The Norton Anthology of Western Literature

Eighth Edition

VOLUME 2

The Norton Anthology
of Western Literature

Eighth Edition

Sarah Lawall, *General Editor*

PROFESSOR EMERITA OF COMPARATIVE LITERATURE,
UNIVERSITY OF MASSACHUSETTS, AMHERST

VOLUME 2
The Enlightenment through the Twentieth Century

W • W • NORTON & COMPANY • *New York* • *London*

W. W. Norton & Company has been independent since its founding in 1923, when William Warder Norton and Mary D. Herter Norton first published lectures delivered at the People's Institute, the adult education division of New York City's Cooper Union. The Nortons soon expanded their program beyond the Institute, publishing books by celebrated academics from America and abroad. By mid-century, the two major pillars of Norton's publishing program—trade books and college texts—were firmly established. In the 1950s, the Norton family transferred control of the company to its employees, and today—with a staff of four hundred and a comparable number of trade, college, and professional titles published each year—W. W. Norton & Company stands as the largest and oldest publishing house owned wholly by its employees.

Editor: Peter Simon
Managing Editor, College: Marian Johnson
Developmental Editor: Carol Flechner
Electronic Media and Ancillaries Editor: Eileen Connell
Editorial Assistants: Robert Bellinger, Simone Gubar
Permission Manager: Nancy Rodwan
Production Manager: Diane O'Connor
Book Designer: Antonina Krass
Art Research: Neil Ryder Hoos

The text of this book is composed in Fairfield Medium with the display set in Bernhard Modern.
Composition by Binghamton Valley Composition.
Manufacturing by R. R. Donnelley & Sons.

Cover illustration: *Self-Portrait* by Vincent Van Gogh. 1889. National Gallery of Art, Washington, D.C. Collection of Mr. and Mrs. John Hay Whitney (1998.74.5). Photo © 2004 Board of Trustees, National Gallery of Art, Washington, D.C.

ISBN 0-393-92616-8 (pbk.)

W. W. Norton & Company, Inc., 500 Fifth Avenue, New York, NY 10110
www.wwnorton.com

W. W. Norton & Company Ltd., Castle House, 75/76 Wells Street, London W1T 3QT

1 2 3 4 5 6 7 8 9 0

Contents

The Enlightenment

The Nineteenth Century: Romanticism

The Nineteenth Century: Realism and Symbolism

The Twentieth Century: Modernisms and Modernity

Preface to the Eighth Edition

The literature of the Western tradition is a celebrated stream of rich and diverse texts that have brought enjoyment and wisdom to readers for—in some cases—thousands of years. As the tradition has evolved and expanded over time, certain authors have been read and reread with remarkable continuity, even as perspectives on their work have changed with changing cultural attitudes. These authors—such as Homer, Sappho, and the Greek dramatists; Virgil and Dante; Cervantes, Shakespeare, and Molière; Goethe, Tolstoy, Flaubert, and Proust—and dozens of others still appear in *The Norton Anthology of Western Literature*, many with additional selections and in vivid new translations. As we have done in the past, the editors have made a number of additions to the list of celebrated authors in the anthology. New authors to this edition include Hesiod, Apuleius, Chrétien de Troyes, Jean de la Fontaine, Lord Byron, Mikhail Lermontov, Nikolai Gogol, Giovanni Verga, Guy de Maupassant, Joseph Conrad, Constantine Cavafy, Alfonsina Storni, Pablo Neruda, Italo Calvino, and Derek Walcott, among others.

This edition improves upon its predecessors in an important new dimension as well: the presence of numerous texts—historical, philosophical, political, and religious—that provide cultural contexts and illuminate patterns of thought. Grouped in thematic clusters for ease of reference and as points of departure for classroom discussion, these texts are more than mere historical documentation. They show how different thinkers viewed the events and central issues of their times. These events and issues resonate with, and sometimes even appear within, the literary works that surround each thematic cluster. Together, the documents reprinted in these clusters comprise a polyphonic tradition of different voices and concepts of reality: they display divergent images of social, political, ethnic, and gendered identity as well as competing concepts of human nature, the nature of the universe, ethical values, and the proper organization of society. Some of the authors are famous: Herodotus, Thucydides, Joan of Arc, Christopher Columbus, Charles Darwin, Karl Marx, and Jean-Paul Sartre, for example. Others—Lucretius, Theophrastus, Christine de Pizan, Madame de Staël, Mona Caird, Giuseppe Garibaldi, Sol T. Plaatje, and Frantz Fanon—are significant but less widely known figures. Reading these cultural texts in conjunction with texts ruled by the artistic imagination richly illuminates a shared world of experience and brings alive the complex reality of a literary-cultural tradition in which all are embedded. Complementing the written texts are sixteen colored plates in each volume, each with a caption situating its subject in cultural history.

Throughout *The Norton Anthology of Western Literature*, you will recognize many other changes, both large and small. What follows is a section-by-section overview of these changes.

The Ancient World. The epic of *Gilgamesh* is brought into sharp focus by the juxtaposition of two differing translations of Tablet XI (the story of the Flood and Gilgamesh's return home), one by noted Near Eastern scholar Benjamin Foster and the other by contemporary poet and translator Stephen Mitchell. The passages from Genesis and Exodus in the Hebrew Bible are newly translated by Robert Alter and now include the story of Abraham and Sarah, and of Moses receiving the Law. Job is newly translated by Raymond Scheindlin. The familiar and influential cadence of the King James Version is retained in our selections from the Psalms and the Song of Songs. Aeschylus's trilogy the *Oresteia* now appears complete with the inclusion of *The Libation Bearers*. *Antigone* has been added to Sophocles' *Oedipus the King*, and a new author, the Carthaginian writer Apuleius, is represented by selections from his comic masterpiece *The Golden Ass*. Book I of Virgil's *Aeneid* is now included, as is the creation myth in Ovid's *Metamorphoses*—and Ovid is newly translated by Charles Martin. Other new translations appear throughout. Homer is represented by Stanley Lombardo's *Iliad*, a realistic rendering that has been enormously successful in the classroom, and by Robert Fagles's well-known translation of the *Odyssey*. Sappho's lyrics are translated by Anne Carson, and Plato's *Apology* by C. D. C. Reeve. Classicist Jeffrey Henderson gives us a new translation of Aristophanes' unforgettable *Lysistrata*. Richmond Lattimore translates the selections from the New Testament. Complementing these and other works in this section is a cluster that describes the competing belief systems in Greece and Rome, ranging from a traditional faith in the Olympian gods to various secular, scientific, and philosophical inquiries. Plato, Aristotle, and Aeschylus, as well as five new authors—Hesiod, Herodotus, Thucydides, Lucretius, and Seneca—contribute their perspectives in a span that ranges over eight centuries.

The Middle Ages. The Middle Ages are not known for their charitable view of women, and another cluster, "Medieval Women," explores this reputation in ten selections, all new to this volume, and concludes that the period was far more divided on the issue than is generally recognized. Passages from Tertullian, St. John Chrysostom, Theophrastus, Heloise, Andreas Capellanus, Guillaume de Mailly, the anonymous Southern Passion, Christine de Pizan, legal records in England, and a transcript of the trial of Joan of Arc furnish passionate arguments on both sides of a debate that reaches back into the ancient world and has not yet disappeared. Echoes of these attitudes appear throughout the most popular works of the period—for example, in Boccaccio's *Decameron*, Chaucer's *Canterbury Tales*, the *lais* of Marie de France, Dante's *Divine Comedy*, and many of the lyric poems printed here. Several new works appear in this section: *The Story of the Grail* by Chrétien de Troyes, "The Story of the Fisherman and the Demon" in *The Thousand and One Nights*, the Prologue to Boccaccio's *Decameron*, and seven new suras added to the existing selections from the Koran. There are also two new translations of note: Seamus Heaney's acclaimed rendering of *Beowulf*, and Mark Musa's *Divine Comedy*.

The Renaissance. Shakespeare's *Hamlet*, found indispensable by many of our readers, returns to the Renaissance section, joined by a group of poems by John Donne, three new stories from *The Heptameron* of Marguerite de Navarre, and additional passages from Cervantes's *Don Quixote* and Milton's *Paradise Lost*. Lope de Vega's *Fuente Ovejuna* appears in a new translation by Gwynne Edwards, and several new translations by Mark Musa round out the selection of Petrarch's sonnets. A major addition to this section consists in an eminently teachable set of three thematically organized clusters of lyric poetry: love poetry in the Petrarchan tradition, "carpe diem" poetry, and a wider range of metaphysical poetry. Leading poets of several national traditions are reunited in these groupings, which demonstrate the power of artistic ideas to cross national boundaries and reinvent themselves in a new setting. For lyric poetry after Petrarch, we have Michelangelo Buonarroti, Francesco Berni, Maurice Scève, Sir Thomas Wyatt, Veronica Franco, Edmund Spenser, Sir Philip Sidney, and Giambattista Marino; for those trying to persuade their loved one to "seize the day," there is Lorenzo de' Medici, Angelo Poliziano, Torquato Tasso, Christopher Marlowe, Sir Walter Raleigh, Edmund Spenser, Sir Philip Sidney, John Donne, Ben Jonson, Robert Herrick, Martin Opitz, and Andrew Marvell. The other metaphysicals are represented by Guy Le Fèvre de la Boderie, San Juan de la Cruz, Agrippa d'Aubigné, George Herbert, Francisco de Queveda, and Constantijn Huygens. Finally, a cluster of prose texts in "Travel and Discovery" run the gamut from fantastic voyages to tales of conquest and subsequently a bleak critique of that conquest, setting side by side the voyagers' assumed (European) norms for human behavior and the challenging reality of contact with other cultures. The spirit of inquiry and self-interrogation shown variously in the writings of Sir John Mandeville, Christopher Columbus, Hernán Cortés, Bernal Díaz, Hans Staden, Bartolomé de Las Casas, and Captain John Smith recur throughout Renaissance writings (notably in Montaigne's celebrated essay *On Cannibals*) and take on new life in nineteenth- and twentieth-century debates over colonization and globalization.

The Enlightenment. The situation of women is the subject of our Enlightenment cluster, with energetic testimony from Judith Drake, Theodor Gottlieb von Hippel, Mary Robinson, Hannah More, and Olympe de Gouges as well as a passage from Jean-Jacques Rousseau's narrative treatise on education, *Émile*. One of the most passionately sought rights for women was the opportunity to receive a full (and not merely "practical") education, and the debate initiated so forcefully here continues well into the nineteenth and twentieth centuries (see Mona Caird and Virginia Woolf, later in this anthology). Also new to this section is a series of celebrated fables by the French classical author Jean de La Fontaine.

The Nineteenth Century: Romanticism. Rousseau, although living in the eighteenth century, is usually discussed as a precursor of nineteenth-century Romanticism, and the new translation of his *Confessions* by J. M. Cohen launches the next section. We are pleased to be able to offer, in addition, Martin Greenberg's remarkable new translation of *Faust*, Part I. Poems by Lord Byron have been added to current selections from Blake, Wordsworth, Coleridge, Shelley, and Keats to form an overview of English Romantic lyrics that corresponds to the section on Continental Romantic lyrics, which itself has expanded to include the Frenchman Gérard de Nerval and the Russian Mikhail Lermontov. The cluster "Revolutionary Moments" focuses on a contrast of American and French figures in the revolutionary period: Governor

Thomas Hutchinson of the Massachusetts Bay Colony, John and Abigail Adams, Mercy Otis Warren, Madame de Staël, Thomas Paine, Jean-Paul Marat (whose death is depicted by Jacques-Louis David in the color insert), and various participants in the French Revolution.

The Nineteenth Century: Realism and Symbolism. This section adds short stories by three celebrated and influential authors who have been claimed at different times for both realism and naturalism: Guy de Maupassant, with *Hautot and His Son;* Giovanni Verga, co-founder of the Italian movement of *verismo* (truthful representation), with *Freedom;* and Nikolai Gogol (paradoxically, also a master of the grotesque) with his tragicomic *The Overcoat.* A new translation of Ibsen's *Hedda Gabler,* by Rick Davis and Brian Johnston, is also offered. To the selections of Symbolist poetry we have added short prose works by Baudelaire, Mallarmé, and Rimbaud that clarify crucial aspects of their poetry: Baudelaire's *The Queen of Faculties* from his *Salon of 1859;* Mallarmé, in passages from an interview and in *Crisis in Poetry;* and Rimbaud, in his letter to Paul Demeny known as the *Letter of the Seer.* Two clusters—"Revolutionary Principles" and "Perspectives on European Empire"—present major texts in intellectual and political history. The former focuses on influential ideas that challenged accepted wisdom and structures of authority: Charles Darwin's evolutionary theory in *The Origin of Species* and *The Descent of Man;* Karl Marx and Friedrich Engels's definitions of "Bourgeois and Proletarians" from the *Manifesto of the Communist Party;* Émile Zola's famous letter *J'Accuse,* denouncing governmental corruption and anti-Semitism in the Dreyfus case; Friedrich Nietzsche's attack on the West's moral decay in *The Gay Science;* and Mona Caird's description of patriarchal marriage as a system of legalized slavery in *The Emancipation of the Family.* "Perspectives on European Empire," focusing especially on the history of colonialism and racist policies, cites documents from various positions of power or vulnerability: Thomas Babington Macaulay's influential *Minute on Indian Education,* prescribing English as the language of instruction in India; the Yao chief Machemba, protesting invasions by German soldiers; the British imperialist Cecil Rhodes, urging the exploitation of Africa for the benefit of Europe; the South African Olive Schreiner, urging a similar development for the benefit of colonists; a fascinating account of her travels in West Africa by the intrepid Victorian ethnologist Mary Kingsley; the diary of an African civil servant, Sol T. Plaatje, set in the siege of Mafeking during the Boer War; and a surprising (and unsuccessful) proposal by international revolutionary Giuseppe Garibaldi to restructure European government in a way that foreshadows the next century's European Union.

The Twentieth Century. The first of many new works in the twentieth-century section is Joseph Conrad's *Heart of Darkness,* which echoes themes of the preceding cluster and can profitably be read in conjunction with it. Other new entries include evocative lyrics by the chief modern Greek poet Constantine Cavafy; the short story *Flowering Judas* by Katherine Anne Porter; poems by the Argentinian writer Alfonsina Storni; selections from the Chilean poet Pablo Neruda, including sections VI through XII of his epic *The Heights of Macchu Picchu* from *General Song;* an intriguing chapter from *Invisible Cities* by the Italian fantasist Italo Calvino; and selections from *Omeros* by the Caribbean poet Derek Walcott. Virginia Woolf's *A Room of One's Own* now contains the addition of Chapter One and is appropriately accompanied by the short story *An Unwritten Novel*. William Faulkner is represented by two favorite short stories: *Barn Burning* and *Spotted Horses*. *The Hollow Men* has been added to the selections by T. S. Eliot. *Borges and I*, Borges's short meditation on textual and personal identity, now accompanies the author's *The Garden of Forking Paths*. The Proust selection from *Swann's Way* appears in a celebrated new translation by Lydia Davis, and Kafka's *Metamorphosis* is now offered in a translation by J. A. Underwood.

Three thematic clusters—"Civilization on Trial," "Freedom and Responsibility at Mid-Century," and "On Being a Cultural Other"—document important issues in twentieth-century thought. Doubts about the status of European civilization begin to be aired at the turn of the century and strengthen after World War I, as is shown in the first cluster with Max Weber's *The Protestant Ethic and the Spirit of Capitalism*, the entry *Civilization* from the famous eleventh edition of the *Encyclopaedia Britannica*, Oswald Spengler's bleak assessment in *The Decline of the West*, Paul Valéry's letter-essay *The Crisis of the Mind*, and two works by Sigmund Freud: *The Future of an Illusion* and *Civilization and Its Discontents*. By mid-century, directly following World War II, attention turned to the role played by individual choice in human affairs, and our second cluster presents analyses by the existentialist philosopher Jean-Paul Sartre (*Being and Nothingness*), the social philosopher Hannah Arendt (*Organized Guilt and Universal Responsibility*), and the novelist and essayist George Orwell (*The Prevention of Literature*). Finally, recapitulating the emphasis on cultural identity that has, in one or another form, permeated the century, the third cluster invokes a range of speakers who remind us—from their own experience—that easy definitions have little validity in real life. Included are selections from René Ménil, *Concerning Colonial Exoticism*; Simone de Beauvoir, *The Second Sex*; Frantz Fanon, *The Wretched of the Earth*; Chinua Achebe, *Named for Victoria, Queen of England*; Audre Lorde, *Age, Race, Class, and Sex: Women Redefining Difference*; Edward Said, *Orientalism*; Trinh T. Minh-ha, *Woman, Native, Other: Writing Postcoloniality and Feminism*; and Salman Rushdie's recent *Step across This Line*.

The new Eighth Edition contains all of the pedagogical support to which our users are accustomed: maps, time lines, pronunciation glossaries, and, of course, the informative introductions and notes, written by editors who are themselves experienced teachers and who often incorporate suggestions from our users. The sixteen color plates new to this volume are captioned and broadly coordinated with each period. In addition, *The Norton Anthology of Western Literature* now provides students and teachers access to a new online resource for students of literature—Norton Literature Online. More information about Norton Literature Online can be found inside the back cover of this anthology.

Each section of *The Norton Anthology of Western Literature* has added new material to old favorites, allowing the teacher to keep tried-and-true works and also to experiment with different contexts and combinations. Some links are suggested by the organization of the table of contents, but there is no prescribed way of using the anthology, and we are confident that the materials presented here offer a wealth of viable options to support customized syllabi geared to specific student needs. A separate *Instructor's Guide*, with further suggestions and helpful guidance for new and experienced instructors alike, is available from the publisher on request.

In closing, we want to pay tribute to Jerome Wright Clinton, professor of Near Eastern Studies at Princeton University, who died in 2003. Professor Clinton, a translator of classical Persian literature and a scholar of great learning and humanity, was the Near Eastern editor for the *Norton Anthology of World Literature* and edited the entries for the Koran and *The Thousand and One Nights* in this edition. A generous colleague and friend, he will be missed.

Acknowledgments

In preparing the texts and contextual clusters of this Eighth Edition, we have called on many colleagues and friends for expert advice in matters that range from linguistic subtleties to cultural expectations at a given place or time. For special help, which has often included related remarks on classroom experience, we are pleased to thank Clifford Ando (University of Southern California); Anthony Boyle (University of Southern California); Jenny Strauss Clay (University of Virginia); Anthony Edwards (University of California, San Diego); Lori Ann Ferrell (Claremont Graduate University); Elizabeth Fitzpatrick (University of Massachusetts); Karen Polinger Foster (Yale University); Andrea Frisch (University of Maryland, Baltimore County); Thomas Habinek (University of Southern California); Peter Mancall (University of Southern California); Richard Martin (Stanford University); Nicholas Moschovakis (Reed College); Anthony Parr (University of the Western Cape); Steven Reece (St. Olaf College); Kathryn Ridenour (University of Massachusetts); Robert Rothstein (University of Massachusetts); Seth Schein (University of California, Davis); Eva Schiffer (University of Massachusetts); Laura Slatkin (New York University); and Robert Sullivan (University of Massachusetts).

In addition, we wish to recognize the contribution of a team of undergraduates at the University of Southern California who reviewed and commented on various editorial introductions and annotations: Phil Taylor (project coordinator), Anne Aubert-Santelli, Monika Lind, and Bryce McFerran. Their perspective as student readers and respondents was invaluable and much appreciated.

In the spring of 2003, W. W. Norton & Company solicited advice from instructors who had contacted the publisher over the years with suggestions for improvement. We are especially grateful to the following, who replied with helpful and thought-provoking responses: Susan Ahern (University of Houston); Heidi E. Ajrami (Victoria College); Allison Alison (Southeastern Community College); Elaine Ancekewicz (Long Island University, C. W. Post Campus); Chris Anderson (Oregon State University); Francis Auld (University of South Florida); Warren G. Babilot (Pueblo Community College); Jim Barnes (Truman State University); Juluette F. Bartlett-Pack (Texas Southern University); Martha Bartter (Truman State University); Patti Bates (California Polytechnic State University); Bridget Beaver (Connors State College); Lee Bedell (Cuesta College); James Bednarz (Long Island University, C. W. Post Campus); Albert J. Bekus (Austin Peay State University); Deb Belt (Hillsdale College); Craig Bennett (Valley Forge Military Academy and College); Paul Benson (Dallas County Community College); Boyd M. Berry (Virginia Commonwealth University); Barbara Bird (St. Petersburg College); Angela Bisong (Texas Southern University); Raymond J. Biziorek (Baker College); Kristin Bluemel (Monmouth University); Richard Bodek

(College of Charleston); Scott Boltwood (Emory & Henry College); David Bordelon (Ocean County College); Marilyn Boutwell (Long Island University); Terence Bowers (College of Charleston); Stephen Boyer (Camden County College); Deborah E. Brassard (Marywood University); John Brinegar (Virginia Commonwealth University); Dan Brooks (Aquinas College); Addison Bross (Lehigh University); Devin Brown (Asbury College); Gayle Brown (University of Florida); Sarah Brown (Schreiner University); Dana Burbank (University of North Alabama); John Burke (University of Alabama); Ann M. Bush (Marywood University); A. Thorpe Butler (Texas Southern University); Lynn Butler (University of Northern Alabama); Catherine Calloway (Arkansas State University); Joseph F. Caputo (Marywood University); Thomas Carabas (Community College of Southern Nevada); Terri Carine; Peter J. Casagrande (University of Kansas); Allen J. Christenson (Brigham Young University); Patricia Cleary-Miller (Rockhurst University); Debra Rae Cohen (University of Arkansas); Adrienne Condon (University of South Florida); William Conlogue (Marywood University); Sharon Coolidge (Wheaton College); Stephen Cooper (Troy State University); Thomas A. Copeland (Youngstown State University); Connie Corbett-Whittier (Friends University); Peter Cortland (Quinnipiac University); Robert Cosgrove (Saddleback College); Catherine Cox (Texas A&M University—Corpus Christi); Sandra Coyle (College of St. Joseph in Vermont); Marcel M. Crespil (Texas Southern University); Phyllis S. Dallas (Georgia Southern University); Dennis Danvers (Virginia Commonwealth University); Lesley Danziger (Orange Coast College); James Davis (Troy State University); James Day (Troy State University); Andrew P. Debicki (University of Kansas); Dorothy Deering (Purdue University); Margaret Del Guercio (Monmouth University); John A. Dern (Gwynedd-Mercy College); Thomas Deveny (McDaniel College); Emily Dial-Driver (Rogers State University); Christopher Dick (Tabor College); Donald R. Dickson (Texas A&M University); Sheila Diecidue (University of South Florida); John DiGaetani (Hofstra University); Joseph M. Ditta (Dakota Wesleyan University); Sharon S. Drake (Texarkana College); David L. Dudley (Georgia Southern University); Alexander Dunlop (Auburn University); Alice T. Duxbury (Palm Beach Community College); Michael Dzanko (College Misericordia); Marilyn Edelstein (Santa Clara University); William Edinger (University of Maryland); Christina Elvidge (Marywood University); Ann W. Engar (University of Utah); Chad Engbers (Calvin College); Renee Epstein (Baruch College, CUNY); Heide Estes (Monmouth University); Prescott Evarts (Monmouth University); Alex Fagan (Virginia Commonwealth University); Chris Fahy (Boston University); Tom Fahy (California Polytechnic State University); Gerald Farber (San Diego State University); Thomas J. Farrell (University of Minnesota, Duluth); Joan Ferrell (Southeastern Illinois College); Shelly Fischer (Community College of Southern Nevada); Randy Fisher (Chapman University, Coachella Valley); Irene Fizer (Hofstra University); Robert Forman (St. John's University); Beverly Forsyth (Odessa College); Marjorie Francoeur (Rivier College); Bruce Gans (Wilbur Wright College); Maria Garcia (Texas Southern University); Elaine Gardiner (William Paterson University); Brian Garvey (Monmouth University); Julie Gates (Angelo State University); Mary Geer (Monmouth University); Jerry D. Gibbens (Williams Baptist College); Virginia Gilbert (Alabama A&M University); John Gillen (Vermont State College, Castleton);

Haydn Gilmore (Marywood University); Janice Glor (University of Northern Alabama); Al Glover (Troy State University); Carolyn Gordon (Mineral Area College); Jonna Gormely Semeiks (Long Island University, C. W. Post Campus); Susan Goulding (Monmouth University); Genie Greavu-Comley (Gainesville College); David Greene (Long Island University, C. W. Post Campus); Ronald Greene (Guilford Technical Community College); Julia B. Griffin (Georgia Southern University); David Gross (University of Oklahoma); Loren C. Gruber (Missouri Valley College); Susan A. Hagedorn (Virginia Polytechnic Institute and State University); Joyce Haines (Friends University); Keith Hale (South Texas Community College); Mary Theresa Hall (Thiel College); Margaret Hallissy (Long Island University, C. W. Post Campus); Jan Haluska (Southern Adventist University); Carol E. Harding (Western Oregon University); Mary Ellen Harje (Angelo State University); Allison Harl (University of Arkansas Community College); Donna Harmon (Texas Southern University); Kent Harrelson (Dalton State College); Charles Harrison (San Jacinto College South); Sarah H. Harrison (Tyler Junior College); Thomas Harrison (Macon State College); John Heath (Santa Clara University); Gloria Henderson (Gordon College); John Henderson (Central Texas College); Dennis E. Hensley (Taylor University Fort Wayne); Deborah Hicks (Troy State University); Adam Hill (California Polytechnic State University); Jack Himmelblau (University of Texas at San Antonio); Susanna Hoeness-Krupsaw (University of Southern Indiana); Michael Holden (Delaware State University); Gail Holian (Georgian Court College); Thomasita Homan (Benedictine College); Glenn Hopp (Howard Payne University); Greg Horn (Southwest Virginia Community College); Barbara Horwitz (Long Island University, C. W. Post Campus); Carolina Hospital (Miami Dade College); Alan Howell (California Polytechnic State University); Dennis J. Humphrey (Arkansas State University—Beebe); John Hussey (Fairmont State Community & Technical College); Collin Hutchison (San Jacinto College South); Ursula Irwin (Mount Hood Community College); Nalini Iyer (Seattle University); Scott Jarvis (Hofstra University); Arbolina L. Jennings (Texas Southern University); Melba M. Johnson (Texas Southern University); Eileen Johnston (United States Naval Academy); Lars R. Jones (Florida Institute of Technology); Debbie Jones (Maranatha Baptist Bible College); Julie Kane (Northwestern State University); Veena Kasbekar (Ohio University—Chillicothe); Robert Keane (Hofstra University); Jill Keller (Middlesex Community College); Joseph Khoury; Geoffrey Kimball (Our Lady of Holy Cross College); Donna K. Kimble (Texas Southern University); John Kingsbury (University of North Alabama); Pam Kingsbury (University of North Alabama); Mark Knoernschild (Fullerton College); Neal Kramer (Brigham Young University); Norbert Krapf (Long Island University, C. W. Post Campus); Richard Krause (Somerset Community College); Bob Kroll (Luzerne County Community College); Ken Kuzmich (Albertus Magnus College); Barb Laman (Dickinson State University); Roger Lathbury (George Mason University); Michael Leddy (Eastern Illinois University); Anthony Leuzzi (Monroe Community College); Lan Lipscomb (Troy State University Montgomery); John Thomas Lloyd (Georgia Southern University); Jon Loessin (Wharton County Junior College); Laura Long (Sul Ross State University); Thomas L. Long (Thomas Nelson Community College); Susan Lorsch (Hofstra University); Gerald Lucas (Macon State College); Scott Lucas (The Citadel); Rob Luscher (University of Nebraska at Kearney); Gary McAllister (Central Baptist College); Patrick A. McCarthy (University of Miami); John L. McCraney (Georgia Military College, Augusta Community College); Sheila McDonald (Long Island University, C. W. Post Campus); Ruth McDowell (Milligan College); Joyce J. McEwing (Texas Southern University); Maria McGarrity (Long Island University); Sherry McGuire (Boise State University); Judith S. McKay (Arkansas State University—Beebe); Rebecca McNeer (Ohio University Southern Campus); William N. MacPherson (Essex County College); Kelley Mahoney (Dalton State College); Dominic Manganiello (University of Ottowa); Kelly Marsh (Mississippi State University); Timothy Martin (Rutgers University); Delinda X. Marzette (Texas Southern University); Jim Matthews (Fairmont State Community & Technical College); David Mead (Texas A&M University, Corpus Christi); Lewis Meyers (Hunter College, CUNY); Brett Millan (South Texas Community College); Arthur Miller (New College of Florida); Edmund Miller (Long Island University, C. W. Post Campus); Nelson Miller (Macon State College); Edward Milowicki (Mills College); Rob Modica (Pima Community College); Todd Moffett (Community College of Southern Nevada); Michael Montgomery (Life University); Theron Montgomery (Troy State University); Janice Townley Moore (Young Harris College); Shirley W. Moore (Texas Southern University); Ken Moss (Marist College); Eric R. Nelson (Georgia Southern University); John H. Newell (College of Charleston); Ronald Newman (University of Miami); Laura K. Noell (Northern Virginia Community College); Michael O'Donnell (United States Naval Academy); Louis J. Oldani (Rockhurst University); Catherine Olson (Tomball College); Jill Onega (University of Alabama in Huntsville); Sherry Organ (Harding University); Michael Orlofsky (Troy State University); Sam Overstreet (Maryville College); John Pagano (Barnard College; Manhattan School of Music); Richard Paris (Monmouth University); Jane Parks (Dalton State College); David Partenheimer (Truman State University); Craig Payne (Indian Hills Community College); S. L. Pearce; Meg F. Pearson (University of Maryland); Allene Phy-Olsen (Austin Peay State University); David Pinault (Santa Clara University); Bruce Plourde (Temple University); Michael W. Price (Grove City College); Richard Priebe (Virginia Commonwealth University); Nichelle Puder (Texas Southern University); Maria A. Quintana (Texas Southern University); Diane Rayor (Grand Valley State University); Lana L. Reese (Texas Southern University); Thomas J. Reiter (Monmouth University); Stuart Richman (Cheney University); Mark Roberts (California Polytechnic State University); David Wayne Robinson (Georgia Southern University); David M. Rogers (Seton Hall University); Clifford Ronan (Southwest Texas State University); Sherry Rosenthal (Community College of Southern Nevada); Alan M. Rosiene (Florida Institute of Technology); Jennifer Rosti (Roanoke College); Lance Rubin (Arapahoe Community College); Ted Ruml (California State University, San Bernardino); Carl Runyon (Owensboro Community College); Craig Rustici (Hofstra University); Robert Ryan (Rutgers University); Steven Ryan (Austin Peay State University); Rhonda Saldivar (Texas Southern University); Ronald C. Samples (Texas Southern University); Frederick K. Sanders (Georgia Southern University); Mark Sandona (Hood College); Rhonda Sanford (Fairmont State Community & Technical College); Tom Sauret (Gainsville College); Rita Saylors (Texas Southern University);

Bill Scalia (Hillsdale College); Tracy Schaelen (Southwestern College); John Scheckter (Long Island University, C. W. Post Campus); Mary Jane Schenck (University of Tampa); James D. Schiavoni (Tennessee Wesleyan College); Owen Schur (Seton Hall University); John Scott (Western Baptist College); Evan Seymour (Community College of Philadelphia); Nick Sharp (Virginia Commonwealth University); Sandra D. Shattuck (Alabama A&M University); Lisa Shoemaker (State Fair Community College); Ellen S. Silber (Marymount College of Fordham University); B. D. Sinclair (University of Nebraska at Kearney); Deborah Sinnreich-Levi (Stevens Institute of Technology); Lynn Siracusa (Monmouth University); Tim Sistrunk (California State University, Chico); Diane Smith (Farmingdale State University of New York); Myrna Smith (Raritan Valley Community College); Wendy Smith (Miramar College); Michael D. Sollars (Texas Southern University); Karen Soreson (Austin Peay State University); David Southmayd (Vanier College); Julie Sparks (University of Arkansas—Monticello); Betty Spitzmiller (Rochester Community and Technical College); James R. Sprouse (Pensacola Christian College); Scott T. Starbuck (San Diego Mesa College); Matthew Stewart (Boston University); Ron Stormer (Culver-Stockton College); David T. Stout (Luzerne County Community College); Chris Sullivan (San Diego Mesa College); John Sweeney (Seton Hall University); Jenny Tabb (Pace University); Phyllis Talmadge (Troy State University); Philip J. Tama (Marywood University); Betty Taylor-Thompson (Texas Southern University); Joan Templeton (Long Island University, Brooklyn Campus); Colette Tennant (Western Baptist College); Burt Thorp (University of North Dakota); John Tucker (Nassau Community College); Billy J. Turner (Texas Southern University); W. Ulmer (University of Alabama); Paul Varner (Oklahoma Christian University); Patricia Vazquez (Community College of Southern Nevada); Beert Verstraete (Acadia University); Cory Wade (Santa Clara University); Joyce S. Walker (Everett Community College); Patricia Ward (College of Charleston); Ward Welty (Alabama A&M University); Marian Wernicke (Pensacola Junior College); Bryan West (Spokane Falls Community College); David Whalen (Hillsdale College); Timothy D. Whelan (Georgia Southern University); Toby Widdicombe (University of Alaska Anchorage); Katherine Ann Wildt (Missouri Valley College); Benjamin Wiley (St. Petersburg College); Dan M. Wiley (Hastings College); Ned Williams (Brigham Young University—Hawaii); Thomas L. Wilmeth (Concordia University Wisconsin); Jean Wilson (McMaster University); Carol Y. Wilson (Lander University); Rodney Wilson (Community College of Southern Nevada); Leigh Winser (Seton Hall University); Timothy Winters (Austin Peay State University); Carl Wooton (California Polytechnic State University); Alok Yadav (George Mason University); Linda Yakle (St. Petersburg College); James Yard (Delaware Valley College); Martha Zamorano (Miami-Dade Community College); David Zehr (Santa Monica College); John Ziebell (Community College of Southern Nevada); Jeffrey Zorn (Santa Clara University).

Phonetic Equivalents

For use with the Pronouncing Glossaries preceding
most selections in this volume.

a as in *cat*
ah as in *father*
ai as in *light*
aw as in *raw*
ay as in *day*
e as in *pet*
ee as in *street*
ehr as in *air*
er as in *bird*
eu as in *lurk*
g as in *good*
i as in *sit*
j as in *joke*
nh a nasal sound (as in French *vin, vẽ*)
o as in *pot*
oh as in *no*
oo as in *boot*
or as in *bore*
ow as in *now*
oy as in *toy*
s as in *mess*
ts as in *ants*
u as in *us*
zh as in *vision*

The Norton Anthology
of Western Literature

Eighth Edition

VOLUME 2

Europe
ca. 1740

The Enlightenment

Is the latest thing always, usually, or ever the best? On the whole, Western citizens of the twenty-first century assume the probability of progress. Our means of travel are far more efficient—and certainly more comfortable—than those of our grandparents. Thus, for many it follows that the newest books, the newest ideas, even the newest political candidates seem to be the most advanced and exciting, if not necessarily the best.

Yet many would disagree. Consider, for instance, the stereotypical attitude of parents toward their teenage children's taste in music. Generation after generation, adults resist, even with horror, young people's music, clothes, language, and adornment. Such conflicts appear relatively trivial, although during the Enlightenment, when the clashes were about ideas, they felt momentous and were by no means entirely generational.

The quarrel between "ancients" and "moderns"—those who believed, respectively, that old ideas or new ones were likely to prove superior to any alternatives—proved especially virulent in France and England. This was not a clash of fuddy-duddies and new spirits. Those who espoused the cause of the ancients feared—with reason—the social alienation, unscrupulous self-seeking, and lack of moral responsibility that might attend the new commitment to individualism. Believing in the universality of truth, they wished to uphold established values, not to invent new ones. On the other side, the moderns upheld the importance of individual autonomy, broad education for women, and intellectual and geographical exploration. They stood for the new and are the recognizable forebears of what we even now call "modernity."

On both sides of the ancient/modern divide, thinkers believed in reason as a dependable guide. Hence the term *Enlightenment* used to express the gaining of illumination by means of the power of the human mind. "He that thinks reasonably must think morally," Dr. Johnson wrote. Reason, in other words, would lead human beings back to eternal truths. But reason also, for others, could provide a means for discovering fresh solutions to scientific, philosophical and political questions. The possibilities seemed endless. Yet commitment to reason as an ideal did not necessarily enable men and women to behave reasonably.

The late seventeenth century, when the Enlightenment began, was a period of great turmoil, and turmoil persisted at intervals throughout the succeeding century. Civil war in England had ended in the king's execution in 1649; the French would guillotine their ruler before the end of the eighteenth century. The notion of divine right, the belief that monarchs governed with authority from God, had been effectively destroyed.

If reason led to the conclusion that sovereigns were ordinary mortals, that conclusion implied new kinds of uncertainty. God seemed to be moving further away. More and more people found it hard to assume the primacy of religion. The fierce strife between Protestants and Catholics lapsed into relative quiescence by the end of the seventeenth century, although the Protestant English deposed their king, James II, in 1688 because of his marriage to a Catholic princess and their fear of a Catholic dynasty, and in France Louis XIV, in 1685, revoked the Edict of Nantes, which had granted religious toleration to Protestants. In other words, religion still figured as a political reality, as it did in the struggle of Cavaliers and Puritans in England, which ended with the restoration of Charles II to the throne in 1660. But religious differ-

1

ences as public problems now became translated into divisions of social class and of political conviction—divisions no less powerful for lacking any claim of God-given authority. To England, the eighteenth century brought two unsuccessful but bitter rebellions on behalf of the deposed Stuart succession as well as the cataclysmic American Revolution. Throughout the eighteenth century, wars erupted over succession to European thrones and over nationalistic claims, although no fighting took place on a scale comparable to the devastating Thirty Years' War (1618–48). Internal divisions in France and England assumed greater importance than struggles between nations.

All these events illustrate that belief in reason did not—and does not—necessarily make human beings reasonable, a point not lost on Enlightenment thinkers. The philosophers who, like René Descartes ("I think, therefore I am"), declared the mind the source of individual being soon came to realize the possibility of the mind's isolation in its own constructions. Perhaps, Gottfried Wilhelm Leibniz suggested, no real communication can take place between one consciousness and another. Possibly, according to David Hume, the idea of individual identity itself derives from the mind's efforts to manufacture continuity out of discontinuous memories. Philosophers pointed out the impossibility of knowing for sure even the reality of the external world: the only certainty is that we think it exists. If contemplating the nature of human reason thus led philosophic skeptics to restrict severely the area of what we can know with certainty, other thoughts induced other thinkers to insist on the existence, beyond ourselves, of an entirely rational physical and moral universe. Isaac Newton's demonstrations of the order of natural law greatly encouraged this line of thought. The fullness and complexity of the perceived physical world testified, as many wrote, to the sublime rationality of a divine plan. The Planner, however, did not necessarily supervise the day-to-day operations of His arrangements; He was seen, rather, as a watchmaker who winds a watch and leaves it running.

Deism, evoking a depersonalized deity, insisted on the logicality of the universe and encouraged the separation of ethics from religion. Ethics, too, could be understood as a matter of reason. Reason might guide human beings to truth, although it rarely seemed to do so. As Enlightenment thinkers could not fail to recognize, men and women embody a capacity for passion as well as reason. Life could be understood as a struggle between rationality and emotion, with feeling frequently exercising controlling force. Those who believed in the desirability of reason's governance could not always perceive its actuality. For them as for us, the gap between the ideal and the actual caused frustration and often despair.

SOCIETY

Despite the social instability that produced revolution and civil war, the *idea* of society retained great power during this period. Seventeenth-century English philosopher Thomas Hobbes, who believed that in the state of nature—the presocietal condition—human life was inevitably "nasty, mean, brutish, and short," thought that men and women had originally banded together for the sake of preservation and progress. By the late seventeenth century in England and on the Continent, social organization had evolved into elaborate hierarchical structures with the aristocracy at the apex. Just below the aristocrats were the educated gentry—clergymen, lawyers, men of leisure with landed property. Below them were masses of workers of various kinds, many of them illiterate. Although literacy rates grew dramatically during the eighteenth century, those who wrote (and, for a long time, those who read) belonged almost entirely to the two upper classes.

As members of the privileged classes, men had many opportunities: for education, for service in government or diplomacy, for the exercise of political and economic power. For the most part, both men and women accepted as necessary the subordination of women, who, even in the upper classes, had few opportunities for education and occupation beyond the household. But the increasing value attached to individualism had implications for women as well as men. In the late seventeenth century, Sor Juana Inés de la Cruz, a Mexican nun, articulated her own passion for thought and reading, and became an eloquent advocate of the right of women to education and a life of the mind. During the next century, a number of women and an occasional man made the same case. It became increasingly obvious that the relegation of women solely to childbearing and child rearing did not conform to the dictates of reason. However one defined reason, it was clearly the possession of all of humankind, not just the males. (There was some dispute over whether women had souls; but, in general, even misogynists had to admit that females were capable of reasoning.) The emphasis on education in virtually all of the period's tracts about women provides proof that the concept of rational progress offered a device that could be used to gain at least some rights for women—if not civil rights, which were long in coming, at least the right to thought and knowledge.

Women of the upper classes occupied a more important place in French society than in English, presiding over "salons," gatherings whose participants engaged in intellectual as well as frivolous conversation. By the late eighteenth century, at least a few equivalent groups had developed in England, where intellectual women known as "bluestockings" conducted their own social assemblies. Women had also begun writing novels. In France, before the end of the seventeenth century, Marie de la Vergne de La Fayette produced *The Princess of Clèves*, a work immediately and lastingly popular, one rich in subtle moral discriminations. Female novelists proliferated in England during the eighteenth century, their books widely read by men and women alike. Although novels by women often focused attention on the domestic scene, they also ranged further. The most prolific writers of Gothic fiction, for instance, were women. Women published translations from the Greek as well as volumes of literary criticism. Even if society as a whole did not acknowledge their full intellectual and moral capacities, individual women were beginning to claim for themselves more rights than those of motherhood.

Society in this period operated, as societies always do, by means of well-defined codes of behavior. Such social masks might provide disguises for deviance: the thoughts of the woman who at all times says exactly what she should may be quite different from what is spoken. Commentators at the time frequently showed themselves troubled by the possibility of sharp discrepancies between social appearance and characterological actuality: Molière's *Tartuffe* provides a vivid example, with its investigation of religious sham. De La Fayette, considering the dilemma of a woman whose sense of propriety wars with her desire; Swift, lashing the English for institutionalized hypocrisy; Pope, calling attention to ambiguities inherent in sexual mores; Voltaire and Johnson, sending naive fictional protagonists to encounter the world's inconsistencies of profession and practice—all of these writers call attention to the deceptiveness and the possible misuses of social norms as well as to their necessity. None suggests that the codes themselves are at fault. If people lived up to what they profess, the world would be a better place; ideally, they would modify not their standards of behavior but their tendency to hide behind them.

In fiction, drama, poetry, and prose satire, writers of the Enlightenment in one way or another make society their subject. On occasion, especially in France, they use domestic situations to provide microcosms of a wider social universe. Marriage, an institution at once social and personal, provides a useful image for human relationship as social and emotional fact. The developing eighteenth-century novel, in England and France alike, would assume marriage as the normal goal for men and women; Molière, Racine, and de La Fayette, writing before the turn of the century, examine economic, psychological, moral, and social implications of specific imagined marriages. The sexual alliances of rulers, Racine's subject in *Phaedra,* have literal consequences far beyond the individuals involved. Molière evokes a private family to suggest how professed sentiment can obscure the operations of ambition; de La Fayette depicts intricate social and emotional pressures impinging on men and women of good will. All three understand marriage as representing a society in miniature, not merely as a structure for fulfillment of personal desire.

In England, writers in genres other than the novel typically focus on a broader panorama. Pope, Swift, and Johnson, like Voltaire satirists of the human scene, consider varied operations of social law and pressure. In *The Rape of the Lock,* Pope uses a card party to epitomize social structures. Swift imagines idealized forms of social institutions ranging from marriage to Parliament, contrasting the ideals with recreations of their actual English counterparts; or he fantasizes the horrifying consequences of venture capitalism in the processing of infants for food. Johnson's and Voltaire's world tourists witness and participate in a vast range of sobering experiences. In general, women fill subordinate roles in the harsh social environments evoked by these satiric works. Dr. Johnson praised Shakespeare because the playwright did not make love the only spring of action; other passions, Johnson suggested, more powerfully motivate human activity. As the social scene in *Rasselas* widens, erotic love plays a less important part and the position of women becomes increasingly insignificant: women's sphere is the home, and home life matters less than does public life. It is perhaps relevant to note that no work in this section (with the horrifying exception of *A Modest Proposal*) describes or evokes children. Only in adulthood do people assume social responsibility; only then do they provide interesting substance for social commentary.

HUMANITY AND NATURE

If the subject of human beings' relation to society occupied many writers, the problem of humankind's relation to the universe also caused perplexity. Deism, which attracted many during this period, assumed the existence of a God who provided evidence of Himself only in His created works. Studying the natural world, therefore, might be understood as a religious act; the powers of reason would enable fruitful study. But how, exactly, should humanity's position in the created universe be understood? Alexander Pope, who in *An Essay on Man* investigates his subject in relation both to society and to the universe, understood creation as a great continuum, with man at the apex of the animal world. This view, sometimes described as belief in a Great Chain of Being, was widely shared. But if one turned the eye of reason on generic man himself, his dominance might seem questionable. Pope describes the inner life of human beings as a "Chaos of Thought and Passion, all confused," and sums up man as "the glory, jest, and riddle of the world." Glory? Perhaps. But when one adds the ideas of jest and riddle, human preeminence seems less obvious.

Across the English Channel, Jean de La Fontaine wrote, in the late seventeenth century, a brilliant and extensive series of beast fables that subtly challenged the notion of humankind's dominance. Taking his subjects from Aesop and from familiar folktales, he versifies them afresh in ways that insist on uncomfortable connections between humanity and the "lower" animals. Pigeons and cicadas, wolves, lions, crows, foxes, and mice populate his fables. They sound very much like men and women. The point of a beast fable, of course, lies just there: in making animals talk and think and feel like people. The greed and selfishness and cruelty of an imaginary wolf, perhaps, will make a reader stop to reflect on the baseness of such qualities—"subhuman" qualities—in actual persons. If animals resemble people, presumably people resemble animals.

But La Fontaine's animal characters exhibit virtues as well as vices. Although the pigeon who goes out to see the world suffers from the carelessness and brutality of other animals, he never loses the devotion of his sibling. The rat spared by a lion in turn rescues the great beast. Again, though, in positive as well as negative respects, the alleged similarity between animals and humans raises questions about human dominion. Is it all a matter of point of view? The eighteenth-century English poet John Gay, in one of *his* beast fables, suggests just this. Man proudly asserts that all things are made for his use; however, a "pampered goose" replies that man serves his needs. The goose is being fattened for slaughter, but all beings die; meanwhile, it is living a life of total indulgence and can imagine its utter power over its human environment. Perhaps the elevated position of humanity in the hierarchy of creation is equally a fantasy. La Fontaine's sly hints raise that possibility.

Yet the natural order—however incomplete human understanding of it—remains, and remains a comfort. It suggests a *system*, a structure of relationships that at some theoretical level necessarily makes sense; thus, it provides an assumed substructure of rationality for all irrational experience. It supplies a means of evaluating the natural world: every flower, every minnow, has meaning beyond itself as part of the great pattern. The passion with which the period's thinkers cling to belief in such a system suggests anxiety about what human reason could not do. Human beings create a vision of something at once sublimely reasonable and beyond reason's grasp to reassure themselves that the limits of the rational need not coincide with the limits of the human.

The notion of a permanent natural order corresponds to the notion of a permanent human nature, as conceived in the eighteenth century. In other words, it was generally believed that human nature remains in all times and places the same. Thus, Racine could re-present a fable from Greek tragedy, using classical setting and characters, with complete assurance that his imagining of Phaedra's conflict and suffering would speak to his contemporaries without falsifying the classical original. Despite social differences, fundamental aspects of personality do in fact remain constant: all people hope and fear, are envious and lustful, and possess the capacity to reason. All suffer loss, all face death. Thinkers of the Enlightenment emphasized these common aspects of humanity far more than they considered cultural dissimilarities. Readers and writers alike could draw on this conviction about universality. It provided a test of excellence: if an author's imagining of character failed to conform to what eighteenth-century readers understood as human nature, a work might be securely judged inadequate. Conversely, the idea of a constant human nature held out the hope of longevity for writers who successfully evoked it. Moral philosophers could define human obligation and possibility, convinced that they, too, wrote for all time; ethical standards would never change. Like the vision of order in the physical universe, the notion of constancy in human nature provided bedrock.

CONVENTION AND AUTHORITY

Like all societies, eighteenth-century society operated—and its literary figures wrote—using established conventions. Manners are social conventions: agreed-on systems of behavior declared appropriate for specific situations. Guides to manners proliferated in the eighteenth century, emphasizing the idea that commitment to decorum helped preserve society's important standards. Literary conventions—agreed-on systems of verbal behavior—served comparable purposes in another sphere. Like established codes of manners, such conventions provide continuity between present and past.

The literary conventions of the past, like outmoded manners or styles of dress, may strike the twentieth-century reader as antiquated and artificial. A woman who curtsied in a modern living room or a man who appeared in a wig would seem to us ridiculous, even insane; but, of course, a young woman in jeans would strike our predecessors as equally perverse. The plaintive lyrics of current country music, like the extravagances of rap, operate within restrictive conventions that affect their hearers as "natural" only because they are familiar. Eighteenth-century writers had at their disposal an established set of conventions for every traditional literary genre. As the repetitive rhythms of the country ballad tell listeners what to expect, these literary conventions provided readers with clues about the kind of experience they could anticipate in a given poem or play.

Underlying all specific conventions was the classical assumption that literature existed to delight and instruct its readers. The various genres of this period embody such belief in literature's dual function. Stage comedy and tragedy, the early novel, satire in prose and verse, didactic poetry, the philosophical tale: each form developed its own set of devices for creating pleasure as well as for involving audiences and readers in situations requiring moral choice. The insistence in drama on unity of time and place (stage action occupying no more time than its representation, with no change of scene) exemplifies one such set, intended to facilitate in audiences the kind of belief encouraging maximum emotional and moral effect. The elevated diction of the *Essay on Man* ("Mark how it mounts, to Man's imperial race, / From the green myriads in the peopled grass"), like the mannered but less dignified language of *The Rape of the Lock* ("Here thou, great Anna! whom three realms obey, / Dost sometimes counsel take—and sometimes tea"), and the two-dimensional characters of Johnson's and Voltaire's tales: such (to us) unfamiliar aspects of these texts provide signals about authorial intention and about anticipated reader response.

One dominant convention of twenty-first-century poetry and prose is something we call "realism." In fiction, verse, and drama, writers often attempt to convey the literal feel of experience, the shape in which events actually occur in the world, the way people really talk. Racine, Pope, and Voltaire pursued no such goal. Despite their concern with permanent patterns of thought and feeling, they employed artifice to emphasize and to obscure. The rapidity with which de La Fayette summarizes crucial events (as when her heroine's mother reports some thirty years of court history in two or three pages), like the sonorous verse in which Racine's characters reflect on their passions ("I hate my life, abominate my lust; / Longing by death to rescue my good name / And hide my black love from the light of day"), embodies a form of stylization. Artistic transformation of life, the period's writers believed, involves imposing formal order on the endless flux of event and feeling. The formalities of this literature constitute part of its meaning: what experience shows as unstable, art makes stable.

By relying on convention, eighteenth-century writers could be seen as trying to control an unstable world. The classical past, for many, provided an emblem of that stability, a standard of permanence. But some felt that the high valuing of the past was problematic, the problem epitomized by the quarrel of ancients versus moderns in England and France. At stake in this controversy was, among other things, the value of permanence as opposed to the value of change. Proponents of the ancients believed that the giants of Greece and Rome had not only established standards applicable to all subsequent accomplishment but had provided models of achievement never to be excelled. Homer wrote the first great epics; subsequent endeavors in the same genre could only imitate him. When innovation came, it came by making the old new, as Pope makes a woman's dressing for conquest new by comparing it to the arming of Achilles. Moderns who valued originality for its own sake, who multiplied worthless publications, who claimed significance for what time had not tested thereby testified to their own inadequacies and their foolish pride.

Those proud to be moderns, on the other hand, held that men (possibly even women) standing on the shoulders of the ancients could see further than their predecessors. The new was conceivably more valuable than the old. One might discover flaws even in revered figures of the classic past. And not everything had yet been accomplished. This view, of course, corresponds to one widely current since the eighteenth century, but it did not triumph easily: many powerful thinkers of the late seventeenth and early eighteenth centuries adhered to the more conservative position.

Also at issue in this debate was the question of authority. What position should be assumed by one who hoped to write and be read? Did authority reside only in tradition? If so, one must write in classical forms, rely on classical allusions. Until late in the eighteenth century, virtually all important writers attempted to ally themselves with the authority of tradition, declaring themselves part of a community extending through time as well as space. The problems of authority became particularly important in connection with satire, a popular Enlightenment form. Satire involves criticism of vice and folly; Molière, Pope, Swift, Voltaire, and Johnson at least on occasion wrote in the satiric mode. To establish the right to criticize human behavior, the satirist must establish a rhetorical ascendancy comparable to the one that the pulpit gives the priest—an ascendancy most readily obtained by at least implicit alliance with literary and moral tradition. The satirist, like the moral philosopher, cannot afford to seem idiosyncratic when prescribing and condemning the behavior of others. The fact that satire flourished so richly in this period suggests another version of the central conflict between reason and passion: that of the forces of stability and of instability. In its heightened description of the world (people eating babies, young women initiating epic battles over the loss of a lock of hair), satire calls attention to the powerful presence of the irrational, opposing that presence with the clarity of the satirist's own claim to reason and tradition. As it chastises human beings for their eruptions of passion, urging resistance and control, satire reminds its readers of the universality of the irrational as well as of opposition to it. The effort "to correct and moderate men's [and women's] passions," as Molière put it, that great theme of the Enlightenment, can equally generate hope or despair—opposed moods richly expressed throughout this period.

THE ENLIGHTENMENT

TEXTS	CONTEXTS
	1660 Civil War in England ends with Charles II's ascension to the throne (the "Restoration").
1664 Jean-Baptiste Poquelin Molière, *Tartuffe*.	
1665 François de La Rochefoucauld, *Reflections*.	1666 Isaac Newton uncovers laws of gravity • London, already stricken by plague, is destroyed in the Great Fire and subsequently rebuilt in more orderly fashion.
1667 Publication of John Milton's *Paradise Lost*.	
1668–1694 Jean de La Fontaine, *Fables*.	1670 The London-based Hudson's Bay Company is incorporated by royal charter to trade in North America.
1677 Jean Racine, *Phaedra*.	
1678 Marie de la Vergne de La Fayette, *The Princess of Clèves*.	
1690 John Locke, *Essay Concerning Human Understanding*.	
1691 Sor Juana Inés de la Cruz, **Reply to Sor Filotea de la Cruz**.	1694 Bank of England is chartered, forerunner of modern national banks and treasury systems; London Stock Exchange follows in 1698.
1696 Judith Drake, **An Essay in Defense of the Female Sex**.	
	1697 Russian czar Peter the Great visits Western Europe and England, resolves to Westernize Russia.
	1707 Kingdom of Great Britain formed by union of England and Scotland.
	1709 Up to 100,000 slaves a year cross the Atlantic, 20,000 to Britain's Caribbean colonies alone.
1710 First British copyright law, transferring rights of property in a published work from publisher to author.	
1717 Alexander Pope, **The Rape of the Lock**.	
1719 Daniel Defoe publishes *Robinson Crusoe*, often called the first true novel in English.	1721 J. S. Bach, *The Brandenburg Concertos*.
1726 Jonathan Swift, **Gulliver's Travels**.	

Boldface titles indicate works in the anthology.

THE ENLIGHTENMENT

TEXTS	CONTEXTS
1729 Swift, *A Modest Proposal*.	
1733–1734 Alexander Pope, *An Essay on Man*.	
1739 "Sophia," *Women Not Inferior to Man*.	
1751 First edition of French *Encyclopédie*, edited by Denis Diderot.	
1755 Samuel Johnson publishes the *Dictionary of the English Language*, the first comprehensive English dictionary on historical principles.	1753 British Museum founded.
1759 François-Marie Arouet de Voltaire, *Candide* • Samuel Johnson, *The History of Rasselas, Prince of Abissinia*.	1756–1763 Seven Years' War, involving nine European powers; Britain acquires Canada and Florida, Spain gets Cuba and the Philippines, France wins colonies in India and Africa as well as Guadeloupe and Martinique.
1762 Jean-Jacques Rousseau, *Émile; or, On Education*.	
	1769 James Watt, a Scot, invents the steam engine, first in a series of mechanical innovations ushering in the Industrial Revolution.
1771 First publication of *Encyclopaedia Britannica* and complete French *Encyclopédie* testify to characteristic "Enlightenment" impulse to organize knowledge.	1775–1783 American War of Independence; Declaration of Independence, 1776 • Constitution of the United States, 1787, the year of Mozart's opera *Don Giovanni*.
1791 Olympe de Gouges, *The Rights of Woman*.	1789 French Revolution begins; French National Assembly adopts the Declaration of the Rights of Man.
1792 Mary Wollstonecraft, *Vindication of the Rights of Woman*, makes feminist case for female equality • Theodor Gottlieb von Hippel, *On Improving the Status of Women*.	
1799 Mary Robinson, *A Letter to the Women of England, on the Injustice of Mental Subordination* • Hannah More, *Strictures on the Modern System of Female Education*.	1799 After successful conquests throughout Europe, Napoleon Bonaparte becomes first consul—in effect, dictator—of France • Ludwig van Beethoven writes first symphony (1799–1800).

JEAN-BAPTISTE POQUELIN MOLIÈRE
1622–1673

Son of a prosperous Paris merchant, Jean-Baptiste Molière (originally named Poquelin) devoted his entire adult life to the creation of stage illusion, as playwright and as actor. At about the age of twenty-five, he joined a company of traveling players established by the Béjart family; with them he toured the provinces for about twelve years. In 1658 the company was ordered to perform for Louis XIV in Paris; a year later, Molière's first great success, *The High-Brow Ladies (Les Précieuses ridicules)*, was produced. The theatrical company to which he belonged, patronized by the king, became increasingly successful, developing finally (1680) into the Comédie-Française. In 1662, Molière married Armande Béjart. He died in 1673, a few hours after performing the lead role in his own play *The Imaginary Invalid*.

Molière wrote both broad farce and comedies of character, in which he caricatured some form of vice or folly by embodying it in a single figure. His targets included the miser, the aspiring but vulgar middle class, female would-be intellectuals, the hypochondriac, and, in *Tartuffe,* the religious hypocrite.

In *Tartuffe* (1664), as in his other plays, Molière employs classic comic devices of plot and character—here, a foolish, stubborn father blocking the course of young love; an impudent servant commenting on her superiors' actions; a happy ending involving a marriage facilitated by implausible means. He often uses such devices, however, to comment on his own immediate social scene, imagining how universal patterns play themselves out in a specific historical context. *Tartuffe* had contemporary relevance so transparent that the Catholic Church forced the king to ban it, although Molière managed to have it published and produced once more by 1669.

The play's emotional energy derives not from the simple discrepancy of man and mask in Tartuffe ("Is not a face quite different from a mask?" inquires the normative character Cléante, who has no trouble making such distinctions), but from the struggle for erotic, psychic, and economic power in which people employ their masks. One can readily imagine modern equivalents for the stresses and strains within Orgon's family. Orgon, an aging man with grown children, seeks ways to preserve control. His mother, Madame Pernelle, encourages his efforts, thus fostering her illusion that *she* still runs things. Orgon identifies his own interests with those of the hypocritical Tartuffe, toward whom he plays a benevolent role. Because Tartuffe fulsomely hails him as benefactor, Orgon feels utterly powerful in relation to his fawning dependent. When he orders his passive daughter Mariane to marry Tartuffe, he reveals his vision of complete domestic autocracy. Tartuffe's lust, one of those passions forever eluding human mastery, disturbs Orgon's arrangements; in the end, the will of the offstage king orders everything, as though a benevolent god had intervened.

To make Tartuffe a specifically religious hypocrite is an act of inventive daring. Orgon, like his mother, conceals from himself his will to power by verbally subordinating himself to that divinity which Tartuffe, too, invokes. Although one may easily accept Molière's defense of his intentions (not to mock faith but to attack its misuse), it is not hard to see why the play might trouble religious authorities. Molière suggests how readily religious faith lends itself to misuse, how high-sounding pieties allow men and women to evade self-examination and immediate responsibilities. Tartuffe deceives others by his grandiosities of mortification ("Hang up my hair shirt") and charity; he encourages his victims in their own grandiosities. Orgon can indulge a fantasy of self-subordination (remarking of Tartuffe, "He guides our lives") at the same time that he furthers his more hidden desire for power. Religion offers ready justification for a course manifestly destructive as well as self-seeking.

Cléante, before he meets Tartuffe, claims (accurately) to understand him by his effects on others. Throughout the play, Cléante speaks in the voice of wisdom, counseling moderation, common sense, and self-control, calling attention to folly. More important, he emphasizes how the issues Molière examines in this comedy relate to dominant late seventeenth-century themes:

> Ah, Brother, man's a strangely fashioned creature
> Who seldom is content to follow Nature,
> But recklessly pursues his inclination
> Beyond the narrow bounds of moderation,
> And often, by transgressing Reason's laws,
> Perverts a lofty aim or noble cause.

To follow Nature means to act appropriately to the human situation in the created universe. Humankind occupies a middle position, between beasts and angels; such aspirations as Orgon's desire to control his daughter completely or his apparent wish to submit himself absolutely to Tartuffe's claim of heavenly wisdom imply a hope to surpass limitations inherent in the human condition. As Cléante's observations suggest, "to follow Nature," given the rationality of the universe, implies adherence to "Reason's laws." All transgression involves failure to submit to reason's dictates. Molière, with his stylized comic plot, makes that point as insistently as does Racine, who depicts grand passions and cataclysmic effects from them.

Cléante understands and can enunciate the principles of proper conduct, but his wisdom has no direct effect on the play's action. Although the comedy suggests a social world in which women exist in utter subordination to fathers and husbands, in the plot, two women bring about the clarifications that unmask the villain. The virtuous wife, Elmire, object of Tartuffe's lust, and the articulate servant girl, Dorine, confront the immediate situation with pragmatic inventiveness. Dorine goads others to response; Elmire encourages Tartuffe to play out his sexual fantasies before a hidden audience. Both women have a clear sense of right and wrong, although they express it in less resounding terms than does Cléante. Their concrete insistence on facing what is really going on, cutting through all obfuscation, rescues the men from entanglement in their own abstract formulations.

The women's clarifications, however, do not resolve the comedy's dilemmas. Suddenly the context shifts: economic terms replace erotic ones. It is as though Tartuffe were only playing in his attempt to seduce Elmire; now we get to what really matters: money. For all his claims of disinterestedness, Tartuffe has managed to get control of his dupe's property. Control of property, the action gradually reveals, amounts to power over life itself: prison threatens Orgon, and the prospect of expulsion from their home menaces him and his family alike. Only the convenient and ostentatious artifice of royal intervention rescues the victims and punishes their betrayer.

Comedies conventionally end in the restoration of order, declaring that good inevitably triumphs; rationality renews itself despite the temporary deviations of the foolish and vicious. At the end of *Tartuffe*, Orgon and his mother have been chastened by revelation of their favorite's depravity, Mariane has been allowed to marry her lover, Tartuffe has been judged, and the king's power and justice have reasserted themselves and been acknowledged. In the organization of family and nation (metaphorically a larger family), order reassumes dominion. Yet the arbitrary intervention of the king leaves a disturbing emotional residue. The play has demonstrated that Tartuffe's corrupt will to power (as opposed to Orgon's merely foolish will) can ruthlessly aggrandize itself. Money speaks, in Orgon's society as in ours; possession of wealth implies total control over others. Only a kind of miracle can save Orgon. The miracle occurs, given the benign world of comedy, but the play reminds its readers of the extreme precariousness with which reason finally triumphs, even given the presence of such reasonable people as Cléante and Elmire. Tartuffe's monstrous lust—for women, money, power—genuinely endangers the social structure. *Tartuffe* enforces recognition of the constant threats to rationality, of how much we have at stake in trying to use reason as principle of action.

PRONOUNCING GLOSSARY

The following list uses common English syllables and stress accents to provide rough equivalents of selected words whose pronunciation may be unfamiliar to the general reader.

Cléante: *clay-ahnt'*

Damis: *dah-meece'*

Dorine: *do-reen'*

Elmire: *el-meer'*

Flipote: *flee-pot'*

Laurent: *lor-awnh'*

Loyal: *lwah-yal'*

Molière: *moh-lyehr'*

Orante: *oh-rahnt'*

Orgon: *or-gohnh'*

Pernelle: *payr-nel'*

Tartuffe: *tahr-tewf'*

Valère: *vah-lehr'*

Vincennes: *vanh-sen'*

Tartuffe[1]

Preface

Here is a comedy that has excited a good deal of discussion and that has been under attack for a long time; and the persons who are mocked by it have made it plain that they are more powerful in France than all whom my plays have satirized up to this time. Noblemen, ladies of fashion, cuckolds, and doctors all kindly consented to their presentation, which they themselves seemed to enjoy along with everyone else; but hypocrites do not understand banter: they became angry at once, and found it strange that I was bold enough to represent their actions and to care to describe a profession shared by so many good men. This is a crime for which they cannot forgive me, and they have taken up arms against my comedy in a terrible rage. They were careful not to attack it at the point that had wounded them: they are too crafty for that and too clever to reveal their true character. In keeping with their lofty custom, they have used the cause of God to mask their private interests; and *Tartuffe*, they say, is a play that offends piety: it is filled with abominations from beginning to end, and nowhere is there a line that does not deserve to be burned. Every syllable is wicked, the very gestures are criminal, and the slightest glance, turn of the head, or step from right to left conceals mysteries that they are able to explain to my disadvantage. In vain did I submit the play to the criticism of my friends and the scrutiny of the public: all the corrections I could make, the judgment of the king and queen[2] who saw the play, the approval of great princes and ministers of state who honored it with their presence, the opinion of good men who found it worthwhile, all this did not help. They will not let go of their prey, and every day of the week they have pious zealots abusing me in public and damning me out of charity.

I would care very little about all they might say except that their devices make enemies of men whom I respect and gain the support of genuinely good men, whose faith they know and who, because of the warmth of their

---

1. Translated by Richard Wilbur. The first version of *Tartuffe* was performed in 1664 and the second in 1667. When a second edition of the third version was printed in June 1669, Molière added his three petitions to Louis XIV; they follow the "Preface." 2. Louis XIV was married to Marie-Thérèse of Austria.

piety, readily accept the impressions that others present to them. And it is this which forces me to defend myself. Especially to the truly devout do I wish to vindicate my play, and I beg of them with all my heart not to condemn it before seeing it, to rid themselves of preconceptions, and not aid the cause of men dishonored by their actions.

If one takes the trouble to examine my comedy in good faith, he will surely see that my intentions are innocent throughout, and tend in no way to make fun of what men revere; that I have presented the subject with all the precautions that its delicacy imposes; and that I have used all the art and skill that I could to distinguish clearly the character of the hypocrite from that of the truly devout man. For that purpose I used two whole acts to prepare the appearance of my scoundrel. Never is there a moment's doubt about his character; he is known at once from the qualities I have given him; and from one end of the play to the other, he does not say a word, he does not perform an action which does not depict to the audience the character of a wicked man, and which does not bring out in sharp relief the character of the truly good man which I oppose to it.

I know full well that by way of reply, these gentlemen try to insinuate that it is not the role of the theater to speak of these matters; but with their permission, I ask them on what do they base this fine doctrine. It is a proposition they advance as no more than a supposition, for which they offer not a shred of proof; and surely it would not be difficult to show them that comedy, for the ancients, had its origin in religion and constituted a part of its ceremonies; that our neighbors, the Spaniards, have hardly a single holiday celebration in which a comedy is not a part; and that even here in France, it owes its birth to the efforts of a religious brotherhood who still own the Hôtel de Bourgogne, where the most important mystery plays of our faith were presented;[3] that you can still find comedies printed in gothic letters under the name of a learned doctor[4] of the Sorbonne; and without going so far, in our own day the religious dramas of Pierre Corneille[5] have been performed to the admiration of all France.

If the function of comedy is to correct men's vices, I do not see why any should be exempt. Such a condition in our society would be much more dangerous than the thing itself; and we have seen that the theater is admirably suited to provide correction. The most forceful lines of a serious moral statement are usually less powerful than those of satire; and nothing will reform most men better than the depiction of their faults. It is a vigorous blow to vices to expose them to public laughter. Criticism is taken lightly, but men will not tolerate satire. They are quite willing to be mean, but they never like to be ridiculed.

I have been attacked for having placed words of piety in the mouth of my impostor. Could I avoid doing so in order to represent properly the character of a hypocrite? It seemed to me sufficient to reveal the criminal motives which make him speak as he does, and I have eliminated all ceremonial phrases, which nonetheless he would not have been found using incorrectly.

3. A reference to the *Confrérie de la Passion et Résurrection de Notre-Seigneur* (Fraternity of the passion and resurrection of our Savior), founded in 1402. The Hôtel de Bourgogne was a theater in rivalry with Molière's. 4. Probably Maistre Jehan Michel, a medical doctor who wrote mystery plays. 5. Corneille (1606–1684) and Racine were France's two greatest writers of classic tragedy. The two dramas that Molière doubtlessly had in mind were *Polyeucte* (1643) and *Théodore, vierge et martyre* (1646).

Yet some say that in the fourth act he sets forth a vicious morality; but is not this a morality which everyone has heard again and again? Does my comedy say anything new here? And is there any fear that ideas so thoroughly detested by everyone can make an impression on men's minds; that I make them dangerous by presenting them in the theater; that they acquire authority from the lips of a scoundrel? There is not the slightest suggestion of any of this; and one must either approve the comedy of *Tartuffe* or condemn all comedies in general.

This has indeed been done in a furious way for some time now, and never was the theater so much abused.[6] I cannot deny that there were Church Fathers who condemned comedy; but neither will it be denied me that there were some who looked on it somewhat more favorably. Thus authority, on which censure is supposed to depend, is destroyed by this disagreement; and the only conclusion that can be drawn from this difference of opinion among men enlightened by the same wisdom is that they viewed comedy in different ways, and that some considered it in its purity, while others regarded it in its corruption and confused it with all those wretched performances which have been rightly called performances of filth.

And in fact, since we should talk about things rather than words, and since most misunderstanding comes from including contrary notions in the same word, we need only to remove the veil of ambiguity and look at comedy in itself to see if it warrants condemnation. It will surely be recognized that as it is nothing more than a clever poem which corrects men's faults by means of agreeable lessons, it cannot be condemned without injustice. And if we listened to the voice of ancient times on this matter, it would tell us that its most famous philosophers have praised comedy—they who professed so austere a wisdom and who ceaselessly denounced the vices of their times. It would tell us that Aristotle spent his evenings at the theater[7] and took the trouble to reduce the art of making comedies to rules. It would tell us that some of its greatest and most honored men took pride in writing comedies themselves;[8] and that others did not disdain to recite them in public; that Greece expressed its admiration for this art by means of handsome prizes and magnificent theaters to honor it; and finally, that in Rome this same art also received extraordinary honors; I do not speak of Rome run riot under the license of the emperors, but of disciplined Rome, governed by the wisdom of the consuls, and in the age of the full vigor of Roman dignity.

I admit that there have been times when comedy became corrupt. And what do men not corrupt every day? There is nothing so innocent that men cannot turn it to crime; nothing so beneficial that its values cannot be reversed; nothing so good in itself that it cannot be put to bad uses. Medical knowledge benefits mankind and is revered as one of our most wonderful possessions; and yet there was a time when it fell into discredit, and was often used to poison men. Philosophy is a gift of Heaven; it has been given to us to bring us to the knowledge of a God by contemplating the wonders of nature; and yet we know that often it has been turned away from its

6. Molière had in mind Pierre Nicole's two attacks on the theater: *Visionnaires* (1666) and *Traité de la Comédie* (1667), as well as the prince de Conti's *Traité de la Comédie* (1666).   7. A reference to Aristotle's *Poetics* (composed between 335 and 322 B.C.E., the year of his death).   8. Scipio Africanus Minor (ca. 185–129 B.C.E.), the Roman consul and general responsible for the final destruction of Carthage in 146 B.C.E., collaborated with Terence (Publius Terentius Afer, ca. 195 or 185–ca. 159 B.C.E.), a writer of comedies.

function and has been used openly in support of impiety. Even the holiest of things are not immune from human corruption, and every day we see scoundrels who use and abuse piety, and wickedly make it serve the greatest of crimes. But this does not prevent one from making the necessary distinctions. We do not confuse in the same false inference the goodness of things that are corrupted with the wickedness of the corrupt. The function of an art is always distinguished from its misuse; and as medicine is not forbidden because it was banned in Rome,[9] nor philosophy because it was publicly condemned in Athens,[1] we should not suppress comedy simply because it has been condemned at certain times. This censure was justified then for reasons which no longer apply today; it was limited to what was then seen; and we should not seize on these limits, apply them more rigidly than is necessary, and include in our condemnation the innocent along with the guilty. The comedy that this censure attacked is in no way the comedy that we want to defend. We must be careful not to confuse the one with the other. There may be two persons whose morals may be completely different. They may have no resemblance to one another except in their names, and it would be a terrible injustice to want to condemn Olympia, who is a good woman, because there is also an Olympia who is lewd. Such procedures would make for great confusion everywhere. Everything under the sun would be condemned; now since this rigor is not applied to the countless instances of abuse we see every day, the same should hold for comedy, and those plays should be approved in which instruction and virtue reign supreme.

I know there are some so delicate that they cannot tolerate a comedy, who say that the most decent are the most dangerous, that the passions they present are all the more moving because they are virtuous, and that men's feelings are stirred by these presentations. I do not see what great crime it is to be affected by the sight of a generous passion; and this utter insensitivity to which they would lead us is indeed a high degree of virtue! I wonder if so great a perfection resides within the strength of human nature, and I wonder if it is not better to try to correct and moderate men's passions than to try to suppress them altogether. I grant that there are places better to visit than the theater; and if we want to condemn every single thing that does not bear directly on God and our salvation, it is right that comedy be included, and I should willingly grant that it be condemned along with everything else. But if we admit, as is in fact true, that the exercise of piety will permit interruptions, and that men need amusement, I maintain that there is none more innocent than comedy. I have dwelled too long on this matter. Let me finish with the words of a great prince on the comedy, *Tartuffe*.[2]

Eight days after it had been banned, a play called *Scaramouche the Hermit*[3] was performed before the court; and the king, on his way out, said to this great prince: "I should really like to know why the persons who make so much noise about Molière's comedy do not say a word about *Scaramouche*." To which the prince replied, "It is because the comedy of *Scaramouche* makes fun of Heaven and religion, which these gentlemen do not care about

---

9. Pliny the Elder says that the Romans expelled their doctors at the same time that the Greeks did theirs.
1. An allusion to Socrates' condemnation to death.   2. One of Molière's benefactors who liked the play was the prince de Condé; de Condé had *Tartuffe* read to him and also privately performed for him.   3. A troupe of Italian comedians had just performed the licentious farce, in which a hermit dressed as a monk makes love to a married woman, announcing that *questo e per mortificar la carne* ("this is to mortify the flesh").

at all, but that of Molière makes fun of *them,* and that is what they cannot bear."

THE AUTHOR

FIRST PETITION[4]

(Presented to the King on the Comedy of Tartuffe)

Sire,

As the duty of comedy is to correct men by amusing them, I believed that in my occupation I could do nothing better than attack the vices of my age by making them ridiculous; and as hypocrisy is undoubtedly one of the most common, most improper, and most dangerous, I thought, Sire, that I would perform a service for all good men of your kingdom if I wrote a comedy which denounced hypocrites and placed in proper view all of the contrived poses of these incredibly virtuous men, all of the concealed villainies of these counterfeit believers who would trap others with a fraudulent piety and a pretended virtue.

I have written this comedy, Sire, with all the care and caution that the delicacy of the subject demands; and so as to maintain all the more properly the admiration and respect due to truly devout men, I have delineated my character as sharply as I could; I have left no room for doubt; I have removed all that might confuse good with evil, and have used for this painting only the specific colors and essential lines that make one instantly recognize a true and brazen hypocrite.

Nevertheless, all my precautions have been to no avail. Others have taken advantage of the delicacy of your feelings on religious matters, and they have been able to deceive you on the only side of your character which lies open to deception: your respect for holy things. By underhanded means, the Tartuffes have skillfully gained Your Majesty's favor, and the models have succeeded in eliminating the copy, no matter how innocent it may have been and no matter what resemblance was found between them.

Although the suppression of this work was a serious blow for me, my misfortune was nonetheless softened by the way in which Your Majesty explained his attitude on the matter; and I believed, Sire, that Your Majesty removed any cause I had for complaint, as you were kind enough to declare that you found nothing in this comedy that you would forbid me to present in public.

Yet, despite this glorious declaration of the greatest and most enlightened king in the world, despite the approval of the Papal Legate[5] and of most of our churchmen, all of whom, at private readings of my work, agreed with the views of Your Majesty, despite all this, a book has appeared by a certain priest[6] which boldly contradicts all of these noble judgments. Your Majesty expressed himself in vain, and the Papal Legate and churchmen gave their opinion to no avail: sight unseen, my comedy is diabolical, and so is my brain;

---

4. The first of the three *petitions* or *placets* to Louis XIV concerning the play. On May 12, 1664, *Tartuffe*—or at least the first three acts roughly as they now stand—was performed at Versailles. A cabal unfavorable to Molière, including the archbishop of Paris, Hardouin de Perefixe, Queen Mother Anne of Austria, certain influential courtiers, and the Brotherhood or Company of the Holy Sacrament (formed in 1627 to enforce morality), arranged that the play be banned and Molière censured.   5. Cardinal Legate Agostino Chigi, nephew of Pope Alexander VII, heard a reading of *Tartuffe* at Fontainebleau on August 4, 1664.   6. Pierre Roullé, the curate of St. Barthélemy, who wrote a scathing attack on the play and sent his book to the king.

I am a devil garbed in flesh and disguised as a man,[7] a libertine, a disbeliever who deserves a punishment that will set an example. It is not enough that fire expiate my crime in public, for that would be letting me off too easily: the generous piety of this good man will not stop there; he will not allow me to find any mercy in the sight of God; he demands that I be damned, and that will settle the matter.

This book, Sire, was presented to Your Majesty; and I am sure that you see for yourself how unpleasant it is for me to be exposed daily to the insults of these gentlemen, what harm these abuses will do my reputation if they must be tolerated, and finally, how important it is for me to clear myself of these false charges and let the public know that my comedy is nothing more than what they want it to be. I will not ask, Sire, for what I need for the sake of my reputation and the innocence of my work: enlightened kings such as you do not need to be told what is wished of them; like God, they see what we need and know better than we what they should give us. It is enough for me to place my interests in Your Majesty's hands, and I respectfully await whatever you may care to command.

(August, 1664)

SECOND PETITION[8]

(Presented to the King in His Camp Before the City of Lille, in Flanders)

Sire,

It is bold indeed for me to ask a favor of a great monarch in the midst of his glorious victories; but in my present situation, Sire, where will I find protection anywhere but where I seek it, and to whom can I appeal against the authority of the power[9] that crushes me, if not to the source of power and authority, the just dispenser of absolute law, the sovereign judge and master of all?

My comedy, Sire, has not enjoyed the kindnesses of Your Majesty. All to no avail, I produced it under the title of *The Hypocrite* and disguised the principal character as a man of the world; in vain I gave him a little hat, long hair, a wide collar, a sword, and lace clothing,[1] softened the action and carefully eliminated all that I thought might provide even the shadow of grounds for discontent on the part of the famous models of the portrait I wished to present; nothing did any good. The conspiracy of opposition revived even at mere conjecture of what the play would be like. They found a way of persuading those who in all other matters plainly insist that they are not to be deceived. No sooner did my comedy appear than it was struck down by the very power which should impose respect; and all that I could do to save myself from the fury of this tempest was to say that Your Majesty had given me permission to present the play and I did not think it was necessary to ask this permission of others, since only Your Majesty could have refused it.

I have no doubt, Sire, that the men whom I depict in my comedy will

7. Molière took some of these phrases from Roullé.   8. On August 5, 1667, *Tartuffe* was performed at the Palais-Royal. The opposition—headed by the first president of parliament—brought in the police, and the play was stopped. Since Louis was campaigning in Flanders, friends of Molière brought the second *placet* to Lille. Louis had always been favorable toward the playwright; in August 1665 Molière's company, the Troupe de Monsieur (nominally sponsored by Louis's brother Philippe, duc d'Orléans), had become the Troupe du Roi.   9. President de Lanvignon, in charge of the Paris police.   1. There is evidence that in 1664 Tartuffe played his role dressed in a cassock, thus allying him more directly to the clergy.

employ every means possible to influence Your Majesty, and will use, as they have used already, those truly good men who are all the more easily deceived because they judge of others by themselves.[2] They know how to display all of their aims in the most favorable light; yet, no matter how pious they may seem, it is surely not the interests of God which stir them; they have proven this often enough in the comedies they have allowed to be performed hundreds of times without making the least objection. Those plays attacked only piety and religion, for which they care very little; but this play attacks and makes fun of them, and that is what they cannot bear. They will never forgive me for unmasking their hypocrisy in the eyes of everyone. And I am sure that they will not neglect to tell Your Majesty that people are shocked by my comedy. But the simple truth, Sire, is that all Paris is shocked only by its ban, that the most scrupulous persons have found its presentation worthwhile, and men are astounded that individuals of such known integrity should show so great a deference to people whom everyone should abominate and who are so clearly opposed to the true piety which they profess.

I respectfully await the judgment that Your Majesty will deign to pronounce: but it's certain, Sire, that I need not think of writing comedies if the Tartuffes are triumphant, if they thereby seize the right to persecute me more than ever, and find fault with even the most innocent lines that flow from my pen.

Let your goodness, Sire, give me protection against their envenomed rage, and allow me, at your return from so glorious a campaign, to relieve Your Majesty from the fatigue of his conquests, give him innocent pleasures after such noble accomplishments, and make the monarch laugh who makes all Europe tremble!

(August, 1667)

THIRD PETITION

(Presented to the King)

Sire,

A very honest doctor[3] whose patient I have the honor to be, promises and will legally contract to make me live another thirty years if I can obtain a favor for him from Your Majesty. I told him of his promise that I do not deserve so much, and that I should be glad to help him if he will merely agree not to kill me. This favor, Sire, is a post of canon at your royal chapel of Vincennes, made vacant by death.

May I dare to ask for this favor from Your Majesty on the very day of the glorious resurrection of Tartuffe, brought back to life by your goodness? By this first favor I have been reconciled with the devout, and the second will reconcile me with the doctors.[4] Undoubtedly this would be too much grace for me at one time, but perhaps it would not be too much for Your Majesty, and I await your answer to my petition with respectful hope.

(February, 1669)

---

2. Molière apparently did not know that de Lanvignon had been affiliated with the Company of the Holy Sacrament for the previous ten years.　3. A physician friend, M. de Mauvillain, who helped Molière with some of the medical details of Le Malade imaginaire.　4. Doctors are ridiculed to varying degrees in earlier plays of Molière: Dom Juan, L'Amour médecin, and Le Médecin malgré lui.

CHARACTERS[5]

MADAME PERNELLE, *Orgon's mother*
ORGON, *Elmire's husband*
ELMIRE, *Orgon's wife*
DAMIS, *Orgon's son, Elmire's stepson*
MARIANE, *Orgon's daughter, Elmire's
 stepdaughter, in love with Valère*

VALÈRE, *in love with Mariane*
CLÉANTE, *Orgon's brother-in-law*
TARTUFFE, *a hypocrite*
DORINE, *Mariane's lady's-maid*
M. LOYAL, *a bailiff*
A POLICE OFFICER
FLIPOTE, *Mme Pernelle's maid*

The scene throughout: ORGON's *house in Paris.*

Act I

SCENE 1[6]

MADAME PERNELLE *and* FLIPOTE, *her maid*, ELMIRE,
MARIANE, DORINE, DAMIS, CLÉANTE

MADAME PERNELLE   Come, come, Flipote; it's time I left this place.
ELMIRE   I can't keep up, you walk at such a pace.
MADAME PERNELLE   Don't trouble, child; no need to show me out.
   It's not your manners I'm concerned about.
ELMIRE   We merely pay you the respect we owe.   5
   But, Mother, why this hurry? Must you go?
MADAME PERNELLE   I must. This house appals me. No one in it
   Will pay attention for a single minute.   *She gets no attention*
   I offer good advice, but you won't hear it.
   Children, I take my leave much vexed in spirit.   10
   You all break in and chatter on and on.
   It's like a madhouse with the keeper gone.
DORINE   If . . .
MADAME PERNELLE
           Girl, you talk too much, and I'm afraid   → *rhyming*
   You're far too saucy for a lady's-maid.
   You push in everywhere and have your say.   15
DAMIS   But . . .
MADAME PERNELLE
           You, boy, grow more foolish every day.
   To think my grandson should be such a dunce!
   I've said a hundred times, if I've said it once,
   That if you keep the course on which you've started,
   You'll leave your worthy father broken-hearted.   20
MARIANE   I think . . .
MADAME PERNELLE   And you, his sister, seem so pure,
   So shy, so innocent, and so demure.

5. The name Tartuffe has been traced back to an older word associated with liar or charlatan: *truffer*, "to deceive" or "to cheat." Then there was also the Italian actor Tartufo, physically deformed and truffle-shaped. Most of the other names are typical of this genre of court comedy and possess rather elegant connotations of pastoral and *bergerie*. Dorine would be a *demoiselle de compagne* and not a mere maid—that is, a female companion to Mariane of roughly the same social status. This in part accounts for the liberties she takes in conversation with Orgon, Madame Pernelle, and others. Her name is short for Théodorine.   6. In French drama, the scene changes every time a character enters or exits.

But you know what they say about still waters. *[margin note: Still waters run deep?]*
I pity parents with secretive daughters.

ELMIRE   Now, Mother . . .

MADAME PERNELLE   And as for you, child, let me add   25
That your behavior is extremely bad,
And a poor example for these children, too.
Their dear, dead mother did far better than you.
You're much too free with money, and I'm distressed
To see you so elaborately dressed.   30
When it's one's husband that one aims to please,
One has no need of costly fripperies.

CLÉANTE   Oh, Madam, really . . .

MADAME PERNELLE   You are her brother, Sir,
And I respect and love you; yet if I were
My son, this lady's good and pious spouse,   35
I wouldn't make you welcome in my house.
You're full of worldly counsels which, I fear,
Aren't suitable for decent folk to hear.
I've spoken bluntly, Sir; but it behooves us
Not to mince words when righteous fervor moves us.   40

DAMIS   Your man Tartuffe is full of holy speeches . . .

MADAME PERNELLE   And practises precisely what he preaches.
He's a fine man, and should be listened to.
I will not hear him mocked by fools like you.

DAMIS   Good God! Do you expect me to submit   45
To the tyranny of that carping hypocrite? *[margin note: Tartuffe seen as a hypocrite.]*
Must we forgo all joys and satisfactions
Because that bigot censures all our actions?

DORINE   To hear him talk—and he talks all the time—
There's nothing one can do that's not a crime. *[margin note: He condemns all]*   50
He rails at everything, your dear Tartuffe.

MADAME PERNELLE   Whatever he reproves deserves reproof.
He's out to save your souls, and all of you
Must love him, as my son would have you do. *[margin note: She believes he is righteous.]*

DAMIS   Ah no, Grandmother, I could never take   55
To such a rascal, even for my father's sake.
That's how I feel, and I shall not dissemble.
His every action makes me seethe and tremble
With helpless anger, and I have no doubt *[margin note: Damis is angered by Tartuffe & won't heed him.]*
That he and I will shortly have it out.   60

DORINE   Surely it is a shame and a disgrace
To see this man usurp the master's place— *[margin note: God's place?]*
To see this beggar who, when first he came,
Had not a shoe or shoestring to his name
So far forget himself that he behaves   65
As if the house were his, and we his slaves.

MADAME PERNELLE   Well, mark my words, your souls would fare far better
If you obeyed his precepts to the letter.

DORINE   You see him as a saint. I'm far less awed;
In fact, I see right through him. He's a fraud.   70

[left margin note: He likes to hear himself talk (pride)]

[left margin note: Madame Pernelle is blindly toward the truth about Tartuffe; Dorine sees the fraud behind the facade]

MADAME PERNELLE   Nonsense!

DORINE   His man Laurent's the same, or worse;
  I'd not trust either with a penny purse.   *The maid doesn't trust Turtuffe's servant.*

MADAME PERNELLE   I can't say what his servant's morals may be;
  His own great goodness I can guarantee.
  You all regard him with distaste and fear   75
  Because he tells you what you're loath to hear,   → *She thinks others*
  Condemns your sins, points out your moral flaws,   *dislike Turtuffe's*
  And humbly strives to further Heaven's cause.   *instructions becaus*
                                                       the people are
DORINE   If sin is all that bothers him, why is it *immoral*
  He's so upset when folk drop in to visit?   80
  Is Heaven so outraged by a social call
  That he must prophesy against us all?   ← *Turtuffe doesn't like*
  I'll tell you what I think: if you ask me,   *unannounced visitors.*
  He's jealous of my mistress' company.

MADAME PERNELLE   Rubbish!
  [To ELMIRE.]
                              He's not alone, child, in complaining   85
  Of all of your promiscuous entertaining.
  Why, the whole neighborhood's upset, I know,
  By all these carriages that come and go,
  With crowds of guests parading in and out
  And noisy servants loitering about.   90
  In all of this, I'm sure there's nothing vicious;
  But why give people cause to be suspicious?

CLÉANTE   They need no cause; they'll talk in any case.
  Madam, this world would be a joyless place
  If, fearing what malicious tongues might say,   95
  We locked our doors and turned our friends away.
  And even if one did so dreary a thing,
  D' you think those tongues would cease their chattering?
  One can't fight slander; it's a losing battle;
  Let us instead ignore their tittle-tattle.   → *One should live rightly*
  Let's strive to live by conscience' clear decrees, *and without fear*   100
  And let the gossips gossip as they please.   *of slander,*

DORINE   If there is talk against us, I know the source:
  It's Daphne and her little husband, of course.
  Those who have greatest cause for guilt and shame   105
  Are quickest to besmirch a neighbor's name.
  When there's a chance for libel, they never miss it;   → *They tell other*
  When something can be made to seem illicit   *gossip*
  They're off at once to spread the joyous news,
  Adding to fact what fantasies they choose.   110
  By talking up their neighbor's indiscretions
  They seek to camouflage their own transgressions,
  Hoping that others' innocent affairs
  Will lend a hue of innocence to theirs,
  Or that their own black guilt will come to seem   115
  Part of a general shady color-scheme.

MADAME PERNELLE   All this is quite irrelevant. I doubt

That anyone's more virtuous and devout
Than dear Orante; and I'm informed that she
Condemns your mode of life most vehemently.   120
DORINE   Oh, yes, she's strict, devout, and has no taint
Of worldliness; in short, she seems a saint.
But it was time which taught her that disguise;
She's thus because she can't be otherwise.
So long as her attractions could enthrall,   125
She flounced and flirted and enjoyed it all,
But now that they're no longer what they were
She quits a world which fast is quitting her,
And wears a veil of virtue to conceal
Her bankrupt beauty and her lost appeal.   130
That's what becomes of old coquettes today:
Distressed when all their lovers fall away,
They see no recourse but to play the prude,
And so confer a style on solitude.
Thereafter, they're severe with everyone,   135
Condemning all our actions, pardoning none,
And claiming to be pure, austere, and zealous
When, if the truth were known, they're merely jealous,
And cannot bear to see another know
The pleasures time has forced them to forgo.   140
MADAME PERNELLE [Initially to ELMIRE.]
That sort of talk[7] is what you like to hear;
Therefore you'd have us all keep still, my dear,
While Madam rattles on the livelong day.
Nevertheless, I mean to have my say.
I tell you that you're blest to have Tartuffe   145
Dwelling, as my son's guest, beneath this roof;
That Heaven has sent him to forestall its wrath
By leading you, once more, to the true path;
That all he reprehends is reprehensible,
And that you'd better heed him, and be sensible.   150
These visits, balls, and parties in which you revel
Are nothing but inventions of the Devil.
One never hears a word that's edifying:
Nothing but chaff and foolishness and lying,
As well as vicious gossip in which one's neighbor   155
Is cut to bits with épée, foil, and saber.
People of sense are driven half-insane
At such affairs, where noise and folly reign
And reputations perish thick and fast.
As a wise preacher said on Sunday last,   160
Parties are Towers of Babylon,[8] because
The guests all babble on with never a pause;
And then he told a story which, I think . . .

---

7. In the original, a reference to a collection of novels about chivalry found in *La Bibliothèque bleue* (The Blue Library), written for children.   8. Tower of Babel. Madame Pernelle's malapropism is the cause of Cléante's laughter.

[Handwritten marginalia:]
Orante — She has to be a hypocrite because she wouldn't appear to be good otherwise.
She veils her own corruption.
They act one way to disguise what they feel. (Jealousy)

[*To* CLÉANTE.] I heard that laugh, Sir, and I saw that wink!
Go find your silly friends and laugh some more!   165
Enough; I'm going; don't show me to the door.
I leave this household much dismayed and vexed;
I cannot say when I shall see you next.
      [*Slapping* FLIPOTE.]
Wake up, don't stand there gaping into space!
I'll slap some sense into that stupid face.   170
Move, move, you slut.

SCENE 2

CLÉANTE, DORINE

CLÉANTE   I think I'll stay behind;
I want no further pieces of her mind.
How that old lady . . .
DORINE   Oh, what wouldn't she say
If she could hear you speak of her that way!
She'd thank you for the *lady,* but I'm sure   5
She'd find the *old* a little premature.
CLÉANTE   My, what a scene she made, and what a din!
And how this man Tartuffe has taken her in!
DORINE   Yes, but her son is even worse deceived;
His folly must be seen to be believed.   10
In the late troubles,[9] he played an able part
And served his king with wise and loyal heart,
But he's quite lost his senses since he fell
Beneath Tartuffe's infatuating spell.
He calls him brother, and loves him as his life,   15
Preferring him to mother, child, or wife.
In him and him alone will he confide;
He's made him his confessor and his guide;
He pets and pampers him with love more tender
Than any pretty maiden could engender,   20
Gives him the place of honor when they dine,
Delights to see him gorging like a swine,
Stuffs him with dainties till his guts distend,
And when he belches, cries "God bless you, friend!"
In short, he's mad; he worships him; he dotes;   25
His deeds he marvels at, his words, he quotes,
Thinking each act a miracle, each word
Oracular as those that Moses heard.
Tartuffe, much pleased to find so easy a victim,
Has in a hundred ways beguiled and tricked him,   30
Milked him of money, and with his permission
Established here a sort of Inquisition.

---

9. A series of political disturbances during the minority of Louis XIV. Specifically, these consisted of the *Fronde* ("opposition") of the Parlement (1648–49) and the *Fronde* of the Princes (1650–53). Orgon is depicted as supporting Louis XIV in these outbreaks and their resolution.

Tartuffe's servant is bad as well

Even Laurent, his lackey, dares to give
Us arrogant advice on how to live;
He sermonizes us in thundering tones   35
And confiscates our ribbons and colognes.
Last week he tore a kerchief into pieces
Because he found it pressed in a *Life of Jesus*:
He said it was a sin to juxtapose
Unholy vanities and holy prose.   40

SCENE 3

ELMIRE, MARIANE, DAMIS, CLÉANTE, DORINE

ELMIRE [*To* CLÉANTE.]   You did well not to follow; she stood in the door
And said *verbatim* all she'd said before.
I saw my husband coming. I think I'd best
Go upstairs now, and take a little rest.
CLÉANTE   I'll wait and greet him here; then I must go.   5
I've really only time to say hello.
DAMIS   Sound him about my sister's wedding, please.
I think Tartuffe's against it, and that he's
Been urging Father to withdraw his blessing.
As you well know, I'd find that most distressing.   10
Unless my sister and Valère can marry,
My hopes to wed *his* sister will miscarry.
And I'm determined . . .
DORINE   He's coming.

SCENE 4

ORGON, CLÉANTE, DORINE

ORGON   Ah, Brother, good-day.
CLÉANTE   Well, welcome back, I'm sorry I can't stay.
How was the country? Blooming, I trust, and green?
ORGON   Excuse me, Brother; just one moment.
[*To* DORINE.]   Dorine . . .
[*To* CLÉANTE.] To put my mind at rest, I always learn   5
The household news the moment I return.
[*To* DORINE.] Has all been well, these two days I've been gone?
How are the family? What's been going on?
DORINE   Your wife, two days ago, had a bad fever,
And a fierce headache which refused to leave her.   10
ORGON   Ah. And Tartuffe?
DORINE   Tartuffe? Why, he's round and red.
Bursting with health, and excellently fed.
ORGON   Poor fellow!
DORINE   That night, the mistress was unable
To take a single bite at the dinner-table.
Her headache-pains, she said, were simply hellish.   15

ORGON   Ah. And Tartuffe?

DORINE   He ate his meal with relish,
  And zealously devoured in her presence
  A leg of mutton and a brace of pheasants.

ORGON   Poor fellow!

DORINE   Well, the pains continued strong,
  And so she tossed and tossed the whole night long,   20
  Now icy-cold, now burning like a flame.
  We sat beside her bed till morning came.

ORGON   Ah. And Tartuffe?

DORINE   Why, having eaten, he rose
  And sought his room, already in a doze,
  Got into his warm bed, and snored away   25
  In perfect peace until the break of day.

ORGON   Poor fellow!

DORINE   After much ado, we talked her
  Into dispatching someone for the doctor.
  He bled her, and the fever quickly fell.

ORGON   Ah. And Tartuffe?

DORINE   He bore it very well.   30
  To keep his cheerfulness at any cost,
  And make up for the blood Madame had lost,
  He drank, at lunch, four beakers full of port.

ORGON   Poor fellow.

DORINE   Both are doing well, in short.
  I'll go and tell Madame that you've expressed
  Keen sympathy and anxious interest.   35

SCENE 5

ORGON, CLÉANTE

CLÉANTE   That girl was laughing in your face, and though
  I've no wish to offend you, even so
  I'm bound to say that she had some excuse.
  How can you possibly be such a goose?
  Are you so dazed by this man's hocus-pocus   5
  That all the world, save him, is out of focus?
  You've given him clothing, shelter, food, and care;
  Why must you also . . .

ORGON   Brother, stop right there.
  You do not know the man of whom you speak.

CLÉANTE   I grant you that. But my judgment's not so weak   10
  That I can't tell, by his effect on others . . .

ORGON   Ah, when you meet him, you two will be like brothers!
  There's been no loftier soul since time began.
  He is a man who . . . a man who. . . . an excellent man.
  To keep his precepts is to be reborn,   15
  And view this dunghill of a world with scorn.
  Yes, thanks to him I'm a changed man indeed.

[Handwritten margin notes: "Four times Orgon asks about Tartuffe but seems unconcerned about his wife." "Orgon is more concerned about Tartuffe than his wife's illness" "Cleante approaches his brother Orgon about his unwholesome alliance with the hypocrite Tartuffe."]

Under his tutelage my soul's been freed
From earthly loves, and every human tie:
My mother, children, brother, and wife could die,   20
And I'd not feel a single moment's pain.
CLÉANTE   That's a fine sentiment, Brother; most humane.
ORGON   Oh, had you seen Tartuffe as I first knew him,
Your heart, like mine, would have surrendered to him.
He used to come into our church each day   25
And humbly kneel nearby, and start to pray.
He'd draw the eyes of everybody there
By the deep fervor of his heartfelt prayer;
He'd sigh and weep, and sometimes with a sound
Of rapture he would bend and kiss the ground;   30
And when I rose to go, he'd run before
To offer me holy-water at the door.
His serving-man, no less devout than he,
Informed me of his master's poverty;
I gave him gifts, but in his humbleness   35
He'd beg me every time to give him less.
"Oh, that's too much," he'd cry, "too much by twice!
I don't deserve it. The half, Sir, would suffice."
And when I wouldn't take it back, he'd share
Half of it with the poor, right then and there.   40
At length, Heaven prompted me to take him in
To dwell with us, and free our souls from sin.
He guides our lives, and to protect my honor
Stays by my wife, and keeps an eye upon her;
He tells me whom she sees, and all she does,   45
And seems more jealous than I ever was!
And how austere he is! Why, he can detect
A moral sin where you would least suspect;
In smallest trifles, he's extremely strict.
Last week, his conscience was severely pricked   50
Because, while praying, he had caught a flea
And killed it, so he felt, too wrathfully.[1]
CLÉANTE   Good God, man! Have you lost your common sense—
Or is this all some joke at my expense?
How can you stand there and in all sobriety . . .   55
ORGON   Brother, your language savors of impiety.
Too much free-thinking's made your faith unsteady,
And as I've warned you many times already,
'Twill get you into trouble before you're through.
CLÉANTE   So I've been told before by dupes like you: 60
Being blind, you'd have all others blind as well;
The clear-eyed man you call an infidel,
And he who sees through humbug and pretense
Is charged, by you, with want of reverence.

1. In the *Golden Legend* (*Legenda aurea*), a popular collection of the lives of the saints written in the thirteenth century, it is said of St. Macarius the Elder (d. 390) that he dwelt naked in the desert for six months, a penance he felt appropriate for having killed a flea.

Spare me your warnings, Brother; I have no fear   65
Of speaking out, for you and Heaven to hear,
Against affected zeal and pious knavery.
There's true and false in piety, as in bravery,
And just as those whose courage shines the most
In battle, are the least inclined to boast,   70
So those whose hearts are truly pure and lowly
Don't make a flashy show of being holy.
There's a vast difference, so it seems to me,
Between true piety and hypocrisy:
How do you fail to see it, may I ask?   75
Is not a face quite different from a mask?
Cannot sincerity and cunning art,
Reality and semblance, be told apart?
Are scarecrows just like men, and do you hold
That a false coin is just as good as gold?   80
Ah, Brother, man's a strangely fashioned creature
Who seldom is content to follow Nature,
But recklessly pursues his inclination
Beyond the narrow bounds of moderation,
And often, by transgressing Reason's laws,   85
Perverts a lofty aim or noble cause.
A passing observation, but it applies.
ORGON   I see, dear Brother, that you're profoundly wise;
You harbor all the insight of the age.
You are our one clear mind, our only sage,   90
The era's oracle, its Cato[2] too,
And all mankind are fools compared to you.
CLÉANTE   Brother, I don't pretend to be a sage,
Nor have I all the wisdom of the age.
There's just one insight I would dare to claim: 95
I know that true and false are not the same;
And just as there is nothing I more revere
Than a soul whose faith is steadfast and sincere,
Nothing that I more cherish and admire
Than honest zeal and true religious fire,   100
So there is nothing that I find more base
Than specious piety's dishonest face—
Than these bold mountebanks, these histrios
Whose impious mummeries and hollow shows
Exploit our love of Heaven, and make a jest   105
Of all that men think holiest and best;
These calculating souls who offer prayers
Not to their Maker, but as public wares,
And seek to buy respect and reputation
With lifted eyes and sighs of exaltation;   110
These charlatans, I say, whose pilgrim souls
Proceed, by way of Heaven, toward earthly goals,

2. Roman statesman (95–46 B.C.E.) with an enduring reputation for honesty and incorruptibility.

Who weep and pray and swindle and extort,
Who preach the monkish life, but haunt the court,
Who make their zeal the partner of their vice—   115
Such men are vengeful, sly, and cold as ice,
And when there is an enemy to defame
They cloak their spite in fair religion's name,
Their private spleen and malice being made
To seem a high and virtuous crusade,   120
Until, to mankind's reverent applause,
They crucify their foe in Heaven's cause.
Such knaves are all too common; yet, for the wise,
True piety isn't hard to recognize,
And, happily, these present times provide us   125
With bright examples to instruct and guide us.
Consider Ariston and Périandre;
Look at Oronte, Alcidamas, Clitandre;[3]
Their virtue is acknowledged; who could doubt it?
But you won't hear them beat the drum about it.   130
They're never ostentatious, never vain,
And their religion's moderate and humane;
It's not their way to criticize and chide:
They think censoriousness a mark of pride,
And therefore, letting others preach and rave,   135
They show, by deeds, how Christians should behave.
They think no evil of their fellow man,
But judge of him as kindly as they can.
They don't intrigue and wangle and conspire;
To lead a good life is their one desire;   140
The sinner wakes no rancorous hate in them;
It is the sin alone which they condemn;
Nor do they try to show a fiercer zeal
For Heaven's cause than Heaven itself could feel.
These men I honor, these men I advocate   145
As models for us all to emulate.
Your man is not their sort at all, I fear:
And, while your praise of him is quite sincere,
I think that you've been dreadfully deluded.
ORGON   Now then, dear Brother, is your speech concluded?   150
CLÉANTE   Why, yes.
ORGON   Your servant, Sir.
         [*He turns to go.*]
CLÉANTE   No, Brother; wait.
There's one more matter. You agreed of late
That young Valère might have your daughter's hand.
ORGON   I did.
CLÉANTE   And set the date, I understand.
ORGON   Quite so.
CLÉANTE   You've now postponed it; is that true?   155

---

3. Vaguely Greek and Roman names derived from the elegant literature of the day.

ORGON   No doubt.

CLÉANTE   The match no longer pleases you?

ORGON   Who knows?

CLÉANTE   D'you mean to go back on your word?

ORGON   I won't say that.

CLÉANTE   Has anything occurred
  Which might entitle you to break your pledge?

ORGON   Perhaps.

CLÉANTE   Why must you hem, and haw, and hedge?   160
  The boy asked me to sound you in this affair . . . .

ORGON   It's been a pleasure.

CLÉANTE   But what shall I tell Valère?

ORGON   Whatever you like.

CLÉANTE   But what have you decided?
  What are your plans?

ORGON   I plan, Sir, to be guided
  By Heaven's will.

CLÉANTE   Come, Brother, don't talk rot.   165
  You've given Valère your word; will you keep it, or not?

ORGON   Good day.

CLÉANTE   This looks like poor Valère's undoing;
  I'll go and warn him that there's trouble brewing.

Cléante suspects his brother Orgon of scheming.

Act II

SCENE 1

ORGON, MARIANE

ORGON   Mariane.

MARIANE.   Yes, Father?

ORGON   A word with you; come here.

MARIANE   What are you looking for?

ORGON [*Peering into a small closet.*]   Eavesdroppers, dear.
  I'm making sure we shan't be overheard.
  Someone in there could catch our every word.
  Ah, good, we're safe. Now, Mariane, my child,   5
  You're a sweet girl who's tractable and mild,
  Whom I hold dear, and think most highly of.

Orgon is suspicious

MARIANE   I'm deeply grateful, Father, for your love.

ORGON   That's well said, Daughter; and you can repay me
  If, in all things, you'll cheerfully obey me.   10

MARIANE   To please you, Sir, is what delights me best.

ORGON   Good, good. Now, what d'you think of Tartuffe, our guest?

MARIANE   I, Sir?

ORGON   Yes. Weigh your answer; think it through.

MARIANE   Oh, dear. I'll say whatever you wish me to.

ORGON   That's wisely said, my Daughter. Say of him, then,   15
  That he's the very worthiest of men,
  And that you're fond of him, and would rejoice

Orgon tells Mariane what to say.

In being his wife, if that should be my choice.
Well?
MARIANE   What?
ORGON   What's that?
MARIANE   I . . .
ORGON   Well?
MARIANE   Forgive me, pray.
ORGON   Did you not hear me?
MARIANE   Of *whom*, Sir, must I say   20
That I am fond of him, and would rejoice
In being his wife, if that should be your choice?
ORGON   Why, of Tartuffe.
MARIANE   But, Father, that's false, you know.
Why would you have me say what isn't so?
ORGON   Because I am resolved it shall be true.   25
That it's my wish should be enough for you.
MARIANE   You can't mean, Father . . .
ORGON   Yes, Tartuffe shall be
Allied by marriage[4] to this family,
And he's to be your husband, is that clear?
It's a father's privilege . . .   30

SCENE 2

DORINE, ORGON, MARIANE

ORGON [*To* DORINE.]   What are you doing in here?
Is curiosity so fierce a passion
With you, that you must eavesdrop in this fashion?
DORINE   There's lately been a rumor going about—
Based on some hunch or chance remark, no doubt—   5
That you mean Mariane to wed Tartuffe.
I've laughed it off, of course, as just a spoof.
ORGON   You find it so incredible?
DORINE   Yes, I do.
I won't accept that story, even from you.
ORGON   Well, you'll believe it when the thing is done.   10
DORINE   Yes, yes, of course. Go on and have your fun.
ORGON   I've never been more serious in my life.
DORINE   Ha!
ORGON   Daughter, I mean it; you're to be his wife.
DORINE   No, don't believe your father; it's all a hoax.
ORGON   See here, young woman . . .
DORINE   Come, Sir, no more jokes;   15
You can't fool us.
ORGON   How dare you talk that way?

4. This assertion is important and more than a mere device in the plot of the day. The second *placet*, or petition, insists that Tartuffe be costumed as a layman, and Orgon's plan for him to marry again asserts Tartuffe's position in the laity. In the 1664 version of the play Tartuffe had been dressed in a cassock, suggesting the priesthood, and Molière was now anxious to avoid any suggestion of this kind.

DORINE All right, then: we believe you, sad to say.
　　　But how a man like you, who looks so wise
　　　And wears a moustache of such splendid size,
　　　Can be so foolish as to . . .
ORGON　　　　　　　　　Silence, please!　　　　　　20
　　　My girl, you take too many liberties.
　　　I'm master here, as you must not forget.
DORINE Do let's discuss this calmly; don't be upset.
　　　You can't be serious, Sir, about this plan.
　　　What should that bigot want with Mariane?　　　25
　　　Praying and fasting ought to keep him busy.
　　　And then, in terms of wealth and rank, what is he?
　　　Why should a man of property like you
　　　Pick out a beggar son-in-law?
ORGON　　　　　　　　　　That will do.
　　　Speak of his poverty with reverence.　　　　30
　　　His is a pure and saintly indigence
　　　Which far transcends all worldly pride and pelf.
　　　He lost his fortune, as he says himself, ← *Tartuffe claims to be penniless*
　　　Because he cared for Heaven alone, and so
　　　Was careless of his interests here below.　　　35
　　　I mean to get him out of his present straits
　　　And help him to recover his estates—
　　　Which, in his part of the world, have no small fame.
　　　Poor though he is, he's a gentleman just the same.
DORINE Yes, so he tells us; and, Sir, it seems to me　　40
　　　Such pride goes very ill with piety.
　　　A man whose spirit spurns this dungy earth
　　　Ought not to brag of lands and noble birth;
　　　Such worldly arrogance will hardly square
　　　With meek devotion and the life of prayer.　　　45
　　　. . . But this approach, I see, has drawn a blank;
　　　Let's speak, then, of his person, not his rank.
　　　Doesn't it seem to you a trifle grim
　　　To give a girl like her to a man like him?
　　　When two are so ill-suited, can't you see　　　50
　　　What the sad consequence is bound to be?
　　　A young girl's virtue is imperilled, Sir,
　　　When such a marriage is imposed on her;
　　　For if one's bridegroom isn't to one's taste,
　　　It's hardly an inducement to be chaste,　　　55
　　　And many a man with horns upon his brow
　　　Has made his wife the thing that she is now.
　　　It's hard to be a faithful wife, in short,
　　　To certain husbands of a certain sort,
　　　And he who gives his daughter to a man she hates　　60
　　　Must answer for her sins at Heaven's gates.
　　　Think, Sir, before you play so risky a role.
ORGON This servant-girl presumes to save my soul!
DORINE You would do well to ponder what I've said.

ORGON   Daughter, we'll disregard this dunderhead.   65
  Just trust your father's judgment. Oh, I'm aware
  That I once promised you to young Valère;
  But now I hear he gambles, which greatly shocks me;
  What's more, I've doubts about his orthodoxy.
  His visits to church, I note, are very few.   70
DORINE   Would you have him go at the same hours as you,
  And kneel nearby, to be sure of being seen?
ORGON   I can dispense with such remarks, Dorine.
  [*To* MARIANE.] Tartuffe, however, is sure of Heaven's blessing.
  And that's the only treasure worth possessing.   75
  This match will bring you joys beyond all measure;
  Your cup will overflow with every pleasure;
  You two will interchange your faithful loves
  Like two sweet cherubs, or two turtle-doves.
  No harsh word shall be heard, no frown be seen,   80
  And he shall make you happy as a queen.
DORINE   And she'll make him a cuckold, just wait and see.
ORGON   What language!
DORINE   Oh, he's a man of destiny;
  He's *made* for horns, and what the stars demand
  Your daughter's virtue surely can't withstand.   85
ORGON   Don't interrupt me further. Why can't you learn
  That certain things are none of your concern?
DORINE   It's for your own sake that I interfere.
      [*She repeatedly interrupts* ORGON *just as he is turning to speak to his*
      daughter.]
ORGON   Most kind of you. Now, hold your tongue, d'you hear?
DORINE   If I didn't love you . . .
ORGON   Spare me your affection.   90
DORINE   I'll love you, Sir, in spite of your objection.
ORGON   Blast!
DORINE   I can't bear, Sir, for your honor's sake,
  To let you make this ludicrous mistake.
ORGON   You mean to go on talking?
DORINE   If I didn't protest
  This sinful marriage, my conscience couldn't rest.   95
ORGON   If you don't hold your tongue, you little shrew . . .
DORINE   What, lost your temper? A pious man like you?
ORGON   Yes! Yes! You talk and talk. I'm maddened by it.
  Once and for all, I tell you to be quiet.
DORINE   Well, I'll be quiet. But I'll be thinking hard.   100
ORGON   Think all you like, but you had better guard
  That saucy tongue of yours, or I'll . . .
  [*Turning back to* MARIANE.]   Now, child,
  I've weighed this matter fully.
DORINE [*Aside.*]   It drives me wild
  That I can't speak.
      [ORGON *turns his head, and she is silent.*]
ORGON   Tartuffe is no young dandy,
  But, still, his person . . .

[handwritten marginal notes:] Dorine compelled to do/say what she wants. Orgon loses his temper. He is not entirely as pious as he thinks.

DORINE [*Aside.*]   Is as sweet as candy.   105
ORGON   Is such that, even if you shouldn't care
  For his other merits . . .
        [*He turns and stands facing* DORINE, *arms crossed.*]
DORINE [*Aside.*]   They'll make a lovely pair.
  If I were she, no man would marry me
  Against my inclination, and go scot-free.
  He'd learn, before the wedding-day was over,   110
  How readily a wife can find a lover.
ORGON [*To* DORINE.]   It seems you treat my orders as a joke.
DORINE   Why, what's the matter? 'Twas not to you I spoke.
ORGON   What *were* you doing?
DORINE   Talking to myself, that's all.
ORGON   Ah! [*Aside.*] One more bit of impudence and gall,   115
  And I shall give her a good slap in the face.
        [*He puts himself in position to slap her;* DORINE, *whenever he glances at
        her, stands immobile and silent.*]
  Daughter, you shall accept, and with good grace,
  The husband I've selected . . . Your wedding-day . . .
  [*To* DORINE.] Why don't you talk to yourself?
DORINE   I've nothing to say.
ORGON   Come, just one word.
DORINE   No thank you, Sir. I pass.   120
ORGON   Come, speak; I'm waiting.
DORINE   I'd not be such an ass.
ORGON [*Turning to* MARIANE.]
  In short, dear Daughter, I mean to be obeyed,
  And you must bow to the sound choice I've made.
DORINE [*Moving away.*]   I'd not wed such a monster, even in jest.
        [ORGON *attempts to slap her, but misses.*]
ORGON   Daughter, that maid of yours is a thorough pest;   125
  She makes me sinfully annoyed and nettled.
  I can't speak further; my nerves are too unsettled.
  She's so upset me by her insolent talk,
  I'll calm myself by going for a walk.

SCENE 3

DORINE, MARIANE

DORINE [*Returning.*]   Well, have you lost your tongue, girl? Must I play
  Your part, and say the lines you ought to say?
  Faced with a fate so hideous and absurd,
  Can you not utter one dissenting word?
MARIANE   What good would it do? A father's power is great.
DORINE   Resist him now, or it will be too late.   5
MARIANE   But . . .
DORINE   Tell him one cannot love at a father's whim;
  That you shall marry for yourself, not him;
  That since it's you who are to be the bride,
  It's you, not he, who must be satisfied;   10

[Handwritten marginal notes:]
Dorine would spurn Tartuffe if she were Mariane
Orgon acts physically violent toward the maid
Orgon can see he has been roused
Does Mariane see resisting as futile?

And that if his Tartuffe is so sublime,
He's free to marry him at any time.

MARIANE   I've bowed so long to Father's strict control,
I couldn't oppose him now, to save my soul.

DORINE   Come, come, Mariane. Do listen to reason, won't you?   15
Valère has asked your hand. Do you love him, or don't you?

MARIANE   Oh, how unjust of you! What can you mean
By asking such a question, dear Dorine?
You know the depth of my affection for him;
I've told you a hundred times how I adore him.   20

DORINE   I don't believe in everything I hear;
Who knows if your professions were sincere?

MARIANE   They were, Dorine, and you do me wrong to doubt it;
Heaven knows that I've been all too frank about it.

DORINE   You love him, then?

MARIANE   Oh, more than I can express.   25

DORINE   And he, I take it, cares for you no less?

MARIANE   I think so.

DORINE   And you both, with equal fire,
Burn to be married?

MARIANE   That is our one desire.

DORINE   What of Tartuffe, then? What of your father's plan?

MARIANE   I'll kill myself, if I'm forced to wed that man.   30

DORINE   I hadn't thought of that recourse. How splendid!
Just die, and all your troubles will be ended!
A fine solution. Oh, it maddens me
To hear you talk in that self-pitying key.

MARIANE   Dorine, how harsh you are! It's most unfair.   35
You have no sympathy for my despair.

DORINE   I've none at all for people who talk drivel
And, faced with difficulties, whine and snivel.

MARIANE   No doubt I'm timid, but it would be wrong . . .

DORINE   True love requires a heart that's firm and strong.   40

MARIANE   I'm strong in my affection for Valère,
But coping with my father is his affair.

DORINE   But if your father's brain has grown so cracked
Over his dear Tartuffe that he can retract
His blessing, though your wedding-day was named,   45
It's surely not Valère who's to be blamed.

MARIANE   If I defied my father, as you suggest,
Would it not seem unmaidenly, at best?
Shall I defend my love at the expense
Of brazenness and disobedience?   50
Shall I parade my heart's desires, and flaunt . . .

DORINE   No, I ask nothing of you. Clearly you want
To be Madame Tartuffe, and I feel bound
Not to oppose a wish so very sound.
What right have I to criticize the match?   55
Indeed, my dear, the man's a brilliant catch.
Monsieur Tartuffe! Now, there's a man of weight!

Yes, yes, Monsieur Tartuffe, I'm bound to state,
Is quite a person; that's not to be denied;
'Twill be no little thing to be his bride.   60
The world already rings with his renown;
He's a great noble—in his native town;
His ears are red, he has a pink complexion,
And all in all, he'll suit you to perfection.

MARIANE Dear God!

DORINE   Oh, how triumphant you will feel   65
At having caught a husband so ideal!

MARIANE Oh, do stop teasing, and use your cleverness
To get me out of this appalling mess.
Advise me, and I'll do whatever you say.

Mariane seeks Dorine's advice about what she should do.

DORINE Ah, no, a dutiful daughter must obey   70
Her father, even if he weds her to an ape.
You've a bright future; why struggle to escape?
Tartuffe will take you back where his family lives,
To a small town aswarm with relatives—
Uncles and cousins whom you'll be charmed to meet.   75
You'll be received at once by the elite,
Calling upon the bailiff's[5] wife, no less—
Even, perhaps, upon the mayoress,[6]
Who'll sit you down in the *best* kitchen chair.[7]
Then, once a year, you'll dance at the village fair   80
To the drone of bagpipes—two of them, in fact—
And see a puppet-show, or an animal act.[8]
Your husband . . .

MARIANE   Oh, you turn my blood to ice!
Stop torturing me, and give me your advice.

DORINE [*Threatening to go.*]
Your servant, Madam.

MARIANE   Dorine, I beg of you . . .   85

DORINE No, you deserve it; this marriage must go through.

MARIANE Dorine!

MARIANE   No.

MARIANE   Not Tartuffe! You know I think him . . .

DORINE Tartuffe's your cup of tea, and you shall drink him.

MARIANE I've always told you everything, and relied . . .

DORINE No. You deserve to be tartuffified.   90

MARIANE Well, since you mock me and refuse to care,
I'll henceforth seek my solace in despair:
Despair shall be my counsellor and friend,
And help me bring my sorrows to an end. [*She starts to leave.*]

DORINE There now, come back; my anger has subsided.   95
You do deserve some pity, I've decided.

Dorine tests Mariane's distaste for Tartuffe.

5. A high-ranking official in the judiciary, not simply a sheriff's deputy, as today.   6. The wife of a tax collector (*élue*), an important official controlling imports, elected by the Estates-General.   7. In elegant society of Molière's day, there was a hierarchy of seats, and the use of each was determined by rank. The seats descended from *fauteuils* to *chaises, perroquets, tabourets*, and *pliants*. Thus, Mariane would get the lowest seat in the room.   8. In the original, *fagotin*, literally "a monkey dressed up in a man's clothing."

MARIANE   Dorine, if Father makes me undergo *mariane will die*
This dreadful martyrdom, I'll die, I know.
DORINE   Don't fret; it won't be difficult to discover
Some plan of action . . . But here's Valère, your lover.   100

SCENE 4

VALÈRE, MARIANE, DORINE

VALÈRE   Madam, I've just received some wondrous news
Regarding which I'd like to hear your views.
MARIANE   What news?
VALÈRE   You're marrying Tartuffe.
MARIANE   I find
That Father does have such a match in mind.
VALÈRE   Your father, Madam . . .
MARIANE   . . . has just this minute said   5
That it's Tartuffe he wishes me to wed.
VALÈRE   Can he be serious?
MARIANE   Oh, indeed he can;
He's clearly set his heart upon the plan.
VALÈRE   And what position do you propose to take,
Madam?
MARIANE   Why—I don't know.
VALÈRE   For heaven's sake—   10
You don't know?
MARIANE   No.
VALÈRE   Well, well!
MARIANE   Advise me, do.
VALÈRE   Marry the man. That's my advice to you.
MARIANE   That's your advice?
VALÈRE   Yes.
MARIANE   Truly?
VALÈRE   Oh, absolutely.
You couldn't choose more wisely, more astutely.   *Valère acts sarcastically?*
MARIANE   Thanks for this counsel; I'll follow it, of course.   15
VALÈRE   Do, do; I'm sure 'twill cost you no remorse.
MARIANE   To give it didn't cause your heart to break.
VALÈRE   I gave it, Madam, only for your sake.
MARIANE   And it's for your sake that I take it, Sir.
DORINE   [*Withdrawing to the rear of the stage.*]
Let's see which fool will prove the stubborner.   20
VALÈRE   So I am nothing to you, and it was flat
Deception when you . . .
MARIANE   Please, enough of that.
You've told me plainly that I should agree
To wed the man my father's chosen for me,
And since you've deigned to counsel me so wisely,   25
I promise, Sir, to do as you advise me.

VALÈRE Ah, no, 'twas not by me that you were swayed.
No, your decision was already made;
Though now, to save appearances, you protest
That you're betraying me at my behest.   30
MARIANE Just as you say.
VALÈRE   Quite so. And I now see
That you were never truly in love with me.
MARIANE Alas, you're free to think so if you choose.
VALÈRE I choose to think so, and here's a bit of news:
You've spurned my hand, but I know where to turn   35
For kinder treatment, as you shall quickly learn.
MARIANE I'm sure you do. Your noble qualities
Inspire affection . . .
VALÈRE   Forget my qualities, please.
They don't inspire you overmuch, I find.
But there's another lady I have in mind   40
Whose sweet and generous nature will not scorn
To compensate me for the loss I've borne.
MARIANE I'm no great loss, and I'm sure that you'll transfer
Your heart quite painlessly from me to her.
VALÈRE I'll do my best to take it in my stride.   45
The pain I feel at being cast aside
Time and forgetfulness may put an end to.
Or if I can't forget, I shall pretend to.
No self-respecting person is expected
To go on loving once he's been rejected.   50
MARIANE Now, that's a fine, high-minded sentiment.
VALÈRE One to which any sane man would assent.
Would you prefer it if I pined away
In hopeless passion till my dying day?
Am I to yield you to a rival's arms   55
And not console myself with other charms?
MARIANE Go then; console yourself; don't hesitate.
I wish you to; indeed, I cannot wait.
VALÈRE You wish me to?
MARIANE   Yes.
VALÈRE   That's the final straw.
Madam, farewell. Your wish shall be my law.   60
      [He starts to leave, and then returns: this repeatedly.]
MARIANE Splendid.
VALÈRE [Coming back again.] This breach, remember, is of your making;
It's you who've driven me to the step I'm taking.
MARIANE Of course.
VALÈRE [Coming back again.] Remember, too, that I am merely
Following your example.
MARIANE   I see that clearly.
VALÈRE Enough. I'll go and do your bidding, then.   65
MARIANE Good.
VALÈRE [Coming back again.] You shall never see my face again.

[handwritten marginal note:] ← Valère already has a lady in mind to weed in place of Mariane?

He hesitates in leaving as all may to give Mariane a second chance

MARIANE   Excellent.

VALÈRE [*Walking to the door, then turning about.*]
                              Yes?

MARIANE   What?

VALÈRE   What's that? What did you say?

MARIANE   Nothing. You're dreaming.

VALÈRE   Ah. Well, I'm on my way.
    Farewell, Madame.
            [*He moves slowly away.*]

MARIANE   Farewell.

DORINE [*To* MARIANE.]   If you ask me,
    Both of you are as mad as mad can be.   70
    Do stop this nonsense, now. I've only let you
    Squabble so long to see where it would get you.
    Whoa there, Monsieur Valère!
            [*She goes and seizes* VALÈRE *by the arm; he makes a great show of resistance.*]

VALÈRE   What's this, Dorine?

DORINE   Come here.

VALÈRE   No, no, my heart's too full of spleen.
    Don't hold me back; her wish must be obeyed.   75

DORINE   Stop!

VALÈRE   It's too late now; my decision's made.

DORINE   Oh, pooh!

MARIANE [*Aside.*]   He hates the sight of me, that's plain.
    I'll go, and so deliver him from pain.

DORINE [*Leaving* VALÈRE, *running after* MARIANE.]
    And now *you* run away! Come back.

MARIANE   No, no.
    Nothing you say will keep me here. Let go!   80

VALÈRE [*Aside.*]   She cannot bear my presence, I perceive.
    To spare her further torment, I shall leave.

DORINE [*Leaving* MARIANE, *running after* VALÈRE.]
    Again! You'll not escape, Sir; don't you try it.
    Come here, you two. Stop fussing and be quiet.
            [*She takes* VALÈRE *by the hand, then* MARIANE, *and draws them together.*]

VALÈRE [*To* DORINE.]   What do you want of me?   85

MARIANE [*To* DORINE.]   What is the point of this?

DORINE   We're going to have a little armistice.
    [*To* VALÈRE.] Now, weren't you silly to get so overheated?

VALÈRE   Didn't you see how badly I was treated?

DORINE [*To* MARIANE.]   Aren't you a simpleton, to have lost your head? 90

MARIANE   Didn't you hear the hateful things he said?

DORINE [*To* VALÈRE.]   You're both great fools. Her sole desire, Valère,
    Is to be yours in marriage. To that I'll swear.
    [*To* MARIANE.] He loves you only, and he wants no wife
    But you, Mariane. On that I'll stake my life.   95

MARIANE [*To* VALÈRE.]   Then why you advised me so, I cannot see.

VALÈRE [*To* MARIANE.]   On such a question, why ask advice of *me*?

DORINE   Oh, you're impossible. Give me your hands, you two.
  [*To* VALÈRE.] Yours first.
VALÈRE [*Giving* DORINE *his hand.*]   But why?
DORINE [*To* MARIANE.]   And now a hand from you.   100
MARIANE [*Also giving* DORINE *her hand.*]
  What are you doing?
DORINE   There: a perfect fit.
  You suit each other better than you'll admit.
      [VALÈRE *and* MARIANE *hold hands for some time without looking at each
      other.*]
VALÈRE [*Turning toward* MARIANE.]
  Ah, come, don't be so haughty. Give a man
  A look of kindness, won't you, Mariane?
      [MARIANE *turns toward* VALÈRE *and smiles.*]
DORINE   I tell you, lovers are completely mad!   105
VALÈRE [*To* MARIANE.]   Now come, confess that you were very bad
  To hurt my feelings as you did just now.
  I have a just complaint, you must allow.
MARIANE   *You* must allow that you were most unpleasant . . .
DORINE   Let's table that discussion for the present;   110
  Your father has a plan which must be stopped.
MARIANE   Advise us, then; what means must we adopt?
DORINE   We'll use all manner of means, and all at once.
  [*To* MARIANE.] Your father's addled; he's acting like a dunce.
  Therefore you'd better humor the old fossil.   115
  Pretend to yield to him, be sweet and docile,
  And then postpone, as often as necessary,
  The day on which you have agreed to marry.
  You'll thus gain time, and time will turn the trick.
  Sometimes, for instance, you'll be taken sick,   120
  And that will seem good reason for delay;
  Or some bad omen will make you change the day—
  You'll dream of muddy water, or you'll pass
  A dead man's hearse, or break a looking-glass.
  If all else fails, no man can marry you   125
  Unless you take his ring and say "I do."
  But now, let's separate. If they should find
  Us talking here, our plot might be divined.
  [*To* VALÈRE.] Go to your friends, and tell them what's occurred,
  And have them urge her father to keep his word.   130
  Meanwhile, we'll stir her brother into action,
  And get Elmire,⁹ as well, to join our faction.
  Good-bye.
VALÈRE [*To* MARIANE.]   Though each of us will do his best,
  It's your true heart on which my hopes shall rest.   135
MARIANE [*To* VALÈRE.]   Regardless of what Father may decide,
  None but Valère shall claim me as his bride.

9. Orgon's second wife.

VALÈRE Oh, how those words content me! Come what will . . .
DORINE Oh, lovers, lovers! Their tongues are never still.
  Be off, now.
VALÈRE [*Turning to go, then turning back.*
            One last word . . .
DORINE   No time to chat: 140
  You leave by this door; and *you* leave by that.
      [DORINE *pushes them, by the shoulders, toward opposing doors.*]

Act III

SCENE 1

DAMIS, DORINE

DAMIS May lightning strike me even as I speak,
  May all men call me cowardly and weak,
  If any fear or scruple holds me back
  From settling things, at once, with that great quack!
DORINE Now, don't give way to violent emotion.   5
  Your father's merely talked about this notion,
  And words and deeds are far from being one.
  Much that is talked about is never done.
DAMIS No, I must stop that scoundrel's machinations;
  I'll go and tell him off; I'm out of patience.   10
DORINE Do calm down and be practical. I had rather
  My mistress dealt with him—and with your father.
  She has some influence with Tartuffe, I've noted.
  He hangs upon her words, seems most devoted,
  And may, indeed, be smitten by her charm.   15
  Pray Heaven it's true! 'Twould do our cause no harm.
  She sent for him, just now, to sound him out
  On this affair you're so incensed about;
  She'll find out where he stands, and tell him, too,
  What dreadful strife and trouble will ensue   20
  If he lends countenance to your father's plan.
  I couldn't get in to see him, but his man
  Says that he's almost finished with his prayers.
  Go, now. I'll catch him when he comes downstairs.
DAMIS I want to hear this conference, and I will.   25
DORINE No, they must be alone.
DAMIS   Oh, I'll keep still.
DORINE Not you. I know your temper. You'd start a brawl,
  And shout and stamp your foot and spoil it all.
  Go on.
DAMIS I won't; I have a perfect right . . .
DORINE Lord, you're a nuisance! He's coming; get out of sight. 30
      [DAMIS *conceals himself in a closet at the rear of the stage.*]

SCENE 2

TARTUFFE, DORINE

TARTUFFE [*Observing* DORINE, *and calling to his manservant off-stage.*]
  Hang up my hair-shirt, put my scourge in place,
  And pray, Laurent, for Heaven's perpetual grace.
  I'm going to the prison now, to share
  My last few coins with the poor wretches there.
DORINE [*Aside.*] Dear God, what affectation! What a fake!   5
TARTUFFE You wished to see me?
DORINE   Yes . . .
TARTUFFE [*Taking a handkerchief from his pocket.*]
                      For mercy's sake,
  Please take this handkerchief, before you speak.
DORINE What?
TARTUFFE   Cover that bosom,[1] girl. The flesh is weak.
  And unclean thoughts are difficult to control.
  Such sights as that can undermine the soul.   10
DORINE Your soul, it seems, has very poor defenses,
  And flesh makes quite an impact on your senses.
  It's strange that you're so easily excited;
  My own desires are not so soon ignited,
  And if I saw you naked as a beast,   15
  Not all your hide would tempt me in the least.
TARTUFFE Girl, speak more modestly; unless you do,
  I shall be forced to take my leave of you.
DORINE Oh, no, it's I who must be on my way;
  I've just one little message to convey.   20
  Madame is coming down, and begs you, Sir,
  To wait and have a word or two with her.
TARTUFFE Gladly.
DORINE [*Aside.*] *That* had a softening effect!
  I think my guess about him was correct.
TARTUFFE Will she be long?
DORINE   No: that's her step I hear.   25
  Ah, here she is, and I shall disappear.

SCENE 3

ELMIRE, TARTUFFE

TARTUFFE May Heaven, whose infinite goodness we adore,
  Preserve your body and soul forevermore,
  And bless your days, and answer thus the plea
  Of one who is its humblest votary.

---

1. The Brotherhood of the Holy Sacrament practiced alms giving to prisoners and kept a careful, censorious check on women's clothing, if they deemed it lascivious. Thus, Molière's audience would have identified Tartuffe as sympathetic—hypocritically—to the aims of the organization.

ELMIRE   I thank you for that pious wish. But please,   5
Do take a chair and let's be more at ease.
        [*They sit down.*]
TARTUFFE   I trust that you are once more well and strong?
ELMIRE   Oh, yes: the fever didn't last for long.
TARTUFFE   My prayers are too unworthy, I am sure,
To have gained from Heaven this most gracious cure;   10
But lately, Madam, my every supplication
Has had for object your recuperation.
ELMIRE   You shouldn't have troubled so. I don't deserve it.
TARTUFFE   Your health is priceless, Madam, and to preserve it
I'd gladly give my own, in all sincerity.   15
ELMIRE   Sir, you outdo us all in Christian charity.
You've been most kind. I count myself your debtor.
TARTUFFE   'Twas nothing, Madam. I long to serve you better.
ELMIRE   There's a private matter I'm anxious to discuss.
I'm glad there's no one here to hinder us.   20
TARTUFFE   I too am glad; it floods my heart with bliss
To find myself alone with you like this.
For just this chance I've prayed with all my power—
But prayed in vain, until this happy hour.
ELMIRE   This won't take long, Sir, and I hope you'll be   25
Entirely frank and unconstrained with me.
TARTUFFE   Indeed, there's nothing I had rather do
Than bare my inmost heart and soul to you.
First, let me say that what remarks I've made
About the constant visits you are paid   30
Were prompted not by any mean emotion,
But rather by a pure and deep devotion,
A fervent zeal . . .
ELMIRE   No need for explanation.
Your sole concern, I'm sure, was my salvation.
TARTUFFE [*Taking* ELMIRE's *hand and pressing her fingertips.*]
Quite so; and such great fervor do I feel . . .   35
ELMIRE   Ooh! Please! You're pinching!
TARTUFFE   'Twas from excess of zeal.
I never meant to cause you pain, I swear.
I'd rather . . .
        [*He places his hand on* ELMIRE's *knee.*]
ELMIRE   What can your hand be doing there?
TARTUFFE   Feeling your gown: what soft, fine-woven stuff!
ELMIRE   Please, I'm extremely ticklish. That's enough.   40
        [*She draws her chair away;* TARTUFFE *pulls his after her.*]
TARTUFFE [*Fondling the lace collar of her gown.*]
My, my, what lovely lacework on your dress!
The workmanship's miraculous, no less.
I've not seen anything to equal it.
ELMIRE   Yes, quite. But let's talk business for a bit.
They say my husband means to break his word   45
And give his daughter to you, Sir. Had you heard?

TARTUFFE   He did once mention it. But I confess
   I dream of quite a different happiness.
   It's elsewhere, Madam, that my eyes discern
   The promise of that bliss for which I yearn.   50
ELMIRE   I see: you care for nothing here below.
TARTUFFE   Ah, well—my heart's not made of stone, you know.
ELMIRE   All your desires mount heavenward, I'm sure,
   In scorn of all that's earthly and impure.
TARTUFFE   A love of heavenly beauty does not preclude   55
   A proper love for earthly pulchritude;
   Our senses are quite rightly captivated
   By perfect works our Maker has created.
   Some glory clings to all that Heaven has made;
   In you, all Heaven's marvels are displayed.   60
   On that fair face, such beauties have been lavished,
   The eyes are dazzled and the heart is ravished;
   How could I look on you, O flawless creature,
   And not adore the Author of all Nature,
   Feeling a love both passionate and pure   65
   For you, his triumph of self-portraiture?
   At first, I trembled lest that love should be
   A subtle snare that Hell had laid for me;
   I vowed to flee the sight of you, eschewing
   A rapture that might prove my soul's undoing;   70
   But soon, fair being, I became aware
   That my deep passion could be made to square
   With rectitude, and with my bounden duty,
   I thereupon surrendered to your beauty.
   It is, I know, presumptuous on my part   75
   To bring you this poor offering of my heart,
   And it is not my merit, Heaven knows,
   But your compassion on which my hopes repose.
   You are my peace, my solace, my salvation;
   On you depends my bliss—or desolation;   80
   I bide your judgment and, as you think best,
   I shall be either miserable or blest.
ELMIRE   Your declaration is most gallant, Sir,
   But don't you think it's out of character?
   You'd have done better to restrain your passion   85
   And think before you spoke in such a fashion.
   It ill becomes a pious man like you . . .
TARTUFFE   I may be pious, but I'm human too:
   With your celestial charms before his eyes,
   A man has not the power to be wise.   90
   I know such words sound strangely, coming from me,
   But I'm no angel, nor was meant to be,
   And if you blame my passion, you must needs
   Reproach as well the charms on which it feeds.
   Your loveliness I had no sooner seen   95
   Than you became my soul's unrivalled queen;

Tartuffe's heart
is impure and
uncontrolled

Before your seraph glance, divinely sweet,
My heart's defenses crumbled in defeat,
And nothing fasting, prayer, or tears might do
Could stay my spirit from adoring you.　　　　　　　100
My eyes, my sighs have told you in the past
What now my lips make bold to say at last,
And if, in your great goodness, you will deign
To look upon your slave, and ease his pain,—
If, in compassion for my soul's distress,　　　　　　105
You'll stoop to comfort my unworthiness,
I'll raise to you, in thanks for that sweet manna,
An endless hymn, an infinite hosanna.
With me, of course, there need be no anxiety,
No fear of scandal or of notoriety.　　　　　　　110
These young court gallants, whom all the ladies fancy,
Are vain in speech, in action rash and chancy;
When they succeed in love, the world soon knows it;
No favor's granted them but they disclose it
And by the looseness of their tongues profane　　　115
The very altar where their hearts have lain.
Men of my sort, however, love discreetly,
And one may trust our reticence completely.
My keen concern for my good name insures
The absolute security of yours;　　　　　　　120
In short, I offer you, my dear Elmire,　　*Tartuffe's*
Love without scandal, pleasure without fear.　　*adulterous*
　　　　　　　　　　　　　　　　　　　　　intentions
ELMIRE　I've heard your well-turned speeches to the end,
　　And what you urge I clearly apprehend.
　　Aren't you afraid that I may take a notion　　　125
　　To tell my husband of your warm devotion,
　　And that, supposing he were duly told,
　　His feelings toward you might grow rather cold?
TARTUFFE　I know, dear lady, that your exceeding charity
　　Will lead your heart to pardon my temerity;　　130
　　That you'll excuse my violent affection
　　As human weakness, human imperfection;
　　And that—O fairest!—you will bear in mind
　　That I'm but flesh and blood, and am not blind.
ELMIRE　Some women might do otherwise, perhaps,　　135
　　But I shall be discreet about your lapse;
　　I'll tell my husband nothing of what's occurred
　　If, in return, you'll give your solemn word
　　To advocate as forcefully as you can
　　The marriage of Valère and Mariane,　　　140
　　Renouncing all desire to dispossess
　　Another of his rightful happiness,
　　And . . .

She would
make a bargain
for her
silence

SCENE 4

DAMIS, ELMIRE, TARTUFFE

DAMIS [*Emerging from the closet where he has been hiding.*]
    No! We'll not hush up this vile affair;
I heard it all inside that closet there,
Where Heaven, in order to confound the pride
Of this great rascal, prompted me to hide.
Ah, now I have my long-awaited chance   5
To punish his deceit and arrogance,
And give my father clear and shocking proof
Of the black character of his dear Tartuffe.
ELMIRE Ah no, Damis; I'll be content if he
Will study to deserve my leniency.   10
I've promised silence—don't make me break my word;
To make a scandal would be too absurd.
Good wives laugh off such trifles, and forget them;
Why should they tell their husbands, and upset them?
DAMIS You have your reasons for taking such a course,   15
And I have reasons, too, of equal force.
To spare him now would be insanely wrong. *Damis has righteous*
I've swallowed my just wrath for far too long *anger toward Tartuffe*
And watched this insolent bigot bringing strife
And bitterness into our family life.   20
Too long he's meddled in my father's affairs,
Thwarting my marriage-hopes, and poor Valère's.
It's high time that my father was undeceived,
And now I've proof that can't be disbelieved—
Proof that was furnished me by Heaven above.   25
It's too good not to take advantage of.
This is my chance, and I deserve to lose it
If, for one moment, I hesitate to use it.
ELMIRE Damis . . .
DAMIS   No, I must do what I think right.
Madam, my heart is bursting with delight,   30
And, say whatever you will, I'll not consent
To lose the sweet revenge on which I'm bent.
I'll settle matters without more ado;
And here, most opportunely, is my cue.[2]

SCENE 5

ORGON, DAMIS, TARTUFFE, ELMIRE

DAMIS Father, I'm glad you've joined us. Let us advise you
Of some fresh news which doubtless will surprise you.

---

2. In the original stage directions, Tartuffe now reads silently from his breviary—in the Roman Catholic Church, the book containing the Divine Office for each day, which those in holy orders are required to recite.

You've just now been repaid with interest
For all your loving-kindness to our guest.
He's proved his warm and grateful feelings toward you;   5
It's with a pair of horns he would reward you.
Yes, I surprised him with your wife, and heard
His whole adulterous offer, every word.
She, with her all too gentle disposition,
Would not have told you of his proposition;   10
But I shall not make terms with brazen lechery,
And feel that not to tell you would be treachery.

ELMIRE   And I hold that one's husband's peace of mind
Should not be spoilt by tattle of this kind.
One's honor doesn't require it: to be proficient   15
In keeping men at bay is quite sufficient.
These are my sentiments, and I wish, Damis,
That you had heeded me and held your peace.

SCENE 6

ORGON, DAMIS, TARTUFFE

ORGON   Can it be true, this dreadful thing I hear?
TARTUFFE   Yes, Brother, I'm a wicked man, I fear:
A wretched sinner, all depraved and twisted,
The greatest villain that has ever existed.
My life's one heap of crimes, which grows each minute;   5
There's naught but foulness and corruption in it;
And I perceive that Heaven, outraged by me,
Has chosen this occasion to mortify me.
Charge me with any deed you wish to name;
I'll not defend myself, but take the blame.   10
Believe what you are told, and drive Tartuffe
Like some base criminal from beneath your roof;
Yes, drive me hence, and with a parting curse:
I shan't protest, for I deserve far worse.
ORGON [To DAMIS.]   Ah, you deceitful boy, how dare you try   15
To stain his purity with so foul a lie?
DAMIS   What! Are you taken in by such a fluff?
Did you not hear . . . ?
ORGON   Enough, you rogue, enough!
TARTUFFE   Ah, Brother, let him speak: you're being unjust.
Believe his story; the boy deserves your trust.   20
Why, after all, should you have faith in me?
How can you know what I might do, or be?
Is it on my good actions that you base
Your favor? Do you trust my pious face?
Ah, no, don't be deceived by hollow shows;   25
I'm far, alas, from being what men suppose;
Though the world takes me for a man of worth,
I'm truly the most worthless man on earth.
[To DAMIS] Yes, my dear son, speak out now: call me the chief

Of sinners, a wretch, a murderer, a thief;   30
Load me with all the names men most abhor;
I'll not complain; I've earned them all, and more;
I'll kneel here while you pour them on my head
As a just punishment for the life I've led.

ORGON [*To* TARTUFFE.]
This is too much, dear Brother.

    [*To* DAMIS.]   Have you no heart?   35

DAMIS   Are you so hoodwinked by this rascal's art . . . ?

ORGON   Be still, you monster.

    [*To* TARTUFFE.]   Brother, I pray you, rise.

    [*To* DAMIS.] Villain!

DAMIS   But . . .

ORGON   Silence!

DAMIS   Can't you realize . . . ?

ORGON   Just one word more, and I'll tear you limb from limb.

TARTUFFE   In God's name, Brother, don't be harsh with him.   40
I'd rather far be tortured at the stake
Than see him bear one scratch for my poor sake.

ORGON [*To* DAMIS.]   Ingrate!

TARTUFFE   If I must beg you, on bended knee,
To pardon him . . .

ORGON [*Falling to his knees, addressing* TARTUFFE.]
               Such goodness cannot be!

    [*To* DAMIS.] Now, *there's* true charity!

DAMIS   What, you . . . ?

ORGON   Villain, be still!   45
I know your motives; I know you wish him ill:
Yes, all of you—wife, children, servants, all—
Conspire against him and desire his fall,
Employing every shameful trick you can
To alienate me from this saintly man.   50
Ah, but the more you seek to drive him away,
The more I'll do to keep him. Without delay,
I'll spite this household and confound its pride
By giving him my daughter as his bride.

DAMIS   You're going to force her to accept his hand?   55

ORGON   Yes, and this very night, d'you understand?
I shall defy you all, and make it clear
That I'm the one who gives the orders here.
Come, wretch, kneel down and clasp his blessed feet,
And ask his pardon for your black deceit.   60

DAMIS   I ask that swindler's pardon? Why, I'd rather . . .

ORGON   So! You insult him, and defy your father!
A stick! A stick! [*To* TARTUFFE.] No, no—release me, do.
[*To* DAMIS.] Out of my house this minute! Be off with you,
And never dare set foot in it again.   65

DAMIS   Well, I shall go, but . . .

ORGON   Well, go quickly, then.
I disinherit you; an empty purse
Is all you'll get from me—except my curse!

SCENE 7

ORGON, TARTUFFE

ORGON   How he blasphemed your goodness! What a son!

TARTUFFE   Forgive him, Lord, as I've already done.
[*To* ORGON.] You can't know how it hurts when someone tries
To blacken me in my dear brother's eyes.

ORGON   Ahh!

TARTUFFE   The mere thought of such ingratitude   5
Plunges my soul into so dark a mood . . .
Such horror grips my heart . . . I gasp for breath,
And cannot speak, and feel myself near death.

ORGON [*He runs, in tears, to the door through which he has just driven his
    son.*]
You blackguard! Why did I spare you? Why did I not
Break you in little pieces on the spot?   10
Compose yourself, and don't be hurt, dear friend.

TARTUFFE   These scenes, these dreadful quarrels, have got to end.
I've much upset your household, and I perceive
That the best thing will be for me to leave.

ORGON   What are you saying!

TARTUFFE   They're all against me here;   15
They'd have you think me false and insincere.

ORGON   Ah, what of that? Have I ceased believing in you?

TARTUFFE   Their adverse talk will certainly continue,
And charges which you now repudiate
You may find credible at a later date.   20

ORGON   No, Brother, never.

TARTUFFE   Brother, a wife can sway
Her husband's mind in many a subtle way.

ORGON   No, no.

TARTUFFE   To leave at once is the solution;
Thus only can I end their persecution.

ORGON   No, no, I'll not allow it; you shall remain.   25

TARTUFFE   Ah, well; 'twill mean much martyrdom and pain,
But if you wish it . . .

ORGON   Ah!

TARTUFFE   Enough; so be it.
But one thing must be settled, as I see it.
For your dear honor, and for our friendship's sake,
There's one precaution I feel bound to take.   30
I shall avoid your wife, and keep away . . .

ORGON   No, you shall not, whatever they may say.
It pleases me to vex them, and for spite
I'd have them see you with her day and night.
What's more, I'm going to drive them to despair   35
By making you my only son and heir;
This very day, I'll give to you alone
Clear deed and title to everything I own.

A dear, good friend and son-in-law-to-be
Is more than wife, or child, or kin to me.   40
Will you accept my offer, dearest son?
TARTUFFE   In all things, let the will of Heaven be done.
ORGON   Poor fellow! Come, we'll go draw up the deed.
Then let them burst with disappointed greed!

Act IV

SCENE 1

CLÉANTE, TARTUFFE

CLÉANTE   Yes, all the town's discussing it, and truly,
Their comments do not flatter you unduly.
I'm glad we've met, Sir, and I'll give my view
Of this sad matter in a word or two.
As for who's guilty, that I shan't discuss;   5
Let's say it was Damis who caused the fuss;
Assuming, then, that you have been ill-used
By young Damis, and groundlessly accused,
Ought not a Christian to forgive, and ought
He not to stifle every vengeful thought?   10
Should you stand by and watch a father make
His only son an exile for your sake?
Again I tell you frankly, be advised:
The whole town, high and low, is scandalized;
This quarrel must be mended, and my advice is   15
Not to push matters to a further crisis.
No, sacrifice your wrath to God above,
And help Damis regain his father's love.
TARTUFFE   Alas, for my part I should take great joy
In doing so. I've nothing against the boy.   20
I pardon all, I harbor no resentment;
To serve him would afford me much contentment.
But Heaven's interest will not have it so:
If he comes back, then I shall have to go.
After his conduct—so extreme, so vicious—   25
Our further intercourse would look suspicious.
God knows what people would think! Why, they'd describe
My goodness to him as a sort of bribe;
They'd say that out of guilt I made pretense
Of loving-kindness and benevolence—   30
That, fearing my accuser's tongue, I strove
To buy his silence with a show of love.
CLÉANTE   Your reasoning is badly warped and stretched,
And these excuses, Sir, are most far-fetched.
Why put yourself in charge of Heaven's cause?   35
Does Heaven need our help to enforce its laws?
Leave vengeance to the Lord, Sir; while we live,

Our duty's not to punish, but forgive;
And what the Lord commands, we should obey
Without regard to what the world may say.   40
What! Shall the fear of being misunderstood
Prevent our doing what is right and good?
No, no: let's simply do what Heaven ordains,
And let no other thoughts perplex our brains.

TARTUFFE   Again, Sir, let me say that I've forgiven   45
Damis, and thus obeyed the laws of Heaven;
But I am not commanded by the Bible
To live with one who smears my name with libel.

CLÉANTE   Were you commanded, Sir, to indulge the whim
Of poor Orgon, and to encourage him   50
In suddenly transferring to your name
A large estate to which you have no claim?

TARTUFFE   'Twould never occur to those who know me best
To think I acted from self-interest.
The treasures of this world I quite despise;   55
Their specious glitter does not charm my eyes;
And if I have resigned myself to taking
The gift which my dear Brother insists on making,
I do so only, as he well understands,
Lest so much wealth fall into wicked hands,   60
Lest those to whom it might descend in time
Turn it to purposes of sin and crime,
And not, as I shall do, make use of it
For Heaven's glory and mankind's benefit.

CLÉANTE   Forget these trumped-up fears. Your argument   65
Is one the rightful heir might well resent;
It *is* a moral burden to inherit
Such wealth, but give Damis a chance to bear it.
And would it not be worse to be accused
Of swindling, than to see that wealth misused?   70
I'm shocked that you allowed Orgon to broach
This matter, and that you feel no self-reproach;
Does true religion teach that lawful heirs
May freely be deprived of what is theirs?
And if the Lord has told you in your heart   75
That you and young Damis must dwell apart,
Would it not be the decent thing to beat
A generous and honorable retreat,
Rather than let the son of the house be sent,
For your convenience, into banishment?   80
Sir, if you wish to prove the honesty
Of your intentions . . .

TARTUFFE   Sir, it is a half past three.
I've certain pious duties to attend to,
And hope my prompt departure won't offend you.

CLÉANTE [*Alone.*]   Damn.

SCENE 2

ELMIRE, MARIANE, CLÉANTE, DORINE

DORINE   Stay, Sir, and help Mariane, for Heaven's sake!
  She's suffering so, I fear her heart will break.
  Her father's plan to marry her off tonight
  Has put the poor child in a desperate plight.
  I hear him coming. Let's stand together, now,   5
  And see if we can't change his mind, somehow,
  About this match we all deplore and fear.

SCENE 3

ORGON, ELMIRE, MARIANE, CLÉANTE, DORINE

ORGON   Hah! Glad to find you all assembled here.
  [*To* MARIANE.] This contract, child, contains your happiness,
  And what it says I think your heart can guess.
MARIANE [*Falling to her knees.*]
  Sir, by that Heaven which sees me here distressed,
  And by whatever else can move your breast,   5
  Do not employ a father's power, I pray you,
  To crush my heart and force it to obey you,
  Nor by your harsh commands oppress me so
  That I'll begrudge the duty which I owe—
  And do not so embitter and enslave me   10
  That I shall hate the very life you gave me.
  If my sweet hopes must perish, if you refuse
  To give me to the one I've dared to choose,
  Spare me at least—I beg you, I implore—
  The pain of wedding one whom I abhor;   15
  And do not, by a heartless use of force,
  Drive me to contemplate some desperate course.
ORGON [*Feeling himself touched by her.*]
  Be firm, my soul. No human weakness, now.   *Orgon won't be moved by*
MARIANE   I don't resent your love for him. Allow   *his love for his daughter*
  Your heart free rein, Sir; give him your property,   20
  And if that's not enough, take mine from me;
  He's welcome to my money; take it, do,
  But don't, I pray, include my person too.
  Spare me, I beg you; and let me end the tale
  Of my sad days behind a convent veil.   25
ORGON   A convent! Hah! When crossed in their amours,
  All lovesick girls have the same thought as yours.
  Get up! The more you loathe the man, and dread him,
  The more ennobling it will be to wed him.
  Marry Tartuffe, and mortify your flesh!   30
  Enough; don't start that whimpering afresh.

DORINE   But why . . . ?

ORGON   Be still, there. Speak when you're spoken to.
   Not one more bit of impudence out of you.

CLÉANTE   If I may offer a word of counsel here . . .

ORGON   Brother, in counselling you have no peer;   35
   All your advice is forceful, sound, and clever;
   I don't propose to follow it, however.

ELMIRE [To ORGON.]   I am amazed, and don't know what to say;
   Your blindness simply takes my breath away.
   You are indeed bewitched, to take no warning   40
   From our account of what occurred this morning.

ORGON   Madam, I know a few plain facts, and one
   Is that you're partial to my rascal son;
   Hence, when he sought to make Tartuffe the victim
   Of a base lie, you dared not contradict him.   45
   Ah, but you underplayed your part, my pet;
   You should have looked more angry, more upset.

ELMIRE   When men make overtures, must we reply
   With righteous anger and a battle-cry?
   Must we turn back their amorous advances   50
   With sharp reproaches and with fiery glances?
   Myself, I find such offers merely amusing,
   And make no scenes and fusses in refusing;
   My taste is for good-natured rectitude,
   And I dislike the savage sort of prude   55
   Who guards her virtue with her teeth and claws,
   And tears men's eyes out for the slightest cause:
   The Lord preserve me from such honor as that,
   Which bites and scratches like an alley-cat!
   I've found that a polite and cool rebuff   60
   Discourages a lover quite enough.

ORGON   I know the facts, and I shall not be shaken.

ELMIRE   I marvel at your power to be mistaken.
   Would it, I wonder, carry weight with you
   If I could show you that our tale was true?   65

ORGON   Show me?

ELMIRE   Yes.

ORGON   Rot.

ELMIRE   Come, what if I found a way
   To make you see the facts as plain as day?

ORGON   Nonsense.

ELMIRE   Do answer me; don't be absurd.
   I'm not now asking you to trust our word.
   Suppose that from some hiding-place in here   70
   You learned the whole sad truth by eye and ear—
   What would you say of your good friend, after that?

ORGON   Why, I'd say . . . nothing, by Jehoshaphat!
   It can't be true.

ELMIRE   You've been too long deceived,
   I'm quite tired of being disbelieved.   75

Come now: let's put my statements to the test,
And you shall see the truth made manifest.

Elmire will devise a plot to show what Tartuffe's really like!!

ORGON   I'll take that challenge. Now do your uttermost.
We'll see how you make good your empty boast.

organ doubts

ELMIRE [*To* DORINE.]   Send him to me.

DORINE   He's crafty; it may be hard   80
To catch the cunning scoundrel off his guard.

ELMIRE   No, amorous men are gullible. Their conceit
So blinds them that they're never hard to cheat.
Have him come down.

Tartuffe can be blinded by his own failing).

[*To* CLÉANTE *and* MARIANE.] Please leave us, for a bit.

SCENE 4

ELMIRE, ORGON

ELMIRE   Pull up this table, and get under it.

ORGON   What?

ELMIRE   It's essential that you be well-hidden.

ORGON   Why there?

ELMIRE   Oh, Heavens! Just do as you are bidden.
I have my plans; we'll soon see how they fare.
Under the table, now; and once you're there,   5
Take care that you are neither seen nor heard.

ORGON   Well, I'll indulge you, since I gave my word
To see you through this infantile charade.

ELMIRE   Once it is over, you'll be glad we played.
[*To her husband, who is now under the table.*]
I'm going to act quite strangely, now, and you   10
Must not be shocked at anything I do.
Whatever I may say, you must excuse
As part of that deceit I'm forced to use.
I shall employ sweet speeches in the task
Of making that impostor drop his mask;   15
I'll give encouragement to his bold desires,
And furnish fuel to his amorous fires.
Since it's for your sake, and for his destruction,
That I shall seem to yield to his seduction,
I'll gladly stop whenever you decide   20
That all your doubts are fully satisfied.
I'll count on you, as soon as you have seen
What sort of man he is, to intervene,
And not expose me to his odious lust
One moment longer than you feel you must.   25
Remember: you're to save me from my plight
Whenever . . . He's coming! Hush! Keep out of sight!

SCENE 5

TARTUFFE, ELMIRE, ORGON

TARTUFFE   You wish to have a word with me, I'm told.
ELMIRE   Yes, I've a little secret to unfold.
  Before I speak, however, it would be wise
  To close that door, and look about for spies.
      [TARTUFFE *goes to the door, closes it, and returns.*]
  The very last thing that must happen now   5
  Is a repetition of this morning's row.
  I've never been so badly caught off guard.
  Oh, how I feared for you! You saw how hard
  I tried to make that troublesome Damis
  Control his dreadful temper, and hold his peace.   10
  In my confusion, I didn't have the sense
  Simply to contradict his evidence;
  But as it happened, that was for the best,
  And all has worked out in our interest.
  This storm has only bettered your position;   15
  My husband doesn't have the least suspicion,
  And now, in mockery of those who do,
  He bids me be continually with you.
  And that is why, quite fearless of reproof,
  I now can be alone with my Tartuffe,   20
  And why my heart—perhaps too quick to yield—
  Feels free to let its passion be revealed.
TARTUFFE   Madam, your words confuse me. Not long ago,
  You spoke in quite a different style, you know.
ELMIRE   Ah, Sir, if that refusal made you smart,   25
  It's little that you know of woman's heart,
  Or what that heart is trying to convey
  When it resists in such a feeble way!
  Always, at first, our modesty prevents
  The frank avowal of tender sentiments;   30
  However high the passion which inflames us,
  Still, to confess its power somehow shames us.
  Thus we reluct, at first, yet in a tone
  Which tells you that our heart is overthrown,
  That what our lips deny, our pulse confesses,   35
  And that, in time, all noes will turn to yesses.
  I fear my words are all too frank and free,
  And a poor proof of woman's modesty;
  But since I'm started, tell me, if you will—
  Would I have tried to make Damis be still,   40
  Would I have listened, calm and unoffended,
  Until your lengthy offer of love was ended,
  And been so very mild in my reaction,
  Had your sweet words not given me satisfaction?
  And when I tried to force you to undo   45

The marriage-plans my husband has in view,
What did my urgent pleading signify
If not that I admired you, and that I
Deplored the thought that someone else might own
Part of a heart I wished for mine alone?   50
TARTUFFE   Madam, no happiness is so complete
As when, from lips we love, come words so sweet;
Their nectar floods my every sense, and drains
In honeyed rivulets through all my veins.
To please you is my joy, my only goal;   55
Your love is the restorer of my soul;
And yet I must beg leave, now, to confess
Some lingering doubts as to my happiness.
Might this not be a trick? Might not the catch
Be that you wish me to break off the match   60
With Mariane, and so have feigned to love me?
I shan't quite trust your fond opinion of me
Until the feelings you've expressed so sweetly
Are demonstrated somewhat more concretely,
And you have shown, by certain kind concessions,   65
That I may put my faith in your professions
ELMIRE [*She coughs, to warn her husband.*]
Why be in such a hurry? Must my heart
Exhaust its bounty at the very start?
To make that sweet admission cost me dear,
But you'll not be content, it would appear,   70
Unless my store of favors is disbursed
To the last farthing, and at the very first.
TARTUFFE   The less we merit, the less we dare to hope,
And with our doubts, mere words can never cope.
We trust no promised bliss till we receive it;   75
Not till a joy is ours can we believe it.
I, who so little merit your esteem,
Can't credit this fulfillment of my dream,
And shan't believe it, Madam, until I savor
Some palpable assurance of your favor.   80
ELMIRE   My, how tyrannical your love can be,
And how it flusters and perplexes me!
How furiously you take one's heart in hand,
And make your every wish a fierce command!
Come, must you hound and harry me to death?   85
Will you not give me time to catch my breath?
Can it be right to press me with such force,
Give me no quarter, show me no remorse,
And take advantage, by your stern insistence,
Of the fond feelings which weaken my resistance?   90
TARTUFFE   Well, if you look with favor upon my love,
Why, then, begrudge me some clear proof thereof?
ELMIRE   But how can I consent without offense
To Heaven, toward which you feel such reverence?

TARTUFFE   If Heaven is all that holds you back, don't worry.   95
  I can remove that hindrance in a hurry.
  Nothing of that sort need obstruct our path.
ELMIRE   Must one not be afraid of Heaven's wrath?
TARTUFFE   Madam, forget such fears, and be my pupil,
  And I shall teach you how to conquer scruple.   100
  Some joys, it's true, are wrong in Heaven's eyes;
  Yet Heaven is not averse to compromise;
  There is a science, lately formulated,
  Whereby one's conscience may be liberated,[3]
  And any wrongful act you care to mention   105
  May be redeemed by purity of intention.
  I'll teach you, Madam, the secrets of that science;
  Meanwhile, just place on me your full reliance.
  Assuage my keen desires, and feel no dread:
  The sin, if any, shall be on my head.   110
      [ELMIRE *coughs, this time more loudly.*]
  You've a bad cough.
ELMIRE   Yes, yes, It's bad indeed.
TARTUFFE [*Producing a little paper bag.*]
  A bit of licorice may be what you need.
ELMIRE   No, I've a stubborn cold, it seems. I'm sure it
  Will take much more than licorice to cure it.
TARTUFFE   How aggravating.
ELMIRE   Oh, more than I can say.   115
TARTUFFE   If you're still troubled, think of things this way:
  No one shall know our joys, save us alone,
  And there's no evil till the act is known;
  It's scandal, Madam, which makes it an offense,
  And it's no sin to sin in confidence.   120
ELMIRE [*Having coughed once more.*]
  Well, clearly I must do as you require,
  And yield to your importunate desire.
  It is apparent, now, that nothing less
  Will satisfy you, and so I acquiesce.
  To go so far is much against my will;   125
  I'm vexed that it should come to this; but still,
  Since you are so determined on it, since you
  Will not allow mere language to convince you,
  And since you ask for concrete evidence, I
  See nothing for it, now, but to comply.   130
  If this is sinful, if I'm wrong to do it,
  So much the worse for him who drove me to it.
  The fault can surely not be charged to me.
TARTUFFE   Madam, the fault is mine, if fault there be,
  And . . .
ELMIRE   Open the door a little, and peek out;   135
  I wouldn't want my husband poking about.

---

3. Molière created his own footnote to this line: "It is a scoundrel who speaks."

TARTUFFE   Why worry about the man? Each day he grows
   More gullible; one can lead him by the nose.
   To find us here would fill him with delight,
   And if he saw the worst, he'd doubt his sight.   140
ELMIRE   Nevertheless, do step out for a minute
   Into the hall, and see that no one's in it.

Orgon's gullibility admitted by Tartuffe

SCENE 6

ORGON, ELMIRE

ORGON [*Coming out from under the table.*]
   That man's a perfect monster, I must admit!
   I'm simply stunned. I can't get over it.
ELMIRE   What, coming out so soon? How premature!
   Get back in hiding, and wait until you're sure.
   Stay till the end, and be convinced completely;   5
   We mustn't stop till things are proved concretely.
ORGON   Hell never harbored anything so vicious!   *Orgon sees the truth*
ELMIRE   Tut, don't be hasty. Try to be judicious.
   Wait, and be certain that there's no mistake.
   No jumping to conclusions, for Heaven's sake!   10
   [*She places* ORGON *behind her, as* TARTUFFE *re-enters.*]

SCENE 7

TARTUFFE, ELMIRE, ORGON

TARTUFFE [*Not seeing* ORGON.]
   Madam, all things have worked out to perfection;
   I've given the neighboring rooms a full inspection;
   No one's about; and now I may at last . . .
ORGON [*Intercepting him.*]   Hold on, my passionate fellow, not so fast!
   I should advise a little more restraint.   5
   Well, so you thought you'd fool me, my dear saint!
   How soon you wearied of the saintly life—
   Wedding my daughter, and coveting my wife!
   I've long suspected you, and had a feeling
   That soon I'd catch you at your double-dealing.   10
   Just now, you've given me evidence galore;
   It's quite enough; I have no wish for more.
ELMIRE [*To* TARTUFFE.]   I'm sorry to have treated you so slyly,
   But circumstances forced me to be wily.
TARTUFFE   Brother, you can't think . . .
ORGON   No more talk from you;   15
   Just leave this household, without more ado.
TARTUFFE   What I intended . . .
ORGON   That seems fairly clear.
   Spare me your falsehoods and get out of here.
TARTUFFE   No, I'm the master, and you're the one to go!

This house belongs to me, I'll have you know,   20
And I shall show you that you can't hurt *me*
By this contemptible conspiracy,
That those who cross me know not what they do,
And that I've means to expose and punish you,
Avenge offended Heaven, and make you grieve   25
That ever you dared order me to leave.

SCENE 8

ELMIRE, ORGON

ELMIRE   What was the point of all that angry chatter?
ORGON   Dear God, I'm worried. This is no laughing matter.
ELMIRE   How so?
ORGON   I fear I understood his drift.
  I'm much disturbed about that deed of gift.
ELMIRE   You gave him . . . ?
ORGON   Yes, it's all been drawn and signed.   5
  But one thing more is weighing on my mind.
ELMIRE   What's that?
ORGON   I'll tell you; but first let's see if there's
  A certain strong-box in his room upstairs.

Act V

SCENE 1

ORGON, CLÉANTE

CLÉANTE   Where are you going so fast?
ORGON   God knows!
CLÉANTE   Then wait;
  Let's have a conference, and deliberate
  On how this situation's to be met.
ORGON   That strong-box has me utterly upset;
  This is the worst of many, many shocks.   5
CLÉANTE   Is there some fearful mystery in that box?
ORGON   My poor friend Argas brought that box to me
  With his own hands, in utmost secrecy;
  'Twas on the very morning of his flight.
  It's full of papers which, if they came to light,   10
  Would ruin him—or such is my impression.
CLÉANTE   Then why did you let it out of your possession?
ORGON   Those papers vexed my conscience, and it seemed best
  To ask the counsel of my pious guest.
  The cunning scoundrel got me to agree   15
  To leave the strong-box in his custody,
  So that, in case of an investigation,
  I could employ a slight equivocation
  And swear I didn't have it, and thereby,
  At no expense to conscience, tell a lie.   20

CLÉANTE   It looks to me as if you're out on a limb.
  Trusting him with that box, and offering him
  That deed of gift, were actions of a kind
  Which scarcely indicate a prudent mind.
  With two such weapons, he has the upper hand,   25
  And since you're vulnerable, as matters stand,
  You erred once more in bringing him to bay.
  You should have acted in some subtler way.
ORGON   Just think of it: behind that fervent face,
  A heart so wicked, and a soul so base!   30
  I took him in, a hungry beggar, and then . . .
  Enough, by God! I'm through with pious men:
  Henceforth I'll hate the whole false brotherhood,
  And persecute them worse than Satan could.
CLÉANTE   Ah, there you go—extravagant as ever!   35
  Why can you not be rational? You never
  Manage to take the middle course, it seems,
  But jump, instead, between absurd extremes.
  You've recognized your recent grave mistake
  In falling victim to a pious fake;   40
  Now, to correct that error, must you embrace
  An even greater error in its place,
  And judge our worthy neighbors as a whole
  By what you've learned of one corrupted soul?
  Come, just because one rascal made you swallow   45
  A show of zeal which turned out to be hollow,
  Shall you conclude that all men are deceivers,
  And that, today, there are no true believers?
  Let atheists make that foolish inference;
  Learn to distinguish virtue from pretense,   50
  Be cautious in bestowing admiration,
  And cultivate a sober moderation.
  Don't humor fraud, but also don't asperse
  True piety; the latter fault is worse,
  And it is best to err, if err one must,   55
  As you have done, upon the side of trust.

SCENE 2

DAMIS, ORGON, CLÉANTE

DAMIS   Father, I hear that scoundrel's uttered threats
  Against you; that he pridefully forgets
  How, in his need, he was befriended by you,
  And means to use your gifts to crucify you.
ORGON   It's true, my boy. I'm too distressed for tears.   5
DAMIS   Leave it to me, Sir; let me trim his ears.
  Faced with such insolence, we must not waver.
  I shall rejoice in doing you the favor
  Of cutting short his life, and your distress.
CLÉANTE   What a display of young hotheadedness!   10

Do learn to moderate your fits of rage.
In this just kingdom, this enlightened age,
One does not settle things by violence.

SCENE 3

MADAME PERNELLE, MARIANE, ELMIRE, DORINE, DAMIS, ORGON, CLÉANTE

MADAME PERNELLE   I hear strange tales of very strange events.
ORGON   Yes, strange events which these two eyes beheld.
The man's ingratitude is unparalleled.
I save a wretched pauper from starvation,
House him, and treat him like a blood relation,   5
Shower him every day with my largesse,
Give him my daughter, and all that I possess;
And meanwhile the unconscionable knave
Tries to induce my wife to misbehave;
And not content with such extreme rascality,   10
Now threatens me with my own liberality,
And aims, by taking base advantage of
The gifts I gave him out of Christian love,
To drive me from my house, a ruined man,
And make me end a pauper, as he began.   15
DORINE   Poor fellow!
MADAME PERNELLE   No, my son, I'll never bring
Myself to think him guilty of such a thing.
ORGON   How's that?
MADAME PERNELLE   The righteous always were maligned.
ORGON   Speak clearly, Mother. Say what's on your mind.   20
MADAME PERNELLE   I mean that I can smell a rat, my dear.
You know how everybody hates him, here.
ORGON   That has no bearing on the case at all.
MADAME PERNELLE   I told you a hundred times, when you were small,
That virtue in this world is hated ever;   25
Malicious men may die, but malice never.
ORGON   No doubt that's true, but how does it apply?
MADAME PERNELLE   They've turned you against him by a clever lie.
ORGON   I've told you, I was there and saw it done.
MADAME PERNELLE   Ah, slanderers will stop at nothing, Son.   30
ORGON   Mother, I'll lose my temper . . . For the last time,
I tell you I was witness to the crime.
MADAME PERNELLE   The tongues of spite are busy night and noon,
And to their venom no man is immune.
ORGON   You're talking nonsense. Can't you realize   35
I saw it; saw it; saw it with my eyes?
Saw, do you understand me? Must I shout it
Into your ears before you'll cease to doubt it?
MADAME PERNELLE   Appearances can deceive, my son. Dear me,
We cannot always judge by what we see.   40

ORGON   Drat! Drat!

MADAME PERNELLE   One often interprets things awry;
  Good can seem evil to a suspicious eye.

ORGON   Was I to see his pawing at Elmire
  As an act of charity?

MADAME PERNELLE   Till his guilt is clear,   45
  A man deserves the benefit of the doubt.
  You should have waited, to see how things turned out.

ORGON   Great God in Heaven, what more proof did I need?
  Was I to sit there, watching, until he'd . . .
  You drive me to the brink of impropriety.   50

MADAME PERNELLE   No, no, a man of such surpassing piety
  Could not do such a thing. You cannot shake me.
  I don't believe it, and you shall not make me.

ORGON   You vex me so that, if you weren't my mother,
  I'd say to you . . . some dreadful thing or other.   55

DORINE   It's your turn now, Sir, not to be listened to;
  You'd not trust us, and now she won't trust you.

Orgon gets back what he gave.

CLÉANTE   My friends, we're wasting time which should be spent
  In facing up to our predicament.
  I fear that scoundrel's threats weren't made in sport.   60

DAMIS   Do you think he'd have the nerve to go to court?

ELMIRE   I'm sure he won't: they'd find it all too crude
  A case of swindling and ingratitude.

CLÉANTE   Don't be too sure. He won't be at a loss
  To give his claims a high and righteous gloss;   65
  And clever rogues with far less valid cause
  Have trapped their victims in a web of laws.
  I say again that to antagonize
  A man so strongly armed was most unwise.

ORGON   I know it; but the man's appalling cheek   70
  Outraged me so, I couldn't control my pique.

CLÉANTE   I wish to Heaven that we could devise
  Some truce between you, or some compromise.

ELMIRE   If I had known what cards he held, I'd not
  Have roused his anger by my little plot.   75

ORGON [*To* DORINE, *as* M. LOYAL *enters.*]
  What is that fellow looking for? Who is he?
  Go talk to him—and tell him that I'm busy.

SCENE 4

MONSIEUR LOYAL, MADAME PERNELLE, ORGON, DAMIS, MARIANE, DORINE,
ELMIRE, CLÉANTE

MONSIEUR LOYAL   Good day, dear sister. Kindly let me see
  Your master.

DORINE   He's involved with company,
  And cannot be disturbed just now, I fear.

MONSIEUR LOYAL   I hate to intrude; but what has brought me here

Will not disturb your master, in any event.   5
Indeed, my news will make him most content.

DORINE   Your name?

MONSIEUR LOYAL   Just say that I bring greetings from
Monsieur Tartuffe, on whose behalf I've come.

DORINE [*To* ORGON.]   Sir, he's a very gracious man, and bears
A message from Tartuffe, which, he declares,   10
Will make you most content.

CLÉANTE   Upon my word,
I think this man had best be seen, and heard.

ORGON   Perhaps he has some settlement to suggest.
How shall I treat him? What manner would be best?

CLÉANTE   Control your anger, and if he should mention   15
Some fair adjustment, give him your full attention.

MONSIEUR LOYAL   Good health to you, good Sir. May Heaven confound
Your enemies, and may your joys abound.

ORGON [*Aside, to* CLÉANTE.]   A gentle salutation: it confirms
My guess that he is here to offer terms.   20

MONSIEUR LOYAL   I've always held your family most dear;
I served your father, Sir, for many a year.

ORGON   Sir, I must ask your pardon; to my shame,
I cannot now recall your face or name.

MONSIEUR LOYAL   Loyal's my name; I come from Normandy,   25
And I'm a bailiff, in all modesty.
For forty years, praise God, it's been my boast
To serve with honor in that vital post,
And I am here, Sir, if you will permit
The liberty, to serve you with this writ . . .   30

ORGON   To—*what?*

MONSIEUR LOYAL   Now, please, Sir, let us have no friction:
It's nothing but an order of eviction.
You are to move your goods and family out
And make way for new occupants, without
Deferment or delay, and give the keys . . .   35

ORGON   I? Leave this house?

MONSIEUR LOYAL   Why yes, Sir, if you please.
This house, Sir, from the cellar to the roof,
Belongs now to the good Monsieur Tartuffe,
And he is lord and master of your estate
By virtue of a deed of present date,   40
Drawn in due form, with clearest legal phrasing . . .

DAMIS   Your insolence is utterly amazing!

MONSIEUR LOYAL   Young man, my business here is not with you
But with your wise and temperate father, who,
Like every worthy citizen, stands in awe   45
Of justice, and would never obstruct the law.

ORGON   But . . .

MONSIEUR LOYAL   Not for a million, Sir, would you rebel
Against authority; I know that well.
You'll not make trouble, Sir, or interfere
With the execution of my duties here.   50

DAMIS   Someone may execute a smart tattoo
  On that black jacket[4] of yours, before you're through.
MONSIEUR LOYAL   Sir, bid your son be silent. I'd much regret
  Having to mention such a nasty threat
  Of violence, in writing my report.   55
DORINE [*Aside.*]   This man Loyal's a most disloyal sort!
MONSIEUR LOYAL   I love all men of upright character,
  And when I agreed to serve these papers, Sir,
  It was your feelings that I had in mind.
  I couldn't bear to see the case assigned   60
  To someone else, who might esteem you less
  And so subject you to unpleasantness.
ORGON   What's more unpleasant than telling a man to leave
  His house and home?
MONSIEUR LOYAL   You'd like a short reprieve?
  If you desire it, Sir, I shall not press you,   65
  But wait until tomorrow to dispossess you.
  Splendid. I'll come and spend the night here, then,
  Most quietly, with half a score of men.
  For form's sake, you might bring me, just before
  You go to bed, the keys to the front door.   70
  My men, I promise, will be on their best
  Behavior, and will not disturb your rest.
  But bright and early, Sir, you must be quick
  And move out all your furniture, every stick:
  The men I've chosen are both young and strong,   75
  And with their help it shouldn't take you long.
  In short, I'll make things pleasant and convenient,
  And since I'm being so extremely lenient,
  Please show me, Sir, a like consideration,
  And give me your entire cooperation.   80
ORGON [*Aside.*]   I may be all but bankrupt, but I vow
  I'd give a hundred louis, here and now,
  Just for the pleasure of landing one good clout
  Right on the end of that complacent snout.
CLÉANTE   Careful; don't make things worse.
DAMIS   My bootsole itches   85
  To give that beggar a good kick in the breeches.
DORINE   Monsieur Loyal, I'd love to hear the whack
  Of a stout stick across your fine broad back.
MONSIEUR LOYAL   Take care: a woman too may go to jail if
  She uses threatening language to a bailiff.   90
CLÉANTE   Enough, enough, Sir. This must not go on.
  Give me that paper, please, and then begone.
MONSIEUR LOYAL   Well, *au revoir*. God give you all good cheer!
ORGON   May God confound you, and him who sent you here!

---

4. In the original, *justaucorps à longues basques,* a close-fitting, long black coat with skirts, the customary dress of a bailiff.

SCENE 5

ORGON, CLÉANTE, MARIANE, ELMIRE, MADAME PERNELLE, DORINE, DAMIS

ORGON   Now, Mother, was I right or not? This writ
   Should change your notion of Tartuffe a bit.
   Do you perceive his villainy at last?
MADAME PERNELLE   I'm thunderstruck. I'm utterly aghast.
DORINE   Oh, come, be fair. You mustn't take offense   5
   At this new proof of his benevolence.
   He's acting out of selfless love, I know.
   Material things enslave the soul, and so
   He kindly has arranged your liberation
   From all that might endanger your salvation.   10
ORGON   Will you not ever hold your tongue, you dunce?
CLÉANTE   Come, you must take some action, and at once.
ELMIRE   Go tell the world of the low trick he's tried.
   The deed of gift is surely nullified
   By such behavior, and public rage will not   15
   Permit the wretch to carry out his plot.

SCENE 6

VALÈRE, ORGON, CLÉANTE, ELMIRE, MARIANE, MADAME PERNELLE,
DAMIS, DORINE

VALÈRE   Sir, though I hate to bring you more bad news,
   Such is the danger that I cannot choose.
   A friend who is extremely close to me
   And knows my interest in your family
   Has, for my sake, presumed to violate   5
   The secrecy that's due to things of state,
   And sends me word that you are in a plight
   From which your one salvation lies in flight.
   That scoundrel who's imposed upon you so
   Denounced you to the King an hour ago   10
   And, as supporting evidence, displayed
   The strong-box of a certain renegade
   Whose secret papers, so he testified,
   You had disloyally agreed to hide.
   I don't know just what charges may be pressed,   15
   But there's a warrant out for your arrest;
   Tartuffe has been instructed, furthermore,
   To guide the arresting officer to your door.
CLÉANTE   He's clearly done this to facilitate
   His seizure of your house and your estate.   20
ORGON   That man, I must say, is a vicious beast!
VALÈRE   You can't afford to delay, Sir, in the least.
   My carriage is outside, to take you hence;
   This thousand louis should cover all expense.

Let's lose no time, or you shall be undone;   25
The sole defense, in this case, is to run.
I shall go with you all the way, and place you
In a safe refuge to which they'll never trace you.
ORGON   Alas, dear boy, I wish that I could show you
My gratitude for everything I owe you.   30
But now is not the time; I pray the Lord
That I may live to give you your reward.
Farewell, my dears; be careful . . .
CLÉANTE   Brother, hurry.
We shall take care of things; you needn't worry.

SCENE 7

The OFFICER, TARTUFFE, VALÈRE, ORGON, ELMIRE, MARIANE,
MADAME PERNELLE, DORINE, CLÉANTE, DAMIS

TARTUFFE   Gently, Sir, gently; stay right where you are.
No need for haste; your lodging isn't far.
You're off to prison, by order of the Prince.
ORGON   This is the crowning blow, you wretch; and since
It means my total ruin and defeat,   5
Your villainy is now at last complete.
TARTUFFE   You needn't try to provoke me; it's no use.
Those who serve Heaven must expect abuse.
CLÉANTE   You are indeed most patient, sweet, and blameless.
DORINE   How he exploits the name of Heaven! It's shameless.   10
TARTUFFE   Your taunts and mockeries are all for naught;
To do my duty is my only thought.
MARIANE   Your love of duty is most meritorious,
And what you've done is little short of glorious.
TARTUFFE   All deeds are glorious, Madam, which obey   15
The sovereign prince who sent me here today.
ORGON   I rescued you when you were destitute;
Have you forgotten that, you thankless brute?
TARTUFFE   No, no, I well remember everything;
But my first duty is to serve my King.   20
That obligation is so paramount
That other claims, beside it, do not count;
And for it I would sacrifice my wife,
My family, my friend, or my own life.
ELMIRE   Hypocrite!
DORINE   All that we most revere, he uses   25
To cloak his plots and camouflage his ruses.
CLÉANTE   If it is true that you are animated
By pure and loyal zeal, as you have stated,
Why was this zeal not roused until you'd sought
To make Orgon a cuckold, and been caught?   30
Why weren't you moved to give your evidence
Until your outraged host had driven you hence?

I shan't say that the gift of all his treasure
Ought to have damped your zeal in any measure;
But if he is a traitor, as you declare,   35
How could you condescend to be his heir?

TARTUFFE [*To the* OFFICER.]
Sir, spare me all this clamor; it's growing shrill.
Please carry out your orders, if you will.

OFFICER[5]   Yes, I've delayed too long, Sir. Thank you kindly.
You're just the proper person to remind me.   40
Come, you are off to join the other boarders
In the King's prison, according to his orders.

TARTUFFE   Who? I, Sir?
OFFICER   Yes.
TARTUFFE   To prison? This can't be true!
OFFICER   I owe an explanation, but not to you.
     [*To* ORGON.] Sir, all is well; rest easy, and be grateful.   45
We serve a Prince to whom all sham is hateful,
A Prince who sees into our inmost hearts,
And can't be fooled by any trickster's arts.
His royal soul, though generous and human,
Views all things with discernment and acumen;   50
His sovereign reason is not lightly swayed,
And all his judgments are discreetly weighed.
He honors righteous men of every kind,
And yet his zeal for virtue is not blind,
Nor does his love of piety numb his wits   55
And make him tolerant of hypocrites.
'Twas hardly likely that this man could cozen
A King who's foiled such liars by the dozen.
With one keen glance, the King perceived the whole
Perverseness and corruption of his soul,   60
And thus high Heaven's justice was displayed:
Betraying you, the rogue stood self-betrayed.
The King soon recognized Tartuffe as one
Notorious by another name, who'd done
So many vicious crimes that one could fill   65
Ten volumes with them, and be writing still.
But to be brief: our sovereign was appalled
By this man's treachery toward you, which he called
The last, worst villainy of a vile career,
And bade me follow the impostor here   70
To see how gross his impudence could be,
And force him to restore your property.
Your private papers, by the King's command,
I hereby seize and give into your hand.
The King, by royal order, invalidates   75
The deed which gave this rascal your estates,

---

5. In the original, *un exempt.* He would actually have been a gentleman from the king's personal bodyguard with the rank of lieutenant colonel or "master of the camp."

And pardons, furthermore, your grave offense
In harboring an exile's documents.
By these decrees, our Prince rewards you for
Your loyal deeds in the late civil war,[6]   80
And shows how heartfelt is his satisfaction
In recompensing any worthy action,
How much he prizes merit, and how he makes
More of men's virtues than of their mistakes.

DORINE   Heaven be praised!

MADAME PERNELLE.   I breathe again, at last.   85

ELMIRE   We're safe.

MARIANE   I can't believe the danger's past.

ORGON [*To* TARTUFFE.]   Well, traitor, now you see . . .

CLÉANTE   Ah, brother, please
Let's not descend to such indignities.
Leave the poor wretch to his unhappy fate,
And don't say anything to aggravate   90
His present woes; but rather hope that he
Will soon embrace an honest piety,
And mend his ways, and by a true repentance
Move our just King to moderate his sentence.
Meanwhile, go kneel before your sovereign's throne   95
And thank him for the mercies he has shown.

ORGON   Well said: let's go at once and, gladly kneeling,
Express the gratitude which all are feeling.
Then, when that first great duty has been done,
We'll turn with pleasure to a second one,   100
And give Valère, whose love has proven so true,
The wedded happiness which is his due.

6. A reference to Orgon's role in supporting the king during the *Frondes*.

MARIE DE LA VERGNE DE LA FAYETTE
1634–1693

The Princess of Clèves, Marie de La Fayette's masterpiece, is generally agreed to be the first important French novel. Out of the psychological situation of a woman who rejects romantic love, it generates fiction of compelling interest.

The author of this singular work had an unusual career. At the age of twenty-two, Marie de la Vergne married the comte de La Fayette, who thereupon took her to one of his estates in rural Auvergne. The young woman, born in Paris, had always lived in the metropolis, where her mother and her stepfather (her father had died when she was sixteen) frequented intellectual circles on the fringe of the court. Until 1659, de La Fayette remained in the country, bearing and raising two sons; then she returned alone to Paris, where she handled some of her husband's business affairs, became hostess of an important literary salon whose frequenters included Madame de Sévigné and the duc de La Rochefoucauld, and developed friendships with important figures at court. She wrote five novels and *Memoirs of the French Court for the Years 1688 and 1689*, a historical work reporting both such public events as the English revolution that deposed James II and the private affairs of figures more or less directly connected with important happenings. She outlived her husband by thirteen years.

The Princess of Clèves, first published (anonymously) in 1678, won instantaneous popular success. Set in the sixteenth-century French court, it incorporated the names and on occasion the histories of real people; even the prince of Clèves, in this novel the heroine's husband, once actually lived (d. 1564). (In reality he never married.) However, its immediate interest, as well as its lasting appeal, depend not on its historical allusions but on its psychological profundity. At a time when virtually all French fiction took the form of long, fanciful romances, it inaugurated a new novelistic tradition involving character development and narrative economy.

The single event in *The Princess of Clèves* that most intensely interested de La Fayette's contemporaries involved the heroine's confession to her husband of her interest in another man. The princess acknowledges her attraction to the duke of Nemours not to justify it but to ask for help in combating it. She wishes to remain a faithful wife, although many around her at court happily conduct adulterous love affairs; she yearns to retreat to the country to avoid constant anguishing temptation. Her husband finds this confession as astonishing as de La Fayette's readers did; her would-be lover, who overhears it, is equally amazed. The remarkable action calls attention to the princess's overwhelming desire to keep her integrity as a person, which her desire would destroy. At no time does she deviate significantly from her yearning after virtue.

The novelist provides a psychological history of her heroine's devotion to goodness, reporting the young woman's early relation to her mother and that mother's undeviating insistence on the importance of female chastity and fidelity. When the mother dies, the orphaned daughter incorporates more strongly than ever the doctrines her parent has taught. Her acceptance of such standards appears a form of repression: she feels no erotic passion for her devoted husband, and the narrative provides no reason to expect her to develop capacity for such feeling. When a handsome, brave, courteous, intelligent, kind, and witty aristocrat falls in love with her, when the princess realizes that she now feels that passion she has never experienced, the stage is set for a conventional conflict of love and duty. The novel renders exactly this conflict—but in ways far from conventional.

The Princess of Clèves is not, as it may seem, only a story of female self-abnegation. It is relevant to remember that the princess's lover, for his beloved's sake, gives up his chance to marry the queen of England, a bit of *male* abnegation, and an indication of the female protagonist's emotional power. The heroine suppresses erotic impulse—or, at any rate, such impulse's expression—but she allows herself gratification compatible with her goodness: the satisfaction of the dominance she achieves by her steady withholding of response. She does not consciously experience her situation as one of mastery; the reader, however, may realize her innocent force.

The twenty-first-century reader, like de La Fayette's contemporaries, finds himself or herself caught up in knotty problems of psychological interpretation. Is the princess honorable or needlessly cruel in confessing to her husband? Does she behave like a child or like a mature woman? Does she reject her lover at last out of virtue or (as she herself suggests) from fear of his eventual infidelity? Does she consolidate or yield her power by this rejection? Does she choose happiness or misery in committing herself to celibate widowhood?

The reader's problem of understanding and interpreting the protagonist duplicates that of the fictional characters. In the confined social and political world depicted here, shifting sexual alliances often prefigure movements of power. Royal marriages dictate national policy; royal love affairs may have equally potent effects; the sexual arrangements of those near the throne imply political consequences. Hence the effort to understand people's sexual behavior involves, by extension, matters of public importance. For the princess herself, however, love remains an intensely personal matter, despite her full awareness that personal meanings can have wider implications. The princess thinks about her virtue, her commitments, her feelings. And she thinks about how to protect those feelings from the knowledge of the avid watchers and interpreters who compose her society.

Everyone watches everyone else in the court of Henri II, where "what appears is seldom the truth." For the princess and the duke, looking at one another, in the flesh or in some form of representation, is their most fulfilling erotic activity. The duke steals a miniature of his beloved, who watches him doing so. The princess, alone in her pavilion, gazes at a painted battle scene including a depiction of the duke. Outside her window, the duke, himself unseen, watches her looking at his picture. At the edge of the park, another watcher, sent by the princess's husband, seeks to comprehend the duke's activities. This third watcher represents the social world constantly impinging on individual desire; the duke's watching, like the princess's contemplation of his image, epitomizes desire. Similarly, in a late episode (after the prince's death), the duke watches the princess from a distant window. She in turn watches his window from her own apartment, her erotic imagination aroused by the idea that her lover seeks opportunity merely to look at her. But she can allow herself no satisfaction beyond this attenuated variety. As she says proudly in her final interview with the duke, "You have seen that my feelings did not guide my actions."

The court's obsessive watching generates an atmosphere of tension. Every appearance provides matter for speculation: the colors a nobleman wears in a tournament, a letter falling out of someone's pocket, the degree of splendor with which a lady dresses for a ball. Often watchers make mistakes, which then become part of the dense social texture enveloping everyone. The princess would like to remove herself from the arena of watchers, but proper social behavior demands participation, as object or as subject.

The woman at the novel's center initiates little action. She provides an interesting contrast with Racine's Phaedra, also central to an imaginative work, a woman torn by passion and forever acting to disastrous effect. But the princess of Clèves, more passive, only allows herself to be loved. The prince, her husband, feels intense passion for her; she keeps it alive by never reciprocating it; he dies partly of grief over her imagined infidelity. The duke who loves her wins her acknowledged love in return, but she will not marry him after her husband dies: withholding herself, she cannot become vulnerable to the possible diminution of his passion. Her beauty has the greater power over observers because she refuses to bestow it.

The princess's restraint, although she gains power from it, derives from no desire for power. On the contrary, it declares a woman's experience of powerlessness. Her mother, emphasizing love's dangers, urges chastity; she explains "how insincere men are, how false and deceitful." In a society where "love was always mixed with politics, and politics with love," where "ambition and gallantry were the sole occupation of the court," the princess's self-protection is sensible. Although *The Princess of Clèves,* like other works of its period, endorses the control of passion by reason, it also reveals the costs of such control. And it suggests that actual—as opposed to ideal—social orders reflect the shape of individual passion more clearly than they indicate the organizing force of reason.

The array of characters in the opening pages of *The Princess of Clèves* may seem forbidding; it is difficult for modern readers to keep them straight or to remember their connections with one another. In fact, the novel provides necessary information as it goes along, and one need not know historical facts to enjoy the fictional arrangement of them. A preliminary summary of the situation and characters specified in the first section may, however, be helpful. Henri II of France (1519–1559), known as a patron of the arts and as a brave soldier, heads the court. The queen, Catherine de Médicis (1519–1589), has less social and political power than does the king's long-time mistress, Diane de Poitiers, duchess of Valentinois (1499–1566). Also politically important is the woman usually referred to as "Madame," the king's sister, Marguerite (1525–1574). The two dominant factions at court are headed by the duke of Montmorency, constable of France (1492–1567), member of an enormously powerful family, and François de Lorraine, chevalier of Guise (d. 1562). Various marital alliances link the families of these persons with the duchess of Valentinois, to whose patronage all aspire.

The title character, the princess, and her mother are fictional, but they are said to belong to the family of another historical character, the powerful François de Vendôme, vidame of Chartres (1522–1560). Both the prince, whom the protagonist marries, and Jacques de Savoie, duke of Nemours (1531–1585), whom she loves, actually existed.

The most important historical facts to keep in mind are the rivalries between the duchess of Valentinois and the queen and between the Montmorency and Guise families. The court intrigues reported in the novel mainly stem from these oppositions.

PRONOUNCING GLOSSARY

The following list uses common English syllables and stress accents to provide rough equivalents of selected words whose pronunciation may be unfamiliar to the general reader.

Châtelart: *sha'-te-lahr*

Chevalier de Guise: *she-vah'-lyay deu geez*

Clèves: *klev*

de La Fayette: *deu lah fai-et'*

Lignerolles: *leen-ye-rohl'*

Nemours: *neu-moor'*

Nevers: *neu-vehr'*

Orléans: *ohr-lay-onh'*

Piennes: *pee-en'*

Poitiers: *pwah-tyay'*

Randan: *rahn-dahnh'*

Savoie: *sah-vwah'*

Tournon: *toor-nohnh'*

Valentinois: *vahl-ahn-ti-nwah'*

Vendôme: *vahn-dohm'*

Vidame of Chartres: *vee-dahm' of shahr'-treu*

The Princess of Clèves[1]

Part I

There never was in France so brilliant a display of magnificence and gallantry as during the last years of the reign of Henri II. This monarch was gallant, handsome, and susceptible; although his love for Diane de Poitiers, Duchess of Valentinois, had lasted twenty years, its ardor had not diminished, as his conduct testified.

He was remarkably skilful in physical exercises, and devoted much attention to them; every day was filled with hunting and tennis, dancing, running at the ring,[2] and sports of that kind. The favorite colors and the initials of Madame de Valentinois were to be seen everywhere, and she herself used to appear dressed as richly as Mademoiselle de la Marck, her granddaughter, who was then about to be married.

The fact that the queen was there, accounted for her presence. This prin-

---

1. Translated by Thomas Sergeant Perry.   2. A court game in which men, mounted on horseback, competed to carry away a suspended metal ring on the point of a lance.

cess, although she had passed her first youth, was still beautiful; she was fond of splendor, magnificence, and pleasure. The king had married her while still Duke of Orléans, in the lifetime of his elder brother, the dauphin, who afterward died at Tournon, mourned as a worthy heir to the position of Francis I, his father.

The queen's ambition made her like to reign. She seemed indifferent to the king's attachment to the Duchess of Valentinois, and never betrayed any jealousy; but she was so skilled a dissembler that it was hard to discover her real feelings, and she was compelled by policy to keep the duchess near her if she wanted to see anything of the king. As for him, he liked the society of women, even of those with whom he was not at all in love. He was with the queen every day at her audience,[3] when all the most attractive lords and ladies were sure to appear.

At no court had there ever been gathered together so many lovely women and brave men. It seemed as if Nature had made an effort to show her highest beauty in the greatest lords and ladies. Madame Elisabeth of France, afterwards queen of Spain, began to show her wonderful intelligence and that unrivalled beauty which was so fatal to her. Mary Stuart, the queen of Scotland, who had just married the dauphin and was called the crown princess, or dauphiness, was faultless in mind and body. She had been brought up at the French court and had acquired all its polish; she was endowed by Nature with so strong a love for the softer graces that in spite of her youth she admired and understood them perfectly. Her mother-in-law, the queen, and Madame, the king's sister, were also fond of poetry, of comedy, and of music. The interest which King Francis I had felt in poetry and letters still prevailed in France and since the king, his son, was devoted to physical exercise, pleasures of all sorts were to be found at the court. But what rendered the court especially fine and majestic was the great number of princes and lords of exceptional merit; those I am about to name were, in their different ways, the ornament and the admiration of their age.

The King of Navarre inspired universal respect by his exalted rank and his royal bearing. He excelled in the art of war; but the Duke of Guise had shown himself so strong a rival that he had often laid aside his command to enter the duke's service as a private soldier in the most dangerous battles. This duke had manifested such admirable bravery with such remarkable success that he was an object of envy to every great commander. He had many conspicuous qualities besides his personal courage,—he possessed a vast and profound intelligence, a noble, lofty mind, and equal capacity for war and affairs. His brother, the Cardinal of Lorraine, was born with an unbridled ambition, and had acquired vast learning; this he turned to his profit by using it in defence of Catholicism, which had begun to be attacked. The Chevalier de Guise, afterwards known as the Grand Prior, was loved by all; he was handsome, witty, clever, and his courage was renowned throughout Europe. The short, ill-favored body of the Prince of Condé held a great and haughty soul, and an intelligence that endeared him to even the most beautiful women. The Duke of Nevers, famous for his military prowess and his important services to the state, though somewhat advanced in years was adored by all the court. He had three handsome sons,—the second, known as the Prince of Clèves, was worthy to bear that proud title; he was brave and grand,

3. A formal gathering.

and was withal endowed with a prudence rare in the young. The Vidame[4] of Chartres, a scion of the old house of Vendôme, a name not despised by princes of the blood, had won equal triumphs in war and gallantry; he was handsome, attractive, brave, hardy, generous; all his good qualities were distinct and striking,—in short, he was the only man fit to be compared, if such comparison be possible, with the Duke of Nemours. This nobleman was a masterpiece of Nature; the least of his fascinations was his extreme beauty; he was the handsomest man in the world. What made him superior to every one else was his unrivalled courage and a charm manifested in his mind, his expression, and his actions, such as no other showed. He possessed a certain playfulness that was equally attractive to men and women; he was unusually skilful in physical exercises; and he dressed in a way that every one tried in vain to imitate; moreover, his bearing was such that all eyes followed him whenever he appeared. There was no lady in the court who would not have been flattered by his attentions; few of those to whom he had devoted himself could boast of having resisted him; and even many in whom he had shown no interest made very clear their affection for him. He was so gentle and courteous that he could not refuse some attentions to those who tried to please him,—hence he had many mistresses; but it was hard to say whom he really loved. He was often to be seen with the dauphiness; her beauty, her gentleness, her desire to please every one, and the especial regard she showed for this prince, made some imagine that he dared to raise his eyes to her. The Guises, whose niece she was, had acquired influence and position by her marriage; they aspired to an equality with the princes of the blood and to a share of the power exercised by the Constable[5] of Montmorency. It was to the constable that the king confided the greater part of the cares of state, while he treated the Duke of Guise and the Marshal of Saint-André as his favorites. But those attached to his person by favor or position could only keep their place by submitting to the Duchess of Valentinois, who, although no longer young or beautiful, ruled him so despotically that she may be said to have been the mistress of his person and of the state.

The king had always loved the constable, and at the beginning of his reign had summoned him from the exile into which he had been sent by Francis I. The court was divided between the Guises and the constable, who was the favorite of the princes of the blood. Both parties had always struggled for the favor of the Duchess of Valentinois. The Duke of Aumale, brother of the Duke of Guise, had married one of her daughters. The constable aspired to the same alliance, not satisfied with having married his eldest son to Madame Diane, a daughter of the king by a lady of Piedmont who entered a convent after the birth of her child. The promises which Monsieur de Montmorency had made to Mademoiselle de Piennes, one of the queen's maids-of-honor, had proved a serious obstacle to this match; and although the king had removed it with extreme patience and kindness, the constable still felt insecure until he had won over the Duchess of Valentinois and had separated her from the Guises, whose greatness had begun to alarm her. She had delayed in every way in her power the marriage between the dauphin and the Queen of Scotland; this young queen's beauty and intelligence, and the

---

4. A title that designated the lay representative of a bishop and the commander of the bishop's troops.
5. A title that designated the highest-ranking official of the court.

position given to the Guises by this marriage, were very odious to her. She especially detested the Cardinal of Lorraine, who had addressed her in bitter, even contemptuous terms. She saw that he was intriguing with the queen; hence the constable found her ready to join forces with him by bringing about the marriage of Mademoiselle de la Marck, her granddaughter, to Monsieur d'Anville, his second son, who succeeded to his post in the reign of Charles IX. The constable did not expect that Monsieur d'Anville would have any objections to this marriage, as had been the case with Monsieur de Montmorency; but though the reasons were more hidden, the difficulties were no less obstinate. Monsieur d'Anville was desperately in love with the crown princess; and although his passion was hopeless, he could not persuade himself to contract other ties. The Marshal of Saint-André was almost the only courtier who had taken sides with neither faction; he was one of the favorites, but this position he held simply by his own merits. Ever since he had been the dauphin, the king had been attached to this nobleman, and later had made him marshal of France, at an age when men are satisfied with lesser honors. His advance gave him a distinction which he maintained by his personal worth and charm, by a costly table and rich surroundings, and by more splendor than any private individual had yet displayed. The king's generosity warranted this sumptuousness. There was no limit to this monarch's generosity to those he loved. He did not possess every great quality, but he had many, and among them the love of war and a good knowledge of it. This accounted for his many successes; and if we except the battle of St. Quentin, his reign was an unbroken series of victories. He had won the battle of Renty in person, Piedmont had been conquered, the English had been driven from France, and the Emperor Charles V had seen his good fortune desert him before the city of Metz,[6] which he had besieged in vain with all the forces of the Empire and of Spain. Nevertheless, since the defeat of St. Quentin had diminished our hope of conquest, and fortune seemed to favor one king as much as the other, they were gradually led to favor peace.

The Dowager Duchess of Lorraine had begun to lead the way to a cessation of hostilities at the time of the dauphin's marriage, and ever since then there had been secret negotiations. At last Cercamp, in the Province of Artois, was chosen as the place of meeting. The Cardinal of Lorraine, the constable, and the Marshal of Saint-André appeared in behalf of the King of France; the Duke of Alva and the Prince of Orange in behalf of Philip II. The Duke and Duchess of Lorraine were the mediators. The leading articles were the marriage of Madame Elisabeth of France to Don Carlos, Infanta of Spain, and that of Madame, the king's sister, with Monsieur de Savoie.

Meanwhile the king remained on the frontier, and there heard of the death of Mary, queen of England. He sent the Count of Randan to Elizabeth to congratulate her on ascending the throne. She was very glad to receive him, because her rights were so insecure that it was of great service to her to have them acknowledged by the king. The count found her well informed about the interests of France and the capabilities of those who composed the court, but especially familiar with the reputation of the Duke of Nemours. She

6. Henri II had continued the struggle of his father, Francis I, against Charles V, leader of the Holy Roman Empire, for supremacy in Europe and particularly for control in Italy. The battles mentioned here belong to that struggle. The French armies were defeated at St. Quentin in 1557. The French drove the English from Calais in 1558. The French captured Metz in 1552.

spoke of this nobleman so often and with such warmth that when Monsieur de Randan returned and recounted his journey to the king, he told him that there was nothing to which Monsieur de Nemours could not aspire, and that she would be capable of marrying him. That very evening the king spoke to this nobleman, and made Monsieur de Randan repeat to him his conversation with Elizabeth, urging him to essay this great fortune. At first Monsieur de Nemours thought that the king was jesting; but when he saw his mistake he said,—

"At any rate, sire, if I undertake a fantastic enterprise under the advice and in behalf of your Majesty, I beg of you to keep it secret until success shall justify me before the public, and to guard me from appearing vain enough to suppose that a queen who has never seen me should wish to marry me from love."

The king promised to speak of the plan to no one but the constable, and agreed that secrecy was essential for its success. Monsieur de Randan advised Monsieur de Nemours to visit England as a simple traveller; but the latter could not make up his mind to do this. He sent Lignerolles, an intelligent young man, one of his favorites, to ascertain the queen's feeling and to try to open the matter. Meanwhile he went to see the Duke of Savoy, who was then at Brussels with the King of Spain. The death of Mary of England[7] raised great obstacles to any treaty of peace; the commission broke up at the end of November, and the king returned to Paris.

At that moment there appeared at court a young lady to whom all eyes were turned, and we may well believe that she was possessed of faultless beauty, since she aroused admiration where all were well accustomed to the sight of handsome women. Of the same family as the Vidame of Chartres, she was one of the greatest heiresses in France. Her father had died young, leaving her under the charge of his wife, Madame de Chartres, whose kindness, virtue, and worth were beyond praise. After her husband's death she had withdrawn from court for many years; during this period she had devoted herself to the education of her daughter, not merely cultivating her mind and her beauty, but also seeking to inspire her with the love of virtue and to make her attractive. Most mothers imagine that it is enough never to speak of gallantry to their daughters to guard them from it forever. Madame de Chartres was of a very different opinion; she often drew pictures of love to her daughter, showing her its fascinations, in order to give her a better understanding of its perils. She told her how insincere men are, how false and deceitful; she described the domestic miseries which illicit love-affairs entail, and, on the other hand, pictured to her the peaceful happiness of a virtuous woman's life, as well as the distinction and elevation which virtue gives to a woman of rank and beauty. She taught her, too, how hard it was to preserve this virtue without extreme care, and without that one sure means of securing a wife's happiness, which is to love her husband and to be loved by him.

This heiress was, then, one of the greatest matches in France, and although she was very young, many propositions of marriage had been made to her. Madame de Chartres, who was extremely proud, found almost nothing worthy of her daughter, and the girl being in her sixteenth year, she was anxious to take her to court. The Vidame went to welcome her on her arrival,

7. Mary Tudor (1516–1558), "Bloody Mary," wife of Philip II of Spain.

and was much struck by the marvellous beauty of Mademoiselle de Chartres,—and with good reason: her delicate complexion and her blond hair
gave her a unique brilliancy; her features were regular, and her face and
person were full of grace and charm.

The day after her arrival she went to match some precious stones at the
house of an Italian who dealt in them. He had come from Florence with the
queen, and had grown so rich by his business that his house seemed that of
some great nobleman rather than of a merchant. The Prince of Clèves happened to come in while she was there; he was so struck by her beauty that
he could not conceal his surprise, and Mademoiselle de Chartres could not
keep from blushing when she saw his astonishment: she succeeded, however,
in regaining her composure without paying any further attention to the
prince than civility required for a man of his evident importance. Monsieur
de Clèves gazed at her admiringly, wondering who this beauty was whom he
did not know. He perceived from her bearing and her suite[8] that she must
be a lady of high rank. She was so young that he thought she must be unmarried; but since she had not her mother with her, and the Italian, who did not
know her, addressed her as "madame," he was in great doubt, and stared at
her with continual surprise. He saw that his glances embarrassed her, unlike
most young women, who always take pleasure in seeing the effect of their
beauty; it even seemed to him that his presence made her anxious to go
away, and in fact she left very soon. Monsieur de Clèves consoled himself
for her departure with the hope of finding out who she was, and was much
disappointed to learn that no one knew. He was so struck by her beauty and
evident modesty that from that moment he conceived for her the greatest
love and esteem. That evening he called on Madame, the king's sister.

This princess was held in high esteem on account of her influence with
the king, her brother; and this influence was so great that when the king
made peace he consented to restore Piedmont to enable her to marry Monsieur de Savoie. Although she had always meant to marry, she had determined to give her hand to none but a sovereign, and had for that reason
refused the King of Navarre when he was Duke of Vendôme, and had always
felt an interest in Monsieur de Savoie after seeing him at Nice on the occasion of the interview between Francis I and Pope Paul III.[9] Since she possessed great intelligence and a fine taste, she drew pleasant persons about
her, and at certain hours the whole court used to visit her.

Thither Monsieur de Clèves went, as was his habit. He was so full of the
wit and beauty of Mademoiselle de Chartres that he could speak of nothing
else; he talked freely of his adventure, and set no limit to his praise of the
young woman he had seen but did not know. Madame said to him that there
was no such person as he described, and that if there were, every one would
have known about her. Madame de Dampierre, her lady-in-waiting and a
friend of Madame de Chartres, when she heard the conversation moved near
the princess and said to her in a low voice that doubtless it was Mademoiselle
de Chartres whom Monsieur de Clèves had seen. Madame turned towards
him and said that if he would return the next day, she would show him this
beauty who had so impressed him. Mademoiselle de Chartres made her

---

8. Group of attendants or servants.   9. The meeting took place in 1538. The pope helped arrange a ten-
year truce between France and the empire.

appearance the next day. The queen received her with every imaginable attention, and she was greeted with such admiration by every one that she heard around her nothing but praise. This she received with such noble modesty that she seemed not to hear it, or at least not to be affected by it. Then she visited the apartments of Madame, the king's sister. The princess, after praising her beauty, told her the surprise she had given to Monsieur de Clèves. A moment after, that person appeared.

"Come," she said to him, "see if I have not kept my word, and if, when I point out Mademoiselle de Chartres to you, I do not show you the beauty you sought; at any rate, thank me for telling her how much you already admire her."

Monsieur de Clèves was filled with joy to find that this young woman whom he had found so attractive was of a rank proportionate to her beauty. He went up to her and asked her to remember that he had been the first to admire her, and that without knowing her he had felt all the respect and esteem that were her due.

The Chevalier de Guise, his friend, and he left the house together. At first they praised Mademoiselle de Chartres without stint; then they found that they were praising her too much, and both stopped saying what they thought of her: but they were compelled to talk about her on the following days wherever they met. This new beauty was for a long time the general subject of conversation. The queen praised her warmly and showed an extraordinary regard for her; the dauphiness made her one of her favorites, and begged Madame de Chartres to bring her to see her very often; the daughters of the king invited her to all their entertainments,—in short, she was loved and admired by the whole court, except by Madame de Valentinois. It was not that this new beauty gave her any uneasiness,—her long experience had made her sure of the king,—but she so hated the Vidame of Chartres, whom she had desired to ally with herself by the marriage of one of her daughters, while he had joined the queen's party, that she could not look with favor on any one who bore his name and seemed to enjoy his friendship.

The Prince of Clèves fell passionately in love with Mademoiselle de Chartres, and was eager to marry her; but he feared lest the pride of Madame de Chartres should prevent her from giving her daughter to a man who was not the eldest of his family. Yet this family was so distinguished, and the Count of Eu, who was the head of the house, had just married a woman so near to royalty, that it was timidity rather than any true reason that inspired the fear of Monsieur de Clèves. He had many rivals; the Chevalier de Guise seemed to him the most formidable, on account of his birth, his ability, and the brilliant position of his family. This prince had fallen in love with Mademoiselle de Chartres the first day he saw her; he had noticed the passion of Monsieur de Clèves just as the latter had noticed his. Though the two men were friends, the separation which resulted from this rivalry gave them no chance to explain themselves, and their friendship cooled without their having courage to come to an understanding. The good fortune of Monsieur de Clèves in being the first to see Mademoiselle de Chartres seemed to him a happy omen, and to promise him some advantage over his rivals; but he foresaw serious obstacles on the part of the Duke of Nevers, his father. This duke was bound to the Duchess of Valentinois by many ties; she was an enemy of the Vidame, and this was reason enough to prevent the Duke of

Nevers from consenting that his son should think of that nobleman's niece.

Madame de Chartres, who had already taken such pains to fill her daughter with a love of virtue, did not remit them in this place where they were still so necessary, and bad examples were so frequent. Ambition and gallantry were the sole occupation of the court, busying men and women alike. There were so many interests and so many different intrigues in which women took part that love was always mingled with politics, and politics with love. No one was calm or indifferent; every one sought to rise, to please, to serve, or to injure; no one was weary or idle, every one was taken up with pleasure or intrigue. The ladies had their special interest in the queen, in the crown princess, in the Queen of Navarre, in Madame the king's sister, or in the Duchess of Valentinois, according to their inclinations, their sense of right, or their humor. Those who had passed their first youth and assumed an austere virtue, were devoted to the queen; those who were younger and sought pleasure and gallantry, paid their court to the crown princess. The Queen of Navarre had her favorites; she was young, and had much influence over her husband the king,[1] who was allied with the constable, and hence highly esteemed. Madame the king's sister still preserved some of her beauty, and gathered several ladies about herself. The Duchess of Valentinois was sought by all those whom she deigned to regard; but the women she liked were few, and with the exception of those who enjoyed her intimacy and confidence, and whose disposition bore some likeness to her own, she received only on the days when she assumed to hold a court like the queen.

All these different cliques were separated by rivalry and envy. Then, too, the women who belonged to each one of them were also jealous of one another, either about their chances of advancement, or about their lovers; often their interests were complicated by other pettier, but no less important questions. Hence there was in this court a sort of well-ordered agitation, which rendered it very charming, but also very dangerous, for a young woman. Madame de Chartres saw this peril, and thought only of protecting her daughter from it. She besought her, not as a mother, but as a friend, to confide to her all the sweet speeches that might be made to her, and promised her aid in all those matters which so often embarrass the young.

The Chevalier de Guise made his feelings for Mademoiselle de Chartres and his intentions so manifest that every one could see them; yet he well knew the very grave difficulties that stood in his way. He was aware that he was not a desirable match, because his fortune was too small for his rank. He knew, too, that his brothers would disapprove of his marrying, through fear of the loss of position which sometimes befalls great families through the marriage of younger sons. The Cardinal of Lorraine soon proved to him that his fears were well grounded, for he denounced the chevalier's love for Mademoiselle de Chartres very warmly, though he concealed his true reasons. The cardinal nourished a hatred for the Vidame, which was hidden at the time, and only broke out later. He would have preferred to see his brother ally himself with any other family than that of the Vidame, and gave such public expression to his dislike that Madame de Chartres was plainly offended. She took great pains to show that the Cardinal of Lorraine had no cause for fear, and that she herself never contemplated the match. The

---

1. Antoine de Bourbon (1518–1562), king of Navarre, father of Henri IV of France.

Vidame adopted the same course, and with a better understanding of the cardinal's objection, because he knew the underlying reason.

The Prince of Clèves had concealed his passion quite as little as had the Chevalier de Guise. The Duke of Nevers was sorry to hear of this attachment, but thought that his son would forget it at a word from him; great was his surprise when he found him determined to marry Mademoiselle de Chartres. He opposed this determination with a warmth so ill concealed that the whole court soon had wind of it, and it came to the knowledge of her mother. She had never doubted that Monsieur de Nevers would regard this match as an advantageous one for his son, and was much surprised that both the house of Clèves and that of Guise dreaded the alliance instead of desiring it. She was so chagrined that she sought to marry her daughter to some one who could raise her above those who fancied themselves superior to her; and after carefully going over the ground, pitched on the prince dauphin, the son of the Duke of Montpensier. He was of the right age to marry, and held the highest position at court. Since Madame de Chartres was a very clever woman, and was aided by the Vidame, who at that time had great influence, while her daughter was in every way a good match, she played her cards so cleverly and successfully that Monsieur de Montpensier appeared to desire the marriage, and it seemed as if nothing could stand in its way.

The Vidame, though aware of Monsieur d'Anville's devotion to the crown princess, still thought that he might make use of the influence which she had over him to induce him to speak well of Mademoiselle de Chartres to the king and to the Prince of Montpensier, whose intimate friend he was. He mentioned this to the princess, who took up the matter eagerly, since it promised advancement to a young woman of whom she had become very fond. This she told the Vidame, assuring him that though she knew she should offend her uncle, the Cardinal of Lorraine, this would be no objection, because she had good grounds for disliking him, since he every day furthered the queen's interests in opposition to her own.

Persons in love are always glad of any excuse for talking about the object of their affection. As soon as the Vidame had gone, the crown princess ordered Châtelart, the favorite of Monsieur d'Anville and the confidant of his love for her, to tell him to be at the queen's reception that evening. Châtelart received this command with great delight. He belonged to a good family of Dauphiné, but his merit and intelligence had raised him to a higher place than his birth warranted. He was received and treated with kindness by all the great lords at the court, and the favor of the family of Montmorency had attached him especially to Monsieur d'Anville. He was handsome and skilled in all physical exercises; he sang agreeably, wrote verses, and had a gallant, ardent nature, which so attracted Monsieur d'Anville that he made him a confidant of his love for the crown princess. The confidence brought him into the society of that lady, and thus began that unhappy passion, which robbed him of his reason and finally cost him his life.

Monsieur d'Anville did not fail to make his appearance that evening in the queen's drawing-room; he was pleased that the dauphiness had chosen him to aid her, and he promised faithfully to obey her commands. But Madame de Valentinois had heard of the contemplated marriage and had laid her plans to thwart it; she had been so successful in arousing the king's opposition that when Monsieur d'Anville spoke of it, he showed his disapproval, and commanded him to apprise the Prince of Montpensier of it. It is easy to imagine the feelings of Madame de Chartres at the failure of a plan she had so much desired, especially when her ill-success gave so great an advantage to her enemies and did so much harm to her daughter.

The crown princess kindly expressed to Mademoiselle de Chartres her regrets at not being able to further her interests. "You see," she said, "I have but very little power; I am so detested by the queen and the Duchess of Valentinois that they or their attendants always oppose everything I desire. Still," she added, "I have always tried to please them, and they hate me only on account of my mother, who used to fill them with uneasiness and jealousy. The king had been in love with her before he loved Madame de Valentinois, and in his early married life, before he had any children, though he loved this duchess, he seemed bent on dissolving that marriage to marry the queen my mother. Madame de Valentinois dreaded the woman he had loved so well, lest her wit and beauty should diminish her own power, and entered into an alliance with the constable, who was also opposed to the king's marrying a sister of the Guises. They won over the late king; and though he hated the Duchess of Valentinois as much as he loved the queen, he joined with them in preventing the king from dissolving his marriage. In order to make this impossible, they arranged my mother's marriage with the King of Scotland, whose first wife had been Madame Magdeleine, the king's sister,—this they did because it was the first thing that offered; though they broke the promises that had been made to the King of England, who was deeply in love with her. In fact, this matter nearly caused a falling out between the two kings. Henry VIII could not be consoled for not marrying my mother; and whenever any other French princess was proposed to him, he used to say that she would never take the place of the one they had taken from him. It is true that my mother was a perfect beauty, and it is remarkable that when she was the widow of a duke of Longueville, three kings should have wanted to marry her. It was her misfortune to be married to the least important of them all, and to be sent to a kingdom where she has found nothing but unhappiness. I am told that I am like her; I dread the same sad fate, and whatever happiness seems to be awaiting me, I doubt if I ever enjoy it."

Mademoiselle de Chartres assured the crown princess that these gloomy presentiments were so fantastic that they could not long disturb her, and that she ought not to doubt that her good fortune would give the lie to her fears.

Henceforth no one dared to think of Mademoiselle de Chartres, through fear of displeasing the king or of not succeeding in winning a young woman who had aspired to a prince of the blood. None of these considerations moved Monsieur de Clèves. The death of his father, the Duke of Nevers, which happened at that time, left him free to follow his own inclinations, and as soon as the period of mourning had passed, he thought of nothing but marrying Mademoiselle de Chartres. He was glad to make his proposal at a time when circumstances had driven away all rivals and when he felt almost sure that she would not refuse him. What dimmed his joy was the fear of not being agreeable to her; and he would have preferred the happiness of pleasing her to the certainty of marrying her when she did not love him.

The Chevalier de Guise had somewhat aroused his jealousy; but since this was inspired more by his rival's merits than by the conduct of Mademoiselle de Chartres, he thought of nothing but ascertaining whether by good fortune she would approve of his designs. He met her only at the queen's rooms or in company, yet he managed to speak to her of his intentions and hopes in the most respectful way; he begged her to let him know how she felt towards him, and told her that his feelings for her were such that he should be forever unhappy if she obeyed her mother only from a sense of duty.

Mademoiselle de Chartres, having a very noble heart, was really grateful to the Prince of Clèves for what he did. This gratitude lent to her answer a certain gentleness, which was quite sufficient to feed the hope of a man as much in love as he was, and he counted on attaining at least a part of what he desired.

Mademoiselle repeated this conversation to her mother, who said that Monsieur de Clèves was of such high birth, possessed so many fine qualities, and seemed so discreet for a man of his age, that if she inclined to marry him she would herself gladly give her consent. Mademoiselle de Chartres replied that she had noticed the same fine qualities, and that she would rather marry him than any one else, but that she had no special love for him.

The next day the prince had his offer formally made to Madame de Chartres; she accepted it, being willing to give her daughter a husband she did not love. The marriage settlement was drawn up, the king was told of it, and the marriage became known to every one.

Monsieur de Clèves was very happy, although not perfectly satisfied; it gave him much pain to see that what Mademoiselle de Chartres felt for him was only esteem and gratitude, and he could not flatter himself that she nourished any warmer feeling; for had she done so, she would have readily shown it in their closer intimacy. Within a few days he complained to her of this.

"Is it possible," he said, "that I may not be happy in my marriage? Yet assuredly I am not happy. You have a sort of kindly feeling for me which cannot satisfy me; you are not impatient, uneasy, or grieved: you are as indifferent to my love as if this were given to your purse, and not to your charms."

"You do wrong to complain," she replied. "I do not know what more you can ask; it seems to me that you have no right to demand anything more."

"It is true," he said, "that you have a certain air with which I should be satisfied if there were anything behind it; but instead of your being restrained by a sense of propriety, it is a sense of propriety which inspires your actions. I do not touch your feelings or your heart; my presence causes you neither pleasure nor pain."

"You cannot doubt," she made answer, "that I am glad to see you, and I blush so often when I do see you that you may be sure that the sight of you affects me."

"I am not deceived by your blushes," he urged; "they come from modesty, and not from any thrill of your heart, and I do not exaggerate their importance."

Mademoiselle de Chartres did not know what to answer; these distinctions were outside of her experience. Monsieur de Clèves saw only too well how far removed she was from feeling for him as he should have liked, when he saw that she had no idea of what that feeling was.

The Chevalier de Guise returned from a journey a few days before the wedding. He had seen so many insurmountable obstacles in the way of his marrying Mademoiselle de Chartres that he knew he had no chance of success; yet he was evidently distressed at seeing her become the wife of another. This grief did not extinguish his passion, and he remained quite as much in love as before. Mademoiselle de Chartres had not been ignorant of his devotion. On his return he let her know that she was the cause of the deep gloom that marked his face; and he had so much merit and charm that it was almost impossible to make him unhappy without regretting it. Hence she was depressed; but this pity went no further, and she told her mother how much pain this prince's love caused her.

Madame de Chartres admired her daughter's frankness, and with good reason, for it could not be fuller or simpler; she regretted, however, that her heart was not touched, especially when she saw that the prince had not affected it any more than the others. Hence she took great pains to attach her to her future husband, and to impress upon her what she owed him for the interest he had taken in her before he knew who she was, and for the proof he had given of his love in choosing her at a time when no one else ventured to think of her.

The marriage ceremony took place at the Louvre,[2] and in the evening the king and queen, with all the court, supped at the house of Madame de Chartres, who received them with great splendor. The Chevalier de Guise did not venture to make himself conspicuous by staying away, but his dejection was evident.

Monsieur de Clèves did not find that Mademoiselle de Chartres had altered her feelings when she changed her name. His position as her husband gave him greater privileges, but no different place in her heart. Though he had married her, he did not cease to be her lover,[3] because there was always left something for him to desire; and though she lived on the best of terms with him, he was not yet perfectly happy. He preserved for her a violent and restless passion, which marred his joy. Jealousy had no part in it, for never had a husband been further from feeling it, or a wife from inspiring it. Yet she was exposed to all the temptations of the court, visiting the queen and the king's sister every day. All the young and fashionable men met her at her own house and at that of her brother-in-law, the Duke of Nevers, whose doors were always open; but she always had an air that inspired respect, and seemed so remote from gallantry that the Marshal of Saint-André, though bold and protected by the king's favor, was touched by her beauty without venturing to show it except by delicate attentions. There were many others who felt as did the marshal; and Madame de Chartres added to her daughter's natural modesty such a keen sense of propriety that she made her seem like a woman to be sighed for in vain.

The Duchess of Lorraine, while trying to bring about peace, had also tried to arrange the marriage of her son, the Duke of Lorraine, and had succeeded; he was to marry Madame Claude of France, the king's second daughter. The wedding had been settled for the month of February.

Meanwhile the Duke of Nemours had remained at Brussels, completely taken up with his plans for England. He was always sending and receiving messengers. His hopes grew from day to day, and at last Lignerolles told him that it was time for him to appear and finish in person what had been so well

---

2. At this time, a royal residence.   3. I.e., he continued to love her.

begun. He received this news with all the satisfaction that an ambitious man can feel at seeing himself raised to a throne simply through his reputation. He had gradually grown so accustomed to the contemplation of this great piece of good fortune that whereas at first he had regarded it as an impossibility, all difficulties had vanished, and he foresaw no obstacles.

He at once despatched to Paris orders for a magnificent outfit, that he might make his appearance in England with a splendor proportionate to his designs, and also hastened to court to be present at the wedding of the Duke of Lorraine. He arrived the day before the formal betrothal, and that same evening went to report to the king the condition of affairs and to receive his advice and commands about his future conduct. Thence he went to pay his respects to the queens. Madame de Clèves was not there, so that she did not see him, and was not even aware of his arrival. She had heard every one speak of this prince as the handsomest and most agreeable man at court, and Madame the Dauphiness had spoken of him so often and in such terms that she felt some curiosity to see him.

Madame de Clèves spent the day of the betrothal at home dressing herself for the ball in the evening at the Louvre. When she made her appearance, her beauty and the splendor of her dress aroused general admiration. The ball opened, and while she was dancing with Monsieur de Guise, there was a certain commotion at the door of the ballroom, as if some one were entering for whom way was being made. Madame de Clèves finished her dance, and while she was looking about for another partner, the king called out to her to take the gentleman who had just arrived. She turned, and saw a man, who she thought must be Monsieur de Nemours, stepping over some seats to reach the place where the dancing was going on. No one ever saw this prince for the first time without amazement; and this evening he was more striking than ever in the rich attire which set off his natural beauty to such great advantage; and it was also hard to see Madame de Clèves for the first time without astonishment.

Monsieur de Nemours was so amazed by her beauty that when he drew near her and bowed to her he could not conceal his wonder and delight. When they began their dance, a murmur of admiration ran through the ballroom. The king and the queens remembered that the pair had never met, and saw how strange it was that they should be dancing together without being acquainted. They summoned them when they had finished the set, and without giving them a chance to speak to any one, asked if each would not like to know who the other was, and whether either had any idea.

"As for me, Madame," said Monsieur de Nemours, "I have no doubts; but since Madame de Clèves has not the same reasons for guessing who I am that I have for recognizing her, I must beg your Majesty to be good enough to tell her my name."

"I fancy," said the dauphiness, "that she knows it as well as you know hers."

"I assure you, Madame," said Madame de Clèves, who seemed a little embarrassed, "that I cannot guess so well as you think."

"You can guess very well," replied the dauphiness, "and you are very kind to Monsieur de Nemours in your unwillingness to acknowledge that you recognize him without ever having seen him before."

The queen interrupted the conversation, that the ball might go on, and

Monsieur de Nemours danced with the dauphiness. This lady was a perfect beauty, and had always appeared to be one in the eyes of Monsieur de Nemours before he went to Flanders; but all that evening he admired no one but Madame de Clèves.

The Chevalier de Guise, who never ceased worshipping her, was standing near, and this incident caused him evident pain. He regarded it as a sure sign that fate meant that Monsieur de Nemours should fall in love with Madame de Clèves; and whether it was that he saw something in her face, or that jealousy sharpened his fears, he believed that she had been moved by the sight of this prince, and he could not keep from telling her that Monsieur de Nemours was very fortunate in making her acquaintance in such a gallant and unusual way.

Madame de Clèves went home so full of what had happened at the ball that though it was very late, she went to her mother's room to tell her about it; and she praised Monsieur de Nemours with a certain air that made Madame de Chartres entertain the same suspicion as the Chevalier de Guise.

The next day the wedding took place; Madame de Clèves there saw the Duke of Nemours, and was even more struck by his admirable grace and dignity than before.

On succeeding days she met him at the drawing-room of the dauphiness, saw him playing tennis with the king and riding at the ring, and heard him talk; and she always found him so superior to every one else, and so much outshining all in conversation wherever he might be, by the grace of his person and the charm of his wit, that he soon made a deep impression on her heart.

Then, too, the desire to please made the Duke of Nemours, who was already deeply interested, more charming than ever; and since they met often, and found each other more attractive than any one else at court, they naturally experienced great delight in being together.

The Duchess of Valentinois took part in all the merry-making, and the king showed her all the interest and attention that he had done when first in love with her. Madame de Clèves, who was then of an age at which it is usual to believe that no woman can ever be loved after she is twenty-five years old, regarded with great amazement the king's attachment to this duchess, who was a grandmother and had just married[4] her granddaughter. She often spoke of it to Madame de Chartres. "Is it possible," she asked, "that the king has been in love so long? How could he get interested in a woman much older than himself, and who had been his father's mistress, as well as that of a great many other men, as I have heard?"

"It is true," was the answer, "that neither merit nor fidelity inspired the king's passion, or has kept it alive. And this is something which is scarcely to be excused; for had this woman had youth and beauty as well as rank, had she loved no one else, had she loved the king with untiring constancy, for himself alone, and not solely for his wealth and position, and had she used her power for worthy objects such as the king desired, it would have been easy to admire his great devotion to her. If," Madame de Chartres went on, "I were not afraid that you would say of me what is always said of women of my age, that we like to talk about old times, I would tell you the beginning

4. Married off.

of the king's love for this duchess; and many things that happened at the court of the late king bear much resemblance to what is now going on."

"So far from accusing you of repeating old stories," said Madame de Clèves, "I regret that you have told me so little about the present, and that you have not taught me the different interests and intrigues of the court. I am so ignorant of them that a few days ago I thought the constable was on the best of terms with the queen."

"You were very far from the truth," replied Madame de Chartres. "The queen hates the constable, and if she ever gets any power he will learn it very quickly. She knows that he has often told the king that of all his children it is only his bastards who look like him."

"I should never have imagined this hatred," interrupted Madame de Clèves, "after seeing the zeal with which the queen wrote to the constable when he was in prison, the joy she manifested at his return, and the familiarity of her address as regards him."

"If you judge from appearances here," replied Madame de Chartres, "you will be often mistaken; what appears is seldom the truth.

"But to return to Madame de Valentinois: you know her name is Diane de Poitiers. She is of illustrious family, being descended from the old dukes of Aquitaine; her grandmother was a natural daughter of Louis XI,—in short, there is no common blood in her veins. Saint-Vallier, her father, was implicated in the affair of the Constable of Bourbon, of which you have heard, was condemned to be beheaded, and was led to the scaffold. His daughter, who was remarkably beautiful, and had already pleased the late king, managed, I don't know how, to save her father's life. His pardon was granted him when he was expecting the mortal stroke; but fear had so possessed him that he did not recover consciousness, but died a few days later. His daughter made her appearance at court as the king's mistress. His journey to Italy and his imprisonment interrupted this passion. When he returned from Spain and Madame Regénte went to meet him at Bayonne, she had with her all her young women, among whom was Mademoiselle de Pisseleu, afterwards Duchess of Estampes. The king fell in love with her, though she was inferior in birth, beauty, and intelligence to Madame de Valentinois: the only advantage she had was that she was younger. I have often heard her say that she was born on the day that Diane de Poitiers was married; but that remark was more malicious than truthful, for I am much mistaken if the Duchess of Valentinois did not marry Monsieur de Brézé, grand seneschal of Normandy, at the same time that the king fell in love with Madame d'Estampes. Never was there fiercer hatred than existed between those two women. The Duchess of Valentinois could not forgive Madame d'Estampes for depriving her of the title of the king's mistress. Madame d'Estampes was madly jealous of Madame de Valentinois because the king maintained his relations with her. This king was never rigorously faithful to his mistresses; there was always one who had the title and the honors, but the ladies of what was called the little band shared his attentions. The death of his oldest son, it was supposed by poison, at Tournon, was a great blow to him. He had much less love for his second son, the present king, who was in every way far less to his taste, and whom he even regarded as lacking courage and spirit. He was lamenting this one day to Madame de Valentinois, whereupon she said she would like to make him fall in love with her, that he might become livelier and more agreeable. She succeeded, as you know. This love has lasted more than twenty years, without being dimmed by time or circumstances.

"At first the late king objected to it,—whether because he was still enough in love with Madame de Valentinois to feel jealous, or because he was influenced by Madame d'Estampes, who was in despair when the dauphin became attached to her enemy, is uncertain; however that may be, he viewed this passion with an anger and a disapproval that were apparent every day. His son feared neither his wrath nor his hate; and since nothing could induce him to abate or to conceal his attachment, the king was forced to endure it as best he could. His son's opposition to his wishes estranged him still more, and attached him more closely to the Duke of Orléans, his third son. This prince was handsome, energetic, ambitious, of a somewhat tempestuous nature, which needed to be controlled, but who in time would become a really fine man.

"The elder son's rank as dauphin and the father's preference for the Duke of Orléans inspired a rivalry between them which amounted to hatred. This rivalry had begun in their childhood, and lasted until the death of the latter. When the emperor entered French territory[5] he gave his whole preference to the Duke of Orléans. This so pained the dauphin that when the emperor was at Chantilly he tried to compel the constable to arrest him, without waiting for the king's orders; but the constable refused. Afterward the king blamed him for not following his son's advice; and this had a good deal to do with his leaving the court.

"The division between the two brothers induced the Duchess of Estampes to rely on the Duke of Orléans for protection against the influence which Madame de Valentinois had over the king. In this she succeeded; the duke, without falling in love with her, was as warm in defence of her interests as was the dauphin in defence of those of Madame de Valentinois. Hence there were two cabals in the court such as you can imagine; but the intrigues were not limited to two women's quarrels.

"The emperor, who had maintained his friendship for the Duke of Orléans, had frequently offered him the duchy of Milan. In the subsequent negotiations about peace, he raised hopes in the breast of the duke that he would give him the seventeen provinces[6] and his daughter's hand. The dauphin, however, desired neither peace nor this marriage. He made use of the constable, whom he had always loved, to convince the king how important it was not to give to his successor a brother so powerful as would be the Duke of Orléans in alliance with the emperor and governing the seventeen provinces. The constable agreed the more heartily with the dauphin's views because he also opposed those of Madame d'Estampes, who was his avowed enemy, and ardently desired that the power of the Duke of Orléans should be increased.

"At that time the dauphin was in command of the king's army in Champagne, and had reduced that of the emperor to such extremities that it would have utterly perished had not the Duchess of Estampes, fearing that too great success would prevent our granting peace and consenting to the marriage, secretly sent word to the enemy to surprise Epernay and Château-Thierry, which were full of supplies. This they did, and thereby saved their whole army.

"This duchess did not long profit by her treason. Soon afterward the Duke

5. Despite the enmity between France and the empire, Charles V was allowed to cross France in 1539 on his way to put down a revolt in the Netherlands.   6. The Spanish Netherlands, which included most of modern Belgium and Holland.

of Orléans died at Farmoutier of some contagious disease. He loved one of the most beautiful women of the court, and was beloved by her. I shall not tell you who it was, because her life since that time has been most decorous; and she has tried so hard to have her affection for the prince forgotten that she deserves to have her reputation left untarnished. It so happened that she heard of her husband's death on the same day that she heard of that of Monsieur d'Orléans; consequently she was able to conceal her real grief without an effort.

"The king did not long survive his son's decease,—he died two years later. He urged the dauphin to make use of the services of the Cardinal of Tournon and of the Amiral d'Annebauld, without saying a word about the constable, who at that time was banished to Chantilly. Nevertheless, the first thing the present king did after his father's death was to call the constable back and intrust him with the management of affairs.

"Madame d'Estampes was sent away, and became the victim of all the ill-treatment she might have expected from an all-powerful enemy. The Duchess of Valentinois took full vengeance on this duchess and on all who had displeased her. Her power over the king seemed the greater because it had not appeared while he was dauphin. During the twelve years of his reign she has been in everything absolute mistress. She disposes of places and controls affairs of every sort; she secured the dismissal of the Cardinal of Tournon, of the Chancelier Olivier, and of Villeroy. Those who have endeavored to open the king's eyes to her conduct have been ruined for their pains. The Count of Taix, commander-in-chief of the artillery, who did not like her, could not keep from talking about her love affairs, and especially about one with the Count of Brissac, of whom the king was already very jealous. Yet she managed so well that the Count of Taix was disgraced and deprived of his position; and impossible as it may sound, he was succeeded by the Count of Brissac, whom she afterward made a marshal of France. Still, the king's jealousy became so violent that he could not endure having this marshal remain at court; but though usually jealousy is a hot and violent passion, it is modified and tempered in him by his extreme respect for his mistress, so that the only means he ventured to use to rid himself of his rival was by intrusting to him the government of Piedmont. There he has spent several years; last winter, however, he returned, under the pretext of asking for men and supplies for the army under his command. Possibly the desire of seeing Madame de Valentinois and dread of being forgotten had something to do with this journey. The king received him very coldly. The Guises, who do not like him, did not dare betray their feelings, on account of Madame de Valentinois, so they made use of the Vidame, his open enemy, to prevent his getting any of the things he wanted. It was not hard to injure him. The king hated him, and was made uneasy by his presence; consequently he was obliged to go back without getting any advantage from his journey,—unless, possibly, he had rekindled in the heart of Madame de Valentinois feelings which absence had nearly extinguished. The king has had many other grounds for jealousy, but either he has not known them, or he has not dared to complain.

"I am not sure, my dear," added Madame de Chartres, "that you may not think I have told you more than you cared to hear."

"Not at all," answered Madame de Clèves; "and if I were not afraid of tiring you, I should ask you many more questions."

Monsieur de Nemours' love for Madame de Clèves was at first so violent that he lost all interest in those he had formerly loved, and with whom he had kept up relations during his absence. He not merely did not seek any excuses for deserting them, he would not even listen to their complaints or reply to their reproaches. The dauphiness, for whom he had nourished very warm feelings, was soon forgotten by the side of Madame de Clèves. His impatience for his journey to England began to abate, and he ceased to hasten his preparations for departure. He often visited the crown princess, because Madame de Clèves was frequently in her apartments, and he was not unwilling to give some justification to the widespread suspicions about his feelings for the dauphiness. Madame de Clèves seemed to him so rare a prize that he decided to conceal all signs of his love rather than let it be generally known. He never spoke of it even to his intimate friend the Vidame de Chartres, to whom he usually confided everything. He was so cautious and discreet that no one suspected his love for Madame de Clèves except the Chevalier de Guise; and the lady herself would scarcely have perceived it had not her own interest in him made her watch him very closely, so that she became sure of it.

Madame de Clèves did not find herself so disposed to tell her mother what she thought of this prince's feelings as had been the case with her other lovers; and without definitely deciding on reserve, she yet never spoke of the subject. But Madame de Chartres soon perceived this, as well as her daughter's interest in him. This knowledge gave her distinct pain, for she well understood how dangerous it was for Madame de Clèves to be loved by a man like Monsieur de Nemours, especially when she was already disposed to admire him. An incident that happened a few days later confirmed her suspicions of this liking.

The Marshal of Saint-André, who was always on the look-out for opportunities to display his magnificence, made a pretext of desiring to show his house, which had just been finished, and invited the king to do him the honor of supping there with the queens. The marshal was also glad to be able to show to Madame de Clèves his lavish splendor.

A few days before the one of the supper, the dauphin, whose health was delicate, had been ailing and had seen no one. His wife, the crown princess, had spent the whole day with him, and toward evening, as he felt better, he received all the persons of quality who were in his ante-chamber. The crown princess went to her own apartment, where she found Madame de Clèves and a few other ladies with whom she was most intimate.

Since it was already late, and the crown princess was not dressed, she did not go to the queen, but sent word she could not come; she then had her jewels brought, to decide what she should wear at the Marshal of Saint-André's ball, and to give some, according to a promise she had made, to Madame de Clèves. While they were thus occupied, the Prince of Condé, whose rank gave him free admission everywhere, entered. The crown princess said to him that he doubtless came from her husband, and asked what was going on in his apartments.

"They are having a discussion, Madame, with Monsieur de Nemours," he answered. "He defends the side he has taken so eagerly that he must have a personal interest in it. I fancy he has a mistress who makes him uneasy when she goes to a ball, for he maintains that it makes a lover unhappy to see the woman he loves at such a place."

"What!" said the dauphiness, "Monsieur de Nemours does not want his mistress to go to a ball? I thought husbands might object, but I never supposed that lovers could have such a feeling."

"Monsieur de Nemours," replied the Prince of Condé, "declares that a ball is most distressing to lovers, whether they are loved or not. He says if their love is returned, they have the pain of being loved less for several days; that there is not a woman in the world who is not prevented from thinking of her lover by the demands of her toilet,[7] which entirely engrosses her attention; that women dress for every one as well as for those they love; that when they are at the ball they are anxious to please all who look at them; that when they are proud of their beauty, they feel a pleasure in which the lover plays but a small part. He says, too, that one who sighs in vain suffers even more when he sees his mistress at an entertainment; that the more she is admired by the public, the more one suffers at not being loved, through fear lest her beauty should kindle some love happier than his own; finally, that there is no pain so keen as seeing one's mistress at a ball, except knowing that she is there while absent one's self."

Madame de Clèves, though pretending not to hear what the Prince of Condé was saying, listened attentively. She readily understood her share in the opinion expressed by Monsieur de Nemours, especially when he spoke of his grief at not being at the ball with his mistress, because he was not to be at that given by the Marshal of Saint-André, being ordered by the king to go to meet the Duke of Ferrara.

The crown princess laughed with the Prince of Condé, and expressed her disapproval of the views of Monsieur de Nemours. "There is only one condition, Madame," said the prince, "on which Monsieur de Nemours is willing that his mistress should go to a ball, and that is that he himself should give her permission. He said that last year when he gave a ball to your Majesty, he thought that his mistress did him a great favor in coming to it, though she seemed to be there only as one of your suite; that it is always a kindness to a lover to take part in any entertainment that he gives; and that it is also agreeable to a lover to have his mistress see him the host of the whole court and doing the honors fittingly."

"Monsieur de Nemours did well," said the dauphiness, with a smile, "to let his mistress go to that ball; for so many women claimed that position that if they had not come, there would have been scarcely any one there."

As soon as the Prince of Condé had begun to speak of what Monsieur de Nemours thought of the ball, Madame de Clèves was very anxious not to go to that of the Marshal of Saint-André. She readily agreed that it was not fitting for a woman to go to the house of a man who was in love with her, and she was glad to have so good a reason for doing a kindness to Monsieur de Nemours. Nevertheless, she took away the jewels which the crown princess had given her; that evening, however, when she showed them to her mother, she told her that she did not mean to wear them, that the Marshal of Saint-André had made his love for her so manifest that she felt sure he meant to have it thought that she was to have some part in the entertainment he was to give to the king, and that under the pretext of doing honor to the king he would pay her attentions which might perhaps prove embarrassing.

7. The process of dressing.

Madame de Chartres argued for some time against her daughter's decision, which she thought singular, but at last yielded, and told her she must pretend to be ill, in order to have a good excuse for not going, because her real reasons would not be approved and should not be suspected. Madame de Clèves gladly consented to stay at home for a few days, in order not to meet Monsieur de Nemours, who left without having the pleasure of knowing that she was not going to the ball.

The duke returned the day after the ball, and heard that she had not been there; but inasmuch as he did not know that his talk with the dauphin had been repeated to her, he was far from thinking that he was fortunate enough to be the cause of her absence.

The next day, when Monsieur de Nemours was calling on the queen and talking with the dauphiness, Madame de Chartres and Madame de Clèves happened to come in and approached this princess. Madame de Clèves was not in full dress, as if she were not very well, though her countenance belied her attire.

"You look so well," said the crown princess, "that I can scarcely believe that you have been ill. I fancy that the Prince of Condé, when he told you what Monsieur de Nemours thought about the ball, convinced you that you would do a kindness to the Marshal of Saint-André by going to his ball, and that that was the reason you stayed away."

Madame de Clèves blushed at the dauphiness's accurate guess which she thus expressed before Monsieur de Nemours.

Madame de Chartres saw at once why her daughter did not go to the ball, and in order to throw Monsieur de Nemours off the track, she at once addressed the dauphiness with an air of sincerity. "I assure you, Madame," she said, "that your Majesty pays an honor to my daughter which she does not deserve. She was really ill; but I am sure that if I had not forbidden it, she would have accompanied you, unfit as she was, to have the pleasure of seeing the wonderful entertainment last evening."

The dauphiness believed what Madame de Chartres said, and Monsieur de Nemours was vexed to see how probable her story was; nevertheless the confusion of Madame de Clèves made him suspect that the dauphiness's conjecture was not without some foundation in fact. At first Madame de Clèves had been annoyed because Monsieur de Nemours had reason to suppose that it was he who had kept her from going to the ball, and then she felt regret that her mother had entirely removed the grounds for this supposition.

Although the attempt to make peace at Cercamp had failed, negotiations still continued, and matters had assumed such a shape that toward the end of February a meeting was held at Cateau-Cambrésis.[8] The same commissioners had assembled there, and the departure of the Marshal of Saint-André freed Monsieur de Nemours from a rival who was more to be dreaded on account of his close observation of all those who approached Madame de Clèves than from any real success of his own.

Madame de Chartres did not wish to let her daughter see that she knew her feeling for this prince, lest she should make her suspicious of the advice

8. Negotiations were beginning toward a peace treaty between France and the empire. The death of Queen Mary of England ended the preliminary meetings that had begun at Cercamp in 1558; they resumed the next year and ended with the Treaty of Cateau-Cambrésis.

she wanted to give her. One day she began to talk about him. She spoke of him in warm terms, but craftily praised his discretion in being unable to fall really in love and in seeking only pleasure, not a serious attachment, in his relations with women. "To be sure," she went on, "he has been suspected of a great passion for the dauphiness; I notice that he visits her very often, and I advise you to avoid talking with him as much as possible, especially in private, because you are on such terms with the crown princess that people would say that you were their confidant, and you know how disagreeable that would be. I think that if the report continues, you would do well to see less of the crown princess, that you may not be connected with love-affairs of that sort."

Madame de Clèves had never heard Monsieur de Nemours and the dauphiness talked about, and was much surprised by what her mother said. She was so sure that she had misunderstood the prince's feelings for her that she changed color. Madame de Chartres noticed this, but company coming in at that moment, Madame de Clèves went home and locked herself up in her room.

It is impossible to express her grief when her mother's words opened her eyes to the interest she took in Monsieur de Nemours; she had never dared to acknowledge it to herself. Then she saw that her feelings for him were what Monsieur de Clèves had so often supplicated, and she felt the mortification of having them for another than a husband who so well deserved them. She felt hurt and embarrassed, fearing that Monsieur de Nemours might have used her as a pretext for seeing the dauphiness; and this thought decided her to tell Madame de Chartres what she had hitherto kept secret.

The next morning she went to her mother to carry out this decision; but Madame de Chartres was a little feverish, and did not care to talk with her. The illness seemed so slight, however, that Madame de Clèves called on the dauphiness after dinner, and found her in her room with two or three ladies with whom she was on intimate terms.

"We were talking about Monsieur de Nemours," said the queen when she saw her, "and were surprised to see how much he is changed since his return from Brussels; before he went, he had an infinite number of mistresses, and it was a positive disadvantage to him, because he used to be kind both to those who were worthy and to those who were not. Since his return, however, he will have nothing to do with any of them. There has never been such a change. His spirits, moreover, seem to be affected, as he is much less cheerful than usual."

Madame de Clèves made no answer; she thought with a sense of shame that she would have taken all that they said about the change in him for a proof of his passion if she had not been undeceived. She was somewhat vexed with the dauphiness for trying to explain and for expressing surprise at something of which she must know the real reason better than any one else. She could not keep from showing her annoyance, and when the other ladies withdrew, she went up to the crown princess and said in a low voice,—

"Is it for my benefit that you have just spoken, and do you want to hide from me that you are the cause of the altered conduct of Monsieur de Nemours?"

"You are unjust," said the crown princess; "you know that I never keep anything from you. It is true that before he went to Brussels, Monsieur de Nemours meant to have me understand that he did not hate me; but since his return he seems to have forgotten all about it, and I confess that I am a little curious about the reason of this change. I shall probably find it out," she went on, "as the Vidame de Chartres, his intimate friend, is in love with a young woman over whom I have some power, and I shall know from her what has made this change."

The dauphiness spoke with an air that carried conviction to Madame de Clèves, who found herself calmer and happier than she had been before. When she went back to her mother, she found her much worse than when she had left her. She was more feverish, and for some days it seemed as if she were going to be really ill. Madame de Clèves was in great distress, and did not leave her mother's room. Monsieur de Clèves spent nearly all his time there too, both to comfort his wife and to have the pleasure of seeing her: his love had not lessened.

Monsieur de Nemours, who had always been one of his friends, had not neglected him since his return from Brussels. During the illness of Madame de Chartres he found it possible to see Madame de Clèves very often, under pretence of calling on her husband or of stopping to take him to walk. He even sought him at hours when he knew he was not in; then he would say that he would wait for him, and used to stay in the ante-chamber of Madame de Chartres, where were assembled many persons of quality. Madame de Clèves would often look in, and although she was in great anxiety, she seemed no less beautiful to Monsieur de Nemours. He showed her how much he sympathized with her distress, and soon convinced her that it was not with the dauphiness that he was in love.

She could not keep from being embarrassed, and yet delighted to see him; but when he was out of her sight and she remembered that this pleasure was the beginning of an unhappy passion, she felt she almost hated him, so much did the idea of guilty love pain her.

Madame de Chartres rapidly grew worse, and soon her life was despaired of; she heard the doctors' opinion of her danger with a courage proportionate to her virtue and piety. After they had left her, she dismissed all who were present, and sent for Madame de Clèves.

"We have to part, my daughter," she said, holding out her hand; "and the peril in which you are and the need you have of me, double my pain in leaving you. You have an affection for Monsieur de Nemours; I do not ask you to confess it, as I am no longer able to make use of your sincerity in order to guide you. It is long since I perceived this affection, but I have been averse to speaking to you about it, lest you should become aware of it yourself. Now you know it only too well. You are on the edge of a precipice: a great effort, a violent struggle, alone can save you. Think of what you owe your husband, think of what you owe yourself, and remember that you are in danger of losing that reputation which you have acquired and which I have so ardently desired for you. Take strength and courage, my daughter: withdraw from the court; compel your husband to take you away. Do not be afraid of making a difficult decision. Terrible as it may appear at first, it will in the end be pleasanter than the consequences of a love-affair. If any other reasons than virtue and duty can persuade you to what I wish, let me say that if anything is capable of destroying the happiness I hope for in another world, it would be seeing you fall like so many women; but if this misfortune must come to you, I welcome death that I may not see it."

Madame de Clèves' tears fell on her mother's hand, which she held clasped in her own, and Madame de Chartres saw that she was moved. "Good-by, my daughter," she said; "let us put an end to a conversation which moves us both too deeply, and remember, if you can, all I have just said to you."

With these words she turned away and bade her daughter call her women, without hearing or saying more. Madame de Clèves left her mother's room in a state that may be imagined, and Madame de Chartres thought of nothing but preparing herself for death. She lingered two days more, but refused again to see her daughter,—the only person she loved.

Madame de Clèves was in sore distress; her husband never left her side, and as soon as Madame de Chartres had died, he took her into the country, to get her away from a place which continually renewed her grief, which was intense. Although her love and gratitude to her mother counted for a great deal, the need she felt of her support against Monsieur de Nemours made the blow even more painful. She lamented being left to herself when she had her emotions so little under control, and when she so needed some one to pity her and give her strength. Her husband's kindness made her wish more than ever to be always true to him. She showed him more affection and kindliness than she had ever done before, and she wanted him always by her side; for it seemed to her that her attachment to him would prove a defence against Monsieur de Nemours.

This prince went to visit Monsieur de Clèves in the country, and did his best to see Madame de Clèves; but she declined to receive him, knowing that she could not fail to find him charming. Moreover, she resolutely determined to avoid every occasion of meeting him, so far as she was able.

Monsieur de Clèves repaired[9] to Paris to pay his respects at court, promising his wife to return the next day; but he did not return till the day after.

"I expected you all day yesterday," Madame de Clèves said to him when he arrived, "and I ought to find fault with you for not returning when you promised. You know that if I could feel a new sorrow in the state I am in, it would be at the death of Madame de Tournon, of which I heard this morning. I should have been distressed by it even if I had not known her. It is always painful when a young and beautiful woman like her dies after an illness of only two days, and much more so when it is one of the persons I liked best in the world, and who seemed as modest as she was worthy."

"I was sorry not to return yesterday," answered Monsieur de Clèves; "but it was so imperatively necessary that I should console an unhappy man that I could not possibly leave him. As for Madame de Tournon, I advise you not to be too profoundly distressed, if you mourn her as an upright woman who deserved your esteem."

"You surprise me," said Madame de Clèves, "as I have often heard you say that there was no woman at court whom you esteemed more highly."

"That is true," he answered; "but women are incomprehensible, and the more I see of them, the happier I feel that I have married you, and I cannot be sufficiently grateful for my good fortune."

"You think better of me than I deserve," exclaimed Madame de Clèves,

---

9. Went.

with a sigh, "and it is much too soon to think me worthy of you. But tell me, please, what has undeceived you about Madame de Tournon."

"I have long been undeceived in regard to her," he replied, "and have long known that she loved the Count of Sancerre, to whom she held out hopes that she would marry him."

"I can scarcely believe," interrupted Madame de Clèves, "that Madame de Tournon, after the extraordinary reluctance to matrimony which she showed after she became a widow, and after her public assertions that she would never marry again, should have given Sancerre any hopes."

"If she had given them only to him," replied Monsieur de Clèves, "there would be little occasion for surprise; but what is astounding is that she also gave them to Estouteville at the same time, and I will tell you the whole story."

Part II

"You know," Monsieur de Clèves continued, "what good friends Sancerre and I are; yet when, about two years ago, he fell in love with Madame de Tournon, he took great pains to conceal it from me, as well as from every one else, and I was far from suspecting it. Madame de Tournon appeared still inconsolable for her husband's death, and was still living in the most absolute retirement. Sancerre's sister was almost the only person she saw, and it was at her house that the count fell in love with her.

"One evening when there was to be a play at the Louvre, and while they were waiting for the king and Madame de Valentinois in order to begin, word was brought that she was ill and that the king would not come. Every one guessed that the duchess's illness was some quarrel with the king. We knew how jealous he had been of the Marshal of Brissac during his stay at court; but the marshal had gone back to Piedmont a few days before, and we could not imagine the cause of this falling-out.

"While I was talking about it with Sancerre, Monsieur d'Anville came into the hall and whispered to me that the king was in a state of distress and anger most piteous to see; that when he and Madame de Valentinois were reconciled a few days before, after their quarrels about the Marshal of Brissac, the king had given her a ring and asked her to wear it. While she was dressing for the play, he had noticed its absence, and had asked her the reason. She seemed surprised to miss it, and asked her women for it; but they, unfortunately, perhaps because they had not been put on their guard, said that it was some four or five days since they had seen it.

"'That exactly corresponded with the date of the Marshal of Brissac's departure,' Monsieur d'Anville went on; 'and the king is convinced that she gave him the ring when she bade him good-by. This thought has so aroused all his jealousy, which was by no means wholly extinguished, that, contrary to his usual custom, he flew into a rage and reproached her bitterly. He has gone back to his room in great distress, whether because he thinks that Madame de Valentinois has given away his ring, or because he fears that he has displeased her by his wrath, I do not know.'

"As soon as Monsieur d'Anville had finished, I went up to Sancerre to tell him the news, assuring him that it was a secret that had just been told me, and was to go no farther.

"The next morning I called rather early on my sister-in-law, and found Madame de Tournon there. She did not like Madame de Valentinois, and knew very well that my sister-in-law also had no reason for being fond of her. Sancerre had seen her when he left the play, and had told her about the king's quarrel with the duchess; this she had come to repeat to my sister-in-law, either not knowing or not remembering that it was I who had told her lover.

"When I came in, my sister-in-law said to Madame de Tournon that I could be trusted with what she had just told her, and without waiting for permission she repeated to me word for word everything I had told Sancerre the previous evening. You will understand my surprise. I looked at Madame de Tournon, who seemed embarrassed, and her embarrassment aroused my suspicions. I had mentioned the matter to no one but Sancerre, who had left me after the play, without saying where he was going; but I remembered hearing him praise Madame de Tournon very warmly. All these things opened my eyes, and I soon decided that there was a love-affair between them, and that he had seen her after he left me.

"I was so annoyed to find that he kept the matter secret from me that I said a good many things that made it clear to Madame de Tournon that she had been imprudent; as I handed her to her carriage, I assured her that I envied the happiness of the person who had informed her of the falling-out of the king and Madame de Valentinois.

"At once I went to see Sancerre; I reproached him, and said that I knew of his passion for Madame de Tournon, but I did not say how I had found it out. He felt obliged to make a complete confession. I then told him how it was I had discovered his secret, and he told me all about the affair; he said that inasmuch as he was a younger son, and far from having any claims to such an honor, she was yet determined to marry him. No one could be more surprised than I was. I urged Sancerre to hasten his marriage, and told him that he would be justified in fearing anything from a woman who was so full of craft that she could play so false a part before the public. He said in reply that her grief had been sincere, but that it had yielded before her affection for him, and that she could not suddenly make this great change manifest. He brought up many other things in her defence, which showed me clearly how much in love he was; he assured me that he would persuade her to let me know all about the passion he had for her, since it was she who had let out the secret,—and in fact he compelled her to consent, though with much difficulty, and I was from that time fully admitted to their confidence.

"I have never seen a woman so honorable and agreeable toward her lover; yet I was always pained by her affectation of grief. Sancerre was so much in love, and so well satisfied with the way she treated him, that he was almost afraid to urge their marriage, lest she should think that he was moved thereto by interest rather than passion. Still, he often talked to her about it, and she seemed to have decided to marry him; she even began to leave her retirement and to reappear in the world,—she used to come to my sister-in-law's at the time when part of the court used to be there. Sancerre came very seldom; but those who were there every evening and met her often, found her very charming.

"Shortly after she began to come out again into society, Sancerre imagined that he detected some coolness in her love for him. He spoke to me about it several times without rousing any anxiety in me by his complaints; but when at length he told me that instead of hastening, she seemed to be postponing their marriage, I began to think that he had good grounds for uneasiness. I said that even if Madame de Tournon's passion should lessen after lasting for two years, he ought not to be surprised; that even if it did not lessen, and though it should not be strong enough to persuade her to marry him, he ought not to complain; since their marriage would injure her much in the eyes of the public, not only because he was not a very good match for her, but because it would affect her reputation: hence that all he could reasonably desire was that she should not deceive him and feed him with false hopes. I also said that if she had not the courage to marry him, or if she should confess that she loved some one else, he ought not to be angry or complain, but preserve his esteem and gratitude for her.

" 'I give you the advice,' I said to him, 'which I should take myself; for I am so touched by sincerity that I believe that if my mistress, or my wife, were to confess that any one pleased her, I should be distressed without being angered, and should lay aside the character of lover or husband to advise and sympathize with her.' "

At these words Madame de Clèves blushed, finding a certain likeness to her own condition which surprised her and distressed her for some time.

"Sancerre spoke to Madame de Tournon," Monsieur de Clèves went on, "telling her everything I had advised; but she reassured him with such tact and seemed so pained by his suspicions that she entirely dispelled them. Nevertheless she postponed their marriage until after a long journey which he was about to make; but her conduct was so discreet up to the time of his departure, and she seemed so grieved at parting with him, that I, as well as he, believed that she truly loved him. He went away about three months ago. During his absence I saw Madame de Tournon very seldom; you have taken up all my time, and I only knew that Sancerre was to return soon.

"The day before yesterday, on my arrival in Paris, I heard that she was dead. I at once sent to his house to find out if they had heard from him, and was told that he had arrived the day before,—the very day of Madame de Tournon's death. I went at once to see him, knowing very well in what a state I should find him; but his agony far exceeded what I had imagined. Never have I seen such deep and tender grief. As soon as he saw me, he embraced me, bursting into tears. 'I shall never see her again,' he said, 'I shall never see her again; she is dead! I was not worthy of her; but I shall soon follow her.'

"After that he was silent; then from time to time he repeated: 'She is dead, and I shall never see her again!' Thereupon he would again burst into tears, and seemed out of his head. He told me he had received but few letters from her while away, but that this did not surprise him, because he well knew her aversion to running any risk in writing letters. He had no doubt that she would have married him on his return; and he looked upon her as the most amiable and faithful woman who had ever lived; he believed that she loved him tenderly, and that he had lost her at the moment when he made sure of winning her forever. These thoughts plunged him into the deepest distress, by which he was wholly overcome, and I confess that I was deeply moved.

"Nevertheless, I was obliged to leave him to go to the king, but I promised to return soon. This I did; but imagine my surprise when I found that he was in an entirely different mood. He was pacing up and down his room with a wild face, and he stopped as if he were beside himself and said: 'Come, come! see the most desperate man in the world; I am ten thousand times unhappier than I was before, and what I have just heard of Madame de Tournon is worse than her death.'

"I thought that his grief had crazed him, for I could imagine nothing more terrible than the death of a loved mistress who returns one's love. I told him that so long as his grief had been within bounds I had understood and sympathized with it; but that I should cease to pity him if he gave way to despair and lost his mind. 'I wish I could lose it, and my life too,' he exclaimed. 'Madame de Tournon was unfaithful to me; and I ascertained her infidelity and treachery the day after I heard of her death, at a time when my soul was filled with the deepest grief and the tenderest love that were ever felt,—at a time when my heart was filled with the thought of her as the most perfect creature that had ever lived, and the most generous to me. I find that I was mistaken in her, and that she does not deserve my tears; nevertheless, I have the same grief from her death as if she had been faithful to me, and I suffer from her infidelity as if she were not dead. Had I known of her changed feeling before she died, I should have been wild with wrath and jealousy, and should have been in some way hardened against the blow of her death; but now I can get no consolation from it or hate her.'

"You may judge of my surprise at what Sancerre told me; I asked him how he found this out. He told me that the moment I had left his room, Estouteville, an intimate friend of his, though he knew nothing of his love for Madame de Tournon, had come to see him; that as soon as he had sat down, he burst into tears and said he begged his pardon for not having told him before what he was about to say; that he had come to open his heart to him; and that he saw before him a man utterly crushed by the death of Madame de Tournon.

" 'That name,' said Sancerre, 'surprised me so that my first impulse was to tell him that I was much more distressed than he; but I was unable to speak a word. He went on and told me that he had been in love with her for six months; that he had always meant to tell me, but she had forbidden it so firmly that he had not dared to disobey her; that almost ever since he fell in love with her she had taken a tender interest in him; that he only visited her secretly; that he had had the pleasure of consoling her for the loss of her husband; and, finally, that he was on the point of marrying her at the time of her death, but that this marriage, which would have been one of love, would have appeared to be one of duty and obedience, because she had won over her father to command this marriage, in order that there should not be any great change in her conduct, which had indicated an unwillingness to contract a second marriage.

" 'While Estouteville was speaking,' Sancerre went on, 'I fully believed him, because what he said seemed likely, and the time he had mentioned as that when he fell in love with Madame de Tournon coincided with that of her altered treatment of me. But a moment after, I thought him a liar, or at least out of his senses, and I was ready to tell him so. I thought, however, I would first make sure; hence I began to question him and to show that I had my doubts. At last I was so persistent in the search of my unhappiness that he asked if I knew Madame de Tournon's handwriting, and placed on my bed four of her letters and her portrait. My brother happened to come in at that moment. Estouteville's face was so stained with tears that he had to go away in order not to be seen in that state; he told me that he would come back that evening to get the things he left. I sent my brother away, pretending that I was not feeling well, being impatient to read the letters, and still hoping to find something which would convince me that Estouteville was mistaken. But, alas, what did I not find! What tenderness, what protestations, what promises to marry him, what letters! She had never written me any like them. So,' he went on, 'I suffer at the same time grief for her death and for her faithlessness,—two misfortunes which have often been compared, but have never been felt at the same time by one person. I confess, to my shame, that I feel much more keenly her death than her change; I cannot find her guilty enough to deserve to die. If she were still alive, I should have the pleasure of reproaching her, of avenging myself by showing her how great was her injustice. But I shall never see her again.' He repeated, 'I shall never see her again,—that is the bitterest blow of all; I would gladly give up my life for hers. What a wish! If she were to return, she would live for Estouteville. How happy I was yesterday!' he exclaimed, 'how happy I was then! I was the most sorely distressed man in the world; but my distress was in the order of nature, and I drew some comfort from the thought that I could never be consoled. To-day all my feelings are false ones; I pay to the pretended love she felt for me the same tribute that I thought due to a real affection. I can neither hate nor love her memory; I am incapable of consolation or of grief. At least,' he said, turning suddenly toward me, 'let me, I beg of you, never see Estouteville again; his very name fills me with horror. I know very well that I have no reason to blame him; it is my own fault for concealing from him my love for Madame de Tournon: if he had known of it, he would perhaps have never cared for her, and she would not have been unfaithful to me. He came to see me to confide his grief; I really pity him. Yes, and with good reason,' he exclaimed; 'he loved Madame de Tournon and was loved by her. He will never see her again; yet I feel that I cannot keep from hating him. Once more, I beg of you never to let me see him again.'

"Thereupon Sancerre burst again into tears, mourning Madame de Tournon, saying to her the tenderest things imaginable; thence he changed to hatred, complaints, reproaches, and denunciations of her conduct. When I saw him in this desperate state I knew that I should need some aid in calming him, so I sent for his brother, whom I had just left with the king. I went out to speak to him in the hall before he came in, and I told him what a state Sancerre was in. We gave orders that he was not to see Estouteville, and spent a good part of the night trying to persuade him to listen to reason. This morning I found him in still deeper distress; his brother is staying with him, and I have returned to you."

"No one could be more surprised than I am," said Madame de Clèves, "for I thought Madame de Tournon incapable of both love and deception."

"Address and dissimulation,"[1] answered Monsieur de Clèves, "could not go further. Notice that when Sancerre thought she had changed toward him, she really had, and had begun to love Estouteville. She told her new lover that he consoled her for her husband's death, and that it was he who was

---

1. Skill and tact.

the cause of her returning to society; while it seemed to Sancerre that it was because we had decided that she should no longer appear to be in such deep affliction. She was able to persuade Estouteville to conceal their relations, and to seem obliged to marry him by her father's orders, as if it were the result of her care for her reputation,—and this in order to abandon Sancerre without leaving him ground for complaint. I must go back," continued Monsieur de Clèves, "to see this unhappy man, and I think you had better return to Paris. It is time for you to see company and to begin to receive the number of visits that await you."

Madame de Clèves gave her consent, and they returned the next day. She found herself more tranquil about Monsieur de Nemours than she had been; Madame de Chartres' dying words and her deep grief had for a time dulled her feelings, and she thought they had entirely changed.

The evening of Madame de Clèves' arrival the dauphiness came to see her, and after expressing her sympathy with her affliction, said that in order to drive away her sad thoughts she would tell her everything that had taken place at court during her absence, and narrated many incidents. "But what I most want to tell you," she added, "is that it is certain that Monsieur de Nemours is passionately in love, and that his most intimate friends are not only not in his confidence, but they can't even guess whom it is whom he loves. Yet this love is strong enough to make him neglect, or rather give up, the hope of a crown."

The dauphiness then told Madame de Clèves the whole plan about England. "I heard what I have just told you," she went on, "from Monsieur d'Anville; and he said to me this morning that the king sent last evening for Monsieur de Nemours, after reading some letters from Lignerolles, who is anxious to return, and had written to the king that he was unable to explain to the Queen of England Monsieur de Nemours' delay; that she is beginning to be offended; and that although she has given no positive answer, she had said enough to warrant him in starting. The king read this letter to Monsieur de Nemours, who instead of talking seriously, as he had done in the beginning, only laughed and joked about Lignerolles' hopes. He said that the whole of Europe would blame his imprudence if he were to presume to go to England as a claimant for the queen's hand without being assured of success. 'It seems to me too,' he went on, 'that I should not choose the present time for my journey, when the King of Spain is doing his best to marry her.[2] In a love-affair he would not be a very formidable rival; but I think that in a question of marrying, your Majesty would not advise me to try my chances against him.' 'I do advise you so in the present circumstances,' answered the king. 'But you have no occasion to fear him. I know that he has other thoughts, and even if he had not, Queen Mary was too unhappy under the Spanish yoke for one to believe that her sister wishes to assume it, or would let herself be dazzled by the splendor of so many united crowns.' 'If she does not let herself be dazzled by them,' went on Monsieur de Nemours, 'probably she will wish to marry for love; she has loved Lord Courtenay for several years. Queen Mary also loved him, and she would have married him, with the consent of the whole of England, had she not known that the youth and

2. At the death of his wife, Mary Tudor, in 1558, Philip II of Spain (1527–1598) considered marrying her sister, Elizabeth of England.

beauty of her sister Elizabeth attracted him more than the desire of reigning. Your Majesty knows that her violent jealousy caused her to throw them both into prison, then to exile Lord Courtenay, and finally decided her to marry the King of Spain. I believe that Elizabeth, now that she is on the throne, will soon recall this lord and thus choose a man she has loved, who is very attractive, and who has suffered so much for her, rather than another whom she has never seen.' 'I should agree with you,' replied the king, 'if Courtenay were still living; but some days ago I heard that he had died at Padua, where he was living in banishment. I see very well,' he added, as he left Monsieur de Nemours, 'that it will be necessary to celebrate your marriage as we should celebrate the dauphin's, by sending ambassadors to marry the Queen of England by procuration.'

"Monsieur d'Anville and the Vidame, who were present while the king was talking with Monsieur de Nemours, are convinced that it is this great passion which has dissuaded him from this plan. The Vidame, who is more intimate than any one with him, said to Madame de Martigues that the prince is changed beyond recognition; and what amazes him still more is that he never finds him engaged or absent, so that he supposes he never meets the woman he loves; and what is so surprising, is to see Monsieur de Nemours in love with a woman who does not return his passion."

All this story that the dauphiness told her was as poison to Madame de Clèves. It was impossible for her not to feel sure that she was the woman whose name was unknown; and she was overwhelmed with gratitude and tenderness when she learned from one who had the best means of knowing that this prince, who had already aroused her interest, hid his passion from every one, and for love of her gave up his chances of a crown. It is impossible to describe her agitation. If the dauphiness had observed her with any care, she would at once have seen that the story she had just repeated was by no means without interest to her; but having no suspicion of the truth, she went on without noticing her. "Monsieur d'Anville," she added, "who, as I said, told me all this, thinks that I know more about it than he does, and he has so high an opinion of my charms that he is convinced that I am the only person who can make such a great change in Monsieur de Nemours."

Madame de Clèves was agitated by this last remark of the crown princess, though not in the same way as a few moments before. "I should readily agree with Monsieur d'Anville," she replied, "and it is certainly probable, Madame, that no one but a princess like you could make him indifferent to the Queen of England."

"I should at once acknowledge it," said the dauphiness, "if I knew that was the case, and I should know if it were true. Love-affairs of that sort do not escape the notice of those who inspire them; they are the first to perceive them. Monsieur de Nemours has never paid me any but the most insignificant attentions; but there is nevertheless so great a difference between his way with me and his present conduct that I can assure you I am not the cause of the indifference he shows for the crown of England.

"I forget everything while I am with you," she went on, "and it had slipped my mind that I must go to see Madame Elisabeth.[3] You know that peace is

---

3. Elizabeth of France (1545–1568), daughter of Henri II. Philip indeed married her; although she was "inconsolable" about the idea, she was in fact happy with him.

nearly concluded, but what you don't know is that the King of Spain would not agree to a single article except on the condition that he, instead of the prince Don Carlos, his son, should marry this princess. The king had great difficulty in agreeing to this; at last he yielded, and has gone to tell Madame. I fancy she will be inconsolable; it certainly cannot be pleasant to marry a man of the age and temper of the King of Spain, especially for her, who, in all the pride of youth and beauty, expected to marry a young prince for whom she has a fancy, though she has never seen him. I don't know whether the king will find her as docile as he wishes, and he has asked me to go to see her; for he knows that she is fond of me, and imagines that I have some influence over her. I shall then make a very different visit, for I must go to congratulate Madame, the king's sister. Everything is arranged for her marriage with Monsieur de Savoie, and he will be here shortly. Never was a person of the age of that princess so glad to marry. The court will be finer and larger than it has ever been, and in spite of your afflictions you must come and help us show the foreigners that we have some famous beauties here."

Then the dauphiness left Madame de Clèves, and the next day Madame Elisabeth's marriage was known to every one. A few days later the king and the queens called on Madame de Clèves. Monsieur de Nemours, who had awaited her return with extreme impatience, and was very desirous of speaking to her alone, put off his call until every one should have left and it was unlikely that others would come in. His plan was successful, and he arrived just as the latest visitors were taking their departure.

The princess was still lying down;[4] it was warm, and the sight of Monsieur de Nemours gave her face an additional color, which did not lessen her beauty. He sat down opposite her with the timidity and shyness that real passion gives. It was some time before he spoke; Madame de Clèves was equally confused, so that they kept a long silence. At last Monsieur de Nemours took courage, and expressed his sympathy with her grief. Madame de Clèves, who was glad to keep the conversation on this safe topic, spoke for some time about the loss she had experienced; and finally she said that when time should have dimmed the intensity of her grief, it would still leave a deep and lasting impression, and that her whole nature had been changed by it.

"Great afflictions and violent passions," replied Monsieur de Nemours, "do greatly alter people; as for me, I am entirely changed since I returned from Flanders. Many persons have noticed this alteration, and even the dauphiness spoke of it last evening."

"It is true," said Madame de Clèves, "that she has noticed it, and I think I have heard her say something about it."

"I am not sorry, Madame," Monsieur de Nemours continued, "that she perceived it, but I should prefer that she should not be the only one to notice it. There are persons to whom one does not dare to give any other marks of the love one feels for them than those which do not affect them in any but an indirect way; and since one does not dare to show one's love, one would at least desire that they should see that one wishes not to be loved by any one else. One would like to have them know that there is no beauty, of

---

4. It was common at this period for women to receive visitors in their bedroom.

whatever rank, whom one would not regard with indifference, and that there is no crown which one would wish to buy at the price of never seeing them. Women generally judge the love one has for them," he went on, "by the pains one takes to please them and to pursue them; but that is an easy matter, provided they are charming. What is difficult is not to yield to the pleasure of pursuing them—it is to avoid them, from fear of showing to the public or to them one's feelings; and the most distinctive mark of a true attachment is to become entirely different from what one was, to be indifferent to ambition or pleasure after having devoted one's whole life to one or the other."

Madame de Clèves readily understood the reference to her in these words. It seemed to her that she ought to answer them and express her disapproval; it also seemed to her that she ought not to listen to them or show that she took his remarks to herself: she believed that she ought to speak, and also that she ought to say nothing. The remarks of Monsieur de Nemours pleased and offended her equally; she saw in them a confirmation of what the crown princess had made her think,—she found them full of gallantry and respect, but also bold and only too clear. Her interest in the prince caused an agitation which she could not control. The vaguest words of a man one likes produce more emotion than the open declarations of a man one does not like. Hence she sat without saying a word, and Monsieur de Nemours noticed her silence, which would have seemed to him a happy omen, if the arrival of Monsieur de Clèves had not put an end to the talk and to his visit.

The Prince de Clèves had come to tell his wife the latest news about Sancerre; but she had no great curiosity about the rest of that affair. She was so interested in what had just happened that she could hardly hide her inattention. When she was able to think it all over, she perceived that she had been mistaken when she fancied that she had become indifferent to Monsieur de Nemours. His words had made all the impression he could desire, and had thoroughly convinced her of his passion. His actions harmonized too well with his words for her to have any further doubts on the subject. She did not any longer indulge in the hope of not loving him; she merely determined to give him no further sign of it. This was a difficult undertaking,—how difficult she knew already. She was aware that her only chance of success lay in avoiding the prince, and her mourning enabled her to live in retirement; she made it a pretext for not going to places where she might meet him. She was in great dejection; her mother's death appeared to be the cause, and she sought no other.

Monsieur de Nemours was in despair at not seeing her oftener; and knowing that he should not meet her at any assembly or entertainment at which the whole court was present, he could not make up his mind to go to them; he pretended a great interest in hunting, and made up hunting-parties on the days of the queens' assemblies. For a long time a slight indisposition served as a pretext for staying at home, and thus escaping going to places where he knew that Madame de Clèves would not be.

Monsieur de Clèves was ailing at nearly the same time, and Madame de Clèves never left his room during his illness; but when he was better and began to see company, and among others Monsieur de Nemours, who, under the pretext of being still weak, used to spend a good part of every day with him, she determined not to stay there. Nevertheless, she could not make up her mind to leave during his first visits; it was so long since she had seen him that she was anxious to meet him again. He too managed to make her listen to him, by what seemed like general talk; though she understood, from its reference to what he had said in his previous visit to her, that he went hunting to get an opportunity for meditation, and that he stayed away from the assemblies because she was not there.

At last Madame de Clèves put into execution her decision to leave her husband's room when the duke should be there, though she found it a difficult task: Monsieur de Nemours observed that she avoided him, and was much pained.

Monsieur de Clèves did not at first notice his wife's conduct; but at last he saw that she was unwilling to stay in his room when company was present. He spoke to her about it, and she replied that she did not think it quite proper that she should meet every evening all the young men of the court. She begged him to let her lead a more retired life than she had done before, because the presence of her mother, who was renowned for her virtue, had authorized many things impossible for a woman of her age.

Monsieur de Clèves, who was generally kind and pleasant to his wife, was not so on this occasion; he told her he was averse to any change in her conduct. She was tempted to tell him that there was a report that Monsieur de Nemours was in love with her; but she did not feel able to mention his name. She was also ashamed to assign a false reason, and to hide the truth from a man who had so good an opinion of her.

A few days later, the king happened to be with the queen when she was receiving, and the company was talking about horoscopes and predictions. Opinions were divided about the credence that ought to be given to them. The queen was inclined to believe in them; she maintained that after so many predictions had come true, it was impossible to doubt the exactness of this science. Others again held that the small number of lucky hits out of the numerous predictions that were made, proved that they were merely the result of chance.

"In former times," said the king, "I was very curious about the future; but I was told so much that was false or improbable that I became convinced that we can know nothing certain. A few years ago a famous astrologer came here. Every one went to see him, I as well as the rest, but without saying who I was; and I carried with me Monsieur de Guise and D'Escars, sending them into the room in front of me. Nevertheless the astrologer addressed me first, as if he thought I was their master; perhaps he knew me, although he said something to me which seemed to show that he did not know who I was. He prophesied that I should be killed in a duel; then he told Monsieur de Guise that he would be killed from behind, and D'Escars that he would have his skull broken by a kick from a horse. Monsieur de Guise was almost angry at hearing this,—as if he were accused of running away; D'Escars was no more pleased at learning that he was going to perish by such an unfortunate accident,—so that we all left the astrologer in extreme discontent. I have no idea what will happen to Monsieur de Guise or to D'Escars, but it is very unlikely that I shall be killed in a duel. The King of Spain and I have just made peace; and even if we had not, I doubt if we should resort to a personal combat, and it seems unlikely that I should challenge him, as my father challenged Charles V."

After the king had mentioned the unhappy end which had been foretold him, those who had supported astrology gave up and agreed that it was unworthy of belief. "For my part," said Monsieur de Nemours, "I am the last man in the world to place any confidence in it;" and turning to Madame de Clèves, near whom he was, he said in a low voice: "I was told that I should be made happy by the kindness of the woman for whom I should have the most violent and the most respectful passion. You may judge, Madame, whether I ought to believe in predictions."

The dauphiness, who fancied, from what Monsieur de Nemours had said aloud, that he was mentioning some absurd prophecy that had been made about him, asked him what he was saying to Madame de Clèves. He would have been embarrassed by this question if he had had less presence of mind; but he answered without hesitation: "I was saying, Madame, that it had been predicted about me that I should rise to a lofty position to which I should not even dare to aspire."

"If that is the only prediction that has been made about you," replied the dauphiness, smiling, and thinking of the English scheme, "I do not advise you to denounce astrology; you might find good reasons for supporting it."

Madame de Clèves understood what the crown princess referred to; but she also understood that the happiness of which Monsieur de Nemours spoke was not that of being king of England.

As it was some time since her mother's death, Madame de Clèves had to appear again in society and to resume her visits at court. She met Monsieur de Nemours at the dauphiness's and at her own house, whither he often came with young nobles of his own age, in order not to be talked about; but she never saw him without an agitation which he readily perceived.

In spite of the care she took to escape his glances and to talk less with him than with others, certain things inadvertently escaped her which convinced this prince that she was not indifferent to him. A less observant man than he would not, perhaps, have noticed them; but so many women had been in love with him that it was hard for him not to know when he was loved. He perceived that the Chevalier de Guise was his rival, and that prince knew that Monsieur de Nemours was his. He was the only man at court who would have discovered this truth; his interest had rendered him more clear-sighted than the others. The knowledge they had of each other's feelings so embittered their relations that although there was no open breach, they were opposed in everything. In running at the ring and in all the amusements in which the king took part they were always on different sides, and their rivalry was too intense to be hidden.

The English scheme often recurred to Madame de Clèves, and she felt that Monsieur de Nemours would not be able to withstand the king's advice and Lignerolles' urging. She noticed with pain that this last had not yet returned, and she awaited him with impatience. If she had followed his movements, she would have learned the condition of that matter; but the same feeling that inspired her curiosity compelled her to conceal it, and she contented herself with making inquiries about the beauty, intelligence, and character of Queen Elizabeth. A portrait of her was carried to the palace, and she found Elizabeth more beautiful than was pleasant to her, and she could not refrain from saying that it must flatter her.

"I don't think so," replied the dauphiness, who was present. "Elizabeth has a great reputation as a beauty and as the possessor of a mind far above the common, and I know that all my life she has been held up to me as an example. She ought to be attractive if she is like Anne Boleyn, her mother. Never was there a more amiable woman or one more charming both in appearance and disposition. I have been told that her face was exceptionally vivacious, and that she in no way resembled most English beauties."

"It seems to me," said Madame de Clèves, "that I have heard that she was born in France."

"Those who think so," replied the crown princess, "are in error, and I will tell you her history in a few words. She was born of a good English family. Henry VIII had been in love with her sister and her mother, and it had even been suspected that she was his daughter. She came here with the sister of Henry VII, who married Louis XII. This young and gallant princess found it very hard to leave the court of France after her husband's death; but Anne Boleyn, who shared her mistress's feelings, decided to stay. The late king was in love with her, and she remained as maid of honor to Queen Claude. This queen died, and Madame Marguerite, the king's sister, the Duchess of Alençon, since then Queen of Navarre, whose stories you have seen, added Anne to her suite; it was from her that this queen received her inclination toward the new religion. Then Anne returned to England, where she delighted every one. She had French manners, which please all nations; she sang well, and danced charmingly. She was made a lady in waiting to Queen Catherine of Aragon, and King Henry VIII fell desperately in love with her.

"Cardinal Wolsey, his favorite and prime minister, desired to be made pope; and being dissatisfied with the emperor for not supporting his claims, he resolved to avenge himself by allying the king his master with France. He suggested to Henry VIII that his marriage with the emperor's aunt was null and void, and proposed to him to marry the Duchess of Alençon, whose husband had just died. Anne Boleyn, being an ambitious woman, looked on this divorce as a possible step to the throne. She began to instill into the King of England the principles of Lutheranism, and persuaded the late king to urge at Rome Henry's divorce, in the hope of his marriage with Madame d'Alençon. Cardinal Wolsey contrived to be sent to France on other pretexts to arrange this affair; but his master would not consent to have the proposition made, and sent orders to Calais that this marriage was not to be mentioned.

"On his return from France, Cardinal Wolsey was received with honors equal to those paid to the king himself; never did a favorite display such haughtiness and vanity. He arranged an interview between the two kings, which took place at Boulogne. Francis I offered his hand to Henry VIII, who was unwilling to take it; they treated each other with great splendor, each giving the other clothes like those he himself wore. I remember having heard that those the late king sent to the King of England were of crimson satin trimmed with pearls and diamonds arranged in triangles, the cloak of white velvet embroidered with gold. After spending a few days at Boulogne, they went to Calais. Anne Boleyn was quartered in the house with Henry VIII in the queen's suite, and Francis I made her the same presents and paid her the same honors as if she had been a queen herself. At last, after being in love with her for nine years, Henry married her, without waiting for the annulment of his first marriage, which he had long been asking of Rome. The pope at once excommunicated him; this so enraged Henry that he declared himself the head of the Church, and carried all England into the unhappy change of religion in which you now see it.

"Anne Boleyn did not long enjoy her grandeur, for one day, when she thought her position assured by the death of Catherine of Aragon, she happened to be present with all the court when the Viscount Rochford, her brother, was running at the ring. The king was suddenly overwhelmed by such an access of jealousy that he instantly left the spot, hastened to London, and gave orders for the arrest of the queen, the Viscount Rochford, and many others whom he believed to be the queen's lovers or confidants. Although this jealousy seemed the work of a moment, it had for some time been instigated by the Viscountess Rochford, who could not endure her husband's intimacy with the queen, and represented it to the king as criminal intimacy; consequently he, being already in love with Jane Seymour, thought only of getting rid of Anne Boleyn. In less than three weeks he succeeded in having the queen and her brother brought to trial and beheaded, and he married Jane Seymour. He had afterward several wives, whom he either divorced or put to death, among others Catherine Howard, who had been the confidante of the Viscountess of Rochford, and was beheaded with her. Hence she was punished for the crimes with which she had blackened Anne Boleyn, and Henry VIII, having reached a monstrous size, died."

All the ladies present thanked the dauphiness for teaching them so much about the English court, and among others Madame de Clèves, who could not refrain from asking more questions about Queen Elizabeth.

The dauphiness had miniatures painted of all the beauties of the court to send to the queen her mother. The day when that of Madame de Clèves was receiving the last touches the crown princess came to spend the afternoon with her. Monsieur de Nemours was also there, for he neglected no opportunity of seeing Madame de Clèves, although he never seemed to court her society. She was so beautiful that day that he would surely have fallen in love with her then if he had not done so already; but he did not dare to sit with his eyes fixed on her, while she feared lest he should show too plainly the pleasure he found in looking at her.

The crown princess asked Monsieur de Clèves for a miniature he had of his wife, to compare it with the one that was painting. All who were there expressed their opinion of both, and Madame de Clèves asked the painter to make a little correction in the hair of the old one. The artist took the miniature out of its case, and after working on it, set it down on the table.

For a long time Monsieur de Nemours had been desiring to have a portrait of Madame de Clèves. When he saw this one, though it belonged to her husband, whom he tenderly loved, he could not resist the temptation to steal it; he thought that among the many persons present he should not be suspected.

The dauphiness was seated on the bed, speaking low to Madame de Clèves, who was standing in front of her. One of the curtains was only partly closed, and Madame de Clèves was able to see Monsieur de Nemours, whose back was against the table at the foot of the bed, without turning his head pick up something from this table. She at once guessed that it was her portrait, and she was so embarrassed that the crown princess noticed she was not listening to her, and asked her what she was looking at. At these words Monsieur de Nemours turned round and met Madame de Clèves' eyes fastened on him; he felt sure that she must have seen what he had just done.

Madame de Clèves was greatly embarrassed. Her reason bade her ask for her portrait; but if she asked for it openly, she would announce to every one the prince's feelings for her, and by asking for it privately, she would give him an opportunity to speak to her of his love, so that at last she judged it better to let him keep it,—and she was very glad to be able to grant him a favor without his knowing that she did it of her own choice. Monsieur de Nemours, who observed her embarrassment and guessed its cause, came up to her and said in a low voice: "If you saw what I ventured to do, be good enough, Madame, to let me suppose that you know nothing about it; I do not dare to ask anything more." Then he went away, without waiting for an answer.

The dauphiness, accompanied by all her ladies, went out for a walk. Monsieur de Nemours locked himself up in his own room, being unable to contain his joy at having in his possession a portrait of Madame de Clèves. He felt all the happiness that love can give. He loved the most charming woman of the court, and felt that in spite of herself she loved him; he saw in everything she did the agitation and embarrassment which love evokes in the innocence of early youth.

That evening every one looked carefully for the portrait; when they found the case, no one supposed that it had been stolen, but that it had been dropped somewhere. Monsieur de Clèves was distressed at its loss, and after hunting for it in vain, told his wife, but evidently in jest, that she doubtless had some mysterious lover to whom she had given the portrait, or who had stolen it, for no one but a lover would care for the portrait without the case.

Although these words were not said seriously, they made a deep impression on the mind of Madame de Clèves and filled her with remorse. She thought of the violence of her love for Monsieur de Nemours, and perceived that she could not control either her words or her face. She reflected that Lignerolles had returned, and that the English scheme had no terrors for her; that she had no longer grounds for suspecting the dauphiness; and finally, that, as she was without further defence, her only safety was in flight. Since, however, she knew she could not go away, she saw that she was in a most perilous condition, and ready to fall into what she judged to be the greatest possible misfortune,—namely, betraying to Monsieur de Nemours the interest she felt in him. She recalled everything her mother had said to her on her death-bed, and her advice to try everything rather than enter upon a love-affair. She remembered what her husband had said about her sincerity when he was speaking about Madame de Tournon, and it seemed to her that it was her duty to confess her passion for Monsieur de Nemours. She pondered over this for a long time; then she was astonished that the thought occurred to her: she deemed it madness, and fell back into the agony of indecision.

Part III

When peace was signed,[5] Madame Elisabeth, though with great repugnance, determined to obey her father the king. The Duke of Alva had been deputed to marry her in the name of the Catholic king, and he was expected to arrive

5. The peace treaty of Cateau-Cambrésis (April 1559).

shortly. The Duke of Savoy was also expected; he was to marry Madame the king's sister, and the two weddings were to take place at the same time. The king thought of nothing but making these events illustrious by entertainments at which he could display all the brilliancy and splendor of his court. It was suggested that plays and ballets should be sumptuously set upon the stage; but the king thought that too meagre a form of entertainment, and desired something more magnificent. He determined to have a tournament at which the foreigners might enter, and to admit the populace as spectators. All the princes and young noblemen gladly furthered the king's plan, and especially the Duke of Ferrara, Monsieur de Guise, and Monsieur de Nemours, who surpassed all others in exercises of this sort. The king chose them to be, with himself, the four champions of the tournament.

It was announced throughout the whole kingdom that a tournament would be opened in the city of Paris on the fifteenth day of June by His Very Christian Majesty and by the Prince Alphonso of Este Duke of Ferrara, Francis of Lorraine Duke of Guise, and James of Savoy Duke of Nemours, who were ready to meet all comers. The first combat was to be on horseback, with four antagonists, with four assaults with the lance, and one for the ladies; the second combat with swords, either singly or in couples, as should be determined; the third combat on foot, three assaults with the pike, and six with the sword. The champions were to supply the lances, swords, and pikes, from which the assailants might choose their weapons. Any one striking a horse in the attack was to be put out of the ranks. There would be four masters of the camp who should have command, and those of the assailants who should be most successful would receive a prize, of a value to be determined by the judges. All the assailants, French or foreign, were to be obliged to come and touch one or more of the shields hanging by the steps at the end of the lists; there they would find an officer to receive and enroll them according to their rank and the shields they had touched. The assailants were to have a gentleman bring their shields with their arms, to be hung by the steps three days before the beginning of the tournament, otherwise they would not be received without the permission of the champions.

A great field was made ready near the Bastile, extending from the caste of Tournelles, across the Rue St. Antoine, to the royal mews. On each side scaffolding was raised, with rows of seats and covered boxes and galleries, fine to look upon, and capable of holding a vast number of spectators. All the princes and lords were thinking of nothing but their preparations to make a magnificent appearance, and were busily occupied in working some device into their initials or mottoes that should flatter the woman they loved.

A few days before the Duke of Alva's arrival the king went to play tennis with Monsieur de Nemours, the Chevalier de Guise, and the Vidame of Chartres. The queens went with their suites, and Madame de Clèves among the others, to watch the game. After it was over, and they were leaving the court, Châtelart went up to the dauphiness and told her that he had just found a love-letter that had fallen from Monsieur de Nemours' pocket. The crown princess, who was always curious about everything that concerned that prince, told Châtelart to give it to her; she took it, and followed the queen her mother-in-law, who was going with the king to see the preparations for the tournament. After they had been there some time the king sent for some horses which he had recently bought. Though they had not been broken, he wanted to mount them, and he also had them saddled for the gentlemen with him. The king and Monsieur de Nemours got on the most fiery ones, and they tried to spring at one another. Monsieur de Nemours, fearful of injuring the king, backed his horse suddenly against a post with such violence that he was dismounted. The attendants ran up to him and thought he was seriously injured; Madame de Clèves thought him more hurt than did the others. Her interest in him inspired an agitation which she did not think of concealing; she went up to him with the queens, and her color was so changed that a man less interested than the Chevalier de Guise would have noticed it. He remarked it at once, and gave much more attention to the condition of Madame de Clèves than to that of Monsieur de Nemours. This prince was so stunned by the fall that his head had to be supported by those about him. When he came to himself, the first person he saw was Madame de Clèves; he read on her face all the pity she felt, and his expression showed that he was grateful. He then thanked the queens for their kindness, and apologized for appearing before them in such a state. The king ordered him to go home and lie down.

After Madame had recovered from her fright she began to recall the way she had betrayed it. The Chevalier de Guise did not leave her long to enjoy the hope that no one had observed it. As he gave her his hand to lead her from the field, he said: "I am more to be pitied, Madame, than Monsieur de Nemours. Pardon me if I abandon the profound reserve which I have always shown in regard to you, and if I betray the keen grief I feel at what I have just seen; it is the first time that I have been bold enough to speak to you, and it will be the last. Death, or at any rate an eternal separation, will remove me from a place where I cannot live, now that I have lost the sad consolation of believing that all those who dare to look upon you are as unhappy as I."

Madame de Clèves answered with a few disjointed words, as if she did not understand what the Chevalier de Guise meant. At any other time she would have been offended at his speaking of his feelings for her; but at that moment she thought only of her pain at perceiving that he had detected her own for Monsieur de Nemours. The Chevalier de Guise was so overwhelmed and pained by this discovery that he at once resolved never to think of winning Madame de Clèves' love; but the abandonment of a design which had seemed so difficult and glorious required one of equal moment to take its place, hence he thought of going to take Rhodes,[6]—a plan he had already meditated. When he died, in the flower of his youth, just when he had acquired a reputation as one of the greatest princes of his century, his only regret was that he had not been able to carry out that noble project, which seemed on the point of accomplishment.

Madame de Clèves at once went to the queen, with her mind intent on what had just happened. Monsieur de Nemours came there soon afterward, in magnificent attire, as if he had forgotten what had just happened. He appeared even gayer than usual, and his delight at what he thought he had seen added to his content. Every one was surprised to see him, and asked him how he felt, except Madame de Clèves, who remained by the fire-place, as if she did not see him. The king came out of his room, and observing him

---

6. The Turks had recaptured the island of Rhodes from the Christians in 1523. François de Lorraine, chevalier de Guise, in fact later led an expedition there. He was killed at the battle of Dreux in the religious wars against the Huguenots in 1563, at the age of twenty-nine.

there, called him to ask about his mishap. As Monsieur de Nemours passed by Madame de Clèves, he said in a low voice: "I have received to-day, Madame, tokens of your pity, but not those I most deserve." Madame de Clèves had suspected that the prince had noticed her emotion at his accident, and his words showed her that she was not mistaken. She was deeply pained to see that she could not control her emotions, and had even made them manifest to the Chevalier de Guise. It distressed her, too, to perceive that Monsieur de Nemours had read them; but this distress was tempered by a certain pleasure.

The dauphiness, who was impatient to know what was in the letter that Châtelart had given her, went up to Madame de Clèves. "Read this letter," she said; "it is addressed to Monsieur de Nemours, and apparently is from that mistress for whom he has left all the others. If you cannot read it now, keep it; come to me this evening and give it back to me, and tell me whether you know the handwriting." With these words the crown princess turned away from Madame de Clèves, leaving her so astonished and agitated that she could scarcely move. Her emotion and impatience were so great that she could not stay longer with the queen, and she went home, though it was much earlier than her usual hour of leaving. Her hands, in which she held the letter, trembled; her thoughts were all confused, and she felt an unendurable pain such as she had never known. As soon as she was safe in her room she opened the letter, and read as follows:—

"I love you too much to let you think that the change you see in me is the result of my fickleness; I want you to know that the real cause is your infidelity. You are surprised that I say your 'infidelity'; you have concealed it so craftily, and I have taken such pains to hide from you my knowledge of it, that you are naturally astonished that I should have detected it. I am myself surprised that I have been able to keep it from you. Never was there any grief like mine; I imagined that you felt for me a violent passion. I did not conceal what I felt for you, and at the time when I let you see it, I learned that you were deceiving me, that you loved another, and, according to all appearances, were sacrificing me to a new mistress. I knew it the day of the running at the ring, and that is why I was not there. I pretended to be ill, in order to conceal my emotion; but I really became so, for my body could not stand the intense agitation. When I began to get better, I pretended to be still suffering, in order to have an excuse for not seeing or writing to you; I wanted time to decide how I should act toward you. Twenty times at least I formed and changed my decision; but at last I judged you unworthy to see my grief, and I determined to hide it from you. I wished to wound your pride by letting you see my love for you fade away. I thought thus to diminish the price of the sacrifice you made of it; I did not wish you to have the pleasure of showing how much I loved you in order to appear more amiable. I resolved to write to you indifferent, dull letters, to suggest to the woman to whom you gave them that you were loved less. I did not wish her to have the pleasure of learning that I knew of her triumph over me, or to add to her triumph by my despair and reproaches. I thought I could not punish you sufficiently by breaking with you, and that I should inflict but a slight pain if I ceased to love you when you had ceased to love me. I thought you must love me, if you were to know the pang of not being loved, which tormented me so sorely.

I thought that if anything could rekindle the feelings you had had for me, it was by showing that my own were changed, but to show this by pretending to hide it from you, as if I had not strength to tell you. I decided on this; but how hard it was to do so, and when I saw you, how almost impossible to carry it out! Hundreds of times I was ready to spoil all with my reproaches and tears. The state of my health helped me to conceal my emotion and distress. Afterward I was borne up by the pleasure of dissimulating to you as you dissimulated to me; nevertheless I did myself such violence to tell you and to write to you that I loved you, that you saw sooner than I had intended that I had not meant to let you see that my feelings were altered. You were wounded, and complained to me. I tried to reassure you, but in such an artificial way that you were more convinced than ever that I did not love you. At last I succeeded in what I had meant to do. The capriciousness of your heart made you turn again toward me when you saw me leaving you. I have tasted all the joy of vengeance; it has seemed to me that you loved me better than ever, and I have shown you that I did not love you. I have had reason to believe that you had entirely abandoned her for whom you had left me. I have also had grounds for supposing that you never spoke to her of me. But your return and your desertion have not been able to make good your fickleness; your heart has been divided between me and another; you have deceived me: that is enough to deprive me of the pleasure of being loved by you as I thought I deserved, and to fix me in the resolution that I had formed never to see you again, which so surprises you."

Madame de Clèves read and re-read this letter several times without understanding it; all that she made out was that Monsieur de Nemours did not love her as she had thought, and that he loved other women, whom he deceived as he did her. This was a grievous blow to a woman of her character, who was deeply in love, and had just shown this to a man whom she deemed unworthy, in sight of another whom she maltreated for love of his rival. Never was sorrow more bitter! It seemed to her that what had happened that day gave it a special sting, and that if Monsieur de Nemours had not had reason to suppose that she loved him, she would not care whether he had loved another woman. But she deceived herself; the pang she found so unendurable was that of jealousy, with all its hideous accompaniments. This letter showed her that Monsieur de Nemours had had a love affair for some time. She thought that it attested the writer's cleverness and worth, and she seemed a woman who deserved to be loved. She appeared to have more courage than herself, and she envied her the strength of character she showed in concealing her feelings from Monsieur de Nemours. The end of the letter showed that the woman thought herself still loved; she imagined that his constant discretion, which had so touched her, was perhaps only the effect of his love for the other, whom he feared to offend. In a word, all her thoughts only fed her grief and despair. How often she thought of herself; how often of her mother's counsels! How bitterly she regretted that she had not withdrawn from the world, in spite of Monsieur de Clèves, or that she had not followed her plan of confessing to him her feeling for Monsieur de Nemours! She judged that she would have done better to tell everything to a husband whose generosity she knew, and who would be interested in keeping her secret, than to betray it to a man unworthy of it, who was moved to love of her by no other feeling than pride or vanity. In a word, she deemed every evil that could befall her, every misery to which she might be reduced, insignificant by the side of letting Monsieur de Nemours see that she loved him, and knowing that he loved another woman. Her only consolation was that henceforth she need have no fear of herself, and that she was entirely cured of her love for him.

She gave no thought to the dauphiness's command to come to her that evening; she went to bed and pretended to be indisposed, so that when Monsieur de Clèves came back from seeing the king, he was told that she was asleep. But she was far from enjoying the calmness that induces sleep. She spent the night in self-reproach and in reading over the letter.

Madame de Clèves was not the only person whose rest was disturbed by this letter. The Vidame of Chartres, who had lost it, not Monsieur de Nemours, was very uneasy about it. He had spent the evening with Monsieur de Guise, who had given a grand supper to his brother-in-law, the Duke of Ferrara, and all the young men of the court. It so happened that during the supper the conversation turned to bright letters, and the Vidame said he had in his pocket the brightest letter that ever was written. He was asked to show it to them, but he refused. Monsieur de Nemours thereupon declared that he had never had it, and was only boasting. The Vidame replied that he tempted him to commit an indiscretion, but he would not show the letter, though he would read a few passages that would prove that few men ever received one like it. At the same time he felt for the letter, but could not find it; he sought everywhere in vain. They laughed at his discomfiture, but he seemed so uneasy that they soon stopped talking about it. He left before the others, hastening home to see if he had left the missing letter there. While he was still hunting for it, a first *valet de chambre*[7] of the queen came to tell him that the Vicomtesse d'Uzès thought it well to let him know that they were talking at the queen's apartment about a love-letter he had dropped from his pocket while he was playing tennis; that they had repeated a good deal that was in the letter; that the queen had expressed a strong desire to see it; that she had asked one of her gentlemen-in-waiting for it; but he had answered that he had given it to Châtelart.

The *valet de chambre* said many other things to the Vidame which only added to his distress. He went out at once to see a gentleman who was a great friend of Châtelart; he made him get out of bed, although it was very late, to go and ask for the letter, without telling him who wanted it or who had written it. Châtelart, who was confident that it had been written to Monsieur de Nemours, and that he was in love with the dauphiness, felt sure that he knew who had asked for it. He replied, with malicious joy, that he had handed the letter to the dauphiness. The gentleman brought this answer back to the Vidame of Chartres; it gave him only fresh uneasiness. After long hesitation about what he should do, he decided that Monsieur de Nemours was the only man who could aid him.

The Vidame thereupon went to the house of the duke, and entered his bedroom at about daybreak. The prince was sleeping calmly; what he had seen that day of Madame de Clèves gave him only agreeable thoughts. He was much surprised when he was awakened by the Vidame, and he asked

---

7. A personal manservant.

him whether this had been done out of revenge for what he had said at the supper. The Vidame's countenance showed that he had come on some serious matter. "I have come," he said, "to confide to you the most important event of my life. I know very well that you have no cause to be grateful, because I do this at a moment when I need your aid; but I know that I should have sunk in your esteem if without being compelled by necessity I had told you what I am about to say. Some time yesterday I dropped the letter of which I was speaking last evening; it is of extreme importance that no one should know that it was written to me. It has been seen by a number of persons who were at the tennis-court when I dropped it. Now, you were there too, and I beg of you to say that it was you who lost it."

"You must suppose that I am not in love with any woman," answered Monsieur de Nemours, smiling, "to make such a proposition to me, and to imagine that there is no one with whom I might fall out if I let it be thought that I receive letters of that sort."

"I beg you," said the Vidame, "to listen to me seriously. If you have a mistress, as I do not doubt, though I have no idea who she is, it will be easy for you to explain yourself, and I will tell you how to do it. Even if you do not have an explanation with her, your falling-out will last but a few moments; whereas I by this mischance bring dishonor to a woman who has loved me passionately, and is one of the most estimable women in the world; and moreover, from another quarter I bring upon myself an implacable hatred, which will certainly cost me my fortune, and may cost me something more."

"I do not understand what you tell me," replied Monsieur de Nemours; "but you imply that the current rumors about the interest a great princess takes in you are not entirely without foundation."

"They are not," exclaimed the Vidame; "but would to God they were! In that case I should not be in my present trouble. But I must tell you what has happened, to give you an idea of what I have to fear.

"Ever since I have been at court, the queen has always treated me with much distinction and amiability, and I have reason to believe that she has had a kindly feeling for me; yet there was nothing marked about it, and I had never dreamed of other feelings toward me than those of respect. I was even much in love with Madame de Themines; the sight of her is enough to prove that a man can have a great deal of love for her when she loves him,—and she loved me. Nearly two years ago, when the court was at Fontainebleau, I happened to talk with the queen two or three times when very few people were there. It seemed to me that I pleased her, and that she was interested in all that I said. One day especially we were talking about confidence. I said I did not confide wholly in any one; that one always repented absolute unreserve sooner or later; and that I knew a number of things of which I had never spoken to any one. The queen said that she thought better of me for that; that she had not found any one in France who had any reserve; and that this had troubled her greatly, because it had prevented her confiding in any one; that one must have somebody to talk to, especially persons of her rank. The following days she several times resumed the same conversation, and told me many tolerably secret things that were happening. At last it seemed to me that she wanted to test my reserve, and that she wished to intrust me with some of her own secrets. This thought attached me to her;

I was flattered by the distinction, and I paid her my court with more assiduity than usual. One evening, when the king and all the ladies had gone out to ride in the forest, she remained at home, because she did not feel well, and I stayed with her. She went down to the edge of the pond and let go of the equerry's hand, to walk more freely. After she had made a few turns, she came near me and bade me follow her. 'I want to speak to you,' she said, 'and you will see from what I wish to say that I am a friend of yours.' Then she stopped and gazed at me intently. 'You are in love,' she went on, 'and because you do not confide in any one, you think that your love is not known; but it is known even to the persons interested. You are watched; it is known where you see your mistress: a plan has been made to surprise you. I do not know who she is, I do not ask you; I only wish to save you from the misfortunes into which you may fall.' Observe, please, the snare the queen set for me, and how difficult it was to escape it. She wanted to find out whether I was in love; and by not asking with whom, and by showing that her sole intention was to aid me, she prevented my thinking that she was speaking to me from curiosity or with premeditation.

"Nevertheless, in the face of all appearances I made out the truth. I was in love with Madame de Themines; but though she loved me, I was not fortunate enough to meet her in any private place where we could be surprised, hence I saw that it was not she whom the queen meant. I knew too that I had a love-affair with a woman less beautiful and less severe than Madame de Themines, and it was not impossible that the place where I used to meet her had been discovered; but since I took but little interest in her, it was easy for me to escape from perils of that sort by ceasing to see her. Hence I decided to confess nothing to the queen, but to assure her that I had long since given up the desire to win the love of such women as might smile on me, because I deemed them unworthy of an honorable man's devotion, and it would take women far above them to fascinate me. 'You are not frank,' replied the queen; 'I know the opposite of what you say. The way in which I speak to you binds you to conceal nothing from me. I want you to be one of my friends,' she went on; 'but when I give you that place, I must know all your ties. Consider whether you care to purchase it at the price of informing me; I give you two days to think it over. But be careful what you say to me at the expiration of that time, and remember that if I find out afterward that you have deceived me, I shall never pardon you so long as I live.' Thereupon the queen left me, without awaiting my reply.

"You may well imagine that I was much impressed by what she had just said. The two days she had given me for consideration did not seem to me too long. I perceived that she wished to know whether I was in love, and hoped that I was not. I saw the importance of the decision I was about to make. My vanity was not a little flattered by a love-affair with a queen, and a queen who was still so charming. To be sure, I love Madame de Themines, and although I was unfaithful to her in a way with that other woman I mentioned, I could not make up my mind to break with her. I also saw the danger to which I exposed myself in deceiving the queen, and how hard it would be to deceive her; yet I could not decide to refuse what fortune offered me, and I determined to risk the consequences of my evil conduct. I broke with that woman with whom my relations might be discovered, and I hoped to conceal those I had with Madame de Themines.

"At the expiration of the two days that the queen had granted me, as I was entering a room where all her ladies were assembled, she said to me aloud, with a seriousness that surprised me,—

" 'Have you thought over that matter of which I spoke to you, and do you know the truth about it?'

" 'Yes, Madame,' I replied, 'and it is as I told your Majesty.'

" 'Come this evening at the hour that I shall write to you, and I will give you the rest of my orders.'

"I made a deep bow, without answering, and did not fail to appear at the hour set. I found her in the gallery with her secretary and some of her ladies. As soon as she saw me, she came up to me and led me to the other end of the gallery.

" 'Well!' she said, 'is it after due reflection that you have nothing to say to me, and does not my treatment of you deserve that you should speak to me frankly?'

" 'It is because I am frank with you, Madame,' I replied, 'that I have nothing to tell you; and I swear to your Majesty, with all the respect I owe you, that I am not in love with any lady of the court.'

" 'I am willing to believe it,' resumed the queen, 'because I wish to; and I wish it because I desire that you should be unreservedly attached to me; and I could not possibly be satisfied with your friendship if you were in love. One may trust those who are, but it is impossible to have confidence in their secrecy. They are too inattentive and have too many distractions; their mistress is their main interest,—and that would not suit the way in which I want you to be attached to me. Remember, it is on account of your oath that you are free that I choose you for the recipient of my confidence. Remember that I wish yours without reserve, that I want you to have no friend, man or woman, except such as shall be agreeable to me, and that you will give up every aim except pleasing me. I shall not let harm come to your fortune,—I shall look after that more zealously than you do; and whatever I do for you, I shall consider myself more than paid if I find that you are to me what I hope. I choose you in order to confide in you all my anxieties, and to help me endure them. You will see that they are not light. To all appearance I suffer no pain from the king's attachment to Madame de Valentinois; but I can scarcely bear it. She controls the king; she is false to him; she despises me; all my people are devoted to her. My daughter-in-law, the crown princess, is vain of her beauty and of her uncle's power, and pays no respect to me. The Constable of Montmorency is master of the king and of the kingdom; he hates me, and has given me tokens of his hatred which I can never forget. The Marshal of Saint-André is an audacious young favorite, who treats me no better than do the others. The full list of my sufferings would arouse your compassion. Hitherto I have not dared to trust any one; I do put confidence in you: act in such a way that I shall not repent of it, and be my sole consolation.'

"The queen's eyes filled with tears as she said these last words, and I was on the point of throwing myself at her feet, so deeply was I moved by the kindness she showed me. Since that day she has had perfect confidence in me; she never takes a step without talking it over with me, and my alliance with her still lasts.

Part IV

"Still, though much taken up by my new intimacy with the queen, I was bound to Madame de Themines by a feeling which I could not overcome. It seemed to me that her love for me was waning; and although if I had been wise I should have taken advantage of this change I saw in her to try to forget her, as it was, my love for her redoubled, and I managed so ill that the queen in time learned something about this attachment. Persons of her nation[8] are always inclined to jealousy, and possibly her feelings toward me were warmer than she herself supposed. But at last the report that I was in love gave her such distress and grief that I very often felt sure that I had wholly lost her favor. I reassured her by my attentions, submissiveness, and by many false oaths; but I could not have long deceived her if Madame de Themines' altered demeanor had not at last set me free in spite of myself. She made me see that she loved me no longer, and I was so sure of this that I felt compelled to cease persecuting her with my attentions. Some time after, she wrote me the letter that I have lost. That told me that she knew about my relations with the other woman I mentioned, and that this was the reason of the change. Since, then, there was no one to divide my attentions, the queen was tolerably satisfied with me; but inasmuch as my feeling for her was not of a sort to render me incapable of another attachment, and it is impossible for a man to control his heart by force of will, I fell in love with Madame de Martigues, in whom I had been much interested before, when she was a Villemontais[9] and maid-of-honor to the dauphiness. I had reason for believing that she did not hate me, and that she was pleased with my discreet conduct, although she did not understand all its reasons. The queen has no suspicions about this affair, but there is another which torments her a great deal. Since Madame de Martigues is always with the crown princess, I go there oftener than usual. The queen has taken it into her head that it is with this princess that I am in love. The dauphiness's rank, which is equal to her own, and her advantages of youth and beauty, inspire a jealousy which amounts to madness, and she cannot conceal her hatred of her daughter-in-law. The Cardinal of Lorraine, who seems to me to have been for a long time an aspirant for the queen's good graces, and who sees me occupying a place that he would like to fill, under the pretence of bringing about a reconciliation between her and the crown princess is looking into the causes of their dissension. I do not doubt that he has found out the real cause of the queen's bitterness, and I fancy that he has done me many an evil turn, though without showing his hand. That is the state of affairs now. Judge then what will be the effect of the letter I lost when I was unfortunate enough to put it into my pocket to return it to Madame de Themines. If the queen sees this letter, she will know that I have deceived her, and that at almost the same time when I was false to her on account of Madame de Themines, I was false to Madame de Themines on account of another woman. Judge then what sort of an opinion she will have of me, and whether she will ever believe me again. If she does not see this letter, what shall I say to her? She knows that it has been in the dauphiness's hands; she will think that Châtelart recog-

8. Italy.   9. I.e., before her marriage: Villemontais was her maiden name.

nized that princess's handwriting, and that the letter is from her; she will imagine that she is perhaps the woman whose jealousy is mentioned,—in a word, there is nothing which she may not think, and there is nothing I may not fear from her thoughts. Add to this that I am sincerely interested in Madame de Martigues, that the crown princess will certainly show her this letter, and that she will believe it was written very recently. So I shall be embroiled both with the woman I love best in the world and with the woman from whom I have most to fear. Consider now whether I am not justified in begging you to say that the letter is yours and in asking you as a favor to try to get it from the dauphiness."

"It is very plain," said Monsieur de Nemours, "that one could hardly be in more serious perplexity than you are; and you must confess that you got into it by your own fault. I have been accused of being a faithless lover and of carrying on several love-affairs at the same time; but I am nothing by the side of you, for I should never have dreamed of doing what you have done. Could you suppose it possible to keep on good terms with Madame de Themines when you formed your alliance with the queen; and did you hope to become intimate with the queen and yet succeed deceiving her? She is an Italian and a queen, and hence suspicious, jealous, and haughty. When your good luck rather than your good conduct got you out of one entanglement, you got into a new one, and imagined that here, amid the whole court, you could love Madame de Martigues without the queen's knowing anything about it. You could not have been too careful to rid her of the mortification of having taken the first steps. She has a violent passion for you. You are too discreet to say so, and I am too discreet to ask any questions; but she loves you, she distrusts you, and the facts justify her."

"Is it for you to overwhelm me with reproaches?" interrupted the Vidame. "Ought not your experience to make you indulgent to my faults? Still, I am willing to confess that I did wrong; but consider, I beg of you, how to get me out of my present complications. It seems to me that you must see the crown princess as soon as she is up, and ask her for the letter as if it were yours."

"I have already told you," replied Monsieur de Nemours, "that this is a somewhat extraordinary request, and one that, the circumstances being what they are, I do not find very easy to grant. Then, too, if the letter was seen to fall from your pocket, how can I convince them that it fell from mine?"

"I thought I had said that they told the dauphiness that it was from yours that it fell."

"What!" said Monsieur de Nemours with some asperity, for he saw at once that this mistake might complicate matters with Madame de Cleves. "So the dauphiness has been told that I dropped this letter?"

"Yes," answered the Vidame; "that is what they told her,—and the mistake arose in this way: there were several of the queen's gentlemen in one of the rooms by the tennis-court where our clothes were hanging, and when we sent for them the letter dropped; these gentlemen took it up and read it aloud. Some thought it was written to you; others, that it was written to me. Chatelart, who took it, and from whom I have just tried to get it, said he had given it to the crown princess as a letter of yours; those who mentioned it to the queen unfortunately said it was mine,—so you can easily do what I wish, and get me out of this terrible complication."

Monsieur de Nemours had always been very fond of the Vidame of Chartres, and his relationship to Madame de Clèves rendered him still dearer. Nevertheless, he could not make up his mind to run the risk of her hearing of this letter as something in which he was concerned. He began to meditate profoundly, and the Vidame, guessing the nature of his thoughts, said: "I really believe you are afraid of falling out with your mistress; and I should be inclined to think that it is about the dauphiness that you are anxious, were it not that your freedom from any jealousy of Monsieur d'Anville forbids the thought. But however that may be, you must not sacrifice your peace of mind to mine, and I will make it possible for you to prove to the woman you love that this letter was written to me, and not to you. Here is a note from Madame d'Amboise; she is a friend of Madame de Themines, and to her she has confided all her feelings about me. In this note she asks me for her friend's letter,—the one I lost. My name is on the note, and its contents prove beyond the possibility of doubt that the letter she asks for is the one that has been picked up. I intrust this note to you, and I am willing that you should show it to your mistress in order to clear yourself. I beg of you not to lose a moment, but to go to the dauphiness this morning."

Monsieur de Nemours gave his promise to the Vidame of Chartres and took Madame d'Amboise's note. But his intention was not to see the crown princess; he thought he had something more urgent to do. He felt sure that she had already spoken about this letter to Madame de Clèves, and he could not endure that a woman he loved so much should have any reason for thinking that he was attached to any other.

He went to her house as soon as he thought she might be awake, and sent up word that he would not ask to have the honor at such an extraordinary hour if it were not on very important business. Madame de Clèves was not yet up; she was much embittered and agitated by the gloomy thoughts that had tormented her all night. She was extremely surprised when she heard that Monsieur de Nemours wanted to see her. Grieved as she was, she did not hesitate to send him word that she was ill, and unable to see him.

He was not pained by this refusal; an act of coolness at a time when she might be jealous was no unfavorable omen. He went to Monsieur de Clèves' apartments and told him that he had just called on his wife; that he was very sorry he could not see her, because he wished to speak to her of a matter of importance in which the Vidame of Chartres was interested. In a few words he told Monsieur de Clèves how serious the matter was, and Monsieur de Clèves took him at once to his wife's room. Nothing but the darkness enabled her to hide her agitation and surprise at seeing Monsieur de Nemours brought into her room by her husband. Monsieur de Clèves said that there was some question about a letter, and the Vidame's interests required her aid; he added that Monsieur de Nemours would tell her what was to be done, and that he should go to the king, who had just sent for him.

Monsieur de Nemours was left alone with Madame de Clèves,—which was exactly what he wanted. "I have come, Madame," he began, "to ask you if the dauphiness has not spoken to you about a letter which Châtelart gave her."

"She said something about it to me," answered Madame de Clèves; "but I don't understand how this letter concerns my uncle, and I am able to assure you that his name is not mentioned in it."

"True, Madame," Monsieur de Nemours went on, "his name is not mentioned; nevertheless, it was written to him, and it is of the utmost importance to him that you should get it out of her hands."

"I fail to understand," said Madame de Clèves, "how it concerns him that this letter should not be seen, and why it should be asked for in his name."

"If you will kindly listen to me," said Monsieur de Nemours, "I will speedily explain the matter to you, and you will soon see that the Vidame is so implicated that I should not have said anything about it even to the Prince of Clèves if I had not needed his assistance in order to have the honor of seeing you."

"I think that all that you might take the trouble to say to me would be useless," replied Madame de Clèves, somewhat tartly; "and it is much better that you should go to the crown princess and tell her frankly your interest in this letter, since it has been said that it belongs to you."

The vexation that Monsieur de Nemours saw in Madame de Clèves gave him the keenest pleasure he had yet known, and fully consoled him for his impatience to explain himself. "I do not know, Madame," he began, "what may have been said to the dauphiness; but this letter does not concern me personally, and it was written to the Vidame."

"That I believe," replied Madame de Clèves; "but the dauphiness has been told the contrary, and it will not seem to her likely that the Vidame's letters should fall out of your pockets. That is why, unless you have some good reason for concealing the truth from her, I advise you to confess it to her."

"I have nothing to confess to her," he went on; "the letter is none of mine, and if there is any one I wish to convince of this, it is not the crown princess. But, Madame, since the Vidame's fate is at stake, permit me to tell you some things which you will find quite worth listening to."

The silence of Madame de Clèves showed that she was willing to listen, and Monsieur de Nemours repeated in as few words as possible what the Vidame had told him. Although this might well have surprised, or at least interested, her, Madame de Clèves listened with such marked indifference that she seemed to doubt it or to find it unworthy of her attention. She maintained this indifference until Monsieur de Nemours mentioned Madame d'Amboise's note to the Vidame of Chartres, which was the proof of all he had just been saying. Since Madame de Clèves knew that she was a friend of Madame de Themines, it seemed to her possible that Monsieur de Nemours had been speaking the truth, and she began to think that possibly the letter in question had not been written to him. This thought suddenly dispelled her indifference. The prince read her the note, which exonerated him completely, and then handed it to her for examination, telling her that perhaps she knew the handwriting; she was compelled to take it and to read the address, and indeed every word, in order to make sure that the letter asked for was the one in her possession. Monsieur de Nemours said everything he could think of to convince her; and since a pleasant truth is readily believed, he succeeded in proving to Madame de Clèves that he had no part whatsoever in the letter.

Then she began to reflect on the Vidame's troubles and danger, to blame his evil conduct, and to desire means to aid him. She was surprised at the queen's behavior; she confessed to Monsieur de Nemours that the letter was in her possession,—in a word, so soon as she thought him innocent, she interested herself at once with the utmost cordiality in the very things that at first left her perfectly indifferent. They agreed that it was not necessary to return the letter to the crown princess, lest she should show it to Madame de Martigues, who knew Madame de Themines' handwriting, and would at once have guessed, from her interest in the Vidame, that the letter had been written to him. They also thought that it was better not to confide to the dauphiness the part concerning her mother-in-law, the queen. Madame de Clèves, under the pretext of her concern for her uncle's affairs, gladly promised to keep every secret that Monsieur de Nemours might intrust to her.

This prince would have talked with her about other things than the Vidame's affairs, and would have taken advantage of this opportunity to speak to her with greater freedom than he had ever done, were it not that word was brought to Madame de Clèves that the dauphiness had sent for her; Monsieur de Nemours consequently was obliged to withdraw. He went to see the Vidame, to tell him that after leaving him he had thought it better to see his niece, Madame de Clèves, than to go straight to the dauphiness. He brought forward many good arguments in support of what he had done and to make success seem probable.

Meanwhile Madame de Clèves dressed in all haste to go to the crown princess. She had scarcely entered the room when the dauphiness called her to her, and said in a low voice,—

"I have been waiting two hours for you, and never had more difficulty in concealing the truth than I have had this morning. The queen has heard about the letter I gave you yesterday, and thinks it was the Vidame of Chartres who dropped it; you know she takes a good deal of interest in him. She wanted to see the letter, and sent to ask Châtelart for it; he told her he had given it to me, and then they came to ask me for it, under the pretext that it was a very bright letter, which the queen was anxious to see. I did not dare say that you had it; I feared she would think that it had been placed in your hands because the Vidame is your uncle, and that there was some understanding between you and me. It has already occurred to me that she did not like his seeing me often; so I said the letter was in the pocket of the clothes I wore yesterday, and that those who had the key of the room in which they were locked had gone out. So give me the letter at once, that I may send it to her; and let me look at it before I send it, to see if I know the handwriting."

Madame de Clèves was even more embarrassed than she had expected. "I don't know, Madame," she answered, "what you will do; for Monsieur de Clèves, to whom I had given it, gave it back to Monsieur de Nemours, who came this morning to get him to ask you to return it to him. Monsieur de Clèves was imprudent enough to say that it was in his possession, and weak enough to yield to Monsieur de Nemours' entreaties and to give it to him."

"You have put me in the greatest possible embarrassment," said the dauphiness, "and you did very wrong to return the letter to Monsieur de Nemours; since I gave it you, you ought not to have returned it without my permission. What can I say to the queen, and what will she think? She will believe, and on good grounds, that this letter concerns me, and that there is something between the Vidame and me. She will never believe that the letter belongs to Monsieur de Nemours."

"I am extremely sorry," answered Madame de Clèves, "for the trouble I have caused,—I see just how great it is; but it is Monsieur de Clèves' fault, not mine."

"It is yours," retorted the dauphiness, "because you gave him the letter.

There is not another woman in the world who would confide to her husband everything she knows."

"I acknowledge that I was wrong, Madame," said Madame de Clèves; "but think rather of repairing than of discussing my fault."

"Don't you remember pretty well what was in the letter?" asked the crown princess.

"Yes, Madame," was the reply; "I remember it, for I read it over more than once."

"In that case, you must go at once and write it in a disguised hand. This copy I will send to the queen. She will not show it to any one who has seen the original; and even if she should, I shall always maintain that it was the one that Châtelart gave me, and he will not dare to deny it."

Madame de Clèves agreed to this plan, and all the more readily because she thought she would send for Monsieur de Nemours to let her have the letter again, in order to copy it word for word, and so far as possible imitate the handwriting; in this way she thought the queen could not fail to be deceived. As soon as she got home she told her husband about the dauphiness's embarrassment, and begged him to send for Monsieur de Nemours; this was done, and he came at once. Madame de Clèves repeated to him what she had just told her husband, and asked him for the letter. Monsieur de Nemours replied that he had already given it back to the Vidame de Chartres, who was so glad to see it again and to be out of danger that he had at once sent it to Madame de Themines. Madame de Clèves was in new trouble; but at last, after discussing the matter together, they determined to write the letter from memory. They locked themselves up to work, left word at the door that no one was to be let in, and sent off Monsieur de Nemours' servants. This appearance of mystery and of confidence was far from unpleasant to this prince, and even to Madame de Clèves. The presence of her husband and the thought that she was furthering the Vidame's interests almost calmed her scruples. She felt only the pleasure of seeing Monsieur de Nemours; it was a fuller and purer joy than any she had ever felt, and it inspired her with a liveliness and ease that Monsieur de Nemours had never seen in her, and his love for her was only deepened. Since he had never before had such pleasant moments, his own spirits rose, and when Madame de Clèves wanted to recall the letter and to write, he, instead of aiding her seriously, did nothing but interrupt her with idle jests. Madame de Clèves was quite as merry; so that they had been long shut up together, and twice word had come from the dauphiness urging Madame de Clèves to make haste, before half the letter was written.

Monsieur de Nemours was only too happy to prolong so pleasant a visit, and forgot his friend's interests. Madame de Clèves was amusing herself, and forgot those of her uncle. At last, at four o'clock, the letter was hardly finished, and the handwriting was so unlike that of the original that it was impossible that the queen should not at once detect the truth; and she was not deceived by it. Although they did their best to convince her that the letter was written to Monsieur de Nemours, she remained convinced, not only that it was addressed to the Vidame de Chartres, but that the dauphiness had something to do with it, and that there was some understanding between him and her. This thought so intensified her hatred of this princess that she never forgave her, and persecuted her till she drove her from France.

As for the Vidame of Chartres, he was ruined so far as she was concerned; and whether it was that the Cardinal of Lorraine had already acquired an ascendency over her, or that the affair of this letter, in which she saw that she had been deceived, opened her eyes to the other deceptions of which the Vidame had been guilty, it is certain that he could never bring about a satisfactory reconciliation. Their intimacy was at an end, and she accomplished his ruin afterward at the time of the conspiracy of Amboise,[1] in which he was implicated.

After the letter had been sent to the crown princess, Monsieur de Clèves and Monsieur de Nemours went away. Madame de Clèves was left alone; and as soon as she was deprived of the presence of the man she loved, she seemed to awaken from a dream. She thought with surprise of the difference between her state of mind the previous evening and that she then felt; she pictured the coldness and harshness she had shown to Monsieur de Nemours so long as she had supposed that Madame de Themines' letter had been written to him, and the tranquillity and happiness that had succeeded them when he had proved to her that this letter in no way concerned him. When she recalled that the day before she had reproached herself, as if it were a crime, for having shown an interest that mere compassion had called forth, and that by her harshness she had betrayed a feeling of jealousy,—a certain proof of affection,—she scarcely recognized herself. When she thought further that Monsieur de Nemours saw that she was aware of his love; when he saw that, in spite of this, she treated him with perfect cordiality in her husband's presence,—indeed that she had treated him with more kindness than ever before, that she was the cause of her husband's sending for him, and that they had just passed an afternoon together privately,—she saw that there was an understanding between herself and Monsieur de Nemours; that she was deceiving a husband who deserved to be deceived less than any husband in the world; and she was ashamed to appear so unworthy of esteem even before the eyes of her lover. But what pained her more than all the rest was the memory of the state in which she had passed the night, and the acute grief she had suffered from the thought that Monsieur de Nemours loved another and that she had been deceived.

Up to that time she had not known the stings of mistrust and jealousy; her only thought had been to keep from loving Monsieur de Nemours, and she had not yet begun to fear that he loved another. Although the suspicions that this letter had aroused were wholly removed, they opened her eyes to the danger of being deceived, and gave her impressions of mistrust and jealousy such as she had never felt before. She was astounded that she had never yet thought how improbable it was that a man like Monsieur de Nemours, who had always treated women with such fickleness, should be capable of a sincere and lasting attachment. She thought it almost impossible that she could ever be satisfied with his love. "But if I could be," she asked herself, "what could I do with it? Do I wish it? Could I return it? Do I wish to begin a love-affair? Do I wish to fail in my duty to Monsieur de Clèves? Do I wish to expose myself to the cruel repentance and mortal anguish that are inseparable from love? I am overwhelmed by an affection which carries me away

---

1. A 1560 conspiracy led by Louis de Bourbon, prince of Condé, and the Huguenot party in an effort to destroy the influence of the Guises over King Francis II. The plot failed.

in spite of myself; all my resolutions are vain; I thought yesterday what I think to-day, and I act to-day in direct contradiction to my resolutions of yesterday. I must tear myself away from the society of Monsieur de Nemours; I must go to the country, strange as the trip may seem; and if Monsieur de Clèves persists in opposing it, or in demanding my reasons, perhaps I shall do him and myself the wrong of telling them to him." She held firm to this resolution, and spent the evening at home, instead of going to find out from the dauphiness what had become of the Vidame's pretended letter.

When Monsieur de Clèves came home she told him she wanted to go into the country; that she was not feeling well, and needed a change of air. Monsieur de Clèves, who felt sure from her appearance that there was nothing serious ailed her, at first laughed at the proposed trip, and told her that she forgot the approaching marriages of the princesses and the tournament, and that she would not have time enough to make her preparations for appearing in due splendor alongside the other ladies. Her husband's arguments did not move her; she begged him, when he went to Compiègne with the king, to let her go to Coulommiers,[2]—a country-house they were building at a day's journey from Paris. Monsieur de Clèves gave his consent; so she went off with the intention of not returning at once, and the king left for a short stay at Compiègne.

Monsieur de Nemours felt very bad at not seeing Madame de Clèves again after the pleasant afternoon he had spent with her, which had so fired his hopes. His impatience to meet her once more left him no peace; so that when the king returned to Paris he determined to make a visit to his sister, the Duchess of Mercœur, who lived in the country not far from Coulommiers. He proposed to the Vidame to go with him; the latter gladly consented, to the delight of Monsieur de Nemours, who hoped to make sure of seeing Madame de Clèves by calling in company with the Vidame.

Madame de Mercœur was delighted to see them, and at once began to devise plans for their amusement. While they were deer-hunting, Monsieur de Nemours lost his way in the forest; and when he asked what road he should take, he was told that he was near Coulommiers. When he heard this word, "Coulommiers," he at once, without thinking, without forming any plan, dashed off in that direction. He got once more into the forest, and followed such paths as seemed to him to lead to the castle. These paths led to a summer-house, which consisted of a large room with two closets,[3] one opening on a flower-garden separated from the forest by a fence, and the other opening on one of the walks of the park. He entered the summer-house, and was about to stop and admire it, when he saw Monsieur and Madame de Clèves coming along the path, followed by a number of servants. Surprised at seeing Monsieur de Clèves, whom he had left with the king, his first impulse was to hide. He entered the closet near the flower-garden, with the intention of escaping by a door opening into the forest; but when he saw Madame de Clèves and her husband sitting in the summer-house, while their servants stayed in the park, whence they could not reach him without coming by Monsieur and Madame de Clèves, he could not resist the temptation to watch her, or overcome his curiosity to listen to her conversation with her husband, of whom he was more jealous than of any of his rivals.

2. About twenty-five miles east of Paris.   3. Small private rooms for reading or meditation.

He heard Monsieur de Clèves say to his wife: "But why don't you wish to return to Paris? What can keep you in the country? For some time you have had a taste for solitude which surprises me and pains me, because it keeps us apart. I find you in even lower spirits than usual, and I am afraid something distresses you."

"I have nothing on my mind," she answered, with some embarrassment; "but the bustle of a court is so great, and our house is always so thronged, that it is impossible for mind and body not to be tired and to need rest."

"Rest," he answered, "is not needed by persons of your age. Neither at home nor at court do you get tired, and I should be rather inclined to fear that you are glad to get away from me."

"If you thought that, you would do me great injustice," she replied, with ever-growing embarrassment; "but I beg of you to leave me here. If you could stay too I should be very glad, provided you would stay alone, and did not care for the throng of people who almost never leave you."

"Ah, Madame," exclaimed Monsieur de Clèves, "your air and your words show me that you have reasons for wishing to be alone which I don't know, and which I beg of you to tell me."

For a long time the prince besought her to tell him the reason, but in vain; and after she had refused in a way that only redoubled his curiosity, she stood for a time silent, with eyes cast down; then, raising her eyes to his, she said suddenly,—

"Don't compel me to confess something which I have often meant to tell you, but had not the strength. Only remember that prudence does not require that a woman of my age, who is mistress of her actions, should remain exposed to the temptations of the court."

"What is it you suggest, Madame?" exclaimed Monsieur de Clèves. "I should not dare to say, for fear of offending you."

Madame de Clèves did not answer, and her silence confirming her husband's suspicions, he went on,—

"You are silent, and your silence tells me I am not mistaken."

"Well, sir," she answered, falling on her knees, "I am going to make you a confession such as no woman has ever made to her husband; the innocence of my actions and of my intentions gives me strength to do so. It is true that I have reasons for keeping aloof from the court, and I wish to avoid the perils that sometimes beset women of my age. I have never given the slightest sign of weakness, and I should never fear displaying any, if you would leave me free to withdraw from court, or if Madame de Chartres still lived to guide my actions. Whatever the dangers of the course I take, I pursue it with pleasure, in order to keep myself worthy of you. I beg your pardon a thousand times if my feelings offend you; at any rate I shall never offend you by my actions. Remember that to do what I am now doing requires more friendship and esteem for a husband than any one has ever had. Guide me, take pity on me, love me, if you can."

All the time she was speaking, Monsieur de Clèves sat with his head in his hands; he was really beside himself, and did not once think of lifting his wife up. But when she had finished, and he looked down and saw her, her face wet with tears, and yet so beautiful, he thought he should die of grief. He kissed her, and helped her to her feet.

"Do you, Madame, take pity on me," he said, "for I deserve it; and excuse me if in the first moments of a grief so poignant as mine I do not respond as I should to your appeal. You seem to me worthier of esteem and admiration than any woman that ever lived; but I also regard myself as the unhappiest of men. The first moment that I saw you, I was filled with love of you; neither your indifference to me nor the fact that you are my wife has cooled it: it still lives. I have never been able to make you love me, and I see that you fear you love another. And who, Madame, is the happy man that inspires this fear? Since when has he charmed you? What has he done to please you? What was the road he took to your heart? I found some consolation for not having touched it in the thought that it was beyond any one's reach; but another has succeeded where I have failed. I have all the jealousy of a husband and of a lover; but it is impossible to suffer as a husband after what you have told me. Your noble conduct makes me feel perfectly secure, and even consoles me as a lover. Your confidence and your sincerity are infinitely dear to me; you think well enough of me not to suppose that I shall take any unfair advantage of this confession. You are right, Madame,—I shall not; and I shall not love you less. You make me happy by the greatest proof of fidelity that a woman ever gave her husband; but, Madame, go on and tell me who it is you are trying to avoid."

"I entreat you, do not ask me," she replied; "I have determined not to tell you, and I think that the more prudent course."

"Have no fear, Madame," said Monsieur de Clèves; "I know the world too well to suppose that respect for a husband ever prevents men falling in love with his wife. He ought to hate those who do so, but without complaining; so once more, Madame, I beg of you to tell me what I want to know."

"You would urge me in vain," she answered; "I have strength enough to keep back what I think I ought not to say. My avowal is not the result of weakness, and it requires more courage to confess this truth than to undertake to hide it."

Monsieur de Nemours lost not a single word of this conversation, and Madame de Clèves' last remark made him quite as jealous as it made her husband. He was himself so desperately in love with her that he supposed every one else was just as much so. It was true in fact that he had many rivals, but he imagined even more than there were; and he began to wonder whom Madame de Clèves could mean. He had often believed that she did not dislike him, and he had formed this opinion from things which now seemed so slight that he could not imagine he had kindled a love so intense that it called for this desperate remedy. He was almost beside himself with excitement, and could not forgive Monsieur de Clèves for not insisting on knowing the name his wife was hiding.

Monsieur de Clèves, however, was doing his best to find it out, and after he had entreated her in vain, she said: "It seems to me that you ought to be satisfied with my sincerity; do not ask me anything more, and do not give me reason to repent what I have just done. Content yourself with the assurance I give you that no one of my actions has betrayed my feelings, and that not a word has ever been said to me at which I could take offence."

"Ah, Madame," Monsieur de Clèves suddenly exclaimed, "I cannot believe you! I remember your embarrassment the day your portrait was lost. You gave it away, Madame,—you gave away that portrait which was so dear to me, and belonged to me so legitimately. You could not hide your feelings; it is known that you are in love: your virtue has so far preserved you from the rest."

"Is it possible," the princess burst forth, "that you could suspect any misrepresentation in a confession like mine, which there was no ground for my making? Believe what I say: I purchase at a high price the confidence that I ask of you. I beg of you, believe that I did not give away the portrait; it is true that I saw it taken, but I did not wish to show that I saw it, lest I should be exposed to hearing things which no one had yet dared to say."

"How then did you see his love?" asked Monsieur de Clèves. "What marks of love were given to you?"

"Spare me the mortification," was her answer, "of repeating all the details which I am ashamed to have noticed, and have only convinced me of my weakness."

"You are right, Madame," he said, "I am unjust. Deny me when I shall ask such things, but do not be angry if I ask them."

At this moment some of the servants who were without, came to tell Monsieur de Clèves that a gentleman had come with a command from the king that he should be in Paris that evening. Monsieur de Clèves was obliged to leave at once, and he could say to his wife nothing except that he begged her to return the next day, and besought her to believe that though he was sorely distressed, he felt for her an affection and esteem which ought to satisfy her.

When he had gone, and Madame de Clèves was alone and began to think of what she had done, she was so amazed that she could scarcely believe it true. She thought that she had wholly alienated her husband's love and esteem, and had thrown herself into an abyss from which escape was impossible. She asked herself why she had done this perilous thing, and saw that she had stumbled into it without intention. The strangeness of such a confession, for which she knew no precedent, showed her all her danger.

But when she began to think that this remedy, violent as it was, was the only one that could protect her against Monsieur de Nemours, she felt that she could not regret it, and that she had not gone too far. She spent the whole night in uncertainty, anxiety, and fear; but at last she grew calm. She felt a vague satisfaction in having given this proof of fidelity to a husband who so well deserved it, who had such affection and esteem for her, and who had just shown these by the way in which he had received her avowal.

Meanwhile Monsieur de Nemours had left the place where he had overheard a conversation which touched him keenly, and had hastened into the forest. What Madame de Clèves had said about the portrait gave him new life, by showing him that it was he whom she did not hate. He first gave himself up to this joy; but it was not of long duration, for he reflected that the same thing which showed him that he had touched the heart of Madame de Clèves, ought to convince him that he would never receive any token of it, and that it was impossible to gain any influence over a woman who resorted to so strange a remedy. He felt, nevertheless, great pleasure in having brought her to this extremity. He felt a certain pride in making himself loved by a woman so different from all others of her sex,—in a word, he felt a hundred times happier and unhappier. Night came upon him in the forest, and he had great difficulty in finding the way back to Madame de Mercœur's.

He reached there at daybreak. He found it very hard to explain what had delayed him, but he made the best excuses he could, and returned to Paris that same day with the Vidame.

Monsieur de Nemours was so full of his passion and so surprised by what he had heard that he committed a very common imprudence,—that of speaking in general terms of his own feelings and of describing his own adventures under borrowed names. On his way back he turned the conversation to love: he spoke of the pleasure of being in love with a worthy woman; he mentioned the singular effects of this passion; and, finally, not being able to keep to himself his astonishment at what Madame de Clèves had done, he told the whole story to the Vidame, without naming her and without saying that he had any part in it. But he manifested such warmth and admiration that the Vidame at once suspected that the story concerned the prince himself. He urged him strongly to acknowledge this; he said that he had long known that he nourished a violent passion, and that it was wrong not to trust in a man who had confided to him the secret of his life. Monsieur de Nemours was too much in love to acknowledge his love; he had always hidden it from the Vidame, though he loved him better than any man at court. He answered that one of his friends had told him this adventure, and had made him promise not to speak of it, and he besought him to keep his secret. The Vidame promised not to speak of it; nevertheless, Monsieur de Nemours repented having told him.

Meanwhile, Monsieur de Clèves had gone to the king, his heart sick with a mortal wound. Never had a husband felt warmer love or higher respect for his wife. What he had heard had not lessened his respect, but this had assumed a new form. His most earnest desire was to know who had succeeded in pleasing her. Monsieur de Nemours was the first to occur to him, as the most fascinating man at court, and the Chevalier de Guise and the Marshal of Saint-André as two men who had tried to please her and had paid her much attention; so that he decided it must be one of these three. He reached the Louvre, and the king took him into his study to tell him that he had chosen him to carry Madame to Spain; that he had thought that the prince would discharge this duty better than any one; and that no one would do so much credit to France as Madame de Clèves. Monsieur de Clèves accepted this appointment with due respect, and even looked upon it as something that would remove his wife from court without attracting any attention; but the date of their departure was still too remote to relieve his present embarrassment. He wrote at once to Madame de Clèves to tell her what the king had said, and added that he was very anxious that she should come to Paris. She returned in obedience to his request, and when they met, each found the other in the deepest gloom.

Monsieur de Clèves addressed her in the most honorable terms, and seemed well worthy of the confidence she had placed in him.

"I have no uneasiness about your conduct," he said; "you have more strength and virtue than you think. It is not dread of the future that distresses me; I am only distressed at seeing that you have for another feelings that I have not been able to inspire in you."

"I do not know how to answer you," she said; "I am ready to die with shame when I speak to you. Spare me, I beg of you, these painful conversations. Regulate my conduct; let me see no one,—that is all I ask; but permit me never to speak of a thing which makes me seem so little worthy of you, and which I regard as so unworthy of me."

"You are right, Madame," he answered; "I abuse your gentleness and your confidence. But do you too take some pity on the state into which you have cast me, and remember that whatever you have told me, you conceal from me a name which excites an unendurable curiosity. Still, I do not ask you to gratify it; but I must say that I believe the man I must envy to be the Marshal of Saint-André, the Duke of Nemours, or the Chevalier de Guise."

"I shall not answer," she said, blushing, "and I shall give you no occasion for lessening or strengthening your suspicions; but if you try to find out by watching me, you will surely make me so embarrassed that every one will notice it. In Heaven's name," she went on, "invent some illness, that I may see no one!"

"No, Madame," he replied, "it would soon be found that it was not real; and moreover I want to place my confidence in you alone,—that is the course my heart recommends, and my reason too. In your present mood, by leaving you free, I protect you by a closer guard than I could persuade myself to set about you."

Monsieur de Clèves was right; the confidence he showed in his wife proved a stronger protection against Monsieur de Nemours and inspired her to make austerer resolutions than any form of constraint could have done. She went to the Louvre and visited the dauphiness as usual; but she avoided Monsieur de Nemours with so much care that she took away nearly all his happiness at thinking that she loved him. He saw nothing in her actions which did not prove the contrary. He was almost ready to believe that what he had heard was a dream, so unlikely did it appear. The only thing that assured him that he was not mistaken was the extreme sadness of Madame de Clèves, in spite of all her efforts to conceal it. Possibly kind words and glances would not have so fanned Monsieur de Nemours' love as did this austere conduct.

One evening, when Monsieur and Madame de Clèves were with the queen, some one said that it was reported that the king was going to name another nobleman of the court to accompany Madame to Spain. Monsieur de Clèves fixed his eyes on his wife when the speaker added that it would be either the Chevalier de Guise or the Marshal of Saint-André. He noticed that she showed no agitation at either of these names, or at the mention of their joining the party. This led him to think that it was neither of these that she dreaded to see; and wishing to determine the matter, he went to the room where the king was. After a short absence he returned to his wife and whispered to her that he had just learned that it would be Monsieur de Nemours who would go with them to Spain.

The name of Monsieur de Nemours and the thought of seeing him every day during a long journey, in her husband's presence, so agitated Madame de Clèves that she could not conceal it, and wishing to assign other reasons, she answered,—

"The choice of that gentleman will be very disagreeable for you; he will divide all the honors, and I think you ought to try to have some one else appointed."

"It is not love of glory, Madame," said Monsieur de Clèves, "that makes you dread that Monsieur de Nemours should come with me. Your regret springs from another cause. This regret tells me what another woman would have told by her delight. But do not be alarmed; what I have just told you is not true: I made it up to make sure of a thing which I had only too long inclined to believe." With these words he went away, not wishing by his presence to add to his wife's evident embarrassment.

At that moment Monsieur de Nemours entered, and at once noticed Madame de Clèves' condition. He went up to her, and said in a low voice that he respected her too much to ask what made her so thoughtful. His voice aroused her from her revery; and looking at him, without hearing what he said, full of her own thoughts and fearful that her husband would see him by her side, she said: "In Heaven's name, leave me alone!"

"Alas! Madame," he replied, "I leave you only too much alone. Of what can you complain? I do not dare to speak to you, or even to look at you; I never come near you without trembling. How have I brought such a remark on myself, and why do you make me seem to have something to do with the depression in which I find you?"

Madame de Clèves deeply regretted that she had given Monsieur de Nemours an opportunity to speak to her more frankly than he had ever done. She left him without giving him any answer, and went home in a state of agitation such as she had never known. Her husband soon noticed this; he perceived that she was afraid lest he should speak to her about what had just happened. He followed her into her room and said to her,—

"Do not try to avoid me, Madame; I shall say nothing that could displease you. I beg your pardon for surprising you as I did; I am sufficiently punished by what I learned. Monsieur de Nemours was the man whom I most feared. I see your danger: control yourself for your own sake, and, if possible, for mine. I do not ask this as your husband, but as a man, all of whose happiness you make, and who feels for you a tenderer and stronger love than he whom your heart prefers." Monsieur de Clèves nearly broke down at these last words, which he could hardly utter. His wife was much moved, and bursting into tears, she embraced him with a gentleness and a sorrow that almost brought him to the same condition. They remained for some time perfectly silent, and separated without having strength to utter a word.

The preparations for Madame Elisabeth's marriage were completed, and the Duke of Alva[4] arrived for the ceremony. He was received with all the pomp and formality that the occasion required. The king sent the Prince of Condé, the Cardinals of Lorraine and Guise, the Dukes of Lorraine, Ferrara, Aumale, Bouillon, Guise, and Nemours to meet him. They were accompanied by many gentlemen and a great number of pages wearing their liveries. The king himself received the Duke of Alva at the first door of the Louvre with two hundred gentlemen in waiting, with the constable at their head. As the duke drew near the king, he wished to embrace his knees;[5] but the king prevented him, and made him walk by his side to call on the queen and on Madame Elisabeth, to whom the Duke of Alva brought a magnificent present from his master. He then called on Madame Marguerite, the king's sister, to convey to her the compliments of Monsieur de Savoie, and to assure her that he would arrive in a few days. There were large receptions at the Louvre, to show the Duke of Alva and the Prince of Orange, who accompanied him, the beauties of the court.

Madame de Clèves did not dare to stay away, much as she desired it,

4. He acted as a stand-in for Philip II at the marriage. 5. An act of homage.

through fear of displeasing her husband, who gave her special orders to go. What made him even more determined was the absence of Monsieur de Nemours. He had gone to meet Monsieur de Savoie, and after that prince's arrival he was obliged to be with him almost all the time, to help him in his preparations for the wedding ceremonies; hence Madame de Clèves did not meet him so often as usual, and she was able to enjoy a little peace.

The Vidame of Chartres had not forgotten the talk he had had with Monsieur de Nemours. He had made up his mind that the adventure this prince had told him was his own, and he watched him so closely that perhaps he would have made out the truth, had not the arrival of the Duke of Alva and of Monsieur de Savoie so changed and busied the court that he had no further opportunity. His desire for more information, or, rather, the natural tendency to tell all one knows to the woman one loves, made him mention to Madame de Martigues the extraordinary conduct of the woman who had confessed to her husband the love she felt for another man. He assured her that it was Monsieur de Nemours who had inspired this violent passion, and he besought her to aid him in observing this prince. Madame de Martigues was greatly interested in what the Vidame had told her, and her curiosity about the dauphiness's relations with Monsieur de Nemours made her more anxious than ever to get to the bottom of the affair.

A few days before the one set for the wedding the crown princess gave a supper to her father-in-law the king and the Duchess of Valentinois. Madame de Clèves, who was delayed in dressing, started for the Louvre a little later than usual, and on her way met a gentleman coming from the dauphiness to fetch her. When she entered the room the crown princess called out to her from the bed on which she was lying that she had been waiting for her with the utmost impatience.

"I fancy, Madame," she replied, "that I have no cause to be grateful to you for this impatience; it is doubtless for some other reason that you were eager to see me."

"You are right," said the dauphiness; "but, nevertheless, you ought to be obliged to me, for I am going to tell you something that I am sure you will be very glad to hear."

Madame de Clèves knelt down by the side of the bed in such a way that, fortunately for her, her face was in the dark. "You know," said the crown princess, "how anxious we have been to find out the cause of the change in the Duke of Nemours; I think I have found out, and it is something that will surprise you. He is desperately in love with one of the most beautiful women of the court, and the lady returns his love."

These words, which Madame de Clèves could not take to herself, because she thought that no one knew of her love for this prince, gave her a pang that may be easily imagined.

"I see nothing in that," she replied, "which is surprising for a man of his age and appearance."

"But that," resumed the dauphiness, "is not the surprising part; what is amazing is the fact that this woman who loves Monsieur de Nemours has never given him any token of it, and that her fear that she may not always be able to control her passion has caused her to confess it to her husband to persuade him to take her away from court. And it is Monsieur de Nemours himself who is the authority for what I say."

If Madame de Clèves had been grieved at first by thinking that the affair in no way concerned her, these last words of the dauphiness filled her with despair, since they made it sure that it did concern her only too deeply. She could make no reply, but remained with her head resting on the bed while the dauphiness went on talking, too much taken up with what she was saying to notice her embarrassment. When Madame de Clèves had recovered some of her self-control, she answered,—

"This does not sound like a very probable story, and I wonder who told it to you."

"It was Madame de Martigues, who heard it from the Vidame. You know he is her lover; he told it to her as a secret, as he heard it from the Duke of Nemours. It is true that the Duke of Nemours did not mention the lady's name and did not even acknowledge that it was he who was loved; but the Vidame de Chartres has no doubt about that."

As the dauphiness pronounced these last words, some one drew near the bed. Madame de Clèves was turned away so that she could not see who it was; but she knew when the dauphiness exclaimed, with an air of surprise and amusement, "There he is himself, and I am going to ask how much truth there is in it."

Madame de Clèves knew that it must be the Duke of Nemours, and so it was. Without turning toward him, she leaned over to the crown princess and whispered to her to be careful not to say a word about this adventure, that he had told it to the Vidame in confidence, and that this would very possibly set them by the ears. The dauphiness answered laughingly that she was absurdly prudent, and turned toward Monsieur de Nemours. He was arrayed for the evening entertainment, and addressed her with all his usual grace.

"I believe, Madame," he began, "that I can think, without impertinence, that you were talking about me when I came in, that you wanted to ask me something, and that Madame de Clèves objected."

"You are right," replied the dauphiness; "but I shall not be as obliging to her as I usually am. I want to know whether a story I have heard is true, and whether you are the man who is in love with and is loved by a lady of the court who carefully conceals her passion from you and has confessed it to her husband."

Madame de Clèves' agitation and embarrassment cannot be conceived, and she would have welcomed death as an escape from her sufferings; but Monsieur de Nemours was even more embarrassed, if that is possible. This statement from the lips of the dauphiness, who, he had reason to believe, did not hate him, in the presence of Madame de Clèves, whom he loved better than any woman at court, and who also loved him, so overwhelmed him that he could not control his face. The embarrassment into which his blunder had plunged Madame de Clèves, and the thought of the good reason he gave her to hate him, made it impossible for him to answer. The dauphiness, noticing his intense confusion, said to Madame de Clèves: "Look at him, look at him, and see whether this is not his own story!"

Meanwhile Monsieur de Nemours, recovering from his first agitation, and recognizing the importance of escaping from this dangerous complication, suddenly recovered his presence of mind and regained his composure.

"I must acknowledge, Madame," he said, "that no one could be more surprised and distressed than I am by the Vidame de Chartres' treachery in repeating the adventure of one of my friends which I told to him in confidence. I might easily revenge myself," he went on, smiling in a way that almost dispelled the dauphiness's suspicions; "since he has confided to me matters of considerable importance. But I fail to understand why you do me the honor of implicating me in this affair. The Vidame cannot say that it concerns me, because I told him the very opposite. It may do very well to represent me as a man in love; but it will hardly do to represent me as a man who is loved,—which, Madame, is what you do."

Monsieur de Nemours was very glad to say something to the dauphiness which had some connection with his appearance in former times, in order to divert her thoughts. She caught his meaning; but without referring to these last words of his, she continued to harp on his evident confusion.

"I was embarrassed, Madame," he replied, "out of zeal for my friend and from fear of the reproaches he would be justified in making to me for repeating a thing dearer to him than life. Nevertheless, he only told me half, and did not mention the name of the woman he loves. I simply know that he is more in love and more to be pitied than any man in the world."

"Do you find him so worthy of pity," asked the crown princess, "because he is loved?"

"Are you sure that he is?" he answered; "and do you think that a woman who felt a real love would confide it to her husband? This woman, I am sure, knows nothing about love, and has mistaken for it a faint feeling of gratitude for his devotion to her. My friend cannot nourish any hope; but, wretched as he is, he has at least the consolation of having made her fearful of loving him, and he would not change his fate for that of any man in the world."

"Your friend's love is easily satisfied," said the crown princess, "and I begin to think that you can't be talking about yourself; I am inclined to agree with Madame de Clèves, who maintains that there can be no truth in the whole story."

"I don't think there can be," said Madame de Clèves, who had not yet said a word; "and if it were true, how could it become known? It is extremely unlikely that a woman capable of such an extraordinary thing would have the weakness to tell of it. Evidently a husband would not think of doing such a thing, unless he were a husband very unworthy of the confidence that was placed in him."

Monsieur de Nemours, who saw that Madame de Clèves' suspicions had fallen on her husband, was very glad to strengthen them; he knew that he was his strongest rival.

"Jealousy," he replied, "and the desire to find out more than he had been told, may induce a husband to commit a great many indiscretions."

Madame de Clèves was at the end of her strength; and being unable to carry on the conversation further, she was about to say that she did not feel well, when, fortunately for her, the Duchess of Valentinois came in to tell the dauphiness that the king would arrive very soon. The crown princess accordingly went into her room to dress; whereupon Monsieur de Nemours came up to Madame de Clèves as she was about to follow her, and said,—

"Madame, I would give my life to speak to you a moment; but of all the important things I should have to say to you, nothing seems to me more important than to beg you to believe that if I have said anything which might seem to refer to the dauphiness, I have done so for reasons which do not concern her."

Madame de Clèves pretended not to hear him, but moved away without looking at him and joined the suite of the king, who had just come in. There being a great crowd present, her foot caught in her dress, and she made a misstep; she took advantage of this excuse to leave a place where she had no strength to stay longer, and went away pretending that she could not stand.

Monsieur de Clèves went to the Louvre, and being surprised not to see his wife, he was told of the accident that had just happened to her. He left at once, to find out how she was; he found her in bed, and she told him that she was but slightly hurt. When he had been with her for some time he saw that she was exceedingly sad; this surprised him, and he asked her, "What is the matter? You seem to suffer in some other way than that you have told me."

"I could not be in greater distress than I am," she answered. "What use did you make of the extraordinary, I might say foolish, confidence I had in you? Was I not worthy of secrecy on your part? And even if I was unworthy of it, did not your own interest urge it? Was it necessary that your curiosity to know a name which I ought not to tell you, could force you to confide in any one else in order to discover it? Nothing but curiosity could have led you to commit such an imprudence. The consequences have been most disastrous; the story is known, and has just been told to me, without any notion that I was the person most concerned."

"What do you say, Madame?" he replied. "You accuse me of having repeated what passed between us, and you tell me the story is known! I shall not defend myself from the charge of repeating it; you can't believe it, and you must have taken to yourself something said about some other woman."

"Oh, sir," she said, "in the whole world there is not another case like mine; there is not another woman capable of doing what I have done! Chance could not make any one invent it; no one has ever imagined it,—the very thought never entered any one's mind but mine. The dauphiness has just told me the whole story; she heard it from the Vidame of Chartres, and he had it from Monsieur de Nemours."

"Monsieur de Nemours!" exclaimed Monsieur de Clèves, with a gesture expressive of the wildest despair. "What, Monsieur de Nemours knows that you love him and that I know it!"

"You always want to fix on Monsieur de Nemours rather than any one else," she replied; "I told you that I should never say anything about your suspicions. I cannot say whether Monsieur de Nemours knows my share in this affair, or the part you assign to him; but he told it to the Vidame de Chartres, saying that he had it from one of his friends, who did not give the name of the woman. This friend of Monsieur de Nemours must be one of your friends, and you must have told the story to him in an effort to get some information."

"Is there a friend in the world," he exclaimed, "to whom any one would make a confidence of that sort? And would any one try to confirm his suspicions by telling another what one would wish to hide from one's self? Consider rather to whom you have spoken. It is more likely that the secret got out from you than from me. You could not endure your misery alone, and you sought solace in making a confidant of some friend who has played you false."

"Do not torment me further," she burst forth, "and do not be so cruel as to charge me with a fault which you have committed. Could you suspect me of that? And because I was capable of speaking to you, am I capable of speaking of it to any one else?"

His wife's confession had so convinced Monsieur de Clèves of her frankness, and she so warmly denied having mentioned the incident to any one, that Monsieur de Clèves did not know what to think. For his own part, he was sure that he had repeated nothing; it was something nobody could have guessed: it was known, and it must have become known through one of them. But what caused the liveliest grief was the knowledge that this secret was in somebody's hands, and apparently would be soon divulged.

Madame de Clèves' thoughts were nearly the same; she held it equally impossible that her husband should have spoken and should not have spoken. What Monsieur de Nemours had said, that curiosity might make a husband indiscreet, seemed to apply so well to just the state of mind in which Monsieur de Clèves was, that she could not think it was a mere strange coincidence; and this probability compelled her to believe that Monsieur de Clèves had abused her confidence in him. They were both so busy with their thoughts that they for a long time did not speak, and when they broke the silence, it was but to repeat what they had already said very often, and they felt farther apart than they had ever been.

It is easy to picture the way they passed the night. Monsieur de Clèves' constancy had been nearly worn out by his effort to endure the unhappiness of seeing his wife, whom he adored, touched with love for another man. His courage was wellnigh exhausted; he even doubted whether this was an opportunity to make use of it, in a matter in which his pride and honor were so sorely wounded. He no longer knew what to think of his wife; he could not decide what course of action he should urge her to take nor how he should himself act; on all sides he saw nothing but precipices and steep abysses. At last, after long distress and uncertainty, reflecting that he should soon have to go to Spain, he made up his mind to do nothing that should confirm any one's suspicions or knowledge of his unhappy condition. He went to Madame de Clèves and told her that it was not worth while to discuss which of them had betrayed their secret, but that it was very important to prove that the story that had been told was a mere invention in no way referring to her; that it depended on her to convince Monsieur de Nemours and the rest of this; that she had only to treat him with the severity and coldness which she ought to have for a man who made love to her, and that in this way she would soon dispel the notion that she had any interest in him. Hence, he argued, there was no need of her distressing herself about what he might have thought, because if henceforth she should betray no weakness, his opinion would necessarily change; and above all, he urged upon her the necessity of going to the palace and into the world as much as usual.

When he had finished, Monsieur de Clèves left his wife without awaiting her answer. She thought what he had said very reasonable, and her indignation against Monsieur de Nemours made her think it would be very easy to carry it out; but she found it very hard to appear at all the wedding festivities with a calm face and an easy mind. Nevertheless, since she had been selected to carry the train of the dauphiness's dress,—a special honor to her alone of all the princesses,—she could not decline it without exciting much attention and wonder. Hence she resolved to make a great effort to control herself; but the rest of the day she devoted to preparations and to indulging the feelings that harassed her. She shut herself up alone in her room. What most distressed her was to have grounds for complaint against Monsieur de Nemours, with no chance of excusing him. She felt sure that he had told the story to the Vidame,—this he had acknowledged; and she felt sure too, from the way in which he spoke of it, that he knew that she was implicated. What excuse could be found for so great a piece of imprudence, and what had become of the prince's discretion, that had once so touched her? "He was discreet," she said to herself, "so long as he thought himself unhappy; but the mere thought of happiness, vague as it was, put an end to his discretion. He could not imagine that he was loved without wishing it to be known. He has said everything he could say. I have not confessed that it was he whom I loved; he suspected it, and showed his suspicions. If he had been sure of it, he would have done the same thing. I did wrong to think that there ever was a man capable of concealing what flattered his vanity. Yet it is for this man, whom I thought so different from other men, that I find myself in the same plight as other women whom I so little resemble. I have lost the love and esteem of a husband who ought to make me happy; soon every one will look upon me as a woman possessed by a mad and violent passion. The man for whom I feel it is no longer ignorant of it, and it is to escape just these evils that I have imperilled all my peace of mind, and even my life." These sad reflections were followed by a torrent of tears; but whatever the grief by which she felt herself overwhelmed, she knew that she could have endured it if she had been satisfied with Monsieur de Nemours.

This prince's state of mind was no more tranquil. His imprudence in unbosoming himself to the Vidame of Chartres, and the cruel results of this imprudence, caused him great pain. He could not without intense mortification recall Madame de Clèves' agitation and embarrassment. He could not forgive himself for having spoken about that affair in terms which, though courteous in themselves, must have seemed coarse and impolite, since they had implied to Madame de Clèves that he knew that she was the woman who was deeply in love, and with him. All that he could wish was a conversation with her; but he thought this more to be dreaded than desired. "What should I have to say to her?" he exclaimed. "Should I once more undertake to tell her what I have already made too clear to her? Shall I let her see that I know she loves me,—I, who have never dared to tell her that I loved her? Shall I begin by speaking to her openly of my passion, in order to appear like a man emboldened by hope? Can I think merely of going near her, and should I dare to embarrass her by my presence? How could I justify myself? I have no excuse, I am unworthy to appear before Madame de Clèves, and I do not venture to hope that she will ever look at me again. By my own fault, I have given her a better protection against me than any she sought, and sought perhaps in vain. By my imprudence I have lost the happiness and pride of being loved by the most charming and estimable woman in the world. If I had lost this happiness without her suffering, without having inflicted on her a bitter blow, that would be some consolation; and at this moment I feel more keenly the harm I have done her than I did when I was in her presence."

Monsieur de Nemours long tortured himself with these thoughts. The desire to see Madame de Clèves perpetually haunted him, and he began to look about for means of communicating with her. He thought of writing to her; but he considered, after his blunder, and in view of her character, that the best thing he could do would be to show his profound respect, and by silence and evident distress to make it clear that he did not dare to meet her, and to wait until time, chance, or her own interest in him should work in his favor. He resolved also to forbear from reproaching the Vidame of Chartres for his treachery, lest he should confirm his suspicions.

The betrothal of Madame Elisabeth, which was to take place on the morrow, and the wedding, which was to be celebrated on the following day, so occupied the court that Madame de Clèves and Monsieur de Nemours had no difficulty in concealing their grief and annoyance from the public. The dauphiness referred only lightly to their talk with Monsieur de Nemours, and Monsieur de Clèves took pains not to say anything more to his wife about what had happened, so that soon she found herself more at ease than she had supposed possible.

The betrothal was celebrated at the Louvre; and after the banquet and the ball, the whole royal household went to the bishop's palace to pass the night, as was the custom. The next morning the Duke of Alva, who always dressed very simply, put on a coat of cloth of gold, mingled with red, yellow, and black, and all covered with precious stones; on his head he wore a crown. The Prince of Orange, arrayed in equal splendor, came with his servants, and all the Spaniards with theirs, to fetch the Duke of Alva from the Villeroy mansion, where he was staying; and they started, walking four abreast, for the bishop's palace. As soon as they arrived, they went in due order to the church. The king conducted Madame Elisabeth, who also wore a crown; her dress was held by Mesdemoiselles de Montpensier and De Longueville; then came the queen, but not wearing a crown; after her came the dauphiness, the king's sister, Madame de Lorraine, and the Queen of Navarre, with princesses holding their trains. The queens and princesses had all their maids-of-honor magnificently dressed in the same colors that they themselves wore, so that the maids-of-honor could be at once distinguished by the colors of their dresses. They ascended the platform set up in the church, and the wedding ceremony took place. Then they returned to dinner at the bishop's palace, and at about five left for the palace, to be present at the banquet to which the parliament, the sovereign courts,[6] and the city officials had been invited. The king, the queens, the princes, and princesses ate at the marble table in the great hall of the palace, the Duke of Alva being seated near the new Queen of Spain. Below the steps of the marble table, on the king's right hand, was a table for the ambassadors, the archbishops, and the knights of the order,[7] and on the other side a table for the members of parliament.

The Duke of Guise, dressed in a robe of cloth of gold, was the king's majordomo, the Prince of Condé his head butler, the Duke of Nemours his cupbearer.[8] After the tables were removed, the ball began; it was interrupted by the ballets and by extraordinary shows; then it was renewed, until, after midnight, the king and all the court returned to the Louvre. Though Madame de Clèves was very much depressed, she yet appeared in the eyes of every one, and especially in those of Monsieur de Nemours, incomparably beautiful. He did not dare to speak to her, although the confusion of the ceremony

6. Legal courts of appeal. The Parliament of Paris was essentially a judicial body.　　7. The Order of the Knights of Malta, a military religious order that had led many battles against the Turks.　　8. The positions of butler and cupbearer were honorific designations only for the duration of the ceremonies.

gave him many opportunities; but his demeanor was so dejected, and he showed such fear of approaching her, that she began to deem him less blameworthy, though he had not said a word in excuse of his conduct. His behavior was the same on the succeeding days, and continued to produce the same impression on Madame de Clèves.

At last the day of the tournament came. The queens betook themselves to the galleries and the raised seats set apart for them. The four champions appeared at the end of the lists, with a number of horses and servants, who formed the most magnificent spectacle ever seen in France.

The king's colors were plain black and white, which he always wore for the sake of Madame de Valentinois, who was a widow. The Duke of Ferrara and all his suite wore yellow and red. Monsieur de Guise appeared in pink and white: no one knew why he wore these colors; but it was remembered that they were those of a beautiful woman whom he had loved before she was married, and still loved, though he did not dare to show it. Monsieur de Nemours wore yellow and black,—why, no one knew. Madame de Clèves, however, had no difficulty in guessing: she remembered telling him one day that she liked yellow, and was sorry she was a blonde, because she could never wear that color. He believed that he could appear in it without indiscretion, because since Madame de Clèves never wore it, no one could suspect that it was hers.

Never was there seen greater skill than the four champions displayed. Although the king was the best horseman in the kingdom, it was hard to know to whom to give the palm.[9] Monsieur de Nemours showed a grace in all he did that inclined in his favor women less interested than Madame de Clèves. As soon as she saw him at the end of the lists she felt an unusual emotion, and every time he ran she could scarcely conceal her joy when he escaped without harm.

Toward evening, when all was nearly over, and the company on the point of withdrawing, the evil fate of the country made the king wish to break another lance. He ordered the Count of Montgomery, who was very skilful, to enter the lists. The count begged the king to excuse him, and made every apology he could think of; but the king, with some annoyance, sent him word that he insisted upon it. The queen sent a message to the king beseeching him not to run again, saying that he had done so well he ought to be satisfied, and that she entreated him to come to her. He answered that it was for love of her that he was going to run again, and entered the field. She sent Monsieur de Savoie to beg him again to come; but all was in vain. He started, the lances broke, and a splinter from that of the Count of Montgomery struck him in the eye and remained in it. He fell at once to the ground. His equerries and Monsieur de Montgomery, one of the marshals of the field, ran up to him, and were alarmed to see him so severely wounded. The king was not alarmed; he said it was a slight matter, and that he forgave the count. It is easy to conceive the excitement and distress caused by this unhappy accident after a day devoted to merry-making. As soon as the king had been carried to his bed the surgeons examined his wound, which they found very serious. The constable at that moment recalled the prediction made to the king that he should be slain in single combat, and he had no doubt that the prophecy would come true.

9. An ancient symbol of victory. Here, award the victory.

As soon as the King of Spain, who was then in Brussels, heard of this accident, he sent his physician, a man of vast experience; but he thought the king's state desperate.

The court, thus distracted and torn by conflicting interests, was much excited on the eve of this great event; but all dissensions were quieted, and there seemed to be no other cause of anxiety than the king's health. The queens, the princes, and the princesses scarcely left his ante-chamber.

Madame de Clèves, knowing that she was compelled to be there and to meet Monsieur de Nemours, and that she could not hide from her husband the embarrassment that the sight of him would produce; knowing too that the mere presence of this prince would excuse him and overthrow all her plans,—decided to feign illness. The court was too busy to notice her conduct or to make out how much was true and how much feigned in her illness. Her husband alone could know the truth; but she was not sorry to have him know it, so she remained at home, thinking little of the great change that was impending, and perfectly free to indulge in her own reflections. Every one was with the king. Monsieur de Clèves came at certain hours to tell her the news. He treated her as he had always done, except that when they were alone his manner was a little colder and stiffer. He never spoke to her again about what had happened, and she lacked the strength and deemed it unwise to reopen the subject.

Monsieur de Nemours, who had expected to find a few moments to speak to Madame de Clèves, was much surprised and pained not to have even the pleasure of seeing her. The king grew so much worse that on the seventh day his physicians gave him up. He received the news of his approaching death with wonderful firmness, all the more admirable because he died by such an unfortunate accident, in the prime of life, full of happiness, adored by his subjects, and loved by a mistress whom he madly worshipped. The evening before his death he had Madame his sister married with Monsieur de Savoie, very quietly.

It is easy to conceive in what state was Madame de Valentinois. The queen did not permit her to see the king, and sent to her to ask for the king's seals and for the crown jewels, which were in her keeping. The duchess asked if the king was dead; and when they told her no, she said: "Then I have no master, and no one can compel me to return what he intrusted to my hands."

As soon as he had died, at the castle of Tournelles, the Duke of Ferrara, the Duke of Guise, and the Duke of Nemours conducted to the Louvre the queen-dowager, the king, and his wife the queen.[1] Monsieur de Nemours escorted the queen-dowager. Just as they were starting, she drew back a little and told her daughter-in-law she was to go first; but it was easy to see that there was more vexation than politeness in this compliment.

Part V

The Cardinal of Lorraine had acquired complete ascendency over the mind of the queen-dowager; the Vidame de Chartres had completely fallen from her good graces, but his love for Madame de Martigues and his enjoyment of his freedom had prevented him from suffering from this change as much

---

1. The new king, Francis II, married to Mary Stuart, who became Mary, queen of Scots, after her husband's death in 1560. *The queen-dowager:* former king's widow, Catherine de Médicis.

as he might have done. During the ten days of the king's illness the cardinal had had abundant leisure to form his plans and to persuade the queen to take measures in conformity with his projects; hence as soon as the king was dead, the queen ordered the constable to remain at the castle of Tournelles to keep watch by the body of the late king and to take charge of the customary ceremonies. This order kept him aloof from everything, and prevented all action on his part. He sent a messenger to the king of Navarre to summon him in all diligence, in order that they might combine to oppose the promotion that evidently awaited the Guises. The command of the army was given to the Duke of Guise; that of the treasury to the Cardinal of Lorraine; the Duchess of Valentinois was driven from the court; the Cardinal of Tournon, the avowed enemy of the constable, was recalled, as well as the Chancelier Olivier, the open enemy of the Duchess of Valentinois, so that the aspect of the court was completely changed. The Duke of Guise was made equal to the princes of the blood, and allowed to carry the king's mantle at the funeral; he and his brothers were placed high in authority, not merely through the cardinal's influence over the queen, but also because she believed that she could overthrow them if they should offend her, while she would not be able to overthrow the constable, who was supported by the princes of the blood.

After the funeral the constable went to the Louvre, but met with a cold reception from the king. He desired to speak with the king in private; but the king called the Guises and told him in their presence that he advised him to seek retirement, that the treasury and the command of the army were already disposed of, and that whenever he might need his counsels he should summon him. The queen-dowager received him even more coldly than the king; she went so far as to remind him of his insulting remark to the late king about his children not looking like him. The King of Navarre arrived, and was received no better. The Prince of Condé, who was less patient than his brother, complained bitterly, but all in vain; he was exiled from court under the pretext of sending him to Flanders to sign the ratification of the treaty of peace.[2] The King of Navarre was shown a forged letter of the King of Spain which accused him of making attempts on his territory, and he was made to fear for his own possessions, and induced to return to his kingdom. The queen made this easy for him by assigning to him the duty of escorting Madame Elisabeth; she even obliged him to start before her, so that there was no one left at court to oppose the power of the household of Guise.

Although it was most unfortunate for Monsieur de Clèves that he could not escort Madame Elisabeth, he still could not complain, in view of the lofty rank of the man who was preferred; but the deprivation of the dignity was not what pained him, but rather that his wife lost an opportunity of absenting herself from court without exciting comment.

A few days after the king's death it was decided that the court should go to Rheims for the coronation. Madame de Clèves, who had hitherto stayed at home under pretence of illness, begged her husband to excuse her from accompanying the court, and to let her go to Coulommiers to get strength from the change of air. He replied that he would not ask her whether it was care for her health that compelled her to give up the journey, but that he

---

2. Again, the Treaty of Cateau-Cambrésis, in which France gave up its claims in Italy.

was willing she should not take it. He readily consented to a plan he had already decided on. High as was his opinion of his wife's virtue, he saw very clearly that it was not well for her to be exposed longer to meeting a man she loved.

Monsieur de Nemours soon learned that Madame de Clèves was not to accompany the court. He could not bear to think of leaving without seeing her; and the day before he was to start he called on her as late as he could, in order to find her alone. Fortune favored him, and as he entered the court-yard he met Madame de Nevers and Madame de Martigues coming out. They told him they had left her alone. He went upstairs in a state of agitation that can only be compared with that of Madame de Clèves when his name was announced. Her fear that he would mention his love; her apprehension lest she should give him a favorable answer; the anxiety that this visit would give her husband; the difficulty of repeating or concealing everything that happened,—all crowded on her mind at once, and so embarrassed her that she determined to avoid the thing she desired most in the world. She sent one of her maids to Monsieur de Nemours, who was in the hall, to tell him that she was not feeling well, and much regretted that she could not have the honor of receiving him. It was a grievous blow to him that he could not see Madame de Clèves because she was unwilling to receive him. He was to leave the next day, and there was no chance of his meeting her. He had not spoken to her since their conversation at the crown princess's, and he had reason to believe that his mistake in speaking to the Vidame had shattered all his hopes; consequently, he went away in deep rejection.

As soon as Madame de Clèves had somewhat recovered from the agitation of the prince's threatened visit, all the arguments that had made her decline it vanished from her mind; she even thought she had made a mistake, and if she had dared, and there had still been time, she would have called him back.

Madame de Nevers and Madame de Martigues, after leaving her, went to the crown princess's and found Monsieur de Clèves there. The princess asked them where they had been. They said they had just come from Madame de Clèves', where they had spent the afternoon with a number of persons, and that they had left no one there except Monsieur de Nemours. These words, which they thought thoroughly insignificant, were quite the opposite for Monsieur de Clèves, although it must have been evident to him that Monsieur de Nemours could easily find opportunities to speak to his wife. Nevertheless, the thought that he was with her alone, and able to speak to her of his love, seemed to him at that moment such a new and unendurable thing that his jealousy flamed out with greater fury than ever. He was not able to stay longer with the dauphiness, but left, not knowing why he did so, or whether he meant to interrupt Monsieur de Nemours. As soon as he got home he looked to see if that gentleman was still there; and when he had the consolation of finding him gone, he rejoiced to think that he could not have stayed long. He fancied that perhaps it was not Monsieur de Nemours of whom he ought to be jealous; and although he did not really doubt it, he tried his best to do so: but so many things pointed in that direction that he could not long enjoy the happiness of uncertainty. He went straight to his wife's room, and after a little talk on indifferent matters, he could not refrain from asking her what she had done and whom she had seen. Observing that she did not mention Monsieur de Nemours, he asked her, trembling with excitement, if those were all she had seen, in order to give her an opportunity to mention him, and thus save him from the pain of thinking she was capable of deception. Since she had not seen him, she said nothing about him; whereupon Monsieur de Clèves, in a tone that betrayed his distress, asked:

"And Monsieur de Nemours, didn't you see him, or have you forgotten him?"

"I did not see him, in point of fact; I was not feeling well, and I sent my regrets by one of my maids."

"Then you were ill for him alone," he went on, "since you received everybody else? Why this difference for him? Why is he not the same to you as all the rest? Why should you dread meeting him? Why do you show him that you make use of the power his passion gives you over him? Would you dare to refuse to see him if you did not know that he is able to distinguish your severity from incivility? Why should you be severe to him? From a person in your position, Madame, everything is a favor except indifference."

"I never thought," answered Madame de Clèves, "that however suspicious you might be of Monsieur de Nemours, you would reproach me for not seeing him."

"I do, however," he went on, "and with good cause. Why do you decline to see him, if he has not said anything to you? But, Madame, he has spoken to you; had his silence been the only sign of his passion, it would have made no such deep impression. You have not been able to tell me the whole truth; you have even repented telling me the little you did, and you have not the strength to go on. I am more unhappy than I supposed,—I am the unhappiest of men. You are my wife, I love you devotedly, and I see you love another man! He is the most fascinating man at court, he sees you every day, he knows that you love him. And I," he exclaimed,—"I could bring myself to believe that you would overcome your passion for him! I must have lost my reason when I imagined such a thing possible."

"I don't know," replied Madame de Clèves, sadly, "whether you were wrong in judging such extraordinary conduct as mine so favorably; I don't feel sure that I was right in thinking that you would do me justice."

"Do not doubt it Madame," said Monsieur de Clèves. "You were mistaken; you expected of me things quite as impossible as what I expected of you. How could you expect me to retain my self-control? Have you forgotten that I loved you madly and that I was your husband? Either case is enough to drive a man wild: what must it be when the two combine? And see what they do! I am torn by wild and uncertain feelings that I cannot control; I find myself no longer worthy of you,—you seem no more worthy of me. I adore you, and I hate you; I offend you, and I beg your pardon; I admire you, and I am ashamed of my admiration,—in a word, I have lost all my calmness, all my reason. I do not know how I have been able to live since you spoke with me at Coulommiers, and since the day when you learned from the dauphiness that your adventure was known. I cannot conjecture how it came out, or what passed between Monsieur de Nemours and you on this subject. You will never tell me, and I don't ask you to tell me; I beg of you only to remember that you have made me the unhappiest man in the world."

With those words Monsieur de Clèves left his wife's room, and went away the next morning without seeing her, although he wrote her a letter full of grief, consideration, and gentleness. She wrote him a touching answer, containing such assurances about her past and future conduct that, since they sprang from the truth and were her real feelings, the letter carried great weight with Monsieur de Clèves and calmed him somewhat. Moreover, since Monsieur de Nemours was also on his way to join the king, her husband had the consolation of knowing that he was separated from Madame de Clèves. Whenever she spoke with her husband, the love he showed her, the uprightness of his treatment of her, her own affection for him, and her sense of duty, made an impression on her heart which effaced all thought of Monsieur de Nemours. But this was only for a time; the remembrance of him soon returned with greater force than ever.

The first days after that prince had left, she scarcely noticed his absence; then it began to appear painful,—for since she began to love him, hardly a day had passed in which she had not either feared or hoped to see him; and it was to her a melancholy thought that chance could no longer make her meet him.

She went to Coulommiers, taking with her copies she had had made of the large pictures with which Madame de Valentinois had adorned her fine house at Anet.[3] All the memorable events of the king's reign were represented in these pictures. Among others was one of the Siege of Metz, with excellent likenesses of the principal officers, among whom was Monsieur de Nemours; and that was perhaps why Madame de Clèves cared for the pictures.

Madame de Martigues, having been unable to accompany the court, promised to spend a few days with her at Coulommiers. The queen's favor, which they both enjoyed, did not make them jealous or hostile; they were good friends, although they did not confide to each other everything. Madame de Clèves knew that Madame de Martigues loved the Vidame, but Madame de Martigues did not know that Madame de Clèves loved Monsieur de Nemours and was loved by him. The fact that she was a niece of the Vidame endeared her to Madame de Martigues; and Madame de Clèves was drawn toward her as a woman who, like herself, was in love, and with her lover's most intimate friend.

Madame de Martigues kept her promise, and went to Coulommiers. She found Madame de Clèves leading a most retired life,—indeed, she had sought absolute solitude, spending her evenings in the gardens, unaccompanied by her servants. She used to go into the summer-house where Monsieur de Nemours had overheard her talking with her husband, and enter the closet which opened on the garden. Her women and the servants would stay in the summer-house or in the other closet, coming to her only when they were called. Madame de Martigues had never seen Coulommiers; she was delighted with all the loveliness she found there, and especially with the comfort of this summer-house, in which she and Madame de Clèves spent every evening. Their solitude after dark, in the most beautiful place in the world, made easy prolonged talks between these two young women, who were both in love; and although they did not confide in each other, they delighted in talking together. Madame de Martigues would have been very sorry to leave Coulommiers if she had not been going to meet the Vidame; she went to Chambord, where was the whole court.

3. A château, about forty miles east of Paris, built for her by Henri II.

The new king was crowned at Rheims by the Cardinal of Lorraine, and the rest of the summer was to be spent at the castle of Chambord, then newly built. The queen manifested great pleasure at seeing Madame de Martigues again; and after giving expression to her joy, she asked after Madame de Clèves and what she was doing in the country. Monsieur de Nemours and Monsieur de Clèves were then with the queen. Madame de Martigues, who had been delighted with Coulommiers, described its beauty, and spoke at great length of the summer-house in the wood and of the pleasant evenings she had passed there with Madame de Clèves. Monsieur de Nemours, who was sufficiently familiar with the place to know what Madame de Martigues was talking about, thought that it might be possible to see Madame de Clèves there without being seen by her. He questioned Madame de Martigues, in order to get further information; and Monsieur de Clèves, who had kept his eyes on him while Madame de Martigues was talking, fancied that he detected his design. The questions that Monsieur de Nemours asked only strengthened his suspicions, so that he felt sure the duke intended to go to see his wife. He was right; this plan so attracted Monsieur de Nemours that after spending the night in devising plans to carry it into execution, the next morning he asked leave of the king to go to Paris on some pretext he had invented.

Monsieur de Clèves had no doubt about his reasons for going away, but he determined to seek information on his wife's conduct, and no longer to remain in cruel uncertainty. He desired to leave at the same time with Monsieur de Nemours, and from some place of concealment to discover what success he might have; but he feared lest their simultaneous absence might attract attention, or that Monsieur de Nemours might get wind of it and adopt other measures; so he determined to rely on one of the gentlemen in his suite, in whose fidelity and intelligence he felt confidence. He told him in what trouble he was, and what Madame de Clèves' virtue had been hitherto, and ordered him to follow in Monsieur de Nemours' footsteps, to watch him closely, and to see if he did not go to Coulommiers and enter the garden by night.

This gentleman, who was well suited for the duty, discharged it with the utmost exactness. He followed Monsieur de Nemours to a village half a league from Coulommiers, where the prince stopped, and the gentleman easily guessed that this was to await the approach of night. He did not think it well to wait there too, but passed through the village and made his way into the forest, to a spot which he thought Monsieur de Nemours would have to pass. He was not mistaken; as soon as night had fallen, he heard footsteps, and though it was dark, he easily recognized Monsieur de Nemours. He saw him walk about the garden as if to find out if he could hear some one, and to choose the most convenient spot for entering it. The palings were very high, and there were some beyond to bar the way, so that it was not easy to get in; nevertheless, Monsieur de Nemours succeeded. As soon as he had made his way into the garden, he had no difficulty in making out where Madame de Clèves was, as he saw many lights in the closet. All the windows were open; and creeping along the palings, he approached it with an emotion that can easily be imagined. He hid behind one of the long windows by which one entered the closet, to see what Madame de Clèves was doing. He saw that she was alone; she was so beautiful that he could scarcely control his rapture at the spectacle. It was warm, and her head and shoulders had no other covering than her loosely fastened hair. She was on a couch behind a table, on which were many baskets of ribbons; she was picking some out, and Monsieur de Nemours observed that they were of the same colors that he had worn in the tournament. He saw that she was fastening bows on a very peculiar stick that he had carried for some time and had given to his sister, from whom Madame de Clèves had taken it, without seeming to recognize it as belonging to Monsieur de Nemours. When she had finished her work with a grace and gentleness that reflected on her face the feelings that filled her heart, she took a light and drew near to a large table opposite the picture of the Siege of Metz, in which was the portrait of Monsieur de Nemours; then she sat down and gazed at this portrait with a rapt attention such as love alone could give.

It would be impossible to describe everything that Monsieur de Nemours felt at this moment. To see, in the deep night, in the most beautiful spot in the world, the woman he adored; to see her without her seeing him, busied with things that bore reference to him and to the hidden love she felt for him,—all that is something no other lover ever enjoyed or imagined.

Monsieur de Nemours was so entranced that he stood motionless, contemplating Madame de Clèves, without remembering that every moment was precious. When he had come to his senses again, he thought he ought to wait till she came into the garden before speaking to her; this he reflected would be safer, because then she would be farther from her maids. When, however, he saw that she remained in the closet, he decided to go in there. When he tried to do it, he was overwhelmed with agitation and with the fear of displeasing her. He could not bear the thought of seeing the face, just before so gentle, suddenly darken with anger and surprise.

He thought it madness, not his undertaking to see Madame de Clèves without being seen, but to think of showing himself; he saw everything that he had not before thought of. It seemed to him foolhardy to surprise at midnight a woman to whom he had never spoken of his love. He thought he had no right to assume that she would consent to listen to him, and he knew she would have good grounds for indignation at the danger to which he exposed her from the possible consequences of his acts. All his courage abandoned him, and more than once he was on the point of deciding that he would go back without seeing her. But he was so anxious to speak to her, and so encouraged by what he had seen, that he pushed on a few steps, though in such agitation that his scarf caught on the window and made a noise. Madame de Clèves turned her head; and whether it was that her mind was full of this prince, or that his face was actually in the light, she thought that she recognized him; and without hesitation or turning toward him, she rejoined her maids. She was so agitated that she had to trump up an excuse of not feeling well; and she said it also to attract their attention and thus give Monsieur de Nemours time to beat a retreat. After a little reflection she decided that she had been mistaken, and that the vision of Monsieur de Nemours was a mere illusion. She knew that he had been at Chambord, and she judged it extremely unlikely that he could have undertaken so perilous an enterprise; several times she was on the point of going back into the closet to see if there was any one in the garden. Perhaps she hoped as much as she feared to find Monsieur de Nemours there; but at last reason and prudence prevailed over every other feeling, and she decided that she should do better to stay where she was than to seek any further information. She was long in making up her mind to leave a place near which he might be, and it was almost morning when she returned to the castle.

Monsieur de Nemours stayed in the garden as long as he saw a light. He had not given up all hope of seeing Madame de Clèves again, although he was sure that she had recognized him and had only left in order to avoid him; but when he saw the servants locking the doors, he knew that he had no further chance. He retraced his steps, passing by the place where the friend of Monsieur de Clèves was in waiting. This gentleman followed him to the village, whence he had started in the evening. Monsieur de Nemours determined to spend the whole day there, in order to return to Coulommiers that night, to see if Madame de Clèves would be cruel enough to flee from him, or not to let him look at her. Although he was highly delighted to find that her mind was occupied with him, he was deeply pained to see her so instinctively taking flight.

Never was there a tenderer or intenser love than that which animated this prince. He strolled beneath the willows beside a little brook which ran behind the house in which he was concealed. He kept himself out of sight as much as possible, that no one might know of his presence. He gave himself up to the transports of love, and his heart was so full that he could not keep from shedding a few tears; but these were not of grief, they were tempered with all the sweetness that only love can give.

He recalled all Madame de Clèves' actions since he had fallen in love with her,—the honorable and modest severity with which she had treated him, although she loved him. "For she does indeed love me," he exclaimed; "she loves me,—I cannot doubt it. The most fervent protestations, the greatest favors, are no surer tokens than those I have received; and yet she treats me with the same austerity as if she hated me. I thought time would bring a change, but I can expect nothing more from it; I see her always on her guard against me and against herself. If she did not love me, I should try to please her; but I do please her, she loves me, and hides her love. What then am I to hope,—what change in my fate can I expect. What! the most charming woman in the world loves me, and I cannot enjoy the supreme happiness that comes from the first certainty of being loved, except in the agony of being ill-treated! Show, fair princess," he called aloud, "that you love me; show me that you really feel! If you will only once let me hear from you what your feelings are, I am willing that you should resume for ever the severity with which you overwhelm me. At least look at me with those eyes that I saw gazing at my portrait. Could you look at it with such gentleness, and then flee from me so cruelly? What do you fear? Why do you so dread my love? You love me, and you hide your love to no purpose; you have yourself given me tokens of its unawares. I know my good fortune: let me enjoy it, and cease making me unhappy. Is it possible that Madame de Clèves loves me, and I am still unhappy? How beautiful she was last night! How could I resist my longing to fling myself at her feet? Had I done so, I might have prevented her flight; my respectful bearing would have reassured her. But perhaps she did not recognize me,—I distress myself more than I should; and the sight of a man at such an extraordinary hour frightened her."

These thoughts haunted Monsieur de Nemours all day. He awaited the night with impatience, and when it had come he took once more the road to Coulommiers. The friend of Monsieur de Clèves, having assumed a disguise to avoid being recognized, followed him as he had done the previous evening, and saw him enter the same garden. Then Monsieur de Nemours perceived that Madame de Clèves was unwilling to run the risk of his trying to see her; every entrance was closed. He wandered in every direction to find some light, but his search was vain.

Madame de Clèves, suspecting that Monsieur de Nemours might come back, stayed in her own room; she feared lest strength to flee should be denied her, and she did not wish to risk the possibility of speaking to him in a manner that might contradict her previous conduct. Although Monsieur de Nemours had no hope of seeing her, he could not make up his mind to leave at once a place where she had been so often. He spent the whole night in the garden, finding some slight consolation in at least gazing on the same objects which she saw every day. The sun had risen before he thought of leaving; but at last the fear of being observed compelled him to go.

It was impossible for him to return without seeing Madame de Clèves; hence he went to see Madame de Mercœur, who was then living in her house not far from Coulommiers. She was extremely surprised at her brother's arrival. He invented some specious excuse for his journey, which completely deceived her, and at last managed so cleverly that she herself proposed their calling on Madame de Clèves. This plan they carried out that very day, and Monsieur de Nemours told his sister that he would leave her at Coulommiers to return with all speed to the king. He devised this plan of parting from her at Coulommiers in the hope that she would be the first to leave; in this way he imagined he could not fail to have an opportunity of speaking to Madame de Clèves.

When they reached Coulommiers, they found Madame de Clèves walking in a broad path along the edge of the flower-garden. The sight of Monsieur de Nemours embarrassed her not a little, and made her sure that it was he whom she had seen the previous night. This conviction filled her with anger that he should have been so bold and imprudent. He noticed with pain her evident coldness. The talk ran on insignificant subjects, and yet he succeeded in displaying so much wit and amiability, and so much admiration for Madame de Clèves, that he finally dispelled some of her coolness, in spite of her determination not to be appeased.

When he had got over his first timidity, he expressed great curiosity to see the summer-house in the wood; he described it as the most delightful spot in the world, and with so many details that Madame de Mercœur said he must have often seen it, to be so familiar with all its beauty.

"Still, I do not believe," answered Madame de Clèves, "that Monsieur de Nemours has ever been in it; it has been finished only a very short time."

"It is not long, either, since I was there," he retorted, looking at her; "and I do not know whether I ought not to be very glad that you have forgotten having seen me there."

Madame de Mercœur, who was busy looking at the garden, paid no attention to what her brother was saying. Madame de Clèves, blushing, and casting down her eyes so as not to see Monsieur de Nemours, said:

"I do not remember ever having seen you there, and if you ever have been there, it was without my knowledge."

"It is true, Madame," he said, "that I have been there without your permission, and I have spent there the most blissful and the most wretched moments of my life."

Madame de Clèves knew only too well what he meant; but she made no answer. She was thinking how she should keep Madame de Mercœur from going into the closet which contained the portrait of Monsieur de Nemours: this she did not want her to see. She succeeded so well that the time passed imperceptibly, and Madame de Mercœur spoke of leaving; but when Madame de Clèves noticed that Madame de Mercœur and her brother were not going away together, she saw the impending danger, and was as much embarrassed as she had been in Paris, and she decided on the same course. Her fear lest this visit should only confirm her husband's suspicions helped her to form this decision, and in order to prevent Monsieur de Nemours from being alone with her, she told Madame de Mercœur that she would accompany her to the edge of the forest, and ordered her carriage to follow her. This prince's grief at finding Madame de Clèves as austere as ever was so keen that he turned pale. Madame de Mercœur asked him if he was ill; but he looked at Madame de Clèves without being seen by any one, and let her see that he was suffering from nothing but despair. Nevertheless, he was compelled to let them go without daring to follow them; and after what he had said, he could not go back with his sister. He returned to Paris, and left it the next day.

Monsieur de Clèves' friend had watched him all the while. He also returned to Paris; and when he saw that Monsieur de Nemours had left for Chambord, he took the post in order to get there before him, and to make his report about his expedition. His master was awaiting his return to determine his life's unhappiness.

As soon as Monsieur de Clèves saw him, he read in his expression and his silence that he had brought only bad news. He remained for some time overwhelmed with grief, his head bowed, unable to speak; then he motioned to him to withdraw. "Go," he said; "I see what you have to tell me, but I am not strong enough to hear it."

"I have nothing to report," answered the gentleman, "from which it is possible to form an accurate judgment. It is true that Monsieur de Nemours entered the garden in the woods two nights running, and called at Coulommiers the next day with Madame de Mercœur."

"That is enough," replied Monsieur de Clèves, "that is enough;" and then, again motioning to him to leave, he added, "I have no need of further information."

The gentleman was forced to leave his master plunged in despair. Never, perhaps, has there been more poignant grief, and few men who possessed so much spirit and so affectionate a heart as Monsieur de Clèves have suffered the agony of discovering at the same time a wife's infidelity and the mortification of being deceived by a woman.

Monsieur de Clèves was overwhelmed by this grievous blow. That same night he was seized with a fever of such severity that at once his life was in peril. Word was sent to Madame de Clèves, and she went to him with all speed. He was worse when she reached him, and she noticed something cold and icy in his manner toward her that greatly surprised and pained her. He even seemed to be annoyed at the attention she paid him; but at last she thought this was perhaps a result of his illness.

As soon as Madame de Clèves had arrived at Blois, where the court was at that time, Monsieur de Nemours was filled with joy at knowing that she was in the same place as himself. He tried to see her, and called at the house every day, under pretext of inquiring after Monsieur de Clèves; but it was all in vain. She never left her husband's room, and was very anxious about him. Monsieur de Nemours regretted that she suffered so much; he readily saw how this grief would be likely to rekindle her love for Monsieur de Clèves, and how this affection would prove a dangerous foe to the love she bore in her heart. This feeling depressed him for some time; but the extreme seriousness of Monsieur de Clèves' illness soon gave him new hopes. He saw that Madame de Clèves would soon be free to follow her own wishes, and that in the future he might find lasting happiness. This thought filled him with almost painful rapture, and he banished it from his mind, lest he should be too miserable if his hopes were disappointed.

Meanwhile Monsieur de Clèves was almost given up. One of the last days of his illness, after he had passed a very bad night, he said, toward morning, that he would like to rest. Madame de Clèves alone stayed in his room. It seemed to her that, instead of resting, he was very uneasy; she went up to him and knelt down by his bed, with her face covered with tears. Monsieur de Clèves had made up his mind to say nothing about his grievance against her; but her attentions and her sorrow, which seemed genuine, and which he sometimes regarded as tokens of deceit and treachery, produced such conflicting and painful feelings that he could not repress them.

"You, Madame," he said, "are shedding a great many tears for a death of which you are the cause, and which cannot give you the sorrow which you display. I am no longer able to reproach you," he went on, in a voice weakened by illness and grief, "but I am dying of the cruel suffering you have inflicted on me. Was it necessary that so extraordinary an action as that of speaking to me as you did at Coulommiers should have so little result? Why confide to me your love for Monsieur de Nemours, if your virtue was not strong enough to resist it? I loved you so that I was glad to be deceived,—I confess it to my shame; I have since longed for the false tranquillity of which you robbed me. Why did you not leave me in the calm blindness in which so many husbands are happy? I should perhaps have never known that you loved Monsieur de Nemours. I am dying," he went on; "but bear it in mind that you make me welcome death, and that since you have robbed me of the love and esteem I felt for you, I dread living. What would life be to me, if I had to spend it with a woman I have loved so much and who has so cruelly deceived me, or if I had to live apart from her, after a scene of violence utterly repugnant to my disposition and to the love I bear you? My love for you, Madame, has been far deeper than you know; I have concealed the greater part of it, from fear of tormenting you or of lessening your esteem by a manner unbecoming to a husband; I really deserved your affection. I say it once more: I die without regret, since I could not win this, and now can no longer wish for it. Farewell, Madame. Some day you will mourn a man who had for you a true and lawful love. You will know the misery that overtakes women who fall into these entanglements, and you will learn the difference between being loved as I loved you, and being loved by men who, while protesting their love, seek only the honor of misleading you. But my death will leave you free, and you will be able to make Monsieur de Nemours happy without doing anything criminal. What do I care what may happen when I shall be no more? Must I be weak enough to look upon it?"

Madame de Clèves was so far from imagining that her husband could suspect her that she listened to him without understanding what he was saying, and supposing that he was blaming her interest in Monsieur de Nemours. At last, suddenly grasping his meaning, she exclaimed,—

"I a criminal! The very thought of it never entered my head. The severest virtue could command no different course of conduct than mine, and I have not done one thing of which I should not be glad to have you an eye-witness."

"Should you have been glad," asked Monsieur de Clèves, looking at her somewhat disdainfully, "to have had me for an eye-witness of the nights you spent with Monsieur de Nemours? Ah! Madame, am I speaking of you when I speak of a woman who has spent nights with a man?"

"No," she answered, "no; it is not of me that you are speaking,—I have never passed nights or moments with Monsieur de Nemours; he has never seen me in private; I have never had anything to do with him or listened to him, and I will swear—"

"Say no more," interrupted Monsieur de Clèves; "false oaths or a confession would give me equal pain."

Madame de Clèves could not answer; her tears and her grief choked her. At last, making a great effort, she said: "Look at me, at least; listen to me. If it concerned me alone, I should endure these reproaches; but it is your life that is at stake. Listen to me for your own sake; it is impossible that, with all the truth on my side, I should not convince you of my innocence."

"Would to God that you could convince me!" he exclaimed. "But what can you say to me? Was not Monsieur de Nemours at Coulommiers with his sister, and had he not passed the two previous nights with you in the garden in the forest?"

"If that is my crime," she replied, "I can clear myself easily. I don't ask you to believe me, but believe your servants: ask them if I was in the garden the evening Monsieur de Nemours came to Coulommiers, and if I didn't leave it the evening before, two hours earlier than usual."

She then told him how she had imagined she saw some one in the garden, and confessed that she had thought it was Monsieur de Nemours. She spoke with such earnestness, and the truth, even when improbable, carries such weight, that Monsieur de Clèves was almost convinced of her innocence.

"I do not know," he said, "whether I dare believe you; I am so near death that I do not want to see anything that might make me long to live. Your explanation comes too late; but it will always be a consolation to think that you are worthy of the esteem I have had for you. I beg of you to let me have the additional consolation of knowing that my memory will be dear to you, and that if it had depended on you, you would have had for me the feeling you have had for another."

He wanted to go on; but a sudden faintness made it impossible, and Madame de Clèves summoned the physicians. They found him almost lifeless. Nevertheless he lingered a few days longer, and at last died, having displayed admirable firmness.

Madame de Clèves was almost crazed by the intensity of her grief. The queen at once came to see her, and carried her to a convent, without her knowing whither she was going. Her sisters-in-law brought her to Paris before she was yet able to realize her afflictions. When she began to be strong enough to think about it, and saw what a husband she had lost, and reflected that she was the cause of his death by means of her love for another man, the horror she felt at herself and at Monsieur de Nemours cannot be described.

At first this prince did not venture to pay her any other attentions than such as etiquette required. He knew Madame de Clèves well enough to be sure that anything more marked would displease her; but what he learned later assured him that he would have to maintain this reserve for a long time. One of his equerries told him that Monsieur de Clèves' gentleman,[4] a friend of his, had told him, in his deep regret for the loss of his master, that Monsieur de Nemours' trip to Coulommiers was the cause of his death. Monsieur de Nemours was extremely surprised to hear this; but on thinking it over, he made out a part of the truth, and conjectured what would be the feelings of Madame de Clèves, and how she would detest him if she thought her husband's illness had been due to jealousy. He thought that the best thing would be not to have his name brought to her notice, and he regulated his conduct accordingly, painful as he found it.

The prince went to Paris, and could not refrain from calling on Madame de Clèves to ask how she was. He was informed that she saw no one, and had even given orders that she was not to be told who had inquired after her. Possibly these rigid orders were given solely on account of the prince, and to avoid hearing his name mentioned. But Monsieur de Nemours was too desperately in love to be able to live with absolutely no chance of seeing Madame de Clèves. He resolved to try every means, no matter how difficult, to escape from such an unendurable condition of affairs.

The princess's grief passed all bounds of reason. Her dying husband,—dying for her sake, and filled with such tender love for her,—was never sent from her mind; she continually recalled everything she owed him, and blamed herself for not having loved him,—as if that were a thing that depended on her will. Her sole consolation was the thought that she mourned him as he deserved, and that for the rest of her life she would only do what he would have approved if he had lived.

She had often wondered how he knew that Monsieur de Nemours had come to Coulommiers; she did not suspect that the prince had spoken of it, and it even seemed to her that it was immaterial whether he had said anything about it, so thoroughly rid of her passion did she feel. Nevertheless, she was deeply distressed to think that he was the cause of her husband's death, and she remembered with sorrow the fear that had tormented Monsieur de Clèves on his deathbed lest she should marry him; but all these various sources of grief were lost in that over her husband's death, and the others sank into insignificance.

After many months had passed, she recovered from her violent grief, becoming sad and languid. Madame de Martigues made a visit to Paris, and saw her repeatedly during her stay there. She talked with her about the court and of all that had happened; and although Madame de Clèves seemed to take no interest, Madame de Martigues went on talking in order to divert her. She told her all about the Vidame, Monsieur de Guise, and all the other men of note.

---

4. Attendant. *Equerries:* personal attendants.

"As for Monsieur de Nemours," she said, "I do not know whether his occupations have taken the place of gallantry, but he is less cheerful than he used to be; he shuns the society of women; he continually runs up to Paris, and I believe is here now."

Monsieur de Nemours' name surprised Madame de Clèves and made her blush; she changed the subject, and Madame de Martigues did not notice her confusion.

The next day, the princess, being anxious to find some occupation suitable for her condition, went to see a man living close by who worked in silk in a peculiar way, with the intention of undertaking something of the sort herself. After looking at what he had to show, her eyes fell on the door of a room in which she thought there were some more, and asked to have it opened. The man replied that he did not have the key, and that it was occupied by a man who came there sometimes to draw the fine houses and gardens to be seen from the windows. "He is the handsomest man in the world," he went on, "and does not seem obliged to support himself by his work. Whenever he comes here, I see him always looking at the houses and gardens, but I have never seen him at work."

Madame de Clèves listened with great attention; what Madame de Martigues had said about Monsieur de Nemours coming some times to Paris, as well as her vision of this handsome man who had taken quarters near her house, made her think of that prince, and suggested that he was trying to see her. This thought produced in her an agitation which she could not understand. She went to the windows to see on what they looked, and saw that it was on her garden and her own apartment; and when she was in her room she saw the same window to which she had been told that the stranger used to come. The conjecture that it was Monsieur de Nemours entirely altered the current of her thoughts; she no longer felt the sad tranquillity which she had begun to enjoy,—she was uneasy and agitated. At last, unable to endure her loneliness, she went out to take the air in a garden in the faubourgs,[5] where she expected to find solitude. At first she supposed no one was there; the place seemed deserted, and she strolled about for some little time.

After passing through a little thicket, she saw at the end of the path, in the most retired part of the garden, a sort of summer-house open on all sides, and she turned in that direction. When she had got near it, she saw a man lying on the benches who seemed sunk in deep thought, and she recognized Monsieur de Nemours. At the sight of him she stopped short; but her servants, who were following her, made some noise that aroused him. Without looking at them, he arose, to avoid their company, and turned into another path, bowing deeply, so that he was unable to see whom he was saluting.

Had Monsieur de Nemours known from whom he was running away, he would have eagerly retraced his steps; but as it was, he followed the path and went out by a sidegate, at which his carriage was waiting. This incident made a deep impression on Madame de Clèves' heart; all her love was suddenly rekindled with its former fervor. She went on and sat down in the place which Monsieur de Nemours had just left, and there she remained, completely overwhelmed. Her mind was full of this prince, more fascinating than any man in the world; loving her long with respect and constancy; giving up

5. Suburbs.

everything for her; respecting even her grief; trying to see her, without himself being seen; abandoning the court, where he was a favorite, to look upon the walls behind which she was immured, to come and muse in places where he could not hope to meet her,—in short, a man worthy to be loved for his love alone, and for whom she felt a passion so violent that she would have loved him even if he had not loved her, and one moreover of a lofty nature perfectly in harmony with her own. Duty and virtue could not restrain her emotions; every obstacle vanished; and of all her past she remembered nothing but her love for Monsieur de Nemours and his for her.

All these thoughts were new to the princess; she had been so lost in grief for her husband's death that she had given them no attention. With the sight of Monsieur de Nemours they all recurred to her. But when they came fastest, and she remembered that this same man whom now she thought of as able to marry her was the one she had loved during her husband's lifetime and was the cause of his death; that on his deathbed he had manifested his fear lest she should marry him,—her rigid virtue was so pained by the thought that it seemed to her quite as grievous a crime to marry Monsieur de Nemours as it had been to love him while her husband was living. She gave herself up to these reflections, which were so hostile to her happiness, and confirmed them by many arguments concerning her peace of mind and the evils she foresaw in case she married him. At last, after spending two hours there, she returned home, convinced that she ought to avoid the sight of him as a real obstacle to her duty.

But this conviction, the product of reason and virtue, did not control her heart, which remained attached to Monsieur de Nemours with a violence that reduced her to a most restless and pitiable state. That night was one of the unhappiest she had ever known. In the morning her first thought was to go to see if there was any one at the window which commanded her house; she looked out and saw Monsieur de Nemours. This surprised her, and she drew back so quickly that he felt sure she must have recognized him. This he had long wished might happen, since he had devised this method of seeing her; and when it seemed hopeless, he used to go and meditate in the garden where she had seen him.

Worn out at last by grief and uncertainty, the duke made up his mind to find some way of determining his fate. "Why should I wait?" he asked. "I have long known she loved me; she is free, and duty no longer stands in her way. Why should she force me to see her without being seen by her and with no chance to speak to her? Can love have so absolutely destroyed my reason and my boldness that I am not what I was when in love before? I was bound to respect Madame de Clèves' grief; but I have respected it too long, and I am giving her time to forget the affection she feels for me."

Thereupon he began to devise some way of seeing her. He fancied that there was no good reason for concealing his love from the Vidame of Chartres, and he resolved to speak to him and to confide to him his plans about his niece. The Vidame was then in Paris, like all the rest of the court, who had come to town to make their preparations for accompanying the king, who was to escort the Queen of Spain. Accordingly, Monsieur de Nemours called on the Vidame and frankly told him everything he had kept hidden until then, except Madame de Clèves' feelings, which he did not wish to appear to know.

The Vidame heard him with great pleasure, and answered that, with no knowledge of his feelings, he had often, since Madame de Clèves had become a widow, thought that she was the only woman worthy of him. Monsieur de Nemours besought his aid in getting a chance to address her, in order to find out her intentions.

The Vidame proposed taking him to call on her; but Monsieur de Nemours feared that she would not like this, because she did not yet see any one. They decided that the Vidame should invite her to come and see him on some pretext or other, and that Monsieur de Nemours should enter by a hidden staircase, in order not to be seen. This was carried out according to their plans. Madame de Clèves came; the Vidame went to receive her, and led her into a small room at the end of his apartment. Shortly after, Monsieur de Nemours came in, as if by chance. Madame de Clèves was much surprised to see him; she blushed, and tried to hide her blushes. The Vidame began to talk about unimportant subjects, and then went away, under the pretext of having some orders to give. He asked Madame de Clèves to do the honors in his place, and said he should return in a moment.

It would be impossible to express the feelings of Monsieur de Nemours and Madame de Clèves when they for the first time found themselves alone and free to talk. They remained for a long time without a word; then at last Monsieur de Nemours broke the silence. "Will you, Madame, forgive the Vidame," he said, "for having given me an opportunity to see you and to speak with you, which you have always cruelly denied me?"

"I ought not to forgive him," she replied, "for having forgotten my position and to what he exposes my reputation." As she uttered these words she started to leave; but Monsieur de Nemours delayed her, saying:

"Do not be alarmed, Madame; no one knows that I am here, and there is no danger. Listen to me, Madame,—if not through kindness, at least through love of yourself, and in order to protect yourself against the extravagances to which I shall certainly be led by an uncontrollable passion."

For the first time Madame de Clèves yielded to her tenderness for Monsieur de Nemours, and looking at him with eyes full of gentleness and charm, she said: "But what do you hope from the kindness that you ask of me? You would certainly regret obtaining it, and I should regret granting it. You deserve a happier fate than you have yet had, and can have in the future, unless you seek it elsewhere."

"I, Madame, find such happiness elsewhere! Is there any other happiness than winning your love? Although I have never spoken with you, I cannot think that you are ignorant of my affection, or that you do not know that it is truer and warmer than ever. How much it has been tried by events unknown to you, and how much by your severity!"

"Since you wish me to speak, and I decide it best," answered Madame de Clèves, sitting down, "I will do so, with a frankness that you will not always find in women. I shall not tell you that I have not noticed your attachment to me,—perhaps you could not believe me if I were to say so; I confess, then, not only that I have noticed it, but also just as you wished it to appear."

"And, Madame, if you have seen it," he interrupted, "is it possible that you have not been touched by it; and may I venture to ask if it has made no impression on your heart?"

"You should have judged of that from my conduct," she replied; "but I should be glad to know what you have thought of it."

"I should have to be in a happier condition to dare to tell you," he answered, "and my fate has too little relation with what I should say. All that I can tell you, Madame, is that you would not have confessed to Monsieur de Clèves what you concealed from me, and that you would have concealed from him what you would have let me see."

"How were you able to find out," she asked, blushing, "that I confessed anything to Monsieur de Clèves?"

"I heard it from your own lips, Madame," he replied; "but as an excuse for my boldness in listening to you, consider whether I misused what I had heard, whether my hopes were strengthened by it, whether I became bold enough to speak to you."

He began to tell her how he had heard her conversation with Monsieur de Clèves: but she interrupted him in the middle.

"Say no more," she said; "I now see how you came to know too much: that you did, was very plain to me at the dauphiness's when she had heard the story from those to whom you had told it."

Monsieur de Nemours then explained to her how that had happened.

"Do not apologize," she resumed; "I forgave you a long time ago, before you told me how it occurred. But since you have yourself heard from me what I had meant to keep a secret from you all my life, I confess that you have inspired me with emotions unknown before I saw you, and so unfamiliar to me that they filled me with a surprise which greatly added to the agitation they produced. I confess this with the less shame because I may now do it innocently, and you have seen that my feelings did not guide my actions."

"Do you believe, Madame," exclaimed Monsieur de Nemours, falling on his knees, "that I am not ready to die at your feet with joy and rapture?"

"I only tell you," she answered, smiling, "what you already know only too well."

"Ah! Madame," he said, "what a difference between finding something out by accident, and hearing it from you, and seeing that you wish me to know it."

"It is true," said she, "that I wish you to know it, and that I take pleasure in telling you. I am not certain that I do not tell it more from love of myself than from love of you; for certainly this avowal will have no consequences, and I shall follow the rigid rules that my condition imposes."

"You will not think of such a thing, Madame," replied Monsieur de Nemours; "you are bound by no further duty; you are free; and if I dared, I should even tell you that it depends on you so to act that your duty shall some day oblige you to preserve the feelings that you have for me."

"My duty," she replied, "forbids my ever thinking of any one, and of you last of all, for reasons unknown to you."

"Perhaps they are not, Madame," he pleaded; "but those are no true reasons. I have reason to believe that Monsieur de Clèves thought me happier than I was, and imagined that you approved of mad freaks of mine which my passion suggested without your knowledge."

"Let us not speak of that affair," she said. "I cannot bear the thought of it; it fills me with shame, and its consequences were too painful. It is only too likely that you are the cause of Monsieur de Clèves' death; the suspicions you aroused, your inconsiderate conduct, cost him his life as truly as if you had taken it with your own hands. Think of what I should do if you had come to such extremities and the same unhappy result had followed. I know very well this is not the same thing in the eyes of the world; but in mine there is no difference, for I know it was from you he got his death, and on account of me."

"Oh! Madame," interposed Monsieur de Nemours, "what phantom of duty do you oppose to my happiness? What! Madame, a vain and baseless fancy can prevent your making happy a man you do not hate, when he has conceived the hope of passing his life with you, his fate leading him to love you as the best woman in the world, finding in you every charming trait, incurring not your hatred, and seeing in you everything that best becomes a woman,—for, Madame, there is no other woman who combines what you do. Men who marry their mistresses who love them, tremble from fear lest they should renew their misconduct with others; but nothing of the sort is to be feared in you: you are only to be admired. Can I have foreseen such felicity only to find you raising obstacles? Ah! Madame, you forget that you chose me from other men,—or rather, you did not; you made a mistake, and I have flattered myself."

"You did not flatter yourself," she replied; "the reasons for my acting as I do would not, perhaps, seem to me so strong, had I not chosen you as you suspect,—and that is what makes me foresee unhappiness if I should take an interest in you."

"I have no answer," he said, "when you show me that you fear unhappiness; but I confess that, after all you have been good enough to say to me, I did not expect to be opposed by such a cruel argument." "It is so far from uncomplimentary to you," she answered, "that I shall even find it hard to tell it to you."

"Alas! Madame, what can you fear will flatter me too much after what you have just said to me?"

"I wish still to speak to you as frankly as I began," she explained, "and I want to dispense with all the reserve and formalities that I should respect in a first conversation; but I beg of you to listen to me without interruption.

"I think it but a slight reward for your affection that I should hide from you none of my feelings, but should let you see them exactly as they are. This probably will be the only time in my life that I shall take the liberty of letting you see them; nevertheless, I cannot confess to you without deep shame that the certainty of not being loved by you as I am, seems to me a horrible misfortune; that if there were not already insurmountable claims of duty, I doubt if I could make up my mind to risk this unhappiness. I know that you are free, as I am, and that we are so situated that the world would probably blame neither of us if we should marry; but do men keep their love in these permanent unions? Ought I to expect a miracle in my case, and can I run the risk of seeing this passion, which would be my only happiness, fade away? Monsieur de Clèves was perhaps the only man in the world capable of keeping his love after marriage. My fate forbade my enjoying this blessing. Perhaps, too, his love only survived because he found none in me. But I should not have the same way of preserving yours; I believe that the obstacles you have met have made you constant; those were enough to make you yearn to conquer them, and my involuntary actions,—things you learned by chance,—gave you enough hope to keep you interested."

"Oh! Madame," replied Monsieur de Nemours, "I can no longer maintain the silence you impose on me; you do me too much injustice, and you let me see how far you are from being prejudiced in my favor."

"I confess," she said, "that I may be moved by my emotions, but they cannot blind me; nothing can prevent my seeing that you are born with every disposition for gallantry, and with all the qualities proper to secure speedy success. You have already been in love several times,—you would be again very often. I should not make you happy; I should see you interested in another as you have been in me: this would inflict on me a mortal blow, and I should never feel sure that I should not be jealous. I have said too much to try to hide from you that you have already made me feel this passion, and that I suffered cruel tortures that evening when the queen gave me that letter from Madame de Themines which was said to be directed to you, and that the impression left on me is that jealousy is the greatest unhappiness in the world.

"Vanity or taste makes all women try to secure you; there are few whom you do not please,—my own experience teaches me that there are few whom you might not please. I should always imagine that you were loved and in love, and I should not be often wrong. Yet in this condition I could only suffer,—I should not dare to complain. One may make reproaches to a lover, but can a woman reproach her husband for ceasing to love her? If I could become hardened to that misfortune, could I become hardened to imagining that I saw Monsieur de Clèves charging you with his death, reproaching me for loving you, and showing the difference between his affection and yours? It is impossible to resist such arguments; I must remain in my present position and in my immovable determination never to leave it."

"But do you think you can, Madame?" exclaimed Monsieur de Nemours. "Do you think that your resolutions can hold out against a man who worships you and is fortunate enough to please you? It is harder than you think, Madame, to resist what pleases us and one who loves us. You have done it by an austere virtue which is almost without a precedent; but this virtue no longer conflicts with your emotions, and these I hope you will follow, in spite of yourself."

"I know that there is nothing harder than what I undertake; I mistrust my own strength, supported by all my arguments. What I think due to the memory of Monsieur de Clèves would be ineffectual, if it were not reinforced by my anxiety for my own peace of mind; and these arguments need to be strengthened by those of duty. But though I mistrust myself, I think I shall never overcome my scruples, and I do not hope to overcome my interest in you. It will make me unhappy, and I shall deny myself the pleasure of seeing you, whatever pain this may cost me. I am in a position which makes that a crime which at any other time would be permissible, and mere etiquette forbids that we should meet."

Monsieur de Nemours flung himself at her feet and gave expression to all the emotion that filled him. He manifested, by his words and tears, the liveliest and tenderest passion that heart ever felt. Madame de Clèves was not unmoved; and looking at Monsieur de Nemours with eyes heavy with tears, she exclaimed,—

"Why must I charge you with the death of Monsieur de Clèves? Why did I not learn to know you when I was free; or why did I not know you before I was married? Why does fate divide us by such an insuperable obstacle?"

"There is no obstacle," pleaded Monsieur de Nemours; "you alone thwart my happiness, you alone impose a law which virtue and reason could not impose."

"It is true," she replied, "that I make a great sacrifice to a duty which exists only in my imagination. Wait to see what time will do. Monsieur de Clèves has but just died, and that fatal event is too recent for me to judge clearly. Meanwhile you have the pleasure of having won the love of a woman who would never have loved had she not seen you; be sure that my feelings for you will never change and will always survive, whatever I do.

"Good by," she said. "This conversation fills me with shame. Repeat it to the Vidame; I give my consent,—nay, I beg of you to do so."

With these words she left the room, Monsieur de Nemours being unable to prevent her. She found the Vidame in the next room. He saw her so agitated that he did not dare to speak to her, and he handed her to her carriage without a word. He went back to Monsieur de Nemours, who was in such a whirl of joy, sadness, surprise, and admiration,—in short, so possessed by all the emotions that spring from a passion full of hope and dread,—that he seemed beside himself. It was long before the Vidame got any clear notion of what they had said; finally, however, he succeeded; and Monsieur de Chartres, without being the least in love, had no less admiration for the virtue, intelligence, and worth of Madame de Clèves than had Monsieur de Nemours himself. They tried to determine the prince's probable chances; and whatever the fears that love might arouse, the prince agreed with the Vidame that it was impossible that Madame de Clèves should persist in her resolutions. Nevertheless, they agreed to follow her orders, from fear lest, if the duke's love for her should become known, she should in some way bind herself, and would not change from fear of its being thought that she had loved him while her husband was living.

Monsieur de Nemours determined to join the king, as he could no longer stay away, and he made up his mind to start without even trying to see Madame de Clèves again. He begged the Vidame to speak to her. He told him a number of things to say to her, and suggested countless arguments with which to overcome her scruples. At last a good part of the night was gone before Monsieur de Nemours thought of leaving to seek repose.

Madame de Clèves was in no condition to find rest; it was for her such a new thing to lay aside the reserve which she had imposed upon herself, to permit a man to tell her that he loved her, to confess that she too was in love, that she did not recognize herself. She was amazed at what she had done, and repented it bitterly; she was also made happy by it,—she was completely upset by love and agitation. She went over once more the arguments in defence of her duty which stood in the way of her happiness; she lamented their strength, and regretted having stated them so strongly to Monsieur de Nemours. Although the thought of marrying him had occurred to her the moment she saw him again in the garden, it had not made so deep an impression on her as had her talk with him; and at moments she could scarcely believe that she would be unhappy if she should marry him. She would have liked to be able to say that she was wrong both in her scruples about the past and in her fears for the future. At other moments reason and duty convinced her of the opposite, and decided her not to marry again or ever to see Monsieur de Nemours; but this resolution was extremely repugnant to her when her heart was so much moved and had so recently seen the joys of love. At last, in order to allay her agitation, she thought it was not necessary for her to do herself the violence of forming a decision,—etiquette left her still much time for making up her mind; but she resolved to abide by her determination to have nothing to do with Monsieur de Nemours meanwhile.

The Vidame came to see her, and pleaded his friend's cause with all possible skill and earnestness; but he could not persuade her to modify her own conduct or that which she had imposed on Monsieur de Nemours. She told him that she did not mean to change her present condition, that she knew it would be hard for her to carry out this intention, but that she hoped she should be strong enough to do so. She showed him how firmly convinced she was that Monsieur de Nemours had caused her husband's death, and that she should do wrong in marrying him; so that the Vidame feared it would not be easy to convince her of the opposite. He did not confide to this prince what he thought, and when he reported his talk with her, he let him enjoy all the hope that reason can awaken in a man who is loved.

The next day they left to join the king. The Vidame, at the request of Monsieur de Nemours, wrote to Madame de Clèves, in order to speak of him; and in a second letter, which soon followed, Monsieur de Nemours added a few lines himself. But Madame de Clèves, who did not wish to infringe her rules, and who feared the perils of correspondence, told the Vidame that she should decline to receive his letters if he continued to write about Monsieur de Nemours; and this she said so earnestly that this prince himself begged his friend never to mention his name.

The court left to escort the Queen of Spain as far as Poitou. Madame de Clèves was left to herself during their absence, and the farther she was removed from Monsieur de Nemours and from anything that could remind her of him, the more she recalled the memory of Monsieur de Clèves, which she was bent on keeping ever present before her. Her reasons for not marrying Monsieur de Nemours seemed strong so far as her duty, and irrefutable so far as her tranquillity, was concerned. The fading of his love after marriage, and all the pangs of jealousy, which she regarded as certain, showed her the misery to which she would expose herself; but she saw too that she had assumed an impossible task in undertaking to resist the most fascinating of men, whom she loved and who loved her, in a matter which offended neither virtue nor propriety. She decided that only separation could give her strength; and this she felt that she needed, not merely to maintain her determination not to marry, but also to protect herself from the sight of Monsieur de Nemours. Hence she resolved to make a long journey during the time that etiquette forced her to spend in retirement. Some large estates that she owned in the Pyrénées seemed to her the best place she could choose. She started a few days before the court returned; and just before leaving, she wrote to the Vidame to beg that no one should inquire after her or write to her.

Monsieur de Nemours was as much afflicted by her absence as another man would have been by the death of the woman he loved. The thought of this long separation from Madame de Clèves was a constant source of suffering, especially after he had tasted the pleasure of meeting her and seeing that she loved him. He could do nothing but grieve, and his grief increased daily. Madame de Clèves, as a result of all her agitation, fell seriously ill after her arrival at her country place, and news of this reached the court. Monsieur de Nemours was inconsolable, and fell into the most unbounded despair. The Vidame had great difficulty in keeping him from letting his love be seen, as well as from following after her to find out how she was. The Vidame's relationship and intimacy served as a pretext for sending constant letters. At last word came that she had passed the turning point of her dangerous illness, but was still so weak that all were very anxious.

This long and near view of death enabled Madame de Clèves to judge mundane matters in a very different spirit from that of health. Her imminent peril taught her indifference to everything, and the length of her illness enforced this upon her. Yet when she had recovered, she found that she had not wholly forgotten Monsieur de Nemours; but she summoned to her aid every argument she could devise against marrying him. The conflict was a stern one; but at last she conquered what was left of this passion, which was already diminished by her reflections during her illness. The thought of death had revived her memory of Monsieur de Clèves; and this, harmonizing with her sense of duty, made a strong impression on her heart. The affections and ties of the world appeared to her as they appear to persons of enlarged views. Her health, which was still delicate, helped her to preserve those feelings; but knowing how circumstances affect the wisest resolutions, she was unwilling to run the risk of seeing her own altered, or of returning to the place where lived the man she had loved. Under the pretext of needing change of air, she withdrew to a religious house, without making known her determination to leave the court.

When Monsieur de Nemours heard of this, he at once saw what a decisive step it was, and feared that he had no more ground for hope. Yet the destruction of his hopes did not prevent his doing his utmost to bring about her return; he made the queen write to her, and even persuaded the Vidame to visit her: but it was all to no purpose. The Vidame saw her; she did not tell him that she had resolved upon this, but he decided that she would never return. At last Monsieur de Nemours went himself, under the pretext of going to the baths.[6] She was much moved and astonished when she heard that he had come. She sent him a message by one of her trusty companions that she begged him not to be surprised if she was unwilling to run the risk of seeing him again and of having the feelings she felt bound to maintain swept away by his presence; that she wanted him to know that having found her duty and her peace of mind unalterably opposed to her interest in him, everything else in the world seemed so indifferent that she had abandoned it entirely, had given all her thoughts to another life, and had no other feeling left but her desire to have him share the same sentiments.

Monsieur de Nemours thought he should die of grief in the presence of the woman who brought this message. He begged her twenty times to go back to Madame de Clèves, to entreat her to let him see her; but she told him that Madame de Clèves had forbidden her, not only to bring her any message from him, but even to repeat to her what he might say. At last he had to leave, as completely overwhelmed with grief as a man could be who had lost all hopes of ever seeing again a woman whom he loved with the

---

6. At a resort or spa where bathing, usually in natural springs, is part of the medical treatment.

most violent and the most natural passion possible. Yet he did not yield even then; he did everything he could to induce her to alter her decision. At last, when years had passed, time and separation allayed his grief and extinguished his passion. Madame de Clèves led such a life that it was evident she meant never to go into the world again; part of each year she spent in this religious house, and the other part at home, but in retirement, busied with severer tasks than those of the austerest convents. Her life, which was not long, furnished examples of the loftiest virtue.

JEAN RACINE
1639–1699

Jean Racine's capacity to communicate intense passion in tragedies marked by formal decorum and an elevated tone gave him immediate and lasting fame among French dramatists. He brings to material adapted from classic texts psychological insight to which twenty-first-century audiences readily respond.

Born into the family of a government official in the Valois district, eighty miles from Paris, Racine attended the Collège de Beauvais. Later (1655–59), he studied in the Jansenist center of Port-Royal des Champs. (Jansenism, a strict Catholic movement emphasizing moral self-examination and severely controlled conduct, exercised a profound influence on Racine.) In 1660, encouraged by the poet and fabulist Jean de La Fontaine, Racine came to Paris, where his early plays failed, driving him into seclusion in Provence. When he returned to Paris in 1663, however, the court and the nobility patronized him, and he rapidly developed a reputation as a major playwright. In 1677 he left Paris and returned to Port-Royal, an environment conducive to his increasing interest in religion. He married Catherine de Romanet, with whom he had seven children, most of whom became nuns or priests. Remaining in the country, he wrote history, made short trips to Paris, and traveled as a royal historian with Louis XIV on his campaigns. Buried at Port-Royal, his body was exhumed in 1711 and reburied next to Pascal at the church of St. Étienne-du-Mont in Paris.

Only one of Racine's twelve plays, an early comedy, deviated from the tragic mode. His first tragedies imitated the work of his contemporary, Pierre Corneille; later, he chose biblical and classical models. *Phaedra* (1677) adapts, with new emphasis, Euripides' *Hippolytus,* making the guilty woman rather than the relatively passive man the protagonist and using the highly charged sexual situation between the two to generate the psychological tension. To twenty-first-century readers, the play's most immediately obvious characteristic may be its conventional formalities: the long declamatory speeches, the stylized exchanges in compressed half lines, the artificiality of conveying such complicated relationships and histories within the time span of a single day. Such devices, however—which would have seemed as artificial to seventeenth-century audiences as they do to us, although more familiar—intensify the impact of the central characters' anguish and their desperate attempts to deal with it. If the play's surface is formal, its depths seethe with passion.

Passion, of course, is the subject of *Phaedra.* The conflict between reason and passion that preoccupied many thinkers of the late seventeenth and early eighteenth centuries—that conflict resolved on the side of reason at such great cost to the princess of Clèves—here plays itself out with stark urgency. Passion triumphs, in *Phaedra,* over all principles of control, bringing death to the two central characters and misery to their survivors. As in Greek tragedy, although by different means, the reader feels not only the self-destructiveness of the human psyche but the pathos and heroism of the doomed effort to transcend the limits of the given.

The play opens not with Phaedra herself but with Hippolytus, meditating about his heroic father, Theseus. Like Molière, Racine uses the family as a microcosm of larger social orders, but the intense conflicts that throb beneath the surface in many real-life families here undergo no comic transformation. Hippolytus has his own problems, quite apart from Phaedra. Blessed and burdened with a larger-than-life father, he must choose whether to try to imitate that father or to seek other ways of being a man. "I sucked that pride which seems so strange to you / From an Amazonian mother," he tells his friend Theramenes, alluding to the "austere and proud / Persuasions" that have prevented him from feeling interest in any woman. But matters cannot remain so simple. Theseus has distinguished himself in two ways: by heroic womanizing (he leaves a trail of women behind him wherever he goes) and by heroic action, the conquering and destruction of monsters human and inhuman. As the play opens, Hippolytus acknowledges in himself the first incursions of love. No longer can his adolescent defense, his refusal of any resemblance to his father, serve him. When Theseus returns, Hippolytus will beg permission to seek his own heroism:

> Before you'd lived as long as I have done,
> More than one tyrant, monsters more than one
> Had felt your strength of arm, your sword's keen blade . . .
> Let me at long last show my courage.

He wants, he says, even by death to "prove to all the world I was your son." By the time he makes this plea, however, his innocent desire to prove his manhood, to declare his separateness from and worthiness of his father, has been overwhelmed by darker forces.

Phaedra's impulses are less innocent—less "natural," she suggests. In a poignant passage, she imagines Hippolytus and his youthful beloved, Aricia, expressing their love in a natural setting, themselves a part of the natural world. She understands her own sin as an internal war between feeling and control; she speaks of desperately seeking her "lost reason" in the entrails of sacrifices she makes to Venus, trying to avert her fate. Never does she excuse herself, never does she believe herself justified in loving the son of the man who kidnapped her into marriage. When Theseus is thought dead, Phaedra declares herself unworthy to rule a nation because she cannot rule herself. Yet such moral awareness fails to help her: knowing her sin, she continues to enact it, at least in feeling. The play evokes the full torment of such experience.

As for powerful Theseus, conqueror of women, defier of the supernatural, ally of Neptune—this kingly figure returns to find himself powerless at home. The son and wife who by social convention exist in utter subordination to him turn into enemies he has no capacity to master. First his wife's nurse tells him that his son has attempted to seduce Phaedra. The rivalry of sons and fathers runs deep: if sons fear they can never equal their fathers, fathers fear that the young necessarily overcome the old. Theseus believes the nurse's bare assertion, unsupported by substantial evidence. He banishes his son and invokes Neptune's power to destroy him. Then Aricia's hints lead him to suspect his wife, who confesses her own emotional sin while already on the verge of self-inflicted death. Theseus remains alone, bereft, his tyrannical impulse now devoid of domestic object. His own passions, too quickly fired—jealous possessiveness of his wife, jealous rivalry with his son—have deprived him of two beings he loved.

The play provides no villains. Phaedra, in some versions of the story a monster of lust, here becomes a woman struggling against her nature, as profoundly committed to standards of control as to the violent feelings that overthrow them. Hippolytus, in the process of self-discovery, at a delicate balance point between youth and maturity, cannot protect himself against the alternations of closely linked love and hate in a woman whose passions, and whose self-awareness, far exceed his. Theseus, in the ignorance of success, fails to understand himself, his wife, or his son. All three exemplify the pathos and dignity of the human struggle to be human.

Phaedra dies with the word "purity" on her lips, seeking self-purification in death, the only course now possible to her. Hippolytus dies in the beauty of his youth, deprived of age's suffering and fulfillment. Theseus lives to try once more to rule adequately, perhaps chastened by suffering into greater awareness. The names of the Greek gods survive in this drama: Aphrodite torments Phaedra; Neptune serves Theseus's impetuous will. But the gods now function as projections of human passion: Phaedra's sexual lust; Theseus's lust for power. Phaedra's torment suggests a Christian effort at purification, a Christian ideal of self-denial. The drama, in Racine's handling of the ancient story, projects on a giant screen conflicts that all men and women undergo, the surge of feeling that wars with the ideal of self-restraint. By concentrating the play of passions within a small family group and a confined space of time, while recalling connections between the characters' feelings and historical events that lie behind them; by giving Theseus and Phaedra heroic dignity and stature; by linking this family with the fate of nations, Racine forces his readers to feel the intensity and the large significance of feelings and happenings that might in other treatments seem merely sordid. He gives his characters timeless reality—speaking to his time and to ours.

To translate Racine into English is particularly difficult since the French alexandrine couplet, composed of twelve-syllable lines, does not adapt naturally to English verse. Richard Wilbur's version uses the common English pentameter, the ten-syllable line, to construct fluent, pointed, and dignified verse. His couplets, by their formal elegance, remind the reader steadily of the discipline that the play embodies and celebrates.

PRONOUNCING GLOSSARY

The following list uses common English syllables and stress accents to provide rough equivalents of selected words whose pronunciation may be unfamiliar to the general reader.

Acheron: *ah'-ker-awn*	Panope: *pah'-no-pe*
Ariadne: *ah-ree-ahd'-ne*	Pasiphaë: *pa-si'-fa-ee*
Aricia: *ah-ree'-sha*	Peirithous: *pay-rith'-oo-uhs*
Cocytus: *coh-sai'-tuhs*	Peloponnesus: *pel-luh-puh-nee'-suhs*
Euripides: *yoo-rip'-uh-deez*	Phaedra: *fee'-drah*
Hippolytus: *hip-pol'-i-tuhs*	Scythia: *si'-thee-uh*
Ismene: *is-mee'-ne*	Taenarus: *ten'-a-ruhs*
Medea: *me-dee'-a*	Theramenes: *the-ram'-uh-neez*
Mycenae: *mai-see'-nee*	Theseus: *thee'-see-uhs*
Oenone: *ee-noh'-ne*	Troezen: *troh'-zen*

Phaedra[1]

CHARACTERS

THESEUS, *son of Aegeus, King of Athens*

PHAEDRA, *wife of Theseus, daughter of Minos and Pasiphaë*

HIPPOLYTUS, *son of Theseus and Antiope, Queen of the Amazons*

ARICIA, *princess of the blood royal of Athens*

THERAMENES, *Hippolytus' tutor*

OENONE, *Phaedra's nurse and confidante*

ISMENE, *Aricia's confidante*

PANOPE, *lady-in-waiting to Phaedra*

GUARDS

The action takes place within and without a palace at Troezen, a town in the Peloponnesus.

Act I

SCENE 1

HIPPOLYTUS, THERAMENES

HIPPOLYTUS   No, dear Theramenes, I've too long delayed
In pleasant Troezen; my decision's made.
I'm off; in my anxiety, I commence
To tax myself with shameful indolence.
My father has been gone six months and more,
And yet I do not know what distant shore
Now hides him, or what trials he now may bear.
THERAMENES   You'll go in search of him, my lord? But where?
Already, to appease your fears, I've plied   10
The seas which lie on Corinth's either side;
I've asked for Theseus among tribes who dwell
Where Acheron[2] goes plunging into Hell;
Elis I've searched and, from Taenarus[3] bound,
Reached even that sea where Icarus[4] was drowned.   15
In what fresh hope, in what unthought-of places,
Do you set out to find your father's traces?
Who knows, indeed, if he wants the truth about
His long, mysterious absence to come out,
And whether, while we tremble for him, he's   20
Not fondling some new conquest at his ease
And planning to deceive her like the rest? . . .
HIPPOLYTUS   Enough, Theramenes. In King Theseus' breast,
The foolish fires of youth have ceased to burn;
No tawdry dalliance hinders his return.
Phaedra need fear no rivals now; the King   25

---

1. Translated by Richard Wilbur.   2. A river that flows into Hades; Charon ferried the dead across it.
3. A point of land in southern Greece, near Sparta. Elis is a district of Greece on the west coast of the Peloponnesus.   4. Son of Daedalus. Escaping from Crete by means of wings made by his father, Icarus flew so high that the sun melted the wax holding his wings together, and he fell to his death.

Long since, for her sake, ceased philandering.
I go then, out of duty—and as a way
To flee a place in which I dare not stay.

THERAMENES   Since when, my lord, have you begun to fear
This peaceful place your childhood held so dear,   30
And which I've often known you to prefer
To Athens' court, with all its pomp and stir?
What danger or affliction drives you hence?

Theramenes thinks Hippolytus must fear something.

HIPPOLYTUS   Those happy times are gone. All's altered since
The Gods dispatched to us across the sea   35
The child of Minos and Pasiphaë.[5]

THERAMENES   Ah. Then it's Phaedra's presence in this place
That weighs on you. She'd hardly seen your face
When, as the King's new consort, she required
Your banishment, and got what she desired.   40
But now her hatred for you, once so great,
Has vanished, or has cooled, at any rate.
And why, my lord, should you feel threatened by
A dying woman who desires to die?
Sick unto death—with what, she will not say,   45
Weary of life and of the light of day,
Could Phaedra plot to do you any harm?

HIPPOLYTUS   Her vain hostility gives me no alarm.
It is, I own, another enemy.
The young Aricia, from whom I flee,   50
Last of a line which sought to overthrow
Our house.

THERAMENES   What! Will you also be her foe?
That gentle maiden, though of Pallas' line,
Had no part in her brothers' base design.[6]
If she is guiltless, why should you hate her, Sir?   55

HIPPOLYTUS   I would not flee her if I hated her.

Hippolytus won't flee Aricia out of fear.

THERAMENES   Dare I surmise, then, why you're leaving us?
Are you no longer that Hippolytus
Who spurned love's dictates and refused with scorn
The yoke which Theseus has so often borne?   60
Has Venus, long offended by your pride,
Contrived to see her Theseus justified
By making you confess her power divine
And bow, like other men, before her shrine?
Are you in love, Sir?

Theramenes wonders if Hippolytus, his pupil, is in love with Aricia

HIPPOLYTUS   What do you mean, dear man   65
You who have known me since my life began?
How can you wish that my austere and proud
Persuasions be so basely disvowed?
I sucked that pride which seems so strange to you

---

5. Phaedra was the daughter of King Minos of Crete and Pasiphaë, sister to Circe. Enamored of a white bull sent by Poseidon, Pasiphaë consequently gave birth to the Minotaur, the Cretan monster later killed by Theseus. Phaedra was thus half-sister to the Minotaur.   **6.** Theseus killed all fifty sons of Pallas because they threatened his kingdom of Athens. Aricia is Pallas's daughter.

From an Amazonian mother,[7] and when I grew   70
To riper years, and knew myself, I thought
My given nature to be nobly wrought.
You then, devoted friend, instructed me
In all my father's brilliant history,
And you recall how glowingly I heard   75
His exploits, how I hung on every word
As you portrayed a sire whose deeds appease
Men's longing for another Hercules—
Those monsters slain, those brigands all undone,
Procrustes, Sciron, Sinis, Cercyon,—   80
The Epidaurian giant's scattered bones,
The Minotaur's foul blood on Cretan stones!
But when you told me of less glorious feats,
His far-flung chain of amorous deceits,
Helen of Sparta[8] kidnapped as a maid;   85
Sad Periboea[9] in Salamis betrayed;
Others, whose very names escape him now,
Too-trusting hearts, deceived by sigh and vow;
Wronged Ariadne,[1] telling the rocks her moan,
Phaedra abducted, though to grace a throne,—   90
You know how, loathing stories of that sort,
I begged you oftentimes to cut them short,
And wished posterity might never hear
The worser half of Theseus' great career.
Shall I, in my turn, be subjected so   95
To passion, by the Gods be brought so low—
The more disgraced because I cannot claim
Such honors as redeem King Theseus' name,
And have not, by the blood of monsters, won
The right to trespass as my sire has done?   100
And even if my pride laid down its arms,
Could I surrender to Aricia's charms?
Would not my wayward passions heed the ban
Forbidding her to me, or any man?
The King's no friend to her, and has decreed   105
That she not keep alive her brothers' seed;
Fearing some new shoot from their guilty stem,
He wants her death to be the end of them;
For her, the nuptial torch shall never blaze,
He's doomed her to be single all her days.   110
Shall I take up her cause then, brave his rage,
Set a rebellious pattern for the age,
Commit my youth to love's delirium . . . ?

---

7. Hippolytus's mother was Antiope, sister of Hippolyta, queen of the Amazons.   8. Daughter of Zeus and Leda, later the wife of Menelaus of Sparta (and the cause of the Trojan War). In her girlhood she was abducted by Theseus and Peirithoüs; her brothers rescued her and brought her back home.   9. The mother of Ajax, one of the women Theseus seduced and abandoned.   1. Phaedra's sister, who was abandoned by Theseus on the island of Naxos after she rescued him from the Minotaur.

THERAMENES   Ah, Sir, if love's appointed hour has come,
It's vain to reason; Heaven will not hear.
What Theseus bans, he makes you hold more dear.
His hate for her but stirs your flames the more,
And lends new grace to her whom you adore.   115
Why fear, my lord, a love that's true and chaste?
Of what's so sweet, will you not dare to taste?
Shall timid scruples make your blood congeal?   120
What Hercules once felt, may you not feel?
What hearts has Venus' power failed to sway?
Where would you be, who strive with her today,
If fierce Antiope had not grown tame[2]   125
And loved king Theseus with a virtuous flame?
But come, my lord, why posture and debate?
Admit that you have changed, and that of late
You're seen less often, in your lonely pride,
Racing your chariot by the oceanside,   130
Or deftly using Neptune's[3] art to train
Some charger to obey the curb and rein.
The woods less often echo to our cries.
A secret fire burns in your heavy eyes.
No question of it: you're sick with love, you feel   135
A wasting passion which you would conceal.
Has fair Aricia wakened your desire?
HIPPOLYTUS   I'm off, Theramenes, to find my sire.
THERAMENES   Will you not see the Queen before you go,
My lord?
HIPPOLYTUS
            I mean to. You may tell her so.   140
Duty requires it of me. Ah, but here's
Her dear Oenone; what new grief prompts her tears?

SCENE 2

HIPPOLYTUS, OENONE, THERAMENES

OENONE   Alas, my lord, what grief could equal mine?
The Queen has gone into a swift decline.
I nurse her, tend her day and night, but she
Is dying of some nameless malady.
Disorder rules within her heart and head.   5
A restless pain has dragged her from her bed;
She longs to see the light; but in her keen
Distress she is unwilling to be seen. . . .
She's coming.
HIPPOLYTUS   I understand, and I shall go.
My hated face would but increase her woe.   10

2. As an Amazon, Antiope was committed to chastity.   3. Or Poseidon, god of the sea, who was also
identified with Hippios, god of horses.

SCENE 3

PHAEDRA, OENONE

PHAEDRA   Let's go no farther; stay, Oenone dear.
    I'm faint; my strength abandons me, I fear.
    My eyes are blinded by the glare of day,
    And now I feel my trembling knees give way.
    Alas!

[*She sits.*]

OENONE   O Gods, abate our misery!   5
PHAEDRA   These veils, these baubles, how they burden me!
    What meddling hand has twined my hair, and made
    Upon my brow so intricate a braid?
    All things oppress me, vex me, do me ill.
OENONE   Her wishes war against each other still.   10
    'Twas you who, full of self-reproach, just now
    Insisted that our hands adorn your brow;
    You who called back your strength so that you might
    Come forth again and once more see the light.
    Yet, seeing it, you all but turn and flee,   15
    Hating the light which you came forth to see.
PHAEDRA   Founder of our sad race, bright god of fire,
    You whom my mother dared to boast her sire,[4]
    Who blush perhaps to see my wretched case,
    For the last time, O Sun, I see your face.   20
OENONE   Can't you shake off that morbid wish? Must I
    Forever hear you laying plans to die?
    What is this pact with death which you have made?
PHAEDRA   Oh, to be sitting in the woods' deep shade!
    When shall I witness, through a golden wrack   25
    Of dust, a chariot flying down the track?
OENONE   What, Madam?
PHAEDRA   Where am I? Madness! What did I say?
    Where have I let my hankering senses stray?
    The Gods have robbed me of my wits. A rush
    Of shame, Oenone, causes me to blush.   30
    I make my guilty torments all too plain.
    My eyes, despite me, fill with tears of pain.
OENONE   If you must blush, then blush for your perverse
    Silence, which only makes your sickness worse.
    Spurning our care, and deaf to all we say—   35
    Is it your cruel design to die this way?
    What madness dooms your life in middle course?
    What spell, what poison has dried up its source?
    Three times the night has overrun the skies
    Since sleep last visited your hollow eyes,   40
    And thrice the day has made dim night retreat

4. Helios, the sun god, was the father of Phaedra's mother, Pasiphaë.

Since you, though starving, have refused to eat.
What frightful evil does your heart intend?
What right have you to plot your own life's end?
You thereby wrong the Gods who authored you;   45
Betray the spouse to whom your faith is due;
Betray your children by the selfsame stroke,
And thrust their necks beneath a heavy yoke.
Yes, on the day their mother's life is done,
Proud hopes will stir in someone else's son—   50
Your foe, the foe of all your lineage, whom
An Amazon once carried in her womb:
Hippolytus . . .
PHAEDRA   Gods!
OENONE   My words strike home at last.
PHAEDRA   Oh, wretched woman, what was that name which passed
    Your lips?
OENONE   Ah, now you're roused to anger. Good.   55
    That name has made you shudder, as it should.
    Live, then. Let love and duty fire your spirit.
    Live, lest a Scythian's[5] son should disinherit
    Your children, lest he crush the noblest fruit
    Of Greece and of the Gods beneath his boot.   60
    But lose no time; each moment now could cost
    Your life; retrieve the strength that you have lost,
    While still your feeble fires, which sink so low,
    Smoulder and may be fanned into a glow.
PHAEDRA   Alas, my guilty flame has burnt too long.   65
OENONE   Come, what remorse can flay you so? What wrong
    Can you have done to be so crushed with guilt?
    There is no innocent blood your hands have spilt.
PHAEDRA   My hands, thank Heaven, are guiltless, as you say.
    Gods! That my heart were innocent as they!   70
OENONE   What fearful notion can your thoughts have bred
    So that your heart still shrinks from it in dread?
PHAEDRA   I've said enough, Oenone. Spare me the rest.
    I die, to keep that horror unconfessed.
OENONE   Then die, and keep your heartless silence, do;   75
    But someone else must close your eyes for you.
    Although your flickering life has all but fled,
    I shall go down before you to the dead.
    There are a thousand roads that travel there;
    I'll choose the shortest, in my just despair.   80
    O cruel mistress! When have I failed or grieved you?
    Remember: at your birth, these arms received you.
    For you I left my country, children, kin:
    Is this the prize my faithfulness should win?
PHAEDRA   What can you gain by this? Why rant and scold?   85
    You'd shake with terror if the truth were told.

5. Scythia, home of the Amazons, was, to the Greeks, associated with barbarians.

*Oenone
doubts
her
surprise*

OENONE   Great Gods! What words could match the terror I
Must daily suffer as I watch you die?

PHAEDRA   When you have learnt my crime, my fate, my shame,
I'll die no less, but with a guiltier name.   90

OENONE   My lady, by the tears which stain my face,
And by your trembling knees which I embrace,
Enlighten me; deliver me from doubt.

PHAEDRA   You've asked it. Rise.

OENONE   I'm listening. Come, speak out.

PHAEDRA   O Gods! What shall I say to her? Where shall I start?   95

OENONE   Speak, speak. Your hesitations wound my heart.

PHAEDRA   Alas, how Venus hates us! As Love's thrall,
Into what vileness did my mother fall!

OENONE   Dear Queen, forget it; to the end of time
Let silence shroud the memory of that crime.   100

PHAEDRA   O sister Ariadne! Through love, once more,
You died abandoned on a barren shore![6]

OENONE   Madame, what's this? What anguish makes you trace
So bitterly the tale of all your race?

PHAEDRA   And now, since Venus wills it, I must pine   105
And die, the last of our accursèd line.

OENONE   You are in love?

PHAEDRA   I feel love's raging thirst.

OENONE   For whom?

PHAEDRA   Of all dire things, now hear the worst.
I love . . . From that dread name I shrink, undone;
I love . . .

OENONE   Whom?

PHAEDRA   Think of a Scythian woman's son,   110
A prince I long ill-used and heaped with blame.

OENONE   Hippolytus? Gods!

PHAEDRA   'Twas you who spoke his name.

OENONE   Just Heaven! All my blood begins to freeze.
O crime, despair, most curst of families!
Why did we voyage to this ill-starred land   115
And set our feet upon its treacherous strand?

PHAEDRA   My ills began far earlier. Scarcely had I
Pledged with Aegeus' son our marriage-tie,
Secure in that sweet joy a bride should know,
When I, in Athens, met my haughty foe.   120
I stared, I blushed, I paled, beholding him;
A sudden turmoil set my mind aswim;
My eyes no longer saw, my lips were dumb;
My body burned, and yet was cold and numb.
I knew myself possessed by Venus, whose   125
Fierce flames torment the quarry she pursues.
I thought to appease her then by constant prayer,
And built for her a temple, decked with care.

---

6. Ariadne died on Naxos after Theseus's desertion of her.

I made continual sacrifice, and sought
In entrails[7] for a spirit less distraught—   130
But what could cure a lovesick soul like mine?
In vain my hands burnt incense at her shrine:
Though I invoked the Goddess' name, 'twas he
I worshipped; I saw his image constantly,
And even as I fed the altar's flame   135
Made offering to a god I dared not name.
I shunned him; but—O horror and disgrace!—
My eyes beheld him in his father's face.
At last I knew that I must act, must urge
Myself, despite myself, to be his scourge.   140
To rid me of the foe I loved, I feigned
A harsh stepmother's malice, and obtained
By ceaseless cries my wish that he be sent
From home and father into banishment.
I breathed once more, Oenone; once he was gone,   145
My blameless days could flow more smoothly on.
I hid my grief, was faithful to my spouse,
And reared the offspring of our luckless vows.
Ah, mocking Fate! What use was all my care?
Brought by my spouse himself to Troezen, there   150
I yet again beheld my exiled foe:
My unhealed wound began once more to flow.
Love hides no longer in these veins, at bay:
Great Venus fastens on her helpless prey.
I look with horror on my crime; I hate   155
My life; my passion I abominate.
I hoped by death to keep my honor bright,
And hide so dark a flame from day's pure light;
Yet, yielding to your tearful argument,
I've told you all; of that I'll not repent   160
Provided you do not, as death draws near,
Pour more unjust reproaches in my ear,
Or seek once more in vain to fan a fire
Which flickers and is ready to expire.

SCENE 4

PHAEDRA, OENONE, PANOPE

PANOPE   Madam, there's grievous news which I'd withhold
   If I were able; but it must be told.
   Death's claimed your lord, who feared no other foe—
   Of which great loss you are the last to know.
OENONE   You tell us, Panope . . . ?
PANOPE   That the Queen in vain   5
   Prays for her Theseus to return again;

---

7. Examining the entrails of an animal sacrifice was a means of prophecy.

That mariners have come to port, from whom
Hippolytus has learned his father's doom.

PHAEDRA   Gods!

PANOPE   Who'll succeed him, Athens can't agree.
The Prince your son commands much loyalty,   10
My lady; yet, despite their country's laws,[8]
Some make the alien woman's son their cause;
Some plot, they say, to put in Theseus' place
Aricia, the last of Pallas' race.
Of both these threats I thought that you should know.   15
Hippolytus has rigged his ship to go,
And if, in Athens' ferment, he appeared,
The fickle mob might back him, it is feared.

OENONE   Enough. The Queen has heard you. She'll give thought
To these momentous tidings you have brought.   20

SCENE 5

PHAEDRA, OENONE

OENONE   Mistress, I'd ceased to urge you not to die;
I thought to follow you to the grave, since my
Dissuasions had no longer any force:
But this dark news prescribes a change of course.
Your destiny now wears a different face: 5
The King is dead, and you must take his place.
He leaves a son who needs your sheltering wing—
A slave without you; if you live, a king.
Who else will soothe his orphan sorrows, pray?
If you are dead, who'll wipe his tears away?   10
His innocent cries, borne up to Heaven, will make
The Gods, his forebears, curse you for his sake.
Live, then: there's nothing now you're guilty of.
Your love's become like any other love.
With Theseus' death, those bonds exist no more   15
Which made your passion something to abhor.
Hippolytus need no longer cause you fear;
Seeing him now, your conscience can be clear.
Perhaps, convinced that you're his bitter foe,
He means to lead the rebels. Make him know   20
His error; win him over; stay his hand.
He's king, by right, of Troezen's pleasant land;
But as for bright Minerva's[9] citadel,
It is your son's by law, as he knows well.
You should, indeed, join forces, you and he: 25
Aricia is your common enemy.

PHAEDRA   So be it. By your advice I shall be led;

---

8. Athenian law made the son of an Athenian and a non-Greek woman illegitimate. As noted, Hippolytus's
mother was an Amazon. It is not clear why Phaedra's children are not similarly classified.   9. The Greek
goddess Athene, protector of Athens.

I'll live, if I can come back from the dead,
And if my mother-love still has the power
To rouse my weakened spirits in this hour.   30

Act II

SCENE 1

ARICIA, ISMENE

ARICIA   Hippolytus asks to see me? Can this be?
He seeks me out to take his leave of me?
There's no mistake, Ismene?

[handwritten note: Aricia is surprised that Hippolytus seeks her audience before he leaves.]

ISMENE   Indeed, there's not.
This shows how Theseus' death has changed your lot.
Expect now to receive from every side
The homage which, through him, you've been denied.   5
At last, Aricia rules her destiny;
Soon, at her feet, all Greece shall bend the knee.
ARICIA   This is no doubtful rumor, then? I've shed
The bonds of slavery? My oppressor's dead?   10
ISMENE   The Gods relent, my lady. It is so.
Theseus has joined your brothers' shades below.
ARICIA   And by what mishap did he come to grief?
ISMENE   The tales are many, and they strain belief.

[handwritten note: The tales of Theseus's death are numerous and varied.]

Some say that he, abducting from her home
A new beloved, was swallowed by the foam.   15
It's even thought, as many tongues now tell,
That, faring with Pirithoüs down to Hell,[1]
He walked alive amid the dusky ranks
Of souls, and saw Cocytus'[2] dismal banks,
But found himself a prisoner in that stern   20
Domain from which no mortal can return.
ARICIA   Shall I believe that, while he still draws breath,
A man can penetrate the realms of death?
What spell could lure him to that fearsome tract?

[handwritten note: All but Aricia believe that Theseus is dead.]

ISMENE   Theseus is dead. You, only, doubt the fact.   25
All Athens grieves; the news was scarcely known
When Troezen raised Hippolytus to its throne.
Here in this palace, trembling for her son,
Phaedra confers on what must now be done.
ARICIA   You think Hippolytus will be more kind   30
Than Theseus was to me, that he'll unbind
My chains, and show me pity?

[handwritten note: Theseus has acted harshly with Aricia.]

ISMENE   Madam, I do.
ARICIA   Isn't the man's cold nature known to you?
What makes you think that, scorning women, he   35

---

1. Theseus went to Hades with Pentithoüs, king of the Lapiths—with whom he had earlier abducted
Helen—to help his friend steal Persephone. Hercules freed Theseus, whom the god Hades had imprisoned,
but could not free Pentithoüs, who was later killed.   2. River in Hades, tributary to Acheron.

Will yet show pity and respect to me?
He long has shunned us, and as you well know
Haunts just those places where we do not go.

ISMENE He's called, I know, the most austere of men,
But I have seen him in your presence, when,   40
Intrigued by his repute, I thought to observe
His celebrated pride and cold reserve.
His manner contradicted all I'd heard:
At your first glance, I saw him flushed and stirred.
His eyes, already full of languor, tried   45
To leave your face, but could not turn aside.
He has, though love's a thing he may despise,
If not a lover's tongue, a lover's eyes.

ARICIA Ismene, how your words delight my ear!
Even if baseless, they are sweet to hear.   50
O you who know me, can you believe of me,
Sad plaything of a ruthless destiny,
Forever fed on tears and bitterness,
That love could touch me, and its dear distress?
Last offspring of that king whom Earth once bore,[3]   55
I only have escaped the rage of war.
I lost six brothers, young and fresh as May,
In whom the hopes of our great lineage lay:
The sharp sword reaped them all; Earth, soaked and red,
Drank sadly what Erectheus' heirs had shed.   60
You know that, since their death, a harsh decree
Forbids all Greeks to pay their court to me,
Lest, through my progeny, I should revive
My brothers' ashes, and keep their cause alive.
But you know too with what disdain I bore   65
The ban of our suspicious conqueror.
You know how I, a lifelong enemy
Of love, gave thanks for Theseus' tyranny,
Since he forbade what I was glad to shun.
But then . . . but then I had not seen his son.   70
Not that my eyes alone, charmed by his grace,
Have made me love him for his form or face,
Mere natural gifts for which he seems to care
But little, or of which he's unaware.
I find in him far nobler gifts than these—   75
His father's strengths, without his frailties.
I love, I own, a heart that's never bowed
Beneath Love's yoke, but stayed aloof and proud.
Small glory Phaedra gained from Theseus' sighs!
More proud than she, I spurn the easy prize   80
Of love-words said a thousand times before,
And of a heart that's like an open door.
Ah, but to move a heart that's firm as stone,

Handwritten margin notes: Ismene has observed Hyppolytus love for Aricia

Handwritten margin note: Aricia is glad to think Hyppolytus may love her.

Handwritten margin note: Aricia loves Hyppolytus

---

3. Erectheus, their ancestor, son of Earth and reared by Athene.

To teach it pangs which it has never known,
To bind my baffled captive in a chain   85
Against whose sweet constraint he strives in vain:
There's what excites me in Hippolytus; he's
A harder conquest than was Hercules,
Whose heart, so often vanquished and inflamed,
Less honored those by whom he had been tamed.   90
But, dear Ismene, how rashly I have talked!
My hopes may all too easily be balked,
And I may humbly grieve in future days
Because of that same pride which now I praise.
Of fortune can it be . . . ?

ISMENE   You'll shortly learn;   95
He's coming.

SCENE 2

HIPPOLYTUS, ARICIA, ISMENE

HIPPOLYTUS   Madam, I felt, ere leaving here,
That I should make your altered fortunes clear.
My sire is dead. My fears divined, alas,
By his long absence, what had come to pass.
Death only, ending all his feats and frays,   5
Could hide him from the world so many days.
The Gods have yielded to destroying Fate
Hercules' heir[4] and friend and battle-mate.
Although you hated him, I trust that you
Do not begrudge such praise as was his due.   10
One thought, however, soothes my mortal grief:
I now may offer you a just relief,
Revoking the most cruel of decrees.
Your heart, your hand, bestow them as you please;
For here in Troezen, where I now shall reign,   15
Which was my grandsire Pittheus' domain,
And which with one voice gives its throne to me,
I make you free as I; indeed, more free.
ARICIA   Your goodness stuns me, Sir. By this excess
Of noble sympathy for my distress,   20
You leave me, more than you could dream, still yoked
By those strict laws which you have just revoked.
HIPPOLYTUS   Athens, unsure of who should rule, divides
'Twixt you and me, and the Queen's son besides.
ARICIA   They speak of *me*?
HIPPOLYTUS   Their laws, I'm well aware,   25
Would seem to void my claim as Theseus' heir,
Because an alien bore me. But if my one
Opponent were my brother, Phaedra's son,

Hippolytus wishes to free Aricia from laws she's bound to.

---

4. *Heir* in the sense of being, like Hercules, a destroyer of monsters.

I would, my lady, have the better cause,
And would contest those smug and foolish laws.
What checks me is a truer claim, your own;   30
I yield, or, rather, give you back, a throne
And scepter which your sires inherited
From that great mortal whom the Earth once bred.

(margin: Hippolytus gives back Aricia's rightful throne.)

Aegeus,[5] though adopted, took their crown.   35
Theseus, his son, enlarged the state, cast down
Her foes, and was the choice of everyone,
Leaving your brothers in oblivion.
Now Athens calls you back within her walls.
Too long she's grieved for these dynastic brawls;   40
Too long your kinsmen's blood has drenched her earth,
Rising in steam from fields which gave it birth.
Troezen is mine, then. The domain of Crete
Offers to Phaedra's son a rich retreat.
Athens is yours. I go now to combine   45
In your cause all your partisans and mine.

ARICIA   These words so daze me that I almost fear
Some dream, some fancy has deceived my ear.
Am I awake? This plan which you have wrought—

(margin: Aricia can't believe the good fortune.)

What god, what god inspired you with the thought?   50
How just that, everywhere, men praise your name!
And how the truth, my lord, exceeds your fame!
You'll press my claims, against your interest?
'Twas kind enough that you should not detest
My house and me, should not be governed by   55
Old hatreds. . . .

HIPPOLYTUS   Hate you, Princess? No, not I.
I'm counted rough and proud, but don't assume
That I'm the issue of some monster's womb.
What hate-filled heart, what brute however wild
Could look upon your face and not grow mild?   60
Could I withstand your sweet, beguiling spell?

(margin: Aricia's beauty will soften the most immovable of hearts.)

ARICIA   What's this, my lord?

HIPPOLYTUS   I've said too much. Ah, well.
My reason can't rein in my heart, I see.
Since I have spoken thus impetuously,
I must go on, my lady, and make plain   65
A secret I no longer can contain.

(margin: Hippolytus had formerly spurned love.)

You see before you a most sorry prince,
A signal case of blind conceit. I wince
To think how I, Love's enemy, long disdained
Its bonds, and all whom passion had enchained;   70
How, pitying poor storm-tossed fools, I swore
Ever to view such tempests from the shore;
And now, like common men, for all my pride,

---

5. Pandion's son by adoption, and Theseus's father.

Am lost to reason in a raging tide.
One moment saw my vain defenses fall: 75
My haughty spirit is at last in thrall.
For six months now, ashamed and in despair,
I've borne Love's piercing arrow everywhere;
I've striven with you, and with myself, and though
I shun you, you are everywhere I go;   80
In the deep woods, your image haunts my sight;
The light of day, the shadows of the night,
All things call up your charms before my eyes
And vie to make my rebel heart your prize.
What use to struggle? I am not as before: 85
I seek myself, and find myself no more.
My bow, my javelins and my chariot pall;
What Neptune taught me once, I can't recall;
My idle steeds forget the voice they've known,
And the woods echo to my plaints alone.   90
You blush, perhaps, for so uncouth a love
As you have caused, and which I tell you of.
What a rude offer of my heart I make!
How strange a captive does your beauty take!
Yet that should make my offering seem more rich.   95
Remember, it's an unknown tongue in which
I speak; don't scorn these words, so poorly turned,
Which, but for you, my lips had never learned.

Aricia overcomes all of Hippolytus's life

← He finds only her.

SCENE 3

HIPPOLYTUS, ARICIA, THERAMENES, ISMENE

THERAMENES   My lord: the Queen, they tell me, comes this way.
   It's you she seeks.
HIPPOLYTUS   Me?
THERAMENES   Why, I cannot say.
   But Phaedra's sent ahead to let you know
   That she must speak with you before you go.
HIPPOLYTUS   I, talk with Phaedra? What should we talk about?   5
ARICIA   My lord, you can't refuse to hear her out.
   Malignant toward you as the Queen appears,
   You owe some pity to her widow's tears.
HIPPOLYTUS   But now you'll leave me! And I shall sail before
   I learn my fate from her whom I adore,   10
   And in whose hands I leave this heart of mine. . . .
ARICIA   Go, Prince; pursue your generous design.
   Make Athens subject to my royal sway.
   All of your gifts I gladly take this day.
   But that great empire, glorious though it be,   15
   Is not the offering most dear to me.

The empire is not the most supreme in Aricia's heart.

SCENE 4

HIPPOLYTUS, THERAMENES

HIPPOLYTUS   Are we ready, friend? But the Queen's coming: hark.
Go, bid them trim our vessel; we soon embark.
Quick, give the order and return, that you
May free me from a vexing interview.

SCENE 5

PHAEDRA, HIPPOLYTUS, OENONE

PHAEDRA [*To* OENONE, *at stage rear*].
He's here. Blood rushes to my heart: I'm weak,
And can't recall the words I meant to speak.
OENONE   Think of your son, whose one hope rests with you.
PHAEDRA   My lord, they say you leave us. Before you do,
I've come to join your sorrows and my tears,   5
And tell you also of a mother's fears.
My son now lacks a father; and he will learn
Ere long that death has claimed me in my turn.
A thousand foes already seek to end
His hopes, which you, you only, can defend.   10
Yet I've a guilty fear that I have made
Your ears indifferent to his cries for aid.
I tremble lest you visit on my son
Your righteous wrath at what his mother's done.
HIPPOLYTUS   So base a thought I could not entertain.   15
PHAEDRA   Were you to hate me, I could not complain,
My lord. You've seen me bent on hurting you,
Though what was in my heart you never knew.
I sought your enmity. I would not stand
Your dwelling with me in the selfsame land.   20
I vilified you, and did not feel free
Till oceans separated you and me.
I went so far, indeed, as to proclaim
That none should, in my hearing, speak your name.
Yet if the crime prescribes the culprit's fate,   25
If I must hate you to have earned your hate,
Never did woman more deserve, my lord,
Your pity, or less deserve to be abhorred.
HIPPOLYTUS   It's common, Madam, that a mother spites
The stepson who might claim her children's rights.   30
I know that in a second marriage-bed
Anxiety and mistrust are often bred.
Another woman would have wished me ill
As you have, and perhaps been harsher still.
PHAEDRA   Ah, Prince! The Gods, by whom I swear it, saw   35
Fit to except me from that general law.

By what a different care am I beset!
HIPPOLYTUS   My lady, don't give way to anguish yet.
　　Your husband still may see the light of day;
　　Heaven may hear us, and guide his sail this way.
　　Neptune protects him, and that deity   40
　　Will never fail to heed my father's plea.
PHAEDRA   No one goes twice among the dead; and since
　　Theseus has seen those gloomy regions, Prince,
　　No god will bring him back, hope though you may,   45
　　Nor greedy Acheron yield up his prey.
　　But no! He is not dead; he breathes in you.
　　My husband still seems present to my view.
　　I see him, speak with him . . . Ah, my lord, I feel
　　Crazed with a passion which I can't conceal.   50
HIPPOLYTUS   In your strong love, what wondrous power lies!
　　Theseus, though dead, appears before your eyes.
　　For love of him your soul is still on fire.
PHAEDRA   Yes, Prince, I burn for him with starved desire,
　　Though not as he was seen among the shades,   55
　　The fickle worshiper of a thousand maids,
　　Intent on cuckolding the King of Hell;
　　But constant, proud, a little shy as well,
　　Young, charming, irresistible, much as we
　　Depict our Gods, or as you look to me.   60
　　He had your eyes, your voice, your virile grace,
　　It was your noble blush that tinged his face
　　When, crossing on the waves, he came to Crete
　　And made the hearts of Minos' daughters[6] beat.
　　Where were you then? Why no Hippolytus   65
　　Among the flower of Greece he chose for us?
　　Why were you yet too young to join that band
　　Of heroes whom he brought to Minos' land?
　　You would have slain the Cretan monster then,
　　Despite the endless windings of his den.[7]   70
　　My sister would have armed you with a skein
　　Of thread, to lead you from that dark domain.
　　But no: I'd first have thought of that design,
　　Inspired by love; the plan would have been mine.
　　It's I who would have helped you solve the maze,   75
　　My Prince, and taught you all its twisting ways.
　　What I'd have done to save that charming head!
　　My love would not have trusted to a thread.
　　No, Phaedra would have wished to share with you
　　Your perils, would have wished to lead you through   80
　　The Labyrinth, and thence have side by side
　　Returned with you; or else, with you, have died.
HIPPOLYTUS   Gods! What are you saying, Madam? Is Theseus not

Does Hippolytus believe his father may yet live?

---

6. Phaedra and Ariadne.　7. The Minotaur inhabited the heart of a maze. Ariadne provided Theseus with a ball of thread, by which he left a trail behind him and could retrace his steps after killing the monster.

Your husband, and my sire? Have you forgot?

PHAEDRA   You think that I forget those things? For shame,   85
My lord. Have I no care for my good name?

HIPPOLYTUS   Forgive me, Madam. I blush to have misread
The innocent intent of what you said.
I'm too abashed to face you; I shall take
My leave. . . .

PHAEDRA   Ah, cruel Prince, 'twas no mistake.   90
You understood; my words were all too plain.
Behold then Phaedra as she is, insane
With love for you. Don't think that I'm content
To be so, that I think it innocent,
Or that by weak compliance I have fed   95
The baneful love that clouds my heart and head.
Poor victim that I am of Heaven's curse,[8]
I loathe myself; you could not hate me worse.
The Gods could tell how in this breast of mine
They lit the flame that's tortured all my line,   100
Those cruel Gods for whom it is but play
To lead a feeble woman's heart astray.
You too could bear me out; remember, do,
How I not only shunned but banished you.
I wanted to be odious in your sight;   105
To balk my love, I sought to earn your spite.
But what was gained by all of that distress?
You hated me the more; I loved no less,
And what you suffered made you still more dear.
I pined, I withered, scorched by many a tear.   110
That what I say is true, your eyes could see
If for a moment they could look at me.
What have I said? Do you suppose I came
To tell, of my free will, this tale of shame?
No, anxious for a son I dared not fail,   115
I came to beg you not to hate him. Frail
Indeed the heart is that's consumed by love!
Alas, it's only you I've spoken of.
Avenge yourself, now; punish my foul desire.
Come, rid the world, like your heroic sire,   120
Of one more monster; do as he'd have done.
Shall Theseus' widow dare to love his son?
No, such a monster is too vile to spare.
Here is my heart. Your blade must pierce me there.
In haste to expiate its wicked lust,   125
My heart already leaps to meet your thrust.
Strike, then. Or if your hatred and disdain
Refuse me such a blow, so sweet a pain,
If you'll not stain your hand with my abhorred
And tainted blood, lend me at least your sword.   130

Her own devices couldn't conquer her fault

Phaedra wishes to Hippolytus to kill her

8. Phaedra feels herself a victim of Venus, the goddess of love; she loves Hippolytus against her will.

Give it to me!

OENONE   Just Gods! What's this, my Queen?
   Someone is coming. You must not be seen.
   Quick! Flee! You'll be disgraced if you delay.

SCENE 6

HIPPOLYTUS, THERAMENES

THERAMENES   Did I see Phaedra vanish, dragged away?
   Why do I find you pale and overcome?
   Where is your sword, Sir? Why are you stricken dumb?
HIPPOLYTUS   Theramenes, I'm staggered. Let's go in haste.
   I view myself with horror and distaste.   5
   Phaedra . . . but no, great Gods! This thing must not
   Be told, but ever buried and forgot.
THERAMENES   Sir, if you wish to sail, our ship's prepared.
   But Athens' choice already is declared.
   Her clans have all conferred; their leaders name   10
   Your brother; Phaedra has achieved her aim.
HIPPOLYTUS   Phaedra?
THERAMENES   A herald's come at their command
   To give the reins of state into her hand.
   Her son is king.
HIPPOLYTUS   Gods, what she is you know;
   Is it her virtue you've rewarded so?   15
THERAMENES   Meanwhile, it's rumored that the King's not dead,
   That in Epirus he has shown his head.
   But I, who searched that land, know well, my lord . . .
HIPPOLYTUS   No, let all clues be weighed, and none ignored.
   We'll track this rumor down. Should it appear   20
   Too insubstantial to detain us here,
   We'll sail, and at whatever cost obtain
   Great Athens' crown for one who's fit to reign.

Act III

SCENE 1

PHAEDRA, OENONE

PHAEDRA   Ah, let their honors deck some other brow.
   Why urge me? How can I let them see me now?
   D'you think to soothe my anguished heart with such
   Vain solace? Hide me, rather. I've said too much.
   My frenzied love's burst forth in act and word.   5
   I've spoken what should never have been heard.
   And how he heard me! How, with many a shift,
   The brute pretended not to catch my drift!
   How ardently he longed to turn and go!
   And how his blushes caused my shame to grow!   10

She was shamed by him?

Why did you come between my death and me?
Ah, when his sword-point neared my breast, did he
Turn pale with horror, and snatch back the blade?
No. I had touched it, and that touch had made
Him see it as a thing defiled and stained,   15
By which his pure hand must not be profaned.
OENONE   Dwelling like this on all you're grieved about,
You feed a flame which best were beaten out.
Would it not suit King Minos' child to find
In loftier concerns her peace of mind,   20
To flee an ingrate whom you love in vain,
Assume the conduct of the State, and reign?
PHAEDRA   I, reign? You'd trust the State to my control,
When reason rules no longer in my soul?
When passion's overthrown me? When, from the weight   25
Of shame I bear, I almost suffocate?
When I am dying?
OENONE   Flee him.
PHAEDRA   How could I? How?
OENONE   You once could banish him; can't you shun him now?
PHAEDRA   Too late. He knows what frenzy burns in me.
I've gone beyond the bounds of modesty.   30
My conqueror has heard my shame confessed,
And hope, despite me, has crept into my breast.
'Twas you who, when my life was near eclipse
And my last breath was fluttering on my lips,
Revived me with sweet lies that took me in.   35
You said that now my love was free of sin.
OENONE   Ah, whether or not your woes are on my head,
To save you, what would I not have done or said?
But if an insult ever roused your spleen,
How can you pardon his disdainful mien?   40
How stonily, and with what cold conceit
He saw you all but grovel at his feet!
Oh, but his arrogance was rude and raw!
Why did not Phaedra see the man I saw?
PHAEDRA   This arrogance which irks you may grow less.   45
Bred in the forests, he has their ruggedness,
And, trained in harsh pursuits since he was young,
Has never heard, till now, love's gentle tongue.
No doubt it was surprise which made him mute,
And we do wrong to take him for a brute.   50
OENONE   Remember that an Amazon gave him life.
PHAEDRA   True: yet she learned to love like any wife.
OENONE   He has a savage hate for womankind.
PHAEDRA   No fear of rivals, then, need plague my mind.
Enough. Your counsels now are out of season.   55
Oenone, serve my madness, not my reason.
His heart is armored against love; let's seek

Some point where his defenses may be weak.
Imperial rule was in his thoughts, I feel;
He wanted Athens; that he could not conceal;   60
His vessels' prows already pointed there,
With sails all set and flapping in the air.
Go in my name, then; find this ambitious boy;
Dangle the crown before him like a toy.
His be the sacred diadem; in its stead   65
I ask no honor but to crown his head,
And yield a power I cannot hold. He'll school
My son in princely arts, teach him to rule,
And play for him, perhaps, a father's role.
Both mother and son I yield to his control.   70
Sway him, Oenone, by every wile that's known:
Your words will please him better than my own.
Sigh, groan, harangue him; picture me as dying;
Make use of supplication and of crying;
I'll sanction all you say. Go. I shall find,   75
When you return, what fate I am assigned.

[handwritten margin note: She would entice him with the promise of power.]

[handwritten margin note: She will use treachery to try to get what she wants.]

SCENE 2

PHAEDRA, alone

PHAEDRA   O you who see to what I have descended,
Implacable Venus, is your vengeance ended?
Your shafts have all struck home; your victory's
Complete; what need for further cruelties?
If you would prove your pitiless force anew,   5
Attack a foe who's more averse to you.
Hippolytus flouts you; braving your divine
Wrath, he has never knelt before your shrine.
His proud ears seem offended by your name.
Take vengeance, Goddess; our causes are the same.   10
Force him to love . . . Oenone! You've returned
So soon? He hates me, then; your words were spurned.

SCENE 3

PHAEDRA, OENONE

OENONE   Madam, your hopeless love must be suppressed.
Call back the virtue which you once possessed.
The King, whom all thought dead, will soon be here;
Theseus has landed; Theseus is drawing near.
His people rush to see him, rapturous.   5
I'd just gone out to seek Hippolytus
When a great cry went up on every hand. . . .
PHAEDRA   My husband lives, Oenone; I understand.

I have confessed a love he will abhor.
He lives, and I have wronged him. Say no more.   10
OENONE   What?
PHAEDRA   I foresaw this, but you changed my course.
Your tears won out over my just remorse.
I might have died this morning, mourned and chaste;
I took your counsels, and I die disgraced.
OENONE   You die?
PHAEDRA   Just Heaven! Think what I have done!   15
My husband's coming; with him will be his son.
I'll see the witness of my vile desire
Watch with what countenance I can greet his sire,
My heart still heavy with rejected sighs,
And tears which could not move him in my eyes.   20
Mindful of Theseus' honor, will he conceal
The scandal of my passion, do you feel,
Deceiving both his sire and king? Will he
Contain the horror that he feels for me?
His silence would be vain. What ill I've done   25
I know, Oenone, and I am not one
Of those bold women who, at ease in crime,
Are never seen to blush at any time.
I know my mad deeds, I recall them all.
I think that in this place each vault, each wall   30
Can speak, and that, impatient to accuse,
They wait to give my trusting spouse their news.
I'll die, then; from these horrors I'll be free.
It is so sad a thing to cease to be?
Death is not fearful to a suffering mind.   35
My only fear's the name I leave behind.
For my poor children, what a dire bequest!
Each has the blood of Jove within his breast,
But whatsoever pride of blood they share,
A mother's crime's a heavy thing to bear.   40
I tremble lest—alas, too truly!—they
Be chided for their mother's guilt some day.
I tremble lest, befouled by such a stain,
Neither should dare to lift his head again.
OENONE   I pity both of them; you could not be   45
More justified in your anxiety.
But why expose them to such insult? Why
Witness against yourself? You've but to die,
And folk will say that Phaedra, having strayed
From virtue, flees the husband she betrayed.   50
Hippolytus will rejoice that, cutting short
Your days, you lend his charges your support.
How shall I answer your accuser? He
Will have no trouble in refuting me.
I'll watch him gloating hatefully, and hear   55

Him pour your shame in every listening ear.
Let Heaven's fire consume me ere I do!
But come, speak frankly; is he still dear to you?
How do you see this prince so full of pride?

PHAEDRA   I see a monster, of whom I'm terrified.   60

OENONE   Then why should he triumph, when all can be reversed?
You fear the man. Dare to accuse him first
Of that which he might charge you with today.
What could belie you? The facts all point his way:
The sword which by good chance he left behind,   65
Your past mistrust, your present anguished mind,
His sire long cautioned by your warning voice,
And he sent into exile by your choice.

PHAEDRA   I, charge an innocent man with doing ill?

OENONE   Trust to my zeal. You've only to be still.   70
Like you I tremble, and feel a sharp regret.
I'd sooner face a thousand deaths. And yet
Since, lacking this sad remedy, you'll perish;
Since, above all, it is your life I cherish,
I'll speak to Theseus. He will do no more   75
Than doom his son to exile, as before.
A sire, when he must punish, is still a sire;
A lenient sentence will appease his ire.
But even if guiltless blood must flow, the cost
Were less than if your honor should be lost.   80
That honor is too dear to risk; its cause
Is priceless, and its dictates are your laws.
You must give up, since honor is at stake,
Everything, even virtue, for its sake.
Ah! Here comes Theseus.

PHAEDRA   And Hippolytus, he   85
In whose cold eyes I read the end of me.
Do what you will; I yield myself to you.
In my confusion, I know not what to do.

SCENE 4

THESEUS, HIPPOLYTUS, PHAEDRA, OENONE, THERAMENES

THESEUS   Fortune has blessed me after long delay,
And in your arms, my lady . . .

PHAEDRA   Theseus, stay,
And don't profane the love those words express.
I am not worthy of your tenderness.
You have been wronged. Fortune or bitter fate   5
Did not, while you were absent, spare your mate.
Unfit to please you, or to be at your side,
Henceforth my only thought must be to hide.

[handwritten margin notes:] Oenone would have Phaedra lie to cover her evilness.

Phaedra questions Oenone's advice

SCENE 5

THESEUS, HIPPOLYTUS, THERAMENES

THESEUS   Why am I welcomed in this curious vein?

HIPPOLYTUS   That, Father, only Phaedra can explain.
But if my prayers can move you, grant me, Sir,
Never again to set my eyes on her.
Allow Hippolytus to say farewell   5
To any region where your wife may dwell.

THESEUS   Then you, my son, would leave me?

HIPPOLYTUS   I never sought her
When to this land she came, 'twas you who brought her.
Yes, you, my lord, when last you left us, bore
Aricia and the Queen to Troezen's shore.   10
You bade me be their guardian then; but how
Should any duties here detain me now?
Too long my youthful skill's been thrown away
Amidst these woods, upon ignoble prey.
May I not flee my idle pastimes here   15
To stain with worthier blood my sword or spear?
Before you'd lived as long as I have done,
More than one tyrant, monsters more than one
Had felt your strength of arm, your sword's keen blade;
Already, scourging such as sack and raid,   20
You had made safe the coasts of either sea.
The traveler lost his fears of banditry,
And Hercules, to whom your fame was known,
Welcomed your toils, and rested from his own.
But I, the unknown son of such a sire,   25
Lack even the fame my mother's deeds inspire.[9]
Let me at long last show my courage, and,
If any monster has escaped your hand,
Bring back its pelt and lay it at your feet,
Or let me by a glorious death complete   30
A life that will defy oblivion
And prove to all the world I was your son.

THESEUS   What have I found? What horror fills this place,
And makes my family flee before my face?
If my unwished return makes all grow pale,   35
Why, Heaven, did you free me from my jail?
I'd one dear friend. He had a hankering
To steal the consort of Epirus'[1] king.
I joined his amorous plot, though somewhat loath;
But outraged Fate brought blindness on us both.   40

He never wants to see Phaedra again.

Hippolytus has yet to do a noble deed which will establish his fame.

---

9. Hippolytus's mother also performed brave deeds.   1. A district in western Greece on the Ionian Sea.

The tyrant caught me, unarmed and by surprise.
I saw Pirithoüs with my weeping eyes
Flung by the barbarous king to monsters then,
Fierce beasts who drink the blood of luckless men.
Me he confined where never light invades,   45
In caverns near the empire of the shades.
After six months, Heaven pitied my mischance.
Escaping from my guardians' vigilance,
I cleansed the world of one more fiend, and threw
To his own beasts the bloody corpse to chew.
But now when, joyful, I return to see   50
The dearest whom the Gods have left to me;
Now, when my spirits, glad once more and light,
Would feast again upon that cherished sight,
I'm met with shudders and with frightened faces;   55
All flee me, all deny me their embraces.
Touched by the very terror I beget,
I wish I were Epirus' prisoner yet.
Speak! Phaedra says that I've been wronged. By whom?
Why has the culprit not yet met his doom?   60
Has Greece, so often sheltered by my arm,
Chosen to shield this criminal from harm?
You're silent. Is my own son, if you please,
In some alliance with my enemies?
I shall go in, and end this maddening doubt.   65
Both crime and culprit must be rooted out,
And Phaedra tell why she is so distraught.

SCENE 6

HIPPOLYTUS, THERAMENES

HIPPOLYTUS   How her words chilled me! What was in her thought?
Will Phaedra, who is still her frenzy's prey,
Accuse herself, and throw her life away?
What will the King say? Gods! What love has done
To poison all this house while he was gone!   5
And I, who burn for one who bears his curse,
Am altered in his sight, and for the worse!
I've dark forebodings; something ill draws near.
Yet surely innocence need never fear.
Come, let's consider now how I may best   10
Revive the kindness in my father's breast,
And tell him of a love which he may take
Amiss, but all his power cannot shake.

Act IV

SCENE 1

THESEUS, OENONE

THESEUS   What do I hear? How bold and treacherous
   To plot against his father's honor thus!
   How sternly you pursue me, Destiny!
   Where shall I turn? I know not. Where can I be?
   O love and kindness not repaid in kind!   5
   Outrageous scheme of a degenerate mind!
   To seek his lustful end he had recourse,
   Like any blackguard, to the use of force.
   I recognize the sword his passion drew—
   My gift, bestowed with nobler deeds in view.   10
   Why did our ties of blood prove no restraint?
   Why too did Phaedra make no prompt complaint?
   Was it to spare the culprit?
OENONE   It was rather
   That she, in pity, wished to spare his father.
   Ashamed because her beauty had begot   15
   So foul a passion, and so fierce a plot,
   By her own hand, my lord, she sought to die,
   And darken thus the pure light of her eye.
   I saw her raise her arm; to me you owe
   Her life, because I ran and stayed the blow.   20
   Now, pitying both her torment and your fears,
   I have, against my will, spelled out her tears.
THESEUS   The traitor! Ah, no wonder he turned pale.
   When first he sighted me, I saw him quail.
   'Twas strange to see no greeting in his face.   25
   My heart was frozen by his cold embrace.
   But did he, even in Athens, manifest
   This guilty love by which he is possessed?
OENONE   The Queen, remember, could not tolerate him.
   It was his infamous love which made her hate him.   30
THESEUS   That love, I take it, was rekindled here
   In Troezen?
OENONE   I've told you all, my lord. I fear
   I've left the Queen too long in mortal grief.
   Let me now haste to bring her some relief.

SCENE 2

THESEUS, HIPPOLYTUS

THESEUS   Ah, here he comes. Gods! By that noble mien
   What eye would not be duped, as mine has been!
   Why must the brow of an adulterer
   Be stamped with virtue's sacred character?

Should there not be clear signs by which one can   5
Divine the heart of a perfidious man?

HIPPOLYTUS   May I enquire what louring cloud obscures,
  My lord, that royal countenance of yours?
  Dare you entrust the secret to your son?

THESEUS   Dare you appear before me, treacherous one?   10
  Monster, at whom Jove's thunder should be hurled!
  Foul brigand, like those of whom I cleaned the world!
  Now that your vile, unnatural love has led
  You even to attempt your father's bed,
  How dare you show your hated self to me   15
  Here in the precincts of your infamy,
  Rather than seek some unknown land where fame
  Has never brought the tidings of my name?
  Fly, wretch. Don't brave the hate which fills my soul,
  Or tempt a wrath it pains me to control.   20
  I've earned, forevermore, enough disgrace
  By fathering one who'd do a deed so base,
  Without your death upon my hands, to soil
  A noble history of heroic toil.
  Fly, and unless you wish to join the band   25
  Of knaves who've met quick justice at my hand,
  Take care lest by the sun's eye you be found
  Setting an insolent foot upon this ground.
  Now, never to return, be off; take flight;
  Cleanse all my realms of your abhorrent sight.   30
  And you, O Neptune, if by courage I
  Once cleared your shores of murderers, hear my cry.
  Recall that, as reward for that great task,
  You swore to grant the first thing I should ask.
  Pent in a cruel jail for endless hours,   35
  I never called on your immortal powers.
  I've hoarded up the aid you promised me
  Till greater need should justify my plea.
  I make it now. Avenge a father's wrong.
  Seize on this traitor, and let your rage be strong.   40
  Drown in his blood his brazen lust. I'll know
  Your favor by the fury that you show.

HIPPOLYTUS   Phaedra accuses me of lust? I'm weak
  With horror at the thought, and cannot speak;
  By all these sudden blows I'm overcome;   45
  They leave me stupefied, and stricken dumb.

THESEUS   Scoundrel, you thought that Phaedra'd be afraid
  To tell of the depraved assault you made.
  You should have wrested from her hands the hilt
  Of the sharp sword that points now to your guilt;   50
  Or, better, crowned your outrage of my wife
  By robbing her at once of speech and life.

HIPPOLYTUS   In just resentment of so black a lie,
  I might well let the truth be known, but I

[handwritten annotation: Hippolytus is surprised at Phaedra's slander]

Suppress what comes too near your heart. Approve,   55
My lord, a silence which bespeaks my love.
Restrain, as well, your mounting rage and woe:
Review my life; recall the son you know.
Great crimes grow out of small ones. If today
A man first oversteps the bounds, he may   60
Abuse in time all laws and sanctities;
For crime, like virtue, ripens by degrees;
But when has one seen innocence, in a trice,
So change as to embrace the ways of vice?
Not in a single day could time transmute   65
A virtuous man to an incestuous brute.
I had an Amazon mother, brave and chaste,
Whose noble blood my life has not debased.
And when I left her hands, 'twas Pitteus,[2] thought
Earth's wisest man, by whom my youth was taught.   70
I shall not vaunt such merits as I've got,
But if one virtue's fallen to my lot,
It is, my lord, a fierce antipathy
To just that vice imputed now to me.
It is for that Hippolytus is known   75
In Greece—for virtue cold and hard as stone.
By harsh austerity I am set apart.
The daylight is not purer than my heart.
Yet I, it's charged, consumed by lechery . . .
THESEUS   This very boast betrays your guilt. I see   80
What all your vaunted coldness signifies:
Phaedra alone could please your lustful eyes;
No other woman moved you, or could inspire
Your scornful heart with innocent desire.
HIPPOLYTUS   No, Father: hear what it's time I told you of;   85
I have not scorned to feel a blameless love.
I here confess my only true misdeed:
I am in love, despite what you decreed.
Aricia has enslaved me; my heart is won,
And Pallas' daughter has subdued your son.   90
I worship her against your orders, Sir,
Nor could I burn or sigh except for her.
THESEUS   You love her? Gods! But no, I see your game.
You play the criminal to clear your name.
HIPPOLYTUS   Six months I've shunned her whom my heart adored.   95
I came in fear to tell you this, my lord.
Why must you be so stubbornly mistaken?
To win your trust, what great oath must be taken?
By Earth, and Heaven, and all the things that be . . .
THESEUS   A rascal never shrinks from perjury.   100

2. The most learned man of his age, Theseus's guardian. After marrying Phaedra, Theseus sent Hippolytus
to Pitteus (or Pitheus), who had adopted him as heir to the throne of Troezen.

Cease now to weary me with sly discourse,
If your false virtue has but that resource.
HIPPOLYTUS   My virtue may seem false and sly to you,
But Phaedra has good cause to know it true.
THESEUS   Ah, how your impudence makes my temper boil!   105
HIPPOLYTUS   How long shall I be banished? On what soil?
THESEUS   Were you beyond Alcides' pillars,[3] I
Would think yet that a rogue was too nearby.
HIPPOLYTUS   Who will befriend me now—a man suspected
Of such a crime, by such a sire rejected?   110
THESEUS   Go look for friends who think adultery cause
For accolades, and incest for applause,
Yes, ingrates, traitors, to law and honor blind,
Fit to protect a blackguard of your kind.
HIPPOLYTUS   Incest! Adultery! Are these still your themes?   115
I'll say no more. Yet Phaedra's mother, it seems,
And, as you know, Sir, all of Phaedra's line
Knew more about such horrors than did mine.
THESEUS   So! You dare storm and rage before my face?
I tell you for the last time: leave this place.   120
Be off, before I'm roused to violence
And have you, in dishonor, driven hence.

SCENE 3

THESEUS, *alone*

THESEUS   Poor wretch, the path you take will end in blood.
What Neptune swore by Styx, that darkest flood
Which frights the Gods themselves, he'll surely do.
And none escapes when vengeful Gods pursue.
I loved you; and in spite of what you've done,   5
I mourn your coming agonies, my son.
But you have all too well deserved my curse.
When was a father ever outraged worse?
Just Gods, who see this grief which drives me wild,
How could I father such a wicked child?   10

SCENE 4

PHAEDRA, THESEUS

PHAEDRA   My lord, I hasten to you, full of dread.
I heard your threatening voice, and what it said.   *Phaedra has been listening*
Pray Heaven no deed has followed on your threat.
I beg you, if there is time to save him yet,
To spare your son; spare me the dreadful sound   5   *Her love for Hippolytus moves her.*

---

3. The Pillars of Hercules, the two points of land on either side of the Strait of Gibraltar, at the western
end of the Mediterranean and thus representing one edge of the known world.

Of blood, your own blood, crying from the ground.
Do not impose on me the endless woe
Of having caused your hand to make it flow.
THESEUS   No, Madam, my blood's not on my hands. But he,
The thankless knave, has not escaped from me.   10
A God's great hand will be his nemesis
And your avenger. Neptune owes me this.
PHAEDRA   Neptune! And will your angry prayers be heard?
THESEUS   What! Are you fearful lest he keep his word?
No, rather join me in my righteous pleas.   15
Recount to me my son's black treacheries;
Stir up my sluggish wrath, that's still too cold.
He has done crimes of which you've not been told:
Enraged at you, he slanders your good name:
Your mouth is full of lies, he dares to claim;   20
He states that heart and soul, his love is pledged
To Aricia.
PHAEDRA   What, my lord!
THESEUS   So he alleged;
But I saw through so obvious a trick.
Let's hope that Neptune's justice will be quick.
I go now to his altars, to implore   25
A prompt fulfillment of the oath he swore.

SCENE 5

PHAEDRA, alone

PHAEDRA   He's gone. What news assails my ear? What ill-
Extinguished fire flares in my bosom still?
By what a thunderbolt I am undone!
I'd flown here with one thought, to save his son.
Escaping from Oenone's arms by force,   5
I'd yielded to my torturing remorse.
How far I might have gone, I cannot guess.
Guilt might perhaps have driven me to confess.
Perhaps, had shock not caused my voice to fail,
I might have blurted out my hideous tale.   10
Hippolytus can feel, but not for me!
Aricia has his love, his loyalty!
Gods! When he steeled himself against my sighs
With that forbidding brow, those scornful eyes,
I thought his heart, which love-darts could not strike,   15
Was armed against all womankind alike.
And yet another's made his pride surrender;
Another's made his cruel eyes grow tender.
Perhaps his heart is easy to ensnare.
It's me, alone of women, he cannot bear!   20
Shall I defend a man by whom I'm spurned?

SCENE 6

PHAEDRA, OENONE

PHAEDRA   Oenone dear, do you know what I have learned?
OENONE   No, but in truth I'm quaking still with fear
  Of the wild urge that sent you rushing here:
  I feared some blunder fatally adverse.
PHAEDRA   I had a rival. Who would have thought it, Nurse?   5
OENONE   What?
PHAEDRA   Yes, Hippolytus is in love; it's true.
  That savage creature no one could subdue,
  Who scorned regard, who heard no lovers' pleas,
  That tiger whom I viewed with trembling knees,
  Is tame now, broken by a woman's art: 10
  Aricia's found the way into his heart.
OENONE   Aricia?
PHAEDRA   O pain I never felt before!
  What new, sharp torments have I kept in store!
  All that I've suffered—frenzies, fears, the dire
  Oppression of remorse, my heart on fire,   15
  The merciless rebuff he gave to me—
  All were but foretastes of this agony.
  They love each other! By what magic, then,
  Did they beguile me? Where did they meet, and when?
  You knew. Why did you keep me unaware,   20
  Deceived as to their furtive love-affair?
  Were they much seen together? Were they known
  To haunt the deep woods, so as to be alone?
  Alas, they'd perfect liberty to meet.
  Heaven smiled on hearts so innocent and sweet;   25
  Without remorse, they savored love's delight;
  For them, each dawn arose serene and bright—
  While I, creation's outcast, hid away
  From the Sun's eye, and fled the light of day.
  Death was the only God I dared implore.   30
  I longed for him; I prayed to be no more.
  Quenching my thirst with tears, and fed on gall,
  Yet in my woe too closely watched by all,
  I dared not weep and grieve in fullest measure;
  I sipped in secret at that bitter pleasure;   35
  And often, wearing a serene disguise,
  I kept my pain from welling in my eyes.
OENONE   What will their love avail them? They will never
  Meet again.
PHAEDRA   But they will love forever.
  Even as I speak—ah, deadly thought!—they dare   40
  To mock my crazed desire and my despair.
  Despite this exile which will make them part,

[handwritten marginal notes:] Oenone feared Phaedra would tell her secret

[handwritten marginal notes:] She knows that the love of aricia and Hippolytus is true and faithful

They swear forever to be joined in heart.

Their hearts are one

No, no, their bliss I cannot tolerate,
Oenone. Take pity on my jealous hate.   45
Aricia must die. Her odious house
Must once more feel the anger of my spouse.
Nor can the penalty be light, for her
Misdeeds are darker than her brothers' were.
In my wild jealousy I will plead with him.   50
I'll what? Has my poor reason grown so dim? ← *a sign that Phaedra is mad*
I, jealous! And it's with Theseus I would plead!
My husband lives, and still my passions feed
On whom? Toward whom do all my wishes tend?
At every word, my hair stands up on end.   55
The measure of my crimes is now replete.   *Her hands will now be as corrupted as her heart,*
I foul the air with incest and deceit.
My murderous hands are itching to be stained
With innocent blood, that vengeance be obtained.
Wretch that I am, how can I live, how face   60
That sacred Sun, great elder of my race?
My grandsire was, of all the Gods, most high;
My forebears fill the world, and all the sky.
Where can I hide? For Hades' night I yearn.
No, there my father holds the dreadful urn   65
Entrusted to his hands by Fate, it's said:
There Minos judges all the ashen dead.
Ah, how his shade will tremble with surprise
To see his daughter brought before his eyes—
Forced to confess a throng of sins, to tell   70
Of crimes perhaps unheard of yet in Hell!
What will you say then, Father? As in a dream,
I see you drop the fearful urn;[4] you seem
To ponder some new torment fit for her,
Yourself become your own child's torturer.   75
Forgive me. A cruel God destroys your line;
Behold her hand in these mad deeds of mine.
My heart, alas! not once enjoyed the fruit
Of its dark, shameful crime. In fierce pursuit,
Misfortune dogs me till, with my last breath,   80
My sad life shall, in torments, yield to death.

OENONE   My lady, don't give in to needless terror.
Look freshly at your pardonable error.
You love. But who can conquer Destiny? ← *Destiny acts as to will.*
Lured by a fatal spell, you were not free.   85
Is that a marvel hitherto unknown?
Has Love entrapped no heart but yours alone?
Weakness is natural to us, is it not?
You are a mortal; accept your mortal lot.

---

4. After his death, Minos of Crete became, along with his brother Rhadamanthus, one of the judges of souls in the underworld. The urn held the lots determining to what abode in the underworld the souls of the dead were to be sent.

The wishes to destroy her rival

To chafe against our frail estate is vain.   90
Even the Gods who on Olympus reign,
And with their thunders chasten men for crime,
Have felt illicit passions many a time.

PHAEDRA   Ah, what corrupting counsels do I hear?
Wretch! Will you pour such poison in my ear   95
Right to the end? Look how you've ruined me.
You dragged me back to all I sought to flee.
You blinded me to duty; called it no wrong
To see Hippolytus, whom I'd shunned so long.
Ah, meddling creature, why did your sinful tongue   100
Falsely accuse a soul so pure and young?
He'll die, it may be, if the Gods can bear
To grant his maddened father's impious prayer.
No, say no more. Go, monster whom I hate.
Go, let me face at last my own sad fate.   105
May Heaven reward you for your deeds! And may
Your punishment forever give dismay
To all who, like yourself, by servile arts
Nourish the weaknesses of princes' hearts,
Incline them to pursue the baser path,   110
And smooth for them the way to sin and wrath—
Accursèd flatterers, the worst of things
That Heaven's anger can bestow on kings!

OENONE   I've given my life to her. Ah, Gods! It hurts
To be thus thanked. Yet I have my just deserts.   115

Act V

SCENE 1

HIPPOLYTUS, ARICIA

ARICIA   Come, in this mortal danger, will you not make
Your loving sire aware of his mistake?
If, scorning all my tears, you can consent
To parting and an endless banishment,
Go, leave Aricia in her life alone.   5
But first assure the safety of your own.
Defend your honor against a foul attack,
And force your sire to call his prayers back.
There yet is time. What moves you, if you please,
Not to contest Queen Phaedra's calumnies?   10
Tell Theseus the truth.

HIPPOLYTUS   What more should I
Have told him? How she smirched their marriage-tie?
How could I, by disclosing everything,
Humiliate my father and my king?
It's you alone I've told these horrors to.   15
I've bared my heart but to the Gods and you.

Judge of my love, which forced me to confide
What even from myself I wished to hide.
But, mind you, keep this secret ever sealed.
Forget, if possible, all that I've revealed,   20
And never let those pure lips part to bear
Witness, my lady, to this vile affair.
Let us rely upon the Gods' high laws:
Their honor binds them to defend my cause;
And Phaedra, sooner or later brought to book,   25
Will blush for crimes their justice cannot brook.
To that restraint I ask you to agree.
In all things else, just anger makes me free.
Come, break away from this, your slavish plight;
Dare follow me, dare join me in my flight;   30
Be quit of an accursèd country where
Virtue must breathe a foul and poisoned air.
Under the cover of this turbulence
Which my disfavor brings, slip quickly hence.
I can assure a safe escape for you.   35
Your only guards are of my retinue.
Strong states will champion us; upon our side
Is Sparta; Argos' arms are open wide:
Let's plead then to these friends our righteous case,
Lest Phaedra, profiting by our disgrace,   40
Deny our lineal claims to either throne,
And pledge her son my birthright and your own.
Come, let us seize the moment; we mustn't wait.
What holds you back? You seem to hesitate.
It's zeal for you that moves me to be bold.   45
When I am all on fire, what makes you cold?
Are you afraid to join a banished man?
ARICIA   Alas, my lord, how sweet to share that ban!
What deep delight, as partner of your lot,
To live with you, by all the world forgot!   50
But since no blessèd tie unites us two,
Can I, in honor, flee this land with you?
The sternest code, I know, would not deny
My right to break your father's bonds and fly;
I'd grieve no loving parents thus; I'm free,   55
As all are, to escape from tyranny.
But, Sir, you love me, and my fear of shame . . .
HIPPOLYTUS   Ah, never doubt my care for your good name.
It is a nobler plan that I propose:
Flee with your husband from our common foes.   60
Freed my mischance, since Heaven so commands,
We need no man's consent to join our hands.
Not every nuptial needs the torch's light.
At Troezen's gate, amidst that burial site
Where stand our princes' ancient sepulchers,   65
There is a temple feared by perjurers.

No man there dares to break his faith, on pain
Of instant doom, or swear an oath in vain;
There all deceivers, lest they surely die,
Bridle their tongues and are afraid to lie.   70
There, if you trust me, we will go, and of
Our own accord shall pledge eternal love;
The temple's God will witness to our oath;
We'll pray that he be father to us both.
I shall invoke all deities pure and just.   75
The chaste Diana, Juno[5] the august,
And all the Gods who know my faithfulness
Will guarantee the vows I shall profess.
ARICIA   The king is coming. Go, Prince, make no delay.
To cloak my own departure, I'll briefly stay.   80
Go, go; but leave with me some faithful guide
Who'll lead my timid footsteps to your side.

SCENE 2

THESEUS, ARICIA, ISMENE

THESEUS   O Gods, bring light into my troubled mind;
Show me the truth which I've come here to find.
ARICIA   Make ready for our flight, Ismene dear.

SCENE 3

THESEUS, ARICIA

THESEUS   Your color changes, Madame, and you appear
Confused. Why was Hippolytus here with you?
ARICIA   He came, my lord, to say a last adieu.
THESEUS   Ah, yes. You've tamed his heart, which none could capture.
And taught his stubborn lips to sigh with rapture.   5
ARICIA   I shan't deny the truth, my lord. No, he
Did not inherit your malignity,
Nor treat me as a criminal, in your fashion.
THESEUS   I see. He's sworn, no doubt, eternal passion.
Put no reliance on the vows of such   10
A fickle lover. He's promised others as much.
ARICIA   He, Sir?
THESEUS   You should have taught him not to stray.
How could you share his love in that base way?
ARICIA   How could you let a shameful lie besmear
The stainless honor of his young career?   15
Have you so little knowledge of his heart?
Can't you tell sin and innocence apart?
Must some black cloud bedim your eyes alone
To the bright virtue for which your son is known?

5. The wife of Jupiter and queen of the gods. Diana was goddess of the moon and of chastity.

Shall slander ruin him? That were too much to bear.   20
Turn back: repent now of your murderous prayer.
Fear, my lord, fear lest the stern deities
So hate you as to grant your wrathful pleas.
Our sacrifices anger Heaven at times;
Its gifts are often sent to scourge our crimes.   25

THESEUS   Your words can't cover up that sin of his:
Love's blinded you to what the scoundrel is.
But I've sure proofs on which I may rely:
I have seen tears—yes, tears which could not lie.

ARICIA   Take care, my lord. You have, in many lands,   30
Slain countless monsters with your conquering hands;
But all are not destroyed; there still lives one
Who . . . No, I am sworn to silence by your son.
Knowing his wish to shield your honor, I'd
Afflict him if I further testified.   35
I'll imitate his reticence, and flee
Your presence, lest the truth should burst from me.

SCENE 4

THESEUS, *alone*

THESEUS   What does she mean? These speeches which begin
And then break off—what are they keeping in?
Is this some sham those two have figured out?
Have they conspired to torture me with doubt?
But I myself, despite my stern control—   5
What plaintive voice cries from my inmost soul?
I feel a secret pity, a surge of pain.
Oenone must be questioned once again.
I'll have more light on this. Not all is known.
Guards, go and bring Oenone here, alone.   10

SCENE 5

THESEUS, PANOPE

PANOPE   I don't know what the Queen may contemplate,
My lord, but she is in a frightening state.
Mortal despair is what her looks bespeak;
Death's pallor is already on her cheek.
Oenone, driven from her in disgrace,   5
Has thrown herself into the sea's embrace.
None knows what madness caused the thing she did;
Beneath the waves she lies forever hid.

THESEUS   What do you tell me?

PANOPE   This death has left the Queen
No calmer; her distraction grows more keen.   10
At moments, to allay her dark unrest,

She clasps her children, weeping, to her breast;
Then, with a sudden horror, she will shove
Them both away, and starve her mother-love. → *She is acting mad.*
She wanders aimlessly about the floor;   15
Her blank eye does not know us any more.
Thrice she has written; and thrice, before she'd done,
Torn up the letter which she had begun.
We cannot help her. I beg you, Sire, to try.
THESEUS   Oenone's dead? And Phaedra wants to die?   20
O bring me back my son, and let him clear
His name! If he'll but speak, I now will hear.
O Neptune, let your gifts not be conferred
Too swiftly; let my prayers go unheard.
Too much I've trusted what may not be true,   25
Too quickly raised my cruel hands to you.
How I'd despair if what I asked were done!

SCENE 6

THESEUS, THERAMENES

THESEUS   Is it you, Theramenes? Where have you left my son?
You've been his mentor since his tenderest years.
But why do I behold you drenched in tears?
Where's my dear son?
THERAMENES   Too late, Sire, you restore
Your love to him. Hippolytus is no more.   5
THESEUS   Gods!
pfoTHERAMENES
                    I have seen the best of mortals slain,
My lord, and the least guilty, I maintain.
THESEUS   My son is dead? What! Just when I extend
My arms to him, Heaven's haste has caused his end?
What thunderbolt bereaved me? What was his fate?   10
THERAMENES   Scarcely had we emerged from Troezen's gate:
He drove his chariot, and his soldiery
Were ranged about him, mute and grave as he.
Brooding, he headed toward Mycenae. Lax
In his hands, the reins lay on his horses' backs.   15
His haughty chargers, quick once to obey
His voice, and give their noble spirits play,
Now, with hung head and mournful eye, seemed part
Of the sad thoughts that filled their master's heart.
Out of the sea-deeps then a frightful cry   20
Arose, to tear the quiet of the sky,
And a dread voice from far beneath the ground
Replies in groans to that appalling sound.
Our hearts congeal; blood freezes in our veins.
The horses, hearing, bristle up their manes.   25
And now there rises from the sea's calm breast

Hippolytus was unjustly slain

A liquid mountain with a seething crest.
The wave approaches, breaks, and spews before
Our eyes a raging monster on the shore.
His huge brow's armed with horns; the spray unveils   30
A body covered all with yellow scales;
Half bull he is, half dragon; fiery, bold;
His thrashing tail contorts in fold on fold.
With echoing bellows now he shakes the strand.
The sky, aghast, beholds him; he makes the land   35
Shudder; his foul breath chokes the atmosphere;
The wave which brought him in recoils in fear.
All flee, and in a nearby temple save
Their lives, since it is hopeless to be brave.
Hippolytus alone dares make a stand.   40
He checks his chargers, javelins in hand,
Has at the monster and, with a sure-aimed throw,
Pierces his flank: a great wound starts to flow.
In rage and pain the beast makes one dread spring,
Falls near the horses' feet, still bellowing,   45
Rolls over toward them, with fiery throat takes aim
And covers them with smoke and blood and flame.
Sheer panic takes them; deaf now, they pay no heed
To voice or curb, but bolt in full stampede;
Their master strives to hold them back, in vain.   50
A bloody slaver drips from bit and rein.
It's said that, in that tumult, some caught sight
Of a God who spurred those dusty flanks to flight.
Fear drives them over rocks; the axletree
Screeches and breaks. The intrepid Prince must see   55
His chariot dashed to bits, for all his pains;
He falls at last, entangled in the reins.
Forgive my grief. That cruel sight will be
An everlasting source of tears for me.
I've seen, my lord, the heroic son you bred   60
Dragged by the horses which his hand had fed.
His shouts to them but make their fear more strong.
His body seems but one great wound, ere long.
The plain re-echoes to our cries of woe.
At last, their headlong fury starts to slow: 65
They stop, then, near that graveyard which contains,
In royal tombs, his forebears' cold remains.
I run to him in tears; his guards are led
By the bright trail of noble blood he shed;
The rocks are red with it; the briars bear   70
Their red and dripping trophies of his hair.
I reach him; speak his name; his hand seeks mine;
His eyelids lift a moment, then decline.
"Heaven takes," he says, "my innocent life away.
Protect my sad Aricia, I pray.   75
If ever, friend, my sire is disabused,
And mourns his son who falsely was accused,

Bid him appease my blood and plaintive shade
By dealing gently with that captive maid.
Let him restore . . ." His voice then died away,   80
And in my arms a mangled body lay
Which the God's wrath had claimed, a sorry prize
Which even his father would not recognize.

THESEUS   My son, dear hope whom folly made me kill!
O ruthless Gods, too well you did my will!   85
I'll henceforth be the brokenest of men.

THERAMENES   Upon this scene came shy Aricia then,
Fleeing your wrath, and ready to espouse
Your son before the Gods by holy vows.
She comes, and sees the red and steaming grass;   90
She sees—no sight for loving eyes, alas!—
Hippolytus sprawled there, lacking form or hue.
At first, she won't believe her loss is true.
Not recognizing her beloved, she
Both looks at him and asks where he may be.   95
At last she knows too well what's lying there;
She lifts to the Gods a sad, accusing stare;
Then, moaning, cold, and all but dead, the sweet
Maid drops unconscious at her lover's feet.
Ismene, weeping, kneels and seeks to bring   100
Her back to life—a life of suffering.
And I, my lord, have come, who now detest
This world, to bring a hero's last request,
And so perform the bitter embassy
Which, with his dying breath, he asked of me.   105
But look: his mortal enemy comes this way.

SCENE 7

THESEUS, PHAEDRA, THERAMENES, PANOPE, GUARDS

THESEUS   Well, Madam, my son's no more; you've won the day!
Ah, but what qualms I feel! What doubts torment
My heart, and plead that he was innocent!
But, madam, claim your victim. He is dead.
Enjoy his death, unjust or merited.   5
I'm willing to be evermore deceived.
You've called him guilty; let it be believed.
His death is grief enough for me to bear
Without my further probing this affair,
Which could not bring his dear life back again   10
And might perhaps but aggravate my pain.
No, far from you and Troezen, I shall flee
My dead son's torn and bloody memory.
It will pursue me ever, like a curse:
Would I were banished from the universe!   15
All seems to chide my wicked wrathfulness.
My very fame now adds to my distress.

How shall I hide, who have a name so great?
Even the Gods' high patronage I hate.
I go to mourn this murderous gift of theirs,   20
Nor trouble them again with useless prayers.
Do for me what they might, it could not pay
For what their deadly favor took away.

PHAEDRA   Theseus, my wrongful silence must be ended.
Your guiltless son must be at last defended.   25
He did no ill.

THESEUS   How curst a father am I!
I doomed him, trusting in your heartless lie!
Do you think to be excused for such a crime?

PHAEDRA   Hear me, my lord. I have but little time.
I was the lustful and incestuous one   30
Who dared desire your chaste and loyal son.
Heaven lit a fatal blaze within my breast.
Detestable Oenone did the rest.
She, fearing lest Hippolytus, who knew
Of my vile passion, might make it known to you,   35
Abused my weakness and, by a vicious ruse,
Made haste to be the first one to accuse.
For that she's paid; fleeing my wrath, she found
Too mild a death, and in the waves is drowned.
Much though I wished to die then by the sword,   40
Your son's pure name cried out to be restored.
That my remorse be told, I chose instead
A slower road that leads down to the dead.
I drank, to give my burning veins some peace,
A poison which Medea[6] brought to Greece.   45
Already, to my heart, the venom gives
An alien coldness, so that it scarcely lives;
Already, to my sight, all clouds and fades—
The sky, my spouse, the world my life degrades;
Death dims my eyes, which soiled what they could see,   50
Restoring to the light its purity.

PANOPE   She's dead, my lord!

THESEUS   Would that I could inter
The memory of her black misdeeds with her!
Let's go, since now my error's all too clear,
And mix my poor son's blood with many a tear,   55
Embrace his dear remains, and expiate
The fury of a prayer which now I hate.
To his great worth all honor shall be paid,
And, further to appease his angry shade,
Aricia, despite her brothers' offense,   60
Shall be my daughter from this moment hence.

---

6. A sorceress who helped Jason get the Golden Fleece; later, deserted by him, she killed her rival and her own children and burned her palace before fleeing to Athens. According to one legend, she tried to poison Theseus.

JEAN DE LA FONTAINE
1621–1695

Although the stories that La Fontaine tells in his fables may already be familiar from other sources, his telling makes them new. He narrates the familiar fables not only with a deft pointedness that makes them seem up to date even now, but with a high degree of narrative economy so that their impact is quick and sharp.

Born into a bourgeois family at Château-Thierry, in northern France, La Fontaine settled in Paris, where he had completed his schooling. There he soon attracted financial patronage by virtue of his literary accomplishments. His personal life, however, was fairly chaotic: he lived apart from his wife and child for most of his adult life; he was constantly in debt and existed in a state of financial dependency. On the other hand, he was widely admired and ultimately elected to the Académie Française. He is now generally agreed to be France's most important poet.

La Fontaine's fables, 230 of them, were first published from 1668 to 1694. Mainly based on Aesop's tales, they were immediately popular with children and adults alike. He also published a series of volumes called, in English, *Tales and Novels in Verse* (1664–74), in which he versified comic, sometimes bawdy, tales from Boccaccio and Ariosto, among others. He wrote poetry in several different genres, including opera librettos, but the collection of fables is still considered his masterpiece.

The wit of beast fables depends on an analogy between human beings and animals. To encounter a cicada talking like a man-about-town has an immediate comic effect. But the analogy also has serious implications: if a cicada resembles a man, a man must resemble a cicada. Satiric energy lurks beneath the playful representations of various species. Fables such as "The Wolf and the Lamb," with its ostensible moral "Might is right," expose the cruelty of the powerful. Many fables suggest the eagerness with which people take advantage of one another as well as the delusiveness of claimed self-understanding. La Fontaine, however, also shows himself capable of exploring the more positive aspects of human nature—sometimes openly, as in "The Two Pigeons," a tale of love and loyalty as well as cruelty; sometimes subtly, as in "The Cicada and the Ant," where the wastrel cicada, a singer of songs, seems more attractive than the smug and contemptuous ant.

The traditional association between fables and teaching may mislead careless readers into thinking that these tales are simple. After all, many of the fables state their morals openly, and those morals tend to be obvious and perhaps even uninteresting. But La Fontaine is usually up to much more than presenting a simple moral. The subtleties of his characterization and the economy and grace of his verse often deliberately undermine the proclaimed moral. "The Wolf and the Lamb" provides an obvious example. One may suspect from the beginning that "Might is right" isn't really the message, but the fable illustrates precisely what is wrong with such a doctrine. The wolf, as he offers rationalizations for what he proposes to do with or without rationalization, seems more and more frightening, more and more recognizable. By the end, the reader understands the danger of self-justification as well as the terror of powerlessness. The reader also probably understands that "Might is right" indeed serves as the guiding principle for many in the world. "Might *isn't* right" could be the moral. But such a doctrine must be qualified by awareness that, whether it is or isn't right, might makes the worse appear the better reason for itself.

Fables[1]

The Cicada and the Ant

The cicada,[2] having chirped her song
    All summer long,
Found herself bitterly deprived
    When the north wind arrived—
Not a mouthful of worm or fly.   5
    Whereupon in her want
She rushed round to her neighbor the ant
    And begged her to supply
Some crumbs on loan to keep body and soul together
Till next spring. "On my word as an animal   10
    I swear," she said, "to repay
With interest before the harvest ends."
Of the ant's few faults the minimal
    Is that she never lends.
"What were you doing during the hot weather?"   15
She asked the importunate insect.
        "With all respect,
    I was singing night and day
For the pleasure of anyone whom chance
    Sent my way."   20
        "Singing, did you say?
I'm delighted to hear it. Now you can dance!"

The Crow and the Fox

Mr. Crow, perched in a tree, held in his beak
    A piece of cheese.
Mr. Fox, attracted by the smell,
    Began to speak
    In terms roughly like these: 5
    "Hullo!
I mean, good morning, honorable Crow,
    You look uncommonly well,
Indeed you look a veritable Romeo.
Honestly, if it were not for one thing   10
You would be the phoenix[1] of our woodland birds:
Your feathers are gorgeous—but how well can you sing?"
    At these words
The crow, beside himself with pleasure,
Opened his big mouth to show off, and dropped his treasure.   15
    The fox snapped it up in a trice,
    Remarking: "My dear sir, learn the hard way
        That all flatterers live

---

1. James Michie is the translator of all the fables appearing here except for "The Two Pigeons," which was translated by Francis Duke.   2. A grasshopper-like insect.   1. A legendary bird of great beauty that is supposed to live five hundred years and then regenerate itself from the ashes of its funeral pyre.

At the expense of those with a credulous ear to give—
A lesson cheap, surely, at the price   20
    Of your lost cheese-slice."
    Mortified and confused,
The crow vowed (rather late in the day)
Never again to be so abused.

The Wolf and the Lamb

Might is right: the verdict goes to the strong.
To prove the point won't take me very long.

    A lamb was once drinking
From a clear stream when a foraging wolf came slinking
    Out of the woods, drawn to that quarter   5
    Of the countryside by hunger.
    "How dare you muddy my drinking water!"
    Said the beast of prey in anger.
"You shall be punished for your insolence."
    "Your Majesty," answered the lamb,   10
"I beg you not to be angry but to think
    Calmly about it. Here I am,
    Relieving my throat's dryness
At least twenty yards downstream from your Highness,
    And in consequence   15
    I cannot be in the least
    Guilty of sullying your royal drink."
    "But you are," said the pitiless beast.
"Besides, I know you spoke ill of me last year."
"How could I have done? I wasn't even here,"   20
The lamb replied. "I'm still at the teat of my mother."
"If it wasn't you, it must have been your brother."
"I haven't got one." "Well, then, one of you sheep;
For you and your shepherds and damned dogs keep
Making it harder and harder for me to eat.   25
But now revenge is mine—and revenge is sweet!"
    Whereupon he dragged the lamb deep
    Into the forest and had his meal.
    There was no right of appeal.

The Oak and the Reed

One day the oak said to the reed:
"You have good cause indeed
To accuse Nature of being unkind.
To you a wren must seem
An intolerable burden, and the least puff of wind   5
That chances to wrinkle the face of the stream

Forces your head low; whereas I,
Huge as a Caucasian peak, defy
Not only the sun's glare, but the worst the weather can do.
What seems a breeze to me is a gale for you.   10
Had you been born in the lee of my leaf-sheltered ground,
You would have suffered less, I should have kept you warm;
But you reeds are usually found
On the moist borders of the kingdom of the storm.
It strikes me that to you Nature has been unfair."   15
"Your pity," the plant replied, "springs from a kind heart.
But please don't be anxious on my part.
Your fear of the winds ought to be greater than mine.
I bend, but I never break. You, till now, have been able to bear
Their fearful buffets without flexing your spine.   20
But let us wait and see." Even as he spoke,
From the horizon's nethermost gloom
The worst storm the north had ever bred in its womb
    Furiously awoke.
The tree stood firm, the reed began to bend.   25
The wind redoubled its efforts to blow—
    So much so
    That in the end
It uprooted the one that had touched the sky with its head,
But whose feet reached to the region of the dead.   30

The Lion and the Rat

    In this world we must do our best
      To oblige others; for we all
      Occasionally have need to call
    On the services of the weak and small.
      This truth two fables attest: 5
    Indeed proofs of all such truths abound.

    Rashly popping from a hole in the ground,
    A rat came up between a lion's paws.
    The king of beasts, sheathing his claws,
    In this instance showed his royal nature   10
      And spared the little creature.
    The kindness wasn't wasted. . . . But a rat
      Paying a lion back a debt—
      Could anyone credit that?
    And yet it happened. On the fringe of the jungle   15
    The same lion was later caught in a net
    Which all his roars were powerless to untangle.
      Up ran Sir Rat and set
    To work with his teeth, gnawing and fretting,
    Till, mesh by mesh, he'd unpicked all the netting.   20

    Patience and perseverance at length
    Accomplish more than anger and brute strength.

The Fox and the Grapes

A starving fox—a Gascon, Normans[1] claim,
But Gascons say a Norman—saw a cluster
Of luscious-looking grapes of purplish luster
Dangling above him on a trellis-frame.
He would have dearly liked them for his lunch,   5
But when he tried and failed to reach the bunch:
"Ah well, it's more than likely they're not sweet—
    Good only for green fools to eat!"

Wasn't he wise to say they were unripe
    Rather than whine and gripe?   10

The Rooster and the Fox

A shrewd, wily old rooster
Was keeping look-out on a bough
When a fox, in the nicest voice he could muster,
    Addressed him: "Brother,
We are no longer at war with each other: 5
I've come to announce that it's peace now,
Total peace! Descend and accept my embrace.
    But for goodness' sake
Don't keep me waiting—today I'm in a hurry,
With twenty different calls to make.   10
From now on you and your race
Can go about your business free of worry—
We shall treat you as brothers. Let us light
    Jubilee bonfires tonight.
Meanwhile come and receive a fraternal kiss."   15
"My friend," the rooster replied, "I couldn't have heard
Better or more welcome news than this.
    Peace is a wonderful word,
    And to me it's a double delight
    To hear it from you. But wait!   20
I see two hounds—they must be envoys sent
Expressly to attend this great event.
They'll be here in a moment, to judge by their pace.
Then I'll get down and we can all four embrace."
"Goodbye," said the fox. "I've a long day ahead.   25
    We'll have to celebrate
    Tomorrow, or the day after. . . ."
    Whereupon, sick
    At the failure of his trick,
That gentleman hitched his trousers up and fled.   30
The old cock watched his panicky retreat

---

1. Normandy and Gascony, home of Normans and Gascons, respectively, are different regions of France that are sometimes in competition with one another.

With silent laughter;
For the pleasure is twice as sweet
When you cheat a cheat.

The Two Pigeons

Two Pigeons shared a tender love;
But one, being bored with life at home,
Made up his foolish mind to rove
Away, and through the world to roam.
"What shall you do?" exclaimed the other.   5
"Why must you desert your brother?
Absence is the worst of blows;
But, cruel, not to you! Would that a wanderer's woes,
And risks, and cares, might serve for you
A little to amend your view;   10
And later in the year you might fare better too!
Wait till the zephyrs¹ stir; who's goading you? A crow
Just now croaked warning that some bird would be brought low.
I'll dream of nothing but of travelers distressed
And hawks, and nets. I'll say: 'Dear, but the weather's wet;   15
And are my brother's wants all met,
Hot supper, warm bed, and the rest?' "
This plea brought turmoil to the heart
That on so mad a voyage would start;
But curiosity and restlessness at last   20
Prevailed, and he responded: "Wipe your tears away,
For I'll have had enough before three days have passed.
I'll soon be back, and in a circumstantial way
I'll tell my brother my adventures
For his pleasure. Anyone who nothing ventures   25
Can't make conversation either. When you know
My tale, you'll find it royal fare.
I'll say: 'That's where I was; this happened thus and so'—
You'll think you actually are there."
Upon these words they wept, and said a fond good-bye.   30
The wanderer wings away. And now a cloud sails near,
And makes him seek some safer hiding-spot close by.
He finds a tree such that the tempest even here
Lashed at the Pigeon through the leaves. The air grows clear,
Until, with feathers sodden, he flies on ahead;   35
And as he flies, he does his best to dry the wet.
His eyes fall on a lonely field where wheat lies spread,
And where a pigeon pecks, his appetite to whet.
Alighting, he falls prisoner to a noose, await
Beneath the wheat's delusive bait.   40

---

1. Gentle spring breezes.

The noose was frayed, and so the bird, with beating wing,
And busy feet and bill, at last has broken loose
With only feathers lost. But fate allows no truce:
A certain sharp-clawed hawk, above him hovering,
Descries our luckless victim trailing bits of string   45
That as he flies he carries still about him draped,
  As might a convict just escaped.
The hawk being poised to strike, down out of clouds descended
Now an eagle with yet fiercer claws extended.
Profiting from this dispute of thief with thief,   50
The Pigeon flees, escapes, lands near a peasant's hut,
  And hopes that now perhaps his grief
  May end with this adventure. But
A vagrant boy (that age is heartless), with his sling
And pebblestones, came very near to murdering   55
  The hapless feathered flyer, who came,
 With curses on himself for an idle fling,
  And one foot dragging, and one wing,
  Half dead and more than halfway lame,
  Back to his home, which he contrived   60
  Somehow to reach, and so arrived
  Secure at last from ill luck's aim;
And so the two unite. I leave it to be guessed
With what extreme delight their sorrows they allay.

O lovers, happy lovers, must you fly the nest?   65
  Fly, then, but never far away.
Fly to a world of beauty fixed between you two,
  Forever different and new.
Be all things each to each, what though all else default.
There was a time when I too loved; and when I did,   70
  For all the Louvre[2] and all it hid,
And all the starry firmament and Heaven's vault,
  I'd not have given the woodland dell
Trod by the light step, and whereon the bright glance fell,
  Of that young shepherdess who'd won   75
  My heart—for whom, by Cythera's son[3]
Commanded, I served out my youth's first vows. But when,
Alas, shall moments such as those return again?
Must objects so beguiling and so charming, then,
Abandon me a victim to my spirit's thirst?   80
Ah, that love's flame still flared within my heart! Must I
Be warmed no more by charms that kept me young at first?
  Can love perhaps have passed me by?

---

2. The greatest French art museum, located in Paris. 3. Cupid.

SOR JUANA INÉS DE LA CRUZ
1648–1695

One hardly expects to find a spirited defense of women's intellectual rights issuing from the pen of a seventeenth-century Mexican nun, but *Reply to Sor Filotea de la Cruz,* by Sister Juana Inés de la Cruz, is exactly that. In the guise of declaring her humility and her religious subordination, this nun manages to advance claims for her sex more far-reaching and profound than any previously offered.

Born into an upper-class family, Sister Juana in her teens served as lady-in-waiting at the viceregal court. She soon took the veil, however; her *Reply* suggests as a reason her desire for a safe environment in which to pursue her intellectual interests. Religious vocation did not prevent her from writing in secular forms: lyric poetry and drama. Indeed, she achieved an important literary reputation, later coming to be known throughout the Spanish-speaking world as the "Tenth Muse." Since her religious superiors intermittently rebuked her for her worldly interests, however, she appears to have developed a powerful sense of guilt. And the natural disturbances and disasters—a solar eclipse, storms, and famine—plaguing Mexico City in the 1690s may have intensified her guilt; in 1694, she reaffirmed her faith, signing the statement in her own blood with the words "I, Sister Juana Inés de la Cruz, the worst in the world." She died after nursing the sick in an epidemic.

The *Reply* stems directly from Sister Juana's venture into theological polemic. In 1690 she wrote a commentary on a sermon delivered forty years earlier by the Portuguese Jesuit Antonio Vieira, a sermon in which he disputed with St. Augustine and St. Thomas about the nature of Christ's greatest expression of love at His life's end. Her commentary, in the form of a letter, was published, without her consent, by the bishop of Puebla. The bishop provided the title *Athenagoric Letter,* or "letter worthy of the wisdom of Athena," but he also prefixed his own letter to Sister Juana, signed with the pseudonym "Filotea de la Cruz." Here he advised the nun to focus her attention and her talents more on religious matters. In her *Reply* (1691), she nominally accepted the bishop's rebuke; the smooth surface of her elegant prose, however, conceals both rage and determination to assert her right—and that of other women— to a fully realized life of the mind.

The artistry of this piece of self-defense demonstrates Sister Juana's powers and thus constitutes part of her justification. Systematically refusing to make any overt claims for herself, she declares her desire to do whatever her associates wish or demand of her. While asserting her own unimportance, she illustrates the range of her knowledge and of her rhetorical skill. The sheer abundance of her biblical allusions and of her quotations from theological texts, for instance, proves that she has mastered a large body of religious material and that she has not sacrificed religious to secular study. Her elaborate protestations of deference, her vocabulary of insignificance, her narrative of subservience, all show the verbal dexterity that enables her to achieve her own rhetorical ends even as she denies her commitment to purely personal goals.

If she acknowledges no self-seeking, she nevertheless declares and demonstrates her ungovernable passion for the life of the mind. She tells of how she joined the convent despite fears that the community "would intrude upon the peaceful silence of my books." "Certain learned persons," however, explained to her that her desire for solitary intellectual experience constituted "temptation." She, therefore, entered the religious life, believing, she says, "that I was fleeing from myself, but—wretch that I am!—I brought with me my worst enemy, my inclination, which I do not know whether to consider a gift or a punishment from Heaven; for once dimmed and encumbered by the many activities common to Religion, that inclination exploded in me like gunpowder." Although this sentence explicitly labels her intellectual inclinations her worst enemy and suggests that they might be considered divine punishment, the same sentence dramatizes the uncontrollable, explosive force of those inclinations and hints at the negative potential of religious experience, which dims and encumbers the mind. No matter how often Sister Juana admits that her longings amount to a form of "vice," she embodies in her prose the energy and the vividness that they generate and makes her audience feel their positive weight.

The autobiographical aspects of Sister Juana's self-defense give it special immediacy for modern readers, who may recognize themselves in her narrative. Of course, girls no longer have to trick their way into learning or plead for permission to dress in boy's clothes to go to a university. But even young women of the twenty-first century have been known to experience the kind of hostility Sister Juana reports as the response to her remarkable achievement. More recognizable is the nun's stated ability to respond to others, indicating a "tender and affable nature," one that causes the other nuns, she says, to hold her "in great affection." She insists that she fills all the responsibilities of a woman as well as displays qualities more generally associated with men, and she performs her womanly and her religious duties *first*, reserving her scholarly pursuits for leisure hours.

But, of course, her larger argument depends on her insistance that intelligence or a thirst for knowledge is not a sex-linked characteristic. She draws on history for evidence of female intellectual power; one may feel the irony of the fact that her list of female worthies requires so much annotation today—the names of these notable women have hardly become household words. Still, these names, these histories, do exist, providing powerful support for Sister Juana's position. Even more forceful is the testimony of her own experience: her account of how, deprived of books, she finds matter for intellectual inquiry everywhere—in the yolk of an egg, the spinning of a top, the reading of the Bible. This is, the reader comes to believe, a woman born to think. If she arouses uneasiness when she implicitly equates herself, as object of persecution, with Christ, she also makes one feel directly the horror of women's official exclusion, in the past, from intellectual pursuits.

PRONOUNCING GLOSSARY

The following list uses common English syllables and stress accents to provide rough equivalents of selected words whose pronunciation may be unfamiliar to the general reader.

Albertus Magnus: *ahl-bayrl'-tus mahg'-noos*

Arete: *ah-ray'-tee*

Atenagórica: *ah-tay-nah-goh'-ree-kah*

Duquesa of Abeyro: *doo-kay'-zah of ah-bay'-roh*

Machiavelli: *mah-kee-ah-vel'-ee*

señora: *sen-yoh'-rah*

sueño: *swayn'-yoh*

Reply to Sor Filotea de la Cruz[1]

My most illustrious *señora*, dear lady. It has not been my will, my poor health, or my justifiable apprehension that for so many days delayed my response. How could I write, considering that at my very first step my clumsy pen encountered two obstructions in its path? The first (and, for me, the most uncompromising) is to know how to reply to your most learned, most prudent, most holy, and most loving letter. For I recall that when Saint Thomas,

---

1. Translated by Margaret Sayers Peden.

the Angelic Doctor of Scholasticism, was asked about his silence regarding his teacher Albertus Magnus,[2] he replied that he had not spoken because he knew no words worthy of Albertus. With so much greater reason, must not I too be silent? Not, like the Saint, out of humility, but because in reality I know nothing I can say that is worthy of you. The second obstruction is to know how to express my appreciation for a favor as unexpected as extreme, for having my scribblings printed, a gift so immeasurable as to surpass my most ambitious aspiration, my most fervent desire, which even as an entity of reason never entered my thoughts. Yours was a kindness, finally, of such magnitude that words cannot express my gratitude, a kindness exceeding the bounds of appreciation, as great as it was unexpected—which is as Quintilian[3] said: *aspirations engender minor glory; benefices,[4] major.* To such a degree as to impose silence on the receiver.

When the blessedly sterile—that she might miraculously become fecund— Mother of John the Baptist saw in her house such an extraordinary visitor as the Mother of the Word, her reason became clouded and her speech deserted her; and thus, in the place of thanks, she burst out with doubts and questions: *And whence is to me [that the mother of my Lord should come to me?][5]* And whence cometh such a thing to *me?* And so also it fell to Saul when he found himself the chosen, the anointed, King of Israel: *Am I not a son of Jemini, of the least tribe of Israel, and my kindred the last among all the families of the tribe of Benjamin? Why then hast thou spoken this word to me?[6]* And thus say I, most honorable lady. Why do I receive such favor? By chance, am I other than an humble nun, the lowliest creature of the world, the most unworthy to occupy your attention? "Wherefore then speakest thou so to me?" "And whence is this to me?" Nor to the first obstruction do I have any response other than I am little worthy of your eyes; nor to the second, other than wonder, in the stead of thanks, saying that I am not capable of thanking you for the smallest part of that which I owe you. This is not pretended modesty, lady, but the simplest truth issuing from the depths of my heart, that when the letter which with propriety you called *Atenagórica[7]* reached my hands, in print, I burst into tears of confusion (withal, that tears do not come easily to me) because it seemed to me that your favor was but a remonstrance God made against the wrong I have committed, and that in the same way He corrects others with punishment He wishes to subject me with benefices, with this special favor for which I know myself to be myself to be His debtor, as for an infinitude of others from His boundless kindness. I looked upon this favor as a particular way to shame and confound me, it being the most exquisite means of castigation, that of causing me, by my own intellect, to be the judge who pronounces sentence and who denounces my ingratitude. And thus, when here in my solitude I think on these things, I am wont to say: Blessed art Thou, oh Lord, for Thou hast not chosen to place in the hands of others my judgment, nor yet in mine, but hast reserved that to Thy own, and freed me from myself, and from the necessity to sit in judgment on myself, which judgment, forced from my own intellect, could be no less

---

2. St. Albert the Great (1193?–1280), scholastic philosopher, called the Universal Doctor; he exercised great influence on his student Thomas Aquinas.   3. Marcus Fabius Quintilianus (ca. 35–100 C.E.), born in Spain, became a famous Roman orator and wrote on rhetoric.   4. I.e., good works.   5. Luke 1.43. 6. 1 Samuel 9.21.   7. Sister Juana's letter criticizing Father Vieira's sermon was retitled by the bishop *Carta Atenagórica* (Letter worthy of Athena). Athena was the Greek goddess of wisdom.

than condemnation, but Thou hast reserved me to Thy mercy, because Thou lovest me more than I can love myself.

I beg you, lady, to forgive this digression to which I was drawn by the power of truth, and, if I am to confess all the truth, I shall confess that I cast about for some manner by which I might flee the difficulty of a reply, and was sorely tempted to take refuge in silence. But as silence is a negative thing, though it explains a great deal through the very stress of not explaining, we must assign some meaning to it that we may understand what the silence is intended to say, for if not, silence will say nothing, as that is its very office: *to say nothing.* The holy Chosen Vessel, Saint Paul, having been caught up into paradise, and having heard the arcane secrets of God, *heard secret words, which it is not granted to man to utter.*[8] He does not say what he heard; he says that he cannot say it. So that of things one cannot say, it is needful to say at least that they cannot be said, so that it may be understood that not speaking is not the same as having nothing to say, but rather being unable to express the many things there are to say. Saint John says that if all the marvels our Redeemer wrought "were written every one, the world itself, I think, would not be able to contain the books that should be written."[9] And Vieyra[1] says on this point that in this single phrase the Evangelist said more than in all else he wrote; and this same Lusitanian[2] Phoenix speaks well (but when does he not speak well, even when he does not speak well of others?) because in those words Saint John said everything left unsaid and expressed all that was left to be expressed. And thus I, lady, shall respond only that I do not know how to respond; I shall thank you in saying only that I am incapable of thanking you; and I shall say, through the indication of what I leave to silence, that it is only with the confidence of one who is favored and with the protection of one who is honorable that I presume to address your magnificence, and if this be folly, be forgiving of it, for folly may be good fortune, and in this manner I shall provide further occasion for your benignity and you will better shape my intellect.

Because he was halting of speech, Moses thought himself unworthy to speak with Pharaoh, but after he found himself highly favored of God, and thus inspired, he not only spoke with God Almighty but dared ask the impossible: *shew me thy face.*[3] In this same manner, lady, and in view of how you favor me, I no longer see as impossible the obstructions I posed in the beginning: for who was it who had my letter printed unbeknownst to me? Who entitled it, who bore the cost, who honored it, it being so unworthy in itself, and in its author? What will such a person not do, not pardon? What would he fail to do, or fail to pardon? And thus, based on the supposition that I speak under the safe-conduct of your favor, and with the assurance of your benignity, and with the knowledge that like a second Ahasuerus[4] you have offered to me to kiss the top of the golden scepter of your affection as a sign of conceding to me your benevolent license to speak and offer judgments in your exalted presence, I say to you that I have taken to heart your most holy admonition that I apply myself to the study of the Sacred Books, which,

---

8. 2 Corinthians 12.4.   9. John 21.25.   1. Antonio Vieira (1608–1697), author of the sermon that Sister Juana had earlier criticized, was a Portuguese ecclesiastic whose most important work was converting the Indians of Brazil.   2. Roman name for Portugal.   3. Exodus 33.13.   4. King of Persia, who stretched out his gold scepter to his queen, Esther, and said he would grant her whatever she wished (Esther 5.2–3).

though it comes in the guise of counsel, will have for me the authority of a precept, but with the not insignificant consolation that even before your counsel I was disposed to obey your pastoral suggestion as your direction, which may be inferred from the premise and argument of my Letter. For I know well that your most sensible warning is not directed against it, but rather against those worldly matters of which I have written.[5] And thus I had hoped with the Letter to make amends for any lack of application you may (with great reason) have inferred from others of my writings; and, speaking more particularly, I confess to you with all the candor of which you are deserving, and with the truth and clarity which are the natural custom in me, that my not having written often of sacred matters was not caused by disaffection or by want of application, but by the abundant fear and reverence due those Sacred Letters, knowing myself incapable of their comprehension and unworthy of their employment. Always resounding in my ears, with no little horror, I hear God's threat and prohibition to sinners like myself. *Why dost thou declare my justices, and take my covenant in thy mouth?*[6] This question, as well as the knowledge that even learned men are forbidden to read the Canticle of Canticles[7] until they have passed thirty years of age, or even Genesis—the latter for its obscurity; the former in order that the sweetness of those epithalamia not serve as occasion for imprudent youth to transmute their meaning into carnal emotion, as borne out by my exalted Father Saint Jerome,[8] who ordered that these be the last verses to be studied, and for the same reason: *And finally, one may read without peril the Song of Songs, for if it is read one may suffer harm through not understanding those Epithalamia of the spiritual wedding which is expressed in carnal terms.* And Seneca[9] says: *In the early years the faith is dim.* For how then would I have dared take in my unworthy hands these verses, defying gender, age, and, above all, custom? And thus I confess that many times this fear has plucked my pen from my hand and has turned my thoughts back toward the very same reason from which they had wished to be born: which obstacle did not impinge upon profane matters, for a heresy against art is not punished by the Holy Office but by the judicious with derision, and by critics with censure, and censure, *just or unjust, is not to be feared,* as it does not forbid the taking of communion or hearing of mass, and offers me little or no cause for anxiety, because in the opinion of those who defame my art, I have neither the obligation to know nor the aptitude to triumph. If, then, I err, I suffer neither blame nor discredit: I suffer no blame, as I have no obligation; no discredit, as I have no possibility of triumphing—*and no one is obliged to do the impossible.* And, in truth, I have written nothing except when compelled and constrained, and then only to give pleasure to others; not alone without pleasure of my own, but with absolute repugnance, for I have never deemed myself one who has any worth in letters or the wit necessity demands of one who would write; and thus my customary response to those who press me, above all in sacred matters, is, what capacity of reason have I? what application? what resources? what rudimentary knowledge of

5. Sister Juana had published secular poetry and drama.   6. Psalms 50.16.   7. The Song of Solomon (also called Song of Songs), which employs erotic imagery.   8. Eusebius Sophronius Hieronymus (ca. 342–420), ascetic and scholar, most learned of the Latin Church Fathers, a prolific author of treatises and commentaries. Sister Juana belonged to a Jeronymite convent; Jerome had founded the order.   9. Lucius Annaeus Seneca (ca. 3 B.C.E.–63 C.E.), Roman playwright, philosopher, and orator.

such matters beyond that of the most superficial scholarly degrees? Leave these matters to those who understand them; I wish no quarrel with the Holy Office, for I am ignorant, and I tremble that I may express some proposition that will cause offense or twist the true meaning of some scripture. I do not study to write, even less to teach—which in one like myself were unseemly pride—but only to the end that if I study, I will be ignorant of less. This is my response, and these are my feelings.

I have never written of my own choice, but at the urging of others, to whom with reason I might say, *You have compelled me.*[1] But one truth I shall not deny (first, because it is well-known to all, and second, because although it has not worked in my favor, God has granted me the mercy of loving truth above all else), which is that from the moment I was first illuminated by the light of reason, my inclination toward letters has been so vehement, so overpowering, that not even the admonitions of others—and I have suffered many—nor my own meditations—and they have not been few—have been sufficient to cause me to forswear this natural impulse that God placed in me: the Lord God knows why, and for what purpose. And He knows that I have prayed that He dim the light of my reason, leaving only that which is needed to keep His Law, for there are those who would say that all else is unwanted in a woman, and there are even those who would hold that such knowledge does injury. And my Holy Father knows too that as I have been unable to achieve this (my prayer has not been answered), I have sought to veil the light of my reason—along with my name—and to offer it up only to Him who bestowed it upon me, and He knows that none other was the cause of my entering into Religion, notwithstanding that the spiritual exercises and company of a community were repugnant to the freedom and quiet I desired for my studious endeavors. And later, in that community, the Lord God knows—and, in the world, only the one who must know[2]—how diligently I sought to obscure my name, and how this was not permitted, saying it was temptation: and so it would have been. If it were in my power, lady, to repay you in some part what I owe you, it might be done by telling you this thing which has never before passed my lips, except to be spoken to the one who should hear it. It is my hope that by having opened wide to you the doors of my heart, by having made patent to you its most deeply-hidden secrets, you will deem my confidence not unworthy of the debt I owe to your most august person and to your most uncommon favors.

Continuing the narrations of my inclinations, of which I wish to give you a thorough account, I will tell you that I was not yet three years old when my mother determined to send one of my elder sisters to learn to read at a school for girls we call the *Amigas.* Affection, and mischief, caused me to follow her, and when I observed how she was being taught her lessons I was so inflamed with the desire to know how to read, that deceiving—for so I knew it to be—the mistress, I told her that my mother had meant for me to have lessons too. She did not believe it, as it was little to be believed, but, to humour me, she acceded. I continued to go there, and she continued to teach me, but now, as experience had disabused her, with all seriousness; and I learned so quickly that before my mother knew of it I could already read, for my teacher had kept it from her in order to reveal the surprise and

1. 2 Corinthians 12.11.   2. Presumably her confessor, Father Antonio Núñez.

reap the reward at one and the same time. And I, you may be sure, kept the secret, fearing that I would be whipped for having acted without permission. The woman who taught me, may God bless and keep her, is still alive and can bear witness to all I say. I also remember that in those days, my tastes being those common to that age, I abstained from eating cheese because I had heard that it made one slow of wits, for in me the desire for learning was stronger than the desire for eating—as powerful as that is in children. When later, being six or seven, and having learned how to read and write, along with all the other skills of needlework and household arts that girls learn, it came to my attention that in Mexico City there were Schools, and a University, in which one studied the sciences. The moment I heard this, I began to plague my mother with insistent and importunate pleas: she should dress me in boy's clothing and send me to Mexico City to live with relatives, to study and be tutored at the University. She would not permit it, and she was wise, but I assuaged my disappointment by reading the many and varied books belonging to my grandfather, and there were not enough punishments, nor reprimands, to prevent me from reading: so that when I came to the city many marveled, not so much at my natural wit, as at my memory, and at the amount of learning I had mastered at an age when many have scarcely learned to speak well.

I began to study Latin grammar—in all, I believe, I had no more than twenty lessons—and so intense was my concern that though among women (especially a woman in the flower of her youth) the natural adornment of one's hair is held in such high esteem, I cut off mine to the breadth of some four to six fingers, measuring the place it had reached, and imposing upon myself the condition that if by the time it had again grown to that length I had not learned such and such a thing I had set for myself to learn while my hair was growing, I would again cut it off as punishment for being so slow-witted. And it did happen that my hair grew out and still I had not learned what I had set for myself—because my hair grew quickly and I learned slowly—and in fact I did cut it in punishment for such stupidity: for there seemed to me no cause for a head to be adorned with hair and naked of learning—which was the more desired embellishment. And so I entered the religious order, knowing that life there entailed certain conditions (I refer to superficial, and not fundamental, regards) most repugnant to my nature; but given the total antipathy I felt for marriage, I deemed convent life the least unsuitable and the most honorable I could elect if I were to insure my salvation. Working against that end, first (as, finally, the most important) was the matter of all the trivial aspects of my nature which nourished my pride, such as wishing to live alone, and wishing to have no obligatory occupation that would inhibit the freedom of my studies, nor the sounds of a community that would intrude upon the peaceful silence of my books. These desires caused me to falter some while in my decision, until certain learned persons enlightened me, explaining that they were temptation, and, with divine favor, I overcame them, and took upon myself the state which now so unworthily I hold. I believed that I was fleeing from myself, but—wretch that I am!—I brought with me my worst enemy, my inclination, which I do not know whether to consider a gift or a punishment from Heaven, for once dimmed and encumbered by the many activities common to Religion, that inclination exploded in me like gunpowder, proving how *privation is the source of appetite.*

I turned again (which is badly put, for I never ceased), I continued, then, in my studious endeavour (which for me was respite during those moments not occupied by my duties) of reading and more reading, of study and more study, with no teachers but my books. Thus I learned how difficult it is to study those soulless letters, lacking a human voice or the explication of a teacher. But I suffered this labor happily for my love of learning. Oh, had it only been for love of God, which were proper, how worthwhile it would have been! I strove mightily to elevate these studies, to dedicate them to His service, as the goal to which I aspired was to study Theology—it seeming to me debilitating for a Catholic not to know everything in this life of the Divine Mysteries that can be learned through natural means—and, being a nun and not a layperson, it was seemly that I profess my vows to learning through ecclesiastical channels; and especially, being a daughter of a Saint Jerome and a Saint Paula,[3] it was essential that such erudite parents not be shamed by a witless daughter. This is the argument I proposed to myself, and it seemed to me well-reasoned. It was, however (and this cannot be denied) merely glorification and approbation of my inclination, and enjoyment of it offered as justification. And so I continued, as I have said, directing the course of my studies toward the peak of Sacred Theology, it seeming necessary to me, in order to scale those heights, to climb the steps of the human sciences and arts; for how could one undertake the study of the Queen of Sciences if first one had not come to know her servants?

How, without Logic, could I be apprised of the general and specific way in which the Holy Scripture is written? How, without Rhetoric, could I understand its figures, its tropes, its locutions? How, without Physics,[4] so many innate questions concerning the nature of animals, their sacrifices, wherein exist so many symbols, many already declared, many still to be discovered? How should I know whether Saul's being refreshed by the sound of David's harp was due to the virtue and natural power of Music, or to a transcendent power God wished to place in David? How, without Arithmetic, could one understand the computations of the years, days, months, hours, those mysterious weeks communicated by Gabriel to Daniel,[5] and others for whose understanding one must know the nature, concordance, and properties of numbers? How, without Geometry, could one measure the Holy Ark of the Covenant and the Holy City of Jerusalem, whose mysterious measures are foursquare in their dimensions, as well as the miraculous proportions of all their parts? How, without Architecture, could one know the great Temple of Solomon, of which God Himself was the Author who conceived the disposition and the design, and the Wise King but the overseer who executed it, of which temple there was no foundation without mystery, no column without symbolism, no cornice without allusion, no architrave without significance; and similarly others of its parts, of which the least fillet was never intended solely for the service and complement of Art, but as symbol of greater things? How, without great knowledge of the laws and parts of which History is comprised, could one understand historical Books? Or those recapitulations in which many times what happened first is seen in the narrated account to have happened later? How, without great learning in Canon and

---

3. A Roman woman (d. 404), converted to Christianity after her daughter's death, who founded a nunnery next to St. Jerome's monastery at Bethlehem and helped Jerome in his studies.   4. I.e., physic, or medicine.   5. While Daniel was praying, Gabriel came to him to interpret, in great chronological detail, a vision Daniel had previously had (Daniel 9.21–27).

Civil Law, could one understand Legal Books? How, without great erudition, could one apprehend the secular histories of which the Holy Scripture makes mention, such as the many customs of the Gentiles, their many rites, their many ways of speaking? How without the abundant laws and lessons of the Holy Fathers could one understand the obscure lesson of the Prophets? And without being expert in Music, how could one understand the exquisite precision of the musical proportions that grace so many Scriptures, particularly those in which Abraham beseeches God in defense of the Cities,[6] asking whether He would spare the place were there but fifty just men therein; and then Abraham reduced that number to five less than fifty, forty-five, which is a ninth, and is as Mi to Re; then to forty, which is a tone, and is as Re to Mi; from forty to thirty, which is a diatessaron, the interval of the perfect fourth; from thirty to twenty, which is the perfect fifth; and from twenty to ten, which is the octave, the diapason; and as there are no further harmonic proportions, made no further reductions. How might one understand this without Music? And there in the Book of Job, God says to Job: *Shalt thou be able to join together the shining stars the Pleiades, or canst thou stop the turning about of Arcturus? Canst thou bring forth the day star in its time, and make the evening star to rise upon the children of the earth?*[7] Which message, without knowledge of Astrology, would be impossible to apprehend. And not only these noble sciences; there is no applied art that is not mentioned. And, finally, in consideration of the Book that comprises all books, and the Science in which all sciences are embraced, and for whose comprehension all sciences serve, and even after knowing them all (which we now see is not easy, nor even possible), there is one condition that takes precedence over all the rest, which is uninterrupted prayer and purity of life, that one may entreat of God that purgation of spirit and illumination of mind necessary for the understanding of such elevated matters: and if that be lacking, none of the aforesaid will have been of any purpose.

Of the Angelic Doctor Saint Thomas[8] the Church affirms: *When reading the most difficult passages of the Holy Scripture, he joined fast with prayer. And he was wont to say to his companion Brother Reginald that all he knew derived not so much from study or his own labor as from the grace of God.* How then should I—so lacking in virtue and so poorly read—find courage to write? But as I had acquired the rudiments of learning, I continued to study ceaselessly divers subjects, having for none any particular inclination, but for all in general; and having studied some more than others was not owing to preference, but to the chance that more books on certain subjects had fallen into my hands, causing the election of them through no discretion of my own. And as I was not directed by preference, nor, forced by the need to fulfill certain scholarly requirements, constrained by time in the pursuit of any subject, I found myself free to study numerous topics at the same time, or to leave some for others; although in this scheme some order was observed, for some I deigned[9] study and others diversion, and in the latter I found respite from the former. From which it follows that though I have studied many things I know nothing, as some have inhibited the learning of others. I speak specifically of the practical aspect of those arts that allow practice, because it is clear that when the pen moves the compass must lie idle, and

6. Abraham beseeches God to save Sodom for the sake of its just inhabitants (Genesis 18.23–33).   7. Job 38.31–32.   8. Thomas Aquinas (ca. 1225–1274), Dominican theologian, author of *Summa Theologica* (ca. 1266), and for centuries the most important authority on Church doctrine.   9. Deemed, considered.

while the harp is played the organ is stilled, *et sic de caeteris*.[1] And because much practice is required of one who would acquire facility, none who divides his interest among various exercises may reach perfection. Whereas in the formal and theoretical arts the contrary is true, and I would hope to persuade all with my experience, which is that one need not inhibit the other, but, in fact, each may illuminate and open the way to others, by nature of their variations and their hidden links, which were placed in this universal chain by the wisdom of their Author in such a way that they conform and are joined together with admirable unity and harmony. This is the very chain the ancients believed did issue from the mouth of Jupiter, from which were suspended all things linked one with another, as is demonstrated by the Reverend Father Athanasius Kircher[2] in his curious book, *De Magnate*. All things issue from God, Who is at once the center and the circumference from which and in which all lines begin and end.

I myself can affirm that what I have not understood in an author in one branch of knowledge I may understand in a second in a branch that seems remote from the first. And authors, in their elucidation, may suggest metaphorical examples in other arts: as when logicians say that to prove whether parts are equal, the means is to the extremes as a determined measure to two equidistant bodies; or in stating how the argument of the logician moves, in the manner of a straight line, along the shortest route, while that of the rhetorician moves as a curve, by the longest, but that both finally arrive at the same point. And similarly, as it is when they say that the Exegetes are like an open hand, and the Scholastics like a closed fist.[3] And thus it is no apology, nor do I offer it as such, to say that I have studied many subjects, seeing that each augments the other; but that I have not profited is the fault of my own ineptitude and the inadequacy of my intelligence, not the fault of the variety. But what may be offered as exoneration is that I undertook this great task without benefit of teacher, or fellow students with whom to confer and discuss, having for a master no other than a mute book, and for a colleague, an insentient inkwell; and in the stead of explication and exercise, many obstructions, not merely those of my religious obligations (for it is already known how useful and advantageous is the time employed in them), rather, all the attendant details of living in a community: how I might be reading, and those in the adjoining cell would wish to play their instruments, and sing; how I might be studying, and two servants who had quarreled would select me to judge their dispute; or how I might be writing, and a friend come to visit me, doing me no favor but with the best of will, at which time one must not only accept the inconvenience, but be grateful for the hurt. And such occurrences are the normal state of affairs, for as the times I set apart for study are those remaining after the ordinary duties of the community are fulfilled, they are the same moments available to my sisters, in which they may come to interrupt my labor; and only those who have experience of such a community will know how true this is, and how it is only the strength of my vocation that allows me happiness; that, and the great love existing between me and my beloved sisters, for as love is union, it knows no extremes of distance.

With this I confess how interminable has been my labor; and how I am

---

1. And so for other things (Latin). 2. German Jesuit scientist (1601?–1680), author of *Magnes sive de arte magnetica* (The magnet; or, of the magnetic science). 3. The Exegetes emphasized interpretation; the Scholastics, logic.

unable to say what I have with envy heard others state—that they have not been plagued by the thirst for knowledge: blessed are they. For me, not the knowing (for still I do not know), merely the desiring to know, has been such torment that I can say, as has my Father Saint Jerome (although not with his accomplishment) . . . *my conscience is witness to what effort I have expended, what difficulties I have suffered, how many times I have despaired, how often I have ceased my labors and turned to them again, driven by the hunger for knowledge; my conscience is witness, and that of those who have lived beside me.* With the exception of the companions and witnesses (for I have been denied even this consolation), I can attest to the truth of these words. And to the fact that even so, my black inclination has been so great that it has conquered all else!

It has been my fortune that, among other benefices,[4] I owe to God a most tender and affable nature, and because of it my sisters (who being good women do not take note of my faults) hold me in great affection, and take pleasure in my company; and knowing this, and moved by the great love I hold for them—having greater reason than they—I enjoy even more *their* company. Thus I was wont in our rare idle moments to visit among them, offering them consolation and entertaining myself in their conversation. I could not help but note, however, that in these times I was neglecting my study, and I made a vow not to enter any cell unless obliged by obedience or charity; for without such a compelling constraint—the constraint of mere intention not being sufficient—my love would be more powerful than my will. I would (knowing well my frailty) make this vow for the period of a few weeks, or a month; and when that time had expired, I would allow myself a brief respite of a day or two before renewing it, using that time not so much for rest (for *not* studying has never been restful for me) as to assure that I not be deemed cold, remote, or ungrateful in the little-deserved affection of my dearest sisters.

In this practice one may recognize the strength of my inclination. I give thanks to God, Who willed that such an ungovernable force be turned toward letters and not to some other vice. From this it may also be inferred how obdurately against the current my poor studies have sailed (more accurately, have foundered). For still to be related is the most arduous of my difficulties—those mentioned until now, either compulsory or fortuitous, being merely tangential—and still unreported the more directly aimed slings and arrows that have acted to impede and prevent the exercise of my study. Who would have doubted, having witnessed such general approbation, that I sailed before the wind across calm seas, amid the laurels of widespread acclaim. But our Lord God knows that it has not been so; He knows how from amongst the blossoms of this very acclaim emerged such a number of aroused vipers, hissing their emulation and their persecution, that one could not count them. But the most noxious, those who most deeply wounded me, have not been those who persecuted me with open loathing and malice, but rather those who in loving me and desiring my well-being (and who are deserving of God's blessing for their good intent) have mortified and tormented me more than those others with their abhorrence. "Such studies are not in conformity with sacred innocence; surely she will be lost; surely she will, by

4. Benefits or kindnesses.

cause of her very perspicacity and acuity, grow heady at such exalted heights." How was I to endure? An uncommon sort of martyrdom in which I was both martyr and executioner. And for my (in me, twice hapless) facility in making verses, even though they be sacred verses, what sorrows have I not suffered? What sorrows not ceased to suffer? Be assured, lady, it is often that I have meditated on how one who distinguishes himself—or one on whom God chooses to confer distinction, for it is only He who may do so—is received as a common enemy, because it seems to some that he usurps the applause they deserve, or that he dams up the admiration to which they aspired, and so they persecute that person.

That politically barbaric law of Athens by which any person who excelled by cause of his natural gifts and virtues was exiled from his Republic in order that he not threaten the public freedom still endures, is still observed in our day, although not for the reasons held by the Athenians. Those reasons have been replaced by another, no less efficient though not as well founded, seeming, rather, a maxim more appropriate to that impious Machiavelli[5]—which is to abhor one who excels, because he deprives others of regard. And thus it happens, and thus it has always happened.

For if not, what was the cause of the rage and loathing the Pharisees[6] directed against Christ, there being so many reasons to love Him? If we behold His presence, what is more to be loved than that Divine beauty? What more powerful to stir one's heart? For if ordinary human beauty holds sway over strength of will, and is able to subdue it with tender and enticing vehemence, what power would Divine beauty exert, with all its prerogatives and sovereign endowments? What might move, what effect, what not move and not effect, such incomprehensible beauty, that beauteous face through which, as through a polished crystal, were diffused the rays of Divinity? What would not be moved by that semblance which beyond incomparable human perfections revealed Divine illuminations? If the visage of Moses, merely from conversation with God, caused men to fear to come near him,[7] how much finer must be the face of God-made-flesh? And among other virtues, what more to be loved than that celestial modesty? That sweetness and kindness disseminating mercy in every movement? That profound humility and gentleness? Those words of eternal life and eternal wisdom? How therefore is it possible that such beauty did not stir their souls, that they did not follow after Him, enamored and enlightened?

The Holy Mother, my Mother Teresa,[8] says that when she beheld the beauty of Christ never again was she inclined toward any human creature, for she saw nothing that was not ugliness compared to such beauty. How was it then that in men it engendered such contrary reactions? For although they were uncouth and vile and had no knowledge or appreciation of His perfections, not even as they might profit from them, how was it they were not moved by the many advantages of such benefices as He performed for them, healing the sick, resurrecting the dead, restoring those possessed of the devil? How was it they did not love Him? But God is witness that it was

5. Niccolò Machiavelli (1469–1527), Italian statesman whose writings (notably *The Prince*) advocated political unscrupulousness.   6. The Pharisees, members of a strict Jewish sect that emphasized conformity to the law, were, according to the New Testament, prominent in plotting the death of Jesus (Mark 3.6, John 11.47–57).   7. Exodus 34.30.   8. St. Teresa of Ávila (1515–1582), a mystical writer, responsible for a great awakening of religious fervor.

for these very acts they did not love Him, that they despised Him. As they themselves testified.

They gather together in their council and say: *What do we? for this man doth many miracles.*[9] Can this be cause? If they had said: here is an evil-doer, a transgressor of the law, a rabble-rouser who with deceit stirs up the populace, they would have lied—as they did indeed lie when they spoke these things. But there were more apposite reasons for effecting what they desired, which was to take His life; and to give as reason that he had performed wondrous deeds seems not befitting learned men, for such were the Pharisees. Thus it is that in the heat of passion learned men erupt with such irrelevancies; for we know it as truth that only for this reason was it determined that Christ should die. Oh, men, if men you may be called, being so like to brutes, what is the cause of so cruel a determination? Their only response is that "this man doth many miracles." May God forgive them. Then is performing signal deeds cause enough that one should die? This "he doth many miracles" evokes *the root of Jesse, who standeth for an ensign of the people,*[1] and that *and for a sign which shall be contradicted.*[2] He is a sign? Then He shall die. He excels? Then He shall suffer, for that is the reward for one who excels.

Often on the crest of temples are placed as adornment figures of the winds and of fame, and to defend them from the birds, they are covered with iron barbs; this appears to be in defense, but is in truth obligatory propriety: the figure thus elevated cannot survive without the very barbs that prick it; there on high is found the animosity of the air, on high the ferocity of the elements, on high is unleashed the anger of the thunderbolt, on high stands the target for slings and arrows. Oh unhappy eminence, exposed to such uncounted perils. Oh sign, become the target of envy and the butt of contradiction. Whatever eminence, whether that of dignity, nobility, riches, beauty, or science, must suffer this burden; but the eminence that undergoes the most severe attack is that of reason. First, because it is the most defenseless, for riches and power strike out against those who dare attack them; but not so reason, for while it is the greater it is more modest and long-suffering, and defends itself less. Second, as Gracián[3] stated so eruditely, *favors in man's reason are favors in his nature.*

For no other cause except that the angel is superior in reason is the angel above man; for no other cause does man stand above the beast but by his reason; and thus, as no one wishes to be lower than another, neither does he confess that another is superior in reason, as reason is a consequence of being superior. One will abide, and will confess that another is nobler than he, that another is richer, more handsome, and even that he is more learned, but that another is richer in reason scarcely any will confess: *Rare is he who will concede genius.* That is why the assault against this virtue works to such profit.

When the soldiers mocked, made entertainment and diversion of our Lord Jesus Christ, they brought Him a worn purple garment and a hollow reed, and a crown of thorns to crown Him King of Fools.[4] But though the reed and the purple were an affront, they did not cause suffering. Why does only

9. John 11.47. 1. Isaiah 11.10. 2. Luke 2.34. 3. Baltasar Gracián (1601–1658), Spanish Jesuit philosopher. 4. Matthew 27.28–31.

the crown give pain? Is it not enough that like the other emblems the crown was a symbol of ridicule and ignominy, as that was its intent? No. Because the sacred head of Christ and His divine intellect were the depository of wisdom, and the world is not satisfied for wisdom to be the object of mere ridicule, it must also be done injury and harm. A head that is a storehouse of wisdom can expect nothing but a crown of thorns. What garland may human wisdom expect when it is known what was bestowed on that divine wisdom? Roman pride crowned the many achievements of their Captains with many crowns: he who defended the city received the civic crown; he who fought his way into the hostile camp received the camp crown; he who scaled the wall, the mural;[5] he who liberated a beseiged city, or any army besieged either in the field or in the enemy camp, received the obsidional, the siege, crown; other feats were crowned with naval, ovation, or triumphal crowns, as described by Pliny and Aulus Gellius.[6] Observing so many and varied crowns, I debated as to which Christ's crown must have been, and determined that it was the siege crown, for (as well you know, lady) that was the most honored crown and was called obsidional after *obsidio*, which means siege; which crown was made not from gold, or silver, but from the leaves and grasses flourishing on the field where the feat was achieved. And as the heroic feat of Christ was to break the siege of the Prince of Darkness, who had laid siege to all the earth, as is told in the Book of Job, quoting Satan: *I have gone round about the earth, and walked through it,*[7] and as St. Peter says: *As a roaring lion, goeth about seeking whom he may devour.*[8] And our Master came and caused him to lift the siege: *Now shall the prince of this world be cast out.*[9] So the soldiers crowned Him not with gold or silver but with the natural fruit of the world, which was the field of battle—and which, after the curse *Thorns also and thistles shall it bring forth to thee,*[1] produced only thorns—and thus it was a most fitting crown for the courageous and wise Conqueror, with which His mother Synagogue crowned Him. And the daughters of Zion, weeping, came out to witness the sorrowful triumph,[2] as they had come rejoicing for the triumph of Solomon,[3] because the triumph of the wise is earned with sorrow and celebrated with weeping, which is the manner of the triumph of wisdom; and as Christ is the King of wisdom, He was the first to wear that crown; and as it was sanctified on His brow, it removed all fear and dread from those who are wise, for they know they need aspire to no other honor.

The Living Word, Life, wished to restore life to Lazarus, who was dead. His disciples did not know His purpose and they said to Him: *Rabbi, the Jews but now sought to stone thee; and goest thou thither again?* And the Redeemer calmed their fear: *Are there not twelve hours of the day?*[4] It seems they feared because there had been those who wished to stone Him when He rebuked them, calling them thieves and not shepherds of sheep.[5] And thus the disciples feared that if He returned to the same place—for even though rebukes be just, they are often badly received—He would be risking his life. But once having been disabused and having realized that He was setting forth to raise

---

5. Pertaining to walls; the word *crown* is understood.   6. Latin writer (second century C.E.), author of *Noctes Atticae,* valuable for its quotations from lost works. Pliny the Younger (62?–ca. 113) was a Roman orator and statesman, and author of well-known letters about Roman life.   7. Job 1.7.   8. 1 Peter 5.8.   9. John 12.31.   1. The curse on Adam and Eve after the Fall (Genesis 3.18).   2. Luke 23.27–28.   3. Song of Solomon 3.11.   4. John 11.8–9.   5. John 10.1–31.

up Lazarus from the dead, what was it that caused Thomas, like Peter in the Garden, to say *Let us also go, that we may die with him*?[6] What say you, Sainted Apostle? The Lord does not go out to die; whence your misgiving? For Christ goes not to rebuke, but to work an act of mercy, and therefore they will do Him no harm. These same Jews could have assured you, for when He reproved those who wished to stone Him, *Many good works I have shewed you from my Father; for which of those works do you stone me?* they replied: *For a good work we stone thee not; but for blasphemy.*[7] And as they say they will not stone Him for doing good works, and now He goes to do a work so great as to raise up Lazarus from the dead, whence your misgiving? Why do you fear? Were it not better to say: let us go to gather the fruits of appreciation for the good work our Master is about to do; to see him lauded and applauded for His benefice; to see men marvel at His miracle. Why speak words seemingly so alien to the circumstance as *Let us also go*? Ah, woe, the Saint feared as a prudent man and spoke as an Apostle. Does Christ not go to work a miracle? Why, what *greater* peril? It is less to be suffered that pride endure rebukes than envy witness miracles. In all the above, most honored lady, I do not wish to say (nor is such folly to be found in me) that I have been persecuted for my wisdom, but merely for my love of wisdom and letters, having achieved neither one nor the other.

At one time even the Prince of the Apostles was very far from wisdom, as is emphasized in that *But Peter followed afar off*.[8] Very distant from the laurels of a learned man is one so little in his judgment that he was *Not knowing what he said*.[9] And being questioned on his mastery of wisdom, he himself was witness that he had not achieved the first measure: *But he denied him, saying: Woman, I know him not.*[1] And what becomes of him? We find that having this reputation of ignorance, he did not enjoy its good fortune, but, rather, the affliction of being taken for wise. And why? There was no other motive but: *This man also was with him*[2] He was fond of wisdom, it filled His heart, He followed after it, He prided himself as a pursuer and lover of wisdom; and although He followed from so *afar off* that He neither understood nor achieved it, His love for it was sufficient that He incur its torments. And there was present that soldier to cause Him distress, and a certain maidservant to cause Him grief. I confess that I find myself very distant from the goals of wisdom, for all that I have desired to follow it, even from *afar off*. But in this I have been brought closer to the fire of persecution, to the crucible of torment, and to such lengths that they have asked that study be forbidden to me.

At one time this was achieved through the offices of a very saintly and ingenuous Abbess who believed that study was a thing of the Inquisition, who commanded me not to study. I obeyed her (the three some[3] months her power to command endured) in that I did not take up a book; but that I study not at all is not within my power to achieve, and this I could not obey, for though I did not study in books, I studied all the things that God had wrought, reading in them, as in writing and in books, all the workings of the universe. I looked on nothing without reflection; I heard nothing without meditation, even in the most minute and imperfect things; because as there

---

6. John 11.16.   **7.** John 10.32–33.   **8.** Luke 22.54.   **9.** Refers to Peter (Luke 9.33).   **1.** Luke 22.57.   **2.** A serving maid says this of Peter, who thereupon denies knowing Jesus (Luke 22.56). **3.** I.e., "the three or so."

is no creature, however lowly, in which one cannot recognize that *God made me,* there is none that does not astound reason, if properly meditated on. Thus, I reiterate, I saw and admired all things; so that even the very persons with whom I spoke, and the things they said, were cause for a thousand meditations. Whence the variety of genius and wit, being all of a single species? Which the temperaments and hidden qualities that occasioned such variety? If I saw a figure, I was forever combining the proportion of its lines and measuring it with my reason and reducing it to new proportions. Occasionally as I walked along the far wall of one of our dormitories (which is a most capacious room) I observed that though the lines of the two sides were parallel and the ceiling perfectly level, in my sight they were distorted, the lines seeming to incline toward one another, the ceiling seeming lower in the distance than in proximity: from which I inferred that *visual* lines run straight but not parallel, forming a pyramidal figure. I pondered whether this might not be the reason that caused the ancients to question whether the world were spherical. Because, although it so seems, this could be a deception of vision, suggesting concavities where possibly none existed.

This manner of reflection has always been my habit, and is quite beyond my will to control; on the contrary, I am wont to become vexed that my intellect makes me weary; and I believed that it was so with everyone, as well as making verses, until experience taught me otherwise; and it is so strong in me this nature, or custom, that I look at nothing without giving it further examination. Once in my presence two young girls were spinning a top and scarcely had I seen the motion and the figure described, when I began, out of this madness of mine, to meditate on the effortless *motus*[4] of the spherical form, and how the impulse persisted even when free and independent of its cause—for the top continued to dance even at some distance from the child's hand, which was the causal force. And not content with this, I had flour brought and sprinkled about, so that as the top danced one might learn whether these were perfect circles it described with its movement; and I found that they were not, but, rather, spiral lines that lost their circularity as the impetus declined. Other girls sat playing at spillikins[5] (surely the most frivolous game that children play); I walked closer to observe the figures they formed, and seeing that by chance three lay in a triangle, I set to joining one with another, recalling that this was said to be the form of the mysterious ring of Solomon,[6] in which he was able to see the distant splendor and images of the Holy Trinity, by virtue of which the ring worked such prodigies and marvels. And the same shape was said to form David's harp, and that is why Saul was refreshed at its sound; and harps today largely conserve that shape.

And what shall I tell you, lady, of the natural secrets I have discovered while cooking? I see that an egg holds together and fries in butter or in oil, but, on the contrary, in syrup shrivels into shreds; observe that to keep sugar in a liquid state one need only add a drop or two of water in which a quince or other bitter fruit has been soaked; observe that the yolk and the white of one egg are so dissimilar that each with sugar produces a result not obtainable with both together. I do not wish to weary you with such inconsequential matters, and make mention of them only to give you full notice of my nature,

4. Motion. 5. Jackstraws, or pickup sticks. 6. It may, like Solomon's seal, have contained the image of the Star of David, composed of triangles.

for I believe they will be occasion for laughter. But, lady, as women, what wisdom may be ours if not the philosophies of the kitchen? Lupercio Leonardo[7] spoke well when he said: how well one may philosophize when preparing dinner. And I often say, when observing these trivial details: had Aristotle prepared victuals, he would have written more. And pursuing the manner of my cogitations, I tell you that this process is so continuous in me that I have no need for books. And on one occasion, when because of a grave upset of the stomach the physicians forbade me to study, I passed thus some days, but then I proposed that it would be less harmful if they allowed me books, because so vigorous and vehement were my cogitations that my spirit was consumed more greatly in a quarter of an hour than in four days' studying books. And thus they were persuaded to allow me to read. And moreover, lady, not even have my dreams been excluded from this ceaseless agitation of my imagination; indeed, in dreams it is wont to work more freely and less encumbered, collating with greater clarity and calm the gleanings of the day, arguing and making verses, of which I could offer you an extended catalogue, as well as of some arguments and inventions that I have better achieved sleeping than awake. I relinquish this subject in order not to tire you, for the above is sufficient to allow your discretion and acuity to penetrate perfectly and perceive my nature, as well as the beginnings, the methods, and the present state of my studies.

Even, lady, were these merits (and I see them celebrated as such in men), they would not have been so in me, for I cannot but study. If they are faults, then, for the same reasons, I believe I have none. Nevertheless, I live always with so little confidence in myself that neither in my study, nor in any other thing, do I trust my judgment; and thus I remit the decision to your sovereign genius, submitting myself to whatever sentence you may bestow, without controversy, without reluctance, for I have wished here only to present you with a simple narration of my inclination toward letters.

I confess, too, that though it is true, as I have stated, that I had no need of books, it is nonetheless also true that they have been no little inspiration, in divine as in human letters. Because I find a Debbora[8] administering the law, both military and political, and governing a people among whom there were many learned men. I find a most wise Queen of Saba,[9] so learned that she dares to challenge with hard questions the wisdom of the greatest of all wise men, without being reprimanded for doing so, but, rather, as a consequence, to judge unbelievers. I see many and illustrious women; some blessed with the gift of prophecy, like Abigail, others of persuasion, like Esther; others with pity, like Rehab; others with perseverance, like Anna,[1] the mother of Samuel; and an infinite number of others, with divers gifts and virtues.

If I again turn to the Gentiles, the first I encounter are the Sibyls,[2] those women chosen by God to prophesy the principal mysteries of our Faith, and

---

7. Lupercio Leonardo de Argensola (1559–1613), poet, playwright, and historian.   8. Or Deborah, a prophetess who judged the Israelites (Judges 4.4–14).   9. Or Sheba, who tested King Solomon with questions (1 Kings 10.1–3).   1. Or Hannah, who after years of childlessness received the answer to her prayers in the birth of Samuel (1 Samuel 1.1–20). Abigail was the wife of a surly husband, Nabal. After Nabal insulted King David, she went to the king with presents and prophesied his future triumphs, thus saving her husband's life (1 Samuel 25.2–35). Esther persuaded her husband, King Ahasuerus, to protect the Jews (Esther 5–9). Rehab, or Rahab, was a harlot who protected two Israelites from the king of Jericho (Joshua 2.1–7).   2. Female prophets of the ancient world.

with learned and elegant verses that surpass admiration. I see adored as a goddess of the sciences a woman like Minerva,[3] the daughter of the first Jupiter and mistress over all the wisdom of Athens. I see a Polla Argentaria, who helped Lucan, her husband, write his epic *Pharsalia*.[4] I see the daughter of the divine Tiresias, more learned than her father. I see a Zenobia, Queen of the Palmyrans, as wise as she was valiant. An Arete, most learned daughter of Aristippus.[5] A Nicostrate,[6] framer of Latin verses and most erudite in Greek. An Aspasia Milesia, who taught philosophy and rhetoric, and who was a teacher of the philosopher Pericles. An Hypatia, who taught astrology, and studied many years in Alexandria. A Leontium, a Greek woman, who questioned the philosopher Theophrastus, and convinced him. A Julia, a Corinna, a Cornelia;[7] and, finally, a great throng of women deserving to be named, some as Greeks, some as muses, some as seers; for all were nothing more than learned women, held, and celebrated—and venerated as well—as such by antiquity. Without mentioning an infinity of other women whose names fill books. For example, I find the Egyptian Catherine,[8] studying and influencing the wisdom of all the wise men of Egypt. I see a Gertrudis[9] studying, writing, and teaching. And not to overlook examples close to home, I see my most holy mother Paula, learned in Hebrew, Greek, and Latin, and most able in interpreting the Scriptures. And what greater praise than, having as her chronicler a Jeronimus Maximus,[1] that Saint scarcely found himself competent for his task, and says, with that weighty deliberation and energetic precision with which he so well expressed himself: "If all the members of my body were tongues, they still would not be sufficient to proclaim the wisdom and virtue of Paula." Similarly praiseworthy was the widow Blesilla; also, the illustrious virgin Eustochium,[2] both daughters of this same saint; especially the second, who, for her knowledge, was called the Prodigy of the World. The Roman Fabiola[3] was most well-versed in the Holy Scripture. Proba Falconia, a Roman woman, wrote elegant centos,[4] containing verses from Virgil, about the mysteries of Our Holy Faith. It is well-known by all that Queen Isabel,[5] wife of the tenth Alfonso, wrote about astrology. Many others I do not list, out of the desire not merely to transcribe what others have said (a vice I have always abominated); and many are flourishing today, as witness Christina Alexandra, Queen of Sweden,[6] as learned as she is valiant and magnanimous, and the Most Honorable Ladies, the Duquesa of Abeyro and the Condesa of Villaumbrosa.

The venerable Doctor Arce[7] (by his virtue and learning a worthy teacher of the Scriptures) in his scholarly *Bibliorum* raises this question: *Is it per-*

---

3. Or Athena, goddess of wisdom.   4. Epic poem on the civil war between Caesar and Pompey, properly called *Bellum Civile* (ca. 62–65 C.E.).   5. Greek philosopher (ca. 435–ca. 360 B.C.E.). Tiresias was a legendary blind Theban seer. His daughter was Manto, known for her skill in divination by fire. Zenobia, the learned widow of Odenathus, declared her independence from Rome and expanded the Middle Eastern territory under her rule, naming herself Augusta, empress of Rome. She was finally defeated and captured in 272 B.C.E.   6. Or Carmentis, legendary daughter of Pallas, king of Arcadia, and (in legend) inventor of the Roman alphabet.   7. Noted for her devotion to her children's education after her husband's death (2nd century B.C.E.); she was the second daughter of Scipio Africanus and wife of Tiberius Sempronius Gracchus. Julia Domna (2nd century C.E.), wife of the Roman emperor Septimius Severus, known for her learning as Julia the Philosopher. Corinna (ca. 500? B.C.E.), a lyric poet of Tanagra who wrote for a group of women.   8. St. Catherine of Alexandria (4th century?), allegedly so wise she could refute fifty philosophers at once.   9. St. Gertrude (d. 1302), Benedictine nun and visionary, an important mystic.   1. St. Jerome.   2. Blesilla and Eustochium were daughters of St. Paula and, like her, were taught by St. Jerome.   3. One of Jerome's disciples.   4. Compositions made up of verses from other authors.   5. Of Spain, wife of Alfonso X, Alfonso the Wise (1221–1284).   6. She attracted many scholars and artists to her court (1626–1689).   7. Juan Díaz de Arce (1594–1653), author of theological books.

missible for women to dedicate themselves to the study of the Holy Scriptures, and to their interpretation? and he offers as negative arguments the opinions of many saints, especially that of the Apostle: *Let women keep silence in the churches; for it is not permitted them to speak,* etc.[8] He later cites other opinions and, from the same Apostle, verses from his letter to Titus: *The aged women in like manner, in holy attire . . . teaching well,*[9] with interpretations by the Holy Fathers. Finally he resolves, with all prudence, that teaching publicly from a University chair, or preaching from the pulpit, is not permissible for women; but that to study, write, and teach privately not only is permissible, but most advantageous and useful. It is evident that this is not to be the case with all women, but with those to whom God may have granted special virtue and prudence, and who may be well advanced in learning, and having the essential talent and requisites for such a sacred calling. This view is indeed just, so much so that not only women, who are held to be so inept, but also men, who merely for being men believe they are wise, should be prohibited from interpreting the Sacred Word if they are not learned and virtuous and of gentle and well-inclined natures; that this is not so has been, I believe, at the root of so much sectarianism and so many heresies. For there are many who study but are ignorant, especially those who are in spirit arrogant, troubled, and proud, so eager for new interpretations of the Word (which itself rejects new interpretations) that merely for the sake of saying what no one else has said they speak a heresy, and even then are not content. Of these the Holy Spirit says: *For wisdom will not enter into a malicious soul.*[1] To such as these more harm results from knowing than from ignorance. A wise man has said: he who does not know Latin is not a complete fool; but he who knows it is well qualified to be.[2] And I would add that a fool may reach perfection (if ignorance may tolerate perfection) by having studied his tittle of philosophy and theology and by having some learning of tongues, by which he may be a fool in many sciences and languages: a great fool cannot be contained solely in his mother tongue.

For such as these, I reiterate, study is harmful, because it is as if to place a sword in the hands of a madman; which, though a most noble instrument for defense, is in his hands his own death and that of many others. So were the Divine Scriptures in the possession of the evil Pelagius and the intractable Arius, of the evil Luther, and the other heresiarchs like our own Doctor (who was neither ours nor a doctor) Cazalla.[3] To these men, wisdom was harmful, although it is the greatest nourishment and the life of the soul; in the same way that in a stomach of sickly constitution and adulterated complexion, the finer the nourishment it receives, the more arid, fermented, and perverse are the humors it produces; thus these evil men: the more they study, the worse opinions they engender, their reason being obstructed with the very substance meant to nourish it, and they study much and digest little, exceeding the limits of the vessel of their reason. Of which the Apostle says: *For I say, by the grace that is given me, to all that are among you, not to be*

8. 1 Corinthians 14.34.   9. Titus 2.3–5.   1. Book of Wisdom 1.4 (in the Apocrypha).   2. Alludes to the Spanish proverb "A fool, unless he knows Latin, is never a great fool."   3. Augustino Cazallo (1510–1559), Spanish Protestant executed by the Inquisition for promulgating Lutheran doctrine. Pelagius was a heretical monk (ca. 355–ca. 425) who taught that people do not need divine grace since they have a natural tendency to seek the good. Arius was a Libyan theologian (ca. 256–336), founder of the Arian heresy that declared that Christ was neither eternal nor equal with God. Martin Luther (1483–1546) was the German leader of the Protestant Reformation and, from Sister Juana's point of view, another heretic.

more wise than it behoveth to be wise, but to be wise unto sobriety, and according as God hath divided to every one the measure of faith.[4] And in truth, the Apostle did not direct these words to women, but to men; and that *keep silence* is intended not only for women, but for *all* incompetents. If I desire to know as much, or more, than Aristotle or Saint Augustine, and if I have not the aptitude of Saint Augustine or Aristotle, though I study more than either, not only will I not achieve learning, but I will weaken and dull the workings of my feeble reason with the disproportionateness of the goal.

Oh, that each of us—I, being ignorant, the first—should take the measure of our talents before we study, or, more importantly, write, with the covetous ambition to equal and even surpass others, how little spirit we should have for it, and how many errors we should avoid, and how many tortured intellects of which we have experience, we should have had no experience! And I place my own ignorance in the forefront of all these, for if I knew all I should, I would not write. And I protest that I do so only to obey you; and with such apprehension that you owe me more that I have taken up my pen in fear than you would have owed had I presented you more perfect works. But it is well that they go to your correction. Cross them out, tear them up, reprove me, and I shall appreciate that more than all the vain applause others may offer. *That just men shall correct me in mercy, and shall reprove me; but let not the oil of the sinner fatten my head.*[5] And returning again to our Arce, I say that in affirmation of his opinion he cites the words of my father, Saint Jerome: *To Leta, Upon the Education of Her Daughter.* Where he says: *Accustom her tongue, still young, to the sweetness of the Psalms. Even the names through which little by little she will become accustomed to form her phrases should not be chosen by chance, but selected and repeated with care; the prophets must be included, of course, and the apostles, as well, and all the Patriarchs beginning with Adam and down to Matthew and Luke, so that as she practices other things she will be readying her memory for the future. Let your daily task be taken from the flower of the Scriptures.* And if this Saint desired that a young girl scarcely beginning to talk be educated in this fashion, what would he desire for his nuns and his spiritual daughters? These beliefs are illustrated in the examples of the previously mentioned Eustochium and Fabiola, and Marcella, her sister, and Pacatula, and others whom the Saint honors in his epistles, exhorting them to this sacred exercise, as they are recognized in the epistle I cited, *Let your daily task . . .* which is affirmation of and agreement with the *aged women . . . teaching well* of Saint Paul. My illustrious Father's *Let your daily task . . .* makes clear that the teacher of the child is to be Leta herself, the child's mother.

Oh, how much injury might have been avoided in our land if our aged women had been learned, as was Leta, and had they known how to instruct as directed by Saint Paul and by my Father, Saint Jerome. And failing this, and because of the considerable idleness to which our poor women have been relegated, if a father desires to provide his daughters with more than ordinary learning, he is forced by necessity, and by the absence of wise elder women, to bring men to teach the skills of reading, writing, counting, the playing of musical instruments, and other accomplishments, from which no little harm results, as is experienced every day in doleful examples of perilous

4. Romans 12.3.   5. Psalms 141.5.

association, because through the immediacy of contact and the intimacy born from the passage of time, what one may never have thought possible is easily accomplished. For which reason many prefer to leave their daughters unpolished and uncultured rather than to expose them to such notorious peril as that of familiarity with men, which quandary could be prevented if there were learned elder women, as Saint Paul wished to see, and if the teaching were handed down from one to another, as is the custom with domestic crafts and all other traditional skills.

For what objection can there be that an older woman, learned in letters and in sacred conversation and customs, have in her charge the education of young girls? This would prevent these girls being lost either for lack of instruction or for hesitating to offer instruction through such dangerous means as male teachers, for even when there is no greater risk of indecency than to seat beside a modest woman (who still may blush when her own father looks directly at her) a strange man who treats her as if he were a member of the household and with the authority of an intimate, the modesty demanded in interchange with men, and in conversation with them, is sufficient reason that such an arrangement not be permitted. For I do not find that the custom of men teaching women is without its peril, lest it be in the severe tribunal of the confessional, or from the remote decency of the pulpit, or in the distant learning of books—never in the personal contact of immediacy. And the world knows this is true; and, notwithstanding, it is permitted solely from the want of learned elder women. Then is it not detrimental, the lack of such women? This question should be addressed by those who, bound to that *Let women keep silence in the church,* say that it is blasphemy for women to learn and teach, as if it were not the Apostle himself who said: *The aged women . . . teaching well.* As well as the fact that this prohibition touches upon historical fact as reported by Eusebium:[6] which is that in the early Church, women were charged with teaching the doctrine to one another in the temples and the sound of this teaching caused confusion as the Apostles were preaching and this is the reason they were ordered to be silent; and even today, while the homilist is preaching, one does not pray aloud.

Who will argue that for the comprehension of many Scriptures one must be familiar with the history, customs, ceremonies, proverbs, and even the manners of speaking of those times in which they were written, if one is to apprehend the references and allusions of more than a few passages of the Holy Word. *And rend your heart and not your garments.*[7] Is this not a reference to the ceremony in which Hebrews rent their garments as a sign of grief, as did the evil pontiff when he said that Christ had blasphemed? In many scriptures the Apostle writes of succour for widows; did they not refer to the customs of those times? Does not the example of the valiant woman, *Her husband is honourable in the gates,*[8] allude to the fact that the tribunals of the judges were at the gates of the cities? That *Dare terram Deo,* give of your land to God, did that not mean to make some votive offering? And did they not call the public sinners *hiemantes,* those who endure the winter, because they made their penance in the open air instead of at a town gate

6. Probably Eusebius of Caesarea (ca. 263–339?), an early Church historian. 7. Joel 2.13. 8. Proverbs 31.23.

as others did? And Christ's plaint to that Pharisee who had neither kissed him nor given him water for his feet,[9] was that not because it was the Jews' usual custom to offer these acts of hospitality? And we find an infinite number of additional instances not only in the Divine Letters, but human, as well, such as *adorate purpuram,* venerate the purple, which meant obey the King; *manumittere eum,* manumit them, alluding to the custom and ceremony of striking the slave with one's hand to signify his freedom. That *intonuit coelum,* heaven thundered, in Virgil, which alludes to the augury of thunder from the west, which was held to be good.[1] Martial's *tu nunquam leporem edisti,*[2] you never ate hare, has not only the wit of ambiguity in its *leporem,*[3] but, as well, the allusion to the reputed propensity of hares [to bless with beauty those who dine on them]. That proverb, *maleam legens, que sunt domi obliviscere,* to sail along the shore of Malia is to forget what one has at home, alludes to the great peril of the promontory of Laconia.[4] That chaste matron's response to the unwanted suit of her pretender: "the hinge-pins shall not be oiled for my sake, nor shall the torches blaze," meaning that she did not want to marry, alluded to the ceremony of anointing the doorways with oils and lighting the nuptial torches in the wedding ceremony, as if now we would say, they shall not prepare the thirteen coins for my dowry, nor shall the priest invoke the blessing. And thus it is with many comments of Virgil and Homer and all the poets and orators. In addition, how many are the difficulties found even in the grammar of the Holy Scripture, such as writing a plural for a singular, or changing from the second to third persons, as in the Psalms, *Let him kiss me with the kiss of his mouth, for thy breasts are better than wine.*[5] Or placing adjectives in the genitive instead of the accusative, as in *Calicem salutaris accipiam,* I will take the chalice of salvation.[6] Or to replace the feminine with the masculine, and, in contrast, to call any sin adultery.

All this demands more investigation than some believe, who strictly as grammarians, or, at most, employing the four principles of applied logic, attempt to interpret the Scriptures while clinging to that *Let the women keep silence in the church,* not knowing how it is to be interpreted. As well as that other verse, *Let the women learn in silence.*[7] For this latter scripture works more to women's favor than their disfavor, as it commands them to learn; and it is only natural that they must maintain silence while they learn. And it is also written, *Hear, oh Israel, and be silent.*[8] Which addresses the entire congregation of men and women, commanding all to silence, because if one is to hear and learn, it is with good reason that he attend and be silent. And if it is not so, I would want these interpreters and expositors of Saint Paul to explain to me how they interpret that scripture, *Let the women keep silence in the church.* For either they must understand it to refer to the material church, that is the church of pulpits and cathedras,[9] or to the spiritual, the community of the faithful, which is the Church. If they understand it to be the former, which, in my opinion, is its true interpretation, then we see that if in fact it is not permitted of women to read publicly in church, nor preach,

9. Luke 7.44–45.   1. Sister Juana possibly misremembers *Aeneid* 2.693: "thunder on the left." 2. Marcus Valerius Martialis (ca. 40–ca. 104), Roman epigrammatic poet; "Edisti numquam, Gellia, tu leporem" (*Epigrams* 5.29).   3. This word can also mean charm, grace, attractiveness.   4. The site of ancient Sparta, conquered by Macedonia in the 4th century B.C.E.   5. Song of Solomon 1.2. 6. Psalms 116.13.   7. 1 Timothy 2.11.   8. Not a biblical quotation.   9. The cathedra is the throne of the bishop in his church.

why do they censure those who study privately? And if they understand the latter, and wish that the prohibition of the Apostle be applied transcendentally—that not even in private are women to be permitted to write or study—how are we to view the fact that the Church permitted a Gertrudis, a Santa Teresa, a Saint Birgitta, the Nun of Agreda,[1] and so many others, to write? And if they say to me that these women were saints, they speak the truth; but this poses no obstacle to my argument. First, because Saint Paul's proposition is absolute, and encompasses all women not excepting saints, as Martha and Mary, Marcella, Mary, mother of Jacob, and Salome,[2] all were in their time, and many other zealous women of the early church. But we see, too, that the Church allows women who are not saints to write, for the Nun of Agreda and Sor María de la Antigua[3] are not canonized, yet their writings are circulated. And when Santa Teresa and the others were writing, they were not as yet canonized. In which case, Saint Paul's prohibition was directed solely to the public office of the pulpit, for if the Apostle had forbidden women to write, the Church would not have allowed it. Now I do not make so bold as to teach—which in me would be excessively presumptuous—and as for writing, that requires a greater talent than mine, and serious reflection. As Saint Cyprian[4] says: *The things we write require most conscientious consideration.* I have desired to study that I might be ignorant of less; for (according to Saint Augustine[5]) some things are learned to be enacted and others only to be known: *We learn some things to know them, others, to do them.* Then, where is the offense to be found if even what is licit to women—which is to teach by writing—I do not perform, as I know that I am lacking in means, following the counsel of Quintilian: *Let each person learn not only from the precepts of others, but also let him reap counsel from his own nature.*

If the offense is to be found in the *Atenagórica* letter, was that letter anything other than the simple expression of my feeling, written with the implicit permission of our Holy Mother Church? For if the Church, in her most sacred authority, does not forbid it, why must others do so? That I proffered an opinion contrary to that of de Vieyra was audacious, but, as a Father, was it not audacious that he speak against the three Holy Fathers of the Church? My reason, such as it is, is it not as unfettered as his, as both issue from the same source? Is his opinion to be considered as a revelation, as a principle of the Holy Faith, that we must accept blindly? Furthermore, I maintained at all times the respect due such a virtuous man, a respect in which his defender was sadly wanting, ignoring the phrase of Titus Lucius:[6] *Respect is companion to the arts.* I did not touch a thread of the robes of the Society of Jesus; nor did I write for other than the consideration of the person who suggested that I write. And, according to Pliny, *how different the condition of one who writes from that of one who merely speaks.* Had I believed the letter

---

1. Maria de Agreda (1602–1665), Spanish Franciscan nun, author of *The Mystical City of God* (1670), a work allegedly divinely inspired. Birgitta, or Bridget (1303–1373), of Sweden. 2. In the King James Bible, Mary, the mother of James (or Jacob), and Salome came to the empty sepulcher to anoint Jesus' body (Mark 16.1). Martha and Mary were sisters. Mary anointed Jesus' feet (John 12.3). Martha was preoccupied with household tasks (Luke 10.40–42). Marcella was one of the women taught by Jerome. 3. Spanish nun (1544–1617). 4. Thaschus Caecilius Cyprianus (ca. 200–258), one of the Church Fathers, known for his efforts to enforce Church discipline. 5. Aurelius Augustinus (354–430), baptized by St. Ambrose in 387, author of *De Civitate Dei*, a vindication of the Church that long possessed great authority. 6. Better known as Saturantius Apuleius, greatly celebrated in his time (2nd century C.E.) for eloquence.

was to be published I would not have been so inattentive. If, as the censor says, the letter is heretical, why does he not denounce it? And with that he would be avenged, and I content, for, which is only seemly, I esteem more highly my reputation as a Catholic and obedient daughter of the Holy Mother Church than all the approbation due a learned woman. If the letter is rash, and he does well to criticize it, then laugh, even if with the laugh of the rabbit, for I have not asked that he approve; as I was free to dissent from de Vieyra, so will anyone be free to oppose my opinion.

But how I have strayed, lady. None of this pertains here, nor is it intended for your ears, but as I was discussing my accusers I remembered the words of one that recently have appeared, and, though my intent was to speak in general, my pen, unbidden, slipped, and began to respond in particular. And so, returning to our Arce, he says that he knew in this city two nuns: one in the Convent of the Regina, who had so thoroughly committed the Breviary to memory that with the greatest promptitude and propriety she applied in her conversation its verses, psalms, and maxims of saintly homilies. The other, in the Convent of the Conception, was so accustomed to reading the Epistles of my Father Saint Jerome, and the Locutions of this Saint, that Arce says, *It seemed I was listening to Saint Jerome himself, speaking in Spanish*. And of this latter woman he says that after her death he learned that she had translated these Epistles into the Spanish language. What pity that such talents could not have been employed in major studies with scientific principles. He does not give the name of either, although he offers these women as confirmation of his opinion, which is that not only is it licit, but most useful and essential for women to study the Holy Word, and even more essential for nuns; and that study is the very thing to which your wisdom exhorts me, and in which so many arguments concur.

Then if I turn my eyes to the oft-chastized faculty of making verses—which is in me so natural that I must discipline myself that even this letter not be written in that form—I might cite those lines, *All I wished to express took the form of verse*.[7] And seeing that so many condemn and criticize this ability, I have conscientiously sought to find what harm may be in it, and I have not found it, but, rather, I see verse acclaimed in the mouths of the Sibyls; sanctified in the pens of the Prophets, especially King David, of whom the exalted Expositor my beloved Father[8] says (explicating the measure of his meters): *in the manner of Horace and Pindar, now it hurries along in iambs, now it rings in alcaic, now swells in sapphic, then arrives in broken feet*. The greater part of the Holy Books are in meter, as is the Book of Moses; and those of Job (as Saint Isidore[9] states in his *Etymologiae*) are in heroic verse. Solomon wrote the Canticle of Canticles in verse; and Jeremias, his *Lamentations*. And so, says Cassiodorus:[1] *All poetic expression had as its source the Holy Scriptures*. For not only does our Catholic Church not disdain verse, it employs verse in its hymns, and recites the lines of Saint Ambrose,[2] Saint Thomas, Saint Isidore, and others. Saint Bonaventure[3] was so taken with verse that he writes scarcely a page where it does not appear. It is readily apparent that Saint Paul had studied verse, for he quotes and translates

7. Ovid's *Tristia* 4.10.25 ff.   8. Jerome.   9. Spanish archbishop (ca. 560–636), who helped organize the Church in Spain.   1. Flavius Magnus Aurelius Cassiodorus (ca. 485–ca. 580), Roman monk and author of *Institutiones*, a course of studies for monks.   2. Bishop of Milan (339–397), who had an important share in the conversion of St. Augustine.   3. Franciscan bishop and cardinal (1221–1274), who preached the importance of study.

verses of Aratus: *For in him we live, and move, and are.*[4] And he quotes also that verse of Parmenides: *The Cretians are always liars, evil beasts, slothful bellies.*[5] Saint Gregory Nazianzen[6] argues in elegant verses the questions of matrimony and virginity. And, how should I tire? The Queen of Wisdom, Our Lady, with Her sacred lips, intoned the Canticle of the Magnificat;[7] and having brought forth this example, it would be offensive to add others that were profane, even those of the most serious and learned men, for this alone is more than sufficient confirmation; and even though Hebrew elegance could not be compressed into Latin measure, for which reason, although the sacred translator, more attentive to the importance of the meaning, omitted the verse, the Psalms retain the number and divisions of verses, and what harm is to be found in them? For misuse is not the blame of art, but rather of the evil teacher who perverts the arts, making of them the snare of the devil; and this occurs in all the arts and sciences.

And if the evil is attributed to the fact that a woman employs them, we have seen how many have done so in praiseworthy fashion; what then is the evil in my being a woman? I confess openly my own baseness and meanness; but I judge that no couplet of mine has been deemed indecent. Furthermore, I have never written of my own will, but under the pleas and injunctions of others; to such a degree that the only piece I remember having written for my own pleasure was a little trifle they called *El sueño*.[8] That letter, lady, which you so greatly honored, I wrote more with repugnance than any other emotion; both by reason of the fact that it treated sacred matters, for which (as I have stated) I hold such reverent awe, and because it seems to wish to impugn, a practice for which I have natural aversion; and I believe that had I foreseen the blessed destiny to which it was fated—for like a second Moses I had set it adrift, naked, on the waters of the Nile of silence, where you, a princess, found and cherished it[9]—I believe, I reiterate, that had I known, the very hands of which it was born would have drowned it, out of the fear that these clumsy scribblings from my ignorance appear before the light of your great wisdom; by which one knows the munificence of your kindness, for your goodwill applauds precisely what your reason must wish to reject. For as fate cast it before your doors, so exposed, so orphaned, that it fell to you even to give it a name, I must lament that among other deformities it also bears the blemish of haste; both because of the unrelenting ill-health I suffer, and for the profusion of duties imposed on me by obedience, as well as the want of anyone to guide me in my writing and the need that it all come from my hand, and, finally, because the writing went against my nature and I wished only to keep my promise to one whom I could not disobey, I could not find the time to finish properly, and thus I failed to include whole treatises and many arguments that presented themselves to me, but which I omitted in order to put an end to the writing—many, that had I known the letter was to be printed, I would not have excluded, even if merely to satisfy some objections that have since arisen and which could have been refuted. But I shall not be so ill-mannered as to place such indecent objects before

4. Acts 17.28.   5. Titus 1.12.   6. Gregorius Nazianzenus, bishop of Constantinople and associate of Jerome. The allusion is to the first of his forty moral poems, 732 lines eulogizing virginity.   7. Luke 1.46–55.   8. *The Dream*, one of Sister Juana's best-known poems, which tells of the flight of her soul toward learning.   9. Because Pharaoh had ordered all male Hebrew infants killed, Moses' mother placed him in a basket by the Nile, where he was found and rescued by Pharaoh's daughter (Exodus 2.1–10).

the purity of your eyes, for it is enough that my ignorance be an offense in your sight, without need of entrusting to it the effronteries of others. If they should wing your way (and they are of such little weight that this will happen), then you will command what I am to do; for, if it does not run contrary to your will, my defense shall be not to take up my pen, for I deem that one affront need not occasion another, if one recognizes the error in the very place it lies concealed. As my Father Saint Jerome says, *good discourse seeks not things*, and Saint Ambrose, *it is the nature of a guilty conscience to lie concealed.* Nor do I consider that I have been impugned, for one statute of the Law states: *An accusation will not endure unless nurtured by the person who brought it forth.* What *is* a matter to be weighed is the effort spent in copying the accusation. A strange madness, to expend more effort in denying acclaim than in earning it! I, lady, have chosen not to respond (although others did so without my knowledge); it suffices that I have seen certain treatises, among them one so learned I send it to you so that reading it will compensate in part for the time you squandered on my writing. If, lady, you wish that I act contrary to what I have proposed here for your judgment and opinion, the merest indication of your desire will, as is seemly, countermand my inclination, which, as I have told you, is to be silent, for although Saint John Chrysostom[1] says, *those who slander must be refuted, and those who question, taught,* I know also that Saint Gregory[2] says, *It is no less a victory to tolerate enemies than to overcome them.* And that patience conquers by tolerating and triumphs by suffering. And if among the Roman Gentiles it was the custom when their captains were at the highest peak of glory—when returning triumphant from other nations, robed in purple and wreathed with laurel, crowned-but-conquered kings pulling their carriages in the stead of beasts, accompanied by the spoils of the riches of all the world, the conquering troops adorned with the insignia of their heroic feats, hearing the plaudits of the people who showered them with titles of honor and renown such as Fathers of the Nation, Columns of the Empire, Walls of Rome, Shelter of the Republic, and other glorious names—a soldier went before these captains in this moment of the supreme apogee of glory and human happiness crying out in a loud voice to the conqueror (by his consent and order of the Senate): Behold how you are mortal; behold how you have this or that defect, not excepting the most shameful, as happened in the triumph of Caesar, when the vilest soldiers clamored in his ear: *Beware, Romans, for we bring you the bald adulterer.* Which was done so that in the midst of such honor the conquerers not be swelled up with pride, and that the ballast of these insults act as counterweight to the bellying sails of such approbation, and that the ship of good judgment not founder amidst the winds of acclamation. If this, I say, was the practice among Gentiles, who knew only the light of Natural Law, how much might we Catholics, under the injunction to love our enemies, achieve by tolerating them? And in my own behalf I can attest that calumny has often mortified me, but never harmed me, being that I hold as a great fool one who having occasion to receive credit suffers the difficulty and loses the credit, as it is with those who do not resign themselves to death, but, in the end, die anyway, their resistance not having prevented

---

1. Syrian prelate (ca. 347–407), known as the greatest orator of the Church, author of many homilies and treatises.   2. Gregory the Great (ca. 540–604), pope from 590, deeply concerned with the reformation of the Church.

death, but merely deprived them of the credit of resignation and caused them to die badly when they might have died well. And thus, lady, I believe these experiences do more good than harm, and I hold as greater the jeopardy of applause to human weakness, as we are wont to appropriate praise that is not our own, and must be ever watchful, and carry graven on our hearts those words of the Apostle: *Or what hast thou that thou hast not received? And if thou hast received, why doest thou glory as if thou hadst not received it?*[3] so that these words serve as a shield to fend off the sharp barbs of commendations, which are as spears which when not attributed to God (whose they are), claim our lives and cause us to be thieves of God's honor and usurpers of the talents He bestowed on us and the gifts that He lent to us, for which we must give the most strict accounting. And thus, lady, I fear applause more than calumny, because the latter, with but the simple act of patience becomes gain, while the former requires many acts of reflection and humility and proper recognition so that it not become harm. And I know and recognize that it is by special favor of God that I know this, as it enables me in either instance to act in accord with the words of Saint Augustine: *One must believe neither the friend who praises nor the enemy who detracts.* Although most often I squander God's favor, or vitiate with such defects and imperfections that I spoil what, being His, was good. And thus in what little of mine that has been printed, neither the use of my name, nor even consent for the printing, was given by my own counsel, but by the license of another who lies outside my domain, as was also true with the printing of the *Atenagórica* letter, and only a few *Exercises of the Incarnation* and *Offerings of the Sorrow* were printed for public devotions with my pleasure, but without my name; of which I am sending some few copies that (if you so desire) you may distribute them among our sisters, the nuns of that holy community, as well as in that city. I send but one copy of the *Sorrows* because the others have been exhausted and I could find no other copy. I wrote them long ago, solely for the devotions of my sisters, and later they were spread abroad; and their contents are disproportionate as regards my unworthiness and my ignorance, and they profited that they touched on matters of our exalted Queen; for I cannot explain what it is that inflames the coldest heart when one refers to the Most Holy Mary. It is my only desire, esteemed lady, to remit to you works worthy of your virtue and wisdom; as the poet said: *Though strength may falter, good will must be praised. In this, I believe, the gods will be content.*

If ever I write again, my scribbling will always find its way to the haven of your holy feet and the certainty of your correction, for I have no other jewel with which to pay you, and, in the lament of Seneca, he who has once bestowed benefices has committed himself to continue; and so you must be repaid out of your own munificence, for only in this way shall I with dignity be freed from debt and avoid that the words of that same Seneca come to pass: *It is contemptible to be surpassed in benefices.*[4] For in his gallantry the generous creditor gives to the poor debtor the means to satisfy his debt. So God gave his gift to a world unable to repay Him: He gave his son that He be offered a recompense worthy of Him.

If, most venerable lady, the tone of this letter may not have seemed right and proper, I ask forgiveness for its homely familiarity, and the less than

---

3. Corinthians 11.4.   4. *On Benefits* 5.2.1.

seemly respect in which by treating you as a nun, one of my sisters, I have lost sight of the remoteness of your most illustrious person; which, had I seen you without your veil, would never have occurred; but you in all your prudence and mercy will supplement or amend the language, and if you find unsuitable the *Vos* of the address I have employed, believing that for the reverence I owe you, Your Reverence seemed little reverent, modify it in whatever manner seems appropriate to your due, for I have not dared exceed the limits of your custom, nor transgress the boundary of your modesty.

And hold me in your grace, and entreat for me divine grace, of which the Lord God grant you large measure, and keep you, as I pray Him, and am needful. From this convent of our Father Saint Jerome in Mexico City, the first day of the month of March of sixteen hundred and ninety-one. Allow me to kiss your hand, your most favored

Juana Inés de la Cruz

The Situation of Women

Many late-twentieth-century feminist ideas appeared in the writings of eighteenth-century women (and occasionally men). The equality of the sexes and even the possible superiority of women to men in some respects; the putative aptitude of women for virtually any occupation; the iniquity of relegating women entirely to childbearing and child rearing, on the one hand, and, on the other, the worth and dignity of child rearing: early feminists enunciated such ideas with clarity and force, often with considerable wit, and frequently with obvious indignation.

The concepts of what we now call "feminism" had appeared in the West long before the late seventeenth century. Think, for instance, of Chaucer's Wife of Bath. But forceful statements about the situation of women began to multiply toward the beginning of the eighteenth century, at the same time that people were more and more being seen as individuals. At the center of most discussions was the question of female education. Like Sor Juana, many perceived the need for more serious forms of schooling for women. Writers as different from one another as Mary Wollstonecraft, a fiery radical, and Hannah More, a proud and pious conservative, united in their belief that existing systems of girls' education encouraged superficiality, frivolity, and excessive worldliness. Indeed, both boarding-school and home education of females generally specialized in inculcating "accomplishments": minimal competence in drawing, dancing, and singing and playing music; perhaps a superficial knowledge of French. As a young woman, the novelist Frances Burney, when Dr. Johnson offered to teach her Latin, responded immediately with concern lest others discover that she had adopted so presumptuous a course. Real learning was not ladylike.

To be sure, learned women existed, rare though they were. Again, Sor Juana represents the type. Henry Fielding, among many others, wrote a diatribe against them—in his last novel, *Amelia*. Most of those who wished to reform the existing system, though, supported not education in the dead languages for its own sake, but education to supply substance and exercise for women's minds. Such education would, at the very least, make women better companions for men and better guides for their own children. Even Jean-Jacques Rousseau, who believed that women's primary function was to please men, wanted his ideal girl, Sophie, to receive some intellectual grounding. More daring thinkers like "Sophia" claimed that women could study whatever men studied and could perform as well as men in most professions.

Awareness of inequities for women mounted as the eighteenth century continued, moving toward the great revolutions in America and France that created heightened consciousness of "inalienable" human rights and of principles of equality—for men. Toward the century's end, Theodor Gottlieb von Hippel in Germany, like Olympe de Gouges in France, called attention to the illogical distinctions made between men and women when it came to civil rights. Women could be executed in France, but they could not vote. Such violations of rational principle, advanced thinkers maintained, should not be tolerated in nations that claimed to believe in liberty and justice for all.

As this point suggests, the gathering concern about women rose not only from developing individualism, but from the Enlightenment commitment to reason as guiding principle. It was difficult to justify the social inequalities between men and women on rational grounds, even if one believed, as Rousseau and Hannah More did, that the two sexes were designed for radically different functions. But no national government was yet willing to allow women equal civil rights. America, England, France, Germany: none granted suffrage to women; none fostered systems of education that established equivalence between boys and girls.

In practical terms, then, the polemics about the situation of women had little visible effect. Yet they presumably made a difference to their writers, each of whom worked out a systematic structure of thought about subjects habitually ignored. And they probably made a difference, however immeasurable, in the consciousness of their readers. They laid the groundwork for change that would occur only gradually and belatedly. But it would, in fact, occur in the long run.

JUDITH DRAKE
seventeenth century

Nothing is known of Judith Drake. Her name survives only because the publisher Edmund Curll, in a catalogue of his publications and of secondhand books sold after 1741, listed a copy of *An Essay in Defense of the Female Sex* as written by her, an attribution tentatively confirmed by an old annotation in a British Museum copy. She is thought to have been a sister of Dr. James Drake, who saw to the publication of the original version of the *Essay*.

An Essay in Defense of the Female Sex has sometimes been attributed to Mary Astell, a well-known feminist who wrote in the same period. Its frequently satiric tone and its occasionally liberal ideas about relations between the sexes, however, do not correspond to Astell's attitudes, and it often contradicts positions that Astell had taken in print. We are left, therefore, with only a name to identify the author of this vigorous early polemic.

The argument about conversation that is printed here is unusual among early feminist tracts in its claim that women can and do give pleasure to men in other than sexual ways. One purpose of better education of females, the essay argues, might be to increase the pleasure that women provide by their talk as well as the good they do. The undervaluing of the capacity of women, in other words, harms those who undervalue.

From An Essay in Defense of the Female Sex

* * *

I shall not enter into any dispute, whether men, or women be generally more ingenious, or learned; that Point must be given up to the advantages men have over us by their education, freedom of converse, and variety of business and company. But when any comparison is made between them, great allowances must be made for the disparity of those circumstances. Neither shall I contest about the preeminence of our virtues; I know there are too many vicious, and I hope there are a great many virtuous of both sexes. Yet this I may say, that whatever vices are found amongst us, have in general both their source, and encouragement from them.[1]

The question I shall at present handle is, whether the time an ingenious gentleman spends in the company of women, may justly be said to be misemployed, or not? I put the question in general terms; because whoever holds the affirmative must maintain it so, or the sex is no way concerned to oppose him. On the other side I shall not maintain the negative, but with some restrictions and limitations; because I will not be bound to justify those women, whose vices and ill conduct expose them deservedly to the censure of the other sex, as well as of their own. The question being thus stated, let us consider the end and purposes, for which conversation was at first instituted, and is yet desirable; and then we shall see, whether they may not all be found in the company of women. These ends, I take it, are the same with those we aim at in all our other actions, in general only two, profit or pleasure. These are divided into those of the mind, and those of the body. Of the latter I shall take no further notice, as having no relation to the present subject; but shall confine my self wholly to the mind, the profit of which is the improvement of the understanding, and the pleasure is the diversion, and relaxation of its cares and passions. Now if either of these ends be attainable by the society of women, I have gained my point, However, I hope to make it appear, that they are not only both to be met with in the conversation of women, but one of them more generally, and in greater measure than in men's.

Our company is generally by our adversaries represented as unprofitable and irksome to men of sense, and by some of the more vehement sticklers against us, as criminal. These imputations as they are unjust, especially the latter, so they savor strongly of the malice, arrogance and sottishness of those, that most frequently urge them; who are commonly either conceited fops, whose success in their pretenses to the favor of our sex has been no greater than their merit, and fallen very far short of their

Some advantages to be allowed to the disparity of education.

1. Men.

vanity and presumption, or a sort of morose, ill-bred, unthinking fellows, who appear to be men only by their habit and beards, and are scarce distinguishable from brutes by their figure and risibility. But I shall wave[2] these reflections at present, however, just, and come closer to our argument. If women are not qualified for the conversation of ingenious men, or, to go yet further, their friendship, it must be because they want some one condition, or more, necessarily requisite to either. The necessary conditions of these are sense, and good nature, to which must be added, for friendship, fidelity and integrity. Now if any of these be wanting to our sex, it must be either because nature has not been so liberal as to bestow them upon us; or because due care has not been taken to cultivate those gifts to a competent measure in us.

The first of these causes is that, which is most generally urged against us, whether it be in raillery, or spite. I might easily cut this part of the controversy short by an irrefragable argument, which is, that the express intent, and reason for which woman was created, was to be a companion, and helpmeet to man; and that consequently those, that deny them to be so, must argue a mistake in Providence, and think themselves wiser than their Creator. But these gentlemen are generally such passionate admirers of themselves, and have such a profound value and reverence for their own parts,[3] that they are ready at any time to sacrifice their religion to the reputation of their wit, and rather than lose their point, deny the truth of the history. There are others, that though they allow the story yet affirm, that the propagation, and continuance of mankind, was the only reason for which we were made; as if the wisdom that first made man, could not without trouble have continued the species by the same or any other method, had not this been most conducive to his happiness, which was the gracious and only end of his creation. But these superficial gentlemen wear their understandings like their clothes, always set and formal, and would no more talk than dress out of fashion; beaus that, rather than any part of their outward figure should be damaged, would wipe the dirt of their shoes with their handkercher,[4] and that value themselves infinitely more upon modish nonsense, than upon the best sense against the fashion. But since I do not intend to make this a religious argument, I shall leave all further considerations of this nature to the divines, whose more immediate business and study it is to assert the wisdom of Providence in the order, and distribution of this world, against all that shall oppose it.

To proceed therefore: if we be naturally defective, the defect must be either in soul or body. In the soul it can't be, if what I have heard some learned men maintain, be true, that all souls are equal, and alike, and that consequently there is no such distinction, as male and female souls; that there are no innate *ideas*, but that all the notions we have, are derived from our external

No distinction of sexes in souls.

2. Waive.   3. Intellectual capacities.   4. Handkerchief.

senses, either immediately, or by reflection. These metaphysical speculations, I must own Madam, require much more learning and a stronger head, than I can pretend to be mistress of, to be considered as they ought: Yet so bold I may be, as to undertake the defense of these opinions, when any of our jingling opponents think fit to refute 'em.

Neither can it be in the body, (if I may credit the report of learned physicians) for there is no difference in the organization of those parts, which have any relation to, or influence over the minds; but the brain, and all other parts (which I am not anatomist enough to name) are contrived as well for the plentiful conveyance of spirits, which are held to be the immediate instruments of sensation, in women, as men. I see therefore no natural impediment in the structure of our bodies; nor does experience, or observation argue any: we use all our natural faculties, as well as men, nay and our rational too, deducting only for the advantages before mentioned. *No advantage in the organization of their bodies.*

Let us appeal yet further to experience, and observe those creatures that deviate least from simple nature, and see if we can find any difference in sense, or understanding between males and females. In these we may see nature plainest, who lie under no constraint of custom or laws, but those of passion or appetite, which are Nature's, and know no difference of education, nor receive any bias by prejudice. We see great distance in degrees of understanding, wit, cunning and docility (call them what you please) between the several species of brutes. An ape, a dog, a fox, are by daily observation found to be more docile, and more subtle than an ox, a swine, or a sheep. But a she ape is as full of, and as ready at imitation as a he; a bitch will learn as many tricks in as short a time as a dog, a female fox has as many wiles as a male. A thousand instances of this kind might be produced; but I think these are so plain, that to instance more were a superfluous labor; I shall only once more take notice, that in brutes and other animals there is no difference betwixt male and female in point of sagacity, notwithstanding there is the same distinction of sexes, that is between men and women. I have read, that some philosophers have held brutes to be no more than meer machines, a sort of divine clockwork, that act only by the force of nice unseen springs without sensation, and cry out without feeling pain, eat without hunger, drink without thirst, fawn upon their keepers without seeing them, hunt hares without smelling, etc. Here Madam is cover for our antagonists against the last argument so thick, that there is no beating them out.[5] For my part, I shall not envy them their refuge, let them lie like the wild *Irish* secure within their bogs; the field is at least ours, so long as they keep to their fastnesses. But to quit this topic, I shall only add, that if the learnedest he of them all can convince me of the *Confirmed from experience of brutes.*

---

5. The metaphor is from hunting: like hares secure in underbrush, Drake's "antagonist," men, take refuge in philosophers' arguments and cannot be beaten out, as a hare might be beaten out by huntsmen.

truth of this opinion, he will very much stagger my faith; for hitherto I have been able to observe no difference between our knowledge and theirs, but a gradual one; and depend upon revelation alone, that our souls are immortal, and theirs not.

But if an argument from brutes and other animals shall not be allowed as conclusive, (though I can't see, why such an inference should not be valid, since the parity of reason is the same on both sides in this case) I shall desire those, that hold against us to observe the country people, I mean the inferior sort of them, such as not having stocks to follow husbandry upon their own score, subsist upon their daily labor. For amongst these, though not so equal as that of the brutes, yet the condition of the two sexes is more level, than amongst gentlemen, city traders, or rich yeomen. Examine them in their several businesses, and their capacities will appear equal; but talk to them of things indifferent, and out of the road of their constant employment, and the balance will fall on our side, the women will be found the more ready and polite. Let us look a little further, and view our sex in a state of more improvement, amongst our neighbors the *Dutch*. There we shall find them managing not only the domestic affairs of the family, but making and receiving all payments as well great as small, keeping the books, balancing the accounts, and doing all the business, even the nicest[6] of merchants, with as much dexterity and exactness as their, or our men can do. And I have often heared some of our considerable merchants blame the conduct of our countrymen in this point; that they breed our women so ignorant of business; whereas were they taught arithmetic, and other arts which require not much bodily strength, they might supply the places of abundance of lusty men now employed in sedentary business; which would be a mighty profit to the nation by sending those men to employments, where hands and strength are more required, especially at this time when we are in such want of people.[7] Beside that it might prevent the ruin of many families, which is often occasioned by the death of merchants in full business, and leaving their accounts perplexed, and embroiled to a widow and orphans, who understanding nothing of the husband or father's business occasions the rending, and oftentimes the utter confounding a fair estate; which might be prevented, did the wife but understand merchants' accounts, and were made acquainted with the books.

I have yet another argument from Nature, which is, that the very make and temper of our bodies shew that we were never designed for fatigue; and the vivacity of our wits, and readiness of our invention (which are confessed even by our adversaries) demonstrate that we were chiefly intended for thought and the exercise of the mind. Whereas on the contrary it is apparent from the strength and size of their limbs, the vigor and hardiness of

Experience of mankind.

---

6. Most precise.   7. The male population had perhaps been depleted as a result of 17th-century wars (e.g., the War of the League of Augsburg, 1689–1697), and workers were needed for increased and increasing mercantile activity in England.

their constitutions, that men were purposely framed and contrived for action, and labor. And herein the wisdom and contrivance of Providence is abundantly manifested; for as the one sex is fortified with courage and ability to undergo the necessary drudgery of providing materials for the sustenance of life in both; so the other is furnished with ingenuity and prudence for the orderly management and distribution of it, for the relief and comfort of a family; and is over and above enriched with a peculiar tenderness and care requisite to the cherishing their poor helpless offspring. I know our opposers usually miscall our quickness of thought, fancy and flash, and christen their own heaviness by the specious names of judgment and solidity; but it is easy to retort upon them the reproachful ones of dullness and stupidity with more justice. I shall pursue this point no further, but continue firm in my persuasion, that Nature has not been so niggardly to us, as our adversaries would insinuate, till I see better cause to the contrary, than I have hitherto at any time done. Yet I am ready to yield to conviction, whoever offers it; which I don't suddenly expect.

It remains then for us to enquire, whether the bounty of Nature be wholly neglected, or stifled by us, or so far as to make us unworthy the company of men? Or whether our education (as bad as it is) be not sufficient to make us a useful, nay a necessary part of society for the greatest part of mankind. This cause is seldom indeed urged against us by the men, though it be the only one, that gives them any advantage over us in understanding. But it does not serve their pride, there is no honor to be gained by it: for a man ought no more to value himself upon being wiser than a woman, if he owe his advantage to a better education, and greater means of information, then he ought to boast of his courage, for beating a man, when his hands were bound. Nay it would be so far from honorable to contend for preference upon this score, that they would thereby at once argue themselves guilty both of tyranny, and of fear: I think I need not have mentioned the latter; for none can be tyrants but cowards. For nothing makes one party slavishly depress another, but their fear that they may at one time or other become strong or couragious enough to make themselves equal to, if not superior to their masters. This is our case; for men being sensible as well of the abilities of mind in our sex, as of the strength of body in their own, began to grow jealous, that we, who in the infancy of the world were their equals and partners in dominion, might in process of time, by subtlety and stratagem, become their superiors; and therefore began in good time to make use of force (the origin of power) to compel us to a subjection, Nature never meant; and made use of Nature's liberality to them to take the benefit of her kindness from us. From that time they have endeavored to train us up altogether to ease and ignorance; as conquerors use to do to those, they reduce by force, that so they may disarm them, both of courage and wit; and consequently make them tamely give up their liberty, and

Women industriously kept in ignorance.

abjectly submit their necks to a slavish yoke. As the world grew more populous, and men's necessities whetted their inventions, so it increased their jealousy, and sharpened their tyranny over us, till by degrees, it came to that height of severity, I may say cruelty, it is now at in all the eastern parts of the world, where the women, like our Negroes in our western plantations, are born slaves, and live prisoners all their lives.[8] Nay, so far has this barbarous humor prevailed, and spread itself, that in some parts of *Europe*, which pretend to be most refined and civilized, in spite of Christianity, and the zeal for religion which they so much affect, our condition is not very much better. And even in *France*, a country that treats our sex with more respect than most do, we are by the *Salique law*[9] excluded from sovereign power. The *French* are an ingenious people, and the contrivers of that law knew well enough, that we were no less capable of reigning, and governing well, than themselves; but they were suspicious, that if the regal power should fall often into the hands of women, they would favor their own sex, and might in time restore them to their primitive liberty and equality with the men, and so break the neck of that unreasonable authority they so much affect over us; and therefore made this law to prevent it. The historians indeed tell us other reasons, but they can't agree among themselves, and as men are parties against us, and therefore their evidence may justly be rejected. To say the truth Madam, I can't tell how to prove all this from ancient records; for if any histories were anciently written by women, time, and the malice of men have effectually conspired to suppress them; and it is not reasonable to think that men should transmit, or suffer to be transmitted to posterity, anything that might shew the weakness and illegality of their title to a power they still exercise so arbitrarily, and are so fond of. But since daily experience shews, and their own histories tell us, how earnestly they endeavor, and what they act, and suffer to put the same trick upon one another, 'tis natural to suppose they took the same measures with us at first, which now they have effected, like the rebels in our last civil wars,[1] when they had brought the royal party under, they fall together by the ears about the dividend. The sacred history takes no notice of any such authority they had before the flood, and their own confess that whole nations have rejected it since, and not suffered a man to live amongst them, which could be for no other reason, than their tyranny. For upon less provocation the women would never have been so foolish, as to deprive themselves of the benefit of that ease and security, which a good agreement with their men might have afforded them. 'Tis true the same histories tell us, that there were whole countries where were none but

Original of the Salique law.

Amazons; why they rejected the society of men.

---

8. I.e., in harems. Drake argues that the situation of women in the West is not significantly better than that of Asian women confined to harems all their lives.   9. Salic law, a rule of succession in European royal and noble families that forbade females and those descended from the female line to succeed to family titles or offices.   1. I.e., the civil war (1642–1646) between adherents of King Charles I and supporters of Parliament, mainly Puritans. The Parliamentarians won, but their victory was soon followed by disagreements between Parliament and the army.

men, which bordered upon them. But this makes still for us; for it shews that the conditions of their society were not so easy, as to engage their women to stay amongst them; but as liberty presented itself, they withdrew and retired to the *Amazons*.[2] But since our sex can hardly boast of so great privileges, and so easy a servitude anywhere as in *England,* I cut this ungrateful digression short in acknowledgment; though fetters of gold are still fetters, and the softest lining can never make them so easy, as liberty.

*　　*　　*

2. The mythological tribes of warlike women who lived in a matriarchal society in Asia Minor; the men performed household tasks while the women fought and governed.

"SOPHIA"
eighteenth century

"Sophia" has never been identified. The title page of *Woman Not Inferior to Man* claims her to be "A Person of Quality," but the claim is not necessarily true. The name *Sophia* denotes wisdom, but evidence of the author's wisdom consists only in her books. All we know about her is her ideas, ideas specifically about women.

A year after *Woman Not Inferior to Man*, another work written by "Sophia" appeared: *Woman's Superior Excellence over Man* (1740). As this title suggests, the author—if, indeed, it was the same author—intensified her argument about the undervalued powers of women. Despite their radical claims, her books were popular, perhaps because of their sprightly style and tone. The ideas they contained were not new: French and English writers alike had argued strongly that women's apparent inferiority to men derived from their inferior educations rather than from any inherent intellectual deficiency. "Sophia" makes the same case, but she does so by means of jokes, verbal extravagance, and vigorous colloquial language. Even two and two-thirds centuries after their writing, her polemics still make good reading.

Woman Not Inferior to Man

CHAP. II.

In what esteem the women are held by the men, and how justly.

Was every individual *man* to divulge his thoughts of our sex, they would all be found unanimous in thinking, that we are made only for their use, that we are fit only to breed and nurse children in their tender years, to mind household affairs, and to obey, serve, and please our masters, that is, themselves forsooth. All this is very fine, and, amidst a seraglio of slaves, could not but sound mighty big from a mussulman's[1] mouth. Yet I cannot help

1. Muslim's.

thinking it of a stamp with all those fantastical expressions which are more easily advanced than proved.

Men seem to conclude, that all other creatures were made for them, because they themselves were not created till all were in readiness for them. How far this reasoning will hold good I will not take upon me to say. But if it has any weight at all, I am sure it must equally prove, that the *men* were made for our use rather than we for theirs. That the province of breeding children belongs to us is as certain, as that the office of getting them is wholly theirs. And if the latter entitles them to any degree of public esteem and respect, surely the former entitles us to an equal share of both; since the immediate concurrence of both is so essentially necessary for the propagation of human nature, that either without the other would be entirely useless. Where then is the reason for underrating us, or claiming a superiority over us, for an office in life, in which they bear so equal a proportion with us? It is too well known to be dissembled, that the office of nursing children is held by the *men* in a despicable light, as something low and degrading. Whereas had they nature for their guide, they would not need to be told, that there is no employment in a commonwealth which deserves more honor, or greater thanks and rewards. Let it but be considered, what are the advantages accruing to mankind from it, and its merit must stand immediately confessed. Nay, I know not whether it may not appear to render *women* deserving the first places in civil society.

Why, or to what end, do the individuals of human species associate together, but for the better preservation of life, and the peaceable enjoyment of everything conducive to that purpose? Do not such then as contribute the most to this public advantage deserve the greatest share of public esteem? And who are these but the *women*, in the generous disinterested employ of nursing the *men* in their infancy?

It is from this principle that princes are considered as the chief persons in the state, and in quality of such receive the first honors of it, because they are at least supposed to have the greatest share of toil, care, and foresight, for the prosperity of the public weal; so in proportion we pay more or less of that respect to such as are under him at a lesser or greater distance from him, because the nearer or farther off they are from sharing with him in the fatigues of serving the public, the more or less useful to society they must be considered. For the same reason we are apt to prefer soldiers to gownsmen,[2] because they are supposed to stand as a bulwark between us and our enemies. And all mankind give to persons such a degree of respect, as they suppose them to merit by being useful. And since this is the case throughout life, are not the *women*, by the very same rule, entitled to the greatest share in public esteem, who are incomparably the greatest contributors to the public good? *Men* can absolutely dispense with princess, merchants, soldiers, lawyers, etc. as they did in the beginning of time, and as savages do still. But can they in their infancy do without nurses? And since they themselves are too awkward for that important office, are not *women* indispensably wanted? In a peaceful, orderly state, the major part of *men* are useless in their office, with all their authority. But *women* will never cease to be useful, while there are *men*, and those *men* have children. Of what other use are judges, mag-

2. Lawyers or academics.

istrates, and their dependent officers in the execution of justice, any more than to secure their property to persons, who, if they were not forbidden, would perhaps be able to do themselves justice in a more exact and expeditious manner? But *women*, more truly useful, are employed in preserving their lives to enjoy that property. Soldiers are esteemed and rewarded because engaged in defending full-grown *men*, who are equally and often more capable of defending themselves. How much more then is our sex worthy their esteem and gratitude, who labor in their defense, when as yet they know not what they are, are unable to distinguish between friends and foes, and are naked of every defense but that of tears! If their princes and statesmen sometimes exert themselves in the service of the public, ambition is their motive, and power, riches, or splendor, the point in view. But our more generous souls are biased only by the good we do to the children we breed and nurse; daily experience reminding us, that all the return we can hope for from the unnatural creatures, for the almost infinite pains, anxieties, care, and assiduities to which we expose ourselves on their account, and which cannot be matched in any other state of civil society, is ungrateful treatment of ourselves, and the basest contempt of our sex in general. Such the generous offices we do them: such the ungenerous use they make of them.

Surely then nothing but a corrupt imagination can make *men* look upon an office of such high importance to them as mean and contemptible, or as less valuable than it really is. How largely are they rewarded who succeed in taming a tiger, an elephant, or such like animals, and shall *women* be neglected for spending years in the taming that *fiercer animal* MAN? If the source of this unjust partiality be examined into we shall find, that the only true cause, why these important services, done by our sex, have so little value set upon them, is their being so frequent, and usual.

However, as the pleasure which the generosity of our sex makes us take in that office, is sufficient to make us discharge ourselves of it with the utmost tenderness, without any view of reward; I do not here mean to complain of our receiving none. I would only beg leave to say, that our being so much more capable than the male kind to execute that office well, no ways proves us unqualified to execute any other. Indeed, the *men* themselves seem tacitly agreed to acknowledge as much: but then, according to their wonted disinterestedness, they are still for confining all our other talents to the pleasant limits of obeying, serving, and pleasing our masters. That they are our masters, they take it for granted; but by what title they are so, not one of them is able to make out. And yet so universally received is this notion among them, that it everywhere prevails, from the prince to the peasant. Nay, I myself was accidentally witness to the diverting scene of a journeyman tailor's beating his wife about the ears with a neck of mutton, to make her know, as he said, her *sovereign lord* and *master*. And yet this, perhaps, is as strong an argument as the best of their sex is able to produce, though conveyed in a greasy light.

But be this as it may, whether nature designed them for our masters or not, if their injunctions were the sober dictates of sound reason, we should find the yoke of obedience an agreeable weight; since obeying them we should but submit our will to *reason*, and act like those intelligent beings we know ourselves to be. And that, generally speaking, the *women* are more inclined so to do than the *men*, where every circumstance is parallel, is too well known to admit of a doubt. But then it would be putting ourselves upon the level with brutes, to descend to a compliance with the generality of their commands, since that alone would suffice to degrade us, and render us as despicable as the upright unfeathered animals who lay them upon us.

Masters then, or not masters, they have but one of these two means to choose in exerting their pretended authority: either let them, as usual, suit their commands to their *passions*, in opposition to *reason*; and then none but *women*, as irrational as themselves, will obey them, a pre-eminence which no *woman* of sense will envy them: or let *reason* speak in their orders, and all *Women* of *sense* will listen to it; though the *Men* should tickle themselves with the notion, that our obedience is paid to them.

Were the *men* to make choice of the *latter*, we would indulge them the innocent liberty of fancying themselves masters, while we, pleased with seeing all the authority placed in *reason*, where it should be, must know that each sex would have the privilege of conveying its influences to the other in their turns; and if *man* had steadiness enough to conform all his injunctions to *woman*, to the dictates of *reason*, the same steadiness would induce him to yield to those dictates when *woman* was the means of conveying them. No matter by what mouth *reason* speaks: if *men* were strictly attached to it; whether we or themselves were the vehicles of its influence, we should on both sides be equally determined by it. But the case is at present quite otherwise. The *men* who cannot deny us to be rational creatures, would have us justify their irrational opinion and treatment of us, by descending to a mean compliance with their irrational expectations. But I hope, while *women* have any spirit left, they will exert it all, in shewing how worthy they are of better usage, by not submitting tamely to such misplaced arrogance.

To stoop to some regard for the strutting things is not enough; to humor them more than we could children, with any tolerable decency, is too little; they must be served forsooth. Pretty creatures indeed! How worthy do they appear of this boasted pre-eminence: to exact a servitude they want the courage themselves to submit to, from those whom their vanity stigmatizes with the character of weaker vessels; and to require us to be their drudges, whom they are forced to court and decoy into their power by the most pitiful cringes? Upon what title do they build their claim to our services, greater than we can shew to theirs? Have they half so plausible a plea over us, as over those hapless savages, whose unsuspecting innocence has robbed them of the power of guarding against their unnatural violence and injustice? And yet are not the generality of our sex, when weak enough to yield ourselves, in pity to their fawning, affected despair, a prey to their dissimulation, made the dupes of our credulous good-nature and innocence? Where is there a *woman*, who having generously trusted her liberty with a husband, does not immediately find the *spaniel* metamorphosed into a *tiger*, or has not reason to envy the lesser misery of a bond-slave to a merciless tyrant?

If brutal strength, in which we acknowledge their pre-eminence, is a sufficient plea, for their trampling upon us, the lion has a much better title over the whole creation. But that is a more generous kind of brute than those we are speaking of, though not quite so fierce and ungovernable. And therefore, he scorns to exert his strength, where he finds too great a disproportion in even an adversary.

I allow indeed, we ought to make it part of our business to please the poor things, if the attempt were likely to succeed. It would be quite barbarous to let a child cry, if a rattle would keep it quiet. But the misfortune is, that it is a study for life to find out a means of pleasing these greater, more stubborn brats. I have heard, it is a vulgar proverb, that *the Devil is good-humored when he is pleased*, and if this proverb, like others, be founded on experience, it is a proof, the Devil can be pleased sometimes. I wish as good an argument could be brought to prove that the *men* can ever be pleased. But such is the fantastical composition of their nature, that the more pains is taken in endeavoring to please them, the less, generally speaking, is the labor like to prove successful; and if ever it does succeed, the reward never pays the expense. And surely the *women* were created by Heaven for some better end, than to labor in vain their whole life long.

I foresee it may be urged, that we cannot be said to spend our lives in vain, while we are answering the end of our creation: And as we were created for no other end than for the *men's* use, our only business is to be subject to, and please them: neither shall we be answerable for neglecting everything else, because God has not given us a capacity for more. But this must appear, from what I have already said, and shall hereafter shew, begging the question; and supposing what should, but cannot be proved.

There are some however more condescending, and gracious enough to confess, that many *women* have wit and conduct; but yet they are of opinion, that even such of us as are most remarkable for either or both, still betray something which speaks the imbecility of our sex. Stale, threadbare notions, which long since sunked[3] with their own weight; and the extreme weakness of which seemed to condemn to perpetual oblivion; till an ingenious writer, for want of something better to employ his pen about, was pleased lately to revive them in one of the weekly papers,[4] lest this age should be ignorant what fools there have been among his sex in former ones.

To give us a sample then of the wisdom of his sex, he tells us, that it was always the opinion of the wisest among them, that *women* are never to be indulged the sweets of liberty; but ought to pass their whole lives in a state of subordination to the *men*, and in an absolute dependence upon them. And the reason assigned for so extravagant an assertion, is our not having a sufficient capacity to govern ourselves. It must be observed, that so bold a tenet ought to have better proofs to support it, than the bare word of the persons who advance it; as their being *parties* so immediately concerned, must render all they say of this kind highly suspect. However, since we are as suspect on that account as they are, it must be to as little purpose for us to deny it, unless it be to put them upon the proof. And doubtless, creatures of such profound wisdom as these *men* are, if we take their own word, would never attempt to assert anything so positively, without being able to back it with the best of proofs. Let us see then upon what grounds they build these extravagant notions of our sex, and how far they will stand the test of *truth* and *reason*; that we may give into their opinion or reject it.

---

3. Sank.   4. The author's note identifies the paper as *Common-Sense*, Sept. 1, 1739.

CHAP. III.

Whether women are inferior to men in their intellectual capacity, or not.

In the first place then, according to them, "the greatest part of our sex have but short, lucid intervals; ——but sudden flashes of reason which vanish in a minute; ——we have a resemblance of that planet, which is dark of itself, and only shines by borrowed light; ——our wit has but a false luster, more fit to surprise admiration than deserve it; ——we are enemies to reflection; ——the majority of us only reason at hazard, think by sallies, and discourse by rote." A heavy charge this, to be laid against the majority of *women*. But granting it, for argument's sake, to be literally true, is it not as undeniably true, that the very same charge may be equally retorted on the majority of *men*? And yet would they not triumphantly allege it as a proof of our weak sense, were we wisely to conclude, in their way, that therefore all the *men* ought to be perpetually under guardianship to us? A little experience is sufficient to demonstrate how much fitter we are to be guardians over them, than they are to be such over us. Every young *maiden* is qualified to be the mistress and manager of a family, at an age when the *men* are scarce susceptible of the precepts of a master. And the only sure expedient to reclaim a young fellow from his excesses, and to render him useful to society, is to give him for *guardian* a *wife*, who may reform him by her example, moderate his passions by her prudence, and win him from his debaucheries by her engaging behavior.

So far then are the *men* from proving their principle by practice, when their interest is concerned. When their own profound wisdom is too weak to curb the more unruly among them, they have no other recourse than to shelter them under our tutelage: thus contradicting in fact, what they advance in words. But it is the fear of making us too proud of ourselves, which makes them contend, that we have neither solidity nor constancy, much less that depth of judgment which they very humbly ascribe to themselves. Wherefore they as wisely conclude, that it must absolutely have been a joint effect of divine providence, and their own sovereign sense, which debarred us of *sciences*, *government*, and *public offices*.

Whether there be any solidity in this, will best appear upon an unprejudiced examination. To know then, whether the *women* are less capable of the sciences than the *men* or not, we must consider what is the *principle* by which *sciences* are attained; and if that be wanting in *women*, or less perfect, there will be no more required to demonstrate that the *men* are in the right. But if that *principle* should appear to be as perfect in the *one* as it is in the *other*, then there will be great reason to suspect the *men* of *jealousy*; and it cannot be rash to say, that their only reason for locking up from us all the avenues to knowledge, is the fear of our excelling them in it.

It is a known truth, that the difference of sexes regards only the body, and that merely as it relates to the propagation of human nature. But the soul concurring to it only by consent, actuates all after the same manner, so that in *that* there is *no sex* at all. There is no more difference to be discerned between the souls of a dunce, and a man of wit, or of an illiterate and an experienced one, than between a boy of four, and a man of forty years of age. And since there is not at most any greater difference between the souls of *women* and *men,* there can be no real diversity contracted from the body: all the diversity then must come from *education, exercise,* and the *impressions* of those external objects which surround us in different circumstances.

The same Creator, by the same laws, unites the souls of *women* and *men* to their respective bodies. The same sentiments, passions, and propensions,[5] cement that union in both. And the soul operating in the same manner in the one and the other, is capable of the very same functions in both.

To render this still more evident, we need only consider the texture of the head, the seat of the sciences, and the part where the soul exerts itself most. All the researches of anatomy, have not yet been able to shew us the least difference in this part between *men* and *women.* Our brain is perfectly like theirs, we receive the impressions of sense as they do, we martial[6] and pre-serve ideas for imagination and memory as they do, and we have all the organs they have, and apply them to the same purposes as they do. We hear with ears, see with eyes, and taste with a tongue as well as they. Nor can there be any difference pointed out between any of our organs and theirs, but that ours are more delicate, and consequently fitter to answer the ends they were made for, than theirs.

Even among the *men* it is universally observed, that the more gross and lumpish are commonly stupid; and the more delicate, are on the other hand, ever the most sprightly. The reason is plain: The soul, while confined to the body, is dependent on its organs in all its operations; and therefore the more free or clogged those organs are, the more or less must the soul be at liberty to exert itself. Now it is too well known to need any support, that the organs in our sex are of a much finer, and more delicate temperature than in theirs; and therefore, had we the same advantages of study allowed us which the *men* have, there is no room to doubt but we should at least keep pace with them in the *sciences,* and every useful knowledge.

It can only then be a mean dastardly jealousy in them to exclude us from those advantages, in which we have so natural a right to emulate them. Their pretext for so doing, that study and learning would make *women* proud and vicious, is pitiful, capricious, and of a piece with their practice. No: false knowledge, and superficial learning only can produce so bad an effect. For true knowledge, and solid learning must, cannot but, make *women,* as well as *men,* both more humble, and more virtuous. And it must be owned, that if a little superficial knowledge has rendered some of our sex vain, it equally renders many of theirs insupportable. But that is no reason, why solid learn-ing should be denied, or not instilled into, either; rather ought the greater pains to be taken to improve, in both, every disposition to the sciences, into a true relish for, and a deep knowledge of them; according to the advice of one of their brightest writers, as applicable to any science as to poetry:

> *A little learning is a dangerous thing;*
> *Drink deep, or taste not the* Pierian *spring:*
> *There shallow drafts intoxicate the brain,*
> *And drinking largely sobers us again.*[7]

It is a common received notion that mankind need not be knowing to be virtuous: which proceeds from this, that we see many persons who are

5. Propensities.   6. Marshal.   7. Alexander Pope, *Essay on Criticism,* lines 215–18.

reputed men of sense, of very immoral characters: and therefore is it falsely concluded, that knowledge is not only unprofitable in itself to virtue, but even frequently destructive to it: whereas it would be no arduous task to prove, that the knowledge of ourselves and many other things, is highly requisite to corroborate our persuasion of our moral obligations. Since the chief reason which is to be assigned for so many persons falling into vice and folly so precipitately, or practicing virtue so faintly, is their being ignorant of themselves, and the objects which strike them: and how shall they remove this ignorance but by *science* and *study?*

If there have been some of our sex so affected with their learning as to become assuming;[8] their fault carries its excuse with it. Either they have been such as had not drank deep enough to learn to be humble: or the uncommoness of this advantage in our sex, and the difficulties they must have surmounted who have attained to it, will apologize for the little vanity they may have shewn. As a person of low rank, whose merit and industry has raised him to an unusual eminence, may be excused, if, seeing himself advanced above the sphere of his equals, he should be seized with some degree of giddiness. Besides that, if it be a fault, as its wanting an apology proves it to be, it is a fault which the *men* themselves daily fall into. And yet neither in the *men* nor in the *women* ought it to be imputed, as a blemish, to the *sciences* they may possess. The real cause of it is, that they who are versed in any science, look upon themselves as possessed of something, which is a mystery to the generality of the world. But let the matter be how it will, it is more than probable, that, since the vanity of the learned *men* greatly surpasses that of the learned of our sex, as appears from the frothy titles the former arrogate to themselves; if *women* were admitted to an equal share of the sciences, and the advantages leading to, and flowing from, them, they would be much less subject to the vanity, they are apt to occasion.

It is a very great absurdity, to argue that learning is useless to *women*, because forsooth they have not a share in public offices, which is the end for which *men* apply themselves to it. *Virtue* and *felicity* are equally requisite in a private, as well as in a public station, and *learning* is a necessary means to both. It is by that, we acquire an exactness of thought, a propriety of speech, and a justness of actions: without that we can never have a right knowledge of ourselves; it is that which enables us to distinguish between right and wrong, true and false: and finally, that alone can give us skill to regulate our passions by teaching us, that true happiness and virtue consist not so much in enlarging our possessions as in contracting our desires.

Besides let it be observed, what a wretched circle this poor way of reasoning among the *men* draws them insensibly into. Why is *learning* useless to us? Because we have no share in public offices. And why have we no share in public offices? Because we have no *learning.* They are sensible of the injustice they do us, and therefore are reduced to the mean shift of cloaking it at the expense of their own reason. But let truth speak for once: Why are they so industrious to debar us that learning we have an equal right to with themselves, but for fear of our sharing with, and outshining them in, those public offices they fill so miserably? The same sordid selfishness which urged them to engross all power and dignity to themselves, prompted them

8. Presumptuous.

to shut up from us that knowledge which would have made us their competitors.

As nature seems to have designed the *men* for our drudges, I could easily forgive them the usurpation by which they first took the trouble of public employments off our hands, if their injustice were content with stopping there. But as one abyss calls on another, and vices seldom go single, they are not satisfied with engrossing all authority into their hands, but are confident enough to assert that they possess it by right, because we were formed by nature to be under perpetual subjection to them, for want of abilities to share with them in *government* and *public offices*. To confute this *mannish* extravagance, it will be necessary to sap it from the foundation on which it is built.

CHAP. IV.

Whether the men are better qualified to govern than women, or not.

If you are doting enough to hold upon trust what the *men* themselves say, you are to take it for granted, that *women* are such senseless mortals by nature, as to be absolutely incapable of taking the least care of themselves. "It is therefore," say they, "a cruel tenderness, a false complaisance, to abandon the fair-sex to their own conduct. The more they are made to please and charm, the more it imports them to fly from those dangers, to which they are exposed by being so." A plain proof of their speaking from their hearts, is their imagining us weak enough to be wheedled out of our liberty and property, by such jingling, empty stuff. But where have they proved that we are not as capable of guarding ourselves from dangers, as they are of guarding us; had we the same power and advantages allowed us, which they have? Again, are we safer under their conduct than our own? Is it not manifestly launching from *Scylla* to *Charybdis*,[9] to fly to their protection from danger? There is scarce an instance in a million among *women*, of *one woman* of a middling capacity, who does not, or would not, govern herself better than most *men* in parallel circumstances, if the circumvention, treachery, and baseness of that sex did not interfere. Whereas for *one woman*, who is bettered in understanding or morality under their tuition, many millions are betrayed into inevitable ruin. As this is undeniable matter of fact, it needs no proofs to support it. Neither will it bear retorting upon us. For granting some few *men* to have suffered by petticoat-government, the number is extremely small in proportion. And were it equal, the *women's* conduct, in this case, is to be charged wholly to the *men's* account, for having robbed them of those advantages of education, which would have enabled them to act better, which they were susceptible of, and which they had a natural right to. The same apology cannot be made for the *men's* misconduct in governing us: they have all the advantages requisite to qualify them; and, if, spite of all, we are worse under their government than under our own; the consequence speaks itself, that either they have a natural want of capacity, or want of honesty. They are at liberty to choose which imputation pleases them best: though without judging rashly, I might venture to say, they have

9. From one danger to another. Scylla was a rock on the Italian coast directly opposite the whirlpool Charybdis.

a right to both. If they imagine they can elude the force of this truth, by saying that the *men*, whom this accusation regards, have not made use of the advantages which their sex in general has, and therefore might as well have been without them; that no ways lessens the truth of what I have advanced; that most *women* are ruined, instead of being improved in heart or mind under the conduct of the *men*. And therefore, since we are at most in no greater safety under their government than our own, there can be no solid reason assigned why we should be subject to it.

But it seems we are already condemned to it by a judge of their own erecting, a blubbering dotard, too conceited of his own sense, to be improved by that of his wife; *Cato*, the *wise Cato*,[1] who grown obstinate in wrong by age and humored prejudice, chose rather to die a fool of his own making, than live a man of sense by a wife's advice; this *Cato* has pronounced sentence against us. And so disinterested a judge, we cannot surely except against. Let us hear then what this oracle says.

"Let us treat *women* as our equals," (*says he*) "and they will immediately want to become our mistresses."[2] 'Tis *Cato* says it, and therefore there needs no proof. Besides, to oblige men to prove all they advance by reason, would be imposing silence upon them; a grievance to which they are perhaps full as unequal as they pretend we are. But granting *Cato* to be infallible in his assertions, what then? Have not *women* as much right to be mistresses, as the *men* have to be masters? No, says *Cato*. But why? *Because they have not.* Such convincing arguments must make us fond of hearing him farther. If we make the *women* our *equals*, "they will demand that tomorrow as a tribute, which they receive today as a grace." But where is the grace in granting us a share in what we have an equal right to? Have not the *women* an equal claim to power and dignity with the *men*? If we have; the wise *Cato* nods:[3] if we have not; *Cato* would have been wise indeed, to convince us of it. But supposing it to be a favor, a grace, what he pleased to call it; would not the *men* reap the chief benefit of it? The reserve peculiar to our sex, proves, that knowing how to curb ourselves, we are qualified to govern them, and the meekness and tenderness which make part of our characteristic, are sufficient to persuade them that our yoke would not be heavy. But no, *says Cato*, "we may thank ourselves for that sweetness and reserve which they shew in our presence. ——This shadow of virtue is owing to the necessity we impose upon them of dissembling." Then *Cato* is forced at last to own that the subjection we are kept under by that arrogant sex, is the effect of violence and imposition? This he does to compliment his own sex, with attributing all our merit to them. A sorry compliment, considering the ungrateful truth it extorts from him. And yet how against his grain is it to own any merit in us. No, we have but the shadow of virtue, and all their impositions and violence can only induce us to dissemble. Is not this calling all his own sex fools? For surely nothing can be a greater proof of folly in the *men* than to use violence and imposition, and to take perpetual pains to support both, only to make us act with affectation, when much less labor would make us shew ourselves in a more natural light; especially since it is impossible ever to govern subjects rightly, without knowing as well what they really are as what they only

---

1. Cato the Elder (234–149 B.C.E.), Roman statesman and moralist. The specific passages quoted here have not been identified.   2. Female superiors or rulers.   3. Falls asleep for a moment.

seem; which the *men* can never be supposed to do, while they labor to force *women* to live in constant masquerade. So that either all the *men* are downright changelings, by *Cato's* own consession, or this mighty oracle himself is a driveler, and to be heeded by none but such.

I should not myself have thought him worth so much notice as I have here taken of him; but that the *men* are weak enough in general, to suffer their sense to be led away captive, by such half-thinking retailers of sentences. Among whom, this is particular, was he worth the pains, might be easily proved to have been often grossly in the wrong in other matters as well as in the present case; and therefore, when he happens to be in the right, the merit of it is more to be imputed to blind chance than to his wisdom: since the greatest fools, when active, may blunder into the right sometimes: and great talkers among many absurdities, must here and there drop a good saying, when they least design it. Of this stamp, are the generality of evidence brought against us. Men aversed to the labor of thinking; who found reason a drudgery, and therefore, rather chose to prostitute than wed it; who have gained all their reputation by a pretty gimness[4] of expressions, which would no more bear examination than their heads, their hearts, or their faces; and who (to mimic this sage) would rather see *common sense* in confusion, than *a word* misplaced in one of their *sentences*. Yet these are sages among the *men*, and their sentences are so many divine oracles; whereas perhaps, had we lived in their own times, to have heard the many more foolish things they said than sensible ones, we should have found them as auffish[5] as the dupes who revere them. And though perhaps we might have been more surprised to hear such dotards talk sometimes rationally, than we now are, to read their sayings; we should have had reason still to think them more fit to extort our admiration than deserve it. Care has been taken to hand down to us the best of their sentences, many of which nevertheless are weak enough: But had the same care been taken to register all their absurdities, how great a share of their present applause would they have lost! As the infidel observed to the priest of *Neptune*, when proving the god's divinity from the trophies in his temple.

> *'Tis true their pictures who escaped you keep,*
> *But where are they who perished in the deep?*[6]

But we have a more formidable set of enemies than these laconic gentlemen; *men* who pretend to build their assertions upon very good grounds, and who would scorn, say they, to exclude us from power, dignity, and public offices, if they could not shew us the best of reasons. It will be proper therefore to hear their reasons, before we undertake to say they are in the wrong.

FROM CHAP. V.

Whether the women are fit for public offices, or not.

It is enough for the *men* to find a thing established to make them believe it well grounded. In all countries we are seen in subjection and absolute dependence on the *men*, without being admitted to the advantages of sciences, or

---

4. Glibness?　**5.** Oafish.　**6.** Unidentified.

the opportunity of exerting our capacity in a public station. Hence the *men*, according to their usual talent of arguing from seemings, conclude that we ought to be so. But supposing it to be true, that *women* had ever been excluded from *public offices*, is it therefore necessarily true that they ought to be so? God has always been more or less resisted by ungrateful man, a fine conclusion it would be then to infer, that therefore he ought to be so.

But why do the *men* persuade themselves that we are less fit for public employments than they are? Can they give any better reason than custom and prejudice formed in them by external appearances, for want of a closer examination? If they did but give themselves the leisure to trace things back to their fountainhead, and judge of the sentiments and practices of *men* in former ages, from what they discover in their own times, they would not be so open as they are to errors and absurdities in all their opinions. And particularly with regard to *women*, they would be able to see that, if we have been subjected to their authority, it has been by no other law than that of the stronger: and that we have not been excluded from a share in the power and privileges which lift their sex above ours, for want of natural capacity, or merit, but for want of an equal spirit of violence, shameless injustice, and lawless oppression, with theirs.

Nevertheless, so weak are their intellectuals, and so untuned are their organs to the voice of reason, that custom makes more absolute slaves of their senses than they can make of us. They are so accustomed to see things as they now are, that they cannot represent to themselves how they can be otherwise. It would be extremely odd they think to see a *woman* at the head of an army giving battle, or at the helm of a nation giving laws; pleading causes in quality of counsel; administering justice in a court of judicature; preceded in the street with sword, mace, and other ensigns of authority; as magistrates; or teaching rhetoric, medicine, philosophy, and divinity, in quality of university professors.

If by oddity they understand something in its nature opposite to the genuine, unbiased rules of good sense; I believe the *men* will find it a difficult task, to prove any oddity in such a sight, or any real inconsistence in it with *rectified reason*. For if *women* are but considered as rational creatures, abstracted from the disadvantages imposed upon them by the unjust usurpation and tyranny of the *men*, they will be found, to the full, as capable as the *men*, of filling these offices.

I must own indeed in this age, to see a *woman*, however well qualified, exert herself in any of these employments, could not but as greatly surprize us as to see a man or woman dressed in the garb in vogue at the time of Queen *Bess*.[7] And yet our wonder in either case would be the sole effect of novelty, or of the revival of an obsolete custom new to us. If from immemorable time, the *men* had been so little envious, and so very impartial, as to do justice to our talents, by admitting us to our right of sharing with them in public action; they would have been as accustomed to see us filling public offices, as we are to see them disgrace them; and to see a lady at a bar, or on a bench,[8] would have been no more strange than it is now, to see a grave judge whimpering at his maid's knees; or, a lord embroidering his wife's

---

7. Queen Elizabeth I of England (1533–1603), who reigned during England's Golden Age.   8. Acting as a lawyer or judge.

petticoat: a *Schurman*,[9] with a thesis in her hand, displaying nature in its most innocent useful lights, would have been as familiar a sight, as a physician in his chariot, conning *Ovid*'s Art of Love: and an *Amazon*, with a helmet on her head, animating her embattled troops, would have been no more a matter of surprise than a milliner behind a counter with a thimble on her finger; or than a peer of *Great Britain* playing with his *garter*.[1] Not reason then, but error and ignorance cased in custom, makes these superficial creatures think it an unnatural sight.

There are few nations, beside our own, which think *women* capable of holding the scepter; but *England* has learned by repeated experience, how much happier a kingdom is, when under the protection and rule of *a woman*, than it can hope to be under the government of a *man*. Matter of fact then plainly points out the absurdity of the contrary prejudice. How many ladies have there been, and still are, who deserve place among the learned; and who are more capable of *teaching* the *sciences* than those who now fill most of the *university chairs*? The age we live in has produced as many, as any heretofore; though their modesty prevents their making any public shew of it. And as our sex, when it applies to learning, may be said at least to keep pace with the *men*, so are they more to be esteemed for their learning than the latter: since they are under a necessity of surmounting the softness they were educated in; of renouncing the pleasure and indolence to which cruel custom seemed to condemn them; to overcome the external impediments in their way to study; and to conquer the disadvantageous notions, which the vulgar of both sexes entertain of learning in *women*. And whether it be that these difficulties add any keenness to a female understanding, or that nature has given *women*, a quicker, more penetrating genius, than to *men*; it is self-evident, that many of our sex have far outstript the *men*.* * *

9. Anna Maria van Schurman (1607–1678) was the author of a defense of women's right to learning (*The Learned Maid*, 1659) and an expert in learned languages.   1. The badge of the Order of the Garter, the highest order of British knighthood.

JEAN-JACQUES ROUSSEAU
1712–1778

If Rousseau believed that he himself had been shaped by the beneficent influence of nature and of good people around him, he believed also that the powers that formed him might likewise improve others. The ideas about education that he set forth in *Émile* promoted a mode of teaching and learning that systematized his own experience. These ideas would have a powerful effect on educational theory for the next century or more. When first enunciated, though, they were seen as heretical. Church authorities had copies of *Émile* burned both in Paris and in Geneva, where the author had lived.

The life that Rousseau narrates in *Confessions* (see pp. 500–521), a life of responsiveness to his own feelings, suggests his model for the good man. His educational project demanded, however, that he think as well about the development of the good woman. He chose for *Émile* a quasi-fictional form, following the early life of a boy whom he imagines from birth onward. *Émile* must eventually have a mate; Rousseau imagines the rearing of that ideal mate, Sophie. Through his imagining, he delineates his idea of what women should be and do.

Unlike most of the other writers on women in this section, Rousseau understands women as "naturally" subordinate to men. He feels no uncertainty about the naturalness of female desire for adornment, predilection for dolls, or concern with pleasing others. As his principles for a boy's education build on what he considers the natural strengths of males, his notions of a girl's training focuses on heightening their natural qualities. "Girls realize that they are made for obedience," he points out, and their guides should emphasize the urgency of consistent compliance. In other words, although he believes in the importance of female education, his concept of what such education should include bears little relation to modern assumptions.

For biographical details, see pages 498–499.

Émile[1]

From Marriage

DIFFERENCES IN EDUCATION

Once it has been shown that men and women are essentially different in character and temperament, it follows that they ought not to have the same education. In accordance with the direction of nature they ought to cooperate in action, but not to do the same things. To complete the attempt we have been making to form the man of nature, we must now go on to consider how the fitting mate for him is to be formed.

If you want right guidance, always follow the leadings of nature. Everything that characterizes sex should be respected as established by nature. Men's pride leads them astray when, comparing women with themselves, they say, as they are continually doing, that women have this or that defect, which is absent in men. What would be defects in men are good qualities in women, which are necessary to make things go on well. Women on their side never stop complaining that we men make coquettes of them and keep amusing them with trifles in order to maintain our ascendency. What a foolish idea! When have men ever had to do with the education of girls? Who prevents the mothers bringing up their daughters as they please? Are we men to blame if girls please us by their beauty and attract us by the art they have learned from their mothers? Well, try to educate them like men. They will be quite willing. But the more they resemble men the less will be their power over men, and the greater their own subjection.

The faculties common to the sexes are not equally shared between them; but take them all in all, they are well balanced. The more womanly a woman is, the better. Whenever she exercises her own proper powers she gains by it: when she tries to usurp ours she becomes our inferior. Believe me, wise mother, it is a mistake to bring up your daughter to be like a good man. Make her a good woman, and you can be sure that she will be worth more for herself and for us. This does not mean that she should be brought up in utter ignorance and confined to domestic tasks. A man does not want to make his companion a servant and deprive himself of the peculiar charms

1. Translated by William Boyd.

of her company. That is quite against the teaching of nature, which has endowed women with quick pleasing minds. Nature means them to think, to judge, to love, to know and to cultivate the mind as well as the countenance. This is the equipment nature has given them to compensate for their lack of strength and enable them to direct the strength of men.

As I see it, the special functions of women, their inclinations and their duties, combine to suggest the kind of education they require. Men and women are made for each other but they differ in the measure of their dependence on each other. We could get on better without women than women could get on without us. To play their part in life they must have our willing help, and for that they must earn our esteem. By the very law of nature women are at the mercy of men's judgments both for themselves and for their children. It is not enough that they should be estimable: they must be esteemed. It is not enough that they should be beautiful: they must be pleasing. It is not enough that they should be wise: their wisdom must be recognized. Their honor does not rest on their conduct but on their reputation. Hence the kind of education they get should be the very opposite of men's in this respect. Public opinion is the tomb of man's virtue but the throne of a woman's.

On the good constitution of the mothers depends that of the children and the early education of men is in their hands. On women too depend the morals, the passions, the tastes, the pleasures, aye and the happiness of men. For this reason their education must be wholly directed to their relations with men. To give them pleasure, to be useful to them, to win their love and esteem, to train them in their childhood, to care for them when they grow up, to give them counsel and consolation, to make life sweet and agreeable for them: these are the tasks of women in all times for which they should be trained from childhood.

Training for Womanhood (1) To the Age of Ten

PHYSICAL TRAINING FOR GRACE

From the beginning little girls are fond of dress. Not content with being pretty they want notice taken of them. It is evident from their little airs that they have already got this concern. Almost as soon as they can understand what is said to them they can be controlled by telling them what people think of them. It would be foolish to speak that way to little boys and it would not have the same effect. Provided they are left free to enjoy their games boys care very little about what anybody thinks of them. It takes much time and effort to bring them under the same control.

However girls get this first lesson, it is a very good one. The body, one might say is born before the mind and for that reason must be trained first. That applies to both sexes but with a difference. In the boys the object of the training is the development of strength, in the girls the development of graces. Not that these qualities should be confined to one sex or the other but that they should differ in the importance attached to them. Women should have enough strength to do all they have to do gracefully: men enough skill to do what they have to do with ease.

Excessive softness in women makes men soft. They should not be sturdy like men but for them, so that they may be the mothers of sturdy males. From this point of view convents and boarding schools where the children get homely food and can run about and play freely in the open air and garden are preferable to the home where a delicately nurtured girl, always seated in a stuffy room under her mother's eye, dare not get up to walk or talk or breathe and is never free for a moment to jump or run or shout or give way to the natural petulance of her age. This is against all reason. It can only result in the ruin of both heart and body.

Everything that checks and constrains nature is in bad taste. This applies to the finery that bedecks the body as much as to the ornaments of the mind. Life, health, sanity, comfort ought to come first. There can be no grace without freedom and no charm in languor and illness. Suffering excites pity but it is the bloom of health that gives pleasure and delight.

THE DRESSING OF THE DOLL LEADING TO DRAWING, COUNTING, READING AND WRITING

Children of the two sexes have many amusements in common, and that is right since it will be the same when they grow up. But they have also distinctive tastes. Boys like movement and noise: their toys are drums, tops and go-carts. Girls would rather have things that look well and serve for adornment: mirrors, jewels, dress materials and most of all dolls. The doll is the special plaything of the sex. Here the girl's liking is plainly directed towards her lifework. For her the art of pleasing finds its physical expression in dress. That is all a child can acquire of this art.

Look at the little girl, busy with her doll all day long, changing its trappings, dressing and undressing it hundreds of times, always on the outlook for new ways of decoration whether good or bad. Her fingers are clumsy and her taste unformed, but already her bent is evident. "But," you may say, "she is dressing her doll, not herself." No doubt! The fact is that she sees her doll and not herself. For the time being she herself does not matter. She is absorbed in the doll and her coquetry is expressed through it. But the time will come when she will be her own doll.

Here then right at the beginning is a well-marked taste. You have only to follow it up and give it direction. What the little one wishes most of all is to decorate her doll, to make bows, tippets,[2] sashes, lacework for it. In all this she has to depend on the good will of others for help and it would be more convenient in every way if she could do it herself. Here is a motive for the first lessons given to her. They are not tasks prescribed for her but favors conferred. As a matter of fact nearly all little girls greatly dislike learning to read and write but they are always willing to learn to use the needle. They imagine themselves grown up and think happily of the time when they will be using their talents in adorning themselves.

The first open road is easy to follow. Tapestry which is the amusement of women is not much to the liking of girls, and furnishings, having nothing to do with the person, are remote from their interests. But needlework, embroidery and lacemaking come readily to them. The same willing prog-

2. Scarves.

ress leads on easily to drawing, for this art is not unrelated to that of dressing one's self with good taste. I would not have girls taught to draw landscape or to do figure painting. It will be enough if they draw leaves, flowers, fruit, draperies, anything that can add to the elegance of dress and enable them to make their own embroidery patterns. If it is important for men to confine their studies in the main to everyday knowledge, it is even more important for women whose way of life, though less laborious, does not permit them to devote themselves to the talent of their choice at the expense of their duties.

Whatever the humorists may say, good sense is common to the two sexes. Girls are generally more docile than boys and in any case have more need to be brought under authority. But this does not mean that they should be required to do things without seeing the use of them. The maternal art is to make evident the purpose of everything that is prescribed to them; and this is all the easier to do since the girl's intelligence is more precocious than the boy's. This principle excludes for both boys and girls not only studies which serve no obvious purpose but even those which only become useful at a later stage. If it is wrong to urge a boy to learn to read it is even worse to compel little girls to do so before making them realize the value of reading. After all what need have girls to read and write at an early age? They are not going to have a household to manage for a long time to come. All of them have curiosity enough to make sure that they will learn without compulsion when leisure and the occasion come. Possibly they should learn to count first of all. Counting has an obvious utility at all stages and much practice is required to avoid errors in calculation. I guarantee that if a little girl does not get cherries at tea time till she has performed some arithmetical exercise she will very soon learn to count.

THE PREVENTION OF IDLENESS AND INDOCILITY

Always justify the tasks you impose on young girls but impose them all the same. Idleness and indocility are their most dangerous faults and are most difficult to cure once they are contracted. Not only should girls be careful and industrious but they should be kept under control from an early age. This hardship, if it be a hardship, is inseparable from their sex. All their lives they will be under the hard, unceasing constraints of the proprieties. They must be disciplined to endure them till they come to take them as a matter of course and learn to overcome caprice and bow to authority. If they are inclined to be always busy they should sometimes be compelled to do nothing whatever. To save them from dissipation, caprice and fickleness they must learn above all to master themselves.

Do not let girls get bored with their occupations and turn too keen on their amusements, as happens in the ordinary education where, as Fénelon[3] says, all the boredom is on the one side and all the pleasure on the other. A girl will only be bored with her tasks if she gets on badly with the people around her. A little one who loves her mother or some darling friend will work in their company day in day out and never become tired. The constraint put on the child, so far from weakening the affection she has for her mother,

---

3. François de Salignac de la Mothe-Fénelon (1651–1715), French theologian, wrote about both male and female education.

will make it stronger; for dependence is a state natural to women, and girls realize that they are made for obedience.

And just because they have, or ought to have, little freedom, they carry the freedom they have to excess. Extreme in all things, they devote themselves to their play with greater zeal than boys. This is the second defect. This zeal must be kept within bounds. It is the cause of several vices peculiar to women, among others the capricious changing of their tastes from day to day. Do not deprive them of mirth, laughter, noise and romping games, but prevent them tiring of one game and turning to another. They must get used to being stopped in the middle of their play and put to other tasks without protest on their part. This daily constraint will produce the docility that women need all their lives. The first and most important quality of a woman is sweetness. Being destined to obey a being so imperfect as man (often with many vices and always with many shortcomings), she must learn to submit uncomplainingly to unjust treatment and marital wrongs. Not for his sake but for her own she must preserve her sweetness.

Girls should always be submissive, but mothers should not always be inexorable. To make a young person docile there is no call to make her unhappy. Indeed I should not be sorry if sometimes she were allowed to exercise a little cunning, not to elude punishment but to escape having to obey. Guile is a natural gift of her sex; and being convinced that all natural dispositions are good and right in themselves I think that this one should be cultivated like the rest. The characteristic cunning with which women are endowed is an equitable compensation for their lesser strength. Without it women would not be the comrade of man but his slave. This talent gives her the superiority that keeps her his equal and enables her to rule him even while she obeys.

Training for Womanhood (2) After the Age of Ten

ADORNMENT AND THE ARTS OF PLEASING

Fine dress may make a woman outstanding, but it is only the person herself that pleases. The attire that is least noticeable often makes its wearer most noticed. The education of young girls in this respect is utterly wrong. They are promised ornaments for rewards, and taught to love gorgeous apparel. "How beautiful she is," people say when a girl is all dressed up. This is quite wrong. Girls should learn that so much finery is only put on to hide defects, and that the triumph of beauty is to shine by itself. If I saw a young girl strutting like a peacock in gay garments I should show myself disturbed by this disguising of her figure. I should remark: "What a pity she is so overdressed. Do you not think she could do with something simpler? Is she pretty enough to dispense with this or that?" Perhaps she would then be the first to want the ornamentation removed so that she might be judged on her merits.

The first thing that young persons notice as they grow up is that external adornment is not enough, if they lack accomplishments of their own. They cannot make themselves beautiful, and it is too soon for them to play the coquette; but they are old enough to have graceful gestures, an attractive accent, a self-possessed bearing, a light step, and gracious manners. At this stage the voice improves in range, strength and tone, the arms develop, the movements become more confident; and with all this comes the discovery that there is an art by which they can win attention in any situation. From this point sewing and industry no longer suffice of themselves. New talents make their appearance and their usefulness is recognised.

I know that austere teachers are against teaching girls singing or dancing or any of the arts of pleasing. Secular songs, they say, are wicked. Dancing is an invention of the devil. A young girl should find entertainment enough in work and prayer. Strange entertainments these for a child of ten! For my part I greatly fear that the little saints who have been compelled to spend their childhood in prayer will occupy their youth in quite different ways and make up for what they missed in girlhood when they marry. We should consider what befits age as well as befits sex. A young girl should not live like her grandmother. She should be lively and merry. She should dance and sing as much as she likes and enjoy all the innocent pleasures of her age.

The agreeable accomplishments have been made too formal with maxims and precepts, and what ought to be only lighthearted games have been made burdensome for young people. Take music, for example. Is written music really necessary? Is it not possible to make the voice flexible and true and to teach expressive singing without the knowledge of a single note? Is the same kind of song suitable for all voices? Does the same method suit every temperament? I just do not believe that the same poses, steps, gestures, dances can befit a lively little brunette and a big blonde beauty with languishing eyes. So when I see a teacher giving the same lessons to two such people I say: "The man is following a routine. He knows nothing of his art."

The question is sometimes raised whether girls should be taught by masters or mistresses. Personally I would rather they had no need for either but should learn of themselves what they are strongly inclined to learn. In the arts which have pleasure as their object anyone can teach a young girl— father or mother, sister or brother, girlfriends, governesses, her mirror, above all her own taste. Taste is formed by industry and the natural gifts. By its means the mind is gradually opened to the idea of beauty in all its forms, and ultimately to those moral notions allied to beauty. This is perhaps one reason why the sentiments of decency and propriety are acquired by girls sooner than by boys. They certainly do not come from their governesses.

The art of speech takes first place among the pleasing arts. It is the mind with its succession of feelings and ideas that imparts life and variety to the countenance and inspires the talk that keeps the attention fixed on one object. That, I believe, is why young girls so quickly learn to chatter agreeably and put expression into their talk, even before they feel it. And that is why men find it amusing to listen to them so soon: they are waiting for the first gleam of intelligence to break through feeling.

The chatter of girls should not be curbed by the hard question that one puts to boys. "What's the good of that?" but rather by the other question that is no more easy to answer: "What will be the effect of that?" In the early years before they can distinguish good and evil, or pass judgment on other people, girls should make it a rule for themselves to say only agreeable things to those with whom they are talking. What makes this rule difficult in practice is that it must always be kept subordinate to our first rule: "Never tell a lie."

RELIGION

It is obvious that if male children cannot form any true idea of religion it is still more beyond the comprehension of girls. For that very reason I would speak to them about it at an earlier age, for if it were necessary to wait till they were able to discuss these profound questions the chances are that they would never be mentioned at all. Just as a woman's conduct is subject to public opinion, so is her faith subject to authority. Every girl should have her mother's religion, and every woman her husband's. Not being able to judge for themselves in such matters, they should accept the conviction of fathers and husbands as they accept that of the church.

* * *

Sophie

THE OUTCOME OF THE RIGHT EDUCATION

Let us now look at the picture of Sophie which has been put before Émile, the image he has of the woman who can make him happy.

Sophie is well born and has a good natural disposition. She has a feeling heart which sometimes makes her imagination difficult to control. Her mind is acute rather than precise: her temper easy but variable; her person ordinary but pleasing. Her countenance gives indication of a soul—with truth. Some girls have good qualities she lacks and others have the qualities she possesses in fuller measure; but none has these qualities better combined in a happy character. Without being very striking, she interests and charms, and it is difficult to say why.

Sophie is fond of dress and has taste enough to dress well. She dislikes rich clothes and her own always combine simplicity with elegance. She does not know which are the fashionable colors, but she knows to perfection those that suit herself. No girl gives less sign of careful dressing and yet no piece of hers has been selected casually. Her dress is modest in appearance but coquettish in effect. She does not display her charms, but hides them in such a way as to appeal to the imagination.

Sophie has natural talents. She is aware of them and has not neglected them. But not having been in a position to give much thought to their cultivation, she has been content to exercise her sweet voice in singing with truth and taste, and her little feet in walking with an easy grace. She has had no singing teacher but her father, and no dancing mistress but her mother. A neighboring organist has given her a few lessons in playing accompaniments on the harpsichord, which she has practiced alone. But music for her is a taste rather than a talent, and she cannot play a tune by note.

What Sophie knows best and has been most carefully taught are the tasks of her own sex, even those like dressmaking, not usually thought necessary. There is no kind of needlework she cannot do, but she has a special preference for lace making because it calls for a pleasing pose, as well as grace and lightness in the fingers. She has also applied herself to all the details of the household. She understands cookery and kitchen work. She knows the prices of provisions and can judge their qualities. She can keep accounts and is her mother's housekeeper. At the same time, she does not take equal pleasure in all her duties. For example, though she likes nice food she is not fond of cooking, and is rather disgusted with some of its details. For the same reason she has always been unwilling to inspect the garden. The soil seems to her dirty, and when she sees the dunghill she imagines she feels a smell. This defect she owes to her mother, according to whom cleanliness is one of the first obligations imposed on a woman by nature. The result is that cleaning takes up an undue amount of Sophie's time.

* * *

THEODOR GOTTLIEB VON HIPPEL
1741–1796

Theodor Gottlieb von Hippel, deeply committed to Enlightenment principles of rationality, belongs to the relatively small group of men supporting the rights of women in the late eighteenth century. Reason led him to the position that women should have the same privileges as men; he went so far as to claim that they should be allowed to serve as clergy. His views on women were as progressive as those of his most radical female contemporaries.

Born in East Prussia to a socially modest family (his father was a school superintendent; his mother came from a family of artisans), von Hippel followed two brilliant career paths: as a writer, working at nights and on holidays; and as a public administrator. He had begun by studying theology, but association with men of learning and high reputation led him to prefer a secular occupation. With great determination he succeeded in earning a law degree, after which he rose rapidly in the public bureaucracy. At the age of thirty-nine, he became governing mayor of Königsberg, the most important city in East Prussia; he also served the country in various ways.

Von Hippel wrote prolifically in several genres: sentimental fiction, poetry, hymns, and moral and social treatises. One of his most important publications was the literary sensation *Über die Ehe* (*On Marriage*, 1774; the author himself never married). The book went through several editions and showed evidence of the author's changing attitudes along the way: by the third edition of 1792, he had gone from assuming male supremacy to arguing for equality in marriage. *On Improving the Status of Women* appeared in 1792, the same year as that third edition. Like all von Hippel's work, it was published anonymously—presumably to avoid the public demands of an author's life, which might interfere with his official career.

Like many of the woman writers in this section, von Hippel allows himself an intermittent tone of indignation, even outrage, as he details the implicit injustices of being female. His rhetoric, though, depends largely on questions, abundant questions about the current state of things, the implicit answers to which should be self-evident.

On Improving the Status of Women[1]

FROM V

Suggestions for Improvement

Is the opposite sex always to remain as it has been and is? Are the human rights so basely taken away from the women, the civil rights so indecently withheld from them to be lost forever? Are the women never to attain an absolute value *in* and *for* the state, but always to possess mere relative worth? Are they never to take a direct part in the founding and preservation of the state? Are they never to think and act *for* and *by* themselves? Will we seek the answers to these questions in a subtle and sophisticated Roman legal fiction or in ancient and traditional property rights and statutes of limitation, so that we may again reject such questions and force them into a state of distasteful silence? Will we even soothe our masculine consciences with misgivings concerning the possible consequences, with further abuses, or with whatever other bugbears people use to frighten children and thus put off and put off again this concern of the entire human race? If so, then the glorious morning of redemption is not yet at hand. Will we be able to refrain from still calling ourselves Vandals and Goths[2]—the names of our forefathers of old—if we do not seek to rectify this injustice, and the sooner the better?

Abuse of a right does not cause its disappearance. Human rights can never be lost; civil rights only through a felony. This latter term, derived from feudal law (not a particularly exotic ancestry), designates all sins of omission or commission in the relationship between a vassal and his liege lord, according to their particular contract. Since both the vassal and the lord possess certain rights and duties in relation to each other, not only the former but also the latter is capable of committing a felony. And is the fief[3] itself lost merely because of a sin of omission or commission? Rather, is not the feudal lord, since he is nothing more or less than a human being, bound to hold the vassal to the performance of the deeds required by the contract and to the avoidance of those which run contrary to the contract, as well as to petition for damages if the contract is broken? Are contracts weakened when penalties for contravention are added to them, or are they not rather strengthened? Can the actions of one person ever be ascribed to another? And if the vassal loses his fief because of a felony, is the feudal lord not duty-bound to return it after his death to whomever inherits it from the vassal guilty of the felony and declared unworthy of holding a fief? Can a fief ever cease to exist because of a felony? And who made the man a feudal lord and the woman a vassal? Do they not both hold their fiefs from God? The earth could perhaps sooner be called a woman's fief than a man's, and is a very mixed fief at best. Let us put this felony against woman—of which neither nature nor history has the slightest comprehension—back in its place and not forget that God

---

1. Translated by Timothy F. Sellner.   2. Members of primitive tribes, at this time thought to have been barbaric.   3. A feudal estate.

entrusted the fief of the world to the first human couple, whom He (O, the worth of mankind) himself created, and that between His feudal law and the shoddiness of human law no comparison is imaginable. So much for *civil* rights! In matters of *human* rights only God can act as judge; and to fall into His hands—how comforting that is when compared to our own petty concerns here on earth!

Is it perhaps fear, or merely a grimace[4] of the same, which we pretend to in order to evade in a dignified way this well-founded and legally valid demand? "Become as little children"[5] is a well-intentioned piece of advice, for it is only a childlike fear which is not unmanly. It consists in taking care to avoid that which is contrary to the eternal laws of the True and the Good. That servile fear of punishment which arises when we do what these laws require and avoid what they prohibit is the truly unmanly one. Do we wish to fear a sex which was created to love, and which, even when it becomes angry, seldom lets the sun set on its anger? A sex which, except in one particular point (and here we are speaking of a sin against the Holy Spirit of the sex itself)[6] comes to meet its accuser even three-quarters of the way in order to offer him reconciliation! How much more cause do we have to fear ourselves than a sex which, if we were to restore it to its rights, would owe us good will, if not gratitude, and would strive with the very nature of its being to pay this debt gladly!

It is said that we can hardly hope that the human race, which has had the impertinence to have removed itself so far from nature, which will not allow itself be guided by religious sentiments of any sort, and which will not let itself be blinded by the deceptions of the state—that we can hardly hope it will conform its behavior to eternal laws either, and that consequently our fears and apprehensions are not so completely out of the question as one might generally think. My dear fellow! How can you require that the human race remain forever content to be led about as if on a leash? Do not both the deceptions of the state and religious sentiments, whenever the latter are not founded on fundamental principles, give rise all by themselves to disbelief and skepticism with regard to these laws? Is man never to be brought to a respect for duty? Is he never to attain to the main principle of life: "be reasonable"? Does sensuality mean more to him than moral reason and moral law? Will he never raise himself high enough to be worthy of his spiritual nature and to render respect and esteem also unto that which he cannot see? Should mere meekness of temperament determine our inclinations? Or is there such a thing, besides inclination of temperament, which, if it were to be distilled and refined, could be called an inclination of the heart? And is there not also, besides these two, an inclination of the mind, just as there are pleasures of the mind? Proud man does not long honor what he can perceive with his senses—he familiarizes himself with it, and it becomes a part of him. The single means which great heroes and scholars possess to survive in the face of extraordinary honor (and what is it really worth?) is to withdraw into themselves. As soon as we reveal ourselves for inspection, we

---

4. Affectation, sham.   5. Matthew 18.3.   6. The unforgivable sin against the Holy Spirit consists of rejection of its grace; von Hippel suggests that, analogously, rejection of the female sex to the point of allowing it no effect on the heart constitutes another unforgivable sin.

sell ourselves more cheaply. The greater the tension, the faster the recoil. Man must learn everything except dying. He can accustom himself to anything, good or bad. One leads a shy horse back to the object which has frightened it. And here, where the highest goal of his honor and dignity is at stake—is he to renounce his vigor and force? By no means! We can and shall come to the point where we will honor the divinity of the laws in their sanctuary, in our soul, and win our heart over by means of the beliefs of our mind. To be sure, at the present any legislator would be guilty of the grossest miscalculation if he formulated his laws on the basis of a firm confidence in the reasoning power and wisdom of his constituents. But will humanity never grow up? If not, then everything remains but a patch job on the old edifice of injustice, and man ought to be ashamed to call himself human.

If, however, mankind is capable of rising to that degree of perfection which it imagines is possible for itself; of exercising those virtues which in their ideal form give it pleasure, then let us do away with the mist of deception by means of which people were taken in who sooner or later will come to use their powers of reason and find themselves deceived. Men, would you not consider that fear to be barbarous and inhuman which took away all your liberty merely because it could be misused in part? What kind of name will you give to that fear which keeps you from giving the opposite sex back its honor? The times have passed for convincing the opposite sex that a state of guardianship like the one which has existed up to now is advantageous to them, and that this guardianship allows them to be more comfortable and carefree than emancipation, wherein they would be burdened with responsibilities, cares, anxiety, and a thousand other unpleasantries of civic life which they now hardly have the good fortune to be able to call by name. This is truly a shabby piece of trickery from that inhuman despot of whom we have been speaking, whereby he wishes to lighten the heavy chains of his cowardly slaves. As if liberty, with all her discomfort, were not to be preferred to the most comfortable slavery! "Do not think that the land of Württemberg was created merely on your account," wrote Frederick the Great to the present Duke of Württemberg. "But understand that Providence had you born in order to make your people happy." And men! do you wish to believe that half the world exists for your *bon plaisir*,[7] at your behest—that is, translated, for your own self-interest? Animals behave; people act. Why should the woman not be able to express her own *ego*?—truly a gentle word to those who understand ungrudging *nature*. Whoever understands only *art* is jealous and does not betray in himself the hand of the Master.

Is it not the greatest of human prerogatives that we are able to understand ourselves? Our price is our own matter; our value is the concern of God and righteous men. Did God make a mistake with the opposite sex? Or was it the men who sinned against the will of the Creator with regard to this sex? Why should women not be considered as persons? Why do we not know the difference between: "that is good," and "that is good for me"; or "that is right," and "that works to my advantage"?

Even now France is terrorizing with liberty those powers which threaten to restrict the excessive decrees of the National Assembly.[8] God help us! At

---

7. Pleasure.   8. The French, believing that the Austrians and Prussians threatened to interfere with their internal affairs, had declared war against Austria and Prussia.

the end of the eighteenth century, where no specter, even one of some considerable stature, a poltergeist for example, any longer has an effect, can people terrorize with *liberty*? Has it come to that? Why, even those who were raised in chains are now illuminated by the radiance from this word! Liberty, this divine spark by means of which we are what we are, and which renders us not so much unbridled and unrestrained as it binds us more firmly than anything else to the holy sanctuary of the eternal laws. The female sex was deprived of its *human* rights through no fault of its own, but merely through the great strides forward taken by all human activity and affairs in their advancement toward civilization. Moreover, it has not made any effort to regain, either by negotiation or by force, the *civil* rights which it lost at the time of the formation of smaller family-states and still awaits today, with complete self-abnegation, from our sense of justice and magnanimity. Do we wish to let it wait in vain? Will we reject the petition which nature submits on behalf of the female sex with a clear and straightforward "nay" at a time when human rights are being preached loudly from the housetops?[9]

The new French constitution deserves a repetition of my reproaches, because it has considered it sufficient not to make mention of an entire half of a nation, even though it did grant the rights of active citizenship to a smaller part of this nation—that is, to those who already enjoyed the right to religious toleration.[1] All human beings have the same rights—all the French, men and women alike, should be free and enjoy citizens' rights. Proposals for a *degradation civique*, a public ceremony in which men are declared unworthy of citizenship in the French state because of criminal acts, have not been extended to include the female sex. In such cases, women are merely to have the following curse spoken over them: "Your fatherland has found you guilty of an infamous act."

Mirabeau,[2] who perhaps had lost confidence in the present generation, finally came, like all great men of action, to place his hope for the future in education. In his posthumous work *Travail sur l'education publique*, published by his friend and physician, Cabanis, he assigns to the woman domesticity and the quiet and gentle virtues (is not every virtue quiet and gentle?) on which in the final analysis the happiness of the state is so dependent. Without getting involved myself in the dispute which has been conducted among his friends and enemies with such gross exaggeration concerning count or "no count" Mirabeau, may I be permitted at this point to contradict the assertion that a person who is a miserable wretch in his private life is capable of being the most virtuous citizen in public life, let alone the highest example of public life, a competent state official? An individual who is capable of indifference toward all that is good or bad, just or unjust, simply cannot be an upright citizen. And since the opposite sex is accustomed to drawing conclusions about a man's public life from his private life and very quickly learns to size up role players who do not act according to basic principles, but merely as the situation and circumstances seem to require, is it any wonder that these fortune and misfortune hunters seek to cast away the opposite sex as they do?

9. The phrase comes from Matthew 10.27: "What ye hear in the ear, that preach ye upon the housetops."
1. By an edict of 1787, the civil rights of Protestants had been reinstated in France.   2. Honoré-Gabriel Riqueti, comte de Mirabeau (1749–1791), had served as spokesman for the people in France during the Revolution.

We err if we let ourselves be convinced that women have no feeling for humanity's affair of honor, for the fight for freedom against absolute authority. Not only by their vociferous approval have they shown that they understand the value of liberty and that its flame is still able to blaze brightly among them, they have even worked themselves to break the fetters in which the nation lay, and probably are not to be held altogether responsible for the fact that they have only been allowed to play supporting roles in this drama.

That famous author of the history of Queen Elizabeth, Madame Kéralio,[3] has been defending the rights of humanity with candor, truth, and vigor ever since the Revolution in her *Journal d'État et du citoyen*. Women felt that snub, that profound silence on so glorious an occasion, that rejection when it came to serving the state. One among them dared to allow her indignation to become vocal. In a letter addressed to the National Assembly she made the observation that there was not a single word in the Constitution concerning women, although mothers would logically have had to be considered citizens of the state.[4] She then requested that mothers be allowed in the presence of the proper civil authorities to take the ceremonious oath of citizenship. This sacred ceremony certainly would have made it worthwhile to be a mother. History has not recorded what the representatives of the nation decided to do concerning this request from a noble Frenchwoman. It is with sadness that today, the 18th of March, 1792, I celebrate her memory, for I read in the newspapers that the French, unmoved by this suggestion, have let it come to pass that the opposite sex is now more urgently demanding these rights. It would have been much better if the men had come first with their offer of citizenship and given women no cause for the embarrassment of appearing ridiculous in this very serious matter. And would all those lamppost spectacles[5] have taken place if women had been legal voters in France?

Nevertheless, the question remains whether the fashionable ladies of Paris can overcome themselves and return far enough back to nature to be able to ponder the matter in humane and homely[6] fashion. Surely we can have more faith in the women of Germany. Does not God, who gives us our strength, also give us the right to use it? Should a woman wrap her talent in a handkerchief and bury it in the ground, thus deriving no interest from it— interest which would bring the state fruits, some perhaps of a thousandfold?[7]

It is up to human reason and its masterpiece, human society, to determine whether this strength should be given freer rein, or whether it is to be curtailed; however, the state may at no time take steps to suppress it completely. Could the state dare rob us of our liberty when the safeguarding of this very entity constitutes the chief reason for its existence? If members of a certain social class can only be represented by their peers; if even our ancestors had justice meted out to them and laws interpreted for them by those of equal rank, how can we exclude women from service to the state, insofar as legislation and the administration of laws is concerned? Do we wish to deny women initiation into these mysteries to keep them from seeing that our true

---

3. Louise-Félicité Guinement de Kéralio (1738–1821), a minor novelist who had helped to edit the journal that von Hippel refers to (and that, however, ceased publication).   4. Mothers had been officially granted equality in the family; therefore, they should logically have an equivalent position in the state.   5. Lawless executions carried out by Parisian mobs by means of hangings from public lampposts.   6. Familiar, friendly.   7. See the parable of the talents, Matthew 25.14–30.

weakness lies precisely at that point where we pretend our greatest strength by means of hieroglyphic rituals and incantations? Most officials of the state are nothing more than midwives to a mountain giving birth to a mouse, a mouse which nevertheless is baptized with the most glorious names and brought before the public with almost more fanfare than if a writer were to review his own books. Whoever has had the good fortune to have lived in close proximity to those who govern the state will readily grasp my meaning. What sweat of the brow!—councils and boards, assemblies and committees, tribunals and commissions! What great quantities of paper are carried about, written upon, and read! Stockbrokers of merely another sort—paper dealers of a higher dignity! And yet it seems as if everything is against everyone, because everyone is warring against everyone else.[8]

Are these the high and mighty committees and organizations from which the fair sex is excluded? One really ought to take the women in, just as in the Free Imperial cities political tub-thumpers and outright agitators were made members of the council in order to keep them quiet. And perhaps this little stratagem would already have been put into practice if we had been able to rely on the women a little more to keep their silence. Truly, in order for us to get our bearings once more we ought to allow women a voice in the matters of the state, to which they have an indisputable divine calling—which is more than can be said for most of the ne'er-do-wells whom we now call our high-ranking public officials.

Can it be denied that in every code of laws one can and must proceed from the basic premise of a natural equality and begin with the Garden of Eden—provided, of course, that one does not forget thereby the Fall of Man? Yet, such a promise of natural equality will and must, when applied to the state, have as a consequence political inequality among its citizens.[9] The opposite sex stands to gain from this natural equality, of course; nonetheless, it is simply not possible for the resulting political inequality to proclaim an entire sex—in which there are perhaps more who are of age than in our own—as unworthy for perhaps no other reason than the fact that the business of making laws rests entirely in the hands of the men. Should I add that I am not speaking here merely of using mouth and tongue to vote, but of using soul and heart as well? As soon as the time comes when physical strength, the notion of male superiority, and outmoded tradition play no part in the making of laws—and woe to the state which lays such cornerstones into its foundation—as soon as every normal society exists for the express purpose of bringing such natural preponderances into equilibrium once again, the women will have a right to demand of the state that it show them justice and not lose sight of their strength of soul in the face of their physical weakness, which for the most part is a result of blind prejudice. For is not the soul the chief part of man?

Natural equality necessitates political inequality, for the elevation of the natural worth of the human race is only possible through a reciprocal political contract between its members, and because outstanding men must be held in check by laws, just as genius must be subject to rules. But can this

---

8. A reference to the English philosopher Thomas Hobbes (1588–1679), who in *Leviathan* (1651) referred to the war of all against all.   9. At the beginning of the next paragraph, von Hippel explains this obscure comment.

fundamental principle, not contradictory in and of itself, be applied to an entire sex? Is it just, reasonable, advisable, or even humane that our entire sex be elevated and viewed as the center point around which the other is to revolve?

There are but two entities of which we can truly have any notion: nature and liberty—and for both natural science and ethics women have undeniable talent. And if we wished to have a visual representation of nature or liberty, both would have to assume the form of a woman. So what is it that stands in their way? Civil law? No book of laws, even if it were to speak with the tongues of angels, can become a Formula of Concord or an Augsburg Confession.[1] Laws educate men, but when men come of age, the laws must be educated by them. Assuming women are in fact physically weak—assuming!—what in that case would be the duty of the law? To be mighty on the side of the weak! It is not the strong who have need of the physician, but the weak.

Am I not aware that many women are still perfectly content with their relationship to their husbands? Nevertheless, whatever is based on personal sentiment must by its very nature be subject to change; and it is therefore necessary that, even in the face of the most tolerant of sentiments within the state, no intolerant passages remain in the law books. Who will stand up for those who come after us? Women know how to convince their men that they have no will of their own. But it is precisely when they seem to be denying their will in the most convincing way that they become the most autocratic—without mitigating in any way the belief of the men that these alone rule the roost. Women rule not by force (*vi*), but clandestinely and by way of request (*clam et precario*).[2]

The admirer of a woman believes himself to be in the service of a goddess who has the power to confer divinity the way university faculties confer doctoral degrees. The happy loved one believes himself to be at least half god himself, because he is so fortunate as to serve such a goddess. But if he wakes from this dream after a short while, behold! The caterpillar is transformed not into a butterfly, but into a harsh taskmaster, and his wife, deprived of all her divine attributes, becomes his slave. The bridegroom becomes not a husband, but a marital steward. In like manner, our monarchs have given up their status as gods and condescended to descend to the level of men—but in order to maintain their superiority over the rest of humanity they relegated the rest of humanity to a step below their former standing as human beings. Half-truth is more dangerous than total lie; the latter is more easily recognized than the former, which is accustomed to disguising itself with appearances in order to deceive doubly. Men, let us call mankind what God created as mankind! "Let us make man in our own image," it is written, and "in the image of God created he him; male and female created he them." They are bone of our bones, flesh of our flesh[3]—and why not citizens like us? Why not, for they lack neither the mind nor the strength for the virtues of citizenship, and it is but a matter of educating them to this role! True, as they are now—molded to be playthings for men—if they were suddenly to

1. Fundamental statements of Lutheran doctrine.   2. Von Hippel alludes to a Roman legal expression meaning "by stealth, force, or importunity"; women, he says, rule by stealth and importunity.   3. Genesis 1.26–27.

leave the gynaeceum[4] for the great marketplace of everyday life, which is such very unfamiliar soil for them in body and soul, and where they would be expected to play roles now filled by men, they would hardly make a tolerable debut. But who is asking this either of their heads or their hands? They should tread the paths we have trod, cross the deserts which were so difficult for us on our own way to Canaan;[5] only through education, instruction, and experience are they to reach that goal of which they are so worthy. It takes light nearly eight minutes to come from the sun to us, and thus we see any changes which occur in that body eight minutes after the fact. Pythagoras[6] required silence from all his pupils before their philosophical tongues could be loosened. Let the following serve as a rule of thumb for both men and women: for the *latter*, not to lay claim to the privileges of the master craftsman before they have the requisite years of apprenticeship behind them; for the *former*, not to demand fruits before their time from a sex which has been neglected for so long. Nature and the human mind very easily enter into proper harmony; and if the means appear insignificant—if, indeed, they are in fact so—who would judge them on their own merit and not rather on the magnitude of the ends which can be attained through them? An oak of no mean age can still be considered young when a shrub of the same age or a flowering plant at the base of its great trunk are at the end of their years. Not in individual cases, but in every case; not in individuals, but in the entire sex the dignity and the purpose of humanity are revealed.

Why the difference now in the upbringing of the two sexes, which begins at the cradle and ends at the bier? Why such a significant difference, as if the two sexes had not but one origin, were not made of the same stuff, were not born to a single destiny? Let the wall which divides us be broken apart— let us raise citizens for the state without regard to sex and leave that which women must know as housewives and mothers to separate instruction, and all will return to the order of nature. Child rearing is still far from what it could and should be. Only at a very late stage did it occur to us how we should have begun—that is, by determining first the purpose of child rearing, and then seeking out our goals and turning our course in their direction. Instead of straying far afield without plan or purpose like lost sheep, it should be our first concern to return home to nature and not seek the answers outside ourselves. For what is a man profited, if he shall gain the whole world, and lose his own soul? If child rearing has no purpose the bond which holds each of its individual phases together will loosen—and in our children lies the kingdom of God.

To be sure, we have of late begun to take this important need of the state to heart—but we have hardly just begun. The nations as a whole and even their representatives, whose primary and most important concern ought to be the education of the people, seem either not to perceive this need sufficiently, or in fact believe it their duty to place obstacles in the way of attempts to educate their citizens. If the leaders of the people would consider the fact that nothing but a proper education can safeguard forever their possession

4. The women's quarters in a Greek house.   5. The promised land of the biblical Israelites.   6. Pre-Socratic Greek philosopher and mathematician (ca. 582–ca. 507 B.C.E.).

of legal privileges based on contract, they would at the same time be reflecting upon what it is that insures their peace of mind. Formal instruction and child rearing, so different in form and purpose, have long been considered as one. For a long time we encouraged teachers, who as a rule had not been raised properly themselves, to bring our children up as well as teach them—and we then professed not to understand how a person could be educated and yet deficient in manners and morals. We firmly believed the golden proverb that art and morality are sister and brother, and it never occurred to anybody to investigate whether the two were instead related to each other in terms of cause and effect.

If we add to these deficiencies the fact that half of the human race was educated incorrectly or remained without any education whatsoever, and that precisely this half was entrusted with the most important phases of child rearing, then it is almost a miracle that we are human beings at all. Nevertheless, there can be no doubt that nature destined the opposite sex for the noble business of education and endowed it with all the talents and faculties necessary to fulfill this great calling: with the most receptive senses; with the most refined sensibilities for distinguishing, even in trivial matters and chance occurrences, between the true and the false, the genuine and that which is merely pretense.

The Socratic method, which Socrates learned from his mother, a midwife (*sage femme*), whereby he aimed at the delivery of souls[7] and became a philosopher (*homme sage*) in the process, is doubtless peculiar to the opposite sex, which never, even when dealing with voracious intellectual appetites in their children, overstuffs their bellies with facts, but supplies them with each new concept singly, transforming it as much as possible into a sense perception. Women give to each mental concept a body; they seek to clothe it and lend it perceptible form. Robinet[8] is of the opinion that Mother Nature endowed women with talkativeness so that they might be enabled all the better to pre-digest for their children that verbal fare which is too highly seasoned for them. Thus when we speak derisively of this tendency to talkativeness—is that not tantamount to giving a wonderful gift of nature a bad name? Rousseau once said to Grétry,[9] who offered him his hand to help him over a pile of stones: "Let me use my own strength." And for whom is the development of those ideas which lie hidden in the souls of children more natural than for this sex? It spins them out like webs, and binds the sensual and perceptible to mental concepts by means of images and parables. We ourselves prefer more heroic methods—yet does not in every case a feeling of emptiness follow the *aria di bravura*,[1] because a single impression which is too vivid tends to destroy the effect of the whole? It is not simply a matter of inducing accurate perception, but of extracting the sum and then concentrating one's efforts upon this sum. And how important here is the matter of *when* and *how!* The wanderer's every path leads him but to a single destination; every stream wends its way to the sea.

But how is it possible that women will be able to do justice to this profession, when these talents and capabilities are being so little developed? When we not only ignore them, but actually suppress them intentionally? The child

7. The characterization of Socrates as a midwife of souls comes from Plato's dialogue *Theaetetus* (ca. 369 B.C.E.). 8. Jean-Baptiste Robinet (1735–1820), French naturalist and philosopher. 9. Andre-Ernest-Modeste Grétry (1741–1813), French composer. 1. A florid aria demanding brilliant execution (Italian).

is sexless; why, then, do we seek to get the jump on nature, who is wiser than we are? Why have we begun to separate the sexes earlier than nature tells us we should? A child is sociable not because it is compelled to be so by a particular drive, but out of need and a desire to be active. It is certainly not moral sensibility—that capacity for feeling which bonds the adult to his peers so that he may communicate with them, so that he may grind off the sharp corners of his character and fulfill himself through others—which causes the child to be sociable. What does it know other than its own needs? It wishes but to be fed and amused—it is sociable out of a desire to pass the time pleasantly. Whenever this goal is attained, it is happy; differences in sex or in moral or intellectual capacity do not play any role whatsoever in its choice of a companion.

In European countries, it is not until around the age of twelve that the sex drive begins to develop in the female and bring about the awakening of an unaccustomed unrest, presentiments previously unnoticed, and yearnings of a gentle nature. Up to this time everything, excepting clothing, should remain the same, for this is the way nature would have it. Upbringing, instruction, and pastimes can be the same for both sexes, for during this period education should concern itself merely with the human being and the development of his capabilities, disregarding all further vocations except this first and most important one: to be a human being according to the original and authentic interpretation given him by nature. This single purpose should be the aim of all pedagogical endeavors; by serving in the role of midwife to young children, they should seek to extend the latitude for the first efforts of the child's awakening powers, and only gradually and with great care attempt to control the luxuriant outgrowth of these powers, thus giving proper but unobtrusive direction to the natural drives. During this period of time, instruction need not take differences in sex into account any more than it would acknowledge future relationships within the state. Has the child of this age even the slightest inkling of what is to come, not to mention a hard and fast notion of this? And does not all such instruction remain knowledge of the most useless sort, until in the course of nature an awareness develops for such teachings? All instruction during this period must be limited to that which we must believe, know, and do as *human beings*.

Why this difference between male and female instruction, since man and woman have not yet been born? Are children's games what they could and should be? Only recently, now that people are taking greater interest in the art of child rearing, have we begun to perceive the great influence of this facet of life; yet have we not, as usual, made poor use of these games by raising play to the level of a general technique of instruction? Games must never become teaching methods, although they can serve very well as incentives for enriching the memory and training the powers of reason. Yet, whenever they are used to facilitate instruction, their value is and will remain purely subjective. With children's games we must always keep the goal in mind of preoccupying children in a way which is commensurate with their capabilities and their age. The children themselves, however, must never guess this intention, for otherwise the game loses its meaning. Children must become accustomed from an early age to differentiating between play and business in order that they may come to respect and love the latter, while learning to renounce the former—if they are not to remain children forever.

Yet why should I go on about a matter which is the object of every other word of our writers and which is preached from every housetop? I shall return to my point with the suggestion that until the child becomes a young man or woman it should remain in the hands and under the supervision of the female sex. Both the state and the women would gain thereby. All children's schools should have women as teachers and supervisors, for nature has richly endowed this sex with excellent faculties for such work. Purity, a requisite so important in the care of children; tenderness, patience, endurance in the face of seemingly trivial endeavors; sympathy, talkativeness, and other such character traits indispensable for the educating of children appear to be inherent in the female sex, and merely artificially acquired skills in the male. As nature is to art, so would a system of child rearing and education by women be to the present educational system. Even now the part they play is great; what would we be capable of without their assistance? O, what wonderful training for mothers of the middle class it is when a household of crying and screaming children tests their patience, and the questions of curious, bashful young girls and impudent boys confuse and embarrass them. It is incomprehensible to me how a good woman is able to handle so many heterogeneous matters simultaneously—here she wrests knife, fork, and scissors out of the hand of little Field Marshal James; there she pulls harmful objects from the mouth of the omnivorous Bishop Peter; now she shoos the flies from little sleeping Henrietta; and how difficult it is to pacify the young madcap Karl, who jumps continuously from one pastime to another! How many vigils and how many daily cares are their share and inheritance within the family duties which fall to their lot! And does not even the lady of high station, who according to the custom and tradition of the land possesses the harsh right to treat her little ones as foundlings[2] and is herself hardly busy at all—does she not still have much more to occupy her time than her officious lazybones of a husband, who, overburdened as he is with affairs of enormous inconsequence and elegant infirmities, nevertheless finds time to spin so many other such webs outside the spinning rooms of his own council chambers, webs which almost always wind up complicating simple matters and attempting to impart an air of significance to things frivolous?

But what is that you say? Would women not, by virtue of their timidity and an awareness of their own weakness, pamper and coddle the children and make the human race even more feeble and delicate than it already is? This is an objection which seems to have some basis in truth; but in fact it is nothing more than an apparition which strikes our imaginations with terror, and which must necessarily vanish the closer women approach to their goal. Tenderness, or even actual weakness of the constitution, is frequently congenital and much less often a consequence of delicate upbringing. In the latter case the skill of the teacher can often restore in boyhood and early manhood whatever well-intentioned, but poorly understood delicacy of upbringing ruined in the child. This fear will vanish only when the order of nature which we have reversed is once again brought back to its previous state, and we decide once and for all to give the opposite sex some guidance in this matter. We have already partially given up turning children into dolls and smothering them with soft feathers, and then, when they availed them-

2. Upper-class women in France sent their infants to a wet nurse to be suckled.

selves of their lungs, the only way out of their predicament, anesthetizing them with soothing syrup[3] or a gentle box on the ears; we will also surely cease to keep children away from water and fresh air as soon as women begin to feel more comfortable dealing with the influence of these two elements.[4] Attempts have already been made to cast suspicion on the type of clothing children have worn up to now, and to criticize it for that constraint and pressure which causes the effect of oxygen on the entire body to be lost, the child's ability to exhale to be impaired, his chest to constrict, his heart to be crushed, his strength and vitality to slacken before its time and the whole machine, in effect, to become overwrought. The tyranny of fashion! Even our painters and sculptors are for their own part exposed to the unfortunate embarrassment of having to portray their subjects in some sort of idealized costume simply because the altar of true good taste has no place for the absurdities of fashion—an act of the most exquisite revenge by nature on those who would disdain her! And while we are in the process of improving the status of women, nothing would be easier than to bring about some sort of clothing regulations based both on physical and moral considerations, then to produce such clothing cheaply, naturally, and simply, and thus to remove from the matter all the exaggeration and foppery now associated with it. Only from unpampered, stable, and solid *children* can we obtain unpampered, stable, and solid *adults!* Let women first feel strong themselves, then they will bear with their bodies children who are strong in both body and soul, and with the power of their spirit they will continually "re-bear" them their whole life long—that is, they will bring them into the world and educate them as well.

*   *   *

3. Which characteristically contained opiates.   4. Previously, women were not allowed to enjoy the open air themselves.

HANNAH MORE
1745–1833

A writer and thinker of enormous influence in her own time, Hannah More identified herself firmly as a conservative. She always wrote from the perspective of Evangelical piety, grounding her educational and philosophical theories in her understanding of Christian imperatives. Thus, she brought to the subject of the female in contemporary society a point of view not widely represented at the time.

An avid learner, More was educated, and later taught, at her sisters' school for girls in Bristol. She became engaged at the age of twenty-two to one William Turner, who on three occasions broke the engagement. Finally, as payment for breach of promise, he gave her an annuity that made her financially independent. Income from her writing soon abundantly supplemented this money. More never married.

She wrote plays, a didactic novel, and many works of social commentary. *Strictures on the Modern System of Female Education,* published in the last year of the eighteenth century, resembled other radical treatments of women's education in its emphasis on the destructiveness of existing systems of female education. But More disclaimed any feminist intention. She recommended, however, a solid system of content-based education that would more highly develop the intellectual capacity of women than was currently the norm.

Strictures on the Modern System of Female Education

Introduction

It is a singular injustice which is often exercised towards women, first to give them a very defective Education, and then to expect from them the most undeviating purity of conduct;—to train them in such a manner as shall lay them open to the most dangerous faults, and then to censure them for not proving faultless. Is it not unreasonable and unjust, to express disappointment if our daughters should, in their subsequent lives, turn out precisely that very kind of character for which it would be evident to an unprejudiced bystander that the whole scope and tenor of their instruction had been systematically preparing them?

Some reflections on the present erroneous system are here with great deference submitted to public consideration. The Author is apprehensive that she shall be accused of betraying the interests of her sex by laying open their defects: but surely, an earnest wish to turn their attention to objects calculated to promote their true dignity, is not the office of an enemy. So to expose the weakness of the land as to suggest the necessity of internal improvement, and to point out the means of effectual defense, is not treachery, but patriotism.

Again, it may be objected to this little work, that many errors are here ascribed to women which by no means belong to them *exclusively,* and that it seems to confine to the sex those faults which are common to the species: but this is in some measure unavoidable. In speaking on the qualities of one sex, the moralist is somewhat in the situation of the Geographer, who is treating on the nature of one country:—the air, soil, and produce of the land which he is describing, cannot fail in many essential points to resemble those of other countries under the same parallel;[1] yet it is his business to descant on the one without adverting to the other: and though in drawing his map he may happen to introduce some of the neighboring coast, yet his principal attention must be confined to that country which he proposes to describe, without taking into account the resembling circumstances of the adjacent shores.

It may be also objected that the opinion here suggested on the state of manners among the higher classes of our countrywomen, may seem to controvert the just encomiums of modern travelers, who generally concur in ascribing a decided superiority to the ladies of this country over those of every other. But such is the state of foreign manners, that the comparative praise is almost an injury to *English* women. To be flattered for excelling those whose

1. At the same latitude.

standard of excellence is very low, is but a degrading kind of commendation; for the value of all praise derived from superiority depends on the worth of the competitor. The character of British ladies, with all the unparalleled advantages they possess, must never be determined by a comparison with the women of other nations, but by what they themselves might be if all their talents and unrivaled opportunities were turned to the best account.

Again, it may be said, that the Author is less disposed to expatiate on excellence than error: but the office of the historian of human manners is delineation rather than panegyric. Were the end in view eulogium[2] and not improvement, eulogium would have been far more gratifying, nor would just objects for praise have been difficult to find. Even in her own limited sphere of observation, the Author is acquainted with much excellence in the class of which she treats;—with women who, possessing learning which would be thought extensive in the other sex, set an example of deep humility to their own;—women who, distinguished for wit and genius, are eminent for domestic qualities;—who, excelling in the fine arts, have carefully enriched their understandings;—who, enjoying great affluence, devote it to the glory of God;—who, possessing elevated rank, think their noblest style and title is that of a Christian.—

That there is also much worth which is little known, she is persuaded; for it is the modest nature of goodness to exert itself quietly, while a few characters of the opposite cast seem, by the rumor of their exploits, to fill the world; and by their noise to multiply their numbers. It often happens that a very small party of people, by occupying the foreground, so seize the public attention, and monopolize the public talk, that *they* appear to be the great body: and a few active spirits, provided their activity take the wrong turn and support the wrong cause, seem to fill the scene; and a few disturbers of order, who have the talent of thus exciting a false idea of their multitudes by their mischiefs, actually gain strength and swell their numbers by this fallacious arithmetic.

But the present work is no more intended for a panegyric on those purer characters who seek not human praise because they act from a higher motive, than for a satire on the avowedly licentious, who, urged by the impulse of the moment or led away by the love of fashion, dislike not censure, so it may serve to rescue them from neglect or oblivion.

There are, however, multitudes of the young and the well-disposed, who have as yet taken no decided part, who are just launching on the ocean of life, just about to lose their own right convictions, and to counteract their better propensities, unreluctantly yielding themselves to be carried down the tide of popular practices, sanguine and confident of safety.—To these the Author would gently hint, that, when once embarked, it will be no longer easy to say to their passions, or even to their principles, "Thus far shall ye go, and no further."

Should any reader revolt at what is conceived to be unwarranted strictness in this little book, let it not be thrown by in disgust before the following short consideration be weighed.—If in this Christian country we are actually beginning to regard the solemn office of Baptism as merely furnishing an

2. Eulogy, praise.

article to[3] the parish register;—if we are learning from our indefatigable Teachers, to consider this Christian rite as a legal ceremony retained for the sole purpose of recording the *age* of our children;—then, indeed, the prevailing System of Education and Manners on which these volumes presume to animadvert, may be adopted with propriety and persisted in with safety, without entailing on our children or on our ourselves the peril of broken promises or the guilt of violated vows.— —But, if the obligation which Christian Baptism imposes be really binding;—if the ordinance have, indeed, a meaning beyond a mere secular transaction, beyond a record of names and dates;—if it be an institution by which the child is solemnly devoted to God as his Father, to Jesus Christ as his Savior, and to the Holy Spirit as his Sanctifier; if there be no definite period assigned when the obligation of fulfilling the duties it enjoins shall be superseded;—if, having once dedicated our offspring to their Creator, we no longer dare to mock Him by bringing them up in ignorance of His Will and neglect of His Laws;—if, after having enlisted them under the banners of Christ, to fight manfully against the three great enemies of mankind,[4] we are no longer at liberty to let them lay down their arms; much less to lead them to act as if in alliance instead of hostility with these enemies;—if after having promised that they shall renounce the vanities of the world, we are not allowed to invalidate the engagement;—if after such a covenant we should tremble to make these renounced vanities the supreme object of our own pursuit or of *their* instruction;—if all this be really so, then the Strictures on Modern Education in the first of these Volumes, and on the Habits of polished Life in the second, will not be found so repugnant to truth, and reason, and common sense, as may on a first view be supposed.

But if on candidly summing up the evidence, the design and scope of the Author be fairly judged, not by the customs or opinions of the worldly, (for every English subject has a right to object to a suspected or prejudiced jury,) but by an appeal to that divine law which is the only infallible rule of judgment; if on such an appeal her views and principles shall be found censurable for their rigor, absurd in their requisitions, or preposterous in their restrictions, she will have no right to complain of such a verdict, because she will then stand condemned by that court to whose decision she implicitly submits.

Let it not be suspected that the Author arrogantly conceives herself to be exempt from that natural corruption of the heart which it is one chief object of this slight work to exhibit; that she superciliously erects herself into the impeccable censor of her sex and of the world; as if from the critic's chair she were coldly pointing out the faults and errors of another order of beings, in whose welfare she had not that lively interest which can only flow from the tender and intimate participation of fellow feeling.

With a deep self-abasement arising from a strong conviction of being indeed a partaker in the same corrupt nature; together with a full persuasion of the many and great defects of these Volumes, and a sincere consciousness of her inability to do justice to a subject which, however, a sense of duty impelled her to undertake, she commits herself to the candor of that Public

3. Entry in.   4. The world, the flesh, and the devil.

which has so frequently, in her instance, accepted a right intention as a substitute for a powerful performance.

Bath,
March 14, 1799.

OLYMPE DE GOUGES
1748–1793

Born Marie Gouzes in the south of France, her father a butcher, her mother a servant, Olympe de Gouges reinvented herself after the birth of her son and the death of her husband, a man much older than she, to whom she had been married at sixteen. At this point, she changed her name and announced her intention of not remarrying. She went to Paris, circulated in intellectual society, and began to write plays. Just before the French Revolution, she became interested in politics. She advanced highly progressive ideas, including the emancipation of slaves and the rights of orphans and unwed mothers. *The Rights of Woman* was one of many articles and pamphlets in which she demanded equality for women. Since the fashionable circles in which she had moved found her much less appealing in her new political guise, de Gouges was no longer widely accepted socially.

The Rights of Woman is unusual for the specificity and pragmatism of its recommendations. Its author thinks precisely about how existing social structures reinforce inequality, and she addresses the kinds of legalities that must be considered in order to change such structures. Women can legally be guillotined, she observes; they should be allowed to make public speeches as well. She herself provided an example of the flaw in this argument: allowed freedom of public utterance, she was guillotined as a direct consequence. She proved too radical even for the revolutionaries, who executed her as a "public enemy."

The Rights of Woman[1]

Man, are you capable of being just? It is a WOMAN who asks you this question; you will not deprive her at least of this right. Tell me what gave you the supreme authority to oppress my sex? Your strength? Your talents? Observe the creator in his wisdom; Go through nature in all its grandeur, to which you seem to wish to be close. And if you dare, give me one example of this tyrannical empire. Go back to the animals, consult the elements, study plant life, and finally cast a glance, on all modifications in organized matter; and bow down before the evidence when I offer you the means to do so. Search, dig deeper and try to distinguish, if you can, sex in nature's administration. Everywhere you will find them indistinct; everywhere they cooperate in a harmonious whole in this immortal masterpiece.

---

1. Translated under the direction of Nirupama Rastogi.

Man alone is in principle tied down to this exception. Bizarre, blind, bloated with science and degenerated, in this century of enlightenment and wisdom, in the crassest of ignorance. He wishes to rule as a despot over a sex that is endowed with all intellectual faculties; he claims to enjoy the revolution and reclaim his rights to equality, in order to say nothing more.

The Rights of Woman

Declaration of the Rights of Woman and of the Woman-Citizen

To be decreed by the National Assembly in its last sessions or in those of the next legislature.

PREAMBLE

Mothers, daughters, sisters, representatives of the nation, demand to be constituted into a national assembly, considering that ignorance, forgetfulness or contempt of the rights of the WOMAN, are the sole causes of public miseries, and of the corruption of governments, have resolved to set forth in a solemn declaration, the natural inalienable and sacred rights of the WOMAN, in order that this declaration, being ever present to all members of the social body, may unceasingly remind them of their rights and duties, in order that the acts of the power of women, and those of the power of men may at each moment be compared with the aim of all political institutions and thereby be more respected, in order that the demands of women-citizens henceforth founded on simple and incontestable principles, may always turn to maintaining the constitution, good mores, and the happiness of all. In consequence, the sex superior in beauty as in courage, in maternal sufferings, recognizes and declares, in the presence and under the auspices of the Supreme Being, the following Rights of the Woman and of the Woman-Citizen.

I

Woman is born free and remains equal to man in rights. Social distinctions can be based only upon common utility.

II

The aim of every political association is the preservation of the natural and unwritten rights of woman and of man: these rights are liberty, prosperity, security and especially resistance to oppression.

III

The principle of all sovereignty resides essentially in the Nation, which is nothing but the coming together of woman and man: no body, no individual can exercise any authority that does not expressly emanate from it.

IV

Liberty and justice consist in restoring all that which belongs to others: accordingly the exercise of the natural rights of the woman has for its only limits the perpetual tyranny that man imposes on her; these limits must be reformed according to the laws of nature and of reason.

V

The laws of nature and of reason prohibit all actions injurious to society: all that is not forbidden by these wise and divine laws, cannot be prohibited, and no one can be constrained to do what they do not order.

VI

Law must be the expression of the general will; all women and male citizens must take part, personally, or through their representatives in its formation; it must be the same for all: all women and male citizens, being equal in its eyes, must be equally eligible to all dignities, places and public offices, according to their capacities, and without other distinctions than those of their virtues and talents.

VII

No woman is an exception; she is accused, arrested and detained according to cases determined by law. Women obey, just as men, this rigorous law.

VIII

The law must establish only penalties that are strictly and obviously necessary, and no one can be punished except by virtue of a law established and promulgated prior to the offence and legally applicable to women.

IX

Any woman being declared guilty, all severity is exercised by the law.

X

No one ought to be harmed on account of his opinions, even the fundamental ones. Woman has the right to mount the scaffold; she must also have the right to take to the rostrum;[2] provided her manifestations do not disturb the public order established by law.

XI

The free communication of thought and of opinion is one of the most precious rights of women, as this liberty assures the legitimacy of fathers in relation to children. Every woman-citizen can therefore say freely, I am the mother of the child that belongs to you without having to conceal the truth due to a barbarous prejudice only to respond to the abuse of this liberty in cases determined by law.

---

2. Women can be executed; they should also be allowed to make speeches.

XII

The guarantee of the rights of women and the woman-citizen requires a major service, this guarantee must be instituted for the advantage of all, and not for the specific utility of the women to whom it is entrusted.

XIII

For the maintenance of the public force, and for administrative expenditure, the contribution of women and men is equal; she has a share in all chores, in all painful tasks; she should therefore have the same share in the distribution of posts, employment, responsibilities, dignities and industry.

XIV

Women and men-citizens have the right to ascertain, for themselves, or through their representatives, the necessity for a public fund. Women-citizens can become members only if they are eligible for an equal share, not only in fortune, but even in public administration, and to establish the quota, the taxable property, the collection and the duration of the tax.

XV

The mass of women along with men contributing to the public fund, have the right to ask for an account, from every public agent and its administration.

XVI

Every society, where guarantee of rights is not assured, nor the separation of powers determined, has no constitution: the constitution is nothing if the majority of the individuals who constitute the nation, has not cooperated in its drafting.

XVII

Properties belong to all sexes united or separated; they are for everyone an inviolable and sacred right; no one can be deprived of it as a true heritage of nature, unless a public necessity, legally established, evidently demands it, and under the condition of a just and prior indemnity.

POSTAMBULE

Women, rouse yourself, the tolling of the bell of reason can be heard throughout the universe; recognize your rights. Nature's mighty empire is no longer encircled by prejudices, fanaticism, superstition and lies. Truth's flaming torch has dispelled all clouds of foolishness and usurpation. Man-slave has multiplied his strengths and he needs to resort to yours to break his shackles. Once free, he has become unjust towards his companion. O women! Women, when will you cease to be blind? What are the benefits that you have reaped from the revolution? A contempt all the more marked, a disdain all the more evident. During centuries of corruption you have only reigned over the weakness of men. Your empire is destroyed, what then are you left with? The conviction of man's injustices, the demand for your heritage, founded on wise decrees of nature; what would you have to fear for in such a beautiful enterprise? The wit of the legislator in the marriage of Cana?[3] Are you afraid that our French legislators, correctors of these morals, hanging for long to the branches of politics, but which are no longer in season, will repeat to you: WOMEN, what is common between you and us? Everything, you would have to answer. If they persisted stubbornly in their weaknesses, in putting this thoughtlessness in contradiction with their principles; oppose courageously with the force of reason the vain pretensions of superiority; assemble under the banner of philosophy; unfurl all the energy of your character, and you will soon see these arrogant ones become your servile worshippers, cringing at your feet, but proud to share with you the treasures of the Supreme Being. Whatever be the barriers against you, it is within your power to cross them; you only have to wish it. Let us move on now to the appalling picture of what you have been in society, and since there is talk, at this moment, of a national education, let us see if our wise legislators will think soundly about women's education.

Women have done more harm than good. Constraint and dissimulation have been their lot. What force took from them, has been returned to them by guile; they have resorted to all the resources of their charms, and the most irreproachable man could not resist them. Poison, chains, everything was subjugated to them; they controlled crime as well as virtue. The French government specially, for centuries, depended on the nocturnal administration of women,[4] the cabinet had no secrets to be indiscreet about. Be it the embassy, the armed forces, the ministry, the presidency, the pontificate or the cardinalship; in short all that characterizes the stupidity of men, secular or religious, all was submitted to the cupidity and to the ambition of this sex earlier disdainful and respected, and since the revolution, respectable and disdained.

In this sort of antithesis, how many remarks do I not have to offer! I only have a moment to make them, but this moment will arrest the attention of the most remote posterity. Under the Ancien Régime,[5] all was perverted, all guilty; but could we not notice an improvement of things in the very substance of vices? A woman only needed to be beautiful or pleasant; when she possessed these two qualities, she saw a hundred fortunes at her feet. If she did not take advantage of them, she had a bizarre personality, or a less common philosophy, which led her to scorn riches, thus she was only considered headstrong. The most indecent woman made herself respected with gold. Trade in women was a kind of industry accepted in the highest classes and which, henceforth, will have no credit. If it yet had any, the REVOLUTION would be lost, and under new relationships, we would still be corrupt. However, can reason conceal the fact that any other path to fortune is closed to the woman bought by man, like a slave on the African coast? The difference is considerable, we know it. The slave has command over the master, but if the master gives her freedom without reward, and at an age when the slave has lost all her charms, what becomes of this unfortunate woman? The toy

3. At which Jesus performed his first miracle, turning water into wine.　4. The manipulations of women at night, presumably through "pillow talk."　5. The old monarchical, hierarchical system.

of contempt; the very doors of charity are shut for her; she is poor and old one says; why did she not know how to become rich? Other examples, even more touching, come to the mind. A young woman without any experience, seduced by the man she loves, will abandon her parents to follow him; the ungrateful man will leave her after a few years, and the more she has aged with him, the more inhuman his fickleness will be; if she has children he will abandon her all the same. If he is rich, he will think himself exempted from sharing his fortune with his noble victims. If some commitment binds him to his duties, he will violate its power, but hope for everything from the law. If he is married, all other commitments lose their force. What laws remain then to be formed in order to extirpate vice from its very roots? That of sharing wealth between men and women, and that of public administration. One can easily imagine that a woman born in a rich family earns a lot with equal sharing. But she who is born in a poor family, with merits and virtues, what is her lot? Poverty and opprobrium. If she does not excel precisely in music or in painting, she cannot be admitted to any public function even if she is fully capable. I will speak at length about them in the new edition of all my political writings, which I propose to give to the public in a few days' time, with notes.

I take up my text concerning mores.[6] Marriage is the tomb of confidence and love. The married woman can with impunity give bastards to her husband, and fortune which does not belong to them. The unmarried one, has but one weak right; the old and inhuman laws refused her and her children this right in the name and property of the father, and no new laws have been made on this subject. If an attempt to give an honorable and just place to my sex is, at this moment, considered as a paradox on my part and as attempting the impossible, I leave to future men the glory of treating this subject; but in the meanwhile, it can be prepared through national education by restoring customs and conjugal conventions.

---

6. Morally binding customs.

MARY ROBINSON
1758–1800

Author of a famous scandalous memoir largely about her affair with the Prince of Wales, Mary Robinson distinguished herself as an actress and a woman of fashion in addition to pursuing an extensive career as a writer. She wrote mainly sentimental novels and poetry. Her *Letter to the Women of England, on the Injustice of Mental Subordination* came nearly at the end of her life; it suggests that she felt she had paid a high cost for her glamorous existence.

Born Mary Darby, daughter of a wealthy family, Robinson had a happy childhood, which abruptly ended when her father, after using all of his money to establish a whale fishery, left his family, taking his mistress with him. The deserted wife and her children thereafter struggled with poverty. Mary married Thomas Robinson under the impression that he had a rich and elderly uncle who would soon make him financially secure. But Thomas Robinson was in fact the illegitimate son of a Welshman. He was also a gambler who squandered whatever money his family obtained.

Mary Robinson spent fifteen months in debtors' prison with her husband and her infant daughter. Thereafter, she made for herself a more prosperous life, first of all as a successful actress. Her liaison with the Prince of Wales was also financially advantageous. And she made money by writing several popular novels as well as volumes of poems.

A *Letter to the Women of England* rings with personal feeling. Like some of Robinson's novels, it emphasizes the treachery of men. However, it attacks not only men as unreasonable and unjust beings, but the entire system of oppressive social custom. The author seems less concerned about appealing to readers than simply expressing her own passionately held views, the product of hard experience.

From A Letter to the Women of England, on the Injustice of Mental Subordination

* * *

Prejudice (or policy) has endeavored, and indeed too successfully, to cast an odium on what is called a *masculine* woman; or, to explain the meaning of the word, a woman of enlightened understanding. Such a being is too formidable in the circle of society to be endured, much less sanctioned. Man is a despot by nature; he can bear no equal, he dreads the power of woman, because he knows that already half the felicities of life depend on her; and that if she be permitted to demand an equal share in the regulations of social order, she will become omnipotent.

I again recur to the prominent subject of my letter, viz. that woman is denied the first privilege of nature, the power of SELF-DEFENSE. There are lords of the creation, who would not hesitate to rob a credulous woman of fortune, happiness, and reputation, yet they would deem themselves justified in punishing a petty thief, who took from them a watch or a pocket handkerchief. *Man* is not to be deprived of *his* property; *he* is not to be pilfered of the most trifling article, which custom has told him is necessary to *his* ideas of luxury. But WOMAN is to be robbed of that peace of mind which depended on the purity of her character; *she* is to be duped out of all the proud consolations of independence; defrauded of her repose, wounded in the sensibilities of her heart; and, because she is of the *weaker* sex, she is to bear her injuries with *fortitude*.

If a man is stopped on the highway, he may shoot the depredator: and he will receive the thanks of society. If a WOMAN were to act upon the same principle, respecting the more atrocious robber who has deprived her of all that rendered life desirable, she would be punished as a *murderer*. Because the highwayman only takes that which the traveler can afford to lose, and the loss of which he will scarcely feel; and the WOMAN is rendered a complete bankrupt of all that rendered life supportable. The swindler and the cheat are shut out from society; but the avowed libertine, the very worst of defrauders, is tolerated and countenanced by our most fastidious British females.

This is one of the causes why the manners of the age are so unblushingly licentious: *men* will be profligate, as long as *women* uphold them in the practice of seduction.

If, in the common affairs of life, a man be guilty of perjury, on conviction he is sentenced to undergo the penalty of his crime, even though the motive for committing it, were unimportant to the community at large, and only acting against the plea of individual interest. But if a man takes an oath, knowing and premeditatedly resolved to break it, at the altar of the Divinity, his crime is tolerated, and he pleads the force of example, in extenuation of his apostasy. Man swears to love and to cherish his wife, never to forsake her in sickness, or in health, in poverty or wealth, and to keep to her *alone* so long as they both shall live. Let me ask these lawmakers, and these law-*breakers*, these sacriligious oath takers, whether nine out of ten, are not conscious of committing perjury at the moment when they make a vow so universally broken? But man is permitted to *forswear* himself, even at the altar dedicated to the Supreme Being! He is allowed, even *there*, to consider the *most* sacred of ceremonies as merely a political institution, of which he may exclusively avail himself as far as it tends to the promotion of his interest, while neither the publicity, nor the number of his infidelities, attach the badge of worldly censure to his conduct. He is still the lordly reveler; the master of his pleasures; the tolerated breaker of his oath: he pleads the frailty of human nature, though he, as the stronger creature, is supposed to possess an omnipotent source of mental power; he urges the sovereignty of the passions, the dominion of the senses, the sanction of long established custom. He is a man of universal gallantry; he is consequently courted and idolized by the generality of women, though all his days and all his actions prove, that woman is the victim of his falsehood.

Now examine the destiny of the *weaker* sex, under similar circumstances. Woman is to endure neglect, infidelity, and scorn: she is to endure them patiently. She is not allowed to plead the frailty of human nature; she is to have no passions, no affections; and if she chance to overstep the boundaries of chastity, (whatever witcheries and machinations are employed to mislead her;) if she violates that oath, which, perhaps the pride of her kindred, family interest, ambition, or compulsion, extorted from her, custom, that pliant and convenient friend to man, declares her infamous. While women, who are accessories to her disgrace, by countenancing her husband's infidelities, condemn the wife with all the vehemence of indignation; because woman is the weaker creature, and most subjected to temptation! because man errs voluntarily; and woman is seduced, by art and by persecution, from the paths of Virtue.

There is scarcely an event in human existence, in which the oppression of woman is not tolerated. The laws are made by man; and self-preservation is, *by them*, deemed the primary law of nature. Hence, woman is destined to be the passive creature: she is to yield obedience, and to depend for support upon a being who is perpetually authorized to deceive her. If a woman be married, her property becomes her husband's; and yet she is amenable to the laws, if she contracts debts beyond what that husband and those laws pronounce the necessaries of existence. If the comforts, or even the conveniences of woman's life rest on the mercy of her ruler, they will be limited indeed. We have seen innumerable instances, in cases of divorce, where the weaker, the defenseless partner is allotted a scanty pittance, upon which she is expected to live *honorably;* while the husband, the lord of the creation, in the very plenitude of wealth, in the very zenith of splendor, is permitted openly to indulge in every *dishonorable* propensity. Yet, he is commiserated as the injured party; and she is branded with the name of infamous: though he is deemed the *stronger,* and she the *weaker* creature.

Frailty, through all the stages of social intercourse, appears to be most enormous in those who are supposed to have least fortitude to sustain the powers of self-resistance. Yet, such is the force of prejudice, the law of custom, against woman, that she is expected to *act* like a philosopher, though she is not allowed to *think* like one. If she pleads the weakness of her sex, her plea is not admitted; if she professes an equal portion of mental strength with man, she is condemned for arrogance. Yet, if a General be sent into the field of battle with a force inferior to that of the enemy, and is vanquished, the plea of inequality in resisting powers is admitted, and *his* honor is exonerated from every imputation: WOMAN encounters an all-commanding enemy; *she* is subdued;—and *she* is eternally dishonored!

The laws of man have long since decreed, that the jewel, Chastity, and the purity of uncontaminated morals, are the brightest ornaments of the female sex. Yet, the framers of those laws are indefatigable in promoting their violation. Man says to woman, without chastity you are declared infamous; and at the same moment, by a subtle and gradual process, he undermines the purity of her heart, by a bold defiance of all that tends to the support of religion and morality. Man thus commits a kind of mental suicide; while he levels that image to the lowest debasement, which he has ostentatiously set up for universal idolatry.

It is not by precept, but by example, that conviction strikes deeply into the thinking mind. Man is supposed to be the more wise and more rational creature; his faculties are more liberally expanded by classical education: he is supposed to be more enlightened by an unlimited intercourse with society. He is permitted to assert the dignity of his character; to punish those who assail his reputation; and to assume a superiority over all his fellow creatures. He is not accountable to any mortal for the actions of his life; he may revel in the follies, indulge the vices of his *superior* nature. He pursues the pleasures or the eccentricities of his imagination, with an avidity insatiable: and he perpetually *proves* that human passions subjugate *him* to the degradations of human frailty; while woman, the *weaker* animal, she whose enjoyments are limited, whose education, knowledge, and actions are circumscribed by the potent rule of prejudice, she is expected to *resist* temptation; to be invincible in fortitude; strong in prescient and reflecting powers; subtle in the defense of her own honor; and forbearing under all the conflicts of the passions. Man first degrades, and then deserts her. Yet, if driven by famine, insult, shame, and persecution, she rushes forth like the wolf for prey; if, like Milwood,[1] she finds it "necessary to be rich" in this sordid, selfish world, she is shunned, abhorred, condemned to the very lowest scenes of vile debasement; to exist in misery, or to perish unlamented. No kindred breast will pity her misfortunes: no pious tear embalm her ashes: she rushes into

---

1. The wicked woman in George Lillo's (1693–1739) play, *The London Merchant* (1731), who lures the young man, George Barnwell, to his destruction.

the arms of death, as her last, her only asylum from the monsters who have destroyed her.

Woman is destined to pursue no path in which she does not find an enemy. If she is liberal, generous, careless of wealth, friendly to the unfortunate, and bountiful to persecuted merit, she is deemed prodigal, and overmuch profuse; all the good she does every tear she steals from the downcast eye of modest worth, every sigh she converts into a throb of joy, in grateful bosoms, is, by the world, forgotten: while the ingenuous liberality of her soul excites the imputation of folly and extravagance. If, on the contrary, she is wary, shrewd, thrifty, economical, and eager to procure and to preserve the advantages of independence; she is condemned as narrow-minded, mean, unfeeling, artful, mercenary, and base: in either case she is exposed to censure. If liberal, unpitied; if sordid, execrated! In a few words, a generous woman is termed a *fool*; a prudent one, a *prodigal*.

If WOMAN is not permitted to assert a majesty of mind, why fatigue her faculties with the labors of any species of education? why give her books, if she is not to profit by the wisdom they inculcate? The parent, or the preceptress, who enlightened her understanding, like the dark lantern, to spread its rays internally only, puts into her grasp a weapon of defense against the perils of existence; and at the same moment commands her not to use it. Man says you *may* read, and you *will* think, but you shall not evince your knowledge, or employ your thoughts, beyond the boundaries which we have set up around you. Then wherefore burthen the young mind with a gaudy outline which man darkens with shades indelible? why expand the female heart, merely to render it more conscious that it is, by the tyranny of custom, rendered vulnerable? Let man remember, that

A little learning is a dangerous thing.[2]

Let him not hope for a luxurious mental harvest, where the sun of cultivation is obscured by impenetrable prejudice; that cloud which has too long spread over the mind of woman a desolating darkness. So situated, woman is taught to discriminate just sufficiently to know her own unhappiness. She, like Tantalus,[3] is placed in a situation where the intellectual blessing she sighs for is within her view; but she is not permitted to attain it: she is conscious of possessing equally strong mental powers; but she is obliged to yield, as the weaker creature. Man says, "you shall be initiated in all the arts of pleasing; but you shall, in vain, hope that we will contribute to your happiness one iota beyond the principle which constitutes our own." Sensual Egotists! woman is absolutely necessary to your felicity; nay, even to your existence: yet she must not arrogate to herself the power to interest your actions. You idolize her personal attractions, as long as they influence your senses; when they begin to pall, the magic is dissolved; and prejudice is ever eager to condemn what passion has degraded.

* * *

2. Alexander Pope, *An Essay on Criticism*, line 217. 3. The legendary king of Lydia condemned in Hades to stand in a pool of water up to his chin and under a tree laden with fruit, but to have the water and fruit recede when he tried to drink or eat.

JONATHAN SWIFT
1667–1745

In virtually all his writing, Jonathan Swift displays his gift for making other people uncomfortable. He makes us uneasy by making us aware of our own moral inadequacies and, by his wit, energy, and inventiveness, compels us to enjoy the process of being brought to such awareness.

Born in Dublin to English parents, Swift was educated at Trinity College, Dublin. In 1689, the young man went to England, where he served as secretary to the statesman Sir William Temple. During his residence at Moor Park, Sir William's estate, Swift became friendly with Esther Johnson, daughter of the steward there; he remained on close terms with her for the rest of his life. (His playful, intimate letters to her—he used the name "Stella"—were published in a collection called *Journal to Stella*.) In 1692, Swift received an M.A. from Oxford University; three years later, he took orders, becoming a clergyman in the Anglican Church but continuing in Sir William's employ, although with intermittent stays in Ireland. Early in the eighteenth century, he began his career of political journalism; he also published brilliant satiric works, including *A Tale of a Tub* (1704), of which he is supposed to have said, late in his life, "What a genius I had when I composed that book!" Although he had hoped for church advancement in England, as a reward for his writings in the Tory cause, in 1713 he was instead named dean of St. Patrick's Cathedral, Dublin. He spent the rest of his life in Ireland (save for two brief visits to friends in England) writing passionately on behalf of the oppressed Irish people. In his final years, he was declared mentally incompetent, suffering, presumably, from senility. As he had prophesied in his verses *On the Death of Dr. Swift*, "He gave what little wealth he had / To build a house for fools and mad"; the mental hospital founded by his legacy still exists in Dublin.

For *Gulliver's Travels* (1726) Swift used the travel book, a form hovering between fact and fiction, as his model. Lemuel Gulliver, ship's surgeon, travels into four imagined nations. The first book takes him to Lilliput, where he duly observes the customs and traditions of a race of people six inches high. The narrative of their preoccupations and procedures mocks the pettiness of the English, although Gulliver, himself involved in the intrigues of his tiny hosts, fails to note the resemblance between Lilliput and his native land. His simple patriotism survives through the second book, where Gulliver encounters the giants of Brobdingnag, whose benevolent king, after hearing Gulliver's patriotic account of England, comments, "I cannot but conclude the bulk of your natives, to be the most pernicious race of little odious vermin that nature ever suffered to crawl upon the surface of the earth." The third book is more various, and Gulliver seems less gullible in his encounters with the ludicrous or dangerous results of abstract speculation divorced from practical concerns (philosophers, for instance, so deeply involved in the process of reasoning that they have to be attended by "flappers," servants who "flap" them back to reality), with the ghosts of great men from the past who stress the lies of historians and the moral and physical decline of their descendants, and with the terrifying Struldbrugs, who grow old but live forever in horrible senility.

Book Four, printed here, has always presented problems to critics. More directly than any other imaginative work of its period, it confronts problems inherent in the idealization of reason as sufficient guide to human conduct. It is easy enough to see that Swift has here imagined an absolute separation between the animal and the rational aspects of human nature. As Gulliver gradually and with horror realizes (taking the reader with him), the disgusting Yahoos manifest degraded human form and embody characteristics of human beings deprived of all rational capacity. They act on the basis of pure—and ugly—passion: lust, envy, avarice, greed, rage. The

Houyhnhnms, the governing class of horses, treat them as beasts, but consider them more ungovernable than other creatures; Gulliver, looking at them, sees a horrifying version of the human become (by the absence of reason) subhuman.

As for the Houyhnhnms, those noble horses exemplify pure rationality. They lead monotonous, orderly lives, with no need for disagreement (the truth being self-evident to rational creatures) or excitement. Under their influence, Gulliver wants to stay forever in this land without literal or metaphorical salt. After the Houyhnhnms expel him, Gulliver can make no distinction among human beings: he condemns the benevolent Pedro Mendez as a Yahoo, resents his connection with his own wife and children, and spends as much time as possible in his stable. Life with the Houyhnhnms has driven him mad: he cannot adjust to the reality of life in England.

The question is, Why? By one interpretation, Gulliver rightly perceives his fellow human beings as essentially Yahoos. His Houyhnhnm master concludes, Gulliver says, that humans are "a sort of animals to whose share . . . some small pittance of reason had fallen, whereof we made no other use than by its assistance to aggravate our natural corruptions, and to acquire new ones which nature had not given us." Perhaps the Houyhnhnms do exemplify an ideal to which human beings should aspire, although they can never reach it; to call attention to the monotony of their lives or the failure of their curiosity only reveals the reader's participation in human depravity. Pedro Mendez is a good man, as men go, but the gulf between the best of humans and a Houyhnhnm is so huge that Gulliver is correct to detest all humans. If he implicitly excepts himself, he thus acknowledges the difference his education by Houyhnhnms has made: at least he knows the gulf's existence.

According to another view, the Houyhnhnms exemplify a way of being utterly irrelevant to humankind as well as deeply boring. To hate the animal and glorify the rational denies the inextricable mixture of our nature. Gulliver's pride leads him to aspire to an essentially inhuman state; he wishes, sinfully, to exceed ordained natural limits. Moreover, he ignores the Christian virtue of charity, the command to love one's neighbors. Captain Mendez demonstrates that virtue; Gulliver cannot perceive the moral distinction between the generous captain and the bloodthirsty natives who shoot the Englishman with an arrow shortly after he leaves the Houyhnhnms, producing a lasting scar. Gulliver's condemnation of pride in others emphasizes his blindness to his own flaws.

A compromise position reminds us that declaring the Houyhnhnms irrelevant may leave the reader in too comfortable a position, considering Swift's declared intention "to vex the world rather than divert it." *Gulliver's Travels,* this comment implies, involves serious attack. We can perhaps dismiss the Houyhnhnms as boring (they have virtually nothing to talk about) or heartless (they make no distinctions of parentage; they expel Gulliver despite his ardent desire to remain) because our natures include more than reason and we appropriately value principles of conduct beyond the rational. Gulliver becomes crazy when he returns to England, unable to accept his full human nature and to make necessary distinctions; given the limits of the human condition, men and women must find the way to operate within them. Gulliver fails and, failing, reminds us of necessities to which we must adapt. The Houyhnhnms provide no solution to human problems: their extirpation of passion, their narrow commitment to reason, prove "inhumane." (They are, after all, horses!) Humankind, as Swift suggested in a letter, is only capable of reason, not fully reasonable; perhaps the spontaneous generosity of the Portuguese captain exemplifies the greatest good to which human beings should aspire.

On the other hand, we claim to value reason; Gulliver has seen in pure form an ideal to which we pay lip service. His realization of the enormous discrepancy between ideal and actual has made it impossible for him to function in his own society. It has given him a harsh perspective by which he sees how morally intolerable social arrangements in fact are. The readiness of most people to compromise, given social necessity, shows how far they are from taking seriously the values they profess. Swift calls our attention to the discrepancies between what we say we believe and how we actually behave. The reality of reason exceeds human capacities; *Gulliver's Travels* reminds us that we live by hypocrisies. The Houyhnhnms thus tell us something about ourselves despite their lack of humanity.

The problems in interpreting *Gulliver's Travels* come partly from the fact that we receive all information about Gulliver's experience from the traveler himself, an untrustworthy source. In reading his narrative, we must assess his understanding— a slippery process since we lack a point of reference. *Gulliver's Travels* abounds in allusions to such phenomena as corrupt lawyers and politicians, avaricious doctors, mass slaughter in wars over trivial pretexts—aspects of our experience and of Gulliver's, and reminders that this narrative has something to do with us. The necessity of arriving at a coherent judgment of Gulliver and his experiences implicates the reader in the moral problem of how to judge—and perhaps change—society.

And this typifies an important aspect of satire. *A Modest Proposal* (1729), Swift's attack on the economic oppression of the Irish by the English, keeps the reader constantly off balance, trying to understand exactly who is being criticized and why. Swift is writing out of his firsthand awareness of the suffering caused by English policies in Ireland. Absentee landlords who never saw the actual situation of their tenants, British politicians who made policy at a distance, presumably did not know that Ireland had become a land of the starving. In Swift's view, however, the Irish people, by their apathy, collaborated with the oppressors. In *A Modest Proposal*, he attacks English and Irish alike.

Even more emphatically than Gulliver, the nameless speaker in *A Modest Proposal* proves an undependable guide, tempting us to identify with his tone of rationality and compassion, only to reveal that his plausible economic orientation leads to advocacy of cannibalism. He offers a series of morally sound and economically feasible solutions to Ireland's problems but draws back immediately, declaring them impossible since no one will put them in practice. The satire indicts the English for inhumanity, the Irish for passivity, and the economically oriented proposer of remedies for moral blindness. But it also reaches out to criticize the reader as representative of all who endure calmly the intolerable actuality in the world (but not, perhaps, where we have to see it ourselves) of our own inhumanity to our fellow human beings. Swift's self-chosen epitaph, on his tomb, may be translated, "Where fierce indignation no longer tears the heart." *A Modest Proposal* exemplifies the lacerating power of that indignation.

PRONOUNCING GLOSSARY

The following list uses common English syllables and stress accents to provide rough equivalents of selected words whose pronunciation may be unfamiliar to the general reader.

Brobdingrag: *brahb'-ding-rag*   Lilliput: *lil'-ee-put*

Houyhnhnm: *whin'-im*   Psalmanazar: *sahl-mahn'-ah-zahr*

Gulliver's Travels[1]

A Letter from Captain Gulliver to His Cousin Sympson[2]

I hope you will be ready to own publicly, whenever you shall be called to it, that by your great and frequent urgency you prevailed on me to publish a very loose and uncorrect account of my travels; with direction to hire some young gentlemen of either University to put them in order, and correct the style, as my Cousin Dampier[3] did by my advice, in his book called *A Voyage round the World.* But I do not remember I gave you power to consent that anything should be omitted, and much less that anything should be inserted: therefore, as to the latter, I do here renounce everything of that kind; particularly a paragraph about her Majesty the late Queen Anne, of most pious and glorious memory; although I did reverence and esteem her more than any of human species. But you, or your interpolator, ought to have considered that as it was not my inclination, so was it not decent to praise any animal of our composition before my master Houyhnhnm; and besides, the fact was altogether false; for to my knowledge, being in England during some part of her Majesty's reign, she did govern by a chief Minister; nay, even by two successively; the first whereof was the Lord of Godolphin, and the second the Lord of Oxford; so that you have made me *say the thing that was not.* Likewise, in the account of the Academy of Projectors, and several passages of my discourse to my master Houyhnhnm, you have either omitted some material circumstances, or minced or changed them in such a manner, that I do hardly know mine own work. When I formerly hinted to you something of this in a letter, you were pleased to answer that you were afraid of giving offense; that people in power were very watchful over the press; and apt not only to interpret, but to punish everything which looked like an *inuendo* (as I think you called it). But pray, how could that which I spoke so many years ago, and at above five thousand leagues distance, in another reign, be applied to any of the Yahoos, who now are said to govern the herd; especially, at a time when I little thought on or feared the unhappiness of living under them. Have not I the most reason to complain, when I see these very Yahoos carried by Houyhnhnms in a vehicle, as if these were brutes, and those the rational creatures? And, indeed, to avoid so monstrous and detestable a sight was one principal motive of my retirement hither.[4]

Thus much I thought proper to tell you in relation to yourself, and to the trust I reposed in you.

I do in the next place complain of my own great want of judgment, in being prevailed upon by the intreaties and false reasonings of you and some others, very much against mine own opinion, to suffer my travels to be published. Pray bring to your mind how often I desired you to consider, when you insisted on the motive of public good, that the Yahoos were a species of animals utterly incapable of amendment by precepts or examples; and so it hath proved; for instead of seeing a full stop put to all abuses and corruptions,

---

1. Swift's full title for this work was *Travels into Several Remote Nations of the World. In Four Parts. By Lemuel Gulliver, First a Surgeon, and then a Captain of several Ships.* The text is based on the Dublin edition of Swift's work (1735). 2. In this letter, first published in 1735, Swift complains, among other matters, of the alterations in his original text made by the publisher, Benjamin Motte, in the interest of what he considered political discretion. 3. William Dampier (1652–1715), the explorer, whose account of his circumnavigation of the globe Swift had read. 4. To Nottinghamshire in central England.

at least in this little island, as I had reason to expect, behold, after above six months warning. I cannot learn that my book hath produced one single effect according to mine intentions; I desired you would let me know by a letter, when party and faction were extinguished; judges learned and upright; pleaders honest and modest, with some tincture of common sense; and Smithfield[5] blazing with pyramids of law books; the young nobility's education entirely changed; the physicians banished; the female Yahoos abounding in virtue, honor, truth, and good sense; courts and levees of great ministers thoroughly weeded and swept; wit, merit, and learning rewarded; all disgracers of the press in prose and verse, condemned to eat nothing but their own cotton,[6] and quench their thirst with their own ink. These, and a thousand other reformations, I firmly counted upon by your encouragement; as indeed they were plainly deducible from the precepts delivered in my book. And, it must be owned that seven months were a sufficient time to correct every vice and folly to which Yahoos are subject; if their natures had been capable of the least disposition to virtue or wisdom; yet so far have you been from answering mine expectation in any of your letters, that on the contrary, you are loading our carrier every week with libels, and keys, and reflections, and memoirs, and second parts; wherein I see myself accused of reflecting upon great statesfolk; of degrading human nature (for so they have still the confidence to style it) and of abusing the female sex. I find likewise, that the writers of those bundles are not agreed among themselves; for some of them will not allow me to be author of mine own travels; and others make me author of books to which I am wholly a stranger.

I find likewise that your printer hath been so careless as to confound the times, and mistake the dates of my several voyages and returns; neither assigning the true year, or the true month, or day of the month; and I hear the original manuscript is all destroyed, since the publication of my book. Neither have I any copy left; however, I have sent you some corrections, which you may insert, if ever there should be a second edition; and yet I cannot stand to them, but shall leave that matter to my judicious and candid readers, to adjust it as they please.

I hear some of our sea Yahoos find fault with my sea language, as not proper in many parts, nor now in use. I cannot help it. In my first voyages, while I was young, I was instructed by the oldest mariners, and learned to speak as they did. But I have since found that the sea Yahoos are apt, like the land ones, to become new fangled in their words; which the latter change every year; insomuch, as I remember upon each return to mine own country, their old dialect was so altered, that I could hardly understand the new. And I observe, when any Yahoo comes from London out of curiosity to visit me at mine own house, we neither of us are able to deliver our conceptions in a manner intelligible to the other.

If the censure of Yahoos could any way affect me, I should have great reason to complain that some of them are so bold as to think my book of travels a mere fiction out of mine own brain; and have gone so far as to drop hints that the Houyhnhnms and Yahoos have no more existence than the inhabitants of Utopia.

Indeed I must confess that as to the people of Lilliput, Brobdingrag (for

5. An area of London, used in the 16th century for burning heretics, that should now be used (Swift implies) to burn the incentives to litigation.   6. The fiber favored for paper making.

so the word should have been spelled, and not erroneously Brobdingnag) and Laputa, I have never yet heard of any Yahoo so presumptuous as to dispute their being, or the facts I have related concerning them; because the truth immediately strikes every reader with conviction. And, is there less probability in my account of the Houyhnhnms or Yahoos, when it is manifest as to the latter, there are so many thousands even in this city, who only differ from their brother brutes in Houyhnhnmland, because they use a sort of a jabber, and do not go naked. I wrote for their amendment, and not their approbation. The united praise of the whole race would be of less consequence to me, than the neighing of those two degenerate Houyhnhnms I keep in my stable; because, from these, degenerate as they are, I still improve in some virtues, without any mixture of vice.

Do these miserable animals presume to think that I am so far degenerated as to defend my veracity; Yahoo as I am, it is well known through all Houyhnhnmland, that by the instructions and example of my illustrious master, I was able in the compass of two years (although I confess with the utmost difficulty) to remove that infernal habit of lying, shuffling, deceiving, and equivocating, so deeply rooted in the very souls of all my species; especially the Europeans.

I have other complaints to make upon this vexatious occasion; but I forbear troubling myself or you any further. I must freely confess that since my last return, some corruptions of my Yahoo nature have revived in me by conversing with a few of your species, and particularly those of mine own family, by an unavoidable necessity; else I should never have attempted so absurd a project as that of reforming the Yahoo race in this kingdom; but I have now done with all such visionary schemes for ever.

The Publisher to the Reader

The author of these travels, Mr. Lemuel Gulliver, is my ancient and intimate friend; there is likewise some relation between us by the mother's side. About three years ago Mr. Gulliver, growing weary of the concourse of curious people coming to him at his house in Redriff,[7] made a small purchase of land, with a convenient house, near Newark, in Nottinghamshire, his native country; where he now lives retired, yet in good esteem among his neighbors.

Although Mr. Gulliver were born in Nottinghamshire, where his father dwelt, yet I have heard him say his family came from Oxfordshire; to confirm which, I have observed in the churchyard at Banbury, in that county, several tombs and monuments of the Gullivers.

Before he quitted Redriff, he left the custody of the following papers in my hands, with the liberty to dispose of them as I should think fit. I have carefully perused them three times; the style is very plain and simple; and the only fault I find is that the author, after the manner of travelers, is a little too circumstantial. There is an air of truth apparent through the whole; and indeed the author was so distinguished for his veracity, that it became a sort of proverb among his neighbors at Redriff, when anyone affirmed a thing, to say, it was as true as if Mr. Gulliver had spoke it.

By the advice of several worthy persons, to whom, with the author's per-

---

7. Rotherhithe, a district in south London then frequented by sailors.

mission, I communicated these papers, I now venture to send them into the world; hoping they may be, at least for some time, a better entertainment to our young noblemen, than the common scribbles of politics and party.

This volume would have been at least twice as large, if I had not made bold to strike out innumerable passages relating to the winds and tides, as well as to the variations and bearings in the several voyages; together with the minute descriptions of the management of the ship in storms, in the style of sailors; likewise the account of the longitudes and latitudes, wherein I have reason to apprehend that Mr. Gulliver may be a little dissatisfied; but I was resolved to fit the work as much as possible to the general capacity of readers. However, if my own ignorance in sea affairs shall have led me to commit some mistakes, I alone am answerable for them; and if any traveler hath a curiosity to see the whole work at large, as it came from the hand of the author, I will be ready to gratify him.

As for any further particulars relating to the author, the reader will receive satisfaction from the first pages of the book.

RICHARD SYMPSON

Part IV

A Voyage to the Country of the Houyhnhnms[8]

CHAPTER I

The Author sets out as Captain of a ship. His men conspire against him, confine him a long time to his cabin, set him on shore in an unknown land. He travels up into the country. The Yahoos, a strange sort of animal, described. The Author meets two Houyhnhnms.

I continued at home with my wife and children about five months in a very happy condition, if I could have learned the lesson of knowing when I was well. I left my poor wife big with child, and accepted an advantageous offer made me to be Captain of the *Adventure*, a stout merchantman of 350 tons; for I understood navigation well, and being grown weary of a surgeon's employment at sea, which however I could exercise upon occasion, I took a skillful young man of that calling, one Robert Purefoy, into my ship. We set sail from Portsmouth upon the 7th day of September, 1710; on the 14th we met with Captain Pocock of Bristol, at Tenariff, who was going to the Bay of Campeachy[9] to cut logwood. On the 16th he was parted from us by a storm; I heard since my return that his ship foundered and none escaped, but one cabin boy. He was an honest man and a good sailor, but a little too positive in his own opinions, which was the cause of his destruction, as it hath been of several others. For if he had followed my advice, he might at this time have been safe at home with his family as well as myself.

I had several men died in my ship of calentures,[1] so that I was forced to

8. The word suggests the sound of a horse neighing.   9. Probably Campeche, in southeast Mexico, on the western side of the Yucatán Peninsula. Tenariff (now Tenerife) is the largest of the Canary Islands, off northwest Africa in the Atlantic.   1. Tropical fever.

get recruits out of Barbadoes and the Leeward Islands,[2] where I touched by the direction of the merchants who employed me; which I had soon too much cause to repent, for I found afterwards that most of them had been bucca-neers. I had fifty hands on board; and my orders were that I should trade with the Indians in the South Sea, and make what discoveries I could. These rogues whom I had picked up debauched my other men, and they all formed a conspiracy to seize the ship and secure me; which they did one morning, rushing into my cabin, and binding me hand and foot, threatening to throw me overboard, if I offered to stir. I told them I was their prisoner, and would submit. This they made me swear to do, and then unbound me, only fasten-ing one of my legs with a chair near my bed, and placed a sentry at my door with his piece charged, who was commanded to shoot me dead if I attempted my liberty. They sent me down victuals and drink, and took the government of the ship to themselves. Their design was to turn pirates and plunder the Spaniards, which they could not do, till they got more men. But first they resolved to sell the goods in the ship, and then go to Madagascar for recruits, several among them having died since my confinement. They sailed many weeks, and traded with the Indians; but I knew not what course they took, being kept close prisoner in my cabin, and expecting nothing less than to be murdered, as they often threatened me.

Upon the 9th day of May, 1711, one James Welch came down to my cabin; and said he had orders from the Captain to set me ashore. I expostulated with him, but in vain; neither would he so much as tell me who their new Captain was. They forced me into the longboat, letting me put on my best suit of clothes, which were as good as new, and a small bundle of linen, but no arms except my hanger;[3] and they were so civil as not to search my pock-ets, into which I conveyed what money I had, with some other little neces-saries. They rowed about a league, and then set me down on a strand. I desired them to tell me what country it was; they all swore, they knew no more than myself, but said that the Captain (as they called him) was resolved, after they had sold the lading, to get rid of me in the first place where they discovered land. They pushed off immediately, advising me to make haste, for fear of being overtaken by the tide, and bade me farewell.

In this desolate condition I advanced forward, and soon got upon firm ground, where I sat down on a bank to rest myself, and consider what I had best to do. When I was a little refreshed, I went up into the country, resolving to deliver myself to the first savages I should meet, and purchase my life from them by some bracelets, glass rings, and other toys, which sailors usu-ally provide themselves with in those voyages, and whereof I had some about me. The land was divided by long rows of trees, not regularly planted, but naturally growing; there was great plenty of grass, and several fields of oats. I walked very circumspectly for fear of being surprised, or suddenly shot with an arrow from behind, or on either side. I fell into a beaten road, where I saw many tracks of human feet, and some of cows, but most of horses. At last I beheld several animals in a field, and one or two of the same kind sitting in trees. Their shape was very singular, and deformed, which a little discomposed me, so that I lay down behind a thicket to observe them better.

---

2. The northern group of the Lesser Antilles in the West Indies, extending southeast from Puerto Rico. Barbados is the easternmost of the West Indies.   3. A small sword.

Some of them coming forward near the place where I lay, gave me an opportunity of distinctly marking their form. Their heads and breasts were covered with a thick hair, some frizzled and others lank; they had beards like goats, and a long ridge of hair down their backs, and the fore parts of their legs and feet; but the rest of their bodies were bare, so that I might see their skins, which were of a brown buff color. They had no tails, nor any hair at all on their buttocks, except about the anus; which, I presume Nature had placed there to defend them as they sat on the ground; for this posture they used, as well as lying down, and often stood on their hind feet. They climbed high trees, as nimbly as a squirrel, for they had strong extended claws before and behind, terminating in sharp points, and hooded.[4] They would often spring, and bound, and leap with prodigious agility. The females were not so large as the males; they had long lank hair on their heads, and only a sort of down on the rest of their bodies, except about the anus, and pudenda. Their dugs hung between their forefeet, and often reached almost to the ground as they walked. The hair of both sexes was of several colors, brown, red, black, and yellow. Upon the whole, I never beheld in all my travels so disagreeable an animal, or one against which I naturally conceived so strong an antipathy. So that thinking I had seen enough, full of contempt and aversion, I got up and pursued the beaten road, hoping it might direct me to the cabin of some Indian: I had not gone far when I met one of these creatures full in my way, and coming up directly to me. The ugly monster, when he saw me, distorted several ways every feature of his visage, and stared as at an object he had never seen before; then approaching nearer, lifted up his forepaw, whether out of curiosity or mischief, I could not tell; but I drew my hanger, and gave him a good blow with the flat side of it; for I durst not strike him with the edge, fearing the inhabitants might be provoked against me, if they should come to know that I had killed or maimed any of their cattle. When the beast felt the smart, he drew back, and roared so loud, that a herd of at least forty came flocking about me from the next field, howling and making odious faces; but I ran to the body of a tree, and leaning my back against it, kept them off, by waving my hanger. Several of this cursed brood getting hold of the branches behind, leaped up into the tree, from whence they began to discharge their excrements on my head; however, I escaped pretty well, by sticking close to the stem of the tree, but was almost stifled with the filth, which fell about me on every side.

In the midst of this distress, I observed them all to run away on a sudden as fast as they could; at which I ventured to leave the tree, and pursue the road, wondering what it was that could put them into this fright. But looking on my left hand, I saw a horse walking softly in the field; which my persecutors having sooner discovered, was the cause of their flight. The horse started a little when he came near me, but soon recovering himself, looked full in my face with manifest tokens of wonder; he viewed my hands and feet, walking round me several times. I would have pursued my journey, but he placed himself directly in the way, yet looking with a very mild aspect, never offering the least violence. We stood gazing at each other for some time; at last I took the boldness, to reach my hand towards his neck, with a design to stroke it; using the common style and whistle of jockies when they

4. Concealed, or sheathed by flesh.

are going to handle a strange horse. But, this animal seeming to receive my civilities with disdain, shook his head, and bent his brows, softly raising up his left forefoot to remove my hand. Then he neighed three or four times, but in so different a cadence, that I almost began to think he was speaking to himself in some language of his own.

While he and I were thus employed, another horse came up; who applying himself to the first in a very formal manner, they gently struck each other's right hoof before, neighing several times by turns, and varying the sound, which seemed to be almost articulate. They went some paces off, as if it were to confer together, walking side by side, backward and forward, like persons deliberating upon some affair of weight; but often turning their eyes towards me, as it were to watch that I might not escape. I was amazed to see such actions and behavior in brute beasts; and concluded with myself that if the inhabitants of this country were endued with a proportionable degree of reason, they must needs be the wisest people upon earth. This thought gave me so much comfort, that I resolved to go forward until I could discover some house or village, or meet with any of the natives, leaving the two horses to discourse together as they pleased. But the first, who was a dapple grey, observing me to steal off, neighed after me in so expressive a tone that I fancied myself to understand what he meant; whereupon I turned back, and came near him, to expect his farther commands; but concealing my fear as much as I could; for I began to be in some pain, how this adventure might terminate; and the reader will easily believe I did not much like my present situation.

The two horses came up close to me, looking with great earnestness upon my face and hands. The grey steed rubbed my hat all round with his right fore hoof, and discomposed it so much that I was forced to adjust it better, by taking it off, and settling it again; whereat both he and his companion (who was a brown bay) appeared to be much surprised; the latter felt the lappet of my coat, and finding it to hang loose about me, they both looked with new signs of wonder. He stroked my right hand, seeming to admire the softness, and color; but he squeezed it so hard between his hoof and his pastern,[5] that I was forced to roar; after which they both touched me with all possible tenderness. They were under great perplexity about my shoes and stockings, which they felt very often, neighing to each other, and using various gestures, not unlike those of a philosopher, when he would attempt to solve some new and difficult phenomenon.

Upon the whole, the behavior of these animals was so orderly and rational, so acute and judicious, that I at last concluded, they must needs be magicians, who had thus metamorphosed themselves upon some design; and seeing a stranger in the way, were resolved to divert themselves with him; or perhaps were really amazed at the sight of a man so very different in habit, feature, and complexion from those who might probably live in so remote a climate. Upon the strength of this reasoning, I ventured to address them in the following manner: "Gentlemen, if you be conjurers, as I have good cause to believe, you can understand any language; therefore I make bold to let your worships know that I am a poor distressed Englishman, driven by his misfortunes upon your coast; and I entreat one of you, to let me ride upon

5. The part of a horse's foot between the joint at the rear and the hoof.

his back, as if he were a real horse, to some house or village, where I can be relieved. In return of which favor, I will make you a present of this knife and bracelet" (taking them out of my pocket). The two creatures stood silent while I spoke, seeming to listen with great attention; and when I had ended, they neighed frequently towards each other, as if they were engaged in serious conversation. I plainly observed, that their language expressed the passions very well, and the words might with little pains be resolved into an alphabet more easily than the Chinese.

I could frequently distinguish the word *Yahoo*, which was repeated by each of them several times; and although it were impossible for me to conjecture what it meant, yet while the two horses were busy in conversation, I endeavored to practice this word upon my tongue; and as soon as they were silent, I boldly pronounced "Yahoo" in a loud voice, imitating, at the same time, as near as I could, the neighing of a horse; at which they were both visibly surprised, and the grey repeated the same word twice, as if he meant to teach me the right accent, wherein I spoke after him as well as I could, and found myself perceivably to improve every time, although very far from any degree of perfection. Then the bay tried me with a second word, much harder to be pronounced; but reducing it to the English orthography, may be spelt thus *Houyhnhnm*. I did not succeed in this so well as the former, but after two or three farther trials, I had better fortune; and they both appeared amazed at my capacity.

After some farther discourse, which I then conjectured might relate to me, the two friends took their leaves, with the same compliment of striking each other's hoof; and the grey made me signs that I should walk before him; wherein I thought it prudent to comply, till I could find a better director. When I offered to slacken my pace, he would cry, "Hhuun, Hhuun"; I guessed his meaning, and gave him to understand, as well as I could that I was weary, and not able to walk faster; upon which, he would stand a while to let me rest.

CHAPTER II

The Author conducted by a Houyhnhnm to his house. The house described. The Author's reception. The food of the Houyhnhnms. The Author in distress for want of meat is at last relieved. His manner of feeding in that country.

Having traveled about three miles, we came to a long kind of building, made of timber, stuck in the ground, and wattled across; the roof was low, and covered with straw. I now began to be a little comforted, and took out some toys, which travelers usually carry for presents to the savage Indians of America and other parts, in hopes the people of the house would be thereby encouraged to receive me kindly. The horse made me a sign to go in first; it was a large room with a smooth clay floor, and a rack and manger extending the whole length on one side. There were three nags, and two mares, not eating, but some of them sitting down upon their hams, which I very much wondered at; but wondered more to see the rest employed in domestic business; the last seemed but ordinary cattle; however this confirmed my first opinion, that a people who could so far civilize brute animals must needs excel in wisdom all the nations of the world. The grey came in just after, and thereby prevented any ill treatment, which the others might have given me. He neighed to them several times in a style of authority, and received answers.

Beyond this room there were three others, reaching the length of the house, to which you passed through three doors, opposite to each other, in the manner of a vista; we went through the second room towards the third; here the grey walked in first, beckoning me to attend; I waited in the second room, and got ready my presents, for the master and mistress of the house; they were two knives, three bracelets of false pearl, a small looking glass and a bead necklace. The horse neighed three or four times, and I waited to hear some answers in a human voice, but I heard no other returns than in the same dialect, only one or two a little shriller than his. I began to think that this house must belong to some person of great note among them, because there appeared so much ceremony before I could gain admittance. But, that a man of quality should be served all by horses, was beyond my comprehension. I feared my brain was disturbed by my sufferings and misfortunes; I roused myself, and looked about me in the room where I was left alone; this was furnished as the first, only after a more elegant manner. I rubbed my eyes often, but the same objects still occurred. I pinched my arms and sides, to awake myself, hoping I might be in a dream. I then absolutely concluded that all these appearances could be nothing else but necromancy and magic. But I had no time to pursue these reflections; for the grey horse came to the door, and made me a sign to follow him into the third room; where I saw a very comely mare, together with a colt and foal, sitting on their haunches, upon mats of straw, not unartfully made, and perfectly neat and clean.

The mare soon after my entrance, rose from her mat, and coming up close, after having nicely observed my hands and face, gave me a most contemptuous look; then turning to the horse, I heard the word Yahoo often repeated betwixt them; the meaning of which word I could not then comprehend, although it were the first I had learned to pronounce; but I was soon better informed, to my everlasting mortification: for the horse beckoning to me with his head, and repeating the word, "Hhuun, Hhuun," as he did upon the road, which I understood was to attend him, led me out into a kind of court, where was another building at some distance from the house. Here we entered, and I saw three of those detestable creatures, which I first met after my landing, feeding upon roots, and the flesh of some animals, which I afterwards found to be that of asses and dogs, and now and then a cow dead by accident or disease. They were all tied by the neck with strong withes,[6] fastened to a beam; they held their food between the claws of their forefeet, and tore it with their teeth.

The master horse ordered a sorrel nag, one of his servants, to untie the largest of these animals, and take him into a yard. The beast and I were brought close together; and our countenances diligently compared, both by master and servant, who thereupon repeated several times the word "Yahoo." My horror and astonishment are not to be described, when I observed, in this abominable animal, a perfect human figure; the face of it indeed was flat and broad, the nose depressed, the lips large, and the mouth wide; but these differences are common to all savage nations, where the lineaments of

6. Fibers braided into rope.

the countenance are distorted by the natives suffering their infants to lie groveling on the earth, or by carrying them on their backs, nuzzling with their face against the mother's shoulders. The forefeet of the Yahoo differed from my hands in nothing else but the length of the nails, the coarseness and brownness of the palms, and the hairiness on the backs. There was the same resemblance between our feet, with the same differences, which I knew very well, although the horses did not, because of my shoes and stockings; the same in every part of our bodies, except as to hairiness and color, which I have already described.

The great difficulty that seemed to stick with the two horses was to see the rest of my body so very different from that of a Yahoo, for which I was obliged to my clothes, whereof they had no conception; the sorrel nag offered me a root, which he held (after their manner, as we shall describe in its proper place) between his hoof and pastern; I took it in my hand, and having smelled it, returned it to him again as civilly as I could. He brought out of the Yahoo's kennel a piece of ass's flesh, but it smelled so offensively that I turned from it with loathing; he then threw it to the Yahoo, by whom it was greedily devoured. He afterwards showed me a wisp of hay, and a fetlock[7] full of oats; but I shook my head, to signify that neither of these were food for me. And indeed, I now apprehended that I must absolutely starve, if I did not get to some of my own species; for as to those filthy Yahoos, although there were few greater lovers of mankind, at that time, than myself, yet I confess I never saw any sensitive being so detestable on all accounts; and the more I came near them, the more hateful they grew, while I stayed in that country. This the master horse observed by my behavior, and therefore sent the Yahoo back to his kennel. He then put his forehoof to his mouth, at which I was much surprised, although he did it with ease, and with a motion that appeared perfectly natural; and made other signs to know what I would eat; but I could not return him such an answer as he was able to apprehend; and if he had understood me, I did not see how it was possible to contrive any way for finding myself nourishment. While we were thus engaged, I observed a cow passing by; whereupon I pointed to her, and expressed a desire to let me go and milk her. This had its effect; for he led me back into the house, and ordered a mare-servant to open a room, where a good store of milk lay in earthen and wooden vessels, after a very orderly and cleanly manner. She gave me a large bowl full, of which I drank very heartily, and found myself well refreshed.

About noon I saw coming towards the house a kind of vehicle, drawn like a sledge by four Yahoos. There was in it an old steed, who seemed to be of quality; he alighted with his hind feet forward, having by accident got a hurt in his left forefoot. He came to dine with our horse, who received him with great civility. They dined in the best room, and had oats boiled in milk for the second course, which the old horse eat warm, but the rest cold. Their mangers were placed circular in the middle of the room, and divided into several partitions, round which they sat on their haunches upon bosses of straw. In the middle was a large rack with angles answering to every partition of the manger. So that each horse and mare eat their own hay, and their own mash of oats and milk, with much decency and regularity. The behavior

7. The joint at the back of a horse's foot, just above the hoof, in which the Houyhnhnm holds the oats.

of the young colt and foal appeared very modest; and that of the master and mistress extremely cheerful and complaisant to their guest. The grey ordered me to stand by him; and much discourse passed between him and his friend concerning me, as I found by the stranger's often looking on me, and the frequent repetition of the word Yahoo.

I happened to wear my gloves; which the master grey observing, seemed perplexed; discovering signs of wonder what I had done to my forefeet; he put his hoof three or four times to them, as if he would signify, that I should reduce them to their former shape, which I presently did, pulling off both my gloves, and putting them into my pocket. This occasioned farther talk, and I saw the company was pleased with my behavior, whereof I soon found the good effects. I was ordered to speak the few words I understood; and while they were at dinner, the master taught me the names for oats, milk, fire, water, and some others which I could readily pronounce after him, having from my youth a great facility in learning languages.

When dinner was done, the master horse took me aside, and by signs and words made me understand the concern he was in that I had nothing to eat. Oats in their tongue are called *hlunnh*. This word I pronounced two or three times; for although I had refused them at first, yet upon second thoughts, I considered that I could contrive to make a kind of bread, which might be sufficient with milk to keep me alive, till I could make my escape to some other country, and to creatures of my own species. The horse immediately ordered a white mare-servant of his family to bring me a good quantity of oats in a sort of wooden tray. These I heated before the fire as well as I could, and rubbed them till the husks came off, which I made a shift to winnow from the grain; I ground and beat them between two stones, then took water, and made them into a paste or cake, which I toasted at the fire, and eat warm with milk. It was at first a very insipid diet, although common enough in many parts of Europe, but grew tolerable by time; and having been often reduced to hard fare in my life, this was not the first experiment I had made how easily nature is satisfied. And I cannot but observe that I never had one hour's sickness, while I staid in this island. It is true, I sometimes made a shift to catch a rabbit, or bird, by springes made of Yahoos' hairs; and I often gathered wholesome herbs, which I boiled, or ate as salads with my bread; and now and then, for a rarity, I made a little butter, and drank the whey. I was at first at a great loss for salt; but custom soon reconciled the want of it; and I am confident that the frequent use of salt among us is an effect of luxury, and was first introduced only as a provocative to drink; except where it is necessary for preserving of flesh in long voyages, or in places remote from great markets. For we observe no animal to be fond of it but man;[8] and as to myself, when I left this country, it was a great while before I could endure the taste of it in anything that I eat.

This is enough to say upon the subject of my diet, wherewith other travelers fill their books, as if the readers were personally concerned whether we fare well or ill. However, it was necessary to mention this matter, lest the world should think it impossible that I could find sustenance for three years in such a country, and among such inhabitants.

When it grew towards evening, the master horse ordered a place for me

8. Gulliver's error; many animals are very fond of salt.

to lodge in; it was but six yards from the house, and separated from the stable of the Yahoos. Here I got some straw, and covering myself with my own clothes, slept very sound. But I was in a short time better accommodated, as the reader shall know hereafter, when I come to treat more particularly about my way of living.

CHAPTER III

The Author studious to learn the language, the Houyhnhnm his master assists in teaching him. The language described. Several Houyhnhnms of quality come out of curiosity to see the Author. He gives his master a short account of his voyage.

My principal endeavor was to learn the language, which my master (for so I shall henceforth call him) and his children, and every servant of his house were desirous to teach me. For they looked upon it as a prodigy, that a brute animal should discover such marks of a rational creature. I pointed to everything, and enquired the name of it, which I wrote down in my journal book when I was alone, and corrected my bad accent, by desiring those of the family to pronounce it often. In this employment, a sorrel nag, one of the under servants, was very ready to assist me.

In speaking, they pronounce through the nose and throat, and their language approaches nearest to the High Dutch or German, of any I know in Europe; but is much more graceful and significant. The Emperor Charles V made almost the same observation, when he said, that if he were to speak to his horse, it should be in High Dutch.[9]

The curiosity and impatience of my master were so great, that he spent many hours of his leisure to instruct me. He was convinced (as he afterwards told me) that I must be a Yahoo, but my teachableness, civility, and cleanliness astonished him; which were qualities altogether so opposite to those animals. He was most perplexed about my clothes, reasoning sometimes with himself whether they were a part of my body; for I never pulled them off till the family were asleep, and got them on before they waked in the morning. My master was eager to learn from whence I came; how I acquired those appearances of reason, which I discovered in all my actions; and to know my story from my own mouth, which he hoped he should soon do by the great proficiency I made in learning and pronouncing their words and sentences. To help my memory, I formed all I learned into the English alphabet, and writ the words down with the translations. This last, after some time, I ventured to do in my master's presence. It cost me much trouble to explain to him what I was doing; for the inhabitants have not the least idea of books or literature.

In about ten weeks time I was able to understand most of his questions; and in three months could give him some tolerable answers. He was extremely curious to know from what part of the country I came, and how I was taught to imitate a rational creature; because the Yahoos (whom he saw I exactly resembled in my head, hands, and face, that were only visible) with some appearance of cunning, and the strongest disposition to mischief, were observed to be the most unteachable of all brutes. I answered that I came

9. Charles was reputed to have said he would address God in Spanish, women in Italian, men in French, and his horse in German.

over the sea, from a far place, with many others of my own kind, in a great hollow vessel made of the bodies of trees; that my companions forced me to land on this coast, and then left me to shift for myself. It was with some difficulty, and by the help of many signs, that I brought him to understand me. He replied that I must needs be mistaken, or that I *said the thing which was not*. (For they have no word in their language to express lying or false-hood.) He knew it was impossible that there could be a country beyond the sea, or that a parcel of brutes could move a wooden vessel whither they pleased upon water. He was sure no Houyhnhnm alive could make such a vessel, or would trust Yahoos to manage it.

The word Houyhnhnm, in their tongue, signifies a Horse; and in its ety-mology, the Perfection of Nature. I told my master that I was at a loss for expression, but would improve as fast as I could; and hoped in a short time I should be able to tell him wonders; he was pleased to direct his own mare, his colt, and foal, and the servants of the family to take all opportunities of instructing me; and every day for two or three hours, he was at the same pains himself; several horses and mares of quality in the neighborhood came often to our house, upon the report spread of a wonderful Yahoo, that could speak like a Houyhnhnm, and seemed in his words and actions to discover some glimmerings of reason. These delighted to converse with me; they put many questions, and received such answers as I was able to return. By all which advantages, I made so great a progress, that in five months from my arrival, I understood whatever was spoke, and could express myself tolerably well.

The Houyhnhnms who came to visit my master, out of a design of seeing and talking with me, could hardly believe me to be a right Yahoo, because my body had a different covering from others of my kind. They were aston-ished to observe me without the usual hair or skin, except on my head, face, and hands; but I discovered that secret to my master, upon an accident, which happened about a fortnight before.

I have already told the reader, that every night when the family were gone to bed, it was my custom to strip and cover myself with my clothes; it hap-pened one morning early, that my master sent for me, by the sorrel nag, who was his valet; when he came, I was fast asleep, my clothes fallen off on one side, and my shirt above my waist. I awaked at the noise he made, and observed him to deliver his message in some disorder; after which he went to my master, and in a great fright gave him a very confused account of what he had seen; this I presently discovered; for going as soon as I was dressed, to pay my attendance upon his honor, he asked me the meaning of what his servant had reported; that I was not the same thing when I slept as I appeared to be at other times; that his valet assured him, some part of me was white, some yellow, at least not so white, and some brown.

I had hitherto concealed the secret of my dress, in order to distinguish myself as much as possible, from that cursed race of Yahoos; but now I found it in vain to do so any longer. Besides, I considered that my clothes and shoes would soon wear out, which already were in a declining condition, and must be supplied by some contrivance from the hides of Yahoos, or other brutes; whereby the whole secret would be known. I therefore told my master, that in the country from whence I came, those of my kind always covered their bodies with the hairs of certain animals prepared by art, as well for decency, as to avoid inclemencies of air both hot and cold; of which, as to my own person I would give him immediate conviction, if he pleased to command me; only desiring this excuse, if I did not expose those parts that nature taught us to conceal. He said, my discourse was all very strange, but especially the last part; for he could not understand why Nature should teach us to conceal what Nature had given. That neither himself nor family were ashamed of any parts of their bodies; but however I might do as I pleased. Whereupon, I first unbuttoned my coat, and pulled it off. I did the same with my waistcoat; I drew off my shoes, stockings, and breeches. I let my shirt down to my waist, and drew up the bottom, fastening it like a girdle about my middle to hide my nakedness.

My master observed the whole performance with great signs of curiosity and admiration. He took up all my clothes in his pastern, one piece after another, and examined them diligently; he then stroked my body very gently, and looked round me several times; after which he said, it was plain I must be a perfect Yahoo; but that I differed very much from the rest of my species, in the whiteness and smoothness of my skin, my want of hair in several parts of my body, the shape and shortness of my claws behind and before, and my affectation of walking continually on my two hinder feet. He desired to see no more; and gave me leave to put on my clothes again, for I was shuddering with cold.

I expressed my uneasiness at his giving me so often the appellation of Yahoo, an odious animal, for which I had so utter an hatred and contempt. I begged he would forbear applying that word to me, and take the same order in his family, and among his friends whom he suffered to see me. I requested likewise, that the secret of my having a false covering to my body might be known to none but himself, at least as long as my present clothing should last; for as to what the sorrel nag his valet had observed, his honor might command him to conceal it.

All this my master very graciously consented to; and thus the secret was kept till my clothes began to wear out, which I was forced to supply by several contrivances, that shall hereafter be mentioned. In the meantime, he desired I would go on with my utmost diligence to learn their language, because he was more astonished at my capacity for speech and reason, than at the figure of my body, whether it were covered or no; adding that he waited with some impatience to hear the wonders which I promised to tell him.

From thenceforward he doubled the pains he had been at to instruct me; he brought me into all company, and made them treat me with civility, because, as he told them privately, this would put me into good humor, and make me more diverting.

Every day when I waited on him, beside the trouble he was at in teaching, he would ask me several questions concerning myself, which I answered as well as I could; and by those means he had already received some general ideas, although very imperfect. It would be tedious to relate the several steps, by which I advanced to a more regular conversation, but the first account I gave of myself in any order and length was to this purpose:

That, I came from a very far country, as I already had attempted to tell him, with about fifty more of my own species; that we traveled upon the seas, in a great hollow vessel made of wood, and larger than his honor's house. I described the ship to him in the best terms I could; and explained by the help of my handkerchief displayed, how it was driven forward by the wind. That, upon a quarrel among us, I was set on shore on this coast, where I walked forward without knowing whither, till he delivered me from the persecution of those execrable Yahoos. He asked me who made the ship, and how it was possible that the Houyhnhnms of my country would leave it to the management of brutes? My answer was that I durst proceed no farther in my relation, unless he would give me his word and honor that he would not be offended; and then I would tell him the wonders I had so often promised. He agreed; and I went on by assuring him, that the ship was made by creatures like myself, who in all the countries I had traveled, as well as in my own, were the only governing, rational animals; and that upon my arrival hither, I was as much astonished to see the Houyhnhnms act like rational beings, as he or his friends could be in finding some marks of reason in a creature he was pleased to call a Yahoo; to which I owned my resemblance in every part, but could not account for their degenerate and brutal nature. I said farther, that if good fortune ever restored me to my native country, to relate my travels hither, as I resolved to do; everybody would believe that I *said the thing which was not*; that I invented the story out of my own head; and with all possible respect to himself, his family, and friends, and under his promise of not being offended, our countrymen would hardly think it probable, that a Houyhnhnm should be the presiding creature of a nation, and a Yahoo the brute.

CHAPTER IV

The Houyhnhnms' notion of truth and falsehood. The author's discourse disapproved by his master. The author gives a more particular account of himself, and the accidents of his voyages.

My master heard me with great appearances of uneasiness in his countenance; because *doubting* or *not believing* are so little known in this country, that the inhabitants cannot tell how to behave themselves under such circumstances. And I remember in frequent discourses with my master concerning the nature of manhood, in other parts of the world, having occasion to talk of *lying* and *false representation*, it was with much difficulty that he comprehended what I meant; although he had otherwise a most acute judgment. For he argued thus: that the use of speech was to make us understand one another, and to receive information of facts; now if anyone *said the thing which was not*, these ends were defeated; because I cannot properly be said to understand him; and I am so far from receiving information, that he leaves me worse than in ignorance; for I am led to believe a thing *black* when it is *white*, and *short* when it is *long*. And these were all the notions he had concerning that faculty of *lying*, so perfectly well understood, and so universally practiced among human creatures.

To return from this digression; when I asserted that the Yahoos were the only governing animals in my country, which my master said was altogether past his conception, he desired to know, whether we had Houyhnhnms among us, and what was their employment; I told him we had great numbers; that in summer they grazed in the fields, and in winter were kept in houses, with hay and oats, where Yahoo servants were employed to rub their skins smooth, comb their manes, pick their feet, serve them with food, and make their beds. "I understand you well," said my master; "it is now very plain from all you have spoken, that whatever share of reason the Yahoos pretend to, the Houyhnhnms are your masters; I heartily wish our Yahoos would be so tractable." I begged his honor would please to excuse me from proceeding any farther, because I was very certain that the account he expected from me would be highly displeasing. But he insisted in commanding me to let him know the best and the worst; I told him he should be obeyed. I owned that the Houyhnhnms among us, whom we called Horses, were the most generous[1] and comely animal we had; that they excelled in strength and swiftness; and when they belonged to persons of quality, employed in traveling, racing, and drawing chariots, they were treated with much kindness and care, till they fell into diseases, or became foundered in the feet; but then they were sold, and used to all kind of drudgery till they died; after which their skins were stripped and sold for what they were worth, and their bodies left to be devoured by dogs and birds of prey. But the common race of horses had not so good fortune, being kept by farmers and carriers, and other mean people, who put them to greater labor, and fed them worse. I described as well as I could, our way of riding; the shape and use of a bridle, a saddle, a spur, and a whip; of harness and wheels. I added, that we fastened plates of a certain hard substance called iron at the bottom of their feet, to preserve their hoofs from being broken by the stony ways on which we often traveled.

My master, after some expressions of great indignation, wondered how we dared to venture upon a Houyhnhnm's back; for he was sure, that the weakest servant in his house would be able to shake off the strongest Yahoo; or by lying down, and rolling upon his back, squeeze the brute to death. I answered that our horses were trained up from three or four years old to the several uses we intended them for; that if any of them proved intolerably vicious, they were employed for carriages; that they were severely beaten while they were young for any mischievous tricks; that the males, designed for the common use of riding or draught, were generally castrated about two years after their birth, to take down their spirits, and make them more tame and gentle; that they were indeed sensible of rewards and punishments; but his honor would please to consider that they had not the least tincture of reason any more than the Yahoos in this country.

It put me to the pains of many circumlocutions to give my master a right idea of what I spoke; for their language doth not abound in variety of words, because their wants and passions are fewer than among us. But it is impossible to express his noble resentment at our savage treatment of the Houyhnhnm race; particularly after I had explained the manner and use of castrating horses among us, to hinder them from propagating their kind, and to render them more servile. He said, if it were possible there could be any country where Yahoos alone were endued with reason, they certainly must be the governing animal, because reason will in time always prevail against brutal strength. But, considering the frame of our bodies, and especially of mine, he thought no creature of equal bulk was so ill-contrived for employing that reason in the common offices of life; whereupon he desired to know

1. Noble.

whether those among whom I lived resembled me or the Yahoos of his country. I assured him that I was as well shaped as most of my age; but the younger
and the females were much more soft and tender, and the skins of the latter
generally as white as milk. He said I differed indeed from other Yahoos, being
much more cleanly, and not altogether so deformed; but in point of real
advantage, he thought I differed for the worse. That my nails were of no use
either to my fore or hinder feet; as to my forefeet, he could not properly call
them by that name, for he never observed me to walk upon them; that they
were too soft to bear the ground; that I generally went with them uncovered,
neither was the covering I sometimes wore on them of the same shape, or
so strong as that on my feet behind. That I could not walk with any security;
for if either of my hinder feet slipped, I must inevitably fall. He then began
to find fault with other parts of my body; the flatness of my face, the prominence of my nose, my eyes placed directly in front, so that I could not look
on either side without turning my head; that I was not able to feed myself
without lifting one of my forefeet to my mouth; and therefore nature had
placed those joints to answer that necessity. He knew not what could be the
use of those several clefts and divisions in my feet behind; that these were
too soft to bear the hardness and sharpness of stones without a covering
made from the skin of some other brute; that my whole body wanted a fence
against heat and cold, which I was forced to put on and off every day with
tediousness and trouble. And lastly, that he observed every animal in his
country naturally to abhor the Yahoos, whom the weaker avoided, and the
stronger drove from them. So that supposing us to have the gift of reason,
he could not see how it were possible to cure that natural antipathy which
every creature discovered against us; nor consequently, how we could tame
and render them serviceable. However, he would (as he said) debate the
matter no farther, because he was more desirous to know my own story, the
country where I was born, and the several actions and events of my life before
I came hither.

I assured him how extremely desirous I was that he should be satisfied in
every point; but I doubted much whether it would be possible for me to
explain myself on several subjects whereof his honor could have no conception, because I saw nothing in his country to which I could resemble them.
That however, I would do my best, and strive to express myself by similitudes,
humbly desiring his assistance when I wanted proper words; which he was
pleased to promise me.

I said, my birth was of honest parents, in an island called England, which
was remote from this country, as many days journey as the strongest of his
honor's servants could travel in the annual course of the sun. That I was
bred a surgeon, whose trade it is to cure wounds and hurts in the body, got
by accident or violence. That my country was governed by a female man,
whom we called a queen.[2] That I left it to get riches, whereby I might maintain myself and family when I should return. That in my last voyage, I was
Commander of the ship and had about fifty Yahoos under me, many of which
died at sea, and I was forced to supply them by others picked out from several
nations. That our ship was twice in danger of being sunk; the first time by a
great storm, and the second, by striking against a rock. Here my master

---

2. Queen Anne (1665–1714), the last Stuart ruler.

interposed, by asking me, how I could persuade strangers out of different countries to venture with me, after the losses I had sustained, and the hazards I had run. I said, they were fellows of desperate fortunes, forced to fly from the places of their birth, on account of their poverty or their crimes. Some were undone by lawsuits; others spent all they had in drinking, whoring, and gaming; others fled for treason; many for murder, theft, poisoning, robbery, perjury, forgery, coining false money; for committing rapes or sodomy; for flying from their colors, or deserting to the enemy; and most of them had broken prison. None of these durst return to their native countries for fear of being hanged, or of starving in a jail; and therefore were under a necessity of seeking livelihood in other places.

During this discourse, my master was pleased often to interrupt me. I had made use of many circumlocutions in describing to him the nature of the several crimes, for which most of our crew had been forced to fly their country. This labor took up several days conversation before he was able to comprehend me. He was wholly at a loss to know what could be the use or necessity of practicing those vices. To clear up which I endeavored to give him some ideas of the desire of power and riches; of the terrible effects of lust, intemperance, malice, and envy. All this I was forced to define and describe by putting of cases, and making suppositions. After which, like one whose imagination was struck with something never seen or heard of before, he would lift up his eyes with amazement and indignation. Power, government, war, law, punishment, and a thousand other things had no terms, wherein that language could express them; which made the difficulty almost insuperable to give my master any conception of what I meant; but being of an excellent understanding, much improved by contemplation and converse, he at last arrived at a competent knowledge of what human nature in our parts of the world is capable to perform; and desired I would give him some particular account of that land, which we call Europe, especially, of my own country.

CHAPTER V

The Author, at his master's commands, informs him of the state of England. The causes of war among the princes of Europe. The Author begins to explain the English Constitution.

The reader may please to observe that the following extract of many conversations I had with my master contains a summary of the most material points, which were discoursed at several times for above two years; his honor often desiring fuller satisfaction as I farther improved in the Houyhnhnm tongue. I laid before him, as well as I could, the whole state of Europe; I discoursed of trade and manufactures, of arts and sciences; and the answers I gave to all the questions he made, as they arose upon several subjects, were a fund of conversation not to be exhausted. But I shall here only set down the substance of what passed between us concerning my own country, reducing it into order as well as I can, without any regard to time or other circumstances, while I strictly adhere to truth. My only concern is that I shall hardly be able to do justice to my master's arguments and expressions; which must needs suffer by my want of capacity, as well as by a translation into our barbarous English.

In obedience therefore to his honor's commands, I related to him the Revolution under the Prince of Orange; the long war with France entered into by the said Prince, and renewed by his successor the present queen; wherein the greatest powers of Christendom were engaged, and which still continued. I computed at his request, that about a million of Yahoos might have been killed in the whole progress of it; and perhaps a hundred or more cities taken, and five times as many ships burned or sunk.[3]

He asked me what were the usual causes or motives that made one country to go to war with another. I answered, they were innumerable; but I should only mention a few of the chief. Sometimes the ambition of princes, who never think they have land or people enough to govern; sometimes the corruption of ministers, who engage their master in a war in order to stifle or divert the clamor of the subjects against their evil administration. Difference in opinions hath cost many millions of lives; for instance, whether flesh be bread, or bread be flesh; whether the juice of a certain berry be blood or wine; whether whistling be a vice or a virtue; whether it be better to kiss a post, or throw it into the fire; what is the best color for a coat, whether black, white, red, or grey; and whether it should be long or short, narrow or wide, dirty or clean;[4] with many more. Neither are any wars so furious and bloody, or of so long continuance, as those occasioned by difference in opinion, especially if it be in things indifferent.

Sometimes the quarrel between two princes is to decide which of them shall dispossess a third of his dominions, where neither of them pretend to any right. Sometimes one prince quarreleth with another, for fear the other should quarrel with him. Sometimes a war is entered upon, because the enemy is too strong, and sometimes because he is too weak. Sometimes our neighbors want the things which we have, or have the things which we want; and we both fight, till they take ours or give us theirs. It is a very justifiable cause of war to invade a country after the people have been wasted by famine, destroyed by pestilence, or embroiled by factions amongst themselves. It is justifiable to enter into a war against our nearest ally, when one of his towns lies convenient for us, or a territory of land, that would render our dominions round and compact. If a prince send forces into a nation, where the people are poor and ignorant, he may lawfully put half of them to death, and make slaves of the rest, in order to civilize and reduce them from their barbarous way of living. It is a very kingly, honorable, and frequent practice, when one prince desires the assistance of another to secure him against an invasion, that the assistant, when he hath driven out the invader, should seize on the dominions himself, and kill, imprison, or banish the prince he came to relieve. Alliance by blood or marriage is a sufficient cause of war between princes; and the nearer the kindred is, the greater is their disposition to quarrel; poor nations are hungry, and rich nations are proud; and pride and hunger will ever be at variance. For these reasons, the trade of a soldier is held the most honorable of all others: because a soldier is a Yahoo hired to kill in cold blood as many of his own species, who have never offended him, as possibly he can.

3. Gulliver relates recent English history: the Glorious Revolution of 1688 and the War of the Spanish Succession (1703–13). He greatly exaggerates the casualties in the war.   4. Gulliver refers to the religious controversies of the Reformation and Counter-Reformation: the doctrine of transubstantiation, the use of music in church services, the veneration of the crucifix, and the wearing of priestly vestments.

There is likewise a kind of beggarly princes in Europe, not able to make war by themselves, who hire out their troops to richer nations for so much a day to each man; of which they keep three fourths to themselves, and it is the best part of their maintenance; such are those in many northern parts of Europe.

"What you have told me," said my master, "upon the subject of war, doth indeed discover most admirably the effects of that reason you pretend to; however, it is happy that the shame is greater than the danger; and that Nature hath left you utterly uncapable of doing much mischief; for your mouths lying flat with your faces, you can hardly bite each other to any purpose, unless by consent. Then, as to the claws upon your feet before and behind, they are so short and tender, that one of our Yahoos would drive a dozen of yours before him. And therefore in recounting the numbers of those who have been killed in battle, I cannot but think that you have *said the thing which is not.*"

I could not forebear shaking my head and smiling a little at his ignorance. And, being no stranger to the art of war, I gave him a description of cannons, culverins, muskets, carabines, pistols, bullets, powder, swords, bayonets, battles, sieges, retreats, attacks, undermines, countermines, bombardments, sea fights; ships sunk with a thousand men; twenty thousand killed on each side; dying groans, limbs flying in the air; smoke, noise, confusion, trampling to death under horses' feet; flight, pursuit, victory; fields strewed with carcasses left for food to dogs, and wolves, and birds of prey; plundering, stripping, ravishing, burning, and destroying. And, to set forth the valor of my own dear countrymen, I assured him that I had seen them blow up a hundred enemies at once in a siege, and as many in a ship; and beheld the dead bodies drop down in pieces from the clouds, to the great diversion of all the spectators.

I was going on to more particulars, when my master commanded me silence. He said, whoever understood the nature of Yahoos might easily believe it possible for so vile an animal, to be capable of every action I had named, if their strength and cunning equaled their malice. But, as my discourse had increased his abhorrence of the whole species, so he found it gave him a disturbance in his mind, to which he was wholly a stranger before. He thought his ears being used to such abominable words, might by degrees admit them with less detestation. That, although he hated the Yahoos of this country, yet he no more blamed them for their odious qualities, than he did a *gnnayh* (a bird of prey) for its cruelty, or a sharp stone for cutting his hoof. But, when a creature pretending to reason could be capable of such enormities, he dreaded lest the corruption of that faculty might be worse than brutality itself. He seemed therefore confident, that instead of reason, we were only possessed of some quality fitted to increase our natural vices; as the reflection from a troubled stream returns the image of an ill-shapen body, not only larger, but more distorted.

He added that he had heard too much upon the subject of war, both in this and some former discourses. There was another point which a little perplexed him at present. I had said that some of our crew left their country on account of being ruined by law: that I had already explained the meaning of the word; but he was at a loss how it should come to pass, that the law which was intended for every man's preservation, should be any man's ruin. Therefore he desired to be farther satisfied what I meant by law, and the dispensers thereof, according to the present practice in my own country; because he thought nature and reason were sufficient guides for a reasonable animal, as we pretended to be, in showing us what we ought to do, and what to avoid.

I assured his honor that law was a science wherein I had not much conversed, further than by employing advocates, in vain, upon some injustices that had been done me. However, I would give him all the satisfaction I was able.

I said there was a society of men among us, bred up from their youth in the art of proving by words multiplied for the purpose, that white is black, and black is white, according as they are paid. To this society all the rest of the people are slaves.

"For example. If my neighbor hath a mind to my cow, he hires a lawyer to prove that he ought to have my cow from me. I must then hire another to defend my right; it being against all rules of law that any man should be allowed to speak for himself. Now in this case, I who am the true owner lie under two great disadvantages. First, my lawyer being practiced almost from his cradle in defending falsehood is quite out of his element when he would be an advocate for justice, which as an office unnatural, he always attempts with great awkwardness, if not with ill-will. The second disadvantage is that my lawyer must proceed with great caution, or else he will be reprimanded by the judges, and abhorred by his breathren, as one who would lessen the practice of the law. And therefore I have but two methods to preserve my cow. The first is to gain over my adversary's lawyer with a double fee; who will then betray his client, by insinuating that he hath justice on his side. The second way is for my lawyer to make my cause appear as unjust as he can; by allowing the cow to belong to my adversary; and this if it be skillfully done, will certainly bespeak the favor of the bench.

"Now, your honor is to know that these judges are persons appointed to decide all controversies of property, as well as for the trial of criminals; and picked out from the most dextrous lawyers who are grown old or lazy; and having been biased all their lives against truth and equity, lie under such a fatal necessity of favoring fraud, perjury, and oppression, that I have known some of them to have refused a large bribe from the side where justice lay, rather than injure the faculty,[5] by doing anything unbecoming their nature or their office.

"It is a maxim among these lawyers, that whatever hath been done before may legally be done again; and therefore they take special care to record all the decisions formerly made against common justice and the general reason of mankind. These, under the name of *precedents*, they produce as authorities to justify the most iniquitous opinions; and the judges never fail of directing accordingly.

"In pleading, they studiously avoid entering into the merits of the cause; but are loud, violent, and tedious in dwelling upon all circumstances which are not to the purpose. For instance, in the case already mentioned, they never desire to know what claim or title my adversary hath to my cow; but whether the said cow were red or black; her horns long or short; whether the field I graze her in be round or square; whether she were milked at home or abroad; what diseases she is subject to, and the like. After which they

5. Profession.

consult precedents, adjourn the cause, from time to time, and in ten, twenty, or thirty years come to an issue.

"It is likewise to be observed, that this society hath a peculiar cant and jargon of their own, that no other mortal can understand, and wherein all their laws are written, which they take special care to multiply; whereby they have wholly confounded the very essence of truth and falsehood, of right and wrong; so that it will take thirty years to decide whether the field, left me by my ancestors for six generations, belong to me, or to a stranger three hundred miles off.

"In the trial of persons accused for crimes against the state, the method is much more short and commendable: the judge first sends to sound the disposition of those in power; after which he can easily hang or save the criminal, strictly preserving all the forms of law."

Here my master interposing said it was a pity that creatures endowed with such prodigious abilities of mind as these lawyers, by the description I gave of them must certainly be, were not rather encouraged to be instructors of others in wisdom and knowledge. In answer to which, I assured his honor that in all points out of their own trade, they were usually the most ignorant and stupid generation among us, the most despicable in common conversation, avowed enemies to all knowledge and learning; and equally disposed to pervert the general reason of mankind, in every other subject of discourse as in that of their own profession.

CHAPTER VI

A continuation of the state of England, under Queen Anne. The character of a first minister in the courts of Europe.

My master was yet wholly at a loss to understand what motives could incite this race of lawyers to perplex, disquiet, and weary themselves by engaging in a confederacy of injustice, merely for the sake of injuring their fellow animals; neither could he comprehend what I meant in saying they did it for hire. Whereupon I was at much pains to describe to him the use of money, the materials it was made of, and the value of the metals; that when a Yahoo had got a great store of this precious substance, he was able to purchase whatever he had a mind to; the finest clothing, the noblest houses, great tracts of land, the most costly meats and drinks; and have his choice of the most beautiful females. Therefore since money alone was able to perform all these feats, our Yahoos thought they could never have enough of it to spend or to save, as they found themselves inclined from their natural bent either to profusion or avarice. That the rich man enjoyed the fruit of the poor man's labor, and the latter were a thousand to one in proportion to the former. That the bulk of our people was forced to live miserably, by laboring every day for small wages to make a few live plentifully. I enlarged myself much on these and many other particulars to the same purpose, but his honor was still to seek, for he went upon a supposition that all animals had a title to their share in the productions of the earth; and especially those who presided over the rest. Therefore he desired I would let him know what these costly meats were, and how any of us happened to want[6] them. Whereupon I enu-

6. Lack.

merated as many sorts as came into my head, with the various methods of dressing them, which could not be done without sending vessels by sea to every part of the world, as well for liquors to drink, as for sauces, and innumerable other conveniencies. I assured him, that this whole globe of earth must be at least three times gone round, before one of our better female Yahoos could get her breakfast, or a cup to put it in. He said, "That must needs be a miserable country which cannot furnish food for its own inhabitants." But what he chiefly wondered at, was how such vast tracts of ground as I described, should be wholly without fresh water, and the people put to the necessity of sending over the sea for drink. I replied that England (the dear place of my nativity) was computed to produce three times the quantity of food, more than its inhabitants are able to consume, as well as liquors extracted from grain, or pressed out of the fruit of certain trees, which made excellent drink; and the same proportion in every other convenience of life. But, in order to feed the luxury and intemperance of the males, and the vanity of the females, we sent away the greatest part of our necessary things to other countries, from whence in return we brought the materials of diseases, folly, and vice, to spend among ourselves. Hence it follows of necessity, that vast numbers of our people are compelled to seek their livelihood by begging, robbing, stealing, cheating, pimping, foreswearing, flattering, suborning, forging, gaming, lying, fawning, hectoring, voting, scribbling, star gazing, poisoning, whoring, canting, libeling, freethinking, and the like occupations; every one of which terms, I was at much pains to make him understand.

That, wine was not imported among us from foreign countries, to supply the want of water or other drinks, but because it was a sort of liquid which made us merry, by putting us out of our senses; diverted all melancholy thoughts, begat wild extravagant imaginations in the brain, raised our hopes, and banished our fears; suspended every office of reason for a time, and deprived us of the use of our limbs, until we fell into a profound sleep; although it must be confessed, that we always awaked sick and dispirited; and that the use of this liquor filled us with diseases, which made our lives uncomfortable and short.

But beside all this, the bulk of our people supported themselves by furnishing the necessities or conveniencies of life to the rich, and to each other. For instance, when I am at home and dressed as I ought to be, I carry on my body the workmanship of an hundred tradesmen; the building and furniture of my house employ as many more; and five times the number to adorn my wife.

I was going on to tell him of another sort of people, who get their livelihood by attending the sick; having upon some occasions informed his honor that many of my crew had died of diseases. But here it was with the utmost difficulty that I brought him to apprehend what I meant. He could easily conceive that a Houyhnhnm grew weak and heavy a few days before his death; or by some accident might hurt a limb. But that nature, who worketh all things to perfection, should suffer any pains to breed in our bodies, he thought impossible; and desired to know the reason of so unaccountable an evil. I told him, we fed on a thousand things which operated contrary to each other; that we eat when we were not hungry, and drank without the provocation of thirst; that we sat whole nights drinking strong liquors without eating a bit, which disposed us to sloth, inflamed our bodies, and precipitated or prevented digestion. That, prostitute female Yahoos acquired a certain malady, which bred rottenness in the bones of those who fell into their embraces; that this and many other diseases were propagated from father to son; so that great numbers come into the world with complicated maladies upon them; that it would be endless to give him a catalogue of all diseases incident to human bodies; for they could not be fewer than five or six hundred, spread over every limb, and joint; in short, every part, external and intestine, having diseases appropriated to each. To remedy which, there was a sort of people bred up among us, in the profession or pretense of curing the sick. And because I had some skill in the faculty, I would in gratitude to his honor let him know the whole mystery and method by which they proceed.

Their fundamental is that all diseases arise from repletion; from whence they conclude, that a great evacuation of the body is necessary, either through the natural passage, or upwards at the mouth. Their next business is, from herbs, minerals, gums, oils, shells, salts, juices, seaweed, excrements, barks of trees, serpents, toads, frogs, spiders, dead men's flesh and bones, birds, beasts and fishes, to form a composition for smell and taste the most abominable, nauseous, and detestable, that they can possibly contrive, which the stomach immediately rejects with loathing, and this they call a vomit. Or else from the same storehouse, with some other poisonous additions, they command us to take in at the orifice above or below (just as the physician then happens to be disposed) a medicine equally annoying and disgustful to the bowels; which relaxing the belly, drives down all before it; and this they call a purge, or a clyster. For nature (as the physicians allege) having intended the superior anterior orifice only for the intromission of solids and liquids, and the inferior posterior for ejection, these artists ingeniously considering that in all diseases nature is forced out of her seat; therefore to replace her in it, the body must be treated in a manner directly contrary, but interchanging the use of each orifice; forcing solids and liquids in at the anus, and making evacuations at the mouth.

But, besides real diseases, we are subject to many that are only imaginary, for which the physicians have invented imaginary cures; these have their several names, and so have the drugs that are proper for them; and with these our female Yahoos are always infested.

One great excellency in this tribe is their skill at prognostics, wherein they seldom fail; their predictions in real diseases, when they rise to any degree of malignity, generally portending death, which is always in their power, when recovery is not, and therefore, upon any unexpected signs of amendment, after they have pronounced their sentence, rather than be accused as false prophets, they know how to approve[7] their sagacity to the world by a seasonable dose.

They are likewise of special use to husbands and wives, who are grown weary of their mates; to eldest sons, to great ministers of state, and often to princes.

I had formerly upon occasion discoursed with my master upon the nature of government in general, and particularly of our own excellent constitution,

7. Prove.

deservedly the wonder and envy of the whole world. But having here accidentally mentioned a minister of state, he commanded me some time after to inform him what species of Yahoo I particularly meant by that appellation.

I told him that a first or chief minister of state, whom I intended to describe, was a creature wholly exempt from joy and grief, love and hatred, pity and anger; at least makes use of no other passions but a violent desire of wealth, power, and titles; that he applies his words to all uses, except to the indication of his mind; that he never tells a truth, but with an intent that you should take it for a lie; nor a lie, but with a design that you should take it for a truth; that those he speaks worst of behind their backs are in the surest way to preferment; and whenever he begins to praise you to others or to yourself, you are from that day forlorn. The worst mark you can receive is a promise, especially when it is confirmed with an oath; after which every wise man retires, and gives over all hopes.

There are three methods by which a man may rise to be chief minister: the first is by knowing how with prudence to dispose of a wife, a daughter, or a sister; the second, by betraying or undermining his predecessor; and the third is by a furious zeal in public assemblies against the corruptions of the court. But a wise prince would rather choose to employ those who practice the last of these methods; because such zealots prove always the most obsequious and subservient to the will and passions of their master. That, these ministers having all employments at their disposal, preserve themselves in power by bribing the majority of a senate or great council; and at last by an expedient called an Act of Indemnity (whereof I described the nature to him) they secure themselves from after-reckonings, and retire from the public, laden with the spoils of the nation.

The palace of a chief minister is a seminary to breed up others in his own trade; the pages, lackies, and porter, by imitating their master, become ministers of state in their several districts, and learn to excel in the three principal ingredients, of insolence, lying, and bribery. Accordingly, they have a subaltern court paid to them by persons of the best rank; and sometimes by the force of dexterity and impudence, arrive through several gradations to be successors to their lord.

He is usually governed by a decayed wench, or favorite footman, who are the tunnels through which all graces are conveyed, and may properly be called, in the last resort, the governors of the kingdom.

One day, my master, having heard me mention the nobility of my country, was pleased to make me a compliment which I could not pretend to deserve: that, he was sure, I must have been born of some noble family, because I far exceeded in shape, color, and cleanliness, all the Yahoos of his nation, although I seemed to fail in strength, and agility, which must be imputed to my different way of living from those other brutes; and besides, I was not only endowed with the faculty of speech, but likewise with some rudiments of reason, to a degree, that with all his acquaintance I passed for a prodigy.

He made me observe, that among the Houyhnhnms, the white, the sorrel, and the iron grey were not so exactly shaped as the bay, the dapple grey, and the black; nor born with equal talents of mind, or a capacity to improve them; and therefore continued always in the condition of servants, without ever aspiring to match out of their own race, which in that country would be reckoned monstrous and unnatural.

I made his honor my most humble acknowledgements for the good opinion he was pleased to conceive of me; but assured him at the same time, that my birth was of the lower sort, having been born of plain, honest parents, who were just able to give me a tolerable education; that, nobility among us was altogether a different thing from the idea he had of it; that, our young noblemen are bred from their childhood in idleness and luxury; that, as soon as years will permit, they consume their vigor, and contract odious diseases among lewd females; and when their fortunes are almost ruined, they marry some woman of mean birth, disagreeable person, and unsound constitution, merely for the sake of money, whom they hate and despise. That, the productions of such marriages are generally scrofulous, rickety or deformed children; by which means the family seldom continues above three generations, unless the wife take care to provide a healthy father among her neighbors, or domestics, in order to improve and continue the breed. That a weak diseased body, a meager countenance, and sallow complexion are the true marks of noble blood; and a healthy robust appearance is so disgraceful in a man of quality, that the world concludes his real father to have been a groom or a coachman. The imperfections of his mind run parallel with those of his body; being a composition of spleen, dullness, ignorance, caprice, sensuality, and pride.

Without the consent of this illustrious body, no law can be enacted, repealed, or altered, and these nobles have likewise the decision of all our possessions without appeal.

CHAPTER VII

The Author's great love of his native country. His master's observations upon the constitution and administration of England, as described by the Author, with parallel cases and comparisons. His master's observations upon human nature.

The reader may be disposed to wonder how I could prevail on myself to give so free a representation of my own species, among a race of mortals who were already too apt to conceive the vilest opinion of humankind, from that entire congruity betwixt me and their Yahoos. But I must freely confess that the many virtues of those excellent quadrupeds placed in opposite view to human corruptions had so far opened my eyes, and enlarged my understanding, that I began to view the actions and passions of man in a very different light; and to think the honor of my own kind not worth managing; which, besides, it was impossible for me to do before a person of so acute a judgment as my master, who daily convinced me of a thousand faults in myself, whereof I had not the least perception before, and which with us would never be numbered even among human infirmities. I had likewise learned from his example an utter detestation of all falsehood or disguise; and truth appeared so amiable to me, that I determined upon sacrificing everything to it.

Let me deal so candidly with the reader as to confess that there was yet a much stronger motive for the freedom I took in my representation of things. I had not been a year in this country, before I contracted such a love and veneration for the inhabitants, that I entered on a firm resolution never to return to humankind, but to pass the rest of my life among these admirable Houyhnhnms in the contemplation and practice of every virtue; where I could have no example or incitement to vice. But it was decreed by fortune, my perpetual enemy, that so great a felicity should not fall to my share. However, it is now some comfort to reflect that in what I said of my countrymen, I extenuated their faults as much as I durst before so strict an examiner; and upon every article, gave as favorable a turn as the matter would bear. For, indeed, who is there alive that will not be swayed by his bias and partiality to the place of his birth?

I have related the substance of several conversations I had with my master, during the greatest part of the time I had the honor to be in his service; but have indeed for brevity sake omitted much more than is here set down.

When I had answered all his questions, and his curiosity seemed to be fully satisfied; he sent for me one morning early, and commanding me to sit down at some distance (an honor which he had never before conferred upon me), he said he had been very seriously considering my whole story, as far as it related both to myself and my country; that, he looked upon us as a sort of animal to whose share, by what accident he could not conjecture, some small pittance of reason had fallen, whereof we made no other use than by its assistance to aggravate our natural corruptions, and to acquire new ones which nature had not given us. That we disarmed ourselves of the few abilities she had bestowed; had been very successful in multiplying our original wants, and seemed to spend our whole lives in vain endeavors to supply them by our own inventions. That, as to myself, it was manifest I had neither the strength or agility of a common Yahoo; that I walked infirmly on my hinder feet; had found out a contrivance to make my claws of no use or defense, and to remove the hair from my chin, which was intended as a shelter from the sun and the weather. Lastly, that I could neither run with speed, nor climb trees like my brethren (as he called them) the Yahoos in this country.

That our institutions of government and law were plainly owing to our gross defects in reason, and by consequence, in virtue; because reason alone is sufficient to govern a rational creature; which was therefore a character we had no pretense to challenge, even from the account I had given of my own people; although he manifestly perceived, that in order to favor them, I had concealed many particulars, and often *said the thing which was not.*

He was the more confirmed in this opinion, because he observed that I agreed in every feature of my body with other Yahoos, except where it was to my real disadvantage in point of strength, speed, and activity, the shortness of my claws, and some other particulars where nature had no part; so, from the representation I had given him of our lives, our manners, and our actions, he found as near a resemblance in the disposition of our minds. He said the Yahoos were known to hate one another more than they did any different species of animals; and the reason usually assigned was the odiousness of their own shapes, which all could see in the rest, but not in themselves. He had therefore begun to think it not unwise in us to cover our bodies, and by that invention, conceal many of our deformities from each other, which would else be hardly supportable. But he now found he had been mistaken; and that the dissentions of those brutes in his country were owing to the same cause with ours, as I had described them. For, if (said he) you throw among five Yahoos as much food as would be sufficient for fifty, they will, instead of eating peaceably, fall together by the ears, each single one impatient to have all to itself; and therefore a servant was usually employed to stand by while they were feeding abroad, and those kept at home were tied at a distance from each other. That, if a cow died of age or accident, before a Houyhnhnm could secure it for his own Yahoos, those in the neighborhood would come in herds to seize it, and then would ensue such a battle as I had described, with terrible wounds made by their claws on both sides, although they seldom were able to kill one another, for want of such convenient instruments of death as we had invented. At other times the like battles have been fought between the Yahoos of several neighborhoods without any visible cause; those of one district watching all opportunities to surprise the next before they are prepared. But if they find their project hath miscarried, they return home, and for want of enemies, engage in what I call a civil war among themselves.

That, in some fields of his country, there are certain shining stones of several colors, whereof the Yahoos are violently fond; and when part of these stones are fixed in the earth, as it sometimes happeneth, they will dig with their claws for whole days to get them out, and carry them away, and hide them by heaps in their kennels; but still looking round with great caution, for fear their comrades should find out their treasure. My master said he could never discover the reason of this unnatural appetite, or how these stones could be of any use to a Yahoo; but now he believed it might proceed from the same principle of avarice, which I had ascribed to mankind. That he had once, by way of experiment, privately removed a heap of these stones from the place where one of his Yahoos had buried it, whereupon, the sordid animal missing his treasure, by his loud lamenting brought the whole herd to the place, there miserably howled, then fell to biting and tearing the rest; began to pine away, would neither eat nor sleep, nor work, till he ordered a servant privately to convey the stones into the same hole, and hide them as before; which when his Yahoo had found, he presently recovered his spirits and good humor; but took care to remove them to a better hiding place; and hath ever since been a very serviceable brute.

My master farther assured me, which I also observed myself; that in the fields where these shining stones abound, the fiercest and most frequent battles are fought, occasioned by perpetual inroads of the neighboring Yahoos.

He said it was common when two Yahoos discovered such a stone in a field, and were contending which of them should be the proprietor, a third would take the advantage, and carry it away from them both; which my master would needs contend to have some resemblance with our suits at law; wherein I thought it for our credit not to undeceive him; since the decision he mentioned was much more equitable than many decrees among us; because the plaintiff and defendant there lost nothing beside the stone they contended for; whereas our courts of equity would never have dismissed the cause while either of them had anything left.

My master continuing his discourse said there was nothing that rendered the Yahoos more odious, than their undistinguished appetite to devour everything that came in their way, whether herbs, roots, berries, corrupted flesh of animals, or all mingled together; and it was peculiar in their temper, that they were fonder of what they could get by rapine or stealth at a greater distance, than much better food provided for them at home. If their prey held out, they would eat till they were ready to burst, after which nature had pointed out to them a certain root that gave them a general evacuation.

There was also another kind of root very juicy, but something rare and difficult to be found, which the Yahoos fought for with much eagerness, and would suck it with great delight; it produced the same effects that wine hath upon us. It would make them sometimes hug, and sometimes tear one another; they would howl and grin, and chatter, and reel, and tumble, and then fall asleep in the mud.

I did indeed observe that the Yahoos were the only animals in this country subject to any diseases; which however, were much fewer than horses have among us, and contracted not by any ill treatment they meet with, but by the nastiness and greediness of that sordid brute. Neither has their language any more than a general appellation for those maladies; which is borrowed from the name of the beast, and called *Hnea Yahoo*, or the Yahoo's Evil; and the cure prescribed is a mixture of their own dung and urine, forcibly put down the Yahoo's throat. This I have since often known to have been taken with success, and do here freely recommend it to my countrymen, for the public good, as an admirable specific against all diseases produced by repletion.

As to learning, government, arts, manufactures, and the like, my master confessed he could find little or no resemblance between the Yahoos of that country and those in ours. For he only meant to observe what parity there was in our natures. He had heard indeed some curious Houyhnhnms observe that in most herds there was a sort of ruling Yahoo (as among us there is generally some leading or principal stag in a park) who was always more deformed in body, and mischievous in disposition, than any of the rest. That this leader had usually a favorite as like himself as he could get, whose employment was to lick his master's feet and posteriors, and drive the female Yahoos to his kennel; for which he was now and then rewarded with a piece of ass's flesh. This favorite is hated by the whole herd; and therefore to protect himself, keeps always near the person of his leader. He usually continues in office till a worse can be found; but the very moment he is discarded, his successor, at the head of all the Yahoos in that district, young and old, male and female, come in a body, and discharge their excrements upon him from head to foot. But how far this might be applicable to our courts and favorites, and ministers of state, my master said I could best determine.

I durst make no return to this malicious insinuation, which debased human understanding below the sagacity of a common hound, who hath judgment enough to distinguish and follow the cry of the ablest dog in the pack, without being ever mistaken.

My master told me there were some qualities remarkable in the Yahoos, which he had not observed me to mention, or at least very slightly, in the accounts I had given him of humankind. He said, those animals, like other brutes, had their females in common; but in this differed, that the she-Yahoo would admit the male while she was pregnant; and that the hes would quarrel and fight with the females as fiercely as with each other. Both which practices were such degrees of infamous brutality, that no other sensitive creature ever arrived at.

Another thing he wondered at in the Yahoos was their strange disposition to nastiness and dirt; whereas there appears to be a natural love of cleanliness in all other animals. As to the two former accusations, I was glad to let them pass without any reply, because I had not a word to offer upon them in defense of my species, which otherwise I certainly had done from my own inclinations. But I could have easily vindicated humankind from the imputation of singularity upon the last article, if there had been any swine in that country (as unluckily for me there were not) which although it may be a sweeter quadruped than a Yahoo, cannot I humbly conceive in justice pretend to more cleanliness; and so his honor himself must have owned, if he had seen their filthy way of feeding, and their custom of wallowing and sleeping in the mud.

My master likewise mentioned another quality, which his servants had discovered in several Yahoos, and to him was wholly unaccountable. He said, a fancy would sometimes take a Yahoo, to retire into a corner, to lie down and howl, and groan, and spurn away all that came near him, although he were young and fat, and wanted neither food nor water; nor did the servants imagine what could possibly ail him. And the only remedy they found was to set him to hard work, after which he would infallibly come to himself. To this I was silent out of partiality to my own kind; yet here I could plainly discover the true seeds of spleen,[8] which only seizeth on the lazy, the luxurious, and the rich; who, if they were forced to undergo the same regimen, I would undertake for the cure.

His Honor had farther observed, that a female Yahoo would often stand behind a bank or a bush, to gaze on the young males passing by, and then appear, and hide, using many antic gestures and grimaces; at which time it was observed, that she had a most offensive smell; and when any of the males advanced, would slowly retire, looking back, and with a counterfeit show of fear, run off into some convenient place where she knew the male would follow her.

At other times, if a female stranger came among them, three or four of her own sex would get about her, and stare and chatter, and grin, and smell her all over; and then turn off with gestures that seemed to express contempt and disdain.

Perhaps my master might refine a little in these speculations, which he had drawn from what he observed himself, or had been told by others; however, I could not reflect without some amazement, and much sorrow, that the rudiments of lewdness, coquetry, censure, and scandal, should have place by instinct in womankind.

I expected every moment that my master would accuse the Yahoos of those unnatural appetites in both sexes, so common among us. But nature it seems hath not been so expert a school-mistress; and these politer pleasures are entirely the productions of art and reason, on our side of the globe.

CHAPTER VIII

The Author relateth several particulars of the Yahoos. The great virtues of the Houyhnhnms. The education and exercises of their youth. Their general assembly.

8. Hypochondria.

As I ought to have understood human nature much better than I supposed it possible for my master to do, so it was easy to apply the character he gave of the Yahoos to myself and my countrymen; and I believed I could yet make farther discoveries from my own observation. I therefore often begged his honor to let me go among the herds of Yahoos in the neighborhood; to which he always very graciously consented, being perfectly convinced that the hatred I bore those brutes would never suffer me to be corrupted by them; and his honor ordered one of his servants, a strong sorrel nag, very honest and good-natured, to be my guard; without whose protection I durst not undertake such adventures. For I have already told the reader how much I was pestered by those odious animals upon my first arrival. I afterwards failed very narrowly three or four times of falling into their clutches, when I happened to stray at any distance without my hanger. And I have reason to believe, they had some imagination that I was of their own species, which I often assisted myself, by stripping up my sleeves, and shewing my naked arms and breast in their sight, when my protector was with me; at which times they would approach as near as they durst, and imitate my actions after the manner of monkeys, but ever with great signs of hatred; as a tame jackdaw with cap and stockings is always persecuted by the wild ones, when he happens to be got among them.

They are prodigiously nimble from their infancy; however, I once caught a young male of three years old, and endeavored by all marks of tenderness to make it quiet; but the little imp fell a squalling, scratching, and biting with such violence, that I was forced to let it go; and it was high time, for a whole troop of old ones came about us at the noise; but finding the cub was safe (for away it ran) and my sorrel nag being by, they durst not venture near us. I observed the young animal's flesh to smell very rank, and the stink was somewhat between a weasel and a fox, but much more disagreeable. I forgot another circumstance (and perhaps I might have the reader's pardon, if it were wholly omitted) that while I held the odious vermin in my hands, it voided its filthy excrements of a yellow liquid substance, all over my clothes; but by good fortune there was a small brook hard by, where I washed myself as clean as I could; although I durst not come into my master's presence until I were sufficiently aired.

By what I could discover, the Yahoos appear to be the most unteachable of all animals, their capacities never reaching higher than to draw or carry burdens. Yet I am of opinion, this defect ariseth chiefly from a perverse, restive disposition. For they are cunning, malicious, treacherous and revengeful. They are strong and hardy, but of a cowardly spirit, and by consequence insolent, abject, and cruel. It is observed that the red-haired of both sexes are more libidinous and mischievous than the rest, whom yet they much exceed in strength and activity.

The Houyhnhnms keep the Yahoos for present use in huts not far from the house; but the rest are sent abroad to certain fields, where they dig up roots, eat several kinds of herbs, and search about for carrion, or sometimes catch weasels and *luhimuhs* (a sort of wild rat) which they greedily devour. Nature hath taught them to dig deep holes with their nails on the side of a rising ground, wherein they lie by themselves; only the kennels of the females are larger, sufficient to hold two or three cubs.

They swim from their infancy like frogs, and are able to continue long

under water, where they often take fish, which the females carry home to
their young. And upon this occasion, I hope the reader will pardon my relating an odd adventure.

Being one day abroad with my protector the sorrel nag, and the weather
exceeding hot, I entreated him to let me bathe in a river that was near. He
consented, and I immediately stripped myself stark naked, and went down
softly into the stream. It happened that a young female Yahoo standing
behind a bank, saw the whole proceeding; and inflamed by desire, as the nag
and I conjectured, came running with all speed, and leaped into the water
within five yards of the place where I bathed. I was never in my life so terribly
frighted; the nag was grazing at some distance, not suspecting any harm; she
embraced me after a most fulsome manner; I roared as loud as I could, and
the nag came galloping towards me, whereupon she quitted her grasp, with
the utmost reluctancy, and leaped upon the opposite bank, where she stood
gazing and howling all the time I was putting on my clothes.

This was matter of diversion to my master and his family, as well as of
mortification to myself. For now I could no longer deny that I was a real
Yahoo, in every limb and feature, since the females had a natural propensity
to me as one of their own species; neither was the hair of this brute of a red
color (which might have been some excuse for an appetite a little irregular)
but black as a sole, and her countenance did not make an appearance altogether so hideous as the rest of the kind; for I think, she could not be above
eleven years old.

Having already lived three years in this country, the reader I suppose will
expect that I should, like other travelers, give him some account of the manners and customs of its inhabitants, which it was indeed my principal study
to learn.

As these noble Houyhnhnms are endowed by Nature with a general disposition to all virtues, and have no conceptions or ideas of what is evil in a
rational creature; so their grand maxim is to cultivate reason, and to be wholly
governed by it. Neither is reason among them a point problematical as with
us, where men can argue with plausibility on both sides of a question; but
strikes you with immediate conviction; as it must needs do where it is not
mingled, obscured, or discolored by passion and interest. I remember it was
with extreme difficulty that I could bring my master to understand the meaning of the word "opinion," or how a point could be disputable; because reason
taught us to affirm or deny only where we are certain; and beyond our knowledge we cannot do either. So that controversies, wranglings, disputes, and
positiveness in false or dubious propositions are evils unknown among the
Houyhnhnms. In the like manner when I used to explain to him our several
systems of natural philosophy, he would laugh that a creature pretending to
reason should value itself upon the knowledge of other people's conjectures,
and in things, where that knowledge, if it were certain, could be of no use.
Wherein he agreed entirely with the sentiments of Socrates, as Plato delivers
them, which I mention as the highest honor I can do that prince of philosophers. I have often since reflected what destruction such a doctrine would
make in the libraries of Europe; and how many paths to fame would be then
shut up in the learned world.

Friendship and benevolence are the two principal virtues among the
Houyhnhnms; and these not confined to particular objects, but universal to

the whole race. For a stranger from the remotest part is equally treated with the nearest neighbor, and wherever he goes, looks upon himself as at home. They preserve decency and civility in the highest degrees, but are altogether ignorant of ceremony. They have no fondness for[9] their colts or foals; but the care they take in educating them proceedeth entirely from the dictates of reason. And I observed my master to show the same affection to his neighbor's issue that he had for his own. They will have it that nature teaches them to love the whole species, and it is reason only that maketh a distinction of persons, where there is a superior degree of virtue.

When the matron Houyhnhnms have produced one of each sex, they no longer accompany with their consorts, except they lose one of their issue by some casualty, which very seldom happens; but in such a case they meet again; or when the like accident befalls a person whose wife is past bearing, some other couple bestows on him one of their own colts, and then go together a second time, until the mother be pregnant. This caution is necessary to prevent the country from being overburdened with numbers. But the race of inferior Houyhnhnms bred up to be servants is not so strictly limited upon this article; these are allowed to produce three of each sex, to be domestics in the noble families.

In their marriages they are exactly careful to choose such colors as will not make any disagreeable mixture in the breed. Strength is chiefly valued in the male, and comeliness in the female; not upon the account of love, but to preserve the race from degenerating; for, where a female happens to excel in strength, a consort is chosen with regard to comeliness. Courtship, love, presents, jointures, settlements, have no place in their thoughts, or terms whereby to express them in their language. The young couple meet and are joined, merely because it is the determination of their parents and friends; it is what they see done every day; and they look upon it as one of the necessary actions in a reasonable being. But the violation of marriage, or any other unchastity, was never heard of; and the married pair pass their lives with the same friendship and mutual benevolence that they bear to all others of the same species who come in their way, without jealousy, fondness, quarreling, or discontent.

In educating the youth of both sexes, their method is admirable, and highly deserveth our imitation. These are not suffered to taste a grain of oats, except upon certain days, till eighteen years old; nor milk, but very rarely; and in summer they graze two hours in the morning, and as many in the evening, which their parents likewise observe; but the servants are not allowed above half that time; and a great part of the grass is brought home, which they eat at the most convenient hours, when they can be best spared from work.

Temperance, industry, exercise, and cleanliness are the lessons equally enjoined to the young ones of both sexes; and my master thought it monstrous in us to give the females a different kind of education from the males, except in some articles of domestic management; whereby, as he truly observed, one half of our natives were good for nothing but bringing children into the world; and to trust the care of their children to such useless animals, he said was yet a greater instance of brutality.

But the Houyhnhnms train up their youth to strength, speed, and hard-

9. Attachment to.

iness, by exercising them in running races up and down steep hills, or over hard stony grounds; and when they are all in a sweat, they are ordered to leap over head and ears into a pond or a river. Four times a year the youth of certain districts meet to show their proficiency in running, and leaping, and other feats of strength or agility; where the victor is rewarded with a song made in his or her praise. On this festival the servants drive a herd of Yahoos into the field, laden with hay, and oats, and milk for a repast to the Houyhnhnms; after which these brutes are immediately driven back again, for fear of being noisome to the assembly.

Every fourth year, at the vernal equinox, there is a representative council of the whole nation, which meets in a plain about twenty miles from our house, and continueth about five or six days. Here they inquire into the state and condition of the several districts; whether they abound or be deficient in hay or oats, or cows or Yahoos? And wherever there is any want (which is but seldom) it is immediately supplied by unanimous consent and contribution. Here likewise the regulation of children is settled: as for instance, if a Houyhnhnm hath two males, he changeth one of them with another who hath two females, and when a child hath been lost by any casualty, where the mother is past breeding, it is determined what family in the district shall breed another to supply the loss.

CHAPTER IX

A grand debate at the general assembly of the Houyhnhnms, and how it was determined. The learning of the Houyhnhnms. Their buildings. Their manner of burials. The defectiveness of their language.

One of these grand assemblies was held in my time, about three months before my departure, whither my master went as the representative of our district. In this council was resumed their old debate, and indeed, the only debate that ever happened in their country; whereof my master after his return gave me a very particular account.

The question to be debated was whether the Yahoos should be exterminated from the face of the earth. One of the members for the affirmative offered several arguments of great strength and weight, alleging that, as the Yahoos were the most filthy, noisome, and deformed animal which nature ever produced, so they were the most restive and indocile, mischievous, and malicious; they would privately suck the teats of the Houyhnhnms' cows; kill and devour their cats, trample down their oats and grass, if they were not continually watched; and commit a thousand other extravagancies. He took notice of a general tradition, that Yahoos had not been always in their country, but that many ages ago, two of these brutes appeared together upon a mountain; whether produced by the heat of the sun upon corrupted mud and slime, or from the ooze and froth of the sea, was never known. That these Yahoos engendered, and their brood in a short time grew so numerous as to overrun and infest the whole nation. That the Houyhnhnms to get rid of this evil, made a general hunting, and at last enclosed the whole herd; and destroying the older, every Houyhnhnm kept two young ones in a kennel, and brought them to such a degree of tameness as an animal so savage by nature can be capable of acquiring, using them for draft and carriage. That there seemed to be much truth in this tradition, and that those creatures could not be *ylnhniamshy* (or aborigines of the land) because of the violent hatred the Houyhnhnms as well as all other animals bore them; which although their evil disposition sufficiently deserved, could never have arrived at so high a degree, if they had been aborigines, or else they would have long since been rooted out. That the inhabitants taking a fancy to use the service of the Yahoos, had very imprudently neglected to cultivate the breed of asses, which were a comely animal, easily kept, more tame and orderly, without any offensive smell, strong enough for labor, although they yield to the other in agility of body; and if their braying be no agreeable sound, it is far preferable to the horrible howlings of the Yahoos.

Several others declared their sentiments to the same purpose, when my master proposed an expedient to the assembly, whereof he had indeed borrowed the hint from me. He approved of the tradition, mentioned by the honorable member, who spoke before; and affirmed, that the two Yahoos said to be first seen among them, had been driven thither over the sea; that coming to land, and being forsaken by their companions, they retired to the mountains, and degenerating by degrees, became in process of time much more savage than those of their own species in the country from whence these two originals came. The reason of his assertion was that he had now in his possession a certain wonderful Yahoo (meaning myself) which most of them had heard of, and many of them had seen. He then related to them how he first found me; that my body was all covered with an artificial composure of the skins and hairs of other animals; that I spoke in a language of my own, and had thoroughly learned theirs; that I had related to him the accidents which brought me thither; that when he saw me without my covering, I was an exact Yahoo in every part, only of a whiter color, less hairy and with shorter claws. He added how I had endeavored to persuade him that in my own and other countries the Yahoos acted as the governing, rational animal, and held the Houyhnhnms in servitude; that he observed in me all the qualities of a Yahoo, only a little more civilized by some tincture of reason, which however was in a degree as far inferior to the Houyhnhnm race as the Yahoos of their country were to me; that among other things, I mentioned a custom we had of castrating Houyhnhnms when they were young, in order to render them tame; that the operation was easy and safe; that it was no shame to learn wisdom from brutes, as industry is taught by the ant, and building by the swallow (for so I translate the world *lyhannh*, although it be a much larger fowl). That this invention might be practiced upon the younger Yahoos here, which, besides rendering them tractable and fitter for use, would in an age put an end to the whole species without destroying life. That in the meantime the Houyhnhnms should be exhorted to cultivate the breed of asses, which, as they are in all respects more valuable brutes, so they have this advantage, to be fit for service at five years old, which the others are not till twelve.

This was all my master thought fit to tell me at that time, of what passed in the grand council. But he was pleased to conceal one particular, which related personally to myself, whereof I soon felt the unhappy effect, as the reader will know in its proper place, and from whence I date all the succeeding misfortunes of my life.

The Houyhnhnms have no letters, and consequently, their knowledge is all traditional. But there happening few events of any moment among a people so well united, naturally disposed to every virtue, wholly governed by reason, and cut off from all commerce with other nations, the historical part is easily preserved without burdening their memories. I have already observed that they are subject to no diseases, and therefore can have no need of physicians. However, they have excellent medicines composed of herbs, to cure accidental bruises and cuts in the pastern or frog of the foot by sharp stones, as well as other maims and hurts in the several parts of the body.

They calculate the year by the revolution of the sun and the moon, but use no subdivisions into weeks. They are well enough acquainted with the motions of those two luminaries, and understand the nature of eclipses; and this is the utmost progress of their astronomy.

In poetry they must be allowed to excel all other mortals; wherein the justness of their similes, and the minuteness, as well as exactness of their descriptions, are indeed inimitable. Their verses abound very much in both of these, and usually contain either some exalted notions of friendship and benevolence, or the praises of those who were victors in races and other bodily exercises. Their buildings, although very rude and simple, are not inconvenient, but well contrived to defend them from all injuries of cold and heat. They have a kind of tree, which at forty years old loosens in the root, and falls with the first storm; it grows very straight, and being pointed like stakes with a sharp stone (for the Houyhnhnms know not the use of iron), they stick them erect in the ground about ten inches asunder, and then weave in oat straw, or sometimes wattles, betwixt them. The roof is made after the same manner, and so are the doors.

The Houyhnhnms use the hollow part between the pastern and the hoof of their forefeet as we do our hands, and this with greater dexterity than I could at first imagine. I have seen a white mare of our family thread a needle (which I lent her on purpose) with that joint. They milk their cows, reap their oats, and do all the work which requires hands in the same manner. They have a kind of hard flints, which by grinding against other stones they form into instruments that serve instead of wedges, axes, and hammers. With tools made of these flints, they likewise cut their hay, and reap their oats, which there groweth naturally in several fields; the Yahoos draw home the sheaves in carriages, and the servants tread them in certain covered huts, to get out the grain, which is kept in stores. They make a rude kind of earthen and wooden vessels, and bake the former in the sun.

If they can avoid casualties, they die only of old age, and are buried in the obscurest places that can be found, their friends and relations expressing neither joy nor grief at their departure; nor does the dying person discover the least regret that he is leaving the world, any more than if he were upon returning home from a visit to one of his neighbors; I remember my master having once made an appointment with a friend and his family to come to his house upon some affair of importance; on the day fixed, the mistress and her two children came very late; she made two excuses, first for her husband, who, as she said, happened that very morning to *lhnuwnh*. The word is strongly expressive in their language, but not easily rendered into English; it signifies, *to retire to his first Mother.* Her excuse for not coming sooner was that her husband dying late in the morning, she was a good while consulting her servants about a convenient place where his body should be laid; and I observed she behaved herself at our house, as cheerfully as the rest; she died about three months after.

They live generally to seventy or seventy-five years, very seldom to four-score; some weeks before their death they feel a gradual decay, but without pain. During this time they are much visited by their friends, because they cannot go abroad with their usual ease and satisfaction. However, about ten days before their death, which they seldom fail in computing, they return the visits that have been made by those who are nearest in the neighborhood, being carried in a convenient sledge drawn by Yahoos; which vehicle they use, not only upon this occasion, but when they grow old, upon long journeys, or when they are lamed by any accident. And therefore when the dying Houyhnhnms return those visits, they take a solemn leave of their friends, as if they were going to some remote part of the country, where they designed to pass the rest of their lives.

I know not whether it may be worth observing, that the Houyhnhnms have no word in their language to express anything that is evil, except what they borrow from the deformities or ill qualities of the Yahoos. Thus they denote the folly of a servant, an omission of a child, a stone that cuts their feet, a continuance of foul or unseasonable weather, and the like, by adding to each the epithet of Yahoo. For instance, *hhnm Yahoo, whnaholm Yahoo, ynlhmnd-wihlma Yahoo,* and an ill-contrived house, *ynholmhnmrohlnw Yahoo.*

I could with great pleasure enlarge farther upon the manners and virtues of this excellent people; but intending in a short time to publish a volume by itself expressly upon that subject, I refer the reader thither. And in the meantime, proceed to relate my own sad catastrophe.

CHAPTER X

The Author's economy, and happy life among the Houyhnhnms. His great improvement in virtue, by conversing with them. Their conversations. The Author hath notice given him by his master that he must depart from the country. He falls into a swoon for grief, but submits. He contrives and finishes a canoe, by the help of a fellow servant, and puts to sea at a venture.

I had settled my little economy to my own heart's content. My master had ordered a room to be made for me after their manner, about six yards from the house; the sides and floors of which I plastered with clay, and covered with rush mats of my own contriving; I had beaten hemp, which there grows wild, and made of it a sort of ticking; this I filled with the feathers of several birds I had taken with springes made of Yahoos' hairs, and were excellent food. I had worked two chairs with my knife, the sorrel nag helping me in the grosser and more laborious part. When my clothes were worn to rags, I made myself others with the skins of rabbits, and of a certain beautiful animal about the same size, called *nnuhnoh,* the skin of which is covered with a fine down. Of these I likewise made very tolerable stockings. I soled my shoes with wood which I cut from a tree, and fitted to the upper leather, and when this was worn out, I supplied it with the skins of Yahoos, dried in the sun. I often got honey out of hollow trees, which I mingled with water, or eat it with my bread. No man could more verify the truth of these two maxims, that *Nature is very easily satisfied;* and, that *Necessity is the mother of invention.* I enjoyed perfect health of body, and tranquility of mind; I did not feel the treachery or inconstancy of a friend, nor the inquiries of a secret or open enemy. I had no occasion of bribing, flattering, or pimping to procure the favor of any great man, or of his minion. I wanted no fence against fraud or oppression; here was neither physician to destroy my body, nor lawyer to ruin my fortune; no informer to watch my words and actions, or forge accusations against me for hire; here were no gibers, censurers, backbiters, pickpockets, highwaymen, housebreakers, attorneys, bawds, buffoons, gamesters, politicians, wits, splenetics, tedious talkers, controvertists, ravishers, murderers, robbers, virtuosos; no leaders or followers of party and faction; no encouragers to vice, by seducement or examples; no dungeons, axes, gibbets, whipping posts, or pillories; no cheating shopkeepers or mechanics; no pride, vanity or affectation; no fops, bullies, drunkards, strolling whores, or poxes; no ranting, lewd, expensive wives; no stupid, proud pedants; no importunate, overbearing, quarrelsome, noisy, roaring, empty, conceited, swearing companions; no scoundrels raised from the dust upon the merit of their vices; or nobility thrown into it on account of their virtues; no lords, fiddlers, judges, or dancing masters.

I had the favor of being admitted to several Houyhnhnms, who came to visit or dine with my master; where his honor graciously suffered me to wait in the room, and listen to their discourse. Both he and his company would often descend to ask me questions, and receive my answers. I had also sometimes the honor of attending my master in his visits to others. I never presumed to speak, except in answer to a question; and then I did it with inward regret, because it was a loss of so much time for improving myself; but I was infinitely delighted with the station of an humble auditor in such conversations, where nothing passed but what was useful, expressed in the fewest and most significant words; where (as I have already said) the greatest decency was observed, without the least degree of ceremony; where no person spoke without being pleased himself, and pleasing his companions; where there was no interruption, tediousness, heat, or difference of sentiments. They have a notion, that when people are met together, a short silence doth much improve conversation; this I found to be true; for during those little intermissions of talk, new ideas would arise in their minds, which very much enlivened the discourse. Their subjects are generally on friendship and benevolence; on order and economy; sometimes upon the visible operations of nature, or ancient traditions; upon the bounds and limits of virtue; upon the unerring rules of reason; or upon some determinations, to be taken at the next great assembly; and often upon the various excellencies of poetry. I may add, without vanity, that my presence often gave them sufficient matter for discourse, because it afforded my master an occasion of letting his friends into the history of me and my country, upon which they were all pleased to discant in a manner not very advantageous to human kind; and for that reason I shall not repeat what they said; only I may be allowed to observe that his honor, to my great admiration, appeared to understand the nature of Yahoos much better than myself. He went through all our vices and follies, and discovered many which I had never mentioned to him; by only supposing what qualities a Yahoo of their country, with a small proportion of reason, might be capable of exerting; and concluded, with too much probability, how vile as well as miserable such a creature must be.

I freely confess, that all the little knowledge I have of any value was acquired by the lectures I received from my master, and from hearing the discourses of him and his friends; to which I should be prouder to listen, than to dictate to the greatest and wisest assembly in Europe. I admired the strength, comeliness, and speed of the inhabitants; and such a constellation of virtues in such amiable persons produced in me the highest veneration. At first, indeed, I did not feel that natural awe which the Yahoos and all other animals bear towards them; but it grew upon me by degrees, much sooner than I imagined, and was mingled with a respectful love and gratitude, that they would condescend to distinguish me from the rest of my species.

When I thought of my family, my friends, my countrymen, or human race in general, I considered them as they really were, Yahoos in shape and disposition, perhaps a little more civilized, and qualified with the gift of speech; but making no other use of reason than to improve and multiply those vices, whereof their brethren in this country had only the share that nature allotted them. When I happened to behold the reflection of my own form in a lake or fountain, I turned away my face in horror and detestation of myself, and could better endure the sight of a common Yahoo than of my own person. By conversing with the Houyhnhnms, and looking upon them with delight, I fell to imitate their gait and gesture, which is now grown into a habit; and my friends often tell me in a blunt way, that I trot like a horse; which, however, I take for a great compliment; neither shall I disown, that in speaking I am apt to fall into the voice and manner of the Houyhnhnms, and hear myself ridiculed on that account without the least mortification.

In the midst of this happiness, when I looked upon myself to be fully settled for life, my master sent for me one morning a little earlier than his usual hour. I observed by his countenance that he was in some perplexity, and at a loss how to begin what he had to speak. After a short silence, he told me, he did not know how I would take what he was going to say; that, in the last general assembly, when the affair of the Yahoos was entered upon, the representatives had taken offense at his keeping a Yahoo (meaning myself) in his family more like a Houyhnhnm than a brute animal. That he was known frequently to converse with me, as if he could receive some advantage of pleasure in my company; that such a practice was not agreeable to reason or nature, or a thing ever heard of before among them. The assembly did therefore exhort him, either to employ me like the rest of my species, or command me to swim back to the place from whence I came. That the first of these expedients was utterly rejected by all the Houyhnhnms who had ever seen me at his house or their own; for, they alleged, that because I had some rudiments of reason, added to the natural pravity of those animals, it was to be feared, I might be able to seduce them into the woody and mountainous parts of the country, and bring them in troops by night to destroy the Houyhnhnms' cattle, as being naturally of the ravenous kind, and averse from labor.

My master added that he was daily pressed by the Houyhnhnms of the neighborhood to have the assembly's exhortation executed, which he could not put off much longer. He doubted[1] it would be impossible for me to swim to another country; and therefore wished I would contrive some sort of vehi-

1. Suspected.

cle resembling those I had described to him, that might carry me on the sea; in which work I should have the assistance of his own servants, as well as those of his neighbors. He concluded that for his own part he could have been content to keep me in his service as long as I lived; because he found I had cured myself of some bad habits and dispositions, by endeavoring, as far as my inferior nature was capable, to imitate the Houyhnhnms.

I should here observe to the reader, that a decree of the general assembly in this country is expressed by the word *hnhloayn,* which signifies an exhortation, as near as I can render it; for they have no conception how a rational creature can be compelled, but only advised, or exhorted; because no person can disobey reason without giving up his claim to be a rational creature.

I was struck with the utmost grief and despair at my master's discourse; and being unable to support the agonies I was under, I fell into a swoon at his feet; when I came to myself, he told me that he concluded I had been dead (for these people are subject to no such imbecilities of nature). I answered, in a faint voice, that death would have been too great an happiness; that although I could not blame the assembly's exhortation, or the urgency of his friends; yet in my weak and corrupt judgment, I thought it might consist with reason to have been less rigorous. That I could not swim a league, and probably the nearest land to theirs might be distant above an hundred; that many materials, necessary for making a small vessel to carry me off, were wholly wanting in this country, which, however, I would attempt in obedience and gratitude to his honor, although I concluded the thing to be impossible, and therefore looked on myself as already devoted[2] to destruction. That the certain prospect of an unnatural death was the least of my evils; for, supposing I should escape with life by some strange adventure, how could I think with temper[3] of passing my days among Yahoos, and relapsing into my old corruptions, for want of examples to lead and keep me within the paths of virtue. That I knew too well upon what solid reasons all the determinations of the wise Houyhnhnms were founded, not to be shaken by arguments of mine, a miserable Yahoo; and therefore after presenting him with my humble thanks for the offer of his servants' assistance in making a vessel, and desiring a reasonable time for so difficult a work, I told him I would endeavor to preserve a wretched being; and, if ever I returned to England, was not without hopes of being useful to my own species by celebrating the praises of the renowned Houyhnhnms, and proposing their virtues to the imitation of mankind.

My master in a few words made me a very gracious reply, allowed me the space of two months to finish my boat, and ordered the sorrel nag, my fellow servant (for so at this distance I may presume to call him), to follow my instructions, because I told my master that his help would be sufficient, and I knew he had a tenderness for me.

In his company my first business was to go to that part of the coast where my rebellious crew had ordered me to be set on shore. I got upon a height, and looking on every side into the sea, fancied I saw a small island towards the northeast; I took out my pocket glass, and could then clearly distinguish it about five leagues off, as I computed; but it appeared to the sorrel nag to

2. Doomed.   3. Equanimity.

be only a blue cloud; for, as he had no conception of any country besides his own, so he could not be as expert in distinguishing remote objects at sea, as we who so much converse in that element.

After I had discovered this island, I considered no farther; but resolved, it should, if possible, be the first place of my banishment, leaving the consequence to fortune.

I returned home, and consulting with the sorrel nag, we went into a copse at some distance, where I with my knife, and he with a sharp flint fastened very artificially,[4] after their manner, to a wooden handle, cut down several oak wattles about the thickness of a walking staff, and some larger pieces. But I shall not trouble the reader with a particular description of my own mechanics; let it suffice to say, that in six weeks time, with the help of the sorrel nag, who performed the parts that required most labor, I finished a sort of Indian canoe; but much larger, covering it with the skins of Yahoos, well stitched together, with hempen threads of my own making. My sail was likewise composed of the skins of the same animal; but I made use of the youngest I could get, the older being too tough and thick; and I likewise provided myself with four paddles. I laid in a stock of boiled flesh, of rabbits and fowls; and took with me two vessels, one filled with milk, and the other with water.

I tried my canoe in a large pond near my master's house, and then corrected in it what was amiss, stopping all the chinks with Yahoo's tallow, till I found it staunch, and able to bear me and my freight. And when it was as complete as I could possibly make it, I had it drawn on a carriage very gently by Yahoos, to the seaside, under the conduct of the sorrel nag and another servant.

When all was ready, and the day came for my departure, I took leave of my master and lady, and the whole family, my eyes flowing with tears and my heart quite sunk with grief. But his honor, out of curiosity, and perhaps (if I may speak it without vanity) partly out of kindness, was determined to see me in my canoe; and got several of his neighboring friends to accompany him. I was forced to wait above an hour for the tide, and then observing the wind very fortunately bearing towards the island to which I intended to steer my course, I took a second leave of my master; but as I was going to prostrate myself to kiss his hoof, he did me the honor to raise it gently to my mouth. I am not ignorant how much I have been censured for mentioning this last particular. Detractors are pleased to think it improbable that so illustrious a person should descend to give so great a mark of distinction to a creature so inferior as I. Neither have I forgot how apt some travelers are to boast of extraordinary favors they have received. But, if these censurers were better acquainted with the noble and courteous disposition of the Houyhnhnms, they would soon change their opinion. I paid my respects to the rest of the Houyhnhnms in his honor's company; then getting into my canoe, I pushed off from shore.

CHAPTER XI

The Author's dangerous voyage. He arrives at New Holland, hoping to settle there. Is wounded with an arrow by one of the natives. Is seized and carried by force into a Portuguese ship. The great civilities of the Captain. The Author arrives at England.

4. Adroitly.

I began this desperate voyage on February 15, 1714/5,[5] at 9 o'clock in the morning. The wind was very favorable; however, I made use at first only of my paddles; but considering I should soon be weary, and that the wind might probably chop about, I ventured to set up my little sail; and thus, with the help of the tide, I went at the rate of a league and a half an hour, as near as I could guess. My master and his friends continued on the shore, till I was almost out of sight; and I often heard the sorrel nag (who always loved me) crying out, *"Hnuy illa nyha maiah Yahoo"* ("Take care of thyself, gentle Yahoo").

My design was, if possible, to discover some small island uninhabited, yet sufficient by my labor to furnish me with necessaries of life, which I would have thought a greater happiness than to be first minister in the politest court of Europe, so horrible was the idea I conceived of returning to live in the society and under the government of Yahoos. For in such a solitude as I desired, I could at least enjoy my own thoughts, and reflect with delight on the virtues of those inimitable Houyhnhnms, without any opportunity of degenerating into the vices and corruptions of my own species.

The reader may remember what I related when my crew conspired against me, and confined me to my cabin, how I continued there several weeks, without knowing what course we took; and when I was put ashore in the longboat, how the sailors told me with oaths, whether true or false, that they knew not in what part of the world we were. However, I did then believe us to be about 10 degrees southward of the Cape of Good Hope, or about 45 degrees southern latitude, as I gathered from some general words I overheard among them, being I supposed to the southeast in their intended voyage to Madagascar. And although this were but little better than conjecture, yet I resolved to steer my course eastward, hoping to reach the southwest coast of New Holland, and perhaps some such island as I desired, lying westward of it. The wind was full west, and by six in the evening I computed I had gone eastward at least eighteen leagues; when I spied a very small island about half a league off, which I soon reached. It was nothing but a rock with one creek,[6] naturally arched by the force of tempests. Here I put in my canoe, and climbing a part of the rock, I could plainly discover land to the east, extending from south to north. I lay all night in my canoe; and repeating my voyage early in the morning, I arrived in seven hours to the southeast point of New Holland.[7] This confirmed me in the opinion I have long entertained, that the maps and charts place this country at least three degrees more to the east than it really is; which thought I communicated many years ago to my worthy friend Mr. Herman Moll,[8] and gave him my reasons for it, although he hath rather chosen to follow other authors.

I saw no inhabitants in the place where I landed; and being unarmed, I was afraid of venturing far into the country. I found some shellfish on the shore, and eat them raw, not daring to kindle a fire, for fear of being discovered by the natives. I continued three days feeding on oysters and limpets, to save my own provisions; and I fortunately found a brook of excellent water, which gave me great relief.

On the fourth day, venturing out early a little too far, I saw twenty or thirty natives upon a height, not above five hundred yards from me. They were

5. I.e., 1714. The year began on March 25.   6. A bay.   7. Present-day Republic of South Africa.
8. A famous contemporary mapmaker.

stark naked, men, women, and children round a fire, as I could discover by the smoke. One of them spied me, and gave notice to the rest; five of them advanced towards me, leaving the women and children at the fire. I made what haste I could to the shore, and getting into my canoe, shoved off; the savages observing me retreat, ran after me; and before I could get far enough into the sea, discharged an arrow, which wounded me deeply on the inside of my left knee. (I shall carry the mark to my grave.) I apprehended the arrow might be poisoned; and paddling out of the reach of their darts (being a calm day) I made a shift to suck the wound, and dress it as well as I could.

I was at a loss what to do, for I durst not return to the same landing place, but stood to the north, and was forced to paddle; for the wind, although very gentle, was against me, blowing northwest. As I was looking about for a secure landing place, I saw a sail to the north northeast, which appearing every minute more visible, I was in some doubt whether I should wait for them or no; but at last my detestation of the Yahoo race prevailed; and turning my canoe, I sailed and paddled together to the south, and got into the same creek from whence I set out in the morning, choosing rather to trust myself among these barbarians than live with European Yahoos. I drew up my canoe as close as I could to the shore, and hid myself behind a stone by the little brook, which, as I have already said, was excellent water.

The ship came within half a league of this creek, and sent out her longboat with vessels to take in fresh water (for the place it seems was very well known), but I did not observe it until the boat was almost on shore; and it was too late to seek another hiding place. The seamen at their landing observed my canoe, and rummaging it all over, easily conjectured that the owner could not be far off. Four of them well armed searched every cranny and lurking hole, till at last they found me flat on my face behind the stone. They gazed a while in admiration at my strange uncouth dress; my coat made of skins, my wooden-soled shoes, and my furred stockings; from whence, however, they concluded I was not a native of the place, who all go naked. One of the seamen in Portuguese bid me rise, and asked who I was. I understood that language very well, and getting upon my feet, said I was a poor Yahoo, banished from the Houyhnhnms, and desired they would please to let me depart. They admired to hear me answer them in their own tongue, and saw by my complexion I must be an European; but were at a loss to know what I meant by Yahoos and Houyhnhnms, and at the same time fell a laughing at my strange tone in speaking, which resembled the neighing of a horse. I trembled all the while betwixt fear and hatred; I again desired leave to depart, and was gently moving to my canoe; but they laid hold on me, desiring to know what country I was of? whence I came? with many other questions. I told them I was born in England, from whence I came about five years ago, and then their country and ours was at peace. I therefore hoped they would not treat me as an enemy, since I meant them no harm, but was a poor Yahoo, seeking some desolate place where to pass the remainder of his unfortunate life.

When they began to talk, I thought I never heard or saw any thing so unnatural; for it appeared to me as monstrous as if a dog or a cow should speak in England, or a Yahoo in Houyhnhnmland. The honest Portuguese were equally amazed at my strange dress, and the odd manner of delivering my words, which however they understood very well. They spoke to me with great humanity, and said they were sure their Captain would carry me *gratis* to Lisbon, from whence I might return to my own country; that two of the seamen would go back to the ship, to inform the Captain of what they had seen, and receive his orders; in the meantime, unless I would give my solemn oath not to fly, they would secure me by force. I thought it best to comply with their proposal. They were very curious to know my story, but I gave them very little satisfaction; and they all conjectured, that my misfortunes had impaired my reason. In two hours the boat, which went laden with vessels of water, returned with the Captain's commands to fetch me on board. I fell on my knees to preserve my liberty; but all was in vain, and the men having tied me with cords, heaved me into the boat, from whence I was taken into the ship, and from thence into the Captain's cabin.

His name was Pedro de Mendez; he was a very courteous and generous person; he entreated me to give some account of myself, and desired to know what I would eat or drink; said I should be used as well as himself, and spoke so many obliging things, that I wondered to find such civilities from a Yahoo. However, I remained silent and sullen; I was ready to faint at the very smell of him and his men. At last I desired something to eat out of my own canoe; but he ordered me a chicken and some excellent wine, and then directed that I should be put to bed in a very clean cabin. I would not undress myself, but lay on the bedclothes; and in half an hour stole out, when I thought the crew was at dinner; and getting to the side of the ship, was going to leap into the sea, and swim for my life, rather than continue among Yahoos. But one of the seamen prevented me, and having informed the Captain, I was chained to my cabin.

After dinner Don Pedro came to me, and desired to know my reason for so desperate an attempt; assured me he only meant to do me all the service he was able; and spoke so very movingly, that at last I descended to treat him like an animal which had some little portion of reason. I gave him a very short relation of my voyage; of the conspiracy against me by my own men; of the country where they set me on shore, and of my five years residence there. All which he looked upon as if it were a dream or a vision; whereat I took great offense; for I had quite forgot the faculty of lying, so peculiar to Yahoos in all countries where they preside, and consequently the disposition of suspecting truth in others of their own species. I asked him whether it were the custom of his country to *say the thing that was not?* I assured him I had almost forgot what he meant by falsehood; and if I had lived a thousand years in Houyhnhnmland, I should never have heard a lie from the meanest servant. That I was altogether indifferent whether he believed me or no; but however, in return for his favors, I would give so much allowance to the corruption of his nature, as to answer any objection he would please to make; and he might easily discover the truth.

The Captain, a wise man, after many endeavors to catch me tripping in some part of my story, at last began to have a better opinion of my veracity. But he added that since I professed so inviolable an attachment to truth, I must give him my word of honor to bear him company in this voyage without attempting anything against my life; or else he would continue me a prisoner till we arrived at Lisbon. I gave him the promise he required; but at the same time protested that I would suffer the greatest hardships rather than return to live among Yahoos.

Our voyage passed without any considerable accident. In gratitude to the Captain I sometimes sat with him at his earnest request, and strove to conceal my antipathy against humankind, although it often broke out; which he suffered to pass without observation. But the greatest part of the day, I confined myself to my cabin, to avoid seeing any of the crew. The Captain had often entreated me to strip myself of my savage dress, and offered to lend me the best suit of clothes he had. This I would not be prevailed on to accept, abhorring to cover myself with anything that had been on the back of a Yahoo. I only desired he would lend me two clean shirts, which having been washed since he wore them, I believed would not so much defile me. These I changed every second day, and washed them myself.

We arrived at Lisbon, Nov. 5, 1715. At our landing, the Captain forced me to cover myself with his cloak, to prevent the rabble from crowding about me. I was conveyed to his own house; and at my earnest request, he led me up to the highest room backwards.[9] I conjured him to conceal from all persons what I had told him of the Houyhnhnms; because the least hint of such a story would not only draw numbers of people to see me, but probably put me in danger of being imprisoned, or burned by the Inquisition. The Captain persuaded me to accept a suit of clothes newly made; but I would not suffer the tailor to take my measure; however, Don Pedro being almost of my size, they fitted me well enough. He accoutred me with other necessaries, all new, which I aired for twenty-four hours before I would use them.

The Captain had no wife, nor above three servants, none of which were suffered to attend at meals; and his whole deportment was so obliging, added to very good human understanding, that I really began to tolerate his company. He gained so far upon me, that I ventured to look out of the back window. By degrees I was brought into another room, from whence I peeped into the street, but drew my head back in a fright. In a week's time he seduced me down to the door. I found my terror gradually lessened, but my hatred and contempt seemed to increase. I was at last bold enough to walk the street in his company, but kept my nose well stopped with rue, or sometimes with tobacco.

In ten days, Don Pedro, to whom I had given some account of my domestic affairs, put it upon me as a point of honor and conscience that I ought to return to my native country, and live at home with my wife and children. He told me there was an English ship in the port just ready to sail, and he would furnish me with all things necessary. It would be tedious to repeat his arguments, and my contradictions. He said it was altogether impossible to find such a solitary island as I had desired to live in; but I might command in my own house, and pass my time in a manner as recluse as I pleased.

I complied at last, finding I could not do better. I left Lisbon the 24th day of November, in an English merchantman, but who was the Master I never inquired. Don Pedro accompanied me to the ship, and lent me twenty pounds. He took kind leave of me, and embraced me at parting; which I bore as well as I could. During this last voyage I had no commerce with the Master, or any of his men; but pretending I was sick kept close in my cabin. On the fifth of December, 1715, we cast anchor in the Downs about nine in the morning, and at three in the afternoon I got safe to my house at Redriff.

9. At the rear.

My wife and family received me with great surprise and joy, because they concluded me certainly dead; but I must freely confess, the sight of them filled me only with hatred, disgust, and contempt; and the more, by reflecting on the near alliance I had to them. For, although since my unfortunate exile from the Houyhnhnm country, I had compelled myself to tolerate the sight of Yahoos, and to converse with Don Pedro de Mendez; yet my memory and imaginations were perpetually filled with the virtues and ideas of those exalted Houyhnhnms. And when I began to consider that by copulating with one of the Yahoo species, I had become a parent of more, it struck me with the utmost shame, confusion, and horror.

As soon as I entered the house, my wife took me in her arms, and kissed me; at which, having not been used to the touch of that odious animal for so many years, I fell in a swoon for almost an hour. At the time I am writing, it is five years since my last return to England; during the first year I could not endure my wife or children in my presence, the very smell of them was intolerable; much less could I suffer them to eat in the same room. To this hour they dare not presume to touch my bread, or drink out of the same cup; neither was I ever able to let one of them take me by the hand. The first money I laid out was to buy two young stone-horses,[1] which I keep in a good stable, and next to them the groom is my greatest favorite; for I feel my spirits revived by the smell he contracts in the stable. My horses understand me tolerably well; I converse with them at least four hours every day. They are strangers to bridle or saddle; they live in great amity with me, and friendship to each other.

CHAPTER XII

The Author's veracity. His design in publishing this work. His censure of those travelers who swerve from the truth. The Author clears himself from any sinister ends in writing. An objection answered. The method of planting colonies. His native country commended. The right of the crown to those countries described by the Author is justified. The difficulty of conquering them. The Author takes his last leave of the reader; proposeth his manner of living for the future; gives good advice, and concludeth.

Thus, gentle reader, I have given thee a faithful history of my travels for sixteen years, and above seven months; wherein I have not been so studious of ornament as of truth. I could perhaps like others have astonished thee with strange improbable tales; but I rather chose to relate plain matter of fact in the simplest manner and style; because my principal design was to inform, and not to amuse thee.

It is easy for us who travel into remote countries, which are seldom visited by Englishmen or other Europeans, to form descriptions of wonderful animals both at sea and land. Whereas a traveler's chief aim should be to make men wiser and better, and to improve their minds by the bad as well as good example of what they deliver concerning foreign places.

I could heartily wish a law were enacted, that every traveler, before he were permitted to publish his voyages, should be obliged to make oath before the Lord High Chancellor that all he intended to print was absolutely true to the best of his knowledge; for then the world would no longer be deceived

1. Stallions.

as it usually is, while some writers, to make their works pass the better upon the public, impose the grossest falsities on the unwary reader. I have perused several books of travels with great delight in my younger days; but, having since gone over most parts of the globe, and been able to contradict many fabulous accounts from my own observation, it hath given me a great disgust against this part of reading, and some indignation to see the credulity of mankind so impudently abused. Therefore, since my acquaintance were pleased to think my poor endeavors might not be unacceptable to my country; I imposed on myself as a maxim, never to be swerved from, that I would *strictly adhere to truth*; neither indeed can I be ever under the least temptation to vary from it, while I retain in my mind the lectures and example of my noble master, and the other illustrious Houyhnhnms, of whom I had so long the honor to be an humble hearer.

> ——*Nec si miserum Fortuna Sinonem*
> *Finxit, vanum etiam, mendacemque improba finget.*[2]

I know very well how little reputation is to be got by writings which require neither genius nor learning, nor indeed any other talent, except a good memory, or an exact *Journal*. I know likewise, that writers of travels, like dictionary-makers, are sunk into oblivion by the weight and bulk of those who come last, and therefore lie uppermost. And it is highly probable that such travelers who shall hereafter visit the countries described in this work of mine, may be detecting my errors (if there be any) and adding many new discoveries of their own, jostle me out of vogue, and stand in my place, making the world forget that ever I was an author. This indeed would be too great a mortification if I wrote for fame; but, as my sole intention was the PUBLIC GOOD, I cannot be altogether disappointed. For, who can read the virtues I have mentioned in the glorious Houyhnhnms, without being ashamed of his own vices, when he considers himself as the reasoning, governing animal of his country? I shall say nothing of those remote nations where Yahoos preside; amongst which the least corrupted are the Brobdingnagians, whose wise maxims in morality and government it would be our happiness to observe. But I forbear descanting further, and rather leave the judicious reader to his own remarks and applications.

I am not a little pleased that this work of mine can possibly meet with no censurers; for what objections can be made against a writer who relates only plain facts that happened in such distant countries, where we have not the least interest with respect either to trade or negotiations? I have carefully avoided every fault with which common writers of travels are often too justly charged. Besides, I meddle not the least with any party, but write without passion, prejudice, or ill-will against any man or number of men whatsoever. I write for the noblest end, to inform and instruct mankind, over whom I may, without breach of modesty, pretend to some superiority, from the advantages I received by conversing so long among the most accomplished Houyhnhnms. I write without any view towards profit or praise. I never suffer a word to pass that may look like reflection, or possibly give the least offense even to those who are most ready to take it. So that, I hope, I may with

---

2. Fortune has made a derelict of Sinon / but the bitch won't make an empty liar of him, too (Latin; from Virgil's *Aeneid* 2).

justice pronounce myself an Author perfectly blameless; against whom the tribes of answerers, considerers, observers, reflectors, detecters, remarkers will never be able to find matter for exercising their talents.

I confess it was whispered to me that I was bound in duty as a subject of England, to have given in a memorial to a secretary of state, at my first coming over; because, whatever lands are discovered by a subject, belong to the Crown. But I doubt whether our conquests in the countries I treat of would be as easy as those of Ferdinando Cortez[3] over the naked Americans. The Lilliputians, I think, are hardly worth the charge of a fleet and army to reduce them; and I question whether it might be prudent or safe to attempt the Brobdingnagians; or, whether an English army would be much at their ease with the Flying Island over their heads. The Houyhnhnms, indeed, appear not to be so well prepared for war, a science to which they are perfect strangers, and especially against missive weapons. However, supposing myself to be a minister of state, I could never give my advice for invading them. Their prudence, unanimity, unacquaintedness with fear, and their love of their country would amply supply all defects in the military art. Imagine twenty thousand of them breaking into the midst of an European army, confounding the ranks, overturning the carriages, battering the warriors' faces into mummy, by terrible yerks[4] from their hinder hoofs: for they would well deserve the character given to Augustus, *Recalcitrat undique tutus*.[5] But instead of proposals for conquering that magnanimous nation, I rather wish they were in a capacity or disposition to send a sufficient number of their inhabitants for civilizing Europe; by teaching us the first principles of Honor, Justice, Truth, Temperance, Public Spirit, Fortitude, Chastity, Friendship, Benevolence, and Fidelity. The names of all which Virtues are still retained among us in most languages, and are to be met with in modern as well as ancient authors, which I am able to assert from my own small reading.

But I had another reason which made me less forward to enlarge his majesty's dominions by my discoveries: to say the truth, I had conceived a few scruples with relation to the distributive justice of princes upon those occasions. For instance, a crew of pirates are driven by a storm they know not whither; at length a boy discovers land from the topmast; they go on shore to rob and plunder; they see an harmless people, are entertained with kindness, they give the country a new name, they take formal possession of it for the king, they set up a rotten plank or a stone for a memorial, they murder two or three dozen of the natives, bring away a couple more by force for a sample, return home, and get their pardon. Here commences a new dominion acquired with a title by Divine Right. Ships are sent with the first opportunity; the natives driven out or destroyed, their princes tortured to discover their gold; a free license given to all acts of inhumanity and lust; the earth reeking with the blood of its inhabitants: and this execrable crew of butchers employed in so pious an expedition is a *modern colony* sent to convert and civilize an idolatrous and barbarous people.

But this description, I confess, doth by no means affect the British nation, who may be an example to the whole world for their wisdom, care, and justice in planting colonies; their liberal endowments for the advancement of reli-

---

3. Hernán Cortés (1485–1547), the conquistador who destroyed the Aztec Empire. 4. Kicks. *Mummy:* pulp. 5. He kicks backward, at every point on his guard (Latin; Horace's *Satires* 2.20).

gion and learning; their choice of devout and able pastors to propagate Christianity; their caution in stocking their provinces with people of sober lives and conversations from this the Mother Kingdom; their strict regard to the distribution of justice, in supplying the civil administration through all their colonies with officers of the greatest abilities, utter strangers to corruption: and to crown all, by sending the most vigilant and virtuous governors, who have no other views than the happiness of the people over whom they preside, and the honor of the king their master.

But, as those countries which I have described do not appear to have any desire of being conquered, and enslaved, murdered, or driven out by colonies, nor abound either in gold, silver, sugar, or tobacco, I did humbly conceive they were by no means proper objects of our zeal, our valor, or our interest. However, if those whom it may concern, think fit to be of another opinion, I am ready to depose, when I shall be lawfully called, that no European did ever visit these countries before me. I mean, if the inhabitants ought to be believed.

But, as to the formality of taking possession in my sovereign's name, it never came once into my thoughts; and if it had, yet as my affairs then stood, I should perhaps in point of prudence and self-preservation have put it off to a better opportunity.

Having thus answered the only objection that can be raised against me as a traveler, I here take a final leave of my courteous readers, and return to enjoy my own speculations in my little garden at Redriff; to apply those excellent lessons of virtue which I learned among the Houyhnhnms; to instruct the Yahoos of my own family as far as I shall find them docible animals; to behold my figure often in a glass, and thus if possible habituate myself by time to tolerate the sight of a human creature; to lament the brutality of Houyhnhnms in my own country, but always treat their persons with respect, for the sake of my noble master, his family, his friends, and the whole Houyhnhnm race, whom these of ours have the honor to resemble in all their lineaments, however their intellectuals came to degenerate.

I began last week to permit my wife to sit at dinner with me, at the farthest end of a long table; and to answer (but with the utmost brevity) the few questions I ask her. Yet the smell of a Yahoo continuing very offensive, I always keep my nose well stopped with rue, lavender, or tobacco leaves. And although it be hard for a man late in life to remove old habits, I am not altogether out of hopes in some time to suffer a neighbor Yahoo in my company, without the apprehensions I am yet under of his teeth or his claws.

My reconcilement to the Yahoo kind in general might not be so difficult, if they would be content with those vices and follies only which nature hath entitled them to. I am not in the least provoked at the sight of a lawyer, a pickpocket, a colonel, a fool, a lord, a gamester, politician, a whoremonger, a physician, an evidence, a suborner, an attorney, a traitor, or the like: this is all according to the due course of things. But when I behold a lump of deformity, and diseases both in body and mind, smitten with pride, it immediately breaks all the measures of my patience; neither shall I be ever able to comprehend how such an animal and such a vice could tally together. The wise and virtuous Houyhnhnms, who abound in all excellencies that can adorn a rational creature, have no name for this vice in their language, which hath no terms to express anything that is evil, except those whereby they describe the detestable qualities of their Yahoos, among which they were not able to distinguish this of pride, for want of thoroughly understanding human nature, as it showeth itself in other countries, where that animal presides. But I, who had more experience, could plainly observe some rudiments of it among the wild Yahoos.

But the Houyhnhnms, who live under the government of reason, are no more proud of the good qualities they possess, than I should be for not wanting a leg or an arm, which no man in his wits would boast of, although he must be miserable without them. I dwell the longer upon this subject from the desire I have to make the society of an English Yahoo by any means not insupportable; and therefore I here entreat those who have any tincture of this absurd vice, that they will not presume to appear in my sight.

A Modest Proposal[1]

for Preventing the Children of poor People in Ireland, *from being a Burden to their Parents or Country; and for making them beneficial to the Publick.*

Written in the year 1729

It is a melancholy object to those who walk through this great town,[2] or travel in the country, when they see the streets, the roads, and cabin-doors crowded with beggars of the female sex, followed by three, four, or six children, all in rags, and importuning every passenger for an alms. These mothers, instead of being able to work for their honest livelihood, are forced to employ all their time in strolling to beg sustenance for their helpless infants: who, as they grow up, either turn thieves for want of work, or leave their dear native country to fight for the Pretender in Spain, or sell themselves to the Barbadoes.[3]

I think it is agreed by all parties, that this prodigious number of children in the arms, or on the backs, or at the heels of their mothers, and frequently of their fathers, is, in the present deplorable state of the kingdom, a very great additional grievance; and, therefore, whoever could find out a fair, cheap, and easy method of making these children sound and useful members of the commonwealth, would deserve so well of the public, as to have his statue set up for a preserver of the nation.

But my intention is very far from being confined to provide only for the children of professed beggars; it is of a much greater extent, and shall take in the whole number of infants at a certain age, who are born of parents in effect as little able to support them as those who demand our charity in the streets.

As to my own part, having turned my thoughts for many years upon this

1. The complete text edited by Herbert Davis.   2. Dublin.   3. At this time a British possession, with a prosperous sugar industry. Workers were needed in the sugar plantations. *The Pretender:* James Edward (1688–1766), son of the Catholic king James II of England, called the "Old Pretender" (in distinction to his son Charles, nine years old at the time of this work, called the "Young Pretender"). Many thought him a legitimate claimant to the throne.

important subject, and maturely weighed the several schemes of other projectors,[4] I have always found them grossly mistaken in their computation. It is true, a child, just dropped from its dam, may be supported by her milk for a solar year with little other nourishment; at most, not above the value of two shillings, which the mother may certainly get, or the value in scraps, by her lawful occupation of begging; and it is exactly at one year old that I propose to provide for them in such a manner, as, instead of being a charge upon their parents or the parish, or wanting food and raiment for the rest of their lives, they shall, on the contrary, contribute to the feeding, and partly to the clothing, of many thousands.

There is likewise another advantage in my scheme, that it will prevent those voluntary abortions, and that horrid practice of women murdering their bastard children, alas, too frequent among us, sacrificing the poor innocent babes, I doubt more to avoid the expense than the shame, which would move tears and pity in the most savage and inhuman breast.

The number of souls in this kingdom being usually reckoned one million and a half, of these I calculate there may be about two hundred thousand couple whose wives are breeders; from which number I subtract thirty thousand couple, who are able to maintain their own children (although I apprehend there cannot be so many, under the present distresses of the kingdom); but this being granted, there will remain an hundred and seventy thousand breeders. I again subtract fifty thousand for those women who miscarry, or whose children die by accident or disease within the year. There only remain a hundred and twenty thousand children of poor parents annually born. The question therefore is how this number shall be reared and provided for? which, as I have already said, under the present situation of affairs, is utterly impossible by all the methods hitherto proposed. For we can neither employ them in handicraft or agriculture; we neither build houses (I mean in the country) nor cultivate land: they can very seldom pick up a livelihood by stealing until they arrive at six years old, except where they are of towardly parts;[5] although I confess they learn the rudiments much earlier; during which time they can, however, be properly looked upon only as probationers; as I have been informed by a principal gentleman in the county of Cavan, who protested to me, that he never knew above one or two instances under the age of six, even in a part of the kingdom so renowned for the quickest proficiency in that art.

I am assured by our merchants that a boy or a girl before twelve years old is no saleable commodity; and even when they come to this age they will not yield above three pounds or three pounds and half-a-crown at most, on the exchange; which cannot turn to account either to the parents or kingdom, the charge of nutriment and rags having been at least four times that value.

I shall now, therefore, humbly propose my own thoughts, which I hope will not be liable to the least objection.

I have been assured by a very knowing American of my acquaintance in London, that a young healthy child, well nursed, is, at a year old, a most delicious, nourishing, and wholesome food, whether stewed, roasted, baked, or boiled; and I make no doubt that it will equally serve in a fricassee or a ragout.

4. Planners.   5. Particularly talented, unusually gifted.

I do therefore humbly offer it to public consideration, that of the hundred and twenty thousand children already computed, twenty thousand may be reserved for breed, whereof only one-fourth part to be males; which is more than we allow to sheep, black cattle, or swine; and my reason is, that these children are seldom the fruits of marriage, a circumstance not much regarded by our savages, therefore one male will be sufficient to serve four females. That the remaining hundred thousand may, at a year old, be offered in sale to the persons of quality and fortune through the kingdom; always advising the mother to let them suck plentifully in the last month, so as to render them plump and fat for a good table. A child will make two dishes at an entertainment for friends; and when the family dines alone, the fore or hind quarter will make a reasonable dish, and, seasoned with a little pepper or salt, will be very good boiled on the fourth day, especially in winter.

I have reckoned, upon a medium,[6] that a child just born will weigh twelve pounds, and in a solar year, if tolerably nursed, increaseth to twenty-eight pounds.

I grant this food will be somewhat dear,[7] and therefore very proper for landlords, who, as they have already devoured most of the parents, seem to have the best title to the children.

Infants' flesh will be in season throughout the year, but more plentifully in March, and a little before and after: for we are told by a grave author, an eminent French physician,[8] that fish being a prolific diet, there are more children born in Roman Catholic countries about nine months after Lent than at any other season; therefore, reckoning a year after Lent, the markets will be more glutted than usual, because the number of popish infants is at least three to one in this kingdom; and therefore it will have one other collateral advantage, by lessening the number of papists among us.

I have already computed the charge of nursing a beggar's child (in which list I reckon all cottagers, labourers, and four-fifths of the farmers) to be about two shillings per annum,[9] rags included; and I believe no gentleman would repine to give ten shillings for the carcass of a good fat child, which, as I have said, will make four dishes of excellent nutritive meat, when he has only some particular friend, or his own family, to dine with him. Thus the squire will learn to be a good landlord, and grow popular among his tenants; the mother will have eight shillings net profit, and be fit for work till she produces another child.

Those who are more thrifty (as I must confess the times require) may flay the carcass; the skin of which, artificially dressed, will make admirable gloves for ladies, and summer-boots for fine gentlemen.

As to our city of Dublin, shambles[1] may be appointed for this purpose in the most convenient parts of it, and butchers we may be assured will not be wanting; although I rather recommend buying the children alive, and dressing them hot from the knife, as we do roasting pigs.

A very worthy person, a true lover of his country, and whose virtues I highly esteem, was lately pleased, in discoursing on this matter, to offer a refinement upon my scheme. He said, that many gentlemen of this kingdom, having of late destroyed their deer, he conceived that the want of venison

6. Average.   7. Expensive.   8. François Rabelais (1494?–1553), French satirist and author of *Gargantua and Pantagruel* (1532–52).   9. Per year.   1. Slaughterhouses.

might be well supplied by the bodies of young lads and maidens, not exceeding fourteen years of age, nor under twelve; so great a number of both sexes in every country being now ready to starve for want of work and service; and these to be disposed of by their parents, if alive, or otherwise by their nearest relations. But, with due deference to so excellent a friend, and so deserving a patriot, I cannot be altogether in his sentiments; for as to the males, my American acquaintance assured me from frequent experience, that their flesh was generally tough and lean, like that of our schoolboys, by continual exercise, and their taste disagreeable; and to fatten them would not answer the charge. Then as to the females, it would, I think, with humble submission, be a loss to the public, because they soon would become breeders themselves: and besides, it is not improbable that some scrupulous people might be apt to censure such a practice (although indeed very unjustly) as a little bordering upon cruelty; which, I confess hath always been with me the strongest objection against any project, how well soever intended.

But in order to justify my friend, he confessed that this expedient was put into his head by the famous Psalmanazar,[2] a native of the island Formosa, who came from thence to London above twenty years ago; and in conversation told my friend, that in his country, when any young person happened to be put to death, the executioner sold the carcass to persons of quality as a prime dainty; and that in his time the body of a plump girl of fifteen, who was crucified for an attempt to poison the emperor, was sold to his Imperial Majesty's prime minister of state, and other great mandarins of the court, in joints from the gibbet,[3] at four hundred crowns. Neither indeed can I deny, that if the same use were made of several plump young girls in this town, who, without one single groat to their fortunes, cannot stir abroad without a chair,[4] and appear at playhouse and assemblies in foreign fineries which they never will pay for, the kingdom would not be the worse.

Some persons of a desponding spirit are in great concern about the vast number of poor people who are aged, diseased, or maimed; and I have been desired to employ my thoughts what course may be taken to ease the nation of so grievous an encumbrance. But I am not in the least pain upon that matter, because it is very well known, that they are every day dying, and rotting, by cold and famine, and filth and vermin, as fast as can be reasonably expected. And as to the younger labourers, they are now in almost as hopeful a condition: they cannot get work, and consequently pine away for want of nourishment, to a degree, that if at any time they are accidentally hired to common labour, they have not strength to perform it; and thus the country and themselves are happily delivered from the evils to come.

I have too long digressed, and therefore shall return to my subject. I think the advantages by the proposal which I have made are obvious and many, as well as of the highest importance.

For first, as I have already observed, it would greatly lessen the number of papists, with whom we are yearly overrun, being the principal breeders of the nation as well as our most dangerous enemies; and who stay at home on

---

2. George Psalmanazar (1679?–1763), a literary impostor born in southern France who claimed to be a native of Formosa and a recent Christian convert. He published a catechism in an invented language that he called Formosan, as well as a description of Formosa with an introductory autobiography.   3. The post from which the bodies of criminals were hung in chains after execution. *Joints:* portions of a carcass carved up by a butcher.   4. I.e., a sedan chair, an enclosed seat carried on poles by men.

purpose with a design to deliver the kingdom to the Pretender, hoping to take their advantage by the absence of so many good Protestants, who have chosen rather to leave their country than stay at home and pay tithes against their conscience to an idolatrous Episcopal curate.

Secondly, the poorer tenants will have something valuable of their own, which by law may be made liable to distress,[5] and help to pay their landlord's rent; their corn and cattle being already seized, and money a thing unknown.

Thirdly, whereas the maintenance of an hundred thousand children, from two years old and upwards, cannot be computed at less than ten shillings a piece per annum, the nation's stock will be thereby increased fifty thousand pounds per annum; besides the profit of a new dish introduced to the tables of all gentlemen of fortune in the kingdom who have any refinement in taste. And the money will circulate among ourselves, the goods being entirely of our own growth and manufacture.

Fourthly, the constant breeders, besides the gain of eight shillings sterling per annum by the sale of their children, will be rid of the charge of maintaining them after the first year.

Fifthly, this food would likewise bring great custom to taverns; where the vinters will certainly be so prudent as to procure the best receipts[6] for dressing it to perfection, and, consequently, have their houses frequented by all the fine gentlemen, who justly value themselves upon their knowledge in good eating: and a skilful cook, who understands how to oblige his guests, will contrive to make it as expensive as they please.

Sixthly, this would be a great inducement to marriage, which all wise nations have either encouraged by rewards, or enforced by laws and penalties. It would increase the care and tenderness of mothers towards their children, when they were sure of a settlement for life to the poor babes, provided in some sort by the public, to their annual profit instead of expense. We should soon see an honest emulation among the married women, which of them could bring the fattest child to the market. Men would become as fond of their wives during the time of their pregnancy, as they are now of their mares in foal, their cows in calf, or sows when they are ready to farrow; nor offer to beat or kick them (as is too frequent a practice) for fear of a miscarriage.

Many other advantages might be enumerated. For instance, the addition of some thousand carcasses in our exportation of barrelled beef; the propagation of swine's flesh, and improvement in the art of making good bacon, so much wanted among us by the great destruction of pigs, too frequent at our tables, which are no way comparable in taste or magnificence to a well-grown, fat yearling child, which, roasted whole, will make a considerable figure at a Lord Mayor's feast, or any other public entertainment. But this, and many others, I omit, being studious of brevity.

Supposing that one thousand families in this city would be constant customers for infants' flesh, besides others who might have it at merry meetings, particularly weddings and christenings. I compute that Dublin would take off annually about twenty thousand carcasses; and the rest of the kingdom (where probably they will be sold somewhat cheaper) the remaining eighty thousand.

5. The legal seizing of goods to satisfy a debt, particularly for unpaid rent.   6. Recipes.

I can think of no one objection that will possibly be raised against this proposal, unless it should be urged, that the number of people will be thereby much lessened in the kingdom. This I freely own, and it was indeed one principal design in offering it to the world. I desire the reader will observe that I calculate my remedy *for this one individual kingdom of Ireland, and for no other that ever was, is, or I think ever can be, upon earth.* Therefore let no man talk to me of other expedients: *of taxing our absentees at five shillings a pound: of using neither clothes nor household-furniture except what is of our own growth and manufacture: of utterly rejecting the materials and instruments that promote foreign luxury: of curing the expensiveness of pride, vanity, idleness, and gaming in our women; of introducing a vein of parsimony, prudence, and temperance: of learning to love our country, wherein we differ even from Laplanders, and the inhabitants of Topinamboo:*[7] of quitting our animosities and factions, nor act any longer like the Jews,[8] who were murdering one another at the very moment their city was taken: of being a little cautious not to sell our country and consciences for nothing: of teaching landlords to have at least one degree of mercy towards their tenants: lastly, of putting a spirit of honesty, industry, and skill into our shopkeepers; who, if a resolution could now be taken to buy only our native goods, would immediately unite to cheat and exact upon us in the price, the measure, and the goodness, nor could ever yet be brought to make one fair proposal of just dealing, though often and earnestly invited to it.[9]

Therefore I repeat, let no man talk to me of these and the like expedients, till he hath at least some glimpse of hope that there will ever be some hearty and sincere attempts to put them in practice.

But, as to myself, having been wearied out for many years with offering vain, idle, visionary thoughts, and at length utterly despairing of success, I fortunately fell upon this proposal; which, as it is wholly new, so it hath something solid and real, of no expense and little trouble, full in our own power, and whereby we can incur no danger in disobliging England. For this kind of commodity will not bear exportation, the flesh being of too tender a consistence to admit a long continuance in salt, although perhaps I could name a country[1] which would be glad to eat up our whole nation without it.

After all, I am not so violently bent upon my own opinion as to reject any offer proposed by wise men which shall be found equally innocent, cheap, easy, and effectual. But before something of that kind shall be advanced in contradiction to my scheme, and offering a better, I desire the author, or authors, will be pleased maturely to consider two points. First, as things now stand, how they will be able to find food and raiment for a hundred thousand useless mouths and backs? And, secondly, there being a round million of creatures in human figure throughout this kingdom, whose whole subsistence put into a common stock would leave them in debt two millions of pounds sterling, adding those who are beggars by profession, to the bulk of farmers, cottagers, and labourers, with the wives and children who are beggars in effect; I desire those politicians who dislike my overture, and may perhaps be so bold as to attempt an answer, that they will first ask the parents of these mortals, whether they would not at this day think it a great happiness

---

7. In Brazil.   8. Referring to the factionalism under Herod Agrippa II at the time of the destruction of Jerusalem by the Roman emperor Titus.   9. The italicized proposals are Swift's serious suggestions for remedying the situation of Ireland.   1. England.

to have been sold for food at a year old, in the manner I prescribe, and thereby have avoided such a perpetual scene of misfortunes as they have since gone through, by the oppression of landlords, the impossibility of paying rent without money or trade, the want of common sustenance, with neither house nor clothes to cover them from the inclemencies of weather, and the most inevitable prospect of entailing the like, or greater miseries, upon their breed for ever.

I profess, in the sincerity of my heart, that I have not the least personal interest in endeavouring to promote this necessary work, having no other motive than the public good of my country, by advancing our trade, providing for infants, relieving the poor, and giving some pleasure to the rich. I have no children by which I can propose to get a single penny; the youngest being nine years old, and my wife past child-bearing.

ALEXANDER POPE
1688–1744

"If Pope be not a poet, where is poetry to be found?" Samuel Johnson inquired. Transmuting the commonplace, claiming as subject matter everything from the minutiae of social existence to speculation about the nature of universal order, Alexander Pope transformed unlikely raw material into brilliant poetry.

Born to Roman Catholic parents in the year of the Glorious Revolution, which deposed Catholic James II in favor of Protestant William and Mary, Pope lived when Catholics were oppressed financially, educationally, professionally, and residentially. He could not attend a university or hold public employment; he had to live ten miles outside London. Sickly and undersized (he probably had tuberculosis as an infant), he was educated largely at home. Also, beginning in his youth, he developed literary friendships; and throughout his life, he enjoyed close associations with other men and a few women, in particular his neighbor and intimate friend Martha Blount, to whom he left his estate. Increasingly, he won wealth and reputation by his writing, notably his translations of Homer. Following Candide's course of cultivating his garden, he perfected his grounds and grotto at Twickenham, living in retirement from the city. He died of asthma and edema.

Pope's work ranged through most of the poetic genres of his period. Beginning, as Virgil had done, with pastorals, he later produced An Essay on Criticism (1711), versified advice about proper literary and critical procedure, and went on to publish a great philosophic poem, An Essay on Man, and to edit Shakespeare's plays. The bulk of his verse, however, was satiric. In The Dunciad (1728; 1743), he provided a satiric epic for his age, a history of the progress of dullness.

Writing to a woman friend, Pope described The Rape of the Lock (1717) as "at once the most a satire, and the most inoffensive, of anything of mine. . . . 'Tis a sort of writing very like tickling." He thus suggests the tonal complexity of a work that conveys serious social criticism through a fanciful and playful fable narrated in verse of surpassing grace and elegance. The joke of the poem, as well as its serious point, derives from the cataclysmic disturbance a young woman makes over her loss of a lock of hair. Pope adapts epic conventions to his narrative of trivia, including even a supernatural species—the sylphs—parodying the functions of the Greek gods. These reminders of the epic, a genre by definition concerned with important matters, emphasize the poet's consciousness of the relative triviality of eighteenth-century high-society preoccupations. The world Belinda inhabits confuses small things with great; "Puffs, powders, patches, Bibles, billet-doux" occupy her dressing table in indiscriminate assembly. Members of this society take their own pleasure more seriously than anything else: "wretches hang that jurymen may dine." Men and women coexist in fascinated tension, tension that, given even slight provocation, explodes into hostilities. Sexual issues govern the conflict: women guard their "honor," the reputation of chastity, more intently than they preserve their physical purity; men seek to violate both. The ideals of good sense and good humor, expressed in the poem by Clarissa, govern no one in action. Instead, both sexes value beauty (which, as Clarissa points out, fades) and accept it as an excuse for emotional self-indulgence (the theme of Umbriel's excursion to the Cave of Spleen). In its accounts of moral and psychological confusion, of hysterical fits and battles, the poem employs the familiar satiric techniques of exaggeration and distortion intended to reveal the truth and to inspire reform.

But *The Rape of the Lock* celebrates as well as criticizes. The delicacy and grace of the verse, the ethereal beauty of the sylphs, recapitulate Belinda's genuine grace and beauty: "If to her share some female errors fall, / Look on her face, and you'll forget 'em all." Belinda's world operates mainly on the basis of style. In its separation of style from moral substance, the society demands criticism; but the beauty it values—elegant conversation, boat trips on the Thames, magnificent women—like the beauty the poet creates, has meaning in itself. When the disputed lock of hair ascends to the constellations, when the poet calls attention to his own preservation of Belinda's beauty and fame, *The Rape of the Lock* reminds us that praise and blame sometimes appropriately attach to the same objects. Its mixture of playfulness and seriousness, of beauty and harshness, mark the poem's unique achievement.

In *An Essay on Man* (1733–34), a very different work, Pope set out to consider, in successive epistles, humanity in relation to the universe, to itself, to society, and to happiness—an enterprise of ambition almost comparable to Milton's in *Paradise Lost*. Indeed, in the first section of the poem Pope alludes specifically to his predecessor, describing the world as a "Garden, tempting with forbidden fruit" and declaring his own intention to "vindicate [Milton had used *justify*] the ways of God to man." Unlike Milton, Pope pursues this goal not through a dramatic fable but by an extended versified meditation on the philosophical issues involved. That meditation, however, generates its own drama.

Pope draws on a number of intellectual traditions to define the human condition in both cosmic and social terms. The breadth of his reference—to Catholic and Protestant theology, to Platonic and Stoic philosophy, to his period's notions of plenitude and natural order—reinforces the assumption of universal, unchanging human nature. The poet evokes a timeless vision of humanity in the universe, poised at the middle of the Great Chain of Being that extends from God to the most minute forms of life, with the fullest possible range of being above and below humankind. Complaints that the poem's philosophy is shallow ignore the complexity of its synthesis and the seriousness of its ideas. The resounding assertion that concludes the first epistle, for instance ("One truth is clear, WHATEVER IS, IS RIGHT"), implies no unawareness of human misery or evil. Abundant examples of both have been presented in the text. The point is, rather, that the nature of God's plan—by definition not fully comprehensible to human reason—must allow evil for the sake of larger good. And human beings, to possess free will, must have available to them the choice of evil. Such assumptions belong to the intellectual position called "philosophical optimism"—by no means equivalent to what we usually think of as optimism, the faith that everything will turn out well in the long run. The belief expounded in *An Essay on Man*, on the contrary, allows the possibility that matters may turn out badly for individual men and women but assumes that personal misfortune takes its place in a larger, essentially benign, pattern.

The first epistle of the poem, printed here, progresses through ten logically connected sections. It begins by insisting on the necessary limitation of human judgment: we see only parts, not the whole. Nonetheless, this fact does not imply the imperfection of humankind; it means, rather, that we are adapted to our position in the general order of things. Our ignorance of future events and our hope for eternal life give us the possibility of happiness. The poem then indicts human beings for pride and impiety (we claim more power of judgment and more knowledge than we can have), for the absurdity of assuming themselves the center of the created universe, and for the unreasonableness of complaints against the providential order (we demand, the poet suggests, both the perfection of angels and the physical sensitivities of animals, although increase in our capacities would bring misery). Turning to the nature of the universal order, the argument insists on the gradations of faculties from the lower animals to humankind, then suggests that this order extends further than we can know: any interference with it would destroy the whole. Even the speculative possibility of such interference suggests the insanity of human pride. Our only proper course is absolute submission to Providence.

This logical sequence structures the *Essay on Man,* but we should not read the poem only as a versified handbook of eighteenth-century philosophy. Here, as in *The Rape of the Lock,* Pope displays his poetic brilliance, infusing philosophical argument with a rich emotional and intellectual texture. He draws us into the poem by addressing us directly, reminding us of our own tendencies to presumption, our own inevitable desire to understand the universe as revolving around us. "In Pride, in reasoning Pride, our error lies": we all share bewilderment at our situation, we all need to interpret it, and we all face, every day, our necessary limitations. The poet rapidly shifts tone, sometimes berating his readers, sometimes reminding us (and himself) of his own participation in the universal dilemma, sometimes assuming a godlike perspective and suggesting his superior knowledge. By his changing voice, his changing forms of address, he makes dramatic the futile yet noble effort to understand what only the deity can fully comprehend.

At its best, *An Essay on Man* transforms philosophy into emotional experience. It generates drama out of shifting, intersecting perspectives: the lamb licking the hand of its butcher, the Indian looking forward to a Heaven his dog will share, the scientist trying to interpret the physical universe. It also makes the abstract vividly specific and concrete, as when reflection on the necessary limitation of human faculties produces the penetrating image of someone dying "of a rose in aromatic pain." Pope's imagination summons up a vast range of concrete reference, and it does not avoid the disturbing: we are invited to think of the human condition in the universe as comparable to that of the ox, which tills the fields, goes to slaughter, or finds itself worshipped as a god, according to accidents of situation. The fly's "microscopic eye" excels our powers; we resemble weeds more than oaks. Yet the poet, ranging from the conversational ease of his opening lines to the ringing certainties of his conclusion, incorporates perceptions of human inadequacy into assertions of a grand scheme, which he makes not only rational but exciting.

PRONOUNCING GLOSSARY

The following list uses common English syllables and stress accents to provide rough equivalents of selected words whose pronunciation may be unfamiliar to the general reader.

Borgia: *bohr'-jah*

Le Comte de Gabalis: *leu kahmt du gah'-bah-lee*

Rosicrucian: *roh-zee-kru'-shan*

Scylla: *sil'-h*

The Rape of the Lock[1]

An Heroi-Comical Poem

Nolueram, Belinda, tuos violare capillos;
sed juvat hoc precibus me tribuisse tuis.[2]
—MARTIAL

TO MRS. ARABELLA FERMOR

MADAM,

It will be in vain to deny that I have some regard for this piece, since I dedicate it to you. Yet you may bear me witness, it was intended only to divert a few young ladies, who have good sense and good humor enough to laugh not only at their sex's little unguarded follies, but at their own. But as it was communicated with the air of a secret, it soon found its way into the world. An imperfect copy having been offered to a bookseller, you had the good nature for my sake to consent to the publication of one more correct; this I was forced to, before I had executed half my design, for the machinery was entirely wanting to complete it.

The machinery, Madam, is a term invented by the critics, to signify that part which the deities, angels, or demons are made to act in a poem; for the ancient poets are in one respect like many modern ladies: let an action be never so trivial in itself, they always make it appear of the utmost importance. These machines I determined to raise on a very new and odd foundation, the Rosicrucian[3] doctrine of spirits.

I know how disagreeable it is to make use of hard words before a lady; but 'tis so much the concern of a poet to have his works understood, and particularly by your sex, that you must give me leave to explain two or three difficult terms.

The Rosicrucians are a people I must bring you acquainted with. The best account I know of them is in a French book called *Le Comte de Gabalis*,[4] which both in its title and size is so like a novel, that many of the fair sex have read it for one by mistake. According to these gentlemen, the four elements are inhabited by spirits, which they call Sylphs, Gnomes, Nymphs, and Salamanders. The Gnomes or Demons of earth delight in mischief; but the Sylphs, whose habitation is in the air, are the best-conditioned creatures imaginable. For they say, any mortals may enjoy the most intimate familiarities with these gentle spirits, upon a condition very easy to all true adepts, an inviolate preservation of chastity.

As to the following cantos, all the passages of them are as fabulous as the vision at the beginning, or the transformation at the end; (except the loss of your hair, which I always mention with reverence). The human persons are as fictitious as the airy ones; and the character of Belinda, as it is now managed, resembles you in nothing but in beauty.

If this poem had as many graces as there are in your person, or in your

---

1. Text and notes by Samuel Holt Monk.   2. "I was unwilling, Belinda, to ravish your locks; but I rejoice to have conceded this to your prayers" (Martial, *Epigrams* XII.lxxxiv.1–2). Pope substituted his heroine for Martial's Polytimus. The epigraph is intended to suggest that the poem was published at Miss Fermor's request.   3. A system of arcane philosophy introduced into England from Germany in the 17th century.
4. By the Abbé de Montfaucon de Villars, published in 1670.

mind, yet I could never hope it should pass through the world half so uncensured as you have done. But let its fortune be what it will, mine is happy enough, to have given me this occasion of assuring you that I am, with the truest esteem,

MADAM,
Your most obedient, humble servant,

A. POPE

CANTO I

What dire offense from amorous causes springs,
What mighty contests rise from trivial things,
I sing—This verse to Caryll,[5] Muse! is due:
This, even Belinda may vouchsafe to view:
Slight is the subject, but not so the praise,   5
If she inspire, and he approve my lays.
  Say what strange motive, Goddess! could compel
A well-bred lord t' assault a gentle belle?
Oh, say what stranger cause, yet unexplored,
Could make a gentle belle reject a lord?   10
In tasks so bold can little men engage,
And in soft bosoms dwells such mighty rage?
  Sol through white curtains shot a timorous ray,
And oped those eyes that must eclipse the day.
Now lapdogs give themselves the rousing shake,   15
And sleepless lovers just at twelve awake:
Thrice rung the bell, the slipper knocked the ground,
And the pressed watch[6] returned a silver sound.
Belinda still her downy pillow pressed,
Her guardian Sylph prolonged the balmy rest: 20
'Twas he had summoned to her silent bed
The morning dream that hovered o'er her head.
A youth more glittering than a birthnight beau[7]
(That even in slumber caused her cheek to glow)
Seemed to her ear his winning lips to lay,   25
And thus in whispers said, or seemed to say:
  "Fairest of mortals, thou distinguished care
Of thousand bright inhabitants of air!
If e'er one vision touched thy infant thought,
Of all the nurse and all the priest have taught,   30
Of airy elves by moonlight shadows seen,
The silver token, and the circled green,[8]
Or virgins visited by angel powers,
With golden crowns and wreaths of heavenly flowers,
Hear and believe! thy own importance know,   35

5. John Caryll (1666?–1736), a close friend of Pope's who suggested that he write this poem. 6. A watch that chimes the hour and the quarter hour when the stem is pressed down. *Thrice rung the bell:* Belinda thus summons her maid. 7. Courtiers wore especially fine clothes on the sovereign's birthday. 8. According to popular belief, fairies skim off the cream from jugs of milk left standing overnight and leave a coin in payment. *The circled green:* rings of bright green grass, which are common in England even in winter, were held to be due to the round dances of fairies.

Nor bound thy narrow views to things below.
Some secret truths, from learned pride concealed,
To maids alone and children are revealed:
What though no credit doubting wits may give?
The fair and innocent shall still believe.   40
Know, then, unnumbered spirits round thee fly,
The light militia of the lower sky:
These, though unseen, are ever on the wing,
Hang o'er the box,[9] and hover round the Ring.
Think what an equipage thou hast in air,   45
And view with scorn two pages and a chair.[1]
As now your own, our beings were of old,
And once enclosed in woman's beauteous mold
Thence, by a soft transition, we repair
From earthly vehicles to these of air.   50
Think not, when woman's transient breath is fled,
That all her vanities at once are dead:
Succeeding vanities she still regards,
And though she plays no more o'erlooks the cards.
Her joy in gilded chariots, when alive,   55
And love of ombre,[2] after death survive.
For when the Fair in all their pride expire,
To their first elements[3] their souls retire:
The sprites of fiery termagants in flame
Mount up, and take a Salamander's name.[4]   60
Soft yielding minds to water glide away,
And sip, with Nymphs, their elemental tea.[5]
The graver prude sinks downward to a Gnome,
In search of mischief still on earth to roam.
The light coquettes in Sylphs aloft repair,   65
And sport and flutter in the fields of air.
    "Know further yet; whoever fair and chaste
Rejects mankind, is by some Sylph embraced:
For spirits, freed from mortal laws, with ease
Assume what sexes and what shapes they please.   70
What guards the purity of melting maids,
In courtly balls, and midnight masquerades,
Safe from the treacherous friend, the daring spark,
The glance by day, the whisper in the dark,
When kind occasion prompts their warm desires,   75
When music softens, and when dancing fires?
'Tis but their Sylph, the wise Celestials know,
Though Honor is the word with men below.
    "Some nymphs there are, too conscious of their face,
For life predestined to the Gnomes' embrace.   80
These swell their prospects and exalt their pride,

---

9. *Box* in the theater and the fashionable circular drive (*Ring*) in Hyde Park.   1. Sedan chair.   2. The
popular card game. See III.27 ff. and note.   3. The four elements out of which all things were believed
to have been made were fire, water, earth, and air. One or another of these elements was supposed to be
predominant in both the physical and psychological makeup of each human being. In this context they are
spoken of as "humors."   4. Pope borrowed his supernatural beings from Rosicrucian mythology. Each
element was inhabited by a spirit, as the following lines explain. The salamander is a lizardlike animal, in
antiquity believed to live in fire.   5. Pronounced *tay*.

When offers are disdained, and love denied:
Then gay ideas[6] crowd the vacant brain,
While peers, and dukes, and all their sweeping train,
And garters, stars, and coronets appear,   85
And in soft sounds, 'your Grace' salutes their ear.
'Tis these that early taint the female soul,
Instruct the eyes of young coquettes to roll,
Teach infant cheeks a bidden blush to know,
And little hearts to flutter at a beau.   90
   "Oft, when the world imagine women stray,
The Sylphs through mystic mazes guide their way,
Through all the giddy circle they pursue,
And old impertinence expel by new.
What tender maid but must a victim fall   95
To one man's treat, but for another's ball?
When Florio speaks what virgin could withstand,
If gentle Damon did not squeeze her hand?
With varying vanities, from every part,
They shift the moving toyshop[7] of their heart;   100
Where wigs with wigs, with sword-knots sword-knots strive,
Beaux banish beaux, and coaches coaches drive.
This erring mortals levity may call;
Oh, blind to truth! the Sylphs contrive it all.
   "Of these am I, who thy protection claim,   105
A watchful sprite, and Ariel is my name.
Late, as I ranged the crystal wilds of air,
In the clear mirror of thy ruling star
I saw, alas! some dread event impend,
Ere to the main this morning sun descend,   110
But Heaven reveals not what, or how, or where:
Warned by thy Sylph, O pious maid, beware!
This to disclose is all thy guardian can:
Beware of all, but most beware of Man!"
   He said; when Shock,[8] who thought she slept too long,   115
Leaped up, and waked his mistress with his tongue.
'Twas then, Belinda, if report say true,
Thy eyes first opened on a billet-doux;
Wounds, charms, and ardors were no sooner read,
But all the vision vanished from thy head.   120
   And now, unveiled, the toilet stands displayed,
Each silver vase in mystic order laid.
First, robed in white, the nymph intent adores,
With head uncovered, the cosmetic powers.
A heavenly image in the glass appears;   125
To that she bends, to that her eyes she rears.
The inferior priestess, at her altar's side,
Trembling begins the sacred rites of Pride.
Unnumbered treasures ope at once, and here
The various offerings of the world appear;   130
From each she nicely culls with curious toil,

---

6. Images.   7. A shop stocked with baubles and trifles.   8. Belinda's lapdog.

And decks the goddess with the glittering spoil.
This casket India's glowing gems unlocks,
And all Arabia breathes from yonder box.
The tortoise here and elephant unite,   135
Transformed to combs, the speckled and the white.
Here files of pins extend their shining rows,
Puffs, powders, patches, Bibles, billet-doux.
Now awful Beauty puts on all its arms;
The fair each moment rises in her charms,   140
Repairs her smiles, awakens every grace,
And calls forth all the wonders of her face;
Sees by degrees a purer blush arise,
And keener lightnings quicken in her eyes.
The busy Sylphs surround their darling care,   145
These set the head, and those divide the hair,
Some fold the sleeve, whilst others plait the gown;
And Betty's[9] praised for labors not her own.

CANTO II

Not with more glories, in the ethereal plain,
The sun first rises o'er the purpled main,
Than, issuing forth, the rival of his beams
Launched on the bosom of the silver Thames.
Fair nymphs and well-dressed youths around her shone,   5
But every eye was fixed on her alone.
On her white breast a sparkling cross she wore,
Which Jews might kiss, and infidels adore.
Her lively looks a sprightly mind disclose,
Quick as her eyes, and as unfixed as those: 10
Favors to none, to all she smiles extends;
Oft she rejects, but never once offends.
Bright as the sun, her eyes the gazers strike,
And, like the sun, they shine on all alike.
Yet graceful ease, and sweetness void of pride,   15
Might hide her faults, if belles had faults to hide:
If to her share some female errors fall,
Look on her face, and you'll forget 'em all.
This nymph, to the destruction of mankind,
Nourished two locks which graceful hung behind   20
In equal curls, and well conspired to deck
With shining ringlets the smooth ivory neck.
Love in these labyrinths his slaves detains,
And mighty hearts are held in slender chains.
With hairy springes we the birds betray,   25
Slight lines of hair surprise the finny prey,
Fair tresses man's imperial race ensnare,
And beauty draws us with a single hair.
The adventurous Baron the bright locks admired,
He saw, he wished, and to the prize aspired.   30

---

9. Belinda's maid, the "inferior priestess" mentioned in line 127.

Resolved to win, he meditates the way,
By force to ravish, or by fraud betray;
For when success a lover's toil attends,
Few ask if fraud or force attained his ends.
   For this, ere Phoebus rose, he had implored   35
Propitious Heaven, and every power adored,
But chiefly Love—to Love an altar built,
Of twelve vast French romances, neatly gilt.
There lay three garters, half a pair of gloves,
And all the trophies of his former loves.   40
With tender billet-doux he lights the pyre,
And breathes three amorous sighs to raise the fire.
Then prostrate falls, and begs with ardent eyes
Soon to obtain, and long possess the prize:
The powers gave ear, and granted half his prayer,   45
The rest the winds dispersed in empty air.
   But now secure the painted vessel glides,
The sunbeams trembling on the floating tides,
While melting music steals upon the sky,
And softened sounds along the waters die.   50
Smooth flow the waves, the zephyrs gently play,
Belinda smiled, and all the world was gay.
All but the Sylph—with careful thoughts oppressed,
The impending woe sat heavy on his breast.
He summons straight his denizens of air;   55
The lucid squadrons round the sails repair:
Soft o'er the shrouds aërial whispers breathe
That seemed but zephyrs to the train beneath.
Some to the sun their insect-wings unfold,
Waft on the breeze, or sink in clouds of gold.   60
Transparent forms too fine for mortal sight,
Their fluid bodies half dissolved in light,
Loose to the wind their airy garments flew,
Thin glittering textures of the filmy dew,
Dipped in the richest tincture of the skies,   65
Where light disports in ever-mingling dyes,
While every beam new transient colors flings,
Colors that change whene'er they wave their wings.
Amid the circle, on the gilded mast,
Superior by the head was Ariel placed;   70
His purple[1] pinions opening to the sun,
He raised his azure wand, and thus begun:
   "Ye Sylphs and Sylphids, to your chief give ear!
Fays, Fairies, Genii, Elves, and Daemons, hear!
Ye know the spheres and various tasks assigned   75
By laws eternal to the aërial kind.
Some in the fields of purest ether play,
And bask and whiten in the blaze of day.
Some guide the course of wandering orbs on high,

---

1. In 18th-century poetic diction, the word might mean "blood-red," "purple," or simply (as is likely here) "brightly colored." The word derives from Virgil, *Eclogue* IX.40, *pupureus*.

Or roll the planets through the boundless sky.   80
Some less refined, beneath the moon's pale light
Pursue the stars that shoot athwart the night,
Or suck the mists in grosser air below,
Or dip their pinions in the painted bow,
Or brew fierce tempests on the wintry main,   85
Or o'er the glebe distill the kindly rain.
Others on earth o'er human race preside,
Watch all their ways, and all their actions guide:
Of these the chief the care of nations own,
And guard with arms divine the British Throne.   90
     "Our humbler province is to tend the Fair,
Not a less pleasing, though less glorious care:
To save the powder from too rude a gale,
Nor let the imprisoned essences exhale;
To draw fresh colors from the vernal flowers   95
To steal from rainbows e'er they drop in showers
A brighter wash;² to curl their waving hairs,
Assist their blushes, and inspire their airs;
Nay oft, in dreams invention we bestow,
To change a flounce, or add a furbelow.   100
     "This day black omens threat the brightest fair,
That e'er deserved a watchful spirit's care;
Some dire disaster, or by force or slight,
But what, or where, the Fates have wrapped in night:
Whether the nymph shall break Diana's³ law,   105
Or some frail china jar receive a flaw,
Or stain her honor or her new brocade,
Forget her prayers, or miss a masquerade,
Or lose her heart, or necklace, at a ball;
Or whether Heaven has doomed that Shock must fall.   110
Haste, then, ye spirits! to your charge repair:
The fluttering fan be Zephyretta's care;
The drops⁴ to thee, Brillante, we consign;
And, Momentilla, let the watch be thine;
Do thou, Crispissa,⁵ tend her favorite Lock;   115
Ariel himself shall be the guard of Shock.
     "To fifty chosen Sylphs, of special note,
We trust the important charge, the petticoat;
Oft have we known that sevenfold fence to fail,
Though stiff with hoops, and armed with ribs of whale.   120
Form a strong line about the silver bound,
And guard the wide circumference around.
     "Whatever spirit, careless of his charge,
His post neglects, or leaves the fair at large,
Shall feel sharp vengeance soon o'ertake his sins,   125
Be stopped in vials, or transfixed with pins,
Or plunged in lakes of bitter washes lie,
Or wedged whole ages in a bodkin's eye;⁶

2. Cosmetic lotion.   3. Diana was the goddess of chastity.   4. Diamond earrings.   5. From Latin *crispere*, to curl.   6. A blunt needle with a large eye, used for drawing ribbon through eyelets in the edging of women's garments.

Gums and pomatums shall his flight restrain,
While clogged he beats his silken wings in vain, 130
Or alum styptics with contracting power
Shrink his thin essence like a riveled[7] flower:
Or, as Ixion fixed,[8] the wretch shall feel
The giddy motion of the whirling mill,
In fumes of burning chocolate shall glow, 135
And tremble at the sea that froths below!"
　　He spoke; the spirits from the sails descend;
Some, orb in orb, around the nymph extend;
Some thread the mazy ringlets of her hair;
Some hang upon the pendants of her ear: 140
With beating hearts the dire event they wait,
Anxious, and trembling for the birth of Fate.

CANTO III

　　Close by those meads, forever crowned with flowers,
Where Thames with pride surveys his rising towers,
There stands a structure of majestic frame,
Which from the neighboring Hampton[9] takes its name.
Here Britain's statesmen oft the fall foredoom 5
Of foreign tyrants and of nymphs at home;
Here thou, great Anna! whom three realms obey,
Dost sometimes counsel take—and sometimes tea.
　　Hither the heroes and the nymphs resort,
To taste awhile the pleasures of a court; 10
In various talk the instructive hours they passed,
Who gave the ball, or paid the visit last;
One speaks the glory of the British Queen,
And one describes a charming Indian screen;
A third interprets motions, looks, and eyes; 15
At every word a reputation dies.
Snuff, or the fan, supply each pause of chat,
With singing, laughing, ogling, and all that.
　　Meanwhile, declining from the noon of day,
The sun obliquely shoots his burning ray; 20
The hungry judges soon the sentence sign,
And wretches hang that jurymen may dine;
The merchant from the Exchange returns in peace,
And the long labors of the toilet cease.
Belinda now, whom thirst of fame invites, 25
Burns to encounter two adventurous knights,
At ombre[1] singly to decide their doom
And swells her breast with conquests yet to come.

---

7. To "rivel" is to "contract into wrinkles and corrugations" (Johnson's *Dictionary*).　8. In the Greek myth, Ixion was punished in the underworld by being bound on an ever-turning wheel.　9. Hampton Court, the royal palace, about fifteen miles up the Thames from London.　1. The game that Belinda plays against the baron and another young man is too complicated for complete explication here. Pope has carefully arranged the cards so that Belinda wins. The baron's hand is strong enough to be a threat, but the third player's is of little account. The hand is played exactly according to the rules of ombre, and Pope's description of the cards is equally accurate. Each player holds nine cards (line 30). The "Matadores" (line 33), when spades are trumps, are "Spadillio" (line 49), the ace of spades; "Manillio" (line 51), the two of spades; "Basto" (line 53), the ace of clubs; Belinda holds all three of these.

Straight the three bands prepare in arms to join,
Each band the number of the sacred nine.   30
Soon as she spreads her hand, the aërial guard
Descend, and sit on each important card:
First Ariel perched upon a Matadore,
Then each according to the rank they bore;
For Sylphs, yet mindful of their ancient race,   35
Are, as when women, wondrous fond of place.
    Behold, four Kings in majesty revered,
With hoary whiskers and a forky beard;
And four fair Queens whose hands sustain a flower,
The expressive emblem of their softer power;   40
Four Knaves in garbs succinct,[2] a trusty band,
Caps on their heads, and halberts in their hand;
And parti-colored troops, a shining train,
Draw forth to combat on the velvet plain.
The skillful nymph reviews her force with care;   45
"Let Spades be trumps!" she said, and trumps they were.
    Now move to war her sable Matadores,
In show like leaders of the swarthy Moors.
Spadillio first, unconquerable lord!
Led off two captive trumps, and swept the board.   50
As many more Manillio forced to yield,
And marched a victor from the verdant field.
Him Basto followed, but his fate more hard
Gained but one trump and one plebeian card.
With his broad saber next, a chief in years,   55
The hoary Majesty of Spades appears,
Puts forth one manly leg, to sight revealed,
The rest his many-colored robe concealed.
The rebel Knave, who dares his prince engage,
Proves the just victim of his royal rage.   60
Even mighty Pam,[3] that kings and queens o'erthrew
And mowed down armies in the fights of loo,
Sad chance of war! now destitute of aid,
Falls undistinguished by the victor Spade.
    Thus far both armies to Belinda yield;   65
Now to the Baron fate inclines the field.
His warlike amazon her host invades,
The imperial consort of the crown of Spades.
The Club's black tyrant first her victim died,
Spite of his haughty mien and barbarous pride.   70
What boots the regal circle on his head,
His giant limbs, in state unwieldy spread?
That long behind he trails his pompous robe,
And of all monarchs only grasps the globe?
    The Baron now his Diamonds pours apace;   75
The embroidered King who shows but half his face,
And his refulgent Queen, with powers combined
Of broken troops an easy conquest find.

2. Girded up.   3. The knave of clubs, the highest trump in the game of loo.

Clubs, Diamonds, Hearts, in wild disorder seen,
With throngs promiscuous strew the level green. 80
Thus when dispersed a routed army runs,
Of Asia's troops, and Afric's sable sons,
With like confusion different nations fly,
Of various habit, and of various dye,
The pierced battalions disunited fall 85
In heaps on heaps; one fate o'erwhelms them all.
  The Knave of Diamonds tries his wily arts,
And wins (oh, shameful chance!) the Queen of Hearts.
At this, the blood the virgin's cheek forsook,
A livid paleness spreads o'er all her look; 90
She sees, and trembles at the approaching ill,
Just in the jaws of ruin, and Codille,[4]
And now (as oft in some distempered state)
On one nice trick depends the general fate.
An Ace of Hearts steps forth: the King unseen 95
Lurked in her hand, and mourned his captive Queen.
He springs to vengeance with an eager pace,
And falls like thunder on the prostrate Ace.
The nymph exulting fills with shouts the sky,
The walls, the woods, and long canals reply. 100
  O thoughtless mortals! ever blind to fate,
Too soon dejected, and too soon elate:
Sudden these honors shall be snatched away,
And cursed forever this victorious day.
  For lo! the board with cups and spoons is crowned, 105
The berries crackle, and the mill turns round;[5]
On shining altars of Japan[6] they raise
The silver lamp; the fiery spirits blaze:
From silver spouts the grateful liquors glide,
While China's earth receives the smoking tide. 110
At once they gratify their scent and taste,
And frequent cups prolong the rich repast.
Straight hover round the fair her airy band;
Some, as she sipped, the fuming liquor fanned,
Some o'er her lap their careful plumes displayed, 115
Trembling, and conscious of the rich brocade.
Coffee (which makes the politician wise,
And see through all things with his half-shut eyes)
Sent up in vapors to the Baron's brain
New stratagems, the radiant Lock to gain. 120
Ah, cease, rash youth! desist ere 'tis too late,
Fear the just Gods, and think of Scylla's fate![7]
Changed to a bird, and sent to flit in air,
She dearly pays for Nisus' injured hair!
  But when to mischief mortals bend their will, 125

4. The term applied to losing a hand at cards.   5. That is, coffee is roasted and ground.   6. That is, small, lacquered tables. The word "altars" suggests the ritualistic character of coffee drinking in Belinda's world.   7. Scylla, daughter of Nisus, was turned into a seabird because, for the sake of her love for Minos of Crete, who was besieging her father's city of Megara, she cut from her father's head the purple lock on which his safety depended. She is not the Scylla of the "Scylla and Charybdis" episode in the *Odyssey*.

How soon they find fit instruments of ill!
Just then, Clarissa drew with tempting grace
A two-edged weapon from her shining case:
So ladies in romance assist their knight,
Present the spear, and arm him for the fight.   130
He takes the gift with reverence, and extends
The little engine on his fingers' ends;
This just behind Belinda's neck he spread,
As o'er the fragrant steams she bends her head.
Swift to the Lock a thousand sprites repair,   135
A thousand wings, by turns, blow back the hair,
And thrice they twitched the diamond in her ear,
Thrice she looked back, and thrice the foe drew near.
Just in that instant, anxious Ariel sought
The close recesses of the virgin's thought;   140
As on the nosegay in her breast reclined,
He watched the ideas rising in her mind,
Sudden he viewed, in spite of all her art,
An earthly lover lurking at her heart.
Amazed, confused, he found his power expired,   145
Resigned to fate, and with a sigh retired.
      The Peer now spreads the glittering forfex[8] wide,
T' enclose the Lock; now joins it, to divide.
Even then, before the fatal engine closed,
A wretched Sylph too fondly interposed;   150
Fate urged the shears, and cut the Sylph in twain
(But airy substance soon unites again):
The meeting points the sacred hair dissever
From the fair head, forever, and forever!
      Then flashed the living lightning from her eyes,   155
And screams of horror rend the affrighted skies.
Not louder shrieks to pitying heaven are cast,
When husbands, or when lapdogs breathe their last;
Or when rich china vessels fallen from high,
In glittering dust and painted fragments lie!   160
"Let wreaths of triumph now my temples twine,"
The victor cried, "the glorious prize is mine!
While fish in streams, or birds delight in air,
Or in a coach and six the British Fair,
As long as Atalantis[9] shall be read,   165
Or the small pillow grace a lady's bed,
While visits shall be paid on solemn days,
When numerous wax-lights in bright order blaze,
While nymphs take treats, or assignations give,
So long my honor, name, and praise shall live!   170
What Time would spare, from Steel receives its date,
And monuments, like men, submit to fate!
Steel could the labor of the Gods destroy,
And strike to dust the imperial towers of Troy;

8. Scissors.   9. Mrs. Manley's New Atalantis (1709) was notorious for its thinly concealed allusions to contemporary scandals.

Steel could the works of mortal pride confound,   175
And hew triumphal arches to the ground.
What wonder then, fair nymph! thy hairs should feel,
The conquering force of unresisted Steel?"

CANTO IV

But anxious cares the pensive nymph oppressed,
And secret passions labored in her breast.
Not youthful kings in battle seized alive,
Not scornful virgins who their charms survive,
Not ardent lovers robbed of all their bliss,   5
Not ancient ladies when refused a kiss,
Not tyrants fierce that unrepenting die,
Not Cynthia when her manteau's¹ pinned awry,
E'er felt such rage, resentment, and despair,
As thou, sad virgin! for thy ravished hair.   10
    For, that sad moment, when the Sylphs withdrew
And Ariel weeping from Belinda flew,
Umbriel,² a dusky, melancholy sprite
As ever sullied the fair face of light,
Down to the central earth, his proper scene,   15
Repaired to search the gloomy Cave of Spleen.³
    Swift on his sooty pinions flits the Gnome,
And in a vapor⁴ reached the dismal dome.
No cheerful breeze this sullen region knows,
The dreaded east is all the wind that blows.   20
Here in a grotto, sheltered close from air,
And screened in shades from day's detested glare,
She sighs forever on her pensive bed,
Pain at her side, and Megrim⁵ at her head.
    Two handmaids wait the throne: alike in place,   25
But differing far in figure and in face.
Here stood Ill-Nature like an ancient maid,
Her wrinkled form in black and white arrayed;
With store of prayers for mornings, nights, and noons,
Her hand is filled; her bosom with lampoons.   30
    There Affectation, with a sickly mien,
Shows in her cheek the roses of eighteen,
Practiced to lisp, and hang the head aside,
Faints into airs, and languishes with pride,
On the rich quilt sinks with becoming woe,   35
Wrapped in a gown, for sickness and for show.
The fair ones feel such maladies as these,
When each new nightdress gives a new disease.
    A constant vapor⁶ o'er the palace flies,
Strange phantoms rising as the mists arise;   40
Dreadful as hermit's dreams in haunted shades,

---

1. Negligee, or loose robe.   2. The name suggests shade and darkness.   3. Ill humor.   4. Punning
on *vapor* as (1) mist and (2) an excessively emotional (even peevish) state of mind, appropriate to the realm
of "spleen."   5. Headache.   6. Emblematic of "the vapors"—hypochondria, melancholy, peevishness,
often affected by fashionable women.

Or bright as visions of expiring maids.
Now glaring fiends, and snakes on rolling spires,[7]
Pale specters, gaping tombs, and purple fires;
Now lakes of liquid gold, Elysian scenes,   45
And crystal domes, and angels in machines.[8]
   Unnumbered throngs on every side are seen
Of bodies changed to various forms by Spleen.
Here living teapots stand, one arm held out,
One bent; the handle this, and that the spout: 50
A pipkin[9] there, like Homer's tripod, walks;
Here sighs a jar, and there a goose pie talks;
Men prove with child, as powerful fancy works,
And maids, turned bottles, call aloud for corks.
   Safe passed the Gnome through this fantastic band,   55
A branch of healing spleenwort[1] in his hand.
Then thus addressed the Power: "Hail, wayward Queen!
Who rule the sex to fifty from fifteen:
Parent of vapors and of female wit,
Who give the hysteric or poetic fit,   60
On various tempers act by various ways,
Make some take physic, others scribble plays;
Who cause the proud their visits to delay,
And send the godly in a pet to pray.
A nymph there is that all your power disdains,   65
And thousands more in equal mirth maintains.
But oh! if e'er thy Gnome could spoil a grace,
Or raise a pimple on a beauteous face,
Like citron-waters[2] matrons' cheeks inflame,
Or change complexions at a losing game;   70
If e'er with airy horns[3] I planted heads,
Or rumpled petticoats, or tumbled beds,
Or caused suspicion when no soul was rude,
Or discomposed the headdress of a prude,
Or e'er to costive lapdog gave disease,   75
Which not the tears of brightest eyes could ease,
Hear me, and touch Belinda with chagrin:[4]
That single act gives half the world the spleen."
   The Goddess with a discontented air
Seems to reject him though she grants his prayer.   80
A wondrous bag with both her hands she binds,
Like that where once Ulysses held the winds;[5]
There she collects the force of female lungs,
Sighs, sobs, and passions, and the war of tongues.
A vial next she fills with fainting fears,   85

---

7. Coils.   8. Mechanical devices used in the theaters for spectacular effects. The fantasies of neurotic women here merge with the sensational stage effects popular with contemporary audiences.   9. An earthen pot. In *Iliad* XVIII.434–40, Vulcan furnishes the gods with self-propelling "tripods" (three-legged stools).   1. An herb, efficacious against the spleen. Pope alludes to the golden bough that Aeneas and the Cumaean sybil carry with them for protection into the underworld in *Aeneid* VI.   2. Brandy flavored with orange or lemon peel.   3. The symbol of the cuckold; here "airy," because they exist only in the jealous suspicions of the husband, the victim of the mischievous Umbriel.   4. Ill humor.   5. Aeolus (later conceived of as god of the winds) gave Ulysses a bag containing all the winds adverse to his voyage home. When his ship was in sight of Ithaca, his companions opened the bag, and the storms that ensued drove Ulysses far away (*Odyssey* X.19 ff.).

Soft sorrows, melting griefs, and flowing tears.
The Gnome rejoicing bears her gifts away,
Spreads his black wings, and slowly mounts to day.
    Sunk in Thalestris'[6] arms the nymph he found,
Her eyes dejected and her hair unbound.   90
Full o'er their heads the swelling bag he rent,
And all the Furies issued at the vent.
Belinda burns with more than mortal ire,
And fierce Thalestris fans the rising fire.
"O wretched maid!" she spread her hands, and cried   95
(While Hampton's echoes, "Wretched maid!" replied),
"Was it for this you took such constant care
The bodkin, comb, and essence to prepare?
For this your locks in paper durance bound,
For this with torturing irons wreathed around?   100
For this with fillets strained your tender head,
And bravely bore the double loads of lead?[7]
Gods! shall the ravisher display your hair,
While the fops envy, and the ladies stare!
Honor forbid! at whose unrivaled shrine   105
Ease, pleasure, virtue, all, our sex resign.
Methinks already I your tears survey,
Already hear the horrid things they say,
Already see you a degraded toast,
And all your honor in a whisper lost!   110
How shall I, then, your helpless fame defend?
'Twill then be infamy to seem your friend!
And shall this prize, the inestimable prize,
Exposed through crystal to the gazing eyes,
And heightened by the diamond's circling rays,   115
On that rapacious hand forever blaze?
Sooner shall grass in Hyde Park Circus grow,
And wits take lodgings in the sound of Bow;[8]
Sooner let earth, air, sea, to chaos fall,
Men, monkeys, lapdogs, parrots, perish all!"   120
    She said; then raging to Sir Plume repairs,
And bids her beau demand the precious hairs
(Sir Plume of amber snuffbox justly vain,
And the nice conduct of a clouded cane).
With earnest eyes, and round unthinking face,   125
He first the snuffbox opened, then the case,
And thus broke out—"My Lord, why, what the devil!
Z—ds! damn the lock! 'fore Gad, you must be civil!
Plague on't! 'tis past a jest—nay prithee, pox!
Give her the hair'—he spoke, and rapped his box.   130
    "It grieves me much," replied the Peer again,
"Who speaks so well should ever speak in vain.

---

6. The name is borrowed from a queen of the Amazons—hence, a fierce and warlike woman. Thalestris, according to legend, traveled thirty days in order to have a child by Alexander the Great. Plutarch denies the story.   7. The frame on which the elaborate coiffures of the day were arranged.   8. A person born within sound of the bells of St. Mary-le-Bow in Cheapside is said to be a cockney. No fashionable wit would have so vulgar an address.

But by this Lock, this sacred Lock I swear
Which never more shall join its parted hair;
Which never more its honors shall renew,   135
Clipped from the lovely head where late it grew),
That while my nostrils draw the vital air,
This hand, which won it, shall forever wear."
He spoke, and speaking, in proud triumph spread
The long-contended honors⁹ of her head.   140
    But Umbriel, hateful Gnome, forbears not so;
He breaks the vial whence the sorrows flow.
Then see! the nymph in beauteous grief appears,
Her eyes half languishing, half drowned in tears;
On her heaved bosom hung her drooping head,   145
Which with a sigh she raised, and thus she said:
    "Forever cursed be this detested day,
Which snatched my best, my favorite curl away!
Happy! ah, ten times happy had I been,
If Hampton Court these eyes had never seen!   150
Yet am not I the first mistaken maid,
By love of courts to numerous ills betrayed.
Oh, had I rather unadmired remained
In some lone isle, or distant northern land;
Where the gilt chariot never marks the way,   155
Where none learn ombre, none e'er taste bohea!¹
There kept my charms concealed from mortal eye,
Like roses that in deserts bloom and die.
What moved my mind with youthful lords to roam?
Oh, had I stayed, and said my prayers at home!   160
'Twas this the morning omens seemed to tell,
Thrice from my trembling hand the patch box² fell;
The tottering china shook without a wind,
Nay, Poll sat mute, and Shock was most unkind!
A Sylph too warned me of the threats of fate,   165
In mystic visions, now believed too late!
See the poor remnants of these slighted hairs!
My hands shall rend what e'en thy rapine spares.
These in two sable ringlets taught to break,
Once gave new beauties to the snowy neck;   170
The sister lock now sits uncouth, alone,
And in its fellow's fate foresees its own;
Uncurled it hangs, the fatal shears demands,
And tempts once more thy sacrilegious hands.
Oh, hadst thou, cruel! been content to seize   175
Hairs less in sight, or any hairs but these!"

CANTO V

She said: the pitying audience melt in tears.
But Fate and Jove had stopped the Baron's ears.
In vain Thalestris with reproach assails,

---

9. Ornaments—hence—locks; a Latinism.   1. A costly sort of tea.   2. A box to hold the ornamental
patches of court plaster worn on the face by both sexes. Cf. *Spectator* 81.

For who can move when fair Belinda fails?
Not half so fixed the Trojan[3] could remain,   5
While Anna begged and Dido raged in vain.
Then grave Clarissa graceful waved her fan;
Silence ensued, and thus the nymph began:
    "Say why are beauties praised and honored most,
The wise man's passion, and the vain man's toast?   10
Why decked with all that land and sea afford,
Why angels called, and angel-like adored?
Why round our coaches crowd the white-gloved beaux,
Why bows the side box from its inmost rows?
How vain are all these glories, all our pains,   15
Unless good sense preserve what beauty gains;
That men may say when we the front box grace,
'Behold the first in virtue as in face!'
Oh! if to dance all night, and dress all day,
Charmed the smallpox, or chased old age away,   20
Who would not scorn what housewife's cares produce,
Or who would learn one earthly thing of use?
To patch, nay ogle, might become a saint,
Nor could it sure be such a sin to paint.
But since, alas! frail beauty must decay,   25
Curled or uncurled, since locks will turn to gray;
Since painted, or not painted, all shall fade,
And she who scorns a man must die a maid;
What then remains but well our power to use,
And keep good humor still whate'er we lose?   30
And trust me, dear, good humor can prevail
When airs, and flights, and screams, and scolding fail.
Beauties in vain their pretty eyes may roll;
Charms strike the sight, but merit wins the soul."[4]
    So spoke the dame, but no applause ensued;   35
Belinda frowned, Thalestris called her prude.
"To arms, to arms!" the fierce virago cries,
And swift as lightning to the combat flies.
All side in parties, and begin the attack;
Fans clap, silks rustle, and tough whalebones crack;   40
Heroes' and heroines' shouts confusedly rise,
And bass and treble voices strike the skies.
No common weapons in their hands are found,
Like Gods they fight, nor dread a mortal wound.
    So when bold Homer makes the Gods engage,   45
And heavenly breasts with human passions rage;
'Gainst Pallas, Mars; Latona, Hermes arms;
And all Olympus rings with loud alarms:
Jove's thunder roars, heaven trembles all around,
Blue Neptune storms, the bellowing deeps resound: 50
Earth shakes her nodding towers, the ground gives way,

3. Aeneas, who forsook Dido at the bidding of the gods, despite her reproaches and the supplications of
her sister Anna. Virgil compares him to a steadfast oak that withstands a storm (*Aeneid* IV.437–43).
4. The speech is a close parody of Pope's own translation of the speech of Sarpedon to Glaucus, first
published in 1709 and slightly revised in his version of the *Iliad* (XII.371–96).

And the pale ghosts start at the flash of day!
   Triumphant Umbriel on a sconce's height
Clapped his glad wings, and sat to view the fight:
Propped on their bodkin spears, the sprites survey   55
The growing combat, or assist the fray.
   While through the press enraged Thalestris flies,
And scatters death around from both her eyes,
A beau and witling perished in the throng,
One died in metaphor, and one in song.   60
"O cruel nymph! a living death I bear,"
Cried Dapperwit, and sunk beside his chair.
A mournful glance Sir Fopling upwards cast,
"Those eyes are made so killing"—was his last.
Thus on Maeander's flowery margin lies   65
The expiring swan, and as he sings he dies.
   When bold Sir Plume had drawn Clarissa down,
Chloe stepped in, and killed him with a frown;
She smiled to see the doughty hero slain,
But, at her smile, the beau revived again.   70
Now Jove suspends his golden scales in air,
Weighs the men's wits against the lady's hair;
The doubtful beam long nods from side to side;
At length the wits mount up, the hairs subside.
   See, fierce Belinda on the Baron flies,   75
With more than usual lightning in her eyes;
Nor feared the chief the unequal fight to try,
Who sought no more than on his foe to die.
   But this bold lord with manly strength endued,
She with one finger and a thumb subdued: 80
Just where the breath of life his nostrils drew,
A charge of snuff the wily virgin threw;
The Gnomes direct, to every atom just,
The pungent grains of titillating dust.
Sudden, with starting tears each eye o'erflows,   85
And the high dome re-echoes to his nose.
   "Now meet thy fate," incensed Belinda cried,
And drew a deadly bodkin[5] from her side.
(The same, his ancient personage to deck,
Her great-great-grandsire wore about his neck,   90
In three seal rings; which after, melted down,
Formed a vast buckle for his widow's gown:
Her infant grandame's whistle next it grew,
The bells she jingled, and the whistle blew;
Then in a bodkin graced her mother's hairs,   95
Which long she wore, and now Belinda wears.)
   "Boast not my fall," he cried, "insulting foe!
Thou by some other shalt be laid as low.
Nor think to die dejects my lofty mind:
All that I dread is leaving you behind!   100
Rather than so, ah, let me still survive,

5. An ornamental pin shaped like a dagger, to be worn in the hair.

And burn in Cupid's flames—but burn alive."
   "Restore the Lock!" she cries; and all around
"Restore the Lock!" the vaulted roofs rebound.
Not fierce Othello in so loud a strain
Roared for the handkerchief that caused his pain.[6]   105
But see how oft ambitious aims are crossed,
And chiefs contend till all the prize is lost!
The lock, obtained with guilt, and kept with pain,
In every place is sought, but sought in vain: 110
With such a prize no mortal must be blessed,
So Heaven decrees! with Heaven who can contest?
   Some thought it mounted to the lunar sphere,
Since all things lost on earth are treasured there.
There heroes' wits are kept in ponderous vases,   115
And beaux' in snuffboxes and tweezer cases.
There broken vows and deathbed alms are found,
And lovers' hearts with ends of riband bound,
The courtier's promises, and sick man's prayers,
The smiles of harlots, and the tears of heirs,   120
Cages for gnats, and chains to yoke a flea,
Dried butterflies, and tomes of casuistry.
   But trust the Muse—she saw it upward rise,
Though marked by none but quick, poetic eyes
(So Rome's great founder[7] to the heavens withdrew,   125
To Proculus alone confessed in view);
A sudden star, it shot through liquid air,
And drew behind a radiant trail of hair.
Not Berenice's[8] locks first rose so bright,
The heavens bespangling with disheveled light.   130
The Sylphs behold it kindling as it flies,
And pleased pursue its progress through the skies.
   This the beau monde shall from the Mall[9] survey,
And hail with music its propitious ray.
This the blest lover shall for Venus take,   135
And send up vows from Rosamonda's Lake.[1]
This Partridge soon shall view in cloudless skies,
When next he looks through Galileo's eyes;[2]
And hence the egregious wizard shall foredoom
The fate of Louis, and the fall of Rome.   140
   Then cease, bright nymph! to mourn thy ravished hair,
Which adds new glory to the shining sphere!
Not all the tresses that fair head can boast,
Shall draw such envy as the Lock you lost.
For, after all the murders of your eye,   145
When, after millions slain, yourself shall die:
When those fair suns shall set, as set they must,
And all those tresses shall be laid in dust,

---

6. *Othello* III.4.   7. Romulus, the "founder" and first king of Rome, was snatched to heaven in a storm cloud while reviewing his army in the Campus Martius (Livy I.16).   8. Berenice, the wife of Ptolemy III, dedicated a lock of her hair to the gods to ensure her husband's safe return from war. It was turned into a constellation.   9. A walk laid out by Charles II in St. James's Park, a resort for strollers of all sorts. 1. In St. James's Park; associated with unhappy lovers.   2. A telescope. John Partridge was an astrologer whose annually published predictions had been amusingly satirized by Swift and other wits in 1708.

This Lock the Muse shall consecrate to fame,
And 'midst the stars inscribe Belinda's name.   150

An Essay on Man

To Henry St. John, Lord Bolingbroke

EPISTLE I

ARGUMENT OF THE NATURE AND STATE OF MAN, WITH RESPECT TO THE UNI-
VERSE. Of man in the abstract—I. That we can judge only with regard to our
own system, being ignorant of the relations of systems and things, ver. 17,
&c.—II. That man is not to be deemed imperfect, but a being suited to his
place and rank in the creation, agreeable to the general order of things, and
conformable to ends and relations to him unknown, ver. 35, &c.—III. That
it is partly upon his ignorance of future events, and partly upon the hope of
a future state, that all his happiness in the present depends, ver. 77, &c.—
IV. The pride of aiming at more knowledge, and pretending to more perfection, the cause of man's error and misery. The impiety of putting himself in
the place of God, and judging of the fitness or unfitness, perfection or imperfection, justice or injustice of his dispensations, ver. 113, &c.—V. The absurdity of conceiting himself the final cause of the creation, or expecting that
perfection in the moral world which is not in the natural, ver. 131, &c.—VI.
The unreasonableness of his complaints against Providence, while on the
one hand he demands the perfections of the angels, and on the other the
bodily qualifications of the brutes; though, to possess any of the sensitive
faculties in a higher degree, would render him miserable, ver. 173, &c.—
VII. That throughout the whole visible world, an universal order and gradation in the sensual and mental faculties is observed, which causes a
subordination of creature to creature, and of all creatures to man. The gradations of sense, instinct, thought, reflection, reason: that reason alone
countervails all the other faculties, ver. 207.—VIII. How much further this
order and subordination of living creatures may extend, above and below us;
were any part of which broken, not that part only, but the whole connected
creation must be destroyed, ver. 233—IX. The extravagance, madness, and
pride of such a desire, ver. 259.—X. The consequence of all, the absolute
submission due to Providence, both as to our present and future state, ver.
281, &c., to the end.

Awake, my St. John![1] leave all meaner things
To low ambition, and the pride of Kings.
Let us (since Life can little more supply
Than just to look about us and to die)
Expatiate free o'er all this scene of Man;   5
A mighty maze! but not without a plan;

---

1. Henry St. John, Viscount Bolingbroke, Pope's friend, who had thus far neglected to keep his part of
their friendly bargain: Pope was to write his philosophical speculations in verse; Bolingbroke was to write
his in prose.

A Wild, where weeds and flowers promiscuous shoot;
Or Garden, tempting with forbidden fruit.
Together let us beat this ample field,
Try what the open, what the covert yield; 10
The latent tracts, the giddy heights, explore
Of all who blindly creep, or sightless soar;
Eye Nature's walks, shoot Folly as it flies,
And catch the Manners living as they rise;
Laugh where we must, be candid where we can; 15
But vindicate the ways of God to man.²

    I. Say first, of God above, or Man below,
What can we reason, but from what we know?
Of Man, what see we but his station here,
From which to reason, or to which refer? 20
Through worlds unnumbered though the God be known,
'Tis ours to trace him only in our own.
He, who through vast immensity can pierce,
See worlds on worlds compose one universe,
Observe how system into system runs, 25
What other planets circle other suns,
What varied Being peoples every star,
May tell why Heaven has made us as we are.
But of this frame the bearings, and the ties,
The strong connections, nice dependencies, 30
Gradations just, has thy pervading soul
Looked through? or can a part contain the whole?
    Is the great chain,³ that draws all to agree,
And drawn supports, upheld by God, or thee?

    II. Presumptuous Man! the reason wouldst thou find, 35
Why formed so weak, so little, and so blind?
First, if thou canst, the harder reason guess,
Why formed no weaker, blinder, and no less?
Ask of thy mother earth, why oaks are made
Taller or stronger than the weeds they shade? 40
Or ask of yonder argent fields above,
Why Jove's satellites⁴ are less than Jove?
    Of Systems possible, if 'tis confest.
That Wisdom infinite must form the best,
Where all must full⁵ or not coherent be, 45
And all that rises, rise in due degree;
Then, in the scale of reasoning life, 'tis plain,
There must be, somewhere, such a rank as Man:
And all the question (wrangle e'er so long)
Is only this, if God has placed him wrong? 50
    Respecting Man, whatever wrong we call,

2. Cf. Milton's *Paradise Lost* I.26. Pope's theme is essentially the same as Milton's, and even the opening image of the garden reminds one of the earlier poet's Paradise. 3. A reference to the popular 18th-century notion of the Great Chain of Being, in which elements of the universe took their places in a hierarchy ranging from the lowest matter to God. 4. Here pronounced *satéllites*. 5. According to the principle of plenitude, there can be no gaps in the Chain.

May, must be right, as relative to all.
In human works, though laboured on with pain,
A thousand movements scarce one purpose gain;
In God's, one single can its end produce;   55
Yet serves to second too some other use.
So Man, who here seems principal alone,
Perhaps acts second to some sphere unknown,
Touches some wheel, or verges to some goal;
'Tis but a part we see, and not a whole.   60
    When the proud steed shall know why Man restrains
His fiery course, or drives him o'er the plains;
When the dull Ox, why now he breaks the clod,
Is now a victim, and now Egypt's God:
Then shall Man's pride and dullness comprehend   65
His actions', passions', being's use and end;
Why doing, suffering, checked, impelled; and why
This hour a slave, the next a deity.
    Then say not Man's imperfect, Heaven in fault;
Say rather, Man's as perfect as he ought: 70
His knowledge measured to his state and place;
His time a moment, and a point his space.
If to be perfect in a certain sphere,
What matter, soon or late, or here or there?
The blest to-day is as completely so,   75
As who began a thousand years ago.

    III. Heaven from all creatures hides the book of Fate,
All but the page prescribed, their present state:
From brutes what men, from men what spirits know:
Or who could suffer Being here below?   80
The lamb thy riot dooms to bleed to-day,
Had he thy Reason, would he skip and play?
Pleased to the last, he crops the flowery food,
And licks the hand just raised to shed his blood.
Oh blindness to the future! kindly given,   85
That each may fill the circle marked by Heaven:
Who sees with equal eye, as God of all,
A hero perish, or a sparrow fall,
Atoms or systems into ruin hurled,
And now a bubble burst, and now a world.   90
    Hope humbly then; with trembling pinions soar;
Wait the great teacher Death; and God adore.
What future bliss, he gives not thee to know,
But gives that Hope to be thy blessing now.
Hope springs eternal in the human breast: 95
Man never Is, but always To be blest:
The soul, uneasy and confined from home,
Rests and expatiates in a life to come.
    Lo, the poor Indian! whose untutored mind
Sees God in clouds, or hears him in the wind;   100
His soul, proud Science never taught to stray
Far as the solar walk, or milky way;

Yet simple Nature to his hope has given,
Behind the cloud-topt hill, an humbler heaven;
Some safer world in depth of woods embraced, 105
Some happier island in the watery waste,
Where slaves once more their native land behold,
No fiends torment, no Christians thirst for gold.
To Be, contents his natural desire,
He asks no Angel's wing, no Seraph's fire; 110
But thinks, admitted to that equal sky,
His faithful dog shall bear him company.

IV. Go, wiser thou! and, in thy scale of sense,
Weigh thy Opinion against Providence;
Call imperfection what thou fanciest such, 115
Say, here he gives too little, there too much:
Destroy all Creatures for thy sport or gust,
Yet cry, If Man's unhappy, God's unjust;
If Man alone engross not Heaven's high care,
Alone made perfect here, immortal there: 120
Snatch from his hand the balance and the rod,
Re-judge his justice, be the GOD OF GOD.
In Pride, in reasoning Pride, our error lies;
All quit their sphere, and rush into the skies.
Pride still is aiming at the blest abodes, 125
Men would be Angels, Angels would be Gods.
Aspiring to be Gods, if Angels fell,
Aspiring to be Angels, Men rebel:
And who but wishes to invert the laws
Of ORDER, sins against the Eternal Cause. 130

V. Ask for what end the heavenly bodies shine,
Earth for whose use? Pride answers, " 'Tis for mine:
For me kind Nature wakes her genial Power,
Suckles each herb, and spreads out ev'ry flower;
Annual for me, the grape, the rose, renew, 135
The juice nectareous, and the balmy dew;
For me, the mine a thousand treasures brings;
For me, health gushes from a thousand springs;
Seas roll to waft me, suns to light me rise;
My footstool earth, my canopy the skies." 140
But errs not Nature from this gracious end,
From burning suns when livid deaths descend,
When earthquakes swallow, or when tempests sweep
Towns to one grave, whole nations to the deep?
"No," 'tis replied, "the first Almighty Cause 145
Acts not by partial, but by general laws;
The exceptions few; some change since all began:
And what created perfect?"—Why then Man?
If the great end be human happiness,
Then Nature deviates; and can man do less? 150
As much that end a constant course requires
Of showers and sunshine, as of man's desires;

As much eternal springs and cloudless skies,
As Men forever temperate, calm, and wise.
If plagues or earthquakes break not Heaven's design,   155
Why then a Borgia, or a Catiline?[6]
Who knows but He whose hand the lightning forms,
Who heaves old Ocean, and who wings the storms;
Pours fierce Ambition in a Caesar's mind,
Or turns young Ammon[7] loose to scourge mankind?   160
From pride, from pride, our very reasoning springs;
Account for moral, as for natural things:
Why charge we Heaven in those, in these acquit?
In both, to reason right is to submit.

    Better for Us, perhaps, it might appear,   165
Where there all harmony, all virtue here;
That never air or ocean felt the wind;
That never passion discomposed the mind.
But ALL subsists by elemental strife;
And Passions are the elements of Life.   170
The general ORDER, since the whole began,
Is kept in Nature, and is kept in Man.

    VI. What would this Man? Now upward will he soar,
And little less than Angel, would be more;
Now looking downwards, just as grieved appears   175
To want the strength of bulls, the fur of bears.
Made for his use all creatures if he call,
Say what their use, had he the powers of all?
Nature to these, without profusion, kind,
The proper organs, proper powers assigned;   180
Each seeming want compénsated of course,
Here with degrees of swiftness, there of force;
All in exact proportion to the state;
Nothing to add, and nothing to abate.
Each beast, each insect, happy in its own: 185
Is Heaven unkind to Man, and Man alone?
Shall he alone, whom rational we call,
Be pleased with nothing, if not blessed with all?
    The bliss of Man (could Pride that blessing find)
Is not to act or think beyond mankind;   190
No powers of body or of soul to share,
But what his nature and his state can bear.
Why has not Man a microscopic eye?
For this plain reason, Man is not a Fly.
Say what the use, were finer optics[8] given,   195
T' inspect a mite, not comprehend the heaven?
Or touch, if tremblingly alive all o'er,
To smart and agonize at every pore?
Or quick effluvia[9] darting through the brain,
Die of a rose in aromatic pain?   200
If nature thundered in his opening ears,

---

6. Roman who conspired against the state in 63 B.C.E. Cesare Borgia (1476–1507), an Italian prince notorious for his crimes.   7. Alexander the Great, who when he visited the oracle of Zeus Ammon in Egypt was hailed by the priest there as son of the god.   8. Eyes.   9. Stream of minute particles.

And stunned him with the music of the spheres,[1]
How would he wish that Heaven had left him still
The whispering Zephyr, and the purling rill?
Who finds not Providence all good and wise,   205
Alike in what it gives, and what denies?

   VII. Far as Creation's ample range extends,
The scale of sensual, mental powers ascends:
Mark how it mounts, to Man's imperial race,
From the green myriads in the peopled grass: 210
What modes of sight betwixt each wide extreme,
The mole's dim curtain, and the lynx's[2] beam:
Of smell, the headlong lioness between,
And hound sagacious[3] on the tainted green:
Of hearing, from the life that fills the Flood,   215
To that which warbles through the vernal wood:
The spider's touch, how exquisitely fine!
Feels at each thread, and lives along the line:
In the nice bee, what sense so subtly true
From poisonous herbs extracts the healing dew?   220
How Instinct varies in the grovelling swine,
Compared, half-reasoning elephant, with thine!
'Twixt that, and Reason, what a nice barriér,
For ever separate, yet for ever near!
Remembrance and Reflection how allied;   225
What thin partitions Sense from Thought divide:
And Middle natures,[4] how they long to join,
Yet never pass the insuperable line!
Without this just gradation, could they be
Subjected, these to those, or all to thee?   230
The powers of all subdued by thee alone,
Is not thy Reason all these powers in one?

   VIII. See, through this air, this ocean, and this earth,
All matter quick, and bursting into birth.
Above, how high, progressive life may go!   235
Around, how wide! how deep extend below!
Vast chain of Being! which from God began,
Natures ethereal, human, angel, man,
Beast, bird, fish, insect, what no eye can see,
No glass can reach; from Infinite to thee,   240
From thee to Nothing.—On superior powers
Were we to press, inferior might on ours:
Or in the full creation leave a void,
Where, one step broken, the great scale's destroyed:
From Nature's chain whatever link you strike,   245
Tenth or ten thousandth, breaks the chain alike.
   And, if each system in gradation roll

---

1. The old notion that the movement of the planets created a "higher" music.   2. According to legend, one of the keenest sighted animals. *Dim curtain*: the mole's poor vision.   3. Here, exceptionally quick of scent.   4. Animals that seem to share the characteristics of several different classes—e.g., the duck-billed platypus.

Alike essential to the amazing Whole,
The least confusion but in one, not all
That system only, but the Whole must fall.   250
Let Earth unbalanced from her orbit fly,
Planets and Suns run lawless through the sky;
Let ruling angels from their spheres be hurled,
Being on Being wrecked, and world on world;
Heaven's whole foundations to their center nod,   255
And Nature tremble to the throne of God.
All this dread ORDER break—for whom? for thee?
Vile worm!—oh Madness! Pride! Impiety!

    IX. What if the foot, ordained the dust to tread,
Or hand, to toil, aspired to be the head?   260
What if the head, the eye, or ear repined
To serve mere engines to the ruling Mind?
Just as absurd for any part to claim
To be another, in this general frame:
Just as absurd, to mourn the tasks or pains,   265
The great directing MIND OF ALL ordains.
    All are but parts of one stupendous whole,
Whose body Nature is, and God the soul;
That, changed through all, and yet in all the same;
Great in the earth, as in the ethereal frame;   270
Warms in the sun, refreshes in the breeze,
Glows in the stars, and blossoms in the trees,
Lives through all life, extends through all extent,
Spreads undivided, operates unspent;
Breathes in our soul, informs our mortal part,   275
As full, as perfect, in a hair as heart;
As full, as perfect, in vile Man that mourns,
As the rapt Seraph that adores and burns:
To him no high, no low, no great, no small;
He fills, he bounds, connects, and equals all.   280

    X. Cease then, nor ORDER imperfection name:
Our proper bliss depends on what we blame.
Know thy own point: this kind, this due degree
Of blindness, weakness, Heaven bestows on thee.
Submit.—In this, or any other sphere,   285
Secure to be as blest as thou canst bear:
Safe in the hand of one disposing Power,
Or in the natal, or the mortal hour.
All Nature is but Art, unknown to thee;
All Chance, Direction, which thou canst not see;   290
All Discord, Harmony not understood;
All partial Evil, universal Good:
And, spite of Pride, in erring Reason's spite,
One truth is clear, WHATEVER IS, IS RIGHT.[5]

---

5. Epistle II deals with "the Nature and State of Man with respect to himself, as an Individual"; Epistle
III examines "the Nature and State of Man with respect to Society"; and the last epistle concerns "the
Nature and State of Man with Respect to Happiness."

FRANÇOIS-MARIE AROUET DE VOLTAIRE
1694–1778

Voltaire's *Candide* (1759) brings to near perfection the art of black comedy. It subjects its characters to an accumulation of horrors so bizarre that they provoke a bewildered response of laughter as self-protection even while they demand that the reader pay attention to the serious implications of such extravagance.

Voltaire had prepared himself to write such a work by varied experience—including that of political imprisonment. He was born François-Marie Arouet, son of a minor treasury official in Paris. After attending a Jesuit school, he studied law, which, however, he soon abandoned. In his early twenties (1717–18), he spent eleven months in the Bastille for writing satiric verses about the aristocracy. His incarceration did not dissuade him from a literary career; by 1718 he was using the name *Voltaire* and beginning to acquire a literary and social reputation—as well as some wealth (his speculations in the Compagnie des Indes made him rich by 1726). Money, however, did not protect him from spending more time in the Bastille during that year; after his release, he passed three years in exile, mainly in England. From 1734 to 1749, he studied widely, living with Madame du Châtelet on her estate at Cirey. For the next three years he stayed with Frederick the Great of Prussia at his Potsdam court; after that arrangement collapsed, Voltaire bought property in Switzerland and in adjacent France, settling first at his own château, Les Délices, outside Geneva, and later at nearby Ferney, in France. His international reputation as writer and social critic steadily increased; in the year of his death, he returned triumphantly to Paris.

Like his English contemporary Samuel Johnson, Voltaire wrote in many important genres: tragedy, epic, history, philosophy, fiction. His *Philosophical Dictionary* (1764), with its witty and penetrating definitions, typifies his range and acumen and his participation in his period's effort to take control of experience by intellect. While still a young man, Voltaire wrote a *History of Charles XII* of Sweden (1731), a work unusual for its time in its novelistic technique and its assumption that "history" includes the personal lives of powerful individuals and has nothing to do with divine intervention. Before *Candide*, he had published another philosophic tale, *Zadig* (1748), following the pattern of Oriental narrative. Like Candide, Zadig goes through an experiential education; it teaches him inconclusive lessons about life's unforeseeable contingencies.

Candide mocks both the artificial order of fiction (through its ludicrously multiplied recognition scenes and its symmetrical division of the protagonist's travels into three equal parts) and what Voltaire suggests is the equally artificial order posited by philosophic optimists. The view of the universe suggested by Pope's *Essay on Man,* for instance, insists on the rationality of a pattern ungraspable by human reason. *Candide* implicitly argues, however, that it does so only by attending to the abstract and undemonstrable, and ignoring the omnipresent pain of immediate experience. Gottfried Wilhelm Leibniz, the German philosopher, provides Voltaire's most specific target in *Candide,* with the complexities of his version of optimism reduced for satiric purposes to the facile formula "Everything is for the best in this best of all possible worlds." The formulation is, of course, unfair to Leibniz, whose philosophic optimism, like Pope's, implies belief in an unknowable universal order—roughly equivalent to Christian Providence—but no lack of awareness about the actual misery and depravity that human beings experience.

The exuberance and extravagance of Voltaire's imagination force us to laugh at what we may feel embarrassed to laugh at: the plight of the woman whose buttock has been cut off to make rump steak for her hungry companions; the weeping of two girls whose monkey lovers have been killed; the situation of six exiled, poverty-stricken kings. Like Swift, Voltaire keeps his readers off balance. Raped, cut to pieces, hanged, stabbed in the belly, the central characters of *Candide* keep coming back to life at opportune moments, as though no disaster could have permanent or ultimately destructive effects. Such reassuring fantasy suggests that we don't need to worry; it is all a joke, an outpouring of fertile fancy designed to ridicule an outmoded philosophical system with no particular relevance to us. On the other hand, historical reality keeps intruding. Those six hungry kings are real figures, actually dispossessed. Candide sees Admiral Byng executed—an admiral who really lived and really died by firing squad for not engaging an enemy with sufficient ferocity. The Lisbon earthquake actually occurred—30,000 to 40,000 people lost their lives in it. The extravagances of reality equal those of the storyteller; Voltaire demands that the reader imaginatively confront and somehow come to terms with horrors that surround us still.

The real problem, *Candide* suggests, is not natural or human disaster as much as human complacency. When Candide sees Admiral Byng shot, he comments on the injustice of the execution. "That's perfectly true, came the answer; but in this country it is useful from time to time to kill one admiral in order to encourage the others." Early in the nineteenth century, William Wordsworth wrote, "Much it grieved my heart to think / What man has made of man." His tone and perspective differ dramatically from Voltaire's, but his point is the same: human beings use their faculties to increase corruption. Failure to take seriously any human death is a form of moral corruption; failure to acknowledge the intolerability of war, in all its concrete detail of rape and butchery, epitomizes such corruption at its worst.

In a late chapter of *Candide,* the central character, less naïve than he once was, inquires about whether people have always massacred one another. Have they, he asks, "always been liars, traitors, ingrates, thieves, weaklings, sneaks, cowards, backbiters, gluttons, drunkards, misers, climbers, killers, calumniators, sensualists, fanatics, hypocrites, and fools?" His interlocutor, Martin, responds that, just as hawks have always devoured pigeons, human beings have always manifested the same vices. This ironic variation on the period's conviction of the universality and continuity of human nature epitomizes Voltaire's sense of outrage, which in some respects parallels Swift's in the fourth part of *Gulliver's Travels*. Swift demonstrates the implications of "reason" considered as an ideal and shows its irrelevance to actual human behavior; Voltaire shows how the claim of a rational universal order avoids the hard problems of living in a world where human beings have become liars, traitors, and so on. His Swiftian catalog of vice and folly expresses the moral insufficiency and perversity of humankind. Martin's cynical assumption that people are naturally corrupt, as hawks naturally eat smaller birds, constitutes another form of avoidance. The assumed inevitability of vice, like belief that all is for the best, justifies passivity. Nothing *can* be done, nothing *should* be done, or nothing *matters* (the view of Lord Pococurante, another figure Candide encounters). So the characters of this fiction, including Candide himself, mainly pursue self-gratification. Even this course they do not follow judiciously: when Candide and Cacambo find themselves in the earthly paradise of Eldorado, "the two happy men resolved to be so no longer," driven by fantasies of improving their condition. Yet, unlike Gulliver, they acquire wisdom at last, learning to withstand "three great evils, boredom, vice, and poverty," by working hard at what comes to hand and avoiding futile theorizing about the nature of the universe.

Although Voltaire's picture of the human condition reveals the same indignation that marks Swift's, he allows at least conditional hope for moderate satisfaction in this life. Candide's beloved Cunégonde loses all her beauty, but she becomes an accomplished pastry cook; Candide possesses a garden he can cultivate. Greed, malice, and lust do not comprise the total possibility for humankind. If Voltaire's tone sometimes expresses outrage, at other times it verges on the playful. When, for example, he mocks the improbabilities of romance by his characters' miraculous resuscitations or parodies the restrictions of classical form by sending Candide and his friends on an epic journey, one can feel his amused awareness of our human need to make order and our human desire to comfort ourselves by fictions. But as he insists that much of the order we claim to perceive itself comprises a comforting fiction, as he uses satire's fierce energies to challenge our complacencies, he reveals once more the underside of the Enlightenment ideal of reason. That we human beings have reason, Voltaire tells us, is no ground on which to flatter ourselves; rightly used, it exposes our insufficiencies.

PRONOUNCING GLOSSARY

The following list uses common English syllables and stress accents to provide rough equivalents of selected words whose pronunciation may be unfamiliar to the general reader.

Abare: *a-bahr'*   Pangloss: *pan-glaws'*

Cacambo: *ka-kahm'-bo*   Paquette: *pah-ket'*

Candide: *kahn-deed'*   Pococurante: *poh-koh-ku-rahnt'*

Cunégonde: *kew-nay-gohnd'*   Thunder-Ten-Tronckh: *tun-dayr'–ten–trawnk*

Giroflée: *zhee-roh-flay'*

Issachar: *ee-sah-shahr'*

Candide, or Optimism[1]

translated from the German of Doctor Ralph with the additions which were found in the Doctor's pocket when he died at Minden in the Year of Our Lord 1759

CHAPTER 1

How Candide Was Brought up in a Fine Castle and How He Was Driven Therefrom

There lived in Westphalia,[2] in the castle of the Baron of Thunder-Ten-Tronckh, a young man on whom nature had bestowed the perfection of gentle manners. His features admirably expressed his soul; he combined an honest mind with great simplicity of heart; and I think it was for this reason that they called him Candide. The old servants of the house suspected that he was the son of the Baron's sister by a respectable, honest gentleman of the neighborhood, whom she had refused to marry because he could prove only seventy-one quarterings,[3] the rest of his family tree having been lost in the passage of time.

The Baron was one of the most mighty lords of Westphalia, for his castle had a door and windows. His great hall was even hung with a tapestry. The dogs of his courtyard made up a hunting pack on occasion, with the stable-

[handwritten marginal notes: "He is a good character" and "He is suspected to be illegitimate"]

---

1. Translated and with notes by Robert M. Adams.   2. A province of western Germany, near Holland and the lower Rhineland. Flat, boggy, and drab, it is noted chiefly for its excellent ham. In a letter to his niece, written during his German expedition of 1750, Voltaire described the "vast, sad, sterile, detestable countryside of Westphalia."   3. Genealogical divisions of one's family tree. Seventy-one of them is a grotesque number to have, representing over 2,000 years of uninterrupted nobility.

boys as huntsmen; the village priest was his grand almoner. They all called him "My Lord," and laughed at his stories.

The Baroness, who weighed in the neighborhood of three hundred and fifty pounds, was greatly respected for that reason, and did the honors of the house with a dignity which rendered her even more imposing. Her daughter Cunégonde,[4] aged seventeen, was a ruddy-cheeked girl, fresh, plump, and desirable. The Baron's son seemed in every way worthy of his father. The tutor Pangloss was the oracle of the household, and little Candide listened to his lectures with all the good faith of his age and character.

Pangloss gave instruction in metaphysico-theologico-cosmoloonigology.[5] He proved admirably that there cannot possibly be an effect without a cause and that in this best of all possible worlds the Baron's castle was the best of all castles and his wife the best of all possible Baronesses.

—It is clear, said he, that things cannot be otherwise than they are, for since everything is made to serve an end, everything necessarily serves the best end. Observe: noses were made to support spectacles, hence we have spectacles. Legs, as anyone can plainly see, were made to be breeched, and so we have breeches. Stones were made to be shaped and to build castles with; thus My Lord has a fine castle, for the greatest Baron in the province should have the finest house; and since pigs were made to be eaten, we eat pork all year round.[6] Consequently, those who say everything is well are uttering mere stupidities; they should say everything is for the best.

Candide listened attentively and believed implicitly; for he found Miss Cunégonde exceedingly pretty, though he never had the courage to tell her so. He decided that after the happiness of being born Baron of Thunder-Ten-Tronckh, the second order of happiness was to be Miss Cunégonde; the third was seeing her every day, and the fourth was listening to Master Pangloss, the greatest philosopher in the province and consequently in the entire world.

One day, while Cunégonde was walking near the castle in the little woods that they called a park, she saw Dr. Pangloss in the underbrush; he was giving a lesson in experimental physics to her mother's maid, a very attractive and obedient brunette. As Miss Cunégonde had a natural bent for the sciences, she watched breathlessly the repeated experiments which were going on; she saw clearly the doctor's sufficient reason, observed both cause and effect, and returned to the house in a distracted and pensive frame of mind, yearning for knowledge and dreaming that she might be the sufficient reason of young Candide—who might also be hers.

As she was returning to the castle, she met Candide, and blushed; Candide blushed too. She greeted him in a faltering tone of voice; and Candide talked to her without knowing what he was saying. Next day, as everyone was rising from the dinner table, Cunégonde and Candide found themselves behind a screen; Cunégonde dropped her handkerchief, Candide picked it up; she

---

4. Cunégonde gets her odd name from Kunigunda (wife to Emperor Henry II), who walked barefoot and blindfolded on red-hot irons to prove her chastity; Pangloss gets his name from Greek words meaning all-tongue.   5. The "looney" buried in this burlesque word corresponds to a buried *nigaud*—"booby" in the French. Christian Wolff, disciple of Leibniz, invented and popularized the word "cosmology." The catch phrases in the following sentence, echoed by popularizers of Leibniz, make reference to the determinism of his system, its linking of cause with effect, and its optimism.   6. The argument from design supposes that everything in this world exists for a specific reason; Voltaire objects not to the argument as a whole, but to the abuse of it.

held his hand quite innocently, he kissed her hand quite innocently with remarkable vivacity and emotion; their lips met, their eyes lit up, their knees trembled, their hands wandered. The Baron of Thunder-Ten-Tronckh passed by the screen and, taking note of this cause and this effect, drove Candide out of the castle by kicking him vigorously on the backside. Cunégonde fainted; as soon as she recovered, the Baroness slapped her face; and everything was confusion in the most beautiful and agreeable of all possible castles.

CHAPTER 2

What Happened to Candide Among the Bulgars[7]

Candide, ejected from the earthly paradise, wandered for a long time without knowing where he was going, weeping, raising his eyes to heaven, and gazing back frequently on the most beautiful of castles which contained the most beautiful of Baron's daughters. He slept without eating, in a furrow of a plowed field, while the snow drifted over him; next morning, numb with cold, he dragged himself into the neighboring village, which was called Waldberghoff-trarbk-dikdorff; he was penniless, famished, and exhausted. At the door of a tavern he paused forlornly. Two men dressed in blue[8] took note of him:

—Look, chum, said one of them, there's a likely young fellow of just about the right size.

They approached Candide and invited him very politely to dine with them.

—Gentlemen, Candide replied with charming modesty, I'm honored by your invitation, but I really don't have enough money to pay my share.

—My dear sir, said one of the blues, people of your appearance and your merit don't have to pay; aren't you five feet five inches tall?

—Yes, gentlemen, that is indeed my stature, said he, making a bow.

—Then, sir, you must be seated at once; not only will we pay your bill this time, we will never allow a man like you to be short of money; for men were made only to render one another mutual aid.

—You are quite right, said Candide; it is just as Dr. Pangloss always told me, and I see clearly that everything is for the best.

They beg him to accept a couple of crowns, he takes them, and offers an I.O.U.; they won't hear of it, and all sit down at table together.

—Don't you love dearly . . . ?

—I do indeed, says he, I dearly love Miss Cunégonde.

—No, no, says one of the gentlemen, we are asking if you don't love dearly the King of the Bulgars.

—Not in the least, says he, I never laid eyes on him.

—What's that you say? He's the most charming of kings, and we must drink his health.

—Oh, gladly, gentlemen; and he drinks.

—That will do, they tell him; you are now the bulwark, the support, the

---

7. Voltaire chose this name to represent the Prussian troops of Frederick the Great because he wanted to make an insinuation of pederasty against both the soldiers and their master. Cf. French *bougre*, English "bugger." 8. The recruiting officers of Frederick the Great, much feared in 18th-century Europe, wore blue uniforms. Frederick had a passion for sorting out his soldiers by size; several of his regiments would accept only six-footers.

defender, the hero of the Bulgars; your fortune is made and your future assured.

Promptly they slip irons on his legs and lead him to the regiment. There they cause him to right face, left face, present arms, order arms, aim, fire, doubletime, and they give him thirty strokes of the rod. Next day he does the drill a little less awkwardly and gets only twenty strokes; the third day, they give him only ten, and he is regarded by his comrades as a prodigy.

Candide, quite thunderstruck, did not yet understand very clearly how he was a hero. One fine spring morning he took it into his head to go for a walk, stepping straight out as if it were a privilege of the human race, as of animals in general, to use his legs as he chose.[9] He had scarcely covered two leagues when four other heroes, each six feet tall, overtook him, bound him, and threw him into a dungeon. At the court-martial they asked which he preferred, to be flogged thirty-six times by the entire regiment or to receive summarily a dozen bullets in the brain. In vain did he argue that the human will is free and insist that he preferred neither alternative; he had to choose; by virtue of the divine gift called "liberty" he decided to run the gauntlet thirty-six times, and actually endured two floggings. The regiment was composed of two thousand men. That made four thousand strokes, which laid open every muscle and nerve from his nape to his butt. As they were preparing for the third beating, Candide, who could endure no more, begged as a special favor that they would have the goodness to smash his head. His plea was granted; they bandaged his eyes and made him kneel down. The King of the Bulgars, passing by at this moment, was told of the culprit's crime; and as this king had a rare genius, he understood, from everything they told him of Candide, that this was a young metaphysician, extremely ignorant of the ways of the world, so he granted his royal pardon, with a generosity which will be praised in every newspaper in every age. A worthy surgeon cured Candide in three weeks with the ointments described by Dioscorides.[1] He already had a bit of skin back and was able to walk when the King of the Bulgars went to war with the King of the Abares.[2]

CHAPTER 3

How Candide Escaped from the Bulgars, and What Became of Him

Nothing could have been so fine, so brisk, so brilliant, so well-drilled as the two armies. The trumpets, the fifes, the oboes, the drums, and the cannon produced such a harmony as was never heard in hell. First the cannons battered down about six thousand men on each side; then volleys of musket fire removed from the best of worlds about nine or ten thousand rascals who

9. This episode was suggested by the experience of the Frenchman Courtilz, who had deserted from the Prussian army and been bastinadoed for it. Voltaire intervened with Frederick to gain his release. But it also reflects the story about Wolff, Leibniz's disciple, who got into trouble with Frederick's father when someone reported that his doctrine denying free will had encouraged several soldiers to desert. "The argument of the grenadier," who was said to have pleaded preestablished harmony to justify his desertion, so infuriated the king that he had Wolff expelled from the country.   1. Dioscorides' treatise on *materia medica* ("medical matters"), dating from the 1st century C.E., was not the most up to date.   2. A tribe of semicivilized Scythians, who might be supposed at war with the Bulgars; allegorically, the Abares are the French, who opposed the Prussians in the Seven Years' War (1756–63). According to the title page of 1761, "Doctor Ralph," the dummy author of *Candide*, himself perished at the battle of Minden (Westphalia) in 1759.

were cluttering up its surface. The bayonet was a sufficient reason for the demise of several thousand others. Total casualties might well amount to thirty thousand men or so. Candide, who was trembling like a philosopher, hid himself as best he could while this heroic butchery was going on. ⟶ *He takes no part in the butchery*

Finally, while the two kings in their respective camps celebrated the victory by having *Te Deums* sung, Candide undertook to do his reasoning of cause and effect somewhere else. Passing by mounds of the dead and dying, he came to a nearby village which had been burnt to the ground. It was an Abare village, which the Bulgars had burned, in strict accordance with the laws of war. Here old men, stunned from beatings, watched the last agonies of their butchered wives, who still clutched their infants to their bleeding breasts; there, disemboweled girls, who had first satisfied the natural needs of various heroes, breathed their last; others, half-scorched in the flames, begged for their death stroke. Scattered brains and severed limbs littered the ground. *The carnage is terrible*

Candide fled as fast as he could to another village; this one belonged to the Bulgars, and the heroes of the Abare cause had given it the same treatment. Climbing over ruins and stumbling over corpses, Candide finally made his way out of the war area, carrying a little food in his knapsack and never ceasing to dream of Miss Cunégonde. His supplies gave out when he reached Holland; but having heard that everyone in that country was rich and a Christian, he felt confident of being treated as well as he had been in the castle of the Baron before he was kicked out for the love of Miss Cunégonde. *In spite of all, through all, are still of miss Cunégonde*

He asked alms of several grave personages, who all told him that if he continued to beg, he would be shut up in a house of correction and set to hard labor.

Finally he approached a man who had just been talking to a large crowd for an hour on end; the topic was charity. Looking doubtfully at him, the orator demanded:

—What are you doing here? Are you here to serve the good cause?

—There is no effect without a cause, said Candide modestly; all events are linked by the chain of necessity and arranged for the best. I had to be driven away from Miss Cunégonde, I had to run the gauntlet, I have to beg my bread until I can earn it; none of this could have happened otherwise.

—Look here, friend, said the orator, do you think the Pope is Antichrist?[3]

—I haven't considered the matter, said Candide; but whether he is or not, I'm in need of bread.

—You don't deserve any, said the other; away with you, you rascal, you rogue, never come near me as long as you live.

Meanwhile, the orator's wife had put her head out of the window, and, seeing a man who was not sure the Pope was Antichrist, emptied over his head a pot full of——Scandalous! The excesses into which women are led by religious zeal! *Voltaire's obvious distaste for the Catholic church*

A man who had never been baptized, a good Anabaptist[4] named Jacques, saw this cruel and heartless treatment being inflicted on one of his fellow

3. Voltaire is satirizing extreme Protestant sects that have sometimes seemed to make hatred of Rome the sum and substance of their creed.   4. Holland, as the home of religious liberty, had offered asylum to the Anabaptists, whose radical views on property and religious discipline had made them unpopular during the 16th century. Granted tolerance, they settled down into respectable burghers. Since this behavior confirmed some of Voltaire's major theses, he had a high opinion of contemporary Anabaptists.

creatures, a featherless biped possessing a soul;[5] he took Candide home with him, washed him off, gave him bread and beer, presented him with two florins, and even undertook to give him a job in his Persian-rug factory—for these items are widely manufactured in Holland. Candide, in an ecstasy of gratitude, cried out:

—Master Pangloss was right indeed when he told me everything is for the best in this world; for I am touched by your kindness far more than by the harshness of that black-coated gentleman and his wife.

Next day, while taking a stroll about town, he met a beggar who was covered with pustules, his eyes were sunken, the end of his nose rotted off, his mouth twisted, his teeth black, he had a croaking voice and a hacking cough, and spat a tooth every time he tried to speak.

CHAPTER 4

How Candide Met His Old Philosophy Tutor, Doctor Pangloss, and What Came of It

Candide, more touched by compassion even than by horror, gave this ghastly beggar the two florins that he himself had received from his honest Anabaptist friend Jacques. The phantom stared at him, burst into tears, and fell on his neck. Candide drew back in terror.

—Alas, said one wretch to the other, don't you recognize your dear Pangloss any more?

—What are you saying? You, my dear master! you, in this horrible condition? What misfortune has befallen you? Why are you no longer in the most beautiful of castles? What has happened to Miss Cunégonde, that pearl among young ladies, that masterpiece of Nature?

—I am perishing, said Pangloss.

Candide promptly led him into the Anabaptist's stable, where he gave him a crust of bread, and when he had recovered:—Well, said he, Cunégonde?

—Dead, said the other.

Candide fainted. His friend brought him around with a bit of sour vinegar which happened to be in the stable. Candide opened his eyes.

—Cunégonde, dead! Ah, best of worlds, what's become of you now? But how did she die? It wasn't of grief at seeing me kicked out of her noble father's elegant castle?

—Not at all, said Pangloss; she was disemboweled by the Bulgar soldiers, after having been raped to the absolute limit of human endurance; they smashed the Baron's head when he tried to defend her, cut the Baroness to bits, and treated my poor pupil exactly like his sister. As for the castle, not one stone was left on another, not a shed, not a sheep, not a duck, not a tree; but we had the satisfaction of revenge, for the Abares did exactly the same thing to a nearby barony belonging to a Bulgar nobleman.

At this tale Candide fainted again; but having returned to his senses and said everything appropriate to the occasion, he asked about the cause and effect, the sufficient reason, which had reduced Pangloss to his present pitiful state.

---

5. Plato's famous minimal definition of man, which he corrected by the addition of a soul to distinguish man from a plucked chicken.

—Alas, said he, it was love; love, the consolation of the human race, the preservative of the universe, the soul of all sensitive beings, love, gentle love.

—Unhappy man, said Candide, I too have had some experience of this love, the sovereign of hearts, the soul of our souls; and it never got me anything but a single kiss and twenty kicks in the rear. How could this lovely cause produce in you such a disgusting effect?

Pangloss replied as follows:—My dear Candide! you knew Paquette, that pretty maidservant to our august Baroness. In her arms I tasted the delights of paradise, which directly caused these torments of hell, from which I am now suffering. She was infected with the disease, and has perhaps died of it. Paquette received this present from an erudite Franciscan, who took the pains to trace it back to its source; for he had it from an elderly countess, who picked it up from a captain of cavalry, who acquired it from a marquise, who caught it from a page, who had received it from a Jesuit, who during his novitiate got it directly from one of the companions of Christopher Columbus. As for me, I shall not give it to anyone, for I am a dying man.

—Oh, Pangloss, cried Candide, that's a very strange genealogy. Isn't the devil at the root of the whole thing?

—Not at all, replied that great man; it's an indispensable part of the best of worlds, a necessary ingredient; if Columbus had not caught, on an American island, this sickness which attacks the source of generation and some-times prevents generation entirely—which thus strikes at and defeats the greatest end of Nature herself—we should have neither chocolate nor coch-ineal. It must also be noted that until the present time this malady, like religious controversy, has been wholly confined to the continent of Europe. Turks, Indians, Persians, Chinese, Siamese, and Japanese know nothing of it as yet; but there is a sufficient reason for which they in turn will make its acquaintance in a couple of centuries. Meanwhile, it has made splendid progress among us, especially among those big armies of honest, well-trained mercenaries who decide the destinies of nations. You can be sure that when thirty thousand men fight a pitched battle against the same number of the enemy, there will be about twenty thousand with the pox on either side.

—Remarkable indeed, said Candide, but we must see about curing you.

—And how can I do that, said Pangloss, seeing I don't have a cent to my name? There's not a doctor in the whole world who will let your blood or give you an enema without demanding a fee. If you can't pay yourself, you must find someone to pay for you.

These last words decided Candide; he hastened to implore the help of his charitable Anabaptist, Jacques, and painted such a moving picture of his friend's wretched state that the good man did not hesitate to take in Pangloss and have him cured at his own expense. In the course of the cure, Pangloss lost only an eye and an ear. Since he wrote a fine hand and knew arithmetic, the Anabaptist made him his bookkeeper. At the end of two months, being obliged to go to Lisbon on business, he took his two philosophers on the boat with him. Pangloss still maintained that everything was for the best, but Jacques didn't agree with him.

—It must be, said he, that men have corrupted Nature, for they are not born wolves, yet that is what they become. God gave them neither twenty-four-pound cannon nor bayonets, yet they have manufactured both in order to destroy themselves. Bankruptcies have the same effect, and so does the justice which seizes the goods of bankrupts in order to prevent the creditors from getting them.[6]

—It was all indispensable, replied the one-eyed doctor, since private misfortunes make for public welfare, and therefore the more private misfortunes there are, the better everything is.

While he was reasoning, the air grew dark, the winds blew from all directions, and the vessel was attacked by a horrible tempest within sight of Lisbon harbor.

CHAPTER 5

Tempest, Shipwreck, Earthquake, and What Happened to Doctor Pangloss, Candide, and the Anabaptist, Jacques

Half of the passengers, weakened by the frightful anguish of seasickness and the distress of tossing about on stormy waters, were incapable of noticing their danger. The other half shrieked aloud and fell to their prayers, the sails were ripped to shreds, the masts snapped, the vessel opened at the seams. Everyone worked who could stir, nobody listened for orders or issued them. The Anabaptist was lending a hand in the after part of the ship when a frantic sailor struck him and knocked him to the deck; but just at that moment, the sailor lurched so violently that he fell head first over the side, where he hung, clutching a fragment of the broken mast. The good Jacques ran to his aid, and helped him to climb back on board, but in the process was himself thrown into the sea under the very eyes of the sailor, who allowed him to drown without even glancing at him. Candide rushed to the rail, and saw his benefactor rise for a moment to the surface, then sink forever. He wanted to dive to his rescue; but the philosopher Pangloss prevented him by proving that the bay of Lisbon had been formed expressly for this Anabaptist to drown in. While he was proving the point *a priori,* the vessel opened up and everyone perished except for Pangloss, Candide, and the brutal sailor who had caused the virtuous Anabaptist to drown; this rascal swam easily to shore, while Pangloss and Candide drifted there on a plank.

When they had recovered a bit of energy, they set out for Lisbon; they still had a little money with which they hoped to stave off hunger after escaping the storm.

Scarcely had they set foot in the town, still bewailing the loss of their benefactor, when they felt the earth quake underfoot; the sea was lashed to a froth, burst into the port, and smashed all the vessels lying at anchor there. Whirlwinds of fire and ash swirled through the streets and public squares; houses crumbled, roofs came crashing down on foundations, foundations split; thirty thousand inhabitants of every age and either sex were crushed in the ruins.[7] The sailor whistled through his teeth, and said with an oath:— There'll be something to pick up here.

—What can be the sufficient reason of this phenomenon? asked Pangloss.

—The Last Judgment is here, cried Candide.

But the sailor ran directly into the middle of the ruins, heedless of danger in his eagerness for gain; he found some money, laid violent hands on it, got

---

6. Voltaire had suffered losses from various bankruptcy proceedings.   7. The great Lisbon earthquake and fire occurred on November 1, 1755; between 30,000 and 40,000 deaths resulted.

drunk, and, having slept off his wine, bought the favors of the first street-walker he could find amid the ruins of smashed houses, amid corpses and suffering victims on every hand. Pangloss however tugged at his sleeve.

—My friend, said he, this is not good form at all; your behavior falls short of that required by the universal reason; it's untimely, to say the least.

—Bloody hell, said the other, I'm a sailor, born in Batavia; I've been four times to Japan and stamped four times on the crucifix;[8] get out of here with your universal reason.

Some falling stonework had struck Candide; he lay prostrate in the street, covered with rubble, and calling to Pangloss:—For pity's sake bring me a little wine and oil; I'm dying.

—This earthquake is nothing novel, Pangloss replied; the city of Lima, in South America, underwent much the same sort of tremor, last year; same causes, same effects; there is surely a vein of sulphur under the earth's surface reaching from Lima to Lisbon.

—Nothing is more probable, said Candide; but, for God's sake, a little oil and wine.

—What do you mean, probable? replied the philosopher; I regard the case as proved.

Candide fainted and Pangloss brought him some water from a nearby fountain.

Next day, as they wandered amid the ruins, they found a little food which restored some of their strength. Then they fell to work like the others, bringing relief to those of the inhabitants who had escaped death. Some of the citizens whom they rescued gave them a dinner as good as was possible under the circumstances; it is true that the meal was a melancholy one, and the guests watered their bread with tears; but Pangloss consoled them by proving that things could not possibly be otherwise.

—For, said he, all this is for the best, since if there is a volcano at Lisbon, it cannot be somewhere else, since it is unthinkable that things should not be where they are, since everything is well.

A little man in black, an officer of the Inquisition,[9] who was sitting beside him, politely took up the question, and said:—It would seem that the gentleman does not believe in original sin, since if everything is for the best, man has not fallen and is not liable to eternal punishment.

—I most humbly beg pardon of your excellency, Pangloss answered, even more politely, but the fall of man and the curse of original sin entered necessarily into the best of all possible worlds.

—Then you do not believe in free will? said the officer.

—Your excellency must excuse me, said Pangloss; free will agrees very well with absolute necessity, for it was necessary that we should be free, since a will which is determined . . .

Pangloss was in the middle of his sentence, when the officer nodded significantly to the attendant who was pouring him a glass of port, or Oporto, wine.

---

8. The Japanese, originally receptive to foreign visitors, grew fearful that priests and proselytizers were merely advance agents of empire and expelled both the Portuguese and Spanish early in the 17th century. Only the Dutch were allowed to retain a small foothold, under humiliating conditions, of which the notion of stamping on the crucifix is symbolic. It was never what Voltaire suggests here, an actual requirement for entering the country.　9. Specifically, a *familier* or *poursuivant,* an undercover agent with powers of arrest.

CHAPTER 6

How They Made a Fine Auto-da-Fé to Prevent Earthquakes, and How Candide Was Whipped

After the earthquake had wiped out three quarters of Lisbon, the learned men of the land could find no more effective way of averting total destruction than to give the people a fine auto-da-fé;[1] the University of Coimbra had established that the spectacle of several persons being roasted over a slow fire with full ceremonial rites is an infallible specific against earthquakes.

In consequence, the authorities had rounded up a Biscayan convicted of marrying a woman who had stood godmother to his child, and two Portuguese who while eating a chicken had set aside a bit of bacon used for seasoning.[2] After dinner, men came with ropes to tie up Doctor Pangloss and his disciple Candide, one for talking and the other for listening with an air of approval; both were taken separately to a set of remarkably cool apartments, where the glare of the sun is never bothersome; eight days later they were both dressed in *san-benitos* and crowned with paper mitres;[3] Candide's mitre and *san-benito* were decorated with inverted flames and with devils who had neither tails nor claws; but Pangloss's devils had both tails and claws, and his flames stood upright. Wearing these costumes, they marched in a procession, and listened to a very touching sermon, followed by a beautiful concert of plainsong. Candide was flogged in cadence to the music; the Biscayan and the two men who had avoided bacon were burned, and Pangloss was hanged, though hanging is not customary. On the same day there was another earthquake, causing frightful damage.[4]

Candide, stunned, stupefied, despairing, bleeding, trembling, said to himself:—If this is the best of all possible worlds, what are the others like? The flogging is not so bad, I was flogged by the Bulgars. But oh my dear Pangloss, greatest of philosophers, was it necessary for me to watch you being hanged, for no reason that I can see? Oh my dear Anabaptist, best of men, was it necessary that you should be drowned in the port? Oh Miss Cunégonde, pearl of young ladies, was it necessary that you should have your belly slit open?

He was being led away, barely able to stand, lectured, lashed, absolved, and blessed, when an old woman approached and said,—My son, be of good cheer and follow me.

CHAPTER 7

How an Old Woman Took Care of Candide, and How He Regained What He Loved

Candide was of very bad cheer, but he followed the old woman to a shanty; she gave him a jar of ointment to rub himself, left him food and drink; she showed him a tidy little bed; next to it was a suit of clothing.

1. Literally, "act of faith," a public ceremony of repentance and humiliation. Such an auto-da-fé was actually held in Lisbon, June 20, 1756. 2. The Biscayan's fault lay in marrying someone within the forbidden bounds of relationship, an act of spiritual incest. The men who declined pork or bacon were understood to be crypto-Jews. 3. The cone-shaped paper cap (intended to resemble a bishop's miter) and flowing yellow cape were customary garb for those pleading before the Inquisition. 4. In fact, the second quake occurred December 21, 1755.

—Eat, drink, sleep, she said; and may Our Lady of Atocha, Our Lord St. Anthony of Padua, and Our Lord St. James of Compostela watch over you. I will be back tomorrow.

Candide, still completely astonished by everything he had seen and suffered, and even more by the old woman's kindness, offered to kiss her hand.

—It's not *my* hand you should be kissing, said she. I'll be back tomorrow; rub yourself with the ointment, eat and sleep.

In spite of his many sufferings, Candide ate and slept. Next day the old woman returned bringing breakfast; she looked at his back and rubbed it herself with another ointment; she came back with lunch; and then she returned in the evening, bringing supper. Next day she repeated the same routine.

—Who are you? Candide asked continually. Who told you to be so kind to me? How can I ever repay you?

The good woman answered not a word; she returned in the evening, and without food.

—Come with me, says she, and don't speak a word.

Taking him by the hand, she walks out into the countryside with him for about a quarter of a mile; they reach an isolated house, quite surrounded by gardens and ditches. The old woman knocks at a little gate, it opens. She takes Candide up a secret stairway to a gilded room furnished with a fine brocaded sofa; there she leaves him, closes the door, disappears. Candide stood as if entranced; his life, which had seemed like a nightmare so far, was now starting to look like a delightful dream.

a small regaining of Candide's happiness

Soon the old woman returned; on her feeble shoulder leaned a trembling woman, of a splendid figure, glittering in diamonds, and veiled.

—Remove the veil, said the old woman to Candide.

The young man stepped timidly forward, and lifted the veil. What an event! What a surprise! Could it be Miss Cunégonde? Yes, it really was! She herself! His knees give way, speech fails him, he falls at her feet, Cunégonde collapses on the sofa. The old woman plies them with brandy, they return to their senses, they exchange words. At first they could utter only broken phrases, questions and answers at cross purposes, sighs, tears, exclamations. The old woman warned them not to make too much noise, and left them alone.

—Then it's really you, said Candide, you're alive, I've found you again in Portugal. Then you never were raped? You never had your belly ripped open, as the philosopher Pangloss assured me?

—Oh yes, said the lovely Cunégonde, but one doesn't always die of these two accidents.

—But your father and mother were murdered then?

—All too true, said Cunégonde, in tears.

—And your brother?

—Killed too.

—And why are you in Portugal? and how did you know I was here? and by what device did you have me brought to this house?

—I shall tell you everything, the lady replied; but first you must tell me what has happened to you since that first innocent kiss we exchanged and the kicking you got because of it.

Candide obeyed her with profound respect; and though he was overcome, though his voice was weak and hesitant, though he still had twinges of pain from his beating, he described as simply as possible everything that had happened to him since the time of their separation. Cunégonde lifted her eyes to heaven; she wept at the death of the good Anabaptist and at that of Pangloss; after which she told the following story to Candide, who listened to every word while he gazed on her with hungry eyes.

CHAPTER 8

Cunégonde's Story

—I was in my bed and fast asleep when heaven chose to send the Bulgars into our castle of Thunder-Ten-Tronckh. They butchered my father and brother, and hacked my mother to bits. An enormous Bulgar, six feet tall, seeing that I had swooned from horror at the scene, set about raping me; at that I recovered my senses, I screamed and scratched, bit and fought, I tried to tear the eyes out of that big Bulgar—not realizing that everything which had happened in my father's castle was a mere matter of routine. The brute then stabbed me with a knife on my left thigh, where I still bear the scar.

—What a pity! I should very much like to see it, said the simple Candide.

—You shall, said Cunégonde; but shall I go on?

—Please do, said Candide.

So she took up the thread of her tale:—A Bulgar captain appeared, he saw me covered with blood and the soldier too intent to get up. Shocked by the monster's failure to come to attention, the captain killed him on my body. He then had my wound dressed, and took me off to his quarters, as a prisoner of war. I laundered his few shirts and did his cooking; he found me attractive, I confess it, and I won't deny that he was a handsome fellow, with a smooth, white skin; apart from that, however, little wit, little philosophical training; it was evident that he had not been brought up by Doctor Pangloss. After three months, he had lost all his money and grown sick of me; so he sold me to a Jew named Don Issachar, who traded in Holland and Portugal, and who was mad after women. This Jew developed a mighty passion for my person, but he got nowhere with it; I held him off better than I had done with the Bulgar soldier; for though a person of honor may be raped once, her virtue is only strengthened by the experience. In order to keep me hidden, the Jew brought me to his country house, which you see here. Till then I had thought there was nothing on earth so beautiful as the castle of Thunder-Ten-Tronckh; I was now undeceived.

—One day the Grand Inquisitor took notice of me at mass; he ogled me a good deal, and made known that he must talk to me on a matter of secret business. I was taken to his palace; I told him of my rank; he pointed out that it was beneath my dignity to belong to an Israelite. A suggestion was then conveyed to Don Issachar that he should turn me over to My Lord the Inquisitor. Don Issachar, who is court banker and a man of standing, refused out of hand. The inquisitor threatened him with an auto-da-fé. Finally my Jew, fearing for his life, struck a bargain by which the house and I would belong to both of them as joint tenants; the Jew would get Mondays, Wednesdays, and the Sabbath, the inquisitor would get the other days of the week. That has been the arrangement for six months now. There have been quarrels; sometimes it has not been clear whether the night from Saturday to Sunday belonged to the old or the new dispensation. For my part, I have so far been able to hold both of them off; and that, I think, is why they are both still in love with me.

—Finally, in order to avert further divine punishment by earthquake, and to terrify Don Issachar, My Lord the Inquisitor chose to celebrate an auto-da-fé. He did me the honor of inviting me to attend. I had an excellent seat; the ladies were served with refreshments between the mass and the execution. To tell you the truth, I was horrified to see them burn alive those two Jews and that decent Biscayan who had married his child's godmother; but what was my surprise, my terror, my grief, when I saw, huddled in a *san-benito* and wearing a mitre, someone who looked like Pangloss! I rubbed my eyes, I watched his every move, I saw him hanged; and I fell back in a swoon. Scarcely had I come to my senses again, when I saw you stripped for the lash; that was the peak of my horror, consternation, grief, and despair. I may tell you, by the way, that your skin is even whiter and more delicate than that of my Bulgar captain. Seeing you, then, redoubled the torments which were already overwhelming me. I shrieked aloud, I wanted to call out, 'Let him go, you brutes!' but my voice died within me, and my cries would have been useless. When you had been thoroughly thrashed: 'How can it be,' I asked myself, 'that agreeable Candide and wise Pangloss have come to Lisbon, one to receive a hundred whiplashes, the other to be hanged by order of My Lord the Inquisitor, whose mistress I am? Pangloss must have deceived me cruelly when he told me that all is for the best in this world.'

—Frantic, exhausted, half out of my senses, and ready to die of weakness, I felt as if my mind were choked with the massacre of my father, my mother, my brother, with the arrogance of that ugly Bulgar soldier, with the knife slash he inflicted on me, my slavery, my cookery, my Bulgar captain, my nasty Don Issachar, my abominable inquisitor, with the hanging of Doctor Pangloss, with that great plainsong *miserere* which they sang while they flogged you—and above all, my mind was full of the kiss which I gave you behind the screen, on the day I saw you for the last time. I praised God, who had brought you back to me after so many trials. I asked my old woman to look out for you, and to bring you here as soon as she could. She did just as I asked; I have had the indescribable joy of seeing you again, hearing you and talking with you once more. But you must be frightfully hungry; I am, myself; let us begin with a dinner.

So then and there they sat down to table; and after dinner, they adjourned to that fine brocaded sofa, which has already been mentioned; and there they were when the eminent Don Issachar, one of the masters of the house, appeared. It was the day of the Sabbath; he was arriving to assert his rights and express his tender passion.

CHAPTER 9

What Happened to Cunégonde, Candide, the Grand Inquisitor,
and a Jew

This Issachar was the most choleric Hebrew seen in Israel since the Babylonian captivity.

—What's this, says he, you bitch of a Christian, you're not satisfied with the Grand Inquisitor? Do I have to share you with this rascal, too?

So saying, he drew a long dagger, with which he always went armed, and, supposing his opponent defenceless, flung himself on Candide. But our good Westphalian had received from the old woman, along with his suit of clothes, a fine sword. Out it came, and though his manners were of the gentlest, in short order he laid the Israelite stiff and cold on the floor, at the feet of the lovely Cunégonde.

—Holy Virgin! she cried. What will become of me now? A man killed in my house! If the police find out, we're done for.

—If Pangloss had not been hanged, said Candide, he would give us good advice in this hour of need, for he was a great philosopher. Lacking him, let's ask the old woman.

She was a sensible body, and was just starting to give her opinion of the situation, when another little door opened. It was just one o'clock in the morning, Sunday morning. This day belonged to the inquisitor. In he came, and found the whipped Candide with a sword in his hand, a corpse at his feet, Cunégonde in terror, and an old woman giving them both good advice.

Here now is what passed through Candide's mind in this instant of time; this is how he reasoned:—If this holy man calls for help, he will certainly have me burned, and perhaps Cunégonde as well; he has already had me whipped without mercy; he is my rival; I have already killed once; why hesitate?

It was a quick, clear chain of reasoning; without giving the inquisitor time to recover from his surprise, he ran him through, and laid him beside the Jew.

—Here you've done it again, said Cunégonde; there's no hope for us now. We'll be excommunicated, our last hour has come. How is it that you, who were born so gentle, could kill in two minutes a Jew and a prelate?

—My dear girl, replied Candide, when a man is in love, jealous, and just whipped by the Inquisition, he is no longer himself.

The old woman now spoke up and said:—There are three Andalusian steeds in the stable, with their saddles and bridles; our brave Candide must get them ready: my lady has some gold coin and diamonds; let's take to horse at once, though I can only ride on one buttock; we will go to Cadiz. The weather is as fine as can be, and it is pleasant to travel in the cool of the evening.

Promptly, Candide saddled the three horses. Cunégonde, the old woman, and he covered thirty miles without a stop. While they were fleeing, the Holy Brotherhood[5] came to investigate the house; they buried the inquisitor in a fine church, and threw Issachar on the dunghill.

Candide, Cunégonde, and the old woman were already in the little town of Avacena, in the middle of the Sierra Morena; and there, as they sat in a country inn, they had this conversation.

---

5. A semireligious order with police powers, very active in 18th-century Spain.

CHAPTER 10

*In Deep Distress, Candide, Cunégonde, and the Old Woman Reach Cadiz;
They Put to Sea*

—Who then could have robbed me of my gold and diamonds? said Cunégonde, in tears. How shall we live? what shall we do? where shall I find other
inquisitors and Jews to give me some more?

—Ah, said the old woman, I strongly suspect that reverend Franciscan
friar who shared the inn with us yesterday at Badajoz. God save me from
judging him unfairly! But he came into our room twice, and he left long
before us.

—Alas, said Candide, the good Pangloss often proved to me that the fruits
of the earth are a common heritage of all, to which each man has equal right.
On these principles, the Franciscan should at least have left us enough to
finish our journey. You have nothing at all, my dear Cunégonde?

—Not a maravedi, said she.

—What to do? said Candide.

—We'll sell one of the horses, said the old woman; I'll ride on the croup
behind my mistress, though only on one buttock, and so we will get to Cadiz.

There was in the same inn a Benedictine prior; he bought the horse cheap.
Candide, Cunégonde, and the old woman passed through Lucena, Chillas,
and Lebrixa, and finally reached Cadiz. There a fleet was being fitted out and
an army assembled, to reason with the Jesuit fathers in Paraguay, who were
accused of fomenting among their flock a revolt against the kings of Spain
and Portugal near the town of St. Sacrement.[6] Candide, having served in the
Bulgar army, performed the Bulgar manual of arms before the general of the
little army with such grace, swiftness, dexterity, fire, and agility, that they
gave him a company of infantry to command. So here he is, a captain; and
off he sails with Miss Cunégonde, the old woman, two valets, and the two
Andalusian steeds which had belonged to My Lord the Grand Inquisitor of
Portugal.

Throughout the crossing, they spent a great deal of time reasoning about
the philosophy of poor Pangloss.

—We are destined, in the end, for another universe, said Candide;
no doubt that is the one where everything is well. For in this one, it must
be admitted, there is some reason to grieve over our physical and moral
state.

—I love you with all my heart, said Cunégonde; but my soul is still harrowed by thoughts of what I have seen and suffered.

—All will be well, replied Candide; the sea of this new world is already
better than those of Europe, calmer and with steadier winds. Surely it is the
New World which is the best of all possible worlds.

—God grant it, said Cunégonde; but I have been so horribly unhappy in
the world so far, that my heart is almost dead to hope.

---

6. Actually, Colonia del Sacramento. Voltaire took great interest in the Jesuit role in Paraguay, which he
has much oversimplified and largely misrepresented here in the interests of his satire. In 1750 they did,
however, offer armed resistance to an agreement made between Spain and Portugal. They were subdued
and expelled in 1769.

The old lady has known great sorrow.

—You pity yourselves, the old woman told them; but you have had no such misfortunes as mine.

Cunégonde nearly broke out laughing; she found the old woman comic in pretending to be more unhappy than she.

—Ah, you poor old thing, said she, unless you've been raped by two Bulgars, been stabbed twice in the belly, seen two of your castles destroyed, witnessed the murder of two of your mothers and two of your fathers, and watched two of your lovers being whipped in an auto-da-fé, I do not see how you can have had it worse than me. Besides, I was born a baroness, with seventy-two quarterings, and I have worked in a scullery.

—My lady, replied the old woman, you do not know my birth and rank; and if I showed you my rear end, you would not talk as you do, you might even speak with less assurance.

These words inspired great curiosity in Candide and Cunégonde, which the old woman satisfied with this story.

Cunégonde judges before she knows the truth

CHAPTER 11

The Old Woman's Story

She has fallen to a station lower than her birth.

—My eyes were not always bloodshot and red-rimmed, my nose did not always touch my chin, and I was not born a servant. I am in fact the daughter of Pope Urban the Tenth and the Princess of Palestrina.[7] Till the age of fourteen, I lived in a palace so splendid that all the castles of all your German barons would not have served it as a stable; a single one of my dresses was worth more than all the assembled magnificence of Westphalia. I grew in beauty, in charm, in talent, surrounded by pleasures, dignities, and glowing visions of the future. Already I was inspiring the young men to love; my breast was formed—and what a breast! white, firm, with the shape of the Venus de Medici; and what eyes! what lashes, what black brows! What fire flashed from my glances and outshone the glitter of the stars, as the local poets used to tell me! The women who helped me dress and undress fell into ecstasies, whether they looked at me from in front or behind; and all the men wanted to be in their place.

Her future had looked bright.

—I was engaged to the ruling prince of Massa-Carrara; and what a prince he was! as handsome as I, softness and charm compounded, brilliantly witty, and madly in love with me. I loved him in return as one loves for the first time, with a devotion approaching idolatry. The wedding preparations had been made, with a splendor and magnificence never heard of before; nothing but celebrations, masks, and comic operas, uninterruptedly; and all Italy composed in my honor sonnets of which not one was even passable. I had almost attained the very peak of bliss, when an old marquise who had been the mistress of my prince invited him to her house for a cup of chocolate. He died in less than two hours, amid horrifying convulsions. But that was only a trifle. My mother, in complete despair (though less afflicted than I), wished to escape for a while the oppressive atmosphere of grief. She owned a handsome property near Gaeta.[8] We embarked on a papal galley gilded like

She had known love.

7. Voltaire left behind a comment on this passage, a note first published in 1829: "Note the extreme discretion of the author; hitherto there has never been a pope named Urban X; he avoided attributing a bastard to a known pope. What circumspection! what an exquisite conscience!" 8. About halfway between Rome and Naples.

the altar of St. Peter's in Rome. Suddenly a pirate ship from Salé swept down and boarded us. Our soldiers defended themselves as papal troops usually do; falling on their knees and throwing down their arms, they begged of the corsair absolution *in articulo mortis.*[9]

—They were promptly stripped as naked as monkeys, and so was my mother, and so were our maids of honor, and so was I too. It's a very remarkable thing, the energy these gentlemen put into stripping people. But what surprised me even more was that they stuck their fingers in a place where we women usually admit only a syringe. This ceremony seemed a bit odd to me, as foreign usages always do when one hasn't traveled. They only wanted to see if we didn't have some diamonds hidden there; and I soon learned that it's a custom of long standing among the genteel folk who swarm the seas. I learned that my lords the very religious knights of Malta never overlook this ceremony when they capture Turks, whether male or female; it's one of those international laws which have never been questioned.

—I won't try to explain how painful it is for a young princess to be carried off into slavery in Morocco with her mother. You can imagine everything we had to suffer on the pirate ship. My mother was still very beautiful; our maids of honor, our mere chambermaids, were more charming than anything one could find in all Africa. As for myself, I was ravishing, I was loveliness and grace supreme, and I was a virgin. I did not remain so for long; the flower which had been kept for the handsome prince of Massa-Carrara was plucked by the corsair captain; he was an abominable negro, who thought he was doing me a great favor. My Lady the Princess of Palestrina and I must have been strong indeed to bear what we did during our journey to Morocco. But on with my story; these are such common matters that they are not worth describing.

—Morocco was knee deep in blood when we arrived. Of the fifty sons of the emperor Muley-Ismael,[1] each had his faction, which produced in effect fifty civil wars, of blacks against blacks, of blacks against browns, halfbreeds against halfbreeds; throughout the length and breadth of the empire, nothing but one continual carnage.

—Scarcely had we stepped ashore, when some negroes of a faction hostile to my captor arrived to take charge of his plunder. After the diamonds and gold, we women were the most prized possessions. I was now witness of a struggle such as you never see in the temperate climate of Europe. Northern people don't have hot blood; they don't feel the absolute fury for women which is common in Africa. Europeans seem to have milk in their veins; it is vitriol or liquid fire which pulses through these people around Mount Atlas. The fight for possession of us raged with the fury of the lions, tigers, and poisonous vipers of that land. A Moor snatched my mother by the right arm, the first mate held her by the left; a Moorish soldier grabbed one leg, one of our pirates the other. In a moment's time almost all our girls were being dragged four different ways. My captain held me behind him while with his scimitar he killed everyone who braved his fury. At last I saw all our Italian women, including my mother, torn to pieces, cut to bits, murdered by the monsters who were fighting over them. My captive companions, their

9. Literally, when at the point of death. Absolution from a corsair in the act of murdering one is of very dubious validity.   1. Having reigned for more than fifty years, a potent and ruthless sultan of Morocco, he died in 1727 and left his kingdom in much the condition described.

captors, soldiers, sailors, blacks, browns, whites, mulattoes, and at last my captain, all were killed, and I remained half dead on a mountain of corpses. Similar scenes were occurring, as is well known, for more than three hundred leagues around, without anyone skimping on the five prayers a day decreed by Mohammed.

—With great pain, I untangled myself from this vast heap of bleeding bodies, and dragged myself under a great orange tree by a neighboring brook, where I collapsed, from terror, exhaustion, horror, despair, and hunger. Shortly, my weary mind surrendered to a sleep which was more of a swoon than a rest. I was in this state of weakness and languor, between life and death, when I felt myself touched by something which moved over my body. Opening my eyes, I saw a white man, rather attractive, who was groaning and saying under his breath: 'O che sciagura d'essere senza coglioni!'[2]

CHAPTER 12

The Old Woman's Story Continued

—Amazed and delighted to hear my native tongue, and no less surprised by what this man was saying, I told him that there were worse evils than those he was complaining of. In a few words, I described to him the horrors I had undergone, and then fainted again. He carried me to a nearby house, put me to bed, gave me something to eat, served me, flattered me, comforted me, told me he had never seen anyone so lovely, and added that he had never before regretted so much the loss of what nobody could give him back.

'I was born at Naples,' he told me, 'where they caponize two or three thousand children every year; some die of it, others acquire a voice more beautiful than any woman's, still others go on to become governors of kingdoms.[3] The operation was a great success with me, and I became court musician to the Princess of Palestrina . . .'

'Of my mother,' I exclaimed.

'Of your mother,' cried he, bursting into tears; 'then you must be the princess whom I raised till she was six, and who already gave promise of becoming as beautiful as you are now!'

'I am that very princess; my mother lies dead, not a hundred yards from here, buried under a pile of corpses.'

—I told him my adventures, he told me his: that he had been sent by a Christian power to the King of Morocco, to conclude a treaty granting him gunpowder, cannon, and ships with which to liquidate the traders of the other Christian powers.

'My mission is concluded,' said this honest eunuch; 'I shall take ship at Ceuta and bring you back to Italy. Ma che sciagura d'essere senza coglioni!'

—I thanked him with tears of gratitude, and instead of returning me to Italy, he took me to Algiers and sold me to the dey of that country. Hardly had the sale taken place, when that plague which has made the rounds of

2. "Oh what a misfortune to have no testicles!"   3. The castrato Farinelli (1705–1782), originally a singer, came to exercise considerable political influence over the kings of Spain, Philip V and Ferdinand VI.

Africa, Asia, and Europe broke out in full fury at Algiers. You have seen earthquakes; but tell me, young lady, have you ever had the plague?

—Never, replied the baroness.

—If you had had it, said the old woman, you would agree that it is far worse than an earthquake. It is very frequent in Africa, and I had it. Imagine, if you will, the situation of a pope's daughter, fifteen years old, who in three months' time had experienced poverty, slavery, had been raped almost every day, had seen her mother quartered, had suffered from famine and war, and who now was dying of pestilence in Algiers. As a matter of fact, I did not die; but the eunuch and the dey and nearly the entire seraglio of Algiers perished.

—When the first horrors of this ghastly plague had passed, the slaves of the dey were sold. A merchant bought me and took me to Tunis; there he sold me to another merchant, who resold me at Tripoli; from Tripoli I was sold to Alexandria, from Alexandria resold to Smyrna, from Smyrna to Constantinople. I ended by belonging to an aga of janizaries, who was shortly ordered to defend Azov against the besieging Russians.[4]

—The aga, who was a gallant soldier, took his whole seraglio with him, and established us in a little fort amid the Maeotian marshes,[5] guarded by two black eunuchs and twenty soldiers. Our side killed a prodigious number of Russians, but they paid us back nicely. Azov was put to fire and sword without respect for age or sex; only our little fort continued to resist, and the enemy determined to starve us out. The twenty janizaries had sworn never to surrender. Reduced to the last extremities of hunger, they were forced to eat our two eunuchs, lest they violate their oaths. After several more days, they decided to eat the women too.

—We had an imam,[6] very pious and sympathetic, who delivered an excellent sermon, persuading them not to kill us altogether.

'Just cut off a single rumpsteak from each of these ladies,' he said, 'and you'll have a fine meal. Then if you should need another, you can come back in a few days and have as much again; heaven will bless your charitable action, and you will be saved.'

—His eloquence was splendid, and he persuaded them. We underwent this horrible operation. The imam treated us all with the ointment that they use on newly circumcised children. We were at the point of death.

—Scarcely had the janizaries finished the meal for which we furnished the materials, when the Russians appeared in flat-bottomed boats; not a janizary escaped. The Russians paid no attention to the state we were in; but there are French physicians everywhere, and one of them, who knew his trade, took care of us. He cured us, and I shall remember all my life that when my wounds were healed, he made me a proposition. For the rest, he counselled us simply to have patience, assuring us that the same thing had happened in several other sieges, and that it was according to the laws of war.

—As soon as my companions could walk, we were herded off to Moscow. In the division of booty, I fell to a boyar who made me work in his garden, and gave me twenty whiplashes a day; but when he was broken on the wheel

---

4. Azov, near the mouth of the Don, was besieged by the Russians under Peter the Great in 1695–96. *Janizaries:* an elite corps of the Ottoman armies.   5. The Roman name of the so-called Sea of Azov, a shallow, swampy lake near the town.   6. In effect, a chaplain.

after about two years, with thirty other boyars, over some little court intrigue,[7] I seized the occasion; I ran away; I crossed all Russia; I was for a long time a chambermaid in Riga, then at Rostock, Vismara, Leipzig, Cassel, Utrecht, Leyden, The Hague, Rotterdam; I grew old in misery and shame, having only half a backside and remembering always that I was the daughter of a Pope; a hundred times I wanted to kill myself, but always I loved life more. This ridiculous weakness is perhaps one of our worst instincts; is anything more stupid than choosing to carry a burden that really one wants to cast on the ground? to hold existence in horror, and yet to cling to it? to fondle the serpent which devours us till it has eaten out our heart?

—In the countries through which I have been forced to wander, in the taverns where I have had to work, I have seen a vast number of people who hated their existence; but I never saw more than a dozen who deliberately put an end to their own misery: three negroes, four Englishmen, four Genevans, and a German professor named Robeck.[8] My last post was as servant to the Jew Don Issachar; he attached me to your service, my lovely one; and I attached myself to your destiny, till I have become more concerned with your fate than with my own. I would not even have mentioned my own misfortunes, if you had not irked me a bit, and if it weren't the custom, on shipboard, to pass the time with stories. In a word, my lady, I have had some experience of the world, I know it; why not try this diversion? Ask every passenger on this ship to tell you his story, and if you find a single one who has not often cursed the day of his birth, who has not often told himself that he is the most miserable of men, then you may throw me overboard head first.

CHAPTER 13

How Candide Was Forced to Leave the Lovely Cunégonde and the Old Woman

Having heard out the old woman's story, the lovely Cunégonde paid her the respects which were appropriate to a person of her rank and merit. She took up the wager as well, and got all the passengers, one after another, to tell her their adventures. She and Candide had to agree that the old woman had been right.

—It's certainly too bad, said Candide, that the wise Pangloss was hanged, contrary to the custom of autos-da-fé; he would have admirable things to say of the physical evil and moral evil which cover land and sea, and I might feel within me the impulse to dare to raise several polite objections.

As the passengers recited their stories, the boat made steady progress, and presently landed at Buenos Aires. Cunégonde, Captain Candide, and the old woman went to call on the governor, Don Fernando d'Ibaraa y Figueroa y Mascarenes y Lampourdos y Souza. This nobleman had the pride appropriate to a man with so many names. He addressed everyone with the most aristocratic disdain, pointing his nose so loftily, raising his voice so mercilessly, lording it so splendidly, and assuming so arrogant a pose, that everyone who

7. Voltaire had in mind an ineffectual conspiracy against Peter the Great known as the "revolt of the streltsy" or musketeers, which took place in 1698. Though easily put down, it provoked from the emperor a massive and atrocious program of reprisals.   8. Johann Robeck (1672–1739) published a treatise advocating suicide and showed his conviction by drowning himself at the age of sixty-seven.

met him wanted to kick him. He loved women to the point of fury; and Cunégonde seemed to him the most beautiful creature he had ever seen. The first thing he did was to ask directly if she were the captain's wife. His manner of asking this question disturbed Candide; he did not dare say she was his wife, because in fact she was not; he did not dare say she was his sister, because she wasn't that either; and though this polite lie was once ~biblical reference~ common enough among the ancients,[9] and sometimes serves moderns very well, he was too pure of heart to tell a lie. ~Candide's honest character~

—Miss Cunégonde, said he, is betrothed to me, and we humbly beg your excellency to perform the ceremony for us.

Don Fernando d'Ibaraa y Figueroa y Mascarenes y Lampourdos y Souza twirled his moustache, smiled sardonically, and ordered Captain Candide to go drill his company. Candide obeyed. Left alone with My Lady Cunégonde, the governor declared his passion, and protested that he would marry her tomorrow, in church or in any other manner, as it pleased her charming self. Cunégonde asked for a quarter-hour to collect herself, consult the old woman, and make up her mind.

The old woman said to Cunégonde:—My lady, you have seventy-two quarterings and not one penny; if you wish, you may be the wife of the greatest lord in South America, who has a really handsome moustache; are you going to insist on your absolute fidelity? You have already been raped by the Bulgars; a Jew and an inquisitor have enjoyed your favors; miseries entitle one to privileges. I assure you that in your position I would make no scruple of marrying My Lord the Governor, and making the fortune of Captain Candide.

While the old woman was talking with all the prudence of age and experience, there came into the harbor a small ship bearing an alcalde and some alguazils.[1] This is what had happened.

As the old woman had very shrewdly guessed, it was a long-sleeved Franciscan who stole Cunégonde's gold and jewels in the town of Badajoz, when she and Candide were in flight. The monk tried to sell some of the gems to a jeweler, who recognized them as belonging to the Grand Inquisitor. Before he was hanged, the Franciscan confessed that he had stolen them, indicating who his victims were and where they were going. The flight of Cunégonde and Candide was already known. They were traced to Cadiz, and a vessel was hastily dispatched in pursuit of them. This vessel was now in the port of Buenos Aires. The rumor spread that an alcalde was aboard, in pursuit of the murderers of My Lord the Grand Inquisitor. The shrewd old woman saw at once what was to be done.

—You cannot escape, she told Cunégonde, and you have nothing to fear. You are not the one who killed my lord, and, besides, the governor, who is in love with you, won't let you be mistreated. Sit tight.

And then she ran straight to Candide:—Get out of town, she said, or you'll be burned within the hour.

There was not a moment to lose; but how to leave Cunégonde, and where to go?

9. Voltaire has in mind Abraham's adventures with Sarah (Genesis 12) and Isaac's with Rebecca (Genesis 26).   1. Police officers.

CHAPTER 14

How Candide and Cacambo Were Received by the Jesuits of Paraguay

Candide had brought from Cadiz a valet of the type one often finds in the provinces of Spain and in the colonies. He was one quarter Spanish, son of a halfbreed in the Tucuman;[2] he had been choirboy, sacristan, sailor, monk, merchant, soldier, and lackey. His name was Cacambo, and he was very fond of his master because his master was a very good man. In hot haste he saddled the two Andalusian steeds.

—Hurry, master, do as the old woman says; let's get going and leave this town without a backward look.

Candide wept:—O my beloved Cunégonde! must I leave you now, just when the governor is about to marry us! Cunégonde, brought from so far, what will ever become of you?

—She'll become what she can, said Cacambo; women can always find something to do with themselves; God sees to it; let's get going.

—Where are you taking me? where are we going? what will we do without Cunégonde? said Candide.

—By Saint James of Compostela, said Cacambo, you were going to make war against the Jesuits, now we'll go make war for them. I know the roads pretty well, I'll bring you to their country, they will be delighted to have a captain who knows the Bulgar drill; you'll make a prodigious fortune. If you don't get your rights in one world, you will find them in another. And isn't it pleasant to see new things and do new things?

—Then you've already been in Paraguay? said Candide.

—Indeed I have, replied Cacambo; I was cook in the College of the Assumption, and I know the government of Los Padres[3] as I know the streets of Cadiz. It's an admirable thing, this government. The kingdom is more than three hundred leagues across; it is divided into thirty provinces. Los Padres own everything in it, and the people nothing; it's a masterpiece of reason and justice. I myself know nothing so wonderful as Los Padres, who in this hemisphere make war on the kings of Spain and Portugal, but in Europe hear their confessions; who kill Spaniards here, and in Madrid send them to heaven; that really tickles me; let's get moving, you're going to be the happiest of men. Won't Los Padres be delighted when they learn they have a captain who knows the Bulgar drill!

As soon as they reached the first barricade, Cacambo told the frontier guard that a captain wished to speak with My Lord the Commander. A Paraguayan officer ran to inform headquarters by laying the news at the feet of the commander. Candide and Cacambo were first disarmed and deprived of their Andalusian horses. They were then placed between two files of soldiers; the commander was at the end, his three-cornered hat on his head, his cassock drawn up, a sword at his side, and a pike in his hand. He nods, and twenty-four soldiers surround the newcomers. A sergeant then informs them that they must wait, that the commander cannot talk to them, since the reverend father provincial has forbidden all Spaniards from speaking, except in his presence, and from remaining more than three hours in the country.

2. A province of Argentina, to the northwest of Buenos Aires.   3. The Jesuit fathers.

—And where is the reverend father provincial? says Cacambo.

—He is reviewing his troops after having said mass, the sergeant replies, and you'll only be able to kiss his spurs in three hours.

—But, says Cacambo, my master the captain, who, like me, is dying from hunger, is not Spanish at all, he is German; can't we have some breakfast while waiting for his reverence?

The sergeant promptly went off to report this speech to the commander.

—God be praised, said this worthy; since he is German, I can talk to him; bring him into my bower.

Candide was immediately led into a leafy nook surrounded by a handsome colonnade of green and gold marble and trellises amid which sported parrots, birds of paradise,[4] hummingbirds, guinea fowl, and all the rarest species of birds. An excellent breakfast was prepared in golden vessels; and while the Paraguayans ate corn out of wooden bowls in the open fields under the glare of the sun, the reverend father commander entered into his bower.

He was a very handsome young man, with an open face, rather blonde in coloring, with ruddy complexion, arched eyebrows, liquid eyes, pink ears, bright red lips, and an air of pride, but a pride somehow different from that of a Spaniard or a Jesuit. Their confiscated weapons were restored to Candide and Cacambo, as well as their Andalusian horses; Cacambo fed them oats alongside the bower, always keeping an eye on them for fear of an ambush.

First Candide kissed the hem of the commander's cassock, then they sat down at the table.

—So you are German? said the Jesuit, speaking in that language.

—Yes, your reverence, said Candide.

As they spoke these words, both men looked at one another with great surprise, and another emotion which they could not control.

—From what part of Germany do you come? said the Jesuit.

—From the nasty province of Westphalia, said Candide; I was born in the castle of Thunder-Ten-Tronckh.

—Merciful heavens! cries the commander. Is it possible?

—What a miracle! exclaims Candide.

—Can it be you? asks the commander.

—It's impossible, says Candide.

They both fall back in their chairs, they embrace, they shed streams of tears.

—What, can it be you, reverend father! you, the brother of the lovely Cunégonde! you, who were killed by the Bulgars! you, the son of My Lord the Baron! you, a Jesuit in Paraguay! It's a mad world, indeed it is. Oh, Pangloss! Pangloss! how happy you would be, if you hadn't been hanged.

The commander dismissed his negro slaves and the Paraguayans who served his drink in crystal goblets. He thanked God and Saint Ignatius a thousand times, he clasped Candide in his arms, their faces were bathed in tears.

—You would be even more astonished, even more delighted, even more

4. In this passage and several later ones, Voltaire uses in conjunction two words, both of which mean hummingbird. The French system of classifying hummingbirds, based on the work of the celebrated Buffon, distinguishes *oiseaux-mouches* with straight bills from *colibris* with curved bills. This distinction is wholly fallacious. Hummingbirds have all manner of shaped bills, and the division of species must be made on other grounds entirely. At the expense of ornithological accuracy, I have therefore introduced birds of paradise to get the requisite sense of glitter and sheen.

beside yourself, said Candide, if I told you that My Lady Cunégonde, your sister, who you thought was disemboweled, is enjoying good health.

—Where?

—Not far from here, in the house of the governor of Buenos Aires; and to think that I came to make war on you!

Each word they spoke in this long conversation added another miracle. Their souls danced on their tongues, hung eagerly at their ears, glittered in their eyes. As they were Germans, they sat a long time at table, waiting for the reverend father provincial; and the commander spoke in these terms to his dear Candide.

CHAPTER 15

How Candide Killed the Brother of His Dear Cunégonde

—All my life long I shall remember the horrible day when I saw my father and mother murdered and my sister raped. When the Bulgars left, that adorable sister of mine was nowhere to be found; so they loaded a cart with my mother, my father, myself, two serving girls, and three little murdered boys, to carry us all off for burial in a Jesuit chapel some two leagues from our ancestral castle. A Jesuit sprinkled us with holy water; it was horribly salty, and a few drops got into my eyes; the father noticed that my lid made a little tremor; putting his hand on my heart, he felt it beat; I was rescued, and at the end of three weeks was as good as new. You know, my dear Candide, that I was a very pretty boy; I became even more so; the reverend father Croust,[5] superior of the abbey, conceived a most tender friendship for me; he accepted me as a novice, and shortly after, I was sent to Rome. The Father General had need of a resupply of young German Jesuits. The rulers of Paraguay accept as few Spanish Jesuits as they can; they prefer foreigners, whom they think they can control better. I was judged fit, by the Father General, to labor in this vineyard. So we set off, a Pole, a Tyrolean, and myself. Upon our arrival, I was honored with the posts of subdeacon and lieutenant; today I am a colonel and a priest. We are giving a vigorous reception to the King of Spain's men; I assure you they will be excommunicated as well as trounced on the battlefield. Providence has sent you to help us. But is it really true that my dear sister, Cunégonde, is in the neighborhood, with the governor of Buenos Aires?

Candide reassured him with a solemn oath that nothing could be more true. Their tears began to flow again.

The baron could not weary of embracing Candide; he called him his brother, his savior.

—Ah, my dear Candide, said he, maybe together we will be able to enter the town as conquerors, and be united with my sister Cunégonde.

—That is all I desire, said Candide; I was expecting to marry her, and I still hope to.

—You insolent dog, replied the baron, you would have the effrontery to marry my sister, who has seventy-two quarterings! It's a piece of presumption for you even to mention such a crazy project in my presence.

Candide, terrified by this speech, answered:—Most reverend father, all

---

5. A Jesuit rector at Colmar with whom Voltaire had quarreled in 1754.

the quarterings in the world don't affect this case; I have rescued your sister out of the arms of a Jew and an inquisitor; she has many obligations to me, she wants to marry me. Master Pangloss always taught me that men are equal; and I shall certainly marry her.

—We'll see about that, you scoundrel, said the Jesuit baron of Thunder-Ten-Tronckh; and so saying, he gave him a blow across the face with the flat of his sword. Candide immediately drew his own sword and thrust it up to the hilt in the baron's belly; but as he drew it forth all dripping, he began to weep.

—Alas, dear God! said he, I have killed my old master, my friend, my brother-in-law; I am the best man in the world, and here are three men I've killed already, and two of the three were priests.

Cacambo, who was standing guard at the entry of the bower, came running.

—We can do nothing but sell our lives dearly, said his master; someone will certainly come; we must die fighting.

Cacambo, who had been in similar scrapes before, did not lose his head; he took the Jesuit's cassock, which the commander had been wearing, and put it on Candide; he stuck the dead man's square hat on Candide's head, and forced him onto horseback. Everything was done in the wink of an eye.

—Let's ride, master; everyone will take you for a Jesuit on his way to deliver orders; and we will have passed the frontier before anyone can come after us.

Even as he was pronouncing these words, he charged off, crying in Spanish:—Way, make way for the reverend father colonel!

CHAPTER 16

What Happened to the Two Travelers with Two Girls, Two Monkeys, and the Savages Named Biglugs

Candide and his valet were over the frontier before anyone in the camp knew of the death of the German Jesuit. Foresighted Cacambo had taken care to fill his satchel with bread, chocolate, ham, fruit, and several bottles of wine. They pushed their Andalusian horses forward into unknown country, where there were no roads. Finally a broad prairie divided by several streams opened before them. Our two travelers turned their horses loose to graze; Cacambo suggested that they eat too, and promptly set the example. But Candide said:—How can you expect me to eat ham when I have killed the son of My Lord the Baron, and am now condemned never to see the lovely Cunégonde for the rest of my life? Why should I drag out my miserable days, since I must exist far from her in the depths of despair and remorse? And what will the *Journal de Trévoux*[6] say of all this?

Though he talked this way, he did not neglect the food. Night fell. The two wanderers heard a few weak cries which seemed to be voiced by women. They could not tell whether the cries expressed grief or joy; but they leaped at once to their feet, with that uneasy suspicion which one always feels in an unknown country. The outcry arose from two girls, completely naked,

[handwritten margin note: Candide's rage excites him to murder again.]

6. Founded in 1701 and consistently hostile to Voltaire, this newspaper was published by the Jesuit order.

who were running swiftly along the edge of the meadow, pursued by two monkeys who snapped at their buttocks. Candide was moved to pity; he had learned marksmanship with the Bulgars, and could have knocked a nut off a bush without touching the leaves. He raised his Spanish rifle, fired twice, and killed the two monkeys.

—God be praised, my dear Cacambo! I've saved these two poor creatures from great danger. Though I committed a sin in killing an inquisitor and a Jesuit, I've redeemed myself by saving the lives of two girls. Perhaps they are two ladies of rank, and this good deed may gain us special advantages in the country.

[margin handwriting: He thinks a good deed can cover his transgressions]

He had more to say, but his mouth shut suddenly when he saw the girls embracing the monkeys tenderly, weeping over their bodies, and filling the air with lamentations.

—I wasn't looking for quite so much generosity of spirit, said he to Cacambo; the latter replied:—You've really fixed things this time, master; you've killed the two lovers of these young ladies.

—Their lovers! Impossible! You must be joking, Cacambo; how can I believe you?

—My dear master, Cacambo replied, you're always astonished by everything. Why do you think it so strange that in some countries monkeys succeed in obtaining the good graces of women? They are one quarter human, just as I am one quarter Spanish.

—Alas, Candide replied, I do remember now hearing Master Pangloss say that such things used to happen, and that from these mixtures there arose pans, fauns, and satyrs, and that these creatures had appeared to various grand figures of antiquity; but I took all that for fables.

—You should be convinced now, said Cacambo; it's true, and you see how people make mistakes who haven't received a measure of education. But what I fear is that these girls may get us into real trouble.

These sensible reflections led Candide to leave the field and to hide in a wood. There he dined with Cacambo; and there both of them, having duly cursed the inquisitor of Portugal, the governor of Buenos Aires, and the baron, went to sleep on a bed of moss. When they woke up, they found themselves unable to move; the reason was that during the night the Biglugs,[7] natives of the country, to whom the girls had complained of them, had tied them down with cords of bark. They were surrounded by fifty naked Biglugs, armed with arrows, clubs, and stone axes. Some were boiling a caldron of water, others were preparing spits, and all cried out:—It's a Jesuit, a Jesuit! We'll be revenged and have a good meal; let's eat some Jesuit, eat some Jesuit!

—I told you, my dear master, said Cacambo sadly, I said those two girls would play us a dirty trick.

Candide, noting the caldron and spits, cried out:—We are surely going to be roasted or boiled. Ah, what would Master Pangloss say if he could see these men in a state of nature? All is for the best, I agree; but I must say it seems hard to have lost Miss Cunégonde and to be stuck on a spit by the Biglugs.

Cacambo did not lose his head.

---

7. Voltaire's name is "Oreillons" from Spanish "Orejones," a name mentioned in Garcilaso de la Vega's *Historia General del Perú* (1609), on which Voltaire drew for many of the details in his picture of South America.

—Don't give up hope, said he to the disconsolate Candide; I understand a little of the jargon these people speak, and I'm going to talk to them.

—Don't forget to remind them, said Candide, of the frightful inhumanity of eating their fellow men, and that Christian ethics forbid it.

—Gentlemen, said Cacambo, you have a mind to eat a Jesuit today? An excellent idea; nothing is more proper than to treat one's enemies so. Indeed, the law of nature teaches us to kill our neighbor, and that's how men behave the whole world over. Though we Europeans don't exercise our right to eat our neighbors, the reason is simply that we find it easy to get a good meal elsewhere; but you don't have our resources, and we certainly agree that it's better to eat your enemies than to let the crows and vultures have the fruit of your victory. But, gentlemen, you wouldn't want to eat your friends. You think you will be spitting a Jesuit, and it's your defender, the enemy of your enemies, whom you will be roasting. For my part, I was born in your country; the gentleman whom you see is my master, and far from being a Jesuit, he has just killed a Jesuit, the robe he is wearing was stripped from him; that's why you have taken a dislike to him. To prove that I am telling the truth, take his robe and bring it to the nearest frontier of the kingdom of Los Padres; find out for yourselves if my master didn't kill a Jesuit officer. It won't take long; if you find that I have lied, you can still eat us. But if I've told the truth, you know too well the principles of public justice, customs, and laws, not to spare our lives.

Cacambo appeals to their pride, he flatters them.

The Biglugs found this discourse perfectly reasonable; they appointed chiefs to go posthaste and find out the truth; the two messengers performed their task like men of sense, and quickly returned bringing good news. The Biglugs untied their two prisoners, treated them with great politeness, offered them girls, gave them refreshments, and led them back to the border of their state, crying joyously:—He isn't a Jesuit, he isn't a Jesuit!

Candide could not weary of exclaiming over his preservation.

—What a people! he said. What men! what customs! If I had not had the good luck to run a sword through the body of Miss Cunégonde's brother, I would have been eaten on the spot! But, after all, it seems that uncorrupted nature is good, since these folk, instead of eating me, showed me a thousand kindnesses as soon as they knew I was not a Jesuit.

CHAPTER 17

Arrival of Candide and His Servant at the Country of Eldorado, and That They Saw There

When they were out of the land of the Biglugs, Cacambo said to Candide:—You see that this hemisphere is no better than the other; take my advice, and let's get back to Europe as soon as possible.

—How to get back, asked Candide, and where to go? If I go to my own land, the Bulgars and Abares are murdering everyone in sight; if I go to Portugal, they'll burn me alive; if we stay here, we risk being skewered any day. But how can I ever leave that part of the world where Miss Cunégonde lives?

—Let's go toward Cayenne, said Cacambo, we shall find some Frenchmen there, for they go all over the world; they can help us; perhaps God will take pity on us.

To get to Cayenne was not easy; they knew more or less which way to go, but mountains, rivers, cliffs, robbers, and savages obstructed the way everywhere. Their horses died of weariness; their food was eaten; they subsisted for one whole month on wild fruits, and at last they found themselves by a little river fringed with coconut trees, which gave them both life and hope.

Cacambo, who was as full of good advice as the old woman, said to Candide:—We can go no further, we've walked ourselves out; I see an abandoned canoe on the bank, let's fill it with coconuts, get into the boat, and float with the current; a river always leads to some inhabited spot or other. If we don't find anything pleasant, at least we may find something new.

—Let's go, said Candide, and let Providence be our guide.

They floated some leagues between banks sometimes flowery, sometimes sandy, now steep, now level. The river widened steadily; finally it disappeared into a chasm of frightful rocks that rose high into the heavens. The two travelers had the audacity to float with the current into this chasm. The river, narrowly confined, drove them onward with horrible speed and a fearful roar. After twenty-four hours, they saw daylight once more; but their canoe was smashed on the snags. They had to drag themselves from rock to rock for an entire league; at last they emerged to an immense horizon, ringed with remote mountains. The countryside was tended for pleasure as well as profit; everywhere the useful was joined to the agreeable. The roads were covered, or rather decorated, with elegantly shaped carriages made of a glittering material, carrying men and women of singular beauty, and drawn by great red sheep which were faster than the finest horses of Andalusia, Tetuan, and Mequinez.

—Here now, said Candide, is a country that's better than Westphalia.

Along with Cacambo, he climbed out of the river at the first village he could see. Some children of the town, dressed in rags of gold brocade, were playing quoits at the village gate; our two men from the other world paused to watch them; their quoits were rather large, yellow, red, and green, and they glittered with a singular luster. On a whim, the travelers picked up several; they were of gold, emeralds, and rubies, and the least of them would have been the greatest ornament of the Great Mogul's throne.

—Surely, said Cacambo, these quoit players are the children of the king of the country.

The village schoolmaster appeared at that moment, to call them back to school.

—And there, said Candide, is the tutor of the royal household.

The little rascals quickly gave up their game, leaving on the ground their quoits and playthings. Candide picked them up, ran to the schoolmaster, and presented them to him humbly, giving him to understand by sign language that their royal highnesses had forgotten their gold and jewels. With a smile, the schoolmaster tossed them to the ground, glanced quickly but with great surprise at Candide's face, and went his way.

The travelers did not fail to pick up the gold, rubies, and emeralds.

—Where in the world are we? cried Candide. The children of this land must be well trained, since they are taught contempt for gold and jewels.

Cacambo was as much surprised as Candide. At last they came to the finest house of the village; it was built like a European palace. A crowd of people surrounded the door, and even more were in the entry; delightful music was heard, and a delicious aroma of cooking filled the air. Cacambo went up to the door, listened, and reported that they were talking Peruvian; that was his native language, for every reader must know that Cacambo was born in Tucuman, in a village where they talk that language exclusively.

—I'll act as interpreter, he told Candide; it's an hotel, let's go in.

Promptly two boys and two girls of the staff, dressed in cloth of gold, and wearing ribbons in their hair, invited them to sit at the host's table. The meal consisted of four soups, each one garnished with a brace of parakeets, a boiled condor which weighed two hundred pounds, two roast monkeys of an excellent flavor, three hundred birds of paradise in one dish and six hundred hummingbirds in another, exquisite stews, delicious pastries, the whole thing served up in plates of what looked like rock crystal. The boys and girls of the staff poured them various beverages made from sugar cane.

The diners were for the most part merchants and travelers, all extremely polite, who questioned Cacambo with the most discreet circumspection, and answered his questions very directly.

When the meal was over, Cacambo as well as Candide supposed he could settle his bill handsomely by tossing onto the table two of those big pieces of gold which they had picked up; but the host and hostess burst out laughing, and for a long time nearly split their sides. Finally they subsided.

—Gentlemen, said the host, we see clearly that you're foreigners; we don't meet many of you here. Please excuse our laughing when you offered us in payment a couple of pebbles from the roadside. No doubt you don't have any of our local currency, but you don't need it to eat here. All the hotels established for the promotion of commerce are maintained by the state. You have had meager entertainment here, for we are only a poor town; but everywhere else you will be given the sort of welcome you deserve.

Cacambo translated for Candide all the host's explanations, and Candide listened to them with the same admiration and astonishment that his friend Cacambo showed in reporting them.

—What is this country, then, said they to one another, unknown to the rest of the world, and where nature itself is so different from our own? This probably is the country where everything is for the best; for it's absolutely necessary that such a country should exist somewhere. And whatever Master Pangloss said of the matter, I have often had occasion to notice that things went badly in Westphalia.

CHAPTER 18

What They Saw in the Land of Eldorado

Cacambo revealed his curiosity to the host, and the host told him:—I am an ignorant man and content to remain so; but we have here an old man, retired from the court, who is the most knowing person in the kingdom, and the most talkative.

Thereupon he brought Cacambo to the old man's house. Candide now played second fiddle, and acted as servant to his own valet. They entered an austere little house, for the door was merely of silver and the paneling of the rooms was only gold, though so tastefully wrought that the finest paneling would not surpass it. If the truth must be told, the lobby was only decorated with rubies and emeralds; but the patterns in which they were arranged atoned for the extreme simplicity.

The old man received the two strangers on a sofa stuffed with bird-of-paradise feathers, and offered them several drinks in diamond carafes; then he satisfied their curiosity in these terms.

—I am a hundred and seventy-two years old, and I heard from my late father, who was liveryman to the king, about the astonishing revolutions in Peru which he had seen. Our land here was formerly part of the kingdom of the Incas, who rashly left it in order to conquer another part of the world, and who were ultimately destroyed by the Spaniards. The wisest princes of their house were those who had never left their native valley; they decreed, with the consent of the nation, that henceforth no inhabitant of our little kingdom should ever leave it; and this rule is what has preserved our innocence and our happiness. The Spaniards heard vague rumors about this land, they called it El Dorado;[8] and an English knight named Raleigh even came somewhere close to it about a hundred years ago; but as we are surrounded by unscalable mountains and precipices, we have managed so far to remain hidden from the rapacity of the European nations, who have an inconceivable rage for the pebbles and mud of our land, and who, in order to get some, would butcher us all to the last man.

The conversation was a long one; it turned on the form of the government, the national customs, on women, public shows, the arts. At last Candide, whose taste always ran to metaphysics, told Cacambo to ask if the country had any religion.

The old man grew a bit red.

—How's that? he said. Can you have any doubt of it? Do you suppose we are altogether thankless scoundrels?

Cacambo asked meekly what was the religion of Eldorado. The old man flushed again.

—Can there be two religions? he asked. I suppose our religion is the same as everyone's, we worship God from morning to evening.

—Then you worship a single deity? said Cacambo, who acted throughout as interpreter of the questions of Candide.

—It's obvious, said the old man, that there aren't two or three or four of them. I must say the people of your world ask very remarkable questions.

Candide could not weary of putting questions to this good old man; he wanted to know how the people of Eldorado prayed to God.

—We don't pray to him at all, said the good and respectable sage; we have nothing to ask him for, since everything we need has already been granted; we thank God continually.

Candide was interested in seeing the priests; he had Cacambo ask where they were. The old gentleman smiled.

—My friends, said he, we are all priests; the king and all the heads of household sing formal psalms of thanksgiving every morning, and five or six thousand voices accompany them.

—What! you have no monks to teach, argue, govern, intrigue, and burn at the stake everyone who disagrees with them?

—We should have to be mad, said the old man; here we are all of the same mind, and we don't understand what you're up to with your monks.

Candide was overjoyed at all these speeches, and said to himself:—This is

---

8. The myth of this land of gold somewhere in Central or South America had been widespread since the 16th century. *The Discovery of Guiana*, published in 1595, described Sir Walter Ralegh's infatuation with the myth of Eldorado and served to spread the story still further.

very different from Westphalia and the castle of My Lord the Baron; if our friend Pangloss had seen Eldorado, he wouldn't have called the castle of Thunder-Ten-Tronckh the finest thing on earth; to know the world one must travel.

After this long conversation, the old gentleman ordered a carriage with six sheep made ready, and gave the two travelers twelve of his servants for their journey to the court.

—Excuse me, said he, if old age deprives me of the honor of accompanying you. The king will receive you after a style which will not altogether displease you, and you will doubtless make allowance for the customs of the country if there are any you do not like.

Candide and Cacambo climbed into the coach; the six sheep flew like the wind, and in less than four hours they reached the king's palace at the edge of the capital. The entryway was two hundred and twenty feet high and a hundred wide; it is impossible to describe all the materials of which it was made. But you can imagine how much finer it was than those pebbles and sand which we call gold and jewels.

Twenty beautiful girls of the guard detail welcomed Candide and Cacambo as they stepped from the carriage, took them to the baths, and dressed them in robes woven of hummingbird feathers; then the high officials of the crown, both male and female, led them to the royal chamber between two long lines, each of a thousand musicians, as is customary. As they approached the throne room, Cacambo asked an officer what was the proper method of greeting his majesty: if one fell to one's knees or on one's belly; if one put one's hands on one's head or on one's rear; if one licked up the dust of the earth—in a word, what was the proper form?[9]

—The ceremony, said the officer, is to embrace the king and kiss him on both cheeks.

Candide and Cacambo fell on the neck of his majesty, who received them with all the dignity imaginable, and asked them politely to dine.

In the interim, they were taken about to see the city, the public buildings rising to the clouds, the public markets and arcades, the fountains of pure water and of rose water, those of sugar cane liquors which flowed perpetually in the great plazas paved with a sort of stone which gave off odors of gilly-flower and rose petals. Candide asked to see the supreme court and the hall of parliament; they told him there was no such thing, that lawsuits were unknown. He asked if there were prisons, and was told there were not. What surprised him more, and gave him most pleasure, was the palace of sciences, in which he saw a gallery two thousand paces long, entirely filled with mathematical and physical instruments.

Having passed the whole afternoon seeing only a thousandth part of the city, they returned to the king's palace. Candide sat down to dinner with his majesty, his own valet Cacambo, and several ladies. Never was better food served, and never did a host preside more jovially than his majesty. Cacambo explained the king's witty sayings to Candide, and even when translated they still seemed witty. Of all the things which astonished Candide, this was not, in his eyes, the least astonishing.

[handwritten margin notes: Candide's scientific mind rejoices; Candide is surprised by the place.]

9. Candide's questions are probably derived from those of Gulliver on a similar occasion, in the third part of *Gulliver's Travels*.

They passed a month in this refuge. Candide never tired of saying to Cacambo:—It's true, my friend, I'll say it again, the castle where I was born does not compare with the land where we now are; but Miss Cunégonde is not here, and you doubtless have a mistress somewhere in Europe. If we stay here, we shall be just like everybody else, whereas if we go back to our own world, taking with us just a dozen sheep loaded with Eldorado pebbles, we shall be richer than all the kings put together, we shall have no more inquisitors to fear, and we shall easily be able to retake Miss Cunégonde.

This harangue pleased Cacambo; wandering is such pleasure, it gives a man such prestige at home to be able to talk of what he has seen abroad, that the two happy men resolved to be so no longer, but to take their leave of his majesty.

—You are making a foolish mistake, the king told them; I know very well that my kingdom is nothing much; but when you are pretty comfortable somewhere, you had better stay there. Of course I have no right to keep strangers against their will, that sort of tyranny is not in keeping with our laws or our customs; all men are free; depart when you will, but the way out is very difficult. You cannot possibly go up the river by which you miraculously came; it runs too swiftly through its underground caves. The mountains which surround my land are ten thousand feet high, and steep as walls; each one is more than ten leagues across; the only way down is over precipices. But since you really must go, I shall order my engineers to make a machine which can carry you conveniently. When we take you over the mountains, nobody will be able to go with you, for my subjects have sworn never to leave their refuge, and they are too sensible to break their vows. Other than that, ask of me what you please.

—We only request of your majesty, Cacambo said, a few sheep loaded with provisions, some pebbles, and some of the mud of your country.

The king laughed.

—I simply can't understand, said he, the passion you Europeans have for our yellow mud; but take all you want, and much good may it do you.

He promptly gave orders to his technicians to make a machine for lifting these two extraordinary men out of his kingdom. Three thousand good physicists worked at the problem; the machine was ready in two weeks' time, and cost no more than twenty million pounds sterling, in the money of the country. Cacambo and Candide were placed in the machine; there were two great sheep, saddled and bridled to serve them as steeds when they had cleared the mountains, twenty pack sheep with provisions, thirty which carried presents consisting of the rarities of the country, and fifty loaded with gold, jewels, and diamonds. The king bade tender farewell to the two vagabonds.

It made a fine spectacle, their departure, and the ingenious way in which they were hoisted with their sheep up to the top of the mountains. The technicians bade them good-bye after bringing them to safety, and Candide had now no other desire and no other object than to go and present his sheep to Miss Cunégonde.

—We have, said he, enough to pay off the governor of Buenos Aires—if, indeed, a price can be placed on Miss Cunégonde. Let us go to Cayenne, take ship there, and then see what kingdom we can find to buy up.

CHAPTER 19

What Happened to Them at Surinam, and How Candide Got to Know Martin

The first day was pleasant enough for our travelers. They were encouraged by the idea of possessing more treasures than Asia, Europe, and Africa could bring together. Candide, in transports, carved the name of Cunégonde on the trees. On the second day two of their sheep bogged down in a swamp and were lost with their loads; two other sheep died of fatigue a few days later; seven or eight others starved to death in a desert; still others fell, a little after, from precipices. Finally, after a hundred days' march, they had only two sheep left. Candide told Cacambo:—My friend, you see how the riches of this world are fleeting; the only solid things are virtue and the joy of seeing Miss Cunégonde again.

—I agree, said Cacambo, but we still have two sheep, laden with more treasure than the king of Spain will ever have; and I see in the distance a town which I suspect is Surinam; it belongs to the Dutch. We are at the end of our trials and on the threshold of our happiness.

As they drew near the town, they discovered a negro stretched on the ground with only half his clothes left, that is, a pair of blue drawers; the poor fellow was also missing his left leg and his right hand.

—Good Lord, said Candide in Dutch, what are you doing in that horrible condition, my friend?

—I am waiting for my master, Mr. Vanderdendur,[1] the famous merchant, answered the negro.

—Is Mr. Vanderdendur, Candide asked, the man who treated you this way?

—Yes, sir, said the negro, that's how things are around here. Twice a year we get a pair of linen drawers to wear. If we catch a finger in the sugar mill where we work, they cut off our hand; if we try to run away, they cut off our leg: I have undergone both these experiences. This is the price of the sugar you eat in Europe. And yet, when my mother sold me for ten Patagonian crowns on the coast of Guinea, she said to me: 'My dear child, bless our witch doctors, reverence them always, they will make your life happy; you have the honor of being a slave to our white masters, and in this way you are making the fortune of your father and mother.' Alas! I don't know if I made their fortunes, but they certainly did not make mine. The dogs, monkeys, and parrots are a thousand times less unhappy than we are. The Dutch witch doctors who converted me tell me every Sunday that we are all sons of Adam, black and white alike. I am no genealogist; but if these preachers are right, we must all be remote cousins; and you must admit no one could treat his own flesh and blood in a more horrible fashion.

—Oh Pangloss! cried Candide, you had no notion of these abominations! I'm through, I must give up your optimism after all.

—What's optimism? said Cacambo.

---

1. A name perhaps intended to suggest VanDuren, a Dutch bookseller with whom Voltaire had quarreled. In particular, the incident of gradually raising one's price recalls VanDuren, to whom Voltaire had successively offered 1,000, 1,500, 2,000, and 3,000 florins for the return of the manuscript of Frederick the Great's *Anti-Machiavel*.

—Alas, said Candide, it is a mania for saying things are well when one is in hell.

And he shed bitter tears as he looked at this negro, and he was still weeping as he entered Surinam.

The first thing they asked was if there was not some vessel in port which could be sent to Buenos Aires. The man they asked was a Spanish merchant who undertook to make an honest bargain with them. They arranged to meet in a café; Candide and the faithful Cacambo, with their two sheep, went there to meet with him.

Candide, who always said exactly what was in his heart, told the Spaniard of his adventures, and confessed that he wanted to recapture Miss Cunégonde.

—I shall take good care *not* to send you to Buenos Aires, said the merchant; I should be hanged, and so would you. The lovely Cunégonde is his lordship's favorite mistress.

This was a thunderstroke for Candide; he wept for a long time; finally he drew Cacambo aside.

—Here, my friend, said he, is what you must do. Each one of us has in his pockets five or six millions' worth of diamonds; you are cleverer than I; go get Miss Cunégonde in Buenos Aires. If the governor makes a fuss, give him a million; if that doesn't convince him, give him two millions; you never killed an inquisitor, nobody will suspect you. I'll fit out another boat and go wait for you in Venice. That is a free country, where one need have no fear either of Bulgars or Abares or Jews or inquisitors.

Cacambo approved of this wise decision. He was in despair at leaving a good master who had become a bosom friend; but the pleasure of serving him overcame the grief of leaving him. They embraced, and shed a few tears; Candide urged him not to forget the good old woman. Cacambo departed that very same day; he was a very good fellow, that Cacambo.

Candide remained for some time in Surinam, waiting for another merchant to take him to Italy, along with the two sheep which were left him. He hired servants and bought everything necessary for the long voyage; finally Mr. Vanderdendur, master of a big ship, came calling.

—How much will you charge, Candide asked this man, to take me to Venice—myself, my servants, my luggage, and those two sheep over there?

The merchant set a price of ten thousand piastres; Candide did not blink an eye.

—Oh, ho, said the prudent Vanderdendur to himself, this stranger pays out ten thousand piastres at once, he must be pretty well fixed.

Then, returning a moment later, he made known that he could not set sail under twenty thousand.

—All right, you shall have them, said Candide.

—Whew, said the merchant softly to himself, this man gives twenty thousand piastres as easily as ten.

He came back again to say he could not go to Venice for less than thirty thousand piastres.

—All right, thirty then, said Candide.

—Ah ha, said the Dutch merchant, again speaking to himself; so thirty thousand piastres mean nothing to this man; no doubt the two sheep are loaded with immense treasures; let's say no more; we'll pick up the thirty thousand piastres first, and then we'll see.

Candide sold two little diamonds, the least of which was worth more than all the money demanded by the merchant. He paid him in advance. The two sheep were taken aboard. Candide followed in a little boat, to board the vessel at its anchorage. The merchant bides his time, sets sail, and makes his escape with a favoring wind. Candide, aghast and stupefied, soon loses him from view.

Candide acts too quickly and loses all.

—Alas, he cries, now there is a trick worthy of the old world!

He returns to shore sunk in misery; for he had lost riches enough to make the fortunes of twenty monarchs.

Now he rushes to the house of the Dutch magistrate, and, being a bit disturbed, he knocks loudly at the door; goes in, tells the story of what happened, and shouts a bit louder than is customary. The judge begins by fining him ten thousand piastres for making such a racket; then he listens patiently to the story, promises to look into the matter as soon as the merchant comes back, and charges another ten thousand piastres as the costs of the hearing.

This legal proceeding completed the despair of Candide. In fact he had experienced miseries a thousand times more painful, but the coldness of the judge, and that of the merchant who had robbed him, roused his bile and plunged him into a black melancholy. The malice of men rose up before his spirit in all its ugliness, and his mind dwelt only on gloomy thoughts. Finally, when a French vessel was ready to leave for Bordeaux, since he had no more diamond-laden sheep to transport, he took a cabin at a fair price, and made it known in the town that he would pay passage and keep, plus two thousand piastres, to any honest man who wanted to make the journey with him, on condition that this man must be the most disgusted with his own condition and the most unhappy man in the province.

His optimism is gone.

This drew such a crowd of applicants as a fleet could not have held. Candide wanted to choose among the leading candidates, so he picked out about twenty who seemed companionable enough, and of whom each pretended to be more miserable than all the others. He brought them together at his inn and gave them a dinner, on condition that each would swear to tell truthfully his entire history. He would select as his companion the most truly miserable and rightly discontented man, and among the others he would distribute various gifts.

The meeting lasted till four in the morning. Candide, as he listened to all the stories, remembered what the old woman had told him on the trip to Buenos Aires, and of the wager she had made, that there was nobody on the boat who had not undergone great misfortunes. At every story that was told him, he thought of Pangloss.

—That Pangloss, he said, would be hard put to prove his system. I wish he was here. Certainly if everything goes well, it is in Eldorado and not in the rest of the world.

At last he decided in favor of a poor scholar who had worked ten years for the booksellers of Amsterdam. He decided that there was no trade in the world with which one should be more disgusted.

This scholar, who was in fact a good man, had been robbed by his wife, beaten by his son, and deserted by his daughter, who had got herself abducted by a Portuguese. He had just been fired from the little job on which he existed; and the preachers of Surinam were persecuting him because they took him for a Socinian.[2] The others, it is true, were at least as unhappy as he, but Candide hoped the scholar would prove more amusing on the voyage. All his rivals declared that Candide was doing them a great injustice, but he pacified them with a hundred piastres apiece.

CHAPTER 20
What Happened to Candide and Martin at Sea

The old scholar, whose name was Martin, now set sail with Candide for Bordeaux. Both men had seen and suffered much; and even if the vessel had been sailing from Surinam to Japan via the Cape of Good Hope, they would have been able to keep themselves amused with instances of moral evil and physical evil during the entire trip.

However, Candide had one great advantage over Martin, that he still hoped to see Miss Cunégonde again, and Martin had nothing to hope for; besides, he had gold and diamonds, and though he had lost a hundred big red sheep loaded with the greatest treasures of the earth, though he had always at his heart a memory of the Dutch merchant's villainy, yet, when he thought of the wealth that remained in his hands, and when he talked of Cunégonde, especially just after a good dinner, he still inclined to the system of Pangloss.

—But what about you, Monsieur Martin, he asked the scholar, what do you think of all that? What is your idea of moral evil and physical evil?

—Sir, answered Martin, those priests accused me of being a Socinian, but the truth is that I am a Manichee.[3]

—You're joking, said Candide; there aren't any more Manichees in the world.

—There's me, said Martin; I don't know what to do about it, but I can't think otherwise.

—You must be possessed of the devil, said Candide.

—He's mixed up with so many things of this world, said Martin, that he may be in me as well as elsewhere; but I assure you, as I survey this globe, or globule, I think that God has abandoned it to some evil spirit—all of it except Eldorado. I have scarcely seen one town which did not wish to destroy its neighboring town, no family which did not wish to exterminate some other family. Everywhere the weak loathe the powerful, before whom they cringe, and the powerful treat them like brute cattle, to be sold for their meat and fleece. A million regimented assassins roam Europe from one end to the other, plying the trades of murder and robbery in an organized way for a living, because there is no more honest form of work for them; and in the cities which seem to enjoy peace and where the arts are flourishing, men are devoured by more envy, cares, and anxieties than a whole town experiences

2. A follower of Faustus and Laelius Socinus, 16th-century Italian theologians, who proposed a form of "rational" Christianity which exalted the rational conscience and minimized such mysteries as the Trinity. The Socinians, by a special irony, were vigorous optimists.   3. Mani, a Persian sage and philosopher of the 3rd century C.E., taught (probably under the influence of traditions stemming from Zoroaster and the worshippers of the sun god Mithra) that the earth is a field of dispute between two almost equal powers, one of light and one of darkness, both of which must be propitiated.

when it's under siege. Private griefs are worse even than public trials. In a word, I have seen so much and suffered so much, that I am a Manichee.

—Still there is some good, said Candide.

—That may be, said Martin, but I don't know it. *Martin doesn't believe that good still exists.*

In the middle of this discussion, the rumble of cannon was heard. From minute to minute the noise grew louder. Everyone reached for his spyglass. At a distance of some three miles they saw two vessels fighting; the wind brought both of them so close to the French vessel that they had a pleasantly comfortable seat to watch the fight. Presently one of the vessels caught the other with a broadside so low and so square as to send it to the bottom. Candide and Martin saw clearly a hundred men on the deck of the sinking ship; they all raised their hands to heaven, uttering fearful shrieks; and in a moment everything was swallowed up.

—Well, said Martin, that is how men treat one another.

—It is true, said Candide, there's something devilish in this business.

As they chatted, he noticed something of a striking red color floating near the sunken vessel. They sent out a boat to investigate; it was one of his sheep. Candide was more joyful to recover this one sheep than he had been afflicted to lose a hundred of them, all loaded with big Eldorado diamonds.

The French captain soon learned that the captain of the victorious vessel was Spanish and that of the sunken vessel was a Dutch pirate. It was the same man who had robbed Candide. The enormous riches which this rascal had stolen were sunk beside him in the sea, and nothing was saved but a single sheep.

—You see, said Candide to Martin, crime is punished sometimes; this scoundrel of a Dutch merchant has met the fate he deserved. *He sees the bad only.*

—Yes, said Martin; but did the passengers aboard his ship have to perish too? God punished the scoundrel, and the devil drowned the others.

Meanwhile the French and Spanish vessels continued on their journey, and Candide continued his talks with Martin. They disputed for fifteen days in a row, and at the end of that time were just as much in agreement as at the beginning. But at least they were talking, they exchanged their ideas, they consoled one another. Candide caressed his sheep.

—Since I have found you again, said he, I may well rediscover Miss Cunégonde. *Candide still hopes*

CHAPTER 21

Candide and Martin Approach the Coast of France: They Reason Together

At last the coast of France came in view.

—Have you ever been in France, Monsieur Martin? asked Candide.

—Yes, said Martin, I have visited several provinces. There are some where half the inhabitants are crazy, others where they are too sly, still others where they are quite gentle and stupid, some where they venture on wit; in all of them the principal occupation is love-making, the second is slander, and the third stupid talk.

—But, Monsieur Martin, were you ever in Paris?

—Yes, I've been in Paris; it contains specimens of all these types; it is a chaos, a mob, in which everyone is seeking pleasure and where hardly anyone finds it, at least from what I have seen. I did not live there for long; as I arrived, I was robbed of everything I possessed by thieves at the fair of St. Germain; I myself was taken for a thief, and spent eight days in jail, after which I took a proofreader's job to earn enough money to return on foot to Holland. I knew the writing gang, the intriguing gang, the gang with fits and convulsions.[4] They say there are some very civilized people in that town; I'd like to think so.

—I myself have no desire to visit France, said Candide; you no doubt realize that when one has spent a month in Eldorado, there is nothing else on earth one wants to see, except Miss Cunégonde. I am going to wait for her at Venice; we will cross France simply to get to Italy; wouldn't you like to come with me?

—Gladly, said Martin; they say Venice is good only for the Venetian nobles, but that on the other hand they treat foreigners very well when they have plenty of money. I don't have any; you do, so I'll follow you anywhere.

—By the way, said Candide, do you believe the earth was originally all ocean, as they assure us in that big book belonging to the ship's captain?[5]

—I don't believe that stuff, said Martin, nor any of the dreams which people have been peddling for some time now.

—But why, then, was this world formed at all? asked Candide.

—To drive us mad, answered Martin.

—Aren't you astonished, Candide went on, at the love which those two girls showed for the monkeys in the land of the Biglugs that I told you about?

—Not at all, said Martin, I see nothing strange in these sentiments; I have seen so many extraordinary things that nothing seems extraordinary any more.

—Do you believe, asked Candide, that men have always massacred one another as they do today? That they have always been liars, traitors, ingrates, thieves, weaklings, sneaks, cowards, backbiters, gluttons, drunkards, misers, climbers, killers, calumniators, sensualists, fanatics, hypocrites, and fools?

—Do you believe, said Martin, that hawks have always eaten pigeons when they could get them?

—Of course, said Candide.

—Well, said Martin, if hawks have always had the same character, why do you suppose that men have changed?

—Oh, said Candide, there's a great deal of difference, because freedom of the will . . .

As they were disputing in this manner, they reached Bordeaux.

CHAPTER 22

What Happened in France to Candide and Martin

Candide paused in Bordeaux only long enough to sell a couple of Dorado pebbles and to fit himself out with a fine two-seater carriage, for he could no longer do without his philosopher Martin; only he was very unhappy to part with his sheep, which he left to the academy of science in Bordeaux.

4. The Jansenists, a sect of strict Catholics, became notorious for spiritual ecstasies. Their public displays reached a height during the 1720s, and Voltaire described them in *Le Siècle de Louis XIV* (chap. 37), as well as in the article "Convulsions" in the *Philosophical Dictionary*.   5. The Bible: Genesis 1.

They proposed, as the theme of that year's prize contest, the discovery of why the wool of the sheep was red; and the prize was awarded to a northern scholar[6] who demonstrated by A plus B minus C divided by Z that the sheep ought to be red and die of sheep rot.

But all the travelers with whom Candide talked in the roadside inns told him:—We are going to Paris.

This general consensus finally inspired in him too a desire to see the capital; it was not much out of his road to Venice.

He entered through the Faubourg Saint-Marceau,[7] and thought he was in the meanest village of Westphalia.

Scarcely was Candide in his hotel, when he came down with a mild illness caused by exhaustion. As he was wearing an enormous diamond ring, and people had noticed among his luggage a tremendously heavy safe, he soon found at his bedside two doctors whom he had not called, several intimate friends who never left him alone, and two pious ladies who helped to warm his broth. Martin said:—I remember that I too was ill on my first trip to Paris; I was very poor; and as I had neither friends, pious ladies, nor doctors, I got well.

Voltaire's thought about the part of medicine.

However, as a result of medicines and bleedings, Candide's illness became serious. A resident of the neighborhood came to ask him politely to fill out a ticket, to be delivered to the porter of the other world.[8] Candide wanted nothing to do with it. The pious ladies assured him it was a new fashion; Candide replied that he wasn't a man of fashion. Martin wanted to throw the resident out the window. The cleric swore that without the ticket they wouldn't bury Candide. Martin swore that he would bury the cleric if he continued to be a nuisance. The quarrel grew heated; Martin took him by the shoulders and threw him bodily out the door; all of which caused a great scandal, from which developed a legal case.

Candide got better; and during his convalescence he had very good company in to dine. They played cards for money; and Candide was quite surprised that none of the aces were ever dealt to him, and Martin was not surprised at all.

Among those who did the honors of the town for Candide there was a little abbé from Perigord, one of those busy fellows, always bright, always useful, assured, obsequious, and obliging, who waylay passing strangers, tell them the scandal of the town, and offer them pleasures at any price they want to pay. This fellow first took Candide and Martin to the theatre. A new tragedy was being played. Candide found himself seated next to a group of wits. That did not keep him from shedding a few tears in the course of some perfectly played scenes. One of the commentators beside him remarked during the intermission:—You are quite mistaken to weep, this actress is very bad indeed; the actor who plays with her is even worse; and the play is even worse than the actors in it. The author knows not a word of Arabic, though the action takes place in Arabia; and besides, he is a man who doesn't believe

---

6. Maupertuis Le Lapon, philosopher and mathematician, whom Voltaire had accused of trying to adduce mathematical proofs of the existence of God.   7. A district on the left bank, notably grubby in the 18th century. "As I entered [Paris] through the Faubourg Saint-Marceau, I saw nothing but dirty stinking little streets, ugly black houses, a general air of squalor and poverty, beggars, carters, menders of clothes, sellers of herb-drinks and old hats." Jean-Jacques Rousseau, *Confessions*, Book IV.   8. In the middle of the 18th century, it became customary to require persons who were grievously ill to sign *billets de confession*, without which they could not be given absolution, admitted to the last sacraments, or buried in consecrated ground.

in innate ideas. Tomorrow I will show you twenty pamphlets written against him.

—Tell me, sir, said Candide to the abbé, how many plays are there for performance in France?

—Five or six thousand, replied the other.

—That's a lot, said Candide; how many of them are any good?

—Fifteen or sixteen, was the answer.

—That's a lot, said Martin.

Candide was very pleased with an actress who took the part of Queen Elizabeth in a rather dull tragedy[9] that still gets played from time to time.

—I like this actress very much, he said to Martin, she bears a slight resemblance to Miss Cunégonde; I should like to meet her.

The abbé from Perigord offered to introduce him. Candide, raised in Germany, asked what was the protocol, how one behaved in France with queens of England.

—You must distinguish, said the abbé; in the provinces, you take them to an inn; at Paris they are respected while still attractive, and thrown on the dunghill when they are dead.[1]

—Queens on the dunghill! said Candide.

—Yes indeed, said Martin, the abbé is right; I was in Paris when Miss Monime herself[2] passed, as they say, from this life to the other; she was refused what these folk call 'the honors of burial,' that is, the right to rot with all the beggars of the district in a dirty cemetery; she was buried all alone by her troupe at the corner of the Rue de Bourgogne; this must have been very disagreeable to her, for she had a noble character.

—That was extremely rude, said Candide.

—What do you expect? said Martin; that is how these folk are. Imagine all the contradictions, all the incompatibilities you can, and you will see them in the government, the courts, the churches, and the plays of this crazy nation.

—Is it true that they are always laughing in Paris? asked Candide.

—Yes, said the abbé, but with a kind of rage too; when people complain of things, they do so amid explosions of laughter; they even laugh as they perform the most detestable actions.

—Who was that fat swine, said Candide, who spoke so nastily about the play over which I was weeping, and the actors who gave me so much pleasure?

—He is a living illness, answered the abbé, who makes a business of slandering all the plays and books; he hates the successful ones, as eunuchs hate successful lovers; he's one of those literary snakes who live on filth and venom; he's a folliculator . . .

—What's this word *folliculator*? asked Candide.

—It's a folio filler, said the abbé, a Fréron.[3]

It was after this fashion that Candide, Martin, and the abbé from Perigord chatted on the stairway as they watched the crowd leaving the theatre.

—Although I'm in a great hurry to see Miss Cunégonde again, said Can-

9. *Le Comte d'Essex* by Thomas Corneille.   1. Voltaire engaged in a long and vigorous campaign against the rule that actors and actresses could not be buried in consecrated ground. The superstition probably arose from a feeling that by assuming false identities they drained their own souls.   2. Adrienne Lecouvreur (1692–1730), so called because she made her debut as Monime in Racine's *Mithridate*. Voltaire had assisted at her secret midnight funeral and wrote an indignant poem about it.   3. A successful and popular journalist, who had attacked several of Voltaire's plays, including *Tancrède*.

dide, I would very much like to dine with Miss Clairon,[4] for she seemed to me admirable.

The abbé was not the man to approach Miss Clairon, who saw only good company.

—She has an engagement tonight, he said; but I shall have the honor of introducing you to a lady of quality, and there you will get to know Paris as if you had lived here for years.

Candide, who was curious by nature, allowed himself to be brought to the lady's house, in the depths of the Faubourg St.-Honoré; they were playing faro;[5] twelve melancholy punters held in their hands a little sheaf of cards, blank summaries of their bad luck. Silence reigned supreme, the punters were pallid, the banker uneasy; and the lady of the house, seated beside the pitiless banker, watched with the eyes of a lynx for the various illegal redoublings and bets at long odds which the players tried to signal by folding the corners of their cards; she had them unfolded with a determination which was severe but polite, and concealed her anger lest she lose her customers. The lady caused herself to be known as the Marquise of Parolignac.[6] Her daughter, fifteen years old, sat among the punters and tipped off her mother with a wink to the sharp practices of these unhappy players when they tried to recoup their losses. The abbé from Perigord, Candide, and Martin came in; nobody arose or greeted them or looked at them; all were lost in the study of their cards.

—My Lady the Baroness of Thunder-Ten-Tronckh was more civil, thought Candide.

However, the abbé whispered in the ear of the marquise, who, half rising, honored Candide with a gracious smile and Martin with a truly noble nod; she gave a seat and dealt a hand of cards to Candide, who lost fifty thousand francs in two turns; after which they had a very merry supper. Everyone was amazed that Candide was not upset over his losses; the lackeys, talking together in their usual lackey language, said:—He must be some English milord.

The supper was like most Parisian suppers: first silence, then an indistinguishable rush of words; then jokes, mostly insipid, false news, bad logic, a little politics, a great deal of malice. They even talked of new books.

—Have you seen the new novel by Dr. Gauchat, the theologian?[7] asked the abbé from Perigord.

—Oh yes, answered one of the guests; but I couldn't finish it. We have a horde of impudent scribblers nowadays, but all of them put together don't match the impudence of this Gauchat, this doctor of theology. I have been so struck by the enormous number of detestable books which are swamping us that I have taken up punting at faro.

—And the *Collected Essays* of Archdeacon T———[8] asked the abbé, what do you think of them?

—Ah, said Madame de Parolignac, what a frightful bore he is! He takes

4. Actually Claire Leris (1723–1803). She had played the lead role in *Tancrède* and was for many years a leading figure on the Paris stage.   5. A game of cards, about which it is necessary to know only that a number of punters play against a banker or dealer. The pack is dealt out two cards at a time, and each player may bet on any card as much as he pleases. The sharp practices of the punters consist essentially of tricks for increasing their winnings without corresponding risks.   6. A *paroli* is an illegal redoubling of one's bet; her name therefore implies a title grounded in cardsharping.   7. He had written against Voltaire, and Voltaire suspected him (wrongly) of having written the novel *L'Oracle des nouveaux philosophes*. 8. His name was Trublet, and he had said, among other disagreeable things, that Voltaire's epic poem, the *Henriade,* made him yawn and that Voltaire's genius was "the perfection of mediocrity."

such pains to tell you what everyone knows; he discourses so learnedly on matters which aren't worth a casual remark! He plunders, and not even wittily, the wit of other people! He spoils what he plunders, he's disgusting! But he'll never disgust me again; a couple of pages of the archdeacon have been enough for me. *Voltaire pokes fun at the church again.*

There was at table a man of learning and taste, who supported the marquise on this point. They talked next of tragedies; the lady asked why there were tragedies which played well enough but which were wholly unreadable. The man of taste explained very clearly how a play could have a certain interest and yet little merit otherwise; he showed succinctly that it was not enough to conduct a couple of intrigues, such as one can find in any novel, and which never fail to excite the spectator's interest; but that one must be new without being grotesque, frequently touch the sublime but never depart from the natural; that one must know the human heart and give it words; that one must be a great poet without allowing any character in the play to sound like a poet; and that one must know the language perfectly, speak it purely, and maintain a continual harmony without ever sacrificing sense to mere sound.

—Whoever, he added, does not observe all these rules may write one or two tragedies which succeed in the theatre, but he will never be ranked among the good writers; there are very few good tragedies; some are idylls in well-written, well-rhymed dialogue, others are political arguments which put the audience to sleep, or revolting pomposities; still others are the fantasies of enthusiasts, barbarous in style, incoherent in logic, full of long speeches to the gods because the author does not know how to address men, full of false maxims and emphatic commonplaces.

Candide listened attentively to this speech and conceived a high opinion of the speaker; and as the marquise had placed him by her side, he turned to ask her who was this man who spoke so well.

—He is a scholar, said the lady, who never plays cards and whom the abbé sometimes brings to my house for supper; he knows all about tragedies and books, and has himself written a tragedy that was hissed from the stage and a book, the only copy of which ever seen outside his publisher's office was dedicated to me.

—What a great man, said Candide, he's Pangloss all over.

Then, turning to him, he said:—Sir, you doubtless think everything is for the best in the physical as well as the moral universe, and that nothing could be otherwise than as it is?

—Not at all, sir, replied the scholar, I believe nothing of the sort. I find that everything goes wrong in our world; that nobody knows his place in society or his duty, what he's doing or what he ought to be doing, and that outside of mealtimes, which are cheerful and congenial enough, all the rest of the day is spent in useless quarrels, as of Jansenists against Molinists,[9] parliament-men against churchmen, literary men against literary men, courtiers against courtiers, financiers against the plebs, wives against husbands, relatives against relatives—it's one unending warfare.

Candide answered:—I have seen worse; but a wise man, who has since had the misfortune to be hanged, taught me that everything was marvelously

9. The Jansenists (from Corneille Jansen, 1585–1638) were a relatively strict party of religious reform; the Molinists (from Luis Molina, 1535–1600) were the party of the Jesuits. Their central issue of controversy was the relative importance of divine grace and human will to the salvation of man.

well arranged. <u>Troubles are just the shadows in a beautiful picture.</u> ⇐ *Candide sees troubles as a normal part of life.*

—Your hanged philosopher was joking, said Martin; the shadows are horrible ugly blots.

—It is human beings who make the blots, said Candide, and they can't do otherwise.

—Then it isn't their fault, said Martin.

Most of the faro players, who understood this sort of talk not at all, kept on drinking; Martin disputed with the scholar, and Candide told part of his story to the lady of the house.

After supper, the marquise brought Candide into her room and sat him down on a divan.

—Well, she said to him, are you still madly in love with Miss Cunégonde of Thunder-Ten-Tronckh?

—Yes, ma'am, replied Candide. The marquise turned upon him a tender smile.

—You answer like a young man of Westphalia, said she; a Frenchman would have told me: 'It is true that I have been in love with Miss Cunégonde; but since seeing you, madame, I fear that I love her no longer.'

—Alas, ma'am, said Candide, I will answer any way you want.

—Your passion for her, said the marquise, began when you picked up her handkerchief; I prefer that you should pick up my garter.

—Gladly, said Candide, and picked it up.

—But I also want you to put it back on, said the lady; and Candide put it on again.

—Look you now, said the lady, you are a foreigner; my Paris lovers I sometimes cause to languish for two weeks or so, but to you I surrender the very first night, because we must render the honors of the country to a young man from Westphalia.

The beauty, who had seen two enormous diamonds on the two hands of her young friend, praised them so sincerely that from the fingers of Candide they passed over to the fingers of the marquise. *Candide is flattered and gives away jewels*

As he returned home with his Perigord abbé, Candide felt some remorse at having been unfaithful to Miss Cunégonde; the abbé sympathized with his grief; he had only a small share in the fifty thousand francs which Candide lost at cards, and in the proceeds of the two diamonds which had been half-given, half-extorted. His scheme was to profit, as much as he could, from the advantage of knowing Candide. He spoke at length of Cunégonde, and Candide told him that he would beg forgiveness for his beloved for his infidelity when he met her at Venice.

The Perigordian overflowed with politeness and unction, taking a tender interest in everything Candide said, everything he did, and everything he wanted to do.

—Well, sir, said he, so you have an assignation at Venice?

—Yes indeed, sir, I do, said Candide; it is absolutely imperative that I go there to find Miss Cunégonde.

And then, carried away by the pleasure of talking about his love, he recounted, as he often did, a part of his adventures with that illustrious lady of Westphalia.

—I suppose, said the abbé, that Miss Cunégonde has a fine wit and writes charming letters.

—I never received a single letter from her, said Candide; for, as you can imagine, after being driven out of the castle for love of her, I couldn't write; shortly I learned that she was dead; then I rediscovered her; then I lost her again, and I have now sent, to a place more than twenty-five hundred leagues from here, a special agent whose return I am expecting.

The abbé listened carefully, and looked a bit dreamy. He soon took his leave of the two strangers, after embracing them tenderly. Next day Candide, when he woke up, received a letter, to the following effect:

—Dear sir, my very dear lover, I have been lying sick in this town for a week, I have just learned that you are here. I would fly to your arms if I could move. I heard that you had passed through Bordeaux; that was where I left the faithful Cacambo and the old woman, who are soon to follow me here. The governor of Buenos Aires took everything, but left me your heart. Come; your presence will either return me to life or cause me to die of joy.

This charming letter, coming so unexpectedly, filled Candide with inexpressible delight, while the illness of his dear Cunégonde covered him with grief. Torn between these two feelings, he took gold and diamonds, and had himself brought, with Martin, to the hotel where Miss Cunégonde was lodging. Trembling with emotion, he enters the room; his heart thumps, his voice breaks. He tries to open the curtains of the bed, he asks to have some lights.

—Absolutely forbidden, says the serving girl; light will be the death of her. And abruptly she pulls shut the curtain.

—My dear Cunégonde, says Candide in tears, how are you feeling? If you can't see me, won't you at least speak to me?

—She can't talk, says the servant.

But then she draws forth from the bed a plump hand, over which Candide weeps a long time, and which he fills with diamonds, meanwhile leaving a bag of gold on the chair.

Amid his transports, there arrives a bailiff followed by the abbé from Perigord and a strong-arm squad.

—These here are the suspicious foreigners? says the officer; and he has them seized and orders his bullies to drag them off to jail.

—They don't treat visitors like this in Eldorado, says Candide.

—I am more a Manichee than ever, says Martin.

—But, please sir, where are you taking us? says Candide.

—To the lowest hole in the dungeons, says the bailiff.

Martin, having regained his self-possession, decided that the lady who pretended to be Cunégonde was a cheat, the abbé from Perigord was another cheat who had imposed on Candide's innocence, and the bailiff still another cheat, of whom it would be easy to get rid.

Rather than submit to the forms of justice, Candide, enlightened by Martin's advice and eager for his own part to see the real Cunégonde again, offered the bailiff three little diamonds worth about three thousand pistoles apiece.

—Ah, my dear sir! cried the man with the ivory staff, even if you have committed every crime imaginable, you are the most honest man in the world. Three diamonds! each one worth three thousand pistoles! My dear sir! I would gladly die for you, rather than take you to jail. All foreigners get arrested here; but let me manage it; I have a brother at Dieppe in Normandy; I'll take you to him; and if you have a bit of a diamond to give him, he'll take care of you, just like me.

—And why do they arrest all foreigners? asked Candide.

The abbé from Perigord spoke up and said:—It's because a beggar from Atrebatum[1] listened to some stupidities; that made him commit a parricide, not like the one of May, 1610, but like the one of December, 1594, much on the order of several other crimes committed in other years and other months by other beggars who had listened to stupidities.

The bailiff then explained what it was all about.[2]

—Foh! what beasts! cried Candide. What! monstrous behavior of this sort from a people who sing and dance? As soon as I can, let me get out of this country, where the monkeys provoke the tigers. In my own country I've lived with bears; only in Eldorado are there proper men. In the name of God, sir bailiff, get me to Venice where I can wait for Miss Cunégonde.

—I can only get you to Lower Normandy, said the guardsman.

He had the irons removed at once, said there had been a mistake, dismissed his gang, and took Candide and Martin to Dieppe, where he left them with his brother. There was a little Dutch ship at anchor. The Norman, changed by three more diamonds into the most helpful of men, put Candide and his people aboard the vessel, which was bound for Portsmouth in England. It wasn't on the way to Venice, but Candide felt like a man just let out of hell; and he hoped to get back on the road to Venice at the first possible occasion.

CHAPTER 23

Candide and Martin Pass the Shores of England; What They See There

—Ah, Pangloss! Pangloss! Ah, Martin! Martin! Ah, my darling Cunégonde! What is this world of ours? sighed Candide on the Dutch vessel.

—Something crazy, something abominable, Martin replied.

—You have been in England; are people as crazy there as in France?

—It's a different sort of crazy, said Martin. You know that these two nations have been at war over a few acres of snow near Canada, and that they are spending on this fine struggle more than Canada itself is worth.[3] As for telling you if there are more people in one country or the other who need a strait jacket, that is a judgment too fine for my understanding; I know only that the people we are going to visit are eaten up with melancholy.

As they chatted thus, the vessel touched at Portsmouth. A multitude of people covered the shore, watching closely a rather bulky man who was kneeling, his eyes blindfolded, on the deck of a man-of-war. Four soldiers, stationed directly in front of this man, fired three bullets apiece into his brain, as peaceably as you would want; and the whole assemblage went home, in great satisfaction.[4]

1. The Latin name for the district of Artois, from which came Robert-François Damiens, who tried to stab Louis XV in 1757. The assassination failed, like that of Châtel, who tried to kill Henri IV in 1594, but unlike that of Ravaillac, who succeeded in killing him in 1610. 2. The point, in fact, is not too clear since arresting foreigners is an indirect way at best to guard against homegrown fanatics, and the position of the abbé from Périgord in the whole transaction remains confused. Has he called in the officer just to get rid of Candide? If so, why is he sardonic about the very suspicions he is trying to foster? Candide's reaction is to the notion that Frenchmen should be capable of political assassination at all; it seems excessive. 3. The wars of the French and English over Canada dragged intermittently through the 18th century until the peace of Paris sealed England's conquest (1763). Voltaire thought the French should concentrate on developing Louisiana, where the Jesuit influence was less marked. 4. Candide has witnessed the execution of Admiral John Byng, defeated off Minorca by the French fleet under Galisonnière and executed by firing squad on March 14, 1757. Voltaire had intervened to avert the execution.

—What's all this about? asked Candide. What devil is everywhere at work?

He asked who was that big man who had just been killed with so much ceremony.

—It was an admiral, they told him.

—And why kill this admiral?

—The reason, they told him, is that he didn't kill enough people; he gave battle to a French admiral, and it was found that he didn't get close enough to him.

—But, said Candide, the French admiral was just as far from the English admiral as the English admiral was from the French admiral.

—That's perfectly true, came the answer; but in this country it is useful from time to time to kill one admiral in order to encourage the others.

Candide was so stunned and shocked at what he saw and heard, that he would not even set foot ashore; he arranged with the Dutch merchant (without even caring if he was robbed, as at Surinam) to be taken forthwith to Venice.

The merchant was ready in two days; they coasted along France, they passed within sight of Lisbon, and Candide quivered. They entered the straits, crossed the Mediterranean, and finally landed at Venice.

—God be praised, said Candide, embracing Martin; here I shall recover the lovely Cunégonde. I trust Cacambo as I would myself. All is well, all goes well, all goes as well as possible.

CHAPTER 24

About Paquette and Brother Giroflée

As soon as he was in Venice, he had a search made for Cacambo in all the inns, all the cafés, all the stews—and found no trace of him. Every day he sent to investigate the vessels and coastal traders; no news of Cacambo.

—How's this? said he to Martin. I have had time to go from Surinam to Bordeaux, from Bordeaux to Paris, from Paris to Dieppe, from Dieppe to Portsmouth, to skirt Portugal and Spain, cross the Mediterranean, and spend several months at Venice—and the lovely Cunégonde has not come yet! In her place, I have met only that impersonator and that abbé from Perigord. Cunégonde is dead, without a doubt; and nothing remains for me too but death. Oh, it would have been better to stay in the earthly paradise of Eldorado than to return to this accursed Europe. How right you are, my dear Martin; all is but illusion and disaster.

He fell into a black melancholy, and refused to attend the fashionable operas or take part in the other diversions of the carnival season; not a single lady tempted him in the slightest. Martin told him:—You're a real simpleton if you think a half-breed valet with five or six millions in his pockets will go to the end of the world to get your mistress and bring her to Venice for you. If he finds her, he'll take her for himself; if he doesn't, he'll take another. I advise you to forget about your servant Cacambo and your mistress Cunégonde.

Martin was not very comforting. Candide's melancholy increased, and Martin never wearied of showing him that there is little virtue and little happiness on this earth, except perhaps in Eldorado, where nobody can go.

While they were discussing this important matter and still waiting for Cunégonde, Candide noticed in St. Mark's Square a young Theatine[5] monk who had given his arm to a girl. The Theatine seemed fresh, plump, and flourishing; his eyes were bright, his manner cocky, his glance brilliant, his step proud. The girl was very pretty, and singing aloud; she glanced lovingly at her Theatine, and from time to time pinched his plump cheeks.

—At least you must admit, said Candide to Martin, that these people are happy. Until now I have not found in the whole inhabited earth, except Eldorado, anything but miserable people. But this girl and this monk, I'd be willing to bet, are very happy creatures.

—I'll bet they aren't, said Martin.

—We have only to ask them to dinner, said Candide, and we'll find out if I'm wrong.

Promptly he approached them, made his compliments, and invited them to his inn for a meal of macaroni, Lombardy partridges, and caviar, washed down with wine from Montepulciano, Cyprus, and Samos, and some Lacrima Christi. The girl blushed but the Theatine accepted gladly, and the girl followed him, watching Candide with an expression of surprise and confusion, darkened by several tears. Scarcely had she entered the room when she said to Candide:—What, can it be that Master Candide no longer knows Paquette?

At these words Candide, who had not yet looked carefully at her because he was preoccupied with Cunégonde, said to her:—Ah, my poor child! so you are the one who put Doctor Pangloss in the fine fix where I last saw him.

—Alas, sir, I was the one, said Paquette; I see you know all about it. I heard of the horrible misfortunes which befell the whole household of My Lady the Baroness and the lovely Cunégonde. I swear to you that my own fate has been just as unhappy. I was perfectly innocent when you knew me. A Franciscan, who was my confessor, easily seduced me. The consequences were frightful; shortly after My Lord the Baron had driven you out with great kicks on the backside, I too was forced to leave the castle. If a famous doctor had not taken pity on me, I would have died. Out of gratitude, I became for some time the mistress of this doctor. His wife, who was jealous to the point of frenzy, beat me mercilessly every day; she was a gorgon. The doctor was the ugliest of men, and I the most miserable creature on earth, being continually beaten for a man I did not love. You will understand, sir, how dangerous it is for a nagging woman to be married to a doctor. This man, enraged by his wife's ways, one day gave her as a cold cure a medicine so potent that in two hours' time she died amid horrible convulsions. Her relatives brought suit against the bereaved husband; he fled the country, and I was put in prison. My innocence would never have saved me if I had not been rather pretty. The judge set me free on condition that he should become the doctor's successor. I was shortly replaced in this post by another girl, dismissed without any payment, and obliged to continue this abominable trade which you men find so pleasant and which for us is nothing but a bottomless pit of misery. I went to ply the trade in Venice. Ah, my dear sir, if you could imagine what it is like to have to caress indiscriminately an old merchant, a lawyer,

---

5. A Catholic order founded in 1524 by Cardinal Cajetan and G. P. Carafa, later Pope Paul IV.

a monk, a gondolier, an abbé; to be subjected to every sort of insult and outrage; to be reduced, time and again, to borrowing a skirt in order to go have it lifted by some disgusting man; to be robbed by this fellow of what one has gained from that; to be shaken down by the police, and to have before one only the prospect of a hideous old age, a hospital, and a dunghill, you will conclude that I am one of the most miserable creatures in the world.

Thus Paquette poured forth her heart to the good Candide in a hotel room, while Martin sat listening nearby. At last he said to Candide:—You see, I've already won half my bet.

Brother Giroflée[6] had remained in the dining room, and was having a drink before dinner.

—But how's this? said Candide to Paquette. You looked so happy, so joyous, when I met you; you were singing, you caressed the Theatine with such a natural air of delight; you seemed to me just as happy as you now say you are miserable.

—Ah, sir, replied Paquette, that's another one of the miseries of this business; yesterday I was robbed and beaten by an officer, and today I have to seem in good humor in order to please a monk.

Candide wanted no more; he conceded that Martin was right. They sat down to table with Paquette and the Theatine; the meal was amusing enough, and when it was over, the company spoke out among themselves with some frankness.

—Father, said Candide to the monk, you seem to me a man whom all the world might envy; the flower of health glows in your cheek, your features radiate pleasure; you have a pretty girl for your diversion, and you seem very happy with your life as a Theatine.

—Upon my word, sir, said Brother Giroflée, I wish that all the Theatines were at the bottom of the sea. A hundred times I have been tempted to set fire to my convent, and go turn Turk. My parents forced me, when I was fifteen years old, to put on this detestable robe, so they could leave more money to a cursed older brother of mine, may God confound him! Jealousy, faction, and fury spring up, by natural law, within the walls of convents. It is true, I have preached a few bad sermons which earned me a little money, half of which the prior stole from me; the remainder serves to keep me in girls. But when I have to go back to the monastery at night, I'm ready to smash my head against the walls of my cell; and all my fellow monks are in the same fix.

Martin turned to Candide and said with his customary coolness:

—Well, haven't I won the whole bet?

Candide gave two thousand piastres to Paquette and a thousand to Brother Giroflée.

—I assure you, said he, that with that they will be happy.

—I don't believe so, said Martin; your piastres may make them even more unhappy than they were before.

—That may be, said Candide; but one thing comforts me, I note that people often turn up whom one never expected to see again; it may well be that, having rediscovered my red sheep and Paquette, I will also rediscover Cunégonde.

6. His name means "carnation," and *Paquette* means "daisy."

—I hope, said Martin, that she will some day make you happy; but I very much doubt it.

—You're a hard man, said Candide.

—I've lived, said Martin.

—But look at these gondoliers, said Candide; aren't they always singing?

—You don't see them at home, said Martin, with their wives and squalling children. The doge has his troubles, the gondoliers theirs. It's true that on the whole one is better off as a gondolier than as a doge; but the difference is so slight, I don't suppose it's worth the trouble of discussing.

—There's a lot of talk here, said Candide, of this Senator Pococurante,[7] who has a fine palace on the Brenta and is hospitable to foreigners. They say he is a man who has never known a moment's grief.

—I'd like to see such a rare specimen, said Martin.

Candide promptly sent to Lord Pococurante, asking permission to call on him tomorrow.

CHAPTER 25

Visit to Lord Pococurante, Venetian Nobleman

Candide and Martin took a gondola on the Brenta, and soon reached the palace of the noble Pococurante. The gardens were large and filled with beautiful marble statues; the palace was handsomely designed. The master of the house, sixty years old and very rich, received his two inquisitive visitors perfectly politely, but with very little warmth; Candide was disconcerted and Martin not at all displeased.

First two pretty and neatly dressed girls served chocolate, which they whipped to a froth. Candide could not forbear praising their beauty, their grace, their skill.

—They are pretty good creatures, said Pococurante; I sometimes have them into my bed, for I'm tired of the ladies of the town, with their stupid tricks, quarrels, jealousies, fits of ill humor and petty pride, and all the sonnets one has to make or order for them; but, after all, these two girls are starting to bore me too.

After lunch, Candide strolled through a long gallery, and was amazed at the beauty of the pictures. He asked who was the painter of the two finest.

—They are by Raphael, said the senator; I bought them for a lot of money, out of vanity, some years ago; people say they're the finest in Italy, but they don't please me at all; the colors have all turned brown, the figures aren't well modeled and don't stand out enough, the draperies bear no resemblance to real cloth. In a word, whatever people may say, I don't find in them a real imitation of nature. I like a picture only when I can see in it a touch of nature itself, and there are none of this sort. I have many paintings, but I no longer look at them.

As they waited for dinner, Pococurante ordered a concerto performed. Candide found the music delightful.

—That noise? said Pococurante. It may amuse you for half an hour, but if it goes on any longer, it tires everybody though no one dares to admit it.

---

7. His name means "small care."

Music today is only the art of performing difficult pieces, and what is merely difficult cannot please for long. Perhaps I should prefer the opera, if they had not found ways to make it revolting and monstrous. Anyone who likes bad tragedies set to music is welcome to them; in these performances the scenes serve only to introduce, inappropriately, two or three ridiculous songs designed to show off the actress's sound box. Anyone who wants to, or who can, is welcome to swoon with pleasure at the sight of a castrate wriggling through the role of Caesar or Cato, and strutting awkwardly about the stage. For my part, I have long since given up these paltry trifles which are called the glory of modern Italy, and for which monarchs pay such ruinous prices.

Candide argued a bit, but timidly; Martin was entirely of a mind with the senator.

They sat down to dinner, and after an excellent meal adjourned to the library. Candide, seeing a copy of Homer in a splendid binding, complimented the noble lord on his good taste.

—That is an author, said he, who was the special delight of great Pangloss, the best philosopher in all Germany.

—He's no special delight of mine, said Pococurante coldly. I was once made to believe that I took pleasure in reading him; but that constant recital of fights which are all alike, those gods who are always interfering but never decisively, that Helen who is the cause of the war and then scarcely takes any part in the story, that Troy which is always under siege and never taken— all that bores me to tears. I have sometimes asked scholars if reading it bored them as much as it bores me; everyone who answered frankly told me the book dropped from his hands like lead, but that they had to have it in their libraries as a monument of antiquity, like those old rusty coins which can't be used in real trade.

Your Excellence doesn't hold the same opinion of Virgil? said Candide.

—I concede, said Pococurante, that the second, fourth, and sixth books of his *Aeneid* are fine; but as for his pious Aeneas, and strong Cloanthes, and faithful Achates, and little Ascanius, and that imbecile King Latinus, and middle-class Amata, and insipid Lavinia, I don't suppose there was ever anything so cold and unpleasant. I prefer Tasso and those sleepwalkers' stories of Ariosto.

—Dare I ask, sir, said Candide, if you don't get great enjoyment from reading Horace?

—There are some maxims there, said Pococurante, from which a man of the world can profit, and which, because they are formed into vigorous couplets, are more easily remembered; but I care very little for his trip to Brindisi, his description of a bad dinner, or his account of a quibblers' squabble between some fellow Pupilus, whose words he says *were full of pus*, and another whose words *were full of vinegar*.[8] I feel nothing but extreme disgust at his verses against old women and witches; and I can't see what's so great in his telling his friend Maecenas that if he is raised by him to the ranks of lyric poets, he will strike the stars with his lofty forehead. Fools admire everything in a well-known author. I read only for my own pleasure; I like only what is in my style.

8. *Satires* I.vii; Pococurante, with gentlemanly negligence, has corrupted Rupilius to Pupilus. Horace's poems against witches are *Epodes* V, VIII, XII; the one about striking the stars with his lofty forehead is *Odes* I.i.

Contrast in the way Candide and Martin think

Pococurante's arrogance

Candide, who had been trained never to judge for himself, was much astonished by what he heard; and Martin found Pococurante's way of thinking quite rational.

—Oh, here is a copy of Cicero, said Candide. Now this great man I suppose you're never tired of reading.

—I never read him at all, replied the Venetian. What do I care whether he pleaded for Rabirius or Cluentius? As a judge, I have my hands full of lawsuits. I might like his philosophical works better, but when I saw that he had doubts about everything, I concluded that I knew as much as he did, and that I needed no help to be ignorant.

—Ah, here are eighty volumes of collected papers from a scientific academy, cried Martin; maybe there is something good in them.

—There would be indeed, said Pococurante, if one of these silly authors had merely discovered a new way of making pins; but in all those volumes there is nothing but empty systems, not a single useful discovery.

—What a lot of stage plays I see over there, said Candide, some in Italian, some in Spanish and French.

—Yes, said the senator, three thousand of them, and not three dozen good ones. As for those collections of sermons, which all together are not worth a page of Seneca, and all these heavy volumes of theology, you may be sure I never open them, nor does anybody else.

Martin noticed some shelves full of English books.

—I suppose, said he, that a republican must delight in most of these books written in the land of liberty.

—Yes, replied Pococurante, it's a fine thing to write as you think; it is mankind's privilege. In all our Italy, people write only what they do not think; men who inhabit the land of the Caesars and Antonines dare not have an idea without the permission of a Dominican. I would rejoice in the freedom that breathes through English genius, if partisan passions did not corrupt all that is good in that precious freedom.

Candide, noting a Milton, asked if he did not consider this author a great man.

—Who? said Pococurante. That barbarian who made a long commentary on the first chapter of Genesis in ten books of crabbed verse?[9] That clumsy imitator of the Greeks, who disfigures creation itself, and while Moses represents the eternal being as creating the world with a word, has the messiah take a big compass out of a heavenly cupboard in order to design his work? You expect me to admire the man who spoiled Tasso's hell and devil? who disguises Lucifer now as a toad, now as a pigmy? who makes him rehash the same arguments a hundred times over? who makes him argue theology? and who, taking seriously Ariosto's comic story of the invention of firearms, has the devils shooting off cannon in heaven? Neither I nor anyone else in Italy has been able to enjoy these gloomy extravagances. The marriage of Sin and Death, and the monster that Sin gives birth to, will nauseate any man whose taste is at all refined; and his long description of a hospital is good only for a gravedigger. This obscure, extravagant, and disgusting poem was despised at its birth; I treat it today as it was treated in its own country by its contem-

9. The first edition of *Paradise Lost* had ten books, which Milton later expanded to twelve.

poraries. Anyhow, I say what I think, and care very little whether other people agree with me. ← *This is a very accurate statement.*

Candide was a little cast down by this speech; he respected Homer, and had a little affection for Milton.

—Alas, he said under his breath to Martin, I'm afraid this man will have a supreme contempt for our German poets.

—No harm in that, said Martin.

—Oh what a superior man, said Candide, still speaking softly, what a great genius this Pococurante must be! Nothing can please him.

Having thus looked over all the books, they went down into the garden. Candide praised its many beauties.

—I know nothing in such bad taste, said the master of the house; we have nothing but trifles here; tomorrow I am going to have one set out on a nobler design.

When the two visitors had taken leave of his excellency:—Well now, said Candide to Martin, you must agree that this was the happiest of all men, for he is superior to everything he possesses.

—Don't you see, said Martin, that he is disgusted with everything he possesses? Plato said, a long time ago, that the best stomachs are not those which refuse all food.

—But, said Candide, isn't there pleasure in criticizing everything, in seeing faults where other people think they see beauties?

—That is to say, Martin replied, that there's pleasure in having no pleasure?

—Oh well, said Candide, then I am the only happy man . . . or will be, when I see Miss Cunégonde again.

—It's always a good thing to have hope, said Martin.

But the days and the weeks slipped past; Cacambo did not come back, and Candide was so buried in his grief, that he did not even notice that Paquette and Brother Giroflée had neglected to come and thank him.

Pococurante is never satisfied

Candide's bit of sarcasm.

CHAPTER 26

About a Supper that Candide and Martin Had with Six Strangers, and Who They Were

One evening when Candide, accompanied by Martin, was about to sit down for dinner with the strangers staying in his hotel, a man with a soot-colored face came up behind him, took him by the arm, and said:—Be ready to leave with us, don't miss out.

He turned and saw Cacambo. Only the sight of Cunégonde could have astonished and pleased him more. He nearly went mad with joy. He embraced his dear friend.

—Cunégonde is here, no doubt? Where is she? Bring me to her, let me die of joy in her presence.

—Cunégonde is not here at all, said Cacambo, she is at Constantinople.

—Good Heavens, at Constantinople! but if she were in China, I must fly there, let's go.

—We will leave after supper, said Cacambo; I can tell you no more; I am a slave, my owner is looking for me, I must go wait on him at table; mum's the word; eat your supper and be prepared.

Candide, torn between joy and grief, delighted to have seen his faithful agent again, astonished to find him a slave, full of the idea of recovering his mistress, his heart in a turmoil, his mind in a whirl, sat down to eat with Martin, who was watching all these events coolly, and with six strangers who had come to pass the carnival season at Venice.

Cacambo, who was pouring wine for one of the strangers, leaned respect-fully over his master at the end of the meal, and said to him:—Sire, Your Majesty may leave when he pleases, the vessel is ready.

Having said these words, he exited. The diners looked at one another in silent amazement, when another servant, approaching his master, said to him:—Sire, Your Majesty's litter is at Padua, and the bark awaits you.

The master nodded, and the servant vanished. All the diners looked at one another again, and the general amazement redoubled. A third servant, approaching a third stranger, said to him:—Sire, take my word for it, Your Majesty must stay here no longer; I shall get everything ready.

Then he too disappeared.

Candide and Martin had no doubt, now, that it was a carnival masquerade. A fourth servant spoke to a fourth master:—Your Majesty will leave when he pleases—and went out like the others. A fifth followed suit. But the sixth servant spoke differently to the sixth stranger, who sat next to Candide. He said:—My word, sire, they'll give no more credit to Your Majesty, nor to me either; we could very well spend the night in the lockup, you and I. I've got to look out for myself, so good-bye to you.

When all the servants had left, the six strangers, Candide, and Martin remained under a pall of silence. Finally Candide broke it.

—Gentlemen, said he, here's a funny kind of joke. Why are you all royalty? I assure you that Martin and I aren't.

Cacambo's master spoke up gravely then, and said in Italian:—This is no joke, my name is Achmet the Third.[1] I was grand sultan for several years; then, as I had dethroned my brother, my nephew dethroned me. My viziers had their throats cut; I was allowed to end my days in the old seraglio. My nephew, the Grand Sultan Mahmoud, sometimes lets me travel for my health; and I have come to spend the carnival season at Venice.

A young man who sat next to Achmet spoke after him, and said:—My name is Ivan; I was once emperor of all the Russias.[2] I was dethroned while still in my cradle; my father and mother were locked up, and I was raised in prison; I sometimes have permission to travel, though always under guard, and I have come to spend the carnival season at Venice.

The third said:—I am Charles Edward, king of England;[3] my father yielded me his rights to the kingdom, and I fought to uphold them; but they tore out the hearts of eight hundred of my partisans, and flung them in their faces. I have been in prison; now I am going to Rome, to visit the king, my father, dethroned like me and my grandfather; and I have come to pass the carnival season at Venice.

The fourth king then spoke up, and said:—I am a king of the Poles;[4] the

1. Ottoman ruler (1673–1736); he was deposed in 1730. 2. Ivan VI reigned from his birth in 1740 until 1756, then was confined in the Schlusselberg, and executed in 1764. 3. This is the Young Pre-tender (1720–1788), known to his supporters as Bonnie Prince Charlie. The defeat so theatrically described took place at Culloden, April 16, 1746. 4. Augustus III (1696–1763), elector of Saxony and king of Poland, dethroned by Frederick the Great in 1756.

luck of war has deprived me of my hereditary estates; my father suffered the same losses; I submit to Providence like Sultan Achmet, Emperor Ivan, and King Charles Edward, to whom I hope heaven grants long lives; and I have come to pass the carnival season at Venice.

The fifth said:—I too am a king of the Poles;[5] I lost my kingdom twice, but Providence gave me another state, in which I have been able to do more good than all the Sarmatian kings ever managed to do on the banks of the Vistula. I too have submitted to Providence, and I have come to pass the carnival season at Venice.

It remained for the sixth monarch to speak.

—Gentlemen, said he, I am no such great lord as you, but I have in fact been a king like any other. I am Theodore; I was elected king of Corsica.[6] People used to call me *Your Majesty,* and now they barely call me *Sir;* I used to coin currency, and now I don't have a cent; I used to have two secretaries of state, and now I scarcely have a valet; I have sat on a throne, and for a long time in London I was in jail, on the straw; and I may well be treated the same way here, though I have come, like your majesties, to pass the carnival season at Venice.

The five other kings listened to his story with noble compassion. Each one of them gave twenty sequins to King Theodore, so that he might buy a suit and some shirts; Candide gave him a diamond worth two thousand sequins.

—Who in the world, said the five kings, is this private citizen who is in a position to give a hundred times as much as any of us, and who actually gives it?[7]

Just as they were rising from dinner, there arrived at the same establishment four most serene highnesses, who had also lost their kingdoms through the luck of war, and who came to spend the rest of the carnival season at Venice. But Candide never bothered even to look at these newcomers because he was only concerned to go find his dear Cunégonde at Constantinople.

CHAPTER 27

Candide's Trip to Constantinople

Faithful Cacambo had already arranged with the Turkish captain who was returning Sultan Achmet to Constantinople to make room for Candide and Martin on board. Both men boarded ship after prostrating themselves before his miserable highness. On the way, Candide said to Martin:—Six dethroned kings that we had dinner with! and yet among those six there was one on

---

5. Stanisław Leszczyński (1677–1766), father-in-law of Louis XV, who abdicated the throne of Poland in 1736, was made duke of Lorraine and in that capacity befriended Voltaire.   **6.** Theodore, Baron von Neuhof (1690–1756), an authentic Westphalian, an adventurer, and a soldier of fortune, who in 1736 was (for about eight months) the elected king of Corsica. He spent time in an Amsterdam as well as a London debtor's prison.   **7.** A late correction of Voltaire's makes this passage read:

"—Who is this man who is in a position to give a hundred times as much as any of us, and who actually gives it? Are you a king too, sir?

"—No, gentlemen, and I have no desire to be."

But this reading, though Voltaire's on good authority, produces a conflict with Candide's previous remark: "—Why are you all royalty? I assure you that Martin and I aren't."

Thus, it has seemed better for literary reasons to follow an earlier reading. Voltaire was very conscious of his situation as a man richer than many princes; in 1758 he had money on loan to no fewer than three highnesses, Charles Eugene, duke of Wurtemburg; Charles Theodore, Elector Palatine; and the duke of Saxe-Gotha.

whom I had to bestow charity! Perhaps there are other princes even more unfortunate. I myself have only lost a hundred sheep, and now I am flying to the arms of Cunégonde. My dear Martin, once again Pangloss is proved right, all is for the best. *[handwritten: Often, Candide's optimism is premature]*

—I hope so, said Martin.

—But, said Candide, that was a most unlikely experience we had at Venice. Nobody ever saw, or heard tell of, six dethroned kings eating together at an inn.

—It is no more extraordinary, said Martin, than most of the things that have happened to us. Kings are frequently dethroned; and as for the honor we had from dining with them, that's a trifle which doesn't deserve our notice.[8]

Scarcely was Candide on board than he fell on the neck of his former servant, his friend Cacambo.

—Well! said he, what is Cunégonde doing? Is she still a marvel of beauty? Does she still love me? How is her health? No doubt you have bought her a palace at Constantinople.

—My dear master, answered Cacambo, Cunégonde is washing dishes on the shores of the Propontis, in the house of a prince who has very few dishes to wash; she is a slave in the house of a onetime king named Ragotski,[9] to whom the Great Turk allows three crowns a day in his exile; but, what is worse than all this, she has lost all her beauty and become horribly ugly. *[handwritten: Cunégonde has met a terrible fate.]*

—Ah, beautiful or ugly, said Candide, I am an honest man, and my duty is to love her forever. But how can she be reduced to this wretched state with the five or six millions that you had? *[handwritten: He says he will love her in spite of all.]*

—All right, said Cacambo, didn't I have to give two millions to Señor don Fernando d'Ibaraa y Figueroa y Mascarenes y Lampourdos y Souza, governor of Buenos Aires, for his permission to carry off Miss Cunégonde? And didn't a pirate cleverly strip us of the rest? And didn't this pirate carry us off to Cape Matapan, to Melos, Nicaria, Samos, Petra, to the Dardanelles, Marmora, Scutari? Cunégonde and the old woman are working for the prince I told you about, and I am the slave of the dethroned sultan.

—What a lot of fearful calamities linked one to the other, said Candide. But after all, I still have a few diamonds, I shall easily deliver Cunégonde. What a pity that she's become so ugly! *[handwritten: He is sorry her beauty's gone.]*

Then, turning toward Martin, he asked:—Who in your opinion is more to be pitied, the Emperor Achmet, the Emperor Ivan, King Charles Edward, or myself?

—I have no idea, said Martin; I would have to enter your hearts in order to tell.

—Ah, said Candide, if Pangloss were here, he would know and he would tell us.

—I can't imagine, said Martin, what scales your Pangloss would use to weigh out the miseries of men and value their griefs. All I will venture is that the earth holds millions of men who deserve our pity a hundred times more than King Charles Edward, Emperor Ivan, or Sultan Achmet. *[handwritten: Candide's plight may not be the worse of all.]*

—You may well be right, said Candide.

<hr>

8. Another late change adds the following question: "—*What does it matter whom you dine with as long as you fare well at table?*" I have omitted it, again on literary grounds.   9. Francis Leopold Rakoczy (1676–1735), who was briefly king of Transylvania in the early 18th century. After 1720 he was interned in Turkey.

In a few days they arrived at the Black Sea canal. Candide began by repurchasing Cacambo at an exorbitant price; then, without losing an instant, he flung himself and his companions into a galley to go search out Cunégonde on the shores of Propontis, however ugly she might be.

There were in the chain gang two convicts who bent clumsily to the oar, and on whose bare shoulders the Levantine[1] captain delivered from time to time a few lashes with a bullwhip. Candide naturally noticed them more than the other galley slaves, and out of pity came closer to them. Certain features of their disfigured faces seemed to him to bear a slight resemblance to Pangloss and to that wretched Jesuit, that baron, that brother of Miss Cunégonde. The notion stirred and saddened him. He looked at them more closely.

—To tell you the truth, he said to Cacambo, if I hadn't seen Master Pangloss hanged, and if I hadn't been so miserable as to murder the baron, I should think they were rowing in this very galley.

At the names of 'baron' and 'Pangloss' the two convicts gave a great cry, sat still on their bench, and dropped their oars. The Levantine captain came running, and the bullwhip lashes redoubled.

—Stop, stop, captain, cried Candide. I'll give you as much money as you want.

—What, can it be Candide? cried one of the convicts.

—What, can it be Candide? cried the other.

—Is this a dream? said Candide. Am I awake or asleep? Am I in this galley? Is that My Lord the Baron, whom I killed? Is that Master Pangloss, whom I saw hanged?

—It is indeed, they replied.

—What, is that the great philosopher? said Martin.

—Now, sir, Mr. Levantine Captain, said Candide, how much money do you want for the ransom of My Lord Thunder-Ten-Tronckh, one of the first barons of the empire, and Master Pangloss, the deepest metaphysician in all Germany?

—Dog of a Christian, replied the Levantine captain, since these two dogs of Christian convicts are barons and metaphysicians, which is no doubt a great honor in their country, you will give me fifty thousand sequins for them.

—You shall have them, sir, take me back to Constantinople and you shall be paid on the spot. Or no, take me to Miss Cunégonde.

The Levantine captain, at Candide's first word, had turned his bow toward the town, and he had them rowed there as swiftly as a bird cleaves the air. A hundred times Candide embraced the baron and Pangloss.

—And how does it happen I didn't kill you, my dear baron? and my dear Pangloss, how can you be alive after being hanged? and why are you both rowing in the galleys of Turkey?

—Is it really true that my dear sister is in this country? asked the baron.

—Yes, answered Cacambo.

—And do I really see again my dear Candide? cried Pangloss.

Candide introduced Martin and Cacambo. They all embraced; they all talked at once. The galley flew, already they were back in port. A Jew was called, and Candide sold him for fifty thousand sequins a diamond worth a

---

1. From the eastern Mediterranean.

hundred thousand, while he protested by Abraham that he could not possibly give more for it. Candide immediately ransomed the baron and Pangloss. The latter threw himself at the feet of his liberator, and bathed them with tears; the former thanked him with a nod, and promised to repay this bit of money at the first opportunity.

—But is it really possible that my sister is in Turkey? said he.

—Nothing is more possible, replied Cacambo, since she is a dishwasher in the house of a prince of Transylvania.

At once two more Jews were called; Candide sold some more diamonds; and they all departed in another galley to the rescue of Cunégonde.

CHAPTER 28

What Happened to Candide, Cunégonde, Pangloss, Martin, &c.

—Let me beg your pardon once more, said Candide to the baron, pardon me, reverend father, for having run you through the body with my sword.

—Don't mention it, replied the baron. I was a little too hasty myself, I confess it; but since you want to know the misfortune which brought me to the galleys, I'll tell you. After being cured of my wound by the brother who was apothecary to the college, I was attacked and abducted by a Spanish raiding party; they jailed me in Buenos Aires at the time when my sister had just left. I asked to be sent to Rome, to the father general. Instead, I was named to serve as almoner in Constantinople, under the French ambassador. I had not been a week on this job when I chanced one evening on a very handsome young ichoglan.[2] The evening was hot; the young man wanted to take a swim; I seized the occasion, and went with him. I did not know that it is a capital offense for a Christian to be found naked with a young Moslem. A cadi sentenced me to receive a hundred blows with a cane on the soles of my feet, and then to be sent to the galleys. I don't suppose there was ever such a horrible miscarriage of justice. But I would like to know why my sister is in the kitchen of a Transylvanian king exiled among Turks.

—But how about you, my dear Pangloss, said Candide; how is it possible that we have met again?

—It is true, said Pangloss, that you saw me hanged; in the normal course of things, I should have been burned, but you recall that a cloudburst occurred just as they were about to roast me. So much rain fell that they despaired of lighting the fire; thus I was hanged, for lack of anything better to do with me. A surgeon bought my body, carried me off to his house, and dissected me. First he made a cross-shaped incision in me, from the navel to the clavicle. No one could have been worse hanged than I was. In fact, the executioner of the high ceremonials of the Holy Inquisition, who was a subdeacon, burned people marvelously well, but he was not in the way of hanging them. The rope was wet, and tightened badly; it caught on a knot; in short, I was still breathing. The cross-shaped incision made me scream so loudly that the surgeon fell over backwards; he thought he was dissecting the devil, fled in an agony of fear, and fell downstairs in his flight. His wife ran in, at the noise, from a nearby room; she found me stretched out on the table with my cross-shaped incision, was even more frightened than her hus-

2. A page to the sultan.

band, fled, and fell over him. When they had recovered a little, I heard her say to him: 'My dear, what were you thinking of, trying to dissect a heretic? Don't you know those people are always possessed of the devil? I'm going to get the priest and have him exorcised.' At these words, I shuddered, and collected my last remaining energies to cry: 'Have mercy on me!' At last the Portuguese barber[3] took courage; he sewed me up again; his wife even nursed me; in two weeks I was up and about. The barber found me a job and made me lackey to a Knight of Malta who was going to Venice; and when this master could no longer pay me, I took service under a Venetian merchant, whom I followed to Constantinople.

—One day it occurred to me to enter a mosque; no one was there but an old imam and a very attractive young worshipper who was saying her prayers. Her bosom was completely bare; and between her two breasts she had a lovely bouquet of tulips, roses, anemones, buttercups, hyacinths, and prim-roses. She dropped her bouquet, I picked it up, and returned it to her with the most respectful attentions. I was so long getting it back in place that the imam grew angry, and, seeing that I was a Christian, he called the guard. They took me before the cadi, who sentenced me to receive a hundred blows with a cane on the soles of my feet, and then to be sent to the galleys. I was chained to the same galley and precisely the same bench as My Lord the Baron. There were in this galley four young fellows from Marseilles, five Neapolitan priests, and two Corfu monks, who assured us that these things happen every day. My Lord the Baron asserted that he had suffered a greater injustice than I; I, on the other hand, proposed that it was much more per-missible to replace a bouquet in a bosom than to be found naked with an ichoglan. We were arguing the point continually, and getting twenty lashes a day with the bullwhip, when the chain of events within this universe brought you to our galley, and you ransomed us.

—Well, my dear Pangloss, Candide said to him, now that you have been hanged, dissected, beaten to a pulp, and sentenced to the galleys, do you still think everything is for the best in this world?

—I am still of my first opinion, replied Pangloss; for after all I am a phi-losopher, and it would not be right for me to recant since Leibniz could not possibly be wrong, and besides pre-established harmony is the finest notion in the world, like the plenum and subtle matter.[4]

CHAPTER 29

How Candide Found Cunégonde and the Old Woman Again

While Candide, the baron, Pangloss, Martin, and Cacambo were telling one another their stories, while they were disputing over the contingent or non-contingent events of this universe, while they were arguing over effects and causes, over moral evil and physical evil, over liberty and necessity, and over the consolations available to one in a Turkish galley, they arrived at the

---

3. The two callings of barber and surgeon, since they both involved sharp instruments, were interchange-able in the early days of medicine.　4. Rigorous determinism requires that there be no empty spaces in the universe. So wherever it seems empty, one posits the existence of the "plenum." "Subtle matter" describes the soul, the mind, and all spiritual agencies—which can, therefore, supposedly be subject to the influence and control of the great world machine, which is, of course, visibly material. Both are concepts needed to round out the system of optimistic determinism.

shores of Propontis and the house of the prince of Transylvania. The first sight to meet their eyes was Cunégonde and the old woman, who were hanging out towels on lines to dry.

The baron paled at what he saw. The tender lover Candide, seeing his lovely Cunégonde with her skin weathered, her eyes bloodshot, her breasts fallen, her cheeks seamed, her arms red and scaly, recoiled three steps in horror, and then advanced only out of politeness. She embraced Candide and her brother; everyone embraced the old woman; Candide ransomed them both.

There was a little farm in the neighborhood; the old woman suggested that Candide occupy it until some better fate should befall the group. Cunégonde did not know she was ugly, no one had told her; she reminded Candide of his promises in so firm a tone that the good Candide did not dare to refuse her. So he went to tell the baron that he was going to marry his sister.

—Never will I endure, said the baron, such baseness on her part, such insolence on yours; this shame at least I will not put up with; why, my sister's children would not be able to enter the Chapters in Germany.[5] No, my sister will never marry anyone but a baron of the empire.

Cunégonde threw herself at his feet, and bathed them with her tears; he was inflexible.

—You absolute idiot, Candide told him, I rescued you from the galleys, I paid your ransom, I paid your sister's; she was washing dishes, she is ugly, I am good enough to make her my wife, and you still presume to oppose it! If I followed my impulses, I would kill you all over again.

—You may kill me again, said the baron, but you will not marry my sister while I am alive.

CHAPTER 30
Conclusion

At heart, Candide had no real wish to marry Cunégonde; but the baron's extreme impertinence decided him in favor of the marriage, and Cunégonde was so eager for it that he could not back out. He consulted Pangloss, Martin, and the faithful Cacambo. Pangloss drew up a fine treatise, in which he proved that the baron had no right over his sister and that she could, according to all the laws of the empire, marry Candide morganatically.[6] Martin said they should throw the baron into the sea. Cacambo thought they should send him back to the Levantine captain to finish his time in the galleys, and then send him to the father general in Rome by the first vessel. This seemed the best idea; the old woman approved, and nothing was said to his sister; the plan was executed, at modest expense, and they had the double pleasure of snaring a Jesuit and punishing the pride of a German baron.

It is quite natural to suppose that after so many misfortunes, Candide, married to his mistress, and living with the philosopher Pangloss, the philosopher Martin, the prudent Cacambo, and the old woman—having, besides, brought back so many diamonds from the land of the ancient Incas—must have led the most agreeable life in the world. But he was so

5. Knightly assemblies.   6. A morganatic marriage confers no rights on the partner of lower rank or on the offspring.

cheated by the Jews[7] that nothing was left but his little farm; his wife, growing every day more ugly, became sour-tempered and insupportable; the old woman was ailing and even more ill-humored than Cunégonde. Cacambo, who worked in the garden and went into Constantinople to sell vegetables, was worn out with toil, and cursed his fate. Pangloss was in despair at being unable to shine in some German university. As for Martin, he was firmly persuaded that things are just as bad wherever you are; he endured in patience. Candide, Martin, and Pangloss sometimes argued over metaphysics and morals. Before the windows of the farmhouse they often watched the passage of boats bearing effendis, pashas, and cadis into exile on Lemnos, Mytilene, and Erzeroum; they saw other cadis, other pashas, other effendis coming, to take the place of the exiles and to be exiled in their turn. They saw various heads, neatly impaled, to be set up at the Sublime Porte.[8] These sights gave fresh impetus to their discussions; and when they were not arguing, the boredom was so fierce that one day the old woman ventured to say:—

I should like to know which is worse, being raped a hundred times by negro pirates, having a buttock cut off, running the gauntlet in the Bulgar army, being flogged and hanged in an auto-da-fé, being dissected and rowing in the galleys—experiencing, in a word, all the miseries through which we have passed—or else just sitting here and doing nothing?

—It's a hard question, said Candide.

These words gave rise to new reflections, and Martin in particular concluded that man was bound to live either in convulsions of misery or in the lethargy of boredom. Candide did not agree, but expressed no positive opinion. Pangloss asserted that he had always suffered horribly; but having once declared that everything was marvelously well, he continued to repeat the opinion and didn't believe a word of it.

One thing served to confirm Martin in his detestable opinions, to make Candide hesitate more than ever, and to embarrass Pangloss. It was the arrival one day at their farm of Paquette and Brother Giroflée, who were in the last stages of misery. They had quickly run through their three thousand piastres, had split up, made up, quarreled, been jailed, escaped, and finally Brother Giroflée had turned Turk. Paquette continued to ply her trade everywhere, and no longer made any money at it.

—I told you, said Martin to Candide, that your gifts would soon be squandered and would only render them more unhappy. You have spent millions of piastres, you and Cacambo, and you are no more happy than Brother Giroflée and Paquette.

—Ah ha, said Pangloss to Paquette, so destiny has brought you back in our midst, my poor girl! Do you realize you cost me the end of my nose, one eye, and an ear? And look at you now! eh! what a world it is, after all!

This new adventure caused them to philosophize more than ever.

There was in the neighborhood a very famous dervish, who was said to be the best philosopher in Turkey; they went to ask his advice. Pangloss was spokesman, and he said:—Master, we have come to ask you to tell us why such a strange animal as man was created.

7. Voltaire's anti-Semitism, derived from various unhappy experiences with Jewish financiers, is not the most attractive aspect of his personality.   8. The gate of the sultan's palace is often used by extension to describe his government as a whole. But it was in fact a real gate where the heads of traitors and public enemies were gruesomely exposed.

—What are you getting into? answered the dervish. Is it any of your business?

—But, reverend father, said Candide, there's a horrible lot of evil on the face of the earth.

—What does it matter, said the dervish, whether there's good or evil? When his highness sends a ship to Egypt, does he worry whether the mice on board are comfortable or not?

—What shall we do then? asked Pangloss.

—Hold your tongue, said the dervish.

—I had hoped, said Pangloss, to reason a while with you concerning effects and causes, the best of possible worlds, the origin of evil, the nature of the soul, and pre-established harmony.

At these words, the dervish slammed the door in their faces.

During this interview, word was spreading that at Constantinople they had just strangled two viziers of the divan,[9] as well as the mufti, and impaled several of their friends. This catastrophe made a great and general sensation for several hours. Pangloss, Candide, and Martin, as they returned to their little farm, passed a good old man who was enjoying the cool of the day at his doorstep under a grove of orange trees. Pangloss, who was as inquisitive as he was explanatory, asked the name of the mufti who had been strangled.

—I know nothing of it, said the good man, and I have never cared to know the name of a single mufti or vizier. I am completely ignorant of the episode you are discussing. I presume that in general those who meddle in public business sometimes perish miserably, and that they deserve their fate; but I never listen to the news from Constantinople; I am satisfied with sending the fruits of my garden to be sold there.

Having spoken these words, he asked the strangers into his house; his two daughters and two sons offered them various sherbets which they had made themselves, Turkish cream flavored with candied citron, orange, lemon, lime, pineapple, pistachio, and mocha coffee uncontaminated by the inferior coffee of Batavia and the East Indies. After which the two daughters of this good Moslem perfumed the beards of Candide, Pangloss, and Martin.

—You must possess, Candide said to the Turk, an enormous and splendid property?

I have only twenty acres, replied the Turk; I cultivate them with my children, and the work keeps us from three great evils, boredom, vice, and poverty.

Candide, as he walked back to his farm, meditated deeply over the words of the Turk. He said to Pangloss and Martin:—This good old man seems to have found himself a fate preferable to that of the six kings with whom we had the honor of dining.

—Great place, said Pangloss, is very perilous in the judgment of all the philosophers; for, after all, Eglon, king of the Moabites, was murdered by Ehud; Absalom was hung up by the hair and pierced with three darts; King Nadab, son of Jeroboam, was killed by Baasha; King Elah by Zimri; Ahaziah by Jehu; Athaliah by Jehoiada; and Kings Jehoiakim, Jeconiah, and Zedekiah were enslaved. You know how death came to Croesus, Astyages, Darius, Dionysius of Syracuse, Pyrrhus, Perseus, Hannibal, Jugurtha, Ariovistus,

9. Intimate advisers of the sultan.

Caesar, Pompey, Nero, Otho, Vitellius, Domitian, Richard II of England, Edward II, Henry VI, Richard III, Mary Stuart, Charles I, the three Henrys of France, and the Emperor Henry IV? You know . . .

—I know also, said Candide, that we must cultivate our garden.

—You are perfectly right, said Pangloss; for when man was put into the garden of Eden, he was put there *ut operaretur eum,* so that he should work it; this proves that man was not born to take his ease.

—Let's work without speculating, said Martin; it's the only way of rendering life bearable.

The whole little group entered into this laudable scheme; each one began to exercise his talents. The little plot yielded fine crops. Cunégonde was, to tell the truth, remarkably ugly; but she became an excellent pastry cook. Paquette took up embroidery; the old woman did the laundry. Everyone, down even to Brother Giroflée, did something useful; he became a very adequate carpenter, and even an honest man; and Pangloss sometimes used to say to Candide:—All events are linked together in the best of possible worlds; for, after all, if you had not been driven from a fine castle by being kicked in the backside for love of Miss Cunégonde, if you hadn't been sent before the Inquisition, if you hadn't traveled across America on foot, if you hadn't given a good sword thrust to the baron, if you hadn't lost all your sheep from the good land of Eldorado, you wouldn't be sitting here eating candied citron and pistachios.

—That is very well put, said Candide, but we must cultivate our garden.

SAMUEL JOHNSON
1709–1784

In *The History of Rasselas, Prince of Abissinia* (1759), his longest philosophical tale, Samuel Johnson offers a dignified but moving account of the futility of human endeavor. The narrative, written hastily and allegedly published to defray his mother's funeral expenses, distills the melancholy reflections of a fifty-year-old man whose observations and experience alike convince him that human happiness depends mainly on the preservation of illusion.

Son of a Lichfield bookseller, Johnson received his early education at Lichfield Grammar School. In 1728 he entered Pembroke College, Oxford, but poverty forced him to leave without a degree three years later. An attempt at teaching and, later, a brief period as schoolmaster proved unsuccessful; in 1737 he went to London and began to earn a living by writing for the *Gentleman's Magazine*. He had married, in 1735, a widow much older than he; her death, in 1752, left him desolate.

Before long Johnson became distinguished as a conversationalist and a writer, known particularly for *The Rambler* (a periodical published from 1750 to 1752; Johnson himself wrote all but 4½ of its 208 issues) and the *Dictionary of the English Language* (1755), an almost incredible achievement for one man. In 1762, he was granted a royal pension of £300 a year; in 1775, his old university conferred upon him the degree of Doctor in Civil Laws. Meanwhile, he had formed a close attachment to the Scotsman James Boswell, thirty-one years younger than he, of whom he saw much in London and with whom he traveled through Scotland. (Subsequently, Boswell wrote a life of Johnson.) His second intimate relationship was with Henry Thrale, a London brewer, and his wife, Hester, a woman of strong literary interests. With them Johnson made his only trip abroad, to Paris. A group of other distinguished men joined him in founding The Literary Club (1764), which met regularly for conversation. By the time of Johnson's death in 1784, he was unquestionably the most famous literary figure in England.

Johnson wrote poetic adaptations of the classics; original verse in Latin and in English; a travel book; fiction; a tragic drama; literary criticism; philosophical, satirical, and meditative essays; biography; and a dictionary. He edited Shakespeare's plays, with a preface that defined the playwright's place for the mid-eighteenth-century consciousness and that still speaks eloquently to us today. His final work, *Lives of the Poets* (1779–81), biographical and critical introductions to fifty-two English poets, exemplified at its best his gift for forceful judgment and discrimination. Sometimes he was wrong, by our standards: he disapproved, for example, of Milton's *Lycidas.* More often, he provided definitive statements about poetic careers and accomplishments.

Rasselas, published almost simultaneously with Voltaire's *Candide,* was immediately compared to the French work; Johnson himself found the resemblance striking. Both books employ the fictional device of a naïve protagonist whose travels educate him in the evils of the world. In tone and in implication, though, the two fictions differ greatly. Voltaire's satiric intensity and violence much exceed Johnson's; on the other hand, Candide, after far worse disasters than Rasselas faces, arrives at a more specific course of hopeful action than his English counterpart can discover.

Although Johnson was born eleven years after Voltaire, his point of view derives from an earlier era. The context in which Rasselas learns the futility of human endeavor is that of Christian humanism, which focuses attention on human beings and their moral responsibilities within the context of Christian belief. When the princess, having seen the catacombs, concludes, "To me, . . . the choice of life is become less important; I hope hereafter to think only on the choice of eternity," she reveals the book's underlying assumptions. Human beings, because of their humanity, struggle to attain goals that, won, prove less than satisfactory. They live in illusion, governing themselves by hopes and fears disproportionate to actuality. The reality that should focus their attention, the afterlife of reward and punishment, seldom concerns them; they dwell resolutely in the irrelevant. They lack not only adequate reason, but sufficiently active faith.

Unlike Voltaire's Pangloss, Johnson's characters do not rely on universalizing interpretations. They do not worry about whether theirs is the best or the worst of all possible worlds; their blinkered vision focuses on personal and immediate concerns. Rasselas and his sister, trying to make their own "choice of life," seeking models of fulfillment and happiness, repeatedly find the inadequacy of human effort. Even more important, they discover what a chapter title calls "The Dangerous Prevalence [meaning dominance] of Imagination": the degree to which reason proves subject to desire, as individuals, seeing only what they want to see, beguile themselves into temporary satisfaction. The story ends with the "Conclusion, in Which Nothing Is Concluded"; the travelers, still not free of hopeful fantasy, return to Abyssinia. They have not encountered great natural disasters, striking instances of human malice or lust, or large-scale carnage; but neither have they found much ground for expecting earthly happiness. The satirist's tone, Voltaire's tone, by its very vehemence suggests belief that human beings, once aware of their own corruption, might at least minimally improve. Johnson's elevated, dignified, ponderous utterance, on the other hand, rings with the authority of conviction. The world he describes seems in no way subject to change.

This is not to say, however, that *Rasselas* makes its readers feel hopeless. The vigor and authority of the narrative voice carry comfort, conveying a sense of the possibility of knowledge and understanding. Rasselas and Nekayah, voices rather than developed characters, achieve no dazzling insight as a result of their efforts to understand the choices open to them. Never differentiated in personality, they serve mainly as mouthpieces for positions Johnson wishes to represent. Nonetheless, as instruments of communication, they suggest a way of finding at least conditional value in this world. The fable that contains them implies the importance, the educational potential, of *experience*, exemplified by the travel and the purposeful investigations the characters undertake, and of *talk*. Rasselas and his sister learn not only by looking but by discussing. They talk with their mentor, Imlac, the voice of wisdom within the narrative—wisdom that has been derived from its possessor's previous experience, a fact reinforcing the stress on the moral significance of what the travelers see and do. But Rasselas and Nekayah also talk with one another, discovering the meaning of what they have seen by a process of mutual assessment, of sharing and of questioning. If all faith in the possibility of ultimate earthly satisfaction proves illusory, what the travelers take for granted—their companionship—yet continues to sustain them. The human community contains the saving possibility of communal reassurance; the verbal sharing of experience intensifies its value. And the effort to say precisely what one knows is a self-sufficiently valuable enterprise, an enterprise corroborating the importance of Johnson's writing of the tale: for that, too, is an effort at *saying*.

So *Rasselas*, although somber in its assessments, does not imply despair. Reminding its readers as well as its characters of the vital "choice of eternity," it reiterates Johnson's typical insistence on human life as a condition offering much to endure, little to enjoy. But it also suggests the nature and the importance of the little enjoyment and insight possible to human beings; and it implicitly invites readers to take their own lives seriously, to understand and value the moral possibilities of all experience, and to share the restrained, ambiguous excitement of seeing things as they are.

PRONOUNCING GLOSSARY

The following list uses common English syllables and stress accents to provide rough equivalents of selected words whose pronunciation may be unfamiliar to the general reader.

Nekayah: *ne-ky'-yah*   Rasselas: *ra'-se-las*

Pekuah: *pek-'yoo-ah*

The History of Rasselas, Prince of Abissinia[1]

CHAPTER I

Description of a Palace in a Valley

Ye who listen with credulity to the whispers of fancy, and pursue with eagerness the phantoms of hope; who expect that age will perform the promises of youth, and that the deficiencies of the present day will be supplied by the morrow; attend to the history of Rasselas prince of Abissinia.

Rasselas was the fourth son of the mighty emperor, in whose dominions the Father of waters[2] begins his course; whose bounty pours down the streams of plenty, and scatters over half the world the harvests of Egypt.

---

1. The text is that of the sixth edition (London, 1783), the last version published in Johnson's lifetime.
2. The Nile.

According to the custom which has descended from age to age among the monarchs of the torrid zone, Rasselas was confined in a private palace, with the other sons and daughters of Abissinian royalty, till the order of succession should call him to the throne.

The place, which the wisdom or policy of antiquity had destined for the residence of the Abissinian princes, was a spacious valley in the kingdom of Amhara, surrounded on every side by mountains, of which the summits overhang the middle part. The only passage, by which it could be entered, was a cavern that passed under a rock, of which it has long been disputed whether it was the work of nature or of human industry. The outlet of the cavern was concealed by a thick wood, and the mouth which opened into the valley was closed with gates of iron, forged by the artificers of ancient days, so massy[3] that no man could, without the help of engines,[4] open or shut them.

From the mountains on every side, rivulets descended that filled all the valley with verdure and fertility, and formed a lake in the middle inhabited by fish of every species, and frequented by every fowl whom nature has taught to dip the wing in water. This lake discharged its superfluities by a stream which entered a dark cleft of the mountain on the northern side, and fell with dreadful noise from precipice to precipice till it was heard no more.

The sides of the mountains were covered with trees, the banks of the brooks were diversified with flowers; every blast shook spices from the rocks, and every month dropped fruits upon the ground. All animals that bite the grass, or browse the shrub, whether wild or tame, wandered in this extensive circuit, secured from beasts of prey by the mountains which confined them. On one part were flocks and herds feeding in the pastures, on another all the beasts of chase frisking in the lawns; the spritely kid was bounding on the rocks, the subtle[5] monkey frolicking in the trees, and the solemn elephant reposing in the shade. All the diversities of the world were brought together, the blessings of nature were collected, and its evils extracted and excluded.

The valley, wide and fruitful, supplied its inhabitants with the necessaries of life, and all delights and superfluities were added at the annual visit which the emperor paid his children, when the iron gate was opened to the sound of music; and during eight days everyone that resided in the valley was required to propose whatever might contribute to make seclusion pleasant, to fill up the vacancies of attention, and lessen the tediousness of time. Every desire was immediately granted. All the artificers of pleasure were called to gladden the festivity; the musicians exerted the power of harmony, and the dancers showed their activity before the princes, in hope that they should pass their lives in this blissful captivity, to which these only were admitted whose performance was thought able to add novelty to luxury. Such was the appearance of security and delight which this retirement afforded, that they to whom it was new always desired that it might be perpetual; and as those, on whom the iron gate had once closed, were never suffered[6] to return, the effect of longer experience could not be known. Thus every year produced new schemes of delight, and new competitors for imprisonment.

The palace stood on an eminence raised about thirty paces above the surface of the lake. It was divided into many squares or courts, built with greater or less magnificence according to the rank of those for whom they

3. Massive. 4. Machines. 5. Cunning. 6. Permitted.

were designed. The roofs were turned into arches of massy stone joined with a cement that grew harder by time, and the building stood from century to century, deriding the solstitial rains and equinoctial hurricanes, without need of reparation.

This house, which was so large as to be fully known to none but some ancient officers who successively inherited the secrets of the place, was built as if suspicion herself had dictated the plan. To every room there was an open and secret passage, every square had a communication with the rest, either from the upper stories by private galleries, or by subterranean passages from the lower apartments. Many of the columns had unsuspected cavities, in which a long race of monarchs had reposited their treasures. They then closed up the opening with marble, which was never to be removed but in the utmost exigencies of the kingdom; and recorded their accumulations in a book which was itself concealed in a tower not entered but by the emperor, attended by the prince who stood next in succession.

CHAPTER II

The Discontent of Rasselas in the Happy Valley

Here the sons and daughters of Abissinia lived only to know the soft vicissitudes[7] of pleasure and repose, attended by all that were skillful to delight, and gratified with whatever the senses can enjoy. They wandered in gardens of fragrance, and slept in the fortresses of security. Every art was practiced to make them pleased with their own condition. The sages who instructed them, told them of nothing but the miseries of public life, and described all beyond the mountains as regions of calamity, where discord was always raging, and where man preyed upon man.

To heighten their opinion of their own felicity, they were daily entertained with songs, the subject of which was the *happy valley*. Their appetites were excited by frequent enumerations of different enjoyments, and revelry and merriment was the business of every hour from the dawn of morning to the close of even.

These methods were generally successful; few of the princes had ever wished to enlarge their bounds, but passed their lives in full conviction that they had all within their reach that art or nature could bestow, and pitied those whom fate had excluded from this seat of tranquillity, as the sport of chance, and the slaves of misery.

Thus they rose in the morning, and lay down at night, pleased with each other and with themselves, all but Rasselas, who, in the twenty-sixth year of his age, began to withdraw himself from their pastimes and assemblies, and to delight in solitary walks and silent meditation. He often sat before tables covered with luxury, and forgot to taste the dainties that were placed before him: he rose abruptly in the midst of the song, and hastily retired beyond the sound of music. His attendants observed the change and endeavored to renew his love of pleasure: he neglected their officiousness,[8] repulsed their invitations, and spent day after day on the banks of rivulets sheltered with trees, where he sometimes listened to the birds in the branches, some-

7. Alternations.　　8. Helpfulness.

times observed the fish playing in the stream, and anon cast his eyes upon the pastures and mountains filled with animals, of which some were biting the herbage, and some sleeping among the bushes.

This singularity of his humor made him much observed. One of the sages, in whose conversation he had formerly delighted, followed him secretly, in hope of discovering the cause of his disquiet. Rasselas, who knew not that any one was near him, having for some time fixed his eyes upon the goats that were browsing among the rocks, began to compare their condition with his own.

"What, said he, makes the difference between man and all the rest of the animal creation? Every beast that strays beside me has the same corporal necessities with myself; he is hungry and crops the grass, he is thirsty and drinks the stream, his thirst and hunger are appeased, he is satisfied and sleeps; he rises again and is hungry, he is again fed and is at rest. I am hungry and thirsty like him, but when thirst and hunger cease I am not at rest; I am, like him, pained with want, but am not, like him, satisfied with fullness. The intermediate hours are tedious and gloomy; I long again to be hungry that I may again quicken my attention. The birds peck the berries or the corn, and fly away to the groves where they sit in seeming happiness on the branches, and waste their lives in tuning one unvaried series of sounds. I likewise can call the lutanist and the singer, but the sounds that pleased me yesterday weary me today, and will grow yet more wearisome tomorrow. I can discover within me no power of perception which is not glutted with its proper[9] pleasure, yet I do not feel myself delighted. Man has surely some latent sense for which this place affords no gratification, or he has some desires distinct from sense which must be satisfied before he can be happy."

After this he lifted up his head, and seeing the moon rising, walked towards the palace. As he passed through the fields, and saw the animals around him, "Ye," said he, "are happy, and need not envy me that walk thus among you, burthened with myself; nor do I, ye gentle beings, envy your felicity; for it is not the felicity of man. I have many distresses from which ye are free; I fear pain when I do not feel it; I sometimes shrink at evils recollected, and sometimes start at evils anticipated: surely the equity of providence has balanced peculiar[1] sufferings with peculiar enjoyments."

With observations like these the prince amused himself as he returned, uttering them with a plaintive voice, yet with a look that discovered him to feel some complacence in his own perspicacity, and to receive some solace of the miseries of life, from consciousness of the delicacy with which he felt, and the eloquence with which he bewailed them. He mingled cheerfully in the diversions of the evening, and all rejoiced to find that his heart was lightened.

* * *

[Rasselas remains dissatisfied in the happy valley and attempts to escape by means of wings; the wings, however, drop their inventor in the lake.]

9. Appropriate.   1. Distinctive.

CHAPTER VII

The Prince Finds a Man of Learning

The prince was not much afflicted by this disaster, having suffered himself to hope for a happier event, only because he had no other means of escape in view. He still persisted in his design to leave the happy valley by the first opportunity.

His imagination was now at a stand; he had no prospect of entering into the world; and, notwithstanding all his endeavors to support himself,[2] discontent by degrees preyed upon him, and he began to lose his thoughts in sadness, when the rainy season, which in these countries is periodical, made it inconvenient to wander in the woods.

The rain continued longer and with more violence than had been ever known: the clouds broke on the surrounding mountains, and the torrents streamed into the plain on every side, till the cavern was too narrow to discharge the water. The lake overflowed its banks, and all the level of the valley was covered with the inundation. The eminence, on which the palace was built, and some other spots of rising ground, were all that the eye could now discover. The herds and flocks left the pastures, and both the wild beasts and the tame retreated to the mountains.

This inundation confined all the princes to domestic amusements, and the attention of Rasselas was particularly seized by a poem, which Imlac rehearsed,[3] upon the various conditions of humanity. He commanded the poet to attend him in his apartment, and recite his verses a second time; then entering into familiar talk, he thought himself happy in having found a man who knew the world so well, and could so skillfully paint the scenes of life. He asked a thousand questions about things, to which, though common to all other mortals, his confinement from childhood had kept him a stranger. The poet pitied his ignorance, and loved his curiosity, and entertained him from day to day with novelty and instruction, so that the prince regretted the necessity of sleep, and longed till the morning should renew his pleasure.

As they were sitting together, the prince commanded Imlac to relate his history, and to tell by what accident he was forced, or by what motive induced, to close his life in the happy valley. As he was going to begin his narrative, Rasselas was called to a concert, and obliged to restrain his curiosity till the evening.

CHAPTER VIII

The History of Imlac

The close of the day is, in the regions of the torrid zone, the only season of diversion and entertainment, and it was therefore midnight before the music ceased, and the princesses retired. Rasselas then called for his companion and required him to begin the story of his life.

"Sir," said Imalac, "my history will not be long: the life that is devoted to knowledge passes silently away, and is very little diversified by events. To talk in public, to think in solitude, to read and to hear, to inquire, and answer

---

2. Keep up his spirits.   3. Recited.

inquiries, is the business of a scholar. He wanders about the world without pomp or terror, and is neither known nor valued but by men like himself.

"I was born in the kingdom of Goiama,[4] at no great distance from the fountain of the Nile. My father was a wealthy merchant, who traded between the inland countries of Afric and the ports of the Red Sea. He was honest, frugal and diligent, but of mean[5] sentiments, and narrow comprehension: he desired only to be rich, and to conceal his riches, lest he should be spoiled[6] by the governors of the province."

"Surely," said the prince, "my father must be negligent of his charge, if any man in his dominions dares take that which belongs to another. Does he not know that kings are accountable for injustice permitted as well as done? If I were emperor, not the meanest[7] of my subjects should be oppressed with impunity. My blood boils when I am told that a merchant durst not enjoy his honest gains for fear of losing them by the rapacity of power. Name the governor who robbed the people, that I may declare his crimes to the emperor."

"Sir," said Imlac, "your ardor is the natural effect of virtue animated by youth: the time will come when you will acquit your father, and perhaps hear with less impatience of the governor. Oppression is, in the Abissinian dominions, neither frequent nor tolerated; but no form of government has been yet discovered, by which cruelty can be wholly prevented. Subordination supposes power on one part and subjection on the other; and if power be in the hands of men, it will sometimes be abused. The vigilance of the supreme magistrate may do much, but much will still remain undone. He can never know all the crimes that are committed, and can seldom punish all that he knows."

"This," said the prince, "I do not understand, but I had rather hear thee than dispute. Continue thy narration."

"My father," proceeded Imlac, "originally intended that I should have no other education, than such as might qualify me for commerce; and discovering in me great strength of memory, and quickness of apprehension, often declared his hope that I should be some time the richest man in Abissinia."

"Why," said the prince, "did thy father desire the increase of his wealth, when it was already greater than he durst discover or enjoy? I am unwilling to doubt thy veracity, yet inconsistencies cannot both be true."

"Inconsistencies," answered Imlac, "cannot both be right, but, imputed to man, they may both be true. Yet diversity is not inconsistency. My father might expect a time of greater security. However, some desire is necessary to keep life in motion, and he, whose real wants are supplied, must admit those of fancy."

"This," said the prince, "I can in some measure conceive. I repent that I interrupted thee."

"With this hope," proceeded Imlac, "he sent me to school; but when I had once found the delight of knowledge, and felt the pleasure of intelligence and the pride of invention, I began silently to despise riches, and determined to disappoint the purpose of my father, whose grossness of conception raised my pity. I was twenty years old before his tenderness would expose me to

4. Source. Goiama, or Gojam, a province of ancient Abyssinia, indeed contains the source of the Blue Nile.   5. Ignoble, small-minded.   6. Plundered.   7. Lowliest.

the fatigue of travel, in which time I had been instructed, by successive masters, in all the literature of my native country. As every hour taught me something new, I lived in a continual course of gratifications; but, as I advanced towards manhood, I lost much of the reverence with which I had been used to look on my instructors; because, when the lesson was ended, I did not find them wiser or better than common men.

"At length my father resolved to initiate me in commerce, and, opening one of his subterranean treasuries, counted out ten thousand pieces of gold. 'This, young man,' said he, 'is the stock with which you must negotiate.'[8] I began with less than the fifth part, and you see how diligence and parsimony have increased it. This is your own to waste or to improve. If you squander it by negligence or caprice, you must wait for my death before you will be rich: if, in four years, you double your stock, we will thenceforward let subordination cease, and live together as friends and partners; for he shall always be equal with me, who is equally skilled in the art of growing rich.'

"We laid our money upon camels, concealed in bales of cheap goods, and traveled to the shore of the Red Sea. When I cast my eye on the expanse of waters my heart bounded like that of a prisoner escaped. I felt an unextinguishable curiosity kindle in my mind, and resolved to snatch this opportunity of seeing the manners of other nations, and of learning sciences[9] unknown in Abissinia.

"I remembered that my father had obliged me to the improvement of my stock, not by a promise which I ought not to violate, but by a penalty which I was at liberty to incur; and therefore determined to gratify my predominant desire, and by drinking at the fountains of knowledge, to quench the thirst of curiosity.

"As I was supposed to trade without connection with my father, it was easy for me to become acquainted with the master of a ship, and procure a passage to some other country. I had no motives of choice to regulate my voyage; it was sufficient for me that, wherever I wandered, I should see a country which I had not seen before. I therefore entered a ship bound for Surat,[1] having left a letter for my father declaring my intention."

CHAPTER IX

The History of Imlac Continued

"When I first entered upon the world of waters, and lost sight of land, I looked round about me with pleasing terror, and thinking my soul enlarged by the boundless prospect, imagined that I could gaze round for ever without satiety; but, in a short time, I grew weary of looking on barren uniformity, where I could only see again what I had already seen. I then descended into the ship, and doubted for a while whether all my future pleasures would not end like this in disgust and disappointment. Yet, surely, said I, the ocean and the land are very different; the only variety of water is rest and motion, but the earth has mountains and valleys, deserts and cities: it is inhabited by men of different customs and contrary opinions; and I may hope to find variety in life, though I should miss it in nature.

"With this thought I quieted my mind; and amused myself during the voyage, sometimes by learning from the sailors the art of navigation, which

8. Do business.   9. Forms of knowledge.   1. An Indian port.

I have never practiced, and sometimes by forming schemes for my conduct in different situations, in not one of which I have been ever placed.

"I was almost weary of my naval amusements when we landed safely at Surat. I secured my money, and purchasing some commodities for show, joined myself to a caravan that was passing into the inland country. My companions, for some reason or other, conjecturing that I was rich, and, by my inquiries and admiration,[2] finding that I was ignorant, considered me as a novice whom they had a right to cheat, and who was to learn at the usual expense the art of fraud. They exposed me to the theft of servants, and the exaction of officers, and saw me plundered upon false pretenses, without any advantage to themselves, but that of rejoicing in the superiority of their own knowledge."

"Stop a moment," said the prince. "Is there such depravity in man, as that he should injure another without benefit to himself? I can easily conceive that all are pleased with superiority; but your ignorance was merely accidental, which, being neither your crime nor your folly, could afford them no reason to applaud themselves; and the knowledge which they had, and which you wanted,[3] they might as effectively have shown by warning, as betraying you."

"Pride," said Imlac, "is seldom delicate, it will please itself with very mean advantages; and envy feels not its own happiness, but when it may be compared with the misery of others. They were my enemies because they grieved to think me rich, and my oppressors because they delighted to find me weak."

"Proceed," said the prince: "I doubt not of the facts which you relate, but imagine that you impute them to mistaken motives."

"In this company," said Imlac, "I arrived at Agra, the capital of Indostan, the city in which the great Mogul commonly resides. I applied myself to the language of the country, and in a few months was able to converse with the learned men; some of whom I found morose and reserved, and others easy and communicative; some were unwilling to teach another what they had with difficulty learned themselves; and some showed that the end of their studies was to gain the dignity of instructing.

"To the tutor of the young princes I recommended myself so much, that I was presented to the emperor as a man of uncommon knowledge. The emperor asked me many questions concerning my country and my travels; and though I cannot now recollect anything that he uttered above the power of a common man, he dismissed me astonished at his wisdom, and enamored of his goodness.

"My credit was now so high, that the merchants, with whom I had traveled, applied to me for recommendations to the ladies of the court. I was surprised at their confidence of solicitation, and gently reproached them with their practices on the road. They heard me with cold indifference, and showed no tokens of shame or sorrow.

"They then urged their request with the offer of a bribe; but what I would not do for kindness I would not do for money; and refused them, not because they had injured me, but because I would not enable them to injure others; for I knew they would have made use of my credit to cheat those who should buy their wares.

"Having resided at Agra till there was no more to be learned, I traveled

2. Astonishment.　3. Lacked.

into Persia, where I saw many remains of ancient magnificence, and observed many new accommodations[4] of life. The Persians are a nation eminently social, and their assemblies afforded me daily opportunities of remarking[5] characters and manners, and of tracing human nature through all its variations.

"From Persia I passed into Arabia, where I saw a nation at once pastoral and warlike; who live without any settled habitation; whose only wealth is their flocks and herds; and who have yet carried on, through all ages, an hereditary war with all mankind, though they neither covet nor envy their possessions."

CHAPTER X
Imlac's History Continued. A Dissertation upon Poetry

"Wherever I went, I found that poetry was considered as the highest learning, and regarded with a veneration somewhat approaching to that which man would pay to the angelic nature. And it yet fills me with wonder, that, in almost all countries, the most ancient poets are considered as the best: whether it be that every other kind of knowledge is an acquisition gradually attained, and poetry is a gift conferred at once; or that the first poetry of every nation surprised them as a novelty, and retained the credit by consent which it received by accident at first: or whether, as the province of poetry is to describe nature and passion, which are always the same, the first writers took possession of the most striking objects for description, and the most probable occurrences for fiction, and left nothing to those that followed them, but transcription of the same events, and new combinations of the same images. Whatever be the reason, it is commonly observed that the early writers are in possession of nature, and their followers of art: that the first excel in strength and invention, and the latter in elegance and refinement.

"I was desirous to add my name to this illustrious fraternity. I read all the poets of Persia and Arabia, and was able to repeat by memory the volumes that are suspended in the mosque of Mecca.[6] But I soon found that no man was ever great by imitation. My desire of excellence impelled me to transfer my attention to nature and to life. Nature was to be my subject, and men to be my auditors: I could never describe what I had not seen: I could not hope to move those with delight or terror, whose interests and opinions I did not understand.

"Being now resolved to be a poet, I saw everything with a new purpose; my sphere of attention was suddenly magnified: no kind of knowledge was to be overlooked. I ranged mountains and deserts for images and resemblances, and pictured upon my mind every tree of the forest and flower of the valley. I observed with equal care the crags of the rock and the pinnacles of the palace. Sometimes I wandered along the mazes of the rivulet, and sometimes watched the changes of the summer clouds. To a poet nothing can be useless. Whatever is beautiful, and whatever is dreadful, must be familiar to his imagination: he must be conversant with all that is awfully[7] vast or elegantly little. The plants of the garden, the animals of the wood, the minerals of the earth, and meteors of the sky, must all concur to store

4. Comforts, conveniences. 5. Noting. 6. Because they have won prizes. 7. Impressively.

his mind with inexhaustible variety: for every idea is useful for the enforcement or decoration of moral or religious truth; and he, who knows most, will have most power of diversifying his scenes, and of gratifying his reader with remote allusions and unexpected instruction.

"All the appearances of nature I was therefore careful to study, and every country which I have surveyed has contributed something to my poetical powers."

"In so wide a survey," said the prince, "you must surely have left much unobserved. I have lived, till now, within the circuit of these mountains, and yet cannot walk abroad without the sight of something which I had never beheld before, or never heeded."

"The business of a poet," said Imlac, "is to examine, not the individual, but the species; to remark general properties and large appearances: he does not number the streaks of the tulip, or describe the different shades in the verdure of the forest. He is to exhibit in his portraits of nature such prominent and striking features, as recall the original to every mind; and must neglect the minuter discriminations, which one may have remarked, and another have neglected, for those characteristics which are alike obvious to vigilance and carelessness.

"But the knowledge of nature is only half the task of a poet; he must be acquainted likewise with all the modes of life. His character requires that he estimate the happiness and misery of every condition; observe the power of all the passions in all their combinations, and trace the changes of the human mind as they are modified by various institutions and accidental influences of climate or custom, from the spriteliness of infancy to the despondence of decrepitude. He must divest himself of the prejudices of his age or country; he must consider right and wrong in their abstracted and invariable state; he must disregard present laws and opinions, and rise to general and transcendental truths, which will always be the same: he must therefore content himself with the slow progress of his name; contemn the applause of his own time, and commit his claims to the justice of posterity. He must write as the interpreter of nature, and the legislator of mankind, and consider himself as presiding over the thoughts and manners of future generations; as a being superior to time and place.

"His labor is not yet at an end: he must know many languages and many sciences; and, that his style may be worthy of his thoughts, must, by incessant practice, familiarize to himself every delicacy of speech and grace of harmony."

CHAPTER XI

Imlac's Narrative Continued. A Hint on Pilgrimage

Imlac now felt the enthusiastic fit,[8] and was proceeding to aggrandize his own profession, when the prince cried out, "Enough! Thou hast convinced me, that no human being can ever be a poet. Proceed with thy narration."

"To be a poet," said Imlac, "is indeed very difficult." "So difficult," returned the prince, "that I will at present hear no more of his labors. Tell me whither you went when you had seen Persia."

---

8. A seizure of extravagant emotion.

"From Persia," said the poet, "I traveled through Syria, and for three years resided in Palestine, where I conversed with great numbers of the northern and western nations of Europe; the nations which are now in possession of all power and all knowledge; whose armies are irresistible, and whose fleets command the remotest parts of the globe. When I compared these men with the natives of our own kingdom, and those that surround us, they appeared almost another order of beings. In their countries it is difficult to wish for anything that may not be obtained: a thousand arts, of which we never heard, are continually laboring for their convenience and pleasure; and whatever their own climate has denied them is supplied by their commerce."

"By what means," said the prince, "are the Europeans thus powerful? or why, since they can so easily visit Asia and Africa for trade or conquest, cannot the Asiatics and Africans invade their coasts, plant colonies in their ports, and give laws to their natural princes? The same wind that carries them back would bring us thither."

"They are more powerful, Sir, than we," answered Imlac, "because they are wiser; knowledge will always predominate over ignorance, as man governs the other animals. But why their knowledge is more than ours, I know not what reason can be given, but the unsearchable will of the Supreme Being."

"When," said the prince with a sigh, "shall I be able to visit Palestine, and mingle with this mighty confluence of nations? Till that happy moment shall arrive, let me fill up the time with such representations as thou canst give me. I am not ignorant of the motive that assembles such numbers in that place, and cannot but consider it as the center of wisdom and piety, to which the best and wisest men of every land must be continually resorting."

"There are some nations," said Imlac, "that send few visitants to Palestine; for many numerous and learned sects in Europe, concur to censure pilgrimage as superstitious, or deride it as ridiculous."

"You know," said the prince, "how little my life has made me acquainted with diversity of opinions: it will be too long to hear the arguments on both sides; you, that have considered them, tell me the result."

"Pilgrimage," said Imlac, "like many other acts of piety, may be reasonable or superstitious, according to the principles upon which it is performed. Long journeys in search of truth are not commanded. Truth, such as is necessary to the regulation of life, is always found where it is honestly sought. Change of place is no natural cause of the increase of piety, for it inevitably produces dissipation of mind.[9] Yet, since men go every day to view the fields where great actions have been performed, and return with stronger impressions of the event, curiosity of the same kind may naturally dispose us to view that country whence our religion had its beginning; and I believe no man surveys those awful[1] scenes without some confirmation of holy resolutions. That the Supreme Being may be more easily propitiated in one place than in another, is the dream of idle superstition; but that some places may operate upon our own minds in an uncommon manner, is an opinion which hourly experience will justify. He who supposes that his vices may be more successfully combated in Palestine, will, perhaps, find himself mistaken, yet he may go thither without folly: he who thinks they will be more freely pardoned, dishonors at once his reason and religion."

---

9. Scattering of attention.   1. Awe-inspiring.

"These," said the prince, "are European distinctions. I will consider them another time. What have you found to be the effect of knowledge? Are those nations happier than we?"

"There is so much infelicity," said the poet, "in the world, that scarce any man has leisure from his own distresses to estimate the comparative happiness of others. Knowledge is certainly one of the means of pleasure, as is confessed by the natural desire which every mind feels of increasing its ideas. Ignorance is mere privation, by which nothing can be produced: it is a vacuity in which the soul sits motionless and torpid for want of attraction; and, without knowing why, we always rejoice when we learn, and grieve when we forget. I am therefore inclined to conclude, that, if nothing counteracts the natural consequence of learning, we grow more happy as our minds take a wider range.

"In enumerating the particular comforts of life we shall find many advantages on the side of the Europeans. They cure wounds and diseases with which we languish and perish. We suffer inclemencies of weather which they can obviate. They have engines for the despatch of many laborious works, which we must perform by manual industry. There is such communication between distant places, that one friend can hardly be said to be absent from another. Their policy removes all public inconveniencies: they have roads cut through their mountains, and bridges laid upon their rivers. And, if we descend to the privacies of life, their habitations are more commodious, and their possessions are more secure."

"They are surely happy," said the prince, "who have all these conveniencies, of which I envy none so much as the facility with which separated friends interchange their thoughts."

"The Europeans," answered Imlac, "are less unhappy than we, but they are not happy. Human life is everywhere a state in which much is to be endured, and little to be enjoyed."

CHAPTER XII

The Story of Imlac Continued

"I am not yet willing," said the prince, "to suppose that happiness is so parsimoniously distributed to mortals; nor can believe but that, if I had the choice of life, I should be able to fill every day with pleasure. I would injure no man, and should provoke no resentment: I would relieve every distress, and should enjoy the benedictions of gratitude. I would choose my friends among the wise, and my wife among the virtuous; and therefore should be in no danger from treachery, or unkindness. My children should, by my care, be learned and pious, and would repay to my age what their childhood had received. What would dare to molest him who might call on every side to thousands enriched by his bounty, or assisted by his power? And why should not life glide quietly away in the soft reciprocation of protection and reverence? All this may be done without the help of European refinements, which appear by their effects to be rather specious than useful. Let us leave them and pursue our journey."

"From Palestine," said Imlac, "I passed through many regions of Asia; in the more civilized kingdoms as a trader, and among the Barbarians of the mountains as a pilgrim. At last I began to long for my native country, that I might repose after my travels, and fatigues, in the places where I had spent my earliest years, and gladden my old companions with the recital of my adventures. Often did I figure[2] to myself those, with whom I had sported away the gay hours of dawning life, sitting round me in its evening, wondering at my tales, and listening to my counsels.

"When this thought had taken possession of my mind, I considered every moment as wasted which did not bring me nearer to Abissinia. I hastened into Egypt, and, notwithstanding my impatience, was detained ten months in the contemplation of its ancient magnificence, and in inquiries after the remains of its ancient learning. I found in Cairo a mixture of all nations; some brought thither by the love of knowledge, some by the hope of gain, and many by the desire of living after their own manner without observation, and of lying hid in the obscurity of multitudes: for, in a city, populous as Cairo, it is possible to obtain at the same time the gratifications of society, and the secrecy of solitude.

"From Cairo I traveled to Suez, and embarked on the Red Sea, passing along the coast till I arrived at the port from which I had departed twenty years before. Here I joined myself to a caravan and re-entered my native country.

"I now expected the caresses of my kinsmen, and the congratulations of my friends, and was not without hope that my father, whatever value he had set upon riches, would own[3] with gladness and pride a son who was able to add to the felicity and honor of the nation. But I was soon convinced that my thoughts were vain. My father had been dead fourteen years, having divided his wealth among my brothers, who were removed to some other provinces. Of my companions the greater part was in the grave, of the rest some could with difficulty remember me, and some considered me as one corrupted by foreign manners.

"A man used to vicissitudes is not easily dejected. I forgot, after a time, my disappointment, and endeavoured to recommend myself to the nobles of the kingdom: they admitted me to their tables, heard my story, and dismissed me. I opened a school, and was prohibited to teach. I then resolved to sit down in the quiet of domestic life, and addressed[4] a lady that was fond of my conversation, but rejected my suit, because my father was a merchant.

"Wearied at last with solicitation and repulses, I resolved to hide myself forever from the world, and depend no longer on the opinion or caprice of others. I waited for the time when the gate of the *happy valley* should open, that I might bid farewell to hope and fear: the day came; my performance was distinguished with favor, and I resigned myself with joy to perpetual confinement."

"Hast thou here found happiness at last?" said Rasselas. "Tell me without reserve; art thou content with thy condition? or, dost thou wish to be again wandering and inquiring? All the inhabitants of this valley celebrate their lot, and, at the annual visit of the emperor, invite others to partake of their felicity."

"Great prince," said Imlac, "I shall speak the truth: I know not one of all your attendants who does not lament the hour when he entered this retreat. I am less unhappy than the rest, because I have a mind replete with images,

2. Imagine.   3. Acknowledge.   4. Courted.

which I can vary and combine at pleasure. I can amuse my solitude by the renovation of the knowledge which begins to fade from my memory, and by recollection of the accidents of my past life. Yet all this ends in the sorrowful consideration, that my acquirements are now useless, and that none of my pleasures can be again enjoyed. The rest, whose minds have no impression but of the present moment, are either corroded by malignant passions, or sit stupid in the gloom of perpetual vacancy."

"What passions can infest those," said the prince, "who have no rivals? We are in a place where impotence precludes malice, and where all envy is repressed by community of enjoyments."

"There may be community," said Imlac, "of material possessions, but there can never be community of love or of esteem. It must happen that one will please more than another; he that knows himself despised will always be envious; and still more envious and malevolent, if he is condemned to live in the presence of those who despise him. The invitations, by which they allure others to a state which they feel to be wretched, proceed from the natural malignity of hopeless misery. They are weary of themselves, and of each other, and expect to find relief in new companions. They envy the liberty which their folly has forfeited, and would gladly see all mankind imprisoned like themselves.

"From this crime, however, I am wholly free. No man can say that he is wretched by my persuasion. I look with pity on the crowds who are annually soliciting admission to captivity, and wish that it were lawful for me to warn them of their danger."

"My dear Imlac," said the prince, "I will open to thee my whole heart. I have long meditated an escape from the happy valley. I have examined the mountains on every side, but find myself insuperably barred: teach me the way to break my prison; thou shalt be the companion of my flight, the guide of my rambles, the partner of my fortune, and my sole director in the *choice of life*."

"Sir," answered the poet, "your escape will be difficult, and, perhaps, you may soon repent your curiosity. The world, which you figure to yourself smooth and quiet as the lake in the valley, you will find a sea foaming with tempests, and boiling with whirlpools: you will be sometimes overwhelmed by the waves of violence, and sometimes dashed against the rocks of treachery. Amidst wrongs and frauds, competitions and anxieties, you will wish a thousand times for these seats[5] of quiet, and willingly quit hope to be free from fear."

"Do not seek to deter me from my purpose," said the prince: "I am impatient to see what thou hast seen; and, since thou art thyself weary of the valley, it is evident, that thy former state was better than this. Whatever be the consequence of my experiment, I am resolved to judge with my own eyes of the various conditions of men, and then to make deliberately my *choice of life*."

"I am afraid," said Imlac, "you are hindered by stronger restraints than my persuasions; yet, if your determination is fixed, I do not counsel you to despair. Few things are impossible to diligence and skill."

*   *   *

---

5. Sites, locations.

[With the help of Imlac, Rasselas, joined by his sister, Nekayah, tunnels to freedom.]

CHAPTER XVI

They Enter Cairo, and Find Every Man Happy

As they approached the city, which filled the strangers with astonishment, "This," said Imlac to the prince, "is the place where travelers and merchants assemble from all the corners of the earth. You will here find men of every character, and every occupation. Commerce is here honorable: I will act as a merchant, and you shall live as strangers, who have no other end[6] of travel than curiosity; it will soon be observed that we are rich; our reputation will procure us access to all whom we shall desire to know; you will see all the conditions of humanity, and enable yourself at leisure to make your *choice of life*."

They now entered the town, stunned by the noise, and offended by the crowds. Instruction had not yet so prevailed over habit, but that they wondered to see themselves pass undistinguished along the street, and met by the lowest of the people without reverence or notice. The princess could not at first bear the thought of being leveled with the vulgar,[7] and, for some days, continued in her chamber, where she was served by her favorite Pekuah as in the palace of the valley.

Imlac, who understood traffic,[8] sold part of the jewels the next day, and hired a house, which he adorned with such magnificence, that he was immediately considered as a merchant of great wealth. His politeness attracted many acquaintance, and his generosity made him courted by many dependents. His table was crowded by men of every nation, who all admired his knowledge, and solicited his favor. His companions, not being able to mix in the conversation, could make no discovery[9] of their ignorance or surprise, and were gradually initiated in the world as they gained knowledge of the language.

The prince had, by frequent lectures, been taught the use and nature of money; but the ladies could not, for a long time, comprehend what the merchants did with small pieces of gold and silver, or why things of so little use should be received as equivalent to the necessaries of life.

They studied the language two years, while Imlac was preparing to set before them the various ranks and conditions of mankind. He grew acquainted with all who had anything uncommon in their fortune or conduct. He frequented the voluptuous and the frugal, the idle and the busy, the merchants and the men of learning.

The prince, being now able to converse with fluency, and having learned the caution necessary to be observed in his intercourse with strangers, began to accompany Imlac to places of resort, and to enter into all assemblies, that he might make his *choice of life*.

For some time he thought choice needless, because all appeared to him equally happy. Wherever he went he met gaiety and kindness, and heard the song of joy, or the laugh of carelessness. He began to believe that the world overflowed with universal plenty, and that nothing was withheld either from want or merit; that every hand showered liberality, and every

6. Goal.　7. Common people.　8. Trade.　9. Revelation.

heart melted with benevolence: "and who then," says he, "will be suffered to be wretched?"

Imlac permitted the pleasing delusion, and was unwilling to crush the hope of inexperience; till one day, having sat awhile silent, "I know not," said the prince, "what can be the reason that I am more unhappy than any of our friends. I see them perpetually and unalterably cheerful, but feel my own mind restless and uneasy. I am unsatisfied with those pleasures which I seem most to court; I live in the crowds of jollity, not so much to enjoy company as to shun myself, and am only loud and merry to conceal my sadness."

"Every man," said Imlac, "may, by examining his own mind, guess what passes in the minds of others: when you feel that your own gaiety is counterfeit, it may justly lead you to suspect that of your companions not to be sincere. Envy is commonly reciprocal. We are long before we are convinced that happiness is never to be found, and each believes it possessed by others, to keep alive the hope of obtaining it for himself. In the assembly, where you passed the last night, there appeared such spriteliness of air, and volatility of fancy, as might have suited beings of an higher order, formed to inhabit serener regions inaccessible to care or sorrow: yet, believe me, prince, there was not one who did not dread the moment when solitude should deliver him to the tyranny of reflection."

"This," said the prince, "may be true of others, since it is true of me; yet, whatever be the general infelicity of man, one condition is more happy than another, and wisdom surely directs us to take the least evil in the *choice of life*."

"The causes of good and evil," answered Imlac, "are so various and uncertain, so often entangled with each other, so diversified by various relations, and so much subject to accidents which cannot be foreseen, that he who would fix his condition upon incontestable reasons of preference, must live and die inquiring and deliberating."

"But surely," said Rasselas, "the wise men, to whom we listen with reverence and wonder, chose that mode of life for themselves which they thought most likely to make them happy."

"Very few," said the poet, "live by choice. Every man is placed in his present condition by causes which acted without his foresight, and with which he did not always willingly cooperate; and therefore you will rarely meet one who does not think the lot of his neighbor better than his own."

"I am pleased to think," said the prince, "that my birth has given me at least one advantage over others, by enabling me to determine for myself. I have here the world before me; I will review it at leisure: surely happiness is somewhere to be found."

CHAPTER XVII

The Prince Associates with Young Men of Spirit and Gaiety

Rasselas rose next day, and resolved to begin his experiments upon life. "Youth," cried he, "is the time of gladness: I will join myself to the young men, whose only business is to gratify their desires, and whose time is all spent in a succession of enjoyments."

To such societies he was readily admitted, but a few days brought him back weary and disgusted. Their mirth was without images,[1] their laughter without motive; their pleasures were gross and sensual in which the mind had no part; their conduct was at once wild and mean; they laughed at order and at law, but the frown of power dejected, and the eye of wisdom abashed them.

The prince soon concluded, that he should never be happy in a course of life of which he was ashamed. He thought it unsuitable to a reasonable being to act without a plan, and to be sad or cheerful only by chance. "Happiness," said he, "must be something solid and permanent, without fear and without uncertainty."

But his young companions had gained so much of his regard by their frankness and courtesy, that he could not leave them without warning and remonstrance. "My friends," said he, "I have seriously considered our manners and our prospects, and find that we have mistaken our own interest. The first years of man must make provision for the last. He that never thinks never can be wise. Perpetual levity must end in ignorance; and intemperance, though it may fire the spirits for an hour, will make life short or miserable. Let us consider that youth is of no long duration, and that in maturer age, when the enchantments of fancy shall cease, and phantoms of delight dance no more about us, we shall have no comforts but the esteem of wise men, and the means of doing good. Let us, therefore, stop, while to stop is in our power: let us live as men who are sometime to grow old, and to whom it will be the most dreadful of all evils not to count their past years but by follies, and to be reminded of their former luxuriance of health only by the maladies which riot has produced."

They stared awhile in silence one upon another, and, at last, drove him away by a general chorus of continued laughter.

The consciousness that his sentiments were just, and his intentions kind, was scarcely sufficient to support him against the horror of derision. But he recovered his tranquillity, and pursued his search.

CHAPTER XVIII

The Prince Finds a Wise and Happy Man

As he [Rasselas] was one day walking in the street, he saw a spacious building which all were, by the open doors, invited to enter: he followed the stream of people, and found it a hall or school of declamation, in which professors read lectures to their auditory.[2] He fixed his eye upon a sage raised above the rest, who discoursed with great energy on the government of the passions. His look was venerable, his action graceful, his pronunciation clear, and his diction elegant. He showed, with great strength of sentiment, and variety of illustration, that human nature is degraded and debased, when the lower faculties predominate over the higher; that when fancy, the parent of passion, usurps the domination of the mind, nothing ensues but the natural effect of unlawful government, perturbation and confusion; that she betrays the fortresses of the intellect to rebels, and excites her children to sedition against reason their lawful sovereign. He compared reason to the sun, of which the light is constant, uniform, and lasting; and fancy to a meteor, of

1. Ideas, conceptions.   2. Audience.

bright but transitory luster irregular in its motion, and delusive in its direction.

He then communicated the various precepts given from time to time for the conquest of passion, and displayed the happiness of those who had obtained the important victory, after which man is no longer the slave of fear, nor the fool of hope; is no more emaciated by envy, inflamed by anger, emasculated by tenderness, or depressed by grief; but walks on calmly through the tumults or the privacies of life, as the sun pursues alike his course through the calm or the stormy sky.

He enumerated many examples of heroes immovable by pain or pleasure, who looked with indifference on those modes or accidents to which the vulgar give the names of good and evil. He exhorted his hearers to lay aside their prejudices, and arm themselves against the shafts of malice or misfortune, by invulnerable patience; concluding that this state only was happiness, and that this happiness was in every one's power.

Rasselas listened to him with the veneration due to the instructions of a superior being, and, waiting for him at the door, humbly implored the liberty of visiting so great a master of true wisdom. The lecturer hesitated a moment, when Rasselas put a purse of gold into his hand, which he received with a mixture of joy and wonder.

"I have found," said the prince, at his return to Imlac, "a man who can teach all that is necessary to be known, who, from the unshaken throne of rational fortitude, looks down on the scenes of life changing beneath him. He speaks, and attention watches his lips. He reasons, and conviction closes his periods.[3] This man shall be my future guide: I will learn his doctrines, and imitate his life."

"Be not too hasty," said Imlac, "to trust, or to admire, the teachers of morality: they discourse like angels, but they live like men."

Rasselas, who could not conceive how any man could reason so forcibly without feeling the cogency of his own arguments, paid his visit in a few days, and was denied admission. He had now learned the power of money, and made his way by a piece of gold to the inner apartment, where he found the philosopher in a room half darkened, with his eyes misty, and his face pale. "Sir," said he, "you are come at a time when all human friendship is useless; what I suffer cannot be remedied, what I have lost cannot be supplied. My daughter, my only daughter, from whose tenderness I expected all the comforts of my age, died last night of a fever. My views, my purposes, my hopes are at an end: I am now a lonely being disunited from society."

"Sir," said the prince, "mortality is an event by which a wise man can never be surprised: we know that death is always near, and it should therefore always be expected." "Young man," answered the philosopher, "you speak like one that has never felt the pangs of separation." "Have you then forgot the precepts," said Rasselas, "which you so powerfully enforced? Has wisdom no strength to arm the heart against calamity? Consider, that external things are naturally variable, but truth and reason are always the same." "What comfort," said the mourner, "can truth and reason afford me? Of what effect are they now, but to tell me, that my daughter will not be restored?"

The prince, whose humanity would not suffer him to insult misery with

3. Sentences.

reproof, went away convinced of the emptiness of rhetorical sound, and the inefficacy of polished periods and studied sentences.

CHAPTER XIX

A Glimpse of Pastoral Life

He was still eager upon the same inquiry; and, having heard of a hermit, that lived near the lowest cataract of the Nile, and filled the whole country with the fame of his sanctity, resolved to visit his retreat, and inquire whether that felicity, which public life could not afford, was to be found in solitude; and whether a man, whose age and virtue made him venerable, could teach any peculiar art of shunning evils, or enduring them.

Imlac and the princess agreed to accompany him, and, after the necessary preparations, they began their journey. Their way lay through fields, where shepherds tended their flocks, and the lambs were playing upon the pasture. "This," said the poet, "is the life which has been often celebrated for its innocence and quiet: let us pass the heat of the day among the shepherds' tents, and know whether all our searches are not to terminate in pastoral simplicity."

The proposal pleased them, and they induced the shepherds, by small presents and familiar questions, to tell their opinion of their own state: they were so rude[4] and ignorant, so little able to compare the good with the evil of the occupation, and so indistinct in their narratives and descriptions, that very little could be learned from them. But it was evident that their hearts were cankered with discontent; that they considered themselves as condemned to labor for the luxury of the rich, and looked up with stupid malevolence toward those that were placed above them.

The princess pronounced with vehemence, that she would never suffer these envious savages to be her companions, and that she should not soon be desirous of seeing any more specimens of rustic happiness; but could not believe that all the accounts of primeval pleasures were fabulous, and was yet in doubt whether life had anything that could be justly preferred to the placid gratifications of fields and woods. She hoped that the time would come, when, with a few virtuous and elegant companions, she should gather flowers planted by her own hand, fondle the lambs of her own ewe, and listen, without care, among brooks and breezes, to one of her maidens reading in the shade.

CHAPTER XX

The Danger of Prosperity

On the next day they continued their journey, till the heat compelled them to look round for shelter. At a small distance they saw a thick wood, which they no sooner entered than they perceived that they were approaching the habitations of men. The shrubs were diligently cut away to open walks where the shades were darkest; the boughs of opposite trees were artificially interwoven; seats of flowery turf were raised in vacant spaces, and a rivulet, that wantoned along the side of a winding path, had its banks sometimes opened

4. Unpolished, boorish.

into small basons,[5] and its stream sometimes obstructed by little mounds of stone heaped together to increase its murmurs.

They passed slowly through the wood, delighted with such unexpected accommodations, and entertained each other with conjecturing what, or who, he could be, that, in those rude and unfrequented regions, had leisure and art for such harmless luxury.

As they advanced, they heard the sound of music, and saw youths and virgins dancing in the grove; and, going still further, beheld a stately palace built upon a hill surrounded with woods. The laws of eastern hospitality allowed them to enter, and the master welcomed them like a man liberal and wealthy.

He was skillful enough in appearances soon to discern that they were no common guests, and spread his table with magnificence. The eloquence of Imlac caught his attention, and the lofty courtesy of the princess excited his respect. When they offered to depart he entreated their stay, and was the next day still more unwilling to dismiss them than before. They were easily persuaded to stop, and civility grew up in time to freedom and confidence.

The prince now saw all the domestics cheerful, and all the face of nature smiling round the place, and could not forbear to hope that he should find here what he was seeking; but when he was congratulating the master upon his possessions, he answered with a sigh, "My condition has indeed the appearance of happiness, but appearances are delusive. My prosperity puts my life in danger; the Bassa[6] of Egypt is my enemy, incensed only by my wealth and popularity. I have been hitherto protected against him by the princes of the country; but, as the favor of the great is uncertain, I know not how soon my defenders may be persuaded to share the plunder with the Bassa. I have sent my treasures into a distant country, and, upon the first alarm, am prepared to follow them. Then will my enemies riot in my mansion, and enjoy the gardens which I have planted."

They all joined in lamenting his danger, and deprecating his exile; and the princess was so much disturbed with the tumult of grief and indignation, that she retired to her apartment. They continued with their kind inviter a few days longer, and then went forward to find the hermit.

CHAPTER XXI

The Happiness of Solitude. The Hermit's History

They came on the third day, by the direction of the peasants, to the hermit's cell: it was a cavern in the side of a mountain, overshadowed with palm trees; at such a distance from the cataract, that nothing more was heard than a gentle uniform murmur, such as composed the mind to pensive meditation, especially when it was assisted by the wind whistling among the branches. The first rude essay of nature had been so much improved by human labor, that the cave contained several apartments, appropriated to different uses, and often afforded lodging to travelers, whom darkness or tempests happened to overtake.

The hermit sat on a bench at the door, to enjoy the coolness of the evening. On one side lay a book with pens and papers, on the other mechanical instru-

5. Ponds. 6. A high official.

ments of various kinds. As they approached him unregarded, the princess observed that he had not the countenance of a man that had found, or could teach, the way to happiness.

They saluted him with great respect, which he repaid like a man not unaccustomed to the forms of courts. "My children," said he, "if you have lost your way, you shall be willingly supplied with such conveniences for the night as this cavern will afford. I have all that nature requires, and you will not expect delicacies in a hermit's cell."

They thanked him, and, entering, were pleased with the neatness and regularity of the place. The hermit set flesh and wine before them, though he fed only upon fruits and water. His discourse was cheerful without levity, and pious without enthusiasm.[7] He soon gained the esteem of his guests, and the princess repented of her hasty censure.

At last Imlac began thus: "I do not now wonder that your reputation is so far extended; we have heard at Cairo of your wisdom, and came hither to implore your direction for this young man and maiden in the *choice of life.*"

"To him that lives well," answered the hermit, "every form of life is good; nor can I give any other rule for choice, than to remove from all apparent evil."

"He will remove most certainly from evil," said the prince, "who shall devote himself to that solitude which you have recommended by your example."

"I have indeed lived fifteen years in solitude," said the hermit, "but have no desire that my example should gain any imitators. In my youth I professed arms, and was raised by degrees to the highest military rank. I have traversed wide countries at the head of my troops, and seen many battles and sieges. At last, being disgusted by the preferment of a younger officer, and feeling that my vigor was beginning to decay, I resolved to close my life in peace, having found the world full of snares, discord, and misery. I had once escaped from the pursuit of the enemy by the shelter of this cavern, and therefore chose it for my final residence. I employed artificers to form it into chambers, and stored it with all that I was likely to want.

"For some time after my retreat, I rejoiced like a tempest-beaten sailor at his entrance into the harbor, being delighted with the sudden change of the noise and hurry of war, to stillness and repose. When the pleasure of novelty went away, I employed my hours in examining the plants which grow in the valley, and the minerals which I collected from the rocks. But that inquiry is now grown tasteless and irksome. I have been for some time unsettled and distracted: my mind is disturbed with a thousand perplexities of doubt, and vanities of imagination, which hourly prevail upon me, because I have no opportunities of relaxation or diversion. I am sometimes ashamed to think that I could not secure myself from vice, but by retiring from the exercise of virtue, and begin to suspect that I was rather impelled by resentment, than led by devotion, into solitude. My fancy riots in scenes of folly, and I lament that I have lost so much, and have gained so little. In solitude, if I escape the example of bad men, I want likewise the counsel and conversation of the good. I have been long comparing the evils with the advantages of society, and resolve to return into the world tomorrow. The life of a solitary man will be certainly miserable, but not certainly devout."

7. Excessive ardor.

They heard his resolution with surprise, but, after a short pause, offered to conduct him to Cairo. He dug up a considerable treasure which he had hid among the rocks, and accompanied them to the city, on which, as he approached it, he gazed with rapture.

CHAPTER XXII

The Happiness of a Life Led According to Nature

Rasselas went often to an assembly of learned men, who met at stated times to unbend their minds, and compare their opinions. Their manners were somewhat coarse, but their conversation was instructive, and their disputations acute, though sometimes too violent, and often continued till neither controvertist remembered upon what question they began. Some faults were almost general among them: every one was desirous to dictate to the rest, and every one was pleased to hear the genius or knowledge of another depreciated.

In this assembly Rasselas was relating his interview with the hermit, and the wonder with which he heard him censure a course of life which he had so deliberately chosen, and so laudably followed. The sentiments of the hearers were various. Some were of opinion, that the folly of his choice had been justly punished by condemnation to perpetual perseverance.[8] One of the youngest among them, with great vehemence, pronounced him an hypocrite. Some talked of the right of society to the labor of individuals, and considered retirement as a desertion of duty. Others readily allowed, that there was a time when the claims of the public were satisfied, and when a man might properly sequester himself, to review his life, and purify his heart.

One, who appeared more affected with the narrative than the rest, thought it likely, that the hermit would, in a few years, go back to his retreat, and, perhaps, if shame did not restrain, or death intercept him, return once more from his retreat into the world: "For the hope of happiness," said he, "is so strongly impressed, that the longest experience is not able to efface it. Of the present state, whatever it be, we feel, and are forced to confess, the misery, yet, when the same state is again at a distance, imagination paints it as desirable. But the time will surely come, when desire will be no longer our torment, and no man shall be wretched but by his own fault."

"This," said a philosopher, who had heard him with tokens of great impatience, "is the present condition of a wise man. The time is already come, when none are wretched but by their own fault. Nothing is more idle, than to inquire after happiness, which nature has kindly placed within our reach. The way to be happy is to live according to nature, in obedience to that universal and unalterable law with which every heart is originally impressed; which is not written on it by precept, but engraven by destiny, not instilled by education, but infused at our nativity. He that lives according to nature will suffer nothing from the delusions of hope, or importunities of desire: he will receive and reject with equability of temper; and act or suffer as the reason of things shall alternately prescribe. Other men may amuse themselves with subtle definitions, or intricate raciocination. Let them learn to be wise by easier means: let them observe the hind of the forest, and the linnet of the grove: let them consider the life of animals, whose motions are

---

8. Repetition; hence, monotony.

regulated by instinct; they obey their guide and are happy. Let us therefore, at length, cease to dispute, and learn to live; throw away the incumbrance of precepts, which they who utter them with so much pride and pomp do not understand, and carry with us this simple and intelligible maxim, That deviation from nature is deviation from happiness."

When he had spoken, he looked round him with a placid air, and enjoyed the consciousness of his own beneficence. "Sir," said the prince, with great modesty, "as I, like all the rest of mankind, am desirous of felicity, my closest attention has been fixed upon your discourse: I doubt not the truth of a position which a man so learned has so confidently advanced. Let me only know what it is to live according to nature."

"When I find young men so humble and so docile," said the philosopher, "I can deny them no information which my studies have enabled me to afford. To live according to nature, is to act always with due regard to the fitness arising from the relations and qualities of causes and effects; to concur with the great and unchangeable scheme of universal felicity; to cooperate with the general disposition and tendency of the present system of things."

The prince soon found that this was one of the sages whom he should understand less as he heard him longer. He therefore bowed and was silent, and the philosopher, supposing him satisfied, and the rest vanquished, rose up and departed with the air of a man that had cooperated with the present system.

CHAPTER XXIII

The Prince and His Sister Divide between Them the Work of Observation

Rasselas returned home full of reflections, doubtful how to direct his future steps. Of the way to happiness he found the learned and simple equally ignorant; but, as he was yet young, he flattered himself that he had time remaining for more experiments, and further inquiries. He communicated to Imlac his observations and his doubts, but was answered by him with new doubts, and remarks that gave him no comfort. He therefore discoursed more frequently and freely with his sister, who had yet the same hope with himself, and always assisted him to give some reason why, though he had been hitherto frustrated, he might succeed at last.

"We have hitherto," said she, "known but little of the world: we have never yet been either great or mean. In our own country, though we had royalty, we had no power, and in this we have not yet seen the private recesses of domestic peace. Imlac favors not our search, lest we should in time find him mistaken. We will divide the task between us: you shall try what is to be found in the splendor of courts, and I will range the shades of humbler life. Perhaps command and authority may be the supreme blessings, as they afford most opportunities of doing good: or, perhaps, what this world can give may be found in the modest habitations of middle fortune; too low for great designs, and too high for penury and distress."

CHAPTER XXIV

The Prince Examines the Happiness of High Stations

Rasselas applauded the design, and appeared next day with a splendid retinue at the court of the Bassa. He was soon distinguished for his magnificence, and admitted, as a prince whose curiosity had brought him from distant countries, to an intimacy with the great officers, and frequent conversation with the Bassa himself.

He was at first inclined to believe, that the man must be pleased with his own condition, whom all approached with reverence, and heard with obedience, and who had the power to extend his edicts to a whole kingdom. "There can be no pleasure," said he, "equal to that of feeling at once the joy of thousands all made happy by wise administration. Yet, since, by the law of subordination, this sublime delight can be in one nation but the lot of one, it is surely reasonable to think that there is some satisfaction more popular[9] and accessible, and that millions can hardly be subjected to the will of a single man, only to fill his particular breast with incommunicable content."

These thoughts were often in his mind, and he found no solution of the difficulty. But as presents and civilities gained him more familiarity, he found that almost every man who stood high in employment hated all the rest, and was hated by them, and that their lives were a continual succession of plots and detections, stratagems and escapes, faction and treachery. Many of those, who surrounded the Bassa, were sent only to watch and report his conduct; every tongue was muttering censure and every eye was searching for a fault.

At last the letters of revocation arrived, the Bassa was carried in chains to Constantinople, and his name was mentioned no more.

"What are we now to think of the prerogatives of power," said Rasselas to his sister; "is it without any efficacy to good? or, is the subordinate degree only dangerous, and the supreme safe and glorious? Is the Sultan the only happy man in his dominions? or, is the Sultan himself subject to the torments of suspicion, and the dread of enemies?"

In a short time the second Bassa was deposed. The Sultan, that had advanced him, was murdered by the Janisaries,[1] and his successor had other views and different favorites.

CHAPTER XXV

The Princess Pursues Her Inquiry with More Diligence Than Success

The princess, in the meantime, insinuated herself into many families; for there are few doors, through which liberality, joined with good humor, cannot find its way. The daughters of many houses were airy[2] and cheerful, but Nekayah had been too long accustomed to the conversation of Imlac and her brother to be much pleased with childish levity and prattle which had no meaning. She found their thoughts narrow, their wishes low, and their merriment often artificial. Their pleasures, poor as they were, could not be

---

9. Available to the people as a whole.   1. Turkish guards.   2. Lively.

preserved pure, but were embittered by petty competitions and worthless emulation. They were always jealous of the beauty of each other; of a quality to which solicitude can add nothing, and from which detraction can take nothing away. Many were in love with triflers like themselves, and many fancied that they were in love when in truth they were only idle. Their affection was seldom fixed on sense or virtue, and therefore seldom ended but in vexation. Their grief, however, like their joy, was transient; everything floated in their mind unconnected with the past or future, so that one desire easily gave way to another, as a second stone cast into the water effaces and confounds the circles of the first.

With these girls she played as with inoffensive animals, and found them proud of her countenance,[3] and weary of her company.

But her purpose was to examine more deeply, and her affability easily persuaded the hearts that were swelling with sorrow to discharge their secrets in her ear: and those whom hope flattered, or prosperity delighted, often courted her to partake their pleasures.

The princess and her brother commonly met in the evening in a private summerhouse on the bank of the Nile, and related to each other the occurrences of the day. As they were sitting together, the princess cast her eyes upon the river that flowed before her. "Answer," said she, "great father of waters, thou that rollest thy floods through eighty nations, to the invocations of the daughter of thy native king. Tell me if thou waterest, through all thy course, a single habitation from which thou dost not hear the murmurs of complaint?"

"You are then," said Rasselas, "not more successful in private houses than I have been in courts." "I have, since the last partition of our provinces,"[4] said the princess, "enabled myself to enter familiarly into many families, where there was the fairest show of prosperity and peace, and know not one house that is not haunted by some fury that destroys its quiet.

"I did not seek ease among the poor, because I concluded that there it could not be found. But I saw many poor whom I had supposed to live in affluence. Poverty has, in large cities, very different appearances: it is often concealed in splendor, and often in extravagance. It is the care of a very great part of mankind to conceal their indigence from the rest: they support themselves by temporary expedients, and every day is lost in contriving for the morrow.

"This, however, was an evil, which, though frequent, I saw with less pain, because I could relieve it. Yet some have refused my bounties; more offended with my quickness to detect their wants, than pleased with my readiness to succor them: and others, whose exigencies compelled them to admit my kindness, have never been able to forgive their benefactress. Many, however, have been sincerely grateful without the ostentation of gratitude, or the hope of other favors."

CHAPTER XXVI

The Princess Continues Her Remarks upon Private Life

Nekayah perceiving her brother's attention fixed, proceeded in her narrative.

"In families, where there is or is not poverty, there is commonly discord:

---

3. Favor.   4. Division of assigned tasks.

if a kingdom be, as Imlac tells us, a great family, a family likewise is a little kingdom, torn with factions and exposed to revolutions. An unpracticed observer expects the love of parents and children to be constant and equal; but this kindness seldom continues beyond the years of infancy: in a short time the children become rivals to their parents. Benefits are allayed by reproaches, and gratitude debased by envy.

"Parents and children seldom act in concert: each child endeavors to appropriate the esteem or fondness of the parents, and the parents, with yet less temptation, betray each other to their children; thus some place their confidence in the father, and some in the mother, and, by degrees, the house is filled with artifices and feuds.

"The opinions of children and parents, of the young and the old, are naturally opposite, by the contrary effects of hope and despondence, of expectation and experience, without crime or folly on either side. The colors of life in youth and age appear different, as the face of nature in spring and winter. And how can children credit the assertions of parents, which their own eyes show them to be false?

"Few parents act in such a manner as much to enforce their maxims by the credit of their lives. The old man trusts wholly to slow contrivance and gradual progression: the youth expects to force his way by genius, vigor, and precipitance. The old man pays regard to riches, and the youth reverences virtue. The old man deifies prudence: the youth commits himself to magnanimity and chance. The young man, who intends no ill, believes that none is intended, and therefore acts with openness and candor:[5] but his father, having suffered the injuries of fraud, is impelled to suspect, and too often allured to practice it. Age looks with anger on the temerity of youth, and youth with contempt on the scrupulosity of age. Thus parents and children, for the greatest part, live on to love less and less: and, if those whom nature has thus closely united are the torments of each other, where shall we look for tenderness and consolation?"

"Surely," said the prince, "you must have been unfortunate in your choice of acquaintance: I am unwilling to believe, that the most tender of all relations is thus impeded in its effects by natural necessity."

"Domestic discord," answered she, "is not inevitably and fatally necessary; but yet is not easily avoided. We seldom see that a whole family is virtuous: the good and evil cannot well agree; and the evil can yet less agree with one another: even the virtuous fall sometimes to variance, when their virtues are of different kinds, and tending to extremes. In general, those parents have most reverence who most deserve it: for he that lives well cannot be despised.

"Many other evils infest private life. Some are the slaves of servants whom they have trusted with their affairs. Some are kept in continual anxiety to the caprice of rich relations, whom they cannot please, and dare not offend. Some husbands are imperious, and some wives perverse: and, as it is always more easy to do evil than good, though the wisdom or virtue of one can very rarely make many happy, the folly or vice of one may often make many miserable."

"If such be the general effect of marriage," said the prince, "I shall, for the future, think it dangerous to connect my interest with that of another, lest I should be unhappy by my partner's fault."

5. Generosity.

"I have met," said the princess, "with many who live single for that reason; but I never found that their prudence ought to raise envy. They dream away their time without friendship, without fondness, and are driven to rid themselves of the day, for which they have no use, by childish amusements, or vicious delights. They act as beings under the constant sense of some known inferiority, that fills their minds with rancor, and their tongues with censure. They are peevish at home, and malevolent abroad; and, as the outlaws of human nature, make it their business and their pleasure to disturb that society which debars them from its privileges. To live without feeling or exciting sympathy, to be fortunate without adding to the felicity of others, or afflicted without tasting the balm of pity, is a state more gloomy than solitude: it is not retreat but exclusion from mankind. Marriage has many pains, but celibacy has no pleasures."

"What then is to be done?" said Rasselas; "the more we inquire, the less we can resolve. Surely he is most likely to please himself that has no other inclination to regard."

CHAPTER XXVII
Disquisition upon Greatness

The conversation had a short pause. The prince, having considered his sister's observations, told her, that she had surveyed life with prejudice, and supposed misery where she did not find it. "Your narrative," says he, "throws yet a darker gloom upon the prospects of futurity: the predictions of Imlac were but faint sketches of the evils painted by Nekayah. I have been lately convinced that quiet is not the daughter of grandeur, or of power: that her presence is not to be bought by wealth, nor enforced by conquest. It is evident, that as any man acts in a wider compass, he must be more exposed to opposition from enmity or miscarriage from chance; whoever has many to please or to govern, must use the ministry of many agents, some of whom will be wicked, and some ignorant; by some he will be misled, and by others betrayed. If he gratifies one he will offend another: those that are not favored will think themselves injured; and, since favors can be conferred but upon few, the greater number will be always discontented."

"The discontent," said the princess, "which is thus unreasonable, I hope that I shall always have spirit to despise, and you, power to repress."

"Discontent," answered Rasselas, "will not always be without reason under the most just or vigilant administration of public affairs. None, however attentive, can always discover that merit which indigence or faction may happen to obscure; and none, however powerful, can always reward it. Yet, he that sees inferior desert[6] advanced above him, will naturally impute that preference to partiality or caprice; and, indeed, it can scarcely be hoped that any man, however magnanimous by nature, or exalted by condition, will be able to persist forever in fixed and inexorable justice of distribution: he will sometimes indulge his own affections, and sometimes those of his favorites; he will permit some to please him who can never serve him; he will discover in those whom he loves qualities which in reality they do not possess; and to those, from whom he receives pleasure, he will in his turn endeavor to

---

6. Merit, worth.

give it. Thus will recommendations sometimes prevail which were purchased by money, or by the more destructive bribery of flattery and servility.

"He that has much to do will do something wrong, and of that wrong must suffer the consequences; and, if it were possible that he should always act rightly, yet when such numbers are to judge of his conduct, the bad will censure and obstruct him by malevolence, and the good sometimes by mistake.

"The highest stations cannot therefore hope to be the abodes of happiness, which I would willingly believe to have fled from thrones and palaces to seats[7] of humble privacy and placid obscurity. For what can hinder the satisfaction, or intercept the expectations, of him whose abilities are adequate to his employments, who sees with his own eyes the whole circuit of his influence, who chooses by his own knowledge all whom he trusts, and whom none are tempted to deceive by hope or fear? Surely he has nothing to do but to love and to be loved, to be virtuous and to be happy."

"Whether perfect happiness would be procured by perfect goodness," said Nekayah, "this world will never afford an opportunity of deciding. But this, at least, may be maintained, that we do not always find visible happiness in proportion to visible virtue. All natural and almost all political evils, are incident alike to the bad and good: they are confounded in the misery of a famine, and not much distinguished in the fury of a faction; they sink together in a tempest, and are driven together from their country by invaders. All that virtue can afford is quietness of conscience, a steady prospect of a happier state; this may enable us to endure calamity with patience; but remember that patience must suppose pain."

CHAPTER XXVIII

Rasselas and Nekayah Continue Their Conversation

"Dear princess," said Rasselas, "you fall into the common errors of exaggeratory declamation, by producing, in a familiar disquisition, examples of national calamities, and scenes of extensive misery, which are found in books rather than in the world, and which, as they are horrid, are ordained to be rare. Let us not imagine evils which we do not feel, nor injure life by misrepresentations. I cannot bear that querulous eloquence which threatens every city with a siege like that of Jerusalem,[8] that makes famine attend on every flight of locusts, and suspends pestilence on the wing of every blast that issues from the south.

"On necessary and inevitable evils, which overwhelm kingdoms at once, all disputation is vain: when they happen they must be endured. But it is evident, that these bursts of universal distress are more dreaded than felt: thousands and ten thousands flourish in youth, and wither in age, without the knowledge of any other than domestic evils, and share the same pleasures and vexations whether their kings are mild or cruel, whether the armies of their country pursue their enemies, or retreat before them. While courts are disturbed with intestine[9] competitions, and ambassadors are negotiating in foreign countries, the smith still plies his anvil, and the husbandman drives

---

7. Residences.   8. The siege of 70 C.E., after which Titus captured and destroyed the city.   9. Internal.

his plow forward; the necessaries of life are required and obtained, and the successive business of the seasons continues to make its wonted revolutions.

"Let us cease to consider what, perhaps, may never happen, and what, when it shall happen, will laugh at human speculation. We will not endeavor to modify the motions of the elements, or to fix the destiny of kingdoms. It is our business to consider what beings like us may perform; each laboring for his own happiness, by promoting within his circle, however narrow, the happiness of others.

"Marriage is evidently the dictate of nature; men and women were made to be companions of each other, and therefore I cannot be persuaded but that marriage is one of the means of happiness."

"I know not," said the princess, "whether marriage be more than one of the innumerable modes of human misery. When I see and reckon the various forms of connubial infelicity, the unexpected causes of lasting discord, the diversities of temper, the oppositions of opinion, the rude collisions of contrary desire where both are urged by violent impulses, the obstinate contests of disagreeing virtues, where both are supported by consciousness of good intention, I am sometimes disposed to think with the severer casuists of most nations, that marriage is rather permitted than approved, and that none, but by the instigation of a passion too much indulged, entangle themselves with indissoluble compacts."

"You seem to forget," replied Rasselas, "that you have, even now, represented celibacy as less happy than marriage. Both conditions may be bad, but they cannot both be worst. Thus it happens when wrong opinions are entertained, that they mutually destroy each other, and leave the mind open to truth."

"I did not expect," answered the princess, "to hear that imputed to falsehood which is the consequence only of frailty. To the mind, as to the eye, it is difficult to compare with exactness objects vast in their extent, and various in their parts. Where we see or conceive the whole at once we readily note the discriminations and decide the preference: but of two systems, of which neither can be surveyed by any human being in its full compass of magnitude and multiplicity of complication, where is the wonder, that judging of the whole by parts, I am alternately affected by one and the other as either presses on my memory or fancy? We differ from ourselves just as we differ from each other, when we see only part of the question, as in the multifarious relations of politics and morality: but when we perceive the whole at once, as in numerical computations, all agree in one judgment, and none ever varies his opinion."

"Let us not add," said the prince, "to the other evils of life, the bitterness of controversy, nor endeavor to vie with each other in subtleties of argument. We are employed in a search, of which both are equally to enjoy the success, or suffer by the miscarriage. It is therefore fit that we assist each other. You surely conclude too hastily from the infelicity of marriage against its institution; will not the misery of life prove equally that life cannot be the gift of heaven? The world must be peopled by marriage, or peopled without it."

"How the world is to be peopled," returned Nekayah, "is not my care, and needs not be yours. I see no danger that the present generation should omit to leave successors behind them: we are not now inquiring for the world, but for ourselves."

CHAPTER XXIX

The Debate on Marriage Continued

"The good of the whole," says Rasselas, "is the same with the good of all its parts. If marriage be best for mankind it must be evidently best for individuals, or a permanent and necessary duty must be the cause of evil, and some must be inevitably sacrificed to the convenience of others. In the estimate which you have made of the two states, it appears that the incommodities of a single life are, in a great measure, necessary and certain, but those of the conjugal state accidental and avoidable.

"I cannot forbear to flatter myself that prudence and benevolence will make marriage happy. The general folly of mankind is the cause of general complaint. What can be expected but disappointment and repentance from a choice made in the immaturity of youth, in the ardor of desire, without judgment, without foresight, without inquiry after conformity of opinions, similarity of manners, rectitude of judgment, or purity of sentiment.

"Such is the common process of marriage. A youth and maiden meeting by chance, or brought together by artifice, exchange glances, reciprocate civilities, go home, and dream of one another. Having little to divert attention, or diversify thought, they find themselves uneasy when they are apart, and therefore conclude that they shall be happy together. They marry, and discover what nothing but voluntary blindness had before concealed; they wear out life in altercations, and charge nature with cruelty.

"From those early marriages proceeds likewise the rivalry of parents and children: the son is eager to enjoy the world before the father is willing to forsake it, and there is hardly room at once for two generations. The daughter begins to bloom before the mother can be content to fade, and neither can forbear to wish for the absence of the other.

"Surely all these evils may be avoided by that deliberation and delay which prudence prescribes to irrevocable choice. In the variety and jollity of youthful pleasures life may be well enough supported without the help of a partner. Longer time will increase experience, and wider views will allow better opportunities of inquiry and selection: one advantage, at least, will be certain; the parents will be visibly older than their children."

"What reason cannot collect," said Nekayah, "and what experiment has not yet taught, can be known only from the report of others. I have been told that late marriages are not eminently happy. This is a question too important to be neglected, and I have often proposed it to those, whose accuracy of remark, and comprehensiveness of knowledge, made their suffrages[1] worthy of regard. They have generally determined, that it is dangerous for a man and woman to suspend their fate upon each other, at a time when opinions are fixed, and habits are established; when friendships have been contracted on both sides, when life has been planned into method, and the mind has long enjoyed the contemplation of its own prospects.

"It is scarcely possible that two traveling through the world under the conduct of chance, should have been both directed to the same path, and it will not often happen that either will quit the track which custom has made

---

1. Opinions.

pleasing. When the desultory levity of youth has settled into regularity, it is soon succeeded by pride ashamed to yield, or obstinacy delighting to contend. And even though mutual esteem produces mutual desire to please, time itself, as it modifies unchangeably the external mien, determines likewise the direction of the passions, and gives an inflexible rigidity to the manners. Long customs are not easily broken: he that attempts to change the course of his own life, very often labors in vain; and how shall we do that for others which we are seldom able to do for ourselves?"

"But surely," interposed the prince, "you suppose the chief motive of choice forgotten or neglected. Whenever I shall seek a wife, it shall be my first question, whether she be willing to be led by reason?"

"Thus it is," said Nekayah, "that philosophers are deceived. There are a thousand familiar disputes which reason never can decide; questions that elude investigation, and make logic ridiculous; cases where something must be done, and where little can be said. Consider the state of mankind, and inquire how few can be supposed to act upon any occasions, whether small or great, with all the reasons of action present to their minds. Wretched would be the pair above all names of wretchedness, who should be doomed to adjust by reason every morning all the minute detail of a domestic day.

"Those who marry at an advanced age, will probably escape the encroachments of their children; but, in diminution of this advantage, they will be likely to leave them, ignorant and helpless, to a guardian's mercy: or, if that should not happen, they must at least go out of the world before they see those whom they love best either wise or great.

"From their children, if they have less to fear, they have less also to hope, and they lose, without equivalent, the joys of early love, and the convenience of uniting with manners pliant, and minds susceptible of new impressions, which might wear away their dissimilitudes by long cohabitation, as soft bodies, by continual attrition, conform their surfaces to each other.

"I believe it will be found that those who marry late are best pleased with their children, and those who marry early with their partners."

"The union of these two affections," said Rasselas, "would produce all that could be wished. Perhaps there is a time when marriage might unite them, a time neither too early for the father, nor too late for the husband."

"Every hour," answered the princess, "confirms my prejudice in favor of the position so often uttered by the mouth of Imlac, 'That nature sets her gifts on the right hand and on the left.' Those conditions, which flatter hope and attract desire, are so constituted, that, as we approach one, we recede from another. There are goods so opposed that we cannot seize both, but, by too much prudence, may pass between them at too great a distance to reach either. This is often the fate of long consideration; he does nothing who endeavors to do more than is allowed to humanity. Flatter not yourself with contrarieties of pleasure. Of the blessings set before you make your choice, and be content. No man can taste the fruits of autumn while he is delighting his scent with the flowers of the spring: no man can, at the same time, fill his cup from the source and from the mouth of the Nile."

* * *

[They decide to visit the pyramids, as monuments of the past. Nekayah's attendant, Pekuah, is frightened and remains behind.]

CHAPTER XXXII

They Enter the Pyramid

Pekuah descended to the tents, and the rest entered the pyramid: they passed through the galleries, surveyed the vaults of marble, and examined the chest in which the body of the founder is supposed to have been reposited. They then sat down in one of the most spacious chambers to rest awhile before they attempted to return.

"We have now," said Imlac, "gratified our minds with an exact view of the greatest work of man, except the wall of China."

"Of the wall it is very easy to assign the motives. It secured a wealthy and timorous nation from the incursions of Barbarians, whose unskillfulness in arts made it easier for them to supply their wants by rapine than by industry, and who from time to time poured in upon the habitations of peaceful commerce, as vultures descend upon domestic fowl. Their celerity and fierceness made the wall necessary, and their ignorance made it efficacious.

"But for the pyramids no reason has ever been given adequate to the cost and labor of the work. The narrowness of the chambers proves that it could afford no retreat from enemies, and treasures might have been reposited at far less expense with equal security. It seems to have been erected only in compliance with that hunger of imagination which preys incessantly upon life, and must be always appeased by some employment. Those who have already all that they can enjoy, must enlarge their desires. He that has built for use, till use is supplied, must begin to build for vanity, and extend his plan to the utmost power of human performance, that he may not be soon reduced to form another wish.

"I consider this mighty structure as a monument of the insufficiency of human enjoyments. A king, whose power is unlimited, and whose treasures surmount all real and imaginary wants, is compelled to solace, by the erection of a pyramid, the satiety of dominion and tastelessness of pleasures, and to amuse the tediousness of declining life, by seeing thousands laboring without end, and one stone, for no purpose, laid upon another. Whoever thou art, that, not content with a moderate condition, imaginest happiness in royal magnificence, and dreamest that command or riches can feed the appetite of novelty with perpetual gratifications, survey the pyramids, and confess thy folly!"

* * *

[Pekuah is kidnapped by an Arab, but eventually returns to her friends.]

CHAPTER XL

The History of a Man of Learning

They returned to Cairo, and were so well pleased at finding themselves together, that none of them went much abroad. The prince began to love learning, and one day declared to Imlac, that he intended to devote himself to science,[2] and pass the rest of his days in literary solitude.

---

2. Knowledge.

"Before you make your final choice," answered Imlac, "you ought to examine its hazards, and converse with some of those who are grown old in the company of themselves. I have just left the observatory of one of the most learned astronomers in the world, who has spent forty years in unwearied attention to the motions and appearances of the celestial bodies, and has drawn out his soul in endless calculations. He admits a few friends once a month to hear his deductions and enjoy his discoveries. I was introduced as a man of knowledge worthy of his notice. Men of various ideas and fluent conversation are commonly welcome to those whose thoughts have been long fixed upon a single point, and who find the images of other things stealing away. I delighted him with my remarks, he smiled at the narrative of my travels, and was glad to forget the constellations, and descend for a moment into the lower world.

"On the next day of vacation I renewed my visit, and was so fortunate as to please him again. He relaxed from that time the severity of his rule, and permitted me to enter at my own choice. I found him always busy, and always glad to be relieved. As each knew much which the other was desirous of learning, we exchanged our notions with great delight. I perceived that I had every day more of his confidence, and always found new cause of admiration in the profundity of his mind. His comprehension is vast, his memory capacious and retentive, his discourse is methodical, and his expression clear.

"His integrity and benevolence are equal to his learning. His deepest researches and most favorite studies are willingly interrupted for any opportunity of doing good by his counsel or his riches. To his closest retreat, at his most busy moments, all are admitted that want his assistance: 'For though I exclude idleness and pleasure, I will never,' says he, 'bar my doors against charity. To man is permitted the contemplation of the skies, but the practice of virtue is commanded.' "

"Surely," said the princess, "this man is happy."

"I visited him," said Imlac, "with more and more frequency, and was every time more enamored of his conversation: he was sublime[3] without haughtiness, courteous without formality, and communicative without ostentation. I was at first, great princess, of your opinion, thought him the happiest of mankind, and often congratulated him on the blessing that he enjoyed. He seemed to hear nothing with indifference but the praises of his condition, to which he always returned a general answer, and diverted the conversation to some other topic.

"Amidst this willingness to be pleased, and labor to please, I had quickly reason to imagine that some painful sentiment pressed upon his mind. He often looked up earnestly towards the sun, and let his voice fall in the midst of his discourse. He would sometimes, when we were alone, gaze upon me in silence with the air of a man who longed to speak what he was yet resolved to suppress. He would often send for me with vehement injunctions of haste, though, when I came to him, he had nothing extraordinary to say. And sometimes, when I was leaving him would call me back, pause a few moments and then dismiss me."

---

3. Noble, exalted.

CHAPTER XLI

The Astronomer Discovers the Cause of His Uneasiness

"At last the time came when the secret burst his reserve. We were sitting together last night in the turret of his house, watching the emersion[4] of a satellite of Jupiter. A sudden tempest clouded the sky, and disappointed our observation. We sat awhile silent in the dark, and then he addressed himself to me in these words: 'Imlac, I have long considered thy friendship as the greatest blessing of my life. Integrity without knowledge is weak and useless, and knowledge without integrity is dangerous and dreadful. I have found in thee all the qualities requisite for trust, benevolence, experience, and fortitude. I have long discharged an office which I must soon quit at the call of nature, and shall rejoice in the hour of imbecility and pain to devolve it upon thee.'

"I thought myself honored by this testimony, and protested that whatever could conduce to his happiness would add likewise to mine.

" 'Hear, Imlac, what thou wilt not without difficulty credit. I have possessed for five years the regulation of weather, and the distribution of the seasons: the sun has listened to my dictates, and passed from tropic to tropic by my direction; the clouds, at my call, have poured their waters, and the Nile has overflowed at my command; I have restrained the rage of the Dog Star,[5] and mitigated the fervors of the Crab.[6] The winds alone, of all the elemental powers, have hitherto refused my authority, and multitudes have perished by equinoctial tempests which I found myself unable to prohibit or restrain. I have administered this great office with exact justice, and made to the different nations of the earth an impartial dividend of rain and sunshine. What must have been the misery of half the globe, if I had limited the clouds to particular regions, or confined the sun to either side of the equator?' "

CHAPTER XLII

The Opinion of the Astronomer Is Explained and Justified

"I suppose he discovered in me, through the obscurity of the room, some tokens of amazement and doubt, for, after a short pause, he proceeded thus:

" 'Not to be easily credited will neither surprise nor offend me; for I am, probably, the first of human beings to whom this trust has been imparted. Nor do I know whether to deem this distinction a reward or punishment; since I have possessed it I have been far less happy than before, and nothing but the consciousness of good intention could have enabled me to support the weariness of unremitted vigilance.'

" 'How long, Sir,' said I, 'has this great office been in your hands?'

" 'About ten years ago,' said he, 'my daily observations of the changes of the sky led me to consider, whether, if I had the power of the seasons, I

---

4. Reappearance (after having been obscured, for example, by clouds).   5. Sirius, which rises in late summer and was supposed to cause insanity.   6. The constellation Cancer, associated with the summer solstice.

could confer greater plenty upon the inhabitants of the earth. This contemplation fastened on my mind, and I sat days and nights in imaginary dominion, pouring upon this country and that the showers of fertility, and seconding every fall of rain with a due proportion of sunshine. I had yet only the will to do good, and did not imagine that I should ever have the power.

" 'One day as I was looking on the fields withering with heat, I felt in my mind a sudden wish that I could send rain on the southern mountains, and raise the Nile to an inundation. In the hurry of my imagination I commanded rain to fall, and, by comparing the time of my command, with that of the inundation, I found that the clouds had listened to my lips.'

" 'Might not some other cause,' said I, 'produce this concurrence? The Nile does not always rise on the same day.'

" 'Do not believe,' said he with impatience, 'that such objections could escape me: I reasoned long against my own conviction, and labored against truth with the utmost obstinacy. I sometimes suspected myself of madness, and should not have dared to impart this secret but to a man like you, capable of distinguishing the wonderful from the impossible, and the incredible from the false.'

" 'Why, Sir,' said I, 'do you call that incredible, which you know, or think you know, to be true?'

" 'Because,' said he, 'I cannot prove it by any external evidence; and I know too well the laws of demonstration to think that my conviction ought to influence another, who cannot, like me, be conscious of its force. I, therefore, shall not attempt to gain credit by disputation. It is sufficient that I feel this power, that I have long possessed, and every day exerted it. But the life of man is short, the infirmities of age increase upon me, and the time will soon come when the regulator of the year must mingle with the dust. The care of appointing a successor has long disturbed me; the night and the day have been spent in comparisons of all the characters which have come to my knowledge, and I have yet found none so worthy as thyself.' "

CHAPTER XLIII

The Astronomer Leaves Imlac His Directions

" 'Hear therefore, what I shall impart, with attention, such as the welfare of a world requires. If the task of a king be considered as difficult, who has the care only of a few millions, to whom he cannot do much good or harm, what must be the anxiety of him, on whom depends the action of the elements, and the great gifts of light and heat!—Hear me therefore with attention.

" 'I have diligently considered the position of the earth and sun, and formed innumerable schemes in which I changed their situation. I have sometimes turned aside the axis of the earth, and sometimes varied the ecliptic of the sun: but I have found it impossible to make a disposition by which the world may be advantaged; what one region gains, another loses by any imaginable alteration, even without considering the distant parts of the solar system with which we are unacquainted. Do not, therefore, in thy administration of the year, indulge thy pride by innovation; do not please thyself with thinking that thou canst make thyself renowned of all future ages, by disordering the seasons. The memory of mischief is no desirable fame. Much less will it become thee to let kindness or interest[7] prevail. Never rob other countries of rain to pour it on thine own. For us the Nile is sufficient.'

"I promised that when I possessed the power, I would use it with inflexible integrity, and he dismissed me, pressing my hand. 'My heart,' said he, 'will be now at rest, and my benevolence will no more destroy my quiet: I have found a man of wisdom and virtue, to whom I can cheerfully bequeath the inheritance of the sun.' "

The prince heard this narration with very serious regard, but the princess smiled, and Pekuah convulsed herself with laughter. "Ladies," said Imlac, "to mock the heaviest of human afflictions is neither charitable nor wise. Few can attain this man's knowledge, and few practice his virtues; but all may suffer his calamity. Of the uncertainties of our present state, the most dreadful and alarming is the uncertain continuance of reason."

The princess was recollected, and the favorite was abashed. Rasselas, more deeply affected, inquired of Imlac, whether he thought such maladies of the mind frequent, and how they were contracted.

CHAPTER XLIV
The Dangerous Prevalence of Imagination

"Disorders of intellect," answered Imlac, "happen much more often than superficial observers will easily believe. Perhaps, if we speak with rigorous exactness, no human mind is in its right state. There is no man whose imagination does not sometimes predominate over his reason, who can regulate his attention wholly by his will, and whose ideas will come and go at his command. No man will be found in whose mind airy notions do not sometimes tyrannize, and force him to hope or fear beyond the limits of sober probability. All power of fancy over reason is a degree of insanity; but while this power is such as we can control and repress, it is not visible to others, nor considered as any depravation of the mental faculties: it is not pronounced madness but when it comes[8] ungovernable, and apparently[9] influences speech or action.

"To indulge the power of fiction, and send imagination out upon the wing, is often the sport of those who delight too much in silent speculation. When we are alone we are not always busy; the labor of excogitation is too violent to last long; the ardor of inquiry will sometimes give way to idleness or satiety. He who has nothing external that can divert him, must find pleasure in his own thoughts, and must conceive himself what he is not; for who is pleased with what he is? He then expatiates in boundless futurity, and culls from all imaginable conditions that which for the present moment he should most desire, amuses his desires with impossible enjoyments, and confers upon his pride unattainable dominion. The mind dances from scene to scene, unites all pleasures in all combinations, and riots in delights which nature and fortune, with all their bounty, cannot bestow.

"In time some particular train of ideas fixes the attention, all other intellectual gratifications are rejected, the mind, in weariness or leisure, recurs constantly to the favorite conception, and feasts on the luscious falsehood

7. Self-interest.   8. Becomes.   9. Obviously.

whenever she is offended with the bitterness of truth. By degrees the reign of fancy is confirmed; she grows first imperious, and in time despotic. Then fictions begin to operate as realities, false opinions fasten upon the mind, and life passes in dreams of rapture or of anguish.

"This, Sir, is one of the dangers of solitude, which the hermit has confessed not always to promote goodness, and the astronomer's misery has proved to be not always propitious to wisdom."

"I will no more," said the favorite, "imagine myself the queen of Abissinia. I have often spent the hours, which the princess gave to my own disposal, in adjusting ceremonies and regulating the court; I have repressed the pride of the powerful, and granted the petitions of the poor; I have built new palaces in more happy situations, planted groves upon the tops of mountains, and have exulted in the beneficence of royalty, till, when the princess entered, I had almost forgotten to bow down before her."

"And I," said the princess, "will not allow myself any more to play the shepherdess in my waking dreams. I have often soothed my thoughts with the quiet and innocence of pastoral employments, till I have in my chamber heard the winds whistle, and the sheep bleat; sometimes freed the lamb entangled in the thicket, and sometimes with my crook encountered the wolf. I have a dress like that of the village maids, which I put on to help my imagination, and a pipe on which I play softly, and suppose myself followed by my flocks."

"I will confess," said the prince, "an indulgence of fantastic delight more dangerous than yours. I have frequently endeavored to image the possibility of a perfect government, by which all wrong should be restrained, all vice reformed, and all the subjects preserved in tranquility and innocence. This thought produced innumerable schemes of reformation, and dictated many useful regulations and salutary edicts. This has been the sport and sometimes the labor of my solitude; and I start, when I think with how little anguish I once supposed the death of my father and my brothers."

"Such," says Imlac, "are the effects of visionary schemes: when we first form them we know them to be absurd, but familiarize them by degrees, and in time lose sight of their folly."

CHAPTER XLV

They Discourse with an Old Man

The evening was now far past, and they rose to return home. As they walked along the bank of the Nile, delighted with the beams of the moon quivering on the water, they saw at a small distance an old man, whom the prince had often heard in the assembly of the sages. "Yonder," said he, "is one whose years have calmed his passions, but not clouded his reason: let us close the disquisitions of the night, by inquiring what are his sentiments of his own state, that we may know whether youth alone is to struggle with vexation, and whether any better hope remains for the latter part of life."

Here the sage approached and saluted them. They invited him to join their walk, and prattled[1] awhile as acquaintance that had unexpectedly met one another. The old man was cheerful and talkative, and the way seemed short

1. Chatted.

in his company. He was pleased to find himself not disregarded, accompanied them to their house, and, at the prince's request, entered with them. They placed him in the seat of honor, and set wine and conserves before him.

"Sir," said the princess, "an evening walk must give to a man of learning, like you, pleasures which ignorance and youth can hardly conceive. You know the qualities and the causes of all that you behold, the laws by which the river flows, the periods in which the planets perform their revolutions. Everything must supply you with contemplation, and renew the consciousness of your own dignity."

"Lady," answered he, "let the gay and the vigorous expect pleasure in their excursions, it is enough that age can obtain ease. To me the world has lost its novelty: I look round, and see what I remember to have seen in happier days. I rest against a tree, and consider, that in the same shade I once disputed upon the annual overflow of the Nile with a friend who is now silent in the grave. I cast my eyes upwards, fix them on the changing moon, and think with pain on the vicissitudes of life. I have ceased to take much delight in physical truth; for what have I to do with those things which I am soon to leave?"

"You may at least recreate yourself," said Imlac, "with the recollection of an honorable and useful life, and enjoy the praise which all agree to give you."

"Praise," said the sage, with a sigh, "is to an old man an empty sound. I have neither mother to be delighted with the reputation of her son, nor wife to partake the honors of her husband. I have outlived my friends and my rivals. Nothing is now of much importance; for I cannot extend my interest beyond myself. Youth is delighted with applause, because it is considered as the earnest of some future good, and because the prospect of life is far extended: but to me, who am now declining to decrepitude, there is little to be feared from the malevolence of men, and yet less to be hoped from their affection or esteem. Something they may yet take away, but they can give me nothing. Riches would now be useless, and high employment would be pain. My retrospect of life recalls to my view many opportunities of good neglected, much time squandered upon trifles, and more lost in idleness and vacancy.[2] I leave many great designs unattempted, and many great attempts unfinished. My mind is burthened with no heavy crime, and therefore I compose myself to tranquillity; endeavor to abstract my thoughts from hopes and cares, which, though reason knows them to be vain, still try to keep their old possession of the heart; expect; with serene humility, that hour which nature cannot long delay; and hope to possess in a better state that happiness which here I could not find, and that virtue which here I have not attained."

He rose and went away, leaving his audience not much elated with the hope of long life. The prince consoled himself with remarking, that it was not reasonable to be disappointed by this account; for age had never been considered as the season of felicity, and, if it was possible to be easy in decline and weakness, it was likely that the days of vigor and alacrity might be happy: that the noon of life might be bright, if the evening could be calm.

The princess suspected that age was querulous and malignant, and

2. Inactivity.

delighted to repress the expectations of those who had newly entered the world. She had seen the possessors of estates look with envy on their heirs, and known many who enjoy pleasure no longer than they can confine it to themselves.

Pekuah conjectured, that the man was older than he appeared, and was willing to impute his complaints to delirious dejection; or else supposed that he had been unfortunate, and was therefore discontented: "For nothing," said she, "is more common than to call our own condition, the condition of life."

Imlac, who had no desire to see them depressed, smiled at the comforts which they could so readily procure to themselves, and remembered, that at the same age, he was equally confident of unmingled prosperity, and equally fertile of consolatory expedients. He forbore to force upon them unwelcome knowledge, which time itself would too soon impress. The princess and her lady retired; the madness of the astronomer hung upon their minds, and they desired Imlac to enter upon his office, and delay next morning the rising of the sun.

CHAPTER XLVI

The Princess and Pekuah Visit the Astronomer

The princess and Pekuah having talked in private of Imlac's astronomer, thought his character at once so amiable and so strange, that they could not be satisfied without a nearer knowledge, and Imlac was requested to find the means of bringing them together.

This was somewhat difficult; the philosopher had never received any visits from women, though he lived in a city that had in it many Europeans who followed the manners of their own countries, and many from other parts of the world that lived there with European liberty. The ladies would not be refused, and several schemes were proposed for the accomplishment of their design. It was proposed to introduce them as strangers in distress, to whom the sage was always accessible; but, after some deliberation, it appeared, that by this artifice, no acquaintance could be formed, for their conversation would be short, and they could not decently importune him often. "This," said Rasselas, "is true; but I have yet a stronger objection against the mis-representation of your state. I have always considered it as treason against the great republic of human nature, to make any man's virtues the means of deceiving him, whether on great or little occasions. All imposture weakens confidence and chills benevolence. When the sage finds that you are not what you seemed, he will feel the resentment natural to a man who, con-scious of great abilities, discovers that he has been tricked by understandings meaner than his own, and, perhaps, the distrust, which he can never after-wards wholly lay aside, may stop the voice of counsel, and close the hand of charity; and where will you find the power of restoring his benefactions to mankind, or his peace to himself?"

To this no reply was attempted, and Imlac began to hope that their curi-osity would subside; but, next day, Pekuah told him, she had now found an honest pretense for a visit to the astronomer, for she would solicit permis-sion to continue under him the studies in which she had been initiated by the Arab, and the princess might go with her either as a fellow student, or because a woman could not decently come alone. "I am afraid," said Imlac, "that he will be soon weary of your company: men advanced far in knowledge do not love to repeat the elements of their art, and I am not certain that even of the elements, as he will deliver them connected with inferences, and mingled with reflections, you are a very capable auditress." "That," said Pekuah, "must be my care: I ask of you only to take me thither. My knowledge is, perhaps, more than you imagine it, and by concurring always with his opinions I shall make him think it greater than it is."

The astronomer, in pursuance of this resolution, was told, that a foreign lady, traveling in search of knowledge, had heard of his reputation, and was desirous to become his scholar. The uncommonness of the proposal raised at once his surprise and curiosity, and when, after a short deliberation, he consented to admit her, he could not stay without impatience till the next day.

The ladies dressed themselves magnificently, and were attended by Imlac to the astronomer, who was pleased to see himself approached with respect by persons of so splendid an appearance. In the exchange of the first civilities he was timorous and bashful; but when the talk became regular, he recollected his powers, and justified the character[3] which Imlac had given. Inquiring of Pekuah what could have turned her inclination towards astronomy, he received from her a history of her adventure at the pyramid, and of the time passed in the Arab's island. She told her tale with ease and elegance, and her conversation took possession of his heart. The discourse was then turned to astronomy: Pekuah displayed what she knew: he looked upon her as a prodigy of genius, and entreated her not to desist from a study which she had so happily begun.

They came again and again, and were every time more welcome than before. The sage endeavored to amuse them, that they might prolong their visits, for he found his thoughts grow brighter in their company; the clouds of solicitude vanished by degrees, as he forced himself to entertain them, and he grieved when he was left at their departure to his old employment of regulating the seasons.

The princess and her favorite had now watched his lips for several months, and could not catch a single word from which they could judge whether he continued, or not, in the opinion of his preternatural commission. They often contrived to bring him to an open declaration, but he easily eluded all their attacks, and on which side soever they pressed him escaped from them to some other topic.

As their familiarity increased they invited him often to the house of Imlac, where they distinguished him by extraordinary respect. He began gradually to delight in sublunary pleasures. He came early and departed late; labored to recommend himself by assiduity and compliance; excited their curiosity after new arts, that they might still want his assistance; and when they made any excursion of pleasure or inquiry, entreated to attend them.

By long experience of his integrity and wisdom, the prince and his sister were convinced that he might be trusted without danger; and lest he should draw any false hopes from the civilities which he received, discovered to him their condition, with the motives of their journey, and required his opinion on the choice of life.

"Of the various conditions which the world spreads before you, which you

3. Characterization.

shall prefer," said the sage, "I am not able to instruct you. I can only tell that I have chosen wrong. I have passed my time in study without experience; in the attainment of sciences which can, for the most part, be but remotely useful to mankind. I have purchased knowledge at the expense of all the common comforts of life: I have missed the endearing elegance of female friendship, and the happy commerce[4] of domestic tenderness. If I have obtained any prerogatives above other students, they have been accompanied with fear, disquiet, and scrupulosity; but even of these prerogatives, whatever they were, I have, since my thoughts have been diversified by more inter-course with the world, begun to question the reality. When I have been for a few days lost in pleasing dissipation,[5] I am always tempted to think that my inquiries have ended in error, and that I have suffered much, and suffered it in vain."

Imlac was delighted to find that the sage's understanding was breaking through its mists, and resolved to detain him from the planets till he should forget his task of ruling them, and reason should recover its original influ-ence.

From this time the astronomer was received into familiar friendship, and partook of all their projects and pleasures: his respect kept him attentive, and the activity of Rasselas did not leave much time unengaged. Something was always to be done; the day was spent in making observations which furnished talk for the evening, and the evening was closed with a scheme for the morrow.

The sage confessed to Imlac, that since he had mingled in the gay tumults of life, and divided his hours by a succession of amusements, he found the conviction of his authority over the skies fade gradually from his mind, and began to trust less to an opinion which he never could prove to others, and which he now found subject to variation from causes in which reason had no part. "If I am accidentally left alone for a few hours," said he, "my invet-erate persuasion rushes upon my soul, and my thoughts are chained down by some irresistible violence, but they are soon disentangled by the prince's conversation, and instantaneously released at the entrance of Pekuah. I am like a man habitually afraid of specters, who is set at ease by a lamp, and wonders at the dread which harassed him in the dark, yet, if his lamp be extinguished, feels again the terrors which he knows that when it is light he shall feel no more. But I am sometimes afraid lest I indulge my quiet by criminal negligence, and voluntarily forget the great charge with which I am entrusted. If I favor myself in a known error, or am determined by my own ease in a doubtful question of this importance, how dreadful is my crime!"

"No disease of the imagination," answered Imlac, "is so difficult of cure, as that which is complicated with the dread of guilt: fancy and conscience then act interchangeably upon us, and so often shift their places, that the illusions of one are not distinguished from the dictates of the other. If fancy presents images not moral or religious, the mind drives them away when they give it pain, but when melancholic notions take the form of duty, they lay hold on the faculties without opposition, because we are afraid to exclude or banish them. For this reason the superstitious are often melancholy, and the melancholy almost always superstitious.

4. Exchange.   5. Frivolity.

"But do not let the suggestions of timidity overpower your better reason: the danger of neglect can be but as the probability of the obligation, which, when you consider it with freedom, you find very little, and that little growing every day less. Open your heart to the influence of the light, which, from time to time, breaks in upon you: when scruples importune you, which you in your lucid moments know to be vain, do not stand to parley, but fly to business or to Pekuah, and keep this thought always prevalent, that you are only one atom of the mass of humanity, and have neither such virtue nor vice, as that you should be singled out for supernatural favors or afflictions."

CHAPTER XLVII

The Prince Enters, and Brings a New Topic

"All this," said the astronomer, "I have often thought, but my reason has been so long subjugated by an uncontrollable and overwhelming idea, that it durst not confide in its own decisions. I now see how fatally I betrayed my quiet, by suffering chimeras to prey upon me in secret; but melancholy shrinks from communication, and I never found a man before, to whom I could impart my troubles, though[6] I had been certain of relief. I rejoice to find my own sentiments confirmed by yours, who are not easily deceived, and can have no motive or purpose to deceive. I hope that time and variety will dissipate the gloom that has so long surrounded me, and the latter part of my days will be spent in peace."

"Your learning and virtue," said Imlac, "may justly give you hopes."

Rasselas then entered with the princess and Pekuah, and inquired whether they had contrived any new diversion for the next day. "Such," said Nekayah, "is the state of life, that none are happy but by the anticipation of change: the change itself is nothing; when we have made it, the next wish is to change again. The world is not yet exhausted; let me see something tomorrow which I never saw before."

* * *

[They visit the catacombs, "ancient repositories, in which the bodies of the earliest generations were lodged."]

CHAPTER XLVIII

Imlac Discourses on the Nature of the Soul

"What reason," said the prince, "can be given, why the Egyptians should thus expensively preserve those carcasses which some nations consume with fire, others lay to mingle with the earth, and all agree to remove from their sight, as soon as decent rites can be performed?"

"The original[7] of ancient customs," said Imlac, "is commonly unknown; for the practice often continues when the cause has ceased; and concerning superstitious ceremonies it is vain to conjecture; for what reason did not dictate reason cannot explain. I have long believed that the practice of embalming arose only from tenderness to the remains of relations or friends, and to this opinion I am more inclined, because it seems impossible that this

6. Even if.   7. Origin.

care should have been general: had all the dead been embalmed, their repositories must in time have been more spacious than the dwellings of the living. I suppose only the rich or honorable were secured from corruption, and the rest left to the course of nature.

"But it is commonly supposed that the Egyptians believed the soul to live as long as the body continued undissolved, and therefore tried this method of eluding death."

"Could the wise Egyptians," said Nekayah, "think so grossly of the soul? If the soul could once survive its separation, what could it afterwards receive or suffer from the body?"

"The Egyptians would doubtless think erroneously," said the astronomer, "in the darkness of heathenism, and the first dawn of philosophy. The nature of the soul is still disputed amidst all our opportunities of clearer knowledge: some yet say, that it may be material, who, nevertheless, believe it to be immortal."

"Some," answered Imlac, "have indeed said that the soul is material, but I can scarcely believe that any man has thought it, who knew how to think; for all the conclusions of reason enforce the immateriality of mind, and all the notices of sense and investigations of science concur to prove the unconsciousness of matter.

"It was never supposed that cogitation is inherent in matter, or that every particle is a thinking being. Yet, if any part of matter be devoid of thought, what part can we suppose to think? Matter can differ from matter only in form, density, bulk, motion, and direction of motion: to which of these, however varied or combined, can consciousness be annexed? To be round or square, to be solid or fluid, to be great or little, to be moved slowly or swiftly one way or another, are modes of material existence, all equally alien from the nature of cogitation. If matter be once without thought, it can only be made to think by some new modification, but all the modifications which it can admit are equally unconnected with cogitative powers."

"But the materialists," said the astronomer, "urge that matter may have qualities with which we are unacquainted."

"He who will determine," returned Imlac, "against that which he knows, because there may be something which he knows not; he that can set hypothetical possibility against acknowledged certainty, is not to be admitted among reasonable beings. All that we know of matter is, that matter is inert, senseless and lifeless; and if this conviction cannot be opposed but by referring us to something that we know not, we have all the evidence that human intellect can admit. If that which is known may be overruled by that which is unknown, no being, not omniscient, can arrive at certainty."

"Yet let us not," said the astronomer, "too arrogantly limit the Creator's power."

"It is no limitation of omnipotence," replied the poet, "to suppose that one thing is not consistent with another, that the same proposition cannot be at once true and false, that the same number cannot be even and odd, that cogitation cannot be conferred on that which is created incapable of cogitation."

"I know not," said Nekayah, "any great use of this question. Does that immateriality, which, in my opinion, you have sufficiently proved, necessarily include eternal duration?"

"Of immateriality," said Imlac, "our ideas are negative, and therefore obscure. Immateriality seems to imply a natural power of perpetual duration as a consequence of exemption from all causes of decay: whatever perishes, is destroyed by the solution of its contexture, and separation of its parts; nor can we conceive how that which has no parts, and therefore admits no solution, can be naturally corrupted or impaired."

"I know not," said Rasselas, "how to conceive anything without extension: what is extended must have parts, and you allow, that whatever has parts may be destroyed."

"Consider your own conceptions," replied Imlac, "and the difficulty will be less. You will find substance without extension. An ideal form is no less real than material bulk: yet an ideal form has no extension. It is no less certain, when you think on a pyramid, that your mind possesses the idea of a pyramid, than that the pyramid itself is standing. What space does the idea of a pyramid occupy more than the idea of a grain of corn? or how can either idea suffer laceration? As is the effect such is the cause; as thought is, such is the power that thinks; a power impassive and indiscerptible."[8]

"But the Being," said Nekayah, "whom I fear to name, the Being which made the soul, can destroy it."

"He, surely, can destroy it," answered Imlac, "since, however unperishable, it receives from a superior nature its power of duration. That it will not perish by any inherent cause of decay, or principle of corruption, may be shown by philosophy; but philosophy can tell no more. That it will not be annihilated by him that made it, we must humbly learn from higher authority."

The whole assembly stood awhile silent and collected. "Let us return," said Rasselas, "from this scene of mortality. How gloomy would be these mansions of the dead to him who did not know that he shall never die; that what now acts shall continue its agency, and what now thinks shall think on forever. Those that lie here stretched before us, the wise and the powerful of ancient times, warn us to remember the shortness of our present state: they were, perhaps, snatched away while they were busy, like us, in the choice of life."

"To me," said the princess, "the choice of life is become less important; I hope hereafter to think only on the choice of eternity."

They then hastened out of the caverns, and, under the protection of their guard, returned to Cairo.

CHAPTER XLIX

The Conclusion, in Which Nothing Is Concluded

It was now the time of the inundation of the Nile: a few days after their visit to the catacombs, the river began to rise.

They were confined to their house. The whole region being underwater gave them no invitation to any excursions, and, being well supplied with materials for talk, they diverted themselves with comparisons of the different forms of life which they had observed, and with various schemes of happiness which each of them had formed.

Pekuah was never so much charmed with any place as the convent of St.

8. Indivisible.

Anthony, where the Arab restored her to the princess, and wished only to fill it with pious maidens, and to be made prioress of the order: she was weary of expectation and disgust, and would gladly be fixed in some unvariable state.

The princess thought, that of all sublunary things, knowledge was the best: she desired first to learn all sciences, and then purposed to found a college of learned women, in which she would preside, that, by conversing with the old, and educating the young, she might divide her time between the acquisition and communication of wisdom, and raise up for the next age models of prudence, and patterns of piety.

The prince desired a little kingdom, in which he might administer justice in his own person, and see all the parts of government with his own eyes; but he could never fix the limits of his dominion, and was always adding to the number of his subjects.

Imlac and the astronomer were contented to be driven along the stream of life without directing their course to any particular port.

Of these wishes that they had formed they well knew that none could be obtained. They deliberated awhile what was to be done, and resolved, when the inundation should cease, to return to Abissinia.

FINIS

Europe and
Eastern America

ca. 1866

The Nineteenth Century: Romanticism

"Bliss was it in that dawn to be alive, / But to be young was very heaven." William Wordsworth alludes here to his experience, at the age of seventeen, of the French Revolution. The possibility of referring to a national cataclysm in such terms suggests the remarkable shift in sensibility, in dominant assumptions, and in intellectual pre-occupations that occurred late in the eighteenth century. We call the evidence of that shift "Romanticism"—a designation so grandly inclusive as to defy definition. If our terms for the late seventeenth and early eighteenth centuries ("Enlightenment," "Age of Reason") emphasize one aspect of the prevailing intellectual culture to the exclusion of others equally important, the label *Romanticism* refers to so many cultural manifestations that one can hardly pin it down. In general, it implies new emphases on imagination, on feeling, and on the value of the primitive and untrammeled, especially a narrowing of outlook from the universal to the particular, from humankind or "man" (the subject of Pope's *Essay*) to nation or ethnic group, and from the stability of community to the "fulfillment" of the individual. Such shifts have important political and philosophical as well as literary implications.

In the writings of individuals, one finds lines of continuity between the late and early parts of the eighteenth century; but when it comes to generalizations, all the important truths appear to have reversed themselves. In the middle of the century, reason was the guide to certainty; at the century's end, *feeling* tested authenticity. Earlier, tradition still anchored experience; now, the ideal of joyous liberation implied rejection of traditional authority. Wisdom had long associated itself with maturity, even with old age; by the 1790s, William Blake hinted at the child's superior insight, and Wordsworth openly claimed for the infant holy wisdom inevitably lost in the process of aging. Johnson had valued experience as a vital path to knowledge; at the beginning of the nineteenth century, innocence—in its nature evanescent—provided a more generally treasured resource.

Cause and effect, in such massive shifts of perspective, can never be ascertained. The French Revolution derived from new ideas about the sacredness of the individual; it also helped generate such ideas. Without trying to distinguish causes from effects—indeed, with a strong suspicion that the period's striking phenomena constitute simultaneous causes and effects—one can specify a number of ways that the world appeared to change, as the eighteenth century approached the nineteenth, as well as ways that these changes both solidified themselves and evoked challenges later in the nineteenth century.

NEW AND OLD

The embattled farmers of Concord, Massachusetts, fired the shot heard round the world in 1775; fourteen years later, the Bastille fell. Both the American and the French revolutions developed out of strong convictions about the innate rights of individual human beings—in other words, Protestantism in political form. Those who developed revolutionary theory glimpsed new human possibility. The hope of salvation lay in overturning established institutions. Swift, in *Gulliver's Travels,* had made a clear distinction between institutions as ideal constructions of human reason and their corruption in practice. Lawyers might be a money-grubbing, hypocritical lot; but the idea of law, of a social structure designed to ensure the provision of justice, has its own inherent power. The theory of revolution implied radical assault on virtually all social institutions. Fundamental hierarchies of government, notions of sovereignty and of aristocracy, inherited systems of distinction—all fell. Old conventions, once emblems of social and literary stability, now exemplified the dead hand of the past. Only a few years before, the old, the inherited, and the traditional had embodied truth, its power attested by its survival. But the revolutionaries felt themselves to be originators; the newness of what they proposed gave it the almost religious authority suggested by Wordsworth's allusions to "bliss" and "heaven."

The blessed state evoked by the new political thinkers embodied a sense of infinite possibility. Pope had written, in *An Essay on Man,* "The bliss of Man (could Pride that blessing find) / Is not to act or think beyond mankind." By the century's end, people were doing their best to "think beyond mankind"—or, at any rate, beyond what had been considered normal limitations. Evidence of this fact abounds: in revolutionary sermons preached from pulpits even in England; in writings by such flamboyant defenders of human rights as Thomas Paine; even in the development of a political theory about women's social position. Mary Wollstonecraft was not the first to note the oppression of women; a century before her, Mary Astell had suggested the need for broader female education, and outcries on the subject emerged sporadically even earlier in the seventeenth century. But Wollstonecraft's *Vindication of the Rights of Woman* (1792) offered the first detailed argument to hold that the ideal of fulfilled human possibility for men and women demanded political acknowledgment of women's equality.

The very existence of such a work (which achieved a second edition in the year it was first published) testifies to the atmosphere of political expectancy in which men and women could rethink "self-evident" principles. Replacing the ideal of hierarchy (what Dr. Johnson revered as "subordination"), for example, was the revolutionary notion of human brotherhood. Liberty, equality, and fraternity, the French proclaimed; the new American nation celebrated essentially the same ideals. In practice, though, *fraternity* turned out to involve specifically the citizens of France or of the new United States. The emphasis on individual uniqueness extended itself to national uniqueness. In America particularly, ideas of national character and of national destiny developed almost talismanic force. Although peace generally prevailed among nations in the early nineteenth century, the developing distinctions dividing one country imaginatively from another foretold future danger.

New ideas with massive practical consequences included more than the political. In 1776, Adam Smith published *The Wealth of Nations,* a theory of laissez-faire economics presaging the enormous importance of money in subsequent history. Matters of exchange and acquisition, Smith argued, could be left to regulate themselves—a doctrine behind which still lurked unobtrusively the confidence, expressed in market terms, that Pope had expressed in religious ones: "All Chance, Direction, which thou canst not see, / All Discord, Harmony, not understood." As manufacturing and trade increased in vitality, however, their importance as financial resources in fact heightened discord through growing nationalism. Early in the century, at the end of *Windsor Forest* (1713), Pope had recognized in Britain's trade a form of power. A century later, the acceleration of this power would have astonished Pope. No longer did agriculture provide England's central economic resource. New forms of manufacture provided new substance for trade, generated new fortunes, produced a new social class—a "middle class" with the influence of wealth and without the inherited system of responsibilities, restrictions, and decorums that had helped control aristocratic possessors of wealth in preceding generations. Aristocrats had used their money, on the whole, to enlarge and beautify their estates. The newly monied developed original ideas about what money might do. Reinvested, it could support inno-vation in manufacture and trade. It could educate the children of the uneducated; it could buy them (as it had been doing for a century) husbands and wives from the aristocracy; it could help obviate ancient class distinctions. England's increasing eco-nomic ascendancy in the nineteenth century derived not only from new money but from the development of men willing and able to employ money ingeniously as power.

The expanded possibilities of manufacture testified to practical applications of sci-entific research, another area of activity in which the new overwhelmingly replaced the old. In England and America especially, inventions multiplied: the steam engine, the spinning jenny, the cotton gin. Increasingly often, and in increasing numbers, men and women left their native rural environments to congregate in cities, where opportunities for relatively unskilled workers abounded—and where more and more people lived in congestion, poverty, and misery.

More vividly, perhaps, than ever before, the world was changing—becoming, in fact, the world we ourselves assume, in which *mankind* as an ideal wanes, nations define themselves in psychic and military opposition to one another, money consti-tutes immediate power, and science serves manufacture and, hence, commerce. From the beginning of these crucial changes, certain thinkers and writers realized the destructive possibilities inherent in every form of "progress." Blake, for example, glimpsed London's economic brutality and human wastefulness; his "revolutionary" impulses expressed themselves partly in resistance to the consequences of the new. That is to say, the new gave way to the newer, as it had not previously done on such a scale. No longer did the impulse to conserve past values express itself with the authority and power that Swift and Johnson had brought to the theme. As M. H. Abrams has written, "The Romantic period was eminently an age obsessed with the fact of violent change." Such change might provide ground for fear; it also supplied the substance for hope.

INDIVIDUALISM

Immanuel Kant (1724–1804), a German philosopher whose work influenced virtually all philosophers after him, questioned the power of reason to provide the most sig-nificant forms of knowledge—knowledge of the ultimately real. Feeling, on the other hand, might offer a guide. The individual will must engage itself in ethical struggle to locate and experience the good. Such followers of Kant as Johann Fichte (1762–1814) more clearly suggested an identification between will and what we call ego. The idea of the self took on ever greater importance, for philosophers and poets, for political thinkers, autobiographers, and novelists.

To locate authority in the self rather than in society implies yet another radical break with the assumptions of the previous period. The idea of the self's importance is so familiar to us that it may be difficult to imagine the startling implications of the new focus. "I know my own heart, and understand my fellow man," Jean-Jacques Rousseau writes, at the beginning of his *Confessions*. "I am made unlike anyone I have ever met; I will even venture to say that I am like no one in the whole world." Samuel Johnson would have felt certain that a man who could write such words must be mad, like the astronomer in *Rasselas* who believes himself able to control the weather. Yet faith in the absolute uniqueness of every consciousness became increas-ingly prevalent. Rousseau's significance for his period derives partly from the fact that his stress on the feelings of his heart and on his own specialness aroused recognition in his audience. No longer did the universality of human nature supply comfort to individuals; now they might seek reassurance instead in their uniqueness.

Not only could individuals now see themselves as unique, but they could also understand themselves as *good*. In its earlier forms, Christianity had emphasized the fallen nature of the human soul. Every self, according to this view, contains the potential for violence and destructiveness. One must rely on God's grace for salvation, which cannot depend on human worth. At the secular level, human beings need institutions to provide the controls that save us from anarchy—from the evil latent in ourselves. Rousseau and his successors articulated the opposite position, stressing the essential goodness of human nature and the corresponding danger of institutional restraint. Repressiveness now became the fearful enemy, uniformity the menace. We may recognize the fear of external control today in the slogans of those celebrating the importance of "individual rights," and we still hear the older faith in institutions in the proponents of "law and order."

The new emphasis on the individual opened new possibilities for writers of poetry and prose alike. Even the grotesque and deviant became interesting. Victor Hugo could explore the psychology of Satan, for example: the angel cast out of heaven and falling through the abyss, undergoing a process of increasing horror, enduring the going out of light, but remaining defiant throughout his long ordeal. Unlike John Milton, who directed attention to cosmic drama on a large scale, Hugo concentrated his focus to create an impression of poignance as well as nightmare. In Russia, Alexander Pushkin investigated the psychology (as well as the social arrangements) of a group of people concerned only with money, generating a very different sense of horror.

As these instances suggest, stress on the individual implied revaluation of inner as opposed to outer experience. Previously, life in the public arena had been assumed to test human capacities and to provide meaningful forms of experience. After Rousseau, however, psychic experience could provide the proper measure of an individual's emotional capacity. To place value *there* opened the possibility of taking women as seriously as men, children as seriously as adults, "savages" as seriously as civilized beings. Indeed, women, children, and "primitive" peoples were often thought to exceed cultivated adult males in their capacity both to feel and to express their feelings spontaneously—although the social subordination of such groups continued unchanged.

Even before Rousseau, the novel of sensibility in England and on the Continent revealed interest in highly developed emotional responsiveness. Johann Wolfgang von Goethe's *The Sorrows of Young Werther* (1774) made its author famous and inspired a cult of introverted, melancholy young people. In England, Henry Mackenzie's *The Man of Feeling* (1771) associated intense emotion with benevolent action. By the latter part of the century, the Gothic novel had become an important form—a novelistic mode, often practiced by women, that typically placed a young woman at the center of the action. The heroines of such novels confront a kind of experience (usually involving at least apparent supernatural elements) for which their social training, that important resource of earlier heroines, provides no help; instead, quick intuitions and subtle feelings ensure their triumph over apparently insurmountable obstacles with no loss of feminine delicacy.

Given the view of feeling's centrality, which replaced the earlier stress on passion's fruitful tension with reason, a broader spectrum of feeling drew literary attention. From its beginnings (*The Princess of Clèves* is an early example), the novel had tended to emphasize (usually in decorous terms) love between the sexes. Now romantic love became a central subject of poetry and drama as well. More surprising kinds of emotion also attracted notice. William Blake imagined a chimney sweep's emotional relation to the idea of heaven; Samuel Taylor Coleridge and Percy Bysshe Shelley made poetry of dejection; Alfred, Lord Tennyson, at the midpoint of the nineteenth century, wove his anxieties about the revelations of recent scientific inquiry into the texture of an elegiac poem. Rosalía de Castro wrote of the death of her child; Giacomo Leopardi could produce a lyric called *To Himself*, exploring his personal relation to large ideas; Friedrich Hölderlin, in Germany, like Wordsworth and Coleridge in England, used the making of poetry as a subject for thought and feeling alike. As these examples indicate, painful as well as pleasurable emotion interested readers and writers. The poet, Wordsworth said, is a man speaking to men; poetry originates in recollected emotion and recapitulates lost feeling. Lyric, not epic, typifies poetry for Wordsworth, who understands his genre as a form of emotional communication.

Wordsworth's definition ignores the fact that women, too (including his own sister, Dorothy), write poetry. Emily Brontë, Christina Rossetti, Rosalía de Castro, Anna Petrovna Bunina, Emily Dickinson—such women writing in different countries evoked intense passion in verse. In the Romantic novel also, women excelled in the rendering of powerful feeling. The Brontë sisters, like George Eliot after them in England and the equally passionate George Sand in France, wrote under male pseudonyms but established distinctively female visions of the struggle not only for love but also for freedom and power within a context of social restriction. Mary Shelley (daughter of Mary Wollstonecraft and wife of the poet Shelley) in her eloquent fable of creativity, *Frankenstein* (1818), epitomizes the peculiar intensity of much women's writing in this period.

As the nineteenth century wore on, hope for a new earthly Eden faded. The flourishing of commerce and the innovations of science had negative as well as positive consequences. As the novels of Charles Dickens and William Thackeray insist, the new middle class frequently became the repository of moral mediocrity. The autocracy of money had effects more brutal than those of inherited privilege. Science, once the emblem of progress, began to generate theological confusion. Charles Darwin's *On the Origin of Species* (1859) stated clearly humanity's mean rather than transcendent origins: animal and plant species had evolved over the millennia, adapting themselves to their environment through the process of natural selection. Fossils found in rocks provided supporting evidence for this theory—an assertion troubling to many Christians because it contradicted the biblical account of Creation. Eight years after Darwin's revolutionary work, Karl Marx published *Das Kapital,* with its dialectical theory of history and its vision of capitalism's eventual decay and of the working class's inevitable triumph. In the United States, civil war raged from 1861 to 1865, its central issue states' rights, a topic that, of course, involved the morality of slavery—that byproduct of agricultural capitalism. Neither the making of money nor the effort to fathom natural law seemed merely reassuring.

In the face of history's threats—the menace of Marx's prophecy and of Darwin's biology, the chaos of civil war—to insist on the importance of private experience offered tentative security, a standing place, a temporary source of authority. The voices of blacks and, in increasing numbers, of women could now be heard: placing high value on the personal implied respecting all persons. The American Civil War made African Americans for the first time truly visible to the society that both included and denied them. Slave narratives—sometimes wholly or partly fictional, sometimes entirely authentic renditions of often horrifying experience—provided useful propaganda for the abolitionist cause, the ideology opposed to the institution of slavery. They also opened a new emotional universe. In their typical emphasis, for instance, on the salvationary force of reading and writing (officially forbidden to most slaves), these narratives illuminated a new area of the taken-for-granted, thus extending the enterprise of Romantic poetry.

The capacity for revelatory illumination belonged, according to the dominant nineteenth-century view, to imagination, a mysterious and virtually sacred power of individual consciousness. When Johnson, in *Rasselas,* suggested that the predominance of imagination over reason is insane, he intended, to put it crudely, an antithesis of true and false since imagination, the faculty of generating images, has no necessary anchor in the communal, historical experience that tests truth. For Wordsworth and Coleridge and those who came after them, imagination is a visionary and unifying force (a new incarnation of the seventeenth century's inner light or candle of the Lord) through which the gifted person discovers and communicates new truth.

(Johnson, of course, would have denied the possibility of "new" truth.) As Coleridge wrote,

> from the soul itself must issue forth
> A light, a glory, a fair luminous cloud
> Enveloping the Earth.

Imagination derives from the soul, that aspect of our being that links the human with the eternal. Through it, men and women can transcend earthly limitations, can express high aspiration, can escape—and help one another escape—the dreariness of mortality without necessarily admitting to a life beyond the present one.

A result of the high value attached to creative imagination was a new concern with originality. The notion of "the genius," the man or woman so gifted as to operate by principles unknown to ordinary mortals, developed only in the late eighteenthcentury. Previously, a person *had* genius rather than *was* a genius: the term designated a particular tendency or gift (a genius for cooking, say) rather than a human being with vast creative power. Now the genius was revered for his or her extraordinary difference from others, idealized as a being set apart; and the literary or artistic products of genius, it could be assumed, would correspondingly differ from everything previously produced. Yet the writers of this movement also recorded their anxiety about the claim of specialness implicit in the idea of genius. Goethe's *Faust*, a rewriting of an old legend, emphasizes the danger inherent in the desire to do what no one has ever done, to be what no one has ever been.

Despite all reservations, though, newness now became as never before a measure of value. The language, the themes, the forms of the preceding century would no longer suffice. In the early eighteenth century, literary figures wishing to congratulate themselves and their contemporaries would compare their artistic situation to that of Rome under the benevolent patronage of Augustus Caesar. A hundred years later, the note of self-congratulation would express itself in the claim of an unprecedented situation or unprecedented kinds of accomplishment. John Keats, in a letter, characterized Wordsworth as representing "the egotistical sublime." Such sublimity—authority and grandeur emanating from a unique self still in touch with something beyond itself—was the nineteenth century's special achievement.

NATURE

Nature and nature's laws, the rationally ordered universe, provided the foundation for much early eighteenth-century thought. In the nineteenth century, nature's importance possibly increased, but *nature* now meant something new. *Wuthering Heights* (1847) creates a setting of windswept moors for its romantic lovers—both environment and metaphor for their love. Wordsworth could value a host of daffodils, or fog-enveloped hills, or an icy lake. Lamartine appealed to the landscape to embody the characteristics of his lost love. The physical reality of the natural world, in its varied abundance, became a matter of absorbing interest for poets and novelists. Nature provided an alternative to the human, a possibility for imaginative as well as literal escape. Its imagery—flowers, clouds, ocean—became the common poetic stock. Workers still hastened from the country to the city because the city housed possibilities of wealth; yet educated men and women increasingly declared their nostalgia for rural or sylvan landscapes embodying peace and beauty.

Nature, in the nineteenth-century mind, however, did not consist only in physical details. It also implied a totality, an enveloping whole greater than the sum of its parts, a vast unifying spirit. Wordsworth evokes

> a sense sublime
> Of something far more deeply interfused,
> Whose dwelling is the light of setting suns,
> And the round ocean and the living air,
> And the blue sky, and in the mind of man:
> A motion and a spirit, that impels
> All thinking things, all objects of all thought,
> And rolls through all things.

Coleridge and Shelley, Bécquer and de Castro hint similar visions, vague yet comforting. The unifying whole, as Wordsworth's language suggests, depends less on rational system than on emotional association. Human beings link themselves to the infinite by what Wordsworth elsewhere terms "wise passiveness," the capacity to submit to feeling and be led by it to transcendence. Natural detail, too, acquires value by evoking and symbolizing emotion. Nature belongs to the realm of the nonrational, the superrational. It can be linked, as it is for Anna Petrovna Bunina, to a sense of misery and pain, or it can evoke, as it does for Dorothy Wordsworth, possibilities of utter joy and transcendence.

The idea of the natural can also imply the uncivilized or precivilized. Philosophers have differed dramatically in their hypotheses about what humankind was like in its "natural" state. Thomas Hobbes, in the seventeenth century, argued that the natural human condition was one of conflict. Society developed to curb the violent impulses that human beings would manifest without its restraint. The prevailing nineteenth-century view, on the other hand, made civilization the agent of corruption. Rousseau expounded the crippling effect of institutions. The child raised with the greatest possible freedom, he maintained, would develop in more admirable ways than one subjected to system. By the second half of the eighteenth century, a French novelist could contrast the decadent life of Europe unfavorably with existence on an unspoiled island (Jacques-Henri Bernardin de Saint-Pierre, *Paul and Virginia*, 1788); Thomas Chatterton, before committing suicide in 1770 at the age of eighteen, wrote poems rich in nostalgia for a more primitive stage of social development that he tried to pass off as medieval works; the forged Ossian poems (1760–63) of James Macpherson, purportedly ancient texts, attracted a large and enthusiastic audience. New interest manifested itself in ballads, poetic survivals of the primitive; Romantic poets imitated the form. The interest in a simpler past, a simpler life, continued throughout the nineteenth century: in Victorian England, Tennyson recast Arthurian legend in modern verse; the Pre-Raphaelites evoked the medieval in visual and verbal arts.

The revolutionary fervor of the late eighteenth century had generated a vision of infinite human possibility, political and personal. The escapist implications of the increasing emphasis on nature, the primitive, the uncomplicated past suggest, however, a sense of alienation. Blake, Wordsworth, and Shelley all wrote poems of social protest. "Society" would not help the individual work out his or her salvation; on the contrary, it embodied forces opposed to individual development. Indeed, the word *society* had come to embody the impulses that desecrated nature and oppressed the poor in the interests of industry and "progress." Melancholy marked the Romantic hero (Lord Byron in his poetic self-manifestations and Heathcliff in fiction, for example) and tinged nineteenth-century poetry and fiction. The satiric spirit—that spirit of social reform—was suspended. Hope lay in the individual's separation from, not participation in, society. In the woods and mountains, one might feel free.

The Waste Land (1922), T. S. Eliot's twentieth-century epic, contains the line "In the mountains, there you feel free," a line given complex ironic overtones by its context. It reminds us how ideas that came into currency in the late eighteenth and early nineteenth centuries powerfully survive into our own time. The world of the Romantic period specifically prefigures our own, despite all the differences dividing the two cultures. We have developed more fully important Romantic tendencies: stress on the sacredness of the individual, suspicion of social institutions, belief in expressed feeling as the sign of authenticity, nostalgia for simpler ways of being, faith in genius, valuing of originality and imagination, an ambivalent relation to science. Although Wordsworth and Dickinson and Melville employ vocabularies and use references partly strange to us, they speak directly to the preoccupations of our time. By attending closely to their works, we may learn more about ourselves: not only in the common humanity that we share with all our predecessors but in our special historical situation as both direct heirs of nineteenth-century assumptions and rebels against them. Chronology provides little guide to the Romantic period. Jean-Jacques Rousseau, the first writer included in this section, died before Gustavo Bécquer was born. The Romantic movement, as subsequent critics have defined it, extends from the late eighteenth to the late nineteenth century, but it is overlapped throughout by other sets of literary and philosophic assumptions.

ROMANTICISM

TEXTS	CONTEXTS
1773 Thomas Hutchinson, **Address to the Massachusetts Assembly**	
1781–1788 Jean-Jacques Rousseau, *Confessions*	1781 Immanuel Kant, *Critique of Pure Reason*
	1787 Wolfgang Amadeus Mozart's *Don Giovanni* is first performed
	1789 The National Assembly in France issues its charter, Declaration of the Rights of Man
1791 Germaine de Staël, *The Superiority of Moderation over Extremism*	
1792 Thomas Paine, **Address to the People of France** • Jean-Paul Marat, **Address to the Convention on the Crimes of King Louis XVI**	
1794 William Blake, *Songs of Innocence and of Experience*	
1798 William Wordsworth and Samuel Taylor Coleridge, *Lyrical Ballads* • Dorothy Wordsworth begins her journals	
1800 Novalis, *Hymns to the Night*	
	1801 United Kingdom of Great Britain (England and Scotland) and Ireland established
1802 Coleridge, *Dejection: An Ode*	1803 President Thomas Jefferson purchases French "Louisiana"
	1804 Napoleon has himself crowned emperor of France
1805 Mercy Otis Warren, *History of the Rise, Progress, and Termination of the American Revolution*	
1806 First published lyrics by Anna Petrovna Bunina	
1808 Johann Wolfgang von Goethe, *Faust, Part I* (Part II, 1832)	
1812–1870 Charles Dickens, English novelist	
1812–1818 George Gordon, Lord Byron, *Childe Harold's Pilgrimage*	1815 Battle of Waterloo, ending Napoleon's career
1816 Coleridge, *Kubla Khan* • John Keats, *On First Looking into Chapman's Homer*	

Boldface titles indicate works in the anthology.

ROMANTICISM

TEXTS	CONTEXTS
1818 Germaine de Staël, *Considerations on the Principal Events of the French Revolution*	
1818–1820 Lyrics by Percy Bysshe Shelley and John Keats	
1820 Alphonse de Lamartine, *Poetic Meditations,* his first collection of poems	
1824 Giacomo Leopardi, *Canzoni,* his first collection of poems	
1826 Friedrich Hölderlin, *Gedichte*	
1827 Heinrich Heine, *Book of Songs*	
1828 Victor Hugo, *Odes and Ballads*	
	1831 First preparation of chloroform inaugurates a new medical era
1834 Alexander Sergeyevich Pushkin, *The Queen of Spades*	
1837 Mikhail Yuryevitch Lermontov, *The Poet's Death*	1837 Victoria crowned queen of the United Kingdom • Electric telegraph patented
1840 Percy Bysshe Shelley, *A Defense of Poetry;* published posthumously	
1842 Alfred, Lord Tennyson, *Ulysses*	
1845 Frederick Douglass, *Narrative of the Life of Frederick Douglass, an American Slave*	
1847 Charlotte Brontë, *Jane Eyre* • Emily Brontë, *Wuthering Heights*	
	1848 Karl Marx and Friedrich Engels, *Communist Manifesto* • Revolutions in France, Italy, Austria, Prague • Gold discovered in California
1850 Alfred, Lord Tennyson, *In Memoriam A. H. H.*	
1842–1855 Robert Browning writes poems, including *"Childe Roland to the Dark Tower Came"*	
	1854 Electric lightbulb invented
1855 Walt Whitman, *Song of Myself* • Gérard de Nerval, *Aurélia*	
	1859 Charles Darwin's *On the Origin of Species,* presenting his theory of evolution
1860 Gustavo Adolfo Bécquer, *Rimas*	1861 Serfs emancipated in Russia • Beginning of American Civil War

ROMANTICISM

TEXTS	CONTEXTS
	1863 Emancipation Proclamation frees slaves in the Confederate States of America
	1864 Louis Pasteur, who formulated the germ theory of infection, invents pasteurization
	1865 American Civil War ends • President Abraham Lincoln assassinated • Thirteenth amendment emancipates all slaves in the United States
	1867 Karl Marx, *Das Kapital*
	1874 First Impressionist exhibition, Paris
	1876 Alexander Graham Bell invents the telephone
1884 Rosalía de Castro, *Beside the River Sar*	
1890 Emily Dickinson, *Poems,* published posthumously	
1891 Herman Melville leaves manuscript of *Billy Budd, Sailor* at his death; not published until 1924	
	1895 X rays discovered by Bavarian physicist Wilhelm Röntgen

JEAN-JACQUES ROUSSEAU
1712–1778

It would be difficult to overstate the historical importance of Jean-Jacques Rousseau's *Confessions* (composed between 1765 and 1770, published 1781–88), which inaugurated a new form of autobiography and suggested new ways of thinking about the self and its relation to others. Even for today's readers, the book's sheer audacity compels attention, demanding that we rethink easy assumptions about important and trivial, right and wrong.

The facts of Rousseau's life are unclear partly because the *Confessions,* despite its claim of absolute truthfulness, sometimes appears more concerned to create a self-justifying story than to confine itself strictly to reality. The son of a Geneva watchmaker, Rousseau left home in his teens and lived for some time with Françoise-Louise de Warens, his protector and eventually his mistress, the "mamma" of the *Confessions.* He worked at many occupations, from secretary to government official (under the king of Sardinia). In Paris, where he settled in 1745, he lived with Thérèse le Vasseur; he claims she bore him five children, all consigned to an orphanage, but the claim has never been substantiated (or, for that matter, disproved). At various times, his controversial writing forced Rousseau to leave France, usually for Switzerland; in 1766, he went to England as the guest of the philosopher David Hume. He was allowed to return to Paris in 1770 only on condition that he write nothing against the government or the Church.

Rousseau's social ideas, elaborated in his didactic novels *Julie: or, The New Eloise* (1761) and *Émile* (1762) as well as in his autobiographical writings and political treatises (for example, *The Social Contract,* 1762), stirred much contemporary discussion. He believed in the destructiveness of institutions, the gradual corruption of humankind throughout history, and the importance of nature and of feeling in individual development and, consequently, in society. As he writes in *Émile,* "I hate books; they only teach us to talk about things we know nothing about." He proposes to teach children by immersing them first in the natural, then in the human world, preventing the corruption of their bodies and their feelings. For a time, he was a music teacher, and he published several works on music, including a dictionary, and composed a comic opera called *The Village Soothsayer* (1752).

The *Confessions* presents its subject as a person who always strives to express natural impulses and is recurrently frustrated by society's demands and assumptions. The central figure described here resembles Candide in his naïveté and good feeling. Experience chastens him less than it does Candide, however, although he reports many psychic hard knocks. For Voltaire's didactic purposes, his character's experience was more important than his personality; for Rousseau, his own nature is much more significant than anything that happens to him. His account of that nature becomes ever more complicated as the *Confessions* continues and the writer concerns himself increasingly with the problem of his relation to society at large. His sense of alienation alternates with wistful longing for inclusion as he delineates the dilemmas of the extraordinary individual in a world full of people primarily concerned with accumulating wealth and power.

To read even a few pages of the work reveals how completely Rousseau exemplifies several of his period's dominant values. He describes himself as a being of powerful passions but confused ideas, he makes feeling the guide of conduct, he glorifies imagination and romantic love, he believes the common people morally superior to the upper classes. The emphasis on imagination and passion for him seems not a matter of ideology but of experience: life presents itself to him in this way. The fact emphasizes the degree to which the movement we call Romanticism involved genuine revision. Everything looked different in the late eighteenth century, demanding that categories change from those previously accepted without question. The new way of looking at the world that characterizes the Romantic movement, inasmuch as it implies valuing the inner life of emotion and fancy for its own sake (not for the sake of any insight it might provide), always includes the danger of narcissism, a concentration on the self that shuts out awareness of the reality and integrity of others. Rousseau, in the *Confessions*, vividly expresses the narcissistic side of Romanticism.

Implicit in Rousseau's ways of understanding himself and his life are new moral assumptions as well. Honesty of a particular kind becomes the highest value; however disreputable his behavior, Rousseau can feel comfortable about it because he reports it accurately. What Johnson or Pope would see as self-indulgence, care exclusively for one's own pleasure, seems acceptable to Rousseau because of the minute, exacting attention devoted to it. The autobiographer examines each nuance of his own happiness, as if to know it fully constitutes moral achievement. To take the self this seriously as subject—not in relation to a progress of education or of salvation, but, merely in its moment-to-moment being—implies belief in self-knowledge (knowledge of feeling, thought, action) as a high moral achievement. This is not the slowly achieved, arduous discipline recommended by Socrates but a more indulgent form of self-contemplation. To connect it, as Rousseau does, with morality conveys the view that self-absorption without self-judgment provides valuable and sufficient insight.

In his presentation of self, Rousseau contrasts vividly with his great predecessor, Montaigne. Rousseau insists on his uniqueness: "I am made unlike any one I have ever met; I will even venture to say that I am like no one in the whole world." He presents himself for the reader's contemplation as a remarkable phenomenon. Montaigne, on the other hand, reminds us constantly of what author and reader (and humankind in general) have in common. "Not only does the wind of accidents stir me according to its blowing, but I am also stirred and troubled by the instability of my attitude; and he who examines himself closely will seldom find himself twice in the same state." The movement within the sentence from *I* to the universalizing *he* characterizes a more outward-looking mode.

It must be said, however, that the intensity of Rousseau's self-concentration makes his subject compelling for others as well. However distasteful one might find his obsessive focus, it is difficult to stop reading. The writer hints—makes us believe— that he will reveal all the secrets about himself; and learning such secrets, despite Rousseau's insistence on his own uniqueness, tells us of human weakness, inconsistency, power, scope—tells us, therefore, something about ourselves. Moreover, the writer's self-absorption causes him to examine minute shades of thought and feeling, thus depicting a personality of great subtlety and complexity. Rousseau is unafraid of exposing contradictions in his attitudes, unafraid of revealing sexual peculiarities, unafraid of acknowledging odd relationships. He makes vivid, in almost novelistic fashion, the intricacies of motivation and purpose.

The novel, already flourishing during the eighteenth century, would turn in the nineteenth century toward the psychological analysis of large groups of characters. Rousseau, making himself a "character," exemplifies a narrator's way of bringing personality to life as he not only examines himself but sketches the others who impinge upon him, often with flashes of brilliant selectivity. His art of detail and introspection provided a model for autobiographers and novelists alike.

PRONOUNCING GLOSSARY

The following list uses common English syllables and stress accents to provide rough equivalents of selected words whose pronunciation may be unfamiliar to the general reader.

de Vulson: *deu vyewl-sohnh'*   Lausanne: *loh-zahn'*

de Warens: *deu vah-rahnh'*   Montaigne: *mohn-ten'*

Nyon: *nee-yohnh'*

Jean-Jacques Rousseau: *zhahnh-zhahk roo-soh'*

St. Marceau: *sanh mahr-soh'*

Saône: *sohn*

Turin: *tyew-ranh'*

Vaud: *voh*

Vévay: *vay-vay'*

Confessions[1]

Part I

FROM BOOK ONE

[The Years 1712–1723]

I have resolved on an enterprise which has no precedent, and which, once complete, will have no imitator. My purpose is to display to my kind a portrait in every way true to nature, and the man I shall portray will be myself.

Simply myself. I know my own heart and understand my fellow man. But I am made unlike any one I have ever met; I will even venture to say that I am like no one in the whole world. I may be no better, but at least I am different. Whether Nature did well or ill in breaking the mold in which she formed me, is a question which can only be resolved after the reading of my book.

Let the last trump sound when it will, I shall come forward with this work in my hand, to present myself before my Sovereign Judge, and proclaim aloud: "Here is what I have done, and if by chance I have used some immaterial embellishment it has been only to fill a void due to a defect of memory. I may have taken for fact what was no more than probability, but I have never put down as true what I knew to be false. I have displayed myself as I was, as vile and despicable when my behavior was such, as good, generous, and noble when I was so. I have bared my secret soul as Thou thyself hast seen it, Eternal Being! So let the numberless legion of my fellow men gather round me, and hear my confessions. Let them groan at my depravities, and blush for my misdeeds. But let each one of them reveal his heart at the foot of Thy throne with equal sincerity, and may any man who dares, say 'I was a better man than he.'"

* * *

I felt before I thought: which is the common lot of man, though more pronounced in my case than in another's. I know nothing of myself till I was five or six. I do not know how I learnt to read. I only remember my first books and their effect upon me; it is from my earliest reading that I date the unbroken consciousness of my own existence. My mother had possessed some novels, and my father and I began to read them after our supper. At first it was only to give me some practice in reading. But soon my interest in this

---

1. Translated by J. M. Cohen.

entertaining literature became so strong that we read by turns continuously, and spent whole nights so engaged. For we could never leave off till the end of the book. Sometimes my father would say with shame as we heard the morning larks: "Come, let us go to bed. I am more of a child than you are."

In a short time I acquired by this dangerous method, not only an extreme facility in reading and expressing myself, but a singular insight for my age into the passions. I had no idea of the facts, but I was already familiar with every feeling. I had grasped nothing; I had sensed everything. These confused emotions which I experienced one after another, did not warp my reasoning powers in any way, for as yet I had none. But they shaped them after a special pattern, giving me the strangest and most romantic notions about human life, which neither experience nor reflection has ever succeeded in curing me of.

*   *   *

I had one brother seven years older than myself, who was learning my father's trade. The extraordinary affection lavished upon me led to his being somewhat neglected, which I consider very wrong. Moreover his education had suffered by this neglect, and he was acquiring low habits even before he arrived at an age at which he could in fact indulge them. He was apprenticed to another master, with whom he took the same liberties as he had taken at home. I hardly ever saw him. Indeed, I can hardly say that I ever knew him, but I did not cease to love him dearly, and he loved me as well as a scoundrel can love. I remember once when my father was correcting him severely and angrily, throwing myself impetuously between them, and clasping my arms tightly around him. Thus I covered him with my body, and received the blows intended for him. So obstinately did I maintain my hold that, either as a result of my tearful cries or so as not to hurt me more than him, my father let him off his punishment. In the end my brother became so bad that he ran away and completely disappeared. We heard some time later that he was in Germany. But he did not write at all, and we had no more news of him after that. So it was that I became an only son.

But if that poor lad's upbringing was neglected, it was a different matter with his brother. No royal child could be more scrupulously cared for than I was in my early years. I was idolized by everyone around me and, what is rarer, always treated as a beloved son, never as a spoiled child. Never once, until I left my father's house, was I allowed to run out alone into the road with the other children. They never had to repress or to indulge in me any of those wayward humors that are usually attributed to Nature, but which are all the product of education alone. I had the faults of my years. I was a chatterer, I was greedy, and sometimes I lied. I would have stolen fruit or sweets or any kind of eatable; but I never took delight in being naughty or destructive, or in accusing other people or torturing poor animals. However, I do remember once having made water in one of our neighbor's cooking-pots while she was at church; her name was Mme Clot. I will even admit that the thought of it still makes me laugh, because Mme Clot, although a good woman on the whole, was the grumpiest old body I have ever met. And that is a brief and truthful account of all my childish misdeeds.

How could I have turned out wicked when I had nothing but examples of kindliness before my eyes, none but the best people in the world around me?

His desires are impartial

She music still effects him

My father, my aunt, my nurse, our friends and relations and everyone near me, may not have done my every bidding, but they did love me, and I loved them in return. My desires were so rarely excited and so rarely thwarted, that it never came into my head to have any. I could swear indeed that until I was put under a master I did not so much as know what it was to want my own way. When I was not reading or writing with my father, or going out for walks with my nurse, I spent all my time with my aunt, watching her embroider, hearing her sing, always sitting or standing beside her; and I was happy. Her cheerfulness and kindness and her pleasant face have left such an impression upon me that I can still remember her manner, her attitude and the way she looked. I recall too her affectionate little remarks, and I could still describe her clothes and her headdress, not forgetting the two curls of black hair she combed over her temples in the fashion of the day.

I am quite sure that it is to her I owe my taste, or rather my passion, for music, though it did not develop in me till long afterwards. She knew an enormous number of songs and tunes which she sang in a thin voice, that was very sweet. Such was the serenity of this excellent woman that it kept melancholy and sadness away, not only from her but from anyone who came near her; and such delight did I take in her singing that not only have many of her songs remained in my memory, but even now that I have lost her, others which I had completely forgotten since my childhood come back to me as I grow older, with a charm that I cannot express. It may seem incredible but, old dotard that I am, eaten up with cares and infirmities, I still find myself weeping like a child as I hum her little airs in my broken, tremulous voice.

* * *

The simplicity of this rural existence brought me one invaluable benefit; it opened my heart to friendship. Up to that time I had known nothing but lofty and theoretical emotions. Living peacefully side by side with my cousin Bernard gave me a bond of affection with him, and in a very short time I felt a greater attachment for him than I had ever felt for my brother, an attachment that has never disappeared. He was a tall, lank, sickly boy, as mild in spirit as he was weak in body, and he never abused his favored position in the house as my guardian's son. We shared the same studies, the same amusements, and the same tastes; we were on our own and of the same age, and each of us needed a companion; to be separated would have broken our hearts. Seldom though we had the opportunity of proving our attachment to one another, it was extremely strong. For not only could we not have lived one moment apart, but we never imagined that we could ever be parted. Being both of a nature easily swayed by affection, and tractable so long as there was no attempt at constraint, we were always in agreement on all subjects, and if the favor of our guardians gave him some advantage when they were present, the ascendancy was mine when we were alone—which redressed the balance. At our lessons I prompted him if he broke down; and when I had written my exercise I helped him with his. In our sports too I was the more active, and always took the lead. In fact our two natures agreed so well, and our friendship was so mutual and wholehearted that for five complete years, both at Bossey and at Geneva, we were almost inseparable. We often fought, I confess, but no one ever had to part us. Not one of our quarrels lasted more than a quarter of an hour, and not once did either of us complain of the other. It may be said that these observations are puerile, but the relationship they describe is perhaps a unique one in all the history of childhood.

The manner of my life at Bossey suited me so well that if only it had lasted longer it could not have failed to fix my character forever. It was founded on the affectionate, tender, and peaceable emotions. There was never, I believe, a creature of our kind with less vanity than I. By sudden transports I achieved moments of bliss, but immediately afterwards I relapsed into languor. My strongest desire was to be loved by everyone who came near me. I was gentle, so was my cousin, and so were our guardians. For a whole two years I was neither the witness nor the victim of any violence. Everything served to strengthen the natural disposition of my heart. Nothing seemed to me so delightful as to see everyone pleased with me and with everything. I shall always remember repeating my catechism in my church, where nothing upset me more than the grieved and anxious look on Mlle Lambercier's face when I hesitated. This made me unhappier than did my shame at faltering in public, though that too distressed me exceedingly. For although I was not very susceptible to praise, I was always extremely sensitive to disgrace. But I may say now that the expectation of a scolding from Mlle Lambercier alarmed me less than the fear of annoying her.

Neither she nor her brother was lacking in severity when necessary. But as their severity was almost always just and never excessive, I took it to heart and never resented it. I was more upset at displeasing them, however, than at being punished; and a word of rebuke was more painful to me than a blow. It embarrasses me to be more explicit, but it is necessary nevertheless. How differently people would treat children if only they saw the eventual results of the indiscriminate, and often culpable, methods of punishment they employ! The magnitude of the lesson to be derived from so common and unfortunate a case as my own has resolved me to write it down.

Since Mlle Lambercier treated us with a mother's love, she had also a mother's authority, which she exercised sometimes by inflicting on us such childish chastisements as we had earned. For a long while she confined herself to threats, and the threat of a punishment entirely unknown to me frightened me sufficiently. But when in the end I was beaten I found the experience less dreadful in fact than in anticipation; and the very strange thing was that this punishment increased my affection for the inflicter. It required all the strength of my devotion and all my natural gentleness to prevent my deliberately earning another beating; I had discovered in the shame and pain of the punishment an admixture of sensuality which had left me rather eager than otherwise for a repetition by the same hand. No doubt, there being some degree of precocious sexuality in all this, the same punishment at the hands of her brother would not have seemed pleasant at all. But he was of too kindly a disposition to be likely to take over this duty; and so, if I refrained from earning a fresh punishment, it was only out of fear of annoying Mlle Lambercier; so much am I swayed by kindness, even by kindness that is based on sensuality, that it has always prevailed with me over sensuality itself.

The next occasion, which I postponed, although not through fear, occurred through no fault of mine—that is to say I did not act deliberately.

But I may say that I took advantage of it with an easy conscience. This second occasion, however, was also the last. For Mlle Lambercier had no doubt detected signs that this punishment was not having the desired effect. She announced, therefore, that she would abandon it, since she found it too exhausting. Hitherto we had always slept in her room, and sometimes, in winter, in her bed. Two days afterwards we were made to sleep in another room, and henceforward I had the honor, willingly though I would have dispensed with it, of being treated as a big boy.

Who could have supposed that this childish punishment, received at the age of eight at the hands of a woman of thirty, would determine my tastes and desires, my passions, my very self for the rest of my life, and that in a sense diametrically opposed to the one in which they should normally have developed. At the moment when my senses were aroused my desires took a false turn and, confining themselves to this early experience, never set about seeking a different one. With sensuality burning in my blood almost from my birth, I kept myself pure and unsullied up to an age when even the coldest and most backward natures have developed. Tormented for a long while by I knew not what, I feasted feverish eyes on lovely women, recalling them ceaselessly to my imagination, but only to make use of them in my own fashion as so many Mlle Lamberciers.

My morals might well have been impaired by these strange tastes, which persisted with a depraved and insane intensity. But in fact they kept me pure even after the age of puberty. If ever education was chaste and decent, mine was. My three aunts were not only women of remarkable virtue, but examples of a modesty that has long since disappeared from womankind. My father was a pleasure lover, but a gallant of the old school, and never made a remark in the hearing of those women he loved most that would have brought a blush to a virgin's cheek; and never was the respect due to children more scrupulously observed than in my family and in my case. I did not find the slightest difference in this respect at M. Lambercier's; a very good servant maid was dismissed for a dubious word pronounced in our hearing. Not only had I not till adolescence any clear ideas concerning sexual intercourse, but my muddled thoughts on the subject always assumed odious and disgusting shapes. I had a horror of prostitutes which has never left me, and I could not look on a debauchee without contempt and even fear. Such had been my horror of immorality, even since the day when, on my way to Petit Saconex along the sunken road, I saw the holes in the earth on either side where I was told such people performed their fornications. When I thought of this I was always reminded of the coupling of dogs, and my stomach turned over at the very thought.

These adolescent prejudices would themselves have been sufficient to retard the first explosions of an inflammable temperament. But they were reinforced, as I have said, by the effect upon me of the promptings of sensuality. Imagining no pleasures other than those I had known, I could not, for all the restless tinglings in my veins, direct my desires towards any other form of gratification. Always I stopped short of imagining those satisfactions which I had been taught to loathe, and which, little though I suspected it, were in fact not so far divorced from those I envisaged. In my crazy fantasies, my wild fits of eroticism, and in the strange behavior which they sometimes drove me to, I always invoked, imaginatively, the aid of the opposite sex, without so much as dreaming that a woman could serve any other purpose than the one I lusted for.

Not only, therefore, did I, though ardent, lascivious, and precocious by nature, pass the age of puberty without desiring or knowing any other sensual pleasures than those which Mlle Lambercier had, in all innocence, acquainted me with; but when finally, in the course of years, I became a man I was preserved by that very perversity which might have been my undoing. My old childish tastes did not vanish, but became so intimately associated with those of maturity that I could never, when sensually aroused, keep the two apart. This peculiarity, together with my natural timidity, has always made me very backward with women, since I have never had the courage to be frank or the power to get what I wanted, it being impossible for the kind of pleasure I desired—to which the other kind is no more than a consummation—to be taken by him who wants it, or to be guessed at by the woman who could grant it. So I have spent my days in silent longing in the presence of those I most loved. I never dared to reveal my strange taste, but at least I got some pleasure from situations which pandered to the thought of it. To fall on my knees before a masterful mistress, to obey her commands, to have to beg for her forgiveness, have been to me the most delicate of pleasures; and the more my vivid imagination heated my blood the more like a spellbound lover I looked. As can be imagined, this way of making love does not lead to rapid progress, and is not very dangerous to the virtue of the desired object. Consequently I have possessed few women, but I have not failed to get a great deal of satisfaction in my own way, that is to say imaginatively. So it is that my sensibility, combined with my timidity and my romantic nature, have preserved the purity of my feelings and my morals, by the aid of those same tastes which might, with a little more boldness, have plunged me into the most brutal sensuality.

Now I have made the first and most painful step in the dark and miry maze of my confessions. It is the ridiculous and the shameful, not one's criminal actions, that it is hardest to confess. But henceforth I am certain of myself; after what I have just had the courage to say, nothing else will defeat me. How much it has cost me to make such revelations can be judged when I say that though sometimes laboring under passions that have robbed me of sight, of hearing, and of my senses, though sometimes trembling convulsively in my whole body in the presence of the woman I loved, I have never, during the whole course of my life, been able to force myself, even in moments of extreme intimacy, to confess my peculiarities and implore her to grant the one favor which was lacking. That confession I was only able to make once, when I was a child to a child of my own age, and then it was she who made the first overtures.

When I trace my nature back in this way to its earliest manifestations, I find features which may appear incompatible, but which have nevertheless combined to form a strong, simple, and uniform whole. I find other features, however, which, though similar in appearance, have formed by a concatenation of circumstances combinations so different that one could never suppose them to be in any way related to one another. Who would imagine, for instance, that I owe one of the most vigorous elements in my character to the same origins as the weakness and sensuality that flows in my veins? Before we leave the subject I have been dwelling on, I will show it under a very different light.

One day I was learning my lessons alone in the room next to the kitchen, where the servant had left Mlle Lambercier's combs to dry on the stove top. Now when she came to take them off, she discovered that the teeth of one were broken off, all down one side. Who was to be blamed for this? I was the only person who had been in the room; but I said I had not touched it. M. and Mlle Lambercier jointly lectured, pressed, and threatened me; but I stubbornly maintained my denial. Appearances were too strong for me, however, and all my protests were overruled, although this was the first time that I had been convicted of a downright lie. They took the matter seriously, as it deserved. The mischief, the untruth, and my persistent denials, all seemed to deserve a punishment; but this time it was not Mlle Lambercier who inflicted it. They wrote to my Uncle Bernard, and he came. My cousin was accused of another crime no less grave; we were awarded the same chastisement, which was a severe one. If they had intended to allay my depraved tastes for ever by using the evil as its own remedy, they could not have gone about it in a better way. For a long time my desires left me in peace.

They were unable to force from me the confession they required. Though the punishment was several times repeated and I was reduced to the most deplorable condition, I remained inflexible. I would have died rather than give in, and I was resolved to. So force had to yield before the diabolical obstinacy of a child. For that is what they called my persistence. But finally I emerged from that cruel ordeal shattered but triumphant.

It is now nearly fifty years since this occurrence, and I have no fear of a fresh punishment for the offense. But I declare before Heaven that I was not guilty. I had not broken, nor so much as touched, the comb. I had not gone near the stove, nor so much as thought of doing so. But do not ask me how the mischief occurred. I have no idea, and I cannot understand it. But I do most positively know that I was innocent.

Imagine a person timid and docile in ordinary life, but proud, fiery, and inflexible when roused, a child who has always been controlled by the voice of reason, always treated with kindness, fairness, and indulgence, a creature without a thought of injustice, now for the first time suffering a most grave one at the hands of the people he loves best and mostly deeply respects. Imagine the revolution in his ideas, the violent change of his feelings, the confusion in his heart and brain, in his small intellectual and moral being! I say, imagine all this if you can. For myself I do not feel capable of unraveling the strands, or even remotely following all that happened at that time within me.

I had not yet sufficient reasoning power to realize the extent to which appearances were against me, to put myself in my elders' position. I clung to my own, and all I felt was the cruelty of an appalling punishment for a crime I had not committed. The physical pain was bad enough, but I hardly noticed it; what I felt was indignation, rage, and despair. My cousin was in a more or less similar case; he had been punished for what had only been a mistake but was taken for a premeditated crime, and he, following my example, got into a rage, and so to speak, worked himself up to the same pitch as myself. Lying together in the same bed, we embraced wildly, almost stifling one another; and when our young hearts were somewhat assuaged and we could give voice to our anger, we sat up and shouted a hundred times in unison at the tops of our voices: "Carnifex! carnifex! carnifex!"[2]

I feel my pulse beat faster once more as I write. I shall always remember that time if I live to be a thousand. That first meeting with violence and injustice has remained so deeply engraved on my heart that any thought which recalls it summons back this first emotion. The feeling was only a personal one in its origins, but it has since assumed such a consistency and has become so divorced from personal interests that my blood boils at the sight or the tale of any injustice, whoever may be the sufferer and wherever it may have taken place, in just the same way as if I were myself its victim. When I read of the cruelties of a fierce tyrant, of the subtle machinations of a rascally priest, I would gladly go and stab the wretch myself, even if it were to cost me my life a hundred times over. I have often run till I dropped, flinging stones at some cock or cow or dog, or any animal that I saw tormenting another because it felt itself the stronger. This is perhaps an innate characteristic in me. Indeed I think it is. But the memory of the first injustice I suffered was so painful, so persistent, and so intricately bound up with it that, however strong my initial bent in that direction, this youthful experience must certainly have powerfully reinforced it.

There ended the serenity of my childish life. From that moment I never again enjoyed pure happiness, and even today I am conscious that memory of childhood's delights stops short at that point. We stayed some months longer at Bossey. We lived as we are told the first man lived in the earthly paradise, but we no longer enjoyed it; in appearance our situation was unchanged, but in reality it was an entirely different kind of existence. No longer were we young people bound by ties of respect, intimacy, and confidence to our guardians; we no longer looked on them as gods who read our hearts; we were less ashamed of wrongdoing, and more afraid of being caught; we began to be secretive, to rebel, and to lie. All the vices of our years began to corrupt our innocence and to give an ugly turn to our amusements. Even the country no longer had for us those sweet and simple charms that touch the heart; it seemed to our eyes depressing and empty, as if it had been covered by a veil that cloaked its beauties. We gave up tending our little gardens, our herbs and flowers. We no longer went out to scratch the surface of the ground and shout with delight at finding one of the seeds we had sown beginning to sprout. We grew to dislike that life; and they grew to dislike us. So my uncle took us away, and we left M. and Mme Lambercier, with few regrets on either side, each party having grown weary of the other.

* * *

FROM BOOK TWO
[The Years 1728–1731]

Before I go further I must present my reader with an apology, or rather a justification, for the petty details I have just been entering into, and for those I shall enter into later, none of which may appear interesting in his eyes.

2. Torturer! torturer! torturer! (Latin).

Since I have undertaken to reveal myself absolutely to the public, nothing about me must remain hidden or obscure. I must remain incessantly beneath his gaze, so that he may follow me in all the extravagances of my heart and into every least corner of my life. Indeed, he must never lose sight of me for a single instant, for if he finds the slightest gap in my story, the smallest hiatus, he may wonder what I was doing at that moment and accuse me of refusing to tell the whole truth. I am laying myself sufficiently open to human malice by telling my story, without rendering myself more vulnerable by any silence.

* * *

Mine was no true childhood; I always felt and thought like a man. Only as I grew up did I become my true age, which I had not been at my birth. You may laugh at my modestly setting myself up as a prodigy. Very well, but when you have had your laugh, find a child who is attracted by novels at six, who is interested and moved by them to the point of weeping hot tears. Then I shall admit to being absurdly vain, and agree that I am wrong.

So, when I said that one should not talk to children about religion if one hopes that one day they will have some, and that they are incapable of knowing God, even in our imperfect way, I was basing my conviction on my observations, but not on my own experience. For I knew that my experience did not apply to others. Find me a Jean-Jacques Rousseau of six, talk to him of God at seven, and I promise you that you will be taking no risks.[3]

* * *

But, alas, I have not said all that I have to say about my time at Mme de Vercellis's. For though my condition was apparently unchanged I did not leave her house as I had entered it. I took away with me lasting memories of a crime and the unbearable weight of a remorse which, even after forty years, still burdens my conscience. In fact the bitter memory of it, far from fading, grows more painful with the years. Who would suppose that a child's wickedness could have such cruel results? It is for these only too probable consequences that I can find no consolation. I may have ruined a nice, honest, and decent girl, who was certainly worth a great deal more than I, and doomed her to disgrace and misery.

It is almost inevitable that the breaking up of an establishment should cause some confusion in the house, and that various things should be mislaid. But so honest were the servants and so vigilant were M. and Mme Lorenzi that nothing was found missing when the inventory was taken. Only Mlle Pontal lost a little pink and silver ribbon, which was quite old. Plenty of better things were within my reach, but this ribbon alone tempted me. I stole it, and as I hardly troubled to conceal it it was soon found. They inquired how I had got hold of it. I grew confused, stammered, and finally said with a blush that it was Marion who had given it to me. Marion was a young girl from the Maurienne whom Mme de Vercellis had taken as her cook when she had ceased to give dinners and had discharged her chef, since she had more need of good soup than of fine stews. Marion was not only

---

3. That is, of turning the child into an atheist or agnostic since, if possessed of such exceptional gifts as Rousseau, he will not be susceptible. At this point in the narrative, Rousseau reports his own conversion to Catholicism and tells of his experience in Turin, where he eventually took service as a valet with Mme. de Vercellis.

pretty. She had that fresh complexion that one never finds except in the mountains, and such a sweet and modest air that one had only to see her to love her. What is more she was a good girl, sensible and absolutely trustworthy. They were extremely surprised when I mentioned her name. But they had no less confidence in me than in her, and decided that it was important to find which of us was a thief. She was sent for, to face a considerable number of people, including the Comte de la Roque himself. When she came she was shown the ribbon. I boldly accused her. She was confused, did not utter a word, and threw me a glance that would have disarmed the devil, but my cruel heart resisted. In the end she firmly denied the theft. But she did not get indignant. She merely turned to me, and begged me to remember myself and not disgrace an innocent girl who had never done me any harm. But, with infernal impudence, I repeated my accusation, and declared to her face that she had given me the ribbon. The poor girl started to cry, but all she said to me was, "Oh, Rousseau, I thought you were a good fellow. You make me very sad, but I should not like to be in your place." That is all. She continued to defend herself with equal firmness and sincerity, but never allowed herself any reproaches against me. This moderation, contrasted with my decided tone, prejudiced her case. It did not seem natural to suppose such diabolical audacity on one side and such angelic sweetness on the other. They seemed unable to come to a definite decision, but they were prepossessed in my favor. In the confusion of the moment they had not time to get to the bottom of the business; and the Comte de la Roque, in dismissing us both, contented himself with saying that the guilty one's conscience would amply avenge the innocent. His prediction was not wide of the mark. Not a day passes on which it is not fulfilled.

I do not know what happened to the victim of my calumny, but she cannot possibly have found it easy to get a good situation after that. The imputation against her honor was cruel in every respect. The theft was only a trifle, but after all, it was a theft and, what is worse, had been committed in order to lead a boy astray. Theft, lying, and obstinacy—what hope was there for a girl in whom so many vices were combined? I do not even consider misery and friendlessness the worst dangers to which she was exposed. Who can tell to what extremes the depressed feeling of injured innocence might have carried her at her age? And if my remorse at having perhaps made her unhappy is unbearable, what can be said of my grief at perhaps having made her worse than myself?

This cruel memory troubles me at times and so disturbs me that in my sleepless hours I see this poor girl coming to reproach me for my crime, as if I had committed it only yesterday. So long as I have lived in peace it has tortured me less, but in the midst of a stormy life it deprives me of that sweet consolation which the innocent feel under persecution. It brings home to me indeed what I think I have written in one of my books, that remorse sleeps while fate is kind but grows sharp in adversity. Nevertheless I have never been able to bring myself to relieve my heart by revealing this in private to a friend. Not with the most intimate friend, not even with Mme de Warens,[4] has this been possible. The most that I could do was to

---

4. Françoise-Louise de Warens, whom Rousseau also refers to as "mamma." Rousseau had originally been sent to her home at Annecy, a town in southeastern France, in order that she, herself a recent convert to Catholicism, should help him toward his own conversion. The two became devoted to one another.

confess that I had a terrible deed on my conscience, but I have never said in what it consisted. The burden, therefore, has rested till this day on my conscience without any relief; and I can affirm that the desire to some extent to rid myself of it has greatly contributed to my resolution of writing these *Confessions*.

I have been absolutely frank in the account I have just given, and no one will accuse me, I am certain, of palliating the heinousness of my offense. But I should not fulfill the aim of this book if I did not at the same time reveal my inner feelings and hesitated to put up such excuses for myself as I honestly could. Never was deliberate wickedness further from my intention than at that cruel moment. When I accused that poor girl, it is strange but true that my friendship for her was the cause. She was present in my thoughts, and I threw the blame on the first person who occurred to me. I accused her of having done what I intended to do myself. I said that she had given the ribbon to me because I meant to give it to her. When afterwards I saw her in the flesh my heart was torn. But the presence of all those people prevailed over my repentance. I was not much afraid of punishment, I was only afraid of disgrace. But that I feared more than death, more than crime, more than anything in the world. I should have rejoiced if the earth had swallowed me up and stifled me in the abyss. But my invincible sense of shame prevailed over everything. It was my shame that made me impudent, and the more wickedly I behaved the bolder my fear of confession made me. I saw nothing but the horror of being found out, of being publicly proclaimed, to my face, as a thief, a liar, and a slanderer. Utter confusion robbed me of all other feeling. If I had been allowed time to come to my senses, I should most certainly have admitted everything. If M. de la Roque had taken me aside and said: "Do not ruin that poor girl. If you are guilty tell me so," I should immediately have thrown myself at his feet, I am perfectly sure. But all they did was to frighten me, when what I needed was encouragement. My age also should be taken into account. I was scarcely more than a child. Indeed I still was one. In youth real crimes are even more reprehensible than in riper years; but what is no more than weakness is much less blameworthy, and really my crime amounted to no more than weakness. So the memory tortures me less on account of the crime itself than because of its possible evil consequences. But I have derived some benefit from the terrible impression left with me by the sole offense I have committed. For it has secured me for the rest of my life against any act that might prove criminal in its results. I think also that my loathing of untruth derives to a large extent from my having told that one wicked lie. If this is a crime that can be expiated, as I venture to believe, it must have been atoned for by all the misfortunes that have crowded the end of my life, by forty years of honest and upright behavior under difficult circumstances. Poor Marion finds so many avengers in this world that, however great my offense against her may have been, I have little fear of carrying the sin on my conscience at death. That is all I have to say on the subject. May I never have to speak of it again.

* * *

FROM BOOK THREE

[*The Years 1731–1732*]

So there I was, settled at last in her[5] house. This, however, was still not the moment from which I date the happy period of my life, but it served to pave the way for it. Although the emotional sensibility that gives rise to real joy is a work of Nature, and perhaps innate in our constitutions, it stands in need of situations in which it can develop. Lacking the right circumstances, a man born with acute sensibility would feel nothing, and would die without ever having known his true nature. I had been more or less in that condition till then, and should have been so always perhaps had I never met Mme de Warens, or even, having known her, if I had not lived close to her for long enough to contract the sweet habit of affection with which she inspired me. I will venture to say that anyone who feels no more than love misses the sweetest thing in life. For I know another feeling, less impetuous perhaps but a thousand times more delightful, which is sometimes joined with love and sometimes separate from it. This feeling is something other than friendship, something less temperate and more tender. I do not think that it can be felt for anyone of the same sex. I have known friendship, at least, if ever a man has, and I have never had this feeling for any of my friends. This statement is obscure, but it will become clear in the sequel. Feelings can only be described in terms of their effects.

Mme de Warens lived in an old house, large enough to contain a fine spare room which she used as a drawing room, and it was here that I was put. It gave on to the passage * * * in which our first interview took place, and from it, on the far side of the stream and the gardens, one could see the country. This view was not a matter of indifference to the room's young occupant. Now, for the first time since Bossey, I had green fields outside my windows. Always shut in by walls, I had had nothing on which to gaze but the roofs of houses and the gray of the streets. I was truly sensitive, therefore, to the charm and novelty of my new situation, which greatly increased my suscep-tibility to tender feelings. I thought of this charming landscape as an addi-tional gift from my dear patroness, who seemed to have placed it there deliberately for me. There I took my place peacefully beside her, and saw her everywhere among the flowers and the greenery. Her charms and the charms of spring became one in my eyes. My heart, constricted till then, felt more free before this open prospect, and among the orchards my sighs found easier vent.

* * *

She ran her household in exactly the way I should have chosen myself, and naturally I was only too pleased to take advantage of it. What somewhat displeased me, however, was having to spend a long time over meals. At the first smell of the soup and of the other dishes she almost fell into a faint. Indeed she could hardly bear these smells at all, and took some time to recover from her nausea. But little by little she felt better. Then she began to talk, but ate nothing. It would be half an hour before she would take her

---

5. He has returned to Mme. de Warens.

first mouthful. I could have eaten my dinner three times over in this time. My meal was finished long before she had started hers. So I began again, to keep her company, and ate enough for two, without feeling any the worse for it.

In a word, I gave myself up to the sweet sense of well-being I felt in her company, a state of mind which was undisturbed by any concern as to the means of preserving it. Not being as yet in her close confidence, I supposed that the present state of affairs was likely always to continue. I found the same comforts again in her house in later days. But, knowing the true situation better, and seeing that she was anticipating her revenue,[6] I was not able to enjoy them so calmly. Looking ahead always ruins my enjoyment. It is never any good foreseeing the future. I have never known how to avoid it.

From the first day the sweetest intimacy was established between us, and it continued to prevail during the rest of her life. "Little one" was my name, hers was "Mamma," and we always remained "Little one" and "Mamma," even when the passage of the years had almost effaced the difference between our ages. The two names, I find, admirably express the tone of our behavior, the simplicity of our habits and, what is more, the relation between our hearts. To me she was the most tender of mothers, who never thought of her own pleasure but always of my good. And if there was a sensual side of my attachment to her, that did not alter its character, but only made it more enchanting. I was intoxicated with delight at having a young and pretty mamma whom I loved to caress. I use caress in the strict sense of the word, for she never thought of grudging me kisses or the tender caresses of a mother, and it never entered my thoughts to abuse them. It will be objected that we had in the end a relationship of a different character. I agree. But wait, I cannot tell everything at the same time.

The sudden moment of our first meeting was the only truly passionate one she ever made me feel. But that moment was the product of surprise. My glances never went wandering indiscreetly beneath her kerchief, though an ill-concealed plumpness in that region might well have attracted them. I felt neither emotions nor desires in her presence; my state was one of blissful calm, in which I enjoyed I knew not what. I could have spent my life like that and eternity as well, without a moment's boredom. She is the only person with whom I never suffered from that inability to find words that makes the maintenance of conversation such a penance to me. Our time together was spent less in conversation than in one interminable gossip, which required an interruption to bring it to an end. I needed no compulsion to talk; it almost needed compulsion to silence me. As she often thought over her plans, she often fell into reveries. I let her dream on. I gazed on her in silence and was the happiest of men. I had another singular habit. I never claimed the favor of being alone with her, but I ceaselessly sought opportunities for private interviews, which I enjoyed with a passion that turned to fury whenever troublesome visitors came to disturb us. As soon as anyone arrived—whether man or woman, it did not matter which—I went out grumbling, for I could never bear to remain with a third party. Then I would stay in her antechamber, counting the minutes and continually cursing her eternal visitors, quite

---

6. Spending her money before she had it—that is, living on credit.

unable to conceive how they could have so much to say since I had so much more.

I only felt the full strength of my attachment to her when she was out of my sight. When I could see her I was merely happy. But my disquiet when she was away became almost painful. My inability to live without her caused me outbreaks of tenderness which often concluded with tears. I shall always remember how, on a Saint's day, while she was at vespers, I went for a walk outside the town, with my heart full of the thought of her and with a burning desire to spend my days beside her. I had sense enough to see that for the present this was impossible, that a happiness so deeply enjoyed must needs be short. This gave my thoughts a sad tinge, but not a gloomy one. For it was tempered by a flattering hope. The sound of the bells, which has always singularly moved me, the song of the birds, the beauty of the day, the calm of the countryside, the scattered country dwellings, one of which I fancifully pictured as our common home—all these produced so vivid an impression upon me, raised in me so tender, sad, and touching a mood, that I saw myself ecstatically transported into that happy time and place in which my heart would possess everything it could desire and in which I should enjoy it all with indescribable rapture, yet without so much as a thought of sensual pleasure. I do not remember ever having leapt into the future with greater force and illusion than I did then. And what has struck me most about my memory of this dream, now that it has been realized, is that eventually I found things exactly as I imagined them. If ever a waking man's dream seemed like a prophetic vision, that reverie of mine did. I was only deceived in my dream's seeming duration. For in it days and years and a whole life passed in changeless tranquillity, whilst in reality the whole experience was only a momentary one. Alas, my most lasting happiness was in a dream. Its fruition was almost immediately succeeded by my awakening.

I should never finish were I to describe in detail all the follies which the memory of my dear Mamma caused me to commit when I was out of her sight. How often have I kissed my bed because she had slept in it; my curtains, all the furniture of my room, since they belonged to her and her fair hand had touched them; even the floor on to which I threw myself, calling to mind how she had walked there! Sometimes even in her presence I fell into extravagances that seemed as if they could only have been inspired by the most violent love. One day at table, just as she had put some food into her mouth, I cried out that I had seen a hair in it. She spat the morsel back on her plate, whereupon I seized it greedily and swallowed it. In a word, there was but one difference between myself and the most passionate of lovers. But that difference was an essential one, and sufficient to render my whole condition inexplicable in the light of reason.

*　*　*

In me are united two almost irreconcilable characteristics, though in what way I cannot imagine. I have a passionate temperament, and lively and headstrong emotions. Yet my thoughts arise slowly and confusedly, and are never ready till too late. It is as if my heart and my brain did not belong to the same person. Feelings come quicker than lightning and fill my soul, but they bring me no illumination; they burn me and dazzle me. I feel everything and I see nothing; I am excited but stupid; if I want to think I must be cool. The astonishing thing is, though, that I have considerable tact, some understanding, and a certain skill with people so long as they will wait for me. I can make excellent replies impromptu, if I have a moment to think, but on the spur of the moment I can never say or do anything right. I could conduct a most delightful conversation by post, as they say the Spaniards play chess. When I read the story of that Duke of Savoy who turned round on his homeward journey to cry, "Mind out, my fine Paris merchant!" I recognize myself.

But I do not suffer from this combination of quick emotion and slow thoughts only in company. I know it too when I am alone and when I am working. Ideas take shape in my head with the most incredible difficulty. They go round in dull circles and ferment, agitating me and overheating me till my heart palpitates. During this stir of emotion I can see nothing clearly, and cannot write a word; I have to wait. Insensibly all this tumult grows quiet, the chaos subsides, and everything falls into place, but slowly, and after long and confused perturbations. Have you ever been to the opera in Italy? During changes of scenery wild and prolonged disorder reigns in their great theaters. The furniture is higgledy-piggledy; on all sides things are being shifted and everything seems upside down; it is as if they were bent on universal destruction; but little by little everything falls into place, nothing is missing, and, to one's surprise, all the long tumult is succeeded by a delightful spectacle. That is almost exactly the process that takes place in my brain when I want to write. If I had known in the past how to wait and then put down in all their beauty the scenes that painted themselves in my imagination, few authors would have surpassed me.

This is the explanation of the extreme difficulty I have in writing. My blotted, scratched, confused, illegible manuscripts attest to the pain they have cost me. There is not one that I have not had to rewrite four or five times before sending it to the printer. I have never been able to do anything with my pen in my hand, and my desk and paper before me; it is on my walks, among the rocks and trees, it is at night in my bed when I lie awake, that I compose in my head; and you can imagine how slowly, for I am completely without verbal memory and have never been able to memorize half a dozen verses in my life. Some of my paragraphs I have shaped and reshaped mentally for five or six nights before they were fit to be put down on paper. It is for that reason that I am more successful in works that demand labor than in things which need a light touch. I have never caught the knack of letter writing, for instance; it is a real torture to me. I never write a letter on the most trivial subject that does not cost me hours of weariness. For if I try to put down immediately what comes to me, I do not know how to begin or end; my letter is a long, muddled rigmarole, and scarcely understandable when it is read.

But not only do I find ideas difficult to express, I find them equally difficult to take in. I have studied men, and I think I am a fairly good observer. But all the same I do not know how to see what is before my eyes; I can only see clearly in retrospect, it is only in my memories that my mind can work. I have neither feeling nor understanding for anything that is said or done or that happens before my eyes. All that strikes me is the external manifestation. But afterwards it all comes back to me, I remember the place and the time, the tone of voice and look, the gesture and situation; nothing escapes me.

Then from what a man has done or said I can read his thoughts, and I am rarely mistaken.

Seeing that I am so little master of myself when I am alone, imagine what I am like in conversation, when in order to speak to the point one must think promptly of a dozen things at a time. The mere thought of all the conventions, of which I am sure to forget at least one, is enough to frighten me. I cannot understand how a man can have the confidence to speak in company. For not a word should be uttered without taking everyone present into account, without knowing their characters and their histories, in order to be certain of not offending anyone. In that respect men who live in society are at a great advantage. Knowing better what not to say, they are more certain of what they say. But even then they often make blunders. Consider then the predicament of a man who has come in out of the blue: it is almost impossible for him to talk for a moment without blundering.

In private conversation there is another difficulty, which I consider worse, the necessity of always talking. You have to reply each time you are spoken to, and if the conversation fails, to set it going again. This unbearable constraint would be enough in itself to disgust me with society. I can think of no greater torture than to be obliged to talk continually and without a moment for reflection. I do not know whether this is just an aspect of my mortal aversion to any sort of compulsion, but I have only to be absolutely required to speak and I infallibly say something stupid. But what is even more fatal is that, instead of keeping quiet when I have nothing to say, it is at just those times that I have a furious desire to chatter. In my anxiety to fulfill my obligations as quickly as possible I hastily gabble a few ill-considered words, and am only too glad if they mean nothing at all. So anxious am I to conquer or hide my ineptitude that I rarely fail to make it apparent. Among countless examples which I could cite I will relate one, which does not belong to my youth but to a time when I had lived for some while in society. By then I should have acquired a social manner and ease if that had been possible. One evening I was with two fine ladies and one gentleman whom I can name; it was the Duke de Gontaut. There was no one else in the room, and I compelled myself to contribute a few words—goodness knows what—to a four-cornered conversation, in which the other three had certainly no need of my help. The mistress of the house sent for a laudanum draft which she took twice a day for her digestion. The other lady, seeing her make a wry face, asked with a laugh, "Is that from Doctor Tronchin's prescription?" "I don't think so," answered the first lady in the same light tone. "That's about as good as she deserves," put in the gallant Rousseau in his witty way. Everyone was speechless; there was not a word, there was not a smile, and the next moment the conversation took another turn. Addressed to anyone else this blunder might have been only silly, but said to a lady too charming not to have some stories attached to her name, a lady whom I had certainly no wish to offend, it was dreadful; and I think the two witnesses of my discomfiture had all they could do not to burst out laughing. That is the kind of witticism I produce when I feel I must speak, but have nothing to say. It will be a long time before I forget that occasion. For not only is it very vivid in itself, but it had consequences that remain in my head to remind me of it only too often.

Some people think him a fool

I think that I have sufficiently explained why, though I am not a fool, I am very often taken for one, even by people in a good position to judge.

* * *

FROM BOOK FOUR

[The Year 1732]

It is a very strange thing that my imagination never works more delightfully than when my situation is the reverse of delightful, and that, on the other hand, it is never less cheerful than when all is cheerful around me. My poor head can never submit itself to facts. It cannot beautify; it must create. It can depict real objects only more or less as they are, reserving its embellishments for the things of the imagination. If I want to describe the spring it must be in winter; if I want to describe a fine landscape I must be within doors; and as I have said a hundred times, if ever I were confined in the Bastille, there I would draw the picture of liberty. On leaving Lyons I could see none but agreeable prospects; I was as cheerful—and I had cause to be— as I had been the reverse when I set out from Paris. During this journey, however, I enjoyed none of those delicious daydreams that had accompanied me on my last trip. My heart was light, and that was all. I felt some emotion as I drew nearer to my excellent friend whom I was now to see again. I enjoyed some foretaste of the pleasure of living in her company, but I was not beside myself. I had always expected this; it was as if nothing new had happened. I felt a little anxious about my future employment, as if that had been a matter for much anxiety. My thoughts were calm and peaceful; they were not heavenly or ecstatic. Objects caught my eye. I observed the different landscapes I passed through. I noticed the trees, the houses, and the streams. I deliberated at crossroads. I was afraid of getting lost, but did not lose myself even once. In a word, I was no longer in the clouds. Sometimes I was where I was, sometimes already at my destination, but never did I soar off into the distance.

In telling the story of my travels, as in traveling itself, I never know how to stop.

* * *

He is still childish

These long details of my early youth may well seem extremely childish, and I am sorry for it. Although in certain respects I have been a man since birth, I was for a long time, and still am, a child in many others. I never promised to present the public with a great personage. I promised to depict myself as I am; and to know me in my latter years it is necessary to have known me well in my youth. As objects generally make less impression on me than does the memory of them, and as all my ideas take pictorial form, the first features to engrave themselves on my mind have remained there, and such as have subsequently imprinted themselves have combined with these rather than obliterated them. There is a certain sequence of impressions and ideas which modify those that follow them, and it is necessary to know the original set before passing any judgments. I endeavor in all cases to explain the prime causes, in order to convey the interrelation of results. I should like in some way to make my soul transparent to the reader's eye, and for that purpose I am trying to present it from all points of view, to show it in all lights, and to contrive that none of its movements shall escape his notice, so that he may judge for himself of the principle which has produced them.

If I made myself responsible for the result and said to him, "Such is my character," he might suppose, if not that I am deceiving him, at least that I am deceiving myself. But by relating to him in simple detail all that has happened to me, all that I have done, all that I have felt, I cannot lead him into error, unless willfully; and even if I wish to, I shall not easily succeed by this method. His task is to assemble these elements and to assess the being who is made up of them. The summing up must be his, and if he comes to wrong conclusions, the fault will be of his own making. But, with this in view, it is not enough for my story to be truthful, it must be detailed as well. It is not for me to judge of the relative importance of events; I must relate them all, and leave the selection to him. That is the task to which I have devoted myself up to this point with all my courage, and I shall not relax in the sequel. But memories of middle age are always less sharp than those of early youth. So I have begun by making the best possible use of the former. If the latter come back to me in the same strength, impatient readers will perhaps be bored, but I shall not be displeased with my labors. I have only one thing to fear in this enterprise; not that I may say too much or tell untruths, but that I may not tell everything and may conceal the truth.

He fears not confessing all. [handwritten marginal note]

* * *

FROM BOOK FIVE

[The Years 1732–1738]

At Chambéry[7] I often saw a Jacobin[8] who was professor of physics, a good-natured friar whose name I have forgotten, who frequently made small experiments that greatly amused me. Following his example, and with the assistance of Ozanam's *Mathematical Recreations*, I tried to make some sympathetic ink;[9] to which purpose I more than half-filled a bottle with quicklime, sulphide of arsenic, and water, and corked it tightly. Almost instantaneously the effervescence began most violently. I ran to the bottle to uncork it, but I was not in time; it burst in my face like a bomb. I swallowed so much of the sulphide and lime that it almost killed me. I was blinded for six weeks, and in that way I learnt not to meddle in experimental physics without knowing the rudiments of that science.

This accident came at an awkward moment, since for some time my health had been sensibly deteriorating. I do not know how it was, but, though of a sound constitution and indulging in no sort of excesses, I was visibly on the decline. I am pretty well built, my chest is broad and my lungs have room enough to expand. Nevertheless I was short of breath, felt constricted across the chest, gasped involuntarily, had palpitations and spat blood. On top of all this came a lingering fever which I have never entirely thrown off. How

---

7. The town in eastern France where Mme. de Warens was now living. 8. A member of a political group originally moderate, but becoming increasingly radical. 9. Ink that produces writing that remains invisible until a reagent is applied.

He lives and dies by his passions

can a man fall into such a state in the flower of his youth, without any internal injury and having done nothing to destroy his health?

The sword wears out its sheath, as is sometimes said. That is my story. My passions have made me live, and my passions have killed me. What passions, it may be asked. Trifles, the most childish things in the world. Yet they affected me as much as if the possession of Helen,[1] or of the throne of the Universe, had been at stake. In the first place, women. When I possessed one my senses were quiet, but my heart never. At the height of my pleasure the need for love devoured me. I had a tender mother, a dear friend; but I needed a mistress. In my imagination I put one in Mamma's place, endowing her with a thousand shapes in order to deceive myself. If I had thought I was holding Mamma in my arms when I embraced her, my embraces would have been just as tender, but all my desires would have died. I should have sobbed with affection but I should have had no physical pleasure. Physical pleasure! Is it the lot of man to enjoy it? Ah, if ever in all my life I had once tasted the delights of love to the full, I do not think that my frail existence could have endured them; I should have died on the spot.

So I was burning with love for no object, and it is perhaps love of this sort that is the most exhausting. I was restless, worried by the bad state of my poor Mamma's affairs and by her reckless conduct, which could not fail to bring on her ruin within a short time. My cruel imagination, which always outleaps my misfortunes, repeatedly showed me the approaching tragedy in all its hideous extent and with all its consequences. I already saw myself forcibly separated by poverty from one to whom I had consecrated my life, and without whom I could not enjoy it. That is why my soul was always disturbed. I was devoured alternately by desires and by fears.

* * *

FROM BOOK SIX

[*The Year 1738*]

Here begins the short period of my life's happiness; here I come to those peaceful but transient moments that have given me the right to say I have lived. Precious and ever-regretted moments, begin to run your charming course again for me! Flow one after another through my memory, more slowly, if you can, than you did in your fugitive reality! What shall I do to prolong this touching and simple tale, as I should like to; endlessly to repeat the same words, and no more to weary my readers by their repetition than I wearied myself by beginning them for ever afresh? Indeed if it all consisted of facts, deeds, and words, I could describe it and in a sense convey its meaning. But how can I tell what was neither said, nor done, nor even thought, but only relished and felt, when I cannot adduce any other cause for my happiness but just this feeling? I rose with the sun, and I was happy; I went for walks, and I was happy; I saw Mamma, and I was happy; I left her, and I was happy; I strolled through the woods and over the hills, I wandered in the valleys, I read, I lazed, I worked in the garden, I picked the fruit, I helped in the household, and happiness followed me everywhere; it

---

1. Helen of Troy, a woman of legendary beauty about whom the Trojan War was fought.

lay in no definable object, it was entirely within me; it would not leave me for a single moment.

Nothing that happened to me during that delightful time, nothing that I did, said, or thought all the while it lasted, has slipped from my memory. The period preceding it and following it recur to me at intervals; I recall them irregularly and confusedly; but I recall that time in its entirety, as if it existed still. My imagination, which in my youth always looked forward but now looks back, compensates me with these sweet memories for the hope I have lost for ever. I no longer see anything in the future to attract me; only a return into the past can please me, and these vivid and precise returns into the period of which I am speaking often give me moments of happiness in spite of my misfortunes.[2]

I will present a single example of these memories, which will give some idea of their strength and precision. The first day we went out to sleep at Les Charmettes Mamma was in a sedan chair, and I followed on foot. The road climbed; she was rather heavy and, being afraid of overtiring her porters, she insisted on getting out at about halfway and completing the journey on foot. As she walked she saw something blue in the hedge, and said to me: "Look! There are some periwinkle still in flower." I had never seen a periwinkle, I did not stoop to examine it, and I am too shortsighted to distinguish plants on the ground without doing so. I merely gave it a passing glance, and nearly thirty years elapsed before I saw any periwinkle again, or at least before I noticed any. In 1764, when I was at Cressier with my friend M. du Peyrou, we were climbing a hill, on the top of which he has built a pretty little look out which he rightly calls Belle Vue. I was then beginning to botanize a little and, as I climbed and looked among the bushes, I gave a shout of joy: "Look, there are some periwinkle!," as in fact they were. Du Peyrou noticed my delight, but he did not know its cause; he will learn it, I hope, when one day he reads this. The reader can judge by the effect on me of something so small, the degree to which I have been moved by everything which relates to that stage in my life.

* * *

I should like to know whether such childish notions pass through other men's hearts as sometimes pass through mine. In the midst of my studies and of a life as innocent as any man could lead, I was still frequently disturbed by the fear of Hell, no matter what anyone might say. "In what state am I?" I asked myself. "If I were to die at this moment, should I be damned?" According to my Jansenists[3] the matter was past all doubt; but according to my conscience it seemed quite otherwise. Being always fearful, and now a prey to this cruel uncertainty, I resorted to the most ludicrous expedients to overcome it. I should not hesitate, in fact, to have a man shut up in a madhouse if I saw him acting as I did. One day, when brooding on this melancholy subject, I began throwing stones at the tree trunks, and this with my usual skill, which meant that I hardly hit one. While engaged in this noble exercise, it occurred to me to draw a sort of omen from it, to allay my anxiety. "I am going to throw this stone," I said to myself, "at the tree facing me. If

---

2. Rousseau considered himself persecuted for his writing and his beliefs.   3. Proponents of Jansenism, a doctrine of moral determinism considered heretical by the Catholic Church.

I hit it, it is a sign that I am saved; if I miss it I am damned." As I said this I threw my stone with a trembling hand and a terrible throbbing of the heart, but so accurately that it hit the tree full in the middle; which really was not very difficult, since I had taken care to choose a very large tree very near to me. Since then I have never again doubted my salvation. But as I recall this incident I do not know whether I ought to laugh or weep. You great men, who are most certainly laughing, are welcome to congratulate yourselves. But do not insult my misery, for I feel it most deeply, I assure you.

These troubles and alarms, however, though perhaps an inevitable part of the religious life, were not a permanent state. In general I was calm enough, and the effect on my mind of the prospect of early death was not so much one of sadness as of peaceful languor, which even had its charms. I have recently discovered amongst some old papers a kind of exhortation that I made for myself, congratulating myself upon dying at an age when a man has enough courage in his heart to envisage death, and without having suffered any great physical or mental ills in the course of my life. How right I was! I was frightened by the presentiment of living on only to suffer. It was as if I foresaw the fate that awaited me in my old age. I have never been so near to wisdom as during those happy days. Since I had no great remorse for the past, and was free of all care for the future, the dominant feeling in my heart was a constant enjoyment of the present. Religious people ordinarily possess a limited but very keen sensuality which makes them savor to the full such innocent pleasures as they are allowed. The worldly call this a crime, I do not know why; or rather I know very well. It is because they envy them the enjoyment of simple pleasures for which they have themselves lost the taste. I had that taste, and it delighted me to satisfy it with an easy conscience. My heart, which was still fresh, gave itself to everything with the joy of a child, or rather, if I may say so, with the rapture of an angel; for these quiet pleasures are in very truth as serene as the joys of Paradise. Picnic dinners at Montagnole, suppers in the arbor, the fruit picking, the grape harvest, the evenings stripping the hemp with our servants; all these were for us so many festivals, in which Mamma took as much pleasure as I. Our more solitary walks had a still greater charm, for the heart had then more freedom for its outpourings. One in particular forms a landmark in my memory. It is one which we took on a Saint Louis' day, which was Mamma's name day. We set out alone together in the early morning, after a mass that had been read by a visiting Carmelite at daybreak in a chapel belonging to the house. I had suggested walking along the opposite slope of the valley, where we had not yet been. We had sent our provisions on ahead, for the expedition was to take all day. Mamma, although somewhat round and fat, was not a bad walker, and we went from hill to hill and from wood to wood, sometimes in the sun and sometimes in the shade, resting from time to time and forgetting our cares for hours on end, talking of ourselves, of our relationship, and of the sweetness of our lot, and offering up prayers for its continuance, which were not granted. Everything seemed to conspire to add to the day's happiness. It had rained a short while before. There was no dust, and the streams were full. A little fresh wind shook the leaves. The air was clear and the horizon free from clouds. Serenity prevailed in the heavens, as it prevailed in our hearts. We took our dinner in a peasant's hut, sharing it with his family, who gave us their heartfelt blessings. These poor Savoyards are such good creatures! After dinner we went into the shade of some large trees where Mamma amused herself by botanizing amongst the undergrowth while I gathered dry twigs to boil our coffee. Then she took flowers from the bunch I had gathered for her on the way, and showed me a thousand curious details about their formation. This pleased me greatly and should have given me a taste for botany but the moment had not arrived. I was preoccupied with too many other studies. An idea struck me which diverted my mind from flowers and plants. The state of mind I was in, everything that we had said and done that day, all the objects which had caught my attention, combined to call to my mind the waking dream I had had at Annecy seven or eight years before, which I have already described in its place. The similarities were so striking that as I thought of it I was moved to tears. In an access of emotion I embraced my dear friend. "Mamma, Mamma," I cried passionately. "This day has long been promised to me, I can imagine nothing more beautiful. Thanks to you, my happiness is at its height. May it not decline hereafter! May it last as long as I continue to desire it, and it will only end with my life."

* * *

JOHANN WOLFGANG VON GOETHE
1749–1832

Recasting the ancient legend of Faust, Johann Wolfgang von Goethe created a powerful symbol of the Romantic imagination in all its aspiration and anxiety. Faust himself, central character of the epic drama, emerges as a Romantic hero, ever testing the limits of possibility. Yet to achieve his ends he must make a contract with the Devil—as if to say that giving full scope to imagination necessarily partakes of sin.

Goethe's *Faust* (Part I, 1808; Part II, 1832) constituted the crowning masterpiece of a life rich in achievement. Goethe exemplifies the nineteenth-century meaning of *genius*. Accomplished as poet, dramatist, novelist, and autobiographer, he also practiced law, served as a diplomat, and pursued scientific research. He had a happy childhood in Frankfurt, after which he studied law at Leipzig and then at Strasbourg, where in 1770–71 he met Johann Gottfried von Herder, a leader of a new literary movement called Sturm und Drang (Storm and Stress). Participants in this movement emphasized the importance of revolt against established standards; they interested Goethe in such newly discovered forms as the folk song and in the literary vitality of Shakespeare, as opposed to more formally constricted writers.

During the brief period when he practiced law, after an unhappy love affair, Goethe wrote *The Sorrows of Young Werther* (1774), a novel of immense influence in establishing the image of the introspective, self-pitying, melancholy Romantic hero. In 1775 he accepted an invitation to the court of Charles Augustus, duke of Saxe-Weimar. He remained in Weimar for the rest of his life, for ten years serving the duke as chief minister. A trip to Italy from 1786 to 1788 aroused his interest in classic sources. He wrote dramas based on classic texts, most notably *Iphigenia in Tauris* (1787); novels (for example, *Elective Affinities*, 1809) that pointed the way to the psychological novel; lyric poetry; and an important autobiography, *Poetry and Truth*

(1811–33). He also did significant work in botany and physiology. Increasingly famous, he became in his own lifetime a legendary figure; all Europe flocked to Weimar to visit him.

The legend of Dr. Faustus (the real Johannes Faustus, a scholar, lived from 1480 to 1540), in most versions a seeker after forbidden knowledge, had attracted other writers before Goethe. The most important previous literary embodiment of the tale was Christopher Marlowe's *Doctor Faustus* (ca. 1588), a drama ending in its protagonist's damnation as a result of his search for illegitimate power through learning. Goethe's Faust meets no such fate. Pursuing not knowledge but experience, he embodies the ideal of limitless aspiration in all its glamour and danger. His contract with Mephistopheles provides that he will die at the moment he declares himself satisfied, content to rest in the present; he stakes his life and his salvation on his capacity ever to yearn for something beyond.

In Part I of Goethe's play, the protagonist's vision of the impossible locates itself specifically in the figure of Margarete (or its diminutive, *Gretchen*), the simple, innocent girl whom he possesses physically but with whom he can never attain total union. In a speech epitomizing Romantic attitudes toward nature and toward emotion (especially the emotion of romantic love), Faust responds to his beloved's question "Do you believe in God?"

> The sky it arches over us,
> The earth stands firm beneath our feet,
> And don't the stars, looking with friendly eyes,
> Eternally mount aloft?
> And don't I look at you, don't
> Our eyes meet and mingle?
> And all there is, all things, don't they
> Strain yearningly toward you,
> Acting and working invisibly,
> Yet visible all around you,
> An everlasting mystery?
> Fill heart with it until heart overflows
> In an ecstasy of blissful feeling,
> Which then call what you please,
> Happiness or love or heart or God!
> I know no name for it;
> Feeling is everything,
> The name just noise, just vapor,
> Dimming the heavenly fire.

The idea of happiness here identifies an unnameable feeling derived from experience of nature and of romantic love, possibly identical with God, but valued partly for its very vagueness.

Modern readers may feel that Faust bullies Margarete, allowing her no reality except as instrument for his desires. In a poignant moment early in the play, interrupting Faust's rhapsody about her "meekness" and "lowliness," Margarete says, "You'll think of me for a moment or two." Faust seems incapable of any such awareness, too busy inventing his loved one to see her as she is. He dramatically represents the "egotistical sublime," with a kind of imaginative grandeur inseparable from his utter absorption in the wonder of his own being, his own experience.

Yet the action of Part I turns on Faust's development of just that consciousness of another's reality that seemed impossible for him, and Margarete is the agent of his development. In the great final scene—Margarete in prison, intermittently mad, condemned to death for murdering her illegitimate child by Faust—the woman again appeals to the man to think about her, to *know* her: "Have you any idea who you're letting go free?" Her anguish, his responsibility for it, force themselves on Faust. He wishes he had never been born: his lust for experience has resulted in this terrible culpability, this agonizing loss. At the final moment of separation, with Margaret's spiritual redemption proclaimed from above, Faust implicitly acknowledges the full reality of the woman he has lost and thus, even though he departs with Mephistopheles, distinguishes himself from his satanic mentor. Mephistopheles in his nature cannot grasp a reality utterly apart from his own; he can recognize only what belongs to him. Faust, at least fleetingly, realizes the otherness of the woman and the value of what he has lost.

Mephistopheles, at the outset witty and powerful in his own imagination, gradually reveals his limitations. In the "Prologue in Heaven," the Devil seems energetic, perceptive, enterprising, fearless: as the Lord says, a "railer," apparently more "trying" than malign. His bargain with the Lord turns on his belief in the essentially "beastly" nature of humankind: like Gulliver's Houyhnhnm master, he emphasizes the human misuse of reason. Although the scene is modeled on the interchange between God and Satan in the Book of Job, it differs significantly in that the Lord gives an explicit reason for allowing the Tempter to function. "As long as man strives, he is bound to err," He says, but He adds that Mephistopheles's value is in prodding humanity into action. The introductory scene thus suggests that Mephistopheles will function as an agent of salvation rather than damnation. The Devil's subsequent exchanges with Faust, in Mephistopheles's mind predicated on his own superior knowledge and comprehension, gradually make one realize that the man in significant respects knows more than does the Devil. Mephistopheles, for example, can understand Faust's desire for Margarete only in sexual terms. His witty cynicism seems more and more inadequate to the actual situation. By the end of Part I, Faust's suffering has enlarged him; but from the beginning, his capacity for sympathy marks his potential superiority to the Devil.

The "Walpurgis Night" section, with the "Walpurgis Night's Dream," marks a stage in Faust's education and an extreme moment in the play's dramatic structure. Goethe here allows himself to indulge in unrestrained fantasy—grotesque, obscene, comic, with an explosion of satiric energy in the dream. The shifting tone and reference of these passages embody ways in which the diabolic might be thought to operate in human terms. While Margarete suffers the consequences of her sin, Faust experiences the ambiguous freedom of the imagination, always at the edge of horror.

The pattern of Faust's moral development in Part I prepares the reader for a nontragic denouement to the drama as a whole. In Part II, which he worked on for some thirty years, completing it only the year before his death, Goethe moves from the individual to the social. Faust marries Helen of Troy, who gives birth to Euphorion, symbol of new humanity. He turns soldier to save a kingdom; he reclaims land from the sea; finally, he rests contented in a vision of happy community generated by the industry of humankind. Mephistopheles thinks this his moment of victory: now Faust has declared himself satisfied. But since his satisfaction depends still on aspiration, on a dream of the future, the angels rescue him at last and take him to heaven.

One cannot read *Faust* with twenty-first-century expectations of what a play should be like. This is above all *poetic* drama, to be read with pleasure in the richness of its language, the fertility and daring of its imagination. Although its cast of characters natural and supernatural and its sequence of supernaturally generated events are far from "realistic," it addresses problems still very much with us. How can individual ambition and desire be reconciled with responsibility to others? Does a powerful imagination—an artist's, say, or a scientist's—justify its possessor in ignoring social obligations? Goethe investigates such perplexing issues in symbolic terms, drawing his readers into personal involvement by playing on their emotions even as he questions the proper functions and limitations of commitment to desire—that form of emotional energy that leads to the greatest human achievements but involves the constant danger of debilitating narcissism.

PRONOUNCING GLOSSARY

The following list uses common English syllables and stress accents to provide rough equivalents of selected words whose pronunciation may be unfamiliar to the general reader.

Altmayer: *ahlt'-maier*

Auerbach: *aw'-er-bahk*

Elend: *ay'-lend*

encheirisis naturae: *en-kai-ray'-sis nah-tu'-rai*

Euphorion: *oy-foh'-ree-on*

Faust: *fowst*

Goethe: *gur'te*

Leipzig: *laip'-zig*

Proktophantasmist: *prohk-toh-fan-tas'-mist*

Schierke: *sheer'ke*

Sturm und Drang: *shturm unt drahng*

Te Deum: *tay day'-um*

Wagner: *vahg'-ner*

Walpurgis: *vahl-poor'-gis*

Werther: *vayr'-ter*

Zenien: *tsay'-nee-en*

Faust[1]

Prologue in Heaven[2]

THE LORD. THE HEAVENLY HOST. Then MEPHISTOPHELES.[3] *The three Archangels advance to front.*

RAPHAEL   The sun blares out his age-old music
In contest with each brother sphere,
Marching around and around, with steps of thunder,
His appointed circuit, year after year.
To see him lends us angels strength,   5
But what he *is*, oh who can say?
The inconceivably great works are great
As on the first creating day.

GABRIEL   And swift, past all conception swift,
The jeweled globe spins on its axletree,   10
Celestial brightness alternating
With shuddering night's obscurity.
Against earth's deep-based precipices
The broad-running ocean tides are hurled,
And rock and sea together hurtle   15
With the eternally turning world.

MICHAEL   And hurricanes, contending, roar
From sea to land, from land to sea,
Linking in tremendous circuit
A chain of blazing energy.   20
The lightning bolt makes ready for

---

1. Translated by Martin Greenberg.   2. The scene is patterned on Job 1.6–12 and 2.1–6.   3. The origin of the name remains debatable. It may come from Hebrew, Persian, or Greek, with such meanings as "destroyer-liar," "no friend of Faust," and "no friend of light."

The thunderclap a ruinous way—
Yet Lord, your servants reverence
The stiller motions of your day.

ALL THREE　From seeing this we draw our strength,　25
For what You *are*, oh who can say?
And all your great works are as great
As on the first creating day.

MEPHISTOPHELES　Lord, since you've stopped by here again, wanting to
　　　know
How all of us are doing, for which we're grateful,　30
And since you've never made me feel *de trop,*
Well, here I am too with your other people.
I hope you will excuse my lack of eloquence,
Though this whole host, I'm sure, will think me stupid;
Coming from me, high-sounding sentiments　35
Would only make you laugh—that is, provided
Laughing was a thing that you still did.
About suns and worlds I don't know beans, what I
Know is, how men and women find it hard to live.
Earth's little god's shaped out of the same old clay,　40
He's the same queer fish he was on the first day.
He'd be much better off, in my opinion, without
The bit of Heavenly Light you dealt him out.
He calls it Reason, and the use he puts it to?
To act more beastly than beasts ever do.　45
To me he seems, begging Your Worship's pardon,
Like a long-legged grasshopper all of whose leaping
Only lands him back in the grass again chirping
The tune he's always chirped. And if only he'd
Stay put in the grass! But no! It's an absolute need　50
With him to creep and crawl and strain and sweat
And stick his nose in every pile of dirt.

THE LORD　Is that all you have got to say to me?
Is that all you can do, accuse eternally?
Is nothing ever right for you down there, sir?　55

MEPHISTOPHELES　No, nothing, Lord—all's just as bad as ever.
I really pity humanity's myriad miseries,
I swear I hate tormenting the poor ninnies.

THE LORD　Do you know Faust?

MEPHISTOPHELES　　　　　　　　The Doctor?[4]

THE LORD　　　　　　　　　　　　My good servant!

MEPHISTOPHELES　You[5] don't say! Well, he serves you in a funny way,　60
Finds meat and drink, the fool, in nothing earthly,
The ferment in him drives him on incessantly,
He himself is half aware he's crazy;
From Heaven he must have the brightest stars,
From earth the most ecstatic raptures,　65
And all that's near at hand or far and wide

---

4. Of philosophy.　5. In the German text, Mephistopheles shifts from *du* to *ihr*, indicating his lack of respect for God.

Leaves your good servant quite unsatisfied.
THE LORD   If today he's still confused, a soul astray,
My light shall lead him into the true way.
When the sapling greens, the gardener can feel certain   70
Flower and fruit will follow in due season.
MEPHISTOPHELES   Would you care to bet on that? You'll lose, I tell you,
If you'll just give me leave to lead the fellow
Gently down my broad, my primrose path.
THE LORD   As long as Faustus walks the earth   75
I won't, I promise, interfere.
As long as man strives, he is bound to err.
MEPHISTOPHELES   Well thanks, Lord, for it's not the dead and gone
I like dealing with. What I prefer, oh much,
Are round and rosy cheeks. When corpses come   80
A-knocking, pardon me, I'm out to lunch;
My way of working's the cat's way with a mouse.
THE LORD   So it's agreed, you have my full consent.
Induce this soul to defect from its true source
And if you're able, lead him along, Hell bent   85
With you, upon the downward course—
Then blush for shame when you find you must admit:
Stumbling along as he must, through darkness and confusion,
A good man still knows which road is the right one.
MEPHISTOPHELES   Of course, of course! Yet I'll seduce him from it   90
Soon enough. I'm not afraid I'll lose my bet.
And after I have won it,
You won't, I trust, begrudge me
My whoops of triumph, shouts of victory.
Dust he'll eat   95
And find that he enjoys it, exactly like
That old aunt of mine, the famous snake.
THE LORD   There too you may feel free, you have carte blanche.
You know, I've never hated fellows like yourself.
I find, of all the spirits of negation,   100
You railers the least trying to my patience.
Man's very quick to slacken in his effort,
What he likes best is Sunday peace and quiet;
So I'm glad to give him a devil—for his own good,
To prod and poke and incite him as a devil should.   105
[To the ANGELS] But you who are God's true and faithful children—
Delight in the world's wealth of living beauty!
May that which moves all, ever changing, living,
Ring you around with smiling love, benignly,
And the fitfulness, the inconstancy, of appearance,   110
Seize it in thoughts that raise it into permanence.
        [The Heavens close, the ARCHANGELS withdraw.]
MEPHISTOPHELES   I like to see the Old Man now and then,
And take good care I don't fall out with him.
How very decent of a Lord Celestial
To talk man to man with the Devil of all people.   115

Part I

NIGHT

In a narrow, high-vaulted Gothic room, FAUST, *seated restlessly in an armchair at his desk.*

FAUST I've studied, alas, philosophy,
    Law and medicine, recto and verso,
    And how I regret it, theology also,
    Oh God, how hard I've slaved away,
    With what result? Poor fool that I am,   120
    I'm no whit wiser than when I began!
    I've got a Master of Arts degree,
    On top of that a Ph.D.,
    For ten long years, around and about,
    Upstairs, downstairs, in and out,   125
    I've led my students by the nose
    To what conclusion?—that nobody knows,
    Or ever can know, the tiniest crumb!
    Which is why I feel completely undone.
        Of course I'm cleverer than these stuffed shirts,   130
    These Doctors, Masters, Jurists, Priests;
    I'm not bothered by a doubt or a scruple,
    I'm not afraid of Hell or the Devil—
    But the consequence is, my mirth's all gone;
    No longer can I fool myself   135
    I am able to teach men
    How to be better, love true worth;
    I've got no money or property,
    Worldly honors or celebrity;
    A dog wouldn't put up with this life!   140
    Which is why I've turned to magic,
    Seeking to know, by ways occult,
    From ghostly mouths, many a secret;
    So I no longer need to sweat
    Painfully explaining what   145
    I don't know anything about;
    So I may penetrate the power
    That holds the universe together,
    Behold the source whence all proceeds
    And deal no more in words, words, words.   150

    O full moon, melancholy-bright,
    Friend I've watched for, many a night,
    Till your quiet-shining face
    Appeared above my high-piled desk—
    If this were only the last time   155
    You looked down on my pain!
    If only I might stray at will

Beneath your light, high on the hill,
Haunt with spirits upland hollows,
Fade with you in dim-lit meadows,   160
And soul no longer gasping in
The stink of learning's midnight lamp,
Bathe in your dews till well again!

But oh, unhappy man that I am,
Isn't this your familiar prison?   165
Damned musty-smelling hole in the wall
Where even the golden light of Heaven
Must struggle hard to force its way through
The dim panes of the stained-glass window.
Yes, here you sit walled in by books   170
Stacked up to the shadowy vault,
Books worm-eaten, covered with dust,
With rolls of paper, all smoke-blackened,
Pushed and wedged and stuck between them,
With vessels, flasks, retorts, and beakers   175
Filling all the shelves and drawers,
And adding to the dense confusion
Your family's ancient furnishings.
Call this a world, this world you live in?

Can you still wonder why your heart   180
Should tighten in your breast so anxiously?
Why your every impulse is stopped short
By an inexplicable misery?
Instead of the living house of Nature
God created man to dwell in,   185
Dust, mold, they are what surround you,
Dogs' bones, a human skeleton.

Escape outdoors! Breathe the fresh air!
And this strange book of secret lore
By Nostradamus'[6] own hand—   190
What better help to master the secrets
Of how the stars turn in their orbits,
From Nature learn to understand
The spirits' power to speak to spirits.
Sitting here and racking your brains   195
To puzzle out the sacred signs—
What a sterile, futile business!
Spirits, I feel your presence around me:
Announce yourselves if you hear me!
      [*He opens the book and his eye encounters the sign of the Macrocosm.*[7]]

6. The Latin name of the French astrologer and physician Michel de Notredame (1503–1566). His collection of rhymed prophecies, *The Centuries*, appeared in 1555.   7. The great world (literal trans.); the universe as a whole. It represents the ordered, harmonious universe in its totality.

The pure bliss flooding all my senses 200
Seeing this! Through every nerve and vein
I feel youth's fiery, fresh spirit race again.
Was it a god marked out these signs
By which my agitated bosom's stilled,
By which my bleak heart's filled with joy, 205
By whose mysterious agency
The powers of Nature all around me stand revealed?
Am *I* a god? All's bright as day!
By these pure brush strokes I can see,
At my soul's feet, great Nature unconcealed. 210
And the sage's words—I understand them, finally:
"The spirit world is not barred shut,
It's your own mind, your dead heart!
Stand up unappalled, my scholar,
And bathe your breast in the rose of Aurora!" 215
[*He contemplates the sign.*]
How all is woven one, uniting,
Each in the other living, working!
How Heavenly Powers rise, descend,
Passing gold vessels from hand to hand!
On wings that scatter sweet-smelling blessings, 220
Everywhere they post in earth
And make a universal harmony sound forth!
Oh, what a sight! But a sight, and no more!
How seize you and hold you, infinite Nature?
Find the life-giving fountains, your breasts, that sustain 225
Both the earth and the heavens, breasts at which my breast,
So dried up, a desert, is yearning to nurse—
You flow, *overflow*, yet I go on thirsting in vain.
[*Morosely, he turns the pages of the book and comes on the sign of the*
SPIRIT OF EARTH.[8]]
What a different effect this sign has on me!
You, Spirit of Earth, are closer to me, 230
Already fresh lifeblood pours through every vein,
Already I glow as if from new wine—
Now I have the courage to dare
To go out into the world and bear
The ill and well of life, to battle 235
Storms, and when the ship splits, not to tremble.

How the air grows thick overhead—
The moon's put out her light,
The lamp flame looks like dying.
Vapors eddy and drift— 240
Red flashes, leaping, dazzle—

8. This figure seems to be a symbol for the energy of terrestrial nature—neither good nor bad, merely powerful.

Fear, shuddering down from the vault,
Seizes me by the throat!
Spirit I have invoked, hovering near:
Reveal yourself! 245
How all my senses fumble toward, founder in
Never-experienced feelings!
Spirit, I feel I am yours, body and breath!
Appear! Oh, you must! Though it costs me my life!
    [*He seizes the book and pronounces the* SPIRIT's *mystic spell. A red flame*
    flashes, in the midst of which the SPIRIT *appears.*]

SPIRIT   Who's calling? 250
FAUST [*Averting his face*]   Overpowering! Dreadful!
SPIRIT   Potently you've drawn me here,
   A parched mouth sucking at my sphere.
   And now—?
FAUST   Oh, you're unbearable!
SPIRIT   You're breathless from your implorations 255
   To see my face, to hear me speak,
   I've yielded to your supplications
   And here I am.—Well, in a funk
   I find the superman! I come at your bidding
   And you're struck dumb! Is this the mind 260
   That builds a whole interior world, doting
   On its own creation, puffed to find
   Itself quite on a par, the equal,
   Of us spirits? Wherever is that Faust
   Who urged himself just now with all 265
   His strength on me, made such a fuss?
   You're Faust? The one who at my breath's
   Least touch, shudders to his depths,
   A worm who wriggles away in terror?
FAUST   I shrink back from you, abject and fearful? 270
   Yes, I'm called so, called Faust—your equal!
SPIRIT   I surge up and down
   In the tides of being,
   Drive forward and back
   In the shocks of men's striving! 275
   I am birth and the grave,
   An eternal ocean,
   A web changing momently,
   A life burning hotly.
   Thus seated at time's whirring loom 280
   I weave the Godhead's living gown.
FAUST   We're equals, I know! I feel so close to you, near,
   You busy spirit ranging everywhere!
SPIRIT   It's your idea of me you're equal to,
   Not me! [*Vanishes.*] 285
FAUST [*Deflated*]   Not you?
  Then who?
  Me, made in God's own image,

Not even equal to you?
    [*A knocking*]
Death! My famulus[9]—I know that knock.   290
Finis my supremest moment—worse luck!
That visions richer than I could have guessed
Should be scattered by a shuffling Dryasdust!
    [WAGNER *in dressing gown and nightcap, carrying a lamp.* FAUST *turns
    around impatiently.*]

WAGNER   Excuse me, sir, but wasn't that
    Your voice I heard declaiming? A Greek tragedy,   295
    I'm sure. Well, that's an art that comes in handy
    Nowadays. I'd love to master it.
    People say, how often I have heard it,
    Actors could really give lessons to the clergy.
FAUST   Yes, when clergymen go in for acting—   300
    Something I have seen in more than one case.
WAGNER   Oh dear, to be so shut up in one's study,
    Seeing the world only now and then, on holiday,
    And only from far off, as if through a spyglass—
    How can one ever teach it what's the right way?   305
FAUST   You can't—unless you speak with feeling's own
    True voice, unless your words are from
    The soul and by their spontaneous power,
    Seize with delight the soul of your hearer.
    But no! Stick in your seats, you fellows!   310
    Paste bits and pieces together, cook up
    A beggar's stew from others' leftovers,
    Over a flame you've sweated to coax up
    From your own little heap of smoldering ashes,
    Filling with wonder all the jackasses,   315
    If that's the kind of stuff your taste favors—
    But you'll never get heart to cleave to heart
    Unless you speak from your own heart.
WAGNER   Still and all, a good delivery is what
    Makes the orator. I'm far behind in that art.   320
FAUST   Advance yourself in an honest way.
    Don't try to be a performing ape!
    Good sense, good understanding, they
    Are quite enough, they are their own art.
    When you have something serious   325
    To say, what need is there to hunt
    Around for fancy words and phrases?
    All those speeches polished up
    With bits and pieces collected out
    Of every tongue and race, are about   330
    As bracing as the foggy autumnal breeze
    Swaying the last leaves on the trees.
WAGNER   Dear God, but art is long

---

9. Assistant to a medieval scholar.

And our life—lots shorter.
Often in the middle of my labor   335
My confidence and courage falter.
How hard it is to master all the stuff
For dealing with each and every source.
And before you've traveled half the course,
Poor devil, you have gone and left this life.   340
FAUST   Parchment, tell me—that's the sacred fount
You drink out of, to slake your eternal thirst?
The only true refreshment that exists
You get from where? Yourself—where all things start.
WAGNER   But sir, it's such a pleasure, isn't it,   345
To enter into another age's spirit,
To see what thinkers long before us thought
And measure how far since then we have got.
FAUST   As far as to the stars, no doubt!
Your history, why, it's a joke;   350
Bygone times are a seven-sealed book.[1]
The thing you call the spirit of the past,
What is it? Nothing but your own poor spirit
With the past reflected in it.
And it's pathetic, what's to be seen in your mirror!   355
One look and I have to beat a quick retreat—
A trash can, strewn attic, junk-filled cellar,
At best it is a blood-and-thunder thriller
Improved with the most high-minded sentiments
Exactly suited for mouthing by marionettes.   360
WAGNER   But the world we're in! The hearts and minds of men!
Surely all of us want to know about them.
FAUST   Yes, know as the world knows knowing!
Who wants to know the real truth, tell me?
Those, few with vision, feeling, understanding,   365
Who failed to stand guard, most unwisely,
Over their tongues, speaking their minds and hearts
For the mob to hear—you know what's been their fate:
They were crucified, burnt, torn to bits.
But we must break off, friend, it's getting late.   370
WAGNER   I love serious conversation; to improve
One's mind so, I'd stay up all night gladly.
But it's Easter Sunday, sir, in the morning,
And perhaps I may ask you a question or two then, if you're willing?
I've studied hard, yes, studied diligently,   375
I know a lot, but still, I aim at knowing everything. [*Exit.*]
FAUST [*Alone*]   How such fellows keep their hopes up is a wonder!
Their attention forever occupied with trivialities,
Digging greedily in the ground for treasure,
And when they've turned a worm up—what ecstacies!   380

---

1. Revelation 5.1.

That banal, commonplace human accents
Should fill air just now filled with spirits' voices!
Still, this one time you've earned my thanks,
You sorriest of human specimens.
You snatched me out of the grip of a dejection   385
So profound, I was nearly driven off
My head. So gigantic was the apparition,
It made me feel no bigger than a dwarf—

Me, the one made in the very image of God,
Fully persuaded the mirror of eternal truth   390
At last lay in his reach, already basking in
The heavenly light and glory, all earthliness cast off;
Me, higher placed than the cherubim, imagining
His own strength already poured freely,
Divinely creative, through Nature's great body! Well, now   395
I must pay for it: a thunderous word and I am laid low.

No, I can't claim we are equals, presumptuously!
Though I was strong enough to draw you down to me,
Holding on to you was another matter entirely.
In that exalted-humbling moment of pure delight   400
I felt myself at once both small and great.
And then you thrust me remorselessly back
Into uncertainty, which is all of humanity's fate.
Who'll teach me what to seek, what to shun?
Yield, should I, to that burning desire of mine?   405
Alas, what we do as much as what's done to us
Cramps and obstructs our entire life's progress.

The noblest thoughts our minds are able to entertain
Are undermined by a corrupting grossness;
When we've managed a bit of the good of this world for ourselves 410
Then the better's dismissed as a fairy tale or confidence game;
Those radiant sentiments which were once life itself to us
Grow pale and expire in the glare of the world's busyness.

There was a time when bold imagination
Pitched her flight as high as God's own station,   415
But now that everything I took such joy in
Has shipwrecked for me in time's maelstrom,
She's quite content to cower in a narrow space.
In our heart of hearts Care has her nesting place
And there she does her worst,   420
Dithering nervously, poisoning pleasure and peace,
Masking herself as genuine concern
For house and home, for wife and children,
In fear of fire and flood, violence and mayhem;
You shrink back in terror from imagined blows   425
And weep over losing what you never in fact lose.

Oh no, I'm no god, only too well do I know it!
A worm's what I am, wriggling through the dust
And finding his nourishment in it,
Whom the wayfarer treads underfoot.   430

These high walls with their shelves and niches—
Dust is what shrinks them to a stifling cell;
This moth-eaten world with its trash and its trinkets—
It is the reason I feel shut up in jail.
And here I'll discover the things I most lack?   435
Devour thousands of books so as to learn, shall I,
Mankind has always been stretched on the rack,
With now and then somebody, somewhere, who's happy?
    You, empty skull there, smirking so, I know why!
Your brain, once as whirling as mine is,   440
Seeking the bright day, longing for truth,
Blundered about, lost in onerous darkness, just as wretchedly.
And all that apparatus—how I feel you are mocking me,
With your wheels and cylinders, cams, and ratchets!
I stood at the door, certain you were the key;   445
But the key, though cut intricately, couldn't unlatch it.
Great Nature, so mysterious even in broad day,
Doesn't let you unveil her, plead how you may.
And if she won't allow you one glimpse of her mystery,
You'll never compel her with all your machinery.   450

Old instruments I've never touched,
You're here, and why?—because my father[2] used you.
And you, old scrolls, have gathered soot
For as long as the lamp's smoked on this table.
Much better to have squandered the little I've got   455
Than find myself sweating under its weight.
It's from our fathers, what we inherit,
To make it ours truly, we've got to earn it.
What's never used weighs like lead;
What's useful responds to a living need.   460

But why do I find I must stare in that corner,
Is that bottle a magnet enchanting my sight?
Why is everything all at once lovely and luminous,
Like woods when the moon's up and floods them with light?

Vial, I salute you, O rare, O precious!   465
And reverently bring you down from the shelf,
Honoring in you man's cunning and craft.
Quintessence of easeful sleeping potions,
Pure distillation of subtle poisons,
Do your master the kindness that lies in your power!   470

2. Later we find that Faust's father was a doctor of medicine.

One look at you and my agony lessens,
One touch and my feverish straining grows calmer
And my tight-stretched spirit bit by bit slackens.
The glassy waters glitter before me,
My way is clear—into Ocean's immensity,   475
A new day is dawning, a new shore beckons.

A fiery chariot, bird-winged, swoops down on me,
I am ready to follow new roads through the ether,
Aloft into new spheres of purest activity.
An existence so exalted, a rapture so godlike—   480
Does the worm of a minute ago deserve it?
No matter. Resolution! Turn your back bravely
On the sunlight, sweet sunlight, of our earth forever!
Fling wide open those dark gates, defiantly,
Which the whole world skulks past with averted heads!   485
The time has come to disprove by deeds,
Because the gods are great, man's a derision,
To cringe back no more from that black pit
Whose unspeakable tortures are your own invention,
To struggle toward that narrow gate   490
Around which all Hellfire's darkly flaming,
To take resolutely the last step,
Even at the risk of utter extinction.

And now let me take this long forgotten
Crystal wine cup down from its case.   495
Once it shone at our family feasts,
Making the solemn guests' faces brighten
When it went round with the lively toasts.
The figures artfully cut in the crystal,
Which it was the duty of all at the table,   500
In turn, to make up rhymes about,
Then drain the cup at a single draught—
How they recall many nights of my youth!
But now there's no passing you on to my neighbor
Or thinking up rhymes to parade my quick wit;[3]   505
Here is a juice that is quick too—to intoxicate,
A brownish liquid, see, filling the beaker,
Chosen by me, by me mixed together,
My last drink! Which now I lift up in festive greeting
To the bright new day I can see dawning!   510

    [*He raises the cup to his lips. Bells peal, a choir bursts into song.*]

CHORUS OF ANGELS
    Christ is arisen!
    Joy to poor mortals
    By their own baleful,

---

3. Faust here alludes to the drinking of toasts. The maker of a toast often produced impromptu rhymes.

    Inherited, subtle
    Failings imprisoned.   515
FAUST What deep-sounding peals, what caroling voices
  Arrest the glass before I can drink?
  Is that solemn ringing already proclaiming
  The glorious advent of Holy Week?
  Already intoning, choirs, are you,   520
  What angels' lips sang, oh comforting chant,
  High above the sepulcher's darkness,
  Certain assurance of a new covenant?
CHORUS OF WOMEN
    With sweet-smelling spices
    We laid out the man,   525
    We, his most faithful ones,
    Here at the tomb;
    In linen we wound him
    And bound up his hair—
    Oh, what do we find now?   530
    Christ is not here.
CHORUS OF ANGELS
    Christ is arisen!
    Blest is the man of love,
    He who in triumph passed
    Earth's hard and bitter test,   535
    Bringing salvation.
FAUST But why do you seek me out in my dust,
  You music of Heaven, mild and magnificent?
  Ring out where men and women are simple,
  I hear your message but can't believe it—   540
  And where belief's lacking, no miracle's possible.
  The spheres whence those glad tidings come
  Are not for me to try and enter—
  Yet all's familiar from when I was young
  And back to life I feel myself summoned.   545
  Years ago the Heavenly Love
  Flew down to me in the Sabbath stillness
  And caught me in His strong embrace;
  Oh, with what meaning the deep bells sounded,
  Praying to Jesus, oh what bliss!   550
  A yearning so sweet it was not to be fathomed
  Drove me out to the woods and the fields,
  Inside my soul a new world opened
  And my cheeks were streaming with scalding tears!
  Your song gave the signal for the sports we rejoiced in   555
  When the holiday springtime gladdened the world:
  Innocent childhood's remembered feelings
  Hold me back from the last step of all.
  O sound away, sound away, sweet songs of Heaven!
  Tears fill my eyes, earth claims me again!   560

CHORUS OF DISCIPLES

    He who was buried
    Is already ascended,
    The one who on this earth
    Lived most sublimely, then
    Rose up in glory   565
    So he may take part in
    The bliss of creating.
    But here on the earth
    We huddle afflicted;
    He has left us, his children,   570
    Desponding, behind—Master,
    Must we bewail your good fortune?

CHORUS OF ANGELS

    Christ is arisen
    From the womb of decay,
    Strike off your fetters   575
    And shout for joy!
    Who praise him with works
    Of loving-kindness
    By feeding the hungry,
    By preaching him east and west,   580
    By promising blessedness—
    You have the Master near,
    You have him here, right here!

OUTSIDE THE CITY GATE

All sorts of PEOPLE *out walking.*

SOME APPRENTICES   Where are you fellows off to?
OTHERS   To the hunters' lodge—over that way.   585
FIRST BUNCH   Well, we're on our way to the old mill.
ONE APPRENTICE   The river inn—that's what I say.
SECOND APPRENTICE   But the walk there's not much of a pleasure.
SECOND BUNCH   And what about you?
THIRD APPRENTICE   I'll stick with the rest of us here.
FOURTH APPRENTICE   Let's go up to the village. There, I can promise
    you   590
    The best-looking girls, the best-tasting beer,
    And some very good roughhousing too.
FIFTH APPRENTICE   My, but aren't you greedy!
    You'd like your hide tanned still a third time?
    I'll never go there, it's too scary.   595
SERVANT GIRL   No, no, I'm turning back, now let me be.
ANOTHER   We're sure to find him at those poplar trees.
FIRST GIRL   Is that supposed to make me jump for joy?
    It's you he wants to walk with, wants to please,
    And you're the one he'll dance with. Fine   600

For you. But what's it to me, your good time?
THE OTHER   He's not alone, I know, today. He said
He'd bring his friend—you know, that curlyhead.
A STUDENT   Those fast-stepping girls there, look at the heft of them!
Into action, old fellow, we're taking out after them.   605
Beer with body, tobacco with a bite,
And red-cheeked housemaids in their Sunday best
Are just the things to make your Hermann happiest.
A BURGHER'S DAUGHTER   Oh look over there, such nice-looking boys!
Really, I think they are so outrageous,   610
They have their pick of the nicest girls
And instead they run after overweight wenches.
SECOND STUDENT [To the first]   Hold up, go slow! I see two more,
And the pair of them dressed so pretty, so proper.
But I know that one! She lives next door,   615
And she, I must tell you, I think I could care for.
They loiter along, eyes lowered decorously,
But after saying no twice, they'll jump at our company.
FIRST STUDENT   No, no—all that bowing and scraping, it makes me feel ill
     at ease,
If we don't get a move on we'll lose our two birds in the bushes!   620
The work-reddened hand that swings the broom Saturdays
On Sundays knows how to give the softest caresses.
A BURGHER   No, you can have him, our new Mayor,
Since he took office he's been a dictator,
All he's done is make the town poorer,   625
Every day I get madder and madder,
When he says a thing's so, not a peep, not a murmur
Dare we express—and the taxes climb higher.
A BEGGAR [Singing]
     Good sirs and all you lovely ladies,
     Healthy in body and handsome in dress,   630
     Turn, oh turn your eyes on me, please,
     And pity the beggarman's distress!
     Must I grind the organ bootlessly?
     Only the charitable know true joy.
     This day when all the world make merry,   635
     Oh make it for me a harvest day.
ANOTHER BURGHER   On a Sunday or holiday nothing in all my experience
Beats talking about war and rumors of war,
When leagues away, in Turkey, for instance,
Armies are wading knee deep in gore.   640
You stand at the window, take long pulls at your schooner,
And watch the gaily colored boats glide past,
And then at sunset go home in the best of humor
And praise God for the blessings of his peace.
THIRD BURGHER   Yes, neighbor, yes, exactly my opinion.   645
Let them go and beat each other's brains in,
Let them turn the whole world upside down,
As long as things are just as always here at home.

OLD CRONE [*To the* BURGHERS' DAUGHTERS]   Well, aren't we the smart ones!
 And so pretty and young!
I'd like to see the man who could resist you.   650
But not so proud, my dears! And never fear—I'm mum.
Oh, I know how to get what you want for you.

BURGHER'S DAUGHTER   Agatha, come, we've got to leave!
I'm afraid of being seen with that witchwoman.
Oh dear, and only last St. Andrew's Eve[4]   655
She showed me in a glass my very own one.

HER FRIEND   And mine she showed me in a crystal ball,
Looking a soldier, with cocky friends around him.
And though I seek him everywhere,
It seems that I shall never find him.   660

SOLDIERS
    Castles have ramparts,
    Great walls and towers,
    Girls turn their noses up
    At soldier-boy lovers—
    We'll make both ours!   665
    Boldly adventure
    And rake in the pay!

    Hear the shrill bugle
    Summon to battle,
    Forward to rapture   670
    Or forward to ruin!
    Oh what a struggle!
    Our life—oh how stirring!
    Haughty girls and great castles,
    We'll make them surrender!   675
    Boldly adventure
    And rake in the pay!
    —And after, the soldiers
    Go marching away.

        FAUST *and* WAGNER

FAUST   The streams put off their icy mantle   680
Under the springtime's kindly smile;
Hope's green banner flies in the valley;
White-bearded winter, old and frail,
Retreats into his mountain fastness,
And still retreating, down he sends   685
Feeble volleys of sleet showers,
Whitening in patches the green plains.
But the sun can bear with white no longer,
When life stirs, shaping all anew,
He wants a scene that has some color,   690

4. St. Andrew's Eve, November 29, the traditional time for young girls to consult fortune-tellers about their future lovers or husbands.

And since there's nowhere yet one flower,
Holiday crowds have got to do.

Now face about, and looking down
From the hilltop at the town,
See the many-colored throng   695
Passing through the arch of stone
Into sunshine, out of gloom.
They celebrate the Resurrection,
For they themselves today are risen:
From airless rooms in huddled houses,   700
From drudgery at counters and benches,
From under cumbrous roofs and gables,
From crowded, suffocating alleys,
From the mouldering dimness of the churches,
All are brought forth into brightness.   705
And look there, how the eager crowd
Scatters through the fields and gardens,
How over the river's length and breadth
Skiffs and sculls are busily darting,
And that last boat, packed near to sinking,   710
Already's pulled a good ways off.
Even from distant mountain slopes
Bright colored clothes wink back at us.
Hear all that village noise and confusion?
There's where you find the people's real heaven.   715
Listen to young and old shouting exultingly.
Oh I feel a man here, here's where I should be!
WAGNER   To go for a walk with you, dear Doctor,
Is a treat for my mind as well as honoring me;
But by myself I'd never come here   720
For I can't abide the least vulgarity.
The screeching fiddles, the shrieking, the playing bowls
For me are all an unbearable uproar,
All scream and shout like possessed souls
And call it music, call it pleasure.   725
PEASANTS [*Singing and dancing under the linden tree*]
The shepherd dressed up in his best,
Pantaloons and flowered vest,
    Oh my, how brave and handsome!
Within the broad-leaved linden's shade
Madly spun both man and maid,   730
    Hooray, hooray,
    Hurrah, hurrah, hooray!
The fiddle bow flew, and then some.
He flung himself into their midst
And seized a young thing round the waist,   735
    While saying, "Care to dance, ma'am?"
The snippy miss she tossed her head,
"You boorish shepherd boy!" she said,

Hooray, hooray,
  Hurrah, hurrah, hooray!   740
"Observe, do, some decorum!"

But round the circle swiftly wheeled,
To right and left the dancers whirled,
 Till all the breath flew from them.
They got so red, they got so warm,   745
They rested, panting, arm in arm,
  Hooray, hooray,
  Hurrah, hurrah, hooray!
And breast to breast—a twosome.

"I'll thank you not to make so free!   750
We girls know well how men betray,
 What snakes lurk in their bosom!"
But still he wheedled her away—
Far off they heard the music play,
  Hooray, hooray,   755
  Hurrah, hurrah, hooray!
The shouting and the dancing.

OLD PEASANT Professor, it's so nice of you
To join us common folk today,
Though such a wise and learned man,   760
Not to scorn our holiday.
So please accept our best cup, filled
With good fresh drink. To you I give
It in the hope, not only will
It quench your thirst, but may you live   765
As many days beyond your lot
As there are drops inside the cup.

FAUST Friends, thanks for this refreshment, I
In turn wish you all health and joy.
  [*The people make a circle around him.*]

OLD PEASANT Indeed it's only right that you   770
Should be with us this happy day,
Who when our times were bitter, proved
Himself our friend in every way.
Many a one stands in his boots here
Whom your good father, the last minute,   775
Snatched from the hot grip of the fever,
That time he quelled the epidemic.[5]
And you yourself, a youngster then,
Never shrank back; every house
The pest went in, you did too.   780
Out they carried many a corpse,
But never yours. Much you went through;
Us you saved, and God saved you.

---

5. Pestilence or plague.

ALL   Health to our tried and trusty friend,
   And may he help us yet again.   785
FAUST   Bow down to him who dwells above,
   Who is our help, commands us love.
   [*He continues on with* WAGNER.]
WAGNER   The gratification you must get from all this,
   From knowing the reverence these people hold you in!
   The man whose gifts can gain him such advantages,   790
   Oh, he's a lucky one in my opinion.
   Who is it, each one asks as he rushes up,
   Fathers point you out to their boys,
   The fiddle stops, the dancers pause,
   And as you pass between the rows   795
   Of people, caps fly in the air, why,
   Next you know they'll all be on their knees
   As if the Host itself[6] were passing by.
FAUST   A few steps more to that rock where we'll rest
   A bit, shall we, from our walk. How often   800
   I would sit alone here, plunged in thought,
   And torture myself with prayers and with fasting.
   So much hope I had then, such firm faith.
   I'd wring my hands, I'd weep, fall on my knees,
   Believing by these means I could force God   805
   To look down from above and stop the disease.
   But now these people's praises seem
   A mockery to me. If you could only
   See into my heart, you'd understand
   How little worthy father and son were really.   810
     My father was an upright man, a solitary,
   Brooding soul who pondered Nature's mysteries
   With honest zeal, yet quite fantastically.
   Together with other alchemical adepts, he gave
   Himself up to the black arts of their kitchen,   815
   Mixing together opposites according
   To innumerable recipes. A bold Red Lion,
   Handsome suitor he, took for wedding
   Partner a pure White Lily, the two uniting
   In a tepid bath; then being tested by fire,   820
   The pair precipitately fled
   From one bridal chamber to another,
   Till there appeared, within the glass,
   The young Queen, dazzlingly dressed
   In every color of the spectrum: 825
   The Great Specific, Sovereign Medicine.
   The patients died; none stopped to inquire
   How many there were who had got better.[7]

---

6. The Eucharist, the consecrated bread and wine of the Sacrament.   7. This confusing sequence evokes a kind of medicine closely allied to magic and inappropriate to the needs of the ill seeking help.

So with our infernal electuary
We killed our way across the country.   830
I poisoned, myself, by prescription, thousands;
They sickened and faded; yet I must live to see
On every side the murderers' fame emblazoned.

WAGNER   But why such violent, such intense emotion?
When a good man follows, with scrupulous devotion,   835
The arts his predecessors practiced,
He does all that can be expected.
A youth who is respectful of his father
Eagerly soaks up all he has to teach;
If later, thanks to him, our science is enriched,   840
His son in turn can carry science further.

FAUST   Oh, he's a happy man who hopes
To keep from drowning in these seas of error!
What we know least about, we need the most,
And what we do know, is no use whatever.   845
        But we mustn't poison with our gloomy thoughts
The sweetness of the present hour!
Look how the sunset's level rays
Gild those cottages in their green bower,
The day fades quietly, the sun departs,   850
Hurrying off to kindle new life elsewhere—
If only I had wings to bear me up
Into the air and follow after!
Then I would see the whole world at my feet.
Quietly shining in the eternal sunset,   855
The peaks ablaze, the valleys gone to sleep,
And every silver stream a golden torrent.
The savage mountain with its yawning rifts
Shouldn't ever thwart my godlike soaring,
And there's the ocean, see, already swelling   860
Before my wondering gaze, with its sun-warmed gulfs.
But finally the bright god looks like sinking,
Whereupon a renewed urgency
Drives me on to drink his eternal light,
The day always before, behind the night,   865
The heavens overhead, below the heaving sea . . .
        A lovely dream!—and meanwhile it grows dark.
Oh dear, oh dear, that our frames should lack
Wings wherewith to match the spirit's wings.
And yet our nature's such that everybody   870
Knows feelings that soar upwards, always straining,
When high above, lost in the blue immensity,
The skylark pours out his shrill rhapsody,
When over fir-clad mountain steeps
The eagle on his broad wings gyres slowly,   875
And passing over prairies, over lakes,
The homeward-bound crane labors steadily.

WAGNER   Well, I've had more than one odd moment, I have,
    But I have never felt those impulses you have.
    Soon enough you get your fill of woods and things;   880
    I don't really envy birds their wings.
    How different are the pleasures of the intellect,
    Sustaining one from page to page, from book to book,
    And warming winter nights with dear employment
    And with the consciousness your life's so lucky.   885
    And goodness, when you spread out an old parchment,
    Heaven's fetched straight down into your study.
FAUST   You know the one great driving force,
    May you never know the other!
    Two souls live in me, alas,   890
    Forever warring with each other.
    One, amorous of the world, with all its might
    Grapples it close, greedy of all its pleasures;
    The other fights to rise out of the dust
    Up, up into the heaven of our great forebears.   895

    You beings of the air, if such exist,
    Holding sway between the skies and earth,
    Come down to me out of the golden haze
    And translate me to a new, a vivid life!
    Oh, if I only had a magic mantle   900
    To bear me off to unknown lands,
    I'd never trade it for the costliest gowns,
    Or for a cloak however rich and royal.
WAGNER   Never call down that familiar swarm
    That swoops and hovers through the middle air,   905
    Bringing mankind every kind of harm
    From every corner of the terrestrial sphere.
    Out of the North, sharp-toothed spirits fall
    On us and grip us with their chill fingers;
    Out of the East, soughing with parched breath,   910
    They suck our lungs dry, shrivel up our innards;
    And when from Southern deserts the hot ones
    Blow, heaping fire on our heads,
    The West ones send for our relief
    Rains to cool, then drown, us and our fields.   915
    Their ears are cocked, alert to trip men up;
    Seem dutiful because they mean to fool us;
    Their pretense is that they are heaven-sent
    And lisp like angels even as they cheat us.
      However, come, let's go, the world's turned chill   920
    And dreary, evening mists are rising!
    Indoors is where you want to be at nightfall.
    But why should you stand still, astonished, staring?
    What can you see in the dusk to find upsetting?
FAUST   Don't you see that black dog in the stubble,   925

Coursing back and forth?
WAGNER   I do. I noticed him.
A while back. What about him?
FAUST   Look again.
What kind of creature is it?
WAGNER   Kind? A poodle—
Who's a nuisance to his master, always
Searching out his track, the way dogs do.
FAUST   Look, he's   930
Circling around us, coming nearer and nearer.
Unless I'm much mistaken, a wake of fire
'S streaming behind him.
WAGNER   I see nothing
But a black-haired poodle. Your eyes are playing
Tricks on you, perhaps.
FAUST   I think I see   935
Him winding a magic snare, quietly,
Around our feet, a noose which he'll pull tight
In the future, when the time is ripe.
WAGNER He's circling us because he's timid and uncertain;
He's missed his master, come on men unknown to him.   940
FAUST The circle's getting tighter, he's much closer!
WAGNER You see!—a dog and no ghost, sir.
He growls suspiciously, he hesitates,
He wags his tail, he sinks down flat—
Never fear, it's all just dog behavior.   945
FAUST Come here, doggie, here, come here!
WAGNER A silly creature, a poor beast.
When you stop, he stops too and waits;
Speak to him, he'll leap and bark;
Throw something and he'll fetch it back,   950
Splash right in the river for your stick.
FAUST I guess you're right, it's just what he's been taught;
I see no sign of anything occult.
WAGNER A dog that's so well-trained, has such good manners,
Why, even a philosopher would like him.   955
His student teachers found him an apt scholar—
Sir, he deserves you should adopt him.
    [*They enter at the City Gate.*]

FAUST'S STUDY [I]

FAUST [*Entering with the poodle*]
Behind me lie the fields and meadows
Underneath the cloak of night,
With a shuddering sense of premonition   960
Our better soul now starts awake.
Our worser one, unruly, reckless,
Quietens and starts to nod;

In me the love of my own fellows
Begins to stir, and the love of God. 965

Poodle, hush! And stop that running!
What makes you sniff so at the door?
Here's my best cushion for you to doze on
Behind the stove, there on the floor.
Just now when we came down the hillside 970
We found you an amusing beast;
I'm glad to take you in and feed you,
You're welcome—as a silent guest.

When a man comes back to his cramped little study,
To the friendly lamplight, the coziness, 975
Oh then it brightens in his bosom
And his heart feels it knows itself.
Again he hears the voice of reason,
And hope revives, it breathes afresh,
He longs to drink the living waters, 980
Mount upwards to our being's source.

You're growling, poodle! Animal noises
Hardly suit the solemn music
Filling my soul to overflowing.
We're used to people ridiculing 985
What they hardly understand,
Grumbling at the good and the beautiful—
It makes them so uncomfortable!
Do dogs now emulate mankind?
    Yet even with the best of will 990
I feel my new contentment fail.
Why must the waters cease so soon
And leave us thirsting once again?
Oh, this has happened much too often!
But there's an answer to it all: 995
I mean the supernatural,
I mean our hope of revelation,
Which nowhere shines so radiant
As here in the New Testament.
I'll look right now at the original[8] 1000
And see if it is possible
For me to put it, with true feeling,
Into my beloved German.
    [*He opens the volume and begins.*]
"In the beginning was the Word"[9]—so goes
The text. And right off I am given pause! 1005
A little help, please, someone! I'm unable
To see the *word* as having supreme value;

8. I.e., the Greek.   9. John 1.1.

If I am filled with the true spirit,
I'll find a better way to say it.
So: "In the beginning, what was?—*mind!*"   1010
Give plenty of thought to that first line,
Rein in your pen, it's too impetuous:
Is it mind that makes and moves the universe?
Once more: "In vital *force* the world began."
Yet even as I write this sentence down   1015
Something tells me it is still not right.
The spirit speaks, I see the light!
Oh, now I'm sure of it: "First was the *act!*"

If this cell's one that we'll be sharing,
Poodle, stop that barking, yelping!   1020
You're giving me a splitting headache,
I can't put up with such a roomate.
I'm sorry to say that one of us
Has got to quit the premises.
It goes against the grain with me   1025
To renege on hospitality,
But there's the door, dog, leave, goodbye.

But what the devil's going on?
What I see's beyond belief!
Is it real, is it a phantom?   1030
My poodle's swelled up huger than life!
Now he's rising ponderously;
That isn't any dog, believe me!
What a dreadful spook I've brought
Out of the night into my house!   1035
He looks, with his fierce eyes and jaws,
Just like a hippopotamus.
But I have got you in my power!
With a demi-imp of Hell, as you are,
Solomon's Key[1] is what is called for.   1040

SPIRITS [*Outside the door*]
        There's someone locked up inside there!
        Don't dare enter, stay right here!
        Like a fox the hunter's snared,
        Old Nick trembles, oh he's scared!
        But keep a sharp lookout,   1045
        Fly this way and that,
        Around and about,
        And you'll see he's soon out.
        If you can help him,
        Don't let him sit there,   1050
        All of us owe him
        For many a favor.

---

1. The *Clavicula Salomonis*, a standard work used by magicians for conjuring. In many medieval legends, Solomon was noted as a great magician.

FAUST   Against such a creature, my first defense:
The Spell of the Four Elements.

> Let Salamander burn,   1055
> Undine wind and turn,
> Sylph melt into thin air,
> Hobgoblin² sweat and swear.

Ignorance
Of the elements,
Their powers and properties,   1060
Denies you all mastery
Over the demonry.

> Vanish in fire,
> Salamander!   1065
> Swirl and stream,
> Water-child Undine!

> Like a meteor burn,
> Aërial Sylph!
> Grind and churn,   1070
> Drudging gnome!
> Come out, come out and let's have done!

None of the four
Is in the cur.
Calmly he lies there, grinning at me;   1075
My spells glance off him harmlessly.
—Now hear me conjure
With something stronger.

> Are you, grim fellow,
> Escaped here from Hell below?   1080
> Then look at this symbol
> Before which the legions
> Of devils and demons
> Fearfully bow.

How his hair bristles, how he swells up now!   1085

> Creature cast into darkness,
> This name then is known to you
> Of the never-begotten one,
> Wholly ineffable one,
> Cruelly pierced in the side one,   1090
> Whose blood in the heavens
> Is everywhere streaming?

---

2. A spirit of the earth. *Salamander:* spirit of fire. *Undine:* spirit of water. *Sylph:* spirit of air.

Behind the stove, spellbound, caught,
The demon puffs up gray and bloat,
Expanding into the whole chamber,   1095
Dissolving himself into vapor.
—Now don't you try going through the ceiling!
Down at my feet, do your master's bidding!
You see, my threats are scarcely idle—
Oh I will flush you out, yes, I will!
Don't drag your feet unless you'd like   1100
My triune light[3] to knock you flat!
Don't drag your feet until you force me
To call on my most potent sorcery.

> [*The smoke clears, and* MEPHISTOPHELES, *dressed as an itinerant student,
> emerges from behind the stove.*]

MEPHISTO   Why all the racket? What's your wish, sir?   1105
FAUST   So you were the one inside the poodle!
  I have to laugh—a wandering scholar!
MEPHISTO   My greetings to you, learned doctor,
  You really had me sweating hard there.
FAUST   And what's your name?
MEPHISTO   Your question's trivial   1110
  From one who finds words superficial,
  Who strives to pass beyond mere seeming
  And penetrate the heart of being.[4]
FAUST   With gentry like yourself, it's common
  To find the name declares what you are   1115
  Very plainly; for example:
  Lord of the Flies,[5] Destroyer, Liar.
  So who are you, I'd like to know?
MEPHISTO   A humble part of that great power
  Which always means evil, always does good.   1120
FAUST   And pray tell what you mean by *that*.
MEPHISTO   I am the spirit that says no, no always!
  And how right I am! For what
  Does everything that comes into existence
  Here on earth deserve, if not   1125
  To be wiped out completely? Much better, surely,
  Nothing ever was. So all that you call sin,
  Catastrophe and ruin—i.e. evil—
  For me's the water I swim in.
FAUST   A part, you say? You look like the whole works to me. 1130
MEPHISTO   I say what's so, it isn't modesty—
  Man in his world of self's a fool,
  He likes to think he's all in all.
  I'm part of the part which was all at first,
  A part of the dark from which light burst forth,   1135
  Arrogant light which now usurps the air

---

3. Perhaps the Trinity or a triangle with divergent rays.   4. Mephistopheles refer to Faust's substitution
of *Act* for *Word* in the passage from John (see line 1004).   5. An almost literal translation of the name
of the Philistine deity Beelzebub.

And seeks to thrust Night from her ancient chair,
To no avail. Since light is one with all
Things bodily, making them beautiful,
Streams from them, from them is reflected,   1140
Since light by matter's manifested—
When by degrees all matter's burnt up and no more,
Why, then light shall not matter any more.

FAUST   Oh, now I understand your office:
Since you can't wreck things all at once,   1145
You're going at it by bits and pieces.

MEPHISTO   And making little headway, I confess.
The opposite of nothing-at-all,
The *something*, this great shambling world,
In spite of how I exert myself against it,   1150
Phlegmatically endures my every onset
By earthquake, fire, tidal wave and storm:
Next day the land and sea again are calm.
And all that *stuff*, those animal and human species—
I can hardly make a dent in them.   1155
The numbers I've already buried, armies!
Yet fresh troops keep on marching up again.
That's how it is, it's enough to drive you crazy!
From air, from water, from the earth
Seeds innumerable sprout forth   1160
In dry and wet and cold and warm!
If I hadn't kept back fire for myself,
What the devil could I call my own?

FAUST   So against the good, the never-resting,
All-powerful creative force   1165
In impotent spite you raise your fist and
Try to arrest life's forward thrust.
Look around for work that's more rewarding,
You singular son of old Chaos!

MEPHISTO   Well, it's a subject for discussion—   1170
At our next meeting. Now I wish
To go. That is, with your permission.

FAUST   But why should you ask me for leave?
We've struck up an acquaintance, we two,
Drop in on me whenever you please.   1175
There's the door and there's the window
And your old reliable, the chimney.

MEPHISTO   Well . . . you see . . . an obstacle
Keeps me from dropping *out*—so sorry!
That witch's foot chalked on your doorsill.   1180

FAUST   The pentagram's[6] the difficulty?
But if it's that that has you stopped,
How did you ever manage an entry?
And how should a spirit like you get trapped?

_____
6. A magic five-pointed star designed to keep away evil spirits.

MEPHISTO   Well, look close and you'll see that   1185
  A corner's open: the outward pointing
  Angle's lines don't quite meet.
FAUST   What a stroke of luck! I'm thinking
  Now you are my prisoner.
  Pure chance has put you in my power!   1190
MEPHISTO   The poodle dashed right in, saw nothing;
  But now the case is the reverse:
  The Devil can't get out of the house!
FAUST   There's the window, why don't you use it?
MEPHISTO   It's an iron law we devils can't flout,   1195
  The way we come in, we've got to go out,
  We're free as to entrée, but not as to exit.
FAUST   So even in Hell there's law and order!
  I'm glad, for then a man might sign
  A contract with you gentlemen.   1200
MEPHISTO   Whatever we promise, you get, full measure,
  There's no cutting corners, no skulduggery—
  But it's not a thing to be done in a hurry;
  Let's save the subject for our next get-together.
  And as for now, I beg you earnestly,   1205
  Release me from the spell that binds me!
FAUST   Why rush off, stay a while, do.
  I'd love to hear some more from you.
MEPHISTO   Let me go now. I swear I'll come back,
  Then you can ask me whatever you like.   1210
FAUST   Don't blame me because you're caught;
  You trapped yourself, it's your own fault.
  Who's nabbed the Devil must keep a tight grip,
  You don't grab him again once he gives you the slip.
MEPHISTO   Oh, all right! To please you I   1215
  Will stay and keep you company;
  Provided with my arts you let me
  Entertain you in my own way.
FAUST   Delighted, go ahead. But please
  Make sure those arts of yours amuse!   1220
MEPHISTO   You'll find, my friend, your senses, in one hour,
  More teased and roused than all the long dull year.
  The songs the fluttering spirits murmur in your ear,
  The visions they unfold of sweet desire,
  Oh they are more than just tricks meant to fool!   1225
  By Arabian scents you'll be delighted,
  Your palate tickled, never sated,
  The ravishing sensations you will feel!
  No preparation's needed, none.
  Here we are. Let the show begin!   1230
SPIRITS   Open, you gloomy
    Vaulted ceiling above him,
    Let the blue ether
    Look benignly in on him,

And dark cloudbanks scatter   1235
So that all is fair for him!
Small stars are glittering,
Milder suns glowing,
Angelic troops shining
In celestial beauty   1240
Hover past smiling,
Swaying and stooping.
Ardent desire
Follows them yearning;
And their robes streaming ribbons   1245
Veil the fields, veil the meadows,
Veil the arbors where lovers
In pensive surrender
Give themselves to each other
For ever and ever.   1250
Arbor on arbor!
Vines clambering and twining!
Their heavy clusters,
Poured into presses,
Pour out purple wines   1255
Which descend in dark streams
Over beds of bright jewels
Down the vineyards' steep slopes
To broaden to lakes
At the foot of green hills.   1260
Birds blissfully drink there,
With beating wings sunwards soar,
Soar towards the golden isles
Shimmering hazily
On the horizon;   1265
Where we hear voices
Chorusing jubilantly,
Where we see dancers
Whirling exuberantly
Over the meadows,   1270
Here, there and everywhere.
Some climb the heights,
Some swim in the lakes,
Others float in the air—
Joying in life, all,   1275
Beneath the paradisal
Stars glowing with love
Afar in the distance.
MEPHISTO   Asleep! Oh bravely done, my airy younglings!
How duly to his slumbers you have sung him!   1280
I am in your debt for this performance.
—As for you, sir, you were never born
To keep the Prince of Darkness down!
Weave a circle of sweet dreams around him,

Drown him in a deep sea of delusion. 1285
But to break the spell that holds me here,
A rat's tooth is what I require.
No need for conjuring long-windedly—
Listen! I hear a rat rustling already.

The lord of flies and rats and mice, 1290
Of frogs and bedbugs, worms and lice,
Commands you forth from your dark hole
To gnaw, beast, for me that doorsill
Whereon I dab this drop of oil!
—And there you are! Begin, begin! 1295
The corner that is pointing in,
That's the one that shuts me in;
One last crunch to clear my way:
Now Faustus, till we meet next—dream away!

FAUST [Awakening]   Again deceived by tricks, am I? 1300
Do all those vanished spirits only mean:
I saw the Devil in a dream,
Took home a dog that ran away?

FAUST'S STUDY [II]

FAUST, MEPHISTOPHELES.

FAUST   A knock, was that? Come in! Who is it this time?
MEPHISTO   Me.
FAUST   Come in!
MEPHISTO   You have to say it still a third time. 1305
FAUST   All right, all right—come in!
MEPHISTO   Good, very good!
We two will get along, I see, just as we should.
I've come here dressed up as a grandee.[7] Why?
To help you drive your blues away!
In a scarlet suit, all over gold braid, 1310
Across my shoulders a stiff silk cape,
A gay cock's feather in my cap,
At my side a gallant's long blade—
And bringing you advice that's short and sweet:
Put fine clothes on like me, cut loose a bit, 1315
Be free and easy, man, throw off your yoke
And find out what real life is like.
FAUST   In any clothes, I'd feel the misery
Of this cramped, suffocating life on earth.
I'm too old to live for amusement only, 1320
Too young to live without desire or wish.

---

7. In the popular plays based on the Faust legend, the Devil often appeared as a monk when the play catered to a Protestant audience and as a noble squire when the audience was predominantly Catholic.

The world—what has it got to say to me?
Renounce all that you long for, all—renounce!
That's the everlasting song-and-dance
Which you're greeted by on every side,   1325
The croak you hear year in, year out;
You can't have what you want, you can't!
I awake each morning, how? Horrified,
On the verge of tears, to confront a day
Which at its close will not have satisfied   1330
One smallest wish of mine, not one. Why,
Even the hope of a bit of pleasure, some pleasantness,
Withers in the atmosphere of mean-spirited fault-finding;
My eager nature's bold expansiveness
Is brought up short by the daily vexations, jeering.   1335
And when the night draws on and all is hushed,
I go to bed not soothed at last, but apprehensively,
Well knowing what awaits me is not rest,
But wild and whirling dreams that terrify me.
The god who thrones inside my bosom,   1340
Able to shake me to the depths, so powerfully,
The lord and master of my powers,
Is impotent to effect a single thing outside me;
And so I find existence burdensome, wretched,
Death eagerly desired, my life hated.   1345
MEPHISTO   Yet the welcome men give death is never wholehearted.
FAUST   Happy the man, even as he conquers gloriously,
Upon whose brow death sets the blood-stained laurel!
Happy the man, after dancing the night through furiously,
Whom it finds out in the white arms of a girl!   1350
If only, overwhelmed by the Spirit's power,
In raptures, I had died right then and there!
MEPHISTO   And yet that very night, I seem to remember,
A fellow didn't down a drink he'd prepared.
FAUST   Spying around, I see, is what you like to do.   1355
MEPHISTO   I don't know everything, but I know a thing or two.
FAUST   If a sweet, familiar strain of music,
When I was staggering, steadied me,
Beguiled what's left of childhood feeling
With echoes of a happier day—   1360
Well, never again! I pronounce a curse on
All tales that snare and cheat the soul,
All false and flattering persuasion
That ties it to this *corpus vile*.
First I curse man's mind, for thinking   1365
Much too well of itself; I curse
The show of things, so dazzling, glittering,
That assails us through our every sense;
Our dreams of fame, of our name's enduring,
Oh what a sham, I curse them too;   1370
I curse as hollow all our having,

Curse wife and child, peasant and plow;
I curse Mammon[8] when he incites us
With dreams of treasure to reckless deeds,
Or plumps the cushions for our pleasure   1375
As we lie lazily at ease;
Curse comfort sucked out of the grape,
Curse love on its pinnacle of bliss,
Curse faith, so false, curse all vain hope,
And patience most of all I curse!   1380

SPIRIT CHORUS [*Invisible*]
    Oh, what a pity,
    Now you've destroyed it!
    The world once so lovely,
    How you have wrecked it!
    Down it goes, smashed   1385
    By a demigod's fist!
    Out of existence
    We sweep its poor remnants,
    Sorrowing over
    Beauty now lost forever.   1390
    —Then build again, better,
    Potent son of the earth,
    Build a new world, a fairer,
    Inside your own self,
    Within your own heart!   1395
    With a mind clear and strong,
    On your lips a new song,
    Come, make a fresh start!

MEPHISTO   Do you hear them, my angels,
My dear little wise ones,   1400
Sagely advising you
To do things, be cheerful?
Their wish is to draw you
Out of the shell you're shut up in,
Out of your torpid stagnation   1405
Into the wide world before you.

Stop making love to your misery,
It gnaws away at you like a vulture;
Even in the meanest company
You'd feel yourself a man like any other.   1410
Not that I'm advising you
To mingle with the multitude;
Among demons I am not a V.I.P.,
But still, if you'll throw in with me,
I'll walk beside you life's long route,   1415
Your good companion. If I suit,

---

8. The Aramaic word for "riches," used in the New Testament of the Bible. Medieval writers interpreted the word as a proper noun, the name of the Devil, as representing covetousness or avarice.

I'm ready to serve you hand and foot.
FAUST   And in return what must I do?
MEPHISTO   There's plenty of time for that, forget it.
FAUST   No, no, the Devil must have his due,   1420
He doesn't do things for the hell of it,
Just to see another fellow through.
So let's hear the terms, what the fine print is;
Having you for a servant's a tricky business.
MEPHISTO   I promise I will serve your wishes—here,   1425
A slave who'll do your bidding faithfully;
But if we meet each other—there,
Why, you must do the same for me.
FAUST   That "there" of yours—it doesn't scare me off;
If you pull this world down about my ears,   1430
Let the other one come on, who cares?
My joys are part and parcel of this earth,
It's under this sun that I suffer,
And once it's goodbye and I've left them
Then let whatever happens happen,   1435
And that is that. About the hereafter
We have had enough palaver,
More than I want to hear, by far:
If still we love and hate each other,
If some stand high and some stand lower,   1440
Et cetera, et cetera.
MEPHISTO   In that case, an agreement's easy.
Come, dare it! Come, your signature!
Oh, how my tricks will tickle your fancy!
I'll show you things no man has seen before.   1445
FAUST   You poor devil, really, what have you got to offer?
The mind of man in its sublime endeavor,
Tell me, have you ever understood it?
Oh yes indeed, you've bread: and when I eat it
I'm hungry still; you've yellow gold: like yellow sand   1450
It runs away fast through the hand;
Games of chance no man can win at, ever;
Girls who wind me in their arms, their lover,
While eyeing up a fresh one over my shoulder;
There's honor, that the noblest minds all thirst for: 1455
It shoots across the sky a second, then it's over—
Oh yes, do show me fruit that rots as you try
To pick it, trees whose leaves bud daily, daily die!
MEPHISTO   Marvels like that? For a devil, not so daunting.
I'm good for whatever you have in mind.   1460
—But friend, the day comes when you find
A share of your own in life's good things,
And peace and quiet, are what you're wanting.
FAUST   If ever you see me loll at ease,
Then it's all yours, you can have it, my life!   1465
If ever you fool me with flatteries
Into feeling satisfied with myself,

Or tempt me with visions of luxuries,
Well, that's my last day on this earth,
   I'll bet you!
MEPHISTO   Done! A bet!
FAUST   A bet—agreed!   1470
If ever I plead with the passing moment,
"Linger awhile, oh how lovely you are!"
Then shut me up in close confinement,
I'll gladly breathe the air no more!
Then let the death bell toll my finis,   1475
Then you are free of all your service,
Let the clock wind down, hands fall to pieces,
And time for me be over and done with!
MEPHISTO   Think twice. Forgetting's not a thing we do.
FAUST   Of course, quite right—a bet's a bet.   1480
This isn't anything I'm rushing into.
But if I stagnate, fall into a rut,
I'm a slave, it doesn't matter who to,
To this one, that one, or to you.
MEPHISTO   My service starts now—no procrastinating!—   1485
At the dinner tonight for the just-made Ph.D.s.
But there's one thing: you know, for emergencies,
I'd like to have our arrangement down in writing.
FAUST   In black and white you want it! Oh, what pedantry!
You've never learnt a *man's* word's your best surety?   1490
It's not enough for you that I'm committed
By what I promise till the end of days?
—Yet the world's a flood sweeps all along before it,
And why should I feel my word must hold always?
A strange idea, but that's the way we are,   1495
And who would want it otherwise?
That man's blessed who keeps his conscience clear,
He'll regret no sacrifice.
But parchment signed and stamped and sealed,
Is a bogey all recoil from, scared.   1500
The pen does in the living word,
Only sealing wax and vellum count: honor must yield.
Base spirit, say what you require!
Brass or marble, parchment or paper?
Shall I write with quill, with stylus, chisel,   1505
I leave it up to you, you devil!
MEPHISTO   Why get so hot, make extravagant speeches?
Ranting away does no good.
A scrap of paper takes care of the business.
And sign it with a drop of blood.   1510
FAUST   Oh, all right. If that's what makes you happy,
I'll go along with the buffoonery.
MEPHISTO   Blood's a very special ink, you know.
FAUST   Are you afraid that I won't keep our bargain?
Till doomsday I will strive, I'll never slacken!   1515
So I've promised, that's what I will do.

I had ideas too big for me,
Your level's mine, that's all I'm good for.
The Spirit laughed derisively;
Nature won't allow me near her.   1520
Thinking's done with, for ever so long
Learning and knowledge have sickened me.
—Then let's unloose our passions, sound
The depths of sensuality!
Bring on your miracles, each one,   1525
Worked by inscrutable sorcery!
We'll plunge into time's racing current,
The vortex of activity,
Where pleasure and distress,
Setbacks and success,   1530
May come as they come, by turn-about, however;
To be always up and doing is man's nature.
MEPHISTO   Go everywhere, sample everything, all sensations,
And what you like, snatch it up on the run,
And may they agree with you, all your pleasant diversions!   1535
Only don't be bashful, wade right in.
FAUST   I told you, I'm not out to enjoy myself, have fun,
I want frenzied excitements, gratifications that are painful,
Love and hatred violently mixed,
Anguish that enlivens, inspiriting trouble.   1540
Cured of my thirst to know at last,
I'll never again shun anything distressful;
From now on my wish is to undergo
All that men everywhere undergo, their whole portion,
Make mine their heights and depths, their weal and woe,   1545
Everything human embrace in my single person,
And so enlarge my soul to encompass all humanity,
And shipwreck with them when all shipwreck finally.
MEPHISTO   Believe me, I have chewed away in vain
At that tough meat, mankind, since long ago,   1550
From birth to death's by far too short a time
For any man to digest such a lump of sourdough!
Only a God can take in all of them,
The whole lot. For He dwells in eternal light,
While we poor devils are stuck down below   1555
In darkness and gloom, lacking even candlelight,
And all *you* qualify for is half day, half night.
FAUST   Nevertheless I will!
MEPHISTO   Bravely proclaimed!
Still, there's one thing worries me.
The time allotted you is very short,   1560
But art has always been around and will be,
So listen, hear what is my thought:
Hire a poet, learn by his instruction.
Let the good gentleman rove through
All the realm of imagination,   1565

And every noble attribute and virtue
He discovers, heap on you, his inspired creation:
>The lion's fierceness,
>Mild hart's swiftness,
>Italian fieriness,   1570
>Northern steadiness.
Let your poet solve that old conundrum,
How to be generous and also cunning;
How, driven by youthful impulsiveness, unrestrained,
To fall in love as beforehand planned.   1575
Such a creature—my, I'd love to know him!—
I'd call him Mr. Microcosm.

FAUST What am I, then, if it can never be:
>The realization of all human possibility,
>That crown my soul so avidly reaches for?   1580

MEPHISTO In the end you are—just what you are.
>Wear wigs high-piled with curls, oh millions,
>Stick your legs in yard-high hessians,
>You're still you, the one you always were.

FAUST I feel it now, how pointless my long grind   1585
>To make mine all the treasures of man's mind;
>When I sit back and interrogate my soul,
>No new powers answer to my call;
>I'm not a hair's breadth more in height,
>A step nearer to the infinite.   1590

MEPHISTO Dear Dr. Faust, your understanding's
>Ordinary, commonplace;
>We have got the see things better
>Or lose our seat at life's rich feast.
>Hell, man, you have hands and feet,   1595
>A headpiece and a pair of balls;
>And pleasures freshly savored, don't
>You have them too? They're no less yours.
>If I can keep six spanking stallions,
>That horsepower's mine, my property,   1600
>My coach bowls on, ain't I the fellow,
>Two dozen legs I've got for me!
>   Sir, come on, quit all that thinking,
>Into the world, the pair of us!
>The man who lives in his head only's   1605
>Like a donkey in the rough
>Led round and round by the bad fairies,
>While green grass grows a stone's throw off.

FAUST And how do we begin?

MEPHISTO   By clearing out—just leaving.
>A torture chamber, that's what this place is!   1610
>You call it living, to be boring
>Yourself and your young men to death?
>Leave that to Dr. Bacon Fat next door!
>Why toil and moil at threshing heaps of straw?

Anyhow, the deepest knowledge you possess   1615
You daren't let on to before your class.
—Oh now I hear one in the passageway!
FAUST   I can't see him—tell him to go away.
MEPHISTO   The poor boy's been so patient, don't be cross;
We mustn't let him leave here *désolé*.   1620
Let's have your cap and gown, Herr Doctor.
Won't I look the fine professor!
       [*Changes clothes.*]
Count on me to know just what to say!
Fifteen minutes's all I need for it—
Meanwhile get ready for our little junket!   1625
                                       [*Exit* FAUST.]
MEPHISTO [*Wearing* FAUST's *gown*]   Despise science, heap contempt on
    reason,
The human race's best possession,
Only let the lying spirit draw you
Over into mumbo-jumbo,
Make-believe and pure illusion—   1630
And then you're mine for sure, I have you,
No matter what we just agreed to.
    Fate's given him a spirit that's relentless,
It drives him on and on, he can't be stopped,
It soars away beyond all earthly pleasures;   1635
Yet I'll seduce him into roistering about,
Where all proves shallow, meaningless,
Till he is limed and thrashes wildly, stuck;
Before his greedy insatiableness
I'll dangle food and drink; he'll shriek   1640
In vain for relief from his torturing dryness!
And even if he weren't the Devil's already,
He'd still be sure to perish miserably.
       [*Enter a student.*]
STUDENT   May I impose, sir, on your kindness?
The object of my visit's to advise with   1645
One whom all the people here
Greatly esteem, indeed revere.
MEPHISTO   I thank you for your courtesy.
But I'm a man, as you can see,
Like any other. Have you perhaps tried elsewhere?   1650
STUDENT   It's you, sir, you, I want for adviser!
I've come here eager and determined,
Anxious to learn whatever's worth learning;
Mother cried to see me go;
I've got an allowance, it's small, but will do.   1655
MEPHISTO   You've come to the right place, my son.
STUDENT   But I'm ready to turn right around and run!
It seems so sad inside these walls,
My heart misgives me; here all's
Confined, shut in; there's nothing green,   1660

Not even a single tree, to be seen.
Oh, I'm unable, in the lecture hall,
To hear or see or think at all!
MEPHISTO   It's a matter of getting used to the place.
At first an infant fights the breast,   1665
But soon it's feeding lustily.
Just so your craving will grow daily
The more you nurse at Wisdom's bosom.
STUDENT   I'll cling tight to her bosom, with pleasure,
But how do I find the way to her?   1670
MEPHISTO   First of all, then—have you chosen
A faculty?
STUDENT   Well, you see,
I'd like to be a learned man.
The earth below, the heavens on high—
All those things I long to understand,   1675
All the sciences; all nature.
MEPHISTO   You've got the right idea; however,
It demands close application.
STUDENT   Oh never fear, I'm in this heart and soul;
But still, a fellow gets so dull   1680
Without time off for recreation,
In the long and lovely days of summer.
MEPHISTO   Time slips away so fast, you need to use it
Rationally and not abuse it.
And for that reason I advise you: 1685
The Principles of Logic *primo*!
We will drill your mind by rote,
Strap it in the Spanish boot
So it never will forget
The road that's been marked out for it   1690
And stray about incautiously,
A will-o'-the-wisp, this way and that way.
Day after day you'll be taught
All you once did just like that,
Like eating and drinking, thoughtlessly,   1695
Now needs a methodology,
Order and system: *A, B, C!*
    Our thinking instrument behaves
Like a loom: a thousand threads,
At a step on the treadle, are set moving,   1700
Back and forth the shuttles fly,
The strands flow too fast for the eye,
A blow of the batten and there's cloth, woven!
Now enter your philosopher, he
Proves all is just as it should be: 1705
A being thus and B also,
Then C and D inevitably follow;
And if there were no A and B,
There'd never be a C and D.

They're struck all of a heap, his admiring hearers, 1710
But still, it doesn't make them weavers.
How do you study something living?
Drive out the spirit, deny it being,
So there're just parts with which to deal,
Gone is that anomalous thing, the soul 1715
With lifeless pieces as the only things real,
The wonder's where's the life of the whole—
Encheiresis naturae,[9] the chemists then call it,
Make fools of themselves and never know it.

STUDENT   I have trouble following what you say. 1720

MEPHISTO   You'll get the hang of it by and by,
When you learn to distinguish and classify.

STUDENT   How stupid all this makes me feel;
It goes around in my head like a mill.

MEPHISTO   Next, my boy, and let me stress it, 1725
You've got to study metaphysic,
Exert your faculties to venture
Beyond the boundaries of our nature,
Gain intelligence the brain
Has difficulty taking in, 1730
And whether it goes in or not,
There's always a big word for it.
    Your first semester, be very sure
To do things right, attend each lecture.
Five of them you'll have daily; 1735
Be in your seat when the bell peals shrilly.
Come to class with your homework done,
The sections memorized, each one,
So you are sure there's no mistake
And no word's said not in the book. 1740
Still, all you hear set down in your notes
As if it came from the Holy Ghost.

STUDENT   No need to tell me that again,
I realize notes help a lot;
What you've got down in black and white 1745
Goes home with you, is yours for certain.

MEPHISTO   But your faculty—you've still not told me!

STUDENT   Well, I don't think the law would suit me.

MEPHISTO   I can't blame you for disliking it,
Jurisprudence's in a dreadful state, 1750
Laws are like a disease we inherit,
Passed down through generations, spread about
From people to people, place to place;
What once made sense in time becomes nonsensical,
What first was beneficial now's a plague. 1755
O grandsons coming after, how I pity you all!

---

9. The natural process by which substances are united into a living organism—a name for an action no one understands.

As for the rights we have from Nature as her heir—
Never a word about *them* will you hear!
STUDENT   I hate the stuff now more than ever!
   How lucky I am to have you for adviser.   1760
   Perhaps I'll take theology.
MEPHISTO   I shouldn't want to lead you astray,
   But it's a science, if you'll allow me to say it,
   Where it's easy to lose your way.
   There's so much poison hidden in it,   1765
   It's very nearly impossible
   To tell what's toxic from what's medicinal.
   Here again it's safer to choose
   One single master and echo his words dutifully—
   As a general rule, put your trust in *words*,   1770
   They'll guide you safely past doubt and dubiety
   Into the Temple of Absolute Certainty.
STUDENT   But shouldn't words convey ideas, a meaning?
MEPHISTO   Of course they should! But why overdo it?
   It's exactly when ideas are lacking   1775
   Words come in so handy as a substitute.
   With words we argue pro and con,
   With words invent a whole system.
   Believe in words! Have faith in them!
   No jot or title shall pass from them.   1780
STUDENT   Forgive me, but I have another query.
   It's my last one and then I'll go.
   Medicine, sir—what might you care to tell me
   About that study I should know?
   Three years, my God, is such a short time,   1785
   And the field so broad, it quite defeats me.
   One or two professional suggestions
   Helps one along in one's studies wonderfully.
MEPHISTO [*Aside*]   I'm sick of playing the Herr Professor—
   Back again to deviltry!   1790
   [*Aloud*] Medicine's an easy art to master.
   Up and down you study the whole world
   Only so as to discover
   In the end it's all up to the Lord.
   Plough your way through all the sciences you please,   1795
   Each learns only what he can;
   But the man who understands his opportunities,
   Now he's the one I call a man!
   You seem a pretty strapping fellow,
   Not one to hang back bashfully;   1800
   If you don't doubt yourself, I know
   Nobody else will doubt you, nobody.
   Above all learn your way with women;
   Their everlasting sighs and groans,
   Their never-ending aches and pains   1805
   Have one sole source, there's where to treat them,

And if you don't do things too crudely
You'll have them all just where you want them.
With an M.D. you enjoy great credit,
Your art, they're sure, beats others' arts;   1810
The doctor, when he pays a visit,
For greeting reaches for those parts
It takes a layman years to come at;
You feel her pulse with extra emphasis,
Fix her, slyly, with burning looks,   1815
And slipping your arm around her slender hips,
See if it's because she's so tight-laced.

STUDENT   Oh, that's much better—practical, down to earth!

MEPHISTO   All theory, my dear fellow, is gray,
And green the golden tree of life.   1820

STUDENT   I swear it seems a dream to me!
Would you allow me to impose on
Your generous kindness another day
And drink still more draughts of your wisdom?

MEPHISTO   I'm glad to help you in whatever way.   1825

STUDENT   I mustn't leave without presenting
You my album. Do write something
In it for me, would you?

MEPHISTO   Gladly.
        [*Writes and hands back the album.*]

STUDENT [*Reading*]   *Eritis sicut Deus, scientes bonum et malum.*[1]
        [*Closes the book reverently and exits.*]

MEPHISTO   Faithfully follow that good old verse,   1830
That favorite line of my aunt's, the snake,
And for all your precious godlikeness,
You'll end up how? A nervous wreck.
        [*Enter* FAUST.]

FAUST   And now where to?

MEPHISTO   Wherever you like.
First we'll mix with little people, then with great.   1835
The pleasure and the profit you will get
From our course—and never pay tuition for it!

FAUST   But me and my long beard—we're hardly suited
For the fast life. I feel myself defeated
Even before we start. I've never been   1840
A fellow to fit in. Among other men
I feel so small, so mortified, so fazed.
Oh, in the world I'm always ill at ease!

MEPHISTO   My friend, that's all soon changed, it doesn't matter;
With confidence comes *savoir-vivre.*   1845

FAUST   But how do we get out of here?
Where are your horses, groom and carriage?

MEPHISTO   The way we're going is by air,

---

1. A slight alteration of the serpent's words to Eve in Genesis: "Ye shall be as God, knowing good and evil" (Latin).

Upon my cloak—you'll enjoy the voyage.
But take care, on so bold a tour,   1850
You're sparing in the matter of luggage.
I'll heat some gas, that way we'll lift
Quickly off the face of earth;
If we're light enough we'll rise right up—
Congratulations, sir, on your new life!   1855

AUERBACH'S CELLAR IN LEIPZIG

Drinkers carousing.

FROSCH   Faces glum and glasses empty?
I don't call this much of a party.
You fellows seem wet straw tonight,
Who always used to blaze so bright.
BRANDER   It's your fault—he just sits there, hardly speaks!   1860
Where's the horseplay, where're the dirty jokes?
FROSCH [*Emptying a glass of wine on his head*]
There! Both at once!
BRANDER   O horse and swine!
FROSCH   You asked for it, so don't complain.
SIEBEL   Out in the street if you want to punch noses!
—Now take a deep breath and roar out a chorus   1865
In praise of the grape and the jolly god Bacchus.
Come, all together with a rollicking round-o!
ALTMAYER   Stop, stop, man, I'm wounded, someone fetch me some cotton,
The terrible fellow has burst me an eardrum!
SIEBEL   Hear the sound rumble above in the vault?   1870
That tells you you're hearing the true bass note.
FROSCH   That's right! Out the door, whoever don't like it!
With a do-re-mi,
ALTMAYER   And a la-ti-do,
FROSCH   We will have us a concert!   1875
[*Sings.*]
Our dear Holy Roman Empire.
How does the damn thing hold together?
BRANDER   Oh, but that's awful, a terrible tune!
A dreary, disgusting *political* song!
Thank the Lord when you wake each morning   1880
You're not the one must keep the Empire going.
It's a blessing I'm grateful for
To be neither Kaiser nor Chancellor.
But we, too, need a chief for our group,
So let's elect ourselves a pope.   1885
To all of us here I'm sure it's well known
What a man must do to sit on that throne.
FROSCH [*Singing*]
Nightingale, fly away, o'er lawn, o'er bower,
Tell her I love her ten thousand times over.

SIEBEL   Enough of that love stuff, it turns my stomach.   1890

FROSCH   Ten thousand times, though it drives you frantic!
>   [*Sings.*]
>   Unbar the door, the night is dark!
>   Unbar the door, my love, awake!
>   Bar up the door now it's daybreak.

SIEBEL   Go on, then, boast about her charms, her favor,   1895
>   But I will have the latest laugh of all.
>   She played me false—just wait, she'll play you falser.
>   A horned imp's what I wish her, straight from Hell,
>   To dawdle with her in the dust of crossroads;
>   And may an old goat stinking from the Brocken   1900
>   Bleat "Goodnight, dearie," to her, galloping homewards.
>   A fellow made of honest flesh and blood
>   For a slut like that is much too good.
>   I know the way I'd send my love to her—and how!
>   With a rock heaved through her kitchen window.   1905

BRANDER [*Banging on the table*]
>   Good fellows, your attention! None here will deny
>   I know what should be done and shouldn't at all.
>   Now we have lovers in our company
>   Whom we must treat in manner suitable
>   To their condition, our jollity,   1910
>   With a song just lately written. So mind the air
>   And come in on the chorus loud and clear!
>   [*He sings.*]
>   A rat lived downstairs in the cellar,
>   Dined every day on lard and butter,
>   His paunch grew round as any burgher's,   1915
>   As round as Dr. Martin Luther's[2]
>   The cook put poison down for it,
>   Oh, how it groaned, the pangs it felt,
>   *As if by Cupid smitten.*

CHORUS [*Loud and clear*]
>   *As if by Cupid smitten!*   1920

BRANDER
>   It rushed upstairs, it raced outdoors
>   And drank from every gutter,
>   It gnawed the woodwork, scratched the floors,
>   Its fever burned still hotter,
>   In agony it hopped and leaped,   1925
>   Oh, piteously the creature squeaked,
>   *As if by Cupid smitten.*

CHORUS
>   *As if by Cupid smitten!*

BRANDER
>   Its torment drove it, in broad day,
>   Out into the kitchen;   1930

---

2. Martin Luther (1483–1546), German leader of the Protestant Reformation, hence an object of distaste for Catholics.

Collapsing on the hearth, it lay
Panting hard and twitching.
But that cruel Borgia only laughed:
Ha, ha, the brute's at its last gasp,
    As if by Cupid smitten.   1935

CHORUS
    As if by Cupid smitten!

SIEBEL   You find it funny, you coarse louts,
  Oh, quite a stunt, so very cunning,
  To put down poison for poor rats!

BRANDER   You feel for them, you find them touching?   1940

ALTMAYER   O big of gut and bald of pate!
  Losing out's subdued the oaf;
  What he sees in the bloated rat
  'S the spitting image of himself.
      [FAUST *and* MEPHISTOPHELES *enter.*]

MEPHISTO   What your case calls for, Doctor, first,   1945
  Is some amusing company,
  To teach you life can be so easy.
  For these men every night's a bout
  And every day a holiday;
  With little wit but lots of noise,   1950
  All spin inside their little orbit
  Like young cats chasing their own tails.
  As long as the landlord grants them credit
  And they are spared a splitting headache,
  They're satisfied and have no cares.   1955

BRANDER   They're travelers, come here from elsewhere,
  You can tell it by their foreign manner—
  They've not been here, I'll bet, an hour.

FROSCH   Right, right! My Leipzig's an attraction, how I love her,
  A little Paris spreading light and culture!   1960

SIEBEL   Who might they be? What's your guess?

FROSCH   Leave it to me. I'll fill their glass,
  Gently extract, as you do a baby's tooth,
  All there is to know about them, the whole truth.
  I'd say we're dealing with nobility,   1965
  They look so proud, so dissatisfied, to me.

BRANDER   They're pitchmen at the Fair, is what I think.

ALTMAYER   Maybe.

FROSCH   Now watch me go to work.

MEPHISTO [*To* FAUST]
  These dolts can't ever recognize Old Nick
  Even when he's got them by the neck.   1970

FAUST   Gentlemen, good day.

SIEBEL   Thank you, the same.
      [*Aside, obliquely studying* MEPHISTOPHELES]
  What the hell, the fellow limps, he's lame![3]

---

3. By tradition, the Devil had a cloven foot, split like a sheep's hoof.

MEPHISTO   We'd like to join you, sirs, if you'll allow it.
  About my landlord's wine I don't feel sanguine,
  So the company shall make up for it.   1975
ALTMAYER   Particular, you are, about your drinking.
FROSCH   Fresh from Dogpatch, right? From supper
  On cabbage soup with Goodman Clodhopper?
MEPHISTO   We couldn't stop on this trip, more's the pity!
  But last time he went on so tenderly   1980
  About his Leipzig kith and kin,
  And sent his very best to you, each one.
                                              [Bowing to FROSCH.]
ALTMAYER [Aside to FROSCH]
      Score one for him. He's got some wit.
SIEBEL   A sly one, he is.
FROSCH   Wait, I'll fix him yet!
MEPHISTO   Unless I err, weren't we just now hearing   1985
  Some well-schooled voices joined in choral singing?
  Voices, I am sure, must resonate
  Inside this vault to very fine effect.
FROSCH   You know music professionally, I think.
MEPHISTO   Oh no—the spirit's eager, but the voice is weak.   1990
ALTMAYER   Give us a song!
MEPHISTO   Whatever you'd like to hear.
SIEBEL   A new one, nothing we ever heard before.
MEPHISTO   Easily done. We've just come back from Spain,
  Land where the air breathes song, the rivers run wine.
      [Sings]
      Once upon a time a King   1995
        Had a flea, a big one—
FROSCH   Did you hear that? A flea, goddamn!
  I'm all for fleas, myself, I am.
MEPHISTO [Sings]
      Once upon a time a King   2000
        Had a flea, a big one,
      Doted fondly on the thing
        With fatherly affection.
      Calling his tailor in, he said,
        Fetch needles, thread and scissors,
      Measure the Baron up for shirts,   2005
        Measure him, too, for trousers.
BRANDER   And make it perfectly clear to the tailor
  He must measure exactly, sew perfect stitches,
  If he's fond of his head, not the least little error,
  Not a wrinkle, you hear, not one, in those breeches!   2010
MEPHISTO
      Glowing satins, gleaming silks
        Now were the flea's attire,
      Upon his chest red ribbons crossed
        And a great star shone like fire,
      In sign of his exalted post   2015

As the King's First Minister.
His sisters, cousins, uncles, aunts
    Enjoyed great influence too—
The bitter torments that that Court's
    Nobility went through!   2020
And the Queen as well, and her lady's maid,
    Though bitten till delirious,
Forbore to squash the fleas, afraid
    To incur the royal animus.
But we free souls, we squash all fleas   2025
    The instant they light on us!

CHORUS [*Loud and clear*]
    But we free souls, we squash all fleas
        The instant they light on us!

FROSCH   Bravo, bravo! That was fine!
SIEBEL   May every flea's fate be the same!   2030
BRANDER   Between finger and nail, then crack! and they're done for.
ALTMAYER   Long live freedom, long live wine!
MEPHISTO   I'd gladly drink a glass in freedom's honor,
    If only your wine was a little better.[4]
SIEBEL   Talk like that around here isn't popular!   2035
MEPHISTO   I'm sure our landlord wouldn't take it kindly,
    Otherwise I'd treat this company
    To wine that's wine—straight out of our own cellar.
SIEBEL   Go on, go on, let the landlord be my worry.
FROSCH   You're princes, you are, if you're able   2040
    To put good wine upon the table;
    But a drop or two, well, that's no trial at all,
    To judge right what I need's a real mouthful.
ALTMAYER [*In an undertone*]   They're from the Rhineland, I would swear.
MEPHISTO   Let's have an auger, please.
BRANDER   What for?   2045
    Don't tell me you've barrels piled outside the door!
ALTMAYER   There's a basket of tools—look, over there.
MEPHISTO [*Picking out an auger, to* FROSCH]
    Now gentlemen, name what you'll have, please.
FROSCH   What do you mean? We have a choice?
MEPHISTO   Whatever you wish, I will produce.   2050
ALTMAYER [*To* FROSCH]   Licking his lips already, he is!
FROSCH   Fine, fine! For me—a Rhine wine any day,
    The best stuff's from the Fatherland, I say.
MEPHISTO [*Boring a hole in the table edge at* FROSCH's *place*]
    Some wax to stop the holes with, quick!
ALTMAYER   Hell, it's just a sideshow trick.   2055
MEPHISTO [*To* BRANDER]
    And you?
BRANDER   The best champagne you have, friend, please,
    With lots of sparkle, lots of fizz.

---

4. I.e., not cursed.

[MEPHISTOPHELES *goes round the table boring holes at all the places, which one of the drinkers stops with bungs made of wax.*]

You can't always avoid what's foreign;
About pleasure I'm nonpartisan.
A man who's a true German can't stand Frenchmen,   2060
But he can stand their wine, oh how he can!

SIEBEL [*As* MEPHISTOPHELES *reaches his place*]
    I confess your dry wines don't
    Please my palate, I'll take sweet.

MEPHISTO   Tokay⁵ for you! Coming up shortly!

ALTMAYER   No, gentlemen! Look at me honestly,   2065
    The whole thing's meant to make fools of us.

MEPHISTO   Come on, my friend, I'm not so obtuse!
    Trying something like that on you would be risky.
    So what's your pleasure, I'm waiting—speak!

ALTMAYER   Whatever you like, just don't take all week.   2070

MEPHISTO [*All the holes are now bored and stopped; gesturing grotesquely*]
    Grapes grow on the vine,
    Horns on the head of the goat,
    O vinestock of hard wood,
    O juice of the tender grape!
    And a wooden table shall,   2075
    When summoned, yield wine as well!
    O depths of Nature, mysterious, secret,
    Here is a miracle—if you believe it!
Now pull the plugs, all, drink and be merry!

ALL [*Drawing the bungs and the wine each drinker asked for gushing into his glass*]
Sweet fountain, flowing for us only!   2080

MEPHISTO   But take good care you don't spill any.
    [*They drink glass after glass.*]

ALL [*Singing*]
    How lovely everything is, I'm dreaming!
    Like cannibals having a feast,
    Like pigs in a pen full of slops!

MEPHISTO   They feel so free, what a time they're having!   2085

FAUST   I'd like to depart now. Might we, perhaps?

MEPHISTO   Before we do, you must admire
    Their swinishness in its full splendor.

SIEBEL [*Spilling wine on the floor, where it bursts into flame*]
    All Hell's afire, I burn, I burn!

MEPHISTO [*Conjuring the flame*]
    Peace, my own element, down, down!   2090
    [*To the drinkers*]
    Only a pinch, for the present, of the purgatorial fire.

---

5. A sweet Hungarian wine.

SIEBEL   What's going on here? For this you'll pay dear!
　You don't seem to know the kind of men you have here.
FROSCH   Once is enough for that kind of business!
ALTMAYER   Throw him out on his ear, but quietly, no fuss!　2095
SIEBEL   You've got your nerve, trying out on us
　Stuff like that—damned hocus-pocus!
MEPHISTO   Quiet, you tub of guts!
SIEBEL　　　　　　　　　　　　Bean pole, you!
　Now he insults us. I know what to do.
BRANDER   A taste of our fists is what: one-two, one-two.　2100
ALTMAYER [*Drawing a bung and flames shooting out at him*]
　I'm on fire, I'm on fire!
SIEBEL　　　　　　　　　　It's witchcraft, no mistaking!
　Stick him, the rogue, he's free for the taking!
　　　[*They draw their knives and fall on* MEPHISTOPHELES.]
MEPHISTO [*Gesturing solemnly*]
　　False words, false shapes
　　Addle wits, muddle senses!
　　Let here and otherwheres　　　　　　　　　2105
　　Change their places!
　　　[*All stand astonished and gape at each other.*]
ALTMAYER   Where am I? What a lovely country!
FROSCH   Such vineyards! Do my eyes deceive me?
SIEBEL   And grapes you only need to reach for!
BRANDER   Just look inside this green arbor!　2110
　What vines, what grapes! Cluster on cluster!
　　　[*He seizes* SIEBEL *by the nose. The others do the same to each other, and
　　raise their knives.*]
MEPHISTO   Unspell, illusion, eyes and ears!
　—Take note the Devil's a jester, my dears!
　　　[*He vanishes with* FAUST; *the drinkers recoil from each other.*]
SIEBEL   What's happened?
ALTMAYER　　　　　　　　What?
FROSCH　　　　　　　　　　　Was that your nose?
BRANDER [*To* SIEBEL]   And I'm still holding on to yours!　2115
ALTMAYER   The shock I felt—in every limb!
　Get me a chair, I'm caving in.
FROSCH   But what the devil was it, tell me.
SIEBEL   If I ever catch that scoundrel,
　He won't go home alive, believe me!　2120
ALTMAYER   I saw him, horsed upon a barrel,
　Vault straight out through the cellar door—
　My feet feel leaden, so unnatural.
　　　[*Turning toward the table.*]
　Well—maybe some wine's still trickling there.
SIEBEL   The whole thing was a fraud, a gyp.　2125
FROSCH   I was drinking wine, I'd swear.
BRANDER   And all those grapes—I can tell a grape!
ALTMAYER   Now try and tell me, you know-it-alls,
　There's no such thing as miracles!

WITCH'S KITCHEN

A low hearth, and on the fire a large cauldron. In the steam rising up from it, various figures can be glimpsed. A SHE-APE *is seated by the cauldron, skimming it to keep it from boiling over. The* MALE *with their young crouches close by, warming himself. Hanging on the walls and from the ceiling are all sorts of strange objects, the household gear of a witch.*

FAUST, MEPHISTOPHELES.

FAUST   Why, it's revolting, all this crazy witchery!   2130
  Are you telling me I'll learn to be a new man
  Stumbling around in this lunatic confusion?
  Is an ancient hag the doctor who will cure me?
  And that stuff that beast's stirring, that's the remedy
  To cancel thirty years, unbow my back?   2135
  If you can do no better, the outlook's black
  For me, the hopes I nursed are dead already.
  Hasn't the mind of man, instructed by Nature,
  Discovered some sort of balm, some potent elixer?
MEPHISTO   Now you're speaking sensibly!   2140
  There *is* a natural way to recover your youth;
  But that's another business entirely
  And not your sort of thing, is my belief.
FAUST   No, no, come on, I want to hear it.
MEPHISTO   All right. It's simple: you don't need to worry   2145
  About money, doctors, necromancy.
  Go out into the fields right now, this minute,
  Start digging and hoeing away, working the land,
  Confine yourself and your thoughts to the narrowest sphere,
  Eat nothing but the plainest kind of fare,   2150
  Live with the cattle as cattle, don't feel ashamed
  To spread dung on the ground with your own hand.
  So there you have it, the sane way, the healthy,
  To keep yourself young till the age of eighty!
FAUST   Yes, not my sort of thing, I'm afraid,   2155
  Humbling myself to work with a spade;
  So straitened a life would never suit me.
MEPHISTO   So it's back to the witch, my friend, are we?
FAUST   That horrible hag—no one else will do?
  Why can't *you* concoct the brew?   2160
MEPHISTO   A nice thing that would be, to waste the time of the Devil
  When his every moment is claimed by the business of evil!
  Please understand. Not only skill and science
  Are called for here, but also patience:
  A mind must keep at it for years, very quietly,   2165
  Only time can supply the mixture its potency.
  Such a deal of stuff goes into the process,
  All very strange, mysterious!

The Devil, it's true, taught her how to do it,
But it's no business of his to brew it.   2170
    [*Seeing the* APES]
See here, those creatures, aren't they pretty!
That one's the housemaid, that one's the flunkey.
    [*To the* APES]
Madam is not at home, it seems?
APES   Flew straight up the chimney
    To dine out with friends.   2175
MEPHISTO   And her feasting, how long does it usually take her?
APES   As long as we warm our paws by the fire.
MEPHISTO [*To Faust*]   What do you think of this elegant troupe?
FAUST   Nauseating—make me want to throw up.
MEPHISTO   Well, just this sort of causerie   2180
Is what I find most entertains me.
    [*To the* APES]
Tell me, you ugly things, oh do,
What's that you're stirring there, that brew?
APES   Beggars' soup, it's thin stuff, goes down easy.
MEPHISTO   Your public's assured—they like what's wishy-washy.   2185
HE-APE [*Sidling up to* MEPHISTOPHELES *fawningly*]
    Oh let the dice roll,
    I need money, and quick,
    Let me win, make me rich
    I'm so down on my luck.
    With a purse full of thaler,   2190
    An ape passes for clever.
MEPHISTO   How very happy that monkey would be
If he could buy chances in the lottery.
    [*Meanwhile the young* APES *have been rolling around a big ball to which
    they now give a push forward.*]
HE-APE   The world, sirs, behold it!
    The up side goes down,   2195
    The down side goes up,
    And there's never a respite.
    Touch it, it'll ring,
    It's like glass, fractures easily.
    When all's said and done,   2200
    A hollow, void thing.
    Here it shines brightly,
    And brighter here—tinsel!
    —Oops, ain't I nimble!
    But you, son, take care   2205
    And keep a safe distance,
    Or surely you'll die.
    The thing's made of clay,
    A knock, and it's fragments.
MEPHISTO   What is that sieve for?   2210
HE-APE [*Taking it down*]
    If you came here to thieve,

It would be my informer.
[*He scampers across to the* SHE-APE *and has her look through it.*]
Look through the sieve!
Now say, do you know him?
Or you don't dare to name him?   2215
MEPHISTO [*Approaching the fire*]   And this pot over here?
APES
Oh, you're a blockhead, sir—
Don't know what a pot's for!
Nor a cauldron neither.
MEPHISTO   What a rude creature!   2220
HE-APE
Here, take this duster,
Sit down in the armchair.
[*Presses* MEPHISTOPHELES *down in the chair.*]
FAUST [*Who meanwhile has been standing in front of a mirror, going forward
to peer into it from close up and then stepping back*]
What do I see? It's a magic mirror!
What a vision of beauty! Love lend me your pinions,
The swiftest you have, so I may speed to her,   2225
Love, show me the way to the heaven she dwells in!
Oh dear, unless I stay fixed to this spot,
If I dare to move the least bit nearer,
Mist blurs the vision and quite obscures her.
Woman unrivaled, beauty absolute!   2230
Can such things be, a creature so lovely?
The body so indolently stretched out there
Surely epitomizes all that is heavenly.
Can such a marvel inhabit down here?
MEPHISTO   Naturally, if God has sweated hard for six whole days, 2235
And on the seventh himself cries Bravo! seeing his works,
You can be sure he's obtained better than average results.
Look all you want now, stare away, gaze;
But I can put your hands on that prize,
And happy the man, his fortune's assured,   2240
Who can bring home such a sweetie to his bed and board.
[FAUST *continues to stare into the mirror, while* MEPHISTOPHELES, *lean-
ing back comfortably in the armchair and toying with the feather duster,
talks on.*]
Here I sit like a king on a throne,
Scepter in hand, all I'm lacking's my crown.
APES [*Who have been performing all sorts of queer, involved movements,
with loud cries bring* MEPHISTOPHELES *a crown*]
Here, your majesty,
If you would,   2245
Glue up the crown
With sweat and blood!
[*Their clumsy handling of the crown causes it to break in two, and they
cavort around with the pieces.*]
Oh there, now it's broken!

We look and we listen,
We chatter, scream curses, 2250
And make up our verses—

FAUST [*Still gazing raptly into the mirror*]
Good God, how my mind reels, it's going to snap!

MEPHISTO [*Nodding toward the* APES]
My own head's starting to spin like a top.

APES
And if by some fluke
The words happen to suit 2255
Then the rhyme makes a thought!

FAUST [*As above*]   I feel as if my insides are on fire!
Come, we've got to get out of here.

MEPHISTO [*Keeping his seat*]   They tell the truth, these poets do,
You've got to give the creatures their due. 2260
[*The cauldron, neglected by the* SHE-APE, *starts to boil over, causing a
great tongue of flame to shoot up in the chimney.* THE WITCH *comes riding
down the flame, shrieking hideously.*]

THE WITCH   It hurts, it hurts!
Monkeys, apes, incompetent brutes!
Forgetting the pot and singeing your mistress—
The servants I have! Utterly brainless!
[*Catching sight of* FAUST *and* MEPHISTOPHELES]
What's this? What's this? 2265
Who are you? Explain!
What's your business?
Sneaking your way in!
Hellfire's pains
Torture your bones! 2270
[*She plunges the spoon into the cauldron and scatters fire over* FAUST,
MEPHISTOPHELES *and the* APES. *The apes whine.*]

MEPHISTOPHELES [*Turning the duster upside down and hitting out violently
among the glasses and jars with the butt end*]
Let's knock things around,
Let's have a good smashup!
It's all in fun, really—
Beating time, you old carcass,
To your melody. 2275
[THE WITCH *starts back in rage and fear.*]
Can't recognize me, can you, rattlebones?
Can't recognize your lord and master?
Why I don't chop up you and your monkey friends
Into the littlest bits and pieces is a wonder!
No respect at all for my red doublet? 2280
And my cock's feather means nothing to you, bedlam?
Is my face masked, or can you plainly see it?
Must I tell *you* of all people who I am?

THE WITCH   Oh sir, forgive my discourteous salute!
But I look in vain for your cloven foot, 2285
And your two ravens, where are they?

MEPHISTO Well, this time you're let off—I remember,
It's been so long since we've seen each other.
Also, the world's grown so cultured today,
Even the Devil's been swept up in it;   2290
The northern bogey has made his departure,
No horns now, no tail, to make people shiver;
And as for my hoof, though I can't do without it,
Socially it would raise too many eyebrows,
And so, like a lot of other young fellows,   2295
I've padded my calves to try and conceal it.
THE WITCH [Dancing with glee]
I'm out of my mind with delight, I am,
My lord Satan's appeared again.
MEPHISTO Woman, that name—I forbid you to speak it!
THE WITCH Why not? Whatever's wrong with it?   2300
MEPHISTO Since God knows when, it belongs to mythology,
But that's hardly improved the temper of humanity.
The Evil One's no more, evil ones more than ever.
Address me as Baron, that will do,
A gentleman of rank like any other.   2305
And if you doubt my blood is blue,
See, here's my house's arms, the noblest ever!
          [He makes an indecent gesture.]
THE WITCH [Laughing excessively]
Ha, ha! It's you, it's you, I swear,
The same old rascal you always were!
MEPHISTO [To FAUST] Observe, friend, my diplomacy   2310
And learn the art of witch-mastery.
THE WITCH Gentlemen, now what's your pleasure?
MEPHISTO A generous glass of your famous liquor.
But please, let it be from your oldest stock:
It doubles in strength as the years mount up.   2315
THE WITCH At once! Here I've got, as it happens, a bottle
From which I myself every now and then tipple,
And what is more, it's lost all its stink.
I'll gladly pour you out a cup.
          [Under her breath]
But if the fellow's unprepared, the drink   2320
Might kill him, you know, before an hour's up.
MEPHISTO I know the man well, he'll thrive on it;
I wish him the best your kitchen affords.
Now draw your circle, say the magic words,
And pour him out a brimming goblet.   2325
          [Making bizarre gestures, THE WITCH draws a circle and sets down an
          assortment of strange objects inside it. All the glasses start to ring and the
          pots to resound, providing a kind of musical accompaniment. Last of all,
          she brings out a great tome and stands the APES in the circle to serve as
          a lectern and to hold up the torches. Then she signals FAUST to approach]
FAUST [To MEPHISTOPHELES]
What's to be hoped from this, would you tell me?

That junk of hers, and her waving her arms crazily,
All the crude deceptions she's practicing—
I know them too well, they fill me with loathing.
MEPHISTO   Nonsense, friend, it's not all that serious;   2330
Really, you're being much too difficult.
She needs a bit of hocus-pocus
For her elixer to produce a result.
    [*He presses* FAUST *inside the circle.*]
THE WITCH [*Declaiming from the book, with great emphasis*]
    Hearken to me!
    From one make ten,   2335
    Now two goes in,
    And after, a three,
    And lo, you are rich!
    Drop the four!
    From five and six,   2340
    So says the witch,
    Make seven and eight,
    And all's complete.
    And nine is one,
    And ten is none,   2345
    And now my witch's table's done.
FAUST   I think the old woman's throwing a fit.
MEPHISTO   We're nowhere near the end of it.
I know the book, it's all like that.
The time I've wasted over it!   2350
For a thoroughgoing paradox is what
Bemuses fools and wise men equally.
The trick's got a beard, yet it's still going strong:
With Three-in-One and One-in-Three[6]
Lies are sown broadcast, truth may go hang.   2355
The Doctor drones on in undisturbed peace:
Who wants to debate and dispute with a fool?
People dutifully think, hearing all that glib speech,
It can't be such big words mean nothing at all.
THE WITCH [*Continuing*]
    The power of wisdom   2360
    From the whole world kept hidden
    Save from those who don't think—
    To them it is given
    Unsought and unbidden,
    It's theirs without sweat.   2365
FAUST   Did you hear that, my God, what nonsense,
It's giving me a headache, phew!
It makes me think I'm listening to
A hundred thousand fools in chorus.
MEPHISTO   Enough, enough, O excellent Sibyl!   2370
Bring on the potion, fill the cup.

6. The Christian doctrine of the Trinity.

Your drink won't give my friend here trouble,
He's earned his Ph.D. in many a bout.

[THE WITCH *very ceremoniously pours the potion into a bowl; when* FAUST
raises it to his lips, a low flame plays over it.]

Drink, now drink, no need to diddle,
It'll put you into a fine glow.   2375
When you've got a sidekick in the Devil,
Why should some fire frighten you so?

[THE WITCH *breaks the circle and* FAUST *steps out.*]

Now let's be off, you mustn't dally.

THE WITCH   I hope that little nip, sir, hits the spot!

MEPHISTO [*To* THE WITCH]   Madam, thanks. If I can help *you* out,   2380
Don't fail, upon Walpurgis Night,[7] to ask me.

THE WITCH [*To* FAUST]   Here is a song, sir, carol it now and then,
You'll find it assists the medicine.

MEPHISTO   Come away quick! You must do as I say.
To soak up the potion body and soul,   2385
A man's got to sweat a bucketful.
And after, I'll teach you the gentleman's way
Of wasting your time expensively.
Soon yours the delight outdelights all things—
Boy Cupid astir in you, stretching his wings.   2390

FAUST   A last look in the mirror, let me—
That woman was so very lovely!

MEPHISTO   No, no, soon enough you'll behold in the flesh
The fairest woman that ever drew breath.

[*Aside*] With that stuff in him, old Jack will   2395
Soon see a Helen in every Jill.

A STREET

FAUST. MARGARETE *passing by.*

FAUST   Pretty lady, here's my arm,
Would you allow me to see you home?

MARGARETE   I'm neither pretty nor a lady,
And I can find my way unaided.   2400

[*She escapes his arm and passes by.*]

FAUST   By God, what a lovely girl,
I've never seen her like, a pearl!
A good girl, too, and quick-witted,
Her behavior modest and yet spirited,
Those glowing cheeks, lips like a rose,   2405
Will haunt me till the end of days!
The way she looked down shamefastly
Touched me to the heart, profoundly;
And bringing me up short, quite speechless—
Oh that was charming, that was priceless!   2410

---

7. May Day Eve (April 30), when witches are supposed to assemble on the Brocken, the highest peak in
the Harz Mountains, which are in central Germany.

[*Enter* MEPHISTOPHELES.]

FAUST Get me that girl, do you hear, you must!

MEPHISTO What girl?

FAUST   The one who just went past.

MEPHISTO Oh, her. She's just been to confession
To be absolved of all her sins.
I sidled near the box to listen: 2415
She could have spared herself her pains,
She is the soul of innocence
And has no reason, none at all,
To visit the confessional.
Her kind is too much for me.   2420

FAUST She's over fourteen, isn't she?

MEPHISTO Well, listen to him, the lady-killer,[8]
Eager to pluck every flower he sees,
Who's quite convinced that every favor
Is his to have, hand it over, please.   2425
But it doesn't go so easy always.

FAUST Dear Doctor of What's Right and Proper,
Spare me your lectures, I can do without.
Let me tell you it straight out:
If I don't hold that darling creature   2430
Tight in my arms this very night,
We're through, we two, at stroke of midnight.

MEPHISTO Impossible! That's out of the question!
I must have two weeks at least
To spy out a propitious occasion.   2435

FAUST With a quiet hour or so, at the most,
I could seduce her handily—
Don't need the Devil to pimp for me.

MEPHISTO You're talking like a Frenchman now.
Calm down, there's no cause for vexation.   2440
You'll find that instant gratification
Disappoints; if you allow
For compliments and billets doux,
Whisperings and rendezvous,
The pleasure's felt so much more keenly.   2445
Italian novels teach you exactly.

FAUST I've no use for your slow-paced courting;
My appetite needs no whetting.

MEPHISTO Please, I'm being serious.
With such a pretty little miss   2450
You mustn't be impetuous
And assault the fortress frontally.
What's called for here is strategy.

FAUST Something of hers, do you hear, I require!
Come, show me the way to the room she sleeps in,   2455
Get me a scarf, a glove, a ribbon,
A garter with which to feed my desire!

---

8. The German reads *Hans Liederlich*, meaning a profligate since *liederlich* means "careless" or "dissolute."

MEPHISTO   To prove to you my earnest intention
    By every means to further your passion,
    Not losing a minute, without delay   2460
    I'll take you to her room today.
FAUST   I'll see her, yes? And have her?
MEPHISTO   No!
    She'll be at a neighbor's—you *must* go slow!
    Meanwhile in her room, alone there,
    You can drink her atmosphere   2465
    And dream of the delights to come.
FAUST   Can we start now?
MEPHISTO   Too soon, too soon!
FAUST   Well, find me a present I can give her.
                               [*Exit.*]
MEPHISTO   Presents already? The man's proving a lover!
    Now for his gift. I know there's treasure   2470
    Buried in many an out-of-the-way corner.
    Off I go to reconnoiter!

EVENING

A small room, very neat and clean.

MARGARETE [*As she braids her hair and puts it up*]
    Who was he, I wonder, that gentleman,
    Who spoke to me this afternoon?
    I wish I knew. He seemed very nice.   2475
    I'm sure he's noble, from some great house;
    His look and manner told you that plainly,
    And who else would speak so boldly?
                                 [*Exit.*]

[MEPHISTOPHELES, FAUST.]
MEPHISTO   Come in now, in!—but quietly.
FAUST [*After a silent interval*]   Leave, would you, I would like to be
    alone.   2480
MEPHISTO [*Sniffing around*]   Not every girl keeps things so neat and clean.
                                 [*Exit.*]
FAUST   Welcome, evening's tender dark,
    Stealing through this holy spot,
    Heart, my heart, learn love's sweet ache,
    That lives upon the dew of hope.   2485
    Stillness reigns here, breathing quietly
    Peace, good order and contentment—
    What riches in this poverty,
    What bliss I feel in this confinement!
      [*He flings himself into a leather armchair by the bed.*]
    How good it is to sink into this chair   2490
    Where many a one, in times gone by, has sat
    Through all life's joys and all of its despair!
    How often children must have crowded round
    This seat where their grandfather sat enthroned!

Here she, perhaps, pleased with her Christmas present,   2495
Pressed her round cheek against his shrunken hand.
Dear girl, I feel where you are, all is comfort,
Where you are, order, goodness all abound;
Instructed by your own maternal spirit,
Your quick hands spread the clean cloth on the table,   2500
Scatter the sand on the floor, housewifely, in a pattern,[9]
Dear hands, so good, so capable,
That change this cottage into very heaven.
And here—!
      [*He lifts a bed curtain.*]
        I tremble, frightened, with delight!
Here I could linger hour after hour.   2505
Here the dear creature, softly dreaming, slept,
Her angel substance slowly shaped by Nature.
Here warm life in her tender bosom swelled,
Here by a pure and holy weaving
Of the strands, there was revealed   2510
The celestial being.

But me? What is it brought me here?
See how shaken, how moved I am!
What do I want? Why is my heart so torn?
Poor Faust, I hardly know you any more.   2515

Has this room put a spell on me?
I came here burning up with lust,
And melt with love now, helplessly.
Are we blown about by every gust?

And suppose she came in now, this minute,   2520
How I would have to atone for it!
The big talker, Herr Professor,
Would dwindle to nothing, grovel before her.
MEPHISTO [*Entering*]   Hurry! I saw her, she's coming up.
FAUST   Hurry indeed, I'll never come here again!   2525
MEPHISTO   Here's a jewel box I snatched up
When I—but who cares how or when.
Put it in the closet there,
She'll jump for joy when she comes on it.
It's got a number of choice things in it,   2530
Meant for another—but I declare,
Girls are girls, they're all the same,
The only thing that matters is the game.
FAUST   Should I, I wonder?
MEPHISTO   *Should* you, you say!
Do you mean to keep it for yourself?   2535
If what you're after's treasure, pelf,
Then I have wasted my whole day,

---

9. Floors were sprinkled with sand after cleaning.

Been put to a lot of needless bother.
I hope you aren't some awful miser—
After all my head-scratching, scheming, labor!   2540
    [*He puts the box in the closet and shuts it.*]
Come on, let's go!
Our aim? Your darling's favor,
So you may do with her as you'd like to do.
—And you stand there
Looking like a lecturer   2545
Who fears he'll find, staring across at him,
Gray Philosophy in person!
Come on, come on!

                                  [*Exit.*]

MARGARETE [*With a lamp*] How close, oppressive it is in here.
    [*She opens the window.*]
And yet outside it isn't warm.   2550
I feel, I don't know why, so queer—
I wish Mother would come home.
I tremble so in every limb—
What a foolish, frightened girl I am!
    [*She sings as she undresses.*]
There was a king in Thule,[1]   2555
No truer man drank up,
To whom his mistress, dying,
Gave a golden cup.

Nothing he held dearer,
And at the loud banquet,   2560
Each time he raised the beaker
All saw his eyes were wet.

And when death knocked, he tallied
His towns and treasure up,
Yielded his heirs all gladly,   2565
All except the cup.

In the great hall of his fathers,
In the castle by the sea,
He and his knights sat down to
Their last revelry.   2570

Up stood the old carouser,
Drank life-warmth one more time,
Then pitched the sacred beaker
Out into the tide.

He saw it fall, fill up and   2575
Founder in the sea.

---

1. The fabled *ultima Thule* of Latin literature—those distant lands just beyond the reach of every explorer. Goethe wrote the ballad in 1774; it was published in 1782 and set to music by several composers.

His eyes glazed over,
And never again drank he.

[*She opens the closet to put her clothes away and sees the jewel box.*]

How did this pretty box get here?
I locked the closet, I'm quite sure.   2580
Whatever's in the box? Maybe
Mother took it in pledge today.
And there's the little key on a ribbon.
I think I'd like to open it!
—Look at all this, God in Heaven!   2585
I've never seen the like of it!
Jewels! And *such* jewels, that a fine lady
Might wear on a great holiday.
How would the necklace look on me?
Who is it owns these wonderful things?   2590

[*She puts the jewelry on and stands in front of the mirror.*]

I wish they were mine, these lovely earrings!
When you put them on, you're changed completely.
But what do youth and beauty amount to?
They are not what men pay mind to.
Praising you, their eyes turn elsewhere,   2595
Money's younger, money's prettier,
Money is the thing they seek, all,
Alas for us, the poor people!

OUT WALKING

FAUST *strolling up and down, thinking. To him* MEPHISTOPHELES.

MEPHISTO   By true love cruelly scorned! By Hellfire black and fiery!
  If only I could think of worse to swear by!   2600
FAUST   What's wrong, what's thrown you into such a turmoil?
  I've never seen you like this till today.
MEPHISTO   The Devil take me, that's what I would say,
  If it didn't so happen I'm the Devil.
FAUST   Are you in your right mind—behaving   2605
  Like a madman, wildly raving?
MEPHISTO   The jewels I got for Gretchen,[2] just imagine—
  A damned priest's gone and made off with them!
  The minute her mother saw them, she
  Began to tremble fearfully.   2610
  The woman has a nose! It's stuck
  Forever in her prayerbook;
  She knows right off, by the smell alone,
  If something's sacred or profane;
  One whiff of the jewelry was enough   2615
  To tell her something's wrong with the stuff.
  My child—she cried—and listen well to me,

---

2. Diminutive of the German *Margarete*. She is given this name through much of the play.

All property obtained unlawfully
Does body and soul a mortal injury.
These jewels we'll consecrate to the Blessed Virgin,   2620
And for reward have showers of manna from Heaven.
Our little Margaret pouted, loath—
Why look a gift horse[3] in the mouth?
And surely the one who gave her it
So generously, was hardly wicked.   2625
Her mother sent for the priest, and he,
When he saw how the land lay,
Was mightily pleased. You've done, he said,
Just as you should, mother and maid;
Who overcometh, is repaid.   2630
The Church's stomach's very capacious,
Gobbles up whole realms, anything precious,
Nor once suffers qualms, not even belches.
The Church alone, dear sister, God has named
Receiver of goods unlawfully obtained.   2635
FAUST   That's the way the whole world over,
From a king to a Jew, so all do, ever.
MEPHISTO   So then he pockets brooches, chains and rings
As if they were quite ordinary things,
And gives the women as much thanks   2640
As a body gets for a handful of nuts;
In Heaven, he says, you'll be compensated—
And makes off leaving them feeling uplifted.
FAUST   And Gretchen?
MEPHISTO   Sits there restlessly,
Her mind confused, her will uncertain,   2645
Thinks about jewels night and day,
Even more about the one who brought them.
FAUST   I can't bear that she should suffer.
Find her new ones immediately!
Poor stuff, those others, anyway.   2650
MEPHISTO   Oh yes indeed! With a snap of the fingers!
FAUST   Do what I say—march, man, don't linger!
Insinuate yourself with her neighbor!
Damn it, devil, you move so sluggishly!
Fetch Gretchen new and better jewelry!   2655
MEPHISTO   Yes, yes, just as Your Majesty prefers.

                                                        [*Exit* FAUST.]

A lovesick fool! To amuse his doxy
He'd blow the world up, sun and moon and stars.

THE NEIGHBOR'S HOUSE

MARTHE [*Alone*]   May God forgive that man of mine,
He's done me wrong—disappeared   2660
Into the night without a word

---

3. Like the wooden horse in which Greek soldiers entered Troy to capture it; an emblem of treachery.

And left me here to sleep alone.
I never gave him cause for grief
But loved him as a faithful wife.
    [*She weeps.*]
Suppose he's dead—oh I feel hopeless!   2665
If only I had an official notice.
    [*Enter* MARGARETE.]

MARGARETE   Frau Marthe!

MARTHE   Gretel, what's wrong, tell me!

MARGARETE   I feel so weak I'm near collapse!
Just now I found another box
Inside my closet. Ebony,   2670
And such things in it, much more splendid
Than the first ones, I'm dumbfounded!

MARTHE   Never a word to your mother about it,
Or the priest will have all the next minute.

MARGARETE   Just look at this, and this, and this here!   2675

MARTHE [*Decking her out in the jewels*]
Oh, what a lucky girl you are!

MARGARETE   But I mustn't be seen in the streets with such jewelry,
And never in church. Oh, it's too cruel!

MARTHE   Come over to me whenever you're able,
Here you can wear them without any worry,   2680
March back and forth in front of the mirror—
Won't we enjoy ourselves together!
And when it's a holiday, some such occasion,
Bit by bit you can start to wear them;
First a necklace, then a pearl earring,   2685
Your mother, I'm sure, won't notice a thing,
And if she does we'll think of something.

MARGARETE   Who put the jewelry in my closet?
There's something that's not right about it.
    [*A knock.*]
Dear God above, can that be Mother?   2690

MARTHE [*Peeping through the curtain*]
Please come in!—No, it's a stranger.
    [*Enter* MEPHISTOPHELES.]

MEPHISTO   With your permission, my good women!
I beg you to excuse the intrusion.
    [*Steps back deferentially from* MARGARETE.]
I'm looking for Frau Marthe Schwerdtlein.

MARTHE   I'm her. And what have you to say, sir?   2695

MEPHISTO [*Under his breath to her*]
Now I know who you are, that's enough.
You have a lady under your roof,
I'll go away and come back later.

MARTHE [*Aloud*]   Goodness, child, you won't believe me,
What the gentleman thinks is, you're a lady!   2700

MARGARETE   A poor girl's what I am, no more.
The gentleman's kind—I thank you, sir.
These jewels don't belong to me.

MEPHISTO Ah, it's not just the jewelry,
    It's the Fräulein herself, so clear-eyed, serene.   2705
    —So delighted I'm allowed to remain.

MARTHE Why are you here, if I may ask?

MEPHISTO I wish my news were pleasanter.
    Don't blame me, the messenger:
    Your husband's dead. He sent his best.   2710

MARTHE The good man's dead, gone, departed?
    Then I'll die too. Oh, I'm broken-hearted!

MARGARETE Marthe dear, it's too violent, your sorrow!

MEPHISTO Hear the sad story I've come to tell you.

MARGARETE As long as I live I'll never love, no,   2715
    It would kill me with grief to lose my man so.

MEPHISTO Joy's latter end is sorrow—and sorrow's joy.

MARTHE Tell me how the dear man died.

MEPHISTO He's buried in Padua, beside
    The blessed saint, sweet Anthony,   2720
    In hallowed ground where he can lie
    In rest eternal, quietly.

MARTHE And nothing else, sir, that is all?

MEPHISTO A last request. He enjoins you solemnly:
    Let three hundred masses be sung for his soul!   2725
    As for anything else, my pocket's empty.

MARTHE What! No gold coin, jewel, souvenir,
    Such as every journeyman keeps in his wallet,
    And would sooner go hungry and beg than sell it?

MEPHISTO Nothing, I'm sorry to say, Madam dear.   2730
    However—he never squandered his money,
    And he sincerely regretted his sins,
    Regretted even more he was so unlucky.

MARGARETE Why must so many be so unhappy!
    I'll pray for him often, say requiems.   2735

MEPHISTO What a lovable creature, there's none dearer!
    What you should have now, right away,
    Is a good husband. It's true what I say.

MARGARETE Oh no, it's not time yet, that must come later.

MEPHISTO If not now a husband, meanwhile a lover.   2740
    What blessing from Heaven, which one of life's charms
    Rivals holding a dear thing like you in one's arms.

MARGARETE With us people here it isn't the custom.

MEPHISTO Custom or not, all the same it is what's done.

MARTHE Go on with your story, sir, go on!   2745

MEPHISTO He lay on a bed of half-rotten straw,
    Better at least than a dunghill; and there
    He died as a Christian, knowing well
    Much remained outstanding on his bill.
    "Oh how," he cried, "I hate myself!   2750
    To abandon my trade, desert my wife!
    It kills me even to think of it.
    If only she would forgive and forget!"

MARTHE [*Weeping*] I did, long ago! The dear man's forgiven!

MEPHISTO "But she's more to blame, God knows, than I am." 2755

MARTHE He's a liar! How shameless! At death's very door!

MEPHISTO His mind wandered as the end drew near,
  If I'm anything of a connoisseur here.
  "No pleasure," he said, "no good times, nor anything nice;
  First getting children, then getting them fed, 2760
  Fed all the time, and not just with food,
  With never a moment for having my bite in peace."

MARTHE How could he forget my love and loyalty,
  My hard work day and night, the drudgery!

MEPHISTO He didn't forget, he remembered all tenderly. 2765
  "When we set sail from Malta's port," he said,
  "For wife and children fervently I prayed.
  And Heaven, hearing, smiled down kindly,
  For we captured a Turkish vessel, stuffed
  With the Sultan's treasure. How we rejoiced! 2770
  Our courage being recompensed,
  I left the ship with a fatter purse
  Than ever I'd owned before in my life."

MARTHE Treasure! Do you think he buried it?

MEPHISTO Who knows what's become of it? 2775
  In Naples, where he wandered about,
  A pretty miss with a kind heart
  Showed the stranger such good will
  Till the day he died he felt it still.

MARTHE The villain! Robbing his children, his wife! 2780
  And for all his misery, dire need,
  He would never give up his scandalous life.

MEPHISTO Well, he's been paid, the man is dead.
  If I were in your shoes, my dear,
  I'd mourn him decently a year 2785
  And meanwhile keep an eye out for another.

MARTHE Dear God, I'm sure it won't be easy
  To find, on this earth, his successor;
  So full of jokes he was, so jolly!
  But he was restless, always straying, 2790
  Loved foreign women, foreign wine,
  And how he loved, drat him, dice-playing.

MEPHISTO Oh well, I'm sure things worked out fine
  If he was equally forgiving.
  With such an arrangement, why, I swear 2795
  I'd marry you myself, my dear!

MARTHE Oh sir, you would? You're joking, I'm sure!

MEPHISTO [*Aside*] Time to leave! This one's an ogress,
  She'd sue the Devil for breach of promise!
    [*To* GRETCHEN]
  And what's your love life like, my charmer? 2800

MARGARETE What do you mean?

MEPHISTO [*Aside*]   Oh you good girl,

All innocence! [*Aloud*] And now farewell.

MARGARETE Farewell.

MARTHE   Quick, one last matter,
  If you would I want to know
  If I might have some proof to show   2805
  How and when my husband died
  And where the poor man now is laid?
  I like to have things right and proper,
  With a notice published in the paper.

MEPHISTO Madam, yes. To attest the truth,   2810
  Two witnesses must swear an oath.
  I know someone, a good man; we
  Will go before the notary.
  I'll introduce you to him.

MARTHE   Do.

MEPHISTO And she'll be here, your young friend, too?—   2815
  A very fine fellow who's been all over,
  So polite to ladies, so urbane his behavior.

MARGARETE I'd blush for shame before the gentleman.

MEPHISTO No, not before a king or any man!

MARTHE We'll wait for you tonight, the two of us,   2820
  Inside my garden, just behind the house.

A STREET

FAUST, MEPHISTOPHELES

FAUST Well? What's doing? When am I going to have her?

MEPHISTO Bravo, bravo, I can see you're all on fire!
  Very shortly Gretchen will be yours.
  This evening you will meet her at her neighbor's.   2825
  Oh, that's a woman made to order
  To play the bawd, our Mistress Marthe.

FAUST Good work.

MEPHISTO   There's something we must do for her, however.

FAUST One good turn deserves another.

MEPHISTO All it is is swear an oath   2830
  Her husband's buried in the earth,
  Interred in consecrated ground at Padua.

FAUST So that means we must make a trip there—very clever!

MEPHISTO Sancta simplicitas![4] Whoever said that?
  Just swear an oath; that's all there's to it.   2835

FAUST If that's your scheme, keep it, I'm through.

MEPHISTO The saintly fellow! Just like you!
  Declaring falsely—Heaven forbid!—
  Is something Faustus never did.
  Haven't you pontificated   2840
  About God and the world, undisconcerted,

---

4. Holy simplicity (Latin).

About man, man's mind and heart and being,
As bold as brass, without blushing?
Look at it closely and what's the truth?
You know as much about those things   2845
As you know about Herr Schwerdtlein's death.

FAUST   You always were a sophist and a liar.

MEPHISTO   Indeed, indeed. If we look ahead a little further,
To tomorrow, what do we see?
You swearing, oh so honorably,   2850
Your soul is Gretchen's—cajoling and deceiving her.

FAUST   My soul, and all my heart as well.

MEPHISTO   Oh wonderful!
You'll swear undying faith and love eternal,
Go on about desire unique and irresistible,
About longing, boundless, infinite: 2855
That, too, with all your heart—I'll bet!

FAUST   With all my heart! And now enough.
What I feel, an emotion of such depth,
Such turbulence—when I try to find
A name for it and nothing comes to mind,   2860
And cast about, search heaven and earth
For words to express its transcendent worth,
And call the fire in which I burn
Eternal, yes, eternal, without end—
Do you really mean to tell me   2865
That's just devil's doing, deception, lying?

MEPHISTO   Say what you please, I'm right.

FAUST   One word more, one only,
And then I'll save my breath. A man who is unyielding,
Sure, absolutely, he's right, and has a tongue in his mouth—
Is right. So come, I'm sick of arguing.   2870
You're right, and the reason's simple enough:
I must do what I must, can't help myself.

A GARDEN

MARGARETE *with* FAUST, *her arm linked with his;* MARTHE *with* MEPHISTOPHELES.
The two couples stroll up and down.

MARGARETE   You are too kind, sir, I am sure it's meant
To spare a simple girl embarrassment.
A traveler finds whatever amusement he can,   2875
You've been all over, you're a gentleman—
How can anything I say
Interest you in any way?

FAUST   I'm more pleased by one word of yours, one look,
Than all the wisdom in the great world's book.   2880
        [*He kisses her hand.*]

MARGARETE   No, no, sir, please, you mustn't! How could you kiss
A hand so ugly—red and coarse?

You can't imagine all the work I have to do;
My mother must have things just so.
    [*They walk on.*]

MARTHE   And you, sir, I believe, you constantly travel?   2885
MEPHISTO   Business, business! It is so demanding!
Leaving a place you like can be so painful,
But there's no help for it, you have to keep on going.
MARTHE   How fine, how free, when you're young and full of ginger,
To travel the world, see everything,   2890
But soon enough worse times arrive and worser;
No one can find it to his liking
To crawl to his grave a lonely bachelor.
MEPHISTO   When I look at what's ahead, I tremble.
MARTHE   Then, sir, bethink yourself while you're still able.   2895
    [*They walk on.*]
MARGARETE   Yes, out of sight is out of mind.
It's second nature with you, gallantry;
But you have heaps and heaps of friends
Cleverer by far, oh much, than me.
FAUST   Dear girl, believe me, what's called cleverness   2900
Is mostly shallowness and vanity.
MARGARETE   What do you mean?
FAUST   God, isn't it a pity
That pure simplicity and innocence
Should never know itself and its own worth,
That meekness, lowliness, those highest gifts   2905
Kindly Nature endows us with—
MARGARETE   You'll think of me for a moment or two,
I'll have hours enough to think of you.
FAUST   You're alone a good deal, are you?
MARGARETE   Our family's very small, it's true,   2910
But still it has to be looked to.
We have no maid, I sweep the floors, I cook and knit
And sew, do all the errands, morning and night;
Mother's very careful about money,
All's accounted for to the last penny.   2915
Not that she really needs to pinch and save;
We could afford much more than many have.
My father left us a good bit,
With a small dwelling added to it,
And a garden just outside the city.   2920
But lately I've lived quietly.
My brother is a soldier. My little sister died.
The trouble that she cost me, the poor child!
But I loved her very much, I'd gladly do
It all again.
FAUST   An angel, if at all like you.   2925
MARGARETE   All the care of her was mine,
And she was very fond of her sister.
My father died before she was born,

And Mother, well, we nearly lost her;
It took so long, oh many months, till she got better. 2930
It was out of the question she should nurse
The poor little crying thing herself,
So I nursed her, on milk and water.
I felt she was my own daughter.
In my arms, upon my lap, 2935
She smiled and kicked, grew round and plump.
FAUST   The happiness it must have given you!
MARGARETE   But it was hard on me so often, too.
Her crib stood at my bedside, near my head,
A slightest movement, cradle's creak, 2940
And instantly I was awake;
I'd give her a bottle, or take her into my bed;
If still she fretted, up I'd get,
Walk up and down with her, swaying and crooning,
And be at the washtub early the next morning; 2945
To market after that, then getting the hearth to blaze,
And so it went, day after day, always.
Not the merriest life you can have, sir, here below,
But your supper tastes good, and at night, what a pleasure, your pillow.
       [They walk on.]
MARTHE   It's very hard on us poor women; 2950
You bachelors are such a problem.
MEPHISTO   What's needed are more charmers like yourself
To bring us bachelors down from off the shelf.
MARTHE   There's never, sir, been anyone? Confess!
You've never lost your heart to one of us? 2955
MEPHISTO   How does the proverb go? A loving wife,
And one's own hearthside, are more worth
Than all the gold that's hidden in the earth.
MARTHE   I mean, you've had no wish, yourself?
MEPHISTO   Oh, everywhere I've been received politely. 2960
MARTHE   No, what I mean is, hasn't there been somebody
Who ever made your heart beat? Seriously?
MEPHISTO   It's never a joking matter with women, believe me.
MARTHE   Oh, you don't understand!
MEPHISTO   So sorry! Still,
I understand that you are—amiable. 2965
       [They walk on.]
FAUST   You recognized me instantly
When I came through the gate into the garden?
MARGARETE   I dropped my eyes. Didn't you see?
FAUST   And you'll forgive the liberty, you'll pardon
My swaggering up in that insulting fashion 2970
When you came out of the church door?
MARGARETE   I was bewildered. Never before
Had I been spoken to in that way.
I'm a good girl. Who would dare
To say a bad thing, ever, about me? 2975

Did he, I wondered, see a suggestion
Of something flaunting in my look?
There's a creature, he seemed to think,
With whom a man might strike a bargain
On the spot. But I'll confess,   2980
Something there was, I don't know what,
Spoke in your favor, here in my breast.
And oh how vexed I felt with myself
To find I wasn't vexed with you in the least.

FAUST   Dear girl!

MARGARETE   Just wait.
　　　[*Picking a daisy and plucking the petals one by one*]

FAUST   What is it for, a bouquet?   2985

MARGARETE   Only a little game of ours.

FAUST   A game, is it?

MARGARETE   Never mind. I'm afraid you'll laugh at me.
　　　[*Murmuring to herself as she plucks the petals*]

FAUST   I can't hear. What is it?

MARGARETE [*under her breath*]
　　　　　　　　　Loves me—loves me not—

FAUST   Oh, what a creature, heavenly!

MARGARETE [*continuing*]   He loves me—not—he loves me—not—   2990
　　　[*Plucking the last petal and crying out delightedly*]
He loves me.

FAUST   Dearest, yes! Yes, let the flower be
The oracle that tells your destiny.
He loves you! Do you understand?
He loves you! Let me take your hand.
　　　[*He takes her hands in his.*]

MARGARETE   I'm trembling with fear.   2995

FAUST   Don't be afraid! Read the look
On my face, feel my hands gripping yours—
They tell you what's impossible
Ever to put in words:
Here is complete surrender, and such rapture   3000
As must never end, must be eternal!
Yes, eternal! It's end would mean
Utter despair!
No; no end! No end!
　　　[MARGARETE *squeezes his hands, frees herself and runs away. He doesn't*
　　　move for a moment, thinking, then follows her.]

MARTHE   It's getting dark.

MEPHISTO   That's right. We have to go.   3005

MARTHE   Please forgive me if I don't invite
You in. But ours is such a nasty-minded street,
You'd think people had no more to do
Than watch their neighbors' every coming and going.
The gossip that goes on here, about nothing!   3010
But where are they, our little couple?

MEPHISTO   Flew.

Up that path like butterflies.

MARTHE   He seems to like her.

MEPHISTO   And she him. Which is the way the world swags ever.

A SUMMERHOUSE

GRETCHEN *runs in and hides behind the door, putting her fingertips to her lips and peeping through a crack.*

MARGARETE   Here he comes!

FAUST   You're teasing me, are you?
I've got you now. [*Kisses her.*]

MARGARETE [*Holding him around and returning the kiss*]
                          I love you, yes, I do!   3015
          [MEPHISTOPHELES *knocks.*]

FAUST [*Stamping his foot*]
Who's there?

MEPHISTO   A friend.

FAUST   A brute!

MEPHISTO   We must be on our way.

MARTHE [*Coming up*]   Yes, sir, it's late.

FAUST   I'd like to walk you home.

MARGARETE   My mother, I'm afraid. . . . Goodbye!

FAUST   So we must say
Goodbye? Goodbye!

MARGARETE   I hope I'll see you soon.
                          [*Exit* FAUST *and* MEPHISTOPHELES.]

Good God, the thoughts that fill the brain   3020
Of such a man, oh it's astounding!
I stand there dumbly, red with shame,
And stammer yes to everything.
I'm such a poor little ignorant fool,
How should I interest him at all?   3025

A CAVERN IN THE FOREST

FAUST [*Alone*]   Sublime Spirit, all that I asked for, all,
You gave me. Not for nothing was it,
The face you showed me, glaring, out of the fire.
You gave me glorious Nature for my kingdom,
With the power to feel, to delight in her—nor as   3030
A spectator only, coolly admiring her wonders,
But seeing deep into her bosom
As a man sees into a friend's heart.
Before me you make pass all living things,
From high to low, and teach me how to know   3035
My brother creatures in the woods, the streams, the air.
And when the shrieking storm winds make the forest
Groan, toppling the giant fir whose fall
Bears nearby branches down with it and crushes

Neighboring trees so that the hill returns   3040
A hollow thunder—oh, then you lead me to
The shelter of this cave, lay bare my being to myself,
And all the mysteries hidden in my depths
Unfold themselves and open to the day.
And after, when the white moon climbs the sky,   3045
Shedding a pure, assuaging light, out
Of the walls of rock, the dripping bushes, drift
Silver figures from antiquity
To relieve reflection's solitary pleasures.

That nothing perfect's ever ours, oh but   3050
I know it now. Together with the rapture
That I owe you, by which I am exalted
Nearer and still nearer to the gods,
Came a companion, one whom I already
Cannot do without, though he's a cold   3055
And shameless devil who drags me down
In my own eyes and with a whispered word
Makes all you granted me to be as nothing.
The longing that I feel for that enchanting
Image of a woman, he busily blows up   3060
Into a leaping flame. And so desire
Whips me, stumbling on, to seize enjoyment,
And once enjoyed, I languish for desire.
     [*Enter* MEPHISTOPHELES.]
MEPHISTO   Aren't you fed up with it by now,
This mooning about? How can it still   3065
Amuse you? You do it for a while,
All right; but enough's enough, on to the new!
FAUST   I wish you'd put your time to better use
Than bedeviling me when I have found some ease.
MEPHISTO   Oh well, a little breather, have it, have it.   3070
But "ease," man, you can't really mean it—
I wouldn't shed tears, losing a companion
Who is so mad, so rude, so sullen.
I have my hands full every minute—
Impossible to tell what pleases you or doesn't.   3075
FAUST   Why, that's just perfect, isn't it?
He pesters me and wants praise for it.
MEPHISTO   You poor earthly creature, would
You ever have managed at all without me?
Whom do you have to thank for being cured   3080
Of your mad ideas, your feverish frenzy?
If not for me you would have disappeared
From off the face of earth already.
What kind of life do you call it, dully moping
Owl-like in caves, or toad-like feeding   3085
On oozing moss and dripping stone?
That's a way to spend your time!

You're still living in your head—I have to say so;
Only the old Dr. Faust would carry on so.
FAUST   Try to understand: my life's renewed   3090
When I wander, musing, in wild Nature.
But even if you could, I know you would
Begrudge me, Devil that you are, my rapture.
MEPHISTO   For sure, your rapture, spiritual, sublime!
Lying in dew and darkness on some mountain,   3095
Embracing earth and heaven in a swoon;
A god no less, so great you've grown, so swollen,
Penetrating the bowels of earth
By sheer force of intuition,
Feeling all Creation, the whole six days' work, inside yourself, 3100
In your pride of strength delighting in—what, I can't imagine,
Ecstatically merging with all there is, all being,
The earthly creature transcended and forgotten—
And how will it end, all your exalted insight?
            [Making a gesture]
I forbid myself to say, it's not polite.   3105
FAUST   For shame!
MEPHISTO   So that's not to your taste at all, sir?
You're right, "shame,"'s right, the moral comment called for.
One mustn't mention, for chaste ears to hear,
What hearts, however chaste, always look out for.
I mean, feel free to fool yourself   3110
As and when it pleases you.
Yet you can't keep on doing as you do,
Already you're a wreck again, sick near to death;
And if you do keep on, quite soon
You'll go mad with fear and gloom.   3115
Enough, I say! Your sweetheart sits down there
And all's a dismal prison for her.
You haunt her mind continually,
She's mad about you, oh completely.
At first your passion, like a freshet,   3120
Poured tumultuously, seething and foaming
And filling her heart to overflowing;
But now the flood's thinned to a streamlet.
Instead of playing monarch of the wood,
My opinion is, dear Doctor,   3125
You should make the little creature
Some return, in gratitude.
For her the hours creep along,
She stands at the window, watching the clouds
Pass slowly over the old town walls,   3130
"Lend me, sweet bird, your wings," is the song
She sings all day and half the night.
Sometimes she's cheerful, mostly she's downhearted,
Sometimes she cries as if brokenhearted,
Then she's calm again and seems all right,   3135

And loves you always in despite.
FAUST   Serpent! Snake!
MEPHISTO [*Aside*]   I'll have you yet!
FAUST   Get away from me, you fiend!
   Don't mention her, so beautiful, to me!   3140
   Don't make my half-crazed senses crave again
   The sweetness of that lovely body!
MEPHISTO   Then what? She thinks you've taken flight,
   And I must say, the girl's half right.
FAUST   However far I wander, I am near her,   3145
   I can't forget her for a minute.
   I even envy the Lord's body
   Her pressing her lips, in church, to it.[5]
MEPHISTO   I understand. I've often envied *you*
   Her pair of roes that feed among the lilies.[6]   3150
FAUST   Pander! I won't hear your blasphemies.
MEPHISTO   Fine! Insult me! And I laugh at you.
   The God that made you girls and boys
   Himself was first to recognize,
   And practice, what's the noblest calling,   3155
   The furnishing of opportunities.
   Away! A crying shame this, never linger!
   You act as if hard fate were dragging
   You to death, not to your truelove's chamber.
FAUST   Heaven's out-heavened when she holds me tight,   3160
   I'm warmed to life upon her bosom—
   But it doesn't matter, still I feel her plight.
   A fugitive is what I am, a beast
   That's houseless, restless, purposeless,
   A furious, impatient cataract   3165
   That plunges down from rock to rock toward the abyss.
   And there she was, half wakened into woman,
   In her quiet cottage on the Alpine meadow,
   Her life the same domestic round
   Within a little world where fell no shadow.   3170
   And I, abhorred by God,
   Was not content to batter
   Rocks to bits, I had
   To undermine her peace and overwhelm her!
   This sacrifice you claimed, Hell, as your due!   3175
   Help me, Devil, please, to shorten
   The anxious time I must go through!
   Let happen quick what has to happen!
   Let her fate fall on me, too, crushingly,
   And both together perish, her and me!   3180
MEPHISTO   All worked up again, all in a sweat!
   On your way, you fool, and comfort her.
   When blockheads think there's no way out,

---

5. When the bread of Communion miraculously turns to the body of Christ.   **6.** Cf. Song of Solomon
4.5: "Thy two breasts are like two young roes that are twins, which feed among the lilies."

Right away they're sure they're done for.
Long live the man who keeps on undeterred!   3185
I'd rate your progress as a devil pretty fair;
But tell me, what is there that's more absurd
Than a moping devil, mewling in despair?

GRETCHEN'S ROOM

GRETCHEN [*Alone at her spinning wheel*]
    My heart's heavy,
    My peace gone,   3190
    I'll never know any
    Peace again.

    All's a grave
    Where he is not,
    The whole world   3195
    Turned sour, spoilt.

    And my poor head—
    I think I'm mad,
    How it goes round
    And round, my mind.   3200

    My heart's heavy,
    My peace gone,
    I'll never know any
    Peace again.

    I look out the window,   3205
    Walk out the door,
    Him, only him,
    I'm looking for.

    His bold step,
    His princely person,   3210
    His smiling lips,
    His eyes' persuasion,

    And his murmuring voice,
    Pure magicalness,
    And his fingers' touch,   3215
    And oh, his kiss!

    My heart's heavy,
    My peace gone,
    I'll never know any
    Peace again.   3220

    With all of me, I
    Strain so toward him,

One thing only
I want, to hold him,

And kiss him and kiss him,   3225
Never ceasing,
Until I die in
His arms kissing.

MARTHE'S GARDEN

MARGARETE, FAUST

MARGARETE   Heinrich,[7] the truth—I have to insist!
FAUST   As far as I'm able.
MARGARETE   Well, tell me, you must,   3230
   About your religion—how do you feel?
   You're such a good man, kind and intelligent,
   But I suspect you are indifferent.
FAUST   Enough of that, my child. You know quite well
   I cherish you so very dearly,   3235
   For those I love I'd give my life up gladly,
   And I never interfere with people's faith.
MARGARETE   That isn't right, you've got to have belief!
FAUST   You do?
MARGARETE   I know you think I am a dunce!
   You don't respect the sacraments.   3240
FAUST   I do respect them.
MARGARETE   Not enough to go to mass.
   And tell me when you last went to confess?
   Do you believe in God?
FAUST   Who, my dear,
   Can say, I believe in God?
   Ask any priest, philosopher,   3245
   And what you get by way of answer
   Sounds like a joke, pure mockery.
MARGARETE   So you don't believe in him?
FAUST   Don't misunderstand me, sweet girl, please.
   Who can give a name to him?   3250
   In good conscience say that he believes?
   And where's the man who truly feels,
   Who has the hardihood to say
   I *don't* believe in him?
   The all-embracing, all-sustaining   3255
   Power of heaven and earth,
   Doesn't he embrace and sustain
   You, me, himself?
   The sky it arches over us,

---

7. I.e., Faust. In the legend, Faust's name was generally Johann (John). Goethe changed it to Heinrich (Henry).

The earth stands firm beneath our feet, 3260
And don't the stars, looking with friendly eyes,
Eternally mount aloft?
And don't I look at you, don't
Our eyes meet and mingle?
And all there is, all things, don't they 3265
Strain yearningly toward you,
Acting and working invisibly,
Yet visible all around you,
An everlasting mystery?
Fill heart with it until heart overflows 3270
In an ecstasy of blissful feeling,
Which then call what you please,
Happiness or love or heart or God!
I know no name for it;
Feeling is everything, 3275
The name just noise, just vapor,
Dimming the heavenly fire.

MARGARETE   I guess what you say is all right,
The priest speaks so, or pretty near,
Except his language isn't yours, not quite. 3280

FAUST   I speak as all do here below,
All souls beneath bright heaven's day,
They use the language that they know,
And I use mine. Why shouldn't I?

MARGARETE   It sounds fine when you put it your way, 3285
But something's wrong, there's still a question;
The truth is, you are not a Christian.

FAUST   Now darling!

MARGARETE   It has made me so uneasy
To see the company you keep.

FAUST   Company? What do you mean by that? 3290

MARGARETE   That man you always have with you,
I loathe him, oh how much I do;
In all my life I can't remember
Anything that's made me shiver
More than his face has, so horrid, hateful! 3295

FAUST   Silly thing, don't be so fearful.

MARGARETE   His presence throws me into such a turmoil.
I like people, most of them indeed;
But even as I long for you,
I think of him with secret dread— 3300
And he's a scoundrel, he is too!
If I'm unjust, forgive me, Lord.

FAUST   It takes all kinds to make a world.

MARGARETE   I wouldn't want to have his kind around me!
His lips curl so sarcastically, 3305
Half angrily,
When he pokes his head inside the door;
You can see there's nothing he cares for;

It's written on his face as plain as day
He loves no one, we're all his enemy.   3310
I'm so happy with your arms around me,
I'm yours, and feel so warm, so free, so easy,
But when he's here it knots up so inside me.

FAUST   You angel, you, atremble with foreboding!

MARGARETE   What I feel's so strong, so overwhelming,   3315
That let him join us anywhere
And right away I almost fear
I don't love you anymore.
And when he's near, my lips refuse to pray,
Which causes me such agony.   3320
Don't you feel the same way too?

FAUST   It's just that you dislike him so.

MARGARETE   I must go now.

FAUST   Shall we never
Pass a quiet time alone together,
Bosom pressed to bosom, two souls one?   3325

MARGARETE   Oh, if I only slept alone!
I'd draw the bolt for you tonight, yes, gladly;
But my mother sleeps so lightly,
And if we were surprised by her
I know I'd die right then and there.   3330

FAUST   Angel, there's no need to worry.
Here's a vial—three drops only
In her cup will subdue nature
And lull her into pleasant slumber.

MARGARETE   What is there that I'd say no to   3335
When you ask?
It won't harm her, though,
There is no risk?

FAUST   If there was anything to fear,
Would I suggest you give it her?   3340

MARGARETE   Let me only look at you
And I don't know, I have to do
Your least wish.
I have gone so far already,
How much farther's left for me to go?   3345
                                                           [Exit.]

        [Enter MEPHISTOPHELES.]

MEPHISTO   The girl's a goose! I hope she's gone.

FAUST   Spying around, are you, again?

MEPHISTO   I heard it all, yes, every bit of it,
How she put the Doctor through his catechism,
From which he'll have, I trust, much benefit.   3350
Does a fellow stick to the old, the true religion?—
That's what all the girls are keen to know.
If he minds there, they think, then he will mind us too.

FAUST   Monster, lacking the least comprehension
How such a soul, so loving, pure,   3355

Whose faith is all in all to her,
The sole means to obtain salvation,
Should be tormented by the fear
The one she loves is damned forever!

MEPHISTO   You transcendental, hot and sensual, Romeo,   3360
See how a little skirt's got you in tow.

FAUST   You misbegotten thing of filth and fire!

MEPHISTO   And she's an expert, too, in physiognomy.
When I come in, she feels—what, she's not sure;
This face I wear hides a dark mystery;   3365
I am genius of some kind, a bad one,
About that she is absolutely certain,
Even the Devil, very possibly.
Now about tonight—?

FAUST   What's that to you?

MEPHISTO   I get my kicks out of it too.   3370

AT THE WELL

GRETCHEN *and* LIESCHEN *carrying pitchers.*

LIESCHEN   You've heard about that Barbara, have you?

GRETCHEN   No, not a word. I hardly see a soul.

LIESCHEN   Sybil told me; yes, the whole thing's true.
She's gone and done it now, the little fool.
You see what comes of being so stuck up!   3375

GRETCHEN   What comes?

LIESCHEN   Oh, it smells bad, I tell you, phew!—
When she eats now, she's feeding two.

GRETCHEN   Oh dear!

LIESCHEN   Serves her right, if you ask me.
How she kept after him, relentlessly;
Gadding about, the pair, and gallivanting   3380
Off to the village for the music, dancing;
She had to be first, she did, all the time,
And he was always there with cakes and wine;
She thought she was a raving beauty,
Accepted his gifts shamelessly.   3385
They hugged and kissed each other by the hour,
Till it was goodbye to her little flower.

GRETCHEN   The poor thing!

LIESCHEN   Poor thing, you say!
While we two sat home spinning the whole day
And mother didn't let us out at night,   3390
That one was outside, hugging her sweetheart
On a bench, or up a dark alley,
And never found an hour passed too slowly.
Well, now the hussy's got to pay for it—
Shiver in church, she must, in her sinner's shift.   3395

GRETCHEN   He'll marry her, I'm sure he will.

LIESCHEN   Not him! The fellow's no such fool,
 He'll find he likes it in another district.
 In fact he's gone.
GRETCHEN   But that's not right, it's wicked!
LIESCHEN   And if he does, she'll rue the day,   3400
 The boys will snatch her bridal wreath away
 And we'll throw dirty straw down in her doorway.[8]

                   [*Exit.*]

GRETCHEN [*Turning to go home*]
 How full of blame I used to be, how scornful
 Of any girl who got herself in trouble!
 I couldn't find words enough to express   3405
 My disgust for others' sinfulness.
 Black as all their misdeeds seemed to be,
 I blackened them still more, so cruelly,
 And still they weren't black enough for me.
 I blessed myself, was smug and proud   3410
 To think I was so very good,
 And who's the sinner now? Me, me, oh God!
 Yet everything that brought me to it,
 God, was so good, oh, was so sweet!

THE CITY WALL

In a niche in the wall, an image of the Mater Dolorosa[9] at the foot of the cross, with pots of flowers before it.

GRETCHEN [*Putting fresh flowers in the pots*]
  Look down at me,   3415
  Lady of sorrows!
  Pity my wretchedness!

  With the sword in your heart,
  Upwards you look
  To your dying son nailed to the cross.   3420

  Up to the Father
  Your sighs race each other,
  For his torment, your torment pleading.

  But who is there knows
  How sharp a pain gnaws   3425
  All through me, through flesh, bone and marrow?
  Knows my heart that's so fearful,
  Knows how it yearns, trembles?
  You only, you only know!

  I go no matter where,   3430

---

8. In Germany, this treatment was reserved for young women who had sexual relations before marriage.
9. Sorrowful mother (Latin; literal trans.); i.e., the Virgin Mary.

The pain goes with me there,
Inside my bosom, aching!
No sooner I'm alone
I cry aloud, I moan—
Mary, my heart is breaking!   3435

From the box outside my window
I picked these, this morning, for you,
My eyes dropping tears as I picked them,
Tears like the morning dew.

Into my room at the dawning   3440
The light of the sun shone red,
It found me bolt upright, sitting
In misery on my bed.

Help! Save me from shame and death!
Look down at me,   3445
Lady of sorrows!
Pity my wretchedness!

NIGHT

The street outside GRETCHEN'*s door.*

VALENTINE [*A soldier,* GRETCHEN'*s brother*]
    Whenever at a bout the boys
    Would fill the tavern with the noise
    Of their loud bragging, swearing Mattie,   3450
    Handsome Kate or blushing Mary,
    The finest girl in all the country,
    Confirming what they said by drinking
    Many a bumper, I'd say nothing,
    My elbows on the table propped,   3455
    Till all their boasting at last stopped.
    And then I'd stroke my beard, and smiling,
    Say there was no point disputing
    About taste; but tell me where
    There was one who could compare,   3460
    A virgin who could hold a candle
    To my beloved sister, Gretel?
    Clink, clank, you heard the tankards rattle
    And voices all round crying out,
    He's right, our Valentine is right,   3465
    Among all her sex she has no equal!
    Which shut the loud mouths up. And now!—
    I could tear my hair out, all,
    Run right up the side of the wall!
    All the drunks are free to crow   3470
    Over me, to needle, sneer,
    And I'm condemned to sitting there

Like a man with debts unpaid
Who sweats should anything be said.
I itch to smash them all, those beggars,   3475
But still that wouldn't make them liars.

Who's sneaking up here? Who is that?
There's two! And one I bet's that rat.
When I lay my hands on him
He won't be going home again!   3480
    [FAUST, MEPHISTOPHELES.]

FAUST   How through the window of the vestry, look,
The flickering altar lamp that's always lit,
Upward throws its light, while dim and weak,
By darkness choked, a gleam dies at our feet.
Just so all's night and gloom within my soul.   3485

MEPHISTO   And I feel like a tomcat on the prowl,
Creeping up a ladder, round a corner,
And how I like it, how it suits my nature,
Which, as you well know, is rather knavish.
Tonight I'm itchy-fingered, lickerish—   3490
That shows Walpurgis Night's already
Spooking up and down inside me.
Still another night of waiting, then
The glorious season's here again
When a fellow finds out waking beats   3495
Sleeping life away between the sheets.

FAUST   That flickering light I see, is that
Buried treasure rising, or what?

MEPHISTO   Very soon you'll have the pleasure
Of lifting out a pot of treasure.   3500
The other day I stole a look—
Such lovely coins, oh you're in luck!

FAUST   No necklace, bracelet, some such thing
My darling can put on, a ring?

MEPHISTO   I think I glimpsed a string of pearls—   3505
Just the thing to please the girls.

FAUST   Good, good. It makes me feel unhappy
When I turn up with my hands empty.

MEPHISTO   Why should you mind it if you can
Enjoy a drink on the house now and then?   3510
Look up, how the heavens sparkle, star-filled,
Time for a song, a cunning one, artful:
I'll sing her a ballad that's moral, proper,
So as to delude the baggage the better.
    [*Sings to the guitar.*]
    What business have you there,   3515
    Before your darling's door,
    Oh, Katherine, my dear,
      In dawning's chill?
    You pretty child, beware,

The maid that enters there,   3520
Out she shall come ne'er
  A maiden still.

Girls, listen, trust no one,
Or when all's said and done,
You'll find you are *undone*   3525
  And smart for it.
Of your good selves take care,
Yield nothing though he swear,
Until your finger wear
  A ring on it.[1]   3530

VALENTINE [*Advancing*]
  What's going on here with that singing?
  Pied Piper you, you damned seducer!
  The devil take that thing you're playing,
  And then take you, you squalling lecher!
MEPHISTO   Smashed my guitar! Now it's no good at all.   3535
VALENTINE   And next what I'll smash is, your thick skull.
MEPHISTO [*To* FAUST]   Hold your ground, Professor! At the ready!
  Stick close to me, I'll show you how.
  Out with your pigsticker now!
  You do the thrusting, I will parry.   3540
VALENTINE   Parry that!
MEPHISTO   Why not?
VALENTINE   And this one too!
MEPHISTO   So delighted, I am, to oblige you.
VALENTINE   It's the Devil I think I'm fighting!
  What's this? My hand is feeling feeble.
MEPHISTO [*To* FAUST]   Stick him!
VALENTINE [*Falling*]   Oh!
MEPHISTO   See how the lout's turned civil. 3545
  What's called for now is legwork. Off and running!
  In no time they will raise a hue and cry.
  I can manage sheriffs without trouble,
  But not the High Judiciary.
                                                     [*Exeunt.*]
MARTHE [*Leaning out of the window*]
  Neighbors, help!
GRETCHEN [*Leaning out of her window*]
                    A light, a light!   3550
MARTHE   Curses, shouting,—it's a fight.
CROWD   Here's one on the ground. He's dead.
MARTHE [*Coming out*]   Where are the murderers? All flown?
GRETCHEN [*Coming out*]
  Who's lying here?
CROWD   Your mother's son.

---

1. Lines 3515–30 are adapted by Goethe from Shakespeare's *Hamlet* 4.5.

GRETCHEN   My God, the horror, O my God!   3555
VALENTINE   I'm dying! Well, it's soon said, that,
  And sooner done. You women, don't
  Stand there blubbering away.
  Come here, I've something I must say.
      [*All gather around him.*]
  Gretchen, look here, you're young yet,   3560
  A green girl, not so smart about
  Managing her business.
  We know it, don't we, you and me,
  You're a whore on the q.t.—
  Go public, don't be shy, miss.   3565
GRETCHEN   My brother! God! What wretchedness!
VALENTINE   You can leave God out of this.
  What's done can't ever be undone.
  And as things went, so they'll go on.
  You let in one at the back door,   3570
  Soon there'll be others, more and more—
  A whole dozen, hot for pleasure,
  And then the whole town for good measure.

  Shame is born in hugger-mugger,
  The lying-in veiled in black night,   3575
  And she is swaddled up so tight
  In hopes the ugly thing will smother.
  But as she thrives, grows bigger, bolder,
  The hussy's eager to step out,
  Though she has grown no prettier.   3580
  The more she's hateful to the sight,
  The more the creature seeks the light.

  I look ahead and I see what?
  The honest people of this place
  Standing back from you, you slut,   3585
  As from a plague-infected corpse.
  When they look you in the face
  You'll cringe with shame, pierced to the heart.
  In church they'll drive you from the altar,
  No wearing gold chains any more,   3590
  No putting on a fine lace collar
  For skipping around on the dance floor.
  You'll hide in dark and dirty corners
  With limping cripples, lousy beggars.
  God may pardon you at last,   3595
  But here on earth you are accurst!
MARTHE   Look up to God and ask his mercy!
  Don't add to all your other sins
  Sacrilege and blasphemy.
VALENTINE   If I could only lay my hands   3600
  On your scrawny, dried up body,

Vile panderer, repulsive bawd,
Then I might hope to find forgiveness
Two times over from the Lord!
GRETCHEN   My brother! Oh, what pain, what anguish!   3605
VALENTINE   Stop your bawling, all your to-do.
When you said goodbye to honor,
That is what gave me the worst blow.
And now I go down in the earth,
Passing through the sleep of death   3610
To God—who in his life was a brave soldier.

[*Dies.*]

THE CATHEDRAL

Requiem mass, organ music, singing. GRETCHEN *among a crowd of worshippers.*
Behind her an EVIL SPIRIT.

EVIL SPIRIT   Oh, but it's different,
Isn't it, Gretchen,
From the days of your childhood
When you used to come here to   3615
The altar and, kneeling,
Prattle out prayers
From the worn little prayerbook,
Half playing a child's game,
Half worshipping God   3620
In your innocent heart,
Oh my Gretchen!
What thought's in your head now,
What crime in your heart?
Do you pray for the soul of your mother,   3625
Who by your contriving slept deep
To wake into agelong punition?
That blood on your doorstep, whose is it?
And under your heart, that faint stirring,
A quickening in you, what is it?—   3630
Affrighting you and itself
With its ominous presence.
GRETCHEN   Oh misery, misery!
These thoughts which race round and round,
To and fro, in me, in spite of myself—   3635
If only they'd leave me in peace!
CHOIR   *Dies irae, dies illa*
Solvet saeclum in favilla.[2]
[*Organ music.*]
EVIL SPIRIT   The wrath of God grips you!
The trumpet blares out!   3640

---

2. Day of wrath, that day that dissolves the world into ashes (Latin). The choir sings a famous mid-
thirteenth-century hymn by Thomas Celano (ca. 1200–ca. 1255).

The graves quake and split!
And your heart lifts its head
From its sleep in the dust
To writhe in the fire.

GRETCHEN   How I wish I were elsewhere!   3645
The pealing organ
Leaves me gasping for breath,
The singing shatters
The heart in my breast.

CHOIR   *Judex ergo cum sedebit,*   3650
Quidquid latet adparebit,
Nil inultum remanebit.[3]

GRETCHEN   How hemmed in I feel here!
The pillars imprison me!
The great dome is pressing   3655
Down on me—air!

EVIL SPIRIT   Hide yourself, try to! Sin and shame
Never stay hidden.
Air, you want, light?
Wretch that you are!   3660

CHOIR   *Quid sum miser tunc dicturus?*
Quem patronum rogaturus,
Cum vix justus sit securus?[4]

EVIL SPIRIT   The blessed avert
Their faces from you.   3665
The pure souls shrink back
Lest their fingertips brush you.

CHOIR   *Quid sum miser tunc dicturus?*

GRETCHEN   Neighbor, your smelling salts!
        [*She swoons.*]

WALPURGIS NIGHT

The Harz Mountains, near Schierke and Elend. FAUST, MEPHISTOPHELES.

MEPHISTO   What you would like now is a broomstick, right?   3670
Myself, give me a tough old billy goat.
We've got a ways to go, still, on this route.

FAUST   While legs hold up and breath comes freely,
This knotty blackthorn's all I want.
Hastening our journey, what's the point?   3675
To loiter through each winding valley,
Then clamber up this rocky slope
Down which that stream there tumbles ceaselessly—
That's what gives the pleasure to our tramp.
The spring has laid her finger on the birch,   3680

---

3. When the judge shall be seated, what is hidden shall appear, nothing shall remain unavenged (Latin).
4. What shall I say in my wretchedness? To whom shall I appeal when scarcely the righteous man is safe (Latin).

Even the fir tree feels her touch,
Then mustn't we, too, feel new energy?

MEPHISTO   Must we! I don't feel that way, not me.
My season's strictly wintertime,
I'd much prefer we went through ice and snow.   3685
The waning moon, making its tardy climb
Up the sky, gives off a reddish glow
So sad and dim, at every step you run
Into a tree or stumble on a stone.
You won't mind me, will you, begging help   3690
Of some quick-flitting will-o'-the-wisp?[5]
I see one yonder, shining merrily.
—Hello there, friend, we'd like your company!
Why blaze away so uselessly, for nothing?
Do us a favor, light up this path we're climbing.   3695

WILL-O'-THE-WISP   I hope the deep respect I hold you in, sir,
Will keep in check my all-too-skittish temper;
The way we go is zigzag, that's our nature.

MEPHISTO   Trying to ape mankind, poor wandering light.
Now listen to me: in the Devil's name, go straight   3700
Or I will blow your puny spark right out!

WILL-O'-THE-WISP   Yes, yes, you give the orders here, quite right;
I'll do what you require, eagerly.
But don't forget, the mountain on this night
Is mad with magic, witchcraft, sorcery,   3705
And if Jack-o'-Lantern is your guide,
Don't expect more than he can provide.

FAUST, MEPHISTOPHELES, WILL-O'-THE-WISP [Singing in turn]
We have entered, as it seems,
Realm of magic, realm of dreams.
Lead us well and win such honor   3710
His to have, bright-shining creature,
By whose flicker we may hasten
Forward through this wide, waste region!

See the trees, one then another,
Spinning past us fast and faster,   3715
And the cliffs impending over,
And the jutting crags, like noses
Winds blow through with snoring noises!

Over stones and through the heather
Rills and runnels downwards hasten.   3720
Is that water splashing, listen,
Is it singing, that soft murmur,
Is it love's sweet voice, lamenting,
From the days when all was heaven?

5. *Ignis fatuus*, a wavering light formed by marsh gas. In German folklore, it was thought to lead travelers
to their destruction.

How our hearts hoped, loving, yearning!   3725
And like a tale, an old, familiar,
Echo once more tells it over.

Hark, the owl's hoot's heard nearer,
Cry of magpie and of plover—
Still not nested, still awake?   3730
Are those lizards in the brake,
Straggle-legged and big-bellied?
And roots, winding every which way
In the rock and sand, send out
Shoots to snare the passing foot;   3735
Tree warts, gross things, swollen, living,
Send their tendrils, dangling, swaying,
Out to catch us. And mice scamper
In great packs of every color
Through the moss and through the heather.   3740
And the glowworms swarm around us
In dense clouds, and only lead us
This way, that way to confuse us.

Tell me, are we standing still, or
Still advancing, climbing higher?   3745
Everything spins round us wildly,
Rocks and trees grin at us madly,
Will-o'-the-wisps, so many, swelling
Themselves up—oh, terrifying!
MEPHISTO   Seize hold of my coattails, quick,   3750
We're coming to a middling peak
Where you'll marvel at the sight
Of Mammon's mountain, burning bright.[6]
FAUST   How strange that light is, there, far down,
Dim and reddish, like the dawn.   3755
Its faint luminescence reaches
Deep into the yawning gorges.
Mist rises here and streams away there,
Penetrated by pale fire.
Now the fire curls and winds in   3760
A gold thread, now like a fountain
Overflows, and spreading out
In branching veins, pours through the valley,
Or squeezed into a narrow gully,
Collects into a pool of light.   3765
Sparks fly about as if a hand
Were scattering golden grains of sand.
And look there, how from base to top
The whole cliffside is lit up.

6. Mammon is imagined as leading a group of fallen angels in digging out gold and gems from the ground
of hell, presumably for Satan's palace, as described in Milton's *Paradise Lost* I.678 ff.

MEPHISTO At holiday time Lord Mammon stages   3770
   Quite a show, don't you agree?
   Oh, you're a lucky man to see this.
   And here the guests come—not so quietly!
FAUST What a gale of wind is blowing,
   Buffeting my back and shoulders!   3775
MEPHISTO Clutch with your fingers that outcropping
   Or you'll fall to your death among the boulders.
   The mist is making it darker than ever.
   Hear how the trees are pitching and tossing!
   Frightened, the owls fly up in a flutter.   3780
   The evergreen palaces' pillars are creaking
   And cracking, boughs snapping and breaking,
   As down the trunks thunder
   With a shriek of roots tearing,
   Piling up on each other   3785
   In a fearful disorder!
   And through the wreckage-strewn ravines
   The hurtling storm blast howls and screams.
   And hear those voices in the air,
   Some far-off and others near?   3790
   That's the witches' wizard singing,
   Along the mountain shrilly ringing.
CHORUS OF WITCHES
      The witches ride up to the Brocken,
      Stubble's yellow, new grain green.
      The great host meets upon the peak, and   3795
      There Urian[7] mounts his throne.
      So over stock and stone go stumping,
      Witches farting, billy goats stinking!
VOICE Here comes Mother Baubo[8] now,
   Riding on an old brood sow.   3800
CHORUS
      Honor to whom honor is due!
      Old Baubo to the head of the queue!
      A fat pig and a fat frau on her,
      And all the witches following after!
VOICE How did you come?
VOICE   Ilsenstein way.   3805
   I peeked in an owl's nest, passing by,
   Eyes like moons stared back at me.
VOICE Too fast, too fast, my bottom's skinned sore!
   Oh, my wounds! Look here, and here!
CHORUS OF WITCHES
      Broad the way and long the road,   3810
      What a pushing, shoving crowd!
      By broomstraw scratched, by pitchfork pricked,

---

7. A name for the Devil. 8. In Greek mythology, the nurse of Demeter, noted for her obscenity and bestiality.

Baby's crushed and belly's ripped.

HALF-CHORUS OF WARLOCKS
    We crawl like snails lugging their whorled shell,
    The women have got a good mile's lead.   3815
    When where you're going's to the Devil,
    It's woman knows how to get up speed.
OTHER HALF-CHORUS
    A mile or so, why should we care?
    Women may get the start of us,
    But for all of their forehandedness,   3820
    One jump carries a man right there.
VOICE [*Above*]   Come along with us, you down at the lake.
VOICE [*From below*]   Is there anything better we would like?
    We scrub ourselves as clean as a whistle,
    But it's no use, still we are sterile.   3825
BOTH CHORUSES
    The wind is still, the stars are fled,
    The moon's relieved to hide her head.
    Rushing, roaring, the mad chorus
    Scatters sparks of fire broadcast.
VOICE [*From below*]   Wait, oh wait!   3830
VOICE [*Above*]   Who's that calling from that cleft?
VOICE [*From below*]   Take me along, don't forget me!
    For three hundred years I've tried to climb
    Up to the summit—all in vain.
    I long for creatures who are like me.   3835
BOTH CHORUSES
    Straddle a broomstick, a pitchfork's fine too,
    Get up on a goat, a plain stick will do.
    Who doesn't bestir himself today
    Forever is done for, and so goodbye.
HALF-WITCH [*From below*]   I trot breathlessly, and yet   3840
    How far ahead the rest have got.
    No peace at all at home, and here
    It's no better. Dear, oh dear!
CHORUS OF WITCHES
    The unction gives us hags a lift,
    A bit of rag will do for a sail,   3845
    Any tub's a fine sky boat—
    Don't fly now and you never will.
BOTH CHORUSES
    And when we've gained the very top,
    Light down, swooping, to a stop.
    We'll darken the heath entirely   3850
    With all our swarming witchery.
        [*They alight.*]
MEPHISTO   What a pushing and shoving, rushing, colliding,
    Tugging and twisting, hissing and gibbering,
    Sparks flying, flames leaping, a burning and stinking—
    We're among witches, no mistaking!   3855

Stick close or we will be parted for sure.
But where are you?
FAUST   Here, over here!
MEPHISTO   Already swept away so far!
I must show who's master here.
Out of the way of Voland the Devil,   3860
Out of the way, you charming rabble!
Doctor, hang on, we'll make a quick dash
And get ourselves out of this terrible crush—
Even for me it's much too much.
Yonder's a light has a funny glisten,   3865
Those bushes attract me for some reason.
Come along quick, we'll sneak into them.
FAUST   Spirit of Contradiction! However,
Lead the way!—He's clever, my devil:
Walpurgis Night up the Brocken we scramble   3870
So as to do what? Hide ourselves in a corner!
MEPHISTO   Just look at that fire there, brightly shining,
Clubmen are having a jolly meeting.
When the company's few, the feeling's friendlier.
FAUST   But I would much prefer to be   3875
On the summit. I can see
A red glow and black smoke swirling,
Satanwards a great crowd's streaming,
And there, I have no doubt at all,
Many a riddle's at last resolved.   3880
MEPHISTO   And many another riddle revealed.
Let the world rush on crazily,
We'll pass the time here cozily;
And following what is now the custom,
Inside the great world make us a little one.   3885
Look there, young witches, all stark naked,
And old ones wisely petticoated.
Don't sulk, be nice, if only to please me;
Much fun at small cost, really it's easy.
I hear music, a damned racket!   3890
You must learn not to mind it.
No backing out now, in with me!
You'll meet a distinguished company
And again be much obliged to me.
—Now what do you think of this place, my friend?   3895
Our eyes can hardly see to its end.
A hundred fires, in a row burning,
People around them dancing, carousing,
Talking and making love—oh, what a party!
Where is there anything better, just show me.   3900
FAUST   And when we enter into the revel,
What part will you play, magician or devil?
MEPHISTO   I travel incognito normally,
But when it comes to celebrations

A man must show his decorations.   3905
The Garter's never been awarded me,[9]
But in these parts the split hoof's much respected.
That snail there, do you see it, creeping forwards,
Its face pushing this way, that way, towards us?
Already I've been smelt out, I'm detected.   3910
Even if deception was my aim,
Here there's no denying who I am.
Come on, we'll go along from fire to fire,
The go-between me, you the cavalier.

    [*Addressing several figures huddled around a fading fire.*]

Old sirs, you keep apart here, what a shame!   3915
Join the fun or sink in my esteem.
You ought to be carousing with the youth,
At home we're all of us alone enough.

GENERAL   Put no trust in nations, for the people,
  In spite of all you've done, are never grateful.   3920
  It's with them always as it is with women,
  The young come first, and we—we are forgotten.

MINISTER OF STATE   The world has got completely off the track.
  Oh, they were men, the older generation!
  When we held every high position,   3925
  That was the golden age, and no mistake.

PARVENU   We were no simpletons ourselves, we weren't,
  And often did the things we shouldn't.
  But everything's turned topsy-turvy now,
  Just when we're foursquare for the status quo.   3930

AUTHOR   Who wants, today, to read a book
  With a modicum of sense or wit?
  And as for our younger folk,
  I've never seen such rude conceit.

MEPHISTO [*Suddenly transformed into an old man*]
  My days of climbing Brocken reach their close,   3935
  The Judgment Day, I feel it near at hand!
  And since my cup of life's drained to the lees,
  The world, too, must be coming to an end.

JUNK-DEALER WITCH   Good sirs, don't pass me unawares,
  Don't miss this opportunity!   3940
  Look here, will you, at my wares,
  What richness, what variety!
  Yet there is not a single item
  Hasn't served to do in someone.
  Nowhere on earth will you find such a stall!   3945
  No dagger here but it has drunk hot blood,
  No cup but from it deadly poison's flowed
  To waste a body once robust and hale,
  No gem but has seduced a loving girl,
  No sword but has betrayed an ally or a friend,   3950

9. I.e., he has no decoration of nobility, such as the Order of the Garter.

Or struck an adversary from behind.

MEPHISTO Auntie, think about the times you live in!
What's past is done, your junk's anachronous.
The new, the latest, that's what you should deal in.
Only novelties appeal to us.   3955

FAUST Am I me, I wonder, I'm so giddy.
This is a fair to beat all fairs, believe me!

MEPHISTO Upwards all the witches surge, half crazed,
You think you're shoving but you're being shoved.

FAUST Who's that there?

MEPHISTO   Take a good look.   3960
Lilith.[1]

FAUST   Lilith? Who is that?

MEPHISTO Adam's wife, his first. Beware of her.
Her beauty's one boast is her dangerous hair.
When Lilith winds it tight around young men
She doesn't soon let go of them again.   3965

FAUST Look, one old witch, one young one, there they sit—
They've waltzed around a lot already, I will bet!

MEPHISTO Tonight's no night for resting. Come,
Another dance is starting, let's join in.

FAUST [Dancing with the YOUNG WITCH]
A lovely dream I dreamt one day: 3970
I saw a green-leaved apple tree,
Two apples swayed upon a stem,
So tempting! I climbed up for them.

THE PRETTY WITCH Ever since the days of Eden
Apples have been man's desire.   3975
How overjoyed I am to think, sir,
Apples grow, too, in my garden.

MEPHISTO [Dancing with the OLD WITCH]
A wicked dream I one day:
I saw a tree split up the middle—
A huge hole, phenomenal!   3980
And yet it pleased me every way.

THE OLD WITCH Welcome, welcome, to you, sire,
Cloven-footed cavalier!
Stand to with a proper stopper,
Unless you fear to come a cropper.   3985

PROCTOPHANTASMIST[2] Accursed tribe, so bold, presumptuous!
Hasn't it been proven past disputing
Spirits all are footless, they lack standing?
And here you're footing like the rest of us!

THE PRETTY WITCH [Dancing]
What's he doing here, at our party?   3990

1. According to rabbinical legend, Adam's first wife; the *female* mentioned in Genesis 1.27: "So God created man in his own image, in the image of God created he him; male and female created he them." After Eve was created, Lilith became a ghost who seduced men and inflicted evil on children. 2. A German coinage meaning "one who exorcises evil spirits by sitting in a pond and applying leeches to his behind" (see lines 4014–17). The figure caricatures Friedrich Nicolai (1733–1811), who opposed modern movements in German thought and literature and had parodied Goethe's *The Sorrows of Young Werther* (1774).

FAUST [*Dancing*]

    Him? You find him everywhere, that killjoy.
    We others dance, he does the criticizing.
    Every step one takes requires analyzing;
    Until it's jawed about, it hasn't really happened.
    What he can't stand is our going forward.   3995
    If you keep going around in the same old circle,
    As he plods year in, year out on his treadmill,
    You might be favored with his good opinion,
    Provided you most humbly beg it of him.

PROCTOPHANTASMIST   Still here, are you? It's an outrage!   4000

    Vanish, ours is the Enlightened Age—
    You devils, no respect for rule and regulation.
    We've grown so wise, yet ghosts still walk in Tegel.[3]
    How long I've toiled to banish superstition,
    Yet it lives on. The whole thing is a scandal!   4005

THE PRETTY WITCH   Stop, stop, you're boring us insufferably!

PROCTOPHANTASMIST   Now listen, all you ghostly freaks,

    I won't endure this tyranny of spooks—
    Lively spirits are too much for me.
        [*They go on dancing.*]
    I see I'm getting nowhere with these devils,   4010
    Still, it will add a chapter to my travels,
    And I hope, before my sands of life run out,
    To put foul fiends and poets all to rout.

MEPHISTO   He'll go and plump himself down in a pond—

    That's his cure for a bedeviled mind—   4015
    And purge away his visions and his wits
    By having leeches feed on where he sits.[4]
        [*To* FAUST, *who has broken off dancing and withdrawn*]
    What's this? You've left your partner in the lurch
    As she was sweetly singing, pretty witch.

FAUST   Ugh! From her mouth a red mouse sprang   4020

    In the very middle of her song.

MEPHISTO   Is that anything to fuss about?

    And anyway it wasn't gray, was it?
    To take on so, to me, seems simply rudeness
    When you are sporting with your Amaryllis.   4025

FAUST   And then I saw—

MEPHISTO   Saw what?

FAUST   Look there, Mephisto,

    At that lovely child, so pale, so wistful,
    Standing by herself. How painfully
    She makes her way along, how slowly,
    As if her feet were chained. To me,   4030
    I must confess, it looks like Gretchen.

MEPHISTO   Let it be!

    It's bad, that thing, a lifeless shape, a wraith

---

3. A town near Berlin where ghosts had been reported.   4. Nicolai claimed that he had been bothered by ghosts but had repelled them by applying leeches to his rump.

No man ever wants to meet up with.
Your blood freezes under her dead stare,
Almost turned to stone, you are.   4035
Medusa,[5] did you ever hear of her?

FAUST   Yes, yes, those are a corpse's eyes
No loving hand was by to close.
That's Gretchen's breast, which she so often
Gave to me to rest my head on,   4040
That shape her dear, her lovely body
She gave to me to enjoy freely.

MEPHISTO   It's all magic, hocus-pocus, idiot!
Her power is, each thinks she is his sweetheart.

FAUST   What rapture! And what suffering!   4045
I stand here spellbound by her look.
How strange, that bit of scarlet string
Which ornaments her lovely neck,
No thicker than a knife blade's back.

MEPHISTO   Right you are. I see it, too.   4050
She's also perfectly able to
Tuck her head beneath her arm
And stroll about. Perseus—remember him?—
He was the one who hacked it off.
—Man, I'd think you'd have enough of   4055
The mad ideas your head is stuffed with!
Come, we'll climb this little hill where
All's as lively as inside the Prater.[6]
And unless somebody has bewitched me,
The thing I see there is a theater.   4060
What's happening?

SERVIBILIS   Our next show's starting shortly,
Last of seven. With us here it's customary
To offer a full repertory.
The playwright's a rank amateur,
So are we all, myself and every actor.   4065
Well, I must hurry off now, please excuse me,
I need to raise the curtain—amateurishly!

MEPHISTO   How right it is that I should find you here, sirs;
The Blocksberg's just the place for amateurs.

WALPURGIS NIGHT'S DREAM;

OR

OBERON AND TITANIA'S GOLDEN WEDDING

INTERMEZZO[7]

STAGE MANAGER [*To crew*]   Today we'll put by paint and canvas,   4070
          Mieding's[8] brave sons, all.
          Nature paints the scene for us:

---

5. The Gorgon with hair of serpents whose glance turned people to stone.   6. A famous park in Vienna.
7. Brief interlude. Oberon and Titania are king and queen of the fairies.   8. Johann Martin Mieding (d.
1782), a master carpenter and scene builder in the Weimar theater.

Gray steep and mist-filled vale.

HERALD   For the wedding to be golden,
    Years must pass, full fifty;   4075
    But if the quarrel is made up, then
    It is golden truly.

OBERON   Spirits hovering all around,
    Appear, dear imps, to me here!
    King and Queen are once more bound   4080
    Lovingly together.

PUCK[9]   Here's Puck, my lord, who spins and whirls
    And cuts a merry caper,
    A hundred follow at his heels,
    Skipping to the measure.   4085

ARIEL[1]   Ariel strikes up his song,
    The notes as pure as silver;
    Philistines all around him throng,
    But those, too, with true culture.   4090

OBERON   Wives and husbands, learn from us
    How two hearts unite:
    To find connubial happiness,
    Only separate.

TITANIA   If Master sulks and Mistress pouts,
    Here is the remedy: 4095
    Send her on a trip down south,
    Send him the other way.

FULL ORCHESTRA [*Fortissimo*]   Buzzing fly and humming gnat
    And all their consanguinity,
    Frog's hoarse croak, cicada's chirp   4100
    Compose our symphony.

SOLO   Here I come, the bagpipes, whose
    Throat swells like a soap bubble.
    Hear me through my stumpy nose
    Go tootle-doodle-doodle.   4105

A BUDDING IMAGINATION   A spider's foot, a green toad's gut,
    Two winglets—though a travesty
    Devoid of life and nature, yet
    It does as nonsense poetry.

A COUPLE   Short steps, smart leaps, all done neatly 4110
    In a pas de deux:
    And though you foot it very featly,
    Never will you soar.

AN INQUIRING TRAVELER   No, no, the whole thing is a fraud,
    Villains, you deceive me!   4115
    Oberon the handsome god
    Has long been dead and buried.

A PIOUS BELIEVER   I don't see claws, nor any tail,
    And yet it's indisputable:
    Like Greece's gods, his dishabille   4120

---

9. A mischievous spirit.   1. A helpful sprite.

Shows he's a pagan devil.

AN ARTIST OF THE NORTH   Here all I see and paint must lack
    Wholeness, harmony.
    But I'm preparing soon to make
    My Italian journey.   4125

A STICKLER FOR DECORUM   I'm here, and most unhappily,
    Where all's impure, improper;
    Among this riotous witchery
    There's only two wear powder.

A YOUNG WITCH   Powder, like a petticoat,   4130
    Is right for wives with gray hair;
    But I'll sit naked on my goat,
    Show off my strapping figure.

A MATRON   We are too well bred by far
    To bandy words about: 4135
    But may you, young thing that you are,
    Drop dead, and soon, cheap tart.

THE CONDUCTOR   Don't crowd so round the naked charmer,
    On with the concerto!
    Frog and blowfly, gnat, cicada—   4140
    Mind you keep the tempo.

A WEATHERCOCK [Pointing one way]
    No better company than maids
    Like these, in such profusion!
    And bachelors to match, old boys
    Agog with expectation.   4145

WEATHERCOCK [Pointing the other way]
    And if the earth don't open up
    And swallow this lewd rabble,
    Off I'll race at a great clip,
    Myself go to the Devil.

SATIRICAL EPIGRAMS [XENIEN[2]]   We are gadflies, plant our sting   4150
    In those hides which deserve them,
    By so doing honoring
    Great Satan, our patron.

HENNINGS[3]   Look there, at the pack of them,
    Like schoolboys, jeering meanly.   4155
    Next, I'm sure, they all will claim
    It's all in fun, friends, really.

MUSAGET[4] ("LEADER OF THE MUSES")
    Among these witches I'd prefer
    To linger out my time;
    I know I'd find it easier   4160
    To lead them, than the Nine.

(A JOURNAL) FORMERLY (ENTITLED) "THE SPIRIT OF THE AGE"[5]

---

2. Literally, polemical verses written by Goethe and Friedrich von Schiller (1759–1805). The characters here are versions of Goethe himself.   3. August Adolf von Hennings (1746–1826), publisher of a journal called *Genius of the Age* that had attacked Schiller.   4. The title of a collection of Hennings's poetry. 5. I.e., former "Genius of the Age"; probably alludes to the journal's change of title in 1800 to *Genius of the Nineteenth Century*.

What counts is knowing the right people,
With me, sir, you'll go places;
The Blocksberg's got a place for all,
Like Germany's Parnassus.[6]   4165

THE INQUIRING TRAVELER   Who's that fellow who's so stiff
And marches so majestical?
He sniffs away for all he's worth,
"Pursuing things Jesuitical."

A CRANE   An earnest fisherman I am,   4170
Above all in troubled waters,
And thus it is a pious man
'S seen hobnobbing with devils.

A CHILD OF THIS WORLD   All occasions serve the godly
In their work. Atop   4175
The Blocksberg, even there, they
Set up religious shop.

A DANCER   What's that drumming, a new group
Of musicians coming?
No, no, they're bitterns in the swamp   4180
Monotonously booming.

THE DANCING MASTER   How cautiously they lift their feet,
All difficulties dodging;
The shifty leap, the ponderous hop,
Heedless how they're looking.   4185

THE FIDDLER   This riffraff's so hate-filled, each lusts
To slit the other's throat;
Orpheus with his lute tamed beasts.[7]
These march to the bagpipes' note.

A DOGMATIST   You can't shake me, it's in vain,   4190
Your doubts and criticism.
The Devil's real, how could the brain
Possibly invent him?

AN IDEALIST   The mind's creative faculty
This time has gone too far.   4195
If all I'm seeing's only me,
I'm crazy, that's for sure.

A REALIST   It's pandemonium, it's mad,
Oh, I feel so cast down;
This is the first time I have stood   4200
On such shaky ground.

A SUPERNATURALIST   The presence of these devils here
Is a comforting assurance.
From the demonical I infer
The angelical's existence.   4205

A SKEPTIC   They see a flickering light and think
There's treasure there, oh surely;
Devil's a word that pairs with doubt,

<hr>

6. A mountain sacred to Apollo and the Muses; hence, figuratively, the locale of poetic excellence.   7. In Greek mythology, Orpheus's music was said to have the power to quiet wild animals.

This is a place that suits me.

CONDUCTOR Buzzing fly and humming gnat—   4210
    What damned amateurs!
    Frog's hoarse croak, cicada's chirp—
    I've not heard worse performers.

THE (POLITICALLY) ADROIT Sans all souci[8] we are, shift
    About with lightning speed;   4215
    When walking on the feet is out,
    We walk upon the head.

THE MALADROIT At court we sat down to free dinners,
    And now, dear God, there's naught!
    We've worn out our dancing slippers   4220
    And limp along barefoot.

WILL-O'-THE-WISPS We're from the bottom lands, the swamps,
    Such is our lowly origin;
    But now we sparkle as gallants
    And dance in the cotillion.   4225

A SHOOTING STAR I shot across the sky's expanse,
    A meteor, blazing bright.
    Now fallen, I sprawl in the grass—
    Who'll help me to my feet?

THE ROUGHNECKS Look out, look out, we're coming through,   4230
    Trampling your lawn,
    We're spirits too, but spirits who
    Have lots of beef and brawn.

PUCK You tramp much too heavily,
    Like young elephants.   4235
    Step light as Puck, Puck's tread today
    Let be the heaviest.

ARIEL If you have wings from kindly Nature,
    Or from your own spirit,
    As I fly, fly close after,   4240
    Up to the rose hill's summit.

ORCHESTRA [*Pianissimo*]
    The shrouding mists and thick-massed clouds
    Lighten in the dawn,
    The wind stirs leaves, it rattles reeds,
    And all is scattered, gone.   4245

AN OVERCAST DAY. A FIELD

FAUST *and* MEPHISTOPHELES.

FAUST In misery! In despair! Stumbling about pitifully over the earth for
so long, and now a prisoner! A condemned criminal, shut up in a dungeon
and suffering horrible torments, the poor unfortunate child! It's come to
this, to this! And not a word about it breathed to me, you treacherous,
odious spirit! Stand there rolling your Devil's eyes around in rage, oh do!

---

8. Without any care or unhappiness (French).

Brazen it out with your intolerable presence! A prisoner! In misery, irremediable misery! Delivered up to evil spirits and the stony-hearted justice of mankind! And meanwhile you distract me with your insipid entertainments, keep her situation, more desperate every day, from me, and leave her to perish helplessly!

MEPHISTO   She's not the first.

FAUST   You dog, you monster! Change him, O you infinite Spirit, change the worm back into a dog, give it back the shape it wore those evenings when it liked to trot ahead of me and roll at the feet of some innocent wayfarer, tripping him up and leaping on him as he fell. Give it back its favorite shape so it can crawl on its belly in the sand before me, and I can kick it as it deserves, the abomination!—Not the first!—Such misery, such misery! It's inconceivable, humanly inconceivable, that more than one creature should ever have plumbed such depths of misery, that the first who did, writhing in her last agony under the eyes of the Eternal Forgiveness, shouldn't have expiated the guilt of all the others who came after! I am cut to the quick, pierced to the marrow, by the suffering of this one being—you grin indifferently at the fate of thousands!

MEPHISTO   So once again we're at our wits' end, are we—reached the point where you fellows start feeling your brain is about to explode? Why did you ever throw in with us if you can't see the thing through? You'd like to fly, but are afraid of getting dizzy. Did we force ourselves on you or you on us?

FAUST   Don't snarl at me that way with those wolfish fangs of yours, it sickens me!—Great and glorious Spirit, Spirit who vouchsafed to appear to me, who knows me in my heart and soul, why did you fasten me to this scoundrel who diets on destruction, delights to hurt?

MEPHISTO   Finished yet?

FAUST   Save her or you'll pay for it! With a curse on you, the dreadfulest there is, for thousands of years to come!

MEPHISTO   I'm powerless to strike off the Great Avenger's chains or draw his bolts.—Save her indeed!—Who's the one who ruined her, I would like to know—you or me?

   [FAUST *looks around wildly.*]

Looking for a thunderbolt, are you? A good thing you wretched mortals weren't given them. That's the tyrant's way of getting out of difficulties—strike down any innocent person who makes an objection, gets in his way.

FAUST   Take me to where she is, you hear? She's got to be set free.

MEPHISTO   In spite of the risk you would run? There's blood guilt on the town because of what you did. Where murder was, there the avenging spirits hover, waiting for the murderer to return.

FAUST   That, from you, that too? Death and destruction, a world's worth, on your head, you monster! Take me there, I say, and set her free!

MEPHISTO   All right, all right, I'll take you there. But hear what I can do—do you think all the powers of heaven and earth are mine? I'll cause the jailer's senses to be befuddled, then you seize his keys and lead her out. Only a human hand can do it. I'll keep watch. The spirit horses are ready. Off I'll carry both of you. That's what I can do.

FAUST   Away then!

NIGHT. OPEN COUNTRY

FAUST *and* MEPHISTOPHELES *going by on black horses at a furious gallop.*

FAUST   What are they doing, there at the gallows block?
MEPHISTO   Doing, brewing something or other, who knows?
FAUST   Swooping back and forth, bowing down, kneeling.
MEPHISTO   A pack of witches.
FAUST   As if strewing and blessing.   4250
MEPHISTO   Keep going, keep going!

A PRISON

FAUST [*With a bunch of keys and carrying a lamp, at a narrow iron door*]
   I shudder as I haven't for so long—
   Oh, how it suffers, our humanity!
   She's shut up inside these dank walls, poor thing,
   And all her crime was love, the brave, the illusory.   4255
   You're hanging back from going in!
   You're afraid of meeting her eyes again!
   In, in, delay means death, you've got to hurry.
      [*He puts the key in the lock.*]
SINGING [*From within*]
         My mother, the whore,
         In the dark of night slew me!   4260
         My father, the knave,
         Made his dinner of me!
         My sister, wee thing,
         Heaped up my bones
         Beneath the green tree,   4265
         Changed into a bird, I sing
         Fly away, fly away!
FAUST [*Unlocking the door*]   She doesn't dream her lover's listening.
   Hears her chains rattle, the straw rustling.
      [*He enters.*]
MARGARETE [*Cowering on her paillasse*]
   They're coming, they're coming! How bitter, death, bitter!   4270
FAUST [*Whispering*]   Hush, dear girl, hush! You'll soon be free.
MARGARETE [*Groveling before him*]
   If your heart's human, think how I suffer.
FAUST   You'll wake the guards. Speak quietly.
      [*Taking hold of the chains to unlock them*]
MARGARETE [*On her knees*]   Headsman, so early, it isn't right.
   Have mercy on me! Too soon, too soon!   4275
   You come for me in the dead of night—
   Isn't it time enough at dawn?
      [*Stands up.*]
   I'm still so young, too young surely—
   Still I must die.
   How pretty I was, that's what undid me.   4280

He held me so close, now he's far away,
My wreath pulled apart, the flowers scattered.
How rough your hands are! Please, won't you spare me?
What did I ever do to you?
Don't let me beg in vain for mercy,   4285
I never before laid eyes on you.

FAUST It's unendurable, her mercy,

MARGARETE What can I do, I'm in your power.
Only let me nurse my baby first.
All night long I hugged the dear creature;   4290
They took it from me out of spite
And now they say I murdered it.
And I'll never be happy, no, never again.
They've made up songs to sing about me. It's wicked of them.
There's an old fairy tale ends that way,   4295
But what has it got to do with me?

FAUST [Falling at her feet] It's me here who loves you, me, at your feet,
To rescue you from this miserable fate.

MARGARETE [Kneeling beside him]
We'll kneel down, that's right, and pray to the saints.
Look, under those steps,   4300
Below the doorsill,
All Hell's a-boil!
The Evil One
In his horrible rage
Makes such a noise.   4305

FAUST [Crying out] Gretchen! Gretchen!

MARGARETE [Listening] That was my darling's own dear voice!
    [She jumps up, the chains fall away.]
I heard him call. Where can he be?
No one may stop me, now I am free!
Into his arms I'll run so fast,   4310
Lie on his breast at last, at last.
Gretchen, he called, from there on the sill.
Through all the wailing and clashing of Hell,
Through the furious, devilish jeering and mockery
I heard his dear voice calling to me.   4315

FAUST It's me!

MARGARETE It's you! Oh, say it again.
    [Catching hold of him.]
It's him! Where is the torture now, it's him!
Where's my fear of the prison, the chains they hung on me?
It's you, it's you! You've come here to save me!
I'm saved!   4320
—I see it before me, so very plainly,
The street I saw you the first time on,
I see Marthe and me where we waited for you
In the sunlit garden.

FAUST [Pulling her toward the door]

Come along, come!

MARGARETE   Oh stay!   4325
I love it so being wherever you are.
  [*Caressing him.*]
FAUST   Hurry!
If you don't hurry,
The price we will pay!
MARGARETE   What? Don't know how to kiss anymore?   4330
Parted from me a short time only
And quite forgotten what lips are for?
Why am I frightened with your arms around me?
Time was, at a word or a look from you,
Straight to heaven I was transported   4335
And you kissed me as if you'd devour me.
Kiss me, kiss me!
Or I'll kiss you!
  [*She embraces him.*]
What cold lips you have,
You don't speak, look dumbly.   4340
What's become of your love?
Who took it from me?
  [*She turns away from him.*]
FAUST   Come, follow me! Darling, be brave!
Oh, the kisses I'll give you, my love—
Only come now, we'll slip through that door.   4345
MARGARETE [*Turning back to him*]
Is it really you? Can I be sure?
FAUST   Yes, it's me—you must come!
MARGARETE   You cast off my chains,
Take me into your arms.
How is it you don't shrink away from me?
Have you any idea who you're letting go free?   4350
FAUST   Hurry, hurry! The night's almost over.
MARGARETE   I murdered my mother,
Drowned my baby—
Weren't both of us given it, you and me?
Given you, too? It's you, I can hardly believe it.   4355
Give me your hand. No, I haven't dreamed it.
Your dear hand!—But your hand is wet!
Wipe it off, there's blood on it!
My God, my God, what did you do?
Put away your sword,   4360
I beg you to!
FAUST   What's past is done, forget it all.
You're killing me.
MARGARETE   No, live on still.
I'll tell you how the graves should be;   4365
Tomorrow you must see to it.
Give my mother the best spot,

My brother put alongside her,
Me, put me some distance off,
Yet not too far, 4370
And at my right breast put my baby.
Nobody else will lie beside me.
When I used to press up close to you,
How sweet it was, pure happiness,
But now I can't, it's over, all such bliss— 4375
I feel it as an effort I must make,
That I must force myself on you,
And you, I feel, resist me, push me back.
And yet it's you, with your good, kind look.

FAUST   If it's me, then come, we mustn't stay. 4380

MARGARETE   Out there?

FAUST   Out there, away!

MARGARETE   If the grave's out there, death waiting for me,
Come, yes, come! The two of us together!
But only to the last place, there, no other.
—You're going now? 4385
I'd go too if I could, Heinrich, believe me!

FAUST   You can! Just say you will, and come!
The way is clear.

MARGARETE   No, I may not; for me all hope is gone.
It's useless, flight. They'd keep, I'm sure, 4390
A sharp watch out. I'd find it dreadful
To have to beg my bread from people,
Beg with a bad conscience, too;
Dreadful to have to wander about
Where all is strange and new, 4395
Only to end up getting caught.

FAUST   But I'll be there with you!

MARGARETE   Quick, be quick!
Save your child, run!
Keep to the path 4400
That goes up by the brook,
Over the bridge,
Into the wood,
Left where the fence is,
There, in the pool— 4405
Reach down and catch it!
It wants to come up,
It's struggling still!
Save it, oh save it!

FAUST   Get hold of yourself! 4410
One step and you're free, dear girl!

MARGARETE   If only we were well past the mountain!
On the rock over there Mother is sitting,
I'm frozen with fear and apprehension!
She sits on the rock, her head heavy, nodding, 4415
Doesn't look, doesn't wave, can't hold it up straight,

Her sleep was so long she will never awake.
She slept so we might have our pleasure.
The happy hours we passed together!

FAUST   If I can't persuade you, if pleading's no use,   4420
I'll have to carry you off by force.

MARGARETE   Let go of me, how dare you compel me!
You're gripping me so brutally!
I always did what you wanted, once.

FAUST   Soon day will be breaking! Darling, darling!   4425

MARGARETE   Day? Yes, day, my last day's dawning,
My wedding day it should have been.
Not a word to a soul you've already been with your Gretchen.
My poor wreath!
Well, everything's finished, it's done.   4430
We'll see one another again,
But not to go dancing.
The crowd's collecting, they don't make a sound.
The square and the streets can hardly contain them.
There goes the bell, now the staff is broken,   4435
I'm seized and I'm bound,
I'm brought to the block.
How it twitches, the skin on each neck,
As the axe-blade's about to strike mine.
Dumb lies the world as the grave.   4440

FAUST   I wish I had never been born!

MEPHISTOPHELES [Appearing outside]
Unless you come you are lost, now come on!
Shilly-shallying, debating and jabbering!
My horses are trembling.
A minute or two and it's day.   4445

MARGARETE   Who's that rising up out of the ground?
It's him, him, oh drive him away!
It's holy here, what does he want?
Me, he wants me!

FAUST   Live, hear me, live!

MARGARETE   It's the judgment of God! I submit!   4450

MEPHISTO   Die both of you, I have to leave.

MARGARETE   In your hands, our Father! Oh, save me!
You angelical hosts, stand around me,
Draw up in your ranks to safeguard me!
I'm afraid of you, Heinrich, afraid!   4455

MEPHISTO   She's condemned, she is lost!

VOICE [From above]
                                   She is saved!

MEPHISTO [To FAUST, peremptorily]
Now come on, I tell you, with me!
        [He disappears with FAUST.]

VOICE [From within, dying away]
Heinrich! Heinrich!

REVOLUTIONARY MOMENTS

We have become accustomed to speaking readily of ideas or products as "revolutionary." We mean, usually, little more than that the idea or gimmick appears to be new. Toward the end of the eighteenth century, in contrast, the revolutions were real: they cost lives. Vast upheavals in America and France had emotional and political consequences throughout the Western world. They also had consequences for those who lived through them, not only as soldiers but as men engaged in political thought and action or as women on the sidelines or trying to be part of the action.

Some men and women, of course, resisted revolution—even in the American colonies, which we tend to think of as unanimously anti-British. Thomas Hutchinson, colonial governor of Massachusetts, speaks passionately in favor of the established order. Subjects owe loyalty to their king—that principle takes precedence, he believes, over all others. The alternative to subordination, he obviously feels, is chaos. Indeed, considerable chaos did ensue as the colonists increasingly resisted government from afar and all its agents.

From the perspective of Americans living more than two centuries after the Revolution, the country's independence seems inevitable and necessary. It did not seem inevitable to those living through the tumult that preceded the actual physical struggle. Indeed, to men and women who had emigrated from England or whose parents had, the dominion of the mother country was as "natural" as the state of independence is to us. An effort of imagination and intellect was required to conceive the possibility of separation. The letters between Abigail and John Adams vividly convey the alternations of feeling, the conflicting impulses, that attended the development of an ideology of liberty and equality. Even writing after the fact, Mercy Otis Warren, who had lived through the events that she recorded as a historian, suggests that the Revolution was as much the product of changing ideas as of physical conflict.

The power of the new ideas articulated in the Declaration of Independence and subsequently in the American Constitution made itself widely felt. When Thomas Paine, almost a quarter of a century after the Declaration, addressed the people of France, he clearly articulated the continuity between the American and the French Revolutions: the first implied the second, in his interpretation. Given the principles that the Americans had enunciated, oppressed people around the world must, he thought, rise up against their oppressors.

The conflict between reason and passion that had preoccupied so many earlier thinkers played itself out dramatically in the events of the French Revolution. The revolutionary leader Jean-Paul Marat, maintaining that Louis XVI should be put on trial, exemplifies the point. He argues against the view that the king should be summarily executed without trial. For Marat, the making of a reasoned case against a corrupt monarch had great importance. He desired and expected the same outcome as those who wished immediately to guillotine the king but felt an urgent need to fully expose the logic of the case. In supporting revolution, Marat, like many other revolutionaries, believed himself to be speaking for principles of the utmost importance to the entire human race. The moderate Madame de Staël resembled such revolutionaries in her insistence on taking a long view of the political implications latent in immediate actions.

When one hears the voices of those most immediately involved in the struggle, though, rationality seems beside the point. Immediate needs and pressing feelings, as well as the powerful influence of mob psychology, governed those who marched on Versailles as part of the crowd and those who tried to control the movements of that crowd. The issues were far from theoretical for such participants, who powerfully declare their positions.

Both eighteenth-century revolutions resulted in the articulation of important principles and the expression of important feelings. As the nineteenth century played itself out, those revolutions would provide the models and the impetus for other uprisings. The year 1848, for instance, saw revolts in Germany, Austria, and Italy as well as in France—revolts that expressed their participants' yearning to partake directly in realizing the glorious principles that the French had earlier defined as liberty, equality, and fraternity. The realization, to be sure, never fully corresponded to the ideal, although the revolts brought various kinds of progress in their wake; and attempts to fulfill the ideals frequently involved injustices along the way. Such is the nature of ideals and their realizations. Yet the period's impulse toward literal revolution reflected, as truly as its lyric poetry, a dynamic of hope and aspiration.

THOMAS HUTCHINSON
1711–1780

A colonial governor of Massachusetts, Thomas Hutchinson was wealthy, learned, and noted for his integrity. Appointed royal governor in 1771, he held a great deal of power in the colonies. His sympathies lay predominantly with the British. Although, for instance, he considered the Stamp Act unwise, he believed in strict enforcement of British law. In 1765, when he held the position of lieutenant governor, his unpopularity caused a mob to sack and burn his mansion. That unpopularity only increased. In 1773, he refused to let tea-laden ships clear Boston Harbor; this action precipitated the Boston Tea Party.

The speech to the Massachusetts Assembly here printed dates from earlier in the same year. It constitutes a principled defense of the Tory position, an argument based on England's legal right to control and govern the colonies and utterly rejecting the notion that "natural law" guarantees individual rights.

[Address to the Massachusetts Assembly]

His Excellency the Governor was pleased to open the Assembly with the following speech to both Houses, viz.
Gentlemen of the Council, and
Gentlemen of the House of Representatives.

I have nothing in special command from his Majesty to lay before you at this time; I have general instructions to recommend to you, at all times, such measures as may tend to promote that peace and order upon which your own happiness and prosperity as well as his Majesty's service very much depend. That the government is at present in a disturbed and disordered state is a truth too evident to be denied. The cause of this disorder appears to me equally evident. I wish I may be able to make it appear so to you, for then I may not doubt that you will agree with me in the proper measures for the removal of it. I have pleased myself, for several years past, with hopes that the cause would cease of itself and the effect with it, but I am disappointed, and I may not any longer, consistent with my duty to the King and my regard to the interest of the province, delay communicating my sentiments to you upon a matter of so great importance. I shall be explicit and treat the subject without reserve. I hope you will receive what I have to say upon it with candor, and, if you shall not agree in sentiments with me, I promise you, with candor likewise, to receive and consider what you may offer in answer.

When our predecessors first took possession of this plantation or colony, under a grant and charter from the Crown of England, it was their sense, and it was the sense of the kingdom, that they were to remain subject to the supreme authority of Parliament. This appears from the charter itself and from other irresistable evidence. This supreme authority has, from time to time, been exercised by Parliament and submitted to by the colony, and hath been, in the most express terms, acknowledged by the legislature and, except about the time of anarchy and confusion in England which preceded the restoration of King Charles the Second, I have not discovered that it has been called in question even by private or particular persons until within seven or eight years last past. Our provincial or local laws have, in numerous instances, had relation to acts of Parliament made to respect the plantations[1] in general and this colony in particular, and in our executive courts both juries and judges have to all intents and purposes, considered such acts as part of our rule of law. Such a constitution, in a plantation, is not peculiar to England but agrees with the principles of the most celebrated writers upon the law of nations that "when a Nation takes Possession of a distant Country and settles there, that Country, though separated from the principal Establishment or Mother Country, naturally becomes a Part of the State equally with its ancient Possessions."[2]

So much however of the spirit of liberty breathes through all parts of the English constitution, that although from the nature of government there must be one supreme authority over the whole, yet this constitution will admit of subordinate powers with legislative and executive authority, greater or less according to local and other circumstances. Thus we see a variety of corporations formed within the kingdom with powers to make and execute such bylaws as are for their immediate use and benefit, the members of such corporations still remaining subject to the general laws of the kingdom. We see also governments established in the plantations which, from their separate and remote situation, require more general and extensive powers of legislation within themselves than those formed within the kingdom, but subject nevertheless, to all such laws of the kingdom as immediately respect them or are designed to extend to them, and accordingly we in this province have, from the first settlement of it, been left to the exercise of our legislative and executive powers, Parliament occasionally though rarely, interposing as in its wisdom has been judged necessary.

Under this constitution, for more than one hundred years, the laws both of the supreme and subordinate authority were in general, duly executed, Offenders against them have been brought to condign punishment, peace and order have been maintained and the people of this province have experienced as largely the advantages of government, as, perhaps, any people

1. Colonies. 2. The quotation comes from Emer de Vattell, *The Law of Nations* (1758), I.xviii.210. First published in France, the book was translated into many European languages and widely circulated throughout the 18th century.

upon the globe, and they have from time to time in the most public manner expressed their sense of it and, once in every year, have offered up their united thanksgivings to God for the enjoyment of these privileges and, as often, their united prayers for the continuance of them.

At length the constitution has been called in question and the authority of the Parliament of Great Britain to make and establish laws for the inhabitants of this province has been, by many, denied. What was, at first, whispered with caution, was soon after openly asserted in print and, of late, a number of inhabitants in several of the principal towns in the province, have assembled together in their respective towns and, having assumed the name of legal town meetings, have passed resolves which they have ordered to be placed upon their town records, and caused to be printed & published in pamphlets and newspapers. I am sorry that it is thus become impossible to conceal what I could wish had never been made public. I will not particularize these resolves or votes and shall only observe to you, in general, that some of them deny the supreme authority of Parliament, and so are repugnant to the principles of the constitution, and that others speak of this supreme authority, of which the king is a constituent part and to every act of which his assent is necessary, in such terms as have a direct tendency to alienate the affections of the people from their sovereign who has ever been most tender of their rights, and whose person, crown and dignity we are under every possible obligation to defend and support. In consequence of these resolves, committees of correspondence are formed, in several of those towns, to maintain the principles upon which they are founded.

I know of no arguments, founded in reason, which will be sufficient to support these principles or to justify the measures taken in consequence of them. It has been urged,[3] that the sole power of making laws is granted by charter to a legislature established in the province, consisting of the king by his representative the governor, the council and the house of representatives—that by this charter there are likewise granted or assured to the inhabitants of the province all the liberties and immunities of free and natural subjects, to all intents constructions and purposes whatsoever, as if they had been born within the realm of England—that it is part of the liberties of English subjects, which has its foundation in nature, to be governed by laws made by their consent in person or by their representative—that the subjects in this province are not and cannot be represented in the Parliament of Great Britain and, consequently, the acts of Parliament cannot be binding upon them.

I do not find, gentlemen, in the charter such an expression as *sole* power or any words which import it. The general court has, by charter, *full* power to make such laws as are not repugnant to the laws of England. A favorable construction has been put upon this clause when it has been allowed to intend such laws of England only as are expressly declared to respect us. Surely then this is by charter a reserve of power and authority to Parliament to bind us by such laws, at least, as are made expressly to refer to us and, consequently, is a limitation of the power given to the general court. Nor can it be contended that by the liberties of free and natural subjects is to be

3. By the town of Boston.

understood an exemption from acts of Parliament because not represented there, seeing it is provided, by the same charter, that such acts shall be in force; and if they that make the objection to such acts will read the charter with attention, they must be convinced that this grant of liberties and immunities is nothing more than a declaration and assurance on the part of the Crown that the place to which their predecessors were about to remove was and would be considered as part of the dominions of the Crown of England, and therefore that the subjects of the Crown so removing, and those born there or in their passage thither or in their passage from thence, would not become aliens but would throughout all parts of the English dominions, wherever they might happen to be, as well within the colony, retain the liberties and immunities of free and natural subjects, their removal from or not being born within the realm notwithstanding. If the plantations be part of the dominions of the Crown, this clause in the charter does not confer or reserve any liberties but what would have been enjoyed without it and what the inhabitants of every other colony do enjoy where they are without a charter. If the plantations are not the dominions of the Crown will not all that are born here be considered as born out of the ligeance of[4] the king of England, and whenever they go into any part of the dominions will they not be deemed aliens to all intents and purposes, this grant in the charter notwithstanding?

They who claim exemption from acts of Parliament by virtue of their rights as Englishmen, should consider that it is impossible the rights of English subjects should be the same, in every respect, in all parts of the dominions. It is one of their rights as English subjects to be governed by laws made by persons in whose election they have, from time to time, a voice—they remove from the kingdom where, perhaps, they were in the full exercise of this right to the plantations where it cannot be exercised or where the exercise of it would be of no benefit to them. Does it follow that the government, by their removal from one part of the dominions to another, loses its authority over that part to which they remove, and that they are freed from the subjection they were under before; or do they expect that government should relinquish its authority because they cannot enjoy this particular right? Will it not rather be said that, by this their voluntary removal, they have relinquished for a time at least, one of the rights of an English subject which they might if they pleased have continued to enjoy and may again enjoy whensoever they will return to the place where it can be exercised?

They who claim exemption, as part of their rights by nature,[5] should consider that every restraint which men are laid under by a state of government is a privation of part of their natural rights, and of all the different forms of government which exist, there can be no two of them in which the departure from natural rights is exactly the same. Even in case of representation by election, do they not give up part of their natural rights when they consent to be represented by such person as shall be chosen by the majority of the electors, although their own voices may be for some other person? And is it

4. Allegiance to. 5. The "natural rights" argument was important to those inclined toward seeking independence from England.

not contrary to their natural rights to be obliged to submit to a representative for seven years, or even one year, after they are dissatisfied with his conduct, although they gave their voices for him when he was elected? This must therefore be considered as an objection against a state of government rather than against any particular form.

If what I have said shall not be sufficient to satisfy such as object to the supreme authority of Parliament over the plantations, there may something further be added to induce them to an acknowledgment of it which I think will well deserve their consideration. I know of no line that can be drawn between the supreme authority of Parliament and the total independence of the colonies: It is impossible there should be two independent legislatures in one and the same state, for although there may be but one head, the king, yet the two legislative bodies will make two governments as distinct as the kingdoms of England and Scotland before the union. If we might be suffered to be altogether independent of Great Britain, could we have any claim to the protection of that government of which we are no longer a part? Without this protection should we not become the prey of one or the other powers of Europe, such as should first seize upon us? Is there any thing which we have more reason to dread than independence? I hope it will never be our misfortune to know by experience the difference between the liberties of an English colonist and those of the Spanish, French or Dutch.

If then the supremacy of Parliament over the whole British dominions shall no longer be denied, it will follow that the *mere* exercise of its authority can be no matter of grievance. If it has been or shall be exercised in such way and manner as shall appear to be grievous, still this cannot be sufficient grounds for immediately denying or renouncing the authority or refusing to submit to it. The acts and doings of authority in the most perfect form of government will not always be thought just and equitable by all the parts of which it consists, but it is the greatest absurdity to admit the several parts to be at liberty to obey or disobey according as the acts of such authority may be approved of or disapproved of by them, for this necessarily works a dissolution of the government. The manner then of obtaining redress must be by representations and endeavors, in such ways and forms as the established rules of the constitution prescribe or allow in order to make any matters alleged to be grievances appear to be really such; but I conceive it is rather the *mere* exercise of this authority which is complained of as a grievance, than any heavy burdens which have been brought upon the people by means of it.

As contentment and order were the happy effects of a constitution strengthened by universal assent and approbation, so discontent and disorder are now the deplorable effects of a constitution enfeebled by contest and opposition. Besides divisions and animosities which disturb the peace of towns and families, the law in some important cases cannot have its course, offenders ordered by advice of His Majesty's council to be prosecuted, escape with impunity and are supported and encouraged to go on offending,—the authority of government is brought into contempt, and there are but small remains of that subordination which was once very conspicious in this colony, and which is essential to a well-regulated state.

When the bands of government are thus weakened, it certainly behoves those with whom the powers of government are intrusted to omit nothing which may tend to strengthen them.

I have disclosed my sentiments to you without reserve. Let me intreat you to consider them calmly and not to be too sudden in your determination. If my principles of government are right let us adhere to them. With the same principles our ancestors were easy and happy for a long course of years together, and I know of no reason to doubt of your being equally easy & happy. The people, influenced by you will forsake their unconstitutional principles and desist from their irregularities which are the consequence of them, they will be convinced that everything which is valuable to them depend upon their connection with their parent state, that this connection cannot be continued in any other way than such as will also continue their dependence upon the supreme authority of the British dominions, and that, notwithstanding this dependance, they will enjoy as great a proportion of those rights to which they have a claim by nature or as Englishmen as can be enjoyed by a plantation or colony.

If I am wrong in my principles of government or in the inferences which I have drawn from them, I wish to be convinced of my error. Independence I may not allow myself to think that you can possibly have in contemplation. If you can conceive of any other constitutional dependence than what I have mentioned, if you are of opinion that upon any other principles our connection with the state from which we sprang can be continued, communicate your sentiments to me with the same freedom and unreservedness as I have communicated mine to you.

I have no desire, gentlemen, by any thing I have said to preclude you from seeking relief, in a constitutional way, in any cases in which you have heretofore or may hereafter suppose that you are aggrieved and, although I should not concur with you in sentiment, I will, notwithstanding, do nothing to lessen the weight which your representations may deserve. I have laid before you what I think are the principles of your constitution: If you do not agree with me I wish to know your objections: They may be convincing to me, or I may be able to satisfy you of the insufficiency of them: In either case I hope, we shall put an end to those irregularities, which ever will be the portion of a government where the supreme authority is controverted, and introduce that tranquillity which seems to have taken place in most of the colonies upon the continent.

The ordinary business of the session I will not now particularly point out to you. To the enacting of any new laws which may be necessary for the more equal and effectual distribution of justice, or for giving further encouragement to our merchandise, fishery, and agriculture, which through the divine favor are already in a very flourishing state, or for promoting any measures which may conduce to the general good of the province I will readily give my assent or concurrence.

Council Chamber   T. Hutchinson
6 January 1773

MERCY OTIS WARREN
1728–1814

As vigorous in her support of the American Revolution as any man, Mercy Otis Warren wrote and published in several genres. Her poetry and plays were widely read, but her *History of the Rise, Progress, and Termination of the American Revolution* (1805), on which she had worked for thirty years, marked her most important intervention in political discourse. She wrote as one who had witnessed many of the events she reported, and she published her work (in three volumes) at a time when women customarily provided manuscripts only for private circulation.

Warren lived her entire life in Massachusetts, first on Cape Cod, then, when she married James Warren, a colonial legislator, in Plymouth. She received no formal education, although her brothers went to Harvard, and late in life she was vociferous about the need to provide better education for women. Although she gave birth to five sons, she found time to develop and express vigorous political views. Like her husband, father, and brothers, she supported the cause of independence and urged the colonies to act in their own interest. She also urged—unsuccessfully—the inclusion in the U.S. Constitution of specifications for equal rights for women. Later, she supported the French Revolution. A friend of such revolutionary notables as Washington, Franklin, and Jefferson, she quarreled with John Adams when he became too conservative for her tastes.

In her account of the Revolution, Warren stresses not only the events of the war but the principles underlying the revolutionary enterprise. A staunch proponent of natural-rights philosophy, which held that the right to equality was part of the natural order, she believed that the colonists were forming political structures that would change the course of Western ideology. The importance of the Revolution, therefore, was more than national, and the exalted rhetoric Warren sometimes employs reflects her belief in this truth.

From History of the Rise, Progress, and Termination of the American Revolution

CHAPTER XVII

[1780]

Distressed Situation of the Army and the Country, from Various Causes • General Gates Sent to the Southward—Surprised and Defeated at Camden by Lord Cornwallis—Superseded • General Greene Appointed to the Command in the Carolinas • Major Ferguson's Defeat • Sir Henry Clinton Makes a Diversion in the Chesapeake, in Favor of Lord Cornwallis • General Arnold Sent There • His Defection and Character • Detection, Trial, and Death of Major Andre • Disposition of the Dutch Republic with Regard to America • Governor Trumbull's Character, and Correspondence with the Baron Van der Capellen • Mr. Laurens appointed to negotiate with the Dutch Republic

The year one thousand seven hundred and eighty, was a year of incident, expectation, and event; a period pregnant with future consequences, interesting in the highest degree to the political happiness of the nations, and perhaps ultimately to the civil institutions of a great part of mankind. We left England in the preceding chapter, in a very perturbed state, arising both from their own internal dissensions, and the dread of foreign combinations, relative to their own island and its former dependencies.

At the same time, neither the pen of the historian, or the imagination of the poet, can fully describe the embarrassments suffered by congress, by the commander in chief, and by men of firmness and principle in the several legislative bodies, through this and the beginning of the next year. The scarcity of specie,[1] the rapid depreciation of paper,[2] which at once sunk the property and corrupted the morals of the people; which destroyed all confidence in public bodies, reduced the old army to the extremes of misery, and seemed to preclude all possibility of raising a new one, sufficient for all the departments; were evils, which neither the wisdom or vigilance of Congress could remedy.

At such a crisis, more penetration and firmness, more judgment, impartiality, and moderation, were requisite in the commander in chief of the American armies, than usually fall within the compass of the genius or ability of man. In the neighborhood of a potent army, General Washington had to guard with a very inadequate force, not only against the arms of his enemies, but the machinations of British emissaries, continually attempting to corrupt the fidelity both of his officers and his troops.

Perhaps no one but himself can describe the complicated sources of anxiety, that at this period pervaded the breast of the first military officer, whose honor, whose life, whose country, hung suspended, not on a single point only, but on many events that quivered in the winds of fortune, chance, or the more uncertain determinations of men. Happy is it to reflect, that these are all under the destination of an unerring hand, that works in secret, ultimately to complete the beneficent designs of Providence.

Some extracts from his own pen, very naturally express the agitations of the mind of General Washington, in the preceding as well as the present year. In one of his letters to a friend[3] he observed,

> Our conflict is not likely to cease so soon as every good man would wish. The measure of iniquity is not yet filled; and unless we can return a little more to first principles, and act a little more upon patriotic ground, I do not know when it will—or—what may be the issue of the contest. Speculation—peculation—engrossing—forestalling[4]—with all their concomitants, afford too many melancholy proofs of the decay of public virtue; and too glaring instances of its being the interest and desire of too many, who would wish to be thought friends, to continue the war.
>
> Nothing, I am convinced, but the depreciation of our currency, proceeding in a great measure from the foregoing causes, aided by stock-jobbing and party dissensions, has fed the hopes of the enemy, and kept the arms of Britain in America until now. They do not scruple to declare this themselves; and add, that we shall be our own conquerors. Cannot our common country (America) possess virtue enough to disappoint them? With you, sir, I think, that the consideration of a little dirty pelf[5] to individuals, is not to be placed in competition with the essential rights and liberties of the present generation, and of millions yet unborn.

1. Coins. 2. I.e., paper money. 3. James Warren, the author's husband, who was then speaker of the Massachusetts assembly. 4. *Peculation—engrossing—forestalling:* embezzling, creating monopolies, preventing fair trade. 5. Money.

Shall a few designing men, for their own aggrandizement, and to gratify their own avarice, overset the goodly fabric[6] we have been rearing at the expense of so much time, blood, and treasure?—and shall we at last become the victims of our own abominable lust of gain?—Forbid it Heaven!—forbid it all, and every state in the union! by enacting and enforcing efficacious laws for checking the growth of these monstrous evils, and restoring matters in some degree, to the pristine state they were in at the commencement of the war.

Our cause is noble,—it is the cause of mankind; and the danger to it springs from ourselves. Shall we slumber and sleep then, when we should be punishing those miscreants who have brought these troubles upon us, and who are aiming to continue us in them? while we should be striving to fill our battalions, and devising ways and means to appreciate the currency, on the credit of which every thing depends?—I hope not.

* * *

Let vigorous measures be adopted to punish speculators—forestallers—and extortioners;—and above all—to sink the money by heavy taxes—to promote public and private economy—encourage manufactures, etc.

Measures of this sort gone heartily into by the several states, will strike at once at the root of all our misfortunes, and give the *coup de grâce* to British hope of subjugating this great continent, either by their arms or their arts. The first, as I have before observed, they acknowledge unequal to the task; the latter I am sure will be so, if we are not lost to everything that is good and virtuous.

A little time now, must unfold in some degree, the enemy's designs. Whether the state of affairs in Europe will permit them to augment their army, with more than recruits for the regiments now in America, and therewith attempt an active and vigorous campaign,—or whether with their Canadian and Florida force, they will aid and abet the Indians in ravaging our western frontier, while their shipping with detachments harass, (and if they mean to prosecute the predatory war threatened by administration through their commissioners,) burn, and destroy our sea-coast,—or whether, contrary to expectation, they are more disposed to negotiate than to either, is more than I can determine. The latter will depend very much on their apprehensions of Spain, and their own foreign alliances. At present, we seem to be in a chaos, but this cannot last long, as I presume the ultimate determinations of the British court will be developed at the meeting of Parliament, after the holidays.

An extract of another letter from General Washington to the governor of Pennsylvania, dated August the twentieth, one thousand seven hundred and eighty, discovers the same anxiety for the fate of the contest, as the above. In this he said,

To me it will appear miraculous if our affairs can maintain themselves much longer, in their present train. If either the temper or the resources of the country will not admit of an alteration, we may soon expect to be

6. Construction.

reduced to the humiliating condition, of seeing the cause of America held up in America by foreign arms. The discontents of the troops have been gradually nurtured to a dangerous extremity. Something satisfactory must be done, or the army must cease to exist at the end of the campaign; or it will exhibit an example of more virtue, fortitude, self-denial, and perseverance, than has perhaps ever been paralleled in the history of human enthusiasm.

While thus impressed with these apprehensions of the depreciation of public virtue, General Washington had to balance the parties, and to meliorate the distresses of the inhabitants, alternately ravaged by all descriptions of soldiers, in the vicinity of both armies. It was impossible for him to strike any capital blow, without money even for daily expenses, without a naval force sufficient to cover any exertions; his battalions incomplete, his army clamorous and discontented, and on the point of mutiny, from the deficiencies in their pay, and the immediate want of every necessary of life.

At the same time, the legislatures of the several states were in the utmost anxiety, to devise ways and means to supply the requisitions of Congress, who had recently laid a tax of many millions on the states, in order to sink the enormous quantity of old paper money. The calls of an army, naked, hungry, and turbulent, even to the discovery of symptoms of revolt, were indeed alarming. The pressing necessities of the army, and the critical exigencies of the times, crowded upon them in every department, and required the utmost wisdom, vigilance, and fortitude.

Nothing depictures the characters, the sentiments, and the feelings of men, more strongly than their private letters at the time. Perhaps this may be evinced, by giving the reader a paragraph of a letter from the speaker[7] of the house of representatives of Massachusetts, to a private friend, at this critical area of embarrassment and perplexity.

> Our public affairs wear a most disagreeable aspect. Embarrassments increase from every quarter. My contemplations are engrossed by day and by night, for the salvation of my country. If we succeed, I shall have pleasure which a fortune cannot give; if we fail, I shall feel consolations that those who are intent only on making fortunes, must envy. In a country abounding with men and provisions, it would torture a Sully[8] to raise and support an army in the field. Everything is resolved into money: but the great question is, how to get it?—Taxes, though so great, and often repeated, do not bring it in fast enough; we cannot borrow, because no one will lend: while the army is in danger of starving or disbanding. If we lay more taxes, the very people who have been used to tender the one-half of their property, or even their all, for the service of their country, will now revolt at the idea of paying a two-hundredth part; and it might perhaps create uneasiness that might break the union. On the other hand, if we do not lay more taxes, for aught I see, there must be an end of the contest. All these difficulties are increased by the successes of the enemy, which clog our measures by dispiriting the army and the people. But I do not despair. One vigorous and grand campaign may yet

---

7. James Warren.   8. Maximilien de Béthune, duc de Sully (1560–1641), restored French prosperity after finding national finances in disorder as a result of Henry III's extravagance and religious wars.

put a glorious period to the war. All depends on proper exertions. We have to choose glory, honor, and happiness, or infamy, disgrace, and misery.

The complicated difficulties already depictured, clearly prove, that such a spirit of avarice and peculation had crept into the public departments, and taken deep hold of the majority of the people, as Americans a few years before, were thought incapable of. The careful observer of human conduct will readily perceive, that a variety of concurring causes led to this sudden change of character. The opulent, who had been used to ease, independence, and generosity, were reduced, dispirited, and deprived of the ability of rendering pecuniary service to their country, by the unavoidable failure of public faith. Great part of the fortunes of the widow, the orphan, and the aged, were sunk in the public funds; so that the nominal income of a year, would scarcely supply the necessities of a day.

The depreciation of paper had been so rapid, that at this time, one hundred and twenty dollars of the paper currency was not an equivalent to one in silver or gold: while at the same time, a sudden accumulation of property by privateering, by speculation, by accident, or fraud, placed many in the lap of affluence, who were without a principle, education, or family. These, from a thoughtless ignorance, and the novelty of splendor to which they had been total strangers, suddenly plunged into every kind of dissipation, and grafted the extravagancies and follies of foreigners, on their own passion for squandering what by them had been so easily acquired.

Thus, avarice without frugality, and profusion without taste, were indulged, and soon banished the simplicity and elegance that had formerly reigned: instead of which, there was spread in America among the rising generation, a thirst for the accumulation of wealth, unknown to their ancestors. A class who had not had the advantages of the best education, and who had paid little attention to the principles of the revolution, took the lead in manners. Sanctioned by the breach of public faith, the private obligations of justice seemed to be little regarded, and the sacred idea of equity in private contracts was annihilated for a time, by the example of public deficiency.

The infantile state of government, the inexperience of its leaders, and the necessity of substituting a medium with only an imaginary value, brought an impeachment on Congress, without voluntary deviations from probity, or willing breaches of faith. Perhaps nothing is more true, than an observation of a member of that body, that *"the necessity of affairs had often obliged them to depart from the purity of their first principles."* The complaint that the foundation was corrupt, was artfully diffused: however that might be, the streams were undoubtedly tainted, and contamination, with few exceptions, seemed to run through the whole body of the people; and a declension of morals was equally rapid with the depreciation of their currency.

But a superintending Providence, that overrules the designs, and defeats the projects of men, remarkably upheld the spirit of the Americans; and caused events that had for a time a very unfavorable aspect, to operate in favor of independence and peace, and to make a new nation of the recent emigrants from the old and proud empire of Britain.

But they had yet many difficulties to struggle with, which will be sufficiently evinced as we follow the *route* of the British army, and detail the transactions in the Carolinas. The embarrassments and distresses, the battles, skirmishes, and disappointments, the alternate successes and defeats, flight and pursuit, that took place between the contending parties there, must be more copiously related, previous to the maneuvers through the state of Virginia, that led to the last capital stroke, which finished with glory and renown the grand contest between Great Britain and her colonies, and sealed the independence of America.

Indeed a considerable time had elapsed, before the distresses of the country; the situation of the army, naked, hungry, and clamorous; the pressing importunity of General Washington; the addresses and declarations of Congress; and the remonstrances of the several legislative bodies, could arouse from the pursuit of private interest, those who thought themselves secure from immediate danger.

Though from many untoward circumstances, a cloud for a time had seemed to hover over the minds of many, the people again awaked, both from the dream of secure enjoyment in some, and the dread apprehensions in others of falling under the British yoke. The patriotic exertions and unshaken firmness of the few in every state, again had their influence on the many, and all seemed ready to suffer anything, but a subjugation to the crown of Britain.

Not the loss of Charleston, a captured army, the destruction of their marine, the sinking state of their medium,[9] the internal ravages of their country, and their seacoast blazing under the fire of their enemies, had the smallest tendency to bend the Americans to a dereliction of their claim to independence. A confidence in their own good fortune, or rather in that Providence, whose fiat points out the rise and marks the boundaries of empire, supported the more thoughtful; while a constitutional hardiness, warmed by enthusiasm, and whetted by innumerable and recent injuries, still buoyed up the hopes of the soldier, the statesman, the legislator, and the people at large, even in the darkest moments.

Immediately after the news reached Congress, that General Lincoln had surrendered Charleston, and that himself and his army were prisoners to the British commander, the baron de Kalb,[1] a brave and experienced Prussian officer, who had been some time in the American service, was ordered to Virginia, with sanguine hopes of checking the further progress of the British arms. Though the baron de Kalb was an officer of great military merit, his command at the southward was only temporary.

General Gates,[2] the successful conqueror in the northern, was vested with the chief command in the southern department. It was an appointment of great responsibility: this might be a reason, in addition to the great respect which this foreign nobleman had for General Gates, that led him to express in all his letters to his friends, the peculiar satisfaction he felt on his arrival to take the chief command. An officer of his name and experience, at once emboldened the friends of their country, and intimidated the wavering and disaffected. The renowned soldier who had captured one proud British gen-

9. Currency.   1. Johann Kalb (1721–1780), American general in the Revolution. Generally known as Baron de Kalb, he had claimed the title for military reasons. Second in command to Horatio Gates in the campaign Warren here describes, he died from wounds received in that campaign.   2. Horatio Gates (c. 1727–1806), born in England, served in the British Army before joining the American cause. As a general, he led the troops that overwhelmingly defeated the British under General John Burgoyne.

eral and his army, was at this time viewed with particular awe and respect by another.

Nor was it long before most of the British commanders were convinced of the delusory nature of those assurances they had received from the loyalists, that a general disgust to the authority of Congress prevailed; that the defection, more particularly in North Carolina, was such, that the people were ready to renounce all *American usurpations*, as soon as the royal standard should be erected among them. But experiment soon convinced them of the futility of such expectations.

The baron de Kalb had been sent on earlier from headquarters: he had with him a detachment of fourteen hundred men. He stayed only a few weeks in Virginia, and moved from thence to Carolina, where he soon after met General Gates. After the junction of General Gates and the baron de Kalb, they, with unexampled patience and fatigue, marched an army of several thousand men through a barren country, that afforded no subsistence except green fruits, and other unwholesome aliments. They reached the borders of South Carolina, and encamped at Clermont the thirteenth of August.

On his arrival in the vicinity of the British headquarters, General Gates published a proclamation, inviting the patriotic inhabitants of South Carolina, "to join heartily in rescuing themselves and their country, from the oppression of a government imposed on them by the ruffian hand of power." In this proclamation he promised forgiveness and perfect security, to such of the unfortunate citizens of the state, as had been induced by the terror of sanguinary punishments, and the arbitrary measures of military domination, apparently to acquiesce under the British government.

He observed,

> that they had been obliged to make a forced declaration of allegiance and support to a tyranny, which the indignant souls of citizens resolved on freedom, inwardly revolted at with horror and detestation: that they might rest satisfied, that the genuine motive which has given energy to the present exertions, is the hope of rescuing them from the iron rod of oppression, and restoring to them those blessings of freedom and independence, which it is the duty and interest of the citizens of these United States, jointly and reciprocally to support and confirm.

The situation of General Gates at Clermont was not very advantageous, but his design was not to continue long there, but by a sudden move to fall unexpectedly on Lord Rawdon, who had fixed his headquarters at Camden. This place was about thirteen miles distant from Clermont, on the borders of the river Santee, from whence the communication was easy to the internal parts of the country.

Lord Cornwallis[3] had gained early intelligence of the movements of the American army, and had arrived at Camden himself, with a similar design, by an unexpected blow, to surprise General Gates and defeat his arrangements. His lordship effected his purpose with a facility beyond his own expectations. The two armies met in the night of the fifteenth of August, one thousand seven hundred and eighty. Mutually surprised by the sudden

---

3. Charles Cornwallis, first Marquess Cornwallis (1738–1805), the English general who was at this time second in command of the British forces in North America.

necessity of action, a loose skirmish was kept up until the morning, when a general engagement commenced.

The British troops were not equal in numbers to those of the Americans, including the militia, while the renowned character of General Gates heightened the ideas of their strength. But the onset on both sides began with equal spirit and bravery, and was continued with valor equally honorary to both parties, until the militia intimidated, particularly those from Virginia and North Carolina, gave ground, threw down their arms, and fled with great precipitation. The order of the army was immediately broken, and fortune no longer favorable, forsook the American veteran, at the moment his reputation courted, and depended on her smiles. His troops were totally routed, and the general himself fled, rather than retreated, in a manner that was thought for a time, in some measure to sully the laurels of Saratoga.

The baron de Kalb, an officer of great military talents and reputation, was mortally wounded in this action. He died rejoicing in the services he had rendered America in her noble struggles for liberty, and gloried with his last breath, in the honor of dying in defense of the rights of man. Before his death he dictated a letter to a friend, expressive of the warmest affection for the Americans, containing the highest encomiums on the valor of the continental troops, of which he had been so recent a witness, and declaring the satisfaction which he then felt, in having been a partaker of their fortune, and having fallen in their cause.[4]

CHAPTER XXX

[The Aftermath of the Revolution]

A Survey of the Situation of America on the Conclusion of the War with Britain • Observations on the Declaration of Independence • Withdraw of the British Troops from New York—A Few Observations on the Detention of the Western Posts • The American Army Disbanded, after the Commander in Chief Had Addressed the Public, and Taken Leave of His Fellow Soldiers—General Washington Resigns His Commission to Congress

We have seen the banners of Albion[5] displayed, and the pendants of her proud navy waving over the waters of the Western world, and threatening terror, servitude, or desolation, to resisting millions. We have seen through the tragic tale of war, all political connection with Great Britain broken off, the authority of the parent state renounced, and the independence of the American states sealed by the definitive treaty. The mind now willingly draws a veil over the unpleasing part of the drama, and indulges the imagination in future prospects of peace and felicity; when the soldier shall retreat from the field, lay by the sword, and resume the implements of husbandry—the mechanic return to his former occupation, and the merchant rejoice in the prosperous view of commerce; when trade shall not be restricted by the unjust or partial regulations of foreigners; and when the ports of America shall

---

4. When Lord Cornwallis was informed of the rank and merits of the baron de Kalb, he directed that his remains should be respectfully interred. He was buried near the village of Camden; but no memorial of the deposite of this distinguished hero has been preserved, though Congress some time afterwards directed a monument should be erected to his memory. Nothing was however done, except planting an ornamental tree at the head of his grave [Warren's note].   5. England.

be thrown open to all the world, and an intercourse kept free, to reap the advantages of commerce extended to all nations.

The young government of this newly established nation had, by the recent articles of peace, a claim to a jurisdiction over a vast territory, reaching from the St. Mary's[6] on the south, to the river St. Croix,[7] the extreme boundary of the east, containing a line of post roads of eighteen hundred miles, exclusive of the northern and western wilds, but partially settled, and whose limits have not yet been explored. Not the Lycian League,[8] nor any of the combinations of the Grecian states, encircled such an extent of territory; nor does modern history furnish any example of a confederacy of equal magnitude and respectability with that of the United States of America.

We look back with astonishment when we reflect, that it was only in the beginning of the seventeenth century, that the first Europeans landed in Virginia, and that nearly at the same time, a few wandering strangers coasted about the unknown bay of Massachusetts, until they found a footing in Plymouth. Only a century and an half had elapsed, before their numbers and their strength accumulated, until they bade defiance to foreign oppression, and stood ready to meet the power of Britain, with courage and magnanimity scarcely paralleled by the progeny of nations, who had been used to every degree of subordination and obedience.

The most vivid imagination cannot realize the contrast, when it surveys the vast surface of America now enrobed with fruitful fields, and the rich herbage of the pastures, which had been so recently covered with a thick mattress of woods; when it beholds the cultivated vista, the orchards and the beautiful gardens which have arisen within the limits of the Atlantic states, where the deep embrowned, melancholy forest, had from time immemorial sheltered only the wandering savage; where the sweet notes of the feathered race, that follow the track of cultivation, had never chanted their melodious songs: the wild waste had been a haunt only for the hoarse birds of prey, and the prowling quadrupeds that filled the forest.

In a country like America, including a vast variety of soil and climate, producing everything necessary for convenience and pleasure, every man might be lord of his own acquisition. It was a country where the standard of freedom had recently been erected, to allure the liberal minded to her shores, and to receive and to protect the persecuted subjects of arbitrary power, who might there seek an asylum from the chains of servitude to which they had been subjected in any part of the globe. Here it might rationally be expected, that beside the natural increase, the emigration to a land of such fair promise of the blessings of plenty, liberty, and peace, to which multitudes would probably resort, there would be exhibited in a few years, a population almost beyond the calculation of figures.

The extensive tract of territory above described, on the borders of the Atlantic, had, as we have seen, been divided into several distinct governments, under the control of the crown of Great Britain; these governments were now united in a strong confederacy, absolutely independent of all foreign domination: the several states retained their own legislative powers; they

6. A river in southern Maryland.   7. A river that rises in Canada and flows to Passamaquoddy Bay in Maine, now forming part of the U.S.–Canada border.   8. An alliance among the twenty-three city-states of ancient Lycia, a country that was formed on the mountainous coastline of western Anatolia, now part of Turkey.

were proud of their individual independence, tenacious of their republican principles, and newly emancipated from the degrading ideas of foreign control, and the sceptered hand of monarchy. With all these distinguished privileges, deeply impressed with the ideas of internal happiness, we shall see they grew jealous of each other, and soon after the peace, even of the powers of the several governments erected by themselves: they were eager for the acquisition of wealth, and the possession of the new advantages dawning on their country, from their friendly connections abroad, and their abundant resources at home.

At the same time that these wayward appearances began early to threaten their internal felicity, the inhabitants of America were in general sensible,[9] that the freedom of the people, the virtue of society, and the stability of their commonwealth, could only be preserved by the strictest union; and that the independence of the United States must be secured by an undeviating adherence to the principles that produced the revolution.

These principles were grounded on the natural equality of man, their right of adopting their own modes of government, the dignity of the people, and that sovereignty which cannot be ceded either to representatives or to kings. But, as a certain writer has expressed it,

> Powers may be delegated for particular purposes; but the omnipotence of society, if any where, is in itself. Princes, senates, or parliaments, are not proprietors or masters; they are subject to the people, who form and support that society, by an eternal law of nature, which has ever subjected a part to the whole.[1]

These were opinions congenial to the feelings, and were disseminated by the pens, of political writers; of Otis, Dickinson, Quincy,[2] and many others, who with pathos and energy had defended the liberties of America, previous to the commencement of hostilities.

On these principles, a due respect must ever be paid to the general will; to the right in the people to dispose of their own monies by a representative voice; and to liberty of conscience without religious tests: on these principles, frequent elections, and rotations of office, were generally thought necessary, without precluding the indispensable subordination and obedience due to rulers of their own choice. From the principles, manners, habits, and education of the Americans, they expected from their rulers, economy in expenditure, (both public and private,) simplicity of manners, pure morals, and undeviating probity. These they considered as the emanations of virtue, grounded on a sense of duty, and a veneration for the Supreme Governor of the universe, to whom the dictates of nature teach all mankind to pay homage, and whom they had been taught to worship according to revelation, and the divine precepts of the Gospel. Their ancestors had rejected and fled from the impositions and restrictions of men, vested either with princely or priestly authority: they equally claimed the exercise of private judgment, and the

9. Aware.   1. David Williams, *Lessons to a Young Prince, by an Old Statesman, on the Present Disposition in Europe to a General Revolution* (1791).   2. Josiah Quincy (1744–1775), lawyer, wrote in support of the American colonists; he died on the way home from a trip to England to argue the American cause. James Otis (1725–1783), colonial political leader, as a lawyer defined and defended colonial rights from a radical point of view. John Dickinson (1732–1808), also a lawyer, held a more conservative position but opposed British actions as well as American radicals.

rights of conscience, unfettered by religious establishments in favor of particular denominations.

They expected a simplification of law; clearly defined distinctions between executive, legislative, and judiciary powers: the right of trial by jury, and a sacred regard to personal liberty and the protection of private property, were opinions embraced by all who had any just ideas of government, law, equity, or morals.

These were the rights of men, the privileges of Englishmen, and the claim of Americans: these were the principles of the Saxon ancestry of the British Empire, and of all the free nations of Europe, previous to the corrupt systems introduced by intriguing and ambitious individuals.

These were the opinions of Ludlow and Sydney, of Milton and Harrington:[3] these were principles defended by the pen of the learned, enlightened, and renowned Locke; and even Judge Blackstone,[4] in his excellent commentaries on the laws of England, has observed, "that trial by jury and the liberties of the people went out together." Indeed, most of the learned and virtuous writers that have adorned the pages of literature from generation to generation, in an island celebrated for the erudite and comprehensive genius of its inhabitants, have enforced these rational and liberal opinions.

These were the principles which the ancestors of the inhabitants of the United States brought with them from the polished shores of Europe, to the dark wilds of America: these opinions were deeply infixed in the bosoms of their posterity, and nurtured with zeal, until necessity obligated them to announce the declaration of the independence of the United States. We have seen that the instrument which announced the final separation of the American colonies from Great Britain, was drawn by the elegant and energetic pen of Jefferson,[5] with that correct judgment, precision, and dignity, which have ever marked his character.

The Declaration of Independence, which has done so much honor to the then existing Congress, to the inhabitants of the United States, and to the genius and heart of the gentleman who drew it, in the belief, and under the awe, of the Divine Providence, ought to be frequently read by the rising youth of the American states, as a palladium of which they should never lose sight, so long as they wish to continue a free and independent people.

This celebrated paper, which will be admired in the annals of every historian, begins with an assertion, that all men are created equal, and endowed by their Creator with certain unalienable rights, which nature and nature's God entitle them to claim; and, after appealing to the Supreme Judge of the world for the rectitude of their intentions, it concludes in the name of the *good people* of the *colonies*, by their representatives assembled in Congress, they publish and declare, that they are, and of right ought to be, free and independent states: in the *name* of the *people*, the fountain of all just author-

3. James Harrington (1611–1677) was an English political writer whose ideas were influential in both the American and the French revolutions. Edmund Ludlow (1617–1692) sympathized with the English Puritans but opposed Oliver Cromwell as well as the restoration of King Charles II. Algernon Sidney (1622–1683), famous for his liberal ideas, also opposed Cromwell and plotted against Charles II. John Milton (1608–1674), the poet, was likewise a notable political thinker, supporting those who had imprisoned King Charles I and continuing to defend Cromwell and his government. **4.** Sir William Blackstone (1723–1780), in *Commentaries on the Laws of England*, 4 vols. (1765–69), clarified the principles and practice of English law. **5.** Thomas Jefferson (1743–1826), author of the Declaration of Independence.

ity, relying on the protection of Divine Providence, they mutually pledged themselves to maintain these rights, with their lives, fortunes, and honor.

These principles the *sons of Columbia*[6] had supported by argument, defended by the sword, and have now secured by negotiation, as far as the pledges of national faith and honor will bind society to a strict adherence to equity. This however is seldom longer than it appears to be the interest of nations, or designing individuals of influence and power. Virtue in the sublimest sense, operates only on the minds of a chosen few: in their breasts it will ever find its own reward.

In all ages, mankind are governed less by reason and justice, than by interest and passion: the caprice of a day, or the impulse of a moment, will blow them about as with a whirlwind, and bear them down the current of folly, until awakened by their misery: by these they are often led to breaches of the most solemn engagements, the consequences of which may involve whole nations in wretchedness. It is devoutly to be hoped, that the conduct of America will never stand upon record as a striking example of the truth of this observation. She has fought for her liberties; she has purchased them by the most costly sacrifices: we have seen her embark in the enterprise, with a spirit that gained her the applause of mankind. The United States have procured their own emancipation from foreign thraldom, by the sacrifice of their heroes and their friends: they are now ushered on to the temple of peace, who holds out her wand, and beckons them to make the wisest improvement of the advantages they had acquired, by their patience, perseverance, and valor.

They had now only to close the scenes of war by a quiet dispersion of their own armies, and to witness the last act of hostile parade, the decampment of the battalions of Britain, and the retirement of the potent fleets that had long infested their coasts. This was to have been done at an earlier day: it was expected that on the ratification of the definitive treaty, there would have been an immediate evacuation of all the posts which had been held by the British, within the limits of the United States.

The seventh article of the treaty expressly stipulated, that

> His Britannic Majesty shall, with all convenient speed, and without causing any destruction, or carrying away any negroes or other property of the American inhabitants, withdraw all his armies, garrisons, and fleets, from the said United States, and from every post, place, and harbor, within the same; leaving in all fortifications the American artillery that may be therein: and shall also order and cause all archives, records, deeds, and papers, belonging to any of the said states, or their citizens, which in the course of the war may have fallen into the hands of his officers, to be forthwith restored and delivered to the proper states and persons to whom they belong.

General Carleton[7] had assigned his reasons for delay relative to the evacuation of New York, in his correspondence with the president of Congress and General Washington. Some satisfactory arrangements were however

---

6. Colonial patriots; *Columbia* designated the new United States.   7. Guy Carleton, Baron Dorchester (1724–1808), British general in command of Canada.

soon after made, relative to the loyalists, the exchange of prisoners, and several other points, for which the reader is referred to the journals of Congress. When this was done, a detachment from the American army, under the command of General Knox,[8] was directed to enter New York, in order to prevent any irregularities, confusion, or insult, among the citizens, on the important movement now about to take place.

On the twenty-fifth of November, one thousand seven hundred and eighty-three, all the British, Hessian, and other foreign troops in the pay of his Britannic majesty, were drawn off from the city of New York: General Carleton embarked the same day; and Admiral Digby sailed for England with the remainder of the British fleet, that had for many years invaded the seacoasts of America. Thus the shores of the Atlantic states, that had so long been alarmed by the terrific thunders of the British navy, and ravaged by hostile squadrons, were left in repose. In consequence of this much desired event, a general joy pervaded the borders, from Georgia to the extreme boundaries of the New England states.

No sufficient apology was however yet made for the detention of the western posts: they were long retained; and this breach of faith was afterwards attended with very important consequences. Under various frivolous pretences of noncompliance on the part of the United States, with some articles stipulated in the definitive treaty of peace, a long line of posts in the western territory were not relinquished.

8. Henry Knox (1750–1806), American general and friend of George Washington.

JOHN ADAMS AND ABIGAIL ADAMS
1735–1826 and 1744–1818

The correspondence between John Adams, second president of the United States, and his wife, Abigail, provides unusual personal perspective on the tumultuous years during which the American colonies moved toward independence. Although Adams, serving at the time of these letters in the Massachusetts legislature, lived a full life of public service, his attachment to his wife and son kept his mind turning toward home. His wife, confined to the domestic sphere, nonetheless felt free to comment on matters of public import. The charm of the letters, however, resides mainly in the sense of free and intimate communication that they convey.

John Adams, educated at Harvard, became a lawyer of outstanding integrity and learning. His opposition to the Stamp Act made him conspicuous in the early years of colonial unrest, and he became a leader of the revolutionary group. He proposed George Washington as commander in chief of the colonists' troops, helped to draft the Declaration of Independence, and argued powerfully for its adoption. Later, he became a diplomat, and, later still, president.

Abigail Adams, born Abigail Smith, was to become a particularly distinguished first lady, a leader of social life, and a powerful influence on her husband's policies. Her letters, to many correspondents, have provided a valuable source of social history.

The letters here printed, from May 1774 to August 1776, record responses to the exciting events that surrounded the Declaration of Independence and provide insight into the lives of those who could only witness or hear of those events rather than participate directly in them.

[Familiar Letters]

Boston, 12 May, 1774.

I am extremely afflicted with the relation your father gave me of the return of your disorder. I fear you have taken some cold. We have had a most pernicious air a great part of this spring. I am sure I have reason to remember it. My cold is the most obstinate and threatening one I ever had in my life. However, I am unwearied in my endeavors to subdue it, and have the pleasure to think I have had some success. I rise at five, walk three miles, keep the air all day, and walk again in the afternoon. These walks have done me more good than anything. My own infirmities, the account of the return of yours, and the public news[1] coming altogether have put my utmost philosophy to the trial.

We live, my dear soul, in an age of trial. What will be the consequence, I know not. The town of Boston, for aught I can see, must suffer martyrdom. It must expire. And our principal consolation is, that it dies in a noble cause—the cause of truth, of virtue, of liberty, and of humanity, and that it will probably have a glorious resurrection to greater wealth, splendor, and power, than ever.

Let me know what is best for us to do. It is expensive keeping a family here, and there is no prospect of any business in my way in this town this whole summer. I don't receive a shilling a week. We must contrive as many ways as we can to save expenses; for we may have calls to contribute very largely, in proportion to our circumstances, to prevent other very honest worthy people from suffering for want, besides our own loss in point of business and profit.

Don't imagine from all this that I am in the dumps. Far otherwise. I can truly say that I have felt more spirits and activity since the arrival of this news than I had done before for years. I look upon this as the last effort of Lord North's[2] despair, and he will as surely be defeated in it, as he was in the project of the tea.

I am, with great anxiety for your health,

Your   John Adams.

York, 1 July, 1774.

I am so idle that I have not an easy moment without my pen in my hand. My time might have been improved to some purpose in mowing grass, raking hay, or hoeing corn, weeding carrots, picking or shelling peas. Much better

---

1. Four merchant ships had just arrived in Boston with news of the British response to the Boston Tea Party. Various repressive measures had been instituted, and a new governor, a general, was on his way from England to enforce them.   2. Frederick, Baron North (1732–1792), at that time prime minister in England. He was the principal author of the stern policies about to be enforced—which actually had the effect of uniting the American colonists against England.

should I have been employed in schooling my children, in teaching them to write, cipher, Latin, French, English, and Greek.

I sometimes think I must come to this—to be the foreman upon my own farm and the schoolmaster to my own children. I confess myself to be full of fears that the ministry and their friends and instruments will prevail, and crush the cause and friends of liberty. The minds of that party are so filled with prejudices against me that they will take all advantages, and do me all the damage they can. These thoughts have their turns in my mind, but in general my hopes are predominant.

Dr. Gardiner, arrived here today from Boston, brings us news of a battle at the town meeting, between Whigs and Tories, in which the Whigs, after a day and a half's obstinate engagement, were finally victorious by two to one. He says the Tories are preparing a flaming protest.

I am determined to be cool, if I can. I have suffered such torments in my mind heretofore as have almost overpowered my constitution, without any advantage. And now I will laugh and be easy if I can, let the contest of parties terminate as it will, let my own estate and interest suffer what it will, nay, whether I stand high or low in the estimation of the world, so long as I keep a conscience void of offense towards God and man. And this I am determined by the will of God to do, let what will become of me or mine, my country or the world.

I shall arouse myself erelong, I believe, and exert an industry, a frugality, a hard labor, that will serve my family, if I can't serve my country. I will not lie down in despair. If I cannot serve my children by the law, I will serve them by agriculture, by trade, by some way or other. I thank God I have a head, and heart, and hands, which, if once fully exerted altogether, will succeed in the world as well as those of the mean-spirited, low-minded, fawning, obsequious scoundrels who have long hoped that my integrity would be an obstacle in my way, and enable them to outstrip me in the race.

But what I want in comparison of them of villainy and servility, I will make up in industry and capacity. If I don't, they shall laugh and triumph. I will not willingly see blockheads, whom I have a right to despise, elevated above me and insolently triumphing over me. Nor shall knavery, through any negligence of mine, get the better of honesty, nor ignorance of knowledge, nor folly of wisdom, nor vice of virtue.

I must entreat you, my dear partner in all the joys and sorrows, prosperity and adversity of my life, to take a part with me in the struggle. I pray God for your health—entreat you to rouse your whole attention to the family, the stock, the farm, the dairy. Let every article of expense which can possibly be spared be retrenched; keep the hands[3] attentive to their business, and [let] the most prudent measures of every kind be adopted and pursued with alacrity and spirit.

[John Adams]

Braintree, 19 August, 1774.

The great distance between us makes the time appear very long to me. It seems already a month since you left me. The great anxiety I feel for my

---

3. Farm hands.

country, for you, and for our family renders the day tedious and the night unpleasant. The rocks and quicksands appear upon every side. What course you can or will take is all wrapped in the bosom of futurity. Uncertainty and expectation leave the mind great scope. Did ever any kingdom or state regain its liberty, when once it was invaded, without bloodshed? I cannot think of it without horror. Yet we are told that all the misfortunes of Sparta were occasioned by their too great solicitude for present tranquillity, and, from an excessive love of peace, they neglected the means of making it sure and lasting. They ought to have reflected, says Polybius, that, "as there is nothing more desirable or advantageous than peace, when founded in justice and honor, so there is nothing more shameful, and at the same time more pernicious, when attained by bad measures and purchased at the price of liberty." I have received a most charming letter from our friend Mrs. Warren.[4] She desires me to tell you that her best wishes attend you through your journey, both as a friend and a patriot,—hopes you will have no uncommon difficulties to surmount, or hostile movements to impede you, but, if the Locrians[5] should interrupt you, she hopes that you will beware, that no future annals may say you chose an ambitious Philip for your leader, who subverted the noble order of the American Amphictyons, and built up a monarchy on the ruins of the happy institution.

I have taken a very great fondness for reading Rollin's Ancient History[6] since you left me. I am determined to go through with it, if possible, in these my days of solitude. I find great pleasure and entertainment from it, and I have persuaded Johnny[7] to read me a page or two every day, and hope he will, from his desire to oblige me, entertain a fondness for it. We have had a charming rain, which lasted twelve hours and has greatly revived the dying fruits of the earth.

I want much to hear from you. I long impatiently to have you upon the stage of action. The first of September, or the month of September, perhaps, may be of as much importance to Great Britain as the Ides of March were to Caesar.[8] I wish you every public as well as private blessing, and that wisdom which is profitable both for instruction and edification, to conduct you in this difficult day. The little flock remember papa, and kindly wish to see him; so does your most affectionate

Abigail Adams.

Philadelphia, 8 September, 1774.

When or where this letter will find you I know not. In what scenes of distress and terror I cannot foresee. We have received a confused account from Boston of a dreadful catastrophe. The particulars we have not heard. We are waiting with the utmost anxiety and impatience for further intelligence. The effect of the news we have, both upon the Congress and the

---

4. I.e., Mercy Otis Warren (see pp. 635–47).   **5.** Abigail Adams here embarks on a series of analogies to ancient times. The Locrians inhabited a central region in ancient Greece; they formed part of the Aetolian League that defeated Philip V of Macedon (238–179 B.C.E.). The Amphictyons, mentioned below, are metaphorical descendants of Amphictyon, son of Deucalion and Pyrrha, who became a symbol of compromise because he succeeded in mixing water and oil.   **6.** *Ancient History* by Charles Rollin (1661–1741) was originally published in a French edition of twelve volumes (1730–38) but was rapidly translated into other languages.   **7.** The Adamses' son, John Quincy Adams (1767–1848), about seven at the time, who was to become the sixth president in his turn (1825–29).   **8.** Caesar is supposed to have been killed on the Ides of March, March 15.

inhabitants of this city, was very great. Great indeed! Every gentleman seems to consider the bombardment of Boston[9] as the bombardment of the capital of his own province. Our deliberations are grave and serious indeed.

It is a great affliction to me that I cannot write to you oftener than I do. But there are so many hindrances that I cannot. It would fill volumes to give you an idea of the scenes I behold, and the characters I converse with. We have so much business, so much ceremony, so much company, so many visits to receive and return, that I have not time to write. And the times are such as to make it imprudent to write freely.

We cannot depart from this place until the business of the Congress is completed, and it is the general disposition to proceed slowly. When I shall be at home I can't say. If there is distress and danger in Boston, pray invite our friends, as many as possible, to take an asylum with you,—Mrs. Cushing and Mrs. Adams, if you can. There is in the Congress a collection of the greatest men upon this continent in point of abilities, virtues, and fortunes. The magnanimity and public spirit which I see here make me blush for the sordid, venal herd which I have seen in my own province. The addressers, and the new councillors[1] are held in universal contempt and abhorrence from one end of the continent to the other.

Be not under any concern for me. There is little danger from anything we shall do at the Congress. There is such a spirit through the colonies, and the members of the Congress are such characters, that no danger can happen to us which will not involve the whole continent in universal desolation; and in that case, who would wish to live? Adieu.

[John Adams]

Braintree, 14 September, 1774.

Five weeks have passed and not one line have I received. I would rather give a dollar for a letter by the post, though the consequence should be that I ate but one meal a day these three weeks to come. Every one I see is inquiring after you, when did I hear. All my intelligence is collected from the newspaper, and I can only reply that I saw by that, you arrived such a day. I know your fondness for writing, and your inclination to let me hear from you by the first safe conveyance, which makes me suspect that some letter or other has miscarried; but I hope, now you have arrived at Philadelphia, you will find means to convey me some intelligence.

We are all well here. I think I enjoy better health than I have done these two years. I have not been to town since I parted with you there. The Governor is making all kinds of warlike preparations, such as mounting cannon upon Beacon Hill, digging intrenchments upon the Neck, placing cannon there, encamping a regiment there, throwing up breastworks, etc. The people are much alarmed, and the selectmen have waited upon him in consequence of it. The County Congress[2] have also sent a committee; all which proceedings you will have a more particular account of than I am able to give you, from the public papers. But as to the movements of this town, perhaps you may not hear them from any other person.

9. Rumors had spread that the British army and navy were firing into the town of Boston.   1. Officials named by England to enforce the new regulations.   2. A meeting of delegates from all parts of Suffolk County, around Boston.

In consequence of the powder being taken from Charlestown, a general alarm spread through many towns and was caught pretty soon here. The report took here on Friday, and on Sunday a soldier was seen lurking about the Common supposed to be a spy, but most likely a deserter. However, intelligence of it was communicated to the other parishes, and about eight o'clock Sunday evening there passed by here about two hundred men, preceded by horse cart, and marched down to the powder house, from whence they took the powder, and carried it into the other parish and there secreted it. I opened the window upon their return. They passed without any noise, not a word among them till they came against this house, when some of them, perceiving me, asked me if I wanted any powder. I replied, No, since it was in so good hands. The reason they gave for taking it was that we had so many Tories here, they dared not trust us with it; they had taken Vinton in their train, and upon their return they stopped between Cleverly's and Etter's, and called upon him to deliver two warrants. Upon his producing them, they put it to vote whether they should burn them, and it passed in the affirmative. They then made a circle and burnt them. They then called a vote whether they should huzza, but, it being Sunday evening, it passed in the negative. They called upon Vinton to swear that he would never be instrumental in carrying into execution any of these new acts. They were not satisfied with his answers; however, they let him rest. A few days afterwards, upon his making some foolish speeches, they assembled to the amount of two or three hundred, and swore vengeance upon him unless he took a solemn oath. Accordingly, they chose a committee and sent it with him to Major Miller's to see that he complied; and they waited his return, which proving satisfactory, they dispersed. This town appears as high as you can well imagine, and, if necessary, would soon be in arms. Not a Tory but hides his head. The church parson thought they were coming after him, and ran up garret; they say another jumped out of his window and hid among the corn, whilst a third crept under his board fence and told his beads.[3]

[Abigail Adams]

16 September 1774

Upon my return at night, Mr. Thaxter met me at the door with your letter, dated at Princeton, New Jersey. It really gave me such a flow of spirits that I was not composed enough to sleep until one o'clock. You make no mention of one I wrote you previous to that you received by Mr. Breck, and sent by Mr. Cunningham. I am rejoiced to hear you are well. I want to know many more particulars than you write me, and hope soon to hear from you again. I dare not trust myself with the thought how long you may perhaps be absent. I only count the weeks already past, and they amount to five. I am not so lonely as I should have been without my two neighbors; we make a tableful at mealtimes. All the rest of their time they spend in the office. Never were two persons who gave a family less trouble than they do. It is at last determined that Mr. Rice keep the school here. Indeed, he has kept ever since he has been here, but not with any expectation that he should be continued; but the people, finding no small difference between him and his predecessor,

---

3. Counted his rosary beads (presumably metaphorically, as an image of fear).

chose he should be continued. I have not sent Johnny. He goes steadily to Mr. Thaxter, who I believe takes very good care of him, and as they seem to have a liking to each other, I believe it will be best to continue him with him. However, when you return, we can consult what will be best. I am certain that, if he does not get so much good, he gets less harm; and I have always thought it of very great importance that children should, in the early part of life, be unaccustomed to such examples as would tend to corrupt the purity of their words and actions, that they may chill with horror at the sound of an oath, and blush with indignation at an obscene expression. These first principles, which grow with their growth, and strengthen with their strength, neither time nor custom can totally eradicate.

You will perhaps be tired. No. Let it serve by way of relaxation from the more important concerns of the day, and be such an amusement as your little hermitage used to afford you here. You have before you, to express myself in the words of the bishop, the greatest national concerns that ever came before any people; and if the prayers and petitions ascend unto heaven which are daily offered for you, wisdom will flow down as a stream, and righteousness as the mighty waters, and your deliberations will make glad the cities of our God.

I was very sorry I did not know of Mr. Cary's going; it would have been so good an opportunity to have sent this, as I lament the loss of. You have heard, no doubt, of the people's preventing the court from sitting in various counties; and last week, in Taunton, Angier urged the court's opening and calling out the actions, but could not effect it. I saw a letter from Miss Eunice, wherein she gives an account of it, and says there were two thousand men assembled round the courthouse, and, by a committee of nine, presented a petition requesting that they would not sit, and with the utmost order waited two hours for their answer, when they dispersed.

You will burn all these letters, lest they should fall from your pocket, and thus expose your most affectionate friend.

[Abigail Adams]

Braintree, 12 November, 1775.

I received yours of 23d October. I want to hear from you every day, and I always feel sorry when I come to the close of a letter. Your time must be greatly engrossed—but little of it to spare to the calls of private friendship, and I have reason to think I have the largest share of it. Winter makes its approaches fast. I hope I shall not be obliged to spend it without my dearest friend. I know not how to think of it.

The intelligence you will receive before this reaches you will, I should think, make a plain path, though a dangerous one, for you. I could not join today in the petitions of our worthy pastor, for a reconciliation between our no longer parent state, but tyrant state, and these colonies. Let us separate; they are unworthy to be our brethren. Let us renounce them; and instead of supplications, as formerly, for their prosperity and happiness, let us beseech the Almighty to blast their counsels and bring to nought all their devices.

I have nothing remarkable to write you. A little skirmish happened last week. The particulars I have endeavored to collect, but whether I have the facts right, I am not certain. A number of cattle were kept at Lechmere's

Point, where two sentinels were placed. In a high tide it is an island. The regulars had observed this, and a scheme was laid to send a number of them over and take off the stock. Accordingly, a number of boats and about four hundred men were sent. They landed, it seems, unperceived by the sentinels, who were asleep; one of whom they killed, and took the other prisoner. As soon as they were perceived, they fired the cannon from Prospect Hill upon them, which sunk one of their boats; but, as the tide was very high, it was difficult getting over, and some time before any alarm was given. A Colonel Thompson, of the riflemen, marched instantly with his men; and, though a very stormy day, they regarded not the tide nor waited for boats, but marched over neck-high in water, and discharged their pieces, when the regulars ran, without waiting to get off their stock, and made the best of their way to the opposite shore. The General sent his thanks in a public manner to the brave officer and his men. Major Mifflin, I hear, was there, and flew about as though he would have raised the whole army. May they never find us deficient in courage and spirit.

Dr. Franklin invited me to spend the winter in Philadelphia. I shall wish to be there unless you return. I have been like a nun in a cloister, ever since you went away, and have not been into any other house than my father's and sister's, except once to Colonel Quincy's. Indeed, I have no inclination for company. My evenings are lonesome and melancholy. In the daytime family affairs take off my attention, but the evenings are spent with my departed parent.[4] I then ruminate upon all her care and tenderness, and am sometimes lost and absorbed in a flood of tenderness ere I am aware of it, or can call to my aid my only prop and support. I must bid you adieu; 'tis late at night.

Most affectionately yours.
[Abigail Adams]

27 November, 1775

Colonel Warren returned last week to Plymouth, so that I shall not hear anything from you until he goes back again, which will not be till the last of this month. He damped my spirits greatly by telling me that the Court[5] had prolonged your stay another month. I was pleasing myself with the thought that you would soon be upon your return. It is in vain to repine. I hope the public will reap what I sacrifice.

I wish I knew what mighty things were fabricating. If a form of government is to be established here, what one will be assumed? Will it be left to our Assemblies to choose one? And will not many men have many minds? And shall we not run into dissensions among ourselves?

I am more and more convinced that man is a dangerous creature; and that power, whether vested in many or a few, is ever grasping, and, like the grave, cries, "Give, give!" The great fish swallow up the small; and he who is most strenuous for the rights of the people, when vested with power, is as eager after the prerogatives of government. You tell me of degrees of perfection to which human nature is capable of arriving, and I believe it, but at the same time lament that our admiration should arise from the scarcity of the instances.

4. Her mother, who had recently died.   5. The legislature.

The building up a great empire, which was only hinted at by my correspondent, may now, I suppose, be realized even by the unbelievers. Yet, will not ten thousand difficulties arise in the formation of it? The reins of government have been so long slackened, that I fear the people will not quietly submit to those restraints which are necessary for the peace and security of the community. If we separate from Britain, what code of laws will be established? How shall we be governed so as to retain our liberties? Can any government be free which is not administered by general stated laws? Who shall frame these laws? Who will give them force and energy? It is true, your resolutions, as a body, have hitherto had the force of laws; but will they continue to have?

When I consider these things, and the prejudices of people in favor of ancient customs and regulations, I feel anxious for the fate of our monarchy, or democracy, or whatever is to take place. I soon get lost in a labyrinth of perplexities; but, whatever occurs, may justice and righteousness be the stability of our times, and order arise out of confusion. Great difficulties may be surmounted by patience and perseverance.

I believe I have tired you with politics. As to news, we have not any at all. I shudder at the approach of winter, when I think I am to remain desolate.

I must bid you good night; 'tis late for me, who am much of an invalid. I was disappointed last week in receiving a packet by the post, and, upon unsealing it, finding only four newspapers. I think you are more cautious than you need be. All letters, I believe, have come safe to hand. I have sixteen from you, and wish I had as many more. Adieu.

Yours.
[Abigail Adams]

Philadelphia, 3 December, 1775.

My best Friend,—Yours of November 12th is before me. I wish I could write you every day, more than once, for although I have a number of friends and many relations who are very dear to me, yet all the friendship I have for others is far unequal to that which warms my heart for you. The most agreeable time that I spend here is in writing to you, and conversing with you, when I am alone. But the call of friendship and of private affection must give place to that of duty and honor. Even private friendship and affections require it.

I am obliged, by the nature of the service I am in, to correspond with many gentlemen, both of the army and of the two houses of Assembly, which takes up much of my time. How I find time to write half the letters I do, I know not, for my whole time seems engrossed with business. The whole Congress is taken up, almost, in different committees, from seven to ten in the morning. From ten to four or sometimes five, we are in Congress, and from six to ten in committees again. I don't mention this to make you think me a man of importance, because it is not I alone, but the whole Congress is thus employed, but to apologize for not writing to you oftener.

Indeed, I know not what to write that is worth your reading. I send you the papers, which inform you of what is public. As to what passes in Congress, I am tied fast by my honor to communicate nothing. I hope the Journal of the Session will be published soon, and then you will see what we have been about in one view, excepting what ought to be excepted. If I could visit the coffee houses in the evening, and the coffee tables of the ladies in the afternoon, I could entertain you with many smart remarks upon dress and air, etc., and give you many sprightly conversations, but my fate, you know, is to be moping over books and papers all the leisure time I have, when I have any.

I hope I shall be excused from coming to Philadelphia again, at least until other gentlemen have taken their turns. But I never will come here again without you, if I can persuade you to come with me. Whom God has joined together ought not to be put asunder so long, with their own consent. We will bring master Johnny with us, you and he shall have the smallpox here, and we will be as happy as Mr. Hancock and his lady. Thank Abby and John for their letters, and kiss Charles and Tom for me. John writes like a hero, glowing with ardor for his country and burning with indignation against her enemies.

As to coming home, I have no thoughts of it; shall stay here till the year is out, for what I know. Affairs are in a critical state, and important steps are now taking every day, so that I could not reconcile it to my own mind to be absent from this place at present. Nothing is expected from the Commissioners, yet we are waiting for them in some respects. The Tories and timids pretend to expect great things from them. But the generality expect nothing but more insults and affronts. Privateering is licensed, and the ports are wide open. As soon as the resolves are printed, which will be tomorrow, I will send them.

[John Adams]

Philadelphia, 3 July, 1776.

Had a Declaration of Independency been made seven months ago, it would have been attended with many great and glorious effects. We might, before this hour, have formed alliances with foreign states. We should have mastered Quebec, and been in possession of Canada. You will perhaps wonder how such a declaration would have influenced our affairs in Canada, but if I could write with freedom, I could easily convince you that it would, and explain to you the manner how. Many gentlemen in high stations, and of great influence, have been duped by the ministerial bubble of Commissioners to treat.[6] And in real, sincere expectation of this event, which they so fondly wished, they have been slow and languid in promoting measures for the reduction of that province. Others there are in the Colonies who really wished that our enterprise in Canada would be defeated, that the Colonies might be brought into danger and distress between two fires, and be thus induced to submit. Others really wished to defeat the expedition to Canada, lest the conquest of it should elevate the minds of the people too much to hearken to those terms of reconciliation which, they believed, would be offered us. These jarring views, wishes, and designs occasioned an opposition to many salutary measures which were proposed for the support of that expe-

---

6. Gentlemen have been tricked by the fantasy of dealing with commissioners appointed by the British government.

dition, and caused obstructions, embarrassments, and studied delays, which have finally lost us the province.

All these causes, however, in conjunction would not have disappointed us, if it had not been for a misfortune which could not be foreseen, and perhaps could not have been prevented; I mean the prevalence of the smallpox among our troops. This fatal pestilence completed our destruction. It is a frown of Providence upon us, which we ought to lay to heart.

But, on the other hand, the delay of this Declaration to this time has many great advantages attending it. The hopes of reconciliation which were fondly entertained by multitudes of honest and well-meaning, though weak and mistaken people, have been gradually, and at last totally extinguished. Time has been given for the whole people maturely to consider the great question of independence, and to ripen their judgment, dissipate their fears, and allure their hopes, by discussing it in newspapers and pamphlets, by debating it in assemblies, conventions, committees of safety and inspection, in town and county meetings, as well as in private conversations, so that the whole people, in every colony of the thirteen, have now adopted it as their own act. This will cement the union, and avoid those heats, and perhaps convulsions, which might have been occasioned by such a Declaration six months ago.

But the day is past. The second day of July, 1776, will be the most memorable epocha in the history of America.[7] I am apt to believe that it will be celebrated by succeeding generations as the great anniversary festival. It ought to be commemorated as the day of deliverance, by solemn acts of devotion to God Almighty. It ought to be solemnized with pomp and parade, with shows, games, sports, guns, bells, bonfires, and illuminations, from one end of this continent to the other, from this time forward forevermore.

You will think me transported with enthusiasm, but I am not. I am well aware of the toil and blood and treasure that it will cost us to maintain this Declaration and support and defend these States. Yet, through all the gloom, I can see the rays of ravishing light and glory. I can see that the end is more than worth all the means. And that posterity will triumph in that day's transaction, even although we should rue it, which I trust in God we shall not.

[John Adams]

14 August, 1776.

Your letter of August 3 came by this day's post. I find it very convenient to be so handy. I can receive a letter at night, sit down and reply to it, and send it off in the morning.

You remark upon the deficiency of education in your countrymen. It never, I believe, was in a worse state, at least for many years. The college is not in the state one could wish. The scholars complain that their professor in philosophy is taken off by public business, to their great detriment. In this town I never saw so great a neglect of education. The poorer sort of children are wholly neglected, and left to range the streets, without schools, without business, given up to all evil. The town is not, as formerly, divided into wards.

---

7. The fourth of July, which has always been celebrated, was the day on which the final form of the Declaration of Independence was agreed to. An agreement in principle had been reached on the second.

There is either too much business left upon the hands of a few, or too little care to do it. We daily see the necessity of a regular government.

You speak of our worthy brother. I often lament it, that a man so peculiarly formed for the education of youth, and so well qualified as he is in many branches of literature, excelling in philosophy and the mathematics, should not be employed in some public station. I know not the person who would make half so good a successor to Dr. Winthrop. He has a peculiar, easy manner of communicating his ideas to youth; and the goodness of his heart and the purity of his morals, without an affected austerity, must have a happy effect upon the minds of pupils.

If you complain of neglect of education in sons, what shall I say with regard to daughters, who every day experience the want of it? With regard to the education of my own children, I find myself soon out of my depth, destitute and deficient in every part of education.

I most sincerely wish that some more liberal plan might be laid and executed for the benefit of the rising generation, and that our new Constitution may be distinguished for encouraging learning and virtue. If we mean to have heroes, statesmen, and philosophers, we should have learned women. The world perhaps would laugh at me and accuse me of vanity, but you, I know, have a mind too enlarged and liberal to disregard the sentiment. If much depends, as is allowed, upon the early education of youth, and the first principles which are instilled take the deepest root, great benefit must arise from literary accomplishments in women.

Excuse me. My pen has run away with me. I have no thoughts of coming to Philadelphia. The length of time I have and shall be detained here would have prevented me, even if you had no thoughts of returning till December; but I live in daily expectation of seeing you here. Your health, I think, requires your immediate return. I expected Mr. G—— would have set off before now, but he perhaps finds it very hard to leave his mistress. I won't say harder than some do to leave their wives. Mr. Gerry stood very high in my esteem. What is meat for one is not for another. No accounting for fancy. She is a queer dame and leads people wild dances.

But hush! Post, don't betray your trust and lose my letter.

Portia.[8]

18 August, 1776.

My letters to you are an odd mixture. They would appear to a stranger like the dish which is sometimes called *omnium gatherum*. This is the first time, I believe, that these two words were ever put together in writing. The literal interpretation I take to be "a collection of all things." But, as I said before, the words having never before been written, it is not possible to be very learned in telling you what the Arabic, Syriac, Chaldaic, Greek, and Roman commentators say upon the subject. Amidst all the rubbish that constitutes the heap, you will see a proportion of affection for my friends, my family, and country, that gives a complexion to the whole. I have a very tender, feeling heart. This country knows not, and never can know, the torments I

---

8. Probably a reference to Shakespeare's Portia, in *The Merchant of Venice*, who acts effectively as a lawyer. Abigail Adams may be joking about her own claims of wisdom as she "lays down the law" about female education.

have endured for its sake. I am glad it never can know, for it would give more pain to the benevolent and humane that I could wish even the wicked and malicious to feel.

I have seen in this world but a little of that pure flame of patriotism which certainly burns in some breasts. There is much of the ostentation and affectation of it. I have known a few who could not bear to entertain a selfish design, nor to be suspected by others of such a meanness; but these are not the most respected by the world. A man must be selfish, even to acquire great popularity. He must grasp for himself, under specious pretenses for the public good, and he must attach himself to his relations, connections, and friends, by becoming a champion for their interests, in order to form a phalanx about him for his own defense, to make them trumpeters of his praise, and sticklers for his fame, fortune, and honor.

My friend Warren, the late Governor Ward, and Mr. Gadsden are three characters in which I have seen the most generous disdain of every spice and species of such meanness. The two last had not great abilities, but they had pure hearts. Yet they had less influence than many others, who had neither so considerable parts nor any share at all of their purity of intention. Warren has both talents and virtues beyond most men in this world, yet his character has never been in proportion. Thus it always is and has been and will be. Nothing has ever given me more mortification than a suspicion that has been propagated of me, that I am actuated by private views and have been aiming at high places. The office of Chief Justice has occasioned this jealousy, and it never will be allayed until I resign it. Let me have my farm, family, and goose quill, and all the honors and offices this world has to bestow may go to those who deserve them better and desire them more. I court them not. There are very few people in this world with whom I can bear to converse. I can treat all with decency and civility, and converse with them, when it is necessary, on points of business. But I am never happy in their company. This has made me a recluse and will one day make me a hermit. I had rather build stone wall upon Penn's hill, than to be the first Prince in Europe, or the first General or first Senator in America.

Our expectations are very high of some great affair at New York.

[John Adams]

THOMAS PAINE
1737–1809

A radical thinker and would-be reformer, Thomas Paine involved himself in both great revolutions of his time. Born in England, son of a Quaker, he emigrated to America in 1774, a moment of high political excitement. The clash between England and the American colonies provoked him to write a hugely successful pamphlet, *Common Sense* (1776), in which he argued for independence. He continued to encourage the colonists' cause throughout the war, after which he returned to his New York farm.

In 1787, Paine returned to England. There he wrote *The Rights of Man* (1791,

1792), a defense of the French Revolution that resulted in a charge of treason and caused him to flee to France. The present selection, written shortly after his arrival in France, responds to his honorary title of "French citizen" and his election to the National Convention, where he was to play a significant role. By late 1793, however, he was imprisoned by the radical Jacobins; in prison, he wrote *The Age of Reason*. After his release, he wrote an attack on George Washington. As a consequence of his political and literary activities, he was treated with contempt when he returned to the United States in 1802; he died in poverty.

The short *Address to the People of France* conveys vividly the idealism, energy, and conviction that marked all of Paine's writing. He understands the French Revolution as resembling the American Revolution in its aspirations for liberty and equality. Although he here writes about France, he implicitly writes also about America as he declares the possibility that commitment to the idea of freedom will spread inexorably throughout the world.

Address to the People of France

Paris, Sept. 25, [1792.]
First Year of the Republic.

Fellow Citizens,

I receive, with affectionate gratitude, the honor which the late National Assembly has conferred upon me, by adopting me a citizen of France: and the additional honor of being elected by my fellow citizens a member of the National Convention.[1] Happily impressed, as I am, by those testimonies of respect shown towards me as an individual, I feel my felicity increased by seeing the barrier broken down that divided patriotism by spots of earth, and limited citizenship to the soil, like vegetation.

Had those honors been conferred in an hour of national tranquillity, they would have afforded no other means of shewing my affection, than to have accepted and enjoyed them; but they come accompanied with circumstances that give me the honorable opportunity of commencing my citizenship in the stormy hour of difficulties. I come not to enjoy repose. Convinced that the cause of France is the cause of all mankind, and that liberty cannot be purchased by a wish, I gladly share with you the dangers and honors necessary to success.

I am well aware that the moment of any great change, such as that accomplished on the 10th of August,[2] is unavoidably the moment of terror and confusion. The mind, highly agitated by hope, suspicion and apprehension, continues without rest till the change be accomplished. But let us now look calmly and confidently forward, and success is certain. It is no longer the paltry cause of kings, or of this, or of that individual, that calls France and her armies into action. It is the great cause of ALL. It is the establishment of a new era, that shall blot despotism from the earth, and fix, on the lasting principles of peace and citizenship, the great Republic of Man.

It has been my fate to have borne a share in the commencement and

---

1. The National Assembly had elected Paine to citizenship along with several other workers for freedom, including George Washington, Alexander Hamilton, and James Madison.   2. When a crowd stormed the Tuileries and the legally elected Commune of Paris was replaced by an insurrectionary commune.

complete establishment of one revolution, (I mean the Revolution of America.) The success and events of that revolution are encouraging to us. The prosperity and happiness that have since flowed to that country, have amply rewarded her for all the hardships she endured and for all the dangers she encountered.

The principles on which that revolution began, have extended themselves to Europe; and an overruling Providence is regenerating the Old World by the principles of the New. The distance of America from all the other parts of the globe, did not admit of her carrying those principles beyond her own situation. It is to the peculiar honor of France, that she now raises the standard of liberty for all nations; and in fighting her own battles, contends for the rights of all mankind.

The same spirit of fortitude that insured success to America; will insure it to France, for it is impossible to conquer a nation determined to be free! The military circumstances that now unite themselves to France, are such as the despots of the earth know nothing of, and can form no calculation upon. They know not what it is to fight against a nation; they have only been accustomed to make war upon each other, and they know, from system and practice, how to calculate the probable success of despot against despot; and here their knowledge and their experience end.

But in a contest like the present a new and boundless variety of circumstances arise, that deranges all such customary calculations. When a whole nation acts as an army, the despot knows not the extent of the power against which he contends. New armies arise against him with the necessity of the moment. It is then that the difficulties of an invading enemy multiply, as in the former case they diminished; and he finds them at their height when he expected them to end.

The only war that has any similarity of circumstances with the present, is the late revolution war in America. On her part, as it now is in France, it was a war of the whole nation:—there it was that the enemy, by beginning to conquer, put himself in a condition of being conquered. His first victories prepared him for defeat. He advanced till he could not retreat, and found himself in the midst of a nation of armies.

Were it now to be proposed to the Austrians and Prussians,[3] to escort them into the middle of France, and there leave them to make the most of such a situation, they would see too much into the dangers of it to accept the offer, and the same dangers would attend them, could they arrive there by any other means. Where, then, is the military policy of their attempting to obtain, by force, that which they would refuse by choice? But to reason with despots is throwing reason away. The best of arguments is a vigorous preparation.

Man is ever a stranger to the ways by which Providence regulates the order of things. The interference of foreign despots may serve to introduce into their own enslaved countries the principles they come to oppose. Liberty and Equality are blessings too great to be the inheritance of France alone. It is an honor to her to be their first champion; and she may now say to her enemies, with a mighty voice, "O! ye Austrians, ye Prussians! ye who now turn your bayonets against us, it is for you, it is for all Europe, it is for all

---

3. The Austrians and Prussians, to whom Louis XVI had appealed, were fighting France.

mankind, and not for France alone, that she raises the standard of Liberty and Equality!"

The public cause has hitherto suffered from the contradictions contained in the Constitution of the Constituent Assembly. Those contradictions have served to divide the opinions of individuals at home, and to obscure the great principles of the Revolution in other countries. But when those contradictions shall be removed, and the Constitution be made conformable to the Declaration of Rights;[4] when the bagatelles of monarchy, royalty, regency, and hereditary succession, shall be exposed, with all their absurdities, a new ray of light will be thrown over the world, and the Revolution will derive new strength by being universally understood.

The scene that now opens itself to France extends far beyond the boundaries of her own dominions. Every nation is becoming her colleague, and every court is become her enemy. It is now the cause of all nations, against the cause of all courts. The terror that despotism felt, clandestinely begot a confederation of despots; and their attack upon France was produced by their fears at home.

In entering on this great scene, greater than any nation has yet been called to act in, let us say to the agitated mind, be calm. Let us punish by instructing, rather than by revenge. Let us begin the new era by a greatness of friendship, and hail the approach of union and success.

Your Fellow Citizen,
Thomas Paine

4. The Declaration of the Rights of Man and Citizen, adopted in 1789, defined the "inalienable rights" of individuals, guaranteeing liberty, property, security, and freedom of speech and of the press. It was, indeed, to be embodied in the constitution of 1791.

JEAN-PAUL MARAT
1743–1793

A doctor, a philosopher, and a journalist, Marat was best known as a revolutionary, an expounder of extreme views who had a gift for arousing the public. Born in Switzerland, he had studied medicine in England but soon moved to Paris. At the beginning of the French Revolution, he founded the journal *L'Ami du peuple* (*The Friend of the People*) as a vehicle for his anti-aristocratic views. Because he fomented violence and aroused public opinion, he was outlawed, twice fleeing to England. In 1792, he was elected to the French Convention, where he led attacks against moderates. He was stabbed to death in his bath by Charlotte Corday, a royalist sympathizer.

Louis XVI, who occupied the throne of France when the Revolution broke out, was the object of much popular hatred. Although he apparently compromised with the demands of the people, he allowed reactionary plotting at the court by members of the nobility, including the queen. In June 1791, he and his family attempted to escape France in disguise. They were brought back to Paris and, in August, imprisoned. Finally, the king was tried by the Convention, found guilty by unanimous vote, and by a narrow margin condemned to death. He was guillotined on January 21, 1793.

Marat's speech about the king, written on December 3, 1792, was never delivered—

he wrote it for the Convention but failed to give it. It was, however, immediately published, both in his own journal and in the official record of the Convention. He argues powerfully in it that the king should be tried for crimes against the nation, seeing the proposed trial as an important forum for articulating publicly the ways in which royalty had betrayed the people.

[Address to the Convention on the Crimes of King Louis XVI][1]

The crimes of Louis XVI are unhappily all too real; they are patent; they are notorious. Need we ask if a nation has the right to judge, and to punish by death, a public official raised to the highest rank, when he has concealed himself behind a mask of hypocrisy the more securely to plot against the nation? when he oppressed his countrymen with the authority confided to him for their protection? when he made of the laws an instrument of violence to crush the partisans of the Revolution? when he robbed the citizens of their gold as a subsidy for their foes, robbed them of their subsistence to feed the barbarian hordes who came to slaughter them? when he caused his hirelings to hoard, to create famine, to dry up the sources of abundance that the people might die from misery and hunger? when he declared himself the leader of traitors and conspirators? when he turned against the nation those arms he had been delivered for its defense? when he wove the plot to have the defenders of liberty slaughtered, to enchain the people once again? It is an insult to reason, an outrage to justice, a perversion of nature. Need we ask if a despot, stained with all possible crimes, if a monster still covered with the blood of those friends of France whose slaughter he had commanded, can be brought to judgment and condemned to death? To ask such a question would be to mock humanity and to renounce all shame.

No, Gentlemen, I will not do you the injury of believing that a single man could be found among you who would question this truth, unless interest led him to do so. If you have made it the basis of the public discussion of the great trial which will soon begin, it is less to illumine a point under question than to furnish patriotic orators a unique occasion to display the absurdity of the sophisms used in the defense of the ex-monarch by his creatures, the partisans of monarchy and the tools of despotism.

Your committee on legislation has made clear by a series of arguments drawn from natural law, from the law of nations, from civil law, that Louis Capet[2] should be brought to judgment. That step was necessary for the instruction of the people; for it is important that all members of the Republic be brought to this conviction by different routes suitable to their different spirits. The representatives of the sovereign people can see the question only in its political aspects.

Among the speakers who preceded me at this rostrum, those who saw the question from this point of view, harking back to a supposed initial contract and arguing for the reciprocity of the conditions stipulated between people and prince, have thence inferred that Louis Capet, having broken his contract by his crimes, has fallen from the throne and can be considered only

1. Translated by Marian Rothstein.   2. Marat refers to the king by his family name rather than his title because of the revolutionary assumption of universal equality.

as a simple citizen: an erroneous conclusion, laboriously deduced from a vain sophism. There was never a contract between the people and their agents, although there was a binding one between the sovereign and its members. A nation which delegates its powers to agents does not contract with them; it assigns them some function in the general interest. They may very well on occasion refuse these functions; yet the agents remain always accountable to the nation, and it can at any time withdraw these functions without their consent. Thus, with whatever luster these duties may be surrounded, they should never be considered as anything but an honorable burden. Such are, Gentlemen, the true bonds which exist between the sovereign and its agents. The original contract which has been cited as the basis for these bonds is completely imaginary. If such a contract exists, it is only among conquering nations; and even then, it can have no effect save when the head of the army, become the chief of state, has found the means to inspire fear or rather, when he is in open war with a nation which he has forced to surrender. What! Shall we take the crimes of a usurper as a starting place to establish his prerogatives, and shall we take as legitimate and sacred rights the usurpation of sovereignty by the first agent of the people? Such, nonetheless, is the odious contract which existed between the French and their princes: an iniquitous contract which the representatives of the French people renewed with Louis Capet, heir to the usurped power of his ancestors, after the excess of his speculations had forced him to assemble the Estates General[3] to fill the abyss which he had dug, and after his last attempt, which caused the nation to rise against the tyranny, forced him to lower himself and ask for mercy. Such a contract is null and void, not only because it offends the dearest interests and the most sacred rights of the people, but because the people have not ratified it. All the many loyal addresses their faithless deputies spread out before their eyes, with such complaisance, as unequivocal proofs of their approbation, had been vilely purchased. Rather, I might say, they had almost all been perfidiously presented by counter-revolutionary administrative bodies.

Let us examine the facts: after thirteen centuries of servitude and tyranny, despotism would have been forever struck down had the nation, too long bent under the yoke, been able to stand strong and erect and to keep vigorously its magnanimous resolution to reclaim its rights. Despotism would have been forever struck down if the representatives of the people had had the courage to profit from the consternation of the despot and his henchmen, to cast him from the throne and to reestablish liberty. But, to our grief, those weak representatives who at first, to remain in their position, gave evidence of resistance to the orders of the tyrant, no sooner saw themselves supported by armed citizens than they compounded with the court and used no more energy than was needed to collect their bribes. Nor did they delay long before setting up a shameful trade in the inalienable rights of the people. Some were even so criminally bold as to confer upon the despot the horrible privilege of disposing of provinces and selling the inhabitants thereof like so many sheep. I shall pass in silence over the long list of injurious, unjust, vexatious, oppressive, and tyrannic decrees passed by a base and corrupt

---

3. A national assembly, organized essentially by social class (clergy, nobles, and common people), which had not met for many years until Louis XVI was forced, in 1788, to call it into existence.

majority, which seemed to have no other end but to shore up despotism under the pretext of regenerating the Empire. Surprised from time to time by a timid minority, these were the fatal decrees which did dishonor to the Constituent Assembly and stained the Constitution; atrocious decrees against which I have so often spoken with bitterness inspired by a holy indignation.

Who does not know the guile with which the faithless delegates of the people piled sophism upon sophism to render the prince sacred and inviolable, to invest in him the supreme executive power, to confer upon him the right to make the principal appointments, to render him the arbiter of the legislature, to raise him above the law, to place in his hands the keys to the national treasury, the care of the public wealth, the disposition of the armed forces, on land and at sea, and the destiny of the state—until the moment when these senators bereft of shame, throwing off their mask and recognizing no further control, undertook with the aid of an organized massacre to turn the public force which they had misled and enchained against the people, designing to have them slaughtered or to forge them new chains. That was the moment when the sham representatives of the sovereign people, on their knees before a simple functionary, substituted for his title of first public official, that of born representative of the nation, invested in him the highest authority, placed all power once again in his hands, and provided a thousand means by which he might, with impunity, effect the ruin of the people and the destruction of liberty by force. And should it be necessary, they provided that he might flee to put himself at the head of enemy armies, suffering no penalty but presumed abdication, to which he might always reply by a simple denial. And that is the monstrous Constitution which, ready to pass like a dream, will nonetheless be forever a source of shame to its authors and which would appear to wise eyes a monument of folly and madness, were it not a monument of venality and villainy. This is the monstrous Constitution which has been made a bulwark for Louis Capet against that nation which he betrayed and whose downfall he so often plotted after having so long been the cause of its distress.

All the same, let us admit for the moment these so called constitutional laws, and let us consider such provisions as must be claimed that the tyrant may elude his bloody deserts. The Constitution declares the person of the king to be inviolable and sacred. But that inviolability, which the legislators were careful to avoid defining clearly, and which is invoked today in favor of Louis the traitor as a certificate of impunity, applied only to the legal acts of the monarch. It was therefore merely the privilege not to be called to account for the choice of means by which the laws were executed. As such, inviolability could have no end but to smooth the course of the political process by preventing constant hindrance to him who was supposed to give it movement and life.

Ridiculous sophists, you have undertaken to cover with the aegis of inviolability the former monarch become traitor, perjurer, and assassin. But your blindness, whatever its nature, cannot be so profound as to lead you to maintain that in rendering Louis Capet inviolable, the legislators conferred upon him the privilege of pillaging the public treasury with impunity; of corrupting those in whom authority had been vested, ministers of the law, representatives of the people; the privilege of supporting legions of spies, of brigands, of assassins; of aiding the enemies of the state with the gold, the munitions, and the arms destined for the defenders of liberty; of conspiring for the ruin of the country and of enjoying afterward the fruits of his crimes. But should the legislators have designed this, was it within their rights? For such is the right which you unthinkingly demand, to benefit the dethroned despot, when you invoke his inviolability to shield him from judgment.

Let us have no illusions. It is only too evident by the ambiguity of the laws in several cases, and by their silence in others, that the Constituent Assembly, especially during revision, had applied itself to arranging all possible means by which the king could conspire with impunity against public liberty.[4] But, thanks to their base natures, the legislators who had prostituted themselves to the court dared not openly consummate these outrages. Thus the Constitution, monstrous as it is, contains nonetheless clauses which are quite precise, so that we may try the tyrant and condemn him.

Those who wish to make a bulwark of the Constitution cite an article of the Declaration of Rights: "That no man can be accused, arrested, or detained, except in cases determined by the law, and according to the forms which the law hath prescribed," whence they assert that no one shall be punished save by virtue of a law prior to his crime. Let us accord them that.

They go further to cite several articles of the Constitution when they conclude that Louis XVI ought not to be punished, or ought to suffer no punishment but forced abdication. Let us look at the texts: "The king, on his accession to the throne, or at the period of his majority, shall take to the nation in the presence of the legislative body, the oath—'to be faithful to the nation and the law,' to employ all the power delegated to him to maintain the Constitution decreed by the constituting national assembly, in the years 1789, 1790 and 1791, and to cause the laws to be executed.

"If, a month after the invitation of the legislative body, the king has not taken the oath; or if, after taking it, he retracts, he shall then be held to have abdicated the royalty.

"If the king put himself at the head of an army, and direct the forces of it against the nation, or if he do not oppose, by a formal act, any such enterprise undertaken in his name, he shall be held to have abdicated.

"After abdication, express or legal, the king shall be in the class of citizens, and may be accused and tried like them, for acts posterior to his abdication."

Yet all these cases consider nothing but the refusal of the king to take the oath of fidelity to the laws, his retraction of that oath, his flight at the head of an army whose forces he would direct against the nation. Nowhere are mentioned plots woven in the very bosom of the state to extinguish liberty, to enchain the people once again, or cause their slaughter; nowhere the seizure of coin and grain; nowhere the plots to lay the way for national bankruptcy and bring famine to the land; nowhere the undermining of the courts of law, and the devices used to corrupt public officials; nowhere the vexations, the crimes, and the murders perpetrated on a multitude of citizens, friends of liberty. Now, in all these cases, about which the Constitution maintained the deepest silence, the monarch could be considered only as an

---

4. After the king's attempted escape, the Constituent Assembly revised the constitution without changing the section on inviolability.

ordinary citizen; since the article which follows immediately on that concerning inviolability cited by the defenders of Louis the traitor, says: "There is no authority in France superior to that of the law. The king reigns only by it; and it is only in the name of the law that he can require obedience." Whence it follows that he was himself subject to the rule of law, like any other citizen.

Article three of the Declaration of Rights says: "That the same crimes shall be subject to the same punishment without any distinction of persons." Laws brought to bear against ordinary citizens must then have their entire execution with respect to Louis Capet, whence it follows that he should suffer the penalties meted to traitors and conspirators.

Finally, if it were true that Louis Capet was above the Constitution in those cases stipulated as royal prerogatives, and that in this respect he had the "exclusive privilege to violate with impunity all laws," it is no less beyond doubt that the articles on which his defense is supposed to be based suffice to cause his condemnation.

The Constitution declares that after his abdication, the king might be accused and judged for his posterior acts. Now, there is an article which clearly states that "He shall be held to have abdicated by the retraction of his oath of fidelity to the nation, and the law; of his oath to use for the maintenance of the Constitution, the authority confided in him."[5] His abdication, therefore, dates from the moment when he conspired the ruin of the nation and began to subvert the Constitution after having accepted it. He can, then, be judged for the treason he has plotted since.

Another article says that "if he do not oppose, by a formal act, any armed force undertaken against the nation in his name, he shall be held to have abdicated." His abdication may also be dated from the moment the Prussians, the Austrians, and the émigré rebels invaded France.[6] And as the Tuileries massacre[7] occurred after their invasion, he must be judged as a traitor to the country and the assassin of several thousand Frenchmen. What will be the result if it is proven, and there is little room for doubt, that he himself raised those hordes of enemy brigands who ravaged France?

There is more here than is needed to silence the officious defenders of Louis Capet who will come, the Constitution in hand, to demand impunity for his atrocious crimes. They will claim that he purchased the exclusive privilege to conspire freely against the state from the faithless representatives of the people. But those infamous law mongers dared not stipulate that impunity with either enough clarity or with enough breadth to shield him from the sword of justice.

As for you, Gentlemen, whom the nation has commissioned not only to wreak vengeance on traitors, but to replace by wise laws the Constitution so long the cause of its unhappiness and nearly, at last, of its ruin. Neither concerted omissions, nor the appalling defects of this shameful monument of servitude will restrain you from leading to judgment a despot cast from the throne, nor keep you from making the tyrant expiate, by an ignominious penalty, the long chain of his misdeeds. On the inalienable law of nations

---

5. This is a combination and paraphrases of several articles.   6. Austria and Prussia attacked France after the king had appealed to them for help.   7. In 1792, a crowd stormed the Tuileries Palace, in Paris, and troops killed many of them.

and on the positive laws of states, you will found the judgment of Louis Capet. There is no doubt that a people has the right to punish its agents if they are guilty. And in what free State do the laws not punish with death princes who conspired for the ruin of the nation? I repeat, it would be an outrage at once to all law to invoke the law in defense of the former monarch. They all condemn him as a peculator, a prevaricator, a traitor, a conspirator; as a tyrant stained with all crimes, as a monster still covered with the blood of his fellow citizens whose slaughter he commanded.

He is already more than punished, his partisans will cry, by the cruel sentence to a life lived among a free nation whose head he was and whose shame he has become. Let him live then, and let him feel every instant the weight of shame and of remorse.

If the Constitution were written and liberty were consolidated, if the wounds of the state were healed, if peace reigned among us, if abundance flowing through its various channels had begun once again to bring life to the Empire, if the nation could rest at last in the shadow of wise laws and look forward to happy days, perhaps then we might be able to remember the scourge of monarchy but as a painful dream; perhaps we might be able to abandon the tyrant to his regret, to the long punishment of life in recompense for the ills he has done us, or rather, for the liberty which followed his attempted crimes. But, Gentlemen, if you were ever able to lend an ear to the sophisms of those who wish to spare his life, while yet subjecting him to the rule of law, concern for the public safety alone should cause you to reject any penalty which is not capital. As long as the former monarch draws breath and an unforeseen event may set him once again at liberty, he will be the center of the conspiracies of all the enemies of France: and if his prison does not become the home of their endless plots, it will become their rallying point. Thus, there will be no liberty, no security, no peace, no rest, no happiness for the French, no hope for other peoples of breaking this yoke, unless the tyrant's head is struck off.

Must I speak to you of the bloody scenes, the disasters, the dissolution of the state, the slaughter of all the friends of liberty, of your own suffering, which would be the result of his dreadful vengeance if he were ever to escape and place himself at the head of enemy armies who even now ready themselves to turn on us? What pen could describe them, what heart so hard that it could bear the thought?

Louis Capet, Gentlemen, did not plot alone for the ruin of the nation; once placed before the bar he will denounce his accomplices, his ministers, his agents, the disloyal deputies, the administrators, the judges, the generals, who conspired with him against public safety. The investigation connected with his trial is therefore the surest means to deliver at last the nation from its most redoubtable enemies, to strike fear into traitors, to cut off their plots at the root, and finally, to assure liberty, tranquillity, and public felicity. Without these, your efforts to reestablish order and prepare for the reign of law will be in vain.

"The former monarch must be judged; that is beyond doubt; but by whom shall he be judged?" I would reply, by an ordinary tribunal of the state, composed of the direct delegates of the people—if one could confide so important a case to an ordinary tribunal and if a prompt decision were not so important for the public safety. Let there be no more doubt: Louis Capet is still the rallying point for the enemies of liberty as he is the subject of their hopes. He can therefore be judged only by the National Convention which represents the nation itself. Do not answer that there will be incompetence of jurisdiction, so as to invoke for the accused the title of born representative of the people; a false and lying title conferred upon him by baseness, perfidy, and craft, to raise him above the law. The monarch was only the foremost public official; for that title he could claim no prerogative.

A final question remains to be examined. How should the former monarch be judged? With pomp and with severity. Far from us those false ideas of clemency and generosity by which the national vanity is flattered! How could we listen to them without calling down upon our heads the blame of the nation and all the ills which would befall the land if we left the former monarch the possibility ever again to plot? Thus, to grant a pardon would be not merely weakness, but treason, wickedness, and perfidy.

On the course you choose, Gentlemen, depends the safety of France, the establishment of the Republic. I conclude from this that the tyrant be judged by the Convention and that his punishment be capital.

GERMAINE DE STAËL
1766–1817

Noted for her intellectual salons—social gatherings marked by the brilliant talk of hostess and guests alike—Madame de Staël made a conspicuous place for herself in Paris society and acquired fame as a writer of fiction, literary criticism, and social commentary. Born in Paris, she married a Swedish diplomat from whom she eventually separated, pursuing thereafter an unconventional amorous life. She sympathized moderately with the French Revolution, about which she writes in the excerpts here, but left France in 1792 to return only after all revolutionary activity had ended. Her book about Germany (De l'Allemagne, 1810) enraged Napoleon, who ordered the first edition destroyed. The threat of Napoleon's enmity caused her to flee to Russia and England; in 1815, she returned to Switzerland, where she had lived for a time.

The passages printed here include an excerpt from Considérations sur les principaux événements de la Révolution française (Considerations on the Principal Events of the French Revolution; published 1818, completed 1816) as well as a self-contained essay from 1791. Both constitute efforts to come to terms with the violence of the Revolution, while reflecting on and supporting the political advances it had enabled. De Staël thinks of political life as an emanation of human character, so her reflections on the political situation imply views about psychology and morality as well.

From Considerations on the Principal Events of the French Revolution[1]

Part One

CHAPTER I

General Remarks

The French Revolution is one of the great occurrences of the social order. Those who consider it an accidental event have looked to neither the past nor the future. They have taken the actors for the play, and passionate wishful thinking has led them to attribute to men of the moment what it took centuries to prepare.

One need only cast a glance upon the principal turning points of history to become convinced that they were all inevitable whenever they were connected in any way with the development of ideas, and that after a struggle and more or less prolonged misfortunes the triumph of enlightenment has always been favorable to the greatness and improvement of mankind.

I would like to speak of the time in which we have lived as if it were already remote from us.

I shall limit myself, in this chapter, to some general remarks on the political progress of European civilization, but only in its relation to the French Revolution.

The two ancient peoples whose literature and history still comprise our main intellectual treasure[2] owed their amazing superiority to nothing but the possession of a free country. But slavery existed among them, and consequently the privileges of and grounds for emulation that ought to have been common to all men were shared exclusively by a few citizens. The Greek and Roman nations disappeared from the world as a result of the barbarous— that is to say, unjust—features of their institutions. The vast regions of Asia are lost in despotism and for the past several centuries such civilization as remained to them has been stagnant. So the great historical change whose results are apparent in the present condition of the modern nations dates from the invasions by the Northern peoples; for the public law of most European states today still rests upon the law of conquest.

It seems to me that we may direct our attention to four eras in which changes, already foreshadowed, became strikingly clear.

The first political era is the one in which the nobles, that is, the conquerors, considered themselves partners in the royal power of their chief, while the nation was divided among the various lords who disposed of it as they pleased. There was at that time neither education, nor industry, nor commerce; landed property[3] was virtually the only known kind. Everything indicates that in this period the great lords were very independent of the kings. They upheld liberty for themselves—if one who imposes servitude on others can himself be free.

---

1. Translated by Morroe Berger.   2. I.e., the Greeks and the Romans.   3. Property consisting of real estate.

The feudal *régime* was much better for the nobles than the status of courtiers to which royal despotism has condemned them. It is now a purely metaphysical question whether the human species would gain more from the independence of one whole class or from oppression exerted mildly but equally over all. The point is simply that the nobles, during their glorious era, enjoyed a kind of political liberty, and that the absolute power of kings was established against them with the support of the populace.

In the second political era, that of partial emancipation, the middle classes of the cities claimed certain rights; for when men unite they thereby gain at least as much wisdom as strength. The German and Italian republics and the municipal privileges of the rest of Europe date from this period. Yet the institutions of these republics reflected the period in which they were established; the rights of individual liberty, assuring the exercise and development of the faculties of all men, were not guaranteed. The period of partial emancipation, as I have just shown it, is no longer clearly noticeable except in the free cities and republics that have subsisted down to our times. Thus, in the history of large modern states we should acknowledge only three entirely distinct eras: feudalism, despotism, and representative government.

For about five centuries independence and enlightenment have been influencing events in all ways and almost by chance, yet royal power has steadily grown from various causes and through various means. Kings, often having reason to fear the arrogance of nobles, sought an alliance with the populace against them. The regular army made the assistance of the nobles less necessary, while the need for taxes forced the sovereigns to have recourse to the third estate.[4] And to obtain direct taxes from it, the sovereigns had to disengage it, more or less, from the control of the nobles. The Renaissance, the invention of printing, the Reformation, the discovery of the New World, and the advance of commerce taught men that there could be a force other than military; and they have realized since then that military force is not the exclusive province of gentlemen.

In the Middle Ages only the clergy had any learning. They rendered great service during the Dark Ages. But when the clergy found themselves attacked by the Reformation, they combated the progress of the human mind instead of helping it. The middle class of society monopolized the sciences, literature, the study of law, and commerce; and thus its importance grew daily. On the other hand, the states became increasingly centralized and governmental resources became greater; and the kings, by using the third estate against the barons and the higher clergy, set up their own despotism, that is, the combination of executive and legislative power in the same hands.

England is the only great European empire that has achieved the final stage of perfection of the social order known to us. The third estate, or rather the nation, as elsewhere, aided the royal power under Henry VIII to curb the nobility and the clergy, and expanded at their expense. But the British nobility were early on more liberal than in any other country, and from the time of the Magna Carta[5] we see the barons making demands in favor of the liberties of the people.

The same impulses among men produced the English revolution, and that

---

4. The common people. The nobility and the clergy constituted the first and second estates.   5. Charter of rights granted in 1215 by King John in England, under compulsion partly from the barons.

of France in 1789. Both belong to the third era of the progress of the social order, to the establishment of representative government, toward which the human spirit is advancing from all sides.

Let us now examine the circumstances peculiar to France, where we have seen the colossal events that in our times have aroused so many hopes and so many fears.

* * *

Part Three

CHAPTER XV

Political Fanaticism

The events we have reviewed up till now are merely the sort of history that may be found anywhere. But an abyss is now about to open in our path. We shall pass as quickly as we can over this ghastly crisis, in which there is no man or event worthy of our regard. Everything is the same but extraordinary, monotonous but horrible. One is almost ashamed to be able to examine these gross atrocities closely enough to describe them in detail. Let us examine only the main principle of these monstrous phenomena, political fanaticism.

Worldly desires have always been a part of religious fanaticism, while, on the other hand, true fidelity to abstract ideas often feeds political fanaticism. The mixture occurs everywhere, but it is its proportion that determines good and evil. The social order is in itself a curious structure, yet it cannot be conceived other than it is. But the compromises into which we must sink so that it may endure rack the noble-minded with pity, satisfy the vanity of some people and arouse the discontent and ambition of most. It is to this state of things, more or less accentuated or tempered by custom and education, that we must attribute the political fanaticism of which we have been the witnesses in France. A kind of fury possessed the poor in the presence of the rich. The honors of the nobility adding to the envy property inspires, the populace took pride in its numbers, and everything that went to make up the power and splendor of the minority seemed to it nothing but a usurpation. The germs of this sentiment have existed at all times, but until the era of the Terror in France[6] human society had not trembled to its foundations. One should not be surprised if this abominable scourge has left deep traces upon us. The only reflection one can make, which the remainder of this book will, I hope, confirm, is that the cure for popular passions lies not in despotism but in the rule of law.

Religious fanaticism offers the kind of infinite future that raises all the hopes of the imagination. But the pleasures of this life appear equally unlimited to those who have not tasted them; men often expose themselves to death in order to live better. As to the wealthy, vanity increases as it defends its advantages; it appears less guilty than those who attack it because even injustices, when they have existed for a long time, come to be regarded as a property right. The two elements of religious fanaticism and political fanat-

---

6. I.e., 1793–94, when enormous numbers of more or less arbitrarily chosen "enemies of the state" were executed.

icism still persist: for those who are at the top of the wheel, the desire to rule; for those at the bottom, the eagerness to make it turn. Such is the basis of all violence: the pretext changes but not the causes, and the mutual fanaticism remains the same.

Massacres no less horrible than those of the Terror have been committed in the name of religion; the human race has for several centuries exhausted itself in useless efforts to compel men to one creed. Such a goal could not be achieved, and the simplest idea, tolerance, such as William Penn[7] professed, has banished forever from North America the fanaticism of which the South[8] has been the dreadful scene. It is the same with political fanaticism; liberty alone can abate it. After a certain time, some truths will no longer be disputed and people will regard obsolete institutions as they do old ideas of physics that have been completely obliterated by factual evidence.

The Superiority of Moderation over Extremism[1]

In a tranquil era this question would be easy to settle, but in the very midst of revolt, which seems to reveal a dominant opinion most vigorously, we must concentrate all our mental powers to distinguish what is momentary from what is enduring, and what fear inspires from what reason prompts, and above all what is born of hatred for the old form of government from what is born of attachment to the new.

The more odious the old government, the more agreement there was to overthrow it, and the more difficult it is to distinguish among the various opinions separating those who, united for destruction, are divided in rebuilding.

The right wing of the Assembly, known as *Aristocrats*, claims that fear stifles the voice of the majority. A section of the left wing, known as the *Jacobins*,[2] blames all opposition it encounters upon an attachment to the old abuses. The two parties agree in professing to submit to the general will. But both wrongly rest (the one with logic completely contrary to the facts and the other with facts completely contrary to logic) upon the existence of a majority that never appears or upon one that is always in rebellion.

In human as in physical nature, there are two all-powerful forces: the tendency to cherish repose and the impulse to seek liberty. Each prevails in turn, but the abiding general will results from both in combination. It is when this problem of combination is solved that we can look for and be sure to find the abiding general will.

During a revolution the party that holds moderate opinions needs, more than any other, courage of soul and breadth of mind. It has two struggles to carry on, two kinds of argument to refute, two dangers to avoid. If leaders in such a party are rare, nothing is more numerous than the army awaiting their direction to learn where to find the common welfare it desires. This large

---

7. William Penn (1644–1718), Quaker founder of Pennsylvania as a colony to be marked by its religious and political freedom. 8. Probably South America. 1. Translated by Morroe Berger. Madame de Staël wrote this essay in 1791, giving it the title *How Can We Determine What Is the Opinion of the Majority of the Nation?* She wanted to support the moderate position that welcomed the Revolution for putting an end to past abuses but wished to retain the monarchy. 2. Extreme radicals.

group of people is neither oppressors nor oppressed. If they had been allied with the enemies of the Revolution, it would have died long ago; if they were for the Jacobins, we would not see that party acting in so many ways to prolong anxiety and persecution in order to retain the effective power of fear and hatred.

Some people heap ridicule upon opinions that are removed equally from two conflicting extremes. It is understandable that the two extreme parties should agree in attacking this common enemy. But it is by no means understandable that anyone should dare to call this way of thinking weak and indecisive. Nor is it understandable that it should be impossible to establish a party somewhere between the aristocratic and the democratic positions that would be stronger, more distinct, and more vigorous than the two opposed extremes. People have the knack of reducing everything to extremes in the belief that these are certain to be preferred. Opinions do exist that we must adopt without modification. But are we to allow every lunatic who discovers a new madness to erect a new barrier to truth?

If it is true that the nation does not agree with any of the excesses of the Jacobins, and that it distinguishes clearly between private interests and public welfare, between the establishment of the Constitution and the ambition of those who are associated in managing it, then, one may argue, why does it not give evidence of this? Because, favoring the Revolution, the people do not yet know if its enemies are sufficiently weakened for them to dare to make a choice among its friends; because the horror the people conceived for the Old Regime makes them still cling strongly to this feeling (as a kind of shield) which, though it has perhaps been retained too long, had at first to be regarded as sacred. Finally both the enemies of the Revolution and those whom they appear to detest seem to agree in making fears endure and to compete in perpetuating threats (on the part of the former) and useless terrors (on the part of the latter); so the people, in doubt, do not dare to feel at ease and still allow to act those radicals who know nothing of liberty but its conquest and who devastate the land they have seized.

I would say to the partisans of the Old Regime, to the Aristocrats (if we may dare still to use a word that so often serves to make inquiry—and even more often ability—unnecessary): Do not regard as secret allies of your party those enlightened men who are dissatisfied with some sections of the Constitution nor those good souls who are rightly indignant at the crimes of the Revolution; the unbridgeable gap that separates you comes from the bottom of their hearts, and if one day you were to be victorious you would realize that it is so.

And you, too, present-day enemies of the common good, you who desecrate all words merely by using them and who, always hiding your deeds with speech, calling one to aid the other in order to deceive men—you do not have as allies all those who are proud to call themselves friends of the Constitution, a title that has nourished your hatred of these individuals much more than your love of the common good. If in disturbed times men and opinions merge, they are separated when peace returns; the more that faith in liberty becomes universal, the more will it be proper not to regard its mere profession as its guarantee and to inquire what kind of conduct is joined to this faith. In such a subject a host of comparisons drawn from religion come to mind. For fanaticism and hypocrisy accompany all the causes by which people have been stirred: the fanaticism theirs, the hypocrisy their leaders'.

By examining the character of the Puritans in the history of England[3] and by observing what is happening in our own time, we can see that a lasting and awesome power over the people can never be gained except by those who appear to have all the virtues. Their very morality makes people a prey to hypocrisy. The earliest successes of hypocrisy are always with people who are at a distance from it; its only enemies are the enlightened men who see it up close. But it is they who, sooner or later, determine reputations in all domains. Public recognition must radiate from the enlightened center, and the kind that originates on the periphery is lost on the way.

So I believe that the majority of the nation wants and will always want equality and liberty, but also that it wants order and holds that the legal authority and the legitimate power of a king are necessary to maintain that order.

The Revolution made more rapid progress possible. Each day yielded a benefit by destroying an abuse. A constitution, however, is a more complicated process, the outcome of so many ideas and intentions that judgments of it must differ. One must seek support with righteousness of mind and heart, which for a long time to come will not be unanimous. This great question must be debated by only two parties. The partisans of the Old Regime, who assert that their status as gentlemen exempts them from thinking, must no longer be regarded as French citizens. We must waste neither time nor precious energy in attacking this futile ghost. There are only two parties, the Royalists and the Republicans: why should not both dare to state their names? What feelings doom the Republicans to hypocrisy and the Royalists to silence? Why does this bizarre contrast persist? Why do they not learn from one another? Why do the Republicans fear the Royalists, who dare not even avow their views, and the Royalists the Republicans, who think they are forced to profess a contrary view? Cannot both of these political positions be upheld? Is there sacrilege in the one and servitude in the other? Is not the time when royalty was made a religion gone forever? Have we not reached the point where we can regard royalty as a political idea whose advantages and disadvantages ought to be weighed like those of every other social institution? Why do all Republicans not dare to attack it? Why do the Royalists not dare to defend it? It is treated as a prejudice, when it ought to be analyzed as a principle; the first yields to words, the second entails consequences.

When this great question is cleared up, two parties may stand forth. People will perhaps attack each other, but they will no longer deceive each other or attack with sophisms that are insults the people must not forget. Let these two parties created to divide the Kingdom and the Assembly raise themselves to that level of truth. The one preferring the monarchy is not slavish, and the one preferring the republic is not seditious. Slaves and the seditious are to be found only among hypocrites. Whoever says what he believes has the entire nation as witness and judge. But it is high time that those who are firmly convinced that the only republic possible in a large state is a federative one and that the unity of the realm can exist only with a king spoke out

---

3. In the English civil war of 1642–48, which marked the struggle between King Charles I and his opponents, the king was defeated and executed. His enemies, predominantly Puritans, set up a republican commonwealth that was, in turn, brought down by supporters of Charles II.

clearly for their views in the National Assembly. Far from rallying to itself feeble and timid souls, this party needs more than any other the courage that braves all kinds of distrust and danger. It must impress by the boldness of its character those whom it heartens by the wisdom of its opinions. It must be itself and not some absurd mixture or an irrelevant alternative to opposed extremes. It must combat them instead of becoming a compromise between them. It must in short demonstrate to all that reason is not a shade of meaning between extremes, but the primary color given off by the purest rays of the sun.

WOMEN IN REVOLUTIONARY PARIS

The collection from which the following excerpts are taken attempts to document the role of women during the French Revolution. The voices one hears in these testimonies are otherwise mainly unknown to history. Although the single male writer here published his recollections, the women "authors" record their experience by means of oral testimony, written down by others, or by petitions possibly composed with the aid of others. The accounts focus on two events: the storming of the Bastille in July 1789 and the capture of the king and queen at Versailles in October of the same year.

MARGUERITE PINAIGRE

The conquest of the Bastille in 1789 was immediately seen as an event of enormous importance. The men involved in the storming gained glory by the action, often listed on official registers as "Vainqueurs [conquerors] de la Bastille." This petition to the National Assembly, by Marguerite Pinaigre, demonstrates that women, too, might feel they had a claim to attention.

[My Role in the Conquest of the Bastille][1]

Legislators:

The person named here, Margueritte Piningre [sic], wife of Sieur Bernard Vener, one of the Vainqueurs de la Bastille, has the honor of appearing today before your august assembly to reclaim the execution of the decree issued by the Constituent Assembly in his [her husband's] favor in 1789. This intrepid citizen, who has the misfortune of being crippled for the rest of his days without ever being able to work again in his life because of wounds received on all parts of his body, yes, Legislators, not only has this dear citizen fought in the conquest of the Bastille with the greatest courage, but fur-

---

1. Translated by Jennifer Westfall.

thermore, his *citoyenne*[2] wife, who is present here, worked equally hard with all her might, both of them having resolved to triumph or to die. It is she who ran to several wineshops to fill her apron with bottles, both broken and unbroken, which she gave to the authorities to be used as shot in the cannon used to break the chain on the drawbridge of the Bastille. Therefore, by virtue of these legitimate claims the petitioner believes herself justified in coming before the National Assembly today to advise it concerning the nonexecution of laws relative to conquerors who were severely maimed, as was the petitioner's husband. This law awards a pension to those who are really crippled and without the means for earning their living. Such is the situation of the latter, who is offering to provide evidence in the form of authentic statements. Nevertheless, he still has not been awarded this pension which he so richly deserves, he as well as his wife, as a consequence of the dangers they faced. The only gratification which this citizen has received is a small sum of four hundred *livres*,[3] which since 1789 has barely sufficed to care for him and to help him get over the severe wounds he suffered.

Under these circumstances, and in the light of such a compelling account, the petitioner dares hope, Messieurs, for your justice and your usual generosity. May you be willing to take under urgent consideration the object of a request which is becoming as pressing as it is urgent,—assuming that surely you would not allow one of the most zealous and intrepid Vainqueurs de la Bastille to languish any longer bent under the weight of the indigence to which he is presently reduced, along with his wife and his children, who expect his every minute to be his last—because from this period [July 14, 1789] on he has always been ill and continues to suffer cruelly every day. The petitioner expects the favor of the representatives of the French nation, to whom she will never cease to offer her most heartfelt gratitude.

[signed] Marguerite Pinaigre

2. "Citizen," the term by which the revolutionaries addressed one another.   3. An old French monetary unit.

CLAUDE FOURNIER L'HÉRITIER, L'AMÉRICAIN
1745–1825

Called "L'Américain," Claude Fournier L'Héritier, son of a poor weaver, went to the Americas to seek his fortune. When he returned to France, he committed himself to the revolutionary cause; his organization of the popular force that marched to Versailles helped to make him well known. He was imprisoned by various governments because of his activities as an agitator and was at one point deported to Guiana. He never settled down to any gainful occupation. In his last years, he became a royalist. The secret memoir from which the following account of women during the October Days is excerpted was composed about four years after the events it narrates.

[The October Days][1]

* * * When I saw my brothers crying with hunger on the fifth of October,[2] I could no longer hold in my feelings. The detestable aristocratic and royalist horde had plotted to submit the nation to slavery by starvation and saw no other way to force this nation to renounce its plans for conquering its liberty. That day, at 7 A.M., I heard cries of general alarm and the tocsin, which was being sounded. I ran to the Hôtel-de-Ville. I found the people there, who, when they saw me, cried out: "Fournier, lead us to Versailles, where we want to go and ask for bread." I answered that I would go if I could assemble a sufficient number of armed troops. The battalion of the Vainqueurs de la Bastille was the first to start moving, and having come to an understanding with the women, it went off to Versailles, where, in the middle of the place d'Armes, it seized despotism's bodyguards and troops, who were posted there.

I felt I shouldn't waste a minute. I ran through Paris rallying the greatest number possible of good citizens.

When I arrived at Sainte-Eustache, I found in command d'Ogny, my successor, under whom the citizens were refusing to march. D'Ogny was base enough to turn to me and urge me to assemble them. The public safety was at stake; I allowed myself no other consideration. I had only to say to my former comrades, "Brothers, do you recognize me?" Immediately all companies took up arms. Will you believe that on the spot d'Ogny had the impudence to station himself beside me, *at the head* of these same companies, which [then] went to the Hôtel-de-Ville? There a fight broke out over whether d'Ogny or I should remain in command. A fair number of citizens and troops went over to my side. Then it was remarked that we were missing a standard for our rally. I went to get the flag with the celebrated motto *Destruction des tyrans.*

When I returned to the Hôtel-de-Ville, I found all the people and the French Guard, who called out to me, "To Versailles, Fournier, lead us!" I sounded the call to arms, and everyone willingly rallied.

Then, d'Ogny came out of the Hôtel-de-Ville. "Who gave you the command to sound the call to arms?" he asked the drummers. "I did," I answered, stepping forward. "Who gave you the order to do that?" he retorted. I told him in the strongest tone: "The tocsin and the sovereign people." Then he uttered some threatening remarks against me which I cut off by going after him with my naked sword. He fled into the Hôtel-de-Ville, where I pursued him.

But reflection caused me to let this coward go so I could busy myself with the sycophant Lafayette,[3] whom I found in one of the suites of the Hôtel-de-Ville at work drafting important motions which were neither mine nor the people's. I addressed him and said: "General, the people are asking for you below, on the Place-de-Grève. You must go out at once; the time has come. The people want to make the trip to Versailles to look for bread. I exhort you not to delay." Lafayette obeyed. I went out immediately. He came

---

1. Translated by Darline Gay Levy, Harriet Branson Applewhite, and Mary Durham Johnson. 2. The date of the march to Versailles, when a Parisian mob, angered by rising food prices, captured the king and queen. 3. Marie-Joseph-Gilbert du Motier, marquis de Lafayette (1757–1834), a French general who served in the American revolutionary army. In France, he tried to moderate opposed opinions but lacked the confidence of the court and the populace alike. A hero to Americans, he appeared to Fournier a government toady.

over to my column, where, addressing me [carrying] a little brochure in his hand, he said: "Fournier, what's this? You, on whom I have counted most heavily for detachments for a forty- or fifty-league hike to search for grain— are you going to let me down today?"

This obvious trap set to divert us from the major objectives on our minds had no hold on me. "Yes, General," I retorted, "I am going to let you down today. We must go to Versailles, and it is time to get started." Having replied, I took up my role as commander. "Attention! Left face! To Versailles! * * *" Right then, two women went over to Lafayette and said, pointing with their fingers at the notorious street lamp, "À Versailles, ou à la lanterne!"[4] After these remarks he left, [and] we left.

But these scoundrels of ours had agreed among themselves to use every means to cause the enterprise to fail. D'Ogny had become Lafayette's lieutenant. He marched at his side. We had only gotten up to the Pont-Neuf when they forced us to make our first stop. The general and d'Ogny came over to me and said: "We must not leave without ammunition. You could go get some at the District Sainte-Eustache." I was very suspicious that this bait covered still another hook. That is why I was on my guard. I consented to go with my first column to look for ammunition, but I told my second [column] to wait for me at the end of the Champs-Elysées, along with the general, and not to lose sight of him.

What a surprise I had when I arrived at Sainte-Eustache to find d'Ogny there and to hear him call out to the troops inside the church and [to those] in battle formation: "Put down your arms! Everyone home! I order you in the name of the general." Indignant, I cried out, "Citizens! Stop where you are!" Immediately, I ripped off my epaulettes, I stamped on them, and I cried out with all my might: "That coward who has just dared order citizens to go home deserves to be stamped on, like this." I reattached my epaulettes and said to my troops: "Citizens, whoever loves me will follow me"; and to the women: "Your children are dying of hunger; if your husbands are perverted and cowardly enough not to want to go look for bread for them, then the only thing left for you to do is to slit their throats."

The effect of this speech was most deadly for d'Ogny. It had scarcely been delivered before the women fell upon him and dealt him so many fist blows and kicks in the stomach that they forced him to march along. He died shortly afterwards, following complications from this treatment, which he had merited only too well.

I went back to the Champs-Elysées to rejoin my detachment, which I had left on the Pont-Neuf, and then it looked as if we were off to Versailles at last.

When we were opposite the manufactory of Sèvres,[5] a carriage came by identifying itself as Lafayette's trains.[6] It was led by eight post-horses. Eight to ten men in the uniform of national cavalry were on the *impériale*,[7] on the seat, and behind. All along our lines, they cried out: "Attention. Coming through. These are the trains of the general." At this word, "of the general," I stopped the carriage and said, "This could be the devil's carriage. I'm stopping it to find out what's inside." Immediately a swarm of *mouchards*[8] and

---

4. The choice offered is between marching to Versailles and being hanged from the lamppost. 5. A factory for making fine porcelain. 6. Retinue. 7. Carriage. 8. Informers.

coupe-jarrets[9] encircled me and let the carriage get through. I ask whether they might not have been mixed up in planning a joint getaway by the king and the general, because at this very hour and minute the ever-active and patriotic National Guard of Versailles and the Vainqueurs de la Bastille, who, as I mentioned earlier, were the first to leave, and out in front, stopped the royal trains at Versailles, just below the Orangerie, and had them returned to a safe place.

The perfidious intentions of this wretched Lafayette cannot be in doubt when it is recalled that he had the armed citizens make five or six stops between Paris and Versailles, in the middle of a downpour of rain and the most awful weather, which made it impossible to get there until sometime between midnight and 1 A.M. That way, d'Estaing[1] was given time to prepare all the criminal maneuvers of the court and the traitor-general. This d'Estaing gave up his post with the National Guard of Versailles with the express intention of making himself more useful at the château. But when I was informed of his treason, I took over the *corps de garde* of the former French Guard and its artillery range, where I established special security. * * *

[Fournier l'Américain goes on to explain that he had tried unsuccessfully to prevent the general massacre on the sixth of October. Later that morning:]

* * * I addressed five or six of these women who, with the name and outward appearance of *poissardes*,[2] conceal moral qualities, and above all, judgment, which always makes it possible for them to value sound advice. I stooped to their level of intelligence and borrowed Père Duchesne's style, and while putting fist to nose, I told them: "Damn my ass, [*Sac * * * b * * * esses*] don't you see that Lafayette and the king are fucking you up [*vous c * * *]* when they tell you they are going to meet in private to get bread for you? Don't you see that it's a ruse to put you off and to give you your chains back, and famine? The whole damned lot should be taken away to Paris. * * *"

No sooner had I spoken these words and followed them up with the gesture of hanging my hat on the tip of my sword, and crying, "To Paris! To Paris with the king!" than fifty thousand voices repeated this same cry, "To Paris!" And then, we left. * * *

We set off again.

I was delegated to go ahead in order to give the municipality of Paris the news that the master of Versailles was arriving in Paris, and that the people, who wanted it that way, were escorting him back.

Women Testify

The following passages comprise three of the twenty-five testimonies offered by women appearing before the Châtelet Commission, convened in 1790 to investigate the October Days. Madelaine Glain had played a fairly conspicuous part, acting as a spokeswoman to the National Assembly and helping to carry decrees of the Assembly to the mayor of Paris. Barré was also a leader among women, Delaissement a less conspicuous participant.

---

9. Bandits or assassins.   1. Charles Hector, comte d'Estaing (1729–1794), French admiral who commanded the National Guard at Versailles when the mob arrived. He would later be guillotined as a royalist. 2. Vulgar women.

MADELAINE GLAIN

Deposition Number 83[1]

Madelaine Glain, forty-two years old, a *faiseuse de ménage*,[2] wife of François Gaillard, an office clerk in the District de l'Oratoire with whom she lives on rue Froidmanteau, no. 40, testifies that, having been forced, as many women were, to follow the crowd that went to Versailles last Monday, October 5, and having arrived at Sèvres near the porcelain manufactory, [and] a gentleman with a black decoration having asked them where they were going, they answered that they were going to ask for bread at Versailles. This gentleman urged them to behave themselves, but a woman whom the declarant knew to be a prostitute and who since then has been living with Lagrement, a soft drink peddler on rue Bailleul, having said that she was going to Versailles to bring back the queen's head, was sharply reproached by the others. Having arrived at the streets leading to Versailles, this same woman stopped a mounted Royal Guardsman, to whom she delivered many insults, threatening him with a bad, rusty sword which she held open in her hand. This Royal Guardsman said that she was a wretch, and in order to [make her] release the bridle of his horse, which she was holding, he struck her a blow which inflicted an arm wound. Having come at last to the Château with the intention of informing His Majesty concerning the motives of their proceedings, she, the declarant, found herself locked in, that is to say, her skirts caught on two spikes of the gate, from which a Swiss Guard released her. After that she went with the other women to the hall of the National Assembly, where they entered, many strong. Some of these women having asked for the four-pound loaf at eight *sols*,[3] and for meat at the same price, she, the declarant, called for silence, and then she said that they were asking that they not be lacking bread, but not [that it be fixed] at the price these women were wanting to have it. She did not go with the deputation to the Chateau but returned with Sieur Maillard and two other women to the Hotel-de-Ville in Paris to bring back the decrees they were given at the National Assembly. Monsieur the mayor and the representatives of the commune were satisfied and received them with joy. Then she, the declarant, was led by the National Guard to the District de l'Oratoire to convey this good news. She cannot give us any news concerning what happened at Versailles on the sixth, but she learned, without being able to say from whom, that someone named Nicolas, a model in the academy, who lived at the home of Poujet, rue Champfleuri, on that day, Tuesday, had cut off the heads of two Royal Guards who had been massacred by the people, and since then the above-mentioned Nicolas has not reappeared in the *quartier*.

---

1. Translated by Philip Dawson. 2. Housewife. 3. Coins of small value.

JEANNE DOROTHÉE DELAISSEMENT

Deposition Number 85[1]

Jeanne Dorothée Delaissement, age twenty-eight, a mistress seamstress, widow of Philippe Brenair, living in Paris, rue Mauconseil, at the house of the wheelwright, opposite rue Française, stated that on last Monday, October 5, in the morning, she, the declarant, was forced to go, as many other women were, with the crowd that wanted to go to Versailles. The women who dragged her in first led her to the Hotel-de-Ville and then to Versailles. She saw nothing worth mentioning along the way. She knows that an individual whom she did not know at that time, but whom she came to know afterwards, named Maillard went to a great deal of trouble to keep order among the women, who were armed with pikes, sticks, pieces of iron, and other things, and that he succeeded in getting them to disarm *en route*. When they arrived at Versailles, a soldier dressed in a blue costume, who she learned was in the Regiment of Flanders, told her, in answer to her questions about people they should be suspicious of, that the Flanders Regiment would do them no harm, but that they must beware of the Royal Guards, who, during a meal, had trampled the *national cockade*. She, the declarant, did not go to the Château or to the meeting hall of the National Assembly, etc.

1. Translated by Philip Dawson.

MARIE-ROSE BARRÉ

Deposition Number 343[1]

June 18, 1790

Marie-Rose Barré, age twenty, unmarried, a lace worker, residing at 61, rue Meslay, upon oath * * *

Deposes that on October 5, last, at about eight o'clock in the morning, going to take back some work, she was stopped at the Pont Notre Dame by about a hundred women, who told her that it was necessary for her to go with them to Versailles to ask for bread there. Not being able to resist this great number of women, she decided to go with them. At the hamlet at the Point-du-Jour, two young men, unknown to her, who were on foot and going their way, told them that they were running a great risk, that there were cannon mounted at the bridge at Saint Cloud. This did not prevent them from continuing on their way. At Sèvres they had some refreshments; then they continued on their way toward Versailles. The two young men of whom she spoke met them near Viroflay and told them that they had escaped at

1. Translated by Philip Dawson.

Saint Cloud but that at Versailles they would be fired on. But they continued on their way. At Versailles they found the King's Guards lined up in three ranks before the palace. A gentleman dressed in the uniform of the King's Guards, who, she was told, was the duc de Guiche, came to ask them what they wanted of the king, recommending peaceful behavior on their part. They answered that they were coming to ask him for bread. This gentleman was absent for a few minutes and then returned to take four of them to introduce them to the king. The deponent was one of the four. Before taking them to the king, he led them to the comte d'Affry, who requested that they be introduced to His Majesty right away, which was done.

They spoke first to M. de Saint-Priest, and then to His Majesty, whom they asked for bread. His Majesty answered them that he was suffering at least as much as they were, to see them lacking it, and that so far as he was able he had taken care to prevent them from experiencing a dearth. Upon the king's response they begged him to be so good as to arrange escorts for the flour transports intended for the provisioning of Paris, because according to what they had been told at the bridge in Sèvres by the two young men of whom she spoke earlier, only two wagons out of seventy intended for Paris actually arrived there. The king promised them to have the flour escorted and said that if it depended on him, they would have bread then and there. They took leave of His Majesty and were led, by a gentleman in a blue uniform with red piping, into the apartments and courts of the palace to the ranks of the Flanders Regiment, to which they called out, "Vive Le Roi!" It was then about nine o'clock. After this they retired into a house on rue Satory and went to bed in a stable. She does not know the names and addresses of the three women introduced to the king with her. Tired from the trip, having a swollen foot, she did not go Tuesday to the palace or the Place d'Armes, knows nothing, as a witness, of what happened there, and came back to Paris between four and five o'clock in the afternoon of that day in a carriage.

She adds that a fortnight later a gentleman whom she heard called M. de Saint-Paul came to her place and asked her to go to a court commissioner to make a formal declaration of what M. de Saint-Priest told her on Monday, October 5, at Versailles, when she presented herself to speak to the king. As the deponent did not know a court commissioner, Saint-Paul suggested Maître Chenu. The deponent remarks that she was then living on rue du Four at the corner of rue des Ciseaux. * * * The commissioner * * * took her declaration * * * in which she sets forth that having heard it said, by the two young men mentioned above, that of seventy wagons of flour intended for Paris only two had arrived, she informed M. de Saint-Priest of this, and he answered that as the grain shortage was equally bad everywhere, it was not surprising that the inhabitants of places where flour passed through stopped it for their supply. Besides, the threshing season had not yet arrived, which caused the provisions to be smaller than they should be. * * * She told the commissioner that the minister did not say to her what was being attributed to him by the public: "When you had only one king, you had bread; now that you have twelve hundred of them, go and ask them for it," that in fact she did not hear the minister say this. Which is all that the dependent said she knows * * * and she has signed. * * *

ENGLISH ROMANTIC LYRICS: A SELECTION

This group of English Romantic poems illustrates the excitement of continuity and variety. The lyrics reinforce one another's effects, both by reiterating common issues and attitudes and by demonstrating how many ways a single theme can be communicated.

In virtually all these works, one can feel the visionary force of poets possessed by a sense of possibility. That sense expresses itself both in outrage at existing conditions and in articulations of alternatives to actuality. Thus William Blake imagines himself wandering through London and seeing everywhere the manifestations of social corruption, as sounds of misery and fear evoke the bondage of human self-distortion and the melancholy of a soldier objectifies itself in blood. But he can also imagine an ancient scene in which Christ walks through England; the poet creates on the basis of that scene a vision of a new Jerusalem that will confirm England as a "green & pleasant Land" and nullify the menace of "dark Satanic Mills." William Wordsworth can remember a youth when "The sounding cataract / Haunted me like a passion" and construct from the memory "a sense sublime" of universal order in which God conveys Himself through nature, which serves as guardian to humanity. Percy Bysshe Shelley specifies in chilling detail the human horrors ("A people starved and stabbed in th' untilled field") of his country at the moment he writes, only to conclude that the political corruption of the present may become a grave from which "a glorious Phantom" bursts to illuminate the scene.

The moral and aesthetic energy of such visions—and their equivalents appear in many other Romantic poems—make them persuasive. We may not believe that Jerusalem will be reconstituted in England or that a benign system operates through the natural world for the benefit of individuals. But the poems create in their readers what Coleridge called "poetic faith": the "willing suspension of disbelief for the moment." The suspension of disbelief is not the same as belief. It implies, rather, a willingness to allow poetry briefly to take over, to make the world anew in the imagination even though reality allows no new worlds. Like all literature, this poetry has designs on us. One of its designs is to renew awareness of possibility.

Lyrics, by definition, draw on personal feeling. One kind of personal feeling produces the visionary fervor so marked in many of these lyrics, but different varieties of emotion abound here. A melancholy note often emerges, providing in one case (Samuel Taylor Coleridge's *Dejection: An Ode*) a poem's announced subject. Coleridge evokes vividly the familiar condition of depression:

> A grief without a pang, void, dark, and drear,
> A stifled, drowsy, unimpassioned grief,
> Which finds no natural outlet, no relief,
> In word, or sigh, or tear—

And then he uses his experience of that condition as the basis for reflecting on joy and imagination, closely allied powers in his conception, and for invoking the blessing of those powers on a friend. But not all expressions of melancholy lead to happy endings. George Gordon, Lord Byron, reflecting on the end of his marriage or the end of a love affair, builds entire poems out of negative emotion. John Keats celebrates melancholy as itself a shaping power (*Ode on Melancholy*) and evokes the somber spirit of autumn ("Season of mists," though also of "mellow fruitfulness") as a source of music as satisfying as that of spring.

It is, of course, literally the poet who has made music out of sadness, and this is an important point. Byron writes *Stanzas for Music,* in which he ostentatiously demonstrates the poet's power to create melody out of language, even with virtually no subject matter. That power can in fact transform any raw material. Keats's *Ode on Melancholy,* despite its subject, does not create a melancholy experience for the reader because melancholy has been transmuted into beauty before we as readers experience it. Even when Byron, in the short poem *Politics in 1813*, sketches a situation containing nothing but violations of social order, by making that situation into a poem he makes it into something different. The economy and wit of his evocation transmute social chaos into poetic order, creating pleasure for the reader by the transmutation.

So the sound of this poetry matters as much as the sense; the sound, indeed, makes part of the sense. Shelley writes,

> The Sun is warm, the sky is clear,
> The waves are dancing fast and bright,
> Blue isles and snowy mountains wear
> The purple noon's transparent might.

The title of the poem containing these lines is *Stanzas Written in Dejection*. The simple rhythms of the lines, though—the speed of the dancing waves yielding to the slow motion of the noon's might—make one feel the countervailing force of poetic melody as part of the meaning of a poem that ponders the nature of feeling. Blake's first poem in *Songs of Innocence* begins,

> Piping down the valleys wild
> Piping songs of pleasant glee
> On a cloud I saw a child,
> And he laughing said to me . . .

The singsong meter, the ballad rhyme scheme, both promise a naïve and readily comprehensible set of verses. The expectation thus established sets up a fruitful tension as the poem continues, raising questions that it fails to answer.

Every reader will discover further areas of commonality and diversity. To mention only one more aspect shared by some of these poems, it is worth noting the self-mythologizing that may attend poetic emphasis on personal feeling. This is perhaps most vivid in Byron's verse, which uses the poet's amorous career not only as a basis for emotion but as a way of re-creating the poet himself in the form of a slightly cynical hero, a survivor of betrayal and abandonment, worldly-wise as a result of his experience yet still pained by it. But one may also feel aspects of self-invention—or at least of self-enlargement, in Shelley ("I am one Whom men love not, and yet regret"; "I fall upon the thorns of life! I bleed!") and in Wordsworth ("For nature then . . . To me was all in all.—I cannot paint What then I was."). Thus the poet uses himself, or an imagined version of himself, in order to construct implicit narratives that lie behind the lyric expression of feeling, giving them intricacy and depth.

WILLIAM BLAKE
1757–1827

Few works so ostentatiously "simple" as William Blake's *Songs of Innocence and of Experience* (1794) can ever have aroused such critical perplexity. Employing uncomplicated vocabulary and, often, variants of traditional ballad structure; describing the experience usually of naïve subjects; supplying no obvious intellectual substance, these short lyrics have long fascinated and baffled their readers.

With no formal education, Blake, son of a London hosier, was at the age of fourteen apprenticed to the engraver James Basire. He developed both as painter and as engraver, partly influenced by the painter Henry Fuseli and the sculptor John Flaxman, both his friends, but remaining always highly individual in style and technique. An acknowledged mystic, he saw visions from the age of four: trees filled with angels, God looking at him through the window. His highly personal view of a world penetrated by the divine helped to form both his visual and his verbal art. In 1800, Blake moved from London to Felpham, where the poet William Hayley was his patron. He returned to London in 1803 and remained there for the rest of his life, married but childless, engaged in writing, printing, and engraving.

Blake felt a close relation between the visual and the verbal; he illustrated the works of many poets, notably Milton and Dante. His first book, *Poetical Sketches* (1783), was conventionally published, but he produced all of his subsequent books himself, combining pictorial engravings with lettering, striking off only a few copies of each work by hand. Gradually, in increasingly long poems, he developed an elaborate private mythology, with important figures appearing in one work after another. His major mythic poems include *The Marriage of Heaven and Hell* (1793), *America* (1793), *The Book of Los* (1795), *Milton* (1804), *Jerusalem* (1804), and *The Four Zoas* (which he never completed).

As his short poem *Mock On, Mock On, Voltaire, Rousseau* testifies, Blake was bitterly opposed to what he thought the destructive and repressive rationalism of the eighteenth century. Voltaire and Rousseau might have been surprised to find themselves thus associated; they belong together, in Blake's view, because both implicitly oppose not only orthodox Christianity but the more private variety of revealed religion so vital to Blake himself. Although, like his contemporaries, Blake idealizes imagination and emotion and believes in the sacredness of the individual, he entirely avoids the "egotistical sublime," neither speaking directly of himself in his poetry, as Wordsworth did, nor, like Goethe, creating self-absorbed characters. In his short lyrics he adopts many different voices; the difficulties of interpretation stem partly from this fact. He insistently deals with metaphysical questions about our place in the universe and with social questions about the nature of human responsibility.

In *Songs of Innocence*, the speaker is often a child: asking questions of a lamb, meditating on his own blackness, describing the experience of a chimney sweep. Ostensibly these children in their innocence feel no anger or bitterness at the realities of the world in which they find themselves. The "little black boy" ensures himself a future when the "little English boy" will resemble him and love him; the child addressing the lamb evokes a realm of pure delight; the chimney sweep comforts himself with conventional morality and with a companion's dream. When an adult observer watches children, as in *Holy Thursday*, he, too, sees a benign arrangement in which children are "flowers of London town," supervised by "agèd men, wise guardians of the poor." In the *Introduction* to the volume, the adult speaker receives empowering advice from a child, who instructs him to write. Everything is for the best in this best of all possible worlds.

But not quite. Disturbing undertones reverberate through even the most "innocent" of these songs. Innocence is, after all, by definition a state automatically lost through experience and impossible to regain. If the children evoked by the text still possess their innocence, the adult reader does not. *The Little Black Boy* suggests the kind of ambiguity evoked by the conjunction between innocent speaker and experienced reader. The poem opens with a situation that the speaker does not entirely understand but one likely to be painfully familiar to the reader. "White as an angel is the English child: / But I am black as if bereaved of light": the child's similes indicate how completely he has incorporated the value judgments of his society, in which white suggests everything good and black means deficiency and deprivation. In this context, the mother's teaching, a comforting myth, becomes comprehensible as a way of dealing with her child's bewilderment and anxiety about his difference. At the end of the poem, the boy extends his mother's story into a prophetic vision in which black means protective power ("I'll shade him from the heat till he can bear / To lean in joy upon our father's knee"), and difference disappears into likeness, hostility into love. The vision evokes an ideal situation located in an imagined afterlife; it has only an antithetical connection to present actuality. Its emphatic divergence from real social conditions creates the subterranean disturbance characteristic of Blake's lyrics, the disturbance that calls attention to the serious social criticism implicit even in lyrics that may appear sweet to the point of blandness.

For all Blake's dislike of the earlier eighteenth century, he shares with his forebears one important assumption: his poetry, too, instructs as well as pleases. The innocent chimney sweep evokes parental death and betrayal, horrifying working conditions (soot and nakedness, darkness and shaved heads), and compensatory dreams. He never complains, but when he ends with the tag "So if all do their duty, they need not fear harm," it generates moral shock. The discrepancy between the child's purity and his brutal exploitation indicts the society that allows such things. Innocence may be its own protection, these poems suggest, but that fact does not obviate social guilt.

If the *Songs of Innocence*, for all their atmosphere of brightness, cheer, and peace, convey outrage at the ways that social institutions harm those whom they should protect, the *Songs of Experience* more directly evoke a world worn, constricted, and burdened with misery created by human beings. Now a new version of *The Chimney Sweeper* openly states what the earlier poem suggested:

> "And because I am happy, & dance & sing,
> They think they have done me no injury,
> And are gone to praise God & his Priest & King,
> Who make up a heaven of our misery."

The child understands the protective self-blinding of adults.

London, in its sixteen lines, sums up many of the collection's implications. Like most of the *Songs of Experience, London* presents an adult speaker, a wanderer through the city, who finds wherever he goes, in every face, "Marks of weakness, marks of woe." The city is the repository of suffering: men and infants and chimney sweepers cry; soldiers sigh; harlots curse. All are victims of corrupt institutions: blackening Church, bloody palace. Marriage and death interpenetrate; the curses of illness and corruption pass through the generations. The speaker reports only what he sees and hears, without commentary. He evokes a society in dreadful decay, and he conveys his despairing rage at a situation he cannot remedy.

Blake's lyrics, in their mixture of the visionary and the observational, strike notes far different from those of satire. Like the visionary observations of Swift and Voltaire, though, they insist on the connection between literature and life. Literature has transformative capacity, but it works with the raw material of actual experience. And its visions have the power to insist on the necessity of change.

Songs of Innocence and of Experience

SHEWING THE TWO CONTRARY STATES OF THE HUMAN SOUL

From *Songs of Innocence*[1]

Introduction

Piping down the valleys wild
Piping songs of pleasant glee
On a cloud I saw a child,
And he laughing said to me,

"Pipe a song about a Lamb";   5
So I piped with merry chear;
"Piper pipe that song again"—
So I piped, he wept to hear.

"Drop thy pipe thy happy pipe
Sing thy songs of happy chear";   10
So I sung the same again
While he wept with joy to hear.

"Piper sit thee down and write
In a book that all may read"—
So he vanished from my sight.   15
And I plucked a hollow reed,

And I made a rural pen,
And I stained the water clear,
And I wrote my happy songs
Every child may joy to hear.   20

The Lamb

Little Lamb, who made thee?
Dost thou know who made thee?
Gave thee life & bid thee feed,
By the stream & o'er the mead;
Gave thee clothing of delight,   5
Softest clothing wooly bright;
Gave thee such a tender voice,

---

1. The text for all of Blake's works is edited by David V. Erdman and Harold Bloom. *Songs of Innocence* (1789) was later combined with *Songs of Experience* (1794), and the poems were etched and accompanied by Blake's illustrations, the process accomplished by copper engravings stamped on paper, then colored by hand.

Making all the vales rejoice!
Little Lamb who made thee?
Dost thou know who made thee?   10

Little Lamb I'll tell thee,
Little Lamb I'll tell thee!
He is callèd by thy name,
For he calls himself a Lamb:
He is meek & he is mild,   15
He became a little child:
I a child & thou a lamb,
We are callèd by his name.[1]
Little Lamb God bless thee.
Little Lamb God bless thee.   20

The Little Black Boy

My mother bore me in the southern wild,
And I am black, but O! my soul is white;
White as an angel is the English child:
But I am black as if bereaved of light.

My mother taught me underneath a tree,   5
And sitting down before the heat of day,
She took me on her lap and kissèd me,
And pointing to the east, began to say:

"Look on the rising sun: there God does live,
And gives his light, and gives his heat away;   10
And flowers and trees and beasts and men receive
Comfort in morning, joy in the noon day.

"And we are put on earth a little space,
That we may learn to bear the beams of love,
And these black bodies and this sun-burnt face   15
Is but a cloud, and like a shady grove.

"For when our souls have learned the heat to bear,
The cloud will vanish; we shall hear his voice,
Saying: 'Come out from the grove, my love & care,
And round my golden tent like lambs rejoice.' "   20

Thus did my mother say, and kissèd me;
And thus I say to little English boy:
When I from black and he from white cloud free,
And round the tent of God like lambs we joy,

I'll shade him from the heat till he can bear   25

---

1. Christians use the name of Christ to designate themselves.

To lean in joy upon our father's knee;
And then I'll stand and stroke his silver hair,
And be like him, and he will then love me.

Holy Thursday[1]

'Twas on a Holy Thursday, their innocent faces clean,
The children walking two & two, in red & blue & green,[2]
Grey headed beadles[3] walked before with wands as white as snow,
Till into the high dome of Paul's they like Thames' waters flow.

O what a multitude they seemed, these flowers of London town!   5
Seated in companies they sit with radiance all their own.
The hum of multitudes was there, but multitudes of lambs,
Thousands of little boys & girls raising their innocent hands.

Now like a mighty wind they raise to heaven the voice of song,
Or like harmonious thunderings the seats of heaven among.   10
Beneath them sit the agèd men, wise guardians[4] of the poor;
Then cherish pity, lest you drive an angel from your door.[5]

The Chimney Sweeper

When my mother died I was very young,
And my father sold me[1] while yet my tongue
Could scarcely cry " 'weep![2] 'weep! 'weep! 'weep!"
So your chimneys I sweep & in soot I sleep.

There's little Tom Dacre, who cried when his head   5
That curled like a lamb's back, was shaved, so I said,
"Hush, Tom! never mind it, for when your head's bare,
You know that the soot cannot spoil your white hair."

And so he was quiet, & that very night,
As Tom was a-sleeping he had such a sight!   10
That thousands of sweepers, Dick, Joe, Ned, & Jack,
Were all of them locked up in coffins of black;

And by came an Angel who had a bright key,
And he opened the coffins & set them all free;
Then down a green plain, leaping, laughing they run,   15
And wash in a river and shine in the Sun;

1. Ascension Day, forty days after Easter, when children from charity schools were marched to St. Paul's Cathedral.   2. Each school had its own distinctive uniform.   3. Ushers and minor functionaries, whose job was to maintain order.   4. The governors of the charity schools.   5. See Hebrews 13.2: "Be not forgetful to entertain strangers: for thereby some have entertained angels unawares."   1. It was common practice in Blake's day for fathers to sell, or indenture, their children to become chimney sweeps. The average age at which such children began working was six or seven; they were generally employed for seven years, until they were too big to ascend the chimneys.   2. The child's lisping effort to say "sweep," as he walks the streets looking for work.

Then naked[3] & white, all their bags left behind,
They rise upon clouds, and sport in the wind.
And the Angel told Tom, if he'd be a good boy,
He'd have God for his father & never want joy.   20

And so Tom awoke; and we rose in the dark
And got with our bags & our brushes to work.
Tho' the morning was cold, Tom was happy & warm;
So if all do their duty, they need not fear harm.

From *Songs of Experience*

Introduction

Hear the voice of the Bard!
Who Present, Past, & Future sees;
Whose ears have heard
The Holy Word
That walked among the ancient trees;[1]   5

Calling the lapsèd Soul
And weeping in the evening dew;[2]
That might control
The starry pole,
And fallen, fallen light renew!   10

"O Earth, O Earth, return!
Arise from out the dewy grass;
Night is worn,
And the morn
Rises from the slumberous mass.   15

"Turn away no more;
Why wilt thou turn away?
The starry floor
The watery shore
Is given thee till the break of day."   20

Earth's Answer

Earth raised up her head,
From the darkness dread & drear.
Her light fled:
Stony dread!
And her locks covered with grey despair.   5

---

3. They climbed up the chimneys naked.   **1.** Genesis 3.8: "And [Adam and Eve] heard the voice of the Lord God walking in the garden in the cool of the day."   **2.** Blake's ambiguous use of pronouns makes for interpretative difficulties. It would seem that *The Holy Word* (Jehovah, a name for God in the Old Testament of the Bible) calls *the lapsèd Soul*, and weeps—not the Bard.

"Prisoned on watery shore
Starry Jealousy does keep my den,
Cold and hoar
Weeping o'er
I hear the Father[1] of the ancient men.   10

"Selfish father of men,
Cruel, jealous, selfish fear!
Can delight
Chained in night
The virgins of youth and morning bear?   15

"Does spring hide its joy
When buds and blossoms grow?
Does the sower
Sow by night,
Or the plowman in darkness plow?   20

"Break this heavy chain
That does freeze my bones around;
Selfish! vain!
Eternal bane!
That free Love with bondage bound."   25

The Tyger

Tyger! Tyger! burning bright
In the forests of the night,
What immortal hand or eye
Could frame thy fearful symmetry?

In what distant deeps or skies   5
Burnt the fire of thine eyes?
On what wings dare he aspire?
What the hand dare seize the fire?

And what shoulder, & what art,
Could twist the sinews of thy heart?   10
And when thy heart began to beat,
What dread hand? & what dread feet?

What the hammer? what the chain?
In what furnace was thy brain?
What the anvil? what dread grasp   15
Dare its deadly terrors clasp?

---

1. In Blake's later prophetic works, one of the four Zoas, representing the four chief faculties of humankind, is Urizen. In general, he stands for the orthodox conception of the Divine Creator, sometimes Jehovah in the Old Testament, often the God conceived by Newton and Locke—in all instances a tyrant associated with excessive rationalism and sexual repression, and the opponent of the imagination and creativity. This may be "the Holy Word" in line 4 of *Introduction* (p. 691).

When the stars threw down their spears,
And watered heaven with their tears,
Did he smile his work to see?
Did he who made the Lamb make thee?   20

Tyger! Tyger! burning bright
In the forests of the night,
What immortal hand or eye
Dare frame thy fearful symmetry?

The Sick Rose

O Rose, thou art sick.
The invisible worm
That flies in the night
In the howling storm

Has found out thy bed   5
Of crimson joy,
And his dark secret love
Does thy life destroy.

London

I wander thro' each chartered[1] street,
Near where the chartered Thames does flow,
And mark in every face I meet
Marks of weakness, marks of woe.

In every cry of every Man,   5
In every Infant's cry of fear,
In every voice, in every ban,
The mind-forged manacles I hear:

How the Chimney-sweeper's cry
Every blackening Church appalls;[2]   10
And the hapless Soldier's sigh
Runs in blood down Palace walls.

But most thro' midnight streets I hear
How the youthful Harlot's curse
Blasts the new-born Infant's tear,[3]   15
And blights with plagues the Marriage hearse.

---

1. Hired (literally). Blake implies that the streets and the river are controlled by commercial interests.
2. Makes white (literally), punning also on *appall* (to dismay) and *pall* (the cloth covering a corpse or bier).
3. The harlot infects the parents with venereal disease, and thus the infant is inflicted with neonatal blindness.

The Chimney Sweeper

A little black thing among the snow
Crying " 'weep, 'weep," in notes of woe!
"Where are thy father & mother? say?"
"They are both gone up to the church to pray.

"Because I was happy upon the heath,   5
And smiled among the winter's snow;
They clothèd me in the clothes of death,
And taught me to sing the notes of woe.

"And because I am happy, & dance & sing,
They think they have done me no injury,   10
And are gone to praise God & his Priest & King,
Who make up a heaven of our misery."

Mock On, Mock On, Voltaire, Rousseau

Mock on, Mock on, Voltaire, Rousseau;
Mock on, Mock on, 'tis all in vain.
You throw the sand against the wind,
And the wind blows it back again.

And every sand becomes a Gem   5
Reflected in the beams divine;
Blown back, they blind the mocking Eye,
But still in Israel's paths they shine.

The Atoms of Democritus[1]
And Newton's Particles of light[2]   10
Are sands upon the Red sea shore,
Where Israel's tents do shine so bright.

And Did Those Feet

And did those feet[1] in ancient time
Walk upon England's mountains green?
And was the holy Lamb of God
On England's pleasant pastures seen?

1. Greek philosopher (460?–362? B.C.E.), who advanced a theory that all things are merely patterns of atoms.
2. Sir Isaac Newton's (1642–1727) corpuscular theory of light. For Blake, both men were condemned as materialists.   1. A reference to an ancient legend that Jesus came to England with Joseph of Arimathea.

And did the Countenance Divine 5
Shine forth upon our clouded hills?
And was Jerusalem builded here,
Among those dark Satanic Mills?[2]

Bring me my Bow of burning gold:
Bring me my Arrows of desire: 10
Bring me my Spear: O clouds unfold!
Bring me my Chariot of fire!

I will not cease from Mental Fight,
Nor shall my Sword sleep in my hand,
Till we have built Jerusalem 15
In England's green & pleasant Land.

2. Possibly industrial England, but *mills* also meant for Blake 18th-century arid, mechanistic philosophy.

WILLIAM WORDSWORTH
1770–1850

William Wordsworth both proclaimed and embodied the *newness* of the Romantic movement. In his preface to the second edition of *Lyrical Ballads* (1800), a collection of poems by him and his friend Samuel Taylor Coleridge, he announced the advent of a poetic revolution. Like other revolutionaries, Wordsworth and Coleridge created their identities by rebelling against and parodying their predecessors. Now no longer would poets write in "dead" forms; now they had discovered a "new" direction, "new" subject matter; now poetry could at last serve as an important form of human communication. Reading Wordsworth's poems with the excitement of that revolution long past, we can still feel the power of his desire to communicate. The human heart is his subject; he writes, in particular, of growth and of memory and of the perplexities inherent in the human condition.

Born at Cockermouth, Cumberland, to the family of an attorney, Wordsworth attended St. John's College, Cambridge, from 1787 to 1791. The next year, early in the French Revolution, he spent in France, where he met Annette Vallon and had a daughter by her. In 1795, Wordsworth met Coleridge; two years later, Wordsworth and his sister, Dorothy, moved to Alfoxden, near Coleridge's home in Nether Stowey, in Somerset. There the two men conceived the idea of collaboration; in 1798, the first edition of their *Lyrical Ballads* appeared, anonymously. The next year, Wordsworth and his sister settled in the Lake District of northwest England. In 1802, the poet married Mary Hutchinson, with whom he had five children. He received the sinecure of stamp distributor in 1813 and in 1843 succeeded Robert Southey as England's poet laureate, having long since abandoned the political radicalism of his youth.

Wordsworth wrote little prose, except for the famous preface of 1800 and another preface in 1815; his accomplishment was almost entirely poetic. His early work employed conventional eighteenth-century techniques, but *Lyrical Ballads* marked a new direction: an effort to employ simple language and to reveal the high significance of simple themes, the transcendent importance of the everyday. Between 1798 and 1805 he composed his nineteenth-century version of an epic, *The Prelude*, an account of the development of a poet's mind—his own. His subsequent work included odes, sonnets, and many poems written to mark specific occasions.

It would be difficult to overestimate the extent of Wordsworth's historical and poetic importance. In *The Prelude,* not published until 1850, he not only made powerful poetry out of his own experience but also specified a way of valuing experience:

> There are in our existence spots of time,
> That with distinct pre-eminence retain
> A renovating virtue, whence, depressed
> By false opinion and contentious thought,
> Or aught of heavier or more deadly weight,
> In trivial occupations, and the round
> Of ordinary intercourse, our minds
> Are nourished and invisibly repaired;
> A virtue, by which pleasure is enhanced,
> That penetrates, enables us to mount
> When high, more high, and lifts us up when fallen.

To take seriously the moment, this passage suggests, enables us to resist the dulling force of everyday life ("trivial occupations") and provides the means of personal salvation.

Wordsworth often uses religious language (a religious reference is hinted in the idea of being lifted up when fallen) to insist on the importance of his doctrine. He inaugurated an attempt—lasting far into the century—to establish and sustain a secular religion to substitute for Christian faith. The attempt was, even for Wordsworth, only intermittently successful. *The Prelude* records experiences of persuasive visionary intensity, as when the poet speaks of seeing a shepherd in the distance:

> Or him have I descried in distant sky,
> A solitary object and sublime,
> Above all height! like an aerial cross
> Stationed alone upon a spiry rock
> Of the Chartreuse, for worship.

But such "spots of time" exist in isolation; it is difficult to maintain a saving faith on their basis.

The two long poems printed here treat the problem of discovering and sustaining faith. *Lines Composed a Few Miles above Tintern Abbey,* first published in *Lyrical Ballads,* and *Ode on Intimations of Immortality,* published in 1807 but written between 1802 and 1806, share a preoccupation with loss and with the saving power of memory. Both speak of personal experience, although the ode, a more formal poem, also generalizes to a hypothetical "we." Both insist that nature—the external world experienced through the senses and the containing pattern assumed beyond that world—offers the possibility of wisdom to combat the pain inherent in human growth.

But it would be a mistake to assume that these works exist to promulgate a doctrine of natural salvation, although some readers have considered the poems' "pantheism" (the belief that God pervades every part of His created universe) their most important aspect. Both poems evoke an intellectual and emotional process, not a conclusion; they sketch dramas of human development.

In *Tintern Abbey,* the speaker conveys his relief at returning to a sylvan scene that has been important to him in memory. His recollections of this natural beauty, he says, have helped sustain him in the confusion and weariness of city life; he thinks that they may also have encouraged him toward goodness and serenity. But this second suggestion, that memories of nature have a moral effect, is only hypothetical, qualified in the text by such words and phrases as "I trust" and "perhaps." Indeed, the poem's next section opens with explicit statement that this may "Be but a vain belief." True or false, though, the belief comforts the speaker, who then

recalls his more direct relation with nature in the past, when "The sounding cataract / Haunted me like a passion." He hopes, but cannot be sure, that his present
awareness of "The still, sad music of humanity" and of the great "presence" that
infuses nature compensates for what he has sacrificed in losing the immediacy of
youthful experience.

The last section of *Tintern Abbey* emphasizes still more that the speaker is struggling with depression over his sense of loss; he observes that the presence of his
"dearest Friend," his sister, would protect his "genial spirits" from decay even without
his faith in what he has learned. That sister now becomes the focus for his thoughts
about nature; he imagines her growth similar to his own, but perfected, and her power
of memory as able to contain not only the beauties of the landscape but his presence
as part of that landscape. The poem thus resolves itself with emphasis on a human
relationship, between the man and his sister, as well as on the importance of nature.
Its emotional power derives partly from its evocation of the *need* to believe in nature
as a form of salvation and of the process of development through which that need
manifests itself.

At about the same time that he wrote the *Ode on Intimations of Immortality*, Wordsworth composed his sonnet *The World Is Too Much with Us*:

> . . . we lay waste our powers
> Little we see in Nature that is ours;
> . . . we are out of tune.

Despite the rhapsodic tone that dominates the ode, it, too, reveals itself as a hard-won
act of faith, an effort to combat the view of the present world conveyed in the sonnet.

The ode opens with insistence on loss: "The things which I have seen I now can
see no more." The speaker feels grief; he tries to deny it because it seems at odds with
the harmony and joy of the natural world. Yet the effort fails: even natural beauty
speaks to him of what he no longer possesses. Stanzas V through VIII emphasize the
association of infancy with natural communion and the inevitable deprivation attending growth. In stanza IX, the speaker attempts to value what still remains to him: it's
all he has; he's grateful for it. In the concluding stanzas, however, he arrives at a new
revelation: now nature acquires value not as a form of unmixed ecstasy, but in connection with the experience of human suffering:

> Though nothing can bring back the hour
> Of splendour in the grass, of glory in the flower;
> We will grieve not, rather find
> Strength in what remains behind; . . .
> In the soothing thoughts that spring
> Out of human suffering . . .

It is "the human heart by which we live" that finally enables the poet to experience
the wonder of a flower, now become the source of "Thoughts that do often lie too
deep for tears."

The view that the processes of maturing involve giving up a kind of wisdom accessible only to children belongs particularly to the Romantic period, but most people
at least occasionally feel that in growing up they have left behind something they
would rather keep. Wordsworth's poetic expression of the effort to come to terms
with such feelings may remind his readers of barely noticed aspects of their own
experience.

PRONOUNCING GLOSSARY

The following list uses common English syllables and stress accents to provide rough equivalents of selected words whose pronunciation may be unfamiliar to the general reader.

Proteus: *proh'-tee-us*   Triton: *try'-tun*

Lines Composed a Few Miles above Tintern Abbey

On Revisiting the Banks of the Wye During a Tour, July 13, 1798

Five years have past; five summers, with the length
Of five long winters! and again I hear
These waters, rolling from their mountain-springs
With a soft inland murmur.—Once again
Do I behold these steep and lofty cliffs,   5
That on a wild secluded scene impress
Thoughts of more deep seclusion; and connect
The landscape with the quiet of the sky.
The day is come when I again repose
Here, under this dark sycamore, and view   10
These plots of cottage-ground, these orchard-tufts,
Which at this season, with their unripe fruits,
Are clad in one green hue, and lose themselves
'Mid groves and copses. Once again I see
These hedge-rows, hardly hedge-rows, little lines   15
Of sportive wood run wild: these pastoral farms,
Green to the very door; and wreaths of smoke
Sent up, in silence, from among the trees!
With some uncertain notice, as might seem
Of vagrant dwellers in the houseless woods,   20
Or of some Hermit's cave, where by his fire
The Hermit sits alone.

              These beauteous forms,
Through a long absence, have not been to me
As is a landscape to a blind man's eye:
But oft, in lonely rooms, and 'mid the din   25
Of towns and cities, I have owed to them,
In hours of weariness, sensations sweet,
Felt in the blood, and felt along the heart;
And passing even into my purer mind,
With tranquil restoration:—feelings too   30
Of unremembered pleasure: such, perhaps,
As have no slight or trivial influence
On that best portion of a good man's life,
His little, nameless, unremembered, acts
Of kindness and of love. Nor less, I trust,   35
To them I may have owed another gift,
Of aspect more sublime; that blessèd mood,
In which the burthen of the mystery,
In which the heavy and the weary weight
Of all this unintelligible world,   40
Is lightened:—that serene and blessèd mood,
In which the affections gently lead us on,—
Until, the breath of this corporeal frame
And even the motion of our human blood
Almost suspended, we are laid asleep   45
In body, and become a living soul:

While with an eye made quiet by the power
Of harmony, and the deep power of joy,
We see into the life of things.

                    If this
Be but a vain belief, yet, oh! how oft—   50
In darkness and amid the many shapes
Of joyless daylight; when the fretful stir
Unprofitable, and the fever of the world,
Have hung upon the beatings of my heart—
How oft, in spirit, have I turned to thee,   55
O sylvan Wye! thou wanderer thro' the woods,
How often has my spirit turned to thee!

    And now, with gleams of half-extinguished thought,
With many recognitions dim and faint,
And somewhat of a sad perplexity,   60
The picture of the mind revives again:
While here I stand, not only with the sense
Of present pleasure, but with pleasing thoughts
That in this moment there is life and food
For future years. And so I dare to hope,   65
Though changed, no doubt, from what I was when first
I came among these hills; when like a roe
I bounded o'er the mountains, by the sides
Of the deep rivers, and the lonely streams,
Wherever nature led: more like a man   70
Flying from something that he dreads, than one
Who sought the thing he loved. For nature then
(The coarser pleasures of my boyish days,
And their glad animal movements all gone by)
To me was all in all.—I cannot paint   75
What then I was. The sounding cataract
Haunted me like a passion: the tall rock,
The mountain, and the deep and gloomy wood,
Their colours and their forms, were then to me
An appetite; a feeling and a love,   80
That had no need of a remoter charm,
By thought supplied, nor any interest
Unborrowed from the eye.—That time is past,
And all its aching joys are now no more,
And all its dizzy raptures. Not for this   85
Faint I, nor mourn nor murmur; other gifts
Have followed; for such loss, I would believe,
Abundant recompense. For I have learned
To look on nature, not as in the hour
Of thoughtless youth; but hearing oftentimes   90
The still, sad music of humanity,
Nor harsh nor grating, though of ample power
To chasten and subdue. And I have felt
A presence that disturbs me with the joy
Of elevated thoughts; a sense sublime   95

Of something far more deeply interfused,
Whose dwelling is the light of setting suns,
And the round ocean and the living air,
And the blue sky, and in the mind of man:
A motion and a spirit, that impels   100
All thinking things, all objects of all thought,
And rolls through all things. Therefore am I still
A lover of the meadows and the woods,
And mountains; and of all that we behold
From this green earth; of all the mighty world   105
Of eye, and ear,—both what they half create,
And what perceive; well pleased to recognise
In nature and the language of the sense,
The anchor of my purest thoughts, the nurse,
The guide, the guardian of my heart, and soul   110
Of all my moral being.

                    Nor perchance,
If I were not thus taught, should I the more
Suffer my genial[1] spirits to decay:
For thou art with me here upon the banks
Of this fair river; thou my dearest Friend,   115
My dear, dear Friend; and in thy voice I catch
The language of my former heart, and read
My former pleasures in the shooting lights
Of thy wild eyes. Oh! yet a little while
May I behold in thee what I was once,   120
My dear, dear Sister! and this prayer I make,
Knowing that Nature never did betray
The heart that loved her; 'tis her privilege,
Through all the years of this our life, to lead
From joy to joy: for she can so inform   125
The mind that is within us, so impress
With quietness and beauty, and so feed
With lofty thoughts, that neither evil tongues,
Rash judgments, nor the sneers of selfish men,
Nor greetings where no kindness is, nor all   130
The dreary intercourse of daily life,
Shall e'er prevail against us, or disturb
Our cheerful faith, that all which we behold
Is full of blessings. Therefore let the moon
Shine on thee in thy solitary walk;   135
And let the misty mountain-winds be free
To blow against thee: and, in after years,
When these wild ecstasies shall be matured
Into a sober pleasure; when thy mind
Shall be a mansion for all lovely forms,   140
Thy memory be as a dwelling-place

1. Generative, creative.

For all sweet sounds and harmonies; oh! then,
If solitude, or fear, or pain, or grief
Should be thy portion, with what healing thoughts
Of tender joy wilt thou remember me,   145
And these my exhortations! Nor, perchance—
If I should be where I no more can hear
Thy voice, nor catch from thy wild eyes these gleams
Of past existence—wilt thou then forget
That on the banks of this delightful stream   150
We stood together; and that I, so long
A worshipper of Nature, hither came
Unwearied in that service; rather say
With warmer love—oh! with far deeper zeal
Of holier love. Nor wilt thou then forget   155
That after many wanderings, many years
Of absence, these steep woods and lofty cliffs,
And this green pastoral landscape, were to me
More dear, both for themselves and for thy sake!

Ode on Intimations of Immortality

From Recollections of Early Childhood

> The Child is father of the Man;
> And I could wish my days to be
> Bound each to each by natural piety.

I

There was a time when meadow, grove, and stream,
The earth, and every common sight,
        To me did seem
    Apparelled in celestial light,
The glory and the freshness of a dream.   5
It is not now as it hath been of yore;—
    Turn wheresoe'er I may,
        By night or day,
The things which I have seen I now can see no more.

II

    The Rainbow comes and goes,   10
    And lovely is the Rose;
    The Moon doth with delight
Look round her when the heavens are bare,
        Waters on a starry night
        Are beautiful and fair;   15
    The sunshine is a glorious birth;
    But yet I know, where'er I go,
That there hath past away a glory from the earth.

III

Now, while the birds thus sing a joyous song,
  And while the young lambs bound   20
    As to the tabor's sound,
To me alone there came a thought of grief:
A timely utterance gave that thought relief,
    And I again am strong:
The cataracts blow their trumpets from the steep;   25
No more shall grief of mine the season wrong;
I hear the Echoes through the mountains throng,
The Winds come to me from the fields of sleep,
    And all the earth is gay;
      Land and sea   30
  Give themselves up to jollity,
    And with the heart of May
Doth every Beast keep holiday;—
    Thou Child of Joy,
Shout round me, let me hear thy shouts, thou happy   35
  Shepherd-boy!

IV

Ye blessèd Creatures, I have heard the call
  Ye to each other make; I see
The heavens laugh with you in your jubilee;
  My heart is at your festival,   40
    My head hath its coronal,
The fulness of your bliss, I feel—I feel it all.
    Oh evil day! if I were sullen
    While Earth herself is adorning,
      This sweet May-morning,   45
    And the Children are culling
      On every side,
  In a thousand valleys far and wide,
  Fresh flowers; while the sun shines warm,
And the Babe leaps up on his Mother's arm:—   50
    I hear, I hear, with joy I hear!
    —But there's a Tree, of many, one,
A single Field which I have looked upon,
Both of them speak of something that is gone:
    The Pansy at my feet   55
    Doth the same tale repeat:
Whither is fled the visionary gleam?
Where is it now, the glory and the dream?

V

Our birth is but a sleep and a forgetting:
The Soul that rises with us, our life's Star,   60
    Hath had elsewhere its setting,
      And cometh from afar:

Not in entire forgetfulness,
   And not in utter nakedness,
But trailing clouds of glory do we come   65
   From God, who is our home:
Heaven lies about us in our infancy!
Shades of the prison-house begin to close
   Upon the growing Boy,
But He beholds the light, and whence it flows,   70
   He sees it in his joy;
The Youth, who daily farther from the east
   Must travel, still is Nature's Priest,
   And by the vision splendid
   Is on his way attended;   75
At length the Man perceives it die away,
And fade into the light of common day.

                    VI

Earth fills her lap with pleasures of her own;
Yearnings she hath in her own natural kind,
And, even with something of a Mother's mind,   80
   And no unworthy aim,
   The homely Nurse doth all she can
To make her Foster-child, her Inmate, Man,
   Forget the glories he hath known,
And that imperial palace whence he came.   85

                    VII

Behold the Child among his new-born blisses,
A six years' Darling of a pigmy size!
See, where 'mid work of his own hand he lies,
Fretted by sallies of his mother's kisses,
With light upon him from his father's eyes!   90
See, at his feet, some little plan or chart,
Some fragment from his dream of human life,
Shaped by himself with newly-learnèd art;
   A wedding or a festival,
   A mourning or a funeral;   95
   And this hath now his heart,
   And unto this he frames his song:
   Then will he fit his tongue
To dialogues of business, love, or strife;
   But it will not be long   100
   Ere this be thrown aside,
   And with new joy and pride
The little Actor cons another part;
Filling from time to time his "humorous stage"
With all the Persons, down to palsied Age,
That Life brings with her in her equipage;   105
   As if his whole vocation
   Were endless imitation.

VIII

Thou, whose exterior semblance doth belie
    Thy Soul's immensity;   110
Thou best Philosopher, who yet dost keep
Thy heritage, thou Eye among the blind,
That, deaf and silent, read'st the eternal deep,
Haunted for ever by the eternal mind,—
    Mighty Prophet! Seer blest!   115
    On whom those truths do rest,
Which we are toiling all our lives to find,
In darkness lost, the darkness of the grave;
Thou, over whom thy Immortality
Broods like the Day, a Master o'er a Slave,   120
A Presence which is not to be put by;
    [To whom the grave
Is but a lonely bed without the sense or sight
    Of day or the warm light,
A place of thought where we in waiting lie;][1]   125
Thou little Child, yet glorious in the might
Of heaven-born freedom on thy being's height,
Why with such earnest pains dost thou provoke
The years to bring the inevitable yoke,
Thus blindly with thy blessedness at strife?   130
Full soon thy Soul shall have her earthly freight,
And custom lie upon thee with a weight,
Heavy as frost, and deep almost as life!

IX

    O joy! that in our embers
    Is something that doth live,   135
    That nature yet remembers
    What was so fugitive!
The thought of our past years in me doth breed
Perpetual benediction: not indeed
For that which is most worthy to be blest;   140
Delight and liberty, the simple creed
Of Childhood, whether busy or at rest,
With new-fledged hope still fluttering in his breast—
    Not for these I raise
    The song of thanks and praise;   145
    But for those obstinate questionings
    Of sense and outward things,
    Fallings from us, vanishings;
    Blank misgivings of a Creature
Moving about in worlds not realized,   150
High instincts before which our mortal Nature
Did tremble like a guilty Thing surprised:

1. The lines within brackets were included in the *Ode* in the 1807 and 1815 editions of Wordsworth's poems but were omitted in the 1820 and subsequent editions, as a result of Coleridge's severe censure of them.

But for those first affections,
    Those shadowy recollections,
        Which, be they what they may,   155
Are yet the fountain-light of all our day,
Are yet a master-light of all our seeing;
    Uphold us, cherish, and have power to make
Our noisy years seem moments in the being
Of the eternal Silence: truths that wake,   160
        To perish never;
Which neither listlessness, nor mad endeavour,
        Nor Man nor Boy,
Nor all that is at enmity with joy,
Can utterly abolish or destroy!   165
    Hence in a season of calm weather
        Though inland far we be,
Our Souls have sight of that immortal sea
        Which brought us hither,
        Can in a moment travel thither,   170
And see the Children sport upon the shore,
And hear the mighty waters rolling evermore.

                        X

Then sing, ye Birds, sing, sing a joyous song!
    And let the young Lambs bound
    As to the tabor's sound!   175
We in thought will join your throng,
    Ye that pipe and ye that play,
    Ye that through your hearts to-day
    Feel the gladness of the May!
What though the radiance which was once so bright   180
Be now for ever taken from my sight,
    Though nothing can bring back the hour
Of splendour in the grass, of glory in the flower;
        We will grieve not, rather find
        Strength in what remains behind;   185
        In the primal sympathy
        Which having been must ever be;
        In the soothing thoughts that spring
        Out of human suffering;
        In the faith that looks through death, 190
In years that bring the philosophic mind.

                        XI

And O, ye Fountains, Meadows, Hills, and Groves,
Forebode not any severing of our loves!
Yet in my heart of hearts I feel your might;
I only have relinquished one delight   195
To live beneath your more habitual sway.
I love the Brooks which down their channels fret,
Even more than when I tripped lightly as they;

The innocent brightness of a new-born Day
    Is lovely yet;   200
The Clouds that gather round the setting sun
Do take a sober colouring from an eye
That hath kept watch o'er man's mortality;
Another race hath been, and other palms are won.
Thanks to the human heart by which we live,   205
Thanks to its tenderness, its joys, and fears,
To me the meanest flower that blows can give
Thoughts that do often lie too deep for tears.

Composed upon Westminster Bridge, September 3, 1802

Earth has not anything to show more fair:
Dull would he be of soul who could pass by
A sight so touching in its majesty;
This City now doth, like a garment, wear
The beauty of the morning; silent, bare,   5
Ships, towers, domes, theatres, and temples lie
Open unto the fields, and to the sky;
All bright and glittering in the smokeless air.
Never did sun more beautifully steep
In his first splendour, valley, rock, or hill;   10
Ne'er saw I, never felt, a calm so deep!
The river glideth at his own sweet will:
Dear God! the very houses seem asleep;
And all that mighty heart is lying still!

The World Is Too Much with Us

The world is too much with us; late and soon,
Getting and spending, we lay waste our powers:
Little we see in Nature that is ours;
We have given our hearts away, a sordid boon![1]
This Sea that bares her bosom to the moon,   5
The winds that will be howling at all hours,
And are up-gathered now like sleeping flowers;
For this, for everything, we are out of tune;
It moves us not.—Great God! I'd rather be
A Pagan suckled in a creed outworn;   10
So might I, standing on this pleasant lea,
Have glimpses that would make me less forlorn;
Have sight of Proteus[2] rising from the sea;
Or hear old Triton[3] blow his wreathèd horn.

We are harmed by our inability to be more by nature

We don't love what we have

---

1. Gift. _Sordid:_ refers to the act of giving the heart away.   2. An old man of the sea who, in the _Odyssey,_ could assume a variety of shapes.   3. A sea deity, usually represented as blowing on a conch shell.

DOROTHY WORDSWORTH
1771–1855

The era inaugurated by Jean-Jacques Rousseau encouraged self-reflection and the development of a highly articulated language of feeling. Among the writers about themselves who flourished during the period of Romanticism, Dorothy Wordsworth occupies a unique position. Her voluminous journals include relatively little open discussion of her personal feelings. Instead, she perfects a technique of indirect self-revelation through intense concentration on details of the world outside her.

In her youth, Dorothy Wordsworth was separated from her four brothers after the death of their mother when Dorothy was seven years old. In 1795, however, her brother William was lent a house in Dorset, where she joined him, acting as home-maker. From that time on, she lived with William, even after he married in 1802. Like William, she became close to Samuel Taylor Coleridge and accompanied the two men to Germany in 1798–99. As the journals reveal, she led a quiet domestic life. After a serious illness in 1829, she was an invalid for the rest of her life.

The Grasmere Journals, from which the selections printed here are taken, record the texture of Dorothy's daily existence with William at Dove Cottage, Grasmere, in the English Lake District. The two of them had moved there in 1799, taking pleasure in the first home they had owned. They lived close to Grasmere Lake, in a landscape of hills, mountains, woods, and water of striking beauty, through which they walked almost every day. They also created a garden, transplanting plants from the wild. William wrote poems; Dorothy copied them out for him. She made bread and pies, sewed, read aloud and to herself. She enjoyed her association with their neighbors as well as the more intense friendship with Coleridge and with the Hutchinson sisters—Mary, whom William married, and Sara, with whom Coleridge, already married and the father of two sons, fell disastrously in love. The journals report these facts in considerable detail.

But they do far more. Wordsworth responded to what she saw with the eye of a poet. She noted the precise aspects of flowers; the names of birds; and the look of the clouds on a summer day, of the fleece on sheep, of the moon in its varying appearances. Seldom does she write in any detail directly of her own emotions. The characteristic sequence of the *Journals* printed here includes only one moment of sharp, open self-revelation: "I shall be beloved—I want no more." Unlike Rousseau, Wordsworth does not appear to consider herself remarkable. But she uses the minute particulars of what she sees as an indirect means of expressing feeling, and the *Journals* convey an emotional life of subtle complexity. Thus she describes crows flying: "We watched the crows at a little distance from us become white as silver as they flew in the sunshine, and when they went still further they looked like shapes of water passing over the green fields." The precision of the observation and the brilliance of the image ("shapes of water") express the passion of the watcher, for whom powerful meaning inheres in the natural world.

Consciously, Dorothy wrote her journals, as she did so much else, for the sake of her brother. William read them and used them as data for his poetry. Dorothy writes of daffodils that they "tossed and reeled and danced and seemed as if they verily laughed with the wind." William, two years later, describes "a jocund company" of daffodils in *I Wandered Lonely as a Cloud*:

> Ten thousand saw I at a glance,
> Tossing their heads in sprightly dance.

Dorothy had provided him with raw material. But the power of her writing does not depend on her brother's conversion of it to verse. In its own right, it expresses a subtle and compelling sensibility.

That sensibility emerges not only in her muted but powerful responses to nature, but in her expressions of feeling about her brother. When he is away, she thinks of him constantly. The sight of an apple that he has bitten rouses her emotion: "O the Darling! here is one of his bitten apples! I can hardly find in my heart to throw it into the fire." When he marries Mary Hutchinson, Dorothy is not surprised, and she declares herself pleased. But her account of the wedding day suggests powerful contending emotions. She gives her brother his wedding ring—which she herself has worn all night. She does not attend the wedding but waits for the news of its completion. When she sees Mary's brothers coming up the walk to bring that news, she "could stand it no longer" and flings herself on the bed, "where I lay in stillness, neither hearing or seeing any thing, till Sara came upstairs to me and said 'They are coming.' " At this point she feels "forced" from the bed; she rushes forward, "faster than my strength could carry me till I met my beloved William and fell upon his bosom."

The intensity of this sequence of responses and the absence of any attempt to explain them makes the passage extraordinarily compelling. In a sense, it stands as a centerpiece to the journal, not because we need William Wordsworth to interpret Dorothy Wordsworth, but because she so clearly needs him to interpret herself. Understanding her life as organized around her brother provides her with the psychic freedom that enables her to react so richly to all she sees in the human and the natural world.

The *Journals* make no ostentatious claim of profundity, but they evoke a consistent vision of unity between inanimate and animate nature, including humankind. One of Wordsworth's characteristic rhetorical devices is the sentence composed largely of miscellaneous nouns, their conjunction evoking a sense of pattern created by the observer but also inherent in the universe. For example: "Lasses spreading dung, a dog's barking now and then, cocks crowing, birds twittering, the snow in patches at the top of the highest hills, yellow palms, purple and green twigs on the birches, ashes with their glittering spikes quite bare." Utterly unpretentious, the lucid prose brings the world alive.

Little effort has been made here to annotate the names of local people and places in the anthologized selections. They have scanty importance for a modern reader, except through what Wordsworth has made of them.

The source of the text is Dorothy Wordsworth, *The Grasmere Journals*, ed. Pamela Woolf (1991).

PRONOUNCING GLOSSARY

The following list uses common English syllables and stress accents to provide rough equivalents of selected words whose pronunciation may be unfamiliar to the general reader.

Eusemere: *yooz'-meer*

Grasmere: *gras'-meer*

Loughrigg: *luf'-rig*

Wytheburn: *waith'-burn*

From The Grasmere Journals

[This selection from the *Journals* begins in mid-February 1802.]

Sunday 14th February

A fine morning the sun shines but it has been a hard frost in the night. There are some little snowdrops that are afraid to pop their white heads quite out, and a few blossoms of hepatica that are half starved.[1] William left me at work altering some passages of the Pedlar,[2] and went into the orchard—the fine day pushed him on to resolve and as soon as I had read a letter to him which I had just received from Mrs. Clarkson he said he would go to Penrith, so Molly was dispatched for the horse—I worked hard, got the backs pasted the writing finished, and all quite trim. I wrote to Mrs. Clarkson and put up some letters for Mary H—and off he went in his blue Spenser[3] and a pair of *new* pantaloons fresh from London. He turned back when he had got as far as Frank's to ask if he had his letters safe, then for some apples—then fairly off. We had money to borrow for him.——It was a pleasant afternoon. I ate a little bit of cold mutton without laying cloth and then sate over the fire reading Ben Jonson's Penshurst,[4] and other things. Before sunset I put on my shawl and walked out. The snow-covered mountains were spotted with rich sunlight, a palish buffish color. The roads were very dirty,[5] for though it was a keen frost the sun had melted the snow and water upon them. I stood at Sara's gate & when I came in view of Rydale I cast a long look upon the mountains beyond. They were very white but I concluded that Wm would have a very safe passage over Kirkstone, and I was quite easy about him.

Sunday 14th February 1802

See the morning former book. After dinner a little before sunset I walked out. About 20 yards above Glowworm Rock I met a carman, a high[land]er I suppose, with 4 carts, the first 3 belonging to himself, the last evidently to a man and his family who had joined company with him and who I guessed to be potters. The carman was cheering his horses and talking to a little lass about 10 years of age who seemed to make him her companion. She ran to the wall and took up a large stone to support the wheel of one of his carts and ran on before with it in her arms to be ready for him. She was a beautiful creature and there was something uncommonly impressive in the lightness and joyousness of her manner. Her business seemed to be all pleasure—pleasure in her own motions—and the man looked at her as if he too was pleased and spoke to her in the same tone in which he spoke to his horses. There was a wildness in her whole figure, not the wildness of a mountain lass but a *road* lass, a traveler from her birth, who had wanted neither food nor clothes. Her mother followed the last cart with a lovely child, perhaps about a year old, at her back and a good-looking girl about 15 years old walked beside her. All the children were like the mother. She had a very fresh complexion, but she was blown[6] with fagging up the hill with the steepness of the hill and the Bairn[7] that she carried. Her husband was helping the horse to drag the cart up by pushing it with his shoulder. I got tea when I reached home and read German till about 9 o'clock. Then Molly went away and I wrote to Coleridge. Went to bed at about 12 o'clock. I slept in Wm's bed, and I slept badly, for my thoughts were full of William.

1. Frozen, withered.   2. Probably the Wordsworth poem published as *The Ruined Cottage*, which later, in altered form, became part of Book I of *The Excursion*.   3. Short jacket.   4. A long poem (1616) in praise of the quality of life provided by a country house.   5. Muddy   6. Exhausted.   7. Child.

Monday 15th February 1802

I was starching small linen all the morning. It snowed a good deal and was terribly cold. After dinner it was fair, but I was obliged to run all the way to the foot of the White Moss to get the least bit of warmth into me. I found a letter from C—he was much better—this was very satisfactory but his letter was not an *answer* to William's which I expected. A letter from Annette.[8] I got tea when I reached home and then set on to reading German. I wrote part of a letter to Coleridge, went late to bed and slept badly.

* * *

Thursday [4th]

Before we had quite finished breakfast Calvert's man brought the horses for Wm. We had a deal to do to shave—pens to make—poems to put in order for writing, to settle the dress pack up [et cetera et cetera.] The man came before the pens were made and he was obliged to leave me with only two— Since he has left me (at half past 11) it is now 2 I have been putting the drawers into order, laid by his clothes which we had thrown here and there and everywhere, filed two months' newspapers and got my dinner 2 boiled eggs and 2 apple tarts. I have set Molly on to clear the garden a little, and I myself have helped. I transplanted some snowdrops—The bees are busy— Wm has a rich bright day—It was hard frost in the night—The robins are singing sweetly—Now for my walk. I *will* be busy, I *will* look well and be well when he comes back to me. O the Darling! here is one of his bitten apples! I can hardly find in my heart to throw it into the fire. I must wash myself, then off—I walked round the two lakes crossed the stepping stones at Rydale foot. Sate down where we always sit I was full of thoughts about my darling. Blessings on him. I came home at the foot of our own lake under Loughrigg. They are making sad ravages in the woods—Benson's Wood is going and the wood above the river. The wind has blown down a small fir tree on the rock that terminates John's path—I suppose the wind of Wednesday night. I read German after my return till tea time. After tea I worked and read the LB,[9] enchanted with the Idiot Boy. Wrote to Wm then went to bed. It snowed when I went to bed.

Friday [5th]

First walked in the garden and orchard—a frosty sunny morning. After dinner I gathered mosses in Easedale. I saw before me sitting in the open field upon his sack of rags the old ragman that I know—his coat is of scarlet in a thousand patches his breeches knees were untied—the Breeches have been given him by someone—he has a round hat pretty good, small crowned but large rimmed. When I came, to me he said Is there a brigg[1] yonder that'll carry me ower t'watter? He seemed half stupid. When I came home Molly had shook the carpet and cleaned everything upstairs. When I see her so

---

8. Annette Vallon, the French woman with whom William Wordsworth had an affair during an early trip to France.   9. *Lyrical Ballads*, containing poems by William Wordsworth and Samuel Taylor Coleridge (1798). "The Idiot Boy" is one of Wordsworth's poems in the collection.   1. Bridge.

happy in her work and exulting in her own importance I often think of that affecting expression which she made use of to me one evening lately—talking of her good luck in being in this house, "Aye Mistress them 'at's low laid would have been a proud creature could they but have [seen] where I is now fra what they thought mud be my Doom."—I was tired when I reached home, I sent Molly Ashburner to Rydale. No letters! I was sadly mortified. I expected one fully from Coleridge—wrote to William. Read the LB, got into sad thoughts, tried at German but could not go on—Read LB.—Blessings on that brother of mine! Beautiful new moon over Silver How.

* * *

Thursday [18th]

A very fine morning the sun shone but it was far colder than yesterday. I felt myself weak, and William charged me not to go to Mrs. Lloyds—I seemed indeed, to myself unfit for it but when he was gone I thought I would get the visit over if I could—so I ate a beefsteak thinking it would strengthen me so it did, and I went off—I had a very pleasant walk. Rydale vale was full of life and motion. The wind blew briskly and the lake was covered all over with bright silver waves that were there each the twinkling of an eye, then others rose up and took their place as fast as they went away. The rocks glittered in the sunshine, the crows and the ravens were busy, and the thrushes and little Birds sang—I went through the fields, and sate half an hour afraid to pass a cow. The cow looked at me and I looked at the cow and whenever I stirred the cow gave over eating. I was not very much tired when I reached Lloyds, I walked in the garden. Charles is all for agriculture. Mrs. Ll. in her kindest way. A parcel came in from Birmingham, with Lamb's play for us and for C. They came with me as far as Rydale. As we came along Ambleside vale in the twilight—it was a grave evening—there was something in the air that compelled me to serious thought—the hills were large, closed in by the sky. It was nearly dark when I parted from the Lloyds that is, night was come on and the moon was overcast. But as I climbed Moss the moon came out from behind a mountain mass of black clouds—O the unutterable darkness of the sky and the earth below the moon! And the glorious brightness of the moon itself! There was a vivid sparkling streak of light at this end of Rydale water but the rest was very dark and Loughrigg fell and Silver How were white and bright as if they were covered with hoar frost. The moon retired again and appeared and disappeared several times before I reached home. Once there was no moonlight to be seen but upon the island house and the promontory of the island where it stands, "That needs must be a holy place" [et cetera—et cetera]. I had many many exquisite feelings when I saw this lowly building in the waters among the dark and lofty hills, with that bright soft light upon it—it made me more than half a poet. I was tired when I reached home I could not sit down to reading and tried to write verses but alas! I gave up expecting William and went soon to bed. Fletcher's carts came home late.

* * *

Wednesday 14th

William did not rise till dinner time. I walked with Mrs. C. I was ill out of spirits—disheartened. Wm and I took a long walk in the rain.

Thursday 15th

It was a threatening misty morning—but mild. We set off after dinner from Eusemere—Mrs. Clarkson went a short way with us but turned back. The wind was furious and we thought we must have returned. We first rested in the large boat-house, then under a furze bush opposite Mr. Clarkson's, saw the plough going in the field. The wind seized our breath; the lake was rough. There was a boat by itself floating in the middle of the bay below Water Millock—We rested again in the Water Millock lane. The hawthorns are black and green, the birches here and there greenish but there is yet more of purple to be seen on the twigs. We got over into a field to avoid some cows—people working, a few primroses by the roadside, woodsorrel flowers, the anemone, scentless violets, strawberries, and that starry yellow flower which Mrs. C calls pile wort.[2] When we were in the woods beyond Gowbarrow park we saw a few daffodils close to the water side, we fancied that the lake had floated the seeds ashore and that the little colony had so sprung up—But as we went along there were more and yet more and at last under the boughs of the trees, we saw that there was a long belt of them along the shore, about the breadth of a country turnpike road. I never saw daffodils so beautiful; they grew among the mossy stones about and about them, some rested their heads upon these stones as on a pillow for weariness and the rest tossed and reeled and danced and seemed as if they verily laughed with the wind that blew upon them over the lake, they looked so gay, ever glancing, ever changing. This wind blew directly over the lake to them. There was here and there a little knot and a few stragglers a few yards higher up but they were so few as not to disturb the simplicity and unity and life of that one busy highway—We rested again and again. The bays were stormy and we heard the waves at different distances and in the middle of the water like the sea—Rain came on, we were wet when we reached Luffs' but we called in. Luckily all was chearless and gloomy so we faced the storm—we *must* have been wet if we had waited—put on dry clothes at Dobson's. I was very kindly treated by a young woman, the landlady looked sour but it is her way. She gave us a goodish supper, excellent ham and potatoes. We paid 7 /[3] when we came away. William was sitting by a bright fire when I came downstairs. He soon made his way to the library piled up in a corner of the window. He brought out a volume of Enfield's Speaker, another miscellany, and an odd volume of Congreve's[4] plays. We had a glass of warm rum and water—we enjoyed ourselves and wished for Mary.[5] It rained and blew when we went to bed. N.B. deer in Gowbarrow park like to skeletons.

---

2. I.e., the lesser celandine.   **3.** I.e., 7 shillings, approximately $28. In a subsequent note, Wordsworth wrote that they had paid 1 shilling more than they should have,   **4.** William Congreve (1670–1729), Restoration dramatist, best known for his witty comedies. *Speaker: The Speaker; or, Miscellaneous Pieces Selected from the Best English Writers, and Disposed under Proper Heads, for the Improvement of Youth in Reading and Speaking* (1778), compiled by William Enfield.   **5.** Mary Hutchinson (1770–1859), whom William later married.

Friday 16th April (Good Friday)

When I undrew my curtains in the morning, I was much affected by the beauty of the prospect and the change. The sun shone, the wind had passed away, the hills looked chearful. The river was very bright as it flowed into the lake. The church rises up behind a little knot of rocks, the steeple not so high as an ordinary three story house. Bees, in a row in the garden under the wall. After Wm had shaved we set forward. The valley is at first broken by little rocky woody knolls that make retiring places, fairy valleys in the vale, the river winds along under these hills travelling not in a bustle but not slowly to the lake. We saw a fisherman in the flat meadow on the other side of the water; he came towards us and threw his line over the two-arched bridge. It is a bridge of a heavy construction, almost bending inwards in the middle, but it is grey and there is a look of ancientry in the architecture of it that pleased me. As we go on the vale opens out more into one vale with somewhat of a cradle bed. Cottages with groups of trees on the side of the hills. We passed a pair of twin children two years old—and sate on the next bridge which we crossed, a single arch, we rested again upon the turf and looked at the same bridge—we observed arches in the water occasioned by the large stones sending it down in two streams—a sheep came plunging through the river, stumbled up the bank and passed close to us, it had been frightened by an insignificant little dog on the other side, its fleece dropped a glittering shower under its belly—primroses by the roadside, pile wort that shone like stars of gold in the sun, violets, strawberries, retired and half buried among the grass. When we came to the foot of Brothers' Water I left William sitting on the bridge and went along the path on the right side of the lake through the wood—I was delighted with what I saw—the water under the boughs of the bare old trees, the simplicity of the mountains and the exquisite beauty of the path. There was one grey cottage. I repeated "The Glowworm"[6] as I walked along—I hung over the gate, and thought I could have stayed for ever. When I returned I found William writing a poem descriptive of the sights and sounds we saw and heard. There was the gentle flowing of the stream, the glittering lively lake, green fields without a living creature to be seen on them, behind us, a flat pasture with forty-two cattle feeding, to our left the road leading to the hamlet, no smoke there, the sun shone on the bare roofs. The people were at work ploughing, harrowing and sowing—lasses spreading dung, a dog's barking now and then, cocks crowing, birds twittering, the snow in patches at the top of the highest hills, yellow palms, purple and green twigs on the birches, ashes[7] with their glittering spikes quite bare. The hawthorn a bright green with black stems under, the oak and the moss of the oak glossy. We then went on, passed two sisters at work, *they first passed us*, one with two pitch forks in her hand. The other had a spade. We had some talk with them. They laughed aloud after we were gone, perhaps half in wantonness, half boldness. William finished his poem before we got to the foot of Kirkstone. There were hundreds of cattle in the vale. There we ate our dinner. The walk up Kirkstone was very interesting. The becks[8] among the rocks were all alive—Wm showed me the little mossy streamlet which he had before loved when he saw its bright green track in the snow.

---

6. *Among All Lovely Things My Love Had Been.*   7. I.e., ash trees.   8. Creeks, small streams.

The view above Ambleside, very beautiful. There we sate and looked down on the green vale. We watched the crows at a little distance from us become white as silver as they flew in the sunshine, and when they went still further they looked like shapes of water passing over the green fields. The whitening of Ambleside Church is a great deduction from the beauty of it seen from this point. We called at the Luffs', the Boddingtons there, did not go in and went round by the fields. I pulled off, my stockings intending to wade the beck but I was obliged to put them on and we climbed over the wall at the bridge. The post[9] passed us. No letters! Rydale Lake was in its own evening brightness, the islands and points distinct. Jane Ashburner came up to us when we were sitting upon the wall—we rode in her cart to Tom Dawson's— all well. The garden looked pretty in the half moonlight half daylight. As we went up the vale of Brothers' Water more and more cattle feeding, one hundred of them.

Saturday 17th

A mild warm rain. We sate in the garden all the morning. William dug a little. I transplanted a honey suckle. The lake was still, the sheep on the island reflected in the water, like the grey deer we saw in Gowbarrow park. We walked after tea by moonlight. I had been in bed in the afternoon and William had slept in his chair. We walked towards Rydale first then backwards and forwards below Mr. Olliff's. The village was beautiful in the moonlight—Helm Crag we observed very distinct. The dead hedge round Benson's field bound together at the top by an interlacing of ash sticks which made a chain of silver when we faced the moon—a letter from C, and also from S. H.[1] I saw a robin chacing a scarlet butterfly this morning.

Sunday 18th

I lay in bed late. Again a mild grey morning with rising vapours we sate in the orchard—William wrote the poem on the robin and the butterfly. I went to drink tea at Luff's but as we did not dine till six o'clock it was late. It was mist and small[2] rain all the way but very pleasant. William met me at Rydale—Aggy[3] accompanied me thither. We sate up late. He met me with the conclusion of the poem of the robin.[4] I read it to him in bed. We left out some lines.

Monday 19th

A mild rain, very warm. Wm worked in the garden, I made pies and bread. After dinner the mist cleared away and sun shone. William walked to Luff's. I was not very well and went to bed. Wm came home pale and tired. I could not rest when I got to bed.

Tuesday 20th

A beautiful morning, the sun shone—William wrote a conclusion to the poem of the butterfly, "I've watch'd you now a full half-hour." I was quite

9. Mailman.   1. Sara Hutchinson, sister of Mary. C: Samuel Taylor Coleridge (1772–1834), the Wordsworths' fellow poet and close friend.   2. Light.   3. Agnes Fisher, a friend.   4. *The Redbreast and the Butterfly*.

out of spirits and went into the orchard—When I came in he had finished the poem. We sate in the orchard after dinner, it was a beautiful afternoon. The sun shone upon the level fields and they grew greener beneath the eye— houses, village all chearful, people at work. We sate in the orchard and repeated "The Glowworm" and other poems. Just when William came to a well or a trough which there is in Lord Darlington's Park he began to write that poem of the glow-worm, not being able to ride[5] upon the long trot— interrupted in going through the Town of Staindrop. Finished it about two miles and a half beyond Staindrop—he did not feel the jogging of the horse while he was writing but when he had done he felt the effect of it and his fingers were cold with his gloves. His horse fell with him on the other side of St. Helen's, Auckland.—So much for "The Glowworm": It was written coming from Middleham on Monday, April 12th, 1802. On Tuesday 20th when we were sitting after tea Coleridge came to the door. I started Wm with my voice—C came up palish but I afterwards found he looked well. William was not well and I was in low spirits.

Wednesday 21st

William and I sauntered a little in the garden. Coleridge came to us and repeated the verses he wrote to Sara—I was affected with them and was on the whole, not being well, in miserable spirits. The sunshine—the green fields and the fair sky made me sadder; even the little happy sporting lambs seemed but sorrowful to me. The pile wort spread out on the grass a thousand shining stars, the primroses were there and the remains of a few daffodils. The well which we cleaned out last night is still but a little muddy pond, though full of water. I went to bed after dinner, could not sleep, went to bed again. Read Ferguson's life[6] and a poem or two—fell asleep for five minutes and awoke better. We got tea. Sate comfortably in the evening. I went to bed early.

Thursday 22nd

A fine mild morning—we walked into Easedale. The sun shone. Coleridge talked of his plan of sowing the laburnum in the woods—The waters were high for there had been a great quantity of rain in the night. I was tired and sate under the shade of a holly tree that grows upon a rock—I sate there and looked down the stream. I then went to the single holly behind that single rock in the field and sate upon the grass till they came from the waterfall. I saw them there and heard Wm flinging stones into the river whose roaring was loud even where I was. When they returned William was repeating the poem "I have thoughts that are fed by the Sun."[7] It had been called to his mind by the dying away of the stunning of the waterfall when he came behind a stone. When we had got into the vale a heavy rain came on. We saw a family of little children sheltering themselves under a wall before the rain came on, they sate in a row making a canopy for each other of their clothes. The servant lass was planting potatoes near them. Coleridge changed his

---

5. A mistake for "write." William could write only when the horse was walking. 6. David Irving, *Poetical Works of Robert Fergusson with the Life of the Author* (1800). 7. A poem that William had recently written; he never published it.

clothes—we were all wet—Wilkinson[8] came in while we were at dinner. Coleridge and I after dinner drank black currants and water.

Friday 23rd April 1802

It being a beautiful morning we set off at eleven o'clock intending to stay out of doors all the morning. We went towards Rydale and before we got to Tom Dawson's we determined to go under Nab Scar.[9] Thither we went. The sun shone and we were lazy. Coleridge pitched upon several places to sit down upon but we could not be all of one mind respecting sun and shade so we pushed on to the foot of the scar. It was very grand when we looked up, very stony, here and there a budding tree. William observed that the umbrella yew tree that breasts the wind had lost its character as a tree and had become something like to solid wood. Coleridge and I pushed on before. We left William sitting on the stones feasting with silence—and C and I sate down upon a rock seat—a couch it might be under the bower of William's eglantine, Andrew's broom.[1] He was below us and we could see him—he came to us and repeated his poems while we sate beside him upon the ground. He had made himself a seat in the crumbly ground. After we had lingered long looking into the vales—Ambleside vale with the copses, the village under the hill and the green fields—Rydale with a lake all alive and glittering yet but little stirred by breezes, and our own dear Grasmere first making a little round lake of nature's own with never a house never a green field—but the copses and the bare hills, enclosing it and the river flowing out of it. Above rose the Coniston Fells in their own shape and colour—not man's hills but all for themselves, the sky and the clouds and a few wild creatures. C went to search for something new. We saw him climbing up towards a rock, he called us and we found him in a bower, the sweetest that was ever seen—the rock on one side is very high and all covered with ivy which hung loosely about and bore bunches of brown berries. On the other side it was higher than my head. We looked down upon the Ambleside vale that seemed to wind away from us, the village *lying* under the hill. The fir tree island was reflected beautifully—we now first saw that the trees are planted in rows. About this bower there is mountain ash, common ash, yew tree, ivy, holly, hawthorn, mosses and flowers, and a carpet of moss—Above at the top of the rock there is another spot—it is scarce a bower, a little parlour, one not *enclosed* by walls but shaped out for a resting place by the rocks and the ground rising about it. It had a sweet moss carpet—We resolved to go and plant flowers in both these places tomorrow. We wished for Mary and Sara. Dined late. After dinner Wm and I worked in the garden. C read. A letter from Sara.

Saturday 24th

A very wet day. William called me out to see a waterfall behind the barberry tree—We walked in the evening to Rydale—Coleridge and I lingered

---

8. Probably the Reverend Joseph Wilkinson (1764–1831).   9. Rock or crag (obsolete). Nab Scar was a large local crag.   1. Allusion to two of William's poems from 1800. In *The Waterfall and the Eglantine*, an eglantine grows too close to a waterfall and is swept away in the wintertime. In *The Oak and the Broom*, narrated by the shepherd Andrew, an oak is struck by lightning in a storm while the smaller, carefree broom plant survives.

behind—C stopped up the little runner[2] by the road side to make a lake. We all stood to look at Glowworm Rock—a primrose that grew there and just looked out on the road from its own sheltered bower. The clouds moved as William observed in one regular body like a multitude in motion, a sky all clouds over, not one cloud. On our return it broke a little out and we saw here and there a star. One appeared but for a moment in a lake—pale blue sky.

Sunday 25th April

After breakfast we set off with Coleridge towards Keswick. Wilkinson over-took us near the Potters' and interrupted our discourse. C got into a gig with Mr. Beck, and drove away from us. A shower came on but it was soon over—we spent the morning in the orchard. Read the Prothalamium[3] of Spenser—walked backwards and forwards. Mr. Simpson[4] drank tea with us. I was not well before tea. Mr. S sent us some quills by Molly Ashburner and his brother's book.[5] The Luffs called at the door.

Monday 26th

I copied Wm's poems for Coleridge. Letters from Peggy[6] and Mary H—wrote to Peggy and Coleridge. A terrible rain and wind all day. Went to bed at twelve o'clock.

Tuesday 27th

A fine morning. Mrs. Luff called. I walked with her to the boat-house—William met me at the top of the hill with his fishing-rod in his hand. I turned with him and we sate on the hill looking to Rydale. I left him intending to join him but he came home, and said his line would not stand the pulling—he had had several bites. He sate in the orchard, I made bread. Miss Simpson called. I walked with her to Goans. When I came back I found that he and John Fisher had cleaned out the well—John had sodden[7] about the bee-stand. In the evening Wm began to write "The Tinker."[8] We had a letter and verses from Coleridge.

Wednesday 28th April

A fine sunny but coldish morning. I copied the Prioress's tale.[9] Wm was in the orchard—I went to him—he worked away at his poem, though he was ill and tired—I happened to say that when I was a child I would not have

2. Rivulet.   3. A poem celebrating an aristocratic marriage (1596), by Edmund Spenser (1522–1599).
4. Probably Bartholomew Simpson, an old man at this time.   5. *Science Revived; or, The Vision of Alfred: A Poem in Eight Books* (1802), by the Reverend Joseph Simpson.   6. Once a servant of the Wordsworths; her last name is unknown.   7. Laid sod.   8. Unpublished.   9. William had translated Geoffrey Chaucer's tale into modern English.

pulled a strawberry blossom. I left him and wrote out the Manciple's Tale.[1] At dinner-time he came in with the poem of "Children gathering flowers"[2]— but it was not quite finished and it kept him long off his dinner. It is now done, he is working at "The Tinker," he promised me he would get his tea and do no more but I have got mine an hour and a quarter and he has scarcely begun his. I am not quite well—We have let the bright sun go down without walking—now a heavy shower comes on and I guess we shall not walk at all—I wrote a few lines to Coleridge. Then we walked backwards and forwards between our house and Olliff's. We talked about T Hutchinson and Bell Addison.[3] William left me sitting on a stone. When we came in we corrected the Chaucers but I could not finish them tonight, went to bed.

Thursday 29th

A beautiful morning. The sun shone and all was pleasant. We sent off our parcel to Coleridge by the waggon. Mr. Simpson heard the cuckow today. Before we went out, after I had written down "The Tinker" which William finished this morning, Luff called. He was very lame, limped into the kitchen—he came on a little pony. We then went to Johns Grove, sate a while at first. Afterwards William lay, and I lay in the trench under the fence—he with his eyes shut and listening to the waterfalls and the birds. There was no one waterfall above another—it was a sound of waters in the air—the voice of the air. William heard me breathing and rustling now and then but we both lay still, and unseen by one another—he thought that it would be as sweet thus to lie so in the grave, to hear the *peaceful* sounds of the earth and just to know that one's dear friends were near. The lake was still; there was a boat out. Silver how reflected with delicate purple and yellowish hues as I have seen spar[4]—Lambs on the island and running races together by the half dozen in the round field near us. The copses green*ish*, hawthorn green.—Came home to dinner then went to Mr. Simpson. We rested a long time under a wall. Sheep and lambs were in the field—cottages smoking. As I lay down on the grass, I observed the glittering silver line on the ridges of the backs of the sheep, owing to their situation respecting the sun—which made them look beautiful but with something of strangeness, like animals of another kind—as if belonging to a more splendid world. Met old Mr. S at the door—Mrs. S poorly—I got mullens and pansies—I was sick and ill[5] and obliged to come home soon. We went to bed immediately—I slept up stairs. The air coldish where it was felt somewhat frosty.

Friday April 30th

We came into the orchard directly after breakfast, and sate there. The lake was calm—the sky cloudy. We saw two fishermen by the lake side. William began to write the poem of the Celandine.[6] I wrote to Mary H—sitting on

---

1. Another of Chaucer's *Canterbury Tales* that William had translated.   2. Later published as *Foresight*.
3. Isabella Addison (1784–1807), who married the Hutchinsons' cousin John Monkhouse. Tom Hutchinson (1773–1849), brother of Sara and Mary.   4. A crystalline mineral that shines in the sun.
5. Nauseated and generally did not feel well. *Muellens:* mulleins, plants of the snapdragon family.   6. *To the Lesser Celandine.*

the fur gown. Walked backwards and forwards with William—he repeated his poem to me—then he got to work again and would not give over[7]—he had not finished his dinner till five o'clock. After dinner we took up the fur gowns into The Hollins[8] above. We found a sweet seat and thither we will often go. We spread the gown, put on each a cloak and there we lay—William fell asleep—he had a bad head ache owing to his having been disturbed the night before with reading C's letter which Fletcher had brought to the door— I did not sleep but I lay with half shut eyes, looking at the prospect as in a vision almost I was so resigned to it—Loughrigg Fell was the most distant hill, then came the lake slipping in between the copses and above the copse the round swelling field, nearer to me a wild intermixture of rocks, trees, and slacks[9] of grassy ground.—When we turned the corner of our little shelter we saw the church and the whole vale. It is a blessed place. The birds were about us on all sides—skobbys,[1] robins, bullfinches. Crows now and then flew over our heads as we were warned by the sound of the beating of the air above. We stayed till the light of day was going and the little birds had begun to settle their singing—But there was a thrush not far off that seemed to sing louder and clearer than the thrushes had sung when it was quite day. We came in at eight o'clock, got tea. Wrote to Coleridge, and I wrote to Mrs. Clarkson[2] part of a letter. We went to bed at twenty minutes past eleven with prayers that Wm might sleep well.

Saturday May 1st

Rose not till half past eight—a heavenly morning—as soon as breakfast was over we went into the garden and sowed the scarlet beans about the house. It was a clear sky, a heavenly morning. I sowed the flowers. William helped me. We then went and sate in the orchard till dinnertime, it was very hot. William wrote "The Celandine." We planned a shed, for the sun was too much for us. After dinner we went again to our old resting place in the Hollins under the rock. We first lay under a holly where we saw nothing but the holly tree and a budding elm mossed with[3] and the sky above our heads. But that holly tree had a beauty about it more than its own, knowing as we did where we were. When the sun had got low enough we went to the rock shade—Oh the overwhelming beauty of the vale below—greener than green. Two ravens flew high high in the sky and the sun shone upon their bellys and their wings long after there was none of his light to be seen but a little space on the top of Loughrigg Fell. We went down to tea at eight o'clock— had lost the poem[4] and returned after tea. The landscape was fading, sheep and lambs quiet among the rocks. We walked towards King's[5] and backwards and forwards. The sky was perfectly cloudless. N.B. is it often so? three solitary stars in the middle of the blue vault, one or two on the points of the high hills. Wm wrote "The Celandine" second part tonight. Heard the cuckow today this first of May.

---

7. Stop.   8. A wood full of holly trees near the Wordsworths' house.   9. Hollows, dips in the ground.
1. Or scobbies, a north-country name for chaffinches, which are small birds.   2. Catherine Clarkson (1772–1856), a close neighbor and friend.   3. A word has apparently been left out here.   4. Not the one William had been writing in the morning but the idea for a second poem on the celandine: *Pleasures newly found are sweet.* The idea returned to him in the evening.   5. Thomas King (1772–1831), who had a house in Grasmere, not far away.

Sunday 2nd May

Again a heavenly morning—Letter from Coleridge.

Tuesday May 4th

William had slept pretty well and though he went to bed nervous and jaded
in the extreme he rose refreshed. I wrote "The Leech Gatherer"[6] for him
which he had begun the night before and of which he wrote several stanzas
in bed this Monday morning. It was very hot, we called at Mr. Simpson's
door as we passed but did not go in. We rested several times by the way, read
and repeated "The Leech gatherer." We were almost melted before we were
at the top of the hill. We saw Coleridge on the Wytheburn side of the water,
he crossed the beck to us. Mr. Simpson was fishing there. William and I ate
a luncheon, then went on towards the waterfall. It is a glorious wild solitude
under that lofty purple crag. It stood upright by itself. Its own self and its
shadow below, one mass—all else was sunshine. We went on further. A bird
at the top of the crags was flying round and round and looked in thinness
and transparency, shape and motion, like a moth. We climbed the hill but
looked in vain for a shade except at the foot of the great waterfall, and there
we did not like to stay on account of the loose stones above our heads. We
came down and rested upon a moss covered rock, rising out of the bed of
the river. There we lay, ate our dinner and stayed there till about four o'clock
or later—Wm and C repeated and read verses. I drank a little brandy and
water and was in heaven. The stags horn[7] is very beautiful and fresh springing
upon the fells. Mountain ashes, green. We drank tea at a farm house. The
woman had not a pleasant countenance, but was civil enough. She had a
pretty boy a year old whom she suckled. We parted from Coleridge at Sara's
Crag after having looked at the letters which C carved in the morning. I
kissed them all. Wm deepened the T with C's penknife.[8] We sate afterwards
on the wall, seeing the sun go down and the reflections in the still water. C
looked well and parted from us chearfully, hopping up upon the side stones.
On the Rays we met a woman with two little girls, one in her arms, the other
about four years old walking by her side, a pretty little thing, but half starved.
She had on a pair of slippers that had belonged to some gentleman's child,
down at the heels, but it was not easy to keep them on—but, poor thing!
young as she was, she walked carefully with them. Alas too young for such
cares and such travels—The mother when we accosted her told us that her
husband had left her and gone off with another woman and how she "*pursued*" them. Then her fury kindled and her eyes rolled about. She changed
again to tears. She was a Cockermouth woman—thirty years of age a child
at Cockermouth when I was—I was moved and gave her a shilling, I believe
6d[9] more than I ought to have given. We had the crescent moon with the
"auld moon in her arms"[1]—We rested often:—always upon the bridges.
Reached home at about ten o'clock. The Lloyds had been here in our

6. Later published as *Resolution and Independence*. Wrote: i.e., wrote out, copied. 7. A type of moss.
8. Coleridge had carved their initials in the rock. The *T* that William deepened is Coleridge's middle initial.
9. A sixpence or half a shilling; perhaps roughly equivalent to two dollars now. 1. *The Ballad of Sir
Patrick Spens.*

absence. We went soon to bed. I repeated verses to William while he was in bed—he was soothed and I left him. "This is the Spot"[2] over and over again.

Wednesday 5th May 1802

A very fine morning rather cooler than yesterday. We planted three-fourths of the bower. I made bread—we sate in the orchard. The thrush sang all day as he always sings. I wrote to the Hutchinsons and to Coleridge, packed off *Thalaba*.[3] William had kept off work till near bedtime when we returned from our walk—then he began again and went to bed very nervous—we walked in the twilight and walked till night came on—the moon had the old moon in her arms but not so plain to be seen as the night before. When we went to bed it was a boat without the circle.[4] I read "The Lover's Complaint"[5] to Wm in bed and left him composed.

6th May Thursday 1802

A sweet morning. We have put the finishing stroke to our bower and here we are sitting in the orchard. It is one o'clock. We are sitting upon a seat under the wall which I found my brother building up when I came to him with his apple—he had intended that it should have been done before I came. It is a nice cool shady spot. The small birds are singing—Lambs bleating, cuckow calling—The thrush sings by fits, Thomas Ashburner's axe is going quietly (without passion) in the orchard—Hens are cackling, flies humming, the women talking together at their doors—Plumb and pear trees are in blossom, apple trees greenish—the opposite woods green, the crows are caw-ing. We have heard ravens. The ash trees are in blossom, birds flying all about us. The stitchwort is coming out, there is one budding lychnis.[6] The primroses are passing their prime. Celandine, violets and wood sorrel for ever more—little geranium and pansies on the wall. We walked in the eve-ning to Tail End to enquire about hurdles[7] for the orchard shed and about Mr. Luff's flower—The flower dead—no hurdles. I went to look at the falling wood—Wm also, when he had been at Benson's went with me. They have left a good many small oak trees but we dare not hope that they are all to remain. The ladies are come to Mr. Gell's cottage; we saw them as we went and their light when we returned. When we came in we found a magazine and review and a letter from Coleridge with verses to Hartley[8] and Sara H. We read the review etc. The moon was a perfect boat, a silver boat, when we were out in the evening. The birch tree is all over green in *small* leaf. More light and elegant than when it is full out. It bent to the breezes as if for the love of its own delightful motions. Sloe thorns and hawthorns in the hedges.

Friday 7th May

William had slept uncommonly well so, feeling himself strong, he fell to work at "The Leech Gatherer"—he wrote hard at it till dinner time, then he gave

---

2. Lines that William had written two years earlier; he published them only in part.   3. Robert Southey, *Thalaba the Destroyer* (1801), an epic poem in twelve books.   4. I.e., the moon appeared thus.   5. By Shakespeare.   6. Cuckoo flower or ragged robin. *Stitchwort*: stellaria, a flower with large white blossoms; it was supposed to alleviate stitches, or pains in the side.   7. Withes and stakes for enclosures. 8. Coleridge's son. The poem is *Do you ask what the birds say?*

over tired to death—he had finished the poem. I was making Derwent's frocks.[9] After dinner we sate in the orchard. It was a thick hazy dull air. The thrush sang almost continually—the little birds were more than usually busy with their voices. The sparrows are now full fledged. The nest is so full that they lie upon one another, they sit quietly in their nest with closed mouths. I walked to Rydale after tea, which we drank by the kitchen fire. The evening very dull—a terrible kind of threatening brightness at sunset above Easedale. The sloe thorn beautiful in the hedges, and in the wild spots higher up among the hawthorns. No letters. William met me—he had been digging in my absence and cleaning the well. We walked up beyond Lewthwaites. A very dull sky, coolish crescent moon now and then. I had a letter brought me from Mrs. Clarkson. While we were walking in the orchard I observed the sorrel leaves opening at about nine o'clock—William went to bed tired with thinking about a poem.

Saturday Morning May 8th 1802

We sowed the scarlet beans in the orchard. I read _Henry V_[1] there—William lay on his back on the seat. "Wept, For names, sounds paths delights and duties lost"—Taken from a poem upon Cowley's wish to retire to the plantations, read in the review.[2] I finished Derwent's frocks—after dinner William added a step to the orchard steps.

Sunday Morning May 9th 1802

The air considerably colder today but the sun shone all day—William worked at "The Leech Gatherer" almost incessantly from morning till tea-time. I copied "The Leech-Gatherer" and other poems for Coleridge—I was oppressed and sick at heart for he wearied himself to death. After tea he wrote two stanzas in the manner of Thomson's _Castle of Indolence_[3]—and was tired out. Bad news of Coleridge.

Monday May 10th

A fine clear morning but coldish—William is still at work though it is past ten o'clock—he will be tired out I am sure—My heart fails in me—he worked a little at odd things, but after dinner he gave over—an affecting letter from Mary H. We sate in the orchard before dinner. Old Joyce spent the day. I wrote to Mary H. Mrs. Jameson and Miss Simpson called just when William was going to bed at eight o'clock. I wrote to Coleridge, sent off reviews and poems, went to bed at twelve o'clock. William did not sleep till three o'clock.

Tuesday May 11th

A cool air. William finished the stanzas[4] about C and himself—he did not go out today. Miss. Simpson came in to tea which was lucky enough for it

---

9. Garments for Coleridge's infant son.   1. By Shakespeare.   2. From an anonymous poem, published in the March 1802 _Monthly Review_, that imagines the seventeenth-century poet Abraham Cowley on an American plantation.   3. A poem in Spenserian stanzas (1748) by the Scottish poet James Thomson (1700–1748).   4. William wrote them in the manner of _The Castle of Indolence_.

interrupted his labours. I walked with her to Rydale—the evening cool—the moon only now and then to be seen—the lake purple as we went—primroses still in abundance. William did not meet me, he completely finished his poems. I finished Derwent's frocks. We went to bed at twelve o'clock. Wm pretty well he looked very well, he complains that he gets cold in his chest.

Wednesday 12th

A sunshiny but coldish morning—we walked into Easedale and returned by George Rownson's and the lane. We brought home heckberry blossom, crab blossom—the anemone nemorosa—marsh marygold—speedwell, that beautiful blue one the colour of the blue-stone or glass used in jewellery, with its beautiful pearl-like chives—anemones are in abundance and still the dear dear primroses violets in beds, pansies in abundance, and the little celandine. I pulled a branch of the taller celandine. Butterflies of all colours—I often see some small ones of a pale purple lilac or emperor's eye colour[5] something of the colour of that large geranium which grows by the lake side. Wm observed the beauty of Geordy Green's house. We see it from our orchard. Wm pulled ivy with beautiful berries—I put it over the chimney piece—sate in the orchard the hour before dinner, coldish. We have now dined. My head aches—William is sleeping in the window. In the evening we were sitting at the table, writing, when we were rouzed by Coleridge's voice below—he had walked, looked palish but was not much tired. We sate up till one o'clock all together. Then William went to bed and I sate with C in the sitting room (where he slept) till quarter past two o'clock. Wrote to MH.

13th May Thursday 1802

The day was very cold, with snow showers. Coleridge had intended going in the morning to Keswick but the cold and showers hindered him. We went with him after tea as far as the plantations by the roadside descending to Wytheburn—he did not look very well when we parted from him.—We sate an hour at Mr. Simpson's.

Friday May 14th 1802

A very cold morning—hail and snow showers all day. We went to Brothers' Wood, intending to get plants and to go along the shore of the lake to the foot. We did go a part of the way, but there was no pleasure in stepping along that difficult sauntering road in this ungenial weather. We turned again and walked backwards and forwards in Brothers' Wood. William teased himself with seeking an epithet for the cuckow. I sate a while upon my last summer's seat, the mossy stone—William's unemployed beside me, and the space between where Coleridge has so often lain. The oak trees are just putting forth yellow knots of leaves. The ashes with their flowers passing away and leaves coming out. The blue hyacinth is not quite full blown—gowans[6] are coming out—marsh marygolds in full glory—the little star plant a star without a flower. We took home a great load of gowans and planted

---

5. I.e., the color of the purple emperor butterfly.   6. Daisylike field flowers.

them in the cold about the orchard. After dinner I worked[7] bread then came and mended stockings beside William. He fell asleep. After tea I walked to Rydale for letters. It was a strange night. The hills were covered over with a slight covering of hail or snow, just so as to give them a hoary winter look with the black rocks—The woods looked miserable, the coppices green as grass which looked quite unnatural and they seemed half shrivelled up as if they shrunk from the air. O thought I! what a beautiful thing God has made winter to be by stripping the trees and letting us see their shapes and forms. What a freedom does it seem to give to the storms! There were several new flowers out but I had no pleasure in looking at them—I walked as fast as I could back again with my letter from S. H. which I skimmed over at Tommy Fleming's. Met Wm at the top of White Moss. We walked a little beyond Olliff's—near ten when we came in. Wm and Molly had dug the ground and planted potatoes in my absence. We wrote to Coleridge—sent off a letter to Annette,[8] bread and frocks to the C's—Went to bed at half past eleven, William very nervous—after he was in bed haunted with altering "The Rainbow."[9]

Saturday Morning [15th]

It is now quarter past ten and he is not up. Miss Simpson called when I was in bed—I have been in the garden. It looks fresh and neat in spite of the frost. Molly tells me they had thick ice on a jug at their door last night.

Saturday 15th

A very cold and cheerless morning. I sate mending stockings all the morning. I read in Shakespeare. William lay very late because he slept till last night. It snowed this morning just like Christmas. We had a melancholy letter from Coleridge just at bed-time—. It distressed me very much and I resolved upon going to Keswick[1] the next day.

[The following is written on the blotting-paper opposite this date:]

S T Coleridge

Dorothy Wordsworth   William Wordsworth

Mary Hutchinson   Sara Hutchinson

William Coleridge Mary

Dorothy Sara

16th May

1802

John Wordsworth[2]

Sunday 16th

William was at work all the morning. I did not go to Keswick. A sunny cold frosty day a snow-shower at night. We were a good while in the orchard in the morning.

7. Kneaded.   8. Annette Vallon (1766–1841), a Frenchwoman from Blois, who had borne William an illegitimate daughter after his visit to France in 1791–92.   9. Probably *My heart leaps up*, composed March 26, 1802.   1. Where Coleridge lived.   2. Dorothy and William's brother (1772–1805).

Monday 17th May

William was not well—he went with me to Wytheburn Water. He left me in a post chaise. Hail showers, snow and cold attacked me. The people were graving peats[3] under Nadel Fell.—A lark and thrush singing near Coleridge's house—Barcrofts[4] there. A letter from MH.

Tuesday 18th May

Terribly cold. Coleridge not well. Froude called, Wilkinsons called, I not well. C and I walked in the evening in the Garden warmer in the evening wrote to M and S.[5]

Wednesday 19th May 1802

A grey morning—not quite so cold. C and I set off at half past nine o'clock. Met William, near the six mile stone. We sate down by the road side, and then went to Wytheburn Water. Longed to be at the island, sate in the sun, Coleridge's bowels bad, mine also. We drank tea at John Stanley's—the evening cold and clear, a glorious light on Skiddaw. I was tired—brought a cloak down from Mr. Simpsons. Packed up books for Coleridge then got supper and went to bed.

Thursday 20th May

A frosty clear morning. I lay in bed late—William got to work. I was somewhat tired. We sate in the orchard sheltered all the morning. In the evening there was a fine rain. We received a letter from Coleridge, telling us that he wished us not to go to Keswick.

Friday 21st May

A very warm gentle morning—a little rain. Wm wrote two sonnets on Buonaparte after I had read Milton's sonnets to him. In the evening he went with Mr. Simpson with Borwick's boat to gather ling[6] in Bainriggs. I planted about the well—was much heated and I think I caught cold.

Saturday 22nd May

A very hot morning, a hot wind as if coming from a sand desert. We met Coleridge, he was sitting under Sara's rock when we reached him—he turned with us—we sate a long time under the wall of a sheep-fold, had some interesting melancholy talk about his private affairs. We drank tea at a farm house. The woman was very kind. There was a woman with three children travelling from Workington to Manchester. The woman served them liberally. Afterwards she said that she never suffered any to go away without a trifle "sec as we have." The woman at whose house we drank tea the last

3. Carving peat moss for use as fuel.   4. The Barcroft family lived in Keswick.   5. Mary and Sara Hutchinson.   6. Heather.

time was rich and senseless—she said "she never served any but their own poor"—C came home with us. We sate some time in the orchard. Then they came in to supper—mutton chops and potatoes. Letters from S & MH.

Sunday [23rd]

I sate with C in the orchard all the morning. William was very nervous. I was ill in the afternoon, took laudanum. We walked in Bainriggs after tea, saw the juniper—umbrella shaped.—C went to S & M Points,[7] joined us on White Moss.

Monday 24th May 1802

A very hot morning. We were ready to go off with Coleridge, but foolishly sauntered and Miss Taylor and Miss Stanley called. William and Coleridge and I went afterwards to the top of the Rays. I was ill and left them, lay down at Mrs. Simpsons. I had sent off a letter to Mary by C. I wrote again and to C, then went to bed. William slept not till five o'clock.

Tuesday 25th

Very hot—I went to bed after dinner—We walked in the evening. Papers and short note from C—again no sleep for Wm.

Wednesday 26th

I was very unwell—went to bed again after dinner. We walked a long time backwards and forwards between Johns Grove and the lane upon the turf—a beautiful night, not cloudless, it has never been so since May day.

Thursday 27th

I was in bed all day—very ill. William wrote to Rd, Cʳ and Cook.[8] Wm went after tea into the orchard. I slept in his bed—he slept downstairs. He slept better than before.

Friday 28th

I was much better than yesterday, though poorly. Wm tired himself with hammering at a passage. I was out of spirits. After dinner he was better and I grew better. We sate in the orchard. The sky cloudy, the air sweet and cool. The young bullfinches in their party coloured[9] raiment bustle about among the blossoms and poize themselves like wire dancers or tumblers, shaking the twigs and dashing off the blossoms. There is yet one primrose in the orchard—the stitchwort is fading—the wild columbines are coming into beauty—the vetches are in abundance blossoming and seeding. That pretty little waxy looking dial-like yellow flower, the speedwell, and some others

7. Rocks that they had named for Mary and Sara Hutchinson.   8. Their brothers Richard (the eldest, 1768–1816), a lawyer, and Christopher (1774–1846), a clergyman. Richard Cooke was Richard Wordsworth's legal associate.   9. Or particolored; showing different colors.

whose names I do not yet know. The wild columbines are coming into beauty—some of the gowans fading. In the garden we have lilies and many other flowers. The scarlet beans are up in crowds. It is now between eight and nine o'clock. It has rained sweetly for two hours and a half—the air is very mild. The heckberry blossoms are dropping off fast, almost gone—barberries are in beauty—snowballs coming forward—May roses blossoming.

Saturday 29th

I was much better. I made bread and a wee rhubarb tart and batter pudding for William. We sate in the orchard after dinner William finished his poem on Going for Mary. I wrote it out—I wrote to Mary H, having received a letter from her in the evening. A sweet day. We nailed up the honeysuckles, and hoed the scarlet beans.

Sunday 30th May 1802

I wrote to Mrs. Clarkson. It was a clear but cold day. The Simpsons called in the evening. I had been obliged to go to bed before tea and was unwell all day. Gooseberries a present from Peggy Hodgson. I wrote to my Aunt Cookson.

Monday 31st

I was much better. We sate out all the day. Mary Jameson dined. I wrote out the poem on "Our Departure" which he seemed to have finished. In the evening Miss Simpson brought us a letter from MH and a complimentary and critical letter to W from John Wilson of Glasgow post paid.[1] I went a little way with Miss S. My tooth broke today. They will soon be gone. Let that pass. I shall be beloved—I want no more.

Tuesday [1st]

A very sweet day, but a sad want of rain. We went into the orchard before dinner after I had written to MH. Then on to Mr. Olliff's intakes—we found some torn birds' nests. The columbine was growing upon the rocks, here and there a solitary plant—sheltered and shaded by the tufts and bowers of trees. It is a graceful slender creature, a female seeking retirement and growing freest and most graceful where it is most alone. I observed that the more shaded plants were always the tallest—a short note and gooseberries from Coleridge.

Wednesday 2nd June 1802

In the morning we observed that the scarlet beans were drooping in the leaves in great numbers owing, we guess to an insect. We sate a while in the orchard—then we went to the old carpenter's about the hurdles. Yesterday an old man called, a grey-headed man, above seventy years of age; he said

1. It was customary for the recipients of letters to pay the postage.

he had been a soldier, that his wife and children had died in Jamaica. He had a beggar's wallet over his shoulders, a coat of shreds and patches altogether of a drab colour—he was tall and though his body was bent he had the look of one used to have been upright. I talked a while to him, and then gave him a piece of cold bacon and a penny—said he "You're a fine woman!" I could not help smiling. I suppose he meant "You're a kind woman!" Afterwards a woman called travelling to Glasgow. After dinner William was very unwell. We went into Frank's field, crawled up the little glen and planned a seat, then went to Mr. Olliff's Hollins and sate there—found a beautiful shell-like purple fungus in Frank's field. After tea we walked to Butterlip How and backwards and forwards there. All the young oak tree leaves are dry as powder. A cold south wind portending rain. After we came in we sate in deep silence at the window—I on a chair and William with his hand on my shoulder. We were deep in silence and love, a blessed hour. We drew to the fire before bed-time and ate some broth for our suppers. I ought to have said that on Tuesday evening, namely June 1st, we walked upon the turf near John's Grove. It was a lovely night. The clouds of the western sky reflected a saffron light upon the upper end of the lake—all was still—We went to look at Rydale. There was an alpine fire-like red upon the tops of the mountains. This was gone when we came in view of the lake. But we saw the lake in a new and most beautiful point of view between two little rocks, and behind a small ridge that had concealed it from us.—This White Moss a place made for all kinds of beautiful works of art and nature, woods and valleys, fairy valleys and fairy tairns,[2] miniature mountains, alps above alps. Little John Dawson[3] came past us from the woods with a huge stick over his shoulder.

Thursday 3rd June 1802

A very fine rain. I lay in bed till ten o'clock. William much better than yesterday—We walked into Easedale, sheltered in a cow-house. Came home wet—the cuckow sang and we watched the little birds as we sate at the door of the cow-house—the oak copses are brown as in autumn, with the late frosts—scattered over with green trees, birches or hazels—the ashes are coming into full leaf—some of them injured. We came home quite wet. We have been reading the Life and some of the writings of poor Logan[4] since dinner. "And everlasting Longings for the lost." It is an affecting line. There are many affecting lines and passages in his poems. William is now sleeping—with the window open, lying on the window seat. The thrush is singing. There are I do believe a thousand buds on the honeysuckle tree, all small and far from blowing[5] save one that is retired behind the twigs close to the wall and as snug as a bird's nest. John's rose tree is very beautiful blended with the honeysuckle.

On Tuesday evening when we were among the rocks we saw in the woods what seemed to be a man, resting or looking about him. He had a piece of wood near him. William was on before me when we returned, and as I was going up to him, I found that this supposed man was John Dawson. I spoke

2. Or tarns, pools. 3. A three-year-old child. 4. John Logan (1748–1788), a poet whose life William and Dorothy read in *The Works of the British Poets with Prefaces, Biographical and Critical* (1795), ed. Robert Anderson. 5. Blossoming.

to him and I suppose he thought I asked him what my brother had said to him before, for he replied, "*William* asks me how my head is"—Poor fellow!—he says it is worse and worse and he walks as if he were afraid of putting his body in motion.

Yesterday morning William walked as far as the Swan with Aggy Fisher. She was going to attend upon Goan's dying infant. She said "There are many heavier crosses than the death of an infant," and went on "There was a woman in this vale who buried four grown-up children in one year, and I have heard her say when many years were gone by that she had more pleasure in thinking of these four than of her living children, for as children get up and have families of their own their duty to their parents 'wears out and weakens.' She could trip lightly by the graves of those who died when they were young—with a light step, as she went to church on a Sunday."

Thursday June 3rd

We walked while dinner was getting ready up into Mr. King's Hollins. I was weak and made my way down alone, for Wm took a difficult way. After dinner we walked upon the turf path—a showery afternoon. A very affecting letter came from MH while I was sitting in the window reading Milton's "Penseroso"[6] to William. I answered this letter before I went to bed.

Friday June 4th

It was a very sweet morning, there had been much rain in the night. William had slept miserably—but knowing this I lay in bed while he got some sleep but was much disordered, he shaved himself then we went into the orchard—dined late. In the evening we walked on our favorite path. Then we came in and sate in the orchard. The evening was dark and warm—a tranquil night—I left William in the orchard. I read "Mother Hubbard's Tale"[7] before I went to bed.

Saturday 5th

A fine showery morning. I made both pies and bread, but we first walked into Easedale, and sate under the oak trees upon the mossy stones. There were one or two slight showers. The gowans were flourishing along the banks of the stream. The strawberry flower (geum)[8] hanging over the brook—all things soft and green.—In the afternoon William sate in the orchard. I went there, was tired and fell asleep. Mr. Simpson drank tea, Mrs. Smith called with her daughter. We walked late in the evening upon our path. We began the letter to John Wilson.

Sunday 6th June 1802

A showery morning. We were writing the letter to John Wilson when Ellen came—Molly at Goan's child's funeral. After dinner I walked into John

6. *Il Penseroso* (1645), by John Milton. 7. *Prosopopoeia; or, Mother Hubbard's Tale*, by Edmund Spenser (1591). 8. A small rosaceous plant.

Fisher's intake with Ellen. She brought us letters from Coleridge, Mrs. Clarkson and Sara Hutchinson. William went out in the evening and sate in the orchard, it was a showery day. In the evening there was one of the heaviest showers I ever remember.

Monday June 7th

I wrote to Mary H. this morning, sent the C Indolence poem. Copied the letter to John Wilson, and wrote to my brother Richard and Mrs. Coleridge. In the evening I walked with Ellen to Butterlip How and to George Mackareth's for the horse—it was a very sweet evening—there was the cuckow and the little birds—the copses still injured, but the trees in general looked most soft and beautiful in tufts. William was walking when we came in—he had slept miserably for two nights past so we all went to bed soon. I went with Ellen in the morning to Rydale Falls. Letters from Annette, Mary H and Cook.

Tuesday June 8th

Ellen and I rode to Windermere. We had a fine sunny day, neither hot nor cold. I mounted the horse at the quarry—we had no difficulties or delays but at the gates. I was enchanted with some of the views. From the High Ray the view is very delightful, rich and festive, water and wood, houses, groves, hedgerows, green fields, and mountains—white houses large and small—We passed two or three nice looking statesmen's houses. Mr. Curwen's shrubberies looked pitiful enough under the native trees. We put up our horses, ate our dinner by the water-side and walked up to the station. Then we went to the island, walked round it, and crossed the lake with our horse in the ferry. The shrubs have been cut away in some parts of the island. I observed to the boatman that I did not think it improved—he replied—"We think it is for one could hardly see the house before." It seems to me to be, however, no better than it was. They have made no natural glades, it is merely a lawn with a few miserable young trees standing as if they were half starved. There are no sheep no cattle upon these lawns. It is neither one thing or another—neither *natural* nor wholly cultivated and artificial which it was before, and that great house! Mercy upon us! If it *could* be concealed it would be well for all who are pained to see the pleasantest of earthly spots deformed by man. But it *cannot* be covered. Even the tallest of our old oak trees would not reach to the top of it. When we went into the boat there were two men standing at the landing place. One seemed to be about sixty, a man with a jolly red face—he looked as if he might have lived many years in Mr. Curwen's house. He wore a blue jacket and trowsers, as the people who live close by Windermere particularly at the places of chief resort in affectation, I suppose. He looked significantly at our boatman just as we were rowing off and said "Thomas mind you take off the directions off that cask. You know what I mean. It will serve as a blind for them, *you* know. It was a blind business both for you and the coachman and me and all of us. Mind you take off the directions—A wink's as good as a nod with some folks"—and then he turned round looking at his companion with such an air of self-satisfaction and deep insight into unknown things!—I could hardly help laughing outright at him. The laburnums blossom freely at the island and in the shrubberies on the shore—they are blighted everywhere else. Roses of various sorts were out. The brooms were in full glory everywhere, "veins of gold"[9] among the copses. The hawthorns in the valley fading away—beautiful upon the hills. We reached home at three o'clock. After tea William went out and walked and wrote that poem,[1]

"The sun has long been set" etc.—

He first went up to G Mackareths with the horse. Afterwards he walked on our own path and wrote the lines, he called me into the orchard and there repeated them to me—he then stayed there till eleven o'clock.

Wednesday June 9th

Wm slept ill. A soaking all-day rain. We should have gone to Mr. Simpson's to tea but we walked up after tea. Lloyds called. The hawthorns on the mountain sides like orchards in blossom. Brought rhubarb down. It rained hard. Ambleside Fair. I wrote to Christopher and MH.

Thursday June 10th

I wrote to Mrs. Clarkson and Luff—went with Ellen to Rydale. Coleridge came in with a sack-full of books etc. and a branch of mountain ash. He had been attacked by a cow—he came over by Grisdale—a furious wind. Mr. Simpson drank tea. William very poorly—we went to bed latish. I slept in sitting room.

Friday June 11th

A wet day. William had slept very ill. Wm and C walked out—I went to bed after dinner not well. I was tired with making beds cooking etc.—Molly being very ill.

Saturday June 12th

A rainy morning. C set off before dinner. We went with him to the Rays but it rained so we went no further—sheltered under a wall—He would be sadly wet for a furious shower came on just when we parted.—We got no dinner, but gooseberry pie to our tea. I baked both pies and bread, and walked with William first on our own path but it was too wet there, next over the rocks to the road, and backward and forward, and last of all up to Mr. King's. Miss Simpson and Robert had called. Letters from Sara and Annette.

Sunday June 13th

A fine morning. Sunshiny and bright, but with rainy clouds. William had slept better—but not well—he has been altering the poem to Mary this

---

9. From William's poem *To Joanna* (1800).   1. The poem was published in 1807, with the first line as its title.

morning, he is now washing his feet. I wrote out poems for our journey and I wrote a letter to my Uncle Cookson. Mr. Simpson came when we were in the orchard in the morning and brought us a beautiful drawing which he had done. In the evening we walked first on our own path. There we walked a good while—It was a silent night. The stars were out by ones and twos but no cuckow, no little birds, the air was not warm, and we have observed that since Tuesday 8th when William wrote, "The sun has long been set," that we have had no birds singing after the evening is fairly set in. We walked to our new view of Rydale, but it put on a sullen face. There was an owl hooting in Bainriggs. Its first halloo was so like a human shout that I was surprized when it made its second call, tremulous and lengthened out, to find that the shout had come from an owl. The full moon (not quite full) was among a company of steady island clouds, and the sky bluer about it than the natural sky blue. William observed that the full moon above a dark fir grove is a fine image of the descent of a superior being. There was a shower which drove us into John's grove before we had quitted our favorite path—we walked upon John's path before we went to view Rydale. We went to bed immediately on our return home.

Monday June 14th

I was very unwell—went to bed before I drank my tea—was sick and afterwards almost asleep when Wm brought me a letter from Mary which he read to me sitting by the bed-side—Wm wrote to Mary and Sara about "The Leech Gatherer." I wrote to both of them in one and to Annette, to Coleridge also. I was better after tea.—I walked with Wm—when I had put up my parcel on our own path—we were driven away by the horses that go on the commons. Then we went to look at Rydale, walked a little in the fir grove, went again to the top of the hill and came home—a mild and sweet night—Wm stayed behind me. I threw him the cloak out of the window, the moon overcast, he sate a few minutes in the orchard, came in sleepy, and hurried to bed—I carried him his bread and butter.

Tuesday 15th

A sweet grey mild morning the birds sing soft and low—William has not slept all night. It wants only ten minutes of ten and he is in bed yet. After William rose we went and sate in the orchard till dinner time. We walked a long time in the evening upon our favorite path—the owls hooted, the night-hawk sang to itself incessantly, but there were no little birds, no thrushes. I left William writing a few lines about the night-hawk and other images of the evening, and went to seek for letters—none were come.—We walked backwards and forwards a little, after I returned to William, and then up as far as Mr. King's. Came in. There was a basket of lettuces, a letter from MH about the delay of mine and telling of one she had sent by the other post, one from Wade and one from Sara to C—William did not read them—MH growing fat.

Wednesday 16th

We walked towards Rydale for letters—met Frank Baty with the expected one from Mary. We went up into Rydale woods and read it there, we sate near an old wall which fenced a hazel grove, which Wm said was exactly like the filbert grove at Middleham. It is a beautiful spot, a sloping or rather steep piece of ground, with hazels growing "tall and erect,"[2] in clumps at distances almost seeming regular as if they had been planted. We returned to dinner. I wrote to Mary after dinner while Wm sate in the orchard. Old Mr. Simpson drank tea with us. When Mr. S was gone I read my letter to William, speaking to Mary about having a cat. I spoke of the little birds keeping us company— and William told me that that very morning a bird had perched upon his leg—he had been lying very still and had watched this little creature, it had come under the bench where he was sitting and then flew up to his leg, he thoughtlessly stirred himself to look further at it and it flew onto the apple tree above him. It was a little young creature, that had just left its nest, equally unacquainted with man and unaccustomed to struggle against storms and winds. While it was upon the apple tree the wind blew about the stiff boughs and the bird seemed bemazed and not strong enough to strive with it. The swallows come to the sitting-room window as if wishing to build but I am afraid they will not have courage for it, but I believe they will build at my room window. They twitter and make a bustle and a little chearful song hanging against the panes of glass, with their soft white bellies close to the glass, and their forked fish-like tails. They swim round and round and again they come.—It was a sweet evening. We first walked to the top of the hill to look at Rydale and then to Butterlip How—I do not now see the brownness that was in the coppices. The lower hawthorn blossoms passed away, those on the hills are a faint white. The wild guelder rose is coming out, and the wild roses. I have seen no honeysuckles yet except our own one nestling and a tree of the yellow kind at Mrs. Townley's the day I went with Ellen to Windermere. Foxgloves are now frequent, the first I saw was that day with Ellen, and the first ripe strawberries—a letter from Coleridge. I read the first Canto of *The Fairy Queen*[3] to William. William went to bed immediately.

Thursday 17th

William had slept well. I took castor oil and lay in bed till twelve o'clock. William injured himself with working a little.—When I got up we sate in the orchard, a sweet mild day. Miss Hudson called. I went with her to the top of the hill. When I came home I found William at work, attempting to alter a stanza in the poem on our going for Mary which I convinced him did not need altering—We sate in the house after dinner. In the evening walked on our favorite path, a short letter from Coleridge. William added a little to the ode[4] he is writing.

Friday June 18th

When we were sitting after breakfast, William about to shave, Luff came in. It was a sweet morning. He had rode over the fells—he brought news about Lord Lowther's intention to pay all debts[5] etc. and a letter from Mr. Clarkson.

---

2. From William's poem *Nutting* (1800).   3. *The Faerie Queene* (1590, 1596), by Edmund Spenser.
4. *Ode: Intimations of Immortality*, completed in 1804.   5. Sir James Lowther, earl of Lonsdale (1736–1802), had owed £4,500 to the Wordsworths' father for legal services. A lawsuit to recover the money had been unsuccessful. When his cousin Sir William Lowther (1757–1844) succeeded him, he agreed to pay his predecessor's debts. The Wordsworths received £8,500 (including interest) in 1804.

He saw our garden, was astonished at the scarlet beans etc. When he was gone he wrote to Coleridge, MH, and my brother Richard about the affair. Wm determined to go to Eusemere on Monday. In the afternoon we walked to Rydale with our letters, found no letters there. A sweet evening, I had a woful headache and was ill in stomach from agitation of mind—went to bed at nine o'clock but did not sleep till late.

Saturday 19th

The swallows were very busy under my window this morning—I slept pretty well, but William has got no sleep. It is after eleven and he is still in bed— a fine morning—Coleridge when he was last here, told us that for many years there being no Quaker meeting held at Keswick, a single old Quaker woman used to go regularly alone every Sunday, to attend the meeting-house and there used to sit and perform her worship, alone, in that beautiful place among those fir-trees, in that spacious vale, under the great mountain Skiddaw!!! Poor old Willy—we never pass by his grave close to the churchyard gate without thinking of him and having his figure brought back to our minds. He formerly was an ostler[6] at Hawkshead, having spent a little estate. In his old age he was boarded or as they say *let* by the parish. A boy of the house that hired him was riding one morning pretty briskly beside John Fisher's, "Hallo! has aught particular happened," said John to the boy "Nay naught at aw nobbut auld Willy's dead." He was going to order the passing bell to be told.[7]—On Thursday morning Miss Hudson of Workington called. She said "O! I love flowers! I sow flowers in the parks several miles from home and my mother and I visit them and watch them how they grow." This may show that botanists may be often deceived when they find rare flowers growing far from houses. This was a very ordinary young woman, such as in any town in the north of England one may find a score. I sate up a while after William— he then called me down to him. (I was writing to Mary H.) I read Churchill's *Rosciad*[8] returned again to my writing and did not go to bed till he called to me. The shutters were closed, but I heard the birds singing. There was our own thrush shouting with an impatient shout—so it sounded to me. The morning was still, the twittering of the little birds was very gloomy. The owls had hooted a quarter of an hour before. Now the cocks were crowing. It was near daylight. I put out my candle and went to bed. In a little time I thought I heard William snoring, so I composed myself to sleep—Charles Lloyd called—"Smiling at my sweet Brother."[9]

Sunday 20th

He had slept better than I could have expected but he was far from well all day; we were in the orchard a great part of the morning. After tea we walked upon our own path for a long time. We talked sweetly together about the disposal of our riches. We lay upon the sloping turf. Earth and sky were so lovely that they melted our very hearts. The sky to the north was of a chastened yet rich yellow fading into pale blue and streaked and scattered over

---

6. Hostler, one who takes care of horses. 7. Tolled. 8. *The Rosciad* (1761), a satiric poem by Charles Churchill. 9. Quotation unidentified.

with steady islands of purple melting away into shades of pink. It made my heart almost feel like a vision to me. We afterwards took our cloaks and sate in the orchard. Mr. and Miss Simpson called. We told them of our expected good fortune. We were astonished and somewhat hurt to see how coldly Mr. Simpson received it—Miss S seemed very glad. We went into the house when they left us, and Wm went to bed. I sate up about an hour, he then called me to talk to him—he could not fall asleep. I wrote to Montagu.

October 1802

* * * We dressed ourselves immediately and got tea—the garden looked gay with asters and sweet peas—I looked at everything with tranquillity and happiness but I was ill both on Saturday and Sunday and continued to be poorly most of the time of our stay. Jack and George[1] came on Friday evening 1st October. On Saturday 2nd we rode to Hackness, William Jack George and Sara single, I behind Tom. On Sunday 3rd Mary and Sara were busy packing. On Monday 4th October 1802, my brother William was married to Mary Hutchinson. I slept a good deal of the night and rose fresh and well in the morning—at a little after 8 o clock I saw them go down the avenue towards the church. William had parted from me upstairs. I gave him the wedding ring—with how deep a blessing! I took it from my forefinger where I had worn it the whole of the night before—he slipped it again onto my finger and blessed me fervently. When they were absent my dear little Sara prepared the breakfast. I kept myself as quiet as I could, but when I saw the two men[2] running up the walk, coming to tell us it was over, I could stand it no longer and threw myself on the bed where I lay in stillness, neither hearing or seeing anything, till Sara came upstairs to me and said "They are coming." This forced me from the bed where I lay and I moved I knew not how straight forward, faster than my strength could carry me till I met my beloved William and fell upon his bosom. He and John Hutchinson led me to the house and there I stayed to welcome my dear Mary. As soon as we had breakfasted we departed. It rained when we set off. Poor Mary was much agitated when she parted from her brothers and sisters and her home. Nothing particular occurred till we reached Kirby. We had sunshine and showers, pleasant talk, love and cheerfulness. We were obliged to stay two hours at K. while the horses were feeding. We wrote a few lines to Sara and then walked out, the sun shone and we went to the churchyard, after we had put a letter into the post office for the York Herald. We sauntered about and read the gravestones. There was one to the memory of 5 children, who had all died within 5 years, and the longest-lived had only lived 4 years. There was another stone erected to the memory of an unfortunate woman (as we supposed, by a stranger). The verses engraved upon it expressed that she had been neglected by her relations and counseled the readers of those words to look within and recollect their own frailties. We left Kirby at about half past 2. There is not much variety of prospect from K. to Helmsely but the country is very pleasant, being rich and woody, and Helmsely itself stands very sweetly at the foot of the rising grounds of Duncombe Park which is scattered

---

1. The bride's brothers.   2. The brothers again.

over with tall woods and lifting itself above the common buildings of the town stands Helmsely Castle, now a ruin, formerly inhabited by the gay Duke of Buckingham.[3] Every foot of the road was, of itself interesting to us, for we had traveled along it on foot Wm and I when we went to fetch our dear Mary, and had sate upon the turf by the roadside more than once. Before we reached Helmsely our driver told us that he could not take us any further, so we stopped at the same inn where we had slept before. My heart danced at the sight of its cleanly outside, bright yellow walls, casements over-shadowed with jasmine and its low, double gavel-ended front. We were not shewn into the same parlor where Wm and I were, it was a small room with a drawing over the chimney piece which the woman told us had been bought at a sale. Mary and I warmed ourselves at the kitchen fire [;] we then walked into the garden, and looked over a gate up to the old ruin which stands at the top of a mount, and round about it the moats are grown up into soft green cradles, hollows surrounded with green grassy hillocks and these are overshadowed by old trees, chiefly ashes. I prevailed upon William to go up with me to the ruins [;] we left Mary sitting by the kitchen fire. The sun shone, it was warm and very pleasant. One part of the castle seems to be inhabited. There was a man mowing nettles in the open space which had most likely once been the castle court. There is one gateway exceedingly beautiful—children were playing upon the sloping ground. We came home by the street. After about an hour's delay we set forward again, had an excel-lent driver who opened the gates so dexterously that the horses never stopped. Mary was very much delighted with the view of the castle from the point where we had seen it before. I was pleased to see again the little path which we had walked upon, the gate I had climbed over, and the road down which we had seen the two little boys drag a log of wood, and a team of horses struggle under the weight of a great load of timber. We had felt com-passion for the poor horses that were under the governance of oppressive and ill-judging drivers, and for the poor boys who seemed of an age to have been able to have dragged the log of wood merely out of the love of their own activity, but from poverty and bad food they panted for weakness and were obliged to fetch their father from the town to help them. Duncombe House looks well from the road—a large building, though I believe only two-thirds of the original design are completed. We rode down a very steep hill to Ryvaux valley, with woods all round us. We stopped upon the bridge to look at the abbey and again when we had crossed it. Dear Mary had never seen a ruined abbey before except Whitby. We recognized the cottages, houses, and the little valleys as we went along. We walked up a long hill, the road carrying us up the cleft or valley with woody hills on each side of us. When we *went* to GH[4] I had walked down this valley alone. Wm followed me. It was not dark evening when we passed the little public house, but before we had crossed the Hambledon Hills and reached the point over-looking Yorkshire it was quite dark. We had not wanted,[5] however, fair pros-pects before us, as we drove along the flat plain of the high hill, far far off

---

3. I.e., George Villiers, duke of Buckingham (1628–1687). Helmsley, his estate, had to be sold after his death to pay his debts.   4. I.e., Gallows Hill, where she and her brother had walked during the summer.   5. Lacked.

us, in the western sky, we saw shapes of castles, ruins among groves, a great, spreading wood, rocks, and single trees, a minster with its tower unusually distinct, minarets in another quarter, and a round Grecian temple also—the colors of the sky of a bright grey and the forms of a sober grey, with a dome. As we descended the hill there was no distinct view, but of a great space, only near us, we saw the wild and (as the people say) bottomless tarn[6] in the hollow at the side of the hill. It seemed to be made visible to us only by its own light, for all the hill about us was dark. Before we reached Thirsk we saw a light before us which we at first thought was the moon, then lime kilns, but when we drove into the marketplace it proved a large bonfire with lads dancing round it, which is a sight I dearly love. The inn was like an illuminated house—every room full. We asked the cause, and were told by the girl that it was "Mr John Bell's Birthday, that he had heired his Estate." The landlady was very civil. She did not recognize the despised foot-travelers.[7] We rode nicely in the dark, and reached Leming Lane at 11 o'clock. I am always sorry to get out of a chaise[8] when it is night. The people of the house were going to bed and we were not very well treated though we got a hot supper. We breakfasted the next morning and set off at about half past 8 o'clock. It was a chearful sunny morning. We soon turned out of Leming Lane and passed a nice village with a beautiful church. We had a few showers, but when we came to the green fields of Wensley, the sun shone upon them all, and the Eure in its many windings glittered as it flowed along under the green slopes of Middleham and Middleham Castle. Mary looked about for her friend Mr. Place, and thought she had him sure on the contrary side of the vale from that on which we afterwards found that he lived. We went to a new built house at Leyburn, the same village where Wm and I had dined with George Hutchinson on our road to Grasmere 2 years and three-quarters ago, but not the same house. The landlady was very civil, giving us cake and wine but the horses being out we were detained at least 2 hours and did not set off till 2 o'clock. We paid for 35 miles, i.e. to Sedbergh, but the landlady did not encourage us to hope to get beyond Hawes. A shower came on just after we left the inn while the rain beat against the windows we ate our dinners which M and W heartily enjoyed—I was not quite well. When we passed through the village of Wensley my heart was melted away with dear recollections, the bridge, the little waterspout[,] the steep hill[,] the church—They are among the most vivid of my own inner visions, for they were the first objects that I saw after we were left to ourselves, and had turned our whole hearts to Grasmere as a home in which we were to rest. The vale looked most beautiful each way. To the left the bright silver stream inlaid the flat and very green meadows, winding like a serpent. To the right we did not see it so far, it was lost among trees and little hills. I could not help observing as we went along how much more *varied* the prospects of Wensley Dale are in the summertime than I could have thought possible in the winter.

* * *

6. Lake. *Bottomless Tarn:* Lake Gormire.　7. From the previous summer.　8. A light two-wheeled carriage, intended for one or two passengers.

SAMUEL TAYLOR COLERIDGE
1772–1834

For Samuel Taylor Coleridge, the mystery of the imagination provided the most compelling and perplexing of subjects. In prose and in verse, by reasoned discussion and by poetic symbol making, he explored the subject, affirming imagination's virtually divine status as a creative power and suggesting his own emotional dependence on it.

Son of an English clergyman, Coleridge attended Jesus College, Cambridge, from 1791 to 1793. In 1795, he married Sara Fricker; that same year, he met Wordsworth and began the fruitful collaboration leading to *Lyrical Ballads*. In 1810, his period of greatest poetic creativity already over, he separated from his wife; subsequently, he became increasingly addicted to opium. Known for his brilliant conversation, he spent much time talking and lecturing as well as writing.

The most intellectual of the English Romantics, Coleridge, after an early trip to Germany, was strongly influenced by the German Idealist philosophers, notably Immanuel Kant and Johann Gottlieb Fichte. His best-known critical work, *Biographia Literaria* (1817), in which he develops most fully and explicitly his theory of imagination, contains many borrowings from German sources. His output of poetry was relatively small. In some of his most important poems (such as *The Rime of the Ancient Mariner*), he tries to incorporate the supernatural into essentially psychological narrative. He was also interested in the native English ballad tradition, which on occasion influenced his choice of stanzaic form and meter.

Like other Romantic poets, Coleridge was fascinated by the aeolian harp (it figures in the first stanza of *Dejection: An Ode*), an instrument that makes music without human intervention, by the action of wind on its strings. *Kubla Khan,* a poem recording (according to Coleridge's prefatory note) what the writer remembered of a dream stimulated by opium, is a kind of poetic equivalent for the aeolian harp: a work for which its author disclaims conscious responsibility. It simply came to his mind, he says, to be broken off when he was interrupted by a person from Porlock. The poem, therefore, makes no claim to rational coherence; however, this has not stopped many from providing critical interpretations. Evoking a lush and splendid setting, it yet contains ominous suggestions: the ruler who presides over the magnificence of landscape ("deep romantic chasm," river, caves, incense-bearing trees) and building, hears "Ancestral voices prophesying war." The theme of mingled beauty and danger intensifies as the poem focuses on the figure of a singer, a "damsel with a dulcimer," whose power the poem's speaker wishes to "revive" within himself. Then he could re-create the vision of Kubla Khan's domain, and people would respond to him with "holy dread," recognizing his association with the magic, the sacred, the dangerous, the unpredictable and uncontrollable power of imagination. Thus the singer becomes an image for the poet, and we are reminded that the uncannily evocative scene of the poem's opening section itself issues from the poetic imagination, which creates for its possessor and for his readers a new version of reality, closer to the heart's desire than our workaday world, but not without danger—including the danger of becoming lost in it.

In *Dejection: An Ode,* Coleridge concerns himself with the same theme in more extended personal terms. Paradoxically, this poem—mourning his loss of creative imagination—demonstrates the active presence of that quality whose absence it deplores, as it creates out of the dullness of depression a rich emotional and psychological texture. Like Wordsworth's *Ode on Intimations of Immortality, Dejection* confronts the speaker's sense of diminishing power. He has lost the "joy" that he associates with the spontaneity of youth. More emphatically than Wordsworth, Coleridge attributes even the beauty of nature to the human imagination:

> O Lady! we receive but what we give,
> And in our life alone does Nature live: . . .
> Ah! from the soul itself must issue forth
> A light, a glory, a fair luminous cloud
> Enveloping the Earth—

One cannot hope for inspiration from nature, cannot expect to receive from without that reassurance and pleasure whose sources are within. As the poem develops, it demonstrates how the imagination gives meaning to the external world—meaning related to human action and suffering—in the sound of wind and storm. The imaginative activity provides its own solace; although the speaker never ceases to assert his dejection, he, like Wordsworth, can finally displace his vision of joy, harmony, and peace onto the figure of a woman who will embody all that he now feels impossible for himself.

In its emphasis on the "shaping spirit of Imagination," that presiding power of Romantic poetry, *Dejection* makes a strong statement of Coleridge's central concern. By its capacity to evoke emotional complexity—longing for what is lost, resentment at its passing, struggle to repossess what is mourned—and to demonstrate the patterns in which the mind deals with its own problems, it exemplifies the subtlety and the force of his poetic achievement.

PRONOUNCING GLOSSARY

The following list uses common English syllables and stress accents to provide rough equivalents of selected words whose pronunciation may be unfamiliar to the general reader.

Aeolian: *ee-oh'-lee-an*

Purchas: *pur'-chus*

Xanadu: *zan'-a-doo*

Kubla Khan

Or, a Vision in a Dream. A Fragment

The following fragment is here published at the request of a poet of great and deserved celebrity [Lord Byron], and, as far as the Author's own opinions are concerned, rather as a psychological curiosity, than on the ground of any supposed *poetic* merits.

In the summer of the year 1797, the Author, then in ill health, had retired to a lonely farm-house between Porlock and Linton, on the Exmoor confines of Somerset and Devonshire.[1] In consequence of a slight indisposition, an anodyne had been prescribed, from the effects of which he fell asleep in his chair at the moment that he was reading the following sentence, or words of the same substance, in "Purchas's Pilgrimage":[2] "Here the Khan Kubla commanded a palace to be built, and a stately garden thereunto. And thus ten miles of fertile ground were inclosed with a wall." The Author continued for about three hours in a profound sleep, at least of the external senses,

---

1. A high moorland shared by the two southwestern counties in England.   2. Samuel Purchas (1575?–1626) published *Purchas, his Pilgrimage; or, Relations of the World and the Religions observed in all Ages* in 1613. The passage in Purchas is slightly different: "In Xamdu did Cublai Can build a stately Palace, encompassing sixteene miles of plaine ground with a wall, wherein are fertile meddowes, pleasant Springs, delightfull Streames, and all sorts of beasts of chase and game, and in the middest thereof a sumptuous house of pleasure, which may be removed from place to place" (IV.13).

during which time he has the most vivid confidence, that he could not have composed less than from two to three hundred lines; if that indeed can be called composition in which all the images rose up before him as *things,* with a parallel production of the correspondent expressions, without any sensation or consciousness of effort.[3] On awaking he appeared to himself to have a distinct recollection of the whole, and taking his pen, ink, and paper, instantly and eagerly wrote down the lines that are here preserved. At this moment he was unfortunately called out by a person on business from Porlock, and detained by him above an hour, and on his return to his room, found, to his no small surprise and mortification, that though he still retained some vague and dim recollection of the general purport of the vision, yet, with the exception of some eight or ten scattered lines and images, all the rest had passed away like the images on the surface of a stream into which a stone has been cast, but, alas! without the after restoration of the latter!

>   Then all the charm
> Is broken—all that phantom-world so fair
> Vanishes, and a thousand circlets spread,
> And each mis-shape[s] the other. Stay awhile,
> Poor youth! who scarcely dar'st lift up thine eyes—
> The stream will soon renew its smoothness, soon
> The visions will return! And lo, he stays,
> And soon the fragments dim of lovely forms
> Come trembling back, unite, and now once more
> The pool becomes a mirror.[4]

Yet from the still surviving recollections in his mind, the Author has frequently purposed to finish for himself what had been originally, as it were, given to him. Σαμερον αδιον ασω:[5] but the to-morrow is yet to come. . . .

> In Xanadu did Kubla Khan[6]
> A stately pleasure-dome decree:
> Where Alph,[7] the sacred river, ran
> Through caverns measureless to man
>   Down to a sunless sea.   5
> So twice five miles of fertile ground
> With walls and towers were girdled round:
> And there were gardens bright with sinuous rills,
> Where blossomed many an incense-bearing tree;
> And here were forests ancient as the hills,   10
> Enfolding sunny spots of greenery.
>
> But oh! that deep romantic chasm which slanted
> Down the green hill athwart a cedarn cover!
> A savage place! as holy and enchanted
> As e'er beneath a waning moon was haunted   15

3. Coleridge's statement that he dreamed the poem and wrote down what he could later remember verbatim has been queried, most recently by medical opinion. The belief that opium produces special dreams or even any dreams at all lacks confirmation.   **4.** From Coleridge's poem *The Picture; or, The Lover's Resolution,* lines 91–100.   **5.** From Theocritus's *Idylls* 1.145: "I'll sing a sweeter song tomorrow" (Greek). **6.** Mongol emperor (1215?–1294), visited by Marco Polo.   **7.** J. L. Lowes, in *The Road to Xanadu* (1927), thinks that Coleridge may have had in mind the river Alpheus—linked with the Nile—mentioned by Virgil.

By woman wailing for her demon-lover!
And from this chasm, with ceaseless turmoil seething,
As if this earth in fast thick pants were breathing,
A mighty fountain momently was forced:
Amid whose swift half-intermitted burst 20
Huge fragments vaulted like rebounding hail,
Or chaffy grain beneath the thresher's flail:
And 'mid these dancing rocks at once and ever
It flung up momently the sacred river.
Five miles meandering with a mazy motion 25
Through wood and dale the sacred river ran,
Then reached the caverns measureless to man,
And sank in tumult to a lifeless ocean:
And 'mid this tumult Kubla heard from far
Ancestral voices prophesying war! 30
 The shadow of the dome of pleasure
  Floated midway on the waves;
  Where was heard the mingled measure
  From the fountain and the caves.
It was a miracle of rare device, 35
A sunny pleasure-dome with caves of ice!
 A damsel with a dulcimer
  In a vision once I saw:
  It was an Abyssinian maid,
  And on her dulcimer she played, 40
  Singing of Mount Abora.[8]
 Could I revive within me
  Her symphony and song,
  To such a deep delight 'twould win me,
That with music loud and long, 45
I would build that dome in air,
That sunny dome! those caves of ice!
And all who heard should see them there,
And all should cry, Beware! Beware!
His flashing eyes, his floating hair! 50
Weave a circle round him thrice,
And close your eyes with holy dread,
For he on honey-dew hath fed,
And drunk the milk of Paradise.

Dejection: An Ode

  Late, late yestreen I saw the new Moon,
  With the old Moon in her arms;
  And I fear, I fear, my Master dear!
  We shall have a deadly storm.
     Ballad of Sir Patrick Spence

---

8. Lowes argues that this may have been "Mt. Amara," mentioned by Milton in *Paradise Lost* (4.28), or Amhara in Samuel Johnson's *Rasselas*.

I

Well! If the Bard was weather-wise, who made
   The grand old ballad of Sir Patrick Spence,
   This night, so tranquil now, will not go hence
Unroused by winds, that ply a busier trade
Than those which mould yon cloud in lazy flakes,   5
Or the dull sobbing draft, that moans and rakes
Upon the strings of this Aeolian lute,[1]
     Which better far were mute.
    For lo! the New-moon winter-bright!
    And overspread with phantom light,   10
    (With swimming phantom light o'erspread
    But rimmed and circled by a silver thread)
I see the old Moon in her lap, foretelling
   The coming-on of rain and squally blast.
And oh! that even now the gust were swelling,   15
   And the slant night-shower driving loud and fast!
Those sounds which oft have raised me, whilst they awed,
    And sent my soul abroad,
Might now perhaps their wonted impulse give,
Might startle this dull pain, and make it move and live!   20

II

A grief without a pang, void, dark, and drear,
   A stifled, drowsy, unimpassioned grief,
   Which finds no natural outlet, no relief,
    In word, or sigh, or tear—
O Lady! in this wan and heartless mood,   25
To other thoughts by yonder throstle[2] woo'd,
   All this long eve, so balmy and serene,
Have I been gazing on the western sky,
   And its peculiar tint of yellow green:
And still I gaze—and with how blank an eye!   30
And those thin clouds above, in flakes and bars,
That give away their motion to the stars;
Those stars, that glide behind them or between,
Now sparkling, now bedimmed, but always seen:
Yon crescent Moon, as fixed as if it grew   35
In its own cloudless, starless lake of blue;
I see them all so excellently fair,
I see, not feel, how beautiful they are!

---

1. A frame fitted with strings or wires that produce musical tones when the wind hits them. Named after Aeolus, god of the winds.   **2.** The song thrush.

III

My genial spirits[3] fail;
    And what can these avail
To lift the smothering weight from off my breast?
    It were a vain endeavour,
    Though I should gaze forever
On that green light that lingers in the west:
I may not hope from outward forms to win
The passion and the life, whose fountains are within.

IV

O Lady! we receive but what we give,
And in our life alone does Nature live:
Ours is her wedding garment, ours her shroud!
    And would we aught behold of higher worth,
Than that inanimate cold world allowed
To the poor loveless ever-anxious crowd,
    Ah! from the soul itself must issue forth
A light, a glory, a fair luminous cloud
        Enveloping the Earth—
And from the soul itself must there be sent
    A sweet and potent voice, of its own birth,
Of all sweet sounds the life and element!

V

O pure of heart! thou need'st not ask of me
What this strong music in the soul may be!
What, and wherein it doth exist,
This light, this glory, this fair luminous mist,
This beautiful and beauty-making power.
    Joy, virtuous Lady! Joy that ne'er was given,
Save to the pure, and in their purest hour,
Life, and Life's effluence, cloud at once and shower,
Joy, Lady! is the spirit and the power,
Which wedding Nature to us gives in dower
    A new Earth and new Heaven,
Undreamt of by the sensual and the proud—
Joy is the sweet voice, Joy the luminous cloud—
    We in ourselves rejoice!
And thence flows all that charms or ear or sight,
    All melodies the echoes of that voice,
All colours a suffusion from that light.

---

3. Generative spirits; creativity. This poem was written soon after Wordsworth had composed the first four stanzas of the Ode on Intimations of Immortality, and the themes are similar.

VI

There was a time when, though my path was rough,
   This joy within me dallied with distress,
And all misfortunes were but as the stuff
   Whence Fancy made me dreams of happiness:
For hope grew round me, like the twining vine,   80
And fruits, and foliage, not my own, seemed mine.
But now afflictions bow me down to earth:
Nor care I that they rob me of my mirth;
   But oh! each visitation[4]
Suspends what nature gave me at my birth,   85
   My shaping spirit of Imagination.[5]
For not to think of what I needs must feel,
   But to be still and patient, all I can;
And haply by abstruse research to steal
   From my own nature all the natural man—   90
   This was my sole resource, my only plan:
Till that which suits a part infects the whole,
And now is almost grown the habit of my soul.

VII

Hence, viper thoughts, that coil around my mind,
   Reality's dark dream!   95
I turn from you, and listen to the wind,
   Which long has raved unnoticed. What a scream
Of agony by torture lengthened out
That lute sent forth! Thou Wind that rav'st without,
   Bare crag, or mountain-tairn,[6] or blasted tree,   100
Or pine-grove whither woodman never clomb,
Or lonely house, long held the witches' home,
   Methinks were fitter instruments for thee,
Mad Lutanist![7] who in this month of showers,
Of dark-brown gardens, and of peeping flowers,   105
Mak'st Devils' yule[8] with worse than wintry song,
The blossoms, buds, and timorous leaves among.
   Thou Actor, perfect in all tragic sounds!
Thou mighty Poet, e'en to frenzy bold!
   What tell'st thou now about?   110
   'Tis of the rushing of an host in rout,
With groans, of trampled men, with smarting wounds—
At once they groan with pain, and shudder with the cold!
But hush! there is a pause of deepest silence!
   And all that noise, as of a rushing crowd,   115
With groans, and tremulous shudderings—all is over—
   It tells another tale,[9] with sounds less deep and loud!
   A tale of less affright,

---

4. Of the *misfortunes* (line 78) and *afflictions* (line 82).   **5.** Coleridge made much of the distinction between *Fancy* (line 79) and *Imagination*. Fancy makes pleasant combinations of images; Imagination is a higher faculty of the mind that combines images in such a way that they create a higher reality, a poetic "truth" more valid than that which is perceived by the ordinary senses.   **6.** I.e., tarn; small mountain lake. **7.** The storm wind in line 99.   **8.** Originally, a heathen feast.   **9.** The story of Wordsworth's *Lucy Gray*.

And tempered with delight,
As Otway's self[1] had framed the tender lay,— 120
   'Tis of a little child
   Upon a lonesome wild,
Not far from home, but she hath lost her way:
And now moans low in bitter grief and fear,
And now screams loud, and hopes to make her mother hear. 125

VIII

'Tis midnight, but small thoughts have I of sleep.
Full seldom may my friend such vigils keep!
Visit her, gentle Sleep! with wings of healing,
   And may this storm be but a mountain birth,
May all the stars hang bright above her dwelling, 130
   Silent as though they watched the sleeping Earth!
     With light heart may she rise,
     Gay fancy, cheerful eyes,
   Joy lift her spirit, joy attune her voice;
To her may all things live, from pole to pole, 135
Their life the eddying of her living soul!
     O simple spirit, guided from above,
Dear Lady! friend devoutest of my choice,
Thus mayest thou ever, evermore rejoice.

---

1. Originally, "William's," referring to Wordsworth. *As:* as if. Thomas Otway (1652–1685), a tragic dramatist, admired for his mastery of pathos.

GEORGE GORDON, LORD BYRON
1788–1824

Renowned as much for his life as for his work, Byron epitomized the Romantic hero he often wrote about. He cultivated the persona of the solitary sufferer as well as the dashing adventurer. Highly attractive to women (despite his clubfoot, about which he was very sensitive), Byron had several liaisons; was separated from his wife, probably as a result of her discovery of his affair with his stepsister; and provided substance for titillating gossip all over Europe. He was also, for a time, enormously popular as both poet and person. By 1816 a social outcast after the separation, he left England for good, settling in Venice. He interested himself in the cause of Greek independence from the Turks and died of a fever in Missolonghi, where he was working for that cause.

Byron wrote in many verse modes: short lyrics; long oriental tales; satire; a melancholy long poem (*Childe Harold's Pilgrimage*), taken at the time to be autobiographical; and mock epic. His link to eighteenth-century verse satire, such as Pope's, is often as evident as is his expression of Romantic ideology. In the lyrics represented here, he frequently appears to allude to biographically verifiable events in his own life. All over Europe, poets imitated him. His capacity to find images in the external world that correspond to complex emotions and his ability to create rich musical effects in verse make his lyrics immediately moving. They captured a wide audience in his own time and have remained popular ever since.

[Again Deceived! Again Betrayed!]

> I pull in resolution and begin
> To doubt the equivocation of the fiend
> That lies like truth.
>   Macbeth

[1.]

Again deceived! again betrayed![1]
  In manhood as in youth,
The dupe of every smiling maid
  That ever "lied like truth".—

2.

Well, dearly was the lesson bought   5
  The present and the past,
What Love some twenty times has taught
  We needs must learn at last.

3.

In turn deceiving or deceived
  The wayward Passion roves,   10
Beguiled by her we most believed,
  Or leaving her who loves.

4.

Oh thou! for whom my heart must bleed,
  From whom this anguish springs,
Thy Love was genuine Love indeed,   15
  And showed it in his wings.

5.

His pinions, had he deigned to stay,
  I only meant to borrow.
I wish thy love remained today
  To fly with mine tomorrow.   20

                                  1812

---

1. This probably alludes to Byron's infatuation with a Welsh servant girl named Susan Vaughan. He discovered that she had been unfaithful to him in his absence.

[Politics in 1813. To Lady Melbourne][1]

'Tis said *Indifference* marks the present time,
Then hear the reason—though 'tis told in rhyme—
A King who *can't*—a Prince of Wales who *don't*—[2]
Patriots who *shan't*, and Ministers who *won't*—
What matters who are *in* or *out* of place[3]
The *Mad*—the *Bad*—the *Useless*—or the *Base*?

[1813]

Stanzas for Music

There be none of Beauty's daughters
  With a magic like thee;
And like music on the waters
  Is thy sweet voice to me:
When, as if its sound were causing   5
The charmed ocean's pausing,
The waves lie still and gleaming,
And the lulled winds seem dreaming.

And the midnight moon is weaving
  Her bright chain o'er the deep;   10
Whose breast is gently heaving,
  As an infant's asleep.
So the spirit bows before thee,
To listen and adore thee;
With a full but soft emotion,   15
Like the swell of Summer's ocean.

[1816]

Fare Thee Well!

Alas! they had been friends in Youth;
But whispering tongues can poison truth;
And constancy lives in realms above:
And Life is thorny; and youth is vain:
And to be wroth with one we love,
Doth work like madness in the brain:

*   *   *   *   *   *   *   *   *   *
But never either found another
To free the hollow heart from paining—
They stood aloof, the scars remaining,

---

1. Elizabeth, Lady Melbourne (1751–1818), mistress of the prince regent; mother-in-law of Caroline Lamb, with whom Byron had an affair, and confidante of Byron.   2. The king, George III, was insane; his son, the prince of Wales, was acting as prince regent. This was a time of social unrest; the government was doing nothing to remedy it.   3. Position of status and power.

> Like cliffs, which had been rent asunder;
> A dreary sea now flows between,
> But neither heat, nor frost, nor thunder
> Shall wholly do away, I ween,
> The marks of that which once hath been.
> *Coleridge's Christabel* [408–13, 419–26].

Fare thee well! and if for ever—
  Still for ever, fare *thee well*—[1]
Even though unforgiving, never
  'Gainst thee shall my heart rebel.—
Would that breast were bared before thee   5
  Where they head so oft hath lain,
While that placid sleep came o'er thee
  Which thou ne'er can'st know again:
Would that breast by thee glanc'd over,
  Every inmost thought could show!   10
Then, thou would'st at last discover
  'Twas not well to spurn it so—
Though the world for this commend thee—
  Though it smile upon the blow,
Even its praises must offend thee,   15
  Founded on another's woe—
Though my many faults defaced me,
  Could no other arm be found
Than the one which once embraced me,
  To inflict a cureless wound!   20
Yet—oh, yet—thyself deceive not—
  Love may sink by slow decay,
But by sudden wrench, believe not,
  Hearts can thus be torn away;
Still thine own its life retaineth—   25
  Still must mine—though bleeding—beat,
And the undying thought which paineth
  Is—that we no more may meet.—
These are words of deeper sorrow
  Than the wail above the dead,   30
Both shall live—but every morrow
  Wake us from a widowed bed.—
And when thou wouldst solace gather—
  When our child's first accents flow—[2]
Wilt thou teach her to say—"Father!"   35
  Though his care she must forgo?
When her little hands shall press thee—
  When her lip to thine is prest—
Think of him whose prayer shall bless thee—
  Think of him thy love had bless'd.   40
Should her lineaments resemble
  Those thou never more may'st see—
Then thy heart will softly tremble

---

1. This poem was written in 1816 the day after the signing of the preliminary separation agreement between Lord and Lady Byron.   2. Byron's daughter, Augusta Ada, had been born at the end of 1815.

With a pulse yet true to me.—
All my faults—perchance thou knowest— 45
All my madness—none can know;
All my hopes—where'er thou goest—
Wither—yet with *thee* they go.—
Every feeling hath been shaken,
Pride—which not a world could bow— 50
Bows to thee—by thee forsaken
Even my soul forsakes me now.—
But 'tis done—all words are idle—
Words from me are vainer still;
But the thoughts we cannot bridle 55
Force their way without the will.—
Fare thee well!—thus disunited—
Torn from every nearer tie—
Seared in heart—and lone—and blighted—
More than this, I scarce can die.

[1816]

When We Two Parted

1.

When we two parted
   In silence and tears,
Half broken-hearted
   To sever for years,
Pale grew thy cheek and cold, 5
   Colder thy kiss;
Truly that hour foretold
   Sorrow to this.

2.

The dew of the morning
   Sunk chill on my brow— 10
It felt like the warning
   Of what I feel now.
Thy vows are all broken,
   And light is thy fame;
I hear thy name spoken, 15
   And share in its shame.

3.

They name thee before me,
   A knell to mine ear;
A shudder comes o'er me—
   Why wert thou so dear? 20
They know not I knew thee,

Who knew thee too well:—
   Long, long shall I rue thee,
   Too deeply to tell.

4.

In secret we met—   25
   In silence I grieve,
That thy heart could forget,
   Thy spirit deceive.
If I should meet thee
   After long years,
How should I greet thee!—   30
   With silence and tears.

[1815]

PERCY BYSSHE SHELLEY
1792–1822

A longing for alternatives to things as they are dominates much of Shelley's poetry. Whether he writes of his own dejection, of the energizing force of the west wind, or of the political situation of England, he writes often from the conviction that matters could and should be better.

Son of a country squire in Sussex, Shelley led a privileged early life, attending Eton and Oxford. He was, however, expelled from Oxford after a single year for writing *The Necessity of Atheism*: already he had begun to defy convention. He dramatized his defiance yet more forcefully in 1814, when, after three years of marriage (and two children) with Harriet Westbrook, he eloped with Mary Wollstonecraft Godwin, daughter of two advanced social thinkers. Harriet committed suicide; the lovers married and had several children. Shelley was on friendly terms with other important Romantic writers; in Italy, where he moved in 1818, he associated closely with Byron. He was drowned while sailing off the Italian coast.

Productive as a poet, Shelley mastered tones ranging from the satiric to the prophetic. His most important works include *Prometheus Unbound* (1820), a philosophic-visionary-revolutionary expansion of a classical theme; *Epipsychidon* (1821), a defense of free love; and the elegy *Adonais* (1821), for the death of Keats. He also wrote a verse play having to do with the incest of a father and daughter, *The Cenci* (1819).

At the end of his essay *A Defense of Poetry*, posthumously published in 1840, Shelley insists on poetry's necessary connection with the future. Poets, he says, are "the mirrors of the gigantic shadows which futurity casts upon the present . . . : the influence which is moved not, but moves. Poets are the unacknowledged legislators of the World." His own lyrics corroborate such grandiose claims by insistently establishing images of the possible. The sonnet *England in 1819*, for example, after twelve lines of nouns and noun clauses about the political and social horrors of the current English situation, concludes that all these phenomena "Are graves from which a glorious Phantom may / Burst, to illumine our tempestuous day." The possibility— never the certainty—of good coming from evil always exists.

Like Coleridge, Shelley writes about his own dejection, interspersing penetrating images of natural beauty with detailed presentation of his painful psychic state. In *Stanzas Written in Dejection,* the speaker dreams of death as a kind of mild fulfillment, a reabsorption into nature. The ending of the poem, however, has less dismal implications. Finally, the speaker compares himself with the dying day as a presence in memory. Men do not love him but would regret his passing; the day, which he has enjoyed, will linger "like joy in Memory." The comparison, which at first appears to sustain the mood of self-pity, also transcends that self-perpetuating emotion: it reminds the speaker of the capacity for enjoyment that he retains even in his bleakest mood. While he fancies his own easeful death, he still takes pleasure in the scene around him; that pleasure remains a lasting element in memory.

Ode to the West Wind makes a particularly emphatic statement of the good-from-evil theme. Images of violence and sinister power ("Thou, from whose unseen presence the leaves dead / Are driven, like ghosts from an enchanter fleeing") dominate the early part of the poem. The third section creates an atmosphere of luxurious beauty but ends with the depths of the sea growing suddenly "grey with fear" at the wind's advent. In the next section, however, the speaker places himself in relation with the natural force he has described, begging to be lifted, to "share / The impulse of thy strength." Finally, in imagination, the poet becomes the "lyre" (in effect, Coleridge's aeolian harp) of the wind, now revealed as a force of inspiration and change, which enables him to function as "The trumpet of a prophecy!" *Defense of Poetry* describes poets as "the trumpets which sing to battle"; in *Ode to the West Wind,* Shelley suggests that they acquire such inspirational capacity by imaginative union with nature and, particularly, as in the west wind blowing away the remnants of the past year, with the forces of regeneration and reform.

PRONOUNCING GLOSSARY

The following list uses common English syllables and stress accents to provide rough equivalents of selected words whose pronunciation may be unfamiliar to the general reader.

Baiæ: *by'-ee*   Mænad: *mee'-nad*

Stanzas Written in Dejection— December 1818, near Naples

The Sun is warm, the sky is clear,
The waves are dancing fast and bright,
Blue isles and snowy mountains wear
The purple noon's transparent might,
The breath of the moist earth is light   5
Around its unexpanded buds;
Like many a voice of one delight,
The winds, the birds, the Ocean-floods,
The City's voice, itself is soft like Solitude's.

I see the Deep's untrampled floor   10
With green and purple seaweeds strown;
I see the waves upon the shore
Like light dissolved in star-showers, thrown;
I sit upon the sands alone;

The lightning of the noontide Ocean   15
Is flashing round me, and a tone
Arises from its measured motion,
How sweet! did any heart now share in my emotion.

Alas, I have nor hope nor health
Nor peace within nor calm around,   20
Nor that content surpassing wealth
The sage in meditation found,
And walked with inward glory crowned;
Nor fame nor power nor love nor leisure—
Others I see whom these surround,   25
Smiling they live and call life pleasure:
To me that cup has been dealt in another measure.

Yet now despair itself is mild,
Even as the winds and waters are;
I could lie down like a tired child   30
And weep away the life of care
Which I have borne and yet must bear
Till Death like Sleep might steal on me,
And I might feel in the warm air
My cheek grow cold, and hear the Sea   35
Breathe o'er my dying brain its last monotony.

Some might lament that I were cold,
As I, when this sweet day is gone,
Which my lost heart, too soon grown old,
Insults with this untimely moan—   40
They might lament,—for I am one
Whom men love not, and yet regret;
Unlike this day, which, when the Sun
Shall on its stainless glory set,
Will linger though enjoyed, like joy in Memory yet.   45

England in 1819

An old, mad, blind, despised, and dying King;[1]
Princes,[2] the dregs of their dull race, who flow
Through public scorn,—mud from a muddy spring;
Rulers who neither see nor feel nor know,
But leechlike to their fainting country cling   5
Till they drop, blind in blood, without a blow.
A people starved and stabbed in th' untilled field;
An army, whom liberticide and prey

---

1. George III (1738–1820).   2. The King's sons, including the prince regent, whose dissolute behavior gave rise to public scandals.

Makes as a two-edged sword to all who wield;
Golden and sanguine[3] laws which tempt and slay;   10
Religion Christless, Godless—a book sealed;
A senate, Time's worst statute,[4] unrepealed—
Are graves from which a glorious Phantom may
Burst, to illumine our tempestuous day.

Ode to the West Wind

I

O wild West Wind, thou breath of Autumn's being,
Thou, from whose unseen presence the leaves dead
Are driven, like ghosts from an enchanter fleeing,

Yellow, and black, and pale, and hectic red,
Pestilence-stricken multitudes: O Thou,   5
Who chariotest to their dark wintry bed

The winged seeds, where they lie cold and low,
Each like a corpse within its grave, until
Thine azure sister of the Spring shall blow

Her clarion o'er the dreaming earth, and fill   10
(Driving sweet buds like flocks to feed in air)
With living hues and odours plain and hill:

Wild Spirit, which art moving everywhere;
Destroyer and Preserver; hear, O hear!

II

Thou on whose stream, 'mid the steep sky's commotion,   15
Loose clouds like Earth's decaying leaves are shed,
Shook from the tangled boughs of Heaven and Ocean,

Angels of rain and lightning; there are spread
On the blue surface of thine aery surge,
Like the bright hair uplifted from the head   20

Of some fierce Mænad,[1] even from the dim verge
Of the horizon to the zenith's height,
The locks of the approaching storm. Thou Dirge

---

3. Bloody, causing bloodshed. *Golden*: bought. The laws favor the rich and powerful.   4. The law by
which the civil liberties of Roman Catholics and dissenters from the state religion (Anglicanism) were
restricted.   1. Ecstatic female worshipper of Bacchus, Greek god of wine.

Of the dying year, to which this closing night
Will be the dome of a vast sepulchre,   25
Vaulted with all thy congregated might
Of vapors, from whose solid atmosphere
Black rain and fire and hail will burst: O hear!

III

Thou who didst waken from his summer dreams
The blue Mediterranean, where he lay,   30
Lulled by the coil of his crystalline streams,

Beside a pumice isle in Baiæ's bay,[2]
And saw in sleep old palaces and towers
Quivering within the wave's intenser day,

All overgrown with azure moss and flowers   35
So sweet, the sense faints picturing them! Thou
For whose path the Atlantic's level powers

Cleave themselves into chasms, while far below
The sea-blooms and the oozy woods which wear
The sapless foliage of the ocean, know   40

Thy voice, and suddenly grow grey with fear,
And tremble and despoil themselves: O hear!

IV

If I were a dead leaf thou mightest bear;
If I were a swift cloud to fly with thee;
A wave to pant beneath thy power, and share   45

The impulse of thy strength, only less free
Than thou, O Uncontrollable! If even
I were as in my boyhood, and could be

The comrade of thy wanderings over Heaven,
As then, when to outstrip thy skiey speed   50
Scarce seemed a vision; I would ne'er have striven

As thus with thee in prayer in my sore need.
Oh! lift me as a wave, a leaf, a cloud!
I fall upon the thorns of life! I bleed!

A heavy weight of hours has chained and bowed   55
One too like thee: tameless, and swift, and proud.

2. West of Naples; the Roman emperors built villas there.

V

Make me thy lyre,[3] even as the forest is:
What if my leaves are falling like its own!
The tumult of thy mighty harmonies

Will take from both a deep, autumnal tone,   60
Sweet though in sadness. Be thou, Spirit fierce,
My spirit! Be thou me, impetuous one!

Drive my dead thoughts over the universe
Like withered leaves to quicken a new birth!
And, by the incantation of this verse,   65

Scatter, as from an unextinguished hearth
Ashes and sparks, my words among mankind!
Be through my lips to unawakened Earth

The trumpet of a prophecy! O Wind,
If Winter comes, can Spring be far behind?   70

A Defense of Poetry

[Conclusion]

* * * Poetry is the record of the best and happiest moments of the happiest
and best minds. We are aware of evanescent visitations of thought and feeling sometimes associated with place or person, sometimes regarding our own
mind alone, and always arising unforeseen and departing unbidden, but elevating and delightful beyond all expression: so that even in the desire and
the regret they leave, there cannot but be pleasure, participating as it does
in the nature of its object. It is as it were the interpenetration of a diviner
nature through our own; but its footsteps are like those of a wind over a sea,
which the coming calm erases, and whose traces remain only as on the wrinkled sand which paves it. These and corresponding conditions of being are
experienced principally by those of the most delicate sensibility and the most
enlarged imagination; and the state of mind produced by them is at war with
every base desire. The enthusiasm of virtue, love, patriotism, and friendship
is essentially linked with these emotions, and whilst they last, self appears
as what it is, an atom to a Universe. Poets are not only subject to these
experiences as spirits of the most refined organization, but they can colour
all that they combine with the evanescent hues of this ethereal world; a word,
or a trait in the representation of a scene or a passion, will touch the
enchanted chord, and reanimate, in those who have ever experienced these
emotions, the sleeping, the cold, the buried image of the past. Poetry thus
makes immortal all that is best and most beautiful in the world; it arrests
the vanishing apparitions which haunt the interlunations of life, and veiling

---

3. Ancient harp. The allusion is also to the aeolian harp, an instrument played by the wind and a frequent
image for the poet played by inspiration.

them or[1] in language or in form sends them forth among mankind, bearing sweet news of kindred joy to those with whom their sisters abide—abide, because there is no portal of expression from the caverns of the spirit which they inhabit into the universe of things. Poetry redeems from decay the visitations of the divinity in man.

* * *

The first part of these remarks has related to Poetry in its elements and principles; and it has been shown, as well as the narrow limits assigned them would permit, that what is called poetry, in a restricted sense, has a common source with all other forms of order and of beauty according to which the materials of human life are susceptible of being arranged, and which is poetry in an universal sense.

The second part[2] will have for its object an application of these principles to the present state of the cultivation of Poetry, and a defense of the attempt to idealize the modern forms of manners and opinion, and compel them into a subordination to the imaginative and creative faculty. For the literature of England, an energetic development of which has ever preceded or accompanied a great and free development of the national will, has arisen as it were from a new birth. In spite of the low-thoughted envy which would undervalue contemporary merit, our own will be a memorable age in intellectual achievements, and we live among such philosophers and poets as surpass beyond comparison any who have appeared since the last national struggle for civil and religious liberty.[3] The most unfailing herald, companion, and follower of the awakening of a great people to work a beneficial change in opinion or institution, is Poetry. At such periods there is an accumulation of the power of communicating and receiving intense and impassioned conceptions respecting man and nature. The persons in whom this power resides, may often, as far as regards many portions of their nature, have little apparent correspondence with that spirit of good of which they are the ministers. But even whilst they deny and abjure, they are yet compelled to serve, the Power which is seated upon the throne of their own soul. It is impossible to read the compositions of the most celebrated writers of the present day without being startled with the electric life which burns within their words. They measure the circumference and sound the depths of human nature with a comprehensive and all-penetrating spirit, and they are themselves perhaps the most sincerely astonished at its manifestations, for it is less their spirit than the spirit of the age. Poets are the hierophants[4] of an unapprehended inspiration, the mirrors of the gigantic shadows which futurity casts upon the present, the words which express what they understand not; the trumpets which sing to battle, and feel not what they inspire: the influence which is moved not, but moves. Poets are the unacknowledged legislators of the World.

---

1. Either. *Interlunations*: dark periods between the old and new moon.   2. The second part was never written.   3. The English Civil War. The great poet of that age was Milton.   4. Interpreters, in the role of priests who interpret sacred mysteries.

JOHN KEATS
1795–1821

A poet "half in love with easeful Death," to quote a line from his *Ode to a Nightingale*, John Keats expressed with compelling intensity the Romantic longing for the unattainable, a concept that he defined in ways very different from Goethe's. In a series of brilliant lyrics, he explored subtle links between the passion for absolute beauty, which provides an imagined alternative to the everyday world's sordidness and disappointment, and the desire to melt into extinction, another form of that alternative.

At the age of sixteen, Keats was apprenticed to a druggist and surgeon; in 1816, he was licensed as an apothecary—but almost immediately abandoned medicine for poetry. Son of a hostler (a groom for horses) at a London inn, he had earlier attended school at Enfield, where he manifested an interest in literature encouraged by his friend Charles Cowden Clarke, the headmaster's son. Through political radical, poet, and critic Leigh Hunt, whose literary circle he joined in 1816, Keats came to know Percy Bysshe Shelley, William Hazlitt, and Charles Lamb, important members of the Romantic movement. He had a brief love affair with Fanny Brawne, to whom he became engaged in 1819; the next year he went to Italy, seeking a cure for his tuberculosis, only to die in Rome.

Although his first book, *Poems* (1817), met with some critical success, the long mythological poem *Endymion*, which he published a year later, became an object of attack by conservative literary reviews (*Blackwood's* and the *Quarterly*). Shelley, in his elegy for Keats (*Adonais*, 1821), encouraged the myth that the harsh reviews caused the poet's death. In fact, Keats lived long enough to publish his most important volume—written scarcely five years after he first tried his hand at poetry—*Lamia, Isabella, The Eve of St. Agnes, and Other Poems* (1820), which won critical applause and contained most of the poems for which he is remembered today.

Some of Keats's greatest works return to a form popular in the eighteenth century: the ode addressed to an abstraction (for example, melancholy) or another nonhuman object (for example, a nightingale or an urn). Although the basic literary device seems highly artificial, Keats uses it powerfully to express his characteristic sense of beauty so intensely experienced that it almost corresponds to pain.

> My heart aches, and a drowsy numbness pains
> My sense, as though of hemlock I had drunk . . .
> 'Tis not through envy of thy happy lot,
> But being too happy in thy happiness. . . .

Ode on Melancholy, in its sharp contrast to Coleridge's and Shelley's poems on dejection as well as to seventeenth- and eighteenth-century evocations of melancholy, illustrates particularly well Keats's special exemplification of the Romantic sensibility. In the first stanza, the speaker explicitly rejects traditional accompaniments of melancholy—yew, the death's-head moth, the owl—because such associations suggest a kind of passivity or inertia that might "drown the wakeful anguish of the soul," interfering with the immediate and intense experience of melancholy that he actively seeks. Instead, he advocates trying to live as completely as possible in the immediacy of emotion. Melancholy, he continues, dwells with beauty and joy and pleasure, all in their nature evanescent. To fully feel the wonder of beauty or happiness implies awareness that it will soon vanish. Only those capable of active participation in their own positive emotions can hope to know melancholy; paradoxically, the result of energetic commitment to the life of feeling is the utter submission to melancholy's power: one can hope to "be among her cloudy trophies hung."

Prose summary of such an argument risks sounding ridiculous or incomprehensible, for Keats's emotional logic inheres in the imagery and the music of his poems, which exert their own compelling force. Without any previous belief in the desirability of melancholy as an emotion, the reader, absorbed into a rich sequence of images, feels swept into an experience comparable to that which the poem endorses. The ode generates its own sense of beauty and of melancholy, and of the close relation between the two. Its brilliantly evocative specificity of physical reference always suggests more than is directly said, more than paraphrase can encompass:

> Aye, in the very temple of Delight
>   Veiled Melancholy has her sovereign shrine,
>   Though seen of none save him whose strenuous tongue
>   Can burst Joy's grape against his palate fine . . .

Everyone can recall the sensuous pleasure of a grape releasing its juice into the mouth, but it would be difficult to elucidate the full implications of the "strenuous tongue" or of "Joy's grape." Keat's great poetic gift manifests itself most unmistakably in his extraordinary power of suggestion—not only in the odes, but in the ballad imitation *La Belle Dame sans Merci*, with its haunting, half-told story, and in the understated sonnets, asserting the speaker's feeling but always hinting more emotion than they directly affirm.

PRONOUNCING GLOSSARY

The following list uses common English syllables and stress accents to provide rough equivalents of selected words whose pronunciation may be unfamiliar to the general reader.

Arcady: *ahr'-kah-dee*

Darien: *day'-ree-en*

Hippocrene: *hip'-oh-kreen*

La Belle Dame sans Merci: *lah bel dahm sahnh mayr-see'*

Lethe: *lee'-thee*

Proserpine: *pro'-ser-pain*

Provençal: *proh-vahn-sahl'*

Tempe: *tem'-pee*

On First Looking into Chapman's Homer[1]

Much have I traveled in the realms of gold,
  And many goodly states and kingdoms seen;
  Round many western islands have I been
Which bards in fealty to Apollo[2] hold.
Oft of one wide expanse had I been told   5
  That deep-browed Homer ruled as his demesne;[3]
  Yet did I never breathe its pure serene
Till I heard Chapman speak out loud and bold:
Then felt I like some watcher of the skies
  When a new planet swims into his ken;   10
Or like stout Cortez[4] when with eagle eyes
  He stared at the Pacific—and all his men
Looked at each other with a wild surmise—
  Silent, upon a peak in Darien.

---

1. Keats's friend and former teacher Charles Cowden Clarke had introduced Keats to George Chapman's (1559?–1634) translations of the *Iliad* (1611) and the *Odyssey* (1616) the night before this poem was written.   2. The Greek god of poetic inspiration.   3. Realm, kingdom.   4. In fact, Vasco Núñez de Balboa (ca. 1475–1519), Spanish conquistador, not Hernando Cortés (1485–1547), another Spaniard, was the European explorer who first saw the Pacific from Darién, Panama.

Bright Star

Bright star, would I were steadfast as thou art—
   Not in lone splendor hung aloft the night,
And watching, with eternal lids apart,
   Like nature's patient, sleepless Eremite,[1]
The moving waters at their priestlike task   5
   Of pure ablution round earth's human shores,
Or gazing on the new soft fallen mask
   Of snow upon the mountains and the moors—
No—yet still steadfast, still unchangeable,
   Pillowed upon my fair love's ripening breast,   10
To feel forever its soft fall and swell,
   Awake forever in a sweet unrest,
Still, still to hear her tender-taken breath,
And so live ever—or else swoon to death.

La Belle Dame sans Merci[1]

I

O what can ail thee, knight at arms,
   Alone and palely loitering?
The sedge has withered from the lake
   And no birds sing!

II

O what can ail thee, knight at arms,   5
   So haggard, and so woebegone?
The squirrel's granary is full
   And the harvest's done.

III

I see a lily on thy brow
   With anguish moist and fever dew,   10
And on thy cheeks a fading rose
   Fast withereth too.

IV

I met a lady in the meads,[2]
   Full beautiful, a faery's child,
Her hair was long, her foot was light   15
   And her eyes were wild.

1. Hermit.   1. The beautiful lady without pity (French); from a medieval poem by Alain Chartier.
2. Meadows. Here the knight answers the question asked in lines 5–6.

V

I made a garland for her head,
    And bracelets too, and fragrant zone;[3]
She looked at me as she did love
    And made sweet moan.   20

VI

I set her on my pacing steed
    And nothing else saw all day long,
For sidelong would she bend and sing
    A faery's song.

VII

She found me roots of relish sweet,   25
    And honey wild, and manna[4] dew,
And sure in language strange she said
    "I love thee true."

VIII

She took me to her elfin grot[5]
    And there she wept and sighed full sore,[6]   30
And there I shut her wild wild eyes
    With kisses four.

IX

And there she lullèd me asleep,
    And there I dreamed, ah woe betide!
The latest[7] dream I ever dreamt   35
    On the cold hill's side.

X

I saw pale kings, and princes too,
    Pale warriors, death-pale were they all;
They cried, "La belle dame sans merci
    Thee hath in thrall!"[8]   40

XI

I saw their starved lips in the gloam[9]
    With horrid warning gapèd wide,
And I awoke, and found me here
    On the cold hill's side.

---

3. Girdle.   4. The supernatural substance with which God fed the children of Israel in the wilderness (Exodus 16 and Joshua 5.12).   5. Cavern.   6. With great grief.   7. Last.   8. Bondage.
9. Twilight.

XII

And this is why I sojourn here,   45
   Alone and palely loitering;
Though the sedge withered from the lake
   And no birds sing.

Ode on a Grecian Urn

I

Thou still unravished bride of quietness,
   Thou foster-child of silence and slow time, *They could tell*
Sylvan historian, who canst thus express ← *and immaculate*
   A flowery tale more sweetly than our rhyme: *tale.*
What leaf-fringed legend haunts about thy shape   5
   Of deities or mortals, or of both,
      In Tempe or the dales of Arcady?[1]
What men or gods are these? What maidens loth?
What mad pursuit? What struggle to escape?
      What pipes and timbrels? What wild ecstasy?   10

II

Heard melodies are sweet, but those unheard
   Are sweeter; therefore, ye soft pipes, play on;
Not to the sensual ear, but, more endeared,
   Pipe to the spirit ditties of no tone:
Fair youth, beneath the trees, thou canst not leave   15
   Thy song, nor ever can those trees be bare;
      Bold lover, never, never canst thou kiss,
Though winning near the goal—yet, do not grieve;
      She cannot fade, though thou hast not thy bliss,
      For ever wilt thou love, and she be fair!   20

III

Ah, happy, happy boughs! that cannot shed
   Your leaves, nor ever bid the Spring adieu;
And, happy melodist, unwearièd,
   For ever piping songs for ever new;
More happy love! more happy, happy love!   25
   For ever warm and still to be enjoyed,
      For ever panting, and for ever young;
All breathing human passion far above,
   That leaves a heart high-sorrowful and cloyed,
      A burning forehead, and a parching tongue.   30

---

1. A mountainous region in the Peloponnese, traditionally regarded as the place of ideal rustic, bucolic contentment. *Tempe*: a valley in Thessaly between Mount Olympus and Mount Ossa.

IV

Who are these coming to the sacrifice?
   To what green altar, O mysterious priest,
Lead'st thou that heifer lowing at the skies,
   And all her silken flanks with garlands drest?
What little town by river or sea shore,   35
   Or mountain-built with peaceful citadel,
      Is emptied of this folk, this pious morn?
And, little town, thy streets for evermore
Will silent be; and not a soul to tell
      Why thou art desolate, can e'er return.   40

V

O Attic shape! Fair attitude! with brede[2]
   Of marble men and maidens overwrought,
With forest branches and the trodden weed;
   Thou, silent form, dost tease us out of thought
As doth eternity: Cold Pastoral!   45
   When old age shall this generation waste,
      Thou shalt remain, in midst of other woe
Than ours, a friend to man, to whom thou say'st,
   "Beauty is truth, truth beauty,"—that is all
      Ye know on earth, and all ye need to know.   50

Ode to a Nightingale

I

My heart aches, and a drowsy numbness pains
   My sense, as though of hemlock I had drunk,
Or emptied some dull opiate to the drains
   One minute past, and Lethe-wards[1] had sunk:
'Tis not through envy of thy happy lot,   5
   But being too happy in thy happiness,
      That thou, light-winged Dryad[2] of the trees,
         In some melodious plot
Of beechen green, and shadows numberless,
      Singest of summer in full-throated ease.   10

II

O for a draught of vintage! that hath been
   Cooled a long age in the deep-delvèd earth,
Tasting of Flora[3] and the country green,

---

2. Pattern. *Attic:* classical (literally, Athenian).   1. I.e., toward Lethe, the river of forgetfulness in Greek mythology.   2. Wood nymph.   3. The goddess of flowers and spring; here, flowers.

Dance, and Provençal[4] song, and sunburnt mirth!
O for a beaker full of the warm South!   15
   Full of the true, the blushful Hippocrene,[5]
      With beaded bubbles winking at the brim,
         And purple-stainèd mouth;
   That I might drink, and leave the world unseen,
      And with thee fade away into the forest dim: 20

III

Fade far away, dissolve, and quite forget
   What thou among the leaves hast never known,
The weariness, the fever, and the fret
   Here, where men sit and hear each other groan;
Where palsy shakes a few, sad, last gray hairs,   25
   Where youth grows pale, and spectre-thin, and dies;
      Where but to think is to be full of sorrow
         And leaden-eyed despairs;
   Where beauty cannot keep her lustrous eyes,
      Or new love pine at them beyond tomorrow.   30

IV

Away! away! for I will fly to thee,
   Not charioted by Bacchus and his pards,[6]
But on the viewless wings of Poesy,
   Though the dull brain perplexes and retards:
Already with thee! tender is the night,   35
   And haply[7] the Queen-Moon is on her throne,
      Clustered around by all her starry Fays;[8]
         But here there is no light,
   Save what from heaven is with the breezes blown
      Through verdurous glooms and winding mossy ways.   40

V

I cannot see what flowers are at my feet,
   Nor what soft incense hangs upon the boughs,
But, in embalmèd darkness, guess each sweet
   Wherewith the seasonable month endows
The grass, the thicket, and the fruit-tree wild;   45
   White hawthorn, and the pastoral eglantine;
      Fast-fading violets covered up in leaves;
         And mid-May's eldest child,
   The coming musk-rose, full of dewy wine,
      The murmurous haunt of flies on summer eves.   50

---

4. From Provence, the district in France associated with the troubadours.   **5.** The fountain on Mount Helicon, in Greece, sacred to the muse of poetry.   **6.** Leopards. Bacchus (Dionysus) was traditionally supposed to be accompanied by leopards, lions, goats, and so on.   **7.** Perhaps.   **8.** Fairies.

VI

Darkling[9] I listen; and for many a time
　　I have been half in love with easeful Death,
Called him soft names in many a musèd rhyme,
　　To take into the air my quiet breath;
Now more than ever seems it rich to die,　　　　　　　55
　　To cease upon the midnight with no pain,
　　　　While thou art pouring forth thy soul abroad
　　　　　　In such an ecstasy!
Still wouldst thou sing, and I have ears in vain—
　　To thy high requiem become a sod.[1]　　　　　　60

VII

Thou wast not born for death, immortal Bird!
　　No hungry generations tread thee down;
The voice I hear this passing night was heard
　　In ancient days by emperor and clown:
Perhaps the self-same song that found a path　　　　65
　　Through the sad heart of Ruth, when, sick for home,
　　　　She stood in tears amid the alien corn;[2]
　　　　　　The same that ofttimes hath
Charmed magic casements, opening on the foam
　　Of perilous seas, in faery lands forlorn.　　　　　70

VIII

Forlorn! the very word is like a bell
　　To toll me back from thee to my sole self!
Adieu! the fancy cannot cheat so well
　　As she is famed to do, deceiving elf.
Adieu! adieu! thy plaintive anthem fades　　　　　75
　　Past the near meadows, over the still stream,
　　　　Up the hill-side; and now 'tis buried deep
　　　　　　In the next valley-glades:
Was it a vision, or a waking dream?
　　Fled is that music:—do I wake or sleep?　　　　　80

Ode on Melancholy

I

No, no, go not to Lethe,[1] neither twist
　　Wolfsbane, tight-rooted, for its poisonous wine;
Nor suffer thy pale forehead to be kissed

---

9. In the dark.   1. I.e., like dirt, unable to hear.   2. See the Book of Ruth. After her Ephrathite husband died, she returned to his native land with her mother-in-law.   1. The river of forgetfulness in Hades.

By nightshade, ruby grape of Proserpine;[2]
Make not your rosary of yew-berries,[3]   5
   Nor let the beetle, nor the death-moth[4] be
   Your mournful Psyche,[5] nor the downy owl
A partner in your sorrow's mysteries;
   For shade to shade will come too drowsily,
   And drown the wakeful anguish of the soul.   10

II

But when the melancholy fit shall fall
   Sudden from heaven like a weeping cloud,
That fosters the droop-headed flowers all,
   And hides the green hill in an April shroud;
Then glut thy sorrow on a morning rose,   15
   Or on the rainbow of the salt sand-wave,
   Or on the wealth of globèd peonies;
Or if thy mistress some rich anger shows,
   Imprison her soft hand, and let her rave,
   And feed deep, deep upon her peerless eyes.   20

III

She[6] dwells with Beauty—Beauty that must die;
   And Joy, whose hand is ever at his lips
Bidding adieu; and aching Pleasure nigh,
   Turning to Poison while the bee-mouth sips:
Aye, in the very temple of Delight   25
   Veiled Melancholy has her sovereign shrine,
     Though seen of none save him whose strenuous tongue
   Can burst Joy's grape against his palate fine;
His soul shall taste the sadness of her might,
   And be among her cloudy trophies hung.[7]   30

To Autumn

I

Season of mists and mellow fruitfulness,
   Close bosom-friend of the maturing sun;
Conspiring with him how to load and bless
   With fruit the vines that round the thatch-eaves run;
To bend with apples the mossed cottage-trees,   5
   And fill all fruit with ripeness to the core;
     To swell the gourd, and plump the hazel shells
With a sweet kernel; to set budding more,

---

2. Wife of Pluto, queen of the underworld.   3. Wolfsbane, nightshade, and yew berries are all poisonous.
4. The death's-head moth has markings that resemble a skull. The scarab beetle, depicted in Egyptian tombs, was an emblem of death.   5. The soul, portrayed by the Greeks as a butterfly.   6. Melancholy.
7. The Greeks placed war trophies in their temples to commemorate victories.

And still more, later flowers for the bees,
Until they think warm days will never cease,   10
   For Summer has o'er-brimmed their clammy cells.

II

Who hath not seen thee oft amid thy store?
   Sometimes whoever seeks abroad may find
Thee sitting careless on a granary floor,
   Thy hair soft-lifted by the winnowing wind;   15
Or on a half-reaped furrow sound asleep,
   Drowsed with the fume of poppies, while thy hook
     Spares the next swath and all its twinèd flowers:
And sometimes like a gleaner thou dost keep
   Steady thy laden head across a brook;   20
   Or by a cyder-press, with patient look,
     Thou watchest the last oozings hours by hours.

III

Where are the songs of Spring? Ay, where are they?
   Think not of them, thou hast thy music too,—
While barrèd clouds bloom the soft-dying day,   25
   And touch the stubble-plains with rosy hue;
Then in a wailful choir the small gnats mourn
   Among the river sallows,[8] borne aloft
     Or sinking as the light wind lives or dies;
And full-grown lambs loud bleat from hilly bourn;   30
   Hedge-crickets sing; and now with treble soft
The red-breast whistles from a garden-croft;
   And gathering swallows twitter in the skies.

8. Willows.

CONTINENTAL ROMANTIC LYRICS: A SELECTION

This group of poems from five European countries exemplifies both the scope and the consistency of the Romantic imagination. Like their English counterparts, the writers represented here concern themselves with time, death, nature, and love and with the connections among these vast subjects. They express emotions ranging from extreme depression to exhilaration. As one can see even in translation, these poets explore a broad spectrum of metrical possibilities. Although they write mainly in the first person, they consistently focus on, explicitly or implicitly, the links between the self and the world—both the natural world and that composed of other people (including, in Heinrich Heine's *The Silesian Weavers,* the political realm). In their insistence on feeling's importance and complexity, its capacity to guide the individual toward profound insight, they reveal why Romantic poetry continues to communicate directly with readers who live long after the era of its writing.

   This poetry characteristically reveals a spiritual dimension even when its ostensible concerns appear relatively trivial. Thus Rosalía de Castro, feeling the heat of a summer day, finds herself aware of "the anguish of the soul," and Friedrich Hölderlin, also contemplating a summer scene, perceives the water into which swans dip their heads as "holy." Often, though, the poets directly confront metaphysical issues. Like Wordsworth, they may feel themselves united with the natural universe (see, for example, Gustavo Adolfo Bécquer's *Nameless Spirit*). But they also explore the emotional reverberations of Christianity. The German poet known as Novalis (born Friedrich von Hardenberg) unites his preoccupation with time and his sense of loss with his Christian convictions, imagining Jesus not only as the type of perfection but as the representative of vanished serenity and nobility of spirit. Victor Hugo, employing the lyric impulse to illuminate a narrative plot, evokes the almost inconceivable emotional experience of Satan falling from heaven to hell. Whether writing openly or covertly of religious feeling, Romantic poets consciously and often triumphantly stretch the limits of the expressible.

Particularly striking in this group of selections, as in the entire body of Romantic lyrics, is the complex symbolic use made of material from the natural world. Anna Petrovna Bunina, for instance, an early nineteenth-century Russian poet, begins *From the Seashore* with a scene of calm natural beauty—quiet sea, shining sky, birds in their nests. The poem then mutates into an equally peaceful domestic scene, only to return to a new figuration of the sea, invoked now as a prospective grave. The shift calls attention to the way that human beings attach meanings to nature in accord with mutable psychic conditions.

The French poet Alphonse de Lamartine, in his long lyric *The Lake,* explores more fully the assignment of meaning to nature, using his memory of being in a boat with his beloved on an idyllic summer evening to reflect on the ineluctable passing of time. Now the woman he loves is dying. In the earlier time, she spoke to him about the need to live intensely, given the flight of the moments, using the boat trip as a metaphor:

> "We have no port, time itself has no shore;
> It glides by, and we pass away."

Now, the speaker can only hope that the beauty of the lake and its surroundings will survive as a symbol of their love, possessing a kind of permanence that human beings cannot attain.

Yet more mysterious are the allusions to nature in Heine's lyrics, which rely on subtle suggestion rather than overt statement. Writing, for instance, of a pine tree in the north that dreams during the winter of a faraway palm tree, he evokes the omnipresence of human longing without ever mentioning the human. "Death is like the long cool night," he writes in another poem, without explaining, but his allusion to young nightingales singing in the trees captures a sense of death as beautiful, remote, and haunting.

Gérard de Nerval, who, writing about nature, explicitly stresses its connection with his feelings, also succeeds in treating products of civilization as though they were part of the natural world. Thus he writes of waking up in a carriage and seeing rows of little houses marching like sheep. Most memorably, he imagines the cathedral of Notre-Dame at some distant time in the future, falling into decay like an ox felled by a wolf, its great bones contemplated by human beings as though they were a natural spectacle.

For the human, too, can figure as subject matter for Romantic poets. Mikhail Lermontov, who explicitly compares himself with Byron (if only to affirm that he is *not* Byron), like the Englishman writes about women and his relations with them. He also writes, in a particularly famous early poem, about the death of a fellow poet, Pushkin, in a duel. Just as Nerval uses the figure of a woman glimpsed in the street as a pretext for fantasizing about himself in relation to her, Lermontov employs the fact of Pushkin's death as an opportunity to discuss the situation of the poet in a hostile community. His vivid anger, ostensibly about the loss of another poet, obviously concerns his own predicament as well.

These lyricists value the inexpressibility of powerful feeling. At the same time, they set themselves the impossible task of communicating precisely what defies expression. The sheer musicality of their verse helps to convey emotion, as they create powerful (and often untranslatable) verbal melodies through the rhythms of their stanzaic forms and the varied movement of their lines. By strategies of indirection, they often succeed in persuading their readers that lyric verse can, after all, convey the kinds of feeling that most of us lock within ourselves. The poems collected here investigate experience both commonplace and extraordinary; interrogate the universe; but, most important, explore and imagine the depths of human emotion.

FRIEDRICH HÖLDERLIN
1770–1843

Important partly for his capacity to combine classical and Romantic sensibility, the German poet Friedrich Hölderlin (*freed'-rick hul'der-lin*) wrote his considerable body of lyric verse early in his life, before becoming incurably schizophrenic at the age of thirty-six. He had prepared himself for the ministry but decided that he was unsuited for such a vocation and found work—not very successfully—as a tutor. In his lyrics, which have become celebrated since the twentieth century, he records and evokes intensities of personal feeling, with particular emphasis, as the selections printed here reveal, on what it means for human beings to live in time.

The poems are translated by Christopher Middleton, who successfully evokes Hölderlin's range of tones and meters.

The Half of Life

With yellow pears the country,
Brimming with wild roses,
Hangs into the lake,
You gracious swans,
And drunk with kisses   5
Your heads you dip
Into the holy lucid water.

Where, ah where shall I find,
When winter comes, the flowers,
And where the sunshine   10
And shadows of the earth?
Walls stand
Speechless and cold, in the wind
The weathervanes clatter.

Hyperion's[1] Song of Fate

You walk up there in the light
On floors like velvet, blissful spirits.
Shining winds divine
Touch you lightly
As a harper touches holy   5
Strings with her fingers.

Fateless as babes asleep
They breathe, the celestials.
Chastely kept
In a simple bud,   10
For them the spirit
Flowers eternal,
And in bliss their eyes
Gaze in eternal
Calm clarity.   15

But to us it is given
To find no resting place,
We faint, we fall,
Suffering, human,
Blindly from one   20
To the next moment
Like water flung
From rock to rock down
Long years into uncertainty.

Brevity

Why make it so short? Have you lost your old liking
For song? Why, in days of hope, when young,
You sang and sang,
There scarce was an end of it.

My song is short as my luck was. Who'd go   5
Gaily swimming at sundown? It's gone, earth's cold,
And the annoying nightbird
Flits, close, blocking your vision.

---

1. In Greek mythology, a Titan, father of Aurora, goddess of dawn.

To the Fates

Grant me a single summer, you lords of all,
  A single autumn, for the fullgrown song,
    So that, with such sweet playing sated,
      Then my heart may die more willing.

The soul, in life robbed of its godly right,   5
  Rests not, even in Orcus[1] down below;
    Yet should I once achieve my heart's
      First holy concern, the poem,

Welcome then, O stillness of the shadow world!
  Even if down I go without my   10
    Music, I shall be satisfied; once
      Like gods I shall have lived, more I need not.

1. Hades.

NOVALIS (FRIEDRICH VON HARDENBERG)
1772–1801

Born into a family of the German nobility, Friedrich von Hardenberg assumed the pseudonym Novalis on the basis of his family's earlier use of the name "de Novali." He studied first law, then mining, and ended his career as a mine inspector at a saltworks. His achievement as poet and philosopher, however, despite his short life (he died of tuberculosis), powerfully influenced later Romantic thought. *Hymns to the Night,* from which the selection printed here is taken, expressed his grief over the death, also from tuberculosis, of the young girl to whom he had been engaged. In the hymns, Novalis insists that death provides the entrance into a higher life, and he anticipates his eventual union with his fiancée and with the universe as a whole.

The translator is Charles E. Passage, who attempts to convey Novalis's characteristic combination of mystical and sentimental feeling.

PRONOUNCING GLOSSARY

The following list uses common English syllables and stress accents to provide rough equivalents of selected words whose pronunciation may be unfamiliar to the general reader.

Friedrich von Hardenberg: *freed'-rick*   Novalis: *noh-vahl'-is*
  fon hahr'-den-berg

Yearning for Death

Down now into the dark earth's womb,
From Light's domain away!
Wild rage of grief and pangs of gloom
Mark glad departure's day.
In narrow barque[1] we swiftly ply   5
To land along the shores of sky.

Praised be the everlasting Night,
Praised be eternal slumber!
Day's heat has withered us, and blight
Of sorrows without number.   10
For alien lands we no more yearn,
To our Father's house we would return.

In this world what can us betide
Our love and constancy?
When old things have been put aside   15
What use can new things be?
O! lonely stands and all undone
Whoever loves the times foregone.

The times foregone, when in bright dance
High spirits flamed, and when   20
The Father's hand and countenance
Were still in mankind's ken,
And nobly, simply, many bore
The lofty image that he bore.

The times foregone, when full-bloom-blowing   25
Primaeval races throve,
And children toward God's kingdom going
For death and torment strove;
And when, though life and pleasure spoke,
Yet many hearts, for loving, broke.   30

Those times, when God himself revealed
Himself with youthful ardor,
And with love's strength his sweet life sealed
In young death as a martyr,
Refusing not the smart and pain,   35
That it might be our dearer gain.

We see them now, with anxious yearning,
Shrouded in dark of night;
In temporal life our hot thirst's burning
Will not be slaked outright;   40

---

1. Boat.

Unto our homeland we must go
That we that holy time may know.

What holds up our return? To rest
Our loved ones are long laid.
At their graves closes our lives' quest,   45
Sad are we and afraid.
There is no more for us to seek,
The heart is sated, the world is bleak.

A mystic shudder, sweet, unbounded,
Now courses through our marrow;   50
Methinks from the far distance sounded
An echo of our sorrow.
Perhaps our loved ones likewise longing
Have wafted us this sigh of longing.

Down to the sweet bride[2] come away,   55
To Jesus whom we love!
Good cheer! The evening dawn shows gray
On them who grieve and love.
Dream bursts our bonds and sinks us free
To our Father's arms eternally.   60

2. Jesus, as the bride of humankind.

ANNA PETROVNA BUNINA
1774–1829

One of the first woman poets to be published in Russia, Anna Petrovna Bunina (*ah'-na pet-rohv'-na boo-nee'-na*) insisted, in the face of her parents' disapproval, on pursuing a literary career and on developing her intellectual capacities. She had inherited a small amount of money, which made it possible for her initially to hire tutors and to spend her time writing, demonstrating a gift for lyric verse that drew on details of the natural world as a means of expressing personal feeling. After she began publishing poetry (in 1806), she acquired literary supporters who tried to ease her financial and physical circumstances when she developed cancer in 1815. She died of the disease.

In the poem printed here, Bunina begins with a deceptively calm natural scene, lovingly evoking the appearance and mood of the sea just after sunset. The poem gradually builds intensity as it turns to the experience of human misery, ending with an appeal to the sea to abandon its calm to better respond to the speaker's mood. Like many other Romantic lyrics, the poem draws on the idea of harmony between humanity and nature—but only to declare the insufficiency of nature to the personal anguish in which "Poison flows / In my veins."

Pamela Perkins translated this selection.

From the Seashore

The bright sea
Flowed from the sky,
In quiet the waves
Lap along the shore,
Brief ripples   5
Faintly tremble.

The sun's gone down,
There is no moon,
In the scarlet glow
The west is shining,   10
Birds in their nests,
Flocks in the tree-crests.

Everything suddenly fell silent,
Everything in its place.
In the room it is quiet,   15
There is no rustle;
The children are nestled
Modestly in the corners.

Lina touched
The strings of the harp;   20
The golden harp
Gave voice;
Sounds in harmony
Sing with Lina.

In a rose flame   25
The hearth gives light;
The bright fire
Leaps along the coals;
The smoke dark-silver
Curls in a column.   30

The fierce flame
scorches the soul;
The heart languishes,
Everything has withered;
Poison flows   35
In my veins.

Tears ran dry
In troubled eyes,
Sighs stopped
The chest from heaving,   40
Speech dies down
On cold lips.

Sea, start to churn!
Be a grave for me!
Golden harp,   45
Strike like thunder!
Fire, flow,
Warm this poor woman!

ALPHONSE DE LAMARTINE
1790–1869

Celebrated among the French Romantics for his "poetry of the soul," lyric meditations that united passion, philosophy, and religious humanism, Alphonse de Lamartine was also a novelist and statesman who served in various diplomatic and elected positions before retiring in disgust at Louis-Napoléon's coup d'état in 1851. His father was an aristocrat who had narrowly escaped the guillotine in the French Revolution; he himself had early royalist sympathies but became a liberal and a prominent opposition figure in the revolution of 1848, even holding a top position in the short-lived provisional government.

Poetry, Lamartine said, echoes our deepest intuitions and intelligence: it is a sincere expression of the whole human being. He boasted that he had "brought poetry down from Parnassus" and taught it to express human emotions. Much of his own poetry draws on personal life, and *The Lake,* whose lyrical passion inspired a generation of French romantics, recalls a brief but intense love affair between the poet and a young married woman, Julie Charles. Meeting one summer when both were at a health resort on Lake Bourget in the French Alps, they separated over the winter but promised to meet again the next year. When the poet returned to the lake, however, Julie was already dying and he found himself alone. *The Lake* is Lamartine's elegy to his lost love, a melodious complaint that moves from the intimate situation of two lovers to a meditation on nature and time.

Andrea Moorhead's remarkably faithful translation suggests Lamartine's lyrical yet philosophical voice.

PRONOUNCING GLOSSARY

The following list uses common English syllables and stress accents to provide rough equivalents of selected words whose pronunciation may be unfamiliar to the general reader.

Bourget: *boor-zhay'*   Lamartine: *lah-mahr-teen'*

The Lake

And thus, forever driven towards new shores,
Swept into eternal night without return,
Will we never, for even one day, drop anchor
    On time's vast ocean?

O lake! Only a year has now gone by,[1]   5
And to these dear waves she would have seen again,
Look! I'm returning alone to rest on the very rock
    Where you last saw her rest!

Then as now, you rumbled under these great rocks;
Then as now, you broke against their torn flanks;   10
The wind hurling the foam from your waves
    Onto her adored feet.

One evening, you recall? We drifted in silence;
Far off on the water and under the stars hearing
Only the rhythmic sound of oars striking   15
    Your melodious waves.

Suddenly strains unknown on earth
Echoed from the enchanted shore;
The water paid heed, and the voice so dear
    To me spoke these words: 20

"O time, suspend your flight! and you, blessed hours,
    Suspend your swift passage.
Allow us to savor the fleeting delights
    Of our most happy days!

So many wretched people beseech you: 25
    Flow, flow quickly for them;
Take away the cares devouring them;
    Overlook the happy.

But I ask in vain for just a few more moments,
    Time escaping me flees;   30
While I beg the night: 'Slow down,' already
    It fades into the dawn.

Then let us love, let us love! And the fleeting hours
    Let us hasten to enjoy.
We have no port, time itself has no shore;   35
    It glides by, and we pass away."

Jealous time, will these moments of such intoxication,
Love flooding us with overwhelming bliss,
Fly past us with the same speed
    As dark and painful days?   40

What! will we not keep at least the trace of them?
What! They are gone forever? Totally lost?
This time that gave them and is obliterating them,
    Will it never return them to us?

---

1. They met in October 1816; it is now August 1817.

Eternity, nothingness, past, somber abysses,   45
What are you doing with the days you swallow up?
Speak: will you ever give back the sublime bliss
    You stole from us?

O lake! silent rocks! shaded grottoes! dark forest!
You whom time can spare or even rejuvenate,   50
Preserve, noble nature, preserve from this night
    At least the memory!

May it live in your peace, may it be in your storms,
Beautiful lake, and in the light of your glad slopes,
And in these tall dark firs and in these savage rocks,   55
    Overhanging your waves.

May it be in the trembling zephyr passing by,
In the endless sounds that carry from shore to shore
In the silver faced star[2] that whitens your surface
    With its softened brilliance.   60

May the moaning wind and sighing reed,
May the delicate scent of your fragrant breeze,
May everything that we hear and see and breathe,
    Awaken the memory of—their love!

2. The moon.

HEINRICH HEINE
1797–1856

Born in Germany of Jewish parents, Heinrich Heine is most famous as a lyric poet, although he also composed drama, narrative poetry, political commentary, and literary criticism. As *The Silesian Weavers* suggests, he had strong revolutionary sympathies, which drew him to Paris in 1831. There he died, after a prolonged illness.

    Simple diction and frequent reliance on the metrical patterns of traditional ballads characterize many of Heine's lyrics, which have frequently been set to music. Naïve though the lyrics often seem, they have dark undertones. When Heine openly confronts political actualities, one ground for his despair becomes apparent: he sees German society as divided between the uncaring and tyrannical rich and the profoundly oppressed poor, and he finds the structure of social inequity intolerable.

    Hal Draper translated the selections printed here.

PRONOUNCING GLOSSARY

The following list uses common English syllables and stress accents to provide rough equivalents of selected words whose pronunciation may be unfamiliar to the general reader.

Heinrich Heine: *hain'-rik hai'-ne*   Silesian: *sai-lee'-zhahn*

[A Pine Is Standing Lonely]

A pine is standing lonely
In the North on a bare plateau.
He sleeps; a bright white blanket
Enshrouds him in ice and snow.

He's dreaming of a palm tree   5
Far away in the Eastern land
Lonely and silently mourning
On a sunburnt rocky strand.

[A Young Man Loves a Maiden]

A young man loves a maiden
Who chooses another instead;
This other loves still another
And these two haply wed.

The maiden out of anger   5
Marries, with no regard,
The first good man she runs into—
The young lad takes it hard.

It is so old a story,
Yet somehow always new;   10
And he that has just lived it,
It breaks his heart in two.

[Ah, Death Is Like the Long Cool Night]

Ah, death is like the long cool night,
    And life is like the sultry day.
        Dusk falls now; I grow sleepy;
The day makes me tired of light.

Over my bed there's a tree that gleams—   5
    Young nightingales are singing there,
        Of love, love only, singing—
I hear it even in dreams.

The Silesian Weavers[1]

In somber eyes no tears of grieving;
Grinding their teeth, they sit at their weaving;
"O Germany, at your shroud we sit,
We're weaving a threefold curse in it—
    We're weaving, we're weaving!   5

"A curse on the god we prayed to, kneeling
With cold in our bones, with hunger reeling;
We waited and hoped, in vain persevered,
He scorned us and duped us, mocked and jeered—
    We're weaving, we're weaving!   10

"A curse on the king[2] of the rich man's nation
Who hardens his heart at our supplication,
Who wrings the last penny out of our hides
And lets us be shot like dogs besides—
    We're weaving, we're weaving!   15

"A curse on this false fatherland, teeming
With nothing but shame and dirty scheming,
Where every flower is crushed in a day,
Where worms are regaled on rot and decay—
    We're weaving, we're weaving!   20

"The shuttle flies, the loom creaks loud,
Night and day we weave your shroud—
Old Germany, at your shroud we sit,
We're weaving a threefold curse in it,
    We're weaving, we're weaving!"   25

1. Silesia was a province of the kingdom of Prussia in northeast Germany. This poem was occasioned by violent uprisings of weavers protesting intolerable working conditions during June 1844. 2. Friedrich Wilhelm IV (1795–1861). Heine's poem is prophetic: in 1848 the king, though not deposed, was forced by revolution to grant a constitution to Prussia.

GIACOMO LEOPARDI
1798–1837

The product of a rigid upbringing by aristocratic parents, the Italian Giacomo Leopardi (*jah'-koh-moh lay-oh-pahr'-dee*) grew to adulthood plagued by many ailments, a hunchback close to blindness. But his intellectual powers were highly developed, and he soon attained a fine reputation as scholar, poet, and translator. His poetry characteristically expresses a poignant sensitivity to the beauty and promise of every-day life, as well as despair at its inevitable destruction with the passage of time. Only the poetic imagination, which allows Leopardi to grasp and transcend his own mortality, offers an escape: "And sweet to me the foundering in this sea [of eternity]," he writes in *The Infinite*.

Ottavio M. Casale translated the selections printed here, skillfully conveying the rhythms of Leopardi's free verse.

The Infinite

This lonely hill has always been so dear
To me, and dear the hedge which hides away
The reaches of the sky. But sitting here
And wondering, I fashion in my mind
The endless spaces far beyond, the more   5
Than human silences, and deepest peace;
So that the heart is on the edge of fear.
And when I hear the wind come blowing through
The trees, I pit its voice against that boundless
Silence and summon up eternity,   10
And the dead seasons, and the present one,
Alive with all its sound. And thus it is
In this immensity my thought is drowned:
And sweet to me the foundering in this sea.

To Himself

Now you may rest forever,
My tired heart. The last illusion is dead
That I believed eternal. Dead. I can
So clearly see—not only hope is gone
But the desire to be deceived as well.   5
Rest, rest forever.
You have beaten long enough. Nothing is worth
Your smallest motion, nor the earth your sighs.
This life is bitterness
And vacuum, nothing else. The world is mud.   10
From now on calm yourself.
Despair for the last time. The only gift
Fate gave our kind was death. Henceforth, heap scorn
Upon yourself, Nature, the ugly force
That, hidden, orders universal ruin,   15
And the boundless emptiness of everything.

To Sylvia

Sylvia. Do you remember still
The moments of your mortal lifetime here,
When such a loveliness
Shone in the elusive laughter of your eyes,
And you, contemplative and gay, climbed toward   5
The summit of your youth?

The tranquil chambers held,
The paths re-echoed, your perpetual song,
When at your woman's tasks
You sat, content to concentrate upon   10
The future beckoning within your mind.
It was the fragrant May,
And thus you passed your time.

I often used to leave
The dear, belabored pages which consumed   15
So much of me and of my youth, and from
Ancestral balconies
Would lean to hear the music of your voice,
Your fingers humming through
The intricacies of the weaving work.   20
And I would gaze upon
The blue surrounding sky,
The paths and gardens golden in the sun,
And there the far-off sea, and here the mountain.
No human tongue can tell   25
What I felt then within my brimming heart.

What tendernesses then,
What hopes, what hearts were ours, O Sylvia mine!
How large a thing seemed life, and destiny!
When I recall those bright anticipations,   30
Bitterness invades,
And I turn once again to mourn my lot.
O Nature, Nature, why
Do you not keep the promises you gave?
Why trick the children so?   35

Before the winter struck the summer grass,
You died, my gentle girl,
Besieged by hidden illness and possessed.
You never saw the flowering of your years.
Your heart was never melted by the praise   40
Of your dark hair, your shy,
Enamoured eyes. Nor did you with your friends
Conspire on holidays to talk of love.

The expectation failed
As soon for me, and fate denied my youth.   45
Ah how gone by, gone by,
You dear companion of my dawning time,
The hope that I lament!
Is this the world we knew? And these the joys
The love, the labors, happenings we shared?   50
And this the destiny
Of human beings? My poor one, when
The truth rose up, you fell,
And from afar you pointed me the way
To coldest death and the stark sepulchre.   55

The Village Saturday

The sun is falling as the peasant girl
Returns from the open fields,
Bearing a swathe of grass and in her hand
Her customary bunch of violets
And roses which will grace   5
Her hair and breast the coming holiday.
And, spinning, the old woman sits upon
The steps among her neighbors,
Their faces turned against the dying light;
And she tells tales of her green days, when she   10
Adorned her body for the holidays
And, slenderly robust,
Would dance the night away
Among the companions of her lovely prime.
The very air seems now to deepen, the sky   15
Turns darker blue. Down from the hills and roofs
Returning shadows fall
At the whitening of the moon.

Now bells declare the time
Is near, the festive day,   20
The hour of heart's renewal.
The shouting lads invade
The village square in troops,
Leaping now here, now there,
Making such happy chatter.   25
Meanwhile the whistling laborer comes back
To take his meager meal
And ruminate about his day of rest.

And then, when every other lamp is out
And other sounds are stilled—   30
Listen—a pounding hammer and a saw:
It is the carpenter,

Awake and hurrying by lanternlight
Inside his shuttered shop
To end his task before the morning breaks.   35

Of all the seven days this is the one
Most cherished, full of joy and expectation.
The passing hours will bring tomorrow soon,
And tedium and sadness,
When each shall turn inside   40
His mind to his habitual travail.

O playful little boy,
Your flowering time is like a day of grace,
So brightly blue,
Anticipating the great feast of life.   45
My child, enjoy the season.
I will not tell you more; but if the day
Seems slow in coming, do not grieve too much.

VICTOR HUGO
1802–1885

Celebrated as poet, dramatist, and novelist, Victor Hugo was a towering figure in his
generation of French literary figures. He wrote in virtually every available genre and
explored an enormous range of subjects and feelings, helping throughout to articulate
the principles of Romanticism. His various political allegiances determined some of
his actions: for twenty years he exiled himself to the island of Guernsey (a possession
of the British Crown), believing his life in danger after President Louis-Napoléon
seized power. Always, though, he devoted himself to writing. *Et nox facta est*, printed
here, is the first section of the epic *The End of Satan* and depicts the fallen angel's
defiant plunge from heaven. Hugo's portrait of Satan demonstrates both psychological
acuity and powerful identification with the figure of a rebel. The poem makes one
feel both the terror and the ugliness of Satan's nay-saying and the splendor of his
refusal.

The translator is Mary Ann Caws, who has evoked the dignity and the intensity of
Hugo's verse.

PRONOUNCING GLOSSARY

The following list uses common English syllables and stress accents to provide rough equivalents of selected words whose pronunciation may be unfamiliar to the general reader.

Victor Hugo: *vik-tor' ew-goh'*

Et nox facta est[1]

I

He[2] had been falling in the abyss some four thousand years.

Never had he yet managed to grasp a peak,
Nor lift even once his towering forehead.
He sank deeper in the dark and the mist, aghast,
Alone, and behind him, in the eternal nights,   5
His wing feathers fell more slowly still.
He fell dumbfounded, grim, and silent,
Sad, his mouth open and his feet towards the heavens,
The horror of the chasm imprinted on his livid face.
He cried: "Death!" his fists stretched out in the empty dark.   10
Later this word was man and was named Cain.[3]

He was falling. A rock struck his hand quite suddenly;
He held on to it, as a dead man holds on to his tomb,
And stopped. Someone, from on high, cried out to him: "Fall!
The suns will go out around you, accursed!"   15
And the voice was lost in the immensity of horror.
And pale, he looked toward the eternal dawn.
The suns were far off, but shone still.
Satan raised his head and spoke, his arms in the air:
"You lie!" This word was later the soul of Judas.[4]   20

Like the gods of bronze erect upon their pilasters,
He waited a thousand years, eyes fixed upon the stars.
The suns were far off, but were still shining.
The thunder then rumbled in the skies unhearing, cold.
Satan laughed, and spat towards the thunder.   25
Filled by the visionary shadow, the immensity
Shivered. This spitting out was later Barabbas.[5]

A passing breath made him fall lower still.

II

The fall of the damned one began once again.—Terrible,
Somber, and pierced with holes luminous as a sieve,   30
The sky full of suns withdrew, brightness
Trembled, and in the night the great fallen one,
Naked, sinister, and pulled by the weight of his crime,
Fell, and his head wedging the abyss apart.
Lower! Lower, and still lower! Everything presently   35

---

1. Written as part of *The End of Satan*, an epic poem never completed. The Latin title (And there was night) contrasts with the biblical "And there was light" (Genesis 1.3).   2. Satan, formerly the rebellious archangel Lucifer, thrown out of heaven by God (Revelation 12.7–9 and Isaiah 14.12).   3. The first murderer, son of Adam and brother of Abel, the victim (Genesis 4.1–15).   4. Judas Iscariot, the apostle who betrayed Jesus (Matthew 26.47–50, 27.3–5).   5. The condemned criminal who was freed instead of Jesus (Mark 15.6–15).

Fled from him; no obstacle to seize in passing,
No mountain, no crumbling rock, no stone,
Nothing, shadow! and from fright he closed his eyes.

And when they opened, three suns only
Shone, and shadow had eaten away the firmament.   40
All the other suns had perished.

III

A rock
Emerged from blackest mist like some arm approaching.
He grasped it, and his feet touched summits.

Then the dreadful being called Never
Dreamed. His forehead sank between his guilty hands.   45
The three suns, far off, like three great eyes,
Watched him, and he watched them not.
Space resembled our earthly plains,
At evening, when the horizon sinking, retreating,
Blackens under the white eyes of the ghostly twilight.   50
Long rays entwined the feet of the great exile.
Behind him his shadow filled the infinite.
The peaks of chaos mingled in themselves.
In an instant he felt some horrendous growth of wings;
He felt himself become a monster, and that the angel in him   55
Was dying, and the rebel then knew regret.
He felt his shoulder, so bright before,
Quiver in the hideous cold of membraned wing,
And folding his arms with his head lifted high,
This bandit, as if grown greater through affront,   60
Alone in these depths that only ruin inhabits,
Looked steadily at the shadow's cave.
The noiseless darkness grew in the nothingness.
Obscure opacity closed off the gaping sky;
And making beyond the last promontory   65
A triple crack in the black pane,
The three suns mingled their three lights.
You would have thought them three wheels of a chariot of fire,
Broken after some battle in the high firmament.
Like prows, the mountains from the mist emerged.   70
"So," cried Satan, "so be it! still I can see!
He shall have the blue sky, the black sky is mine.
Does he think I will come weeping to his door?
I hate him. Three suns suffice. What do I care?
I hate the day, the blueness, fragrance and the light."   75

Suddenly he shivered; there remained only one.

IV

The abyss was fading. Nothing kept its shape.
Darkness seemed to swell its giant wave.

Something nameless and submerged, something
That is no longer, takes its leave, falls silent; 80
And no one could have said, in this deep horror,
If this frightful remnant of a mystery or a world,
Like the vague mist where the dream takes flight,
Was called shipwreck or was called night;
And the archangel felt himself become a phantom. 85
He shouted: "Hell!" This word later made Sodom.[6]

And the voice repeated slowly on his forehead:
"Accursed! all about you the stars will go dark."

And already the sun was only a star.

V

And all disappeared slowly under a veil. 90
Then the archangel quaked; Satan learned to shiver.
Toward the star trembling livid on the horizon
He hurled himself, leaping from peak to peak.
Then, although with horror at the wings of a beast,
Although it was the clothing of emprisonment, 95
Like a bird going from bush to bush,
Horrendous he took his flight from mount to mount,
And this convict began running in his cell.
He ran, he flew, he shouted: "Star of gold! Brother![7]
Wait for me! I'm running! Don't go out yet! 100
Don't leave me alone!"

Thus the monster
Crossed the first lakes of the dead immensity,
Former chaos, emptied and already stagnant,
And into the lugubrious depths he plunged.

Now the star was only a spark. 105

He went down further in universal shadow,
Sank further, cast himself wallowing in the night,
Climbed the filthy mountains, their damp gleaming front,
Whose base is unsteady in the cesspool deeps,
And trembling stared before him.

The spark 110
Was only a red dot in the depth of the dark abyss.

VI

As between two battlements the archer leans
On the wall, when twilight has reached his keep,
Wild he leaned from the mountain top,

---

6. Biblical city, with Gomorrah a symbol of corruption and decadence. Both were destroyed by God (Genesis 18.20–19.28). 7. Lucifer means "Light Bearer."

And upon the star, hoping to arouse its flame,   115
He started to blow as upon some ember.
And anguish caused his fierce nostrils to swell.
The breath rushing from his chest
Is now upon earth and called hurricane.

With his breath a great noise stirred the shadow, an ocean   120
No being dwells in and no fires illumine.
The mountains found nearby took their flight,
The monstrous chaos full of fright arose
And began to shriek: Jehovah Jehovah!
The infinite opened, rent apart like a cloth,   125
But nothing moved in the lugubrious star;
And the damned one, crying: "Don't go out yet! I'll go on!
I'll get there!" resumed again his desperate flight.
And the glaciers mingled with the nights resembling them
Turned on their backs like frightened beasts,   130
And the black tornadoes and the hideous chasms
Bent in terror, while above them,
Flying toward the star like some arrow to the goal,
There passed, wild and haggard, this terrible supplicant.

And ever since it has seen this frightening flight,   135
This bitter abyss, aghast like a fleeing man
Retains forever the horror and the craze,
So monstrous was it to see, in the shadow immense,
Opening his atrocious wing far from the heavens,
This bat flying from his eternal prison!   140

VII

He flew for ten thousand years.

For ten thousand years,
Stretching forth his livid neck and his frenzied hands,
He flew without finding a peak on which to rest.
The star seemed sometimes to fade and to go out,   145
And the horror of the tomb caused the angel to shiver;
Then a pale brightness, vague, strange, uncertain,
Reappeared: and in joy, he cried: "Onward!"
Around him hovered the north wind birds.
He was flying. The infinite never ceases to start again.   150
His flight circled immense in that sea.
The night watched his horrible talons fleeing.
As a cloud feels its whirlwinds fall,
He felt his strength crumble in the chasm.
The winter murmured: tremble! and the shadow said: suffer!   155

Finally he perceived a black peak far off
Which a fearsome reflection in the shadow inflamed.
Satan, like a swimmer in his effort supreme,
Stretched out his wing, with claws and bald, and specter-pale,

Panting, broken, tired, and smoking with sweat,   160
He sank down on the edge of the abrupt descent.[8]

VIII

There was the sun dying in the abyss.
The star, in the deepest fog had no air to revive it,
Grew cold, dim, and was slowly destroyed.
Its sinister round was seen in the night;   165
And in this somber silence its fiery ulcers were seen
Subsiding under a leprosy of dark.
Coal of a world put out! torch blown out by God!
Its crevices still showed a trace of fire,
As if the soul could be seen through holes in the skull.   170
At the center there quivered and flickered a flame
Now and then licking the outermost edge,
And from each crater flashes came
Shivering like flaming swords,
And fading noiselessly as dreams.   175
The star was almost black. The archangel was tired
Beyond voice or breath, a pity to see.
And the star in death throes under his savage glance,
Was dying, doing battle. With its somber apertures
Into the cold darkness it spewed now and again   180
Burning streams, crimson lumps, and smoking hills,
Rocks foaming with initial brightness:
As if this giant of life and light
Engulfed by the mist where all is fading,
Had refused to die without insulting the night   185
And spitting its lava in the shadow's face.
About it time and space and number,
Form, and noise expired, making
The forbidding and black oneness of void.
Then the specter Nothing[9] raised its head from the abyss.   190

Suddenly, from the heart of the star, a jet of sulphur
Sharp, clamorous like one dying in delirium,
Burst sudden, shining, splendid with surprise,
And lighting from far a thousand deathly forms,
Massive, pierced to the shadow's depths   195
The monstrous porches of endless deep.
Night and immensity formed
Their angels. Satan, wild and out of breath,
His vision dazzled and full of this flashing,
Beat with his wing, opened his hands and then shivered   200
And cried: "Despair! see it growing pale!"

The archangel understood, as does the mast in its sinking,
That he was the drowned man of the shadows' flood;
He furled once more his wing with its granite nails,
And wrung his hands. And the star went out.   205

---

8. Literally, escarpment, the steep wall before a fortification or cliff.   9. Satan.

IX

Now, near the skies, at chasm's edge where nothing changes,
One feather escaped from the archangel's wing
Remained and quivered, pure and white.
The angel on whose forehead the dazzling dawn is born
Saw and grasped it, observing the sublime sky: 210
"Lord, must it too fall into the abyss?"
God turned about, absorbed in being and in Life,
And said "Do not discard what has not fallen."[1]

* * *

Black caves of the past, porches of time passed
With no date and no radiance, somber, unmeasured,   215
Cycles previous to man, chaos, heavens,
World terrible and rich in prodigious beings,
Oh fearful fog where the preadamites
Appeared, standing in limitless shadow.
Who could fathom you, oh chasms, oh unknown times.   220
The thinker barefoot like the poor,
Through respect for the One unseen, the sage,
Digs in the depths of origin and age,
Fathoms and seeks beyond the colossi,[2] further
Than the facts witnessed by the present sky,   225
Reaches with pale visage suspected things,
And finds, lifting the darkness of years
And the layers of days, worlds, voids,
Gigantic centuries dead beneath giants of centuries.
And thus the wise man dreams in the deep of the night   230
His face illumined by glints of the abyss.

1. In the second part of *The End of Satan—Satan's Feather*—the feather is brought to life by a divine glance and becomes the female spirit Liberty. She wins God's permission to plunge into hell in an attempt to redeem her father (part 3), and in part 4 the repentant archangel is released and re-created as Lucifer.
2. Giants of preadamic time.

GÉRARD DE NERVAL
1808–1855

Born Gérard Labrunie, the son of an army doctor, Nerval almost never lived with his father until he was twelve years old. After his mother died, when the child was two, he was sent to live with an uncle in the country, near Rousseau's final home at Ermenonville, near Paris. Rousseau exerted an imaginative influence on him as did the French countryside. As a young man, however, he moved to Paris, where he indulged in various forms of Romantic excess. He also traveled widely and made many literary friends, especially among other Romantic poets. His behavior was sometimes sufficiently bizarre to cause his confinement in a mental hospital, which he inhabited in 1840–41, 1851–52, and 1853–54. Even after his final release, he hardly curbed his predilection for oddness. For instance, he paraded a lobster attached to a pale blue ribbon down the boulevards of Paris, explaining that the lobster was an ideal pet. It didn't bark, and it "knew the secrets of the deep." In 1805, he hanged himself.

Nerval's writing included such extravagant works as *Aurélia*, a fantastic spiritual autobiography, but also much solid accomplishment. He translated *Faust* as well as other German works; he published numerous short stories and travel sketches; and he wrote love poetry, nature poetry, and poetry of precise observation. The five sonnets included here, as translated by Geoffrey Wagner, suggest the range of his lyric voice.

Notre-Dame[1]

Notre-Dame is very old; yet eventually perhaps
We shall see her bury the city she saw born, Paris.
Still, in some millenium, time will make her topple,
This heavy carcass, like a wolf makes an ox,
It will twist her iron sinews and with insensible tooth   5
Sadly corrode her old bones of rock.

Many men of every country on earth will come
To contemplate this austere ruin,
Dreaming, reading again that book by Victor . . . .[2]
—Thus they will think to see the old basilica,   10
Just as she used to be, powerful and splendid,
Rising before them like the shade of one dead!

Awakening in the Carriage

This is what I saw—On the road the trees fleeing,
All intermingled, like a defeated army:
Underneath the ground swaying in the high wind
Like rolling waves of clod and paving-stone.

Among the green plains the steeples seemed to lead   5
Hamlets of plaster houses, tile-roofed,
Which trotted along like flocks
Of white sheep, marked in red on their backs.

And the drunken mountains tottered: the river,
Like a boa constrictor stretched over   10
The whole valley, darted out to wrap itself around them . . .
I was in the carriage, having just awoken!

1. Notre-Dame de Paris, Paris's cathedral church, constructed in the 12th and 13th centuries.   2. Victor
Hugo (1802–1885), a friend of Nerval, wrote the novel called in French *Notre-Dame de Paris* (in English,
The Hunchback of Notre-Dame).

A Lane in the Luxembourg

And now the girl has passed me by,
Quick and nimble as a bird:
In her hand a dazzling flower,
On her lips a song unheard.

Perhaps she is the only one   5
Whose heart would answer mine,
Who with a single look would shine
And light my lonely night.

But no—my youth has gone . . .
Farewell, soft and illuminating ray,   10
Perfume, young girl, harmony . . .
Fortune fades,—has fled away.

April

Already there are fine days and dust,
Already a blazing, azure sky,
The walls are on fire, the evenings lengthening,
And the green going; little by little
A reddish reflection decorates   5
The towering trees with their black branches.

This fine weather weighs me down and wearies me.
It is only after rainy days
That spring should surge up,
A picture going green and rose-colored,   10
Brought out like a new nymph
Who steps from the water, smiling.

Grandmother

It is three years now since grandmother died,
The dear soul: and when she was buried,
Everyone, parents and friends, wept for her,
With a sorrow that was very real and very bitter.

Only I wandered through the house,   5
Feeling surprise rather than sadness; and as I went close
To her coffin, they told me I ought not to see it
Without wanting to cry.

Vociferous sorrow is soon over:
For three years, other emotions,   10
Good and evil, even revolutions,
Have erased this memory from the minds of men.

Only I think of it and weep for her often;
For three years now, taking strength from time,
Like a name engraved in the bark of a tree,   15
Her memory sinks more deeply into me.

MIKHAIL YURYEVICH LERMONTOV
1814–1841

Destined in his short life to win great fame as a writer, Lermontov began producing poetry at fourteen. He was born in Moscow, at two and a half, he was consigned to the care of his maternal grandmother because his mother had died. Lermontov was educated by tutors and at boarding school, briefly attended the University of Moscow, and spent two years in the Russian School of Military Cadets, becoming an ensign in 1834. He was punished for an early duel and was killed in a later one after a quarrel of unknown cause with a fellow officer.

Lermontov wrote narrative poems, drama, a novel, and many lyrics. He first attracted widespread attention with his poem (included here) *The Poet's Death,* which protests the death of the great Russian writer Pushkin in a duel and expresses familiar Romantic attitudes about the alienation of the artist from an uncomprehending and insensitive public. Writing in a lyrical mode in the first person, he conveys a sense of himself, too, as one set apart from others. His poems, here translated by Anatoly Liberman, communicate deep commitment to a life of feeling as well as acknowledgment of the pain involved in such commitment and a claim of value in the pain.

[I Do Not Love You]

I do not love you; I have shed
The weight of longing and remorse.
But still your image is not dead:
It lives in me, devoid of force.
And in the passions' later play   5
I thought of you as only mine;
Thus to the fallen gods we pray
And kneel at a forsaken shrine.

1831

[No, I Am Not Byron]

No, I am not Byron, though I and he
Were both exposed to fame and danger;
'Mid men a wanderer and stranger,
I have a Russian soul in me.
I started young, I'll finish sooner,   5
In vain my mind for wisdom gropes;
My soul is like a shipwrecked schooner
That sank with all its broken hopes.
Who will, oh sea! your secrets fathom?
Who will you of your treasure rob?   10
And so my thoughts: alone I have them—
Myself and God, but not the mob.

1832

To

I ask you to restrain your feeling,
Forget what happened long before:
I've hidden nothing worth revealing
For which you could have loved me more.
I would be sad if you insisted   5
And probed the man you love so well;
My soul, believe me, would be twisted
If you should see its blackest hell.
Your happiness I will not shatter,
I will not come to you and say   10
That things I treasure do not matter,
That for my peace you must not pray,
That I have taught my heart to smother
Old love, affections, wishes—all!
That more than to a friend or brother   15
It clings to sufferings and gall.
For just one word of yours so tender
Demand my life and all I've won—
But not my past; its sole defender,
I'll sell its grief and pain to none.   20

1832

[Her Face Is Not the Face of Venus]

Her face is not the face of Venus,[1]
That we should stand around in awe,

---

1. Roman goddess of love, associated with beauty. Lermontov here follows the convention of mocking poetic conventions about how to represent a beloved woman.

And she has hardly ever seen us
Extol her, worship, and adore.
A shapely nymph is more appealing,   5
Her breast is not a heaving wave,
So no one swept by violent feeling
Will kneel before her like a slave.
And yet her every little motion,
Her speech, her laughter, and her face—   10
All is exuberant emotion,
All is inimitable grace.
Her voice breaks through the soul's defenses,
As sunrays break through winter chill,
And once again revives the senses   15
And stirs the heart against its will.

1832

The Poet's Death[1]

   Retaliation, Sire, retaliation!
   You see me at your feet:
   Be fair and let the murderer be punished,
   And may his death in centuries to come
   Proclaim to all posterity your justice,
   That villains should not ever dare to kill
           (From a tragedy)[2]

The poet fell, maligned by scandal,
Fell with a bullet in his breast,
Expired like a resplendent candle,
A slave to chivalry's behest.
He could not bear the shameless babble,   5
So, with a thirst for vengeance filled,
He threw his gauntlet to the rabble
And was dispassionately killed.
Killed, killed . . . you say your hearts are bleeding,
You praise in chorus, simper, prate . . .   10
Who needs your mumbling, childish pleading,
As if the murderer were fate!
Or were you not forever planning
To soil his genius and his name
And for your mean amusement fanning   15
A spark into a roaring flame?
Well! You can triumph: to his tortures
The man preferred eternal gloom;
Exult, for you extinguish torches
And smother fragrant wreaths in bloom.[3]   20

1. Alexander Sergeyevich Pushkin (1799–1837), Russian poet and dramatist, was killed in a duel that Lermontov sees as an emblem for public hostility to the artist.   2. Unidentified.   3. I.e., destroy the symbols of poetic aspiration and achievement.

The slayer, unmoved by the disaster,
Has taken aim—the deed is done;
His empty heart does not beat faster,
His hand is steady with the gun.

Small wonder! From across the border,   25
Like many others lacking pluck,
In search of money, rank, and luck,
He came to us, consumed with boredom.
He mocked the alien tongue and mind,
And at that moment, grim and gory,   30
He was not shaken, was not sorry
To point his gun at Russia's glory—
He was to fame and glory blind.

He is killed and closed to consolation,
Like someone else, a child of his creation,   35
A victim of the cold and cruel—
A singer of poetic inspiration,
Cut off like him in a relentless duel.

Why did he leave behind the joys of adolescence?
Why did he want to learn the mortal lessons   40
And live with people treacherous and vile?
Why did he think—how could he think of running
With petty slanderers, unscrupulous and cunning,
He, who had always seen through every guile?

They took away his crown and gladly made it rougher,   45
They put a laurel wreath with thorns upon his head
And left him all alone to suffer,
For no one wiped the brow that bled.
Until the very end he saw the spurious glitter
And heard the falsehoods that had killed his art,   50
And so he died, his sweetness turning bitter,
His thirst for vengeance drying up his heart.
We'll never learn, we'll never know it,
What other songs he could have sung;
Deep in the ground they laid the poet,   55
They sealed his lips and stopped his tongue.

*

And you, so arrogant and bloated,
Whose fathers' villainy has carried far and wide,
You trample underfoot the clans on which you doted
The moment fortune brushes them aside.   60
You, greedy, hungry pack, corrupters of the palace,
You, murderers of Freedom, Genius, Fame!
The laws you write have made you bold and callous,
Both truth and justice are for you a game!
But God will judge you all for every crime committed,   65
Yes, He will judge: He waits;

He will not be by you outwitted:
This time your clinking gold will not avert your fate.
In vain you will pretend that you are smart and clever,
    This will not help you anymore;   70
In all eternity, your loathsome blood will never
    Wash off the poet's righteous gore!

1837

GUSTAVO ADOLFO BÉCQUER
1836–1870

Although his major literary reputation developed only after his death, Gustavo Adolfo Bécquer (*goo-stah'-voh ah-dol'-foh beh-hay'*), a pseudonym for Gustavo Adolfo Dominguez Bastida, is now generally considered the most important of the Spanish Romantic poets. Born in Seville, he was orphaned at the age of nine. He made his living—supporting a wife and two sons—by various means (government official, translator, journalist), but he always thought of himself as a writer, producing not only poetry but prose fiction and nonfiction. His early death resulted from tuberculosis.

Bécquer's poetry often attempts to express the ineffable, to convey his sense of spiritual exhilaration in the natural world. But the poet relies most often on simple, direct diction in an attempt to familiarize grand ideas.

The selections printed here were translated by Bruce Phenix, who attempts both to offer as literal a rendition as possible of Bécquer's meaning and to convey the rhythm and movement of the Spanish text. These poems come from *Rimas*, a collection of Bécquer's verse in which individual poems are assigned only numbers, not titles. First lines have been used as titles in this anthology.

[I Know a Strange, Gigantic Hymn]

I know a strange, gigantic hymn
that heralds a dawn in the night of the soul,
and these pages are cadences of this hymn
that the air carries abroad in the shadows.

I should like to write it, subduing   5
the rebel against man, impoverished language,
in words that were at the same time
sighs and laughs, colours and notes.

But in vain is the struggle; for there is no cipher
capable of containing it, and scarcely, oh beautiful one!   10
holding your hands in mine,
could I sing it, by ear, to you alone.

[Nameless Spirit]

Nameless spirit,
indefinable essence,
I live with the formless
life of idea.

I swim in the void,   5
I quiver in the bonfire of the sun,
I palpitate among the shadows
and I float with the mists.

I am the gold braid
of the distant star;   10
I am the lukewarm, serene light
of the high moon.

I am the burning cloud
that undulates in the west:
I am the luminous wake   15
of the wandering star.

I am snow on the peaks,
I am fire on the sands,
a blue wave on the seas,
and foam on the shores.   20

I am a note in the lute,
perfume in the violet,
a fleeting flame in the tombs,
and ivy in the ruins.

I deafen in the torrent,   25
and I hiss in the lightning,
and I blind in the flash,
and I roar in the storm.

I laugh in the hills,
I whisper in the tall grass,   30
I sigh in the pure wave,
and I weep in the dead leaf.

I undulate with the atoms
of the smoke that rises,
and slowly goes up to the sky   35
in an immense spiral.

I, on the gilded threads
that the insects hang,
swing between the trees
in the fiery noonday heat.   40

I run after the nymphs
who in the cool stream
of the crystalline brook
frolic naked.

I, in forests of corals   45
carpeted by white pearls,
pursue in the ocean
the swift naiads.

I, in the hollow caverns
where the sun never penetrates,   50
mingling with the gnomes
observe their riches.

I look for the now obliterated
traces of the centuries,
and I know of those empires   55
of which not even the name is left.

I follow in rapid giddiness
the worlds that revolve,
and my pupil[1] embraces
the whole of creation.   60

I know of those regions
both where no noise reaches,
and where formless stars
wait for the breath of life.

I am the bridge that crosses   65
over the abyss,
I am the unknown ladder
that joins Heaven to the Earth.

I am the invisible
ring that fastens   70
the world of form
to the world of idea.

I, in short, am that spirit,
unfamiliar essence,
mysterious perfume,   75
of which the poet is the vessel.

---

1. Eye.

ROSALÍA DE CASTRO
1837–1885

An illegitimate child of a priest, who, of course, could not acknowledge her, the Spanish writer Rosalía de Castro (*roh-za-lee'-a day kahs'-troh*) frequently expresses in her verse a sense of despair that may, critics have speculated, derive from the ambiguities of her birth. She began writing poetry as a child and published her first volume at the age of twenty. A year later, she married, subsequently giving birth to seven children. She died of cancer.

Beside the River Sar (1884), from which the selections printed here come, was the last volume published in de Castro's lifetime. Predominantly melancholy in tone, the poems express spiritual questioning, sorrow, and intense responsiveness to the environment. They are characteristically modest (note, for example, *As I Composed This Little Book*). At times they reveal the author's intimate reactions to her own experience, as in *Mild Was the Air,* a lyric about the death of one of her infant children.

These poems were translated by S. Griswold Morley.

[As I Composed This Little Book]

As I composed this little book, I thought:
Although my songs may never bring me fame,
    Simple they are and brief,
And may achieve, perhaps, my longed-for aim.
For they can be sure-fixed in memory   5
As are the prayers and rituals of belief,
Fervent though short, we learned in infancy.
Those we do not forget, in spite of grief
And time and distance and the destroying flame
Of passion. That is why my songs are brief   10
And simple,—though they may not bring me fame.

[Mild Was the Air]

    Mild was the air
    And still the day;
    The rain fell gently
    With never a stay.
    I hushed my sobs   5
    And softly wept;—
    My child was dying
    As he slept.
He left this world, and peace was in his heart;
I watched his going, and mine was torn apart!   10

Throw earth upon the unburied body . . . earth!
Before corruption fastens on his flesh!
Be calm; the grave is covered now. Quite soon
Up from the newly broken clods the grass
Will push; it will be green and fresh.   15

What are you seeking, you of the roving glance
And cloudy thought, prowling about that tomb?
With what is there to dust returning, fret
Not yourself. He'll not offend you more
Or love you more, who rests within that room.   20

Oh, never, never more! Can it be true
That all is ended now forever? No,
Surely immensity can have no end,
Eternity can never cease to flow.

You have left me forever; but my soul   25
Yearns with the eagerness of love to greet
My darling. You will come, or I shall go,
    Whither we twain can meet.

Within my body something of you remains
    That cannot die,   30
And God, because He is just and because He is good,
    Will never try
To take it from me. Somewhere—on earth, in Heaven,
Beyond all sounded space—you will find me,
I shall find you. For certainly I know   35
Immensity can never have an end,
Eternity can never cease to flow.

But . . . he is gone, gone never to return!
Ay, that is true. To man, guest of a day
In this our world, nothing eternal is.   40
Within its circle he is born and lives and dies,
As every creature is born and lives and dies;
    It is the earthly way.

[A Glowworm Scatters Flashes through the Moss]

A glowworm scatters flashes through the moss;
A star gleams in its high remote domain.
Abyss above, and in the depths abyss:
What things come to an end and what remain?
    Man's thought—we call it science!—peers and pries   5
Into the soundless dark. But it is vain:
When all is done, we still are ignorant
Of what things reach an end, and what remain.

Kneeling before an image rudely carved,
I sink my spirit in the Infinite,   10
And—is it impious?—I vacillate
And tremble, questioning Heaven and Hell of it.

My Deity, shattered in a thousand bits,
Has fallen to chasms where I cannot see.
I rush to seek Him, and my groping meets   15
A solitary vast vacuity.

When lo! from their lofty marble niches,
Angels gazed down in sorrow; and in my ears
Murmured a gentle voice: "Unhappy soul,
     Take hope; pour out thy tears   20
Before the feet of the Most High;
But well remember this: No insolent cry
     To Heaven makes its way
From one whose heart adores material things,
Who makes an idol out of Adam's clay."   25

[The Feet of Spring Are on the Stair]

The feet of Spring are on the stair;
Her breath is sweet and warm and rare;
Beneath the soil in amorous heat
Seeds are astir with restless beat,
And atoms drifting in the air,   5
Afloat and silent, pair by pair,
     Kiss as they meet.

Youth's blood is eager, youth's heart is hot,
Its courage leaps, its bold mad thought
Believes that man—oh, dreams of youth!—   10
Is, like the gods, immortal. What
If dreams are lies? This much is truth:
Unblest are they who dreamless draw their breath,
And fortunate who in a dream find death.

How swift the passage of each thing   15
     In our sad world!
By a wild giant, quivering
     Our lives are whirled!
Yesterday bud, today a rose,
And then the sun-scorched blossom goes   20
     As Summer masters Spring.

[Candescent[1] Lies the Air]

Candescent lies the air.
A fox explores the unfrequented road.
The brook which cleanly flowed
As crystal, turns now noisome, where
    A pine, motionless, misses   5
The breeze and its inconstant kisses.

A stifling silence quells the countryside.
    Only the insect's drone,
    Persistent, shrilling
Over the breathless landscape, filling   10
The shadows moist and wide,
Like a low death-rattle, makes a monotone.

In summer, to the fighter worn and dull,
    The midmost hour of day
    Is best called night.   15
    Then more than ever weigh
Upon him the unconquerable might
Of matter, and the anguish of the soul.

Return, return, ye chill wild nights of winter,
Our well-tried friends of a not distant time!   20
Give us again your nipping frost and rime,
To cool the blood inflamed by sorry summer,
Insufferable with its flaming rays—
Yes, sorry! though it bring the fruited wheat!

[The Ailing Woman Felt Her Forces Ebb]

The ailing woman felt her forces ebb
With summer, and knew her time was imminent.
    "In autumn I shall die,"
She thought, half-melancholy, half-content,
"And I shall feel the leaves, that will be dead   5
Like me, drop on the grave in which I lie."

Not even Death would do her so much pleasure.
    Cruel to her he too,
In winter spared her life, and when anew
The earth was being born in blossoming,   10
Slew her by inches to the joyous hymns
    Of fair and merry spring!

---

1. Glowing or dazzling as from great heat.

ALEXANDER SERGEYEVICH PUSHKIN
1799–1837

In his best-known story, *The Queen of Spades*, Alexander Pushkin combines familiar elements of Romantic fiction—the penniless young woman; the ambitious, passionate young man; the decayed beauty; the ghost—in a tale with intense ironic overtones, a tale later a favorite of the great Russian novelist Fyodor Dostoevsky. Pushkin's own life story sounds like a Romantic novel. Born into an aristocratic Russian family, neglected by his parents, he early began an extensive amatory and poetic career, publishing his first poem at the age of fifteen and becoming notorious about the same time for his many erotic involvements. At eighteen he graduated from a distinguished boarding school and accepted appointment in the Foreign Service; six years later, the various instances of his defiance of authority resulted in expulsion from the service and confinement, under police surveillance, on a paternal estate. After the death of Czar Alexander I and the abortive military uprising that followed (one involving several of Pushkin's friends, five of whom were subsequently hanged), Pushkin—by then a well-known poet—was befriended (1826) by the new czar, Nicholas. He moved back to Moscow, then to Petersburg, leading a moneyed and relatively carefree life. In 1831, however, he married a nineteen-year-old woman, whose apparently flirtatious behavior embittered his subsequent life. He died after a duel with his wife's putative lover.

Producing short lyrics, narrative poems, a great novel in verse (*Eugene Onegin*), lyrical drama (notably *Boris Gudonov*), versified folktales, and prose fiction, Pushkin established himself as one of Russia's greatest writers. His interest in his nation's past, his tendency to challenge authority, his fascination with the character and situation of strong individuals—such obsessive concerns link his work with that of his Romantic contemporaries elsewhere in Europe. Goethe, Byron, and early nineteenth-century French novelists had a marked influence on him. He retained also, however, the kind of clarity, discipline, and ironic distance more often associated with the literature of the preceding century.

The treatment of love and sexuality in *The Queen of Spades* exemplifies the complexity of Pushkin's approach. First of all we hear the story of the "Muscovite Venus," the beautiful young gambler who pays her debts by learning the secret of three infallible cards. Then we encounter a young woman suffering in her dependent position and longing for a "deliverer." Hermann, the immediate object of Lisaveta's dreams, has his own sexual fantasies: himself a young man, he imagines becoming the lover of the eighty-seven-year-old countess. At this point, if not before, the reader begins to realize that something's wrong here: this is not the kind of romantic tale we're used to. Describing Hermann's first glimpse of Lisaveta, Pushkin writes, "Hermann saw a small, fresh face and a pair of dark eyes. That moment decided his fate." A Romantic cliché—except that the young man sees Lisaveta not as an object of devotion but as a means to an end. He sends her a love letter, copied word for word from a German novel. His rapidly developing passion focuses on financial, not erotic, gain.

Lisaveta's character is more ambiguous. The narrator invokes sympathy for her plight: she is at the mercy of a tyrannical employer who makes endless irrational demands and who never pays her. Her situation prohibits her from enjoying the kinds of amorous gratification other young women can expect. We can understand, therefore, why her dreams should concentrate specifically on a deliverer. Like Hermann, although far less unscrupulous, she may indulge in intrigues as a means to an end—in her case, not money but liberty.

The Queen of Spades contains no completely attractive characters. If Lisaveta's victimization arouses compassion, her lack of moral force or determination may also provoke irritation. Hermann's will to succeed, on the other hand, makes him a potential hero; but his obsession with money and his mean-spirited expediency alienate most readers. The countess, old and approaching death, uses the power of her money and rank with utter disregard for the needs or feelings of others. Even such a minor figure as the countess's grandson, Tomsky, playing with Lisaveta's feelings, going through his ritualized flirtation with Princess Polina, seems thoroughly contaminated by the values of the world he inhabits.

Indeed, those values provide the central subject of this tale. Pushkin employs conventions of the kind of ghost story common in folktales to convey serious criticism of a social structure corrupted by universal concentration on money. Gambling provides not only the chief male activity but also the central metaphor of the story. Everyone is out for what he or she can get. The countess, whose days at the card table are past, uses her money to buy subservience; Lisaveta is willing to risk her reputation, maybe even her chastity, for the possibility of escaping servitude; Hermann frightens someone to death in an effort to make his fortune; Tomsky plays elaborate social games of advance and retreat, trying to get his princess. The queen of spades is a conventional symbol of death; the kind of death most important in Pushkin's story is not literal—not the countess's demise—but figurative: it is the spiritual death suffered by the other characters, over whose world the countess / queen of spades metaphorically presides.

The "Conclusion" of *The Queen of Spades,* a deadpan summary of the characters' future careers, epitomizes the story's central concerns. Hermann's madness dramatizes the financial obsession he has displayed from the beginning; Lisaveta's marriage, to an anonymous "very agreeable young man" with a good position "somewhere," emphasizes the degree to which she has always wished for marriage as rescue, not as attachment to a particular beloved other. In her married state, Lisaveta, ironically, "is bringing up a poor relative," recapitulating the structure of exploitation from which she herself suffered. Tomsky, relatively unimportant to the plot line, supplies the subject for the story's concluding sentence: his promotion and his "good" marriage remind us that everyone in the society here described seeks personal advantage at all costs. Hermann has simply paid the cost in the most dramatic way.

PRONOUNCING GLOSSARY

The following list uses common English syllables and stress accents to provide rough equivalents of selected words whose pronunciation may be unfamiliar to the general reader.

Chekalinsky: *che-kah-leen'-skee*

Eletskaya: *ye-lyet'-skah-yuh*

Fedotovna: *fye-daw'-tuv-nuh*

Ilyitch: *il-yeech'*

Lisaveta Ivanovna: *lyee-zah-vye'-tuh ee-vah'-nuv-nuh*

Richelieu: *ree'-she-lyeuh*

St-Germain: *sanh-zher-manh'*

The Queen of Spades[1]

CHAPTER ONE

And on rainy days
They gathered
Often;
Their stakes—God help them!—
Wavered from fifty
To a hundred,
And they won

---

1. Translated by Gillon R. Aitken.

And marked up their winnings
With chalk.
Thus on rainy days
Were they
Busy.[2]

There was a card party one day in the rooms of Narumov, an officer of the Horse Guards. The long winter evening slipped by unnoticed; it was five o'clock in the morning before the assembly sat down to supper. Those who had won ate with a big appetite; the others sat distractedly before their empty plates. But champagne was brought in, the conversation became more lively, and everyone took a part in it.

"And how did you get on, Surin?" asked the host.

"As usual, I lost. I must confess, I have no luck: I never vary my stake, never get heated, never lose my head, and yet I always lose!"

"And weren't you tempted even once to back[3] on a series . . . ? Your strength of mind astonishes me."

"What about Hermann then," said one of the guests, pointing at the young Engineer.[4] "He's never held a card in his hand, never doubled a single stake in his life, and yet he sits up until five in the morning watching us play."

"The game fascinates me," said Hermann, "but I am not in the position to sacrifice the essentials of life in the hope of acquiring the luxuries."

"Hermann's a German: he's cautious—that's all," Tomsky observed. "But if there's one person I can't understand, it's my grandmother, the Countess Anna Fedotovna."

"How? Why?" the guests inquired noisily.

"I can't understand why it is," Tomsky continued, "that my grandmother doesn't gamble."

"But what's so astonishing about an old lady of eighty not gambling?" asked Narumov.

"Then you don't know . . . ?"

"No, indeed; I know nothing."

"Oh well, listen then:

"You must know that about sixty years ago my grandmother went to Paris, where she made something of a hit. People used to chase after her to catch a glimpse of la vénus moscovite; Richelieu[5] paid court to her, and my grandmother vouches that he almost shot himself on account of her cruelty. At that time ladies used to play faro.[6] On one occasion at the Court, my grandmother lost a very great deal of money on credit to the Duke of Orleans. Returning home, she removed the patches[7] from her face, took off her hooped petticoat, announced her loss to my grandfather and ordered him to pay back the money. My late grandfather, as far as I can remember, was a sort of lackey to my grandmother. He feared her like fire; on hearing of such a disgraceful loss, however, he completely lost his temper; he produced his accounts, showed her that she had spent half a million francs in six months, pointed out that neither their Moscow nor their Saratov estates were in Paris,

---

2. Like most of the chapter epigraphs, this was presumably written by Pushkin himself.   3. Bet.   4. A member of the Corps of Engineers, concerned with fortifications.   5. Louis-François-Armand de Vignerod du Plessis, duc de Richelieu (1696–1788), French aristocrat renowned throughout the 18th century for both his military and his sexual exploits. La vénus moscovite: the Venus of Moscow (French). Venus was the Roman goddess of love.   6. A card game much used for gambling.   7. I.e., beauty patches, artificial "beauty marks" made of black silk or court plaster and worn on the face or neck.

and refused point-blank to pay the debt. My grandmother gave him a box on the ear and went off to sleep on her own as an indication of her displeasure. In the hope that this domestic infliction would have had some effect on him, she sent for her husband the next day; she found him unshakeable. For the first time in her life she approached him with argument and explanation, thinking that she could bring him to reason by pointing out that there are debts and debts, that there is a big difference between a Prince and a coach-maker. But my grandfather remained adamant, and flatly refused to discuss the subject any further. My grandmother did not know what to do. A little while before, she had become acquainted with a very remarkable man. You have heard of Count St-Germain,[8] about whom so many marvellous stories are related. You know that he held himself out to be the Wandering Jew, and the inventor of the elixir of life, the philosopher's stone and so forth. Some ridiculed him as a charlatan and in his memoirs Casanova declares that he was a spy. However, St-Germain, in spite of the mystery which surrounded him, was a person of venerable appearance and much in demand in society. My grandmother is still quite infatuated with him and becomes quite angry if anyone speaks of him with disrespect. My grandmother knew that he had large sums of money at his disposal. She decided to have recourse to him, and wrote asking him to visit her without delay. The eccentric old man at once called on her and found her in a state of terrible grief. She depicted her husband's barbarity in the blackest light, and ended by saying that she pinned all her hopes on his friendship and kindness.

"St-Germain reflected. 'I could let you have this sum,' he said, 'but I know that you would not be at peace while in my debt, and I have no wish to bring fresh troubles upon your head. There is another solution—you can win back the money.'

" 'But, my dear Count,' my grandmother replied, 'I tell you—we have no money at all.'

" 'In this case money is not essential,' St-Germain replied. 'Be good enough to hear me out.'

"And at this point he revealed to her the secret for which any one of us here would give a very great deal . . ."

The young gamblers listened with still great attention. Tomsky lit his pipe, drew on it and continued:

"That same evening my grandmother went to Versailles, *au jeu de la Reine*.[9] The Duke of Orleans kept the bank; inventing some small tale, my grandmother lightly excused herself for not having brought her debt, and began to play against him. She chose three cards and played them one after the other: all three won and my grandmother recouped herself completely."

"Pure luck!" said one of the guests.

"A fairy-tale," observed Hermann.

"Perhaps the cards were marked!" said a third.

"I don't think so," Tomsky replied gravely.

"What!" cried Narumov. "You have a grandmother who can guess three cards in succession, and you haven't yet contrived to learn her secret."

"No, not much hope of that!" replied Tomsky. "She had four sons, includ-

---

8. A celebrated adventurer (ca. 1710–1784?) who frequented the French, German, and Russian courts.
9. To the queen's game (French).

ing my father; all four were desperate gamblers, and yet she did not reveal her secret to a single one of them, although it would have been a good thing if she had told them—told me, even. But this is what I heard from my uncle, Count Ivan Ilyitch, and he gave me his word for its truth. The late Chaplitsky—the same who died a pauper after squandering millions—in his youth once lost nearly 300,000 roubles—to Zoritch, if I remember rightly. He was in despair. My grandmother, who was most strict in her attitude towards the extravagances of young men, for some reason took pity on Chaplitsky. She told him the three cards on condition that he played them in order; and at the same time she exacted his solemn promise that he would never play again as long as he lived. Chaplitsky appeared before his victor; they sat down to play. On the first card Chaplitsky staked 50,000 roubles and won straight off; he doubled his stake, redoubled—and won back more than he had lost. . . .

"But it's time to go to bed; it's already a quarter to six."

Indeed, the day was already beginning to break. The young men drained their glasses and dispersed.

CHAPTER TWO

"Il paraît que monsieur est décidément pour les suivantes."
"Que voulez-vous, madame? Elles sont plus fraîches."
FASHIONABLE CONVERSATION

The old Countess * * *[1] was seated before the looking-glass in her dressing-room. Three lady's maids stood by her. One held a jar of rouge, another a box of hairpins, and the third a tall bonnet with flame-coloured ribbons. The Countess no longer had the slightest pretensions to beauty, which had long since faded from her face, but she still preserved all the habits of her youth, paid strict regard to the fashions of the seventies, and devoted to her dress the same time and attention as she had done sixty years before. At an embroidery frame by the window sat a young lady, her ward.

"Good morning, grand'maman!" said a young officer as he entered the room. "Bonjour, mademoiselle Lise. Grand'maman,[2] I have a request to make of you."

"What is it, Paul?"

"I want you to let me introduce one of my friends to you, and to allow me to bring him to the ball on Friday."

"Bring him straight to the ball and introduce him to me there. Were you at * * *'s yesterday?"

"Of course. It was very gay; we danced until five in the morning. How charming Eletskaya was!"

"But, my dear, what's charming about her? Isn't she like her grandmother, the Princess Darya Petrovna . . . ? By the way, I dare say she's grown very old now, the Princess Darya Petrovna?"

1. Asterisks in this selection are the author's and are intended to suggest that the proper name of an actual person has been omitted. The epigram can be translated as: "It appears that the gentleman is decidedly in favor of servant girls." "What would you have me do, Madam? They are fresher [than upper-class women]" (French).   2. Russian aristocrats often spoke French. Lisaveta is here called by the French name Lise, and Pavel, Paul.

"What do you mean, 'grown old'?" asked Tomsky thoughtlessly. "She's been dead for seven years."

The young lady raised her head and made a sign to the young man. He remembered then that the death of any of her contemporaries was kept secret from the old Countess, and he bit his lip. But the Countess heard the news, previously unknown to her, with the greatest indifference.

"Dead!" she said. "And I didn't know it. We were maids of honour together, and when we were presented, the Empress . . ."

And for the hundredth time the Countess related the anecdote to her grandson.

"Come, Paul," she said when she had finished her story, "help me to stand up. Lisanka, where's my snuff-box?"

And with her three maids the Countess went behind a screen to complete her dress. Tomsky was left alone with the young lady.

"Whom do you wish to introduce?" Lisaveta Ivanovna asked softly.

"Narumov. Do you know him?"

"No. Is he a soldier or a civilian?"

"A soldier."

"An Engineer?"

"No, he's in the Cavalry. What made you think he was an Engineer?"

The young lady smiled but made no reply.

"Paul!" cried the Countess from behind the screen. "Bring along a new novel with you some time, will you, only please not one of those modern ones."

"What do you mean, *grand'maman?*"

"I mean not the sort of novel in which the hero strangles either of his parents or in which someone is drowned.[3] I have a great horror of drowned people."

"Such novels don't exist nowadays. Wouldn't you like a Russian one?"

"Are there such things? Send me one, my dear, please send me one."

"Will you excuse me now, *grand'maman*, I'm in a hurry. Good-bye, Lisaveta Ivanovna. What made you think that Narumov was in the Engineers?"

And Tomsky left the dressing-room.

Lisaveta Ivanovna was left on her own; she put aside her work and began to look out of the window. Presently a young officer appeared from behind the corner house on the other side of the street. A flush spread over her cheeks; she took up her work again and lowered her head over the frame. At this moment, the Countess returned, fully dressed.

"Order the carriage, Lisanka," she said, "and we'll go for a drive."

Lisanka got up from behind her frame and began to put away her work.

"What's the matter with you, my child? Are you deaf?" shouted the Countess. "Order the carriage this minute."

"I'll do so at once," the young lady replied softly and hastened into the ante-room.

A servant entered the room and handed the Countess some books from the Prince Pavel Alexandrovitch.

---

3. Novels of the sort the countess does not wish to read were typical of the then current decadent movement in French literature.

"Good, thank him," said the Countess. "Lisanka, Lisanka, where are you running to?"

"To get dressed."

"Plenty of time for that, my dear. Sit down. Open the first volume and read to me."

The young lady took up the book and read a few lines.

"Louder!" said the Countess. "What's the matter with you, my child? Have you lost your voice, or what . . . ? Wait . . . move that footstool up to me . . . nearer . . . that's right!"

Lisaveta Ivanovna read a further two pages. The Countess yawned.

"Put the book down," she said; "what rubbish! Have it returned to Prince Pavel with my thanks. . . . But where is the carriage?"

"The carriage is ready," said Lisaveta Ivanovna, looking out into the street.

"Then why aren't you dressed?" asked the Countess. "I'm always having to wait for you—it's intolerable, my dear!"

Lisa ran up to her room. Not two minutes elapsed before the Countess began to ring with all her might. The three lady's maids came running in through one door and the valet through another.

"Why don't you come when you're called?" the Countess asked them. "Tell Lisaveta Ivanovna that I'm waiting for her."

Lisaveta Ivanovna entered the room wearing her hat and cloak.

"At last, my child!" said the Countess. "But what clothes you're wearing . . . ! Whom are you hoping to catch? What's the weather like? It seems windy."

"There's not a breath of wind, your Ladyship," replied the valet.

"You never know what you're talking about! Open that small window. There; as I thought: windy and bitterly cold. Unharness the horses. Lisaveta, we're not going out—there was no need to dress up like that."

"And this is my life," thought Lisaveta Ivanovna.

And indeed Lisaveta Ivanovna was a most unfortunate creature. As Dante says: "You shall learn the salt taste of another's bread, and the hard path up and down his stairs";[4] and who better to know the bitterness of dependence than the poor ward of a well-born old lady? The Countess * * * was far from being wicked, but she had the capriciousness of a woman who has been spoiled by the world, and the miserliness and cold-hearted egotism of all old people who have done with loving and whose thoughts lie with the past. She took part in all the vanities of the *haut-monde*;[5] she dragged herself to balls, where she sat in a corner, rouged and dressed in old-fashioned style, like some misshapen but essential ornament of the ball-room; on arrival, the guests would approach her with low bows, as if in accordance with an established rite, but after that, they would pay no further attention to her. She received the whole town at her house, and although no longer able to recognise the faces of her guests, she observed the strictest etiquette. Her numerous servants, grown fat and grey in her hall and servants' room, did exactly as they pleased, vying with one another in stealing from the dying old lady. Lisaveta Ivanovna was the household martyr. She poured out the tea, and was reprimanded for putting in too much sugar; she read novels aloud, and was held guilty of all the faults of the authors; she accompanied the Countess

---

4. *Paradiso* 17.59.   5. High society (French).

on her walks, and was made responsible for the state of the weather and the pavement. There was a salary attached to her position, but it was never paid; meanwhile, it was demanded of her to be dressed like everybody else—that is, like the very few who could afford to dress well. In society she played the most pitiable role. Everybody knew her, but nobody took any notice of her; at balls she danced only when there was a partner short, and ladies only took her arm when they needed to go to the dressing-room to make some adjustment to their dress. She was proud and felt her position keenly, and looked around her in impatient expectation of a deliverer; but the young men, calculating in their flightiness, did not honour her with their attention, despite the fact that Lisaveta Ivanovna was a hundred times prettier than the cold, arrogant but more eligible young ladies on whom they danced attendance. Many a time did she creep softly away from the bright but wearisome drawing-room to go and cry in her own poor room, where stood a papered screen, a chest of drawers, a small looking-glass and a painted bedstead, and where a tallow candle burned dimly in its copper candle-stick.

One day—two days after the evening described at the beginning of this story, and about a week previous to the events just recorded—Lisaveta Ivanovna was sitting at her embroidery frame by the window, when, happening to glance out into the street, she saw a young Engineer, standing motionless with his eyes fixed upon her window. She lowered her head and continued with her work; five minutes later she looked out again—the young officer was still standing in the same place. Not being in the habit of flirting with passing officers, she ceased to look out of the window, and sewed for about two hours without raising her head. Dinner was announced. She got up and began to put away her frame, and, glancing casually out into the street, she saw the officer again. She was considerably puzzled by this. After dinner, she approached the window with a feeling of some disquiet, but the officer was no longer outside, and she thought no more of him.

Two days later, while preparing to enter the carriage with the Countess, she saw him again. He was standing just by the front-door, his face concealed by a beaver collar; his dark eyes shone from beneath his cap. Without knowing why, Lisaveta Ivanovna felt afraid, and an unaccountable trembling came over her as she sat down in the carriage.

On her return home, she hastened to the window—the officer was standing in the same place as before, his eyes fixed upon her; she drew back, tormented by curiosity and agitated by a feeling that was quite new to her.

Since then, not a day had passed without the young man appearing at the customary hour beneath the windows of their house. A sort of mute acquaintance grew up between them. At work in her seat, she used to feel him approaching, and would raise her head to look at him—for longer and longer each day. The young man seemed to be grateful to her for this: she saw, with the sharp eye of youth, how a sudden flush would spread across his pale cheeks on each occasion that their glances met. After a week she smiled at him. . . .

When Tomsky asked leave of the Countess to introduce one of his friends to her; the poor girl's heart beat fast. But on learning that Narumov was in the Horse Guards, and not in the Engineers, she was sorry that, by an indiscreet question, she had betrayed her secret to the light-hearted Tomsky.

Hermann was the son of a Russianised German, from whom he had inherited a small amount of money. Being firmly convinced of the necessity of ensuring his independence, Hermann did not draw on the income that this yielded, but lived on his pay, forbidding himself the slightest extravagance. Moreover, he was secretive and ambitious, and his companions rarely had occasion to laugh at his excessive thrift. He had strong passions and a fiery imagination, but his tenacity of spirit saved him from the usual errors of youth. Thus, for example, although at heart a gambler, he never took a card in his hand, for he reckoned that his position did not allow him (as he put it) "to sacrifice the essentials of life in the hope of acquiring the luxuries"—and meanwhile, he would sit up at the card table for whole nights at a time, and follow the different turns of the game with feverish anxiety.

The story of the three cards had made a strong impression on his imagination, and he could think of nothing else all night.

"What if the old Countess should reveal her secret to me?" he thought the following evening as he wandered through the streets of Petersburg. "What if she should tell me the names of those three winning cards? Why not try my luck . . . ? Become introduced to her, try to win her favour, perhaps become her lover . . . ? But all that demands time, and she's eighty-seven; she might die in a week, in two days . . . ! And the story itself . . . ? Can one really believe it . . . ? No! Economy, moderation and industry; these are my three winning cards, these will treble my capital, increase it sevenfold, and earn for me ease and independence!"

Reasoning thus, he found himself in one of the principal streets of Petersburg, before a house of old-fashioned architecture. The street was crowded with vehicles; one after another, carriages rolled up to the lighted entrance. From them there emerged, now the shapely little foot of some beautiful young woman, now a rattling jack-boot, now the striped stocking and elegant shoe of a diplomat. Furs and capes flitted past the majestic hall-porter. Hermann stopped.

"Whose house is this?" he asked the watchman at the corner.

"The Countess * * *'s," the watchman replied.

Hermann started. His imagination was again fired by the amazing story of the three cards. He began to walk around near the house, thinking of its owner and her mysterious faculty. It was late when he returned to his humble rooms; for a long time he could not sleep; and when at last he did drop off, cards, a green table,[6] heaps of banknotes and piles of golden coins appeared to him in his dreams. He played one card after the other, doubled his stake decisively, won unceasingly, and raked in the golden coins and stuffed his pockets with the banknotes. Waking up late, he sighed at the loss of his imaginary fortune, again went out to wander about the town and again found himself outside the house of the Countess * * *. Some unknown power seemed to have attracted him to it. He stopped and began to look at the windows. At one he saw a head with long black hair, probably bent down over a book or a piece of work. The head was raised. Hermann saw a small, fresh face and a pair of dark eyes. That moment decided his fate.

6. Tables on which gambling took place were typically covered with green baize.

CHAPTER THREE

*Vous m'écrivez, mon ange, des lettres de
quatre pages plus vite que je ne puis
les lire.*[7]

CORRESPONDENCE

Scarcely had Lisaveta Ivanovna taken off her hat and cloak when the Countess sent for her and again ordered her to have the horses harnessed. They went out to take their seats in the carriage. At the same moment as the old lady was being helped through the carriage doors by two footmen, Lisaveta Ivanovna saw her Engineer standing close by the wheel; he seized her hand; before she could recover from her fright, the young man had disappeared—leaving a letter in her hand. She hid it in her glove and throughout the whole of the drive neither heard nor saw a thing. As was her custom when riding in her carriage, the Countess kept up a ceaseless flow of questions: "Who was it who met us just now? What's this bridge called? What's written on that signboard?" This time Lisaveta Ivanovna's answers were so vague and inappropriate that the Countess became angry.

"What's the matter with you, my child? Are you in a trance or something? Don't you hear me or understand what I'm saying . . . ? Heaven be thanked that I'm still sane enough to speak clearly."

Lisaveta Ivanovna did not listen to her. On returning home, she ran up to her room and drew the letter out of her glove; it was unsealed. Lisaveta Ivanovna read it through. The letter contained a confession of love; it was tender, respectful and taken word for word from a German novel. But Lisaveta Ivanovna had no knowledge of German and was most pleased by it.

Nevertheless, the letter made her feel extremely uneasy. For the first time in her life she was entering into a secret and confidential relationship with a young man. His audacity shocked her. She reproached herself for her imprudent behaviour, and did not know what to do. Should she stop sitting at the window and by a show of indifference cool off the young man's desire for further acquaintance? Should she send the letter back to him? Or answer it with cold-hearted finality? There was nobody to whom she could turn for advice: she had no friend or preceptress. Lisaveta Ivanovna resolved to answer the letter.

She sat down at her small writing-table, took a pen and some paper, and lost herself in thought. Several times she began her letter—and then tore it up; her manner of expression seemed to her to be either too condescending or too heartless. At last she succeeded in writing a few lines that satisfied her:

> *I am sure that your intentions are honourable, and that you did not wish to offend me by your rash behaviour, but our acquaintance must not begin in this way. I return your letter to you and hope that in the future I shall have no cause to complain of undeserved disrespect.*

The next day, as soon as she saw Hermann approach, Lisaveta Ivanovna rose from behind her frame, went into the ante-room, opened a small window, and threw her letter into the street, trusting to the agility of the young officer

7. My angel, you write me four-page-long letters faster than I can read them (French).

to pick it up. Hermann ran forward, took hold of the letter and went into a confectioner's shop. Breaking the seal of the envelope, he found his own letter and Lisaveta Ivanovna's answer. It was as he had expected, and he returned home, deeply preoccupied with his intrigue.

Three days afterwards, a bright-eyed young girl brought Lisaveta Ivanovna a letter from a milliner's shop. Lisaveta Ivanovna opened it uneasily, envisaging a demand for money, but she suddenly recognised Hermann's handwriting.

"You have made a mistake, my dear," she said; "this letter is not for me."

"Oh, but it is!" the girl answered cheekily and without concealing a sly smile. "Read it."

Lisaveta Ivanovna ran her eyes over the note. Hermann demanded a meeting.

"It cannot be," said Lisaveta Ivanovna, frightened at the haste of his demand and the way in which it was made: "this is certainly not for me."

And she tore the letter up into tiny pieces.

"If the letter wasn't for you, why did you tear it up?" asked the girl. "I would have returned it to the person who sent it."

"Please, my dear," Lisaveta Ivanovna said, flushing at the remark, "don't bring me any more letters in the future. And tell the person who sent you that he should be ashamed of . . ."

But Hermann was not put off. By some means or other, he sent a letter to Lisaveta Ivanovna every day. The letters were no longer translated from the German. Hermann wrote them inspired by passion, and used a language true to his character; these letters were the expression of his obsessive desires and the disorder of his unfettered imagination. Lisaveta Ivanovna no longer thought of returning them to him: she revelled in them, began to answer them, and with each day, her replies became longer and more tender. Finally, she threw out of the window the following letter:

> This evening there is a ball at the * * * Embassy. The Countess will be there. We will stay until about two o'clock. Here is your chance to see me alone. As soon as the Countess has left the house, the servants will probably go to their quarters—with the exception of the hall-porter, who normally goes out to his closet anyway. Come at half-past eleven. Walk straight upstairs. If you meet anybody in the ante-room, ask whether the Countess is at home. You will be told 'No'—and there will be nothing you can do but go away. But it is unlikely that you will meet anybody. The lady's maids sit by themselves, all in the one room. On leaving the hall, turn to the left and walk straight on until you come to the Countess' bedroom. In the bedroom, behind a screen, you will see two small doors: the one on the right leads into the study, which the Countess never goes into; the one on the left leads into a corridor and thence to a narrow winding staircase: this staircase leads to my bedroom.

Hermann quivered like a tiger as he awaited the appointed hour. He was already outside the Countess' house at ten o'clock. The weather was terrible; the wind howled, and a wet snow fell in large flakes upon the deserted streets, where the lamps shone dimly. Occasionally a passing cab-driver leaned forward over his scrawny nag, on the look-out for a late passenger. Feeling neither wind nor snow, Hermann waited, dressed only in his frock-coat. At last the Countess' carriage was brought round. Hermann saw two footmen carry out in their arms the bent old lady, wrapped in a sable fur, and immediately following her, the figure of Lisaveta Ivanovna, clad in a light cloak, and with her head adorned with fresh flowers. The doors were slammed and the carriage rolled heavily away along the soft snow. The hall-porter closed the front door. The windows became dark. Hermann began to walk about near the deserted house; he went up to a lamp and looked at his watch; it was twenty minutes past eleven. He remained beneath the lamp; his eyes fixed upon the hands of his watch, waiting for the remaining minutes to pass. At exactly half-past eleven, Hermann ascended the steps of the Countess' house and reached the brightly-lit porch. The hall-porter was not there. Hermann ran up the stairs, opened the door into the ante-room and saw a servant asleep by the lamp in a soiled antique armchair. With a light, firm tread Hermann stepped past him. The drawing-room and reception-room were in darkness, but the lamp in the ante-room sent through a feeble light. Hermann passed through into the bedroom. Before an icon-case, filled with old-fashioned images,[8] glowed a gold sanctuary lamp. Faded brocade armchairs and dull gilt divans with soft cushions were ranged in sad symmetry around the room, the walls of which were hung with Chinese silk. Two portraits, painted in Paris by Madame Lebrun,[9] were hung from one of the walls. One of these featured a plump, red-faced man of about forty, in a light-green uniform and with a star pinned to his breast; the other—a beautiful young woman with an aquiline nose and powdered hair, brushed back at the temples and adorned with a rose. In the corners of the room stood porcelain shepherdesses, table clocks from the workshop of the celebrated Leroy, little boxes, roulettes,[1] fans and the various lady's playthings which had been popular at the end of the last century, when the Montgolfiers' balloon and Mesmer's magnetism[2] were invented. Hermann went behind the screen, where stood a small iron bedstead; on the right was the door leading to the study; on the left the one which led to the corridor. Hermann opened the latter, and saw the narrow, winding staircase which led to the poor ward's room. . . . But he turned back and stepped into the dark study.

The time passed slowly. Everything was quiet. The clock in the drawing-room struck twelve; one by one the clocks in all the other rooms sounded the same hour, and then all was quiet again. Hermann stood leaning against the cold stove. He was calm; his heart beat evenly, like that of a man who has decided upon some dangerous but necessary action. One o'clock sounded; two o'clock; he heard the distant rattle of the carriage. He was seized by an involuntary agitation. The carriage drew near and stopped. He heard the sound of the carriage-steps being let down. The house suddenly came alive. Servants ran here and there, voices echoed through the house and the rooms were lit. Three old maid-servants hastened into the bedroom, followed by the Countess, who, tired to death, lowered herself into a Voltairean armchair.[3] Hermann peeped through a crack. Lisaveta Ivanovna went

---

8. I.e., religious images.　9. Marie-Louise-Élisabeth Vigée-Lebrun (1755–1842), French portrait painter, particularly of the aristocracy and royalty.　1. Little balls; or possibly portable devices for playing the gambling game of roulette. Julien Leroy (1686–1759), famous French clockmaker.　2. Franz Anton Mesmer (1734–1815) argued that a person can transmit personal force to others in the form of "animal magnetism." Joseph-Michel (1740–1810) and Jacques-Étienne (1745–1799) Montgolfier, French brothers, helped develop the hot-air balloon and conducted the first untethered flights.　3. A large armchair with a high back.

past him. Hermann heard her hurried steps as she went up the narrow staircase. In his heart there echoed something like the voice of conscience, but it grew silent, and his heart once more turned to stone.

The Countess began to undress before the looking-glass. Her rose-bedecked cap was unfastened; her powdered wig was removed from her grey, closely-cropped hair. Pins fell in showers around her. Her yellow dress, embroidered with silver, fell at her swollen feet. Hermann witnessed all the loathsome mysteries of her dress; at last the Countess stood in her dressing-gown and night-cap; in this attire, more suitable to her age, she seemed less hideous and revolting.

Like most old people, the Countess suffered from insomnia. Having undressed, she sat down by the window in the Voltairean armchair and dismissed her maidservants. The candles were carried out; once again the room was lit by a single sanctuary lamp. Looking quite yellow, the Countess sat rocking to and fro in her chair, her flabby lips moving. Her dim eyes reflected a complete absence of thought and, looking at her, one would have thought that the awful old woman's rocking came not of her own volition, but by the action of some hidden galvanism.

Suddenly, an indescribable change came over her death-like face. Her lips ceased to move, her eyes came to life: before the Countess stood an unknown man.

"Don't be alarmed, for God's sake, don't be alarmed," he said in a clear, low voice. "I have no intention of harming you; I have come to beseech a favour of you."

The old woman looked at him in silence, as if she had not heard him. Hermann imagined that she was deaf, and bending right down over her ear, he repeated what he had said. The old woman kept silent as before.

"You can ensure the happiness of my life," Hermann continued, "and it will cost you nothing: I know that you can guess three cards in succession. . . ."

Hermann stopped. The Countess appeared to understand what was demanded of her; she seemed to be seeking words for her reply.

"It was a joke," she said at last. "I swear to you, it was a joke."

"There's no joking about it," Hermann retorted angrily. "Remember Chaplitsky whom you helped to win."

The Countess was visibly disconcerted, and her features expressed strong emotion; but she quickly resumed her former impassivity.

"Can you name these three winning cards?" Hermann continued.

The Countess was silent. Hermann went on:

"For whom do you keep your secret? For your grandsons? They are rich and they can do without it; they don't know the value of money. Your three cards will not help a spendthrift. He who cannot keep his paternal inheritance will die in want, even if he has the devil at his side. I am not a spendthrift; I know the value of money. Your three cards will not be lost on me. Come . . . !"

He stopped and awaited her answer with trepidation. The Countess was silent. Hermann fell upon his knees.

"If your heart has ever known the feeling of love," he said, "if you remember its ecstasies, if you ever smiled at the wailing of your new-born son, if ever any human feeling has run through your breast, I entreat you by the feelings of a wife, a lover, a mother, by everything that is sacred in life, not to deny my request! Reveal your secret to me! What is it to you . . . ? Perhaps it is bound up with some dreadful sin, with the loss of eternal bliss, with some contract made with the devil . . . Consider: you are old; you have not long to live—I am prepared to take your sins on my own soul. Only reveal to me your secret. Realise that the happiness of a man is in your hands, that not only I, but my children, my grandchildren, my great-grandchildren will bless your memory and will revere it as something sacred. . . ."

The old woman answered not a word.

Hermann stood up.

"You old witch!" he said, clenching his teeth. "I'll force you to answer. . . ."

With these words he drew a pistol from his pocket. At the sight of the pistol, the Countess, for the second time, exhibited signs of strong emotion. She shook her head and raising her hand as though to shield herself from the shot, she rolled over on her back and remained motionless.

"Stop this childish behaviour now," Hermann said, taking her hand. "I ask you for the last time: will you name your three cards or won't you?"

The Countess made no reply. Hermann saw that she was dead.

CHAPTER FOUR

*7 Mai 18**
Homme sans moeurs et sans religion!*[4]
CORRESPONDENCE

Still in her ball dress, Lisaveta Ivanovna sat in her room, lost in thought. On her arrival home, she had quickly dismissed the sleepy maid who had reluctantly offered her services, had said that she would undress herself, and with a tremulous heart had gone up to her room, expecting to find Hermann there and yet hoping not to find him. Her first glance assured her of his absence and she thanked her fate for the obstacle that had prevented their meeting. She sat down, without undressing, and began to recall all the circumstances which had lured her so far in so short a time. It was not three weeks since she had first seen the young man from the window—and yet she was already in correspondence with him, and already he had managed to persuade her to grant him a nocturnal meeting! She knew his name only because some of his letters had been signed; she had never spoken to him, nor heard his voice, nor heard anything about him . . . until that very evening. Strange thing! That very evening, Tomsky, vexed with the Princess Polina * * * for not flirting with him as she usually did, had wished to revenge himself by a show of indifference: he had therefore summoned Lisaveta Ivanovna and together they had danced an endless mazurka. All the time they were dancing, he had teased her about her partiality to officers of the Engineers, had assured her that he knew far more than she would have supposed possible, and indeed, some of his jests were so successfully aimed that on several occasions Lisaveta Ivanovna had thought that her secret was known to him.

"From whom have you discovered all this?" she asked, laughing.

"From a friend of the person whom you know so well," Tomsky answered; "from a most remarkable man!"

"Who is this remarkable man?"

4. A man without morals and without religion! (French).

"He is called Hermann."

Lisaveta made no reply, but her hands and feet turned quite numb.

"This Hermann," Tomsky continued, "is a truly romantic figure: he has the profile of a Napoleon, and the soul of a Mephistopheles. I should think that he has at least three crimes on his conscience. . . . How pale you have turned. . . . !"

"I have a headache. . . . What did this Hermann—or whatever his name is—tell you?"

"Hermann is most displeased with his friend: he says that he would act quite differently in his place . . . I even think that Hermann himself has designs on you; at any rate he listens to the exclamations of his enamoured friend with anything but indifference."

"But where has he seen me?"

"At church, perhaps; on a walk—God only knows! Perhaps in your room, whilst you were asleep: he's quite capable of it . . ."

Three ladies approaching him with the question: *oublie ou regret?*[5] interrupted the conversation which had become so agonisingly interesting to Lisaveta Ivanovna.

The lady chosen by Tomsky was the Princess Polina * * * herself. She succeeded in clearing up the misunderstanding between them during the many turns and movements of the dance, after which he conducted her to her chair. Tomsky returned to his own place. He no longer had any thoughts for Hermann or Lisaveta Ivanovna, who desperately wanted to renew her interrupted conversation; but the mazurka came to an end and shortly afterwards the old Countess left.

Tomsky's words were nothing but ball-room chatter, but they made a deep impression upon the mind of the young dreamer. The portrait, sketched by Tomsky, resembled the image she herself had formed of Hermann, and thanks to the latest romantic novels, Hermann's quite commonplace face took on attributes that both frightened and captivated her imagination. Now she sat, her uncovered arms crossed, her head, still adorned with flowers, bent over her bare shoulders. . . . Suddenly the door opened, and Hermann entered. She shuddered.

"Where have you been?" she asked in a frightened whisper.

"In the old Countess' bedroom," Hermann answered: "I have just left it. The Countess is dead."

"Good God! What are you saying?"

"And it seems," Hermann continued, "that I am the cause of her death."

Lisaveta Ivanovna looked at him, and the words of Tomsky echoed in her mind: "he has at least three crimes on his conscience"! Hermann sat down beside her on the window sill and told her everything.

Lisaveta Ivanovna listened to him with horror. So those passionate letters, those ardent demands, the whole impertinent and obstinate pursuit—all that was not love! Money—that was what his soul craved for! It was not she who could satisfy his desire and make him happy! The poor ward had been nothing but the unknowing assistant of a brigand, of the murderer of her aged benefactress! . . . She wept bitterly, in an agony of belated repentance.

---

5. The ladies cut in, offering the man a choice: *oublie* (forgetting) or *regret*. He does not know which lady is which. He chooses correctly the one with whom he wants to dance.

Hermann looked at her in silence; his heart was also tormented; but neither the tears of the poor girl nor the astounding charm of her grief disturbed his hardened soul. He felt no remorse at the thought of the dead old lady. He felt dismay for only one thing: the irretrievable loss of the secret upon which he had relied for enrichment.

"You are a monster!" Lisaveta Ivanovna said at last.

"I did not wish for her death," Hermann answered. "My pistol wasn't loaded."

They were silent.

The day began to break. Lisaveta Ivanovna extinguished the flickering candle. A pale light lit up her room. She wiped her tear-stained eyes and raised them to Hermann: he sat by the window, his arms folded and with a grim frown on his face. In this position he bore an astonishing resemblance to a portrait of Napoleon. Even Lisaveta Ivanovna was struck by the likeness.

"How am I going to get you out of the house?" Lisaveta Ivanovna said at last. "I had thought of leading you along the secret staircase, but that would mean going past the Countess' bedroom, and I am afraid."

"Tell me how to find this secret staircase; I'll go on my own."

Lisaveta Ivanovna stood up, took a key from her chest of drawers, handed it to Hermann, and gave him detailed instructions. Hermann pressed her cold, unresponsive hand, kissed her bowed head and left.

He descended the winding staircase and once more entered the Countess' bedroom. The dead old lady sat as if turned to stone; her face expressed a deep calm. Hermann stopped before her and gazed at her for a long time, as if wishing to assure himself of the dreadful truth; finally, he went into the study, felt for the door behind the silk wall hangings, and, agitated by strange feelings, he began to descend the dark staircase.

"Along this very staircase," he thought, "perhaps at this same hour sixty years ago, in an embroidered coat, his hair dressed à l'oiseau royal,[6] his three-cornered hat pressed to his heart, there may have crept into this very bedroom a young and happy man now long since turned to dust in his grave—and to-day the aged heart of his mistress ceased to beat."

At the bottom of the staircase Hermann found a door, which he opened with the key Lisaveta Ivanovna had given him, and he found himself in a corridor which led into the street.

CHAPTER FIVE

That evening there appeared before me
the figure of the late Baroness von V**.
She was all in white and she said to me:
"How are you, Mr. Councillor!"
SWEDENBORG[7]

Three days after the fateful night, at nine o'clock in the morning, Hermann set out for the * * * monastery, where a funeral service for the dead Countess was going to be held. Although unrepentant, he could not altogether silence the voice of conscience, which kept on repeating: "You are the murderer of

6. In the style of the royal bird (French, literal trans.); an antiquated and elaborate hairstyle. 7. Emanuel Swedenborg (1688–1772), Swedish theologian, believed that he had several experiences of divine revelation, some involving appearances to him of the dead.

the old woman!" Having little true religious belief, he was extremely superstitious. He believed that the dead Countess could exercise a harmful influence on his life, and he had therefore resolved to be present at the funeral, in order to ask her forgiveness.

The church was full. Hermann could scarcely make his way through the crowd of people. The coffin stood on a rich catafalque beneath a velvet canopy. Within it lay the dead woman, her arms folded upon her chest, and dressed in a white satin robe, with a lace cap on her head. Around her stood the members of her household: servants in black coats, with armorial ribbons upon their shoulders and candles in their hands; the relatives—children, grandchildren, great-grandchildren—in deep mourning. Nobody cried; tears would have been *une affectation*. The Countess was so old that her death could have surprised nobody, and her relatives had long considered her as having outlived herself. A young bishop pronounced the funeral sermon. In simple, moving words, he described the peaceful end of the righteous woman, who for many years had been in quiet and touching preparation for a Christian end. "The angel of death found her," the speaker said, "waiting for the midnight bridegroom, vigilant in godly meditation." The service was completed with sad decorum. The relatives were the first to take leave of the body. Then the numerous guests went up to pay final homage to her who had so long participated in their frivolous amusements. They were followed by all the members of the Countess' household, the last of whom was an old housekeeper of the same age as the Countess. She was supported by two young girls who led her up to the coffin. She had not the strength to bow down to the ground—and merely shed a few tears as she kissed the cold hand of her mistress. After that, Hermann decided to approach the coffin. He knelt down and for several minutes lay on the cold floor, which was strewn with fir branches; at last he got up, as pale as the dead woman herself; he went up the steps of the catafalque and bent his head over the body of the Countess. . . . At that very moment it seemed to him that the dead woman gave him a mocking glance, and winked at him. Hermann, hurriedly stepping back, missed his footing, and crashed on his back against the ground. He was helped to his feet. At the same moment, Lisaveta Ivanovna was carried out in a faint to the porch of the church. These events disturbed the solemnity of the gloomy ceremony for a few moments. A subdued murmur rose among the congregation, and a tall, thin chamberlain, a near relative of the dead woman, whispered in the ear of an Englishman standing by him that the young officer was the Countess' illegitimate son, to which the Englishman replied coldly: "Oh?"

For the whole of that day Hermann was exceedingly troubled. He went to a secluded inn for dinner and, contrary to his usual custom and in the hope of silencing his inward agitation, he drank heavily. But the wine fired his imagination still more. Returning home, he threw himself on to his bed without undressing, and fell into a heavy sleep.

It was already night when he awoke: the moon lit up his room. He glanced at his watch; it was a quarter to three. He found he could not go back to sleep; he sat down on his bed and thought about the funeral of the old Countess.

At that moment somebody in the street glanced in at his window, and immediately went away again. Hermann paid no attention to the incident. A minute or so later, he heard the door into the front room being opened. Hermann imagined that it was his orderly, drunk as usual, returning from some nocturnal outing. But he heard unfamiliar footsteps and the soft shuffling of slippers. The door opened: a woman in a white dress entered. Hermann mistook her for his old wet-nurse and wondered what could have brought her out at that time of the night. But the woman in white glided across the room and suddenly appeared before him—and Hermann recognised the Countess!

"I have come to you against my will," she said in a firm voice, "but I have been ordered to fulfill your request. Three, seven, ace, played in that order, will win for you, but only on condition that you play not more than one card in twenty-four hours, and that you never play again for the rest of your life. I'll forgive you my death if you marry my ward, Lisaveta Ivanovna. . . ."

With these words, she turned round quietly, walked towards the door and disappeared, her slippers shuffling. Herman heard the door in the hall bang, and again saw somebody look in at him through the window.

For a long time Hermann could not collect his senses. He went out into the next room. His orderly was lying asleep on the floor; Hermann could scarcely wake him. The orderly was, as usual, drunk, and it was impossible to get any sense out of him. The door into the hall was locked. Hermann returned to his room, lit a candle, and recorded the details of his vision.

CHAPTER SIX

"Attendez!"[8]
"How dare you say to me: 'Attendez'?"
"Your Excellency, I said: 'Attendez, sir'!"

Two fixed ideas can no more exist in one mind than, in the physical sense, two bodies can occupy one and the same place. "Three, seven, ace" soon eclipsed from Hermann's mind the form of the dead old lady. "Three, seven, ace" never left his thoughts, were constantly on his lips. At the sight of a young girl, he would say: "How shapely she is! Just like the three of hearts." When asked the time, he would reply: "About seven." Every pot-bellied man he saw reminded him of an ace. "Three, seven, ace," assuming all possible shapes, persecuted him in his sleep: the three bloomed before him in the shape of some luxuriant flower, the seven took on the appearance of a Gothic gateway, the ace—of an enormous spider. To the exclusion of all others, one thought alone occupied his mind—making use of the secret which had cost him so much. He began to think of retirement and of travel. He wanted to try his luck in the public gaming-houses of Paris. Chance spared him the trouble.

There was in Moscow a society of rich gamblers, presided over by the celebrated Chekalinsky, a man whose whole life had been spent at the card-table, and who had amassed millions long ago, accepting his winnings in the form of promissory notes and paying his losses with ready money. His long experience had earned him the confidence of his companions, and his open house, his famous cook and his friendliness and gaiety had won him great

---

8. Wait! (French). Attendants at the gaming table called "Attendez" to indicate the end of the period to place bets.

public respect. He arrived in Petersburg. The younger generation flocked to his house, forgetting balls for cards, and preferring the enticements of faro to the fascinations of courtship. Narumov took Hermann to meet him.

They passed through a succession of magnificent rooms, full of polite and attentive waiters. Several generals and privy councillors were playing whist; young men, sprawled out on brocade divans, were eating ices and smoking their pipes. In the drawing-room, seated at the head of a long table, around which were crowded about twenty players, the host kept bank. He was a most respectable-looking man of about sixty; his head was covered with silvery grey hair, and his full, fresh face expressed good nature; his eyes, enlivened by a perpetual smile, shone brightly. Narumov introduced Hermann to him. Chekalinsky shook his hand warmly, requested him not to stand on ceremony, and went on dealing.

The game lasted a long time. More than thirty cards lay on the table. Chekalinsky paused after each round in order to give the players time to arrange their cards, wrote down their losses, listened politely to their demands, and more politely still allowed them to retract any stake accidentally left on the table. At last the game finished. Chekalinsky shuffled the cards and prepared to deal again.

"Allow me to place a stake," Hermann said, stretching out his hand from behind a fat gentleman who was punting[9] there.

Chekalinsky smiled and nodded silently, as a sign of his consent. Narumov laughingly congratulated Hermann on forswearing a longstanding principle and wished him a lucky beginning.

"I've staked," Hermann said, as he chalked up the amount, which was very considerable, on the back of his card.

"How much is it?" asked the banker, screwing up his eyes. "Forgive me, but I can't make it out."

"47,000 roubles," Hermann replied.

At these words every head in the room turned, and all eyes were fixed on Hermann.

"He's gone out of his mind!" Narumov thought.

"Allow me to observe to you," Chekalinsky said with his invariable smile, "that your stake is extremely high: nobody here has ever put more than 275 roubles on any single card."

"What of it?" retorted Hermann. "Do you take me or not?"

Chekalinsky, bowing, humbly accepted the stake.

"However, I would like to say," he said, "that, being judged worthy of the confidence of my friends, I can only bank against ready money. For my own part, of course, I am sure that your word is enough, but for the sake of the order of the game and of the accounts, I must ask you to place your money on the card."

Hermann drew a banknote from his pocket and handed it to Chekalinsky who, giving it a cursory glance, put it on Hermann's card.

He began to deal. On the right a nine turned up, on the left a three.[1]

"The three wins," said Hermann, showing his card.

9. Betting against the dealer.   1. Bets in faro are made on the positions of cards. A player selects a card and places it facedown in front of him or her; if the card turns up on the dealer's left, the player wins; if on the right, the dealer wins.

A murmur arose among the players. Chekalinsky frowned, but instantly the smile returned to his face.

"Do you wish to take the money now?" he asked Hermann.

"If you would be so kind."

Chekalinsky drew a number of banknotes from his pocket and settled up immediately. Hermann took up his money and left the table. Narumov was too astounded even to think. Hermann drank a glass of lemonade and went home.

The next evening he again appeared at Chekalinsky's. The host was dealing. Hermann walked up to the table; the players already there immediately gave way to him. Chekalinsky bowed graciously.

Hermann waited for the next deal, took a card and placed on it his 47,000 roubles together with the winnings of the previous evening.

Chekalinsky began to deal. A knave turned up on the right, a seven on the left.

Hermann showed his seven.

There was a general cry of surprise, and Chekalinsky was clearly disconcerted. He counted out 94,000 roubles and handed them to Hermann, who pocketed them coolly and immediately withdrew.

The following evening Hermann again appeared at the table. Everyone was expecting him; the generals and privy councillors abandoned their whist in order to watch such unusual play. The young officers jumped up from their divans; all the waiters gathered in the drawing-room. Hermann was surrounded by a crowd of people. The other players held back their cards, impatient to see how Hermann would get on. Hermann stood at the table and prepared to play alone against the pale but still smiling Chekalinsky. Each unsealed a pack of cards. Chekalinsky shuffled. Hermann drew and placed his card, covering it with a heap of banknotes. It was like a duel. A deep silence reigned all around.

His hands shaking, Chekalinsky began to deal. On the right lay a queen, on the left an ace.

"The ace wins," said Hermann and showed his card.

"Your queen has lost," Chekalinsky said kindly.

Hermann started: indeed, instead of an ace, before him lay the queen of spades. He could not believe his eyes, could not understand how he could have slipped up.

At that moment it seemed to him that the queen of spades winked at him and smiled. He was struck by an unusual likeness. . . .

"The old woman!" he shouted in terror.

Chekalinsky gathered up his winnings. Hermann stood motionless. When he left the table, people began to converse noisily.

"Famously punted!" the players said.

Chekalinsky shuffled the cards afresh; play went on as usual.

CONCLUSION

Hermann went mad. He is now installed in Room 17 at the Obukhov Hospital; he answers no questions, but merely mutters with unusual rapidity: "Three, seven, ace! Three, seven, queen!"

Lisaveta Ivanovna has married a very agreeable young man, who has a good position in the service somewhere; he is the son of the former steward of the old Countess. Lisaveta Ivanovna is bringing up a poor relative.

Tomsky has been promoted to the rank of Captain, and is going to marry Princess Polina.

ALFRED, LORD TENNYSON
1809–1892

Tennyson's poetry expresses a conflict—characteristic of his historical period but also of human experience generally—between the tendency to despair and the desire to hope. Hope locates itself, for Tennyson, in the human capacity to struggle toward future goals and, on occasion, in religious faith. Mortality causes despair: the death of others, the inevitable sense of increasing weakness as one ages, the scientific discovery that whole species have disappeared in the world's history. It is Tennyson's ability to remind us of both contradictory emotions, and of the degree to which they inevitably coexist and alternate, that makes his poetry compelling.

The poet's pervasive melancholy came partly from experience. Son of an Anglican clergyman, he spent four unhappy years in school before his father consented to allow him to be tutored at home. He attended Trinity College, Cambridge, where, with his friend Arthur Hallam, he belonged to an undergraduate society called The Apostles, whose members discussed contemporary social, religious, scientific, and literary issues. The friendship with Hallam retained its intensity after his undergraduate years; by 1830, Hallam had become engaged to Tennyson's sister. Three years later, however, at the age of twenty-two, Hallam died suddenly in Vienna. The loss acutely affected Tennyson, who during the next seventeen years gradually composed the long elegiac poem *In Memoriam A. H. H.* to record the profound emotional and intellectual effects on him of his friend's death.

In 1836, Tennyson became engaged to Emily Sellwood; but, largely because of financial difficulties, he did not marry her until 1850, the year in which, after the publication of *In Memoriam*, he was made poet laureate. Five years earlier, he had received a pension. He lived quietly for the rest of his life, increasingly famous; in 1884, he was created first Baron Tennyson.

Tennyson's earliest independent collections of poems (1830 and 1833; he had published a collaborative volume with his brother in 1827) were the target of fierce critical attack, another cause for melancholy. He published nothing more until 1842, when a collection called simply *Poems* met great critical success. Subsequently revered as a kind of national spokesman, Tennyson won popularity particularly with *The Princess* (1847; revised 1855), *Maud* (1855), and *The Idylls of the King* (1859, 1885), a retelling of the legends of King Arthur.

In *Ulysses* (1842), Tennyson, imagining the situation of the Greek hero after his return to domestic peace, evokes the excitement and moral grandeur of the human capacity for aspiration:

> that which we are, we are;
> One equal temper of heroic hearts
> Made weak by time and fate, but strong in will
> To strive, to seek, to find, and not to yield.

In another meditation on classic themes, *Tithonus* (published in 1860, written in 1833), he puts the other side of the case. "The woods decay, the woods decay and fall," the poem begins; its imagined speaker, a man who has been granted immortality at his own request, wishes to return the gift. "Why should a man desire in any way / To vary from the kindly race of men?" Ulysses insists on the specialness of his sort of man; Tithonus knows the burden of specialness. In conjunction, the two poems call attention to the fact that neither the Enlightenment nor the early Romantic view of experience seems entirely adequate to this poet. Tithonus's desire to share the common fate of humankind throbs with melancholy; he feels that fate as doom, although he equally experiences his exemption from it as doom. Ulysses' condescension to his prudent son ("Most blameless is he. . . . / He works his work, I mine") underlines the sense of desperation in his insistent striving. No alternative form of action or commitment satisfies the imagination.

In Memoriam, Tennyson's most ambitious work, suggests reasons for the poet's inability to imagine fulfillment. The problem is not merely temperament, but the effect on his consciousness of intellectual and social actuality as well as the loss and the possibility of loss made palpable to him by Hallam's death.

> Are God and Nature then at strife,
>   That Nature lends such evil dreams?
>   So careful of the type she seems,
> So careless of the single life.

That stanza comes from number 55 of the 125 linked poems that make up the whole. The next in the series begins,

> "So careful of the type?" but no. . . .
>   She [Nature] cries, "A thousand types are gone;
>   I care for nothing, all shall go."

Reality offers not the slightest assurance of survival; contemporary scientists, studying fossils, had revealed the extinction of entire species. "Man, [Nature's] last work, who seemed so fair, / Such splendid purpose in his eyes"—with a Ulysses' capacity for fine imaginings—even man, humankind in general, may face extinction (a possibility that today looks ever more compelling). Number 55 concludes with the faintest possible religious hope:

> O life as futile, then, as frail!
>   O for thy voice to soothe and bless!
>   What hope of answer, or redress?
> Behind the veil, behind the veil.

By the end of the entire sequence, the poet has arrived at a more affirmative vision; he claims to have discovered God through his own pain and through the processes of feeling, which he asserts as more revelatory than those of logic. Indeed, *In Memoriam* persuasively evokes the slow reconciliation of mourning, giving its readers vicarious experience of the despair, the false starts, the inconsistencies of grief. The poem's power, however, derives not only from its record of personal emotional experience but from its demonstration, its embodiment, of how the intellectual and the emotional intertwine. The private loss of a friend assimilates itself to a more general loss of faith and certainty characteristic of the Victorian period. The determination to strive, to seek, to find, and not to yield generated scientific discovery, industrial and mercantile development. As early as 1850, though, such achievements threatened established social and theological orders. Tennyson re-creates for us what such threats felt like to those actually experiencing them. He writes an elegy not only for Arthur Hallam but for the larger losses of his moment in history.

PRONOUNCING GLOSSARY

The following list uses common English syllables and stress accents to provide rough equivalents of selected words whose pronunciation may be unfamiliar to the general reader.

Aeonian: *ay-ohn'-ee-an* Hyades: *hai'-u-deez*

Arcady: *ahr'-kah-dee* Telemachus: *tel-em'-u-kus*

Argive: *ahr-gaive* Tithonus: *ti-thoh'-nus*

Ulysses

It little profits that an idle king,
By this still hearth, among these barren crags,
Matched with an agèd wife, I mete and dole
Unequal laws unto a savage race,
That hoard, and sleep, and feed, and know not me.   5
    I cannot rest from travel; I will drink
Life to the lees. All times I have enjoyed
Greatly, have suffered greatly, both with those
That loved me, and alone; on shore, and when
Through scudding drifts the rainy Hyades[1]   10
Vexed the dim sea. I am become a name;
For always roaming with a hungry heart
Much have I seen and known,—cities of men
And manners, climates, councils, governments,
Myself not least, but honored of them all,—   15
And drunk delight of battle with my peers,
Far on the ringing plains of windy Troy.
I am a part of all that I have met;
Yet all experience is an arch wherethrough
Gleams that untravelled world whose margin fades   20
Forever and forever when I move.
How dull it is to pause, to make an end,
To rust unburnished, not to shine in use!
As though to breathe were life! Life piled on life
Were all too little, and of one to me   25
Little remains; but every hour is saved
From that eternal silence, something more,
A bringer of new things; and vile it were
For some three suns to store and hoard myself,
And this gray spirit yearning in desire   30
To follow knowledge like a sinking star,
Beyond the utmost bound of human thought.
    This is my son, mine own Telemachus,
To whom I leave the scepter and the isle[2]—
Well-loved of me, discerning to fulfill   35
This labor, by slow prudence to make mild
A rugged people, and through soft degrees

1. A cluster of seven stars in the constellation of Taurus. The ancients supposed that when Hyades rose with the sun, rainy weather would follow.   2. Ithaca.

Subdue them to the useful and the good.
Most blameless is he, centered in the sphere
Of common duties, decent not to fail   40
In offices of tenderness, and pay
Meet adoration to my household gods,
When I am gone. He works his work, I mine.
   There lies the port; the vessel puffs her sail;
There gloom the dark, broad seas. My mariners,   45
Souls that have toiled, and wrought, and thought with me—
That ever with a frolic welcome took
The thunder and the sunshine, and opposed
Free hearts, free foreheads—you and I are old;
Old age hath yet his honor and his toil;   50
Death closes all. But something ere the end,
Some work of noble note, may yet be done,
Not unbecoming men that strove with gods.
The lights begin to twinkle from the rocks;
The long day wanes; the slow moon climbs; the deep   55
Moans round with many voices. Come, my friends,
'Tis not too late to seek a newer world.
Push off, and sitting well in order smite
The sounding furrows; for my purpose holds
To sail beyond the sunset, and the baths   60
Of all the western stars, until I die.
It may be that the gulfs will wash us down;
It may be we shall touch the Happy Isles,[3]
And see the great Achilles,[4] whom we knew.
Though much is taken, much abides; and though   65
We are not now that strength which in old days
Moved earth and heaven, that which we are, we are;
One equal temper of heroic hearts,
Made weak by time and fate, but strong in will
To strive, to seek, to find, and not to yield.   70

Tithonus[1]

   The woods decay, the woods decay and fall,
The vapors weep their burthen to the ground,
Man comes and tills the field and lies beneath,
And after many a summer dies the swan.
Me only cruel immortality[2]   5
Consumes; I wither slowly in thine arms,
Here at the quiet limit of the world,
A white-haired shadow roaming like a dream
The ever-silent spaces of the East,
Far-folded mists, and gleaming halls of morn.   10

---

3. In Greek myth, the abode of the warriors after death.   4. Comrade-in-arms of Ulysses at Troy.   1. A prince of Troy loved by Aurora, goddess of dawn, in whose palace he is depicted as living.   2. From Zeus, Aurora obtained for Tithonus the gift of immortality but not of eternal youth.

Alas! for this gray shadow, once a man—
So glorious in his beauty and thy choice,
Who madest him thy chosen, that he seemed
To his great heart none other than a God!
I asked thee, "Give me immortality."   15
Then didst thou grant mine asking with a smile,
Like wealthy men who care not how they give.
But thy strong Hours[3] indignant worked their wills,
And beat me down and marred and wasted me,
And though they could not end me, left me maimed   20
To dwell in presence of immortal youth,
Immortal age beside immortal youth,
And all I was in ashes. Can thy love,
Thy beauty, make amends, though even now,
Close over us, the silver star,[4] thy guide,   25
Shines in those tremulous eyes that fill with tears
To hear me? Let me go; take back thy gift.
Why should a man desire in any way
To vary from the kindly race of men,
Or pass beyond the goal of ordinance   30
Where all should pause, as is most meet[5] for all?
   A soft air fans the cloud apart; there comes
A glimpse of that dark world where I was born.
Once more the old mysterious glimmer steals
From thy pure brows, and from thy shoulders pure,   35
And bosom beating with a heart renewed.
Thy cheek begins to redden through the gloom,
Thy sweet eyes brighten slowly close to mine,
Ere yet they blind the stars, and the wild team[6]
Which love thee, yearning for thy yoke, arise,   40
And shake the darkness from their loosened manes,
And beat the twilight into flakes of fire.
   Lo! ever thus thou growest beautiful
In silence, then before thine answer given
Departest, and thy tears are on my cheek.   45
   Why wilt thou ever scare me with thy tears,
And make me tremble lest a saying learnt,
In days far-off, on that dark earth, be true?
"The Gods themselves cannot recall their gifts."
   Ay me! ay me! with what another heart   50
In days far-off, and with what other eyes
I used to watch—if I be he that watched—
The lucid outline forming round thee; saw
The dim curls kindle into sunny rings;
Changed with thy mystic change, and felt my blood   55
Glow with the glow that slowly crimsoned all
Thy presence and thy portals, while I lay,
Mouth, forehead, eyelids, growing dewy-warm

---

3. Or Horae, goddesses of the seasons and of growth and decay.   4. The morning star that precedes the
dawn.   5. Suitable.   6. Of supernatural horses; they draw Aurora's chariot into the sky at dawn.

With kisses balmier than half-opening buds
Of April, and could hear the lips that kissed   60
Whispering I knew not what of wild and sweet,
Like that strange song I heard Apollo[7] sing,
While Ilion like a mist rose into towers.[8]
    Yet hold me not forever in thine East;
How can my nature longer mix with thine?   65
Coldly thy rosy shadows bathe me, cold
Are all thy lights, and cold my wrinkled feet
Upon thy glimmering thresholds, when the steam
Floats up from those dim fields about the homes
Of happy men that have the power to die,   70
And grassy barrows[9] of the happier dead.
Release me, and restore me to the ground.
Thou seest all things, thou wilt see my grave;
Thou wilt renew thy beauty morn by morn,
I earth in earth forget these empty courts,   75
And thee returning on thy silver wheels.

From *In Memoriam A. H. H.*

Obit. MDCCCXXXIII

[PROLOGUE]

Strong Son of God, immortal Love,[1]
  Whom we, that have not seen thy face,
  By faith, and faith alone, embrace,
Believing where we cannot prove;

Thine are these orbs of light and shade;[2]   5
  Thou madest Life in man and brute;
  Thou madest Death; and lo, thy foot
Is on the skull which thou hast made.[3]

Thou wilt not leave us in the dust:
  Thou madest man, he knows not why,   10
  He thinks he was not made to die;
And thou hast made him: thou art just.

Thou seemest human and divine,
  The highest, holiest manhood, thou.
  Our wills are ours, we know not how;   15
Our wills are ours, to make them thine.

---

7. Greek god of music and patron of Troy.   8. According to legend, the walls of Troy (Ilion) were raised by the sound of Apollo's song.   9. Burial mounds.   1. 1 John 4.8: "He that loveth not knoweth not God; for God is love." 1 John 4.15: "Whosoever shall confess that Jesus is the Son of God, God dwelleth in him, and he in God."   2. I.e., the Earth and the planets, part of each of which is sunlit, the rest in shadow.   3. I.e., Jesus crushes Death underfoot, a common motif in painting and sculpture.

Our little systems have their day;
　　They have their day and cease to be;[4]
　　They are but broken lights of thee,[5]
And thou, O Lord, art more than they.　　　　　　　20

We have but faith: we cannot know,
　　For knowledge is of things we see;
　　And yet we trust it comes from thee,
A beam in darkness: let it grow.

Let knowledge grow from more to more,　　　　　　25
　　But more of reverence in us dwell;
　　That mind and soul, according well,
May make one music as before,

But vaster. We are fools and slight;
　　We mock thee when we do not fear:　　　　　　30
　　But help thy foolish ones to bear;
Help thy vain worlds to bear thy light.

Forgive what seemed my sin in me,
　　What seemed my worth since I began;
　　For merit lives from man to man,　　　　　　35
And not from man, O Lord, to thee.

Forgive my grief for one removed,
　　Thy creature, whom I found so fair.
　　I trust he lives in thee, and there
I find him worthier to be loved.　　　　　　40

Forgive these wild and wandering cries,
　　Confusions of a wasted[6] youth;
　　Forgive them where they fail in truth,
And in thy wisdom make me wise.

1

I held it truth, with him[7] who sings
　　To one clear harp in divers[8] tones,
　　That men may rise on stepping-stones
Of their dead selves to higher things.

But who shall so forecast the years　　　　　　5
　　And find in loss a gain to match?
　　Or reach a hand through time to catch
The far-off interest of tears?

---

4. Transient theological and philosophical systems, contrasted with the enduring systems of the stars.
5. Refracted, as by a prism.　6. Laid waste (by Hallam's loss).　7. Goethe, who in the second part of *Faust* and elsewhere voices his conception of spiritual progress through the outgrowing of one's former selves.　8. Various.

Let Love clasp Grief lest both be drowned,
  Let darkness keep her raven gloss.   10
  Ah, sweeter to be drunk with loss,
To dance with Death, to beat the ground,

Than that the victor Hours[9] should scorn
  The long result of love, and boast,
  "Behold the man that loved and lost,   15
But all he was is overworn."[1]

2

Old yew,[2] which graspest at the stones
  That name the underlying dead,
  Thy fibers net the dreamless head,
Thy roots are wrapped about the bones.

The seasons bring the flower again,   5
  And bring the firstling[3] to the flock;
  And in the dusk of thee the clock
Beats out the little lives of men.

O, not for thee the glow, the bloom,
  Who changest not in any gale,   10
  Nor branding summer suns avail
To touch thy thousand years of gloom;

And gazing on thee, sullen tree,
  Sick for thy stubborn hardihood,
  I seem to fail from out my blood   15
And grow incorporate into thee.

3

O Sorrow, cruel fellowship,
  O Priestess in the vaults of Death,
  O sweet and bitter in a breath,
What whispers from thy lying lip?

"The stars," she whispers, "blindly run;   5
  A web is woven across the sky;
  From out waste places comes a cry,
And murmurs from the dying sun;

"And all the phantom, Nature, stands—
  With all the music in her tone,
  A hollow echo of my own,—   10
A hollow form with empty hands."

---

9. Or Horae, goddesses of the seasons and of growth and decay.   1. Worn out, exhausted.   2. Evergreen capable of reaching great age. It is often planted in graveyards as a symbol of immortality.   3. First-born.

And shall I take a thing so blind,
   Embrace her as my natural good;
   Or crush her, like a vice of blood,   15
Upon the threshold of the mind?

*   *   *

5

Our words reveal what our hearts

I sometimes hold it half a sin
   To put in words the grief I feel;
   For words, like Nature, half reveal
And half conceal the Soul within.

But, for the unquiet heart and brain,   5
   A use in measured language lies;
   The sad mechanic exercise,
Like dull narcotics, numbing pain.

In words, like weeds,[4] I'll wrap me o'er,
   Like coarsest clothes against the cold;   10
   But that large grief which these enfold
Is given in outline and no more.

*   *   *

7

Dark house,[5] by which once more I stand
   Here in the long unlovely street,
   Doors, where my heart was used to beat
So quickly, waiting for a hand,

A hand that can be clasped no more—   5
   Behold me, for I cannot sleep,
   And like a guilty thing I creep
At earliest morning to the door.

He is not here; but far away
   The noise of life begins again,   10
   And ghastly through the drizzling rain
On the bald street breaks the blank day.

*   *   *

10

I hear the noise about thy keel;[6]
   I hear the bell struck in the night;
   I see the cabin-window bright;
   I see the sailor at the wheel.

4. Garments (with allusion to mourning garments).   5. The Hallam family residence.   6. Of the ship bringing Hallam's body back from Vienna.

Thou bring'st the sailor to his wife,   5
   And traveled men from foreign lands;
   And letters unto trembling hands;
And, thy dark freight, a vanished life.

So bring him; we have idle dreams;
   This look of quiet flatters thus   10
   Our home-bred fancies. O, to us,
The fools of habit, sweeter seems

To rest beneath the clover sod,
   That takes the sunshine and the rains,
   Or where the kneeling hamlet drains   15
The chalice of the grapes of God;[7]

Than if with thee the roaring wells
   Should gulf him fathom-deep in brine,
   And hands so often clasped in mine,
Should toss with tangle[8] and with shells.   20

11

Calm is the morn without a sound,
   Calm as to suit a calmer grief,
   And only through the faded leaf
The chestnut pattering to the ground;[9]

Calm and deep peace on this high wold,[1]   5
   And on these dews that drench the furze,
   And all the silvery gossamers
That twinkle into green and gold;

Calm and still light on yon great plain
   That sweeps with all its autumn bowers,   10
   And crowded farms and lessening towers,
To mingle with the bounding main;

Calm and deep peace in this wide air,
   These leaves that redden to the fall,
   And in my heart, if calm at all,   15
If any calm, a calm despair;

Calm on the seas, and silver sleep,
   And waves that sway themselves in rest,
   And dead calm in that noble breast
Which heaves but with the heaving deep.   20

*   *   *

7. This stanza mentions alternate modes of burial: in the churchyard or under the chancel where worshipers kneel for the Sacrament.   8. Seaweed.   9. The time is September, when Hallam's body is still en route.   1. Open uplands; i.e., Tennyson is at his home in Somersby, Lincolnshire.

15

Tonight the winds begin to rise
  And roar from yonder dropping day;
  The last red leaf is whirled away,
The rooks[2] are blown about the skies;

The forest cracked, the waters curled,   5
  The cattle huddled on the lea;[3]
  And wildly dashed on tower and tree
The sunbeam strikes along the world:

And but for fancies, which aver
  That all thy motions gently pass   10
  Athwart a plane of molten glass,
I scarce could brook the strain and stir

That makes the barren branches loud;
  And but for fear it is not so,
  The wild unrest that lives in woe   15
Would dote and pore on yonder cloud[4]

That rises upward always higher,
  And onward drags a laboring breast,
  And topples round the dreary west,
A looming bastion fringed with fire.   20

16

What words are these have fall'n from me?
  Can calm despair and wild unrest
  Be tenants of a single breast,
Or Sorrow such a changeling be?

Or doth she only seem to take   5
  The touch of change in calm or storm,
  But knows no more of transient form
In her deep self, than some dead lake

That holds the shadow of a lark
  Hung in the shadow of a heaven?   10
  Or has the shock, so harshly given,
Confused me like the unhappy bark[5]

That strikes by night a craggy shelf,
  And staggers blindly ere she sink?

---

2. European crowlike birds.   **3.** Pasture.   **4.** In the midst of a gathering storm, the poet's imagination soothes him with the fancy that Hallam's ship moves gently toward England on a glass-calm sea. Only a fear that this fancy may delude him (and Hallam's crossing be really in danger) prevents the stormy unrest within him from romantically luxuriating in the stormy sunset all around him.   **5.** Ship.

And stunned me from my power to think   15
And all my knowledge of myself;

And made me that delirious man
    Whose fancy fuses old and new,
    And flashes into false and true,
And mingles all without a plan?   20

*   *   *

19

The Danube to the Severn[6] gave
    The darkened heart that beat no more;
    They laid him by the pleasant shore,
And in the hearing of the wave.[7]

There twice a day the Severn fills;   5
    The salt sea-water passes by,
    And hushes half the babbling Wye,[8]
And makes a silence in the hills.

The Wye is hushed nor moved along,
    And hushed my deepest grief of all,   10
    When filled with tears that cannot fall,
I brim with sorrow drowning song.

The tide flows down, the wave again
    Is vocal in its wooded walls;
    My deeper anguish also falls,   15
And I can speak a little then.

*   *   *

21

I sing to him that rests below,
    And, since the grasses round me wave,
    I take the grasses of the grave,
And make them pipes[9] whereon to blow.

The traveler hears me now and then,   5
    And sometimes harshly will he speak:
    "This fellow would make weakness weak,
And melt the waxen hearts of men."

Some would think his extreme grief is a weakness

6. The church at Clevedon, Somerset, where Hallam was buried, is on the Severn. Vienna, where he died, is on the Danube.   7. Tennyson was not present at the funeral and did not learn until years later that Hallam had been buried in the church, not in the graveyard by the river.   8. The tides reach far up the Bristol Channel into the Severn and the Wye, its tributary.   9. Alluding to the pipes of mourning shepherds in pastoral elegy, the genre to which *In Memoriam* in part belongs.

Another answers: "Let him be,
   He loves to make parade of pain,
   That with his piping he may gain
The praise that comes to constancy."   10

A third is wroth:[1] "Is this an hour
   For private sorrow's barren song,
   When more and more the people throng   15
The chairs and thrones of civil power?

"A time to sicken and to swoon,
   When Science reaches forth her arms
   To feel from world to world, and charms
Her secret from the latest moon?"[2]   20

Behold, ye speak an idle thing;
   Ye never knew the sacred dust.
   I do but sing because I must,
And pipe but as the linnets sing;

And one is glad; her note is gay,   25
   For now her little ones have ranged;
   And one is sad; her note is changed,
Because her brood is stolen away.

22

The path by which we twain did go,
   Which led by tracts that pleased us well,
   Through four sweet years arose and fell,
From flower to flower, from snow to snow;

And we with singing cheered the way,   5
   And, crowned with all the season lent,
   From April on to April went,
And glad at heart from May to May.

But where the path we walked began
   To slant the fifth autumnal slope,
   As we descended following Hope,   10
There sat the Shadow feared of man;

Who broke our fair companionship,
   And spread his mantle dark and cold,
   And wrapt thee formless in the fold,   15
And dulled the murmur on thy lip,

And bore thee where I could not see
   Nor follow, though I walk in haste,

1. Very angry.   2. From 1846 to 1848, astronomers discovered the planet Neptune and one of its moons, some of the satellites of Uranus, and the eighth moon of Saturn.

And think that somewhere in the waste[3]
   The Shadow sits and waits for me.   20

23

Now, sometimes in my sorrow shut,
   Or breaking into song by fits,
   Alone, alone, to where he sits,
The Shadow cloaked from head to foot,

Who keeps the keys of all the creeds,   5
   I wander, often falling lame,
   And looking back to whence I came,
Or on to where the pathway leads;

And cry, How changed from where it ran
   Through lands where not a leaf was dumb,   10
   But all the lavish hills would hum
The murmur of a happy Pan;[4]

When each by turns was guide to each,
   And Fancy light from Fancy caught,
   And Thought leapt out to wed with Thought   15
Ere Thought could wed itself with Speech;

And all we met was fair and good,
   And all was good that Time could bring,
   And all the secret of the Spring
Moved in the chambers of the blood;   20

And many an old philosophy
   On Argive heights divinely sang,
   And round us all the thicket rang
To many a flute of Arcady.[5]

*   *   *

27

I envy not in any moods
   The captive void of noble rage,
   The linnet born within the cage,
That never knew the summer woods;

I envy not the beast that takes   5
   His license in the field of time,
   Unfettered by the sense of crime,
To whom a conscience never wakes;

3. Wasteland.   4. Greek god of flocks and shepherds, and hence of pastoral poetry.   5. I.e., they were like shepherds on the hills of Greece when what is now "old philosophy" was brand new or on the plains of Arcady (home of pastoral poetry) when pastoral poetry was young.

> Nor, what may count itself as blest,
>   The heart that never plighted troth[6]
>   But stagnates in the weeds of sloth;
> Nor any want-begotten rest.[7]

> I hold it true, whate'er befall;
>   I feel it, when I sorrow most;
>   'Tis better to have loved and lost
> Than never to have loved at all.

[handwritten margin note: A life of having not loved by sorrowful]

28

> The time draws near the birth of Christ.
>   The moon is hid, the night is still;
>   The Christmas bells from hill to hill
> Answer each other in the mist.

> Four voices of four hamlets round,
>   From far and near, on mead and moor,
>   Swell out and fail, as if a door
> Were shut between me and the sound;

> Each voice four changes on the wind,
>   That now dilate, and now decrease,
>   Peace and goodwill, goodwill and peace,
> Peace and goodwill, to all mankind.

> This year I slept and woke with pain,
>   I almost wished no more to wake,
>   And that my hold on life would break
> Before I heard those bells again;

[handwritten margin note: His sorrow is so great that he wished to]

> But they my troubled spirit rule,
>   For they controlled me when a boy;
>   They bring me sorrow touched with joy,
> The merry, merry bells of Yule.

* * *

50

> Be near me when my light is low,
>   When the blood creeps, and the nerves prick
>   And tingle; and the heart is sick,
> And all the wheels of being slow.

> Be near me when the sensuous frame
>   Is racked with pangs that conquer trust;
>   And Time, a maniac scattering dust,[8]
> And Life, a Fury slinging flame.[9]

6. Became engaged to be married.   7. I.e., any rest that comes from a lack or deficiency—specifically, from a failure to be fully human, a state that would entail vulnerability.   8. I.e., the dust from which life comes and to which it returns.   9. The Furies, avenging deities of Greek myth, carry torches.

Be near me when my faith is dry,
　　And men the flies of latter spring,　　　　　　　　10
　　That lay their eggs, and sting and sing
And weave their petty cells and die.

Be near me when I fade away,
　　To point the term of human strife,
　　And on the low dark verge of life　　　　　　　　15
The twilight of eternal day.

* * *

54

O, yet we trust that somehow good
　　Will be the final goal of ill,
　　To pangs of nature, sins of will,
Defects of doubt, and taints of blood;

That nothing walks with aimless feet;　　　　　　　5
　　That not one life shall be destroyed,
　　Or cast as rubbish to the void,
When God hath made the pile complete;

That not a worm is cloven in vain;
　　That not a moth with vain desire　　　　　　　　10
　　Is shriveled in a fruitless fire,
Or but subserves another's gain.

Behold, we know not anything;
　　I can but trust that good shall fall
　　At last—far off—at last, to all,　　　　　　　　15
And every winter change to spring.

So runs my dream; but what am I?
　　An infant crying in the night;
　　An infant crying for the light,
And with no language but a cry.　　　　　　　　　20

55

The wish, that of the living whole
　　No life may fail beyond the grave,
　　Derives it not from what we have
The likest God within the soul?

Are God and Nature then at strife,　　　　　　　　5
　　That Nature lends such evil dreams?
　　So careful of the type[1] she seems,
So careless of the single life,[2]

---

1. Species.　2. The significance of nature's prodigality and destructiveness was widely debated during
Tennyson's lifetime.

That I, considering everywhere
    Her secret meaning in her deeds   10
    And finding that of fifty seeds
She often brings but one to bear,

I falter where I firmly trod,
    And falling with my weight of cares
    Upon the great world's altar-stairs   15
That slope through darkness up to God,

I stretch lame hands of faith, and grope,
    And gather dust and chaff, and call
    To what I feel is Lord of all,
And faintly trust the larger hope.   20

56

"So careful of the type?" but no.
    From scarpèd[3] cliff and quarried stone
    She cries, "A thousand types are gone;[4]
I care for nothing, all shall go.

"Thou makest thine appeal to me: 5
    I bring to life, I bring to death;
    The spirit does but mean the breath:
I know no more." And he, shall he,

Man, her last work, who seemed so fair,
    Such splendid purpose in his eyes,   10
    Who rolled the psalm to wintry skies,
Who built him fanes[5] of fruitless prayer,

Who trusted God was love indeed
    And love Creation's final law—
    Though Nature, red in tooth and claw   15
With ravin,[6] shrieked against his creed—

Who loved, who suffered countless ills,
    Who battled for the True, the Just,
    Be blown about the desert dust,
Or sealed within the iron hills?   20

No more? A monster then, a dream,
    A discord. Dragons of the prime,[7]
    That tear each other in their slime,
Were mellow music matched with him.

---

3. Shorn away vertically to expose the rock strata of different ages.   4. That whole species had disappeared, not merely individuals, had become evident from Charles Lyell's researches, published in his *Principles of Geology* (1830–33) and *Elements of Geology* (1838).   5. Temples.   6. Prey.   7. Prehistoric creatures.

O life as futile, then, as frail!   25
    O for thy[8] voice to soothe and bless!
    What hope of answer, or redress?
Behind the veil,[9] behind the veil.

*   *   *

78

Again at Christmas did we weave
    The holly round the Christmas hearth;
    The silent snow possessed the earth,
And calmly fell our Christmas-eve:

The yule-clog[1] sparkled keen with frost,   5
    No wing of wind the region swept,
    But over all things brooding slept
The quiet sense of something lost.

As in the winters left behind,
    Again our ancient games had place,   10
    The mimic picture's[2] breathing grace,
And dance and song and hoodman-blind.[3]

Who showed a token of distress?
    No single tear, no mark of pain:
    O sorrow, then can sorrow wane?   15
O grief, can grief be changed to less?

O last regret, regret can die!
    No—mixed with all this mystic frame,
    Her deep relations are the same,
But with long use her tears are dry.   20

*   *   *

95

By night we lingered on the lawn,
    For underfoot the herb was dry;
    And genial warmth; and o'er the sky
The silvery haze of summer drawn;

And calm that let the tapers burn   5
    Unwavering; not a cricket chirred;
    The brook alone far-off was heard,
And on the board the fluttering urn.[4]

And bats went round in fragrant skies,
    And wheeled or lit the filmy shapes   10

___

8. Hallam's. 9. Death. 1. Yule log. 2. The game may be charades. 3. Blindman's buff.
4. Boiling tea urn. *Board*: table.

That haunt the dusk, with ermine capes
And woolly breasts and beaded eyes;

While now we sang old songs that pealed
  From knoll to knoll, where, couched at ease,
  The white kine[5] glimmered, and the trees   15
Laid their dark arms about the field.

But when those others, one by one,
  Withdrew themselves from me and night,
  And in the house light after light
Went out, and I was all alone,   20

A hunger seized my heart; I read
  Of that glad year which once had been,
  In those fall'n leaves which kept their green,
The noble letters of the dead.

And strangely on the silence broke   25
  The silent-speaking words, and strange
  Was love's dumb cry defying change
To test his worth; and strangely spoke

The faith, the vigor, bold to dwell
  On doubts that drive the coward back,   30
  And keen through wordy snares to track
Suggestion to her inmost cell.

So word by word, and line by line,
  The dead man touched me from the past,
  And all at once it seemed at last   35
The living soul was flashed on mine,

And mine in this was wound, and whirled
  About empyreal[6] heights of thought,
  And came on that which is, and caught
The deep pulsations of the world,   40

Æonian[7] music measuring out
  The steps of Time—the shocks of Chance—
  The blows of Death. At length my trance
Was canceled, stricken through with doubt.

Vague words! but ah, how hard to frame   45
  In matter-molded forms of speech,
  Or even for intellect to reach
Through memory that which I became;

5. Cattle. 6. Sublime. 7. Age-old.

Till now the doubtful dusk revealed
   The knolls once more where, couched at ease,   50
   The white kine glimmered, and the trees
Laid their dark arms about the field;

And sucked from out the distant gloom
   A breeze began to tremble o'er
   The large leaves of the sycamore,   55
And fluctuate all the still perfume,

And gathering freshlier overhead,
   Rocked the full-foliaged elms, and swung
   The heavy-folded rose, and flung
The lilies to and fro, and said,   60

"The dawn, the dawn," and died away;
   And East and West, without a breath,
   Mixt their dim lights, like life and death,
To broaden into boundless day.

*   *   *

106

Ring out, wild bells, to the wild sky,
   The flying cloud, the frosty light:
   The year is dying in the night;
Ring out, wild bells, and let him die.

Ring out the old, ring in the new,   5
   Ring, happy bells, across the snow:
   The year is going, let him go;
Ring out the false, ring in the true.

Ring out the grief that saps the mind,
   For those that here we see no more;   10
   Ring out the feud of rich and poor,
Ring in redress to all mankind.

Ring out a slowly dying cause,
   And ancient forms of party strife;
   Ring in the nobler modes of life,   15
With sweeter manners, purer laws.

Ring out the want, the care, the sin,
   The faithless coldness of the times;
   Ring out, ring out my mournful rhymes,
But ring the fuller minstrel in.   20

Ring out false pride in place and blood,
   The civic slander and the spite;

Ring in the love of truth and right,
Ring in the common love of good.

Ring out old shapes of foul disease;   25
    Ring out the narrowing lust of gold;
    Ring out the thousand wars of old,
Ring in the thousand years of peace.[8]

Ring in the valiant man and free,
    The larger heart, the kindlier hand;   30
    Ring out the darkness of the land,
Ring in the Christ that is to be.

*   *   *

118

Contèmplate all this work of Time,
    The giant laboring in his youth;
    Nor dream of human love and truth,
As dying Nature's earth and lime;[9]

But trust that those we call the dead   5
    Are breathers of an ampler day
    For ever nobler ends. They say,
The solid earth whereon we tread

In tracts of fluent heat began,
    And grew to seeming-random forms,   10
    The seeming prey of cyclic storms,
Till at the last arose the man;

Who throve and branched from clime to clime,
    The herald of a higher race,
    And of himself in higher place,   15
If so he type[1] this work of time

Within himself, from more to more;
    Or, crowned with attributes of woe
    Like glories, move his course, and show
That life is not as idle ore,   20

But iron dug from central gloom,
    And heated hot with burning fears,
    And dipped in baths of hissing tears,
And battered with the shocks of doom

To shape and use. Arise and fly   25
    The reeling Faun, the sensual feast;

8. The poet has in mind Revelation 20, where it is said that Satan will be bound in chains for a thousand years, during which time the martyrs will be "priest of God and of Christ, and shall reign with him." 9. The products of the decay of flesh and bone.   1. Copy, emulate.

Move upward, working out the beast,
    And let the ape and tiger die.

*   *   *

124

That which we dare invoke to bless;
    Our dearest faith; our ghastliest doubt;
    He, They, One, All;[2] within, without;
The Power in darkness whom we guess,—

I found Him not in world or sun,   5
    Or eagle's wing, or insect's eye,
    Nor through the questions men may try,
The petty cobwebs we have spun.

If e'er when faith had fallen asleep,
    I heard a voice, "believe no more,"   10
    And heard an ever-breaking shore
That tumbled in the Godless deep,

A warmth within the breast would melt
    The freezing reason's colder part,
    And like a man in wrath the heart   15
Stood up and answered, "I have felt."

No, like a child in doubt and fear:
    But that blind clamor made me wise;
    Then was I as a child that cries,
But, crying, knows his father near;   20

And what I am beheld again
    What is, and no man understands;
    And out of darkness came the hands
That reach through nature, molding men.

[EPILOGUE][3]

*   *   *

Today the grave is bright for me,
    For them[4] the light of life increased,
    Who stay to share the morning feast,
Who rest tonight beside the sea.

Let all my genial spirits advance   5
    To meet and greet a whiter[5] sun;
    My drooping memory will not shun
The foaming grape[6] of eastern France.

---

2. Christ, as part of the Trinity, seen as three elements and as indivisible.   3. The Epilogue celebrates the wedding of Tennyson's sister Cecilia to his friend Edmund Lushington (October 10, 1842) and brings the poem of mourning full circle to its conclusion in a marriage and in the prospect of a new birth.   4. The new husband and wife.   5. More joyous and hopeful because of the marriage.   6. Champagne.

The hope of coming happiness

It circles round, and fancy plays,
  And hearts are warmed and faces bloom,
  As drinking health to bride and groom   10
We wish them store of happy days.

Nor count me all to blame if I
  Conjecture of a stiller guest,
  Perchance, perchance, among the rest,   15
And, though in silence, wishing joy.

But they must go, the time draws on,
  And those white-favored[7] horses wait;
  They rise, but linger; it is late;
Farewell, we kiss, and they are gone.   20

A shade falls on us like the dark
  From little cloudlets on the grass,
  But sweeps away as out we pass
To range the woods, to roam the park,

Discussing how their courtship grew,   25
  And talk of others that are wed,
  And how she looked, and what he said,
And back we come at fall of dew.

Again the feast, the speech, the glee,
  The shade of passing thought, the wealth   30
  Of words and wit, the double health,
The crowning cup, the three-times-three,[8]

And last the dance;—till I retire.
  Dumb is that tower[9] which spake so loud,
  And high in heaven the streaming cloud,   35
And on the downs a rising fire:

And rise, O moon, from yonder down,
  Till over down and over dale
  All night the shining vapor sail
And pass the silent-lighted town,   40

The white-faced halls, the glancing rills,
  And catch at every mountain head,
  And o'er the friths[1] that branch and spread
Their sleeping silver through the hills;

And touch with shade the bridal doors,   45
  With tender gloom the roof, the wall;
  And breaking let the splendor fall
To spangle all the happy shores

---

7. Wearing white ribbons for the wedding.   8. Rousing cheers.   9. The church tower where wedding
bells recently rang.   1. Narrow bays of the sea.

By which they rest, and ocean sounds,
  And, star and system rolling past,   50
  A soul shall draw from out the vast
And strike his being into bounds,

And, moved through life of lower phase,
  Result in man, be born and think,
  And act and love, a closer link   55
Betwixt us and the crowning race

Of those that, eye to eye, shall look
  On knowledge; under whose command
  Is Earth and Earth's, and in their hand
Is Nature like an open book;   60

No longer half-akin to brute,
  For all we thought and loved and did,
  And hoped, and suffered, is but seed
Of what in them is flower and fruit;

Whereof the man that with me trod   65
  This planet was a noble type
  Appearing ere the times were ripe,
That friend of mine who lives in God,

That God, which ever lives and loves,   *In love, God*
  One God, one law, one element,   *Controls the*   70
  And one far-off divine event,   *universe*
To which the whole creation moves.

ROBERT BROWNING
1812–1889

The pleasure of reading Robert Browning's dramatic monologues—the poems for which he is best known—not only involves the delight of encountering a vividly realized personality but is also, often, the kind of enjoyment one gets from detective fiction. An imaginary speaker utters words designed to generate a specific effect; from these words, typically, one can deduce a story never actually told. The poet allows us the enjoyment of figuring out what has really happened as well as more familiar poetic pleasures.

Browning was the son of a bank clerk who later became a prosperous banker. After attending the University of London, he traveled on the Continent. Back in England, he became friendly with other important Victorian literary figures: Charles Dickens, Thomas Carlyle, and Leigh Hunt, for example. His romance with the semi-invalid Elizabeth Barrett, also a poet, eventuated in marriage in 1846; the two lived mainly in Italy for the remaining fifteen years of her life. Although Browning returned to England after his wife's death, he made frequent visits to the Continent and died in Venice.

Browning wrote verse plays and introspective Shelleyan lyrics, but his most popular poems have always been the dramatic monologues, originally included in such volumes as *Bells and Pomegranates* (1841–46), *Men and Women* (1855), and *Dramatis Personae* (1864). His most ambitious work was *The Ring and the Book* (1868–69), a linked series of blank verse dramatic monologues based on a Renaissance murder trial. In this long poem, in the course of which several people report the same events from very different points of view, Browning most clearly concentrates on the problem implicit in all his monologues—that of perspective. The nature of a story depends on who tells it: Browning's verse insistently reminds us of this fact.

My Last Duchess (1842), probably Browning's best-known and most popular monologue, in fifty-six lines exemplifies the characteristic technique. The speaker, a duke, prefers his wife's portrait to her corporeal existence, having put an end to her life because he found her gaiety and spiritual generosity offensive to his aristocratic pride. He explains his attitude to an envoy with whom he is negotiating for a new bride, with no awareness that his story reflects badly on himself. The pleasure of reading the poem derives largely from experiencing simultaneous communications: the story the duke thinks he tells—of offended dignity—and the story he really tells—of narcissistic self-indulgence.

The Bishop Orders His Tomb at Saint Praxed's Church (1845) invites more complicated responses to the personality it evokes. The imagined sixteenth-century bishop reveals his lack of real allegiance to the Church he nominally serves. He has violated his vows of celibacy, having had at least one mistress and several children. He feels powerful competitive impulses, as well as rage and envy, toward his predecessor as bishop. Even on his deathbed, he remains utterly absorbed in the things of this world: the lump of lapis lazuli he has buried, the splendor of the marble he imagines for his tomb. The mass itself exists in his memory and imagination only as a sensuous experience:

> And then how I shall lie through centuries,
> And hear the blessed mutter of the mass,
> And see God made and eaten all day long,
> And feel the steady candle-flame, and taste
> Good strong thick stupefying incense-smoke!

If one wished to summarize this bishop in abstract terms, one might allude to "the corruption of the Church." Indeed, he exemplifies such corruption in many different ways, by what he fails to say as well as by what he says. "And thence ye may perceive the world's a dream": occasionally such tag lines erupt in his speech, but his lack of real religious feeling is all too apparent. He imagines himself lying in his tomb in his church through eternity; he does not think of an afterlife in heaven—or, for that matter, in hell, perhaps his more likely destination. Browning, however, implicitly insists on the difference between people and abstractions. To sum up this bishop in terms of ecclesiastical corruption would leave out the fact of his enormous vitality, a vitality that informs the entire poem. The dramatic monologue makes the bishop's feeling come alive, makes the reader sympathetically understand his reluctance to leave behind beauty he has valued all his life.

Browning uses the superficially remote situation he has evoked to reiterate the great Romantic theme—we have encountered it most vividly in Wordsworth and in Keats—of the poignance and the inevitability of loss. Instead of considering the problem of loss in autobiographical terms, he enters imaginatively into the experience of an invented character.

> She, men would have to be your mother once,
> Old Gandolf envied me, so fair she was!
> What's done is done, and she is dead beside,
> Dead long ago, and I am Bishop since,
> And as she died so must we die ourselves.

The dying man's emotions recapitulate a feeling we have all had: the sadness of memory, even memory of happy experiences (in this case, love of a woman and triumph over an enemy), when it tells us of what is irretrievably gone. The bishop holds on still to what he knows he must lose. His speech, as Browning captures it, expresses in its rhythms and its idiom the enduring vigor of his personality, even on the edge of death.

> Ah, ye hope
> To revel down my villas while I gasp
> Bricked o'er with beggar's mouldy travertine
> Which Gandolf from his tomb-top chuckles at!

This is not a man who has given up: he insists on the preoccupations of his life as he faces his death. The poem, demanding no judgment of the bishop, suggests, rather, the inadequacy of judgment as a reaction to the intricacies of any single human being.

Browning's greatest gift as a poet is his capacity to convey an energetic sense of pleasure in the reality of experience. "Grow old along with me, / The best is yet to be," urges a character in one of his poems. But he also recognizes the cost of such intense living as that which the bishop enjoys, since all human existence involves loss. The tonal complexity of *The Bishop Orders His Tomb* suggests the kind of richness typical of the Victorian period, with its faith and hope in the possibilities of human accomplishment mingled with doubt about what it all means in the end.

"*Childe Roland to the Dark Tower Came*" (1855), on the other hand, supplies little faith or hope. A nightmare vision that lends itself to no ready rational explanation, the poem narrates, in the first person, the experience of a quester who understands neither the purpose nor the meaning of his quest. (Nor can the reader deduce purpose or meaning.) The speaker finds himself in a landscape of despair; he remembers the failures of those who have preceded him. Increasingly conscious of loss and failure, he yet finally blows on his horn a call of challenge, not knowing what he challenges or why. The affirmation implicit in that final challenge promises no cheerful outcome. It constitutes a kind of existential defiance of impossibility. The poem's peculiar appeal for twenty-first-century readers depends on its acknowledgment of the kind of dark consciousness that can afflict anyone. Browning here explains nothing away. Indeed, he explains nothing at all.

PRONOUNCING GLOSSARY

The following list uses common English syllables and stress accents to provide rough equivalents of selected words whose pronunciation may be unfamiliar to the general reader.

Apollyon: *a-pol'-yon*

Elucescebat: *ay-loo-say-say'-but*

Frascati: *frah-skah'-tee*

Tophet: *toh'-fet*

My Last Duchess

Ferrara

That's my last Duchess painted on the wall,
Looking as if she were alive. I call
That piece a wonder, now: Frà Pandolf's hands
Worked busily a day, and there she stands.
Will't please you sit and look at her? I said   5

'Frà Pandolf' by design, for never read
Strangers like you that pictured countenance,
The depth and passion of its earnest glance,
But to myself they turned (since none puts by
The curtain I have drawn for you, but I)   10
And seemed as they would ask me, if they durst,
How such a glance came there; so, not the first
Are you to turn and ask thus. Sir, 'twas not
Her husband's presence only, called that spot
Of joy into the Duchess' cheek: perhaps   15
Frà Pandolf chanced to say 'Her mantle laps
Over my lady's wrist too much,' or 'Paint
Must never hope to reproduce the faint
Half-flush that dies along her throat:' such stuff
Was courtesy, she thought, and cause enough   20
For calling up that spot of joy. She had
A heart—how shall I say?—too soon made glad,
Too easily impressed; she liked whate'er
She looked on, and her looks went everywhere.
Sir, 'twas all one! My favour at her breast,   25
The dropping of the daylight in the West,
The bough of cherries some officious fool
Broke in the orchard for her, the white mule
She rode with round the terrace—all and each
Would draw from her alike the approving speech,   30
Or blush, at least. She thanked men,—good! but thanked
Somehow—I know not how—as if she ranked
My gift of a nine-hundred-years-old name
With anybody's gift. Who'd stoop to blame
This sort of trifling? Even had you skill   35
In speech—(which I have not)—to make your will
Quite clear to such an one, and say, 'Just this
Or that in you disgusts me; here you miss,
Or there exceed the mark'—and if she let
Herself be lessoned so, nor plainly set   40
Her wits to yours, forsooth, and make excuse,
—E'en then would be some stooping; and I choose
Never to stoop. Oh sir, she smiled, no doubt,
Whene'er I passed her; but who passed without
Much the same smile? This grew; I gave commands;   45
Then all smiles stopped together. There she stands
As if alive. Will't please you rise? We'll meet
The company below, then. I repeat,
The Count your master's known munificence
Is ample warrant that no just pretence   50
Of mine for dowry will be disallowed;
Though his fair daughter's self, as I avowed
At starting, is my object. Nay, we'll go
Together down, sir. Notice Neptune, though,
Taming a sea-horse, thought a rarity,   55
Which Clause of Innsbruck cast in bronze for me!

The Bishop Orders His Tomb at Saint Praxed's Church[1]

Rome, 15—

Vanity, saith the preacher, vanity![2]
Draw round my bed: is Anselm keeping back?
Nephews—sons mine . . . ah God, I know not! Well—
She, men would have to be your mother once,
Old Gandolf[3] envied me, so fair she was!   5
What's done is done, and she is dead beside,
Dead long ago, and I am Bishop since,
And as she died so must we die ourselves,
And thence ye may perceive the world's a dream.
Life, how and what is it? As here I lie   10
In this state-chamber, dying by degrees,
Hours and long hours in the dead night, I ask
"Do I live, am I dead?" Peace, peace seems all.
Saint Praxed's ever was the church for peace;
And so, about this tomb of mine. I fought   15
With tooth and nail to save my niche, ye know:
—Old Gandolf cozened me, despite my care;
Shrewd was that snatch from out the corner south
He graced his carrion with, God curse the same!
Yet still my niche is not so cramped but thence   20
One sees the pulpit o' the epistle-side,[4]
And somewhat of the choir, those silent seats,
And up into the aery dome where live
The angels, and a sunbeam's sure to lurk:
And I shall fill my slab of basalt there,   25
And 'neath my tabernacle[5] take my rest,
With those nine columns round me, two and two,
The odd one at my feet where Anselm stands:
Peach-blossom marble all, the rare, the ripe
As fresh-poured red wine of a mighty pulse.   30
—Old Gandolf with his paltry onion-stone,[6]
Put me where I may look at him! True peach,
Rosy and flawless: how I earned the prize!
Draw close: that conflagration of my church
—What then? So much was saved if aught were missed!   35
My sons, ye would not be my death? Go dig
The white-grape vineyard where the oil-press stood,
Drop water gently till the surface sink,
And if ye find . . . Ah God, I know not, I! . . .
Bedded in store of rotten fig-leaves soft,   40
And corded up in a tight olive-frail,[7]

1. The bishop, his tomb, and the character Gandolf are all fictional. Saint Praxed's church, seen by Browning in 1844, is named after a second-century Roman virgin.   2. Ecclesiastes 1.2.   3. The bishop's predecessor.   4. I.e., the right side as the congregation faces the altar, from which during the service some portion of St. Paul's Epistles is read.   5. Here, the canopy over his tomb.   6. A lesser grade of green marble.   7. Basket made of rushes, for figs, raisins, olives, and so on.

Some lump, ah God, of lapis lazuli,[8]
Big as a Jew's head cut off at the nape,
Blue as a vein o'er the Madonna's breast. . . .
Sons, all have I bequeathed you, villas, all,   45
That brave Frascati[9] villa with its bath,
So, let the blue lump poise between my knees,
Like God the Father's globe on both his hands
Ye worship in the Jesu Church[1] so gay,
For Gandolf shall not choose but see and burst!   50
Swift as a weaver's shuttle[2] fleet our years:
Man goeth to the grave, and where is he?
Did I say basalt for my slab, sons? Black—
'Twas ever antique-black[3] I meant! How else
Shall ye contrast my frieze to come beneath?   55
The bas-relief in bronze ye promised me,
Those Pans and Nymphs ye wot[4] of, and perchance
Some tripod, thyrsus,[5] with a vase or so,
The Saviour at his sermon on the mount,
Saint Praxed in a glory, and one Pan   60
Ready to twitch the Nymph's last garment off,
And Moses with the tables[6] . . . but I know
Ye mark me not! What do they whisper thee,
Child of my bowels, Anselm? Ah, ye hope
To revel down my villas while I gasp   65
Bricked o'er with beggar's mouldy travertine[7]
Which Gandolf from his tomb-top chuckles at!
Nay, boys, ye love me—all of jasper,[8] then!
'Tis jasper ye stand pledged to, lest I grieve.
My bath must needs be left behind, alas!   70
One block, pure green as a pistachio-nut,
There's plenty jasper somewhere in the world—
And have I not Saint Praxed's ear to pray
Horses for ye, and brown Greek manuscripts,
And mistresses with great smooth marbly limbs?   75
—That's if ye carve my epitaph aright,
Choice Latin, picked phrase, Tully's[9] every word,
No gaudy ware like Gandolf's second line—
Tully, my masters? Ulpian[1] serves his need!
And then how I shall lie through centuries,   80
And hear the blessed mutter of the mass,
And see God made and eaten[2] all day long,
And feel the steady candle-flame, and taste
Good strong thick stupefying incense-smoke!
For as I lie here, hours of the dead night,   85
Dying in state and by such slow degrees,

---

8. A bright blue semiprecious stone.   9. A wealthy Roman suburb.   1. The principal Jesuit church in Rome.   2. Job 7.6.   3. A grade of good marble.   4. Know. Pans and nymphs were Greek nature deities.   5. A staff tipped with a pinecone, associated with the Greek god Bacchus.   6. The stone tablets on which the Ten Commandments were inscribed.   7. A cheap, flaky Italian building stone. 8. Reddish quartz.   9. Marcus Tullius Cicero (106–43 B.C.E.), Roman writer and master of Latin prose style.   1. Ulpianus Domitius (A.D., ca. 170–228), lawyer, secretary to Emperor Alexander Severus, writer of nonclassical Latin.   2. A reference to the Sacrament of Communion.

I fold my arms as if they clasped a crook,[3]
And stretch my feet forth straight as stone can point,
And let the bedclothes, for a mortcloth,[4] drop
Into great laps and folds of sculptor's-work: 90
And as yon tapers dwindle, and strange thoughts
Grow, with a certain humming in my ears,
About the life before I lived this life,
And this life too, popes, cardinals, and priests,
Saint Praxed at his[5] sermon on the mount,   95
Your tall pale mother with her talking eyes,
And new-found agate urns as fresh as day,
And marble's language, Latin pure, discreet,
—Aha, *Elucescebat*[6] quoth our friend?
No Tully, said I, Ulpian at the best!   100
Evil and brief hath been my pilgrimage.
All lapis, all, sons! Else I give the Pope
My villas! Will ye ever eat my heart?
Ever your eyes were as a lizard's quick,
They glitter like your mother's for my soul,   105
Or ye would heighten my impoverished frieze,
Piece out its starved design, and fill my vase
With grapes, and add a vizor and a Term,[7]
And to the tripod ye would tie a lynx
That in his struggle throws the thyrsus down,   110
To comfort me on my entablature
Whereon I am to lie till I must ask
'Do I live, am I dead?' There, leave me, there!
For ye have stabbed me with ingratitude
To death—ye wish it—God, ye wish it! Stone—   115
Gritstone,[8] a-crumble! Clammy squares which sweat
As if the corpse they keep were oozing through—
And no more lapis to delight the world!
Well go! I bless ye. Fewer tapers there,
But in a row: and, going, turn your backs   120
—Ay, like departing altar-ministrants,
And leave me in my church, the church for peace,
That I may watch at leisure if he leers—
Old Gandolf, at me, from his onion-stone,
As still he envied me, so fair she was!   125

---

3. The bishop's crosier.   **4.** Funeral pall or winding sheet.   **5.** Roger Cruik interprets the drowsy
bishop as conflating the two allusions of lines 59–60, to Christ's Sermon on the Mount and to the (female)
St. Prassede.   **6.** "He was illustrious," or "famous." In classical Latin the word would be *elucebat*. *Elucescebat* is an example of the less elegant Latin associated with Ulpian's era.   **7.** A pillar bearing a statue
or a bust. *Vizor*: a masked figure.   **8.** Sandstone, a cheap substitute for marble.

"Childe Roland to the Dark Tower Came"

(See Edgar's Song in *Lear*)[1]

I

My first thought was, he lied in every word,
    That hoary cripple, with malicious eye
    Askance to watch the working of his lie
On mine, and mouth scarce able to afford
Suppression of the glee, that pursed and scored   5
    Its edge, at one more victim gained thereby.

II

What else should he be set for, with his staff?
    What, save to waylay with his lies, ensnare
    All travellers who might find him posted there,
And ask the road? I guessed what skull-like laugh   10
Would break, what crutch 'gin[2] write my epitaph
    For pastime in the dusty thoroughfare,

III

If at his counsel I should turn aside
    Into that ominous tract which, all agree,
    Hides the Dark Tower. Yet acquiescingly   15
I did turn as he pointed: neither pride
Nor hope rekindling at the end descried,
    So much as gladness that some end might be.

IV

For, what with my whole world-wide wandering,
    What with my search drawn out through years, my hope   20
    Dwindled into a ghost not fit to cope
With that obstreperous joy success would bring,—
I hardly tried now to rebuke the spring
    My heart made, finding failure in its scope.

V

As when a sick man very near to death   25
    Seems dead indeed, and feels begin and end
    The tears and takes the farewell of each friend,
And hears one bid the other go, draw breath
Freelier outside, ("since all is o'er," he saith,
    "And the blow fallen no grieving can amend");   30

---

1. Shakespeare's *King Lear* 3.4.173.   2. Begin to.

VI

While some discuss if near the other graves
   Be room enough for this, and when a day
   Suits best for carrying the corpse away,
With care about the banners, scarves and staves:
And still the man hears all, and only craves   35
   He may not shame such tender love and stay.

VII

Thus, I had so long suffered in this quest,
   Heard failure prophesied so oft, been writ
   So many times among "The Band"—to wit,
The knights who to the Dark Tower's search addressed   40
Their steps—that just to fail as they, seemed best,
   And all the doubt was now—should I be fit?

VIII

So, quiet as despair, I turned from him,
   That hateful cripple, out of his highway
   Into the path he pointed. All the day   45
Had been a dreary one at best, and dim
Was settling to its close, yet shot one grim
   Red leer to see the plain catch its estray.[3]

IX

For mark! no sooner was I fairly found
   Pledged to the plain, after a pace or two,   50
   Than, pausing to throw backward a last view
O'er the safe road, 'twas gone; grey plain all round:
Nothing but plain to the horizon's bound.
   I might go on; nought else remained to do.

X

So, on I went. I think I never saw   55
   Such starved ignoble nature; nothing throve:
   For flowers—as well expect a cedar grove!
But cockle, spurge, according to their law
Might propagate their kind, with none to awe,
   You'd think; a burr had been a treasure-trove.   60

XI

No! penury, inertness and grimace,
   In some strange sort, were the land's portion. "See
   Or shut your eyes," said Nature peevishly,
"It nothing skills: I cannot help my case:

---

3. In law, a stray and unclaimed domestic animal.

'Tis the Last Judgment's fire must cure this place,
    Calcine its clods and set my prisoners free." 65

XII

If there pushed any ragged thistle-stalk
    Above its mates, the head was chopped; the bents[4]
    Were jealous else. What made those holes and rents
In the dock's[5] harsh swarth leaves, bruised as to baulk 70
All hope of greenness? 'tis a brute must walk
    Pashing their life out, with a brute's intents.

XIII

As for the grass, it grew as scant as hair
    In leprosy; thin dry blades pricked the mud
    Which underneath looked kneaded up with blood. 75
One stiff blind horse, his every bone a-stare,
Stood stupefied, however he came there:
    Thrust out past service from the devil's stud!

XIV

Alive? he might be dead for aught I know,
    With that red gaunt and colloped[6] neck a-strain, 80
    And shut eyes underneath the rusty mane;
Seldom went such grotesqueness with such woe;
I never saw a brute I hated so;
    He must be wicked to deserve such pain.

XV

I shut my eyes and turned them on my heart. 85
    As a man calls for wine before he fights,
    I asked one draught of earlier, happier sights,
Ere fitly I could hope to play my part.
Think first, fight afterwards—the soldier's art:
    One taste of the old time sets all to rights. 90

XVI

Not it! I fancied Cuthbert's reddening face
    Beneath its garniture of curly gold,
    Dear fellow, till I almost felt him fold
An arm in mine to fix me to the place,
That way he used. Alas, one night's disgrace! 95
    Out went my heart's new fire and left it cold.

XVII

Giles then, the soul of honour—there he stands
    Frank as ten years ago when knighted first.

---

4. Coarse grasses.   5. Any of several coarse weeds of the buckwheat family.   6. Ridged.

What honest men should dare (he said) he durst.
Good—but the scene shifts—faugh! what hangman-hands   100
Pin to his breast a parchment?[7] his own bands
    Read it. Poor traitor, spit upon and curst!

XVIII

Better this present than a past like that;
    Back therefore to my darkening path again!
    No sound, no sight as far as eye could strain.   105
Will the night send a howlet[8] or a bat?
I asked: when something on the dismal flat
    Came to arrest my thoughts and change their train.

XIX

A sudden little river crossed my path
    As unexpected as a serpent comes.
    No sluggish tide congenial to the glooms;   110
This, as it frothed by, might have been a bath
For the fiend's glowing hoof—to see the wrath
    Of its black eddy bespate[9] with flakes and spumes.

XX

So petty yet so spiteful! All along,   115
    Low scrubby alders kneeled down over it;
    Drenched willows flung them headlong in a fit
Of mute despair, a suicidal throng:
The river which had done them all the wrong,
    Whate'er that was, rolled by, deterred no whit.   120

XXI

Which, while I forded,—good saints, how I feared
    To set my foot upon a dead man's cheek,
    Each step, or feel the spear I thrust to seek
For hollows, tangled in his hair or beard!
—It may have been a water-rat I speared,   125
    But, ugh! it sounded like a baby's shriek.

XXII

Glad was I when I reached the other bank.
    Now for a better country. Vain presage!
    Who were the strugglers, what war did they wage,
Whose savage trample thus could pad the dank   130
Soil to a plash? Toads in a poisoned tank,
    Or wild cats in a red-hot iron cage—

7. Containing an account of the crime for which he is condemned.   8. Owl.   9. Spattered.

XXIII

The fight must so have seemed in that fell[1] cirque.
    What penned them there, with all the plain to choose?
    No foot-print leading to the horrid mews,   135
None out of it. Mad brewage set to work
Their brains, no doubt, like galley-slaves the Turk
    Pits for his pastime, Christians against Jews.

XXIV

And more than that—a furlong on—why, there!
    What bad use was that engine for, that wheel,   140
    Or brake, not wheel—that harrow fit to reel
Men's bodies out like silk? with all the air
Of Tophet's[2] tool, on earth left unaware,
    Or brought to sharpen its rusty teeth of steel.

XXV

Then came a bit of stubbed ground, once a wood,   145
    Next a marsh, it would seem, and now mere earth
    Desperate and done with; (so a fool finds mirth,
Makes a thing and then mars it, till his mood
Changes and off he goes!) within a rood[3]—
    Bog, clay and rubble, sand and stark black dearth.   150

XXVI

Now blotches rankling, coloured gray and grim,
    Now patches where some leanness of the soul's
    Broke into moss or substances like boils;
Then came some palsied oak, a cleft in him
Like a distorted mouth that splits its rim   155
    Gaping at death, and dies while it recoils.

XXVII

And just as far as ever from the end!
    Nought in the distance but the evening, nought
    To point my footstep further! At the thought,
A great black bird. Apollyon's[4] bosom-friend,   160
Sailed past, nor beat his wide wing dragon-penned[5]
    That brushed my cap—perchance the guide I sought.

XXVIII

For, looking up, aware I somehow grew,
    'Spite of the dusk, the plain had given place
    All round to mountains—with such name to grace   165

---

1. Cruel, terrible.   2. Hell (Hebrew).   3. Quarter acre (40 square rods).   4. "The angel of the bottomless pit" (Revelation 9.11).   5. Dragon-winged.

Mere ugly heights and heaps now stolen in view
How thus they had surprised me,—solve it, you![6]
    How to get from them was no clearer case.

XXIX

Yet half I seemed to recognize some brick
    Of mischief happened to me, God knows when—   170
    In a bad dream perhaps. Here ended, then,
Progress this way. When, in the very nick
Of giving up, one time more, came a click
    As when a trap shuts—you're inside the den!

XXX

Burningly it came on me all at once,   175
    This was the place! those two hills on the right,
    Crouched like two bulls locked horn in horn in fight;
While to the left, a tall scalped mountain . . . Dunce,
Dotard, a-dozing at the very nonce,[7]
    After a life spent training for the sight!   180

XXXI

What in the midst lay but the Tower itself?
    The round squat turret, blind as the fool's heart,
    Built of brown stone, without a counterpart
In the whole world. The tempest's mocking elf
Points[8] to the shipman thus the unseen shelf   185
    He strikes on, only when the timbers start.

XXXII

Not see? because of night perhaps?—why, day
    Came back again for that! before it left,
    The dying sunset kindled through a cleft:
The hills, like giants at a hunting, lay,   190
Chin upon hand, to see the game at bay,—
    "Now stab and end the creature—to the heft!"

XXXIII

Not hear? when noise was everywhere! it tolled
    Increasing like a bell. Names in my ears
    Of all the lost adventurers my peers,—   195
How such a one was strong, and such was bold,
And such was fortunate, yet each of old
    Lost, lost! one moment knelled the woe of years.

6. The speaker addresses an imaginary listener—or the reader of the poem.   7. Occasion.   8. Points out.

XXXIV

There they stood, ranged along the hill-sides, met
　　To view the last of me, a living frame　　　　　　　　　　　200
　　For one more picture! in a sheet of flame
I saw them and I knew them all. And yet
Dauntless the slug-horn[9] to my lips I set,
　　And blew. *"Childe Roland to the Dark Tower came."*

9. Trumpet; the word was apparently invented by the poet Thomas Chatterton (1752–1770).

FREDERICK DOUGLASS
1818?–1895

The *Narrative of the Life of Frederick Douglass, an American Slave* (1845) powerfully details the struggle for identity of a black man who, in the mid-nineteenth century, came to realize his own exclusion from the American myth of liberty and justice for all. His autobiographical record epitomizes the experience of many pre–Civil War slaves, but in its narrative skill it also suggests how the writer's effort to achieve selfhood and freedom partakes of a more nearly universal pattern, incident to men and women of whatever color.

Virtually everything that is known of Douglass's early life comes from the *Narrative* itself, which ends half a century before his death. The book became an immediate best seller but also a subject of controversy when accusations of fraud (promptly refuted) were made against it by a man who claimed to have known Douglass as a slave and to know him incapable of writing such a book. Because the autobiography's publication endangered its author, who might have been returned to slavery, Douglass subsequently went to Great Britain for two years of highly successful lecture appearances. At the end of 1846, two Englishwomen purchased his freedom from his old master, Hugh Auld, and Douglass returned to the United States in March 1847. He then began a journalistic career, writing and publishing a series of newspapers and making himself a leader of his people who continued to locate and to proclaim the injustices to which blacks were subject. Late in his life, he held a number of diplomatic posts, including minister resident and consul general to the Republic of Haiti and chargé d'affaires for Santo Domingo. He died in Washington, D.C., and was buried in Rochester, New York.

Douglass gradually enlarged and elaborated his *Narrative*, which exists in three subsequent versions: *My Bondage and My Freedom* (1855) and two different editions of *Life and Times of Frederick Douglass* (1881, 1892). The earliest, shortest form has the greatest narrative integrity and clarity. For literary as well as historical reasons (its status as an important document in the abolitionist crusade), it merits reprinting. It belongs to a genre familiar in its time: thousands of slave narratives were published in America—and in many cases translated into European languages—between the end of the eighteenth century and the beginning of the American Civil War. They won a large, enthusiastic readership; by making the horrors of slavery emotionally immediate, they intensified abolitionist sentiment. From the first publication of Douglass's work, it was acknowledged as unusually forceful by virtue of its rhetorical control and its narrative skill.

Douglass casts his autobiography as an account of self-discovery. The contrast between the openings of the *Narrative* and of Rousseau's *Confessions* is instructive. Rousseau begins by proclaiming that he differs importantly from everyone else in his unique and early established personality and character. Douglass, on the other hand, starts by reporting what he does *not* know of himself. He must guess his own age, he doesn't know his birthday, he has only rumor to tell him his father's identity. Although he knows his mother, he spends virtually no time with her; she comes to him and leaves him in the dark. Most children develop their sense of who they are by precisely the clues missing in Douglass's experience: age, parentage, such ritual occasions as birthdays. Douglass has only a generic identity: slave. Like other slave children, he wears nothing but a shirt—not the trousers that would symbolize his maleness, not shoes to protect his feet, nothing to differentiate him from others of his kind. Like the other children, he eats cornmeal mush from a trough on the floor, thus, as he notes, treated like a pig and reduced to animality. Everything in Douglass's experience denies his individuality and declares his lack of particularized identity.

The narrative constructed by a man who has finally, arduously, discovered his self-hood recapitulates the process of that discovery: a process with language at its heart. The book ends with its author claiming his name: "I subscribe myself, FREDERICK DOUGLASS." The name itself is a triumph, not his father's or his mother's but the freshly bestowed name of his freedom. The author has won with difficulty the power to subscribe himself, to sign his name, for it involves the capacity to read and write as well as the claim to a name. Each step of the winning—learning to read, learning to write, acquiring a name—involves painful self-testing, but the *word* proves for Douglass literally a means to salvation.

Douglass believes his arrival in Baltimore, to serve the Aulds, a sign of Providential intervention: in Baltimore he learns to read. Mrs. Auld, wife of his master, begins to teach the boy the alphabet; her husband warns her to desist. Reading, he says, "would forever unfit him to be a slave." Douglass comments: "It was a new and special revelation, explaining dark and mysterious things, with which my youthful understanding had struggled, but struggled in vain." The word *revelation* has almost religious force: the child's vision of reading as the key to freedom saves his soul. From this point on in his story—and he is only about eight years old at the time—words lead Douglass to succeeding revelations. He defies all efforts to shut him up "in mental darkness." From little white street urchins he acquires the sustaining "bread of knowledge." At the age of twelve or thereabouts, he reads a book called *The Columbian Orator,* which contains forceful antislavery arguments, and is thus enabled for the first time to utter his thoughts. Without the authority of the written word, the contact through it with other minds, he could not know how to articulate what he thinks, could hardly know what it is he thinks. He puzzles over the word *abolitionist,* hearing but not understanding it. When he figures out its meaning, he has passed another milestone. A slave's thoughts must be free, this account suggests, before he can hope for meaningful freedom of body; and freedom of thought comes only through knowledge of the word.

We know that the writer successfully achieves freedom, but he makes gripping drama out of the gradual reporting of how he does so. First he must painfully learn to write, another step toward taking possession of language. For his first, agonizingly abortive attempt at escape, he writes passes for himself and his friends, briefly preempting the glory of being his own master. Subjected subsequently to more brutalized conditions, he sustains himself by making an imaginary speech, in what he remembers as elaborate literary language, to the fleet of ships he sees on Chesapeake Bay, images of freedom. He defies his brutal overseer, claims his manhood, teaches fellow slaves to read; finally, as though by magic, he escapes. (He withholds details of the escape to protect others; the effect of this suppression on the narrative is to suggest that the escape occurs almost as the inevitable, natural culmination of the process of self-discovery.) A friendly white man gives him a new name. And finally Douglass discovers his own voice and his own words: the *Narrative* concludes with his assuming the role of orator on behalf of his people.

Despite its emphasis on the power of language, the autobiography reminds us also that language cannot express everything. Rousseau exhaustively explores his own feelings; Douglass recurrently comments on the inexpressibility of his deepest feelings. At the end of Chapter I, Frederick, a small child, watches his aunt whipped until she is covered with blood. "It was a most terrible spectacle. I wish I could commit to paper the feelings with which I beheld it." His feelings exceed the possibility of verbal representation. Other episodes of comparable brutality elicit the same response: the narrator feels more than he can say. The reader is recurrently reminded that the horrible reality to which Douglass's words refer is in fact a reality beyond words.

Douglass's development of identity, his ultimate subscription of his new name as the sign of his self, leads to no claim of uniqueness. On the contrary, the identity he claims is partly *communal*. "Sincerely and earnestly hoping that this little book may do something toward throwing light on the American slave system, and hastening the glad day of deliverance to the millions of my brethren in bonds—faithfully relying upon the power of truth, love, and justice, for success in my humble efforts—and solemnly pledging my self anew to the sacred cause,—I subscribe myself, FREDERICK DOUGLASS." The "little book" exists not to establish Douglass's difference but to declare his unity. Now he possesses his own name, his own differentiating clothes, his own wife, his own self-defined occupation; but as much as when he was a half-naked child gobbling mush with the others, he feels part of a group. His love for fellow slaves, a recurrent theme of his story, provides the foundation for his identity—not, like Rousseau, emotionally isolated, but part of a sustaining community.

His language, both in the final paragraph just quoted and elsewhere, suggests that he partakes also of an even wider community. He evokes "truth" and "justice," proclaimed ideals of the American nation. He quotes John Greenleaf Whittier, "the slaves' poet," to express feelings he finds it hard to state for himself. Everywhere his prose rings with biblical rhythms and allusions. Frederick Douglass is not only a slave, not only an ex-slave; he is a literary man, an American, a Christian, claiming, relying on, and valuing these larger forms of communion as well as his union with his race— and implicitly demanding that others who call themselves Americans or Christians acknowledge his participation with them and accept the responsibility such acknowledgment implies.

Narrative of the Life of Frederick Douglass, an American Slave[1]

CHAPTER I

I was born in Tuckahoe, near Hillsborough, and about twelve miles from Easton, in Talbot county, Maryland. I have no accurate knowledge of my age, never having seen any authentic record containing it. By far the larger part of the slaves know as little of their ages as horses know of theirs, and it is the wish of most masters within my knowledge to keep their slaves thus ignorant. I do not remember to have ever met a slave who could tell of his birthday. They seldom come nearer to it than planting-time, harvest-time, cherry-time, spring-time, or fall-time. A want of information concerning my own was a source of unhappiness to me even during childhood. The white

1. The text, printed in its entirety, is that of the first American edition, published by the Massachusetts Anti-Slavery Society in Boston in 1845.

children could tell their ages. I could not tell why I ought to be deprived of the same privilege. I was not allowed to make any inquiries of my master concerning it. He deemed all such inquiries on the part of a slave improper and impertinent, and evidence of a restless spirit. The nearest estimate I can give makes me now between twenty-seven and twenty-eight years of age. I come to this, from hearing my master say, some time during 1835, I was about seventeen years old.

My mother was named Harriet Bailey. She was the daughter of Isaac and Betsey Bailey, both colored, and quite dark. My mother was of a darker complexion than either my grandmother or grandfather.

My father was a white man. He was admitted to be such by all I ever heard speak of my parentage. The opinion was also whispered that my master was my father; but of the correctness of this opinion, I know nothing; the means of knowing was withheld from me. My mother and I were separated when I was but an infant—before I knew her as my mother. It is a common custom, in the part of Maryland from which I ran away, to part children from their mothers at a very early age. Frequently, before the child has reached its twelfth month, its mother is taken from it, and hired out on some farm a considerable distance off, and the child is placed under the care of an old woman, too old for field labor. For what this separation is done, I do not know, unless it be to hinder the development of the child's affection toward its mother, and to blunt and destroy the natural affection of the mother for the child. This is the inevitable result.

I never saw my mother, to know her as such, more than four or five times in my life; and each of those times was very short in duration, and at night. She was hired by a Mr. Stewart, who lived about twelve miles from my home. She made her journeys to see me in the night, travelling the whole distance on foot, after the performance of her day's work. She was a field hand, and a whipping is the penalty of not being in the field at sunrise, unless a slave has special permission from his or her master to the contrary—a permission which they seldom get, and one that gives to him that gives it the proud name of being a kind master. I do not recollect of ever seeing my mother by the light of day. She was with me in the night. She would lie down with me, and get me to sleep, but long before I waked she was gone. Very little communication ever took place between us. Death soon ended what little we could have while she lived, and with it her hardships and suffering. She died when I was about seven years old, on one of my master's farms, near Lee's Mill. I was not allowed to be present during her illness, at her death, or burial. She was gone long before I knew anything about it. Never having enjoyed, to any considerable extent, her soothing presence, her tender and watchful care, I received the tidings of her death with much the same emotions I should have probably felt at the death of a stranger.

Called thus suddenly away, she left me without the slightest intimation of who my father was. The whisper that my master was my father, may or may not be true; and, true or false, it is of but little consequence to my purpose whilst the fact remains, in all its glaring odiousness, that slaveholders have ordained, and by law established, that the children of slave women shall in all cases follow the condition of their mothers; and this is done too obviously to administer to their own lusts, and make a gratification of their wicked desires profitable as well as pleasurable; for by this cunning arrangement, the slaveholder, in cases not a few, sustains to his slaves the double relation of master and father.

I know of such cases; and it is worthy of remark that such slaves invariably suffer greater hardships, and have more to contend with, than others. They are, in the first place, a constant offence to their mistress. She is ever disposed to find fault with them; they can seldom do any thing to please her; she is never better pleased than when she sees them under the lash, especially when she suspects her husband of showing to his mulatto children favors which he withholds from his black slaves. The master is frequently compelled to sell this class of his slaves, out of deference to the feelings of his white wife; and, cruel as the deed may strike any one to be, for a man to sell his own children to human flesh-mongers, it is often the dictate of humanity for him to do so; for, unless he does this, he must not only whip them himself, but must stand by and see one white son tie up his brother, of but few shades darker complexion than himself, and ply the gory lash to his naked back; and if he lisp one word of disapproval, it is set down to his parental partiality, and only makes a bad matter worse, both for himself and the slave whom he would protect and defend.

Every year brings with it multitudes of this class of slaves. It was doubtless in consequence of a knowledge of this fact, that one great statesman of the south predicted the downfall of slavery by the inevitable laws of population. Whether this prophecy is ever fulfilled or not, it is nevertheless plain that a very different-looking class of people are springing up at the south, and are now held in slavery, from those originally brought to this country from Africa; and if their increase will do no other good, it will do away the force of the argument, that God cursed Ham,[2] and therefore American slavery is right. If the lineal descendants of Ham are alone to be scripturally enslaved, it is certain that slavery at the south must soon become unscriptural; for thousands are ushered into the world, annually, who, like myself, owe their existence to white fathers, and those fathers most frequently their own masters.

I have had two masters. My first master's name was Anthony. I do not remember his first name. He was generally called Captain Anthony—a title which, I presume, he acquired by sailing a craft on the Chesapeake Bay. He was not considered a rich slaveholder. He owned two or three farms, and about thirty slaves. His farms and slaves were under the care of an overseer. The overseer's name was Plummer. Mr. Plummer was a miserable drunkard, a profane swearer, and a savage monster. He always went armed with a cowskin and a heavy cudgel. I have known him to cut and slash the women's heads so horribly, that even master would be enraged at his cruelty, and would threaten to whip him if he did not mind himself. Master, however, was not a humane slaveholder. It required extraordinary barbarity on the part of an overseer to affect him. He was a cruel man, hardened by a long life of slaveholding. He would at times seem to take great pleasure in whipping a slave. I have often been awakened at the dawn of day by the most heart-rending shrieks of an own aunt of mine, whom he used to tie up to a joist,

2. It was thought that Noah cursed his second son, Ham, for mocking him; that black skin resulted from the curse; and that all black people descended from Ham. In fact, according to Genesis 9.20–27 and 10.6–14, Noah cursed not Ham but Ham's son Canaan, while Ham's son Cush was black.

and whip upon her naked back till she was literally covered with blood. No words, no tears, no prayers, from his gory victim, seemed to move his iron heart from its bloody purpose. The louder she screamed, the harder he whipped; and where the blood ran fastest, there he whipped longest. He would whip her to make her scream, and whip her to make her hush; and not until overcome by fatigue, would he cease to swing the blood-clotted cowskin. I remember the first time I ever witnessed this horrible exhibition. I was quite a child, but I well remember it. I never shall forget it whilst I remember any thing. It was the first of a long series of such outrages, of which I was doomed to be a witness and a participant. It struck me with awful force. It was the blood-stained gate, the entrance to the hell of slavery, through which I was about to pass. It was a most terrible spectacle. I wish I could commit to paper the feelings with which I beheld it.

This occurrence took place very soon after I went to live with my old master, and under the following circumstances. Aunt Hester went out one night,—where or for what I do not know,—and happened to be absent when my master desired her presence. He had ordered her not to go out evenings, and warned her that she must never let him catch her in company with a young man, who was paying attention to her, belonging to Colonel Lloyd. The young man's name was Ned Roberts, generally called Lloyd's Ned. Why master was so careful of her, may be safely left to conjecture. She was a woman of noble form, and of graceful proportions, having very few equals, and fewer superiors, in personal appearance, among the colored or white women of our neighborhood.

Aunt Hester had not only disobeyed his orders in going out, but had been found in company with Lloyd's Ned; which circumstance, I found, from what he said while whipping her, was the chief offence. Had he been a man of pure morals himself, he might have been thought interested in protecting the innocence of my aunt; but those who knew him will not suspect him of any such virtue. Before he commenced whipping Aunt Hester, he took her into the kitchen, and stripped her from neck to waist, leaving her neck, shoulders, and back, entirely naked. He then told her to cross her hands, calling her at the same time a d——d b———h. After crossing her hands, he tied them with a strong rope, and led her to a stool under a large hook in the joist, put in for the purpose. He made her get upon the stool, and tied her hands to the hook. She now stood fair for his infernal purpose. Her arms were stretched up at their full length, so that she stood upon the ends of her toes. He then said to her, "Now, you d——d b———h, I'll learn you how to disobey my orders!" and after rolling up his sleeves, he commenced to lay on the heavy cowskin, and soon the warm, red blood (amid heart-rending shrieks from her, and horrid oaths from him) came dripping to the floor. I was so terrified and horror-stricken at the sight, that I hid myself in a closet, and dared not venture out till long after the bloody transaction was over. I expected it would be my turn next. It was all new to me. I had never seen any thing like it before. I had always lived with my grandmother on the outskirts of the plantation, where she was put to raise the children of the younger women. I had therefore been, until now, out of the way of the bloody scenes that often occurred on the plantation.

CHAPTER II

My master's family consisted of two sons, Andrew and Richard; one daughter, Lucretia, and her husband, Captain Thomas Auld. They lived in one house, upon the home plantation of Colonel Edward Lloyd. My master was Colonel Lloyd's clerk and superintendent. He was what might be called the overseer of the overseers. I spent two years of childhood on this plantation in my old master's family. It was here that I witnessed the bloody transaction recorded in the first chapter; and as I received my first impressions of slavery on this plantation, I will give some description of it, and of slavery as it there existed. The plantation is about twelve miles north of Easton, in Talbot county, and is situated on the border of Miles River. The principal products raised upon it were tobacco, corn, and wheat. These were raised in great abundance; so that, with the products of this and the other farms belonging to him, he was able to keep in almost constant employment a large sloop, in carrying them to market at Baltimore. This sloop was named *Sally Lloyd,* in honor of one of the colonel's daughters. My master's son-in-law, Captain Auld, was master of the vessel; she was otherwise manned by the colonel's own slaves. Their names were Peter, Isaac, Rich, and Jake. These were esteemed very highly by the other slaves, and looked upon as the privileged ones of the plantation; for it was no small affair, in the eyes of the slaves, to be allowed to see Baltimore.

Colonel Lloyd kept from three to four hundred slaves on his home plantation, and owned a large number more on the neighboring farms belonging to him. The names of the farms nearest to the home plantation were Wye Town and New Design. "Wye Town" was under the overseership of a man named Noah Willis. New Design was under the overseership of a Mr. Townsend. The overseers of these, and all the rest of the farms, numbering over twenty, received advice and direction from the managers of the home plantation. This was the great business place. It was the seat of government for the whole twenty farms. All disputes among the overseers were settled here. If a slave was convicted of any high misdemeanor, became unmanageable, or evinced a determination to run away, he was brought immediately here, severely whipped, put on board the sloop, carried to Baltimore, and sold to Austin Woolfolk, or some other slave-trader, as a warning to the slaves remaining.

Here, too, the slaves of all the other farms received their monthly allowance of food, and their yearly clothing. The men and women slaves received, as their monthly allowance of food, eight pounds of pork, or its equivalent in fish, and one bushel of corn meal. Their yearly clothing consisted of two coarse linen shirts, one pair of linen trousers, like the shirts, one jacket, one pair of trousers for winter, made of coarse negro cloth, one pair of stockings, and one pair of shoes; the whole of which could not have cost more than seven dollars. The allowance of the slave children was given to their mothers, or the old women having the care of them. The children unable to work in the field had neither shoes, stockings, jackets, nor trousers, given to them; their clothing consisted of two coarse linen shirts per year. When these failed them, they went naked until the next allowance-day. Children from seven to ten years old, of both sexes, almost naked, might be seen at all seasons of the year.

There were no beds given the slaves, unless one coarse blanket be considered such, and none but the men and women had these. This, however, is not considered a very great privation. They find less difficulty from the want of beds, than from the want of time to sleep; for when their day's work in the field is done, the most of them having their washing, mending, and cooking to do, and having few or none of the ordinary facilities for doing either of these, very many of their sleeping hours are consumed in preparing for the field the coming day; and when this is done, old and young, male and female, married and single, drop down side by side, on one common bed,—the cold, damp floor,—each covering himself or herself with their miserable blankets; and here they sleep till they are summoned to the field by the driver's horn. At the sound of this, all must rise, and be off to the field. There must be no halting; every one must be at his or her post; and woe betides them who hear not this morning summons to the field; for if they are not awakened by the sense of hearing, they are by the sense of feeling: no age nor sex finds any favor. Mr. Severe, the overseer, used to stand by the door of the quarter, armed with a large hickory stick and heavy cowskin, ready to whip any one who was so unfortunate as not to hear, or, from any other cause, was prevented from being ready to start for the field at the sound of the horn.

Mr. Severe was rightly named: he was a cruel man. I have seen him whip a woman, causing the blood to run half an hour at the time; and this, too, in the midst of her crying children, pleading for their mother's release. He seemed to take pleasure in manifesting his fiendish barbarity. Added to his cruelty, he was a profane swearer. It was enough to chill the blood and stiffen the hair of an ordinary man to hear him talk. Scarce a sentence escaped him but that was commenced or concluded by some horrid oath. The field was the place to witness his cruelty and profanity. His presence made it both the field of blood and of blasphemy. From the rising till the going down of the sun, he was cursing, raving, cutting, and slashing among the slaves of the field, in the most frightful manner. His career was short. He died very soon after I went to Colonel Lloyd's; and he died as he lived, uttering, with his dying groans, bitter curses and horrid oaths. His death was regarded by the slaves as the result of a merciful providence.

Mr. Severe's place was filled by a Mr. Hopkins. He was a very different man. He was less cruel, less profane, and made less noise, than Mr. Severe. His course was characterized by no extraordinary demonstrations of cruelty. He whipped, but seemed to take no pleasure in it. He was called by the slaves a good overseer.

The home plantation of Colonel Lloyd wore the appearance of a country village. All the mechanical operations for all the farms were performed here. The shoemaking and mending, the blacksmithing, cartwrighting, coopering, weaving, and grain-grinding, were all performed by the slaves on the home plantation. The whole place wore a business-like aspect very unlike the neighboring farms. The number of houses, too, conspired to give it advantage over the neighboring farms. It was called by the slaves the *Great House Farm*. Few privileges were esteemed higher, by the slaves of the out-farms, than that of being selected to do errands at the Great House Farm. It was associated in their minds with greatness. A representative could not be prouder of his election to a seat in the American Congress, than a slave on one of the out-farms would be of his election to do errands at the Great House Farm. They regarded it as evidence of great confidence reposed in them by their overseers; and it was on this account, as well as a constant desire to be out of the field from under the driver's lash, that they esteemed it a high privilege, one worth careful living for. He was called the smartest and most trusty fellow, who had this honor conferred upon him the most frequently. The competitors for this office sought as diligently to please their overseers, as the office-seekers in the political parties seek to please and deceive the people. The same traits of character might be seen in Colonel Lloyd's slaves, as are seen in the slaves of the political parties.

The slaves selected to go to the Great House Farm, for the monthly allowance for themselves and their fellow-slaves, were peculiarly enthusiastic. While on their way, they would make the dense old woods, for miles around, reverberate with their wild songs, revealing at once the highest joy and the deepest sadness. They would compose and sing as they went along, consulting neither time nor tune. The thought that came up, came out—if not in the word, in the sound;—and as frequently in the one as in the other. They would sometimes sing the most pathetic sentiment in the most rapturous tone, and the most rapturous sentiment in the most pathetic tone. Into all of their songs they would manage to weave something of the Great House Farm. Especially would they do this, when leaving home. They would then sing most exultingly the following words:—

> "I am going away to the Great House Farm!
> O, yea! O, yea! O!"

This they would sing, as a chorus, to words which to many would seem unmeaning jargon, but which, nevertheless, were full of meaning to themselves. I have sometimes thought that the mere hearing of those songs would do more to impress some minds with the horrible character of slavery, than the reading of whole volumes of philosophy on the subject could do.

I did not, when a slave, understand the deep meaning of those rude and apparently incoherent songs. I was myself within the circle; so that I neither saw nor heard as those without might see and hear. They told a tale of woe which was then altogether beyond my feeble comprehension; they were tones loud, long, and deep; they breathed the prayer and complaint of souls boiling over with the bitterest anguish. Every tone was a testimony against slavery, and a prayer to God for deliverance from chains. The hearing of those wild notes always depressed my spirit, and filled me with ineffable sadness. I have frequently found myself in tears while hearing them. The mere recurrence to those songs, even now, afflicts me; and while I am writing these lines, an expression of feeling has already found its way down my cheek. To those songs I trace my first glimmering conception of the dehumanizing character of slavery. I can never get rid of that conception. Those songs still follow me, to deepen my hatred of slavery, and quicken my sympathies for my brethren in bonds. If any one wishes to be impressed with the soul-killing effects of slavery, let him go to Colonel Lloyd's plantation, and, on allowance-day, place himself in the deep pine woods, and there let him, in silence, analyze the sounds that shall pass through the chambers of his soul,—and if he is not thus impressed, it will only be because "there is no flesh in his obdurate heart."

I have often been utterly astonished, since I came to the north, to find persons who could speak of the singing, among slaves, as evidence of their contentment and happiness. It is impossible to conceive of a greater mistake. Slaves sing most when they are most unhappy. The songs of the slave represent the sorrows of his heart; and he is relieved by them, only as an aching heart is relieved by its tears. At least, such is my experience. I have often sung to drown my sorrow, but seldom to express my happiness. Crying for joy, and singing for joy, were alike uncommon to me while in the jaws of slavery. The singing of a man cast away upon a desolate island might be as appropriately considered as evidence of contentment and happiness, as the singing of a slave; the songs of the one and of the other are prompted by the same emotion.

CHAPTER III

Colonel Lloyd kept a large and finely cultivated garden, which afforded almost constant employment for four men, besides the chief gardener, (Mr. M'Durmond). This garden was probably the greatest attraction of the place. During the summer months, people came from far and near—from Baltimore, Easton, and Annapolis—to see it. It abounded in fruits of almost every description, from the hardy apple of the north to the delicate orange of the south. This garden was not the least source of trouble on the plantation. Its excellent fruit was quite a temptation to the hungry swarms of boys, as well as the older slaves, belonging to the colonel, few of whom had the virtue or the vice to resist it. Scarcely a day passed, during the summer, but that some slave had to take the lash for stealing fruit. The colonel had to resort to all kinds of stratagems to keep his slaves out of the garden. The last and most successful one was that of tarring his fence all around; after which, if a slave was caught with tar upon his person, it was deemed sufficient proof that he had either been into the garden, or had tried to get in. In either case, he was severely whipped by the chief gardener. This plan worked well; the slaves became as fearful of tar as of the lash. They seemed to realize the impossibility of touching *tar* without being defiled.[3]

The colonel also kept a splendid riding equipage. His stable and carriage-house presented the appearance of some of our large city livery establishments. His horses were of the finest form and noblest blood. His carriage-house contained three splendid coaches, three or four gigs, besides dearborns and barouches[4] of the most fashionable style.

This establishment was under the care of two slaves—old Barney and young Barney—father and son. To attend to this establishment was their sole work. But it was by no means an easy employment; for in nothing was Colonel Lloyd more particular than in the management of his horses. The slightest inattention to these was unpardonable, and was visited upon those, under whose care they were placed, with the severest punishment; no excuse could shield them, if the colonel only suspected any want of attention to his horses—a supposition which he frequently indulged, and one which, of course, made the office of old and young Barney a very trying one. They never knew when they were safe from punishment. They were frequently

---

3. Compare the proverb "He who touches pitch shall be defiled."   4. Light four-wheeled carriages (*dearborns*) and carriages with a front seat for the driver and two facing back seats for couples (*barouches*).

whipped when least deserving, and escaped whipping when most deserving it. Every thing depended upon the looks of the horses, and the state of Colonel Lloyd's own mind when his horses were brought to him for use. If a horse did not move fast enough, or hold his head high enough, it was owing to some fault of his keepers. It was painful to stand near the stable-door, and hear the various complaints against the keepers when a horse was taken out for use. "This horse has not had proper attention. He has not been sufficiently rubbed and curried, or he has not been properly fed; his food was too wet or too dry; he got it too soon or too late; he was too hot or too cold; he had too much hay, and not enough of grain; or he had too much grain, and not enough of hay; instead of old Barney's attending to the horse, he had very improperly left it to his son." To all these complaints, no matter how unjust, the slave must answer never a word. Colonel Lloyd could not brook any contradiction from a slave. When he spoke, a slave must stand, listen, and tremble; and such was literally the case. I have seen Colonel Lloyd make old Barney, a man between fifty and sixty years of age, uncover his bald head, kneel down upon the cold, damp ground, and receive upon his naked and toil-worn shoulders more than thirty lashes at the time. Colonel Lloyd had three sons—Edward, Murray, and Daniel,—and three sons-in-law, Mr. Winder, Mr. Nicholson, and Mr. Lowndes. All of these lived at the Great House Farm, and enjoyed the luxury of whipping the servants when they pleased, from old Barney down to William Wilkes, the coach-driver. I have seen Winder make one of the house-servants stand off from him a suitable distance to be touched with the end of his whip, and at every stroke raise great ridges upon his back.

To describe the wealth of Colonel Lloyd would be almost equal to describing the riches of Job.[5] He kept from ten to fifteen house-servants. He was said to own a thousand slaves, and I think this estimate quite within the truth. Colonel Lloyd owned so many that he did not know them when he saw them; nor did all the slaves of the out-farms know him. It is reported of him, that, while riding along the road one day, he met a colored man, and addressed him in the usual manner of speaking to colored people on the public highways of the south: "Well, boy, whom do you belong to?" "To Colonel Lloyd," replied the slave. "Well, does the colonel treat you well?" "No, sir," was the ready reply. "What, does he work you too hard?" "Yes, sir." "Well, don't he give you enough to eat?" "Yes, sir, he gives me enough, such as it is."

The colonel, after ascertaining where the slave belonged, rode on; the man also went on about his business, not dreaming that he had been conversing with his master. He thought, said, and heard nothing more of the matter, until two or three weeks afterwards. The poor man was then informed by his overseer that, for having found fault with his master, he was now to be sold to a Georgia trader. He was immediately chained and handcuffed; and thus, without a moment's warning, he was snatched away, and forever sundered, from his family and friends, by a hand more unrelenting than death. This is the penalty of telling the truth, of telling the simple truth, in answer to a series of plain questions.

5. Job 1.3: "His substance also was seven thousand sheep, and three thousand camels, and five hundred yoke of oxen, and five hundred she asses, and a very great household; so that this man was the greatest of all the men of the east."

It is partly in consequence of such facts, that slaves, when inquired of as to their condition and the character of their masters, almost universally say they are contented, and that their masters are kind. The slaveholders have been known to send in spies among their slaves, to ascertain their views and feelings in regard to their condition. The frequency of this has had the effect to establish among the slaves the maxim, that a still tongue makes a wise head. They suppress the truth rather than take the consequences of telling it, and in so doing prove themselves a part of the human family. If they have any thing to say of their masters, it is generally in their masters' favor, especially when speaking to an untried man. I have been frequently asked, when a slave, if I had a kind master, and do not remember ever to have given a negative answer; nor did I, in pursuing this course, consider myself as uttering what was absolutely false; for I always measured the kindness of my master by the standard of kindness set up among slaveholders around us. Moreover, slaves are like other people, and imbibe prejudices quite common to others. They think their own better than that of others. Many, under the influence of this prejudice, think their own masters are better than the masters of other slaves; and this, too, in some cases, when the very reverse is true. Indeed, it is not uncommon for slaves even to fall out and quarrel among themselves about the relative goodness of their masters, each contending for the superior goodness of his own over that of the others. At the very same time, they mutually execrate their masters when viewed separately. It was so on our plantation. When Colonel Lloyd's slaves met the slaves of Jacob Jepson, they seldom parted without a quarrel about their masters; Colonel Lloyd's slaves contending that he was the richest, and Mr. Jepson's slaves that he was the smartest, and most of a man. Colonel Lloyd's slaves would boast his ability to buy and sell Jacob Jepson. Mr. Jepson's slaves would boast his ability to whip Colonel Lloyd. These quarrels would almost always end in a fight between the parties, and those that whipped were supposed to have gained the point at issue. They seemed to think that the greatness of their masters was transferable to themselves. It was considered as being bad enough to be a slave; but to be a poor man's slave was deemed a disgrace indeed!

CHAPTER IV

Mr. Hopkins remained but a short time in the office of overseer. Why his career was so short, I do not know, but suppose he lacked the necessary severity to suit Colonel Lloyd. Mr. Hopkins was succeeded by Mr. Austin Gore, a man possessing, in an eminent degree, all those traits of character indispensable to what is called a first-rate overseer. Mr. Gore had served Colonel Lloyd, in the capacity of overseer, upon one of the out-farms, and had shown himself worthy of the high station of overseer upon the home or Great House Farm.

Mr. Gore was proud, ambitious, and persevering. He was artful, cruel, and obdurate. He was just the man for such a place, and it was just the place for such a man. It afforded scope for the full exercise of all his powers, and he seemed to be perfectly at home in it. He was one of those who could torture the slightest look, word, or gesture, on the part of the slave, into impudence, and would treat it accordingly. There must be no answering back to him; no explanation was allowed a slave, showing himself to have been wrongfully accused. Mr. Gore acted fully up to the maxim laid down by slaveholders,— "It is better that a dozen slaves suffer under the lash, than that the overseer should be convicted, in the presence of the slaves, of having been at fault." No matter how innocent a slave might be—it availed him nothing, when accused by Mr. Gore of any misdemeanor. To be accused was to be convicted, and to be convicted was to be punished; the one always following the other with immutable certainty. To escape punishment was to escape accusation; and few slaves had the fortune to do either, under the overseership of Mr. Gore. He was just proud enough to demand the most debasing homage of the slave, and quite servile enough to crouch, himself, at the feet of the master. He was ambitious enough to be contented with nothing short of the highest rank of overseers, and persevering enough to reach the height of his ambition. He was cruel enough to inflict the severest punishment, artful enough to descend to the lowest trickery, and obdurate enough to be insensible to the voice of a reproving conscience. He was, of all the overseers, the most dreaded by the slaves. His presence was painful; his eye flashed confusion; and seldom was his sharp, shrill voice heard, without producing horror and trembling in their ranks.

Mr. Gore was a grave man, and, though a young man, he indulged in no jokes, said no funny words, seldom smiled. His words were in perfect keeping with his looks, and his looks were in perfect keeping with his words. Overseers will sometimes indulge in a witty word, even with the slaves; not so with Mr. Gore. He spoke but to command, and commanded but to be obeyed; he dealt sparingly with his words, and bountifully with his whip, never using the former where the latter would answer as well. When he whipped, he seemed to do so from a sense of duty, and feared no consequences. He did nothing reluctantly, no matter how disagreeable; always at his post, never inconsistent. He never promised but to fulfil. He was, in a word, a man of the most inflexible firmness and stone-like coolness.

His savage barbarity was equalled only by the consummate coolness with which he committed the grossest and most savage deeds upon the slaves under his charge. Mr. Gore once undertook to whip one of Colonel Lloyd's slaves, by the name of Demby. He had given Demby but few stripes, when, to get rid of the scourging, he ran and plunged himself into a creek, and stood there at the depth of his shoulders, refusing to come out. Mr. Gore told him that he would give him three calls, and that, if he did not come out at the third call, he would shoot him. The first call was given. Demby made no response, but stood his ground. The second and third calls were given with the same result. Mr. Gore then, without consultation or deliberation with any one, not even giving Demby an additional call, raised his musket to his face, taking deadly aim at his standing victim, and in an instant poor Demby was no more. His mangled body sank out of sight, and blood and brains marked the water where he had stood.

A thrill of horror flashed through every soul upon the plantation, excepting Mr. Gore. He alone seemed cool and collected. He was asked by Colonel Lloyd and my old master, why he resorted to this extraordinary expedient. His reply was, (as well as I can remember,) that Demby had become unmanageable. He was setting a dangerous example to the other slaves,—one which, if suffered to pass without some such demonstration on his part, would finally lead to the total subversion of all rule and order upon the plantation. He argued that if one slave refused to be corrected, and escaped with his life, the other slaves would soon copy the example; the result of which would be, the freedom of the slaves, and the enslavement of the whites. Mr. Gore's defence was satisfactory. He was continued in his station as overseer upon the home plantation. His fame as an overseer went abroad. His horrid crime was not even submitted to judicial investigation. It was committed in the presence of slaves, and they of course could neither institute a suit, nor testify against him; and thus the guilty perpetrator of one of the bloodiest and most foul murders goes unwhipped of justice, and uncensured by the community in which he lives. Mr. Gore lived in St. Michael's, Talbot county, Maryland, when I left there; and if he is still alive, he very probably lives there now; and if so, he is now, as he was then, as highly esteemed and as much respected as though his guilty soul had not been stained with his brother's blood.

I speak advisedly when I say this,—that killing a slave, or any colored person, in Talbot county, Maryland, is not treated as a crime, either by the courts or the community. Mr. Thomas Lanman, of St. Michael's, killed two slaves, one of whom he killed with a hatchet, by knocking his brains out. He used to boast of the commission of the awful and bloody deed. I have heard him do so laughingly, saying, among other things, that he was the only benefactor of his country in the company, and that when others would do as much as he had done, we should be relieved of "the d———d niggers."

The wife of Mr. Giles Hicks, living but a short distance from where I used to live, murdered my wife's cousin, a young girl between fifteen and sixteen years of age, mangling her person in the most horrible manner, breaking her nose and breastbone with a stick, so that the poor girl expired in a few hours afterward. She was immediately buried, but had not been in her untimely grave but a few hours before she was taken up and examined by the coroner, who decided that she had come to her death by severe beating. The offence for which this girl was thus murdered was this:—She had been set that night to mind Mrs. Hicks's baby, and during the night she fell asleep, and the baby cried. She, having lost her rest for several nights previous, did not hear the crying. They were both in the room with Mrs. Hicks. Mrs. Hicks, finding the girl slow to move, jumped from her bed, seized an oak stick of wood by the fireplace, and with it broke the girl's nose and breastbone, and thus ended her life. I will not say that this most horrid murder produced no sensation in the community. It did produce sensation, but not enough to bring the murderess to punishment. There was a warrant issued for her arrest, but it was never served. Thus she escaped not only punishment, but even the pain of being arraigned before a court for her horrid crime.

Whilst I am detailing bloody deeds which took place during my stay on Colonel Lloyd's plantation, I will briefly narrate another, which occurred about the same time as the murder of Demby by Mr. Gore.

Colonel Lloyd's slaves were in the habit of spending a part of their nights and Sundays in fishing for oysters, and in this way made up the deficiency of their scanty allowance. An old man belonging to Colonel Lloyd, while thus engaged, happened to get beyond the limits of Colonel Lloyd's, and on the premises of Mr. Beal Bondly. At this trespass, Mr. Bondly took offence, and with his musket came down to the shore, and blew its deadly contents into the poor old man.

Mr. Bondly came over to see Colonel Lloyd the next day, whether to pay him for his property, or to justify himself in what he had done, I know not. At any rate, this whole fiendish transaction was soon hushed up. There was very little said about it at all, and nothing done. It was a common saying, even among little white boys, that it was worth a half-cent to kill a "nigger," and a half-cent to bury one.

CHAPTER V

As to my own treatment while I lived on Colonel Lloyd's plantation, it was very similar to that of the other slave children. I was not old enough to work in the field, and there being little else than field work to do, I had a great deal of leisure time. The most I had to do was to drive up the cows at evening, keep the fowls out of the garden, keep the front yard clean, and run off errands for my old master's daughter, Mrs. Lucretia Auld. The most of my leisure time I spent in helping Master Daniel Lloyd in finding his birds, after he had shot them. My connection with Master Daniel was of some advantage to me. He became quite attached to me, and was a sort of protector of me. He would not allow the older boys to impose upon me, and would divide his cakes with me.

I was seldom whipped by my old master, and suffered little from any thing else than hunger and cold. I suffered much from hunger, but much more from cold. In hottest summer and coldest winter, I was kept almost naked— no shoes, no stockings, no jacket, no trousers, nothing on but a coarse tow linen shirt, reaching only to my knees. I had no bed. I must have perished with cold, but that, the coldest nights, I used to steal a bag which was used for carrying corn to the mill. I would crawl into this bag, and there sleep on the cold, damp, clay floor, with my head in and feet out. My feet had been so cracked with the frost, that the pen with which I am writing might be laid in the gashes.

We were not regularly allowanced. Our food was coarse corn meal boiled. This was called *mush*. It was put into a large wooden tray or trough, and set down upon the ground. The children were then called, like so many pigs, and like so many pigs they would come and devour the mush; some with oystershells, others with pieces of shingle, some with naked hands, and none with spoons. He that ate fastest got most; he that was strongest secured the best place; and few left the trough satisfied.

I was probably between seven and eight years old when I left Colonel Lloyd's plantation. I left it with joy. I shall never forget the ecstasy with which I received the intelligence that my old master (Anthony) had determined to let me go to Baltimore, to live with Mr. Hugh Auld, brother to my old master's son-in-law, Captain Thomas Auld. I received this information about three days before my departure. They were three of the happiest days I ever enjoyed. I spent the most part of all these three days in the creek, washing off the plantation scurf, and preparing myself for my departure.

The pride of appearance which this would indicate was not my own. I spent the time in washing, not so much because I wished to, but because Mrs. Lucretia had told me I must get all the dead skin off my feet and knees before I could go to Baltimore; for the people in Baltimore were very cleanly, and would laugh at me if I looked dirty. Besides, she was going to give me a pair of trousers, which I should not put on unless I got all the dirt off me. The thought of owning a pair of trousers was great indeed! It was almost a sufficient motive, not only to make me take off what would be called by pig-drovers the mange, but the skin itself. I went at it in good earnest, working for the first time with the hope of reward.

The ties that ordinarily bind children to their homes were all suspended in my case. I found no severe trial in my departure. My home was charmless; it was not home to me; on parting from it, I could not feel that I was leaving any thing which I could have enjoyed by staying. My mother was dead, my grandmother lived far off, so that I seldom saw her. I had two sisters and one brother, that lived in the same house with me; but the early separation of us from our mother had well nigh blotted the fact of our relationship from our memories. I looked for home elsewhere, and was confident of finding none which I should relish less than the one which I was leaving. If, however, I found in my new home hardship, hunger, whipping, and nakedness, I had the consolation that I should not have escaped any one of them by staying. Having already had more than a taste of them in the house of my old master, and having endured them there, I very naturally inferred my ability to endure them elsewhere, and especially at Baltimore; for I had something of the feeling about Baltimore that is expressed in the proverb, that "being hanged in England is preferable to dying a natural death in Ireland." I had the strongest desire to see Baltimore. Cousin Tom, though not fluent in speech, had inspired me with that desire by his eloquent description of the place. I could never point out any thing at the Great House, no matter how beautiful or powerful, but that he had seen something at Baltimore far exceeding, both in beauty and strength, the object which I pointed out to him. Even the Great House itself, with all its pictures, was far inferior to many buildings in Baltimore. So strong was my desire, that I thought a gratification of it would fully compensate for whatever loss of comforts I should sustain by the exchange. I left without a regret, and with the highest hopes of future happiness.

We sailed out of Miles River for Baltimore on a Saturday morning. I remember only the day of the week, for at that time I had no knowledge of the days of the month, nor the months of the year. On setting sail, I walked aft, and gave to Colonel Lloyd's plantation what I hoped would be the last look. I then placed myself in the bows of the sloop, and there spent the remainder of the day in looking ahead, interesting myself in what was in the distance rather than in things near by or behind.

In the afternoon of that day, we reached Annapolis, the capital of the State. We stopped but a few moments, so that I had no time to go on shore. It was the first large town that I had ever seen, and though it would look small compared with some of our New England factory villages, I thought it a wonderful place for its size—more imposing even than the Great House Farm!

We arrived at Baltimore early on Sunday morning, landing at Smith's Wharf, not far from Bowley's Wharf. We had on board the sloop a large flock of sheep; and after aiding in driving them to the slaughterhouse of Mr. Curtis on Louden Slater's Hill, I was conducted by Rich, one of the hands belonging on board of the sloop, to my new home in Alliciana Street, near Mr. Gardner's ship-yard, on Fells Point.

Mr. and Mrs. Auld were both at home, and met me at the door with their little son Thomas, to take care of whom I had been given. And here I saw what I had never seen before; it was a white face beaming with the most kindly emotions; it was the face of my new mistress, Sophia Auld. I wish I could describe the rapture that flashed through my soul as I beheld it. It was a new and strange sight to me, brightening up my pathway with the light of happiness. Little Thomas was told, there was his Freddy,—and I was told to take care of little Thomas; and thus I entered upon the duties of my new home with the most cheering prospect ahead.

I look upon my departure from Colonel Lloyd's plantation as one of the most interesting events of my life. It is possible, and even quite probable, that but for the mere circumstance of being removed from that plantation to Baltimore, I should have to-day, instead of being here seated by my own table, in the enjoyment of freedom and the happiness of home, writing this Narrative, been confined in the galling chains of slavery. Going to live at Baltimore laid the foundation, and opened the gateway, to all my subsequent prosperity. I have ever regarded it as the first plain manifestation of that kind providence which has ever since attended me, and marked my life with so many favors. I regarded the selection of myself as being somewhat remarkable. There were a number of slave children that might have been sent from the plantation to Baltimore. There were those younger, those older, and those of the same age. I was chosen from among them all, and was the first, last, and only choice.

I may be deemed superstitious, and even egotistical, in regarding this event as a special interposition of divine Providence in my favor. But I should be false to the earliest sentiments of my soul, if I suppressed the opinion. I prefer to be true to myself, even at the hazard of incurring the ridicule of others, rather than to be false, and incur my own abhorrence. From my earliest recollection, I date the entertainment of a deep conviction that slavery would not always be able to hold me within its foul embrace; and in the darkest hours of my career in slavery, this living word of faith and spirit of hope departed not from me, but remained like ministering angels to cheer me through the gloom. This good spirit was from God, and to him I offer thanksgiving and praise.

CHAPTER VI

My new mistress proved to be all she appeared when I first met her at the door,—a woman of the kindest heart and finest feelings. She had never had a slave under her control previously to myself, and prior to her marriage she had been dependent upon her own industry for a living. She was by trade a weaver; and by constant application to her business, she had been in a good degree preserved from the blighting and dehumanizing effects of slavery. I was utterly astonished at her goodness. I scarcely knew how to behave towards her. She was entirely unlike any other white woman I had ever seen. I could not approach her as I was accustomed to approach other white ladies. My early instruction was all out of place. The crouching servility, usually so acceptable a quality in a slave, did not answer when manifested toward her.

Her favor was not gained by it; she seemed to be disturbed by it. She did not deem it impudent or unmannerly for a slave to look her in the face. The meanest slave was put fully at ease in her presence, and none left without feeling better for having seen her. Her face was made of heavenly smiles, and her voice of tranquil music.

But, alas! this kind heart had but a short time to remain such. The fatal poison of irresponsible power was already in her hands, and soon commenced its infernal work. That cheerful eye, under the influence of slavery, soon became red with rage; that voice, made all of sweet accord, changed to one of harsh and horrid discord; and that angelic face gave place to that of a demon.

Very soon after I went to live with Mr. and Mrs. Auld, she very kindly commenced to teach me the A, B, C. After I had learned this, she assisted me in learning to spell words of three or four letters. Just at this point of my progress, Mr. Auld found out what was going on, and at once forbade Mrs. Auld to instruct me further, telling her, among other things, that it was unlawful, as well as unsafe, to teach a slave to read. To use his own words, further, he said, "If you give a nigger an inch, he will take an ell. A nigger should know nothing but to obey his master—to do as he is told to do. Learning would *spoil* the best nigger in the world. Now," said he, "if you teach that nigger (speaking of myself) how to read, there would be no keeping him. It would forever unfit him to be a slave. He would at once become unmanageable, and of no value to his master. As to himself, it could do him no good, but a great deal of harm. It would make him discontented and unhappy." These words sank deep into my heart, stirred up sentiments within that lay slumbering, and called into existence an entirely new train of thought. It was a new and special revelation, explaining dark and mysterious things, with which my youthful understanding had struggled, but struggled in vain. I now understood what had been to me a most perplexing difficulty—to wit, the white man's power to enslave the black man. It was a grand achievement, and I prized it highly. From that moment, I understood the pathway from slavery to freedom. It was just what I wanted, and I got it at a time when I the least expected it. Whilst I was saddened by the thought of losing the aid of my kind mistress, I was gladdened by the invaluable instruction which, by the merest accident, I had gained from my master. Though conscious of the difficulty of learning without a teacher, I set out with high hope, and a fixed purpose, at whatever cost of trouble, to learn how to read. The very decided manner with which he spoke, and strove to impress his wife with the evil consequences of giving me instruction, served to convince me that he was deeply sensible of the truths he was uttering. It gave me the best assurance that I might rely with the utmost confidence on the results which, he said, would flow from teaching me to read. What he most dreaded, that I most desired. What he most loved, that I most hated. That which to him was a great evil, to be carefully shunned, was to me a great good, to be diligently sought; and the argument which he so warmly urged, against my learning to read, only served to inspire me with a desire and determination to learn. In learning to read, I owe almost as much to the bitter opposition of my master, as to the kindly aid of my mistress. I acknowledge the benefit of both.

I had resided but a short time in Baltimore before I observed a marked difference, in the treatment of slaves, from that which I had witnessed in the country. A city slave is almost a freeman, compared with a slave on the plantation. He is much better fed and clothed, and enjoys privileges altogether unknown to the slave on the plantation. There is a vestige of decency, a sense of shame, that does much to curb and check those out-breaks of atrocious cruelty so commonly enacted upon the plantation. He is a desperate slaveholder, who will shock the humanity of his nonslaveholding neighbors with the cries of his lacerated slave. Few are willing to incur the odium attaching to the reputation of being a cruel master; and above all things, they would not be known as not giving a slave enough to eat. Every city slaveholder is anxious to have it known of him, that he feeds his slaves well; and it is due to them to say, that most of them do give their slaves enough to eat. There are, however, some painful exceptions to this rule. Directly opposite to us, on Philpot Street, lived Mr. Thomas Hamilton. He owned two slaves. Their names were Henrietta and Mary. Henrietta was about twenty-two years of age, Mary was about fourteen; and of all the mangled and emaciated creatures I ever looked upon, these two were the most so. His heart must be harder than stone, that could look upon these unmoved. The head, neck, and shoulders of Mary were literally cut to pieces. I have frequently felt her head, and found it nearly covered with festering sores, caused by the lash of her cruel mistress. I do not know that her master ever whipped her, but I have been an eye-witness to the cruelty of Mrs. Hamilton. I used to be in Mr. Hamilton's house nearly every day. Mrs. Ham-ilton used to sit in a large chair in the middle of the room, with a heavy cowskin always by her side, and scarce an hour passed during the day but was marked by the blood of one of these slaves. The girls seldom passed her without her saying, "Move faster, you *black gip!*"[6] at the same time giving them a blow with the cowskin over the head or shoulders, often drawing the blood. She would then say, "Take that, you *black gip!*"—continuing, "If you don't move faster, I'll move you!" Added to the cruel lashings to which these slaves were subjected, they were kept nearly half-starved. They seldom knew what it was to eat a full meal. I have seen Mary contending with the pigs for the offal thrown into the street. So much was Mary kicked and cut to pieces, that she was oftener called *"pecked"* than by her name.

CHAPTER VII

I lived in Master Hugh's family about seven years. During this time, I succeeded in learning to read and write. In accomplishing this, I was com-pelled to resort to various stratagems. I had no regular teacher. My mistress, who had kindly commenced to instruct me, had, in compliance with the advice and direction of her husband, not only ceased to instruct, but had set her face against my being instructed by any one else. It is due, however, to my mistress to say of her, that she did not adopt this course of treatment immediately. She at first lacked the depravity indispensable to shutting me up in mental darkness. It was at least necessary for her to have some training in the exercise of irresponsible power, to make her equal to the task of treat-ing me as though I were a brute.

My mistress was, as I have said, a kind and tender-hearted woman; and in

---

6. Cheat, swindler.

the simplicity of her soul she commenced, when I first went to live with her, to treat me as she supposed one human being ought to treat another. In entering upon the duties of a slaveholder, she did not seem to perceive that I sustained to her the relation of a mere chattel, and that for her to treat me as a human being was not only wrong, but dangerously so. Slavery proved as injurious to her as it did to me. When I went there, she was a pious, warm, and tender-hearted woman. There was no sorrow or suffering for which she had not a tear. She had bread for the hungry, clothes for the naked, and comfort for every mourner that came within her reach. Slavery soon proved its ability to divest her of these heavenly qualities. Under its influence, the tender heart became stone, and the lamblike disposition gave way to one of tiger-like fierceness. The first step in her downward course was in her ceasing to instruct me. She now commenced to practise her husband's precepts. She finally became even more violent in her opposition than her husband himself. She was not satisfied with simply doing as well as he had commanded; she seemed anxious to do better. Nothing seemed to make her more angry than to see me with a newspaper. She seemed to think that here lay the danger. I have had her rush at me with a face made all up of fury, and snatch from me a newspaper, in a manner that fully revealed her apprehension. She was an apt woman; and a little experience soon demonstrated, to her satisfaction, that education and slavery were incompatible with each other.

From this time I was most narrowly watched. If I was in a separate room any considerable length of time, I was sure to be suspected of having a book, and was at once called to give an account of myself. All this, however, was too late. The first step had been taken. Mistress, in teaching me the alphabet, had given me the *inch*, and no precaution could prevent me from taking the *ell*.

The plan which I adopted, and the one by which I was most successful, was that of making friends of all the little white boys whom I met in the street. As many of these as I could, I converted into teachers. With their kindly aid, obtained at different times and in different places, I finally succeeded in learning to read. When I was sent of errands, I always took my book with me, and by going one part of my errand quickly, I found time to get a lesson before my return. I used also to carry bread with me, enough of which was always in the house, and to which I was always welcome; for I was much better off in this regard than many of the poor white children in our neighborhood. This bread I used to bestow upon the hungry little urchins, who, in return, would give me that more valuable bread of knowledge. I am strongly tempted to give the names of two or three of those little boys, as a testimonial of the gratitude and affection I bear them; but prudence forbids;—not that it would injure me, but it might embarrass them; for it is almost an unpardonable offence to teach slaves to read in this Christian country. It is enough to say of the dear little fellows, that they lived on Philpot Street, very near Durgin and Bailey's ship-yard. I used to talk this matter of slavery over with them. I would sometimes say to them, I wished I could be as free as they would be when they got to be men. "You will be free as soon as you are twenty-one, *but I am a slave for life!* Have not I as good a right to be free as you have?" These words used to trouble them; they would express for me the liveliest sympathy, and console me with the hope that something would occur by which I might be free.

I was now about twelve years old, and the thought of being *a slave for life* began to bear heavily upon my heart. Just about this time, I got hold of a book entitled "The Columbian Orator."[7] Every opportunity I got, I used to read this book. Among much of other interesting matter, I found in it a dialogue between a master and his slave. The slave was represented as having run away from his master three times. The dialogue represented the conversation which took place between them, when the slave was retaken the third time. In this dialogue, the whole argument in behalf of slavery was brought forward by the master, all of which was disposed of by the slave. The slave was made to say some very smart as well as impressive things in reply to his master—things which had the desired though unexpected effect; for the conversation resulted in the voluntary emancipation of the slave on the part of the master.

In the same book, I met with one of Sheridan's[8] mighty speeches on and in behalf of Catholic emancipation. These were choice documents to me. I read them over and over again with unabated interest. They gave tongue to interesting thoughts of my own soul, which had frequently flashed through my mind, and died away for want of utterance. The moral which I gained from the dialogue was the power of truth over the conscience of even a slaveholder. What I got from Sheridan was a bold denunciation of slavery, and a powerful vindication of human rights. The reading of these documents enabled me to utter my thoughts, and to meet the arguments brought forward to sustain slavery; but while they relieved me of one difficulty, they brought on another even more painful than the one of which I was relieved. The more I read, the more I was led to abhor and detest my enslavers. I could regard them in no other light than a band of successful robbers, who had left their homes, and gone to Africa, and stolen us from our homes, and in a strange land reduced us to slavery. I loathed them as being the meanest as well as the most wicked of men. As I read and contemplated the subject, behold! that very discontentment which Master Hugh had predicted would follow my learning to read had already come, to torment and sting my soul to unutterable anguish. As I writhed under it, I would at times feel that learning to read had been a curse rather than a blessing. It had given me a view of my wretched condition, without the remedy. It opened my eyes to the horrible pit, but to no ladder upon which to get out. In moments of agony, I envied my fellow-slaves for their stupidity. I have often wished myself a beast. I preferred the condition of the meanest reptile to my own. Any thing, no matter what, to get rid of thinking! It was this everlasting thinking of my condition that tormented me. There was no getting rid of it. It was pressed upon me by every object within sight or hearing, animate or inanimate. The silver trump of freedom had roused my soul to eternal wakefulness. Freedom now appeared, to disappear no more forever. It was heard in every sound, and seen in every thing. It was ever present to torment me with a sense of my wretched condition. I saw nothing without seeing it, I heard nothing without hearing it, and felt nothing without feeling it. It looked from every star, it smiled in every calm, breathed in every wind, and moved in every storm.

I often found myself regretting my own existence, and wishing myself dead;

7. Caleb Bingham, *The Columbian Orator: Containing a Variety of Original and Selected Pieces, Together with Rules, Calculated to Improve Youth and Others in the Ornamental and Useful Art of Eloquence*, 8th ed. (1807).   8. Thomas Sheridan (1719–1788), lecturer and writer on elocution.

and but for the hope of being free, I have no doubt but that I should have killed myself, or done something for which I should have been killed. While in this state of mind, I was eager to hear any one speak of slavery. I was a ready listener. Every little while, I could hear something about the abolitionists. It was some time before I found what the word meant. It was always used in such connections as to make it an interesting word to me. If a slave ran away and succeeded in getting clear, or if a slave killed his master, set fire to a barn, or did any thing very wrong in the mind of a slaveholder, it was spoken of as the fruit of *abolition*. Hearing the word in this connection very often, I set about learning what it meant. The dictionary afforded me little or no help. I found it was "the act of abolishing;" but then I did not know what was to be abolished. Here I was perplexed. I did not dare to ask any one about its meaning, for I was satisfied that it was something they wanted me to know very little about. After a patient waiting, I got one of our city papers, containing an account of the number of petitions from the north, praying for the abolition of slavery in the District of Columbia, and of the slave trade between the States. From this time I understood the words *abolition* and *abolitionist,* and always drew near when that word was spoken, expecting to hear something of importance to myself and fellow-slaves. The light broke in upon me by degrees. I went one day down on the wharf of Mr. Waters; and seeing two Irishmen unloading a scow of stone, I went, unasked, and helped them. When we had finished, one of them came to me and asked me if I were a slave. I told him I was. He asked, "Are ye a slave for life?" I told him that I was. The good Irishman seemed to be deeply affected by the statement. He said to the other that it was a pity so fine a little fellow as myself should be a slave for life. He said it was a shame to hold me. They both advised me to run away to the north; that I should find friends there, and that I should be free. I pretended not to be interested in what they said, and treated them as if I did not understand them; for I feared they might be treacherous. White men have been known to encourage slaves to escape, and then, to get the reward, catch them and return them to their masters. I was afraid that these seemingly good men might use me so; but I nevertheless remembered their advice, and from that time I resolved to run away. I looked forward to a time at which it would be safe for me to escape. I was too young to think of doing so immediately; besides, I wished to learn how to write, as I might have occasion to write my own pass. I consoled myself with the hope that I should one day find a good chance. Meanwhile, I would learn to write.

The idea as to how I might learn to write was suggested to me by being in Durgin and Bailey's ship-yard, and frequently seeing the ship carpenters, after hewing, and getting a piece of timber ready for use, write on the timber the name of that part of the ship for which it was intended. When a piece of timber was intended for the larboard side, it would be marked thus—"L." When a piece was for the starboard side, it would be marked thus—"S." A piece for the larboard forward, would be marked thus—"L.F." When a piece was for starboard side forward, it would be marked thus—"S.F." For larboard aft, it would be marked thus—"L.A." For starboard aft, it would be marked thus—"S.A." I soon learned the names of these letters, and for what they were intended when placed upon a piece of timber in the ship-yard. I immediately commenced copying them, and in a short time was able to make the four letters named. After that, when I met with any boy who I knew could write, I would tell him I could write as well as he. The next word would be, "I don't believe you. Let me see you try it." I would then make the letters which I had been so fortunate as to learn, and ask him to beat that. In this way I got a good many lessons in writing, which it is quite possible I should never have gotten in any other way. During this time, my copy-book was the board fence, brick wall, and pavement; my pen and ink was a lump of chalk. With these, I learned mainly how to write. I then commenced and continued copying the Italics in Webster's Spelling Book, until I could make them all without looking on the book. By this time, my little Master Thomas had gone to school, and learned how to write, and had written over a number of copy-books. These had been brought home, and shown to some of our near neighbors, and then laid aside. My mistress used to go to class meeting at the Wilk Street meetinghouse every Monday afternoon, and leave me to take care of the house. When left thus, I used to spend the time in writing in the spaces left in Master Thomas's copy-book, copying what he had written. I continued to do this until I could write a hand very similar to that of Master Thomas. Thus, after a long, tedious effort for years, I finally succeeded in learning how to write.

CHAPTER VIII

In a very short time after I went to live at Baltimore, my old master's youngest son Richard died; and in about three years and six months after his death, my old master, Captain Anthony, died, leaving only his son, Andrew, and daughter, Lucretia, to share his estate. He died while on a visit to see his daughter at Hillsborough. Cut off thus unexpectedly, he left no will as to the disposal of his property. It was therefore necessary to have a valuation of the property, that it might be equally divided between Mrs. Lucretia and Master Andrew. I was immediately sent for, to be valued with the other property. Here again my feelings rose up in detestation of slavery. I had now a new conception of my degraded condition. Prior to this, I had become, if not insensible to my lot, at least partly so. I left Baltimore with a young heart overborne with sadness, and a soul full of apprehension. I took passage with Captain Rowe, in the schooner *Wild Cat*, and, after a sail of about twenty-four hours, I found myself near the place of my birth. I had now been absent from it almost, if not quite, five years. I, however, remembered the place very well. I was only about five years old when I left it, to go and live with my old master on Colonel Lloyd's plantation; so that I was now between ten and eleven years old.

We were all ranked together at the valuation. Men and women, old and young, married and single, were ranked with horses, sheep, and swine. There were horses and men, cattle and women, pigs and children, all holding the same rank in the scale of being, and all were subjected to the same narrow examination. Silvery-headed age and sprightly youth, maids and matrons, had to undergo the same indelicate inspection. At this moment, I saw more clearly than ever the brutalizing effects of slavery upon both slave and slaveholder.

After the valuation, then came the division. I have no language to express the high excitement and deep anxiety which were felt among us poor slaves during this time. Our fate for life was now to be decided. We had no more voice in that decision than the brutes among whom we were ranked. A single word from the white men was enough—against all our wishes, prayers, and entreaties—to sunder forever the dearest friends, dearest kindred, and strongest ties known to human beings. In addition to the pain of separation, there was the horrid dread of falling into the hands of Master Andrew. He was known to us all as being a most cruel wretch,—a common drunkard, who had, by his reckless mismanagement and profligate dissipation, already wasted a large portion of his father's property. We all felt that we might as well be sold at once to the Georgia traders, as to pass into his hands; for we knew that that would be our inevitable condition,—a condition held by us all in the utmost horror and dread.

I suffered more anxiety than most of my fellow-slaves. I had known what it was to be kindly treated; they had known nothing of the kind. They had seen little or nothing of the world. They were in very deed men and women of sorrow, and acquainted with grief.[9] Their backs had been made familiar with the bloody lash, so that they had become callous; mine was yet tender; for while at Baltimore I got few whippings, and few slaves could boast of a kinder master and mistress than myself; and the thought of passing out of their hands into those of Master Andrew—a man who, but a few days before, to give me a sample of his bloody disposition, took my little brother by the throat, threw him on the ground, and with the heel of his boot stamped upon his head till the blood gushed from his nose and ears—was well calculated to make me anxious as to my fate. After he had committed this savage outrage upon my brother, he turned to me, and said that was the way he meant to serve me one of these days,—meaning, I suppose, when I came into his possession.

Thanks to a kind Providence, I fell to the portion of Mrs. Lucretia, and was sent immediately back to Baltimore, to live again in the family of Master Hugh. Their joy at my return equalled their sorrow at my departure. It was a glad day to me. I had escaped a [fate] worse than lion's jaws. I was absent from Baltimore, for the purpose of valuation and division, just about one month, and it seemed to have been six.

Very soon after my return to Baltimore, my mistress, Lucretia, died, leaving her husband and one child, Amanda; and in a very short time after her death, Master Andrew died. Now all the property of my old master, slaves included, was in the hands of strangers,—strangers who had had nothing to do with accumulating it. Not a slave was left free. All remained slaves, from the youngest to the oldest. If any one thing in my experience, more than another, served to deepen my conviction of the infernal character of slavery, and to fill me with unutterable loathing of slaveholders, it was their base ingratitude to my poor old grandmother. She had served my old master faithfully from youth to old age. She had been the source of all his wealth; she had peopled his plantation with slaves; she had become a great grandmother in his service. She had rocked him in infancy, attended him in childhood, served him through life, and at his death wiped from his icy brow the cold death-sweat, and closed his eyes forever. She was nevertheless left a slave—a slave for life—a slave in the hands of strangers; and in their hands she saw her children, her grandchildren, and her great-grandchildren, divided, like

---

9. In Isaiah 53.3, the Lord's servant is described as "a man of sorrows, and acquainted with grief."

so many sheep, without being gratified with the small privilege of a single word, as to their or her own destiny. And, to cap the climax of their base ingratitude and fiendish barbarity, my grandmother, who was now very old, having outlived my old master and all his children, having seen the beginning and end of all of them, and her present owners finding she was of but little value, her frame already racked with the pains of old age, and complete helplessness fast stealing over her once active limbs, they took her to the woods, built her a little hut, put up a little mud-chimney, and then made her welcome to the privilege of supporting herself there in perfect loneliness; thus virtually turning her out to die! If my poor old grandmother now lives, she lives to suffer in utter loneliness; she lives to remember and mourn over the loss of children, the loss of grandchildren, and the loss of great-grandchildren. They are, in the language of the slave's poet, Whittier,—

> "Gone, gone, sold and gone
> To the rice swamp dank and lone,
> Where the slave-whip ceaseless swings,
> Where the noisome insect stings,
> Where the fever-demon strews
> Poison with the falling dews,
> Where the sickly sunbeams glare
> Through the hot and misty air:—
> Gone, gone, sold and gone
> To the rice swamp dank and lone,
> From Virginia hills and waters—
> Woe is me, my stolen daughters!"[1]

The hearth is desolate. The children, the unconscious children, who once sang and danced in her presence, are gone. She gropes her way, in the darkness of age, for a drink of water. Instead of the voices of her children, she hears by day the moans of the dove, and by night the screams of the hideous owl. All is gloom. The grave is at the door. And now, when weighed down by the pains and aches of old age, when the head inclines to the feet, when the beginning and ending of human existence meet, and helpless infancy and painful old age combine together—at this time, this most needful time, the time for the exercise of that tenderness and affection which children only can exercise towards a declining parent—my poor old grandmother, the devoted mother of twelve children, is left all alone, in yonder little hut, before a few dim embers. She stands—she sits—she staggers—she falls—she groans—she dies—and there are none of her children or grandchildren present, to wipe from her wrinkled brow the cold sweat of death, or to place beneath the sod her fallen remains. Will not a righteous God visit[2] for these things?

In about two years after the death of Mrs. Lucretia, Master Thomas married his second wife. Her name was Rowena Hamilton. She was the eldest daughter of Mr. William Hamilton. Master now lived in St. Michael's. Not long after his marriage, a misunderstanding took place between himself and Master Hugh; and as a means of punishing his brother, he took me from

---

1. John Greenleaf Whittier, American poet (1807–1892), wrote a large group of antislavery poems. This one is *The Farewell of a Virginia Slave Mother to Her Daughters Sold into Southern Bondage.*   2. I.e., visit vengeance. Compare Exodus 32.34: "Nevertheless, in the day when I visit their sin upon them."

him to live with himself at St. Michael's. Here I underwent another most painful separation. It, however, was not so severe as the one I dreaded at the division of property; for, during this interval, a great change had taken place in Master Hugh and his once kind and affectionate wife. The influence of brandy upon him, and of slavery upon her, had effected a disastrous change in the characters of both; so that, as far as they were concerned, I thought I had little to lose by the change. But it was not to them that I was attached. It was to those little Baltimore boys that I felt the strongest attachment. I had received many good lessons from them, and was still receiving them, and the thought of leaving them was painful indeed. I was leaving, too, without the hope of ever being allowed to return. Master Thomas had said he would never let me return again. The barrier betwixt himself and brother he considered impassable.

I then had to regret that I did not at least make the attempt to carry out my resolution to run away; for the chances of success are tenfold greater from the city than from the country.

I sailed from Baltimore for St. Michael's in the sloop *Amanda*, Captain Edward Dodson. On my passage, I paid particular attention to the direction which the steamboats took to go to Philadelphia. I found, instead of going down, on reaching North Point they went up the bay, in a north-easterly direction. I deemed this knowledge of the utmost importance. My determination to run away was again revived. I resolved to wait only so long as the offering of a favorable opportunity. When that came, I was determined to be off.

CHAPTER IX

I have now reached a period of my life when I can give dates. I left Baltimore, and went to live with Master Thomas Auld, at St. Michael's, in March, 1832. It was now more than seven years since I lived with him in the family of my old master, on Colonel Lloyd's plantation. We of course were now almost entire strangers to each other. He was to me a new master, and I to him a new slave. I was ignorant of his temper and disposition; he was equally so of mine. A very short time, however, brought us into full acquaintance with each other. I was made acquainted with his wife not less than with himself. They were well matched, being equally mean and cruel. I was now, for the first time during a space of more than seven years, made to feel the painful gnawings of hunger—a something which I had not experienced before since I left Colonel Lloyd's plantation. It went hard enough with me then, when I could look back to no period at which I had enjoyed a sufficiency. It was tenfold harder after living in Master Hugh's family, where I had always had enough to eat, and of that which was good. I have said Master Thomas was a mean man. He was so. Not to give a slave enough to eat, is regarded as the most aggravated development of meanness even among slaveholders. The rule is, no matter how coarse the food, only let there be enough of it. This is the theory; and in the part of Maryland from which I came, it is the general practice,—though there are many exceptions. Master Thomas gave us enough of neither coarse nor fine food. There were four of us slaves in the kitchen—my sister Eliza, my aunt Priscilla, Henny, and myself; and we were allowed less than a half of a bushel of corn-meal per week, and very little else, either in the shape of meat or vegetables. It was not enough for us to subsist upon. We were therefore reduced to the wretched necessity of living at the expense of our neighbors. This we did by begging and stealing, whichever came handy in the time of need, the one being considered as legitimate as the other. A great many times have we poor creatures been nearly perishing with hunger, when food in abundance lay mouldering in the safe and smoke-house, and our pious mistress was aware of the fact; and yet that mistress and her husband would kneel every morning, and pray that God would bless them in basket and store!

Bad as all slaveholders are, we seldom meet one destitute of every element of character commanding respect. My master was one of this rare sort. I do not know of one single noble act ever performed by him. The leading trait in his character was meanness; and if there were any other element in his nature, it was made subject to this. He was mean; and, like most other mean men, he lacked the ability to conceal his meanness. Captain Auld was not born a slaveholder. He had been a poor man, master only of a Bay craft. He came into possession of all his slaves by marriage; and of all men, adopted slaveholders are the worst. He was cruel, but cowardly. He commanded without firmness. In the enforcement of his rules, he was at times rigid, and at times lax. At times, he spoke to his slaves with the firmness of Napoleon and the fury of a demon; at other times, he might well be mistaken for an inquirer who had lost his way. He did nothing of himself. He might have passed for a lion, but for his ears.[3] In all things noble which he attempted, his own meanness shone most conspicuous. His airs, words, and actions, were the airs, words, and actions of born slaveholders, and, being assumed, were awkward enough. He was not even a good imitator. He possessed all the disposition to deceive, but wanted the power. Having no resources within himself, he was compelled to be the copyist of many, and being such, he was forever the victim of inconsistency; and of consequence he was an object of contempt, and was held as such even by his slaves. The luxury of having slaves of his own to wait upon him was something new and unprepared for. He was a slaveholder without the ability to hold slaves. He found himself incapable of managing his slaves either by force, fear, or fraud. We seldom called him "master;" we generally called him "Captain Auld," and were hardly disposed to title him at all. I doubt not that our conduct had much to do with making him appear awkward, and of consequence fretful. Our want of reverence for him must have perplexed him greatly. He wished to have us call him master, but lacked the firmness necessary to command us to do so. His wife used to insist upon our calling him so, but to no purpose. In August, 1832, my master attended a Methodist camp-meeting held in the Bay-side, Talbot county, and there experienced religion. I indulged a faint hope that his conversion would lead him to emancipate his slaves, and that, if he did not do this, it would, at any rate, make him more kind and humane. I was disappointed in both these respects. It neither made him to be humane to his slaves, nor to emancipate them. If it had any effect on his character, it made him more cruel and hateful in all his ways; for I believe him to have been a much worse man after his conversion than before. Prior to his conversion, he relied upon his

3. A variation on Aesop's fable of the ass in the lion's skin, in which the fox says, "I should have been frightened too, if I had heard you bray."

own depravity to shield and sustain him in his savage barbarity; but after his conversion, he found religious sanction and support for his slaveholding cruelty. He made the greatest pretensions to piety. His house was the house of prayer. He prayed morning, noon, and night. He very soon distinguished himself among his brethren, and was soon made a class-leader and exhorter. His activity in revivals was great, and he proved himself an instrument in the hands of the church in converting many souls. His house was the preachers' home. They used to take great pleasure in coming there to put up; for while he starved us, he stuffed them. We have had three or four preachers there at a time. The names of those who used to come most frequently while I lived there, were Mr. Storks, Mr. Ewery, Mr. Humphry, and Mr. Hickey. I have also seen Mr. George Cookman at our house. We slaves loved Mr. Cookman. We believed him to be a good man. We thought him instrumental in getting Mr. Samuel Harrison, a very rich slaveholder, to emancipate his slaves; and by some means got the impression that he was laboring to effect the emancipation of all the slaves. When he was at our house, we were sure to be called in to prayers. When the others were there, we were sometimes called in and sometimes not. Mr. Cookman took more notice of us than either of the other ministers. He could not come among us without betraying his sympathy for us, and, stupid as we were, we had the sagacity to see it.

While I lived with my master in St. Michael's, there was a white young man, a Mr. Wilson, who proposed to keep a Sabbath school for the instruction of such slaves as might be disposed to learn to read the New Testament. We met but three times, when Mr. West and Mr. Fairbanks, both class-leaders, with many others, came upon us with sticks and other missiles, drove us off, and forbade us to meet again. Thus ended our little Sabbath school in the pious town of St. Michael's.

I have said my master found religious sanction for his cruelty. As an example, I will state one of many facts going to prove the charge. I have seen him tie up a lame young woman, and whip her with a heavy cowskin upon her naked shoulders, causing the warm red blood to drip; and, in justification of the bloody deed, he would quote this passage of Scripture—"He that knoweth his master's will, and doeth it not, shall be beaten with many stripes."[4]

Master would keep this lacerated young woman tied up in this horrid situation four or five hours at a time. I have known him to tie her up early in the morning, and whip her before breakfast; leave her, go to his store, return to dinner, and whip her again, cutting her in the places already made raw with his cruel lash. The secret of master's cruelty toward "Henny" is found in the fact of her being almost helpless. When quite a child, she fell into the fire, and burned herself horribly. Her hands were so burnt that she never got the use of them. She could do very little but bear heavy burdens. She was to master a bill of expense; and as he was a mean man, she was a constant offence to him. He seemed desirous of getting the poor girl out of existence. He gave her away once to his sister; but, being a poor gift, she was not disposed to keep her. Finally, my benevolent master, to use his own words, "set her adrift to take care of herself." Here was a recently-converted man, holding on upon the mother, and at the same time turning out her helpless child, to starve and die! Master Thomas was one of the many pious

4. Luke 12.47.

slaveholders who hold slaves for the very charitable purpose of taking care of them.

My master and myself had quite a number of differences. He found me unsuitable to his purpose. My city life, he said, had had a very pernicious effect upon me. It had almost ruined me for every good purpose, and fitted me for every thing which was bad. One of my greatest faults was that of letting his horse run away, and go down to his father-in-law's farm, which was about five miles from St. Michael's. I would then have to go after it. My reason for this kind of carelessness, or carefulness, was, that I could always get something to eat when I went there. Master William Hamilton, my master's father-in-law, always gave his slaves enough to eat. I never left there hungry, no matter how great the need of my speedy return. Master Thomas at length said he would stand it no longer. I had lived with him nine months, during which time he had given me a number of severe whippings, all to no good purpose. He resolved to put me out, as he said, to be broken; and, for this purpose, he let me for one year to a man named Edward Covey. Mr. Covey was a poor man, a farm-renter. He rented the place upon which he lived, as also the hands with which he tilled it. Mr. Covey had acquired a very high reputation for breaking young slaves, and this reputation was of immense value to him. It enabled him to get his farm tilled with much less expense to himself than he could have had it done without such a reputation. Some slaveholders thought it not much loss to allow Mr. Covey to have their slaves one year, for the sake of the training to which they were subjected, without any other compensation. He could hire young help with great ease, in consequence of this reputation. Added to the natural good qualities of Mr. Covey, he was a professor of religion—a pious soul—a member and a class-leader in the Methodist church. All of this added weight to his reputation as a "nigger-breaker." I was aware of all the facts, having been made acquainted with them by a young man who had lived there. I nevertheless made the change gladly; for I was sure of getting enough to eat, which is not the smallest consideration to a hungry man.

CHAPTER X

I left Master Thomas's house, and went to live with Mr. Covey, on the 1st of January, 1833. I was now, for the first time in my life, a field hand. In my new employment, I found myself even more awkward than a country boy appeared to be in a large city. I had been at my new home but one week before Mr. Covey gave me a very severe whipping, cutting my back, causing the blood to run, and raising ridges on my flesh as large as my little finger. The details of this affair are as follows: Mr. Covey sent me, very early in the morning of one of our coldest days in the month of January, to the woods, to get a load of wood. He gave me a team of unbroken oxen. He told me which was the in-hand ox, and which the off-hand ox. He then tied the end of a large rope around the horns of the in-hand ox, and gave me the other end of it, and told me, if the oxen started to run, that I must hold on upon the rope. I had never driven oxen before, and of course I was very awkward. I, however, succeeded in getting to the edge of the woods with little difficulty; but I had got a very few rods into the woods, when the oxen took fright, and started full tilt, carrying the cart against trees, and over stumps, in the most frightful manner. I expected every moment that my brains would be dashed out against the trees. After running thus for a considerable distance, they finally upset the cart, dashing it with great force against a tree, and threw themselves into a dense thicket. How I escaped death, I do not know. There I was, entirely alone, in a thick wood, in a place new to me. My cart was upset and shattered, my oxen were entangled among the young trees, and there was none to help me. After a long spell of effort, I succeeded in getting my cart righted, my oxen disentangled, and again yoked to the cart. I now proceeded with my team to the place where I had, the day before, been chopping wood, and loaded my cart pretty heavily, thinking in this way to tame my oxen. I then proceeded on my way home. I had now consumed one half of the day. I got out of the woods safely, and now felt out of danger. I stopped my oxen to open the woods gate; and just as I did so, before I could get hold of my ox-rope, the oxen again started, rushed through the gate, catching it between the wheel and the body of the cart, tearing it to pieces, and coming within a few inches of crushing me against the gate-post. Thus twice, in one short day, I escaped death by the merest chance. On my return, I told Mr. Covey what had happened, and how it happened. He ordered me to return to the woods again immediately. I did so, and he followed on after me. Just as I got into the woods, he came up and told me to stop my cart, and that he would teach me how to trifle away my time, and break gates. He then went to a large gum-tree, and with his axe cut three large switches, and, after trimming them up neatly with his pocket-knife, he ordered me to take off my clothes. I made him no answer, but stood with my clothes on. He repeated his order. I still made him no answer, nor did I move to strip myself. Upon this he rushed at me with the fierceness of a tiger, tore off my clothes, and lashed me till he had worn out his switches, cutting me so savagely as to leave the marks visible for a long time after. This whipping was the first of a number just like it, and for similar offences.

I lived with Mr. Covey one year. During the first six months, of that year, scarce a week passed without his whipping me. I was seldom free from a sore back. My awkwardness was almost always his excuse for whipping me. We were worked fully up to the point of endurance. Long before day we were up, our horses fed, and by the first approach of day we were off to the field with our hoes and ploughing teams. Mr. Covey gave us enough to eat, but scarce time to eat it. We were often less than five minutes taking our meals. We were often in the field from the first approach of day till its last lingering ray had left us; and at saving-fodder time, midnight often caught us in the field binding blades.[5]

Covey would be out with us. The way he used to stand it was this. He would spend the most of his afternoons in bed. He would then come out fresh in the evening, ready to urge us on with his words, example, and frequently with the whip. Mr. Covey was one of the few slaveholders who could and did work with his hands. He was a hard-working man. He knew by himself just what a man or a boy could do. There was no deceiving him. His work went on in his absence almost as well as in his presence; and he had the faculty of making us feel that he was ever present with us. This he did by surprising us. He seldom approached the spot where we were at work

5. Gathering cut grain into bundles or sheaves.

openly, if he could do it secretly. He always aimed at taking us by surprise. Such was his cunning, that we used to call him, among ourselves, "the snake." When we were at work in the cornfield, he would sometimes crawl on his hands and knees to avoid detection, and all at once he would rise nearly in our midst, and scream out, "Ha, ha! Come, come! Dash on, dash on!" This being his mode of attack, it was never safe to stop a single minute. His comings were like a thief in the night. He appeared to us as being ever at hand. He was under every tree, behind every stump, in every bush, and at every window, on the plantation. He would sometimes mount his horse, as if bound to St. Michael's, a distance of seven miles, and in half an hour afterwards you would see him coiled up in the corner of the wood-fence, watching every motion of the slaves. He would, for this purpose, leave his horse tied up in the woods. Again, he would sometimes walk up to us, and give us orders as though he was upon the point of starting on a long journey, turn his back upon us, and make as though he was going to the house to get ready; and, before he would get half way thither, he would turn short and crawl into a fence-corner, or behind some tree, and there watch us till the going down of the sun.

Mr. Covey's *forte* consisted in his power to deceive. His life was devoted to planning and perpetrating the grossest deceptions. Every thing he possessed in the shape of learning or religion, he made conform to his disposition to deceive. He seemed to think himself equal to deceiving the Almighty. He would make a short prayer in the morning, and a long prayer at night; and, strange as it may seem, few men would at times appear more devotional than he. The exercises of his family devotions were always commenced with singing; and, as he was a very poor singer himself, the duty of raising the hymn generally came upon me. He would read his hymn, and nod at me to commence. I would at times do so; at others, I would not. My non-compliance would almost always produce much confusion. To show himself independent of me, he would start and stagger through with his hymn in the most discordant manner. In this state of mind, he prayed with more than ordinary spirit. Poor man! such was his disposition, and success at deceiving, I do verily believe that he sometimes deceived himself into the solemn belief, that he was a sincere worshipper of the most high God; and this, too, at a time when he may be said to have been guilty of compelling his woman slave to commit the sin of adultery. The facts in the case are these: Mr. Covey was a poor man; he was just commencing in life; he was only able to buy one slave; and, shocking as is the fact, he bought her, as he said, for a *breeder*. This woman was named Caroline. Mr. Covey bought her from Mr. Thomas Lowe, about six miles from St. Michael's. She was a large, able-bodied woman, about twenty years old. She had already given birth to one child, which proved her to be just what he wanted. After buying her, he hired a married man of Mr. Samuel Harrison, to live with him one year; and him he used to fasten up with her every night! The result was, that, at the end of the year, the miserable woman gave birth to twins. At this result Mr. Covey seemed to be highly pleased, both with the man and the wretched woman. Such was his joy, and that of his wife, that nothing they could do for Caroline during her confinement was too good, or too hard, to be done. The children were regarded as being quite an addition to his wealth.

If at any one time of my life more than another, I was made to drink the bitterest dregs of slavery, that time was during the first six months of my stay with Mr. Covey. We were worked in all weathers. It was never too hot or too cold; it could never rain, blow, hail, or snow, too hard for us to work in the field. Work, work, work, was scarcely more the order of the day than of the night. The longest days were too short for him, and the shortest nights too long for him. I was somewhat unmanageable when I first went there, but a few months of this discipline tamed me. Mr. Covey succeeded in breaking me. I was broken in body, soul, and spirit. My natural elasticity was crushed, my intellect languished, the disposition to read departed, the cheerful spark that lingered about my eye died; the dark night of slavery closed in upon me; and behold a man transformed into a brute!

Sunday was my only leisure time. I spent this in a sort of beast-like stupor, between sleep and wake, under some large tree. At times I would rise up, a flash of energetic freedom would dart through my soul, accompanied with a faint beam of hope, that flickered for a moment, and then vanished. I sank down again, mourning over my wretched condition. I was sometimes prompted to take my life, and that of Covey, but was prevented by a combination of hope and fear. My sufferings on this plantation seem now like a dream rather than a stern reality.

Our house stood within a few rods of the Chesapeake Bay, whose broad bosom was ever white with sails from every quarter of the habitable globe. Those beautiful vessels, robed in purest white, so delightful to the eye of freemen, were to me so many shrouded ghosts, to terrify and torment me with thoughts of my wretched condition. I have often, in the deep stillness of a summer's Sabbath, stood all alone upon the lofty banks of that noble bay, and traced, with saddened heart and tearful eye, the countless number of sails moving off to the mighty ocean. The sight of these always affected me powerfully. My thoughts would compel utterance; and there, with no audience but the Almighty, I would pour out my soul's complaint, in my rude way, with an apostrophe[6] to the moving multitude of ships:—

"You are loosed from your moorings, and are free; I am fast in my chains, and am a slave! You move merrily before the gentle gale, and I sadly before the bloody whip! You are freedom's swift-winged angels, that fly round the world; I am confined in bands of iron! O that I were free! O, that I were on one of your gallant decks, and under your protecting wing! Alas! betwixt me and you, the turbid waters roll. Go on, go on. O that I could also go! Could I but swim! If I could fly! O, why was I born a man, of whom to make a brute! The glad ship is gone; she hides in the dim distance. I am left in the hottest hell of unending slavery. O God, save me! God, deliver me! Let me be free! Is there any God? Why am I a slave? I will run away. I will not stand it. Get caught, or get clear, I'll try it. I had as well die with ague as the fever. I have only one life to lose. I had as well be killed running as die standing. Only think of it; one hundred miles straight north, and I am free! Try it? Yes! God helping me, I will. It cannot be that I shall live and die a slave. I will take to the water. This very bay shall bear me into freedom. The steam boats steered in a north-east course from North Point. I will do the same; and when I get to the head of the bay, I will turn my canoe adrift, and walk straight through Delaware into Pennsylvania. When I get there, I shall not be required to

6. An exclamatory form of address.

have a pass; I can travel without being disturbed. Let but the first opportunity offer, and, come what will, I am off. Meanwhile, I will try to bear up under the yoke. I am not the only slave in the world. Why should I fret? I can bear as much as any of them. Besides, I am but a boy, and all boys are bound to some one. It may be that my misery in slavery will only increase my happiness when I get free. There is a better day coming."

Thus I used to think, and thus I used to speak to myself; goaded almost to madness at one moment, and at the next reconciling myself to my wretched lot.

I have already intimated that my condition was much worse, during the first six months of my stay at Mr. Covey's, than in the last six. The circumstances leading to the change in Mr. Covey's course toward me form an epoch in my humble history. You have seen how a man was made a slave; you shall see how a slave was made a man. On one of the hottest days of the month of August, 1833, Bill Smith, William Hughes, a slave named Eli, and myself, were engaged in fanning wheat.[7] Hughes was clearing the fanned wheat from before the fan, Eli was turning, Smith was feeding, and I was carrying wheat to the fan. The work was simple, requiring strength rather than intellect; yet, to one entirely unused to such work, it came very hard. About three o'clock of that day, I broke down; my strength failed me; I was seized with a violent aching of the head, attended with extreme dizziness; I trembled in every limb. Finding what was coming, I nerved myself up, feeling it would never do to stop work. I stood as long as I could stagger to the hopper with grain. When I could stand no longer, I fell, and felt as if held down by an immense weight. The fan of course stopped; every one had his own work to do; and no one could do the work of the other, and have his own go on at the same time.

Mr. Covey was at the house, about one hundred yards from the treading-yard where we were fanning. On hearing the fan stop, he left immediately, and came to the spot where we were. He hastily inquired what the matter was. Bill answered that I was sick, and there was no one to bring wheat to the fan. I had by this time crawled away under the side of the post and rail-fence by which the yard was enclosed, hoping to find relief by getting out of the sun. He then asked where I was. He was told by one of the hands. He came to the spot, and, after looking at me awhile, asked me what was the matter. I told him as well as I could, for I scarce had strength to speak. He then gave me a savage kick in the side, and told me to get up. I tried to do so, but fell back in the attempt. He gave me another kick, and again told me to rise. I again tried, and succeeded in gaining my feet; but, stooping to get the tub with which I was feeding the fan, I again staggered and fell. While down in this situation, Mr. Covey took up the hickory slat with which Hughes had been striking off the half-bushel measure, and with it gave me a heavy blow upon the head, making a large wound, and the blood ran freely; and with this again told me to get up. I made no effort to comply, having now made up my mind to let him do his worst. In a short time after receiving this blow, my head grew better. Mr. Covey had now left me to my fate. At this moment I resolved, for the first time, to go to my master, enter a complaint, and ask his protection. In order to [do] this, I must that afternoon walk seven

7. Separating the grain from the chaff.

miles; and this, under the circumstances, was truly a severe undertaking. I was exceedingly feeble; made so as much by the kicks and blows which I received, as by the severe fit of sickness to which I had been subjected. I, however, watched my chance, while Covey was looking in an opposite direction, and started for St. Michael's. I succeeded in getting a considerable distance on my way to the woods, when Covey discovered me, and called after me to come back, threatening what he would do if I did not come. I disregarded both his calls and his threats, and made my way to the woods as fast as my feeble state would allow; and thinking I might be overhauled by him if I kept the road, I walked through the woods, keeping far enough from the road to avoid detection, and near enough to prevent losing my way. I had not gone far before my little strength again failed me. I could go no farther. I fell down, and lay for a considerable time. The blood was yet oozing from the wound on my head. For a time I thought I should bleed to death; and think now that I should have done so, but that the blood so matted my hair as to stop the wound. After lying there about three quarters of an hour, I nerved myself up again, and started on my way, through bogs and briers, barefooted and bareheaded, tearing my feet sometimes at nearly every step; and after a journey of about seven miles, occupying some five hours to perform it, I arrived at master's store. I then presented an appearance enough to affect any but a heart of iron. From the crown of my head to my feet, I was covered with blood. My hair was all clotted with dust and blood; my shirt was stiff with blood. My legs and feet were torn in sundry places with briers and thorns, and were also covered with blood. I suppose I looked like a man who had escaped a den of wild beasts, and barely escaped them. In this state I appeared before my master, humbly entreating him to interpose his authority for my protection. I told him all the circumstances as well as I could, and it seemed, as I spoke, at times to affect him. He would then walk the floor, and seek to justify Covey by saying he expected I deserved it. He asked me what I wanted. I told him, to let me get a new home; that as sure as I lived with Mr. Covey again, I should live with but to die with him; that Covey would surely kill me; he was in a fair way for it. Master Thomas ridiculed the idea that there was any danger of Mr. Covey's killing me, and said that he knew Mr. Covey; that he was a good man, and that he could not think of taking me from him; that, should he do so, he would lose the whole year's wages; that I belonged to Mr. Covey for one year, and that I must go back to him, come what might; and that I must not trouble him with any more stories, or that he would himself *get hold of me.* After threatening me thus, he gave me a very large dose of salts, telling me that I might remain in St. Michael's that night, (it being quite late) but that I must be off back to Mr. Covey's early in the morning; and that if I did not, he would *get hold of me,* which meant that he would whip me. I remained all night, and, according to his orders, I started off to Covey's in the morning, (Saturday morning), wearied in body and broken in spirit. I got no supper that night, or breakfast that morning. I reached Covey's about nine o'clock; and just as I was getting over the fence that divided Mrs. Kemp's fields from ours, out ran Covey with his cowskin, to give me another whipping. Before he could reach me, I succeeded in getting to the cornfield; and as the corn was very high, it afforded me the means of hiding. He seemed very angry, and searched for me a long time. My behavior was altogether unaccountable. He finally gave up the chase, thinking, I suppose, that I must come home for something to eat; he would give himself no further trouble in looking for me. I spent that day mostly in the woods, having the alternative before me,—to go home and be whipped to death, or stay in the woods and be starved to death. That night, I fell in with Sandy Jenkins, a slave with whom I was somewhat acquainted. Sandy had a free wife who lived about four miles from Mr. Covey's; and it being Saturday, he was on his way to see her. I told him my circumstances, and he very kindly invited me to go home with him. I went home with him, and talked this whole matter over, and got his advice as to what course it was best for me to pursue. I found Sandy an old adviser. He told me, with great solemnity, I must go back to Covey; but that before I went, I must go with him into another part of the woods, where there was a certain *root*, which, if I would take some of it with me, carrying it *always on my right side*, would render it impossible for Mr. Covey, or any other white man, to whip me. He said he had carried it for years; and since he had done so, he had never received a blow, and never expected to while he carried it. I at first rejected the idea, that the simple carrying of a root in my pocket would have any such effect as he had said, and was not disposed to take it; but Sandy impressed the necessity with much earnestness, telling me it could do no harm, if it did no good. To please him, I at length took the root, and, according to his direction, carried it upon my right side. This was Sunday morning. I immediately started for home; and upon entering the yard gate, out came Mr. Covey on his way to meeting. He spoke to me very kindly, bade me drive the pigs from a lot near by, and passed on towards the church. Now, this singular conduct of Mr. Covey really made me begin to think that there was something in the *root* which Sandy had given me; and had it been on any other day than Sunday, I could have attributed the conduct to no other cause than the influence of that root; and as it was, I was half inclined to think the *root* to be something more than I at first had taken it to be. All went well till Monday morning. On this morning, the virtue of the *root* was fully tested. Long before daylight, I was called to go and rub, curry, and feed, the horses. I obeyed, and was glad to obey. But whilst thus engaged, whilst in the act of throwing down some blades from the loft, Mr. Covey entered the stable with a long rope; and just as I was half out of the loft, he caught hold of my legs, and was about tying me. As soon as I found what he was up to, I gave a sudden spring, and as I did so, he holding to my legs, I was brought sprawling on the stable floor. Mr. Covey seemed now to think he had me, and could do what he pleased; but at this moment—from whence came the spirit I don't know—I resolved to fight; and, suiting my action to the resolution, I seized Covey hard by the throat; and as I did so, I rose. He held on to me, and I to him. My resistance was so entirely unexpected, that Covey seemed taken all aback. He trembled like a leaf. This gave me assurance, and I held him uneasy, causing the blood to run where I touched him with the ends of my fingers. Mr. Covey soon called out to Hughes for help. Hughes came, and, while Covey held me, attempted to tie my right hand. While he was in the act of doing so, I watched my chance, and gave him a heavy kick close under the ribs. This kick fairly sickened Hughes, so that he left me in the hands of Mr. Covey. This kick had the effect of not only weakening Hughes, but Covey also. When he saw Hughes bending over with pain, his courage quailed. He asked me if I meant to persist in my resistance. I told him I did, come what might; that he had used me like a brute for six months, and that I was determined to be used so no longer. With that, he strove to drag me to a stick that was lying just out of the stable door. He meant to knock me down. But just as he was leaning over to get the stick, I seized him with both hands by his collar, and brought him by a sudden snatch to the ground. By this time, Bill came. Covey called upon him for assistance. Bill wanted to know what he could do. Covey said, "Take hold of him, take hold of him!" Bill said his master hired him out to work, and not to help to whip me; so he left Covey and myself to fight our own battle out. We were at it for nearly two hours. Covey at length let me go, puffing and blowing at a great rate, saying that if I had not resisted, he would not have whipped me half so much. The truth was, that he had not whipped me at all. I considered him as getting entirely the worst end of the bargain; for he had drawn no blood from me, but I had from him. The whole six months afterwards, that I spent with Mr. Covey, he never laid the weight of his finger upon me in anger. He would occasionally say, he didn't want to get hold of me again. "No," thought I, "you need not; for you will come off worse than you did before."

This battle with Mr. Covey was the turning-point in my career as a slave. It rekindled the few expiring embers of freedom, and revived within me a sense of my own manhood. It recalled the departed self-confidence, and inspired me again with a determination to be free. The gratification afforded by the triumph was a full compensation for whatever else might follow, even death itself. He only can understand the deep satisfaction which I experienced, who has himself repelled by force the bloody arm of slavery. I felt as I never felt before. It was a glorious resurrection, from the tomb of slavery, to the heaven of freedom. My long-crushed spirit rose, cowardice departed, bold defiance took its place; and I now resolved that, however long I might remain a slave in form, the day had passed forever when I could be a slave in fact. I did not hesitate to let it be known of me, that the white man who expected to succeed in whipping, must also succeed in killing me.

From this time I was never again what might be called fairly whipped, though I remained a slave four years afterwards. I had several fights, but was never whipped.

It was for a long time a matter of surprise to me why Mr. Covey did not immediately have me taken by the constable to the whipping-post, and there regularly whipped for the crime of raising my hand against a white man in defence of myself. And the only explanation I can now think of does not entirely satisfy me; but such as it is, I will give it. Mr. Covey enjoyed the most unbounded reputation for being a first-rate overseer and negro-breaker. It was of considerable importance to him. That reputation was at stake; and had he sent me—a boy about sixteen years old—to the public whipping-post, his reputation would have been lost; so, to save his reputation, he suffered me to go unpunished.

My term of actual service to Mr. Edward Covey ended on Christmas day, 1833. The days between Christmas and New Year's day are allowed as holidays; and, accordingly, we were not required to perform any labor, more than to feed and take care of the stock. This time we regarded as our own, by the grace of our masters; and we therefore used or abused it nearly as we pleased. Those of us who had families at a distance, were generally allowed to spend the whole six days in their society. This time, however, was spent in various ways. The staid, sober, thinking and industrious ones of our number would employ themselves in making corn-brooms, mats, horse-collars, and baskets; and another class of us would spend the time in hunting opossums, hares, and coons. But by far the larger part engaged in such sports and merriments as playing ball, wrestling, running foot-races, fiddling, dancing, and drinking whisky; and this latter mode of spending the time was by far the most agreeable to the feelings of our masters. A slave who would work during the holidays was considered by our masters as scarcely deserving them. He was regarded as one who rejected the favor of his master. It was deemed a disgrace not to get drunk at Christmas; and he was regarded as lazy indeed, who had not provided himself with the necessary means, during the year, to get whisky enough to last him through Christmas.

From what I know of the effect of these holidays upon the slave, I believe them to be among the most effective means in the hands of the slaveholder in keeping down the spirit of insurrection. Were the slaveholders at once to abandon this practice, I have not the slightest doubt it would lead to an immediate insurrection among the slaves. These holidays serve as conductors, or safety-valves, to carry off the rebellious spirit of enslaved humanity. But for these, the slave would be forced up to the wildest desperation; and woe betide the slaveholder, the day he ventures to remove or hinder the operation of those conductors! I warn him that, in such an event, a spirit will go forth in their midst, more to be dreaded than the most appalling earthquake.

The holidays are part and parcel of the gross fraud, wrong, and inhumanity of slavery. They are professedly a custom established by the benevolence of the slaveholders; but I undertake to say, it is the result of selfishness, and one of the grossest frauds committed upon the down-trodden slave. They do not give the slaves this time because they would not like to have their work during its continuance, but because they know it would be unsafe to deprive them of it. This will be seen by the fact, that the slaveholders like to have their slaves spend those days just in such a manner as to make them as glad of their ending as of their beginning. Their object seems to be, to disgust their slaves with freedom, by plunging them into the lowest depths of dissipation. For instance, the slaveholders not only like to see the slave drink of his own accord, but will adopt various plans to make him drunk. One plan is, to make bets on their slaves, as to who can drink the most whisky without getting drunk; and in this way they succeed in getting whole multitudes to drink to excess. Thus, when the slave asks for virtuous freedom, the cunning slaveholder, knowing his ignorance, cheats him with a dose of vicious dissipation, artfully labelled with the name of liberty. The most of us used to drink it down, and the result was just what might be supposed: many of us were led to think that there was little to choose between liberty and slavery. We felt, and very properly too, that we had almost as well be slaves to man as to rum. So, when the holidays ended, we staggered up from the filth of our wallowing, took a long breath, and marched to the field,—feeling, upon the whole, rather glad to go, from what our master had deceived us into a belief was freedom, back to the arms of slavery.

I have said that this mode of treatment is a part of the whole system of fraud and inhumanity of slavery. It is so. The mode here adopted to disgust the slave with freedom, by allowing him to see only the abuse of it, is carried out in other things. For instance, a slave loves molasses; he steals some. His master, in many cases, goes off to town, and buys a large quantity; he returns, takes his whip, and commands the slave to eat the molasses, until the poor fellow is made sick at the very mention of it. The same mode is sometimes adopted to make the slaves refrain from asking for more food than their regular allowance. A slave runs through his allowance, and applies for more. His master is enraged at him; but, not willing to send him off without food, gives him more than is necessary, and compels him to eat it within a given time. Then, if he complains that he cannot eat it, he is said to be satisfied neither full nor fasting, and is whipped for being hard to please! I have an abundance of such illustrations of the same principle, drawn from my own observation, but think the cases I have cited sufficient. The practice is a very common one.

On the first of January, 1834, I left Mr. Covey, and went to live with Mr. William Freeland, who lived about three miles from St. Michael's. I soon found Mr. Freeland a very different man from Mr. Covey. Though not rich, he was what would be called an educated southern gentleman. Mr. Covey, as I have shown, was a well-trained negro-breaker and slave-driver. The former (slaveholder though he was) seemed to possess some regard for honor, some reverence for justice, and some respect for humanity. The latter seemed totally insensible to all such sentiments. Mr. Freeland had many of the faults peculiar to slaveholders, such as being very passionate and fretful; but I must do him the justice to say, that he was exceedingly free from those degrading vices to which Mr. Covey was constantly addicted. The one was open and frank, and we always knew where to find him. The other was a most artful deceiver, and could be understood only by such as were skilful enough to detect his cunningly-devised frauds. Another advantage I gained in my new master was, he made no pretensions to, or profession of, religion; and this, in my opinion, was truly a great advantage. I assert most unhesitatingly, that the religion of the south is a mere covering for the most horrid crimes,—a justifier of the most appalling barbarity,—a sanctifier of the most hateful frauds,—and a dark shelter under which the darkest, foulest, grossest, and most infernal deeds of slaveholders find the strongest protection. Were I to be again reduced to the chains of slavery, next to that enslavement, I should regard being the slave of a religious master the greatest calamity that could befall me. For of all slaveholders with whom I have ever met, religious slaveholders are the worst. I have ever found them the meanest and basest, the most cruel and cowardly, of all others. It was my unhappy lot not only to belong to a religious slaveholder, but to live in a community of such religionists. Very near Mr. Freeland lived the Rev. Daniel Weeden, and in the same neighborhood lived the Rev. Rigby Hopkins. These were members and ministers in the Reformed Methodist Church. Mr. Weeden owned, among others, a woman slave, whose name I have forgotten. This woman's back, for weeks, was kept literally raw, made so by the lash of this merciless, *religious* wretch. He used to hire hands. His maxim was, Behave well or behave ill, it is the duty of a master occasionally to whip a slave, to remind him of his master's authority. Such was his theory, and such his practice.

Mr. Hopkins was even worse than Mr. Weeden. His chief boast was his ability to manage slaves. The peculiar feature of his government was that of whipping slaves in advance of deserving it. He always managed to have one or more of his slaves to whip every Monday morning. He did this to alarm their fears, and strike terror into those who escaped. His plan was to whip for the smallest offences, to prevent the commission of large ones. Mr. Hopkins could always find some excuse for whipping a slave. It would astonish one, unaccustomed to a slaveholding life, to see with what wonderful ease a slaveholder can find things, of which to make occasion to whip a slave. A mere look, word, or motion,—a mistake, accident, or want of power,—are all matters for which a slave may be whipped at any time. Does a slave look dissatisfied? It is said, he has the devil in him, and it must be whipped out. Does he speak loudly when spoken to by his master? Then he is getting highminded, and should be taken down a button-hole lower. Does he forget to pull off his hat at the approach of a white person? Then he is wanting in reverence, and should be whipped for it. Does he ever venture to vindicate his conduct, when censured for it? Then he is guilty of impudence,—one of the greatest crimes of which a slave can be guilty. Does he ever venture to suggest a different mode of doing things from that pointed out by his master? He is indeed presumptuous, and getting above himself; and nothing less than a flogging will do for him. Does he, while ploughing, break a plough,—or, while hoeing, break a hoe? It is owing to his carelessness, and for it a slave must always be whipped. Mr. Hopkins could always find something of this sort to justify the use of the lash, and he seldom failed to embrace such opportunities. There was not a man in the whole county, with whom the slaves who had the getting their own home, would not prefer to live, rather than with this Rev. Mr. Hopkins. And yet there was not a man any where round, who made higher professions of religion, or was more active in revivals,—more attentive to the class, love-feast, prayer and preaching meetings, or more devotional in his family,—that prayed earlier, later, louder, and longer,—than this same reverend slave-driver, Rigby Hopkins.

But to return to Mr. Freeland, and to my experience while in his employment. He, like Mr. Covey, gave us enough to eat; but, unlike Mr. Covey, he also gave us sufficient time to take our meals. He worked us hard, but always between sunrise and sunset. He required a good deal of work to be done, but gave us good tools with which to work. His farm was large, but he employed hands enough to work it, and with ease, compared with many of his neighbors. My treatment, while in his employment, was heavenly, compared with what I experienced at the hands of Mr. Edward Covey.

Mr. Freeland was himself the owner of but two slaves. Their names were Henry Harris and John Harris. The rest of his hands he hired. These consisted of myself, Sandy Jenkins,[8] and Handy Caldwell. Henry and John were quite intelligent, and in a very little while after I went there, I succeeded in creating in them a strong desire to learn how to read. This desire soon sprang up in the others also. They very soon mustered up some old spelling-books, and nothing would do but that I must keep a Sabbath school. I agreed to do so, and accordingly devoted my Sundays to teaching these my loved fellowslaves how to read. Neither of them knew his letters when I went there. Some of the slaves of the neighboring farms found what was going on, and

---

8. This is the same man who gave me the roots to prevent my being whipped by Mr. Covey. He was "a clever soul." We used frequently to talk about the fight with Covey, and as often as we did so, he would claim my success as the result of the roots which he gave me. This superstition is very common among the more ignorant slaves. A slave seldom dies but that his death is attributed to trickery [Douglass's note].

also availed themselves of this little opportunity to learn to read. It was understood, among all who came, that there must be as little display about it as possible. It was necessary to keep our religious masters at St. Michael's unacquainted with the fact, that, instead of spending the Sabbath in wrestling, boxing, and drinking whiskey, we were trying to learn how to read the will of God; for they had much rather see us engaged in those degrading sports, than to see us behaving like intellectual, moral, and accountable beings. My blood boils as I think of the bloody manner in which Messrs. Wright Fairbanks and Garrison West, both class-leaders, in connection with many others, rushed in upon us with sticks and stones, and broke up our virtuous little Sabbath school, at St. Michael's—all calling themselves Christians! humble followers of the Lord Jesus Christ! But I am again digressing.

I held my Sabbath school at the house of a free colored man, whose name I deem it imprudent to mention; for should it be known, it might embarrass him greatly, though the crime of holding the school was committed ten years ago. I had at one time over forty scholars, and those of the right sort, ardently desiring to learn. They were of all ages, though mostly men and women. I look back to those Sundays with an amount of pleasure not to be expressed. They were great days to my soul. The work of instructing my dear fellow-slaves was the sweetest engagement with which I was ever blessed. We loved each other, and to leave them at the close of the Sabbath was a severe cross indeed. When I think that those precious souls are to-day shut up in the prison-house of slavery, my feelings overcome me, and I am almost ready to ask, "Does a righteous God govern the universe? and for what does he hold the thunders in his right hand, if not to smite the oppressor, and deliver the spoiled out of the hand of the spoiler?" These dear souls came not to Sabbath school because it was popular to do so, nor did I teach them because it was reputable to be thus engaged. Every moment they spent in that school, they were liable to be taken up, and given thirty-nine lashes. They came because they wished to learn. Their minds had been starved by their cruel masters. They had been shut up in mental darkness. I taught them, because it was the delight of my soul to be doing something that looked like bettering the condition of my race. I kept up my school nearly the whole year I lived with Mr. Freeland; and, beside my Sabbath school, I devoted three evenings in the week, during the winter, to teaching the slaves at home. And I have the happiness to know, that several of those who came to Sabbath school learned how to read; and that one, at least, is now free through my agency.

The year passed off smoothly. It seemed only about half as long as the year which preceded it. I went through it without receiving a single blow. I will give Mr. Freeland the credit of being the best master I ever had, *till I became my own master.* For the ease with which I passed the year, I was, however, somewhat indebted to the society of my fellow-slaves. They were noble souls; they not only possessed loving hearts, but brave ones. We were linked and interlinked with each other. I loved them with a love stronger than any thing I have experienced since. It is sometimes said that we slaves do not love and confide in each other. In answer to this assertion, I can say, I never loved any or confided in any people more than my fellow-slaves, and especially those with whom I lived at Mr. Freeland's. I believe we would have died for each other. We never undertook to do any thing, of any importance, without a mutual consultation. We never moved separately. We were one; and as much so by our tempers and dispositions, as by the mutual hardships to which we were necessarily subjected by our condition as slaves.

At the close of the year 1834, Mr. Freeland again hired me of my master, for the year 1835. But, by this time, I began to want to live *upon free land* as well as *with Freeland*; and I was no longer content, therefore, to live with him or any other slaveholder. I began, with the commencement of the year, to prepare myself for a final struggle, which should decide my fate one way or the other. My tendency was upward. I was fast approaching manhood, and year after year had passed, and I was still a slave. These thoughts roused me—I must do something. I therefore resolved that 1835 should not pass without witnessing an attempt, on my part, to secure my liberty. But I was not willing to cherish this determination alone. My fellow-slaves were dear to me. I was anxious to have them participate with me in this, my life-giving determination. I therefore, though with great prudence, commenced early to ascertain their views and feelings in regard to their condition, and to imbue their minds with thoughts of freedom. I bent myself to devising ways and means for our escape, and meanwhile strove, on all fitting occasions, to impress them with the gross fraud and inhumanity of slavery. I went first to Henry, next to John, then to the others. I found, in them all, warm hearts and noble spirits. They were ready to hear, and ready to act when a feasible plan should be proposed. This was what I wanted. I talked to them of our want of manhood, if we submitted to our enslavement without at least one noble effort to be free. We met often, and consulted frequently, and told our hopes and fears, recounted the difficulties, real and imagined, which we should be called on to meet. At times we were almost disposed to give up, and try to content ourselves with our wretched lot; at others, we were firm and unbending in our determination to go. Whenever we suggested any plan, there was shrinking—the odds were fearful. Our path was beset with the greatest obstacles; and if we succeeded in gaining the end of it, our right to be free was yet questionable—we were yet liable to be returned to bondage. We could see no spot, this side of the ocean, where we could be free. We knew nothing about Canada. Our knowledge of the north did not extend farther than New York; and to go there, and be forever harassed with the frightful liability of being returned to slavery—with the certainty of being treated tenfold worse than before—the thought was truly a horrible one, and one which it was not easy to overcome. The case sometimes stood thus: At every gate through which we were to pass, we saw a watchman—at every ferry a guard—on every bridge a sentinel—and in every wood a patrol. We were hemmed in upon every side. Here were the difficulties, real or imagined—the good to be sought, and the evil to be shunned. On the one hand, there stood slavery, a stern reality, glaring frightfully upon us,—its robes already crimsoned with the blood of millions, and even now feasting itself greedily upon our own flesh. On the other hand, away back in the dim distance, under the flickering light of the north star, behind some craggy hill or snow-covered mountain, stood a doubtful freedom—half frozen—beckoning us to come and share its hospitality. This in itself was sometimes enough to stagger us; but when we permitted ourselves to survey the road, we were frequently appalled. Upon either side we saw grim death, assuming the most horrid shapes. Now it was starvation, causing us to eat our own flesh;—now we were contending with the waves, and were drowned;—now

we were overtaken, and torn to pieces by the fangs of the terrible blood-
hound. We were stung by scorpions, chased by wild beasts, bitten by snakes,
and finally, after having nearly reached the desired spot,—after swimming
rivers, encountering wild beasts, sleeping in the woods, suffering hunger and
nakedness,—we were overtaken by our pursuers, and, in our resistance, we
were shot dead upon the spot! I say, this picture sometimes appalled us, and
made us

> "rather bear those ills we had,
> Than fly to others, that we knew not of."[9]

In coming to a fixed determination to run away, we did more than Patrick
Henry,[1] when he resolved upon liberty or death. With us it was a doubtful
liberty at most, and almost certain death if we failed. For my part, I should
prefer death to hopeless bondage.

Sandy, one of our number, gave up the notion, but still encouraged us.
Our company then consisted of Henry Harris, John Harris, Henry Bailey,
Charles Roberts, and myself. Henry Bailey was my uncle, and belonged to
my master. Charles married my aunt: he belonged to my master's father-in-
law, Mr. William Hamilton.

The plan we finally concluded upon was, to get a large canoe belonging
to Mr. Hamilton, and upon the Saturday night previous to Easter holidays,
paddle directly up the Chesapeake Bay. On our arrival at the head of the
bay, a distance of seventy or eighty miles from where we lived, it was our
purpose to turn our canoe adrift, and follow the guidance of the north star
till we got beyond the limits of Maryland. Our reason for taking the water
route was, that we were less liable to be suspected as runaways; we hoped
to be regarded as fishermen; whereas, if we should take the land route, we
should be subjected to interruptions of almost every kind. Any one having a
white face, and being so disposed, could stop us, and subject us to examination.

The week before our intended start, I wrote several protections, one for
each of us. As well as I can remember, they were in the following words, to
wit:—

> "This is to certify that I, the undersigned, have given the bearer, my
> servant, full liberty to go to Baltimore, and spend the Easter holidays.
> Written with mine own hand, &c., 1835.
>
> "WILLIAM HAMILTON,
> "Near St. Michael's, in Talbot county, Maryland."

We were not going to Baltimore; but, in going up the bay, we went toward
Baltimore, and these protections were only intended to protect us while on
the bay.

As the time drew near for our departure, our anxiety became more and
more intense. It was truly a matter of life and death with us. The strength
of our determination was about to be fully tested. At this time, I was very
active in explaining every difficulty, removing every doubt, dispelling every
fear, and inspiring all with the firmness indispensable to success in our

9. Shakespeare's *Hamlet* 3.1.81–82: "rather bear those ills we have, / Than fly to others, that we know not
of."   1. American statesman and orator (1736–1799) whose most famous utterance was "Give me liberty
or give me death."

undertaking; assuring them that half was gained the instant we made the move; we had talked long enough; we were now ready to move; if not now, we never should be; and if we did not intend to move now, we had as well fold our arms, sit down, and acknowledge ourselves fit only to be slaves. This, none of us were prepared to acknowledge. Every man stood firm; and at our last meeting, we pledged ourselves afresh, in the most solemn manner, that, at the time appointed, we would certainly start in pursuit of freedom. This was in the middle of the week, at the end of which we were to be off. We went, as usual, to our several fields of labor, but with bosoms highly agitated with thoughts of our truly hazardous undertaking. We tried to conceal our feelings as much as possible; and I think we succeeded very well.

After a painful waiting, the Saturday morning, whose night was to witness our departure, came. I hailed it with joy, bring what of sadness it might. Friday night was a sleepless one for me. I was, by common consent, at the head of the whole affair. The responsibility of success or failure lay heavily upon me. The glory of the one, and the confusion of the other, were alike mine. The first two hours of that morning were such as I never experienced before, and hope never to again. Early in the morning, we went, as usual, to the field. We were spreading manure; and all at once, while thus engaged, I was overwhelmed with an indescribable feeling, in the fulness of which I turned to Sandy, who was near by, and said, "We are betrayed!" "Well," said he, "that thought has this moment struck me." We said no more. I was never more certain of any thing.

The horn was blown as usual, and we went up from the field to the house for breakfast. I went for the form, more than for want of any thing to eat that morning. Just as I got to the house, in looking out at the lane gate, I saw four white men, with two colored men. The white men were on horseback, and the colored ones were walking behind, as if tied. I watched them a few moments till they got up to our lane gate. Here they halted, and tied the colored men to the gate-post. I was not yet certain as to what the matter was. In a few moments, in rode Mr. Hamilton, with a speed betokening great excitement. He came to the door, and inquired if Master William was in. He was told he was at the barn. Mr. Hamilton, without dismounting, rode up to the barn with extraordinary speed. In a few moments, he and Mr. Freeland returned to the house. By this time, the three constables rode up, and in great haste dismounted, tied their horses, and met Master William and Mr. Hamilton returning from the barn; and after talking awhile, they all walked up to the kitchen door. There was no one in the kitchen but myself and John. Henry and Sandy were up at the barn. Mr. Freeland put his head in at the door, and called me by name, saying, there were some gentlemen at the door who wished to see me. I stepped to the door, and inquired what they wanted. They at once seized me, and, without giving me any satisfaction, tied me—lashing my hands closely together. I insisted upon knowing what the matter was. They at length said, that they had learned I had been in a "scrape," and that I was to be examined before my master; and if their information proved false, I should not be hurt.

In a few moments, they succeeded in tying John. They then turned to Henry, who had by this time returned, and commanded him to cross his hands. "I won't!" said Henry, in a firm tone, indicating his readiness to meet the consequences of his refusal. "Won't you?" said Tom Graham, the constable. "No, I won't!" said Henry, in a still stronger tone. With this, two of the constables pulled out their shining pistols, and swore, by their Creator, that they would make him cross his hands or kill him. Each cocked his pistol, and, with fingers on the trigger, walked up to Henry, saying, at the same time, if he did not cross his hands, they would blow his damned heart out. "Shoot me, shoot me!" said Henry; "you can't kill me but once. Shoot, shoot,—and be damned! *I won't be tied!*" This he said in a tone of loud defiance; and at the same time, with a motion as quick as lightning, he with one single stroke dashed the pistols from the hand of each constable. As he did this, all hands fell upon him, and, after beating him some time, they finally overpowered him, and got him tied.

During the scuffle, I managed, I know not how, to get my pass out, and, without being discovered, put it into the fire. We were all now tied; and just as we were to leave for Easton jail, Betsy Freeland, mother of William Free-land, came to the door with her hands full of biscuits, and divided them between Henry and John. She then delivered herself of a speech, to the following effect:—addressing herself to me, she said, *"You devil! You yellow devil!* it was you that put it into the heads of Henry and John to run away. But for you, you long-legged mulatto devil! Henry nor John would never have thought of such a thing." I made no reply, and was immediately hurried off towards St. Michael's. Just a moment previous to the scuffle with Henry, Mr. Hamilton suggested the propriety of making a search for the protections which he had understood Frederick had written for himself and the rest. But, just at the moment he was about carrying his proposal into effect, his aid was needed in helping to tie Henry; and the excitement attending the scuffle caused them either to forget, or to deem it unsafe, under the circumstances, to search. So we were not yet convicted of the intention to run away.

When we got about half way to St. Michael's, while the constables having us in charge were looking ahead, Henry inquired of me what he should do with his pass. I told him to eat it with his biscuit, and own nothing; and we passed the word around, *"Own nothing"*; and *"Own nothing!"* said we all. Our confidence in each other was unshaken. We were resolved to succeed or fail together, after the calamity had befallen us as much as before. We were now prepared for any thing. We were to be dragged that morning fifteen miles behind horses, and then to be placed in the Easton jail. When we reached St. Michael's, we underwent a sort of examination. We all denied that we ever intended to run away. We did this more to bring out the evidence against us, than from any hope of getting clear of being sold; for, as I have said, we were ready for that. The fact was, we cared but little where we went, so we went together. Our greatest concern was about separation. We dreaded that more than any thing this side of death. We found the evidence against us to be the testimony of one person; our master would not tell who it was; but we came to a unanimous decision among ourselves as to who their informant was. We were sent off to the jail at Easton. When we got there, we were delivered up to the sheriff, Mr. Joseph Graham, and by him placed in jail. Henry, John, and myself, were placed in one room together—Charles, and Henry Bailey, in another. Their object in separating us was to hinder concert.

We had been in jail scarcely twenty minutes, when a swarm of slave traders, and agents for slave traders, flocked into jail to look at us, and to ascertain if we were for sale. Such a set of beings I never saw before! I felt myself surrounded by so many fiends from perdition. A band of pirates never looked more like their father, the devil. They laughed and grinned over us, saying, "Ah, my boys! we have got you, haven't we?" And after taunting us in various ways, they one by one went into an examination of us, with intent to ascertain our value. They would impudently ask us if we would not like to have them for our masters. We would make them no answer, and leave them to find out as best they could. Then they would curse and swear at us, telling us that they could take the devil out of us in a very little while, if we were only in their hands.

While in jail, we found ourselves in much more comfortable quarters than we expected when we went there. We did not get much to eat, nor that which was very good; but we had a good clean room, from the windows of which we could see what was going on in the street, which was very much better than though we had been placed in one of the dark, damp cells. Upon the whole, we got along very well, so far as the jail and its keeper were concerned. Immediately after the holidays were over, contrary to all our expectations, Mr. Hamilton and Mr. Freeland came up to Easton, and took Charles, the two Henrys, and John, out of jail, and carried them home, leaving me alone. I regarded this separation as a final one. It caused me more pain than any thing else in the whole transaction. I was ready for any thing rather than separation. I supposed that they had consulted together, and had decided that, as I was the whole cause of the intention of the others to run away, it was hard to make the innocent suffer with the guilty; and that they had, therefore, concluded to take the others home, and sell me, as a warning to the others that remained. It is due to the noble Henry to say, he seemed almost as reluctant at leaving the prison as at leaving home to come to the prison. But we knew we should, in all probability, be separated, if we were sold; and since he was in their hands, he concluded to go peaceably home.

I was now left to my fate. I was all alone, and within the walls of a stone prison. But a few days before, and I was full of hope. I expected to have been safe in a land of freedom; but now I was covered with gloom, sunk down to the utmost despair. I thought the possibility of freedom was gone. I was kept in this way about one week, at the end of which, Captain Auld, my master, to my surprise and utter astonishment, came up, and took me out, with the intention of sending me, with a gentleman of his acquaintance, into Alabama. But, from some cause or other, he did not send me to Alabama, but concluded to send me back to Baltimore, to live again with his brother Hugh, and to learn a trade.

Thus, after an absence of three years and one month, I was once more permitted to return to my old home at Baltimore. My master sent me away, because there existed against me a very great prejudice in the community, and he feared I might be killed.

In a few weeks after I went to Baltimore, Master Hugh hired me to Mr. William Gardner, an extensive ship-builder, on Fell's Point. I was put there to learn how to calk. It, however, proved a very unfavorable place for the accomplishment of this object. Mr. Gardner was engaged that spring in building two large man-of-war brigs, professedly for the Mexican government. The vessels were to be launched in the July of that year, and in failure thereof, Mr. Gardner was to lose a considerable sum; so that when I entered, all was hurry. There was no time to learn any thing. Every man had to do that which he knew how to do. In entering the shipyard, my orders from Mr. Gardner were, to do whatever the carpenters commanded me to do. This was placing me at the beck and call of about seventy-five men. I was to regard all these as masters. Their word was to be my law. My situation was a most trying one. At times I needed a dozen pair of hands. I was called a dozen ways in the space of a single minute. Three or four voices would strike my ear at the same moment. It was—"Fred., come help me to cant this timber here."—"Fred., come carry this timber yonder."—"Fred., bring that roller here."—"Fred., go get a fresh can of water."—"Fred., come help saw off the end of this timber."—"Fred., go quick, and get the crowbar."—"Fred., hold on the end of this fall."—"Fred., go to the blacksmith's shop, and get a new punch."—"Hurra,[2] Fred.! run and bring me a cold chisel."—"I say, Fred., bear a hand, and get up a fire as quick as lightning under that steam-box."— "Halloo, nigger! come, turn this grindstone."—"Come, come! move, move! and *bowse*[3] this timber forward."—"I say, darky, blast your eyes, why don't you heat up some pitch?"—"Halloo! halloo! halloo!" (Three voices at the same time.) "Come here!—Go there!—Hold on where you are! Damn you, if you move, I'll knock your brains out!"

This was my school for eight months, and I might have remained there longer, but for a most horrid fight I had with four of the white apprentices, in which my left eye was nearly knocked out, and I was horribly mangled in other respects. The facts in the case were these: Until a very little while after I went there, white and black ship-carpenters worked side by side, and no one seemed to see any impropriety in it. All hands seemed to be very well satisfied. Many of the black carpenters were freemen. Things seemed to be going on very well. All at once, the white carpenters knocked off, and said they would not work with free colored workmen. Their reason for this, as alleged, was, that if free colored carpenters were encouraged, they would soon take the trade into their own hands, and poor white men would be thrown out of employment. They therefore felt called upon at once to put a stop to it. And, taking advantage of Mr. Gardner's necessities, they broke off, swearing they would work no longer, unless he would discharge his black carpenters. Now, though this did not extend to me in form, it did reach me in fact. My fellow-apprentices very soon began to feel it degrading to them to work with me. They began to put on airs, and talk about the "niggers" taking the country, saying we all ought to be killed; and, being encouraged by the journeymen, they commenced making my condition as hard as they could, by hectoring me around, and sometimes striking me. I, of course, kept the vow I made after the fight with Mr. Covey, and struck back again, regardless of consequences; and while I kept them from combining, I succeeded very well; for I could whip the whole of them, taking them separately. They, however, at length combined, and came upon me, armed with sticks, stones, and heavy handspikes. One came in front with a half brick. There was one at each side of me, and one behind me. While I was attending to those in front, and on either side, the one behind ran up with the handspike, and struck me a heavy blow upon the head. It stunned me. I fell, and with this they all ran upon me, and fell to beating me with their fists. I let them lay on for a while, gathering strength. In an instant, I gave a sudden surge, and

2. Hurry.   3. Lift or haul (usually with the help of block and tackle.)

rose to my hands and knees. Just as I did that, one of their number gave me, with his heavy boot, a powerful kick in the left eye. My eyeball seemed to have burst. When they saw my eye closed, and badly swollen, they left me. With this I seized the handspike, and for a time pursued them. But here the carpenters interfered, and I thought I might as well give it up. It was impossible to stand my hand against so many. All this took place in sight of not less than fifty white ship-carpenters, and not one interposed a friendly word; but some cried, "Kill the damned nigger! Kill him! kill him! He struck a white person." I found my only chance for life was in flight. I succeeded in getting away without an additional blow, and barely so; for to strike a white man is death by Lynch law,—and that was the law in Mr. Gardner's ship-yard; nor is there much of any other out of Mr. Gardner's ship-yard.

I went directly home, and told the story of my wrongs to Master Hugh; and I am happy to say of him, irreligious as he was, his conduct was heavenly, compared with that of his brother Thomas under similar circumstances. He listened attentively to my narration of the circumstances leading to the savage outrage, and gave many proofs of his strong indignation of it. The heart of my once overkind mistress was again melted into pity. My puffed-out eye and blood-covered face moved her to tears. She took a chair by me, washed the blood from my face, and, with a mother's tenderness, bound up my head, covering the wounded eye with a lean piece of fresh beef. It was almost compensation for my suffering to witness, once more, a manifestation of kindness from this, my once affectionate old mistress. Master Hugh was very much enraged. He gave expression to his feelings by pouring out curses upon the heads of those who did the deed. As soon as I got a little the better of my bruises, he took me with him to Esquire Watson's, on Bond Street, to see what could be done about the matter. Mr. Watson inquired who saw the assault committed. Master Hugh told him it was done in Mr. Gardner's ship-yard, at midday, where there were a large company of men at work. "As to that," he said, "the deed was done, and there was no question as to who did it." His answer was, he could do nothing in the case, unless some white man would come forward and testify. He could issue no warrant on my word. If I had been killed in the presence of a thousand colored people, their testimony combined would have been insufficient to have arrested one of the murderers. Master Hugh, for once, was compelled to say this state of things was too bad. Of course, it was impossible to get any white man to volunteer his testimony in my behalf, and against the white young men. Even those who may have sympathized with me were not prepared to do this. It required a degree of courage unknown to them to do so; for just at that time, the slightest manifestation of humanity toward a colored person was denounced as abolitionism, and that name subjected its bearer to frightful liabilities. The watchwords of the bloody-minded in that region, and in those days, were, "Damn the abolitionists!" and "Damn the niggers!" There was nothing done, and probably nothing would have been done if I had been killed. Such was, and such remains, the state of things in the Christian city of Baltimore.

Master Hugh, finding he could get no redress, refused to let me go back again to Mr. Gardner. He kept me himself, and his wife dressed my wound till I was again restored to health. He then took me into the ship-yard of which he was foreman, in the employment of Mr. Walter Price. There I was immediately set to calking, and very soon learned the art of using my mallet and irons. In the course of one year from the time I left Mr. Gardner's, I was able to command the highest wages given to the most experienced calkers. I was now of some importance to my master. I was bringing him from six to seven dollars per week. I sometimes brought him nine dollars per week: my wages were a dollar and a half a day. After learning how to calk, I sought my own employment, made my own contracts, and collected the money which I earned. My pathway became much more smooth than before; my condition was now much more comfortable. When I could get no calking to do, I did nothing. During these leisure times, those old notions about freedom would steal over me again. When in Mr. Gardner's employment, I was kept in such a perpetual whirl of excitement, I could think of nothing, scarcely, but my life; and in thinking of my life, I almost forgot my liberty. I have observed this in my experience of slavery,—that whenever my condition was improved, instead of its increasing my contentment, it only increased my desire to be free, and set me to thinking of plans to gain my freedom. I have found that, to make a contented slave, it is necessary to make a thoughtless one. It is necessary to darken his moral and mental vision, and, as far as possible, to annihilate the power of reason. He must be made to feel that slavery is right; and he can be brought to that only when he ceases to be a man.

I was now getting, as I have said, one dollar and fifty cents per day. I contracted for it; I earned it; it was paid to me; it was rightfully my own; yet, upon each returning Saturday night, I was compelled to deliver every cent of that money to Master Hugh. And why? Not because he earned it,—not because he had any hand in earning it,—not because I owed it to him,—nor because he possessed the slightest shadow of a right to it; but solely because he had the power to compel me to give it up. The right of the grim-visaged pirate upon the high seas is exactly the same.

CHAPTER XI

I now come to that part of my life during which I planned, and finally succeeded in making, my escape from slavery. But before narrating any of the peculiar circumstances, I deem it proper to make known my intention not to state all the facts connected with the transaction. My reasons for pursuing this course may be understood from the following: First, were I to give a minute statement of all the facts, it is not only possible, but quite probable, that others would thereby be involved in the most embarrassing difficulties. Secondly, such a statement would most undoubtedly induce greater vigilance on the part of slaveholders than has existed heretofore among them; which would, of course, be the means of guarding a door whereby some dear brother bondman might escape his galling chains. I deeply regret the necessity that impels me to suppress any thing of importance connected with my experience in slavery. It would afford me great pleasure indeed, as well as materially add to the interest of my narrative, were I at liberty to gratify a curiosity, which I know exists in the minds of many, by an accurate statement of all the facts pertaining to my most fortunate escape. But I must deprive myself of this pleasure, and the curious of the gratification which such a statement would afford. I would allow myself to suffer under the greatest imputations which evil-minded men might suggest, rather than exculpate myself, and thereby run the hazard of closing the slightest avenue by which a brother slave might clear himself of the chains and fetters of slavery.

I have never approved of the very public manner in which some of our western friends have conducted what they call the *underground railroad*,[4] but which, I think, by their open declarations, has been made most emphatically the *upperground railroad*. I honor those good men and women for their noble daring, and applaud them for willingly subjecting themselves to bloody persecution, by openly avowing their participation in the escape of slaves. I, however, can see very little good resulting from such a course, either to themselves or the slaves escaping; while, upon the other hand, I see and feel assured that those open declarations are a positive evil to the slaves remaining, who are seeking to escape. They do nothing towards enlightening the slave, whilst they do much towards enlightening the master. They stimulate him to greater watchfulness, and enhance his power to capture his slave. We owe something to the slaves south of the line[5] as well as to those north of it; and in aiding the latter on their way to freedom, we should be careful to do nothing which would be likely to hinder the former from escaping from slavery. I would keep the merciless slaveholder profoundly ignorant of the means of flight adopted by the slave. I would leave him to imagine himself surrounded by myriads of invisible tormentors, ever ready to snatch from his infernal grasp his trembling prey. Let him be left to feel his way in the dark; let darkness commensurate with his crime hover over him; and let him feel that at every step he takes, in pursuit of the flying bondman, he is running the frightful risk of having his hot brains dashed out by an invisible agency. Let us render the tyrant no aid; let us not hold the light by which he can trace the footprints of our flying brother. But enough of this. I will now proceed to the statement of those facts, connected with my escape, for which I am alone responsible, and for which no one can be made to suffer but myself.

In the early part of the year 1838, I became quite restless. I could see no reason why I should, at the end of each week, pour the reward of my toil into the purse of my master. When I carried to him my weekly wages, he would, after counting the money, look me in the face with a robber-like fierceness, and ask, "Is this all?" He was satisfied with nothing less than the last cent. He would, however, when I made him six dollars, sometimes give me six cents, to encourage me. It had the opposite effect. I regarded it as a sort of admission of my right to the whole. The fact that he gave me any part of my wages was proof, to my mind, that he believed me entitled to the whole of them. I always felt worse for having received any thing; for I feared that the giving me a few cents would ease his conscience, and make him feel himself to be a pretty honorable sort of robber. My discontent grew upon me. I was ever on the look-out for means of escape; and, finding no direct means, I determined to try to hire my time, with a view of getting money with which to make my escape. In the spring of 1838, when Master Thomas came to Baltimore to purchase his spring goods, I got an opportunity, and applied to him to allow me to hire my time. He unhesitatingly refused my request, and told me this was another stratagem by which to escape. He told

4. A system set up by opponents of slavery to help fugitive slaves from the South escape to free states and to Canada.   5. The Mason-Dixon Line, the boundary between Pennsylvania and Maryland and between slave and free states.

me I could go nowhere but that he could get me; and that, in the event of my running away, he should spare no pains in his efforts to catch me. He exhorted me to content myself, and be obedient. He told me, if I would be happy, I must lay out no plans for the future. He said, if I behaved myself properly, he would take care of me. Indeed, he advised me to complete thoughtlessness of the future, and taught me to depend solely upon him for happiness. He seemed to see fully the pressing necessity of setting aside my intellectual nature, in order to [insure] contentment in slavery. But in spite of him, and even in spite of myself, I continued to think, and to think about the injustice of my enslavement, and the means of escape.

About two months after this, I applied to Master Hugh for the privilege of hiring my time. He was not acquainted with the fact that I had applied to Master Thomas, and had been refused. He too, at first, seemed disposed to refuse; but, after some reflection, he granted me the privilege, and proposed the following terms: I was to be allowed all my time, make all contracts with those for whom I worked, and find my own employment; and, in return for this liberty, I was to pay him three dollars at the end of each week; find myself in calking tools, and in board and clothing. My board was two dollars and a half per week. This, with the wear and tear of clothing and calking tools, made my regular expenses about six dollars per week. This amount I was compelled to make up, or relinquish the privilege of hiring my time. Rain or shine, work or no work, at the end of each week the money must be forthcoming, or I must give up my privilege. This arrangement, it will be perceived, was decidedly in my master's favor. It relieved him of all need of looking after me. His money was sure. He received all the benefits of slave-holding without its evils; while I endured all the evils of a slave, and suffered all the care and anxiety of a freeman. I found it a hard bargain. But, hard as it was, I thought it better than the old mode of getting along. It was a step towards freedom to be allowed to bear the responsibilities of a freeman, and I was determined to hold on upon it. I bent myself to the work of making money. I was ready to work at night as well as day, and by the most untiring perseverance and industry, I made enough to meet my expenses, and lay up a little money every week. I went on thus from May till August. Master Hugh then refused to allow me to hire my time longer. The ground for his refusal was a failure on my part, one Saturday night, to pay him for my week's time. This failure was occasioned by my attending a camp meeting about ten miles from Baltimore. During the week, I had entered into an engagement with a number of young friends to start from Baltimore to the camp ground early Saturday evening; and being detained by my employer, I was unable to get down to Master Hugh's without disappointing the company. I knew that Master Hugh was in no special need of the money that night. I therefore decided to go to camp meeting, and upon my return pay him the three dollars. I staid at the camp meeting one day longer than I intended when I left. But as soon as I returned, I called upon him to pay him what he con-sidered his due. I found him very angry; he could scarce restrain his wrath. He said he had a great mind to give me a severe whipping. He wished to know how I dared go out of the city without asking his permission. I told him I hired my time, and while I paid him the price which he asked for it, I did not know that I was bound to ask him when and where I should go. This reply troubled him; and, after reflecting a few moments, he turned to me, and said I should hire my time no longer; that the next thing he should know of, I would be running away. Upon the same plea, he told me to bring my tools and clothing home forthwith. I did so; but instead of seeking work, as I had been accustomed to do previously to hiring my time, I spent the whole week without the performance of a single stroke of work. I did this in retaliation. Saturday night, he called upon me as usual for my week's wages. I told him I had no wages; I had done no work that week. Here we were upon the point of coming to blows. He raved, and swore his determination to get hold of me. I did not allow myself a single word; but was resolved, if he laid the weight of his hand upon me, it should be blow for blow. He did not strike me, but told me that he would find me in constant employment in future. I thought the matter over during the next day, Sunday, and finally resolved upon the third day of September, as the day upon which I would make a second attempt to secure my freedom. I now had three weeks during which to prepare for my journey. Early on Monday morning, before Master Hugh had time to make any engagement for me, I went out and got employment of Mr. Butler, at his ship-yard near the draw-bridge, upon what is called the City Block, thus making it unnecessary for him to seek employment for me. At the end of the week, I brought him between eight and nine dollars. He seemed very well pleased, and asked me why I did not do the same the week before. He little knew what my plans were. My object in working steadily was to remove any suspicion he might entertain of my intent to run away; and in this I succeeded admirably. I suppose he thought I was never better satisfied with my condition than at the very time during which I was planning my escape. The second week passed, and again I carried him my full wages; and so well pleased was he, that he gave me twenty-five cents, (quite a large sum for a slaveholder to give a slave,) and bade me to make a good use of it. I told him I would.

Things went on without very smoothly indeed, but within there was trouble. It is impossible for me to describe my feelings as the time of my contemplated start drew near. I had a number of warm-hearted friends in Baltimore,—friends that I loved almost as I did my life,—and the thought of being separated from them forever was painful beyond expression. It is my opinion that thousands would escape from slavery, who now remain, but for the strong cords of affection that bind them to their friends. The thought of leaving my friends was decidedly the most painful thought with which I had to contend. The love of them was my tender point, and shook my decision more than all things else. Besides the pain of separation, the dread and apprehension of a failure exceeded what I had experienced at my first attempt. The appalling defeat I then sustained returned to torment me. I felt assured that, if I failed in this attempt, my case would be a hopeless one—it would seal my fate as a slave forever. I could not hope to get off with any thing less than the severest punishment, and being placed beyond the means of escape. It required no very vivid imagination to depict the most frightful scenes through which I should have to pass, in case I failed. The wretchedness of slavery, and the blessedness of freedom, were perpetually before me. It was life and death with me. But I remained firm, and, according to my resolution, on the third day of September, 1838, I left my chains, and succeeded in reaching New York without the slightest interruption of any kind. How I did so,—what means I adopted,—what direction I travelled, and by what mode of conveyance,—I must leave unexplained, for the reasons before mentioned.

I have been frequently asked how I felt when I found myself in a free State. I have never been able to answer the question with any satisfaction to myself. It was a moment of the highest excitement I ever experienced. I suppose I felt as one may imagine the unarmed mariner to feel when he is rescued by a friendly man-of-war from the pursuit of a pirate. In writing to a dear friend, immediately after my arrival at New York, I said I felt like one who had escaped a den of hungry lions. This state of mind, however, very soon subsided; and I was again seized with a feeling of great insecurity and loneliness. I was yet liable to be taken back, and subjected to all the tortures of slavery. This in itself was enough to damp the ardor of my enthusiasm. But the loneliness overcame me. There I was in the midst of thousands, and yet a perfect stranger; without home and without friends, in the midst of thousands of my own brethren—children of a common Father, and yet I dared not to unfold to any one of them my sad condition. I was afraid to speak to any one for fear of speaking to the wrong one, and thereby falling into the hands of money-loving kidnappers, whose business it was to lie in wait for the panting fugitive, as the ferocious beasts of the forest lie in wait for their prey. The motto which I adopted when I started from slavery was this—"Trust no man!" I saw in every white man an enemy, and in almost every colored man cause for distrust. It was a most painful situation; and, to understand it, one must needs experience it, or imagine himself in similar circumstances. Let him be a fugitive slave in a strange land—a land given up to be the hunting-ground for slaveholders—whose inhabitants are legalized kidnappers—where he is every moment subjected to the terrible liability of being seized upon by his fellow-men, as the hideous crocodile seizes upon his prey!—I say, let him place himself in my situation—without home or friends—without money or credit—wanting shelter, and no one to give it—wanting bread, and no money to buy it,—and at the same time let him feel that he is pursued by merciless men-hunters, and in total darkness as to what to do, where to go, or where to stay,—perfectly helpless both as to the means of defence and means of escape,—in the midst of plenty, yet suffering the terrible gnawings of hunger,—in the midst of houses, yet having no home,—among fellow-men, yet feeling as if in the midst of wild beasts, whose greediness to swallow up the trembling and half-famished fugitive is only equalled by that with which the monsters of the deep swallow up the helpless fish upon which they subsist,—I say, let him be placed in this most trying situation,—the situation in which I was placed,—then, and not till then, will he fully appreciate the hardships of, and know how to sympathize with, the toil-worn and whip-scarred fugitive slave.

Thank Heaven, I remained but a short time in this distressed situation. I was relieved from it by the humane hand of Mr. DAVID RUGGLES,[6] whose vigilance, kindness, and perseverance, I shall never forget. I am glad of an opportunity to express, as far as words can, the love and gratitude I bear him. Mr. Ruggles is now afflicted with blindness, and is himself in need of the same kind offices which he was once so forward in the performance of toward others. I had been in New York but a few days, when Mr. Ruggles sought

6. A black abolitionist (1810–1849), at this time living in New York, who helped many slaves to escape.

me out, and very kindly took me to his boarding-house at the corner of Church and Lespenard Streets. Mr. Ruggles was then very deeply engaged in the memorable *Darg* case, as well as attending to a number of other fugitive slaves, devising ways and means for their successful escape; and, though watched and hemmed in on almost every side, he seemed to be more than a match for his enemies. Very soon after I went to Mr. Ruggles, he wished to know of me where I wanted to go; as he deemed it unsafe for me to remain in New York. I told him I was a calker, and should like to go where I could get work. I thought of going to Canada; but he decided against it, and in favor of my going to New Bedford, thinking I should be able to get work there at my trade. At this time, Anna,[7] my intended wife, came on; for I wrote to her immediately after my arrival at New York, (notwithstanding my homeless, houseless, and helpless condition,) informing her of my successful flight, and wishing her to come on forthwith. In a few days after her arrival, Mr. Ruggles called in the Rev. J. W. C. Pennington, who, in the presence of Mr. Ruggles, Mrs. Michaels, and two or three others, performed the marriage ceremony, and gave us a certificate, of which the following is an exact copy:—

"THIS may certify, that I joined together in holy matrimony Frederick Johnson[8] and Anna Murray, as man and wife, in the presence of Mr. David Ruggles and Mrs. Michaels.

"JAMES W. C. PENNINGTON.

"*New York, Sept.* 15, 1838."

Upon receiving this certificate, and a five-dollar bill from Mr. Ruggles, I shouldered one part of our baggage, and Anna took up the other, and we set out forthwith to take passage on board of the steamboat John W. Richmond for Newport, on our way to New Bedford. Mr. Ruggles gave me a letter to a Mr. Shaw in Newport, and told me, in case my money did not serve me to New Bedford, to stop in Newport and obtain further assistance; but upon our arrival at Newport, we were so anxious to get to a place of safety, that, notwithstanding we lacked the necessary money to pay our fare, we decided to take seats in the stage, and promise to pay when we got to New Bedford. We were encouraged to do this by two excellent gentlemen, residents of New Bedford, whose names I afterward ascertained to be Joseph Ricketson and William C. Taber. They seemed at once to understand our circumstances, and gave us such assurance of their friendliness as put us fully at ease in their presence. It was good indeed to meet with such friends, at such a time. Upon reaching New Bedford, we were directed to the house of Mr. Nathan Johnson, by whom we were kindly received, and hospitably provided for. Both Mr. and Mrs. Johnson took a deep and lively interest in our welfare. They proved themselves quite worthy of the name of abolitionists. When the stage-driver found us unable to pay our fare, he held on upon our baggage as security for the debt. I had but to mention the fact to Mr. Johnson, and he forthwith advanced the money.

We now began to feel a degree of safety, and to prepare ourselves for the duties and responsibilities of a life of freedom. On the morning after our

7. She was free [Douglass's note].   8. I had changed my name from Frederick *Bailey* to that of *Johnson* [Douglass's note].

arrival at New Bedford, while at the breakfast-table, the question arose as to what name I should be called by. The name given me by my mother was, "Frederick Augustus Washington Bailey." I, however, had dispensed with the two middle names long before I left Maryland so that I was generally known by the name of "Frederick Bailey." I started from Baltimore bearing the name of "Stanley." When I got to New York, I again changed my name to "Frederick Johnson," and thought that would be the last change. But when I got to New Bedford, I found it necessary again to change my name. The reason of this necessity was, that there were so many Johnsons in New Bedford, it was already quite difficult to distinguish between them. I gave Mr. Johnson the privilege of choosing me a name, but told him he must not take from me the name of "Frederick." I must hold on to that, to preserve a sense of my identity. Mr. Johnson had just been reading the "Lady of the Lake,"[9] and at once suggested that my name be "Douglass." From that time until now I have been called "Frederick Douglass;" and as I am more widely known by that name than by either of the others, I shall continue to use it as my own.

I was quite disappointed at the general appearance of things in New Bedford. The impression which I had received respecting the character and condition of the people of the north, I found to be singularly erroneous. I had very strangely supposed, while in slavery, that few of the comforts, and scarcely any of the luxuries, of life were enjoyed at the north, compared with what were enjoyed by the slaveholders of the south. I probably came to this conclusion from the fact that northern people owned no slaves. I supposed that they were about upon a level with the non-slaveholding population of the south. I knew *they* were exceedingly poor, and I had been accustomed to regard their poverty as the necessary consequence of their being non-slaveholders. I had somehow imbibed the opinion that, in the absence of slaves, there could be no wealth, and very little refinement. And upon coming to the north, I expected to meet with a rough, hard-handed, and uncultivated population, living in the most Spartan-like simplicity, knowing nothing of the ease, luxury, pomp, and grandeur of southern slaveholders. Such being my conjectures, any one acquainted with the appearance of New Bedford may very readily infer how palpably I must have seen my mistake.

In the afternoon of the day when I reached New Bedford, I visited the wharves, to take a view of the shipping. Here I found myself surrounded with the strongest proofs of wealth. Lying at the wharves, and riding in the stream, I saw many ships of the finest model, in the best order, and of the largest size. Upon the right and left, I was walled in by granite warehouses of the widest dimensions, stowed to their utmost capacity with the necessaries and comforts of life. Added to this, almost every body seemed to be at work, but noiselessly so, compared with what I had been accustomed to in Baltimore. There were no loud songs heard from those engaged in loading and unloading ships. I heard no deep oaths or horrid curses on the laborer. I saw no whipping of men; but all seemed to go smoothly on. Every man appeared to understand his work, and went at it with a sober, yet cheerful earnestness, which betokened the deep interest which he felt in what he was doing, as well as a sense of his own dignity as a man. To me this looked exceedingly strange. From the wharves I strolled around and over the town, gazing with

9. A narrative poem by Sir Walter Scott (1810) about the fortunes of the Douglas clan in Scotland.

wonder and admiration at the splendid churches, beautiful dwellings, and finely-cultivated gardens; evincing an amount of wealth, comfort, taste, and refinement, such as I had never seen in any part of slaveholding Maryland.

Every thing looked clean, new, and beautiful. I saw few or no dilapidated houses, with poverty-stricken inmates; no half-naked children and bare-footed women, such as I had been accustomed to see in Hillsborough, Easton, St. Michael's, and Baltimore. The people looked more able, stronger, healthier, and happier, than those of Maryland. I was for once made glad by a view of extreme wealth, without being saddened by seeing extreme poverty. But the most astonishing as well as the most interesting thing to me was the condition of the colored people, a great many of whom, like myself, had escaped thither as a refuge from the hunters of men. I found many, who had not been seven years out of their chains, living in finer houses, and evidently enjoying more of the comforts of life, than the average of slave-holders in Maryland. I will venture to assert that my friend Mr. Nathan Johnson (of whom I can say with a grateful heart, "I was hungry, and he gave me meat; I was thirsty, and he gave me drink; I was a stranger, and he took me in")[1] lived in a neater house; dined at a better table; took, paid for, and read, more newspapers; better understood the moral, religious, and political character of the nation,—than nine tenths of the slaveholders in Talbot county Maryland. Yet Mr. Johnson was a working man. His hands were hardened by toil, and not his alone, but those also of Mrs. Johnson. I found the colored people much more spirited than I had supposed they would be. I found among them a determination to protect each other from the blood-thirsty kidnapper, at all hazards. Soon after my arrival, I was told of a circumstance which illustrated their spirit. A colored man and a fugitive slave were on unfriendly terms. The former was heard to threaten the latter with informing his master of his whereabouts. Straightway a meeting was called among the colored people, under the stereotyped notice, "Business of importance!" The betrayer was invited to attend. The people came at the appointed hour, and organized the meeting by appointing a very religious old gentleman as president, who, I believe, made a prayer, after which he addressed the meeting as follows: *"Friends, we have got him here, and I would recommend that you young men just take him outside the door, and kill him!"* With this, a number of them bolted at him; but they were intercepted by some more timid than them-selves, and the betrayer escaped their vengeance, and has not been seen in New Bedford since. I believe there have been no more such threats, and should there be hereafter, I doubt not that death would be the consequence.

I found employment, the third day after my arrival, in stowing a sloop with a load of oil. It was new, dirty, and hard work for me; but I went at it with a glad heart and a willing hand. I was now my own master. It was a happy moment, the rapture of which can be understood only by those who have been slaves. It was the first work, the reward of which was to be entirely my own. There was no Master Hugh standing ready, the moment I earned the money, to rob me of it. I worked that day with a pleasure I had never before experienced. I was at work for myself and newly-married wife. It was to me the starting-point of a new existence. When I got through with that job, I

1. Matthew 25.35: "For I was an hungered, and ye gave me meat: I was thirsty, and ye gave me drink: I was a stranger, and ye took me in."

went in pursuit of a job of calking; but such was the strength of prejudice against color, among the white calkers, that they refused to work with me, and of course I could get no employment.[2] Finding my trade of no immediate benefit, I threw off my calking habiliments, and prepared myself to do any kind of work I could get to do. Mr. Johnson kindly let me have his wood-horse and saw, and I very soon found myself a plenty of work. There was no work too hard—none too dirty. I was ready to saw wood, shovel coal, carry the hod, sweep the chimney, or roll oil casks,—all of which I did for nearly three years in New Bedford, before I became known to the anti-slavery world.

In about four months after I went to New Bedford there came a young man to me, and inquired if I did not wish to take the "Liberator."[3] I told him I did; but, just having made my escape from slavery, I remarked that I was unable to pay for it then. I, however, finally became a subscriber to it. The paper came, and I read it from week to week with such feelings as it would be quite idle for me to attempt to describe. The paper became my meat and my drink. My soul was set all on fire. Its sympathy for my brethren in bonds—its scathing denunciations of slaveholders—its faithful exposures of slavery—and its powerful attacks upon the upholders of the institution—sent a thrill of joy through my soul, such as I had never felt before!

I had not long been a reader of the "Liberator," before I got a pretty correct idea of the principles, measures and spirit of the anti-slavery reform. I took right hold of the cause. I could do but little; but what I could, I did with a joyful heart, and never felt happier than when in an anti-slavery meeting. I seldom had much to say at the meetings, because what I wanted to say was said so much better by others. But, while attending an anti-slavery convention at Nantucket, on the 11th of August, 1841, I felt strongly moved to speak, and was at the same time much urged to do so by Mr. William C. Coffin, a gentleman who had heard me speak in the colored people's meeting at New Bedford. It was a severe cross, and I took it up reluctantly. The truth was, I felt myself a slave, and the idea of speaking to white people weighed me down. I spoke but a few moments, when I felt a degree of freedom, and said what I desired with considerable ease. From that time until now, I have been engaged in pleading the cause of my brethren—with what success, and with what devotion, I leave those acquainted with my labors to decide.

APPENDIX

I find, since reading over the foregoing Narrative, that I have, in several instances, spoken in such a tone and manner, respecting religion, as may possibly lead those unacquainted with my religious views to suppose me an opponent of all religion. To remove the liability of such misapprehension, I deem it proper to append the following brief explanation. What I have said respecting and against religion, I mean strictly to apply to the *slaveholding religion* of this land, and with no possible reference to Christianity proper; for, between the Christianity of this land, and the Christianity of Christ, I recognize the widest possible difference—so wide, that to receive the one as good, pure, and holy, is of necessity to reject the other as bad, corrupt, and

2. I am told that colored persons can now get employment at calking in New Bedford—a result of anti-slavery effort [Douglass's note].   3. William Lloyd Garrison's antislavery newspaper, which began publication in 1831.

wicked. To be the friend of the one, is of necessity to be the enemy of the other. I love the pure, peaceable, and impartial Christianity of Christ: I therefore hate the corrupt, slaveholding, women-whipping, cradle-plundering, partial and hypocritical Christianity of this land. Indeed, I can see no reason, but the most deceitful one, for calling the religion of this land Christianity. I look upon it as the climax of all misnomers, the boldest of all frauds, and the grossest of all libels. Never was there a clearer case of "stealing the livery of the court of heaven to serve the devil in." I am filled with unutterable loathing when I contemplate the religious pomp and show, together with the horrible inconsistencies, which every where surround me. We have men-stealers for ministers, women-whippers for missionaries, and cradle-plunderers for church members. The man who wields the blood-clotted cowskin during the week fills the pulpit on Sunday, and claims to be a minister of the meek and lowly Jesus. The man who robs me of my earnings at the end of each week meets me as a class-leader on Sunday morning, to show me the way of life, and the path of salvation. He who sells my sister, for purposes of prostitution, stands forth as the pious advocate of purity. He who proclaims it a religious duty to read the Bible denies me the right of learning to read the name of the God who made me. He who is the religious advocate of marriage robs whole millions of its sacred influence, and leaves them to the ravages of wholesale pollution. The warm defender of the sacredness of the family relation is the same that scatters whole families,— sundering husbands and wives, parents and children, sisters and brothers,— leaving the hut vacant, and the hearth desolate. We see the thief preaching against theft, and the adulterer against adultery. We have men sold to build churches, women sold to support the gospel, and babes sold to purchase Bibles for the *poor heathen! all for the glory of God and the good of souls!* The slave auctioneer's bell and the church-going bell chime in with each other, and the bitter cries of the heart-broken slave are drowned in the religious shouts of his pious master. Revivals of religion and revivals in the slave-trade go hand in hand together. The slave prison and the church stand near each other. The clanking of fetters and the rattling of chains in the prison, and the pious psalm and solemn prayer in the church, may be heard at the same time. The dealers in the bodies and souls of men erect their stand in the presence of the pulpit, and they mutually help each other. The dealer gives his blood-stained gold to support the pulpit, and the pulpit, in return, covers his infernal business with the garb of Christianity. Here we have religion and robbery the allies of each other—devils dressed in angels' robes, and hell presenting the semblance of paradise.

> "Just God! and these are they,
>   Who minister at thine altar, God of right!
> Men who their hands, with prayer and blessing, lay
>   On Israel's ark of light.
>
> "What! preach, and kidnap men?
>   Give thanks, and rob thy own afflicted poor?
> Talk of thy glorious liberty, and then
>   Bolt hard the captive's door?
>
> "What! servants of thy own
>   Merciful Son, who came to seek and save

> The homeless and the outcast, fettering down
> The tasked and plundered slave!
>
> "Pilate and Herod friends!
> Chief priests and rulers, as of old, combine!
> Just God and holy! is that church which lends
> Strength to the spoiler thine?"

The Christianity of America is a Christianity, of whose votaries it may be as truly said, as it was of the ancient scribes and Pharisees, "They bind heavy burdens, and grievous to be borne, and lay them on men's shoulders, but they themselves will not move them with one of their fingers. All their works they do for to be seen of men.——They love the uppermost rooms at feasts, and the chief seats in the synagogues, ... and to be called of men, Rabbi, Rabbi.——But woe unto you, scribes and Pharisees, hypocrites! for ye neither go in yourselves, neither suffer ye them that are entering to go in. Ye devour widows' houses, and for a pretence make long prayers; therefore ye shall receive the greater damnation. Ye compass sea and land to make one proselyte, and when he is made, ye make him twofold more the child of hell than yourselves.——Woe unto you, scribes and Pharisees, hypocrites! for ye pay tithe of mint, and anise, and cumin, and have omitted the weightier matters of the law, judgment, mercy, and faith; these ought ye to have done, and not to leave the other undone. Ye blind guides! which strain at a gnat, and swallow a camel. Woe unto you, scribes and Pharisees, hypocrites! for ye make clean the outside of the cup and of the platter; but within, they are full of extortion and excess.——Woe unto you, scribes and Pharisees, hypocrites! for ye are like unto whited sepulchres, which indeed appear beautiful outward, but are within full of dead men's bones, and of all uncleanness. Even so ye also outwardly appear righteous unto men, but within ye are full of hypocrisy and iniquity."[4]

Dark and terrible as is this picture, I hold it to be strictly true of the overwhelming mass of professed Christians in America. They strain at a gnat, and swallow a camel. Could any thing be more true of our churches? They would be shocked at the proposition of fellowshipping a *sheep*-stealer; and at the same time they hug to their communion a *man*-stealer, and brand me with being an infidel, if I find fault with them for it. They attend with Pharisaical strictness to the outward forms of religion, and at the same time neglect the weightier matters of the law, judgment, mercy, and faith. They are always ready to sacrifice, but seldom to show mercy. They are they who are represented as professing to love God whom they have not seen, whilst they hate their brother whom they have seen. They love the heathen on the other side of the globe. They can pray for him, pay money to have the Bible put into his hand, and missionaries to instruct him; while they despise and totally neglect the heathen at their own doors.

Such is, very briefly, my view of the religion of this land; and to avoid any misunderstanding, growing out of the use of general terms, I mean, by the religion of this land, that which is revealed in the words, deeds, and actions, of those bodies, north and south, calling themselves Christian churches, and yet in union with slaveholders. It is against religion, as presented by these bodies, that I have felt it my duty to testify.

---

4. Matthew 23.

I conclude these remarks by copying the following portrait of the religion of the south, (which is, by communion and fellowship, the religion of the north) which I soberly affirm is "true to the life," and without caricature or the slightest exaggeration. It is said to have been drawn, several years before the present anti-slavery agitation began, by a northern Methodist preacher, who, while residing at the south, had an opportunity to see slaveholding morals, manners, and piety, with his own eyes. "Shall I not visit for these things? saith the Lord. Shall not my soul be avenged on such a nation as this?"[5]

"A Parody.

"Come, saints and sinners, hear me tell
How pious priests whip Jack and Nell,
And women buy and children sell,
And preach all sinners down to hell,
    And sing of heavenly union.

"They'll bleat and baa, dona[6] like goats,
Gorge down black sheep, and strain at motes,
Array their backs in fine black coats,
Then seize their negroes by their throats,
    And choke, for heavenly union.

"They'll church you if you sip a dram,
And damn you if you steal a lamb;
Yet rob old Tony, Doll, and Sam,
Of human rights, and bread and ham;
    Kidnapper's heavenly union.

"They'll loudly talk of Christ's reward,
And bind his image with a cord,
And scold, and swing the lash abhorred,
And sell their brother in the Lord
    To handcuffed heavenly union.

"They'll read and sing a sacred song,
And make a prayer both loud and long,
And teach the right and do the wrong,
Hailing the brother, sister throng,
    With words of heavenly union.

"We wonder how such saints can sing,
Or praise the Lord upon the wing,
Who roar, and scold, and whip, and sting,
And to their slaves and mammon cling,
    In guilty conscience union.

5. Jeremiah 5.9.   6. Believed to be a printer's error in the original edition for "go on" or "go n-a-a-ah."

"They'll raise tobacco, corn, and rye,
And drive, and thieve, and cheat, and lie,
And lay up treasures in the sky,
By making switch and cowskin fly,
    In hope of heavenly union.

"They'll crack old Tony on the skull,
And preach and roar like Bashan bull,
Or braying ass, of mischief full,
Then seize old Jacob by the wool,
    And pull for heavenly union.

"A roaring, ranting, sleek man-thief,
Who lived on mutton, veal, and beef,
Yet never would afford relief
To needy, sable sons of grief,
    Was big with heavenly union.

" 'Love not the world,' the preacher said,
And winked his eye, and shook his head;
He seized on Tom, and Dick, and Ned,
Cut short their meat, and clothes, and bread,
    Yet still loved heavenly union.

"Another preacher whining spoke
Of One whose heart for sinners broke:
He tied old Nanny to an oak,
And drew the blood at every stroke,
    And prayed for heavenly union.

"Two others oped their iron jaws,
And waved their children-stealing paws;
There sat their children in gewgaws;
By stinting negroes' backs and maws,
    They kept up heavenly union.

"All good from Jack another takes,
And entertains their flirts and rakes,
Who dress as sleek as glossy snakes,
And cram their mouths with sweetened cakes;
    And this goes down for union."

    Sincerely and earnestly hoping that this little book may do something toward throwing light on the American slave system, and hastening the glad day of deliverance to the millions of my brethren in bonds—faithfully relying upon the power of truth, love, and justice, for success in my humble efforts—and solemnly pledging my self anew to the sacred cause,—I subscribe myself,

                FREDERICK DOUGLASS.

Lynn, Mass., April 28, 1845.

WALT WHITMAN
1819–1892

As insistently as Rousseau, but with a far richer sense of the nature and the importance of his social context, Walt Whitman in his poetry makes himself the center of the universe. He brings to his emphatic self-presentation a detailed, partly ironic, partly celebratory sense of what it means to be an American; his poetry suggests something of what life in the United States must have felt like in the middle of the nineteenth century.

Born on New York's Long Island, Whitman in his childhood moved with his family to Brooklyn. He was christened Walter, but shortened his first name to distinguish himself from his father. As a young man, he worked as schoolteacher, builder, bookstore owner, journalist, and poet, before moving to Washington, D.C., to work as a government clerk. There he also served as a volunteer nurse, helping to care for the Civil War wounded. In 1873 he settled in Camden, New Jersey, where he remained for the rest of his life.

Whitman began writing in his youth, producing a good deal of bad poetry and a novel, a fictionalized temperance tract. He first published *Leaves of Grass* in 1855, after having become an admirer of Emerson and a Jeffersonian Democrat; he continued enlarging and revising the book for the rest of his life. In 1865, he published *Drum Taps,* poems derived from his Civil War experiences; in 1871, *Democratic Vistas,* a collection of political and philosophical essays.

Whitman's shifting diction—familiar, even slangy, to formal and rhetorical—makes possible a large range of tones in *Song of Myself.* In a single section (21), for example, these two sequences occur in close conjunction:

> I chant the chant of dilation or pride,
> We have had ducking and deprecating about enough,
> I show that size is only development.

> Smile O voluptuous cool-breathed earth!
> Earth of the slumbering and liquid trees!
> Earth of departed sunset—earth of the mountains misty-topt!
> Earth of the vitreous pour of the full moon just tinged with blue!

The first three-line passage, after its formal opening, falls into a pattern like that of colloquial speech. "About enough" belongs to an informal vocabulary; the final line, turning on the word *only,* makes the kind of joke one might make in conversation. ("Size doesn't matter, really, it only comes from growing.") The speaker's claim that he does not endorse conventional judgments, by which bigger is better, and his slightly mocking tone declare his independence and his willingness not to take himself with undue seriousness. Only a few lines later, when he turns to the "voluptuous cool-breathed earth," he sounds like a different person, entirely serious, almost grandiose, about his personal perceptions. Now his rhapsodic tone unites him with the Romantic poets, although his vocabulary still insists on his individuality. The conjunction of "voluptuous" with "cool-breathed," the use of "vitreous" (glasslike) to modify "pour" used as a noun, the idea of "liquid trees": such choices demand the reader's close attention to figure out exactly what the poem is saying, and they emphasize a fresh way of seeing, a precise attention to the look of things. But they also sound like poetry, in a sense familiar to readers of earlier nineteenth-century works—unlike the lines quoted just before, which resemble colloquial prose.

The range of tones used in the above example helps to communicate an important theme of Whitman's poem: the tension and exchange between desire for individuality and for community. *Narrative of the Life of Frederick Douglass* directly and without apparent conflict expresses a sense of community as part of a sense of personal identity. *Song of Myself,* on the other hand, alternates between assertions of specialness and of identification with others.

> I am of old and young, of the foolish as much as the wise,. . . .
> One of the Nation of many nations, the smallest the same and the largest the
>   same,
> A Southerner soon as a Northerner, a planter nonchalant and hospitable down by
>   the Oconee I live, . . .
> At home on Kanadian snow-shoes or up in the bush, or with fishermen off New-
>   foundland,
> At home in the fleet of ice-boats, sailing with the rest and tacking.

Declaring his union not, like Wordsworth, with the natural universe, but with the society of his compatriots, Whitman identifies himself with the enormous variety he perceives and celebrates in his country. But his poem opens "I celebrate myself, and sing myself, / And what I assume you shall assume," insisting on his uniqueness and dominance. Toward the end, these two lines occur: "I too am not a bit tamed, I too am untranslatable, / I sound my barbaric yawp over the roofs of the world." One hears the note of defiant specialness, another characteristic aspect of *Song of Myself.* The poem's power derives partly from its capacity to embody both feelings, the feeling of uniqueness and the sense of shared humanity, feelings that most people experience, sometimes in confusing conjunction. Like his Romantic predecessors, Whitman values emotion, every kind of emotion, for its own sake. He suggests the irrelevance of the notion of contradiction to any understanding of inner life. In the realm of emotion, everything coexists. *Song of Myself* attempts to include all of it.

    The poetic daring of *Song of Myself* expresses itself not only in choice of subject matter but in poetic technique. Whitman's lines are unrhymed and avoid the blank verse that had been the norm, instead establishing a new sort of rhythm—one that proved of crucial importance to twentieth-century American poets, who adapted it to their own purposes. Not metrical in any familiar sense, the verse establishes its own hypnotic rhythms, evoking an individual speaking voice, an individual idiom. It even risks the prosaic in its insistence that poetry implies, above all, personal perception and personal voice: "everything" can be included in technique as well as in material.

    Out of the Cradle Endlessly Rocking, another of Whitman's best-known pre–Civil War poems, develops a child's imaginative relation with nature in a way that Wordsworth might have approved. A man hears a birdsong that evokes for him a past experience—just as, at the beginning of *Remembrance of Things Past,* Proust's narrator finds his childhood returning to his memory at the taste of a madeleine. Reduced to tears by the song and the memory, the speaker, "chanter of pains and joys, uniter of here and hereafter," records and explores his youthful revelation of lyric power, achieved by identification with the bird mourning the loss of its mate.

> Now in a moment I know what I am for, I awake,
> And already a thousand singers, a thousand songs, clearer, louder and more
>   sorrowful than yours,
> A thousand warbling echoes have started to life within me, never to die.

The poem concludes with the adult speaker meditating on the nature of his creative force in terms recalling Keats's in *Ode to a Nightingale.* Whitman, too, muses about the attraction of death, feels the demonic and the beautiful united in the song that inspires him. His own songs merge in his imagination with the "strong and delicious word" spoken by the sea, another aspect of nature and one traditionally associated with death (as well as with birth). In poetry marked, like *Song of Myself,* by his powerfully individual rhythm and meter, Whitman reminds us once more of a great Romantic theme: the mystery of creativity.

From Song of Myself[1]

1

I celebrate myself, and sing myself,
And what I assume you shall assume,
For every atom belonging to me as good belongs to you.

I loafe and invite my soul,
I lean and loafe at my ease observing a spear of summer grass.   5

My tongue, every atom of my blood, formed from this soil, this air,
Born here of parents born here from parents the same, and their parents
    the same,
I, now thirty-seven years old in perfect health begin,
Hoping to cease not till death.

Creeds and schools in abeyance,   10
Retiring back a while sufficed at what they are, but never forgotten,
I harbor for good or bad, I permit to speak at every hazard,
Nature without check with original energy.

* * *

4

Trippers and askers surround me,
People I meet, the effect upon me of my early life or the ward and city I
    live in, or the nation,
The latest dates, discoveries, inventions, societies, authors old and new,
My dinner, dress, associates, looks, compliments, dues,
The real or fancied indifference of some man or woman I love,   5
The sickness of one of my folks or of myself, or ill-doing or loss or lack
    of money, or depressions or exaltations,
Battles, the horrors of fratricidal war, the fever of doubtful news, the
    fitful events;
These come to me days and nights and go from me again,
But they are not the Me myself.

Apart from the pulling and hauling stands what I am,   10
Stands amused, complacent, compassionating, idle, unitary,
Looks down, is erect, or bends an arm on an impalpable certain rest,
Looking with side-curved head curious what will come next,
Both in and out of the game and watching and wondering at it.

Backward I see in my own days where I sweated through fog with
    linguists and contenders,   15
I have no mockings or arguments, I witness and wait.

* * *

---

1. First published in 1855. This text is from the 1891–92 edition of *Leaves of Grass*, the so-called Deathbed
Edition.

7

Has any one supposed it lucky to be born?
I hasten to inform him or her it is just as lucky to die, and I know it.

He seems indifferent about life and dea...

I pass death with the dying and birth with the new-washed babe, and am
    not contained between my hat and boots,
And peruse manifold objects, no two alike and every one good,
The earth good and the stars good, and their adjuncts all good.

He thinks everything is good.

5

I am not an earth nor an adjunct of an earth,
I am the mate and companion of people, all just as immortal and
    fathomless as myself,
(They do not know how immortal, but I know.)

Every kind for itself and its own, for me mine male and female,
For me those that have been boys and that love women,   10
For me the man that is proud and feels how it stings to be slighted,
For me the sweet-heart and the old maid, for me mothers and the mothers
    of mothers,
For me lips that have smiled, eyes that have shed tears,
For me children and the begetters of children.

Undrape! you are not guilty to me, nor stale nor discarded,   15
I see through the broadcloth and gingham whether or no,
And am around, tenacious, acquisitive, tireless, and cannot be shaken
    away.

*   *   *

16

I am of old and young, of the foolish as much as the wise,
Regardless of others, ever regardful of others,
Maternal as well as paternal, a child as well as a man,
Stuffed with the stuff that is coarse and stuffed with the stuff that is fine,
One of the Nation of many nations, the smallest the same and the
    largest the same,   5
A Southerner soon as a Northerner, a planter nonchalant and hospitable
    down by the Oconee[2] I live,
A Yankee bound my own was ready for trade, my joints the limberest joints
    on earth and the sternest joints on earth,
A Kentuckian walking the vale of the Elkhorn in my deer-skin leggings,
    a Louisianian or Georgian,
A boatman over lakes or bays or along coasts, a Hoosier, Badger,
    Buckeye;
At home on Kanadian snow-shoes or up in the bush, or with fishermen off
    Newfoundland,   10
At home in the fleet of ice-boats, sailing with the rest and tacking,

2. River in Georgia.

At home on the hills of Vermont or in the woods of Maine, or the
    Texan ranch,
Comrade of Californians, comrade of free North-Westerners, (loving their
    big proportions,)
Comrade of raftsmen and coalmen, comrade of all who shake hands
    and welcome to drink and meat,
A learner with the simplest, a teacher of the thoughtfullest,   15
A novice beginning yet experient of myriads of seasons,
Of every hue and caste am I, of every rank and religion,
A farmer, mechanic, artist, gentleman, sailor, quaker,
Prisoner, fancy-man, rowdy, lawyer, physician, priest.

I resist any thing better than my own diversity,   20
Breathe the air but leave plenty after me,
And am not stuck up, and am in my place.

(The moth and the fish-eggs are in their place,
The bright suns I see and the dark suns I cannot see are in their place,
The palpable is in its place and the impalpable is in its place.)   25

*   *   *

21

I am the poet of the Body and I am the poet of the Soul,
The pleasures of heaven are with me and the pains of hell are with me,
The first I graft and increase upon myself, the latter I translate into a
    new tongue.

I am the poet of the woman the same as the man,
And I say it is as great to be a woman as to be a man,   5
And I say there is nothing greater than the mother of men.

I chant the chant of dilation or pride,
We have had ducking and deprecating about enough,
I show that size is only development.

Have you outstript the rest? are you the President?   10
It is a trifle, they will more than arrive there every one, and still pass on.

I am he that walks with the tender and growing night,
I call to the earth and sea half-held by the night.

Press close bare-bosomed night—press close magnetic nourishing night!
Night of south winds—night of the large few stars!   15
Still nodding night—mad naked summer night.

Smile O voluptuous cool-breathed earth!
Earth of the slumbering and liquid trees!
Earth of departed sunset—earth of the mountains misty-topt!
Earth of the vitreous pour of the full moon just tinged with blue!   20

Earth of shine and dark mottling the tide of the river!
Earth of the limpid gray of clouds brighter and clearer for my sake!
Far-swooping elbowed earth—rich apple-blossomed earth!
Smile, for your lover comes.

Prodigal, you have given me love—therefore I to you give love!   25
O unspeakable passionate love.

* * *

24

Walt Whitman, a kosmos, of Manhattan the son,
Turbulent, fleshy, sensual, eating, drinking and breeding,
No sentimentalist, no stander above men and women or apart from them,
No more modest than immodest.   *He believes his is equally all things*

Unscrew the locks from the doors!   5
Unscrew the doors themselves from their jambs!

Whoever degrades another degrades me,
And whatever is done or said returns at last to me.

Through me the afflatus surging and surging, through me the current and
    index.

I speak the pass-word primeval, I give the sign of democracy,   10
By God! I will accept nothing which all cannot have their counterpart
    of on the same terms.

* * *

32

I think I could turn and live with animals, they are so placid and self-
    contained,
I stand and look at them long and long.

They do not sweat and whine about their condition,
They do not lie awake in the dark and weep for their sins,
They do not make me sick discussing their duty to God,   *His dispose for humans and God*   5
Not one is dissatisfied, not one is demented with the mania of owning
    things,
Not one kneels to another, nor to his kind that lived thousands of years
    ago,
Not one is respectable or unhappy over the whole earth.

So they show their relations to me and I accept them,
They bring me tokens of myself, they evince them plainly in their
    possession.   10

I wonder where they get those tokens,
Did I pass that way huge times ago and negligently drop them?

Myself moving forward then and now and forever,
Gathering and showing more always and with velocity,
Infinite and omnigenous,[3] and the like of these among them, 15
Not too exclusive toward the reachers of my remembrancers,
Picking out here one that I love, and now go with him on brotherly terms.

A gigantic beauty of a stallion, fresh and responsive to my caresses,
Head high in the forehead, wide between the ears,
Limbs glossy and supple, tail dusting the ground, 20
Eyes full of sparkling wickedness, ears finely cut, flexibly moving.

His nostrils dilate as my heels embrace him,
His well-built limbs tremble with pleasure as we race around and return.

I but use you a minute, then I resign you, stallion,
Why do I need your paces when I myself out-gallop them? 25
Even as I stand or sit passing faster than you.

*   *   *

46

I know I have the best of time and space, and was never measured and
      never will be measured.

I tramp a perpetual journey, (come listen all!)
My signs are a rain-proof coat, good shoes, and a staff cut from the woods,
No friend of mine takes his ease in my chair,
I have no chair, no church, no philosophy, 5
I lead no man to a dinner-table, library, exchange,
But each man and each woman of you I lead upon a knoll,
My left hand hooking you round the waist,
My right hand pointing to landscapes of continents and the public road.
Not I, not any one else can travel that road for you, 10
You must travel it for yourself.

It is not far, it is within reach,
Perhaps you have been on it since you were born and did not know,
Perhaps it is everywhere on water and on land.

Shoulder your duds dear son, and I will mine, and let us hasten forth, 15
Wonderful cities and free nations we shall fetch as we go.

*   *   *

---

3. Belonging to all races.

51

The past and present wilt—I have filled them, emptied them,
And proceed to fill my next fold of the future.

Listener up there! what have you to confide to me?
Look in my face while I snuff the sidle of evening,[4]
(Talk honestly, no one else hears you, and I stay only a minute longer.)   5

Do I contradict myself?
Very well then I contradict myself,
(I am large, I contain multitudes.)

I concentrate toward them that are nigh, I wait on the door-slab.

Who has done his day's work? who will soonest be through with his
    supper?   10
Who wishes to walk with me?

Will you speak before I am gone? will you prove already too late?

52

The spotted hawk swoops by and accuses me, he complains of my gab and
    my loitering.

I too am not a bit tamed, I too am untranslatable,   *He is a law*
I sound my barbaric yawp over the roofs of the world. *unto himself.*

The last scud of day holds back for me,
It flings my likeness after the rest and true as any on the shadowed
    wilds,   5
It coaxes me to the vapor and the dusk.

I depart as air, I shake my white locks at the runaway sun,
I effuse my flesh in eddies, and drift it in lacy jags.

I bequeath myself to the dirt to grow from the grass I love,
If you want me again look for me under your boot-soles.   10

You will hardly know who I am or what I mean,
But I shall be good health to you nevertheless,
And filter and fibre your blood.

Failing to fetch me at first keep encouraged,
Missing me one place search another,   15
I stop somewhere waiting for you.

4. I.e., smell the fragrance of the slowly descending evening.

Out of the Cradle Endlessly Rocking

Out of the cradle endlessly rocking,
Out of the mocking-bird's throat, the musical shuttle,
Out of the Ninth-month[1] midnight,
Over the sterile sands and the fields beyond, where the child leaving
    his bed wandered alone, bareheaded, barefoot,
Down from the showered halo,   5
Up from the mystic play of shadows twining and twisting as if they
    were alive,
Out from the patches of briers and blackberries,
From the memories of the bird that chanted to me,
From your memories sad brother, from the fitful risings and fallings I
    heard,
From under that yellow half-moon late-risen and swollen as if with
    tears,   10
From those beginning notes of yearning and love there in the mist,
From the thousand responses of my heart never to cease,
From the myriad thence-aroused words,
From the word stronger and more delicious than any,
From such as now they start the scene revisiting,   15
As a flock, twittering, rising, or overhead passing,
Borne hither, ere all eludes me, hurriedly,
A man, yet by these tears a little boy again,
Throwing myself on the sand, confronting the waves,
I, chanter of pains and joys, uniter of here and hereafter,   20
Taking all hints to use them, but swiftly leaping beyond them,
A reminiscence sing.

Once Paumanok,[2]
When the lilac-scent was in the air and Fifth-month[3] grass was growing,
Up this seashore in some briers,   25
Two feathered guests from Alabama, two together,
And their nest, and four light-green eggs spotted with brown,
And every day the he-bird to and fro near at hand,
And every day the she-bird crouched on her nest, silent, with bright eyes,
And every day I, a curious boy, never too close, never disturbing them,   30
Cautiously peering, absorbing, translating.

Shine! shine! shine!
Pour down your warmth, great sun!
While we bask, we two together.

Two together!   35
Winds blow south, or winds blow north,
Day come white, or night come black,

Home, or rivers and mountains from home,
Singing all time, minding no time,
While we two keep together.   40

1. September, in Quaker usage.   2. Pronounced *paw-mah'-nok*. The Native American name for Long
Island, where Whitman grew up.   3. May.

Till of a sudden,
Maybe killed, unknown to her mate,
One forenoon the she-bird crouched not on the nest,
Nor returned that afternoon, nor the next,
Nor ever appeared again. 45

And thenceforward all summer in the sound of the sea,
And at night under the full of the moon in calmer weather,
Over the hoarse surging of the sea,
Or flitting from brier to brier by day,
I saw, I heard at intervals the remaining one, the he-bird, 50
The solitary guest from Alabama.

Blow! blow! blow!
Blow up sea-winds along Paumanok's shore;
I wait and I wait till you blow my mate to me.

Yes, when the stars glistened, 55
All night long on the prong of a moss-scalloped stake,
Down almost amid the slapping waves,
Sat the lone singer wonderful causing tears.

He called on his mate,
He poured forth the meanings which I of all men know. 60

Yes my brother I know,
The rest might not, but I have treasured every note,
For more than once dimly down to the beach gliding,
Silent, avoiding the moonbeams, blending myself with the shadows,
Recalling now the obscure shapes, the echoes, the sounds and sights
after their sorts, 65
The white arms out in the breakers tirelessly tossing,
I, with bare feet, a child, the wind wafting my hair,
Listened long and long.

Listened to keep, to sing, now translating the notes,
Following you my brother. 70

Soothe! soothe! soothe!
Close on its wave soothes the wave behind,
And again another behind embracing and lapping, every one close,
But my love soothes not me, not me.

Low hangs the moon, it rose late, 75
It is lagging—O I think it is heavy with love, with love.

O madly the sea pushes upon the land,
With love, with love.

O night! do I not see my love fluttering out among the breakers?
What is that little black thing I see there in the white? 80

Loud! loud! loud!
Loud I call to you, my love!
High and clear I shoot my voice over the waves,
Surely you must know who is here, is here,
You must know who I am, my love.   85

Low-hanging moon!
What is that dusky spot in your brown yellow?
O it is the shape, the shape of my mate!
O moon do not keep her from me any longer.

Land! land! O land!   90
Whichever way I turn, O I think you could give me my mate back again
    if you only would,
For I am almost sure I see her dimly whichever way I look.

O rising stars!
Perhaps the one I want so much will rise, will rise with some of you.

O throat! O trembling throat!   95
Sound clearer through the atmosphere!
Pierce the woods, the earth,
Somewhere listening to catch you must be the one I want.

Shake out carols!
Solitary here, the night's carols!   100
Carols of lonesome love! death's carols!
Carols under that lagging, yellow, waning moon!
O under that moon where she droops almost down into the sea!
O reckless despairing carols.

But soft! sink low!   105
Soft! let me just murmur,
And do you wait a moment you husky-noised sea,
For somewhere I believe I heard my mate responding to me,
So faint, I must be still, be still to listen,
But not altogether still, for then she might not come immediately to me.   110

Hither my love!
Here I am! here!
With this just-sustained note I announce myself to you,
This gentle call is for you my love, for you.

Do not be decoyed elsewhere,   115
That is the whistle of the wind, it is not my voice,
That is the fluttering, the fluttering of the spray,
Those are the shadows of leaves.

O darkness! O in vain!
O I am very sick and sorrowful.   120

O brown halo in the sky near the moon, drooping upon the sea!
O troubled reflection in the sea!

O throat! O throbbing heart!
And I singing uselessly, uselessly all the night.

O past! O happy life! O songs of joy! 125
In the air, in the woods, over fields,
Loved! loved! loved! loved! loved!
But my mate no more, no more with me!
We two together no more.

The aria sinking, 130
All else continuing, the stars shining,
The winds blowing, the notes of the bird continuous echoing,
With angry moans the fierce old mother incessantly moaning,
On the sands of Paumanok's shore gray and rustling,
The yellow half-moon enlarged, sagging down, drooping, the face of
    the sea almost touching, 135
The boy ecstatic, with his bare feet the waves, with his hair the
    atmosphere dallying,
The love in the heart long pent, now loose, now at last tumultuously
    bursting,
The aria's meaning, the ears, the soul, swiftly depositing,
The strange tears down the cheeks coursing,
The colloquy there, the trio, each uttering, 140
The undertone, the savage old mother incessantly crying,
To the boy's soul's questions sullenly timing, some drowned secret hissing,
To the outsetting bard.

Demon or bird! (said the boy's soul,)
Is it indeed toward your mate you sing? or is it really to me? 145
For I, that was a child, my tongue's use sleeping, now I have heard you,
Now in a moment I know what I am for, I awake,
And already a thousand singers, a thousand songs, clearer, louder and
    more sorrowful than yours,
A thousand warbling echoes have started to life within me, never to die.

O you singer solitary, singing by yourself, projecting me, 150
O solitary me listening, never more shall I cease perpetuating you,
Never more shall I escape, never more the reverberations,
Never more the cries of unsatisfied love be absent from me,
Never again leave me to be the peaceful child I was before what there
    in the night,
By the sea under the yellow and sagging moon, 155
The messenger there aroused, the fire, the sweet hell within,
The unknown want, the destiny of me.

O give me the clue! (it lurks in the night here somewhere,)
O if I am to have so much, let me have more!

A word then, (for I will conquer it,) 160
The word final, superior to all,
Subtle, sent up—what is it?—I listen;
Are you whispering it, and have been all the time, you sea-waves?
Is that it from your liquid rims and wet sands?

Whereto answering, the sea,   165
Delaying not, hurrying not,
Whispered me through the night, and very plainly before daybreak,
Lisped to me the low and delicious word death,
And again death, death, death, death,
Hissing melodious, neither like the bird nor like my aroused child's
        heart,   170
But edging near as privately for me rustling at my feet,
Creeping thence steadily up to my ears and laving me softly all over.
Death, death, death, death, death.

Which I do not forget,
But fuse the song of my dusky demon and brother,   175
That he sang to me in the moonlight on Paumanok's gray beach,
With the thousand responsive songs at random,
My own songs awaked from that hour,
And with them the key, the word up from the waves,
The word of the sweetest song and all songs,   180
That strong and delicious word which, creeping to my feet,
(Or like some old crone rocking the cradle, swathed in sweet garments,
        bending aside,)
The sea whispered me.

HERMAN MELVILLE
1819–1891

Herman Melville's *Billy Budd, Sailor* has always absorbed and puzzled its readers. Its story appears to deal with the eternal struggle of good and evil as manifested in mortal affairs, but critics disagree about who or what the author considered "good." It has something to say about the nature of justice and of the individual's relation to society—but what? Commentators have asserted that the book affirms Melville's final serene acceptance of life as it is but also that it documents his ironic defiance. We don't know whether Melville had completed the work before he died, or what he intended its title to be. The challenging experience of becoming implicated in the novel's dilemmas, of confronting its perplexing characters, of trying to follow its moral logic, may lead to no firm conclusions, but it can hardly fail to generate imaginative excitement.

Melville's father died when the boy was thirteen, leaving the family in near poverty. This fact helps to account for young Melville's varied moneymaking enterprises. He taught school, kept a store, and clerked in a bank; at the age of twenty, he for the first time shipped out as a sailor. Subsequent ventures at sea included several whaling expeditions. On one of these, he jumped ship in the South Pacific, living for a month on an island in the Marquesas; on another whaling trip, he participated in a mutiny. In 1847, Melville married Elizabeth Shaw. The couple settled in Pittsfield, Massachusetts, where Melville spent his time writing. He attempted in vain to get an appointment to a foreign consulate as a means of support; his lecture tours, also intended to make money, were unsuccessful. Finally, with his wife and four children, he moved to New York City, where in 1867 he obtained a position at the Custom House, which he held for the next eighteen years.

Melville's first novels, including *Typee* (1846) and *Omoo* (1847), seafaring adventure stories based on his own experience, won popular success. His masterpiece, *Moby-Dick* (1851), however, puzzled readers by its allegorical obscurity, its apparent shapelessness, and its highly elaborate language. Melville thought it his best work and felt disappointed and somewhat embittered by its critical failure. Although he continued writing and publishing short stories, novels, and poems, none of his later works achieved popularity.

Billy Budd, Sailor existed only in a heavily revised and at some points barely comprehensible manuscript at the time of the novelist's death. It was printed for the first time, in an imperfect version (*Billy Budd, Foretopman*), in a 1924 edition of Melville's works. In 1948, Frederick Barron Freeman re-edited the novel as *Billy Budd*; his text was supplemented in 1956 by emendations from the manuscript by Elizabeth Treeman. In 1962, *Billy Budd, Sailor*, source of the text printed here, was produced by Harrison Hayford and Merton M. Sealts Jr., who returned to the original manuscript, distinguished Elizabeth Melville's handwriting in it from her husband's, and generated a version substantially different from its predecessors. Although the nature of Melville's intention must remain impossible to ascertain, this careful effort to recapture what the novelist actually wrote at least has clear authority for every editorial choice.

The issues raised by the French Revolution, so vivid a part of literary consciousness at the beginning of the nineteenth century, once more provide a novelistic theme at the century's end—but with a new perspective. The events reported in *Billy Budd, Sailor* are said to occur in 1797. The narrator speaks of "those invading waters of novel opinion social, political, and otherwise, which carried away as in a torrent no few minds in those days." His metaphor suggests disapproval of the "novel opinion" that so greatly excited the early Romantics. Captain Vere, an important character whose name associates him with truth ("verity"), utterly resists the "invading waters." The only direct evidence, within the novel, of the actual effects of revolution is the reported mutinies, of which the narrator also appears to disapprove. Such evidence suggests a negative view of the French Revolution in its moral and political effects.

On the other hand, the narrator provides evidence of abundant cause for mutiny, particularly in the brutal practice of impressment, by which men were removed forcibly from nonnaval ships (or from their hometown streets, or their farms) and pressed into navy service, with no legal or practical recourse. When Billy Budd says goodbye to his ship, *Rights-of-Man,* he intends no irony, but others hear irony, as well they may: the concept of human rights is violated in every instance of impressment. Captain Vere's absolute devotion to legality and rule, his lack of openness to new possibility, arguably amount to extreme rigidity, even, possibly, to insanity. The narrator's wariness about "invading waters" may, like Billy's good-bye, be heard as ironic.

The conflicting claims of this series of statements, all supportable, need not be resolved; the important point is that by the end of the nineteenth century, everything that seemed true and exciting at the beginning had been called into question—not refuted, only made dubious. One can readily multiply examples from *Billy Budd, Sailor.* Billy, powerfully associated with images of innocence, resembles a child; a baby, even; a friendly dog; a big horse; Adam before the Fall. A hundred years earlier, Blake had suggested the perceptive power of the innocent, the child who points out that the emperor wears no clothes (or that chimney sweepers must rely on dreams and a black child on his mother's wishful stories to compensate for social injustice). Billy's innocence, on the other hand, has ambiguous implications. What does it mean to be an unfallen man in a fallen world? Billy can neither acquire from experience nor learn from others the knowledge that might make him capable of self-protective suspicion. His utter helplessness indicts his society but also raises troubling questions about the desirability of innocence.

Of course, one might argue that we in the twenty-first-century, "cynical" in the same sense as the old Dansker in the novel, are suspicious of such figures as Billy and Captain Vere in ways that our forebears would not be. Perhaps; yet virtually all the questions suggested in the last two paragraphs appear more or less directly in the novelistic text. The narrator reflects about troubling aspects of Billy's innocence; the surgeon raises the possibility that Captain Vere is "unhinged." At many points, the narrative's symbolic language calls insistent attention to itself. It, too, however, typically leaves one poised between interpretive alternatives. Here, for instance, is the description of Billy's hanging. "At the same moment it chanced that the vapory fleece hanging low in the East was shot through with a soft glory as of the fleece of the Lamb of God seen in mystical vision, and simultaneously therewith, watched by the wedged mass of upturned faces, Billy ascended; and, ascending, took the full rose of dawn." Are we to take seriously the implicit identification of Billy with Christ? Billy has willingly taken guilt upon himself, has forgiven his condemner, dies in his innocence, and "ascends." On the other hand, he ascends not to heaven but to the yardarm, not in resurrection but in death. Is this a form of transcendence? Or is it irony again, at the expense of those who comfort themselves for social injustice by religious sentimentality?

Possibilities for interpretation depend, the novel tells us, on who formulates the story and who receives it. The book's subtitle, "An Inside Narrative," proves as ambiguous as everything else about it. This account, it suggests, will tell what really happened, as opposed to the newspaper report quoted late in the narrative that makes Billy into a suspicious foreigner who nefariously stabs the noble English Claggart. The storyteller returns intermittently to his insistence that he deals with facts; hence he draws back from the climactic scene between Billy and Captain Vere. Because no one else was present, the narrator can only speculate; in this instance, we will never know what really happened. The dialogue between the purser and the surgeon about the physical peculiarities of the hanging exemplifies the universal difficulty of interpretation. The storyteller is only one more interpreter, with his own biases. Educating us in mistrust by the nature of his story, he leaves us no certainties. The last word on Billy is presented in the sailor's ballad at the end, in which Billy's execution becomes a matter of pathos, not of moral speculation. Perhaps this story does not after all involve the conflict of good and evil; maybe it only provides a record of social contingency. This final possibility explains events as adequately—and as inadequately—as any other hypothesis.

In its questioning of the Romantic verities, revolution and innocence, as in its possibly ironic use of nature ("a soft glory as of the fleece of the Lamb of God"), Melville's novel reminds us how much can happen over time. It may also remind us how insistently the nineteenth century foretells the twentieth and twenty-first. We are accustomed to feeling that we never get enough dependable information to make accurate judgments in matters of morality; we often distrust, if we think about it, the reliability of the "news" we are lavishly offered. *Billy Budd, Sailor* evokes a world that feels in many troubling respects like our own.

PRONOUNCING GLOSSARY

The following list uses common English syllables and stress accents to provide rough equivalents of selected words whose pronunciation may be unfamiliar to the general reader.

Aldebaran: *al-deb'-ar-an*

Anacharsis: *an-u-kahr'-sis*

Ananias: *a-nu-nai'-us*

Athée: *ah-tay'*

Bucephalus: *boo-sef'-u-lus*

Chiron: *kai'-ron*

Erebus: *ay-ray'-bus*

Hesperides: *hes-payr'-i-deez*

Montaigne: *mohn-ten'-yu*

Murat: *myoo-rah'*

Tecumseh: *tay-kum'-se*

Trafalgar: *trah-fahl'-gar*

Billy Budd, Sailor[1]

(An Inside Narrative)

1

In the time before steamships, or then more frequently than now, a stroller along the docks of any considerable seaport would occasionally have his attention arrested by a group of bronzed mariners, man-of-war's men or merchant sailors in holiday attire, ashore on liberty. In certain instances they would flank, or like a bodyguard quite surround, some superior figure of their own class, moving along with them like Aldebaran[2] among the lesser lights of his constellation. That signal object was the 'Handsome Sailor' of the less prosaic time alike of the military and merchant navies. With no perceptible trace of the vainglorious about him, rather with the offhand unaffectedness of natural regality, he seemed to accept the spontaneous homage of his shipmates.

A somewhat remarkable instance recurs to me. In Liverpool, now half a century ago, I saw under the shadow of the great dingy street-wall of Prince's Dock (an obstruction long since removed) a common sailor so intensely black that he must needs have been a native African of the unadulterate blood of Ham[3]—a symmetric figure much above the average height. The two ends of a gay silk handkerchief thrown loose about the neck danced upon the displayed ebony of his chest, in his ears were big hoops of gold, and a Highland bonnet with a tartan band set off his shapely head. It was a hot noon in July; and his face, lustrous with perspiration, beamed with barbaric good humor. In jovial sallies right and left, his white teeth flashing into view, he rollicked along, the center of a company of his shipmates. These were made up of such an assortment of tribes and complexions as would have well fitted them to be marched up by Anacharsis Cloots[4] before the bar of the first French Assembly as Representatives of the Human Race. At each spontaneous tribute rendered by the wayfarers to this black pagod[5] of a fellow—the tribute of a pause and stare, and less frequently an exclamation—the motley retinue showed that they took that sort of pride in the evoker of it which the Assyrian priests doubtless showed for their grand sculptured Bull when the faithful prostrated themselves.

To return. If in some cases a bit of a nautical Murat[6] in setting forth his person ashore, the Handsome Sailor of the period in question evinced nothing of the dandified Billy-be-Dam, an amusing character all but extinct now, but occasionally to be encountered, and in a form yet more amusing than the original, at the tiller of the boats on the tempestuous Erie Canal or, more likely, vaporing in the groggeries[7] along the towpath. Invariably a proficient in his perilous calling, he was also more or less of a mighty boxer or wrestler.

1. Edited by Harrison Hayford and Merton M. Sealts Jr.   2. A star of the first magnitude in the constellation of Taurus, the Bull, frequently used in navigation.   3. It was thought that Noah cursed his second son, Ham, for mocking him; that black skin resulted from the curse; and that all black people descended from Ham. In fact, according to Genesis 9.20–27 and 10.6–14, Noah cursed not Ham but Ham's son Canaan, while Ham's son Cush was black.   4. Jean-Baptiste du Val-de-Grâce, baron de Cloots, or Clootz (1755–1794), assembled a crowd of assorted nationalities and introduced them at the French National Assembly during the Revolution; he was popularly called "Anacharsis."   5. Meaning not only a pagoda but "an image of a deity, an idol" (*Oxford English Dictionary*).   6. Joachim Murat (1767–1815), marshal of France and king of Naples, Napoleon's brother-in-law, famous as a dandy.   7. Taverns. *Vaporing*: boasting or blustering.

It was strength and beauty. Tales of his prowess were recited. Ashore he was the champion; afloat the spokesman; on every suitable occasion always foremost. Close-reefing topsails in a gale, there he was, astride the weather yardarm-end, foot in the Flemish horse[8] as stirrup, both hands tugging at the earing as at a bridle, in very much the attitude of young Alexander curbing the fiery Bucephalus.[9] A superb figure, tossed up as by the horns of Taurus against the thunderous sky, cheerily hallooing to the strenuous file along the spar.

The moral nature was seldom out of keeping with the physical make. Indeed, except as toned by the former, the comeliness and power, always attractive in masculine conjunction, hardly could have drawn the sort of honest homage the Handsome Sailor in some examples received from his less gifted associates.

Such a cynosure, at least in aspect, and something such too in nature, though with important variations made apparent as the story proceeds, was welkin-eyed[1] Billy Budd—or Baby Budd, as more familiarly, under circumstances hereafter to be given, he at last came to be called—aged twenty-one, a foretopman[2] of the British fleet toward the close of the last decade of the eighteenth century. It was not very long prior to the time of the narration that follows that he had entered the King's service, having been impressed on the Narrow Seas from a homeward-bound English merchantman into a seventy-four[3] outward bound, H.M.S. *Bellipotent;* which ship, as was not unusual in those hurried days, having been obliged to put to sea short of her proper complement of men. Plump upon Billy at first sight in the gangway the boarding officer, Lieutenant Ratcliffe, pounced, even before the merchantman's crew was formally mustered on the quarter-deck for his deliberate inspection. And him only he elected. For whether it was because the other men when ranged before him showed to ill advantage after Billy, or whether he had some scruples in view of the merchantman's being rather short-handed, however it might be, the officer contented himself with his first spontaneous choice. To the surprise of the ship's company, though much to the lieutenant's satisfaction, Billy made no demur. But, indeed, any demur would have been as idle as the protest of a goldfinch popped into a cage.

Noting this uncomplaining acquiescence, all but cheerful, one might say, the shipmaster turned a surprised glance of silent reproach at the sailor. The shipmaster was one of those worthy mortals found in every vocation, even the humbler ones—the sort of person whom everybody agrees in calling 'a respectable man.' And—nor so strange to report as it may appear to be—though a ploughman of the troubled waters, lifelong contending with the intractable elements, there was nothing this honest soul at heart loved better than simple peace and quiet. For the rest, he was fifty or thereabouts, a little inclined to corpulence, a prepossessing face, unwhiskered, and of an agreeable color—a rather full face, humanely intelligent in expression. On a fair day with a fair wind and all going well, a certain musical chime in his voice

8. A hazardous activity: sailors go out on a yardarm (a spar supporting a sail) by means of foot ropes, one of which is called the *Flemish horse.*   9. Alexander the Great's warhorse.   1. Blue-eyed (*welkin:* sky). 2. Junior to a maintopman like Jack Chase, to whom the book is dedicated.   3. A third-rate ship of the line, equivalent to a light cruiser today. The designation refers to the number of guns the ship carried. *Narrow Seas:* the English Channel and the waters between England and Ireland.

seemed to be the veritable unobstructed outcome of the innermost man. He had much prudence, much conscientiousness, and there were occasions when these virtues were the cause of overmuch disquietude in him. On a passage, so long as his craft was in any proximity to land, no sleep for Captain Graveling. He took to heart those serious responsibilities not so heavily borne by some shipmasters.

Now while Billy Budd was down in the forecastle getting his kit together, the *Bellipotent's* lieutenant, burly and bluff, nowise disconcerted by Captain Graveling's omitting to proffer the customary hospitalities on an occasion so unwelcome to him, an omission simply caused by preoccupation of thought, unceremoniously invited himself into the cabin, and also to a flask from the spirit locker, a receptacle which his experienced eye instantly discovered. In fact he was one of those sea dogs in whom all the hardship and peril of naval life in the great prolonged wars of his time never impaired the natural instinct for sensuous enjoyment. His duty he always faithfully did; but duty is sometimes a dry obligation, and he was for irrigating its aridity, whensoever possible, with a fertilizing decoction of strong waters. For the cabin's proprietor there was nothing left but to play the part of the enforced host with whatever grace and alacrity were practicable. As necessary adjuncts to the flask, he silently placed tumbler and water jug before the irrepressible guest. But excusing himself from partaking just then, he dismally watched the unembarrassed officer deliberately diluting his grog[4] a little, then tossing it off in three swallows, pushing the empty tumbler away, yet not so far as to be beyond easy reach, at the same time settling himself in his seat and smacking his lips with high satisfaction, looking straight at the host.

These proceedings over, the master broke the silence; and there lurked a rueful reproach in the tone of his voice: 'Lieutenant, you are going to take my best man from me, the jewel of 'em.'

'Yes, I know,' rejoined the other, immediately drawing back the tumbler preliminary to a replenishing. 'Yes, I know. Sorry.'

'Beg pardon, but you don't understand, Lieutenant. See here, now. Before I shipped that young fellow, my forecastle was a rat-pit of quarrels. It was black times, I tell you, aboard the *Rights* here. I was worried to that degree my pipe had no comfort for me. But Billy came; and it was like a Catholic priest striking peace in an Irish shindy.[5] Not that he preached to them or said or did anything in particular; but a virtue went out of him, sugaring the sour ones. They took to him like hornets to treacle; all but the buffer[6] of the gang, the big shaggy chap with the fire-red whiskers. He indeed, out of envy, perhaps, of the newcomer, and thinking such a "sweet and pleasant fellow," as he mockingly designated him to the others, could hardly have the spirit of a gamecock, must needs bestir himself in trying to get up an ugly row with him. Billy forebore with him and reasoned with him in a pleasant way—he is something like myself, Lieutenant, to whom aught like a quarrel is hateful—but nothing served. So, in the second dogwatch[7] one day, the Red Whiskers in presence of the others, under pretense of showing Billy just whence a sirloin steak was cut—for the fellow had once been a butcher—insultingly gave him a dig under the ribs. Quick as lightning Billy let fly his arm. I dare say he never meant to do quite so much as he did, but anyhow he gave the burly fool a terrible drubbing. It took about half a minute, I should think. And lord bless you, the lubber was astonished at the celerity. And will you believe it, Lieutenant, the Red Whiskers now really loves Billy—loves him, or is the biggest hypocrite that ever I heard of. But they all love him. Some of 'em do his washing, darn his old trousers for him; the carpenter is at odd times making a pretty little chest of drawers for him. Anybody will do anything for Billy Budd; and it's the happy family here. But now, Lieutenant, if that young fellow goes—I know how it will be aboard the *Rights*. Not again very soon shall I, coming up from dinner, lean over the capstan smoking a quiet pipe—no, not very soon again, I think. Ay, Lieutenant, you are going to take away the jewel of 'em; you are going to take away my peacemaker!' And with that the good soul had really some ado in checking a rising sob.

'Well,' said the lieutenant, who had listened with amused interest to all this and now was waxing merry with his tipple: 'well, blessed are the peacemakers, especially the fighting peacemakers. And such are the seventy-four beauties some of which you see poking their noses out of the portholes of yonder warship lying to for me,' pointing through the cabin window at the *Bellipotent*. 'But courage! Don't look so downhearted, man. Why, I pledge you in advance the royal approbation. Rest assured that His Majesty will be delighted to know that in a time when his hardtack is not sought for by sailors with such avidity as should be, a time also when some shipmasters privily resent the borrowing from them a tar[8] or two for the service; His Majesty, I say, will be delighted to learn that *one* shipmaster at least cheerfully surrenders to the King the flower of his flock, a sailor who with equal loyalty makes no dissent.—But where's my beauty? Ah,' looking through the cabin's open door, 'here he comes; and, by Jove, lugging along his chest—Apollo with his portmanteau!—My man,' stepping out to him, 'you can't take that big box aboard a warship. The boxes there are mostly shot boxes. Put your duds in a bag, lad. Boot and saddle for the cavalryman, bag and hammock for the man-of-war's man.'

The transfer from chest to bag was made. And, after seeing his man into the cutter and then following him down, the lieutenant pushed off from the *Rights-of-Man*. That was the merchant ship's name, though by her master and crew abbreviated in sailor fashion into the *Rights*. The hardheaded Dundee owner was a staunch admirer of Thomas Paine,[9] whose book in rejoinder to Burke's arraignment of the French Revolution had then been published for some time and had gone everywhere. In christening his vessel after the title of Paine's volume the man of Dundee was something like his contemporary ship-owner, Stephen Girard[1] of Philadelphia, whose sympathies, alike with his native land and its liberal philosophers, he evinced by naming his ships after Voltaire, Diderot, and so forth.

But now, when the boat swept under the merchantman's stern, and officer and oarsmen were noting—some bitterly and others with a grin—the name emblazoned there; just then it was that the new recruit jumped up from the bow where the coxswain had directed him to sit, and waving hat to his silent shipmates sorrowfully looking over at him from the taffrail, bade the lads a

---

8. Sailor. 9. American Revolutionary patriot (1737–1809), born in England, published *The Rights of Man* in 1791 as a response to Edmund Burke's *Reflections on the Revolution in France* (1790). Dundee is a seaport in Scotland. 1. Merchant, banker, and philanthropist (1750–1831), a native of France who emigrated at the age of twenty-seven.

genial good-bye. Then, making a salutation as to the ship herself, 'And good-bye to you too, old *Rights-of-Man*.'

'Down, sir!' roared the lieutenant, instantly assuming all the rigor of his rank, though with difficulty repressing a smile.

To be sure, Billy's action was a terrible breach of naval decorum. But in that decorum he had never been instructed; in consideration of which the lieutenant would hardly have been so energetic in reproof but for the concluding farewell to the ship. This he rather took as meant to convey a covert sally on the new recruit's part, a sly slur at impressment in general, and that of himself in especial. And yet, more likely, if satire it was in effect, it was hardly so by intention, for Billy, though happily endowed with the gaiety of high health, youth, and a free heart, was yet by no means of a satirical turn. The will to it and the sinister dexterity were alike wanting. To deal in double meanings and insinuations of any sort was quite foreign to his nature.

As to his enforced enlistment, that he seemed to take pretty much as he was wont to take any vicissitude of weather. Like the animals, though no philosopher, he was, without knowing it, practically a fatalist. And it may be that he rather liked this adventurous turn in his affairs, which promised an opening into novel scenes and martial excitements.

Aboard the *Bellipotent* our merchant sailor was forthwith rated as an able seaman and assigned to the starboard watch of the foretop. He was soon at home in the service, not at all disliked for his unpretentious good looks and a sort of genial happy-go-lucky air. No merrier man in his mess: in marked contrast to certain other individuals included like himself among the impressed portion of the ship's company; for these when not actively employed were sometimes, and more particularly in the last dogwatch when the drawing near of twilight induced revery, apt to fall into a saddish mood which in some partook of sullenness. But they were not so young as our foretopman, and no few of them must have known a hearth of some sort, others may have had wives and children left, too probably, in uncertain circumstances, and hardly any but must have had acknowledged kith and kin, while for Billy, as will shortly be seen, his entire family was practically invested in himself.

2

Though our new-made foretopman was well received in the top and on the gun decks, hardly here was he that cynosure he had previously been among those minor ship's companies of the merchant marine, with which companies only had he hitherto consorted.

He was young; and despite his all but fully developed frame, in aspect looked even younger than he really was, owing to a lingering adolescent expression in the as yet smooth face all but feminine in purity of natural complexion but where, thanks to his seagoing, the lily was quite suppressed and the rose had some ado visibly to flush through the tan.

To one essentially such a novice in the complexities of factitious life, the abrupt transition from his former and simpler sphere to the ampler and more knowing world of a great warship; this might well have abashed him had there been any conceit or vanity in his composition. Among her miscellaneous multitude, the *Bellipotent* mustered several individuals who however inferior in grade were of no common natural stamp, sailors more signally susceptive of that air which continuous martial discipline and repeated presence in battle can in some degree impart even to the average man. As the Handsome Sailor, Billy Budd's position aboard the seventy-four was something analogous to that of a rustic beauty transplanted from the provinces and brought into competition with the highborn dames of the court. But this change of circumstances he scarce noted. As little did he observe that something about him provoked an ambiguous smile in one or two harder faces among the bluejackets. Nor less unaware was he of the peculiar favorable effect his person and demeanor had upon the more intelligent gentlemen of the quarter-deck. Nor could this well have been otherwise. Cast in a mold peculiar to the finest physical examples of those Englishmen in whom the Saxon strain would seem not at all to partake of any Norman or other admixture, he showed in face that humane look of reposeful good nature which the Greek sculptor in some instances gave to his heroic strong man, Hercules. But this again was subtly modified by another and pervasive quality. The ear, small and shapely, the arch of the foot, the curve in mouth and nostril, even the indurated hand dyed to the orange-tawny of the toucan's bill, a hand telling alike of the halyards and tar bucket; but, above all, something in the mobile expression, and every chance attitude and movement, something suggestive of a mother eminently favored by Love and the Graces; all this strangely indicated a lineage in direct contradiction to his lot. The mysteriousness here became less mysterious through a matter of fact elicited when Billy at the capstan was being formally mustered into the service. Asked by the officer, a small, brisk little gentleman as it chanced, among other questions, his place of birth, he replied, 'Please, sir, I don't know.'

'Don't know where you were born? Who was your father?'

'God knows, sir.'

Struck by the straightforward simplicity of these replies, the officer next asked, 'Do you know anything about your beginning?'

'No, sir. But I have heard that I was found in a pretty silk-lined basket hanging one morning from the knocker of a good man's door in Bristol.'

'Found, say you? Well,' throwing back his head and looking up and down the new recruit; 'well, it turns out to have been a pretty good find. Hope they'll find some more like you, my man; the fleet sadly needs them.'

Yes, Billy Budd was a foundling, a presumable by-blow, and, evidently, no ignoble one. Noble descent was as evident in him as in a blood horse.

For the rest, with little or no sharpness of faculty or any trace of the wisdom of the serpent, nor yet quite a dove, he possessed that kind and degree of intelligence going along with the unconventional rectitude of a sound human creature, one to whom not yet has been proffered the questionable apple of knowledge. He was illiterate; he could not read, but he could sing, and like the illiterate nightingale was sometimes the composer of his own song.

Of self-consciousness he seemed to have little or none, or about as much as we may reasonably impute to a dog of Saint Bernard's breed.

Habitually living with the elements and knowing little more of the land than as a beach, or, rather, that portion of the terraqueous globe providentially set apart for dance-houses, doxies, and tapsters, in short what sailors call a 'fiddler's green,'[2] his simple nature remained unsophisticated by those moral obliquities which are not in every case incompatible with that manufacturable thing known as respectability. But are sailors, frequenters of fiddler's greens, without vices? No; but less often than with landsmen do their vices, so called, partake of crookedness of heart, seeming less to proceed from viciousness than exuberance of vitality after long constraint: frank manifestations in accordance with natural law. By his original constitution aided by the co-operating influences of his lot, Billy in many respects was little more than a sort of upright barbarian, much such perhaps as Adam presumably might have been ere the urbane Serpent wriggled himself into his company.

And here be it submitted that apparently going to corroborate the doctrine of man's Fall, a doctrine now popularly ignored, it is observable that where certain virtues pristine and unadulterate peculiarly characterize anybody in the external uniform of civilization, they will upon scrutiny seem not to be derived from custom or convention, but rather to be out of keeping with these, as if indeed exceptionally transmitted from a period prior to Cain's city[3] and citified man. The character marked by such qualities has to an unvitiated taste an untampered-with flavor like that of berries, while the man thoroughly civilized, even in a fair specimen of the breed, has to the same moral palate a questionable smack as of a compounded wine. To any stray inheritor of these primitive qualities found, like Caspar Hauser,[4] wandering dazed in any Christian capital of our time, the good-natured poet's famous invocation, near two thousand years ago, of the good rustic out of his latitude in the Rome of the Caesars, still appropriately holds:

> Honest and poor, faithful in word and thought,
> What hath thee, Fabian, to the city brought?[5]

Though our Handsome Sailor had as much of masculine beauty as one can expect anywhere to see; nevertheless, like the beautiful woman in one of Hawthorne's minor tales,[6] there was just one thing amiss in him. No visible blemish indeed, as with the lady; no, but an occasional liability to a vocal defect. Though in the hour of elemental uproar or peril he was everything that a sailor should be, yet under sudden provocation of strong heart-feeling his voice, otherwise singularly musical, as if expressive of the harmony within, was apt to develop an organic hesitancy, in fact more or less of a stutter or even worse. In this particular Billy was a striking instance that the arch interferer, the envious marplot of Eden, still has more or less to do with every human consignment to this planet of Earth. In every case, one way or another he is sure to slip in his little card, as much as to remind us—I too have a hand here.

The avowal of such an imperfection in the Handsome Sailor should be evidence not alone that he is not presented as a conventional hero, but also that the story in which he is the main figure is no romance.

2. A sailor's utopia.   3. I.e., in the time of the Garden of Eden. Cain "builded a city" in Genesis 4.16–17.   4. A German foundling (1812?–1833) who claimed to have been brought up in a primitive wilderness.   5. Martial's *Epigrams* 1.4.1–2, from Cowley's translation in the Bohn edition.   6. *The Birthmark*, in which the *blemish* is on the lady's cheek.

3

At the time of Billy Budd's arbitrary enlistment into the *Bellipotent* that ship was on her way to join the Mediterranean fleet. No long time elapsed before the junction was effected. As one of that fleet the seventy-four participated in its movements, though at times on account of her superior sailing qualities, in the absence of frigates, dispatched on separate duty as a scout and at times on less temporary service. But with all this the story has little concernment, restricted as it is to the inner life of one particular ship and the career of an individual sailor.

It was the summer of 1797. In the April of that year had occurred the commotion at Spithead followed in May by a second and yet more serious outbreak in the fleet at the Nore. The latter is known, and without exaggeration in the epithet, as 'the Great Mutiny.' It was indeed a demonstration more menacing to England than the contemporary manifestoes and conquering and proselyting armies of the French Directory.[7] To the British Empire the Nore Mutiny was what a strike in the fire brigade would be to London threatened by general arson. In a crisis when the kingdom might well have anticipated the famous signal that some years later published along the naval line of battle what it was that upon occasion England expected of Englishmen;[8] *that* was the time when at the mastheads of the three-deckers and seventy-fours moored in her own roadstead—a fleet the right arm of a Power then all but the sole free conservative one of the Old World—the bluejackets, to be numbered by thousands, ran up with huzzas the British colors with the union and cross[9] wiped out; by that cancellation transmuting the flag of founded law and freedom defined, into the enemy's red meteor of unbridled and unbounded revolt. Reasonable discontent growing out of practical grievances in the fleet had been ignited into irrational combustion as by live cinders blown across the Channel from France in flames.

The event converted into irony for a time those spirited strains of Dibdin[1]—as a song-writer no mean auxiliary to the English government at that European conjuncture—strains celebrating, among other things, the patriotic devotion of the British tar: 'And as for my life, 'tis the King's!'

Such an episode in the Island's grand naval story her naval historians naturally abridge, one of them (William James)[2] candidly acknowledging that fain would he pass it over did not 'impartiality forbid fastidiousness.' And yet his mention is less a narration than a reference, having to do hardly at all with details. Nor are these readily to be found in the libraries. Like some other events in every age befalling states everywhere, including America, the Great Mutiny was of such character that national pride along with views of policy would fain shade it off into the historical background. Such events cannot be ignored, but there is a considerate way of historically treating them. If a well-constituted individual refrains from blazoning aught amiss or

---

7. The five directors who governed France from 1795 to 1799, during the Revolution.   8. "England expects every man to do his duty!": Lord Nelson, before the battle at Trafalgar, October 21, 1805.   9. The British Union Jack, or national flag, carries the crosses of St. Andrew, St. George, and St. Patrick, patron saints of Scotland, England, and Ireland.   1. Charles Dibdin (1745–1814), English dramatist, chiefly remembered for his sea chanteys. The ballad quoted is "Poor Jack."   2. *The Naval History of Great Britain* (1860). Melville mistakenly wrote "G. P. R. James."

calamitous in his family, a nation in the like circumstance may without reproach be equally discreet.

Though after parleyings between government and the ringleaders, and concessions by the former as to some glaring abuses, the first uprising—that at Spithead—with difficulty was put down, or matters for the time pacified; yet at the Nore the unforeseen renewal of insurrection on a yet larger scale, and emphasized in the conferences that ensued by demands deemed by the authorities not only inadmissible but aggressively insolent, indicated—if the Red Flag did not sufficiently do so—what was the spirit animating the men. Final suppression, however, there was; but only made possible perhaps by the unswerving loyalty of the marine corps and a voluntary resumption of loyalty among influential sections of the crews.

To some extent the Nore Mutiny may be regarded as analogous to the distempering irruption of contagious fever in a frame constitutionally sound, and which anon throws it off.

At all events, of these thousands of mutineers were some of the tars who not so very long afterwards—whether wholly prompted thereto by patriotism, or pugnacious instinct, or by both—helped to win a coronet for Nelson at the Nile, and the naval crown of crowns for him at Trafalgar.[3] To the mutineers, those battles and especially Trafalgar were a plenary absolution and a grand one. For all that goes to make up scenic naval display and heroic magnificence in arms, those battles, especially Trafalgar, stand unmatched in human annals.

4

In this matter of writing, resolve as one may to keep to the main road, some bypaths have an enticement not readily to be withstood. I am going to err into such a bypath. If the reader will keep me company I shall be glad. At the least, we can promise ourselves that pleasure which is wickedly said to be in sinning, for a literary sin the divergence will be.

Very likely it is no new remark that the inventions of our time have at last brought about a change in sea warfare in degree corresponding to the revolution in all warfare effected by the original introduction from China into Europe of gunpowder. The first European firearm, a clumsy contrivance, was, as is well known, scouted[4] by no few of the knights as a base implement, good enough peradventure for weavers too craven to stand up crossing steel with steel in frank fight. But as ashore knightly valor, though shorn of its blazonry, did not cease with the knights, neither on the sea—though nowadays in encounters there a certain kind of displayed gallantry be fallen out of date as hardly applicable under changed circumstances—did the nobler qualities of such naval magnates as Don John of Austria, Doria, Van Tromp, Jean Bart, the long line of British admirals, and the American Decaturs of 1812 become obsolete with their wooden walls.[5]

3. Nelson was made a baronet for his victory over the French at Aboukir in 1798; his 1805 victory at Trafalgar is considered one of the greatest in naval history.   4. Scoffed at.   5. A reference to the wooden ships made obsolete by ironclads. Don Juan of Austria (1547–1578) commanded a fleet against the Turks at Lepanto in 1571, the last major sea battle in which oared ships predominated. Andrea Doria (1468–1560) liberated Genoa from the French. Maarten Van Tromp (1596–1653), Dutch admiral, fought successfully against the English. Jean Bart (1651?–1702), a French captain, battled the Dutch. Stephen Decatur (1779–1820) won victories over the Barbary Coast pirates at Tripoli and over the British in the War of 1812.

Nevertheless, to anybody who can hold the Present at its worth without being inappreciative of the Past, it may be forgiven, if to such an one the solitary old hulk at Portsmouth, Nelson's *Victory*, seems to float there, not alone as the decaying monument of a fame incorruptible, but also as a poetic reproach, softened by its picturesqueness, to the *Monitors*[6] and yet mightier hulls of the European ironclads. And this not altogether because such craft are unsightly, unavoidably lacking the symmetry and grand lines of the old battleships, but equally for other reasons.

There are some, perhaps, who while not altogether inaccessible to that poetic reproach just alluded to, may yet on behalf of the new order be disposed to parry it; and this to the extent of iconoclasm, if need be. For example, prompted by the sight of the star inserted in the *Victory*'s quarter-deck designating the spot where the Great Sailor fell, these martial utilitarians may suggest considerations implying that Nelson's ornate publication of his person in battle was not only unnecessary, but not military, nay, savored of foolhardiness and vanity. They may add, too, that at Trafalgar it was in effect nothing less than a challenge to death; and death came; and that but for his bravado the victorious admiral might possibly have survived the battle, and so, instead of having his sagacious dying injunctions overruled by his immediate successor in command, he himself when the contest was decided might have brought his shattered fleet to anchor, a proceeding which might have averted the deplorable loss of life by shipwreck in the elemental tempest that followed the martial one.

Well, should we set aside the more than disputable point whether for various reasons it was possible to anchor the fleet, then plausibly enough the Benthamites[7] of war may urge the above. But the *might-have-been* is but boggy ground to build on. And, certainly, in foresight as to the larger issue of an encounter, and anxious preparations for it—buoying the deadly way and mapping it out, as at Copenhagen[8]—few commanders have been so painstakingly circumspect as this same reckless declarer of his person in fight.

Personal prudence, even when dictated by quite other than selfish considerations, surely is no special virtue in a military man; while an excessive love of glory, impassioning a less burning impulse, the honest sense of duty, is the first. If the name *Wellington* is not so much of a trumpet to the blood as the simpler name *Nelson*, the reason for this may perhaps be inferred from the above. Alfred in his funeral ode on the victory of Waterloo ventures not to call him the greatest soldier of all time, though in the same ode he invokes Nelson as 'the greatest sailor since our world began.'[9]

At Trafalgar Nelson on the brink of opening the fight sat down and wrote his last brief will and testament. If under the presentiment of the most magnificent of all victories to be crowned by his own glorious death, a sort of priestly motive led him to dress his person in the jewelled vouchers of his own shining deeds; if thus to have adorned himself for the altar and the sacrifice were indeed vainglory, then affectation and fustian is each more

---

6. The *Monitor* was an ironclad launched in 1862 to fight the Confederate *Virginia* (formerly the frigate *Merrimack*) in a battle effectively ending the era of wooden ships.   7. Utilitarian thinkers and followers of Jeremy Bentham (1748–1832), who believed in the greatest good for the greatest number.   8. Where Nelson's careful planning defeated the Danish on April 2, 1801.   9. The quotation comes from Tennyson's *Ode on the Death of the Duke of Wellington* (1852) 6.7.

heroic line in the great epics and dramas, since in such lines the poet but embodies in verse those exaltations of sentiment that a nature like Nelson, the opportunity being given, vitalizes into acts.

5

Yes, the outbreak at the Nore was put down. But not every grievance was redressed. If the contractors, for example, were no longer permitted to ply some practices peculiar to their tribe everywhere, such as providing shoddy cloth, rations not sound, or false in the measure; not the less impressment, for one thing, went on. By custom sanctioned for centuries, and judicially maintained by a Lord Chancellor as late as Mansfield,[1] that mode of manning the fleet, a mode now fallen into a sort of abeyance but never formally renounced, it was not practicable to give up in those years. Its abrogation would have crippled the indispensable fleet, one wholly under canvas, no steam power, its innumerable sails and thousands of cannon, everything in short, worked by muscle alone; a fleet the more insatiate in demand for men, because then multiplying its ships of all grades against contingencies present and to come of the convulsed Continent.

Discontent foreran the Two Mutinies, and more or less it lurkingly survived them. Hence it was not unreasonable to apprehend some return of trouble sporadic or general. One instance of such apprehensions: In the same year with this story, Nelson, then Rear Admiral Sir Horatio, being with the fleet off the Spanish coast, was directed by the admiral in command to shift his pennant from the *Captain* to the *Theseus*; and for this reason: that the latter ship having newly arrived on the station from home, where it had taken part in the Great Mutiny, danger was apprehended from the temper of the men; and it was thought that an officer like Nelson was the one, not indeed to terrorize the crew into base subjection, but to win them, by force of his mere presence and heroic personality, back to an allegiance if not as enthusiastic as his own yet as true.

So it was that for a time, on more than one quarter-deck, anxiety did exist. At sea, precautionary vigilance was strained against relapse. At short notice an engagement might come on. When it did, the lieutenants assigned to batteries felt it incumbent on them, in some instances, to stand with drawn swords behind the men working the guns.

6

But on board the seventy-four in which Billy now swung his hammock, very little in the manner of the men and nothing obvious in the demeanor of the officers would have suggested to an ordinary observer that the Great Mutiny was a recent event. In their general bearing and conduct the commissioned officers of a warship naturally take their tone from the commander, that is if he have that ascendancy of character that ought to be his.

Captain the Honorable Edward Fairfax Vere, to give his full title, was a bachelor of forty or thereabouts, a sailor of distinction even in a time prolific of renowned seamen. Though allied to the higher nobility, his advancement

1. William Murray, Baron Mansfield (1705–1793), lord chief justice of Great Britain from 1756 to 1788.

had not been altogether owing to influences connected with that circumstance. He had seen much service, been in various engagements, always
acquitting himself as an officer mindful of the welfare of his men, but never
tolerating an infraction of discipline; thoroughly versed in the science of his
profession, and intrepid to the verge of temerity, though never injudiciously
so. For his gallantry in the West Indian waters as flag lietutenant under
Rodney in that admiral's crowning victory over De Grasse,[2] he was made a
post captain.

Ashore, in the garb of a civilian, scarce anyone would have taken him for
a sailor, more especially that he never garnished unprofessional talk with
nautical terms, and grave in his bearing, evinced little appreciation of mere
humor. It was not out of keeping with these traits that on a passage when
nothing demanded his paramount action, he was the most undemonstrative
of men. Any landsman observing this gentleman not conspicuous by his stature and wearing no pronounced insignia, emerging from his cabin to the
open deck, and noting the silent deference of the officers retiring to leeward,
might have taken him for the King's guest, a civilian aboard the King's ship,
some highly honorable discreet envoy on his way to an important post. But
in fact this unobtrusiveness of demeanor may have proceeded from a certain
unaffected modesty of manhood sometimes accompanying a resolute nature,
a modesty evinced at all times not calling for pronounced action, which
shown in any rank of life suggests a virtue aristocratic in kind. As with some
others engaged in various departments of the world's more heroic activities,
Captain Vere though practical enough upon occasion would at times betray
a certain dreaminess of mood. Standing alone on the weather side of the
quarter-deck, one hand holding by the rigging, he would absently gaze off at
the blank sea. At the presentation to him then of some minor matter interrupting the current of his thoughts, he would show more or less irascibility;
but instantly he would control it.

In the navy he was popularly known by the appellation 'Starry Vere.' How
such a designation happened to fall upon one who whatever his sterling
qualities was without any brilliant ones, was in this wise: A favorite kinsman,
Lord Denton, a freehearted fellow, had been the first to meet and congratulate him upon his return to England from his West Indian cruise; and but
the day previous turning over a copy of Andrew Marvell's[3] poems had lighted,
not for the first time, however, upon the lines entitled 'Appleton House,' the
name of one of the seats of their common ancestor, a hero in the German
wars of the seventeenth century, in which poem occur the lines:

> This 'tis to have been from the first
> In a domestic heaven nursed,
> Under the discipline severe
> Of Fairfax and the starry Vere.

And so, upon embracing his cousin fresh from Rodney's great victory wherein
he had played so gallant a part, brimming over with just family pride in the
sailor of their house, he exuberantly exclaimed, 'Give ye joy, Ed; give ye joy,
my starry Vere!' This got currency, and the novel prefix serving in familiar

---

2. The British admiral George Brydges, Baron Rodney (1719–1792), defeated the French admiral de
Grasse off Dominica, in the Leeward Islands, in 1782.   3. English lyric poet (1621–1678).

parlance readily to distinguish the *Bellipotent*'s captain from another Vere his senior, a distant relative, an officer of like rank in the navy, it remained permanently attached to the surname.

7

In view of the part that the commander of the *Bellipotent* plays in scenes shortly to follow, it may be well to fill out that sketch of him outlined in the previous chapter.

Aside from his qualities as a sea officer Captain Vere was an exceptional character. Unlike no few of England's renowned sailors, long and arduous service with signal devotion to it had not resulted in absorbing and *salting* the entire man. He had a marked leaning toward everything intellectual. He loved books, never going to sea without a newly replenished library, compact but of the best. The isolated leisure, in some cases so wearisome, falling at intervals to commanders even during a war cruise, never was tedious to Captain Vere. With nothing of that literary taste which less heeds the thing conveyed than the vehicle, his bias was toward those books to which every serious mind of superior order occupying any active post of authority in the world naturally inclines: books treating of actual men and events no matter of what era—history, biography, and unconventional writers like Montaigne,[4] who, free from cant and convention, honestly and in the spirit of common sense philosophize upon realities. In this line of reading he found confirmation of his own more reserved thoughts—confirmation which he had vainly sought in social converse, so that as touching most fundamental topics, there had got to be established in him some positive convictions which he forefelt would abide in him essentially unmodified so long as his intelligent part remained unimpaired. In view of the troubled period in which his lot was cast, this was well for him. His settled convictions were as a dike against those invading waters of novel opinion social, political, and otherwise, which carried away as in a torrent no few minds in those days, minds by nature not inferior to his own. While other members of that aristocracy to which by birth he belonged were incensed at the innovators mainly because their theories were inimical to the privileged classes, Captain Vere disinterestedly opposed them not alone because they seemed to him insusceptible of embodiment in lasting institutions, but at war with the peace of the world and the true welfare of mankind.

With minds less stored than his and less earnest, some officers of his rank, with whom at times he would necessarily consort, found him lacking in the companionable quality, a dry and bookish gentleman, as they deemed. Upon any chance withdrawal from their company one would be apt to say to another something like this: 'Vere is a noble fellow, Starry Vere. 'Spite the gazettes,[5] Sir Horatio' (meaning him who became Lord Nelson) 'is at bottom scarce a better seaman or fighter. But between you and me now, don't you think there is a queer streak of the pedantic running through him? Yes, like the King's yarn in a coil of navy rope?'[6]

Some apparent ground there was for this sort of confidential criticism;

4. Michel Eyquem de Montaigne (1533–1592), French essayist.   5. Official gazettes that printed accounts of naval careers and honors.   6. A thread was worked into hempen cable to mark it as belonging to the Royal Navy.

since not only did the captain's discourse never fall into the jocosely familiar, but in illustrating of any point touching the stirring personages and events of the time he would be as apt to cite some historic character or incident of antiquity as he would be to cite from the moderns. He seemed unmindful of the circumstance that to his bluff company such remote allusions, however pertinent they might really be, were altogether alien to men whose reading was mainly confined to the journals. But considerateness in such matters is not easy to natures constituted like Captain Vere's. Their honesty prescribes to them directness, sometimes far-reaching like that of a migratory fowl that in its flight never heeds when it crosses a frontier.

8

The lieutenants and other commissioned gentlemen forming Captain Vere's staff it is not necessary here to particularize, nor needs it to make any mention of any of the warrant officers. But among the petty officers[7] was one who, having much to do with the story, may as well be forthwith introduced. His portrait I essay, but shall never hit it. This was John Claggart, the master-at-arms. But that sea title may to landsmen seem somewhat equivocal. Originally, doubtless, that petty officer's function was the instruction of the men in the use of arms, sword or cutlass. But very long ago, owing to the advance in gunnery making hand-to-hand encounters less frequent and giving to niter and sulphur the pre-eminence over steel, that function ceased; the master-at-arms of a great warship becoming a sort of chief of police charged among other matters with the duty of preserving order on the populous lower gun decks.

Claggart was a man about five-and-thirty, somewhat spare and tall, yet of no ill figure upon the whole. His hand was too small and shapely to have been accustomed to hard toil. The face was a notable one, the features all except the chin cleanly cut as those on a Greek medallion; yet the chin, beardless as Tecumseh's,[8] had something of strange protuberant broadness in its make that recalled the prints of the Reverend Dr Titus Oates,[9] the historic deponent with the clerical drawl in the time of Charles II and the fraud of the alleged Popish Plot. It served Claggart in his office that his eye could cast a tutoring glance. His brow was of the sort phrenologically associated with more than average intellect; silken jet curls partly clustering over it, making a foil to the pallor below, a pallor tinged with a faint shade of amber akin to the hue of time-tinted marbles of old. This complexion, singularly contrasting with the red or deeply bronzed visages of the sailors, and in part the result of his official seclusion from the sunlight, though it was not exactly displeasing, nevertheless seemed to hint of something defective or abnormal in the constitution and blood. But his general aspect and manner were so suggestive of an education and career incongruous with his naval function that when not actively engaged in it he looked like a man of high quality, social and moral, who for reasons of his own was keeping incog.[1] Nothing was known of his former life. It might be that he was an Englishman;

7. Enlisted men corresponding in rank to noncommissioned officers in the army. *Warrant officers*: ranked above petty and just below commissioned officers.   8. Shawnee chief (1768?–1813) who attempted to unite the American Indians against the United States.   9. In 1678 Oates (1649–1705) invented a plot accusing Jesuits of planning to assassinate Charles II, burn London, and slaughter English Protestants. 1. Incognito, unrecognized.

and yet there lurked a bit of accent in his speech suggesting that possibly he was not such by birth, but through naturalization in early childhood. Among certain grizzled sea gossips of the gun decks and forecastle went a rumor perdue[2] that the master-at-arms was a *chevalier*[3] who had volunteered into the King's navy by way of compounding for some mysterious swindle whereof he had been arraigned at the King's Bench.[4] The fact that nobody could substantiate this report was, of course, nothing against its secret currency. Such a rumor once started on the gun decks in reference to almost anyone below the rank of a commissioned officer would, during the period assigned to this narrative, have seemed not altogether wanting in credibility to the tarry old wiseacres of a man-of-war crew. And indeed a man of Claggart's accomplishments, without prior nautical experience entering the navy at mature life, as he did, and necessarily allotted at the start to the lowest grade in it; a man too who never made allusion to his previous life ashore; these were circumstances which in the dearth of exact knowledge as to his true antecedents opened to the invidious a vague field for unfavorable surmise.

But the sailors' dogwatch gossip concerning him derived a vague plausibility from the fact that now for some period the British navy could so little afford to be squeamish in the matter of keeping up the muster rolls, that not only were press gangs notoriously abroad both afloat and ashore, but there was little or no secret about another matter, namely, that the London police were at liberty to capture any able-bodied suspect, any questionable fellow at large, and summarily ship him to the dockyard or fleet. Furthermore, even among voluntary enlistments there were instances where the motive thereto partook neither of patriotic impulse nor yet of a random desire to experience a bit of sea life and martial adventure. Insolvent debtors of minor grade, together with the promiscuous lame ducks of morality, found in the navy a convenient and secure refuge, secure because, once enlisted aboard a King's ship, they were as much in sanctuary as the transgressor of the Middle Ages harboring himself under the shadow of the altar. Such sanctioned irregularities, which for obvious reasons the government would hardly think to parade at the time and which consequently, and as affecting the least influential class of mankind, have all but dropped into oblivion, lend color[5] to something for the truth whereof I do not vouch, and hence have some scruple in stating; something I remember having seen in print though the book I cannot recall; but the same thing was personally communicated to me now more than forty years ago by an old pensioner in a cocked hat with whom I had a most interesting talk on the terrace at Greenwich, a Baltimore Negro, a Trafalgar man.[6] It was to this effect: In the case of a warship short of hands whose speedy sailing was imperative, the deficient quota, in lack of any other way of making it good, would be eked out by drafts culled direct from the jails. For reasons previously suggested it would not perhaps be easy at the present day directly to prove or disprove the allegation. But allowed as a verity, how significant would it be of England's straits at the time confronted by those wars which like a flight of harpies rose shrieking from the din and dust of the fallen Bastille.[7] That era appears measurably clear to us who look back

2. Surreptitious.   3. A man of high rank.   4. Formerly the supreme court of common law in Great Britain.   5. Appearance of truth.   6. A veteran of the Battle of Trafalgar. *Greenwich*: a hospital near London, a home for retired personnel.   7. The fall of the Bastille (July 14, 1789) signaled the beginning of the French Revolution.

at it, and but read of it. But to the grandfathers of us graybeards, the more thoughtful of them, the genius of it presented an aspect like that of Camoëns' Spirit of the Cape,[8] an eclipsing menace mysterious and prodigious. Not America was exempt from apprehension. At the height of Napoleon's unexampled conquests, there were Americans who had fought at Bunker Hill who looked forward to the possibility that the Atlantic might prove no barrier against the ultimate schemes of this French portentous upstart from the revolutionary chaos who seemed in act of fulfilling judgment prefigured in the Apocalypse.

But the less credence was to be given to the gun-deck talk touching Claggart, seeing that no man holding his office in a man-of-war can ever hope to be popular with the crew. Besides, in derogatory comments upon anyone against whom they have a grudge, or for any reason or no reason mislike, sailors are much like landsmen: they are apt to exaggerate or romance it.

About as much was really known to the *Bellipotent*'s tars of the master-at-arms' career before entering the service as an astronomer knows about a comet's travels prior to its first observable appearance in the sky. The verdict of the sea quidnuncs[9] has been cited only by way of showing what sort of moral impression the man made upon rude uncultivated natures whose conceptions of human wickedness were necessarily of the narrowest, limited to ideas of vulgar rascality—a thief among the swinging hammocks during a night watch, or the man-brokers and land-sharks of the seaports.

It was no gossip, however, but fact that though, as before hinted, Claggart upon his entrance into the navy was, as a novice, assigned to the least honorable section of a man-of-war's crew, embracing the drudgery, he did not long remain there. The superior capacity he immediately evinced, his constitutional sobriety, an ingratiating deference to superiors, together with a peculiar ferreting genius manifested on a singular occasion; all this, capped by a certain austere patriotism, abruptly advanced him to the position of master-at-arms.

Of this maritime chief of police the ship's corporals, so called, were the immediate subordinates, and compliant ones; and this, as is to be noted in some business departments ashore, almost to a degree inconsistent with entire moral volition. His place put various converging wires of underground influence under the chief's control, capable when astutely worked through his understrappers of operating to the mysterious discomfort, if nothing worse, of any of the sea commonalty.

9

Life in the foretop well agreed with Billy Budd. There, when not actually engaged on the yards yet higher aloft, the topmen, who as such had been picked out for youth and activity, constituted an aerial club lounging at ease against the smaller stun'sails[1] rolled up into cushions, spinning yarns like the lazy gods, and frequently amused with what was going on in the busy world of the decks below. No wonder then that a young fellow of Billy's

8. The Portuguese poet Luiz Vaz de Camoëns (1524?–1580) describes in his epic poem, the *Lusiads*, a monster named Adamastor who attempts to destroy Vasco da Gama and his crew.   9. What now (Latin, literal trans.); a busybody.   1. Studding sails (small auxiliaries to the mainsails).

disposition was well content in such society. Giving no cause of offense to anybody, he was always alert at a call. So in the merchant service it had been with him. But now such a punctiliousness in duty was shown that his topmates would sometimes good-naturedly laugh at him for it. This heightened alacrity had its cause, namely, the impression made upon him by the first formal gangway-punishment he had ever witnessed, which befell the day following his impressment. It had been incurred by a little fellow, young, a novice afterguardsman absent from his assigned post when the ship was being put about; a dereliction resulting in a rather serious hitch to that maneuver, one demanding instantaneous promptitude in letting go and making fast. When Billy saw the culprit's naked back under the scourge, gridironed with red welts and worse, when he marked the dire expression in the liberated man's face as with his woolen shirt flung over him by the executioner he rushed forward from the spot to bury himself in the crowd, Billy was horrified. He resolved that never through remissness would he make himself liable to such a visitation or do or omit aught that might merit even verbal reproof. What then was his surprise and concern when ultimately he found himself getting into petty trouble occasionally about such matters as the stowage of his bag or something amiss in his hammock, matters under the police oversight of the ship's corporals of the lower decks, and which brought down on him a vague threat from one of them.

So heedful in all things as he was, how could this be? He could not understand it, and it more than vexed him. When he spoke to his young topmates about it they were either lightly incredulous or found something comical in his unconcealed anxiety. 'Is it your bag, Billy?' said one. 'Well, sew yourself up in it, bully boy, and then you'll be sure to know if anybody meddles with it.'

Now there was a veteran aboard who because his years began to disqualify him for more active work had been recently assigned duty as mainmastman in his watch, looking to the gear belayed[2] at the rail roundabout that great spar near the deck. At off-times the foretopman had picked up some acquaintance with him, and now in his trouble it occurred to him that he might be the sort of person to go to for wise counsel. He was an old Dansker[3] long anglicized in the service, of few words, many wrinkles, and some honorable scars. His wizened face, time-tinted and weather-stained to the complexion of an antique parchment, was here and there peppered blue by the chance explosion of a gun cartridge in action.

He was an *Agamemnon* man, some two years prior to the time of this story having served under Nelson when still captain in that ship immortal in naval memory, which dismantled and in part broken up to her bare ribs is seen a grand skeleton in Haden's etching.[4] As one of a boarding party from the *Agamemnon* he had received a cut slantwise along one temple and cheek leaving a long pale scar like a streak of dawn's light falling athwart the dark visage. It was on account of that scar and the affair in which it was known that he had received it, as well as from his blue-peppered complexion, that the Dansker went among the *Bellipotent*'s crew by the name of 'Board-Her-in-the-Smoke.'

---

2. Stowed. 3. Dane. 4. *The Breaking Up of the Agamemnon*, the masterpiece of Sir Francis Seymour Haden (1818–1910).

Now the first time that his small weasel eyes happened to light on Billy Budd, a certain grim internal merriment set all his ancient wrinkles into antic play. Was it that his eccentric unsentimental old sapience, primitive in its kind, saw or thought it saw something which in contrast with the warship's environment looked oddly incongruous in the Handsome Sailor? But after slyly studying him at intervals, the old Merlin's[5] equivocal merriment was modified; for now when the twain would meet, it would start in his face a quizzing[6] sort of look, but it would be but momentary and sometimes replaced by an expression of speculative query as to what might eventually befall a nature like that, dropped into a world not without some mantraps and against whose subtleties simple courage lacking experience and address,[7] and without any touch of defensive ugliness, is of little avail; and where such innocence as man is capable of does yet in a moral emergency not always sharpen the faculties or enlighten the will.

However it was, the Dansker in his ascetic way rather took to Billy. Nor was this only because of a certain philosophic interest in such a character. There was another cause. While the old man's eccentricities, sometimes bordering on the ursine, repelled the juniors, Billy, undeterred thereby, revering him as a salt hero, would make advances, never passing the old *Agamemnon* man without a salutation marked by that respect which is seldom lost on the aged, however crabbed at times or whatever their station in life.

There was a vein of dry humor, or what not, in the mastman; and, whether in freak of patriarchal irony touching Billy's youth and athletic frame, or for some other and more recondite reason, from the first in addressing him he always substituted *Baby* for Billy, the Dansker in fact being the originator of the name by which the foretopman eventually became known aboard ship.

Well then, in his mysterious little difficulty going in quest of the wrinkled one, Billy found him off duty in a dogwatch ruminating by himself, seated on a shot box of the upper gun deck, now and then surveying with a somewhat cynical regard certain of the more swaggering promenaders there. Billy recounted his trouble, again wondering how it all happened. The salt seer attentively listened, accompanying the foretopman's recital with queer twitchings of his wrinkles and problematical little sparkles of his small ferret eyes. Making an end of his story, the foretopman asked, 'And now, Dansker, do tell me what you think of it.'

The old man, shoving up the front of his tarpaulin and deliberately rubbing the long slant scar at the point where it entered the thin hair, laconically said, 'Baby Budd, *Jemmy Legs*'[8] (meaning the master-at-arms) 'is down on you.'

'*Jemmy Legs!*' ejaculated Billy, his welkin eyes expanding.

'What for? Why, he calls me "the sweet and pleasant young fellow," they tell me.'

'Does he so?' grinned the grizzled one; then said, 'Ay, Baby lad, a sweet voice has Jemmy Legs.'

'No, not always. But to me he has. I seldom pass him but there comes a pleasant word.'

---

5. King Arthur's court magician.   6. Mocking.   7. Skill and tact in handling situations.   8. A disparaging nickname for the master-at-arms, still used in the American navy.

'And that's because he's down upon you, Baby Budd.'

Such reiteration, along with the manner of it, incomprehensible to a novice, disturbed Billy almost as much as the mystery for which he had sought explanation. Something less unpleasingly oracular he tried to extract; but the old sea Chiron,[9] thinking perhaps that for the nonce he had sufficiently instructed his young Achilles, pursed his lips, gathered all his wrinkles together, and would commit himself to nothing further.

Years, and those experiences which befall certain shrewder men subordinated lifelong to the will of superiors, all this had developed in the Dansker the pithy guarded cynicism that was his leading characteristic.

10

The next day an incident served to confirm Billy Budd in his incredulity as to the Dansker's strange summing up of the case submitted. The ship at noon, going large before the wind, was rolling on her course, and he below at dinner and engaged in some sportful talk with the members of his mess, chanced in a sudden lurch to spill the entire contents of his soup pan upon the new-scrubbed deck. Claggart, the master-at-arms, official rattan[1] in hand, happened to be passing along the battery in a bay of which the mess was lodged, and the greasy liquid streamed just across his path. Stepping over it, he was proceeding on his way without comment, since the matter was nothing to take notice of under the circumstances, when he happened to observe who it was that had done the spilling. His countenance changed. Pausing, he was about to ejaculate something hasty at the sailor, but checked himself, and pointing down to the streaming soup, playfully tapped him from behind with his rattan, saying in a low musical voice peculiar to him at times, 'Handsomely done, my lad! And handsome is as handsome did it, too!' And with that passed on. Not noted by Billy as not coming within his view was the involuntary smile, or rather grimace, that accompanied Claggart's equivocal words. Aridly it drew down the thin corners of his shapely mouth. But everybody taking his remark as meant for humorous, and at which therefore as coming from a superior they were bound to laugh 'with counterfeited glee,'[2] acted accordingly; and Billy, tickled, it may be, by the allusion to his being the Handsome Sailor, merrily joined in; then addressing his messmates exclaimed, 'There now, who says that Jemmy Legs is down on me!'

'And who said he was, Beauty?' demanded one Donald with some surprise. Whereat the foretopman looked a little foolish, recalling that it was only one person, Board-Her-in-the-Smoke, who had suggested what to him was the smoky idea that his master-at-arms was in any peculiar way hostile to him. Meantime that functionary, resuming his path, must have momentarily worn some expression less guarded than that of the bitter smile, usurping the face from the heart—some distorting expression perhaps, for a drummer-boy heedlessly frolicking along from the opposite direction and chancing to come into light collision with his person was strangely disconcerted by his aspect. Nor was the impression lessened when the official, impetuously giving him a sharp cut with the rattan, vehemently exclaimed, 'Look where you go!'

9. A centaur, half man and half horse, skilled in healing and the wisest of his species; he taught the Greek heroes Achilles, Hercules, and Aesculapius.　1. Swagger stick, light whip.　2. Oliver Goldsmith (1730–1774), *The Deserted Village*, line 201, alluding to the response of students to a severe choolmaster.

11

What was the matter with the master-at-arms? And, be the matter what it might, how could it have direct relation to Billy Budd, with whom prior to the affair of the spilled soup he had never come into any special contact official or otherwise? What indeed could the trouble have to do with one so little inclined to give offense as the merchantship's 'peacemaker,' even him who in Claggart's own phrase was 'the sweet and pleasant young fellow'? Yes, why should Jemmy Legs, to borrow the Dansker's expression, be 'down' on the Handsome Sailor? But, at heart and not for nothing, as the late chance encounter may indicate to the discerning, down on him, secretly down on him, he assuredly was.

Now to invent something touching the more private career of Claggart, something involving Billy Budd, of which something the latter should be wholly ignorant, some romantic incident implying that Claggart's knowledge of the young bluejacket began at some period anterior to catching sight of him on board the seventy-four—all this, not so difficult to do, might avail in a way more or less interesting to account for whatever of enigma may appear to lurk in the case. But in fact there was nothing of the sort. And yet the cause necessarily to be assumed as the sole one assignable is in its very realism as much charged with that prime element of Radcliffian romance, the mysterious, as any that the ingenuity of the author of *The Mysteries of Udolpho*[3] would devise. For what can more partake of the mysterious than an antipathy spontaneous and profound such as is evoked in certain exceptional mortals by the mere aspect of some other mortal, however harmless he may be, if not called forth by this very harmlessness itself?

Now there can exist no irritating juxtaposition of dissimilar personalities comparable to that which is possible aboard a great warship fully manned and at sea. There, every day among all ranks, almost every man comes into more or less of contact with almost every other man. Wholly there to avoid even the sight of an aggravating object one must needs give it Jonah's toss[4] or jump overboard himself. Imagine how all this might eventually operate on some peculiar human creature the direct reverse of a saint!

But for the adequate comprehending of Claggart by a normal nature these hints are insufficient. To pass from a normal nature to him one must cross 'the deadly space between.' And this is best done by indirection.

Long ago an honest scholar, my senior, said to me in reference to one who like himself is now no more, a man so unimpeachably respectable that against him nothing was ever openly said though among the few something was whispered, 'Yes, X—is a nut not to be cracked by the tap of a lady's fan. You are aware that I am the adherent of no organized religion, much less of any philosophy built into a system. Well, for all that, I think that to try and get into X—, enter his labyrinth and get out again, without a clue derived from some source other than what is known as "knowledge of the world"— that were hardly possible, at least for me.'

'Why,' said I, 'X—, however singular a study to some, is yet human, and

---

3. An immensely popular Gothic novel by Ann Radcliffe (1764–1823).   4. Jonah 1.15: "So they took up Jonah, and cast him forth into the sea." A nautical expression when an unlucky object or person is put overboard.

knowledge of the world assuredly implies the knowledge of human nature, and in most of its varieties.'

'Yes, but a superficial knowledge of it, serving ordinary purposes. But for anything deeper, I am not certain whether to know the world and to know human nature be not two distinct branches of knowledge, which while they may co-exist in the same heart, yet either may exist with little or nothing of the other. Nay, in an average man of the world, his constant rubbing with it blunts that finer spiritual insight indispensable to the understanding of the essential in certain exceptional characters, whether evil ones or good. In a matter of some importance I have seen a girl wind an old lawyer about her little finger. Nor was it the dotage of senile love. Nothing of the sort. But he knew law better than he knew the girl's heart. Coke and Blackstone[5] hardly shed so much light into obscure spiritual places as the Hebrew prophets. And who were they? Mostly recluses.'

At the time, my inexperience was such that I did not quite see the drift of all this. It may be that I see it now. And, indeed, if that lexicon which is based on Holy Writ were any longer popular, one might with less difficulty define and denominate certain phenomenal men. As it is, one must turn to some authority not liable to the charge of being tinctured with the biblical element.

In a list of definitions included in the authentic translation of Plato, a list attributed to him, occurs this: 'Natural Depravity: a depravity according to nature,' a definition which, though savoring of Calvinism,[6] by no means involves Calvin's dogma as to total mankind. Evidently its intent makes it applicable but to individuals. Not many are the examples of this depravity which the gallows and jail supply. At any rate, for notable instances, since these have no vulgar alloy of the brute in them, but invariably are dominated by intellectuality, one must go elsewhere. Civilization, especially if of the austerer sort, is auspicious to it. It folds itself in the mantle of respectability. It has certain negative virtues serving as silent auxiliaries. It never allows wine to get within its guard. It is not going too far to say that it is without vices or small sins. There is a phenomenal pride in it that excludes them. It is never mercenary or avaricious. In short, the depravity here meant partakes nothing of the sordid or sensual. It is serious, but free from acerbity. Though no flatterer of mankind it never speaks ill of it.

But the thing which in eminent instances signalizes so exceptional a nature is this: Though the man's even temper and discreet bearing would seem to intimate a mind peculiarly subject to the law of reason, not the less in heart he would seem to riot in complete exemption from that law, having apparently little to do with reason further than to employ it as an ambidexter[7] implement for effecting the irrational. That is to say: Toward the accomplishment of an aim which in wantonness of atrocity would seem to partake of the insane, he will direct a cool judgment sagacious and sound. These men are madmen, and of the most dangerous sort, for their lunacy is not continuous, but occasional, evoked by some special object; it is protectively secretive, which is as much as to say it is self-contained, so that when, moreover, most active it is to the average mind not distinguishable from sanity, and for

5. Sir Edward Coke (1552–1634) and Sir William Blackstone (1723–1780), noted British jurists and writers on the law.   6. The religious system founded by John Calvin (1509–1564), which emphasizes predestination.   7. Two-handed.

the reason above suggested: that whatever its aims may be—and the aim is never declared—the method and the outward proceeding are always perfectly rational.

Now something such an one was Claggart, in whom was the mania of an evil nature, not engendered by vicious training or corrupting books or licentious living, but born with him and innate, in short 'a depravity according to nature.'

Dark sayings are these, some will say. But why? Is it because they somewhat savor of Holy Writ in its phrase 'mystery of iniquity'?[8] If they do, such savor was far enough from being intended, for little will it commend these pages to many a reader of today.

The point of the present story turning on the hidden nature of the master-at-arms has necessitated this chapter. With an added hint or two in connection with the incident at the mess, the resumed narrative must be left to vindicate, as it may, its own credibility.

12

That Claggart's figure was not amiss, and his face, save the chin, well molded, has already been said. Of these favorable points he seemed not insensible, for he was not only neat but careful in his dress. But the form of Billy Budd was heroic; and if his face was without the intellectual look of the pallid Claggart's, not the less was it lit, like his, from within, though from a different source. The bonfire in his heart made luminous the rose-tan in his cheek.

In view of the marked contrast between the persons of the twain, it is more than probable that when the master-at-arms in the scene last given applied to the sailor the proverb 'Handsome is as handsome does,' he there let escape an ironic inkling, not caught by the young sailors who heard it, as to what it was that had first moved him against Billy, namely, his significant personal beauty.

Now envy and antipathy, passions irreconcilable in reason, nevertheless in fact may spring conjoined like Chang and Eng[9] in one birth. Is Envy then such a monster? Well, though many an arraigned mortal has in hopes of mitigated penalty pleaded guilty to horrible actions, did ever anybody seriously confess to envy? Something there is in it universally felt to be more shameful than even felonious crime. And not only does everybody disown it, but the better sort are inclined to incredulity when it is in earnest imputed to an intelligent man. But since its lodgment is in the heart not the brain, no degree of intellect supplies a guarantee against it. But Claggart's was no vulgar form of the passion. Nor, as directed toward Billy Budd, did it partake of that streak of apprehensive jealousy that marred Saul's visage perturbedly brooding on the comely young David.[1] Claggart's envy struck deeper. If askance he eyed the good looks, cheery health, and frank enjoyment of young life in Billy Budd, it was because these went along with a nature that, as Claggart magnetically felt, had in its simplicity never willed malice or experienced the reactionary bite of that serpent. To him, the spirit lodged within Billy, and looking out from his welkin eyes as from windows, that ineffability

8. 2 Thessalonians 2.7.   9. Famous Siamese twins (1811–1874) who toured the United States.
1. David's comeliness and Saul's jealousy are described in 1 Samuel 16.18, 18.8 ff.

it was which made the dimple in his dyed cheek, suppled his joints, and dancing in his yellow curls made him pre-eminently the Handsome Sailor. One person excepted, the master-at-arms was perhaps the only man in the ship intellectually capable of adequately appreciating the moral phenomenon presented in Billy Budd. And the insight but intensified his passion, which assuming various secret forms within him, at times assumed that of cynic disdain, disdain of innocence—to be nothing more than innocent! Yet in an aesthetic way he saw the charm of it, the courageous free-and-easy temper of it, and fain would have shared it, but he despaired of it.

With no power to annul the elemental evil in him, though readily enough he could hide it; apprehending the good, but powerless to be it; a nature like Claggart's, surcharged with energy as such natures almost invariably are, what recourse is left to it but to recoil upon itself and, like the scorpion for which the Creator alone is responsible, act out to the end the part allotted it.

13

Passion, and passion in its profoundest, is not a thing demanding a palatial stage whereon to play its part. Down among the groundlings,[2] among the beggars and rakers of the garbage, profound passion is enacted. And the circumstances that provoke it, however trivial or mean, are no measure of its power. In the present instance the stage is a scrubbed gun deck, and one of the external provocations a man-of-war's man's spilled soup.

Now when the master-at-arms noticed whence came that greasy fluid streaming before his feet, he must have taken it—to some extent wilfully, perhaps—not for the mere accident it assuredly was, but for the sly escape of a spontaneous feeling on Billy's part more or less answering to the antipathy on his own. In effect a foolish demonstration, he must have thought, and very harmless, like the futile kick of a heifer, which yet were the heifer a shod stallion would not be so harmless. Even so was it that into the gall of Claggart's envy he infused the vitriol of his contempt. But the incident confirmed to him certain telltale reports purveyed to his ear by 'Squeak,' one of his more cunning corporals, a grizzled little man, so nicknamed by the sailors on account of his squeaky voice and sharp visage ferreting about the dark corners of the lower decks after interlopers, satirically suggesting to them the idea of a rat in a cellar.

From his chief's employing him as an implicit tool in laying little traps for the worriment of the foretopman—for it was from the master-at-arms that the petty persecutions heretofore adverted to had proceeded—the corporal, having naturally enough concluded that his master could have no love for the sailor, made it his business, faithful understrapper that he was, to foment the ill blood by perverting to his chief certain innocent frolics of the good-natured foretopman, besides inventing for his mouth sundry contumelious epithets he claimed to have overheard him let fall. The master-at-arms never suspected the veracity of these reports, more especially as to the epithets, for he well knew how secretly unpopular may become a master-at-arms, at least a master-at-arms of those days, zealous in his function, and how the blue-jackets shoot at him in private their raillery and wit; the nickname by which

2. The part of the audience that stood on the ground in an Elizabethan theater; the poorest spectators.

he goes among them (Jemmy Legs) implying under the form of merriment their cherished disrespect and dislike. But in view of the greediness of hate for pabulum[3] it hardly needed a purveyor to feed Claggart's passion.

An uncommon prudence is habitual with the subtler depravity, for it has everything to hide. And in case of an injury but suspected, its secretiveness voluntarily cuts it off from enlightenment or disillusion; and, not unreluctantly, action is taken upon surmise as upon certainty. And the retaliation is apt to be in monstrous disproportion to the supposed offense; for when in anybody was revenge in its exactions aught else but an inordinate usurer? But how with Claggart's conscience? For though consciences are unlike as foreheads, every intelligence, not excluding the scriptural devils who 'believe and tremble,'[4] has one. But Claggart's conscience being but the lawyer to his will, made ogres of trifles, probably arguing that the motive imputed to Billy in spilling the soup just when he did, together with the epithets alleged, these, if nothing more, made a strong case against him; nay, justified animosity into a sort of retributive righteousness. The Pharisee is the Guy Fawkes[5] prowling in the hid chambers underlying some natures like Claggart's. And they can really form no conception of an unreciprocated malice. Probably the master-at-arms' clandestine persecution of Billy was started to try the temper of the man; but it had not developed any quality in him that enmity could make official use of or even pervert into plausible self-justification; so that the occurrence at the mess, petty if it were, was a welcome one to that peculiar conscience assigned to be the private mentor of Claggart; and, for the rest, not improbably it put him upon new experiments.

14

Not many days after the last incident narrated, something befell Billy Budd that more graveled him than aught that had previously occurred.

It was a warm night for the latitude; and the foretopman, whose watch at the time was properly below, was dozing on the uppermost deck whither he had ascended from his hot hammock, one of hundreds suspended so closely wedged together over a lower gun deck that there was little or no swing to them. He lay as in the shadow of a hillside, stretched under the lee of the booms, a piled ridge of spare spars amidships between foremast and mainmast among which the ship's largest boat, the launch, was stowed. Alongside of three other slumberers from below, he lay near that end of the booms which approaches the foremast; his station aloft on duty as a foretopman being just over the deckstation of the forecastlemen, entitling him according to usage to make himself more or less at home in that neighborhood.

Presently he was stirred into semiconsciousness by somebody, who must have previously sounded the sleep of the others, touching his shoulder, and then, as the foretopman raised his head, breathing into his ear in a quick whisper, 'Slip into the lee forechains, Billy; there is something in the wind. Don't speak. Quick, I will meet you there,' and disappearing.

Now Billy, like sundry other essentially good-natured ones, had some of

3. Sustenance.   4. James 2.19: "The devils also believe, and tremble."   5. Instigator of the Gunpowder Plot, the plan to blow up the Houses of Parliament and King James I on November 5, 1605. *Pharisee:* follower of a Jewish sect known for its strict observance of the Torah; hence anyone extremely rigid and dogmatic.

the weaknesses inseparable from essential good nature; and among these was a reluctance, almost an incapacity of plumply[6] saying *no* to an abrupt proposition not obviously absurd on the face of it, nor obviously unfriendly, nor iniquitous. And being of warm blood, he had not the phlegm[7] tacitly to negative any proposition by unresponsive inaction. Like his sense of fear, his apprehension as to aught outside of the honest and natural was seldom very quick. Besides, upon the present occasion, the drowse from his sleep still hung upon him.

However it was, he mechanically rose and, sleepily wondering what could be in the wind, betook himself to the designated place, a narrow platform, one of six, outside of the high bulwarks and screened by the great deadeyes and multiple columned lanyards of the shrouds and backstays; and, in a great warship of that time, of dimensions commensurate to the hull's magnitude; a tarry balcony in short, overhanging the sea, and so secluded that one mariner of the *Bellipotent,* a Nonconformist[8] old tar of a serious turn, made it even in daytime his private oratory.[9]

In this retired nook the stranger soon joined Billy Budd. There was no moon as yet; a haze obscured the starlight. He could not distinctly see the stranger's face. Yet from something in the outline and carriage, Billy took him, and correctly, for one of the afterguard.

'Hist! Billy,' said the man, in the same quick cautionary whisper as before. 'You were impressed, weren't you? Well, so was I'; and he paused, as to mark the effect. But Billy, not knowing exactly what to make of this, said nothing. Then the other: 'We are not the only impressed ones, Billy. There's a gang of us.—Couldn't you—help—at a pinch?'

'What do you mean?' demanded Billy, here thoroughly shaking off his drowse.

'Hist, hist!' the hurried whisper now growing husky. 'See here,' and the man held up two small objects faintly twinkling in the night-light; 'see, they are yours, Billy, if you'll only—'

But Billy broke in, and in his resentful eagerness to deliver himself his vocal infirmity somewhat intruded. 'D—d—damme, I don't know what you are d—d—driving at, or what you mean, but you had better g—g—go where you belong!' For the moment the fellow, as confounded, did not stir; and Billy, springing to his feet, said, 'If you d—don't start, I'll t—t—toss you back over the r—rail!' There was no mistaking this, and the mysterious emissary decamped, disappearing in the direction of the mainmast in the shadow of the booms.

'Hallo, what's the matter?' here came growling from a forecastleman awakened from his deck-doze by Billy's raised voice. And as the foretopman reappeared and was recognized by him: 'Ah, Beauty, is it you? Well, something must have been the matter, for you st—st—stuttered.'

'Oh,' rejoined Billy, now mastering the impediment, 'I found an afterguardsman in our part of the ship here, and I bid him be off where he belongs.'

'And is that all you did about it, Foretopman?' gruffly demanded another, an irascible old fellow of brick-colored visage and hair who was known to his

6. Bluntly.   7. Sluggishness, apathy.   8. A Protestant dissenter from the Church of England.   9. A small chapel, especially for private prayer.

associate forecastlemen as 'Red Pepper.' 'Such sneaks I should like to marry to the gunner's daughter!'—by that expression meaning that he would like to subject them to disciplinary castigation over a gun.

However, Billy's rendering of the matter satisfactorily accounted to these inquirers for the brief commotion, since of all the sections of a ship's company the forecastlemen, veterans for the most part and bigoted in their sea prejudices, are the most jealous in resenting territorial encroachments, especially on the part of any of the afterguard, of whom they have but a sorry opinion—chiefly landsmen, never going aloft except to reef or furl the mainsail, and in no wise competent to handle a marlinspike or turn in a deadeye, say.

15

This incident sorely puzzled Billy Budd. It was an entirely new experience, the first time in his life that he had ever been personally approached in underhand intriguing fashion. Prior to this encounter he had known nothing of the afterguardsman, the two men being stationed wide apart, one forward and aloft during his watch, the other on deck and aft.

What could it mean? And could they really be guineas,[1] those two glittering objects the interloper had held up to his (Billy's) eyes? Where could the fellow get guineas? Why, even spare buttons are not so plentiful at sea. The more he turned the matter over, the more he was nonplussed, and made uneasy and discomfited. In his disgustful recoil from an overture which, though he but ill comprehended, he instinctively knew must involve evil of some sort, Billy Budd was like a young horse fresh from the pasture suddenly inhaling a vile whiff from some chemical factory, and by repeated snortings trying to get it out of his nostrils and lungs. This frame of mind barred all desire of holding further parley with the fellow, even were it but for the purpose of gaining some enlightenment as to his design in approaching him. And yet he was not without natural curiosity to see how such a visitor in the dark would look in broad day.

He espied him the following afternoon in his first dogwatch below, one of the smokers on that forward part of the upper gun deck allotted to the pipe. He recognized him by his general cut and build more than by his round freckled face and glassy eyes of pale blue, veiled with lashes all but white. And yet Billy was a bit uncertain whether indeed it were he—yonder chap about his own age chatting and laughing in freehearted way, leaning against a gun; a genial young fellow enough to look at, and something of a rattlebrain, to all appearance. Rather chubby too for a sailor, even an afterguardsman. In short, the last man in the world, one would think, to be overburdened with thoughts, especially those perilous thoughts that must needs belong to a conspirator in any serious project, or even to the underling of such a conspirator.

Although Billy was not aware of it, the fellow, with a sidelong watchful glance, had perceived Billy first, and then noting that Billy was looking at him, thereupon nodded a familiar sort of friendly recognition as to an old acquaintance, without interrupting the talk he was engaged in with the group

---

1. English gold coins, not minted after 1813, worth 21 shillings (approximately $84).

of smokers. A day or two afterwards, chancing in the evening promenade on a gun deck to pass Billy, he offered a flying word of good-fellowship, as it were, which by its unexpectedness, and equivocalness under the circumstances, so embarrassed Billy that he knew not how to respond to it, and let it go unnoticed.

Billy was now left more at a loss than before. The ineffectual speculations into which he was led were so disturbingly alien to him that he did his best to smother them. It never entered his mind that here was a matter which, from its extreme questionableness, it was his duty as a loyal bluejacket to report in the proper quarter. And, probably, had such a step been suggested to him, he would have been deterred from taking it by the thought, one of novice magnanimity, that it would savor overmuch of the dirty work of a telltale. He kept the thing to himself. Yet upon one occasion he could not forebear a little disburdening himself to the old Dansker, tempted thereto perhaps by the influence of a balmy night when the ship lay becalmed; the twain, silent for the most part, sitting together on deck, their heads propped against the bulwarks. But it was only a partial and anonymous account that Billy gave, the unfounded scruples above referred to preventing full disclosure to anybody. Upon hearing Billy's version, the sage Dansker seemed to divine more than he was told; and after a little meditation, during which his wrinkles were pursed as into a point, quite effacing for the time that quizzing expression his face sometimes wore: 'Didn't I say so, Baby Budd?'

'Say what?' demanded Billy.

'Why, *Jemmy Legs* is *down* on you.'

'And what,' rejoined Billy in amazement, 'has *Jemmy Legs* to do with that cracked afterguardsman?'

'Ho, it was an afterguardsman, then. A cat's-paw,[2] a cat's-paw!' And with that exclamation, whether it had reference to a light puff of air just then coming over the calm sea, or a subtler relation to the afterguardsman, there is no telling, the old Merlin gave a twisting wrench with his black teeth at his plug of tobacco, vouchsafing no reply to Billy's impetuous question, though now repeated, for it was his wont to relapse into grim silence when interrogated in skeptical sort as to any of his sententious oracles, not always very clear ones, rather partaking of that obscurity which invests most Delphic[3] deliverances from any quarter.

Long experience had very likely brought this old man to that bitter prudence which never interferes in aught and never gives advice.

16

Yes, despite the Dansker's pithy insistence as to the master-at-arms being at the bottom of these strange experiences of Billy on board the *Bellipotent*, the young sailor was ready to ascribe them to almost anybody but the man who, to use Billy's own expression, 'always had a pleasant word for him.' This is to be wondered at. Yet not so much to be wondered at. In certain matters, some sailors even in mature life remain unsophisticated enough. But a young seafarer of the disposition of our athletic foretopman is much of a child-man.

---

2. Either a light wind perceived by its impressions on the sea or a seaman employed to entice volunteers.
3. Literally, issuing from the ancient Greek oracle of Apollo at Delphi, which made ambiguous prophecies; hence, obscure in meaning, ambiguous.

And yet a child's utter innocence is but its blank ignorance, and the innocence more or less wanes as intelligence waxes. But in Billy Budd intelligence, such as it was, had advanced while yet his simple-mindedness remained for the most part unaffected. Experience is a teacher indeed; yet did Billy's years make his experience small. Besides, he had none of that intuitive knowledge of the bad which in natures not good or incompletely so foreruns experience, and therefore may pertain, as in some instances it too clearly does pertain, even to youth.

And what could Billy know of man except of man as a mere sailor? And the old-fashioned sailor, the veritable man before the mast, the sailor from boyhood up, he, though indeed of the same species as a landsman, is in some respects singularly distinct from him. The sailor is frankness, the landsman is finesse. Life is not a game with the sailor, demanding the long head—no intricate game of chess where few moves are made in straightforwardness and ends are attained by indirection, an oblique, tedious, barren game hardly worth that poor candle burnt out in playing it.

Yes, as a class, sailors are in character a juvenile race. Even their deviations are marked by juvenility, this more especially holding true with the sailors of Billy's time. Then too, certain things which apply to all sailors do more pointedly operate here and there upon the junior one. Every sailor, too, is accustomed to obey orders without debating them; his life afloat is externally ruled for him; he is not brought into that promiscuous[4] commerce with mankind where unobstructed free agency on equal terms—equal superficially, at least—soon teaches one that unless upon occasion he exercise a distrust keen in proportion to the fairness of the appearance, some foul turn maybe served him. A ruled undemonstrative distrustfulness is so habitual, not with businessmen so much as with men who know their kind in less shallow relations than business, namely, certain men of the world, that they come at last to employ it all but unconsciously; and some of them would very likely feel real surprise at being charged with it as one of their general characteristics.

17

But after the little matter at the mess Billy Budd no more found himself in strange trouble at times about his hammock or his clothes bag or what not. As to that smile that occasionally sunned him, and the pleasant passing word, these were, if not more frequent, yet if anything more pronounced than before.

But for all that, there were certain other demonstrations now. When Claggart's unobserved glance happened to light on belted Billy rolling along the upper gun deck in the leisure of the second dogwatch, exchanging passing broadsides of fun with other young promenaders in the crowd, that glance would follow the cheerful sea Hyperion[5] with a settled meditative and melancholy expression, his eyes strangely suffused with incipient feverish tears. Then would Claggart look like the man of sorrows.[6] Yes, and sometimes the melancholy expression would have in it a touch of soft yearning, as if Claggart

---

4. Indiscriminate.   5. In Greek mythology, the Titan god who came to be identified with Apollo, god of youth and beauty.   6. In Isaiah 53.3, the Lord's servant is described as "despised and rejected of men; a man of sorrows, and acquainted with grief."

could even have loved Billy but for fate and ban. But this was an evanescence, and quickly repented of, as it were, by an immitigable look, pinching and shriveling the visage into the momentary semblance of a wrinkled walnut. But sometimes catching sight in advance of the foretopman coming in his direction, he would, upon their nearing, step aside a little to let him pass, dwelling upon Billy for the moment with the glittering dental satire of a Guise.[7] But upon any abrupt unforeseen encounter a red light would flash forth from his eye like a spark from an anvil in a dusk smithy. That quick, fierce light was a strange one, darted from orbs which in repose were of a color nearest approaching a deeper violet, the softest of shades.

Though some of these caprices of the pit[8] could not but be observed by their object, yet were they beyond the construing of such a nature. And the thews of Billy were hardly compatible with that sort of sensitive spiritual organization which in some cases instinctively conveys to ignorant innocence an admonition of the proximity of the malign. He thought the master-at-arms acted in a manner rather queer at times. That was all. But the occasional frank air and pleasant word went for what they purported to be, the young sailor never having heard as yet of the 'too fair-spoken man.'

Had the foretopman been conscious of having done or said anything to provoke the ill will of the official, it would have been different with him, and his sight might have been purged if not sharpened. As it was, innocence was his blinder.

So was it with him in yet another matter. Two minor officers, the armorer and captain of the hold, with whom he had never exchanged a word, his position in the ship not bringing him into contact with them, these men now for the first began to cast upon Billy, when they chanced to encounter him, that peculiar glance which evidences that the man from whom it comes has been some way tampered with, and to the prejudice of him upon whom the glance lights. Never did it occur to Billy as a thing to be noted or a thing suspicious, though he well knew the fact, that the armorer and captain of the hold, with the ship's yeoman, apothecary, and others of that grade, were by naval usage messmates of the master-at-arms, men with ears convenient to his confidential tongue.

But the general popularity that came from our Handsome Sailor's manly forwardness upon occasion and irresistible good nature, indicating no mental superiority tending to excite an invidious feeling, this good will on the part of most of his shipmates made him the less to concern himself about such mute aspects toward him as those whereto allusion has just been made, aspects he could not so fathom as to infer their whole import.

As to the afterguardsman, though Billy for reasons already given necessarily saw little of him, yet when the two did happen to meet, invariably came the fellow's offhand cheerful recognition, sometimes accompanied by a passing pleasant word or two. Whatever that equivocal young person's original design may really have been, or the design of which he might have been the deputy, certain it was from his manner upon these occasions that he had wholly dropped it.

It was as if his precocity of crookedness (and every vulgar villain is pre-

---

7. Henri de Guise (1550–1588), a famed conspirator who could smile throughout his villainy.   8. Of hell.

cocious) had for once deceived him, and the man he had sought to entrap as a simpleton had through his very simplicity ignominiously baffled him.

But shrewd ones may opine that it was hardly possible for Billy to refrain from going up to the afterguardsman and bluntly demanding to know his purpose in the initial interview so abruptly closed in the forechains. Shrewd ones may also think it but natural in Billy to set about sounding some of the other impressed men of the ship in order to discover what basis, if any, there was for the emissary's obscure suggestions as to plotting disaffection aboard. Yes, shrewd ones may so think. But something more, or rather something else than mere shrewdness is perhaps needful for the due understanding of such a character as Billy Budd's.

As to Claggart, the monomania in the man—if that indeed it were—as involuntarily disclosed by starts in the manifestations detailed, yet in general covered over by his self-contained and rational demeanor; this, like a subterranean fire, was eating its way deeper and deeper in him. Something decisive must come of it.

18

After the mysterious interview in the forechains, the one so abruptly ended there by Billy, nothing especially germane to the story occurred until the events now about to be narrated.

Elsewhere it has been said that in the lack of frigates (of course better sailers than line-of-battle ships) in the English squadron up the Straits at that period, the *Bellipotent* 74 was occasionally employed not only as an available substitute for a scout, but at times on detached service of more important kind. This was not alone because of her sailing qualities, not common in a ship of her rate,[9] but quite as much, probably, that the character of her commander, it was thought, specially adapted him for any duty where under unforeseen difficulties a prompt initiative might have to be taken in some matter demanding knowledge and ability in addition to those qualities implied in good seamanship. It was on an expedition of the latter sort, a somewhat distant one, and when the *Bellipotent* was almost at her furthest remove from the fleet, that in the latter part of an afternoon watch she unexpectedly came in sight of a ship of the enemy. It proved to be a frigate. The latter, perceiving through the glass that the weight of men and metal would be heavily against her, invoking her light heels crowded sail to get away. After a chase urged almost against hope and lasting until about the middle of the first dogwatch, she signally succeeded in effecting her escape.

Not long after the pursuit had been given up, and ere the excitement incident thereto had altogether waned away, the master-at-arms, ascending from his cavernous sphere, made his appearance cap in hand by the mainmast respectfully waiting the notice of Captain Vere, then solitary walking the weather side of the quarter-deck, doubtless somewhat chafed at the failure of the pursuit. The spot where Claggart stood was the place allotted to men of lesser grades seeking some more particular interview either with the officer of the deck or the captain himself. But from the latter it was not often that a sailor or petty officer of those days would seek a hearing; only some

9. Classification.

exceptional cause would, according to established custom, have warranted that.

Presently, just as the commander, absorbed in his reflections, was on the point of turning aft in his promenade, he became sensible of Claggart's presence, and saw the doffed cap held in deferential expectancy. Here be it said that Captain Vere's personal knowledge of his petty officer had only begun at the time of the ship's last sailing from home, Claggart then for the first, in transfer from a ship detained for repairs, supplying on board the *Bellipotent* the place of a previous master-at-arms disabled and ashore.

No sooner did the commander observe who it was that now deferentially stood awaiting his notice than a peculiar expression came over him. It was not unlike that which uncontrollably will flit across the countenance of one at unawares encountering a person who, though known to him indeed, has hardly been long enough known for thorough knowledge, but something in whose aspect nevertheless now for the first provokes a vaguely repellent distaste. But coming to a stand and resuming much of his wonted official manner, save that a sort of impatience lurked in the intonation of the opening word, he said, 'Well? What is it, Master-at-arms?'

With the air of a subordinate grieved at the necessity of being a messenger of ill tidings, and while conscientiously determined to be frank yet equally resolved upon shunning overstatement, Claggart at this invitation, or rather summons to disburden, spoke up. What he said, conveyed in the language of no uneducated man, was to the effect following, if not altogether in these words, namely, that during the chase and preparations for the possible encounter he had seen enough to convince him that at least one sailor aboard was a dangerous character in a ship mustering some who not only had taken a guilty part in the late serious troubles, but others also who, like the man in question, had entered His Majesty's service under another form than enlistment.

At this point Captain Vere with some impatience interrupted him: 'Be direct, man; say *impressed men*.'

Claggart made a gesture of subservience, and proceeded. Quite lately he (Claggart) had begun to suspect that on the gun decks some sort of movement prompted by the sailor in question was covertly going on, but he had not thought himself warranted in reporting the suspicion so long as it remained indistinct. But from what he had that afternoon observed in the man referred to, the suspicion of something clandestine going on had advanced to a point less removed from certainty. He deeply felt, he added, the serious responsibility assumed in making a report involving such possible consequences to the individual mainly concerned, besides tending to augment those natural anxieties which every naval commander must feel in view of extraordinary outbreaks so recent as those which, he sorrowfully said it, it needed not to name.

Now at the first broaching of the matter Captain Vere, taken by surprise, could not wholly dissemble his disquietude. But as Claggart went on, the former's aspect changed into restiveness under something in the testifier's manner in giving his testimony. However, he refrained from interrupting him. And Claggart, continuing, concluded with this: 'God forbid, your honor, that the *Bellipotent*'s should be the experience of the—'

'Never mind that!' here peremptorily broke in the superior, his face altering with anger, instinctively divining the ship that the other was about to name, one in which the Nore Mutiny had assumed a singularly tragical character that for a time jeopardized the life of its commander. Under the circumstances he was indignant at the purposed allusion. When the commissioned officers themselves were on all occasions very heedful how they referred to the recent events in the fleet, for a petty officer unnecessarily to allude to them in the presence of his captain, this struck him as a most immodest presumption. Besides, to his quick sense of self-respect it even looked under the circumstances something like an attempt to alarm him. Nor at first was he without some surprise that one who so far as he had hitherto come under his notice had shown considerable tact in his function should in this particular evince such lack of it.

But these thoughts and kindred dubious ones flitting across his mind were suddenly replaced by an intuitional surmise which, though as yet obscure in form, served practically to affect his reception of the ill tidings. Certain it is that, long versed in everything pertaining to the complicated gun-deck life, which like every other form of life has its secret mines and dubious side, the side popularly disclaimed, Captain Vere did not permit himself to be unduly disturbed by the general tenor of his subordinate's report.

Furthermore, if in view of recent events prompt action should be taken at the first palpable sign of recurring insubordination, for all that, not judicious would it be, he thought, to keep the idea of lingering disaffection alive by undue forwardness in crediting an informer, even if his own subordinate and charged among other things with police surveillance of the crew. This feeling would not perhaps have so prevailed with him were it not that upon a prior occasion the patriotic zeal officially evinced by Claggart had somewhat irritated him as appearing rather supersensible and strained. Furthermore something even in the official's self-possessed and somewhat ostentatious manner in making his specifications strangely reminded him of a bandsman,[1] a perjurous witness in a capital case before a courtmartial ashore of which when a lieutenant he (Captain Vere) had been a member.

Now the peremptory check given to Claggart in the matter of the arrested allusion was quickly followed up by this: 'You say that there is at least one dangerous man aboard. Name him.'

'William Budd, a foretopman, your honor.'

'William Budd!' repeated Captain Vere with unfeigned astonishment. 'And mean you the man that Lieutenant Ratcliffe took from the merchantman not very long ago, the young fellow who seems to be so popular with the men—Billy the Handsome Sailor, as they call him?'

'The same, your honor; but for all his youth and good looks, a deep one. Not for nothing does he insinuate himself into the good will of his shipmates, since at the least they will at a pinch say—all hands will—a good word for him, and at all hazards. Did Lieutenant Ratcliffe happen to tell your honor of that adroit fling of Budd's, jumping up in the cutter's bow under the merchantman's stern when he was being taken off? It is even masked by that sort of good-humored air that at heart he resents his impressment. You have but noted his fair cheek. A mantrap may be under the ruddy-tipped daisies.'

Now the Handsome Sailor as a signal figure among the crew had naturally

1. Crewman charged with the task of stitching bands of canvas into sails to strengthen them.

enough attracted the captain's attention from the first. Though in general not very demonstrative to his officers, he had congratulated Lieutenant Ratcliffe upon his good fortune in lighting on such a fine specimen of the *genus homo,* who in the nude might have posed for a statue of a young Adam before the Fall. As to Billy's adieu to the ship *Rights-of-Man,* which the boarding lieutenant had indeed reported to him, but, in a deferential way, more as a good story than aught else, Captain Vere, though mistakenly understanding it as a satiric sally, had but thought so much the better of the impressed man for it; as a military sailor, admiring the spirit that could take an arbitrary enlistment so merrily and sensibly. The foretopman's conduct, too, so far as it had fallen under the captain's notice, had confirmed the first happy augury, while the new recruit's qualities as a 'sailor-man' seemed to be such that he had thought of recommending him to the executive officer for promotion to a place that would more frequently bring him under his own observation, namely, the captaincy of the mizzentop, replacing there in the starboard watch a man not so young whom partly for that reason he deemed less fitted for the post. Be it parenthesized here that since the mizzentopmen have not to handle such breadths of heavy canvas as the lower sails on the mainmast and foremast, a young man if of the right stuff not only seems best adapted to duty there, but in fact is generally selected for the captaincy of that top, and the company under him are light hands and often but striplings. In sum, Captain Vere had from the beginning deemed Billy Budd to be what in the naval parlance of the time was called a 'King's bargain': that is to say, for His Britannic Majesty's navy a capital investment at small outlay or none at all.

After a brief pause, during which the reminiscences above mentioned passed vividly through his mind and he weighed the import of Claggart's last suggestion conveyed in the phrase 'mantrap under the daisies,' and the more he weighed it the less reliance he felt in the informer's good faith, suddenly he turned upon him and in a low voice demanded: 'Do you come to me, Master-at-arms, with so foggy a tale? As to Budd, cite me an act or spoken word of his confirmatory of what you in general charge against him. Stay,' drawing nearer to him; 'heed what you speak. Just now, and in a case like this, there is a yardarm-end for the false witness.'

'Ah, your honor!' sighed Claggart, mildly shaking his shapely head as in sad deprecation of such unmerited severity of tone. Then, bridling—erecting himself as in virtuous self-assertion—he circumstantially alleged certain words and acts which collectively, if credited, led to presumptions morally inculpating Budd. And for some of these averments, he added, substantiating proof was not far.

With gray eyes impatient and distrustful essaying to fathom to the bottom Claggart's calm violet ones, Captain Vere again heard him out; then for the moment stood ruminating. The mood he evinced, Claggart—himself for the time liberated from the other's scrutiny—steadily regarded with a look difficult to render: a look curious of the operation of his tactics, a look such as might have been that of the spokesman of the envious children of Jacob deceptively imposing upon the troubled patriarch the blood-dyed coat of young Joseph.[2]

2. Genesis 37.31–32: "And they took Joseph's coat, and killed a kid of the goats, and dipped the coat in the blood; And they sent the coat of many colours, and they brought it to their father; and said, This have we found: know now whether it be thy son's coat or no."

Though something exceptional in the moral quality of Captain Vere made him, in earnest encounter with a fellow man, a veritable touchstone of that man's essential nature, yet now as to Claggart and what was really going on in him his feeling partook less of intuitional conviction than of strong suspicion clogged by strange dubieties. The perplexity he evinced proceeded less from aught touching the man informed against—as Claggart doubtless opined—than from considerations how best to act in regard to the informer. At first, indeed, he was naturally for summoning that substantiation of his allegations which Claggart said was at hand. But such a proceeding would result in the matter at once getting abroad, which in the present stage of it, he thought, might undesirably affect the ship's company. If Claggart was a false witness—that closed the affair. And therefore, before trying the accusation, he would first practically test the accuser; and he thought this could be done in a quiet, undemonstrative way.

The measure he determined upon involved a shifting of the scene, a transfer to a place less exposed to observation than the broad quarter-deck. For although the few gunroom officers there at the time had, in due observance of naval etiquette, withdrawn to leeward the moment Captain Vere had begun his promenade on the deck's weather side; and though during the colloquy with Claggart they of course ventured not to diminish the distance; and though throughout the interview Captain Vere's voice was far from him, and Claggart's silvery and low; and the wind in the cordage and the wash of the sea helped the more to put them beyond earshot; nevertheless, the interview's continuance already had attracted observation from some topmen aloft and other sailors in the waist or further forward.

Having determined upon his measures, Captain Vere forthwith took action. Abruptly turning to Claggart, he asked, 'Master-at-arms, is it now Budd's watch aloft?'

'No, your honor.'

Whereupon, 'Mr Wilkes!' summoning the nearest midshipman. 'Tell Albert to come to me.' Albert was the captain's hammock-boy, a sort of sea valet in whose discretion and fidelity his master had much confidence. The lad appeared.

'You know Budd, the foretopman?'

'I do, sir.'

'Go find him. It is his watch off. Manage to tell him out of earshot that he is wanted aft. Contrive it that he speaks to nobody. Keep him in talk yourself. And not till you get well aft here, not till then let him know that the place where he is wanted is my cabin. You understand. Go.—Master-at-arms, show yourself on the decks below, and when you think it time for Albert to be coming with his man, stand by quietly to follow the sailor in.'

19

Now when the foretopman found himself in the cabin, closeted there, as it were, with the captain and Claggart, he was surprised enough. But it was a surprise unaccompanied by apprehension or distrust. To an immature nature essentially honest and humane, forewarning intimations of subtler danger from one's kind come tardily if at all. The only thing that took shape in the young sailor's mind was this: Yes, the captain, I have always thought, looks kindly upon me. Wonder if he's going to make me his coxswain. I should like that. And may be now he is going to ask the master-at-arms about me.

'Shut the door there, sentry,' said the commander; 'stand without, and let nobody come in.—Now, Master-at-arms, tell this man to his face what you told of him to me,' and stood prepared to scrutinize the mutually confronting visages.

With the measured step and calm collected air of an asylum physician approaching in the public hall some patient beginning to show indications of a coming paroxysm, Claggart deliberately advanced within short range of Billy and, mesmerically looking him in the eye, briefly recapitulated the accusation.

Not at first did Billy take it in. When he did, the rose-tan of his cheek looked struck as by white leprosy. He stood like one impaled and gagged. Meanwhile the accuser's eyes, removing not as yet from the blue dilated ones, underwent a phenomenal change, their wonted rich violet color blurring into a muddy purple. Those lights of human intelligence, losing human expression, were gelidly protruding like the alien eyes of certain uncatalogued creatures of the deep. The first mesmeristic glance was one of serpent fascination; the last was as the paralyzing lurch of the torpedo fish.

'Speak, man!' said Captain Vere to the transfixed one, struck by his aspect even more than by Claggart's. 'Speak! Defend yourself!' Which appeal caused but a strange dumb gesturing and gurgling in Billy; amazement at such an accusation so suddenly sprung on inexperienced nonage; this, and, it may be, horror of the accuser's eyes, serving to bring out his lurking defect and in this instance for the time intensifying it into a convulsed tongue-tie; while the intent head and entire form straining forward in an agony of ineffectual eagerness to obey the injunction to speak and defend himself, gave an expression to the face like that of a condemned vestal priestess in the moment of being buried alive, and in the first struggle against suffocation.[3]

Though at the time Captain Vere was quite ignorant of Billy's liability to vocal impediment, he now immediately divined it, since vividly Billy's aspect recalled to him that of a bright young schoolmate of his whom he had once seen struck by much the same startling impotence in the act of eagerly rising in the class to be foremost in response to a testing question put to it by the master. Going close up to the young sailor, and laying a soothing hand on his shoulder, he said, 'There is no hurry, my boy. Take your time, take your time.' Contrary to the effect intended, these words so fatherly in tone, doubtless touching Billy's heart to the quick, prompted yet more violent efforts at utterance—efforts soon ending for the time in confirming the paralysis, and bringing to his face an expression which was as a crucifixion to behold. The next instant, quick as the flame from a discharged cannon at night, his right arm shot out, and Claggart dropped to the deck. Whether intentionally or but owing to the young athlete's superior height, the blow had taken effect full upon the forehead, so shapely and intellectual-looking a feature in the master-at-arms; so that the body fell over lengthwise, like a heavy plank tilted from erectness. A gasp or two, and he lay motionless.

'Fated boy,' breathed Captain Vere in tone so low as to be almost a whisper, 'what have you done! But here, help me.'

The twain raised the felled one from the loins up into a sitting position.

3. Vestal virgins in Rome were buried alive if they violated their vows.

The spare form flexibly acquiesced, but inertly. It was like handling a dead snake. They lowered it back. Regaining erectness, Captain Vere with one hand covering his face stood to all appearance as impassive as the object at his feet. Was he absorbed in taking in all the bearings of the event and what was best not only now at once to be done, but also in the sequel? Slowly he uncovered his face; and the effect was as if the moon emerging from eclipse should reappear with quite another aspect than that which had gone into hiding. The father in him, manifested towards Billy thus far in the scene, was replaced by the military disciplinarian. In his official tone he bade the foretopman retire to a stateroom aft (pointing it out), and there remain till thence summoned. This order Billy in silence mechanically obeyed. Then going to the cabin door where it opened on the quarter-deck, Captain Vere said to the sentry without, 'Tell somebody to send Albert here.' When the lad appeared, his master so contrived it that he should not catch sight of the prone one. 'Albert,' he said to him, 'tell the surgeon I wish to see him. You need not come back till called.'

When the surgeon entered—a self-poised character of that grave sense and experience that hardly anything could take him aback—Captain Vere advanced to meet him, thus unconsciously intercepting his view of Claggart, and interrupting the other's wonted ceremonious salutation, said, 'Nay. Tell me how it is with yonder man,' directing his attention to the prostrate one.

The surgeon looked, and for all his self-command somewhat started at the abrupt revelation. On Claggart's always pallid complexion, thick black blood was now oozing from nostril and ear. To the gazer's professional eye it was unmistakably no living man that he saw.

'Is it so, then?' said Captain Vere, intently watching him. 'I thought it. But verify it.' Whereupon the customary tests confirmed the surgeon's first glance, who now, looking up in unfeigned concern, cast a look of intense inquisitiveness upon his superior. But Captain Vere, with one hand to his brow, was standing motionless. Suddenly, catching the surgeon's arm convulsively, he exclaimed, pointing down to the body, 'It is the divine judgment on Ananias![4] Look!'

Disturbed by the excited manner he had never before observed in the *Bellipotent*'s captain, and as yet wholly ignorant of the affair, the prudent surgeon nevertheless held his peace, only again looking an earnest interrogatory as to what it was that had resulted in such a tragedy.

But Captain Vere was now again motionless, standing absorbed in thought. Again starting, he vehemently exclaimed, 'Struck dead by an angel of God! Yet the angel must hang!'

At these passionate interjections, mere incoherences to the listener as yet unapprised of the antecedents, the surgeon was profoundly discomposed. But now, as recollecting himself, Captain Vere in less passionate tone briefly related the circumstances leading up to the event. 'But come, we must dispatch,' he added. 'Help me to remove him' (meaning the body) 'to yonder compartment,' designating one opposite that where the foretopman remained immured. Anew disturbed by a request that, as implying a desire for secrecy, seemed unaccountably strange to him, there was nothing for the subordinate to do but comply.

4. Acts 5.3–5: "Peter said, Ananias . . . thou hast not lied unto men, but unto God. And Ananias hearing these words fell down, and gave up the ghost."

'Go now,' said Captain Vere with something of his wonted manner. 'Go now. I presently shall call a drumhead court.[5] Tell the lieutenants what has happened, and tell Mr Mordant' (meaning the captain of marines), 'and charge them to keep the matter to themselves.'

20

Full of disquietude and misgiving, the surgeon left the cabin. Was Captain Vere suddenly affected in his mind, or was it but a transient excitement, brought about by so strange and extraordinary a tragedy? As to the drumhead court, it struck the surgeon as impolitic, if nothing more. The thing to do, he thought, was to place Billy Budd in confinement, and in a way dictated by usage, and postpone further action in so extraordinary a case to such time as they should rejoin the squadron, and then refer it to the admiral. He recalled the unwonted agitation of Captain Vere and his excited exclamations, so at variance with his normal manner. Was he unhinged?

But assuming that he is, it is not so susceptible of proof. What then can the surgeon do? No more trying situation is conceivable than that of an officer subordinate under a captain whom he suspects to be not mad, indeed, but yet not quite unaffected in his intellects. To argue his order to him would be insolence. To resist him would be mutiny.

In obedience to Captain Vere, he communicated what had happened to the lieutenants and captain of marines, saying nothing as to the captain's state. They fully shared his own surprise and concern. Like him too, they seemed to think that such a matter should be referred to the admiral.

21

Who in the rainbow can draw the line where the violet tint ends and the orange tint begins? Distinctly we see the difference of the colors, but where exactly does the one first blendingly enter into the other? So with sanity and insanity. In pronounced cases there is no question about them. But in some supposed cases, in various degrees supposedly less pronounced, to draw the exact line of demarcation few will undertake, though for a fee becoming considerate some professional experts will. There is nothing nameable but that some men will, or undertake to, do it for pay.

Whether Captain Vere, as the surgeon professionally and privately surmised, was really the sudden victim of any degree of aberration, every one must determine for himself by such light as this narrative may afford.

That the unhappy event which has been narrated could not have happened at a worse juncture was but too true. For it was close on the heel of the suppressed insurrections, an aftertime very critical to naval authority, demanding from every English sea commander two qualities not readily interfusable—prudence and rigor. Moreover, there was something crucial in the case.

In the jugglery of circumstances preceding and attending the event on board the *Bellipotent,* and in the light of that martial code whereby it was formally to be judged, innocence and guilt personified in Claggart and Budd in effect changed places. In a legal view the apparent victim of the tragedy

5. A court-martial, originally held around an upturned drum, to try offenses committed during military operations.

was he who had sought to victimize a man blameless; and the indisputable deed of the latter, navally regarded, constituted the most heinous of military crimes. Yet more. The essential right and wrong involved in the matter, the clearer that might be, so much the worse for the responsibility of a loyal sea commander, inasmuch as he was not authorized to determine the matter on that primitive basis.

Small wonder then that the *Bellipotent*'s captain, though in general a man of rapid decision, felt that circumspectness not less than promptitude was necessary. Until he could decide upon his course, and in each detail; and not only so, but until the concluding measure was upon the point of being enacted, he deemed it advisable, in view of all the circumstances, to guard as much as possible against publicity. Here he may or may not have erred. Certain it is, however, that subsequently in the confidential talk of more than one or two gun rooms and cabins he was not a little criticized by some officers, a fact imputed by his friends and vehemently by his cousin Jack Denton to professional jealousy of Starry Vere. Some imaginative ground for invidious comment there was. The maintenance of secrecy in the matter, the confining all knowledge of it for a time to the place where the homicide occurred, the quarter-deck cabin; in these particulars lurked some resemblance to the policy adopted in those tragedies of the palace which have occurred more than once in the capital founded by Peter the Barbarian.[6]

The case indeed was such that fain would the *Bellipotent*'s captain have deferred taking any action whatever respecting it further than to keep the foretopman a close prisoner till the ship rejoined the squadron and then submitting the matter to the judgment of his admiral.

But a true military officer is in one particular like a true monk. Not with more of self-abnegation will the latter keep his vows of monastic obedience than the former his vows of allegiance to martial duty.

Feeling that unless quick action was taken on it, the deed of the foretopman, so soon as it should be known on the gun decks, would tend to awaken any slumbering embers of the Nore among the crew, a sense of the urgency of the case overruled in Captain Vere every other consideration. But though a conscientious disciplinarian, he was no lover of authority for mere authority's sake. Very far was he from embracing opportunities for monopolizing to himself the perils of moral responsibility, none at least that could properly be referred to an official superior or shared with him by his official equals or even subordinates. So thinking, he was glad it would not be at variance with usage to turn the matter over to a summary court of his own officers, reserving to himself, as the one on whom the ultimate accountability would rest, the right of maintaining a supervision of it, or formally or informally interposing at need. Accordingly a drum-head court was summarily convened, he electing the individuals composing it: the first lieutenant, the captain of marines, and the sailing master.

In associating an officer of marines with the sea lieutenant and the sailing master in a case having to do with a sailor, the commander perhaps deviated from general custom. He was prompted thereto by the circumstance that he took that soldier to be a judicious person, thoughtful, and not altogether incapable of grappling with a difficult case unprecedented in his prior expe-

6. St. Petersburg, founded by Peter the Great (1672–1725) in 1703.

rience. Yet even as to him he was not without some latent misgiving, for withal he was an extremely good-natured man, an enjoyer of his dinner, a sound sleeper, and inclined to obesity—a man who though he would always maintain his manhood in battle might not prove altogether reliable in a moral dilemma involving aught of the tragic. As to the first lieutenant and the sailing master, Captain Vere could not but be aware that though honest natures, of approved gallantry upon occasion, their intelligence was mostly confined to the matter of active seamanship and the fighting demands of their profession.

The court was held in the same cabin where the unfortunate affair had taken place. This cabin, the commander's, embraced the entire area under the poop deck. Aft, and on either side, was a small stateroom, the one now temporarily a jail and the other a dead-house, and a yet smaller compartment, leaving a space between expanding forward into a goodly oblong of length coinciding with the ship's beam. A skylight of moderate dimension was overhead, and at each end of the oblong space were two sashed porthole windows easily convertible back into embrasures for short carronades.[7]

All being quickly in readiness, Billy Budd was arraigned, Captain Vere necessarily appearing as the sole witness in the case, and as such temporarily sinking his rank, though singularly maintaining it in a matter apparently trivial, namely, that he testified from the ship's weather side, with that object having caused the court to sit on the lee side. Concisely he narrated all that had led up to the catastrophe, omitting nothing in Claggart's accusation and deposing as to the manner in which the prisoner had received it. At this testimony the three officers glanced with no little surprise at Billy Budd, the last man they would have suspected either of the mutinous design alleged by Claggart or the undeniable deed he himself had done. The first lieutenant, taking judicial primacy and turning toward the prisoner, said, 'Captain Vere has spoken. Is it or is it not as Captain Vere says?'

In response came syllables not so much impeded in the utterance as might have been anticipated. They were these: 'Captain Vere tells the truth. It is just as Captain Vere says, but it is not as the master-at-arms said. I have eaten the King's bread and I am true to the King.'

'I believe you, my man,' said the witness, his voice indicating a suppressed emotion not otherwise betrayed.

'God will bless you for that, your honor!' not without stammering said Billy, and all but broke down. But immediately he was recalled to self-control by another question, to which with the same emotional difficulty of utterance he said, 'No, there was no malice between us. I never bore malice against the master-at-arms. I am sorry that he is dead. I did not mean to kill him. Could I have used my tongue I would not have struck him. But he foully lied to my face and in presence of my captain, and I had to say something, and I could only say it with a blow, God help me!'

In the impulsive aboveboard manner of the frank one the court saw confirmed all that was implied in words that just previously had perplexed them, coming as they did from the testifier to the tragedy and promptly following Billy's impassioned disclaimer of mutinous intent—Captain Vere's words, 'I believe you, my man.'

7. Large pieces of artillery.

Next it was asked of him whether he knew of or suspected aught savoring of incipient trouble (meaning mutiny, though the explicit term was avoided) going on in any section of the ship's company.

The reply lingered. This was naturally imputed by the court to the same vocal embarrassment which had retarded or obstructed previous answers. But in main it was otherwise here, the question immediately recalling to Billy's mind the interview with the afterguardsman in the forechains. But an innate repugnance to playing a part at all approaching that of an informer against one's own shipmates—the same erring sense of uninstructed honor which had stood in the way of his reporting the matter at the time, though as a loyal man-of-war's man it was incumbent on him, and failure so to do, if charged against him and proven, would have subjected him to the heaviest of penalties; this, with the blind feeling now his that nothing really was being hatched, prevailed with him. When the answer came it was a negative.

'One question more,' said the officer of marines, now first speaking and with a troubled earnestness. 'You tell us that what the master-at-arms said against you was a lie. Now why should he have so lied, so maliciously lied, since you declare there was no malice between you?'

At that question, unintentionally touching on a spiritual sphere wholly obscure to Billy's thoughts, he was nonplussed, evincing a confusion indeed that some observers, such as can readily be imagined, would have construed into involuntary evidence of hidden guilt. Nevertheless, he strove some way to answer, but all at once relinquished the vain endeavor, at the same time turning an appealing glance towards Captain Vere as deeming him his best helper and friend. Captain Vere, who had been seated for a time, rose to his feet, addressing the interrogator. 'The question you put to him comes naturally enough. But how can he rightly answer it?—or anybody else, unless indeed it be he who lies within there,' designating the compartment where lay the corpse. 'But the prone one there will not rise to our summons. In effect, though, as it seems to me, the point you make is hardly material. Quite aside from any conceivable motive actuating the master-at-arms, and irrespective of the provocation to the blow, a martial court must needs in the present case confine its attention to the blow's consequence, which consequence justly is to be deemed not otherwise than as the striker's deed.'

This utterance, the full significance of which it was not at all likely that Billy took in, nevertheless caused him to turn a wistful interrogative look toward the speaker, a look in its dumb expressiveness not unlike that which a dog of generous breed might turn upon his master, seeking in his face some elucidation of a previous gesture ambiguous to the canine intelligence. Nor was the same utterance without marked effect upon the three officers, more especially the soldier. Couched in it seemed to them a meaning unanticipated, involving a prejudgment on the speaker's part. It served to augment a mental disturbance previously evident enough.

The soldier once more spoke, in a tone of suggestive dubiety addressing at once his associates and Captain Vere: 'Nobody is present—none of the ship's company, I mean—who might shed lateral light, if any is to be had, upon what remains mysterious in this matter.'

'That is thoughtfully put,' said Captain Vere; 'I see your drift. Ay, there is a mystery; but, to use a scriptural phrase, it is a "mystery of iniquity," a matter for psychologic theologians to discuss. But what has a military court to do with it? Not to add that for us any possible investigation of it is cut off by the lasting tongue-tie of—him—in yonder,' again designating the mortuary stateroom. 'The prisoner's deed—with that alone we have to do.'

To this, and particularly the closing reiteration, the marine soldier, knowing not how aptly to reply, sadly abstained from saying aught. The first lieutenant, who at the outset had not unnaturally assumed primacy in the court, now overrulingly instructed by a glance from Captain Vere, a glance more effective than words, resumed that primacy. Turning to the prisoner, 'Budd,' he said, and scarce in equable tones, 'Budd, if you have aught further to say for yourself, say it now.'

Upon this the young sailor turned another quick glance toward Captain Vere; then, as taking a hint from that aspect, a hint confirming his own instinct that silence was now best, replied to the lieutenant, 'I have said all, sir.'

The marine—the same who had been the sentinel without the cabin door at the time that the foretopman, followed by the master-at-arms, entered it— he, standing by the sailor throughout these judicial proceedings was now directed to take him back to the after compartment originally assigned to the prisoner and his custodian. As the twain disappeared from view, the three officers, as partially liberated from some inward constraint associated with Billy's mere presence, simultaneously stirred in their seats. They exchanged looks of troubled indecision, yet feeling that decide they must and without long delay. For Captain Vere, he for the time stood—unconsciously with his back toward them, apparently in one of his absent fits—gazing out from a sashed porthole to windward upon the monotonous blank of the twilight sea. But the court's silence continuing, broken only at moments by brief consultations, in low earnest tones, this served to arouse him and energize him. Turning, he to-and-fro paced the cabin athwart; in the returning ascent to windward climbing the slant deck in the ship's lee roll, without knowing it symbolizing thus in his action a mind resolute to surmount difficulties even if against primitive instincts strong as the wind and the sea. Presently he came to a stand before the three. After scanning their faces he stood less as mustering his thoughts for expression than as one inly deliberating how best to put them to well-meaning men not intellectually mature, men with whom it was necessary to demonstrate certain principles that were axioms to himself. Similar impatience as to talking is perhaps one reason that deters some minds from addressing any popular assemblies.

When speak he did, something, both in the substance of what he said and his manner of saying it, showed the influence of unshared studies modifying and tempering the practical training of an active career. This, along with his phraseology, now and then was suggestive of the grounds whereon rested that imputation of a certain pedantry socially alleged against him by certain naval men of wholly practical cast, captains who nevertheless would frankly concede that His Majesty's navy mustered no more efficient officer of their grade than Starry Vere.

What he said was to this effect: 'Hitherto I have been but the witness, little more; and I should hardly think now to take another tone, that of your coadjutor for the time, did I not perceive in you—at the crisis too—a troubled hesitancy, proceeding, I doubt not, from the clash of military duty with moral scruple—scruple vitalized by compassion. For the compassion, how can I otherwise than share it? But, mindful of paramount obligations, I strive against scruples that may tend to enervate decision. Not, gentlemen, that I hide from myself that the case is an exceptional one. Speculatively regarded, it well might be referred to a jury of casuists. But for us here, acting not as casuists or moralists, it is a case practical, and under martial law practically to be dealt with.

'But your scruples: do they move as in a dusk? Challenge them. Make them advance and declare themselves. Come now; do they import something like this: If, mindless of palliating circumstances, we are bound to regard the death of the master-at-arms as the prisoner's deed, then does that deed constitute a capital crime whereof the penalty is a mortal one. But in natural justice is nothing but the prisoner's overt act to be considered? How can we adjudge to summary and shameful death a fellow creature innocent before God, and whom we feel to be so?—Does that state it aright? You sign sad assent. Well, I too feel that, the full force of that. It is Nature. But do these buttons that we wear attest that our allegiance is to Nature? No, to the King. Though the ocean, which is inviolate Nature primeval, though this be the element where we move and have our being as sailors, yet as the King's officers lies our duty in a sphere correspondingly natural? So little is that true, that in receiving our commissions we in the most important regards ceased to be natural free agents. When war is declared are we the commissioned fighters previously consulted? We fight at command. If our judgments approve the war, that is but coincidence. So in other particulars. So now. For suppose condemnation to follow these present proceedings. Would it be so much we ourselves that would condemn as it would be martial law operating through us? For that law and the rigor of it, we are not responsibile. Our vowed responsibility is in this: That however pitilessly that law may operate in any instances, we nevertheless adhere to it and administer it.

'But the exceptional in the matter moves the hearts within you. Even so too is mine moved. But let not warm hearts betray heads that should be cool. Ashore in a criminal case, will an upright judge allow himself off the bench to be waylaid by some tender kinswoman of the accused seeking to touch him with her tearful plea? Well, the heart here, sometimes the feminine in man, is as that piteous woman, and hard though it be, she must here be ruled out.'

He paused, earnestly studying them for a moment; then resumed.

'But something in your aspect seems to urge that it is not solely the heart that moves in you, but also the conscience, the private conscience. But tell me whether or not, occupying the position we do, private conscience should not yield to that imperial one formulated in the code under which alone we officially proceed?'

Here the three men moved in their seats, less convinced than agitated by the course of an argument troubling but the more the spontaneous conflict within.

Perceiving which, the speaker paused for a moment; then abruptly changing his tone, went on.

'To steady us a bit, let us recur to the facts.—In wartime at sea a man-of-war's man strikes his superior in grade, and the blow kills. Apart from its effect the blow itself is, according to the Articles of War, a capital crime. Furthermore—'

'Ay, sir,' emotionally broke in the officer of marines, 'in one sense it was. But surely Budd proposed neither mutiny nor homicide.'

'Surely not, my good man. And before a court less arbitrary and more merciful than a martial one, that plea would largely extenuate. At the Last Assizes[8] it shall acquit. But how here? We proceed under the law of the Mutiny Act.[9] In feature no child can resemble his father more than that Act resembles in spirit the thing from which it derives—War. In His Majesty's service—in this ship, indeed—there are Englishmen forced to fight for the King against their will. Against their conscience, for aught we know. Though as their fellow creatures some of us may appreciate their position, yet as navy officers what reck we of it? Still less recks the enemy. Our impressed men he would fain cut down in the same swath with our volunteers. As regards the enemy's naval conscripts, some of whom may even share our own abhorrence of the regicidal French Directory, it is the same on our side. War looks but to the frontage, the appearance. And the Mutiny Act, War's child, takes after the father. Budd's intent or non-intent is nothing to the purpose.

'But while, put to it by those anxieties in you which I cannot but respect, I only repeat myself—while thus strangely we prolong proceedings that should be summary—the enemy may be sighted and an engagement result. We must do; and one of two things must we do—condemn or let go.'

'Can we not convict and yet mitigate the penalty?' asked the sailing master, here speaking, and falteringly, for the first.

'Gentlemen, were that clearly lawful for us under the circumstances, consider the consequences of such clemency. The people' (meaning the ship's company) 'have native sense; most of them are familiar with our naval usage and tradition; and how would they take it? Even could you explain to them— which our official position forbids—they, long molded by arbitrary discipline, have not that kind of intelligent responsiveness that might qualify them to comprehend and discriminate. No, to the people the foretopman's deed, however it be worded in the announcement, will be plain homicide committed in a flagrant act of mutiny. What penalty for that should follow, they know. But it does not follow. *Why?* they will ruminate. You know what sailors are. Will they not revert to the recent outbreak at the Nore? Ay. They know the well-founded alarm—the panic it struck throughout England. Your clement sentence they would account pusillanimous. They would think that we flinch, that we are afraid of them—afraid of practicing a lawful rigor singularly demanded at this juncture, lest it should provoke new troubles. What shame to us such a conjecture on their part, and how deadly to discipline. You see then, whither, prompted by duty and the law, I steadfastly drive. But I beseech you, my friends, do not take me amiss. I feel as you do for this unfortunate boy. But did he know our hearts, I take him to be of that generous nature that he would feel even for us on whom in this military necessity so heavy a compulsion is laid.'

With that, crossing the deck he resumed his place by the sashed porthole, tacitly leaving the three to come to a decision. On the cabin's opposite side the troubled court sat silent. Loyal lieges, plain and practical, though at bottom they dissented from some points Captain Vere had put to them, they

---

8. The highest courts of appeal in Great Britain. Melville refers here to the Last Judgment.   9. First passed in 1689; the act and its successors applied only to the army. The navy followed the King's Regulations and Admiralty Instructions of 1772.

were without the faculty, hardly had the inclination, to gainsay one whom they felt to be an earnest man, one too not less their superior in mind than in naval rank. But it is not improbable that even such of his words as were not without influence over them, less came home to them than his closing appeal to their instinct as sea officers: in the forethought he threw out as to the practical consequences to discipline, considering the unconfirmed tone of the fleet at the time, should a man-of-war's man's violent killing at sea of a superior in grade be allowed to pass for aught else than a capital crime demanding prompt infliction of the penalty.

Not unlikely they were brought to something more or less akin to that harassed frame of mind which in the year 1842 actuated the commander of the U.S. brig-of-war *Somers* to resolve, under the so-called Articles of War, Articles modeled upon the English Mutiny Act, to resolve upon the execution at sea of a midshipman and two sailors as mutineers designing the seizure of the brig.[1] Which resolution was carried out though in a time of peace and within not many days' sail of home. An act vindicated by a naval court of inquiry subsequently convened ashore. History, and here cited without comment. True, the circumstances on board the *Somers* were different from those on board the *Bellipotent*. But the urgency felt, well-warranted or otherwise, was much the same.

Says a writer whom few know,[2] 'Forty years after a battle it is easy for a noncombatant to reason about how it ought to have been fought. It is another thing personally and under fire to have to direct the fighting while involved in the obscuring smoke of it. Much so with respect to other emergencies involving considerations both practical and moral, and when it is imperative promptly to act. The greater the fog the more it imperils the steamer, and speed is put on though at the hazard of running somebody down. Little ween the snug card players in the cabin of the responsibilities of the sleepless man on the bridge.'

In brief, Billy Budd was formally convicted and sentenced to be hung at the yardarm in the early morning watch, it being now night. Otherwise, as is customary in such cases, the sentence would forthwith have been carried out. In wartime on the field or in the fleet, a mortal punishment decreed by a drumhead court—on the field sometimes decreed by but a nod from the general—follows without delay on the heel of conviction, without appeal.

22

It was Captain Vere himself who of his own motion communicated the finding of the court to the prisoner, for that purpose going to the compartment where he was in custody and bidding the marine there to withdraw for the time.

Beyond the communication of the sentence, what took place at this interview was never known. But in view of the character of the twain briefly closeted in that stateroom, each radically sharing in the rarer qualities of our nature—so rare indeed as to be all but incredible to average minds however much cultivated—some conjectures may be ventured.

It would have been in consonance with the spirit of Captain Vere should

1. Melville's cousin, Guert Gansevoort, was first lieutenant of the *Somers* at the time of a mutiny. The incident may have been in the back of Melville's mind when he wrote *Billy Budd*. 2. Melville himself.

he on this occasion have concealed nothing from the condemned one—should he indeed have frankly disclosed to him the part he himself had played in bringing about the decision, at the same time revealing his actuating motives. On Billy's side it is not improbable that such a confession would have been received in much the same spirit that prompted it. Not without a sort of joy, indeed, he might have appreciated the brave[3] opinion of him implied in his captain's making such a confidant of him. Nor, as to the sentence itself, could he have been insensible that it was imparted to him as to one not afraid to die. Even more may have been. Captain Vere in end may have developed the passion sometimes latent under an exterior stoical or indifferent. He was old enough to have been Billy's father. The austere devotee of military duty, letting himself melt back into what remains primeval in our formalized humanity, may in end have caught Billy to his heart, even as Abraham may have caught young Isaac on the brink of resolutely offering him up in obedience to the exacting behest.[4] But there is no telling the sacrament, seldom if in any case revealed to the gadding world, wherever under circumstances at all akin to those here attempted to be set forth two of great Nature's nobler order embrace. There is privacy at the time, inviolable to the survivor; and holy oblivion, the sequel to each diviner magnanimity, providentially covers all at last.

The first to encounter Captain Vere in act of leaving the compartment was the senior lieutenant. The face he beheld, for the moment one expressive of the agony of the strong, was to that officer, though a man of fifty, a startling revelation. That the condemned one suffered less than he who mainly had effected the condemnation was apparently indicated by the former's exclamation in the scene soon perforce to be touched upon.

23

Of a series of incidents within a brief term rapidly following each other, the adequate narration may take up a term less brief, especially if explanation or comment here and there seem requisite to the better understanding of such incidents. Between the entrance into the cabin of him who never left it alive, and him who when he did leave it left it as one condemned to die; between this and the closeted interview just given, less than an hour and a half had elapsed. It was an interval long enough, however, to awaken speculations among no few of the ship's company as to what it was that could be detaining in the cabin the master-at-arms and the sailor; for a rumor that both of them had been seen to enter it and neither of them had been seen to emerge, this rumor had got abroad upon the gun decks and in the tops, the people of a great warship being in one respect like villagers, taking microscopic note of every outward movement or non-movement going on. When therefore, in weather not at all tempestuous, all hands were called in the second dogwatch, a summons under such circumstances not usual in those hours, the crew were not wholly unprepared for some announcement extraor-

3. Fine, superior. 4. Genesis 22.1–18: "God did tempt Abraham, and said . . . Take now thy son, thine only son Isaac, whom thou lovest . . . and offer him . . . for a burnt offering. . . . And Abraham . . . bound Isaac his son, and laid him on the altar upon the wood. And Abraham stretched forth his hand, and took the knife to slay his son. And the angel of the Lord . . . said, Lay not thine hand upon the lad, neither do thou anything unto him: for now I know that thou fearest God. . . . And the angel of the Lord . . . said, . . . I will bless thee . . . because thou hast obeyed my voice."

dinary, one having connection too with the continued absence of the two men from their wonted haunts.

There was a moderate sea at the time; and the moon, newly risen and near to being at its full, silvered the white spar deck wherever not blotted by the clear-cut shadows horizontally thrown of fixtures and moving men. On either side the quarter-deck the marine guard under arms was drawn up; and Captain Vere, standing in his place surrounded by all the wardroom officers, addressed his men. In so doing, his manner showed neither more nor less than that properly pertaining to his supreme position aboard his own ship. In clear terms and concise he told them what had taken place in the cabin: that the master-at-arms was dead, that he who had killed him had been already tried by a summary court and condemned to death, and that the execution would take place in the early morning watch. The word *mutiny* was not named in what he said. He refrained too from making the occasion an opportunity for any preachment as to the maintenance of discipline, thinking perhaps that under existing circumstances in the navy the consequence of violating discipline shoud be made to speak for itself.

Their captain's announcement was listened to by the throng of standing sailors in a dumbness like that of a seated congregation of believers in hell listening to the clergyman's announcement of his Calvinistic text.

At the close, however, a confused murmur went up. It began to wax. All but instantly, then, at a sign, it was pierced and suppressed by shrill whistles of the boatswain and his mates. The word was given to about ship.

To be prepared for burial Claggart's body was delivered to certain petty officers of his mess. And here, not to clog the sequel with lateral matters, it may be added that at a suitable hour, the master-at-arms was committed to the sea with every funeral honor properly belonging to his naval grade.

In this proceeding as in every public one growing out of the tragedy strict adherence to usage was observed. Nor in any point could it have been at all deviated from, either with respect to Claggart or Billy Budd, without begetting undersirable speculations in the ship's company, sailors, and more particularly men-of-war's men, being of all men the greatest sticklers for usage. For similar cause, all communication between Captain Vere and the condemned one ended with the closeted interview already given, the latter being now surrendered to the ordinary routine preliminary to the end. His transfer under guard from the captain's quarters was effected without unusual precautions—at least no visible ones. If possible, not to let the men so much as surmise that their officers anticipate aught amiss from them is the tacit rule in a military ship. And the more that some sort of trouble should really be apprehended, the more do the officers keep that apprehension to themselves, though not the less unostentatious vigilance may be augmented. In the present instance, the sentry placed over the prisoner had strict orders to let no one have communication with him but the chaplain. And certain unobtrusive measures were taken absolutely to insure this point.

24

In a seventy-four of the old order the deck known as the upper gun deck was the one covered over by the spar deck, which last, though not without its armament, was for the most part exposed to the weather. In general it was at all hours free from hammocks; those of the crew swinging on the lower gun deck and berth deck, the latter being not only a dormitory but also the place for the stowing of the sailors' bags, and on both sides lined with the large chests or movable pantries of the many messes of the men.

On the starboard side of the *Bellipotent's* upper gun deck, behold Billy Budd under sentry lying prone in irons in one of the bays formed by the regular spacing of the guns comprising the batteries on either side. All these pieces were of the heavier caliber of that period. Mounted on lumbering wooden carriages, they were hampered with cumbersome harness of breeching and strong side-tackles for running them out. Guns and carriages, together with the long rammers and shorter linstocks lodged in loops overhead—all these, as customary, were painted black; and the heavy hempen breechings, tarred to the same tint, wore the like livery of the undertakers. In contrast with the funereal hue of these surroundings, the prone sailor's exterior apparel, white jumper and white duck trousers, each more or less soiled, dimly glimmered in the obscure light of the bay like a patch of discolored snow in early April lingering at some upland cave's black mouth. In effect he is already in his shroud, or the garments that shall serve him in lieu of one. Over him but scarce illuminating him, two battle lanterns swing from two massive beams of the deck above. Fed with the oil supplied by the war contractors (whose gains, honest or otherwise, are in every land an anticipated portion of the harvest of death), with flickering splashes of dirty yellow light they pollute the pale moonshine all but ineffectually struggling in obstructed flecks through the open ports from which the tampioned[5] cannon protrude. Other lanterns at intervals serve but to bring out somewhat the obscurer bays which, like small confessionals or side-chapels in a cathedral, branch from the long dim-vistaed broad aisle between the two batteries of that covered tier.

Such was the deck where now lay the Handsome Sailor. Through the rose-tan of his complexion no pallor could have shown. It would have taken days of sequestration from the winds and the sun to have brought about the effacement of that. But the skeleton in the cheekbone at the point of its angle was just beginning delicately to be defined under the warm-tinted skin. In fervid hearts self-contained, some brief experiences devour our human tissue as secret fire in a ship's hold consumes cotton in the bale.

But now lying between the two guns, as nipped in the vice of fate, Billy's agony, mainly proceeding from a generous young heart's virgin experience of the diabolical incarnate and effective in some men—the tension of that agony was over now. It survived not the something healing in the closeted interview with Captain Vere. Without movement, he lay as in a trance, that adolescent expression previously noted as his taking on something akin to the look of a slumbering child in the cradle when the warm hearthglow of the still chamber at night plays on the dimples that at whiles mysteriously form in the cheek, silently coming and going there. For now and then in the gyved[6] one's trance a serene happy light born of some wandering reminiscence or dream would diffuse itself over his face, and then wane away only anew to return.

The chaplain, coming to see him and finding him thus, and perceiving no

5. Plugged with a tampion, which fits into the muzzle of a gun not in use.   6. Shackled, chained.

sign that he was conscious of his presence, attentively regarded him for a space, then slipping aside, withdrew for the time, peradventure feeling that even he, the minister of Christ though receiving his stipend from Mars,[7] had no consolation to proffer which could result in a peace transcending that which he beheld. But in the small hours he came again. And the prisoner, now awake to his surroundings, noticed his approach, and civilly, all but cheerfully, welcomed him. But it was to little purpose that in the interview following, the good man sought to bring Billy Budd to some godly understanding that he must die, and at dawn. True, Billy himself freely referred to his death as a thing close at hand; but it was something in the way that children will refer to death in general, who yet among their other sports will play a funeral with hearse and mourners.

Not that like children Billy was incapable of conceiving what death really is. No, but he was wholly without irrational fear of it, a fear more prevalent in highly civilized communities than those so-called barbarous ones which in all respects stand nearer to unadulterate Nature. And, as elsewhere said, a barbarian Billy radically was—as much so, for all the costume, as his countrymen the British captives, living trophies, made to march in the Roman triumph of Germanicus.[8] Quite as much so as those later barbarians, young men probably, and picked specimens among the earlier British converts to Christianity, at least nominally such, taken to Rome (as today converts from lesser isles of the sea may be taken to London), of whom the Pope at that time, admiring the strangeness of their personal beauty so unlike the Italian stamp, their clear ruddy complexion and curled flaxen locks, exclaimed, 'Angles' (meaning *English,* the modern derivative), 'Angles, do you call them? And is it because they look so like angels?'[9] Had it been later in time, one would think that the Pope had in mind Fra Angelico's seraphs, some of whom, plucking apples in gardens of the Hesperides,[1] have the faint rosebud complexion of the more beautiful English girls.

If in vain the good chaplain sought to impress the young barbarian with ideas of death akin to those conveyed in the skull, dial, and crossbones on old tombstones, equally futile to all appearance were his efforts to bring home to him the thought of salvation and a Savior. Billy listened, but less out of awe or reverence, perhaps, than from a certain natural politeness, doubtless at bottom regarding all that in much the same way that most mariners of his class take any discourse abstract or out of the common tone of the workaday world. And this sailor way of taking clerical discourse is not wholly unlike the way in which the primer of Christianity, full of transcendent miracles, was received long ago on tropic isles by any superior *savage,* so called—a Tahitian, say, of Captain Cook's time or shortly after that time.[2] Out of a natural courtesy he received, but did not appropriate. It was like a gift placed in the palm of an outreached hand upon which the fingers do not close.

But the *Bellipotent*'s chaplain was a discreet man possessing the good sense of a good heart. So he insisted not in his vocation here. At the instance

7. The god of war. I.e., paid by the navy.   8. Germanicus Caesar (15 B.C.E.–19 C.E.), granted a triumph in Rome in 17 C.E.   9. Bede's *Ecclesiastical History of the English People* tells this anecdote about Pope Gregory the Great (540?–604).   1. Daughters of Atlas who guarded a tree bearing golden apples on an enchanted island in the western sea. Fra Angelico (ca. 1387–1455), the Florentine painter Giovanni da Fiesole.   2. James Cook (1728–1779) was in Tahiti in 1769 and from 1772 to 1775.

of Captain Vere, a lieutenant had apprised him of pretty much everything as to Billy; and since he felt that innocence was even a better thing than religion wherewith to go to Judgment, he reluctantly withdrew; but in his emotion not without first performing an act strange enough in an Englishman, and under the circumstances yet more so in any regular priest. Stooping over, he kissed on the fair cheek his fellow man, a felon in martial law, one whom though on the confines of death he felt he could never convert to a dogma; nor for all that did he fear for his future.

Marvel not that having been made acquainted with the young sailor's essential innocence the worthy man lifted not a finger to avert the doom of such a martyr to martial discipline. So to do would not only have been as idle as invoking the desert, but would also have been an audacious transgression of the bounds of his function, one as exactly prescribed to him by military law as that of the boatswain or any other naval officer. Bluntly put, a chaplain is the minister of the Prince of Peace serving in the host of the God of War—Mars. As such, he is as incongruous as a musket would be on the altar at Christmas. Why, then, is he there? Because he indirectly subserves the purpose attested by the cannon; because too he lends the sanction of the religion of the meek to that which practically is the abrogation of everything but brute Force.

25

The night so luminous on the spar deck, but otherwise on the cavernous ones below, levels so like the tiered galleries in a coal mine—the luminous night passed away. But like the prophet in the chariot disappearing in heaven and dropping his mantle to Elisha,[3] the withdrawing night transferred its pale robe to the breaking day. A meek, shy light appeared in the East, where stretched a diaphanous fleece of white furrowed vapor. That light slowly waxed. Suddenly *eight bells* was struck aft, responded to by one louder metallic stroke from forward. It was four o'clock in the morning. Instantly the silver whistles were heard summoning all hands to witness punishment. Up through the great hatchways rimmed with racks of heavy shot the watch below came pouring, overspreading with the watch already on deck the space between the mainmast and foremast including that occupied by the capacious launch and the black booms tiered on either side of it, boat and booms making a summit of observation for the powder-boys and younger tars. A different group comprising one watch of topmen leaned over the rail of that sea balcony, no small one in a seventy-four, looking down on the crowd below. Man or boy, none spake but in whisper, and few spake at all. Captain Vere—as before, the central figure among the assembled commissioned officers—stood nigh the break of the poop deck facing forward. Just below him on the quarter-deck the marines in full equipment were drawn up much as at the scene of the promulgated sentence.

At sea in the old time, the execution by halter of a military sailor was generally from the foreyard. In the present instance, for special reasons[4] the

---

3. 2 Kings 2.11–13: "There appeared a chariot of fire, and horses of fire, and parted them both asunder; and Elijah went up by a whirlwind into heaven. And Elisha . . . took up . . . the mantle of Elijah that fell from him."   4. The *special reasons* remain obscure. The text editors suggest that the captain's motives were precautionary; the phrase, an insertion, previously read, "for strategic reasons."

mainyard was assigned. Under an arm of that yard the prisoner was presently brought up, the chaplain attending him. It was noted at the time, and remarked upon afterwards, that in this final scene the good man evinced little or nothing of the perfunctory. Brief speech indeed he had with the condemned one, but the genuine Gospel was less on his tongue than in his aspect and manner towards him. The final preparations personal to the latter being speedily brought to an end by two boatswain's mates, the consummation impended. Billy stood facing aft. At the penultimate moment, his words, his only ones, words wholly unobstructed in the utterance, were these: 'God bless Captain Vere!' Syllables so unanticipated coming from one with the ignominious hemp about his neck—a conventional felon's benediction[5] directed aft towards the quarters of honor; syllables too delivered in the clear melody of a singing bird on the point of launching from the twig— had a phenomenal effect, not unenhanced by the rare personal beauty of the young sailor, spiritualized now through late experiences so poignantly profound.

Without volition, as it were, as if indeed the ship's populace were but the vehicles of some vocal current electric, with one voice from alow and aloft came a resonant sympathetic echo: 'God bless Captain Vere!' And yet at that instant Billy alone must have been in their hearts, even as in their eyes.

At the pronounced words and the spontaneous echo that voluminously rebounded them, Captain Vere, either through stoic self-control or a sort of momentary paralysis induced by emotional shock, stood erectly rigid as a musket in the ship-armorer's rack.

The hull, deliberately recovering from the periodic roll to leeward, was just regaining an even keel when the last signal, a preconcerted dumb one, was given. At the same moment it chanced that the vapory fleece hanging low in the East was shot through with a soft glory as of the fleece of the Lamb of God seen in mystical vision, and simultaneously therewith, watched by the wedged mass of upturned faces, Billy ascended; and, ascending, took the full rose of the dawn.

In the pinioned figure arrived at the yard-end, to the wonder of all no motion was apparent, none save that created by the slow roll of the hull in moderate weather, so majestic in a great ship ponderously cannoned.

26

When some days afterwards, in reference to the singularity just mentioned, the purser, a rather ruddy, rotund person more accurate as an accountant than profound as a philosopher, said at mess to the surgeon, "What testimony to the force lodged in will power," the latter, saturnine, spare, and tall, one in whom a discreet causticity went along with a manner less genial than polite, replied. 'Your pardon, Mr Purser. In a hanging scientifically conducted—and under special orders I myself directed how Budd's was to be effected—any movement following the completed suspension and originating in the body suspended, such movement indicates mechanical spasm in the muscular system. Hence the absence of that is no more attributable to will power, as you call it, than to horsepower—begging your pardon.'

5. It is a traditional ritual for the condemned man to forgive the official compelled by duty to order his death.

'But this muscular spasm you speak of, is not that in a degree more or less invariable in these cases?'

'Assuredly so, Mr Purser.'

'How then, my good sir, do you account for its absence in this instance?'

'Mr Purser, it is clear that your sense of the singularity in this matter equals not mine. You account for it by what you call will power—a term not yet included in the lexicon of science. For me, I do not, with my present knowledge, pretend to account for it at all. Even should we assume the hypothesis that at the first touch of the halyards the action of Budd's heart, intensified by extraordinary emotion at its climax, abruptly stopped—much like a watch when in carelessly winding it up you strain at the finish, thus snapping the chain—even under that hypothesis how account for the phenomenon that followed?'

'You admit, then, that the absence of spasmodic movement was phenomenal.'

'It was phenomenal, Mr Purser, in the sense that it was an appearance the cause of which is not immediately to be assigned.'

'But tell me, my dear sir,' pertinaciously continued the other, 'was the man's death effected by the halter, or was it a species of euthanasia?'[6]

'*Euthanasia*, Mr Purser, is something like your *will power*: I doubt its authenticity as a scientific term—begging your pardon again. It is at once imaginative and metaphysical—in short, Greek.—But,' abruptly changing his tone, 'there is a case in the sick bay that I do not care to leave to my assistants. Beg your pardon, but excuse me.' And rising from the mess he formally withdrew.

27

The silence at the moment of execution and for a moment or two continuing thereafter, a silence but emphasized by the regular wash of the sea against the hull or the flutter of a sail caused by the helmsman's eyes being tempted astray, this emphasized silence was gradually disturbed by a sound not easily to be verbally rendered. Whoever has heard the freshet-wave of a torrent suddenly swelled by pouring showers in tropical mountains, showers not shared by the plain; whoever has heard the first muffled murmur of its sloping advance through precipitous woods may form some conception of the sound now heard. The seeming remoteness of its source was because of its murmurous indistinctness, since it came from close by, even from the men massed on the ship's open deck. Being inarticulate, it was dubious in significance further than it seemed to indicate some capricious revulsion of thought or feeling such as mobs ashore are liable to, in the present instance possibly implying a sullen revocation on the men's part of their involuntary echoing of Billy's benediction. But ere the murmur had time to wax into clamor it was met by a strategic command, the more telling that it came with abrupt unexpectedness: 'Pipe down the starboard watch, Boatswain, and see that they go.'

Shrill as the shriek of the sea hawk, the silver whistles of the boatswain and his mates pierced that ominous low sound, dissipating it; and yielding

---

6. A quiet and easy death.

to the mechanism of discipline the throng was thinned by one-half. For the remainder, most of them were set to temporary employments connected with trimming the yards and so forth, business readily to be got up to serve occasion by any officer of the deck.

Now each proceeding that follows a mortal sentence pronounced at sea by a drumhead court is characterized by promptitude not perceptibly merging into hurry, though bordering that. The hammock, the one which had been Billy's bed when alive, having already been ballasted with shot and otherwise prepared to serve for his canvas coffin, the last offices of the sea undertakers, the sailmakers' mates, were now speedily completed. When everything was in readiness a second call for all hands, made necessary by the strategic movement before mentioned, was sounded, now to witness burial.

The details of this closing formality it needs not to give. But when the tilted plank let slide its freight into the sea, a second strange human murmur was heard, blended now with another inarticulate sound proceeding from certain larger seafowl who, their attention having been attracted by the peculiar commotion in the water resulting from the heavy sloped dive of the shotted hammock into the sea, flew screaming to the spot. So near the hull did they come, that the stridor or bony creak of their gaunt double-jointed pinions was audible. As the ship under light airs passed on, leaving the burial spot astern, they still kept circling it low down with the moving shadow of their outstretched wings and the croaked requiem of their cries.

Upon sailors as superstitious as those of the age preceding ours, men-of-war's men too who had just beheld the prodigy of repose in the form suspended in air, and now foundering in the deeps; to such mariners the action of the seafowl, though dictated by mere animal greed for prey, was big with no prosaic significance. An uncertain movement began among them, in which some encroachment was made. It was tolerated but for a moment. For suddenly the drum beat to quarters,[7] which familiar sound happening at least twice every day, had upon the present occasion a signal peremptoriness in it. True martial discipline long continued superinduces in average man a sort of impulse whose operation at the official word of command much resembles in its promptitude the effect of an instinct.

The drumbeat dissolved the multitude, distributing most of them along the batteries of the two covered gun decks. There, as wonted, the guns' crew stood by their respective cannon erect and silent. In due course the first officer, sword under arm and standing in his place on the quarter-deck, formally received the successive reports of the sworded lieutenants commanding the sections of batteries below; the last of which reports being made, the summed report he delivered with the customary salute to the commander. All this occupied time, which in the present case was the object in beating to quarters at an hour prior to the customary one. That such variance from usage was authorized by an officer like Captain Vere, a martinet as some deemed him, was evidence of the necessity for unusual action implied in what he deemed to be temporarily the mood of his men. 'With mankind,' he would say, 'forms, measured forms, are everything; and this is the import couched in the story of Orpheus with his lyre spellbinding the wild denizens of the wood.'[8] And this he once applied to

7. The signal for the sailors to return to their assigned stations.   8. When Orpheus, in Greek mythology, played his lyre and sang, wild animals were charmed, trees and stones followed him, fish left the water in which they swam, and birds flew about his head.

the disruption of forms going on across the Channel and the consequences thereof.

At this unwonted muster at quarters, all proceeded as at the regular hour. The band on the quarter-deck played a sacred air, after which the chaplain went through the customary morning service. That done, the drum beat the retreat; and toned by music and religious rites subserving the discipline and purposes of war, the men in their wonted orderly manner dispersed to the places allotted them when not at the guns.

And now it was full day. The fleece of low-hanging vapor had vanished, licked up by the sun that late had so glorified it. And the circumambient air in the clearness of its serenity was like smooth white marble in the polished block not yet removed from the marble-dealer's yard.

28

The symmetry of form attainable in pure fiction cannot so readily be achieved in a narration essentially having less to do with fable than with fact. Truth uncompromisingly told will always have its ragged edges; hence the conclusion of such a narration is apt to be less finished than an architectural finial.

How it fared with the Handsome Sailor during the year of the Great Mutiny has been faithfully given. But though properly the story ends with his life, something in way of sequel will not be amiss. Three brief chapters will suffice.

In the general rechristening under the Directory of the craft originally forming the navy of the French monarchy, the *St. Louis* line-of-battle ship was named the *Athée* (the *Atheist*). Such a name, like some other substituted ones in the Revolutionary fleet, while proclaiming the infidel audacity of the ruling power, was yet, though not so intended to be, the aptest name, if one consider it, ever given to a warship; far more so indeed than the *Devastation*, the *Erebus* (the *Hell*), and similar names bestowed upon fighting ships.

On the return passage to the English fleet from the detached cruise during which occurred the events already recorded, the *Bellipotent* fell in with the *Athée*. An engagement ensued, during which Captain Vere, in the act of putting his ship alongside the enemy with a view of throwing his boarders across her bulwarks, was hit by a musket ball from a porthole of the enemy's main cabin. More than disabled, he dropped to the deck and was carried below to the same cockpit where some of his men already lay. The senior lieutenant took command. Under him the enemy was finally captured, and though much crippled was by rare good fortune successfully taken into Gibraltar, an English port not very distant from the scene of the fight. There, Captain Vere with the rest of the wounded was put ashore. He lingered for some days, but the end came. Unhappily he was cut off too early for the Nile and Trafalgar. The spirit that 'spite its philosophic austerity may yet have indulged in the most secret of all passions, ambition, never attained to the fulness of fame.

Not long before death, while lying under the influence of that magical drug[9] which, soothing the physical frame, mysteriously operates on the subtler element in man, he was heard to murmur words inexplicable to his

9. Opium.

attendant: 'Billy Budd, Billy Budd.' That these were not the accents of remorse would seem clear from what the attendant said to the *Bellipotent*'s senior officer of marines, who, as the most reluctant to condemn of the members of the drumhead court, too well knew, though here he kept the knowledge to himself, who Billy Budd was.

29

Some few weeks after the execution, among other matters under the head of 'News from the Mediterranean,' there appeared in a naval chronicle of the time, an authorized weekly publication, an account of the affair. It was doubtless for the most part written in good faith, though the medium, partly rumor, through which the facts must have reached the writer served to deflect and in part falsify them. The account was as follows:

'On the tenth of the last month a deplorable occurrence took place on board H.M.S. *Bellipotent*. John Claggart, the ship's master-at-arms, discovering that some sort of plot was incipient among an inferior section of the ship's company, and that the ringleader was one William Budd; he, Claggart, in the act of arraigning the man before the captain, was vindictively stabbed to the heart by the suddenly drawn sheath knife of Budd.

'The deed and the implement employed sufficiently suggest that though mustered into the service under an English name the assassin was no Englishman, but one of those aliens adopting English cognomens whom the present extraordinary necessities of the service have caused to be admitted into it in considerable number.

'The enormity of the crime and the extreme depravity of the criminal appear the greater in view of the character of the victim, a middle-aged man respectable and discreet, belonging to that minor official grade, the petty officers, upon whom, as none know better than the commissioned gentlemen, the efficiency of His Majesty's navy so largely depends. His function was a responsible one, at once onerous and thankless; and his fidelity in it the greater because of his strong patriotic impulse. In this instance as in so many other instances in these days, the character of this unfortunate man signally refutes, if refutation were needed, that peevish saying attributed to the late Dr Johnson, that patriotism is the last refuge of a scoundrel.[1]

'The criminal paid the penalty of his crime. The promptitude of the punishment has proved salutary. Nothing amiss is now apprehended aboard H.M.S. *Bellipotent*.'

The above, appearing in a publication now long ago superannuated and forgotten, is all that hitherto has stood in human record to attest what manner of men respectively were John Claggart and Billy Budd.

30

Everything is for a term venerated in navies. Any tangible object associated with some striking incident of the service is converted into a monument. The spar from which the foretopman was suspended was for some few years kept trace of by the bluejackets. Their knowledges followed it from ship to dockyard and again from dockyard to ship, still pursuing it even when at last

---

1. The saying is quoted in James Boswell's *Life of Samuel Johnson Ll. D.* (1791).

reduced to a mere dockyard boom. To them a chip of it was as a piece of the Cross. Ignorant though they were of the secret facts of the tragedy, and not thinking but that the penalty was somehow unavoidably inflicted from the naval point of view, for all that, they instinctively felt that Billy was a sort of man as incapable of mutiny as of wilful murder. They recalled the fresh young image of the Handsome Sailor, that face never deformed by a sneer or subtler vile freak of the heart within. This impression of him was doubtless deepened by the fact that he was gone, and in a measure mysteriously gone. On the gun decks of the *Bellipotent* the general estimate of his nature and its unconscious simplicity eventually found rude utterance from another foretopman, one of his own watch, gifted, as some sailors are, with an artless *poetic* temperament. The tarry hand made some lines which, after circulating among the shipboard crews for a while, finally got rudely printed at Portsmouth as a ballad. The title given to it was the sailor's.

Billy in the Darbies[2]

Good of the chaplain to enter Lone Bay
And down on his marrowbones here and pray
For the likes just o' me, Billy Budd.—But, look:
Through the port comes the moonshine astray!
It tips the guard's cutlass and silvers this nook;   5
But 'twill die in the dawning of Billy's last day.
A jewel-block[3] they'll make of me tomorrow,
Pendant pearl from the yardarm-end
Like the eardrop I gave to Bristol Molly—
O, 'tis me, not the sentence they'll suspend.   10
Ay, ay, all is up; and I must up too,
Early in the morning, aloft from alow.
On an empty stomach now never it would do.
They'll give me a nibble—bit o' biscuit ere I go.
Sure, a messmate will reach me the last parting cup;   15
But, turning heads away from the hoist and the belay,
Heaven knows who will have the running of me up!
No pipe to those halyards.—But aren't it all sham?
A blur's in my eyes; it is dreaming that I am.
A hatchet to my hawser? All adrift to go?   20
The drum roll to grog, and Billy never know?
But Donald he has promised to stand by the plank;
So I'll shake a friendly hand ere I sink.
But—no! It is dead then I'll be, come to think.
I remember Taff the Welshman when he sank.   25
And his cheek it was like the budding pink.
But me they'll lash in hammock, drop me deep.
Fathoms down, fathoms down, how I'll dream fast asleep.
I feel it stealing now. Sentry, are you there?
Just ease these darbies at the wrist,   30
And roll me over fair!
I am sleepy, and the oozy weeds about me twist.

---

2. Handcuffs or fetters.   3. Carries a studding-sail to the very end of the yard where it is hoisted.

EMILY DICKINSON
1830–1886

Emily Dickinson forces her readers to acknowledge the startling aspects of ordinary life. "Ordinary life" includes the mysterious actuality of death, but it also includes birds and woods and oceans, arguments between people, the weight of depression. In small facts and large, Dickinson perceives enormous meaning.

The poet's life, like her verse, was somewhat mysterious. Born to a prosperous and prominent Amherst, Massachusetts, family (her father, a lawyer, was also treasurer of Amherst College), Dickinson attended Amherst Academy and later, for a year, the Mount Holyoke Female Seminary. Thereafter, however, she remained almost entirely in her father's house, leading the life of a recluse. She had close family attachments and a few close friendships, pursued mainly through correspondence. The most important of these relationships, from a literary point of view, was with the Boston writer and critic Thomas Wentworth Higginson, who eventually published her poems. She had begun writing verse in the late 1850s; in 1862, after seeing an essay of Higginson's in the *Atlantic Monthly,* Dickinson wrote him to ask his opinion of her poems, about three hundred of them in existence by this time. The correspondence thus begun continued to the end of Dickinson's life; Higginson also visited her in Amherst.

At Dickinson's death, 1,775 poems survived; only seven had been published, anonymously. With the help of another friend, Mabel Todd Loomis, Higginson selected poems for a volume, published in 1890, which proved extremely popular. Further selections continued to appear, but not until 1955 did Dickinson's entire body of work reach print.

By 1843, the English poet Elizabeth Barrett Browning had written in verse an exhortation to social reform (*The Cry of the Children*); in 1857, she published a long poem, *Aurora Leigh,* commenting on the oppressed situation of women. Christina Rossetti, born the same year as Dickinson and like her unmarried, in poems like *Goblin Market* (1862) found indirect ways to meditate on female predicaments. Dickinson, on the other hand, seems only peripherally aware of social facts. She alludes to church services, locomotives, female costume; very occasionally (for example, in "My Life had stood—a Loaded Gun—") she refers to the way a woman's life is defined in relation to a man's. More centrally, she finds brilliant and provocative formulations of the emotional import of universal phenomena. We may feel already that death amounts to an incomprehensible and indigestible fact, but we are unlikely to have imagined conversations within a tomb or a personified version of death as carriage driver. By using such images, Dickinson disarmingly suggests a kind of playful innocence. Only gradually does one realize that the naïve, childlike perception, devoid of obviously ominous suggestion, conceals a complex, disturbing sense of human self-deception and reluctance to face the truth of experience.

Truth is an important word in Dickinson's poetry. "Tell all the Truth but tell it slant," she advises, pointing out that "The Truth must dazzle gradually / Or every man be blind—." She tells of a man who preaches about " 'Truth' until it proclaimed him a Liar—": truth remains an absolute, both challenging and judging us all. In one of her most haunting poems, she claims the identity of Beauty and Truth (an identity tellingly asserted earlier in Keats's *Ode on a Grecian Urn*) through the fiction of two dead people discussing their profound commitments:

> I died for Beauty—but was scarce
> Adjusted in the Tomb
> When One who died for Truth, was lain
> In an adjoining Room—

Her neighbor asks her why she "failed"; when she explains, he says that beauty and truth "are One":

And so, as Kinsmen, met a Night—
We talked between the Rooms—
Until the Moss had reached our lips—
And covered up—our names—

Until the last two lines, about the moss, the poem appears to evoke a rather cozy vision of death: neighbors amiably conversing from one room to another, as though at a slumber party ("met a Night"), two "Kinsmen" dedicated to noble abstractions and comforted by the companionship of their dedication. Only the word *failed* (meaning "died") disturbs the comfortable atmosphere, by suggesting a view of death as defeat.

The Keats poem that ends by asserting the identity of truth and beauty implies the permanence of both, as embodied in the work of art, the Grecian urn that stimulates the poet's reflections. Dickinson's poem concludes with troubling suggestions of impermanence. Talk of beauty and truth may reassure the talkers, but death necessarily implies forgetfulness: the dead forget and are forgotten, their very identities ("names") lost, their capacity for communication eliminated. Death *is* defeat; the high Romanticism of Keats's ode, on which this poem implicitly comments, blurs that fact. Despite Dickinson's fanciful images and allegories, her poems insist on their own kind of uncompromising realism. They speak of the universal human effort to imagine experience in reassuring terms, but they do not suggest that reality offers much in the way of reassurance: only brief experiences of natural beauty; and even those challenge human constructions. "I started Early—Took my dog—" a poem about visiting the sea begins; but it ends with the sea encountering "the Solid Town—/ No One He seemed to know—" and withdrawing.

Dickinson's eccentric punctuation, with dashes as the chief mark of emphasis and interruption, emphasizes the movements of consciousness in her lyrics. In their early publication, the poems were typically given conventional punctuation; only in 1955 did the body of work appear as Dickinson wrote it. The highly personal mode of punctuation emphasizes the fact that this verse contains also a personal and demanding vision.

216

Safe in their Alabaster Chambers—
Untouched by Morning
And untouched by Noon—
Sleep the meek members of the Resurrection—
Rafter of satin,   5
And Roof of stone.

Light laughs the breeze
In her Castle above them—
Babbles the Bee in a stolid Ear,
Pipe the Sweet Birds in ignorant cadence—   10
Ah, what sagacity perished here!

258

There's a certain Slant of light,
Winter Afternoons—
That oppresses, like the Heft
Of Cathedral Tunes—

Heavenly Hurt, it gives us—   5
We can find no scar,
But internal difference,
Where the Meanings, are—

None may teach it—Any—
'Tis the Seal Despair—   10
An imperial affliction
Sent us of the Air—

When it comes, the Landscape listens—
Shadows—hold their breath—
When it goes, 'tis like the Distance   15
On the look of Death—

303

The Soul selects her own Society—
Then—shuts the Door—
To her divine Majority—
Present no more—

Unmoved—she notes the Chariots—pausing   5
At her low Gate—
Unmoved—an Emperor be kneeling
Upon her Mat—

I've known her—from an ample nation—
Choose One—   10
Then—close the Valves of her attention—
Like Stone—

328

A Bird came down the Walk—
He did not know I saw—
He bit an Angleworm in halves
And ate the fellow, raw,

And then he drank a Dew 5
From a convenient Grass—
And then hopped sidewise to the Wall
To let a Beetle pass—

He glanced with rapid eyes
That hurried all around— 10
They looked like frightened Beads, I thought—
He stirred his Velvet Head

Like one in danger, Cautious,
I offered him a Crumb
And he unrolled his feathers 15
And rowed him softer home—

Than Oars divide the Ocean,
Too silver for a seam—
Or Butterflies, off Banks of Noon
Leap, plashless as they swim. 20

341

After great pain, a formal feeling comes—
The Nerves sit ceremonious, like Tombs—
The stiff Heart questions was it He, that bore,
And Yesterday, or Centuries before?

The Feet, mechanical, go round— 5
Of Ground, or Air, or Ought[1]—
A Wooden way
Regardless grown,
A Quartz contentment, like a stone—

This is the Hour of Lead— 10
Remembered, if outlived,
As Freezing persons, recollect the Snow—
First—Chill—then Stupor—then the letting go—

435

Much Madness is divinest Sense—
To a discerning Eye—
Much Sense—the starkest Madness—
'Tis the Majority

---

1. Zero.

In this, as All, prevail—   5
Assent—and you are sane—
Demur—you're straightway dangerous—
And handled with a Chain—

449

I died for Beauty—but was scarce
Adjusted in the Tomb
When One who died for Truth, was lain
In an adjoining Room—

He questioned softly "Why I failed"?   5
"For Beauty", I replied—
"And I—for Truth—Themself are One—
We Brethren, are", He said—

And so, as Kinsmen, met a Night—
We talked between the Rooms—   10
Until the Moss had reached our lips—
And covered up—our names—

465

I heard a Fly buzz—when I died—
The Stillness in the Room
Was like the Stillness in the Air—
Between the Heaves of Storm—

The Eyes around—had wrung them dry—   5
And Breaths were gathering firm
For that last Onset—when the King
Be witnessed—in the Room—

I willed my Keepsakes—Signed away
What portion of me be   10
Assignable—and then it was
There interposed a Fly—

With Blue—uncertain stumbling Buzz—
Between the light—and me—
And then the Windows failed—and then   15
I could not see to see—

519

'Twas warm—at first—like Us—
Until there crept upon
A Chill—like frost upon a Glass—
Till all the scene—be gone.

The Forehead copied Stone—   5
The Fingers grew too cold
To ache—and like a Skater's Brook—
The busy eyes—congealed—

It straightened—that was all—
It crowded Cold to Cold   10
It multiplied indifference—
As[1] Pride were all it could—

And even when with Cords—
'Twas lowered, like a Weight—
It made no Signal, nor demurred,   15
But dropped like Adamant.

585

I like to see it lap the Miles—
And lick the Valleys up—
And stop to feed itself at Tanks—
And then—prodigious step

Around a Pile of Mountains—   5
And supercilious peer
In Shanties—by the sides of Roads—
And then a Quarry pare

To fit its Ribs
And crawl between   10
Complaining all the while
In horrid—hooting stanza—
Then chase itself down Hill—

And neigh like Boanerges[2]—
Then—punctual as a Star   15
Stop—docile and omnipotent
At its own stable door—

1. As if.   2. "Sons of thunder," name given by Jesus to the brothers and disciples James and John, presumably because they were thunderous preachers.

632

The Brain—is wider than the Sky—
For—put them side by side—
The one the other will contain
With ease—and You—beside—

The Brain is deeper than the sea—   5
For—hold them—Blue to Blue—
The one the other will absorb—
As Sponges—Buckets—do—

The Brain is just the weight of God—
For—Heft them—Pound for Pound—   10
And they will differ—if they do—
As Syllable from Sound—

657

I dwell in Possibility—
A fairer House than Prose—
More numerous of Windows—
Superior—for Doors—

Of Chambers as the Cedars—   5
Impregnable of Eye—
And for an Everlasting Roof
The Gambrels[1] of the Sky—

Of Visitors—the fairest—
For Occupation—This—   10
The spreading wide my narrow Hands
To gather Paradise—

712

Because I could not stop for Death—
He kindly stopped for me—
The Carriage held but just Ourselves—
And Immortality.

---

1. Slopes, as in the large, arched roofs often seen on barns.

We slowly drove—He knew no haste   5
And I had put away
My labor and my leisure too,
For His Civility—

We passed the School, where Children strove
At Recess—in the Ring—   10
We passed the Fields of Gazing Grain—
We passed the Setting Sun—

Or rather—He passed Us—
The Dews drew quivering and chill—
For only Gossamer, my Gown—   15
My Tippet—only Tulle¹—

We paused before a House that seemed
A Swelling of the Ground—
The Roof was scarcely visible—
The Cornice—in the Ground—   20

Since then—'tis Centuries—and yet
Feels shorter than the Day
I first surmised the Horses' Heads
Were toward Eternity—

754

My Life had stood—a Loaded Gun—
In Corners—till a Day
The Owner passed—identified—
And carried Me away—

And now We roam in Sovereign Woods—   5
And now We hunt the Doe—
And every time I speak for Him—
The Mountains straight reply—

And do I smile, such cordial light
Upon the Valley glow—   10
It is as a Vesuvian face²
Had let its pleasure through—

And when at Night—Our good Day done—
I guard My Master's Head—
'Tis better than the Eider-Duck's   15
Deep Pillow—to have shared—

---

1. Fine, silken netting. *Tippet:* a scarf.   2. A face glowing with light like that from an erupting volcano.

To foe of His—I'm deadly foe—
None stir the second time—
On whom I lay a Yellow Eye—
Or an emphatic Thumb—   20

Though I than He—may longer live
He longer must—than I—
For I have but the power to kill,
Without—the power to die—

1084

At Half past Three, a single Bird
Unto a silent Sky
Propounded but a single term
Of cautious melody.

At Half past Four, Experiment   5
Had subjugated test
And lo, Her silver Principle
Supplanted all the rest.

At Half past Seven, Element
Nor Implement, be seen—   10
And Place was where the Presence was
Circumference between.

1129

Tell all the Truth but tell it slant—
Success in Circuit lies
Too bright for our infirm Delight
The Truth's superb surprise

As Lightning to the Children eased   5
With explanation kind
The Truth must dazzle gradually
Or every man be blind—

1207

He preached upon "Breadth" till it argued him narrow—
The Broad are too broad to define
And of "Truth" until it proclaimed him a Liar—
The Truth never flaunted a Sign—

Simplicity fled from his counterfeit presence   5
As Gold the Pyrites[1] would shun—
What confusion would cover the innocent Jesus
To meet so enabled[2] a Man!

1564

Pass to thy Rendezvous of Light,
Pangless except for us—
Who slowly ford the Mystery
Which thou hast leaped across!

1593

There came a Wind like a Bugle—
It quivered through the Grass
And a Green Chill upon the Heat
So ominous did pass
We barred the Windows and the Doors   5
As from an Emerald Ghost—
The Doom's electric Moccasin[1]
That very instant passed—
On a strange Mob of panting Trees
And Fences fled away   10
And Rivers where the Houses ran
Those looked that lived—that Day—
The Bell within the steeple wild
The flying tidings told—
How much can come   15
And much can go,
And yet abide the World!

---

1. Iron bisulfide, sometimes called fool's gold.   **2.** Competent.   **1.** I.e., water moccasin, a poisonous
snake.

CHAZAUD

Europe
ca. 1870

RUSSIA

Volga

Don

Dnieper

• Moscow

Black Sea

Yalta •

Constantinople •

OTTOMAN EMPIRE

Cyprus

Crete

St. Petersburg •

FINLAND

Baltic Sea

SWEDEN

NORWAY

Oslo •

DENMARK

Vistula

Berlin •

Elbe

GERMANY

Rhine

NETH.

BELG.

Paris • Seine

Pont-l'Évêque •

Touques R.

FRANCE

Loire

Ebro

Madrid •

SPAIN

Tagus

PORTUGAL

AUSTRIA

Vienna •

Danube

HUNGARY

SWITZ.

ITALY

Rome •

Corsica

Sardinia

Sicily

Adriatic Sea

Mediterranean Sea

MOROCCO

ALGERIA

TUNIS

North Sea

GREAT BRITAIN

London •

IRELAND

ATLANTIC OCEAN

0   500   1000 km

0   300   600 miles

Trade routes

Nineteenth-Century Colonial Expansion

The Nineteenth Century:
Realism and Symbolism

The nineteenth century saw enormous changes in the history of Western civilization. The upheavals following the French Revolution broke up the old order of Europe. The Holy Roman Empire and the Papal States were dissolved. Nationalism, nourished by the political and social aspirations of the middle classes, grew by leaps and bounds. Colonial empires were created and vast sections of the globe opened up forcibly to Western trade. "Liberty" became the dominant political slogan of the century, although the various calls for liberty focused on Western society and not on the colonies. In different countries and in different decades, *liberty* meant different things: here liberation from the rule of the foreigner, there the emancipation of the serf; here the removal of economic restrictions on trade and manufacturing, there the introduction of a constitution, free speech, parliamentary institutions, and agitation for the rights of women. Almost everywhere in Europe, the middle classes established their effective rule, though revolutions in 1830 and 1848 were crushed across Europe and monarchs remained in more or less nominal power. Two large European countries, Germany and Italy, achieved their centuries-old dream of political unification. The predominance of France, still marked at the beginning of the century, was broken, and England—or, rather, Great Britain—ruled the seas throughout the century. The smaller European nations, especially in the Balkans, began to emancipate themselves from foreign rule.

These major political changes were caused by—and, in their turn, caused—great social and economic changes. The Industrial Revolution, which had begun in England in the eighteenth century, spread throughout the Continent and transformed living conditions radically. The enormous increase in the speed and availability of transportation due to the development of railroads and steamships as well as the rapid urbanization following the establishment of industries changed the pattern of human life in most countries and caused, within a century, an unprecedented increase in population (as much as threefold in most of Europe), which was also fostered by advances in medicine and hygiene. The development of transportation and communication systems brought the world closer and prepared the way for global economic and political systems. The existence of widespread wealth and prosperity is undeniable, although it coexisted with wretched living conditions and other hardships for the early factory workers, many of them women. As the social and political power of the aristocracy declined, the barriers between the social classes also diminished. Middle-class values dominated, and the industrial laborer began to be felt as a political force.

These social and economic changes were closely bound up with shifts in prevailing outlooks and philosophies. Technological innovation is impossible without scientific discoveries. The scientific viewpoint, hitherto dominant only in a comparatively limited area, spread widely and permeated almost all fields of human thought and endeavor. It raised enormous hopes for the future betterment of humankind, especially when Darwin's evolutionary theories fortified the earlier, vaguer faith in unlimited progress. "Liberty," "science," "progress," and "evolution" are the concepts that define the mental atmosphere of the nineteenth century in Europe.

But tendencies hostile to these were by no means absent. Feudal or Catholic conservatism succeeded, especially in Austria-Hungary, Russia, and much of southern Europe, in preserving old regimes, and the philosophies of a conservative and religious society were reformulated in modern terms. At the same time in England, the very assumptions of the new industrial middle-class society were powerfully attacked by writers such as Carlyle and Ruskin, who recommended a return to medieval forms of social cooperation and handicraft. The industrial civilization of the nineteenth century was also opposed by the fierce individualism of many artists and thinkers who were unhappy in the ugly, commercial, and "Philistine" society of the age. The writings of Nietzsche, toward the end of the century, and the whole movement of art for art's sake, which asserted the independence of the artist from society, are the most obvious symptoms of this revolt. The free-enterprise system and the liberalism of the ruling middle classes also clashed early with the rising proletariat; diverse forms of socialism developed, preaching a new collectivism that stressed equality. Socialism could have Christian or romantic motivations, or it could become "scientific" and revolutionary, as Marx's brand of socialism (a certain stage of which he called "communism") claimed to be.

While up through the eighteenth century religion was, at least in name, a major force in European civilization, in the nineteenth century there was a marked decrease in its influence on both intellectual leaders and ordinary people. Local, intense revivals of religious consciousness, such as the Oxford movement in England, did occur, and the traditional religious institutions were preserved everywhere; but the impact of science on religion was such that many tenets of the old faiths crumbled or were severely weakened. The discoveries of astronomy, geology, evolutionary biology, and archaeology as well as biblical criticism forced, almost everywhere, a restatement of the old creeds. Religion, especially in Protestant countries, was frequently confined to an inner feeling of religiosity or to a system of morality that preserved the ancient Christian virtues. In Germany during the early nineteenth century, Hegel and his predecessors and followers tried to interpret the world in spiritual terms, outside the bounds of traditional religion. There were many attempts even late in the century to restate this view, but the methods and discoveries of science seemed to invalidate it, and various formulas that took science as their base in building new lay religions of hope in humanity gained popularity. French positivism, English utilitarianism, the evolutionism of Herbert Spencer are some of the best-known examples. Meanwhile, for the first time in history—at least in Europe—profoundly pessimistic and atheistic philosophies arose, of which Schopenhauer's was the most subtle, while extreme materialism was the most widespread. Thus the whole gamut of views of the universe was represented during the century in new and impressive formulations.

The visual arts did not show a similar vitality. For a long time in most countries, painting and architecture floundered in a sterile eclecticism—in a bewildering variety of historical masquerades in which the neo-Gothic style was replaced by the neo-Renaissance and that by the neo-Baroque and other decorative revivals of past forms. Only in France did painting (with the Impressionists) find a new style that was genuinely original. In music, the highly Romantic art of Richard Wagner attracted the most attention. Wagner's concept of the *Gesamtkunstwerk* (ge-zamt-koonst'-vehrk)— the "total work," combining music, drama, poetry, and spectacle—influenced Symbolist writers and encouraged the tendency to break down distinctions between genres. Otherwise, the individual national schools either continued in their tradition, like Italian opera (Verdi), or founded an idiom of their own, often based on a revival of folklore, as in Russia (Tchaikovsky), Poland (Chopin), Bohemia (Dvořák), and Norway (Grieg).

But literature was the most representative and most widely influential art of nineteenth-century Europe. It found new forms and methods, and expressed the social and intellectual situation of the time most fully and memorably. It was this literature, moreover, that served as a model for many non-Western writers seeking to modernize their own literary traditions on the basis of European masterworks. Nowadays, many writers are unwilling to emulate foreign models and seek instead to rediscover an earlier, precolonial tradition. The literature of nineteenth-century Europe continues nonetheless to be read and admired in its own right.

REALISM

After the great wave of Romanticism had spent its force in the fourth decade of the nineteenth century, European literature moved in the direction of what is usually called *realism*. Realism was not a coherent general movement that established itself unchallenged for a long period of time, as classicism had done during the eighteenth century. Exceptions and reservations there were, and debates over the best way of reproducing reality. But still, in retrospect, the nineteenth century appears as the period of the great realistic writers: Flaubert in France, Dostoevsky and Tolstoy in Russia, Dickens in England, James in America, Ibsen in Norway.

What is meant by *realism*? The term, in literary use (there is a much older philosophical use), apparently dates back to the Germans at the turn of the nineteenth century—to Friedrich Schiller and August and Friedrich Schlegel. It cropped up in France as early as 1826 but became a commonly accepted literary and artistic slogan only in the 1850s. When an academically minded jury rejected Gustave Courbet's painting *The Artist's Studio* for Paris's Exposition Universelle of 1855, the artist exhibited a collection of his paintings separately as "realist" art and wrote a preface to the exhibit catalog that became an unofficial manifesto for realist art. In the following year, a review called *Réalisme* began publication, and in 1857 a novelist and critic, Champfleury (the pseudonym of Jules-François-Félix Husson), published a volume of critical articles with the title *Le Réalisme*. Since then, the word has been bandied about, discussed, analyzed, and abused, as all slogans are. It is frequently confused with *naturalism*, an ancient philosophical term for materialism, epicureanism, or any secularism. As a specifically literary term, *naturalism* crystallized only in France, where it meant simply the study of nature, and the analogy between the writer and the naturalist was ready at hand. Émile Zola, in an essay called *The Experimental Novel*, derived a method of naturalist writing from Dr. Claude Bernard's principles of experimental medicine and claimed that his early novel *Thérèse Raquin* (1866), was "an analytical labor on two living bodies like that of a surgeon on corpses."

The program of the groups of writers and critics who used these terms can be easily summarized. Realists like Flaubert and Maupassant wanted a truthful representation of reality—that is, the reality of contemporary life and manners. They thought of their method as inductive, observational, and, hence, "objective." The personality of the author was to be suppressed or was at least to recede into the background since reality was to be seen "as it is." The naturalistic program, as formulated by Zola, was substantially the same, except that Zola put greater stress on the analogies to science, considering the procedure of the novelist as identical with that of the experimenting scientist. He also more definitely and exclusively embraced the philosophy of scientific materialism, with its deterministic implications and its stress on heredity and environment, while the older realists were not always as clear in drawing the philosophical consequences.

These French theories were anticipated, paralleled, or imitated all over the world of Western literature. In Germany, the movement called Young Germany, with which Heine was associated, had propounded a substantially anti-Romantic realistic program as early as the 1830s, but versions of the French theories definitely triumphed there only in the 1880s. In Russia, as early as the 1840s, the most prominent critic of the time, Vissarion Belinsky, praised the early Gogol as a "poet of reality" and later supported the "natural" school of Russian fiction, which described contemporary Russia with fidelity. In Italy, Giovanni Verga and Luigi Capuana founded an analogous movement called *verismo*. The English-speaking countries were the last to adopt the critical programs and slogans of the Continent: George Moore and George Gissing brought the French theories to England in the late 1880s, and in the United States William Dean Howells began his campaign for realism in 1886, when he became editor of *Harper's Magazine*. Realistic and naturalistic theories of literature have since been widely accepted, either as the basis of writing or as a standard against which later generations rebel. The officially promoted doctrine of Soviet Russia was called "socialist realism," a combination of factual observation and implied socialist message; the realistic novel in the United States is usually considered naturalistic and judged by the standards of nature and truth. Yet twentieth-century novelists in Europe and America also pushed realism to an extreme in the "literature of fact," in documentary novels, and in narratives that foreground a series of undifferentiated "objective" perceptions.

The slogans "realism" and "naturalism" were thus new to the nineteenth century and served as effective formulas directed against the Romantic creed. Truth, contemporaneity, and objectivity were the obvious counterparts of Romantic imagination, of Romantic historicism and its glorification of the past, and of Romantic subjectivity, the exaltation of the ego and the individual. But, of course, the emphasis on truth and objectivity was not really new: these qualities had been demanded by many older, classical theories of imitation, and in the eighteenth century there were great writers such as Denis Diderot who wanted a literal "imitation of life" even on the stage.

The practice of realism, it could be argued, is very old indeed. There are realistic scenes in the *Iliad* and *Odyssey*, and there is plenty of realism in ancient comedy and satire, in medieval stories (*fabliaux*) like some of Chaucer's and Boccaccio's, in many Elizabethan plays, in the Spanish rogue novels, in the English eighteenth-century novel beginning with Daniel Defoe, and so on almost ad infinitum. But while it would be easy to find in early literature anticipations of almost every element of modern realism, still the systematic description of contemporary society, with a serious purpose, often even with a tragic tone, and with sympathy for heroes drawn from the middle and lower classes, was a real innovation of the nineteenth century.

It is usually rash to explain a literary movement in social and political terms. But the new realistic art surely had something to do with the triumph of the middle classes in France after the July Revolution in 1830 and in England after the passage of the Reform Bill in 1832, and with the increasing influence of the middle classes in almost every country. Russia is an exception since no large middle class could develop there during the nineteenth century. An absolute feudal régime continued in power, and the special character of most of Russian literature must be the result of this distinction. But even in Russia, there emerged an "intelligentsia" (the term comes from Russia) that was open to Western ideas and was highly critical of the czarist regime and its official ideology.

Although much nineteenth-century literature reflects the triumph of the middle classes, it would be wrong to think of the great realistic writers as spokespeople or mouthpieces of the middle-class society they described. Honoré de Balzac was politically a Catholic monarchist who applauded the Bourbon restoration after the fall of Napoleon, but he had an extraordinary imaginative insight into the processes leading to the victory of the middle classes. Both Flaubert and Maupassant despised the middle-class society of the Third Empire with an intense hatred and the pride of a self-conscious artist. Dickens became increasingly critical of the middle classes and the assumptions of industrial civilization. Dostoevsky, even though he took part in a conspiracy against the Russian government early in his life and spent ten years in exile in Siberia, became the propounder of an extremely conservative nationalistic and religious creed that was definitely directed against the revolutionary forces in Russia. Tolstoy, himself a count and a landowner, was violent in his criticism of the czarist regime, especially later in his life, but he cannot be described as friendly to the middle classes, to the aims of the democratic movements in Western Europe, or to the science of the time. Ibsen's political attitude was that of a proud individualist who condemns the "compact majority" and its tyranny. Possibly all art is critical of its society. But in the nineteenth century, this criticism became much more explicit, as social and political issues became much more urgent or, at least, were regarded as more urgent by those writing about or within them. To a far greater degree than in earlier centuries, writers felt their isolation from society, viewed the structure and problems of the prevailing order as debatable and reformable, and, in spite of all demands for objectivity, became in many cases social propagandists and reformers in their own right.

The program of realism, while defensible enough as a reaction against Romanticism, raises many critical questions. What is meant by *truth of representation?* Photographic copying? This seems the implication of many famous pronouncements: "A novel is a mirror walking along the road," said Stendhal (the pseudonym of Marie-Henri Beyle) as early as 1830. But such statements can hardly be taken literally. All art must select and represent; it cannot be, and has never been, a simple transcript of reality. What such analogies are intended to convey is rather a claim for an all-inclusiveness of subject matter, a protest against the exclusion of themes that before were considered low, sordid, or trivial (like the puddles on the road along which the mirror walks). Chekhov formulated this protest with the usual parallel between the scientist and the writer: "To a chemist nothing on earth is unclean. A writer must be as objective as a chemist; he must abandon the subjective line: he must know that dung heaps play a very respectable part in a landscape, and that evil passions are as inherent in life as good ones." Thus the truth of realistic art includes the sordid, the low, the disgusting, and the evil; and the implication is that the subject is treated objectively, without interference and falsification by the artist's personality and his own desires.

But in practice, while realistic art succeeded in expanding the themes of art, it could not fulfill the demand for total objectivity. Works of art are written by human beings and inevitably express their personalities and their points of view. As Joseph Conrad admitted, "Even the most artful of writers will give himself (and his morality) away in about every third sentence." Objectivity, in the sense that Zola had in mind when he proposed a scientific method in the writing of novels and conceived of the novelist as a sociologist collecting human documents, is impossible in practice. Surely Maupassant was right when he said that it "would be impossible to describe everything, for you would need at least a book a day to list the multitude of trivial incidents that fill our existence," and concluded that the writer must select and organize details to give the *impression* of truth. The demand for objectivity can be understood only as a demand for a specific method of narration in which the author does not interfere explicitly, in his or her own name, and as a rejection of personal themes of introspection and reverie.

The realistic program, while it made innumerable new subjects available to art, also implied a narrowing of its themes and methods to exclude anything that did not seem a direct representation of reality. Romantic art could, without offending its readers, use coincidences, improbabilities, and even impossibilities that were not, theoretically at least, tolerated in realistic art. Realism professes to present us with a slice of life, but one should recognize that both realism and naturalism are artistic methods and conventions like any other mode of writing. The complete representation of reality in literature is unachievable and not merely because it would take too long: like all art, literature is a *making,* a creating of a world of symbols that differs radically from the world that we call reality. The value of realism lies in its negation of the conventions of Romanticism, its expansion of the themes of art, and its new demonstration (never forgotten by artists) that literature has to deal also with its time and society and has, at its best, an insight into reality (not only social reality) that is not necessarily identical with that of science. Many of the great writers make us realize the world of their time, evoke an imaginative picture of it that seems truer and will last longer than that of historians and sociologists. But this achievement is due to their imagination and to their art or craft, two requisites that realistic theory tended to forget or minimize. One could assert, in short, that all the great realists were simply artists who created worlds of imagination and knew (at least instinctively) that in art one can say something about reality only through language.

SYMBOLISM

Where prose fiction and drama faced outward, aiming to mirror the real world, Symbolist poetry turned its attention to the mirror itself: to the *words* that reflect reality. Symbolist poets found their own way to address the same questions of truth and reality that preoccupied the novelists, and they embarked on an exploration of language that would influence all forms of twentieth-century literature. Preserving the Romantic notion of the poet as seer or visionary but experimenting with language to communicate that vision, they played with multiple and shifting perspectives in a manner that heralded not only modern free verse, prose poems, and spatial poetry, but also the innovative language of novelists such as James Joyce, William Faulkner, Alain Robbe-Grillet, and Marguerite Duras.

The evolution was gradual until the middle of the century. In England, the Pre-Raphaelite movement upheld a Romantic, escapist, and antirealist program. In France, a large and diverse group of Parnassians retained Romantic themes while focusing on a precise and delicate use of detail. The most important writer at mid-century is Charles Baudelaire (1821–1867), whose poetry and writings on art deeply influenced the course of European poetry. Baudelaire's major collection of poems, *The Flowers of Evil*, was published in 1857, the same year that Flaubert was brought to trial for *Madame Bovary*. His art criticism is justly famous, and the selection on the creative imagination, printed here, comes from the *Salon of 1859*, his review of an exhibition of paintings. Inspiring a poetic movement that would later be called Symbolism, Baudelaire remains today the French poet most widely read outside France. Oddly enough, the great poets who are usually called Symbolist (Baudelaire, Mallarmé, Verlaine, Rimbaud) are more accurately "pre-Symbolist" since they were writing well before the official Symbolist movement and the Symbolist Manifesto of 1886. Yet there are elements in common, and the precursors of Symbolism are often discussed in the same breath as their descendants.

Symbolist poetry generally tries to organize patterns of association and allusion to evoke another set of meanings hidden behind appearances. A "symbol" here is not a linear substitution (of the type $A = B$ or *a rose = love*) but is more likely to be an image or group of images created to suggest, as a *whole*, another dimension, a plane of reality, that cannot be expressed in more direct, rational terms. In Baudelaire's poem *Correspondences*, for example, the five senses fuse to evoke a primitive level of being, a preconscious world where colors have taste, sights have physical texture, sounds have odors, and so on. (This fusion is called *synesthesia*.) Baudelaire's poetry may lead to abstract or visionary conclusions, but it is firmly based in images as realistic as a rotting carcass (*A Carcass*), logs falling on the pavement (*Song of Autumn I*), and a mangy cat trying to find a comfortable spot in rainy weather (*Spleen LXXVIII*). The imagined scene is not an escape from natural reality as much as a transformation of it, the creation of a new world reassembled in the mind from pieces of the old.

After Symbolic allusion, the second great theme of Symbolist poetry is language— as a means of communication and as the necessary, but flawed, tool of poetic creation.

Like Flaubert seeking *le mot juste* ("the exact word"), Symbolist poets are haunted by the difficulty of writing: Baudelaire described his exhausted brain as a graveyard; Stéphane Mallarmé felt paralyzed by "the empty paper whose whiteness defends it." The difficulty for the Symbolists is that their ideal poetic language must be distilled out of ordinary language through a totally controlled arrangement of all possible levels of form. Sound patterns, image clusters, and intertwined systems of logical and psychological associations act to create a complex architecture of inner reference. It is the relationship of words that counts, not just their dictionary definitions; the artist is, in a sense, a technician. The extraordinary self-consciousness of the Symbolist poet soon became an accepted element of the poem itself. Some poems focused on difficulties of communication (a characteristic Romantic theme); others, like Baudelaire's *Windows*, asserted the joy of using language to imagine other existences and to gain, in return, a better sense of their own reality. The Symbolists' acute awareness of the possibilities and limitations of language influenced both philosophers of language and literary theorists in the twentieth century.

Symbolist writers frequently compared their poetry to music, whose characteristics they tried to reproduce; Paul Verlaine (1844–1896) is especially known for the musicality of his verse. Both poetry and music were felt to be pure arts in which line and harmony (including calculated dissonance) meant more than separate notes or the definitions of individual words. They saw analogies, too, between their art and painting, where distinctive new methods of depicting reality were being developed. Symbolist poetry and Impressionist art both represented moves away from the conventional realistic representation of reality; and in the poetic as in the art world, they both outraged the average citizen by their apparent betrayal of common sense.

Baudelaire's most important successors were very different figures: an English teacher, Stéphane Mallarmé (1842–1898); a sometime clerk and French teacher, Paul Verlaine; and the adolescent prodigy Arthur Rimbaud (1854–1891). In a short and violent literary career between the ages of fifteen and twenty, Rimbaud attempted to become a seer or *voyant* through hallucinatory writing expressing the "disorder of all the senses." The *Letter of the Seer,* passages of which are printed here, was written when Rimbaud was only sixteen. His rebellion against home and authority, his experiments with drugs and alcohol, his love affair with Verlaine, and his search for a transfigured condition beyond ordinary experience are all expressed in his poetry. Ultimately, Rimbaud became disenchanted with his magical or "alchemical" art. He abruptly stopped writing poetry and left for Africa, where he spent the last eighteen years of his life trying to make a living. A good deal of Rimbaud's legend comes from this extraordinary example of a great poet who simply did not find what he sought in literature and, therefore, ceased to write. Rimbaud's work and the integrity of his spiritual commitment had enormous influence on later writers, especially the Surrealists.

Paul Verlaine, conversely, had an immediate influence on the new generation of French poets for whom his revolutionary verse forms held a fascination almost equaled by the scandalous figure of the poet himself. Verlaine's *Art of Poetry* (1884) recommended music, nuance, and ambiguity instead of the conventionally prized intellect, clarity, and force; and his own poetry emphasized emotion and mood rather than philosophy or moral persuasion. He introduced short, impressionistic sketches that establish a mood, usually melancholy alienation, and strengthened that mood by creating a related music of word sounds and rhythm. Unlike previous classical poetry with its regular alexandrines (twelve-syllable lines), Verlaine's poems used shorter, irregular, continuous, and almost conversational lines that echo the rhythms of speech. Although his example directly inspired the free verse of later Symbolist and modern poetry, he himself cherished the musicality achieved by patterns of rhythm and rhyme.

Stéphane Mallarmé was a quiet, scholarly poet who spent his life in a search for absolute poetry *in language*. Mallarmé loved words and distrusted the sloppiness of everyday speech. He envisaged a special poetic language that would be built out of the precisely planned interaction of ordinary words, in poems that would "give a purer sense to the words of the crowd." Mallarmé's long poem *Dice Thrown*, with its startling arrangement of different type sizes and words scattered to create patterns on the page, heralded concrete poetry and other modern attempts to use the silence of blank space as part of poetry. Toward the end of his life, he considered everything he produced to be a fragment of an ultimate "Book" that he feared he would never be able to write: a massively interrelated composition of pure poetry whose function would be to assert the dignity of human imagination in the face of universal nothingness. Mallarmé uses Symbolist tactics in that he prefers allusion and suggestion to direct speech, or—a specifically Mallarméan theme—potentiality and absence to a fixed and limited reality. Material objects like a bracelet, a fan, a harp, or a lace curtain, are described so as to evoke other elements in another realm of being. A carved angel's wing gilded by the sun evokes a harp. The harp exists only in the imagination, however, and its implied music is doubly unreal because the source is merely suggested, not represented. This music is even more ambiguous than Keats's "melodies . . . unheard," for it is a musical *silence*.

It is paradoxical that none of these poets—Baudelaire, Mallarmé, Rimbaud, or Verlaine—was a member of the Symbolist movement. Symbolist doctrine as such dates to a manifesto issued in 1886 by a minor poet, Jean Moréas (Yánnis Papadiamantópoulos, 1856–1910). In many ways, the movement is a systematization and popularization of ideas gleaned from Baudelaire, Rimbaud, Mallarmé, and Verlaine; especially influential were Verlaine's essays in 1884 describing Rimbaud, Mallarmé, and Tristan Corbière (1845–1875) as outcast or "accursed poets." A number of young poets (often called "Decadents") were attracted to Symbolist ideas and proclaimed Verlaine their master; their publication and literary reviews flourished around the turn of the century. Symbolism as a movement, however, had less of an impact than the major poets from whom it sprang; and it was the example of these earlier poets that especially influenced writers such as W. B. Yeats, T. S. Eliot, Marcel Proust, Rainer Maria Rilke, Wallace Stevens, and others around the world for whom Symbolist poetry became the model for contemporary poetry and poetics.

A NOTE ON FRENCH POETRY

English poetry receives its rhythm from the accent or stress in words, and the most common English line is iambic pentameter ("Whatever is begotten, born, and dies"). In contrast, the rhythm of French poetry is based on *quantity*—on the number and pattern of syllables in a line. The most common French line is the twelve-syllable, or alexandrine, verse, usually divided into balanced segments of six or four syllables. Baudelaire's *Correspondences* (given also in French on page 1547) is a sonnet written in alexandrines that displays many of the conventions of French poetry.

Syllables are divided to reflect the sound of the line when read aloud; thus, every syllable should begin with a consonant whenever possible ("Na / tu / re . . . con / fu / ses / pa / roles.") In traditional French poetry, the unaccented or mute *e* counts as a syllable and is pronounced when it occurs before a sounded consonant (but not otherwise): thus, "Com / *me* / les / prai / ries" (line 10) sounds the mute *e*, but "La / Na / tu / *re est* / un / tem / *ple où*" (line 1) does not. The subtle use of the mute *e* provides rich sonorous effects that are evident only in reading aloud.

French rhymes are categorized as rich, sufficient, or weak and also as masculine or feminine. Weak rhymes have only one accented vowel in common: prair*ies* / infi*nies* (the *ee* sound). Sufficient rhymes have two elements in common: en*fants* / triom*phants*. A rich rhyme has three or more elements in common: p*iliers* / fam*iliers* (*i*, *l*, and the diphthong *ier*). A variety of rhymes is desirable. Feminine rhymes end in the sound of a mute *e: paroles / symboles* or *rose / chose*. All other rhymes are masculine. After the sixteenth century, most poets alternated masculine and feminine rhymes. In *Correspondances*, Baudelaire uses the Petrarchan sonnet form (two quatrains, two tercets) with a rhyme scheme alternating masculine and feminine rhymes as follows: *mffm fmmf mfm fmm*. The intricacy of these and other poetic effects makes clear why later poets revered Baudelaire as a master of classical form as well as a visionary.

PRONOUNCING GLOSSARY

The following list uses common English syllables and stress accents to provide rough equivalents of selected words whose pronunciation may be unfamiliar to the general reader.

Balzac: *bahl-zahk'*

Baudelaire: *boh-d'lair'*

Champfleury: *shom-fler-ee'*

Chekhov: *cheh'-hoff*

Corbière: *cohr-bee-ehr'*

Courbet: *coor-bay'*

Dostoevsky: *dos-toy-eff'-skee*

fabliaux: *fah-blee-oh'*

Flaubert: *floh-bair'*

Mallarmé: *mahl-ahr-may'*

Moréas: *moh-ray-ahs'*

Proust: *Proost*

réalisme: *ray-al-eezm'*

Rilke: *ril'-kuh*

Rimbaud: *ram-boh'*

Schlegel: *shlay'-gel*

Stendhal: *ston-dahl'*

verismo: *vehr-eez'-moh*

Verlaine: *vehr-len'*

Wagner: *vahg'-ner*

Zola: *zoh-lah'*

REALISM AND SYMBOLISM

TEXTS	CONTEXTS
1835 Thomas Babington Macaulay, *[Minute on Indian Education, February 2, 1835]*	
1842 Nikolai Gogol, *Dead Souls* and *The Overcoat*	
1848 Karl Marx and Friedrich Engels, *Manifesto of the Communist Party*	
1856 Gustave Flaubert, *Madame Bovary*	
1857 Charles Baudelaire, *The Flowers of Evil*	
1859 Charles Darwin, *The Origin of Species*	
1860 Giuseppe Garibaldi, *Memorandum* to the heads of Europe	**1861** Serfs emancipated in Russia
	1861–1865 Civil War in the United States
1864 Fyodor Dostoyevsky, *Notes from Underground*	
1866 Fyodor Dostoyevsky, *Crime and Punishment* • Émile Zola's essay *The Experimental Novel* argues for a "naturalist" style analogous to methods in experimental science	
1867 Karl Marx, *Capital*	**1869** Suez Canal completed
1869 Leo Tolstoy, *War and Peace*	
1870 Ernest Renan's *Life of Jesus* offers a historical approach to the New Testament	
1871 George Eliot (Mary Ann Evans), *Middlemarch* • Charles Darwin, *The Descent of Man*	
1874 Paul Verlaine, *Songs without Words*	**1874** Claude Monet's painting *Impression: Rising Sun* launches Impressionism as a style
	1876 Invention of the telephone
1876 Stéphane Mallarmé, *The Afternoon of a Faun*	
1882 Friedrich Nietzsche, *The Gay Science* (1882–87)	
1883 Giovanni Verga, *Freedom*	**1884–1885** Berlin Conference agrees on procedures for European acquisition of African territory; by 1914, all Africa, except Ethiopia and Liberia, succumbs to European rule

Boldface titles indicate works in the anthology.

TEXTS	CONTEXTS
1886 Arthur Rimbaud, *Illuminations* • Leo Tolstoy, *The Death of Ivan Ilyich* • Friedrich Nietzsche's *Beyond Good and Evil* proclaims a "life force," a "will to power," and a "superman" who embodies these qualities	
	1887 Eiffel Tower built for the 1889 Paris World's Fair • Gottlieb Daimler's internal combustion engine for the automobile
1889 Guy de Maupassant, *Hautot and His Son*	
1890 Henrik Ibsen, *Hedda Gabler* • *Poems* of Emily Dickinson (1830–1886) published posthumously • Chief Machemba of the Yao refuses to accept colonial rule in his *Letter to Major von Wissmann*	
1893 Émile Zola completes a twenty-volume series of naturalist novels begun in 1871, *Les Rougon-Macquart*	
	1894 X rays discovered
	1894–1906 In the Dreyfus Affair, anti-Semitic sentiment polarizes France
1897 Mona Caird, *The Emancipation of the Family* • Mary Kingsley, *Travels in West Africa*	
1898 Émile Zola's *Letter to Félix Faure* denounces governmental corruption in the Dreyfus Case	**1898** Radium discovered by Marie and Pierre Curie • Spanish-American War breaks out
1899 Anton Chekhov, *The Lady with the Dog* • Cecil Rhodes, *Speech at Drill Hall, Cape Town, South Africa,* articulates the imperialist view of African colonialism • Olive Schreiner, *An English–South African's View of the Situation*	
1899–1900 Sol T. Plaatje, *Mafeking Diary,* describes the Boer siege of Mafeking from a black perspective	
1904 Anton Chekhov's *The Cherry Orchard* performed	

NIKOLAI GOGOL
1809–1852

Best known as a great comic writer and a founder of modern Russian prose, Nikolai Gogol scandalized the censor in his day, influenced Russia's "natural school" in its depictions of social reality, and prompted the famous statement (attributed to Dostoevsky) that "we all came out of Gogol's *Overcoat*." A realist for some, an artful master of the grotesque for others, Gogol shapes a complex vision that cannot be pinned down to one mood, nor did he wish it to be: his narrative voice shifts without warning between neutral observation, chatty digressions, open mockery, earthy speech, and lyric interjections as he entertains readers and keeps them off balance. Seldom has a writer been categorized so differently by his admirers. Reformist social critics in Gogol's time claimed him as a "poet of reality" who exposed human weaknesses and attacked social injustice, a view that was supported as "critical realism" in twentieth-century Soviet doctrine. Other readers emphasized his technical artistry, pointing to Gogol's love of ornate language, his use of fantastic or supernatural themes, and the way he distorted reality to create grotesque effects or situations. Gogol's literary reputation is based on stories, plays, essays, and a major comic novel entitled *Dead Souls*, all written and published over only thirteen years. After that time and following a serious illness, he turned in another direction, devoting the last ten years of his life to religious self-purification and to writing a sequel for *Dead Souls* that would inspire a spiritual rebirth for Russian culture. Torn by misgivings, he burned the manuscript shortly before his death.

He was born Nikolai Vasilievich Gogol-Yanovsky in the Mirgorod district of the Ukraine (then part of the Russian Empire) on March 20, 1809, to a family of moderately prosperous landowners whose estate included two hundred and fifty serfs (peasants attached to the land). His father, Vasily Afanasievich Gogol-Yanovsky, was an amateur gardener, poet, and playwright who wrote several comedies, drawing on local folklore and the Ukrainian puppet-theater tradition: Gogol would use both in his own work. Gogol's mother, Maria Ivanovna, was a country woman, devout and narrow in her views, who married very young and pampered her firstborn son. Superstitious and steeped in local folklore, she told him terrifying stories of malicious demons and the horrors of the Last Judgment that sank into his anxious imagination: Gogol's fear of the devil lasted throughout his life.

When the young boy was sent to boarding school at the age of nine, he found it a rough awakening from the protective atmosphere at home. In the high school in Nezhin, his unsympathetic schoolmates called him "the mysterious dwarf," and he responded by emphasizing his difference from them. He joined the student literary club, read widely (including contemporary avant-garde poetry excluded from the curriculum), and wrote poetry and prose. His greatest success in school came not as a writer, however, but as an actor in plays, where his talent at mimicry was widely praised and where he contributed enthusiastically as actor, director, or stagehand. In 1825, his father died, and the already dwindling family fortunes continued to decline. His mother wished him to come home and manage the estate after graduation in 1828, but Gogol had high hopes of making a name for himself in some as yet undefined way: above all, he wanted to avoid being merely an "exister," someone living in plantlike passivity who never made a mark on the world. In St. Petersburg, the glittering capital of the Russian Empire, he hoped to find his way to fame, and after six months at home he set off for the city armed with a recommendation from his uncle, a former minister of justice. He dropped the Polish-sounding Yanovsky from his surname at this time, choosing to retain only the name of aristocratic Russian ancestors.

St. Petersburg was disappointing. He could not afford to live there; his recommendations did not win him a job; he auditioned unsuccessfully for a part as an actor;

and, when he published a long romantic poem, *Hans Küchelgarten*, the reviews were so bad that he burned all the remaining copies and (appropriating a mortgage payment entrusted to him by his mother) fled to Germany to recover. After six weeks, Gogol returned to St. Petersburg and spent fourteen months as a clerk in the lowest level of the civil service, an experience that led him to hate and fear bureaucracy, and provided the material for descriptions of poor clerks in tales like *The Diary of a Madman* and *The Overcoat*. A series of jobs for which he was marginally suited and in which he took little interest—tutor, history teacher at a girls' school, adjunct professor of history at St. Petersburg University—allowed him to support himself while writing articles and stories for literary magazines. He met important literary figures such as the poets Vasily Zhukovsky and Alexander Pushkin, under whose sponsorship he began to be recognized as a striking new talent. Zhukovsky's position as poet laureate and tutor to the royal family enabled Gogol to obtain various governmental grants over the next decade, and Pushkin's encouragement and advice were crucially important for the young writer. Gogol idolized Pushkin throughout his life and later attributed to him the idea for his play *The Inspector General* (also translated as *The Government Inspector*) and for his unfinished epic novel, *Dead Souls*.

Between 1829 and 1836, when he left for Rome, Gogol wrote prolifically and established himself as an innovative stylist and comic genius. His first two collections of stories, *Evenings on a Farm near Dikanka* (1831–32), developed themes and situations from Ukrainian folk culture and were a popular success. Experimenting with diverse narrative voices—melodramatic, comic, horror-filled, and lyrical—he presented the volume as regional tales collected by a garrulous beekeeper, Rudy Panko. A third story cycle, *Mirgorod*, appeared in 1835, as did *Arabesques*, a volume of essays and stories. Gogol's reputation was secure by this date, and in *Mirgorod* he replaced Rudy Panko's name with his own and began to establish a personal voice that changed mood within a single piece, being alternately comic, sympathetic, satiric, or lyrical. It was a complex combination of effects that often caught the reader off guard, and it allowed the storyteller to maintain a certain distance and critical perspective. In this last collection using specifically Ukrainian themes, Gogol ranges from the gently satirical nostalgia of *Old-World Landowners* to the grotesque horrors of the demonic tale *Viy*, the melodramatic legend of a Cossack chief in *Taras Bulba*, and the farcical comedy *How Ivan Ivanovich Quarreled with Ivan Nikiforovich*. The ability to call up different tones and to shift disconcertingly between them would continue to characterize Gogol's work even as he turned away from the world of Ukrainian folktales toward the bleaker stories of St. Petersburg or the adventures of Chichikov in *Dead Souls*.

Gogol had not forgotten his first love of the theater, however. In 1833, he abandoned a comedy called *The Order of Vladimir, Third Class* for fear that its biting social satire would not pass the censor. *The Inspector General*, written in the fall of 1835 and produced the following April, gave full rein to his satirical impulse and indicted greed, dishonesty, and self-delusion at almost every level of society. Corrupt administrators in a small town are terrified when they suspect that a traveler staying at the local inn may be a government inspector in disguise; the stranger, however, is a penniless, low-level clerk who is himself terrified because he cannot pay his bill and expects to be thrown in jail. As the mayor, postmaster, doctor, judge, charity commissioner, school superintendent, police, landowners, and merchants all line up to bribe him, the clerk catches on and exploits the situation with brilliant flights of fancy about his achievements and important connections in the capital. Grotesquely realistic, the play was a harsh, if farcical, exposure of human weakness and the corruption of an entire society seen in microcosm. The imperial censor forbade both the production and the publication of the play, but unexpectedly the czar—who had been entertained by a private reading—gave permission for its performance. Reaction was stormy: this was not a conventional light comedy of manners or romance, and the spectators were divided. Those who felt mocked were enraged; others thought it was a comic masterpiece; and still others—chief among them the influential critic Vissarion Belinsky, who would become Gogol's champion—praised the work as an example of social realism that had not yet been seen in Russia. Gogol was overwhelmed by the controversy and once again fled the country, leaving on June 6, 1836, for Rome and what would become a thirteen-year self-imposed exile.

By the time of his departure, he had completed all but one of a cycle of five tales set in St. Petersburg. *Nevsky Prospect, The Portrait, Diary of a Madman,* and *The Nose* develop various themes: an artist's suicide paired with a would-be seducer's unexpected beating, a painting possessed by the devil, a poor clerk's madness, and a nose that comically disappears from a man's face and takes on a life of its own. But they all have one thing in common—a vision of Petersburg as a large, impersonal, modern city characterized by an extensive bureaucracy and a grinding indifference to individual human needs. The city's dehumanized atmosphere destroys not only personal identity but any sense of social relationships or common humanity in its inhabitants, who are alienated from one another as they pursue their separate ambitions. St. Petersburg attains an almost mythic status in Gogol's imagination, and he describes its soulless presence as both materialist and spiritual: "Greed, selfishness, and covetousness are apparent in all who walk or drive along" the city streets, and "the devil himself lights the street lamps to show everything in false colors." The fifth and most famous St. Petersburg tale, *The Overcoat,* published in 1842 and printed here, pursues varying examples of social alienation as it describes the existence of a poor copy clerk who tries vainly to enlist help in recovering his stolen overcoat.

With the social satire of *The Inspector General* and the St. Petersburg tales, Gogol was moving toward a new focus on modern Russian culture that would become less comic and more evangelical toward the end of his life. Encouraged by Pushkin to compose a major work, he envisaged a multivolume epic novel that would describe every facet of Russian society. "All Russia will be in it," he wrote Zhukovsky. This novel (which he also called a poem and compared in scope to Cervantes's *Don Quixote*) would describe the adventures of an imaginative swindler, Pavel Ivanovich Chichikov, as he traveled throughout Russia buying dead "souls," or serfs, from landowners who would otherwise have to pay poll tax on them until they were taken off the next census. With the record of these purchases and a piece of land to which the serfs would be attached, Chichikov could present himself as a wealthy property owner who qualified for a large mortgage. Full of comic portraits and absurd situations, and displaying all of Gogol's richly innovative use of language, the first volume of *Dead Souls* was published in 1842 under the title *Chichikov's Journeys* since the censor found the idea of a "dead soul" both impossible and heretical. Henceforth, Gogol devoted himself to writing the sequel, although his project had changed radically. Convinced that he had a mission to bring about Russia's spiritual rebirth through his writing, he envisaged succeeding volumes in which Chichikov's reform would constitute a moral example for society.

Gogol saw his task as both personal and literary, and he undertook prayer and ascetic living as a way to purify himself for this undertaking. He found the second volume exceedingly hard to write, however, and burned an early version in 1845. In 1847, he published a didactic *Selected Passages from Correspondence with Friends* that astonished and enraged his readers with its religious proselytizing and politically reactionary views: Belinsky, in particular, felt betrayed in his view of the writer as a social critic and "poet of reality." After a trip to Jerusalem in 1848, Gogol returned to Russia, where he struggled to complete the second volume of *Dead Souls,* an increasingly difficult task insofar as he had fallen under the influence of a fanatic priest who advised extreme fasting and ordered him to give up literature. His health, precarious for several years, deteriorated further, and he began to have hallucinations. On February 11, 1852, after an interview in which the priest threatened him with eternal damnation, he burned the recently completed manuscript of the second volume. He died ten days later. At his funeral, the streets were jammed for three days with mourners coming to pay their respect. But the authorities, who could not forgive Gogol's satire, canceled the publication of his collected works and arrested novelist Ivan Turgenev for publishing a brief eulogy in the newspaper. It would not be long, however, before Gogol's works were back in print and critics began to speak of a "Gogolian period in Russian literature."

The Overcoat has its source in an anecdote that Gogol heard of a poor clerk who became desperate after losing a cherished hunting gun on his first trip out. In that case, there was a happy ending because the clerk's colleagues took up a collection and replaced the gun. Gogol initially planned to change the gun to an overcoat and write a comic tale called The Man Who Stole Overcoats. Instead, he built a new tale around the core theme of attachment and loss, and produced the more somber and complex version we have today.

The Overcoat is emphatically a storyteller's tale: a Gogolian version of the Russian skaz, in which the teller is present throughout the tale and observes, comments, and digresses at will. (Compare the "tall tales" of American literature and Spotted Horses by William Faulkner in this volume.) Any mention of the overcoat or its owner is deferred as the narrator launches into the first of many personal digressions: "In the department of . . . but I had better not mention which department." Quickly and humorously establishing both his knowledge of events and his wariness of mentioning government officials, he includes a ridiculous anecdote about literary censorship and only subsequently introduces the story's hero, Akaky Akakievich Bashmachkin, in a roundabout and playful manner. The source of the clerk's name is discussed at length and in comic detail, and he himself is presented as a one-dimensional caricature: a generic copying clerk whose single-minded devotion to his task makes him seem almost a machine. Mockery subsides for a moment when the downtrodden clerk's protest penetrates the heart of a coworker and elicits an emotional digression from the narrator about human cruelty; but the digression peters out in a rhetorical letdown that is comic in itself. Such reversals are common: Akaky Akakievich's image may be pathetic and even acquire sacrificial overtones, but it never gives up the comic possibilities inherent in a one-sided character.

The clerk's career in the story is a simple one, except that it persists after death. When we first meet him, he is merely a cog in an office bureaucracy with no further ambitions or desires of his own. The world of cleanly copied lines replaces any other world for him, and he seems scarcely to exist on the level of human passions or self-awareness. This routine is interrupted, however, when winter comes and he faces the need to replace his threadbare coat—a tattered garment that his coworkers call the "dressing gown," the butt, like himself, of their jokes. His struggles to purchase and then to recover the overcoat coincide with the discovery of a new phase of existence in which he begins to emerge from his one-dimensional identity and to assert himself as a full human being. His existence seems fuller, "as though he had married" (but the coat is his wifely companion). He becomes "more alive" and self-confident; he nearly makes a mistake in his copying, and he is supremely happy with the overcoat when it arrives. Erotic images begin to crowd his mind: he stares at a suggestive picture in a shop window and nearly runs after a woman walking in the street. This new-found assurance is put to the test when he is mugged and the overcoat stolen, for now he must try to negotiate the labyrinth of St. Petersburg officialdom to find help. Bullied and sent away at every level despite his fledgling attempts at self-assertion, Akaky Akakievich is completely destroyed when a high official—a Person of Consequence—shouts at him merely to impress a visitor. The St. Petersburg climate finishes the job by giving the fleeing clerk a violent chill and flu from which he dies, hallucinating, shortly thereafter.

It is a piteous tale, and Gogol's image of a poor clerk persecuted by impersonal society has made its mark on later literature—notably Kafka's. Yet the shifts in tone continue, and the narrator remarks jarringly: "That's how violent the effects of an appropriate reprimand can be!" A second emotional digression takes place but is soon overwhelmed by its own rhetoric, elaborating image after image before finally dwindling comically away in grand generalizations. As a sad tale, the story should end with Akaky Akakievich's death. Instead, the narrative suddenly takes on new and fantastic life full of gossip, comic effects, and melodramatic touches that recall folktales but not pathos. Akaky Akakievich's corpse snatches overcoats throughout the city until the police are given orders to catch it "dead or alive"; at the end, the timid policeman who retreats precipitously before a larger-than-life figure (who may or may not be Akaky Akakievich) is described as a figure of fun, someone knocked off his feet by a pig. Gogol's world is not to be summed up as either tragic, comic, pathetic, or surreal. With multiple perspectives in play, the storyteller preserves his ambiguity and, with it, the complexity of experience.

PRONOUNCING GLOSSARY

The following list uses common English syllables and stress accents to provide rough equivalents of selected words whose pronunciation may be unfamiliar to the general reader.

Akaky Akakievich Bashmachkin: *ah-kah'-kee ah-kah'-kye-vich bahsh-mach'-kin*

Grigory Petrovich: *gree-gaw'-ree pee-traw'-veech*

Nikolai Gogol: *nee-ku-lai' gaw'-gul*

skaz: skahs

The Overcoat[1]

In the department of . . . but I had better not mention which department. There is nothing in the world more touchy than a department, a regiment, a government office, and, in fact, any sort of official body. Nowadays every private individual considers all society insulted in his person. I have been told that very lately a complaint was lodged by a police inspector of which town I don't remember, and that in this complaint he set forth clearly that the institutions of the State were in danger and that his sacred name was being taken in vain; and, in proof thereof, he appended to his complaint an enormously long volume of some romantic work in which a police inspector appeared on every tenth page, occasionally, indeed, in an intoxicated condition. And so, to avoid any unpleasantness, we had better call the department of which we are speaking "a certain department."

And so, in a *certain department* there was a *certain clerk*; a clerk of whom it cannot be said that he was very remarkable; he was short, somewhat pockmarked, with rather reddish hair and rather dim, bleary eyes, with a small bald patch on the top of his head, with wrinkles on both sides of his cheeks and the sort of complexion which is usually described as hemorrhoidal . . . nothing can be done about that, it is the Petersburg climate. As for his grade in the civil service (for among us a man's rank is what must be established

---

1. Published in 1842. Translated by Constance Garnett; revised by Leonard J. Kent.

first) he was what is called a perpetual titular councillor,[2] a class at which, as we all know, various writers who indulge in the praiseworthy habit of attacking those who cannot defend themselves jeer and jibe to their hearts' content. This clerk's surname was Bashmachkin. From the very name it is clear that it must have been derived from a shoe (*bashmak*); but when and under what circumstances it was derived from a shoe, it is impossible to say. Both his father and his grandfather and even his brother-in-law, and all the Bashmachkins without exception wore boots, which they simply resoled two or three times a year. His name was Akaky Akakievich.[3] Perhaps it may strike the reader as a rather strange and contrived name, but I can assure him that it was not contrived at all, that the circumstances were such that it was quite out of the question to give him any other name. Akaky Akakievich was born toward nightfall, if my memory does not deceive me, on the twenty-third of March. His mother, the wife of a government clerk, a very good woman, made arrangements in due course to christen the child. She was still lying in bed, facing the door, while on her right hand stood the godfather, an excellent man called Ivan Ivanovich Yeroshkin, one of the head clerks in the Senate, and the godmother, the wife of a police official and a woman of rare qualities, Arina Semeonovna Belobriushkova. Three names were offered to the happy mother for selection—Mokky, Sossy, or the name of the martyr Khozdazat. "No," thought the poor lady, "they are all such names!" To satisfy her, they opened the calendar at another page, and the names which turned up were: Trifily, Dula, Varakhasy. "What an infliction!" said the mother. "What names they all are! I really never heard such names. Varadat or Varukh would be bad enough, but Trifily and Varakhasy!" They turned over another page and the names were: Pavsikakhy and Vakhisy. "Well, I see," said the mother, "it is clear that it is his fate. Since that is how it is, he had better be named after his father; his father is Akaky, let the son be Akaky, too." This was how he came to be Akaky Akakievich. The baby was christened and cried and made sour faces during the ceremony, as though he foresaw that he would be a titular councillor. So that was how it all came to pass. We have reported it here so that the reader may see for himself that it happened quite inevitably and that to give him any other name was out of the question.

No one has been able to remember when and how long ago he entered the department, nor who gave him the job. Regardless of how many directors and higher officials of all sorts came and went, he was always seen in the same place, in the same position, at the very same duty, precisely the same copying clerk, so that they used to declare that he must have been born a copying clerk, uniform, bald patch, and all. No respect at all was shown him in the department. The porters, far from getting up from their seats when he came in, took no more notice of him than if a simple fly had flown across the reception room. His superiors treated him with a sort of despotic aloofness. The head clerk's assistant used to throw papers under his nose without even saying "Copy this" or "Here is an interesting, nice little case" or some agreeable remark of the sort, as is usually done in well-bred offices. And he would take it, gazing only at the paper without looking to see who had put

---

2. The ninth rank of the Russian imperial civil service. "Perpetual" is ironic: he will not advance.
3. "Akaky, son of Akaky." Gogol plays with comic-sounding names through this paragraph, and the repeated *kak* in "Akaky Akakievich" recalls *kaka*, a common word for *feces* in several European languages.

it there and whether he had the right to do so; he would take it and at once begin copying it. The young clerks jeered and made jokes at him to the best of their clerkly wit, and told before his face all sorts of stories of their own invention about him; they would say of his landlady, an old woman of seventy, that she beat him, would ask when the wedding was to take place, and would scatter bits of paper on his head, calling them snow. Akaky Akakievich never answered a word, however, but behaved as though there were no one there. It had no influence on his work; in the midst of all this teasing, he never made a single mistake in his copying. It was only when the jokes became too unbearable, when they jolted his arm, and prevented him from going on with his work, that he would say: "Leave me alone! Why do you insult me?" and there was something touching in the words and in the voice in which they were uttered. There was a note in it of something that aroused compassion, so that one young man, new to the office, who, following the example of the rest, had allowed himself to tease him, suddenly stopped as though cut to the heart, and from that time on, everything was, as it were, changed and appeared in a different light to him. Some unseen force seemed to repel him from the companions with whom he had become acquainted because he thought they were well-bred and decent men. And long afterward, during moments of the greatest gaiety, the figure of the humble little clerk with a bald patch on his head appeared before him with his heart-rending words: "Leave me alone! Why do you insult me?" and within those moving words he heard others: "I am your brother." And the poor young man hid his face in his hands, and many times afterward in his life he shuddered, seeing how much inhumanity there is in man, how much savage brutality lies hidden under refined, cultured politeness, and, my God! even in a man whom the world accepts as a gentleman and a man of honor. . . .

It would be hard to find a man who lived for his work as did Akaky Akakievich. To say that he was zealous in his work is not enough; no, he loved his work. In it, in that copying, he found an interesting and pleasant world of his own. There was a look of enjoyment on his face; certain letters were favorites with him, and when he came to them he was delighted; he chuckled to himself and winked and moved his lips, so that it seemed as though every letter his pen was forming could be read in his face. If rewards had been given according to the measure of zeal in the service, he might to his amazement have even found himself a civil councillor; but all he gained in the service, as the wits, his fellow clerks, expressed it, was a button in his buttonhole[4] and hemorrhoids where he sat. It cannot be said, however, that no notice had ever been taken of him. One director, being a good-natured man and anxious to reward him for his long service, sent him something a little more important than his ordinary copying; he was instructed to make some sort of report from a finished document for another office; the work consisted only of altering the headings and in places changing the first person into the third. This cost him so much effort that he was covered with perspiration: he mopped his brow and said at last, "No, I'd rather copy something."

From that time on they left him to his copying forever. It seemed as though nothing in the world existed for him except his copying. He gave no thought

---

4. A button instead of a medal or decoration.

at all to his clothes; his uniform was—well, not green but some sort of rusty, muddy color. His collar was very low and narrow, so that, although his neck was not particularly long, yet, standing out of the collar, it looked as immensely long as those of the dozens of plaster kittens with nodding heads which foreigners carry about on their heads and peddle in Russia. And there were always things sticking to his uniform, either bits of hay or threads; moreover, he had a special knack of passing under a window at the very moment when various garbage was being flung out into the street, and so was continually carrying off bits of melon rind and similar litter on his hat. He had never once in his life noticed what was being done and what was going on in the street, all those things at which, as we all know, his colleagues, the young clerks, always stare, utilizing their keen sight so well that they notice anyone on the other side of the street with a trouser strap hanging loose—an observation which always calls forth a sly grin. Whatever Akaky Akakievich looked at, he saw nothing but his clear, evenly written lines, and it was only perhaps when a horse suddenly appeared from nowhere and placed its head on his shoulder, and with its nostrils blew a real gale upon his cheek, that he would notice that he was not in the middle of his writing, but rather in the middle of the street.

On reaching home, he would sit down at once at the table, hurriedly eat his soup and a piece of beef with an onion; he did not notice the taste at all but ate it all with the flies and anything else that Providence happened to send him. When he felt that his stomach was beginning to be full, he would get up from the table, take out a bottle of ink and begin copying the papers he had brought home with him. When he had none to do, he would make a copy especially for his own pleasure, particularly if the document were remarkable not for the beauty of its style but because it was addressed to some new or distinguished person.

Even at those hours when the gray Petersburg sky is completely overcast and the whole population of clerks have dined and eaten their fill, each as best he can, according to the salary he receives and his personal tastes; when they are all resting after the scratching of pens and bustle of the office, their own necessary work and other people's, and all the tasks that an overzealous man voluntarily sets himself even beyond what is necessary; when the clerks are hastening to devote what is left of their time to pleasure; some more enterprising are flying to the theater, others to the street to spend their leisure staring at women's hats, some to spend the evening paying compliments to some attractive girl, the star of a little official circle, while some—and this is the most frequent of all—go simply to a fellow clerk's apartment on the third or fourth story, two little rooms with a hall or a kitchen, with some pretensions to style, with a lamp or some such article that has cost many sacrifices of dinners and excursions—at the time when all the clerks are scattered about the apartments of their friends, playing a stormy game of whist, sipping tea out of glasses, eating cheap biscuits, sucking in smoke from long pipes, telling, as the cards are dealt, some scandal that has floated down from higher circles, a pleasure which the Russian can never by any possibility deny himself, or, when there is nothing better to talk about, repeating the everlasting anecdote of the commanding officer who was told that the tail had been cut off the horse on the Falconet monument[5]—in short, even when everyone, was eagerly seeking entertainment, Akaky Akakievich did not indulge in any amusement. No one could say that they had ever seen him at an evening party. After working to his heart's content, he would go to bed, smiling at the thought of the next day and wondering what God would send him to copy. So flowed on the peaceful life of a man who knew how to be content with his fate on a salary of four hundred rubles[6] and so perhaps it would have flowed on to extreme old age, had it not been for the various disasters strewn along the road of life, not only of titular, but even of privy, actual, court, and all other councillors,[7] even those who neither give counsel to others nor accept it themselves.

There is in Petersburg a mighty foe of all who receive a salary of about four hundred rubles. That foe is none other than our northern frost, although it is said to be very good for the health. Between eight and nine in the morning, precisely at the hour when the streets are filled with clerks going to their departments, the frost begins indiscriminately giving such sharp and stinging nips at all their noses that the poor fellows don't know what to do with them. At that time, when even those in the higher grade have a pain in their brows and tears in their eyes from the frost, the poor titular councillors are sometimes almost defenseless. Their only protection lies in running as fast as they can through five or six streets in a wretched, thin little overcoat and then warming their feet thoroughly in the porter's room, till all their faculties and talents for their various duties thaw out again after having been frozen on the way. Akaky Akakievich had for some time been feeling that his back and shoulders were particularly nipped by the cold, although he did try to run the regular distance as fast as he could. He wondered at last whether there were any defects in his overcoat. After examining it thoroughly in the privacy of his home, he discovered that in two or three places, on the back and the shoulders, it had become a regular sieve, the cloth was so worn that you could see through it and the lining was coming out. I must note that Akaky Akakievich's overcoat had also served as a butt for the jokes of the clerks. It had even been deprived of the honorable name of overcoat and had been referred to as the "dressing gown." It was indeed of rather a peculiar make. Its collar had been growing smaller year by year as it served to patch the other parts. The patches were not good specimens of the tailor's art, and they certainly looked clumsy and ugly. On seeing what was wrong, Akaky Akakievich decided that he would have to take the overcoat to Petrovich, a tailor who lived on the fourth floor up a back staircase, and, in spite of having only one eye and being pockmarked all over his face, was rather successful in repairing the trousers and coats of clerks and others—that is, when he was sober, be it understood, and had no other enterprise in his mind. Of this tailor I ought not, of course, say much, but since it is now the rule that the character of every person in a novel must be completely described, well, there's nothing I can do but describe Petrovich too. At first he was called simply Grigory, and was a serf belonging to some gentleman or other. He

5. A famous equestrian statue of Peter the Great created by French sculptor Étienne-Maurice Falconet (1716–1791). It was cast in bronze and known as *The Bronze Horseman*. 6. A ruble, is the basic unit of Russian currency. In Gogol's time, four hundred rubles was a small salary. 7. There were fourteen levels in the civil service, each with its own title; distinctions were made between full (actual or active) positions and those that were inactive. Privy councillor was third level, actual (or active) privy councillor second level; and court councillor seventh level.

began to be called Petrovich[8] from the time that he got his freedom and began to drink rather heavily on every holiday, at first only on the main holidays, but afterward, on all church holidays indiscriminately, wherever there was a cross in the calendar. In this he was true to the customs of his forefathers, and when he quarreled with his wife he used to call her a worldly woman and a German.[9] Since we have now mentioned the wife, it will be necessary to say a few words about her, too, but unfortunately not much is known about her, except indeed that Petrovich had a wife and that she wore a cap and not a kerchief, but apparently she could not boast of beauty; anyway, none but soldiers of the guard peered under her cap when they met her, and they twitched their mustaches and gave vent to a rather peculiar sound.

As he climbed the stairs leading to Petrovich's—which, to do them justice, were all soaked with water and slops and saturated through and through with that smell of ammonia which makes the eyes smart, and is, as we all know, inseparable from the backstairs of Petersburg houses—Akaky Akakievich was already wondering how much Petrovich would ask for the job, and inwardly resolving not to give more than two rubles. The door was open, because Petrovich's wife was frying some fish and had so filled the kitchen with smoke that you could not even see the cockroaches. Akaky Akakievich crossed the kitchen unnoticed by the good woman, and walked at last into a room where he saw Petrovich sitting on a big, wooden, unpainted table with his legs tucked under him like a Turkish pasha.[1] The feet, as is usual with tailors when they sit at work, were bare; and the first object that caught Akaky Akakievich's eye was the big toe, with which he was already familiar, with a misshapen nail as thick and strong as the shell of a tortoise. Around Petrovich's neck hung a skein of silk and another of thread and on his knees was a rag of some sort. He had for the last three minutes been trying to thread his needle, but could not get the thread into the eye and so was very angry with the darkness and indeed with the thread itself, muttering in an undertone: "She won't go in, the savage! You wear me out, you bitch." Akaky Akakievich was unhappy that he had come just at the minute when Petrovich was in a bad humor; he liked to give him an order when he was a little "elevated," or, as his wife expressed it, "had fortified himself with vodka, the one-eyed devil." In such circumstances Petrovich was as a rule very ready to give way and agree, and invariably bowed and thanked him. Afterward, it is true, his wife would come wailing that her husband had been drunk and so had asked too little, but adding a single ten-kopek piece would settle that. But on this occasion Petrovich was apparently sober and consequently curt, unwilling to bargain, and the devil knows what price he would be ready to demand. Akaky Akakievich realized this, and was, as the saying is, beating a retreat, but things had gone too far, for Petrovich was screwing up his solitary eye very attentively at him and Akaky Akakievich involuntarily said: "Good day, Petrovich!"

"I wish you a good day, sir," said Petrovich, and squinted at Akaky Akak-

---

8. "Son of Peter." A serf was addressed by his first name; free men could be addressed by their full name or just the patronymic (Petrovich). 9. A woman of suspect morals and a foreigner, both used as disparaging terms. Germans filled many privileged positions (such as doctor) that were not open to Russians, and anti-German bias was common among Russian nationalists. 1. A ruler or high official.

ievich's hands, trying to discover what sort of goods he had brought.

"Here I have come to you, Petrovich, do you see . . . !"

It must be noticed that Akaky Akakievich for the most part explained himself by apologies, vague phrases, and meaningless parts of speech which have absolutely no significance whatever. If the subject were a very difficult one, it was his habit indeed to leave his sentences quite unfinished, so that very often after a sentence had begun with the words, "It really is, don't you know . . ." nothing at all would follow and he himself would be quite oblivious to the fact that he had not finished his thought, supposing he had said all that was necessary.

"What is it?" said Petrovich, and at the same time with his solitary eye he scrutinized his whole uniform from the collar to the sleeves, the back, the skirts, the buttonholes—with all of which he was very familiar since they were all his own work. Such scrutiny is habitual with tailors; it is the first thing they do on meeting one.

"It's like this, Petrovich . . . the overcoat, the cloth . . . you see everywhere else it is quite strong; it's a little dusty and looks as though it were old, but it is new and it is only in one place just a little . . . on the back, and just a little worn on one shoulder and on this shoulder, too, a little . . . do you see? that's all, and it's not much work . . ."

Petrovich took the "dressing gown," first spread it out over the table, examined it for a long time, shook his head, and put his hand out to the window sill for a round snuffbox with a portrait on the lid of some general—which general I can't exactly say, for a finger had been thrust through the spot where a face should have been, and the hole had been pasted over with a square piece of paper. After taking a pinch of snuff, Petrovich held the "dressing gown" up in his hands and looked at it against the light, and again he shook his head; then he turned it with the lining upward and once more shook his head; again he took off the lid with the general pasted up with paper and stuffed a pinch into his nose, shut the box, put it away, and at last said: "No, it can't be repaired; a wretched garment!" Akaky Akakievich's heart sank at those words.

"Why can't it, Petrovich?" he said, almost in the imploring voice of a child. "Why, the only thing is, it is a bit worn on the shoulders; why, you have got some little pieces . . ."

"Yes, the pieces will be found all right," said Petrovich, "but it can't be patched, the stuff is rotten; if you put a needle in it, it would give way."

"Let it give way, but you just put a patch on it."

"There is nothing to put a patch on. There is nothing for it to hold on to; there is a great strain on it; it is not worth calling cloth; it would fly away at a breath of wind."

"Well, then, strengthen it with something—I'm sure, really, this is . . . !"

"No," said Petrovich resolutely, "there is nothing that can be done, the thing is no good at all. You had far better, when the cold winter weather comes, make yourself leg wrappings out of it, for there is no warmth in stockings; the Germans invented them just to make money." (Petrovich enjoyed a dig at the Germans occasionally.) "And as for the overcoat, it is obvious that you will have to have a new one."

At the word "new" there was a mist before Akaky Akakievich's eyes, and everything in the room seemed blurred. He could see nothing clearly but the general with the piece of paper over his face on the lid of Petrovich's snuff-box.

"A new one?" he said, still feeling as though he were in a dream; "why, I haven't the money for it."

"Yes, a new one," Petrovich repeated with barbarous composure.

"Well, and if I did have a new one, how much would it . . . ?"

"You mean what will it cost?"

"Yes."

"Well, at least one hundred and fifty rubles," said Petrovich, and he compressed his lips meaningfully. He was very fond of making an effect; he was fond of suddenly disconcerting a man completely and then squinting sideways to see what sort of a face he made.

"A hundred and fifty rubles for an overcoat!" screamed poor Akaky Akakievich—it was perhaps the first time he had screamed in his life, for he was always distinguished by the softness of his voice.

"Yes," said Petrovich, "and even then it depends on the coat. If I were to put marten on the collar, and add a hood with silk linings, it would come to two hundred."

"Petrovich, please," said Akaky Akakievich in an imploring voice, not hearing and not trying to hear what Petrovich said, and missing all his effects, "repair it somehow, so that it will serve a little longer."

"No, that would be wasting work and spending money for nothing," said Petrovich, and after that Akaky Akakievich went away completely crushed, and when he had gone Petrovich remained standing for a long time with his lips pursed up meaningfully before he began his work again, feeling pleased that he had not demeaned himself or lowered the dignity of the tailor's art.

When he got into the street, Akaky Akakievich felt as though he was in a dream. "So that is how it is," he said to himself. "I really did not think it would be this way . . ." and then after a pause he added, "So that's it! So that's how it is at last! and I really could never have supposed it would be this way. And there . . ." There followed another long silence, after which he said: "So that's it! well, it really is so utterly unexpected . . . who would have thought . . . what a circumstance . . ." Saying this, instead of going home he walked off in quite the opposite direction without suspecting what he was doing. On the way a clumsy chimney sweep brushed the whole of his sooty side against him and blackened his entire shoulder; a whole hatful of plaster scattered upon him from the top of a house that was being built. He noticed nothing of this, and only after he had jostled against a policeman who had set his halberd down beside him and was shaking some snuff out of his horn[2] into his rough fist, he came to himself a little and then only because the policeman said: "Why are you poking yourself right in one's face, haven't you enough room on the street?" This made him look around and turn homeward; only there he began to collect his thoughts, to see his position in a clear and true light, and began talking to himself no longer incoherently but reasonably and openly as with a sensible friend with whom one can discuss the most intimate and vital matters. "No," said Akaky Akakievich, "it is no use talking

---

2. A container made of horn. *Halberd:* a weapon consisting of a long shaft with a blade at the end.

to Petrovich now; just now he really is . . . his wife must have been giving it to him. I had better go to him on Sunday morning; after Saturday night he will have a crossed eye and be sleepy, so he'll want a little drink and his wife won't give him a kopek.[3] I'll slip ten kopeks into his hand and then he will be more accommodating and maybe take the overcoat . . ."

So reasoning with himself, Akaky Akakievich cheered up and waited until the next Sunday; then, seeing from a distance Petrovich's wife leaving the house, he went straight in. Petrovich certainly had a crossed eye after Saturday. He could hardly hold his head up and was very drowsy; but, despite all that, as soon as he heard what Akaky Akakievich was speaking about, it seemed as though the devil had nudged him. "I can't," he said, "you must order a new one." Akaky Akakievich at once slipped a ten-kopek piece into his hand. "I thank you, sir, I will have just a drop to your health, but don't trouble yourself about the overcoat; it is no good for anything. I'll make you a fine new coat; you can have faith in me for that."

Akaky Akakievich would have said more about repairs, but Petrovich, without listening, said: "A new one I'll make you without fail; you can rely on that; I'll do my best. It could even be like the fashion that is popular, with the collar to fasten with silver-plated hooks under a flap."

Then Akaky Akakievich saw that there was no escape from a new overcoat and he was utterly depressed. How indeed, for what, with what money could he get it? Of course he could to some extent rely on the bonus for the coming holiday, but that money had long ago been appropriated and its use determined beforehand. It was needed for new trousers and to pay the cobbler an old debt for putting some new tops on some old boots, and he had to order three shirts from a seamstress as well as two items of undergarments which it is indecent to mention in print; in short, all that money absolutely must be spent, and even if the director were to be so gracious as to give him a holiday bonus of forty-five or even fifty, instead of forty rubles, there would be still left a mere trifle, which would be but a drop in the ocean compared to the fortune needed for an overcoat. Though, of course, he knew that Petrovich had a strange craze for suddenly demanding the devil knows what enormous price, so that at times his own wife could not help crying out: "Why, you are out of your wits, you idiot! Another time he'll undertake a job for nothing, and here the devil has bewitched him to ask more than he is worth himself." Though, of course, he knew that Petrovich would undertake to make it for eighty rubles, still where would he get those eighty rubles? He might manage half of that sum; half of it could be found, perhaps even a little more; but where could he get the other half? . . . But, first of all, the reader ought to know where that first half was to be found. Akaky Akakievich had the habit every time he spent a ruble of putting aside two kopeks in a little box which he kept locked, with a slit in the lid for dropping in the money. At the end of every six months he would inspect the pile of coppers there and change them for small silver. He had done this for a long time, and in the course of many years the sum had mounted up to forty rubles and so he had half the money in his hands, but where was he to get the other half; where was he to get another forty rubles? Akaky Akakievich thought

3. There are 100 kopeks in a ruble.

and thought and decided at last that he would have to diminish his ordinary expenses, at least for a year; give up burning candles in the evening, and if he had to do any work he must go into the landlady's room and work by her candle; that as he walked along the streets he must walk as lightly and carefully as possible, almost on tiptoe, on the cobbles and flagstones, so that his soles might last a little longer than usual; that he must send his linen to the wash less frequently, and that, to preserve it from being worn, he must take it off every day when he came home and sit in a thin cotton dressing gown, a very ancient garment which Time itself had spared. To tell the truth, he found it at first rather difficult to get used to these privations, but after a while it became a habit and went smoothly enough—he even became quite accustomed to being hungry in the evening; on the other hand, he had spiritual nourishment, for he carried ever in his thoughts the idea of his future overcoat. His whole existence had in a sense become fuller, as though he had married, as though some other person were present with him, as though he were no longer alone but an agreeable companion had consented to walk the path of life hand in hand with him, and that companion was none other than the new overcoat with its thick padding and its strong, durable lining. He became, as it were, more alive, even more strong-willed, like a man who has set before himself a definite goal. Uncertainty, indecision, in fact all the hesitating and vague characteristics, vanished from his face and his manners. At times there was a gleam in his eyes; indeed, the most bold and audacious ideas flashed through his mind. Why not really have marten on the collar? Meditation on the subject always made him absent-minded. On one occasion when he was copying a document, he very nearly made a mistake, so that he almost cried out "ough" aloud and crossed himself. At least once every month he went to Petrovich to talk about the overcoat: where it would be best to buy the cloth, and what color it should be, and what price; and, though he returned home a little anxious, he was always pleased at the thought that at last the time was at hand when everything would be bought and the overcoat would be made. Things moved even faster than he had anticipated. Contrary to all expectations, the director bestowed on Akaky Akakievich a bonus of no less than sixty rubles. Whether it was that he had an inkling that Akaky Akakievich needed a coat, or whether it happened by luck, owing to this he found he had twenty rubles extra. This circumstance hastened the course of affairs. Another two or three months of partial starvation and Akaky Akakievich had actually saved up nearly eighty rubles. His heart, as a rule very tranquil, began to throb.

The very first day he set out with Petrovich for the shops. They bought some very good cloth, and no wonder, since they had been thinking of it for more than six months, and scarcely a month had passed without their going out to the shop to compare prices; now Petrovich himself declared that there was no better cloth to be had. For the lining they chose calico, but of such good quality, that in Petrovich's words it was even better than silk, and actually as strong and handsome to look at. Marten they did not buy, because it was too expensive, but instead they chose cat fur, the best to be found in the shop—cat which in the distance might almost be taken for marten. Petrovich was busy making the coat for two weeks, because there was a great deal of quilting; otherwise it would have been ready sooner. Petrovich charged twelve rubles for the work; less than that it hardly could have been; everything was sewn with silk, with fine double seams, and Petrovich went over every seam afterwards with his own teeth, imprinting various patterns with them. It was . . . it is hard to say precisely on what day, but probably on the most triumphant day in the life of Akaky Akakievich, that Petrovich at last brought the overcoat. He brought it in the morning, just before it was time to set off for the department. The overcoat could not have arrived at a more opportune time, because severe frosts were just beginning and seemed threatening to become even harsher. Petrovich brought the coat himself as a good tailor should. There was an expression of importance on his face, such as Akaky Akakievich had never seen there before. He seemed fully conscious of having completed a work of no little importance and of having shown by his own example the gulf that separates tailors who only put in linings and do repairs from those who make new coats. He took the coat out of the huge handkerchief in which he had brought it (the handkerchief had just come home from the wash); he then folded it up and put it in his pocket for future use. After taking out the overcoat, he looked at it with much pride and holding it in both hands, threw it very deftly over Akaky Akakievich shoulders, then pulled it down and smoothed it out behind with his hands; then draped it about Akaky Akakievich somewhat jauntily. Akaky Akakievich, a practical man, wanted to try it with his arms in the sleeves. Petrovich helped him to put it on, and it looked splendid with his arms in the sleeves, too. In fact, it turned out that the overcoat was completely and entirely successful. Petrovich did not let slip the occasion for observing that it was only because he lived in a small street and had no signboard, and because he had known Akaky Akakievich so long, that he had done it so cheaply, and that on Nevsky Prospekt[4] they would have asked him seventy-five rubles for the tailoring alone. Akaky Akakievich had no inclination to discuss this with Petrovich; besides he was frightened of the big sums that Petrovich was fond of flinging airily about in conversation. He paid him, thanked him, and went off, with his new overcoat on, to the department. Petrovich followed him out and stopped in the street, staring for a long time at the coat from a distance and then purposely turned off and, taking a short cut through a side street, came back into the street, and got another view of the coat from the other side, that is, from the front.

Meanwhile Akaky Akakievich walked along in a gay holiday mood. Every second he was conscious that he had a new overcoat on his shoulders, and several times he actually laughed from inward satisfaction. Indeed, it had two advantages: one that it was warm and the other that it was good. He did not notice how far he had walked at all and he suddenly found himself in the department; in the porter's room, he took off the overcoat, looked it over, and entrusted it to the porter's special care. I cannot tell how it happened, but all at once everyone in the department learned that Akaky Akakievich had a new overcoat and that the "dressing gown" no longer existed. They all ran out at once into the cloakroom to look at Akaky Akakievich's new overcoat; they began welcoming him and congratulating him so that at first he could do nothing but smile and then felt positively embarrassed. When, com-

4. The main boulevard in St. Petersburg; a fashionable street and area.

ing up to him, they all began saying that he must "sprinkle" the new overcoat
and that he ought at least to buy them all a supper, Akaky Akakievich lost
his head completely and did not know what to do, how to get out of it, nor
what to answer. A few minutes later, flushing crimson, he even began assuring them with great simplicity that it was not a new overcoat at all, that it
wasn't much, that it was an old overcoat. At last one of the clerks, indeed
the assistant of the head clerk of the room, probably in order to show that
he wasn't too proud to mingle with those beneath him, said: "So be it, I'll
give a party instead of Akaky Akakievich and invite you all to tea with me
this evening; as luck would have it, it is my birthday." The clerks naturally
congratulated the assistant head clerk and eagerly accepted the invitation.
Akaky Akakievich was beginning to make excuses, but they all declared that
it was uncivil of him, that it would be simply a shame and a disgrace and
that he could not possibly refuse. So, he finally relented, and later felt pleased
about it when he remembered that through this he would have the opportunity of going out in the evening, too, in his new overcoat. That whole day
was for Akaky Akakievich the most triumphant and festive day in his life. He
returned home in the happiest frame of mind, took off the overcoat, and
hung it carefully on the wall, admiring the cloth and lining once more, and
then pulled out his old "dressing gown," now completely falling apart, and
put it next to his new overcoat to compare the two. He glanced at it and
laughed: the difference was enormous! And long afterwards he went on
laughing at dinner, as the position in which the "dressing gown" was placed
recurred to his mind. He dined in excellent spirits and after dinner wrote
nothing, no papers at all, but just relaxed for a little while on his bed, till it
got dark; then, without putting things off, he dressed, put on his overcoat,
and went out into the street. Where precisely the clerk who had invited him
lived we regret to say we cannot tell; our memory is beginning to fail sadly,
and everything there in Petersburg, all the streets and houses, are so blurred
and muddled in our head that it is a very difficult business to put anything
in orderly fashion. Regardless of that, there is no doubt that the clerk lived
in the better part of the town and consequently a very long distance from
Akaky Akakievich. At first Akaky Akakievich had to walk through deserted
streets, scantily lighted, but as he approached his destination the streets
became more lively, more full of people, and more brightly lighted; passers-by
began to be more frequent, ladies began to appear, here and there beautifully
dressed, and beaver collars were to be seen on the men. Cabmen with
wooden, railed sledges, studded with brass-topped nails, were less frequently
seen; on the other hand, jaunty drivers in raspberry-colored velvet caps, with
lacquered sledges and bearskin rugs, appeared and carriages with decorated
boxes dashed along the streets, their wheels crunching through the snow.

Akaky Akakievich looked at all this as a novelty; for several years he had
not gone out into the streets in the evening. He stopped with curiosity before
a lighted shop window to look at a picture in which a beautiful woman was
represented in the act of taking off her shoe and displaying as she did so the
whole of a very shapely leg, while behind her back a gentleman with whiskers
and a handsome imperial[5] on his chin was sticking his head in at the door.

5. A narrow pointed beard grown below the lower lip.

Akaky Akakievich shook his head and smiled and then went on his way. Why did he smile? Was it because he had come across something quite unfamiliar to him, though every man retains some instinctive feeling on the subject, or was it that he reflected, like many other clerks, as follows: "Well, those Frenchmen! It's beyond anything! If they go in for anything of the sort, it really is . . . !" Though possibly he did not even think that; there is no creeping into a man's soul and finding out all that he thinks. At last he reached the house in which the assistant head clerk lived in fine style; there was a lamp burning on the stairs, and the apartment was on the second floor. As he went into the hall Akaky Akakievich saw rows of galoshes. Among them in the middle of the room stood a hissing samovar[6] puffing clouds of steam. On the walls hung coats and cloaks among which some actually had beaver collars or velvet lapels. From the other side of the wall there came noise and talk, which suddenly became clear and loud when the door opened and the footman[7] came out with a tray full of empty glasses, a jug of cream, and a basket of biscuits. It was evident that the clerks had arrived long before and had already drunk their first glass of tea. Akaky Akakievich, after hanging up his coat with his own hands, went into the room, and at the same moment there flashed before his eyes a vision of candles, clerks, pipes and card tables, together with the confused sounds of conversation rising up on all sides and the noise of moving chairs. He stopped very awkwardly in the middle of the room, looking about and trying to think of what to do, but he was noticed and received with a shout and they all went at once into the hall and again took a look at his overcoat. Though Akaky Akakievich was somewhat embarrassed, yet, being a simple-hearted man, he could not help being pleased at seeing how they all admired his coat. Then of course they all abandoned him and his coat, and turned their attention as usual to the tables set for whist. All this—the noise, the talk, and the crowd of people—was strange and wonderful to Akaky Akakievich. He simply did not know how to behave, what to do with his arms and legs and his whole body; at last he sat down beside the players, looked at the cards, stared first at one and then at another of the faces, and in a little while, feeling bored, began to yawn—especially since it was long past the time at which he usually went to bed. He tried to say goodbye to his hosts, but they would not let him go, saying that he absolutely must have a glass of champagne in honor of the new coat. An hour later supper was served, consisting of salad, cold veal, pastry pies from the bakery, and champagne. They made Akaky Akakievich drink two glasses, after which he felt that things were much more cheerful, though he could not forget that it was twelve o'clock, and that he ought to have been home long ago. That his host might not take it into his head to detain him, he slipped out of the room, hunted in the hall for his coat, which he found, not without regret, lying on the floor, shook it, removed some fluff from it, put it on, and went down the stairs into the street. It was still light in the streets. Some little grocery shops, those perpetual clubs for servants and all sorts of people, were open; others which were closed showed, however, a long streak of light at every crack of the door, proving that they were not yet deserted, and probably

6. A Russian urn made of metal with a spigot at the bottom, that boils water for tea.   7. A servant, usually one who serves food or runs errands.

maids and menservants were still finishing their conversation and discussion, driving their masters to utter perplexity as to their whereabouts. Akaky Akakievich walked along in a cheerful state of mind; he was even on the point of running, goodness knows why, after a lady of some sort who passed by like lightning with every part of her frame in violent motion. He checked himself at once, however, and again walked along very gently, feeling positively surprised at the inexplicable impulse that had seized him. Soon the deserted streets, which are not particularly cheerful by day and even less so in the evening, stretched before him. Now they were still more dead and deserted; the light of street lamps was scantier, the oil evidently running low; then came wooden houses and fences; not a soul anywhere; only the snow gleamed on the streets and the low-pitched slumbering hovels looked black and gloomy with their closed shutters. He approached the spot where the street was intersected by an endless square, which looked like a fearful desert with its houses scarcely visible on the far side.

In the distance, goodness knows where, there was a gleam of light from some sentry box which seemed to be at the end of the world. Akaky Akakievich's lightheartedness faded. He stepped into the square, not without uneasiness, as though his heart had a premonition of evil. He looked behind him and to both sides—it was as though the sea were all around him. "No, better not look," he thought, and walked on, shutting his eyes, and when he opened them to see whether the end of the square was near, he suddenly saw standing before him, almost under his very nose, some men with mustaches; just what they were like he could not even distinguish. There was a mist before his eyes, and a throbbing in his chest. "Why, that overcoat is mine!" said one of them in a voice like a clap of thunder, seizing him by the collar. Akaky Akakievich was on the point of shouting "Help" when another put a fist the size of a clerk's head against his lips, saying: "You just shout now." Akaky Akakievich felt only that they took the overcoat off, and gave him a kick with their knees, and he fell on his face in the snow and was conscious of nothing more. A few minutes later he recovered consciousness and got up on his feet, but there was no one there. He felt that it was cold on the ground and that he had no overcoat, and began screaming, but it seemed as though his voice would not carry to the end of the square. Overwhelmed with despair and continuing to scream, he ran across the square straight to the sentry box beside which stood a policeman leaning on his halberd and, so it seemed, looking with curiosity to see who the devil the man was who was screaming and running toward him from the distance. As Akaky Akakievich reached him, he began breathlessly shouting that he was asleep and not looking after his duty not to see that a man was being robbed. The policeman answered that he had seen nothing, that he had only seen him stopped in the middle of the square by two men, and supposed that they were his friends, and that, instead of abusing him for nothing, he had better go the next day to the police inspector, who would certainly find out who had taken the overcoat. Akaky Akakievich ran home in a terrible state: his hair, which was still comparatively abundant on his temples and the back of his head, was completely disheveled; his sides and chest and his trousers were all covered with snow. When his old landlady heard a fearful knock at the door, she jumped hurriedly out of bed and, with only one slipper on, ran to open it, modestly holding her chemise over her bosom; but when she opened it she stepped back, seeing in what a state Akaky Akakievich was. When he told her what had happened, she clasped her hands in horror and said that he must go straight to the district commissioner,[8] because the local police inspector would deceive him, make promises and lead him a dance; that it would be best of all to go to the district commissioner, and that she knew him, because Anna, the Finnish girl who was once her cook, was now in service as a nurse at the commissioner's; and that she often saw him himself when he passed by their house, and that he used to be every Sunday at church too, saying his prayers and at the same time looking good-humouredly at everyone, and that therefore by every token he must be a kindhearted man. After listening to this advice, Akaky Akakievich made his way very gloomily to his room, and how he spent that night I leave to the imagination of those who are in the least able to picture the position of others.

Early in the morning he set off to the police commissioner's but was told that he was asleep. He came at ten o'clock, he was told again that he was asleep; he came at eleven and was told that the commissioner was not at home; he came at dinnertime, but the clerks in the anteroom would not let him in, and insisted on knowing what was the matter and what business had brought him and exactly what had happened; so that at last Akaky Akakievich for the first time in his life tried to show the strength of his character and said curtly that he must see the commissioner himself, that they dare not refuse to admit him, that he had come from the department on government business, and that if he made complaint of them they would see. The clerks dared say nothing to this, and one of them went to summon the commissioner. The latter received his story of being robbed of his overcoat in an extremely peculiar manner. Instead of attending to the main point, he began asking Akaky Akakievich questions: why had he been coming home so late? wasn't he going, or hadn't he been, to some bawdy house? so that Akaky Akakievich was overwhelmed with confusion, and went away without knowing whether or not the proper measures would be taken regarding his overcoat. He was absent from the office all that day (the only time that it had happened in his life). Next day he appeared with a pale face, wearing his old "dressing gown" which had become a still more pitiful sight. The news of the theft of the overcoat—though there were clerks who did not let even this chance slip of jeering at Akaky Akakievich—touched many of them. They decided on the spot to get up a collection for him, but collected only a very trifling sum, because the clerks had already spent a good deal contributing to the director's portrait and on the purchase of a book, at the suggestion of the head of their department, who was a friend of the author, and so the total realized was very insignificant. One of the clerks, moved by compassion, ventured at any rate to assist Akaky Akakievich with good advice, telling him not to go to the local police inspector, because, though it might happen that the latter might succeed in finding his overcoat because he wanted to impress his superiors, it would remain in the possession of the police unless he presented legal proofs that it belonged to him; he urged that by far the best

8. The local police commissioner.

thing would be to appeal to a Person of Consequence, that the Person of Consequence, by writing and getting into communication with the proper authorities, could push the matter through more successfully. There was nothing else to do. Akaky Akakievich made up his mind to go to the Person of Consequence. What precisely was the nature of the functions of the Person of Consequence has remained a matter of uncertainty. It must be noted that this Person of Consequence had only lately become a person of consequence, and until recently had been a person of no consequence. Though, indeed, his position even now was not reckoned of consequence in comparison with others of still greater consequence. But there is always to be found a circle of persons to whom a person of little consequence in the eyes of others is a person of consequence. It is true that he did his utmost to increase the consequence of his position in various ways, for instance by insisting that his subordinates should come out onto the stairs to meet him when he arrived at his office; that no one should venture to approach him directly but all proceedings should follow the strictest chain of command; that a collegiate registrar[9] should report the matter to the governmental secretary; and the governmental secretary to the titular councillor or whomsoever it might be, and that business should only reach him through this channel. Everyone in Holy Russia[1] has a craze for imitation; everyone apes and mimics his superiors. I have actually been told that a titular councillor who was put in charge of a small separate office, immediately partitioned off a special room for himself, calling it the head office, and posted lackeys[2] at the door with red collars and gold braid, who took hold of the handle of the door and opened it for everyone who went in, though the "head office" was so tiny that it was with difficulty that an ordinary writing desk could be put into it. The manners and habits of the Person of Consequence were dignified and majestic, but hardly subtle. The chief foundation of his system was strictness; "strictness, strictness, and—strictness!" he used to say, and at the last word he would look very significantly at the person he was addressing, though, indeed, he had no reason to do so, for the dozen clerks who made up the whole administrative mechanism of his office stood in appropriate awe of him; any clerk who saw him in the distance would leave his work and remain standing at attention till his superior had left the room. His conversation with his subordinates was usually marked by severity and almost confined to three phrases: "How dare you? Do you know to whom you are speaking? Do you understand who I am?" He was, however, at heart a good-natured man, pleasant and obliging with his colleagues, but his advancement to a high rank had completely turned his head. When he received it, he was perplexed, thrown off his balance, and quite at a loss as to how to behave. If he chanced to be with his equals, he was still quite a decent man, a very gentlemanly man, in fact, and in many ways even an intelligent man; but as soon as he was in company with men who were even one grade below him, there was simply no doing anything with him: he sat silent and his position excited compassion, the more so as he himself felt that he might have been spending his time to so much more advantage. At times there could be seen in his eyes

---

9. The fourteenth, or lowest, level of the civil service.   1. A conventional epithet for Russia, originating in 11th-century epic poems and religious verse that described the Christian state defending itself against invading pagans.   2. Uniformed servants.

an intense desire to join in some interesting conversation, but he was restrained by the doubt whether it would not be too much on his part, whether it would not be too great a familiarity and lowering of his dignity, and in consequence of these reflections he remained everlastingly in the same mute condition, only uttering from time to time monosyllabic sounds, and in this way he gained the reputation of being a terrible bore.

So this was the Person of Consequence to whom our friend Akaky Akakievich appealed, and he appealed to him at a most unpropitious moment, very unfortunate for himself, though fortunate, indeed, for the Person of Consequence. The latter happened to be in his study, talking in the very best of spirits with an old friend of his childhood who had only just arrived and whom he had not seen for several years. It was at this moment that he was informed that a man called Bashmachkin was asking to see him. He asked abruptly, "What sort of man is he?" and received the answer. "A government clerk." "Ah! he can wait. I haven't time now," said the Person of Consequence. Here I must observe that this was a complete lie on the part of the Person of Consequence; he had time; his friend and he had long ago said all they had to say to each other and their conversation had begun to be broken by very long pauses during which they merely slapped each other on the knee saying, "So that's how things are, Ivan Abramovich!"—"So that's it, Stepan Varlamovich!" but, despite that, he told the clerk to wait in order to show his friend, who had left the civil service some years before and was living at home in the country, how long clerks had to wait for him. At last, after they had talked or rather been silent, to their heart's content and had smoked a cigar in very comfortable armchairs with sloping backs, he seemed suddenly to recollect, and said to the secretary, who was standing at the door with papers for his signature: "Oh, by the way, there is a clerk waiting, isn't there? tell him he can come in." When he saw Akaky Akakievich's meek appearance and old uniform, he turned to him at once and said: "What do you want?" in a firm and abrupt voice, which he had purposely rehearsed in his own room in solitude before the mirror for a week before receiving his present post and the grade of a general. Akaky Akakievich, who was overwhelmed with appropriate awe beforehand, was somewhat confused and, as far as his tongue would allow him, explained to the best of his powers, with even more frequent "ers" than usual, that he had had a perfectly new overcoat and now he had been robbed of it in the most inhuman way, and that now he had come to beg him by his intervention either to correspond with his honor, the head police commissioner, or anybody else, and find the overcoat. This mode of proceeding struck the general for some reason as too familiar. "What next, sir?" he went on abruptly. "Don't you know the way to proceed? To whom are you addressing yourself? Don't you know how things are done? You ought first to have handed in a petition to the office; it would have gone to the head clerk of the room, and to the head clerk of the section; then it would have been handed to the secretary and the secretary would have brought it to me . . ."

"But, your Excellency," said Akaky Akakievich, trying to gather the drop of courage he possessed and feeling at the same time that he was perspiring all over, "I ventured, your Excellency, to trouble you because secretaries . . . er . . . are people you can't depend on . . ."

"What? what? what?" said the Person of Consequence, "where did you get hold of that attitude? where did you pick up such ideas? What insubordination is spreading among young men against their superiors and their chiefs!" The Person of Consequence did not apparently observe that Akaky Akakievich was well over fifty, and therefore if he could have been called a young man it would only have been in comparison with a man of seventy. "Do you know to whom you are speaking? Do you understand who I am? Do you understand that, I ask you?" At this point he stamped, and raised his voice to such a powerful note that Akaky Akakievich was not the only one to be terrified. Akaky Akakievich was positively petrified; he staggered, trembling all over, and could not stand; if the porters had not run up to support him, he would have flopped on the floor; he was led out almost unconscious. The Person of Consequence, pleased that the effect had surpassed his expectations and enchanted at the idea that his words could even deprive a man of consciousness, stole a sideway glance at his friend to see how he was taking it, and perceived not without satisfaction that his friend was feeling very uncertain and even beginning to be a little terrified himself.

How he got downstairs, how he went out into the street—of all that Akaky Akakievich remembered nothing; he had no feeling in his arms or his legs. In all his life he had never been so severely reprimanded by a general, and this was by one of another department, too. He went out into the snowstorm that was whistling through the streets, with his mouth open, and as he went he stumbled off the pavement; the wind, as its way is in Petersburg, blew upon him from all points of the compass and from every side street. In an instant it had blown a quinsy into his throat, and when he got home he was not able to utter a word; he went to bed with a swollen face and throat. That's how violent the effects of an appropriate reprimand can be!

Next day he was in a high fever. Thanks to the gracious assistance of the Petersburg climate, the disease made more rapid progress than could have been expected, and when the doctor came, after feeling his pulse he could find nothing to do but prescribe a poultice, and that simply so that the patient might not be left without the benefit of medical assistance; however, two days later he informed him that his end was at hand, after which he turned to Akaky Akakievich's landlady and said: "And you had better lose no time, my good woman, but order him now a pine coffin, for an oak one will be too expensive for him." Whether Akaky Akakievich heard these fateful words or not, whether they produced a shattering effect upon him, and whether he regretted his pitiful life, no one can tell, for he was constantly in delirium and fever. Apparitions, each stranger than the one before, were continually haunting him: first he saw Petrovich and was ordering him to make an overcoat trimmed with some sort of traps for robbers, who were, he believed, continually under the bed, and he was calling his landlady every minute to pull out a thief who had even got under the quilt; then he kept asking why his old "dressing gown" was hanging before him when he had a new overcoat; then he thought he was standing before the general listening to the appropriate reprimand and saying, "I am sorry, your Excellency"; then finally he became abusive, uttering the most awful language, so that his old landlady positively crossed herself, having never heard anything of the kind from him before, and the more horrified because these dreadful words followed immediately upon the phrase "your Excellency." Later on, his talk was merely a medley of nonsense, so that it was quite unintelligible; all that was evident was that his incoherent words and thoughts were concerned with nothing but the overcoat. At last poor Akaky Akakievich gave up the ghost. No seal was put upon his room[3] nor upon his things, because, in the first place, he had no heirs and, in the second, the property left was very small, to wit, a bundle of quills, a quire[4] of white government paper, three pairs of socks, two or three buttons that had come off his trousers, and the "dressing gown" with which the reader is already familiar. Who came into all this wealth God only knows; even I who tell the tale must admit that I have not bothered to inquire. And Petersburg carried on without Akaky Akakievich, as though, indeed, he had never been in the city. A creature had vanished and departed whose cause no one had championed, who was dear to no one, of interest to no one, who never attracted the attention of a naturalist, though the latter does not disdain to fix a common fly upon a pin and look at him under the microscope—a creature who bore patiently the jeers of the office and for no particular reason went to his grave, though even he at the very end of his life was visited by an exalted guest in the form of an overcoat that for one instant brought color into his poor, drab life—a creature on whom disease fell as it falls upon the heads of the mighty ones of this world . . . !

Several days after his death, a messenger from the department was sent to his lodgings with instructions that he should go at once to the office, for his chief was asking for him; but the messenger was obliged to return without him, explaining that he could not come, and to the inquiry "Why?" he added, "Well, you see, the fact is he is dead; he was buried three days ago." This was how they learned at the office of the death of Akaky Akakievich, and the next day there was sitting in his seat a new clerk who was very much taller and who wrote not in the same straight handwriting but made his letters more slanting and crooked.

But who could have imagined that this was not all there was to tell about Akaky Akakievich, that he was destined for a few days to make his presence felt in the world after his death, as though to make up for his life having been unnoticed by anyone? But so it happened, and our little story unexpectedly finishes with a fantastic ending.

Rumors were suddenly floating about Petersburg that in the neighborhood of the Kalinkin Bridge and for a little distance beyond, a corpse had begun appearing at night in the form of a clerk looking for a stolen overcoat, and stripping from the shoulders of all passersby, regardless of grade and calling, overcoats of all descriptions—trimmed with cat fur or beaver or padded, lined with raccoon, fox, and bear—made, in fact of all sorts of skin which men have adapted for the covering of their own. One of the clerks of the department saw the corpse with his own eyes and at once recognized it as Akaky Akakievich; but it excited in him such terror that he ran away as fast as his legs could carry him and so could not get a very clear view of him, and only saw him hold up his finger threateningly in the distance.

From all sides complaints were continually coming that backs and shoul-

---

3. Seals were usually placed on the room of a dead person in order to safeguard personal possessions for the estate.   4. One-twentieth of a ream of paper, about 25 matching sheets.

ders, not of mere titular councillors, but even of upper court councillors, had been exposed to catching cold, as a result of being stripped of their overcoats. Orders were given to the police to catch the corpse regardless of trouble or expense, dead or alive, and to punish him severely, as an example to others, and, indeed, they very nearly succeeded in doing so. The policeman of one district in Kiryushkin Alley snatched a corpse by the collar on the spot of the crime in the very act of attempting to snatch a frieze overcoat from a retired musician, who used, in his day, to play the flute. Having caught him by the collar, he shouted until he had brought two other policemen whom he ordered to hold the corpse while he felt just a minute in his boot to get out a snuffbox in order to revive his nose which had six times in his life been frostbitten, but the snuff was probably so strong that not even a dead man could stand it. The policeman had hardly had time to put his finger over his right nostril and draw up some snuff in the left when the corpse sneezed violently right into the eyes of all three. While they were putting their fists up to wipe their eyes, the corpse completely vanished, so that they were not even sure whether he had actually been in their hands. From that time forward, the policemen had such a horror of the dead that they were even afraid to seize the living and confined themselves to shouting from the distance: "Hey, you! Move on!" and the clerk's body began to appear even on the other side of the Kalinkin Bridge, terrorizing all timid people.

We have, however, quite neglected the Person of Consequence, who may in reality almost be said to be the cause of the fantastic ending of this perfectly true story. To begin with, my duty requires me to do justice to the Person of Consequence by recording that soon after poor Akaky Akakievich had gone away crushed to powder, he felt something not unlike regret. Sympathy was a feeling not unknown to him; his heart was open to many kindly impulses, although his exalted grade very often prevented them from being shown. As soon as his friend had gone out of his study, he even began brooding over poor Akaky Akakievich, and from that time forward, he was almost every day haunted by the image of the poor clerk who had been unable to survive the official reprimand. The thought of the man so worried him that a week later he actually decided to send a clerk to find out how he was and whether he really could help him in any way. And when they brought him word that Akaky Akakievich had died suddenly in delirium and fever, it made a great impression on him; his conscience reproached him and he was depressed all day. Anxious to distract his mind and to forget the unpleasant incident, he went to spend the evening with one of his friends, where he found respectable company, and what was best of all, almost everyone was of the same grade so that he was able to be quite uninhibited. This had a wonderful effect on his spirits. He let himself go, became affable and genial—in short, spent a very agreeable evening. At supper he drank a couple of glasses of champagne—a proceeding which we all know is not a bad recipe for cheerfulness. The champagne made him inclined to do something unusual, and he decided not to go home yet but to visit a lady of his acquaintance, a certain Karolina Ivanovna—a lady apparently of German extraction, for whom he entertained extremely friendly feelings. It must be noted that the Person of Consequence was a man no longer young. He was an excellent husband, and the respectable father of a family. He had two sons, one already serving in an office, and a nice-looking daughter of sixteen with a rather turned-up, pretty little nose, who used to come every morning to kiss his hand, saying: "*Bonjour,*[5] *Papa.*" His wife, who was still blooming and decidedly good-looking, indeed, used first to give him her hand to kiss and then turning his hand over would kiss it. But though the Person of Consequence was perfectly satisfied with the pleasant amenities of his domestic life, he thought it proper to have a lady friend in another quarter of the town. This lady friend was not a bit better looking nor younger than his wife, but these puzzling things exist in the world and it is not our business to criticize them. And so the Person of Consequence went downstairs, got into his sledge, and said to his coachman, "To Karolina Ivanovna." While luxuriously wrapped in his warm fur coat he remained in that agreeable frame of mind sweeter to a Russian than anything that could be invented, that is, when one thinks of nothing while thoughts come into the mind by themselves, one pleasanter than the other, without your having to bother following them or looking for them. Full of satisfaction, he recalled all the amusing moments of the evening he had spent, all the phrases that had started the intimate circle of friends laughing; many of them he repeated in an undertone and found them as amusing as before, and so, very naturally, laughed very heartily at them again. From time to time, however, he was disturbed by a gust of wind which, blowing suddenly, God knows why or where from, cut him in the face, pelting him with flakes of snow, puffing out his coat collar like a sail, or suddenly flinging it with unnatural force over his head and giving him endless trouble to extricate himself from it. All at once, the Person of Consequence felt that someone had clutched him very tightly by the collar. Turning around he saw a short man in a shabby old uniform, and not without horror recognized him as Akaky Akakievich. The clerk's face was white as snow and looked like that of a corpse, but the horror of the Person of Consequence was beyond all bounds when he saw the mouth of the corpse distorted into speech, and breathing upon him the chill of the grave, it uttered the following words: "Ah, so here you are at last! At last I've . . . er . . . . caught you by the collar. It's your overcoat I want; you refused to help me and abused me into the bargain! So now give me yours!" The poor Person of Consequence very nearly dropped dead. Resolute and determined as he was in his office and before subordinates in general, and though anyone looking at his manly air and figure would have said: "Oh, what a man of character!" yet in this situation he felt, like very many persons of heroic appearance, such terror that not without reason he began to be afraid he would have some sort of fit. He actually flung his overcoat off his shoulders as far as he could and shouted to his coachman in an unnatural voice: "Drive home! Let's get out of here!" The coachman, hearing the tone which he had only heard in critical moments and then accompanied by something even more tangible, hunched his shoulders up to his ears in case of worse following, swung his whip, and flew on like an arrow. In a little over six minutes, the Person of Consequence was at the entrance of his own house. Pale, panic-stricken, and without his overcoat, he arrived home instead of at Karolina Ivanovna's, dragged himself to his own room, and spent the night in great distress, so that next morning

---

5. "Good morning" (French). French, not Russian, was spoken in elegant society.

his daughter said to him at breakfast, "You look very pale today, Papa"; but her papa remained mute and said not a word to anyone of what had happened to him, where he had been, and where he had been going. The incident made a great impression upon him. Indeed, it happened far more rarely that he said to his subordinates, "How dare you? Do you understand who I am?" and he never uttered those words at all until he had first heard all the facts of the case.

What was even more remarkable is that from that time on the apparition of the dead clerk ceased entirely; apparently the general's overcoat had fitted him perfectly; anyway nothing more was heard of overcoats being snatched from anyone. Many restless and anxious people refused, however, to be pacified, and still maintained that in remote parts of the town the dead clerk went on appearing. One policeman, in Kolomna,[6] for instance, saw with his own eyes an apparition appear from behind a house; but being by natural constitution somewhat frail—so much so that on one occasion an ordinary grown-up suckling pig, making a sudden dash out of some private building, knocked him off his feet to the great amusement of the cabmen standing around, whom he fined two kopeks each for snuff for such disrespect—he did not dare to stop it, and so followed it in the dark until the apparition suddenly looked around and, stopping, asked him: "What do you want?" displaying a huge fist such as you never see among the living. The policeman said: "Nothing," and turned back on the spot. This apparition, however, was considerably taller and adorned with immense mustaches, and directing its steps apparently toward Obukhov Bridge,[7] vanished into the darkness of the night.

6. Bigger (or Greater) and Smaller Kolomna make up a large historic area of St. Petersburg. Gogol set many of his stories in the poor residential district of Smaller Kolomna.   7. One of the oldest bridges in St. Petersburg, spanning the Fontanka River. It was rebuilt in stone in 1785 by the contractor Obukhov.

GUSTAVE FLAUBERT
1821–1880

Gustave Flaubert is rightly considered the exemplary realist novelist and *Madame Bovary* his masterpiece. He displays the objectivity, the detachment from his characters, demanded by the theory and is a great virtuoso of the art of composition and of style, while giving a clear picture of the society of his time. It is likewise a picture in which we can see much of ourselves.

Flaubert was born in Rouen, Normandy, on December 12, 1821, to the chief surgeon of the Hôtel Dieu. He was extremely precocious: by the age of sixteen he was writing Romantic stories, which were published only after his death. In 1840 he went to Paris to study law (he had received his baccalaureate from the local *lycée*), but he failed in his examinations and in 1843 suffered a sudden nervous breakdown that kept him at home. In 1846 he moved to Croisset, just outside Rouen on the Seine, where he made his home for the rest of his life, devoting himself to writing. The same year, in Paris Flaubert met Louise Colet, a minor writer and socialite, who became his mistress. In 1849–51 he visited the Levant, traveling extensively in Greece, Syria, and Egypt. After his return he settled down to the writing of *Madame Bovary*, which took him five full years and which, despite accusations of immorality, was a great popular success. The remainder of his life was uneventful. He made occasional trips to Paris and one trip, in 1860, to Tunisia to see the ruins of Carthage in preparation for the writing of his novel *Salammbô* (1862). Three more novels followed: *The Sentimental Education* (1869), *The Temptation of St. Anthony* (1874), and the unfinished *Bouvard and Pécuchet* (1881), as well as *Three Tales* (1877), consisting of *A Simple Heart, The Legend of St. Julian the Hospitaler,* and *Herodias*. Flaubert died in Croisset on May 8, 1880.

Madame Bovary (1856) is deservedly considered the showpiece of French realism. It would be impossible to find a novel, certainly before Flaubert, in which relatively humble persons in a humble setting are treated with such seriousness, restraint, verisimilitude, and imaginative clarity. At first sight, *Madame Bovary* is a solidly documented and clearly visualized account of life in a village of the French province of Normandy sometime in the 1840s. We meet a whole spectrum of social types found in such a time and place: the doctor (actually a "health officer" with a lower degree), a pharmacist, a storekeeper, a notary and his clerk, a tax collector, a woman innkeeper and her stable boy, the priest and his sacristan, a neighboring landowner, and a farmer. We are told the story of a young peasant woman brought up in a convent, who marries a dull man and commits adultery first with a ruthless philanderer and then with a spineless younger man. Overwhelmed by debts concealed from her unsuspecting husband, faced by sudden demands for repayment, disillusioned in love, rebuffed by everybody who might help her, she commits suicide by poisoning herself with arsenic. Nothing seems simpler or more ordinary, and the manner of telling seems completely objective, detached, impersonal. A case is presented that is observed with almost scientific curiosity. The descriptions are obviously accurate, sometimes based on expert knowledge; the clubfoot operation and the effects of arsenic poisoning agree with medical evidence. The setting—the topography of the two villages, the interior of the houses, the inn, the pharmacy, the city of Rouen, the cathedral there, the river landscape, and the particular things and sounds—imprints itself vividly on our memory. Every detail serves its purpose of characterization—from the absurd cap of the schoolboy Charles to the mirror and the crucifix in the deathbed scene; from the sound of Binet's lathe turning out napkin rings to the tap of the stable boy's wooden leg. "The technique of *Madame Bovary* has become the model of all novels" (Albert Thibaudet).

But surely the book could not have kept its grip on modern readers if it were only a superbly accurate description of provincial life in France, as the added subtitle, *Mœurs de province* (Provincial manners) suggests. The book transcends its time and place if one thinks of Emma Bovary as the type of the unfulfilled dreamer, as the failed and foiled romanticist, as a female Don Quixote, corrupted by sentimental reading, caught in a trap of circumstance, pitiful and to be pitied in her horrible self-inflicted death.

This central theme has, however, remained ambiguous. What attracted and shocked readers was the uncertainty about the author's attitude toward Emma, particularly at the time of publication, when readers were accustomed to being told clearly by addresses and comments what they were to think of the actions and morals of the characters of a novel. *Madame Bovary*, at publication, caused a scandal. The *Paris Review*, in which it was published serially, and the author were hauled into court for immorality and blasphemy; and the prosecutor described the book as an incitement to adultery and atheism. In his rebuttal, the defense counsel argued that the novel is, rather, a highly moral work in which adultery is punished, even excessively. Flaubert was acquitted, but neither the prosecutor nor the defending attorney interpreted the book correctly. It is neither a salacious novel nor a didactic tract.

Some parts of the book are frankly satirical (and thus far from purely objective): the gross village priest who cannot even understand the distress of Emma is flanked by the fussy, shallow, pseudoscientific, enlightened, "progressive" pharmacist Homais. Though they argue and quarrel, they are finally reduced to a common level when they eat and snore at the wake next to Emma's corpse. The rightly famous scene of the country fair satirizes and parodies the pompous rhetoric of the officials extolling the glories of agriculture, counterpointing it to the equally platitudinous love talk of Rodolphe and the lowing of the cattle in an amalgam that reduces men and women to a common level of animality. Even Emma is not spared: her sentimental religiosity, her taste for luxury, her financial improvidence are diagnosed as disguised eroticism. She would not have minded if Rodolphe had drawn a pistol against her husband. In her desperate search for escape she asks Léon to steal for her. In the last attempt to get money she is ready to sell herself. She is indifferent to her child, deceitful even in small matters. Her longing for sensual satisfaction becomes, in the scenes with Léon in the hotel at Rouen, frantic and corrupt. The author weighted the scales against her: she married an excessively stupid and insensitive man; she met two callous lovers; she is tricked by a merciless usurer; she is utterly alone at last. When Charles, meeting Rodolphe after her death and after he had discovered her infidelities, tells him, ineptly, awkwardly, "It was the fault of destiny," the author expressly approves of this statement. The novel conveys a sense of inexorable determinism, of the vanity of dreaming, of the impossibility of escape from one's nature and station. It conveys a sense of despair, of alienation in an incomprehensible universe—but also a hatred for all the stupidity, mediocrity and baseness of people there and everywhere. (Flaubert called them bourgeois, but included the proletarian masses in his contempt.) Emma is pitied because she has, at least, a spark of discontent, the yearning to escape the cage of her existence. But baseness triumphs and the book ends with a sudden change to the present tense: "Homais has just received the Cross of the Legion of Honor."

This sense of the inexorable, the fatal, the inescapable is secured also by the precision and firmness of Flaubert's style and the carefully planned architectonics of his composition. If we mean by style the systematic exploitation of the syntactical and lexical possibilities of a language, we must class Flaubert with the great stylists. His keen sense of the exact descriptive epithet, the one right word (le mot juste)—even when he uses the most trivial cliché or the most recondite scientific term—coheres with the skillful modulations and rhythms of the sentences; the organization of the paragraphs; and the divisions of the sections, which are grouped around a series of pictorial scenes: the schoolroom, the rustic wedding, the ball, the visit to the priest, the country fair, the ride in the woods, the clubfoot operation, the opera, the cathedral, the cab ride, the deathbed, to mention only the most memorable.

Madame Bovary is constantly cited as an example for the handling of narrative perspective. The story, which begins in the schoolroom, is ostensibly told by a schoolfellow (the word we is used in the first pages); it shifts then to the narration of an omniscient author and, off and on, narrows to the point of view of Emma. Much is seen only through her eyes, but one cannot say that the author identifies with her or enters her mind sympathetically. He keeps his distance and on occasion conveys his own opinion. He is not averse even to moral judgments: he speaks of Emma's hardhearted and tightfisted peasant nature (p. 1077), he refers to her depravity (p. 1102), and Rodolphe is several times condemned for his brutality and cynicism (pp. 1116, 1154, 1159). In the description of extreme unction (p. 1236) the author pronounces solemnly his forgiveness (which he suggests would be also God's) for her coveting all worldly goods, her greediness "for the warm breeze and scents of love," and even her sensuality and lust. But mostly Flaubert depicts the scenes by simple description or reproduction of speech or imagined silent reflections. Things and people become at times symbolic even in an obtrusive way: the wedding bouquet, the plate of boiled beef, and the apparition of the blind beggar who turns up conveniently at the hour of Emma's death. Much is said about her that she could not have observed herself. The famous saying "Madame Bovary c'est moi" ("I am Madame Bovary") cannot be traced back to an earlier date than 1909, when it is reported on distant hearsay in René Descharmes, *Flaubert before 1857*. There are dozens of passages in the letters during the composition of *Madame Bovary* that express Flaubert's distaste for the "vulgarity of his subject," "the fetid smell of the milieu," and his opinion of Emma Bovary as "a woman of false poetry and false sentiments." Usually he defends his choice of theme as a "prodigious *tour de force*," as "an act of crude willpower," as "a deliberate made-up thing," though we suspect him sometimes of exaggerating his efforts to impress his correspondent in Paris, the facile and prolific novelist and poet, Louise Colet.

Still, the saying "Madame Bovary c'est moi" has been widely quoted and accepted because it contains a kernel of truth. In Emma, Flaubert combats his own vices of daydreaming, romanticism, exoticism, of which he thought he could cure himself by writing this antiromantic book. But the identification with Emma distracts us from noticing Flaubert's deep-seated sympathies with the slow-witted, abused, but honest and loving Charles, who rightly opens and closes the book, and for the other good people: Emma's father, the farmer Rouault, kind and distressed by all he could not foresee; Justin, the pharmacist's apprentice adoring Emma from afar, praying on her grave; the clubfoot stable boy tortured and exploited for a dream of medical reputation; poor neglected Berthe sent to the cotton mill; the old peasant woman at the fair who for fifty-four years of service got a medal worth twenty-five francs; and even the blind beggar with his horrible skin disease. Moreover, there is the admirable Dr. Larivière, who appears fleetingly like an apparition from a saner, loftier world of good sense and professional devotion. Thus it seems unjust of the critic Martin Turnell to say that the novel is "an onslaught on the whole basis of human feeling and on all spiritual and moral values."

In Flaubert's mind, the novel was also an assertion of the redeeming power of art. His long struggle with its composition, which took him more than five years of grinding drudgery—five days in which he had written a single page, five or six pages in a week, twenty-five pages in six weeks, thirteen pages in seven weeks, a whole night spent in hunting for the right adjective; the ruthless pruning to which he subjected his enormous manuscript, eliminating many fine touches, similes, metaphors, and descriptions of elusive mental states (as a study of the manuscripts has shown)—were to him a victory of art over reality, a passionate search for Beauty, which he knew to be an illusion. But one wonders whether the conflict of Flaubert's scientific detachment and cruel observation with the intense adoration of beauty, the thirst for calculated purity and structure, for "style" as perfection can be resolved. He tried to achieve this synthesis in *Madame Bovary*. Watching this struggle between heterogeneous elements, and even opposites, explains some of the fascination of the book.

PRONUNCIATION GLOSSARY

The following list uses common English syllables and stress accents to provide rough equivalents of selected words whose pronunciation may be unfamiliar to the general reader.

Berthe: *behrt*	Guillaumin: *ghee-oh-manh'*
Binet: *bee-nay'*	Homais: *oh-maye'*
Bovary: *boh-vahr-ee'*	huissier: *wee-syay'*
Canivet: *cah-nee-vay'*	Larivière: *lah-ree-vyehr'*
Flaubert: *floh-bair'*	La Vaubyessard: *lah vohb-yes-ahr'*

Léon Dupuis: *lay-ohn' dyew-pwee'*

Les Bertaux: *lay behr-toh'*

Lestiboudois: *les-tee-boo-dwah'*

Lheureux: *leu-reu'*

Rodolphe Boulanger de la Huchette:
   ro-dawlf' boo-lawn-zhay'
   deu la ew-shet'

Rouault: *roo-oh'*

Rouen: *roo-awnh'*

Tostes: *tost*

Vinçart: *vanh-sahr'*

Yonville: *yohnh-veel'*

Yvetot: *eev-toh'*

Madame Bovary[1]

Part One

I

We were in study-hall when the headmaster entered, followed by a new boy not yet in school uniform and by the handyman carrying a large desk. Their arrival disturbed the slumbers of some of us, but we all stood up in our places as though rising from our work.

The headmaster motioned us to be seated; then, turning to the teacher:

"Monsieur Roger," he said in an undertone, "here's a pupil I'd like you to keep your eye on. I'm putting him in the last year of the lower school. If he does good work and behaves himself we'll move him up to where he ought to be at his age."

The newcomer, who was hanging back in the corner so that the door half hid him from view, was a country lad of about fifteen, taller than any of us. He had his hair cut in bangs like a cantor in a village church, and he had a gentle, timid look. He wasn't broad in the shoulders, but his green jacket with its black buttons seemed tight under the arms; and through the vents of his cuffs we could see red wrists that were clearly unaccustomed to being covered. His yellowish breeches were hiked up by his suspenders, and from them emerged a pair of blue-stockinged legs. He wore heavy shoes, hobnailed and badly shined.

We began to recite our lessons. He listened avidly, as though to a sermon—he didn't dare even cross his legs or lean on his elbows; and at two o'clock, when the bell rang for the next class, the teacher had to tell him to line up with the rest of us.

We always flung our caps on the floor when entering a classroom, to free our hands; we hurled them under the seats from the doorway itself, in such a way that they struck the wall and raised a cloud of dust: that was "how it was done."

But whether he had failed to notice this ritual or hadn't dared join in observance of it, his cap was still in his lap when we'd finished reciting our prayer. It was a headgear of composite order, containing elements of an ordinary hat, a hussar's busby, a lancer's cap, a sealskin cap and a nightcap: one of those wretched things whose mute hideousness suggests unplumbed

---

1. Translated by Francis Steegmuller.

depths, like an idiot's face. Ovoid and stiffened with whalebone, it began with three convex strips; then followed alternating lozenges of velvet and rabbit's fur, separated by a red band; then came a kind of bag, terminating in a cardboard-lined polygon intricately decorated with braid. From this hung a long, excessively thin cord ending in a kind of tassel of gold netting. The cap was new; its peak was shiny.

"Stand up," said the teacher.

He rose. His cap dropped to the floor. Everyone began to laugh.

He bent over for it. A boy beside him sent it down again with his elbow. Once again he picked it up.

"How about getting rid of your helmet?" suggested the teacher, who was something of a wit.

Another loud laugh from the students confused the poor fellow. He didn't know whether to keep the cap in his hand, drop it on the floor, or put it on his head. He sat down again and placed it in his lap.

"Stand up," repeated the professor, "and tell me your name."

The new boy mumbled a name that was unintelligible.

"Say it again!"

The same jumble of syllables came out, drowned in the jeers of the class.

"Louder!" cried the teacher. "Louder!"

With desperate resolve the new boy opened a mouth that seemed enormous, and as though calling someone he cried at the top of his lungs the word "Charbovari!"

This touched off a roar that rose *crescendo*, punctuated with shrill screams. There was a shrieking, a banging of desks as everyone yelled, "Charbovari! Charbovari!" Then the din broke up into isolated cries that slowly diminished, occasionally starting up again along a line of desks where a stifled laugh would burst out here and there like a half-spent firecracker.

But a shower of penalties gradually restored order; and the teacher, finally grasping the name Charles Bovary after it had been several times spelled out and repeated and he had read it aloud himself, at once commanded the poor devil to sit in the dunce's seat, at the foot of the platform. He began to move toward it, then hesitated.

"What are you looking for?" the teacher demanded.

"My c—" the new boy said timidly, casting an uneasy glance around him.

"Everybody will stay and write five hundred lines!"

Like Neptune's "*Quos ego,*"[2] those words, furiously uttered, cut short the threat of a new storm. "Quiet!" the indignant teacher continued, mopping his forehead with a handkerchief he took from his toque. "As for you," he said to the new boy, "you'll copy out for me twenty times all the tenses of *ridiculus sum.*"[3]

Then, more gently: "You'll find your cap. No one has stolen it."

All was calm again. Heads bent over copybooks, and for the next two hours the new boy's conduct was exemplary, even though an occasional spitball, sent from the nib of a pen, struck him wetly in the face. He wiped himself each time with his hand, and otherwise sat there motionless, his eyes lowered.

That evening, in study period, he took his sleeveguards from his desk,

---

2. An unfinished threat (Latin: "you whom I . . .") delivered by the sea god Neptune to winds that had caused ocean storms without his permission (*Aeneid* 1.135). 3. I am a fool (Latin).

arranged his meager equipment, and carefully ruled his paper. We saw him working conscientiously, looking up every word in the dictionary, taking great pains. It was doubtless thanks to this display of effort that he was not demoted to a lower form. For while he had a fair knowledge of grammatical rules, his translations lacked elegance. He had begun his Latin with his village priest: his thrifty parents had sent him away to school as late as possible.

His father, Monsieur Charles-Denis-Bartholomé Bovary, had been an army surgeon's aide, forced to leave the service about 1812 as a result of involvement in a conscription scandal. He had then turned his personal charms to advantage, picking up a dowry of 60,000 francs brought to him by a knit-goods dealer's daughter who had fallen in love with his appearance. He was a handsome man, much given to bragging and clanking his spurs. His side whiskers merged with his mustache, his fingers were always loaded with rings, his clothes were flashy: he had the look of a bully and the easy cajoling ways of a traveling salesman. Once married, he lived off his wife's money for two or three years. He ate well, rose late, smoked big porcelain pipes, stayed out every night to see a show, spent much of his time in cafés. His father-in-law died and left very little; this made him indignant, and he "went into textiles" and lost some money. Then he retired to the country, with the intention of "making things pay." But he knew as little about crops as he did about calico; and since he rode his horses instead of working them in the fields, drank his cider bottled instead of selling it by the barrel, ate his best poultry, and greased his hunting boots with the fat from his pigs, he soon realized that he had better give up all idea of profit-making.

So for two hundred francs[4] a year he rented, in a village on the border of Normandy and Picardy, a dwelling that was half farm, half gentleman's residence; and there, surly, eaten by discontent, cursing heaven, envying everyone, he shut himself up at the age of forty-five, disgusted with mankind, he said, and resolved to live in peace.

His wife had been mad about him at the beginning; in her love she had tendered him a thousand servilities that had alienated him all the more. Once sprightly, all outgoing and affectionate, with age she had grown touchy, nagging and nervous, like stale wine turning to vinegar. At first she had suffered uncomplainingly, watching him chase after every trollop in the village and having him come back to her at night from any one of twenty disgusting places surfeited and stinking of drink. Then her pride rebelled. She withdrew into her shell; and swallowing her rage she bore up stoically until her death. She was always busy, always doing things. She was constantly running to lawyers, to the judge, remembering when notes fell due and obtaining renewals; and at home she was forever ironing, sewing, washing, keeping an eye on the hired men, figuring their wages. Monsieur, meanwhile, never lifted a finger. He sat smoking in the chimney corner and spitting into the ashes, continually falling into a grumpy doze and waking to utter uncomplimentary remarks.

When she had a child it had to be placed out with a wet nurse. And then

---

4. It is very difficult to transpose monetary values from 1840 into present-day figures, since relationships between the actual value of the franc, the cost of living, and the relative cost of specific items (e.g., rent and real estate) have undergone fundamental changes. A rough calculation of inflation and exchange rates between the franc and the dollar in 1840 and 2003 gives approximately $51; that would show Mme. Bovary destroyed, at the end of the book, by a debt of $20,324.

later, when the little boy was back with its parents, he was pampered like a prince. His mother stuffed him with jams and jellies; his father let him run barefoot, and fancied himself a disciple of Rousseau to the point of saying he'd be quite willing to have the boy go naked like a young animal. To counter his wife's maternal tendencies he tried to form his son according to a certain virile ideal of childhood and to harden his constitution by subjecting him to strict discipline, Spartan-style. He sent him to bed without a fire, taught him to take great swigs of rum and to ridicule religious processions. But the child was pacific by nature, and such training had little effect. His mother kept him tied to her apron-strings: she made him paper cutouts, told him stories, and conversed with him in endless bitter-sweet monologues full of coaxing chatter. In the isolation of her life she transferred to her baby all her own poor frustrated ambitions. She dreamed of glamorous careers: she saw him tall, handsome, witty, successful—a bridge builder or a judge. She taught him to read, and even, on an old piano she had, to sing two or three senti-mental little songs. But from Monsieur Bovary, who cared little for culture, all this brought merely the comment that it was "useless." Could they ever afford to give him an education, to buy him a practice or a business? Besides, "with enough nerve a man could always get ahead in the world." Madame Bovary pursed her lips, and the boy ran wild in the village.

He followed the hired men and chased crows, pelting them with clods of earth until they flew off. He ate the wild blackberries that grew along the ditches, looked after the turkeys with a long stick, pitched hay, roamed the woods, played hopscotch in the shelter of the church porch when it rained, and on important feast-days begged the sexton to let him toll the bells so that he could hang with his full weight from the heavy rope and feel it sweep him off his feet as it swung in its arc.

He throve like an oak. His hands grew strong and his complexion ruddy.

When he was twelve, his mother had her way: he began his studies. The priest was asked to tutor him. But the lessons were so short and irregular that they served little purpose. They took place at odd hurried moments—in the sacristy between a baptism and a funeral; or else the priest would send for him after the Angelus, when his parish business was over for the day. They would go up to his bedroom and begin, midges and moths fluttering around the candle. There in the warmth the child would fall asleep; and the old man, too, would soon be dozing and snoring, his hands folded over his stomach and his mouth open. Other times, as Monsieur le curé was return-ing from a sickbed with the holy oils, he would catch sight of Charles scam-pering in the fields, and would call him over and lecture him for a few minutes, taking advantage of the occasion to make him conjugate a verb right there, under a tree. Rain would interrupt them, or some passer-by whom they knew. However, he was always satisfied with him, and even said that "the young fellow had a good memory."

Things weren't allowed to stop there. Madame was persistent. Shamed into consent—or, rather, his resistance worn down—Monsieur gave in with-out further struggle. They waited a year, until the boy had made his First Communion, then six months more; and finally Charles was sent to the lycée in Rouen. His father delivered him himself, toward the end of October, during the fortnight of the Saint-Romain fair.

It would be very difficult today for any of us to say what he was like. There was nothing striking about him: he played during recess, worked in study-hall, paid attention in class, slept soundly in the dormitory, ate heartily in the refectory. His local guardian was a wholesale hardware dealer in the rue Ganterie, who called for him one Sunday a month after early closing, sent him for a walk along the riverfront to look at the boats, then brought him back to school by seven, in time for supper. Every Thursday night Charles wrote a long letter to his mother, using red ink and three seals; then he looked over his history notes, or leafed through an old volume of *Anacharsis*[5] that lay around the study-hall. When his class went for outings he talked with the school servant who accompanied them, a countryman like himself.

By working hard he managed to stay about in the middle of the class; once he even got an honorable mention in natural history. But before he finished upper school his parents took him out of the lycée entirely and sent him to study medicine, confident that he could get his baccalaureate degree anyway by making up the intervening years on his own.

His mother choose a room for him, four flights up overlooking the stream called the Eau-de-Robec,[6] in the house of a dyer she knew. She arranged for his board, got him a table and two chairs, and sent home for an old cherry bed; and to keep her darling warm she bought him a small cast-iron stove and a load of wood. Then after a week she went back to her village, urging him a thousand times over to behave himself now that he was on his own.

The curriculum that he read on the bulletin board staggered him. Courses in anatomy, pathology, pharmacy, chemistry, botany, clinical practice, therapeutics, to say nothing of hygiene and materia medica—names of unfamiliar etymology that were like so many doors leading to solemn shadowy sanctuaries.

He understood absolutely nothing of any of it. He listened in vain: he could not grasp it. Even so, he worked. He filled his notebooks, attended every lecture, never missed hospital rounds. In the performance of his daily task he was like a mill-horse that treads blindfolded in a circle, utterly ignorant of what he is grinding.

To save him money, his mother sent him a roast of veal each week by the stagecoach, and off this he lunched when he came in from the hospital, warming his feet by beating them against the wall. Then he had to hurry off to lectures, to the amphitheatre, to another hospital, crossing the entire city again when he returned. At night, after eating the meager dinner his landlord provided, he climbed back up to his room, back to work. Steam rose from his damp clothes as he sat beside the red-hot stove.

On fine summer evenings, at the hour when the warm streets are empty and servant girls play at shuttlecock in front of the houses, he would open his window and lean out. The stream, which makes this part of Rouen a kind of squalid little Venice, flowed just below, stained yellow, purple or blue between its bridges and railings. Workmen from the dye plants, crouching on the bank, washed their arms in the water. Above him, on poles projecting from attics, skeins of cotton were drying in the open. And beyond the roof-

---

5. *Voyage du jeune Anacharsis en Grèce* (The voyage of young Anacharsis in Greece; 1788) was a popular account of ancient Greece as seen by a barbarian, by Jean-Jacques Barthélemy (1716–1795).   6. Small river, now covered up, that flows through the poorest neighborhood of Rouen, used as a sewer by the factories that border it, thus suggesting Flaubert's description as *"une ignoble petite Venise"* (squalid little Venise).

tops stretched the sky, vast and pure, with the red sun setting. How good it must be in the country! How cool in the beech grove! And he opened his nostrils wide, longing for a whiff of the fresh and fragrant air, but none was ever wafted to where he was.

He grew thinner and taller, and his face took on a kind of plaintive expression that almost made it interesting.

The fecklessness that was part of his nature soon led him to break all his good resolutions. One day he skipped rounds; the next, a lecture; idleness, he found, was to his taste, and gradually he stayed away entirely.

He began to go to cafés. Soon he was crazy about dominoes. To spend his evenings shut up in a dirty public room, clinking black-dotted pieces of sheep's bone on a marble table, seemed to him a marvelous assertion of his freedom that raised him in his own esteem. It was like an initiation into the world, admission to a realm of forbidden delights; and every time he entered the café the feel of the doorknob in his hand gave him a pleasure that was almost sensual. Now many things pent up within him burst their bonds; he learned verses by heart and sang them at student gatherings, developed an enthusiasm for Béranger,[7] learned to make punch, and knew, at long last, the joys of love.

Thanks to that kind of preparation he failed completely the examination that would have entitled him to practice medicine as an *officier de santé.*[8] And his parents were waiting for him at home that very night to celebrate his success!

He set out on foot; at the outskirts of the village he stopped, sent someone for his mother, and told her all. She forgave him, laying his downfall to the unfairness of the examiners, and steadied him by promising to make all explanations. (It was five years before Monsieur Bovary learned the truth: by that time it was an old story and he could accept it, especially since he couldn't conceive of his own offspring as being stupid.)

Charles set to work again and crammed ceaselessly, memorizing everything on which he could possibly be questioned. He passed with a fairly good grade. What a wonderful day for his mother! Everyone was asked to dinner.

Where should he practice? At Tostes. In that town there was only one elderly doctor, whose death Madame Bovary had long been waiting for; and the old man hadn't yet breathed his last when Charles moved in across the road as his successor.

But it wasn't enough to have raised her son, sent him into medicine, and discovered Tostes for him to practice in: he had to have a wife. She found him one: a *huissier's*[9] widow in Dieppe, forty-five years old, with twelve hundred francs a year.

Ugly though she was, and thin as a lath, with a face as spotted as a meadow in springtime, Madame Dubuc unquestionably had plenty of suitors to choose from. To gain her ends Madame Bovary had to get rid of all the rivals, and her outwitting of one of them, a butcher whose candidacy was favored by the local clergy, was nothing short of masterly.

---

7. Pierre-Jean de Béranger (1780–1857), an extremely popular writer of songs that often exalt the glories of the empire of Napoleon I.   8. Health officer (French). Instituted during the French Revolution, a kind of second-class medical degree, well below the doctorate. The student was allowed to attend a medical school without having passed the equivalent of the *baccalauréat*, and could practice only in the administrative region in which the diploma had been conferred (Bovary is thus tied down to the vicinity of Rouen) and was not allowed to perform major operations, except in the presence of a full-fledged doctor. This diploma was suppressed in 1892.   9. Bailiff's.

Charles had envisaged marriage as the beginning of a better time, thinking that he would have greater freedom and be able to do as he liked with himself and his money. But it was his wife who ruled: in front of company he had to say certain things and not others, he had to eat fish on Friday, dress the way she wanted, obey her when she ordered him to dun nonpaying patients. She opened his mail, watched his every move, and listened through the thinness of the wall when there were women in his office.

She had to have her cup of chocolate every morning: there was no end to the attentions she required. She complained incessantly of her nerves, of pains in her chest, of depressions and faintnesses. The sound of anyone moving about near her made her ill; when people left her she couldn't bear her loneliness; when they came to see her it was, of course, "to watch her die." When Charles came home in the evening she would bring her long thin arms out from under her bedclothes, twine them around his neck, draw him down beside her on the edge of the bed, and launch into the tale of her woes: he was forgetting her, he was in love with someone else! How right people had been, to warn her that he'd make her unhappy! And she always ended by asking him to give her a new tonic and a little more love.

II

One night about eleven o'clock they were awakened by a noise: a horse had stopped just at their door. The maid opened the attic window and parleyed for some time with a man who stood in the street below. He had been sent to fetch the doctor; he had a letter. Nastasie came downstairs, shivering, turned the key in the lock and pushed back the bolts one by one. The man left his horse, followed the maid, and entered the bedroom at her heels. Out of his gray-tasseled woolen cap he drew a letter wrapped in a piece of cloth, and with a careful gesture handed it to Charles, who raised himself on his pillow to read it. Nastasie stood close to the bed, holding the light. Madame had modestly turned her back and lay facing the wall.

This letter, sealed with a small blue wax seal, begged Monsieur Bovary to come immediately to a farm called Les Bertaux, to set a broken leg. Now, from Tostes to Les Bertaux is at least fifteen miles, going by way of Longueville and Saint-Victor. It was a pitch-black night. Madame Bovary was fearful lest her husband meet with an accident. So it was decided that the stable hand who had brought the letter should start out ahead, and that Charles should follow three hours later: by that time there would be a moon. A boy would be sent out to meet him, to show him the way to the farm and open the field gates.

About four o'clock in the morning Charles set out for Les Bertaux, wrapped in a heavy coat. He was still drowsy from his warm sleep, and the peaceful trot of his mare lulled him like the rocking of a cradle. Whenever she stopped of her own accord in front of one of those spike-edged holes that farmers dig along the roadside to protect their crops, he would wake up with a start, quickly remember the broken leg, and try to recall all the fractures he had ever seen. The rain had stopped; day was breaking, and on the leafless branches of the apple trees birds were perched motionless, ruffling up their little feathers in the cold morning wind. The countryside stretched flat as far as eye could see; and the tufts of trees clustered around the farmhouses were widely spaced dark purple stains on the vast gray surface that merged at the horizon into the dull tone of the sky. From time to time Charles would open his eyes; and then, his senses dimmed by a return of sleep, he would fall again into a drowsiness in which recent sensations became confused with older memories to give him double visions of himself: as husband and as student—lying in bed as he had been only an hour or so before, and walking through a surgical ward as in the past. In his mind the hot smell of poultices mingled with the fresh smell of the dew; he heard at once the rattle of the curtain rings on hospital beds, and the sound of his wife's breathing as she lay asleep. At Vassonville he saw a little boy sitting in the grass beside a ditch.

"Are you the doctor?" the child asked.

And when Charles answered, he took his wooden shoes in his hands and began to run in front of him.

As they continued on their way, the *officier de santé* gathered from what his guide told him that Monsieur Rouault must be a very well-to-do farmer indeed. He had broken his leg the previous evening, on his way back from celebrating Twelfth Night at the home of a neighbor. His wife had been dead for two years. He had with him only his "demoiselle"—his daughter—who kept house for him.

Now the road was more deeply rutted: they were approaching Les Bertaux. The boy slipped through an opening in a hedge, disappeared, then reappeared ahead, opening a farmyard gate from within. The horse was slipping on the wet grass; Charles had to bend low to escape overhanging branches. Kenneled watchdogs were barking, pulling at their chains. As he passed through the gate of Les Bertaux, his horse took fright and shied wildly.

It was a prosperous-looking farm. Through the open upper-halves of the stable doors great plough-horses could be seen placidly feeding from new racks. Next to the outbuildings stood a big manure pile, and in among the chickens and turkeys pecking at its steaming surface were five or six peacocks—favorite show pieces of *cauchois* farmyards.[1] The sheepfold was long, the barn lofty, its walls as smooth as your hand. In the shed were two large carts and four ploughs complete with whips, horse collars and full trappings, the blue wool pads gray under the fine dust that sifted down from the lofts. The farmyard sloped upwards, planted with symmetrically spaced trees, and from near the pond came the merry sound of a flock of geese.

A young woman wearing a blue merino dress with three flounces came to the door of the house to greet Monsieur Bovary, and she ushered him into the kitchen, where a big open fire was blazing. Around its edges the farm hands' breakfast was bubbling in small pots of assorted sizes. Damp clothes were drying inside the vast chimney-opening. The fire shovel, the tongs, and the nose of the bellows, all of colossal proportions, shone like polished steel; and along the walls hung a lavish array of kitchen utensils, glimmering in the bright light of the fire and in the first rays of the sun that were now beginning to come in through the windowpanes.

Charles went upstairs to see the patient. He found him in bed, sweating under blankets, his nightcap lying where he had flung it. He was a stocky little man of fifty, fair-skinned, blue-eyed, bald in front and wearing earrings. On a chair beside him was a big decanter of brandy: he had been pouring

---

1. From the Caux area, a large chalky plateau region in Normandy (northern France).

himself drinks to keep up his courage. But as soon as he saw the doctor he dropped his bluster, and instead of cursing as he had been doing for the past twelve hours he began to groan weakly.

The fracture was a simple one, without complications of any kind. Charles couldn't have wished for anything easier. Then he recalled his teachers' bedside manner in accident cases, and proceeded to cheer up his patient with all kinds of facetious remarks—a truly surgical attention, like the oiling of a scalpel. For splints, they sent someone to bring a bundle of laths from the carriage shed. Charles selected one, cut it into lengths and smoothed it down with a piece of broken window glass, while the maidservant tore sheets for bandages and Mademoiselle Emma tried to sew some pads. She was a long time finding her workbox, and her father showed his impatience. She made no reply; but as she sewed she kept pricking her fingers and raising them to her mouth to suck.

Charles was surprised by the whiteness of her fingernails. They were almond shaped, tapering, as polished and shining as Dieppe ivories. Her hands, however, were not pretty—not pale enough, perhaps, a little rough at the knuckles; and they were too long, without softness of line. The finest thing about her was her eyes. They were brown, but seemed black under the long eyelashes; and she had an open gaze that met yours with fearless candor.

When the binding was done, the doctor was invited by Monsieur Rouault himself to "have something" before he left.

Charles went down to the parlor on the ground floor. At the foot of a great canopied bed, its calico hangings printed with a design of people in Turkish dress, there stood a little table on which places had been laid for two, a silver mug beside each plate. From a tall oaken cupboard facing the window came an odor of orris root and damp sheets. In corners stood rows of grain sacks—the overflow from the granary, which was just adjoining, approached by three stone steps. The room's only decoration, hanging from a nail in the center of the flaking green-painted wall, was a black pencil drawing of a head of Minerva framed in gold and inscribed at the bottom in Gothic letters "To my dear Papa."

They spoke about the patient first, and then about the weather, about the bitter cold, about the wolves that roamed the fields at night. Mademoiselle Rouault didn't enjoy country life, especially now, with almost the full responsibility of the farm on her shoulders. The room was chilly, and she shivered as she ate. Charles noticed that her lips were full, and that she had the habit of biting them in moments of silence.

Her neck rose out of the low fold of a white collar. The two black sweeps of her hair, pulled down from a fine center part that followed the curve of her skull, were so sleek that each seemed to be one piece. Covering all but the very tips of her ears, it was gathered at the back into a large chignon, and toward the temples it waved a bit—a detail that the country doctor now observed for the first time in his life. Her skin was rosy over her cheekbones. A pair of shell-rimmed eyeglasses, like a man's, was tucked between two buttons of her bodice.

When Charles came back downstairs after going up to take leave of Monsieur Rouault, he found her standing with her forehead pressed against the windowpane, looking out at the garden, where the beanpoles had been thrown down by the wind. She turned around.

"Are you looking for something?" she asked.

"For my riding crop," he said.

And he began to rummage on the bed, behind doors, under chairs. It had fallen on the floor between the grain bags and the wall. Mademoiselle Emma caught sight of it and reached for it, bending down across the sacks. Charles hurried over politely, and as he, too, stretched out his arm he felt his body in slight contact with the girl's back, bent there beneath him. She stood up, blushing crimson, and glanced at him over her shoulder as she handed him his crop.

Instead of returning to Les Bertaux three days later, as he had promised, he went back the very next day, then twice a week regularly, not to mention unscheduled calls he made from time to time, as though by chance.

Everything went well; the bone knit according to the rules; and after forty-six days, when Monsieur Rouault was seen trying to get around his farmyard by himself, everyone began to think of Monsieur Bovary as a man of great competence. Monsieur Rouault said he wouldn't have been better mended by the biggest doctors of Yvetot or even Rouen.

As for Charles, he didn't ask himself why he enjoyed going to Les Bertaux. Had he thought of it, he would doubtless have attributed his zeal to the seriousness of the case, or perhaps to the fee he hoped to earn. Still, was that really why his visits to the farm formed so charming a contrast to the drabness of the rest of his life? On such days he would rise early, set off at a gallop, urge his horse; and when he was almost there he would dismount to dust his shoes on the grass, and put on his black gloves. He enjoyed the moment of arrival, the feel of the gate as it yielded against his shoulder; he enjoyed the rooster crowing on the wall, the farm boys coming to greet him. He enjoyed the barn and the stables; he enjoyed Monsieur Rouault, who would clap him in the palm of the hand and call him his "savior"; he enjoyed hearing Mademoiselle Emma's little sabots on the newly washed flagstones of the kitchen floor. With their high heels they made her a little taller; and when she walked in them ahead of him their wooden soles kept coming up with a quick, sharp, tapping sound against the leather of her shoes.

She always accompanied him to the foot of the steps outside the door. If his horse hadn't been brought around she would wait there with him. At such moments they had already said good-bye, and stood there silent; the breeze eddied around her, swirling the stray wisps of hair at her neck, or sending her apron strings flying like streamers around her waist. Once she was standing there on a day of thaw, when the bark of the trees in the farmyard was oozing sap and the snow was melting on the roofs. She went inside for her parasol, and opened it. The parasol was of rosy iridescent silk, and the sun pouring through it painted the white skin of her face with flickering patches of light. Beneath it she smiled at the springlike warmth; and drops of water could be heard falling one by one on the taut moiré.

During the first period of Charles's visits to Les Bertaux, Madame Bovary never failed to ask about the patient's progress; and in her double-entry ledger she had given Monsieur Rouault a fine new page to himself. But when she heard that he had a daughter she began to make inquiries; and she learned that Mademoiselle Rouault had had her schooling in a convent, with the Ursuline nuns—had received, as the saying went, a "fine education," in the course of which she had been taught dancing, geography, drawing, needlework and a little piano. Think of that!

"So that's why he brightens up when he goes there! That's why he wears his new waistcoat, even in the rain! Ah! So she's at the bottom of it!"

Instinctively she hated her. At first she relieved her feelings by making insinuations. Charles didn't get them. Then she let fall parenthetical remarks which he left unanswered out of fear of a storm; and finally she was driven to point-blank reproaches which he didn't know how to answer. Why was it that he kept going back to Les Bertaux, now that Monsieur Rouault was completely mended and hadn't even paid his bill? Ah! Because there was *a certain person* there. Somebody who knew how to talk. Somebody who did embroidery. Somebody clever. That's what he enjoyed: he had to have city girls! And she went on:

"Rouault's daughter, a city girl! Don't make me laugh! The grandfather was a shepherd, and there's a cousin who barely escaped sentence for assault and battery. Scarcely good reasons for giving herself airs, for wearing silk dresses to church like a countess! Besides—her father, poor fellow: if it hadn't been for last year's colza crop he'd have been hard put to it to pay his debts."

For the sake of peace, Charles stopped going to Les Bertaux. Heloise had made him swear—his hand on his prayer book—that he would never go back there again: she had accomplished it after much sobbing and kissing, in the midst of a great amorous explosion. He yielded; but the strength of his desire kept protesting against the servility of his behavior, and with a naïve sort of hypocrisy he told himself that this very prohibition against seeing her implicitly allowed him to love her. And then the widow he was married to was skinny; she was long in the tooth; all year round she wore a little black shawl with a corner hanging down between her shoulder blades; her rigid form was always sheathed in dresses that were like scabbards; they were always too short; they showed her ankles, her big shoes, and her shoelaces crisscrossing their way up her gray stockings.

Charles's mother came to see them from time to time; but after a few days she invariably took on her daughter-in-law's sharpness against her son, and like a pair of knives they kept scarifying him with their comments and criticisms. He oughtn't to eat so much! Why always offer a drink to everyone who called? So pigheaded not to wear flannel underwear!

Early in the spring it happened that a notary in Ingouville, custodian of the Widow Dubuc's capital, sailed away one fine day, taking with him all his clients' money. To be sure, Heloise still owned her house in the rue Saint-François in Dieppe, as well as a six-thousand-franc interest in a certain ship; nevertheless, of the great fortune she'd always talked so much about, nothing except a few bits of furniture and some clothes had ever been seen in the household. Now, inevitably, everything came under investigation. The house in Dieppe, it turned out, was mortgaged up to its eaves; what she had placed with the notary, God only knew; and her share in the boat didn't amount to more than three thousand. So she'd been lying—lying all along, the dear, good lady! In his rage the older Monsieur Bovary dashed a chair to pieces on the floor and accused his wife of ruining their son's life by yoking him to such an ancient nag, whose harness was worth even less than her carcass. They came to Tostes. The four of them had it out. There were scenes. The weeping Heloise threw herself into her husband's arms and appealed to him to defend her against his parents. Charles began to take her part. The others flew into a rage and left.

But—"the fatal blow had been struck." A week later she was hanging out washing in her yard when suddenly she began to spit blood; and the next day, while Charles was looking the other way, drawing the window curtain, she gave a cry, then a sigh, and fainted. She was dead! Who would have believed it?

When everything was over at the cemetery, Charles returned to the house. There was no one downstairs, and he went up to the bedroom. One of her dresses was still hanging in the alcove. He stayed there until dark, leaning against the writing desk, his mind full of sad thoughts. Poor thing! She had loved him, after all.

III

One morning Monsieur Rouault came to pay Charles for setting his leg— seventy-five francs in two-franc pieces, with a turkey thrown in for good measure. He had heard of his bereavement, and offered him what consolation he could.

"I know what it is," he said, patting him on the shoulder. "I've been through just what you're going through. When I lost my wife I went out into the fields to be by myself. I lay down under a tree and cried. I talked to God, told him all kinds of crazy things. I wished I were dead, like the maggoty moles I saw hanging on the branches. And when I thought of how other men were holding their wives in their arms at that very moment, I began to pound my stick on the ground. I was almost out of my mind. I couldn't eat: the very thought of going to a café made me sick—you'd never believe it. Well, you know, what with one day gradually nosing out another, and spring coming on top of winter and then fall after the summer—it passed bit by bit, drop by drop. It just went away; it disappeared; I mean it grew less and less—there's always part of it you never get rid of entirely; you always feel something here." And he put his hand on his chest. "But it happens to us all, and you mustn't let yourself go, you mustn't want to die just because other people are dead. You must brace up, Monsieur Bovary: things will get better. Come and see us. My daughter talks about you every once in a while; she says you've probably forgotten her. Spring will soon be here: you and I'll go out after a rabbit—it will take your mind off things."

Charles took his advice. He went back to Les Bertaux; he found it unchanged since yesterday—since five months before, that is. The pear trees were already in flower; and the sight of Monsieur Rouault coming and going normally around the place made everything livelier.

The farmer seemed to think that the doctor's grief-stricken condition called for a special show of consideration, and he urged him to keep his hat on, addressed him in a low voice as though he were ill, and even pretended to be angry that no one had thought to cook him something special and light, like custard or stewed pears. He told him funny stories. Charles found himself laughing, but then the thought of his wife returned to sober him. By the end of the meal he had forgotten her again.

He thought of her less and less as he grew used to living alone. The novelty and pleasure of being independent soon made solitude more bearable. Now he could change his meal hours at will, come and go without explanation, stretch out across the bed if he was particularly tired. So he pampered and coddled himself and accepted all the comforting everyone offered. Besides, he wife's death had helped him quite a bit professionally: for a month or so everyone had kept saying, "Poor young man! What a tragedy!" His reputation grew; more and more patients came. Now he went to Les Bertaux whenever he pleased. He was aware of a feeling of hope—nothing very specific, a vague happiness: he thought himself better-looking when he stood at the mirror to brush his whiskers.

One day he arrived about three o'clock. Everyone was in the fields. He went into the kitchen, and at first didn't see Emma. The shutters were closed; the sun, streaming in between the slats, patterned the floor with long thin stripes that broke off at the corners of the furniture and quivered on the ceiling. On the table, flies were climbing up the sides of glasses that had recently been used, and buzzing as they struggled to keep from drowning in the cider at the bottom. The light coming down the chimney turned the soot on the fireback to velvet and gave a bluish cast to the cold ashes. Between the window and the hearth Emma sat sewing; her shoulders were bare, beaded with little drops of sweat.

Country-style, she offered him something to drink. He refused, she insisted, and finally suggested with a laugh that he take a liqueur with her. She brought a bottle of curaçao from the cupboard, reached to a high shelf for two liqueur glasses, filled one to the brim and poured a few drops in the other. She touched her glass to his and raised it to her mouth. Because it was almost empty she had to bend backwards to be able to drink; and with her head tilted back, her neck and her lips outstretched, she began to laugh at tasting nothing; and then the tip of her tongue came out from between her small teeth and began daintily to lick the bottom of the glass.

She sat down again and resumed her work—she was darning a white cotton stocking. She sewed with her head bowed, and she did not speak: nor did Charles. A draft was coming in under the door and blowing a little dust across the stone floor; he watched it drift, and was aware of a pulsating sound inside his head—that, and the clucking of a laying hen outside in the yard. From time to time Emma cooled her cheeks with the palms of her hands, and then cooled her hands against the iron knobs of the tall andirons.

She complained that the heat had been giving her dizzy spells, and asked whether sea bathing would help; then she began to talk about her convent school and Charles about his lycée: words came to them both. They went upstairs to her room. She showed him her old music exercise books, and the little volumes and the oak-leaf wreaths—the latter now lying abandoned in the bottom of a cupboard—that she had won as prizes. Then she spoke of her mother, and the cemetery, and took him out to the garden to see the bed where she picked flowers the first Friday of every month to put on her grave. But their gardener had no understanding of such things: farm help was so trying! She would love, if only for the winter, to live in the city—though she had to say that it was really in summer, with the days so long, that the country was most boring of all. Depending on what she talked about, her voice was clear, or shrill, or would grow suddenly languorous and trail off almost into a murmur, as though she were speaking to herself. One moment she would be gay and wide-eyed; the next, she would half shut her eyelids and seem to be drowned in boredom, her thoughts miles away.

That evening, on his homeward ride, Charles went over one by one the things she had said, trying to remember her exact words and sense their implications, in an effort to picture what her life had been like before their meeting. But in his thoughts he could never see her any differently from the way she had been when he had seen her the first time, or as she had been just now, when he left her. Then he wondered what would become of her, whether she would marry, and whom. Alas! Monsieur Rouault was very rich, and she . . . so beautiful! But Emma's face appeared constantly before his eyes, and in his ears there was a monotonous throbbing, like the humming of a top: "But why don't *you* get married! Why don't *you* get married!"

That night he didn't sleep, his throat was tight, he was thirsty; he got up to drink from his water jug and opened the window; the sky was covered with stars, a hot wind was blowing, dogs were barking in the distance. He stared out in the direction of Les Bertaux.

After all, he thought, nothing would be lost by trying; and he resolved to ask his question when the occasion presented itself; but each time it did, the fear of not finding the proper words paralyzed his lips.

Actually, Rouault wouldn't have been a bit displeased to have someone take his daughter off his hands. She was of no use to him on the farm. He didn't really hold it against her, being of the opinion that she was too clever to have anything to do with farming—that accursed occupation that had never yet made a man a millionaire. Far from having grown rich at it, the poor fellow was losing money every year: he more than held his own in the market place, where he relished all the tricks of the trade, but no one was less suited than he to the actual growing of crops and the managing of a farm. He never lifted a finger if he could help it, and never spared any expense in matters of daily living: he insisted on good food, a good fire, and a good bed. He liked his cider hard, his leg of mutton rare, his coffee well laced with brandy. He took his meals in the kitchen, alone, facing the fire, at a little table that was brought in to him already set, like on the stage.

So when he noticed that Charles tended to be flushed in his daughter's presence—meaning that one of these days he would ask for her hand—he pondered every aspect of the question well in advance. Charles was a bit namby-pamby, not his dream of a son-in-law; but he was said to be reliable, thrifty, very well educated; and he probably wouldn't haggle too much over the dowry. Moreover, Rouault was soon going to have to sell twenty-two of his acres: he owed considerable to the mason and considerable to the harness maker, and the cider press needed a new shaft. "If he asks me for her," he said to himself, "I won't refuse."

Toward the beginning of October, Charles spent three days at Les Bertaux. The last day had slipped by like the others, with the big step put off from one minute to the next. Rouault was escorting him on the first lap of his homeward journey; they were walking along a sunken road; they were just about to part—the moment had come. Charles gave himself to the corner of the hedge; and finally, when they had passed it: "Monsieur Rouault," he murmured, "there's something I'd like to say to you."

They stopped. Charles fell silent.

"Well, tell me what's on your mind! I know it already anyway!" Rouault said with a gentle laugh.

"Monsieur Rouault . . . Monsieur Rouault . . ." Charles stammered.

"Personally I wouldn't like anything better," continued the farmer. "I imagine the child agrees with me, but we'd better ask her. I'll leave you here now, and go back to the house. If it's 'Yes'—now listen to what I'm saying—you won't have to come in: there are too many people around, and besides she'd be too upset. But to take you off the anxious seat I'll slam a shutter against the wall: you can look back and see, if you lean over the hedge."

And he went off.

Charles tied his horse to a tree. He hastily stationed himself on the path and waited. Half an hour went by; then he counted nineteen minutes by his watch. Suddenly there was a noise against the wall: the shutter had swung back; the catch was still quivering.

The next morning he was at the farm by nine. Emma blushed when he entered, laughing a little in an attempt to be casual. Rouault embraced his future son-in-law. They postponed all talk of financial arrangements: there was plenty of time, since the wedding couldn't decently take place before the end of Charles's mourning—that is, toward the spring of the next year.

It was a winter of waiting. Mademoiselle Rouault busied herself with her trousseau. Part of it was ordered in Rouen, and she made her slips and nightcaps herself, copying fashion drawings that she borrowed. Whenever Charles visited the farm they spoke about preparations for the wedding, discussing which room the dinner should be served in, wondering how many courses to have and what the entrees should be.

Emma herself would have liked to be married at midnight, by torchlight; but Rouault wouldn't listen to the idea. So there was the usual kind of wedding, with forty-three guests, and everybody was sixteen hours at table, and the festivities began all over again the next day and even carried over a little into the days following.

IV

The invited guests arrived early in a variety of vehicles—one-horse shays, two-wheeled charabancs, old gigs without tops, vans with leather curtains; and the young men from the nearest villages came in farm carts, standing one behind the other along the sides and grasping the rails to keep from being thrown, for the horses trotted briskly and the roads were rough. They came from as far as twenty-five miles away, from Goderville, from Normanville, from Cany. All the relations of both families had been asked, old quarrels had been patched up, letters sent to acquaintances long lost sight of.

From time to time the crack of a whip would be heard behind the hedge, then after a moment the gate would open and a cart would roll in; it would come at a gallop as far as the doorstep, then stop with a lurch, and out would pour its passengers, rubbing their knees and stretching their arms. The ladies wore country-style headdresses and city-style gowns, with gold watch chains, tippets (the ends crossed and tucked into their belts), or small colored fichus[2] attached at the back with pins and leaving the neck bare. The boys, attired exactly like their papas, looked ill at ease in their new clothes (and indeed many of them were wearing leather shoes that day for the first time in their lives); and next to them would be some speechless, gangling girl of fourteen or sixteen, probably their cousin or their older sister, flushed and awkward

2. Triangular scarves. *Tippets:* shoulder capes with hanging ends.

in her white First Communion dress let down for the occasion, her hair sticky with scented pomade, terribly worried lest she dirty her gloves. Since there weren't enough stable hands to unharness all the carriages, the men rolled up their sleeves and went to it themselves. According to their social status, they wore tail coats, frock coats, long jackets or short jackets. The tail coats were worthy garments, each of them a prized family possession taken out of the closet only on great occasions; the frock coats had great flaring skirts that billowed in the wind, cylindrical collars, and pockets as capacious as bags; the long jackets were double-breasted, of coarse wool, and usually worn with a cap of some kind, its peak trimmed with brass; and the short jackets were very short indeed, with two back buttons set close together like a pair of eyes, and stiff tails that looked as though a carpenter had hacked them with his axe out of a single block of wood. A few guests (these, of course, would sit at the foot of the table) wore dress smocks—that is, smocks with turned-down collars, fine pleating at the back, and stitched belts low on the hips.

And the shirts! They bulged like breastplates. Every man was freshly shorn; ears stood out from heads; faces were of a holiday smoothness. Some of the guests from farthest away, who had got up before dawn and had to shave in the dark, had slanting gashes under their noses, or patches of skin the size of a three-franc piece peeled from their jaws. During the journey their wounds had been inflamed by the wind, and as a result red blotches adorned many a big beaming white face.

Since the mayor's office was scarcely more than a mile from the farm, the wedding party went there on foot and came back the same way after the church ceremony. The procession was compact at first, like a bright sash festooning the countryside as it followed the narrow path winding between the green grain fields; but soon it lengthened out and broke up into different groups, which lingered to gossip along the way. The fiddler went first, the scroll of his violin gay with ribbons; then came the bridal pair; then their families; then their friends in no particular order; and last of all the children, having a good time pulling the bell-shaped flowers from the oat stalks or playing among themselves out of sight of their elders. Emma's gown was too long, and trailed a little; from time to time she stopped to pull it up; and at such moments she would carefully pick off the coarse grasses and thistle spikes with her gloved fingers, as Charles waited empty-handed beside her. Rouault, in a new silk hat, the cuffs of his black tail coat coming down over his hands as far as his fingertips, had given his arm to the older Madame Bovary. The older Monsieur Bovary, who looked on all these people with contempt, and had come wearing simply a single-breasted overcoat of military cut, was acting the barroom gallant with a blond young peasant girl. She bobbed and blushed, tongue-tied and confused. The other members of the wedding party discussed matters of business, or played tricks behind each other's backs, their spirits already soaring in anticipation of the fun. If they listened, they could hear the steady scraping of the fiddle in the fields. When the fiddler realized that he had left everyone far behind, he stopped for breath, carefully rubbed his bow with rosin to make his strings squeak all the better, and then set off again on his course, raising and lowering the neck of his violin to keep time. The sound of the instrument frightened away all the birds for a long distance ahead.

The table was set up in the carriage shed. On it were four roasts of beef, six fricassees of chicken, a veal casserole, three legs of mutton, and in the center a charming little suckling pig flanked by four *andouilles à l'oseille*—pork sausages flavored with sorrel. At the corners stood decanters of brandy. The sweet cider foamed up around its corks, and before anyone was seated, every glass had been filled to the brim with wine. Great dishes of yellow custard, their smooth surfaces decorated with the newlyweds' initials in candy-dot arabesques, were set trembling whenever the table was given the slightest knock. The pies and cakes had been ordered from a caterer in Yvetot. Since he was just starting up in the district, he had gone to considerable pains; and when dessert time came he himself brought to the table a wedding cake that drew exclamations from all. Its base was a square of blue cardboard representing a temple with porticos and colonnades and adorned on all sides with stucco statuettes standing in niches spangled with gold-paper stars. The second tier was a medieval castle in *gâteau de Savoie*, surrounded by miniature fortifications of angelica, almonds, raisins, and orange sections. And finally, on the topmost layer—which was a green meadow, with rocks, jelly lakes, and boats of hazelnut shells—a little Cupid was swinging in a chocolate swing. The tips of the two uprights, the highest points of the whole, were two real rosebuds.

The banquet went on till nightfall. Those who grew tired of sitting took a stroll in the yard or played a kind of shuffleboard in the barn; then they returned to table. A few, toward the end, fell asleep and snored. But everything came to life again with the coffee: there were songs, displays of strength. The men lifted weights, played the game of passing their heads under their arms while holding one thumb on the table, tried to raise carts to their shoulders. Dirty jokes were in order; the ladies were kissed. In the evening, when it came time to go, the horses, stuffed with oats to the bursting point, could scarcely be forced between the shafts; they kicked and reared, broke their harness, brought curses or laughs from their masters. And all night long, under the light of the moon on the country roads, runaway carts were bouncing along ditches at a gallop, leaping over gravel piles and crashing into banks, with women leaning out trying desperately to seize the reins.

Those who stayed at Les Bertaux spent the night drinking in the kitchen. The children fell asleep on the floor.

The bride had begged her father that she be spared the usual pranks. However, a fishmonger cousin (who had actually brought a pair of soles as a wedding present) was just beginning to spurt water from his mouth through the keyhole when Rouault came along and stopped him, explaining that the importance of his son-in-law's position didn't permit such unseemliness. The cousin complied very grudgingly. In his heart he accused Rouault of being a snob, and he joined a group of four or five other guests, who had happened several times in succession to be given inferior cuts of meat at table and so considered that they, too, had been badly treated. The whole group sat there whispering derogatory things about their host, and in veiled language expressed hopes for his downfall.

The older Madame Bovary hadn't opened her mouth all day. No one had consulted her about her daughter-in-law's bridal dress, or the arrangements for the party: she went up to bed early. Her husband didn't accompany her; instead, he sent to Saint-Victor for cigars and sat up till dawn smoking and drinking kirsch and hot water. This variety of grog was new to his fellow guests, and made him feel that their respect for him rose all the higher.

Charles was far from being a wag. He had been dull throughout the festivities, responding but feebly to the witticisms, puns, *doubles-entendres,* teasings and dubious jokes that everyone had felt obliged to toss at him from the moment they had sat down to the soup.

The next day, however, he seemed a different man. It was he who gave the impression of having lost his virginity overnight: the bride made not the slightest sign that could be taken to betray anything at all. Even the shrewdest were nonplused, and stared at her with the most intense curiosity whenever she came near. But Charles hid nothing. He addressed her as *"ma femme,"* using the intimate *"tu,"*[3] kept asking everyone where she was and looking for her everywhere, and often took her out into the yard, where he could be glimpsed through the trees with his arm around her waist, leaning over her as they walked, his head rumpling the yoke of her bodice.

Two days after the wedding the bridal pair left: because of his patients Charles could stay away no longer. Rouault had them driven to Tostes in his cart, going with them himself as far as Vassonville. There he kissed his daughter a last time, got out, and retraced his way. When he had walked about a hundred yards he stopped; and the sight of the cart disappearing in the distance, its wheels spinning in the dust, made him utter a deep sigh. He remembered his own wedding, his own earlier days, his wife's first pregnancy. He, too, had been very happy, the day he had taken her from her father's house to his own. She had ridden pillion behind him as their horse trotted over the snow, for it had been close to Christmas and the fields were white; she had clutched him with one arm, her basket hooked over the other; the wind was whipping the long lace streamers of her *coiffure cauchoise*[4] so that at times they blew across his mouth; and by turning his head he could see her rosy little face close behind his shoulder, smiling silently at him under the gold buckle of her bonnet. From time to time she would warm her fingers by sliding them inside his coat. How long ago it all was! Their boy would be thirty if he were alive today! Then he looked back again, and there was nothing to be seen on the road. He felt dismal, like a stripped and empty house; and as tender memories and black thoughts mingled in his brain, dulled by the vapors of the feast, he considered for a moment turning his steps toward the church. But he was afraid that the sight of it might make him even sadder, so he went straight home.

Monsieur and Madame Charles reached Tostes about six o'clock. The neighbors came to their windows to see their doctor's new wife.

The elderly maidservant appeared, greeted them, apologized for not having dinner ready, and suggested that Madame, in the meantime, might like to make a tour of inspection of her house.

v

The brick house-front was exactly flush with the street, or rather the road. Behind the door hung a coat with a short cape, a bridle, and a black leather cap; and on the floor in the corner lay a pair of gaiters still caked with mud.

---

3. The intimate form of "you" (French). *Ma femme:* my wife (French).   4. Cauchois headdress.

To the right was the parlor, which served as both dining and sitting room. A canary yellow wallpaper, set off at the top by a border of pale flowers, rippled everywhere on its loose canvas lining; white calico curtains edged with red braid hung crosswise down the length of the windows; and on the narrow mantelpiece a clock ornamented with a head of Hippocrates stood proudly between two silver-plated candlesticks under oval glass domes. Across the hall was Charles's small consulting room, about eighteen feet wide, with a table, three straight chairs and an office armchair. There was a fir bookcase with six shelves, occupied almost exclusively by a set of the *Dictionary of the Medical Sciences,* its pages uncut but its binding battered by a long succession of owners. Cooking smells seeped through the wall during office hours, and the patients' coughs and confidences were quite audible in the kitchen. In the rear, opening directly into the yard (which contained the stables), was a big ramshackle room with an oven, now serving as woodshed, wine bin and storeroom; it was filled with old junk, empty barrels, broken tools, and a quantity of other objects all dusty and nondescript.

The long narrow garden ran back between two clay walls covered with espaliered apricot trees to the thorn hedge that marked it off from the fields. In the middle was a slate sundial on a stone pedestal. Four beds of scrawny rose bushes were arranged symmetrically around a square plot given over to vegetables. At the far end, under some spruces, a plaster priest stood reading his breviary.

Emma went up to the bedrooms. The first was empty; in the second, the conjugal chamber, a mahogany bed stood in an alcove hung with red draperies. A box made of seashells adorned the chest of drawers; and on the desk near the window, standing in a decanter and tied with white satin ribbon, was a bouquet of orange blossoms—a bride's bouquet: the *other* bride's bouquet! She stared at it. Charles noticed, picked it up, and took it to the attic; and as her boxes and bags were brought up and placed around her, she sat in an armchair and thought of her own bridal bouquet, which was packed in one of those very boxes, wondering what would be done with it if she were to die.

She spent the first few days planning changes in the house. She took the domes off the candlesticks, had the parlor repapered, the stairs painted, and seats made to go around the sundial in the garden. She even made inquiries as to the best way of installing a fountain and a fish pond. And her husband, knowing that she liked to go for drives, bought a secondhand two-wheeled buggy. With new lamps and quilted leather mudguards it looked almost like a tilbury.

He was happy now, without a care in the world. A meal alone with her, a stroll along the highway in the evening, the way she touched her hand to her hair, the sight of her straw hat hanging from a window hasp, and many other things in which it had never occurred to him to look for pleasure—such now formed the steady current of his happiness. In bed in the morning, his head beside hers on the pillow, he would watch the sunlight on the downy gold of her cheeks, half covered by the scalloped tabs of her nightcap. Seen from so close, her eyes appeared larger than life, especially when she opened and shut her eyelids several times on awakening: black when looked at in shadow, dark blue in bright light, they seemed to contain layer upon layer of color, thicker and cloudier beneath, lighter and more transparent toward the lustrous surface. As his own eyes plunged into those depths, he saw himself reflected there in miniature down to his shoulders—his foulard on his head, his nightshirt open. After he had dressed she would go to the window and watch him leave for his rounds; she would lean out between two pots of geraniums, her elbows on the sill, her dressing gown loose around her. In the street, Charles would strap on his spurs at the mounting block; and she would continue to talk to him from above, blowing down to him some bit of flower or leaf she had bitten off in her teeth. It would flutter down hesitantly, weaving semicircles in the air like a bird, and before reaching the ground it would catch in the tangled mane of the old white mare standing motionless at the door. From the saddle Charles would send her a kiss; she would respond with a wave; then she would close the window, and he was off. And on the endless dusty ribbon of the highway, on sunken roads vaulted over by branches, on paths between stands of grain that rose to his knees—the sun on his shoulders and the morning air in his nostrils, his heart full of the night's bliss, his spirit at peace and his flesh content—he would ride on his way ruminating his happiness, like someone who keeps savoring, hours later, the fragrance of the truffles he has eaten for dinner.

Up until now, had there ever been a happy time in his life? His years at the lycée, where he had lived shut in behind high walls, lonely among richer, cleverer schoolmates who laughed at his country accent and made fun of his clothes and whose mothers brought them cookies in their muffs on visiting days? Or later, when he was studying medicine and hadn't enough in his purse to go dancing with some little working girl who might have become his mistress? After that he had lived fourteen months with the widow, whose feet in bed had been like icicles. But now he possessed, and for always, this pretty wife whom he so loved. The universe, for him, went not beyond the silken circuit of her petticoat; and he would reproach himself for not showing her his love, and yearn to be back with her. He would gallop home, rush upstairs, his heart pounding. Emma would be at her dressing table; he would creep up silently behind her and kiss her; she would cry out in surprise.

He couldn't keep from constantly touching her comb, her rings, everything she wore; sometimes he gave her great full-lipped kisses on the cheek, or a whole series of tiny kisses up her bare arm, from her fingertips to her shoulder; and half amused, half annoyed, she would push him away as one does an importunate child.

Before her marriage she had thought that she had love within her grasp; but since the happiness which she had expected this love to bring her hadn't come, she supposed she must have been mistaken. And Emma tried to imagine just what was meant, in life, by the words "bliss," "passion," and "rapture"—words that had seemed so beautiful to her in books.

VI

She had read *Paul and Virginia*,[5] and had dreamed of the bamboo cabin, of the Negro Domingo and the dog Fidèle; and especially she dreamed that she, too, had a sweet little brother for a devoted friend, and that he climbed trees as tall as church steeples to pluck her their crimson fruit, and came running barefoot over the sand to bring her a bird's nest.

5. A 1784 story of the sentimental tragic love of two young people on the tropical island of Île de France (today, Mauritius). It was the most popular work of Bernardin de Saint-Pierre (1737–1814).

When she was thirteen, her father took her to the city to enter her as a boarder in the convent. They stayed at a hotel near Saint-Gervais, where their supper plates were decorated with scenes from the life of Mademoiselle de La Vallière.[6] The explanatory captions, slashed here and there by knife scratches, were all in praise of piety, the sensibilities of the heart, and the splendors of the court.

Far from being unhappy in the convent, at first, she enjoyed the company of the nuns: it was fun when they took her to the chapel, down a long corridor from the refectory. She rarely played during recess, and she was very quick at catechism: it was always Mademoiselle Rouault who answered Monsieur le vicaire's hardest questions. As she continued to live uninterruptedly in the insipid atmosphere of the classrooms, among the white-faced women with their brass crucifixes dangling from their rosaries, she gently succumbed to the mystical languor induced by the perfumes of the altar, the coolness of the holy-water fonts, the gleaming of the candles. Instead of following the Mass she kept her prayer book open at the holy pictures with their sky-blue borders; and she loved the Good Shepherd, the Sacred Heart pierced by sharp arrows, and poor Jesus stumbling and falling under his cross. To mortify herself she tried to go a whole day without eating. She looked for some vow that she might accomplish.

When she went to confession she invented small sins in order to linger on her knees there in the darkness, her hands joined, her face at the grille, the priest whispering just above her. The metaphors constantly used in sermons—"betrothed," "spouse," "heavenly lover," "mystical marriage"— excited her in a thrilling new way.

Every evening before prayers a piece of religious writing was read aloud in study hall. During the week it would be some digest of Biblical history or the Abbé Frayssinous's lectures; on Sunday it was always a passage from the *Génie du Christianisme*,[7] offered as entertainment. How intently she listened, the first times, to the ringing lamentations of that romantic melancholy, echoed and reechoed by all the voices of earth and heaven! Had her childhood been spent in cramped quarters behind some city shop, she might have been open to the lyric appeal of nature—which usually reaches us only by way of literary interpretations. But she knew too much about country life: she was well acquainted with lowing herds, with dairy maids and ploughs. From such familiar, peaceful aspects, she turned to the picturesque. She loved the sea for its storms alone, cared for vegetation only when it grew here and there among ruins. She had to extract a kind of personal advantage from things; and she rejected as useless everything that promised no immediate gratification—for her temperament was more sentimental than artistic, and what she was looking for was emotions, not scenery.

At the convent there was an old spinster who came for a week every month to look after the linen. As a member of an ancient noble family ruined by the Revolution she was a protégée of the archdiocese; and she ate at the nuns' table in the refectory and always stayed for a chat with them before returning upstairs to her work. The girls often slipped out of study-hall to

---

6. One of Louis XIV's mistresses, whose mythologized character is familiar to all readers of Alexandre Dumas's *Le Vicomte de Bragelonne* (a sequel to *The Three Musketeers*). 7. An enormously influential book (1802), by François-René de Chateaubriand, celebrating the truths and beauties of Roman Catholicism, just before Napoleon's concordat with Rome. Denis de Frayssinous (1765–1841) was a popular preacher who wrote *Défense du Christianisme* (1825). Under Louis XVIII (restored to the throne after the fall of Napoleon I) he became a bishop and minister of ecclesiastical affairs.

pay her a visit. She had a repertoire of eighteenth-century love songs, and sang them in a low voice as she sewed. She told stories, kept the girls abreast of the news, did errands for them in the city, and to the older ones would surreptitiously lend one of the novels she always carried in her apron pocket—novels of which the good spinster herself was accustomed to devour long chapters in the intervals of her task. They were invariably about love affairs, lovers, mistresses, harassed ladies swooning in remote pavilions. Couriers were killed at every relay, horses ridden to death on every page; there were gloomy forests, broken hearts, vows, sobs, tears and kisses, skiffs in the moonlight, nightingales in thickets; the noblemen were all brave as lions, gentle as lambs, incredibly virtuous, always beautifully dressed, and wept copiously on every occasion. For six months, when she was fifteen, Emma begrimed her hands with this dust from old lending libraries. Later, reading Walter Scott, she became infatuated with everything historical and dreamed about oaken chests and guardrooms and troubadours. She would have liked to live in some old manor, like those long-waisted chatelaines who spent their days leaning out of fretted Gothic casements, elbow on parapet and chin in hand, watching a white-plumed knight come galloping out of the distance on a black horse. At that time she worshiped Mary Queen of Scots, and venerated women illustrious or ill-starred. In her mind Joan of Arc, Héloise, Agnès Sorel, La Belle Ferronière and Clémence Isaure[8] stood out like comets on the shadowy immensity of history; and here and there (though less clearly outlined than the others against the dim background, and quite unrelated among themselves) were visible also St. Louis and his oak, the dying Bayard, certain atrocities of Louis XI, bits of the Massacre of St. Bartholomew, the plumed crest of Henri IV, and, always, the memory of the hotel plates glorifying Louis XIV.[9]

The sentimental songs she sang in music class were all about little angels with golden wings, madonnas, lagoons, gondoliers—mawkish compositions that allowed her to glimpse, through the silliness of the words and the indiscretions of the music, the alluring, phantasmagoric realm of genuine feeling. Some of her schoolmates brought to the convent the keepsake albums they had received as New Year's gifts. They had to hide them—it was very exciting; they could be read only at night, in the dormitory. Careful not to harm the lovely satin bindings, Emma stared bedazzled at the names of the unknown authors—counts or viscounts, most of them—who had written their signatures under their contributions.

She quivered as she blew back the tissue paper from each engraving: it would curl up into the air, then sink gently down against the page. Behind a balcony railing a young man in a short cloak clasped in his arms a girl in a white dress, a chatelaine bag fastened to her belt; or there were portraits

---

8. A half-fictional lady from Toulouse (14th century), popularized in a novel by Florian as an incarnation of the mystical poetry of the troubadours. Héloise, famous for her love affair with the philosopher Abelard (1101–1164). Agnès Sorel (1422–1450), a mistress of Charles VII, rumored to have been poisoned by the future Louis XI. La Belle Ferronière (d. 1540), one of François I's mistresses, wife of the lawyer Le Ferron, who is said to have contracted syphilis for the mere satisfaction of passing it on to the king.   9. Massacre of the Protestants ordered by Catherine de Medici in the night of August 23, 1572. St. Louis (1215–1270), king of France as Louis IX, led the seventh and eighth crusades and was canonized in 1297. According to tradition, he dispensed justice under an oak tree at Vincennes (near Paris). *Bayard*: Seigneur de Pierre du Terrail (1473–1542), one of the most famous French captains, distinguished himself by feats of bravery during the wars of François I. When dying, he chided the connétable de Bourbon for his treason in a famous speech. Louis XI (b. 1421; ruled 1461–83), ruthlessly suppressed the rebellious noblemen.

of unidentified aristocratic English beauties with blond curls, staring out at you with their wide light-colored eyes from under great straw hats. Some were shown lolling in carriages, gliding through parks; their greyhound ran ahead, and two little grooms in white knee breeches drove the trotting horses. Others, dreaming on sofas, an opened letter lying beside them, gazed at the moon through a window that was half open, half draped with a black curtain. Coy maidens with tears on their cheeks kissed turtledoves through the bars of Gothic bird cages; or, smiling, their cheeks practically touching their own shoulders, they pulled the petals from daisies with pointed fingers that curved up at the ends like Eastern slippers. Then there were sultans with long pipes swooning under arbors in the arms of dancing girls; there were Giaours,[1] Turkish sabres, fezzes. And invariably there were blotchy, pale landscapes of fantastic countries: pines and palms growing together, tigers on the right, a lion on the left, Tartar minarets on the horizon. Roman ruins in the foreground, a few kneeling camels—all of it set in a very neat and orderly virgin forest, with a great perpendicular sunbeam quivering in the water; and standing out on the water's surface—scratched in white on the steel-gray background—a few widely spaced floating swans.

The bracket lamp above Emma's head shone down on those pictures of every corner of the world as she turned them over one by one in the silence of the dormitory, the only sound, coming from the distance, that of some belated cab on the boulevards.

When her mother died, she wept profusely for several days. She had a memorial picture made for herself from the dead woman's hair; and in a letter filled with sorrowful reflections on life that she sent to Les Bertaux, she begged to be buried, when her time came, in the same grave. Her father thought she must be ill, and went to see her. Emma was privately pleased to feel that she had so very quickly attained this ideal of ethereal languor, inaccessible to mediocre spirits. So she let herself meander along Lamartinian[2] paths, listening to the throbbing of harps on lakes, to all the songs of dying swans, to the falling of every leaf, to the flight of pure virgins ascending to heaven, and to the voice of the Eternal speaking in the valleys. Gradually these things began to bore her, but she refused to admit it and continued as before, first out of habit, then out of vanity; until one day she discovered with surprise that the whole mood had evaporated, leaving her heart as free of melancholy as her brow was free of wrinkles.

The good nuns, who had been taking her vocation quite for granted, were greatly surprised to find that Mademoiselle Rouault was apparently slipping out of their control. And indeed they had so deluged her with prayers, retreats, novenas and sermons, preached so constantly the respect due the saints and the martyrs, and given her so much good advice about modest behavior and the saving of her soul, that she reacted like a horse too tightly reined: she balked, and the bit fell from her teeth. In her enthusiasms she had always looked for something tangible: she had loved the church for its flowers, music for its romantic words, literature for its power to stir the passions; and she rebelled before the mysteries of faith just as she grew ever more restive under discipline, which was antipathetic to her nature. When

---

1. Romantic heroes of the outcast desperado type. 2. Alphonse de Lamartine (1790–1869), French Romantic poet whose *Méditations poétiques* (1820) resounds with amorous and religious melancholy.

her father took her out of school no one was sorry to see her go. The Mother Superior, indeed, remarked that she had lately been displaying a certain lack of reverence toward the community.

Back at home, Emma at first enjoyed giving orders to the servants, then grew sick of country life and longed to be back in the convent. By the time Charles first appeared at Les Bertaux she thought that she was cured of illusions—that she had nothing more to learn, and no great emotions to look forward to.

But in her eagerness for a change, or perhaps overstimulated by this man's presence, she easily persuaded herself that love, that marvelous thing which had hitherto been like a great rosy-plumaged bird soaring in the splendors of poetic skies, was at last within her grasp. And now she could not bring herself to believe that the uneventful life she was leading was the happiness of which she had dreamed.

VII

She reflected occasionally that these were, nevertheless, the most beautiful days of her life—the honeymoon days, as people called them. To be sure, their sweetness would be best enjoyed far off, in one of those lands with exciting names where the first weeks of marriage can be savored so much more deliciously and languidly! The post chaise with its blue silk curtains would have climbed slowly up the mountain roads, and the postilion's song would have reechoed among the cliffs, mingling with the tinkling of goat bells and the dull roar of waterfalls. They would have breathed the fragrance of lemon trees at sunset by the shore of some bay; and at night, alone on the terrace of a villa, their fingers intertwined, they would have gazed at the stars and planned their lives. It seemed to her that certain portions of the earth must produce happiness—as though it were a plant native only to those soils and doomed to languish elsewhere. Why couldn't she be leaning over the balcony of some Swiss chalet? Or nursing her melancholy in a cottage in Scotland, with a husband clad in a long black velvet coat and wearing soft leather shoes, a high-crowned hat and fancy cuffs?

She might have been glad to confide all these things to someone. But how speak about so elusive a malaise, one that keeps changing its shape like the clouds and its direction like the winds? She could find no words; and hence neither occasion nor courage came to hand.

Still, if Charles had made the slightest effort, if he had had the slightest inkling, if his glance had a single time divined her thought, it seemed to her that her heart would have been relieved of its fullness as quickly and easily as a tree drops its ripe fruit at the touch of a hand. But even as they were brought closer together by the details of daily life, she was separated from him by a growing sense of inward detachment.

Charles's conversation was flat as a sidewalk, a place of passage for the ideas of everyman; they wore drab everyday clothes, and they inspired neither laughter nor dreams. When he had lived in Rouen, he said, he had never had any interest in going to the theatre to see the Parisian company that was acting there. He couldn't swim or fence or fire a pistol; one day he couldn't tell her the meaning of a riding term she had come upon in a novel.

Wasn't it a man's role, though, to know everything? Shouldn't he be expert at all kinds of things, able to initiate you into the intensities of passion, the refinements of life, all the mysteries? *This* man could teach you nothing; he knew nothing, he wished for nothing. He took it for granted that she was content; and she resented his settled calm, his serene dullness, the very happiness she herself brought him.

She drew occasionally; and Charles enjoyed nothing more than standing beside her watching her bent over her sketchbook, half shutting his eyes the better to see her work, or rolling her bread-crumb erasers between his thumb and finger. As for the piano, the faster her fingers flew the more he marveled. She played with dash, swooping up and down the keyboard without a break. The strings of the old instrument jangled as she pounded, and when the window was open it could be heard to the end of the village. The *huissier's* clerk often stopped to listen as he passed on the road—bareheaded, shuffling along in slippers, holding in his hand the notice he was about to post.

Moreover, Emma knew how to run her house. She let Charles's patients know how much they owed him, writing them nicely phrased letters that didn't sound like bills. When a neighbor came to Sunday dinner she always managed to think up some attractive dish. She would arrange greengages in a pyramid on a bed of vine leaves; she served her jellies not in their jars but neatly turned out on a plate; she spoke of buying finger bowls for dessert. All this redounded greatly to Bovary's credit.

He came to esteem himself the higher for having such a wife. He had two of her pencil sketches framed in wide frames, and hung them proudly in the parlor, at the end of long green cords. Citizens returning from Mass saw him standing on his doorstep, wearing a splendid pair of carpet slippers.

He came home from his rounds late—ten o'clock, sometimes midnight. He was hungry at that hour, and since the servant had gone to bed it was Emma who served him. He would take off his coat to be more comfortable at table, tell her every person he had seen, every village he had been to, every prescription he had written; and he would complacently eat what was left of the stew, pare his cheese, munch an apple, pour himself the last drop of wine. Then he would go up to bed, fall asleep the minute he was stretched on his back, and begin to snore.

He had so long been used to wearing cotton nightcaps that he couldn't get his foulard to stay on his head, and in the morning his hair was all over his face and white with down—the strings of his pillowcase often came undone during the night. He always wore heavy boots, with deep creases slanting from instep to ankle and the rest of the uppers so stiff that they seemed to be made of wood. He said that they were "plenty good enough for the country."

His mother approved his thriftiness. As in the past, she came to visit him whenever there was a particularly violent crisis in her own home; and yet she seemed to be prejudiced against her new daughter-in-law. She considered her "too grand in her tastes for the kind of people they were": the younger Bovarys ran through wood, sugar and candles at the rate of some great establishment; and the amount of charcoal they used would have done the cooking for twenty-five. She rearranged Emma's linen in the closets and taught her to check on the butcher when he delivered the meat. Emma listened to these lectures; Madame Bovary did not stint herself; and all day there would be a tremulous-lipped exchange of *"ma fille"* and *"ma mère,"*[3]

***

3. My mother (French). *Ma fille*: my daughter (French).

each of the ladies uttering the sugary words in a voice that quivered with rage.

In Madame Dubuc's day the older woman had known herself to be the favorite; but now Charles's love for Emma seemed to her a desertion, an invasion of her own right; and she looked on sadly at Charles's happiness, like a ruined man staring through a window at revelers in a house that was once his own. Using the device of "Do you remember?" she reminded him of everything she had suffered and sacrificed for his sake; and contrasting all this with Emma's careless ways she pointed out how wrong he was to adore his wife to the exclusion of herself.

Charles didn't know what to answer. He respected his mother, and his love for his wife was boundless; he considered the former's opinions infallible, and yet Emma seemed to him perfect. After the older Madame Bovary's departure he made a fainthearted attempt to repeat one or two of the milder things he had heard her say, using her own phraseology; but with a word or two Emma convinced him he was wrong, and sent him back to his patients.

Throughout all this, following formulas she believed efficacious, she kept trying to experience love. Under the moonlight in the garden she would recite to Charles all the amorous verses she knew by heart, and sing him soulful sighing songs; but it all left her as unruffled as before, and Charles, too, seemed as little lovesick, as little stirred, as ever.

Having thus failed to produce the slightest spark of love in herself, and since she was incapable of understanding what she didn't experience, or of recognizing anything that wasn't expressed in conventional terms, she reached the conclusion that Charles's desire for her was nothing very extraordinary. His transports had become regularized; he embraced her only at certain times. This had now become a habit like any other—like a dessert that could be counted on to end a monotonous meal.

A gamekeeper whom Monsieur had cured of pneumonia made Madame a present of a little Italian greyhound bitch, and she took her with her whenever she went for a stroll: she did this every now and then, for the sake of a moment's solitude, a momentary relief from the everlasting sight of the back garden and the dusty road.

She would walk to the avenue of beeches at Banneville, near the abandoned pavilion at the corner of the wall along the fields. Rushes grow in the ditch there, tall and sharp edged among the grass.

Once arrived she would look around her, to see whether anything had changed since the last time she had come. The foxgloves and the wallflowers were where they had been; clumps of nettles were still growing around the stones; patches of lichen still clung along the three windows, whose perennially closed shutters were rotting away from their rusty iron bars. Her thoughts would be vague at first, straying like her dog, who would be running in circles, barking at yellow butterflies, chasing field mice, nibbling poppies at the edge of a wheatfield. Then her ideas would gradually focus; and sitting on the grass, jabbing it with little pokes of her parasol, Emma would ask herself again and again: "Why—*why*—did I ever marry?"

She wondered whether some different set of circumstances might not have resulted in her meeting some different man; and she tried to picture those imaginary circumstances, the life they would have brought her, the unknown other husband. However she imagined him, he wasn't a bit like Charles. He might have been handsome, witty, distinguished, magnetic—the kind of man her convent schoolmates had doubtless married. What kind of lives were they leading now? Cities, busy streets, buzzing theatres, brilliant balls—such surroundings afforded them unlimited opportunities for deep emotions and exciting sensations. But *her* life was as cold as an attic facing north; and boredom, like a silent spider, was weaving its web in the shadows, in every corner of her heart. She remembered Prize Days, when she had gone up onto the stage to receive her little wreaths. She had been charming, with her braids, her white dress, her prunella-cloth slippers. Gentlemen had leaned over, when she was back in her seat, and paid her compliments; the courtyard had been full of carriages; guests called good-bye to her as they rolled away; the music teacher with his violin case bowed to her as he passed. How far away it all was! How far!

She would call Djali,[4] take her between her knees, stroke her long delicate head. "Kiss your mistress," she would say, "you happy, carefree thing." The slender Djali would yawn slowly, as a dog does; and the melancholy look in her eyes would touch Emma, and she would liken her to herself, talking to her aloud as though comforting someone in distress.

Sometimes squalls blew up, winds that suddenly swept in from the sea over the plateau of the *pays de Caux*[5] and filled the countryside with fresh, salt-smelling air. The whistling wind would flatten the reeds and rustle the trembling beech leaves, while the tops of the trees swayed and murmured. Emma would pull her shawl close about her shoulders and get up.

Under the double row of trees a green light filtered down through the leaves onto the velvety moss that crunched softly beneath her feet. The sun was setting; the sky showed red between the branches; and the identical trunks of the straight line of trees were like a row of brown columns against a golden backdrop; a terror would seize her, she would call Djali and walk quickly back to Tostes along the highway. There she would sink into an armchair, and sit silent all evening.

Then, late in September, something exceptional happened: she was invited to La Vaubyessard, home of the marquis d'Andervilliers.

The marquis had been a member of the cabinet under the Restoration; and now, hoping to reenter political life, he was paving the way for his candidature to the Chamber of Deputies. He made generous distributions of firewood among the poor in the winter, and in sessions of the departmental council he was always eloquent in demanding better roads for his district. During the hot weather he had had a mouth abscess, which Charles had relieved—miraculously, it seemed—by a timely nick of the scalpel. His steward, sent to Tostes to pay the bill for the operation, reported that evening that he had seen some superb cherries in the doctor's little garden. The cherry trees at La Vaubyessard weren't doing well; Monsieur le marquis asked Charles for a few grafts, made a point of going to thank him personally, saw Emma, and noticed that she had a pretty figure and didn't curtsy like a peasant. So at the château it was decided that the doctor and his young wife could be invited without any transgression of the limits of condescension, and at the same time could be counted on to behave with decorum among their betters.

One Wednesday at three in the afternoon, therefore, Monsieur and

---

4. The name of the little she-goat in Hugo's *Notre Dame de Paris*.   5. Caux country (French; see n. 1, p. 1046).

Madame Bovary set out in their buggy for La Vaubyessard, a large trunk tied on behind and a hatbox in front. Charles had another box between his legs.

They arrived at nightfall, just as lanterns were being lit in the grounds to illuminate the driveway.

VIII

The château, a modern building in the Italian style, with two projecting wings and three entrances along the front, stretched across the far end of a vast expanse of turf where cows grazed in the open spaces between groups of tall trees. Tufts of shrubbery—rhododendrons, syringas and snowballs—made a variegated border along the curving line of the graveled drive. A stream flowed under a bridge; through the evening haze the thatched farm buildings could be seen scattered over a meadow shut in by two gently rising wooded ridges; and at the rear, in among thick plantings of trees, were the two parallel lines of the coach houses and the stables—remains of the original, ancient château that had been torn down.

Charles's buggy drew up before the middle door; servants appeared, then the marquis, who gave the doctor's wife his arm and led her into the entrance hall.

This had a marble floor and a high ceiling; footsteps and voices echoed as in a church. From the far side rose a straight staircase; and to the left a gallery giving on the garden led to the billiard room: the sound of clicking ivory balls could be heard ahead. As she passed through on her way to the drawing room Emma noticed the men around the table: dignified-looking, with cravats reaching up to their chins and decorations on their chests, they smiled silently as they made their shots. On the dark wall-paneling hung great gilded frames, inscribed at the base with names in black letters. "Jean-Antoine d'Andervilliers d'Yverbonville, comte de la Vaubyessard and baron de la Fresnaye, killed at the battle of Coutras,[6] October 20, 1587." Or: "Jean-Antoine-Henry-Guy d'Andervilliers de la Vaubyessard, admiral of the fleet and knight of the order of St. Michael, wounded in the battle of La Hogue, May 29, 1692, died at La Vaubyessard January 23, 1693." The rest were barely visible, for the lamplight was directed down on the green felt of the tables, and much of the room was in shadow. This darkened the row of pictures: only the crackle of their varnish caught an occasional broken gleam, and here and there some detail of painting lighter than the rest stood out from one of the dim, gold-framed rectangles: a pale forehead, two staring eyes, powdered wigs cascading onto red-coated shoulders, a garter buckle high up on a fleshy calf.

The marquis opened the drawing-room door, and one of the ladies rose. It was the marquise, and she came over to Emma, greeted her, drew her down beside her on a settee and talked to her as easily as though they were old acquaintances. She was a woman of forty or so, with fine shoulders, a hooked nose and a drawling voice; on her auburn hair she was wearing a simple bit of lace, the points falling down behind. Close beside her sat a blond young woman in a high-backed chair; and around the fireplace gentlemen with flowers in their buttonholes were chatting with the ladies.

---

6. In the Gironde; the battle was won by Henri de Navarre against the duc de Joyeuse.

Dinner was served at seven. The men, more numerous than the ladies, were put at a table in the entrance hall; the ladies sat down in the dining room, with the marquis and the marquise.

Here the air was warm and fragrant; the scent of flowers and fine linen mingled with the odor of cooked meats and truffles. Candle flames cast long gleams on rounded silver dish-covers; the clouded facets of the cut glass shone palely; there was a row of bouquets all down the table; and on the wide bordered plates the napkins stood like bishops' mitres, each with an oval-shaped roll between its folds. Red lobster claws protruded from platters; oversized fruit was piled up on moss in openwork baskets; quail were served in their plumage; steam rose from open dishes; and the platters of carved meat were brought round by the maître d'hotel himself, grave as a judge in silk stockings, knee breeches, white neckcloth and jabot. He reached them down between the guests, and with a flick of his spoon transferred to each plate the piece desired. Atop the high copper-banded porcelain stove the statue of a woman swathed to the chin in drapery stared down motionless at the company.

Madame Bovary was surprised to notice that several of the ladies had failed to put their gloves in their wineglasses.[7]

At the head of the table, alone among ladies, was an old man. His napkin was tied around his neck like a child's, and he sat hunched over his heaped plate, gravy dribbling from his mouth. The underlids of his eyes hung down and showed red inside, and he wore his hair in a little pigtail wound with black ribbon. This was the marquis's father-in-law, the old duc de Laverdière, favorite of the duc d'Artois in the days of the marquis de Conflans's hunting parties at Le Vaudreuil: he was said to have been Marie-Antoinette's lover between Monsieur de Coigny and Monsieur de Lauzun. He had led a wild, dissipated life, filled with duels, wagers and abductions; he had gone through his money and been the terror of his family. Now, muttering unintelligibly, he pointed his finger at one dish after another, and a servant standing behind his chair shouted their names in his ear. Emma's eyes kept coming back to this pendulous-lipped old man as though he were someone extraordinary, someone august. He had lived at court! He had slept with a queen!

Iced champagne was served, and the feel of the cold wine in her mouth gave Emma a shiver that ran over her from head to toe. She had never seen pomegranates or eaten pineapple. Even the powdered sugar seemed to her whiter and finer than elsewhere.

Then the ladies went up to their rooms to dress for the ball.

Emma devoted herself to her toilette with the meticulous care of an actress the night of her debut. She did her hair as the hairdresser advised, and slipped into her gauzy barège[8] gown, which had been laid out for her on the bed.

Charles's trousers were too tight at the waist. And then, "The shoe straps will interfere with my dancing," he said.

"You? Dance?" Emma cried.

"Of course!"

---

7. The ladies in the provinces, unlike their Paris counterparts, did not drink wine at public dinner parties and signified their intention by putting their gloves in their wineglasses. The fact that they fail to do so suggests to Emma the high degree of sophistication of the company.   8. A filmy fabric.

"But you're crazy! Everybody would laugh. You mustn't. It's not suitable for a doctor, anyway," she added.

Charles said no more. He walked up and down waiting for Emma to be ready.

He saw her from behind in a mirror, between two sconces. Her dark eyes seemed darker than ever. Her hair, drawn down smoothly on both sides and slightly fluffed out over the ears, shone with a blue luster; in her chignon a rose quivered on its flexible stem, with artificial dewdrops at the leaf-tips. Her gown was pale saffron, trimmed with three bunches of pompon roses and green sprays.

Charles came up to kiss her on the shoulder. "Don't!" she cried. "You're rumpling me."

The strains of a violin floated up the stairs; a horn joined in. As Emma went down she had to restrain herself from running.

The quadrilles[9] had begun. More and more guests were arriving; there was something of a crush. Emma stayed near the door on a settee.

When the music stopped, the dance floor was left to the men, who stood there talking in groups, and to the liveried servants, who crossed it with their heavy trays. Along the line of seated women there was a flutter of painted fans; smiles were half hidden behind bouquets; gold-stoppered scent bottles twisted and turned in white-gloved hands, the tight silk binding the wrists and showing the form of the nails. There was a froth of lace around décolletages, a flashing of diamonds at throats; bracelets dangling medals and coins tinkled on bare arms. Hair was sleek and shining in front, twisted and knotted behind; and every coiffure had its wreath or bunch or sprig—of forget-me-nots, jasmine, pomegranate blossoms, wheat-sprays, cornflowers. The dowagers, sitting calm and formidable, wore red headdresses like turbans.

Emma's heart pounded a bit as her partner led her out by the fingertips and she waited in line for the starting signal on the violin. But her nervousness soon wore off, and swaying and nodding in time with the orchestra, she glided forward. She responded with a smile to the violinist's flourishes as he continued to play solo when the other instruments stopped; at such moments the chink of gold pieces came clearly from the gaming tables in the next room; then everything was in full swing again: the cornet blared, once again feet tramped in rhythm, skirts ballooned and brushed together, hands joined and separated; eyes lowered one moment looked intently into yours the next.

Scattered among the dancers or talking in doorways were a number of men—a dozen or so, aged from twenty-five to forty—who were clearly distinguishable from the rest by a certain look of overbreeding common to them all despite differences of age, dress, or feature.

Their coats were better cut and seemed to be of finer cloth; their hair, brought forward in ringlets over the temples, seemed to glisten with more expensive pomades. Their complexion bespoke wealth: they had the pale, very white skin that goes so well with the diaphanous tints of porcelain, the luster of satin, the patina of old wood, and is kept flawless by simple, exquisite fare. These men moved their heads unconstrainedly above low cravats; their long side whiskers drooped onto turned-down collars; they wiped their lips with handkerchiefs that were deliciously scented and monogrammed with

9. A square dance with four couples, fashionable in the 19th century.

huge initials. Those who were beginning to age preserved a youthful look, while the faces of the young had a touch of ripeness. There was an air of indifference about them, a calm produced by the gratification of every passion; and though their manners were suave, one could sense beneath them that special brutality which comes from the habit of breaking down half-hearted resistances that keep one fit and tickle ones vanity—the handling of blooded horses, the pursuit of loose women.

A few steps from Emma a blue-coated gentleman was deep in Italy with a pale young woman in pearls. They were gushing about the massiveness of the piers in St. Peter's, about Tivoli, Vesuvius, Castellamare and the Cascine,[1] the roses in Genoa, the Colosseum by moonlight. And the conversation heard with her other ear was full of words she didn't understand: it was coming from a circle that had formed around a very young man who only the week before had "beaten Miss Arabella and Romulus" and seemed to have won two thousand louis d'or by jumping a certain ditch in England. One of the speakers was complaining that his racers were putting on weight, another that misprints had made the name of his horse unrecognizable in the newspapers.

The air in the ballroom had grown heavy; the lamps were beginning to dim; a number of the men disappeared in the direction of the billiard room. A servant climbed on a chair and broke two panes in a window; at the sound of the smash Madame Bovary turned her head and saw peasants peering in from the garden, their faces pressed against the glass. She thought of Les Bertaux: she saw the farm, the muddy pond, her father in a smock under the apple trees; and she saw herself as she had been there, skimming cream with her finger from the milk jars in the dairy. But amid the splendors of this night her past life, hitherto so vividly present, was vanishing utterly; indeed she was beginning almost to doubt that she had lived it. She was here: and around the brilliant ball was a shadow that veiled all else. She was eating a maraschino ice, at that precise moment, from a gilded silver scallop-shell that she was holding in her left hand; the spoon was between her teeth, her eyes were half shut.

A lady near her dropped her fan just as a gentleman was passing. "Would you be good enough to pick up my fan, Monsieur?" she asked him. "It's there behind the sofa."

The gentleman bowed, and as he stretched out his arm Emma saw the lady toss something into his hat, something white, folded in the shape of a triangle. The gentleman recovered the fan and handed it to the lady respectfully; she thanked him with a nod and began to sniff at her bouquet.

For supper there was an array of Spanish wines and Rhine wines, bisque soup and cream of almond soup. Trafalgar pudding, and platters of all kinds of cold meat in trembling aspic; and after it the carriages began gradually to leave. Drawing back a corner of a muslin curtain, Emma could see their lamps slipping away into the darkness. The settees emptied; some of the card players stayed on; the musicians cooled the tips of their fingers on their tongues; Charles was half asleep, propped up against a door.

At three in the morning the closing cotillion began. Emma had never waltzed. Everyone else was waltzing, including Mademoiselle d'Andervilliers

---

1. A park near Florence. Castellamare is a port south of Naples.

and the marquise; by this time only the hosts and the house guests remained, about a dozen in all. One of the waltzers, whom everyone called simply "Vicomte," and whose very low-cut waistcoat seemed to be molded on his torso, came up to Madame Bovary and for the second time asked her to be his partner. He would lead her, he urged; she'd do very well.

They started out slowly, then quickened their step. They whirled: or, rather, everything—lamps, furniture, walls, floor—whirled around them, like a disc on a spindle. As they passed close to a door the hem of Emma's gown caught on her partner's trousers, and for a moment their legs were all but intertwined; he looked down at her, she up at him; a paralyzing numbness came over her, and she stopped. Then they resumed; and spinning more quickly the vicomte swept her off until they were alone at the very end of the gallery; there, out of breath, she almost fell, and for an instant leaned her head against his chest. Then, still circling, but more slowly, he returned her to her seat. She sank back with her head against the wall, and put her hand over her eyes.

When she opened them, a lady was sitting on a low stool in the middle of the salon, three waltzers on their knees before her. The lady chose the vicomte, and the violin struck up again.

Everyone watched them as they went round and round. She held her body rigid, her head inclined; he maintained the same posture as before, very erect, elbow curved, chin forward. This time he had a partner worthy of him! They danced on and on, long after all the others had dropped out exhausted.

Hosts and guests chatted a few minutes longer; and then, bidding each other good night, or rather good morning, they all went up to bed.

Charles dragged himself up the stairs by the handrail; his legs, he said, were "ready to drop off." He had spent five solid hours on his feet by the card tables watching people play whist, unable to make head or tail of it. So he gave a great sigh of relief when he pulled his shoes off at last.

Emma slipped a shawl over her shoulders, opened the window and leaned out.

The night was very dark. A few drops of rain were falling. She breathed the moist wind, so cooling to her eyeballs. The music was still throbbing in her ears, and she forced herself to stay awake in order to prolong the illusion of this luxurious life she would so soon have to be leaving.

The sky began to lighten. Her glance lingered on the windows of the various rooms as she tried to imagine which of them were occupied by the people she had seen the night before. She longed to know all about their lives, to penetrate into them, to be part of them.

But she was shivering with cold. She undressed and crept into bed beside the sleeping Charles.

Everyone came downstairs for breakfast. The meal lasted ten minutes; to the doctor's surprise, no liqueurs were served. Mademoiselle d'Andervilliers gathered up the remains of the brioches in a basket to feed the swans in the lake; and everyone went for a stroll in the greenhouse, where strange hairy plants were displayed on pyramidal stands, and hanging jars that looked like nests crawling with snakes dripped long, dangling, intertwined green tendrils. From the orangery at the end of the greenhouse a roofed passage led to the outbuildings. To please the young woman the marquis took her to see the stables. Above the basket-shaped racks were porcelain name plates with the horses' names in black letters. Each horse moved restlessly in his stall at the approach of the visitors and the coaxing, clicking sounds they made with their tongues. The boards of the harness-room floor shone like the parquet floor of a drawing room. The carriage harness hung in the middle, on two revolving posts; and the bits, whips, stirrups and curbs were on a line of hooks along the wall.

Charles, meanwhile, had gone to ask a groom to harness his buggy. It was brought around to the front door, and when all the bundles were stowed away, the Bovarys said their thank-yous to the marquis and the marquise and set out for home.

Emma sat silent, watching the turning wheels. Charles drove perched on the edge of the seat, arms wide apart; and the little horse went along at an ambling trot between the overwide shafts. The slack reins slapped against his rump and grew wet with lather; and the case tied on behind thumped heavily and regularly against the body of the buggy.

They were climbing one of the rises near Thibourville when just ahead of them, coming from the opposite direction, there appeared a group of riders, who passed by laughing and smoking cigars. Emma thought she recognized the vicomte; she turned and stared; but all she saw was the bobbing heads of trotting or galloping riders silhouetted against the sky.

Half a mile further along they had to stop: the breeching broke, and Charles mended it with rope. As he was checking his harness he saw something on the ground between the horse's feet, and he picked up a cigar case trimmed with green silk and bearing a crest in the center like a carriage door.

"A couple of cigars in it, too," he said. "I'll smoke them after dinner."

"You've taken up smoking?" Emma demanded.

"Once in a while, when I get the chance."

He put his find in his pocket and gave the pony a flick of the whip.

When they reached home dinner was far from ready. Madame lost her temper. Nastasie talked back.

"It's too much!" Emma cried. "I've had enough of your insolence!" And she gave her notice on the spot.

For dinner there was onion soup and veal with sorrel. Charles, sitting opposite Emma, rubbed his hands with satisfaction: "How good to be home!"

They could hear Nastasie weeping. Charles had an affection for the poor thing. She had kept him company on many an idle evening during his widowerhood. She had been his first patient, his first acquaintance in the village.

"Are you really letting her go?" he finally asked.

"Yes—what's to stop me?"

Then they warmed themselves in the kitchen while their room was made ready. Charles proceeded to smoke. He curled and pursed his lips around the cigar, spat every other minute, shrank back from every puff.

"You're going to make yourself sick," she said scornfully.

He put down his cigar and rushed to the pump for a drink of cold water. Emma snatched the cigar case and quickly flung it to the back of the closet.

The next day was endless. She walked in her garden, up and down the same paths over and over again, stopping to look at the flower beds, the fruit trees, the plaster priest, staring with a kind of amazement at all these things from her past life, things once so familiar. How remote the ball already was! What was it that made tonight seem so very far removed from the day before yesterday? Her visit to La Vaubyessard had opened a breach in her life, like one of those great crevasses that a storm can tear across the face of a mountain in the course of a single night. But there was nothing to do about it. She put her beautiful ball costume reverently away in a drawer—even to her satin slippers, whose soles were yellow from the slippery wax of the dance floor. Her heart was like them: contact with luxury had left an indelible mark on it.

The memory of the ball would not leave her. Every Wednesday she told herself as she woke: "Ah! One week ago . . . two weeks ago . . . three weeks ago, I was there!" Little by little the faces grew confused in her mind; she forgot the tune of the quadrille, the liveries and the splendid rooms became blurred. Some of the details departed—but the yearning remained.

IX

Often when Charles was out she went to the closet and took the green silk cigar case from among the piles of linen where she kept it.

She would look at it, open it, even sniff its lining, fragrant with verbena and tobacco. Whose was it? The vicomte's. A present from his mistress, perhaps. It had been embroidered on some rosewood frame, a charming little piece of furniture kept hidden from prying eyes, over which a pensive girl had bent for hours and hours, her soft curls brushing its surface. Love had breathed through the mesh of the canvas; every stroke of the needle had recorded a hope or a memory; and all these intertwined silken threads bespoke one constant, silent passion. And then one morning the vicomte had taken it away with him. What words had they exchanged as he stood leaning his elbow on one of those elaborate mantelpieces decked with vases of flowers and rococo clocks? She was in Tostes. Whereas he now, was in Paris—in Paris! What was it like, Paris? The very name had such a vastness about it! She repeated it to herself under her breath with a thrill of pleasure; it sounded in her ears like the great bell of a cathedral; it blazed before her eyes everywhere, glamorous even on the labels of her jars of pomade.

At night when the fishmongers passed below her window in their carts, singing *La Marjolaine,* she would awaken; and listening to the sound of the iron-rimmed wheels on the pavement, and then the quick change in the sound as they reached the unpaved road at the end of the village, she would tell herself: "They'll be there tomorrow!"

And she followed them in thought, up and down hills, through villages, along the highway by the light of the stars. Then, somewhere along the way, her dream always petered out.

She bought a map of Paris, and with her fingertip she went for walks. She followed the boulevards, stopping at every corner, between the lines indicating the streets, in front of the white squares that were the houses. Then, closing her tired eyes, she would have a shadowy vision of gas lamps flickering in the wind and carriage steps clattering open in front of theatres.

She subscribed to a women's magazine called *La Corbeille,* and to *Le Sylphe des salons.* She devoured every word of every account of a first night, a horse race, a soirée; she was fascinated by the debut of every new singer, the opening of every new shop. She knew the latest fashions, the addresses of the best tailors, the proper days to go to the Bois[2] and the opera. She pored over the interior decorating details in the novels of Eugène Sue; she read Balzac and George Sand,[3] seeking in their pages vicarious satisfactions for her own desires. She brought her book with her even to meals, and turned the leaves while Charles ate and talked to her. Her readings always brought the vicomte back to her mind: she continually found similarities between him and the fictitious characters. But the circle whose center he was gradually widened; and the halo she had given him spread beyond his image, gilding other dreams.

Paris, city vaster than the ocean, glittered before Emma's eyes in a rosy light. But the teeming life of the tumultuous place was divided into compartments, separated into distinct scenes. Emma was aware of only two or three, which shut out the sight of the others and stood for all of mankind. In drawing rooms with mirrored walls and gleaming floors, around oval tables covered with gold-fringed velvet, moved the world of the ambassadors. It was full of trailing gowns, deep secrets, and unbearable tensions concealed beneath smiles. Then came the circle of the duchesses: here everyone was pale and lay in bed till four; the women—poor darlings!—wore English lace on their petticoat hems; and the men, their true worth unsuspected under their frivolous exteriors, rode horses to death for the fun of it, spent their summers at Baden-Baden,[4] and eventually, when they were about forty, married heiresses. After midnight, the gay, motley world of writers and actresses congregated at candlelit suppers in the private rooms of restaurants. They were profligate as kings, full of idealistic ambitions and fantastic frenzies. They lived on a higher plane than other people, somewhere sublime between heaven and earth, up among the storm clouds. As for the rest of the world, it was in some indeterminate pale beyond the pale; it could scarcely be said to exist. Indeed the closer to her things were, the further away from them her thoughts turned. Everything immediately surrounding her—boring countryside, inane petty bourgeois, the mediocrity of daily life—seemed to her the exception rather than the rule. She had been caught in it all by some accident: out beyond, there stretched as far as eye could see the immense territory of rapture and passions. In her longing she made no difference between the pleasures of luxury and the joys of the heart, between elegant living and sensitive feeling. Didn't love, like Indian plants, require rich soils, special temperatures? Sighs in the moonlight, long embraces, hands bathed in lovers' tears—all the fevers of the flesh and the languors of love—were inseparable from the balconies of great idle-houred castles, from a silk-curtained, thick-carpeted, beflowered boudoir with its bed on a dais, from the sparkle of precious stones and the swank of liveries.

The hired boy at the relay post across the road, who came in every morning to rub down the mare, walked through the hall in his heavy wooden shoes; his smock was in holes, his feet were innocent of stockings. Such was the groom in knee breeches she had to content herself with! When his work was done he left for the day: Charles stabled his horse himself when he returned from his rounds—took off the saddle and attached the halter; and the maid

2. Horse races at the Bois de Boulogne. 3. Pseudonym of Aurore Dudevant (1804–1876), prolific woman novelist. Sue (1804–1857), a popular novelist, was extremely successful at that period, both as a writer and as a fashionable dandy. 4. A fashionable German spa with hot mineral-water springs.

brought a truss of straw and tossed it as best she could into the manger.

To replace Nastasie (who finally departed from Tostes in a torrent of tears) Emma hired a sweet-faced orphan girl of fourteen. She forbade her to wear a cotton nightcap during the day, taught her to address her superiors in the third person, to hand a glass of water on a tray, to knock on doors before entering, and to iron, to starch, to help her dress—tried to turn her into a lady's maid. The girl obeyed without a murmur because she was afraid of losing her place; and since Madame usually left the key in the sideboard, Félicité took a little sugar upstairs with her every night, and ate it by herself in bed after saying her prayers.

Afternoons she sometimes crossed the road for a chat with the postilions while Madame was up in her room.

There Emma wore a shawl-collared dressing gown, open very low over a pleated dicky with three gold buttons. Her belt was a cord with large tassels, and her little garnet-colored slippers had rosettes of wide ribbons at the instep. Though she had no one to write to, she had bought herself a blotter, a writing case, a pen and envelopes; she would dust off her whatnot, look at herself in the mirror, take up a book, and then begin to daydream and let it fall to her lap.

She longed to travel; she longed to go back and live in the convent. She wanted to die. And she wanted to live in Paris.

Charles jogged back and forth across the countryside under snow and rain. He ate omelettes at farmhouse tables, thrust his arm into damp beds, had his face spattered with jets of warm blood at bleedings; he listened to death rattles, examined the contents of basins, handled a lot of soiled underclothing. But every night he came home to a blazing fire, a well-set table, a comfortable chair, and a dainty, prettily dressed wife smelling so sweet that he never quite knew where the scent came from, and half wondered whether it wasn't her skin that was perfuming her slip.

She delighted him by countless little niceties: a new way of making sconces out of paper to catch the wax under candles, a flounce that she changed on her dress, or the fancy name of some very plain dish that the maid hadn't got right but that Charles enjoyed eating every bit of. In Rouen she saw ladies with charms dangling from their watch fobs; she bought some charms. She took a fancy to a pair of large blue glass vases for her mantelpiece, and a little later to an ivory workbox with a silver-gilt thimble. The less Charles understood these refinements, the more alluring he found them. They added something to the pleasure of his senses and the charm of his home. They were like a trickle of golden dust along the petty pathway of his life.

His health was good, his appearance hearty; his reputation was secure. The country people liked him because he gave himself no airs. He always fondled the children and never went to a café; moreover, his morals inspired confidence. He was especially successful in treating catarrhs and chest ailments. Actually, Charles had such a dread of killing his patients that he seldom prescribed anything but sedatives—once in a while an emetic or a foot bath or leeches. Not that surgery held any terrors for him: when he bled a patient he bled him hard, like a horse; and he was famous for his iron grip as a tooth puller.

Eventually, "to keep himself up to date," he took out a subscription to the *La Ruche médicale*, a new publication whose prospectus had been sent him.

He read a little in it after his dinner, but the heat of the room plus digestion resulted in his falling asleep at the end of five minutes; and he sat there under the lamp with his chin in his hands and his hair falling forward like a mane. Emma looked at him and shrugged her shoulders. Why didn't she at least have for a husband one of those silent, dedicated men who spend their nights immersed in books and who by the time they're sixty and rheumatic have acquired a row of decorations to wear on their ill-fitting black coats? She would have liked the name Bovary—her name—to be famous, on display in all the bookshops, constantly mentioned in the newspapers, known all over France. But Charles had no ambition! A doctor from Yvetot with whom he had recently held a consultation had humiliated him right at the sickbed, in front of the assembled relatives. When Charles told her the story that evening, Emma burst out furiously against the other doctor. Charles was so moved that he shed a tear and kissed her on the forehead. But it was shame that had exasperated her: she wanted to strike him. She went into the hall, opened the window and took a breath of fresh air to calm herself.

"It's pathetic!" she whispered to herself, despair in her heart. "What a booby!"

And indeed he got on her nerves more and more. As he grew older he grew coarser: at the end of a meal he whittled the cork of the wine bottle with his dessert knife and cleaned his teeth with his tongue; he made a gulping noise every time he took a mouthful of soup; and as he put on weight his eyes, small to begin with, seemed to be pushed toward his temples by the puffing of his cheeks.

Emma sometimes tucked the red edge of his sweater up under his vest, or straightened his tie, or threw away a pair of faded old gloves he was about to put on; and it was never, as he believed, for his sake that she did it, but for her own, out of exasperated vanity. And sometimes she told him about things she had read—a passage in a novel or a new play, some high-life anecdote recounted in a gossip column, for Charles was a presence, at least, an ear that was always open, a sure source of approval. She confided many a secret to her dog, after all! She could almost have opened her heart to the logs in the fireplace and the pendulum of the clock.

Deep down, all the while, she was waiting for something to happen. Like a sailor in distress, she kept casting desperate glances over the solitary waste of her life, seeking some white sail in the distant mists of the horizon. She had no idea by what wind it would reach her, toward what shore it would bear her, or what kind of craft it would be—tiny boat or towering vessel, laden with heartbreaks or filled to the gunwales with rapture. But every morning when she awoke she hoped that today would be the day; she listened for every sound, gave sudden starts, was surprised when nothing happened; and then, sadder with each succeeding sunset, she longed for tomorrow.

Spring came again. She found it hard to breathe, the first warm days, when the pear trees were bursting into bloom.

From early in July she began to count on her fingers how many weeks there were till October, thinking that the marquis d'Andervilliers might give another ball at La Vaubyessard. But September passed without letters or visitors.

After the pain of this disappointment had gone, her heart stood empty once more; and then the series of identical days began all over again.

So from now on they were going to continue one after the other like this, always the same, innumerable, bringing nothing! Other people's lives, drab though they might be, held at least the possibility of an event. One unexpected happening often set in motion a whole chain of change: the entire setting of one's life could be transformed. But to her nothing happened. It was God's will. The future was a pitch-black tunnel ending in a locked door.

She gave up her music: why should she play? Who was there to listen? There wasn't a chance of her ever giving a concert in a short-sleeved velvet gown, skimming butterfly fingers over the ivory keys of a grand piano, feeling the public's ecstatic murmur flow around her like a breeze—so why go through the tedium of practicing? She left her drawing books and her embroidery in a closet. What was the use of anything? What was the use? She loathed sewing.

"I've read everything there is to read," she told herself.

And so she sat—holding the fire tongs in the fire till they glowed red, or watching the falling of the rain.

How depressed she was on Sundays, when the churchbell tolled for vespers! With a dull awareness she listened to the cracked sound as it rang out again and again. Sometimes a cat walking slowly along one of the roofs outside her window arched its back against the pale rays of the sun. The wind blew trails of dust on the highway. Far off somewhere a dog was howling. And the bell would keep on giving its regular, monotonous peals that died away over the countryside.

People came out of church. Women with their wooden shoes polished, peasant men in new smocks, little children skipping bareheaded in front of them—all moved toward home. And until dark five or six men, always the same ones, stayed playing their shuffleboard game before the main entrance of the inn.

The winter was a cold one. Every morning the windowpanes were frosted over, and the whitish light that came through—as though filtered through ground glass—sometimes didn't vary all day. By four o'clock it was time to light the lamps.

On sunny days she went out into the garden. The dew had garnished the cabbages with silvery lace, and joined head to head with long shining filaments. There was no sound of birds, everything seemed to be sleeping—the espaliered trees under their straw, the vine like a great sick snake under the wall coping, where she could see many-legged wood lice crawling as she came near. In among the spruces near the hedge the priest in a tricorn reading his breviary had lost his right foot, and the scaling of the plaster in the frost had left a white scurf on his face.

Then she would return upstairs, close her door, poke the coals; and languid in the heat of the fire she would feel boredom descend again, heavier than before. She would have liked to go down for a chat with the maid, but self-respect held her back.

Every day at the same time the schoolmaster in his black silk skullcap opened the shutters of his house; every day at the same time the village policeman passed, his sword buckled around his smock. Morning and evening the post horses crossed the road in threes to drink at the pond. Now and again the bell of a café door would tinkle as it opened; and when there was a wind she could hear the little copper basins that formed the barber's shop-sign creaking on their two rods. His window display consisted of an old fashion plate on one of the panes, and a wax bust of a woman with yellow hair. The barber, too, was accustomed to bewail the waste of his talents, his ruined career; and dreaming of a shop in a large city—in Rouen, perhaps, on the river front, or near the theatre—he paced back and forth all day between the mayor's office and the church, gloomily waiting for customers. When Madame Bovary raised her eyes she always saw him there with his cap over one ear, and his short work jacket, like a sentry on duty.

In the afternoon, sometimes, a man's face appeared outside the parlor windows, a swarthy face with black side whiskers and a slow, wide, gentle smile that showed very white teeth. Then would come the strain of a waltz; and in a miniature drawing room on top of the hurdy-gurdy a set of tiny dancers would begin to revolve. Women in pink turbans, Tyrolians in jackets, monkeys in black tailcoats, gentlemen in knee breeches—they all spun around among the armchairs, sofas and tables, and were reflected in bits of mirror glass joined together at the edges by strips of gold paper. As he turned his crank the man would glance to his right, to his left, and toward the windows. Now and then he would let out a spurt of brown saliva against the curb and raise his knee to lift the instrument and ease the heavy shoulder strap; and the music, now doleful and dragging, now merry and quick, came out of the box through a pink taffeta curtain under a fancy brasswork grill. The tunes it played were tunes that were being heard in other places—in theatres, in drawing rooms, under the lighted chandeliers of ballrooms: echoes from the world that reached Emma this way. Sarabands ran on endlessly in her head; and her thoughts, like dancing girls on some flowery carpet, leapt with the notes from dream to dream, from sorrow to sorrow. Then, when the man had caught in his cap the coin she threw him, he would pull down an old blue wool cover, hoist his organ onto his back, and move heavily off. She always watched him till he disappeared.

But it was above all at mealtime that she could bear it no longer—in that small ground-floor room with its smoking stove, its squeaking door, its sweating walls and its damp floor tiles. All the bitterness of life seemed to be served up to her on her plate; and the steam rising from the boiled meat brought gusts of revulsion from the depths of her soul. Charles was a slow eater; she would nibble a few hazelnuts, or lean on her elbow and draw lines on the oilcloth with the point of her table knife.

Now she let everything in the house go, and the older Madame Bovary was amazed by the change she found when she came to spend part of Lent in Tostes. Emma, once so careful and dainty, now went whole days without putting on a dress; she wore gray cotton stockings, lit the house with cheap tallow candles. She kept saying that they had to be careful, since they weren't rich; and she always went on to add that she was very contented, very happy, that she liked Tostes very much; and she made other surprising statements that shut up her mother-in-law. However, she seemed no more inclined than ever to follow her advice. Once, indeed, when Madame Bovary took it into her head to suggest that employers should keep an eye on their servants' religious life, Emma replied with such a terrible look and such a freezing smile that the dear woman henceforth kept her fingers out of things.

Emma was becoming capricious, hard to please. She would order special dishes for herself and then not touch them; one day she would drink nothing but fresh milk; the next, cups of tea by the dozen. Often she refused absolutely to go out; then she would feel stifled, open the windows, change to a light dress. She would give the maid a tongue-lashing and then turn around and give her presents, or time off to visit the neighbors, just as occasionally she would give a beggar all the silver she had in her purse, though she was anything but tenderhearted or sympathetic to other people's troubles. (In this she was like most sons and daughters of country folk: their souls always keep some of the horniness of their fathers' hands.)

Toward the end of February, Monsieur Rouault celebrated the anniversary of his recovery by bringing his son-in-law a magnificent turkey, and he stayed on at Tostes for three days. Charles was out most of the time with his patients, and it was Emma who kept her father company. He smoked in her bedroom, spit on the andirons, talked about crops, calves, cows, chickens and the village council; when he finally left and she had shut the door behind him, her feeling of relief surprised even herself. But then she no longer hid her scorn for anything or anyone; and she was beginning now and then to express peculiar opinions, condemning what everyone else approved and approving things that were perverse or immoral—a way of talking that made her husband stare at her wide-eyed.

Would this wretchedness last forever? Was there no way out? And yet she was every bit as good as all the other women, who lived in contentment! She had seen duchesses at La Vaubyessard who were dumpier and more common than she, and she cursed God for his injustice. She leaned her head against the wall and wept. She thought, with envy of riotous living, of nights spent at masked balls, of shameless revels and all the mysterious raptures they must bring in their train.

She grew pale and developed palpitations. Charles gave her valerian drops and camphor baths. Everything he tried seemed to exacerbate her the more.

Some days she chattered endlessly, almost feverishly; and such a period of overexcitement would suddenly be followed by a torpor in which she neither spoke nor moved. At such times she would revive herself with eau de Cologne, pouring a bottle of it over her arms.

Since she continually complained about Tostes, Charles supposed that the cause of her illness must have something to do with the town's situation; and struck by this idea he thought seriously of settling somewhere else.

As soon as she knew this she began to drink vinegar to lose weight, acquired a little dry cough, and lost her appetite completely.

It was a wrench for Charles to leave Tostes, after living there four years and just when he was beginning to be really established. Still, if it had to be—He took her to Rouen, to see one of his old teachers. The diagnosis was that she was suffering from a nervous illness: a change of air was indicated.

After looking here and there, Charles learned that in the district of Neufchâtel there was a good-sized market town named Yonville-l'Abbaye, whose doctor, a Polish refugee, had decamped just the week before. So he wrote to the local pharmacist and inquired about the population, the distance to the nearest doctor, how much his predecessor had earned a year, etc.; and when the answers were satisfactory he decided to move by spring if Emma's health didn't improve.

One day when she was going through a drawer in preparation for moving, something pricked her finger. It was the wire around her bridal bouquet. The orange-blossom buds were yellow with dust, and the silver-edged satin ribbons were frayed. She tossed it into the fire. It blazed up quicker than dry straw. Then it lay like a red bush on the ashes, slowly consuming itself. She watched it burn. The pasteboard berries burst open, the brass wire curled, the braid melted; and the shriveled paper petals hovered along the fireback like black butterflies and finally flew away up the chimney.

When they left Tostes in March, Madame Bovary was pregnant.

Part Two

I

Yonville-l'Abbaye (even the ruins of the ancient Capuchin friary from which it derives its name are no longer there) is a market town twenty miles from Rouen, between the highways to Abbeville and Beauvais in the valley of the Rieule. This is a small tributary of the Andelle: it turns the wheels of three mills before joining the larger stream, and contains some trout that boys like to fish for on Sundays.

Branching off from the highway at La Boissière, the road to Yonville continues level until it climbs the hill at Les Leux; and from there it commands a view of the valley. This is divided by the Rieule into two contrasting bits of countryside: everything to the left is grazing land, everything to the right is ploughed field. The pastures extend along the base of a chain of low hills and merge at the far end with the meadows of Bray; while eastward the plain rises gently and grows steadily wider, flaunting its golden grainfields as far as eye can see. The stream, flowing along the edge of the grass, is a white line dividing the color of the meadows from that of the ploughed earth: the country thus resembles a great spread-out cloak, its green velvet collar edged with silver braid.

On the horizon, beyond Yonville loom the oaks of the Argueil forest and the escarpments of the bluffs of Saint-Jean, the latter streaked from top to bottom with long, irregular lines of red: these are marks left by rain, and their brickish color, standing out so sharply against the gray rock of the hill, comes from the iron content of the many springs in the country just beyond.

This is where Normandy, Picardy and the Ile-de-France come together, a mongrel region where the speech of the natives is as colorless as the landscape is lacking in character. Here they make the worst Neufchâtel cheeses in the entire district; and here farming calls for considerable investment: great quantities of manure are needed to fertilize the friable, sandy, stony soil.

Up until 1835 no road was kept open to Yonville, but about that time the cross-cut was made that links the Abbeville and Amiens highways and is sometimes used by carters traveling from Rouen to Flanders. Nevertheless, despite its "new avenues for trade," Yonville-l'Abbaye has stood still. Instead of adopting improved methods of farming, the natives stick to their pastures, worn-out though they are; and the lazy town, spurning the farmland, has continued its spontaneous growth in the direction of the river. The sight of it from a distance, stretched out along the bank, brings to mind a cowherd taking a noonday nap beside the stream.

At the foot of the hill the road crosses the Rieule on a bridge, and then, becoming an avenue planted with young aspens, leads in a straight line to the first outlying houses. These are surrounded by hedges, and their yards are full of scattered outbuildings—cider presses, carriage houses and distilling sheds standing here and there under thick trees with ladders and poles leaning against their trunks and scythes hooked over their branches. The thatched roofs hide the top third or so of the low windows like fur caps pulled down over eyes, and each windowpane, thick and convex, has a bull's-eye in its center like the bottom of a bottle. Some of the plastered house walls with their diagonal black timbers are the background for scraggly espaliered pear trees; and the house doors have little swinging gates to keep out the baby chicks, who come to the sill to peck at brown-bread crumbs soaked in cider. Gradually the yards become narrower, houses are closer together, the hedges disappear; occasionally a fern broom put out to dry is seen hanging from a window; there is a blacksmith shop, a cart-maker's with two or three new carts outside half blocking the roadway. Then comes a white house behind an iron fence, its circular lawn adorned by a cupid holding finger to lips. Two cast-iron urns stand at either end of the entrance terrace; brass plates gleam brightly at the door: this is the notary's house, the finest in town.

The church is across the street, twenty yards further on, at the corner of the main square. The little graveyard surrounding it, enclosed by an elbow-high wall, is so full of graves that the old tombstones, lying flat on the ground, form a continuous pavement divided into rectangular blocks by the grass that pushes up between. The church was remodeled during the last years of the reign of Charles X.[5] The wooden vaulting is beginning to rot at the top: black cavities are appearing here and there in the blue paint. Above the door, in the place usually occupied by an organ, is a gallery for the men, reached by a spiral staircase that echoes loudly under the tread of wooden shoes.

Daylight, coming through the windows of plain glass, falls obliquely on the pews; and here and there on the wall from which they jut out at right angles is tacked a bit of straw matting, with the name of the pew holder in large letters below. Beyond, where the nave narrows, stands the confessional, and opposite it a statuette of the Virgin: she is dressed in a satin gown and a tulle veil spangled with silver stars, and her cheeks are daubed red like some idol from the Sandwich Islands.[6] A painting by a copyist, inscribed "Holy Family: Presented by the Minister of the Interior," hangs over the main altar; and there, flanked by four candlesticks, it closes the vista. The cheap fir choir stalls have never been painted.

The market—that is, a tile roof supported by about twenty pillars—takes up approximately half the main square of Yonville. The town hall, designed, as everyone will tell you, "by a Paris architect," is a kind of Greek temple forming one corner of the square, next door to the pharmacy. Its lower story has three Ionic columns; above is a row of arched windows; and the culminating pediment is filled with a figure of the Gallic cock, one of its claws resting on the Constitution[7] and the other holding the scales of justice.

But what catches the eye the most is across the square from the Lion d'Or

5. The last Bourbon king (1757–1836), son of Louis XV. He was expelled by the July Revolution (1830). 6. Old name for Hawaii, after John Montagu, fourth earl of Sandwich (1718–1792), who served as first lord of admiralty when the islands were discovered. 7. The *Charte constitutionelle de la France,* basis of the French constitution after the revolution, bestowed in 1814 by Louis XVIII and revised in 1830, after the downfall of Charles X.

hotel: Monsieur Homais' pharmacy! Especially at night, when his lamp is lit, and the red and green glass jars decorating his window cast the glow of their two colors far out across the roadway! Peering through it, as through the glare of Bengal lights,[8] one can catch a glimpse, at that hour, of the dim figure of the pharmacist himself, bent over his desk. The entire façade of his establishment is plastered from top to bottom with inscriptions—in running script, in round hand, in block capitals: "Vichy, Seltzer and Barèges Waters; Depurative Fruit Essences; Raspail's Remedy; Arabian Racahout; Darcet's Pastilles; Regnauk's Ointment; Bandages, Baths, Laxative Chocolates, etc." And the shop sign, as wide as the shop itself, proclaims in gold letters: "Homais Pharmacy." At the rear of the shop, behind the great scales fastened to the counter, the word "Laboratory" is inscribed above a glass door; and this door itself, halfway up, bears once again the name "Homais," in gold letters on a black ground.

That is as much as there is to see in Yonville. The street (the only street), long as a rifle shot and lined with a few shops, abruptly ceases to be a street at a turn of the road. If you leave it on the right and follow the base of the bluffs of Saint-Jean, you soon reach the cemetery.

This was enlarged the year of the cholera—one wall was torn down and three adjoining acres were added; but all this new portion is almost uninhabited, and new graves continue as in the past to be dug in the crowded area near the gate. The caretaker, who is also gravedigger and sexton at the church (thus profiting doubly from the parish corpses), has taken advantage of the empty land to plant potatoes. Nevertheless, his little field grows smaller every year, and when there is an epidemic he doesn't know whether to rejoice in the deaths or lament the space taken by the new graves.

"You are feeding on the dead, Lestiboudois!" Monsieur le curé told him, one day.

The somber words gave him pause, and for a time he desisted; but today he continues to plant his tubers, coolly telling everyone that they come up by themselves.

Since the events which we are about to relate, absolutely nothing has changed in Yonville. To this day the tin tricolor still turns atop the church tower; the two calico streamers outside the dry-goods shop still blow in the wind; the spongy foetuses in the pharmacy window continue to disintegrate in their cloudy alcohol; and over the main entrance of the hotel the old golden lion, much discolored by the rains, stares down like a curly-headed poodle on passers-by.

The evening the Bovarys were expected at Yonville, Madame Lefrançois, the widow who owned this hotel, was so frantically busy with her saucepans that large beads of sweat stood out on her face. Tomorrow was market-day, and she had to get everything ready in advance—cut the meat, clean the chickens, make soup, roast and grind the coffee. In addition, she had tonight's dinner to get for her regular boarders and for the new doctor and his wife and their maid. Bursts of laughter came from the billiard room; in the small dining room three millers were calling for brandy; logs were blazing, charcoal was crackling, and on the long table in the kitchen, in among the quarters of raw mutton, stood high piles of plates that shook with the chop-

8. Blue flares used in signaling.

ping of the spinach on the chopping-block. From the yard came the squawk-
ing of the chickens that the kitchen maid was chasing with murderous intent.

Warming his back at the fire was a man in green leather slippers, wearing
a velvet skullcap with a gold tassel. His face, slightly pitted by smallpox,
expressed nothing but self-satisfaction, and he seemed as contented with life
as the goldfinch in a wicker cage hanging above his head. This was the
pharmacist.

"Artémise!" cried the mistress of the inn. "Chop some kindling, fill the
decanters, bring some brandy—hurry up! Lord! If I only knew what dessert
to offer these people you're waiting for! Listen to their moving-men starting
up that racket in the billiard room again! They've left their van in the driveway, too: the Hirondelle will probably crash into it. Call 'Polyte and tell him
to put it in the shed! Would you believe it, Monsieur Homais—since this
morning they've played at least fifteen games and drunk eight pots of cider!
But they're going to ruin my table," she said, staring over at them across the
room, her skimming spoon in her hand.

"That wouldn't be much of a loss," replied Monsieur Homais. "You'd buy
another one."

"Another billiard table!" cried the widow.

"But this one's falling apart, Madame Lefrançois! I tell you again; it's shortsighted of you not to invest in a new one! Very shortsighted! Players today
want narrow pockets and heavy cues, you know. They don't play billiards the
way they used to. Everything's changed. We must keep up with the times!
Just look at Tellier . . ."

The hostess flushed with anger.

"Say what you like," the pharmacist went on, "his billiard table is nicer
than yours. And if a patriotic tournament were to be got up, for Polish independence or Lyons flood relief . . ."[9]

"We're not afraid of fly-by-nights like Tellier," the hostess interrupted,
shrugging her heavy shoulders. "Don't worry, Monsieur Homais. As long as
the Lion d'Or exists we'll keep our customers. We're a well-established house.
But the Café Français . . . One of these mornings you'll find it sealed up,
with a nice big notice on the window blinds. A new billiard table?" she went
on, talking as though to herself. "But this one's so handy to stack the washing
on! And in the hunting season it's slept as many as six! . . . But what's keeping
that slowpoke Hivert?"

"You'll wait till he arrives, to give your gentlemen their dinner?" the pharmacist asked.

"Wait? And what about Monsieur Binet? You'll see him come in on the
stroke of six: he's the most punctual man in the world. He always has to sit
at the same place in the little room: he'd die rather than eat his dinner
anywhere else. And finicky! So particular about his cider! Not like Monsieur
Léon! Monsieur Léon sometimes doesn't come in till seven, or even half-
past, and half the time he doesn't even know what he's eating. What a nice
young man! So polite! So soft-spoken!"

"Ah, Madame! There's a great difference, you know, between someone

---

9. The allusion dates the action of the novel as taking place in 1840; during the winter of 1840, the Rhône
overflowed with catastrophic results. At the same time, Louis Philippe was under steady attack for his
failure to offer sufficient assistance to the victims of the repression that followed the insurrection of Warsaw
(1831).

who's been properly brought up and a tax collector who got his only schooling in the army."

The clock struck six. Binet entered.

He was clad in a blue frock coat that hung straight down all around his skinny body; and the raised peak of his leather cap, its earflaps pulled up and fastened at the top, displayed a bald, squashed-looking forehead, deformed by long pressure of a helmet. He was wearing a coarse wool vest, a crinoline collar, gray trousers, and—as he did in every season—well-shined shoes that bulged in two parallel lines over the rising of his two big toes. Not a hair was out of place in the blond chin whisker outlining his jaw: it was like the edging of a flower bed around his long, dreary face with its small eyes and hooked nose. He was a clever card player, a good hunter, and wrote a fine hand. His hobby was making napkin rings on his own lathe: jealous as an artist and stingy as a bourgeois, he cluttered up his house with his handiwork.

He headed for the small room, but the three millers had to be got out before he would go in. While his table was being set he stood next to the stove without saying a word; then he closed the door and took off his cap as usual.

"He won't wear out his tongue with civilities," the pharmacist remarked, as soon as he was alone with the hostess.

"He never talks a bit more than that," she answered. "Last week I had two cloth salesmen here—two of the funniest fellows you ever listened to. They told me stories that made me laugh till I cried. Would you believe it? He sat there like a clam—didn't open his mouth."

"No imagination," pronounced the pharmacist. "Not a hint of a spark! No manners whatever!"

"And yet they say he has something to him," objected the hostess.

"Something to him?" cried Monsieur Homais. "That man? Something to him? Still, in his own line I suppose he may have," he conceded.

And he went on: "Ah! A business man with vast connections, a lawyer, a doctor, a pharmacist—I can understand it if they get so engrossed in their affairs that they become eccentric, even surly: history is full of such examples. But at least they have important affairs to be engrossed in! Take me, for instance: how often I've turned my desk upside down looking for my pen to write some labels, only to find I'd stuck it behind my ear!"

Meanwhile Madame Lefrançois had approached the door to see whether the Hirondelle wasn't in sight, and she started as a black-clad man that moment entered the kitchen. In the last faint light of dusk it was just possible to make out his florid face and athletic figure.

"What can I offer you, Monsieur le curé?" she asked, reaching down a brass candlestick from a row that stood all ready and complete with candles on the mantelpiece. "A drop of cassis? A glass of wine?"

The priest very politely declined. He had come to fetch his umbrella, he said: he had left it at the convent in Ernemont the other day, and had supposed the Hirondelle would have delivered it by now. He asked Madame Lefrançois to have it brought to him at the rectory during the evening, and then left for the church, where the bell was tolling the Angelus.

When the sound of his footsteps in the square had died away, the pharmacist declared that in his opinion the priest's behavior had been most improper. His refusal to take a glass of something was the most revolting kind of hypocrisy: all priests were secret tipplers, he said, and they were all doing their best to bring back the days of the tithe.

The hostess said some words in the curé's defense. "Besides," she went on, "he could take on four like you. Last year he helped our men get in the straw: he carried as many as six bundles at a time—that shows you how strong he is."

"Bravo!" cried the pharmacist. "Go ahead! Keep sending your daughters to confession to strapping fellows like that! But if I were the government I'd have every priest bled once a month. Yes, a fine generous phlebotomy every month, Madame, in the interests of morals and decency."

"That's enough, Monsieur Homais! You've no respect for religion!"

"On the contrary, I'm a very religious man, in my own way, far more so than all these people with their mummeries and their tricks. I worship God, I assure you! I believe in a Supreme Being, a Creator. Whoever he is—and what difference does it make?—he put us here on earth to fulfill our duties as citizens and parents. But I don't have to go into church and kiss silver platters and hand over my money to fatten up a lot of rascals that eat better than you and I! To him, one can do full honor in a forest, a field—or merely by gazing up at the ethereal vault, like the ancients. My God is the God of Socrates, of Franklin, of Voltaire, of Béranger! My credo is the credo of Rousseau![1] I adhere to the immortal principles of '89! I have no use for the kind of God who goes walking in his garden with a stick, sends his friends to live in the bellies of whales, gives up the ghost with a groan and then comes back to life three days later! Those things aren't only absurd in themselves, Madame—they're completely opposed to all physical laws. It goes to prove, by the way, that priests have always wallowed in squalid ignorance and have wanted nothing better than to drag the entire world down to their own level."

As he ended, he glanced about in search of an audience: for a moment, during his outburst, he had had the illusion that he was addressing the village council. But the mistress of the inn was no longer listening to him: her ears had caught a distant sound of wheels. There was the rattle of a coach, the pounding of loose horseshoes on the road; and the Hirondelle drew up before the door at last.

It was a yellow box-shaped affair mounted on two large wheels that came up as high as the top, blocking the passengers' view and spattering their shoulders. When the carriage was closed the tiny panes of its narrow windows rattled in their frames, and there were mud stains here and there on the ancient coating of dust that even heavy rainstorms never washed off completely. It was drawn by three horses, one ahead and two abreast. Its under side bumped against the ground on down grades.

A number of the local inhabitants made their appearance in the square, and all speaking at once they asked for news, for explanations of the delay, for their packages. Hivert didn't know whom to answer first. It was he who attended to things in the city for the Yonvillians. He shopped for them, brought back rolls of leather for the shoemaker, scrap iron for the black-

---

1. Rousseau's declaration (1762) of faith in God, a religion of his heart, coupled with a criticism of revealed religion. It is included in book 4 of his pedagogic treatise *Émile* but was frequently reprinted as an independent pamphlet.

smith, a keg of herrings for Madame Lefrançois his employer, ladies' bonnets from the milliner, wigs from the hairdresser; and all along the road on the way back he distributed his packages, standing up on his seat and hurling them over the farmyard fences with a shout as his horses kept galloping ahead.

An accident had delayed him: Madame Bovary's greyhound had run away—disappeared across the fields. They had whistled for her a good fifteen minutes. Hivert had even turned his coach around and gone back over the road for more than a mile, expecting to come upon her any minute; but they'd had to go on without her. Emma had wept and made a scene, blaming it all on Charles. Monsieur Lheureux, the Yonville dry-goods dealer, who was also in the carriage, had tried to comfort her by citing numerous examples of lost dogs' recognizing their masters many years later. There was a famous one, he said, that had returned to Paris all the way from Constantinople. Another had traveled one hundred twenty-five miles in a straight line, swimming four rivers. And his own father had had a poodle who after being gone for twelve years had suddenly jumped up on his back one night in the street, as he was on his way to a friend's house for dinner.

II

Emma stepped out first, followed by Félicité, Monsieur Lheureux, and a wet nurse; and Charles had to be shaken awake in his corner, where he had dozed off as soon as darkness had fallen.

Homais introduced himself: he paid his compliments to Madame and spoke politely to Monsieur, said he was delighted to have been of service to them, and cordially added that he had taken the liberty of inviting himself to share their dinner, his wife being for the moment out of town.

In the kitchen, Madame Bovary crossed to the fireplace. Reaching halfway down her skirt, she grasped it with the tips of two of her fingers, raised it to her ankles, and stretched out a black-shod foot toward the flame, over the leg of mutton that was turning on the spit. She was standing in the full light of the fire, and by its harsh glare one could see the weave of her dress, the pores of her white skin, even her eyelids when she briefly shut her eyes. Now and again she was flooded by a great flow of red, as a gust of wind blew into the fire from the half-open kitchen door.

From the other side of the fireplace a fair-haired young man was silently watching her.

This was Monsieur Léon Dupuis, the second of the Lion d'Or's regular diners, clerk to Maître Guillaumin the notary. Finding Yonville very dull, he dined as late as possible, in the hope that some traveler might turn up at the inn with whom he could have an evening's conversation. On days where there was no work to detain him at the office, he had no way of filling the interval, and ended up arriving on time and enduring a tête-à-tête with Binet straight through from soup to cheese. So it was with pleasure that he accepted the hostess' suggestion that he dine with the new arrivals, and they all went into the large dining room, where their four places had been set: Madame Lefrançois was making an occasion of it.

Homais asked permission to keep his cap on; he had a dread of head colds. Then, turning to his neighbor: "Madame is a bit tired, I presume? Our old

Hirondelle does such a frightful lot of bumping and shaking!"

"It does," Emma answered. "But I always love traveling anyway. I enjoy a change of scene."

The clerk sighed. "It's so boring to be always stuck in the same place!"

"If you were like me," said Charles, "always having to be on horseback . . ."

"But there's nothing more charming than riding, I think," said the clerk, addressing Madame Bovary. "If you have the opportunity, of course."

"As a matter of fact," said the apothecary, "the practice of medicine isn't particularly arduous in this part of the world. The condition of our roads makes it possible to use a gig, and, generally speaking, payment is good— the farmers are well off. Aside from the usual cases of enteritis, bronchitis, liver complaint, etc., our roster of illnesses includes an occasional intermittent fever at harvest time, but on the whole very little that's serious except for a good deal of scrofula, probably the result of the deplorable hygienic conditions in our countryside. Ah! You'll have to fight many a prejudice, Monsieur Bovary; every day your scientific efforts will be thwarted by the peasant's stubborn adherence to his old ways. Plenty of our people still have recourse to novenas and relics and the priest, instead of doing the natural thing and coming to the doctor or the pharmacist. To tell the truth, however, the climate isn't at all bad: we even have a few nonagenarians. The thermometer—this I can tell you from personal observation—goes down in winter to four degrees, and in the hottest season touches twenty-five or thirty degrees Centigrade at the most—that is, twenty-four degrees Réaumur at a maximum, or, in other words, fifty-four degrees Fahrenheit, to use the English scale—not more! You see, we're sheltered from the north winds by the Argueil forest on the one side and from the west winds by the bluffs of Saint-Jean on the other. However, this warmth, which because of the dampness given off by the river and the number of cattle in the pastures, which themselves exhale, as you know, a great deal of ammonia, that is nitrogen, hydrogen, and oxygen (no, just nitrogen and hydrogen), and which, sucking up the humus from the soil, mixing all these different emanations together— making a package of them, so to speak—and combining also with the electricity in the atmosphere when there is any, could in the long run result in noxious miasmas, as in tropical countries; this warmth, I was saying, is actually moderated from the direction from which it comes, or rather the direction from which it could come, namely, from the south, by southeast winds, which being of course cool themselves as a result of crossing the Seine sometimes burst on us all of a sudden like arctic air from Russia!"

"Are there some nice walks in the neighborhood, at least?" Madame Bovary asked, speaking to the young man.

"Oh, hardly any," he answered. "There's one place, called the Pasture, on top of the bluffs at the edge of the woods. I go there Sundays sometimes with a book and watch the sunset."

"There's nothing I love as much as sunsets," she said. "But my favorite place for them is the seashore."

"Oh, I adore the sea," said Monsieur Léon.

"Don't you have the feeling," asked Madame Bovary, "that something happens to free your spirit in the presence of all that vastness? It raises up my soul to look at it, somehow. It makes me think of the infinite, and all kinds of wonderful things."

"Mountain scenery does the same," said Léon. "A cousin of mine traveled in Switzerland last year, and he told me that no one who hasn't been there can imagine the poetry and charm of the lakes and waterfalls and the majesty of the glaciers. You can look across the rivers there and see pine trees so high you can't believe your eyes. They build their chalets right on the edge of precipices. If you look down you can see whole valleys a thousand feet below you through openings in the clouds. Think what it must do to you to see things like that! I'd fall on my knees, I think. I'd want to pray. I can well understand the famous composer who used to play the piano in such places, to get inspiration."

"Are you a musician?" she asked.

"No, but I love music," he answered.

"Ah, don't listen to him, Madame Bovary," interrupted Homais, leaning across his plate. "He's just being modest. What about the other day, my friend? You were singing *L'Ange gardien*[2] in your room—it was delightful. I heard you from the laboratory; you rendered it like a real actor."

Léon lived at the pharmacist's, in a small third-floor room looking out on the square. He blushed at his landlord's compliment. But the latter had already turned back to the doctor and was briefing him on the leading citizens of Yonville. He told stories about them and gave vital statistics. No one knew for sure how well off the notary was; and then there was the Tuvache family, all of them hard to get on with.

Emma went on: "What is your favorite kind of music?"

"Oh, German music. It's the most inspiring."

"Do you know Italian opera?"

"Not yet—but I'll hear some next year when I go to Paris to finish law school."

"As I was just telling your husband," the pharmacist said, "speaking of our poor runaway friend Yanoda, thanks to his extravagance you're going to enjoy one of the most comfortable houses in Yonville. What's especially convenient about it for a doctor is that it has a door opening on the lane, so that people can come and go without being seen. Besides, it has everything a housekeeper needs: laundry, kitchen and pantry, sitting room, fruit closet, etc. Yanoda didn't care how he spent his money! He built an arbor alongside the river at the foot of the garden, just to drink beer in during the summer! If Madame likes gardening, she'll be able to . . ."

"My wife never gardens," said Charles. "She's been advised to take exercise, but even so she'd much rather stay in her room and read."

"So would I," said Léon. "What's more delightful than an evening beside the fire with a nice bright lamp and a book, listening to the wind beating against the windows . . . ?"

"How true!" she said, her great dark eyes fixed widely on him.

"I'm absolutely removed from the world at such times," he said. "The hours go by without my knowing it. Sitting there I'm wandering in countries I can see every detail of—I'm playing a role in the story I'm reading. I actually feel I'm the characters—I live and breathe with them."

"I know!" she said. "I feel the same!"

---

2. The guardian angel (French). A sentimental romance written by Mme. Pauline Duchambre, author of several such songs that appeared in the keepsakes.

"Have you ever had the experience," Léon went on, "of running across in a book some vague idea you've had, some image that you realize has been lurking all the time in the back of your mind and now seems to express absolutely your most subtle feelings?"

"Indeed I have," she answered.

"That's why I'm especially fond of poetry," he said. "I find it much more affecting than prose. It's much more apt to make me cry."

"Still, it's tiresome in the long run," Emma replied. "Nowadays I'm crazy about a different kind of thing—stories full of suspense, stories that frighten you. I hate to read about low-class heroes and their down-to-earth concerns, the sort of thing the real world's full of."

"You're quite right," the clerk approved. "Writing like that doesn't move you: it seems to me to miss the whole true aim of art. Noble characters and pure affections and happy scenes are very comforting things. They're a refuge from life's disillusionments. As for me, they're my *only* means of relief, living here as I do, cut off from the world. Yonville has so little to offer!"

"It's like Tostes, I suppose," Emma said. "That's why I always subscribed to a lending library."

"If Madame would do me the honor of using it," said the pharmacist, who had heard her last words, "I can offer her a library composed of the best authors—Voltaire, Rousseau, Delille,[3] Walter Scott, the *Echo des Feuilletons*. I subscribe to a number of periodicals, too. The *Fanal de Rouen*[4] comes every day: as a matter of fact I happen to be its local correspondent for Buchy, Forges, Neufchâtel, Yonville and all this vicinity."

They had been at table two hours and a half. Artémise was a wretched waitress: she dragged her cloth slippers over the tile floor, brought plates one by one, forgot everything, paid no attention to what was told her, and constantly left the door of the billiard room ajar so that the latch kept banging against the wall.

As he talked, Léon had unconsciously rested his foot on one of the rungs of Madame Bovary's chair. She was wearing a little blue silk scarf that held her pleated batiste collar stiff as a ruff; and as she moved her head the lower part of her face buried itself in the folds or gently rose out of them. Sitting thus side by side while Charles and the pharmacist chatted, they entered into one of those vague conversations in which every new subject that comes up proves to be one more aspect of a core of shared feelings. The names of plays running in Paris, the titles of novels, new dance tunes, the inaccessible great world, Tostes where she had just come from, Yonville where they both were now—all this they went into and talked about until dinner was over.

When coffee was brought in, Félicité went off to prepare the bedroom in the new house, and soon they all got up from the table. Madame Lefrançois was asleep beside her smoldering fire, and the stable-boy, lantern in hand, was waiting to light Monsieur and Madame Bovary home. There were wisps of straw in his red hair, and his left leg was lame. He took Monsieur le curé's umbrella in his other hand, and the company set out.

---

3. Jacques Delille (1738–1813), who wrote idyllic descriptive poems; *Les Jardins* (1782) is best known.
4. The *Rouen Beacon* (a fictitious newspaper).

The town was asleep. The pillars of the market cast long shadows, and the pallor of the road in the moonlight gave the effect of a summer night.

But the doctor's house was only fifty yards from the inn, and almost at once it was time to say good night and they went their separate ways.

The moment she stepped inside the entrance hall Emma felt the chill from the plaster walls fall on her shoulders, like the touch of a damp cloth. The walls were new and the wooden stairs creaked. Upstairs in the bedroom a whitish light came through the uncurtained windows. She could glimpse the tops of trees, and, beyond them, meadows half drowned in the mist that rose up in the moonlight along the river. In the middle of the room was a heap of bureau drawers, bottles, metal and wooden curtain rods; mattresses lying on chairs, basins strewn over the floor—everything had been left there in disorder by the two moving-men.

It was the fourth time that she had gone to bed in a strange place. The first was the day she entered the convent, the second the day she arrived in Tostes, the third at La Vaubyessard, and now the fourth: each time it had been like the opening of a new phase of her life. She refused to believe that things could be the same in different places; and since what had gone before was so bad, what was to come must certainly be better.

III

The next morning she was barely up when she saw the clerk in the square. She was in her dressing gown. He caught sight of her and bowed. She responded with a brief nod and closed the window.

Léon waited all day for six o'clock to come, but when he entered the inn he found only Monsieur Binet, already at table.

The dinner of the previous evening had been a notable event for him: never before had he spoken for two consecutive hours with a "lady." How did it happen that he had been able to tell her so many things, in words that previously he wouldn't have thought of? He was ordinarily timid, with a reticence that was part modesty, part dissimulation. In Yonville he was thought to have very gentlemanly manners. He listened respectfully to his elders, and seemed not to get excited about politics—a remarkable trait in a young man. Besides, he was talented. He painted in water colors, could read the key of G, and when he didn't play cards after dinner he often took up a book. Monsieur Homais esteemed him because he was educated; Madame Homais liked him because he was helpful: he often spent some time with her children in the garden. They were brats, the Homais children, always dirty, wretchedly brought up, sluggish like their mother. Besides the maid, they were looked after by the pharmacist's apprentice, Justin, a distant cousin of Monsieur Homais, who had been taken in out of charity and was exploited as a servant.

The apothecary proved the best of neighbors. He advised Madame Bovary about tradesmen, had his cider dealer make a special delivery, tasted the brew himself, and saw to it that the barrel was properly installed in the cellar. He told her how to buy butter most advantageously, and made an arrangement for her with Lestiboudois the sacristan, who in addition to his ecclesiastical and funerary functions tended the principal gardens in Yonville by the hour or by the year, depending on the owners' preference.

It wasn't mere kindness that prompted the pharmacist to such obsequious cordiality: there was a scheme behind it.

He had violated the law of 19th Ventôse, Year XI,[5] Article I, which forbids anyone not holding a diploma to practice medicine; and in consequence had been denounced by anonymous informants and summoned to Rouen to the private chambers of the royal prosecutor. The magistrate had received him standing, clad in his robe of office banded at the shoulders with ermine and wearing his high official toque. It was in the morning, before the opening of court. Homais could hear the heavy tread of policemen in the corridor, and in the distance what sounded like heavy locks snapping shut. His ears rang so that he thought he was going to have a stroke; he had a vision of underground dungeons, his family in tears, his pharmacy sold, all his glass jars scattered among strangers; and when the interview was over he had to go to a café and drink a rum and soda to steady his nerves.

Gradually the memory of this warning faded, and he continued as before to give innocuous consultations in his back room. But his relations with the mayor were not good; he had competitors who would rejoice in his ruin: he had to watch his step. By being polite to Monsieur Bovary he could win his gratitude and insure his looking the other way should he notice anything. So every morning Homais brought him "the paper," and often left the pharmacy in the afternoon to call on him for a moment's conversation.

Charles was in a gloomy state: he had no patients. He sat silent for hours on end, took naps in his consulting room, or watched his wife as she sewed. To keep occupied he acted as handyman around the house, even attempting to paint the attic with what the painters had left behind. But he was worried about money. He had spent so much for repairs at Tostes, for dresses for Madame, for the move, that the entire dowry and three thousand écus besides had been swallowed up in two years. Besides, so many things had been broken or lost between Tostes and Yonville! The plaster priest was one of them: a particularly violent bump had thrown it out of the van, and it had been smashed into a thousand pieces on the cobblestones of Quincampoix.

He had another, happier concern—his wife's pregnancy. As her term drew near she became ever dearer to him. Another bond of the flesh was being forged between them, one which gave him an all-pervasive feeling that their union was now closer. The indolence of her gait, the gentle sway of her uncorseted body, her tired way of sitting in a chair, all filled him with uncontrollable happiness: he would go up to her and kiss her, stroke her face, call her "little mother," try to dance with her; and half laughing, half weeping, he would think of a thousand playful endearments to shower her with. The idea of having begotten a child enchanted him. Now he had everything he could ever hope for. He had been granted all that human life had to offer, and he was serenely ready to enjoy it.

Emma's first reaction to her condition was one of great surprise; and then she was eager to be delivered and know what it was like to be a mother. But since she couldn't spend the money she would have liked and buy embroidered baby bonnets and a boat-shaped cradle with pink silk curtains, she

5. The government of the French Republic established a new calendar. The new year began on September 22, 1792; thus the year is 1803. *Ventôse:* windy (French); the sixth month of the new calendar (from February 19 to March 20), making the date March 9.

resentfully gave up her own ideas about the layette and ordered the whole thing from a seamstress in the village without indicating any preferences or discussing any details. Thus she had none of the pleasure she might have had in the preparations that whet the appetite of mother love; and this perhaps did something to blunt her affection from the beginning. But Charles spoke of the baby every time they sat down to a meal, and gradually she became accustomed to the idea.

She wanted a son. He would be strong and dark; she would call him Georges; and this idea of having a male child was like a promise of compensation for all her past frustrations. A man is free, at least—free to range the passions and the world, to surmount obstacles, to taste the rarest pleasures. Whereas a woman is continually thwarted. Inert, compliant, she has to struggle against her physical weakness and legal subjection. Her will, like the veil tied to her hat, quivers with every breeze: there is always a desire that entices, always a convention that restrains.

The baby was born one Sunday morning, about six o'clock, as the sun was rising.

"It's a girl!" cried Charles.

She turned her head away and fainted.

Almost immediately Madame Homais rushed in and kissed her, followed by Madame Lefrançois of the Lion d'Or. The pharmacist, a man of discretion, confined himself to a few provisional words of congratulations, spoken through the half-open door. He asked to see the child and pronounced it well formed.

During her convalescence she gave a great deal of thought to a name for her daughter. First she went over all she could think of that had Italian endings—Clara, Louisa, Amanda, Atala; she was tempted by Galsuinde, too, and even more by Isolde and Léocadie. Charles wanted the child named for its mother; Emma was opposed. They went through the almanac from end to end and asked everyone for suggestions.

"Monsieur Léon," said the pharmacist, "told me the other day he's surprised you haven't decided on Madeleine: it's so very fashionable just now."

But the older Madame Bovary protested loudly against a name so associated with sin. Monsieur Homais' predilection was for names that recalled great men, illustrious deeds or noble thoughts: such had been his guiding principle in baptising his own four children. Napoléon stood for fame, Franklin for liberty; Irma was perhaps a concession to romanticism; but Athalie[6] was a tribute to the most immortal masterpiece of the French stage. For— mind you!—his philosophical convictions didn't interfere with his artistic appreciation: in him, the thinker didn't stifle the man of feeling; he was a man of discrimination, quite capable of differentiating between imagination and fanaticism. In the tragedy in question, for example, he condemned the ideas but admired the style, abhorred the conception but praised all the details, found the characters impossible but their speeches marvelous. When he read the famous passages he was carried away, but the thought that the clergy made use of it all for their own purposes distressed him immensely; and so troubling was his confusion of feelings that he would have liked to

6. A tragedy by Jean Racine, written in 1691 for the pupils of Saint-Cyr. Racine had abandoned the regular stage after a spiritual crisis and wrote two sacred tragedies, *Esther* and *Athalie,* for the young girls of Saint-Cyr.

place a wreath on Racine's brow with his own hands and then have a good long argument with him.

In the end, Emma remembered hearing the marquise at Vaubyessard address a young woman as Berthe, and that promptly became the chosen name. Since Monsieur Rouault was unable to come, Monsieur Homais was asked to be godfather. As presents he brought several items from his pharmaceutical stock, namely, six boxes of jujubes, a full jar of racahout, three packages of marshmallow paste, and six sticks of sugar candy that he found in a cupboard and threw in for good measure. The evening of the ceremony there was a large dinner party. The priest was present: words became rather heated, and with the liqueurs Monsieur Homais broke into Béranger's *Le Dieu des bonnes gens*.[7] Monsieur Léon sang a barcarolle, and the older Madame Bovary (who was godmother) a Napoleonic ballad. Finally the older Monsieur Bovary insisted that the baby be brought down, and proceeded to baptize it with a glass of champagne, pouring the wine over its head. This mockery of the first sacrament brought indignant words from the Abbé Bournisien; the older Monsieur Bovary replied with a quotation from *La Guerre des dieux*;[8] and the priest started to leave. The ladies implored him to stay; Homais intervened; and after considerable persuasion the abbé sat down again in his chair and calmly took up his saucer and his half-finished demitasse.

The older Monsieur Bovary stayed on for a month at Yonville, dazzling the inhabitants with a magnificent silver-braided policeman's cap that he wore mornings when he smoked his pipe in the square. He was used to drinking large quantities of brandy, and often sent the maid to the Lion d'Or to buy a bottle, which was charged to his son's account; and to perfume his foulards he used up his daughter-in-law's entire supply of eau de Cologne.

Emma didn't in the least dislike his company. He had seen the world: he spoke of Berlin, of Vienna, of Strasbourg, of his years as an army officer, of the mistresses he had had, of the official banquets he had attended. Then he would become gallant; and sometimes, on the stairs or in the garden, he would even seize hold of her waist and cry, "Better watch out, Charles!" The older Madame Bovary was alarmed for her son's happiness, and began to urge her husband to take her home, lest in the long run he corrupt the young woman's mind. Possibly her fears went further: Monsieur Bovary was a man to whom nothing was sacred.

One day Emma suddenly felt that she had to see her little daughter, who had been put out to nurse with the cabinetmaker's wife; and without looking at the almanac to see whether the six weeks of the Virgin[9] had elapsed, she made her way toward the house occupied by Rollet, at the end of the village at the foot of the hills, between the main road and the meadows.

It was noon: the houses had their shutters closed, and under the harsh light of the blue sky the ridges of the glittering slate roofs seemed to be shooting sparks. A sultry wind was blowing. Emma felt weak as she walked; the stones of the footpath hurt her feet, and she wondered whether she shouldn't return home or stop in somewhere to rest.

7. The god of good people; a deistic song by Béranger (see n. 7, p. 1044). 8. The war of the gods; a satirical poem by Évariste-Désiré Deforge (later vicomte de Parny; 1753–1814) published in 1799. It ridicules the Christian religion. 9. Originally the six weeks that separate Christmas from Purification (February 2); in those days, the normal period of confinement for a woman after childbirth.

At that moment Monsieur Léon emerged from a nearby door, a sheaf of papers under his arm. He advanced to greet her and stood in the shade in front of Lheureux's store, under the gray awning.

Madame Bovary said that she was on her way to see her child but was beginning to feel tired.

"If . . ." Léon began, and then dared go no further.

"Have you an appointment somewhere?" she asked him.

And when he replied that he hadn't she asked him to accompany her. By evening the news of this had spread throughout Yonville, and Madame Tuvache, the wife of the mayor, said in her maid's presence that Madame Bovary was risking her reputation.

To reach the wet-nurse's house they had to turn left at the end of the village street, as though going to the cemetery, and follow a narrow path that led them past cottages and yards between privet hedges. These were in bloom; and blooming, too, were veronicas and wild roses and nettles and the wild blackberries that thrust out their slender sprays from the thickets. Through holes in the hedges they could see, in the farmyards, a pig on a manure pile or cows in wooden collars rubbing their horns against tree trunks. The two of them walked on slowly side by side, she leaning on his arm and he shortening his step to match hers; in front of them hovered a swarm of flies, buzzing in the warm air.

They recognized the house by an old walnut tree that shaded it. It was low, roofed with brown tiles, and from the attic window hung a string of onions. Brushwood propped up against a thorn hedge formed a fence around a bit of garden given over to lettuce, a few plants of lavender, and sweet peas trained on poles. A trickle of dirty water ran off into the grass, and all around were odds and ends of rags, knitted stockings, a red calico wrapper, a large coarsely woven sheet spread out on the hedge. At the sound of the gate the wet nurse appeared, carrying an infant at her breast. With her other hand she was pulling along a frail, unhappy-looking little boy, his face covered with scrofulous sores—the son of a Rouen knit-goods dealer whom his parents were too busy in their shop to bother with.

"Come in," she said. "Your little girl's asleep inside."

The ground-floor bedroom—the only bedroom in the house—had a wide uncurtained bed standing against its rear wall; the window wall (one pane was mended with a bit of wrapping paper) was taken up by the kneading trough. In the corner behind the door was a raised slab for washing, and under it stood a row of heavy boots with shiny hobnails and a bottle of oil with a feather in its mouth. A Mathieu Laensberg almanac[1] lay on the dusty mantelpiece among gun flints, candle ends and bits of tinder. And as a final bit of clutter there was a figure of Fame blowing her trumpets—a picture probably cut out of a perfume advertisement and now fastened to the wall with six shoe tacks.

Emma's baby was asleep in a wicker cradle on the floor, and she took it up in its little blanket and began to sing softly to it and rock it in her arms.

Léon walked around the room: it seemed to him a strange sight, this elegant lady in her nankeen gown here among all this squalor. Madame Bovary

---

1. A farmer's almanac, begun in 1635 by Laensberg, frequently found in farms and country houses.

blushed; he turned away, fearing that his glance might have been indiscreet; and she put the baby back in its cradle—it had just thrown up over the collar of her dress. The wet nurse quickly wiped off the mess, assuring her it wouldn't show.

"It isn't the first time, you know," she said. "I do nothing but wipe up after her all day long. Would you mind leaving word with Camus the grocer to let me pick up a little soap when I need it? That would be the easiest for you—I wouldn't have to trouble you."

"I will, I will," said Emma. "Good-bye, Madame Rollet."

And she left the house, wiping her feet on the doorsill.

The wet nurse walked with her as far as the gate, talking about how hard it was to have to get up during the night.

"I'm so worn out sometimes I fall asleep in my chair. So couldn't you at least let me have just a pound of ground coffee? It would last me a month; I'd drink it with milk in the morning."

After undergoing a deluge of thanks, Madame Bovary moved on; and then when she had gone a little way down the path there was the sound of sabots and she turned around: it was the wet nurse again.

"What is it now?"

And the peasant woman drew her aside behind an elm and began to talk to her about her husband. He "had only his trade and the six francs a year the captain gave him, so . . ."

"Come to the point!" said Emma brusquely.

"Well, what I mean is," the wet nurse said, sighing after every word, "I'm afraid he wouldn't like it, seeing me sitting there drinking coffee by myself; you know how men are, they . . ."

"But you'll both have coffee!" Emma cried. "I just told you I'd give you some! Leave me alone!"

"Ah, Madame, you see he's had terrible cramps in his chest ever since he was wounded, and he says cider makes him feel worse, and . . ."

"Won't you please let me go?"

"So," she went on, making a curtsy, "if it isn't too much to ask"—she curtsied again—"if you would"—and she gave a beseeching glance—"just a little jug of brandy," she finally got out, "and I'll rub your little girl's feet with it—they're as tender as your tongue."

When she was finally rid of the wet nurse, Emma once again took Monsieur Léon's arm. She walked rapidly for a little while; then she slowed, and her glance fell on the shoulder of the young man she was with. His brown hair, smooth and neatly combed, touched the black velvet collar of his frock coat. She noticed that his fingernails were longer than those of most other inhabitants of Yonville. The clerk spent a great deal of time caring for them: he kept a special penknife in his desk for the purpose.

They returned to Yonville along the river. The summer weather had reduced its flow and left uncovered the river walls and water steps of the gardens along its bank. It ran silently, swift and cold-looking; long fine grasses bent with the current, like masses of loose green hair streaming in its limpid depths. Here and there on the tip of a reed or on a water-lily pad a spidery-legged insect was poised or crawling. Sunbeams pierced the little blue air bubbles that kept forming and breaking on the ripples; branchless old willows mirrored their gray bark in the water; in the distance the meadows seemed empty all around them. It was dinner time on the farms, and as they walked the young woman and her companion heard only the rhythm of their own steps on the earth of the path, the words they themselves were uttering, and the whisper of Emma's dress as it rustled around her.

The garden walls, their copings bristling with broken bits of bottles, were as warm as the glass of a greenhouse. Wallflowers had taken root between the bricks; and as she passed, the edge of Madame Bovary's open parasol crumbled some of their faded flowers into yellow dust; or an overhanging branch of honeysuckle or clematis would catch in the fringe and cling for a moment to the silk.

They talked about a company of Spanish dancers scheduled soon to appear at the theatre in Rouen.

"Are you going?" she asked.

"If I can," he answered.

Had they nothing more to say to each other? Their eyes, certainly, were full of more meaningful talk; and as they made themselves utter banalities they sensed the same languor invading them both: it was like a murmur of the soul, deep and continuous, more clearly audible than the sound of their words. Surprised by a sweetness that was new to them, it didn't occur to them to tell each other how they felt or to wonder why. Future joys are like tropic shores: out into the immensity that lies before them they waft their native softness, a fragrant breeze that drugs the traveler into drowsiness and makes him careless of what awaits him on the horizon beyond his view.

In one spot the ground was boggy from the trampling of cattle, and they had to walk on large green stones that had been laid in the mud. She kept stopping to see where to place her foot; and teetering on an unsteady stone, her arms lifted, her body bent, a hesitant look in her eye, she laughed, fearing lest she fall into the puddles.

When they reached her garden, Madame Bovary pushed open the little gate, ran up the steps and disappeared.

Léon returned to his office. His employer was out; he glanced at the piles of papers, sharpened a quill pen, and then—took up his hat and went out again.

He climbed to the Pasture, on the hilltop at the edge of the Argueil forest, and there he stretched out on the ground under the firs and looked up at the sky through his fingers.

"God!" he said to himself. "What a boring existence!"

He felt that he was much to be pitied for having to live in this village, with Homais for a friend and Maître Guillaumin for a master. The latter, completely taken up with business, wore gold-framed spectacles, red side whiskers and a white tie; fine feelings were a closed book to him, though the stiff British manner he affected had impressed the clerk at first. As for Madame Homais, she was the best wife in Normandy, placid as a sheep and devoted to her children, her father, her mother and her cousins; she wept at others' misfortunes, let everything in the house go, and hated corsets. But she was so slow-moving, so boring to listen to, so common-looking and limited in conversation, that it never occurred to him—though she was thirty and he twenty, and they slept in adjoining rooms and he spoke to her every day— that anyone could look on her as a woman, that she had any attributes of her sex except the dress she wore.

Who was there besides? Binet, a few shopkeepers, two or three tavern keepers, the priest, and lastly, Monsieur Tuvache, the mayor, and his two sons—a comfortably-off, surly, dull-witted trio who farmed their own land, ate huge meals with never a guest, faithful churchgoers for all that, and utterly insufferable in company.

But against the background of all these human faces, Emma's stood out— isolated from them and yet further removed than they, for he sensed that some abyss separated him from her.

At first he had gone to her house several times with the pharmacist. Charles had not seemed too eager to have him; and Léon felt helpless, torn as he was between fear of being indiscreet and desire for an intimacy that he considered all but impossible.

IV

With the coming of cold weather Emma moved out of her bedroom into the parlor, a long low-ceilinged room where a chunky branch of coral stood on the mantelpiece in front of the mirror. Sitting in her armchair beside the window, she could watch the villagers go by on the sidewalk.

Twice a day Léon went from his office to the Lion d'Or. Emma could hear him coming in the distance; she would lean forward as she listened, and the young man would slip past on the other side of the window curtain, always dressed the same, never turning his head. At twilight, when she had put down her embroidery and was sitting there with her chin in her left hand, she often started at the sudden appearance of this gliding shadow. She would jump up, order the maid to set the table.

Monsieur Homais often called during dinner. Tasseled cap in hand, he would tiptoe in so as to disturb no one, and he always gave the same greeting: "Good evening, everybody!" Then, sitting down at the table between them, he would ask the doctor for news of his patients, and Charles would ask him what the chances were of being paid. Then they would talk about what was "in the paper." By this time of day Homais knew it almost by heart, and he would repeat it *in toto,* complete with editorials and the news of each and every disaster that had occurred in France and abroad. When these topics ran dry he never failed to comment on the dishes he saw being served. Sometimes, half rising, he would even considerately point out to Madame the tenderest piece of meat; or, turning to the maid, he would advise her on the preparation of her stews and the use of seasoning from a health point of view: he was quite dazzling on the subject of aromas, osmazomes, juices and gelatines. Indeed, Homais had more recipes in his head than there were bottles in his pharmacy, and he excelled at making all kinds of jellies, vinegars and cordials. He was acquainted with all the latest fuel-saving stoves, and with the arts of preserving cheeses and treating spoiled wine.

At eight o'clock Justin always called for him: it was time to shut the pharmacy. Monsieur Homais would give him a quizzical glance, especially if Félicité were in the room, for he had noticed that his pupil was partial to the doctor's house. "My young man's beginning to get ideas," he would say. "Something tells me he's after your maid!"

And there was worse: despite all rebukes, the boy persisted in his habit of listening to conversations. On Sundays, for instance, Madame Homais would summon him to the parlor to take away the children, who had fallen asleep in armchairs, dragging down the loose calico slip covers, and there was no way of getting him to leave the room.

These soirées at the pharmacist's were not very well attended, for his slanderous tongue and his political opinions had alienated one respectable person after another. The clerk was invariably present. At the sound of the doorbell he would run down to greet Madame Bovary, take her shawl, and stow away under the desk in the pharmacy the overshoes she wore when it snowed.

First they would play a few rounds of *trente-et-un;* then Monsieur Homais would play *écarté*[2] with Emma, Léon standing behind her and giving advice. With his hands on the back of her chair, he would look down and see the teeth of her comb piercing her chignon. Each time she threw down a card the right side of her dress gave an upward twist, and he could follow the gradually paling shadow cast down her neck by the knot of her hair, until it was lost in a darker shadow. Then her dress would drop down on both sides of her chair, swelling out in full folds and spreading to the floor. Sometimes Léon would feel himself touching it with the sole of his shoe, and he would quickly move away, as though he had been treading on someone.

When they finished their cards, the apothecary and the doctor played dominoes; and Emma would move to another chair, lean her elbows on the table and leaf through *L'Illustration,* or take up the fashion magazine she usually brought with her. Léon would sit beside her, and together they would look at the pictures and wait for each other before turning a page. Often she would ask him to read a poem aloud, and Léon would recite it in a languid voice that he carefully let die away at the love passages. But the noise of the dominoes annoyed him: Monsieur Homais was an expert, easily outplaying Charles. When the score reached three hundred the two of them would stretch out before the fireplace and quickly fall asleep. The fire smoldered, the teapot was empty; Léon continued to read, and Emma listened, absentmindedly turning the lampshade, its gauzy surface painted with pierrots in carriages and tightrope dancers balancing with their poles. Léon would stop, indicating with a gesture his sleeping audience; and then they would talk in low voices, their conversation seeming the sweeter for not being overheard.

Thus a kind of intimacy grew up between them, a continual exchange of books and ballads. Monsieur Bovary was not jealous; he found it all quite natural.

For his birthday he received a splendid phrenological head, all marked over with numerals down to the thorax and painted blue. This was an offering from the clerk. He was attentive in many other ways, too, even doing errands for Charles in Rouen. When a new novel launched a craze for exotic plants, Léon bought some for Madame, holding them on his knees in the Hirondelle and pricking his fingers on their spikes.

Emma had a railed shelf installed in her window to hold her flowerpots. The clerk, too, had his hanging garden, and they could look out and see each other tending their blossoms.

2. A card game similar to euchre, in which players win tricks by playing a higher card in the suit. *Trente-et-un:* "Thirty-one" (French), also called "Red and Black": a French gambling game in which cards are dealt in two categories (red and black) until a total of thirty-one or more points is reached; players bet on the winning color.

There was one person in the village who spent even more time at his window than they: from morning till night on Sunday, and every afternoon in good weather, the lean profile of Monsieur Binet could be seen in a dormer bent over his lathe, its monotonous drone audible as far as the Lion d'Or.

One evening when he returned home Léon found in his room a velvet and wool coverlet, with foliage designs on a pale ground. He showed it to Madame Homais, Monsieur Homais, Justin, the children, and the cook, and spoke about it to his employer. Everybody wanted to see it: why should the doctor's wife give presents to the clerk? The whole thing seemed suspicious, and everyone was sure that they must be having an affair.

By speaking incessantly about Emma's charms and intelligence, Léon gave plenty of grounds for the belief. Binet turned on him one day with a snarl: "What's it to me? She doesn't let *me* hang around her!"

He was in agony trying to think of a way of "declaring himself" to her. He was constantly torn between the fear of offending her and shame at his own cowardice; he shed tears of despair and frustrated desire. Every so often he resolved to take energetic action: he wrote letters, only to tear them up; he gave himself time limits, only to extend them. More than once he started out intending to dare all; but in Emma's presence he quickly lost his courage, and if Charles happened to appear at such a moment and invited him to get into the buggy and go with him to see a patient living somewhere nearby, he would accept at once, bow to Madame and drive off. Her husband, after all, was part of herself, was he not?

As for Emma, she never tried to find out whether she was in love with him. Love, to her, was something that comes suddenly, like a blinding flash of lightning—a heaven-sent storm hurled into life, uprooting it, sweeping every will before it like a leaf, engulfing all feelings. It never occurred to her that if the drainpipes of a house are clogged, the rain may collect in pools on the roof; and she suspected no danger until suddenly she discovered a crack in the wall.

V

It was a snowy Sunday afternoon in February.

All of them—Monsieur and Madame Bovary, Homais and Monsieur Léon—had gone to see a new flax mill that was being built in the valley, a mile or so from Yonville. The apothecary had taken Napoléon and Athalie along to give them some exercise, and Justin accompanied them, carrying a supply of umbrellas over his shoulder.

Nothing, however, could have been less interesting than this point of interest. A long rectangular building pierced with innumerable little windows stood in the midst of a large tract of bare land, with a few already rusty gear wheels lying here and there among piles of sand and gravel. It was still unfinished, and the sky could be seen between the rafters. Attached to the ridgepole at the peak of one of the gables was a bouquet of straw and wheat, tied with red, white and blue ribbons that flapped in the wind.

Homais was holding forth. He expatiated to them all on how important the mill was going to be, estimated the strength of the floors and the thickness of the walls, and keenly regretted not owning a carpenter's rule, such as Monsieur Binet possessed for his personal use.

Emma, who had taken his arm, was leaning slightly against his shoulder and looking up at the far-off disc of the sun that was suffusing the mist with its pale brilliance; then she turned her head, and saw—Charles. His cap was pulled down over his eyes; and the quivering of his thick lips in the cold gave him a stupid look. Even his back, his placid back, was irritating to look at: all his dullness was written right there, on his coat.

As she was looking at him, deriving a kind of perverse enjoyment from her very irritation, Léon moved a step closer. White in the cold, his face was more languorous and appealing than ever; a bit of his bare skin showed through a gap in his shirt collar; she could see the tip of one of his ears below a lock of his hair; and his large blue eyes, lifted toward the clouds, seemed to Emma more limpid and lovely than mountain lakes mirroring the sky.

"Stop that!" the apothecary suddenly cried.

And he rushed over to his son, who had just jumped into a heap of lime to whiten his shoes. To his father's scoldings Napoléon replied with howls; Justin scraped off the shoes with a bit of plaster; but a knife was needed, and Charles offered his.

"Ah!" she cried to herself. "He carries a knife around with him, like a peasant!"

The cold was beginning to pinch, and they turned back toward Yonville.

That evening Madame Bovary did not attend her neighbor's soirée; and when Charles had gone and she felt herself alone, the comparison returned to her mind almost with the sharpness of an actual sensation, and with the increased perspective conferred on things by memory. Watching the brightly burning fire from her bed, she saw once again, as at the scene itself, Léon standing there, leaning with one hand on his slender, flexing cane and with the other holding Athalie, who was placidly sucking a piece of ice. She found him charming; she could not take her mind off him; she remembered how he had looked on other occasions, things he had said, the sound of his voice, everything about him; and she kept saying to herself, protruding her lips as though for a kiss: "Charming, charming! . . . Isn't he in love? Who could it be?" she asked herself. "Why—he's in love with me!"

All the evidence burst on her at once; her heart leapt up. The flames in the fireplace cast a merry, flickering light on the ceilings; she lay on her back and stretched out her arms.

Then began the eternal lament: "Oh, if only fate had willed it so! Why didn't it? What stood in the way?"

When Charles came in at midnight she pretended to wake up. He made some noise as he undressed, and she complained of migraine; then she casually asked what had happened during the evening.

"Monsieur Léon went up to his room early," said Charles.

She couldn't help smiling, and she fell asleep filled with new happiness.

At nightfall the next day she had a visit from Monsieur Lheureux, the proprietor of the local dry-goods store. He was a clever man, this tradesman. Born a Gascon, but long settled in Normandy, he combined his southern volubility with the cunning of his adopted region. His fat, flabby, clean-shaven face looked as though it had been dyed with a faint tincture of licorice, and his white hair emphasized the piercing boldness of his small black eyes. What he had been in earlier life was a mystery to all: peddler, some said; and others, banker in Routot. What was certain was that he could do in his head intricate feats of calculation that startled Binet himself. Polite to the point of obsequiousness, he was continually in a semi-bent position, like someone making a bow or extending an invitation.

He left his hat with its black mourning band at the door, placed a green case on the table, and began by complaining, with many civilities, at not having been honored up till now with Madame's patronage. A poor shop like his could scarcely be expected to attract so elegant a lady: he emphasized the adjective. But she had only to give him an order and he would undertake to supply anything she wanted, whether accessories, lingerie, hosiery and other knit goods, or notions, for he went to the city four times a month regularly. He was in constant touch with the biggest firms. She could mention his name at the Trois Frères, at the Barbe d'Or or at the Grand Sauvage: everyone in those places knew all about him. Today he would just like to show Madame a few articles he happened to have with him, thanks to a lucky buy; out of his box he took half a dozen embroidered collars.

Madame Bovary looked them over.

"I don't need anything," she said.

Then Monsieur Lheureux daintily held out for her inspection three Algerian scarves, some packages of English needles, a pair of straw slippers, and finally four coconut-shell egg cups, carved in an openwork design by convicts. Then, both hands on the table, leaning forward, his neck outstretched, he watched Emma open-mouthed, following her gaze as it wandered uncertainly over the merchandise. From time to time, as though to brush off a bit of dust, he gave a flick of a fingernail to the silk of the scarves, lying there unfolded to their full length; and they quivered and rustled under his touch, their gold sequins gleaming like little stars in the greenish light of the dusk.

"How much are they?"

"They're absurdly cheap," he said. "Besides, there's no hurry. Pay whenever you like—we're not Jews!"

She meditated a few moments, then finally told Monsieur Lheureux once more that she didn't want to buy.

"That's quite all right," he answered impassively. "You and I will do business some other time. I've always known how to get along with the ladies—except my wife."

Emma smiled.

"I just want you to know," he said, dropping his facetious tone and assuming an air of candor, "that I'm not worried about the money. In fact, I could let you have some if you needed it."

Emma made a gesture of surprise.

"Ah," he said quickly, in a low voice. "I wouldn't have to go far to find it, believe me!"

Then he turned the conversation to the subject of Monsieur Tellier, proprietor of the Café Français, whom Monsieur Bovary was treating.

"What's his trouble, anyway? He's got a cough that shakes the house. I'm afraid he may soon need a wooden overcoat more than a flannel undershirt! He was a wild one in his younger days! The kind that doesn't know even the meaning of self-control, Madame! He literally burned his insides out with brandy! Still, it's hard to see an old friend go."

And as he tied up his box he talked on about the doctor's patients.

"It must be the weather," he said, scowling at the windowpanes, "that's causing all this illness. I don't feel right myself: one of these days I'll have to come and talk to Monsieur about a pain I have in my back. Well—au revoir, Madame Bovary; at your service, any time."

And he shut the door softly behind him.

Emma had her dinner brought to her in her bedroom on a tray, and ate it beside the fire. She lingered over her food: everything tasted good.

"How sensible I was!" she told herself, as she thought of the scarves.

She heard footsteps on the stairs: it was Léon. She jumped up and snatched the topmost dish towel from a pile she had left for hemming on the chest of drawers. She looked very busy when he came in.

Conversation languished: Madame Bovary kept letting his remarks drop unanswered, and he seemed very ill at ease. He sat in a low chair beside the fire, toying with her ivory needlecase; she continued to sew, occasionally creasing the cloth together with her fingernail. She said nothing, and he, too, was quiet, captivated by her silence as he would have been by her words.

"Poor fellow!" she was thinking.

"What does she dislike about me?" he was wondering.

Finally Léon said that he would be going to Rouen some day soon on office business.

"Your subscription at the music library has run out," he said. "Shall I renew it?"

"No," she answered.

"Why not?"

"Because . . ."

And pursing her lips she slowly drew out a new length of gray thread.

Her sewing irritated Léon: the cloth seemed to be roughening the tips of her fingers. A compliment occurred to him, but he hadn't the courage to utter it.

"You're giving it up?"

"What?" she asked quickly. "Oh, my music? Heavens, yes! Haven't I got my house and my husband to look after—a thousand things—all kinds of duties that come first?"

She looked at the clock. Charles was late. She pretended to be worried. "He's such a good man," she said, two or three times.

The clerk was fond of Monsieur Bovary, but he was unpleasantly surprised to hear her speak so affectionately of him. Nevertheless he continued the praises she had begun, and assured her that he heard them from everyone, especially the pharmacist.

"Ah, Monsieur Homais is a fine man," said Emma.

"He certainly is," said the clerk.

He began to speak of Madame Homais, whose sloppy appearance usually made them laugh.

"What of it?" Emma interrupted. "A good wife and mother doesn't worry about her clothes."

And once again she fell silent.

It was the same the following days: her talk, her manner, everything changed. She immersed herself in household tasks, went regularly to church, and was stricter with the maid.

She took Berthe away from the wet nurse. Félicité brought her in when there was company, and Madame Bovary undressed her to show off her little legs and arms. She adored children, she said: they were her consolation, her joy, her delight; and she accompanied her caresses with gushings that would have reminded anyone except the Yonvillians of Esmeralda's mother in *Notre-Dame de Paris*.[3]

Nowadays when Charles came in, he found his slippers set out to warm by the fire. Now his vests were never without linings, his shirts never without buttons; it was a pleasure to see the piles of cotton nightcaps stacked so neatly in the closet. She no longer frowned at the idea of taking a walk in the garden; she agreed to all his suggestions without trying to understand his reasons. And when Léon saw him beside the fire in the evening, his face flushed from dinner, his hands folded over his stomach, his feet on the andirons, his eyes moist with happiness, the baby crawling on the carpet, and this slender woman leaning over the back of his armchair to kiss him on the forehead—"I must be mad," he told himself. "How can I ever hope to come near her?"

She seemed so virtuous and inaccessible that he lost all hope, even the faintest.

But by thus renouncing her, he transformed her into an extraordinary being. She was divested in his eyes of the earthly attributes that held no promise for him; and in his heart she rose higher and higher, withdrawing further from him in a magnificent, soaring apotheosis. His feeling for her was so pure that it did not interfere with his daily life—it was one of those feelings that are cherished because of their very rarity: the distress caused by their loss would be greater than the happiness given by their possession.

Emma grew thinner: her face became paler, more emaciated. With her smooth black hair, her large eyes, her straight nose, her birdlike movements, her new habit of silence, she seemed all but out of contact with life, bearing on her brow the vague mark of a sublime fate. She was so melancholy and so subdued, so sweet and yet so withdrawn, that in her presence he felt transfixed by a glacial spell—just as in a church the fragrance of flowers and the cold given off by marble will sometimes set us shivering. Even other men were not immune to this seduction. The pharmacist put it this way:

"She's got class! She'd hold her own in Le Havre or Dieppe!"

The village housewives admired her for her thrift; Charles's patients for her politeness; the poor for her charity.

And all this time she was torn by wild desires, by rage, by hatred. The trim folds of her dress hid a heart in turmoil, and her reticent lips told nothing of the storm. She was in love with Léon, and she sought the solitude that allowed her to revel undisturbed in his image. The sight of his person spoiled the voluptuousness of her musings. She trembled at the sound of his footsteps; then, with him before her, the agitation subsided, and she was left with nothing but a vast bewilderment that turned gradually into sadness.

Léon did not know, when he left her house in despair, that she went immediately to the window and watched him disappear down the street. She worried over his every move, watched every expression that crossed his face; she concocted an elaborate story to have a pretext for visiting his room. The pharmacist's wife seemed to her blessed to sleep under the same roof; and her thoughts came continually to rest on that house, like the pigeons from

---

3. A historical novel (1831) by Victor Hugo, in which the mother of Agnes, a girl abducted by gypsies who takes the name Esmeralda, worships a shoe of her stolen child.

the Lion d'Or that alighted there to soak their pink feet and white wings in the eaves-trough. But the more aware Emma became of her love the more she repressed it in an effort to conceal it and weaken it. She would have been glad had Léon guessed; and she kept imagining accidents and disasters that would open his eyes. It was indolence, probably, or fear, that held her back, and a feeling of shame. She had kept him at too great a distance, she decided: now it was too late; the occasion was lost. Besides, the pride and pleasure she derived from thinking of herself as "virtuous" and from wearing an air of resignation as she looked at herself in the mirror consoled her a little for the sacrifice she thought she was making.

Her carnal desires, her cravings for money, and the fits of depression engendered by her love gradually merged into a single torment; and instead of trying to put it out of her mind she cherished it, spurring herself on to suffer, never missing an opportunity to do so. A dish poorly served or a door left ajar grated on her nerves; she sighed thinking of the velvet gowns she didn't own, the happiness that eluded her, her unattainable dreams, her entire cramped existence.

What exasperated her was Charles's total unawareness of her ordeal. His conviction that he was making her happy she took as a stupid insult: such self-righteousness could only mean that he didn't appreciate her. For whose sake, after all, was she being virtuous? Wasn't he the obstacle to every kind of happiness, the cause of all her wretchedness, the sharp-pointed prong of this many-stranded belt that bound her on all sides?

So he became the sole object of her resentment. Her attempts to conquer this feeling served only to strengthen it, for their failure gave her additional cause for despair and deepened her estrangement from her husband. She had moments of revulsion against her own meekness. She reacted to the drabness of her home by indulging in daydreams of luxury, and to matrimonial caresses by adulterous desires. She wished that Charles would beat her: then she would feel more justified in hating him and betraying him out of revenge. Sometimes she was surprised by the horrible possibilities that she imagined; and yet she had to keep smiling, hear herself say time and again that she was happy, pretend to be so, let everyone believe it!

Still, there were times when she could scarcely stomach the hypocrisy. She would be seized with a longing to run off with Léon, escape to some far-off place where they could begin life anew; but at such moments she would shudder, feeling herself at the brink of a terrifying precipice.

"What's the use—he doesn't love me any more," she would decide. What was to become of her? What help could she hope for? What comfort? What relief?

Such a crisis always left her shattered, gasping, prostrate, sobbing to herself, tears streaming down her face.

"Why in the world don't you tell Monsieur?" the maid would ask her, finding her thus distraught.

"It's nerves," Emma would answer. "Don't mention it to him. It would only upset him."

"Ah, yes," Félicité said, one day. "You're just like the daughter of old Guérin, the fisherman at Le Pollet.[4] I knew her at Dieppe before I came to you. She used to be so sad, so terribly sad, that when she stood in her door

---

4. Suburb of Dieppe, where the fishermen live.

she made you think of a funeral pall hanging there. It seems it was some kind of a fog in her head that ailed her. The doctors couldn't do anything for her, or the priest either. When it came over her worst, she'd go off by herself along the beach, and sometimes the customs officer would find her stretched out flat on her face on the pebbles and crying, when he made his rounds. It passed off after she was married, they say."

"With me," said Emma, "it was after I married that it began."

VI

One evening when the window was open and she had been sitting beside it watching Lestiboudois the sacristan trim the boxwood, she suddenly heard the tolling of the Angelus.

It was the beginning of April, primrose time, when soft breezes blow over newly spaded flower beds, and gardens, like women, seem to be primping themselves for the gaieties of summer. Through the slats of the arbor, and all around beyond, she could see the stream flowing through the meadows, winding its vagabond course amid the grass. The evening mist was rising among the bare poplars, blurring their outlines with a tinge of purple that was paler and more transparent than the sheerest gauze caught on their branches. In the distance cattle were moving: neither their steps nor their lowing could be heard, and the steadily sounding church bell sent its peaceful lament into the evening air.

As the ringing continued, the young woman's thoughts began to stray among old memories of girlhood and the convent. She remembered the tall altar candlesticks that soared above the vases full of flowers and the columned tabernacle. She wished she could be again what she once had been, one in the long line of white-veiled girls, black specked here and there by the stiff cowls of the nuns bowed over their *prie-dieus*. Sundays at Mass when she raised her head she used to see the gentle features of the Virgin among the bluish clouds of rising incense. The memory filled her with emotion: she felt limp and passive, like a bit of bird's-down whirling in a storm; and automatically she turned her steps toward the church, ready for any devotion that would enable her to humble her heart and lose herself entirely.

In the square she met Lestiboudois on his way back: in order not to lose pay by cutting his workday short, he preferred to interrupt his gardening and then go back to it, with the result that he rang the Angelus when it suited him. Besides, early ringing served to remind the village boys that it was time for catechism.

Some of them were already there, playing marbles on the slabs in the cemetery. Others, astride the wall, were swinging their legs, their wooden shoes breaking off the tall nettles that grew between the wall itself and the nearest graves. This was the only spot that was green: all the rest was stones, always covered with a fine dust despite the sacristan's sweeping.

Other boys had taken off their sabots and were running about on the stones as though the cemetery were a smooth floor made specially for them. Their shouts could be heard above the dying sounds of the bell; the heavy rope that hung down from the top of the bell tower and trailed on the ground was swaying ever more slowly. Swallows flew past, twittering as they sliced the air with their swift flight, and disappeared into their yellow nests under the eave-tiles. At the far end of the church a lamp was burning—a wick in a hanging glass, whose light seemed from a distance like a whitish spot dancing on the oil. A long shaft of sunlight cutting across the nave deepened the darkness in the side aisles and corners.

"Where is the priest?" Madame Bovary asked a boy who was happily trying to wrench the turnstile loose from its socket.

"He'll be here," he answered.

Just then the door of the rectory creaked open and the abbé Bournisien appeared. The boys fled helter-skelter into the church.

"Won't they ever behave?" he muttered to himself. "No respect for anything." He picked up a tattered catechism that he had almost stepped on. Then he saw Madame Bovary. "Excuse me," he said. "I didn't place you for a minute."

He stuffed the catechism into his pocket and stood swinging the heavy sacristy key between two fingers.

The setting sun was full in his face; and the black cloth of his cassock, shiny at the elbows and frayed at the hem, seemed paler in its glow. Grease spots and snuff stains ran parallel to the row of little buttons on his broad chest; they were thickest below his neckband, which held back the heavy folds of his red skin; this was sprinkled with yellow splotches, half hidden by the bristles of his graying beard. He had just had his dinner, and was breathing heavily.

"How are you?" he went on.

"Poorly," said Emma. "Not well at all."

"Neither am I," the priest answered. "These first hot days take it out of you terribly, don't they? But what can we do? We're born to suffer, as St. Paul says. What does your husband think is the trouble?"

"My husband!" she said, with a scornful gesture.

The country priest looked surprised. "He must have prescribed something for you, hasn't he?"

"Ah!" said Emma. "It isn't earthly remedies that I need."

But the priest kept looking away, into the church, where the boys were kneeling side by side, each shoving his neighbor with his shoulder and all of them falling down like ninepins.

"Could you tell me . . ." she began.

"Just wait, Riboudet!" he shouted furiously. "I'll box your ears when I get hold of you!"

Then, turning to Emma: "That's the son of Boudet the carpenter; his parents don't bother with him, they let him do as he likes. He'd learn fast if he wanted to: he's very bright. Sometimes as a joke I call him Riboudet—you know, from the name of the hill near Maromme; sometimes I say 'mon Riboudet'—Mont Riboudet! Ha! Ha! The other day I told my little joke to the bishop. He laughed. He was good enough to laugh. And Monsieur Bovary—how is he?"

She seemed not to hear him, and he went on: "Always on the move, probably? He and I are certainly the two busiest people in the parish. He takes care of the bodies," he added, with a heavy laugh, "and I look after the souls."

She fastened her imploring eyes upon him. "Yes," she said. "You must be called on to relieve all kinds of suffering."

"Believe me, I am, Madame Bovary! This very morning I had to go to Bas-

Diauville for a cow that had the colic: the peasants thought it was a spell. All their cows, for some reason . . . Excuse me, Madame! Longuemarre! Boudet! Drat you both! Will you cut it out?"

And he rushed into the church.

By now the boys were crowding around the high lectern, climbing up on the cantor's bench and opening the missal; and others, moving stealthily, were about to invade the confessional. But the priest was suddenly upon them, slapping them right and left; seizing them by the coat collar, he lifted them off the ground and then set them on their knees on the stone floor of the choir, pushing them down hard as though he were trying to plant them there.

"Well!" he said, returning to Emma. And then, as he opened his large calico handkerchief, holding a corner of it between his teeth: "As we were saying, farmers have plenty of troubles."

"Other people, too," she answered.

"Of course! Workingmen in the cities, for instance . . ."

"I wasn't thinking of them . . ."

"Ah, but I assure you I've known mothers of families, good women, true saints, who didn't even have a crust of bread."

"I was thinking of women who have bread, Monsieur le curé," Emma said, the corners of her mouth twisting as she spoke, "but who lack . . ."

"Firewood for the winter," the priest anticipated.

"Ah, never mind . . ."

"What do you mean, never mind? It seems to me that to be warm and well fed . . ."

"Oh, my God!" Emma whispered to herself. "My God!"

"Are you feeling ill?" he asked. He looked concerned, and advanced a step. "Something must have disagreed with you. You'd better go home, Madame Bovary, and drink a cup of tea; that will pick you up. Or a glass of water with a little brown sugar."

"What for?"

She looked as though she were emerging from a dream.

"You were holding your hand to your forehead. I thought you must be feeling faint." Then: "But weren't you asking me a question? What was it? I can't recall . . ."

"I? Oh, no, nothing . . . nothing," Emma said.

And her wandering glance came slowly to rest on the old man in his cassock. For a few moments they looked at each other without speaking.

"Well, Madame Bovary," he said, finally, "you'll excuse me, but duty calls. I have to look after my youngsters. First Communion will be here soon: it will be on us before we know it. Time's so short I always keep them an extra hour on Wednesdays after Ascension. Poor things! We can't begin too soon to steer their young souls in the Lord's path—indeed it's what he Himself tells us to do, through the mouth of His divine Son. Keep well, Madame; remember me kindly to your husband!"

And he entered the church, genuflecting just inside the door.

Emma watched him as he disappeared between the double line of pews, treading heavily, his head slightly bent to one side, his half-open hands held with palms outward.

Then she turned stiffly, like a statue on a pivot, and set out for home.

Behind her she heard the booming voice of the priest and the lighter voices of the boys.

"Are you a Christian?"

"Yes, I am a Christian."

"What is a Christian?"

"A Christian is one who, after being baptized . . . baptized . . . baptized . . ."

She climbed her stairs holding tight to the rail, and once in her room she sank heavily into a chair.

The whitish light coming through the windowpanes was slowly fading and ebbing away. The various pieces of furniture seemed to be fixed more firmly in their places, lost in shadow as in an ocean of darkness. The fire was out, the clock kept up its tick-tock; and Emma vaguely marveled that all these things should be so quiet while she herself was in such turmoil. Then little Berthe was in front of her, tottering in her knitted shoes between the window and the sewing table, trying to reach her mother and catch hold of the ends of her apron strings.

"Let me alone!" Emma cried, pushing her away.

But a few moments later the little girl was back, this time coming closer. Leaning her arms on her mother's knees she looked up at her with her big blue eyes, and a thread of clear saliva dripped from her lip onto the silk of the apron.

"Let me alone!" Emma cried again, very much annoyed.

The expression on her face frightened the child, who began to scream.

"Won't you let me alone!" she cried, thrusting her off with her elbow.

Berthe fell just at the foot of the chest of drawers, cutting her cheek on one of its brasses. She began to bleed. Madame Bovary rushed to pick her up, broke the bell-rope, called loudly for the maid; and words of self-reproach were on her lips when Charles appeared. It was dinner time; he had just come in.

"Look what's happened, darling," she said, in an even voice. "The baby fell down and hurt herself playing."

Charles reassured her: it was nothing serious, he said, and he went for some adhesive plaster.

Madame Bovary didn't go downstairs for dinner that evening: she insisted on staying alone with her child. As she watched her lying there asleep, her anxiety, such as it was, gradually wore off; and she thought of herself as having been silly and good-hearted indeed to let herself be upset over so small a matter. Berthe had stopped sobbing; and now the cotton coverlet rose and fell imperceptibly with her regular breathing. A few large tears had gathered in the corners of her half-closed eyelids; through the lashes could be seen the pupils, pale and sunken-looking; the adhesive stuck on her cheek pulled the skin to one side.

"It's a strange thing," Emma thought, "what an ugly child she is."

At eleven o'clock, when Charles came back from the pharmacy, where he had gone after dinner to take back the plaster that was left, he found his wife on her feet beside the cradle.

"Really, believe me—it will be all right," he said, kissing her on the forehead. "Don't worry about it, darling: you'll make yourself ill."

He had stayed out a long time. He had not seemed unduly upset, but even so Monsieur Homais had done his best to cheer him up, "raise his morale." The conversation had then turned on the various dangers that beset children because of the absentmindedness of servants. Madame Homais could speak from experience, bearing as she did to this day on her chest the marks of a panful of burning coals that a cook had dropped inside her pinafore when she was small. No wonder the Homaises went out of their way to be careful with their children! In their house knives were never sharpened, floors never waxed. There were iron grills at the windows and heavy bars across the fireplaces. Though taught to be self-reliant, the Homais children couldn't move a step without someone in attendance; at the slightest sign of a cold their father stuffed them with cough syrups, and well past their fourth birthdays they were all mercilessly made to wear padded caps. This, it must be said, was a pet idea of Madame Homais': her husband was secretly worried about it, fearing lest the intellectual organs suffer as a result of such pressure; and he sometimes went so far as to say:

"Do you want to turn them into Caribs or Botocudos?"[5]

Charles, meanwhile, had tried several times to end the conversation. "I'd like to have a word with you," he whispered in the clerk's ear; and Léon walked downstairs ahead of him.

"Can he be suspecting something?" he wondered. His heart pounded, and he imagined a thousand contingencies.

Charles, after closing the door behind them, asked him to inquire in Rouen as to the price of a good daguerreotype: he was thinking of paying a delicate tribute to his wife by giving her a sentimental surprise—a portrait of himself in his black tail coat. But he wanted to know, first, "what he was letting himself in for." Such inquiries would be no trouble for Monsieur Léon, since he went to the city almost every week.

What was the purpose of these visits? Homais suspected that there was a story there, an intrigue of some kind. But he was mistaken: Léon was not carrying on any amourette. These days his spirits were lower than ever: Madame Lefrançois could tell it from the amount of food he left on his plate. To find out more about it she questioned the tax collector; but Binet rebuffed her, saying that he "wasn't in the pay of the police."

Nevertheless his table companion struck him as exceedingly odd. Léon often lay back in his chair, stretched out his arms and complained vaguely about life.

"That's because you have no hobbies," said the tax collector.

"What would you advise?"

"If I were you I'd buy myself a lathe!"

"But I wouldn't know how to use it," the clerk answered.

"That's so, you wouldn't," said Binet. And he stroked his chin with an air of mingled scorn and satisfaction.

Léon was tired of loving without having anything to show for it, and he was beginning to feel the depression that comes from leading a monotonous life without any guiding interest or buoyant hope. He was so sick of Yonville and the Yonvillians that the sight of certain people and certain buildings irritated him beyond endurance: the pharmacist, worthy soul that he was, he found utterly unbearable. Still, though he longed for a new position, the prospect of change frightened him.

---

5. Two South American peoples.

But now timidity gave way to impatience, and Paris beckoned from afar, with the fanfare of its masked balls, the laughter of its grisettes. Since he would have to finish his law studies there sooner or later, why shouldn't he go now? What was preventing him? And he began to make imaginary plans, sketch out his new existence. He furnished a dream apartment. He would lead an artist's life—take guitar lessons, wear a dressing gown, a Basque beret, blue velvet slippers! And in his mind's eye he particularly admired his overmantel arrangement: a pair of crossed fencing foils, with a skull and the guitar hanging above.

The difficulty lay in obtaining his mother's consent; still, there could scarcely be a more reasonable request. Even his employer was urging him to think of another office, where he could widen his experience. Taking a middle course, therefore, Léon looked for a place as second clerk in Rouen, found nothing, and finally wrote his mother a long detailed letter in which he set forth his reasons for moving to Paris at once. She consented.

He didn't hurry. Every day for a month Hivert transported for him, from Yonville to Rouen and from Rouen to Yonville, trunks, valises and bundles; and after Léon had had his wardrobe restocked and his three armchairs reupholstered and had bought a whole new supply of foulard handkerchiefs—after he had made more preparations than for a trip around the world—he kept putting off his departure from week to week, until he received a second letter from his mother urging him to be on his way, since he wanted to pass his examination before the summer vacation.

When the moment came for farewells, Madame Homais wept and Justin sobbed. Homais hid his emotion as a strong man should, and insisted on carrying his friend's overcoat as far as the notary's. Maître Guillaumin was to drive Léon to Rouen in his carriage.

There was just time to say good-bye to Monsieur Bovary. When Léon reached the top of the stairs he was so breathless that he stood still for a moment. As he entered the room Madame Bovary rose quickly to her feet.

"Here I am again," said Léon.

"I knew you'd come!"

She bit her lip, and the blood rushed under her skin, reddening it from the roots of her hair to the edge of her collar. She remained standing, leaning against the wall paneling.

"Monsieur isn't here?" he said.

"He's out."

He repeated: "He's out."

There was a silence. They looked at each other; and their thoughts clung together in their common anguish like two throbbing hearts.

"I'd love to kiss Berthe," said Léon.

Emma went down a few steps and called Félicité.

He glanced quickly around him, taking in the walls, the tables, the fireplace, as though to record them forever down to their last detail and carry them away in his memory.

Then she was back, and the maid brought in Berthe, who was swinging a pinwheel upside down on a string.

Léon kissed her several times on the neck. "Good-bye, sweetheart! Good-bye!" And he handed her back to her mother.

"You may take her," Emma said to the maid.

They were left alone.

Madame Bovary had turned her back, her face pressed to a window-pane. Léon was holding his cap in his hand and kept brushing it against his thigh.

"It's going to rain," said Emma.

"I have a coat," he answered.

"Ah!"

She half turned to him, her face lowered. The light seemed to glide down her forehead to her arching brows as on a marble statue; and there was no way of knowing what she was gazing at on the horizon or what her deepest thoughts might be.

"Good-bye, then," he said, sighing deeply.

She raised her head with an abrupt movement.

"Yes, good-bye—you must be on your way."

They both stepped forward: he held out his hand; she hesitated.

"A handshake, then—English style," she said, with a forced laugh, putting her hand in his.

Léon felt her moist palm in his grasp, and into it seemed to flow the very essence of his being.

Then he released it; their eyes met again; and he was off.

As he crossed the roofed market he stopped behind a pillar to stare for a last time at the white house with its four green shutters. He thought he saw a shadowy form at the bedroom window; then the curtain, released from its hook as though of its own accord, swung slowly for a moment in long slanting folds and sprang fully out to hang straight and motionless as a plaster wall. Léon set off at a run.

Ahead he saw his employer's gig in the road, and beside it a man in an apron holding the horse. Homais and Maître Guillaumin were talking together, waiting for him.

The apothecary embraced him, tears in his eyes. "Here's your overcoat, my boy: wrap up warm! Look after yourself! Take it easy!"

"Come, Léon—jump in!" said the notary.

Homais leaned over the mudguard, and in a voice broken by sobs gulped the sad, familiar words of parting: *Bon voyage!*

"Bon soir!" replied Maître Guillaumin. "Anchors aweigh!"

They rolled off, and Homais went home.

Madame Bovary had opened her window that gave on to the garden, and was watching the clouds.

They were gathering in the west, in the direction of Rouen, twisting rapidly in black swirls; out from behind them shot great sun rays, like the golden arrows of a hanging trophy; and the rest of the sky was empty, white as porcelain. Then came a gust of wind; the poplars swayed; and suddenly the rain was pattering on the green leaves. But soon the sun came out again; chickens cackled; sparrows fluttered their wings in the wet bushes; and rivulets flowing along the gravel carried away the pink flowers of an acacia.

"Ah, by now he must be far away!" she thought.

Monsieur Homais dropped in as usual at half-past six, during dinner.

"Well," he said, sitting down, "so we've sent our young man on his way, have we?"

"I guess so," said the doctor. And then, turning in his chair: "What's new at your house?"

"Nothing much. Just that my wife wasn't quite herself this afternoon. You know how women are—anything upsets them, mine especially. We've no right to complain: their nervous system is much more impressionable than ours."

"Poor Léon!" said Charles. "How will he get along in Paris, do you think? Will he get used to it?"

Madame Bovary sighed.

"Never fear!" said the pharmacist, making a clicking noise with his tongue. "Think of the gay parties in restaurants, the masked balls! The champagne! Everything will go at a merry pace, I assure you!"

"I don't think he'll do anything wrong," Bovary objected.

"Nor do I," Monsieur Homais said quickly, "but he'll have to go along with the others if he doesn't want to be taken for a Jesuit. You have no idea of the life those bohemians lead in the Latin Quarter with their actresses! You know, students are very highly thought of in Paris. If they have even the slightest social grace they're admitted to the very best circles. They're even fallen in love with sometimes by ladies of the Faubourg Saint-Germain.[6] Some of them make very good marriages."

"But," said the doctor, "I'm afraid that in the city he may . . ."

"You're right," interrupted the apothecary. "It's the reverse of the medal. In the city you've got to keep your hand in your watch pocket every minute. Suppose you're sitting in a park. Some fellow comes up to you—well dressed, perhaps even wearing a decoration—somebody you could take for a diplomat. He addresses you, you talk, he ingratiates himself—offers you a pinch of snuff or picks up your hat for you. Then you get friendlier; he takes you to a café, invites you to visit him in the country, introduces you to all kinds of people over your drinks—and three-quarters of the time it's only to get his hands on your purse or lead you into evil ways."

"That's true," said Charles, "but I was thinking chiefly of diseases—typhoid fever, for example: students from the country are susceptible to it."

Emma shuddered.

"Because of the change of diet," agreed the pharmacist, "and the way it upsets the entire system. And don't forget the Paris water! The dishes they serve in restaurants—all those spicy foods—they overheat the blood: don't let anybody tell you they're worth a good stew. I've always said there's nothing like home cooking: it's better for the health. That was why when I was studying pharmacy in Rouen I went to board in a boarding house: I ate where my teachers ate."

And he continued to expound his general opinions and personal preferences until Justin came to fetch him to make an eggnog for a customer.

"Not a moment's peace!" he cried. "It's grind, grind, grind! I can't leave the shop for a minute. I'm like a plough-horse—sweating blood every second. It's a heavy yoke, my friends!"

And when he was at the door: "By the way," he said, "have you heard the news?"

"What news?"

"It is very likely," Homais announced, raising his eyebrows and looking excessively solemn, "that the annual Agricultural Show of the department of

6. The aristocratic quarter of Paris.

the Seine-Inférieure will be held this year at—Yonville-l'Abbaye. There is, at least, a rumor to that effect. The paper referred to it this morning. An event of the very greatest importance for our district! But we'll talk about it later. I can see, thank you. Justin has the lantern."

VII

The next day was a funereal one for Emma. Everything appeared to her as though shrouded in vague, hovering blackness; and grief swirled into her soul, moaning softly like the winter wind in a deserted castle. She was prey to the brooding brought on by irrevocable partings, to the weariness that follows every consummation, to the pain caused by the breaking off of a confirmed habit or the brusque stopping of a prolonged vibration.

It was like the days following her return from La Vaubyessard, when the dance tunes had kept whirling in her head: she was sunk in the same mournful melancholy, the same torpid despair. Léon seemed taller, handsomer, more charming and less distinct: though he had gone, he had not left her; he was there, and the walls of her house seemed to retain his shadow. She kept staring at the rug he had walked on, the empty chairs he had sat in. The stream at the foot of her garden flowed on as usual, rippling past the slippery bank. They had often strolled there, listening to this same murmur of the water over the moss-covered stones. How they had enjoyed the sun! And the shade, too, afternoons by themselves in the garden! He had read aloud to her, bareheaded on a rustic bench, the cool wind from the meadows ruffling the pages of his book and the nasturtiums on the arbor. . . . And now he was gone, the one bright spot in her life, her one possible hope of happiness! Why hadn't she grasped that good fortune when it had offered itself? And when it had first threatened to slip away—why hadn't she seized it with both hands, implored it on her knees? She cursed herself for not having surrendered to her love for Léon: she thirsted for his lips. She was seized with a longing to run after him, to fling herself into his arms, to cry, "Take me! I'm yours!" But the difficulties of such an enterprise discouraged her in advance; and her longings, increased by regret, became all the more violent.

Thereafter, the image she had of Léon became the center of her distress: it glowed more brightly than a travelers' fire left burning on the snow of a Russian steppe. She ran up to it, crouched beside it, stirred it carefully when it was on the verge of extinction, grasped at everything within reach that might bring it back to life. Distant memories and present-day events, experiences actual and imagined, her starved sensuality, her plans for happiness, blown down like dead branches in the wind, her barren "virtue," the collapse of her hopes, the litter of her domestic life—all these she gathered up and used as fuel for her misery.

Nevertheless the flames did die down—whether exhausted from lack of supplies or choked by excessive feeding. Little by little, love was quenched by absence; regret was smothered by routine; and the fiery glow that had reddened her pale sky grew gray and gradually vanished. In this growing inner twilight she even mistook her recoil from her husband for an aspiration toward her lover, the searing waves of hatred for a rekindling of love. But the storm kept raging, her passion burned itself to ashes, no help was forthcoming, no new sun rose on the horizon. Night closed in completely around her, and she was left alone in a horrible void of piercing cold.

Then the bad days of Tostes began all over again. She considered herself far more unhappy now than she had been then, for now she had experienced grief, and she knew that it would never end.

A woman who had assumed such a burden of sacrifice was certainly entitled to indulge herself a little. She bought herself a Gothic *prie-dieu*, and in a month spent fourteen francs on lemons to blanch her fingernails; she wrote to Rouen for a blue cashmere dress; and at Lheureux's she chose the finest of his scarves. She wound it around her waist over her dressing gown, and thus arrayed she closed the shutters and stretched out on her sofa with a book.

She kept changing her way of wearing her hair: she tried it *à la chinoise*,[7] in soft curls, in braids; she tried parting it on one side and turning it under, like a man's.

She decided to learn Italian: she bought dictionaries, a grammar, a supply of paper. She went in for serious reading—history and philosophy. Sometimes at night Charles would wake up with a start, thinking that someone had come to fetch him to a sickbed. "I'm coming," he would mutter, and it would be the sound of the match that Emma was striking to light her lamp. But her books were like her many pieces of needlepoint: barely begun, they were tossed into the cupboard; she started them, abandoned them, discarded them in favor of new ones.

She had spells in which she would have gone to extremes with very little urging. One day she insisted, Charles to the contrary, that she could drink half a water glass of brandy; and when Charles was foolish enough to dare her, she downed every drop of it.

For all her "flightiness"—that was the Yonville ladies' word for it—Emma did not have a happy look. The corners of her mouth were usually marked with those stiff, pinched lines so often found on the faces of old maids and failures. She was pale, white as a sheet all over; the skin of her nose was drawn down toward the nostrils, and she had a way of staring vacantly at whoever she was talking with. When she discovered two or three gray hairs at her temples she began to talk about growing old.

She often had dizzy spells. One day she even spat blood; and when Charles hovered over her and showed his concern she shrugged. "What of it?" she said.

Charles shut himself in his consulting room, and sitting in his office armchair under the phrenological head he put his elbows on the table and wept.

He wrote his mother asking her to come, and they had long conversations on the subject of Emma.

What course to follow? What could be done, since she refused all treatment?

"Do you know what your wife needs?" said the older Madame Bovary. "She needs to be put to work—hard, manual work. If she had to earn her living like so many other people, she wouldn't have those vapors—they come from all those ideas she stuffs her head with, and the idle life she leads."

"She keeps busy, though," Charles said.

"Busy at what? Reading novels and all kinds of bad books—anti-religious

---

7. Chinese fashion (French).

books that quote Voltaire and ridicule the priests. It's a dangerous business, son: anyone who lacks respect for religion comes to a bad end."

So it was decided to prevent Emma from reading novels. The project presented certain difficulties, but the old lady undertook to carry it out: on her way through Rouen she would personally call on the proprietor of the lending library and tell him that Emma was canceling her subscription. If he nevertheless persisted in spreading his poison, they would certainly have the right to report him to the police.

Farewells between mother-in-law and daughter-in-law were curt. During the three weeks they had been together they hadn't exchanged four words apart from the formal greetings and absolute essentials called for at mealtime and bedtime.

The older Madame Bovary left on a Wednesday—market day at Yonville.

From early morning, one side of the square was taken up with a row of carts—all tipped up on end, with their shafts in the air, stretching along the house fronts from the church to the hotel. On the other side were canvas booths for the sale of cotton goods, woolen blankets and stockings, horse halters, and rolls of blue ribbon whose ends fluttered in the wind. Heavy hardware was spread out on the ground between pyramids of eggs and cheese baskets bristling with sticky straw; and close by the harvesting machines were the flat poultry boxes, with clucking hens sticking their necks out between the slats. The crowd always filled the same corner, unwilling to move on: sometimes it seemed on the point of pushing through the glass of the pharmacy window. On Wednesdays the shop was never empty, and everyone elbowed his way in, less to buy pharmaceutical products than to consult the pharmacist, so celebrated was Monsieur Homais' reputation in the villages round about. His hearty self-confidence bewitched the country folk: to them he was a greater doctor than all the doctors.

Emma was leaning out her window (she often did this: in the provinces windows take the place of boulevards and theaters) watching the crowd of yokels, when she caught sight of a gentleman in a green velvet frock coat. His dressy yellow gloves contrasted with his heavy gaiters, and he was approaching the doctor's house. Behind him was a peasant who followed along with lowered head and decidedly pensive expression.

"May I see Monsieur?" he asked Justin, who was chatting in the doorway with Félicité. And assuming that he was one of the house servants, he added: "Give him my name—Monsieur Rodolphe Boulanger de la Huchette."

The new arrival had added the "de" and the "La Huchette" to his name not out of vanity as a landowner but rather to indicate more clearly who he was. La Huchette was an estate near Yonville, and he had recently bought the château and its two dependent farms. The latter he worked himself— not too seriously. He kept a bachelor establishment and was rumored to have "a private income of at least fifteen thousand francs a year."

Charles came into the parlor, and Monsieur Boulanger introduced his man, who wanted to be bled because "he felt prickly all over." There was no arguing with him: he said it would "clear him out."

So Bovary told the maid to bring a bandage, and a basin that he asked Justin to hold. The peasant turned pale at once. "There's nothing to be afraid of," Charles told him.

"I'm all right," the man said. "Go ahead."

He held out his sturdy arm with an air of bravado. At the prick of the scalpel the blood spurted out and spattered against the mirror.

"Hold the basin closer!" Charles cried.

"Look at that!" said the peasant. "Just like a fountain! I've got real red blood: that's a good sign, isn't it?"

"Sometimes," remarked the *officier de santé*, "they don't feel anything at first, and then they keel over—especially the husky ones, like this one here."

At those words the peasant dropped the scalpel case, which he had been twisting in his fingers. The back of the chair creaked under the heavy impact of his shoulders, and his hat fell to the floor.

"Just what I thought," said Bovary, pressing the vein with his finger.

The basin began to shake in Justin's hands; his knees wobbled and he turned pale.

"Where's my wife?" Charles cried, and he called her loudly. She came rushing down the stairs.

"Vinegar!" he cried. "We've got a pair of them, damn it!"

In his excitement he had trouble applying the compress.

"It's nothing," said Monsieur Boulanger, quite calmly; and he lifted Justin in his arms and propped him up on the table with his back against the wall.

Madame Bovary set about loosening Justin's cravat. There was a knot in the strings that fastened his shirt, and when she had undone it she rubbed his boyish neck lightly for a few minutes; then she moistened her batiste handkerchief in vinegar and patted his forehead with it, blowing gently on it as she did so.

The teamster revived; but Justin remained in his faint, the pupils of his eyes sunk into the whites like blue flowers in milk.

"We'd better not let him see this," said Charles.

Madame Bovary took away the basin. As she bent down to put it under the table, her dress—a long-waisted, full-skirted yellow summer dress with four flounces—belled out around her on the tile floor of the parlor; and as she put out her arms to steady herself the material billowed and settled, revealing the lines of her body. Then she brought in a pitcher of water, and was dissolving sugar in it when the pharmacist arrived. The maid had gone after him in the midst of the fracas, and when he found his apprentice with his eyes open he breathed a sigh of relief. Then he stalked back and forth in front of him, staring him up and down.

"Idiot!" he said. "Idiot, with a capital *I*! A terrible thing, a little bloodletting, isn't it! A fine fearless fellow, too. Just look at him! And yet I've seen him go up a tree after nuts like a squirrel—up to the dizziest heights, *Messieurs et Madame!* Say something, can't you? Tell us how good you are! You'll certainly make a fine pharmacist! Don't you know that some day you may be called on to give important evidence in court? The judges may need your expert opinion. You'll have to keep calm at such times, and know what to say! You'll have to show them you're a man, or else be called a fool!"

Justin made no answer, and the apothecary went on:

"Who asked you to come here anyway? You're always bothering Monsieur and Madame! You know perfectly well I always need you Wednesdays! There are twenty people in the shop right now—I left everything out of consideration for you! Go on! Get back there! Keep an eye on things till I come!"

When Justin had put himself to rights and gone, they talked a little about fainting spells. Madame Bovary had never had one.

"That's unusual for a lady," said Monsieur Boulanger. "But there are men who are extraordinarily susceptible, you know. I've seen a second at a duel lose consciousness at the mere sound of the loading of the pistols."

"I don't mind the sight of other people's blood a bit," said the pharmacist. "But the very idea of shedding my own would be enough to turn my stomach if I thought about it too much."

Meanwhile Monsieur Boulanger sent away his man, urging him to stop worrying now that he'd got what he wanted.

"His whim has afforded me the privilege of making your acquaintance," he said; and as he spoke the words he looked at Emma.

Then he put three francs on the corner of the table, bowed casually, and left.

He was soon on the other side of the river (it was the way back to La Huchette); and Emma saw him crossing the meadow under the poplars, occasionally slowing his pace as though he were pondering something.

"She's very nice," he was saying to himself, "very nice, that wife of the doctor's! Lovely teeth, black eyes, a dainty foot—she's like a real Parisian. Where the devil does she come from? How did such a clodhopper ever get hold of her?"

Monsieur Rodolphe Boulanger was thirty-four. He was brutal and shrewd. He was something of a connoisseur: there had been many women in his life. This one seemed pretty, so the thought of her and her husband stayed with him.

"I have an idea he's stupid. I'll bet she's tired of him. His fingernails are dirty and he hasn't shaved in three days. He trots off to see his patients and leaves her home to darn his socks. How bored she must be! Dying to live in town, to dance the polka every night! Poor little thing! She's gasping for love like a carp on a kitchen table gasping for water. A compliment or two and she'd adore me, I'm positive. She'd be sweet! But—how would I get rid of her later?"

And the thought of the troubles inevitable in such an affair brought to his mind by contrast his present mistress, an actress he kept in Rouen. He found he could not evoke her image without a feeling of satiety, and after a time he said to himself:

"Ah, Madame Bovary is much prettier—and what's more, much fresher. Virginie's certainly growing too fat. She's getting on my nerves with all her enthusiasms. And her mania for shrimps . . . !"

The countryside was deserted, and the only sounds were the regular swish of the tall grass against his gaiters and the chirping of crickets hidden in the distant oats. He thought of Emma in the parlor, dressed as he had seen her, and he undressed her.

"I'll have her!" he said aloud, bringing his stick down on a clod of earth in front of him.

And he immediately began to consider the question of strategy.

"Where could we meet? How could we arrange it? The brat would always be around, and the maid, and the neighbors, and the husband—there'd be a lot of headaches. Bah! It would all take too much time."

Then he began all over again:

"Those eyes really bore into you, though! And that pale complexion . . . God! How I love pale women. . . ."

By the time he had reached the top of the hill his mind was made up.

"The only thing to do now is keep my eyes open for opportunities. I'll call on them occasionally and send them presents—game and chickens. I'll have myself bled, if I have to. We'll get to be friends. I'll invite them to the house. . . . And . . . Oh, yes"—it came to him—"we'll soon be having the show. She'll be there. I'll see her. We'll get started. The approach direct: that's the best."

VIII

The great day arrived at last.

The morning of the Agricultural Show all the Yonvillians were standing on their doorsteps discussing the preparations. The pediment of the town hall had been looped with ivy; a marquee had been set up for the banquet in one of the meadows; and in the middle of the square, in front of the church, stood an antiquated fieldpiece that was to be fired as a signal announcing the arrival of the prefect and the proclamation of the prize winners. The Buchy national guard (Yonville had none) had come to join forces with the fire brigade, commanded by Binet. Today he wore a collar even higher than usual; and his bust, tightly encased in his tunic, was so stiff and inflexible that all his animal fluids seemed to be concentrated in his legs, which rose and fell with the music in rhythmic jerks. Since the tax collector and the colonel were rivals, each showed off his talents by drilling his men separately. First the red epaulettes would march up and down, and then the black breastplates. And then it would begin all over again: there was no end to it. Never had there been such a display of pomp! A number of citizens had washed their housefronts the day before; tricolor flags were hanging from half-open windows; all the cafés were full; and in the perfect weather the headdresses of the women seemed whiter than snow, their gold crosses glittered in the bright sun, and their multicolored neckcloths relieved the somber monotony of the men's frock coats and blue smocks. As the farm women dismounted from their horses they undid the big pins that had held their skirts tucked up away from splashing. The men's concern was for their hats: to protect them they had covered them with large pocket handkerchiefs, holding the corners between their teeth as they rode.

The crowd converged on the main street from both ends of the village, from the paths between the houses, from the lanes, and from the houses themselves; knockers could be heard falling against doors as housewives in cotton gloves emerged to watch the festivities. Particularly admired were the two large illumination frames laden with colored glass lamps that flanked the official grandstand; and against the four columns of the town hall stood four poles, each with a little banner bearing a legend in gold letters on a greenish ground. One said "Commerce," another "Agriculture," the third "Industry," and the fourth "Fine Arts."

But the jubilation brightening all faces seemed to cast a gloom over Madame Lefrançois, the hotel-keeper. She was standing on her kitchen steps muttering to herself:

"It's a crime—a crime, that canvas shack! Do they really think the prefect will enjoy eating his dinner in a tent, like a circus performer? They pretend the whole thing's for the good of this village—so why bring a third-class cook over from Neufchâtel? And who's it all for, anyway? A lot of cowherds and riffraff."

The apothecary came by. He was wearing a black tail coat, yellow nankeen trousers, reverse-calf shoes, and—most exceptionally—a hat: a stiff, low-crowned hat.

"Good morning!" he said. "Forgive me for being in such a hurry."

And as the buxom widow asked him where he was going:

"I imagine it must seem funny to you, doesn't it? Considering that most of the time I can't be pried loose from my laboratory any more than the old man's rat from his cheese."

"What cheese is that?" asked the landlady.

"Oh, nothing, nothing," said Homais. "I was merely referring to the fact, Madame Lefrançois, that I usually stay at home, like a recluse. But today things are different. I must absolutely . . ."

"You don't mean you're going *there?*" she said with a scornful look.

"Of course I'm going there," the apothecary replied, surprised. "Don't you know I'm on the advisory committee?"

Madame Lefrançois looked at him for a moment or two and then answered with a smile:

"That's all right, then. But what have you got to do with farming? Do you know anything about it?"

"Certainly I know something about it, being a pharmacist! A pharmacist is a chemist, Madame Lefrançois; and since the aim of chemistry is to discover the laws governing the reciprocal and molecular action of all natural bodies, it follows that agriculture falls within its domain! Take the composition of manures, the fermentation of liquids, the analysis of gasses, the effects of noxious effluvia—what's all that, I ask you, if it isn't chemistry in the strictest sense of the word?"

The landlady made no reply. Homais went on:

"Do you think that to be an agronomist you must till the soil or fatten chickens with your own hands? No: you have to study the composition of various substances—geological strata, atmospheric phenomena, the properties of the various soils, minerals, types of water, the density of different bodies, their capillary attraction. And a hundred other things. You have to be thoroughly versed in all the principles of hygiene—that's an absolute prerequisite if you're going to serve in a supervisory or consultant capacity in anything relating to the construction of farm buildings, the feeding of livestock, the preparation of meals for hired men. And then you've got to know botany, Madame Lefrançois: be able to tell one plant from another—you know what I mean? Which ones are benign and which ones are poisonous, which ones are unproductive and which ones are nutritive; whether it's a good thing to pull them out here and resow them there, propagate some and destroy others. In short, you've got to keep abreast of science by reading pamphlets and publications; you've got to be always on the alert, always on the lookout for possible improvements. . . ."

All this time the landlady never took her eyes off the door of the Café Français. The pharmacist continued:

"Would to God our farmers were chemists, or at least that they listened more carefully to what science has to say. I myself recently wrote a rather considerable little treatise—a monograph of over seventy-two pages, entitled: *Cider: Its Manufacture and Its Effects; Followed by Certain New Observations on This Subject.* I sent it to the Agronomical Society of Rouen, and it even brought me the honor of being admitted to membership in that body—Agricultural Section, Pomology Division. Now if this work of mine had been made available to the public . . ."

The apothecary broke off: Madame Lefrançois' attention was obviously elsewhere.

"Just look at them," she said. "How can they patronize such a filthy place?"

And with shrugs that stretched her sweater tight over her bosom, she pointed with both hands to her competitor's café, out of which came the sound of singing.

"Anyway, it won't be there much longer," she said. "Just a few days more, and then—*finis.*"

Homais drew back in amazement, and she came down her three steps and put her lips to his ear:

"What! Haven't you heard? They're padlocking it this week. It's Lheureux who's forcing the sale; all those notes Tellier signed were murder."

"What an unutterable catastrophe!" The apothecary always had the proper expression ready, whatever the occasion.

The landlady proceeded to tell him the story, which she had from Théodore, Maître Guillaumin's servant; and although she detested Tellier she had nothing but harsh words for Lheureux. He was a wheedler, a cringer.

"Look—there he is now, in the market," she said. "He's greeting Madame Bovary. She's wearing a green hat. In fact, she's on Monsieur Boulanger's arm."

"Madame Bovary!" cried Homais. "I must go and pay her my respects. She might like to have a seat in the enclosure, under the portico."

And ignoring Madame Lefrançois' attempts to detain him with further details, he hurried off, smiling and with springy step, bestowing innumerable salutations right and left, and taking up a good deal of room with his long black coat tails that streamed in the wind behind him.

Rodolphe had seen him coming and had quickened his pace; but Madame Bovary was out of breath, and he slowed and smiled at her. "I was trying to avoid that bore," he said savagely. "You know, the apothecary."

She nudged him with her elbow.

"What does that mean?" he wondered, glancing at her out of the corner of his eye as they moved on.

Her face, seen in profile, was so calm that it gave him no hint. It stood out against the light, framed in the oval of her bonnet, whose pale ribbons were like streaming reeds. Her eyes with their long curving lashes looked straight ahead: they were fully open, but seemed a little narrowed because of the blood that was pulsing gently under the fine skin of her cheekbones. The rosy flesh between her nostrils was all but transparent in the light. She was inclining her head to one side, and the pearly tips of her white teeth showed between her lips.

"Is she laughing at me?" Rodolphe wondered.

But Emma's nudge had been no more than a warning, for Monsieur Lheureux was walking along beside them, now and then addressing them as though to begin conversation.

"What a marvelous day! Everybody's out! The wind is from the east."

Neither Madame Bovary nor Rodolphe made any reply, though at their slightest movement he edged up to them saying, "Beg your pardon?" and touching his hat.

When they were in front of the blacksmith's, instead of following the road as far as the gate Rodolphe turned abruptly into a side path, drawing Madame Bovary with him.

"Good-bye, Monsieur Lheureux!" he called out. "We'll be seeing you!"

"You certainly got rid of him!" she said, laughing.

"Why should we put up with intruders?" he said. "Today I'm lucky enough to be with you, so . . ."

Emma blushed. He left his sentence unfinished, and talked instead about the fine weather and how pleasant it was to be walking on the grass. A few late daisies were blooming around them.

"They're pretty, aren't they?" he said. "If any of the village girls are in love they can come here for their oracles." And he added: "Maybe I should pick one. What do you think?"

"Are you in love?" she asked, coughing a little.

"Ah, ah! Who knows?" answered Rodolphe.

The meadow was beginning to fill up, and housewives laden with big umbrellas, picnic baskets and babies were bumping into everyone. It was constantly necessary to turn aside, out of the way of long lines of girls— servants from farms, wearing blue stockings, low-heeled shoes and silver rings and smelling of the dairy when they came close. They walked holding hands, forming chains the whole length of the meadow, from the row of aspens to the banquet tent. It was time for the judging, and one after another the farmers were filing into a kind of hippodrome marked off by a long rope hung on stakes.

Here stood the livestock, noses to the rope, rumps of all shapes and sizes forming a ragged line. Lethargic pigs were nuzzling the earth with their snouts; calves were lowing and sheep bleating; cows with their legs folded under them lay on the grass, slowly chewing their cud and blinking their heavy eyelids under the midges buzzing around them. Bare-armed teamsters were holding rearing stallions by the halter: these were neighing loudly in the direction of the mares, who stood there quietly, necks outstretched and manes drooping, as their foals rested in their shadow or came now and again to suck. Above the long undulating line of these massed bodies a white mane would occasionally surge up like a wave in the wind, or a pair of sharp horns would stick out, or men's heads would bob up as they ran. Quite apart, outside the arena, a hundred yards off, was a big black bull with a strap harness and an iron ring through its nose, motionless as a brazen image. A ragged little boy held it by a rope.

Meanwhile a group of gentlemen were solemnly advancing between the two rows, inspecting each animal and then conferring in an undertone. One, who seemed the most important, was writing details in a notebook as he walked. This was the chairman of the jury, Monsieur Derozerays de la Panville. As soon as he recognized Rodolphe he quickly stepped forward and addressed him with a cordial smile: "What's this, Monsieur Boulanger? You've deserted us?"

Rodolphe assured him that he was coming directly. But when the chairman had passed:

"I'll certainly *not* be going," he said to Emma. "I like your company better than his."

And though he kept making fun of the show, Rodolphe displayed his blue pass to the guard so that they could walk about unmolested, and he even stopped from time to time in front of some particularly fine exhibit. It was never anything that Madame Bovary cared about: he noticed this, and began to make jokes about the Yonville ladies and the way they dressed; then he apologized for the carelessness of his own costume. This was a mixture of the casual and the refined—the kind of thing that both fascinates and exasperates the common herd, hinting as it does at an eccentric way of life, indulgence in wild passions and "artistic" affections, and a contempt for social conventions. His batiste shirt (it had pleated cuffs) puffed out from the opening of his gray twill vest at each gust of wind; and his broad-striped trousers ended at nankeen shoes trimmed with patent leather so shiny that the grass was reflected in it. He tramped unconcernedly through horse dung, one thumb in his vest pocket, his straw hat tilted over one ear.

"Anyway," he said, "when you live in the country . . ."

"Any trouble you take is wasted," said Emma.

"Completely," replied Rodolphe. "Think of it: there isn't a single person here today capable of appreciating the cut of a coat."

And they talked about the mediocrity of provincial life, so suffocating, so fatal to all noble dreams.

"So," said Rodolphe, "I just get more and more engulfed in gloom as time goes on. . . ."

"You do!" she cried, in surprise. "I thought of you as being very jolly."

"Of course—that's the impression I give: I've learned to wear a mask of mockery when I'm with other people. But many's the time I've passed a cemetery in the moonlight and asked myself if I wouldn't be better off lying there with the rest. . . ."

"Oh! And what about your friends?" she asked. "Have you no thought for them?"

"My friends? What friends? Have I any? Who cares anything about me?"

And he accompanied those last words with a kind of desperate whistle.

But they had to draw apart to make way for a tall tower of chairs borne by a man coming up behind them. He was so excessively laden that the only parts of him visible were the tips of his wooden shoes and his two outstretched hands. It was Lestiboudois, the gravedigger, who was renting out church seats to the crowd. He was highly inventive where his own interests were concerned, and had thought up this way of profiting from the show. It was a good idea: everyone was hailing him at once. The villagers were hot; they clamored for the straw-seated chairs that gave off a smell of incense, and they leaned back with a certain veneration against the heavy slats stained with candle wax.

Then once again Madame Bovary took Rodolphe's arm, and he went on as though talking to himself:

"Yes, so many things have passed me by! I've always been so alone! Ah! If I'd had a purpose in life, if I'd met anyone with true affection, if I'd found somebody who . . . Oh! Then I wouldn't have spared any effort; I'd have surmounted every obstacle, let nothing stand in my way . . . !"

"It seems to me, though," said Emma, "that you're scarcely to be pitied."

"Oh? You think that?" said Rodolphe.

"Yes," she answered, "because after all you're free"—she hesitated—"rich . . ."

"Don't make fun of me," he begged.

And she was swearing that she was doing nothing of the kind, when a cannon shot resounded and everyone began to hurry toward the village.

It was a false alarm: the prefect wasn't even in sight, and the members of the jury were in a quandary, not knowing whether to begin the proceedings or wait a while longer.

Finally at the far end of the square appeared a big hired landau drawn by two skinny horses who were being furiously whipped on by a white-hatted coachman. Binet had just time to shout, "Fall in!" and the colonel to echo him; there was a rush for the stacked rifles; and in the confusion some of the men forgot to button their collars. But the official coach-and-pair seemed to sense the difficulty, and the emaciated beasts, dawdling on their chain, drew up at a slow trot in front of the portico of the town hall just at the moment when the national guard and the fire brigade were deploying into line to the beating of the drums.

"Mark time!" cried Binet.

"Halt!" cried the colonel. "Left, turn!"

And after a present-arms during which the rattle of the metal bands as they slid down the stocks and barrels sounded like a copper cauldron rolling down a flight of stairs, all the rifles were lowered.

Then there emerged from the carriage a gentleman clad in a short, silver-embroidered coat, his forehead high and bald, the back of his head tufted, his complexion wan and his expression remarkably benign. His eyes, very large and heavy-lidded, half shut as he peered at the multitude; and at the same time he lifted his sharp nose and curved his sunken mouth into a smile. He recognized the mayor by his sash, and explained that the prefect had been unable to come. He himself was a prefectural councilor, and he added a few words of apology. Tuvache replied with compliments, the emissary declared himself unworthy of them; and the two officials stood there face to face, their foreheads almost touching, all about them the members of the jury, the village council, the local elite, the national guard and the crowd. Holding his little black three-cornered hat against his chest, the prefectural councilor reiterated his greetings; and Tuvache, bent like a bow, returned his smiles, stammered, clutched uncertainly for words, protested his devotion to the monarchy and his awareness of the honor that was being bestowed on Yonville.

Hippolyte, the stable-boy at the hotel, came to take the horses from the coachman; and limping on his clubfoot he led them through the gateway of the Lion d'Or, where a crowd of peasants gathered to stare at the carriage. There was a roll of the drums, the howitzer thundered, and the gentlemen filed up and took their seats on the platform in red plush armchairs loaned by Madame Tuvache.

All in this group looked alike. Their flabby, fair-skinned, slightly suntanned faces were the color of new cider, and their bushy side whiskers stuck out over high, stiff collars that were held in place by white cravats tied in wide bows. Every vest was of velvet, with a shawl collar; every watch had an oval carnelian seal at the end of a long ribbon; and every one of the gentlemen sat with his hands planted on his thighs, his legs carefully apart, the hard-finished broadcloth of his trousers shining more brightly than the leather of his heavy shoes.

The invited ladies were seated to the rear, under the portico between the columns, while the ordinary citizens faced the platform, either standing, or sitting on chairs. Lestiboudois had retransported to this new location all those that he had previously taken to the meadow; now he kept bringing still more from the church; and he was crowding the place so with his chair-rental business that it was almost impossible for anyone to reach the few steps leading to the platform.

"In my opinion," said Monsieur Lheureux, addressing the pharmacist, who was passing by on his way to take his seat, "they should have set up a pair of Venetian flagstaffs: trimmed with something rich and not too showy they'd have made a very pretty sight."

"Certainly," said Homais. "But what can you expect? The mayor took everything into his own hands. He hasn't much taste, poor Tuvache: in fact, he's completely devoid of what is known as the artistic sense."

Meanwhile Rodolphe, with Madame Bovary, had gone up to the second floor of the town hall, into the "council chamber": it was quite empty—a perfect place, he said, from which to have a comfortable view of the ceremonies. He took three of the stools that stood around the oval table under the king's bust and moved them over to one of the windows; and there they sat down close together.

There was a certain agitation on the platform—prolonged whisperings and consultations. Finally the prefectural councilor rose to his feet. It had become known that he was called Lieuvain, and his name was repeated from one to another in the crowd. He made sure that his sheets of paper were in proper order, peered at them closely, and began:

"Gentlemen: I should like, with your permission (before speaking to you about the object of today's meeting—and this sentiment, I am sure, will be shared by all of you), I should like, with your permission, to pay tribute to the national administration, to the government, to the monarch, gentlemen, to our sovereign, to the beloved king to whom no branch of public or private prosperity is indifferent, and who, with so firm and yet so wise a hand, guides the chariot of state amidst the constant perils of a stormy sea, maintaining at the same time public respect for peace as well as for war—for industry, for commerce, for agriculture, for the fine arts."

"I ought to move a little further back," said Rodolphe.

"Why?" said Emma.

But at that moment the councilor's voice rose to an extraordinary pitch. He was declaiming:

"Gone forever, gentlemen, are the days when civil discord drenched our streets with blood; when the landlord, the businessman, nay, the worker, sank at night into a peaceful slumber trembling lest they be brutally awakened by the sound of inflammatory tocsins; when the most subversive principles were audaciously undermining the foundations . . ."

"It's just that I might be caught sight of from below," said Rodolphe. "If I were, I'd have to spend the next two weeks apologizing; and what with my bad reputation . . ."

"Oh! You're slandering yourself," said Emma.

"No, no, my reputation's execrable, I assure you."

"But, gentlemen," continued the councilor, "if I dismiss those depressing evocations and turn my eyes to the present situation of our cherished fatherland, what do I see before me? Commerce and the arts are thriving every-where; everywhere new channels of communication, like so many new arteries in the body politic, are multiplying contacts between its various parts; our great manufacturing centers have resumed their activity; religion, its foundations strengthened, appeals to every heart; shipping fills our ports; confidence returns; at long last, France breathes again!"

"Moreover, from the point of view of society it's probably deserved," Ro-dolphe said.

"What do you mean?" she asked.

"Do you really not know," he said, "that there exist souls that are cease-lessly in torment? That are driven now to dreams, now to action, driven from the purest passions to the most orgiastic pleasures? No wonder we fling ourselves into all kinds of fantasies and follies!"

She stared at him as if he were a traveler from mythical lands. "We poor women," she said, "don't have even that escape."

"A poor escape," he said, "since it doesn't bring happiness."

"But do we ever find happiness?" she asked.

"Yes, it comes along one day," he answered.

"And the point has not been lost on you," the councilor was saying. "Not on you, farmers and workers in the fields! Not on you, champions of progress and morality! The point has not been lost on you, I say, that the storms of political strife are truly more to be dreaded than the disorders of the ele-ments!"

"Yes, it comes along one day," Rodolphe repeated. "All of a sudden, just when we've given up hope. Then new horizons open before us: it's like a voice crying, 'Look! It's here!' We feel the need to pour out our hearts to a given person, to surrender, to sacrifice everything. In such a meeting no words are necessary: each senses the other's thoughts. Each is the answer to the other's dreams." He kept staring at her. "There it is, the treasure so long sought for—there before us: it gleams, it sparkles. But still we doubt; we daren't believe; we stand there dazzled, as though we'd come from dark-ness into light."

As he ended, Rodolphe enhanced his words with pantomime. He passed his hand over his face, like someone dazed; then he let it fall on Emma's hand. She withdrew hers. The councilor read on:

"And who is there who would wonder at such a statement, gentlemen? Only one so blind, so sunk (I use the word advisedly), so sunk in the preju-dices of another age as to persist in his misconceptions concerning the spirit of our farming population. Where, I ask you, is there to be found greater patriotism than in rural areas, greater devotion to the common weal, greater—in one word—intelligence? And by intelligence, gentlemen, I do not mean that superficial intelligence that is a futile ornament of idle minds, but rather that profound and moderate intelligence that applies itself above all to useful ends, contributing in this manner to the good of all, to public improvement and the upholding of the state—that intelligence that is the fruit of respect for law and the performance of duty!"

"Ah, there they go again!" said Rodolphe. "Duty, duty, always duty—I'm sick of that word. Listen to them! They're a bunch of doddering old morons and bigoted old church mice with foot warmers and rosaries, always squeak-ing, 'Duty! Duty!' at us. I have my own idea of duty. Our duty is to feel what is great and love what is beautiful—not to accept all the social conventions and the infamies they impose on us."

"Still . . . still . . ." objected Madame Bovary.

"No! Why preach against the passions? Aren't they the only beautiful thing in this world, the source of heroism, enthusiasm, poetry, music, the arts, everything?"

"But still," said Emma, "we have to be guided a little by society's opinions; we have to follow its standards of morality."

"Ah! But there are two moralities," he replied. "The petty one, the conventional one, the one invented by man, the one that keeps changing and screaming its head off—that one's noisy and vulgar, like that crowd of fools you see out there. But the other one, the eternal one . . . Ah! This one's all around us and above us, like the landscape that surrounds us and the blue sky that gives us light."

Monsieur Lieuvain had just wiped his mouth with his pocket handkerchief. He resumed:

"Why should I presume, gentlemen, to prove to you who are here today the usefulness of agriculture? Who is it that supplies our needs, who is it that provisions us, if not the farmer? The farmer, gentlemen, sowing with laborious hand the fertile furrows of our countryside, brings forth the wheat which, having been ground and reduced to powder by means of ingenious machinery, emerges in the form of flour, and from thence, transported to our cities, is presently delivered to the baker, who fashions from it a food for the poor man as well as for the rich. Is it not the farmer, once again, who fattens his plentiful flocks in the pastures to provide us with our clothing? For how would we be clothed, for how would we be nourished, without agriculture? Indeed, gentlemen—is there need to seek so far afield for examples? Who among you has not often given thought to the immense benefit we derive from that modest creature—adornment of our kitchen yards— which provides at one and the same time a downy pillow for our beds, its succulent meat for our tables, and eggs? But I should never end, had I to enumerate one after another the different products which properly cultivated soil lavishes on its children like a generous mother. Here, the grape; there, the cider apple; yonder, the colza;[8] elsewhere, a thousand kinds of cheese. And flax, gentlemen, do not forget flax!—an area in which within the past few years there has been considerable development, and one to which I particularly call your attention."

There was no need for him to "call their attention": every mouth in the crowd was open, as though to drink in his words. Tuvache, sitting beside him, listened wide-eyed; Monsieur Derozerays' lids now and again gently shut; and further along the pharmacist, holding his son Napoléon between his knees, cupped his hand to his ear lest he miss a single syllable. The other members of the jury kept slowly nodding their chins against their vests to express their approval. The fire brigade, at the foot of the platform, leaned on their bayonets; and Binet stood motionless, elbow bent, the tip of his sword in the air. He could hear, perhaps, but he certainly could not see, for the visor of his helmet had fallen forward onto his nose. His lieutenant, who was Monsieur Tuvache's younger son, had gone him one better: the helmet

8. A plant yielding rapeseed or canola oil, used in cooking.

he was wearing was far too big for him and kept teetering on his head and showing a corner of the calico nightcap he had on under it. He was smiling from beneath his headgear as sweetly as a baby; and his small pale face, dripping with sweat, wore an expression of enjoyment, exhaustion and drowsiness.

The square was packed solidly with people as far as the houses. Spectators were leaning out of every window and standing on every doorstep; and Justin, in front of the pharmacy show window, seemed nailed to the spot in contemplation of the spectacle. Despite the crowd's silence, Monsieur Lieuvain's voice didn't carry too well in the open air. What came was fragmentary bits of sentences interrupted here and there by the scraping of chairs; then all at once from behind there would resound the prolonged lowing of an ox, and lambs bleated to one another on the street corners. For the cowherds and shepherds had driven their animals in that close, and from time to time a cow would bellow as her tongue tore off some bit of foliage hanging down over her muzzle.

Rodolphe had come close to Emma and was speaking rapidly in a low voice:

"Don't you think it's disgusting, the way they conspire to ruin everything? Is there a single sentiment that society doesn't condemn? The noblest instincts, the purest sympathies are persecuted and dragged in the mud; and if two poor souls do find one another, everything is organized to keep them apart. They'll try, just the same; they'll beat their wings, they'll call to each other. Oh! Never fear! Sooner or later, in six months or ten years, they'll come together and love one another, because they can't go against fate and because they were born for each other."

He was leaning forward with his arms crossed on his knees, and lifting his face to Emma's he looked at her fixedly from very near. In his eyes she could see tiny golden lines radiating out all around his black pupils, and she could even smell the perfume of the pomade that lent a gloss to his hair. Then a languor came over her; she remembered the vicomte who had waltzed with her at La Vaubyessard and whose beard had given off this same odor of vanilla and lemon; and automatically she half closed her eyes to breathe it more deeply. But as she did this, sitting up straight in her chair, she saw in the distance, on the farthest horizon, the old stagecoach, the Hirondelle, slowly descending the hill of Les Leux, trailing a long plume of dust behind it. It was in this yellow carriage that Léon had so often returned to her; and that was the road he had taken when he had left forever. For a moment she thought she saw him across the square, at his window; then everything became confused, and clouds passed before her eyes; it seemed to her that she was still whirling in the waltz, under the blaze of the chandeliers, in the vicomte's arms, and that Léon was not far off, that he was coming. . . . And yet all the while she was smelling the perfume of Rodolphe's hair beside her. The sweetness of this sensation permeated her earlier desires, and like grains of sand in the wind these whirled about in the subtle fragrance that was filling her soul. She opened her nostrils wide to breathe in the freshness of the ivy festooning the capitals outside the window. She took off her gloves and wiped her hands; then she fanned herself with her handkerchief, hearing above the beating of the pulse in her temples the murmur of the crowd and the councilor's voice as he intoned his periods.

"Persist!" he was saying. "Perservere! Follow neither the beaten tracks of routine nor the rash counsels of reckless empiricism. Apply yourselves above all to the improvement of the soil, to rich fertilizers, to the development of fine breeds—equine, bovine, ovine and porcine. May this exhibition be for you a peaceful arena where the winner, as he leaves, will stretch out his hand to the loser and fraternize with him, wishing him better luck another time! And you, venerable servants, humblest members of the household, whose painful labors have by no government up until today been given the slightest consideration: present yourselves now, and receive the reward of your silent heroism! And rest assured that the state henceforth has its eyes upon you, that it encourages you, that it protects you, that it will honor your just demands, and lighten, to the best of its ability, the burden of your painful sacrifices!"

Monsieur Lieuvain sat down.

Monsieur Derozerays stood up, and began another speech. His was perhaps not quite so flowery as the councilor's; but it had the advantage of being characterized by a more positive style—by a more specialized knowledge, that is, and more pertinent arguments. There was less praise of the government, and more mention of religion and agriculture. He showed the relation between the two and how they had always worked together for the good of civilization. Rodolphe was talking to Madame Bovary about dreams, forebodings, magnetism. Going back to the cradle of human society, the orator depicted the savage ages when men lived off acorns in the depths of the forest. Then they had cast off their animal skins, garbed themselves in cloth, dug the ground and planted the vine. Was this an advance? Didn't this discovery entail more disadvantages than benefits? That was the problem Monsieur Derozerays set himself. From magnetism Rodolphe gradually moved on to affinities; and as the chairman cited Cincinnatus and his plough, Diocletian planting his cabbages[9] and the Chinese emperors celebrating the New Year by sowing seed, the young man was explaining to the young woman that these irresistible attractions had their roots in some earlier existence.

"Take us, for example," he said. "Why should we have met? How did it happen? It can only be that something in our particular inclinations made us come closer and closer across the distance that separated us, the way two rivers flow together."

He took her hand, and this time she did not withdraw it.

"First prize for all-round farming!" cried the chairman.

"Just this morning, for example, when I came to your house . . ."

"To Monsieur Bizet, of Quincampoix."

"Did I have any idea that I'd be coming with you to the show?"

"Seventy francs!"

"A hundred times I was on the point of leaving, and yet I followed you and stayed with you . . ."

"For the best manures."

". . . as I'd stay with you tonight, tomorrow, every day, all my life!"

"To Monsieur Caron, of Argueil, a gold medal!"

"Never have I been so utterly charmed by anyone . . ."

9. Diocletian (245–313 C.E.), Roman emperor from 284 to 305. He resigned in 305 and retired to Salonae (now Split), in Dalmatia, to cultivate his garden. Cincinnatus was a Roman consul (460 B.C.E.) who was supposedly called to his office while found plowing.

"To Monsieur Bain, of Givry-Saint-Martin!"

". . . so that I'll carry the memory of you with me. . . ."

"For a merino ram . . ."

"Whereas you'll forget me: I'll vanish like a shadow."

"To Monsieur Belot, of Notre-Dame . . ."

"No, though! Tell me it isn't so! Tell me I'll have a place in your thoughts, in your life!"

"Hogs: a tie! To Messieurs Lehérissé and Cullembourg, sixty francs!"

Rodolphe squeezed her hand, and he felt it all warm and trembling in his, like a captive dove that longs to fly away; but then, whether in an effort to free it, or in response to his pressure, she moved her fingers.

"Oh! Thank God! You don't repulse me! How sweet, how kind! I'm yours: you know that now! Let me see you! Let me look at you!"

A gust of wind coming in the windows ruffled the cloth on the table; and down in the square all the tall headdresses of the peasant women rose up like fluttering white butterfly wings.

"Use of oil cakes!" continued the chairman.

He was going faster now.

"Flemish fertilizer . . . flax-raising . . . drainage, long-term leases . . . domestic service!"

Rodolphe had stopped speaking. They were staring at each other. As their desire rose to a peak their dry lips quivered; and, languidly, of their own accord, their fingers intertwined.

"Catherine-Nicaise-Elizabeth Leroux, of Sassetot-la-Guerrière, for fifty-four years of service on the same farm, a silver medal, value twenty-five francs!"

"Where is Catherine Leroux?" repeated the councilor.

There was no sign of her, but there was the sound of whispering voices:

"Go ahead!"

"No!"

"To the left!"

"Don't be scared!"

"Stupid old thing!"

"Is she there or isn't she?" cried Tuvache.

"Yes! Here she is!"

"Then send her up!"

Everyone watched her as she climbed to the platform: a frightened-looking little old woman who seemed to have shriveled inside her shabby clothes. On her feet were heavy wooden clogs, and she wore a long blue apron. Her thin face, framed in a simple coif, was more wrinkled than a withered russet, and out of the sleeves of her red blouse hung her large, gnarled hands. Years of barn dust, washing soda and wool grease had left them so crusted and rough and hard that they looked dirty despite all the clear water they'd been rinsed in; and from long habit of service they hung half open, as though offering their own humble testimony to the hardships they had endured. A kind of monklike rigidity gave a certain dignity to her face, but her pale stare was softened by no hint of sadness or human kindness. Living among animals, she had taken on their muteness and placidity. This was the first time she had ever been in the midst of so great a crowd; and inwardly terrified by the flags and the drums, by the gentlemen in tail coats and by the decoration worn by the councilor, she stood still, uncertain whether to move ahead or to turn and run, comprehending neither the urgings of the crowd nor the smiles of the jury. Thus did half a century of servitude stand before these beaming bourgeois.

"Step forward, venerable Catherine-Nicaise-Elizabeth Leroux!" cried the councilor, who had taken the list of prize winners from the chairman.

Looking at the sheet of paper and at the old woman in turn, he kept urging her forward like a father: "Come right here, come ahead!"

"Are you deaf?" cried Tuvache, jumping up from his chair.

And he proceeded to shout into her ear: "Fifty-four years of service! A silver medal! Twenty-five francs! For you!"

She took the medal and stared at it. Then a beatific smile spread over her face, and as she left the platform those nearby could hear her mumble: "I'll give it to our priest and he'll say some Masses for me."

"Such fanaticism!" hissed the pharmacist, bending toward the notary.

The ceremonies were ended; the crowd dispersed; and now that the speeches had been read everyone resumed his rank and everything reverted to normal. Masters bullied their servants, the servants beat their cows and their sheep, and the cows and the sheep—indolent in their triumph—moved slowly back to their sheds, their horns decked with the green wreaths that were their trophies.

Meanwhile the national guard had gone up to the second floor of the town hall: brioches were impaled on their bayonets, and their drummer bore a basketful of bottles. Madame Bovary took Rodolphe's arm; he escorted her home; they said good-bye at her door; and then he went for a stroll in the meadow until it was time for the banquet.

The feast was long, noisy, clumsily served: the guests were so crowded that they could scarcely move their elbows; and the narrow planks that were used for benches threatened to snap under their weight. They ate enormously, each piling his plate high to get full value for his assessment. Sweat poured off every forehead; and over the table, between the hanging lamps, hovered a whitish vapor, like a river mist on an autumn morning. Rodolphe, his back against the cloth side of the tent, was thinking so much about Emma that he was aware of nothing going on around him. Out on the grass behind him servants were stacking dirty plates; his tablemates spoke to him and he didn't answer; someone kept filling his glass, and his mind was filled with stillness despite the growing noise. He was thinking of the things she had said and of the shape of her lips; her face shone out from the plaques on the shakos as from so many magic mirrors; the folds of her dress hung down the walls; and days of lovemaking stretched endlessly ahead in the vistas of the future.

He saw her again that evening, during the fireworks, but she was with her husband and Madame Homais and the pharmacist. The latter was very worried about stray rockets, and constantly left the others to give Binet a word of advice.

Through overprecaution, the fireworks, which had been delivered in care of Monsieur Tuvache, had been stored in his cellar, with the result that the damp powder could scarcely be got to light; and the culminating number, which was to have depicted a dragon swallowing its own tail, was a complete fiasco. Now and then some pathetic little Roman candle would go off and bring a roar from the gaping crowd—a roar amidst which could be heard the screams of women, fair game for ticklers in the darkness. Emma nestled silently against Charles's shoulder, raising her head to follow the bright trail of the rockets in the black sky. Rodolphe watched her in the glow of the colored lamps.

Gradually these went out, the stars gleamed; then came a few drops of rain, and she tied a scarf over her hair.

Just then the councilor's landau drove out of the hotel yard. The drunken coachman chose that moment to collapse; and high above the hood, between the two lamps, everyone could see the mass of his body swaying right and left with the pitching of the springs.

"There ought to be strong measures taken against drunkenness," said the apothecary. "If I had my way, there'd be a special bulletin board put up on the door of the town hall, and every week there'd be a list posted of all who had intoxicated themselves with alcoholic liquors during that period. Such a thing would be very valuable statistically, a public record that might . . . Excuse me!"

And once again he hurried off toward the captain.

The latter was homeward bound. He was looking forward to rejoining his lathe.

"It might not do any harm," said Homais, "to send one of your men, or go yourself, to . . ."

"Get away and leave me alone," replied the tax collector. "Everything's taken care of."

"You can all stop worrying," the apothecary announced when he was back with his friends. "Monsieur Binet guarantees that all necessary measures have been taken. Not a spark has fallen. The pumps are full. We can safely retire to our beds."

"I can certainly do with some sleep," said Madame Homais, with a vast yawn. "Never mind—we had a wonderfully beautiful day for the show."

Rodolphe echoed her words in a low voice, his eyes soft: "Yes, it was: wonderfully beautiful."

They exchanged good-byes and went their respective ways.

Two days later, in the *Fanal de Rouen*, there was a great article about the Agricultural Show. Homais had written it in a burst of inspiration the very next day.

"Why these festoons, these flowers, these garlands? Whither was it bound, this crowd rushing like the billows of a raging sea under a torrential tropic sun that poured its torrid rays upon our fertile meadows?"

Then he went on to speak of the condition of the peasants. The government was doing something, certainly, but not enough. "Be bold!" he cried, addressing the administration. "A thousand reforms are indispensable: let us accomplish them." Then, describing the arrival of the councilor, he didn't forget "the warlike air of our militia," or "our sprightliest village maidens," or the bald-headed old men, veritable patriarchs, "some of whom, survivors of our immortal phalanxes, felt their hearts throb once again to the manly sound of the drums." His own name came quite early in his listing of the members of the jury, and he even reminded his readers in a footnote that Monsieur Homais, the pharmacist, had sent a monograph concerning cider to the Agricultural Society. When he came to the distribution of the prizes, he depicted the joy of the winners in dithyrambic terms. Father embraced son, brother embraced brother, husband embraced wife. More than one worthy rustic proudly displayed his humble medal to the assemblage; and, returning home to his helpmeet, doubtless wept tears of joy as he hung it on the modest wall of his cot.

"About six o'clock the leading participants in the festivities forgathered at a banquet in the pasture belonging to Monsieur Liégeard. The utmost cordiality reigned throughout. A number of toasts were proposed. By Monsieur Lieuvain: 'To the king!' By Monsieur Tuvache: 'To the prefect!' By Monsieur Derozerays: 'To agriculture!' By Monsieur Homais: 'To those twin sisters, industry and the fine arts!' By Monsieur Leplichey: 'To progress!' After nightfall a brilliant display of fireworks all at once illumined the heavens. It was a veritable kaleidoscope, a true stageset for an opera, and for a moment our modest village imagined itself transported into the midst of an Arabian Nights dream.

"We may mention that no untoward incidents arose to disturb this family gathering."

And he added:

"Only the clergy was conspicuous by its absence. Doubtless a totally different idea of progress obtains in the sacristies. Suit yourselves, *messieurs de Loyola!*"[1]

IX

Six weeks went by without further visit from Rodolphe. Then one evening he came.

The day after the show he had admonished himself: "I mustn't go back right away. That would be a mistake." And at the end of the week he had left for a hunting trip.

After his hunting was over he thought he had waited too long. But then: "If she loved me from the first, she must be impatient to see me again," he reasoned. "And this means she must love me all the more by now. So—back to the attack!"

And when he saw Emma turn pale as he entered the parlor he knew he was right.

She was alone. Daylight was fading. The muslin sash curtains deepened the twilight; and the gilt barometer had just caught a ray of sun and was blazing in the mirror between the lacy edges of the coral.

Rodolphe remained standing, and Emma scarcely replied to his first conventionally polite phrases.

"I've been having all kinds of things happen," he said. "I was ill."

"Anything serious?" she cried.

"Well, not really," he said, sitting beside her on a stool. "It was just that I didn't want to come here again."

"Why?"

"Can't you guess?"

He stared at her—this time so intently that she blushed and lowered her head.

"Emma . . ." he said.

---

1. Ignatius of Loyola (1491–1556), a Spaniard, founded the order of the Jesuits in 1534. The Jesuits were expelled from France in 1762.

"Monsieur!" she exclaimed, drawing away a little.

"Ah, you can see for yourself," he said, in a resigned voice, "that I was right not to want to come here again. Your name—my heart's full of it—I spoke it without meaning to, and you stopped me. 'Madame Bovary'! Everyone calls you that, and it's not your name at all. It's somebody else's. Somebody else's," he said a second time; and he buried his face in his hands. "I think of you every minute! The thought of you drives me crazy! Forgive me—I won't stay with you. I'll go away—far away—so far that you'll never hear of me again. But today . . . I don't know what power it was that made me come. We can't fight against fate. There's no resisting when an angel smiles. Once something lovely and charming and adorable has wound itself around your heart. . . ."

It was the first time that Emma had had such things said to her; and her pride, like someone relaxing in a steam bath, stretched luxuriously in the warmth of his words.

"No," he continued. "I didn't come, these past few weeks. I haven't seen you. But everything close to you I've looked at and looked at. At night—night after night—I got up and came here and stared at your house—the roof shining in the moonlight, the trees in the garden swaying at your window, and a little lamp, just a gleam, shining through the windowpanes in the dark. Ah! You little knew that a poor wretch was standing there, so near you and yet so far. . . ."

She turned to him with a sob. "How kind you are . . . !"

"I'm not kind! I love you, that's all! You must know it. Tell me you do: one word! Just one word!"

And Rodolphe was sliding imperceptibly from the stool to his knees when there was a sound of sabots in the kitchen and he saw that the door of the room was ajar.

"You'd be doing me a favor," he said, resuming his position on the stool, "if you'd gratify a whim I have."

The whim was to be taken through her house: he wanted to see it. Madame Bovary saw nothing out of the way in the request, and they were both just rising to their feet when Charles appeared.

"Bonjour, docteur," Rodolphe greeted him.

Flattered to be so addressed, the officier de santé was profusely obsequious, and Rodolphe profited from those few moments to regain some of his composure.

"Madame was talking to me about her health," he began, "and . . ."

Charles interrupted him. He was very worried indeed; his wife was having difficulty breathing again. Rodolphe asked whether horseback riding might not be good for her.

"Certainly it would! Just the thing! An excellent suggestion, darling! You ought to follow it."

She pointed out that she had no horse; Monsieur Rodolphe offered her one of his; she declined; he did not insist; and finally, to explain the purpose of his visit, he told Charles that his teamster, the man who had been bled, was still having dizzy spells.

"I'll stop by and see him," said Bovary.

"No, no, I'll send him to you. We'll come here; that will be easier for you."

"Very good; thank you."

As soon as they were alone:

"Why don't you accept Monsieur Boulanger's suggestions? He's being so gracious."

She pouted, made one excuse after another, and finally said that "it might look strange."

"A lot I care about that!" said Charles, turning on his heel. "Health comes first! You're wrong!"

"But how do you expect me to ride a horse if I have no habit?"

"You must order one," he replied.

It was the riding habit that decided her.

When it was ready, Charles wrote to Monsieur Boulanger that his wife was at his disposition, and that they thanked him in advance for his kindness.

The next day at noon Rodolphe presented himself at Charles's door with two riding horses. One of them had pink pompons decorating its ears and bore a lady's buckskin saddle.

Rodolphe had put on a pair of high soft boots, telling himself that she had probably never seen anything like them; and Emma was indeed charmed with his appearance when he came up to the landing in his velvet frock coat and white tricot riding breeches. She was ready and waiting for him.

Justin ran out of the pharmacy to take a look at her, and the apothecary himself left his work for a few moments. He gave Monsieur Boulanger several bits of advice:

"Accidents happen so quickly! Take care! Your horses may be more spirited than you know!"

She heard a sound above her head: it was Félicité drumming on the windowpanes to amuse little Berthe. The child blew her a kiss, and Emma made a sign with her riding crop in answer.

"Have a good ride!" cried Monsieur Homais. "Be careful! That's the main thing! Careful!"

And he waved his newspaper after them as he watched them ride away.

As soon as it felt soft ground, Emma's horse broke into a gallop. Rodolphe galloped at her side. Now and again they exchanged a word. With her head slightly lowered, her hand raised and her right arm outstretched, she let herself go to the rhythmic rocking motion.

At the foot of the hill Rodolphe gave his horse its head: both horses leapt forward as one, and then at the top they as suddenly stopped, and Emma's large blue veil settled and hung still.

It was early October. There was a mist over the countryside. Wisps of vapor lay along the horizon, following the contours of the hills, and elsewhere they were drifting and rising and evaporating. Now and then as the clouds shifted, a ray of sun would light up the roofs of Yonville in the distance, with its riverside gardens, its yards and its church steeple. Emma half closed her eyes trying to pick out her house, and never had the wretched village she lived in looked so very small. From the height on which they were standing the whole valley was like an immense pale lake, dissolving into thin air: clumps of trees stood out here and there like dark rocks, and the tall lines of poplars piercing the fog were like its leafy banks, swaying in the wind.

To one side, over the turf between the firs, the light was dim and the air mild. The reddish earth, the color of snuff, deadened the sound of the hoofs; and the horses kicked fir cones before them as they walked.

For a time Rodolphe and Emma continued to follow the edge of the wood. Now and then she turned her head away to avoid his eyes, and at such moments she saw only the regularly spaced trunks of the firs, almost dizzying in their unbroken succession. The horses were blowing, and the leather creaked in the saddles.

Then they turned into the forest, and at that moment the sun came out.

"God's watching over us," said Rodolphe.

"You think so?" she said.

"Let's go on!" he said.

He clicked his tongue, and both horses broke into a trot.

Tall ferns growing along the path kept catching in Emma's stirrup, and Rodolphe bent over as he rode and pulled them out. At other times he came close to her to push aside overhanging branches, and she felt his knee brush against her leg. Now the sky was blue, and the leaves were still. There were clearings full of heather in bloom, and the sheets of purple alternated with the multicolored tangle of the trees, gray, fawn and gold. Often a faint rustling and fluttering of wings would come from under the bushes; or there would be the cry, at once raucous and sweet, of crows flying off among the oaks.

They dismounted. Rodolphe tethered the horses. She walked ahead of him on the moss between the cart tracks.

But the long skirt of her habit impeded her, even though she held it up by the end; and Rodolphe, walking behind her, kept staring at her sheer white stocking that showed between the black broadcloth and the black shoe as though it were a bit of her naked flesh.

She stopped.

"I'm tired," she said.

"Just a little further," he said. "Come along, try."

Then a hundred yards further on she stopped again; and the veil that slanted down from her man's hat to below her waist covered her face with a translucent blue film, as though she were swimming under limpid water.

"Where are we going?"

He didn't answer. She was breathing quickly. Rodolphe looked this way and that, biting his mustache.

They came to a larger open space, one that had recently been cleared of saplings. They sat down on a log, and Rodolphe spoke to her of his love.

He was careful not to frighten her, at first, by saying anything overbold: he was calm, serious, melancholy.

She listened to him with lowered head, stirring the wood chips on the ground with the toe of her shoe.

But when he said, "Our lives are bound up together now, aren't they?" she answered, "No—you know they can't be."

She rose to leave. He grasped her wrist. She stood still and gave him a long look, her eyes moist and tender. Then she said hastily:

"Please—let's not talk about it any more. Where are the horses? Let's go back."

A movement of angry displeasure escaped him.

"Where are the horses?" she asked again. "Where are the horses?"

Then, smiling a strange smile, staring fixedly, his teeth clenched, he advanced toward her with arms outstretched. She drew back trembling.

"You're frightening me!" she stammered. "What are you doing? Take me back!"

His expression changed. "Since you insist," he said.

And abruptly he was once more considerate, tender, timid. She took his arm and they turned back.

"What was the matter?" he asked. "What came over you? I don't understand. You must have some mistaken idea. I have you in my heart like a Madonna on a pedestal—in an exalted place, secure, immaculate. But I need you if I'm to go on living! I need your eyes, your voice, your thoughts. I beseech you: be my friend, my sister, my angel!"

And he reached out his arm and put it around her waist. She made a half-hearted effort to free herself, but he kept it there, holding her as they walked.

Now they were so close to the horses that they heard them munching leaves.

"Just a little longer," begged Rodolphe. "Let's not go yet. Wait."

He drew her further on, to the edge of a little pond whose surface was green with duck weed and where faded water lilies lay still among the rushes. At the sound of their steps in the grass, frogs leaped to hiding.

"It's wrong of me," she said. "Wrong. I must be out of my mind to listen to you."

"Why? Emma! Emma!"

"Oh! Rodolphe!" The syllables came out slowly, and she pressed against his shoulder.

The broadcloth of her habit clung to the velvet of his coat. She leaned back her head, her white throat swelled in a sigh, and, her resistance gone, weeping, hiding her face, with a long shudder she gave herself to him.

Evening shadows were falling, and the level rays of the sun streamed through the branches and dazzled her eyes. Here and there, all about her, among the leaves and on the ground, were shimmering patches of light, as though hummingbirds winging by had scattered their feathers. All was silent; a soft sweetness seemed to be seeping from the trees; she felt her heart beating again, and her blood flowing in her flesh like a river of milk. Then from far off, beyond the woods in distant hills, she heard a vague, long, drawn-out cry—a sound that lingered; and she listened silently as it mingled like a strain of music with the last vibrations of her quivering nerves. Rodolphe, a cigar between his teeth, was mending a broken bridle with his penknife.

They returned to Yonville by the same route. In the mud they saw, side by side, the hoof prints left there by their own two horses; they saw the same bushes, the same stones in the grass. Nothing around them had changed: and yet to her something had happened that was more momentous than if mountains had moved. Rodolphe reached over, now and then, and raised her hand to his lips.

She was charming on horseback—erect and slender, her knee bent against the animal's mane, her face flushed a little by the air in the red glow of evening.

As she entered the village she made her horse prance on the stone pavement, and people stared at her from their windows.

Her husband, at dinner, found that she looked well; but she seemed not to hear him when he asked about her ride; and she leaned her elbow on the table beside her plate, between the two lighted candles.

"Emma!" he said.

"What?"

"Well, I called on Monsieur Alexandre this afternoon. He bought a filly a few years ago and she's still in fine shape, just a little broken in the knees; I'm sure I could get her for a hundred écus. . . ."

And he went on:

"I thought you might like to have her, so I reserved her. . . . I bought her. . . . Did I do right? Tell me."

She nodded her head in assent. Then, a quarter of an hour later:

"Are you going out tonight?" she asked.

"Yes, why?"

"Oh, nothing—nothing, dear."

And as soon as she was rid of Charles she went upstairs and shut herself in her room.

At first it was as though she were in a daze: she saw the trees, the paths, the ditches, Rodolphe; once again she felt his arms tighten around her as the leaves were all a-tremble and the reeds whistled in the wind.

Then she caught sight of herself in the mirror, and was amazed by the way she looked. Never had her eyes been so enormous, so dark, so deep: her whole being was transfigured by some subtle emanation.

"I have a lover! I have a lover!" she kept repeating to herself, reveling in the thought as though she were beginning a second puberty. At last she was going to know the joys of love, the fever of the happiness she had despaired of. She was entering a marvelous realm where all would be passion, ecstasy, rapture: she was in the midst of an endless blue expanse, scaling the glittering heights of passion; everyday life had receded, and lay far below, in the shadows between those peaks.

She remembered the heroines of novels she had read, and the lyrical legion of those adulterous women began to sing in her memory with sisterly voices that enchanted her. Now she saw herself as one of those *amoureuses* whom she had so envied: she was becoming, in reality, one of that gallery of fictional figures; the long dream of her youth was coming true. She was full of a delicious sense of vengeance. How she had suffered! But now her hour of triumph had come; and love, so long repressed, was gushing forth in joyful effervescence. She savored it without remorse, without anxiety, without distress.

The next day brought a new delight. They exchanged vows. She told him her sorrows. Rodolphe interrupted her with kisses; and she begged him, gazing at him with half-shut eyes, to say her name again and tell her once more that he loved her. They were in the forest, like the day before, this time in a hut used by sabot-makers. The walls were of straw, and the roof was so low that they could not stand erect. They sat side by side on a bed of dry leaves.

From that day on they wrote each other regularly every night. Emma took her letter out into the garden and slipped it into a crack in the terrace wall beside the river; Rodolphe came, took it, and left one for her—one that was always, she complained, too short.

One morning when Charles had gone out before sunrise she was seized with a longing to see Rodolphe at once. She could go quickly to La Huchette, stay there an hour, and be back in Yonville before anyone was up. The thought made her pant with desire, and soon she was halfway across the meadow, walking fast and not looking back.

Day was just breaking. From far off Emma recognized her lover's farm, with its two swallow-tailed weathervanes silhouetted in black against the pale twilight.

Beyond the farmyard was a building that could only be the château. She entered it as though the walls opened of themselves at her approach. A long straight staircase led to an upper hall. Emma turned the latch of a door, and there at the far end of a room she saw a man asleep. It was Rodolphe. She uttered a cry.

"It's you!" he cried. "You, here! How did you come? Ah! Your dress is wet!"

"I love you!" was her answer; and she flung her arms around his neck.

She had dared and won; and from then on, each time that Charles went out early she quickly dressed and stole down the river stairs.

If the cow plank had been raised she had to follow the garden walls that bordered the stream; the bank was slippery, and to keep from falling she would clutch at tufts of faded wallflowers. Then she would strike out across the plowed fields, sinking in, stumbling, her light shoes getting continually stuck in the soft soil. The scarf she had tied over her head fluttered in the wind as she crossed the meadows; she was afraid of the oxen, and would begin to run; and she would arrive breathless, rosy cheeked, everything about her smelling of sap and verdure and fresh air. Rodolphe would still be asleep. She was like a spring morning entering his room.

The yellow curtains masking the windows let through a soft, dull golden light. Emma would grope her way, squinting, dewdrops clinging to her hair like a halo of topazes around her face. And Rodolphe would laugh and draw her to him and strain her to his heart.

Afterwards she would explore the room, opening drawers, combing her hair with his comb, looking at herself in his shaving mirror. Often she took the stem of his pipe in her teeth—a large pipe that he kept on his night table, beside the lemons and lumps of sugar that were there with his water jug.

It always took them a good quarter of an hour to say good-bye. Emma invariably wept: she wished that she never had to leave him. Some irresistible force kept driving her time and again to his side, until one day when she arrived unexpectedly he frowned as though displeased.

"What's wrong?" she cried. "Are you ill? Tell me!"

After some urging, he declared gravely that her visits were becoming fool-hardy and that she was risking her reputation.

X

As time went on she came to share Rodolphe's fears. Love had intoxicated her at first, and she had had no thought beyond it. But now that life was inconceivable without it she was terrified lest she be deprived of any portion of this love, or even that it be in any way interfered with. Each time she returned from one of her visits she cast uneasy glances about her, peering at every figure moving on the horizon, at every dormer in the village from which she might be seen. Her ears picked up the sound of every footstep, every voice, every plow; and she would stand still, paler and more trembling than the leaves of the swaying poplars overhead.

One morning on her way back she suddenly thought she saw a rifle pointing at her. It was slanting out over the edge of a small barrel half hidden in the grass beside a ditch. She felt faint with fright, but continued to walk ahead, and a man emerged from the barrel like a jack-in-the-box. He wore gaiters buckled up to his knees, and his cap was pulled down over his eyes; his lips were trembling with cold and his nose was red. It was Captain Binet, out after wild duck.

"You should have called!" he cried. "When you see a gun you must always give warning."

That reproach was actually the tax collector's attempt to cover up the fright that Emma had given *him*. There was a police ordinance prohibiting duck shooting except from boats, and for all his respect for the law, Monsieur Binet was in the process of committing a violation. He had been expecting the game warden to appear any minute. But fear had added spice to his enjoyment, and in the solitude of his barrel he had been congratulating himself on his luck and his deviltry.

At the sight of Emma he felt relieved of a great weight, and he opened conversation:

"Chilly, isn't it! Really nippy!"

Emma made no answer.

"You're certainly out bright and early," he went on.

"Yes," she stammered. "I've been to see my baby at the nurse's."

"Ah, I see! As for me, I've been right here where I am now ever since daybreak, but it's such dirty weather that unless you have the bird at the very end of your gun . . ."

"Good-bye, Monsieur Binet," she interrupted, turning away.

"Good-bye, Madame," he answered dryly.

And he went back into his barrel.

Emma regretted having taken such brusque leave of the tax collector. Whatever surmises he made would certainly be to her discredit. What she had said about the wet nurse was the worst possible story she could have invented: everyone in Yonville knew perfectly well that little Berthe had been back with her parents for a year. Besides, no one lived out in that direction; that particular path led only to La Huchette. Binet must certainly have guessed where she was coming from: he wouldn't keep his mouth shut, either; he would gossip, unquestionably. All day she racked her brains, trying to dream up all possible lies; and she brooded incessantly about that fool with his game bag.

After dinner Charles, seeing that she looked worried about something, had the idea of distracting her from whatever it was by taking her to call on the pharmacist; and the first person she saw in the pharmacy was, once again, the tax collector! He was standing at the counter in the glow of the red jar, saying, "Give me a half-ounce of vitriol."

"Justin," called the pharmacist, "bring the sulphuric acid."

Then, to Emma, who was about to go up to Madame Homais' quarters:

"No, don't bother to climb the stairs: she'll be coming down directly. Warm yourself at the stove while you wait. Excuse me . . . *Bonjour, docteur.*" (The pharmacist greatly enjoyed uttering the word *docteur*, as though by applying it to someone else he caused some of the glory it held for him to be reflected on himself.) "But be careful not to knock over the mortars," he called to Justin. "No, no! Go get some of the chairs from the little room! You know perfectly well we never move the parlor armchairs."

And Homais was just bustling out from behind the counter to put his armchair back where it belonged when Binet asked him for a half-ounce of sugar acid.

"Sugar acid?" said the pharmacist scornfully. "I don't know what that is. I never heard of it. You want oxalic acid, perhaps? Oxalic is what you mean, isn't it?"

Binet explained that he needed a corrosive: he wanted to make some metal polish to clean the rust off parts of his hunting gear. Emma stood rigid.

"Yes, the weather is certainly unpropitious," said the pharmacist, "what with all this dampness."

"Still," said the tax collector slyly, "there are people who don't mind it."

She was choking.

"Now give me . . ."

"He'll never go!" she thought.

". . . a half-ounce of rosin and turpentine, four ounces of beeswax, and an ounce and a half of boneblack to clean the patent leather on my outfit."

As the apothecary began cutting the wax, Madame Homais appeared with Irma in her arms, Napoléon beside her and Athalie bringing up the rear. She sat down on the plush-covered bench by the window, while the boy took a stool and his elder sister kept close to the jujube jar, near her dear papa. The latter was pouring things into funnels, corking bottles, gluing labels and wrapping parcels. Everyone watched him in silence: the only sound was an occasional clink of weights in the scales, and a few low-voiced words of advice from the pharmacist to his apprentice.

"How is your little girl?" Madame Homais suddenly asked.

"Quiet!" cried her husband, who was jotting figures on a scratch-pad.

"Why didn't you bring her?" she went on, in an undertone.

"Sh! Sh!" said Emma, pointing to the apothecary.

But Binet, absorbed in checking the pharmacist's arithmetic, seemed to have heard nothing. Then at last he left. Emma gave a deep sigh of relief.

"How heavily you're breathing!" said Madame Homais.

"Don't you find it rather warm?" she answered.

The next day, therefore, Emma and Rodolphe discussed the best way of arranging their meetings. Emma was for bribing her maid with a present, but it would be better if they could find some other, safer place in Yonville. Rodolphe promised to look for one.

From then on, three or four times a week throughout the winter, he came to the garden in the dark of the night. Emma had removed the key from the gate, letting Charles think it was lost.

To announce himself, Rodolphe threw a handful of gravel against the shutters. She always started up; but sometimes she had to wait, for Charles loved to chat beside the fire, and went on and on. She would grow wild with impatience: if she could have accomplished it with a look, she would have flung him out a window. Finally she would begin to get ready for bed, and then she would take up a book and sit quietly reading, as though absorbed. Charles, in bed by this time, would call her.

"Come, Emma," he would say. "It's time."

"Yes, I'm coming," she would answer.

But the candles shone in his eyes, and he would turn to the wall and fall asleep. Then she slipped out, holding her breath, smiling, palpitating, half undressed.

Rodolphe would enfold her in the large full cape he wore and, with his arm around her waist, lead her without a word to the foot of the garden.

It was in the arbor that they spent their time together, on the same dilapidated rustic bench from which Léon used to stare at her so amorously on summer evenings. She scarcely thought of him now.

The stars glittered through the bare branches of the jasmine. Behind them they heard the flowing of the river, and now and again the crackle of dry reeds on the bank. Here and there in the darkness loomed patches of deeper shadow; and sometimes these would suddenly seem to shudder, rear up and then curve downward, like huge black waves threatening to engulf them. In the cold of the night they clasped each other the more tightly, the sighs that came from their lips seemed deeper, their half-seen eyes looked larger; and amidst the silence their soft-spoken words had a crystalline ring that echoed and reechoed in their hearts.

If the night was rainy they sought shelter in the consulting room, between the shed and the stable. She would light a kitchen lamp that she kept hidden behind the books. Rodolphe made himself at home here, as though the place belonged to him. The sight of the bookcase and the desk—indeed the whole room—aroused his hilarity: he couldn't keep from joking about Charles in a way that made Emma uncomfortable. She would have liked him to be more serious—or even more dramatic sometimes, like the night she thought she heard the sound of approaching footsteps in the lane.

"Someone's coming," she whispered.

He blew out the light.

"Have you got your pistols?"

"What for?"

"Why—to defend yourself," said Emma.

"You mean against your husband? That poor . . . ?"

And Rodolphe ended his sentence with a gesture that meant that he could annihilate Charles with a flick of his finger.

This display of fearlessness dazzled her, even though she sensed in it a crudity and bland vulgarity that shocked her.

Rodolphe thought a good deal about that episode of the pistols. If she had spoken in earnest, it was absurd of her, he thought, really an odious thing, for he had no cause to hate poor Charles. He was by no means "devoured by jealousy," as the saying went: and indeed, in this connection, Emma had made him a tremendous vow that he, for his part, thought in rather poor taste.

Besides, she was becoming frightfully sentimental. They had had to exchange miniatures and cut handfuls of each other's hair; and now she was asking for a ring—a real wedding band, as a sign of eternal union. She often talked to him about the "bells of evening," or the "voices of nature"; and then she would go on about her mother and his. Rodolphe's mother had been dead for twenty years, but Emma kept consoling him in the kind of affected language one uses to a bereaved child; and sometimes she would even look at the moon and say to him, "Somewhere up there I'm sure they're both looking down at us and approving of our love."

But she was so pretty! He couldn't remember ever having had so unspoiled a mistress. The purity of her love was something entirely new to him. It was a change from his usual loose habits, and it both flattered his pride and inflamed his senses. Emma's continual raptures, which his bourgeois common sense despised, seemed to him in his heart of hearts charming, since it was he who inspired them.

As time went on he stopped making any effort, secure in the knowledge that he was loved; and imperceptibly his manner changed. No longer did he speak to her, as before, in words so sweet that they made her weep; nor were there any more of those fervid embraces that frenzied her. Their great love, in which she lived completely immersed, seemed to be ebbing away, like the water of a river that was sinking into its own bed; and she saw the mud at the bottom. She refused to believe it; she redoubled her caresses; and Rodolphe hid his indifference less and less.

She didn't know whether she regretted having yielded to him or whether she didn't rather long to love him more dearly. Her humiliating feeling of weakness was turning into resentment: but this melted away in the heat of his embraces. It was not an attachment; it was a kind of permanent seduction. She was in his bondage. It almost frightened her.

Nevertheless, from the outside everything looked more serene than ever, Rodolphe having succeeded in conducting the affair as he pleased; and at the end of six months, when spring came, they were like a married couple peacefully tending to a domestic flame.

It was the time of the year when Monsieur Rouault always sent his turkey, in commemoration of his mended leg. As usual, the present was accompanied by a letter. Emma cut the string tying it to the basket, and read the following:

Dear Children:

I hope these lines find you well and that this one will be up to the others: it seems to me a little tenderer, if I may say so, and meatier. But next time I'll send you a cock for a change, unless you'd rather stick to gobblers, and please send me back the basket along with the last two. I had an accident with the cart shed, one night a heavy wind blew the roof off into the trees. Crops haven't been too good either. I can't tell when I'll come to see you. It's so hard for me to leave the place now that I'm alone.

Here there was a space between the lines, as though the old man had put down his pen to think a while.

As for me, I'm all right, except for a cold I caught the other day at the fair in Yvetot, where I went to hire a shepherd, having got rid of the one I had because he was too particular about his food. All these good-for-nothings give you more trouble than they're worth. This one was disrespectful besides.

I heard from a peddler who stopped in your town to have a tooth drawn that Bovary keeps busy. It doesn't surprise me, and he showed me his tooth; we took a cup of coffee together. I asked if he'd seen you, Emma, he said no, but he'd seen two horses in the stable from which I assume that business is prospering. I'm glad of it, dear children, may the good Lord send you every possible happiness.

It grieves me that I've never seen my beloved granddaughter Berthe Bovary. I've planted a tree of September plums for her under the window of your room and I won't let anybody touch it except to make some jam for her later that I'll keep in the cupboard for her when she comes.

Good-bye, dear children. I kiss you on both cheeks, all three of you.

> I am, with all good wishes,
> Your loving father,
> Théodore Rouault

She sat for a few minutes with the sheet of coarse paper in her hand. The letter was thick with spelling mistakes, and Emma brooded on the affectionate thought that cackled through them like a hen half hidden in a thorn hedge. Her father had dried his writing with ash from the fireplace, for a bit of gray dust drifted out of the letter onto her dress, and she could almost see the old man bending down toward the hearth to take up the tongs. How long it was since she had sat there beside him, on the fireseat, burning the end of a stick in the flame of the crackling furze! She remembered summer evenings, full of sunshine. The foals would whinny when anyone came near, and gallop and gallop to their hearts' content. There had been a beehive under her window, and sometimes the bees, wheeling in the light, would strike against the panes like bouncing golden balls. How happy she had been in those days! How free! How full of hope! How rich in illusions! There were no illusions left now! She had had to part with some each time she had ventured on a new path, in each of her successive conditions—as virgin, as wife, as mistress; all along the course of her life she had been losing them, like a traveler leaving a bit of his fortune in every inn along the road.

But what was making her so unhappy? Where was the extraordinary disaster that had wrought havoc with her life? And she lifted her head and looked about her, as though trying to discover the cause of her suffering.

An April sunbeam was dancing on the china in the whatnot; the fire was burning; she felt the rug soft beneath her slippers; the day was cloudless, the air mild, and she could hear her child shouting with laughter.

The little girl was rolling on the lawn, in the cut grass that Lestiboudois was raking. She was lying on her stomach on a pile that he had got together; Félicité was holding her by the skirt; the gardener was working nearby, and whenever he came close she leaned over toward him, waving her arms in the air.

"Bring her in to me!" her mother cried. And she rushed over and kissed her. "How I love you, darling! How I love you!"

Then, noticing that the tips of the child's ears were a little dirty, she quickly rang for hot water; and she washed her, changed her underclothes, stockings, and shoes, asked a thousand questions about how she felt, as though she were just back from a trip, and finally, giving her more and more kisses, and weeping a little, she handed her back to the maid, who stood gaping at this overflow of affection.

That night Rodolphe found her more reserved than usual.

"It will pass," he thought. "It's some whim."

And on three successive evenings he didn't appear for their rendezvous. When he finally came she was cold, almost disdainful.

"Ah! You'll get nowhere playing that game . . . !" And he pretended not to notice her melancholy sighs or the handkerchief she kept bringing out.

Then Emma's repentance knew no bounds.

She even wondered why she detested Charles, and whether it mightn't be better to try to love him. But there was so little about him to which her resurgent feeling could attach itself that she was at a loss as to how to put her noble resolution into effect. And then one day the apothecary provided the desired opportunity.

XI

Homais had lately read an article extolling a new method of curing club-foot; and since he was on the side of progress he conceived the patriotic idea that Yonville, to keep abreast of the times, should have its own operation for talipes, as he learnedly called the deformity.

"After all," he said to Emma, "what's the risk? Look." And he enumerated on his fingers the advantages that would accrue from the attempt. "Almost sure success, relief and improved appearance for the patient, and for the surgeon a rapid rise to fame. Why shouldn't your husband fix up poor Hippolyte, at the Lion d'Or? The boy would unquestionably talk about his cure to every traveler at the inn, and then"—here Homais lowered his voice and cast a glance about him—"what is there to keep me from sending a little piece about it to the paper? Ah! An article gets around—people talk about it—a thing like that really snowballs. Who can tell? Who can tell?"

He was right: Bovary might very well succeed. Emma had never had any reason to think that he wasn't skillful in his work; and what satisfaction *she* would derive from persuading him to take a step that would increase his fame and fortune! Something more solid than love to lean on would be only too welcome.

Egged on by her and by the apothecary, Charles consented. He sent to Rouen for Doctor Duval's treatise; and every night, his head in his hands, he buried himself in its pages.

He studied talipes in its various forms—equinus, varus and valgus: in other words, the varying malformations of the foot downwards, inwards, or outwards, sometimes scientifically called *strephocatopodia, strephendopodia* and *strephexopodia;* and he studied *strephypopodia* and *strephanopodia*—downward or upward torsion. And meanwhile Monsieur Homais tried to persuade the stable boy to agree to be operated on. He used every possible argument.

"You'll scarcely feel it—there'll be the very slightest pain if any. It's just a prick, like the tiniest bloodletting. Not nearly as bad as cutting out certain kinds of corns."

Hippolyte rolled his eyes stupidly as he thought it over.

"Besides," the pharmacist went on, "it's not for my sake that I'm urging you, but for yours—out of pure humanity. I'd like to see you rid of that ugly limp, my boy, and that swaying in the lumbar region that must interfere seriously with your work, whatever you say."

Then Homais painted a picture of how much more lively and nimble he would feel, and even intimated that he'd be much more successful with women. The stable boy grinned sheepishly at that. Then Homais played on his vanity:

"Are you a man or aren't you? Think what it would have been like if you'd had to serve in the army and go into combat! Ah, Hippolyte!"

And Homais moved off, declaring that such stubbornness, such blindness in refusing the benefits of science were beyond his understanding.

In the end the poor wretch yielded, unable to stand up against what was a veritable conspiracy. Binet, who never meddled in other people's affairs, Madame Lefrançois, Artémise, the neighbors, even the mayor, Monsieur Tuvache—everybody urged him, lectured him, shamed him; but what finally decided him was that it wouldn't cost him anything. Bovary even offered to supply the apparatus that would be used after the operation. Emma had thought up that bit of generosity, and Charles had agreed, inwardly marveling at what an angel his wife was.

Guided by the pharmacist's advice, he finally succeeded on the third try in having the cabinetmaker and the locksmith construct a sort of box weighing about eight pounds—a complicated mass of iron, wood, tin, leather, screws and nuts.

Meanwhile, in order to know which of Hippolyte's tendons had to be cut, he first had to find out what variety of clubfoot his was.

The foot made almost a straight line with the leg, and at the same time was twisted inward, so that it was an equinus with certain characteristics of a varus, or else a varus with strong equinus features. But with his equinus— which actually was as wide across as an equine hoof, with rough skin, stringy tendons, oversized toes, and black nails that were like the nails of a horseshoe—the taliped[2] ran about fleet as a deer from morning to night. He was constantly to be seen in the square, hopping about among the carts, thrusting his clubfoot ahead of him. Actually, the affected leg seemed to be stronger than the other. From its long years of service it had taken on moral qualities, as it were—qualities of patience and energy; and whenever Hippolyte was given a particularly heavy task to do, it was that leg that he threw his weight on.

Since it was an equinus, the Achilles tendon would have to be cut, and then later, perhaps, the anterior tibial muscle, to take care of the varus. Charles didn't dare risk two operations at once, and indeed he was trembling already lest he interfere with some important part of the foot he knew nothing about.

Neither Ambroise Paré, applying an immediate ligature to an artery for the first time since Celsus had done it fifteen centuries before; nor Dupuytren cutting open an abscess through a thick layer of the brain; nor Gensoul, when he performed the first removal of an upper maxillary—none of them, certainly, felt such a beating of the heart, such a quivering of the hand, such a tenseness of the mind, as Monsieur Bovary when he approached Hippolyte with his tenotomy knife. On a table nearby, just as in a hospital, lay a pile of lint, waxed thread, and a quantity of bandages—a veritable pyramid of bandages, the apothecary's entire stock. It was Monsieur Homais who had been making these preparations ever since early morning, as much to dazzle the multitude as to inflate his self-importance. Charles pierced the skin: there was a sharp snap. The tendon was cut; the operation was over. Hippolyte couldn't stop marveling: he bent over Bovary's hands and covered them with kisses.

---

2. A person with clubfoot, or talipes.

"Don't get excited," said the apothecary. "You'll have plenty of occasion to express your gratitude to your benefactor."

And he went out to announce the result to five or six sensation seekers who were waiting in the yard expecting Hippolyte to make his appearance walking normally. Then Charles strapped his patient into the apparatus and went home, where Emma was anxiously awaiting him at the door. She flung her arms around his neck; they sat down at table; he ate heartily, and even asked for a cup of coffee with his dessert—a bit of intemperance he ordinarily allowed himself only on Sunday when there was company.

Their evening together was charming: they spoke of their future, the improvement they expected in their fortunes, changes they would make in their house. He saw himself a man of renown and riches, adored by his wife; and she felt herself pleasantly revived by this new sensation—this noble, wholesome experience of returning at least some of poor Charles's love. For a moment the thought of Rodolphe crossed her mind; but then her eyes swung back to Charles, and she noticed with surprise that his teeth weren't bad at all.

They were in bed when Monsieur Homais suddenly entered their room: he had brushed aside the cook's attempts to announce him, and was holding a newly written sheet of paper. It was the publicity article he had prepared for the *Fanal de Rouen:* he had brought it for them to read.

"You read it to us," said Bovary.

He began:

" 'Despite the network of prejudices that still extends across part of the face of Europe, our country districts are beginning to see the light. Just this Tuesday our small community of Yonville was the scene of a surgical experiment that was also an act of pure philanthropy. Monsieur Bovary, one of our most distinguished practitioners . . . ' "

"That's going too far! Too far!" cried Charles, choked with emotion.

"Not at all! Certainly not! ' . . . performed an operation on a clubfoot. . . .' I didn't use the scientific term—in a newspaper, you know . . . not everybody would understand; the masses have to be . . ."

"You're right," said Bovary. "Go ahead."

"Where was I?" said the pharmacist. "Oh, yes. 'Monsieur Bovary, one of our most distinguished practitioners, performed an operation on a clubfoot. The patient was one Hippolyte Tautain, stable boy for the past twenty-five years at the Lion d'Or hotel, owned by Madame Lefrançois, on the Place d'Armes. The novelty of the enterprise and the interest felt in the patient had attracted such a large throng of our local citizenry that there was a veritable crush outside the establishment. The operation went off like magic, and only a few drops of blood appeared on the skin, as though to announce that the rebellious tendon had finally surrendered to the surgeon's art. The patient, strange though it may seem (we report this fact *de visu*), experienced not the slightest pain. Up to the moment of the present writing, his condition is entirely satisfactory. Everything gives us reason to expect that his convalescence will be rapid. Who knows? At the next village festival we may well see our good friend Hippolyte tripping Bacchic measures amidst a chorus of joyous companions, thus demonstrating to all, by his high spirits and his capers, the completeness of his cure. All honor to our generous men of science! All honor to those tireless benefactors who go without sleep to work for the improvement or the relief of mankind! All honor to them! Now indeed we can proclaim that the blind shall see, the deaf shall hear and the lame shall walk! But what fanaticism promised in times past to the elect, science is now achieving for all men! We shall keep our readers informed concerning the subsequent stages of this remarkable cure.' "

But all that eloquence did not alter the course of events. Five days later Madame Lefrançois rushed into the doctor's house frightened out of her wits, crying: "Help! He's dying! It's driving me mad!"

Charles made a dash for the Lion d'Or; and the pharmacist, catching sight of him as he rushed bareheaded across the square, hurriedly left his pharmacy. He, too, arrived at the hotel breathless, flushed and worried. "What has happened," he inquired of the numerous people climbing the stairs, "to our interesting taliped."

The taliped was writhing—writhing in frightful convulsions, so severe that the apparatus locked around his leg was beating against the wall, threatening to demolish it.

Taking every precaution not to disturb the position of the leg, Charles and Monsieur Homais removed the box—and a terrible sight met their eyes. The foot was completely formless, so immensely swollen that the skin seemed ready to burst; and the entire surface was covered with black and blue spots caused by the much-vaunted apparatus. Hippolyte had been complaining of pain for some time, but no one had paid any attention; now it was clear that he hadn't entirely imagined it, and he was allowed to keep his foot out of the box for several hours. But hardly had the swelling subsided a little than the two experts decided that the treatment should be resumed; and they screwed the apparatus on more tightly than before, to hasten results. Finally, three days later, when Hippolyte could bear it no longer, they removed the box again and were amazed by what they saw. A livid tumescence now extended up the leg, and a dark liquid was oozing from a number of blood blisters. Things were taking a serious turn. Hippolyte had no courage left; and Madame Lefrançois moved him into the small room, just off the kitchen, so that he might at least have some distraction.

But the tax collector, who took his dinner there every evening, complained bitterly of such company, so Hippolyte was moved again, this time into the billiard room.

He lay there, groaning under his heavy blankets, pale, unshaven, hollow eyed, turning and twisting his sweaty head on the dirty, fly-covered pillow. Madame Bovary came to see him. She brought him linen for his poultices, comforted him, tried to cheer him. He had no lack of company, especially on market days, when the peasants crowded around him, playing billiards, dueling with the cues, smoking, drinking, singing, shouting.

"How're you getting along?" they would say, giving him a poke in the shoulder. "You don't look too good. But it's your own fault. You should have . . . ." And they would give their advice, telling him about people who had all been cured by methods quite different from the one that had been used on him. Then they would add, by way of comfort: "You fuss too much! Why don't you get up, instead of having everybody wait on you? Well, never mind, old boy—you certainly stink!"

And indeed the gangrene was climbing higher and higher. Bovary was sick about it. He kept coming in every hour, every few minutes. Hippolyte would look at him with terror-filled eyes, and sob and stammer:

"When will I be cured? Help me! Help me! Oh, God, it's terrible!"

And each time the doctor could only go away again, advising him to eat lightly.

"Don't listen to him," Madame Lefrançois would say, when Bovary had left. "They've made you suffer enough already. You'll lose still more of your strength. Here, swallow this!"

And she would give him some tasty soup, or a slice from a leg of mutton, or a bit of bacon, and now and again a little glass of brandy that he hardly dared drink.

The abbé Bournisien, learning that he was getting worse, came to the hotel and asked to see him. He began by condoling with him on his suffering—declaring, however, that he should rejoice in it, since it was the Lord's will, and lose no time taking advantage of this occasion to become reconciled with heaven.

"You've been a little neglectful of your religious duties," he pointed out in a paternal tone. "I've seldom seen you at Mass. How many years is it since you've been to Communion? It's understandable that your work and other distractions should have made you careless about your eternal salvation. But now is the time to think about it. Don't give way to despair: I've known grievous sinners who implored God's mercy when they were about to appear before Him—I know you haven't reached that point yet—and who certainly made better deaths as a result. Be an example to us, as they were! What's to prevent you from saying a Hail Mary and an Our Father every night and morning just as a precaution? Do it! Do it for me, to oblige me! It doesn't amount to much. Will you promise?"

The poor devil promised. The priest came again the following days. He chatted with the hotel keeper, told stories, made jokes and puns that were over Hippolyte's head. Then, at the first possible opening, he would return to religious matters, his face taking on an appropriate expression as he did so.

His zeal seemed to have some effect, for soon the taliped expressed a wish to make a pilgrimage to Bon-Secours if he was cured—to which the abbé replied that he could see nothing against it: two precautions were better than one. What—as he put it—was the risk?

The apothecary railed against what he called the priest's "maneuvers": they were interfering, he claimed, with Hippolyte's convalescence; and he kept saying to Madame Lefrançois, "Leave him alone! Leave him alone! You're confusing him with all your mysticism!"

But the lady wouldn't listen to him. He was "to blame for everything." And on a nail in the wall at the head of the sickbed she defiantly hung a brimming holy-water font with a sprig of boxwood in it.

However, religion seemed to be of no greater help than surgery, and the gangrenous process continued to extend inexorably upward toward the groin. In vain did they change medications and poultices: each day the muscles rotted a little more, and finally Charles replied with an affirmative nod when Madame Lefrançois asked him whether as a last resort she couldn't call in Monsieur Canivet, a celebrated surgeon in Neufchâtel.

This fellow practitioner, a fifty-year-old M.D. of considerable standing and equal self-assurance, laughed with unconcealed scorn when he saw Hippolyte's leg, by now gangrenous to the knee. Then, after declaring flatly that he would have to amputate, he visited the pharmacist and inveighed against the jackasses capable of reducing an unfortunate man to such a plight. He grasped Monsieur Homais by one of his coat buttons and shook him, shouting:

"New-fangled ideas from Paris! It's like strabismus and chloroform and lithotrity—the government ought to forbid such tomfoolery! But everybody wants to be smart nowadays, and they stuff you full of remedies without caring about the consequences! We don't pretend to be so clever, here in the country. We're not such know-it-alls, such la-di-das! We're practitioners, healers! It doesn't occur to us to operate on somebody who's perfectly well! Straighten a clubfoot! Who ever heard of straightening a clubfoot? It's like wanting to iron out a hunchback!"

Those words were a whiplash to Homais, but he hid his discomfiture under an obsequious smile: it was important to humor Canivet, whose prescriptions were sometimes brought into the pharmacy by Yonvillians, and so he made no defense of Bovary and expressed no opinion; he cast principles to the winds, and sacrificed his dignity to the weightier interests of his business.

It was quite an event in the village, that mid-thigh amputation by Doctor Canivet! All the citizens rose early that morning; and the Grande-Rue, thronged though it was, had something sinister about it, as though it were execution day. At the grocer's, Hippolyte's case was discussed from every angle; none of the stores did any business; and Madame Tuvache, the mayor's wife, didn't budge from her window, so eager was she not to miss the surgeon's arrival.

He drove up in his gig, holding the reins himself. Over the years the right-hand spring had given way under the weight of his corpulence, so that the carriage sagged a little to one side as it rolled along. Beside him, on the higher half of the seat cushion, could be seen a huge red leather case, its three brass clasps gleaming magisterially.

The doctor drew up in the hotel yard with a flourish and called loudly for someone to unharness his mare; and then he went to the stable to see whether she was really being given oats as he had ordered. His first concern, whenever he arrived at a patient's, was always for his mare and his gig. "That Canivet—he's a character!" people said of him; and they thought the more of him for his unshakable self-assurance. The universe might have perished to the last man, and he wouldn't have altered his habits a jot.

Homais made his appearance.

"I'm counting on you," said the doctor. "Are we ready? Let's go!"

But the apothecary blushingly confessed that he was too sensitive to be present at such an operation.

"When you just stand there watching," he said, "your imagination begins to play tricks on you, you know. And I'm of such a nervous temperament anyway that . . ."

"Bah!" interrupted Canivet. "You look more like the apoplectic type to me. It doesn't surprise me, either: you pharmacists are always cooped up in your kitchens—it can't help undermining your constitutions in the long run. Look at me: I'm up every day at four, shave in cold water every season of the year; I'm never chilly, never wear flannel underwear, never catch cold—I'm sound as a bell. I eat well one day, badly the next, however it comes. I take it philosophically. That's why I'm not a bit squeamish, like you. And that's why it's all the same to me whether I carve up a Christian or any old chicken they put in front of me. It's all a question of habit."

Thereupon, with no consideration whatever for Hippolyte, who was sweating with pain and terror under his bedclothes in the billiard room, the two gentlemen proceeded there in the kitchen to engage in a conversation in which the apothecary likened the coolness of a surgeon to that of a general. The comparison pleased Canivet, who expatiated on the demands made by his profession. He looked on it as a kind of sacred charge, even though dishonored nowadays by the activities of the *officiers de santé*. Then, finally giving thought to his patient, he inspected the bandages Homais had brought—the same ones he had furnished the day of the earlier operation—and asked for someone to hold the leg for him while he worked. Lestiboudois was sent for, and Canivet rolled up his sleeves and went into the billiard room. The apothecary stayed outside with Artémise and the landlady, both of the latter whiter than their aprons and all three of them with their ears to the door.

Bovary, meanwhile, didn't dare show himself outside his house. He sat downstairs in the parlor beside the empty fireplace, his chin on his chest, his hands folded, his eyes set. What a misfortune! he was thinking. What a disappointment! Certainly he had taken all conceivable precautions. Fate had played a hand in it. Be that as it may, if Hippolyte were later to die it would be he who would have murdered him. And then—how was he to answer the questions his patients were sure to ask him? What reason could he give for his failure? Perhaps he *had* made some mistake? He sought for what it might be, and failed to find it. The greatest surgeons made mistakes, didn't they? That was something no one would ever believe. Everyone would laugh at him, talk about him. The news would spread to Forges, to Neufchâtel, to Rouen—everywhere! Who knew—other doctors might write letters and articles attacking him! There would be a controversy: he would have to send replies to the newspapers. Hippolyte himself might sue him. He saw himself dishonored, ruined, lost! And his imagination, engendering countless fears, was tossed about like an empty barrel carried out to sea and bobbing on the waves.

Emma, sitting opposite, was watching him. She was not participating in his humiliation. She was experiencing a humiliation of a different sort: the humiliation of having imagined that such a man might be worth something—as though she hadn't twenty times already had full proof of his mediocrity.

Charles began to stride up and down the room. The floor creaked under his heavy boots.

"Sit down!" she said. "You're getting on my nerves!"

He sat down.

How in the world had she managed (she who was so intelligent) to commit yet another blunder? What deplorable mania was it that had made her wreck her life by constant self-sacrifice? She recalled all her desires for luxury, all her spiritual privations, the sordid details of marriage and housekeeping, her dreams mired like wounded swallows, everything she had ever craved for, everything she had denied herself, all the things she might have had. And for whose sake had she given up so much?

The silence that hung over the village was suddenly rent by a scream.

Bovary went deathly pale. For an instant her brows contracted in a nervous frown; then she resumed her brooding. It was for him that she had done it— for this creature here, this man who understood nothing, who felt nothing. He was sitting quite calmly, utterly oblivious of the fact that the ridicule henceforth inseparable from his name would disgrace her as well. And she had tried to love him! She had wept tears of repentance at having given herself to another!

"I wonder—could it perhaps have been a valgus?"[3] The question came abruptly from the musing Charles.

At the sudden impact of those words, crashing into her mind like a leaden bullet into a silver dish, Emma felt herself shudder; and she raised her head, straining to understand what he had meant by them. They looked at each other in silence, almost wonderstruck, each of them, to see that the other was there, so far apart had their thoughts carried them. Charles stared at her with the clouded gaze of a drunken man; motionless in his chair, he was listening to the screams that continued to come from the hotel. One followed after another; each was a long, drawn-out succession of tones, and they were interspersed with short, shrill shrieks; it was all like the howling of some animal being butchered far away. Emma bit her pale lips; and twisting and turning in her fingers a sliver she had broken off the coral, she stared fixedly at Charles with blazing eyes that were like twin fiery arrows. Everything, everything about him exasperated her now—his face, his clothes, what he didn't say, his entire person, his very existence. She repented her virtue of days past as though it had been a crime; and what virtue she had left now crumbled under the furious assault of her pride. Adultery was triumphant; and she reveled in the prospect of its sordid ironies. The thought of her lover made her reel with desire; heart and soul she flung herself into her longing, borne toward him on waves of new rapture; and Charles seemed to her as detached from her life, as irrevocably gone, as impossible and done for, as though he were a dying man, gasping his last before her eyes.

There was a sound of footsteps on the sidewalk. Charles looked through the lowered blind: in the hot sun near the market Doctor Canivet was mopping his forehead with his handkerchief. Behind him was Homais, carrying a large red box, and they were both heading for the pharmacy.

Flooded with sudden tenderness and despondency, Charles turned to his wife. "Kiss me!" he cried. "Kiss me, darling!"

"Don't touch me!" she flared, scarlet with fury.

"What . . . what is it?" he stammered, bewildered. "What's wrong? You're not yourself! You know how I love you! I need you!"

"Stop!" she cried in a terrible voice.

And rushing from the room she slammed the door so violently that the barometer was flung from the wall and broke to pieces on the floor.

Charles sank into his chair, crushed, wondering what her trouble was, fearing some nervous illness, weeping, and vaguely aware that the air about him was heavy with something baleful and incomprehensible.

When Rodolphe came to the garden that night he found his mistress waiting for him on the lowest step of the river stairs. They fell into each other's arms: and all their accumulated resentments melted like snow in the heat of this embrace.

---

3. A twisting of the first toe above or below the other toes.

XII

Once again their love was at high tide.

Now Emma would often take it into her head to write him during the day. Through her window she would signal to Justin, and he would whip off his apron and fly to La Huchette. And when Rodolphe arrived in response to her summons, it was to hear that she was miserable, that her husband was odious, that her life was a torment.

"Can I do anything about it?" he snapped at her one day.

"Ah, if you only would . . ."

She was sitting at his feet staring at nothing, her head between his knees, her hair streaming.

"What could I do?" Rodolphe demanded.

She sighed. "We could go live somewhere else, away from here. . . ."

"You're really crazy!" he said, laughing. "You know it's impossible!"

She tried to pursue the subject, but he pretended not to understand, and spoke of other things.

He saw no reason why there should be all this to-do about so simple a thing as lovemaking.

But for her there was a reason: there was a motive force that gave an additional impetus to her passion. Every day her love for Rodolphe was fanned by her aversion for her husband. The more completely she surrendered to the one, the more intensely she loathed the other: never did Charles seem to her so repulsive, so thick-fingered, so heavy-witted, so common, as when she was alone with him after her meetings with Rodolphe. Acting, at such times, the role of wife, of virtuous woman, she thought feverishly of her lover—of his black hair curling over his tanned forehead, of his body so powerful and yet so elegant, of the cool judgment that went hand in hand with his fiery passion. It was for him that she filed her fingernails with the care of the most exquisite artist, that she kept massaging her skin with cold cream, scenting her handkerchiefs with patchouli. She decked herself with bracelets, rings and necklaces. Whenever he was expected she filled her two big blue glass vases with roses; both her room and herself were made ready for him, as though she were a courtesan awaiting a prince. Félicité was perpetually bleaching lingerie: all day long she was in the kitchen, and Justin often sat there with her, watching her work.

His elbows on the ironing board, he would stare hungrily at all the feminine garments strewn about him—the dimity petticoats, the fichus, the collars, the drawstring pantaloons enormously wide at the waist and narrowing below.

"What is this for?" the boy would ask, touching a crinoline lining or a set of fastenings.

"Don't tell me you've never seen anything!" Félicité would laugh. "As if your Madame Homais didn't wear these same things!"

"Oh, Madame Homais . . ." And he would wonder aloud: "Is she a lady, like Madame?"

But Félicité was getting tired of having him hang around her. She was six years his elder, and Théodore, Maître Guillaumin's servant, was beginning to court her.

"Leave me alone!" she would say, reaching for her starch pot. "Go pound your almonds. You're always fussing around the women. You're a nasty little boy: better wait till you get some hair on your face for that sort of thing."

"Don't be cross. I'll do her shoes for you."

And he would go over to the doorsill and reach for Emma's shoes, all caked with the mud she had brought in from her meetings. It would fall away powdery under his fingers, and he would watch the particles float gently upward in a shaft of sun.

"You act as though you're afraid of spoiling them!" the cook would jeer. She herself wasn't so careful when she cleaned them, for Madame always gave them to her as soon as they looked the least bit worn.

Emma had countless pairs in her wardrobe, and discarded them on the slightest pretext. Charles never said a word.

Nor did he protest at paying three hundred francs for a wooden leg that she felt should be given to Hippolyte. It was cork trimmed and had spring joints—a complicated mechanism hidden under a black trouser leg that ended in a patent-leather shoe. But Hippolyte didn't dare use such a beautiful leg every day, and he begged Madame Bovary to get him another that would be more suitable. Naturally Charles paid for the new one as well.

The stable boy gradually resumed his work. He went about the village as before; and whenever Charles heard the sharp tap of his stick on the cobblestones in the distance, he quickly changed his direction.

It was Monsieur Lheureux, the shopkeeper, who had taken charge of the order. It gave him an opportunity to see a good deal of Emma. He chatted with her about the latest novelties from Paris, about a thousand feminine trifles; he was more than obliging, and never pressed for payment. Emma let herself slide into this easy way of gratifying all her whims. When she decided she wanted to give Rodolphe a handsome riding crop she had seen in an umbrella shop in Rouen, she told Lheureux to get it for her, and he set it on her table a week later.

The next day, however, he appeared with his bill—two hundred and seventy francs, not to mention the centimes. Emma didn't know what to do: all the desk drawers were empty, they owed Lestiboudois two weeks' pay and the maid six months' wages, there were a number of other bills, and Bovary was waiting impatiently for a remittance from Monsieur Derozerays, who usually settled with him once a year, toward the end of June.

She was able to put Lheureux off for a time, but eventually he lost patience: he was hard pressed, he said, his capital was tied up, and if she couldn't give him something on account he'd be forced to take back all the items she had chosen.

"All right, take them!" she said.

"I didn't really mean that," he answered. "Except perhaps for the riding crop. I guess I'll have to ask Monsieur for it back."

"No! No!" she cried.

"Ah ha!" Lheureux thought. "I've got you!"

And feeling sure that he had ferreted out her secret, he left her. "We'll see," he murmured to himself, with his customary little whistle. "We'll see!"

She was wondering how to extricate herself when the cook came in and put a little cylindrical parcel on the mantel. "From Monsieur Derozerays," she said. Emma seized it and opened it. It contained fifteen napoleons—full payment. She heard Charles on the stairs, and she flung the gold pieces into one of her drawers and took the key.

Three days later Lheureux came again.

"I have a suggestion," he said. "If instead of paying the amount we agreed on you'd like to take . . ."

"Here!" she said, and she handed him fourteen napoleons.

The shopkeeper was taken aback. To hide his disappointment he overflowed with apologies and offers of service, all of which Emma declined. When he had left she stood a few moments with her hand in her apron, fingering the two five-franc pieces he had given her in change. She resolved to economize, so that eventually she could pay Charles back. . . .

"Bah!" she said to herself. "He'll never give it a thought."

Besides the riding crop with the silver-gilt knob, Rodolphe had been given a signet ring with the motto *"Amor nel cor"*; also a scarf to use as a muffler, and a cigar case very like the vicomte's that Charles had picked up on the road and Emma still kept.

But he found her presents humiliating, and on several occasions refused them. She was insistent, however, and he gave in, grumbling to himself that she was high-handed and interfering.

Then she had such crazy notions.

"When the bell strikes midnight," she would command him, "think of me."

And if he confessed that he hadn't done so, there were strings of reproaches, always ending with the eternal:

"Do you love me?"

"Of course I love you!"

"Very much?"

"Of course."

"You've never loved anybody else, have you?"

That made him laugh: "Do you think you deflowered me?"

When Emma burst into tears he tried to comfort her, protesting his love and saying things to make her smile.

"It's because I love you," she would interrupt. "I love you so much that I can't do without you—you know that, don't you? Sometimes I want so much to see you that it tears me to pieces. 'Where is he?' I wonder. 'Maybe he's with other women. They're smiling at him, he's going up close to them. . . .' Tell me it isn't true! Tell me you don't like any of them! Some of them are prettier than I am, but none of them can love you the way I do. I'm your slave and your concubine! You're my king, my idol! You're good! You're beautiful! You're wise! You're strong!"

He had had such things said to him so many times that none of them had any freshness for him. Emma was like all his other mistresses; and as the charm of novelty gradually slipped from her like a piece of her clothing, he saw revealed in all its nakedness the eternal monotony of passion, which always assumes the same forms and always speaks the same language. He had no perception—this man of such vast experience—of the dissimilarity of feeling that might underlie similarities of expression. Since he had heard those same words uttered by loose women or prostitutes, he had little belief in their sincerity when he heard them now: the more flowery a person's speech, he thought, the more suspect the feelings, or lack of feelings, it concealed. Whereas the truth is that fullness of soul can sometimes overflow in utter vapidity of language, for none of us can ever express the exact measure of his needs or his thoughts or his sorrows; and human speech is like a cracked kettle on which we tap crude rhythms for bears to dance to, while we long to make music that will melt the stars.

But with the superior acumen of those who keep aloof in any relationship, Rodolphe discovered that the affair offered still further possibilities of sensual gratification. He abandoned every last shred of restraint and consideration. He made her into something compliant, something corrupt. Hers was an infatuation to the point of idiocy; the intensity of her admiration for him was matched by the intensity of her own voluptuous feelings; she was in a blissful torpor, a drunkenness in which her very soul lay drowned and shriveled, like the duke of Clarence in his butt of malmsey.[4]

This constant indulgence had its effect on her daily behavior. Her glance grew bolder, her language freer; she went so far as to be seen smoking a cigarette in public, in Rodolphe's company—"as though," people said, "to show her contempt for propriety." Even those who had given her the benefit of the doubt stopped doing so when they saw her step out of the Hirondelle one day wearing a tight-fitting vest, like a man's. The elder Madame Bovary, who had taken refuge with her son following a particularly unpleasant scene with her husband, was as scandalized as any of the Yonville matrons. There were many other things that she disliked, too: first of all, Charles hadn't followed her advice about the ban on novels; and then she disapproved of "the way the house was run." She took the liberty of saying how she felt, and there were quarrels—one, especially, about Félicité.

Going down the hall the previous night the elder Madame Bovary had surprised her with a man—a man of about forty, with dark chin whiskers, who had slipped out through the kitchen when he had heard her coming. When she reported this, Emma burst out laughing; the older woman lost her temper, declaring that unless one cared nothing for morals oneself, one was bound to keep an eye on the morals of one's servants.

"What kind of social circles do *you* frequent?" Emma retorted, with such an impertinent stare that her mother-in-law asked her whether in taking her servant's part it wasn't really herself that she was defending.

"Get out!" the young woman cried, springing from her chair.

"Emma! Mother!" cried Charles, trying to stop the argument. But in their rage they both rushed from the room.

"What manners!" Emma sneered when he came to her. And she stamped with fury: "What a peasant!"

He hurried to his mother and found her close to hysterics. "Such insolence! She's irresponsible! Maybe worse!"

And she declared she would leave the house at once unless her daughter-in-law came to her and apologized. So Charles sought out his wife again and begged her to give in. He implored her on his knees. "Oh, all right, I'll do it," she said finally.

She held out her hand to her mother-in-law with the dignity of a marquise: "*Excusez-moi, Madame.*" And then in her own room she flung herself flat on the bed and wept like a child, her head buried in the pillow.

She and Rodolphe had agreed that in case of an emergency she would

4. The duke of Clarence was the younger brother of King Edward IV of England and the elder brother of Richard, duke of Gloucester. He was condemned to death for treason and, according to rumor, drowned in a butt of malmsey (a sweet aromatic wine) in February 1478. See Shakespeare's *Richard III* 1.4.155.

fasten a piece of white paper to the blind, so that if he happened to be in Yonville he could go immediately into the lane behind the house. Emma hung out the signal; after waiting three-quarters of an hour she suddenly saw Rodolphe at the corner of the market. She was tempted to open the window and call to him; as she hesitated he disappeared. She sank back hopelessly in her chair.

But after a short time she thought she heard someone on the sidewalk: it must be he. She went downstairs and across the yard. He was outside the gate. She flung herself into his arms.

"Be careful!" he warned.

"Ah, if you knew what I've been through," she breathed.

And she proceeded to tell him everything—hurriedly, disjointedly, exaggerating some facts and inventing others, and putting in so many parentheses that he lost the thread of her story.

"Come, angel, be brave! Cheer up! Be patient!"

"But I've been patient for four years! I've suffered for four years! A love like ours is something to boast of! I'm on the rack, with those people! I can't stand it any longer! Rescue me, for God's sake!"

She clung to him. Her tear-filled eyes were flashing like undersea fires; her breast rose and fell in quick gasps; never had he found her so desirable. He lost his head. "What must we do?" he said. "What do you want me to do?"

"Oh! Take me away!" she cried. "I implore you: take me away!"

And she crushed her lips to his, as though to catch the consent she hadn't dared hope for—the consent that was now breathed out in a kiss.

"But . . ." Rodolphe began.

"What is it?"

"What about your little girl?"

She pondered a few moments; then: "We'll take her with us—it's the only way."

"What a woman!" he thought as he watched her move off. She had quickly slipped back into the garden: someone was calling her.

The elder Madame Bovary was astonished, the next few days, by her daughter-in-law's transformation. Emma was docility itself, deferential to the point of asking her for a recipe for pickles.

Was it her way of covering her tracks more thoroughly? Or was it a kind of voluptuous stoicism—a deliberate, deeper savoring of the bitterness of everything she was about to abandon? Scarcely the latter, for she noticed nothing around her: she was living as though immersed in advance in her future happiness. With Rodolphe she talked of nothing else. She would lean on his shoulder, and murmur:

"Think of what it will be like when we're in the stagecoach! Can you imagine it? Is it possible? The moment I feel the carriage moving, I think I'll have the sensation we're going up in a balloon, sailing up into the clouds. I'm counting the days. Are you?"

Never had Madame Bovary been as beautiful as now. She had that indefinable beauty that comes from happiness, enthusiasm, success—a beauty that is nothing more or less than a harmony of temperament and circumstances. Her desires, her sorrows, her experience of sensuality, her evergreen illusions, had developed her step by step, like a flower nourished by

manure and by the rain, by the wind and the sun; and she was finally blooming in the fullness of her nature. Her eyelids seemed strangely perfect when
she half closed them in a long amorous glance; and each of her deep sighs
dilated her fine nostrils and raised the fleshy corners of her lips, lightly shadowed by dark down. Some artist skilled in corruption seemed to have
designed the knot of her hair: it lay on her neck coiled in a heavy mass,
twisted carelessly and always a little differently, for every day it was loosened
by embraces. Her voice now took on softer inflections; her body, too; something subtle and penetrating emanated from the very folds of her dress, from
the very arch of her foot. Charles found her exquisite and utterly irresistible,
as in the first days of their marriage.

When he returned home in the middle of the night he dared not wake her.
The porcelain night-light cast a trembling circular glow on the ceiling; and
the drawn curtains of the cradle made it look like a tiny white hut swelling
out in the darkness beside the bed. Charles looked at both sleepers. He
thought he could hear the light breathing of his child. She would be growing
rapidly now; every season would bring a change. Already he saw her coming
home from school at the end of the day, laughing, her blouse spotted with
ink, her basket on her arm. Then they would have to send her away to boarding school: that would cost a good deal—how would they manage? He
thought and thought about it. He had the idea of renting a little farm on the
outskirts, one that he could supervise himself mornings, as he rode out to
see his patients. He would put the profits aside, in the savings bank; later he
would buy securities of some kind. Besides, his practice would grow: he was
counting on it, for he wanted Berthe to have a good education; he wanted
her to be accomplished, to take piano lessions. Ah! How pretty she would be
later, at fifteen! She would look just like her mother; and like her, in the
summer, she would wear a great straw hat: from a distance they'd be taken
for sisters. He pictured her sewing at night beside them in the lamplight;
she would embroider slippers for him, and look after the house; she would
fill their lives with her sweetness and her gaiety. And then he would think
about her marriage. They would find her some fine young man with a good
position, who would make her happy. And her happiness would last for ever
and ever.

Emma wasn't asleep at such times. She was only pretending to be; and as
Charles gradually sank into slumber beside her she lay awake dreaming different dreams.

A team of four horses, galloping every day for a week, had been whirling
her and Rodolphe toward a new land from which they would never return.
On and on the carriage bore them, and they sat there, arms entwined, saying
not a word. Often from a mountaintop they would espy some splendid city,
with domes, bridges, ships, forests of lemon trees, and white marble cathedrals whose pointed steeples were crowned with storks' nests. Here the
horses slowed, picking their way over the great paving-stones, and the ground
was strewn with bouquets of flowers tossed at them by women laced in red
bodices. The ringing of bells and the braying of mules mingled with the
murmur of guitars and the sound of gushing fountains; pyramids of fruit
piled at the foot of pale statues were cooled by the flying spray, and the
statues themselves seemed to smile through the streaming water. And then
one night they arrived in a fishing village, where brown nets were drying in

the wind along the cliff and the line of cottages. Here they stopped: this would be their dwelling place. They would live in a low flat-roofed house in the shade of a palm tree, on a bay beside the sea. They would ride in gondolas, swing in hammocks; and their lives would be easy and ample like the silk clothes they wore, warm like the soft nights that enveloped them, starry like the skies they gazed upon. Nothing specific stood out against the vast background of the future that she thus evoked: the days were all of them splendid, and as alike as the waves of the sea; and the whole thing hovered on the horizon, infinite, harmonious, blue and sparkling in the sun. But then the baby would cough in the cradle, or Bovary would give a snore louder than the rest, and Emma wouldn't fall asleep till morning, when dawn was whitening the windowpanes and Justin was already opening the shutters of the pharmacy.

She had sent for Monsieur Lheureux and told him she would be needing a cloak: "A long cloak with a deep collar and a lining."

"You're going on a trip?" he asked.

"No! But . . . Anyway, I can count on you to get it, can't I? Soon?"

He bowed.

"I'll want a trunk, too. Not too heavy, roomy."

"I know the kind you mean. About three feet by a foot and a half, the sort they're making now."

"And an overnight bag."

"A little too much smoke not to mean fire," Lheureux said to himself.

"And here," said Madame Bovary, unfastening her watch from her belt. "Take this: you can pay for the things out of what you get for it."

But the shopkeeper protested. She was wrong to suggest such a thing, he said; they were well acquainted; he trusted her completely. She mustn't be childish. But she insisted that he take at least the chain, and Lheureux had put it in his pocket and was on his way out when she called him back.

"Hold the luggage for me," she said. "As for the cloak"—she pretended to ponder the question—"don't bring that to me, either. But give me the address of the shop and tell them to have it ready for me when I come."

They were to elope the following month. She would leave Yonville as though to go shopping in Rouen. Rodolphe was to arrange for their reservations and their passports, and would write to Paris to make sure that they would have the coach to themselves as far as Marseilles; and there they would buy a barouche and continue straight on toward Genoa. She would send her things to Lheureux's, whence they would be loaded directly onto the Hirondelle, thus arousing no one's suspicions. In all these plans there was never a mention of little Berthe. Rodolphe avoided speaking of her: perhaps Emma had forgotten her.

He said he needed two weeks more, to wind up some affairs; then, at the end of the first of them, he said he would need an additional two; then he said he was sick; then he went on a trip somewhere. The month of August passed. Finally they decided they would leave without fail on the fourth of September, a Monday.

The Saturday night before that Monday, Rodolphe arrived earlier than usual.

"Is everything ready?" she asked him.

"Yes."

They strolled around the flower beds and sat on the terrace wall.

"You seem sad," said Emma.

"No, why?"

But he kept looking at her strangely—with unusual softness and tenderness.

"Is it because you're going away?" she asked. "Leaving everything that's dear to you, everything that makes up your life? I understand that. . . . But I have nothing—nothing in the world. You're my everything. And I'll be yours. I'll be your family, your country; I'll look after you, I'll love you."

"How sweet you are!" he cried, clasping her in his arms.

"Am I really?" she laughed, melting with pleasure. "Do you love me? Swear that you do?"

"Do I love you! Do I! I adore you, darling!"

The moon, a deep red disc, was rising straight out of the earth beyond the meadows. They could see it climb swiftly between the poplar branches that partially screened it like a torn black curtain; and finally, dazzlingly white, it shone high above them in the empty sky illumined by its light. Now, moving more slowly, it poured onto a stretch of the river a great brightness that flashed like a million stars; and this silvery gleam seemed to be writhing in its depths like a headless serpent covered with luminous scales. It looked, too, like a monstrous many-branched candlestick dripping with molten diamonds. The night spread softly around them; patches of shadow hung in the leaves of the trees. Emma, her eyes half closed, drank in the cool breeze with deep sighs. Lost in their revery, they said not a word. Full and silent as the flowing river, languid as the perfume of the syringas, the sweetness they had known in earlier days once again surged up in their hearts, casting on their memories longer and more melancholy shadows than those of the motionless willows on the grass. Now and again some prowling night animal, hedgehog or weasel, disturbed the leaves; or they heard the sound of a ripe peach as it dropped to the ground.

"What a lovely night!" said Rodolphe.

"We'll have many more," Emma answered.

And as though speaking to herself:

"Yes, it will be good to be traveling. . . . But why should I feel sad? Is it fear of the unknown, or the effect of leaving everything I'm used to? No— it's from too much happiness. How weak of me! Forgive me!"

"There's still time," he cried. "Think carefully—you might be sorry!"

"Never!" she answered impetuously.

And moving close to him:

"What harm can come to me? There's not a desert, not a precipice, not an ocean, that I wouldn't cross with you. Living together will be like an embrace that's tighter and more perfect every day. There'll be nothing to bother us, no cares—nothing in our way. We'll be alone, entirely to ourselves, for ever and ever. Say something, darling! Answer me!"

At regular intervals he answered, "Yes . . . yes . . ." Her fingers were in his hair, and through the great tears that were welling from her eyes she kept repeating his name in a childish voice:

"Rodolphe! Rodolphe! Sweet little Rodolphe!"

Midnight struck.

"Midnight!" she said. "Now it's tomorrow! One more day!"

He stood up to go; and as though his movement were the signal for their flight, Emma suddenly brightened.

"You have the passports?"

"Yes."

"You haven't forgotten anything?"

"No."

"You're sure?"

"Absolutely."

"And you'll be waiting for me at the Hotel de Provence at noon?"

He nodded.

"Till tomorrow, then," said Emma, giving him a last caress.

And she watched him go.

He did not turn around. She ran after him, and leaning out over the water among the bushes:

"Till tomorrow!" she cried.

Already he was on the other side of the river, walking quickly across the meadow.

After several minutes Rodolphe stopped; and when he saw her in her white dress gradually vanishing into the shadows like a wraith, his heart began to pound so violently that he leaned against a tree to keep from falling.

"God, what a fool I am!" he muttered with an obscene curse. "But she certainly made a pretty mistress!"

Emma's beauty and all the joys of their love rushed back into his mind; and for a moment he softened. But then he turned against her.

"After all," he cried, gesticulating and talking aloud to himself to strengthen his resolution, "I can't spend the rest of my life abroad! I can't be saddled with a child! All that trouble! All that expense! No! No! Absolutely not! It would be too stupid!"

XIII

As soon as he reached home Rodolphe sat down at his desk, under the stag's-head trophy that hung on the wall. But when he took up his pen he couldn't think of what to write, and he leaned on his elbows and pondered. Emma seemed to have receded into a far-off past, as though the resolution he had just made had put a great distance between them.

In order to recapture some feeling of her he went to the wardrobe at the head of his bed and took out an old Rheims cookie box that was his storage place for letters from women. Out of it came a smell of damp dust and withered roses. The first thing his eye fell on was a handkerchief spotted with faint stains. It was one of Emma's: she had had a nosebleed one day when they were out together—he hadn't remembered it till now. Then he took up something that had been knocking against the sides of the box: it was the miniature she had given him; she looked much too fussily dressed, he thought, and her ogling expression was preposterous. He kept staring at the artist's handiwork in an attempt to evoke the model as he remembered her, and this gradually resulted in Emma's features becoming confused in his memory, as though the real face and the painted face had been rubbing against each other and wearing each other away. Finally he read some of her letters. They were as brief, as technical, as urgent as business letters, filled chiefly with details pertaining to their trip. He wanted to reread the longer ones, the earlier ones; they were further down in the box, and to get at them he had to disarrange everything else. He found himself mechanically going through the pile of letters and other things, turning up a heterogeneous assortment—bouquets, a garter, a black mask, pins, locks of hair. So many locks of hair! Brunette and blond: some of them, catching in the metal hinges of the box, had broken off as he opened it.

He rummaged among his souvenirs, lingering on the differences of hand-writing and style in the letters—as marked as the differences of spelling. There were affectionate letters, jolly letters, facetious letters, melancholy letters; there were some that begged for love and others that begged for money. Now and then a word brought back a face, a gesture, the sound of a voice; certain letters brought back nothing at all.

All those women, thronging into his memory, got in each other's way; none of them stood out above the rest, leveled down as they all were by the mea-sure of his love. He took up handfuls of the various letters and for some minutes amused himself by letting them stream from one hand to another. In the end he lost interest in the game and put the box back into the ward-robe. "What a lot of nonsense!" he said to himself.

This accurately summed up his opinion, for his companions in pleasure, like children playing in a schoolyard, had so trampled his heart that nothing green could grow there; indeed they were more casual than children—they hadn't even scribbled their names on the walls.

"Come now," he said to himself. "Get busy."

He began to write:

"You must be courageous, Emma: the last thing I want to do is ruin your life. . . ."

"That's absolutely true, after all," he assured himself "I'm acting in her interest; I'm only being honest."

"Have you given really serious thought to your decision? Do you realize into what abyss I was about to hurl you, poor darling? You don't, I'm sure. You were going ahead blind and confident, full of faith in happiness, in the future. . . . Ah! Poor wretched, insane creatures that we are!"

Here Rodolphe paused, looking for some good excuse.

"I could tell her that I've lost all my money. . . . No—that wouldn't stop her anyway: I'd have to go through the whole thing again later. Is there any way of making such women come to their senses?"

He thought for a while, then added:

"I'll never forget you—believe me—and I'll always feel the deepest devo-tion to you. But some day sooner or later our passion would have cooled—inevitably—it's the way with everything human. We would have had moments of weariness. Who knows—I might even have had the dreadful anguish of witnessing your remorse—and of sharing in it, since it would have been I who caused it. The very thought of the grief in store for you is a torture to me, Emma! Forget me! Why was it ordained that we should meet? Why were you so beautiful? Is the fault mine? In God's name, no! No! Fate alone is to blame—nothing and no one but fate!"

"That's always an effective word," he remarked to himself.

"Ah! Had you been a shallow-hearted creature like so many others, I could very well have gone ahead and let things happen as they might—purely for what was in it for myself—in that case without danger to you. But that marvelous intensity of feelings you have—such a delight for those who know you, such a source of anguish for yourself!—kept you—adorable woman that you are—from realizing the falsity of the position the future held for us. At first I, too, gave it no thought—I was lying in the shade of that ideal happiness we dreamed of as under a poison tree, without thought for the consequences."

"Maybe she'll think I'm giving her up out of stinginess. . . . What's it to me if she does! Let her. . . . And let's get it over with!"

"The world is cruel, Emma. It would have pursued us everywhere. You'd have been subjected to indiscreet questions—calumny—scorn—even insult, perhaps. You—insulted! Oh, my darling! And I would have been the cause of it—I, who wanted to put you on a throne—I, who shall carry away the thought of you like a talisman! Yes—away—for I am punishing myself for the harm I have done you—I am going into exile! Where? How can I tell? My poor mad brain can give no answer. Adieu, Emma! Continue to be as good as you have always been! Never forget the unfortunate man who lost you! Teach your child my name: tell her to include me in her prayers."

The flames of the two candles were flickering. Rodolphe got up to close the window; and then, back at his desk:

"That's all, I guess," he said to himself. "Oh—just this little bit more, to keep her from coming after me":

"I shall be far away when you read these unhappy lines; I dare not linger—the temptation to see you again is all but irresistible! This is no moment for weakness! I shall come back; and perhaps one day we'll be able to speak of our love with detachment, as a thing of the past. Adieu!"

And he appended one more, last adieu, this time written as two words—"A Dieu!": it seemed to him in excellent taste.

"How shall I sign it?" he wondered. " 'Devotedly'? No . . . 'Your friend'? Yes—that's it."

"Your friend."

He read over his letter and thought it was good.

"Poor little thing!" he thought, suddenly sentimental. "She'll think me as unfeeling as a stone. There ought to be a few tears on it, but weeping's beyond me—what can I do?" He poured some water in a glass, wet a finger, and holding it high above the page shook off a large drop. It made a pale blot on the ink. Then, looking around for something to seal the letter with, his eye fell on the signet ring with the motto "Amor nel cor." "Scarcely appropriate under the circumstances, but what the . . ."

Whereupon he smoked three pipes and went to bed.

When he got up the next day (about two in the afternoon—he slept late) Rodolphe had some apricots picked and arranged in a basket. At the bottom, hidden under some vine leaves, he put the letter; and he ordered Girard, his plough-boy, to deliver it carefully to Madame Bovary. This was his usual way of corresponding with her, sending her fruit or game according to the season.

"If she asks you anything about me," he said, "tell her I've left for a trip. Be sure to give the basket to her personally. Get going, now, and do it right!"

Girard put on his new smock, tied his handkerchief over the apricots, and plodding along in his great hobnailed boots, he set out tranquilly for Yonville.

When he reached Madame Bovary's he found her helping Félicité stack linen on the kitchen table.

"Here," said the plough-boy. "My master sent you this."

A feeling of dread came over her, and as she fumbled in her pocket for some change she stared at the peasant with haggard eyes; he in turn looked at her in bewilderment, failing to understand why anyone should be so upset by such a present. Finally he left. Félicité stayed where she was. The suspense was too great for Emma: she ran into the other room as though for the purpose of carrying in the apricots, dumped them out of the basket, tore away the leaves, found the letter and opened it; and as though she were fleeing from a fire she ran panic-stricken up the stairs toward her room.

Charles had come in: she caught sight of him; he spoke to her; whatever he said, she didn't hear it; and she hurried on up the second flight of stairs, breathless, distracted, reeling, clutching the horrible piece of paper that rattled in her hand like a sheet of tin. At the third-floor landing she stopped outside the closed attic door.

She tried to calm herself: only then did she think of the letter. She must finish it—she didn't dare. Besides, where could she read it? How? She'd be seen.

"I'll be all right in here," she thought; and she pushed open the door and went in.

There the roof slates were throwing down a heat that was all but unbearable; it pressed on her so that she could scarcely breathe. She dragged herself over to the dormer, whose shutters were closed; she pulled back the bolt, and the dazzling sunlight poured in.

Out beyond the rooftops, the open countryside stretched as far as eye could see. Below her the village square was empty; the stone sidewalk glittered; the weathervanes on the houses stood motionless. From the lower floor of a house at the corner came a whirring noise with strident changes of tone: Binet was at his lathe.

Leaning against the window frame she read the letter through, now and then giving an angry sneer. But the more she tried to concentrate, the more confused her thoughts became. She saw Rodolphe, heard his voice, clasped him in her arms; and a series of irregular palpitations, thudding in her breast like great blows from a battering ram, came faster and faster. She cast her eyes about her, longing for the earth to open up. Why not end it all? What was holding her back? She was free to act. And she moved forward. "Do it! Do it!" she ordered herself, peering down at the pavement.

The rays of bright light reflected directly up to her from below were pulling the weight of her body toward the abyss. The surface of the village square seemed to be sliding dizzily up the wall of her house; the floor she was standing on seemed to be tipped up on end, like a pitching ship. Now she was at the very edge, almost hanging out, a great emptiness all around her. The blue of the sky was flooding her; her head felt hollow and filled with the rushing of the wind: all she had to do now was to surrender, yield to the onrush. And the lathe kept whirring, like an angry voice calling her.

But then she heard another voice: "Where are you?" It was Charles. She listened.

"Where are you? Come down!"

The thought that she had just escaped death almost made her faint from terror; she closed her eyes; then she gave a start as she felt the touch of a hand on her sleeve. It was Félicité.

"Monsieur is waiting, Madame. The soup is on the table."

And she had to go down—had to sit through a meal!

She did her best to eat. Each mouthful choked her. She unfolded her napkin as though to inspect the darns, and began really seriously to devote her attention to it and count the stitches. Suddenly the thought of the letter came back to her. Had she lost it? Where would she lay hands on it? But in her exhaustion of mind she could invent no excuse for leaving the table. Besides, she didn't dare: she was terrified of Charles; he knew everything— she was sure he must! And oddly enough he chose that moment to say:

"I gather we shan't be seeing Monsieur Rodolphe for some time."

She started: "Who told you so?"

"Who told me?" he said, surprised by her abrupt tone. "Girard—I saw him a few minutes ago at the door of the Café Français. He's left for a trip, or he's about to leave."

A sob escaped her.

"What's so surprising about it? He's always going off on pleasure trips. Why shouldn't he? When you're a bachelor and well off . . . Besides, he knows how to give himself a good time, our friend. He's a real playboy. Monsieur Langlois once told me . . ."

He decorously broke off as the maid came in.

Félicité gathered up the apricots that lay scattered over the sideboard and put them back into the basket. Unaware that his wife had turned scarlet, Charles asked for them, took one, and bit into it.

"Oh, perfect!" he said. "Try one."

He held the basket out toward her, and she gently pushed it away.

"Smell them: such fragrance!" he said, moving it back and forth before her.

"I'm stifling in here!" she cried, leaping to her feet. But she forced herself to conquer her spasm. "It's nothing," she said. "Nothing. Just nerves. Sit down; eat your fruit."

Her great dread was lest he question her, insist on doing something for her, never leave her to herself.

Charles had obediently sat down and was spitting apricot pits into his hand and transferring them to his plate.

Suddenly a blue tilbury crossed the square at a smart trot. Emma gave a cry, fell abruptly backwards and lay on the floor.

Rodolphe had decided, after a good deal of thought, to leave for Rouen. Since the Yonville road was the only route from La Huchette to Buchy, he had to pass through the village; and Emma had recognized him in the glow of his carriage lights as they flashed in the gathering dusk like a streak of lightning.

The commotion at the Bovarys' brought the pharmacist running. The table had been knocked over and all the plates were on the floor; gravy, meat, knives, the salt cellar and the cruet stand littered the room; Charles was calling for help; Berthe was frightened and in tears; and Félicité with trembling hands was unlacing Madame, whose entire body was racked with convulsions.

"I'll run to my laboratory and get a little aromatic vinegar," said the apothecary.

And when he had returned and held the flacon under her nostrils and she opened her eyes:

"I knew it," he said. "This stuff would resuscitate a corpse."

"Speak to us!" cried Charles. "Say something! Can you hear me? It's Charles—Charles, who loves you. Do you recognize me? See—here's your little girl—kiss her, darling."

The child stretched out her arms toward her mother, trying to clasp them around her neck. But Emma turned her head away. "No, no," she said brokenly. "Leave me alone."

She fainted again, and they carried her to her bed.

She lay there on her back, mouth open, eyes closed, hands flat beside her, motionless, white as a wax statue. Two rivulets of tears trickled slowly from her eyes onto the pillow.

Charles stood at the foot of the bed. At his side the pharmacist was observing the thoughtful silence appropriate to life's solemn occasions. Then:

"I think she'll be all right," he said. "The paroxysm seems to be over."

"Yes, she's resting a little now," Charles answered, watching her sleep. "Poor thing! Poor thing! It's a real relapse."

Then Homais asked for details, and Charles told him how she had been stricken suddenly while eating apricots.

"Extraordinary!" said the pharmacist. "Still, the apricots may very well have caused the syncope. Some natures react so strongly to certain odors! It would be an interesting subject to study, in both its pathological and its physiological aspects. The priests are well aware of the importance of this phenomenon—they've always made use of aromatics in their ceremonies. They employ them deliberately, to deaden the understanding and induce ecstatic states—women lend themselves to it easily, they're so much more delicate than the rest of us. Cases are recorded of women fainting from the smell of burnt horn, fresh bread . . ."

"Take care not to wake her!" Bovary warned softly.

"And it's not only humans who are subject to such anomalies," continued the apothecary. "Animals are, too. You are certainly not ignorant of the intensely aphrodisiac effect produced by *nepeta cataria*, vulgarly called catnip, on the feline species; and to mention another example—one whose authenticity I myself can vouch for—Bridoux, one of my old schoolmates, now in business in the Rue Malpalu, has a dog which has convulsions if you show it a snuffbox. Bridoux sometimes makes him perform for his friends, at his suburban residence in Bois-Guillaume. Would you believe that a simple sternutative could work such havoc in the organism of a quadruped? It's extremely curious, don't you find?"

"Yes," said Charles, who wasn't listening.

"This is but another illustration," said the pharmacist, smiling with an air of benign self-satisfaction, "of the innumerable irregularities of the nervous system. As far as Madame is concerned, I confess she has always seemed to me a genuine sensitive. For that reason, my good friend, I advise you not to use any of those so-called remedies which attack the temperament under the guise of attacking the symptoms. No—no futile medication. Just a regimen. Sedatives, emollients, dulcifiers. And then, don't you think it would be a good thing to rouse her imagination—something striking?"

"How? What?"

"Ah, that's the problem. That is indeed the problem. '*That is the question*,'" he quoted in English, "as I read in the paper recently."

Just then Emma, waking from her sleep, cried: "The letter? Where is the letter?"

They thought her delirious, and from midnight on she was: there could be no doubt that it was brain fever.

For forty-three days Charles did not leave her side. He neglected all his patients; he never lay down; he was constantly feeling her pulse, applying mustard plasters and cold compresses. He sent Justin to Neufchâtel for ice; the ice melted on the way; he sent him back. He called in Doctor Canivet for consultation; he had Doctor Larivière, his old teacher, come from Rouen; he was desperate. What frightened him most was Emma's degree of prostration: she didn't speak, she gave no sign of comprehending or even hearing anything that was said to her; and she seemed to be in no pain. It was as though her body and her soul together had sought rest after all their tribulations. Toward the middle of October she could sit up in bed, propped against pillows. Charles wept when he saw her eat her first slice of bread and jam. Her strength returned; she left her bed for a few hours each afternoon; and one day when she felt better than usual he got her to take his arm and try a walk in the garden. The gravel on the paths was almost hidden under dead leaves; she walked slowly, dragging her slippers; and leaning on Charles's shoulder she smiled continuously.

They made their way to the far end, near the terrace. She drew herself up slowly and held her hand above her eyes: she stared into the distance, the far distance; but on the horizon there were only great grass fires, smoking on the hills.

"You'll tire yourself, darling," said Bovary.

And guiding her gently, trying to induce her to enter the arbor:

"Sit on this bench: you'll be comfortable."

"Oh no! Not there! Not there!" she said in a faltering voice.

Immediately she felt dizzy; and beginning that night there was another onset of her illness. This time it was less clearly identifiable, more complex. Now her heart would pain her, now her chest, now her head, now her limbs. She had vomiting spells, which Charles feared were the first symptoms of cancer.

And as though that were not enough, the poor fellow had money worries!

XIV

To begin with, he didn't know how to make good to Monsieur Homais for all the medicaments that had come from the pharmacy: as a doctor he might have been excused from paying for them, but the obligation embarrassed him. Then, what with the cook acting as mistress, the household expenses were getting to be alarming; there was a deluge of bills; the tradespeople were grumbling; Monsieur Lheureux, especially, was harassing him. The dry-goods dealer, taking advantage of the circumstances to pad his bill, had chosen a moment at the very height of Emma's illness to deliver the cloak, the overnight bag, two trunks instead of one, and a number of other things as well. Charles protested that he had no use for them, but the shopkeeper arrogantly retorted that all those items had been ordered and that he wouldn't take them back. Besides, he said, it would be upsetting to Madame in her convalescence. Monsieur should think it over. In short, he was determined to stand on his rights and carry the matter to court rather than give in. A little later Charles ordered that everything be sent back to the shop; but Félicité forgot; and he had other things on his mind and didn't think of them. Monsieur Lheureux brought the matter up again, and by alternating threats and moans got Charles to sign a six-months' promissory note. No sooner had he signed than he had a bold idea: he would try to borrow a thousand francs from Monsieur Lheureux. So he awkwardly asked whether there was any chance of this, explaining that it would be for one year and at any rate of interest Lheureux might specify. Lheureux ran to his shop, brought back the money, and dictated another promissory note, whereby Bovary promised to pay to his order, the first of the following September, the sum of 1,070 francs. Together with the 180 already stipulated, that came to just 1,250. In this way, loaning at the rate of six percent, plus his commission and at least one-third mark-up on the goods, the whole thing would bring him in a clear 130 francs' profit in twelve months; and he hoped that it wouldn't stop there, that the notes wouldn't be met but renewed, and that his poor little capital, after benefiting from the doctor's care like a patient in a sanatorium, would eventually come back to him considerably plumper, fat enough to burst the bag.

Everything Lheureux touched was successful at this moment. His had been the winning bid for the cider-supply contract at the Neufchâtel public hospital; Maître Guillaumin was promising him some shares in the peatery at Grumesnil; and he was thinking of setting up a new coach service between Argueil and Rouen: such a thing would quickly spell the end of the old rattletrap at the Lion d'Or, and being faster and cheaper and carrying a bigger pay load would give him a monopoly of the Yonville trade.

Charles wondered more than once how he was going to be able to pay back so large a sum the following year; and racking his brains he imagined various expedients, such as applying to his father or selling off something. But his father would turn a deaf ear, and he himself owned nothing that could be sold. The difficulties he foresaw were so formidable that he quickly banished the disagreeable subject from his mind. He reproached himself for having let it distract him from Emma—as though his every thought were her property and he were filching something from her if he took his mind off her for a second.

It was a severe winter. Madame's convalescence was slow. On fine days they pushed her armchair to the window—the one overlooking the square, for she had taken an aversion to the garden, and the blind on that side was always down. She asked that her horse be sold: things that had once given her pleasure she now disliked. She seemed to have no thought for anything beyond her own health. She ate her tiny meals in bed, rang for the maid to ask about her tisanes or just to chat. All this while the snow on the roof of the market filled the room with its monotonous white reflection; then came a spell of rain. And every day Emma looked forward, with a kind of anxious expectation, to the same, unfailingly recurring, trivial events, little though they mattered to her. The greatest of these was the nightly arrival of the Hirondelle, when Madame Lefrançois shouted, other voices replied, and Hippolyte's stable lamp, as he looked for luggage under the hood, shone out like a star in the darkness. At noon Charles always returned from his rounds; after lunch he went out again; then she took a cup of bouillon; and toward five, at the close of day, children passed the house on their way home from school, dragging their wooden shoes along the sidewalk, and invariably, one after the other, hitting their rulers against the shutter hooks.

About this time Monsieur Bournisien usually stopped in. He would ask after her health, give her news, and exhort her to prayer in an affectionate, informal way that wasn't without its charm. Just the sight of his cassock she found comforting.

One day at the height of her sickness, when she thought she was dying, she had asked for Communion; and as her room was made ready for the sacrament—the chest of drawers cleared of its medicine bottles and transformed into an altar, the floor strewn with dahlia blossoms by Félicité—Emma felt something powerful pass over her that rid her of all pain, all perception, all feeling. Her flesh had been relieved of its burdens, even the burden of thought; another life was beginning; it seemed to her that her spirit, ascending to God, was about to find annihilation in this love, like burning incense dissolving in smoke. The sheets of her bed were sprinkled with holy water; the priest drew the white host from the sacred pyx; and she was all but swooning with celestial bliss as she advanced her lips to receive the body of the Saviour. The curtains of her alcove swelled out softly around her like clouds; and the beams of the two wax tapers burning on the chest of drawers seemed to her like dazzling emanations of divine light. Then she let her head fall back: through the vastnesses of space seemed to come the music of seraphic harps; and on a golden throne in an azure sky she thought she saw God the Father in all His glory, surrounded by the saints bearing branches of green palm; He was gesturing majestically, and obedient angels with flaming wings were descending to the earth to bear her to Him in their arms.

This splendid vision, the most beautiful of all possible dreams, stayed in her memory—not eclipsing all else as at the time it occurred, but no less intensely sweet; and she kept straining to recapture the original sensation. Her soul, aching with pride, was at last finding rest in Christian humility; and luxuriating in her own weakness she turned her eyes inward and watched the destruction of her will, which was to open wide the way for an onrush of grace. She was filled with wonderment at the discovery that there was a bliss greater than mere happiness—a love different from and transcending all others—a love without break and without end, a love that increased throughout eternity! Among the illusions born of her hope she glimpsed a realm of purity in which she aspired to dwell: it hovered above the earth, merging with the sky. She conceived the idea of becoming a saint. She bought rosaries and festooned herself with holy medals; she wished she had an emerald-studded reliquary within reach at her bed's head, to kiss every night.

The priest was enchanted by her change of heart, though he was of the opinion that her faith might by its very fervor come to border on heresy and even on extravagance. But not being versed in these matters once they went beyond a certain point, he wrote Monsieur Boulard, the bishop's bookseller, and asked him to send him "something particularly good for a lady who had a very fine mind." As casually as though he were shipping trinkets to savages, the bookseller made up a heterogeneous package of everything just then current in the religious book trade—little question-and-answer manuals, pamphlets couched in the contemptuous language made popular by Monsieur de Maistre,[5] so-called novels in pink bindings and sugary style concocted by romantic-minded seminarists or reformed blue-stockings. There were titles such as *Think It Over Carefully; The Man of the World at the Feet of Mary, by Monsieur de———, recipient of several decorations; The Errors of Voltaire, for the use of the young;* etc.

Madame Bovary wasn't yet sufficiently recovered in mind to apply herself seriously to anything; and besides, she plunged into all this literature far too precipitately. The regulations governing worship annoyed her; she disliked the arrogance of the polemical writings because of their relentless attacks on people she had never heard of; and the secular stories flavored with religion seemed to her written out of such ignorance of the world that she was unwittingly led away from the very truths she was longing to have confirmed. Nevertheless she persisted; and when the volume fell from her hands she was convinced that hers was the most exquisite Catholic melancholy that had ever entered an ethereal soul.

As for the memory of Rodolphe, she had buried it in the depths of her heart; and there it remained, as solemn and motionless as the mummy of a pharaoh in an underground chamber. Her great love that lay thus embalmed gave off a fragrance that permeated everything, adding a touch of tenderness to the immaculate atmosphere in which she longed to live. When she knelt at her Gothic *prie-dieu* she addressed the Lord in the same ardent words she had formerly murmured to her lover in the ecstasies of adultery. It was her way of praying for faith; but heaven showered no joy upon her, and she would rise, her limbs aching, with a vague feeling that it was all a vast fraud. This quest she considered meritorious in itself; and in the pride of her piety Emma likened herself to those great ladies of yore whose fame she had dreamed of while gazing at a portrait of La Vallière: how majestically they had trailed the gorgeous trains of their long gowns, as they withdrew into seclusion to shed at the feet of Christ all the tears of their life-wounded hearts!

Now she became wildly charitable. She sewed clothes for the poor, sent firewood to women in childbed; and one day Charles came home to find three tramps sitting at the kitchen table eating soup. She sent for her daughter—during her illness Charles had left the child with the nurse—and she determined to teach her to read. Berthe wept and wept, but she never lost her temper with her. It was a deliberately adopted attitude of resignation, of indulgence toward all. She used a lofty term whenever she could:

"Is your stomach-ache all gone, my angel?" she would say to her daughter.

The elder Madame Bovary found nothing to reproach her for in all this, except perhaps her mania for knitting undershirts for orphans instead of mending her own dish towels. Harassed by the incessant quarrels in her own home, the old lady enjoyed the peaceful atmosphere of this house; and she prolonged her visit through Easter to escape the jibes of her husband, whose invariable habit it was to order pork sausage on Good Friday.

In addition to the company of her mother-in-law, whom she found a steadying influence because of her unswerving principles and solemn demeanor, Emma nearly every day had other visits—from Madame Langlois, Madame

---

5. A major theorist (1753–1821) of Catholic conservatism. His books, *Du Pape* (1819) and *Soirées de Saint-Petersbourg* (1821), defended the power of the pope and the sovereign king and argued that the reign of evil on Earth has to be curbed by authority.

Caron, Madame Dubreuil, Madame Tuvache, and, regularly from two to five, from Madame Homais, who—good soul that she was—had always refused to believe any of the gossip that was spread about her neighbor. The Homais children visited her, too; Justin brought them. He came with them up into her bedroom and stood quietly near the door, never saying a word. Often while he was there Madame Bovary would start to dress, oblivious of him. She would begin by taking out her comb and tossing her head; and the first time he saw her mass of black hair fall in ringlets to her knees, it was for the boy like the sudden opening of a door upon something marvelous and new, something whose splendor frightened him.

Emma never noticed his silent eagerness or his timidity. She knew only that love had disappeared from her life: she had no suspicion that it was pulsating there so close to her, beneath that coarse shirt, in that adolescent heart so open to the emanations of her beauty. Moreover, her detachment from everything had become so complete, her language was so sweet and the look in her eye so haughty, her behavior was so mercurial, that there was no longer any way of telling where selfishness and corruption ended and charity and virtue began. One night, for instance, she lost her temper with her servant, who was asking permission to go out and stammering some pretended reason. Then:

"So you love him, do you?" Emma suddenly demanded.

And without waiting for the blushing Félicité to answer, she added, resignedly:

"All right—run along! Enjoy yourself!"

When the weather turned mild she had the garden completely dug up and relandscaped. Bovary objected a little, but he was glad to see her finally caring about things, and she gave more and more evidence of this as her strength returned. She forbade the house to Madame Rollet the nurse, who during her convalescence had formed the habit of coming too often to the kitchen with her own two babes and her little boarder, the latter more ravenous than a cannibal. She cut down on visits from the Homaises, discouraged all her other callers, and even went less regularly to church, thus eliciting the apothecary's approval.

"I was afraid you'd been taken in by the mumbo-jumbo," he said amicably.

The abbé Bournisien still came every day, after catechism class. He preferred to sit outdoors in the fresh air—in the "grove," as he called the arbor. This was the hour of Charles's return. Both men would be hot; Félicité would bring them sweet cider, and they would raise their glasses and drink to Madame's complete recovery.

Binet was often there: just below, that is—beside the terrace wall, fishing for crayfish. Bovary would invite him to join them for a drink; he prided himself on being an expert uncorker of cider jugs.

"First," he would say—glancing at his companions complacently and then giving an equally smug look at the landscape—"first you must hold the bottle upright on the table, like this. Then you cut the strings. And then you pry up the cork, a little at a time, gently, gently—the way they open seltzer water in restaurants."

But during this demonstration the cork would often pop out and the cider would splash one or another of them in the face; and the curé never failed to laugh his thick laugh and make his joke:

"Its excellence is certainly *striking!*"

He was a good-hearted fellow—there was no denying it—and he even expressed no objection one day when the pharmacist advised Charles to give Madame a treat and take her to the opera in Rouen, to hear the famous tenor, Lagardy. Homais was surprised at his silence, and asked him how he felt about it; and the priest declared that he considered music less dangerous to morals than literature.

The pharmacist sprang to the defense of letters. The theater, he claimed, served to expose prejudice: it taught virtue under the guise of entertainment:

"*Castigat ridendo mores,*[6] Monsieur Bournisien! Take most of Voltaire's tragedies, for example: it's clever the way he's stuck them full of philosophical remarks—they're a complete education in morals and diplomacy for the people."

"I saw a play once, called the *Gamin de Paris,*[7] said Binet. "There's an old general in it that's absolutely first-class. A rich fellow seduces a working girl and the general slaps him down and at the end . . ."

"Of course," Homais went on, "there's bad literature just as there's bad pharmaceutics. But to make a blanket condemnation of the greatest of the fine arts seems to be a yokelism, a medievalism worthy of that abominable age when they imprisoned Galileo."[8]

"I know perfectly well," objected the priest, "that there are good writers who write good things. Still, the fact alone that people of different sexes are brought together in a glamorous auditorium that's the last word in worldly luxury—and then the heathenish disguises, the painted faces, the footlights, the effeminate voices—it all can't help encouraging a certain licentiousness and inducing evil thoughts and impure temptations. Such, at least, is the opinion of all the church fathers. After all," he added, suddenly assuming an unctuous tone and rolling himself a pinch of snuff, "if the church condemns play-going she has good reason for doing so: we must submit to her decrees."

"Why," demanded the apothecary, "does she excommunicate actors? They used to take part openly in ecclesiastical ceremonies, you know. Yes, they used to act right in the middle of the choir—put on farcical plays called mysteries. These often violated the laws of decency, I may say."

The priest's only answer was a groan, and the pharmacist persisted:

"It's the same in the Bible. There's more than one spicy bit in that book, you know—some pret-ty dar-ing things!"

And as Monsieur Bournisien made a gesture of annoyance:

"Ah! You'll agree that it's no book to give a young person! I'd be sorry if my daughter Athalie . . ."

"But *we* don't recommend the reading of the Bible!" cried the abbé impatiently. "It's the Protestants!"

"It makes no difference," said Homais. "I'm astonished that in this day and age—an age of enlightenment—anyone should persist in forbidding a form of intellectual diversion that's harmless, morally uplifting, and sometimes—isn't it true, Doctor?—even good for the health."

---

6. "It [comedy] reproves the manners, through laughter" (Latin); a slogan for comedy invented by the poet Jean de Santeuil (1630–1697) and given to the harlequin Dominique to put on the curtain of his theater. 7. A comedy by Bayard and Vanderbusch performed in 1836 in Paris. 8. Galileo Galilei (1564–1642), astronomer who was confined to his house in Arcetri (near Florence) after his book propounding the view that the Earth circled around the sun was condemned by the Inquisition (in 1633).

"I guess so." Charles made his answer in a vacant tone—perhaps because he shared Homais' opinion and didn't want to offend the priest, or perhaps because he had no opinion.

The conversation seemed to be at an end, when the pharmacist saw fit to make one last dig.

"I've known priests," he said, "who made a practice of going out in civilian clothes and watching leg shows."

"Come now," said the priest.

"Oh yes, I've known some!"

And once again separating his syllables by way of significant emphasis, Homais repeated:

"I—have—known—some!"

"Well, then, they did wrong," said Bournisien with truly Christian patience.

"I should think so! And that wasn't all they were up to, either!" exclaimed the apothecary.

"*Monsieur!*" The priest jumped to his feet and glared so fiercely that the pharmacist was intimidated.

"All I mean," he said, much more mildly, "is that tolerance is the surest means of bringing souls into the church."

"Quite true, quite true," the curé conceded, sitting down again.

He left a moment or two later, however, and Homais said to the doctor:

"Quite a squabble! How did you like the way I got the better of him? Pretty good, eh? Anyway—follow my advice and take Madame to the opera, if only to give a priest a black eye for once in your life. If I could find a substitute I'd come with you. Don't lose any time getting tickets: Lagardy's giving only one performance—he's scheduled for an English tour at staggering fees. From what they say, he must be quite a lad. He's filthy with money. Everywhere he goes he takes along three mistresses and a cook. All those great artists burn their candles at both ends: they have to lead a wild kind of life—it stimulates their imagination. But they die in the poorhouse, because they haven't the sense to save money when they're young. Well, *bon appétit: à demain!*"

The idea of the opera took rapid root in Bovary's mind. He lost no time suggesting it to his wife. She shook her head, pleading fatigue, trouble and expense; but for once Charles didn't give in, so convinced was he that she would benefit from the excursion. He saw no reason for them not to go: his mother had sent him three hundred francs they had given up hope of getting, their debts of the moment were nothing tremendous, and Lheureux's notes weren't due for so long that there was no use thinking about them. Fancying that Emma was refusing out of consideration for him, Charles insisted the more strongly, and finally she gave in. The next day, at eight in the morning, they bundled themselves into the Hirondelle.

The apothecary, who had nothing in the world to keep him in Yonville, but who was firmly convinced that he couldn't absent himself even briefly, gave a sigh as he watched their departure.

"*Bon voyage!*" he called to them. "Some people have all the luck!"

And to Emma, who was wearing a blue silk dress with four rows of flounces:

"You're pretty as a picture! You'll be the belle of Rouen!"

The coach took them to the Hotel de la Croix-Rouge in the Place Beauvoisine. It was one of those inns such as you find on the edge of every provincial city, with large stables and small bedrooms, and chickens scratching for oats in the coach yard under muddy gigs belonging to traveling salesmen—comfortable, old-fashioned stopovers, with worm-eaten wooden balconies that creak in the wind on winter nights, constantly full of people, bustle and victuals, their blackened tabletops sticky with spilled coffee-and-brandies, their thick windowpanes yellowed by flies, their napkins spotted blue by cheap red wine. They always seem a little rustic, like farmhands in Sunday clothes; on the street side they have a café, and in back—on the country side—a vegetable garden. Charles went at once to buy tickets. He got the stage boxes mixed up with the top balconies, and the rest of the boxes with the orchestra; he asked for explanations, didn't understand them, was sent from the box office to the manager, came back to the hotel, went back to the box office again. All in all, between the theater and the outer boulevard he covered the entire length of the city several times over.

Madame bought herself a hat, gloves and a bouquet. Monsieur was nervous about missing the beginning; and without stopping for as much as a cup of bouillon they arrived at the theater before the doors were even open.

XV

There was a crowd waiting outside, lined up behind railings on both sides of the entrance. At the adjoining street corners huge posters in fancy lettering announced: "*Lucie de Lammermoor* . . . *Lagardy*[9] . . . Opéra . . . etc." It was a fine evening; everyone was hot: many a set of curls was drenched in sweat, and handkerchiefs were out, mopping red brows; now and again a soft breeze blowing from the river gently stirred the edges of the canvas awnings over café doors. But just a short distance away there was a coolness, provided by an icy draft smelling of tallow, leather and oil—the effluvia of the Rue des Charettes, with its great, gloomy, barrel-filled warehouses.

Fearing lest they appear ridiculous, Emma insisted that they stroll a bit along the river front before going in; and Bovary, by way of precaution, kept the tickets in his hand and his hand in his trousers pocket, pressed reassuringly against his stomach.

Her heart began to pound as they entered the foyer. A smile of satisfaction rose involuntarily to her lips at seeing the crowd hurry off to the right down the corridor, while she climbed the stairs leading to the first tier. She took pleasure, like a child, in pushing open the wide upholstered doors with one finger; she filled her lungs with the dusty smell of the corridors; and seated in her box she drew herself up with all the airs of a duchess.

The theater began to fill; opera glasses came out of cases; and subscribers exchanged greetings as they glimpsed one another across the house. The arts, for them, were a relaxation from the worries of buying and selling; that was why they had come; but it was quite impossible for them to forget busi-

9. Fictional tenor who plays Edgar in the opera. *Lucie de Lammermoor:* an opera by Gaetano Donizetti (1797–1848), first performed in Naples in 1835 (in Paris in 1837), based on Walter Scott's novel *The Bride of Lammermoor* (1819). There are substantial differences between the French version, which Flaubert followed, and the original Italian libretto. Here, Edgar of Ravenswood has sworn vengeance on Lord Henry Ashton, his father's killer; Edgar and Ashton's sister Lucie are in love, but Ashton forces her to marry a rich suitor, Lord Arthur; Gilbert is a treacherous servant.

ness even here, and their conversation was about cotton, spirits and indigo. The old men looked blank and placid: with their gray-white hair and gray-white skin they were like silver medals that had been tarnished by lead fumes. The young beaux strutted in the orchestra: the openings of their waistcoats were bright with pink or apple-green cravats; and Madame Bovary looked admiringly down at them as they leaned with tightly yellow-gloved hands on their gold-knobbed walking sticks.

Meanwhile the candles were lighted on the music stands and the chandelier came down from the ceiling, the sparkle of its crystals filling the house with sudden gaiety; then the musicians filed in and there was a long cacophony of booming cellos, scraping violins, blaring horns, and piping flutes and flageolets. Then three heavy blows came from the stage; there was a roll of kettledrums and a series of chords from the brasses; and the curtain rose on an outdoor scene.

It was a crossroad in a forest, on the right a spring shaded by an oak. A group of country folk and nobles, all with tartans over their shoulders, sang a hunting chorus; then a captain strode in and inveighed against an evil spirit, raising both arms to heaven; another character joined him; they both walked off, and the huntsmen repeated their chorus.

She was back in the books she had read as a girl—deep in Walter Scott. She imagined she could hear the sound of Scottish pipes echoing through the mist across the heather. Her recollection of the novel made it easy for her to grasp the libretto; and she followed the plot line by line, elusive, half-forgotten memories drifting into her thoughts only to be dispelled by the onrush of the music. She let herself be lulled by the melodies, feeling herself vibrate to the very fiber of her being, as though the bows of the violins were playing on her nerve strings. She couldn't take in enough of the costumes, the sets, the characters, the painted trees that shook at the slightest footstep, the velvet bonnets, the cloaks, the swords—all those fanciful things that fluttered on waves of music as though in another world. Then a young woman came forward, tossing a purse to a squire in green. She was left alone on the stage, and there came the sound of a flute, like the ripple of a spring or the warbling of a bird. Lucie, looking solemn, began her cavatina[1] in G major: she uttered love laments, begged for wings. And at the moment Emma, too, longed that she might leave life behind and take wing in an embrace. Suddenly Edgar Lagardy came on stage.

He was pale to the point of splendor, with that marmoreal majesty sometimes found among the passionate races of the south. His stalwart figure was clad in a tight brown doublet; a small chased dagger swung at his left hip; and he rolled his eyes about him languorously and flashed his white teeth. People said that a Polish princess had heard him sing one night on the beach at Biarritz,[2] where he was a boat boy, and had fallen in love with him; she had beggared herself for him, and he had left her for other women. This reputation as a ladies' man had done no disservice to his professional career. Shrewd ham actor that he was, he always saw to it that his publicity should include a poetic phrase or two about the charm of his personality and the sensibility of his soul. A fine voice, utter self-possession, more temperament than intelligence, more bombast than feeling—such were the principal

---

1. A short, simple song.   2. A fashionable French resort on the Bay of Biscay.

attributes of this magnificent charlatan. There was a touch of the hairdresser about him, and a touch of the toreador.

He had the audience in transports from the first. He clasped Lucie in his arms, left her, returned to her, seemed in despair: he would shout with rage, then let his voice expire, plaintive and infinitely sweet; and the notes that poured from his bare throat were full of sobs and kisses. Emma strained forward to watch him, her fingernails scratching the plush of her box. Her heart drank its full of the melodious laments that hung suspended in the air against the sound of the double bases like the cries of shipwrecked sailors against the tumult of a storm. Here was the same ecstasy, the same anguish that had brought her to the brink of death. The soprano's voice seemed but the echo of her own soul, and this illusion that held her under its spell a part of her own life. But no one on earth had ever loved her with so great a love. That last moonlight night, when they had told each other, "Till tomorrow! Till tomorrow!" *he* had not wept as Edgar was weeping now. The house was bursting with applause. The whole stretto[3] was repeated: the lover sang about the flowers on their graves, about vows and exile and fate and hope; and when their voices rose in the final farewell, Emma herself uttered a sharp cry that was drowned in the blast of the final chords.

"What's that lord doing, mistreating her like that?" Charles asked.

"No, no," she answered. "That's her lover."

"But he's swearing vengeance on her family, whereas the other one—the one that came on a while ago—said 'I love Lucie and I think she loves me!' Besides, he walked off arm in arm with her father. That is her father, isn't it, the ugly little one with the cock feather in his hat?"

Despite Emma's explanations, Charles got everything mixed up beginning with the duet in recitative in which Gilbert explains his abominable machinations to his master Ashton. The false engagement ring serving to trick Lucie he took to be a love token sent by Edgar. In fact he couldn't follow the story at all, he said, because of the music: it interfered so with the words.

"What difference does it make?" said Emma. "Be quiet!"

"But I like to know what's going on," he persisted, leaning over her shoulder. "You know I do."

"Be quiet! Be quiet!" she whispered impatiently.

Lucie came on, half borne up by her women; there was a wreath of orange blossoms in her hair, and she was paler than the white satin of her gown. Emma thought of her own wedding day: she saw herself walking toward the church along the little path amid the wheatfields. Why in heaven's name hadn't she resisted and entreated, like Lucie? But no—she had been light-hearted, unaware of the abyss she was rushing toward. Ah! If only in the freshness of her beauty, before defiling herself in marriage, before the disillusionments of adultery, she could have found some great and noble heart to be her life's foundation! Then virtue and affection, sensual joys and duty would all have been one; and she would never have fallen from her high felicity. But that kind of happiness was doubtless a lie, invented to make one despair of any love. Now she well knew the true paltriness of the passions that art painted so large. So she did her best to think of the opera in a different light: she resolved to regard this image of her own griefs as a vivid

---

3. A final section of an opera in which voices overlap in fugal style and the tempo is accelerated, all in preparation for the climax.

fantasy, an enjoyable spectacle and nothing more; and she was actually smiling to herself in scornful pity when from behind the velvet curtains at the back of the stage there appeared a man in a black cloak.

A single gesture sent his broad-brimmed Spanish hat to the ground; and the orchestra and the singers abruptly broke into the sextet. Edgar, flashing fury, dominated all the others with his high, clear voice. Ashton flung him his homicidal challenge in solemn tones; Lucie uttered her shrill lament; Arthur sang his asides in middle register; and the chaplain's baritone boomed like an organ while the women, echoing his words, repeated them in delicious chorus. All the characters now formed a single line across the stage; all were gesticulating at once; and rage, vengeance, jealousy, terror, pity and amazement poured simultaneously from their open mouths. The outraged lover brandished his naked sword; his lace collar rose and fell with the heaving of his chest; and he strode up and down, clanking the silver-gilt spurs on his soft, flaring boots. His love, she thought, must be inexhaustible, since he could pour it out in such great quantities on the crowd. Her resolution not to be taken in by the display of false sentiment was swept away by the impact of the singer's eloquence; the fiction that he was embodying drew her to his real life, and she tried to imagine what it was like—that glamorous, fabulous, marvelous life that she, too, might have lived had chance so willed it. They might have met! They might have loved! With him she might have traveled over all the kingdoms of Europe, from capital to capital, sharing his hardships and his triumphs, gathering up the flowers his admirers threw, embroidering his costumes with her own hands; and every night behind the gilded lattice of her box she might have sat open-mouthed, breathing in the outpourings of that divine creature who would be singing for her alone: he would have gazed at her from the stage as he played his role. A mad idea seized her: he was gazing at her now! She was sure of it! She longed to rush into his arms and seek refuge in his strength as in the very incarnation of love; she longed to cry: "Ravish me! Carry me off! Away from here! All my passion and all my dreams are yours—yours alone!"

The curtain fell.

The smell of gas mingled with human exhalations, and the air seemed the more stifling for being stirred up by fans. Emma tried to get out, but there was a crush in the corridors, and she sank back onto a chair, oppressed by palpitations. Charles, fearful lest she fall into a faint, hurried to the bar for a glass of orgeat.[4]

He had a hard time getting back to the box: he held the glass in both hands because his elbows were being jarred at every other step, but even so he spilled three-quarters of it over the shoulders of a Rouen lady in short sleeves, who began to scream like a peacock, as though she were being murdered, when she felt the cold liquid trickling down her spine. While she took her handkerchief to the spots on her beautiful cerise taffeta gown, her mill-owner husband gave poor clumsy Charles a piece of his mind, angrily muttering the words "damages," "cost," and "replacement." Finally Charles made his way to his wife.

"I thought I'd never get out of there," he gasped. "Such a crowd! Such a crowd!"

And he added:

---

4. A cooling drink flavored with almond and orange-flower water.

"Guess who I ran into: Monsieur Léon!"

"Léon?"

"Absolutely. He'll be coming along to pay you his respects."

As he uttered the words the former Yonville clerk entered the box.

He held out his hand with aristocratic casualness; and Madame Bovary automatically extended hers—yielding, no doubt, to the attraction of a stronger will. She hadn't touched it since that spring evening when the rain was falling on the new green leaves—the evening they had said farewell as they stood beside the window. But quickly reminding herself of the social requirements of the situation, she roused herself with an effort from her memories and began to stammer hurried phrases:

"Ah, good evening! You here? How amazing . . . . !"

"Quiet!" cried a voice from the orchestra, for the third act was beginning.

"So you're living in Rouen?"

"Yes."

"Since when?"

"*Sh! Sh!*"

People were turning around at them indignantly, and they fell silent.

But from that moment on Emma no longer listened to the music. The chorus of guests, the scene between Ashton and his attendant, the great duet in D major—for her it all took place at a distance, as though the instruments had lost their sound and the characters had moved away. She recalled the card games at the pharmacist's and the walk to the wet nurse's, their readings under the arbor, the tête-à-têtes beside the fire—the whole poor story of their love, so quiet and so long, so discreet, so tender, and yet discarded from her memory. Why was he returning like this? What combination of events was bringing him back into her life? He sat behind her, leaning a shoulder against the wall of the box; and from time to time she quivered as she felt his warm breath on her hair.

"Are you enjoying this?" he asked, leaning over so close that the tip of his mustache brushed against her cheek.

"Heavens no," she said carelessly, "not particularly."

And he suggested that they leave the theater and go somewhere for an ice.

"Oh, not yet! Let's stay!" said Bovary. "Her hair's down: it looks as though it's going to be tragic."

But the mad scene interested Emma not at all: the soprano, she felt, was overdoing her role.

"She's shrieking too loud," she said, turning toward Charles, who was drinking it in.

"Yes . . . perhaps . . . a little," he replied, torn between the fullness of his enjoyment and the respect he had for his wife's opinions.

"It's so hot. . . ." sighed Léon.

"It is. . . . Unbearable."

"Are you uncomfortable?" asked Bovary.

"Yes, I'm stifling; let's go."

Monsieur Léon carefully laid her long lace shawl over her shoulders, and the three of them walked to the river front and sat down on the outdoor terrace of a café. First they spoke of her sickness, Emma interrupting Charles now and then lest, as she said, he bore Monsieur Léon; and Monsieur Léon told them he had just come to Rouen to spend two years in a large office to familiarize himself with the kind of business carried on in Normandy, which was different from anything he had learned about in Paris. Then he asked about Berthe, the Homais', and Madame Lefrançois; and since they had no more to say to each other in front of Charles the conversation soon died.

People coming from the theater strolled by on the sidewalk, humming or bawling at the top of their voices: *"O bel ange, ma Lucie!"* Léon began to show off his musical knowledge. He had heard Tamburini, Rubini, Persiani, Grisi;[5] and in comparison with them, Lagardy, for all the noise he made, was nothing.

"Still," interrupted Charles, who was eating his rum sherbet a tiny bit at a time, "they say he's wonderful in the last act. I was sorry to leave before the end: I was beginning to like it."

"Don't worry," said the clerk, "he'll be giving another performance soon."

But Charles said they were leaving the next day.

"Unless," he said, turning to his wife, "you'd like to stay on by yourself, sweetheart?"

And changing his tune to suit this unexpected opportunity, the young man sang the praises of Lagardy in the final scenes. He was superb, sublime! Charles insisted:

"You can come home Sunday. Yes, make up your mind to do it. You'd be wrong not to, if you think there's the slightest chance it might do you some good."

Meanwhile the tables around them were emptying; a waiter came and stood discreetly nearby; Charles took the hint and drew out his purse; the clerk put a restraining hand on his arm, paid the bill, and noisily threw down a couple of silver coins for the waiter.

"I'm really embarrassed," murmured Bovary, "at the money that you . . ."

The younger man shrugged him off in a friendly way and took up his hat: "So it's agreed?" he said. "Tomorrow at six?"

Charles repeated that he couldn't stay away that much longer, but that there was nothing to prevent Emma . . .

"Oh," she murmured, smiling a peculiar smile, "I really don't know whether . . ."

"Well, think it over," said Charles. "Sleep on it and we'll decide in the morning."

Then, to Léon, who was walking with them:

"Now that you're back in our part of the world I hope you'll drop in now and then and let us give you dinner?"

The clerk said that he certainly would, especially since he'd soon be going to Yonville anyway on a business matter. They said good night at the corner of the Passage Saint-Herbland as the cathedral clock was striking half past eleven.

Part Three

I

Busy though he had been with his law studies, Monsieur Léon had nevertheless found time to frequent the Chaumière, and in that cabaret he had

---

5. Antonio Tamburini (1800–1876); Gian-Battista Rubini (1794–1854); Fanny Tacchinardi Persiani, who was the first Lucia (1812–1867); and Giulia Grisi (1811–1869) were all famous bel-canto singers who appeared in Paris in the operas of Rossini and Donizetti.

done very well for himself with the grisettes, who considered him "distinguished-looking." He was the best-behaved student imaginable; his hair was neither too long nor too short, he didn't spend his entire quarter's allowance the day he got it, and he kept on good terms with his professors. As for excesses, he had been too timorous as well as too squeamish to go in for them.

Often, when he sat reading in his room, or under the lindens of the Luxembourg[6] in the evening, he let his law book fall to the ground, and the memory of Emma came back to him. But gradually his feeling for her faded, and other sensual appetites supplanted it. Even so, it persisted in the background, for Léon never gave up all hope: it was as though a vague promise kept dangling before him in the future, like a golden fruit hanging from some exotic tree.

Then, seeing her again after three years, his passion revived. This time, he decided he must make up his mind to possess her. Much of his shyness had worn off as a result of the gay company he had kept, and he had returned to the provinces filled with contempt for the local ladies, so different from the trim-shod creatures of the boulevards. Before an elegant Parisienne in the salon of some famous, rich, bemedaled physician, the poor clerk would doubtless have trembled like a child; but here on the Rouen river front, in the presence of this wife of an *officier de santé,* he felt at ease, sure in advance that she would be dazzled. Self-confidence depends on surroundings: the same person talks quite differently in the drawing room and in the garret, and a rich woman's virtue is protected by her banknotes quite as effectively as by any cuirass worn under a corset.

After taking leave of Monsieur and Madame Bovary the previous night, Léon had followed them at a distance in the street; and when he saw them turn into the Croix-Rouge, he retraced his steps and spent the rest of the night working out a plan of action.

The next afternoon about five, pale faced, with a tightness in his throat and with the blind resolution of the panic-stricken, he walked into the inn kitchen.

"Monsieur isn't here," a servant told him.

He took that to be a good omen, and went upstairs.

She received him calmly, and even apologized for having forgotten to mention where they were staying.

"Oh, I guessed!" said Léon.

"How?"

He pretended that he had been led to her by pure chance, a kind of instinct. That made her smile; and, ashamed of his blunder, he quickly told her that he had spent the morning looking for her all over the city, in one hotel after another.

"So you decided to stay?" he asked.

"Yes," she said, "and I was wrong. One can't afford to be self-indulgent if one has a thousand things to attend to."

"Oh, I can imagine . . ."

"No, you can't! You're not a woman."

---

6. The gardens of the Palace of Luxembourg (built between 1615 and 1620 for Marie de Médicis); they are open to the public and much frequented by students, as they are near the Sorbonne.

But men had their troubles, too; and so the conversation got under way, with philosophical reflections. Emma expatiated on the vanity of earthly attachments and on the eternal isolation of every human heart. Either to impress her, or naturally taking on the color of her melancholy, the young man declared that he had found his studies prodigiously frustrating. The technicalities of law irritated him, he was tempted by other careers, and in her letters his mother never stopped pestering him. Indeed, as they talked on they both became more specific in their complaints, and less reserved in their confidences. Occasionally they shrank from giving full expression to their thought, and groped for phrases that would convey it obliquely. But she never disclosed having had another passion, and he said nothing about having forgotten her.

Perhaps he no longer remembered the suppers following fancy-dress balls, with the girls costumed as stevedores; and doubtless she didn't recall those early-morning meetings when she had run through the fields to her lover's château. The sounds of the city reached them only faintly, and the room seemed small, designed with them in mind, to make their solitude the closer. Emma, in a dimity dressing gown, leaned her chignon against the back of the old armchair; the yellow wallpaper was like a gold ground behind her; and her bare head was reflected in the mirror, with the white line of her center part and the tips of her ears peeping out from under the sweeps of her hair.

"But forgive me," she said. "I shouldn't bore you with all my complaints!"

"How can you say that!" he said reproachfully.

"Ah!" she said, lifting her lovely tear-bright eyes to the ceiling. "If you knew all the dreams I've dreamed!"

"It's the same with me! Oh, I had a terrible time! Very often I dropped everything and went out and wandered along the quays, trying to forget my thoughts in the noise of the crowd. But I could never drive out the obsession that haunted me. In the window of a print shop on the boulevard there's an Italian engraving showing one of the Muses. She's draped in a tunic and looking at the moon—her hair's streaming down, with forget-me-nots in it. Something made me go back there over and over again: I used to stand in front of that window for hours on end."

Then, in a trembling voice:

"She looked like you a little."

Madame Bovary averted her face lest he see the smile that she couldn't suppress.

"I kept writing you letters," he said, "and then tearing them up."

She made no answer. He went on:

"I used to imagine we'd meet by chance. I kept thinking I saw you on street corners, and I even ran after cabs sometimes, if I saw a shawl or a veil at the window that looked like yours. . . ."

She seemed determined to let him speak without interruption. Arms crossed and head lowered, she stared at the rosettes on her slippers, now and again moving her toes a little under the satin.

Finally she gave a sigh. "The worst thing of all, it seems to me, is to go on leading a futile life the way I do. If our unhappiness were of use to someone, we could find consolation in the thought of sacrifice!"

He launched into a eulogy of virtue, duty, silent renunciation: he, too, he said, had a fantastic need for selfless dedication that he was unable to satisfy.

"What I should love to do," she said, "would be to join an order of nursing Sisters."

"Alas!" he answered. "No such sacred missions are open to men. I can't think of any calling . . . except maybe becoming a doctor. . . ."

She gave a slight shrug and interrupted him, expressing regret that her illness had not been fatal. What a pity! By now she would be past all suffering. Léon at once chimed in with a longing for "the peace of the grave." One night he had even written out his will, asking to be buried in the beautiful velvet-striped coverlet she had given him.

That was how they would have liked to be: what they were doing was to dream up ideals and then refashion their past lives to match them. Speech is a rolling-machine that always stretches the feelings it expresses!

But:

"Why?" she asked him, at his made-up tale about the coverlet.

"Why?" He hesitated. "Because—I was terribly in love with you."

And congratulating himself on having got over the hurdle, Léon watched her face out of the corner of his eye.

It was like the sky when a gust of wind sweeps away the clouds. The mass of sad thoughts that had darkened her blue eyes seemed to lift: her whole face was radiant.

He waited. Finally she answered:

"I always thought so."

They went over, then, the tiny happenings of that far-off time, whose joys and sorrows had been evoked by a single word. He spoke of the clematis bower, of the dresses she had worn, of the furniture in her room—of everything in the house.

"And our poor cactuses—what's become of them?"

"The cold killed them last winter."

"I've thought about them so often, would you believe it? I've pictured them the way they used to look on summer mornings, with the sun on the blinds and your bare arms in among the flowers."

"Poor boy," she said, holding out her hand.

Léon lost no time pressing it to his lips. Then, after taking a deep breath:

"You were a strange, mysterious, captivating force in my life in those days. There was one time, for example, when I came to call on you . . . . But you probably don't remember."

"Yes, I do. Go on."

"You were downstairs in the hall, ready to go out, standing on the bottom step. I even remember your hat—it had little blue flowers on it. And without your asking me at all I went with you. I couldn't help it. I felt more and more foolish every minute, though, and I kept on walking near you. I didn't dare really follow you, and yet I couldn't bear to go away. When you went into a shop I stayed in the street, watching you through the window take off your gloves and count the change on the counter. Then you rang Madame Tuvache's bell; you went in; and I stood there like an idiot in front of the big heavy door even after it had closed behind you."

As she listened to him, Madame Bovary marveled at how old she was: all those reemerging details made her life seem vaster, as though she had endless emotional experiences to look back on. Her voice low, her eyes half closed, she kept saying:

"Yes, I remember! I remember! I remember . . . !"

They heard eight o'clock strike from several belfries near the Place Beau-voisine, a section of Rouen full of boarding schools, churches and great deserted mansions. They were no longer speaking; but as they looked at one another they felt a throbbing in their heads: it was as though their very glances had set off a physical vibration. Now they had clasped hands; and in the sweetness of their ecstasy everything merged—the past, the future, their memories and their dreams. Night was darkening the walls of the room: still gleaming in the dimness were the garish colors of four prints showing four scenes from *La Tour de Nesle,*[7] with captions below in Spanish and French. Through the sash window they could see a patch of dark sky between peaked roofs.

She rose to light two candles on the chest of drawers, and then sat down again.

"Well . . . ?" said Léon.

"Well . . . ?" she echoed.

And as he wondered how to resume the interrupted conversation, she asked:

"Why has no one ever said such things to me before?"

The clerk assured her warmly that idealistic natures were rarely under-stood. But he had loved her the moment he saw her, and despair filled him whenever he thought of the happiness that might have been theirs. Had fortune been kind, had they met earlier, they would long since have been united indissolubly.

"I've thought about that, sometimes," she said.

"What a dream!" murmured Léon.

And then, gently fingering the blue border of her long white belt:

"What's to prevent us from beginning all over again, now?"

"No, no," she said. "I'm too old . . . you're too young . . . forget me! You'll find other women to love you . . . and to love."

"Not as I do you!" he cried.

"What a child you are! Come, let's be sensible. I want us to be."

And she explained why they couldn't be lovers, why they must continue to be friends—like brother and sister—as in the past.

Did she mean those things she was saying? Doubtless Emma herself couldn't tell, engrossed as she was by the charm of seduction and the need to defend herself. Looking fondly at the young man, she gently repulsed the timid caresses his trembling hands essayed.

"Ah! Forgive me!" he said, drawing back.

And Emma was seized by a vague terror in the face of this timidity, a greater danger for her than Rodolphe's boldness when he had advanced with outstretched arms. Never had any man seemed to her so handsome. There was an exquisite candor about him. His long, fine, curving eyelashes were lowered; the smooth skin of his cheek was flushing with desire for her—so she thought; and she felt an all but invincible longing to touch it with her lips. She leaned away toward the clock, as though to see the time.

"Heavens!" she said. "How late! How we've been chattering!"

He understood, and rose to go.

7. The Nesle Tower (French); a melodrama by Alexandre Dumas the elder (1803–1870) and Gaillardet (1832) in which Marie de Bourgogne, famous for her crimes, is the main heroine.

"I forgot all about the opera! And poor Bovary left me here on purpose to see it! It was all arranged that I was to go with Monsieur and Madame Lormeaux, of the Rue Grand-Pont!"

It was her last chance, too, for she was leaving the next day.

"Really?" said Léon.

"Yes."

"But I must see you again," he said. "I had something to tell you. . . ."

"What?"

"Something . . . something serious, important. No—really: you mustn't go, you mustn't. If you knew . . . Listen . . . You haven't understood me, then? You haven't guessed . . ."

"On the contrary, you have a very clear way of putting things," said Emma.

"Ah! Now you're laughing at me! Please don't! Have pity on me: let me see you again. Once—just once."

"Well . . ."

She paused; then, as though changing her mind:

"Not here, certainly!"

"Wherever you like."

"Will you . . ."

She seemed to ponder; and then, tersely:

"Tomorrow at eleven in the cathedral."

"I'll be there!" he cried. He seized her hands, but she pulled them away.

They were standing close together, he behind and she with lowered head, and he bent over and kissed her long and lingeringly on the nape of the neck.

"You're crazy, crazy!" she cried between short bursts of laughter as he kissed her again and again.

Then, leaning his head over her shoulder, he seemed to be imploring her eyes to say yes, but the gaze he received was icy and aloof.

Léon stepped back; in the doorway he paused, and tremblingly whispered:

"Till tomorrow."

Her only reply was a nod, and like a bird she vanished into the adjoining room.

That night Emma wrote the clerk an endless letter canceling their appointment: everything was over between them, and for the sake of their own happiness they must never meet again. But when she finished the letter she didn't know what to do with it—she hadn't Léon's address.

"I'll give it to him myself," she thought, "when he comes."

Léon, the next morning—humming a tune on his balcony beside his open window—polished his pumps himself, going over them again and again. He donned a pair of white trousers, fine socks, and a green tail coat; he doused his handkerchief with all the perfumes he possessed, had his hair curled, then uncurled it again to make it look more elegantly natural.

"Still too early!" he thought: he was looking at the barber's cuckoo clock, and it pointed to nine.

He read an old fashion magazine, went out, smoked a cigar, walked a few blocks. Finally he decided it was time to go, and set off briskly toward the Parvis Notre-Dame.

It was a fine summer morning. Silver gleamed in jewelers' windows, and the sunlight slanting onto the cathedral flashed on the cut surface of the gray stone; a flock of birds was swirling in the blue sky around the trefoiled turrets; the square, echoing with cries, smelled of the flowers that edged its pavement—roses, jasmine, carnations, narcissus and tuberoses interspersed with well-watered plants of catnip and chickweed. The fountain gurgled in the center; and under great umbrellas, among piles of cantaloupes, bare headed flower women were twisting paper around bunches of violets.

The young man chose one. It was the first time he had bought flowers for a woman; and his chest swelled with pride as he inhaled their fragrance, as though this homage that he intended for another were being paid, instead, to him.

But he was afraid of being seen, and resolutely entered the church.

The verger was just then standing in the left doorway, under the figure of the dancing Salomé. He was in full regalia, with plumed hat, rapier and staff, more majestic than a cardinal, shining like a pyx.

He advanced toward Léon, and with the smiling, bland benignity of a priest questioning a child, he said:

"Monsieur is from out of town, perhaps? Monsieur would like to visit the church?"

"No," said Léon.

He walked down one of the side aisles and up the other, then stood outside and looked over the square; there was no sign of Emma, and he reentered the church and strolled as far as the choir.

The nave was mirrored in the holy-water fonts, with the lower portions of the ogives and some of the stained glass; the reflection of the painted windows broke off at the marble rim only to continue beyond, on the pavement, like a many-colored carpet. Brilliant daylight streamed into the church in three enormous shafts through the three open portals. Now and again a sacristan moved across the far end, dipping before the altar in the half-sidewise genuflection practiced by hurried worshipers. The crystal chandeliers hung motionless. A silver lamp was burning in the choir; and from the side chapels and shadowy corners of the church came an occasional sound like a sigh, and the noise of a metal gate clanging shut and echoing under the lofty vaults.

Léon walked meditatively, keeping near the walls. Never had life seemed so good. Any minute now she would appear, charming, all aquiver, turning around to see whether anyone was looking—with her flounced dress, her gold eyeglass, her dainty shoes, all kinds of feminine elegances he had never had a taste of, and all the ineffable allurement of virtue on the point of yielding. The church was like a gigantic boudoir, suffused by her image: the vaults curved dimly down to breathe in the avowal of her love; the windows were ablaze to cast their splendor on her face; and even the incense burners were lighted, to welcome her like an angel amid clouds of perfume.

But still she didn't come. He took a chair and his eyes rested on a blue stained-glass window showing boatmen carrying baskets. He stared at it fixedly, counting the scales on the fish and the buttonholes in the doublets, his thoughts meanwhile roving in search of Emma.

The verger, standing to one side, was raging inwardly at this person who was taking it upon himself to admire the cathedral on his own. He was behaving monstrously, he considered: he was stealing from him, really—almost committing sacrilege.

Then there was a rustle of silk on the stone pavement, the edge of a hat under a hooded cape. . . . It was she! Léon jumped up and ran to meet her. She was pale. She walked quickly.

"Read this!" she said, holding out a sheet of paper. "Oh, no!"

And abruptly she drew back her hand and turned into the chapel of the Virgin, where she knelt down against a chair and began to pray.

The young man was irritated by this sanctimonious bit of whimsy; then he felt a certain charm at seeing her, in the midst of a love meeting, plunged into devotions like an Andalusian *marquesa*; but he soon grew impatient, for there seemed to be no end to it.

Emma was praying, or rather forcing herself to pray, in the hope that heaven might miraculously send her strength of will; and to draw down divine aid she filled her eyes with the splendors of the tabernacle, she breathed the fragrance of the sweet-rockets, white and lush in their tall vases, and she listened intently to the silence of the church, which only increased the tumult of her heart.

She rose, and they were about to leave when the verger came swiftly over:

"Madame is perhaps from out of town? Madame would like to visit the church?"

"Oh, no!" the clerk cried.

"Why not?" she retorted.

Her desperate attempt to steady her virtue made her clutch at the Virgin, at the sculptures, at the tombs, at anything that came to hand.

Insisting that they must "begin at the beginning," the verger led them outside the entrance door to the edge of the square, and there pointed with his staff to a large circle of black stones in the pavement, devoid of carving or inscription:

"That," he said majestically, "is the circumference of the great Amboise bell. It weighed forty thousand pounds. It was without equal in all Europe. The workman who cast it died of joy. . . ."

"Let's get away from here," said Léon.

The guide moved on; and back in the chapel of the Virgin he extended his arms in a showman's gesture that took in everything, and addressed them more proudly than a gentleman farmer displaying his fruit trees:

"This plain stone marks the resting place of Pierre de Brézé, lord of La Varenne and Brissac, grand marshal of Poitou and governor of Normandy, killed at the battle of Montlhéry, July 16, 1465."

Léon bit his lips in a fury of impatience.

"And on the right the nobleman in full armor on a rearing horse is his grandson Louis de Brézé, lord of Braval and Montchauvet, comte de Maulevrier, baron de Mauny, royal chamberlain, knight of the order and likewise governor of Normandy, who died July 23, 1531, a Sunday, as it says on the inscription; and below, the man about to descend into the tomb represents the same person exactly. Human mortality has never been more perfectly represented."

Madame Bovary raised her eyeglass. Léon stood still and stared at her, no longer even trying to utter a word or make the slightest move, so discouraged was he by this combination of patter and indifference.

The guide droned on:

"Near him, there, that kneeling weeping woman is his wife, Diane de Poitiers, comtesse de Brézé, duchesse de Valentinois, born 1499, died 1566;

and on the left, holding a child, the Holy Virgin. Now face this way: those are the tombs of the Amboises. They were both cardinals and archbishops of Rouen. That one was one of King Louis XII's ministers. He was a great benefactor of the cathedral. In his will he left 30,000 *écus d'or* for the poor."

And immediately, without interrupting his stream of talk, he pushed them into a chapel cluttered with railings, some of which he moved aside to reveal a blockish object that looked like a roughly carved statue.

"This," he said with a deep sigh, "once formed part of the decoration of the tomb of Richard Coeur-de-Lion,[8] king of England and duke of Normandy. It was the Calvinists, Monsieur, who reduced it to the condition in which you see it now. Out of pure malice they buried it in the earth, under Monseigneur's episcopal throne. That door, there, by the way, is the one he uses—Monseigneur, I mean—to reach his residence. Now we'll move on to the gargoyle windows."

But Léon hastily took a silver piece from his pocket and grasped Emma's arm. The verger was taken aback, mystified by such premature munificence: the visitor still had so much to see! He called after him:

"Monsieur! The steeple! The steeple!"[9]

"No, thanks," said Léon.

"Monsieur is wrong! It's going to be four hundred forty feet high, only nine feet lower than the Great Pyramid of Egypt. It's entirely of cast iron, it . . ."

Léon fled, for it seemed to him that his love, after being reduced to stone-like immobility in the church for nearly two hours, was now going to vanish like smoke up that truncated pipe, that elongated cage, that fretwork chimney, or what you will, that perches so precariously and grotesquely atop the cathedral like the wild invention of a crazy metalworker.

"But where are we going?" she asked.

Making no answer, he continued swiftly on, and Madame Bovary was already dipping a finger in the holy water when behind them they heard a sound of heavy panting regularly punctuated by the tapping of a staff. Léon turned around.

"Monsieur!"

"What?"

It was the verger, holding about twenty thick paperbound volumes against his stomach. They were "books about the cathedral."

"Fool!" muttered Léon, hurrying out of the church.

An urchin was playing in the square:

"Go get me a cab!"

The youngster vanished like a shot up the Rue des Quatre-Vents, and for a few minutes they were left alone, face to face and a little constrained.

"Oh, Léon! Really—I don't know whether I should . . . !"

She simpered. Then, in a serious tone:

"It's very improper, you know."

"What's improper about it?" retorted the clerk. "Everybody does it in Paris!"

It was an irresistible and clinching argument.

8. Richard the Lion-Hearted (b. 1157), who was king of England from 1189 to 1199, when he died at the siege of the castle of Châlus.   9. Added to the cathedral of Rouen, which was built in the Gothic style in stages from the 13th century to the early 16th, it is a high cast-iron spire (485 feet), generally considered a tasteless disfigurement. Construction was begun in 1824 but not finished until 1876.

But there was no sign of a cab. Léon was terrified lest she retreat into the church. Finally the cab appeared.

"Drive past the north door, at least!" cried the verger, from the entrance. "Take a look at the Resurrection, the Last Judgment, Paradise, King David, and the souls of the damned in the flames of hell!"

"Where does Monsieur wish to go?" asked the driver.

"Anywhere!" said Léon, pushing Emma into the carriage.

And the lumbering contraption rolled away.

It went down the Rue Grand-Pont, crossed the Place des Arts, the Quai Napoléon and the Pont Neuf, and stopped in front of the statue of Pierre Corneille.

"Keep going!" called a voice from within.

It started off again, and gathering speed on the downgrade beyond the Carrefour Lafayette it came galloping up to the railway station.

"No! Straight on!" cried the same voice.

Rattling out through the station gates, the cab soon turned into the Boulevard, where it proceeded at a gentle trot between the double row of tall elms. The coachman wiped his brow, stowed his leather hat between his legs, and veered the cab off beyond the side lanes to the grass strip along the river front.

It continued along the river on the cobbled towing path for a long time in the direction of Oyssel, leaving the islands behind.

But suddenly it rushed off through Quatre-Mares, Sotteville, the Grande-Chaussée, the Rue d'Elbeuf, and made its third stop—this time at the Jardin des Plantes.

"Drive on!" cried the voice, more furiously.

And abruptly starting off again it went through Saint-Sever, along the Quai des Curandiers and the Quai aux Meules, recrossed the bridge, crossed the Place du Champ-de-Mars and continued on behind the garden of the hospital, where old men in black jackets were strolling in the sun on a terrace green with ivy. It went up the Boulevard Bouvreuil, along the Boulevard Cauchoise, and traversed Mont-Riboudet as far as the hill at Deville.

There it turned back; and from then on it wandered at random, without apparent goal. It was seen at Saint-Pol, at Lescure, at Mont-Gargan, at Rouge-Mare and the Place du Gaillardbois; in the rue Maladrerie, the Rue Dinanderie, and in front of one church after another—Saint-Romain, Saint-Vivien, Saint-Maclou, Saint-Nicaise; in front of the customs house, at the Basse Vieille-Tour, at Trois-Pipes, and at the Cimetière Monumental. From his seat the coachman now and again cast a desperate glance at a café. He couldn't conceive what locomotive frenzy was making these people persist in refusing to stop. He tried a few times, only to hear immediate angry exclamation from behind. So he lashed the more furiously at his two sweating nags, and paid no attention whatever to bumps in the road; he hooked into things right and left; he was past caring—demoralized, and almost weeping from thirst, fatigue, and despair.

Along the river front amidst the trucks and the barrels, along the streets from the shelter of the guard posts, the bourgeois stared wide-eyed at this spectacle unheard of in the provinces—a carriage with drawn shades that kept appearing and reappearing, sealed tighter than a tomb and tossing like a ship.

At a certain moment in the early afternoon, when the sun was blazing down most fiercely on the old silver-plated lamps, a bare hand appeared from under the little yellow cloth curtains and threw out some torn scraps of paper. The wind caught them and scattered them, and they alighted at a distance, like white butterflies, on a field of flowering red clover.

Then, about six o'clock, the carriage stopped in a side street near the Place Beauvoisine. A woman alighted from it and walked off, her veil down, without a backward glance.

II

When she reached the hotel, Madame Bovary was surprised to see no sign of the stagecoach. Hivert had waited for her fifty-three minutes, and then driven off.

Nothing really obliged her to go, even though she had said that she would be back that evening. But Charles would be waiting for her: and in advance her heart was filled with that craven submissiveness with which many women both redeem their adultery and punish themselves for it.

She quickly packed her bag, paid her bill, and hired a gig in the yard. She told the driver to hurry, and kept urging him on and asking him the time and how many miles they had gone. They caught up with the Hirondelle on the outskirts of Quincampoix.

She shut her eyes almost before she was seated in her corner, and opened them at the outskirts of the village: ahead she saw Félicité standing watch outside the blacksmith's. Hivert pulled up the horses, and the cook, standing on tiptoe to address her through the window, said with an air of mystery:

"Madame, you must go straight to Monsieur Homais'. It's something urgent."

The village was silent as usual. Little pink mounds were steaming in the gutters: it was jelly-making time, and everyone in Yonville was putting up the year's supply the same day. The mound in front of the pharmacy was by far the largest and most impressive, and quite properly so: a laboratory must always be superior to home kitchens; a universal demand must always over-shadow mere individual tastes!

She went in. The big armchair was overturned, and—what was more shocking—the *Fanal de Rouen* itself had been left lying on the floor between the two pestles. She pushed open the hall door, and in the middle of the kitchen—amid earthenware jars full of stemmed currants, grated sugar, lump sugar, scales on the table and pans on the fire—she found all the Homais, big and little, swathed to the chin in aprons and wielding forks. Justin was standing there hanging his head, and the pharmacist was shouting:

"Who told you to go get it in the Capharnaum?"

"What is it?" Emma asked. "What's the matter?"

"What's the matter?" replied the apothecary. "We're making jelly. It's on the fire. It threatens to boil over. I call for another pan. And this good-for-nothing, out of sheer laziness, goes and takes—goes into my laboratory and takes off the hook—the key to the Capharnaum!"

Such was the apothecary's name for a small room under the eaves, filled with pharmaceutical utensils and supplies. He often spent long hours there alone, labeling, decanting, repackaging. He considered it not a mere store-room, but a veritable sanctuary, birthplace of all kinds of pills, boluses, tisanes, lotions and potions concocted by himself and destined to spread his renown throughout the countryside. Not another soul ever set foot in it: so fiercely did he respect the place that he even swept it out himself. If the pharmacy, open to all comers, was the arena where he paraded in all his glory, the Capharnaum was the hideaway where he rapturously pursued his favorite occupations in selfish seclusion. No wonder Justin's carelessness seemed to him a monstrous bit of irreverence. His face was redder than the currants as he continued his tirade:

"Yes, the key to the Capharnaum! The key that guards the acids and the caustic alkalis! And to calmly go and take one of the spare pans! A pan with a lid! One I may never use! Every detail is important in an art as precise as ours! Distinctions must be preserved! Pharmaceutical implements mustn't be used for near-domestic tasks! It's like carving a chicken with a scalpel, as though a judge were to . . ."

"Stop exciting yourself!" Madame Homais kept saying.

And Athalie pulled at his frock coat and cried: "Papa! Papa!"

"No! Leave me alone!" ordered the apothecary. "Leave me alone! God! I might as well be a grocer, I swear! Go ahead—go right ahead—*don't* respect anything! Smash! Crash! Let the leeches loose! Burn the marshmallow! Make pickles in the medicine jars! Slash up the bandages!"

"But you had something to . . ." said Emma.

"One moment, Madame!—Do you know the risk you were running? Didn't you notice anything in the corner, on the left, on the third shelf? Open your mouth! Say something!"

"I . . . don't . . . know . . ." stammered the boy.

"Ah! You don't know! Well, *I* know! You saw a bottle, a blue glass bottle sealed with yellow wax, with white powder in it, and that I myself marked *Dangerous!*? Do you know what's in that bottle? Arsenic! And you go med-dling with that! You take a pan that's standing right beside it!"

"Right beside it!" cried Madame Homais, clasping her hands. "Arsenic! You might have poisoned us all!"

And the children began to scream, as though they were already prey to the most frightful gastric pains.

"Or you might have poisoned a patient!" the apothecary persisted. "Do you want me to be hauled into court as a common criminal? Do you want to see me dragged to the scaffold? Don't you know how very careful I am about handling anything, no matter how many million times I may have done it before? Sometimes I'm terrified at the thought of my responsibilities! The government positively hounds us! The legal restrictions are absurd—a veri-table sword of Damocles hanging over our heads!"

Emma had given up any attempt to ask what was wanted of her, and the pharmacist breathlessly continued:

"That's your way of being grateful for all the kindness you've been shown! That's how you repay me for the father's care I've showered on you! Where would you be if it weren't for me? What would you be doing? Who gives you your food and your lodging, and training, and clothing—everything you need to become a respectable member of society someday? But to achieve that you've got to bend your back to the oar—get some calluses on your hands, as the saying goes. *Fabricando fit faber, age quod agis.*"[1]

His rage had sent him into Latin: he would have spouted Chinese or Greenlandic had he been able to, for he was in the throes of one of those crises in which the soul lays bare its every last corner, just as the ocean, in the travail of storm, splits open to display everything from the seaweed on its shores to the sand of its deepest bottom.

And he went on:

"I'm beginning to repent bitterly that I ever took you into my charge! I'd have done far better to leave you as I found you—let you wallow in the misery and filth you were born in! You'll never be fit to do anything except look after the cows! You haven't the makings of a scientist! You're scarcely capable of sticking on a label! And you live here at my expense, gorging yourself like a priest, like a pig in clover!"

Emma turned to Madame Homais:

"I was told to come . . ."

"I know," the lady said, wringing her hands, "but how can I possibly tell you . . . ? It's a calamity . . ."

She left her words unfinished. The apothecary was thundering on:

"Empty it out! Scour it! Take it back! Be quick about it!"

And as he shook Justin by the collar of his overall a book fell out of one of the pockets.

The boy bent down for it, but Homais was quicker, and he picked up the book and stared at it open-mouthed.

"*Conjugal . . . Love!*" he cried, placing a deliberate pause between the two words. "Ah! Very good! *Very good!* Charming, in fact! And with illustrations . . . Really! This goes beyond everything!"

Madame Homais stepped forward as though to look.

"No! Don't touch it!"

The children clamored to see the pictures.

"Leave the room!" he said imperiously.

They left.

First he strode up and down, holding the volume open, rolling his eyes, choking, puffing, apoplectic. Then he walked straight up to his apprentice and stood in front of him, arms folded.

"So you're going in for *all* the vices, are you, you little wretch? Watch out, you're on the downward path! Did it ever occur to you that this wicked book might fall into my children's hands? It might be just the spark that . . . It might sully the purity of Athalie! It might corrupt Napoléon! Physically, he's a man already! Are you sure, at least, that they haven't read it? Can you swear to me . . ."

"Really, Monsieur," said Emma. "Did you have something to tell me?"

"So I did, Madame. . . . Your father-in-law is dead!"

It was true: the elder Bovary had died two days before, very suddenly, from an apoplectic stroke, as he was leaving the table; and Charles, overanxious to spare Emma's sensibilities, had asked Monsieur Homais to acquaint her tactfully with the horrible news.

The pharmacist had devoted much thought to the wording of his

1. The artisan becomes proficient through practice; practice what you are supposed to do (Latin).

announcement. He had rounded it and polished it and given it cadence. It was a masterpiece of discretion and transition, of subtlety and shading. But anger had swept away rhetoric.

Emma, seeing that it was useless to ask for details, left the pharmacy, for Monsieur Homais had resumed his vituperations. He was quieting down, however, and now was grumbling in a fatherly way as he fanned himself with his cap:

"It's not that I disapprove entirely of the book. The author was a doctor. It deals with certain scientific aspects that it does a man no harm to know about—aspects, if I may say so, that a man *has* to know about. But later, later! Wait till you're a man yourself, at least; wait till your character's formed."

The sound of the knocker told the expectant Charles that Emma had arrived, and he came toward her with open arms. There were tears in his voice:

"Ah! *Ma chère amie* . . ."

And he bent down gently to kiss her. But at the touch of his lips the memory of Léon gripped her, and she passed her hand over her face and shuddered.

Nevertheless she answered him. "Yes," she said. "I know . . . I know . . ."

He showed her the letter in which his mother told what had happened, without any sentimental hypocrisy. Her only regret was that her husband had not received the succor of the church: he had died not at home, but at Doudeville, in the street, just outside a café, after a patriotic banquet with some ex-army officers.

Emma handed back the letter. At dinner she pretended a little for the sake of good manners to have no appetite, but when Charles urged her, she proceeded to eat heartily, while he sat opposite her motionless, weighed down by grief.

Now and again he lifted his head and gave her a long, stricken look.

"I wish I could have seen him again!" he sighed.

She made no answer. And finally, when she knew that she must say something:

"How old was your father?"

"Fifty-eight."

"Ah!"

And that was all.

A little later:

"My poor mother!" he said. "What's to become of her now?"

She conveyed with a gesture that she had no idea.

Seeing her so silent, Charles supposed that she, too, was affected, and he forced himself to say no more lest he exacerbate her sorrow, which he found touching. But for a moment he roused himself from his own.

"Did you have a good time yesterday?" he asked.

"Yes."

When the tablecloth was removed, Bovary did not get up, nor did Emma; and as she continued to look at him the monotony of the sight gradually banished all compassion from her heart. He seemed to her insignificant, weak, a nonentity—contemptible in every way. How could she rid herself of him? What an endless evening! She felt torpid, drugged, as though from opium fumes.

From the entry came the sharp tap of a stick on the wooden floor. It was Hippolyte, bringing Madame's bags. To set them down, he swung his wooden leg around in an awkward quarter-circle.

"Charles doesn't even think about him anymore," she remarked to herself as she watched the poor devil, his mop of red hair dripping sweat.

Bovary fumbled in his purse for a coin; and, apparently unaware of the humiliation implicit in the very presence of the man who was standing there, like a living reproach for his incurable ineptitude:

"Oh, you have a pretty bouquet!" he said, noticing Léon's violets on the mantelpiece.

"Yes," she said carelessly. "I bought it just before I left—from a beggar woman."

Charles took up the violets, held their coolness against his tear-reddened eyes, and gently sniffed them. She quickly took them from his hand, and went to put them in a glass of water.

The following day the older Madame Bovary arrived. She and her son did a good deal of weeping. Emma, pleading household duties, kept out of the way. The day after that, they had to consult about mourning, and the three of them sat down together, the ladies with their workboxes, under the arbor on the river bank.

Charles thought about his father, and was surprised to feel so much affection for one whom up till then he had thought he loved but little. The older Madame Bovary thought of her husband. The worst of her times with him seemed desirable now. Everything was submerged in grief, so intensely did she miss the life she was used to; and from time to time as she plied her needle a great tear rolled down her nose and hung there for a moment before dropping. Emma was thinking that scarcely forty-eight hours before they had been together, shut away from the world, in ecstasy, devouring each other with their eyes. She tried to recapture the tiniest details of that vanished day. But the presence of her mother-in-law and her husband interfered. She wished she could hear nothing, see nothing: she wanted merely to be left alone to evoke her love, which depite her best efforts was becoming blurred under the impact of external impressions.

She was ripping the lining of a dress, and scraps of the material lay scattered around her; the older Madame Bovary, never raising her eyes, kept squeaking away with her scissors; and Charles, in his cloth slippers and the old brown frock coat that he used as a dressing gown, kept his hand in his pockets and said no more than the others. Near them, Berthe, in a little white apron, was scraping the gravel of the path with her shovel.

Suddenly they saw Monsieur Lheureux, the dry-goods dealer, push open the gate.

He had come to offer his services "on this very sad occasion." Emma answered that she thought she could do without them. But the shopkeeper did not concede defeat.

"If you'll excuse me," he said, "I'd like to speak to you privately."

And in a low voice:

"It's about that little matter . . . you know what I'm referring to?"

Charles blushed to the roots of his hair.

"Oh, yes . . . of course."

And in his embarrassment he turned to his wife:

"Darling would you take care of . . . ?"

She seemed to understand, for she rose; and Charles said to his mother:

"It's nothing—just some household detail, I imagine."

He didn't want her to learn about the promissory note: he dreaded her comments.

As soon as Emma was alone with Monsieur Lheureux he began to congratulate her rather bluntly on coming into money, and then spoke of indifferent matters—fruit trees, the harvest, and his own health, which was always the same, "so-so, could be worse." He worked like a galley slave, he informed her, and even so, despite what people said about him, he didn't make enough to buy butter for his bread.

Emma let him talk. She had been so prodigiously bored these last two days!

"And you're entirely well again?" he went on. "Your husband was in quite a state, I can tell you! He's a fine fellow, even if we did have a little trouble."

"What trouble?" she asked, for Charles had told her nothing about the dispute over the various items.

"But you know perfectly well!" said Lheureux. "About the little things you wanted—the trunks."

He had pushed his hat forward over his eyes, and with his hands behind his back, smiling, and whistling to himself under his breath, he was staring straight at her in a way she found intolerable. Did he suspect something? She waited in a panic of apprehension. But finally he said:

"We made it up, and I came today to propose another arrangement."

What he proposed was the renewal of the note signed by Bovary. Monsieur should of course do as he pleased: he shouldn't worry, especially now that he was going to have so many other things on his mind.

"He'd really do best to turn it over to somebody else—you, for example. With a power of attorney everything would be very simple, and then you and I could attend to our little affairs together."

She didn't understand. He let the matter drop, and turned the conversation back to dry goods: Madame really couldn't not order something from him. He'd send her a piece of black barège—twelve meters, enough to make a dress.

"The one you have there is all right for the house, but you need another for going out. I saw that the minute I came in. I've got an eye like a Yankee!"

He didn't send the material: he brought it. Then he came again to do the measuring, and again and again on other pretexts, each time putting himself out to be agreeable and helpful—making himself her liegeman, as Homais might have put it—and always slipping in a few words of advice about the power of attorney. He didn't mention the promissory note. It didn't occur to her to think of it: early in her convalescence Charles had, in fact, said something to her about it, but her mind had been so agitated that she had forgotten. Moreover she was careful never to bring up anything about money matters. This surprised her mother-in-law, who attributed her new attitude to the religious sentiments she had acquired during her illness.

But as soon as the older woman left, Emma lost no time in impressing Bovary with her practical good sense. It was up to them, she said, to make inquiries, check on mortgages, see if there were grounds for liquidating the property by auction or otherwise. She used technical terms at random, and impressive words like "order," "the future" and "foresight," and she continually exaggerated the complications attendant on inheritance. Then one day she showed him the draft of a general authorization to "manage and administer his affairs, negotiate all loans, sign and endorse all promissory notes, pay all sums," etc. She had profited from Lheureux's lessons.

Charles naïvely asked her where the document came from.

"From Maître Guillaumin."

And with the greatest coolness imaginable she added:

"I haven't too much confidence in him. You hear such dreadful things about notaries! Perhaps we ought to consult . . . We don't know anyone except . . . We don't know anyone, really."

"Unless Léon . . ." said Charles, who was thinking hard.

But it was difficult to make things clear by letter. So she offered to make the trip. He thanked her but said she mustn't. She insisted. Each outdid the other in consideration. Finally, imitating the pert disobedience of a child, she cried:

"I will, too, go! I will!"

"How good you are!" he said, kissing her on the forehead.

The next morning she set out in the Hirondelle for Rouen to consult Monsieur Léon, and she stayed there three days.

III

They were three full, exquisite, glorious days, a real honeymoon.

They stayed at the Hotel de Boulogne on the river front, living there behind drawn shutters and locked doors; their room was strewn with flowers, and iced fruit drinks were brought up to them all day long.

At dusk they hired a covered boat and went to dine on one of the islands.

From the shipyards came the thumping of caulking irons against hulls. Wisps of tar smoke curled up from among the trees, and on the river floated great oily patches, the color of Florentine bronze, undulating unevenly in the purple glow of the sun.

They drifted downstream amidst anchored craft whose long slanting cables grazed the top of their boat.

The sounds of the city gradually receded—the rattle of wagons, the tumult of voices, the barking of dogs on the decks of ships. As they touched the shore of their island she loosened the silk ribbon of her hat.

They sat in the low-ceilinged room of a restaurant with black fishnets hanging at its door, and ate fried smelts, cream and cherries. Then they stretched out on the grass in an out-of-the-way corner and lay in each other's arms under the poplars: they wished they might live forever, like two Robinson Crusoes, in this little spot that seemed to them in their bliss the most magnificent on earth. It wasn't the first time in their lives that they had seen trees, blue sky and lawn, or heard the flowing of water or the rustle of the breeze in the branches, but never before, certainly, had they looked on it all with such wonder: it was as though nature had not existed before, or had only begun to be beautiful with the slaking of their desires.

At nightfall they returned to the city. The boat followed the shoreline of the islands, and they crouched deep in its shadow, not saying a word. The square-tipped oars clicked in the iron oarlocks: it sounded, in the silence, like the beat of a metronome, and the rope trailing behind kept up its gentle splashing in the water.

One night the moon shone out, and of course they rhapsodized about how melancholy and poetical it was. She even sang a little:

> One night—dost thou remember?—
> We were sailing . . . [2]

Her sweet, small voice died away over the river: borne off on the breeze were the trills that Léon heard flit past him like the fluttering of wings.

She was sitting opposite him, leaning against the wall of the little cabin, the moonlight streaming in on her through an open shutter. In her black dress, its folds spreading out around her like a fan, she looked taller, slimmer. Her head was raised, her hands were clasped, her eyes turned heavenward. One moment she would be hidden by the shadow of some willows; the next, she would suddenly reemerge in the light of the moon like an apparition.

Léon, sitting on the bottom beside her, picked up a bright red ribbon.

The boatman looked at it.

"Oh," he said, "that's probably from a party I took out the other day. They were a jolly lot, all right, the men *and* the girls: they brought along food and champagne and music—the whole works. There was one of them, especially—a big, good-looking fellow with a little mustache—he was a riot. They all kept after him. 'Come on, tell us a story, Adolphe'—or Dodolphe, or some name like that."

She shuddered.

"Don't you feel well?" asked Léon, moving closer to her.

"Oh, it's nothing. Just a chill."

"He was another one who never had to worry about where his women would come from," the old boatman added softly, as a compliment to his present passenger.

Then he spit on his hands and took up his oars.

But finally they had to part. Their farewells were sad. He was to write her in care of Madame Rollet; and she gave him such detailed instructions about using a double envelope that he marveled greatly at her shrewdness in love matters.

"So I have your word for it that everything's in order?" she said, as they kissed for the last time.

"Absolutely—But why the devil," he wondered, as he walked home alone through the streets, "is she so set on having that power of attorney?"

IV

Before long, Léon began to give himself superior airs around the office. He kept aloof from his colleagues and totally neglected his work. He waited for Emma's letters, and read them over and over. He wrote to her. He evoked her image with all the strength of his passion and his memories. Far from being lessened by absence, his longing to see her again increased, until finally one Saturday morning he took the road to Yonville.

---

2. The beginning of Alphonse de Lamartine's *The Lake* (see p. 1061).

When he looked down on the valley from the top of the hill and saw the church steeple with its tin flag turning in the wind, he was filled with an exquisite pleasure: smug satisfaction and selfish sentimentality were mingled in it—it was the feeling that a millionaire must experience on revisiting his boyhood village.

He prowled around her house. A light was burning in the kitchen. He watched for her shadow behind the curtains. Not a soul was to be seen.

Madame Lefrançois uttered loud cries at the sight of him, and said that he was "taller and thinner." Artémise, on the other hand, found that he had grown "heavier and darker."

He took his dinner in the small dining room, just as in the old days, but alone, without the tax collector: for Binet, sick of waiting for the Hirondelle, had permanently changed his mealtime to an hour earlier, and now dined on the stroke of five. Even so he never missed a chance to grumble that "the rusty old clock was slow."

Finally Léon got up his courage and knocked on the doctor's door. Madame was in her room: it was a quarter of an hour before she came down. Monsieur seemed delighted to see him again, but didn't stir from the house all evening or all the next day.

Only late Sunday evening did he see her alone, in the lane behind the garden—in the lane, just like Rodolphe. It was during a thunderstorm, and they talked under an umbrella, with lightning flashing around them.

The thought of parting was unbearable.

"I'd rather die!" said Emma.

She clung convulsively to his arm and wept:

"Adieu! Adieu! When will I see you again?"

They separated, then turned back for a last embrace; and it was at that moment that she promised him to find, soon, no matter how, some way in which they would be able to see each other alone and regularly, at least once a week. Emma had no doubt about succeeding. She looked forward to the future with confidence: the inheritance money would shortly be coming in.

On the strength of it she bought, for her bedroom, a pair of wide-striped yellow curtains that Monsieur Lheureux extolled as a bargain. She said she wished she could have a carpet; and Lheureux, assuring her that she wasn't "reaching for the moon," promised very obligingly to find her one. By now she didn't know how she could get along without him. She sent for him twenty times a day, and he always promptly left whatever he was doing and came, without a word of protest. Nor was it clear to anyone why Madame Rollet lunched at her house every day, and even visited with her privately.

It was about this time—the beginning of winter—that she became intensely musical.

One evening while Charles was listening she started the same piece over again four times, each time expressing annoyance with herself. Charles was unaware of anything wrong. "Bravo!" he cried. "Very good! Why stop? Keep going."

"No, I'm playing abominably. My fingers are rusty."

The next day he asked her to "play him something else."

"Very well, if you like."

Charles had to admit that she seemed a little out of practice. She fumbled, struck wrong notes, and finally broke off abruptly:

"That's enough of that! I should take some lessons, but . . ."

She bit her lips and added: "Twenty francs an hour—it's too expensive."

"Yes, it certainly is . . . a little . . ." said Charles, with a silly giggle. "But it seems to me you ought to be able to find somebody for less. There are plenty of musicians without big names who are better than the celebrities."

"Try and find some," said Emma.

When he came in the next day he gave her a sly look, and finally came out with: "You certainly have a way sometimes of thinking you know better than anybody else. I was at Barfeuchères today and Madame Liégeard told me that her three girls—the three at school at the Miséricorde—take lessons at two and a half francs an hour, and from a marvelous teacher!"

She shrugged, and from then on left her instrument unopened.

But whenever she walked by it she would sigh (if Bovary happened to be there): "Ah, my poor piano!"

And she always made a point of telling visitors that she had given up her music and now couldn't possibly go on with it again, for imperative reasons. Everybody pitied her. What a shame! She had so much talent! People even spoke to Bovary about it. They made him feel ashamed, especially the pharmacist.

"You're making a mistake! Natural faculties must never be let lie fallow! Besides, my friend, look at it this way: by encouraging Madame to take lessons now, you'll save money later on your daughter's lessons. In my opinion, mothers should teach their children themselves. It's an idea of Rousseau's— maybe a little new, still, but bound to prevail eventually, I'm sure, like mother's breast-feeding and vaccination."

So Charles brought up the question of the piano again. Emma answered tartly that they'd better sell it. Poor old piano! It had so often been a source of pride for him, that to see it go would be like watching Emma commit partial suicide.

"If you really want to go ahead with it," he said, "I suppose a lesson now and then wouldn't ruin us."

"But lessons aren't worth taking," she said, "unless they're taken regularly."

That was how she obtained her husband's permission to go to the city once a week to meet her lover. By the end of the first month everyone found that her playing had improved considerably.

V

And so, every Thursday, she rose and dressed without a sound, lest she wake Charles, who would have remarked on her getting ready too early. Then she paced up and down, stood at the windows, looked out at the square. The first light of morning was stealing into the pillared market place; and on the pharmacist's house, its shutters still drawn, the pale tints of dawn were picking out the capital letters of the shop sign.

When the clock said quarter past seven she made her way to the Lion d'Or and was let in by the yawning Artémise. The servant paid her the attention of digging out the smoldering coals from under the ashes, and then left her to herself in the kitchen. From time to time she walked out into the yard. Hivert would be harnessing the horses. He went about it very deliberately, listening as he did so to Madame Lefrançois, who had stuck her head, nightcap and all, out of a window and was briefing him on his errands in a way that anyone else would have found bewildering. Emma tapped her foot on the cobbles.

Finally, when he had downed his bowl of soup, put on his overcoat, lighted his pipe and picked up his whip, he unhurriedly climbed onto the seat.

The Hirondelle set off at a gentle trot, and for the first mile or two kept stopping here and there to take on passengers who stood watching for it along the road, outside their gates. Those who had booked seats the day before kept the coach waiting: some, even, were still in their beds, and Hivert would call, shout, curse, and finally get down from his seat and pound on the doors. The wind whistled in through the cracked blinds.

Gradually the four benches filled up, the coach rattled along, row upon row of apple trees flashed by; and the road, lined on each side by a ditch of yellow water, stretched on and on, narrowing toward the horizon.

Emma knew every inch of it: she knew that after a certain meadow came a road sign, then an elm, a barn, or a road-mender's cabin; sometimes she even shut her eyes, trying to give herself a surprise. But she always knew just how much farther there was to go.

Finally the brick houses crowded closer together, the road rang under the wheels, and now the Hirondelle moved smoothly between gardens: through iron fences were glimpses of statues, artificial mounds crowned by arbors, clipped yews, a swing. Then, all at once, the city came into view.

Sloping downward like an amphitheatre, drowned in mist, it sprawled out shapelessly beyond its bridges. Then open fields swept upward again in a monotonous curve, merging at the top with the uncertain line of the pale sky. Thus seen from above, the whole landscape had the static quality of a painting: ships at anchor were crowded into one corner, the river traced its curve along the foot of the green hills, and on the water the oblong-shaped islands looked like great black fish stopped in their course. From the factory chimneys poured endless trails of brown smoke, their tips continually dissolving in the wind. The roar of foundries mingled with the clear peal of chimes that came from the churches looming in the fog. The leafless trees along the boulevards were like purple thickets in amongst the houses; and the roofs, all of them shiny with rain, gleamed with particular brilliance in the upper reaches of the town. Now and again a gust of wind blew the clouds toward the hill of Sainte-Catherine, like aerial waves breaking soundlessly against a cliff.

A kind of intoxication was wafted up to her from those closely packed lives, and her heart swelled as though the 120,000 souls palpitating below had sent up to her as a collective offering the breath of all the passions she supposed them to be feeling. In the face of the vastness her love grew larger, and was filled with a turmoil that echoed the vague ascending hum. All this love she, in turn, poured out—onto the squares, onto the tree-lined avenues, onto the streets; and to her the old Norman city was like some fabulous capital, a Babylon into which she was making her entry. She leaned far out the window and filled her lungs with air; the three horses galloped on, there was a grinding of stones in the mud beneath the wheels; the coach swayed; Hivert shouted warningly ahead to the wagons he was about to overtake, and businessmen leaving their suburban villas in Bois-Guillaume descended the hill at a respectable pace in their little family carriages.

There was a stop at the city gate: Emma took off her overshoes, changed her gloves, arranged her shawl, and twenty paces farther on she left the Hirondelle.

The city was coming to life. Clerks in caps were polishing shop windows, and women with baskets on their hips stood on street corners uttering loud, regular cries. She walked on, her eyes lowered, keeping close to the house walls and smiling happily under her lowered black veil.

For fear of being seen, she usually didn't take the shortest way. She would plunge into a maze of dark alleys, and emerge, hot and perspiring, close to the fountain at the lower end of the Rue Nationale. This is the part of town near the theater, full of bars and prostitutes. Often a van rumbled by, laden with shaky stage sets. Aproned waiters were sanding the pavement between the tubs of green bushes. There was a smell of absinthe, cigars and oysters.

Then she turned a corner. She recognized him from afar by the way his curly hair hung down below his hat.

He walked ahead on the sidewalk. She followed him to the hotel; he went upstairs, opened the door of the room, went in—What an embrace!

Then, after kisses, came a flood of words. They spoke of the troubles of the week, of their forebodings, their worries about letters; but now they could forget everything, and they looked into each other's eyes, laughing with delight and exchanging loving names.

The bed was a large mahogany one in the form of a boat. Red silk curtains hung from the ceiling and were looped back very low beside the flaring headboard, and there was nothing so lovely in the world as her dark hair and white skin against the deep crimson when she brought her bare arms together in a gesture of modesty, hiding her face in her hands.

The warm room, with its discreet carpet, its pretty knickknacks and its tranquil light, seemed designed for the intimacies of passion. The arrow-tipped curtain rods, the brass ornaments on the furniture and the big knobs on the andirons—all gleamed at once if the sun shone in. Between the candlesticks on the mantelpiece was a pair of those great pink shells that sound like the ocean when you hold them to your ear.

How they loved that sweet, cheerful room, for all its slightly faded splendor! Each piece of furniture was always waiting for them in its place, and sometimes the hairpins she had forgotten the Thursday before were still there, under the pedestal of the clock. They lunched beside the fire, on a little table inlaid with rosewood. Emma carved, murmuring all kinds of endearments as she put the pieces on his plate; and she gave a loud, wanton laugh when the champagne foamed over the fine edge of the glass onto the rings on her fingers. They were so completely lost in their possession of each other that they thought of themselves as being in their own home, destined to live there for the rest of their days, eternal young husband and eternal young wife. They said "our room," "our carpet," "our chairs"; she even said "our slippers," meaning a pair that Léon had given her to gratify a whim. They were of pink satin, trimmed with swansdown. When she sat in his lap her legs swung in the air, not reaching the floor, and the dainty slippers, open all around except at the tip, hung precariously from her bare toes.

He was savoring for the first time the ineffable subtleties of feminine refinement. Never had he encountered this grace of language, this quiet taste in dress, these relaxed, dovelike postures. He marveled at the sublimity of her soul and at the lace on her petticoat. Besides—wasn't she a "lady," and married besides? Everything, in short, that a mistress should be?

With her ever-changing moods, by turns brooding and gay, chattering and silent, fiery and casual, she aroused in him a thousand desires, awakening instincts or memories. She was the *amoureuse* of all the novels, the heroine of all the plays, the vague "she" of all the poetry books. Her shoulders were amber toned, like the bathing odalisques he had seen in pictures; she was long waisted like the feudal chatelaines; she resembled Musset's *"pâle femme de Barcelone,"*[3] too: but at all times she was less woman than angel!

Often, as he looked at her, it seemed to him that his soul, leaving him in quest of her, flowed like a wave around the outline of her head, and then was drawn down into the whiteness of her breast.

He would kneel on the floor before her, and with his elbows on her knees gaze at her smilingly, his face lifted.

She would bend toward him and murmur, as though choking with rapture: "Don't move! Don't say a word! Just look at me! There's something so sweet in your eyes, something that does me so much good!"

She called him "child": "Do you love me, child?"

She never heard his answer, so fast did his lips always rise to meet her mouth.

On the clock there was a little bronze cupid, simpering and curving its arms under a gilded wreath. They often laughed at it, but when it came time to part, everything grew serious.

Motionless, face to face, they would say, over and over: "Till Thursday! Till Thursday!"

Then she would abruptly take his face between her hands, quickly kiss him on the forehead, cry, "Adieu!" and run out into the hall.

She always went to a hairdresser in the Rue de la Comédie and had her hair brushed and put in order. Darkness would be falling; in the shops they would be lighting the gas.

She could hear the bell in the theater summoning the actors to the performance, and across the street she would see white-faced men and shabbily dressed women going in through the stage door.

It was hot in this little place with its too-low ceiling and its stove humming in the midst of wigs and pomades. The smell of the curling irons and the touch of the soft hands at work on her head soon made her drowsy, and she dozed off a little in her dressing gown. Often, as he arranged her hair, the coiffeur would ask her to buy tickets for a masked ball.

Then she was off. She retraced her way through the streets, reached the Croix-Rouge, retrieved the overshoes that she had hidden there that morning under a bench, and squeezed herself in among the impatient passengers. To spare the horses, the men got out at the foot of the hill, leaving Emma alone in the coach.

At each bend of the road more and more of the city lights came into view, making a layer of luminous mist that hung over the mass of the houses. Emma would kneel on the cushions and look back, letting her eyes wander over the brilliance. Sobs would burst from her, she would call Léon's name, and send him sweet words, and kisses that were lost in the wind.

---

3. Pale woman of Barcelona (French). Alfred de Musset (1810–1857) frequently incarnates, for Flaubert, the type of stilted romantic sensibility he despises.

On this hill road was a wretched beggar, who wandered with his stick in the midst of the traffic. His clothes were a mass of rags, and his face was hidden under a battered old felt hat that was turned down all around like a basin; when he took this off, it was to reveal two gaping, bloody sockets in place of eyelids. The flesh continually shredded off in red gobbets, and from it oozed a liquid matter, hardening into greenish scabs that reached down to his nose. His black nostrils sniffled convulsively. Whenever he began to talk, he leaned his head far back and gave an idiot laugh; and at such times his bluish eyeballs, rolling round and round, pushed up against the edges of the live wound.

As he walked beside the coaches he sang a little song:

> A clear day's warmth will often move
> A lass to stray in dreams of love . . .

And the rest of it was all about the birds, the sun, and the leaves on the trees.

Sometimes he would loom up all at once from behind Emma, bareheaded. She would draw back with a cry. Hivert always joked with him, urging him to hire a booth at the Saint-Romain fair, or laughingly asking after the health of his sweetheart.

Often while the coach was moving slowly up the hill his hat would suddenly come through the window, and he would be there, clinging with his other hand to the footboard, between the spattering wheels. His voice, at the outset a mere wail, would grow shrill. It would linger in the darkness like a plaintive cry of distress; and through the jingle of the horse bells, the rustle of the trees and the rumble of the empty coach, there was something eerie about it that gave Emma a shudder of horror. The sound spiraled down into the very depths of her soul, like a whirlwind in an abyss, and swept her off into the reaches of a boundless melancholy. But Hivert would become aware that his vehicle was weighed down on one side, and would strike out savagely at the blind man with his whip. The stinging lash would cut into his wounds, and he would drop off into the mud with a shriek.

One by one the Hirondelle's passengers would fall asleep, some with their mouths open, others with their chins on their chests, leaning on their neighbor's shoulder or with an arm in the strap, all the while rocking steadily with the motion of the coach; and the gleam of the lamp, swaying outside above the rumps of the shaft horses and shining in through the chocolate-colored calico curtains, cast blood-red shadows on all those motionless travelers. Emma, numb with sadness, would shiver under her coat; her feet would grow colder and colder, and she felt like death.

Charles would be at the house, waiting: the Hirondelle was always late on Thursdays. Then at last Madame would arrive! She would scarcely take time to kiss her little girl. Dinner wasn't ready—no matter! She forgave the cook: Félicité seemed to have everything her own way, these days.

Often her husband would notice her pallor, and ask whether she were ill.

"No," Emma would say.

"But you're acting so strangely tonight!"

"Oh, it's nothing! It's nothing!"

Some Thursdays she went up to her room almost the minute she came in. Justin would be there and would busy himself silently, cleverer at helping her than an experienced ladies' maid. He would arrange matches, candle-sticks, a book, lay out her dressing jacket, open her bed.

"Very good," she would tell him. "Now run along."

For he would be standing there, his hands at his sides and his eyes staring, as though a sudden revery had tied him to the spot with a thousand strands.

The next day was always an ordeal, and the days that followed were even more unbearable, so impatient was she to recover her happiness. It was a fierce desire that was kept aflame by the vividness of her memories, and on the seventh day burst forth freely under Léon's caresses. His transports took the form of overflowing wonderment and gratitude. Emma enjoyed this pas-sion in a way that was both deliberate and intense, keeping it alive by every amorous device at her command, and fearing all the while that someday it would come to an end.

Often she would say to him, sweetly and sadly:

"Ah! Sooner or later you'll leave me! You'll marry! You'll be like all the others."

"What others?"

"Why, men—all men."

And, languidly pushing him away, she would add: "You're faithless, every one of you!"

One day when they were having a philosophical discussion about earthly disillusionments, she went so far as to say (whether testing his jealousy, or yielding to an irresistible need to confide) that in the past, before him, she had loved someone else. "Not like you!" she quickly added; and she swore by her daughter that "nothing had happened."

The young man believed her, but nevertheless asked her what kind of man "he" had been.

"He was a sea captain," she told him.

Did she say that, perhaps, to forestall his making any inquiries, and at the same time to exalt herself by making the supposed victim of her charms sound like an imperious kind of man accustomed to having his way?

This impressed upon the clerk the mediocrity of his own status: he longed to have epaulettes, decorations and titles. Such things must be to her liking, he suspected, judging by her spendthrift ways.

There were a number of her wildest ideas, however, that Emma never said a word about, such as her craving to be driven to Rouen in a blue tilbury drawn by an English horse, with a groom in turned-down boots on the seat. It was Justin who had inspired her with this particular fancy, by begging her to take him into her service as footman; and though being deprived of it didn't prevent her from enjoying each weekly arrival in the city, it certainly added to the bitterness of each return to Yonville.

Often, when they spoke of Paris, she would murmur:

"Ah! How happy we'd be, living there!"

"Aren't we happy here?" the young man would softly ask, passing his hand over her hair.

"Of course we are! I'm being foolish. Kiss me!"

With her husband she was more charming than ever; she made him pis-tachio creams and played waltzes for him after dinner. He considered himself the luckiest of mortals, and Emma had no fear of discovery—until suddenly, one evening:

"It is Mademoiselle Lempereur you take lessons from, isn't it?"

"Yes."

"Well, I just saw her," said Charles, "at Madame Liégeard's. I talked to her about you: she doesn't know you."

It was like a thunderbolt. But she answered in a natural tone.

"Oh, she must have forgotten my name."

"Or else maybe there's more than one Mademoiselle Lempereur in Rouen who teaches piano."

"Maybe so."

Then, quickly:

"Besides, it just occurs to me: I have her receipts. Look!"

And she went to the secretary, rummaged in all the drawers, mixed up all the papers, and finally grew so rattled that Charles begged her not to go to so much trouble for a few wretched receipts.

"Oh, I'll find them," she said.

And indeed, the following Friday, while Charles was putting on one of his shoes in the dark dressing room where his clothes were kept, he felt a piece of paper between the sole and his sock, and pulled it out and read:

"Three months' lessons, plus supplies. Sixty-five francs. Paid. Félicité Lempereur, *Professeur de musique*."

"How the devil did this get in my shoe?"

"It probably fell down from the old bill file on the shelf."

From that moment on, she piled lie upon lie, using them as veils to conceal her love.

Lying became a need, a mania, a positive joy—to such a point that if she said that she had walked down the right-hand side of a street the day before, it meant that she had gone down the left.

One morning just after she had gone, rather lightly clad as usual, there was a sudden snowfall; and Charles, looking out the window at the weather, saw Monsieur Bournisien setting out for Rouen in Monsieur Tuvache's buggy. So he ran down with a heavy shawl and asked the priest to give it to Madame as soon as he got to the Croix-Rouge. The moment he reached the inn, Bournisien asked where the wife of the Yonville doctor was. The hotel keeper replied that she spent very little time there. That evening, therefore, finding Madame Bovary in the Hirondelle, the curé told her of the *contretemps*: he seemed to attach little importance to it, however, for he launched into praise of a preacher, the sensation at the cathedral, adored by all the ladies.

Still, though he hadn't asked for explanations, others, in the future, might be less discreet. So she thought it practical to take a room each time at the Croix-Rouge, in order that her fellow villagers might see her there and have no suspicion.

One day, however, Monsieur Lheureux ran into her as she was leaving the Hotel de Boulogne on Léon's arm. She was frightened, thinking that he might talk. He was too smart for that.

But three days later he came into her room, closed the door, and said:

"I'd like some money."

She declared that she had none to give him. Lheureux began to moan, and reminded her of how many times he'd gone out of his way to oblige her.

And indeed, of the two notes signed by Charles, Emma had so far paid off only one. As for the second, the shopkeeper had agreed at her request to replace it with two others, which themselves had been renewed for a very long term. Then he drew out of his pocket a list of goods still unpaid for: the curtains, the carpet, upholstery material for armchairs, several dresses and various toilet articles, totaling about two thousand francs.

She hung her head.

"You may not have any cash," he said, "but you do have some property."

And he mentioned a wretched, tumbledown cottage situated at Barneville, near Aumale, which didn't bring in very much. It had once been part of a small farm that the elder Bovary had sold: Lheureux knew everything, down to the acreage and the neighbors' names.

"If I were you I'd get rid of it," he said. "You'd still have a balance after paying me."

She brought up the difficulty of finding a buyer; he was encouraging about the possibility of locating one. But: "What would I have to do to be able to sell?" she asked.

"Haven't you power of attorney?" he countered.

The words came to her like a breath of fresh air.

"Leave your bill with me," said Emma.

"Oh, it's not worth bothering about," replied Lheureux.

He came again the following week, very proud of having unearthed, after a lot of trouble, a certain Monsieur Langlois, who had been eying the property for a long time without ever mentioning the price he was willing to pay.

"The price doesn't matter!" she cried.

On the contrary, he said: they should take their time, sound Langlois out. The affair was worth the bother of a trip, and since she couldn't make it he offered to go himself and talk things over with Langlois on the spot. On his return he announced that the buyer offered 4,000 francs.

Emma beamed at the news.

"Frankly," he said, "it's a good price."

Half the amount was paid her at once, and when she said that now she'd settle his bill, he told her:

"Honestly, it hurts me to see you hand over every bit of all that money right away."

She stared at the banknotes and had a vision of the countless love-meetings those 2,000 francs represented. "What?" she stammered. "What do you mean?"

"Oh," he said, with a jovial laugh, "there's more than one way of making out a bill. Don't you think I know how it is with married couples?"

And he stared at her, running his fingernails up and down two long sheets of paper he had in his hand. After a long moment he opened his billfold and spread out on the table four more promissory notes, each for a thousand francs.

"Sign these," he said, "and keep all the money."

She gave a choked cry.

"But if I give you the balance," Monsieur Lheureux answered, "don't you see that I'm doing you a service?"

And taking up a pen he wrote at the bottom of the bill: "Received from Madame Bovary the sum of 4,000 francs."

"What's there to worry you? In six months you'll have the rest of the money due on your cottage, and I'll make the last note payable after that date."

She was getting a little mixed up in her arithmetic, and she felt a ringing in her ears as though gold pieces were bursting out of their bags and dropping to the floor all about her. Finally Lheureux explained that he had a friend named Vinçart, a Rouen banker, who would discount these four new notes, following which he himself would pay Madame the balance of what was really owed.

But instead of 2,000 francs, he brought her only 1,800; for his friend Vinçart (as was "only right") had deducted 200, representing commission and discount.

Then he casually asked for a receipt.

"You know . . . in business . . . sometimes . . . And put down the date, please, the date."

A host of things that she could do with the money stretched out before Emma in perspective. She had enough sense to put 3,000 francs aside, and with them she paid, as they came due, the first three notes; but the fourth, as luck would have it, arrived at the house on a Thursday; and Charles, stunned, patiently awaited his wife's return to have it explained to him.

Ah! If she hadn't told him anything about that note it was because she hadn't wanted to bother him with household worries; she sat in his lap, caressed him, cooed at him, and gave a long list of all the indispensables she had bought on credit.

"You'll have to admit," she said, "that considering how many things there were, the bill's not too high."

Charles, at his wits' end, soon had recourse to the inevitable Lheureux, who promised to straighten everything out if Monsieur would sign two more notes, one of them for 700 francs, payable in three months. Charles wrote a pathetic letter to his mother, asking for help. Instead of sending an answer, she came herself; and when Emma asked him if he'd got anything out of her:

"Yes," he answered. "But she insists on seeing the bill."

So early the next morning Emma rushed to Monsieur Lheureux and begged him to make out a different note, for not more than 1,000 francs, for if she were to show the one for 4,000 she would have to say that she had paid off two-thirds of it, and consequently reveal the sale of the cottage. That transaction had been handled very cleverly by the shopkeeper, and never did leak out until later.

Despite the low price of each article, the elder Madame Bovary naturally found such expenditure excessive.

"Couldn't you get along without a carpet? Why re-cover the armchairs? In my day every house had exactly one armchair, for elderly persons—at least, that's the way it was at my mother's, and she was a respectable woman, I assure you. Everybody can't be rich! No amount of money will last if you throw it out the window. It would make me blush to pamper myself the way you do—and I'm an old woman and need looking after. . . . Who's ever seen so much finery? What, silk for linings at two francs when you can find jaconet for half a franc and even less that does perfectly well?"

Emma, stretched out on the settee, answered with the greatest calm:

"That's enough, Madame, that's enough."

Her mother-in-law continued to sermonize, prophesying that they'd end in the poorhouse. Besides, it was all Bovary's fault, she said. At least, though, he'd promised her he'd cancel the power of attorney.

"What!"

"Yes, he's given me his word," said the lady.

Emma opened the window and called Charles in, and the poor fellow had to confess the promise his mother had extracted from him.

Emma disappeared, then quickly returned, majestically holding out to her a large sheet of paper.

"I thank you," said the old woman.

And she threw the power of attorney into the fire.

Emma burst out laughing and didn't stop: her laughter was loud and strident—it was an attack of hysterics.

"Ah, my God!" cried Charles. "You're overdoing things, too! You've no right to come here and make scenes."

His mother shrugged her shoulders and said that "it was all put on."

But Charles, rebellious for the first time in his life, took his wife's part, and the older Madame Bovary said she wanted to go. She departed the next day, and on the doorstep, as he was trying to make her change her mind, she answered:

"No! No! You love her more than you do me, and you're right; that's as it should be. There's nothing I can do about it. You'll see, though . . . Take care of yourself . . . I can promise you it will be a long time before I come back here to 'make scenes,' as you put it."

Nevertheless Charles was very hangdog with Emma, and she didn't hide her resentment at having been distrusted. He had to entreat her many times before she would consent to accept power of attorney again, and he even went with her to Maître Guillaumin to have a new one drawn up, identical with the first.

"I well understand your doing this," said the notary. "A man of science can't be expected to burden himself with the practical details of existence."

Charles felt soothed by those oily words: they flattered his weakness, making it look like preoccupation with lofty things.

What exultation there was the next Thursday in their room at the hotel, with Léon! She laughed, cried, sang, danced, sent for water ices, insisted on smoking cigarettes. He found her wild, but adorable, superb.

He had no idea what it was that was driving her more and more to fling herself into a reckless pursuit of pleasure. She grew irritable, greedy, voluptuous; and she walked boldly with him in the street—unafraid, she said, of compromising herself. There were times, though, when Emma trembled at the sudden thought of meeting Rodolphe, for she suspected that even though they had parted forever, he still retained some of his power over her.

One night she didn't return to Yonville at all. Charles lost his head, and little Berthe, unwilling to go to bed without *maman*, sobbed as though her heart would break. Justin had gone off down the road to look for her. Monsieur Homais actually stepped out of his pharmacy.

Finally, at eleven o'clock, unable to stand it any longer, Charles harnessed his buggy, jumped in, whipped the horse on, and reached the Croix-Rouge at two in the morning. No sign of her. It occurred to him that Léon might have seen her: but where did he live? Luckily, Charles remembered the address of his employer, and he hastened there.

The sky was beginning to lighten. He made out some escutcheons over a door, and knocked. Without opening, someone shouted the information he wanted, together with a good deal of abuse about people who disturb other people at night.

The house the clerk lived in boasted neither bell nor knocker nor doorman. Charles pounded with his fists on the shutters, but just then a policeman came along: this frightened him, and he slunk away.

"I'm crazy," he told himself. "The Lormeauxes probably kept her to dinner."

But the Lormeauxes no longer lived in Rouen.

"She must have stayed to look after Madame Dubreuil. Oh, no—Madame Dubreuil died ten months ago. So where can she be?"

He had an idea. In a café he asked for the directory and looked up Mademoiselle Lempereur: 74 Rue de la Renelle-des-Maroquiniers was her address.

Just as he turned into that street, Emma herself appeared at the other end. It would be wrong to say that he embraced her: he flung himself on her, crying:

"What kept you, yesterday?"

"I was ill."

"Ill? How? Where?"

She passed her hand over her forehead:

"At Mademoiselle Lempereur's."

"I knew it! I was on my way there."

"Well, there's no use going there now. She's just gone out. But after this don't get so excited. I won't feel free to do a thing if I know that the slightest delay upsets you like this."

It was a kind of permit that she was giving herself—a permit to feel completely unhampered in her escapades. And she proceeded to make free and frequent use of it. Whenever she felt like seeing Léon, she would go off, using any excuse that came to mind; and since he wouldn't be expecting her that day, she would call for him at his office.

It was all very joyous, the first few times. But before long he stopped hiding the truth from her: his employer was complaining loudly of these incursions.

"Bah!" she said. "Come along."

And he slipped out.

She demanded that he dress entirely in black and grow a little pointed beard, to make himself look like the portraits of Louis XIII.[4] She asked to see his rooms, and found them very so-so; he reddened at that, but she didn't notice, and advised him to buy curtains like hers. When he objected to the expense:

"Ah! So you pinch your pennies!" she said, laughing.

Each time, Léon had to tell her everything he had done since their last rendezvous. She asked for a poem, a poem for herself, a love piece written in her honor: he could never find a rhyme for the second line, and ended up copying a sonnet from a keepsake.

He did that less out of vanity than out of a desire to please her. He never disputed any of her ideas; he fell in with all her tastes: he was becoming her

4. French king (1601–1643), who ruled 1610–43; the father of Louis XIV.

mistress, far more than she was his. Her sweet words and her kisses swept away his soul. Her depravity was so deep and so dissembled as to be almost intangible: where could she have learned it?

VI

On his trips to see her he had often taken dinner at the pharmacist's, and he felt obliged out of politeness to invite him in return.

"With pleasure!" Homais answered. "A change will do me good: my life here is such a rut. We'll see a show and eat in a restaurant and really go out on the town."

"Out on the town!" Madame Homais' exclamation was affectionate: she was alarmed by the vague perils he was girding himself to meet.

"Why shouldn't I? Don't you think I ruin my health enough, exposing myself to all those drug fumes? That's women for you! They're jealous of Science, and yet they're up in arms at the mention of even the most legitimate distraction. Never mind, I'll be there. One of these days I'll turn up in Rouen, and we'll turn the town upside down."

In the past, the apothecary would have been careful to avoid such an expression; but now he was going in for a daredevil, Parisian kind of language that he considered very à la mode, and like his neighbor Madame Bovary he asked the clerk many searching questions about life in the big city. He even talked slang in order to show off in front of the "bourgeois," using such terms as *turne, bazar, chicard, chicanard,* the English "Breda Street" for Rue de Bréda and *je me la casse* for *je m'en vais.*[5]

So one Thursday Emma was surprised to find, in the kitchen of the Lion d'Or, none other than Monsieur Homais in traveling garb—that is, wrapped in an old cape that no one had ever seen on him before, with a suitcase in one hand and in the other the foot warmer from his shop. He hadn't breathed a word about his trip to anyone, fearing lest the public be made nervous by his absence.

The idea of revisiting the scenes of his youth apparently excited him, for he didn't stop talking all the way. The wheels had barely stopped turning when he leapt from the coach in search of Léon; and despite the clerk's struggles he dragged him off to lunch at the Café de Normandie. Here Monsieur Homais made a majestic entrance: he kept his hat on, considering it highly provincial to uncover in a public place.

Emma waited for Léon three-quarters of an hour, then rushed to his office. She was at a loss as to what could have happened: in her mind she heaped him with reproaches for his indifference and herself for her weakness; all afternoon she stood with her forehead glued to the windowpanes of their room.

At two o'clock Léon and Homais were still facing each other across their table. The big dining room was emptying; the stovepipe, designed to resemble a palm tree, spread out in a circle of gilded fronds on the white ceiling; and near them, just inside the window, in full sun, a little fountain gurgled into a marble basin, where among watercress and asparagus three sluggish lobsters stretched their claws toward a heap of quail.

5. I'm leaving. *Turne:* sweet. *Bazar:* fabulous. *Chicard:* "in." *Chicanard:* con artist. *Je me la casse:* I'm breaking (out). (All these terms are French.)

Homais was in heaven. He found the *luxe* even more intoxicating than the fine food and drink; still, the Pommard went to his head a little; and when the rum omelet made its appearance he advanced certain immoral theories concerning women. What particularly captivated him was the quality of *chic*. He adored an elegant *toilette* in a handsome *décor,* and as for physical qualities, he wasn't averse to a "plump little morsel."

Léon desperately watched the clock. The apothecary kept drinking, eating, talking.

"You must feel quite deprived, here in Rouen," he suddenly remarked. "But then, your lady-love doesn't live *too* far away."

And as Léon blushed:

"Come, be frank! You won't deny, will you, that in Yonville . . ."

The young man began to stammer.

". . . at the Bovarys', you did quite some courting of . . ."

"Of whom?"

"Of the maid!"

Homais wasn't joking. But Léon's vanity got the better of his discretion, and despite himself he protested indignantly. Besides, he said, he liked only brunettes.

"I approve your preference," said the pharmacist. "They have more temperament."

And putting his mouth close to his friend's ear, he enumerated the sure signs of temperament in a woman. He even launched into an ethnographical digression: German women were moody, French women licentious, Italian women passionate.

"What about Negro women?" demanded the clerk.

"Much favored by artists," said Homais. "Waiter—two demitasses!"

"Shall we go?" said Léon finally, his patience at an end.

"*Yes,*" said Homais, in English.

But before leaving he insisted on seeing the manager, and offered him his congratulations.

Léon, in the hope of being left alone, now pleaded a business appointment.

"Ah! I'll go with you!" said Homais.

And as he accompanied him through the streets he talked about his wife, about his children, about their future, about his pharmacy, told him in what a rundown state he had found it and to what a peak of perfection he had brought it.

When they reached the Hotel de Boulogne, Léon brusquely took leave of him, ran upstairs and found his mistress close to hysterics.

The mention of the pharmacist's name put her into a rage. He pleaded his case persuasively: it wasn't his fault—surely she knew Monsieur Homais. Could she think for a moment that he preferred his company? But she turned away; he caught hold of her, and winding his arms around her waist he sank to his knees, languorous, passionate, imploring.

She stood there, solemn, almost terrible, transfixing him with her great blazing eyes. Then tears came to cloud them, she lowered her reddened eyelids, held out her hands, and Léon was just pressing them to his lips when a servant knocked and said that someone was asking for Monsieur.

"You'll come back?" she said.

"Yes."

"When?"

"Right away."

"How do you like my little trick?" said the pharmacist, when Léon appeared. "I wanted to help you get away from your company: you gave me the impression you didn't expect to enjoy it. Let's go to Bridoux's and have a glass of cordial."

Léon insisted that he had to return to his office. The apothecary made facetious remarks about legal papers and legal flummery.

"Forget about Cujas and Barthole[6] for a bit, for heaven's sake. Who's to stop you? Be a sport. Let's go to Bridoux's. You'll see his dog: it's very interesting."

And when the clerk stubbornly held out:

"I'll come, too. I'll read a newspaper while I wait, or look through a law book."

Overcome by Emma's anger, Monsieur Homais' chatter, and perhaps by the heavy lunch, Léon stood undecided, as though under the pharmacist's spell.

"Let's go to Bridoux's!" the latter kept repeating. "It's only a step from here—Rue Malpalu."

Out of cowardice or stupidity, or perhaps yielding to that indefinable impulse that leads us to do the things we most deplore, he let himself be carried off to Bridoux's. They found him in his little yard, superintending three workmen who were pantingly turning the great wheel of a Seltzer-water machine. Homais offered them several bits of advice and embraced Bridoux; they had their cordial. Twenty times Léon started to leave, but the pharmacist caught him by the arm, saying:

"Just a minute! I'm coming. We'll go to the *Fanal de Rouen* and say hello to everybody. I'll introduce you to Thomassin."

He got rid of him, however, and flew to the hotel. Emma was gone.

She had just left in a fury. She hated him. His failure to keep their appointment seemed to her an insult, and she sought additional reasons for seeing no more of him. He was unheroic, weak, commonplace, spineless as a woman, and stingy and timorous to boot.

Gradually, growing calmer, she came to see that she had been unjust to him. But casting aspersions on those we love always does something to loosen our ties. We shouldn't maltreat our idols: the gilt comes off on our hands.

From then on, matters extraneous to their love occupied a greater place in their talk. The letters that Emma sent him were all about flowers, poetry, the moon and the stars: she resorted to these naïve expedients as her passion weakened, trying to keep it alive by artificial means. She continually promised herself that the next rendezvous would carry her to the peak of bliss; but when it was over she had to admit that she had felt nothing extraordinary. Each disappointment quickly gave way to new hope; each time, Emma returned to him more feverish, more avid. She could hardly wait to undress: she pulled so savagely at her corset string that it hissed around her hips like a gliding snake. Then she would tiptoe barefoot to see once again that the door was locked, and in a single movement let fall all her clothes; and, pale,

6. Or Bartole (1313–1357), an Italian jurist in Bologna. Jacques Cujas (1552–1590), a famous jurist who interpreted Roman law in contemporary terms.

silent, solemn, she would fling herself against his body with a long shudder.

There was something mad, though, something strange and sinister, about that cold, sweating forehead, about those stammering lips, those wildly staring eyes, the clasp of those arms—something that seemed to Léon to be creeping between them, subtly, as though to tear them apart.

He didn't dare question her; but realizing how experienced she was, he told himself that she must have known the utmost extremes of suffering and pleasure. What had once charmed him he now found a little frightening. Then, too, he rebelled against the way his personality was increasingly being submerged: he resented her perpetual triumph over him. He even did his best to stop loving her; then at the sound of her footsteps he would feel his will desert him, like a drunkard at the sight of strong liquor.

She made a point, it is true, of showering him with all kinds of attentions— everything from fine foods to coquetries of dress and languorous glances. She brought roses from Yonville in her bosom and tossed them at him; she worried over his health, gave him advice about how to conduct himself; and one day, to bind him the closer, hoping that heaven itself might take a hand in things, she slipped over his head a medal of the Blessed Virgin. Like a virtuous mother, she inquired about his associates:

"Don't see them," she would say. "Don't go out. Just think about us: love me!"

She wished she could keep an eye on him continually, and it occurred to her to have him followed on the street. There was a kind of tramp near the hotel who always accosted travelers and who would certainly be willing to . . . But her pride rebelled.

"What if he does betray me? Do I care?"

One day when they had said farewell earlier than usual, she caught sight of the walls of her convent as she was walking back alone down the boulevard, and she sank onto a bench in the shade of the elms. How peaceful those days had been! How she had longed for that ineffable emotion of love that she had tried to imagine from her books!

The first months of her marriage, her rides in the forest, the vicomte she had waltzed with, Lagardy singing—all passed again before her eyes. And Léon suddenly seemed as far removed as the others.

"I do love him, though!" she told herself.

No matter: she wasn't happy, and never had been. Why was life so unsatisfactory? Why did everything she leaned on crumble instantly to dust? But why, if somewhere there existed a strong and handsome being—a man of valor, sublime in passion and refinement, with a poet's heart and an angel's shape, a man like a lyre with strings of bronze, intoning elegiac epithalamiums to the heavens—why mightn't she have the luck to meet him? Ah, fine chance! Besides, nothing was worth looking for: everything was a lie! Every smile concealed a yawn of boredom; every joy, a curse; every pleasure, its own surfeit; and the sweetest kisses left on one's lips but a vain longing for fuller delight.

Through the air came a hoarse, prolonged metallic groan, and then the clock of the convent struck four. Only four! And it seemed to her that she had been there on that bench since eternity. But an infinity of passions can be compressed into a minute, like a crowd into a little space. Emma's passions were the sole concern of her life: for money she had no more thought than an archduchess.

One day, however, she was visited by an ill-kempt individual, red faced and bald, who said he had been sent by Monsieur Vinçart of Rouen. He pulled out the pins fastening the side pocket of his long green frock coat, stuck them in his sleeve, and politely handed her a document.

It was a note for 500 francs, signed by her, which Lheureux, despite all his promises, had endorsed over to Vinçart.

She sent her maid for Lheureux. He couldn't come.

The stranger had remained standing, dissimulating under his thick blond eyebrows the inquisitive glances that he cast left and right. "What answer am I to give Monsieur Vinçart?" he asked, with an innocent air.

"Well," said Emma, "tell him . . . that I haven't got . . . I'll have it next week. . . . He should wait . . . yes, I'll have it next week."

Whereupon the fellow went off without a word.

But the next day, at noon, she received a protest of nonpayment; and the sight of the official document, bearing the words "Maître Hareng, *huissier* at Buchy" several times in large letters, gave her such a fright that she hurried to the dry-goods merchant.

She found him in his shop tying up a parcel.

"At your service!" he said. "What can I do for you?"

He didn't interrupt his task: his clerk, a slightly hunchbacked girl of thirteen or so, who also did his cooking, was helping him.

Finally he clattered across the shop in his wooden shoes, climbed up ahead of Madame to the second floor, and showed her into a small office. Here on a large fir desk lay several ledgers, fastened down by a padlocked metal bar that stretched across them. A safe could be glimpsed against the wall, under some lengths of calico—a safe of such size that it certainly contained something besides cash and promissory notes. And indeed Monsieur Lheureux did some pawnbroking: it was here that he kept Madame Bovary's gold chain, along with some earrings that had belonged to poor Tellier. The latter had finally had to sell the Café Français, and had since bought a little grocery business in Quincampoix, where he was dying of his catarrh, his face yellower than the tallow candles he sold.

Lheureux sat down in his broad, rush-bottomed armchair.

"What's new?" he asked her.

"Look!"

And she showed him the document.

"Well, what can I do about it?"

She flew into a rage, reminding him that he had promised not to endorse her notes. He admitted it.

"But my hand was forced: my creditors had a knife at my throat."

"And what's going to happen now?" she asked.

"Oh, it's very simple: a court warrant, then execution; there's no way out."

Emma had to restrain herself from hitting him. She asked quietly whether there wasn't some way of appeasing Monsieur Vinçart.

"Ha! Appease Vinçart! You don't know him: he's fiercer than an Arab."

But Monsieur Lheureux *had* to do something about it!

"Now listen!" he said. "It seems to me I've been pretty nice to you so far."

And opening one of his ledgers:
"Look!"

He moved his finger up the page:

"Let's see . . . let's see . . . August 3,200 francs . . . June 17, 150 . . . March 23, 46. In April . . ."

He stopped, as though afraid of making a blunder.

"I won't even mention the notes your husband signed, one for seven hundred francs, another for three hundred. And as for your payments on account, and the interest, there's no end to it. It's a mess. I won't have anything more to do with it."

She wept; she even called him her "dear Monsieur Lheureux." But he kept laying the blame on "that scoundrelly Vinçart." Besides, he himself didn't have a centime: no one was paying him at the moment; his creditors were tearing the clothes from his back; a poor shopkeeper like himself couldn't advance money.

Emma stopped speaking; and Monsieur Lheureux, nibbling the quill of his pen, seemed disturbed by her silence.

"Of course," he said, "if I were to have something come in one of these days I might . . ."

"After all," she said, "as soon as the balance on Barneville . . ."

"What's that?"

And when he heard that Langlois hadn't yet paid he seemed very surprised. Then, in an oily voice:

"And our terms will be . . . ?"

"Oh, anything you say!"

Then he shut his eyes to help himself think, wrote down a few figures, and assuring her that he was making things hard for himself, taking a great risk, "bleeding himself white," he made out four notes for 250 francs each, payable a month apart.

"Let's hope that Vinçart's willing to listen to me! Anyway, you have my word: I don't say one thing and mean another; I'm open and aboveboard."

Afterwards he casually showed her a few items, not one of which, in his opinion, was worthy of Madame.

"When I think of dress goods like this selling at seven sous a meter and guaranteed dye-fast! Everybody believes it, too! And they don't get undeceived. I can assure you." The admission that he swindled others was meant as clinching proof of his frankness with herself.

Then he called her back and showed her several yards of point lace that he had come upon recently "in a vendue."

"Isn't it splendid?" he said. "It's being used a good deal now for antimacassars: it's the last word."

And quicker than a juggler he wrapped up the lace and handed it to Emma.

"At least," she said, "let me know how much it . . ."

"Oh, we'll talk about that later," he answered, turning abruptly away.

That very evening she made Bovary write his mother and ask her to send the balance of his inheritance at once. Her mother-in-law replied that there was nothing to send: the estate was settled, and in addition to Barneville they could count on a yearly income of 600 francs, which she would forward punctually.

So Madame sent bills to two or three patients, and before long she was sending them to many more, so successful did the expedient prove. She was always careful to add, in a postscript: "Don't speak of this to my husband—you know how proud he is. With regrets. Your humble servant." There were a few complaints, but she intercepted them.

To raise money she began to sell her old gloves, her old hats, all kinds of household odds and ends. She drove a hard bargain: her peasant blood stood her in good stead. And on her trips to the city she combed the curiosity shops for knickknacks, telling herself that Monsieur Lheureux, if no one else, would take them off her hands. She brought ostrich feathers, Chinese porcelains, old chests; she borrowed from Félicité, from Madame Lefrançois, from the landlady of the Croix-Rouge, from anyone and everyone. With part of the money she finally got from Barneville, she paid off two notes, the rest—1,500 francs—dribbled away. She signed new notes—always new notes.

Occasionally she tried to add up some figures, but the totals were so enormous that she couldn't believe them. Then she'd begin all over again, quickly become confused, and push it all aside and forget it.

The house was a gloomy place these days. Tradesmen called, and left with angry faces. Handkerchiefs lay strewn about on the stoves; and Madame Homais was shocked to see little Berthe with holes in her stockings. If Charles ventured some timid remark, Emma retorted savagely that *she* certainly wasn't to blame.

Why these fits of rage? He laid it all to her old nervous illness; and, penitent at having mistaken her infirmities for faults, he cursed his selfishness and longed to run up to her and take her in his arms.

"Oh, no!" he told himself. "I'd only annoy her."

And he did nothing.

After dinner he would walk alone in the garden. Then, with little Berthe in his lap and his medical journal open, he would try to teach the child to read. But she had never been given the slightest schooling, and after a few moments her eyes would grow round and sad, and the tears would come. He would comfort her: he filled the watering can to help her make rivulets in the paths, or broke privet branches that she could plant as trees in the flower beds. None of this harmed the garden, particularly—it was so choked with high grass anyway: they owed so many days' pay to Lestiboudois! Then the little girl would feel chilly and ask for her mother.

"Call Félicité," Charles would tell her. "You know *maman* doesn't like to be disturbed."

It was the onset of autumn, and already the leaves were falling—like two years before, when she had been so ill. When would there be an end to all this? And he would walk up and down, his hands behind his back.

Madame was in her room. No one else was admitted. She stayed there all day long in a torpor, not bothering to dress, now and again burning incense that she had bought at an Algerian shop in Rouen. She couldn't stand having Charles lying like a log at her side all night, and her repeated complaints finally drove him to sleep in the attic. She would read till morning—lurid novels full of orgies and bloodshed.

Sometimes, in sudden terror, she screamed; but when Charles ran in she dismissed him:

"Oh, get out."

At other times, seared by that hidden fire which her adultery kept feeding, consumed with longing, feverish with desire, she would open her window, inhale the cold air, let the heavy mass of her hair stream out in the wind: as she gazed at the stars she wished she were loved by a prince. Thoughts of Léon filled her. At such moments she would have given anything for a single one of their trysts—the trysts that sated her lust.

Those were her gala days. She was determined that they be glorious; and when he couldn't pay for everything himself she freely made up the difference. This happened almost every time. He tried to convince her that they would be just as well off elsewhere, in a more modest hotel, but she always objected.

One day she opened her bag, produced six little silver-gilt spoons—they had been her father's wedding present—and asked him to run out and pawn them for her. Léon obeyed, though he disliked the errand: he was afraid it might compromise him.

Thinking it over later, he came to the conclusion that his mistress was certainly beginning to act strangely: maybe the people who were urging him to break with her weren't so mistaken after all.

For indeed someone had sent his mother a long anonymous letter, warning her that he was "ruining himself with a married woman"; and the lady, having visions of the perennial bogey of respectable families—that ill-defined, baleful female, that siren, that fantastic monster forever lurking in the abysses of love—wrote to Maître Bocage, his employer. This gentleman's handling of the matter was flawless. He talked to the young man for three-quarters of an hour, trying to unseal his eyes and warn him of the precipice ahead. Sooner or later, such an affair would harm his career. He begged him to break it off—and if he couldn't make the sacrifice for his own sake, then he should at least do it for his—namely, for the sake of Maître Bocage.

In the end Léon had promised never to see Emma again; and he reproached himself for not having kept his word, especially considering all the trouble and reproaches she still probably held in store for him—not to mention the jokes his fellow clerks cracked every morning around the stove. Besides, he was about to be promoted to head clerk: this was the time to turn over a new leaf. So he gave up playing the flute and said good-bye to exalted sentiments and romantic dreams. There isn't a bourgeois alive who in the ferment of his youth, if only for a day or for a minute, hasn't thought himself capable of boundless passions and noble exploits. The sorriest little woman-chaser has dreamed of Oriental queens; in a corner of every notary's heart lie the moldy remains of a poet.

These days it only bored him when Emma suddenly burst out sobbing on his breast: like people who can stand only a certain amount of music, he was drowsy and apathetic amidst the shrillness of her love; his heart had grown deaf to its subtler overtones.

By now they knew each other too well: no longer did they experience, in their mutual possession, that wonder that multiplies the joy a hundredfold. She was as surfeited with him as he was tired of her. Adultery, Emma was discovering, could be as banal as marriage.

But what way out was there? She felt humiliated by the degradation of such pleasures; but to no avail: she continued to cling to them, out of habit or out of depravity; and every day she pursued them more desperately, destroying all possible happiness by her excessive demands. She blamed Léon for her disappointed hopes, as though he had betrayed her; and she even longed for a catastrophe that would bring about their separation, since she hadn't the courage to bring it about herself.

Still, she continued to write him loving letters, faithful to the idea that a woman must always write her lover.

But as her pen flew over the paper she was aware of the presence of another man, a phantom embodying her most ardent memories, the most beautiful things she had read and her strongest desires. In the end he became so real and accessible that she tingled with excitement, unable though she was to picture him clearly, so hidden was he, godlike, under his manifold attributes. He dwelt in that enchanted realm where silken ladders swing from balconies moon-bright and flower-scented. She felt him near her: he was coming—coming to ravish her entirely in a kiss. And the next moment she would drop back to earth, shattered; for these rapturous love-dreams drained her more than the greatest orgies.

She lived these days in a state of constant and total exhaustion. She was continually receiving writs—official documents that she barely looked at. She wished she were dead, or in a state of continual sleep.

The Thursday night of the mi-carême—the mid-Lenten festivities—she didn't return to Yonville, but went to a masked ball. She wore velvet knee breeches and red stockings and a peruke, and a cocked hat over one ear. She danced all night to the wild sound of trombones; she was the center of an admiring throng; and morning found her under the portico of the theatre with five or six maskers dressed as stevedores and sailors—friends of Léon's, who were wondering where they might have something to eat.

The nearby cafés were all full. On the river front they found a nondescript restaurant whose owner showed them up to a little room on the fifth floor.

The men whispered in a corner, doubtless consulting about the expense. A clerk, two medical students and a shop assistant: what company she was keeping! As for the women, Emma was quickly aware from their voices that most of them must be of the lowest class. That frightened her, and she drew back her chair and lowered her eyes.

The others began to eat. She did not. Her forehead was afire, her eyelids were smarting, her skin was icy cold. In her head she still felt the quaking of the dance floor under the rhythmic tread of a thousand feet. The smell of punch and cigar smoke made her dizzy. She fainted, and they carried her to the window.

Day was beginning to break, and in the pale sky toward Sainte-Catherine a large streak of red was widening. The leaden river shivered in the wind; the bridges were empty; the street lamps were going out.

Gradually she revived, and somehow she thought of Berthe, asleep out there beyond the horizon, in Félicité's room. But a wagon laden with long strips of iron went by, and the impact of its metallic clang shook the house walls.

Abruptly, she left the place. She took off her costume, told Léon she had to go home, and at last was alone in the Hotel de Boulogne. She loathed everything, including herself. She longed to fly away like a bird, to recapture her youth somewhere far away in the immaculate reaches of space.

She went out, followed the boulevard, crossed the Place Cauchoise and walked through the outskirts of the city to an open street overlooking gardens. She walked swiftly; the fresh air calmed her; and gradually the faces of the crowd, the maskers, the quadrilles, the blazing lights, the supper, and those women she had found herself with all disappeared like mist blown off by the wind. Then she returned to the Croix-Rouge and flung herself down on her bed in the little third-floor room with the prints of the Tour de Nesle. At four that afternoon Hivert woke her.

When she arrived home Félicité showed her a gray sheet of paper stuck behind the clock.

"By virtue of an instrument," she read, "duly setting forth the terms of a judgment to be enforced . . ."

What judgment? The previous day, she found, another paper had arrived; she hadn't seen it; and now she was dumbfounded to read these words:

"To Madame Bovary: You are hereby commanded by order of the king, the law and the courts . . ."

Then, skipping several lines, she saw:

"Within twenty-four hours." What was this? "Pay the total amount of 8,000 francs." And lower down: "There to be subjected to all due processes of law, and notably to execution of distraint upon furniture and effects."

What was to be done? In twenty-four hours: tomorrow! Lheureux, she thought, was probably trying to frighten her again. Suddenly she saw through all his schemes; the reason for his amiability burst upon her. What reassured her was the very enormity of the amount.

Nonetheless, as a result of buying and never paying, borrowing, signing notes and then renewing those same notes, which grew larger and larger each time they came due, she had gradually built up a capital for Monsieur Lheureux that he was impatient to lay his hands on to use in his speculations.

She called on him, assuming a nonchalant air.

"You know what's happened? It's a joke, I suppose?"

"No."

"What do you mean?"

He slowly turned his head away and folded his arms.

"Did you think, my dear lady," he said, "that I was going to go on to the end of time being your supplier and banker just for the love of God? I have to get back what I laid out: let's be fair!"

She was indignant about the size of the amount claimed.

"What can I do about it? The court upheld it. There's a judgment. You were notified. Besides, I have nothing to do with it—it's Vinçart."

"Couldn't you . . . ?"

"Absolutely nothing."

"But . . . still . . . let's talk it over."

And she stammered incoherently that she had known nothing about it, that the whole thing had come as a surprise. . . .

"Whose fault is that?" said Lheureux, with an ironic bow. "I work like a slave, and you go out enjoying yourself."

"Ah! No preaching!"

"It never did anybody any harm," he retorted.

She was craven: she pled with him, she even put her pretty slender white hand on his knee.

"None of that! Are you trying to seduce me, or what?"

"You're contemptible!" she cried.

"Oh! Oh! How you go on!" he said, laughing.

"I'll let everybody know what you're like. I'll tell my husband. . . ."

"Will you? I have something to *show* your husband!"

And out of his safe Lheureux took the receipt for 1,800 francs that she had given him for the note discounted by Vinçart.

"Do you think," he said, "that he won't see through your little swindle, the poor dear man?"

She crumpled, as though hit over the head with a club. He paced back and forth between the window and the desk, saying over and over:

"I'll show it to him! I'll show it to him!"

Then he came close to her and said softly:

"It's no fun, I know; but nobody's ever died of it, after all, and since it's the only way you have left of paying me back my money. . . ."

"But where can I find some?" cried Emma, wringing her hands.

"Ah! Bah! A woman like you, with plenty of friends!"

And he transfixed her with a stare so knowing and so terrible that she shuddered to the depths of her being.

"I promise you!" she said. "I'll sign . . ."

"I have enough of your signatures!"

"I'll sell more . . ."

"Face it!" he said, shrugging his shoulders. "You've got nothing left."

And he called through a peephole that communicated with the shop:

"Annette! Don't forget the three cuttings of No. 14."

The servant entered; Emma took the hint, and asked how much money would be required to stop all proceedings.

"It's too late!"

"But if I brought you a few thousand francs—a quarter of the amount, a third, almost all?"

"No—there's no use!"

He pushed her gently toward the stairs.

"I implore you, Monsieur Lheureux—just a few days more!"

She was sobbing.

"Ah! Tears! Very good!"

"You'll drive me to do something desperate!"

"A lot I care!" he said, closing the door behind her.

VII

She was stoical, the next day, when Maître Hareng, the *huissier*, arrived with two witnesses to take inventory of the goods and chattels to be sold.

They began with Bovary's consulting room, and didn't include the phrenological head, which was considered a "professional instrument"; but in the kitchen they counted the plates and the pans, the chairs and the candlesticks, and in the bedroom all the knickknacks on the whatnot. They inspected her dresses, the linen, the *cabinet de toilette*: and her very being, down to its most hidden and intimate details, was laid open, like a dissected corpse, to the stares of those three men.

Maître Hareng, bottomed up in a close-fitting black tail coat, with a white cravat, his shoe straps very tight, kept repeating:

"*Vous permettez,*[7] *Madame? Vous permettez?*"

And frequently he exclaimed:

"Charming! Very pretty!"

Then he would resume his writing, dipping his pen in the inkhorn he held in his left hand.

When they had finished with the various rooms they went up to the attic.

She kept a desk there, where Rodolphe's letters were locked away. They made her open it.

"Ah! Personal papers!" said Maître Hareng, with a discreet smile. "*Mais permettez!* I have to make sure there's nothing else in the box."

And he held the envelopes upside down, very gently, as though expecting them to disgorge gold pieces. She was put into a fury by the sight of that great red hand, with its soft, sluglike fingers, touching those pages that had caused her so many heartthrobs.

They left at last. Félicité came back: she had sent her out to watch for Bovary and keep him away. They quickly installed the watchman in the attic, and he promised to stay there.

Charles, she thought during the evening, looked careworn. She scrutinized him with an agonized stare, reading accusations in the drawn lines of his face. Then, as her eyes roved over the mantelpiece, gay with Chinese fans, over the full curtains, the armchairs, all the things that had tempered the bitterness of her life, she was overcome with remorse, or rather with immense regret; and this, far from eclipsing her passion, only exasperated it. Charles placidly stirred the fire, lounging in his chair.

At one moment the watchman—bored, no doubt, in his hiding place—made a slight noise.

"Is somebody walking around up there?" said Charles.

"No!" she answered. "It's a dormer that's been left open, blowing in the wind."

The next day, Sunday, she left for Rouen, determined to call on every banker she had heard of. Most of them were away in the country or traveling. She persisted, however, and those whom she succeeded in seeing she asked for money, insisting that she must have it, swearing to repay. Some of them laughed in her face; they all refused.

At two o'clock she hurried to Léon's and knocked on his door. No one came to open. Finally he appeared.

"What brings you here?"

"Are you sorry to see me?"

"No . . . but . . ."

And he confessed that his landlord didn't like the tenants to entertain "women."

"I've got to talk to you," she said.

He reached for his key. She stopped him:

"Oh, no—let's go to our place."

And they went to their room in the Hotel de Boulogne.

There she drank a large glass of water. She was very pale.

"Léon," she said to him, "you have to do something for me."

---

7. Permit me (French).

And clutching both his hands tightly in hers, she shook them and said:

"Listen! I've got to have eight thousand francs!"

"But you're out of your mind!"

"Not yet!"

And in a rush she told him all about the execution. She was in desperate straits: Charles had been kept in total ignorance, her mother-in-law hated her, her father could do nothing. He—Léon—must save her. He must go out at once and find her the money that she absolutely had to have.

"How in the world do you expect me . . . ?"

"Don't just stand there, like a spineless fool!"

"You're making things out to be worse than they are," he said stupidly. "You could probably quiet your man with three thousand francs."

All the more reason for trying to do something: it wasn't conceivable that three thousand francs couldn't be found. Besides, Léon's signature could go on the notes instead of hers.

"Go ahead! Try! I've got to have it! Hurry! Oh, try! Try! Then I'll show you how I love you!"

He went out. In an hour he was back.

"I've seen three people," he told her, solemn-faced. "Nothing doing."

They sat face to face across the fire, still and silent. Emma kept shrugging her shoulders, tapping her foot. Then he heard her say, low-voiced:

"If I were in your place I'd know where to find the money!"

"You would? Where?"

"In your office!"

She stared at him.

There was a demonic desperation burning in her eyes, and she narrowed them in a look of lascivious provocation: the young man felt himself giving way before the mute will of this woman who was urging him to crime. He took fright; and to avoid hearing anything further he clapped his hand to his forehead.

"Morel should be back tonight!" he cried. "He won't refuse me, I hope!" (Morel was one of his friends, the son of a wealthy businessman.) "I'll bring it to you tomorrow," he promised.

Emma didn't appear to welcome this hope of relief as joyfully as he had thought. Did she suspect his lie? He blushed as he added:

"But if I'm not back by three, don't wait for me any longer, darling. Now I have to go out. Forgive me! Good-bye!"

He pressed her hand, but it lay inert in his: Emma was drained of all feeling.

Four o'clock struck; and she got up to go back to Yonville, automatic in her obedience to the force of habit.

The day was fine—one of those clear, sharp March days with the sun brilliant in a cloudless sky. Contented-looking Rouennais were strolling in their Sunday best. As she came to the Place du Parvis, vespers in the cathedral had just ended: crowds were pouring out through the three portals, like a river through the three arches of a bridge; and in their midst, immovable as a rock, stood the verger.

She remembered how tremulous she had been, how full of hope, the day she had entered that lofty nave: how it had stretched away before her, on and on—and yet not as infinite as her love! And she kept walking, weeping under her veil, dazed, tottering, almost in a faint.

"Watch out!" The cry came from within a porte-cochère that was swinging open; she stopped, and out came a black horse, prancing between the shafts of a tilbury. A gentleman in sables was holding the reins. Who was he? She knew him. . . . The carriage leapt forward and was gone.

The vicomte! It was the vicomte! She turned to stare: the street was empty. And the encounter left her so crushed, so immeasurably sad, that she leaned against a wall to keep from falling.

Then she thought that she might be mistaken. How could she tell? She had no way of knowing. Everything—everything within her, everything without—was abandoning her. She felt lost, rolling dizzily down into some dark abyss; and she was almost glad, when she reached the Croix-Rouge, to see good old Monsieur Homais. He was watching a case of pharmaceutical supplies being loaded onto the Hirondelle, and in his hand he carried a present for his wife—six *cheminots* wrapped in a foulard handkerchief.

Madame Homais was particularly fond of those heavy turban-shaped rolls, which the Rouennais eat in Lent with salted butter—a last relic of Gothic fare, going back perhaps to the times of the Crusades. The lusty Normans of those days gorged themselves on *cheminots*, picturing them as the heads of Saracens, to be devoured by the light of yellow torches along with flacons of spiced wine and giant slabs of meat. Like those ancients, the apothecary's wife crunched them heroically, despite her wretched teeth; and every time Monsieur Homais made a trip to the city he faithfully brought some back to her, buying them always at the best baker's, in the Rue Massacre.

"Delighted to see you!" he said, offering Emma a hand to help her into the Hirondelle.

Then he put the *cheminots* in the baggage net and sat there hatless, his arms folded, in a pose that was pensive and Napoleonic.

But when the blind beggar made his appearance as usual at the foot of the hill, he exclaimed in indignation:

"I cannot understand why the authorities continue to tolerate such dishonest occupations! All these unfortunates should be put away—and put to work! Progress moves at a snail's pace, no doubt about it: we're still wallowing in the midst of barbarism!"

The blind man held out his hat, and it swung to and fro at the window like a loose piece of upholstery.

"That," pronounced the pharmacist, "is a scrofulous disease."

And though he had often seen the poor devil before, he pretended now to be looking at him for the first time, and he murmured the words "cornea," "opaque cornea," "sclerotic," "facies." Then, in a paternal tone:

"Have you had that frightful affliction long, my friend? You'd do well to follow a diet, instead of getting drunk in cafés."

He urged him to take only good wine and good beer, and to eat good roast meat. The blind man kept singing his song: actually, he seemed fairly close to idiocy. Finally Monsieur Homais took out his purse:

"Here—here's a sou: change it for me and keep half of it for yourself. And don't forget my suggestions—you'll find they help."

Hivert presumed to express certain doubts about their efficacy. But the apothecary swore that he could cure the fellow himself, with an antiphlogistic[8] salve of his own invention, and he gave him his address:

"Monsieur Homais, near the market—ask anyone."

"Come now," said Hivert. "Show the gentleman you're grateful by doing your act."

The blind man squatted on his haunches and threw back his head, and rolling his greenish eyes and sticking out his tongue he rubbed his stomach with both hands, meanwhile uttering a kind of muffled howl, like a famished dog. Emma, shuddering with disgust, flung him a five-franc piece over her shoulder. It was all the money she had in the world: there was something grand, she thought, in thus throwing it away.

The coach was again in motion, when suddenly Monsieur Homais leaned out the window.

"Nothing farinaceous!" he shouted. "No dairy products! Wear woolens next to your skin! Fumigate the diseased areas with the smoke of juniper berries!"

The sight of all the familiar things they passed gradually took Emma's mind off her misery. She was oppressed, crushed with fatigue, and she reached home numb and spiritless, almost asleep.

"Let come what may!" she told herself.

Besides—who knew? Something extraordinary might happen any moment. Lheureux himself might die.

She was awakened the next morning at nine by the sound of voices in the square. People were crowding around the market to read a large notice posted on one of the pillars, and she saw Justin climb on a guard post and deface the notice. Just then the village policeman seized him by the collar. Monsieur Homais came out of his pharmacy, and Madame Lefrançois seemed to be holding forth in the midst of the crowd.

"Madame! Madame!" cried Félicité, rushing in. "It's an outrage!"

And the poor girl, much agitated, showed her a yellow paper she had just torn off the front door. Emma read in a glance that all the contents of her house were subject to sale.

They looked at each other in silence. There were no secrets between mistress and maid. Finally Félicité murmured:

"If I were you, Madame, I'd go see Maître Guillaumin."

"Do you think so?"

"You know all about the Guillaumins from their manservant," the question meant; "does the master mention me, sometimes?"

"Yes, go ahead: it's worth trying."

She put on her black dress and her bonnet with jade beads; and to keep from being seen (there was still quite a crowd in the square) she avoided the village and took the river path.

She was breathless when she reached the notary's gate. The sky was dark; it was snowing a little.

At the sound of her ring Théodore, in a red vest, emerged from the front door; and he opened the gate for her with an air of familiarity, as though she were someone he knew well, and showed her into the dining room.

A large porcelain stove was purring; the niche above it was filled with a cactus plant; and against the oak-grained wallpaper hung Steuben's "Esmer-

---

8. Anti-inflammatory.

alda" and Schopin's "Potiphar,"[9] both in black wood frames. The table set for breakfast, the two silver dish warmers, the crystal doorknobs, the parquet floor and the furniture—all gleamed with a meticulous English spotlessness; in the corners of each of the windows were panes of colored glass.

"This," thought Emma, "is the kind of dining room I should have."

The notary came in. He was wearing a dressing gown with palm designs, which he clutched about him with his left hand; and with his right he doffed and then quickly replaced his brown velvet skullcap. This he wore rakishly tilted to the right, and out from under it emerged the ends of three strands of fair hair that were combed up from the back and drawn carefully over his bald cranium.

After offering her a chair he sat down to his breakfast, apologizing profusely for his discourtesy.

"Monsieur," she said, "I want to ask you . . . ."

"What, Madame? I'm listening."

She told him of her predicament.

It was no news to Maître Guillaumin: he was secretly associated with the dry-goods merchant, who could always be counted on to supply him with capital for the mortgage loans he arranged for his clients.

Thus he knew—far better than she—the long story of the notes, small at first, carrying the names of various endorsers, made out for long terms and continually renewed; he knew how the shopkeeper had gradually accumulated the various protests of nonpayment, and how he had finally had his friend Vinçart institute the necessary legal proceedings in his name, wishing to avoid acquiring a reputation for bloodthirstiness among his fellow villagers.

She interspersed her story with recriminations against Lheureux, and to these the notary returned occasional, empty answers. He ate his chop and drank his tea; his chin kept rubbing against his sky-blue cravat, whose two diamond stickpins were linked by a fine gold chain; and he smiled a strange, sugary, ambiguous smile. Then he noticed that her feet were wet.

"Move closer to the stove! Put them up—higher—against the porcelain."

She was afraid of dirtying it, but his retort was gallant:

"Pretty things never do any harm."

Then she tried to appeal to his emotions: growing emotional herself, she told him about her cramped household budget, her harassments, her needs. He was very sympathetic—an elegant woman like herself!—and without interrupting his meal he gradually turned so that he faced her and his knee brushed against her shoe, whose sole was beginning to curl a little as it steamed in the heat of the stove.

But when she asked him for 3,000 francs he tightened his lips and said that he was very sorry not to have had charge of her capital in the past, for there were a hundred easy ways in which even a lady could invest her money profitably. The Grumesnil peatery, building lots in Le Havre—such speculations were excellent, almost risk-proof; and he let her consume herself with rage at the thought of the fantastic sums she could certainly have made.

9. The official in the court of Egypt who was Joseph's master; the wife of Potiphar tried to seduce him. The painting represents the seduction scene. Karl Steuben (1788–1856), a German history painter. Esmeralda is the gypsy girl in Hugo's *Notre Dame de Paris*. A painting titled *Esmeralda et Quasimodo* was exhibited in 1839. Schopin was the brother of the composer Chopin.

"How come," he asked her, "that you never called on me?"

"I really don't know," she said.

"Why didn't you? Did I seem so very frightening to you? But I'm the one who has cause for complaint: we barely know each other! I feel very warmly toward you, though; you realize that now, I hope?"

He reached out his hand, took hers, pressed it to his lips in a greedy kiss, and then kept it on his knee; and he gently fondled her fingers, murmuring a thousand compliments.

His monotonous voice rustled on like a running brook; his eyes were gleaming through the glitter of his glasses; and his hands crept up inside Emma's sleeve and stroked her arm. She felt a panting breath on her cheek. This man was more than she could stand.

She leapt to her feet.

"Monsieur! I'm waiting!"

"What for?" cried the notary, suddenly extremely pale.

"The money."

"But . . ."

Then, yielding to an irresistible surge of desire:

"Yes! Yes!"

He dragged himself toward her on his knees, careless of his dressing gown.

"Please! Don't go! I love you!"

He seized her by the waist.

A flood of crimson rushed to Madame Bovary's face. She shrank back, and with a terrible look she cried:

"It's shameless of you to take advantage of my distress! I'm to be pitied, but I'm not for sale!"

And she walked out.

The notary sat there dumbfounded, his eyes fixed on his beautiful embroidered slippers. They were a gift from a mistress, and the sight of them gradually comforted him. Anyway, he told himself, such an affair would have involved too many risks.

"What a contemptible, lowdown cad!" she said to herself, as she fled tremulously under the aspens lining the road. Disappointment at having failed made her all the more indignant at the insult offered her honor: it seemed to her that Providence was hounding her relentlessly. She was filled with pride at the way she had acted: never before had she esteemed herself so highly; never had she felt such contempt for everyone else. She was at war with the world, and the thought transported her. She longed to lash out at all men, to spit in their faces, grind them all to dust; and she hurried straight on, pale, trembling, furious, scanning the empty horizon with weeping eyes, almost gloating in the hatred that was choking her.

When she caught sight of her house she felt suddenly paralyzed. She couldn't go on, and yet she had to: what escape was there?

Félicité was waiting for her at the door.

"Well?"

"No," said Emma.

And for a quarter of an hour they discussed who in Yonville might be willing to help her. But every time Félicité mentioned someone, Emma answered:

"Out of the question! They'd refuse!"

"And Monsieur will soon be home!"

"I know. . . . Go away and leave me alone."

She had tried everything. Now there was nothing more to be done; so when Charles appeared there would be only one thing to tell him:

"Don't stay here! The very rug you're walking on isn't ours. Not a piece of all this furniture belongs to you—not a pin, not a wisp of straw; and I'm the one who has ruined you!"

Then he would utter a great sob, and then weep floods of tears; and in the end, once the shock was over, he would forgive her.

"Yes," she muttered, through clenched teeth, *"he'll* forgive *me*—the man *I* wouldn't forgive for setting eyes on me if he offered me a million. . . . Never! Never!"

This thought of Bovary in a position to be condescending put her beside herself. But whether she confessed or not, he would inevitably—sooner or later, today or tomorrow—learn of the disaster; so she could only look forward to that horrible scene and to being subjected to the weight of his magnanimity. Suddenly she felt an urge to try Lheureux once more: but what was the use? Or to write to her father: but it was too late. And perhaps she was regretting, now, not having yielded to the notary, when she heard a horse's trot in the lane. It was Charles: he was opening the gate, his face more ashen than the plaster on the wall. Rushing downstairs, she slipped quickly out into the square; and the mayor's wife, who was chatting in front of the church with Lestiboudois, saw her enter the house of the tax collector.

Madame Tuvache ran to tell Madame Caron. The two ladies climbed up to the latter's attic; and there, hidden behind some laundry that was hanging up to dry, they stood so that they could easily see into Binet's.

He was alone in his garret, busily copying, in wood, one of those ivory ornaments that beggar description, a conglomeration of half-moons and of spheres carved one inside the other, the whole thing standing erect like an obelisk and perfectly useless. He was just beginning on the last section: the end was in sight! In the chiaroscuro of his workshop the golden sawdust flew from his lathe like a spray of sparks under the hooves of a galloping horse; the two wheels spun and whirred; Binet was smiling, chin down and nostrils wide: he looked absorbed, in one of those states of utter bliss such as men seem to find only in humble activities, which divert the mind with easy challenges and gratify it with the most utter and complete success.

"Ah! There she is!" said Madame Tuvache.

But the sound of the lathe made it impossible to know what she was saying.

Finally the two ladies thought they heard the word "francs," and Madame Tuvache whispered:

"She's asking him for a postponement of her taxes."

"Looks like it," said the other.

They saw her pacing up and down the room, looking at the shelves along the wall laden with napkin rings, candlesticks and finials, while Binet contentedly stroked his beard.

"Would she be coming to order something from him?" suggested Madame Tuvache.

"But he never sells anything!" the other reminded her.

The tax collector seemed to be listening, staring as though he didn't understand. She continued to talk, her manner gentle and supplicating. She came close to him; her breast was heaving; now they seemed not to be speaking.

"Is she making advances to him?" said Madame Tuvache.

Binet had gone red to the roots of his hair. She grasped his hands.

"Ah! Just look at that . . . !"

And she must have been suggesting something abominable, for the tax collector—and he was a man of courage: he had fought at Bautzen and Lützen, and taken part in the French campaign,[1] and even been proposed for the Legion of Honor—suddenly recoiled as though he had seen a snake.

"Madame!" he cried. "You must be dreaming!"

"Women like that should be horsewhipped," said Madame Tuvache.

"Where has she gone to?" said Madame Caron.

For even as he was speaking she had vanished. Then they saw her darting down the Grande Rue and turning to the right, as though to reach the cemetery, and they didn't know what to make of it.

"Madame Rollet!" she cried, when she reached the wet nurse's. "I can't breathe! Unlace me!"

She fell sobbing onto the bed. Madame Rollet covered her with a petticoat and stood beside her. Then, when she didn't speak, the peasant woman moved away, took up her wheel and began spinning flax.

"Don't do that!" she murmured: she thought it was Binet's lathe.

"What's the matter with her?" wondered the nurse. "Why did she come here?"

She had come because a kind of terror had sent her—a terror that made her flee her home. Lying on her back, motionless, her eyes vacant, she saw things only in a blur, though she focused her attention on them with idiotic persistence. She stared at the flaking plaster on the wall, at two half-burned sticks smoking end to end in the fireplace, at a large spider crawling overhead in a crack in the rafter. Gradually she collected her thoughts. She remembered . . . one day with Léon . . . Oh, how far away it was . . . ! The sun was shining on the river, and the air was full of the scent of clematis. . . . Then, swept along in her memories as in a raging torrent, she quickly recalled the previous day.

"What time is it?" she asked.

Madame Rollet went out, held up the fingers of her right hand against the brightest part of the sky, and came slowly back, saying:

"Almost three."

"Ah! Thank you! Thank you!"

For he would be coming. There could be no question about it: by now he had found the money. But probably he would go to her house, having no idea that she was here; and she ordered the nurse to run and fetch him.

"Hurry!"

"I'm on my way, dear lady! I'm on my way!"

She marveled, now, at not having thought of him in the first place: yesterday he had given his word; he wouldn't fail her; and already she saw herself at Lheureux's, laying the three banknotes on his desk. Then she'd have to invent some story that would satisfy Bovary. What would it be?

1. The battles in France before the Allies captured Paris and forced the abdication of Napoleon and his banishment to Elba in 1814. Bautzen, in Saxony, was the scene of an 1813 battle in which Napoleon defeated the Prussians and Russians. Lützen, in Saxony, was the scene of another victory by Napoleon.

But the nurse was a long time returning. Still, since there was no clock in the cottage, Emma feared that she might be exaggerating the duration of her absence, and she walked slowly around and around the garden, and down the path by the hedge and quickly back, hoping that the nurse might have returned some other way. Finally, weary of waiting, a prey to suspicions that she resolutely put out of her mind, no longer sure whether she had been there a hundred years or a minute, she sat down in a corner and closed her eyes and put her hands to her ears. The gate squeaked: she leapt up. Before she could speak Madame Rollet said:

"He's not there!"

"What?"

"No, he's not! And Monsieur's crying. He keeps calling your name. Everybody's looking for you."

Emma made no answer. She was gasping and staring wildly about her; the peasant woman, frightened by the expression on her face, instinctively shrank back, thinking her crazed. All at once she clapped her hand to her forehead and gave a cry, for into her mind had come the memory of Rodolphe, like a great lightning-flash in a black night. He was so kind, so sensitive, so generous! And if he should hesitate to help her she'd know how to persuade him: one glance from her eyes would remind him of their lost love. So she set out for La Huchette, unaware that now she was eager to yield to the very thing that had made her so indignant only a short while ago, and totally unconscious that she was prostituting herself.

VIII

As she walked she wondered: "What am I going to say? What shall I tell him first?" Drawing nearer, she recognized the thickets, the trees, the furze on the hill, the château in the distance. She was reliving the sensations of her first love, and at the memory her poor anguished heart swelled tenderly. A warm wind was blowing in her face; melting snow dripped from the leaf buds onto the grass.

She entered, as she always had, by the little park gate, and then came to the main courtyard, planted around with a double row of thick-crowned lindens, their long branches rustling and swaying. All the dogs in the kennel barked, but though their outcry echoed and reechoed, no one came.

She climbed the wide, straight, wooden-banistered stairs that led up to the hall with its paving of dusty flagstones. A row of doors opened onto it, as in a monastery or an inn. His room was at the far end, the last on the left. When her fingers touched the latch her strength suddenly left her: she was afraid that he would not be there—she almost wished that he wouldn't be, and yet he was her only hope, her last chance of salvation. For a minute she collected her thoughts; then, steeling her courage to the present necessity, she entered.

He was smoking a pipe before the fire, his feet against the mantelpiece.

"Oh, it's you!" he said, rising quickly.

"Yes, here I am. . . . Rodolphe, I want . . . I need some advice. . . ."

Despite her best efforts she couldn't go on.

"You haven't changed—you're as charming as ever!"

"Oh, my charms!" she answered bitterly. "They can't amount to much, since you scorned them."

He launched into apology, justifying his conduct in terms that were vague but the best he could muster.

She let herself be taken in—not so much by what he said, as by the sound of his voice and the very sight of him; and she pretended to believe—or perhaps she actually did believe—the reason he gave for their break. It was a secret, he said, involving the honor—the life, even—of a third person.

She looked at him sadly. "Whatever it was," she said, "I suffered a great deal."

He answered philosophically:

"That's how life is!"

"Has it been kind to you, at least," asked Emma, "since we parted?"

"Oh, neither kind nor unkind, particularly."

"Perhaps it would have been better had we stayed together."

"Yes . . . perhaps!"

"Do you really think so?" she said, coming closer.

And she sighed:

"Oh, Rodolphe! If you knew! I loved you very much!"

She took his hand; and for a few moments their fingers were intertwined—like that first day, at the Agricultural Show! Pride made him struggle against giving in to his feelings. But she leaned heavily against him, and said:

"How did you ever think that I could live without you? Happiness is a habit that's hard to break! I was desperate! I thought I'd die! I'll tell you all about it. And you . . . you stayed away from me . . . !"

It was true: for the past three years he had carefully avoided her, out of the natural cowardice that characterizes the stronger sex; and now Emma went on, twisting and turning her head in coaxing little movements that were loving and catlike.

"You have other women—admit it. Oh, I sympathize with them: I don't blame them. You seduced them, the way you seduced me. You're a man! You have everything to make us love you. But you and I'll begin all over again, won't we? We'll love each other! Look—I'm laughing, I'm happy! Speak to me!"

And indeed she was ravishing to see, with a tear trembling in her eye like a raindrop in a blue flower-cup after a storm.

He drew her onto his lap, and with the back of his hand caressed her sleek hair: in the twilight a last sunbeam was gleaming on it like a golden arrow. She lowered her head, and soon he was kissing her on the eyelids, very gently, just brushing them with his lips.

"But you've been crying!" he said. "Why?"

She burst into sobs: Rodolphe thought it was from the violence of her love; when she didn't answer him he interpreted her silence as the ultimate refuge of her womanly modesty, and exclaimed:

"Ah! Forgive me! You're the only one I really care about! I've been stupid and heartless! I love you—I'll always love you. . . . What is it? Tell me!"

He was on his knees.

"Well, then . . . I'm ruined, Rodolphe! You've got to lend me three thousand francs!"

"But . . . but . . . ?" he said, slowly rising, a worried expression coming over his face.

"You know," she went on quickly, "my husband gave his money to a notary to invest, and the notary absconded. We've borrowed, patients haven't paid.

. . . The estate isn't settled yet: we'll be getting something later. But today—just for three thousand francs—they're going to sell us out: now, this very instant. I counted on your friendship. I came to you."

"Ah," thought Rodolphe, suddenly pale. "So that's why she came!"

And after a moment he said, calmly:

"I haven't got it, dear lady."

He wasn't lying. If he had had it he would probably have given it to her, unpleasant though it usually is to make such generous gifts: of all the icy blasts that blow on love, a request for money is the most chilling and havoc wreaking.

For a long moment she stared at him. Then:

"You haven't got it!"

She said it again, several times:

"You haven't got it! I might have spared myself this final humiliation. You never loved me! You're no better than the rest!"

She was giving herself away; she no longer knew what she was saying.

Rodolphe broke in, assuring her that he was "hard up" himself.

"Ah, I pity you!" said Emma. "How I pity you!"

And as her eyes fell on a damascened rifle that glittered in a trophy on the wall:

"When you're as poor as all that you don't put silver on the stock of your gun! You don't buy things with tortoiseshell inlay!" she went on, pointing to the Boulle clock. "Or silver-gilt whistles for your whip!"—she touched them—"or charms for your watch chain! Oh, he has everything! Even a liqueur case in his bedroom! You pamper yourself, you live well, you have a château, farms, woods; you hunt, you make trips to Paris. . . . Why, even things like this," she cried, snatching up his cuff links from the mantelpiece, "the tiniest trifles, you can raise money on . . . ! Oh, I don't want them! Keep them."

And she hurled the two buttons so violently that their gold chain snapped as they struck the wall.

"But I—I'd have given you everything, I'd have sold everything, worked my fingers to the bone, begged in the streets, just for a smile from you, for a look, just to hear you say 'Thank you.' And you sit there calmly in your chair, as though you hadn't made me suffer enough already! If it hadn't been for you I could have been happy! What made you do it? Was it a bet? You loved me, though: you used to say so. . . . And you said so again just now. Ah, you'd have done better to throw me out! My hands are still hot from your kisses; and right there on the rug you swore on your knees that you'd love me forever. You made me believe it: for two years you led me on in a wonderful, marvelous dream. . . . Our plans for going away—you remember? Oh! That letter you wrote me! It tore my heart in two! And now when I come back to him—and find him rich and happy and free—to implore him for help that anybody would give me—come in distress, bringing him all my love—he refuses me, because it would cost him three thousand francs!"

"I haven't got it," answered Rodolphe, with that perfect calm that resigned anger employs as a shield.

She walked out. The walls were quaking, the ceiling was threatening to crush her; and she went back down the long avenue of trees, stumbling against piles of dead leaves that were scattering in the wind. At last she reached the ditch before the gate: she broke her nails on the latch, so frantically did she open it. Then, a hundred yards farther on, out of breath, ready to drop, she paused. She turned: and once again she saw the impassive château, with its park, its gardens, its three courtyards, its many-windowed façade.

She stood there in a daze. Only the pulsing of her veins told her that she was alive: she thought she heard it outside herself, like some deafening music filling the countryside. The earth beneath her feet was as yielding as water, and the furrows seemed to her like immense, dark, breaking waves. All the memories and thoughts in her mind poured out at once, like a thousand fireworks. She saw her father, Lheureux's office, their room in Rouen, another landscape. Madness began to take hold of her; she was frightened, but managed to control herself—without, however, emerging from her confusion, for the cause of her horrible state—the question of money—had faded from her mind. It was only her love that was making her suffer, and she felt her soul leave her at the thought—just as a wounded man, as he lies dying, feels his life flowing out with his blood through the gaping hole.

Night was falling; crows flew overhead.

It suddenly seemed to her that fiery particles were bursting in the air, like bullets exploding as they fell, and spinning and spinning and finally melting in the snow among the tree branches. In the center of each of them appeared Rodolphe's face. They multiplied; they came together; they penetrated her; everything vanished. She recognized the lights of houses, shining far off in the mist.

Suddenly her plight loomed before her, like an abyss. She panted as though her lungs would burst. Then, with a heroic resolve that made her almost happy, she ran down the hill and across the cow plank, ran down the river path and the lane, crossed the square, and came to the pharmacy.

It was empty. She was about to go in, when it occurred to her that the sound of the bell might bring someone; and slipping through the side gate, holding her breath, feeling her way along the walls, she came to the kitchen door. A lighted tallow candle was standing on the stove, and Justin, in shirtsleeves, was just leaving the room carrying a dish.

"Ah, they're at dinner," she said to herself. "Better wait."

Justin returned to the kitchen. She tapped on the window. He came out.

"The key! The one for upstairs, where the . . ."

"What?"

And he stared at her, astounded by the pallor of her face, which stood out white against the blackness of the night. She seemed to him extraordinarily beautiful, majestic as an apparition from another world; without understanding what she wanted, he had a foreboding of something terrible.

But she went on quickly, in a low voice, a voice that was gentle and melting:

"I want it! Give it to me."

The wall was thin, and they could hear the clinking of forks on plates in the dining room.

She pretended she had to kill some rats that were keeping her awake nights.

"I must go ask Monsieur."

"No! Stay here!"

Then, with a casual air:

"There's no use bothering him: I'll tell him later. Come along, give me a light."

She passed into the hall off which opened the laboratory door. There against the wall hung a key marked "capharnaum."

"Justin!" called the apothecary impatiently.

"Let's go up!"

He followed her.

The key turned in the lock, and she went straight to the third shelf—so well did her memory serve her as guide—seized the blue jar, tore out the cork, plunged in her hand, withdrew it full of white powder, and ate greedily.

"Stop!" he cried, flinging himself on her.

"Be quiet! Someone might come. . . ."

He was frantic, wanted to call out.

"Don't say a word about it: all the blame would fall on your master!"

Then she went home, suddenly at peace—almost as serene as though she had done her duty.

When Charles reached home, overwhelmed by the news of the execution, Emma had just left. He called her name, wept, fainted away, but she didn't come back. Where could she be? He sent Félicité to the pharmacist's, to the mayor's, to the dry-goods shop, to the Lion d'Or—everywhere; and whenever his anguish about her momentarily subsided he saw his reputation ruined, all their money gone, Berthe's future wrecked! What was the cause of it all . . . ? Not a word! He waited until six that evening. Finally, unable to bear it any longer, and imagining that she must have gone to Rouen, he went out to the highway, followed it for a mile or so, met no one, waited a while, and returned.

She was back.

"What happened? . . . Why? . . . Tell me!"

She sat down at her desk and wrote a letter, sealed it slowly, and added the date and the hour. Then she said in a solemn tone:

"Read it tomorrow. Till then, please don't ask me a single question—not one!"

"But . . ."

"Oh, leave me alone!"

And she stretched out on her bed.

An acrid taste in her mouth woke her. She caught sight of Charles and reclosed her eyes.

She observed herself with interest, to see whether there was any pain. No—nothing yet. She heard the ticking of the clock, the sound of the fire, and Charles breathing, standing there beside her bed.

"Dying doesn't amount to much!" she thought. "I'll fall asleep, and everything will be over."

She swallowed a mouthful of water and turned to the wall.

There was still that dreadful taste of ink.

"I'm thirsty! I'm so thirsty!" she whispered.

"What's wrong with you, anyway?" said Charles, handing her a glass.

"Nothing! Open the window . . . I'm choking!"

She was seized by an attack of nausea so sudden that she scarcely had time to snatch her handkerchief from under the pillow.

"Get rid of it!" she said quickly. "Throw it out!"

He questioned her, but she made no answer. She lay very still, fearing that the slightest disturbance would make her vomit. Now she felt an icy coldness creeping up from her feet toward her heart.

"Ah! It's beginning!" she murmured.

"What did you say?"

She twisted her head from side to side in a gentle movement expressive of anguish, and kept opening her jaws as though she had something very heavy on her tongue. At eight o'clock the vomiting resumed.

Charles noticed that there was a gritty white deposit on the bottom of the basin, clinging to the porcelain.

"That's extraordinary! That's peculiar!" he kept saying.

"No!" she said loudly. "You're mistaken."

Very gently, almost caressingly, he passed his hand over her stomach. She gave a sharp scream. He drew back in fright.

She began to moan, softly at first. Her shoulders heaved in a great shudder, and she grew whiter than the sheet her clenched fingers were digging into. Her irregular pulse was almost imperceptible now.

Beads of sweat stood out on her face, which had turned blue and rigid, as though from the breath of some metallic vapor. Her teeth chattered, her dilated eyes stared about her vaguely, and her sole answer to questions was a shake of her head; two or three times she even smiled. Gradually her groans grew louder. A muffled scream escaped her; she pretended that she was feeling better and that she'd soon be getting up. But she was seized with convulsions.

"God!" she cried. "It's horrible!"

He flung himself on his knees beside her bed.

"Speak to me! What did you eat? Answer, for heaven's sake!"

And in his eyes she read a love such as she had never known.

"There . . . over there . . ." she said in a faltering voice.

He darted to the secretary, broke open the seal and read aloud: "No one is to blame . . ." He stopped, passed his hand over his eyes, read it again.

"What . . . ! Help! Help!"

He could only repeat the word: "Poisoned! Poisoned!" Félicité ran to Homais, who spoke loudly as he crossed the square; Madame Lefrançois heard him at the Lion d'Or, other citizens left their beds to tell their neighbors, and all night long the village was awake.

Distracted, stammering, close to collapse, Charles walked in circles around the room. He stumbled against the furniture, tore his hair: never had the pharmacist dreamed there could be so frightful a sight.

He went back to his own house and wrote letters to Monsieur Canivet and Doctor Larivière. He couldn't concentrate, had to begin them over fifteen times. Hippolyte left for Neufchâtel, and Justin spurred Bovary's horse so hard that he left it on the hill at Bois-Guillaume, foundered and all but done for.

Charles tried to consult his medical dictionary: he couldn't see; the lines danced before his eyes.

"Don't lose your head!" said the apothecary. "It's just a question of administering some powerful antidote. What poison is it?"

Charles showed him the letter. It was arsenic.

"Well then!" said Homais. "We must make an analysis."

For he knew that an analysis always had to be made in cases of poisoning. Charles, who hadn't understood, answered with a groan:

"Do it! Do it! Save her . . . !"

And returning to her side, he sank down on the carpet and leaned his head on the edge of her bed, sobbing.

"Don't cry!" she said. "I shan't be tormenting you much longer."

"Why did you do it? What made you?"

"It was the only thing," she answered.

"Weren't you happy? Am I to blame? But I did everything I could . . . !"

"Yes . . . I know . . . You're good, you're different. . . ."

She slowly passed her hand through his hair. The sweetness of her touch was more than his grief could bear. He felt his entire being give way to despair at the thought of having to lose her just when she was showing him more love than ever in the past; and he could think of nothing to do—he knew nothing, dared nothing: the need for immediate action took away the last of his presence of mind.

Emma was thinking that now she was through with all the betrayals, the infamies, the countless fierce desires that had racked her. She hated no one, now; a twilight confusion was falling over her thoughts, and of all the world's sounds she heard only the intermittent lament of this poor man beside her, gentle and indistinct, like the last echo of an ever-fainter symphony.

"Bring me my little girl," she said, raising herself on her elbow.

"You're not feeling worse, are you?" Charles asked.

"No! No!"

Berthe was carried in by the maid. Her bare feet peeped out from beneath her long nightdress; she looked serious, still half dreaming. She stared in surprise to see the room in such disorder, and she blinked her eyes, dazzled by the candles that were standing here and there on the furniture. They probably reminded her of other mornings—New Year's day or mi-carême,[2] when she was wakened early in just this same way by candlelight and carried to her mother's bed to be given a shoeful of presents; for she asked:

"Where is it, *maman?*"

And when no one answered:

"I don't see my little shoe!"

Félicité held her over the bed, but she kept looking toward the fireplace.

"Did nurse take it away?" she asked.

At the word "nurse," which brought back her adulteries and her calamities, Madame Bovary averted her head, as though another, stronger, poison had risen to her mouth and filled her with revulsion.

"Oh, how big your eyes are, *maman!*" cried Berthe, whom the maid had put on the bed. "How pale you are! You're sweating . . . !"

Her mother looked at her.

"I'm afraid!" cried the little girl, shrinking back.

Emma took her hand to kiss it; she struggled.

"Enough! Take her away!" cried Charles, sobbing at the foot of the bed.

The symptoms momentarily stopped; she seemed calmer; and at each insignificant word she said, each time she breathed a little more easily, his hope gained ground. When Canivet finally arrived he threw himself in his arms, weeping.

2. Mid-Lent.

"Ah! You've come! Thank you! You're kind! But she's doing better. Here: look at her!"

His colleague was not at all of this opinion. There was no use—as he himself put it—"beating around the bush," and he prescribed an emetic, to empty the stomach completely.

Soon she was vomiting blood. Her lips pressed together more tightly. Her limbs were contorted, her body was covered with brown blotches, her pulse quivered under the doctor's fingers like a taut thread, like a harp string about to snap.

Then she began to scream, horribly. She cursed the poison, railed against it, begged it to be quick; and with her stiffened arms she pushed away everything that Charles, in greater agony than herself, tried to make her drink. He was standing, his handkerchief to his mouth, moaning, weeping, choked by sobs and shaking all over; Félicité rushed about the room; Homais, motionless, kept sighing heavily; and Monsieur Canivet, for all his air of self-assurance, began to manifest some uneasiness:

"What the devil . . . ! But she's purged, and since the cause is removed . . ."

"The effect should subside," said Homais. "It's self-evident."

"Do something to save her!" cried Bovary.

Paying no attention to the pharmacist, who was venturing the hypothesis that "this paroxysm may mark the beginning of improvement," Canivet was about to give her theriaca when there came the crack of a whip, all the windows rattled, and a post chaise drawn at breakneck speed by three mud-covered horses flashed around the corner of the marketplace. It was Doctor Larivière.

The sudden appearance of a god wouldn't have caused greater excitement. Bovary raised both hands, Canivet broke off his preparations, and Homais doffed his cap well before the doctor entered.

He belonged to that great surgical school created by Bichat[3]—that generation, now vanished, of philosopher-practitioners, who cherished their art with fanatical love and applied it with enthusiasm and sagacity. Everyone in his hospital trembled when he was angry; and his students so revered him that the moment they set up for themselves they imitated him as much as they could. There was scarcely a town in the district where one of them couldn't be found, wearing a long merino overcoat and a full black tail coat, exactly like his. Doctor Larivière's unbuttoned cuffs partly covered his fleshy hands—extraordinary hands, always ungloved, as though to be the readier to grapple with suffering. Disdainful of decorations, titles and academies, hospitable, generous, a father to the poor, practicing Christian virtues although an unbeliever, he might have been thought of as a saint if he hadn't been feared as a devil because of the keenness of his mind. His scalpel-sharp glance cut deep into your soul, exposing any lie buried under excuses and reticences. His manner was majestic and genial, conscious as he was of his great gifts and his wealth and the forty years of hard work and blameless living he had behind him.

While he was still in the doorway he frowned, catching sight of Emma's cadaverous face as she lay on her back, her mouth open. Then, seeming to listen to Canivet, he passed his forefinger back and forth beneath his nostrils, repeating:

3. Marie-Françoise-Xavier Bichat (1771–1802), author of an *Anatomie générale* (1801).

"Yes, yes."

But his shoulders lifted in a slow shrug. Bovary noticed it; their eyes met. The sight of a grieving face was no novelty to the doctor, yet he couldn't keep a tear from dropping onto his shirt front.

He asked Canivet to step into the next room. Charles followed him.

"She's very low, isn't she? How about poultices? What else? Can't you think of something? You've saved so many lives!"

Charles put his arms around him, sagged against his chest, and looked at him anxiously and beseechingly.

"Come, my poor boy, be brave! There's nothing to be done."

And Doctor Larivière turned away.

"You're leaving?"

"I'll be back."

He pretended he had something to say to the coachman, and went out with Canivet, who was no more eager than he to watch Emma die.

The pharmacist joined them in the square. He was temperamentally incapable of staying away from celebrities, and he begged Monsieur Larivière to do him the signal honor of being his guest at lunch.

Someone was quickly sent to the Lion d'Or for pigeons, the butcher was stripped of all his chops, Tuvache supplied cream and Lestiboudois eggs. The apothecary himself helped with the preparations, while Madame Homais pulled at her wrapper strings and said:

"I hope you'll forgive us, Monsieur. In this wretched village, if we don't have a full day's warning . . ."

"The stemmed glasses!!!" whispered Homais.

"If we lived in the city we'd at least have stuffed pigs' feet to fall back on."

"Don't talk so much . . . ! Sit down, Doctor!"

After the first few mouthfuls he considered it appropriate to supply a few details concerning the catastrophe.

"First we had a sensation of siccity in the pharynx, then intolerable pain in the epigastrium, superpurgation, coma."

"How did she poison herself?"

"I have no idea, Doctor, and I can't even imagine where she managed to procure that arsenous oxide."

Justin, who was just then carrying in a pile of plates, was seized with a fit of trembling.

"What's the matter with you?" asked the pharmacist.

At the question the young man dropped everything with a great crash.

"Imbecile!" cried Homais. "Clumsy lout! Damned idiot!"

Then, quickly regaining his self-control:

"I wanted to try an analysis, Doctor, and, *primo*, I carefully inserted into a tube . . ."

"It would have been better," said the surgeon, "if you'd inserted your fingers into her throat."

Canivet said nothing, having just a few minutes before been given, in private, a severe rebuke concerning his emetic. Today he was as meek as he had been arrogant and verbose the day he had operated on Hippolyte: his face was fixed in a continual, approving smile.

Homais blossomed in his role of proud host, and the thought of Bovary's distress added something to his pleasure as he selfishly contrasted their lots.

Moreover, the doctor's presence excited him. He displayed all his erudition, dragging in, pell-mell, mention of cantharides, the upas, the manchineel, the bite of the adder.

"I've even read about people being poisoned, Doctor—positively struck down—by blood sausages that had been subjected to excessive fumigation! At least, so it says in a very fine report, written by one of our leading pharmaceutical lights, one of our masters, the illustrious Cadet de Gassicourt!"[4]

Madame Homais reappeared, bearing one of those rickety contraptions that are heated with alcohol, for Homais insisted on brewing his coffee at table—having, needless to say, previously done his own roasting, his own grinding and his own blending.

"*Saccharum,* Doctor?" he said, passing the sugar.

Then he called in all his children, eager to have the surgeon's opinion on their constitutions.

Finally, when Monsieur Larivière was about to leave, Madame Homais asked him to advise her about her husband. His "blood was getting thicker" because of his habit of falling asleep every evening after dinner.

"Oh, he's not thick-*blooded!*"

And smiling a little at his joke, which passed unnoticed, the doctor opened the door. But the pharmacy was thronged, and he had a hard time getting rid of Monsieur Tuvache, who was afraid that his wife would get pneumonia because of her habit of spitting into the fire; then Monsieur Binet complained of often feeling ravenous; Madame Caron had prickling sensations; Lheureux suffered from dizzy spells; Lestiboudois was rheumatic; and Madame Lefrançois had heartburn. Finally the three horses bore him away, and the general verdict was that he had been far from obliging.

Then the attention of the public was distracted by the appearance of Monsieur Bournisien, crossing the market with the holy oils.

Homais paid his debt to his principles by likening priests to ravens: both are attracted by the odor of the dead. Actually, he had a more personal reason for disliking the sight of a priest: a cassock made him think of a shroud, and his execration of the one owed something to his fear of the other.

Nevertheless, not flinching in the face of what he called his "mission," he returned to the Bovary house along with Canivet, whom Monsieur Larivière had urged to stay on to the end. But for his wife's protests, the pharmacist would have taken his two sons along, to inure them to life's great moments, to provide them with a lesson, an example, a momentous spectacle that they would remember later.

The bedroom, as they entered, was mournful and solemn. On the sewing table, now covered with a white napkin, were five or six small wads of cotton in a silver dish, and nearby a large crucifix between two lighted candelabra. Emma lay with her chin sunk on her breast, her eyelids unnaturally wide apart; and her poor hands picked at the sheets in the ghastly and poignant way of the dying, who seem impatient to cover themselves with their shrouds. Pale as a statue, his eyes red as coals, but no longer weeping, Charles stood facing her at the foot of the bed; the priest, on one knee, mumbled under his breath.

4. The pharmacist of Emperor Napoleon I who had considerable trouble under the Restoration because of his liberal ideas.

She slowly turned her face, and seemed overjoyed at suddenly seeing the purple stole—doubtless recognizing in this interval of extraordinary peace, the lost ecstasy of her first mystical flights and the first visions of eternal bliss.

The priest stood up and took the crucifix; she stretched out her head like someone thirsting; and pressing her lips to the body of the God-Man, she imprinted on it, with every ounce of her failing strength, the most passionate love-kiss she had ever given. Then he recited the *Misereatur* and the *Indulgentiam*, dipped his right thumb in the oil, and began the unctions. First he anointed her eyes, once so covetous of all earthly luxuries; then her nostrils, so gluttonous of caressing breezes and amorous scents; then her mouth, so prompt to lie, so defiant in pride, so loud in lust; then her hands, that had thrilled to voluptuous contacts; and finally the soles of her feet, once so swift when she had hastened to slake her desires, and now never to walk again.

The curé wiped his fingers, threw the oil-soaked bits of cotton into the fire, and returned to the dying woman, sitting beside her and telling her that now she must unite her sufferings with Christ's and throw herself on the divine mercy.

As he ended his exhortations he tried to have her grasp a blessed candle, symbol of the celestial glories soon to surround her. Emma was too weak, and couldn't close her fingers: but for Monsieur Bournisien the candle would have fallen to the floor.

Yet she was no longer so pale, and her face was serene, as though the sacrament had cured her.

The priest didn't fail to point this out: he even explained to Bovary that the Lord sometimes prolonged people's lives when He judged it expedient for their salvation; and Charles remembered another day, when, similarly close to death, she had received communion.

"Perhaps there's hope after all," he thought.

And indeed, she looked all about her, slowly, like someone waking from a dream; then, in a distinct voice, she asked for her mirror, and she remained bowed over it for some time, until great tears flowed from her eyes. Then she threw back her head with a sigh, and sank onto the pillow.

At once her breast began to heave rapidly. Her tongue hung at full length from her mouth; her rolling eyes grew dim like the globes of two lamps about to go out; and one might have thought her dead already but for the terrifying, ever-faster movement of her ribs, which were shaken by furious gasps, as though her soul were straining violently to break its fetters. Félicité knelt before the crucifix, and even the pharmacist flexed his knees a little. Monsieur Canivet stared vaguely out into the square. Bournisien had resumed his praying, his face bowed over the edge of the bed and his long black cassock trailing out behind him into the room. Charles was on the other side, on his knees, his arms stretched out toward Emma. He had taken her hands, and was pressing them, shuddering at every beat of her heart, as at the tremors of a falling ruin. As the death-rattle grew louder, the priest speeded his prayers: they mingled with Bovary's stifled sobs, and at moments everything seemed drowned by the monotonous flow of Latin syllables that sounded like the tolling of a bell.

Suddenly from out on the sidewalk came a noise of heavy wooden shoes and the scraping of a stick, and a voice rose up, a raucous voice singing:

A clear day's warmth will often move
A lass to stray in dreams of love.

Emma sat up like a galvanized corpse, her hair streaming, her eyes fixed and gaping.

To gather up the stalks of wheat
The swinging scythe keeps laying by,
Nanette goes stooping in the heat
Along the furrows where they lie.

"The blind man!" she cried.

Emma began to laugh—a horrible, frantic, desperate laugh—fancying that she saw the beggar's hideous face, a figure of terror looming up in the darkness of eternity.

The wind blew very hard that day
And snatched her petticoat away!

A spasm flung her down on the mattress. Everyone drew close. She had ceased to exist.

IX

Anyone's death always releases something like an aura of stupefaction, so difficult is it to grasp this irruption of nothingness and to believe that it has actually taken place. But when Charles realized how still she was, he threw himself on her, crying:

"*Adieu! Adieu!*"

Homais and Canivet led him from the room.

"Control yourself!"

"Let me stay!" he said, struggling. "I'll be reasonable; I won't do anything I shouldn't. But I want to be near her—she's my wife!"

And he wept.

"Weep, weep," said the pharmacist. "Let yourself go: you'll feel the better for it."

Helpless as a child, Charles let himself be taken downstairs to the parlor. Monsieur Homais soon went home.

In the square he was accosted by the blind beggar. Lured by the hope of the antiphlogistic salve, he had dragged himself all the way to Yonville, and now was asking every passer-by where the apothecary lived.

"Good Lord! As though I didn't have other things on my mind! Too bad! Come back later."

He hurried into the pharmacy.

He had to write two letters, prepare a sedative for Bovary, and invent a plausible lie that would cover up the suicide for an article in the *Fanal* and for the crowd that was awaiting him in order to learn the news. When all the Yonvillians had heard his story about the arsenic that Emma had mistaken for sugar while making a custard, Homais returned once more to Bovary.

He found him alone (Canivet had just left), sitting in the armchair beside the window, staring vacantly at the parlor floor.

"Now," said the pharmacist, "what you've got to do is decide on a time for the ceremony."

"Why? What ceremony?"

Then, in a frightened stammer:

"Oh no! I don't have to, do I? I want to keep her!"

To hide his embarrassment Homais took a carafe from the whatnot and began to water the geraniums.

"Ah, thank you!" said Charles. "You're so good!"

He broke off, choked by the flood of memories the pharmacist's action evoked.

To distract him, Homais thought it well to talk about horticulture: plants, he ventured, had to be kept moist. Charles nodded in agreement.

"Anyway, we'll soon be having fine spring weather."

"Ah!" said Bovary.

Not knowing what to say next, the apothecary twitched the sash curtain.

"Ah—there's Monsieur Tuvache going by."

Charles repeated mechanically:

"Monsieur Tuvache going by."

Homais didn't dare broach the subject of funeral arrangements again: it was the priest who eventually made Charles see reason.

He locked himself in his consulting room, took a pen, and after sobbing a while he wrote:

"I want her buried in her bridal dress, with white shoes and a wreath and her hair spread over her shoulders. Three coffins—one oak, one mahogany, one lead. No one has to say anything to me: I'll have the strength to go through with it. Cover her with a large piece of green velvet. I want this done. Do it."

The priest and the pharmacist were much taken aback by Bovary's romantic ideas. Homais expostulated:

"The velvet seems to be supererogatory. Not to mention the expense . . ."

"Is it any concern of yours?" cried Charles. "Leave me alone! You didn't love her! Go away!"

The priest took him by the arm and walked him around the garden, discoursing on the vanity of earthly things. God is all-great, all-good; we must submit to His decrees without complaint; more than that, we must be grateful.

Charles burst into a stream of blasphemy.

"I detest your God!"

"The spirit of rebellion is still in you," sighed the priest.

Bovary had strode away from him and was pacing up and down beside the wall of espaliered fruit trees, grinding his teeth and looking curses at heaven: but not even a leaf stirred in answer.

A fine rain was falling. Charles's shirt was open, and soon he began to shiver. He went back into the house and sat in the kitchen.

At six o'clock there was a clanking in the square. It was the Hirondelle arriving, and he stood with his head against the windowpanes, watching all the passengers get out, one after the other. Félicité put down a mattress for him in the parlor, and he threw himself on it and fell asleep.

Rationalist though he was, Monsieur Homais respected the dead. So, bearing no grudge against poor Charles, he returned that night to watch beside the body. He brought three books with him, and a writing pad for making notes.

He found Monsieur Bournisien already there. Two tall candles were burning at the head of the bed, which had been moved out of the alcove.

The apothecary, oppressed by the silence, soon made a few elegiac remarks concerning "this hapless young woman"; and the priest replied that now there was nothing left to do but pray for her.

"Still," said Homais, "it's one thing or the other: either she died in a state of grace (as the church puts it), and therefore had no need of our prayers; or else she died unrepentant (I believe that is the ecclesiastical term) and in that case . . ."

Bournisien interrupted him, replying testily that prayer was called for nonetheless.

"But," objected the pharmacist, "since God knows all our needs, what purpose can be served by prayer?"

"What?" said the priest. "Prayer? Aren't you a Christian, then?"

"I beg your pardon!" said Homais. "I admire Christianity. It freed the slaves, for one thing; it introduced into the world a moral code that . . ."

"That's not the point! All the texts . . ."

"Oh! Oh! The texts! Look in any history book: everybody knows they were falsified by the Jesuits."

Charles came in, walked up to the bed and slowly parted the curtains.

Emma's head was turned toward her right shoulder. The corner of her open mouth was like a black hole in the lower part of her face; her two thumbs were bent inward toward the palms of her hands; a kind of white dust powdered her lashes; and the outline of her eyes was beginning to disappear in a viscous pallor, as though spiders had been spinning cobwebs over her face. From her breasts to her knees the sheet sagged, rising again at her toes; and it seemed to Charles that some infinite mass, some enormous weight, was pressing on her.

The church clock struck two. The flowing river murmured deeply in the darkness at the foot of the terrace. Now and again Monsieur Bournisien blew his nose loudly, and Homais' pen was scratching on his paper.

"Go back to bed, my friend," he said. "Stop torturing yourself."

When Charles had gone, the pharmacist and the curé resumed their arguments.

"Read Voltaire!" said the one. "Read Holbach! Read the Encyclopedia!"[5]

"Read the Letters of Some Portuguese Jews!" said the other. "Read the Proof of Christianity,[6] by ex-magistrate Nicolas!"

They grew excited and flushed; both spoke at once, neither listening to the other; Bournisien was shocked by such audacity; Homais marveled at such stupidity; and they were on the point of exchanging insults when Charles suddenly reappeared. He couldn't keep away: it was as though a spell kept drawing him upstairs.

He stood at the foot of the bed to see her better, absorbed in contemplation so intense that he no longer felt any pain.

He recalled stories about catalepsy and the miracles of magnetism; and he told himself that by straining his will to the utmost he might resuscitate

5. Paul-Henri Dietrich, baron d'Holbach (1723–1789), friend and disciple of Diderot and one of the most outspoken opponents of religion in the French Enlightenment. The Encyclopedia, a dictionary of the sciences, arts, and letters, edited by Diderot and d'Alembert (1751–72), is the intellectual monument of the French Enlightenment, a fountainhead of later secular and agnostic thought.   6. One of the many books defending Roman Catholicism by Jean-Jacques-Auguste Nicolas (1807–1888). Letters of Some Portuguese Jews (1769) refers to a book by Abbé Antoine Guéné directed against Voltaire.

her. Once he even leaned over toward her and cried very softly "Emma! Emma!" The force of his breath blew the flickering candle flames against the wall.

At daybreak the older Madame Bovary arrived, and as Charles embraced her he had another fit of weeping. Like the pharmacist, she ventured a few remarks about the funeral expenses, but he flew into such a rage that she said no more, and he sent her straight to the city to buy what was needed.

Charles spent all afternoon alone. Berthe had been taken to Madame Homais'; Félicité stayed upstairs in the bedroom with Madame Lefrançois.

That evening, people called. He rose and shook hands with them, unable to speak; each then took a seat alongside the others, gradually forming a wide semicircle in front of the fireplace. Eyes lowered and legs crossed, they dangled their feet, sighing deeply from time to time. Everyone was bored beyond measure, but no one was willing to be the first to leave.

When Homais returned at nine o'clock (during the past two days he had seemed to spend all his time crossing the square) he brought with him a supply of camphor, benzoin and aromatic herbs. He also had a vase full of chlorine water, to "drive out the miasmas." At that moment the maid, Madame Lefrançois and the older Madame Bovary were clustered around Emma, putting the finishing touches to her toilette: they drew down the long, stiff veil, covering her even to her satin shoes.

Félicité sobbed:

"Ah! Poor mistress! Poor mistress!"

"Look at her," said the hotel keeper, with a sigh. "How pretty she still is! You'd swear she'd be getting up any minute."

Then they bent over to put on her wreath.

They had to lift her head a little, and as they did so a black liquid poured out of her mouth like vomit.

"Heavens! Watch out for her dress!" cried Madame Lefrançois. "Help us, won't you?" she said to the pharmacist. "You wouldn't be afraid, would you?"

"I, afraid?" he answered, shrugging his shoulders. "Take it from me: I saw plenty of things like this at the hospital, when I was studying pharmacy. We used to make punch in the dissecting room while we worked. Death holds no terrors for a philosopher. In fact, as I often say, I intend to leave my body to the hospitals, so that it can eventually be of service to science."

When the curé arrived he asked how Monsieur was; and at the apothecary's reply he said:

"Of course: he still hasn't got over the shock."

Homais went on to congratulate him on not being exposed, like other men, to the risk of losing a beloved wife; and there followed a discussion on the celibacy of the clergy.

"After all," said the pharmacist, "it's against nature for a man to do without women. We've all heard of crimes . . ."

"But drat it all!" cried the priest. "How would you expect anyone who was married to be able to keep the secrets of the confessional, for example?"

Homais attacked confession. Bournisien defended it: he dilated on the acts of restitution it was constantly responsible for, told stories about thieves suddenly turning honest. Soldiers, approaching the tribunal of repentance, had felt the scales drop from their eyes. There was a minister at Fribourg . . .

His fellow watcher had fallen asleep. Bournisien found it somewhat hard to breathe, the air of the room was so heavy, and he opened a window. This woke the pharmacist.

"Here," the priest said. "Take a pinch of snuff. Do—it clears the head."

There was a continual barking somewhere in the distance.

"Do you hear a dog howling?" said the pharmacist.

"People say that they scent the dead," answered the priest. "It's like bees: they leave the hive when someone dies."

Homais didn't challenge those superstitions, for once again he had fallen asleep.

Monsieur Bournisien, more resistant, continued for some time to move his lips in a murmur, then his chin sank gradually lower, his thick black book slipped from his hand, and he began to snore.

They sat opposite one another, stomachs out, faces swollen, both of them scowling—united, after so much dissension, in the same human weakness; and they stirred no more than the corpse that was like another sleeper beside them.

Charles's coming didn't wake them. This was the last time. He had come to bid her farewell.

The aromatic herbs were still smoking, and at the window their swirls of bluish vapor mingled with the mist that was blowing in.

There were a few stars. The night was mild.

Great drops of wax were falling onto the bedsheets from the candles. Charles watched them burn, tiring his eyes in the gleam of their yellow flames.

The watered satin of her dress was shimmering with the whiteness of moonbeams. Emma was invisible under it; and it seemed to him as though she were spreading out beyond herself, melting confusedly into the surroundings—the silence, the night, the passing wind, the damp fragrance that rose from the earth.

Then, suddenly, he saw her in the garden at Tostes, on the seat, against the thorn hedge—or in Rouen, in the street—or on the doorstep of their house, in the farmyard at Les Bertaux. Once again he heard the laughter of the merry lads dancing under the apple trees; the wedding chamber was full of the perfume of her hair, and her dress rustled in his arms with a sound of flying sparks. And now she was wearing that very dress!

He stood there a long time thus recalling all his past happiness—her poses, her gestures, the sound of her voice. Wave of despair followed upon wave, endlessly, like the waters of an overflowing tide.

A terrible curiosity came over him: slowly, with the tips of his fingers, his heart pounding, he lifted her veil. He gave a scream of horror that woke the sleepers. They took him downstairs to the parlor.

Then Félicité came up, to say that he was asking for a lock of her hair.

"Cut some!" answered the apothecary.

She didn't dare, and he stepped forward himself, scissors in hand. He trembled so violently that he nicked the skin on the temples in several places. Finally, steeling himself, Homais slashed blindly two or three times, leaving white marks in the beautiful black tresses.

The pharmacist and the curé resumed their respective occupations—not without dozing off now and again and reproaching each other for doing so each time they awoke. Then Monsieur Bournisien would sprinkle the room with holy water and Homais would pour a little chlorine water on the floor.

Félicité had thought to leave a bottle of brandy for them on the chest of drawers, along with a cheese and a big brioche. Finally, about four in the morning, the apothecary could hold out no longer.

"I confess," he sighed, "that I'd gladly partake of some nourishment."

The priest didn't have to be asked twice. He went out, said his Mass, came back; and they proceeded to eat and clink their glasses, chuckling a little without knowing why, prey to that indefinable gaiety that often succeeds periods of gloom. With the last drink of brandy the priest slapped the pharmacist on the back:

"We'll be good friends yet!" he said.

Downstairs in the hall they met the workmen arriving, and for two hours Charles had to suffer the torture of the sound of the hammer on the planks. Then they brought her down in her oaken coffin, which they fitted inside the two others. The outermost was too wide, and they had to stuff the space between with wool from a mattress. Finally, when the three lids had been planed, nailed on and soldered, the bier was exposed at the door. The house was thrown open, and the Yonvillians began to flock in.

Monsieur Rouault arrived. He fell in a faint in the square at the sight of the black cloth.

X

The pharmacist's letter hadn't reached him until thirty-six hours after the event; and to spare his feelings Monsieur Homais had worded it in such a way that it was impossible for him to know what to think.

On reading it he fell to the ground, as though stricken by apoplexy. Then he gathered that she was *not* dead. But she might be . . . He put on his smock and his hat, fastened a spur to his boot, and set off at a gallop; and during the entire length of his breathless ride he was frantic with anguish. At one point he had to stop and dismount: he couldn't see, he heard voices, he thought he was losing his mind.

At daybreak he caught sight of three black hens asleep in a tree, and he shuddered, terrified by the omen. He promised the Holy Virgin three chasubles for the church, and vowed to walk barefoot from the cemetery at Les Bertaux to the chapel at Vassonville.

He rode into Maromme, shouting ahead to the people at the inn, burst open the gate with his shoulder, dashed up to the oats bag, poured a bottle of sweet cider into the manger; then he remounted his nag, and it was off again, striking sparks from all four shoes.

He kept telling himself that she would certainly live: the doctors would find a remedy—there was no question. He reminded himself of all the miraculous recoveries people had told him of.

Then he had a vision of her dead. She was there, before him stretched on her back in the middle of the road. He pulled at the reins, and the hallucination vanished.

At Quincampoix he drank three coffees in a row to fortify himself.

It occurred to him that they might have put the wrong name on the letter. He rummaged for it in his pocket, felt it there, but didn't dare open it.

He even began to imagine that it might be a practical joke, an attempt to get even with him for something, or a wag's idea of a prank. Besides—if she was dead, he'd know it! But no—the countryside was as always: the sky was blue, the trees were swaying; a flock of sheep crossed the road. He caught sight of the village; people saw him racing by, hunched over his horse, beating it furiously, its saddle girths dripping blood.

Then, when he had regained consciousness, he fell weeping into Bovary's arms:

"My daughter! Emma! My baby! Tell me . . ."

Charles answered, sobbing:

"I don't know, I don't know! It's a curse . . ."

The apothecary drew them apart.

"There's no use going into the horrible details. I'll tell Monsieur all about it later. People are coming. Have some dignity, for heaven's sake! Take it like a philosopher!"

Poor Charles made an effort, and repeated several times:

"Yes! . . . Be brave!"

"All right, then, I'll be brave, God damn it to hell!" the old man cried. "I'll stay with her to the end."

The bell was tolling. Everything was ready. It was time to set out.

Sitting side by side in one of the choir stalls, they watched the three cantors continually crossing back and forth in front of them, intoning. The serpent[7] player blew with all his might. Monsieur Bournisien, in full regalia, sang in a shrill voice: he bowed to the tabernacle, raised his hands, stretched out his arms, Lestiboudois moved about the church with his verger's staff; near the lectern stood the coffin, between four rows of candles. Charles had to restrain himself from getting up and putting them out.

He did his best, however, to work himself up into a religious frame of mind, to seize on the hope of a future life in which he would see her again. He tried to imagine that she had gone on a trip—far off—a long time ago. But when he remembered that she was right there, in the coffin, and that everything was over, and that now she was going to be buried, he was filled with a rage that was fierce and black and desperate. At moments he thought he was beyond feeling; and he relished this ebbing of grief, cursing himself in the same breath for a scoundrel.

A sharp, regular noise, like the tapping of a metal-tipped walking stick, was heard on the stone floor. It came from the far end of the church and stopped abruptly in the side aisle. A man in a coarse brown jacket sank painfully to his knees. It was Hippolyte, the stable boy at the Lion d'Or. He had put on his new leg.

One of the cantors came through the nave, taking up the collection, and one after another the heavy coins clattered onto the silver plate.

"Get it over with! I can't stand much more of this!" cried Bovary, angrily throwing him a five-franc piece.

The cantor thanked him with a ceremonious bow.

The singing and the kneeling and the rising went on and on. He remembered that once, early in their marriage, they had attended Mass together, and that they had sat on the other side, at the right, against the wall. The bell began to toll again. There was a great scraping of chairs. The pallbearers

7. A woodwind instrument no longer in use.

slipped their three poles under the bier, and everyone left the church.

At that moment Justin appeared in the doorway of the pharmacy and abruptly retreated, white-faced and trembling.

People stood at their windows to watch the procession. Charles, at the head, held himself very straight. He put on a brave front and nodded to those who came out from the lanes and the doorways to join the crowd.

The six men, three on each side, walked with short steps, panting a little. The priests, the cantors and the two choirboys recited the *De profundis;* and their voices carried over the fields, rising and falling in waves. Sometimes they disappeared from view at a twist of the path; but the great silver cross was always visible, high up among the trees.

At the rear were the women, in their black cloaks with turned-down hoods; each of them carried a thick lighted candle; and Charles felt himself overcome amidst this endless succession of prayers and lights, these cloying odors of wax and cassocks. A cool breeze was blowing, the rye and the colza were sprouting green; dewdrops shimmered on the thorn hedges along the road. All kinds of joyous sounds filled the air—the rattle of a jolting cart in distant ruts, the repeated crowing of a cock, the thudding of a colt as it bolted off under the apple trees. The pure sky was dappled with rosy clouds; wisps of bluish smoke trailed down over the thatched cottages, their roofs abloom with iris. Charles recognized each farmyard as he passed. He remembered leaving them on mornings like this after making sick calls, on his way back home to where she was.

The black pall, embroidered with white tears, flapped up now and again, exposing the coffin beneath. The tired pallbearers were slowing down, and the bier moved forward in a series of jerks, like a boat pitching at every wave.

They reached the cemetery.

The pallbearers continued on to where the grave had been dug in the turf.

Everyone stood around it; and as the priest spoke, the reddish earth, heaped up on the edges, kept sliding down at the corners, noiselessly and continuously.

Then, when the four ropes were in position, the coffin was pushed onto them. He watched it go down. It went down and down.

Finally there was a thud, and the ropes creaked as they came back up. Then Bournisien took the shovel that Lestiboudois held out to him. With his left hand—all the while sprinkling holy water with his right—he vigorously pushed in a large spadeful of earth; and the stones striking the wood of the coffin made that awesome sound that seems to us like the very voice of eternity.

The priest passed his sprinkler to the person beside him. It was Homais. He shook it gravely, then handed it to Charles, who sank on his knees in the pile of earth and threw it into the grave in handfuls, crying, *"Adieu!"* He blew her kisses, and dragged himself toward the grave as though to be swallowed up in it with her.

They led him away, and he soon grew calmer—vaguely relieved, perhaps, like everyone else, that it was all over.

On the way back Monsieur Rouault calmly lit his pipe—a gesture that Homais silently condemned as improper. He noticed, too, that Monsieur Binet had stayed away, that Tuvache had "sneaked off" after the Mass, and that Théodore, the notary's servant, was wearing a blue coat—"as if he couldn't find a black coat, since it's the custom, for heaven's sake!" And he went from group to group communicating his sentiments. Everyone was deploring Emma's death, especially Lheureux, who hadn't failed to attend the funeral.

"Poor little lady! How terrible for her husband!"

"If it hadn't been for me, let me tell you," the apothecary assured him, "he would have tried to do away with himself!"

"Such a good woman! To think that just last Saturday I saw her in my shop!"

"I didn't have the leisure," said Homais, "to prepare a little speech. I'd have liked to say a few words at the grave."

Back home, Charles took off his funeral clothes and Monsieur Rouault got back into his blue smock. It was a new one: all the way from Les Bertaux he had kept wiping his eyes with the sleeve, and the dye had come off on his face, which was still dusty and tear-streaked.

The older Madame Bovary was with them. All three were silent. Finally the old man sighed:

"You remember, my friend, I came to Tostes once, when you had just lost your first wife. That time I tried to comfort you. I could think of something to say; but now . . ."

Then, his chest heaving in a long groan:

"Ah! Everything's over for me! I've seen my wife go . . . then my son . . . and now today my daughter!"

He insisted on leaving immediately for Les Bertaux, saying that he couldn't sleep in that house. He even refused to see his granddaughter.

"No! No! It would be too hard on me. . . . But give her a big kiss for me! Good-bye! . . . You're a good man! And—I'll never forget this!" he said, slapping his thigh. "Don't worry—you'll always get your turkey."

But when he reached the top of the hill he turned around as he had turned around once before, after parting from her on the road to Saint-Victor. The windows of the village were all ablaze in the slanting rays of the sun that was setting beyond the meadow. He shaded his eyes with his hand; and on the horizon he made out a walled enclosure where trees stood in dark clumps here and there among white stones; then he continued on his way at a gentle trot, for his nag was limping.

Weary though they were, Charles and his mother sat up very late that night talking. They spoke of days gone by and of the future: she would come and live in Yonville, she would keep house for him; never again would they be apart. She was astute and ingratiating with him, rejoicing inwardly at the thought of recapturing his affection, which had eluded her for so many years. Midnight struck. The village was silent as usual; and Charles lay awake, thinking ceaselessly of *her*.

Rodolphe, who had spent all day roaming the woods to keep his mind off things, was peacefully asleep in his château; and Léon was sleeping, too, in the distant city.

But there was someone else—someone who was not asleep at that late hour.

On the grave among the firs knelt a young boy, weeping and sobbing in the darkness, his heart overflowing with an immense grief that was tender as the moon and unfathomable as night. Suddenly the gate creaked. It was

Lestiboudois, come to fetch his spade, which he had forgotten a while before. He recognized Justin clambering over the wall: at last he knew who was stealing his potatoes!

XI

The next day Charles sent for Berthe. She asked for *maman:* she was away on a trip, she was told, and would bring her back some toys. She mentioned her again several times, then gradually forgot her. Charles found the little girl's cheerfulness depressing. The pharmacist's consolations, too, were an ordeal.

Before long the question of money came up again. Monsieur Lheureux egged on his friend Vinçart as before, and Charles signed notes for enormous sums: he refused absolutely to consider selling the slightest bit of furniture that had belonged to her. His mother fumed; he flew into an even greater rage. He was a completely changed man. She packed up and left.

Then everyone began to snatch what he could. Mademoiselle Lempereur demanded her fees for six months' lessons. Emma had never taken a single one, despite the receipted bills that she had shown Bovary: the two ladies had concocted this device between them. The lending-library proprietor demanded three years' subscription fees. Madame Rollet demanded postage fees for twenty or so letters, and when Charles asked for an explanation she was tactful enough to answer.

"Oh, I don't know anything about them—some personal matters."

Each debt he paid, Charles thought was the last. Then more came—a continual stream.

He dunned patients for back bills, but they showed him the letters his wife had sent and he had to apologize.

Félicité now wore Madame's dresses. Not all, for he had kept a few and used to shut himself up in her dressing room and look at them. The maid was just about her size, and often when Charles caught sight of her from behind he thought it was Emma, and cried out:

"Oh! Don't go! Don't go!"

But at Pentecost she left Yonville without warning, eloping with Théodore and stealing everything that was left of the wardrobe.

It was about this time that "Madame *veuve* Dupuis" had the honor of announcing to him the "marriage of M. Léon Dupuis, her son, notary at Yvetot, and Mlle. Léocadie Leboeuf, of Bondeville." Charles's letter of congratulation contained the sentence: "How happy this would have made my poor wife!"

One day, wandering aimlessly about the house, he went up to the attic; and through the sole of his slipper he felt a wad of thin paper. He opened it. "You must be courageous, Emma," he read. "The last thing I want to do is ruin your life." It was Rodolphe's letter. It had fallen to the floor in among some boxes and had remained there, and now the draught from the dormer had blown it toward the door. Charles stood there motionless and open-mouthed—in the very spot where Emma, desperate and even paler than he was now, had longed to die. Finally he discovered a small "R" at the bottom of the second page. Who was it? He remembered Rodolphe's attentiveness, his sudden disappearance, and his air of constraint the two or three times they had met since. But the respectful tone of the letter deceived him.

"Perhaps they loved each other platonically," he told himself.

In any case, Charles wasn't one to go to the root of things: he closed his eyes to the evidence, and his hesitant jealousy was drowned in the immensity of his grief.

Everyone must have adored her, he thought. Every man who saw her must certainly have coveted her. This made her the lovelier in his mind; and he conceived a furious desire for her that never stopped; it fed the flames of his despair, and it grew stronger and stronger because now it could never be satisfied.

To please her, as though she were still alive, he adopted her tastes, her ideas: he bought himself patent leather shoes, took to wearing white cravats. He waxed his mustache, and signed—just as she had—more promissory notes. She was corrupting him from beyond the grave.

He was forced to sell the silver piece by piece, then he sold the parlor furniture. But though all the other rooms grew bare, the bedroom—her bedroom—remained as before. Charles went there every day after dinner. He pushed the round table up to the fire, pulled her armchair close to it. He sat opposite. A tallow candle burned in one of the gilded sconces. Berthe, at his side, colored pictures.

It pained him, poor fellow, to see her so shabbily dressed, with her shoes unlaced and the armholes of her smock torn and gaping to below her waist— for the cleaning woman completely neglected her. But she was so sweet and gentle, and she bent her little head so gracefully, letting her fair hair fall against her rosy cheek, that he was flooded with infinite pleasure—an enjoyment that was mixed with bitterness, like an inferior wine tasting of resin. He mended her toys, made puppets for her out of cardboard, sewed up the torn stomachs of her dolls. But the sight of the sewing box, or a bit of loose ribbon, or even a pin caught in a crack in the table, would send him brooding; and then he looked so gloomy that she, too, grew sad.

No one came to see them now, for Justin had run off to Rouen, where he found work as a grocery clerk, and the apothecary's children saw less and less of Berthe. Monsieur Homais was not eager to prolong the intimacy, considering the difference in their social status.

The blind man, whom his salve had not cured, had resumed his beat on the hill at Bois-Guillaume, where he told everyone about the pharmacist's failure—to such a point that Homais, whenever he went to the city, hid behind the Hirondelle's curtains to avoid meeting him face to face. He hated him. He must get rid of him at all costs, he decided, for the sake of his own reputation; and he launched an underhand campaign against him in which he revealed his deep cunning and his criminal vanity. During the next six months paragraphs like the following would appear in the *Fanal de Rouen*:

> Anyone who has ever wended his way toward the fertile fields of Picardy cannot help but have noticed, on the hill at Bois-Guillaume, an unfortunate afflicted with a horrible facial deformity. He pesters travelers, persecutes them, levies a veritable tax upon them. Are we back in the monstrous days of the Middle Ages, when vagabonds were permitted to display, in our public squares, the leprous ulcers and scrofulous sores they brought back from the Crusades?

Or:

> Despite the laws against vagrancy, the approaches to our large cities continue to be infested by bands of beggars. There are some who operate single-handed; and these, perhaps, are not the least dangerous of the lot. What are our Municipal Authorities waiting for?

Sometimes Homais invented ancedotes:

> Yesterday, on the hill at Bois-Guillaume, a skittish horse . . .

And there would follow the story of an accident caused by the blind man. This went on until the beggar was locked up. But he was released. He took up where he had left off. So did Homais. It was a fight to the finish. Homais was victorious: his enemy was committed to an asylum for the rest of his days.

This success emboldened him; and from then on whenever a dog was run over in the district, or a barn set on fire, or a woman beaten, Homais hastened to publicize the event, inspired always by love of progress and hatred of the clergy. He instituted comparisons between public and religious schools, to the detriment of the latter; he referred to Saint Bartholomew's Eve apropos of every hundred-franc subsidy the government granted the church; he denounced abuses, he flashed the rapier of satire. Such, at least, was the way he put it. In short, Homais was "undermining the foundations": he was becoming a dangerous man.

He found the narrow limitations of journalism stifling, however, and soon he felt the need to produce a book, a "work." So he composed his *General Statistics Concerning the Canton of Yonville, Followed by Climatological Observations;* and statistics led him into philosophy. He dealt with burning issues: the social problem, raising the moral standards of the poor, pisciculture,[8] rubber, railroads, etc. In the end, he felt it a disgrace to be a bourgeois. He affected bohemian ways, he even smoked! He bought two rococo statuettes, very *chic,* to decorate his parlor.

Not that he gave up pharmacy. Far from it! He kept up with all the latest discoveries. He followed every stage in the great development of chocolates. He was the first to introduce into the department of the Seine-Inférieure those two great chocolate health foods, Cho-ca and Revalentia. He became an enthusiastic partisan of Pulvermacher electric health belts; he wore one himself, and at night when he took off his flannel undershirt Madame Homais never failed to be dazzled by the golden spiral that almost hid him from view, and her passion redoubled for this man she saw before her swaddled like a Scythian and splendid as a Magian priest.

He had brilliant ideas for Emma's tombstone. First he suggested a broken column with a drapery; then a pyramid, then a Temple of Vesta, a kind of rotunda, or perhaps a romantic pile of ruins. One element was constant in all his plans—a weeping willow, which he considered the obligatory symbol of grief.

Charles and he made a trip to Rouen together to look at tombstones at a burial specialist's, accompanied by an artist named Vaufrilard, a friend of Bridoux's, who never stopped making puns. Finally, after examining a hun-

8. Fish breeding.

dred designs, getting an estimate, and making a second trip to Rouen, Charles decided in favor of a mausoleum whose two principal sides were to be adorned with "a spirit bearing an extinguished torch."

As for the inscription, Homais could think of nothing as eloquent as *Sta viator*. He couldn't get beyond it, rack his brains as he might: he kept repeating *"Sta viator"* to himself over and over again. Finally he had an inspiration— *amabilem conjugem calcas;*[9] and this was adopted.

The strange thing was that Bovary, even though he thought of Emma continually, was forgetting her; and he felt desperate realizing that her image was fading from his memory, struggle as he might to keep it alive. Each night, however, he dreamed of her. It was always the same dream: he approached her, but just when he was about to embrace her she fell into decay in his arms.

The first week, he went to church every evening. Monsieur Bournisien called on him two or three times, then left him alone. The fact is that the priest was becoming decidedly less tolerant—sinking into real fanaticism, as Homais put it. He thundered against the spirit of the modern age, and regularly once a fortnight included in his sermon an account of the last agony of Voltaire—who died eating his own excrement, as everyone knows.

Despite Bovary's frugality, he was quite unable to pay off his old debts. Lheureux refused to renew a single note. Execution was imminent. He had recourse to his mother, who agreed to let him mortgage her house; but she seized the occasion to write him many harsh things about Emma, and in return for her sacrifice she demanded a shawl that had escaped Félicité's depredations. Charles refused to let her have it, and they quarreled.

She made the first overtures toward a reconciliation by offering to take the little girl to live with her: the child could help her in the house. Charles consented. But when the time came for her to leave he couldn't face it, and there was a new break between mother and son, this time irrevocable.

As his bonds with others weakened, his love for his child grew ever stronger. She worried him, however, for occasionally she coughed and had red patches on her cheekbones.

Across the square, in constant view, thriving and jovial, was the family of the pharmacist. He had every reason to be satisfied with his lot. Napoléon helped him in the laboratory, Athalie embroidered him a smoking cap, Irma cut paper circles to cover the jelly jars, and Franklin could recite the multiplication table without stumbling. Homais was the happiest of fathers, the luckiest of men.

Not quite, though! He was eaten with a secret ambition: he wanted the cross of the Legion of Honor. He had plenty of qualifications:

"First: during the cholera epidemic, was conspicuous for devotion above and beyond the call of professional duty. *Second:* have published at my own expense various works of public usefulness, such as . . ." (And he cited his treatise on *Cider: Its Manufacture and Its Effects:* also, some observations on the woolly aphis that he had sent to the Academy; his volume of statistics, and even his pharmacist's thesis.) "Not to mention that I am a member of several learned societies." (He belonged to only one.)

---

9. You are treading on a beloved spouse (Latin). Based on the Latin inscription placed over the spot where the valorous Bavarian field marshal Baron Franz von Mercy died in the Second Battle of Nördlingen (1645): *Sta viator, heroem calcas* (Halt, traveler, you are treading on a hero).

"And even suppose," he said with a caper, "that the only thing I had to my credit was my perfect record as a volunteer fireman!"

Homais proceeded to ingratiate himself with the powers that be; he secretly rendered great services to Monsieur le Préfet during an electoral campaign. In short he sold himself; he prostituted himself. He went so far as to address a petition to the sovereign in which he begged him to "do him justice": he called him "our good king" and compared him to Henri IV.

Every morning the apothecary rushed to the newspaper, hoping to find the news of his nomination, but it didn't come. Finally, in his impatience, he had a star-shaped grass plot designed for his garden, to represent the decoration, with two little tufts of greenery as the ribbon. He would walk around it, his arms folded, pondering on governmental stupidity and human ingratitude.

Out of respect, or to prolong the almost sensual pleasure he took in his investigations, Charles had not yet opened the secret compartment of the rosewood desk that Emma had always used. At last, one day, he sat down at it, turned the key and pressed the spring. All Léon's letters were there. No possible doubt, this time! He devoured every last one of them. Then he rummaged in every corner, every piece of furniture, every drawer, looked for hiding places in the walls: he was sobbing, screaming with rage, beside himself, stark mad. He came upon a box, kicked it open. Rodolphe's picture jumped out at him, and all the love letters spilled out with it.

Everyone was amazed at the depth of his depression. He no longer went out, had no visitors, refused even to call on his patients. Everyone said that he "locked himself up to get drunk."

Now and again someone more curious than the rest would peer over the garden hedge and would be startled at the sight of him, wild-eyed, long-bearded, clad in sordid rags, walking and weeping aloud.

Summer evenings he would take his daughter with him and go to the cemetery. They always came back after dark, when the only light in the square was in Binet's dormer.

Still, he was unable to savor his grief to the full, since he had no one with whom he could share it. From time to time he called on Madame Lefrançois, for the sole purpose of talking about "her." But the innkeeper listened to him with only one ear, having her troubles just as he had his: Monsieur Lheureux had finally established his transportation service, *Les Favorites du commerce,* and Hivert, who enjoyed a considerable reputation for his dependability as doer of errands, was demanding an increase in wages and threatening to go to work for her competitor.

One day, at the market in Argueuil, where he had gone to sell his horse—his last asset—he met Rodolphe.

Both men turned pale when they caught sight of each other, Rodolphe, who had merely sent his card with a message of condolence, began by stammering a few excuses; then he grew bolder, and even had the cheek (it was a very hot August day) to invite him to take a bottle of beer in a café.

Sitting opposite him, his elbows on the table, he chewed his cigar as he talked; and Charles was lost in revery as he looked into the face that she had loved. In it, he felt, he was seeing something of her. It was a revelation. He would have liked to be that man.

Rodolphe talked farming, livestock, fertilizers—making use of banalities to stop up all the gaps through which any compromising reference might creep in. Charles wasn't listening. Rodolphe became aware of this; and in the play of expression on Charles's face he could read the sequence of his thoughts. Gradually it grew crimson; Charles's nostrils fluttered, his lips quivered; at one point, filled with somber fury, he stared fixedly at Rodolphe, who in his fright stopped speaking. But almost at once the other man's features reassumed their habitual expression of mournful weariness.

"I don't hold it against you," he said.

Rodolphe sat speechless. And Charles, his head in his hands, repeated, in a dull voice, with all the resignation of a grief that can never be assuaged:

"No, I don't hold it against you, any more."

And he added a bit of rhetoric, the only such utterance that had ever escaped him:

"No one is to blame. It was decreed by fate."

Rodolphe, who had been the instrument of that fate, thought him very meek indeed for a man in his situation—comical, even, and a little contemptible.

The next day Charles sat down on the bench in the arbor. Rays of light came through the trellis, grape leaves traced their shadow on the gravel, the jasmine was fragrant under the blue sky, bettles buzzed about the flowering lilies. A vaporous flood of love-memories swelled in his sorrowing heart, and he was overcome with emotion, like an adolescent.

At seven o'clock little Berthe, who hadn't seen him all afternoon, came to call him to dinner.

She found him with his head leaning back against the wall, his eyes closed, his mouth open; and there was a long lock of black hair in his hands.

"Papa! Come along!" she said.

She thought that he was playing, and gave him a little push. He fell to the ground. He was dead.

Thirty-six hours later Monsieur Canivet arrived, summoned by the apothecary. He performed an autopsy, but found nothing.

When everything was sold, there remained twelve francs and fifteen centimes—enough to pay Mademoiselle Bovary's coach fare to her grandmother's. The old lady died the same year; and since Monsieur Rouault was now paralyzed, it was an aunt who took charge of her. She is poor, and sends her to work for her living in a cotton mill.

Since Bovary's death, three doctors have succeeded one another in Yonville, and not one of them has gained a foothold, so rapidly and so utterly has Homais routed them. The devil himself doesn't have a greater following than the pharmacist: the authorities treat him considerately, and public opinion is on his side.

He has just been awarded the cross of the Legion of Honor.

FYODOR DOSTOEVSKY
1821–1881

Fyodor Dostoevsky has been a central figure in the formation of the modern sensibility. His works are fundamental to the Western tradition of the novel and a strong influence on modern literature in China and Japan. Dostoevsky formulated in fictional terms, in dramatic and even sensational scenes, some of the central predicaments of our time: the choices between God and atheism, good and evil, freedom and tyranny; the recognition of the limits and even of the fall of humanity against the belief in progress, revolution, and utopia. Most important, he captured unforgettably the enormous contradictions of which our common human nature is capable and by which it is torn.

Fyodor Mikhailovich Dostoevsky was born in Moscow on October 30, 1821. His father was a staff doctor at the Hospital for the Poor. Later he acquired an estate and serfs. In 1839 he was killed by one of his peasants in a quarrel. Dostoevsky was sent to the Military Engineering Academy in St. Petersburg, from which he graduated in 1843. He became a civil servant, a draftsman in the St. Petersburg Engineering Corps, but soon resigned because he feared that he would be transferred to the provinces when his writing was discovered. His first novel, *Poor People* (1845), proved a great success with the critics; his second, *The Double* (1846), which followed immediately, was a failure.

Subsequently, Dostoevsky became involved in the Petrashevsky circle, a secret society with antigovernment and socialist tendencies. He was arrested on April 23, 1849, and condemned to be shot. On December 22 he was led to public execution, but he was reprieved at the last moment and sent to penal servitude in Siberia (near Omsk), where he worked for four years in a stockade, wearing fetters, completely cut off from communications with Russia. On his release in 1854, he was assigned as a common soldier to Semipalatinsk, a small town near the Mongolian frontier. There he received several promotions (eventually becoming an ensign); his rank of nobility, forfeited by his sentence, was restored; and he married the widow of a customs official. In July 1859, Dostoevsky was permitted to return to Russia and, finally, in December 1859, to St. Petersburg—after ten years of his life had been spent in Siberia.

In the last year of his exile, Dostoevsky had resumed writing; and in 1861, shortly after his return, he founded a review, *Time* (*Vremya*). This was suppressed in 1863, even though Dostoevsky had changed his political opinions and was now strongly nationalistic and conservative in outlook. He made his first trip to France and England in 1862 and traveled in Europe again in 1863 and 1865, to follow a young woman friend, Apollinaria Suslova and to gamble. After his wife's death in 1864 and another unsuccessful journalistic venture, *The Epoch* (*Epokha,* 1864–65), Dostoevsky was for a time almost crushed by gambling debts, emotional entanglements, and frequent epileptic seizures. He barely managed to return from Germany in 1865. In the winter of 1866 he wrote *Crime and Punishment* and, before he had finished it, dictated a shorter novel, *The Gambler,* to meet a deadline. He married his secretary, Anna Grigoryevna Snitkina, early in 1867 and left Russia with her to avoid his creditors. For years they wandered through Germany, Italy, and Switzerland, frequently in abject poverty. Their first child died. In 1871, when the initial chapters of *The Possessed* proved a popular success, Dostoevsky returned to St. Petersburg. He was the editor of a weekly, *The Citizen* (*Grazhdanin*), for a short time and then published a periodical written by himself, *The Diary of a Writer* (1876–81), which won great acclaim. His last novel, *The Brothers Karamazov* (1880), was an immense success, and honors and some prosperity came to him at last. At a Pushkin anniversary celebrated in Moscow in 1880 he gave the main speech. But soon after his return to St. Petersburg he died, on January 28, 1881, not yet sixty years old.

Dostoevsky, like every great writer, can be approached in different ways and read on different levels. We can try to understand him as a religious philosopher, a political commentator, a psychologist, and a novelist; and, if we know much about his fascinating and varied life, we might also interpret his works as biographical.

The biographical interpretation is the one that has been pushed furthest. The lurid crimes of Dostoevsky's characters (such as the rape of a young girl) have been ascribed to him, and all his novels have been studied as if they constituted a great personal confession. Dostoevsky certainly did draw from his experiences in his books, as every writer does: he several times describes the feelings of a man facing a firing squad as he himself faced it on December 22, 1849, only to be reprieved at the last moment. His writings also reflect his years in Siberia: four years working in a loghouse, in chains, as he describes it in an oddly impersonal book, *Memoirs from the House of the Dead* (1862), and six more years as a common soldier on the borders of Mongolia, in a small, remote provincial town. Similarly, he used the experience of his disease (epilepsy), ascribing great spiritual significance to the ecstatic rapture preceding the actual seizure. He assigned his disease to both his most angelic "good" man, the "Idiot" Prince Myshkin, and his most diabolical, inhuman figure, the cold-blooded unsexed murderer of the old Karamazov, the flunky Smerdyakov. Dostoevsky also used something of his experiences in Germany, where in the 1860s he succumbed to a passion for gambling, which he overcame only much later, during his second marriage. The short novel *The Gambler* (1866) gives an especially vivid account of this life and its moods.

There are other autobiographical elements in Dostoevsky's works, but it seems a gross misunderstanding of his methods and the procedures of art in general to conclude from his writings (as Thomas Mann has done) that he was a "saint and criminal" in one. Dostoevsky, after all, was an extremely hard worker who wrote and rewrote some twenty volumes. He was a novelist who employed the methods of the French sensational novel; he was constantly on the lookout for the most striking occurrences—the most shocking crimes and the most horrible disasters and scandals—because only in such fictional situations could he exalt his characters to their highest pitch, bringing out the clash of ideas and temperaments, revealing the deepest layers of their souls. But these fictions cannot be taken as literal transcriptions of reality and actual experience.

Whole books have been written to explain Dostoevsky's religious philosophy and conception of human nature. The Russian philosopher Berdyayev concludes his excellent study by saying, "So great is the value of Dostoevsky that to have produced him is by itself sufficient justification for the existence of the Russian people in the world." But there is no need for such extravagance. Dostoevsky's philosophy of religion is rather a personal version of extreme mystical Christianity and assumes flesh and blood only in the context of the novels. Reduced to the bare bones of abstract propositions, it says that humanity is fallen but is free to choose between evil and Christ. And choosing Christ means taking on oneself the burden of humanity in love and pity, since "everybody is guilty for all and before all." Hence in Dostoevsky there is tremendous stress on personal freedom of choice; and his affirmation of the worth of every individual is combined, paradoxically, with an equal insistence on the substantial identity of all human beings, their equality before God, the bond of love that unites them.

Dostoevsky also develops a philosophy of history, with practical political implications, based on this point of view. According to him, the West is in complete decay; only Russia has preserved Christianity in its original form. The West is either Catholic (and Catholicism is condemned by Dostoevsky as an attempt to force salvation by magic and authority) or bourgeois, and hence materialistic and fallen away from Christ, or socialist, and socialism is to Dostoevsky identical with atheism since it dreams of a utopia in which human beings would not be free to choose even at the expense of suffering. Dostoevsky—who himself had belonged to a revolutionary group and come into contact with Russian revolutionaries abroad—had an extraordinary insight into the mentality of the Russian underground. In *The Possessed* (1871–72) he gives a lurid satiric picture of these would-be saviors of Russia and humankind. But although he was afraid of the revolution, Dostoevsky himself hoped and prophesied that Russia would save Europe from the dangers of communism since Russia alone was the uncorrupted Christian land. Put in terms of political propositions (as Dostoevsky himself preaches them in his journal, *The Diary of a Writer*, 1876–81), what he propounds is a conservative Russian nationalism with messianic hopes for Russian Christianity.

When translated into abstractions, Dostoevsky's psychology is as unimpressive as his political theory. It is merely a derivative of theories propounded by German writers about the unconscious, the role of dreams, the ambivalence of human feelings. What makes it electric in the novels is his ability to dramatize it in scenes of sudden revelation, in characters who in today's terminology would be called split personalities, in people twisted by isolation, lust, humiliation, and resentment. The dreams of Raskolnikov may be interpreted according to Freudian psychology; but to the reader without any knowledge of science they are comprehensible in their place in the novel and function as warnings and anticipations.

Dostoevsky was first of all an artist—a novelist who succeeded in using his ideas (many old and venerable, many new and fantastic) and psychological insights for the writing of stories of absorbing interest. As an artist, Dostoevsky treated the novel like a drama, constructing it in large, vivid scenes that end with a scandal or a crime or some act of violence, filling it with unforgettable "stagelike" figures torn by great passions and swayed by great ideas. Then he set this world in an environment of St. Petersburg slums or of towns, monasteries, and country houses, all so vividly realized that we forget how the setting, the figures, and the ideas blend together into one cosmos of the imagination only remotely and obliquely related to any reality of nineteenth-century Russia. We take part in a great drama of pride and humility, good and evil, in a huge allegory of humanity's search for God and itself. We understand and share in this world because it is not merely Russia in the nineteenth century, where people could hardly have talked and behaved as Dostoevsky's people do, but a myth of humanity, universalized as all art is.

Notes from Underground (1864) precedes the four great novels: *Crime and Punishment* (1866), *The Idiot* (1868), *The Possessed* (1871–72), and *The Brothers Karamazov* (1880). The *Notes* can be viewed as a prologue, an important introduction to the cycle of the four novels, an anticipation of the mature Dostoevsky's method and thought. Although it cannot compare in dramatic power and scope with these, the story has its own peculiar and original artistry. It is made up of two parts, at first glance seemingly independent: the monologue of the Underground man and the confession that he makes about himself, called *Apropos of Wet Snow*. The monologue, though it includes no action, is dramatic—a long address to an imaginary hostile reader, whom the Underground man ridicules, defies, jeers at, but also flatters. The confession is an autobiographical reminiscence of the Underground man. It describes events that occurred long before the delivery of the monologue, but it functions as a confirmation in concrete terms of the self-portrait drawn in the monologue and as an explanation of the isolation of the hero.

The narrative of the confession is a comic variation on the old theme of the rescue of a fallen woman from vice, a seesaw series of humiliations permitting Dostoevsky to display all the cruelty of his probing psychology. The hero, out of spite and craving for human company, forces himself into the company of former schoolfellows and is shamefully humiliated by them. He reasserts his ego (since he cannot revenge himself on them) in the company of a humble prostitute by impressing her with florid and moving speeches, which he knows to be insincere, about her horrible future. Ironically, he converts her, but when she comes to him and surprises him in a degrading scene with his servant, he humiliates her again. When, even then, she understands and forgives and thus shows her moral superiority, he crowns his spite by deliberately misunderstanding her and forcing money on her. She is the moral victor, and the Underground man returns to his hideout to jeer at humanity. It is hard not to feel that we are shown a tortured and twisted soul almost too despicable to elicit our compassion.

Still we would completely misunderstand Dostoevsky's story if we were to take the philosophy expounded jeeringly in the long monologue of the first part merely as the irrational railings of a sick personality. The Underground man, though abject and spiteful, represents not only a specific Russian type of the time—the intellectual divorced from the soil and his nation—but also modern humanity, even Everyman, and, strangely enough, even the author, who through the mouth of this despicable character, as through a mask, expresses his boldest and most intimate convictions. In spite of the exaggerated pathos, wild paradox, and mocking irony used by the speaker, his self-criticism and his criticism of society and history must be taken seriously and interpreted patiently if we are to extract the meaning accepted by Dostoevsky.

The Underground man is also the hyperconscious man who examines himself with pitiless candor as if he were seeing himself in a mirror. His very self-consciousness cripples his will and poisons his feelings. He cannot escape from his ego; he knows that he has acted badly toward the woman but cannot help acting as he does. He knows that he is alone, that there is no bridge from him to humanity, that the world is hostile to him, and that he is humiliated by everyone he meets. But even though he resents the humiliation, he cannot help courting it, provoking it, and even enjoying it in his perverse manner. He understands (and knows from his own experience) that something within us all enjoys evil and destruction.

His self-criticism widens, then, into a criticism of the assumptions of modern civilization, of nineteenth-century optimism about human nature and progress, of utilitarianism, and of all kinds of utopias. Although we can identify specific allusions to a contemporary novel by radical socialist and revolutionary Nikolai Chernyshevsky entitled *What Is to Be Done?* (1863), we do not need to know the exact target of Dostoevsky's satire to recognize what he attacks: the view that human nature is good, that we generally seek our enlightened self-interest, that science propounds immutable truths, and that a paradise on Earth will be just around the corner once society is reformed along scientific lines. In a series of vivid symbols these assumptions are represented, parodied, exposed. Science says that "twice two makes four"; but the Underground man laughingly maintains that "twice two makes five is sometimes a very charming thing too." Science means to him (and to Dostoevsky) the victory of the doctrine of fatality, of iron necessity, of determinism, and finally of death. Humanity would become an "organ stop," a "piano key," if deterministic science were valid.

Equally disastrous are the implications of the social philosophy of liberalism and of socialism (which Dostoevsky considers its necessary consequence). In this view, we need only follow our enlightened self-interest, need only be rational, and we will become noble and good and the Earth will be a place of prosperity and peace. But the Underground man knows that this conception of human nature is false. What if humankind does not follow, and never will follow, its own enlightened self-interest, is consciously and purposely irrational, even bloodthirsty and evil? History seems to the Underground man to speak a clear language: "Civilization has made mankind if not more bloodthirsty, at least more vilely, more loathsomely bloodthirsty." Humanity wills the irrational and evil because it does not want to become an organ stop, a piano key, because it wants to be left with the freedom to choose between good and evil. This freedom of choice, even at the expense of chaos and destruction, is what makes us human.

Actually, we love something other than our own well-being and happiness, love even suffering and pain, because we are human and not animals inhabiting some great, organized rational "ant heap." The ant heap, the hen house, the block of tenements, and finally the Crystal Palace (then the newest wonder of architecture, a great hall of iron and glass erected for the Great Exhibition of 1851 in London) are the images used by the Underground man to represent his hated utopia. The heroine of *What Is to Be Done?* had dreamed of a building made of cast iron and glass and placed in the middle of a beautiful garden where there would be eternal spring and summer, eternal joy. Dostoevsky had recognized there the utopian dream of Charles Fourier, the French socialist whom he had admired in his youth and whose ideals he had come to hate with a fierce revulsion. But we must realize that the Underground man—and Dostoevsky—despise this "ant heap," this perfectly organized society of automatons, in the name of something higher: freedom. Dostoevsky does not believe that humanity can achieve freedom and happiness at the same time; happiness can be bought only at the expense of freedom, and all utopian schemes seem to him devices to lure us into the yoke of slavery. This freedom is, of course, not political freedom but freedom of choice, indeterminism, even caprice and willfulness, in the paradoxical formulation of the Underground man.

There are hints at a positive solution only in the one chapter (Part I, Chapter X) that was mutilated by the censor. A letter by Dostoevsky to his brother about the "swine of a censor who let through the passages where I jeered at everything and blasphemed ostensibly" refers to the fact that he "suppressed everything where I drew the conclusion that faith in Christ is needed." In Part I, Chapter XI, of the present text (and Dostoevsky never restored the suppressed passages), the Underground man says merely, "I am lying because I know myself that it is not underground that is better, but something different, quite different, for which I am thirsting, but which I cannot find!" All the other writings of Dostoevsky show this "something . . . quite different" to be the voluntary following of the Christian savior even at the expense of suffering and pain.

In a paradoxical form, through the mouth of one of his vilest characters, Dostoevsky reveals in the story his view of humanity and history—of the evil in human nature and of the blood and tragedy in history—and his criticism of the optimistic, utilitarian, utopian, progressive view of humanity that was spreading to Russia from the West during the nineteenth century and that found its most devoted adherents in the Russian revolutionaries. Preoccupied with criticism, Dostoevsky does not here suggest any positive remedy. But if we understand the *Notes,* we can understand how Raskolnikov, the murderer out of intellect in *Crime and Punishment,* can find salvation at last and how Dmitri, the guilty-guiltless parricide of *The Brothers Karamazov,* can sing his hymn to joy in the Siberian mines. We can even understand the legend of the Grand Inquisitor told by Ivan Karamazov, in which we meet the same criticism of a utopia (this time that of Catholicism) and the same exaltation of human freedom even at the price of suffering.

PRONOUNCING GLOSSARY

The following list uses common English syllables and stress accents to provide rough equivalents of selected words whose pronunciation may be unfamiliar to the general reader.

Anton Antonych: *ahn-tawn' ahn-taw'-nich*

Apollon: *ah-pah-lawn'*

Ferfichkin: *fehr-feech'-keen*

Fyodor Dostoevsky: *fyo'dor dos-toy-eff'-skee*

Karamazov: *kuh-rah-mah'-zuf*

Kolya: *kawl'-yuh*

Podkharzhevsky: *put-khar-zhef'-skee*

Simonov: *see'-muh-nuf*

Trudolyubov: *troo-dah-lyoo'-buf*

Zverkov: *zvyehr-kof'*

Notes from Underground[1]

I

Underground[2]

I

I am a sick man. . . . [3] I am a spiteful man. I am a most unpleasant man. I think my liver is diseased. Then again, I don't know a thing about my illness; I'm not even sure what hurts. I'm not being treated and never have been, though I respect both medicine and doctors. Besides, I'm extremely super- stitious—well at least enough to respect medicine. (I'm sufficiently educated not to be superstitious; but I am, anyway.) No, gentlemen, it's out of spite that I don't wish to be treated. Now then, that's something you probably won't understand. Well, I do. Of course, I won't really be able to explain to you precisely who will be hurt by my spite in this case; I know perfectly well that I can't possibly "get even" with doctors by refusing their treatment; I know better than anyone that all this is going to hurt me alone, and no one else. Even so, if I refuse to be treated, it's out of spite. My liver hurts? Good, let it hurt even more!

I've been living this way for some time—about twenty years. I'm forty now. I used to be in the civil service. But no more. I was a nasty official. I was rude and took pleasure in it. After all, since I didn't accept bribes, at least I had to reward myself in some way. (That's a poor joke, but I won't cross it out. I wrote it thinking that it would be very witty; but now, having realized that I merely wanted to show off disgracefully, I'll make a point of not crossing it out!) When petitioners used to approach my desk for information, I'd gnash my teeth and feel unending pleasure if I succeeded in causing someone distress. I almost always succeeded. For the most part they were all timid people: naturally, since they were petitioners. But among the dan- dies there was a certain officer whom I particularly couldn't bear. He simply refused to be humble, and he clanged his saber in a loathsome manner. I waged war with him over that saber for about a year and a half. At last I prevailed. He stopped clanging. All this, however, happened a long time ago, during my youth. But do you know, gentlemen, what the main component of my spite really was? Why, the whole point, the most disgusting thing, was the fact that I was shamefully aware at every moment, even at the moment of my greatest bitterness, that not only was I not a spiteful man, I was not even an embittered one, and that I was merely scaring sparrows to no effect and consoling myself by doing so. I was foaming at the mouth—but just bring me some trinket to play with, just serve me a nice cup of tea with sugar,

---

1. Translated by Michael Katz. 2. Both the author of these notes and the *Notes* themselves are fictitious, of course. Nevertheless, people like the author of these notes not only may, but actually must exist in our society, considering the general circumstances under which our society was formed. I wanted to bring before the public with more prominence than usual one of the characters of the recent past. He's a rep- resentative of the current generation. In the excerpt entitled "Underground" this person introduces himself and his views, and, as it were, wants to explain the reasons why he appeared and why he had to appear in our midst. The following excerpt [*Apropos of Wet Snow*] contains the actual "notes" of this person about several events in his life [Author's note]. 3. The ellipses are the author's and do not indicate omissions from this text.

and I'd probably have calmed down. My heart might even have been touched, although I'd probably have gnashed my teeth out of shame and then suffered from insomnia for several months afterward. That's just my usual way.

I was lying about myself just now when I said that I was a nasty official. I lied out of spite. I was merely having some fun at the expense of both the petitioners and that officer, but I could never really become spiteful. At all times I was aware of a great many elements in me that were just the opposite of that. I felt how they swarmed inside me, these contradictory elements. I knew that they had been swarming inside me my whole life and were begging to be let out; but I wouldn't let them out, I wouldn't, I deliberately wouldn't let them out. They tormented me to the point of shame; they drove me to convulsions and—and finally I got fed up with them, oh how fed up! Perhaps it seems to you, gentlemen, that I'm repenting about something, that I'm asking your forgiveness for something? I'm sure that's how it seems to you. . . . But really, I can assure you, I don't care if that's how it seems. . . .

Not only couldn't I become spiteful, I couldn't become anything at all: neither spiteful nor good, neither a scoundrel nor an honest man, neither a hero nor an insect. Now I live out my days in my corner, taunting myself with the spiteful and entirely useless consolation that an intelligent man cannot seriously become anything and that only a fool can become something. Yes, sir, an intelligent man in the nineteenth century must be, is morally obliged to be, principally a characterless creature; a man possessing character, a man of action, is fundamentally a limited creature. That's my conviction at the age of forty. I'm forty now; and, after all, forty is an entire lifetime; why it's extreme old age. It's rude to live past forty, it's indecent, immoral! Who lives more than forty years? Answer sincerely, honestly. I'll tell you who: only fools and rascals. I'll tell those old men that right to their faces, all those venerable old men, all those silver-haired and sweet-smelling old men! I'll say it to the whole world right to its face! I have a right to say it because I myself will live to sixty. I'll make it to seventy! Even to eighty! . . . Wait! Let me catch my breath. . . .

You probably think, gentlemen, that I want to amuse you. You're wrong about that, too. I'm not at all the cheerful fellow I seem to be, or that I may seem to be; however, if you're irritated by all this talk (and I can already sense that you are irritated), and if you decide to ask me just who I really am, then I'll tell you: I'm a collegiate assessor. I worked in order to have something to eat (but only for that reason); and last year, when a distant relative of mine left me six thousand rubles in his will, I retired immediately and settled down in this corner. I used to live in this corner before, but now I've settled down in it. My room is nasty, squalid, on the outskirts of town. My servant is an old peasant woman, spiteful out of stupidity; besides, she has a foul smell. I'm told that the Petersburg climate is becoming bad for my health, and that it's very expensive to live in Petersburg with my meager resources. I know all that; I know it better than all those wise and experienced advisers and admonishers. But I shall remain in Petersburg; I shall not leave Petersburg! I shall not leave here because . . . Oh, what difference does it really make whether I leave Petersburg or not?

Now, then, what can a decent man talk about with the greatest pleasure? Answer: about himself.

Well, then, I too will talk about myself.

II

Now I would like to tell you, gentlemen, whether or not you want to hear it, why it is that I couldn't even become an insect. I'll tell you solemnly that I wished to become an insect many times. But not even that wish was granted. I swear to you, gentlemen, that being overly conscious is a disease, a genuine, full-fledged disease. Ordinary human consciousness would be more than sufficient for everyday human needs—that is, even half or a quarter of the amount of consciousness that's available to a cultured man in our unfortunate nineteenth century, especially to one who has the particular misfortune of living in St. Petersburg, the most abstract and premeditated city in the whole world.[4] (Cities can be either premeditated or unpremeditated.) It would have been entirely sufficient, for example, to have the consciousness with which all so-called spontaneous people and men of action are endowed. I'll bet that you think I'm writing all this to show off, to make fun of these men of action, that I'm clanging my saber just like that officer did to show off in bad taste. But, gentlemen, who could possibly be proud of his illnesses and want to show them off?

But what am I saying? Everyone does that; people do take pride in their illnesses, and I, perhaps, more than anyone else. Let's not argue; my objection is absurd. Nevertheless, I remain firmly convinced that not only is being overly conscious a disease, but so is being conscious at all. I insist on it. But let's leave that alone for a moment. Tell me this: why was it, as if on purpose, at the very moment, indeed, at the precise moment that I was most capable of becoming conscious of the subtleties of everything that was "beautiful and sublime,"[5] as we used to say at one time, that I didn't become conscious, and instead did such unseemly things, things that . . . . well, in short, probably everyone does, but it seemed as if they occurred to me deliberately at the precise moment when I was most conscious that they shouldn't be done at all? The more conscious I was of what was good, of everything "beautiful and sublime," the more deeply I sank into the morass and the more capable I was of becoming entirely bogged down in it. But the main thing is that all this didn't seem to be occurring accidentally; rather, it was as if it all had to be so. It was as if this were my most normal condition, not an illness or an affliction at all, so that finally I even lost the desire to struggle against it. It ended when I almost came to believe (perhaps I really did believe) that this might really have been my normal condition. But at first, in the beginning, what agonies I suffered during that struggle! I didn't believe that others were experiencing the same thing; therefore, I kept it a secret about myself all my life. I was ashamed (perhaps I still am even now); I reached the point where I felt some secret, abnormal, despicable little pleasure in returning home to my little corner on some disgusting Petersburg night, acutely aware that once again I'd committed some revolting act that day, that what had been done could not be undone, and I used to gnaw and gnaw at myself inwardly, secretly, nagging away, consuming myself until finally the bitterness turned

4. St. Petersburg was conceived as an imposing city; plans called for regular streets, broad avenues, and spacious squares.   5. This phrase originated in Edmund Burke's (1729–1797) *Philosophical Inquiry into the Origin of Our Ideas of the Sublime and Beautiful* (1756) and was repeated in Immanuel Kant's (1724–1804) *Observations on the Feeling of the Beautiful and the Sublime* (1756). It became a cliché in the writings of Russian critics during the 1830s.

into some kind of shameful, accursed sweetness and at last into genuine, earnest pleasure! Yes, into pleasure, real pleasure! I absolutely mean that. . . . That's why I first began to speak out, because I want to know for certain whether other people share this same pleasure. Let me explain: the pleasure resulted precisely from the overly acute consciousness of one's own humiliation; from the feeling that one had reached the limit; that it was disgusting, but couldn't be otherwise; you had no other choice—you could never become a different person; and that even if there were still time and faith enough for you to change into something else, most likely you wouldn't even want to change, and if you did, you wouldn't have done anything, perhaps because there really was nothing for you to change into. But the main thing and the final point is that all of this was taking place according to normal and fundamental laws of overly acute consciousness and of the inertia which results directly from these laws; consequently, not only couldn't one change, one simply couldn't do anything at all. Hence it follows, for example, as a result of this overly acute consciousness, that one is absolutely right in being a scoundrel, as if this were some consolation to the scoundrel. But enough of this. . . . Oh, my, I've gone on rather a long time, but have I really explained anything? How can I explain this pleasure? But I will explain it! I shall see it through to the end! That's why I've taken up my pen. . . .

For example, I'm terribly proud. I'm as mistrustful and as sensitive as a hunchback or a dwarf; but, in truth, I've experienced some moments when, if someone had slapped my face, I might even have been grateful for it. I'm being serious. I probably would have been able to derive a peculiar sort of pleasure from it—the pleasure of despair, naturally, but the most intense pleasures occur in despair, especially when you're very acutely aware of the hopelessness of your own predicament. As for a slap in the face—why, here the consciousness of being beaten to a pulp would overwhelm you. The main thing is, no matter how I try, it still turns out that I'm always the first to be blamed for everything and, what's even worse, I'm always the innocent victim, so to speak, according to the laws of nature. Therefore, in the first place, I'm guilty inasmuch as I'm smarter than everyone around me. (I've always considered myself smarter than everyone around me, and sometimes, believe me, I've been ashamed of it. At the least, all my life I've looked away and never could look people straight in the eye.) Finally, I'm to blame because even if there were any magnanimity in me, it would only have caused more suffering as a result of my being aware of its utter uselessness. After all, I probably wouldn't have been able to make use of that magnanimity: neither to forgive, as the offender, perhaps, had slapped me in accordance with the laws of nature, and there's no way to forgive the laws of nature; nor to forget, because even if there were any laws of nature, it's offensive nonetheless. Finally, even if I wanted to be entirely unmagnanimous, and had wanted to take revenge on the offender, I couldn't be revenged on anyone for anything because, most likely, I would never have decided to do anything, even if I could have. Why not? I'd like to say a few words about that separately.

III

Let's consider people who know how to take revenge and how to stand up for themselves in general. How, for example, do they do it? Let's suppose that they're seized by an impulse to take revenge—then for a while nothing else remains in their entire being except for that impulse. Such an individual simply rushes toward his goal like an enraged bull with lowered horns; only a wall can stop him. (By the way, when actually faced with a wall such individuals, that is, spontaneous people and men of action, genuinely give up. For them a wall doesn't constitute the evasion that it does for those of us who think and consequently do nothing; it's not an excuse to turn aside from the path, a pretext in which a person like me usually doesn't believe, but one for which he's always extremely grateful. No, they give up in all sincerity. For them the wall possesses some kind of soothing, morally decisive and definitive meaning, perhaps even something mystical . . . But more about the wall later.) Well, then, I consider such a spontaneous individual to be a genuine, normal person, just as tender mother nature wished to see him when she lovingly gave birth to him on earth. I'm green with envy at such a man. He's stupid, I won't argue with you about that; but perhaps a normal man is supposed to be stupid—how do we know? Perhaps it's even very beautiful. And I'm all the more convinced of the suspicion, so to speak, that if, for example, one were to take the antithesis of a normal man—that is, a man of overly acute consciousness, who emerged, of course, not from the bosom of nature, but from a laboratory test tube (this is almost mysticism, gentlemen, but I suspect that it's the case), then this test tube man some-times gives up so completely in the face of his antithesis that he himself, with his overly acute consciousness, honestly considers himself not as a per-son, but a mouse. It may be an acutely conscious mouse, but a mouse none-theless, while the other one is a person and consequently, . . . and so on and so forth. But the main thing is that he, he himself, considers himself to be a mouse; nobody asks him to do so, and that's the important point. Now let's take a look at this mouse in action. Let's assume, for instance, that it feels offended (it almost always feels offended), and that it also wishes to be revenged. It may even contain more accumulated malice than *l'homme de la nature et de la vérité*.[6] The mean, nasty, little desire to pay the offender back with evil may indeed rankle in it even more despicably than in *l'homme de la nature et de la vérité*, because *l'homme de la nature et de la vérité*, with his innate stupidity, considers his revenge nothing more than justice, pure and simple; but the mouse, as a result of its overly acute consciousness, rejects the idea of justice. Finally, we come to the act itself, to the very act of revenge. In addition to its original nastiness, the mouse has already managed to pile up all sorts of other nastiness around itself in the form of hesitations and doubts; so many unresolved questions have emerged from that one single question, that some kind of fatal blow is concocted unwillingly, some kind of stinking mess consisting of doubts, anxieties and, finally, spittle showered upon it by the spontaneous men of action who stand by solemnly as judges and arbiters, roaring with laughter until their sides split. Of course, the only thing left to do is dismiss it with a wave of its paw and a smile of assumed contempt which it doesn't even believe in, and creep ignominiously back into its mousehole. There, in its disgusting, stinking underground, our offended, crushed, and ridiculed mouse immediately plunges into cold, malicious, and,

6. The man of nature and truth (French). The basic idea is borrowed from Jean-Jacques Rousseau's *Con-fessions* (1782–89), namely, that human beings in a state of nature are honest and direct and that they are corrupted only by civilization.

above all, everlasting spitefulness. For forty years on end it will recall its insult down to the last, most shameful detail; and each time it will add more shameful details of its own, spitefully teasing and irritating itself with its own fantasy. It will become ashamed of that fantasy, but it will still remember it, rehearse it again and again, fabricating all sorts of incredible stories about itself under the pretext that they too could have happened; it won't forgive a thing. Perhaps it will even begin to take revenge, but only in little bits and pieces, in trivial ways, from behind the stove, incognito, not believing in its right to be revenged, nor in the success of its own revenge, and knowing in advance that from all its attempts to take revenge, it will suffer a hundred times more than the object of its vengeance, who might not even feel a thing. On its deathbed it will recall everything all over again, with interest compounded over all those years and. . . . But it's precisely in that cold, abominable state of half-despair and half-belief, in that conscious burial of itself alive in the underground for forty years because of its pain, in that powerfully created, yet partly dubious hopelessness of its own predicament, in all that venom of unfulfilled desire turned inward, in all that fever of vacillation, of resolutions adopted once and for all and followed a moment later by repentance—herein precisely lies the essence of that strange enjoyment I was talking about earlier. It's so subtle, sometimes so difficult to analyze, that even slightly limited people, or those who simply have strong nerves, won't understand anything about it. "Perhaps," you'll add with a smirk, "even those who've never received a slap in the face won't understand," and by so doing you'll be hinting to me ever so politely that perhaps during my life I too have received such a slap in the face and that therefore I'm speaking as an expert. I'll bet that's what you're thinking. Well, rest assured, gentlemen, I've never received such a slap, although it's really all the same to me what you think about it. Perhaps I may even regret the fact that I've given so few slaps during my lifetime. But that's enough, not another word about this subject which you find so extremely interesting.

I'll proceed calmly about people with strong nerves who don't understand certain refinements of pleasure. For example, although under particular circumstances these gentlemen may bellow like bulls as loudly as possible, and although, let's suppose, this behavior bestows on them the greatest honor, yet, as I've already said, when confronted with impossibility, they submit immediately. Impossibility—does that mean a stone wall? What kind of stone wall? Why, of course, the laws of nature, the conclusions of natural science and mathematics. As soon as they prove to you, for example, that it's from a monkey you're descended,[7] there's no reason to make faces; just accept it as it is. As soon as they prove to you that in truth one drop of your own fat is dearer to you than the lives of one hundred thousand of your fellow creatures and that this will finally put an end to all the so-called virtues, obligations, and other such similar ravings and prejudices, just accept that too; there's nothing more to do, since two times two is a fact of mathematics. Just you try to object.

"For goodness sake," they'll shout at you, "it's impossible to protest: it's two times two makes four! Nature doesn't ask for your opinion; it doesn't

---

7. A reference to the theory of evolution by natural selection developed by Charles Darwin (1809–1882). A book on the subject was translated into Russian in 1864.

care about your desires or whether you like or dislike its laws. You're obliged to accept it as it is, and consequently, all its conclusions. A wall, you see, is a wall . . . etc. etc." Good Lord, what do I care about the laws of nature and arithmetic when for some reason I dislike all these laws and I dislike the fact that two times two makes four? Of course, I won't break through that wall with my head if I really don't have the strength to do so, nor will I reconcile myself to it just because I'm faced with such a stone wall and lack the strength.

As though such a stone wall actually offered some consolation and contained some real word of conciliation, for the sole reason that it means two times two makes four. Oh, absurdity of absurdities! How much better it is to understand it all, to be aware of everything, all the impossibilities and stone walls; not to be reconciled with any of those impossibilities or stone walls if it so disgusts you; to reach, by using the most inevitable logical combinations, the most revolting conclusions on the eternal theme that you are somehow or other to blame even for that stone wall, even though it's absolutely clear once again that you're in no way to blame, and, as a result of all this, while silently and impotently gnashing your teeth, you sink voluptuously into inertia, musing on the fact that, as it turns out, there's no one to be angry with; that an object cannot be found, and perhaps never will be; that there's been a substitution, some sleight of hand, a bit of cheating, and that it's all a mess—you can't tell who's who or what's what; but in spite of all these uncertainties and sleights-of-hand, it hurts you just the same, and the more you don't know, the more it hurts!

IV

"Ha, ha, ha! Why, you'll be finding enjoyment in a toothache next!" you cry out with a laugh.

"Well, what of it? There is some enjoyment even in a toothache," I reply. I've had a toothache for a whole month; I know what's what. In this instance, of course, people don't rage in silence; they moan. But these moans are insincere; they're malicious, and malice is the whole point. These moans express the sufferer's enjoyment; if he didn't enjoy it, he would never have begun to moan. This is a good example, gentlemen, and I'll develop it. In the first place, these moans express all the aimlessness of the pain which consciousness finds so humiliating, the whole system of natural laws about which you really don't give a damn, but as a result of which you're suffering nonetheless, while nature isn't. They express the consciousness that while there's no real enemy to be identified, the pain exists nonetheless; the awareness that, in spite of all possible Wagenheims,[8] you're still a complete slave to your teeth; that if someone so wishes, your teeth will stop aching, but that if he doesn't so wish, they'll go on aching for three more months; and finally, that if you still disagree and protest, all there's left to do for consolation is flagellate yourself or beat your fist against the wall as hard as you can, and absolutely nothing else. Well, then, it's these bloody insults, these jeers coming from nowhere, that finally generate enjoyment that can sometimes reach the highest degree of voluptuousness. I beseech you, gentle-

8. The *General Address Book of St. Petersburg* listed eight dentists named Wagenheim; contemporary readers would have recognized the name from signs throughout the city.

men, to listen to the moans of an educated man of the nineteenth century who's suffering from a toothache, especially on the second or third day of his distress, when he begins to moan in a very different way than he did on the first day, that is, not simply because his tooth aches; not the way some coarse peasant moans, but as a man affected by progress and European civilization, a man "who's renounced both the soil and the common people," as they say nowadays. His moans become somehow nasty, despicably spiteful, and they go on for days and nights. Yet he himself knows that his moans do him no good; he knows better than anyone else that he's merely irritating himself and others in vain; he knows that the audience for whom he's trying so hard, and his whole family, have now begun to listen to him with loathing; they don't believe him for a second, and they realize full well that he could moan in a different, much simpler way, without all the flourishes and affectation, and that he's only indulging himself out of spite and malice. Well, it's precisely in this awareness and shame that the voluptuousness resides. "It seems I'm disturbing you, tearing at your heart, preventing anyone in the house from getting any sleep. Well, then, you won't sleep; you too must be aware at all times that I have a toothache. I'm no longer the hero I wanted to pass for earlier, but simply a nasty little man, a rogue. So be it! I'm delighted that you've seen through me. Does it make you feel bad to hear my wretched little moans? Well, then, feel bad. Now let me add an even nastier flourish. . . ." You still don't understand, gentlemen? No, it's clear that one has to develop further and become even more conscious in order to understand all the nuances of this voluptuousness! Are you laughing? I'm delighted. Of course my jokes are in bad taste, gentlemen; they're uneven, contradictory, and lacking in self-assurance. But that's because I have no respect for myself. Can a man possessing consciousness ever really respect himself?

V

Well, and is it possible, is it really possible for a man to respect himself if he even presumes to find enjoyment in the feeling of his own humiliation? I'm not saying this out of any feigned repentance. In general I could never bear to say: "I'm sorry, Daddy, and I won't do it again," not because I was incapable of saying it, but, on the contrary, perhaps precisely because I was all too capable, and how! As if on purpose it would happen that I'd get myself into some sort of mess for which I was not to blame in any way whatsoever. That was the most repulsive part of it. What's more, I'd feel touched deep in my soul; I'd repent and shed tears, deceiving even myself of course, though not feigning in the least. It seemed that my heart was somehow playing dirty tricks on me. . . . Here one couldn't even blame the laws of nature, although it was these very laws that continually hurt me during my entire life. It's disgusting to recall all this, and it was disgusting even then. Of course, a moment or so later I would realize in anger that it was all lies, lies, revolting, made-up lies, that is, all that repentance, all that tenderness, all those vows to mend my ways. But you'll ask why I mauled and tortured myself in that way? The answer is because it was so very boring to sit idly by with my arms folded; so I'd get into trouble. That's the way it was. Observe yourselves better, gentlemen; then you'll understand that it's true. I used to think up adventures for myself, inventing a life so that at least I could live. How many times did it happen, well, let's say, for example, that I took offense, deliberately, for no reason at all? All the while I knew there was no reason for it; I put on airs nonetheless, and would take it so far that finally I really did feel offended. I've been drawn into such silly tricks all my life, so that finally I lost control over myself. Another time, even twice, I tried hard to fall in love. I even suffered, gentlemen, I can assure you. In the depths of my soul I really didn't believe that I was suffering; there was a stir of mockery, but suffer I did, and in a genuine, normal way at that; I was jealous, I was beside myself with anger. . . . And all as a result of boredom, gentlemen, sheer boredom; I was overcome by inertia. You see, the direct, legitimate, immediate result of consciousness is inertia, that is, the conscious sitting idly by with one's arms folded. I've referred to this before. I repeat, I repeat emphatically: all spontaneous men and men of action are so active precisely because they're stupid and limited. How can one explain this? Here's how: as a result of their limitations they mistake immediate and secondary causes for primary ones, and thus they're convinced more quickly and easily than other people that they've located an indisputable basis for action, and this puts them at ease; that's the main point. For, in order to begin to act, one must first be absolutely at ease, with no lingering doubts whatsoever. Well, how can I, for example, ever feel at ease? Where are the primary causes I can rely upon, where's the foundation? Where shall I find it? I exercise myself in thinking, and consequently, with me every primary cause drags in another, an even more primary one, and so on to infinity. This is precisely the essence of all consciousness and thought. And here again, it must be the laws of nature. What's the final result? Why, the very same thing. Remember: I was talking about revenge before. (You probably didn't follow.) I said: a man takes revenge because he finds justice in it. That means, he's found a primary cause, a foundation: namely, justice. Therefore, he's completely at ease, and, as a result, he takes revenge peacefully and successfully, convinced that he's performing an honest and just deed. But I don't see any justice here at all, nor do I find any virtue in it whatever; consequently, if I begin to take revenge, it's only out of spite. Of course, spite could overcome everything, all my doubts, and therefore could successfully serve instead of a primary cause precisely because it's not a cause at all. But what do I do if I don't even feel spite (that's where I began before)? After all, as a result of those damned laws of consciousness, my spite is subject to chemical disintegration. You look—and the object vanishes, the arguments evaporate, a guilty party can't be identified, the offense ceases to be one and becomes a matter of fate, something like a toothache for which no one's to blame, and, as a consequence, there remains only the same recourse: that is, to bash the wall even harder. So you throw up your hands because you haven't found a primary cause. Just try to let yourself be carried away blindly by your feelings, without reflection, without a primary cause, suppressing consciousness even for a moment; hate or love, anything, just in order not to sit idly by with your arms folded. The day after tomorrow at the very latest, you'll begin to despise yourself for having deceived yourself knowingly. The result: a soap bubble and inertia. Oh, gentlemen, perhaps I consider myself to be an intelligent man simply because for my whole life I haven't been able to begin or finish anything. All right, suppose I am a babbler, a harmless, annoying babbler, like the rest of us.

But then what is to be done[9] if the direct and single vocation of every intelligent man consists in babbling, that is, in deliberately talking in endless circles?

VI

Oh, if only I did nothing simply as a result of laziness. Lord, how I'd respect myself then. I'd respect myself precisely because at least I'd be capable of being lazy; at least I'd possess one more or less positive trait of which I could be certain. Question: who am I? Answer: a sluggard. Why, it would have been very pleasant to hear that said about oneself. It would mean that I'd been positively identified; it would mean that there was something to be said about me. "A sluggard!" Why, that's a calling and a vocation, a whole career! Don't joke, it's true. Then, by rights I'd be a member of the very best club and would occupy myself exclusively by being able to respect myself continually. I knew a gentleman who prided himself all his life on being a connoisseur of Lafite.[1] He considered it his positive virtue and never doubted himself. He died not merely with a clean conscience, but with a triumphant one, and he was absolutely correct. I should have chosen a career for myself too: I would have been a sluggard and a glutton, not an ordinary one, but one who, for example, sympathized with everything beautiful and sublime. How do you like that? I've dreamt about it for a long time. The "beautiful and sublime" have been a real pain in the neck during my forty years, but then it's been *my* forty years, whereas then—oh, then it would have been otherwise! I would've found myself a suitable activity at once—namely, drinking to everything beautiful and sublime. I would have seized upon every opportunity first to shed a tear into my glass and then drink to everything beautiful and sublime. Then I would have turned everything into the beautiful and sublime; I would have sought out the beautiful and sublime in the nastiest, most indisputable trash. I would have become as tearful as a wet sponge. An artist, for example, has painted a portrait of Ge.[2] At once I drink to the artist who painted that portrait of Ge because I love everything beautiful and sublime. An author has written the words, "Just as you please,"[3] at once I drink to "Just as you please," because I love everything "beautiful and sublime." I'd demand respect for myself in doing this, I'd persecute anyone who didn't pay me any respect. I'd live peacefully and die triumphantly— why, it's charming, perfectly charming! And what a belly I'd have grown by then, what a triple chin I'd have acquired, what a red nose I'd have developed—so that just looking at me any passerby would have said, "Now that's a real plus! That's something really positive!" Say what you like, gentlemen, it's extremely pleasant to hear such comments in our negative age.

VII

But these are all golden dreams. Oh, tell me who was first to announce, first to proclaim that man does nasty things simply because he doesn't know

---

9. An oblique reference to the controversial novel by Nikolai Chernyshevsky (1828–1889) entitled *What Is to Be Done?* (1863). *Notes from Underground* is in part Dostoevsky's polemical response to it.   1. A variety of red wine from Médoc in France.   2. N. N. Ge (1831–1894), Russian artist, whose painting *The Last Supper* was displayed in St. Petersburg during the spring of 1863 and provoked considerable controversy.   3. An attack on the writer M. E. Saltykov-Shchedrin, who published a sympathetic review of Ge's painting titled *Just As You Please.*

his own true interest; and that if he were to be enlightened, if his eyes were to be opened to his true, normal interests, he would stop doing nasty things at once and would immediately become good and noble, because, being so enlightened and understanding his real advantage, he would realize that his own advantage really did lie in the good; and that it's well known that there's not a single man capable of acting knowingly against his own interest; consequently, he would, so to speak, begin to do good out of necessity. Oh, the child! Oh, the pure, innocent babe! Well, in the first place, when was it during all these millennia, that man has ever acted only in his own self interest? What does one do with the millions of facts bearing witness to the one fact that people knowingly, that is, possessing full knowledge of their own true interests, have relegated them to the background and have rushed down a different path, that of risk and chance, compelled by no one and nothing, but merely as if they didn't want to follow the beaten track, and so they stubbornly, willfully forged another way, a difficult and absurd one, searching for it almost in the darkness? Why, then, this means that stubbornness and willfulness were really more pleasing to them than any kind of advantage. . . . Advantage! What is advantage? Will you take it upon yourself to define with absolute precision what constitutes man's advantage? And what if it turns out that man's advantage sometimes not only may, but even must in certain circumstances, consist precisely in his desiring something harmful to himself instead of something advantageous? And if this is so, if this can ever occur, then the whole theory falls to pieces. What do you think, can such a thing happen? You're laughing; laugh, gentlemen, but answer me: have man's advantages ever been calculated with absolute certainty? Aren't there some which don't fit, can't be made to fit into any classification? Why, as far as I know, you gentlemen have derived your list of human advantages from averages of statistical data and from scientific-economic formulas. But your advantages are prosperity, wealth, freedom, peace, and so on and so forth; so that a man who, for example, expressly and knowingly acts in opposition to this whole list, would be, in your opinion, and in mine, too, of course, either an obscurantist or a complete madman, wouldn't he? But now here's what's astonishing: why is it that when all these statisticians, sages, and lovers of humanity enumerate man's advantages, they invariably leave one out? They don't even take it into consideration in the form in which it should be considered, although the entire calculation depends upon it. There would be no great harm in considering it, this advantage, and adding it to the list. But the whole point is that this particular advantage doesn't fit into any classification and can't be found on any list. I have a friend, for instance. . . . But gentlemen! Why, he's your friend, too! In fact, he's everyone's friend! When he's preparing to do something, this gentleman straight away explains to you eloquently and clearly just how he must act according to the laws of nature and truth. And that's not all: with excitement and passion he'll tell you all about genuine, normal human interests; with scorn he'll reproach the shortsighted fools who understand neither their own advantage nor the real meaning of virtue; and then—exactly a quarter of an hour later, without any sudden outside cause, but precisely because of something internal that's stronger than all his interests—he does a complete about-face; that is, he does something which clearly contradicts what he's been saying: it goes against the laws of reason and his own advantage, in a word, against everything. . . . I warn you that my friend is a collective personage; therefore it's rather difficult to blame only him. That's just it, gentlemen; in fact, isn't there something dearer to every man than his own best advantage, or (so as not to violate the rules of logic) isn't there one more advantageous advantage (exactly the one omitted, the one we mentioned before), which is more important and more advantageous than all others and, on behalf of which, a man will, if necessary, go against all laws, that is, against reason, honor, peace, and prosperity—in a word, against all those splendid and useful things, merely in order to attain this fundamental, most advantageous advantage which is dearer to him than everything else?

"Well, it's advantage all the same," you say, interrupting me. Be so kind as to allow me to explain further; besides, the point is not my pun, but the fact that this advantage is remarkable precisely because it destroys all our classifications and constantly demolishes all systems devised by lovers of humanity for the happiness of mankind. In a word, it interferes with everything. But, before I name this advantage, I want to compromise myself personally; therefore I boldly declare that all these splendid systems, all these theories to explain to mankind its real, normal interests so that, by necessarily striving to achieve them, it would immediately become good and noble—are, for the time being, in my opinion, nothing more than logical exercises! Yes, sir, logical exercises! Why, even to maintain a theory of mankind's regeneration through a system of its own advantages, why, in my opinion, that's almost the same as . . . well, claiming, for instance, following Buckle,[4] that man has become kinder as a result of civilization; consequently, he's becoming less bloodthirsty and less inclined to war. Why, logically it all even seems to follow. But man is so partial to systems and abstract conclusions that he's ready to distort the truth intentionally, ready to deny everything that he himself has ever seen and heard, merely in order to justify his own logic. That's why I take this example, because it's such a glaring one. Just look around: rivers of blood are being spilt, and in the most cheerful way, as if it were champagne. Take this entire nineteenth century of ours during which even Buckle lived. Take Napoleon—both the great and the present one.[5] Take North America—that eternal union.[6] Take, finally, that ridiculous Schleswig-Holstein[7]. . . . What is it that civilization makes kinder in us? Civilization merely promotes a wider variety of sensations in man and . . . absolutely nothing else. And through the development of this variety man may even reach the point where he takes pleasure in spilling blood. Why, that's even happened to him already. Haven't you noticed that the most refined bloodshedders are almost always the most civilized gentlemen to whom all these Attila the Huns and Stenka Razins[8] are scarcely fit to hold a candle; and if they're not as conspicuous as Attila and Stenka Razin, it's precisely because they're too common and have become too familiar to us. At least if man hasn't become more bloodthirsty as a result of civilization, surely he's become bloodthirsty in a nastier, more repulsive way than before.

---

4. In his *History of Civilization in England* (1857–61), Henry Thomas Buckle (1821–1862) argued that the development of civilization necessarily leads to the cessation of war. Russia had recently been involved in fierce fighting in the Crimea (1853–56).   **5.** The French emperors Napoleon I (1769–1821) and his nephew Napoleon III (1808–1873), both of whom engaged in numerous wars, though on vastly different scales.   **6.** The United States was in the middle of its Civil War (1861–65).   **7.** The German duchies of Schleswig and Holstein, held by Denmark since 1773, were reunited with Prussia after a brief war in 1864.   **8.** Cossack leader (d. 1671) who organized a peasant rebellion in Russia. Attila (406?–453 C.E.), king of the Huns, who conducted devastating wars against the Roman emperors.

Previously man saw justice in bloodshed and exterminated whomever he wished with a clear conscience; whereas now, though we consider bloodshed to be abominable, we nevertheless engage in this abomination even more than before. Which is worse? Decide for yourselves. They say that Cleopatra (forgive an example from Roman history) loved to stick gold pins into the breasts of her slave girls and take pleasure in their screams and writhing. You'll say that this took place, relatively speaking, in barbaric times; that these are barbaric times too, because (also comparatively speaking), gold pins are used even now; that even now, although man has learned on occasion to see more clearly than in barbaric times, *he's still far from having learned* how to act in accordance with the dictates of reason and science. Nevertheless, you're still absolutely convinced that he will learn how to do so, as soon as he gets rid of some bad, old habits and as soon as common sense and science have completely re-educated human nature and have turned it in the proper direction. You're convinced that then man will voluntarily stop committing blunders, and that he will, so to speak, never willingly set his own will in opposition to his own normal interests. More than that: then, you say, science itself will teach man (though, in my opinion, that's already a luxury) that in fact he possesses neither a will nor any whim of his own, that he never did, and that he himself is nothing more than a kind of piano key or an organ stop;[9] that, moreover, there still exist laws of nature, so that everything he's done has been not in accordance with his own desire, but in and of itself, according to the laws of nature. Consequently, we need only discover these laws of nature, and man will no longer have to answer for his own actions and will find it extremely easy to live. All human actions, it goes without saying, will then be tabulated according to these laws, mathematically, like tables of logarithms up to 108,000, and will be entered on a schedule; or even better, certain edifying works will be published, like our contemporary encyclopedic dictionaries, in which everything will be accurately calculated and specified so that there'll be no more actions or adventures left on earth.

At that time, it's still you speaking, new economic relations will be established, all ready-made, also calculated with mathematical precision, so that all possible questions will disappear in a single instant, simply because all possible answers will have been provided. Then the crystal palace[1] will be built. And then . . . Well, in a word, those will be our halcyon days. Of course, there's no way to guarantee (now this is me talking) that it won't be, for instance, terribly boring then (because there won't be anything left to do, once everything has been calculated according to tables); on the other hand, everything will be extremely rational. Of course, what don't people think up out of boredom! Why, even gold pins get stuck into other people out of boredom, but that wouldn't matter. What's really bad (this is me talking again) is that for all I know, people might even be grateful for those gold pins. For man is stupid, phenomenally stupid. That is, although he's not really stupid at all, he's really so ungrateful that it's hard to find another

---

9. A reference to the last discourse of the French philosopher Denis Diderot (1713–1784) in the *Conversation of D'Alembert and Diderot* (1769).   1. An allusion to the crystal palace described in Vera Pavlovna's fourth dream in Chernyshevsky's *What Is to Be Done?* and to the actual building designed by Sir Joseph Paxton, erected for the Great Exhibition in London in 1851 and at that time admired as the newest wonder of architecture; Dostoevsky described it in *Winter Notes on Summer Impressions* (1863).

being quite like him. Why, I, for example, wouldn't be surprised in the least, if, suddenly, for no reason at all, in the midst of this future, universal rationalism, some gentleman with an offensive, rather, a retrograde and derisive expression on his face were to stand up, put his hands on his hips, and declare to us all: "How about it, gentlemen, what if we knock over all this rationalism with one swift kick for the sole purpose of sending all these logarithms to hell, so that once again we can live according to our own stupid will!" But that wouldn't matter either; what's so annoying is that he would undoubtedly find some followers; such is the way man is made. And all because of the most foolish reason, which, it seems, is hardly worth mentioning: namely, that man, always and everywhere, whoever he is, has preferred to act as he wished, and not at all as reason and advantage have dictated; one might even desire something opposed to one's own advantage, and sometimes (this is now my idea) one *positively must do so*. One's very own free, unfettered desire, one's own whim, no matter how wild, one's own fantasy, even though sometimes roused to the point of madness—all this constitutes precisely that previously omitted, most advantageous advantage which isn't included under any classification and because of which all systems and theories are constantly smashed to smithereens. Where did these sages ever get the idea that man needs any normal, virtuous desire? How did they ever imagine that man needs any kind of rational, advantageous desire? Man needs only one thing—his own *independent* desire, whatever that independence might cost and wherever it might lead. And as far as desire goes, the devil only knows. . . .

VIII

"Ha, ha, ha! But in reality even this desire, if I may say so, doesn't exist!" you interrupt me with a laugh. "Why science has already managed to dissect man so now we know that desire and so-called free choice are nothing more than . . ."

Wait, gentlemen, I myself wanted to begin like that. I must confess that even I got frightened. I was just about to declare that the devil only knows what desire depends on and perhaps we should be grateful for that, but then I remembered about science and I . . . stopped short. But now you've gone and brought it up. Well, after all, what if someday they really do discover the formula for all our desires and whims, that is, the thing that governs them, precise laws that produce them, how exactly they're applied, where they lead in each and every case, and so on and so forth, that is, the genuine mathematical formula—why, then all at once man might stop desiring, yes, indeed, he probably would. Who would want to desire according to some table? And that's not all: he would immediately be transformed from a person into an organ stop or something of that sort; because what is man without desire, without will, and without wishes if not a stop in an organ pipe? What do you think? Let's consider the probabilities—can this really happen or not?

"Hmmm . . . ," you decide, "our desires are mistaken for the most part because of an erroneous view of our own advantage. Consequently, we sometimes desire pure rubbish because, in our own stupidity, we consider it the easiest way to achieve some previously assumed advantage. Well, and when all this has been analyzed, calculated on paper (that's entirely possible, since it's repugnant and senseless to assume in advance that man will never come to understand the laws of nature) then, of course, all so-called desires will no longer exist. For if someday desires are completely reconciled with reason, we'll follow reason instead of desire simply because it would be impossible, for example, while retaining one's reason, to *desire* rubbish, and thus knowingly oppose one's reason, and desire something harmful to oneself. . . . And, since all desires and reasons can really be tabulated, since someday the laws of our so-called free choice are sure to be discovered, then, all joking aside, it may be possible to establish something like a table, so that we could actually desire according to it. If, for example, someday they calculate and demonstrate to me that I made a rude gesture because I couldn't possibly refrain from it, that I had to make precisely that gesture, well, in that case, what sort of *free choice* would there be, especially if I'm a learned man and have completed a course of study somewhere? Why, then I'd be able to calculate in advance my entire life for the next thirty years; in a word, if such a table were to be drawn up, there'd be nothing left for us to do; we'd simply have to accept it. In general, we should be repeating endlessly to ourselves that at such a time and in such circumstances nature certainly won't ask our opinion; that we must accept it as is, and not as we fantasize it, and that if we really aspire to prepare a table, a schedule, and, well . . . well, even a laboratory test tube, there's nothing to be done—one must even accept the test tube! If not, it'll be accepted even without you. . . ."

Yes, but that's just where I hit a snag! Gentlemen, you'll excuse me for all this philosophizing; it's a result of my forty years in the underground! Allow me to fantasize. Don't you see: reason is a fine thing, gentlemen, there's no doubt about it, but it's only reason, and it satisfies only man's rational faculty, whereas desire is a manifestation of all life, that is, of all human life, which includes both reason, as well as all of life's itches and scratches. And although in this manifestation life often turns out to be fairly worthless, it's life all the same, and not merely the extraction of square roots. Why, take me, for instance; I quite naturally want to live in order to satisfy all my faculties of life, not merely my rational faculty, that is, some one-twentieth of all my faculties. What does reason know? Reason knows only what it's managed to learn. (Some things it may never learn; while this offers no comfort, why not admit it openly?) But human nature acts as a whole, with all that it contains, consciously and unconsciously; and although it may tell lies, it's still alive. I suspect, gentlemen, that you're looking at me with compassion; you repeat that an enlightened and cultured man, in a word, man as he will be in the future, cannot knowingly desire something disadvantageous to himself, and that this is pure mathematics. I agree with you: it really is mathematics. But I repeat for the one-hundredth time, there is one case, only one, when a man may intentionally, consciously desire even something harmful to himself, something stupid, even very stupid, namely: in order *to have the right* to desire something even very stupid and not be bound by an obligation to desire only what's smart. After all, this very stupid thing, one's own whim, gentlemen, may in fact be the most advantageous thing on earth for people like me, especially in certain cases. In particular, it may be more advantageous than any other advantage, even in a case where it causes obvious harm and contradicts the most sensible conclusions of reason about advantage—because in any case it preserves for us what's most important and precious, that is, our personality and our individuality. There are some people who maintain that in fact this is more precious to man than anything else; of course, desire can, if it so chooses, coincide with reason, especially if it doesn't abuse this option, and chooses to coincide in moderation; this is useful and sometimes even commendable. But very often, even most of the time, desire absolutely and stubbornly disagrees with reason and . . . and . . . and, do you know, sometimes this is also useful and even very commendable? Let's assume, gentlemen, that man isn't stupid. (And really, this can't possibly be said about him at all, if only because if he's stupid, then who on earth is smart?) But even if he's not stupid, he is, nevertheless, monstrously ungrateful. Phenomenally ungrateful. I even believe that the best definition of man is this: a creature who walks on two legs and is ungrateful. But that's still not all; that's still not his main defect. His main defect is his perpetual misbehavior, perpetual from the time of the Great Flood to the Schleswig-Holstein period of human destiny. Misbehavior, and consequently, imprudence; for it's long been known that imprudence results from nothing else but misbehavior. Just cast a glance at the history of mankind; well, what do you see? Is it majestic? Well, perhaps it's majestic; why, the Colossus of Rhodes,[2] for example—that alone is worth something! Not without reason did Mr Anaevsky[3] report that some people consider it to be the product of human hands, while others maintain that it was created by nature itself. Is it colorful? Well, perhaps it's also colorful; just consider the dress uniforms, both military and civilian, of all nations at all times—why, that alone is worth something, and if you include everyday uniforms, it'll make your eyes bulge; not one historian will be able to sort it all out. Is it monotonous? Well, perhaps it's monotonous, too: men fight and fight; now they're fighting; they fought first and they fought last—you'll agree that it's really much too monotonous. In short, anything can be said about world history, anything that might occur to the most disordered imagination. There's only one thing that can't possibly be said about it—that it's rational. You'll choke on the word. Yet here's just the sort of thing you'll encounter all the time: why, in life you're constantly running up against people who are so well-behaved and so rational, such wise men and lovers of humanity who set themselves the lifelong goal of behaving as morally and rationally as possible, so to speak, to be a beacon for their nearest and dearest, simply in order to prove that it's really possible to live one's life in a moral and rational way. And so what? It's a well-known fact that many of these lovers of humanity, sooner or later, by the end of their lives, have betrayed themselves: they've pulled off some caper, sometimes even quite an indecent one. Now I ask you: what can one expect from man as a creature endowed with such strange qualities? Why, shower him with all sorts of earthly blessings, submerge him in happiness over his head so that only little bubbles appear on the surface of this happiness, as if on water, give him such economic prosperity that he'll have absolutely nothing left to do except sleep, eat gingerbread, and worry about the continuation of world history—even then, out of pure ingratitude, sheer perversity, he'll commit some repulsive act. He'll even risk losing his gingerbread, and will intentionally desire the most wicked rubbish, the most

2. A large bronze statue of the Greek sun god, Helios, built between 292 and 280 B.C.E. in the harbor of Rhodes (an island in the Aegean Sea) and considered one of the Seven Wonders of the Ancient World.
3. A. E. Anaevsky was a critic whose articles were frequently ridiculed in literary polemics of the period.

uneconomical absurdity, simply in order to inject his own pernicious fantastic element into all this positive rationality. He wants to hold onto those most fantastic dreams, his own indecent stupidity solely for the purpose of assuring himself (as if it were necessary) that men are still men and not piano keys, and that even if the laws of nature play upon them with their own hands, they're still threatened by being overplayed until they won't possibly desire anything more than a schedule. But that's not all: even if man really turned out to be a piano key, even if this could be demonstrated to him by natural science and pure mathematics, even then he still won't become reasonable; he'll intentionally do something to the contrary, simply out of ingratitude, merely to have his own way. If he lacks the means, he'll cause destruction and chaos, he'll devise all kinds of suffering and have his own way! He'll leash a curse upon the world; and, since man alone can do so (it's his privilege and the thing that most distinguishes him from other animals), perhaps only through this curse will he achieve his goal, that is, become really convinced that he's a man and not a piano key! If you say that one can also calculate all this according to a table, this chaos and darkness, these curses, so that the mere possibility of calculating it all in advance would stop everything and that reason alone would prevail—in that case man would go insane deliberately in order not to have reason, but to have his own way! I believe this, I vouch for it, because, after all, the whole of man's work seems to consist only in proving to himself constantly that he's a man and not an organ stop! Even if he has to lose his own skin, he'll prove it; even if he has to become a troglodyte, he'll prove it. And after that, how can one not sin, how can one not praise the fact that all this hasn't yet come to pass and that desire still depends on the devil knows what . . . ?

You'll shout at me (if you still choose to favor me with your shouts) that no one's really depriving me of my will; that they're merely attempting to arrange things so that my will, by its own free choice, will coincide with my normal interests, with the laws of nature, and with arithmetic.

But gentlemen, what sort of free choice will there be when it comes down to tables and arithmetic, when all that's left is two times two makes four? Two times two makes four even without my will. Is that what you call free choice?

IX

Gentlemen, I'm joking of course, and I myself know that it's not a very good joke; but, after all, you can't take everything as a joke. Perhaps I'm gnashing my teeth while I joke. I'm tormented by questions, gentlemen; answer them for me. Now, for example, you want to cure man of his old habits and improve his will according to the demands of science and common sense. But how do you know not only whether it's possible, but even if it's *necessary* to remake him in this way? Why do you conclude that human desire *must* undoubtedly be improved? In short, how do you know that such improvement will really be to man's advantage? And, to be perfectly frank, why are you so *absolutely* convinced that not to oppose man's real, normal advantage guaranteed by the conclusions of reason and arithmetic is really always to man's advantage and constitutes a law for all humanity? After all, this is still only an assumption of yours. Let's suppose that it's a law of logic, but perhaps not a law of humanity. Perhaps, gentlemen, you're wondering if I'm insane? Allow me to explain. I agree that man is primarily a creative animal, destined to strive consciously toward a goal and to engage in the art of engineering, that, is, externally and incessantly building new roads for himself *wherever they lead*. But sometimes he may want to swerve aside precisely because he's *compelled* to build these roads, and perhaps also because, no matter how stupid the spontaneous man of action may generally be, nevertheless it sometimes occurs to him that the road, as it turns out, almost always leads *somewhere or other*, and that the main thing isn't so much where it goes, but the fact that it does, and that the well-behaved child, disregarding the art of engineering, shouldn't yield to pernicious idleness which, as is well known, constitutes the mother of all vices. Man loves to create and build roads; that's indisputable. But why is he also so passionately fond of destruction and chaos? Now, then, tell me. But I myself want to say a few words about this separately. Perhaps the reason that he's so fond of destruction and chaos (after all, it's indisputable that he sometimes really loves it, and that's a fact) is that he himself has an instinctive fear of achieving his goal and completing the project under construction? How do you know if perhaps he loves his building only from afar, but not from close up; perhaps he only likes building it, but not living in it, leaving it afterward *aux animaux domestiques*,[4] such as ants or sheep, or so on and so forth. Now ants have altogether different tastes. They have one astonishing structure of a similar type, forever indestructible—the anthill.

The worthy ants began with the anthill, and most likely, they will end with the anthill, which does great credit to their perseverance and steadfastness. But man is a frivolous and unseemly creature and perhaps, like a chess player, he loves only the process of achieving his goal, and not the goal itself. And, who knows (one can't vouch for it), perhaps the only goal on earth toward which mankind is striving consists merely in this incessant process of achieving or to put it another way, in life itself, and not particularly in the goal which, of course, must always be none other than two times two makes four, that is, a formula; after all, two times two makes four is no longer life, gentlemen, but the beginning of death. At least man has always been somewhat afraid of this two times two makes four, and I'm afraid of it now, too. Let's suppose that the only thing man does is search for this two times two makes four; he sails across oceans, sacrifices his own life in the quest; but to seek it out and find it—really and truly, he's very frightened. After all, he feels that as soon as he finds it, there'll be nothing left to search for. Workers, after finishing work, at least receive their wages, go off to a tavern, and then wind up at a police station—now that's a full week's occupation. But where will man go? At any rate a certain awkwardness can be observed each time he approaches the achievement of similar goals. He loves the process, but he's not so fond of the achievement, and that, of course is terribly amusing. In short, man is made in a comical way; obviously there's some sort of catch in all this. But two times two makes four is an insufferable thing, nevertheless. Two times two makes four—why, in my opinion, it's mere insolence. Two times two makes four stands there brazenly with its hands on its hips, blocking your path and spitting at you. I agree that two times two makes four

---

4. To domestic animals (French).

is a splendid thing; but if we're going to lavish praise, then two times two makes five is sometimes also a very charming little thing.

And why are you so firmly, so triumphantly convinced that only the normal and positive—in short, only well-being is advantageous to man? Doesn't reason ever make mistakes about advantage? After all, perhaps man likes something other than well-being? Perhaps he loves suffering just as much? Perhaps suffering is just as advantageous to him as well-being? Man sometimes loves suffering terribly, to the point of passion, and that's a fact. There's no reason to study world history on this point; if indeed you're a man and have lived at all, just ask yourself. As far as my own personal opinion is concerned, to love only well-being is somehow even indecent. Whether good or bad, it's sometimes also very pleasant to demolish something. After all, I'm not standing up for suffering here, nor for well-being, either. I'm standing up for . . . my own whim and for its being guaranteed to me whenever necessary. For instance, suffering is not permitted in vaudevilles,[5] that I know. It's also inconceivable in the crystal palace; suffering is doubt and negation. What sort of crystal palace would it be if any doubt were allowed? Yet, I'm convinced that man will never renounce real suffering, that is, destruction and chaos. After all, suffering is the sole cause of consciousness. Although I stated earlier that in my opinion consciousness is man's greatest misfortune, still I know that man loves it and would not exchange it for any other sort of satisfaction. Consciousness, for example, is infinitely higher than two times two. Of course, after two times two, there's nothing left, not merely nothing to do, but nothing to learn. Then the only thing possible will be to plug up your five senses and plunge into contemplation. Well, even if you reach the same result with consciousness, that is, having nothing left to do, at least you'll be able to flog yourself from time to time, and that will liven things up a bit. Although it may be reactionary, it's still better than nothing.

X[6]

You believe in the crystal palace, eternally indestructible, that is, one at which you can never stick out your tongue furtively nor make a rude gesture, even with your fist hidden away. Well, perhaps I'm so afraid of this building precisely because it's made of crystal and it's eternally indestructible, and because it won't be possible to stick one's tongue out even furtively.

Don't you see: if it were a chicken coop instead of a palace, and if it should rain, then perhaps I could crawl into it so as not to get drenched; but I would still not mistake a chicken coop for a palace out of gratitude, just because it sheltered me from the rain. You're laughing, you're even saying that in this case there's no difference between a chicken coop and a mansion. Yes, I reply, if the only reason for living is to keep from getting drenched.

But what if I've taken it into my head that this is not the only reason for living, and, that if one is to live at all, one might as well live in a mansion? Such is my wish, my desire. You'll expunge it from me only when you've changed my desires. Well, then, change them, tempt me with something else, give me some other ideal. In the meantime, I still won't mistake a

5. A dramatic genre, popular on the Russian stage, consisting of scenes from contemporary life acted with a satirical twist, often in racy dialogue.   6. This chapter was badly mutilated by the censor, as Dostoevsky makes clear in the letter to his brother Mikhail, dated March 26, 1864 (see p. 1256).

chicken coop for a palace. But let's say that the crystal palace is a hoax, that according to the laws of nature it shouldn't exist, and that I've invented it only out of my own stupidity, as a result of certain antiquated, irrational habits of my generation. But what do I care if it doesn't exist? What difference does it make if it exists only in my own desires, or, to be more precise, if it exists as long as my desires exist? Perhaps you're laughing again? Laugh, if you wish; I'll resist all your laughter and I still won't say I'm satiated if I'm really hungry; I know all the same that I won't accept a compromise, an infinitely recurring zero, just because it exists according to the laws of nature and it *really* does exist. I won't accept as the crown of my desires a large building with tenements for poor tenants to be rented for a thousand years and, just in case, with the name of the dentist Wagenheim on the sign. Destroy my desires, eradicate my ideals, show me something better and I'll follow you. You may say, perhaps, that it's not worth getting involved; but, in that case, I'll say the same thing in reply. We're having a serious discussion; if you don't grant me your attention, I won't grovel for it. I still have my underground.

And, as long as I'm still alive and feel desire—may my arm wither away before it contributes even one little brick to that building! Never mind that I myself have just rejected the crystal palace for the sole reason that it won't be possible to tease it by sticking out one's tongue at it. I didn't say that because I'm so fond of sticking out my tongue. Perhaps the only reason I got angry is that among all your buildings there's still not a single one where you don't feel compelled to stick out your tongue. On the contrary, I'd let my tongue be cut off out of sheer gratitude, if only things could be so arranged that I'd no longer want to stick it out. What do I care if things can't be so arranged and if I must settle for some tenements? Why was I made with such desires? Can it be that I was made this way only in order to reach the conclusion that my entire way of being is merely a fraud? Can this be the whole purpose? I don't believe it.

By the way, do you know what? I'm convinced that we underground men should be kept in check. Although capable of sitting around quietly in the underground for some forty years, once he emerges into the light of day and bursts into speech, he talks on and on and on. . . .

XI

The final result, gentlemen, is that it's better to do nothing! Conscious inertia is better! And so, long live the underground! Even though I said that I envy the normal man to the point of exasperation, I still wouldn't want to be him under the circumstances in which I see him (although I still won't keep from envying him. No, no, in any case the underground is more advantageous!) At least there one can . . . Hey, but I'm lying once again! I'm lying because I know myself as surely as two times two, that it isn't really the underground that's better, but something different, altogether different, something that I long for, but I'll never be able to find! To hell with the underground! Why, here's what would be better: if I myself were to believe even a fraction of everything I've written. I swear to you, gentlemen, that I don't believe one word, not one little word of all that I've scribbled. That is,

I do believe it, perhaps, but at the very same time, I don't know why, I feel and suspect that I'm lying like a trooper.

"Then why did you write all this?" you ask me.

"What if I'd shut you up in the underground for forty years with nothing to do and then came back forty years later to see what had become of you? Can a man really be left alone for forty years with nothing to do?"

"Isn't it disgraceful, isn't it humiliating!" you might say, shaking your head in contempt. "You long for life, but you try to solve life's problems by means of a logical tangle. How importunate, how insolent your outbursts, and how frightened you are at the same time! You talk rubbish, but you're constantly afraid of them and make apologies. You maintain that you fear nothing, but at the same time you try to ingratiate yourself with us. You assure us that you're gnashing your teeth, yet at the same time you try to be witty and amuse us. You know that your witticisms are not very clever, but apparently you're pleased by their literary merit. Perhaps you really have suffered, but you don't even respect your own suffering. There's some truth in you, too, but no chastity; out of the pettiest vanity you bring your truth out into the open, into the marketplace, and you shame it. . . . You really want to say something, but you conceal your final word out of fear because you lack the resolve to utter it; you have only cowardly impudence. You boast about your consciousness, but you merely vacillate, because even though your mind is working, your heart has been blackened by depravity, and without a pure heart, there can be no full, genuine consciousness. And how importunate you are; how you force yourself upon others; you behave in such an affected manner. Lies, lies, lies!"

Of course, it was I who just invented all these words for you. That, too, comes from the underground. For forty years in a row I've been listening to all your words through a crack. I've invented them myself, since that's all that's occurred to me. It's no wonder that I've learned it all by heart and that it's taken on such a literary form. . . .

But can you really be so gullible as to imagine that I'll print all this and give it to you to read? And here's another problem I have: why do I keep calling you "gentlemen"? Why do I address you as if you really were my readers? Confessions such as the one I plan to set forth here aren't published and given to other people to read. Anyway, I don't possess sufficient fortitude, nor do I consider it necessary to do so. But don't you see, a certain notion has come into my mind, and I wish to realize it at any cost. Here's the point.

Every man has within his own reminiscences certain things he doesn't reveal to anyone, except, perhaps, to his friends. There are also some that he won't reveal even to his friends, only to himself perhaps, and even then, in secret. Finally, there are some which a man is afraid to reveal even to himself; every decent man has accumulated a fair number of such things. In fact, it can even be said that the more decent the man, the more of these things he's accumulated. Anyway, only recently I myself decided to recall some of my earlier adventures; up to now I've always avoided them, even with a certain anxiety. But having decided not only to recall them, but even to write them down, now is when I wish to try an experiment: is it possible to be absolutely honest even with one's own self and not to fear the whole truth? Incidentally, I'll mention that Heine maintains that faithful autobiographies are almost impossible, and that a man is sure to lie about himself.[7] In Heine's opinion, Rousseau, for example, undoubtedly told untruths about himself in his confession and even lied intentionally, out of vanity. I'm convinced that Heine is correct; I understand perfectly well that sometimes it's possible out of vanity alone to impute all sorts of crimes to oneself, and I can even understand what sort of vanity that might be. But Heine was making judgments about a person who confessed to the public. I, however, am writing for myself alone and declare once and for all that if I write as if I were addressing readers, that's only for show, because it's easier for me to write that way. It's a form, simply a form; I shall never have any readers. I've already stated that. . . . I don't want to be restricted in any way by editing my notes. I won't attempt to introduce any order or system. I'll write down whatever comes to mind.

Well, now, for example, someone might seize upon my words and ask me, if you really aren't counting on any readers, why do you make such compacts with yourself, and on paper no less; that is, if you're not going to introduce any order or system, if you're going to write down whatever comes to mind, etc., etc.? Why do you go on explaining? Why do you keep apologizing?

"Well, imagine that," I reply.

This, by the way, contains an entire psychology. Perhaps it's just that I'm a coward. Or perhaps it's that I imagine an audience before me on purpose, so that I behave more decently when I'm writing things down. There may be a thousand reasons.

But here's something else: why is it that I want to write? If it's not for the public, then why can't I simply recall it all in my own mind and not commit it to paper?

Quite so; but somehow it appears more dignified on paper. There's something more impressive about it; I'll be a better judge of myself; the style will be improved. Besides, perhaps I'll actually experience some relief from the process of writing it all down. Today, for example, I'm particularly oppressed by one very old memory from my distant past. It came to me vividly several days ago and since then it's stayed with me, like an annoying musical motif that doesn't want to leave you alone. And yet you must get rid of it. I have hundreds of such memories; but at times a single one emerges from those hundreds and oppresses me. For some reason I believe that if I write it down I can get rid of it. Why not try?

Lastly, I'm bored, and I never do anything. Writing things down actually seems like work. They say that work makes a man become good and honest. Well, at least there's a chance.

It's snowing today, an almost wet, yellow, dull snow. It was snowing yesterday too, a few days ago as well. I think it was apropos of the wet snow that I recalled this episode and now it doesn't want to leave me alone. And so, let it be a tale apropos of wet snow.

---

7. A reference to the work *On Germany* (1853–54) by the German poet Heinrich Heine (1797–1856), in which on the very first page Heine speaks of Rousseau as lying and inventing disgraceful incidents about himself for his *Confessions*.

II

Apropos of Wet Snow

When from the darkness of delusion
I saved your fallen soul
With ardent words of conviction,
And, full of profound torment,
Wringing your hands, you cursed
The vice that had ensnared you;
When, punishing by recollection
Your forgetful conscience,
You told me the tale
Of all that had happened before,
And, suddenly, covering your face,
Full of shame and horror,
You tearfully resolved,
Indignant, shaken . . .
Etc., etc., etc.
    From the poetry of N. A. Nekrasov[8]

I

At that time I was only twenty-four years old. Even then my life was gloomy, disordered, and solitary to the point of savagery. I didn't associate with anyone; I even avoided talking, and I retreated further and further into my corner. At work in the office I even tried not to look at anyone; I was aware not only that my colleagues considered me eccentric, but that they always seemed to regard me with a kind of loathing. Sometimes I wondered why it was that no one else thinks that others regard him with loathing. One of our office-workers had a repulsive pock-marked face which even appeared somewhat villainous. It seemed to me that with such a disreputable face I'd never have dared look at anyone. Another man had a uniform so worn that there was a foul smell emanating from him. Yet, neither of these two gentlemen was embarrassed—neither because of his clothes, nor his face, nor in any moral way. Neither one imagined that other people regarded him with loathing; and if either had so imagined, it wouldn't have mattered at all, as long as their supervisor chose not to view him that way. It's perfectly clear to me now, because of my unlimited vanity and the great demands I accordingly made on myself, that I frequently regarded myself with a furious dissatisfaction verging on loathing; as a result, I intentionally ascribed my own view to everyone else. For example, I despised my own face; I considered it hideous, and I even suspected that there was something repulsive in its expression. Therefore, every time I arrived at work, I took pains to behave as independently as possible, so that I couldn't be suspected of any malice, and I tried to assume as noble an expression as possible. "It may not be a handsome face," I thought, "but let it be noble, expressive, and above all, extremely *intelligent*." But I was agonizingly certain that my face couldn't possibly express all these virtues. Worst of all, I considered it positively stupid. I'd have been reconciled if it had looked intelligent. In fact, I'd even

---

8. A famous Russian poet and editor of radical sympathies (1821–1878). The poem quoted dates from 1845 and is without title. It ends with the lines "And enter my house bold and free / To become its full mistress!"

have agreed to have it appear repulsive, on the condition that at the same time people would find my face terribly intelligent.

Of course, I hated all my fellow office-workers from the first to the last and despised every one of them; yet, at the same time it was as if I were afraid of them. Sometimes it happened that I would even regard them as superior to me. At this time these changes would suddenly occur: first I would despise them, then I would regard them as superior to me. A cultured and decent man cannot be vain without making unlimited demands on himself and without hating himself, at times to the point of contempt. But, whether hating them or regarding them as superior, I almost always lowered my eyes when meeting anyone. I even conducted experiments: could I endure someone's gaze? I'd always be the first to lower my eyes. This infuriated me to the point of madness. I slavishly worshipped the conventional in everything external. I embraced the common practice and feared any eccentricity with all my soul. But how could I sustain it? I was morbidly refined, as befits any cultured man of our time. All others resembled one another as sheep in a flock. Perhaps I was the only one in the whole office who constantly thought of himself as a coward and a slave; and I thought so precisely because I was so cultured. But not only did I think so, it actually was so: I was a coward and a slave. I say this without any embarrassment. Every decent man of our time is and must be a coward and a slave. This is his normal condition. I'm deeply convinced of it. This is how he's made and what he's meant to be. And not only at the present time, as the result of some accidental circumstance, but in general at all times, a decent man must be a coward and a slave. This is a law of nature for all decent men on earth. If one of them should happen to be brave about something or other, we shouldn't be comforted or distracted: he'll still lose his nerve about something else. That's the single and eternal way out. Only asses and their mongrels are brave, and even then, only until they come up against a wall. It's not worthwhile paying them any attention because they really don't mean anything at all.

There was one more circumstance tormenting me at that time: no one was like me, and I wasn't like anyone else. "I'm alone," I mused, "and they are *everyone*"; and I sank deep into thought.

From all this it's clear that I was still just a boy.

The exact opposite would also occur. Sometimes I would find it repulsive to go to the office: it reached the point where I would often return home from work ill. Then suddenly, for no good reason at all, a flash of skepticism and indifference would set in (everything came to me in flashes); I would laugh at my own intolerance and fastidiousness, and reproach myself for my *romanticism*. Sometimes I didn't even want to talk to anyone; at other times it reached a point where I not only started talking, but I even thought about striking up a friendship with others. All my fastidiousness would suddenly disappear for no good reason at all. Who knows? Perhaps I never really had any, and it was all affected, borrowed from books. I still haven't answered this question, even up to now. And once I really did become friends with others; I began to visit their houses, play préférence,[9] drink vodka, talk about promotions. . . . But allow me to digress.

We Russians, generally speaking, have never had any of those stupid, tran-

9. A card game for three players.

scendent German romantics, or even worse, French romantics, on whom nothing produces any effect whatever: the earth might tremble beneath them, all of France might perish on the barricades, but they remain the same, not even changing for decency's sake; they go on singing their transcendent songs, so to speak, to their dying day, because they're such fools. We here on Russian soil have no fools. It's a well-known fact; that's precisely what distinguishes us from foreigners. Consequently, transcendent natures cannot be found among us in their pure form. That's the result of our "positive" publicists and critics of that period, who hunted for the Kostanzhouglo and the Uncle Pyotr Ivanoviches,[1] foolishly mistaking them for our ideal and slandering our own romantics, considering them to be the same kind of transcendents as one finds in Germany or France. On the contrary, the characteristics of our romantics are absolutely and directly opposed to the transcendent Europeans; not one of those European standards can apply here. (Allow me to use the word "romantic"—it's an old-fashioned little word, well-respected and deserving, familiar to everyone.) The characteristics of our romantics are to understand everything, *to see everything, often to see it much more clearly than our most positive minds*; not to be reconciled with anyone or anything, but, at the same time, not to balk at anything; to circumvent everything, to yield on every point, to treat everyone diplomatically; never to lose sight of some useful, practical goal (an apartment at government expense, a nice pension, a decoration)—to keep an eye on that goal through all his excesses and his volumes of lyrical verse, and, at the same time, to preserve intact the "beautiful and sublime" to the end of their lives; and, incidentally, to preserve themselves as well, wrapped up in cotton like precious jewelry, if only, for example, for the sake of that same "beautiful and sublime." Our romantic has a very broad nature and is the biggest rogue of all, I can assure you of that . . . even by my own experience. Of course, all this is true if the romantic is smart. But what am I saying? A romantic is always smart; I merely wanted to observe that although we've had some romantic fools, they really don't count at all, simply because while still in their prime they would degenerate completely into Germans, and, in order to preserve their precious jewels more comfortably, they'd settle over there, either in Weimar or in the Black Forest. For instance, I genuinely despised my official position and refrained from throwing it over merely out of necessity, because I myself sat there working and received good money for doing it. And, as a result, please note, I still refrained from throwing it over. Our romantic would sooner lose his mind (which, by the way, very rarely occurs) than give it up, if he didn't have another job in mind; nor is he ever kicked out, unless he's hauled off to the insane asylum as the "King of Spain,"[2] and only if he's gone completely mad. Then again, it's really only the weaklings and towheads who go mad in our country. An enormous number of romantics later rise to significant rank. What extraordinary versatility! And what a capacity for the most contradictory sensations! I used to be consoled by these thoughts back then, and still am even nowadays. That's why there are so

1. A character in Ivan Goncharov's novel *A Common Story* (1847); a high bureaucrat, a factory owner who teaches lessons of sobriety and good sense to the romantic hero, Alexander Aduyev. Konstanzhouglo is the ideal efficient landowner in the second part of Nikolai Gogol's novel *Dead Souls* (1852). 2. An allusion to the hero of Gogol's short story *Diary of a Madman* (1835). Poprishchin, a low-ranking civil servant, sees his aspirations crushed by the enormous bureaucracy. He ends by going insane and imagining himself to be king of Spain.

many "broad natures" among us, people who never lose their ideals, no matter how low they fall; even though they never lift a finger for the sake of their ideals, even though they're outrageous villains and thieves, nevertheless they respect their original ideals to the point of tears and are extremely honest men at heart. Yes, only among us Russians can the most outrageous scoundrel be absolutely, even sublimely honest at heart, while at the same time never ceasing to be a scoundrel. I repeat, nearly always do our romantics turn out to be very efficient rascals (I use the word "rascal" affectionately); they suddenly manifest such a sense of reality and positive knowledge that their astonished superiors and the general public can only click their tongues at them in amazement.

Their versatility is really astounding; God only knows what it will turn into, how it will develop under subsequent conditions, and what it holds for us in the future. The material is not all that bad! I'm not saying this out of some ridiculous patriotism or jingoism. However, I'm sure that once again you think I'm joking. But who knows? Perhaps it's quite the contrary, that is, you're convinced that this is what I really think. In any case, gentlemen, I'll consider that both of these opinions constitute an honor and a particular pleasure. And do forgive me for this digression.

Naturally, I didn't sustain any friendships with my colleagues, and soon I severed all relations after quarreling with them; and, because of my youthful inexperience at the same time, I even stopped greeting them, as if I'd cut them off entirely. That, however, happened to me only once. On the whole, I was always alone.

At home I spent most of my time reading. I tried to stifle all that was constantly seething within me with external sensations. And of all external sensations available, only reading was possible for me. Of course, reading helped a great deal—it agitated, delighted, and tormented me. But at times it was terribly boring. I still longed to be active; and suddenly I sank into dark, subterranean, loathsome depravity—more precisely, petty vice. My nasty little passions were sharp and painful as a result of my constant, morbid irritability. I experienced hysterical fits accompanied by tears and convulsions. Besides reading, I had nowhere else to go—that is, there was nothing to respect in my surroundings, nothing to attract me. In addition, I was overwhelmed by depression; I possessed a hysterical craving for contradictions and contrasts; and, as a result, I plunged into depravity. I haven't said all this to justify myself. . . . But, no, I'm lying. I did want to justify myself. It's for myself, gentlemen, that I include this little observation. I don't want to lie. I've given my word.

I indulged in depravity all alone, at night, furtively, timidly, sordidly, with a feeling of shame that never left me even in my most loathsome moments and drove me at such times to the point of profanity. Even then I was carrying around the underground in my soul. I was terribly afraid of being seen, met, recognized. I visited all sorts of dismal places.

Once, passing by some wretched little tavern late at night, I saw through a lighted window some gentlemen fighting with billiard cues; one of them was thrown out the window. At some other time I would have been disgusted; but just then I was overcome by such a mood that I envied the gentleman who'd been tossed out; I envied him so much that I even walked into the tavern and entered the billiard room. "Perhaps," I thought, "I'll get into a fight, and they'll throw me out the window, too."

I wasn't drunk, but what could I do—after all, depression can drive a man to this kind of hysteria. But nothing came of it. It turned out that I was incapable of being tossed out the window; I left without getting into a fight.

As soon as I set foot inside, some officer put me in my place.

I was standing next to the billiard table inadvertently blocking his way as he wanted to get by; he took hold of me by the shoulders and without a word of warning or explanation, moved me from where I was standing to another place, and he went past as if he hadn't even noticed me. I could have forgiven even a beating, but I could never forgive his moving me out of the way and entirely failing to notice me.

The devil knows what I would have given for a genuine, ordinary quarrel, a decent one, a more *literary* one, so to speak. But I'd been treated as if I were a fly. The officer was about six feet tall, while I'm small and scrawny. The quarrel, however, was in my hands; all I had to do was protest, and of course they would've thrown me out the window. But I reconsidered and preferred . . . to withdraw resentfully.

I left the tavern confused and upset and went straight home; the next night I continued my petty vice more timidly, more furtively, more gloomily than before, as if I had tears in my eyes—but I continued nonetheless. Don't conclude, however, that I retreated from that officer as a result of any cowardice; I've never been a coward at heart, although I've constantly acted like one in deed, but—wait before you laugh—I can explain this. I can explain anything, you may rest assured.

Oh, if only this officer had been the kind who'd have agreed to fight a duel! But no, he was precisely one of those types (alas, long gone) who preferred to act with their billiard cues or, like Gogol's Lieutenant Pirogov,[3] by appealing to the authorities. They didn't fight duels; in any case, they'd have considered fighting a duel with someone like me, a lowly civilian, to be indecent. In general, they considered duels to be somehow inconceivable, free-thinking, French, while they themselves, especially if they happened to be six feet tall, offended other people rather frequently.

In this case I retreated not out of any cowardice, but because of my unlimited vanity. I wasn't afraid of his height, nor did I think I'd receive a painful beating and get thrown out the window. In fact, I'd have had sufficient physical courage; it was moral fortitude I lacked. I was afraid that everyone present—from the insolent billiard marker to the foul-smelling, pimply little clerks with greasy collars who used to hang about—wouldn't understand and would laugh when I started to protest and speak to them in literary Russian. Because, to this very day, it's still impossible for us to speak about a point of honor, that is, not about honor itself, but a point of honor (*point d'honneur*), except in literary language. One can't even refer to a "point of honor" in everyday language. I was fully convinced (a sense of reality, in spite of all my romanticism!) that they would all simply split their sides laughing, and that the officer, instead of giving me a simple beating, that is, an inoffensive one, would certainly apply his knee to my back and drive me around the billiard table; only then perhaps would he have the mercy to throw me out the window. Naturally, this wretched story of mine couldn't possibly end with this alone. Afterward I used to meet this officer frequently on the street and I

---

3. One of two main characters in Gogol's short story *Nevsky Prospect* (1835). A shallow and self-satisfied officer, he mistakes the wife of a German artisan for a woman of easy virtue and receives a sound thrashing. He decides to lodge an official complaint but, after consuming a cream-filled pastry, thinks better of it.

observed him very carefully. I don't know whether he ever recognized me. Probably not; I reached that conclusion from various observations. As for me, I stared at him with malice and hatred, and continued to do so for several years! My malice increased and became stronger over time. At first I began to make discreet inquiries about him. This was difficult for me to do, since I had so few acquaintances. But once, as I was following him at a distance as though tied to him, someone called to him on the street: that's how I learned his name. Another time I followed him back to his own apartment and for a ten-kopeck piece learned from the doorman where and how he lived, on what floor, with whom, etc.—in a word, all that could be learned from a doorman. One morning, although I never engaged in literary activities, it suddenly occurred to me to draft a description of this officer as a kind of exposé, a caricature, in the form of a tale. I wrote it with great pleasure. I exposed him; I even slandered him. At first I altered his name only slightly, so that it could be easily recognized; but then, upon careful reflection, I changed it. Then I sent the tale off to *Notes of the Fatherland*.[4] But such exposés were no longer in fashion, and they didn't publish my tale. I was very annoyed by that. At times I simply choked on my spite. Finally, I resolved to challenge my opponent to a duel. I composed a beautiful, charming letter to him, imploring him to apologize to me; in case he refused, I hinted rather strongly at a duel. The letter was composed in such a way that if that officer had possessed even the smallest understanding of the "beautiful and sublime," he would have come running, thrown his arms around me, and offered his friendship. That would have been splendid! We would have led such a wonderful life! Such a life! He would have shielded me with his rank; I would have ennobled him with my culture, and, well, with my ideas. Who knows what might have come of it! Imagine it, two years had already passed since he'd insulted me; my challenge was the most ridiculous anachronism, in spite of all the cleverness of my letter in explaining and disguising that fact. But, thank God (to this day I thank the Almighty with tears in my eyes), I didn't send that letter. A shiver runs up and down my spine when I think what might have happened if I had. Then suddenly . . . suddenly, I got my revenge in the simplest manner, a stroke of genius! A brilliant idea suddenly occurred to me. Sometimes on holidays I used to stroll along Nevsky Prospect at about four o'clock in the afternoon, usually on the sunny side. That is, I didn't really stroll; rather, I experienced innumerable torments, humiliations, and bilious attacks. But that's undoubtedly just what I needed. I darted in and out like a fish among the strollers, constantly stepping aside before generals, cavalry officers, hussars, and young ladies. At those moments I used to experience painful spasms in my heart and a burning sensation in my back merely at the thought of my dismal apparel as well as the wretchedness and vulgarity of my darting little figure. This was sheer torture, uninterrupted and unbearable humiliation at the thought, which soon became an incessant and immediate sensation, that I was a fly in the eyes of society, a disgusting, obscene fly—smarter than the rest, more cultured, even nobler—all that goes without saying, but a fly, nonetheless, who incessantly steps aside, insulted and injured by everyone. For what reason did I inflict this torment on myself? Why did I stroll along Nevsky Prospect? I don't know. But something simply *drew* me there at every opportunity.

---

4. A radical literary and political journal published in St. Petersburg from 1839 to 1867.

Then I began to experience surges of that pleasure about which I've already spoken in the first chapter. After the incident with the officer I was drawn there even more strongly; I used to encounter him along Nevsky most often, and it was there that I could admire him. He would also go there, mostly on holidays. He, too, would give way before generals and individuals of superior rank; he, too, would spin like a top among them. But he would simply trample people like me, or even those slightly superior; he would walk directly toward them, as if there were empty space ahead of him; and under no circumstance would he ever step aside. I revelled in my malice as I observed him, and . . . bitterly stepped aside before him every time. I was tortured by the fact that even on the street I found it impossible to stand on an equal footing with him. "Why is it you're always first to step aside?" I badgered myself in insane hysteria, at times waking up at three in the morning. "Why always you and not he? After all, there's no law about it; it isn't written down anywhere. Let it be equal, as it usually is when people of breeding meet: he steps aside halfway and you halfway, and you pass by showing each other mutual respect." But that was never the case, and I continued to step aside, while he didn't even notice that I was yielding to him. Then a most astounding idea suddenly dawned on me. "What if," I thought, "what if I were to meet him and . . . not step aside? Deliberately not step aside, even if it meant bumping into him: how would that be?" This bold idea gradually took such a hold that it afforded me no peace. I dreamt about it incessantly, horribly, and even went to Nevsky more frequently so that I could imagine more clearly how I would do it. I was in ecstasy. The scheme was becoming more and more possible and even probable to me. "Of course, I wouldn't really collide with him," I thought, already feeling more generous toward him in my joy, "but I simply won't turn aside. I'll bump into him, not very painfully, but just so, shoulder to shoulder, as much as decency allows. I'll bump into him the same amount as he bumps into me." At last I made up my mind completely. But the preparations took a very long time. First, in order to look as presentable as possible during the execution of my scheme, I had to worry about my clothes. "In any case, what if, for example, it should occasion a public scandal? (And the public there was *superflu*:[5] a countess, Princess D., and the entire literary world.) It was essential to be well-dressed; that inspires respect and in a certain sense will place us immediately on an equal footing in the eyes of high society." With that goal in mind I requested my salary in advance, and I purchased a pair of black gloves and a decent hat at Churkin's store. Black gloves seemed to me more dignified, more *bon ton*[6] than the lemon-colored ones I'd considered at first. "That would be too glaring, as if the person wanted to be noticed"; so I didn't buy the lemon-colored ones. I'd already procured a fine shirt with white bone cufflinks; but my overcoat constituted a major obstacle. In and of itself it was not too bad at all; it kept me warm; but it was quilted and had a raccoon collar, the epitome of bad taste. At all costs I had to replace the collar with a beaver one, just like on an officer's coat. For this purpose I began to frequent the Shopping Arcade; and, after several attempts, I turned up some cheap German beaver. Although these German beavers wear out very quickly and soon begin to look shabby, at first, when they're brand new, they look very fine indeed; after all, I only needed it for a single occasion. I asked the price: it was still expensive.

5. Excessively refined (French).   6. In good taste (French).

After considerable reflection I resolved to sell my raccoon collar. I decided to request a loan for the remaining amount—a rather significant sum for me—from Anton Antonych Setochkin, my office chief, a modest man, but a serious and solid one, who never lent money to anyone, but to whom, upon entering the civil service, I'd once been specially recommended by an important person who'd secured the position for me. I suffered terribly. It seemed monstrous and shameful to ask Anton Antonych for money. I didn't sleep for two or three nights in a row; in general I wasn't getting much sleep those days, and I always had a fever. I would have either a vague sinking feeling in my heart, or else my heart would suddenly begin to thump, thump, thump! . . . . At first Anton Antonych was surprised, then he frowned, thought it over, and finally gave me the loan, after securing from me a note authorizing him to deduct the sum from my salary two weeks later. In this way everything was finally ready; the splendid beaver reigned in place of the mangy raccoon, and I gradually began to get down to business. It was impossible to set about it all at once, in a foolhardy way; one had to proceed in this matter very carefully, step by step. But I confess that after many attempts I was ready to despair: we didn't bump into each other, no matter what! No matter how I prepared, no matter how determined I was—it seems that we're just about to bump, when I look up—and once again I've stepped aside while he's gone by without even noticing me. I even used to pray as I approached him that God would grant me determination. One time I'd fully resolved to do it, but the result was that I merely stumbled and fell at his feet because, at the very last moment, only a few inches away from him, I lost my nerve. He stepped over me very calmly, and I bounced to one side like a rubber ball. That night I lay ill with a fever once again and was delirious. Then, everything suddenly ended in the best possible way. The night before I decided once and for all not to go through with my pernicious scheme and to give it all up without success; with that in mind I went to Nevsky Prospect for one last time simply in order to see how I'd abandon the whole thing. Suddenly, three paces away from my enemy, I made up my mind unexpectedly; I closed my eyes and— we bumped into each other forcefully, shoulder to shoulder! I didn't yield an inch and walked by him on a completely equal footing! He didn't even turn around to look at me and pretended that he hadn't even noticed; but he was merely pretending, I'm convinced of that. To this very day I'm convinced of that! Naturally, I got the worst of it; he was stronger, but that wasn't the point. The point was that I'd achieved my goal, I'd maintained my dignity, I hadn't yielded one step, and I'd publicly placed myself on an equal social footing with him. I returned home feeling completely avenged for everything. I was ecstatic. I rejoiced and sang Italian arias. Of course, I won't describe what happened to me three days later; if you've read the first part entitled "Underground," you can guess for yourself. The officer was later transferred somewhere else; I haven't seen him for some fourteen years. I wonder what he's doing nowadays, that dear friend of mine! Whom is he trampling underfoot?

II

But when this phase of my nice, little dissipation ended I felt terribly nauseated. Remorse set in; I tried to drive it away because it was too disgusting. Little by little, however, I got used to that, too. I got used to it all; that is, it wasn't that I got used to it, rather, I somehow voluntarily consented to endure it. But I had a way out that reconciled everything—to escape into "all that was beautiful and sublime," in my dreams, of course. I was a terrible dreamer; I dreamt for three months in a row, tucked away in my little corner. And well you may believe that in those moments I was not at all like the gentleman who, in his faint-hearted anxiety, had sewn a German beaver onto the collar of his old overcoat. I suddenly became a hero. If my six-foot-tall lieutenant had come to see me then, I'd never have admitted him. I couldn't even conceive of him at that time. It's hard to describe now what my dreams consisted of then, and how I could've been so satisfied with them, but I was. Besides, even now I can take pride in them at certain times. My dreams were particularly sweet and vivid after my little debauchery; they were filled with remorse and tears, curses and ecstasy. There were moments of such positive intoxication, such happiness, that I felt not even the slightest trace of mockery within me, really and truly. It was all faith, hope and love. That's just it: at the time I believed blindly that by some kind of miracle, some external circumstance, everything would suddenly open up and expand; a vista of appropriate activity would suddenly appear—beneficent, beautiful, and most of all, *ready-made* (what precisely, I never knew, but, most of all, it had to be ready-made), and that I would suddenly step forth into God's world, almost riding on a white horse and wearing a laurel wreath. I couldn't conceive of a secondary role; and that's precisely why in reality I very quietly took on the lowest one. Either a hero or dirt—there was no middle ground. That was my ruin because in the dirt I consoled myself knowing that at other times I was a hero, and that the hero covered himself with dirt; that is to say, an ordinary man would be ashamed to wallow in filth, but a hero is too noble to become defiled; consequently, he can wallow. It's remarkable that these surges of everything "beautiful and sublime" occurred even during my petty depravity, and precisely when I'd sunk to the lowest depths. They occurred in separate spurts, as if to remind me of themselves; however, they failed to banish my depravity by their appearance. On the contrary, they seemed to add spice to it by means of contrast; they came in just the right amount to serve as a tasty sauce. This sauce consisted of contradictions, suffering, and agonizing internal analysis; all of these torments and trifles lent a certain piquancy, even some meaning to my depravity—in a word, they completely fulfilled the function of a tasty sauce. Nor was all this even lacking in a measure of profundity. Besides, I would never have consented to the simple, tasteless, spontaneous little debauchery of an ordinary clerk and have endured all that filth! How could it have attracted me then and lured me into the street late at night? No, sir, I had a noble loophole for everything. . . .

But how much love, oh Lord, how much love I experienced at times in those dreams of mine, in those "escapes into everything beautiful and sublime." Even though it was fantastic love, even though it was never directed at anything human, there was still so much love that afterward, in reality, I no longer felt any impulse to direct it: that would have been an unnecessary luxury. However, everything always ended in a most satisfactory way by a lazy and intoxicating transition into art, that is, into beautiful forms of being, ready-made, largely borrowed from poets and novelists, and adapted to serve every possible need. For instance, I would triumph over everyone; naturally, everyone else grovelled in the dust and was voluntarily impelled to acknowledge my superiority, while I would forgive them all for everything. Or else, being a famous poet and chamberlain, I would fall in love; I'd receive an enormous fortune and would immediately sacrifice it all for the benefit of humanity, at the same time confessing before all peoples my own infamies, which, needless to say, were not simple infamies, but contained a great amount of "the beautiful and sublime," something in the style of Manfred.[7] Everyone would weep and kiss me (otherwise what idiots they would have been), while I went about barefoot and hungry preaching new ideas and defeating all the reactionaries of Austerlitz.[8] Then a march would be played, a general amnesty declared, and the Pope would agree to leave Rome and go to Brazil;[9] a ball would be hosted for all of Italy at the Villa Borghese on the shores of Lake Como,[1] since Lake Como would have been moved to Rome for this very occasion; then there would be a scene in the bushes, etc., etc.—as if you didn't know. You'll say that it's tasteless and repugnant to drag all this out into the open after all the raptures and tears to which I've confessed. But why is it so repugnant? Do you really think I'm ashamed of all this or that it's any more stupid than anything in your own lives, gentlemen? Besides, you can rest assured that some of it was not at all badly composed. . . . Not everything occurred on the shores of Lake Como. But you're right; in fact, it is tasteless and repugnant. And the most repugnant thing of all is that now I've begun to justify myself before you. And even more repugnant is that now I've made that observation. But enough, otherwise there'll be no end to it: each thing will be more repugnant than the last. . . .

I was never able to dream for more than three months in a row, and I began to feel an irresistible urge to plunge into society. To me plunging into society meant paying a visit to my office chief, Anton Antonych Setochkin. He's the only lasting acquaintance I've made during my lifetime; I too now marvel at this circumstance. But even then I would visit him only when my dreams had reached such a degree of happiness that it was absolutely essential for me to embrace people and all humanity at once; for that reason I needed to have at least one person on hand who actually existed. However, one could only call upon Anton Antonych on Tuesdays (his receiving day); consequently, I always had to adjust the urge to embrace all humanity so that it occurred on Tuesday. This Anton Antonych lived near Five Corners,[2] on the fourth floor, in four small, low-ceilinged rooms, each smaller than the last, all very frugal and yellowish in appearance. He lived with his two daughters and an aunt who used to serve tea. The daughters, one thirteen, the other fourteen, had little snub noses. I was very embarrassed by them because they used to whisper all the time and giggle to each other. The host usually sat in his study on a leather couch in front of a table together with some gray-haired guest, a civil servant either from our office or another one.

<hr />

7. The romantic hero of Byron's poetic tragedy *Manfred* (1817), a lonely, defiant figure whose past conceals some mysterious crime.　8. The site of Napoleon's great victory in December 1805 over the combined armies of the Russian czar Alexander I and the Austrian emperor Francis II.　9. Napoleon announced his annexation of the Papal States to France in 1809 and was promptly excommunicated by Pope Pius VII. The pope was imprisoned and forced to sign a new concordat, but in 1814 he returned to Rome in triumph. 1. Located in the foothills of the Italian Alps in Lombardy. Villa Borghese was the elegant summer palace built by Scipione Cardinal Borghese outside the Porta del Popolo in Rome.　2. A well-known landmark in St. Petersburg.

I never saw more than two or three guests there, and they were always the same ones. They talked about excise taxes, debates in the Senate, salaries, promotions, His Excellency and how to please him, and so on and so forth. I had the patience to sit there like a fool next to these people for four hours or so; I listened without daring to say a word to them or even knowing what to talk about. I sat there in a stupor; several times I broke into a sweat; I felt numbed by paralysis; but it was good and useful. Upon returning home I would postpone for some time my desire to embrace all humanity.

I had one other sort of acquaintance, however, named Simonov, a former schoolmate of mine. In fact, I had a number of schoolmates in Petersburg, but I didn't associate with them, and I'd even stopped greeting them along the street. I might even have transferred into a different department at the office so as not to be with them and to cut myself off from my hated childhood once and for all. Curses on that school and those horrible years of penal servitude. In short, I broke with my schoolmates as soon as I was released. There remained only two or three people whom I would greet upon encountering them. One was Simonov, who hadn't distinguished himself in school in any way; he was even-tempered and quiet, but I detected in him a certain independence of character, even honesty. I don't even think that he was all that limited. At one time he and I experienced some rather bright moments, but they didn't last very long and somehow were suddenly clouded over. Evidently he was burdened by these recollections, and seemed in constant fear that I would lapse into that former mode. I suspect that he found me repulsive, but not being absolutely sure, I used to visit him nonetheless.

So once, on a Thursday, unable to endure my solitude, and knowing that on that day Anton Antonych's door was locked, I remembered Simonov. As I climbed the stairs to his apartment on the fourth floor, I was thinking how burdensome this man found my presence and that my going to see him was rather useless. But since it always turned out, as if on purpose, that such reflections would impel me to put myself even further into an ambiguous situation, I went right in. It had been almost a year since I'd last seen Simonov.

III

I found two more of my former schoolmates there with him. Apparently they were discussing some important matter. None of them paid any attention to me when I entered, which was strange since I hadn't seen them for several years. Evidently they considered me some sort of ordinary house fly. They hadn't even treated me like that when we were in school together, although they'd all hated me. Of course, I understood that they must despise me now for my failure in the service and for the fact that I'd sunk so low, was badly dressed, and so on, which, in their eyes, constituted proof of my ineptitude and insignificance. But I still hadn't expected such a degree of contempt. Simonov was even surprised by my visits. All this disconcerted me; I sat down in some distress and began to listen to what they were saying.

The discussion was serious, even heated, and concerned a farewell dinner which these gentlemen wanted to organize jointly as early as the following day for their friend Zverkov, an army officer who was heading for a distant province. Monsieur Zverkov had also been my schoolmate all along. I'd begun to hate him especially in the upper grades. In the lower grades he was merely an attractive, lively lad whom everyone liked. However, I'd hated him in the lower grades, too, precisely because he was such an attractive, lively lad. He was perpetually a poor student and had gotten worse as time went on; he managed to graduate, however, because he had influential connections. During his last year at school he'd come into an inheritance of some two hundred serfs, and, since almost all the rest of us were poor, he'd even begun to brag. He was an extremely uncouth fellow, but a nice lad nonetheless, even when he was bragging. In spite of our superficial, fantastic, and high-flown notions of honor and pride, all of us, except for a very few, would fawn upon Zverkov, the more so the more he bragged. They didn't fawn for any advantage; they fawned simply because he was a man endowed by nature with gifts. Moreover, we'd somehow come to regard Zverkov as a cunning fellow and an expert on good manners. This latter point particularly infuriated me. I hated the shrill, self-confident tone of his voice, his adoration for his own witticisms, which were terribly stupid in spite of his bold tongue; I hated his handsome, stupid face (for which, however, I'd gladly have exchanged my own intelligent one), and the impudent bearing typical of officers during the 1840s. I hated the way he talked about his future successes with women. (He'd decided not to get involved with them yet, since he still hadn't received his officer's epaulettes; he awaited those epaulettes impatiently.) And he talked about all the duels he'd have to fight. I remember how once, although I was usually very taciturn, I suddenly clashed with Zverkov when, during our free time, he was discussing future exploits with his friends; getting a bit carried away with the game like a little puppy playing in the sun, he suddenly declared that not a single girl in his village would escape his attention—that it was his *droit de seigneur*,[3] and that if the peasants even dared protest, he'd have them all flogged, those bearded rascals; and he'd double their quit-rent.[4] Our louts applauded, but I attacked him—not out of any pity for the poor girls or their fathers, but simply because everyone else was applauding such a little insect. I got the better of him that time, but Zverkov, although stupid, was also cheerful and impudent. Therefore he laughed it off to such an extent that, in fact, I really didn't get the better of him. The laugh remained on his side. Later he got the better of me several times, but without malice, just so, in jest, in passing, in fun. I was filled with spite and hatred, but I didn't respond. After graduation he took a few steps toward me; I didn't object strongly because I found it flattering; but soon we came to a natural parting of the ways. Afterward I heard about his barrack-room successes as a lieutenant and about his *binges*. Then there were other rumors—about his *successes* in the service. He no longer bowed to me on the street; I suspected that he was afraid to compromise himself by acknowledging such an insignificant person as myself. I also saw him in the theater once, in the third tier, already sporting an officer's gold braids. He was fawning and grovelling before the daughters of some aged general. In those three years he'd let himself go, although he was still as handsome and agile as before; he sagged somehow and had begun to put on weight; it was clear that by the age of thirty he'd be totally flabby. So it was for this Zverkov, who was finally ready

3. Lord's privilege (French); the feudal lord's right to spend the first night with the bride of a newly married serf. 4. The annual sum paid in cash or produce by serfs to landowners for the right to farm their land in feudal Russia, as opposed to the *corvée*, a certain amount of labor owed.

to depart, that our schoolmates were organizing a farewell dinner. They'd kept up during these three years, although I'm sure that inwardly they didn't consider themselves on an equal footing with him.

One of Simonov's two guests was Ferfichkin, a Russified German, a short man with a face like a monkey, a fool who made fun of everybody, my bitterest enemy from the lower grades—a despicable, impudent show-off who affected the most ticklish sense of ambition, although, of course, he was a coward at heart. He was one of Zverkov's admirers and played up to him for his own reasons, frequently borrowing money from him. Simonov's other guest, Trudolyubov, was insignificant, a military man, tall, with a cold demeanor, rather honest, who worshipped success of any kind and was capable of talking only about promotions. He was a distant relative of Zverkov's, and that, silly to say, lent him some importance among us. He'd always regarded me as a nonentity; he treated me not altogether politely, but tolerably.

"Well, if each of us contributes seven rubles," said Trudolyubov, "with three of us that makes twenty-one altogether—we can have a good dinner. Of course, Zverkov won't have to pay."

"Naturally," Simonov agreed, "since we're inviting him."

"Do you really think," Ferfichkin broke in arrogantly and excitedly, just like an insolent lackey bragging about his master-the-general's medals, "do you really think Zverkov will let us pay for everything? He'll accept out of decency, but then he'll order *half a dozen bottles* on his own."

"What will the four of us do with half a dozen bottles?" asked Trudolyubov, only taking note of the number.

"So then, three of us plus Zverkov makes four, twenty-one rubles, in the Hôtel de Paris, tomorrow at five o'clock," concluded Simonov definitively, since he'd been chosen to make the arrangements.

"Why only twenty-one?" I asked in trepidation, even, apparently, somewhat offended. "If you count me in, you'll have twenty-eight rubles instead of twenty-one."

It seemed to me that to include myself so suddenly and unexpectedly would appear as quite a splendid gesture and that they'd all be smitten at once and regard me with respect.

"Do you really want to come, too?" Simonov inquired with displeasure, managing somehow to avoid looking at me. He knew me inside out.

It was infuriating that he knew me inside out.

"And why not? After all, I was his schoolmate, too, and I must admit that I even feel a bit offended that you've left me out," I continued, just about to boil over again.

"And how were we supposed to find you?" Ferfichkin interjected rudely.

"You never got along very well with Zverkov," added Trudolyubov frowning. But I'd already latched on and wouldn't let go.

"I think no one has a right to judge that," I objected in a trembling voice, as if God knows what had happened. "Perhaps that's precisely why I want to take part now, since we didn't get along so well before."

"Well, who can figure you out . . . such lofty sentiments . . . ," Trudolyubov said with an ironic smile.

"We'll put your name down," Simonov decided, turning to me. "Tomorrow at five o'clock at the Hôtel de Paris. Don't make any mistakes."

"What about the money?" Ferfichkin started to say in an undertone to Simonov while nodding at me, but he broke off because Simonov looked embarrassed.

"That'll do," Trudolyubov said getting up. "If he really wants to come so much, let him."

"But this is our own circle of friends," Ferfichkin grumbled, also picking up his hat. "It's not an official gathering. Perhaps we really don't want you at all. . . ."

They left. Ferfichkin didn't even say goodbye to me as he went out; Trudolyubov barely nodded without looking at me. Simonov, with whom I was left alone, was irritated and perplexed, and he regarded me in a strange way. He neither sat down nor invited me to.

"Hmmm . . . yes . . . , so, tomorrow. Will you contribute your share of the money now? I'm asking just to know for sure," he muttered in embarrassment.

I flared up; but in doing so, I remembered that I'd owed Simonov fifteen rubles for a very long time, which debt, moreover, I'd forgotten, but had also never repaid.

"You must agree, Simonov, that I couldn't have known when I came here . . . oh, what a nuisance, but I've forgotten. . . ."

He broke off and began to pace around the room in even greater irritation. As he paced, he began to walk on his heels and stomp more loudly.

"I'm not detaining you, am I?" I asked after a few moments of silence.

"Oh, no!" he replied with a start. "That is, in fact, yes. You see, I still have to stop by at . . . It's not very far from here . . . ," he added in an apologetic way with some embarrassment.

"Oh, good heavens! Why didn't you say so?" I exclaimed, seizing my cap; moreover I did so with a surprisingly familiar air, coming from God knows where.

"But it's really not far . . . only a few steps away . . . ," Simonov repeated, accompanying me into the hallway with a bustling air which didn't suit him well at all. "So, then, tomorrow at five o'clock sharp!" he shouted to me on the stairs. He was very pleased that I was leaving. However, I was furious.

"What possessed me, what on earth possessed me to interfere?" I gnashed my teeth as I walked along the street. "And for such a scoundrel, a pig like Zverkov! Naturally, I shouldn't go. Of course, to hell with them. Am I bound to go, or what? Tomorrow I'll inform Simonov by post. . . ."

But the real reason I was so furious was that I was sure I'd go. I'd go on purpose. The more tactless, the more indecent it was for me to go, the more certain I'd be to do it.

There was even a definite impediment to my going: I didn't have any money. All I had was nine rubles. But of those, I had to hand over seven the next day to my servant Apollon for his monthly wages; he lived in and received seven rubles for his meals.

Considering Apollon's character it was impossible not to pay him. But more about that rascal, that plague of mine, later.

In any case, I knew that I wouldn't pay him his wages and that I'd definitely go.

That night I had the most hideous dreams. No wonder: all evening I was burdened with recollections of my years of penal servitude at school and I couldn't get rid of them. I'd been sent off to that school by distant relatives on whom I was dependent and about whom I've heard nothing since. They dispatched me, a lonely boy, crushed by their reproaches, already introspective, taciturn, and regarding everything around him savagely. My schoolmates received me with spiteful and pitiless jibes because I wasn't like any of them. But I couldn't tolerate their jibes; I couldn't possibly get along with them as easily as they got along with each other. I hated them all at once and took refuge from everyone in fearful, wounded and excessive pride. Their crudeness irritated me. Cynically they mocked my face and my awkward build; yet, what stupid faces they all had! Facial expressions at our school somehow degenerated and became particularly stupid. Many attractive lads had come to us, but in a few years they too were repulsive to look at. When I was only sixteen I wondered about them gloomily; even then I was astounded by the pettiness of their thoughts and the stupidity of their studies, games and conversations. They failed to understand essential things and took no interest in important, weighty subjects, so that I couldn't help considering them beneath me. It wasn't my wounded vanity that drove me to it; and, for God's sake, don't repeat any of those nauseating and hackneyed clichés, such as, "I was merely a dreamer, whereas they already understood life." They didn't understand a thing, not one thing about life, and I swear, that's what annoyed me most about them. On the contrary, they accepted the most obvious, glaring reality in a fantastically stupid way, and even then they'd begun to worship nothing but success. Everything that was just, but oppressed and humiliated, they ridiculed hard-heartedly and shamelessly. They mistook rank for intelligence; at the age of sixteen they were already talking about occupying comfortable little niches. Of course, much of this was due to their stupidity and the poor examples that had constantly surrounded them in their childhood and youth. They were monstrously depraved. Naturally, even this was more superficial, more affected cynicism; of course, their youth and a certain freshness shone through their depravity; but even this freshness was unattractive and manifested itself in a kind of rakishness. I hated them terribly, although, perhaps, I was even worse than they were. They returned the feeling and didn't conceal their loathing for me. But I no longer wanted their affection; on the contrary, I constantly longed for their humiliation. In order to avoid their jibes, I began to study as hard as I could on purpose and made my way to the top of the class. That impressed them. In addition, they all began to realize that I'd read certain books which they could never read and that I understood certain things (not included in our special course) about which they'd never even heard. They regarded this with savagery and sarcasm, but they submitted morally, all the more since even the teachers paid me some attention on this account. Their jibes ceased, but their hostility remained, and relations between us became cold and strained. In the end I myself couldn't stand it: as the years went by, my need for people, for friends, increased. I made several attempts to get closer to some of them; but these attempts always turned out to be unnatural and ended of their own accord. Once I even had a friend of sorts. But I was already a despot at heart; I wanted to exercise unlimited power over his soul; I wanted to instill in him contempt for his surroundings; and I demanded from him a disdainful and definitive break with those surroundings. I frightened him with my passionate friendship, and I reduced him to tears and convulsions. He was a naive and giving soul, but as soon as he'd surrendered himself to me totally, I began to despise him and reject him immediately—as if I only needed to achieve a victory over him, merely to subjugate him. But I was unable to conquer them all; my one friend was not at all like them, but rather a rare exception. The first thing I did upon leaving school was abandon the special job in the civil service for which I'd been trained, in order to sever all ties, break with my past, cover it over with dust. . . . The devil only knows why, after all that, I'd dragged myself over to see this Simonov! . . .

Early the next morning I roused myself from bed, jumped up in anxiety, just as if everything was about to start happening all at once. But I believed that some radical change in my life was imminent and was sure to occur that very day. Perhaps because I wasn't used to it, but all my life, at any external event, albeit a trivial one, it always seemed that some sort of radical change would occur. I went off to work as usual, but returned home two hours earlier in order to prepare. The most important thing, I thought, was not to arrive there first, or else they'd all think I was too eager. But there were thousands of most important things, and they all reduced me to the point of impotence. I polished my boots once again with my own hands. Apollon wouldn't polish them twice in one day for anything in the world; he considered it indecent. So I polished them myself, after stealing the brushes from the hallway so that he wouldn't notice and then despise me for it afterward. Next I carefully examined my clothes and found that everything was old, shabby, and worn out. I'd become too slovenly. My uniform was in better shape, but I couldn't go to dinner in a uniform. Worst of all, there was an enormous yellow stain on the knee of my trousers. I had an inkling that the spot alone would rob me of nine-tenths of my dignity. I also knew that it was unseemly for me to think that. "But this isn't the time for thinking. Reality is now looming," I thought, and my heart sank. I also knew perfectly well at that time, that I was monstrously exaggerating all these facts. But what could be done? I was no longer able to control myself, and was shaking with fever. In despair I imagined how haughtily and coldly that "scoundrel" Zverkov would greet me; with what dull and totally relentless contempt that dullard Trudolyubov would regard me; how nastily and impudently that insect Ferfichkin would giggle at me in order to win Zverkov's approval; how well Simonov would understand all this and how he'd despise me for my wretched vanity and cowardice; and worst of all, how petty all this would be, not *literary*, but commonplace. Of course, it would have been better not to go at all. But that was no longer possible; once I began to feel drawn to something, I plunged right in, head first. I'd have reproached myself for the rest of my life: "So, you retreated, you retreated before reality, you retreated!" On the contrary, I desperately wanted to prove to all this "rabble" that I really wasn't the coward I imagined myself to be. But that's not all: in the strongest paroxysm of cowardly fever I dreamt of gaining the upper hand, of conquering them, of carrying them away, compelling them to love me—if only "for the nobility of my thought and my indisputable wit." They would abandon Zverkov; he'd sit by in silence and embarassment, and I'd crush him. Afterward, perhaps, I'd be reconciled with Zverkov and drink to our *friendship*, but what was most spiteful and insulting for me was that I knew even then, I knew completely and for sure, that I didn't need any of this at all; that in fact I really didn't want to crush them, conquer them, or attract them, and that if I could have ever achieved all that, I'd be the first to say that it wasn't worth a damn. Oh, how I prayed to God that this day would pass quickly! With inexpressible anxiety I approached the window, opened the transom,[5] and peered out into the murky mist of the thickly falling wet snow. . . .

At last my worthless old wall clock sputtered out five o'clock. I grabbed my hat, and, trying not to look at Apollon—who'd been waiting since early morning to receive his wages, but didn't want to be the first one to mention it out of pride—I slipped out the door past him and intentionally hired a smart cab with my last half-ruble in order to arrive at the Hôtel de Paris in style.

IV

I knew since the day before that I'd be the first one to arrive. But it was no longer a question of who was first.

Not only was no one else there, but I even had difficulty finding our room. The table hadn't even been set. What did it all mean? After many inquiries I finally learned from the waiters that dinner had been ordered for closer to six o'clock, instead of five. This was also confirmed in the buffet. It was too embarrassing to ask any more questions. It was still only twenty-five minutes past five. If they'd changed the time, they should have let me know; that's what the city mail was for. They shouldn't have subjected me to such "shame" in my own eyes and . . . and, at least not in front of the waiters. I sat down. A waiter began to set the table. I felt even more ashamed in his presence. Toward six o'clock candles were brought into the room in addition to the lighted lamps already there, yet it hadn't occurred to the waiters to bring them in as soon as I'd arrived. In the next room two gloomy customers, angry-looking and silent, were dining at separate tables. In one of the distant rooms there was a great deal of noise, even shouting. One could hear the laughter of a whole crowd of people, including nasty little squeals in French—there were ladies present at that dinner. In short, it was disgusting. Rarely had I passed a more unpleasant hour, so that when they all arrived together precisely at six o'clock, I was initially overjoyed to see them, as if they were my liberators, and I almost forgot that I was supposed to appear offended.

Zverkov, obviously the leader, entered ahead of the rest. Both he and they were laughing; but, upon seeing me, Zverkov drew himself up, approached me unhurriedly, bowed slightly from the waist almost coquettishly, and extended his hand politely, but not too, with a kind of careful civility, almost as if he were a general both offering his hand, but also guarding against something. I'd imagined, on the contrary, that as soon as he entered he'd burst into his former, shrill laughter with occasional squeals, and that he'd immediately launch into his stale jokes and witticisms. I'd been preparing for them since the previous evening; but in no way did I expect such condescension, such courtesy characteristic of a general. Could it be that he now considered himself so immeasurably superior to me in all respects? If he'd merely wanted to offend me by this superior attitude, it wouldn't have been so bad, I thought; I'd manage to pay him back somehow. But what if, without any desire to offend, the notion had crept into his dumb sheep's

---

5. A small hinged pane in the window of a Russian house, used for ventilation especially during the winter when the main part of the window is sealed.

brain that he really was immeasurably superior to me and that he could only treat me in a patronizing way? From this possibility alone I began to gasp for air.

"Have you been waiting long?" Trudolyubov asked.

"I arrived at five o'clock sharp, just as I was told yesterday," I answered loudly and with irritation presaging an imminent explosion.

"Didn't you let him know that we changed the time?" Trudolyubov asked, turning to Simonov.

"No, I didn't. I forgot," he replied, but without any regret; then, not even apologizing to me, he went off to order the hors d'oeuvres.

"So you've been here for a whole hour, you poor fellow!" Zverkov cried sarcastically, because according to his notions, this must really have been terribly amusing. That scoundrel Ferfichkin chimed in after him with nasty, ringing laughter that sounded like a dog's yapping. My situation seemed very amusing and awkward to him, too.

"It's not the least bit funny!" I shouted at Ferfichkin, getting more and more irritated. "The others are to blame, not me. They neglected to inform me. It's, it's, it's . . . simply preposterous."

"It's not only preposterous, it's more than that," muttered Trudolyubov, naively interceding on my behalf. "You're being too kind. It's pure rudeness. Of course, it wasn't intentional. And how could Simonov have . . . hmm!"

"If a trick like that had been played on me," said Ferfichkin, "I'd . . ." "Oh, you'd have ordered yourself something to eat," interrupted Zverkov, "or simply asked to have dinner served without waiting for the rest of us."

"You'll agree that I could've done that without asking anyone's permission," I snapped. "If I did wait, it was only because . . ."

"Let's be seated, gentlemen," cried Simonov upon entering. "Everything's ready. I can vouch for the champagne; it's excellently chilled. . . . Moreover, I didn't know where your apartment was, so how could I find you?" he said turning to me suddenly, but once again not looking directly at me. Obviously he was holding something against me. I suspect he got to thinking after what had happened yesterday.

Everyone sat down; I did, too. The table was round. Trudolyubov sat on my left, Simonov, on my right. Zverkov sat across; Ferfichkin, next to him, between Trudolyubov and him.

"Tell-l-l me now, are you . . . in a government department?" Zverkov continued to attend to me. Seeing that I was embarrassed, he imagined in earnest that he had to be nice to me, encouraging me to speak. "Does he want me to throw a bottle at his head, or what?" I thought in a rage. Unaccustomed as I was to all this, I was unnaturally quick to take offense.

"In such and such an office," I replied abruptly, looking at my plate.

"And . . . is it p-p-profitable? Tell-l-l me, what ma-a-de you decide to leave your previous position?"

"What ma-a-a-de me leave my previous position was simply that I wanted to," I dragged my words out three times longer than he did, hardly able to control myself. Ferfichkin snorted. Simonov looked at me ironically; Trudolyubov stopped eating and began to stare at me with curiosity.

Zverkov was jarred, but didn't want to show it.

"Well-l, and how is the support?"

"What support?"

"I mean, the s-salary?"

"Why are you cross-examining me?"

However, I told him right away what my salary was. I blushed terribly.

"That's not very much," Zverkov observed pompously.

"No, sir, it's not enough to dine in café-restaurants!" added Ferfichkin insolently.

"In my opinion, it's really very little," Trudolyubov observed in earnest.

"And how thin you've grown, how you've changed . . . since . . . ," Zverkov added, with a touch of venom now, and with a kind of impudent sympathy, examining me and my apparel.

"Stop embarrassing him," Ferfichkin cried with a giggle.

"My dear sir, I'll have you know that I'm not embarrassed," I broke in at last. "Listen! I'm dining in this 'café-restaurant' at my own expense, my own, not anyone else's; note that, Monsieur Ferfichkin."

"Wha-at? And who isn't dining at his own expense? You seem to be . . ." Ferfichkin seized hold of my words, turned as red as a lobster, and looked me straight in the eye with fury.

"Just so-o," I replied, feeling that I'd gone a bit too far, "and I suggest that it would be much better if we engaged in more intelligent conversation."

"It seems that you're determined to display your intelligence."

"Don't worry, that would be quite unnecessary here."

"What's all this cackling, my dear sir? Huh? Have you taken leave of your senses in that *duh*-partment of yours?"

"Enough, gentlemen, enough," cried Zverkov authoritatively.

"How stupid this is!" muttered Simonov.

"Really, it is stupid. We're gathered here in a congenial group to have a farewell dinner for our good friend, while you're still settling old scores," Trudolyubov said, rudely addressing only me. "You forced yourself upon us yesterday; don't disturb the general harmony now. . . ."

"Enough, enough," cried Zverkov. "Stop it, gentlemen, this'll never do. Let me tell you instead how I very nearly got married a few days ago . . ."

There followed some scandalous, libelous anecdote about how this gentleman very nearly got married a few days ago. There wasn't one word about marriage, however; instead, generals, colonels, and even gentlemen of the bed chamber figured prominently in the story, while Zverkov played the leading role among them all. Approving laughter followed; Ferfichkin even squealed.

Everyone had abandoned me by now, and I sat there completely crushed and humiliated.

"Good Lord, what kind of company is this for me?" I wondered. "And what a fool I've made of myself in front of them all! But I let Ferfichkin go too far. These numbskulls think they're doing me an honor by allowing me to sit with them at their table, when they don't understand that it's I who's done them the honor, and not the reverse. 'How thin I've grown! What clothes!' Oh, these damned trousers! Zverkov's already noticed the yellow spot on my knee. . . . What's the use? Right now, this very moment, I should stand up, take my hat, and simply leave without saying a single word. . . . Out of contempt! And tomorrow—I'll even be ready for a duel. Scoundrels! It's not the seven rubles I care about. But they may think that . . . To hell with it! I don't care about the seven rubles. I'm leaving at once! . . ."

Of course, I stayed.

In my misery I drank Lafite and sherry by the glassful. Being unaccustomed to it, I got drunk very quickly; the more intoxicated I became, the greater my annoyance. Suddenly I felt like offending them all in the most impudent manner—and then I'd leave. To seize the moment and show them all who I really was—let them say: even though he's ridiculous, he's clever . . . and . . . and . . . in short, to hell with them!

I surveyed them all arrogantly with my dazed eyes. But they seemed to have forgotten all about me. *They* were noisy, boisterous and merry. Zverkov kept on talking. I began to listen. He was talking about some magnificent lady whom he'd finally driven to make a declaration of love. (Of course, he was lying like a trooper.) He said that he'd been assisted in this matter particularly by a certain princeling, the hussar Kolya, who possessed some three thousand serfs.

"And yet, this same Kolya who has three thousand serfs hasn't even come to see you off," I said, breaking into the conversation suddenly. For a moment silence fell.

"You're drunk already," Trudolyubov said, finally deigning to notice me, and glancing contemptuously in my direction. Zverkov examined me in silence as if I were an insect. I lowered my eyes. Simonov quickly began to pour champagne.

Trudolyubov raised his glass, followed by everyone but me.

"To your health and to a good journey!" he cried to Zverkov. "To old times, gentlemen, and to our future, hurrah!"

Everyone drank up and pressed around to exchange kisses with Zverkov. I didn't budge; my full glass stood before me untouched.

"Aren't you going to drink?" Trudolyubov roared at me, having lost his patience and turning to me menacingly.

"I wish to make my own speech, all by myself . . . and then I'll drink, Mr. Trudolyubov."

"Nasty shrew!" Simonov muttered.

I sat up in my chair, feverishly seized hold of my glass, and prepared for something extraordinary, although I didn't know quite what I'd say.

"*Silence!*" cried Ferfichkin. "And now for some real intelligence!" Zverkov waited very gravely, aware of what was coming.

"Mr. Lieutenant Zverkov," I began, "you must know that I detest phrases, phrasemongers, and corsetted waists. . . . That's the first point; the second will follow."

Everyone stirred uncomfortably.

"The second point: I hate obscene stories and the men who tell them.[6] I especially hate the men who tell them!"

"The third point: I love truth, sincerity and honesty," I continued almost automatically, because I was beginning to become numb with horror, not knowing how I could be speaking this way. . . . "I love thought, Monsieur Zverkov. I love genuine comradery, on an equal footing, but not . . . hmmm . . . I love . . . But, after all, why not? I too will drink to your health, Monsieur Zverkov. Seduce those Circassian[7] maidens, shoot the enemies of the father-

---

6. A phrase borrowed from the inveterate liar Nozdryov, one of the provincial landowners in the first volume of Gogol's *Dead Souls* (1842).   7. A Muslim people inhabiting a region in the northern Caucasus.

land, and . . . and . . . To your health, Monsieur Zverkov!"

Zverkov rose from his chair, bowed, and said: "I'm most grateful."

He was terribly offended and had even turned pale.

"To hell with him," Trudolyubov roared, banging his fist down on the table.

"No, sir, people should be whacked in the face for saying such things!" squealed Ferfichkin.

"We ought to throw him out!" muttered Simonov.

"Not a word, gentlemen, not a move!" Zverkov cried triumphantly, putting a stop to this universal indignation. "I'm grateful to you all, but I can show him myself how much I value his words."

"Mr. Ferfichkin, tomorrow you'll give me satisfaction for the words you've just uttered!" I said loudly, turning to Ferfichkin with dignity.

"Do you mean a duel? Very well," he replied, but I must have looked so ridiculous as I issued my challenge, it must have seemed so out of keeping with my entire appearance, that everyone, including Ferfichkin, collapsed into laughter.

"Yes, of course, throw him out! Why, he's quite drunk already," Trudolyubov declared in disgust.

"I shall never forgive myself for letting him join us," Simonov muttered again.

"Now's the time to throw a bottle at the lot of them," I thought. So I grabbed a bottle and . . . poured myself another full glass.

". . . No, it's better to sit it out to the very end!" I went on thinking. "You'd be glad, gentlemen, if I left. But nothing doing! I'll stay here deliberately and keep on drinking to the very end, as a sign that I accord you no importance whatsoever. I'll sit here and drink because this is a tavern, and I've paid good money to get in. I'll sit here and drink because I consider you to be so many pawns, nonexistent pawns. I'll sit here and drink . . . and sing too, if I want to, yes, sir, I'll sing because I have the right to . . . sing . . . hmm."

But I didn't sing. I just tried not to look at any of them; I assumed the most carefree poses and waited impatiently until they would be the first to speak to me. But, alas, they did not. How much, how very much I longed to be reconciled with them at that moment! The clock struck eight, then nine. They moved from the table to the sofa. Zverkov sprawled on the couch, placing one foot on the round table. They brought the wine over, too. He really had ordered three bottles at his own expense. Naturally, he didn't invite me to join them. Everyone surrounded him on the sofa. They listened to him almost with reverence. It was obvious they liked him. "What for? What for?" I wondered to myself. From time to time they were moved to drunken ecstasy and exchanged kisses. They talked about the Caucasus, the nature of true passion, card games, profitable positions in the service; they talked about the income of a certain hussar Podkharzhevsky, whom none of them knew personally, and they rejoiced that his income was so large; they talked about the unusual beauty and charm of Princess D., whom none of them had ever seen; finally, they arrived at the question of Shakespeare's immortality.

I smiled contemptuously and paced up and down the other side of the room, directly behind the sofa, along the wall from the table to the stove and back again. I wanted to show them with all my might that I could get along without them; meanwhile, I deliberately stomped my boots, thumping my heels. But all this was in vain. *They* paid me no attention. I had the forbearance to pace like that, right in front of them, from eight o'clock until eleven, in the very same place, from the table to the stove and from the stove back to the table. "I'm pacing just as I please, and no one can stop me." A waiter who came into the room paused several times to look at me; my head was spinning from all those turns; there were moments when it seemed that I was delirious. During those three hours I broke out in a sweat three times and then dried out. At times I was pierced to the heart with a most profound, venomous thought: ten years would pass, twenty, forty; and still, even after forty years, I'd remember with loathing and humiliation these filthiest, most absurd, and horrendous moments of my entire life. It was impossible to humiliate myself more shamelessly or more willingly, and I fully understood that, fully; nevertheless, I continued to pace from the table to the stove and back again. "Oh, if you only knew what thoughts and feelings I'm capable of, and how cultured I really am!" I thought at moments, mentally addressing the sofa where my enemies were seated. But my enemies behaved as if I weren't even in the room. Once, and only once, they turned to me, precisely when Zverkov started in about Shakespeare, and I suddenly burst into contemptuous laughter. I snorted so affectedly and repulsively that they broke off their conversation immediately and stared at me in silence for about two minutes, in earnest, without laughing, as I paced up and down, from the table to the stove, while *I paid not the slightest bit of attention to them.* But nothing came of it; they didn't speak to me. A few moments later they abandoned me again. The clock struck eleven.

"Gentlemen," exclaimed Zverkov, getting up from the sofa, "Now let's all go *to that place.*"[8]

"Of course, of course!" the others replied.

I turned abruptly to Zverkov. I was so exhausted, so broken, that I'd have slit my own throat to be done with all this! I was feverish; my hair, which had been soaked through with sweat, had dried and now stuck to my forehead and temples.

"Zverkov, I ask your forgiveness," I said harshly and decisively. "Ferfichkin, yours too, and everyone's, everyone's. I've insulted you all!" "Aha! So a duel isn't really your sort of thing!" hissed Ferfichkin venomously.

His remark was like a painful stab to my heart.

"No, I'm not afraid of a duel, Ferfichkin! I'm ready to fight with you tomorrow, even after we're reconciled. I even insist upon it, and you can't refuse me. I want to prove that I'm not afraid of a duel. You'll shoot first, and I'll fire into the air."

"He's amusing himself," Simonov observed.

"He's simply taken leave of his senses!" Trudolyubov added.

"Allow us to pass; why are you blocking our way? . . . Well, what is it you want?" Zverkov asked contemptuously. They were all flushed, their eyes glazed. They'd drunk a great deal.

"I ask for your friendship, Zverkov, I've insulted you, but . . . ."

"Insulted me? You? In-sul-ted me? My dear sir, I want you to know that never, under any circumstances, could you possibly insult *me!*"

"And that's enough from you. Out of the way!" Trudolyubov added. "Let's go."

8. I.e., a brothel.

"Olympia is mine, gentlemen, that's agreed!" cried Zverkov.

"We won't argue, we won't," they replied, laughing.

I stood there as if spat on. The party left the room noisily, and Trudolyubov struck up a stupid song. Simonov remained behind for a brief moment to tip the waiters. All of a sudden I went up to him.

"Simonov! Give me six rubles," I said decisively and desperately.

He looked at me in extreme amazement with his dulled eyes. He was drunk, too.

"Are you really going *to that place* with us?"

"Yes!"

"I have no money!" he snapped; then he laughed contemptuously and headed out of the room.

I grabbed hold of his overcoat. It was a nightmare.

"Simonov! I know that you have some money. Why do you refuse me? Am I really such a scoundrel? Beware of refusing me: if you only knew, if you only knew why I'm asking. Everything depends on it, my entire future, all my plans. . . ."

Simonov took out the money and almost threw it at me.

"Take it, if you have no shame!" he said mercilessly, then ran out to catch up with the others.

I remained behind for a minute. The disorder, the leftovers, a broken glass on the floor, spilled wine, cigarette butts, drunkenness and delirium in my head, agonizing torment in my heart; and finally, a waiter who'd seen and heard everything and who was now looking at me with curiosity.

"*To that place!*" I cried. "Either they'll all fall on their knees, embracing me, begging for my friendship, or . . . or else, I'll give Zverkov a slap in the face."

V

"So here it is, here it is at last, a confrontation with reality," I muttered, rushing headlong down the stairs. "This is no longer the Pope leaving Rome and going to Brazil; this is no ball on the shores of Lake Como!"

"You're a scoundrel," the thought flashed through my mind, "if you laugh at that now."

"So what!" I cried in reply. "Everything is lost now, anyway!"

There was no sign of them, but it didn't matter. I knew where they were going.

At the entrance stood a solitary, late-night cabby in a coarse peasant coat powdered with wet, seemingly warm snow that was still falling. It was steamy and stuffy outside. The little shaggy piebald nag was also dusted with snow and was coughing; I remember that very well. I headed for the rough-hewn sledge; but as soon as I raised one foot to get in, the recollection of how Simonov had just given me six rubles hit me with such force that I tumbled into the sledge like a sack.

"No! There's a lot I have to do to make up for that!" I cried. "But make up for it I will or else I'll perish on the spot this very night. Let's go!" We set off. There was an entire whirlwind spinning around inside my head.

"They won't fall on their knees to beg for my friendship. That's a mirage, an indecent mirage, disgusting, romantic, and fantastic; it's just like the ball on the shores of Lake Como. Consequently, I *must* give Zverkov a slap in the face! I am obligated to do it. And so, it's all decided; I'm rushing there to give him a slap in the face."

"Hurry up!"

The cabby tugged at the reins.

"As soon as I go in, I'll slap him. Should I say a few words first before I slap him in the face? No! I'll simply go in and slap him. They'll all be sitting there in the drawing room; he'll be on the sofa with Olympia. That damned Olympia! She once ridiculed my face and refused me. I'll drag Olympia around by the hair and Zverkov by the ears. No, better grab one ear and lead him around the room like that. Perhaps they'll begin to beat me, and then they'll throw me out. That's even likely. So what? I'll still have slapped him first; the initiative will be mine. According to the laws of honor, that's all that matters. He'll be branded, and nothing can wipe away that slap except a duel.[9] He'll have to fight. So just let them beat me now! Let them, the ingrates! Trudolyubov will hit me hardest, he's so strong. Ferfichkin will sneak up alongside and will undoubtedly grab my hair, I'm sure he will. But let them, let them. That's why I've come. At last these blockheads will be forced to grasp the tragedy in all this! As they drag me to the door, I'll tell them that they really aren't even worth the tip of my little finger!"

"Hurry up, driver, hurry up!" I shouted to the cabby.

He was rather startled and cracked his whip. I'd shouted very savagely.

"We'll fight at daybreak, and that's settled. I'm through with the department. Ferfichkin recently said duh-partment, instead of department. But where will I get pistols? What nonsense! I'll take my salary in advance and buy them. And powder? Bullets? That's what the second will attend to. And how will I manage to do all this by daybreak? And where will I find a second? I have no acquaintances. . . ."

"Nonsense!" I shouted, whipping myself up into even more of a frenzy, "Nonsense!"

"The first person I meet on the street will have to act as my second, just as he would pull a drowning man from the water. The most extraordinary possibilities have to be allowed for. Even if tomorrow I were to ask the director himself to act as my second, he too would have to agree merely out of a sense of chivalry, and he would keep it a secret! Anton Antonych . . ."

The fact of the matter was that at that very moment I was more clearly and vividly aware than anyone else on earth of the disgusting absurdity of my intentions and the whole opposite side of the coin, but . . .

"Hurry up, driver, hurry, you rascal, hurry up!"

"Hey, sir!" that son of the earth replied.

A sudden chill came over me.

"Wouldn't it be better . . . wouldn't it be better . . . to go straight home right now? Oh, my God! Why, why did I invite myself to that dinner yesterday? But no, it's impossible. And my pacing for three hours from the table to the stove? No, they, and no one else will have to pay me back for that pacing! They must wipe out that disgrace!"

"Hurry up!"

"What if they turn me over to the police? They wouldn't dare! They'd be afraid of a scandal. And what if Zverkov refuses the duel out of contempt?

---

9. Duels as a means of resolving points of honor were officially discouraged but still fairly common.

That's even likely; but I'll show them. . . . I'll rush to the posting station when he's supposed to leave tomorrow; I'll grab hold of his leg, tear off his overcoat just as he's about to climb into the carriage. I'll fasten my teeth on his arm and bite him. 'Look, everyone, see what a desperate man can be driven to!' Let him hit me on the head while others hit me from behind. I'll shout to the whole crowd, 'Behold, here's a young puppy who's going off to charm Circassian maidens with my spit on his face!' "

"Naturally, it'll all be over after that. The department will banish me from the face of the earth. They'll arrest me, try me, drive me out of the service, send me to prison; ship me off to Siberia for resettlement. Never mind! Fifteen years later when they let me out of jail, a beggar in rags, I'll drag myself off to see him. I'll find him in some provincial town. He'll be married and happy. He'll have a grown daughter. . . . I'll say, 'Look, you monster, look at my sunken cheeks and my rags. I've lost everything—career, happiness, art, science, a *beloved woman*—all because of you. Here are the pistols. I came here to load my pistol, and . . . and I forgive you.' Then I'll fire into the air, and he'll never hear another word from me again. . . ."

I was actually about to cry, even though I knew for a fact at that very moment that all this was straight out of Silvio and Lermontov's *Masquerade*.[1] Suddenly I felt terribly ashamed, so ashamed that I stopped the horse, climbed out of the sledge, and stood there amidst the snow in the middle of the street. The driver looked at me in amazement and sighed.

What was I to do? I couldn't go there—that was absurd; and I couldn't drop the whole thing, because then it would seem like . . . Oh, Lord! How could I drop it? After such insults!

"No!" I cried, throwing myself back into the sledge. "It's predestined; it's fate! Drive on, hurry up, *to that place!*"

In my impatience, I struck the driver on the neck with my fist.

"What's the matter with you? Why are you hitting me?" cried the poor little peasant, whipping his nag so that she began to kick up her hind legs.

Wet snow was falling in big flakes; I unbuttoned my coat, not caring about the snow. I forgot about everything else because now, having finally resolved on the slap, *I felt with horror that it was imminent* and that *nothing on earth could possibly stop it*. Lonely street lamps shone gloomily in the snowy mist like torches at a funeral. Snow got in under my overcoat, my jacket, and my necktie, and melted there. I didn't button up; after all, everything was lost, anyway. At last we arrived. I jumped out, almost beside myself, ran up the stairs, and began to pound at the door with my hands and feet. My legs, especially my knees, felt terribly weak. The door opened rather quickly; it was as if they knew I was coming. (In fact, Simonov had warned them that there might be someone else, since at this place one had to give notice and in general take precautions. It was one of those "fashionable shops" of the period that have now been eliminated by the police. During the day it really was a shop; but in the evening men with recommendations were able to visit as guests.) I walked rapidly through the darkened shop into a familiar drawing-room where there was only one small lit candle, and I stopped in dismay: there was no one there.

"Where are they?" I asked.

1. A drama by Mikhail Lermontov (1835) about romantic conventions of love and honor. Silvio is the protagonist of Alexander Pushkin's short story *The Shot* (1830), about a man dedicated to revenge. Both works conclude with bizarre twists.

Naturally, by now they'd all dispersed. . . .

Before me stood a person with a stupid smile, the madam herself, who knew me slightly. In a moment a door opened, and another person came in.

Without paying much attention to anything, I walked around the room, and, apparently, was talking to myself. It was as if I'd been delivered from death, and I felt it joyously in my whole being. I'd have given him the slap, certainly, I'd certainly have given him the slap. But now they weren't here and . . . everything had vanished, everything had changed! . . . I looked around. I still couldn't take it all in. I glanced up mechanically at the girl who'd come in: before me there flashed a fresh, young, slightly pale face with straight dark brows and a serious, seemingly astonished look. I liked that immediately; I would have hated her if she'd been smiling. I began to look at her more carefully, as though with some effort: I'd still not managed to collect my thoughts. There was something simple and kind in her face, but somehow it was strangely serious. I was sure that she was at a disadvantage as a result, and that none of those fools had even noticed her. She couldn't be called a beauty, however, even though she was tall, strong, and well built. She was dressed very simply. Something despicable took hold of me; I went up to her. . . .

I happened to glance into a mirror. My overwrought face appeared extremely repulsive: it was pale, spiteful and mean; and my hair was dishevelled. "It doesn't matter. I'm glad," I thought. "In fact, I'm even delighted that I'll seem so repulsive to her; that pleases me. . . ."

VI

Somewhere behind a partition a clock was wheezing as if under some strong pressure, as though someone were strangling it. After this unnaturally prolonged wheezing there followed a thin, nasty, somehow unexpectedly hurried chime, as if someone had suddenly leapt forward. It struck two. I recovered, although I really hadn't been asleep, only lying there half-conscious.

It was almost totally dark in the narrow, cramped, low-ceilinged room, which was crammed with an enormous wardrobe and cluttered with cartons, rags, and all sorts of old clothes. The candle burning on the table at one end of the room flickered faintly from time to time, and almost went out completely. In a few moments total darkness would set in.

It didn't take long for me to come to my senses; all at once, without any effort, everything returned to me, as though it had been lying in ambush ready to pounce on me again. Even in my unconscious state some point had constantly remained in my memory, never to be forgotten, around which my sleepy visions had gloomily revolved. But it was a strange thing: everything that had happened to me that day now seemed, upon awakening, to have occurred in the distant past, as if I'd long since left it all behind.

My mind was in a daze. It was as though something were hanging over me, provoking, agitating, and disturbing me. Misery and bile were welling inside me, seeking an outlet. Suddenly I noticed beside me two wide-open eyes, examining me curiously and persistently. The gaze was coldly detached, sullen, as if belonging to a total stranger. I found it oppressive.

A dismal thought was conceived in my brain and spread throughout my whole body like a nasty sensation, such as one feels upon entering a damp, mouldy underground cellar. It was somehow unnatural that only now these two eyes had decided to examine me. I also recalled that during the course of the last two hours I hadn't said one word to this creature, and that I had considered it quite unnecessary; that had even given me pleasure for some reason. Now I'd suddenly realized starkly how absurd, how revolting as a spider, was the idea of debauchery, which, without love, crudely and shamelessly begins precisely at the point where genuine love is consummated. We looked at each other in this way for some time, but she didn't lower her gaze before mine, nor did she alter her stare, so that finally, for some reason, I felt very uneasy.

"What's your name?" I asked abruptly, to put an end to it quickly.

"Liza," she replied, almost in a whisper, but somehow in a very unfriendly way; and she turned her eyes away.

I remained silent.

"The weather today . . . snow . . . foul!" I observed, almost to myself, drearily placing one arm behind my head and staring at the ceiling.

She didn't answer. The whole thing was obscene.

"Are you from around here?" I asked her a moment later, almost angrily, turning my head slightly toward her.

"No."

"Where are you from?"

"Riga," she answered unwillingly.

"German?"

"No, Russian."

"Have you been here long?"

"Where?"

"In this house."

"Two weeks." She spoke more and more curtly. The candle had gone out completely; I could no longer see her face.

"Are your mother and father still living?"

"Yes . . . no . . . they are."

"Where are they?"

"There . . . in Riga."

"Who are they?"

"Just . . ."

"Just what? What do they do?"

"Tradespeople."

"Have you always lived with them?"

"Yes."

"How old are you?"

"Twenty."

"Why did you leave them?"

"Just because . . ."

That "just because" meant: leave me alone, it makes me sick. We fell silent.

Only God knows why, but I didn't leave. I too started to feel sick and more depressed. Images of the previous day began to come to mind all on their own, without my willing it, in a disordered way. I suddenly recalled a scene that I'd witnessed on the street that morning as I was anxiously hurrying to work. "Today some people were carrying a coffin and nearly dropped it," I suddenly said aloud, having no desire whatever to begin a conversation, but just so, almost accidentally.

"A coffin?"

"Yes, in the Haymarket; they were carrying it up from an underground cellar."

"From a cellar?"

"Not a cellar, but from a basement . . . well, you know . . . from downstairs . . . from a house of ill repute . . . There was such filth all around. . . . Eggshells, garbage . . . it smelled foul . . . it was disgusting."

Silence.

"A nasty day to be buried!" I began again to break the silence.

"Why nasty?"

"Snow, slush . . ." (I yawned.)

"It doesn't matter," she said suddenly after a brief silence.

"No, it's foul. . . ." (I yawned again.) "The grave diggers must have been cursing because they were getting wet out there in the snow. And there must have been water in the grave."

"Why water in the grave?" she asked with some curiosity, but she spoke even more rudely and curtly than before. Something suddenly began to goad me on.

"Naturally, water on the bottom, six inches or so. You can't ever dig a dry grave at Volkovo cemetery."

"Why not?"

"What do you mean, why not? The place is waterlogged. It's all swamp. So they bury them right in the water. I've seen it myself . . . many times. . . ."

(I'd never seen it, and I'd never been to Volkovo cemetery, but I'd heard about it from other people.)

"Doesn't it matter to you if you die?"

"Why should I die?" she replied, as though defending herself.

"Well, someday you'll die; you'll die just like that woman did this morning. She was a . . . she was also a young girl . . . she died of consumption."

"The wench should have died in the hospital. . . ." (She knows all about it, I thought, and she even said "wench" instead of "girl.")

"She owed money to her madam," I retorted, more and more goaded on by the argument. "She worked right up to the end, even though she had consumption. The cabbies standing around were chatting with the soldiers, telling them all about it. Her former acquaintances, most likely. They were all laughing. They were planning to drink to her memory at the tavern." (I invented a great deal of this.)

Silence, deep silence. She didn't even stir.

"Do you think it would be better to die in a hospital?"

"Isn't it just the same? . . . Besides, why should I die?" she added irritably.

"If not now, then later?"

"Well, then later . . ."

"That's what you think! Now you're young and pretty and fresh—that's your value. But after a year of this life, you won't be like that any more; you'll fade."

"In a year?"

"In any case, after a year your price will be lower," I continued, gloating. "You'll move out of here into a worse place, into some other house. And a year later, into a third, each worse and worse, and seven years from now you'll end up in a cellar on the Haymarket. Even that won't be so bad. The real trouble will come when you get some disease, let's say a weakness in the chest . . . or you catch cold or something. In this kind of life it's no laughing matter to get sick. It takes hold of you and may never let go. And so, you die."

"Well, then, I'll die," she answered now quite angrily and stirred quickly.

"That'll be a pity."

"For what?"

"A pity to lose a life."

Silence.

"Did you have a sweetheart? Huh?"

"What's it to you?"

"Oh, I'm not interrogating you. What do I care? Why are you angry? Of course, you may have had your own troubles. What's it to me? Just the same, I'm sorry."

"For whom?"

"I'm sorry for you."

"No need . . . ," she whispered barely audibly and stirred once again.

That provoked me at once. What! I was being so gentle with her, while she . . .

"Well, and what do you think? Are you on the right path then?"

"I don't think anything."

"That's just the trouble—you don't think. Wake up, while there's still time. And there is time. You're still young and pretty; you could fall in love, get married, be happy.[2] . . ."

"Not all married women are happy," she snapped in her former, rude manner.

"Not all, of course, but it's still better than this. A lot better. You can even live without happiness as long as there's love. Even in sorrow life can be good; it's good to be alive, no matter how you live. But what's there besides . . . stench? Phew!"

I turned away in disgust; I was no longer coldly philosophizing. I began to feel what I was saying and grew excited. I'd been longing to expound these cherished *little ideas* that I'd been nurturing in my corner. Something had suddenly caught fire in me, some kind of goal had "manifested itself" before me.

"Pay no attention to the fact that I'm here. I'm no model for you. I may be even worse than you are. Moreover, I was drunk when I came here." I hastened nonetheless to justify myself. "Besides, a man is no example to a woman. It's a different thing altogether; even though I degrade and defile myself, I'm still no one's slave; if I want to leave, I just get up and go. I shake it all off and I'm a different man. But you must realize right from the start that you're a slave. Yes, a slave! You give away everything, all your freedom. Later, if you want to break this chain, you won't be able to; it'll bind you ever more tightly. That's the kind of evil chain it is. I know. I won't say anything else; you might not even understand me. But tell me this, aren't you already in debt to your madam? There, you see!" I added, even though she hadn't answered, but had merely remained silent; but she was listening with all her might. "There's your chain! You'll never buy yourself out. That's the way it's done. It's just like selling your soul to the devil. . . .

"And besides . . . I may be just as unfortunate, how do you know, and I

2. A popular theme treated by Gogol, Chernyshevsky, and Nekrasov, among others. Typically, an innocent and idealistic young man attempts to rehabilitate a prostitute or "fallen" woman.

may be wallowing in mud on purpose, also out of misery. After all, people drink out of misery. Well, I came here out of misery. Now, tell me, what's so good about this place? Here you and I were . . . intimate . . . just a little while ago, and all that time we didn't say one word to each other; afterward you began to examine me like a wild creature, and I did the same. Is that the way people love? Is that how one person is supposed to encounter another? It's a disgrace, that's what it is!"

"Yes!" she agreed with me sharply and hastily. The haste of her answer surprised even me. It meant that perhaps the very same idea was flitting through her head while she'd been examining me earlier. It meant that she too was capable of some thought. . . . "Devil take it; this is odd, this *kinship*," I thought, almost rubbing my hands together. "Surely I can handle such a young soul."

It was the sport that attracted me most of all.

She turned her face closer to mine, and in the darkness it seemed that she propped her head up on her arm. Perhaps she was examining me. I felt sorry that I couldn't see her eyes. I heard her breathing deeply.

"Why did you come here?" I began with some authority.

"Just so . . ."

"But think how nice it would be living in your father's house! There you'd be warm and free; you'd have a nest of your own."

"And what if it's worse than that?"

"I must establish the right tone," flashed through my mind. "I won't get far with sentimentality."

However, that merely flashed through my mind. I swear that she really did interest me. Besides, I was somewhat exhausted and provoked. After all, artifice goes along so easily with feeling.

"Who can say?" I hastened to reply. "All sorts of things can happen. Why, I was sure that someone had wronged you and was more to blame than you are. After all, I know nothing of your life story, but a girl like you doesn't wind up in this sort of place on her own accord. . . ."

"What kind of a girl am I?" she whispered hardly audibly; but I heard it.

"What the hell! Now I'm flattering her. That's disgusting! But, perhaps it's a good thing. . . ." She remained silent.

"You see, Liza, I'll tell you about myself. If I'd had a family when I was growing up, I wouldn't be the person I am now. I think about this often. After all, no matter how bad it is in your own family—it's still your own father and mother, and not enemies or strangers. Even if they show you their love only once a year, you still know that you're at home. I grew up without a family; that must be why I turned out the way I did—so unfeeling."

I waited again.

"She might not understand," I thought. "Besides, it's absurd—all this moralizing."

"If I were a father and had a daughter, I think that I'd have loved her more than my sons, really," I began indirectly, talking about something else in order to distract her. I confess that I was blushing.

"Why's that?"

Ah, so she's listening!

"Just because. I don't know why, Liza. You see, I knew a father who was a stern, strict man, but he would kneel before his daughter and kiss her hands and feet; he couldn't get enough of her, really. She'd go dancing at a party, and he'd stand in one spot for five hours, never taking his eyes off her. He was crazy about her; I can understand that. At night she'd be tired and fall asleep, but he'd wake up, go in to kiss her, and make the sign of the cross over her while she slept. He used to wear a dirty old jacket and was stingy with everyone else, but would spend his last kopeck on her, buying her expensive presents; it afforded him great joy if she liked his presents. A father always loves his daughters more than their mother does. Some girls have a very nice time living at home. I think that I wouldn't even have let my daughter get married."

"Why not?" she asked with a barely perceptible smile.

"I'd be jealous, so help me God. Why, how could she kiss someone else? How could she love a stranger more than her own father? It's even painful to think about it. Of course, it's all nonsense; naturally, everyone finally comes to his senses. But I think that before I'd let her marry, I'd have tortured myself with worry. I'd have found fault with all her suitors. Nevertheless, I'd have ended up by allowing her to marry whomever she loved. After all, the one she loves always seems the worst of all to the father. That's how it is. That causes a lot of trouble in many families."

"Some are glad to sell their daughters, rather than let them marry honorably," she said suddenly.

Aha, so that's it!

"That happens, Liza, in those wretched families where there's neither God nor love," I retorted heatedly. "And where there's no love, there's also no good sense. There are such families, it's true, but I'm not talking about them. Obviously, from the way you talk, you didn't see much kindness in your own family. You must be very unfortunate. Hmm . . . But all this results primarily from poverty."

"And is it any better among the gentry? Honest folk live decently even in poverty."

"Hmmm . . . Yes. Perhaps. There's something else, Liza. Man only likes to count his troubles; he doesn't calculate his happiness. If he figured as he should, he'd see that everyone gets his share. So, let's say that all goes well in a particular family; it enjoys God's blessing, the husband turns out to be a good man, he loves you, cherishes you, and never leaves you. Life is good in that family. Sometimes, even though there's a measure of sorrow, life's still good. Where isn't there sorrow? If you choose to get married, *you'll find out for yourself*. Consider even the first years of a marriage to the one you love: what happiness, what pure bliss there can be sometimes! Almost without exception. At first even quarrels with your husband turn out well. For some women, the more they love their husbands, the more they pick fights with them. It's true; I once knew a woman like that. 'That's how it is,' she'd say. 'I love you very much and I'm tormenting you out of love, so that you'll feel it.' Did you know that one can torment a person intentionally out of love? It's mostly women who do that. Then she thinks to herself, 'I'll love him so much afterward, I'll be so affectionate, it's no sin to torment him a little now.' At home everyone would rejoice over you, and it would be so pleasant, cheerful, serene, and honorable. . . . Some other women are very jealous. If her husband goes away, I knew one like that, she can't stand it; she jumps up at night and goes off on the sly to see. Is he there? Is he in that house? Is he with that one? Now that's bad. Even she herself knows that it's bad; her heart sinks and she suffers because she really loves him. It's all out of love. And how nice it is to make up after a quarrel, to admit one's guilt or forgive him! How nice it is for both of them, how good they both feel at once, just as if they'd met again, married again, and begun their love all over again. No one, no one at all has to know what goes on between a husband and wife, if they love each other. However their quarrel ends, they should never call in either one of their mothers to act as judge or to hear complaints about the other one. They must act as their own judges. Love is God's mystery and should be hidden from other people's eyes, no matter what happens. This makes it holier, much better. They respect each other more, and a great deal is based on this respect. And, if there's been love, if they got married out of love, why should love disappear? Can't it be sustained? It rarely happens that it can't be sustained. If the husband turns out to be a kind and honest man, how can the love disappear? The first phase of married love will pass, that's true, but it's followed by an even better kind of love. Souls are joined together and all their concerns are managed in common; there'll be no secrets from one another. When children arrive, each and every stage, even a very difficult one, will seem happy, as long as there's both love and courage. Even work is cheerful; even when you deny yourself bread for your children's sake, you're still happy. After all, they'll love you for it afterward; you're really saving for your own future. Your children will grow up, and you'll feel that you're a model for them, a support. Even after you die, they'll carry your thoughts and feelings all during their life. They'll take on your image and likeness, since they received it from you. Consequently, it's a great obligation. How can a mother and father keep from growing closer? They say it's difficult to raise children. Who says that? It's heavenly joy! Do you love little children, Liza? I love them dearly. You know—a rosy little boy, suckling at your breast; what husband's heart could turn against his wife seeing her sitting there holding his child? The chubby, rosy little baby sprawls and snuggles; his little hands and feet are plump; his little nails are clean and tiny, so tiny it's even funny to see them; his little eyes look as if he already understood everything. As he suckles, he tugs at your breast playfully with his little hand. When the father approaches, the child lets go of the breast, bends way back, looks at his father, and laughs—as if God only knows how funny it is—and then takes to suckling again. Afterward, when he starts cutting teeth, he'll sometimes bite his mother's breast; looking at her sideways his little eyes seem to say, 'See, I bit you!' Isn't this pure bliss—the three of them, husband, wife, and child, all together? You can forgive a great deal for such moments. No, Liza, I think you must first learn how to live by yourself, and only afterward blame others."

"It's by means of images," I thought to myself, "just such images that I can get to you," although I was speaking with considerable feeling, I swear it; and all at once I blushed. "And what if she suddenly bursts out laughing— where will I hide then?" That thought drove me into a rage. By the end of my speech I'd really become excited, and now my pride was suffering some-how. The silence lasted for a while. I even considered shaking her.

"Somehow you . . ." she began suddenly and then stopped.

But I understood everything already: something was trembling in her voice now, not shrill, rude or unyielding as before, but something soft and timid, so timid that I suddenly was rather ashamed to watch her and felt guilty.

"What?" I asked with tender curiosity.

"Well, you . . ."

"What?"

"You somehow . . . it sounds just like a book," she said, and once again something which was noticeably sarcastic was suddenly heard in her voice.

Her remark wounded me dreadfully. That's not what I'd expected.

Yet, I didn't understand that she was intentionally disguising her feelings with sarcasm; that was usually the last resort of people who are timid and chaste of heart, whose souls have been coarsely and impudently invaded; and who, until the last moment, refuse to yield out of pride and are afraid to express their own feelings to you. I should've guessed it from the timidity with which on several occasions she tried to be sarcastic, until she finally managed to express it. But I hadn't guessed, and a malicious impulse took hold of me.

"Just you wait," I thought.

VII

"That's enough, Liza. What do books have to do with it, when this disgusts me as an outsider? And not only as an outsider. All this has awakened in my heart . . . Can it be, can it really be that you don't find it repulsive here? No, clearly habit means a great deal. The devil only knows what habit can do to a person. But do you seriously think that you'll never grow old, that you'll always be pretty, and that they'll keep you on here forever and ever? I'm not even talking about the filth. . . . Besides, I want to say this about your present life: even though you're still young, good-looking, nice, with soul and feelings, do you know, that when I came to a little while ago, I was immediately disgusted to be here with you! Why, a man has to be drunk to wind up here. But if you were in a different place, living as nice people do, I might not only chase after you, I might actually fall in love with you. I'd rejoice at a look from you, let alone a word; I'd wait for you at the gate and kneel down before you; I'd think of you as my betrothed and even consider that an honor. I wouldn't dare have any impure thoughts about you. But here, I know that I need only whistle, and you, whether you want to or not, will come to me, and that I don't have to do your bidding, whereas you have to do mine. The lowliest peasant may hire himself out as a laborer, but he doesn't make a complete slave of himself; he knows that it's only for a limited term. But what's your term? Just think about it. What are you giving up here? What are you enslaving? Why, you're enslaving your soul, something you don't really own, together with your body! You're giving away your love to be defiled by any drunkard! Love! After all, that's all there is! It's a precious jewel, a maiden's treasure, that's what it is! Why, to earn that love a man might be ready to offer up his own soul, to face death. But what's your love worth now? You've been bought, all of you; and why should anyone strive for your love, when you offer everything even without it? Why, there's no greater insult for a girl, don't you understand? Now, I've heard that they console you foolish girls, they allow you to see your own lovers here. But that's merely child's play, deception, making fun of you, while you believe it. And do you really think he loves you, that lover of yours? I don't believe it. How can he, if he knows that you can be called away from him at any moment? He'd have to be depraved after all that. Does he possess even one drop of respect for you? What do you have in common with him? He's laughing at you and stealing from you at the same time—so much for his love. It's not too bad, as long as he doesn't beat you. But perhaps he does. Go on, ask him, if you have such a lover, whether he'll ever marry you. Why, he'll burst out laughing right in your face, if he doesn't spit at you or smack you. He himself may be worth no more than a few lousy kopecks. And for what, do you think, did you ruin your whole life here? For the coffee they give you to drink, or for the plentiful supply of food? Why do you think they feed you so well? Another girl, an honest one, would choke on every bite, because she'd know why she was being fed so well. You're in debt here, you'll be in debt, and will remain so until the end, until such time comes as the customers begin to spurn you. And that time will come very soon; don't count on your youth. Why, here youth flies by like a stagecoach. They'll kick you out. And they'll not merely kick you out, but for a long time before that they'll pester you, reproach you, and abuse you—as if you hadn't ruined your health for the madam, hadn't given up your youth and your soul for her in vain, but rather, as if you'd ruined her, ravaged her, and robbed her. And don't expect any support. Your friends will also attack you to curry her favor, because they're all in bondage here and have long since lost both conscience and pity. They've become despicable, and there's nothing on earth more despicable, more repulsive, or more insulting than their abuse. You'll lose everything here, everything, without exception—your health, youth, beauty, and hope—and at the age of twenty-two you'll look as if you were thirty-five, and even that won't be too awful if you're not ill. Thank God for that. Why, you probably think that you're not even working, that it's all play! But there's no harder work or more onerous task than this one in the whole world and there never has been. I'd think that one's heart alone would be worn out by crying. Yet you dare not utter one word, not one syllable; when they drive you out, you leave as if you were the guilty one. You'll move to another place, then to a third, then somewhere else, and finally you'll wind up in the Haymarket. And there they'll start beating you for no good reason at all; it's a local custom; the clients there don't know how to be nice without beating you. You don't think it's so disgusting there? Maybe you should go and have a look sometime, and see it with your own eyes. Once, at New Year's, I saw a woman in a doorway. Her own kind had pushed her outside as a joke, to freeze her for a little while because she was wailing too much; they shut the door behind her. At nine o'clock in the morning she was already dead drunk, dishevelled, half-naked, and all beaten up. Her face was powdered, but her eyes were bruised; blood was streaming from her nose and mouth; a certain cabby had just fixed her up. She was sitting on a stone step, holding a piece of salted fish in her hand; she was howling, wailing something about her 'fate,' and slapping the fish against the stone step. Cabbies and drunken soldiers had gathered around the steps and were taunting her. Don't you think you'll wind up the same way? I wouldn't want to believe it myself, but how do you know, perhaps eight or ten years ago this same girl, the one with the salted fish, arrived here from somewhere or other, all fresh like a little cherub, innocent, and pure; she knew no evil and blushed at every word. Perhaps she was just like you— proud, easily offended, unlike all the rest; she looked like a queen and knew that total happiness awaited the man who would love her and whom she would also love. Do you see how it all ended? What if at the very moment she was slapping the fish against that filthy step, dead drunk and dishevelled, what if, even at that very moment she'd recalled her earlier, chaste years in her father's house when she was still going to school, and when her neighbor's son used to wait for her along the path and assure her that he'd love her all his life and devote himself entirely to her, and when they vowed to love one another forever and get married as soon as they grew up! No, Liza, you'd be lucky, very lucky, if you died quickly from consumption somewhere in a corner, in a cellar, like that other girl. In a hospital, you say? All right—they'll take you off, but what if the madam still requires your services? Consumption is quite a disease—it's not like dying from a fever. A person continues to hope right up until the last minute and declares that he's in good health. He consoles himself. Now that's useful for your madam. Don't worry, that's the way it is. You've sold your soul; besides, you owe her money—that means you don't dare say a thing. And while you're dying, they'll all abandon you, turn away from you—because there's nothing left to get from you. They'll even reproach you for taking up space for no good reason and for taking so long to die. You won't even be able to ask for something to drink, without their hurling abuse at you: 'When will you croak, you old bitch? You keep on moaning and don't let us get any sleep—and you drive our customers away.' That's for sure; I've overheard such words myself. And as you're breathing your last, they'll shove you into the filthiest corner of the cellar—into darkness and dampness; lying there alone, what will you think about then? After you die, some stranger will lay you out hurriedly, grumbling all the while, impatiently—no one will bless you, no one will sigh over you; they'll merely want to get rid of you as quickly as possible. They'll buy you a wooden trough and carry you out as they did that poor woman I saw today; then they'll go off to a tavern and drink to your memory. There'll be slush, filth, and wet snow in your grave—why bother for the likes of you? 'Let her down, Vanyukha; after all, it's her fate to go down with her legs up, that's the sort of girl she was. Pull up on that rope, you rascal!' 'It's okay like that.' 'How's it okay? See, it's lying on its side. Was she a human being or not? Oh, never mind, cover it up.' They won't want to spend much time arguing over you. They'll cover your coffin quickly with wet, blue clay and then go off to the tavern. . . . That'll be the end of your memory on earth; for other women, children will visit their graves, fathers, husbands—but for you—no tears, no sighs; no remembrances. No one, absolutely no one in the whole world, will ever come to visit you; your name will disappear from the face of the earth, just as if you'd never been born and had never existed. Mud and filth, no matter how you pound on the lid of your coffin at night when other corpses arise: 'Let me out, kind people, let me live on earth for a little while! I lived, but I didn't really see life; my life went down the drain; they drank it away in a tavern at the Haymarket; let me out, kind people, let me live in the world once again!' "

I was so carried away by my own pathos that I began to feel a lump forming in my throat, and . . . I suddenly stopped, rose up in fright, and, leaning over apprehensively, I began to listen carefully as my own heart pounded. There was cause for dismay.

For a while I felt that I'd turned her soul inside out and had broken her heart; the more I became convinced of this, the more I strived to reach my goal as quickly and forcefully as possible. It was the sport, the sport that attracted me; but it wasn't only the sport. . . .

I knew that I was speaking clumsily, artificially, even bookishly; in short, I didn't know how to speak except "like a book." But that didn't bother me, for I knew, I had a premonition, that I would be understood and that this bookishness itself might even help things along. But now, having achieved this effect, I suddenly lost all my nerve. No, never, never before had I witnessed such despair! She was lying there, her face pressed deep into a pillow she was clutching with her hands. Her heart was bursting. Her young body was shuddering as if she were having convulsions. Suppressed sobs shook her breast, tore her apart, and suddenly burst forth in cries and moans. Then she pressed her face even deeper into the pillow: she didn't want anyone, not one living soul, to hear her anguish and her tears. She bit the pillow; she bit her hand until it bled (I noticed that afterward); or else, thrusting her fingers into her dishevelled hair, she became rigid with the strain, holding her breath and clenching her teeth. I was about to say something, to ask her to calm down; but I felt that I didn't dare. Suddenly, all in a kind of chill, almost in a panic, I groped hurriedly to get out of there as quickly as possible. It was dark: no matter how I tried, I couldn't end it quickly. Suddenly I felt a box of matches and a candlestick with a whole unused candle. As soon as the room was lit up, Liza started suddenly, sat up, and looked at me almost senselessly, with a distorted face and a half-crazy smile. I sat down next to her and took her hands; she came to and threw herself at me, wanting to embrace me, yet not daring to. Then she quietly lowered her head before me.

"Liza, my friend, I shouldn't have . . . you must forgive me," I began, but she squeezed my hands so tightly in her fingers that I realized I was saying the wrong thing and stopped.

"Here's my address, Liza. Come to see me."

"I will," she whispered resolutely, still not lifting her head.

"I'm going now, good-bye . . . until we meet again."

I stood up; she did, too, and suddenly blushed all over, shuddered, seized a shawl lying on a chair, threw it over her shoulders, and wrapped herself up to her chin. After doing this, she smiled again somewhat painfully, blushed, and looked at me strangely. I felt awful. I hastened to leave, to get away.

"Wait," she said suddenly as we were standing in the hallway near the door, and she stopped me by putting her hand on my overcoat. She quickly put the candle down and ran off; obviously she'd remembered something or wanted to show me something. As she left she was blushing all over, her eyes were gleaming, and a smile had appeared on her lips—what on earth did it all mean? I waited against my own will; she returned a moment later with a glance that seemed to beg forgiveness for something. All in all it was no longer the same face or the same glance as before—sullen, distrustful, obstinate. Now her glance was imploring, soft, and, at the same time, trusting, affectionate, and timid. That's how children look at people whom they love very much, or when they're asking for something. Her eyes were light hazel, lovely, full of life, as capable of expressing love as brooding hatred.

Without any explanation, as if I were some kind of higher being who was supposed to know everything, she held a piece of paper out toward me. At that moment her whole face was shining with a most naive, almost childlike triumph. I unfolded the paper. It was a letter to her from some medical student containing a high-flown, flowery, but very respectful declaration of love. I don't remember the exact words now, but I can well recall the genuine emotion that can't be feigned shining through that high style. When I'd finished reading the letter, I met her ardent, curious, and childishly impatient gaze. She'd fixed her eyes on my face and was waiting eagerly to see what I'd say. In a few words, hurriedly, but with some joy and pride, she explained that she'd once been at a dance somewhere, in a private house, at the home of some "very, very good people, *family people*, where they *knew nothing*, nothing at all," because she'd arrived at this place only recently and was just . . . well, she hadn't quite decided whether she'd stay here and she'd certainly leave as soon as she'd paid off her debt. . . . Well, and this student was there; he danced with her all evening and talked to her. It turned out he was from Riga; he'd known her as a child, they'd played together, but that had been a long time ago; he was acquainted with her parents—but he knew nothing, absolutely nothing *about this place* and he didn't even suspect it! And so, the very next day, after the dance, (only some three days ago), he'd sent her this letter through the friend with whom she'd gone to the party . . . and . . . well, that's the whole story."

She lowered her sparkling eyes somewhat bashfully after she finished speaking.

The poor little thing, she'd saved this student's letter as a treasure and had run to fetch this one treasure of hers, not wanting me to leave without knowing that she too was the object of sincere, honest love, and that someone exists who had spoken to her respectfully. Probably that letter was fated to lie in her box without results. But that didn't matter; I'm sure that she'll guard it as a treasure her whole life, as her pride and vindication; and now, at a moment like this, she remembered it and brought it out to exult naively before me, to raise herself in my eyes, so that I could see it for myself and could also think well of her. I didn't say a thing; I shook her hand and left. I really wanted to get away. . . . I walked all the way home in spite of the fact that wet snow was still falling in large flakes. I was exhausted, oppressed, and perplexed. But the truth was already glimmering behind that perplexity. The ugly truth!

VIII

It was some time, however, before I agreed to acknowledge that truth. I awoke the next morning after a few hours of deep, leaden sleep. Instantly recalling the events of the previous day, even I was astonished at my *sentimentality* with Liza last night, at all of yesterday's "horror and pity." "Why, it's an attack of old woman's nervous hysteria, phew!" I decided. "And why on earth did I force my address on her? What if she comes? Then again, let her come, it doesn't make any difference. . . ." But *obviously* that was not the main, most important matter: I had to make haste and rescue at all costs my reputation in the eyes of Zverkov and Simonov. That was my main task. I even forgot all about Liza in the concerns of that morning.

First of all I had to repay last night's debt to Simonov immediately. I resolved on desperate means: I would borrow the sum of fifteen rubles from

Anton Antonych. As luck would have it, he was in a splendid mood that morning and gave me the money at once, at my first request. I was so delighted that I signed a promissory note with a somewhat dashing air, and told him *casually* that on the previous evening "I'd been living it up with some friends at the Hôtel de Paris. We were holding a farewell dinner for a comrade, one might even say, a childhood friend, and, you know—he's a great carouser, very spoiled—well, naturally; he comes from a good family, has considerable wealth and a brilliant career; he's witty and charming, and has affairs with certain ladies, you understand. We drank up an extra 'half-dozen bottles' and . . ." There was nothing to it; I said all this very easily, casually, and complacently.

Upon arriving home I wrote to Simonov at once.

To this very day I recall with admiration the truly gentlemanly, good-natured, candid tone of my letter. Cleverly and nobly, and, above all, without unnecessary words, I blamed myself for everything. I justified myself, "if only I could be allowed to justify myself," by saying that, being so totally unac-customed to wine, I'd gotten drunk with the first glass, which (supposedly) I'd consumed even before their arrival, as I waited for them in the Hôtel de Paris between the hours of five and six o'clock. In particular, I begged for Simonov's pardon; I asked him to convey my apology to all the others, espe-cially to Zverkov, whom, "I recall, as if in a dream," it seems, I'd insulted. I added that I'd have called upon each of them, but was suffering from a bad headache, and, worst of all, I was ashamed. I was particularly satisfied by the "certain lightness," almost casualness (though, still very proper), unex-pectedly reflected in my style; better than all possible arguments, it conveyed to them at once that I regarded "all of last night's unpleasantness" in a rather detached way, and that I was not at all, not in the least struck down on the spot as you, gentlemen, probably suspect. On the contrary, I regard this all serenely, as any self-respecting gentleman would. The true story, as they say, is no reproach to an honest young man.

"Why, there's even a hint of aristocratic playfulness in it," I thought admir-ingly as I reread my note. "And it's all because I'm such a cultured and educated man! Others in my place wouldn't know how to extricate them-selves, but I've gotten out of it, and I'm having a good time once again, all because I'm an 'educated and cultured man of our time.' It may even be true that the whole thing occurred as a result of that wine yesterday. Hmmm . . . well, no, it wasn't really the wine. And I didn't have anything to drink between five and six o'clock when I was waiting for them. I lied to Simonov; it was a bold-faced lie—yet I'm not ashamed of it even now. . . ."

But, to hell with it, anyway! The main thing is, I got out of it.

I put six rubles in the letter, sealed it up, and asked Apollon to take it to Simonov. When he heard that there was money in it, Apollon became more respectful and agreed to deliver it. Toward evening I went out for a stroll. My head was still aching and spinning from the events of the day before. But as evening approached and twilight deepened, my impressions changed and became more confused, as did my thoughts. Something hadn't yet died within me, deep within my heart and conscience; it didn't want to die, and it expressed itself as burning anguish. I jostled my way along the more pop-ulous, commercial streets, along Meshchanskaya, Sadovaya, near the Yusu-pov Garden. I particularly liked to stroll along these streets at twilight, just as they became most crowded with all sorts of pedestrians, merchants, and tradesmen, with faces preoccupied to the point of hostility, on their way home from a hard day's work. It was precisely the cheap bustle that I liked, the crass prosaic quality. But this time all that street bustle irritated me even more. I couldn't get a hold of myself or puzzle out what was wrong. Something was rising, rising up in my soul continually, painfully, and didn't want to settle down. I returned home completely distraught. It was just as if some crime were weighing on my soul.

I was constantly tormented by the thought that Liza might come to see me. It was strange, but from all of yesterday's recollections, the one of her tormented me most, somehow separately from all the others. I'd managed to forget the rest by evening, to shrug everything off, and I still remained completely satisfied with my letter to Simonov. But in regard to Liza, I was not at all satisfied. It was as though I were tormented by her alone. "What if she comes?" I thought continually. "Well, so what? It doesn't matter. Let her come. Hmm. The only unpleasant thing is that she'll see, for instance, how I live. Yesterday I appeared before her such a . . . hero . . . but now, hmm! Besides, it's revolting that I've sunk so low. The squalor of my apartment. And I dared go to dinner last night wearing such clothes! And that oilcloth sofa of mine with its stuffing hanging out! And my dressing gown that doesn't quite cover me! What rags! . . . She'll see it all—and she'll see Apollon. That swine will surely insult her. He'll pick on her, just to be rude to me. Of course, I'll be frightened, as usual. I'll begin to fawn before her, wrap myself up in my dressing gown. I'll start to smile and tell lies. Ugh, the indecency! And that's not even the worst part! There's something even more important, nastier, meaner! Yes, meaner! Once again, I'll put on that dishonest, deceitful mask! . . ."

When I reached this thought, I simply flared up.

"Why deceitful? How deceitful? Yesterday I spoke sincerely. I recall that there was genuine feeling in me, too. I was trying no less than to arouse noble feelings in her . . . and if she wept, that's a good thing; it will have a beneficial effect. . . ."

But I still couldn't calm down.

All that evening, even after I returned home, even after nine o'clock, when by my calculations Liza could no longer have come, her image continued to haunt me, and, what's most important, she always appeared in one and the same form. Of all that had occurred yesterday, it was one moment in particular which stood out most vividly: that was when I lit up the room with a match and saw her pale, distorted face with its tormented gaze. What a pitiful, unnatural, distorted smile she'd had at that moment! But little did I know then that even fifteen years later I'd still picture Liza to myself with that same pitiful, distorted, and unnecessary smile which she'd had at that moment.

The next day I was once again prepared to dismiss all this business as nonsense, as the result of overstimulated nerves; but most of all, as exaggeration. I was well aware of this weakness of mine and sometimes was even afraid of it; "I exaggerate everything, that's my problem," I kept repeating to myself hour after hour. And yet, "yet, Liza may still come, all the same"; that was the refrain which concluded my reflections. I was so distressed that I sometimes became furious. "She'll come! She'll definitely come!" If not today, then tomorrow, she'll seek me out! That's just like the damned romanticism of all these *pure hearts!* Oh, the squalor, the stupidity, the narrowness of these "filthy, sentimental souls!" How could all this not be understood, how on earth could it not be understood? . . ." But at this point I would stop myself, even in the midst of great confusion.

"And how few, how very few words were needed," I thought in passing, "how little idyllic sentiment (what's more, the sentiment was artificial, bookish, composed) was necessary to turn a whole human soul according to my wishes at once. That's innocence for you! That's virgin soil!"

At times the thought occurred that I might go to her myself "to tell her everything," and to beg her not to come to me. But at this thought such venom arose in me that it seemed I'd have crushed that "damned" Liza if she'd suddenly turned up next to me. I'd have insulted her, spat at her, struck her, and chased her away!

One day passed, however, then a second, and a third; she still hadn't come, and I began to calm down. I felt particularly reassured and relaxed after nine o'clock in the evening, and even began to daydream sweetly at times. For instance, I'd save Liza, precisely because she'd come to me, and I'd talk to her. . . . I'd develop her mind, educate her. At last I'd notice that she loved me, loved me passionately. I'd pretend I didn't understand. (For that matter, I didn't know why I'd pretend; most likely just for the effect.) At last, all embarrassed, beautiful, trembling, and sobbing, she'd throw herself at my feet and declare that I was her saviour and she loved me more than anything in the world. I'd be surprised, but . . . "Liza," I'd say, "Do you really think that I haven't noticed your love? I've seen everything. I guessed, but dared not be first to make a claim on your heart because I had such influence over you, and because I was afraid you might deliberately force yourself to respond to my love out of gratitude, that you might forcibly evoke within yourself a feeling that didn't really exist. No, I didn't want that because it would be . . . despotism. . . . It would be indelicate (well, in short, here I launched on some European, George Sandian,[3] inexplicably lofty subtleties . . .). But now, now—you're mine, you're my creation, you're pure and lovely, you're my beautiful wife."

> And enter my house bold and free
> To become its full mistress![4]

"Then we'd begin to live happily together, travel abroad, etc., etc." In short, it began to seem crude even to me, and I ended it all by sticking my tongue out at myself.

"Besides, they won't let her out of there, the 'bitch,' " I thought. "After all, it seems unlikely that they'd release them for strolls, especially in the evening (for some reason I was convinced that she had to report there every evening, precisely at seven o'clock). Moreover, she said that she'd yet to become completely enslaved there, and that she still had certain rights; that means, hmm. Devil take it, she'll come, she's bound to come!"

It was a good thing I was distracted at the time by Apollon's rudeness. He made me lose all patience. He was the bane of my existence, a punishment

---

3. George Sand was the pseudonym of the French woman novelist Aurore Dudevant (1804–1876), famous also as a promoter of feminism.   4. The last lines of the poem by Nekrasov used as the epigraph of Part II of this story (see p. 1279).

inflicted on me by Providence. We'd been squabbling constantly for several years now and I hated him. My God, how I hated him! I think that I never hated anyone in my whole life as much as I hated him, especially at those times. He was an elderly, dignified man who worked part-time as a tailor. But for some unknown reason he despised me, even beyond all measure, and looked down upon me intolerably. However, he looked down on everyone. You need only glance at that flaxen, slicked-down hair, at that single lock brushed over his forehead and greased with vegetable oil, at his strong mouth, always drawn up in the shape of the letter V,[5] and you felt that you were standing before a creature who never doubted himself. He was a pedant of the highest order, the greatest one I'd ever met on earth; in addition he possessed a sense of self-esteem appropriate perhaps only to Alexander the Great, King of Macedonia. He was in love with every one of his buttons, every one of his fingernails—absolutely in love, and he looked it! He treated me quite despotically, spoke to me exceedingly little, and, if he happened to look at me, cast a steady, majestically self-assured, and constantly mocking glance that sometimes infuriated me. He carried out his tasks as if he were doing me the greatest of favors. Moreover, he did almost nothing at all for me; nor did he assume that he was obliged to do anything. There could be no doubt that he considered me the greatest fool on earth, and, that if he "kept me on," it was only because he could receive his wages from me every month. He agreed to "do nothing" for seven rubles a month. I'll be forgiven many of my sins because of him. Sometimes my hatred reached such a point that his gait alone would throw me into convulsions. But the most repulsive thing about him was his lisping. His tongue was a bit larger than normal or something of the sort; as a result, he constantly lisped and hissed. Apparently, he was terribly proud of it, imagining that it endowed him with enormous dignity. He spoke slowly, in measured tones, with his hands behind his back and his eyes fixed on the ground. It particularly infuriated me when he used to read the Psalter to himself behind his partition. I endured many battles on account of it. He was terribly fond of reading during the evening in a slow, even singsong voice, as if chanting over the dead. It's curious, but that's how he ended up: now he hires himself out to recite the Psalter over the dead; in addition, he exterminates rats and makes shoe polish. But at that time I couldn't get rid of him; it was as if he were chemically linked to my own existence. Besides, he'd never have agreed to leave for anything. It was impossible for me to live in a furnished room: my own apartment was my private residence, my shell, my case, where I hid from all humanity. Apollon, the devil only knows why, seemed to belong to this apartment, and for seven long years I couldn't get rid of him.

It was impossible, for example, to delay paying him his wages for even two or three days. He'd make such a fuss that I wouldn't know where to hide. But in those days I was so embittered by everyone that I decided, heaven knows why or for what reason, to *punish* Apollon by not paying him his wages for two whole weeks. I'd been planning to do this for some time now, about two years, simply in order to teach him that he had no right to put on such airs around me, and that if I chose to, I could always withhold his wages. I resolved to say nothing to him about it and even remain silent on purpose,

---

5. The last letter of the old Russian alphabet, triangular in shape.

to conquer his pride and force him to be the first one to mention it. Then I would pull all seven rubles out of a drawer and show him that I actually had the money and had intentionally set it aside, but that "I didn't want to, didn't want to, simply didn't want to pay him his wages, and that I didn't want to simply because *that's what I wanted*," because such was "my will as his master," because he was disrespectful and because he was rude. But, if he were to ask respectfully, then I might relent and pay him; if not, he might have to wait another two weeks, or three, or even a whole month. . . .

But, no matter how angry I was, he still won. I couldn't even hold out for four days. He began as he always did, because there had already been several such cases (and, let me add, I knew all this beforehand; I knew his vile tactics by heart), to wit: he would begin by fixing an extremely severe gaze on me. He would keep it up for several minutes in a row, especially when meeting me or accompanying me outside of the house. If, for example, I held out and pretended not to notice these stares, then he, maintaining his silence as before, would proceed to further tortures. Suddenly, for no reason at all, he'd enter my room quietly and slowly, while I was pacing or reading; he'd stop at the door, place one hand behind his back, thrust one foot forward, and fix his gaze on me, no longer merely severe, but now utterly contemptuous. If I were suddenly to ask him what he wanted, he wouldn't answer at all. He'd continue to stare at me reproachfully for several more seconds; then, compressing his lips in a particular way and assuming a very meaningful air, he'd turn slowly on the spot and slowly withdraw to his own room. Two hours later he'd emerge again and suddenly appear before me in the same way. It's happened sometimes that in my fury I hadn't even asked what he wanted, but simply raised my head sharply and imperiously, and begun to stare reproachfully back at him. We would stare at each other thus for some two minutes or more; at last he'd turn slowly and self-importantly, and withdraw for another few hours.

If all this failed to bring me back to my senses and I continued to rebel, he'd suddenly begin to sigh while staring at me. He'd sigh heavily and deeply, as if trying to measure with each sigh the depth of my moral decline. Naturally, it would end with his complete victory: I'd rage and shout, but I was always forced to do just as he wished on the main point of dispute.

This time his usual maneuvers of "severe stares" had scarcely begun when I lost my temper at once and lashed out at him in a rage. I was irritated enough even without that.

"Wait!" I shouted in a frenzy, as he was slowly and silently turning with one hand behind his back, about to withdraw to his own room. "Wait! Come back, come back, I tell you!" I must have bellowed so unnaturally that he turned around and even began to scrutinize me with a certain amazement. He continued, however, not to utter one word, and that was what infuriated me most of all.

"How dare you come in here without asking permission and stare at me? Answer me!"

But after regarding me serenely for half a minute, he started to turn around again.

"Wait!" I roared, rushing up to him. "Don't move! There! Now answer me: why do you come in here to stare?"

"If you've got any orders for me now, it's my job to do 'em," he replied after

The greatest scientific work of the era we familiarly call "the Enlightenment," and one of the greatest such works in all of human history, is Sir Isaac Newton's *Philosophiae Naturalis Principia Mathematica* (*Mathematical Principles of Natural Philosophy*, 1687), in which he outlined the principles of universal gravitation. By the time Newton published the *Principia*, he had also essentially invented integral and (simultaneously with Wilhelm Leibniz) differential calculus and had made several significant discoveries in optics. (His study of optics led him to propose and construct the world's first reflecting telescope, pictured to the right next to the *Principia* manuscript.) Although many others contributed to the feeling during the seventeenth century that the universe was rational and comprehensible, Newton did more than anyone to provide concrete justification for that view.

Accompanying Europe's intellectual optimism during the Enlightenment was a continued recognition of the contingencies of the human condition. Perhaps no European capital was more aware of these contingencies than London during the 1660s. After having suffered through a severe outbreak of plague during the spring and summer of 1665—an outbreak that killed nearly 15 percent of the city's population—London suffered a devastating fire during early September of 1666, re-created here in a lithograph by the nineteenth-century illustrators Thomas Rowlandson and Augustus Pugin. Nearly three-quarters of the city's buildings were destroyed by the fire, including over twelve thousand houses. Although only six people were reported to have died in the fire, thousands were left without homes, belongings, or livelihoods.

Although only thirty-five paintings can be definitively attributed to him, and despite his relative obscurity until very recently, the Dutch artist Jan Vermeer (1632–1675) produced some of the most revolutionary works of visual art during the seventeenth century. He focused his attention on the well-appointed interiors of the Dutch upper-middle class, and exercised his considerable virtuosity on the difficult visual "problems" of light and color. We know that he used optical tools, including the camera obscura, to help him create the vivid illusion of depth, "true" color, and convincing light that is the hallmark of his work, but the fact that his art benefited from the science and technology of his time doesn't detract from the uniqueness of his achievement.

This particular image, *The Allegory of the Art of Painting* (1670–75), features Vermeer himself in the middle ground with his back toward us as he paints a model outfitted with laurel wreath, trumpet, and book—the traditional accoutrements of Clio, the classical Muse of history.

As the eighteenth century in Europe progressed, "nature" became an ever more problematic concept, especially as intellectuals, writers, and artists grappled with the relationship between Nature—the world around us—and "human nature," whatever that might be. In the previous century, Thomas Hobbes had pessimistically asserted that humanity "in the state of nature" was engaged in a "war of all against all." Later, Jean-Jacques Rousseau declared that human nature was essentially good and noble, and that humanity's innate qualities were the best guide to a just and equitable society.

The painting above, *Pilgrimage to the Isle of Cythera* (1717), by the French artist Jean Antoine Watteau, provides a third and more ambiguous perspective. The idyllic natural setting seems perfectly suited for a procession of lovers on pilgrimage to the island of love (Cythera was the birthplace of Aphrodite). Yet there is a sharp contrast between this Nature, shown as a lush natural landscape, and the human beings who inhabit it. The travelers' gallant poses and formal dress suggest a highly sophisticated society that emphasizes appearances, perhaps at the expense of a more innocent "nature." Building on this visual contradiction, viewers have asked what part of the pilgrimage the painting represents: is the procession setting out for the island of love or preparing to leave it?

When this portrait was painted in 1787, Johann Wolfgang von Goethe had already published the immensely popular and influential novel *The Sorrows of Young Werther*, the work that almost single-handedly established the image of the intro-spective, self-pitying, melancholy Romantic hero. His masterpiece, *Faust*, pub-lished twenty-one years after this portrait, secured Goethe's reputation as an authentic Romantic genius and made him a legendary figure in his own lifetime.

This picture, *Goethe in the Campagna* (the countryside around Rome, shown here with artfully scattered classical ruins), was painted in 1786 by the German classical painter Johann Tischbein during the writer's two-year tour of Italy. Its carefully posed and idealized portrait of the handsome writer meditating in the midst of nature and the ruins of classical antiquity can be seen as the eighteenth-century equivalent of modern celebrity posters and gives a hint of the international adulation that Goethe would enjoy as a quintessential genius during the latter half of his life.

"Bliss was it in that dawn to be alive," wrote William Wordsworth about his feelings witnessing the events of the French Revolution. His enthusiasm for the political transformation of France from an absolute monarchy to a representative republic was shared by many artists and intellectuals of the late eighteenth century, including Jacques-Louis David, a French painter whose images of the Revolution and its aftermath are the most famous visual chronicles of its ideals and tragedies.

The image above, a drawing made by David in preparation for a massive painting that he never managed to complete, celebrates a moment of great courage and idealism at the beginning of the Revolution: the Tennis Court Oath of June 1789. Deputies of the Third Estate (commoners, as distinct from the nobles and the clergy), outraged at being locked out of the meeting hall where they were scheduled to discuss reforms, adjourned to a nearby indoor tennis court. Here, the revolutionaries vowed to remain united as the "National Assembly," until they produced a new constitution for France based on ideals that would soon afterward be made explicit in the Declaration of the Rights of Man: "liberty, property, security, and resistance to oppression."

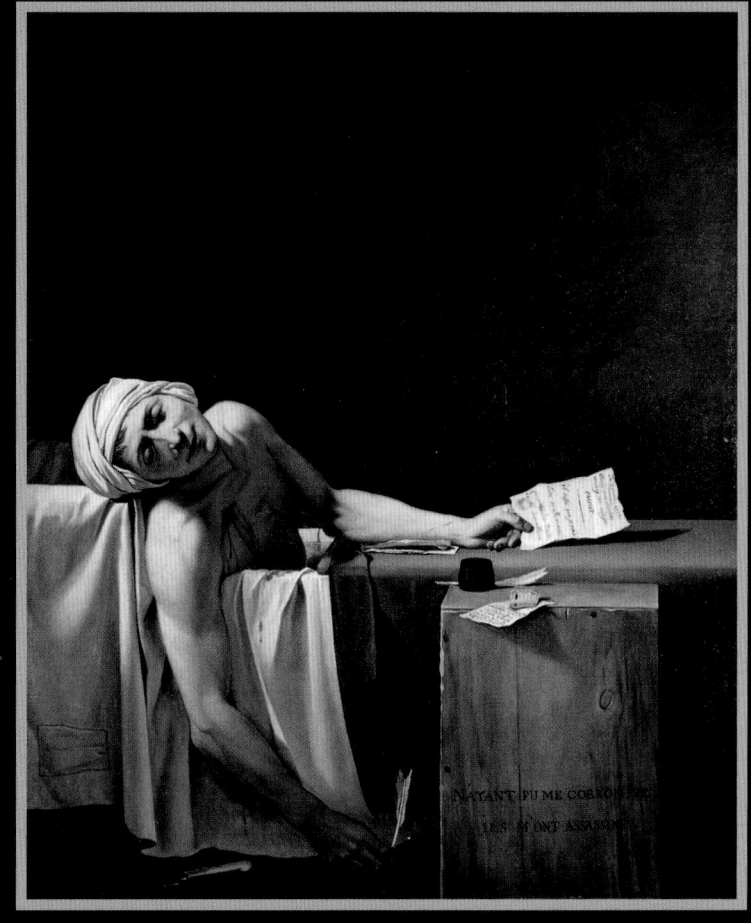

Despite its idealistic and egalitarian beginnings, the French Revolution soon descended into violence and authoritarianism. After a three-year period of factional disputes and suppression of counterrevolutionary forces, the most radical egalitarians—called the Jacobins—gained control of the government in September of 1792. Faced with real and imagined counterrevolutionary threats, however, the Jacobins delayed the introduction of universal male suffrage and consolidated all power in a group of twelve leaders, called the Committee of Public Safety, in order to solidify their revolutionary accomplishments. From the summer of 1793 through the fall of 1794, the Committee authorized over 25,000 executions of people deemed to be enemies of the Revolution.

Among the key Jacobin leaders was the fiery orator Jean-Paul Marat, a physician turned revolutionary who was murdered in the summer of 1793 by a young royalist and was subsequently revered as a martyr of the Revolution. This painting by Jacques-Louis David, *The Death of Marat* (1793), one of the most famous images of the period, shows Marat slumped in his bathtub next to an improvised writing desk (he was forced to spend most of his time in the bath to relieve a chronic skin condition) and holding a note from his assassin, Charlotte Corday. David admired Marat as a man of exceptional civic virtue, and his admiration is shown both in the dead man's idealized appearance and in the homage *À Marat* ("To Marat") written above the painter's signature.

By the mid-nineteenth century, the recently discovered process of photography transformed the visual arts, causing many painters and sculptors to rethink the purpose of their art. Before photography, painting and other visual arts could be appraised and valued based at least in part on the attainment of verisimilitude— the quality of appearing "real" or faithful to a real original. Photography made the criterion of realism seem moot, however, since the images produced with the camera were by definition more faithful to the appearance of the objects or persons they pictured than any painting or sculpture could be.

The image above is an ambrotype (a negative image on glass mounted onto a dark background surface) taken in 1856 of the great orator, autobiographer, journalist, and diplomat Frederick Douglass. Douglass's *Narrative of the Life of Frederick Douglass, an American Slave*, first published in 1845, was a galvanizing document for the abolitionist movement in the United States and also an inspiration to anti-slavery Europeans, who were able to hear him speak during his two-year exile in England from 1845 to 1847.

After the great wave of the international Romantic movement had spent its force in the fourth decade of the nineteenth century, and as photography set a new standard for capturing reality visually, many artists and writers in Europe moved in a direction that we now call *realism*. The realists wanted a truthful representation of contemporary life and manners, and saw their method as inductive, observational, and hence "objective." The realist program in literature and in art aimed at providing a "slice of life," a glimpse into everyday existence that might well include the sordid, the banal, the ugly, and the evil. Artists and writers found interest in the lives of the middle and lower classes, both of which had previously been neglected.

In the visual arts, Honoré Daumier stands a quintessential realist, offering by turns sympathetic views of the lives of those on the bottom rungs of society, as in *Third Class Carriage* (ca. 1860), above, and satirical jabs at the puffery of the privileged, as in his famous illustrations of lawyers, judges, and other members of the professional classes.

Realism introduced to the arts new subject matter and a new approach to familiar subjects. Realist art often met with resistance because both its form and its content offended the sensibilities of those who had been steeped in classical (and Renaissance) aesthetics. For many seeing realist paintings or reading realist novels for the first time, the subject matter and the style of presentation violated age-old ideals of beauty and sublimity. If the Renaissance had focused artistic energies on beauty, realism turned instead to the often cold, hard, and ugly facts of modern life.

Thomas Eakins, an American realist painter whose subjects were mostly landscapes and portraiture, was also fascinated by medical practice of his time. This picture, *The Agnew Clinic*, was commissioned in 1886 by University of Pennsylvania medical students on the occasion of the retirement of Dr. D. Hayes Agnew (standing, in white surgery robe, at left) as head of the university's surgery division.

Impressionism emerged in opposition to the prevailing official styles of realism, which claimed to represent objective reality, and of romanticism, which favored the depiction of human emotions. French artists like Claude Monet and Pierre-August Renoir turned to explorations of light and color and new techniques of painting. Bright colors and combinations of colors, and the manipulation of light and shadow, suggested that reality was not permanent or monolithic but fluid, existing in the viewer's eye and seized moment by moment.

Monet began painting the cathedral at Rouen during a visit in February 1892. Fascinated by the changing appearance of the stone at different times of day, he became obsessed with capturing these moments and created and reworked a series of thirty linked canvases over the next two and a half years. "Everything changes, even stone," he wrote. Monet painted the cathedral in different weather and from morning to night, recording what he called its "enveloppe" of air, light, and color. We see here the west façade first as a "harmony of blue and gold" in the full noon sun and then in gray weather. As with many Impressionist paintings, the images are best viewed at a distance, so that the thick brushstrokes and juxtaposition of myriad colors blend into a single harmonious vision.

[1]

"Postimpressionist" is the name given to a series of late-nineteenth-century European artists who rejected both Impressionist ideals and traditional Academic realism. Developing a range of personal styles, these artists abandoned Impressionist sensitivity and delicate shades to work with vibrant colors, bold, defining lines, and a direct presentation of the subject. Echoing Romantic and Symbolist practice, they evoked moods and emotions, and suggested larger hidden meanings, many of which implied a critique of modern industrial society.

Dreams of exotic escape to a freer, more primitive existence appear in both these pictures, by Paul Gauguin and Henri Rousseau. Gauguin fled Paris for tropical islands, painting idealized scenes of a purer "primitive" life, as in *Tahitian Women/On the Beach* (1891) [1]; Rousseau, whose "naïve" or "primitive" style masks great technical mastery, never left France and painted his fantastic landscapes, such as *The Dream* (1910) [2], on the basis of books and the Paris Zoo.

[2]

1]

estions of perspective began to dominate Western art at the beginning of the
spite recent stylistic innovations, the Renaissance concept of a unified spatia
chor point around which the work of art could be organized in depth—remai
. Pablo Picasso's *Les Demoiselles d'Avignon* (1907) [1], often called the "first
th century," fractures this organizational model, breaking up images (and hun
complex arrangement of planes and geometric shapes. On one level, the pai
rostitutes in a Barcelona brothel; its distorted images also include echoes of C

Bathers, of early Iberia
ture, and—in the two
the right—of African n

The Belgian surreali
Magritte plays with pe
an entirely different m
La Trahison des images
[2], also called *Ceci n'*
pipe (This is not a pipe
moves humorously bac
forth between languag
neither of which comp
tures reality. The paint
a pipe as if in a class ill
yet the sign says it is *n*
and of course it is not

eci n'est pas une pipe.

[1]

Dada-Surrealism put the very nature of the work of art in question. Disillusioned by the collapse of European civilization during World War I, a collapse they blamed on nineteenth-century political and social values, the Surrealists attacked anything that was associated with the old order—including inherited concepts of high art, which they deemed mere institutionalized habit. Marcel Duchamp, a radical innovator whose *Nude Descending a Staircase* caused a scandal at the New York Armory Show in 1913, struggled to eliminate aesthetic qualities from his work by producing a series of "readymades": commercial objects that he declared "art" (or "anti-art") by signing them and putting them on exhibit. *Why not sneeze, Rose Sélavy?* (1921) [1] is an assisted readymade—a grouping of objects—that further unsettles spectators who pick it up and discover the weight of its "sugar cubes" (they are made of heavy white marble). Whether or not viewers consider Dada-Surrealist objects art is an individual choice, but the experience serves to raise questions about the nature of art, of perception, and of the role of expectations in determining our opinions. One of the most famous Surrealist objects is the fur-lined teacup and spoon, *Object* (1936) [2], created in 1936 by Swiss artist Meret Oppenheim, an everyday utensil rendered useless but at the same time mysterious, sensuous, oddly repellent, and invariably fascinating. Viewers examine their reactions to the object, thus responding precisely as the Surrealists wished, whether to "art" or "anti-art."

[2]

An event that united millions in protest and inspired works by some of Europe's best-known writers and artists was the total destruction of a little Basque town, Guernica, by German bombers supporting the Fascist general Francisco Franco and testing weapons that would soon be used in World War II. Five days after the bombing on April 27, 1937, the Spanish artist Pablo Picasso set to work on an enormous commemorative painting, done exclusively in black, white, and gray, that would be exhibited three months later in Paris, at the Spanish Pavilion of the Exposition Universelle. Filled with images of pain and terror, of outstretched arms and gaping mouths, and centered on a screaming horse transfixed by a spear while an enigmatic bull gazes off to the side, *Guernica* (1937) is not a realistic representation but wholly Modernist: it uses Cubist techniques of fragmentation and the expressive power of stretched, distorted forms to convey the agony of death at Guernica. Themes from the artist's earlier work appear: echoes of a Crucifixion, of bullfights, of the Minotaur. The fact that there is no one, all-embracing interpretation of the various figures (and Picasso refused to give one) does not detract from its overall impact but rather—as Picasso suggested—allows viewers to respond individually to the different parts of his work. A reproduction hangs in the United Nations building another pause, lisping softly and deliberately, raising his eyebrows, and calmly shifting his head from one side to the other—what's more, he did all this with horrifying composure.

"That's not it! That's not what I'm asking you about, you executioner!" I shouted, shaking with rage. "I'll tell you myself, you executioner, why you came in here. You know that I haven't paid you your wages, but you're so proud that you don't want to bow down and ask me for them. That's why you came in here to punish me and torment me with your stupid stares, and you don't even sus-s-pect, you torturer, how stupid it all is, how stupid, stupid, stupid, stupid!"

He would have turned around silently once again, but I grabbed hold of him.

"Listen," I shouted to him. "Here's the money, you see! Here it is! (I pulled it out of a drawer.) All seven rubles. But you won't get it, you won't until you come to me respectfully, with your head bowed, to ask my forgiveness. Do you hear?"

"That can't be!" he replied with some kind of unnatural self-confidence.

"It will be!" I shrieked. "I give you my word of honor, it will be!"

"I have nothing to ask your forgiveness for," he said as if he hadn't even noticed my shrieks, "because it was you who called me an 'executioner,' and I can always go lodge a complaint against you at the police station."

"Go! Lodge a complaint!" I roared. "Go at once, this minute, this very second! You're still an executioner! Executioner! Executioner!" But he only looked at me, then turned and, no longer heeding my shouts, calmly withdrew to his own room without looking back.

"If it hadn't been for Liza, none of this would have happened!" I thought to myself. Then, after waiting a minute, pompously and solemnly, but with my heart pounding heavily and forcefully, I went in to see him behind the screen.

"Apollon!" I said softly and deliberately, though gasping for breath, "go at once, without delay to fetch the police supervisor!"

He'd already seated himself at his table, put on his eyeglasses, and picked up something to sew. But, upon hearing my order, he suddenly snorted with laughter.

"At once! Go this very moment! Go, go, or you can't imagine what will happen to you!"

"You're really not in your right mind," he replied, not even lifting his head, lisping just as slowly, and continuing to thread his needle. "Who's ever heard of a man being sent to fetch a policeman against himself? And as for trying to frighten me, you're only wasting your time, because nothing will happen to me."

"Go," I screeched, seizing him by the shoulder. I felt that I might strike him at any moment.

I never even heard the door from the hallway suddenly open at that very moment, quietly and slowly, and that someone walked in, stopped, and began to examine us in bewilderment. I glanced up, almost died from shame, and ran back into my own room. There, clutching my hair with both hands, I leaned my head against the wall and froze in that position.

Two minutes later I heard Apollon's deliberate footsteps.

"There's *some woman* asking for you," he said, staring at me with particular severity; then he stood aside and let her in—it was Liza. He didn't want to leave, and he scrutinized us mockingly.

"Get out, get out!" I commanded him all flustered. At that moment my clock strained, wheezed, and struck seven.

IX

And enter my house bold and free,
To become its full mistress!
From the same poem.[6]

I stood before her, crushed, humiliated, abominably ashamed; I think I was smiling as I tried with all my might to wrap myself up in my tattered, quilted dressing gown—exactly as I'd imagined this scene the other day during a fit of depression. Apollon, after standing over us for a few minutes, left, but that didn't make things any easier for me. Worst of all was that she suddenly became embarrassed too, more than I'd ever expected. At the sight of me, of course.

"Sit down," I said mechanically and moved a chair up to the table for her, while I sat on the sofa. She immediately and obediently sat down, staring at me wide-eyed, and, obviously, expecting something from me at once. This naive expectation infuriated me, but I restrained myself.

She should have tried not to notice anything, as if everything were just as it should be, but she . . . And I vaguely felt that she'd have to pay dearly *for everything*.

"You've found me in an awkward situation, Liza," I began, stammering and realizing that this was precisely the wrong way to begin.

"No, no, don't imagine anything!" I cried, seeing that she'd suddenly blushed. "I'm not ashamed of my poverty. . . . On the contrary, I regard it with pride. I'm poor, but noble. . . . One can be poor and noble," I muttered. "But . . . would you like some tea?"

"No . . . ," she started to say.

"Wait!"

I jumped up and ran to Apollon. I had to get away somehow.

"Apollon," I whispered in feverish haste, tossing down the seven rubles which had been in my fist the whole time, "here are your wages. There, you see, I've given them to you. But now you must rescue me: bring us some tea and a dozen rusks from the tavern at once. If you don't go, you'll make me a very miserable man. You have no idea who this woman is. . . . This means—everything! You may think she's . . . But you've no idea at all who this woman really is!"

Apollon, who'd already sat down to work and had put his glasses on again, at first glanced sideways in silence at the money without abandoning his needle; then, paying no attention to me and making no reply, he continued to fuss with the needle he was still trying to thread. I waited there for about three minutes standing before him with my arms folded *à la Napoleon*.[7] My temples were soaked in sweat. I was pale, I felt that myself. But, thank God, he must have taken pity just looking at me. After finishing with the thread, he stood up slowly from his place, slowly pushed back his chair, slowly took

6. I.e., from the poem quoted on pp. 1279 and 1318.   7. In the style of Napoleon.

off his glasses, slowly counted the money and finally, after inquiring over his shoulder whether he should get a whole pot, slowly walked out of the room. As I was returning to Liza, it occurred to me: shouldn't I run away just as I was, in my shabby dressing gown, no matter where, and let come what may.

I sat down again. She looked at me uneasily. We sat in silence for several minutes.

"I'll kill him." I shouted suddenly, striking the table so hard with my fist that ink splashed out of the inkwell.

"Oh, what are you saying?" she exclaimed, startled.

"I'll kill him, I'll kill him!" I shrieked, striking the table in an absolute frenzy, but understanding full well at the same time how stupid it was to be in such a frenzy.

"You don't understand, Liza, what this executioner is doing to me. He's my executioner. . . . He's just gone out for some rusks; he . . ."

And suddenly I burst into tears. It was a nervous attack. I felt so ashamed amidst my sobs, but I couldn't help it. She got frightened.

"What's the matter? What's wrong with you?" she cried, fussing around me.

"Water, give me some water, over there!" I muttered in a faint voice, realizing full well, however, that I could've done both without the water and without the faint voice. But I was *putting on an act*, as it's called, in order to maintain decorum, although my nervous attack was genuine.

She gave me some water while looking at me like a lost soul. At that very moment Apollon brought in the tea. It suddenly seemed that this ordinary and prosaic tea was horribly inappropriate and trivial after everything that had happened, and I blushed. Liza stared at Apollon with considerable alarm. He left without looking at us.

"Liza, do you despise me?" I asked, looking her straight in the eye, trembling with impatience to find out what she thought.

She was embarrassed and didn't know what to say.

"Have some tea," I said angrily. I was angry at myself, but she was the one who'd have to pay, naturally. A terrible anger against her suddenly welled up in my heart; I think I could've killed her. To take revenge I swore inwardly not to say one more word to her during the rest of her visit. "She's the cause of it all," I thought.

Our silence continued for about five minutes. The tea stood on the table; we didn't touch it. It reached the point of my not wanting to drink on purpose, to make it even more difficult for her; it would be awkward for her to begin alone. Several times she glanced at me in sad perplexity. I stubbornly remained silent. I was the main sufferer, of course, because I was fully aware of the despicable meanness of my own spiteful stupidity; yet, at the same time, I couldn't restrain myself.

"I want to . . . get away from . . . that place . . . once and for all," she began just to break the silence somehow; but, poor girl, that was just the thing she shouldn't have said at that moment, stupid enough as it was to such a person as me, stupid as I was. My own heart even ached with pity for her tactlessness and unnecessary straightforwardness. But something hideous immediately suppressed all my pity; it provoked me even further. Let the whole world go to hell. Another five minutes passed.

"Have I disturbed you?" she began timidly, barely audibly, and started to get up.

But as soon as I saw this first glimpse of injured dignity, I began to shake with rage and immediately exploded.

"Why did you come here? Tell me why, please," I began, gasping and neglecting the logical order of my words. I wanted to say it all at once, without pausing for breath; I didn't even worry about how to begin.

"Why did you come here? Answer me! Answer!" I cried, hardly aware of what I was saying. "I'll tell you, my dear woman, why you came here. You came here because I spoke some *words of pity* to you that time. Now you've softened, and want to hear more 'words of pity.' Well, you should know that I was laughing at you then. And I'm laughing at you now. Why are you trembling? Yes, I was laughing at you! I'd been insulted, just prior to that, at dinner, by those men who arrived just before me that evening. I came intending to thrash one of them, the officer; but I didn't succeed; I couldn't find him; I had to avenge my insult on someone, to get my own back; you turned up and I took my anger out at you, and I laughed at you. I'd been humiliated, and I wanted to humiliate someone else; I'd been treated like a rag, and I wanted to exert some power. . . . That's what it was; you thought that I'd come there on purpose to save you, right? Is that what you thought? Is that it?"

I knew that she might get confused and might not grasp all the details, but I also knew that she'd understand the essence of it very well. That's just what happened. She turned white as a sheet; she wanted to say something. Her lips were painfully twisted, but she collapsed onto a chair just as if she'd been struck down with an ax. Subsequently she listened to me with her mouth gaping, her eyes wide open, shaking with awful fear. It was the cynicism, the cynicism of my words that crushed her. . . .

"To save you!" I continued, jumping up from my chair and rushing up and down the room in front of her, "to save you from what? Why, I may be even worse than you are. When I recited that sermon to you, why didn't you throw it back in my face? You should have said to me, 'Why did you come here? To preach morality or what?' Power, it was the power I needed then, I craved the sport, I wanted to reduce you to tears, humiliation, hysteria—that's what I needed then! But I couldn't have endured it myself, because I'm such a wretch. I got scared. The devil only knows why I foolishly gave you my address. Afterward, even before I got home, I cursed you like nothing on earth on account of that address. I hated you already because I'd lied to you then, because it was all playing with words, dreaming in my own mind. But, do you know what I really want now? For you to get lost, that's what! I need some peace. Why, I'd sell the whole world for a kopeck if people would only stop bothering me. Should the world go to hell, or should I go without my tea? I say, let the world go to hell as long as I can always have my tea. Did you know that or not? And I know perfectly well that I'm a scoundrel, a bastard, an egotist, and a sluggard. I've been shaking from fear for the last three days wondering whether you'd ever come. Do you know what disturbed me most of all these last three days? The fact that I'd appeared to you then as such a hero, and that now you'd suddenly see me in this torn dressing gown, dilapidated and revolting. I said before that I wasn't ashamed of my poverty; well, you should know that I am ashamed, I'm ashamed of it more than anything, more afraid of it than anything, more than if I were a thief, because I'm so vain; it's as if the skin's been stripped away from my body so that even wafts of air cause pain. By now surely even you've guessed that I'll never forgive you for having come upon me in this dressing gown as I was attacking Apollon like a vicious dog. Your saviour, your former hero, behaving like a mangy, shaggy mongrel, attacking his own lackey, while that lackey stood there laughing at me! Nor will I ever forgive you for those tears which, like an embarrassed old woman, I couldn't hold back before you. And I'll never forgive *you* for all that I'm confessing now. Yes—you, you alone must pay for everything because you turned up like this, because I'm a scoundrel, because I'm the nastiest, most ridiculous, pettiest, stupidest, most envious worm of all those living on earth who're no better than me in any way, but who, the devil knows why, never get embarrassed, while all my life I have to endure insults from every louse—that's my fate. What do I care that you don't understand any of this? What do I care, what do I care about you and whether or not you perish there? Why, don't you realize how much I'll hate you now after having said all this with your being here listening to me? After all, a man can only talk like this once in his whole life, and then only in hysteria! . . . What more do you want? Why, after all this, are you still hanging around here tormenting me? Why don't you leave?"

But at this point a very strange thing suddenly occurred.

I'd become so accustomed to inventing and imagining everything according to books, and picturing everything on earth to myself just as I'd conceived of it in my dreams, that at first I couldn't even comprehend the meaning of this strange occurrence. But here's what happened: Liza, insulted and crushed by me, understood much more than I'd imagined. She understood out of all this what a woman always understands first of all, if she sincerely loves—namely, that I myself was unhappy.

The frightened and insulted expression on her face was replaced at first by grieved amazement. When I began to call myself a scoundrel and a bastard, and my tears had begun to flow (I'd pronounced this whole tirade in tears), her whole face was convulsed by a spasm. She wanted to get up and stop me; when I'd finished, she paid no attention to my shouting, "Why are you here? Why don't you leave?" She only noticed that it must have been very painful for me to utter all this. Besides, she was so defenseless, the poor girl. She considered herself immeasurably beneath me. How could she get angry or take offense? Suddenly she jumped up from the chair with a kind of uncontrollable impulse, and yearning toward me, but being too timid and not daring to stir from her place, she extended her arms in my direction. . . . At this moment my heart leapt inside me, too. Then suddenly she threw herself at me, put her arms around my neck, and burst into tears. I, too, couldn't restrain myself and sobbed as I'd never done before.

"They won't let me . . . I can't be . . . good!"[8] I barely managed to say; then I went over to the sofa, fell upon it face down, and sobbed in genuine hysterics for a quarter of an hour. She knelt down, embraced me, and remained motionless in that position.

But the trouble was that my hysterics had to end sometime. And so (after

---

8. This epithet *dobryi* ("good") must be read in combination with that in the second sentence of the work, where the hero describes himself as *zloi*—not only "spiteful" but also "evil."

all, I'm writing the whole loathsome truth), lying there on the sofa and pressing my face firmly into that nasty leather cushion of mine, I began to sense gradually, distantly, involuntarily, but irresistibly, that it would be awkward for me to raise my head and look Liza straight in the eye. What was I ashamed of? I don't know, but I was ashamed. It also occurred to my overwrought brain that now our roles were completely reversed; now she was the heroine, and I was the same sort of humiliated and oppressed creature she'd been in front of me that evening—only four days ago. . . . And all this came to me during those few minutes as I lay face down on the sofa!

My God! Was it possible that I envied her?

I don't know; to this very day I still can't decide. But then, of course, I was even less able to understand it. After all, I couldn't live without exercising power and tyrannizing over another person. . . . But . . . but, then, you really can't explain a thing by reason; consequently, it's useless to try.

However, I regained control of myself and raised my head; I had to sooner or later. . . . And so, I'm convinced to this day that it was precisely because I felt too ashamed to look at her, that another feeling was suddenly kindled and burst into flame in my heart—the feeling of domination and possession. My eyes gleamed with passion; I pressed her hands tightly. How I hated her and felt drawn to her simultaneously! One feeling intensified the other. It was almost like revenge! . . . At first there was a look of something resembling bewilderment, or even fear, on her face, but only for a brief moment. She embraced me warmly and rapturously.

X

A quarter of an hour later I was rushing back and forth across the room in furious impatience, constantly approaching the screen to peer at Liza through the crack. She was sitting on the floor, her head leaning against the bed, and she must have been crying. But she didn't leave, and that's what irritated me. By this time she knew absolutely everything. I'd insulted her once and for all, but . . . there's nothing more to be said. She guessed that my outburst of passion was merely revenge, a new humiliation for her, and that to my former, almost aimless, hatred there was added now a *personal*, *envious* hatred of her. . . . However, I don't think that she understood all this explicitly; on the other hand, she fully understood that I was a despicable man, and, most important, that I was incapable of loving her.

I know that I'll be told this is incredible—that it's impossible to be as spiteful and stupid as I am; you may even add that it was impossible not to return, or at least to appreciate, this love. But why is this so incredible? In the first place, I could no longer love because, I repeat, for me love meant tyrannizing and demonstrating my moral superiority. All my life I could never even conceive of any other kind of love, and I've now reached the point that I sometimes think that love consists precisely in a voluntary gift by the beloved person of the right to tyrannize over him. Even in my underground dreams I couldn't conceive of love in any way other than a struggle. It always began with hatred and ended with moral subjugation; afterward, I could never imagine what to do with the subjugated object. And what's so incredible about that, since I'd previously managed to corrupt myself morally; I'd already become unaccustomed to "real life," and only a short while ago had taken it into my head to reproach her and shame her for having come to hear "words of pity" from me. But I never could've guessed that she'd come not to hear words of pity at all, but to love me, because it's in that kind of love that a woman finds her resurrection, all her salvation from whatever kind of ruin, and her rebirth, as it can't appear in any other form. However, I didn't hate her so much as I rushed around the room and peered through the crack behind the screen. I merely found it unbearably painful that she was still there. I wanted her to disappear. I longed for "peace and quiet"; I wanted to remain alone in my underground. "Real life" oppressed me—so unfamiliar was it—that I even found it hard to breathe.

But several minutes passed, and she still didn't stir, as if she were oblivious. I was shameless enough to tap gently on the screen to remind her. . . . She started suddenly, jumped up, and hurried to find her shawl, hat, and coat, as if she wanted to escape from me. . . . Two minutes later she slowly emerged from behind the screen and looked at me sadly. I smiled spitefully; it was forced, however, for *appearance's sake only*; and I turned away from her look.

"Good-bye," she said, going toward the door.

Suddenly I ran up to her, grabbed her hand, opened it, put something in . . . and closed it again. Then I turned away at once and bolted to the other corner, so that at least I wouldn't be able to see. . . .

I was just about to lie—to write that I'd done all this accidentally, without knowing what I was doing, in complete confusion, out of foolishness. But I don't want to lie; therefore I'll say straight out, that I opened her hand and placed something in it . . . out of spite. It occurred to me to do this while I was rushing back and forth across the room and she was sitting there behind the screen. But here's what I can say for sure: although I did this cruel thing deliberately, it was not from my heart, but from my stupid head. This cruelty of mine was so artificial, cerebral, intentionally invented, *bookish*, that I couldn't stand it myself even for one minute—at first I bolted to the corner so as not to see, and then, out of shame and in despair, I rushed out after Liza. I opened the door into the hallway and listened. "Liza! Liza!" I called down the stairs, but timidly, in a soft voice.

There was no answer; I thought I could hear her footsteps at the bottom of the stairs.

"Liza!" I cried more loudly.

No answer. But at that moment I heard down below the sound of the tight outer glass door opening heavily with a creak and then closing again tightly. The sound rose up the stairs.

She'd gone. I returned to my room deep in thought. I felt horribly oppressed.

I stood by the table near the chair where she'd been sitting and stared senselessly into space. A minute or so passed, then I suddenly started: right before me on the chair I saw . . . in a word, I saw the crumpled blue five-ruble note, the very one I'd thrust into her hand a few moments before. It was the same one; it couldn't be any other; I had none other in my apartment. So she'd managed to toss it down on the table when I'd bolted to the other corner.

So what? I might have expected her to do that. Might have expected it? No. I was such an egotist, in fact, I so lacked respect for other people, that

I couldn't even conceive that she'd ever do that. I couldn't stand it. A moment later, like a madman, I hurried to get dressed. I threw on whatever I happened to find, and rushed headlong after her. She couldn't have gone more than two hundred paces when I ran out on the street.

It was quiet; it was snowing heavily, and the snow was falling almost perpendicularly, blanketing the sidewalk and the deserted street. There were no passers-by; no sound could be heard. The street lights were flickering dismally and vainly. I ran about two hundred paces to the crossroads and stopped.

"Where did she go? And why am I running after her? Why? To fall down before her, sob with remorse, kiss her feet, and beg her forgiveness! That's just what I wanted. My heart was being torn apart; never, never will I recall that moment with indifference. But—why?" I wondered. "Won't I grow to hate her, perhaps as soon as tomorrow, precisely because I'm kissing her feet today? Will I ever be able to make her happy? Haven't I found out once again today, for the hundredth time, what I'm really worth? Won't I torment her?"

I stood in the snow, peering into the murky mist, and thought about all this.

"And wouldn't it be better, wouldn't it," I fantasized once I was home again, stifling the stabbing pain in my heart with such fantasies, "wouldn't it be better if she were to carry away the insult with her forever? Such an insult—after all, is purification; it's the most caustic and painful form of consciousness. Tomorrow I would have defiled her soul and wearied her heart. But now that insult will never die within her; no matter how abominable the filth that awaits her, that insult will elevate and purify her . . . by hatred . . . hmm . . . perhaps by forgiveness as well. But will that make it any easier for her?"

And now, in fact, I'll pose an idle question of my own. Which is better: cheap happiness or sublime suffering? Well, come on, which is better?

These were my thoughts as I sat home that evening, barely alive with the anguish in my soul. I'd never before endured so much suffering and remorse; but could there exist even the slightest doubt that when I went rushing out of my apartment, I'd turn back again after going only halfway? I never met Liza afterward, and I never heard anything more about her. I'll also add that for a long time I remained satisfied with my theory about the use of insults and hatred, in spite of the fact that I myself almost fell ill from anguish at the time.

Even now, after so many years, all this comes back to me as *very unpleasant*. A great deal that comes back to me now is very unpleasant, but . . . perhaps I should end these *Notes* here? I think that I made a mistake in beginning to write them. At least, I was ashamed all the time I was writing this *tale*: consequently, it's not really literature, but corrective punishment. After all, to tell you long stories about how, for example, I ruined my life through moral decay in my corner, by the lack of appropriate surroundings, by isolation from any living beings, and by futile malice in the underground— so help me God, that's not very interesting. A novel needs a hero, whereas here all the traits of an anti-hero have been assembled *deliberately*; but the most important thing is that all this produces an extremely unpleasant impression because we've all become estranged from life, we're all cripples, every one of us, more or less. We've become so estranged that at times we feel some kind of revulsion for genuine "real life," and therefore we can't bear to be reminded of it. Why, we've reached a point where we almost regard "real life" as hard work, as a job, and we've all agreed in private that it's really better in books. And why do we sometimes fuss, indulge in whims, and make demands? We don't know ourselves. It'd be even worse if all our whimsical desires were fulfilled. Go on, try it. Give us, for example, a little more independence; untie the hands of any one of us, broaden our sphere of activity, relax the controls, and . . . I can assure you, we'll immediately ask to have the controls reinstated. I know that you may get angry at me for saying this, you may shout and stamp your feet: "Speak for yourself," you'll say, "and for your own miseries in the underground, but don't you dare say 'all of us.' " If you'll allow me, gentlemen; after all, I'm not trying to justify myself by saying *all of us*. What concerns me in particular, is that in my life I've only taken to an extreme that which you haven't even dared to take halfway; what's more, you've mistaken your cowardice for good sense; and, in so deceiving yourself, you've consoled yourself. So, in fact, I may even be "more alive" than you are. Just take a closer look! Why, we don't even know where this "real life" lives nowadays, what it really is, and what it's called. Leave us alone without books and we'll get confused and lose our way at once—we won't know what to join, what to hold on to, what to love or what to hate, what to respect or what to despise. We're even oppressed by being men— men with real bodies and blood of *our very own*. We're ashamed of it; we consider it a disgrace and we strive to become some kind of impossible "general-human-beings." We're stillborn; for some time now we haven't been conceived by living fathers; we like it more and more. We're developing a taste for it. Soon we'll conceive of a way to be born from ideas. But enough; I don't want to write any more "from Underground. . . ."

However, the "notes" of this paradoxalist don't end here. He couldn't resist and kept on writing. But it also seems to us that we might as well stop here.

LEO TOLSTOY
1828–1910

Count Leo Tolstoy excited the interest of Europe mainly as a public figure: a count owning large estates who decided to give up his wealth and live like a simple Russian peasant—to dress in a blouse, to eat peasant food, and even to plow the fields and make shoes with his own hands. By the time of his death he had become the leader of a religious cult, the propounder of a new religion. It was, in substance, a highly simplified primitive Christianity that he reduced to a few moral commands (such as "Do not resist evil") and from which he drew, with radical consistency, a complete condemnation of modern civilization: the state, courts and law, war, patriotism, marriage, modern art and literature, science and medicine. In debating this Christian anarchism people have tended to forget that Tolstoy established his command of the public ear as a novelist, or they have exaggerated the contrast between the early worldly novelist and the later prophet who repudiated all his early, great novelistic work: *War and Peace*, the enormous epic of the 1812 invasion of Russia, and *Anna*

Karenina, the story of an adulterous love, superbly realized in accurately imagined detail.

Tolstoy was born at Yasnaya Polyana, his mother's estate near Tula (about 130 miles south of Moscow), on August 28, 1828. His father was a retired lieutenant colonel; one of his ancestors, the first count, had served Peter the Great as an ambassador. His mother's father was a Russian general in chief. Tolstoy lost both parents early in his life and was brought up by aunts. He went to the University of Kazan between 1844 and 1847, drifted along aimlessly for a few years after that, and in 1851 became a cadet in the Caucasus. As an artillery officer, he saw action in the wars with the mountain tribes and again, in 1854–55, during the Crimean War against the French and English. Tolstoy had written fictional reminiscences of his childhood while he was in the Caucasus; and during the Crimean War he wrote war stories, which established his literary reputation. For some years he lived on his estate, where he founded and himself taught at an extremely "progressive" school for peasant children. He made two trips to western Europe, in 1857 and in 1860–61. In 1862 he married the daughter of a physician, Sonya Bers, with whom he had thirteen children.

In the first years of his marriage, between 1863 and 1869, he wrote his enormous novel *War and Peace*. The book made him famous in Russia but was not translated into English until long afterward. Superficially, *War and Peace* is an historical novel about the Napoleonic invasion of Russia in 1812, a huge swarming epic of a nation's resistance to the foreigner. Tolstoy himself interprets history in general as a struggle of anonymous collective forces that are moved by unknown irrational impulses, waves of communal feeling. Heroes, great men and women, are actually not heroes but merely insignificant puppets; the best general is the one who does nothing to prevent the unknown course of Providence. But *War and Peace* is not only an impressive and vivid panorama of historical events but also the profound story—centered in two main characters, Pierre Bezukhov and Prince Andrey Bolkonsky—of a search for meaning in life. Andrey finds meaning in love and forgiveness of his enemies. Pierre, at the end of a long, groping struggle, an education by suffering, finds it in an acceptance of ordinary existence, its duties and pleasures, the family, the continuity of the race.

Tolstoy's next long novel, *Anna Karenina* (1875–77), resumes this second thread of *War and Peace*. It is a novel of contemporary manners, a narrative of adultery and suicide. But this vivid story, told with incomparable concrete imagination, is counterpointed and framed by a second story, that of Levin, another seeker after the meaning of life, a figure who represents the author, as Pierre did in the earlier book; the work ends with a promise of salvation, with the ideal of a life in which we should "remember God." Thus *Anna Karenina* also anticipates the approaching crisis in Tolstoy's life. When it came, with the sudden revulsion he describes in *A Confession* (1879), he condemned his earlier books and spent the next years in writing pamphlets and tracts expounding his religion.

Only slowly did Tolstoy return to the writing of fiction, now regarded entirely as a means of presenting his creed. The earlier novels seemed to him unclear in their message, overdetailed in their method. Hence Tolstoy tried to simplify his art; he wrote plays with a thesis, stories that are like fables or parables, and one long, rather inferior novel, *The Resurrection* (1899), his most savage satire on Russian and modern institutions.

In 1901 Tolstoy was excommunicated. A disagreement with his wife about the nature of the good life and about financial matters sharpened into a conflict over his last will, which finally led to a complete break: he left home in the company of a doctor friend. He caught cold on the train journey south and, on November 20, 1910, died in the house of the stationmaster of Astapovo.

If we look back on Tolstoy's work as a whole, we must recognize its continuity. From the very beginning he was a Rousseauist. As early as 1851, when he was in the Caucasus, his diary announced his intention of founding a new, simplified religion.

Even as a young man on his estate he had lived quite simply, like a peasant, except for occasional sprees and debauches. He had been horrified by war from the very beginning, although he admired the heroism of the individual soldier and had remnants of patriotic feeling. All his books concern the same theme—the good life—and they all say that the good life lies outside civilization, near the soil, in simplicity and humility, in love of one's neighbor. Power, the lust for power, luxury are always evil.

Tolstoy's roots as a novelist are part of another, older realistic tradition. He read and knew the English writers of the eighteenth century—and also William Makepeace Thackeray and Anthony Trollope—although he did not care for the recent French writers (he strongly disapproved of Gustave Flaubert) except for Guy de Maupassant, who struck him as truthful and useful in his struggle against hypocrisy. Tolstoy's long novels are loosely plotted even though they have large overall designs. They work by little scenes vividly visualized, by an accumulation of exact detail. Each character is drawn by means of repeated emphasis on certain physical traits, like Pierre's shortsightedness and his hairy, clumsy hands, or Princess Marya's luminous eyes, the red patches on her face, and her shuffling gait. This concretely realized surface, however, everywhere recedes into depths: to the depiction of disease, delirium, and death and to glimpses into eternity. In *War and Peace* the blue sky is the recurrent symbol for the metaphysical spirit within us. Tolstoy is so robust, has his feet so firmly on the ground, presents what he sees with such clarity and objectivity, that one can be easily deluded into considering his dominating quality to be physical, sensual, antithetical to Dostoevsky's spirituality. The contrasts between the two greatest Russian novelists are indeed obvious. While Tolstoy's method can be called epic, Dostoevsky's is dramatic; while Tolstoy's view of humanity is Rousseauistic, Dostoevsky stresses the Fall; while Tolstoy rejects history and status, Dostoevsky appeals to the past and desires a hierarchical society; and so on. But these profound differences should not obscure one basic similarity: the deep spirituality of both writers, their rejection of the basic materialism and the conception of truth propounded by modern science and theorists of realism.

The Death of Ivan Ilyich (1886) was written after Tolstoy's religious conversion, when he slowly returned to fiction writing; it represents a happy medium between his early and late manner. Its story and moral are simple and obvious, as always with Tolstoy (in contrast to Dostoevsky). And it expresses what almost all of his works are intended to convey—that humanity is leading the wrong kind of life, that we should return to essentials, to "nature." In *The Death of Ivan Ilyich* Tolstoy combines a savage satire on the futility and hypocrisy of conventional life with a powerful symbolic presentation of isolation in the struggle with death and of hope for a final resurrection. Ivan Ilyich is a Russian judge, an official, but he is also the average man of the prosperous middle classes of his time and ours and Everyman confronted with disease and dying and death. He is an ordinary person, neither virtuous nor particularly vicious, a "go-getter" in his profession, a "family man," as marriages go, who has children but has drifted apart from his wife. Through his disease, which comes about by a trivial accident in the trivial business of fixing a curtain, Ivan Ilyich is slowly awakened to self-consciousness and a realization of the falsity of his life and ambitions. The isolation that disease imposes on him, the wall of hypocrisy erected around him by his family and his doctors, his suffering and pain, drive him slowly to the recognition of *It:* to a knowledge, not merely theoretical but proved on his pulses, of his own mortality. At first he would like simply to return to his former pleasant and normal life—even in the last days of his illness, knowing he must die, he screams in his agony, "I won't!"—but at the end, struggling in the black sack into which he is being pushed, he sees the light at the bottom. " 'Death is finished,' he said to himself. 'It is no more!' "

The people around him are egotists and hypocrites: his wife, who can remember only how she suffered during his agony; his daughter, who thinks only of the delay in her marriage; his colleagues, who speculate only about the room that his death will make for promotions in the court; the doctors, who think only of the name of the disease and not of the patient; all except his shy and frightened son, Vasya, and the servant Gerasim. Because he is young, near to "nature," and free from hypocrisy, Gerasim is able to make his master more comfortable and even to mention death, while all the others conceal the truth from him. The doctors, especially, are shown as mere specialists, inhuman and selfish. The first doctor is like a judge—like Ivan himself when he sat in court—summing up and cutting off further questions of the patient. The satire at points appears ineffectively harsh in its violence, but it will not seem exceptional to those who know the older Tolstoy's general attitude toward courts, medicine, marriage, and even modern literature. The cult of art is jeered at, in small touches, only incidentally; it belongs, according to Tolstoy, to the falsities of modern civilization, alongside marriage (which merely hides bestial sensuality) and science (which merely hides rapacity and ignorance).

The story is deliberately deprived of any element of suspense, not only by the announcement contained in the title but by the technique of the flashback. We first hear of Ivan Ilyich's death and see the reaction of the widow and friends, and only then listen to the story of his life. The detail, as always in Tolstoy, is superbly concrete and realistic: he does not shy away from the smell of disease, the physical necessity of using a chamber pot, or the sound of screaming. He can employ the creaking of a hassock as a recurrent motif to point out the comedy of hypocrisy played by the widow and her visitor. He can seriously and tragically use the humble image of a black sack or the illusion of the movement of a train.

But all this naturalistic detail serves the one purpose of making us realize, as Ivan Ilyich realizes, that not only is Caius mortal but you and I also, and that the life of "civilized" people is a great lie simply because it disguises and ignores its dark background, the metaphysical abyss, the reality of Death. While the presentation of *The Death of Ivan Ilyich* approaches, at moments, the tone of a legend or fable ("Ivan Ilyich's life had been most simple and most ordinary and therefore most terrible"), Tolstoy in this story manages to stay within the concrete situation of his society and to combine the aesthetic method of realism with the universalizing power of symbolic art.

PRONOUNCING GLOSSARY

The following list uses common English syllables and stress accents to provide rough equivalents of selected words whose pronunciation may be unfamiliar to the general reader.

Fëdor Petrovich: *fyaw'-dur pe-traw'-veech*

Fëdor Vasilievich: *fyaw'-dur vah-seel'-ye-veech*

Gerasim: *gye-rah'-syeem*

Golovin: *guh-lah-veen'*

Ivan Ilyich: *ee-vahn' il-yeech'*

Ivanovich: *ee-vah'-nuh-veech*

Karenina: *kah-re'-nyee-nuh*

The Death of Ivan Ilyich[1]

I

During an interval in the Melvinski trial in the large building of the Law Courts the members and public prosecutor met in Ivan Egorovich Shebek's

1. Translated by Louise Maude and Aylmer Maude.

private room, where the conversation turned on the celebrated Krasovski case. Fëdor Vasilievich warmly maintained that it was not subject to their jurisdiction, Ivan Egorovich maintained the contrary, while Peter Ivanovich, not having entered into the discussion at the start, took no part in it but looked through the *Gazette* which had just been handed in.

"Gentlemen," he said, "Ivan Ilyich has died!"

"You don't say!"

"Here read it yourself," replied Peter Ivanovich, handing Fëdor Vasilievich the paper still damp from the press. Surrounded by a black border were the words: "Praskovya Fëdorovna Golovina, with profound sorrow, informs relatives and friends of the demise of her beloved husband Ivan Ilyich Golovin, Member of the Court of Justice, which occurred on February the 4th of this year 1882. The funeral will take place on Friday at one o'clock in the afternoon."

Ivan Ilyich had been a colleague of the gentlemen present and was liked by them all. He had been ill for some weeks with an illness said to be incurable. His post had been kept open for him, but there had been conjectures that in case of his death Alexeev might receive his appointment, and that either Vinnikov or Shtabel would succeed Alexeev. So on receiving the news of Ivan Ilyich's death the first thought of each of the gentlemen in that private room was of the changes and promotions it might occasion among themselves or their acquaintances.

"I shall be sure to get Shtabel's place or Vinnikov's," thought Fëdor Vasilievich. "I was promised that long ago, and the promotion means an extra eight hundred rubles a year for me besides the allowance."

"Now I must apply for my brother-in-law's transfer from Kaluga," thought Peter Ivanovich. "My wife will be very glad, and then she won't be able to say that I never do anything for her relations."

"I thought he would never leave his bed again," said Peter Ivanovich aloud. "It's very sad."

"But what really was the matter with him?"

"The doctors couldn't say—at least they could, but each of them said something different. When last I saw him I thought he was getting better."

"And I haven't been to see him since the holidays. I always meant to go."

"Had he any property?"

"I think his wife had a little—but something quite trifling."

"We shall have to go to see her, but they live so terribly far away."

"Far away from you, you mean. Everything's far away from your place."

"You see, he never can forgive my living on the other side of the river," said Peter Ivanovich, smiling at Shebek. Then, still talking of the distances between different parts of the city, they returned to the Court.

Besides considerations as to the possible transfers and promotions likely to result from Ivan Ilyich's death, the mere fact of the death of a near acquaintance aroused, as usual, in all who heard of it the complacent feeling that, "it is he who is dead and not I."

Each one thought or felt, "Well, he's dead but I'm alive!" But the more intimate of Ivan Ilyich's acquaintances, his so-called friends, could not help thinking also that they would now have to fulfil the very tiresome demands of propriety by attending the funeral service and paying a visit of condolence to the widow.

Fëdor Vasilievich and Peter Ivanovich had been his nearest acquaintances. Peter Ivanovich had studied law with Ivan Ilyich and had considered himself to be under obligations to him.

Having told his wife at dinner-time of Ivan Ilyich's death, and of his conjecture that it might be possible to get her brother transferred to their circuit, Peter Ivanovich sacrificed his usual nap, put on his evening clothes, and drove to Ivan Ilyich's house.

At the entrance stood a carriage and two cabs. Leaning against the wall in the hall downstairs near the cloak-stand was a coffin-lid covered with cloth of gold, ornamented with gold cord and tassels, that had been polished up with metal powder. Two ladies in black were taking off their fur cloaks. Peter Ivanovich recognized one of them as Ivan Ilyich's sister, but the other was a stranger to him. His colleague Schwartz was just coming downstairs, but on seeing Peter Ivanovich enter he stopped and winked at him, as if to say: "Ivan Ilyich has made a mess of things—not like you and me."

Schwartz's face with his Piccadilly whiskers, and his slim figure in evening dress, had as usual an air of elegant solemnity which contrasted with the playfulness of his character and had a special piquancy here, or so it seemed to Peter Ivanovich.

Peter Ivanovich allowed the ladies to precede him and slowly followed them upstairs. Schwartz did not come down but remained where he was, and Peter Ivanovich understood that he wanted to arrange where they should play bridge that evening. The ladies went upstairs to the widow's room, and Schwartz with seriously compressed lips but a playful look in his eyes, indicated by a twist of his eyebrows the room to the right where the body lay.

Peter Ivanovich, like everyone else on such occasions, entered feeling uncertain what he would have to do. All he knew was that at such times it is always safe to cross oneself. But he was not quite sure whether one should make obeisances while doing so. He therefore adopted a middle course. On entering the room he began crossing himself and made a slight movement resembling a bow. At the same time, as far as the motion of his head and arm allowed, he surveyed the room. Two young men—apparently nephews, one of whom was a high-school pupil—were leaving the room, crossing themselves as they did so. An old woman was standing motionless, and a lady with strangely arched eyebrows was saying something to her in a whisper. A vigorous, resolute Church Reader, in a frock-coat, was reading something in a loud voice with an expression that precluded any contradiction. The butler's assistant, Gerasim, stepping lightly in front of Peter Ivanovich, was strewing something on the floor. Noticing this, Peter Ivanovich was immediately aware of a faint odour of a decomposing body.

The last time he had called on Ivan Ilyich, Peter Ivanovich had seen Gerasim in the study. Ivan Ilyich had been particularly fond of him and he was performing the duty of a sick nurse.

Peter Ivanovich continued to make the sign of the cross slightly inclining his head in an intermediate direction between the coffin, the Reader, and the icons on the table in a corner of the room. Afterwards, when it seemed to him that this movement of his arm in crossing himself had gone on too long, he stopped and began to look at the corpse.

The dead man lay, as dead men always lie, in a specially heavy way, his rigid limbs sunk in the soft cushions of the coffin, with the head forever bowed on the pillow. His yellow waxen brow with bald patches over his sunken temples was thrust up in the way peculiar to the dead, the protruding nose seeming to press on the upper lip. He was much changed and had grown even thinner since Peter Ivanovich had last seen him, but, as is always the case with the dead, his face was handsomer and above all more dignified than when he was alive. The expression on the face said that what was necessary had been accomplished, and accomplished rightly. Besides this there was in that expression a reproach and a warning to the living. This warning seemed to Peter Ivanovich out of place, or at least not applicable to him. He felt a certain discomfort and so he hurriedly crossed himself once more and turned and went out of the door—too hurriedly and too regardless of propriety, as he himself was aware. *He is disconcerted by the dead Ivan*

Schwartz was waiting for him in the adjoining room with legs spread wide apart and both hands toying with his top-hat behind his back. The mere sight of that playful, well-groomed, and elegant figure refreshed Peter Ivanovich. He felt that Schwartz was above all these happenings and could not surrender to any depressing influences. His very look said that this incident of a church service for Ivan Ilyich could not be a sufficient reason for infringing the order of the session—in other words, that it would certainly not prevent his unwrapping a new pack of cards and shuffling them that evening while a footman placed four fresh candles on the table: in fact, that there was no reason for supposing that this incident would hinder their spending the evening agreeably. Indeed he said this in a whisper as Peter Ivanovich passed him, proposing that they should meet for a game at Fëdor Vasilievich's. But apparently Peter Ivanovich was not destined to play bridge that evening. Praskovya Fëdorovna (a short, fat woman who despite all efforts to the contrary had continued to broaden steadily from her shoulders downwards and who had the same extraordinary arched eyebrows as the lady who had been standing by the coffin), dressed all in black, her head covered with lace, came out of her own room with some other ladies, conducted them to the room where the dead body lay, and said: "The service will begin immediately. Please go in."

Schwartz, making an indefinite bow, stood still, evidently neither accepting nor declining this invitation. Praskovya Fëdorovna recognizing Peter Ivanovich, sighed, went close up to him, took his hand, and said: "I know you were a true friend to Ivan Ilyich . . ." and looked at him awaiting some suitable response. And Peter Ivanovich knew that, just as it had been the right thing to cross himself in that room, so what he had to do here was to press her hand, sigh, and say, "Believe me . . ." So he did all this and as he did it felt that the desired result had been achieved: that both he and she were touched.

"Come with me. I want to speak to you before it begins," said the widow. "Give me your arm."

Peter Ivanovich gave her his arm and they went to the inner rooms, passing Schwartz who winked at Peter Ivanovich compassionately.

"That does for our bridge! Don't object if we find another player. Perhaps you can cut in when you do escape," said his playful look.

Peter Ivanovich sighed still more deeply and despondently, and Praskovya Fëdorovna pressed his arm gratefully. When they reached the drawing-room, upholstered in pink cretonne and lighted by a dim lamp, they sat down at the table—she on a sofa and Peter Ivanovich on a low hassock, the springs of which yielded spasmodically under his weight. Praskovya Fëdorovna had been on the point of warning him to take another seat, but felt that such a warning was out of keeping with her present condition and so changed her mind. As he sat down on the hassock Peter Ivanovich recalled how Ivan Ilyich had arranged this room and had consulted him regarding this pink cretonne with green leaves. The whole room was full of furniture and knick-knacks, and on her way to the sofa the lace of the widow's black shawl caught on the carved edge of the table. Peter Ivanovich rose to detach it, and the springs of the hassock, relieved of his weight, rose also and gave him a push. The widow began detaching her shawl herself, and Peter Ivanovich again sat down, suppressing the rebellious springs of the hassock under him. But the widow had not quite freed herself and Peter Ivanovich got up again, and again the hassock rebelled and even creaked. When this was all over she took out a clean cambric handkerchief and began to weep. The episode with the shawl and the struggle with the hassock had cooled Peter Ivanovich's emotions and he sat there with a sullen look on his face. This awkward situation was interrupted by Sokolov, Ivan Ilyich's butler, who came to report that the plot in the cemetery that Praskovya Fëdorovna had chosen would cost two hundred rubles. She stopped weeping and, looking at Peter Ivanovich with the air of a victim, remarked in French that it was very hard for her. Peter Ivanovich made a silent gesture signifying his full conviction that it must indeed be so.

"Please smoke," she said in a magnanimous yet crushed voice, and turned to discuss with Sokolov the price of the plot for the grave.

Peter Ivanovich while lighting his cigarette heard her inquiring very circumstantially into the prices of different plots in the cemetery and finally decide which she would take. When that was done she gave instructions about engaging the choir. Sokolov then left the room.

"I look after everything myself," she told Peter Ivanovich, shifting the albums that lay on the table; and noticing that the table was endangered by his cigarette-ash, she immediately passed him an ashtray, saying as she did so: "I consider it an affectation to say that my grief prevents my attending to practical affairs. On the contrary, if anything can—I won't say console me, but—distract me, it is seeing to everything concerning him." She again took out her handkerchief as if preparing to cry, but suddenly, as if mastering her feeling, she shook herself and began to speak calmly. "But there is something I want to talk to you about."

Peter Ivanovich bowed, keeping control of the springs of the hassock, which immediately began quivering under him.

"He suffered terribly the last few days."

"Did he?" said Peter Ivanovich.

"Oh, terribly! He screamed unceasingly, not for minutes but for hours. For the last three days he screamed incessantly. It was unendurable. I cannot understand how I bore it; you could hear him three rooms off. Oh, what I have suffered!"

"Is it possible that he was conscious all that time?" asked Peter Ivanovich.

"Yes," she whispered. "To the last moment. He took leave of us a quarter of an hour before he died, and asked us to take Vasya away."

The thought of the sufferings of this man he had known so intimately,

He is touched by Ivan's suffering

first as a merry little boy, then as a school-mate, and later as a grown-up colleague, suddenly struck Peter Ivanovich with horror, despite an unpleasant consciousness of his own and this woman's dissimulation. He again saw that brow, and that nose pressing down on the lip, and felt afraid for himself.

"Three days of frightful suffering and then death! Why, that might suddenly, at any time, happen to me," he thought, and for a moment felt terrified. But—he did not himself know how—the customary reflection at once occurred to him that this had happened to Ivan Ilyich and not to him, and that it should not and could not happen to him, and that to think that it could would be yielding to depression which he ought not to do, as Schwartz's expression plainly showed. After which reflection Peter Ivanovich felt reassured, and began to ask with interest about the details of Ivan Ilyich's death, as though death was an accident natural to Ivan Ilyich but certainly not to himself.

After many details of the really dreadful physical sufferings Ivan Ilyich had endured (which details he learnt only from the effect those sufferings had produced on Praskovya Fëdorovna's nerves) the widow apparently found it necessary to get to business.

"Oh, Peter Ivanovich, how hard it is! How terribly, terribly hard!" and she again began to weep.

Peter Ivanovich sighed and waited for her to finish blowing her nose. When she had done so he said, "Believe me . . ." and she again began talking and brought out what was evidently her chief concern with him—namely, to question him as to how she could obtain a grant of money from the government on the occasion of her husband's death. She made it appear that she was asking Peter Ivanovich's advice about her pension, but he soon saw that she already knew about that to the minutest detail, more even than he did himself. She knew how much could be got out of the government in consequence of her husband's death, but wanted to find out whether she could possibly extract something more. Peter Ivanovich tried to think of some means of doing so, but after reflecting for a while and, out of propriety, condemning the government for its niggardliness, he said he thought that nothing more could be got. Then she sighed and evidently began to devise means of getting rid of her visitor. Noticing this, he put out his cigarette, rose, pressed her hand, and went out into the anteroom.

In the dining-room where the clock stood that Ivan Ilyich had liked so much and had bought at an antique shop, Peter Ivanovich met a priest and a few acquaintances who had come to attend the service, and he recognized Ivan Ilyich's daughter, a handsome young woman. She was in black and her slim figure appeared slimmer than ever. She had a gloomy, determined, almost angry expression, and bowed to Peter Ivanovich as though he were in some way to blame. Behind her, with the same offended look, stood a wealthy young man, an examining magistrate, whom Peter Ivanovich also knew and who was her fiancé, as he had heard. He bowed mournfully to them and was about to pass into the death-chamber, when from under the stairs appeared the figure of Ivan Ilyich's schoolboy son, who was extremely like this father. He seemed a little Ivan Ilyich, such as Peter Ivanovich remembered when they studied law together. His tear-stained eyes had in them the look that is seen in the eyes of boys of thirteen or fourteen who are not pure-minded.

When he saw Peter Ivanovich he scowled morosely and shamefacedly. Peter Ivanovich nodded to him and entered the death-chamber. The service began: candles, groans, incense, tears, and sobs. Peter Ivanovich stood looking gloomily down at his feet. He did not look once at the dead man, did not yield to any depressing influence, and was one of the first to leave the room. There was no one in the anteroom, but Gerasim darted out of the dead man's room, rummaged with his strong hands among the fur coats to find Peter Ivanovich's and helped him on with it.

"Well, friend Gerasim," said Peter Ivanovich, so as to say something. "It's a sad affair, isn't it?"

"It's God's will. We shall all come to it some day," said Gerasim, displaying his teeth—the even, white teeth of a healthy peasant—and, like a man in the thick of urgent work, he briskly opened the front door, called the coachman, helped Peter Ivanovich into the sledge, and sprang back to the porch as if in readiness for what he had to do next.

Peter Ivanovich found the fresh air particularly pleasant after the smell of incense, the dead body, and carbolic acid.

"Where to, sir?" asked the coachman.

"It's not too late even now. . . . I'll call round on Fëdor Vasilievich."

He accordingly drove there and found them just finishing the first rubber, so that it was quite convenient for him to cut in.

II

Ivan Ilyich's life had been most simple and most ordinary and therefore most terrible.

He had been a member of the Court of Justice, and died at the age of forty-five. His father had been an official who after serving in various ministries and departments in Petersburg had made the sort of career which brings men to positions from which by reason of their long service they cannot be dismissed, though they are obviously unfit to hold any responsible position, and for whom therefore posts are specially created, which though fictitious, carry salaries of from six to ten thousand rubles that are not fictitious, and in receipt of which they live on to a great age.

Such was the Privy Councillor and superfluous member of various superfluous institutions, Ilya Efimovich Golovin.

He had three sons, of whom Ivan Ilyich was the second. The eldest son was following in his father's footsteps only in another department, and was already approaching that stage in the service at which a similar sinecure would be reached. The third son was a failure. He had ruined his prospects in a number of positions and was now serving in the railway department. His father and brothers, and still more their wives, not merely disliked meeting him, but avoided remembering his existence unless compelled to do so. His sister had married Baron Greff, a Petersburg official of her father's type. Ivan Ilyich was le phénix de la famille[2] as people said. He was neither as cold and formal as his elder brother nor as wild as the younger, but was a happy mean between them—an intelligent, polished, lively and agreeable man. He had studied with his younger brother at the School of Law, but the latter had

2. The phoenix of the family (French). The word phoenix is used here to mean "rare bird," "prodigy."

failed to complete the course and was expelled when he was in the fifth class. Ivan Ilyich finished the course well. Even when he was at the School of Law he was just what he remained for the rest of his life: a capable, cheerful, good-natured, and sociable man, though strict in the fulfilment of what he considered to be his duty: and he considered his duty to be what was so considered by those in authority. Neither as a boy nor as a man was he a toady, but from early youth was by nature attracted to people of high station as a fly is drawn to the light, assimilating their ways and views of life and establishing friendly relations with them. All the enthusiasms of childhood and youth passed without leaving much trace on him; he succumbed to sensuality, to vanity, and latterly among the highest classes to liberalism, but always within limits which his instinct unfailingly indicated to him as correct.

At school he had done things which had formerly seemed to him very horrid and made him feel disgusted with himself when he did them; but when later on he saw that such actions were done by people of good position and that they did not regard them as wrong, he was able not exactly to regard them as right, but to forget about them entirely or not be at all troubled at remembering them.

Having graduated from the School of Law and qualified for the tenth rank of the civil service, and having received money from his father for his equipment, Ivan Ilyich ordered himself clothes at Scharmer's, the fashionable tailor, hung a medallion inscribed *respice finem*[3] on his watch-chain, took leave of his professor and the prince who was patron of the school, had a farewell dinner with his comrades at Donon's first-class restaurant, and with his new and fashionable portmanteau, linen, clothes, shaving and other toilet appliances, and a travelling rug, all purchased at the best shops, he set off for one of the provinces where, through his father's influence, he had been attached to the governor as an official for special service.

In the province Ivan Ilyich soon arranged as easy and agreeable a position for himself as he had at the School of Law. He performed his official tasks, made his career, and at the same time amused himself pleasantly and decorously. Occasionally he paid official visits to country districts, where he behaved with dignity both to his superiors and inferiors, and performed the duties entrusted to him, which related chiefly to the sectarians,[4] with an exactness and incorruptible honesty of which he could not but feel proud.

In official matters, despite his youth and taste for frivolous gaiety, he was exceedingly reserved, punctilious, and even severe; but in society he was often amusing and witty, and always good-natured, correct in his manner, and *bon enfant,* as the governor and his wife—with whom he was like one of the family—used to say of him.

In the province he had an affair with a lady who made advances to the elegant young lawyer, and there was also a milliner; and there were carousals with aides-de-camp who visited the district, and after-supper visits to a certain outlying street of doubtful reputation; and there was too some obsequiousness to his chief and even to his chief's wife, but all this was done with such a tone of good breeding that no hard names could be applied to it. It all came under the heading of the French saying: *"Il faut que jeunesse se*

---

3. Regard the end (a Latin motto).   4. The Old Believers, a large group of Russians (about 25 million in 1900), members of a sect that originated in a break with the Orthodox Church in the 17th century; they were subject to many legal restrictions.

passe."[5] It was all done with clean hands, in clean linen, with French phrases, and above all among people of the best society and consequently with the approval of people of rank.

So Ivan Ilyich served for five years and then came a change in his official life. The new and reformed judicial institutions were introduced, and new men were needed. Ivan Ilyich became such a new man. He was offered the post of Examining Magistrate, and he accepted it though the post was in another province and obliged him to give up the connexions he had formed and to make new ones. His friends met to give him a send-off; they had a group-photograph taken and presented him with a silver cigarette-case, and he set off to his new post.

As examining magistrate Ivan Ilyich was just as *comme il faut* and decorous a man, inspiring general respect and capable of separating his official duties from his private life, as he had been when acting as an official on special service. His duties now as examining magistrate were far more interesting and attractive than before. In his former position it had been pleasant to wear an undress uniform made by Scharmer, and to pass through the crowd of petitioners and officials who were timorously awaiting an audience with the governor, and who envied him as with free and easy gait he went straight into his chief's private room to have a cup of tea and a cigarette with him. But not many people had then been directly dependent on him—only police officials and the sectarians when he went on special missions—and he liked to treat them politely, almost as comrades, as if he were letting them feel that he who had the power to crush them was treating them in this simple, friendly way. There were then but few such people. But now, as an examining magistrate, Ivan Ilyich felt that everyone without exception, even the most important and self-satisfied, was in his power, and that he need only write a few words on a sheet of paper with a certain heading, and this or that important, self-satisfied person would be brought before him in the role of an accused person or a witness, and if he did not choose to allow him to sit down, would have to stand before him and answer his questions. Ivan Ilyich never abused his power; he tried on the contrary to soften its expression, but the consciousness of it and of the possibility of softening its effect, supplied the chief interest and attraction of his office. In his work itself, especially in his examinations, he very soon acquired a method of eliminating all considerations irrelevant to the legal aspect of the case, and reducing even the most complicated case to a form in which it would be presented on paper only in its externals, completely excluding his personal opinion of the matter, while above all observing every prescribed formality. The work was new and Ivan Ilyich was one of the first men to apply the new Code of 1864.[6]

On taking up the post of examining magistrate in a new town, he made new acquaintances and connexions, placed himself on a new footing, and assumed a somewhat different tone. He took up an attitude of rather dignified aloofness towards the provincial authorities, but picked out the best circle of legal gentlemen and wealthy gentry living in the town and assumed a tone of slight dissatisfaction with the government, of moderate liberalism, and of enlightened citizenship. At the same time, without at all altering the

---

5. Youth must have its fling [Translators' note].   6. The emancipation of the serfs in 1861 was followed by a thorough all-round reform of judicial proceedings [Translators' note].

elegance of his toilet, he ceased shaving his chin and allowed his beard to grow as it pleased.

Ivan Ilyich settled down very pleasantly in this new town. The society there, which inclined towards opposition to the governor, was friendly, his salary was larger, and he began to play *vint* [a form of bridge], which he found added not a little to the pleasure of life, for he had a capacity for cards, played good-humouredly, and calculated rapidly and astutely, so that he usually won.

After living there for two years he met his future wife, Praskovya Fëdorovna Mikhel, who was the most attractive, clever, and brilliant girl of the set in which he moved, and among other amusements and relaxations from his labours as examining magistrate, Ivan Ilyich established light and playful relations with her.

While he had been an official on special service he had been accustomed to dance, but now as an examining magistrate it was exceptional for him to do so. If he danced now, he did it as if to show that though he served under the reformed order of things, and had reached the fifth official rank, yet when it came to dancing he could do it better than most people. So at the end of an evening he sometimes danced with Praskovya Fëdorovna, and it was chiefly during these dances that he captivated her. She fell in love with him. Ivan Ilyich had at first no definite intention of marrying, but when the girl fell in love with him he said to himself: "Really, why shouldn't I marry?"

Praskovya Fëdorovna came of a good family, was not bad looking, and had some little property. Ivan Ilyich might have aspired to a more brilliant match, but even this was good. He had his salary, and she, he hoped, would have an equal income. She was well connected, and was a sweet, pretty, and thoroughly correct young woman. To say that Ivan Ilyich married because he fell in love with Praskovya Fëdorovna and found that she sympathized with his views of life would be as incorrect as to say that he married because his social circle approved of the match. He was swayed by both these considerations: the marriage gave him personal satisfaction, and at the same time it was considered the right thing by the most highly placed of his associates.

So Ivan Ilyich got married.

The preparations for marriage and the beginning of married life, with its conjugal caresses, the new furniture, new crockery, and new linen, were very pleasant until his wife became pregnant—so that Ivan Ilyich had begun to think that marriage would not impair the easy, agreeable, gay, and always decorous character of his life, approved of by society and regarded by himself as natural, but would even improve it. But from the first months of his wife's pregnancy, something new, unpleasant, depressing, and unseemly, and from which there was no way of escape, unexpectedly showed itself.

His wife, without any reason—*de gaieté de coeur*[7] as Ivan Ilyich expressed it to himself—began to disturb the pleasure and propriety of their life. She began to be jealous without any cause, expected him to devote his whole attention to her, found fault with everything, and made coarse and ill-mannered scenes.

At first Ivan Ilyich hoped to escape from the unpleasantness of this state

7. From sheer impulsiveness (French).

of affairs by the same easy and decorous relation to life that had served him heretofore: he tried to ignore his wife's disagreeable moods, continued to live in his usual easy and pleasant way, invited friends to his house for a game of cards, and also tried going out to his club or spending his evenings with friends. But one day his wife began upbraiding him so vigorously, using such coarse words, and continued to abuse him every time he did not fulfil her demands, so resolutely and with such evident determination not to give way till he submitted—that is, till he stayed at home and was bored just as she was—that he became alarmed. He now realized that matrimony—at any rate with Praskovya Fëdorovna—was not always conducive to the pleasures and amenities of life, but on the contrary often infringed both comfort and propriety, and that he must therefore entrench himself against such infringement. And Ivan Ilyich began to seek for means of doing so. His official duties were the one thing that imposed upon Praskovya Fëdorovna, and by means of his official work and the duties attached to it he began struggling with his wife to secure his own independence.

With the birth of their child, the attempts to feed it and the various failures in doing so, and with the real and imaginary illnesses of mother and child, in which Ivan Ilyich's sympathy was demanded but about which he understood nothing, the need of securing for himself an existence outside his family life became still more imperative.

As his wife grew more irritable and exacting and Ivan Ilyich transferred the centre of gravity of his life more and more to his official work, so did he grow to like his work better and became more ambitious than before.

Very soon, within a year of his wedding, Ivan Ilyich had realized that marriage, though it may add some comforts to life, is in fact a very intricate and difficult affair towards which in order to perform one's duty, that is, to lead a decorous life approved of by society, one must adopt a definite attitude just as towards one's official duties.

And Ivan Ilyich evolved such an attitude towards married life. He only required of it those conveniences—dinner at home, housewife, and bed—which it could give him, and above all that propriety of external forms required by public opinion. For the rest he looked for light-hearted pleasure and propriety, and was very thankful when he found them, but if he met with antagonism and querulousness he at once retired into his separate fenced-off world of official duties, where he found satisfaction.

Ivan Ilyich was esteemed a good official, and after three years was made Assistant Public Prosecutor. His new duties, their importance, the possibility of indicting and imprisoning anyone he chose, the publicity his speeches received, and the success he had in all these things, made his work still more attractive.

More children came. His wife became more and more querulous and ill-tempered, but the attitude Ivan Ilyich had adopted towards his home life rendered him almost impervious to her grumbling.

After seven years' service in that town he was transferred to another province as Public Prosecutor. They moved, but were short of money and his wife did not like the place they moved to. Though the salary was higher the cost of living was greater, besides which two of their children died and family life became still more unpleasant for him.

Praskovya Fëdorovna blamed her husband for every inconvenience they encountered in their new home. Most of the conversations between husband and wife, especially as to the children's education, led to topics which recalled former disputes, and those disputes were apt to flare up again at any moment. There remained only those rare periods of amorousness which still came to them at times but did not last long. These were islets at which they anchored for a while and then again set out upon that ocean of veiled hostility which showed itself in their aloofness from one another. This aloofness might have grieved Ivan Ilyich had he considered that it ought not to exist, but he now regarded the position as normal, and even made it the goal at which he aimed in family life. His aim was to free himself more and more from those unpleasantnesses and to give them a semblance of harmlessness and propriety. He attained this by spending less and less time with his family, and when obliged to be at home he tried to safeguard his position by the presence of outsiders. The chief thing however was that he had his official duties. The whole interest of his life now centered in the official world and that interest absorbed him. The consciousness of his power, being able to ruin anybody he wished to ruin, the importance, even the external dignity of his entry into court, or meetings with his subordinates, his success with superiors and inferiors, and above all his masterly handling of cases, of which he was conscious—all this gave him pleasure and filled his life, together with chats with his colleagues, dinners, and bridge. So that on the whole Ivan Ilyich's life continued to flow as he considered it should do—pleasantly and properly.

So things continued for another seven years. His eldest daughter was already sixteen, another child had died, and only one son was left, a schoolboy and a subject of dissensions. Ivan Ilyich wanted to put him in the School of Law, but to spite him Praskovya Fëdorovna entered him at the High School. The daughter had been educated at home and had turned out well: the boy did not learn badly either.

III

So Ivan Ilyich lived for seventeen years after his marriage. He was already a Public Prosecutor of long standing, and had declined several proposed transfers while awaiting a more desirable post, when an unanticipated and unpleasant occurrence quite upset the peaceful course of his life. He was expecting to be offered the post of presiding judge in a University town, but Hoppe somehow came to the front and obtained the appointment instead. Ivan Ilyich became irritable, reproached Hoppe, and quarrelled both with him and with his immediate superiors—who became colder to him and again passed him over when other appointments were made.

This was in 1880, the hardest year of Ivan Ilyich's life. It was then that it became evident on the one hand that his salary was insufficient for them to live on, and on the other that he had been forgotten, and not only this, but that what was for him the greatest and most cruel injustice appeared to others a quite ordinary occurrence. Even his father did not consider it his duty to help him. Ivan Ilyich felt himself abandoned by everyone, and that they regarded his position with a salary of 3,500 rubles as quite normal and even fortunate. He alone knew that with the consciousness of the injustices done him, with his wife's incessant nagging, and with the debts he had contracted by living beyond his means his position was far from normal.

In order to save money that summer he obtained leave of absence and went with his wife to live in the country at her brother's place.

In the country, without his work, he experienced *ennui* for the first time in his life, and not only *ennui* but intolerable depression, and he decided that it was impossible to go on living like that, and that it was necessary to take energetic measures.

Having passed a sleepless night pacing up and down the veranda, he decided to go to Petersburg and bestir himself, in order to punish those who had failed to appreciate him and to get transferred to another ministry.

Next day, despite many protests from his wife and her brother, he started for Petersburg with the sole object of obtaining a post with a salary of five thousand rubles a year. He was no longer bent on any particular department, or tendency, or kind of activity. All he now wanted was an appointment to another post with a salary of five thousand rubles, either in the administration, in the banks, with the railways, in one of the Empress Marya's Institutions,[8] or even in the customs—but it had to carry with it a salary of five thousand rubles and be in a ministry other than that in which they had failed to appreciate him.

And this quest of Ivan Ilyich's was crowned with remarkable and unexpected success. At Kursk an acquaintance of his, F. I. Ilyin, got into the first-class carriage, sat down beside Ivan Ilyich, and told him of a telegram just received by the governor of Kursk announcing that a change was about to take place in the ministry: Peter Ivanovich was to be superseded by Ivan Semënovich.

The proposed change, apart from its significance for Russia, had a special significance for Ivan Ilyich, because by bringing forward a new man, Peter Petrovich, and consequently his friend Zachar Ivanovich, it was highly favourable for Ivan Ilyich, since Zachar Ivanovich was a friend and colleague of his.

In Moscow his news was confirmed, and on reaching Petersburg Ivan Ilyich found Zachar Ivanovich and received a definite promise of an appointment in his former department of Justice.

A week later he telegraphed to his wife: "Zachar in Miller's place. I shall receive appointment on presentation of report."

Thanks to this change of personnel, Ivan Ilyich had unexpectedly obtained an appointment in his former ministry which placed him two stages above his former colleagues besides giving him five thousand rubles salary and three thousand five hundred rubles for expenses connected with his removal. All his ill humour towards his former enemies and the whole department vanished, and Ivan Ilyich was completely happy.

He returned to the country more cheerful and contented than he had been for a long time. Praskovya Fëdorovna also cheered up and a truce was arranged between them. Ivan Ilyich told of how he had been fêted by everybody in Petersburg, how all those who had been his enemies were put to shame and now fawned on him, how envious they were of his appointment, and how much everybody in Petersburg had liked him.

8. Reference to the charitable organization founded by the Empress Marya, wife of Paul I, late in the 18th century.

Praskovya Fëdorovna listened to all this and appeared to believe it. She did not contradict anything, but only made plans for their life in the town to which they were going. Ivan Ilyich saw with delight that these plans were his plans, that he and his wife agreed, and that, after a stumble, his life was regaining its due and natural character of pleasant lightheartedness and decorum.

Ivan Ilyich had come back for a short time only, for he had to take up his new duties on the 10th of September. Moreover, he needed time to settle into the new place, to move all his belongings from the province, and to buy and order many additional things: in a word, to make such arrangements as he had resolved on, which were almost exactly what Praskovya Fëdorovna too had decided on.

Now that everything had happened so fortunately, and that he and his wife were at one in their aims and moreover saw so little of one another they got on together better than they had done since the first years of marriage. Ivan Ilyich had thought of taking his family away with him at once, but the insistence of his wife's brother and her sister-in-law, who had suddenly become particularly amiable and friendly to him and his family, induced him to depart alone.

So he departed, and the cheerful state of mind induced by his success and by the harmony between his wife and himself, the one intensifying the other, did not leave him. He found a delightful house, just the thing both he and his wife had dreamt of. Spacious, lofty reception rooms in the old style, a convenient and dignified study, rooms for his wife and daughter, a study for his son—it might have been specially built for them. Ivan Ilyich himself superintended the arrangements, chose the wallpapers, supplemented the furniture (preferably with antiques which he considered particularly *comme il faut*), and supervised the upholstering. Everything progressed and progressed and approached the ideal he had set himself: even when things were only half completed they exceeded his expectations. He saw what a refined and elegant character, free from vulgarity, it would all have when it was ready. On falling asleep he pictured to himself how the reception-room would look. Looking at the yet unfinished drawing-room he could see the fireplace, the screen, the what-not, the little chairs dotted here and there, the dishes and plates on the walls, and the bronzes, as they would be when everything was in place. He was pleased by the thought of how his wife and daughter, who shared his taste in this matter, would be impressed by it. They were certainly not expecting as much. He had been particularly successful in finding, and buying cheaply, antiques which gave a particularly aristocratic character to the whole place. But in his letters he intentionally understated everything in order to be able to surprise them. All this so absorbed him that his new duties—though he liked his official work—interested him less than he had expected. Sometimes he even had moments of absent-mindedness during the Court Sessions, and would consider whether he should have straight or curved cornices for his curtains. He was so interested in it all that he often did things himself, rearranging the furniture, or rehanging the curtains. Once when mounting a step-ladder to show the upholsterer, who did not understand, how he wanted the hangings draped, he made a false step and slipped, but being a strong and agile man he clung on and only knocked his side against the knob of the window frame. The bruised place was painful but the pain soon passed, and he felt particularly bright and well just then. He wrote: "I feel fifteen years younger." He thought he would have everything ready by September, but it dragged on till mid-October. But the result was charming not only in his eyes but to everyone who saw it.

In reality it was just what is usually seen in the houses of people of moderate means who want to appear rich, and therefore succeed only in resembling others like themselves: there were damasks, dark wood, plants, rugs, and dull and polished bronzes—all the things people of a certain class have in order to resemble other people of that class. His house was so like the others that it would never have been noticed, but to him it all seemed to be quite exceptional. He was very happy when he met his family at the station and brought them to the newly furnished house all lit up, where a footman in a white tie opened the door into the hall decorated with plants, and when they went on into the drawing room and the study uttering exclamations of delight. He conducted them everywhere, drank in their praises eagerly, and beamed with pleasure. At tea that evening, when Praskovya Fëdorovna among other things asked him about his fall, he laughed, and showed them how he had gone flying and had frightened the upholsterer.

"It's a good thing I'm a bit of an athlete. Another man might have been killed, but I merely knocked myself, just here; it hurts when it's touched, but it's passing off already—it's only a bruise."

So they began living in their new home—in which, as always happens, when they got thoroughly settled in they found they were just one room short—and with the increased income, which as always was just a little (some five hundred rubles) too little, but it was all very nice.

Things went particularly well at first, before everything was finally arranged and while something had still to be done: this thing bought, that thing ordered, another thing moved, and something else adjusted. Though there were some disputes between husband and wife, they were both so well satisfied and had so much to do that it all passed off without any serious quarrels. When nothing was left to arrange it became rather dull and something seemed to be lacking, but they were then making acquaintances, forming habits, and life was growing fuller.

Ivan Ilyich spent his mornings at the law court and came home to dinner, and at first he was generally in a good humour, though he occasionally became irritable just on account of his house. (Every spot on the tablecloth or the upholstery, and every broken window-blind string, irritated him. He had devoted so much trouble to arranging it all that every disturbance of it distressed him.) But on the whole his life ran its course as he believed life should do: easily, pleasantly, and decorously.

He got up at nine, drank his coffee, read the paper, and then put on his undress uniform and went to the law courts. There the harness in which he worked had already been stretched to fit him and he donned it without a hitch: petitioners, inquiries at the chancery, the chancery itself, and the sittings public and administrative. In all this the thing was to exclude everything fresh and vital, which always disturbs the regular course of official business, and to admit only official relations with people, and then only on official grounds. A man would come, for instance, wanting some information. Ivan Ilyich, as one in whose sphere the matter did not lie, would have nothing to do with him: but if the man had some business with him in his official capacity, something that could be expressed on officially stamped paper, he would do everything, positively everything he could within the limits of such relations, and in doing so would maintain the semblance of friendly human relations, that is, would observe the courtesies of life. As soon as the official relations ended, so did everything else. Ivan Ilyich possessed this capacity to separate his real life from the official side of affairs and not mix the two, in the highest degree, and by long practice and natural aptitude had brought it to such a pitch that sometimes, in the manner of a virtuoso, he would even allow himself to let the human and official relations mingle. He let himself do this just because he felt that he could at any time he chose resume the strictly official attitude again and drop the human relation. And he did it all easily, pleasantly, correctly, and even artistically. In the intervals between the sessions he smoked, drank tea, chatted a little about politics, a little about general topics, a little about cards, but most of all about official appointments. Tired, but with the feelings of a virtuoso—one of the first violins who has played his part in an orchestra with precision—he would return home to find that his wife and daughter had been out paying calls, or had a visitor, and that his son had been to school, had done his homework with his tutor, and was duly learning what is taught at High Schools. Everything was as it should be. After dinner, if they had no visitors, Ivan Ilyich sometimes read a book that was being much discussed at the time, and in the evening settled down to work, that is, read official papers, compared the depositions of witnesses, and noted paragraphs of the Code applying to them. This was neither dull nor amusing. It was dull when he might have been playing bridge, but if no bridge was available it was at any rate better than doing nothing or sitting with his wife. Ivan Ilyich's chief pleasure was giving little dinners to which he invited men and women of good social position, and just as his drawing-room resembled all other drawing-rooms so did his enjoyable little parties resemble all other such parties.

Once they even gave a dance. Ivan Ilyich enjoyed it and everything went off well, except that it led to a violent quarrel with his wife about the cakes and sweets. Praskovya Fëdorovna had made her own plans, but Ivan Ilyich insisted on getting everything from an expensive confectioner and ordered too many cakes, and the quarrel occurred because some of those cakes were left over and the confectioner's bill came to forty-five rubles. It was a great and disagreeable quarrel. Praskovya Fëdorovna called him "a fool and an imbecile," and he clutched at his head and made angry allusions to divorce.

But the dance itself had been enjoyable. The best people were there, and Ivan Ilyich had danced with Princess Trufonova, a sister of the distinguished founder of the Society "Bear my Burden."

The pleasures connected with his work were pleasures of ambition; his social pleasures were those of vanity; but Ivan Ilyich's greatest pleasure was playing bridge. He acknowledged that whatever disagreeable incident happened in his life, the pleasure that beamed like a ray of light above everything else was to sit down to bridge with good players, not noisy partners, and of course to four-handed bridge (with five players it was annoying to have to stand out, though one pretended not to mind), to play a clever and serious game (when the cards allowed it) and then to have supper and drink a glass of wine. After a game of bridge, especially if he had won a little (to win a large sum was unpleasant), Ivan Ilyich went to bed in specially good humour.

So they lived. They formed a circle of acquaintances among the best people and were visited by people of importance and by young folk. In their views as to their acquaintances, husband, wife, and daughter were entirely agreed, and tacitly and unanimously kept at arm's length and shook off the various shabby friends and relations who, with much show of affection, gushed into the drawing-room with its Japanese plates on the walls. Soon these shabby friends ceased to obtrude themselves and only the best people remained in the Golovins' set.

Young men made up to Lisa, and Petrishchev, an examining magistrate and Dmitri Ivanovich Petrischchev's son and sole heir, began to be so attentive to her that Ivan Ilyich had already spoken to Praskovya Fëdorovna about it, and considered whether they should not arrange a party for them, or get up some private theatricals.

So they lived, and all went well, without change, and life flowed pleasantly.

IV

They were all in good health. It could not be called ill health if Ivan Ilyich sometimes said that he had a queer taste in his mouth and felt some discomfort in his left side.

But this discomfort increased and, though not exactly painful, grew into a sense of pressure in his side accompanied by ill humour. And his irritability became worse and worse and began to mar the agreeable, easy, and correct life that had established itself in the Golovin family. Quarrels between husband and wife became more and more frequent, and soon the ease and amenity disappeared and even the decorum was barely maintained. Scenes again became frequent, and very few of those islets remained on which husband and wife could meet without an explosion. Praskovya Fëdorovna now had good reason to say that her husband's temper was trying. With characteristic exaggeration she said he had always had a dreadful temper, and that it had needed all her good nature to put up with it for twenty years. It was true that now the quarrels were started by him. His bursts of temper always came just before dinner, often just as he began to eat his soup. Sometimes he noticed that a plate or dish was chipped, or the food was not right, or his son put his elbow on the table, or his daughter's hair was not done as he liked it, and for all this he blamed Praskovya Fëdorovna. At first she retorted and said disagreeable things to him, but once or twice he fell into such a rage at the beginning of dinner that she realized it was due to some physical derangement brought on by taking food, and so she restrained herself and did not answer, but only hurried to get the dinner over. She regarded this self-restraint as highly praiseworthy. Having come to the conclusion that her husband had a dreadful temper and made her life miserable, she began to feel sorry for herself, and the more she pitied herself the more she hated her husband. She began to wish he would die; yet she did not want him to die because then his salary would cease. And this irritated her against him still more. She considered herself dreadfully unhappy just because not even his death could save her, and though she concealed her exasperation, that hidden exasperation of hers increased his irritation also.

After one scene in which Ivan Ilyich had been particularly unfair and after which he had said in explanation that he certainly was irritable but that it was due to his not being well, she said that if he was ill it should be attended to, and insisted on his going to see a celebrated doctor.

He went. Everything took place as he had expected and as it always does. There was the usual waiting and the important air assumed by the doctor, with which he was so familiar (resembling that which he himself assumed in court), and the sounding and listening, and the questions which called for answers that were foregone conclusions and were evidently unnecessary, and the look of importance which implied that "if only you put yourself in our hands we will arrange everything—we know indubitably how it has to be done, always in the same way for everybody alike." It was all just as it was in the law courts. The doctor put on just the same air towards him as he himself put on towards an accused person.

The doctor said that so-and-so indicated that there was so-and-so inside the patient, but if the investigation of so-and-so did not confirm this, then he must assume that and that. If he assumed that and that, then . . . and so on. To Ivan Ilyich only one question was important: was his case serious or not? But the doctor ignored that inappropriate question. From his point of view it was not the one under consideration, the real question was to decide between a floating kidney, chronic catarrh, or appendicitis. It was not a question of Ivan Ilyich's life or death, but one between a floating kidney and appendicitis. And that question the doctor solved brilliantly, as it seemed to Ivan Ilyich, in favour of the appendix, with the reservation that should an examination of the urine give fresh indications the matter would be reconsidered. All this was just what Ivan Ilyich had himself brilliantly accomplished a thousand times in dealing with men on trial. The doctor summed up just as brilliantly, looking over his spectacles triumphantly and even gaily at the accused. From the doctor's summing up Ivan Ilyich concluded that things were bad, but that for the doctor, and perhaps for everybody else, it was a matter of indifference, though for him it was bad. And this conclusion struck him painfully, arousing in him a great feeling of pity for himself and of bitterness towards the doctor's indifference to a matter of such importance.

He said nothing of this, but rose, placed the doctor's fee on the table, and remarked with a sigh: "We sick people probably often put inappropriate questions. But tell me, in general, is this complaint dangerous or not? . . ."

The doctor looked at him sternly over his spectacles with one eye, as if to say: "Prisoner, if you will not keep to the questions put to you, I shall be obliged to have you removed from the court."

"I have already told you what I consider necessary and proper. The analysis may show something more." And the doctor bowed.

Ivan Ilyich went out slowly, seated himself disconsolately in his sledge, and drove home. All the way home he was going over what the doctor had said, trying to translate those complicated, obscure, scientific phrases into plain language and find in them an answer to the question: "Is my condition bad? Is it very bad? Or is there as yet nothing much wrong?" And it seemed to him that the meaning of what the doctor had said was it was very bad. Everything in the streets seemed depressing. The cabmen, the houses, the passers-by, and the shops, were dismal. His ache, this dull gnawing ache that never ceased for a moment, seemed to have acquired a new and more serious significance from the doctor's dubious remarks. Ivan Ilyich now watched it with a new and oppressive feeling.

He reached home and began to tell his wife about it. She listened, but in the middle of his account his daughter came in with her hat on, ready to go out with her mother. She sat down reluctantly to listen to this tedious story, but could not stand it long, and her mother too did not hear him to the end.

"Well, I am very glad," she said. "Mind now to take your medicine regularly. Give me the prescription and I'll send Gerasim to the chemist's." And she went to get ready to go out.

While she was in the room Ivan Ilyich had hardly taken time to breathe, but he sighed deeply when she left it.

"Well," he thought, "perhaps it isn't so bad after all."

He began taking his medicine and following the doctor's directions, which had been altered after the examination of the urine. But then it happened that there was a contradiction between the indications drawn from the examination of the urine and the symptoms that showed themselves. It turned out that what was happening differed from what the doctor had told him, and that he had either forgotten, or blundered, or hidden something from him. He could not, however, be blamed for that, and Ivan Ilyich still obeyed his orders implicitly and at first derived some comfort from doing so.

From the time of his visit to the doctor, Ivan Ilyich's chief occupation was the exact fulfilment of the doctor's instructions regarding hygiene and the taking of medicine, and the observation of his pain and his excretions. His chief interests came to be people's ailments and people's health. When sickness, deaths, or recoveries were mentioned in his presence, especially when the illness resembled his own, he listened with agitation which he tried to hide, asked questions, and applied what he heard to his own case.

The pain did not grow less, but Ivan Ilyich made efforts to force himself to think that he was better. And he could do this so long as nothing agitated him. But as soon as he had any unpleasantness with his wife, any lack of success in his official work, or held bad cards at bridge, he was at once acutely sensible of his disease. He had formerly borne such mischances, hoping soon to adjust what was wrong, to master it and attain success, or make a grand slam. But now every mischance upset him and plunged him into despair. He would say to himself. "There now, just as I was beginning to get better and the medicine had begun to take effect, comes this accursed misfortune, or unpleasantness . . ." And he was furious with the mishap, or with the people who were causing the unpleasantness and killing him, for he felt that this fury was killing him but could not restrain it. One would have thought that it should have been clear to him that this exasperation with circumstances and people aggravated his illness, and that he ought therefore to ignore unpleasant occurrences. But he drew the very opposite conclusion: he said that he needed peace, and he watched for everything that might disturb it and became irritable at the slightest infringement of it. His condition was rendered worse by the fact that he read medical books and consulted doctors. The progress of his disease was so gradual that he could deceive himself when comparing one day with another—the difference was so slight. But when he consulted the doctors it seemed to him that he was getting worse, and even very rapidly. Yet despite this he was continually consulting them.

That month he went to see another celebrity, who told him almost the same as the first had done but put his questions rather differently, and the interview with this celebrity only increased Ivan Ilyich's doubts and fears. A friend of a friend of his, a very good doctor, diagnosed his illness again quite differently from the others, and though he predicted recovery, his questions and suppositions bewildered Ivan Ilyich still more and increased his doubts. A homeopathist diagnosed the disease in yet another way, and prescribed medicine which Ivan Ilyich took secretly for a week. But after a week, not feeling any improvement and having lost confidence both in the former doctor's treatment and in this one's, he became still more despondent. One day a lady acquaintance mentioned a cure effected by a wonder-working icon. Ivan Ilyich caught himself listening attentively and beginning to believe that it had occurred. This incident alarmed him. "Has my mind really weakened to such an extent?" he asked himself. "Nonsense! It's all rubbish. I mustn't give way to nervous fears but having chosen a doctor must keep strictly to his treatment. That is what I will do. Now it's all settled. I won't think about it, but will follow the treatment seriously till summer, and then we shall see. From now there must be no more of this wavering!" This was easy to say but impossible to carry out. The pain in his side oppressed him and seemed to grow worse and more incessant, while the taste in his mouth grew stranger and stranger. It seemed to him that his breath had a disgusting smell, and he was conscious of a loss of appetite and strength. There was no deceiving himself: something terrible, new, and more important than anything before in his life, was taking place within him of which he alone was aware. Those about him did not understand or would not understand it, but thought everything in the world was going on as usual. That tormented Ivan Ilyich more than anything. He saw that his household, especially his wife and daughter who were in a perfect whirl of visiting, did not understand anything of it and were annoyed that he was so depressed and so exacting, as if he were to blame for it. Though they tried to disguise it he saw that he was an obstacle in their path, and that his wife had adopted a definite line in regard to his illness and kept to it regardless of anything he said or did. Her attitude was this: "You know," she would say to her friends, "Ivan Ilyich can't do as other people do, and keep to the treatment prescribed for him. One day he'll take his drops and keep strictly to his diet and go to bed in good time, but the next day unless I watch him he'll suddenly forget his medicine, eat sturgeon—which is forbidden—and sit up playing cards till one o'clock in the morning."

"Oh, come, when was that?" Ivan Ilyich would ask in vexation. "Only once at Peter Ivanovich's."

"And yesterday with Shebek."

"Well, even if I hadn't stayed up, this pain would have kept me awake."

"Be that as it may you'll never get well like that, but will always make us wretched."

Praskovya Fedorovna's attitude to Ivan Ilyich's illness, as she expressed it both to others and to him, was that it was his own fault and was another of the annoyances he caused her. Ivan Ilyich felt that this opinion escaped her involuntarily—but that did not make it easier for him.

At the law courts too, Ivan Ilyich noticed, or thought he noticed, a strange attitude towards himself. It sometimes seemed to him that people were watching him inquisitively as a man whose place might soon be vacant. Then again, his friends would suddenly begin to chaff him in a friendly way about his low spirits, as if the awful, horrible, and unheard-of thing that was going on within him, incessantly gnawing at him and irresistibly drawing him away, was a very agreeable subject for jests. Schwartz in particular irritated him by his jocularity, vivacity, and *savoir-faire,* which reminded him of what he himself had been ten years ago.

Friends came to make up a set and they sat down to cards. They dealt, bending the new cards to soften them, and he sorted the diamonds in his hand and found he had seven. His partner said "No trumps" and supported him with two diamonds. What more could be wished for? It ought to be jolly and lively. They would make a grand slam. But suddenly Ivan Ilyich was conscious of that gnawing pain, that taste in his mouth, and it seemed ridiculous that in such circumstances he should be pleased to make a grand slam.

He looked at his partner Mikhail Mikhaylovich, who rapped the table with his strong hand and instead of snatching up the tricks pushed the cards courteously and indulgently towards Ivan Ilyich that he might have the pleasure of gathering them up without the trouble of stretching out his hand for them. "Does he think I am too weak to stretch out my arm?" thought Ivan Ilyich, and forgetting what he was doing he over-trumped his partner, missing the grand slam by three tricks. And what was most awful of all was that he saw how upset Mikhail Mikhaylovich was about it but did not himself care. And it was dreadful to realize why he did not care.

They all saw that he was suffering, and said: "We can stop if you are tired. Take a rest." Lie down? No, he was not at all tired, and he finished the rubber. All were gloomy and silent. Ivan Ilyich felt that he had diffused this gloom over them and could not dispel it. They had supper and went away, and Ivan Ilyich was left alone with the consciousness that his life was poisoned and was poisoning the lives of others, and that this poison did not weaken but penetrated more and more deeply into his whole being.

With this consciousness, and with physical pain besides the terror, he must go to bed, often to lie awake the greater part of the night. Next morning he had to get up again, dress, go to the law courts, speak, and write; or if he did not go out, spend at home those twenty-four hours a day each of which was a torture. And he had to live thus all alone on the brink of an abyss, with no one who understood or pitied him.

V

So one month passed and then another. Just before the New Year his brother-in-law came to town and stayed at their house. Ivan Ilyich was at the law courts and Praskovya Fëdorovna had gone shopping. When Ivan Ilyich came home and entered his study he found his brother-in-law there—a healthy, florid man—unpacking his portmanteau himself. He raised his head on hearing Ivan Ilyich's footsteps and looked up at him for a moment without a word. That stare told Ivan everything. His brother-in-law opened his mouth to utter an exclamation of surprise but checked himself, and that action confirmed it all.

"I have changed, eh?"

"Yes, there is a change."

And after that, try as he would to get his brother-in-law to return to the subject of his looks, the latter would say nothing about it. Praskovya Fëdorovna came home and her brother went out to her. Ivan Ilyich locked the door and began to examine himself in the glass, first full face, then in profile. He took up a portrait of himself taken with his wife, and compared it with what he saw in the glass. The change in him was immense. Then he bared his arms to the elbow, looked at them, drew the sleeves down again, sat down on an ottoman, and grew blacker than night.

"No, no, this won't do!" he said to himself, and jumped up, went to the table, took up some law papers and began to read them, but could not continue. He unlocked the door and went into the reception-room. The door leading to the drawing-room was shut. He approached it on tiptoe and listened.

"No, you are exaggerating!" Praskovya Fëdorovna was saying.

"Exaggerating! Don't you see it? Why, he's a dead man! Look at his eyes—there's no light in them. But what is it that is wrong with him?"

The brother in law sees Ivan's dying.

"No one knows. Nikolaevich [that was another doctor] said something, but I don't know what. And Leshchetitsky [this was the celebrated specialist] said quite the contrary . . ."

Ivan Ilyich walked away, went to his own room, lay down and began musing: "The kidney, a floating kidney." He recalled all the doctors had told him of how it detached itself and swayed about. And by an effort of imagination he tried to catch that kidney and arrest it and support it. So little was needed for this, it seemed to him. "No, I'll go to see Peter Ivanovich again." [That was the friend whose friend was a doctor.] He rang, ordered the carriage, and got ready to go.

"Where are you going, *Jean?*" asked his wife, with a specially sad and exceptionally kind look.

This exceptionally kind look irritated him. He looked morosely at her.

"I must go to see Peter Ivanovich."

He went to see Peter Ivanovich, and together they went to see his friend, the doctor. He was in, and Ivan Ilyich had a long talk with him.

Reviewing the anatomical and physiological details of what in the doctor's opinion was going on inside him, he understood it all.

There was something, a small thing, in the vermiform appendix. It might all come right. Only stimulate the energy of one organ and check the activity of another, then absorption would take place and everything would come right. He got home rather late for dinner, ate his dinner, and conversed cheerfully, but could not for a long time bring himself to go back to work in his room. At last, however, he went to his study and did what was necessary, but the consciousness that he had put something aside—an important, intimate matter which he would revert to when his work was done—never left him. When he had finished his work he remembered that this intimate matter was the thought of his vermiform appendix. But he did not give himself up to it, and went to the drawing-room for tea. There were callers there, including the examining magistrate who was a desirable match for his daughter, and they were conversing, playing the piano, and singing. Ivan Ilyich, as Praskovya Fëdorovna remarked, spent that evening more cheerfully than usual, but he never for a moment forgot that he had postponed the important matter of the appendix. At eleven o'clock he said good-night and went to his bedroom. Since his illness he had slept alone in a small room next to his study. He undressed and took up a novel by Zola,[9] but instead of reading it he fell into thought, and in his imagination that desired improvement in the vermiform appendix occurred. There was the absorption and evacuation and the reestablishment of normal activity. "Yes, that's it!" he said to himself. one need only assist nature, that's all." He remembered his medicine, rose, took it, and lay down on his back watching for the beneficent action of the medicine and for it to lessen the pain. "I need only take it regularly and avoid all injurious influences. I am already feeling better, much better." He began touching his side: it was not painful to the touch. "There, I really don't feel it. It's much better already." He put out the light and turned on his side. . . . "The appendix is getting better, absorption is occurring." Suddenly he felt the old, familiar, dull, gnawing pain, stubborn and serious. There was the same familiar loathsome taste in his mouth. His heart sank and he felt dazed. "My God! My God!" he muttered. "Again, again! And it will never cease." And suddenly the matter presented itself in a quite different aspect. "Vermiform appendix! Kidney!" he said to himself. "It's not a question of appendix or kidney, but of life and . . . death. Yes, life was there and now it is going, going and I cannot stop it. Yes. Why deceive myself? Isn't it obvious to everyone but me that I'm dying, and that it's only a question of weeks, days . . . it may happen this moment. There was light and now there is darkness. I was here and now I'm going there! Where?" A chill came over him, his breathing ceased, and he felt only the throbbing of his heart.

"When I am not, what will there be? There will be nothing. Then where shall I be when I am no more? Can this be dying? No, I don't want to!" He jumped up and tried to light the candle, felt for it with trembling hands, dropped candle and candlestick on the floor, and fell back on his pillow.

"What's the use? It makes no difference," he said to himself, staring with wide-open eyes into the darkness. "Death. Yes, death. And none of them know or wish to know it, and they have no pity for me. Now they are playing." (He heard through the door the distant sound of a song and its accompaniment.) "It's all the same to them, but they will die too! Fools! I first, and they later, but it will be the same for them. And now they are merry . . . the beasts!"

Anger choked him and he was agonizingly, unbearably miserable. "It is impossible that all men have been doomed to suffer this awful horror!" He raised himself.

"Something must be wrong. I must calm myself—must think it all over from the beginning." And he again began thinking. "Yes, the beginning of my illness: I knocked my side, but I was still quite well that day and the next. It hurt a little, then rather more. I saw the doctors, then followed despondency and anguish, more doctors, and I drew nearer to the abyss. My strength grew less and I kept coming nearer and nearer, and now I have wasted away and there is no light in my eyes. I think of the appendix—but this is death! I think of mending the appendix, and all the while here is death! Can it really be death!" Again terror seized him and he gasped for breath. He leant down and began feeling for the matches, pressing with his elbow on the stand

He really at last, dying, that he's

He angry at their living while he is dying.

---

9. Émile Zola (1840–1902), French novelist, author of the *Rougon-Macquart* novels (*Nana, Germinal,* and so on). Tolstoy condemned Zola for his naturalistic theories and considered his novels crude and gross.

beside the bed. It was in his way and hurt him, he grew furious with it, pressed on it still harder, and upset it. Breathless and in despair he fell on his back, expecting death to come immediately.

Meanwhile the visitors were leaving. Praskovya Fëdorovna was seeing them off. She heard something fall and came in.

"What has happened?"

"Nothing. I knocked it over accidentally."

She went out and returned with a candle. He lay there panting heavily, like a man who has run a thousand yards, and stared upwards at her with a fixed look.

"What is it, *Jean?*"

"No . . . o . . . thing. I upset it." ("Why speak of it? She won't understand," he thought.)

And in truth she did not understand. She picked up the stand, lit his candle, and hurried away to see another visitor off. When she came back he still lay on his back, looking upwards.

"What is it? Do you feel worse?"

"Yes."

She shook her head and sat down.

"Do you know, *Jean,* I think we must ask Leshchetitsky to come and see you here."

This meant calling in the famous specialist, regardless of expense. He smiled malignantly and said "No." She remained a little longer and then went up to him and kissed his forehead.

While she was kissing him he hated her from the bottom of his soul and with difficulty refrained from pushing her away.

"Good-night. Please God you'll sleep."

"Yes."

VI

Ivan Ilyich saw that he was dying, and he was in continual despair.

In the depth of his heart he knew he was dying, but not only was he not accustomed to the thought, he simply did not and could not grasp it.

The syllogism he had learned from Kiesewetter's *Logic:*[1] "Caius is a man, men are mortal, therefore Caius is mortal," had always seemed to him correct as applied to Caius, but certainly not as applied to himself. That Caius—man in the abstract—was mortal, was perfectly correct, but he was not Caius, not an abstract man, but a creature quite, quite separate from all others. He had been little Vanya, with a mamma and a papa, with Mitya and Volodya, with the toys, a coachman and a nurse, afterwards with Katenka and with all the joys, griefs, and delights of childhood, boyhood, and youth. What did Caius know of the smell of that striped leather ball Vanya had been so fond of? Had Caius kissed his mother's hand like that, and did the silk of her dress rustle so for Caius? Had he rioted like that at school when the pastry was bad? Had Caius been in love like that? Could Caius preside at a session as he did? "Caius really was mortal, and it was right for him to die; but for me, little Vanya, Ivan Ilyich, with all my thoughts and emotions, it's altogether a

---

1. Karl Kiesewetter (1766–1819) was a German popularizer of Kant's philosophy. His *Outline of Logic According to Kantian Principles* (1796) was widely used in Russian adaptations as a schoolbook.

different matter. It cannot be that I ought to die. That would be too terrible."

Such was his feeling.

"If I had to die like Caius I should have known it was so. An inner voice would have told me so, but there was nothing of the sort in me and I and all my friends felt that our case was quite different from that of Caius. And now here it is!" he said to himself. "It can't be. It's impossible! But here it is. How is this? How is one to understand it?"

He could not understand it, and tried to drive this false, incorrect, morbid thought away and to replace it by other proper and healthy thoughts. But that thought, and not the thought only but the reality itself, seemed to come and confront him.

And to replace that thought he called up a succession of others, hoping to find in them some support. He tried to get back into the former current of thoughts that had once screened the thought of death from him. But strange to say, all that had formerly shut off, hidden, and destroyed, his consciousness of death, no longer had that effect. Ivan Ilyich now spent most of his time in attempting to re-establish that old current. He would say to himself: "I will take up my duties again—after all I used to live by them." And banishing all doubts he would go to the law courts, enter into conversation with his colleagues, and sit carelessly as was his wont, scanning the crowd with a thoughtful look and leaning both his emaciated arms on the arms of his oak chair; bending over as usual to a colleague and drawing his papers nearer he would interchange whispers with him, and then suddenly raising his eyes and sitting erect would pronounce certain words and open the proceedings. But suddenly in the midst of those proceedings the pain in his side, regardless of the stage the proceedings had reached, would begin its own gnawing work. Ivan Ilyich would turn his attention to it and try to drive the thought of it away, but without success. *It* would come and stand before him and look at him, and he would be petrified and the light would die out of his eyes, and he would again begin asking himself whether *It* alone was true. And his colleagues and subordinates would see with surprise and distress that he, the brilliant and subtle judge, was becoming confused and making mistakes. He would shake himself, try to pull himself together, manage somehow to bring the sitting to a close, and return home with the sorrowful consciousness that his judicial labours could not as formerly hide from him what he wanted them to hide, and could not deliver him from *It*. And what was worst of all was that *It* drew his attention to itself not in order to make him take some action but only that he should look at *It*, look it straight in the face: look at it without doing anything, suffer inexpressibly.

And to save himself from this condition Ivan Ilyich looked for consolations—new screens—and new screens were found and for a while seemed to save him, but then they immediately fell to pieces or rather became transparent, as *It* penetrated them and nothing could veil *It*.

In these latter days he would go into the drawing-room he had arranged—that drawing-room where he had fallen and for the sake of which (how bitterly ridiculous it seemed) he had sacrificed his life—for he knew that his illness originated with that knock. He would enter and see that something had scratched the polished table. He would look for the cause of this and find that it was the bronze ornamentation of an album, that had got bent. He would take up the expensive album which he had lovingly arranged, and feel vexed with his daughter and her friends for their untidiness—for the album was torn here and there and some of the photographs turned upside down. He would put it carefully in order and bend the ornamentation back into position. Then it would occur to him to place all those things in another corner of the room, near the plants. He would call the footman, but his daughter or wife would contradict him, and he would dispute and grow angry. But that was all right, for then he did not think about *It. It* was invisible.

But then, when he was moving something himself, his wife would say: "Let the servants do it. You will hurt yourself again." And suddenly *It* would flash through the screen and he would see it. It was just a flash, and he hoped it would disappear, but he would involuntarily pay attention to his side. "It sits there as before, gnawing just the same!" And he could no longer forget *It,* but could distinctly see it looking at him from behind the flowers. "What is it all for?"

"It really is so! I lost my life over that curtain as I might have done when storming a fort. Is that possible? How terrible and how stupid. It can't be true! It can't, but it is."

He would go to his study, lie down, and again be alone with *It*: face to face with *It.* And nothing could be done with *It* except to look at it and shudder.

He faces death with fear

VII

How it happened it is impossible to say because it came about step by step, unnoticed, but in the third month of Ivan Ilyich's illness, his wife, his daughter, his son, his acquaintances, the doctors, the servants, and above all he himself, were aware that the whole interest he had for other people was whether he would soon vacate his place, and at last release the living from the discomfort caused by his presence and be himself released from his sufferings.

He slept less and less. He was given opium and hypodermic injections of morphine, but this did not relieve him. The dull depression he experienced in a somnolent condition at first gave him a little relief, but only as something new; afterwards it became as distressing as the pain itself or even more so.

Special foods were prepared for him by the doctors' orders, but all those foods became increasingly distasteful and disgusting to him.

For his excretions also special arrangements had to be made, and this was a torment to him every time—a torment from the uncleanliness, the unseemliness, and the smell, and from knowing that another person had to take part in it.

But just through this most unpleasant matter, Ivan Ilyich obtained comfort. Gerasim, the butler's young assistant, always came in to carry the things out. Gerasim was a clean, fresh peasant lad, grown stout on town food and always cheerful and bright. At first the sight of him, in his clean Russian peasant costume, engaged on that disgusting task embarrassed Ivan Ilyich.

Once when he got up from the commode too weak to draw up his trousers, he dropped into a soft armchair and looked with horror at his bare, enfeebled thighs with the muscles so sharply marked on them.

Gerasim with a firm light tread, his heavy boots emitting a pleasant smell of tar and fresh winter air, came in wearing a clean Hessian apron, the sleeves of his print shirt tucked up over his strong bare young arms; and refraining from looking at his sick master out of consideration for his feelings, and restraining the joy of life that beamed from his face, he went up to the commode.

"Gerasim!" said Ivan Ilyich in a weak voice.

Gerasim started, evidently afraid he might have committed some blunder, and with a rapid movement turned his fresh, kind, simple young face which just showed the first downy sign of a beard.

"Yes, sir?"

"That must be very unpleasant for you. You must forgive me. I am helpless."

"Oh, why, sir," and Gerasim's eyes beamed and he showed his glistening white teeth, "what's a little trouble? It's a case of illness with you, sir."

And his deft strong hands did their accustomed task, and he went out of the room stepping lightly. Five minutes later he as lightly returned.

Ivan Ilyich was still sitting in the same position in the armchair.

"Gerasim," he said when the latter had replaced the freshly-washed utensil. "Please come here and help me." Gerasim went up to him. "Lift me up. It is hard for me to get up, and I have sent Dmitri away."

Gerasim went up to him, grasped his master with his strong arms deftly but gently, in the same way that he stepped—lifted him, supported him with one hand, and with the other drew up his trousers and would have set him down again, but Ivan Ilyich asked to be led to the sofa. Gerasim, without an effort and without apparent pressure, led him, almost lifting him, to the sofa and placed him on it.

"Thank you. How easily and well you do it all!"

Gerasim smiled again and turned to leave the room. But Ivan Ilyich felt his presence such a comfort that he did not want to let him go.

"One thing more, please move up that chair. No, the other one—under my feet. It is easier for me when my feet are raised."

Gerasim brought the chair, set it down gently in place, and raised Ivan Ilyich's legs on to it. It seemed to Ivan Ilyich that he felt better while Gerasim was holding up his legs.

"It's better when my legs are higher," he said. "Place that cushion under them."

Gerasim did so. He again lifted the legs and placed them, and again Ivan Ilyich felt better while Gerasim held his legs. When he set them down Ivan Ilyich fancied he felt worse.

"Gerasim," he said. "Are you busy now?"

"Not at all, sir," said Gerasim, who had learnt from the townsfolk how to speak to gentlefolk.

"What have you still to do?"

"What have I to do? I've done everything except chopping the logs for tomorrow."

"Then hold my legs up a bit higher, can you?"

"Of course I can. Why not?" And Gerasim raised his master's legs higher and Ivan Ilyich thought that in that position he did not feel any pain at all.

"And how about the logs?"

"Don't trouble about that, sir. There's plenty of time."

Ivan Ilyich told Gerasim to sit down and hold his legs, and began to talk to him. And strange to say it seemed to him that he felt better while Gerasim held his legs up.

After that Ivan Ilyich would sometimes call Gerasim and get him to hold his legs on his shoulders, and he liked talking to him. Gerasim did it all easily, willingly, simply, and with a good nature that touched Ivan Ilyich. Health, strength, and vitality in other people were offensive to him, but Gerasim's strength and vitality did not mortify but soothed him.

What tormented Ivan Ilyich most was the deception, the lie, which for some reason they all accepted, that he was not dying but was simply ill, and that he only need keep quiet and undergo a treatment and then something very good would result. He however knew that do what they would nothing would come of it, only still more agonizing suffering and death. This deception tortured him—their not wishing to admit what they all knew and what he knew, but wanting to lie to him concerning his terrible condition, and wishing and forcing him to participate in that lie. Those lies—lies enacted over him on the eve of his death and destined to degrade this awful, solemn act to the level of their visitings, their curtains, their sturgeon for dinner—were a terrible agony for Ivan Ilyich. And strangely enough, many times when they were going through their antics over him he had been within a hair-breadth of calling out to them: "Stop lying! You know and I know that I am dying. Then at least stop lying about it!" But he had never had the spirit to do it. The awful, terrible act of his dying was, he could see, reduced by those about him to the level of a casual, unpleasant, and almost indecorous incident (as if someone entered a drawing-room diffusing an unpleasant odour) and this was done by that very decorum which he had served all his life long. He saw that no one felt for him, because no one even wished to grasp his position. Only Gerasim recognized and pitied him. And so Ivan Ilyich felt at ease only with him. He felt comforted when Gerasim supported his legs (sometimes all night long) and refused to go to bed, saying: "Don't you worry, Ivan Ilyich. I'll get sleep enough later on," or when he suddenly became familiar and exclaimed: "If you weren't sick it would be another matter, but as it is, why should I grudge a little trouble?" Gerasim alone did not lie; everything showed that he alone understood the facts of the case and did not consider it necessary to disguise them, but simply felt sorry for his emaciated and enfeebled master. Once when Ivan Ilyich was sending him away he even said straight out: "We shall all of us die, so why should I grudge a little trouble?"—expressing the fact that he did not think his work burdensome, because he was doing it for a dying man and hoped someone would do the same for him when his time came.

Apart from this lying, or because of it, what most tormented Ivan Ilyich was that no one pitied him as he wished to be pitied. At certain moments after prolonged suffering he wished most of all (though he would have been ashamed to confess it) for someone to pity him as a sick child is pitied. He longed to be petted and comforted. He knew he was an important functionary, that he had a beard turning grey, and that therefore what he longed for was impossible, but still he longed for it. And in Gerasim's attitude towards him there was something akin to what he wished for, and so that attitude comforted him. Ivan Ilyich wanted to weep, wanted to be petted and cried over, and then his colleague Shebek would come, and instead of weeping and being petted, Ivan Ilyich would assume a serious, severe, and profound air, and by force of habit would express his opinion on a decision of the Court of Appeal and would stubbornly insist on that view. This falsity around him and within him did more than anything else to poison his last days.

VIII

It was morning. He knew it was morning because Gerasim had gone, and Peter the footman had come and put out the candles, drawn back one of the curtains, and begun quietly to tidy up. Whether it was morning or evening, Friday or Sunday, made no difference, it was all just the same: the gnawing, unmitigated, agonizing pain, never ceasing for an instant, the consciousness of life inexorably waning but not yet extinguished, the approach of that ever dreaded and hateful Death which was the only reality, and always the same falsity. What were days, weeks, hours, in such a case?

"Will you have some tea, sir?"

"He wants things to be regular, and wishes the gentlefolk to drink tea in the morning," thought Ivan Ilyich, and only said "No."

"Wouldn't you like to move onto the sofa, sir?"

"He wants to tidy up the room, and I'm in the way. I am uncleanliness and disorder," he thought, and said only:

"No, leave me alone."

The man went on bustling about. Ivan Ilyich stretched out his hand. Peter came up, ready to help.

"What is it, sir?"

"My watch."

Peter took the watch which was close at hand and gave it to his master.

"Half-past eight. Are they up?"

"No sir, except Vladimir Ivanich" (the son) "who has gone to school. Praskovya Fëdorovna ordered me to wake her if you asked for her. Shall I do so?"

"No, there's no need to." "Perhaps I'd better have some tea," he thought, and added aloud: "Yes, bring me some tea."

Peter went to the door, but Ivan Ilyich dreaded being left alone. "How can I keep him here? Oh yes, my medicine." "Peter, give me my medicine." "Why not? Perhaps it may still do me some good." He took a spoonful and swallowed it. "No, it won't help. It's all tomfoolery, all deception," he decided as soon as he became aware of the familiar, sickly, hopeless taste. "No, I can't believe in it any longer. But the pain, why this pain? If it would only cease just for a moment!" And he moaned. Peter turned towards him. "It's all right. Go and fetch me some tea."

Peter went out. Left alone Ivan Ilyich groaned not so much with pain, terrible though that was, as from mental anguish. Always and forever the same, always these endless days and nights. If only it would come quicker! If only *what* would come quicker? Death, darkness? . . . No, no! Anything rather than death!

When Peter returned with the tea on a tray, Ivan Ilyich stared at him for a time in perplexity, not realizing who and what he was. Peter was disconcerted by that look and his embarrassment brought Ivan Ilyich to himself.

"Oh, tea! All right, put it down. Only help me to wash and put on a clean shirt."

And Ivan Ilyich began to wash. With pauses for rest, he washed his hands and then his face, cleaned his teeth, brushed his hair, and looked in the glass. He was terrified by what he saw, especially by the limp way in which his hair clung to his pallid forehead.

While his shirt was being changed he knew that he would be still more frightened at the sight of his body, so he avoided looking at it. Finally he was ready. He drew on a dressing-gown, wrapped himself in a plaid, and sat down in the armchair to take his tea. For a moment he felt refreshed, but as soon as he began to drink the tea he was again aware of the same taste, and the pain also returned. He finished it with an effort, and then lay down stretching out his legs, and dismissed Peter.

Always the same. Now a spark of hope flashes up, then a sea of despair rages, and always pain; always pain, always despair, and always the same. When alone he had a dreadful and distressing desire to call someone, but he knew beforehand that with others present it would be still worse. "Another dose of morphine—to lose consciousness. I will tell him, the doctor, that he must think of something else. It's impossible, impossible, to go on like this."

An hour and another pass like that. But now there is a ring at the door bell. Perhaps it's the doctor? It is. He comes in fresh, hearty, plump, and cheerful, with that look on his face that seems to say: "There now, you're in a panic about something, but we'll arrange it all for you directly!" The doctor knows this expression is out of place here, but he has put it on once for all and can't take it off—like a man who has put on a frock-coat in the morning to pay a round of calls.

The doctor rubs his hands vigorously and reassuringly.

"Brr! How cold it is! There's such a sharp frost; just let me warm myself!" he says, as if it were only a matter of waiting till he was warm, and then he would put everything right.

"Well now, how are you?"

Ivan Ilyich feels that the doctor would like to say: "Well, how are our affairs?" but that even he feels that this would not do, and says instead: "What sort of a night have you had?"

Ivan Ilyich looks at him as much as to say: "Are you really never ashamed of lying?" But the doctor does not wish to understand this question, and Ivan Ilyich says: "Just as terrible as ever. The pain never leaves me and never subsides. If only something . . ."

"Yes, you sick people are always like that. . . . There, now I think I'm warm enough. Even Praskovya Fëdorovna, who is so particular, could find no fault with my temperature. Well, now I can say good-morning," and the doctor presses his patient's hand.

Then, dropping his former playfulness, he begins with a most serious face to examine the patient, feeling his pulse and taking his temperature, and then begins the sounding and auscultation.

Ivan Ilyich knows quite well and definitely that all this is nonsense and pure deception, but when the doctor, getting down on his knee, leans over him, putting his ear first higher then lower, and performs various gymnastic movements over him with a significant expression on his face, Ivan Ilyich submits to it all as he used to submit to the speeches of the lawyers, though he knew very well that they were all lying and why they were lying.

The doctor, kneeling on the sofa, is still sounding him when Praskovya Fëdorovna's silk dress rustles at the door and she is heard scolding Peter for not having let her know of the doctor's arrival.

She comes in, kisses her husband, and at once proceeds to prove that she has been up a long time already, and only owing to a misunderstanding failed to be there when the doctor arrived.

Ivan Ilyich looks at her, scans her all over, sets against her the whiteness and plumpness and cleanness of her hands and neck, the gloss of her hair, and the sparkle of her vivacious eyes. He hates her with his whole soul. And the thrill of hatred he feels for her makes him suffer from her touch.

Her attitude towards him and his disease is still the same. Just as the doctor had adopted a certain relation to his patient which he could not abandon, so had she formed one towards him—that he was not doing something he ought to do and was himself to blame, and that she reproached him lovingly for this—and she could not now change that attitude.

"You see he doesn't listen to me and doesn't take his medicine at the proper time. And above all he lies in a position that is no doubt bad for him—with his legs up."

She described how he made Gerasim hold his legs up.

The doctor smiled with a contemptuous affability that said: "What's to be done? These sick people do have foolish fancies of that kind, but we must forgive them."

When the examination was over the doctor looked at his watch, and then Praskovya Fëdorovna announced to Ivan Ilyich that it was of course as he pleased, but she had sent to-day for a celebrated specialist who would examine him and have a consultation with Michael Danilovich (their regular doctor).

"Please don't raise any objections. I am doing this for my own sake," she said ironically, letting it be felt that she was doing it all for his sake and only said this to leave him no right to refuse. He remained silent, knitting his brows. He felt that he was so surrounded and involved in a mesh of falsity that it was hard to unravel anything.

Everything she did for him was entirely for her own sake, and she told him she was doing for herself what she actually was doing for herself, as if that was so incredible that he must understand the opposite.

At half-past eleven the celebrated specialist arrived. Again the sounding began and the significant conversations in his presence and in other rooms, about the kidneys and the appendix, and the questions and answers, with such an air of importance that again, instead of the real question of life and death which now alone confronted him, the question arose of the kidney and the appendix which were not behaving as they ought to and would now be attacked by Michael Danilovich and the specialist and forced to amend their ways.

The celebrated specialist took leave of him with a serious though not hopeless look, and in reply to the timid question in Ivan Ilyich, with eyes glistening with fear and hope, put to him as to whether there was a chance of recovery, said that he could not vouch for it but there was a possibility. The look of hope with which Ivan Ilyich watched the doctor out was so pathetic that Praskovya Fëdorovna, seeing it, even wept as she left the room to hand the doctor his fee.

The gleam of hope kindled by the doctor's encouragement did not last long. The same room, the same pictures, curtains, wallpaper, medicine bottles, were all there, and the same aching suffering body, and Ivan Ilyich began to moan. They gave him a subcutaneous injection and he sank into oblivion.

It was twilight when he came to. They brought him his dinner and he swallowed some beef tea with difficulty, and then everything was the same again and night was coming on.

After dinner, at seven o'clock, Praskovya Fëdorovna came into the room in evening dress, her full bosom pushed up by her corset, and with traces of powder on her face. She had reminded him in the morning that they were going to the theatre. Sarah Bernhardt[2] was visiting the town and they had a box, which he had insisted on their taking. Now he had forgotten about it and her toilet offended him, but he concealed his vexation when he remembered that he had himself insisted on their securing a box and going because it would be an instructive and aesthetic pleasure for the children.

Praskovya Fëdorovna came in, self-satisfied but yet with a rather guilty air. She sat down and asked how he was, but, as he saw, only for the sake of asking and not in order to learn about it, knowing that there was nothing to learn—and then went on to what she really wanted to say: that she would not on any account have gone but that the box had been taken and Helen and their daughter were going, as well as Petrishchev (the examining magistrate, their daughter's fiancé) and that it was out of the question to let them go alone; but that she would have much preferred to sit with him for a while; and he must be sure to follow the doctor's orders while she was away.

"Oh, and Fëdor Petrovich" (the fiancé) "would like to come in. May he? And Lisa?"

"All right."

Their daughter came in in full evening dress, her fresh young flesh exposed (making a show of that very flesh which in his own case caused so much suffering), strong, healthy, evidently in love, and impatient with illness, suffering, and death, because they interfered with her happiness.

Fëdor Petrovich came in too, in evening dress, his hair curled *à la Capoul*, a tight stiff collar round his long sinewy neck, an enormous white shirt-front and narrow black trousers tightly stretched over his strong thighs. He had one white glove tightly drawn on, and was holding his opera hat in his hand.

Following him the schoolboy crept in unnoticed, in a new uniform, poor little fellow, and wearing gloves. Terribly dark shadows showed under his eyes, the meaning of which Ivan Ilyich knew well.

His son had always seemed pathetic to him, and now it was dreadful to see the boy's frightened look of pity. It seemed to Ivan Ilyich that Vasya was the only one besides Gerasim who understood and pitied him.

They all sat down and again asked how he was. A silence followed. Lisa asked her mother about the opera-glasses, and there was an altercation between mother and daughter as to who had taken them and where they had been put. This occasioned some unpleasantness.

Fëdor Petrovich inquired of Ivan Ilyich whether he had ever seen Sarah Bernhardt. Ivan Ilyich did not at first catch the question, but then replied: "No, have you seen her before?"

"Yes, in *Adrienne Lecouvreur*."[3]

Praskovya Fëdorovna mentioned some rôles in which Sarah Bernhardt was particularly good. Her daughter disagreed. Conversation sprang up as to the

2. Stage name of Rosine Bernard (1844–1923), famed for romantic and tragic roles. 3. A play (1849), by the French dramatist Eugène Scribe (1791–1861), in which the heroine was a famous actress of the 18th century. Tolstoy considered Scribe, who wrote over four hundred plays, a shoddy, commercial playwright.

elegance and realism of her acting—the sort of conversation that is always repeated and is always the same.

In the midst of the conversation Fëdor Petrovich glanced at Ivan Ilyich and became silent. The others also looked at him and grew silent. Ivan Ilyich was staring with glittering eyes straight before him, evidently indignant with them. This had to be rectified, but it was impossible to do so. The silence had to be broken, but for a time no one dared to break it and they all became afraid that the conventional deception would suddenly become obvious and the truth become plain to all. Lisa was the first to pluck up courage and break that silence, but by trying to hide what everybody was feeling, she betrayed it.

"Well, if we are going it's time to start," she said, looking at her watch, a present from her father, and with a faint and significant smile at Fëdor Petrovich relating to something known only to them. She got up with a rustle of her dress.

They all rose, said good-night, and went away.

When they had gone it seemed to Ivan Ilyich that he felt better; the falsity had gone with them. But the pain remained—that same pain and that same fear that made everything monotonously alike, nothing harder and nothing easier. Everything was worse.

Again minute followed minute and hour followed hour. Everything remained the same and there was no cessation. And the inevitable end of it all became more and more terrible.

"Yes, send Gerasim here," he replied to a question Peter asked.

IX

His wife returned late at night. She came in on tiptoe, but he heard her, opened his eyes, and made haste to close them again. She wished to send Gerasim away and to sit with him herself, but he opened his eyes and said: "No, go away."

"Are you in great pain?"

"Always the same."

"Take some opium."

He agreed and took some. She went away.

Till about three in the morning he was in a state of stupefied misery. It seemed to him that he and his pain were being thrust into a narrow, deep black sack, but though they were pushed further and further in they could not be pushed to the bottom. And this, terrible enough in itself, was accompanied by suffering. He was frightened yet wanted to fall through the sack, he struggled but yet co-operated. And suddenly he broke through, fell, and regained consciousness. Gerasim was sitting at the foot of the bed dozing quietly and patiently, while he himself lay with his emaciated stockinged legs resting on Gerasim's shoulders; the same shaded candle was there and the same unceasing pain.

"Go away, Gerasim," he whispered.

"It's all right, sir. I'll stay a while."

"No. Go away."

He removed his legs from Gerasim's shoulders, turned sideways onto his arm, and felt sorry for himself. He only waited till Gerasim had gone into the next room and then restrained himself no longer but wept like a child.

He wept on account of his helplessness, his terrible loneliness, the cruelty of man, the cruelty of God, and the absence of God.

"Why hast Thou done all this? Why hast Thou brought me here? Why, dost Thou torment me so terribly?"

He did not expect an answer and yet wept because there was no answer and could be none. The pain again grew more acute, but he did not stir and did not call. He said to himself: "Go on! Strike me! But what is it for? What have I done to Thee? What is it for?"

Then he grew quiet and not only ceased weeping but even held his breath and became all attention. It was as though he were listening not to an audible voice but to a voice of his soul, to the current of thoughts arising within him.

"What is it you want?" was the first clear conception capable of expression in words, that he heard.

"What do you want? What do you want?" he repeated to himself.

"What do I want? To live and not to suffer," he answered.

And again he listened with such concentrated attention that even his pain did not distract him.

"To live? How?" asked his inner voice.

"Why, to live as I used to—well and pleasantly."

"As you lived before, well and pleasantly?" the voice repeated.

And in imagination he began to recall the moments of his pleasant life. But strange to say none of those best moments of his pleasant life now seemed at all what they had then seemed—none of them except the first recollections of childhood. There, in childhood, there had been something really pleasant with which it would be possible to live if it could return. But the child who had experienced that happiness existed no longer, it was like a reminiscence of somebody else.

As soon as the period began which had produced the present Ivan Ilyich, all that had then seemed joys now melted before his sight and turned into something trivial and often nasty.

And the further he departed from childhood and the nearer he came to the present the more worthless and doubtful were the joys. This began with the School of Law. A little that was really good was still found there—there was light-heartedness, friendship, and hope. But in the upper classes there had already been fewer of such good moments. Then during the first years of his official career, when he was in the service of the Governor, some pleasant moments again occurred: they were the memories of love for a woman. Then all became confused and there was still less of what was good; later on again there was still less that was good, and the further he went the less there was. His marriage, a mere accident, then the disenchantment that followed it, his wife's bad breath and the sensuality and hypocrisy: then that deadly official life and those preoccupations about money, a year of it, and two, and ten, and twenty, and always the same thing. And the longer it lasted the more deadly it became. "It is as if I had been going downhill while I imagined I was going up. And that is really what it was. I was going up in public opinion, but to the same extent life was ebbing away from me. And now it is all done and there is only death."

"Then what does it mean? Why? It can't be that life is so senseless and horrible. But if it really has been so horrible and senseless, why must I die and die in agony? There is something wrong!"

"Maybe I did not live as I ought to have done," it suddenly occurred to him. "But how could that be, when I did everything properly?" he replied, and immediately dismissed from his mind this, the sole solution of all the riddles of life and death, as something quite impossible.

"Then what do you want now? To live? Live how? Live as you lived in the law courts when the usher proclaimed 'The judge is coming!' The judge is coming, the judge!" he repeated to himself. "Here he is, the judge. But I am not guilty!" he exclaimed angrily. "What is it for?" And he ceased crying, but turning his face to the wall continued to ponder on the same question: Why, and for what purpose, is there all this horror? But however much he pondered he found no answer. And whenever the thought occurred to him, as it often did, that it all resulted from his not having lived as he ought to have done, he at once recalled the correctness of his whole life, and dismissed so strange an idea.

X

Another fortnight passed. Ivan Ilyich now no longer left his sofa. He would not lie in bed but lay on the sofa, facing the wall nearly all the time. He suffered ever the same unceasing agonies and in his loneliness pondered always on the same insoluble question: "What is this? Can it be that it is Death?" And the inner voice answered: "Yes, it is Death."

"Why these sufferings?" And the voice answered, "For no reason—they just are so." Beyond and besides this there was nothing.

From the very beginning of his illness, ever since he had first been to see the doctor, Ivan Ilyich's life had been divided between two contrary and alternating moods: now it was despair and the expectation of this uncomprehended and terrible death, and now hope and an intently interested observation of the functioning of his organs. Now before his eyes there was only a kidney or an intestine that temporarily evaded its duty, and now only that incomprehensible and dreadful death from which it was impossible to escape.

These two states of mind had alternated from the very beginning of his illness, but the further it progressed the more doubtful and fantastic became the conception of the kidney, and the more real the sense of impending death.

He had but to call to mind what he had been three months before and what he was now, to call to mind with what regularity he had been going downhill, for every possibility of hope to be shattered.

Latterly during that loneliness in which he found himself as he lay facing the back of the sofa, a loneliness in the midst of a populous town and surrounded by numerous acquaintances and relations but that yet could not have been more complete anywhere—either at the bottom of the sea or under the earth—during that terrible loneliness Ivan Ilyich had lived only in memories of the past. Pictures of his past rose before him one after another. They always began with what was nearest in time and then went back to what was most remote—to his childhood—and rested there. If he thought of the stewed prunes that had been offered him that day, his mind went back to the raw shrivelled French plums of his childhood, their peculiar flavour and the flow of saliva when he sucked their stones, and along with the memory of that taste came a whole series of memories of those days: his nurse, his brother, and their toys. "No, I mustn't think of that. . . . It is too painful," Ivan Ilyich said to himself, and brought himself back to the present—to the button on the back of the sofa and the creases in its morocco. "Morocco is expensive, but it does not wear well: there had been a quarrel about it. It was a different kind of quarrel and a different kind of morocco that time when we tore father's portfolio and were punished, and mamma brought us some tarts. . . ." And again his thoughts dwelt on his childhood, and again it was painful and he tried to banish them and fix his mind on something else.

Then again together with that chain of memories another series passed through his mind—of how his illness had progressed and grown worse. There also the further back he looked the more life there had been. There had been more of what was good in life and more of life itself. The two merged together. "Just as the pain went on getting worse and worse, so my life grew worse and worse," he thought. "There is one bright spot there at the back, at the beginning of life, and afterwards all becomes blacker and blacker and proceeds more and more rapidly—in inverse ratio to the square of the distance from death," thought Ivan Ilyich. And the example of a stone falling downwards with increasing velocity entered his mind. Life, a series of increasing sufferings, flies further and further towards its end—the most terrible suffering. "I am flying. . . ." He shuddered, shifted himself, and tried to resist, but was already aware that resistance was impossible, and again with eyes weary of gazing but unable to cease seeing what was before them, he stared at the back of the sofa and waited—awaiting that dreadful fall and shock and destruction.

"Resistance is impossible!" he said to himself. "If I could only understand what it is all for! But that too is impossible. An explanation would be possible if it could be said that I have not lived as I ought to. But it is impossible to say that," and he remembered all the legality, correctitude, and propriety of his life. "That at any rate can certainly not be admitted," he thought, and his lips smiled ironically as if someone could see that smile and be taken in by it. "There is no explanation! Agony, death. . . . What for?"

XI

Another two weeks went by in this way and during that fortnight an event occurred that Ivan Ilyich and his wife had desired. Petrishchev formally proposed. It happened in the evening. The next day Praskovya Fёdorovna came into her husband's room considering how best to inform him of it, but that very night there had been a fresh change for the worse in his condition. She found him still lying on the sofa but in a different position. He lay on his back, groaning and staring fixedly straight in front of him.

She began to remind him of his medicines, but he turned his eyes towards her with such a look that she did not finish what she was saying; so great an animosity, to her in particular, did that look express.

"For Christ's sake let me die in peace!" he said.

She would have gone away, but just then their daughter came in and went up to say good morning. He looked at her as he had done at his wife, and in reply to her inquiry about his health said dryly that he would soon free them all of himself. They were both silent and after sitting with him for a while went away.

"Is it our fault?" Lisa said to her mother. "It's as if we were to blame! I am sorry for papa, but why should we be tortured?"

The doctor came at his usual time. Ivan Ilyich answered "Yes" and "No," never taking his angry eyes from him, and at last said: "You know you can do nothing for me, so leave me alone."

"We can ease your sufferings."

"You can't even do that. Let me be."

The doctor went into the drawing-room and told Praskovya Fëdorovna that the case was very serious and that the only resource left was opium to allay her husband's sufferings, which must be terrible.

It was true, as the doctor said, that Ivan Ilyich's physical sufferings were terrible, but worse than the physical sufferings were his mental sufferings which were his chief torture.

His mental sufferings were due to the fact that that night, as he looked at Gerasim's sleepy, good-natured face with its prominent cheek-bones, the question suddenly occurred to him: "What if my whole life has really been wrong?"

It occurred to him that what had appeared perfectly impossible before, namely that he had not spent his life as he should have done, might after all be true. It occurred to him that his scarcely perceptible attempts to struggle against what was considered good by the most highly placed people, those scarcely noticeable impulses which he had immediately suppressed, might have been the real thing, and all the rest false. And his professional duties and the whole arrangement of his life and of his family, and all his social and official interests, might all have been false. He tried to defend all those things to himself and suddenly felt the weakness of what he was defending. There was nothing to defend.

"But if that is so," he said to himself, "and I am leaving this life with the consciousness that I have lost all that was given me and it is impossible to rectify it—what then?"

He lay on his back and began to pass his life in review in quite a new way. In the morning when he saw first his footman, then his wife, then his daughter, and then the doctor, their every word and movement confirmed to him the awful truth that had been revealed to him during the night. In them he saw himself—all that for which he had lived—and saw clearly that it was not real at all, but a terrible and huge deception which had hidden both life and death. This consciousness intensified his physical suffering tenfold. He groaned and tossed about, and pulled at his clothing which choked and stifled him. And he hated them on that account.

He was given a large dose of opium and became unconscious, but at noon his sufferings began again. He drove everybody away and tossed from side to side.

His wife came to him and said:

"Jean, my dear, do this for me. It can't do any harm and often helps. Healthy people often do it."

He opened his eyes wide.

"What? Take communion? Why? It's unnecessary! However . . ."

She began to cry.

"Yes, do, my dear. I'll send for our priest. He is such a nice man."

"All right. Very well," he muttered.

When the priest came and heard his confession, Ivan Ilyich was softened and seemed to feel a relief from his doubts and consequently from his sufferings, and for a moment there came a ray of hope. He again began to think of the vermiform appendix and the possibility of correcting it. He received the sacrament with tears in his eyes.

When they laid him down again afterwards he felt a moment's ease, and the hope that he might live awoke in him again. He began to think of the operation that had been suggested to him. "To live! I want to live!" he said to himself.

His wife came in to congratulate him after his communion, and when uttering the usual conventional words she added:

"You feel better, don't you?"

Without looking at her he said "Yes."

Her dress, her figure, the expression of her face, the tone of her voice, all revealed the same thing. "This is wrong, it is not as it should be. All you have lived for and still live for is falsehood and deception, hiding life and death from you." And as soon as he admitted that thought, his hatred and his agonizing physical suffering again sprang up, and with that suffering a consciousness of the unavoidable, approaching end. And to this was added a new sensation of grinding shooting pain and a feeling of suffocation.

The expression of his face when he uttered that "yes" was dreadful. Having uttered it, he looked her straight in the eyes, turned on his face with a rapidity extraordinary in his weak state and shouted:

"Go away! Go away and leave me alone!"

XII

From that moment the screaming began that continued for three days, and was so terrible that one could not hear it through two closed doors without horror. At the moment he answered his wife he realized that he was lost, that there was no return, that the end had come, the very end, and his doubts were still unsolved and remained doubts.

"Oh! Oh! Oh!" he cried in various intonations. He had begun by screaming "I won't!" and continued screaming on the letter "o."

For three whole days, during which time did not exist for him, he struggled in that black sack into which he was being thrust by an invisible, resistless force. He struggled as a man condemned to death struggles in the hands of the executioner, knowing that he cannot save himself. And every moment he felt that despite all his efforts he was drawing nearer and nearer to what terrified him. He felt that his agony was due to his being thrust into that black hole and still more to his not being able to get right into it. He was hindered from getting into it by his conviction that his life had been a good one. That very justification of his life held him fast and prevented his moving forward, and it caused him most torment of all.

Suddenly some force struck him in the chest and side, making it still harder to breathe, and he fell through the hole and there at the bottom was a light. What had happened to him was like the sensation one sometimes experiences in a railway carriage when one thinks one is going backwards while one is really going forwards and suddenly becomes aware of the real direction.

"Yes, it was all not the right thing," he said to himself, "but that's no matter. It can be done. But what *is* the right thing?" he asked himself, and suddenly grew quiet.

This occurred at the end of the third day, two hours before his death. Just then his schoolboy son had crept softly in and gone up to the bedside. The dying man was still screaming desperately and waving his arms. His hand fell on the boy's head, and the boy caught it, pressed it to his lips, and began to cry.

At that very moment Ivan Ilyich fell through and caught sight of the light, and it was revealed to him that though his life had not been what it should have been, this could still be rectified. He asked himself, "What *is* the right thing?" and grew still, listening. Then he felt that someone was kissing his hand. He opened his eyes, looked at his son, and felt sorry for him. His wife came up to him and he glanced at her. She was gazing at him open-mouthed, with undried tears on her nose and cheek and a despairing look on her face. He felt sorry for her too.

"Yes, I am making them wretched," he thought. "They are sorry, but it will be better for them when I die." He wished to say this but had not the strength to utter it. "Besides, why speak? I must act," he thought. With a look at his wife he indicated his son and said: "Take him away . . . sorry for him . . . sorry for you too. . . ." He tried to add, "forgive me," but said "forgo" and waved his hand, knowing that He whose understanding mattered would understand.

And suddenly it grew clear to him that what had been oppressing him and would not leave him was all dropping away at once from two sides, from ten sides, and from all sides. He was sorry for them, he must act so as not to hurt them: release them and free himself from these sufferings. "How good and how simple!" he thought. "And the pain?" he asked himself. "What has become of it? Where are you, pain?"

He turned his attention to it.

"Yes, here it is. Well, what of it? Let the pain be."

"And death . . . where is it?"

He sought his former accustomed fear of death and did not find it. "Where is it? What death?" There was no fear because there was no death.

In place of death there was light.

"So that's what it is!" he suddenly exclaimed aloud. "What joy!"

To him all this happened in a single instant, and the meaning of that instant did not change. For those present his agony continued for another two hours. Something rattled in his throat, his emaciated body twitched, then the gasping and rattle became less and less frequent.

"It is finished!" said someone near him.

He heard these words and repeated them in his soul.

"Death is finished," he said to himself. "It is no more!"

He drew in a breath, stopped in the midst of a sigh, stretched out, and died.

REVOLUTIONARY PRINCIPLES

The tumultuous changes of the nineteenth century reflected both a rebellion against established authority and great faith in progress. Each advance in science and technology, each conquest of foreign lands and markets seemed to open up horizons for the enterprising individual or nation. In London in 1851 a vast iron and glass construction known as the Crystal Palace was erected for the Great Exhibition, drawing 14,000 exhibitors (almost half of them foreign) and constant crowds of spectators who flocked to see a promising vision of the future. Wealth was visible, although not all participated, and social changes came rapidly as class distinctions blurred and more people moved to the cities in search of economic opportunity. The middle class was the engine of modern Western society, which it considered the pinnacle of civilization, and it was firmly convinced of the rightness of its own social, scientific, and economic principles. Some, however, had misgivings about aspects of modern thought. They challenged a range of assumptions in science, philosophy, and the structure of society, even going so far as to question established concepts of human identity.

It took a naturalist, Charles Darwin, to focus attention on the way that data about forms of life at various eras and around the globe suggested complex patterns of organic evolution. His conclusions about the structure and origins of coral reefs did not arouse controversy. But when he turned his attention to the way that human beings formed part of a larger, ongoing pattern of evolution, he offended those who followed a literal interpretation of biblical teaching and insisted that the world and all species within it were created as unique life-forms in a single divine gesture. It was not long before scientists accepted Darwin's general principles, but the idea of human beings as part of evolution continued to disturb those who felt that it meant the end of religious belief and moral standards.

More direct assaults came from philosophy and materialist economics. Friedrich Nietzsche declared Western culture a history of moral decay and bourgeois society the antithesis of a free and inquiring mind. Christianity's doctrine of humility and self-sacrifice, he wrote, had sapped the will and aggressive instincts of countless generations, leaving only timid personalities who were afraid of intellectual curiosity and desperate for certainties. A more concrete picture of cultural decline emerged from the writings of Karl Marx and Friedrich Engels, who predicted that the capitalist free-enterprise system that had created the Crystal Palace was now on the verge of collapse and would soon be overturned by the very class of laborers it had created to meet industrial demands. Although the political insurrections of the first half of the nineteenth century were quickly crushed, the prospect of an organized political opposition that crossed national boundaries was indeed—as claimed in the *Manifesto of the Communist Party*—a revolutionary specter that unsettled the ruling class throughout Europe.

To these more general perspectives were added specific critiques of the way that contemporary society carried out its ostensible principles. In England, debates over the rights of women had existed for over a century but had made little progress even in later years owing to the opposition of the conservative queen Victoria. Women's position before the law was confused or at least ambiguous: before marriage, women could own property, earn income, and enter into contracts; after marriage, they lost all legal rights, which were transferred to the husband. The novelist Mona Caird caused a furious controversy when she criticized the virtual slavery to which marriage reduced women and indicted the patriarchal system on which it was based.

In France, the Dreyfus case exposed the depth of anti-Semitism in nineteenth-century society and the ease with which passion could corrupt justice. The gradually accumulating evidence that showed Dreyfus's innocence also showed a cover-up that depended on collusion among elements of the military, the legislature, the courts, and the press, with pressure reaching as far as the president. It is doubtful that all the facts would have been revealed if not for the publicity given to the affair in a series of newspaper articles by novelist Émile Zola, who paid a heavy price over subsequent years for his courage.

The first half of the nineteenth century was marked by a series of unsuccessful political revolutions, rebellions that temporarily threatened the power of traditional monarchies throughout Europe. Yet the nineteenth century's most successful rebellions may have been those of the mind: of revolutionary principles that outlined systematic challenges to accepted ideas in science, philosophy, and society, and that laid the basis for corresponding developments in the following century.

CHARLES DARWIN
1809–1882

As a naturalist, Darwin contributed to many fields; as the author of the *The Origin of Species* (1859) and the *The Descent of Man* (1871), he provoked a reevaluation of what it means to be human by suggesting that all living beings are related. The notes that Darwin took on his five-year voyage as naturalist on the HMS *Beagle* (1831–36) as well as his later researches convinced him that life on earth was much older than had been thought and that the various species had evolved from simpler to more complex organisms through a gradual pattern that fitted survival traits to environmental conditions. Darwin accumulated masses of data about plants, animals, and geological phenomena and scrutinized them for patterns of evolutionary development, signs of what he called the "mutability of species." Most of his contemporaries believed in the fixed identity of all forms of life: that a dog was always a dog, a chimpanzee a chimpanzee, and so on. They were puzzled to see evidence of change and shocked to hear Darwin proclaim that the ancestor of modern human beings was a "hairy, tailed quadruped, probably arboreal in its habits." Not only did the concept lack dignity, but it undermined traditional religious descriptions of human beings as created for all time in the same image; in addition, it made the concept of original sin difficult to uphold. The controversy was bitter, and, although there have been some accommodations, it persists today.

Darwinian thought and, more broadly, "Darwinism" focus on a few basic terms stemming from evolutionary theory. "Mutability of species" is one, and within that concept the notions of "natural selection" and the "survival of the fittest" have found echoes far beyond their original context. For Darwin, natural selection was a factual description of the way that some species evolved traits that allowed them to survive in a hostile environment. Others adapted his concept to describe a "social Darwinism" in which the survival of the fittest meant using force or privilege to prevail. Darwin did not ignore the ethical implications of his model and tried to integrate moral issues into his picture of human evolution and survival. His lasting influence, however, comes from a complex model of organic evolution that still provokes debate in many disciplines and from the patient devotion to evidence and scientific method with which he pursued the truth.

The Origin of Species[1]

FROM CHAPTER XIV

Recapitulation and Conclusion

As each species tends by its geometrical ratio of reproduction to increase inordinately in number; and as the modified descendants of each species will be enabled to increase by so much the more as they become more diversified in habits and structure, so as to be enabled to seize on many and widely different places in the economy of nature, there will be a constant tendency in natural selection to preserve the most divergent offspring of any one species. Hence during a long-continued course of modification, the slight differences, characteristic of varieties of the same species, tend to be augmented into the greater differences characteristic of species of the same genus. New and improved varieties will inevitably supplant and exterminate the older, less improved and intermediate varieties; and thus species are rendered to a large extent defined and distinct objects. Dominant species belonging to the larger groups tend to give birth to new and dominant forms; so that each large group tends to become still larger, and at the same time more divergent in character. But as all groups cannot thus succeed in increasing in size, for the world would not hold them, the more dominant groups beat the less dominant. This tendency in the large groups to go on increasing in size and diverging in character, together with the almost inevitable contingency of much extinction, explains the arrangement of all the forms of life, in groups subordinate to groups, all within a few great classes, which we now see everywhere around us, and which has prevailed throughout all time. This grand fact of the grouping of all organic beings seems to me utterly inexplicable on the theory of creation.[2]

As natural selection acts solely by accumulating slight, successive, favorable variations, it can produce no great or sudden modification; it can act only by very short and slow steps. Hence the canon of "Natura non facit saltum,"[3] which every fresh addition to our knowledge tends to make more strictly correct, is on this theory simply intelligible. We can plainly see why nature is prodigal in variety, though niggard in innovation. But why this should be a law of nature if each species has been independently created, no man can explain.

Many other facts are, as it seems to me, explicable on this theory. How strange it is that a bird, under the form of woodpecker, should have been created to prey on insects on the ground; that upland geese, which never or rarely swim, should have been created with webbed feet; that a thrush should have been created to dive and feed on sub-aquatic insects; and that a petrel should have been created with habits and structure fitting it for the life of an auk or grebe! and so on in endless other cases. But on the view of each species constantly trying to increase in number, with natural selection always ready to adapt the slowly varying descendants of each to any unoccupied or

---

1. Published in 1859. 2. A religious belief according to which the world and all forms of life were divinely created in one moment. The date of creation was calculated as October 23, 4004 B.C.E., by Irish bishop James Ussher (1581–1656). 3. Nature does not make a leap (Latin).

ill-occupied place in nature, these facts cease to be strange, or perhaps might even have been anticipated.

As natural selection acts by competition, it adapts the inhabitants of each country only in relation to the degree of perfection of their associates; so that we need feel no surprise at the inhabitants of any one country, although on the ordinary view supposed to have been specially created and adapted for that country, being beaten and supplanted by the naturalized productions from another land. Nor ought we to marvel if all the contrivances in nature be not, as far as we can judge, absolutely perfect; and if some of them be abhorrent to our ideas of fitness. We need not marvel at the sting of the bee causing the bee's own death; at drones being produced in such vast numbers for one single act, and being then slaughtered by their sterile sisters; at the astonishing waste of pollen by our fir-trees; at the instinctive hatred of the queen bee for her own fertile daughters; at ichneumonidæ[4] feeding within the live bodies of caterpillars; and at other such cases. The wonder indeed is, on the theory of natural selection, that more cases of the want of absolute perfection have not been observed.

The complex and little known laws governing variation are the same, as far as we can see, with the laws which have governed the production of so-called specific forms. In both cases physical conditions seem to have produced but little direct effect; yet when varieties enter any zone, they occasionally assume some of the characters of the species proper to that zone. In both varieties and species, use and disuse seem to have produced some effect; for it is difficult to resist this conclusion when we look, for instance, at the logger-headed duck, which has wings incapable of flight, in nearly the same condition as in the domestic duck; or when we look at the burrowing tucutucu,[5] which is occasionally blind, and then at certain moles, which are habitually blind and have their eyes covered with skin; or when we look at the blind animals inhabiting the dark caves of America and Europe. In both varieties and species correlation of growth seems to have played a most important part, so that when one part has been modified other parts are necessarily modified. In both varieties and species reversions to long-lost characters occur. How inexplicable on the theory of creation is the occasional appearance of stripes on the shoulder and legs of the several species of the horse-genus and in their hybrids! How simply is this fact explained if we believe that these species have descended from a striped progenitor, in the same manner as the several domestic breeds of pigeon have descended from the blue and barred rock-pigeon!

On the ordinary view of each species having been independently created, why should the specific characters, or those by which the species of the same genus differ from each other, be more variable than the generic characters in which they all agree? Why, for instance, should the color of a flower be more likely to vary in any one species of a genus, if the other species, supposed to have been created independently, have differently colored flowers, than if all the species of the genus have the same colored flowers? If species are only well-marked varieties, of which the characters have become in a high degree permanent, we can understand this fact; for they have already

---

4. Ichneumon wasps lay their eggs inside the body of a caterpillar, which subsequently becomes food for the newly hatched larvae.   5. A small burrowing rodent similar to a prairie rat, found in Patagonia and La Plata.

varied since they branched off from a common progenitor in certain characters, by which they have come to be specifically distinct from each other; and therefore these same characters would be more likely still to be variable than the generic characters which have been inherited without change for an enormous period. It is inexplicable on the theory of creation why a part developed in a very unusual manner in any one species of a genus, and therefore, as we may naturally infer, of great importance to the species, should be eminently liable to variation; but, on my view, this part has undergone, since the several species branched off from a common progenitor, an unusual amount of variability and modification, and therefore we might expect this part generally to be still variable. But a part may be developed in the most unusual manner, like the wing of a bat, and yet not be more variable than any other structure, if the part be common to many subordinate forms, that is, if it has been inherited for a very long period; for in this case it will have been rendered constant by long-continued natural selection.

Glancing at instincts, marvelous as some are, they offer no greater difficulty than does corporeal structure on the theory of the natural selection of successive, slight, but profitable modifications. We can thus understand why nature moves by graduated steps in endowing different animals of the same class with their several instincts. I have attempted to show how much light the principle of gradation throws on the admirable architectural powers of the hive-bee. Habit no doubt sometimes comes into play in modifying instincts: but it certainly is not indispensable, as we see, in the case of neuter insects, which leave no progeny to inherit the effects of long-continued habit. On the view of all the species of the same genus having descended from a common parent, and having inherited much in common, we can understand how it is that allied species, when placed under considerably different conditions of life, yet should follow nearly the same instincts; why the thrush of South America, for instance, lines her nest with mud like our British species. On the view of instincts having been slowly acquired through natural selection we need not marvel at some instincts being apparently not perfect and liable to mistakes, and at many instincts causing other animals to suffer.

If species be only well-marked and permanent varieties, we can at once see why their crossed offspring should follow the same complex laws in their degrees and kinds of resemblance to their parents,—in being absorbed into each other by successive crosses, and in other such points,—as do the crossed offspring of acknowledged varieties. On the other hand, these would be strange facts if species have been independently created, and varieties have been produced by secondary laws.

If we admit that the geological record is imperfect in an extreme degree, then such facts as the record gives, support the theory of descent with modification. New species have come on the stage slowly and at successive intervals; and the amount of change, after equal intervals of time, is widely different in different groups. The extinction of species and of whole groups of species, which has played so conspicuous a part in the history of the organic world, almost inevitably follows on the principle of natural selection; for old forms will be supplanted by new and improved forms. Neither single species nor groups of species reappear when the chain of ordinary generation has once been broken.

The fact, as we have seen, that all past and present organic beings constitute one grand natural system, with group subordinate to group, and with extinct groups often falling in between recent groups, is intelligible on the theory of natural selection with its contingencies of extinction and divergence of character. On these same principles we see how it is, that the mutual affinities of the species and genera within each class are so complex and circuitous. We see why certain characters are far more serviceable than others for classification;—why adaptive characters though of paramount importance to the being, are of hardly any importance in classification; why characters derived from rudimentary parts, though of no service to the being, are often of high classificatory value; and why embryological characters are the most valuable of all. The real affinities of all organic beings are due to inheritance or community of descent. The natural system is a genealogical arrangement, in which we have to discover the lines of descent by the most permanent characters, however slight their vital importance may be.

The framework of bones being the same in the hand of a man, wing of a bat, fin of the porpoise, and leg of the horse,—the same number of vertebræ forming the neck of the giraffe and of the elephant,—and innumerable other such facts, at once explain themselves on the theory of descent with slow and slight successive modifications. The similarity of pattern in the wing and leg of a bat, though used for such different purpose,—in the jaws and legs of a crab,—in the petals, stamens, and pistils of a flower, is likewise intelligible on the view of the gradual modification of parts or organs, which were alike in the early progenitor of each class.* * *

* * *Nature may be said to have taken pains to reveal, by rudimentary organs and by homologous structures, her scheme of modification, which it seems that we willfully will not understand.

I have now recapitulated the chief facts and considerations which have thoroughly convinced me that species have changed, and are still slowly changing by the preservation and accumulation of successive slight favorable variations. Why, it may be asked, have all the most eminent living naturalists and geologists rejected this view of the mutability of species? It cannot be asserted that organic beings in a state of nature are subject to no variation; it cannot be proved that the amount of variation in the course of long ages is a limited quantity; no clear distinction has been, or can be, drawn between species and well-marked varieties. It cannot be maintained that species when intercrossed are invariably sterile, and varieties invariably fertile; or that sterility is a special endowment and sign of creation. The belief that species were immutable productions was almost unavoidable as long as the history of the world was thought to be of short duration,[6] and now that we have acquired some idea of the lapse of time, we are too apt to assume, without proof, that the geological record is so perfect that it would have afforded us plain evidence of the mutation of species, if they had undergone mutation.

But the chief cause of our natural unwillingness to admit that one species has given birth to other and distinct species, is that we are always slow in admitting any great change of which we do not see the intermediate steps.

6. That is, in the religious theory of creation.

The difficulty is the same as that felt by so many geologists, when Lyell[7] first insisted that long lines of inland cliffs had been formed, and great valleys excavated, by the slow action of the coast-waves. The mind cannot possibly grasp the full meaning of the term of a hundred million years; it cannot add up and perceive the full effects of many slight variations, accumulated during an almost infinite number of generations.

Although I am fully convinced of the truth of the views given in this volume under the form of an abstract, I by no means expect to convince experienced naturalists whose minds are stocked with a multitude of facts all viewed, during a long course of years, from a point of view directly opposite to mine. It is so easy to hide our ignorance under such expressions as the "plan of creation," "unity of design," et cetera, and to think that we give an explanation when we only restate a fact. Any one whose disposition leads him to attach more weight to unexplained difficulties than to the explanation of a certain number of facts will certainly reject my theory. A few naturalists, endowed with much flexibility of mind, and who have already begun to doubt on the immutability of species, may be influenced by this volume; but I look with confidence to the future, to young and rising naturalists, who will be able to view both sides of the question with impartiality. Whoever is led to believe that species are mutable will do good service by conscientiously expressing his conviction; for only thus can the load of prejudice by which this subject is overwhelmed be removed.

*   *   *

In the distant future I see open fields for far more important researches. Psychology will be based on a new foundation, that of the necessary acquirement of each mental power and capacity by gradation. Light will be thrown on the origin of man and his history.

Authors of the highest eminence seem to be fully satisfied with the view that each species has been independently created. To my mind it accords better with what we know of the laws impressed on matter by the Creator, that the production and extinction of the past and present inhabitants of the world should have been due to secondary causes, like those determining the birth and death of the individual. When I view all beings not as special creations, but as the lineal descendants of some few beings which lived long before the first bed of the Silurian[8] system was deposited, they seem to me to become ennobled. Judging from the past, we may safely infer that not one living species will transmit its unaltered likeness to a distant futurity. And of the species now living very few will transmit progeny of any kind to a far distant futurity; for the manner in which all organic beings are grouped, shows that the greater number of species of each genus, and all the species of many genera, have left no descendants, but have become utterly extinct. We can so far take a prophetic glance into futurity as to foretell that it will be the common and widely-spread species, belonging to the larger and dominant groups, which will ultimately prevail and procreate new and dominant species.* * *

It is interesting to contemplate an entangled bank, clothed with many

<hr/>

7. I.e., Sir Charles Lyell (1797–1875), British geologist and author of the influential three-volume *Principles of Geology* (1830–33).   8. In geology, the third period of the Paleozoic era (405 million to 440 million years ago).

plants of many kinds, with birds singing on the bushes, with various insects flitting about, and with worms crawling through the damp earth, and to reflect that these elaborately constructed forms, so different from each other, and dependent on each other in so complex a manner, have all been produced by laws acting around us. These laws, taken in the largest sense, being Growth with Reproduction; Inheritance which is almost implied by reproduction; Variability from the indirect and direct action of the external conditions of life, and from use and disuse; a Ratio of Increase so high as to lead to a Struggle for Life, and as a consequence to Natural Selection, entailing Divergence of Character and the Extinction of less-improved forms. Thus, from the war of nature, from famine and death, the most exalted object which we are capable of conceiving, namely, the production of the higher animals, directly follows. There is grandeur in this view of life, with its several powers, having been originally breathed into a few forms or into one; and that, whilst this planet has gone cycling on according to the fixed law of gravity, from so simple a beginning endless forms most beautiful and most wonderful have been, and are being, evolved.

The Descent of Man[1]

FROM CHAPTER XXI

General Summary and Conclusion

A brief summary will be sufficient to recall to the reader's mind the more salient points in this work. Many of the views which have been advanced are highly speculative, and some no doubt will prove erroneous; but I have in every case given the reasons which have led me to one view rather than to another. It seemed worth while to try how far the principle of evolution would throw light on some of the more complex problems in the natural history of man. False facts are highly injurious to the progress of science, for they often endure long; but false views, if supported by some evidence, do little harm, for every one takes a salutary pleasure in proving their falseness and when this is done, one path towards error is closed and the road to truth is often at the same time opened.

The main conclusion here arrived at, and now held by many naturalists who are well competent to form a sound judgment, is that man is descended from some less highly organized form. The grounds upon which this conclusion rests will never be shaken, for the close similarity between man and the lower animals in embryonic development, as well as in innumerable points of structure and constitution, both of high and of the most trifling importance,—the rudiments which he retains, and the abnormal reversions to which he is occasionally liable,—are facts which cannot be disputed. They have long been known, but until recently they told us nothing with respect to the origin of man. Now when viewed by the light of our knowledge of the whole organic world, their meaning is unmistakable. The great principle of evolution stands up clear and firm, when these groups or facts are considered

1. Published in 1871.

in connection with others, such as the mutual affinities of the members of the same group, their geographical distribution in past and present times, and their geological succession. It is incredible that all these facts should speak falsely. He who is not content to look, like a savage, at the phenomena of nature as disconnected, cannot any longer believe that man is the work of a separate act of creation. He will be forced to admit that the close resemblance of the embryo of man to that, for instance, of a dog—the construction of his skull, limbs and whole frame on the same plan with that of other mammals, independently of the uses to which the parts may be put—the occasional re-appearance of various structures, for instance of several muscles, which man does not normally possess, but which are common to the Quadrumana[2] and a crowd of analogous facts—all point in the plainest manner to the conclusion that man is the co-descendant with other mammals of a common progenitor.

We have seen that man incessantly presents individual differences in all parts of his body and in his mental faculties. These differences or variations seem to be induced by the same general causes, and to obey the same laws as with the lower animals. In both cases similar laws of inheritance prevail. Man tends to increase at a greater rate than his means of subsistence; consequently he is occasionally subjected to a severe struggle for existence, and natural selection will have effected whatever lies within its scope. A succession of strongly-marked variations of a similar nature is by no means requisite; slight fluctuating differences in the individual suffice for the work of natural selection; not that we have any reason to suppose that in the same species, all parts of the organisation tend to vary to the same degree. We may feel assured that the inherited effects of the long-continued use or disuse of parts will have done much in the same direction with natural selection. Modifications formerly of importance, though no longer of any special use, are long-inherited. When one part is modified, other parts change through the principle of correlation, of which we have instances in many curious cases of correlated monstrosities. Something may be attributed to the direct and definite action of the surrounding conditions of life, such as abundant food, heat or moisture; and lastly, many characters of slight physiological importance, some indeed of considerable importance, have been gained through sexual selection.

* * *

By considering the embryological structure of man,—the homologies which he presents with the lower animals,—the rudiments which he retains,—and the reversions to which he is liable, we can partly recall in imagination the former condition of our early progenitors; and can approximately place them in their proper place in the zoological series. We thus learn that man is descended from a hairy, tailed quadruped, probably arboreal in its habits, and an inhabitant of the Old World. This creature, if its whole structure had been examined by a naturalist, would have been classed amongst the Quadrumana, as surely as the still more ancient progenitor of the Old and New World monkeys. The Quadrumana and all the higher mam-

2. Literally, "four-handed": mammals like monkeys and apes whose four feet possess opposable digits and can, therefore, be used as hands.

mals are probably derived from an ancient marsupial animal, and this through a long series of diversified forms, from some amphibian-like creature, and this again from some fish-like animal. In the dim obscurity of the past we can see that the early progenitor of all the Vertebrata must have been an aquatic animal provided with branchiæ[3] with the two sexes united in the same individual, and with the most important organs of the body (such as the brain and heart) imperfectly or not at all developed. This animal seems to have been more like the larvæ of the existing marine Ascidians[4] than any other known form.

The high standard of our intellectual powers and moral disposition is the greatest difficulty which presents itself, after we have been driven to this conclusion on the origin of man. But every one who admits the principle of evolution, must see that the mental powers of the higher animals, which are the same in kind with those of man, though so different in degree, are capable of advancement. Thus the interval between the mental powers of one of the higher apes and of a fish, or between those of an ant and scale-insect, is immense; yet their development does not offer any special difficulty; for with our domesticated animals, the mental faculties are certainly variable, and the variations are inherited. No one doubts that they are of the utmost importance to animals in a state of nature. Therefore the conditions are favorable for their development through natural selection. The same conclusion may be extended to man; the intellect must have been all-important to him, even at a very remote period, as enabling him to invent and use language, to make weapons, tools, traps, et cetera, whereby with the aid of his social habits, he long ago became the most dominant of all living creatures.

A great stride in the development of the intellect will have followed, as soon as the half-art and half-instinct of language came into use; for the continued use of language will have reacted on the brain and produced an inherited effect; and this again will have reacted on the improvement of language. As Mr. Chauncey Wright[5] has well remarked, the largeness of the brain in man relatively to his body, compared with the lower animals, may be attributed in chief part to the early use of some simple form of language,— that wonderful engine which affixes signs to all sorts of objects and qualities, and excites trains of thought which would never arise from the mere impression of the senses, or if they did arise could not be followed out. The higher intellectual powers of man, such as those of ratiocination, abstraction, self-consciousness, et cetera, probably follow from the continued improvement and exercise of the other mental faculties.

The development of the moral qualities is a more interesting problem. The foundation lies in the social instincts, including under this term the family ties. These instincts are highly complex, and in the case of the lower animals give special tendencies towards certain definite actions; but the more important elements are love, and the distinct emotion of sympathy. Animals endowed with the social instincts take pleasure in one another's company, warn one another of danger, defend and aid one another in many ways. These instincts do not extend to all the individuals of the species, but only to those

---

3. Gills. *Vertebrata*: animals having a backbone or spinal column. 4. Sea squirts. 5. The American philosopher, metaphysician, and mathematician Chauncey Wright (1830–1875) was also an ardent and influential Darwinian on the Harvard scene.

of the same community. As they are highly beneficial to the species, they have in all probability been acquired through natural selection.

A moral being is one who is capable of reflecting on his past actions and their motives—of approving of some and disapproving of others; and the fact that man is the one being who certainly deserves this designation, is the greatest of all distinctions between him and the lower animals. But in the fourth chapter I have endeavored to shew that the moral sense follows, firstly, from the enduring and ever-present nature of the social instincts; secondly, from man's appreciation of the approbation and disapprobation of his fellows; and thirdly, from the high activity of his mental faculties, with past impressions extremely vivid; and in these latter respects he differs from the lower animals. Owing to this condition of mind, man cannot avoid looking both backwards and forwards, and comparing past impressions. Hence after some temporary desire or passion has mastered his social instincts, he reflects and compares the now weakened impression of such past impulses with the ever-present social instincts; and he then feels that sense of dissatisfaction which all unsatisfied instincts leave behind them, he therefore resolves to act differently for the future,—and this is conscience.* * *

Sexual selection has been treated at great length in this work; for, as I have attempted to shew, it has played an important part in the history of the organic world. I am aware that much remains doubtful, but I have endeavored to give a fair view of the whole case. In the lower divisions of the animal kingdom, sexual selection seems to have done nothing: such animals are often affixed for life to the same spot, or have the sexes combined in the same individual, or what is still more important, their perceptive and intellectual faculties are not sufficiently advanced to allow of the feelings of love and jealousy, or of the exertion of choice. When, however, we come to the Arthropoda[6] and Vertebrata, even to the lowest classes in these two great Sub-Kingdoms, sexual selection has effected much.

In the several great classes of the animal kingdom,—in mammals, birds, reptiles, fishes, insects, and even crustaceans,—the differences between the sexes follow nearly the same rules. The males are almost always the wooers; and they alone are armed with special weapons for fighting with their rivals. They are generally stronger and larger than the females, and are endowed with the requisite qualities of courage and pugnacity. They are provided, either exclusively or in a much higher degree than the females, with organs for vocal or instrumental music, and with odoriferous glands. They are ornamental with infinitely diversified appendages, and with the most brilliant or conspicuous colors, often arranged in elegant patterns, whilst the females are unadorned. When the sexes differ in more important structures, it is the male which is provided with special sense-organs for discovering the female, with locomotive organs for reaching her, and often with prehensile organs for holding her. These various structures for charming or securing the female are often developed in the male during only part of the year, namely the breeding-season. They have in many cases been more or less transferred to the females; and in the latter case they often appear in her as mere rudiments. They are lost or never gained by the males after emasculation. Generally they are not developed in the male during early youth, but appear a

6. Invertebrate animals, such as insects, spiders, crustaceans, and myriapods, with segmented feet or limbs.

short time before the age for reproduction. Hence in most cases the young of both sexes resemble each other; and the female somewhat resembles her young offspring throughout life. In almost every great class a few anomalous cases occur, where there has been an almost complete transposition of the characters proper to the two sexes; the females assuming characters which properly belong to the males. This surprising uniformity in the laws regulating the differences between the sexes in so many and such widely separated classes, is intelligible if we admit the action of one common cause, namely sexual selection.

* * *

The belief in the power of sexual selection rests chiefly on the following considerations. Certain characters are confined to one sex; and this alone renders it probable that in most cases they are connected with the act of reproduction. In innumerable instances these characters are fully developed only at maturity, and often during only a part of the year, which is always the breeding-season. The males (passing over a few exceptional cases) are the more active in courtship; they are the better armed, and are rendered the more attractive in various ways. It is to be especially observed that the males display their attractions with elaborate care in the presence of the females; and that they rarely or never display them excepting during the season of love. It is incredible that all this should be purposeless. Lastly we have distinct evidence with some quadrupeds and birds, that the individuals of one sex are capable of feeling a strong antipathy or preference for certain individuals of the other sex.

Bearing in mind these facts, and the marked results of man's unconscious selection, when applied to domesticated animals and cultivated plants, it seems to me almost certain that if the individuals of one sex were during a long series of generations to prefer pairing with certain individuals of the other sex, characterised in some peculiar manner, the offspring would slowly but surely become modified in this same manner.* * *

The reader who has taken the trouble to go through the several chapters devoted to sexual selection, will be able to judge how far the conclusions at which I have arrived are supported by sufficient evidence. If he accepts these conclusions he may, I think, safely extend them to mankind; but it would be superfluous here to repeat what I have so lately said on the manner in which sexual selection apparently has acted on man, both on the male and female side, causing the two sexes to differ in body and mind, and the several races to differ from each other in various characters, as well as from their ancient and lowly-organised progenitors.

He who admits the principle of sexual selection will be led to the remarkable conclusion that the nervous system not only regulates most of the existing functions of the body, but has indirectly influenced the progressive development of various bodily structures and of certain mental qualities. Courage, pugnacity, perseverance, strength and size of body, weapons of all kinds, musical organs, both vocal and instrumental, bright colours and ornamental appendages, have all been indirectly gained by the one sex or the other, through the exertion of choice, the influence of love and jealousy, and the appreciation of the beautiful in sound, color or form; and these powers of the mind manifestly depend on the development of the brain.

* * *

Man may be excused for feeling some pride at having risen, though not through his own exertions, to the very summit of the organic scale; and the fact of his having thus risen, instead of having been aboriginally placed there, may give him hope for a still higher destiny in the distant future. But we are not here concerned with hopes or fears, only with the truth as far as our reason permits us to discover it; and I have given the evidence to the best of my ability. We must, however, acknowledge, as it seems to me, that man with all his noble qualities, with sympathy which feels for the most debased, with benevolence which extends not only to other men but to the humblest living creature, with his god-like intellect which has penetrated into the movements and constitution of the solar system—with all these exalted powers—Man still bears in his bodily frame the indelible stamp of his lowly origin.

KARL MARX AND FRIEDRICH ENGELS
1818–1883 and 1820–1895

"A specter is haunting Europe—the specter of communism." So begins the *Manifesto of the Communist Party,* published by the German socialists Karl Marx and Friedrich Engels in 1848 as a platform for the Communist League. Indeed, the rulers of Europe had reason to see ghosts: the unsuccessful revolutions of 1815 and 1830 had not quelled popular discontent, and in 1847 an economic slump caused widespread unemployment and food shortages in the cities. The year 1848 brought a new wave of democratic revolutions which, although crushed or turned aside within months, nonetheless proved that the old order was vulnerable. The *Manifesto* had little immediate impact on those insurrections, although it later became a founding document; what it did do was define historical change in a way that gave hope to future revolutionaries by making their victory seem inevitable.

Part I, "Bourgeois and Proletarians," introduces the economic and social concepts that underlie all of Marx's work and define them in terms of class struggle. The first sentence, standing alone, makes no concessions: "The history of all hitherto existing society is the history of class struggles." Upper and lower classes, oppressor and oppressed have always existed, although in different ways according to the economic structures of society: the feudal lord and peasant represent an agricultural base with diverse hierarchies, and the relationships of the nineteenth-century bourgeois employer and proletarian employee reflect the different requirements of modern industrial society. Throughout, Marx suggests, economic relationships condition all other aspects of society—social, political, intellectual, and cultural—and these relationships change throughout history as the means of production change.

Marx's economic analysis of the bourgeois mode of production—its pursuit of profit ("surplus value" over the actual cost of production), its reliance on money as an impersonal and easily manipulated medium of exchange, its concentration of resources in large urban centers that process raw material from farther and farther away, and its need to find ever-wider world markets to support increased production and profit—is also a humanistic analysis. He is shocked at the way that the new economic system (capitalism) has reduced previous diversity into two large classes:

one the one hand, workers who have been dehumanized as mere "instruments of labor" and, on the other, bourgeois who mechanically pursue the accumulation of wealth. In the place of "personal worth," he finds "exchange value"; instead of human relations, monetary systems. However, he promises, the end is near; history has prepared a replacement for the dysfunctional bourgeois system. It is the proletariat, brought into existence by "Modern Industry" and now gathering consciousness of their plight. The later sections of the *Manifesto* discuss the relationship of proletarians and communists, different types of socialism, and the position of the communists in relation to other political parties. Although somewhat dated, they mark the move from theory into strategy and action, and thus echo lines from a work written by Marx and Engels two years earlier, *The German Ideology:* "Philosophers have only interpreted the world in various ways. What is really important, is to change it."

From Manifesto of the Communist Party[1]

I.

Bourgeois and Proletarians[2]

The history of all hitherto existing society is the history of class struggles.

Freeman and slave, patrician and plebeian, lord and serf, guild-master[3] and journeyman, in a word, oppressor and oppressed, stood in constant opposition to one another, carried on an uninterrupted, now hidden, now open fight, a fight that each time ended, either in a revolutionary re-constitution of society at large, or in the common ruin of the contending classes.

In the earlier epochs of history, we find almost everywhere a complicated arrangement of society into various orders, a manifold gradation of social rank. In ancient Rome we have patricians, knights, plebeians, slaves; in the Middle Ages, feudal lords, vassals, guild-masters, journeymen, apprentices, serfs; in almost all of these classes, again, subordinate gradations.

The modern bourgeois society that has sprouted from the ruins of feudal society has not done away with clash antagonisms. It has but established new classes, new conditions of oppression, new forms of struggle in place of the old ones.

Our epoch, the epoch of the bourgeoisie, possesses, however, this distinctive feature: it has simplified the class antagonisms: Society as a whole is more and more splitting up into two great hostile camps, into two great classes directly facing each other: Bourgeoisie and Proletariat.

From the serfs of the Middle Ages sprang the chartered burghers of the earliest towns. From these burgesses the first elements of the bourgeoisie[4] were developed.

The discovery of America, the rounding of the Cape, opened up fresh ground for the rising bourgeoisie. The East-Indian and Chinese markets, the colonization of America, trade with the colonies, the increase in the means

---

1. First published in German in 1848. This text is taken from the English edition, published in 1888 and edited by Engels.   2. By bourgeoisie is meant the class of modern capitalists, owners of the means of social production and employers of wage-labor. By proletariat, the class of modern wage-laborers who, having no means of production of their own, are reduced to selling their labor-power in order to live [Engels's note].   3. Guild-master, that is, a full member of a guild, a master within, not a head of a guild [Engels's note]   4. *Burghers, burgesses,* and *bourgeoisie* all stem from the same root meaning "city." Marx focuses on urban society.

of exchange and in commodities generally, gave to commerce, to navigation, to industry, an impulse never before known, and thereby, to the revolutionary element in the tottering feudal society, a rapid development.

The feudal system of industry, under which industrial production was monopolized by closed guilds, now no longer sufficed for the growing wants of the new markets. The manufacturing system took its place. The guildmasters were pushed on one side by the manufacturing middle class; division of labor between the different corporate guilds vanished in the face of division of labor in each single workshop.

Meantime the markets kept ever growing, the demand ever rising. Even manufacture no longer sufficed. Thereupon, steam and machinery revolutionized industrial production. The place of manufacture was taken by the giant, Modern Industry, the place of the industrial middle class, by industrial millionaires, the leaders of whole industrial armies, the modern bourgeois.

Modern industry has established the world-market, for which the discovery of America paved the way. This market has given an immense development to commerce, to navigation, to communication by land. This development has, in its turn, reacted on the extension of industry, and in proportion as industry, commerce, navigation, railways extended, in the same proportion the bourgeoisie developed, increased its capital, and pushed into the background every class handed down from the Middle Ages.

We see, therefore, how the modern bourgeoisie is itself the product of a long course of development, of a series of revolutions in the modes of production and of exchange.

Each step in the development of the bourgeoisie was accompanied by a corresponding political advance of that class. An oppressed class under the sway of the feudal nobility, an armed and self-governing association in the medieval commune, here independent urban republic (as in Italy and Germany), there taxable "third estate" of the monarchy (as in France), afterwards, in the period of manufacture proper, serving either the semi-feudal or the absolute monarchy as a counterpoise against the nobility, and, in fact, corner-stone of the great monarchies in general, the bourgeoisie has at last, since the establishment of Modern Industry and of the world-market, conquered for itself, in the modern representative State, exclusive political sway. The executive of the modern State is but a committee for managing the common affairs of the whole bourgeoisie.

The bourgeoisie, historically, has played a most revolutionary part.

The bourgeoisie, wherever it has got the upper hand, has put an end to all feudal, patriarchal, idyllic relations. It has pitilessly torn asunder the motley feudal ties that bound man to his "natural superiors," and has left remaining no other nexus between man and man than naked self-interest, than callous "cash payment." It has drowned the most heavenly ecstasies of religious fervor, of chivalrous enthusiasm, of philistine sentimentalism, in the icy water of egotistical calculation. It has resolved personal worth into exchange value, and in place of the numberless indefeasible chartered freedoms, has set up that single, unconscionable freedom—Free Trade. In one word, for exploitation, veiled by religious and political illusions, it has substituted naked, shameless, direct, brutal exploitation.

The bourgeoisie has stripped of its halo every occupation hitherto honored and looked up to with reverent awe. It has converted the physician, the lawyer, the priest, the poet, the man of science, into its paid wage-laborers.

The bourgeoisie has torn away from the family its sentimental veil, and has reduced the family relation to a mere money relation.

The bourgeoisie has disclosed how it came to pass that the brutal display of vigor in the Middle Ages, which Reactionists[5] so much admire, found its fitting complement in the most slothful indolence. It has been the first to show what man's activity can bring about. It has accomplished wonders far surpassing Egyptian pyramids, Roman aqueducts, and Gothic cathedrals; it has conducted expeditions that put in the shade all former Exoduses of nations and crusades.

The bourgeoisie cannot exist without constantly revolutionizing the instruments of production, and thereby the relations of production, and with them the whole relations of society. Conservation of the old modes of production in unaltered form, was, on the contrary, the first condition of existence for all earlier industrial classes. Constant revolutionizing of production, uninterrupted disturbance of all social conditions, everlasting uncertainty and agitation distinguish the bourgeois epoch from all earlier ones. All fixed, fast-frozen relations, with their train of ancient and venerable prejudices and opinions, are swept away, all new-formed ones become antiquated before they can ossify. All that is solid melts into air,[6] all that is holy is profaned, and man is at last compelled to face with sober senses, his real conditions of life, and his relations with his kind.

The need of a constantly expanding market for its products chases the bourgeoisie over the whole surface of the globe. It must nestle everywhere, settle everywhere, establish connections everywhere.

The bourgeoisie has through its exploitation of the world-market given a cosmopolitan character to production and consumption in every country. To the great chagrin of Reactionists, it has drawn from under the feet of industry the national ground on which it stood. All old-established national industries have been destroyed or are daily being destroyed. They are dislodged by new industries, whose introduction becomes a life and death question for all civilized nations, by industries that no longer work up indigenous raw material, but raw material drawn from the remotest zones; industries whose products are consumed, not only at home, but in every quarter of the globe. In place of the old wants, satisfied by the productions of the country, we find new wants, requiring for their satisfaction the products of distant lands and climes. In place of the old local and national seclusion and self-sufficiency, we have intercourse in every direction, universal inter-dependence of nations. And as in material, so also in intellectual production. The intellectual creations of individual nations become common property. National one-sidedness and narrow-mindedness become more and more impossible, and from the numerous national and local literatures, there arises a world literature.

The bourgeoisie, by the rapid improvement of all instruments of production, by the immensely facilitated means of communication, draws all, even the most barbarian, nations into civilization. The cheap prices of its commodities are the heavy artillery with which it batters down all Chinese walls,[7]

---

5. Reactionaries.   6. See Prospero's lines in Shakespeare's *The Tempest* 4.1, "These our actors / (as I foretold you) were all spirits, and / are melted into air."   7. A reference to the first Opium War (1839–42), in which England forced China to accept trade with Western countries.

with which it forces the barbarians' intensely obstinate hatred of foreigners to capitulate. It compels all nations, on pain of extinction, to adopt the bourgeois mode of production; it compels them to introduce what it calls civilization into their midst, *i.e.*, to become bourgeois themselves. In one word, it creates a world after its own image.

The bourgeoisie has subjected the country to the rule of the towns. It has created enormous cities, has greatly increased the urban population as compared with the rural, and has thus rescued a considerable part of the population from the idiocy of rural life. Just as it has made the country dependent on the towns, so it has made barbarian and semi-barbarian countries dependent on the civilized ones, nations of peasants on nations of bourgeois, the East on the West.

The bourgeoisie keeps more and more doing away with the scattered state of the population, of the means of production, and of property. It has agglomerated population, centralized means of production, and has concentrated property in a few hands. The necessary consequence of this was political centralization. Independent, or but loosely connected provinces, with separate interests, laws, governments and systems of taxation, became lumped together into one nation, with one government, one code of laws, one national class-interest, one frontier and one customs-tariff.

The bourgeoisie, during its rule of scarce one hundred years, has created more massive and more colossal productive forces than have all preceding generations together. Subjection of Nature's forces to man, machinery, application of chemistry to industry and agriculture, steam-navigation, railways, electric telegraphs, clearing of whole continents for cultivation, canalisation of rivers, whole populations conjured out of the ground—what earlier century had even a presentiment that such productive forces slumbered in the lap of social labor?

We see then: the means of production and of exchange, on whose foundation the bourgeoisie built itself up, were generated in feudal society. At a certain stage in the development of these means of production and of exchange, the conditions under which feudal society produced and exchanged, the feudal organization of agriculture and manufacturing industry, in one word, the feudal relations of property became no longer compatible with the already developed productive forces; they became so many fetters. They had to be burst asunder; they were burst asunder.

Into their place stepped free competition, accompanied by a social and political constitution adapted to it, and by the economical and political sway of the bourgeois class.

A similar movement is going on before our own eyes. Modern bourgeois society with its relations of production, of exchange and of property, a society that has conjured up such gigantic means of production and of exchange, is like the sorcerer, who is no longer able to control the powers of the nether world whom he has called up by his spells. For many a decade past the history of industry and commerce is but the history of the revolt of modern productive forces against modern conditions of production, against the property relations that are the conditions for the existence of the bourgeoisie and of its rule. It is enough to mention the commercial crises that by their periodical return put on its trial, each time more threateningly, the existence of the entire bourgeois society. In these crises a great part not only of the existing products, but also of the previously created productive forces, are periodically destroyed. In these crises there breaks out an epidemic that, in all earlier epochs, would have seemed an absurdity—the epidemic of overproduction. Society suddenly finds itself put back into a state of momentary barbarism; it appears as if a famine, a universal war of devastation had cut off the supply of every means of subsistence; industry and commerce seem to be destroyed; and why? Because there is too much civilisation, too much means of subsistence, too much industry, too much commerce. The productive forces at the disposal of society no longer tend to further the development of the conditions of bourgeois property; on the contrary, they have become too powerful for these conditions, by which they are fettered, and so soon as they overcome these fetters, they bring disorder into the whole of bourgeois society, endanger the existence of bourgeois property. The conditions of bourgeois society are too narrow to comprise the wealth created by them. And how does the bourgeoisie get over these crises? On the one hand by enforced destruction of a mass of productive forces; on the other, by the conquest of new markets, and by the more thorough exploitation of the old ones. That is to say, by paving the way for more extensive and more destructive crises, and by diminishing the means whereby crises are prevented.

The weapons with which the bourgeoisie felled feudalism to the ground are now turned against the bourgeoisie itself.

But not only has the bourgeoisie forged the weapons that bring death to itself; it has also called into existence the men who are to wield those weapons—the modern working class—the proletarians.

In proportion as the bourgeoisie, *i.e.*, capital, is developed, in the same proportion is the proletariat, the modern working class, developed—a class of laborers, who live only so long as they find work, and who find work only so long as their labor increases capital. These laborers, who must sell themselves piece-meal, are a commodity, like every other article of commerce, and are consequently exposed to all the vicissitudes of competition, to all the fluctuations of the market.

Owing to the extensive use of machinery and to division of labor, the work of the proletarians has lost all individual character, and consequently, all charm for the workman. He becomes an appendage of the machine, and it is only the most simple, most monotonous, and most easily acquired knack, that is required of him. Hence, the cost of production of a workman is restricted, almost entirely, to the means of subsistence that he requires for his maintenance, and for the propagation of his race. But the price of a commodity, and therefore also of labor, is equal to its cost of production. In proportion, therefore, as the repulsiveness of the work increases, the wage decreases. Nay more, in proportion as the use of machinery and division of labor increases, in the same proportion the burden of toil also increases, whether by prolongation of the working hours, by increase of the work exacted in a given time or by increased speed of the machinery, etc.

Modern industry has converted the little workshop of the patriarchal master into the great factory of the industrial capitalist. Masses of laborers, crowded into the factory, are organized like soldiers. As privates of the industrial army they are placed under the command of a perfect hierarchy of officers and sergeants. Not only are they slaves of the bourgeois class, and of the bourgeois State; they are daily and hourly enslaved by the machine, by the over-looker, and, above all, by the individual bourgeois manufacturer himself. The more openly this despotism proclaims gain to be its end and aim, the more petty, the more hateful and the more embittering it is.

The less the skill and exertion of strength implied in manual labor, in other words, the more modern industry becomes developed, the more is the labor of men superseded by that of women. Differences of age and sex have no longer any distinctive social validity for the working class. All are instruments of labor, more or less expensive to use, according to their age and sex.

No sooner is the exploitation of the laborer by the manufacturer, so far, at an end, that he receives his wages in cash, than he is set upon by the other portions of the bourgeoisie, the landlord, the shopkeeper, the pawnbroker, etc.

The lower strata of the middle class—the small tradespeople, shopkeepers, and retired tradesmen generally, the handicraftsmen and peasants—all these sink gradually into the proletariat, partly because their diminutive capital does not suffice for the scale on which Modern Industry is carried on, and is swamped in the competition with the large capitalists, partly because their specialized skill is rendered worthless by new methods of production. Thus the proletariat is recruited from all classes of the population.

The proletariat goes through various stages of development. With its birth begins its struggle with the bourgeoisie. At first the contest is carried on by individual laborers, then by the workpeople of a factory, then by the operatives of one trade, in one locality, against the individual bourgeois who directly exploits them. They direct their attacks not against the bourgeois conditions of production, but against the instruments of production themselves; they destroy imported wares that compete with their labor, they smash to pieces machinery, they set factories ablaze, they seek to restore by force the vanished status of the workman of the Middle Ages.

At this stage the laborers still form an incoherent mass scattered over the whole country, and broken up by their mutual competition. If anywhere they unite to form more compact bodies, this is not yet the consequence of their own active union, but of the union of the bourgeoisie, which class, in order to attain its own political ends, is compelled to set the whole proletariat in motion, and is moreover yet, for a time, able to do so. At this stage, therefore, the proletarians do not fight their enemies, but the enemies of their enemies, the remnants of absolute monarchy, the landowners, the non-industrial bourgeois, the petty bourgeoisie. Thus the whole historical movement is concentrated in the hands of the bourgeoisie; every victory so obtained is a victory for the bourgeoisie.

But with the development of industry the proletariat not only increases in number; it becomes concentrated in greater masses, its strength grows, and it feels that strength more. The various interests and conditions of life within the ranks of the proletariat are more and more equalized, in proportion as machinery obliterates all distinctions of labor, and nearly everywhere reduces wages to the same low level. The growing competition among the bourgeois, and the resulting commercial crises, make the wages of the workers ever more fluctuating. The unceasing improvement of machinery, ever more rapidly developing, makes their livelihood more and more precarious; the collisions between individual workmen and individual bourgeois take more and more the character of collisions between two classes. Thereupon the workers begin to form combinations (Trades Unions) against the bourgeois; they club together in order to keep up the rate of wages; they found permanent associations in order to make provision beforehand for these occasional revolts. Here and there the contest breaks out into riots.

Now and then the workers are victorious, but only for a time. The real fruit of their battles lies, not in the immediate result, but in the ever-expanding union of the workers. This union is helped on by the improved means of communication that are created by modern industry and that place the workers of different localities in contact with one another. It was just this contact that was needed to centralise the numerous local struggles, all of the same character, into one national struggle between classes. But every class struggle is a political struggle. And that union, to attain which the burghers of the Middle Ages, with their miserable highways, required centuries, the modern proletarians, thanks to railways, achieve in a few years.

This organization of the proletarians into a class, and consequently into a political party, is continually being upset again by the competition between the workers themselves. But it ever rises up again, stronger, firmer, mightier. It compels legislative recognition of particular interests of the workers, by taking advantage of the divisions among the bourgeoisie itself. Thus the ten-hours' bill in England was carried.[8]

Altogether collisions between the classes of the old society further, in many ways, the course of development of the proletariat. The bourgeoisie finds itself involved in a constant battle. At first with the aristocracy; later on, with those portions of the bourgeoisie itself, whose interests have become antagonistic to the progress of industry; at all times, with the bourgeoisie of foreign countries. In all these battles it sees itself compelled to appeal to the proletariat, to ask for its help, and thus, to drag it into the political arena. The bourgeoisie itself, therefore, supplies the proletariat with its own elements of political and general education, in other words, it furnishes the proletariat with weapons for fighting the bourgeoisie.

Further, as we have already seen, entire sections of the ruling classes are, by the advance of industry, precipitated into the proletariat, or are at least threatened in their conditions of existence. These also supply the proletariat with fresh elements of enlightenment and progress.

Finally, in times when the class struggle nears the decisive hour, the process of dissolution going on within the ruling class, in fact within the whole range of society, assumes such a violent, glaring character, that a small section of the ruling class cuts itself adrift, and joins the revolutionary class, the class that holds the future in its hands. Just as, therefore, at an earlier period, a section of the nobility went over to the bourgeoisie, so now a portion of the bourgeoisie goes over to the proletariat, and in particular, a portion of the bourgeois ideologists, who have raised themselves to the level of comprehending theoretically the historical movement as a whole.

Of all the classes that stand face to face with the bourgeoisie today, the proletariat alone is a really revolutionary class. The other classes decay and finally disappear in the face of Modern Industry; the proletariat is its special and essential product.

8. In 1847, after fierce opposition, a bill was passed in Parliament that limited the time a minor could work to ten hours a day. Minors were defined as persons under eighteen, but far younger children worked in the factories.

The lower middle class, the small manufacturer, the shopkeeper, the artisan, the peasant, all these fight against the bourgeoisie, to save from extinction their existence as fractions of the middle class. They are therefore not revolutionary, but conservative. Nay more, they are reactionary, for they try to roll back the wheel of history. If by chance they are revolutionary, they are so only in view of their impending transfer into the proletariat, they thus defend not their present, but their future interests, they desert their own standpoint to place themselves at that of the proletariat.

The "dangerous class," the social scum, that passively rotting mass thrown off by the lowest layers of old society, may, here and there, be swept into the movement by a proletarian revolution; its conditions of life, however, prepare it far more for the part of a bribed tool of reactionary intrigue.

In the conditions of the proletariat, those of old society at large are already virtually swamped. The proletarian is without property; his relation to his wife and children has no longer anything in common with the bourgeois family-relations; modern industrial labour, modern subjection to capital, the same in England as in France, in America as in Germany, has stripped him of every trace of national character. Law, morality, religion, are to him so many bourgeois prejudices, behind which lurk in ambush just as many bourgeois interests.

All the preceding classes that got the upper hand, sought to fortify their already acquired status by subjecting society at large to their conditions of appropriation. The proletarians cannot become masters of the productive forces of society, except by abolishing their own previous mode of appropriation, and thereby also every other previous mode of appropriation. They have nothing of their own to secure and to fortify; their mission is to destroy all previous securities for, and insurances of, individual property.

All previous historical movements were movements of minorities, or in the interests of minorities. The proletarian movement is the self-conscious, independent movement of the immense majority, in the interests of the immense majority. The proletariat, the lowest stratum of our present society, cannot stir, cannot raise itself up, without the whole superincumbent strata of official society being sprung into the air.

Though not in substance, yet in form, the struggle of the proletariat with the bourgeoisie is at first a national struggle. The proletariat of each country must, of course, first of all settle matters with its own bourgeoisie.

In depicting the most general phases of the development of the proletariat, we traced the more or less veiled civil war, raging within existing society, up to the point where that war breaks out into open revolution, and where the violent overthrow of the bourgeoisie lays the foundation for the sway of the proletariat.

Hitherto, every form of society has been based, as we have already seen, on the antagonism of oppressing and oppressed classes. But in order to oppress a class, certain conditions must be assured to it under which it can, at least, continue its slavish existence. The serf, in the period of serfdom, raised himself to membership in the commune, just as the petty bourgeois, under the yoke of feudal absolutism, managed to develop into a bourgeois. The modern laborer, on the contrary, instead of rising with the progress of industry, sinks deeper and deeper below the conditions of existence of his own class. He becomes a pauper, and pauperism develops more rapidly than population and wealth. And here it becomes evident, that the bourgeoisie is unfit any longer to be the ruling class in society, and to impose its conditions of existence upon society as an over-riding law. It is unfit to rule because it is incompetent to assure an existence to its slave within his slavery, because it cannot help letting him sink into such a state, that it has to feed him, instead of being fed by him. Society can no longer live under this bourgeoisie, in other words, its existence is no longer compatible with society.

The essential condition for the existence, and for the sway of the bourgeois class, is the formation and augmentation of capital; the condition for capital is wage-labor. Wage-labor rests exclusively on competition between the laborers. The advance of industry, whose involuntary promoter is the bourgeoisie, replaces the isolation of the laborers, due to competition, by their revolutionary combination, due to association. The development of Modern Industry, therefore, cuts from under its feet the very foundation on which the bourgeoisie produces and appropriates products. What the bourgeoisie, therefore, produces, above all, is its own grave-diggers. Its fall and the victory of the proletariat are equally inevitable.

ÉMILE ZOLA
1840–1902

The French novelist Émile Zola was at the peak of his reputation as a major writer and public intellectual when he joined the controversy over the conviction of Captain Alfred Dreyfus, a Jewish army office who had been condemned in 1894 after a closed trial and on questionable evidence. Dreyfus continued to protest his innocence. But his family's efforts to have the trial reopened were unsuccessful until the new head of Army intelligence, Major Georges Picquart, discovered further information indicating that someone else—ironically, a member of Army Intelligence—was the culprit. From that point on, the "Dreyfus Affair" proceeded both publicly and behind the scenes: Picquart was reassigned as his superiors tried to cover up their mistake and forged new evidence, and French public opinion became bitterly divided between Dreyfusards (intellectuals, socialists, and antimilitarist republicans) and anti-Dreyfusards (chiefly right-wing militarists and anti-Semites). The military high staff leaked inflammatory statements to the press, and it was in the press that Zola published essays, interviews, and his celebrated open letter in L'Aurore on January 13, 1898. Between 200,000 and 300,000 copies of L'Aurore were sold in Paris the day "J'accuse" appeared, ten times the normal circulation. This popular success only inflamed the opposition, which then dragged both author and newspaper into court.

This was not Zola's first statement about the Dreyfus case—starting on November 25, 1897, he had published five other essays or letters—but it is the most passionate and daring. Two days earlier, the real writer of the memorandum for which Dreyfus had been condemned, a Major Ferdinand Walsin-Esterhazy, had been declared innocent after a closed military trial. Zola takes the occasion to review all the available evidence in an open letter to the president of the French Republic and acts as an unofficial public prosecutor by indicting those responsible. He put not only his reputation at stake, but also his freedom, as he was well aware, for he could be (and subsequently was) prosecuted for libel.

The Dreyfus Affair is often remembered as a famous case about anti-Semitism. However, for Zola (who had already criticized anti-Semitism in unrelated essays), it was more than that: it was a demonstration of the interrelationships of power that permitted public corruption. The military, the courts, the legislature, and even the president had combined to suppress the truth, manipulating the press and public opinion until the resulting religious and political divisions threatened national stability. Zola had shown his sympathy for the poor and downtrodden throughout his fiction; he was deeply patriotic as well, cherishing an image of France as the "cradle of the rights of man." In writing "J'accuse," he issued a revolutionary challenge to the ruling powers. It was a courageous gesture, perhaps even more than he foresaw: he became the subject of vicious campaigns in the press, was threatened by crowds, and lived under the threat of the original lawsuit even after Dreyfus had been pardoned and the true criminals unmasked. The political divisions that he had exposed continued to exist. Zola died on September 29, 1902, and was saluted at his funeral as someone whose destiny was to be "a moment in the conscience of mankind."

PRONOUNCING GLOSSARY

The following list uses common English syllables and stress accents to provide rough equivalents of selected words whose pronunciation may be unfamiliar to the general reader.

Billot: *bee-yoh'*

bordereau: *bor-de-roh'*

Dreyfus: *dray-fyews'* (French) or *drai'-fus* (English)

du Paty de Clam: *dyew pah-tee' deuh clahm'*

Faure: *for*

"J'accuse": *zhah-kyews'*

Mercier: *mehr-syay'*

Picquart: *pee-cahr'*

Émile Zola: *ay-meel' zoh-lah'*

From J'accuse[1]

* * *

Ah, for anyone who knows the true details of the first affair,[2] what a nightmare it is! Major du Paty de Clam arrests Dreyfus and has him placed in solitary confinement. He rushes to the home of Madame Dreyfus and terrifies her, saying that if she speaks up, her husband is lost. Meanwhile the unfortunate man is tearing out his hair, clamoring his innocence. And that is how the investigation proceeded, as in some fifteenth-century chronicle, shrouded in mystery and a wealth of the wildest expedients, and all on the basis of a single, childish accusation, that idiotic bordereau,[3] which was not only a very ordinary kind of treason but also the most impudent kind of swindle, since almost all of the so-called secrets that had supposedly been turned over to the enemy were of no value. I dwell on this point because this is the egg from which the real crime—the dreadful denial of justice which has laid France low—was later to hatch. I would like to make it perfectly clear how the miscarriage of justice came about, how it is the product of

1. From the letter published in the Parisian newspaper *L'Aurore* on January 13, 1898, called "J'accuse" ("I accuse") for the repeated denunciations with which it ends. Translated by Eleanor Levieux.   2. Dreyfus was first accused in October 1894 and tried and convicted in a closed court-martial that December, during which judges were provided a damning "secret file" by the military. He was sentenced to life imprisonment and deported in January 1895 to Devil's Island.   3. Memorandum. The bordereau was a letter addressed to the German military attaché in Paris, Maximilian von Schwartzkoppen, that was discovered by the Army's Intelligence Bureau in September 1894. It described the delivery of national security documents to the Germans and was in fact written by a member of the Intelligence Bureau, Major Ferdinand Walsin-Esterhazy.

Major du Paty de Clam's machinations, how General Mercier and Generals de Boisdeffre and Gonse came to be taken in by it and gradually became responsible for this error and how it is that later they felt they had a duty to impose it as the sacred truth, a truth that will not admit of even the slightest discussion. At the beginning, all they contributed was negligence and lack of intelligence. The worst we can say is that they gave in to the religious passions of the circles they move in and the prejudices wrought by esprit de corps.[4] They let stupidity have its way.

But now, here is Dreyfus summoned before the court martial. The most utter secrecy is demanded. They could not have imposed stricter silence and been more rigorous and mysterious if a traitor had actually opened our borders to the enemy and led the German Emperor straight to Notre Dame. The entire nation is flabbergasted. Terrible deeds are whispered about, monstrous betrayals that scandalize History itself, and of course the nation bows to these rumors. No punishment can be too severe; the nation will applaud the traitor's public humiliation; the nation is adamant: the guilty man shall remain on the remote rock where infamy has placed him and he shall be devoured by remorse.[5] But then, those unspeakable accusations, those dangerous accusations that might inflame all of Europe and had to be so carefully concealed behind the closed doors of a secret session—are they true? No, they are not! There is nothing behind all that but the extravagant, demented flights of fancy of Major du Paty de Clam. It's all a smokescreen with just one purpose: to conceal a cheap novel of the most outlandish sort. And to be convinced of this, one need only examine the formal indictment that was read before the court martial.

How hollow that indictment is! Is it possible a man has been found guilty on the strength of it? Such iniquity is staggering. I challenge decent people to read it: their hearts will leap with indignation and rebellion when they think of the disproportionate price Dreyfus is paying so far away on Devil's Island.[6] So Dreyfus speaks several languages, does he? This is a crime. Not one compromising paper was found in his home? A crime. He occasionally pays a visit to the region he hails from? A crime. He is a hard-working man, eager to know everything? A crime. He does not get flustered? A crime. He does get flustered? A crime. And how naively it is worded! How baseless its claims are! They told us he was indicted on fourteen different counts but in the end there is actually only one: that famous bordereau; and we even find out that the experts did not all agree, that one of them, M. Gobert, was subjected to some military pressure because he dared to come to a different conclusion from the one they wanted him to reach. We were also told that twenty-three officers had come and testified against Dreyfus. We still do not know how they were questioned, but what is certain is that not all of their testimony was negative. Besides, all of them, you will notice, came from the offices of the War Department. This trial is a family conclave; they all *belong*. We must not forget that. It is the General Staff who wanted this trial; it is they who judged Dreyfus; and they have just judged him for the second time.

---

4. Group loyalty (French). *Circles they move in:* The higher ranks in the military were both ardently Catholic and anti-Semitic.   5. In Greek myth, Zeus punished Prometheus for giving fire to human beings by chaining him to a rock and sending an eagle to devour his liver each day.   6. A prison colony situated on an island off French Guiana on the northeast coast of South America. It was known for its extremely harsh conditions.

So all that was left was the bordereau, on which the experts had not agreed. They say that in the council chambers, the judges were naturally leaning towards acquittal. And if that is the case then you can understand why, on the General Staff, they are so desperately insistent today on proclaiming, in order to justify the judgment, that there was a damning but secret document; they cannot reveal it but it makes everything legitimate and we must bow before it, as before an invisible and unknowable God! I deny the existence of any such document, I deny it with all my strength! Some ridiculous piece of paper, possibly; perhaps the one that talks about easy women and mentions a man named D . . . who is becoming too demanding; no doubt some husband or other who feels they're not paying him enough for the use of his wife. But a document that concerns the national defense, a document that would cause war to be declared immediately if ever it was produced? No! No! It's a lie! And what makes the whole business all the more odious and cynical is that they are lying with impunity and there is no way to convict them. They turn France inside out, they shelter behind the legitimate uproar they have caused, they seal mouths by making hearts quake and perverting minds. I know of no greater crime against society.

These, M. le Président, are the facts that explain how a miscarriage of justice has come to be committed. And the evidence as to Dreyfus's character, his financial situation, his lack of motives, the fact that he has never ceased to clamor his innocence—all these demonstrate that he has been a victim of Major du Paty de Clam's overheated imagination, and of the clericalism that prevails in the military circles in which he moves, and of the hysterical hunt for "dirty Jews" that disgraces our times.

Now we come to the Esterhazy affair. Three years have passed. Many people's consciences are still profoundly uneasy; worried, they look further, and ultimately they become convinced that Dreyfus is innocent.

I will not retrace the story of M. Scheurer-Kestner's doubts and then of the certainty he came to feel. But while he was conducting his investigation, very serious events were taking place within the General Staff itself. Colonel Sandherr had died and Lt-Col Picquart had succeeded him at the head of the Intelligence Bureau. And it is in that capacity and in the exercise of his functions that Picquart one day held in his hands a special delivery letter addressed to Major Esterhazy by an agent of a foreign power. It was Picquart's strictest duty to launch an investigation. It is clear that he never acted otherwise than with the consent of his superior officers. So he outlined his suspicions to his hierarchical superiors—General Gonse, then General de Boisdeffre, then General Billot, who had succeeded General Mercier as Minister of War. The famous Picquart file that has been talked about so much was never anything more nor less than the Billot file, by which I mean the file that a subaltern prepared for his Minister, the file that they must still have in the War Ministry. The inquiry lasted from May to September 1896, and two things must be stated in no uncertain terms: General Gonse was convinced that Esterhazy was guilty, and neither General de Boisdeffre nor General Billot questioned the fact that the bordereau was in Esterhazy's handwriting. Lt-Col Picquart's investigation had led to that indubitable conclusion. But feeling ran very high, for if Esterhazy was found guilty, then inevitably the Dreyfus verdict would have to be revised, and that was what the General Staff was determined to avoid at all costs.

* * *

They reached an iniquitous verdict which will forever weigh heavy on all our future courts martial and forever make their future decisions suspect. There may be room for doubt as to whether the first court martial was intelligent but there is no doubt that the second has been criminal. Its excuse, I repeat, is that the commander in chief had spoken and declared the previous verdict unattackable, holy and superior to mere mortals—and how could his subordinates dare to contradict him? They talk to us about the honor of the army; they want us to love the army, respect the army. Oh yes, indeed, if you mean an army that would rise up at the very first hint of danger, that would defend French soil; that army is the French people themselves, and we have nothing but affection and respect for it. But the army that is involved here is not the dignified army that our need for justice calls out for. What we are faced with here is the saber, the master that may be imposed on us tomorrow. Should we kiss the hilt of that saber, that god, with pious devotion? No, we should not!

* * *

It is a crime to lead public opinion astray, to manipulate it for a death-dealing purpose and pervert it to the point of delirium. It is a crime to poison the minds of the humble, ordinary people, to whip reactionary and intolerant passions into a frenzy while sheltering behind the odious bastion of anti-Semitism. France, the great and liberal cradle of the rights of man, will die of anti-Semitism if it is not cured of it. It is a crime to play on patriotism to further the aims of hatred. And it is a crime to worship the saber as a modern god when all of human science is laboring to hasten the triumph of truth and justice.

* * *

That, M. le Président, is the plain truth. It is appalling. It will remain an indelible blot on your term as President. Oh, I know that you are powerless to deal with it, that you are the prisoner of the Constitution and of the people nearest to you. But as a man, your duty is clear, and you will not overlook it, and you will do your duty. Not for one minute do I despair that truth will triumph. I am confident and I repeat, more vehemently even than before, the truth is on the march and nothing shall stop it. The Affair is only just beginning, because only now have the positions become crystal clear: on the one hand, the guilty parties, who do not want the truth to be revealed; on the other, the defenders of justice, who will give their lives to see that justice is done. I have said it elsewhere and I repeat it here: if the truth is buried underground, it swells and grows and becomes so explosive that the day it bursts, it blows everything wide open along with it. Time will tell; we shall see whether we have not prepared, for some later date, the most resounding disaster.

But this letter has been a long one, M. le Président, and it is time to bring it to a close.

I accuse Lt-Col du Paty de Clam of having been the diabolical agent of a miscarriage of justice (though unwittingly, I am willing to believe) and then of having defended his evil deed for the past three years through the most preposterous and most blameworthy machinations.

I accuse General Mercier of having been an accomplice, at least by weak-mindedness, to one of the most iniquitous acts of this century.

I accuse General Billot of having had in his hands undeniable proof that Dreyfus was innocent and of having suppressed it, of having committed this crime against justice and against humanity for political purposes, so that the General Staff, which had been compromised, would not lose face.

I accuse Generals de Boisdeffre and Gonse of having been accomplices to this same crime, one out of intense clerical conviction, no doubt, and the other perhaps because of the esprit de corps which makes the War Office the Holy of Holies and hence unattackable.

I accuse General de Pellieux and Major Ravary of having led a villainous inquiry, by which I mean a most monstrously one-sided inquiry, the report on which, by Ravary, constitutes an imperishable monument of naive audacity.

I accuse the three handwriting experts, Messrs Belhomme, Varinard and Couard, of having submitted fraudulent and deceitful reports—unless a medical examination concludes that their eyesight and their judgment were impaired.

I accuse the War Office of having conducted an abominable campaign in the press (especially in *L'Eclair* and *L'Echo de Paris*) in order to cover up its misdeeds and lead public opinion astray.

Finally, I accuse the first court martial of having violated the law by sentencing a defendant on the basis of a document which remained secret, and I accuse the second court martial of having covered up that illegal action, on orders, by having, in its own turn, committed the judicial crime of knowingly acquitting a guilty man.

In making these accusations, I am fully aware that my action comes under Articles 30 and 31 of the law of 29 July 1881 on the press, which makes libel a punishable offense. I deliberately expose myself to that law.[7]

As for the persons I have accused, I do not know them: I have never seen them; I feel no rancour or hatred towards them. To me, they are mere entities, mere embodiments of social malfeasance. And the action I am taking here is merely a revolutionary means to hasten the revelation of truth and justice.

I have but one goal: that light be shed, in the name of mankind which has suffered so much and has the right to happiness. My ardent protest is merely a cry from my very soul. Let them dare to summon me before a court of law! Let the inquiry be held in broad daylight!

I am waiting.

M. le Président, I beg you to accept the assurance of my most profound respect.

L'Aurore, 13 January 1898

---

7. Zola was convicted on February 23, 1898, and given the maximum sentence for libel: one year in prison and a fine of Fr 3,000. Various appeals and temporary exile in England kept him out of prison, but he died on October 5, 1902, with his case never officially resolved.

FRIEDRICH NIETZSCHE
1844–1900

For a society that believed in progress and saw Western society as the pinnacle of civilization, Friedrich Nietzsche's description of Western culture as a slow history of moral decay must have seemed incomprehensible. The German philosopher explained his meaning in a series of urgently worded poetic volumes, from *The Birth of Tragedy* (1871) to the posthumously published autobiography (*Ecce Homo*) (1908). All our philosophical and religious systems, he said, have been erected solely to hide the fact that we know the world we live in is ungodly, immoral, and "inhuman." There are no absolute truths, and only the lazy-minded and weak-willed keep trying to find them, turning hopefully to religion, philosophy, nationalism, or their apparent opposite, nihilism. Nietzsche described the history of Christianity as a sickening of the will, a socially inspired "vivisection" of our innermost drives in order to preserve society, subordinating natural instincts for the good of civilization (the latter position echoed by Freud in *Civilization and Its Discontents*). Yet modern Christianity, he suggested, lacked the vigor of earlier times. After centuries of scientific discoveries and rationalist thought, people no longer truly believed in a divine universe yet were afraid to forgo its security: out of this hypocrisy came a contemporary culture in which, according to his famous phrase, "God is dead! . . . And we have killed him!"

It is a passionate denunciation, and Nietzsche believes in passion. He is outraged that people would hold ideas (and especially moral questions) at a distance: these are "weak, thin, extinguished personalities" who do not know how to imagine the problem of morality, let alone explore it. Everything must be questioned, including our own values and the premises of our questions (something Nietzsche called perspectival thinking). Only a totally independent mind, a free spirit released from all preexisting ties and dancing precariously on the edge of the abyss, can exercise free will. Such a spirit is the "overman," the next evolutionary stage of humanity. Most people, however, remain tied to the desire for certainty: the certainties of faith and of their place in a social system whose rules they understand.

Although Nietzsche is recognized, along with Darwin and Marx, as one of the founders of modern thought, his reputation suffered greatly in the first half of the twentieth century. During that time, a manufactured image of the philosopher and his ideas was promulgated by others who had their own agendas. Nietzsche had suffered a stroke in January 1889 that left him incapacitated for the last eleven years of his life, during which time he was virtually the prisoner of his sister, Elisabeth. She profited from her control of the invalid (whom she exhibited in his wheelchair to visitors) and of the Nietzsche archives by issuing an edited collection of his writing as well as a posthumously published volume, *The Will to Power* (1901), which she claimed was her brother's work but was in fact her own composition using his notes. Elisabeth's anti-Semitic and fanatically Aryan beliefs shaped *The Will to Power*, and she supported Adolf Hitler from 1933. The Nazis, in turn, simplified and distorted Nietzsche's vision of the overman (or superman) to promote their racist vision of an Aryan superrace. After the end of World War II, scholars were able to reconstruct a truer picture of Nietzsche's complex ideas, which have taken their major—though still controversial—place in the history of modern perspectives on culture.

PRONOUNCING GLOSSARY

The following list uses common English syllables and stress accents to provide rough equivalents of selected names whose pronunciation may be unfamiliar to the general reader.

Mitgefühl: *mit'-ge-fewl*
Mitleiden: *mit'-lai-den*
Friedrich Nietzsche: *free'-drik neet'-chuh*

The Gay Science[1]

From *Book Three*

124

In the horizon of the infinite.—We have forsaken the land and gone to sea! We have destroyed the bridge behind us—more so, we have demolished the land behind us! Now, little ship, look out! Beside you is the ocean; it is true, it does not always roar, and at times it lies there like silk and gold and dreams of goodness. But there will be hours when you realize that it is infinite and that there is nothing more awesome than infinity. Oh, the poor bird that has felt free and now strikes against the walls of this cage! Woe, when homesickness for the land overcomes you, as if there had been more *freedom* there—and there is no more "land"!

125

The madman.—Haven't you heard of that madman who in the bright morning lit a lantern and ran around the marketplace crying incessantly, "I'm looking for God! I'm looking for God!" Since many of those who did not believe in God were standing around together just then, he caused great laughter. Has he been lost, then? asked one. Did he lose his way like a child? asked another. Or is he hiding? Is he afraid of us? Has he gone to sea? Emigrated?—Thus they shouted and laughed, one interrupting the other. The madman jumped into their midst and pierced them with his eyes. "Where is God?" he cried, "I'll tell you! *We have killed him*—you and I! We are all his murderers. But how did we do this? How were we able to drink up the sea? Who gave us the sponge to wipe away the entire horizon? What were we doing when we unchained this earth from its sun? Where is it moving to now? Where are we moving to? Away from all suns? Are we not continually falling? And backwards, sidewards, forwards, in all directions? Is there still an up and a down? Aren't we straying as though through an infinite nothing? Isn't empty space breathing at us? Hasn't it got colder? Isn't night and more night coming again and again? Don't lanterns have to be lit in the morning? Do we still hear nothing of the noise of the grave-diggers who are burying God? Do we still smell nothing of the divine decomposition?—Gods, too, decompose! God is dead! God remains dead! And we have killed him! How can we console ourselves, the murderers of all murderers! The holiest and the mightiest thing the world has ever possessed has bled to death under our knives: who will wipe this blood from us? With what water could we clean ourselves? What festivals of atonement, what holy games will we have to invent for ourselves? Is the magnitude of this deed not too great for us?

---

1. Published in 1882. Translated by Josefine Nauckhoff.

Do we not ourselves have to become gods merely to appear worthy of it? There was never a greater deed—and whoever is born after us will on account of this deed belong to a higher history than all history up to now!" Here the madman fell silent and looked again at his listeners; they too were silent and looked at him disconcertedly. Finally he threw his lantern on the ground so that it broke into pieces and went out. "I come too early," he then said; "my time is not yet. This tremendous event is still on its way, wandering; it has not yet reached the ears of men. Lightning and thunder need time; the light of the stars needs time; deeds need time, even after they are done, in order to be seen and heard. This deed is still more remote to them than the remotest stars—*and yet they have done it themselves!*" It is still recounted how on the same day the madman forced his way into several churches and there started singing his *requiem aeternam deo.*[2] Led out and called to account, he is said always to have replied nothing but, "What then are these churches now if not the tombs and sepulchers of God?"

From *Book Five. We Fearless Ones*

345

Morality as a problem.—The lack of personality always takes its revenge: a weakened, thin, extinguished personality, one that denies itself and its own existence, is no longer good for anything good—least of all for philosophy. "Selflessness" has no value in heaven or on earth; all great problems demand *great love,* and only strong, round, secure minds who have a firm grip on themselves are capable of that. It makes the most telling difference whether a thinker has a personal relationship to his problems and finds in them his destiny, his distress, and his greatest happiness, or an "impersonal" one, meaning he is only able to touch and grasp them with the antennae of cold, curious thought. In the latter case nothing will come of it, that much can be promised; for even if great problems should let themselves be *grasped* by them, they would not allow frogs and weaklings to *hold on* to them; such has been their taste from time immemorial—a taste, incidentally, that they share with all doughty females. Why, then, have I never yet encountered anyone, not even in books, who approached morality in this personal way and who knew morality as a problem, and this problem as his own personal distress, torment, voluptuousness, and passion? It is clear that up to now, morality has been no problem at all but rather that on which, after all mistrust, discord, and contradiction, one could agree—the hallowed place of peace where thinkers took a rest from themselves, took a deep breath, and felt revived. I see no one who has ventured a *critique* of moral valuations; I miss even the slightest attempts of scientific curiosity, of the coddled, experimental imagination of psychologists and historians that easily anticipates a problem and seizes it in flight without knowing what it has caught. I have hardly detected a few meagre preliminary efforts to explore the *history of origins* of these feelings and valuations (which is something quite different from a critique and again different from a history of ethical systems): in one single case I did everything to encourage a sympathy and talent for this kind of history—in

---

2. "Grant God eternal rest" (Latin). Nietzsche substitutes "God" for "them" in the traditional passage from the service for the dead: "Grant them eternal rest."

vain, as it seems to me today. These historians of morality (particularly, the Englishmen) do not amount to much: usually they themselves unsuspectingly stand under the command of a particular morality and, without knowing it, serve as its shield-bearers and followers, for example, by sharing that popular superstition of Christian Europe which people keep repeating so naively to this day, that what is characteristic of morality is selflessness, self-denial, self-sacrifice, or sympathy (*Mitgefühl*) and compassion (*Mitleiden*). Their usual mistaken premise is that they affirm some consensus among peoples, at least among tame peoples, concerning certain moral principles, and then conclude that these principles must be unconditionally binding also for you and me—or, conversely, they see that among different peoples moral valuations are *necessarily* different and infer from this that *no* morality is binding—both of which are equally childish. The mistake of the more subtle among them is that they uncover and criticize the possibly foolish opinions of a people about their morality, or of humanity about all human morality—opinions about its origin, its religious sanction, the myth of the free will and such things—and then think they have criticized the morality itself. But the value of the injunction "Thou Shalt" is still fundamentally different from and independent of such opinions about it and the weeds of error that may have overgrown it—just as surely as the value of a medication for someone sick is totally independent of whether he thinks about medicine scientifically or the way an old woman thinks about it. A morality could even have grown *out of* an error, and the realization of this fact would not as much as touch the problem of its value. Thus no one until now has examined the *value* of that most famous of all medicines called morality; and for that, one must begin by *questioning* it for once. Well then! Precisely that is our task.

346

Our question mark.—But you do not understand this? Indeed, people will have trouble understanding us. We are searching for words, perhaps also for ears. Who are we anyway? If we simply called ourselves godless (to use an old expression), or unbelievers, or even immoralists, we would not think that these words came near to describing us: we are all three of them, at too advanced a stage for anyone to comprehend—for *you* to comprehend, my curious gentlemen—how it feels. No! No longer with the bitterness and passion of the one who has torn himself away and must turn his unbelief into another faith, a goal, a martyrdom! We have become hard-boiled, cold, and tough in the realization that the way of the world is not at all divine—even by human standards it is not rational, merciful, or just. We know it: the world we live in is ungodly, immoral, "inhuman", for far too long we have interpreted it falsely and mendaciously, though according to our wish and will for veneration, that is, according to a *need*. For man is a venerating animal! But he is also a mistrustful one; and that the world is *not* worth what we thought is about the most certain thing our mistrust has finally gotten hold of. The more mistrust, the more philosophy. We take care not to claim that the world is worth *less*; indeed, it would seem laughable to us today if man were to aim at inventing values that were supposed to *surpass* the value of the real world. That is exactly what we have turned away from, as from an extravagant aberration of human vanity and unreason that for long was not recognized as such. It found its final expression in modern pessimism, and an older and stronger expression in the teaching of Buddha; but also Christianity includes it, more doubtfully and ambiguously, to be sure, but not for that reason less seductively. The whole attitude of "man *against* the world," of man as a "world-negating" principle, of man as the measure of the value of things, as judge of the world who finally places existence itself on his scales and finds it too light—the monstrous stupidity of this attitude has finally dawned on us and we are sick of it; we laugh as soon as we encounter the juxtaposition of "man *and* world," separated by the sublime presumptuousness of the little word "and"! But by laughing, haven't we simply taken contempt for man one step further? And thus also pessimism, the contempt for that existence which is knowable to *us*? Have we not exposed ourselves to the suspicion of an opposition—an opposition between the world in which until now we were at home with our venerations—and which may have made it possible for us to *endure* life—and another world *that we ourselves are*: a relentless, fundamental, deepest suspicion concerning ourselves that is steadily gaining more and worse control over us Europeans and that could easily confront coming generations with the terrible Either/Or[3] "Either abolish your venerations or—*yourselves!*" The latter would be nihilism; but would not the former also be—nihilism? That is *our* question mark.

347

Believers and their need to believe.—The extent to which one needs a *faith* in order to flourish, how much that is "firm" and that one does not want shaken because one *clings* to it—that is a measure of the degree of one's strength (or, to speak more clearly, one's weakness). Christianity, it seems to me, is still needed by most people in old Europe even today; hence it still finds believers. For that is how man is: an article of faith could be refuted to him a thousand times; as long as he needed it, he would consider it "true" again and again, in accordance with that famous "proof of strength"[4] of which the Bible speaks. Metaphysics is still needed by some, but so is that impetuous *demand for certainty* that today discharges itself in scientific-positivistic form among great masses—the demand that one *wants* by all means something to be firm (while owing to the fervor of this demand one treats the demonstration of this certainty more lightly and negligently): this is still the demand for foothold, support—in short, the *instinct of weakness* that, to be sure, does not create sundry religions, forms of metaphysics, and convictions but does—preserve them. Indeed, around all these positivistic systems hover the fumes of a certain pessimistic gloom, something of a weariness, fatalism, disappointment, fear of new disappointment—or else self-dramatizing rage, a bad mood, the anarchism of exasperation and whatever other symptoms or masquerades there are of the feeling of weakness. Even the vehemence with which our cleverest contemporaries get lost in pitiful nooks and crevices such as patriotism (I refer to what the French call *chauvinism*[5] and the Germans "German"), or in petty aesthetic creeds such as

---

3. An echo of the ethical questioning and oppositions in Søren Kierkegaard's book *Either/Or* (1843).
4. 1 Corinthians 2.4: "And my spirit and my preaching was not with enticing words of man's wisdom, but in demonstrations of the Spirit and of power" (King James translation). The passage was currently interpreted to mean that belief in Jesus strengthened the believer to overcome all obstacles.   5. Exaggerated and xenophobic nationalism.

French naturalism (which enhances and exposes only the part of nature that simultaneously disgusts and amazes—today one likes to call it *la vérité vraie*—), or in Petersburg-style nihilism[6] (meaning *faith in unbelief* to the point of martyrdom), always indicates primarily the *need* for faith, a foothold, backbone, support . . . Faith is always most desired and most urgently needed where will is lacking; for will, as the affect of command, is the decisive mark of sovereignty and strength. That is, the less someone knows how to command, the more urgently does he desire someone who commands, who commands severely—a god, prince, the social order, doctor, father confessor, dogma, or party conscience. From this one might gather that both world religions, Buddhism and Christianity, may have owed their origin and especially their sudden spread to a tremendous *sickening of the will*. And that is actually what happened: both religions encountered a demand for a "Thou Shalt" that, through a sickening of the will, had increased to an absurd level and bordered on desperation; both religions were teachers of fanaticism in times of a slackening of the will and thereby offered innumerable people support, a new possibility of willing, a delight in willing. For fanaticism is the only "strength of the will" that even the weak and insecure can be brought to attain, as a type of hypnosis of the entire sensual-intellectual system to the benefit of the excessive nourishment (hypertrophy) of a single point of view and feeling which is now dominant—the Christian calls it his *faith*. Once a human being arrives at the basic conviction that he *must* be commanded, he becomes "a believe"; conversely, one could conceive of a delight and power of self-determination, a *freedom* of the will, in which the spirit takes leave of all faith and every wish for certainty, practised as it is in maintaining itself on light ropes and possibilities and dancing even beside abysses. Such a spirit would be the *free spirit* par excellence.

* * *

356

The extent to which things will become ever more "artistic" in Europe.— Even today, in this transitional period in which so many forms of coercion have lost their power, the need to make a living still forces nearly all European men to adopt a particular role—their so-called profession. A few retain the freedom, an apparent freedom, to choose this role themselves; for most of them it is chosen. The result is strange enough. Almost all Europeans, at an advanced age, confuse themselves with their role; they become the victims of their "good performance"; they themselves have forgotten how much they were determined by accidents, moods, and arbitrariness at the time that their "profession" was decided—and how many other roles they may have been *able* to play; for now it is too late! Upon deeper consideration, the role has actually *become* character; and artifice, nature. There were times when men believed with unyielding confidence, even with piety, in their predestination for just this business, just this way of making a living, and utterly refused to acknowledge the element of accident, role, and caprice. With the help of this faith, estates, guilds, and inherited trade privileges were able to establish

---

6. Anarchist beliefs depicted in works by the Russian novelists Ivan Turgenev (1818–1883) and Fyodor Dostoevsky (1821–1881). *La vérité vraie*: true truth or ultimate truth (French).

those monsters, the broad-based social pyramids that distinguished the middle ages and to which one can credit at least one thing: durability (and durability is a first-rank value on earth). But there are contrary ages, the truly democratic ones, in which people unlearn this faith and a certain audacious faith and opposite viewpoint moves steadily into the foreground—the Athenian faith that first became noticeable in the Periclean age;[7] the American faith which is increasingly becoming the European faith as well, where the individual is convinced he can do just about anything *and is up to playing any role;* and everyone experiments with himself, improvises, experiments again, enjoys experimenting, where all nature ends and becomes art . . . When the Greeks had fully accepted this *faith in roles*—the faith of artistes, if you will—they underwent, as is well known, step by step an odd metamorphosis that is not in every respect worthy of imitation: *they really became actors;* as such they captivated and overcame the whole world—finally even the "power that overcame the whole world" itself (for it was not, as innocents tend to say, Greek culture that conquered Rome, but the *graeculus histrio*[8]). But what I fear, what even today one could grasp with one's hands if one felt like grasping it, is that we modern men are pretty much on the same road; and every time man starts to discover the extent to which he is playing a role and the extent to which he *can* be an actor, he *becomes* an actor . . . . With this, a new human flora and fauna emerges that cannot grow in firmer and more limited ages—or that would at least be formally condemned and suspected of lacking honor, it is thus that the most interesting and maddest ages always emerge, in which "the actors," *all* types of actors, are the real masters. Precisely because of this, another human type becomes ever more disadvantaged and is finally made impossible; above all, the great "architects": the strength to build is now paralyzed; the courage to make far-reaching plans is discouraged; the organizational geniuses become scarce—who still dares to undertake works that would *require* millennia to complete? For what is dying out is that fundamental faith on the basis of which someone could calculate, promise, anticipate the future in a plan on that grand scale, and sacrifice the future to his plan—namely, the basic faith that man has worth and sense only in so far as he is *a stone in a great edifice;* to this end he must be *firm* above all, a "stone" . . . above all not an actor! To put it briefly—oh, people will keep silent about it for a long time!—what from now on will never again be built, *can* never again be built, is—a society in the old sense of the term; to build that, everything is lacking, mainly the material. *We are all no longer material for a society;* this is a timely truth! It is a matter of indifference to me that at present the most shortsighted, perhaps the most honest, at any rate the noisiest human type that we have today—our good socialists—believe, hope, dream, and above all shout and write pretty much the opposite. For even now one reads their slogan for the future "free society" on all tables and walls. Free society? Well, well! But surely you know, gentlemen, what one needs to build that? Wooden iron![9] The famous wooden iron! And it need not even be wooden . . .

* * *

---

7. The flourishing of classical Greek culture in mid-5th century B.C.E., a period named for the Athenian leader Pericles.   8. Little Greek actor (Latin).   9. A contradiction in terms.

MONA CAIRD
1854–1931

"Our common respectable marriage," wrote Mona Caird, is "the most hypocritical form of woman-purchase." The British "New Woman" writer published novels and essays over forty-eight years, but it was her fiery article *Marriage* that brought her to public attention in 1888 and launched a long debate over the subordinate and legally circumscribed position of women in Britain. Caird was not so much against marriage per se as against a repressive social system that limited women's options and made marriage and domesticity the only acceptable career. Insufficiently educated and lacking opportunities for respectable work outside the home, women had little choice but to enter into a contract where all the benefits were on one side and the duties and obligations on the other. It is this virtual slavery that particularly dismays Caird, as well as its result—that women who have no control over their own lives rarely develop their own talents or mature as individuals. Ironically, she notes, marriage itself suffers: wives are unhappy, and husbands are bored with the model wife's one-dimensional personality. The fact that Caird's own marriage was a happy one may be attributed to her own independent status: she was educated, earned money through her writings, engaged in activities outside the home, and could travel by herself when she wished. Such options were not available to the women whose lives she described in *The Wing of Azrael* (1889) or in her most famous novel, *The Daughters of Danaus* (1894): they appear with their talents stifled by domesticity and abusive husbands, or frustrated in their attempts to live on their own.

The Morality of Marriage, and Other Essays on the Status and Destiny of Woman (1897), in which the following selection appears, caused a storm of controversy. It not only challenged conventional images of female domesticity but attacked the legal and social structures supporting it and called for an end to the patriarchal system. Caird described the exploitation of women as a modern version of ancient rituals of sacrifice, an "artificial selection of victims for the good—or supposed good—of humanity." The color and force of her arguments made her a leader in the early struggle for equal rights for women.

The Emancipation of the Family[1]
From *The End of the Patriarchal Family*

*   *   *

Meanwhile, the spirit of liberty among women is increasing rapidly, and as soon as an approach to economic independence gives them the power to refuse, without harsh penalty, the terms which men have hitherto been able to dictate to them, in and out of marriage, we shall have some just right to call ourselves a free people. It is then that marriage—at present a mere moldering branch of the patriarchal tree—must alter its nature and its form.

Few seem yet to have realized what the independence of women would actually mean, and how absolutely our present marriage hangs upon their subject condition. Those who have opposed the smallest relaxation of the old laws, who have resisted the education and progress of women, were, from their own point of view, eminently wise; for upon the condition of tutelage

---

1. This essay was first published in 1890.

hung many a cherished belief, many a "sacred institution." It has been easy, hitherto, to maintain stringent forms of marriage, because the real brunt of it has been borne by women. Is it conceivable that when there are, in good sooth, really two to the marriage bargain, one of the parties to it will consent to fetter herself by bonds which the other repudiates? The "contract" can no longer remain unequal, when women have some say in the making of laws which they have to obey, and it remains to be seen how tight and irrevocable men will be willing to make the bond which they, too, must literally carry out. All men who are eloquent about the "sacred institution" will know that it rests upon them to sustain the sacredness which they will then, perhaps, talk less glibly about. They can no longer depute that office to their wives, together with the children and the cares of housekeeping. The "sacredness" which depends on restraints and punishments for its existence can then be fairly considered on its merits.

The "sacredness" which has hitherto hedged round family life can be clearly estimated when we remember the position which the married woman held, as regards her children, before the passing of the Custody of Infants Act in 1886. Before 1886 the father of a legitimate child was, as far as legal rights were concerned, its sole parent, "though the law imposes on the mother, under criminal and other penalties, liabilities and obligations almost equal to those of the father."[2]

The case is reported of a girl who applied to the court for permission to spend her holidays with her mother, the latter being separated from her husband for no fault of her own. The court refused, on the ground that the father's rights were sacred. "With these sacred rights the court has not interfered, and will not interfere." Only in the most extreme cases of cruelty to the child would these rights be set aside. The father, says Lord Chancellor Hardwicke,[3] "is entitled to the care of his own children, by nature and by nurture." This view seemed eminently reasonable to august opponents of the bill, nor do we hear that their grammatical sensibilities were offended. It is amusing to observe their horrified indignation at the bare thought of the father having to act with a guardian appointed by the mother, although the latter, according to law, might be *altogether excluded* from guardianship in favor of some one of her husband's appointment, and the utmost she could expect would be the privilege (in *her* case—in *his* the humiliation) of acting with another guardian.

Even to this day, the mother becomes sole guardian only when no other has been appointed by the father.

She can appoint a guardian to act after her own and her husband's death, but not to act *with* her husband (as he can appoint one or more to act with her) unless he is declared by the court to be unfit to have sole charge. Thus even this bill, fought for so devotedly by its friends, has been deprived of its principle of equality. The fifth clause is supposed to be a great triumph for the mother, because it empowers her, even while living with her husband, to apply to the court on any question regarding the custody of the children,

2. "The Infants' Act, 1886. A Record of a Three Years' Effort for Legislative Reform, with its Results" [Caird's note].   3. Philip Yorke, Lord Hardwicke (1690–1764), lord chancellor from 1737 to 1756 and responsible for an early reform of British marriage law.

or other important matters; and the court is actually directed to have regard to the wishes "as well of the mother as of the father."

Our country is to be congratulated on this achievement, and on the liberality of our law, which discerned fully four years ago that a child generally has two parents, and that one of them, though comparatively unimportant—even verging on the superfluous—might feel hurt if her existence and wishes were altogether ignored. Naturally, there is no necessity to allow this little politeness to interfere with rights more sacred, resting, as Lord Salisbury[4] pointed out, "on far deeper foundations than most of those which we have deemed firmly established." This, at first sight, strikes awe, but the sense of the phrase, under analysis, seems to "softly and suddenly vanish away."

Immense is the benefit which mothers enjoy under that Act of 1886, yet even now their position is subordinate. The woman who bears, suffers, risks her life, rears, trains, watches—of whom, indeed, public opinion *demands* these things, she whose body and soul have been subjected to this terrible service, has still only secondary rights to her children. She must still take the small mercies of the law and be thankful. Indeed, she has reason to be, seeing that four years ago she had no rights at all.

Consider all this in conjunction with the tremendous rigor with which maternal duties are pressed upon a woman; with the demand that she shall surrender to her children health, happiness, and all hope of self-development; with the unbounded, merciless condemnation which is heaped upon her if she prove a neglectful or unenthusiastic mother. In short, so amazing, so overwhelming are the demands made upon the woman, and so meager the rights granted to her, that the sense of the stupendous injustice is almost swallowed by the sense of the stupendous absurdity, and—as fortunately often happens in the study of English law and English opinion—the stress of indignant feeling finds timely relief in a burst of laughter.

Upon gigantic absurdities like these the sacredness of marriage has for centuries been resting. Father and mother are to share pleasantly between them the rights and duties of parenthood—the father having the rights, the mother the duties. No wonder there was opposition to the bill of 1886! They were dear privileges that it attacked.

If we could only realize how fundamental, in our traditions, is the old patriarchal feeling, we should then more clearly see that marriage, with its one-sided obligations, is not a thought-out rational system of sex relationship, but a lineal descendant of barbarian usages, cruel and absurd, even when the warlike condition of society gave them some color of reason, revolting now to all ideas of human justice and of dignity. While the community in other directions has been moving and changing, in this matter it has remained inert. This is the last citadel of the less intelligent kind of conservatism, and it has been defended with the ferocity and jealousy with which one instinctively fights for a last hope.

History and science are rapidly undermining it, by removing those imaginary foundations in the "will of God" or the "ordinance of Nature" on which so many happy theories have been built.

---

4. Robert Arthur Talbot Gascoyne-Cecil, marquess of Salisbury (1830–1903), was prime minister from 1886 to 1892 and from 1895 to 1902.

Since the birth of the comparatively new science of sociology, the favorite satires of men against women lose their brilliancy; they sound stupid and ungenerous as the taunts of gaolers against their half-starved prisoners.

To bring the institution of the family up to date is among the next great tasks of progressive civilization. So very far it has lagged behind, that this proposal sounds like a proposal to break up society altogether. So much the worse for society. We have abandoned *some* of the patriarchal rights; why do we not sweep from our State these remnants of a system which we repudiate utterly, as far as political questions are concerned, but whose influence we still keep warm at the very heart of our life, in the home, where the history of the coming generations is preparing?

The right of private contract is a right very dear to a liberty-loving people; yet in the most important matter of their lives, they have consented to forgo it! So long as the idea holds that a husband or a wife must, in assuming that character, consent to subscribe to a set of conditions decided by some other persons—dead and gone for centuries—and that if these conditions are not assented to, honorable union (as society considers) is impossible, so long will freedom be lacking in the most important relation in life, so long will the right of private contract be denied.

Without irreverence for the Past, we must see that the time has fully come to throw off the tyranny of surviving superstitions which are holding us back, and causing a dislocated social condition, because in public matters, and for one sex, we are working on the principle of individual freedom and the right of private contract; while in all the relations of the family, and for the other sex, we are still molding our life on the worst side of the old patriarchal idea, and denying the principle of private contract.

When domestic life has thus been brought into harmony with civilization, we shall have passed through a bloodless revolution.

Then, and not till then, ought we to regard ourselves as having left behind us the shadows of the Dark Ages; then, and not till then, can the development of science and of education begin to take their full effect upon the race, for then only will the *whole* race be open to all the best influences of the age. Hitherto we have been fostering in our midst a School of Superstition, to which we entrusted the task of fortifying the minds of the rising generation against all the knowledge which the contemporary schools of philosophy and science were laboriously endeavoring to promulgate.

Equal rights for the two sexes; the economic independence of women (hanging in a great measure on the progress of our industrial evolution); the establishment, rapid or gradual, as may prove desirable, of real freedom in the home—this at last would bring us to the end of the patriarchal system.

May we speed the parting guest!

HENRIK IBSEN

1828–1906

Henrik Ibsen was the foremost playwright of his time—treating social themes and ideas and often satirizing the nineteenth-century bourgeoisie—and not only in Norway, his native land. His plays may be viewed historically as the culmination of the bourgeois drama that has flourished fitfully, in France and Germany particularly, since the eighteenth century, when Diderot advocated and wrote plays about the middle classes and their "conditions" and problems. But they may also be seen as the beginning of realistic prose plays about modern life, from George Bernard Shaw and John Galsworthy to a wide range of soap operas on radio and TV. Even in China, Ibsen's drama of domestic and political crisis was immensely popular and influenced a generation of modern playwrights.

Ibsen was born at Skien, in Norway, on March 20, 1828. His family had sunk into poverty and at one point was forced to sell their possessions to pay off creditors. In 1844, at the age of sixteen, he was sent to Grimstad, another small coastal town, as an apothecary's apprentice. There he lived in almost complete isolation and cut himself off from his family, except for his sister Hedvig. In 1850 he managed to get to Oslo (then Christiania) and to enroll at the university. But he never passed his examinations and in the following year left for Bergen, where he had acquired the position of playwright and assistant stage manager at the newly founded Norwegian Theater. Ibsen supplied the small theater with several historical and romantic plays. In 1857 he was appointed artistic director at the Mollergate Theater in Christiania, and a year later he married Susannah Thoresen. *Love's Comedy*, his first major play, caused a scandal when it was published in a journal in 1862. Ibsen was roundly denounced in the press for the play's apparent attack on the institution of marriage, and the Christiana theater refused to stage it. His depression at the attacks on his play increased when Norway refused to support Denmark in its war with Prussia and Austria over Schleswig-Holstein. Ibsen was at that time deeply affected by Scandinavianism, the movement for solidarity of the northern nations, and he was ready to leave Norway when he received a government grant in 1863 to study European art. He settled in Rome with his family and lived for the following twenty-seven years in Rome, Dresden, Munich, and various smaller summer resorts, during which time he wrote all of his later plays.

After a long period of incubation and experimentation with romantic and historical themes, Ibsen wrote a series of "problem" plays, beginning with *The Pillars of Society* (1877), which in their time created a furor by their fearless criticism of the nineteenth-century social scene: the subjection of women, hypocrisy, hereditary disease, seamy politics, and corrupt journalism. He wrote these plays using realistic modes of presentation: ordinary colloquial speech, a simple setting in a drawing room or study, a natural way of introducing or dismissing characters. Ibsen had learned from the "well-made" Parisian play (typified by those of Eugène Scribe) how to confine his action to one climactic situation and how gradually to uncover the past by retrogressive exposition. But he went far beyond Scribe in technical skill and intellectual honesty.

The success of Ibsen's problem plays was international. But we must not forget that he was a Norwegian, the first writer of his small nation (its population at that time was less than 2 million) to win a reputation outside of Norway. Ibsen more than anyone else widened the scope of world literature beyond the confines of the "great" modern nations, which had entered its community roughly in this order: Italy, Spain, France, England, Germany, Russia. Since the time of Ibsen, other small nations have begun to play their part in the concert of world literature. Paradoxically, however, Ibsen rejected his own land. He had dreamed of becoming a great national poet. Instead, the plays he wrote during his voluntary exile depicted Norwegian society as consisting largely of a stuffy, provincial middle class, redeemed by a few upright, even fiery, individuals of initiative and courage. Only in 1891, when he was sixty-three, did Ibsen return to Christiania for good. He was then famous and widely honored, but lived a very retired life. In 1900 he suffered a stroke that made him a complete invalid for the last years of his life. He died on May 23, 1906.

Ibsen could hardly have survived his time if he had been merely a painter of society, a dialectician of social issues, and a magnificent technician of the theater. True, many of his discussions are now dated. We smile at some of what happens in *A Doll's House* (1879) and *Ghosts* (1881). His realistic stagecraft is familiar to modern audiences because it has become part of our dramatic tradition. But Ibsen stays with us because he has more to offer—because he was an artist who managed to create, at his best, works of poetry that, under their mask of sardonic humor, express his dream of humanity reborn by intelligence and self-sacrifice.

Hedda Gabler (1890) surprised and puzzled the large audience all over Europe that Ibsen had won in the 1880s. The play shows nothing of Ibsen's reforming zeal: no general theme emerges that could be used in spreading progressive ideas such as the emancipation of women dramatized in *A Doll's House* (1879), nor is the play an example of Ibsen's peculiar technique of retrospective revelation exhibited in *Rosmersholm* (1886). At first glance it seems mainly a study of a complex, exceptional, and even unique woman. Henry James, reviewing the first English performance, saw it as the picture of "a state of nerves as well as of soul, a state of temper, of health, of chagrin, of despair." Undoubtedly, Hedda is the central figure of the play, but she is no conventional heroine. She behaves atrociously to everyone with whom she comes in contact, and her moral sense is thoroughly defective: she is perverse, egotistical, sadistic, callous, even evil and demonic, truly a *femme fatale*. Still, this impression, while not mistaken, ignores another side of her personality and her situation. The play is, after all, a tragedy (though there are comic touches), and we are to feel pity and terror. Hedda is not simply evil and perverse. Born, she feels, for a greater destiny and imbued with romantic visions of genius that include making one's own life a work of art, she cannot accept the practical compromises and mediocre aspirations with which she is surrounded. We must imagine her as distinguished, well bred, proud, beautiful, and even grand in her defiance of her surroundings and in the final gesture of her suicide. Not for nothing have great actresses excelled in this role. We must pity her as a tortured, tormented creature caught in a web of circumstance, as a victim, in spite of her desperate struggles to dominate and control the fate of those around her.

We are carefully prepared to understand her heritage. She is General Gabler's daughter. Ibsen tells us himself (in a letter to Count Moritz Prozor, dated December 4, 1890) that "I intended to indicate thereby that as a personality she is to be regarded rather as her father's daughter than as her husband's wife." She has inherited an aristocratic view of life. Her father's portrait hangs in her apartment. His pistols tell of the code of honor and the ready escape they offer in a self-inflicted death. Hedda lives in Ibsen's Norway, a stuffy, provincial, middle-class society, and is acutely, even morbidly, afraid of scandal. She has, to her own regret, rejected the advances of Eilert, theatrically threatening him with her father's pistol. She envies Thea for the boldness with which she deserted her husband to follow Eilert. She admires Eilert for his escapades, which she romanticizes with the recurrent metaphor of his returning with "vine leaves in his hair." But she cannot break out of the narrow confines of her society. She is not an emancipated woman.

When she is almost thirty, in reduced circumstances, she accepts a suitable husband, George Tesman. The marriage of convenience turns out to be a ghastly error for which she cannot forgive herself: Tesman is an amiable bore absorbed in his research into the "Domestic Craftsmanship Practices of Medieval Brabant." His expectations of a professorship in his hometown turn out to be uncertain. He has gone into debt, even to his guileless old aunt, in renting an expensive house, and, supreme humiliation for her, Hedda is pregnant by him. The dream of luxury, of becoming a hostess, of keeping thoroughbred horses, is shattered the very first day after their return from the prolonged honeymoon, which for Tesman was also a trip to rummage around in archives. Hedda is deeply stirred by the return of Eilert, her first suitor. She seems vaguely to think of a new relationship, at least, by spoiling his friendship with Thea. She plays with the attentions of Judge Brack. But everything quickly comes to nought: she is trapped in her marriage, unable and unwilling to become unfaithful to her husband; she is deeply disappointed by Eilert's ugly death, saying, "Oh absurdity—! It hangs like a curse over everything I so much as touch." She fears the scandal that will follow when her role in Eilert's suicide is discovered and she is called before the police; she can avoid it only by coming under the power of Judge Brack, who is prepared to blackmail her with his knowledge of the circumstances. Her plot to destroy Thea and Eilert's brainchild is frustrated by Thea's having preserved notes and drafts, which Thea eagerly uses to start to reconstruct with the help of Tesman. Still, while Hedda is in a terrible impasse, her suicide remains a shock, an abrupt, even absurd deed, eliciting the final line from the commonsensical Judge Brack: "But God have mercy—People just don't act that way!" But we must assume that Hedda had pondered suicide long before: the pistol she gave to Eilert implies an unspoken suicide pact. He bungled it; she does it the right way, dying in beauty, shot in the temple and not in the abdomen.

The play is not, however, simply a character study, though Hedda is an extraordinarily complex, contradictory, subtle woman whose portrait, at least on the stage, could not be easily paralleled before Ibsen. It is also an extremely effective, swiftly moving play of action, deftly plotted in its clashes and climaxes. At the end of Act I Hedda seems to have won. The Tesmans, husband and aunt, are put in their place. Thea is lured into making confidences. The scene in Act II in which Hedda appeals to Eilert's pride in his independence and induces him to join in Judge Brack's party is a superb display of Hedda's power and skill. Act II ends with Eilert going off and the two women left alone in their tense though suppressed antagonism. Act III ends with Hedda alone, burning the precious manuscript about the "cultural forces which will shape the future and . . . the future course of civilization," an obvious contrast to Tesman's research into an irrelevant past. (Ibsen himself always believed in progress, in a utopia he called "the Third Empire.")

The action is compressed into about thirty-six hours and located in a house where only the moving of furniture (the piano into the back room) or the change of light or costumes indicates the passing of time. Tesman is something of a fool. He is totally unaware of Hedda's inner turmoil, he obtusely misunderstands allusions to her pregnancy, he comically encourages the advances of Judge Brack, he complacently settles down to the task of assembling the fragments of Eilert's manuscript, recognizing that "finding the order in other people's papers—that's precisely what I'm meant for." Though he seems amiably domestic in his love for his aunts, proud of having won Hedda, ambitious to provide an elegant home for her, his behavior is by no means above reproach. He envies and fears Eilert, gloats over his bad reputation, surreptitiously brings home the lost manuscript, conceals its recovery from Thea; when Hedda tells of its being burned, he is at first shocked, reacting comically with the legal phrase about "criminal appropriation of lost property," but is then easily persuaded to accept it when Hedda tells him that she did it for his sake and is completely won over when she reveals her pregnancy. After Eilert's death he feels, however, some guilt and tries to make up by helping in the reconstruction of the manuscript, now that his rival no longer threatens his career. Tesman is given strong speech mannerisms: the frequent use of "what?"—which Hedda, commenting at the end on the progress of the work on the manuscript, imitates sarcastically—and the use of "Just think." His last inappropriate words, "Shot herself! Shot herself in the temple! Just think!" lend a grotesque touch to the tragic end. Aunt Juliane belongs with him: she is a fussy, kindly person, proud of her nephew, awed by his new wife, eager to help with the expected baby, but also easily consoled after the death of her sister: "Oh, there's always some poor invalid or other who needs care and attention."

The other pair, Eilert Løvborg and Thea Elvsted, are sharply contrasted. Thea had the courage to leave her husband; she is devoted to Eilert and seems to have cured him of his addiction to drink but fears that he cannot resist a new temptation. Eilert tells Hedda unkindly that Thea is "stupid," and there is some truth to that, inasmuch as she is so easily taken in by Hedda. Her quick settling down to work on the manuscript after Eilert's death suggests some obtuseness, though we must, presumably, excuse it as a theatrical foreshortening.

Judge Brack is a "man of the world," a sensualist who hardly conceals his desire to make Hedda his mistress, by blackmail if necessary, and is dismayed when she escapes his clutches: in his facile philosophy, "one can usually learn to live with the inevitable."

Eilert, we must assume, is some kind of genius. His book, we have to take on trust, is an important work. We are told that he had squandered an inheritance, had engaged in orgies, and had regaled Hedda with tales of his exploits before she chased him with her pistol. When he comes back to town, ostensibly reformed, dressed conventionally, he immediately starts courting Hedda again. Stung by her contempt for his abstinence, he rushes off to Brack's party, which degenerates into a disgraceful brawl in a brothel. His relapse and the loss of the manuscript destroy his self-esteem and hope for any future. He accepts Hedda's pistol but dies an ignominious, ugly death. We see Eilert mainly reflected in Hedda's imagination as a figure of pagan freedom who, she thinks, has done something noble, beautiful, and courageous in "to break away from the banquet of life—so soon." She dies in beauty as she wanted Eilert to die.

This aesthetic suicide must seem to us a supremely futile gesture of revolt. Ibsen always admired the great rebels, the fighters for freedom, but *Hedda Gabler* will appear almost a parodic version of his persistent theme: the individual against society, defying it and escaping it in death.

PRONOUNCING GLOSSARY

The following list uses common English syllables and stress accents to provide rough equivalents of selected words whose pronunciation may be unfamiliar to the general reader.

Berta: *behr'-tuh*

Eilert Løvborg: *ai'-lert leuhv'-borg*

fjord: *fyoord*

Rosmersholm: *ross'-merss-holm*

Thea Elvsted: *tay'-ah aelf'-sted*

Hedda Gabler[1]

CHARACTERS

GEORGE TESMAN, *reseach fellow in cultural history*
HEDDA TESMAN, *his wife*
MISS JULIANE TESMAN, *his aunt*
MRS. ELEVSTED
JUDGE BRACK
EILERT LØVBORG
BERTA, *the maid to the Tesmans*

The action takes place in the fashionable west side of Christiania, Norway's capital.

1. Translated by Rick Davis and Brian Johnston.

Act One

A large, pleasantly and tastefully furnished drawing room, decorated in somber tones. In the rear wall is a wide doorway with the curtains pulled back. This doorway leads into a smaller room decorated in the same style. In the right wall of the drawing room is a folding door leading into the hall. In the opposite wall, a glass door, also with its curtains pulled back. Outside, through the windows, part of a covered veranda can be seen, along with trees in their autumn colors. In the foreground, an oval table surrounded by chairs. Downstage, near the right wall, is a broad, dark porcelain stove, a high-backed armchair, a footstool with cushions and two stools. Up in the right-hand corner, a corner-sofa and a small round table. Downstage, on the left side, a little distance from the wall, a sofa. Beyond the glass door, a piano. On both sides of the upstage doorway stand shelves displaying terra cotta and majolica objects. By the back wall of the inner room, a sofa, a table and a couple of chairs can be seen. Above the sofa hangs the portrait of a handsome elderly man in a general's uniform. Above the table, a hanging lamp with an opalescent glass shade. There are many flowers arranged in vases and glasses all around the drawing room. More flowers lie on the tables. The floors of both rooms are covered with thick rugs.

Morning light. The sun shines in through the glass door.

[MISS JULIE TESMAN, *with hat and parasol, comes in from the hall, followed by* BERTA, *who carries a bouquet wrapped in paper.* MISS TESMAN *is a kindly, seemingly good-natured lady of about sixty-five, neatly but simply dressed in a grey visiting outfit.* BERTA *is a housemaid, getting on in years, with a homely and somewhat rustic appearance.*]

MISS TESMAN [*Stops just inside the doorway, listens, and speaks softly.*] Well—I believe they're just now getting up!

BERTA [*Also softly.*] That's what I said, Miss. Just think—the steamer got in so late last night, and then—Lord, the young mistress wanted so much unpacked before she could settle down.

MISS TESMAN Well, well. Let them have a good night's sleep at least. But— they'll have some fresh morning air when they come down. [*She crosses to the glass door and throws it wide open.*]

BERTA [*By the table, perplexed, holding the bouquet.*] Hmm. Bless me if I can find a spot for these. I think I'd better put them down here, Miss. [*Puts the bouquet down on the front of the piano.*]

MISS TESMAN So, Berta dear, now you have a new mistress. As God's my witness, giving you up was a heavy blow.

BERTA And me, Miss—what can I say? I've been in yours and Miss Rina's service for so many blessed years—

MISS TESMAN We must bear it patiently, Berta. Truly, there's no other way. You know George has to have you in the house with him—he simply has to. You've looked after him since he was a little boy.

BERTA Yes, but Miss—I keep worrying about her, lying there at home— so completely helpless, poor thing. And that new girl! She'll never learn how to take care of sick people.

MISS TESMAN Oh, I'll teach her how soon enough. And I'll be doing most of the work myself, you know. Don't you worry about my sister, Berta dear.

BERTA   Yes, but there's something else, Miss. I'm so afraid I won't satisfy the new mistress—

MISS TESMAN   Ffft—Good Lord—there might be a thing or two at first—

BERTA   Because she's so particular about things—

MISS TESMAN   Well, what do you expect? General Gabler's daughter—the way she lived in the general's day! Do you remember how she would go out riding with her father? In that long black outfit, with the feather in her hat?

BERTA   Oh, yes—I remember that all right. But I never thought she'd make a match with our Mr. Tesman.

MISS TESMAN   Neither did I. But—while I'm thinking about it, don't call George "Mister Tesman" any more. Now it's "Doctor Tesman."

BERTA   Yes—that's what the young mistress said as soon as they came in last night. So it's true?

MISS TESMAN   Yes, it's really true. Think of it, Berta—they've made him a doctor. While he was away, you understand. I didn't know a thing about it, until he told me himself, down at the pier.

BERTA   Well, he's so smart he could be anything he wanted to be. But I never thought he'd take up curing people too!

MISS TESMAN   No, no, no. He's not that kind of doctor. [*Nods significantly.*] As far as that goes, you might have to start calling him something even grander soon.

BERTA   Oh no! What could that be?

MISS TESMAN [*Smiling.*]   Hmm—wouldn't you like to know? [*Emotionally.*] Oh, dear God . . . if our sainted Joseph could look up from his grave and see what's become of his little boy. [*She looks around.*] But, Berta—what's this now? Why have you taken all the slipcovers off the furniture?

BERTA   The mistress told me to. She said she can't stand covers on chairs.

MISS TESMAN   But are they going to use this for their everyday living room?

BERTA   Yes, they will. At least she will. He—the doctor—he didn't say anything.

[GEORGE TESMAN *enters, humming, from the right of the inner room, carrying an open, empty suitcase. He is a youthful-looking man of thirty-three, of medium height, with an open, round, and cheerful face, blond hair and beard. He wears glasses and is dressed in comfortable, somewhat disheveled clothes.*]

MISS TESMAN   Good morning, good morning, George!

TESMAN   Aunt Julie! Dear Aunt Julie! [*Goes over and shakes her hand.*] All the way here—so early in the day! Hm!

MISS TESMAN   Yes, you know me—I just had to peek in on you a little.

TESMAN   And after a short night's sleep at that!

MISS TESMAN   Oh, that's nothing at all to me.

TESMAN   So—you got home all right from the pier, hm?

MISS TESMAN   Yes, as it turned out, thanks be to God. The Judge was kind enough to see me right to the door.

TESMAN   We felt so bad that we couldn't take you in the carriage—but you saw how many trunks and boxes Hedda had to bring.

MISS TESMAN   Yes, it was amazing.

BERTA [*To* TESMAN.]   Perhaps I should go in and ask the mistress if there's anything I can help her with.

TESMAN   No, thank you, Berta. You don't have to do that. If she needs you, she'll ring—that's what she said.

BERTA [*Going out to right.*]   Very well.

TESMAN   Ah—but—Berta—take this suitcase with you.

BERTA [*Takes the case.*]   I'll put it in the attic.

TESMAN   Just imagine, Auntie. I'd stuffed that whole suitcase with notes— just notes! The things I managed to collect in those archives—really incredible! Ancient, remarkable things that no one had any inkling of.

MISS TESMAN   Ah yes—you certainly haven't wasted any time on your honeymoon.

TESMAN   Yes—I can really say that's true. But, Auntie, take off your hat— Here, let's see. Let me undo that ribbon, hm?   *He acts kindly*

MISS TESMAN [*While he does so.*]   Ah, dear God—this is just what it was like when you were home with us.

TESMAN [*Examining the hat as he holds it.*]   My, my—isn't this a fine, elegant hat you've got for yourself.

MISS TESMAN   I bought it for Hedda's sake.   *The aunt wants to please Hedda*

TESMAN   For Hedda's—hm?

MISS TESMAN   Yes, so Hedda won't feel ashamed of me if we go out for a walk together.

TESMAN [*Patting her cheek.*]   You think of everything, Auntie Julie, don't you? [*Putting her hat on a chair by the table.*]   And now—let's just settle down here on the sofa until Hedda comes. [*They sit. She puts her parasol down near the sofa.*]

MISS TESMAN [*Takes both his hands and gazes at him.*]   What a blessing to have you here, bright as day, right before my eyes again, George. Sainted Joseph's own boy!

TESMAN   For me too. To see you again, Aunt Julie—who've been both father and mother to me.

MISS TESMAN   Yes, I know you'll always have a soft spot for your old aunts.

TESMAN   But no improvement at all with Rina, hm?

MISS TESMAN   Oh dear no—and none to be expected poor thing. She lies there just as she has all these years. But I pray that Our Lord lets me keep her just a little longer. Otherwise I don't know what I'd do with my life, George. Especially now, you know—when I don't have you to take care of any more.   *George gave importance to her life*

TESMAN [*Patting her on the back.*]   There. There. There.

MISS TESMAN   Oh—just to think that you've become a married man, George. And that you're the one who carried off Hedda Gabler! Beautiful Hedda Gabler. Imagine—with all her suitors.   *Hedda Gabler is a prize*

TESMAN [*Hums a little and smiles complacently.*]   Yes, I believe I have quite a few friends in town who envy me, hm?

MISS TESMAN   And then—you got to take such a long honeymoon—more than five—almost six months . . .

TESMAN   Yes, but it was also part of my research, you know. All those archives I had to wade through—and all the books I had to read!

MISS TESMAN   I suppose you're right. [*Confidentially and more quietly.*]   But listen, George—isn't there something—something extra you want to tell me?

TESMAN   About the trip?

MISS TESMAN   Yes.

TESMAN   No—I can't think of anything I didn't mention in my letters. I was given my doctorate—but I told you that yesterday.

MISS TESMAN So you did. But I mean—whether you might have any—any kind of—prospects—?

TESMAN   Prospects?

MISS TESMAN   Good Lord, George—I'm your old aunt.

TESMAN   Well of course I have prospects.

MISS TESMAN   Aha!

TESMAN   I have excellent prospects of becoming a professor one of these days. But Aunt Julie dear, you already know that.

MISS TESMAN   [*With a little laugh.*]   You're right, I do. [*Changing the subject.*] But about your trip. It must have cost a lot.

TESMAN   Well, thank God, that huge fellowship paid for a good part of it.

MISS TESMAN   But how did you make it last for the both of you?

TESMAN   That's the tricky part, isn't it?

MISS TESMAN   And on top of that, when you're travelling with a lady! That's always going to cost you more, or so I've heard.

TESMAN   You're right—it was a bit more costly. But Hedda just had to have that trip, Auntie. She really had to. There was no choice.

MISS TESMAN   Well, I suppose not. These days a honeymoon trip is essential, it seems. But now tell me—have you had a good look around the house?

TESMAN   Absolutely! I've been up since dawn.

MISS TESMAN   And what do you think about all of it?

TESMAN   It's splendid! Only I can't think of what we'll do with those two empty rooms between the back parlor and Hedda's bedroom.

MISS TESMAN   [*Lightly laughing.*]   My dear George—when the time comes, you'll think of what to do with them.

TESMAN   Oh, of course—as I add to my library, hm?

MISS TESMAN   That's right, my boy—of course I was thinking about your library.

TESMAN   Most of all I'm just so happy for Hedda. Before we got engaged she'd always say how she couldn't imagine living anywhere but here—in Prime Minister Falk's house.

MISS TESMAN   Yes—imagine. And then it came up for sale just after you left for your trip.

TESMAN   Aunt Julie, we really had luck on our side, hm?

MISS TESMAN   But the expense, George. This will all be costly for you.

TESMAN   [*Looks at her disconcertedly.*]   Yes. It might be. It might be, Auntie.

MISS TESMAN   Ah, God only knows.

TESMAN   How much, do you think? Approximately. Hm?

MISS TESMAN   I can't possibly tell before all the bills are in.

TESMAN   Luckily Judge Brack lined up favorable terms for me—he wrote as much to Hedda.

MISS TESMAN   That's right—don't you ever worry about that, my boy. All this furniture, and the carpets? I put up the security for it.

TESMAN   Security? You? Dear Auntie Julie, what kind of security could you give?

MISS TESMAN   I took out a mortgage on our annuity.

TESMAN   What? On your—and Aunt Rina's annuity!

MISS TESMAN   I couldn't think of any other way.

TESMAN [*Standing in front of her.*]   Have you gone completely out of your mind, Auntie? That annuity is all you and Aunt Rina have to live on.

MISS TESMAN   Now, now, take it easy. It's just a formality, you understand. Judge Brack said so. He was good enough to arrange it all for me. Just a formality, he said.

TESMAN   That could very well be, but all the same . . .

MISS TESMAN   You'll be earning your own living now, after all. And, good Lord, so what if we do have to open the purse a little, spend a little bit at first? That would only make us happy.

TESMAN   Auntie . . . you never get tired of sacrificing yourself for me.

MISS TESMAN [*Rises and lays her hands on his shoulders.*]   What joy do I have in the world, my dearest boy, other than smoothing out the path for you? You, without a father or mother to take care of you . . . but we've reached our destination, my dear. Maybe things looked black from time to time. But, praise God, George, you've come out on top!

TESMAN   Yes, it's really amazing how everything has gone according to plan.

MISS TESMAN   And those who were against you—those who would have blocked your way—they're at the bottom of the pit. They've fallen, George. And the most dangerous one, he fell the farthest. Now he just lies there where he fell, the poor sinner.

TESMAN   Have you heard anything about Eilert—since I went away, I mean?

MISS TESMAN   Nothing, except they say he published a new book.

TESMAN   What? Eilert Løvborg? Just recently, hm?

MISS TESMAN   That's what they say. God only knows how there could be anything to it. But when *your* book comes out—now that will be something else again, won't it, George? What's it going to be about?

TESMAN   It will deal with the Domestic Craftsmanship Practices of Medieval Brabant.[2]

MISS TESMAN   Just think—you can write about that kind of thing too.

TESMAN   However, it might be quite a while before that book is ready. I've got all these incredible collections that have to be put in order first.

MISS TESMAN   Ordering and collecting—you're certainly good at that. You're not the son of sainted Joseph for nothing.

TESMAN   And I'm so eager to get going. Especially now that I've got my own snug house and home to work in.

MISS TESMAN   And most of all, now that you've got her—your heart's desire, dear, dear George!

TESMAN [*Embracing her.*]   Yes, Auntie Julie! Hedda . . . that's the most beautiful thing of all! [*Looking toward the doorway.*] I think that's her, hm?

[HEDDA *comes in from the left side of the inner room. She is a lady of*

---

2. In the Middle Ages, Brabant was a duchy located in parts of what are now Belgium and the Netherlands.

twenty-nine. Her face and figure are aristocratic and elegant. Her complexion is pale. Her eyes are steel-grey, cold and clear. Her hair is an attractive medium brown but not particularly full. She is wearing a tasteful, somewhat loose-fitting morning gown.]

MISS TESMAN [*Going to meet* HEDDA.]   Good morning, Hedda, my dear. Good morning.

HEDDA [*Extending her hand.*]   Good morning, Miss Tesman, my dear. You're here so early. How nice of you.

MISS TESMAN [*Looking somewhat embarrassed.*]   Well now, how did the young mistress sleep in her new home?

HEDDA   Fine thanks. Well enough.

TESMAN [*Laughing.*]   Well enough! That's a good one, Hedda. You were sleeping like a log when I got up.

HEDDA   Yes, lucky for me. But of course you have to get used to anything new, Miss Tesman. A little at a time. [*Looks toward the window.*] Uch! Look at that. The maid opened the door. I'm drowning in all this sunlight.

MISS TESMAN [*Going to the door.*]   Well then, let's close it.

HEDDA   No, no, don't do that. Tesman my dear, just close the curtains. That gives a gentler light.

TESMAN [*By the door.*]   All right, all right. Now then, Hedda. You've got both fresh air and sunlight.

HEDDA   Yes, fresh air. That's what I need with all these flowers all over the place. But Miss Tesman, won't you sit down?

MISS TESMAN   No, but thank you. Now that I know everything's all right here, I've got to see about getting home again. Home to that poor dear who's lying there in pain.

TESMAN   Be sure to give her my respects, won't you? And tell her I'll stop by and look in on her later today.

MISS TESMAN   Yes, yes I'll certainly do that. But would you believe it, George? [*She rustles around in the pocket of her skirt.*] I almost forgot. Here, I brought something for you.

TESMAN   And what might that be, Auntie, hm?

MISS TESMAN [*Brings out a flat package wrapped in newspaper and hands it to him.*]   Here you are, my dear boy.

TESMAN [*Opening it.*]   Oh my Lord. You kept them for me, Aunt Julie. Hedda, isn't this touching, hm?

HEDDA   Well, what is it?

TESMAN   My old house slippers. My slippers.

HEDDA   Oh yes, I remember how often you talked about them on our trip.

TESMAN   Yes, well, I really missed them. [*Goes over to her.*] Now you can see them for yourself, Hedda.

HEDDA [*Moves over to the stove.*]   Oh, no thanks, I don't really care to.

TESMAN [*Following after her.*]   Just think, Aunt Rina lying there embroidering for me, sick as she was. Oh, you couldn't possibly believe how many memories are tangled up in these slippers.

HEDDA [*By the table.*]   Not for me.

MISS TESMAN   Hedda's quite right about that, George.

TESMAN   Yes, but now that she's in the family I thought—

HEDDA   That maid won't last, Tesman.

MISS TESMAN   Berta—?

TESMAN   What makes you say that, hm?

HEDDA [*Pointing.*]   Look, she's left her old hat lying there on that chair.

TESMAN [*Terrified, dropping the slippers on the floor.*]   Hedda—!

HEDDA   What if someone came in and saw that.

TESMAN   But Hedda—that's Aunt Julie's hat.

HEDDA   Really?

MISS TESMAN [*Taking the hat.*]   Yes, it really is. And for that matter it's not so old either, my dear little Hedda.

HEDDA   Oh, I really didn't get a good look at it, Miss Tesman.

MISS TESMAN [*Tying the hat on her head.*]   Actually I've never worn it before today—and the good Lord knows that's true.

TESMAN   And an elegant hat it is too. Really magnificent.

MISS TESMAN [*She looks around.*]   Oh that's as may be, George. My parasol? Ah, here it is. [*She takes it.*] That's mine too. [*She mutters.*] Not Berta's.

TESMAN   A new hat and a new parasol. Just think, Hedda.

HEDDA   Very charming, very attractive.

TESMAN   That's true, hm? But Auntie, take a good look at Hedda before you go. Look at how charming and attractive she is.

MISS TESMAN   Oh my dear, that's nothing new. Hedda's been lovely all her life. [*She nods and goes across to the right.*]

TESMAN [*Following her.*]   Yes, but have you noticed how she's blossomed, how well she's filled out on our trip?

HEDDA   Oh, leave it alone!

MISS TESMAN [*Stops and turns.*]   Filled out?

TESMAN   Yes, Aunt Julie. You can't see it so well right now in that gown— but I, who have a little better opportunity to—

HEDDA [*By the glass door impatiently.*]   Oh you don't have the opportunity for anything.

TESMAN   It was that mountain air down in the Tyrol.

HEDDA [*Curtly interrupting.*]   I'm the same as when I left.

TESMAN   You keep saying that. But it's true, isn't it Auntie?

MISS TESMAN [*Folding her hands and gazing at* HEDDA.]   Lovely . . . lovely . . . lovely. That's Hedda. [*She goes over to her and with both her hands takes her head, bends it down, kisses her hair.*]   God bless and keep Hedda Tesman for George's sake.

HEDDA [*Gently freeing herself.*]   Ah—! Let me out!

MISS TESMAN [*With quiet emotion.*]   I'll come look in on you two every single day.

TESMAN   Yes, Auntie, do that, won't you, hm?

MISS TESMAN   Good-bye, good-bye.

[*She goes out through the hall door.* TESMAN *follows her out. The door remains half open.* TESMAN *is heard repeating his greetings to Aunt Rina and his thanks for the slippers. While this is happening,* HEDDA *walks around the room raising her arms and clenching her fists as if in a rage. Then she draws the curtains back from the door, stands there and looks out. After a short time,* TESMAN *comes in and closes the door behind him.*]

TESMAN [*Picking up the slippers from the floor.*]   What are you looking at, Hedda?

HEDDA [*Calm and controlled again.*] Just the leaves. So yellow and so withered.

TESMAN [*Wrapping up the slippers and placing them on the table.*] Yes, well—we're into September now.

HEDDA [*Once more uneasy.*] Yes—It's already—already September.

TESMAN Didn't you think Aunt Julie was acting strange just now, almost formal? What do you suppose got into her?

HEDDA I really don't know her. Isn't that the way she usually is?

TESMAN No, not like today.

HEDDA [*Leaving the glass door.*] Do you think she was upset by the hat business?

TESMAN Not really. Maybe a little, for just a moment—

HEDDA But where did she get her manners, flinging her hat around any way she likes here in the drawing room. People just don't act that way.

TESMAN Well, I'm sure she won't do it again.

HEDDA Anyway, I'll smooth everything over with her soon enough.

TESMAN Yes, Hedda, if you would do that.

HEDDA When you visit them later today, invite her here for the evening.

TESMAN Yes, that's just what I'll do. And there's one more thing you can do that would really make her happy.

HEDDA Well?

TESMAN If you just bring yourself to call her Aunt Julie, for my sake, Hedda, hm?

HEDDA Tesman, for God's sake, don't ask me to do that. I've told you that before. I'll try to call her Aunt once in a while and that's enough.

TESMAN Oh well, I just thought that now that you're part of the family . . .

HEDDA Hmm. I don't know—[*She crosses upstage to the doorway.*]

TESMAN [*After a pause.*] Is something the matter, Hedda?

HEDDA I was just looking at my old piano. It really doesn't go with these other things.

TESMAN As soon as my salary starts coming in, we'll see about trading it in for a new one.

HEDDA Oh, no, don't trade it in. I could never let it go. We'll leave it in the back room instead. And then we'll get a new one to put in here. I mean, as soon as we get the chance.

TESMAN [*A little dejectedly.*] Yes, I suppose we could do that.

HEDDA [*Taking the bouquet from the piano.*] These flowers weren't here when we got in last night.

TESMAN I suppose Aunt Julie brought them.

HEDDA [*Looks into the bouquet.*] Here's a card. [*Takes it out and reads.*] "Will call again later today." Guess who it's from.

TESMAN Who is it, hm?

HEDDA It says Mrs. Elvsted.

TESMAN Really. Mrs. Elvsted. She used to be Miss Rysing.

HEDDA Yes, that's the one. She had all that irritating hair she'd always be fussing with. An old flame of yours, I've heard.

TESMAN [*Laughs.*] Oh, not for long and before I knew you, Hedda. And she's here in town. How about that.

HEDDA Strange that she should come visiting us. I hardly know her except from school.

TESMAN   Yes, and of course I haven't seen her since—well God knows how long. How could she stand it holed up out there so far from everything, hm?

HEDDA [*Reflects a moment and then suddenly speaks.*]   Just a minute, Tesman. Doesn't he live out that way, Eilert Løvborg, I mean?

TESMAN   Yes, right up in that area.

[BERTA *comes in from the hallway.*]

BERTA   Ma'am, she's back again. The lady who came by with the flowers an hour ago. [*Pointing.*] Those you've got in your hand, Ma'am.

HEDDA   Is she then? Please ask her to come in.

[BERTA *opens the door for* MRS. ELVSTED *and then leaves.* MRS. ELVSTED *is slender with soft, pretty features. Her eyes are light blue, large, round and slightly protruding. Her expression is one of alarm and question. Her hair is remarkably light, almost a white gold and exceptionally rich and full. She is a couple of years younger than Hedda. Her costume is a dark visiting dress, tasteful but not of the latest fashion.*]

HEDDA [*Goes to meet her in a friendly manner.*]   Hello my dear Mrs. Elvsted. So delightful to see you again.

MRS. ELVSTED [*Nervous, trying to control herself.*]   Yes, it's been so long since we've seen each other.

TESMAN [*Shakes her hand.*]   And we could say the same, hm?

HEDDA   Thank you for the lovely flowers.

MRS. ELVSTED   I would have come yesterday right away but I heard you were on a trip—

TESMAN   So you've just come into town, hm?

MRS. ELVSTED   Yesterday around noon. I was absolutely desperate when I heard you weren't home.

HEDDA   Desperate, why?

TESMAN   My dear Miss Rysing—I mean Mrs. Elvsted.

HEDDA   There isn't some sort of trouble—?

MRS. ELVSTED   Yes there is—and I don't know another living soul to turn to here in town.

HEDDA [*Sets the flowers down on the table.*]   All right then, let's sit down here on the sofa.

MRS. ELVSTED   Oh no, I'm too upset to sit down.

HEDDA   No you're not. Come over here. [*She draws* MRS. ELVSTED *to the sofa and sits beside her.*]

TESMAN   Well, and now Mrs.—

HEDDA   Did something happen up at your place?

MRS. ELVSTED   Yes—That's it—well, not exactly—Oh, I don't want you to misunderstand me—

HEDDA   Well then the best thing is just to tell it straight out, Mrs. Elvsted—why?

TESMAN   That's why you came here, hm?

MRS. ELVSTED   Yes, of course. So I'd better tell you, if you don't already know, that Eilert Løvborg is in town.

HEDDA   Løvborg?

TESMAN   Eilert Løvborg's back again? Just think, Hedda.

HEDDA   Good Lord, Tesman, I can hear.

MRS. ELVSTED   He's been back now for about a week. The whole week alone here where he can fall in with all kinds of bad company. This town's a dangerous place for him.

HEDDA But my dear Mrs. Elvsted, how does this involve you?

MRS. ELVSTED [*With a scared expression, speaking quickly.*] He was the children's tutor.

HEDDA Your children?

MRS. ELVSTED My husband's. I don't have any.

HEDDA The stepchildren then?

MRS. ELVSTED Yes.

TESMAN [*Somewhat awkwardly.*] But was he sufficiently—I don't know how to say this—sufficiently regular in his habits to be trusted with that kind of job, hm?

MRS. ELVSTED For the past two years no one could say anything against him.

TESMAN Really, nothing. Just think, Hedda.

HEDDA I hear.

MRS. ELVSTED Nothing at all I assure you. Not in any way. But even so, now that I know he's here in the city alone and with money in his pocket I'm deathly afraid for him.

TESMAN But why isn't he up there with you and your husband, hm?

MRS. ELVSTED When the book came out he was too excited to stay up there with us.

TESMAN Yes, that's right. Aunt Julie said he'd come out with a new book.

MRS. ELVSTED Yes, a major new book on the progress of civilization—in its entirely I mean. That was two weeks ago. And it's been selling wonderfully. Everyone's reading it. It's created a huge sensation—why?

TESMAN All that really? Must be something he had lying around from his better days.

MRS. ELVSTED From before, you mean?

TESMAN Yes.

MRS. ELVSTED No, he wrote the whole thing while he was up there living with us. Just in the last year.

TESMAN That's wonderful to hear, Hedda. Just think!

MRS. ELVSTED Yes, if only it continues.

HEDDA Have you met him here in town?

MRS. ELVSTED No, not yet. I had a terrible time hunting down his address but this morning I finally found it.

HEDDA [*Looks searchingly.*] I can't help thinking this is a little odd on your husband's part.

MRS. ELVSTED [*Starts nervously.*] My husband—What?

HEDDA That he'd send you to town on this errand. That he didn't come himself to look for his friend.

MRS. ELVSTED Oh no, no, no. My husband doesn't have time for that. And anyway I had to do some shopping too.

HEDDA [*Smiling slightly.*] Oh well, that's different then.

MRS. ELVSTED [*Gets up quickly, ill at ease.*] And now I beg you, Mr. Tesman, please be kind to Eilert Løvborg if he comes here—and I'm sure he will. You were such good friends in the old days. You have interests in common. The same area of research, as far as I can tell.

TESMAN Yes, that used to be the case anyway.

MRS. ELVSTED   Yes, that's why I'm asking you—from the bottom of my heart to be sure to—that you'll—that you'll keep a watchful eye on him. Oh, Mr. Tesman, will you do that—will you promise me that?

TESMAN   Yes, with all my heart, Mrs. Rysing.

HEDDA   Elvsted.

TESMAN   I'll do anything in my power for Eilert. You can be sure of it.

MRS. ELVSTED   Oh, that is so kind of you. [*She presses his hands.*] Many, many thanks. [*Frightened.*] Because my husband thinks so highly of him.

HEDDA [*Rising.*]   You should write to him, Tesman. He might not come to you on his own.

TESMAN   Yes, that's the way to do it, Hedda, hm?

HEDDA   And the sooner the better. Right now, I think.

MRS. ELVSTED [*Beseechingly.*]   Yes, if you only could.

TESMAN   I'll write to him this moment. Do you have his address, Mrs. Elvsted?

MRS. ELVSTED   Yes. [*She takes a small slip of paper from her pocket and hands it to him.*] Here it is.

TESMAN   Good, good. I'll go write him—[*Looks around just a minute.*]—Where are my slippers? Ah, here they are. [*Takes the packet and is about to leave.*]

HEDDA   Make sure your note is very friendly—nice and long too.

TESMAN   Yes, you can count on me.

MRS. ELVSTED   But please don't say a word about my asking you to do it.

TESMAN   Oh, that goes without saying.

[*TESMAN leaves to the right through the rear room.*]

HEDDA [*Goes over to MRS. ELVSTED, smiles and speaks softly.*]   There, now we've killed two birds with one stone.

MRS. ELVSTED   What do you mean?

HEDDA   Didn't you see that I wanted him out of the way?

MRS. ELVSTED   Yes, to write the letter—

HEDDA   So I could talk to you alone.

MRS. ELVSTED [*Confused.*]   About this thing?

HEDDA   Yes, exactly, about this thing.

MRS. ELVSTED [*Apprehensively.*]   But there's nothing more to it, Mrs. Tesman, really there isn't.

HEDDA   Ah, but there is indeed. There's a great deal more. I can see that much. Come here, let's sit down together. Have a real heart-to-heart talk. [*She forces MRS. ELVSTED into the armchair by the stove and sits down herself on one of the small stools.*]

MRS. ELVSTED [*Nervously looking at her watch.*]   Mrs. Tesman, I was just thinking of leaving.

HEDDA   Now you can't be in such a hurry, can you? Talk to me a little bit about how things are at home.

MRS. ELVSTED   Oh, that's the last thing I want to talk about.

HEDDA   But to me? Good Lord, we went to the same school.

MRS. ELVSTED   Yes, but you were one class ahead of me. Oh, I was so afraid of you then.

HEDDA   Afraid of me?

[handwritten: Mrs. Elvsted disliked Hedda and isn't interested in a private conversation.]

[handwritten margin note: Hedda was a cruel person]

[handwritten margin note: Hedda tries to create a friendship that never existed]

MRS. ELVSTED Horribly afraid. Whenever we'd meet on the stairs you always used to pull my hair.

HEDDA No, did I do that?

MRS. ELVSTED Yes, you did—and once you said you'd burn it off.

HEDDA Oh, just silly talk, you know.

MRS. ELVSTED Yes, but I was so stupid in those days and anyway since then we've gotten to be so distant from each other. Our circles have just been totally different.

HEDDA Well let's see if we can get closer again. Listen now, I know we were good friends in school. We used to call each other by our first names.

MRS. ELVSTED No, no, I think you're mistaken.

HEDDA I certainly am not. I remember it perfectly and so we have to be perfectly open with each other just like in the old days. [*Moves the stool closer.*] There now. [*Kisses her cheek.*] Now you must call me Hedda.

MRS. ELVSTED [*Pressing and patting her hands.*] Oh, you're being so friendly to me. I'm just not used to that.

HEDDA There, there, there. I'll stop being so formal with you and I'll call you my dear Thora.

MRS. ELVSTED My name is Thea.

HEDDA That's right, of course, I meant Thea. [*Looks at her compassionately.*] So you're not used to friendship, Thea, in your own home?

MRS. ELVSTED If I only had a home, but I don't. I've never had one.

HEDDA [*Glances at her.*] I suspected it might be something like that.

MRS. ELVSTED [*Staring helplessly before her.*] Yes, yes, yes.

HEDDA I can't exactly remember now, but didn't you go up to Sheriff Elvsted's as a housekeeper?

MRS. ELVSTED Actually I was supposed to be a governess but his wife—at that time—she was an invalid, mostly bedridden, so I had to take care of the house too.

HEDDA So in the end you became mistress of your own house.

MRS. ELVSTED [*Heavily.*] Yes, that's what I became.

HEDDA Let me see. How long has that been?

MRS. ELVSTED Since I was married?

HEDDA Yes.

MRS. ELVSTED Five years now.

HEDDA That's right, it must be about that.

MRS. ELVSTED Oh these five years——! Or the last two or three anyway—! Ah, Mrs. Tesman, if you could just imagine.

HEDDA [*Slaps her lightly on the hand.*] Mrs. Tesman; really, Thea.

MRS. ELVSTED No, no, of course, I'll try to remember. Anyway, Hedda, if you could only imagine.

HEDDA [*Casually.*] It seems to me that Eilert, Løvborg's been living up there for about three years, hasn't he?

MRS. ELVSTED [*Looks uncertainly at her.*] Eilert Løvborg? Yes, that's about right.

HEDDA Did you know him from before—from here in town?

MRS. ELVSTED Hardly at all. I mean his name of course.

HEDDA But up there he'd come to visit you at the house?

MRS. ELVSTED Yes, every day. He'd read to the children. I couldn't manage everything myself, you see.

HEDDA No, of course not. And what about your husband? His work must take him out of the house quite a bit.

MRS. ELVSTED Yes, as you might imagine. He's the sheriff so he has to go traveling around the whole district.

HEDDA [*Leaning against the arm of the chair.*] Thea, my poor sweet Thea— You've got to tell me everything just the way it is.

MRS. ELVSTED All right, but you've got to ask the questions.

HEDDA So, Thea, what's your husband really like? I mean, you know, to be with? Is he good to you?

MRS. ELVSTED [*Evasively.*] He thinks he does everything for the best.

HEDDA I just think he's a little too old for you. He's twenty years older, isn't he?

MRS. ELVSTED [*Irritatedly.*] There's that too. There's a lot of things. I just can't stand being with him. We don't have a single thought in common, not a single thing in the world, he and I.

HEDDA But doesn't he care for you at all in his own way?

MRS. ELVSTED I can't tell what he feels. I think I'm just useful to him, and it doesn't cost very much to keep me. I'm very inexpensive.

HEDDA That's a mistake.

MRS. ELVSTED [*Shaking her head.*] Can't be any other way, not with him. He only cares about himself and maybe about the children a little.

HEDDA And also for Eilert Løvborg, Thea.

MRS. ELVSTED [*Stares at her.*] For Eilert Løvborg? Why do you think that?

HEDDA Well, my dear, he sent you all the way into town to look for him. [*Smiling almost imperceptibly.*] And besides, you said so yourself, to Tesman.

MRS. ELVSTED [*With a nervous shudder.*] Oh yes, I suppose I did. No, I'd better just tell you the whole thing. It's bound to come to light sooner or later anyway.

HEDDA But my dear Thea.

MRS. ELVSTED All right, short and sweet. My husband doesn't know that I'm gone.

HEDDA What, your husband doesn't know?

MRS. ELVSTED Of course not. Anyway he's not at home. He was out traveling. I just couldn't stand it any longer, Hedda, it was impossible. I would have been so completely alone up there.

HEDDA Well, then what?

MRS. ELVSTED Then I packed some of my things, just the necessities, all in secret, and I left the house.

HEDDA Just like that?

MRS. ELVSTED Yes, and I took the train to town.

HEDDA Oh, my good, dear Thea. You dared to do that!

MRS. ELVSTED [*Gets up and walks across the floor.*] Well, what else could I do?

HEDDA What do you think your husband will say when you go home again?

MRS. ELVSTED [*By the table looking at her.*] Up there to him?

HEDDA Of course, of course.

MRS. ELVSTED I'm never going back up there.

HEDDA [*Gets up and goes closer to her.*] So you've really done it? You've really run away from everything?

MRS. ELVSTED   Yes, I couldn't think of anything else to do.

HEDDA   But you did it—so openly.

MRS. ELVSTED   Oh, you can't keep something like that a secret anyway.

HEDDA   Well, what do you think people will say about you, Thea?

MRS. ELVSTED   They'll say whatever they want, God knows. [*She sits tired and depressed on the sofa.*] But I only did what I had to do.

HEDDA [*After a brief pause.*]   So what will you do with yourself now?

MRS. ELVSTED   I don't know yet. All I know is that I've got to live here where Eilert Løvborg lives if I'm going to live at all.

HEDDA [*Moves a chair closer from the table, sits beside her and strokes her hands.*]   Thea, my dear, how did it come about, this—bond between you and Eilert Løvborg?

MRS. ELVSTED   Oh, it just happened, little by little. I started to have a kind of power over him.

HEDDA   Really?

MRS. ELVSTED   He gave up his old ways—and not because I begged him to. I never dared do that. But he started to notice that those kinds of things upset me, so he gave them up.

HEDDA [*Concealing an involuntary, derisive smile.*]   So you rehabilitated him, as they say. You, little Thea.

MRS. ELVSTED   That's what he said, anyway. And for his part he's made a real human being out of me. Taught me to think, to understand all sorts of things.

HEDDA   So he read to you too, did he?

MRS. ELVSTED   No, not exactly, but he talked to me. Talked without stopping about all sorts of great things. And then there was that wonderful time when I shared in his work, when I helped him.

HEDDA   You got to do that?

MRS. ELVSTED   Yes. Whenever he wrote anything, we had to agree on it first.

HEDDA   Like two good comrades.

MRS. ELVSTED [*Eagerly.*]   Yes, comrades. Imagine, Hedda, that's what he called it too. I should feel so happy, but I can't yet because I don't know how long it will last.

HEDDA   Are you that unsure of him?

MRS. ELVSTED [*Dejectedly.*]   There's the shadow of a woman between Eilert Løvborg and me.

HEDDA [*Stares intently at her.*]   Who could that be?

MRS. ELVSTED   I don't know. Someone from his past. Someone he's never really been able to forget.

HEDDA   What has he told you about all this?

MRS. ELVSTED   He's only talked about it once and very vaguely.

HEDDA   Yes, what did he say?

MRS. ELVSTED   He said that when they broke up she was going to shoot him with a pistol.

HEDDA [*Calm and controlled.*]   That's nonsense, people just don't act that way here.

MRS. ELVSTED   No they don't—so I think it's got to be that red-haired singer that he once—

HEDDA   Yes, that could well be.

MRS. ELVSTED   Because I remember they used to say about her that she went around with loaded pistols.

HEDDA   Well, then it's her, of course.

MRS. ELVSTED [*Wringing her hands.*]   Yes, but Hedda, just think, I hear this singer is in town again. Oh, I'm so afraid.

HEDDA [*Glancing toward the back room.*]   Shh, here comes Tesman. [*She gets up and whispers.*] Now, Thea, all of this is strictly between you and me.

MRS. ELVSTED [*Jumping up.*]   Oh yes, yes, for God's sake!

[GEORGE TESMAN, *a letter in his hand, comes in from the right side of the inner room.*]

TESMAN   There now, the epistle is prepared.

HEDDA   Well done—but Mrs. Elvsted's got to leave now, I think. Just a minute, I'll follow you as far as the garden gate.

TESMAN   Hedda dear, do you think Berta could see to this?

HEDDA [*Takes the letter.*]   I'll instruct her.

[BERTA *comes in from the hall.*]

BERTA   Judge Brack is here. Says he'd like to pay his respects.

HEDDA   Yes, ask the Judge to be so good as to come in, and then—listen here now—Put this letter in the mailbox.

BERTA [*Takes the letter.*]   Yes, ma'am.

[*She opens the door for* JUDGE BRACK *and then goes out.* JUDGE BRACK *is forty-five years old, short, well built and moves easily. He has a round face and an aristocratic profile. His short hair is still almost black. His eyes are lively and ironic. He has thick eyebrows and a thick moustache, trimmed square at the ends. He is wearing outdoor clothing, elegant, but a little too young in style. He has a monocle in one eye. Now and then he lets it drop.*]

BRACK [*Bows with his hat in his hand.*]   Does one dare to call so early?

HEDDA   One does dare.

TESMAN [*Shakes his hand.*]   You're welcome any time. Judge Brack, Mrs. Rysing. [HEDDA *sighs.*]

BRACK [*Bows.*]   Aha, delighted.

HEDDA [*Looks at him laughing.*]   Nice to see you by daylight for a change, Judge.

BRACK   Do I look different?

HEDDA   Yes, younger,

BRACK   You're too kind.

TESMAN   Well, how about Hedda, hm? Doesn't she look fine? Hasn't she filled out?

HEDDA   Stop it now. You should be thanking Judge Brack for all of his hard work—

BRACK   Nonsense. It was my pleasure.

HEDDA   There's a loyal soul. But here's my friend burning to get away. Excuse me, Judge, I'll be right back.

[*Mutual good-byes.* MRS. ELVSTED *and* HEDDA *leave by the hall door.*]

BRACK   Well, now, your wife's satisfied, more or less?

TESMAN   Oh yes, we can't thank you enough. I gather there might be a little more rearrangement here and there and one or two things still missing. A couple of small things yet to be procured.

BRACK Is that so?

TESMAN But nothing for you to worry about. Hedda said that she'd look for everything herself. Let's sit down.

BRACK Thanks. Just for a minute. [*Sits by the table.*] Now, my dear Tesman, there's something we need to talk about.

TESMAN Oh yes, ah, I understand. [*Sits down.*] Time for a new topic. Time for the serious part of the celebration, hm?

BRACK Oh, I wouldn't worry too much about the finances just yet—although I must tell you that it would have been better if we'd managed things a little more frugally.

TESMAN But there was no way to do that. You know Hedda, Judge, you know her well. I couldn't possibly ask her to live in a middle-class house.

BRACK No, that's precisely the problem.

TESMAN And luckily it can't be too long before I get my appointment.[3]

BRACK Well, you know, these things often drag on and on.

TESMAN Have you heard anything further, hm?

BRACK Nothing certain. [*Changing the subject.*] But there is one thing. I've got a piece of news for you.

TESMAN Well?

BRACK Your old friend Eilert Løvborg's back in town.

TESMAN I already know.

BRACK Oh, how did you find out?

TESMAN She told me, that lady who just left with Hedda.

BRACK Oh, I see. I didn't quite get her name.

TESMAN Mrs. Elvsted.

BRACK Ah yes, the sheriff's wife. Yes, he's been staying up there with them.

TESMAN And I'm so glad to hear that he's become a responsible person again.

BRACK Yes, one is given to understand that.

TESMAN And he's come out with a new book, hm?

BRACK He has indeed.

TESMAN And it's caused quite a sensation.

BRACK It's caused an extraordinary sensation.

TESMAN Just think, isn't that wonderful to hear. With all his remarkable talents, I was absolutely certain he was down for good.

BRACK That was certainly the general opinion.

TESMAN But I can't imagine what he'll do with himself now. What will he live on, hm?

[*During these last words,* HEDDA *has entered from the hallway.*]

HEDDA [*To* BRACK, *laughing a little scornfully.*] Tesman is constantly going around worrying about what to live on.

TESMAN My Lord, we're talking about Eilert Løvborg, dear.

HEDDA [*Looking quickly at him.*] Oh yes? [*Sits down in the armchair by the stove and asks casually.*] What's the matter with him?

TESMAN Well, he must have spent his inheritance a long time ago, and he can't really write a new book every year, hm? So I was just asking what was going to become of him.

---

3. Tesman expects to be appointed to a professorship. These positions were much less numerous and more socially prominent than their contemporary American counterparts.

BRACK   Perhaps I can enlighten you on that score.

TESMAN   Oh?

BRACK   You might remember that he has some relatives with more than a little influence.

TESMAN   Unfortunately they've pretty much washed their hands of him.

BRACK   In the old days they thought of him as the family's great shining hope.

TESMAN   Yes, in the old days, possibly, but he took care of that himself.

HEDDA   Who knows? [*Smiles slightly.*] Up at the Elvsteds' he's been the target of a reclamation project.

BRACK   And there's this new book.

TESMAN   Well, God willing, they'll help him out some way or another. I've just written to him, Hedda, asking him to come over this evening.

BRACK   But my dear Tesman, you're coming to my stag party[4] this evening. You promised me on the pier last night.

HEDDA   Had you forgotten, Tesman?

TESMAN   Yes, to be perfectly honest, I had.

BRACK   For that matter, you can be sure he won't come.

TESMAN   Why do you say that, hm?

BRACK   [*Somewhat hesitantly getting up and leaning his hands on the back of his chair.*]   My dear Tesman, you too, Mrs. Tesman, in good conscience I can't let you go on living in ignorance of something like this.

TESMAN   Something about Eilert, hm?

BRACK   About both of you.

TESMAN   My dear Judge, tell me what it is.

BRACK   You ought to prepare yourself for the fact that your appointment might not come through as quickly as you expect.

TESMAN   [*Jumps up in alarm.*]   Has something held it up?

BRACK   The appointment might just possibly be subject to a competition.

TESMAN   A competition! Just think of that, Hedda!

HEDDA   [*Leans further back in her chair.*]   Ah yes—yes.

TESMAN   But who on earth would it—surely not with—?

BRACK   Yes, precisely, with Eilert Løvborg.

TESMAN   [*Clasping his hands together.*]   No, no, this is absolutely unthinkable, absolutely unthinkable, hm?

BRACK   Hmm—well, we might just have to learn to get used to it.

TESMAN   No, but Judge Brack, that would be incredibly inconsiderate. [*Waving his arms.*] Because—well—just look, I'm a married man. We went and got married on this very prospect, Hedda and I. Went and got ourselves heavily into debt. Borrowed money from Aunt Julie too. I mean, good Lord, I was as much as promised the position, hm?

BRACK   Now, now, you'll almost certainly get it but first there'll have to be a contest.

HEDDA   [*Motionless in the armchair.*]   Just think, Tesman, it will be a sort of match.

TESMAN   But Hedda, my dear, how can you be so calm about this?

HEDDA   Oh I'm not, not at all. I can't wait for the final score.

BRACK   In any case, Mrs. Tesman, it's a good thing that you know how

[Margin annotations: "Løvborg wants the same position as Tesman"; "Tesman has gambled and relied on his job prospect"]

---

4. A party for men only, whether single or married.

matters stand. I mean, before you embark on any more of these little purchases I hear you're threatening to make.

HEDDA What's that got to do with this?

BRACK Well, well, that's another matter. Good-bye. [*To* TESMAN.] I'll come by for you when I take my afternoon walk.

TESMAN Oh yes, yes, forgive me—I don't know if I'm coming or going.

HEDDA [*Reclining, stretching out her hand.*] Good-bye, Judge, and do come again.

BRACK Many thanks. Good-bye, good-bye.

TESMAN [*Following him to the door.*] Good-bye, Judge. You'll have to excuse me.

[JUDGE BRACK *goes out through the hallway door.*]

TESMAN [*Pacing about the floor.*] We should never let ourselves get lost in a wonderland, Hedda, hm?

HEDDA [*Looking at him and smiling.*] Do you do that?

TESMAN Yes, well, it can't be denied. It was like living in wonderland to go and get married and set up housekeeping on nothing more than prospects.

HEDDA You may be right about that.

TESMAN Well, at least we have our home, Hedda, our wonderful home. The home both of us dreamt about, that both of us craved, I could almost say, hm?

HEDDA [*Rises slowly and wearily.*] The agreement was that we would live in society, that we would entertain.

TESMAN Yes, good Lord, I was so looking forward to that. Just think, to see you as a hostess in our own circle. Hm. Well, well, well, for the time being at least we'll just have to make do with each other, Hedda. We'll have Aunt Julie here now and then. Oh you, you should have such a completely different—

HEDDA To begin with, I suppose I can't have the liveried footmen.[5]

TESMAN Ah no, unfortunately not. No footmen. We can't even think about that right now.

HEDDA And the horse!

TESMAN [*Horrified.*] The horse.

HEDDA I suppose I mustn't think about that any more.

TESMAN No, God help us, you can see that for yourself.

HEDDA [*Walking across the floor.*] Well, at least I've got one thing to amuse myself with.

TESMAN [*Beaming with pleasure.*] Ah, thank God for that, and what is that, Hedda?

HEDDA [*In the center doorway looking at him with veiled scorn.*] My pistols, George.

TESMAN [*Alarmed.*] Pistols?

HEDDA [*With cold eyes.*] General Gabler's pistols.

[*She goes through the inner room and out to the left.*]

TESMAN [*Running to the center doorway and shouting after her.*] No, for the love of God, Hedda, dearest, don't touch those dangerous things. For my sake, Hedda, hm?

5. Uniformed servants.

Act Two

The TESMANS' *rooms as in the first act except that the piano has been moved out and an elegant little writing table with a bookshelf has been put in its place. Next to the sofa a smaller table has been placed. Most of the bouquets have been removed.* MRS. ELVSTED's *bouquet stands on the larger table in the foreground. It is afternoon.*

[HEDDA, *dressed to receive visitors, is alone in the room. She stands by the open glass door loading a pistol. The matching pistol lies in an open pistol case on the writing table.*]

HEDDA [*Looking down into the garden and calling.*]   Hello again, Judge.

BRACK [*Is heard some distance below.*]   Likewise, Mrs. Tesman.

HEDDA [*Raises the pistol and aims.*]   Now, Judge Brack, I am going to shoot you.

BRACK [*Shouting from below.*]   No, no, no. Don't stand there aiming at me like that.

HEDDA   That's what you get for coming up the back way. [*She shoots.*]

BRACK   Are you out of your mind?

HEDDA   Oh, good Lord, did I hit you?

BRACK [*Still outside.*]   Stop this nonsense.

HEDDA   Then come on in, Judge.

[JUDGE BRACK, *dressed for a bachelor party, comes in through the glass doors. He carries a light overcoat over his arm.*]

BRACK   In the devil's name, are you still playing this game? What were you shooting at?

HEDDA   Oh, I just stand here and shoot at the sky.

BRACK [*Gently taking the pistol out of her hands.*]   With your permission, ma'am? [*Looks at it.*] Ah, this one. I know it well. [*Looks around.*] And where do we keep the case? I see, here it is. [*Puts the pistol inside and shuts the case.*] All right, we're through with these little games for today.

HEDDA   Then what in God's name am I to do with myself?

BRACK   No visitors?

HEDDA [*Closes the glass door.*]   Not a single one. Our circle is still in the country.

BRACK   Tesman's not home either, I suppose.

HEDDA [*At the writing table, locks the pistol case in the drawer.*]   No, as soon as he finished eating he was off to the aunts. He wasn't expecting you so early.

BRACK   Hmm, I never thought of that. Stupid of me.

HEDDA [*Turns her head, looks at him.*]   Why stupid?

BRACK   Then I would have come a little earlier.

HEDDA [*Going across the floor.*]   Then you wouldn't have found anyone here at all. I've been in my dressing room since lunch.

BRACK   Isn't there even one little crack in the door wide enough for a negotiation?

HEDDA   Now that's something you forgot to provide for.

BRACK   That was also stupid of me.

HEDDA So we'll just have to flop down here and wait. Tesman won't be home any time soon.

BRACK Well, well, Lord knows I can be patient.

[HEDDA *sits in the corner of the sofa.* BRACK *lays his overcoat over the back of the nearest chair and sits down, keeps his hat in his hand. Short silence. They look at each other.*]

HEDDA So?

BRACK [*In the same tone.*] So?

HEDDA I asked first.

BRACK [*Leaning a little forward.*] Yes, why don't we allow ourselves a cozy little chat, Mrs. Hedda.

HEDDA [*Leaning further back in the sofa.*] Doesn't it feel like an eternity since we last talked together? A few words last night and this morning, but I don't count them.

BRACK Like this, between ourselves, just the two of us?

HEDDA Well, yes, more or less.

BRACK I wished you were back home every single day.

HEDDA The whole time I was wishing the same thing.

BRACK You, really, Mrs. Hedda? Here I thought you were having a wonderful time on your trip.

HEDDA Oh yes, you can just imagine.

BRACK But that's what Tesman always wrote.

HEDDA Yes, him! He thinks it's the greatest thing in the world to go scratching around in libraries. He loves sitting and copying out old parchments or whatever they are.

BRACK [*Somewhat maliciously.*] Well, that's his calling in the world, at least in part.

HEDDA Yes, so it is, and no doubt it's—but for me, oh dear Judge, I've been so desperately bored.

BRACK [*Sympathetically.*] Do you really mean that? You're serious?

HEDDA Yes, you can imagine it for yourself. Six whole months never meeting with a soul who knew the slightest thing about our circle. No one we could talk with about our kinds of things.

BRACK Ah no, I'd agree with you there. That would be a loss.

HEDDA Then what was most unbearable of all.

BRACK Yes?

HEDDA To be together forever and always—with one and the same person.

BRACK [*Nodding agreement.*] Early and late, yes, night and day, every waking and sleeping hour.

HEDDA That's it, forever and always.

BRACK Yes, all right, but with our excellent Tesman I would have imagined that you might—

HEDDA Tesman is—a specialist, dear Judge.

BRACK Undeniably.

HEDDA And specialists aren't so much fun to travel with. Not for the long run anyway.

BRACK Not even the specialist that one loves?

HEDDA Uch, don't use that syrupy word.

BRACK [*Startled.*] Mrs. Hedda.

HEDDA [*Half laughing, half bitterly.*] Well, give it a try for yourself. Hearing about the history of civilization every hour of the day.

BRACK   Forever and always.

HEDDA   Yes, yes, yes. And then his particular interest, domestic crafts in the Middle Ages. Uch, the most revolting thing of all.

BRACK   [*Looks at her curiously.*]   But, tell me now, I don't quite understand how—hmmm.

HEDDA   That we're together? George Tesman and I, you mean?

BRACK   Well, yes. That's a good way of putting it.

HEDDA   Good Lord, do you think it's so remarkable?

BRACK   I think—yes and no, Mrs. Hedda.

HEDDA   I'd danced myself out, dear Judge. My time was up. [*Shudders slightly.*] Uch, no, I'm not going to say that or even think it.

BRACK   You certainly have no reason to think it.

HEDDA   Ah, reasons—[*Looks watchfully at him.*] And George Tesman? Well, he'd certainly be called a most acceptable man in every way.

BRACK   Acceptable and solid, God knows.

HEDDA   And I can't find anything about him that's actually ridiculous, can you?

BRACK   Ridiculous? No—I wouldn't quite say that.

HEDDA   Hmm. Well, he's a very diligent archivist anyway. Some day he might do something interesting with all of it. Who knows.

BRACK   [*Looking at her uncertainly.*]   I thought you believed, like everyone else, that he'd turn out to be a great man.

HEDDA   [*With a weary expression.*]   Yes, I did. And then when he went around constantly begging with all his strength, begging for permission to let him take care of me, well, I didn't see why I shouldn't take him up on it.

BRACK   Ah well, from that point of view . . . .

HEDDA   It was a great deal more than any of my other admirers were offering.

BRACK   [*Laughing.*]   Well, of course I can't answer for all the others, but as far as I'm concerned you know very well that I've always maintained a certain respect for the marriage bond, that is, in an abstract kind of way, Mrs. Hedda.

HEDDA   [*Playfully.*]   Oh, I never had any hopes for you.

BRACK   All I ask is an intimate circle of good friends, friends I can be of service to in any way necessary. Places where I am allowed to come and go as a trusted friend.

HEDDA   Of the man of the house, you mean.

BRACK   [*Bowing.*]   No, to be honest, of the lady. Of the man as well, you understand, because you know that kind of—how should I put this—that kind of triangular arrangement is really a magnificent convenience for everyone concerned.

HEDDA   Yes, you can't imagine how many times I longed for a third person on that trip. Ach, huddled together alone in a railway compartment.

BRACK   Fortunately, the wedding trip is over now.

HEDDA   [*Shaking her head.*]   Oh no, it's a very long trip. It's nowhere near over. I've only come to a little stopover on the line.

BRACK   Then you should jump out, stretch your legs a little, Mrs. Hedda.

HEDDA   I'd never jump out.

BRACK   Really?

HEDDA   No, because there's always someone at the stop who—

BRACK [*Laughing.*]   Who's looking at your legs, you mean?

HEDDA   Yes, exactly.

BRACK   Yes, but for heaven's sake.

HEDDA [*With a disdainful gesture.*]   I don't hold with that sort of thing. I'd rather remain sitting, just like I am now, a couple alone. On a train.

BRACK   But what if a third man climbed into the compartment with the couple?

HEDDA   Ah yes. Now that's quite different.

BRACK   An understanding friend, a proven friend—

HEDDA   Who can be entertaining on all kinds of topics—

BRACK   And not a specialist in any way!

HEDDA [*With an audible sigh.*]   Yes, that would be a relief.

BRACK [*Hears the front door open and glances toward it.*]   The triangle is complete.

HEDDA [*Half audibly.*]   And there goes the train.

> [GEORGE TESMAN *in a gray walking suit and with a soft felt hat comes in from the hallway. He is carrying a large stack of unbound books under his arm and in his pockets.*]

TESMAN [*Goes to the table by the corner, sofa.*]   Phew—hot work lugging all these here. [*Puts the books down.*] Would you believe I'm actually sweating, Hedda? And you're already here, Judge, hm. Berta didn't mention anything about that.

BRACK [*Getting up.*]   I came up through the garden.

HEDDA   What are all those books you've got there?

TESMAN [*Stands leafing through them.*]   All the new works by my fellow specialists. I've absolutely got to have them.

HEDDA   By your fellow specialists.

BRACK   Ah, the specialists, Mrs. Tesman. [BRACK *and* HEDDA *exchange a knowing smile.*]

HEDDA   You need even more of these specialized works?

TESMAN   Oh, yes, my dear Hedda, you can never have too many of these. You have to keep up with what's being written and published.

HEDDA   Yes, you certainly must do that.

TESMAN [*Searches among the books.*]   And look here, I've got Eilert Løvborg's new book too. (*Holds it out.*) Maybe you'd like to look at it, Hedda, hm?

HEDDA   No thanks—or maybe later.

TESMAN   I skimmed it a little on the way.

HEDDA   And what's your opinion as a specialist?

TESMAN   I think the argument's remarkably thorough. He never wrote like this before. [*Collects the books together*] Now I've got to get all these inside. Oh, it's going to be such fun to cut the pages.[6] Then I'll go and change. [*To* BRACK.] We don't have to leave right away, hm?

BRACK   No, not at all. No hurry at all.

TESMAN   Good, I'll take my time then. [*Leaves with the books but stands in the doorway and turns.*] Oh, Hedda, by the way, Aunt Julie won't be coming over this evening.

---

6. Books used to be sold with the pages folded but uncut; the owner had to cut the pages to read the book.

HEDDA   Really? Because of that hat business?

TESMAN   Not at all. How could you think that of Aunt Julie? No, it's just that Aunt Rina is very ill.

HEDDA   She always is.

TESMAN   Yes, but today she's gotten quite a bit worse.

HEDDA   Well, then it's only right that the other one should stay at home with her. I'll just have to make the best of it.

TESMAN   My dear, you just can't believe how glad Aunt Julie was, in spite of everything, at how healthy and rounded out you looked after the trip.

HEDDA [*Half audibly getting up.*]   Oh, these eternal aunts.

TESMAN   Hm?

HEDDA [*Goes over to the glass door.*]   Nothing.

TESMAN   Oh, all right. [*He goes out through the rear room and to the right.*]

BRACK   What were you saying about a hat?

HEDDA   Oh, just a little run-in with Miss Tesman this morning. She'd put her hat down there on that chair [*Looks at him smiling.*] and I pretended I thought it was the maid's.

BRACK [*Shaking his head.*]   My dear Mrs. Hedda, how could you do such a thing to that harmless old lady.

HEDDA [*Nervously walking across the floor.*]   Oh, you know—these things just come over me like that and I can't resist them. [*Flings herself into the armchair by the stove*.] I can't explain it, even to myself.

BRACK [*Behind the armchair*.]   You're not really happy—that's the heart of it.

HEDDA [*Staring in front of her.*]   And why should I be happy? Maybe you can tell me.

BRACK   Yes. Among other things, be happy you've got the home that you've always longed for.

HEDDA [*Looks up at him and laughs.*]   You also believe that myth?

BRACK   There's nothing to it?

HEDDA   Yes, heavens, there's something to it.

BRACK   So?

HEDDA   And here's what it is. I used George Tesman to walk me home from parties last summer.

BRACK   Yes, regrettably I had to go another way.

HEDDA   Oh yes, you certainly were going a different way last summer.

BRACK [*Laughs.*]   Shame on you, Mrs. Hedda. So you and Tesman . . .

HEDDA   So we walked past here one evening and Tesman, the poor thing, was twisting and turning in his agony because he didn't have the slightest idea what to talk about and I felt sorry that such a learned man—

BRACK [*Smiling skeptically.*]   You did . . .

HEDDA   Yes, if you will, I did, and so just to help him out of his torment I said, without really thinking about it, that this was the house I would love to live in.

BRACK   That was all?

HEDDA   For that evening.

BRACK   But afterward?

HEDDA   Yes, dear Judge, my thoughtlessness has had its consequences.

BRACK   Unfortunately, our thoughtlessness often does, Mrs. Hedda.

HEDDA   Thanks, I'm sure. But it so happens that George Tesman and I found our common ground in this passion for Prime Minister Falk's villa.

And after that it all followed. The engagement, the marriage, the honeymoon and everything else. Yes, yes, Judge, I almost said: you make your bed, you have to lie in it.

BRACK That's priceless. Essentially what you're telling me is you didn't care about any of this here.

HEDDA God knows I didn't.

BRACK What about now, now that we've made it into a lovely home for you?

HEDDA Ach, I feel an air of lavender and dried roses in every room—or maybe Aunt Julie brought that in with her.

BRACK [*Laughing.*] No, I think that's probably a relic of the eminent prime minister's late wife.

HEDDA Yes, that's it, there's something deathly about it. It reminds me of a corsage the day after the ball. [*Folds her hands at the back of her neck, leans back in her chair and gazes at him.*] Oh, my dear Judge, you can't imagine how I'm going to bore myself out here.

BRACK What if life suddenly should offer you some purpose or other, something to live for? What about that, Mrs. Hedda?

HEDDA A purpose? Something really tempting for me?

BRACK Preferably something like that, of course.

HEDDA God knows what sort of purpose that would be. I often wonder if— [*Breaks off.*] No, that wouldn't work out either.

BRACK Who knows. Let me hear.

HEDDA If I could get Tesman to go into politics, I mean.

BRACK [*Laughing.*] Tesman? No, you have to see that politics, anything like that, is not for him. Not in his line at all.

HEDDA No, I can see that. But what if I could get him to try just the same?

BRACK Yes, but why should he do that if he's not up to it? Why would you want him to?

HEDDA Because I'm bored, do you hear me? [*After a pause.*] So you don't think there's any way that Tesman could become a cabinet minister?

BRACK Hmm, you see my dear Mrs. Hedda, that requires a certain amount of wealth in the first place.

HEDDA [*Rises impatiently.*] Yes, that's it, this shabby little world I've ended up in. [*Crosses the floor.*] That's what makes life so contemptible, so completely ridiculous. That's just what it is.

BRACK I think the problem's somewhere else.

HEDDA Where's that?

BRACK You've never had to live through anything that really shakes you up.

HEDDA Anything serious, you mean.

BRACK Yes, you could call it that. Perhaps now, though, it's on its way.

HEDDA [*Tosses her head.*] You mean that competition for that stupid professorship? That's Tesman's business. I'm not going to waste a single thought on it.

BRACK No, forget about that. But when you find yourself facing what one calls in elegant language a profound and solemn calling—[*Smiling.*] a new calling, my dear little Mrs. Hedda.

HEDDA [*Angry.*] Quiet. You'll never see anything like that.

BRACK [*Gently.*] We'll talk about it again in a year's time, at the very latest.

HEDDA [*Curtly.*]   I don't have any talent for that, Judge. I don't want anything to do with that kind of calling.

BRACK   Why shouldn't you, like most other women, have an innate talent for a vocation that—

HEDDA [*Over by the glass door.*]   Oh, please be quiet. I often think I only have one talent, one talent in the world.

BRACK [*Approaching.*]   And what is that may I ask?

HEDDA [*Standing, staring out.*]   Boring the life right out of me. Now you know. [*Turns, glances toward the inner room and laughs.*] Perfect timing; here comes the professor.

BRACK [*Warning softly.*]   Now, now, now, Mrs. Hedda.

    [GEORGE TESMAN, *in evening dress, carrying his gloves and hat, comes in from the right of the rear room.*]

TESMAN   Hedda, no message from Eilert Løvborg?

HEDDA   No.

BRACK   Do you really think he'll come?

TESMAN   Yes, I'm almost certain he will. What you told us this morning was just idle gossip.

BRACK   Oh?

TESMAN   Yes, at least Aunt Julie said she couldn't possibly believe that he would stand in my way anymore. Just think.

BRACK   So, then everything's all right.

TESMAN [*Puts his hat with his gloves inside on a chair to the right.*]   Yes, but I'd like to wait for him as long as I can.

BRACK   We have plenty of time. No one's coming to my place until seven or even half past.

TESMAN   Meanwhile, we can keep Hedda company and see what happens, hm?

HEDDA [*Sets* BRACK's *overcoat and hat on the corner sofa.*]   At the very worst, Mr. Løvborg can stay here with me.

BRACK [*Offering to take his things.*]   At the worst, Mrs. Tesman, what do you mean?

HEDDA   If he won't go out with you and Tesman.

TESMAN [*Looking at her uncertainly.*]   But, Hedda dear, do you think that would be quite right, him staying here with you? Remember, Aunt Julie can't come.

HEDDA   No, but Mrs. Elvsted will be coming and the three of us can have a cup of tea together.

TESMAN   Yes, that's all right then.

BRACK [*Smiling.*]   And I might add, that would be the best plan for him.

HEDDA   Why so?

BRACK   Good Lord, Mrs. Tesman, you've had enough to say about my little bachelor parties in the past. Don't you agree they should be open only to men of the highest principle?

HEDDA   That's just what Mr. Løvborg is now, a reclaimed sinner.

    [BERTA *comes in from the hall doorway.*]

BERTA   Madam, there's a gentleman who wishes to—

HEDDA   Yes, please, show him in.

TESMAN [*Softly.*]   It's got to be him. Just think.

    [EILERT LØVBORG *enters from the hallway. He is slim and lean, the same*

She is endlessly bored.

age as TESMAN, *but he looks older and somewhat haggard. His hair and beard are dark brown. His face is longish, pale, with patches of red over the cheekbones. He is dressed in an elegant suit, black, quite new dark gloves and top hat. He stops just inside the doorway and bows hastily. He seems somewhat embarrassed.*]

TESMAN [*Goes to him and shakes his hands.*]   Oh my dear Eilert, we meet again at long last.

LØVBORG [*Speaks in a low voice.*]   Thanks for the letter, George. [*Approaches* HEDDA.] May I shake your hand also, Mrs. Tesman?

HEDDA [*Takes his hand.*]   Welcome, Mr. Løvborg. [*With a gesture.*] I don't know if you two gentlemen—

LØVBORG [*Bowing.*]   Judge Brack, I believe.

BRACK [*Similarly.*]   Indeed. It's been quite a few years—

TESMAN [*To* LØVBORG, *his hands on his shoulders.*]   And now Eilert, make yourself completely at home. Right, Hedda? I hear you're going to settle down here in town, hm?

LØVBORG   Yes, I will.

TESMAN   Well, that's only sensible. Listen, I got your new book. I haven't really had time to read it yet.

LØVBORG   You can save yourself the trouble.

TESMAN   What do you mean?

LØVBORG   There's not much to it.

TESMAN   How can you say that?

BRACK   But everyone's been praising it so highly.

LØVBORG   Exactly as I intended—so I wrote the sort of book that everyone can agree with.

BRACK   Very clever.

TESMAN   Yes, but my dear Eilert.

LØVBORG   Because I want to reestablish my position, begin again.

TESMAN [*A little downcast.*]   Yes, I suppose you'd want to, hm.

LØVBORG [*Smiling, putting down his hat and pulling a package wrapped in paper from his coat pocket.*]   But when this comes out, George Tesman—this is what you should read. It's the real thing. I've put my whole self into it.

TESMAN   Oh yes? What's it about?

LØVBORG   It's the sequel.

TESMAN   Sequel to what?

LØVBORG   To my book.

TESMAN   The new one?

LØVBORG   Of course.

TESMAN   But my dear Eilert, that one takes us right to the present day.

LØVBORG   So it does—and this one takes us into the future.

TESMAN   The future. Good Lord! We don't know anything about that.

LØVBORG   No, we don't—but there are still one or two things to say about it, just the same. [*Opens the packages.*] Here, you'll see.

TESMAN   That's not your handwriting, is it?

LØVBORG   I dictated it. [*Turns the pages.*] It's written in two sections. The first is about the cultural forces which will shape the future, and this other section [*Turning the pages.*] is about the future course of civilization.

TESMAN   Extraordinary. It would never occur to me to write about something like that.

HEDDA [*By the glass door, drumming on the pane.*]   Hmm, no, no.

LØVBORG [*Puts the papers back in the packet and sets it on the table.*]   I brought it along because I thought I might read some of it to you tonight.

TESMAN   Ah, that was very kind of you, Eilert, but this evening [*Looks at* BRACK.] I'm not sure it can be arranged—

LØVBORG   Some other time then, there's no hurry.

BRACK   I should tell you, Mr. Løvborg, we're having a little party at my place this evening, mostly for Tesman, you understand—

LØVBORG [*Looking for his hat.*]   Aha, well then I'll—

BRACK   No, listen, why don't you join us?

LØVBORG [*Briefly but firmly.*]   No, that I can't do, but many thanks just the same.

BRACK   Oh come now, you certainly can do that. We'll be a small, select circle and I guarantee we'll be "lively," as Mrs. Hed—Mrs. Tesman would say.

LØVBORG   No doubt, but even so—

BRACK   And then you could bring your manuscript along and read it to Tesman at my place. I've got plenty of rooms.

TESMAN   Think about that, Eilert. You could do that, hm?

HEDDA [*Intervening.*]   Now, my dear, Mr. Løvborg simply doesn't want to. I'm quite sure Mr. Løvborg would rather settle down here and have supper with me.

LØVBORG [*Staring at her.*]   With you, Mrs. Tesman?

HEDDA   And with Mrs. Elvsted.

LØVBORG   Ah—[*Casually.*]   I saw her this morning very briefly.

HEDDA   Oh did you? Well, she's coming here; so you might almost say it's essential that you stay here, Mr. Løvborg. Otherwise she'll have no one to see her home.

LØVBORG   That's true. Yes, Mrs. Tesman, many thanks. I'll stay.

HEDDA   I'll go and have a word with the maid.
   [*She goes over to the hall door and rings.* BERTA *enters.* HEDDA *speaks quietly to her and points toward the rear room.* BERTA *nods and goes out again.*]

TESMAN [*At the same time to* LØVBORG.]   Listen, Eilert, your lecture—Is it about this new subject? About the future?

LØVBORG   Yes.

TESMAN   Because I heard down at the bookstore that you'd be giving a lecture series here this fall.

LØVBORG   I plan to. Please don't hold it against me.

TESMAN   No, God forbid, but—?

LØVBORG   I can easily see how this might make things awkward.

TESMAN [*Dejectedly.*]   Oh, for my part, I can't expect you to—

LØVBORG   But I'll wait until you get your appointment.

TESMAN   You will? Yes but—yes but—you won't be competing then?

LØVBORG   No. I only want to conquer you in the marketplace of ideas.

TESMAN   But, good Lord, Aunt Julie was right after all. Oh yes, yes, I was quite sure of it. Hedda, imagine, my dear—Eilert Løvborg won't stand in our way.

HEDDA [*Curtly.*] Our way? Leave me out of it.

[*She goes up toward the rear room where* BERTA *is placing a tray with decanters and glasses on the table.* HEDDA *nods approvingly, comes forward again.* BERTA *goes out.*]

TESMAN [*Meanwhile.*] So, Judge Brack, what do you say about all this?

BRACK Well now, I say that honor and victory, hmm—they have a powerful appeal—

TESMAN Yes, yes, I suppose they do but all the same—

HEDDA [*Looking at* TESMAN *with a cold smile.*] You look like you've been struck by lightning.

TESMAN Yes, that's about it—or something like that, I think—

BRACK That was quite a thunderstorm that passed over us, Mrs. Tesman.

HEDDA [*Pointing toward the rear room.*] Won't you gentlemen go in there and have a glass of punch?

BRACK [*Looking at his watch.*] For the road? Yes, not a bad idea.

TESMAN Wonderful, Hedda, wonderful! And I'm in such a fantastic mood now.

HEDDA You too, Mr. Løvborg, if you please.

LØVBORG [*Dismissively.*] No, thank you, not for me.

BRACK Good Lord, cold punch isn't exactly poison, you know.

LØVBORG Maybe not for everybody.

HEDDA Then I'll keep Mr. Løvborg company in the meantime.

TESMAN Yes, yes, Hedda dear, you do that.

[TESMAN *and* BRACK *go into the rear room, sit down and drink punch, smoking cigarettes and talking animatedly during the following.* EILERT LØVBORG *remains standing by the stove and* HEDDA *goes to the writing table.*]

HEDDA [*In a slightly raised voice.*] Now, if you like, I'll show you some photographs. Tesman and I—we took a trip to the Tyrol on the way home.

[*She comes over with an album and lays it on the table by the sofa, seating herself in the farthest corner.* EILERT LØVBORG *comes closer, stooping and looking at her. Then he takes a chair and sits on her left side with his back to the rear room.*]

HEDDA [*Opening the album.*] Do you see these mountains, Mr. Løvborg? That's the Ortler group. Tesman's written a little caption. Here. "The Ortler group near Meran."[7]

LØVBORG [*Who has not taken his eyes off her from the beginning, says softly and slowly.*] Hedda Gabler.

HEDDA [*Glances quickly at him.*] Shh, now.

LØVBORG [*Repeating softly.*] Hedda Gabler.

HEDDA [*Staring at the album.*] Yes, so I was once, when we knew each other.

LØVBORG And from now—for the rest of my life—do I have to teach myself never to say Hedda Gabler?

HEDDA [*Turning the pages.*] Yes, you have to. And I think you'd better start practicing now. The sooner the better, I'd say.

7. I.e., Merano, a city in the Austrian Tyrol, since 1918 in Italy. The scenic features mentioned here and later are tourist attractions. The Ortler group and the Dolomites are Alpine mountain ranges. The Ampezzo Valley lies beyond the Dolomites to the east. The Brenner Pass is a major route through the Alps to Austria.

LØVBORG [*In a resentful voice.*]   Hedda Gabler married—and then—with George Tesman.

HEDDA   That's how it goes.

LØVBORG   Ah, Hedda, Hedda—how could you have thrown yourself away like that?

HEDDA [*Looks sharply at him.*]   What? Now stop that.

LØVBORG   Stop what, what do you mean?

HEDDA   Calling me Hedda and—[8]

[TESMAN *comes in and goes toward the sofa.*]

HEDDA [*Hears him approaching and says casually.*]   And this one here, Mr. Løvborg, this was taken from the Ampezzo Valley. Would you just look at these mountain peaks. [*Looks warmly up at* TESMAN.] George, dear, what were these extraordinary mountains called?

TESMAN   Let me see. Ah, yes, those are the Dolomites.

HEDDA   Of course. Those, Mr. Løvborg, are the Dolomites.

TESMAN   Hedda, dear, I just wanted to ask you if we should bring some punch in here, for you at least.

HEDDA   Yes, thank you my dear. And a few pastries perhaps.

TESMAN   Any cigarettes?

HEDDA   No.

TESMAN   Good.

[*He goes into the rear room and off to the right.* BRACK *remains sitting, from time to time keeping his eye on* HEDDA *and* LØVBORG.]

LØVBORG [*Quietly, as before.*]   Then answer me, Hedda—how could you go and do such a thing?

HEDDA [*Apparently absorbed in the album.*]   If you keep talking to me that way, I just won't speak to you.

LØVBORG   Not even when we're alone together?

HEDDA   No. You can think whatever you want but you can't talk about it.

LØVBORG   Ah, I see. It offends your love for George Tesman.

HEDDA [*Glances at him and smiles.*]   Love? Don't be absurd.

LØVBORG   Not love then either?

HEDDA   But even so—nothing unfaithful. I will not allow it.

LØVBORG   Answer me just one thing—

HEDDA   Shh.

[TESMAN, *with a tray, enters from the rear room.*]

TESMAN   Here we are, here come the treats. [*He places the tray on the table.*]

HEDDA   Why are you serving us yourself?

TESMAN [*Filling the glasses.*]   I have such a good time waiting on you, Hedda.

HEDDA   But now you've gone and poured two drinks and Mr. Løvborg definitely does not want—

TESMAN   No, but Mrs. Elvsted's coming soon.

HEDDA   Yes, that's right, Mrs. Elvsted.

TESMAN   Did you forget about her?

HEDDA   We were just sitting here so completely wrapped up in these.

---

8. This line is interpolated in an attempt to suggest the difference between the informal *du* (three or thy) and the formal *de* (you) in the Norwegian text. Løvborg has just addressed Hedda in the informal manner and she is warning him not to [Translators' note].

[*Shows him a picture.*] Do you remember this little village?

TESMAN Yes, that's the one below the Brenner Pass. We spent the night there—

HEDDA —and ran into all those lively summer visitors.

TESMAN Ah yes, that was it. Imagine—if you could have been with us, Eilert, just think. [*He goes in again and sits with* BRACK.]

LØVBORG Just answer me one thing—

HEDDA Yes?

LØVBORG In our relationship—wasn't there any love there either? No trace? Not a glimmer of love in any of it?

HEDDA I wonder if there really was. For me it was like we were two good comrades, two really good, faithful friends. [*Smiling.*] I remember you were particularly frank and open.

LØVBORG That's how you wanted it.

HEDDA When I look back on it, there was something really beautiful— something fascinating, something brave about this secret comradeship, this secret intimacy that no living soul had any idea about.

LØVBORG Yes, Hedda, that's true isn't it? That was it. When I'd come to your father's in the afternoon—and the General would sit in the window reading his newspaper with his back toward the room—

HEDDA And us on the corner sofa.

LØVBORG Always with the same illustrated magazine in front of us.

HEDDA Instead of an album, yes.

LØVBORG Yes, Hedda—and when I made all those confessions to you— telling you things about myself that no one else knew in those days. Sat there and told you how I'd lost whole days and nights in drunken frenzy, frenzy that would last for days on end. Ah, Hedda—what kind of power was in you that drew these confessions out of me?

HEDDA You think it was a power in me?

LØVBORG Yes. I can't account for it in any other way. And you'd ask me all those ambiguous leading questions—

HEDDA Which you understood implicity—

LØVBORG How did you sit there and question me so fearlessly?

HEDDA Ambiguously?

LØVBORG Yes, but fearlessly all the same. Questioning me about—About things like that.

HEDDA And how could you answer them, Mr. Løvborg?

LØVBORG Yes, yes. That's just what I don't understand anymore. But now tell me, Hedda, wasn't it love underneath it all? Wasn't that part of it? You wanted to purify me, to cleanse me—when I'd seek you out to make my confessions. Wasn't that it?

HEDDA No, no, not exactly.

LØVBORG Then what drove you?

HEDDA Do you find it so hard to explain that a young girl—when it becomes possible—in secret—

LØVBORG Yes?

HEDDA That she wants a glimpse of a world that—

LØVBORG That—

HEDDA That is not permitted to her.

LØVBORG So that was it.

HEDDA   That too, that too—I almost believe it.

LØVBORG   Comrades in a quest for life. So why couldn't it go on?

HEDDA   That was your own fault.

LØVBORG   You broke it off.

HEDDA   Yes, when it looked like reality threatened to spoil the situation. Shame on you, Eilert Løvborg, how could you do violence to your comrade in arms?

LØVBORG   [*Clenching his hands together.*]   Well, why didn't you do it for real? Why didn't you shoot me dead right then and there like you threatened to?

HEDDA   Oh, I'm much too afraid of scandal.

LØVBORG   Yes, Hedda, underneath it all, you're a coward.

HEDDA   A terrible coward. [*Changes her tone.*] Lucky for you. And now you've got plenty of consolation up there at the Elvsteds'.

LØVBORG   I know what Thea's confided to you.

HEDDA   And no doubt you've confided to her about us.

LØVBORG   Not one word. She's too stupid to understand things like this.

HEDDA   Stupid?

LØVBORG   In things like this she's stupid.

HEDDA   And I'm a coward. [*Leans closer to him without looking him in the eyes and says softly.*] Now I'll confide something to you.

LØVBORG   [*In suspense.*]   What?

HEDDA   My not daring to shoot you—

LØVBORG   Yes?!

HEDDA   —that wasn't my worst cowardice that evening.

LØVBORG   [*Stares at her a moment, understands and whispers passionately.*] Ah, Hedda Gabler, now I see the hidden reason why we're such comrades. This craving for life in you—

HEDDA   [*Quietly, with a sharp glance at him.*]   Watch out, don't believe anything of the sort.

[*It starts to get dark. The hall door is opened by* BERTA.]

HEDDA   [*Clapping the album shut and crying out with a smile.*]   Ah, finally. Thea, darling, do come in.

[MRS. ELVSTED *enters from the hall. She is in evening dress. The door is closed after her.*]

HEDDA   [*On the sofa, stretching out her arms.*]   Thea, my sweet, you can't imagine how I've been expecting you.

[MRS. ELVSTED, *in passing, exchanges a greeting with the gentlemen in the inner room, crosses to the table, shakes* HEDDA's *hand.* EILERT LØVBORG *has risen. He and* MRS. ELVSTED *greet each other with a single nod.*]

MRS. ELVSTED   Perhaps I should go in and have a word with your husband.

HEDDA   Not at all. Let them sit there. They'll be on their way soon.

MRS. ELVSTED   They're leaving?

HEDDA   Yes, they're going out on a little binge.

MRS. ELVSTED   [*Quickly to* LØVBORG.]   You're not?

LØVBORG   No.

HEDDA   Mr. Løvborg . . . he'll stay here with us.

MRS. ELVSTED   [*Takes a chair and sits down beside him.*]   It's so nice to be here.

HEDDA   No, you don't, little Thea, not there. Come right over here next to me. I want to be in the middle between you.

MRS. ELVSTED   All right, whatever you like. [*She goes around the table and sits on the sofa to the right of* HEDDA. LØVBORG *takes his chair again.*]

LØVBORG [*After a brief pause, to* HEDDA.]   Isn't she lovely to look at?

HEDDA [*Gently stroking her hair.*]   Only to look at?

LØVBORG   Yes. We're true comrades, the two of us. We trust each other completely and that's why we can sit here and talk so openly and boldly together.

HEDDA   With no ambiguity, Mr. Løvborg.

LØVBORG   Well—

MRS. ELVSTED [*Softly, clinging to* HEDDA.]   Oh, Hedda, I'm so lucky. Just think, he says I've inspired him too.

HEDDA [*Regards her with a smile.*]   No, dear, does he say that?

LØVBORG   And she has the courage to take action, Mrs. Tesman.

MRS. ELVSTED   Oh God, me, courage?

LØVBORG   Tremendous courage when it comes to comradeship.

HEDDA   Yes, courage—yes! That's the crucial thing.

LØVBORG   Why is that, do you suppose?

HEDDA   Because then—maybe—life has a chance to be lived. [*Suddenly changing her tone.*] But now, my dearest Thea. Why don't you treat yourself to a nice cold glass of punch?

MRS. ELVSTED   No thank you, I never drink anything like that.

HEDDA   Then for you, Mr. Løvborg.

LØVBORG   No thank you, not for me either.

MRS. ELVSTED   No, not for him either.

HEDDA [*Looking steadily at him.*]   But if I insisted.

LØVBORG   Doesn't matter.

HEDDA [*Laughing.*]   Then I have absolutely no power over you? Ah, poor me.

LØVBORG   Not in that area.

HEDDA   But seriously now, I really think you should, for your own sake.

MRS. ELVSTED   No, Hedda—

LØVBORG   Why is that?

HEDDA   Or to be more precise, for others' sakes.

LØVBORG   Oh?

HEDDA   Because otherwise people might get the idea that you don't, deep down inside, feel really bold, really sure of yourself.

LØVBORG   Oh, from now on people can think whatever they like.

MRS. ELVSTED   Yes, that's right, isn't it.

HEDDA   I saw it so clearly with Judge Brack a few minutes ago.

LØVBORG   What did you see?

HEDDA   That condescending little smile when you didn't dare join them at the table.

LØVBORG   Didn't dare? I'd just rather stay here and talk with you, of course.

MRS. ELVSTED   That's only reasonable, Hedda.

HEDDA   How was the Judge supposed to know that? I saw how he smiled and shot a glance at Tesman when you didn't dare join them in their silly little party.

LØVBORG   Didn't dare. You're saying I don't dare.

HEDDA   Oh, I'm not. But that's how Judge Brack sees it.

LØVBORG   Well let him.

HEDDA   So you won't join them?

LØVBORG   I'm staying here with you and Thea.

MRS. ELVSTED   Yes, Hedda, you can be sure he is.

HEDDA   [*Smiling and nodding approvingly to* LØVBORG.]   What a strong foundation you've got. Principles to last a lifetime. That's what a man ought to have. [*Turns to* MRS. ELVSTED.] See now, wasn't that what I told you when you came here this morning in such a panic—

LØVBORG   [*Startled.*]   Panic?

MRS. ELVSTED   [*Terrified.*]   Hedda, Hedda, no.

HEDDA   Just see for yourself. No reason at all to come running here in mortal terror. [*Changing her tone.*] There, now all three of us can be quite jolly.

LØVBORG   [*Shocked.*]   What does this mean, Mrs. Tesman?

MRS. ELVSTED   Oh God, oh God, Hedda. What are you doing? What are you saying?

HEDDA   Keep calm now. That disgusting Judge is sitting there watching you.

LØVBORG   In mortal terror on my account?

MRS. ELVSTED   [*Quietly wailing.*]   Oh, Hedda—

LØVBORG   [*Looks at her steadily for a moment; his face is drawn.*]   So that, then, was how my brave, bold comrade trusted me.

MRS. ELVSTED   [*Pleading.*]   Oh, my dearest friend, listen to me—

LØVBORG   [*Takes one of the glasses of punch, raises it and says in a low, hoarse voice.*]   Your health, Thea. [*Empties the glass, takes another.*]

MRS. ELVSTED   [*Softly.*]   Oh Hedda, Hedda—how could you want this to happen?

HEDDA   Want it? I want this? Are you mad?

LØVBORG   And your health too, Mrs. Tesman. Thanks for the truth. Long may it live. [*He drinks and goes to refill the glass.*]

HEDDA   [*Placing her hand on his arm.*]   That's enough for now. Remember, you're going to the party.

MRS. ELVSTED   No, no, no.

HEDDA   Shh. They're watching us.

LØVBORG   [*Putting down the glass.*]   Thea, be honest with me now.

MRS. ELVSTED   Yes.

LØVBORG   Was your husband told that you came here to look for me?

MRS. ELVSTED   [*Wringing her hands.*]   Oh, Hedda, listen to what he's asking me!

LØVBORG   Did he arrange for you to come to town to spy on me? Maybe he put you up to it himself. Aha, that's it. He needed me back in the office again. Or did he just miss me at the card table?

MRS. ELVSTED   [*Softly moaning.*]   Oh, Løvborg, Løvborg—

LØVBORG   [*Grabs a glass intending to fill it.*]   Skøal to the old Sheriff too.

HEDDA   [*Preventing him.*]   No more now. Remember, you're going out to read to Tesman.

LØVBORG   [*Calmly putting down his glass.*]   Thea, that was stupid of me. What I did just now. Taking it like that I mean. Don't be angry with me, my dear, dear comrade. You'll see. Both of you and everyone else will see that even though I once was fallen—now I've raised myself up again, with your help, Thea.

MRS. ELVSTED [*Radiant with joy.*] Oh God be praised.

    [*Meanwhile* BRACK *has been looking at his watch. He and* TESMAN *get up and come into the drawing room.*]

BRACK [*Taking his hat and overcoat.*] Well, Mrs. Tesman, our time is up.

HEDDA Yes, it must be.

LØVBORG [*Rising.*] Mine too.

MRS. ELVSTED [*Quietly pleading.*] Løvborg, don't do it.

HEDDA [*Pinching her arm.*] They can hear you.

MRS. ELVSTED [*Crying out faintly.*] Ow.

LØVBORG [*To* BRACK.] You were kind enough to ask me along.

BRACK So you're coming after all.

LØVBORG Yes, thanks.

BRACK I'm delighted.

LØVBORG [*Putting the manuscript packet in his pocket and saying to* TESMAN.] I'd really like you to look at one or two things before I send it off.

TESMAN Just think, that will be splendid. But, Hedda dear, how will you get Mrs. Elvsted home?

HEDDA Oh, there's always a way out.

LØVBORG [*Looking at the ladies.*] Mrs. Elvsted? Well, of course, I'll come back for her. [*Coming closer.*] Around ten o'clock, Mrs. Tesman, will that do?

HEDDA Yes, that will be fine.

TESMAN Well, everything's all right then; but don't expect me that early, Hedda.

HEDDA No dear, you stay just as long—as long as you like.

MRS. ELVSTED [*With suppressed anxiety.*] Mr. Løvborg—I'll stay here until you come.

LØVBORG [*His hat in his hand.*] That's understood.

BRACK All aboard then, the party train's pulling out. Gentlemen, I trust it will be a lively trip, as a certain lovely lady suggested.

HEDDA Ah yes, if only that lovely lady could be there—invisible, of course.

BRACK Why invisible?

HEDDA To hear a little of your liveliness, Judge, uncensored.

BRACK [*Laughing.*] Not recommended for the lovely lady.

TESMAN [*Also laughing.*] You really are the limit, Hedda. Think of it.

BRACK Well, well, my ladies. Good night. Good night.

LØVBORG [*Bowing as he leaves.*] Until ten o'clock, then.

    [BRACK, LØVBORG *and* TESMAN *leave through the hall door. At the same time* BERTA *comes in from the rear room with a lighted lamp which she places on the drawing room table, going out the way she came in.*]

MRS. ELVSTED [*Has gotten up and wanders uneasily about the room.*] Oh, Hedda, where is all this going?

HEDDA Ten o'clock—then he'll appear. I see him before me with vine leaves in his hair,[9] burning bright and bold.

MRS. ELVSTED Yes, if only it could be like that.

HEDDA And then you'll see—then he'll have power over himself again. Then he'll be a free man for the rest of his days.

---

9. Like Bacchus, the Greek god of wine, and his followers.

MRS. ELVSTED   Oh God yes—if only he'd come back just the way you see him.

HEDDA   He'll come back just that way and no other. [*Gets up and comes closer.*] You can doubt him as much as you like. I believe in him. And so we'll see—

MRS. ELVSTED   There's something behind this, something else you're trying to do.

HEDDA   Yes, there is. Just once in my life I want to help shape someone's destiny.

MRS. ELVSTED   Don't you do that already?

HEDDA   I don't and I never have.

MRS. ELVSTED   Not even your husband?

HEDDA   Oh yes, that was a real bargain. Oh, if you could only understand how destitute I am while you get to be so rich. [*She passionately throws her arms around her.*] I think I'll burn your hair off after all.

MRS. ELVSTED   Let me go, let me go. I'm afraid of you.

BERTA   [*In the doorway.*]   Tea is ready in the dining room, Madam.

HEDDA   Good. We're on our way.

MRS. ELVSTED   No, no, no! I'd rather go home alone! Right now!

HEDDA   Nonsense! First you're going to have some tea, you little bubble-head, and then—at ten o'clock—Eilert Løvborg—with vine leaves in his hair! [*She pulls* MRS. ELVSTED *toward the doorway almost by force.*]

Act Three

The room at the TESMANS'. *The curtains are drawn across the center doorway and also across the glass door. The lamp covered with a shade burns low on the table. In the stove, with its door standing open, there has been a fire that is almost burned out.*

[MRS. ELVSTED, *wrapped in a large shawl and with her feet on a footstool, sits sunk back in an armchair.* HEDDA, *fully dressed, lies sleeping on the sofa with a rug over her.*]

MRS. ELVSTED   [*After a pause suddenly straightens herself in the chair and listens intently. Then she sinks back wearily and moans softly.*]   Still not back . . . Oh God, oh God . . . Still not back.

> [BERTA *enters tiptoeing carefully through the hall doorway; she has a letter in her hand.*]

MRS. ELVSTED   Ah—did someone come?

BERTA   Yes, a girl came by just now with this letter.

MRS. ELVSTED   [*Quickly stretching out her hand.*]   A letter? Let me have it.

BERTA   No ma'am, it's for the doctor.

MRS. ELVSTED   Oh.

BERTA   It was Miss Tesman's maid who brought it. I'll put it on the table here.

MRS. ELVSTED   Yes, do that.

BERTA   [*Puts down the letter.*]   I'd better put out the lamp; it's starting to smoke.

MRS. ELVSTED   Yes, put it out. It'll be light soon anyway.

BERTA [*Putting out the light.*]   Oh, ma'am, it's already light.

MRS. ELVSTED   So, morning and still not back—!

BERTA   Oh, dear Lord—I knew all along it would go like this.

MRS. ELVSTED   You knew?

BERTA   Yes, when I saw a certain person was back in town. And then when he went off with them—oh we'd heard plenty about that gentleman.

MRS. ELVSTED   Don't speak so loud, you'll wake your mistress.

BERTA [*Looks over to the sofa and sighs.*]   No, dear Lord—let her sleep, poor thing. Shouldn't I build the stove up a little more?

MRS. ELVSTED   Not for me, thanks.

BERTA   Well, well then. [*She goes out quietly through the hall doorway.*]

HEDDA [*Awakened by the closing door, looks up.*]   What's that?

MRS. ELVSTED   Only the maid.

HEDDA [*Looking around.*]   In here—! Oh, now I remember.
   [*Straightens up, stretches sitting on the sofa and rubs her eyes.*]
   What time is it, Thea?

MRS. ELVSTED [*Looks at her watch.*]   It's after seven.

HEDDA   What time did Tesman get in?

MRS. ELVSTED   He hasn't.

HEDDA   Still?

MRS. ELVSTED [*Getting up.*]   No one's come back.

HEDDA   And we sat here waiting and watching until almost four.

MRS. ELVSTED [*Wringing her hands.*]   Waiting for him!

HEDDA [*Yawning and speaking with her hand over her mouth.*]   Oh yes—we could have saved ourselves the trouble.

MRS. ELVSTED   Did you finally manage to sleep?

HEDDA   Yes, I think I slept quite well. Did you?

MRS. ELVSTED   Not a wink. I couldn't, Hedda. It was just impossible for me.

HEDDA [*Gets up and goes over to her.*]   Now, now, now. There's nothing to worry about. I know perfectly well how it all turned out.

MRS. ELVSTED   Yes, what do you think? Can you tell me?

HEDDA   Well, of course they dragged it out dreadfully up at Judge Brack's.

MRS. ELVSTED   Oh God yes—that must be true. But all the same—

HEDDA   And then you see, Tesman didn't want to come home and create a fuss by ringing the bell in the middle of the night. [*Laughing.*] He probably didn't want to show himself either right after a wild party like that.

MRS. ELVSTED   For goodness sake—where would he have gone?

HEDDA   Well, naturally, he went over to his aunt's and laid himself down to sleep there. They still have his old room standing ready for him.

MRS. ELVSTED   No, he's not with them. A letter just came for him from Miss Tesman. It's over there.

HEDDA   Oh? [*Looks at the inscription.*] Yes, that's Aunt Julie's hand all right. So then, he's still over at Judge Brack's and Eilert Løvborg—he's sitting—reading aloud with vine leaves in his hair.

MRS. ELVSTED   Oh, Hedda, you don't even believe what you're saying.

HEDDA   You are such a little noodlehead, Thea.

MRS. ELVSTED   Yes, unfortunately I probably am.

HEDDA   And you look like you're dead on your feet.

MRS. ELVSTED   Yes, I am. Dead on my feet.

HEDDA   And so now you're going to do what I tell you. You'll go into my room and lie down on my bed.

MRS. ELVSTED   Oh no, no—I couldn't get to sleep anyway.

HEDDA   Yes, you certainly will.

MRS. ELVSTED   But your husband's bound to be home any time now and I've got to find out right away—

HEDDA   I'll tell you as soon as he comes.

MRS. ELVSTED   Promise me that, Hedda?

HEDDA   Yes, that you can count on. Now just go in and sleep for a while.

MRS. ELVSTED   Thanks. At least I'll give it a try. [*She goes in through the back room.*]

[HEDDA *goes over to the glass door and draws back the curtains. Full daylight floods the room. She then takes a small hand mirror from the writing table, looks in it and arranges her hair. Then she goes to the hall door and presses the bell. Soon after* BERTA *enters the doorway.*]

BERTA   Did Madam want something?

HEDDA   Yes, build up the stove a little bit. I'm freezing in here.

BERTA   Lord, in no time at all it'll be warm in here. [*She rakes the embers and puts a log inside. She stands and listens.*] There's the front doorbell, Madam.

HEDDA   So, go answer it. I'll take care of the stove myself.

BERTA   It'll be burning soon enough. [*She goes out through the hall door.*]
[HEDDA *kneels on the footstool and puts more logs into the stove. After a brief moment,* GEORGE TESMAN *comes in from the hall. He looks weary and rather serious. He creeps on tiptoes toward the doorway and is about to slip through the curtains.*]

HEDDA   [*By the stove, without looking up.*]   Good morning.

TESMAN   [*Turning around.*]   Hedda. [*Comes nearer.*] What in the world— Up so early, hm?

HEDDA   Yes, up quite early today.

TESMAN   And here I was so sure you'd still be in bed. Just think, Hedda.

HEDDA   Not so loud. Mrs. Elvsted's lying down in my room.

TESMAN   Has Mrs. Elvsted been here all night?

HEDDA   Yes. No one came to pick her up.

TESMAN   No, no, they couldn't have.

HEDDA   [*Shuts the door of the stove and gets up.*]   So, did you have a jolly time at the Judge's?

TESMAN   Were you worried about me?

HEDDA   No, that would never occur to me. I asked if you had a good time.

TESMAN   Yes, I really did, for once, in a manner of speaking—Mostly in the beginning, I'd say. We'd arrived an hour early. How about that? And Brack had so much to get ready. But then Eilert read to me.

HEDDA   [*Sits at the right of the table.*]   So, tell me.

TESMAN   Hedda, you can't imagine what this new work will be like. It's one of the most brilliant things ever written, no doubt about it. Think of that.

HEDDA   Yes, yes, but that's not what I'm interested in.

TESMAN   But I have to confess something, Hedda. After he read—something horrible came over me.

HEDDA   Something horrible?

TESMAN   I sat there envying Eilert for being able to write like that. Think of it, Hedda.

HEDDA   Yes, yes, I'm thinking.

TESMAN   And then, that whole time, knowing that he—even with all the incredible powers at his command—is still beyond redemption.

HEDDA   You mean he's got more of life's courage in him than the others?

TESMAN   No, for heaven sakes—he just has no control over his pleasures.

HEDDA   And what happened then—at the end?

TESMAN   Well, Hedda, I guess you'd have to say it was a bacchanal.

HEDDA   Did he have vine leaves in his hair?

TESMAN   Vine leaves? No, I didn't see anything like that. But he did make a long wild speech for the woman who had inspired him in his work. Yes—that's how he put it.

HEDDA   Did he name her?

TESMAN   No, he didn't, but I can only guess that it must be Mrs. Elvsted. Wouldn't you say?

HEDDA   Hmm—where did you leave him?

TESMAN   On the way back. Most of our group broke up at the same time and Brack came along with us to get a little fresh air. And you see, we agreed to follow Eilert home because—well—he was so far gone.

HEDDA   He must have been.

TESMAN   But here's the strangest part, Hedda! Or maybe I should say the saddest. I'm almost ashamed for Eilert's sake—to tell you——

HEDDA   So?

TESMAN   There we were walking along, you see, and I happened to drop back a bit, just for a couple of minutes, you understand.

HEDDA   Yes, yes, good Lord but——

TESMAN   And then when I was hurrying to catch up—can you guess what I found in the gutter, hm?

HEDDA   How can I possibly guess?

TESMAN   Don't ever tell a soul, Hedda. Do you hear? Promise me that for Eilert's sake. [*Pulls a package out of his coat pocket.*] Just think—this is what I found.

HEDDA   That's the package he had with him here yesterday, isn't it?

TESMAN   That's it. His precious, irreplaceable manuscript—all of it. And he's lost it—without even noticing it. Oh just think, Hedda—the pity of it—

HEDDA   Well, why didn't you give it back to him right away?

TESMAN   Oh, I didn't dare do that—The condition he was in—

HEDDA   You didn't tell any of the others that you found it either?

TESMAN   Absolutely not. I couldn't, you see, for Eilert's sake.

HEDDA   So nobody knows you have Eilert's manuscript? Nobody at all?

TESMAN   No. And they mustn't find out either.

HEDDA   What did you talk to him about later?

TESMAN   I didn't get a chance to talk to him any more. We got to the city limits, and he and a couple of the others went a different direction. Just think—

HEDDA   Aha, they must have followed him home then.

TESMAN   Yes, I suppose so. Brack also went his way.

HEDDA   And, in the meantime, what became of the bacchanal?

TESMAN   Well, I and some of the others followed one of the revelers up to his place and had morning coffee with him—or maybe we should call it morning-after coffee, hm? Now, I'll rest a bit—and as soon as I think Eilert has managed to sleep it off, poor man, then I've got to go over to him with this.

HEDDA   [*Reaching out for the envelope.*]   No, don't give it back. Not yet, I mean. Let me read it first.

TESMAN   Oh no.

HEDDA   Oh, for God's sake.

TESMAN   I don't dare do that.

HEDDA   You don't dare?

TESMAN   No, you can imagine how completely desperate he'll be when he wakes up and realizes he can't find the manuscript. He's got no copy of it. He said so himself.

HEDDA   [*Looks searchingly at him.*]   Couldn't it be written again?

TESMAN   No, I don't believe that could ever be done because the inspiration—you see—

HEDDA   Yes, yes—That's the thing, isn't it? [*Casually.*] But, oh yes—there's a letter here for you.

TESMAN   No, think of that.

HEDDA   [*Hands it to him.*]   It came early this morning.

TESMAN   From Aunt Julie, Hedda. What can it be? [*Puts the manuscript on the other stool, opens the letter and jumps up.*] Oh Hedda—poor Aunt Rina's almost breathing her last.

HEDDA   It's only what's expected.

TESMAN   And if I want to see her one more time, I've got to hurry. I'll charge over there right away.

HEDDA   [*Suppressing a smile.*]   You'll charge?

TESMAN   Oh, Hedda dearest—if you could just bring yourself to follow me. Just think.

HEDDA   [*Rises and says wearily and dismissively.*]   No, no. Don't ask me to do anything like that. I won't look at sickness and death. Let me stay free from everything ugly.

TESMAN   Oh, good Lord, then—[*Darting around.*] My hat—? My overcoat—? Ah, in the hall—Oh, I hope I'm not too late, Hedda, hm?

HEDDA   Then charge right over—
  [BERTA *appears in the hallway.*]

BERTA   Judge Brack is outside.

HEDDA   Ask him to come in.

TESMAN   At a time like this! No, I can't possibly deal with him now.

HEDDA   But I can. [*To* BERTA.] Ask the Judge in.
  [BERTA *goes out.*]

HEDDA   [*In a whisper.*]   The package, Tesman. [*She snatches it off the stool.*]

TESMAN   Yes, give it to me.

HEDDA   No, I'll hide it until you get back.
  [*She goes over to the writing table and sticks the package in the bookcase.* TESMAN *stands flustered, and can't get his gloves on.* BRACK *enters through the hall doorway.*]

HEDDA   [*Nodding to him.*]   Well, you're an early bird.

BRACK   Yes, wouldn't you say. [*To* TESMAN.] You're going out?

TESMAN   Yes, I've got to go over to my aunt's. Just think, the poor dear is dying.

BRACK   Good Lord, is she really? Then don't let me hold you up for even a moment, at a time like this—

TESMAN   Yes, I really must run—Good-bye. Good-bye. [*He hurries through the hall doorway.*]

HEDDA [*Approaches.*]   So, things were livelier than usual at your place last night, Judge.

BRACK   Oh yes, so much so that I haven't even been able to change clothes, Mrs. Hedda.

HEDDA   You too.

BRACK   As you see. But, what has Tesman been telling you about last night's adventures?

HEDDA   Oh, just some boring things. He went someplace to drink coffee.

BRACK   I've already looked into the coffee party. Eilert Løvborg wasn't part of that group, I presume.

HEDDA   No, they followed him home before that.

BRACK   Tesman too?

HEDDA   No, but a couple of others, he said.

BRACK [*Smiles.*]   George Tesman is a very naïve soul, Mrs. Hedda.

HEDDA   God knows, he is. But is there something more behind this?

BRACK   I'd have to say so.

HEDDA   Well then, Judge, let's be seated. Then you can speak freely. [*She sits to the left side of the table,* BRACK *at the long side near her.*] Well, then—

BRACK   I had certain reasons for keeping track of my guests—or, more precisely, some of my guests' movements last night.

HEDDA   For example, Eilert Løvborg?

BRACK   Yes, indeed.

HEDDA   Now I'm hungry for more.

BRACK   Do you know where he and a couple of the others spent the rest of the night, Mrs. Hedda?

HEDDA   Why don't you tell me, if it can be told.

BRACK   Oh, it's certainly worth the telling. It appears that they found their way into a particularly animated soirée.[1]

HEDDA   A lively one?

BRACK   The liveliest.

HEDDA   Tell me more, Judge.

BRACK   Løvborg had received an invitation earlier—I knew all about that. But he declined because, as you know, he's made himself into a new man.

HEDDA   Up at the Elvsteds', yes. But he went just the same?

BRACK   Well, you see, Mrs. Hedda—unfortunately, the spirit really seized him at my place last evening.

HEDDA   Yes, I hear he was quite inspired.

BRACK   Inspired to a rather powerful degree. And so, he started to recon-

---

1. Evening party (French).

sider, I assume, because we men, alas, are not always so true to our principles as we ought to be.

HEDDA Present company excepted, Judge Brack. So, Løvborg—?

BRACK Short and sweet—He ended up at the salon of a certain Miss Diana.

HEDDA Miss Diana?

BRACK Yes, it was Miss Diana's soirée for a select circle of ladies and their admirers.

HEDDA Is she a redhead?

BRACK Exactly.

HEDDA A sort of a—singer?

BRACK Oh, yes—She's also that. And a mighty huntress—of men, Mrs. Hedda. You must have heard of her. Eilert Løvborg was one of her most strenuous admirers—in his better days.

HEDDA And how did all this end?

BRACK Apparently less amicably than it began. Miss Diana, after giving him the warmest of welcomes, soon turned to assault and battery.

HEDDA Against Løvborg?

BRACK Oh, yes. He accused her, or one of her ladies, or robbing him. He insisted that his pocketbook was missing, along with some other things. In short, he seems to have created a dreadful spectacle.

HEDDA And what did that lead to?

BRACK A regular brawl between both the men and the women. Luckily the police finally got there.

HEDDA The police too?

BRACK Yes. It's going to be quite a costly little romp for Eilert Løvborg. What a madman.

HEDDA Well!

BRACK Apparently, he resisted arrest. It seems he struck one of the officers on the ear, and ripped his uniform to shreds, so he had to go to the police station.

HEDDA How do you know all this?

BRACK From the police themselves.

HEDDA [Gazing before her.] So, that's how it ended? He had no vine leaves in his hair.

BRACK Vine leaves, Mrs. Hedda?

HEDDA [Changing her tone.] Tell me now, Judge, why do you go around snooping and spying on Eilert Løvborg?

BRACK For starters, I'm not a completely disinterested party—especially if the hearing uncovers the fact that he came straight from my place.

HEDDA There's going to be a hearing?

BRACK You can count on it. Be that as it may, however—My real concern was my duty as a friend of the house to inform you and Tesman of Løvborg's nocturnal adventures.

HEDDA Why, Judge Brack?

BRACK Well, I have an active suspicion that he'll try to use you as a kind of screen.

HEDDA Oh! What makes you think that?

BRACK Good God—we're not that blind, Mrs. Hedda. Wait and see. This

Mrs. Elvsted—she won't be in such a hurry to leave town again.

HEDDA If there's anything going on between those two, there's plenty of places they can meet.

BRACK Not one single home. Every respectable house will be closed to Eilert Løvborg from now on.

HEDDA And mine should be too—Is that what you're saying?

BRACK Yes. I have to admit it would be more than painful for me if this man secured a foothold here. If this—utterly superfluous—and intrusive individual—were to force himself into—

HEDDA Into the triangle?

BRACK Precisely! It would leave me without a home.

HEDDA [Looks smilingly at him.] I see—The one cock of the walk—That's your goal.

BRACK [Slowly nodding and dropping his voice.] Yes, that's my goal. And it's a goal that I'll fight for—with every means at my disposal.

HEDDA [Her smile fading.] You're really a dangerous man, aren't you— when push comes to shove.

BRACK You think so?

HEDDA Yes, I'm starting to. And that's all right—just as long as you don't have any kind of hold on me.

BRACK [Laughing ambiguously.] Yes, Mrs. Hedda—you might be right about that. Of course, then, who knows whether I might not find some way or other—

HEDDA Now listen, Judge Brack! That sounds like you're threatening me.

BRACK [Gets up.] Oh, far from it. A triangle, you see—is best fortified by free defenders.

HEDDA I think so too.

BRACK Well, I've had my say so I should be getting back. Good-bye, Mrs. Hedda. [He goes toward the glass doors.]

HEDDA Out through the garden?

BRACK Yes, it's shorter for me.

HEDDA And then, it's also the back way.

BRACK That's true. I have nothing against back ways. Sometimes they can be very piquant.

HEDDA When there's sharpshooting.

BRACK [In the doorway, laughing at her.] Oh, no—you never shoot your tame cocks.

HEDDA [Also laughing.] Oh, no, especially when there's only one—

[Laughing and nodding they take their farewells. He leaves. She closes the door after him. HEDDA stands for a while, serious, looking out. Then she goes and peers through the curtains in the back wall. She goes to the writing table, takes Løvborg's package from the bookcase, and is about to leaf through it. BERTA's voice, raised in indignation, is heard out in the hall. HEDDA turns and listens. She quickly locks the package in the drawer and sets the key on the writing table. EILERT LØVBORG, wearing his overcoat and carrying his hat, bursts through the hall doorway. He looks somewhat confused and excited.]

LØVBORG [Turned toward the hallway.] And I'm telling you, I've got to go in! And that's that! [He closes the door, sees HEDDA, controls himself immediately, and bows.]

HEDDA [*By the writing table.*] Well, Mr. Løvborg, it's pretty late to be calling for Thea.

LØVBORG Or a little early to be calling on you. I apologize.

HEDDA How do you know that she's still here?

LØVBORG I went to where she was staying. They told me she'd been out all night.

HEDDA [*Goes to the table.*] Did you notice anything special when they told you that?

LØVBORG [*Looks inquiringly at her.*] Notice anything?

HEDDA I mean—did they seem to have any thought on the subject—one way or the other?

LØVBORG [*Suddenly understanding.*] Oh, of course, it's true. I'm dragging her down with me. Still, I didn't notice anything. Tesman isn't up yet, I suppose?

HEDDA No, I don't think so.

LØVBORG When did he get home?

HEDDA Very late.

LØVBORG Did he tell you anything?

HEDDA Yes. I heard Judge Brack's was very lively.

LØVBORG Nothing else?

HEDDA No, I don't think so. I was terribly tired, though—

[MRS. ELVSTED *comes in through the curtains at the back.*]

MRS. ELVSTED [*Runs toward him.*] Oh, Løvborg—at last!

LØVBORG Yes, at last, and too late.

MRS. ELVSTED [*Looking anxiously at him.*] What's too late?

LØVBORG Everything's too late. I'm finished.

MRS. ELVSTED Oh no, no—Don't say that!

LØVBORG You'll say it too, when you've heard—

MRS. ELVSTED I won't listen—

HEDDA Shall I leave you two alone?

LØVBORG No, stay—You too, I beg you.

MRS. ELVSTED But I won't listen to anything you tell me.

LØVBORG I don't want to talk about last night.

MRS. ELVSTED What is it, then?

LØVBORG We've got to go our separate ways.

MRS. ELVSTED Separate!

HEDDA [*Involuntarily.*] I knew it!

LØVBORG Because I have no more use for you, Thea.

MRS. ELVSTED You can stand there and say that! No more use for me! Can't I help you now, like I did before? Won't we go on working together?

LØVBORG I don't plan to work any more.

MRS. ELVSTED [*Desperately.*] Then what do I have to live for?

LØVBORG Just try to live your life as if you'd never known me.

MRS. ELVSTED I can't do that.

LØVBORG Try, Thea. Try, if you can. Go back home.

MRS. ELVSTED [*Defiantly.*] Where you are, that's where I want to be. I won't let myself be just driven off like this. I want to stay at your side—be with you when the book comes out.

HEDDA [*Half aloud, tensely.*] Ah, the book—Yes.

LØVBORG [*Looking at her.*] Mine and Thea's, because that's what it is.

MRS. ELVSTED   Yes, that's what I feel it is. That's why I have a right to be with you when it comes out. I want to see you covered in honor and glory again, and the joy. I want to share that with you too.

LØVBORG   Thea—our book's never coming out.

HEDDA   Ah!

MRS. ELVSTED   Never coming out?

LØVBORG   It can't ever come out.

MRS. ELVSTED   [*In anxious foreboding.*]   Løvborg, what have you done with the manuscript?

HEDDA   [*Looking intently at him.*]   Yes, the manuscript—?

MRS. ELVSTED   What have you—?

LØVBORG   Oh, Thea, don't ask me that.

MRS. ELVSTED   Yes, yes, I've got to know. I have the right to know.

LØVBORG   The manuscript—all right then, the manuscript—I've ripped it up into a thousand pieces.

MRS. ELVSTED   [*Screams.*]   Oh no, no!

HEDDA   [*Involuntarily.*]   But that's just not—!

LØVBORG   [*Looking at her.*]   Not true, you think?

HEDDA   [*Controls herself.*]   All right then. Of course it is, if you say so. It sounds so ridiculous.

LØVBORG   But it's true, just the same.

MRS. ELVSTED   [*Wringing her hands.*]   Oh God—oh God, Hedda. Torn his own work to pieces.

LØVBORG   I've torn my own life to pieces. I might as well tear up my life's work too—

MRS. ELVSTED   And you did that last night!

LØVBORG   Yes. Do you hear me? A thousand pieces. Scattered them all over the fjord.[2] Way out where there's pure salt water. Let them drift in it. Drift with the current in the wind. Then, after a while, they'll sink. Deeper and deeper. Like me, Thea.

MRS. ELVSTED   You know, Løvborg, all this with the book—? For the rest of my life, it will be just like you'd killed a little child.

LØVBORG   You're right. Like murdering a child.

MRS. ELVSTED   But then, how could you—! That child was partly mine, too.

HEDDA   [*Almost inaudibly.*]   Ah, the child—

MRS. ELVSTED   [*Sighs heavily.*]   So it's finished? All right, Hedda, now I'm going.

HEDDA   You're not going back?

MRS. ELVSTED   Oh, I don't know what I'm going to do. I can't see anything out in front of me. [*She goes out through the hall doorway.*]

HEDDA   [*Standing a while, waiting.*]   Don't you want to see her home, Mr. Løvborg?

LØVBORG   Through the streets? So that people can get a good look at us together?

HEDDA   I don't know what else happened to you last night but if it's so completely beyond redemption—

LØVBORG   It won't stop there. I know that much. And I can't bring myself to live that kind of life again either. Not again. Once I had the courage

2. Inlet of the sea (Norwegian).

to live life to the fullest, to break every rule. But she's taken that out of
me.

HEDDA [*Staring straight ahead.*]   That sweet little fool has gotten hold of a
human destiny. [*Looks at him.*] And you're so heartless to her.

LØVBORG   Don't call it heartless.

HEDDA   To go and destroy the thing that has filled her soul for this whole
long, long time. You don't call that heartless?

LØVBORG   I can tell you the truth, Hedda.

HEDDA   The truth?

LØVBORG   First, promise me—Give me your word that Thea will never find
out what I'm about to confide to you.

HEDDA   You have my word.

LØVBORG   Good. Then I'll tell you—What I stood here and described—It
wasn't true.

HEDDA   About the manuscript?

LØVBORG   Yes. I haven't ripped it up. I didn't throw it in the fjord, either.

HEDDA   No, well—so—Where is it?

LØVBORG   I've destroyed it just the same. Utterly and completely, Hedda!

HEDDA   I don't understand any of this.

LØVBORG   Thea said that what I'd done seemed to her like murdering a
child.

HEDDA   Yes, she did.

LØVBORG   But killing his child—that's not the worst thing a father can do
to it.

HEDDA   Not the worst?

LØVBORG   No. And the worst—that is what I wanted to spare Thea from
hearing.

HEDDA   And what is the worst?

LØVBORG   Imagine, Hedda, a man—in the very early hours of the morning—after a wild night of debauchery, came home to the mother of his
child and said, "Listen—I've been here and there to this place and that
place, and I had our child with me in this place and that place. And the
child got away from me. Just got away. The devil knows whose hands it's
fallen into, who's got a hold of it."

HEDDA   Well—when you get right down to it—it's only a book—

LØVBORG   All of Thea's soul was in that book.

HEDDA   Yes, I can see that.

LØVBORG   And so, you must also see that there's no future for her and me.

HEDDA   So, what will your road be now?

LØVBORG   None. Only to see to it that I put an end to it all. The sooner
the better.

HEDDA [*Comes a step closer.*]   Eilert Løvborg—Listen to me now—Can you
see to it that—that when you do it, you bathe it in beauty?

LØVBORG   In beauty? [*Smiles.*] With vine leaves in my hair, as you used to
imagine?

HEDDA   Ah, no. No vine leaves—I don't believe in them any longer. But
in beauty, yes! For once! Good-bye. You've got to go now. And don't come
here any more.

LØVBORG   Good-bye, Mrs. Tesman. And give my regards to George Tesman. [*He is about to leave.*]

HEDDA   No, wait! Take a souvenir to remember me by.

He admits to Hedda that he lost the manuscript

[*She goes over to the writing table, opens the drawer and the pistol case. She returns to* LØVBORG *with one of the pistols.*]

LØVBORG [*Looks at her.*]   That's the souvenir?

HEDDA [*Nodding slowly.*]   Do you recognize it? It was aimed at you once.

LØVBORG   You should have used it then.

HEDDA   Here, you use it now.

LØVBORG [*Puts the pistol in his breast pocket.*]   Thanks.

HEDDA   In beauty, Eilert Løvborg. Promise me that.

LØVBORG   Good-bye, Hedda Gabler. [*He goes out the hall doorway.*]

[HEDDA *listens a moment at the door. Afterward, she goes to the writing table and takes out the package with the manuscript, looks inside the wrapper, pulls some of the pages half out and looks at them. She then takes it all over to the armchair by the stove and sits down. She has the package in her lap. Soon after she opens the stove door and then opens the package.*]

HEDDA [*Throws one of the sheets into the fire and whispers to herself.*]   Now, I'm burning your child, Thea—You with your curly hair. [*Throws a few more sheets into the fire.*] Your child and Eilert Løvborg's. [*Throws in the rest.*] Now I'm burning—burning the child.

In hate, she destroys the manuscript

Act Four

The same room at the TESMANS'. *It is evening. The drawing room is in darkness. The rear room is lit with a hanging lamp over the table. The curtains are drawn across the glass door.*

[HEDDA, *dressed in black, wanders up and down in the darkened room. Then she goes into the rear room, and over to the left side. Some chords are heard from the piano. Then she emerges again, and goes into the drawing room.* BERTA *comes in from the right of the rear room, with a lighted lamp, which she places on the table in front of the sofa, in the salon. Her eyes show signs of crying, and she has black ribbons on her cap. She goes quietly and carefully to the right.* HEDDA *goes over to the glass door, draws the curtains aside a little, and stares out into the darkness. Soon after,* MISS TESMAN *enters from the hallway dressed in black with a hat and a veil.* HEDDA *goes over to her and shakes her hand.*]

MISS TESMAN   Yes, here I am, Hedda—in mourning black. My poor sister's struggle is over at last.

HEDDA   As you can see, I've already heard. Tesman sent me a note.

MISS TESMAN   Yes, he promised he would but I thought I should bring the news myself. This news of death into this house of life.

HEDDA   That was very kind of you.

MISS TESMAN   Ah, Rina shouldn't have left us right now. Hedda's house is no place for sorrow at a time like this.

HEDDA [*Changing the subject.*]   She died peacefully, Miss Tesman?

MISS TESMAN   Yes, so gently—Such a peaceful release. And she was happy beyond words that she got to see George once more and could say a proper good-bye to him. Is it possible he's not home yet?

HEDDA   No. He wrote saying I shouldn't expect him too early. But, please sit down.

MISS TESMAN   No, thank you, my dear—blessed Hedda. I'd like to, but I have so little time. She'll be dressed and arranged the best that I can. She'll look really splendid when she goes to her grave.

HEDDA   Can I help you with anything?

MISS TESMAN   Oh, don't even think about it. These kinds of things aren't for Hedda Tesman's hands or her thoughts either. Not at this time. No, no.

HEDDA   Ah—thoughts—Now they're not so easy to master—

MISS TESMAN   [Continuing.]   Yes, dear God, that's how this world goes. Over at my house we'll be sewing a linen shroud for Aunt Rina, and here there will be sewing too, but of a whole different kind, praise God.

[GEORGE TESMAN enters through a hall door.]

HEDDA   Well, it's good you're finally here.

TESMAN   You here, Aunt Julie, with Hedda. Just think.

MISS TESMAN   I was just about to go, my dear boy. Well. Did you manage to finish everything you promised to?

TESMAN   No, I'm afraid I've forgotten half of it. I have to run over there tomorrow again. Today my brain is just so confused. I can't keep hold of two thoughts in a row.

MISS TESMAN   George, my dear, you mustn't take it like that.

TESMAN   Oh? How should I take it, do you think?

MISS TESMAN   You must be joyful in your sorrow. You must be glad for what has happened, just as I am.

TESMAN   Ah, yes. You're thinking of Aunt Rina.

HEDDA   You'll be lonely now, Miss Tesman.

MISS TESMAN   For the first few days, yes. But that won't last long, I hope. Our sainted Rina's little room won't stand empty. That much I know.

TESMAN   Really? Who'll be moving in there, hm?

MISS TESMAN   Oh, there's always some poor invalid or other who needs care and attention, unfortunately.

HEDDA   You'd really take on a cross like that again?

MISS TESMAN   Cross? God forgive you child. It's not a cross for me.

HEDDA   But a complete stranger—

MISS TESMAN   It's easy to make friends with sick people. And I so badly need someone to live for. Well, God be praised and thanked—there'll be a thing or two to keep an old aunt busy here in this house soon enough.

HEDDA   Oh, please don't think about us.

TESMAN   Yes. The three of us could be quite cozy here if only—

HEDDA   If only—?

TESMAN   [Uneasily.]   Oh, it's nothing. Everything'll be fine. Let's hope, hm?

MISS TESMAN   Well, well, you two have plenty to talk about, I'm sure. [Smiling.] And Hedda may have something to tell you, George. Now it's home to Rina. [Turning in the doorway.] Dear Lord, isn't it strange to think about. Now Rina's both with me and our sainted Joseph.

TESMAN   Yes, just think, Aunt Julie, hm?

[MISS TESMAN leaves through the hall door.]

HEDDA   [Follows TESMAN with cold, searching eyes.]   I think all this has hit you harder than your aunt.

TESMAN   Oh, it's not just this death. It's Eilert I'm worried about.

HEDDA   [Quickly.]   Any news?

TESMAN   I wanted to run to him this afternoon and tell him that his manuscript was safe—in good hands.

HEDDA   Oh? Did you find him?

TESMAN   No, he wasn't home. But later I met Mrs. Elvsted, and she told me he'd been here early this morning.

HEDDA   Yes, just after you left.

TESMAN   And apparently he said that he'd ripped the manuscript up into a thousand pieces, hm?

HEDDA   That's what he said.

TESMAN   But, good God, he must have been absolutely crazy. So you didn't dare give it back to him, Hedda?

HEDDA   No, he didn't get it back.

TESMAN   But, you told him we had it?

HEDDA   No. [*Quickly.*] Did you tell Mrs. Elvsted?

TESMAN   No, I didn't want to. But you should have told him. What would happen if in his desperation he went and did something to himself? Let me have the manuscript, Hedda. I'll run it over to him right away. Where did you put it?

HEDDA [*Cold and impassively leaning on the armchair.*]   I don't have it any more.

TESMAN   Don't have it! What in the world do you mean?

HEDDA   I burned it up—every page.

TESMAN [*Leaps up in terror.*]   Burned? Burned? Eilert's manuscript!

HEDDA   Don't shout like that. The maid will hear you.

TESMAN   Burned! But good God—! No, no, no—That's absolutely impossible.

HEDDA   Yes, but all the same it's true.

TESMAN   Do you have any idea what you've done, Hedda? That's—that's criminal appropriation of lost property. Think about that. Yes, just ask Judge Brack, then you'll see.

HEDDA   Then it's probably wise for you not to talk about it, isn't it? To the Judge or anyone else.

TESMAN   How could you have gone and done something so appalling? What came over you? Answer me that, Hedda, hm?

HEDDA [*Suppressing an almost imperceptible smile.*]   I did it for your sake, George.

TESMAN   My sake?

HEDDA   Remember you came home this morning and talked about how he had read to you?

TESMAN   Yes, yes.

HEDDA   You confessed that you envied him.

TESMAN   Good God, I didn't mean it literally.

HEDDA   Nevertheless, I couldn't stand the idea that someone would overshadow you.

TESMAN [*Exclaiming between doubt and joy.*]   Hedda—Oh, is this true?— What you're saying?—Yes, but. Yes, but. I never noticed that you loved me this way before. Think of that!

HEDDA   Well, you need to know—that at a time like this—[*Violently breaking off.*] No, no—go and ask your Aunt Julie. She'll provide all the details.

TESMAN   Oh, I almost think I understand you, Hedda. [*Clasps his hands together.*] No, good God—Can it be, hm?

HEDDA   Don't shout like that. The maid can hear you.

TESMAN [*Laughing in extraordinary joy.*]   The maid! Oh, Hedda, you are priceless. The maid—why it's—why it's Berta. I'll go tell Berta myself.

HEDDA [*Clenching her hands as if frantic.*]   Oh, I'm dying—Dying of all this.

TESMAN   All what, Hedda, what?

HEDDA [*Coldly controlled again.*]   All this—absurdity—George.

TESMAN   Absurdity? I'm so incredibly happy. Even so, maybe I shouldn't say anything to Berta.

HEDDA   Oh yes, go ahead. Why not?

TESMAN   No, no. Not right now. But Aunt Julie, yes, absolutely. And then, you're calling me George. Just think. Oh, Aunt Julie will be so happy—so happy.

HEDDA   When she hears I've burned Eilert Løvborg's manuscript for your sake?

TESMAN   No, no, you're right. All this with the manuscript. No. Of course, nobody can find out about that. But, Hedda—you're burning for me—Aunt Julie really must share in that. But I wonder—all this—I wonder if it's typical with young wives, hm?

HEDDA   You'd better ask Aunt Julie about that too.

TESMAN   Oh yes, I certainly will when I get the chance. [*Looking uneasy and thoughtful again.*] No, but, oh no, the manuscript. Good Lord, it's awful to think about poor Eilert, just the same.

[MRS. ELVSTED, *dressed as for her first visit with hat and coat, enters through the hall door.*]

MRS. ELVSTED [*Greets them hurriedly and speaks in agitation.*]   Oh, Hedda, don't be offended that I've come back again.

HEDDA   What happened to you, Thea?

TESMAN   Something about Eilert Løvborg?

MRS. ELVSTED   Oh yes, I'm terrified that he's had an accident.

HEDDA [*Grips her arm.*]   Ah, do you think so?

TESMAN   Good Lord, where did you get that idea, Mrs. Elvsted?

MRS. ELVSTED   I heard them talking at the boarding house—just as I came in. There are the most incredible rumors about him going around town today.

TESMAN   Oh yes, imagine, I heard them too. And still I can swear he went straight home to sleep. Just think.

HEDDA   So—What were they saying at the boarding house?

MRS. ELVSTED   Oh, I couldn't get any details, either because they didn't know or—or they saw me and stopped talking. And I didn't dare ask.

TESMAN [*Uneasily pacing the floor.*]   Let's just hope—you misunderstood.

MRS. ELVSTED   No, I'm sure they were talking about him. Then I heard them say something about the hospital—

TESMAN   Hospital?

HEDDA   No—That's impossible.

MRS. ELVSTED   I'm deathly afraid for him, so I went up to his lodgings and asked about him there.

HEDDA   You dared to do that?

MRS. ELVSTED   What else should I have done? I couldn't stand the uncertainty any longer.

TESMAN   You didn't find him there either, hm?

MRS. ELVSTED   No. And the people there didn't know anything at all. They said he hadn't been home since yesterday afternoon.

TESMAN   Yesterday? How could they say that?

MRS. ELVSTED   It could only mean one thing—Something terrible's happened to him.

TESMAN   You know, Hedda—What if I were to go into town and ask around at different places—?

HEDDA   No! You stay out of this.

[JUDGE BRACK, *carrying his hat, enters through the hall door, which* BERTA *opens and closes after him. He looks serious and bows in silence.*]

TESMAN   Oh, here you are, Judge, hm?

BRACK   Yes, it was essential for me to see you this evening.

TESMAN   I see you got the message from Aunt Julie.

BRACK   Yes, that too.

TESMAN   Isn't it sad, hm?

BRACK   Well, my dear Tesman, that depends on how you look at it.

TESMAN [*Looks at him uneasily.*]   Has anything else happened?

BRACK   Yes, it has.

HEDDA [*Tensely.*]   Something sad, Judge Brack?

BRACK   Once again, it depends on how you look at it, Mrs. Tesman.

MRS. ELVSTED [*In an uncontrollable outburst.*]   It's Eilert Løvborg.

BRACK [*Looks briefly at her.*]   How did you guess, Mrs. Elvsted? Do you already know something—?

MRS. ELVSTED [*Confused.*]   No, no, I don't know anything but—

TESMAN   Well, for God's sake, tell us what it is.

BRACK [*Shrugging his shoulders.*]   Well then—I'm sorry to tell you—that Eilert Løvborg has been taken to the hospital. He is dying.

MRS. ELVSTED [*Crying out.*]   Oh God, oh God.

TESMAN   Dying?

HEDDA [*Involuntarily.*]   So quickly—?

MRS. ELVSTED [*Wailing.*]   And we were quarrelling when we parted, Hedda.

HEDDA [*Whispers.*]   Now, Thea—Thea.

MRS. ELVSTED [*Not noticing her.*]   I'm going to him. I've got to see him alive.

BRACK   It would do you no good, Mrs. Elvsted. No visitors are allowed.

MRS. ELVSTED   At least tell me what happened. What—?

TESMAN   Yes, because he certainly wouldn't have tried to—hm?

HEDDA   Yes, I'm sure that's what he did.

TESMAN   Hedda. How can you—

BRACK [*Who is watching her all the time.*]   Unfortunately, Mrs. Tesman, you've guessed right.

MRS. ELVSTED   Oh, how awful.

TESMAN   To himself, too. Think of it.

HEDDA   Shot himself!

BRACK   Right again, Mrs. Tesman.

MRS. ELVSTED [*Tries to compose herself.*]   When did this happen, Mr. Brack?

BRACK   Just this afternoon, between three and four.

TESMAN Oh, my God—Where did he do it, hm?

BRACK [*Slightly uncertain.*] Where? Oh, I suppose at his lodgings.

MRS. ELVSTED No, that can't be. I was there between six and seven.

BRACK Well then, some other place. I don't know precisely. All I know is that he was found—he'd shot himself—in the chest.

MRS. ELVSTED Oh, how awful to think that he should die like that.

HEDDA [*To* BRACK.] In the chest?

BRACK Yes, like I said.

HEDDA Not through the temple?

BRACK The chest, Mrs. Tesman.

HEDDA Well, well. The chest is also good.

BRACK What was that, Mrs. Tesman?

HEDDA [*Evasively.*] Oh, nothing—nothing.

TESMAN And the wound is fatal, hm?

BRACK The wound is absolutely fatal. In fact, it's probably already over.

MRS. ELVSTED Yes, yes, I can feel it. It's over. It's all over. Oh, Hedda—!

TESMAN Tell me, how did you find out about all this?

BRACK [*Curtly.*] From a police officer. One I spoke with.

HEDDA [*Raising her voice.*] Finally—an action.

TESMAN God help us, Hedda, what are you saying?

HEDDA I'm saying that here, in this—there is beauty.

BRACK Uhm, Mrs. Tesman.

TESMAN Beauty! No, don't even think it.

MRS. ELVSTED Oh, Hedda. How can you talk about beauty?

HEDDA Eilert Løvborg has come to terms with himself. He's had the courage to do what had to be done.

MRS. ELVSTED No, don't ever believe it was anything like that. What he did, he did in a moment of madness.

TESMAN It was desperation.

MRS. ELVSTED Yes, madness. Just like when he tore his book in pieces.

BRACK [*Startled.*] The book. You mean his manuscript? Did he tear it up?

MRS. ELVSTED Yes, last night.

TESMAN [*Whispering softly.*] Oh, Hedda, we'll never get out from under all this.

BRACK Hmm, that's very odd.

TESMAN [*Pacing the floor.*] To think that Eilert Løvborg should leave the world this way. And then not to leave behind the work that would have made his name immortal.

MRS. ELVSTED Oh, what if it could be put together again.

TESMAN Yes—just think—what if it could? I don't know what I wouldn't give—

MRS. ELVSTED Maybe it can, Mr. Tesman.

TESMAN What do you mean?

MRS. ELVSTED [*Searching in the pocket of her skirt.*] See this? I saved all the notes he dictated from.

HEDDA [*A step closer.*] Ah.

TESMAN You saved them, Mrs. Elvsted, hm?

MRS. ELVSTED Yes, they're all here. I brought them with me when I came to town, and here they've been. Tucked away in my pocket—

TESMAN Oh, let me see them.

they want to try to piece the manuscript [handwritten margin note]

MRS. ELVSTED [*Gives him a bundle of small papers.*]   But they're all mixed up, completely out of order.

TESMAN   Just think. What if we could sort them out. Perhaps if the two of us helped each other.

MRS. ELVSTED   Oh yes. Let's at least give it a try—

TESMAN   It will happen. It must happen. I'll give my whole life to this.

HEDDA   You, George, your life?

TESMAN   Yes, or, anyway, all the time I have. Every spare minute. My own research will just have to be put aside. Hedda—you understand, don't you, hm? I owe this to Eilert's memory.

HEDDA   Maybe so.

TESMAN   Now, my dear Mrs. Elvsted, let's pull ourselves together. God knows there's no point brooding about what's happened. We've got to try to find some peace of mind so that—

MRS. ELVSTED   Yes, yes, Mr. Tesman. I'll do my best.

TESMAN   Well. So, come along then. We've got to get started on these notes right away. Where should we sit? Here? No. In the back room. Excuse us, Judge. Come with me, Mrs. Elvsted.

MRS. ELVSTED   Oh God—if only it can be done.

[TESMAN *and* MRS. ELVSTED *go into the rear room. She takes her hat and coat off. Both sit at the table under the hanging lamp and immerse themselves in eager examination of the papers. Hedda goes across to the stove and sits in the armchair. Soon after,* BRACK *goes over to her.*]

HEDDA [*Softly.*]   Ah, Judge—This act of Eilert Løvborg's—there's a sense of liberation in it.

BRACK   Liberation, Mrs. Hedda? Yes, I guess it's a liberation for him, all right.

HEDDA   I mean, for me. It's a liberation for me to know that in this world an act of such courage, done in full, free will, is possible. Something bathed in a bright shaft of sudden beauty.

BRACK [*Smiles.*]   Hmm—Dear Mrs. Hedda—

HEDDA   Oh, I know what you're going to say, because you're a kind of specialist too, after all, just like—Ah well.

BRACK [*Looking steadily at her.*]   Eilert Løvborg meant more to you than you might admit—even to yourself. Or am I wrong?

HEDDA   I don't answer questions like that. All I know is that Eilert Løvborg had the courage to live life his own way, and now—his last great act—bathed in beauty. He—had the will to break away from the banquet of life—so soon.

BRACK   It pains me, Mrs. Hedda—but I'm forced to shatter this pretty illusion of yours.

HEDDA   Illusion?

BRACK   Which would have been taken away from you soon enough.

HEDDA   And what's that?

BRACK   He didn't shoot himself—so freely.

HEDDA   Not freely?

BRACK   No. This whole Eilert Løvborg business didn't come off exactly the way I described it.

HEDDA [*In suspense.*]   Are you hiding something? What is it?

BRACK   I employed a few euphemisms for poor Mrs. Elvsted's sake.

HEDDA Such as—?

BRACK First, of course, he's already dead.

HEDDA At the hospital?

BRACK Yes. And without regaining consciousness.

HEDDA What else?

BRACK The incident took place somewhere other than his room.

HEDDA That's insignificant.

BRACK Not completely. I have to tell you—Eilert Løvborg was found shot in—Miss Diana's boudoir.

HEDDA [*About to jump up but sinks back again.*] That's impossible, Judge. He can't have gone there again today.

BRACK He was there this afternoon. He came to demand the return of something that he said they'd taken from him. He talked crazily about a lost child.

HEDDA Ah, so that's why—

BRACK I thought maybe he was referring to his manuscript but I hear he'd already destroyed that himself so I guess it was his pocketbook.

HEDDA Possibly. So—that's where he was found.

BRACK Right there, with a discharged pistol in his coat pocket, and a fatal bullet wound.

HEDDA In the chest, yes?

BRACK No—lower down.

HEDDA [*Looks up at him with an expression of revulsion.*] That too! Oh absurdity—! It hangs like a curse over everything I so much as touch.

BRACK There's still one more thing, Mrs. Hedda. Also in the ugly category.

HEDDA And what is that?

BRACK The pistol he had with him—

HEDDA [*Breathless.*] Well, what about it?

BRACK He must have stolen it.

HEDDA [*Jumping up.*] Stolen? That's not true. He didn't.

BRACK There's no other explanation possible. He must have stolen it— Shh.

[TESMAN *and* MRS. ELVSTED *have gotten up from the table in the rear room and come into the living room.*]

TESMAN [*With papers in both hands.*] Hedda, my dear—I can hardly see anything in there under that lamp. Just think—

HEDDA I'm thinking.

TESMAN Do you think you might let us sit a while at your desk, hm?

HEDDA Oh, gladly. [*Quickly.*] No, wait. Let me just clean it up a bit first.

TESMAN Oh, not necessary, Hedda. There's plenty of room.

HEDDA No, no, I'll just straighten it up, I'm telling you. I'll just move these things here under the piano for a while.

[*She has pulled an object covered with sheet music out of the bookcase. She adds a few more sheets and carries the whole pile out to the left of the rear room.* TESMAN *puts the papers on the desk and brings over the lamp from the corner table. He and* MRS. ELVSTED *sit and continue their work.*]

HEDDA Well, Thea, my sweet. Are things moving along with the memorial?

MRS. ELVSTED [*Looks up at her dejectedly.*] Oh, God—It's going to be so difficult to find the order in all of this.

TESMAN   But it must be done. There's simply no other choice. And finding the order in other people's papers—that's precisely what I'm meant for.
[HEDDA *goes over to the stove and sits on one of the stools.* BRACK *stands over her, leaning over the armchair.*]

HEDDA [*Whispers.*]   What were you saying about the pistol?

BRACK [*Softly.*]   That he must have stolen it.

HEDDA   Why stolen exactly?

BRACK   Because there shouldn't be any other way to explain it, Mrs. Hedda.

HEDDA   I see.

BRACK [*Looks briefly at her.*]   Eilert Løvborg was here this morning, am I correct?

HEDDA   Yes.

BRACK   Were you alone with him?

HEDDA   Yes, for a while.

BRACK   You didn't leave the room at all while he was here?

HEDDA   No.

BRACK   Think again. Weren't you out of the room, even for one moment?

HEDDA   Yes. Perhaps. Just for a moment—out in the hallway.

BRACK   And where was your pistol case at that time?

HEDDA   I put it under the—

BRACK   Well, Mrs. Hedda—

HEDDA   It was over there on the writing table.

BRACK   Have you looked since then to see if both pistols are there?

HEDDA   No.

BRACK   It's not necessary. I saw the pistol Løvborg had, and I recognized it immediately from yesterday, and from before as well.

HEDDA   Have you got it?

BRACK   No, the police have it.

HEDDA   What will the police do with that pistol?

BRACK   Try to track down its owner.

HEDDA   Do you think they can do that?

BRACK [*Bends over her and whispers.*]   No, Hedda Gabler, not as long as I keep quiet.

HEDDA [*Looking fearfully at him.*]   And what if you don't keep quiet—then what?

BRACK   Then the way out is to claim that the pistol was stolen.

HEDDA   I'd rather die.

BRACK [*Smiling.*]   People make those threats but they don't act on them.

HEDDA [*Without answering.*]   So—let's say the pistol is not stolen and the owner is found out? What happens then?

BRACK   Well, Hedda—then there'll be a scandal.

HEDDA   A scandal?

BRACK   Oh, yes, a scandal. Just what you're so desperately afraid of. You'd have to appear in court, naturally. You and Miss Diana. She'd have to detail how it all occurred. Whether it was an accident or a homicide. Was he trying to draw the pistol to threaten her? Is that when the gun went off? Did she snatch it out of his hands to shoot him, and then put the pistol back in his pocket? That would be thoroughly in character for her. She's a feisty little thing, that Miss Diana.

HEDDA   But all this ugliness has got nothing to do with me.

BRACK   No. But you would have to answer one question. Why did you give the pistol to Eilert Løvborg? And what conclusions would people draw from the fact that you gave it to him?

HEDDA   [*Lowers her head.*]   That's true. I didn't think of that.

BRACK   Well. Fortunately you have nothing to worry about as long as I keep quiet.

HEDDA   [*Looking up at him.*]   So I'm in your power now, Judge. You have a hold over me from now on.

BRACK   [*Whispering more softly.*]   Dearest Hedda—Believe me—I won't abuse my position.

HEDDA   But in your power. Totally subject to your demands—And your will. Not free. Not free at all. [*She gets up silently.*] No, that's one thought I just can't stand. Never!

BRACK   [*Looks mockingly at her.*]   One can usually learn to live with the inevitable.

HEDDA   [*Returning his look.*]   Maybe so. [*She goes over to the writing table, suppressing an involuntary smile and imitating* TESMAN's *intonation.*] Well, George, this is going to work out, hm?

TESMAN   Oh, Lord knows, dear. Anyway, at this rate, it's going to be months of work.

HEDDA   [*As before.*]   No, just think. [*Runs her fingers lightly through* MRS. ELVSTED's *hair.*] Doesn't it seem strange, Thea. Here you are, sitting together with Tesman—just like you used to sit with Eilert Løvborg.

MRS. ELVSTED   Oh, God, if only I could inspire your husband too.

HEDDA   Oh, that will come—in time.

TESMAN   Yes, you know what, Hedda—I really think I'm beginning to feel something like that. But why don't you go over and sit with Judge Brack some more.

HEDDA   Can't you two find any use for me here?

TESMAN   No, nothing in the world. [*Turning his head.*] From now on, my dear Judge, you'll have to be kind enough to keep Hedda company.

BRACK   [*With a glance at* HEDDA.]   That will be an infinite pleasure for me.

HEDDA   Thanks, but I'm tired tonight. I'll go in there and lie down on the sofa for a while.

TESMAN   Yes, do that, Hedda, hm?

[HEDDA *goes into the rear room and draws the curtains after her. Short pause. Suddenly she is heard to play a wild dance melody on the piano.*]

MRS. ELVSTED   [*Jumping up from her chair.*]   Oh—what's that?

TESMAN   [*Running to the doorway.*]   Oh, Hedda, my dear—Don't play dance music tonight. Just think of poor Aunt Rina and of Eilert Løvborg too.

HEDDA   [*Putting her head out from between the curtains.*]   And Aunt Julie and all the rest of them too. From now on I shall be quiet. [*She closes the curtains again.*]

TESMAN   [*At the writing table.*]   This can't be making her very happy— Seeing us at this melancholy work. You know what, Mrs. Elvsted—You're going to move in with Aunt Julie. Then I can come over in the evening, and we can sit and work there, hm?

MRS. ELVSTED   Yes, maybe that would be the best—

HEDDA [*From the rear room.*]   I can hear you perfectly well, Tesman. So, how am I supposed to get through the evenings out here?

TESMAN [*Leafing through the papers.*]   Oh, I'm sure Judge Brack will be good enough to call on you.

BRACK [*In the armchair, shouts merrily.*]   I'd be delighted, Mrs. Tesman. Every evening. Oh, we're going to have some good times together, the two of us.

HEDDA [*Loudly and clearly.*]   Yes, that's what you're hoping for, isn't it, Judge? You, the one and only cock of the walk—

[*A shot is heard within.* TESMAN, MRS. ELVSTED *and* BRACK *all jump to their feet.*]

TESMAN   Oh, she's playing around with those pistols again.

[*He pulls the curtains aside and runs in.* MRS. ELVSTED *follows.* HEDDA *is stretched out lifeless on the sofa. Confusion and cries.* BERTA *comes running in from the right.*]

[*Shrieking to* BRACK.] Shot herself! Shot herself in the temple! Just think!

BRACK [*Half prostrate in the armchair.*]   But God have mercy—People just don't act that way!

END OF PLAY

GIOVANNI VERGA
1840–1922

Giovanni Verga startled European readers with harshly powerful evocations of Sicilian peasant life; in novels and tales, he described the primitive struggles and despair of those who were "the doomed" within a stagnant and unjust social order. Verga is the foremost exponent of a particular style of nineteenth-century realism—Italian *verismo* (truthful representation). Unique among nineteenth-century realist writers, he employs a stripped-down, bare-bones, deceptively simple language that has more in common with many twentieth-century novels than with nineteenth-century tradition. D. H. Lawrence, one of his early translators, wrote to a friend that Verga's work was "one of the genuine emotional extremes of European literature" and that the Italian author was at once "peasant—quite modern—Homeric." Lawrence's multifold appreciation is fitting for a writer who influenced both the twentieth-century experimental playwright Luigi Pirandello and the neorealist filmmaker Luchino Visconti.

He was born Giovanni Carmelo Verga in the university city of Catania, Sicily, on September 2, 1840, to Giovanni Battista Verga, a well-to-do gentleman-landowner, and his wife, Caterina Di Mauro Verga, an educated woman who was interested in current literature and ideas. Catania was not a peaceful region: frequently ravaged by cholera and subject to famines, it had for years been torn by political strife as Sicilian nationalists struggled for independence from the Kingdom of The Two Sicilies, a geographic entity that included Naples on the mainland. Three years before Verga's birth, an antigovernment revolt in Catania was bloodily suppressed, and by the time the young writer left home at twenty-five, the island had undergone a revolution and an invasion before being absorbed into the new kingdom of Italy.

Verga attended one of the few secular schools in Catania, where he read the classic

Italian authors as well as local writers. In 1854–55, a violent cholera epidemic struck Sicily, killing thousands and sending all who could to the countryside to flee contamination. Verga went with his family to their country home in Tiepidi, where he explored the countryside, became acquainted with peasant youths his own age, and learned about local "dramas of passion and distress" that he would later fashion into short stories. His teacher in Catania, Antonio Abate, was both a revolutionary nationalist and an author who favored patriotic themes. Verga's first works—novels—showed Abate's influence. Verga also founded with friends two short-lived political weeklies that discussed contemporary Italian issues, for the young writer was beginning to set his sights on the broader audience outside Sicily. Florence, then Italy's capital, was also its main cultural center and a magnet for aspiring writers who wished to cast off provincial ideas and to purify their use of Italian. Verga moved to Florence in 1865 and, for the next three decades, would divide his time between summers in the Sicilian countryside and winters in the north.

In Florence and Milan, Verga met many important writers, critics, and artists. In Florence, he began a lifelong friendship with Luigi Capuana, who would later become known—with Verga—as the founder of *verismo*. Verga was not yet a realist writer, however, and his novels during this period are chiefly tales of doomed passion, the best-known among them *Storia di una capinera* (Sparrow: The Story of a Songbird) (1871). When he moved to Milan in 1872, Verga became part of a lively bohemian society of artists, writers, and composers who frequented the celebrated salon of Countess Maffei. Here he met musicians like Gioacchino Rossini and Gaetano Donizetti, became friends with the librettist Arrigo Boito, and was introduced to the great French naturalist writer Émile Zola. The novels of the Milan years (*Eva, Eros* and *Tigre reale* [Royal Tigress]) continue to investigate the psychology of unhappy love, but with settings that now include both urban society and the Sicilian countryside.

Verga's style began to change at this time. He had read Flaubert, Maupassant, and Zola, and followed the debates over realist style in the French newspapers. Impressed by his friend Luigi Capuana's experiments with clinically accurate description and by the examples of the French realist and naturalist writers, he decided to express his tales of passion in a more stripped-down, objective manner—recording facts but not openly interpreting them. His first book in the new style was *Vita dei campi* (Life in the Fields) (1880), a collection of Sicilian tales that included the famous *Cavalleria Rusticana* (Rustic Chivalry): a tale of lust, jealousy, and death that was later revised as an internationally popular play and subsequently as an opera with music by Pietro Mascagni. Economic themes began to dominate, as he became more and more convinced of the role played by poverty and wealth in human affairs, and by Darwinian concepts of the struggle for existence. He envisaged a novel cycle, on the model of Balzac's *Human Comedy* or Zola's *Rougon-Macquart*, that would depict the struggle for material wealth at all levels of Italian society. This "Sicilian period" contains Verga's greatest work, including the *Novelle rusticane* (Rustic Tales, 1883), from which our story is taken, and ending with the publication of *Mastro-don Gesualdo* in 1889.

As early as 1878, Verga had sketched out detailed plans for a five-volume series, *I Vinti* (The Vanquished), that would describe successive generations of a Sicilian family, the Malavoglia, in their futile struggles to survive and get ahead. Only two volumes were written—*I Malavoglia* (*The House by the Medlar Tree*) (1881) and *Mastro-don Gesualdo* (1888)—but the author's preface to the first volume outlined the thematic structure of the series and echoed naturalist desires to give a scientifically accurate picture of reality. Verga's version of realism, *verismo*, did not claim to emulate scientific method (as did Zola's), but it did move away from romantic musings on human emotions and emphasized the impersonality of narration—a technique that has been labeled "free indirect discourse" and is seen as a predecessor of the interior monologue. The author as a presence disappears from the text: the "truth" of his characters' lives would be conveyed in their own simple language, almost as though the narrative were generated by characters responding to events in the story. Verga wanted "to see with [his characters'] eyes and to speak in their words," an impractical task since Sicilian dialect could not be understood by a large part of his audience. His job, therefore, became the construction of a new literary language, an *Italian* vernacular that would reproduce his characters' thought patterns and the syntactic patterns of their speech.

Verga's new style shocked and disturbed his readers. It was brusque, wasted no words, emphasized dialogue, and rejected both long descriptions and psychological analysis. Moreover, these stories of the countryside were not pastoral romances but grating accounts of the gulf between rich and poor in a society whose economic, political, and religious corruption destroyed individual lives and offered no prospect of change. The tone was bleak, and events were presented starkly, as bare statements of fact. Such a stripped-down, objective style is familiar to twenty-first-century readers, but it dismayed Verga's contemporaries, who ignored or attacked his new work. He tried to recapture his audience with a novel written in his earlier style (*Il marito di Elena* [Helen's Husband], 1882) but soon returned to the second novel of the Malavoglia cycle, *Mastro-don Gesualdo,* which many critics consider his greatest book. Disappointed at its reception and depressed by an extended lawsuit in which he tried to recover money owed him from performances of the immensely popular opera *Cavalleria rusticana,* the author busied himself with smaller projects and, in 1894 retired to Catania, where he also cared for his deceased brother's family. Here he lived a secluded life, traveling occasionally to collect background material for the third volume in the cycle, *The Duchess of Leyra,* writing a few more stories, and adapting previous works for stage of film.

Over the years, Verga's disturbing novels were accepted as masterworks of modern prose, and he himself became a revered figure of Italian literature. Only after his death on January 27, 1922, did it emerge that he had been unable to complete the third volume of *I Vinti,* despite laboring on it for more than two decades. Verga himself attributed his problems to a difficulty in achieving the right language for his characters—language had always anchored his particular brand of realism—since the new novel was set in the world of Palermo's aristocratic society, a change from the peasant settings and speech of his earlier work.

The story printed here, *Freedom,* is taken from the second volume of Sicilian tales and re-creates a bloody peasant uprising and its numbed aftermath. Land reform had been promised as part of the revolution that unseated the Bourbon monarchy, and after the revolution the peasants expected to share in the new division of property. For them, as the story makes clear, "freedom" meant the right to own a piece of land. In fact, however, the crown lands were sold off to those who could pay the purchase price, and the peasants received nothing. Finding themselves excluded by the new owners even from traditional grazing privileges, they rebelled in 1860 in a series of bloody "massacres of the gentry." Verga was twenty years old when one of the most violent uprisings took place in the town of Bronte, on the western slope of Mount Etna, not far from his home. He would have known about the riot and its repression, and he later used all the techniques of *verismo* to re-create those events.

The story begins in the midst of a violent mob scene, in which local peasants take out their stored-up rage against any member of the upper classes whom they can catch or track down. Background information is supplied indirectly, either by significant images or through explanatory dialogue. The tricolor streamer in the first sentence situates the event after Garibaldi's invasion of Sicily in 1860, an invasion that inspired the peasants because it promised an end to feudalism. Their shouts catalog a range of complaints as the peasants strike down the authority figures who have humiliated and exploited them: baron, priest, rich man, policeman, and gamekeeper. But *verismo* is not merely documentation, and Verga's apparently objective descriptions also utilize selected details that have a strong emotional impact and suggest further dimensions of experience. Don Paolo is wearing "an old cap that his daughter had embroidered for him" when he is killed in front of his family, and the horror of the baroness's flight from room to room ahead of the avenging crowd is magnified by the statement "and there were plenty of rooms for her to run through." It is a scene of horrendous butchery that continues throughout the day. But—as the stony aftermath makes clear—affairs soon return to normal; nothing has really changed. The traditional relationships of rich and poor continue, as do the old resentments. In a final tragicomic moment that shows how little significance the concept of freedom has here, the convicted charcoal burner complains that they can't take him to prison because, although he fought for freedom, he hasn't received even a scrap of land.

PRONOUNCING GLOSSARY

The following list uses common English syllables and stress accents to provide rough equivalents of selected names whose pronunciation may be unfamiliar to the general reader.

Giovanni Verga: *joh-vah'-nee vehr'-gah*

Gnà Lucia: *nyah loo-chee'-ah*

verismo: *vehr-eez'-moh*

Freedom[1]

They unfurled a tricolor streamer above the campanile,[2] rang the bells like merry hell, and began shouting "Hooray for freedom!" in the square.

Like the sea in a storm, the crowd foamed and heaved in front of the bigwigs' club, outside the town hall, on the steps leading up to the church: a solid mass of white headscarves, axes and sickles flashing in the sun. Then they burst into a narrow street.

"You, baron, for a start! That's for getting your farm-watchmen to beat up the people!" At the head of the mob, a harridan with ancient hair sticking straight up, armed only with her fingernails.

"You next, priest of the devil, for sucking away our souls!"

"That's for you, rich pig, who grew so fat on the flesh of the poor that you can't even run away!"

"That's for you, constable, for prosecuting no one except the penniless!"

"And that's for you, woodkeepers, for selling the body and soul of yourselves and your neighbors for a couple of *tarì*[3] a day!"

The smell of blood made them drunk. Sickles, hands, rags, stones were all dripping with it. "Get the bigwigs! Get the felt hats![4] Kill 'em! Kill 'em. Get the felt hats!"

Don Antonio was slipping off home through the back streets. The first blow floored him, face bleeding, on to the pavement. "Why? Why d'you want to kill me?"

"You as well! The devil take you!" A crippled street urchin grabbed his filth-covered hat and spat into it. "Down with the felt hats! Hooray for freedom!"

---

1. Translated by G. H. McWilliam. The story is based on a peasant uprising in the town of Bronte, on Mount Etna, in 1860.   2. A bell tower. *Tricolor*: the flag of Garibaldi's army of liberation was red, green, and white; it would become the national flag of Italy.   3. A tarò is a small coin worth about .85 lira.
4. The upper classes wore felt hats; peasants wore caps or berets.

"Take that! You too!" This to The Reverend who preached that anyone stealing bread would go to Hell.

He was on his way back from saying Mass, with the consecrated Host in his belly. "Please don't kill me! I'm in mortal sin!" Gnà[5] Lucia was the mortal sin he meant. Her father had sold her to The Reverend when she was fourteen, the winter of the famine, and she'd been filling the Cloister Wheel[6] and the streets with starving brats ever since. If all that dog's meat were worth anything to them that day, they could have stuffed themselves with it as they went about carving it up with their sickles in the doorways and the cobbled streets. The same thing happens when a starving wolf turns up in a flock of sheep: it doesn't think of filling its belly, but just slaughters everything in sight from pure rage. First, the Grand Lady's son, who had rushed out to see what was happening; then the chemist[7] as he was shutting up shop in a tearing hurry; and then Don Paolo, who was riding back from the vineyard on his donkey with a couple of saddlebags that looked half-empty. And he was even wearing an old cap that his daughter had embroidered for him ages ago, before the disease struck the vineyard. She saw him fall at the front door, as she was waiting with her five children for the few vegetables he had in his saddlebags to make the minestra.[8] "Paolo! Paolo!"

One of them struck him in the back with a blow from an axe. Another fell upon him with a sickle, and ripped him open as his bloody arm was reaching for the door-knocker.

But the worst moment of all was when the notary's son, an eleven-year-old with a head of golden blond hair, managed somehow to fall in the midst of the crowd. His father had raised his head two or three times and called out, 'Neddu! Neddu!' before dragging himself to die in the gutter.

Neddu was running away in absolute terror, eyes and mouth wide open, unable to utter a sound. He took a tumble, and raised himself on one knee, like his father. The torrent poured over him. One of them put the boot in and smashed his cheek, and the boy still pleading for mercy with clasped hands. No, he didn't want to die in the way he'd seen his father killed! It was heartbreaking! The woodcutter, out of pity, landed him a massive blow with his axe using both hands as if he were felling a fifty-year-old oak, as he lay there shaking like a leaf.

Another one cried out, "What the hell! He would only have grown up a lawyer!"

What did it matter? Now they had their hands covered in so much blood, they had to spill all the rest. Get them all! All the felt hats! It was no longer the hunger, the bullying, the beatings, that were fueling their anger. It was innocent blood. The women were even more ferocious, waving their skinny arms, shrieking with anger in high-pitched voices, their tender flesh showing beneath the rags they were wearing. "So much for you, that came praying to the good Lord in your silk dress! And you, that loathed having to kneel alongside the poor! Take that! Take that!" Into the houses, up the stairs, into the bedrooms, tearing up the silk and the fine curtains. No end of ear-rings decorating those bleeding faces! And what a collection of gold rings on the hands trying to ward off the blows from the axes!

5. Signora, Mrs.—i.e., a grown woman.   6. A revolving horizontal wheel fixed into an opening in the wall of an orphanage (usually a convent). Unwanted babies were left anonymously on the wheel outside, a bell was rung, and someone inside came to collect the child, who was raised by the orphanage until he or she grew old enough to work and could be turned over to an employer.   7. Pharmacist.   8. Vegetable soup.

The baroness had ordered a barricade of wooden beams, country carts, and casks full of wine to be placed behind the main entrance. Her watchmen were firing away from the windows to sell their lives dearly. The crowd kept their heads down against the shotgun pellets, having no weapons of their own to fire back. Before all this, anyone carrying firearms faced the death penalty. "Hooray for freedom!" Once they broke down the door, they charged into the courtyard and up the steps, trampling over the wounded. They left the watchmen alone. "We'll get the watchmen later!" First of all they were after the flesh of the baroness, flesh fattened on partridges and precious wines. She was running from one room to the next with a suckling[9] at her breast, hair disheveled, and there were plenty of rooms for her to run through. You could hear the crowd yelling along the corridors, closing in on her like a river in spate.

Her eldest son, a boy of sixteen with a body still as pale as his mother's, propped up the door with his trembling hands, shouting, "Mother! Mother!" At the first push, they crashed the door down on top of him. He clung on to legs stamping over it, but soon stopped shouting. His mother had taken refuge on the balcony, clinging frantically to the baby with a hand over its mouth to stop it bawling. Staring wildly around him, her other son was trying to shield her with his body, grabbing all those axes by the blades as though he had a hundred hands to do it with. They were separated in a flash. One of them took her by the hair, another by the waist, another by her dress, and they lifted her in the air above the balcony rail. The charcoal-burner seized the suckling baby from her arms. The other brother could see nothing of all this, only black and red everywhere. They were stamping on him and breaking every bone in his body with their hob-nailed boots; he had sunk his teeth into a hand that had him by the throat and refused to let it go. The throng was so tightly packed that they were unable to strike with their axes, that were glistening in the air.

And in that raging carnival of the month of July, amid the drunken shouting of the ravenous mob, the church bell went on tolling furiously away until evening, without either noon or Angelus as if in the land of the Turks.[1] Eventually they began to split up, weary of the slaughter and crept slowly away, each avoiding his companion. By nightfall all the doors were closed out of fear, and in every house a lamp kept vigil. In the narrow streets all you could hear were the dogs, rummaging in the corners, gnawing hungrily away at the bones by the light of the moon, which washed over everything and cast its glow over the wide-open doorways and windows of the empty houses.

Daylight came. It was Sunday, with nobody in the square, and no bell ringing for Mass. The sexton[2] had made himself scarce, there was not a priest to be found anywhere. The first group of people to form in front of the church looked suspiciously at one another, each wondering what his neighbor had on his conscience. Then, once a tidy number had turned up, they started to grumble, saying, "People can't go without their Sunday Mass, like a pack of dogs!" The bigwigs club was boarded up, and no one knew where to go to take the masters' orders for the week to follow. From the campanile the

---

9. A nursing baby.   1. The Angelus, a Roman Catholic devotion, was announced by a church bell that rang in the morning, at noon, and in the evening. It would not be rung in a Muslim country like Turkey.
2. A church employee, one of whose tasks was to ring the bells.

tricolor streamer still dangled flabbily in the stifling midsummer heat.

As the shaded area in front of the church grew gradually smaller, they all crowded together in a corner. Between a pair of shabby-looking houses, at the foot of a narrow lane that sloped down steeply from the square, you could see the parched fields of the plain, and the dark woods on the slopes of Mount Etna.[3] Now it was time for them to share out those woods and those fields. Everyone was adding up on his fingers how big his own portion ought to be, and casting hostile glances at his neighbor.

"Freedom meant there was going to be enough for everyone!" they were saying. "That swine of a Nino, and that Ramurazzo, would like to take over from the felt hats, and carry on the bullying where they left off! With no surveyor left to measure out the land, and no notary to put it down in writing, it's everyone for himself, and the devil take the hindmost!"

"And what if you guzzle up your own share in the tavern? Do we have to divide everything up all over again?"

"You call me a thief, and I'll call you a thief. Now there's freedom, anyone can go for a double helping and live it up like the bigwigs!" The woodcutter waved his arm in the air as if he were still wielding his axe.

Next day they heard the general was coming, the one who frightened the life out of people, to deal out justice. You could see the red shirts[4] of his soldiers making their way slowly up the ravine towards the village. All that was needed was to roll boulders down on them and wipe out the lot. But nobody moved. The women were screaming and tearing out their hair. The men, black as coal and with long beards, waited on the hillside, dangling their hands between their thighs, and watched the young soldiers arriving, bending exhausted beneath their rusty old rifles, with that tiny general on his big black horse riding alone ahead of them.

The general had straw brought into the church, and put his boys to bed like a father. In the morning, before dawn, if they failed to get up at the sound of the trumpet, he would ride into the church on horseback, swearing like a Turk. That was the sort of man he was. The first thing he did was to order five or six to be shot: Pippo, the cripple, Pizzanello, whoever happened to come within reach. The woodcutter, while they were making him kneel against the wall of the cemetery, was crying like a child because of something his mother had said to him, and because of the scream she had let out when they tore him away from her arms. From a distance, in the remotest lanes of the village, behind closed doors, that series of rifle shots sounded like rockets going off at festival time.

Afterwards the real judges arrived, bespectacled gents perched on mules, travel weary, who were still complaining about being overworked as they were questioning the accused in the convent refectory.[5] They were seated side by side on the bench, and letting out a groan every time they changed position. The trial went on and on for ages. The ones they found responsible were led away to the city on foot, chained together in pairs, between two lines of soldiers with muskets at the ready. Their womenfolk ran after them beside the country lanes, across plow-land, through cactus groves, vineyards and golden cornfields, staggering along out of breath, calling out to them by name

---

3. A high volcano on the east coast of Sicily.   4. General Nino Bixio, a lieutenant under Garibaldi, whose army of "red shirts" had entered Catania earlier that year.   5. Dining hall.

every time the road turned a corner, and they could see the prisoners' faces. On reaching the city they were locked up in the great, tall prison, huge as a monastery, dotted all over with tiny barred windows. If the women wanted to see their menfolk, it was Mondays only, in the presence of warders, behind the iron gate. The poor wretches inside became more and more pallid-looking in that eternal half-light, never catching a glimpse of the sun. Monday after Monday they became more reticent, hardly giving an answer, complaining less and less. On the other days of the week, if the women were to buzz around the square by the prison, the sentries would threaten them with their rifles. They had no idea what to do for the best, where to find work in the city, or how to get themselves something to eat. The bed in the stable cost two *soldi*,[6] the white bread was no more than a single mouthful and never filled their stomachs. If they huddled down to spend the night in the doorway of a church, the police arrested them. Gradually they returned to the village, first the wives, then the mothers. One fine-looking young woman disappeared in the city and was never heard of again. All the rest of the villagers had returned to what they were doing before. The bigwigs couldn't work their lands by themselves, and the poor couldn't live without the bigwigs. They declared peace.

The orphan of the chemist stole Neli Pirru's wife from him, and thought it a good way of avenging himself against the man who had killed his father. Now and again, when the woman had qualms because she feared her husband would slash her face when he came out of prison, he would say, "Don't worry, he'll never come out." Nobody gave them a second thought any more, except for a few mothers and a few older men whenever they cast their eyes towards the plain, where the city lay, or else on Sundays, when they saw the others calmly discussing their affairs with the bigwigs in front of the club, cap in hand, which only went to show that the poor always came off worse in the end.

The trial lasted three years! Imagine! Three whole years locked up without a glimpse of the sun. The accused looked like so many corpses dug up from the graveyard, every time they were led handcuffed into the courtroom. Everyone who could manage it dashed in from the village as though to a festival: witnesses, relatives, rubbernecks,[7] so as to take a look at their fellow-villagers cooped up in the dock like so many fattening fowl, which was all they became after such a long time in jail. And there was Neli Pirru, standing face to face with the chemist's son, who had played him such a trick to become his in-law!

They were made to stand up one after the other. "What is your name?" And each of them heard himself spouting it out, name, surname and what he had done. The lawyers fought it out in their broad-sleeved gowns amid the hubbub, getting over-excited and foaming at the mouth, then drying themselves off with their white handkerchiefs and taking a pinch of snuff. The judges were dropping off to sleep so often behind their spectacle lenses that your heart absolutely froze. In the jury-box opposite sat twelve good men and true,[8] so tired and bored by the proceedings that they were yawning,

6. Twenty *soldi* made up 1 lira, the basic unit of Italian currency at the time.   7. Gawking onlookers, stretching their necks so as not to miss anything.   8. *Good men and true*: the traditional English expression for members of the jury. The Italian term is *galantuomini*, "gentlemen," translated as "bigwigs" elsewhere in the story.

scratching their beards, or twittering among themselves. Of course people said it was lucky for them that the good men and true were not from that village up in the hills, when they had struck a blow for freedom. The poor devils in the dock tried to read their faces. Then they went away to have a chat among themselves, and the prisoners waited, pale in the face, their eyes fixed on that closed door. When they came back, the foreman, looking almost as white-faced as the accused, speaking with his hand on his belly, said, "On my honor and on my conscience. . . . !"

As they were putting on his handcuffs again, the charcoal-burner muttered, "Where are you taking me? To prison? What for? I never even got a square meter of land out of it! They told me it was all in the cause of freedom . . . !"

GUY DE MAUPASSANT
1850–1893

In a literary tradition that contains many celebrated storytellers, Guy de Maupassant stands out as a virtuoso of the special economy required by short fiction and a creator of utterly convincing portrayals of human behavior. Although he also wrote poetry, plays, and novels, it is the short stories that made their mark on later generations; they provide the yardstick against which all others are measured. Like his mentor, Gustave Flaubert, Maupassant rejected psychological description and believed in the techniques of objective realism. Instead of trying to delve beneath the surface, writers must rely on external appearances to give a sense of reality—just as portrait painters do and just as we do in real life. The world that Maupassant describes, whether of respectable bourgeois, crafty peasants, cuckolded husbands, or patriotic prostitutes, of greed, deception, ambition, or erotic love, is first of all a physical world described with sensuous detail and alive with human desires. His stories capture a slice of life in which something *happens* and offer small, self-contained episodes that are described elegantly, economically, and with an invariably ironic consciousness.

He was born Henri-René-Albert-Guy de Maupassant on August 5, 1850, reportedly in the Château de Miromesnil, Normandy, which had been rented for the occasion by his parents, Gustave de Maupassant and Laure Le Poittevin de Maupassant. Both parents were well-to-do; the Maupassant family had recently been granted recognition as members of the minor nobility (with the privilege of adding *de* before their name), and Maupassant's mother wished her first child to be born in auspicious circumstances. A brother, Hervé, was born six years later, and the family lived in comfort until 1859, when financial reverses forced the father to take a job in a Paris bank. Guy attended school for a year in Paris before he moved, with his mother and brother, to a house that Madame de Maupassant had bought in the seaside village of Étretat in Normandy. The Maupassant marriage was not harmonious, and his father had many affairs. Guy, taking his mother's side, would remain close to her for the rest of his life. The strong-willed Madame de Maupassant was able to obtain a formal separation in 1863, a rare step at that time, which gave her full oversight of both sons.

Guy continued his education in a Catholic boarding school at Yvetot (whose rigidity he hated and from which he managed to get himself expelled) and at Rouen. When he was not in school, he roamed the outdoors, learning how to handle a boat, a lifelong passion and the setting for many stories. He began to write poetry, and his mother arranged for him to meet the novelist Gustave Flaubert, who was a personal friend and who would later become his literary mentor. It was at this time that Maupassant became sexually active, beginning a period of extreme promiscuity (of which he boasted) during which he contracted syphilis, which ultimately caused his death.

Upon receiving his diploma in 1869, he moved to Paris to study law. But the Franco-Prussian War intervened, and Maupassant enlisted in the army. His experiences during the following year gave him material for many stories, the best known of which are *Boule de suif* (Ball of Fat) and *Mademoiselle Fifi*. After the armistice, he returned to Paris, where he resumed his law studies and found a job in the Naval Ministry and subsequently in the Ministry of Public Education. He performed his duties well and was promoted several times, but neither the jobs nor the law interested him. He abandoned law school in 1875 and spent his free time in solitary rowing; in parties on the Seine in a boat owned jointly with friends, carousing at one of the floating cabarets such as La Grenouillère (depicted in a famous painting by Pierre-Auguste Renoir); or in contemporary martial-arts practice (that is, pistol, fencing, and stick). Observing everything, he filed away a range of portraits that would reappear in his fiction—from bargemen and tramps to holidaying bourgeois. Maupassant began to write prose at twenty-three, encouraged by Flaubert but also by the possibility of making money: the newspapers were paying well for short stories to entertain their readers, and he was living on a very small budget.

It is hard to overestimate Flaubert's importance for the young writer. The novelist, who was at the peak of his fame, took an interest in Maupassant not only for family reasons—Maupassant's uncle had been Flaubert's closest friend before he died, and his mother kept up the friendship—but because he considered the young man, who was clearly talented, his disciple. The older writer read Maupassant's drafts and critiqued them over lunch every Sunday during 1875–76, all the time lecturing him on artistic dedication and the principles of realism. Maupassant later described this training as a search for precision and for the right word. Flaubert also advised him to work more.

It was not merely personal advice that Maupassant received from Flaubert. As a constant visitor, Maupassant met many of the important writers of the day—Ivan Turgenev, Émile Zola, Edmond Goncourt, Catulle Mendès—and was able to establish connections among the younger writers that led to the publication of a group volume in 1880, *Les Soirées de Médan* (Evenings in Médan), which was intended by the group as a manifesto of naturalist writing but perhaps even more as a means of calling attention to themselves. Zola was the most noted contributor to the volume. But Maupassant's *Ball of Fat*, the tale of a patriotic prostitute's sacrifice and ostracism in a coach trip during the Franco-Prussian War, was hailed immediately as a masterpiece and made its author's reputation. Henceforth, his stories were eagerly sought after, and his income soared. He wrote articles and stories for various newspapers, especially *Le Gaulois* and the more literary (and scandalous) *Gil Blas*, and took a series of leaves from the Ministry of Public Education before being let go in 1882. During these years, however, he began to show the first symptoms of syphilis, for which there was no cure at the time, and he traveled widely and consulted many doctors in hope of regaining his health.

Between 1880 and 1890, Maupassant published three hundred stories in a variety of styles, many of them for *Gil Blas*. Some were quite long, revealing Flaubert's influence although the novelist had died in 1880. Others were shorter, lively tales, reviving the traditional French conte and composed to meet the demands of rapid journal publication. Maupassant wrote quickly and vividly, attracting a large audience, and—intent on supporting an increasingly luxurious lifestyle—immediately revised groups of stories for publication as a book. There were stories of the Norman countryside and of outings on the Seine; sketches of crafty peasants and of image-conscious bourgeois; stories set in wartime; tales of libertinage, cuckoldry, and fear of cuckoldry but also sympathetic descriptions of the plight of women; and tales of the supernatural that were also tales of horror and madness.

He soon gained an international reputation for superbly constructed stories that were vivid, objective, sensual, and witty as well as extraordinarily lucid and economical of words. Unfortunately for Maupassant, his work (especially the shorter pieces containing a twist at the end) also provided a model for commercial success, and he was widely imitated, adapted, his identity even being stolen. These imitations and forgeries did considerable damage insofar as they established Maupassant's image, for many readers, as a writer of clever but mechanical fiction. Maupassant's own work, however, contains a great deal of complexity and contextual richness and cannot be reduced to a simple plot line.

The novel, however, was considered more prestigious than the short story during the nineteenth century, and Maupassant wanted to be known as novelist, like his mentor, Flaubert. He develops similar themes at greater length, following the careers of individual characters throughout novels like *Une vie* (A Woman's Life, 1883), whose protagonist is betrayed or exploited by the various men in her life, or *Bel-Ami* (1885), about an opportunistic journalist named Georges Duroy but nick-named "Bel-Ami" for his successes with women. Grounded in historical reality, *Mont-Oriol* (1887) chronicles the discovery of mineralized springs in a small Auvergne town and the subsequent establishment of a thermal station. The larger canvas enabled Maupassant to take up larger political questions such as the abuse of power by the press, or France's colonial policy in northern Africa, or medical quackery and unethical business practices. His best-known novel is *Pierre et Jean* (1888), a psychological exploration of the jealousy and growing alienation of a man who has discovered that his brother—who received a large inheritance from a family friend—is the fruit of their mother's infidelity.

The last years of Maupassant's life were shadowed by the progress of his illness and by the terrifying example of his brother Hervé's insanity and death in 1889. He found it difficult to write: his eyes would not focus, he had frequent migraine headaches and could not concentrate, he took drugs for severe stomach pains, and he suffered from hallucinations. Despite these problems, he kept writing to pay his bills and to support his aging mother and his brother's family. A letter in 1890 wails: "My state is well expressed by the howling of certain dogs—a lamentable complaint addressed to nothing, reaching nowhere, saying nothing, but flinging into the night the cry of chained-up anguish that I should like to utter." He consulted at least twelve doctors without improvement and, after attempting suicide in January 1892, was confined to a mental hospital outside Paris, where his condition deteriorated rapidly. His death from advanced syphilis came on July 6, 1892, a month before his forty-third birthday.

The story printed here, *Hautot and His Son* (Hautot Père et Fils), is taken from *La Main gauche* (The Left Hand, 1889), one of the last two collections published during Maupassant's lifetime. Marriage "on the left hand" is an expression for unrecognized or common-law marriages, like that of Caroline Donet and Hautot senior in this story. *Hautot* is also one of the stories that were pirated and rewritten for a New York newspaper, the *Star*, in 1891, and the pirated version demonstrates the superbly economical construction of Maupassant's original text. Whereas Maupassant's story consists of a taut three-way relationship among the elder Hautot, his son, César, and Caroline Donet, the "English adaptation" by a Philippe Prévost muddles both plot and characters when it adds another woman, whose rejection of César sends him to Caroline. The first story limits itself to three main characters and creates complex psychological and social portraits from the relationship between them. Hautot senior, a forceful and dominating landowner, has tried to raise his son in his own image; but

Hautot junior—obedient, loving, and submissive—is not the same man. What he has become at the end of the story is a question for the reader. Caroline Donet, introduced as Hautot's mistress, is subsequently portrayed as a sympathetic and responsible woman whose quick intelligence immediately (although invisibly and diplomatically) masters the situation; she, like Hautot senior, knows how to take charge. It is worth mentioning that single unattached women found themselves in an impossible economic position at this time: the only respectable jobs open to them were as seamstress or milliner, and, living alone, their moral position was so questionable that they could be arrested at any time on suspicion of prostitution. Maupassant's famous objective style depicts contemporary social contexts in addition to individual psychology and is seen especially well in dialogues—such as that between father and son or Caroline and César—that let the characters define themselves and their relationship without authorial commentary. Indeed, the only place where one can see Maupassant's hand may be in the satirical description of César's embarrassed thoughts as he hesitates before confronting his father's mistress. The author explores many familiar themes: the Norman countryside and the importance given to property; family relationships, including extramarital affairs and questions of illegitimacy; the role of women; and the mockery of bourgeois values. In contrast to Maupassant's harsher stories, this tale is permeated with sympathy for its characters and with an unexpectedly gentle humor.

PRONOUNCING GLOSSARY

The following list uses common English syllables and stress accents to provide rough equivalents of selected names whose pronunciation may be unfamiliar to the general reader.

Caroline Donet: *cah-roh-leen' doh-nay'*   César Hautot: *say-zahr' oh-toh'*
Eperlan: *ay-pehr-lahnh'*   Graindorge: *granh-dorzh'*
Guy de Maupassant: *gee deuh*   Moreau: *Mo-roh'*
      moh-pah-sahnh'   Puysatier: *pwee-zah-tyay'*

Hautot and His Son[1]

I

In front of the building, half farm-house, half manor-house—one of those semi-feudal country dwellings of mixed character now occupied by wealthy farmers—the dogs chained to the apple-trees in the court-yard were barking and howling at the sight of the bags carried by the gamekeepers, and at the mischievous boys. In the large dining-room-kitchen, Hautot and his son, M. Bermont the tax-collector, and M. Mondaru the notary, were having a bite and a mouthful of wine before they went out shooting, for it was the first day of the season.

The elder Hautot, proud of his possessions, was boasting of the game that his guests would find in his shoot. He was a big Norman, one of those powerful, ruddy, big-boned men who can lift a cart-load of apples on to their shoulders. Half peasant, half gentleman, rich, respected, influential, auto-

---

1. Written in 1883; published in 1889. Translated by Margaret Storm Jameson.

cratic, he had first insisted that his son César should work up to the third form[2] so that he might be well informed, and then he had stopped his education for fear of his becoming a fine gentleman without any interest in the farm.

Nearly as tall as his father, but thinner, César Hautot was a good son, docile, contented, full of admiration and respect and regard for the wishes and opinions of the elder Hautot.

M. Bermont, the tax-collector, a short stout man whose red cheeks showed a thin network of violet veins like the tributaries and winding streams of a river on a map, asked:

"And hares—are there any hares?"

The elder Hautot replied:

"As many as you please, especially in the hollows of Puysatier."

"Where shall we begin?" asked the good-natured notary; he was pale and fat, his flesh bulging out in his tight-fitting, brand-new shooting-kit recently bought at Rouen.[3]

"In that direction, through the bottoms. We will drive the partridges into the open and fall upon them."

Hautot got up. The others followed his example, took their guns from the corner, examined the locks, stamped their feet to ease them in their boots, not yet softened by the warmth within. Then they went out, and the dogs straining at the leash barked and beat the air with their paws.

They set out towards the hollows, which were in a little glen, or rather in a long undulating stretch of poor land unfit for cultivation, furrowed with ditches and covered with ferns—an excellent preserve for game.

The sportsmen took their places, Hautot senior to the right, Hautot junior to the left, with the two guests in the center. The keepers and game-bag carriers followed. The solemn moment had come when sportsmen are waiting for the first shot, their hearts beating more rapidly, and their nervous fingers unable to leave the trigger alone.

Suddenly there was a shot. Hautot had fired. They all stopped and saw a partridge, one of a covy flying as swiftly as possible, drop into a ditch covered with thick shrubs. The excited sportsman started to run, taking big strides, dragging aside the briers in his path, and disappeared into the thicket to look for the bird.

Almost immediately a second shot was heard.

"Ha! Ha! the rascal," exclaimed M. Bermont, "he must have started a hare from the undergrowth."

They all waited with eyes fixed on the mass of dense underwood. The notary, making a trumpet of his hands, shouted: "Have you got them?"

As there was no reply from the elder Hautot, César, turning towards the gamekeeper, said: "Go and help him, Joseph. We must keep in line. We'll wait."

And Joseph, a man with an old, lean body and swollen joints, set off at an easy pace down to the ditch, searching for a suitable opening with the caution of a fox. Then, suddenly, he shouted: "Oh, hurry up! Hurry up! There has been an accident!"

They all hurried along and plunged through the briers. Hautot had fallen

---

2. A basic education; third-form pupils were fourteen years old.   3. A major city in Normandy.

on his side in a faint with both hands pressed on his abdomen, from which long trickles of blood flowed on to the grass through his linen jacket torn by a bullet. In letting go of his gun to pick up the dead partridge that lay within reach, he had dropped it and the second discharge going off in the fall had torn open his bowels. They drew him out of the ditch, undressed him and saw a frightful wound through which the intestines protruded. Then after binding him up as well as they could they carried him home and waited for the doctor who had been sent for, as well as the priest.

When the doctor arrived, he shook his head gravely, and turning towards young Hautot, who was sobbing on a chair, he said:

"My poor boy, this looks bad."

But when the wound was dressed, the patient moved his fingers, first opened his mouth, then his eyes, cast around him a troubled, haggard glance, then appeared to be trying to recall, to understand, and he murmured:

"Good God, I am done for."

The doctor held his hand.

"No, no; a question of a few days' rest, it will be all right."

Hautot resumed:

"I am done for! I am torn to bits! I know!"

Then, suddenly:

"I want to talk to my son, if there is time."

In spite of himself, César was weeping, and repeated like a little boy:

"Papa, papa, poor papa!"

But the father said in a more determined tone:

"Come, stop crying, this is no time for tears. I have something to say to you. Sit down there, close to me, it will soon be over, and I shall be easier in my mind. You others, please leave us alone for a minute."

As soon as they were alone:

"Listen, my boy. You are twenty-four, one can talk to you. After all there is not such a mystery about these matters as we attach to them. You know that your mother has been dead seven years and that I am only forty-five, seeing that I married when I was nineteen. Is that not true?"

The son stammered:

"Yes, quite true."

"So then your mother has been dead for seven years, and I am still a widower. Well! a man like me cannot remain a widower at thirty-seven, you agree?"

The son replied:

"That's quite true."

Gasping for breath, very pale and his face drawn with pain, the father continued:

"God! how I suffer! Well, you understand. Man is not made to live alone, but I did not want to give your mother a successor, since I had promised I would not do so. Well . . . you understand?"

"Yes, father."

"Well, I kept a girl at Rouen, number 18 Rue de l'Éperlan, the second door on the third floor—I am telling you all this, don't forget—this young girl has been as nice as nice to me, loving, devoted, a real wife. You understand, my lad?"

"Yes, father."

"Well, if I am taken, I owe her something, something substantial that will place her out of the reach of want. You understand?"

"Yes, father."

"I tell you she is good, really good, and but for you and the memory of your mother and also because we three lived here together in this house, I would have brought her here, and then married her, sure enough . . . listen . . . listen . . . my lad, I might have made a will . . . I have not done so! I did not want to . . . you must never write things down . . . not things of that sort . . . it is bad for the rightful heirs . . . then it muddles up everything . . . it ruins everyone. . . . Look you, never go in for legal documents, never have anything to do with them. If I am rich it is because I have avoided them all my life. You understand, my boy!"

"Yes, father."

"Now listen. . . . Listen attentively. . . . So I have made no will. . . . I did not want to. . . . Besides, I know you, you are kind-hearted, you are not greedy, not stingy. I said to myself that when I saw the end within sight, I would tell you all about it and would beg you not to forget my darling: Caroline Donet, 18 Rue de l'Éperlan, the second door on the right, don't forget. Further, go there directly I am gone—and make such arrangements that she will have no reason to complain. You have plenty. . . . You can spare it.—I am leaving you well provided for. Listen! You won't find her at home on week-days. She works at Madame Moreau's in the Rue Beauvoisine.[4] Go on a Thursday. She always expects me on Thursdays. It has been my day for six years. Poor thing, how she will cry! I tell you all this, my boy, because I know you so well. You cannot tell these things to everybody, either to the notary or to the priest. These things happen, everyone knows that, but no one talks about them except when they are obliged. Then again there must be no outsider in the secret, nobody except the family, because a family is the same as an individual! You understand?"

"Yes, father."

"You promise?"

"Yes, father."

"You swear to this?"

"Yes, father."

"I beg, I pray, do not forget, my boy. It means so much to me."

"No, father."

"You will go yourself. I want you to make sure of everything."

"Yes, father."

"And then, you will see . . . you will see what she says. I can't tell you more about it. You swear?"

"Yes, father."

"That's right, my boy. Embrace me. Adieu, I am done for, I know it. Tell the others they may come in."

The son embraced his father, sobbing as he did so, then, obedient as usual, he opened the door and the priest appeared in a white surplice carrying the holy oils.

But the dying man had closed his eyes and refused to open them again, he would not make any response nor would he make any sign to show that he understood.

4. An actual street in Rouen.

The man had talked enough, he could not continue. Besides, he now felt quiet in his mind and wanted to die in peace. He felt no need to confess to the priest when he had just made his confession to his son who at all events belonged to the family.

Surrounded by his friends and servants on their bended knees, he received the last rites, was purified, and was given absolution, no change of expression on his face showing that he still lived.

He died towards midnight after four hours of convulsive movements indicating terrible suffering.

II

He was buried on Tuesday, the shooting season having opened on Sunday. On returning home from the cemetery César Hautot spent the rest of the day weeping. He scarcely slept that night and felt so sad when he awoke that he wondered how he could manage to go on living.

However, until evening he kept on thinking that in accordance with his father's dying wish he must go to Rouen the following day, and see this girl, Caroline Donet, who lived at 18 Rue de l'Éperlan, the second door on the third story. He went on repeating the blindly obeyed the will of his dead father. But now name and address under his breath—just as a prayer is repeated—so as not to forget, and he ended by stammering them unceasingly, without thinking about anything, to such a point had his mind become obsessed by the set phrase.

Accordingly, about eight o'clock next day he ordered Graindorge to be harnessed to the tilbury and set out at the long, swinging pace of the heavy Norman horse along the high road from Ainville to Rouen. He was wearing a black frock-coat, a silk hat, and trousers strapped under his shoes. Owing to the circumstances he had not put on his flowing blue blouse, so easily taken off at the journey's end, over his black clothes to protect them from dust and dirt.

He got to Rouen just as it was striking ten, put up as usual at the Hôtel des Bons Enfants,[5] in the Rue des Trois-Mares, submitted to being embraced by the landlord, his wife and their five sons, for they had heard the sad news; later on he had to tell them all about the accident, which made him shed tears, repel their offers of service thrust upon him on account of his wealth, and even refuse luncheon, which hurt their feelings.

Having wiped the dust off his hat, brushed his coat and cleaned his boots, he started off to seek the Rue de l'Eperlan without daring to make any inquiries, for fear of being recognized and of arousing suspicion.

At last, unable to find the place, he caught sight of a priest, and trusting to the professional discretion of the priesthood, he asked for help.

It was only about one hundred steps farther on—the second street to the right.

Then he hesitated. Up to the present he had felt agitated, confused, humiliated at the idea of finding himself—he, the son—in the presence of the woman who had been his father's mistress.

All our better feelings developed by centuries of family training, all that he had been taught since early childhood about women of loose character,

5. Literally, the "Good Children's Hotel."

the instinctive distrust that all men feel of these women even when they marry them, all his narrow-minded peasant virtue; all combined to disturb him, to make him hesitate, and fill him with shame.

But he said to himself: "I promised my father. I must not fail." So he pushed the partly-opened door of number 18, discovered a dark staircase, went up three flights, saw first one door, then a second, then found a bell rope, which he pulled.

The ding-dong that sounded in the next room sent a shiver through his body. The door opened and he found himself face to face with a well-dressed young lady, a brunette with rosy cheeks, who gazed at him with eyes full of astonishment.

He did not know what to say, and she, who suspected nothing and was expecting the father, did not invite him in. They looked at each other about thirty seconds until, at last, she said:

"What do you want, sir?"

He muttered:

"I am the young Hautot."

She started, turned pale, and stammered as if she had known him for a long time:

"Monsieur César?"

"Yes."

"Well?"

"I have a message for you from my father."

She exclaimed: "My God!" and moved away so that he might enter. He closed the door and followed her.

Then he caught sight of a little boy of four or five years playing with a cat, seated on the ground in front of a stove from which rose the odor of food being kept hot.

"Sit down," she said.

He sat down. She said: "Well?"

He dare not say anything, he fixed his eyes on the table standing in the middle of the room that was laid for two grown-ups and a child. He looked at the chair with its back to the fire, the plate, the table napkin and glasses, the bottle of red wine already opened, and the bottle of white wine still uncorked. That was his father's chair, with its back to the fire. They were expecting him. That was his bread near the fork, he knew that because the crust had been removed on account of Hautot's bad teeth. Then, raising his eyes, he noticed his father's portrait hanging on the wall, the large photograph taken at Paris the year of the Exhibition,[6] the same one that hung above the bed in the room at Ainville.

The young woman asked again:

"Well, Monsieur César?"

She stared at him. Her face was deathly white with anxiety, and she waited, her hands trembling with fear.

Then he picked up courage:

"Well, Miss, papa died on Sunday, the first day of the season."

She was too overcome to make any movement. After a silence of a few seconds, she faltered almost inaudibly:

---

6. Probably a reference to the upcoming Exposition Universelle (World's Fair) of 1889 in Paris, at which the Eiffel Tower was introduced.

"Oh, it's not possible?"

Then the tears came to her eyes, and covering her face with her hands, she burst out sobbing.

Seeing his mother cry, the little boy turned round and began to roar at the top of his voice. Then, understanding that the sudden grief was caused by the unknown visitor, he threw himself upon César, caught hold of his trousers with one hand and hit his shins as hard as he could with the other. César felt bewildered, deeply affected, thus placed between the woman mourning for his father, and the child who was defending his mother. Their emotion communicated itself to him and his eyes filled with tears, so, to regain his self-control, he began to talk.

"Yes," he said, "the accident occurred on Sunday morning, at eight o'clock." And he told the story in detail, as if she were listening to him, mentioning the most trivial matters with the characteristic thoroughness of the peasant. The child, who had kept on beating César, was now kicking his ankles.

When he reached the point of Hautot's anxiety for her, she heard her name mentioned and, taking her hands from face, asked:

"Excuse me! I was not following you. I would like to know—would it be a bother to you to begin all over again?"

He began the story in the same words: "The accident occurred Sunday morning at eight o'clock."

He repeated everything, at great length, with pauses and occasional reflections of his own. She listened eagerly, feeling with a woman's keen sensitiveness the events as they were unfolded, and, trembling with horror, exclaimed at intervals: "My God!" The boy, thinking that she was all right again, took hold of his mother's hand instead of beating César, and listened attentively as if he understood what was happening.

When the story was finished, young Hautot continued:

"Now, we'll settle matters together according to his wishes. Listen! I am well off, he has left me plenty. I don't want you to have anything to complain about."

She interrupted quickly:

"Oh! Mr. César, not to-day. My heart is . . . Another time . . . another day. . . . No, not to-day. . . . If I accept, listen . . . it is not for myself . . . no, no, no, I swear. It is for the child. Besides, what you give will be placed to his account."

Whereupon César, feeling troubled, guessed the truth and stammered:

"So then . . . it is his . . . the little one?"

"Why, yes," she said.

The young Hautot looked at his brother with confused feelings both intense and painful.

After a long silence, for she was crying again, César, very embarrassed, went on:

"Well, Mam'zelle[7] Donet, I am going. When would you like to talk this over?"

She exclaimed:

"Oh! no, don't go! don't go! Don't leave me all alone with Emile. I would die of grief. I have nobody in the world, nobody but my little one. Oh! what

7. I.e., "Mademoiselle" or "Miss."

misery, what misery, Mr. César. Do sit down. Tell me some more. Tell me how he spent his time at home."

César, accustomed to obey, sat down again.

She drew another chair near to his, in front of the stove on which the food prepared for lunch was bubbling, took Emile on her lap and asked César hundreds of questions about his father—such simple questions about his ordinary everyday life that without reasoning on the subject he felt that she had loved Hautot with all the strength of her aching heart.

And by the natural association of his scanty thoughts he returned to the accident and began to tell her all about it again giving the same details as before.

When he said: "He had a hole in the stomach into which you could put your two fists," she uttered a faint cry and her eyes again filled with tears. Infected by her grief, César began to weep too, and as tears always soften the heart, he bent over Emile, whose forehead was close to his own mouth, and kissed him.

Recovering her breath, the mother murmured:

"Poor boy, he is an orphan now."

"And so am I," said César.

They said no more.

But suddenly the housewife's practical instinct, accustomed to think of everything, reawakened.

"I expect you have had nothing to eat this morning, Mr. César?"

"No, mam'zelle."

"Oh! You must be hungry. You will have a bite?"

"Thank you," he said, "I am not hungry; I have been too worried."

She replied:

"In spite of grief one must go on living, you are surely not going to refuse. Then that will keep you here a little longer. When you are gone, I don't know what I shall do."

He yielded after a little hesitation, and sitting down with his back to the fire, facing her, he ate some of the tripe that was crackling in the oven and drank a glass of red wine. But he would not allow her to uncork the white wine. Several times he wiped the small boy's mouth who had smeared his chin all over with gravy.

As he got up to go, he asked:

"When would you like me to come back to talk the matter over, Mam'zelle Donet?"

"If it is all the same to you, next Thursday, Mr. César. I shall not waste any time that way, as I am always free on Thursdays."

"That will suit me—next Thursday."

"You will come to lunch, won't you?"

"Oh! as for that, I can't promise."

"Well, you know, it is easier to talk when eating. Besides, there is more time."

"Well, all right. At twelve o'clock then."

And off he went after having kissed little Emile and shaken hands with Mademoiselle Donet.

III

The week seemed long to César Hautot. He had never felt so lonely, and the solitude seemed unbearable. Hitherto he had lived with his father, just like his shadow, following him to the fields and superintending the execution of his orders; and when he did leave him for a short time it was only to meet again at dinner. They spent their evenings sitting opposite each other, smoking their pipes and talking about horses, cows or sheep; and the handshake they exchanged every morning was the symbol of deep family affection.

Now César was alone. He strolled about looking on while the harvesters worked, expecting at any moment to see his father's tall gesticulating form at the far end of a field. To kill time he visited his neighbors, telling all about the accident to those who had not already heard it and telling it over again to those who had. Then having reached the end of all that interested him, he would sit down at the side of the road and wonder whether this kind of life would last very long.

He often thought of Mademoiselle Donet. He remembered her with pleasure. He had found her ladylike, gentle and good, exactly as father had described her. Undoubtedly, so far as goodness was concerned, she was good. He was determined to do the thing handsomely and give her two thousand francs a year, settling the capital on the child. He even felt a certain pleasure at the prospect of seeing her again on the following Thursday, and making all the arrangements for her future. Then, although the idea of the brother, the little chap of five—his father's son—did worry and annoy him, it also filled him with a friendly feeling. This illegitimate youngster, though he would never bear the name of Hautot, was, in a sense, a member of the family life, whom he might adopt or abandon as he pleased but who would always remind him of his father.

So that when, on Thursday morning, he was trotting along the road to Rouen on Graindorge's back, he felt lighter-hearted, more at peace than he had done since his bereavement.

On entering Mademoiselle Donet's apartment, he saw the table laid as on the previous Thursday, the only difference being that the crust had been left on the bread.

He shook hands with the young woman, kissed Emile on both cheeks and sat down feeling more or less at home in spite of his heart being heavy. Mademoiselle Donet seemed to him to have grown thinner and paler. She must have wept bitterly. She appeared rather awkward in his presence, as if she now understood what she had not felt the previous week when under the first impression of her loss. She treated him with exaggerated respect, showing stricken humility, and waiting upon him with solicitude as if to repay by her attentions and devotion the kindness he had shown her. The lunch dragged on as they discussed the business that had brought him to the house. She did not want so much money. It was too much, far too much. She earned enough to keep herself and she only wanted Emile to find a small sum awaiting him when he was grown up. César was firm, and even added a present of one thousand francs for her mourning.

When he had finished his coffee, she asked:

"Do you smoke?"

"Yes . . . I have my pipe."

He felt his pocket. Good heavens! he had forgotten it. He was quite miserable until she brought out his father's pipe, which had been put away in a cupboard. He accepted her offer of the pipe, took hold of it, recognized it and smelled it, said what a good one it was, in a voice choked with feeling, filled it with tobacco and lighted it. Then he set Emile astride on his knee and let him play at horses while the mother removed the table-cloth and put the dirty dishes aside in the bottom of the cupboard, intending to wash up as soon as he had gone.

About three o'clock he got up reluctantly, very depressed at the idea of leaving.

"Well, Mademoiselle Donet," he said, "I wish you good afternoon. It has been a pleasure to make your further acquaintance."

She stood before him, blushing, deeply moved, and gazed at him while she thought of the father.

"Shall we never see each other again?" she said.

He replied simply:

"Why, yes, Mademoiselle, if it give you any pleasure."

"Indeed it will, Mr. César. So till next Thursday, if that suits you?"

"Yes, Mademoiselle Donet."

"You will come to lunch, without fail?"

"Well—as you are so kind, I won't refuse."

"It's settled then, next Thursday, at twelve, the same as to-day."

"Thursday at twelve, Mademoiselle Donet!"

ANTON CHEKHOV
1860–1904

In plays and stories Anton Chekhov depicts Russia around the turn of the twentieth century with great pity, gentleness, and kindness of heart. More important, with a deep humanity that has outlasted all the problems of his time, he dramatizes universal and almost timeless feelings rather than ideas that date and pass. He differs sharply from the two giants of Russian literature, Dostoevsky and Tolstoy. For one thing, his work is of smaller scope. With the exception of an immature, forgotten novel and a travel book, he wrote only short stories and plays. He belongs, furthermore, to a very different moral and spiritual atmosphere. Chekhov had studied medicine and practiced it for a time. He shared the scientific outlook of his age and had too skeptical a mind to believe in Christianity or in any metaphysical system. He confessed that an intelligent believer was a puzzle to him. His attitude toward his materials and characters is detached, "objective," and his letters to friends insist that a good writer must present both physical details and a character's state of mind without overt interpretation or judgment. He is thus much more in the stream of Western realism than either Tolstoy or Dostoevsky, and the delicate, precise realism of his short stories has served as a model for later writers in Europe, China, and the United States. But extended reading of Chekhov does convey an impression of his view of life. There is implied in his stories a philosophy of kindness and humanity, a love of beauty, a sense of the unexplainable mystery of life, a sense, especially, of the individual's utter loneliness in this universe and among other people. Chekhov's pessimism has nothing of the defiance of the universe or the horror at it that we meet in other writers with similar attitudes; it is somehow merely sad, often pathetic, and yet also comforting and comfortable.

The Russia depicted in Chekhov's stories and plays is of a later period than that presented by Tolstoy and Dostoevsky. It seems to be nearing its end; there is a sense of decadence and frustration that heralds the approach of catastrophe. The aristocracy still keeps up a beautiful front but is losing its fight without much resistance, resignedly. Officialdom is stupid and venal. The Church is backward and narrow-minded. The intelligentsia are hopelessly ineffectual, futile, lost in the provinces or absorbed in their egos. The peasants live subject to the lowest degradations of poverty and drink, apparently rather aggravated than improved since the much-heralded emancipation of the serfs in 1861. There seems no hope for society except in a gradual spread of enlightenment, good sense, and hygiene, for Chekhov is skeptical of the revolution and revolutionaries as well as of Tolstoy's followers.

Anton Pavlovich Chekhov was born on January 17, 1860, at Taganrog, a small town on the Sea of Azov. His father was a grocer and haberdasher; his grandfather, a serf who had bought his freedom. Chekhov's father went bankrupt in 1876, and the family moved to Moscow, leaving Anton to finish school in his home town. After his graduation in 1879, he followed his family to Moscow, where he studied medicine. To earn additional money for his family and himself, he started to write humorous sketches and stories for magazines. In 1884 he became a doctor and published his first collection of stories, *Tales of Melpomene*. Over the next several years, two collections of light comic tales brought him success and the opportunity to publish serious literature regularly in Moscow's largest daily newspaper, the *New Times*. In 1884, he also had his first hemorrhage. All the rest of his life he struggled against tuberculosis. His first play, *Ivanov*, was performed in 1887; and by 1889 he had written nine volumes of short stories. The next year, he undertook an arduous journey through Siberia to the island of Sakhalin (north of Japan) and back by boat through the Suez Canal. He saw there the Russian penal settlements and wrote a moving account of his trip in *Sakhalin Island* (1892). In 1898 his play *The Sea Gull* was a great success at the Moscow Art Theater. The next year he moved to Yalta, in the Crimea, and in 1901 married the actress Olga Knipper. He died in July 1904 in Badenweiler in the Black Forest.

Chekhov's stories explore small but significant events in ordinary lives, emphasizing the twists and turns of interpersonal relations rather than (for example) the inexorably advancing plot recommended by Edgar Allan Poe. Whether it is a cabdriver's frustrated attempt to tell his fares about his son's recent death (*Misery*), a widow's final happiness in caring for another woman's child (*The Darling*), a retired clerk's delight in his gooseberry bushes (*Gooseberries*), or the aftermath of a businessman's brief affair at a resort (*The Lady with the Dog*), the author focuses on his characters' inner lives. They meditate on their own actions; observe the beauties of nature; wax philosophical about society or human nature; and, most of all, react to the presence of other people. Typically, however, these characters find it hard to communicate with each other and frequently cannot do so at all; isolated in their own private worlds, they rarely make contact with the world of another. Successful or not, these relationships are all-important: they motivate events, illuminate actions, and shape the conclusion, which generally rounds off a stage in the character's life rather than resolving all issues. Chekhov's endings are famously ambiguous, and his conclusions remain—like events in real life—preludes to various possible sequels.

The Lady with the Dog is one of Chekhov's best-known stories. Published in 1899, it tells of a love affair that has sprung up between a man and woman vacationing in Yalta. Both are married, but not to each other, and each expects the affair to be a brief episode; one of many affairs for the banker Dmitri Gurov, and a single experience of romantic love for the dissatisfied Anna Sergeyevna von Diederitz. Anna Sergeyevna, the lady of the title, appears first as a nameless figure known only through local gossip.

She is a tourist, walking her dog at a Crimean resort known for brief liaisons. Married young to an unimaginative minor official in a small town, she is bored, has probably read romantic novels, and is willing to risk anything rather than having her entire life pass without an intense experience. Dmitri Gurov, a prosperous Moscow bank official who likes the company of women, decides on a whim to seduce her and soon succeeds.

The physical seduction is strikingly minimized (quite unlike modern fiction); it happens offstage and is merely indicated through subsequent conversation revealing the couple's different reactions. Chekhov shows Gurov thinking about his various former lovers, and Anna Sergeyevna in self-conscious despair at having passed from the role of "lady with the dog" to that of a "fallen woman." He eats watermelon slices while she weeps (in a later scene, he drinks tea). Despite Anna Sergeyevna's remorse, with which Gurov fails to sympathize and in fact is utterly bored, neither is able to forget the other, and the affair resumes a few months after both have returned home. Anna continues to suffer over her position, and Gurov retreats from emotional entanglement into his role as man-about-town; she cannot bear living a double life, but he enjoys the contrast of public and private roles.

The story does not focus solely on the success or failure of a difficult love affair, nonetheless. As the relationship evolves, the protagonists emerge from the near stereotypes of the beginning to individual personalities possessing a great deal of depth, ambiguity, and—perhaps—openness to change. Gurov's development from a self-satisfied to a self-conscious lover is particularly emphasized; it is his thoughts that we follow as he perceives Anna Sergeyevna first as an object of seduction, later as a woman tragically in love with him, and finally as his true partner. The gulf between the two remains unchanged until he looks in the mirror and realizes his own mortality; suddenly, a feeling of shared vulnerability enables him to reach out to Anna Sergeyevna. Whether or not it enables them to find a satisfactory solution to their dilemma is another question. If the conclusion of the story leaves the lovers' future undecided, it also demonstrates that any sequel we may imagine (and readers usually try to) must take into account both historical possibility and also our idea of what the characters have become.

The plays of Chekhov seem to go furthest in the direction of naturalism, the depiction of a "slice of life," on stage. Compared with Ibsen's plays they seem plotless; they could be described as a succession of little scenes, composed like a mosaic or like the dots or strokes in an Impressionist painting. The characters rarely engage in the usual dialogue; they speak often in little soliloquies, hardly justified by the situation; and they often do not listen to the words of their ostensible partners. They seem alone even in a crowd. Human communication seems difficult and even impossible. There is no clear message, no zeal for social reform; life seems to flow quietly, even sluggishly, until interrupted by some desperate outbreak or even a pistol shot.

Chekhov's last play, *The Cherry Orchard* (written in 1903, first performed at the Moscow Art Theater on January 17, 1904), differs, however, from this pattern in several respects. It has a strongly articulated central theme—the loss of the orchard—and it has a composition that roughly follows the traditional scheme of a well-made play. Arrival and departure from the very same room, the nursery, frame the two other acts: the outdoor idyll of Act II and the dance in Act III. Act III is the turning point of the action: Lopahin appears and announces, somewhat shamefacedly, that he has bought the estate. The orchard was lost from the very beginning—there is no real struggle to prevent its sale—but still the news of Lopahin's purchase is a surprise since he had no intention of buying it but did so only when during the auction sale a rival seemed to have a chance of acquiring it. A leading action runs its course, and many—one may even argue too many—subplots crisscross each other: the shy and awkward love affair of the student Trofimov and the daughter Anya; the love triangle among the three dependents, Yepihodov (the unlucky clerk), Dunyasha (the chambermaid), and Yasha (the conceited and insolent footman). Varya, the practical stepdaughter, has her troubles with Lopahin, and Simeonov-Pishchik is beset by the same financial problems as the owners of the orchard and is rescued by the discovery of some white clay on his estate. The German governess Charlotta drifts around alluding to her obscure origins and past. There are undeveloped references to events preceding the action on stage—the lover in Paris, the drowned boy Grisha—but there is no revelation of the past as in Ibsen, no mystery, no intrigue.

While the events on the stage follow each other naturally, though hardly always in a logical, causal order, a symbolic device is used conspicuously: in Act II after a pause, "suddenly a distant sound is heard, coming from the sky as it were, the sound of a snapping string, mournfully dying away." It occurs again at the very end of the play followed by "the strokes of the ax against a tree far away in the orchard." An attempt is made to explain this sound at its first occurrence as a bucket's fall in a faraway pit or as the cries of a heron or an owl, but the effect is weird and even supernatural; it establishes an ominous mood. Even the orchard carries more than its obvious meaning: it is white, drowned in blossoms when the party arrives in the spring; it is bare and desolate in the autumn when the axes are heard cutting it down. "The old bark on the trees gleams faintly, and the cherry trees seem to be dreaming of things that happened a hundred, two hundred years ago and to be tormented by painful visions," declaims Trofimov, defining his feeling for the orchard as a symbol of repression and serfdom. For Lubov Ranevskaya it is an image of her lost innocence and of the happier past, while Lopahin sees it only as an investment. It seems to draw together the meaning of the play.

But what is this meaning? Can we even decide whether it is a tragedy or a comedy? It has been commonly seen as the tragedy of the downfall of the Russian aristocracy (or more correctly, the landed gentry) victimized by the newly rich, upstart peasantry. One could see the play as depicting the defeat of a group of feckless people at the hand of a ruthless "developer" who destroys nature and natural beauty for profit. Or one could see it as prophesying, through the mouth of the student Trofimov, the approaching end of feudal Russia and the coming happier future. Soviet interpretations and performances leaned that way.

Surely none of these interpretations can withstand inspection in the light of the actual play. They all run counter to Chekhov's professed intentions. He called the play a comedy. In a letter of September 15, 1903, he declared expressly that the play "has not turned out as drama but as comedy, in places even a farce"; and a few days later (September 21, 1903), he wrote that "the whole play is gay and frivolous." Chekhov did not like the staging of the play at the Moscow Art Theater and complained of its tearful tone and its slow pace. He objected that "they obstinately call my play a drama in playbill and newspaper advertisements," while he had called it a comedy (April 10, 1904).

No doubt, there are many comical and even farcical characters and scenes in the play. Charlotta with her nut-eating dog, her card tricks, her ventriloquism, her disappearing acts, is a clownish figure. Gayev, the landowner, though "suave and elegant," is a boor, obsessed by his passion for billiards, constantly popping candy into his mouth, telling the waiters in a restaurant about the "decadents" in Paris. Yepihodov, the clerk, carries a revolver and, threatening suicide, asks foolishly whether you have read Buckle (the English historian) and complains of his ill luck: a spider on his chest, a cockroach in his drink. Simeonov-Pishchik empties a whole bottle of pills; eats half a bucket of pickles; quotes Nietzsche supposedly recommending the forging of banknotes; and, fat as he is, puffs and prances at the dance ordering the "cavaliers à genoux." Even the serious characters are put into ludicrous predicaments: Trofimov falls down the stairs; Lopahin, coming to announce the purchase of the estate, is almost hit with a stick by Varya (and *was* hit in the original version). Lopahin, teasing his intended Varya, "moos like a cow." The ball, the hunting for the galoshes, and the champagne drinking by Yasha in the last act have all a touch of absurdity. The grand speeches, Gayev's addresses to the bookcase and to nature or Trofimov's about "mankind going forward" and "All Russia is our orchard," are undercut by the contrast between words and character: Gayev is callous and shallow; the "perpetual student," Trofimov never did a stitch of work. He is properly ridiculed and insulted by Lubov for his scant beard and his silly professions of being "above love." One can sympathize with Chekhov's irritation at the pervading gloom imposed by the Moscow production.

Still, we cannot, in spite of the author, completely dismiss the genuine pathos of the central situation and of the central figure, Lubov Ranevskaya. Whatever one may say about her recklessness in financial matters and her guilt in relation to her lover in France, we must feel her deep attachment to the house and the orchard, to the past and her lost innocence, clearly and unhumorously expressed in the first act on her arrival, again and again at the impending sale of the estate, and finally at the parting from her house: "Oh, my orchard—my dear, sweet, beautiful orchard! . . . My life, my youth, my happiness—Good-bye!" That Gayev, before the final parting, seems to have overcome the sense of loss and even looks forward to his job in the bank and that Lubov acknowledges that her "nerves are better" and that "she sleeps well" testifies to the indestructible spirit of brother and sister but cannot minimize the sense of loss, the pathos of parting, the nostalgia for happier times. Nor is the conception of Lopahin simple. Chekhov emphasized, in a letter to Konstantin Stanislavsky, who was to play the part, that "Lopahin is a decent person in the full sense of the word, and his bearing must be that of a completely dignified and intelligent man." He is not, he says, a profiteering peasant (*kulachok*, October 30, 1903). He admires Lubov and thinks of her with gratitude. He senses the beauty of the poppies in his fields. Even the scene of the abortive encounter with Varya at the end has its quiet pathos in spite of all its awkwardness and the comic touches such as the reference to the broken thermometer. Firs, the eighty-seven-year-old valet, may be grotesque in his deafness and his nostalgia for the good old days of serfdom, but the very last scene when we see him abandoned in the locked-up house surely ends the play on a note of desolation and even despair.

Chekhov, we must conclude, achieved a highly original and even paradoxical blend of comedy and tragedy, or rather of farce and pathos. Both play and short story present a social picture firmly set in a specific historical time—the dissolution of the landed gentry, the rise of the peasant, the encroachment of the city, newly affluent bourgeoisie and its double standard for women—but they do not propound an obvious social thesis. Chekhov, in his tolerance and tenderness, in his distrust of ideologies and heroics, extends his sympathy to all his characters (with the exception of the crudely ambitious valet Yasha). The glow of his humanity, untrammeled by time and place, keeps *The Cherry Orchard* and *The Lady with the Dog* alive in quite different social and political conditions, as they have the universalizing power of great art.

PRONOUNCING GLOSSARY

The following list uses common English syllables and stress accents to provide rough equivalents of selected words whose pronunciation may be unfamiliar to the general reader.

Anna Sergeyevna von Diederitz: *ahn'-nuh sehr-gay'-ev-nuh fahn dee'-duh-reets*

Anton Chekhov: *ahn-tawn' che'-khuf*

Charlotta Ivanovna: *shar-law'-tuh ee-vah'-nuv-nuh*

Dmitri Gurov: *dmee'-tree goo'-ruf*

Firs: *feers*

Leonid Andreyevich Gayev: *lay-ah-neet' ahn-dray'-uh-veech gah'-yef*

Lubov Andreyevna Ranevskaya: *lyu-bawf' ahn-dray'-uv-nuh rah-nyef'-skah-yuh*

Pyotr Sergeyevich Trofimov: *pyaw'-tr sehr-gay'-eh-veech trah-fee'-muf*

Semyon Yepihodov: *seem-yawn' ye-pee-khaw'-duf*

Simeonov-Pishchik: *see-may-awn'-uf-*
peesh'-cheek

Yermolay Alexeyevich Lopahin:
yehr-mah-lai' ah-lex-ay'-veech lah-
pah'-kheen

The Lady with the Dog[1]

I

People were telling one another that a newcomer had been seen on the promenade—a lady with a dog. Dmitri Dmitrich Gurov had been a fortnight in Yalta,[2] and was accustomed to its ways, and he, too, had begun to take an interest in fresh arrivals. From his seat in Vernet's outdoor café, he caught sight of a young woman in a toque, passing along the promenade; she was fair and not very tall; after her trotted a white Pomeranian.

Later he encountered her in the municipal park and in the square several times a day. She was always alone, wearing the same toque, and the Pomeranian always trotted at her side. Nobody knew who she was, and people referred to her simply as "the lady with the dog."

"If she's here without her husband, and without any friends," thought Gurov, "it wouldn't be a bad idea to make her acquaintance."

He was not yet forty but had a twelve-year-old daughter and two sons in high school. He had been talked into marrying in his second year at college, and his wife now looked nearly twice as old as he did. She was a tall woman with dark eyebrows, erect, dignified, imposing, and, as she said of herself, a "thinker." She was a great reader, omitted the "hard sign"[3] at the end of words in her letters, and called her husband "Dimitry" instead of Dmitry; and though he secretly considered her shallow, narrow-minded, and dowdy, he stood in awe of her, and disliked being at home. He had first begun deceiving her long ago and he was now constantly unfaithful to her, and this was no doubt why he spoke slightingly of women, to whom he referred as *the lower race.*

He considered that the ample lessons he had received from bitter experience entitled him to call them whatever he liked, but without this "lower race" he could not have existed a single day. He was bored and ill-at-ease in the company of men, with whom he was always cold and reserved, but felt quite at home among women, and knew exactly what to say to them, and how to behave; he could even be silent in their company without feeling the slightest awkwardness. There was an elusive charm in his appearance and disposition which attracted women and caught their sympathies. He knew this and was himself attracted to them by some invisible force.

Repeated and bitter experience had taught him that every fresh intimacy, while at first introducing such pleasant variety into everyday life, and offering itself as a charming, light adventure, inevitably developed, among decent people (especially in Moscow, where they are so irresolute and slow to move), into a problem of excessive complication leading to an intolerably irksome

1. Translated by Ivy Litvinov. 2. A fashionable seaside resort in the Crimea. 3. Certain progressive intellectuals, anticipating the reform of the Russian alphabet, omitted the hard sign after consonants in writing; here, however, it is an affectation.

situation. But every time he encountered an attractive woman he forgot all about this experience, the desire for life surged up in him, and everything suddenly seemed simple and amusing.

One evening, then, while he was dining at the restaurant in the park, the lady in the toque came strolling up and took a seat at a neighboring table. Her expression, gait, dress, coiffure, all told him that she was from the upper classes, that she was married, that she was in Yalta for the first time, alone and bored. . . . The accounts of the laxity of morals among visitors to Yalta are greatly exaggerated, and he paid no heed to them, knowing that for the most part they were invented by people who would gladly have transgressed themselves, had they known how to set about it. But when the lady sat down at a neighboring table a few yards away from him, these stories of easy conquests, of excursions to the mountains, came back to him, and the seductive idea of a brisk transitory liaison, an affair with a woman whose very name he did not know, suddenly took possession of his mind.

He snapped his fingers at the Pomeranian and, when it trotted up to him, shook his forefinger at it. The Pomeranian growled. Gurov shook his finger again.

The lady glanced at him and instantly lowered her eyes.

"He doesn't bite," she said, and blushed.

"May I give him a bone?" he asked, and on her nod of consent added in friendly tones: "Have you been long in Yalta?"

"About five days."

"And I am dragging out my second week here."

Neither spoke for a few minutes.

"The days pass quickly, and yet one is so bored here," she said, not looking at him.

"It's the thing to say it's boring here. People never complain of boredom in godforsaken holes like Belyev or Zhizdra, but when they get here it's: 'Oh, the dullness! Oh, the dust!' You'd think they'd come from Granada[4] to say the least."

She laughed. Then they both went on eating in silence, like complete strangers. But after dinner they left the restaurant together, and embarked upon the light, jesting talk of people free and contented, for whom it is all the same where they go, or what they talk about. They strolled along, remarking on the strange light over the sea. The water was a warm, tender purple, the moonlight lay on its surface in a golden strip. They said how close it was, after the hot day. Gurov told her he was from Moscow, that he was really a philologist, but worked in a bank; that he had at one time trained himself to sing in a private opera company, but had given up the idea; that he owned two houses in Moscow. . . . And from her he learned that she had grown up in Petersburg,[5] but had gotten married in the town of S., where she had been living two years, that she would stay another month in Yalta, and that perhaps her husband, who also needed a rest, would join her. She was quite unable to explain whether her husband was a member of the province council, or on the board of the *zemstvo*,[6] and was greatly amused at herself for this. Further, Gurov learned that her name was Anna Sergeyevna.

---

4. A famous medieval city in Spain, once capital of the Moorish kingdom of Granada and now a tourist center known for its art and architecture. Belyev and Zhizdra are small provincial towns.   5. St. Petersburg, the former capital of Russia: an important port and cultural center.   6. District administration.

Back in his own room he thought about her, and felt sure he would meet her the next day. It was inevitable. As he went to bed he reminded himself that only a very short time ago she had been a schoolgirl, like his own daughter, learning her lessons, he remembered how much there was of shyness and constraint in her laughter, in her way of conversing with a stranger—it was probably the first time in her life that she found herself alone, and in a situation in which men could follow her and watch her, and speak to her, all the time with a secret aim she could not fail to divine. He recalled her slender, delicate neck, her fine gray eyes.

"And yet there's something pathetic about her," he thought to himself as he fell asleep.

<h2 style="text-align:center">II</h2>

A week had passed since the beginning of their acquaintance. It was a holiday. Indoors it was stuffy, but the dust rose in clouds out of doors, and people's hats blew off. It was a parching day and Gurov kept going to the outdoor café for fruit drinks and ices to offer Anna Sergeyevna. The heat was overpowering.

In the evening, when the wind had dropped, they walked to the pier to see the steamer come in. There were a great many people strolling about the landing-place; some, bunches of flowers in their hands, were meeting friends. Two peculiarities of the smart Yalta crowd stood out distinctly—the elderly ladies all tried to dress very youthfully, and there seemed to be an inordinate number of generals about.

Owing to the roughness of the sea the steamer arrived late, after the sun had gone down, and it had to maneuver for some time before it could get alongside the pier. Anna Sergeyevna scanned the steamer and passengers through her lorgnette,[7] as if looking for someone she knew, and when she turned to Gurov her eyes were glistening. She talked a great deal, firing off abrupt questions and forgetting immediately what it was she had wanted to know. Then she lost her lorgnette in the crush.

The smart crowd began dispersing, features could no longer be made out, the wind had quite dropped, and Gurov and Anna Sergeyevna stood there as if waiting for someone else to come off the steamer. Anna Sergeyevna had fallen silent, every now and then smelling her flowers, but not looking at Gurov.

"It's turned out a fine evening," he said. "What shall we do? We might go for a drive."

She made no reply.

He looked steadily at her and suddenly took her in his arms and kissed her lips, and the fragrance and dampness of the flowers closed round him, but the next moment he looked behind him in alarm—had anyone seen them?

"Let's go to your room," he murmured.

And they walked off together, very quickly.

Her room was stuffy and smelt of some scent she had bought in the Japanese shop.[8] Gurov looked at her, thinking to himself: "How full of strange encounters life is!" He could remember carefree, good-natured women who

---

7. Small eyeglasses on a short handle.   8. Probably a tourist shop with imported goods.

were exhilarated by love-making and grateful to him for the happiness he gave them, however short-lived; and there had been others—his wife among them—whose caresses were insincere, affected, hysterical, mixed up with a great deal of quite unnecessary talk, and whose expression seemed to say that all this was not just lovemaking or passion, but something much more significant; then there had been two or three beautiful, cold women, over whose features flitted a predatory expression, betraying a determination to wring from life more than it could give, women no longer in their first youth, capricious, irrational, despotic, brainless, and when Gurov had cooled to these, their beauty aroused in him nothing but repulsion, and the lace trimming on their underclothes reminded him of fish-scales.

But here the timidity and awkwardness of youth and inexperience were still apparent; and there was a feeling of embarrassment in the atmosphere, as if someone had just knocked at the door. Anna Sergeyevna, "the lady with the dog," seemed to regard the affair as something very special, very serious, as if she had become a fallen woman, an attitude he found odd and disconcerting. Her features lengthened and drooped, and her long hair hung mournfully on either side of her face. She assumed a pose of dismal meditation, like a repentant sinner in some classical painting.[9]

"It isn't right," she said. "You will never respect me anymore."

On the table was a watermelon. Gurov cut himself a slice from it and began slowly eating it. At least half an hour passed in silence.

Anna Sergeyevna was very touching, revealing the purity of a decent, naïve woman who had seen very little of life. The solitary candle burning on the table scarcely lit up her face, but it was obvious that her heart was heavy.

"Why should I stop respecting you?" asked Gurov. "You don't know what you're saying."

"May God forgive me!" she exclaimed, and her eyes filled with tears. "It's terrible."

"No need to seek to justify yourself."

"How can I justify myself? I'm a wicked, fallen woman, I despise myself and have not the least thought of self-justification. It isn't my husband I have deceived, it's myself. And not only now, I have been deceiving myself for ever so long. My husband is no doubt an honest, worthy man, but he's a flunky. I don't know what it is he does at his office, but I know he's a flunky. I was only twenty when I married him, and I was devoured by curiosity, I wanted something higher. I told myself that there must be a different kind of life I wanted to live, to live. . . . I was burning with curiosity . . . you'll never understand that, but I swear to God I could no longer control myself, nothing could hold me back, I told my husband I was ill, and I came here. . . . And I started going about like one possessed, like a madwoman . . . and now I have become an ordinary, worthless woman, and everyone has the right to despise me."

Gurov listened to her, bored to death. The naïve accents, the remorse, all was so unexpected, so out of place. But for the tears in her eyes, she might have been jesting or play-acting.

"I don't understand," he said gently. "What is it you want?"

---

9. A famous painting of Mary Magdalen (see Luke 7.36–50) by the French classical artist Georges de la Tour (1593–1652) shows her seated at a table meditating, her face and long hair illuminated by a candle.

She hid her face against his breast and pressed closer to him.

"Do believe me, I implore you to believe me," she said. "I love all that is honest and pure in life, vice is revolting to me, I don't know what I'm doing. The common people say they are snared by the Devil. And now I can say that I have been snared by the Devil, too."

"Come, come," he murmured.

He gazed into her fixed, terrified eyes, kissed her, and soothed her with gentle affectionate words, and gradually she calmed down and regained her cheefulness. Soon they were laughing together again.

When, a little later, they went out, there was not a soul on the promenade, the town and its cypresses looked dead, but the sea was still roaring as it dashed against the beach. A solitary fishing-boat tossed on the waves, its lamp blinking sleepily.

They found a carriage and drove to Oreanda.[1]

"I discovered your name in the hall, just now," said Gurov, "written up on the board. Von Diederitz. Is your husband a German?"

"No. His grandfather was, I think, but he belongs to the Orthodox Church himself."

When they got out of the carriage at Oreanda they sat down on a bench not far from the church, and looked down at the sea, without talking. Yalta could be dimly discerned through the morning mist, and white clouds rested motionless on the summits of the mountains. Not a leaf stirred, the grasshoppers chirruped, and the monotonous hollow roar of the sea came up to them, speaking of peace, of the eternal sleep lying in wait for us all. The sea had roared like this long before there was any Yalta or Oreanda, it was roaring now, and it would go on roaring, just as indifferently and hollowly, when we had passed away. And it may be that in this continuity, this utter indifference of life and death, lies the secret of our ultimate salvation, of the stream of life on our planet, and of its never-ceasing movement towards perfection.

Side by side with a young woman, who looked so exquisite in the early light, soothed and enchanted by the sight of all this magical beauty—sea, mountains, clouds and the vast expanse of the sky—Gurov told himself that, when you came to think of it, everything in the world is beautiful really, everything but our own thoughts and actions, when we lose sight of the higher aims of life, and of our dignity as human beings.

Someone approached them—a watchman, probably—looked at them and went away. And there was something mysterious and beautiful even in this. The steamer from Feodosia[2] could be seen coming towards the pier, lit up by the dawn, its lamps out.

"There's dew on the grass," said Anna Sergeyevna, breaking the silence.

"Yes. Time to go home."

They went back to the town.

After this they met every day at noon on the promenade, lunching and dining together, going for walks, and admiring the sea. She complained of sleeplessness, of palpitations, asked the same questions over and over again, alternately surrendering to jealousy and the fear that he did not really respect her. And often, when there was nobody in sight in the square or the park,

---

1. A hotel and beach compound near Yalta; the whole area is known as the Ukrainian Riviera. 2. A coastal town seventy miles northeast of Yalta.

he would draw her to him and kiss her passionately. The utter idleness, these kisses in broad daylight, accompanied by furtive glances and the fear of discovery, the heat, the smell of the sea, and the idle, smart, well-fed people continually crossing their field of vision, seemed to have given him a new lease of life. He told Anna Sergeyevna she was beautiful and seductive, made love to her with impetuous passion, and never left her side, while she was always pensive, always trying to force from him the admission that he did not respect her, that he did not love her a bit, and considered her just an ordinary woman. Almost every night they drove out of town, to Oreanda, the waterfall, or some other beauty-spot. And these excursions were invariably a success, each contributing fresh impressions of majestic beauty.

All this time they kept expecting her husband to arrive. But a letter came in which he told his wife that he was having trouble with his eyes, and implored her to come home as soon as possible. Anna Sergeyevna made hasty preparations for leaving.

"It's a good thing I'm going," she said to Gurov. "It's the intervention of fate."

She left Yalta in a carriage, and he went with her as far as the railway station. The drive took nearly a whole day. When she got into the express train, after the second bell had been rung, she said:

"Let me have one more look at you. . . . One last look. That's right."

She did not weep, but was mournful, and seemed ill, the muscles of her cheeks twitching.

"I shall think of you . . . I shall think of you all the time," she said. "God bless you! Think kindly of me. We are parting forever, it must be so, because we ought never to have met. Good-bye—God bless you."

The train steamed rapidly out of the station, its lights soon disappearing, and a minute later even the sound it made was silenced, as if everything were conspiring to bring this sweet oblivion, this madness, to an end as quickly as possible. And Gurov, standing alone on the platform and gazing into the dark distance, listened to the shrilling of the grasshoppers and the humming of the telegraph wires, with a feeling that he had only just awakened. And he told himself that this had been just one more of the many adventures in his life, and that it, too, was over, leaving nothing but a memory. . . . He was moved and sad, and felt a slight remorse. After all, this young woman whom he would never again see had not been really happy with him. He had been friendly and affectionate with her, but in his whole behaviour, in the tones of his voice, in his very caresses, there had been a shade of irony, the insulting indulgence of the fortunate male, who was, moreover, almost twice her age. She had insisted in calling him good, remarkable, high-minded. Evidently he had appeared to her different from his real self, in a word he had involuntarily deceived her. . . .

There was an autumnal feeling in the air, and the evening was chilly.

"It's time for me to be going north, too," thought Gurov, as he walked away from the platform. "High time!"

III

When he got back to Moscow it was beginning to look like winter; the stoves were heated every day, and it was still dark when the children got up to go to school and drank their tea, so that the nurse had to light the lamp for a short time. Frost had set in. When the first snow falls, and one goes for one's first sleigh-ride, it is pleasant to see the white ground, the white roofs; one breathes freely and lightly, and remembers the days of one's youth. The ancient lime-trees and birches, white with hoarfrost, have a good-natured look, they are closer to the heart than cypresses and palms, and beneath their branches one is no longer haunted by the memory of mountains and the sea.

Gurov had always lived in Moscow, and he returned to Moscow on a fine frosty day, and when he put on his fur-lined overcoat and thick gloves, and sauntered down Petrovka Street, and when, on Saturday evening, he heard the church bells ringing, his recent journey and the places he had visited lost their charm for him. He became gradually immersed in Moscow life, reading with avidity three newspapers a day, while declaring he never read Moscow newspapers on principle. Once more he was caught up in a whirl of restaurants, clubs, banquets, and celebrations, once more he glowed with the flattering consciousness that well-known lawyers and actors came to his house, that he played cards in the Medical Club opposite a professor. He could once again eat a whole serving of Moscow Fish Stew served in a pan.

He had believed that in a month's time Anna Sergeyevna would be nothing but a vague memory, and that hereafter, with her wistful smile, she would only occasionally appear to him in dreams, like others before her. But the month was now well over and winter was in full swing, and all was as clear in his memory as if he had parted with Anna Sergeyevna only the day before. And his recollections grew ever more insistent. When the voices of his children at their lessons reached him in his study through the evening stillness, when he heard a song, or the sounds of a music-box in a restaurant, when the wind howled in the chimney, it all came back to him: early morning on the pier, the misty mountains, the steamer from Feodosia, the kisses. He would pace up and down his room for a long time, smiling at his memories, and then memory turned into dreaming, and what had happened mingled in his imagination with what was going to happen. Anna Sergeyevna did not come to him in his dreams, she accompanied him everywhere, like his shadow, following him everywhere he went. When he closed his eyes, she seemed to stand before him in the flesh, still lovelier, younger, tenderer than she had really been, and looking back, he saw himself, too, as better than he had been in Yalta. In the evenings she looked out at him from the bookshelves, the fireplace, the corner, he could hear her breathing, the sweet rustle of her skirts. In the streets he followed women with his eyes, to see if there were any like her. . . .

He began to feel an overwhelming desire to share his memories with someone. But he could not speak of his love at home, and outside his home who was there for him to confide in? Not the tenants living in his house, and certainly not his colleagues at the bank. And what was there to tell? Was it love that he had felt? Had there been anything exquisite, poetic, anything instructive or even amusing about his relations with Anna Sergeyevna? He had to content himself with uttering vague generalizations about love and women, and nobody guessed what he meant, though his wife's dark eyebrows twitched as she said:

"The role of a coxcomb doesn't suit you a bit, Dimitry."

One evening, leaving the Medical Club with one of his card-partners, a government official, he could not refrain from remarking:

"If you only knew what a charming woman I met in Yalta!"

The official got into his sleigh, and just before driving off, turned and called out:

"Dmitry Dmitrich!"

"Yes?"

"You were quite right, you know—the sturgeon was just a *leetle* off."

These words, in themselves so commonplace, for some reason infuriated Gurov, seemed to him humiliating, gross. What savage manners, what people! What wasted evenings, what tedious, empty days! Frantic card-playing, gluttony, drunkenness, perpetual talk always about the same thing. The greater part of one's time and energy went on business that was no use to anyone, and on discussing the same thing over and over again, and there was nothing to show for it all but a stunted, earth-bound existence and a round of trivialities, and there was nowhere to escape to, you might as well be in a madhouse or a convict settlement.

Gurov lay awake all night, raging, and went about the whole of the next day with a headache. He slept badly on the succeeding nights, too, sitting up in bed, thinking, or pacing the floor of his room. He was sick of his children, sick of the bank, felt not the slightest desire to go anywhere or talk about anything.

When the Christmas holidays came, he packed his things, telling his wife he had to go to Petersburg in the interests of a certain young man, and set off for the town of S. To what end? He hardly knew himself. He only knew that he must see Anna Sergeyevna, must speak to her, arrange a meeting, if possible.

He arrived at S. in the morning and engaged the best suite in the hotel, which had a carpet of gray military frieze, and a dusty ink-pot on the table, surmounted by a headless rider, holding his hat in his raised hand. The hall porter told him what he wanted to know: von Diederitz had a house of his own in Staro-Goncharnaya Street. It wasn't far from the hotel, he lived on a grand scale, luxuriously, kept carriage-horses, the whole town knew him. The hall porter pronounced the name "Drideritz."

Gurov strolled over to Staro-Goncharnaya Street and discovered the house. In front of it was a long gray fence with inverted nails hammered into the tops of the palings.

"A fence like that is enough to make anyone want to run away," thought Gurov, looking at the windows of the house and the fence.

He reasoned that since it was a holiday, Anna's husband would probably be at home. In any case it would be tactless to embarrass her by calling at the house. And a note might fall into the hands of the husband, and bring about catastrophe. The best thing would be to wait about on the chance of seeing her. And he walked up and down the street, hovering in the vicinity of the fence, watching for his chance. A beggar entered the gate, only to be attacked by dogs, then, an hour later, the faint, vague sounds of a piano reached his ears. That would be Anna Sergeyevna playing. Suddenly the front door opened and an old woman came out, followed by a familiar white Pomeranian. Gurov tried to call to it, but his heart beat violently, and in his agitation he could not remember its name.

He walked on, hating the gray fence more and more, and now ready to tell himself irately that Anna Sergeyevna had forgotten him, had already, perhaps, found distraction in another—what could be more natural in a young woman who had to look at this accursed fence from morning to night? He went back to his hotel and sat on the sofa in his suite for some time, not knowing what to do, then he ordered dinner, and after dinner, had a long sleep.

"What a foolish, restless business," he thought, waking up and looking towards the dark windowpanes. It was evening by now. "Well, I've had my sleep out. And what am I to do in the night?"

He sat up in bed, covered by the cheap gray quilt, which reminded him of a hospital blanket, and in his vexation he fell to taunting himself.

"You and your lady with a dog . . . there's adventure for you! See what you get for your pains."

On his arrival at the station that morning he had noticed a poster announcing in enormous letters the first performance at the local theatre of *The Geisha*.[3] Remembering this, he got up and made for the theatre.

"It's highly probable that she goes to first nights," he told himself.

The theatre was full. It was a typical provincial theatre, with a mist collecting over the chandeliers, and the crowd in the gallery fidgeting noisily. In the first row of the stalls the local dandies stood waiting for the curtain to go up, their hands clasped behind them. There, in the front seat of the governor's box, sat the governor's daughter, wearing a boa, the governor himself hiding modestly behind the drapes, so that only his hands were visible. The curtain stirred, the orchestra took a long time tuning up their instruments. Gurov's eyes roamed eagerly over the audience as they filed in and occupied their seats.

Anna Sergeyevna came in, too. She seated herself in the third row of the stalls, and when Gurov's glance fell on her, his heart seemed to stop, and he knew in a flash that the whole world contained no one nearer or dearer to him, no one more important to his happiness. This little woman, lost in the provincial crowd, in no way remarkable, holding a silly lorgnette in her hand, now filled his whole life, was his grief, his joy, all that he desired. Lulled by the sounds coming from the wretched orchestra, with its feeble, amateurish violinists, he thought how beautiful she was . . . thought and dreamed. . . .

Anna Sergeyevna was accompanied by a tall, round-shouldered young man with small whiskers, who nodded at every step before taking the seat beside her and seemed to be continually bowing to someone. This must be her husband, whom, in a fit of bitterness, at Yalta, she had called a "flunky." And there really was something of a lackey's servility in his lanky figure, his sidewhiskers, and the little bald spot on the top of his head. And he smiled sweetly, and the badge of some scientific society gleaming in his buttonhole was like the number on a footman's livery.

The husband went out to smoke in the first interval, and she was left alone in her seat. Gurov, who had taken a seat in the stalls, went up to her and said in a trembling voice, with a forced smile: "How d'you do?"

3. An operetta (1896) by the English composer Sidney Jones.

She glanced up at him and turned pale, then looked at him again in alarm, unable to believe her eyes, squeezing her fan and lorgnette in one hand, evidently struggling to overcome a feeling of faintness. Neither of them said a word. She sat there, and he stood beside her, disconcerted by her embarrassment, and not daring to sit down. The violins and flutes sang out as they were tuned, and there was a tense sensation in the atmosphere, as if they were being watched from all the boxes. At last she got up and moved rapidly towards one of the exits. He followed her and they wandered aimlessly along corridors, up and down stairs; figures flashed by in the uniforms of legal officials, high-school teachers and civil servants, all wearing badges; ladies, coats hanging from pegs flashed by; there was a sharp draft, bringing with it an odor of cigarette butts. And Gurov, whose heart was beating violently, thought:

"What on earth are all these people, this orchestra for? . . ."

The next minute he suddenly remembered how, after seeing Anna Sergeyevna off that evening at the station, he had told himself that all was over, and they would never meet again. And how far away the end seemed to be now!

She stopped on a dark narrow staircase over which was a notice bearing the inscription "To the upper circle."[4]

"How you frightened me!" she said, breathing heavily, still pale and half-stunned. "Oh, how you frightened me! I'm almost dead! Why did you come? Oh, why?"

"But, Anna," he said, in low, hasty tones. "But, Anna. . . . Try to understand . . . do try. . . ."

She cast him a glance of fear, entreaty, love, and then gazed at him steadily, as if to fix his features firmly in her memory.

"I've been so unhappy," she continued, taking no notice of his words. "I could think of nothing but you the whole time, I lived on the thoughts of you. I tried to forget—why, oh, why did you come?"

On the landing above them were two schoolboys, smoking and looking down, but Gurov did not care, and, drawing Anna Sergeyevna towards him, began kissing her face, her lips, her hands.

"What are you doing, oh, what are you doing?" she said in horror, drawing back. "We have both gone mad. Go away this very night, this moment. . . . By all that is sacred, I implore you. . . . Somebody is coming."

Someone was ascending the stairs.

"You must go away," went on Anna Sergeyevna in a whisper. "D'you hear me, Dmitry Dmitrich? I'll come to you in Moscow. I have never been happy, I am unhappy now, and I shall never be happy—never! Do not make me suffer still more! I will come to you in Moscow, I swear it! And now we must part! My dear one, my kind one, my darling, we must part."

She pressed his hand and hurried down the stairs, looking back at him continually, and her eyes showed that she was in truth unhappy. Gurov stood where he was for a short time, listening, and when all was quiet, went to look for his coat, and left the theatre.

---

4. The stalls or back rows; a medium-priced area behind the orchestra seats on the main floor.

IV

And Anna Sergeyevna began going to Moscow to see him. Every two or three months she left the town of S., telling her husband that she was going to consult a specialist on female diseases, and her husband believed her and did not believe her. In Moscow she always stayed at the Slavyanski Bazaar,[5] sending a man in a red cap to Gurov the moment she arrived. Gurov went to her, and no one in Moscow knew anything about it.

One winter morning he went to see her as usual (the messenger had been to him the evening before, but had not found him at home). His daughter was with him, for her school was on the way and he thought he might as well see her to it.

"It is forty degrees," said Gurov to his daughter, "and yet it is snowing. You see it is only above freezing close to the ground, the temperature in the upper layers of the atmosphere is quite different."

"Why doesn't it ever thunder in winter, Papa?"

He explained this, too. As he was speaking, he kept reminding himself that he was going to a rendezvous and that not a living soul knew about it, or, probably, ever would. He led a double life—one in public, in the sight of all whom it concerned, full of conventional truth and conventional deception, exactly like the lives of his friends and acquaintances, and another which flowed in secret. And, owing to some strange, possibly quite accidental chain of circumstances, everything that was important, interesting, essential, everything about which he was sincere and never deceived himself, everything that composed the kernel of his life, went on in secret, while everything that was false in him, everything that composed the husk in which he hid himself and the truth which was in him—his work at the bank, discussions at the club, his "lower race," his attendance at anniversary celebrations with his wife—was on the surface. He began to judge others by himself, no longer believing what he saw, and always assuming that the real, the only interesting life of every individual goes on as under cover of night, secretly. Every individual existence revolves around mystery, and perhaps that is the chief reason that all cultivated individuals insisted so strongly on the respect due to personal secrets.

After leaving his daughter at the door of her school Gurov set off for the Slavyanski Bazaar. Taking off his overcoat in the lobby, he went upstairs and knocked softly on the door. Anna Sergeyevna, wearing the gray dress he liked most, exhausted by her journey and by suspense, had been expecting him since the evening before. She was pale and looked at him without smiling, but was in his arms almost before he was fairly in the room. Their kiss was lingering, prolonged, as if they had not met for years.

"Well, how are you?" he asked. "Anything new?"

"Wait, I'll tell you in a minute. . . . I can't. . . ."

She could not speak, because she was crying. Turning away, she held her handkerchief to her eyes.

"I'll wait till she's had her cry out," he thought, and sank into a chair.

He rang for tea, and a little later, while he was drinking it, she was still standing there, her face to the window. She wept from emotion, from her

5. A luxurious hotel in Moscow.

bitter consciousness of the sadness of their life; they could only see one another in secret, hiding from people, as if they were thieves. Was not their life a broken one?

"Don't cry," he said.

It was quite obvious to him that this love of theirs would not soon come to an end, and that no one could say when this end would be. Anna Sergeyevna loved him ever more fondly, worshipped him, and there would have been no point in telling her that one day it must end. Indeed, she would not have believed him.

He moved over and took her by the shoulders, intending to fondle her with light words, but suddenly he caught sight of himself in the looking-glass.

His hair was already beginning to turn gray. It struck him as strange that he should have aged so much in the last few years. The shoulders on which his hands lay were warm and quivering. He felt a pity for this life, still so warm and exquisite, but probably soon to fade and droop like his own. Why did she love him so? Women had always believed him different from what he really was, had loved in him not himself but the man their imagination pictured him, a man they had sought for eagerly all their lives. And afterwards when they discovered their mistake, they went on loving him just the same. And not one of them had ever been happy with him. Time had passed, he had met one woman after another, become intimate with each, parted with each, but had never loved. There had been all sorts of things between them, but never love.

And only now, when he was gray-haired, had he fallen in love properly, thoroughly, for the first time in his life.

He and Anna Sergeyevna loved one another as people who are very close and intimate, as husband and wife, as dear friends love one another. It seemed to them that fate had intended them for one another, and they could not understand why she should have a husband, and he a wife. They were like two migrating birds, the male and the female, who had been caught and put into separate cages. They forgave one another all that they were ashamed of in the past and in the present, and felt that this love of theirs had changed them both.

Formerly, in moments of melancholy, he had consoled himself by the first argument that came into his head, but now arguments were nothing to him, he felt profound pity, desired to be sincere, tender.

"Stop crying, my dearest," he said. "You've had your cry, now stop. . . . Now let us have a talk, let us try and think what we are to do."

Then they discussed their situation for a long time, trying to think how they could get rid of the necessity for hiding, deception, living in different towns, being so long without meeting. How were they to shake off these intolerable fetters?

"How? How?" he repeated, clutching his head. "How?"

And it seemed to them that they were within an inch of arriving at a decision, and that then a new, beautiful life would begin. And they both realized that the end was still far, far away, and that the hardest, the most complicated part was only just beginning.

The Cherry Orchard[1]

CHARACTERS

LUBOV ANDREYEVNA RANEV-SKAYA, *a landowner*

ANYA, *her seventeen-year-old daughter*

VARYA, *her adopted daughter, twenty-four years old*

LEONID ANDREYEVICH GAYEV, *Mme. Ranevskaya's brother*

YERMOLAY ALEXEYEVICH LOPA-HIN, *a merchant*

PYOTR SERGEYEVICH TROFIMOV, *a student*

SIMEONOV-PISHCHIK, *a land-owner*

CHARLOTTA IVANOVNA, *a governess*

SEMYON YEPIHODOV, *a clerk*

DUNYASHA, *a maid*

FIRS, *a manservant, aged eighty-seven*

YASHA, *a young valet*

A TRAMP

STATIONMASTER

POST OFFICE CLERK

GUESTS

SERVANTS

The action takes place on MME. RANEVSKAYA's *estate.*

Act I

A room that is still called the nursery. One of the doors leads into ANYA's *room. Dawn, the sun will soon rise. It is May, the cherry trees are in blossom, but it is cold in the orchard; there is a morning frost. The windows are shut. Enter* DUN-YASHA *with a candle, and* LOPAHIN *with a book in his hand.*

LOPAHIN The train is in, thank God. What time is it?

DUNYASHA Nearly two. [*Puts out the candle.*] It's light already.

LOPAHIN How late is the train, anyway? Two hours at least. [*Yawns and stretches.*] I'm a fine one! What a fool I've made of myself! I came here on purpose to meet them at the station, and then I went and overslept. I fell asleep in my chair. How annoying! You might have waked me . . .

DUNYASHA I thought you'd left. [*Listens.*] I think they're coming!

LOPAHIN [*Listens.*] No, they've got to get the luggage, and one thing and another . . . [*Pause.*] Lubov Andreyevna spent five years abroad, I don't know what she's like now. . . . She's a fine person—lighthearted, simple. I remember when I was a boy of fifteen, my poor father—he had a shop here in the village then—punched me in the face with his fist and made my nose bleed. We'd come into the yard, I don't know what for, and he'd had a drop too much. Lubov Andreyevna, I remember her as if it were yesterday—she was still young and so slim—led me to the washbasin, in this very room . . . in the nursery. "Don't cry, little peasant," she said, "it'll heal in time for your wedding . . ." [*Pause.*] Little peasant . . . my father was a peasant, it's true, and here I am in a white waistcoat and yellow shoes. A pig in a pastry shop, you might say. It's true I'm rich. I've got a lot

1. Translated by Avrahm Yarmolinsky.

of money. . . . But when you look at it closely, I'm a peasant through and through. [*Pages the book.*] Here I've been reading this book and I didn't understand a word of it. . . . I was reading it and fell asleep . . . [*Pause.*]

DUNYASHA   And the dogs were awake all night, they feel that their masters are coming.

LOPAHIN   Dunyasha, why are you so—

DUNYASHA   My hands are trembling. I'm going to faint.

LOPAHIN   You're too soft, Dunyasha. You dress like a lady, and look at the way you do your hair. That's not right. One should remember one's place.

[*Enter* YEPIHODOV *with a bouquet; he wears a jacket and highly polished boots that squeak badly. He drops the bouquet as he comes in.*]

YEPIHODOV   [*Picking up the bouquet.*]   Here, the gardener sent these, said you're to put them in the dining room. [*Hands the bouquet to* DUNYASHA.]

LOPAHIN   And bring me some kvass.[2]

DUNYASHA   Yes, sir. [*Exits.*]

YEPIHODOV   There's a frost this morning—three degrees below—and yet the cherries are all in blossom. I cannot approve of our climate. [*Sighs.*] I cannot. Our climate does not activate properly. And, Yermolay Alexeyevich, allow me to make a further remark. The other day I bought myself a pair of boots, and I make bold to assure you, they squeak so that it is really intolerable. What should I grease them with?

LOPAHIN   Oh, get out! I'm fed up with you.

YEPIHODOV   Every day I meet with misfortune. And I don't complain, I've got used to it, I even smile.

[DUNYASHA *enters, hands* LOPAHIN *the kvass.*]

YEPIHODOV   I am leaving. [*Stumbles against a chair, which falls over.*] There! [*Triumphantly, as it were.*] There again, you see what sort of circumstance, pardon the expression. . . . It is absolutely phenomenal! [*Exits.*]

DUNYASHA   You know, Yermolay Alexeyevich, I must tell you, Yepihodov has proposed to me.

LOPAHIN   Ah!

DUNYASHA   I simply don't know . . . he's a quiet man, but sometimes when he starts talking, you can't make out what he means. He speaks nicely—and it's touching—but you can't understand it. I sort of like him though, and he is crazy about me. He's an unlucky man . . . every day something happens to him. They tease him about it here . . . they call him, Two-and-Twenty Troubles.

LOPAHIN   [*Listening.*]   There! I think they're coming.

DUNYASHA   They *are* coming! What's the matter with me? I feel cold all over.

LOPAHIN   They really are coming. Let's go and meet them. Will she recognize me? We haven't seen each other for five years.

DUNYASHA   [*In a flutter.*]   I'm going to faint this minute. . . . Oh, I'm going to faint!

[*Two carriages are heard driving up to the house.* LOPAHIN *and* DUNYASHA *go out quickly. The stage is left empty. There is a noise in the adjoining rooms.* FIRS, *who had driven to the station to meet* LUBOV ANDREYEVNA

2. Russian beer, made from rye or barley.

RANEVSKAYA, *crosses the stage hurriedly, leaning on a stick. He is wearing an old-fashioned livery and a tall hat. He mutters to himself indistinctly. The hubbub offstage increases. A* VOICE: *"Come, let's go this way." Enter* LUBOV ANDREYEVNA, ANYA, *and* CHARLOTTA IVANOVNA *with a pet dog on a leash, all in traveling dresses;* VARYA, *wearing a coat and kerchief;* GAYEV, SIMEONOV-PISHCHIK, LOPAHIN, DUNYASHA, *with a bag and an umbrella, servants with luggage. All walk across the room.*]

ANYA   Let's go this way. Do you remember what room this is, Mamma?

MME. RANEVSKAYA [*Joyfully, through her tears.*]   The nursery!

VARYA   How cold it is! My hands are numb. [*To* MME. RANEVSKAYA] Your rooms are just the same as they were, Mamma, the white one and the violet.

MME. RANEVSKAYA   The nursery! My darling, lovely room! I slept here when I was a child . . . [*Cries.*] And here I am, like a child again! [*Kisses her brother and* VARYA, *and then her brother again.*] Varya's just the same as ever, like a nun. And I recognized Dunyasha. [*Kisses* DUNYASHA.]

GAYEV   The train was two hours late. What do you think of that? What a way to manage things!

CHARLOTTA [*To* PISHCHIK.]   My dog eats nuts, too.

PISHCHIK [*In amazement.*]   You don't say!

[*All go out, except* ANYA *and* DUNYASHA.]

DUNYASHA   We've been waiting for you for hours. [*Takes* ANYA's *hat and coat.*]

ANYA   I didn't sleep on the train for four nights and now I'm frozen . . .

DUNYASHA   It was Lent when you left; there was snow and frost, and now . . . My darling! [*Laughs and kisses her.*] I have been waiting for you, my sweet, my darling! But I must tell you something . . . I can't put it off another minute . . .

ANYA [*Listlessly.*]   What now?

DUNYASHA   The clerk, Yepihodov, proposed to me, just after Easter.

ANYA   There you are, at it again . . . [*Straightening her hair.*] I've lost all my hairpins . . . [*She is staggering with exhaustion.*]

DUNYASHA   Really, I don't know what to think. He loves me—he loves me so!

ANYA [*Looking toward the door of her room, tenderly.*]   My own room, my windows, just as though I'd never been away. I'm home! Tomorrow morning I'll get up and run into the orchard. Oh, if I could only get some sleep. I didn't close my eyes during the whole journey—I was so anxious.

DUNYASHA   Pyotr Sergeyevich came the day before yesterday.

ANYA [*Joyfully.*]   Petya!

DUNYASHA   He's asleep in the bathhouse. He has settled there. He said he was afraid of being in the way. [*Looks at her watch.*] I should wake him, but Miss Varya told me not to. "Don't you wake him," she said.

[*Enter* VARYA *with a bunch of keys at her belt.*]

VARYA   Dunyasha, coffee, and be quick. . . . Mamma's asking for coffee.

DUNYASHA   In a minute. [*Exits.*]

VARYA   Well, thank God, you've come. You're home again. [*Fondling* ANYA.] My darling is here again. My pretty one is back.

ANYA   Oh, what I've been through!

VARYA   I can imagine.

ANYA   When we left, it was Holy Week, it was cold then, and all the way
   Charlotta chattered and did her tricks. Why did you have to saddle me
   with Charlotta?
VARYA   You couldn't have travelled all alone, darling—at seventeen!
ANYA   We got to Paris, it was cold there, snowing. My French is dreadful.
   Mamma lived on the fifth floor; I went up there, and found all kinds of
   Frenchmen, ladies, an old priest with a book. The place was full of
   tobacco smoke, and so bleak. Suddenly I felt sorry for Mamma, so sorry,
   I took her head in my arms and hugged her and couldn't let go of her.
   Afterward Mamma kept fondling me and crying. . . .
VARYA   [Through tears.]   Don't speak of it . . . don't.
ANYA   She had already sold her villa at Mentone, she had nothing left,
   nothing. I hadn't a kopeck left either, we had only just enough to get
   home. And Mamma wouldn't understand! When we had dinner at the
   stations, she always ordered the most expensive dishes, and tipped the
   waiters a whole ruble. Charlotta, too. And Yasha kept ordering, too—it
   was simply awful. You know Yasha's Mamma's footman now, we brought
   him here with us.
VARYA   Yes, I've seen the blackguard.
ANYA   Well, tell me—have you paid the interest?
VARYA   How could we?
ANYA   Good heavens, good heavens!
VARYA   In August the estate will be put up for sale.
ANYA   My God!
LOPAHIN   [Peeps in at the door and bleats.]   Meh-h-h.   [Disappears.]
VARYA   [Through tears.]   What I couldn't do to him! [Shakes her fist threat-
   eningly.]
ANYA   [Embracing VARYA gently.]   Varya, has he proposed to you? [VARYA
   shakes her head.] But he loves you. Why don't you come to an under-
   standing? What are you waiting for?
VARYA   Oh, I don't think anything will ever come of it. He's too busy, he
   has no time for me . . . pays no attention to me. I've washed my hands
   of him—I can't bear the sight of him. They all talk about our getting
   married, they all congratulate me—and all the time there's really nothing
   to it—it's all like a dream. [In another tone.] You have a new brooch—
   like a bee.
ANYA   [Sadly.]   Mamma bought it. [She goes into her own room and speaks
   gaily like a child.] And you know, in Paris I went up in a balloon.
VARYA   My darling's home, my pretty one is back. [DUNYASHA returns with
   the coffeepot and prepares coffee. VARYA stands at the door of ANYA's room.]
   All day long, darling, as I go about the house, I keep dreaming. If only
   we could marry you off to a rich man, I should feel at ease. Then I would
   go into a convent, and afterward to Kiev, to Moscow . . . I would spend
   my life going from one holy place to another . . . I'd go on and on. . . .
   What a blessing that would be!
ANYA   The birds are singing in the orchard. What time is it?
VARYA   It must be after two. Time you were asleep, darling. [Goes into
   ANYA's room.] What a blessing that would be!
   [YASHA enters with a plaid and a traveling bag, crosses the stage.]
YASHA   [Finically.]   May I pass this way, please?

DUNYASHA A person could hardly recognize you, Yasha. Your stay abroad has certainly done wonders for you.

YASHA Hm-m . . . and who are you?

DUNYASHA When you went away I was that high—[*Indicating with her hand.*] I'm Dunyasha—Fyodor Kozoyedev's daughter. Don't you remember?

YASHA Hm! What a peach!

[*He looks round and embraces her. She cries out and drops a saucer.* YASHA *leaves quickly.*]

VARYA [*In the doorway, in a tone of annoyance.*] What's going on here?

DUNYASHA [*Through tears.*] I've broken a saucer.

VARYA Well, that's good luck.

ANYA [*Coming out of her room.*] We ought to warn Mamma that Petya's here.

VARYA I left orders not to wake him.

ANYA [*Musingly.*] Six years ago father died. A month later brother Grisha was drowned in the river. . . . Such a pretty little boy he was—only seven. It was more than Mamma could bear, so she went away, went away without looking back . . . [*Shudders.*] How well I understand her, if she only knew! [*Pause.*] And Petya Trofimov was Grisha's tutor, he may remind her of it all . . .

[*Enter* FIRS, *wearing a jacket and a white waistcoat. He goes up to the coffeepot.*]

FIRS [*Anxiously.*] The mistress will have her coffee here. [*Puts on white gloves.*] Is the coffee ready? [*Sternly, to* DUNYASHA.] Here, you! And where's the cream?

DUNYASHA Oh, my God! [*Exits quickly.*]

FIRS [*Fussing over the coffeepot.*] Hah! the addlehead! [*Mutters to himself.*] Home from Paris. And the old master used to go to Paris too . . . by carriage. [*Laughs.*]

VARYA What is it, Firs?

FIRS What is your pleasure, Miss? [*Joyfully.*] My mistress has come home, and I've seen her at last! Now I can die. [*Weeps with joy.*]

[*Enters* RANEVSKAYA, GAYEV, *and* SIMEONOV-PISHCHIK: *The latter is wearing a tight-waisted, pleated coat of fine cloth, and full trousers.* GAYEV, *as he comes in, goes through the motions of a billiard player with his arms and body.*]

MME. RANEVSKAYA Let's see, how does it go? Yellow ball in the corner! Bank shot in the side pocket!

GAYEV I'll tip it in the corner! There was a time, Sister, when you and I used to sleep in this very room and now I'm fifty-one, strange as it may seem.

LOPAHIN Yes, time flies.

GAYEV Who?

LOPAHIN I say, time flies.

GAYEV It smells of patchouli here.

ANYA I'm going to bed. Good night, Mamma. [*Kisses her mother.*]

MME. RANEVSKAYA My darling child! [*Kisses her hands.*] Are you happy to be home? I can't come to my senses.

ANYA Good night, Uncle.

GAYEV [*Kissing her face and hands.*]   God bless you, how like your mother you are! [*To his sister.*] At her age, Luba, you were just like her.

     [ANYA *shakes hands with* LOPAHIN *and* PISHCHIK, *then goes out, shutting the door behind her.*]

MME. RANEVSKAYA   She's very tired.

PISHCHIK   Well, it was a long journey.

VARYA [*To* LOPAHIN *and* PISHCHIK.]   How about it, gentlemen? It's past two o'clock—isn't it time for you to go?

MME. RANEVSKAYA [*Laughs.*]   You're just the same as ever, Varya. [*Draws her close and kisses her.*] I'll have my coffee and then we'll all go. [FIRS *puts a small cushion under her feet.*] Thank you, my dear. I've got used to coffee. I drink it day and night. Thanks, my dear old man. [*Kisses him.*]

VARYA   I'd better see if all the luggage has been brought in. [*Exits.*]

MME. RANEVSKAYA   Can it really be I sitting here? [*Laughs.*] I feel like dancing, waving my arms about. [*Covers her face with her hands.*] But maybe I am dreaming! God knows I love my country, I love it tenderly; I couldn't look out of the window in the train, I kept crying so. [*Through tears.*] But I must have my coffee. Thank you, Firs, thank you, dear old man. I'm so happy that you're still alive.

FIRS   Day before yesterday.

GAYEV   He's hard of hearing.

LOPAHIN   I must go soon, I'm leaving for Kharkov about five o'clock. How annoying! I'd like to have a good look at you, talk to you. . . . You're just as splendid as ever.

PISHCHIK [*Breathing heavily.*]   She's even better-looking. . . . Dressed in the latest Paris fashion. . . . Perish my carriage and all its four wheels. . . .

LOPAHIN   Your brother, Leonid Andreyevich, says I'm a vulgarian and an exploiter. But it's all the same to me—let him talk. I only want you to trust me as you used to. I want you to look at me with your touching, wonderful eyes, as you used to. Dear God! My father was a serf of your father's and grandfather's, but you, you yourself, did so much for me once . . . so much . . . that I've forgotten all about that; I love you as though you were my sister—even more.

MME. RANEVSKAYA   I can't sit still, I simply can't. [*Jumps up and walks about in violent agitation.*] This joy is too much for me. . . . Laugh at me, I'm silly! My own darling bookcase! My darling table! [*Kisses it.*]

GAYEV   While you were away, nurse died.

MME. RANEVSKAYA [*Sits down and takes her coffee.*]   Yes, God rest her soul; they wrote me about it.

GAYEV   And Anastasy is dead. Petrushka Kossoy has left me and has gone into town to work for the police inspector. [*Takes a box of sweets out of his pocket and begins to suck one.*]

PISHCHIK   My daughter Dashenka sends her regards.

LOPAHIN   I'd like to tell you something very pleasant—cheering. [*Glancing at his watch.*] I am leaving directly. There isn't much time to talk. But I will put it in a few words. As you know, your cherry orchard is to be sold to pay your debts. The sale is to be on the twenty-second of August; but don't you worry, my dear, you may sleep in peace; there is a way out. Here is my plan. Give me your attention! Your estate is only fifteen miles from the town; the railway runs close by it; and if the cherry orchard and the land along the riverbank were cut up into lots and these leased for summer cottages, you would have an income of at least 25,000 rubles a year out of it.

GAYEV   Excuse me. . . . What nonsense.

MME. RANEVSKAYA   I don't quite understand you, Yermolay Alexeyevich.

LOPAHIN   You will get an annual rent of at least ten rubles per acre, and if you advertise at once, I'll give you any guarantee you like that you won't have a square foot of ground left by autumn, all the lots will be snapped up. In short, congratulations, you're saved. The location is splendid—by that deep river. . . . Only, of course, the ground must be cleared . . . all the old buildings, for instance, must be torn down, and this house, too, which is useless, and, of course, the old cherry orchard must be cut down.

MME. RANEVSKAYA   Cut down? My dear, forgive me, but you don't know what you're talking about. If there's one thing that's interesting—indeed, remarkable—in the whole province, it's precisely our cherry orchard.

LOPAHIN   The only remarkable thing about this orchard is that it's a very large one. There's a crop of cherries every other year, and you can't do anything with them; no one buys them.

GAYEV   This orchard is even mentioned in the encyclopedia.

LOPAHIN [Glancing at his watch.]   If we can't think of a way out, if we don't come to a decision, on the twenty-second of August the cherry orchard and the whole estate will be sold at auction. Make up your minds! There's no other way out—I swear. None, none.

FIRS   In the old days, forty or fifty years ago, the cherries were dried, soaked, pickled, and made into jam, and we used to—

GAYEV   Keep still, firs.

FIRS   And the dried cherries would be shipped by the cartload. It meant a lot of money! And in those days the dried cherries were soft and juicy, sweet, fragrant. . . . They knew the way to do it, then.

MME. RANEVSKAYA   And why don't they do it that way now?

FIRS   They've forgotten. Nobody remembers it.

PISHCHIK [To MME. RANEVSKAYA.]   What's doing in Paris? Eh? Did you eat frogs there?

MME. RANEVSKAYA   I ate crocodiles.

PISHCHIK   Just imagine!

LOPAHIN   There used to be only landowners and peasants in the country, but now these summer people have appeared on the scene. . . . All the towns, even the small ones, are surrounded by these summer cottages; and in another twenty years, no doubt, the summer population will have grown enormously. Now the summer resident only drinks tea on his porch, but maybe he'll take to working his acre, too, and then your cherry orchard will be a rich, happy, luxuriant place.

GAYEV [Indignantly.]   Poppycock!

[Enter VARYA and YASHA.]

VARYA   There are two telegrams for you, Mamma dear. [Picks a key from the bunch at her belt and noisily opens an old-fashioned bookcase.] Here they are.

MME. RANEVSKAYA   They're from Paris. [Tears them up without reading them.] I'm through with Paris.

GAYEV   Do you know, Luba, how old this bookcase is? Last week I pulled out the bottom drawer and there I found the date burnt in it. It was made exactly a hundred years ago. Think of that! We could celebrate its centenary. True, it's an inanimate object, but nevertheless, a bookcase . . .

PISHCHIK [*Amazed.*]   A hundred years! Just imagine!

GAYEV   Yes. [*Tapping it.*] That's something. . . . Dear, honored bookcase, hail to you who for more than a century have served the glorious ideals of goodness and justice! Your silent summons to fruitful toil has never weakened in all those hundred years [*through tears*], sustaining, through successive generations of our family, courage and faith in a better future, and fostering in us ideals of goodness and social consciousness. [*Pauses.*]

LOPAHIN   Yes . . .

MME. RANEVSKAYA   You haven't changed a bit, Leonid.

GAYEV [*Somewhat embarrassed.*]   I'll play it off the red in the corner! Tip it in the side pocket!

LOPAHIN [*Looking at his watch.*]   Well, it's time for me to go . . .

YASHA [*Handing pillbox to* MME. RANEVSKAYA.]   Perhaps you'll take your pills now.

PISHCHIK   One shouldn't take medicines, dearest lady, they do neither harm nor good. . . . Give them here, my valued friend. [*Takes the pillbox, pours the pills into his palm, blows on them, puts them in his mouth, and washes them down with some kvass.*] There!

MME. RANEVSKAYA [*Frightened.*]   You must be mad!

PISHCHIK   I've taken all the pills.

LOPAHIN   What a glutton!

   [*All laugh.*]

FIRS   The gentleman visited us in Easter week, ate half a bucket of pickles, he did . . . [*Mumbles.*]

MME. RANEVSKAYA   What's he saying?

VARYA   He's been mumbling like that for the last three years—we're used to it.

YASHA   His declining years!

   [CHARLOTTA IVANOVNA, *very thin, tightly laced, dressed in white, a lorgnette at her waist, crosses the stage.*]

LOPAHIN   Forgive me, Charlotta Ivanovna, I've not had time to greet you. [*Tries to kiss her hand.*]

CHARLOTTA [*Pulling away her hand.*]   If I let you kiss my hand, you'll be wanting to kiss my elbow next, and then my shoulder.

LOPAHIN   I've no luck today. [*All laugh.*] Charlotta Ivanovna, show us a trick.

MME. RANEVSKAYA   Yes, Charlotta, do a trick for us.

CHARLOTTA   I don't see the need. I want to sleep. [*Exits.*]

LOPAHIN   In three weeks we'll meet again. [*Kisses* MME. RANEVSKAYA's *hand.*] Good-bye till then. Time's up. [*To* GAYEV.] Bye-bye. [*Kisses* PISHCHIK.] Bye-bye. [*Shakes hands with* VARYA, *then with* FIRS *and* YASHA.] I hate to leave. [*To* MME. RANEVSKAYA.] If you make up your mind about the cottages, let me know; I'll get you a loan of 50,000 rubles.[3] Think it over seriously.

---

3. The basic unit of currency. One ruble is equal to 100 kopecks.

VARYA [*Crossly.*]   Will you never go!

LOPAHIN   I'm going, I'm going. [*Exits.*]

GAYEV   The vulgarian. But, excuse me . . . Varya's going to marry him, he's Varya's fiancé.

VARYA   You talk too much, Uncle.

MME. RANEVSKAYA   Well, Varya, it would make me happy. He's a good man.

PISHCHIK   Yes, one must admit, he's a most estimable man. And my Dashenka . . . she too says that . . . she says . . . lots of things. [*Snores; but wakes up at once.*] All the same, my valued friend, could you oblige me . . . with a loan of 240 rubles? I must pay the interest on the mortgage tomorrow.

VARYA [*Alarmed.*]   We can't, we can't!

MME. RANEVSKAYA   I really haven't any money.

PISHCHIK   It'll turn up. [*Laughs.*] I never lose hope, I thought everything was lost, that I was done for, when lo and behold, the railway ran through my land . . . and I was paid for it. . . . And something else will turn up again, if not today, then tomorrow . . . Dashenka will win two hundred thousand . . . she's got a lottery ticket.

MME. RANEVSKAYA   I've had my coffee, now let's go to bed.

FIRS [*Brushes off* GAYEV; *admonishingly.*]   You've got the wrong trousers on again. What am I to do with you?

VARYA [*Softly.*]   Anya's asleep. [*Gently opens the window.*] The sun's up now, it's not a bit cold. Look, Mamma dear, what wonderful trees. And heavens, what air! The starlings are singing!

GAYEV [*Opens the other window.*]   The orchard is all white. You've not forgotten it? Luba? That's the long alley that runs straight, straight as an arrow; how it shines on moonlight nights, do you remember? You've not forgotten?

MME. RANEVSKAYA [*Looking out of the window into the orchard.*]   Oh, my childhood, my innocent childhood. I used to sleep in this nursery—I used to look out into the orchard, happiness waked with me every morning, the orchard was just the same then . . . nothing has changed. [*Laughs with joy.*] All, all white! Oh, my orchard! After the dark, rainy autumn and the cold winter, you are young again, and full of happiness, the heavenly angels have not left you. . . . If I could free my chest and my shoulders from this rock that weighs on me, if I could only forget the past!

GAYEV   Yes, and the orchard will be sold to pay our debts, strange as it may seem.

MME. RANEVSKAYA   Look! There is our poor mother walking in the orchard . . . all in white . . . [*Laughs with joy.*] It is she!

GAYEV   Where?

VARYA   What are you saying, Mamma dear!

MME. RANEVSKAYA   There's no one there, I just imagined it. To the right, where the path turns toward the arbor, there's a little white tree, leaning over, that looks like a woman . . .

[TROFIMOV *enters, wearing a shabby student's uniform and spectacles.*]

MME. RANEVSKAYA   What an amazing orchard! White masses of blossom, the blue sky . . .

TROFIMOV   Lubov Andreyevna! [*She looks round at him.*] I just want to pay

my respects to you, then I'll leave at once. [*Kisses her hand ardently.*] I
was told to wait until morning, but I hadn't the patience . . .

[MME. RANEVSKAYA *looks at him, perplexed.*]

VARYA [*Through tears.*]   This is Petya Trofimov.

TROFIMOV   Petya Trofimov, formerly your Grisha's tutor. . . . Can I have
changed so much?

[MME. RANEVSKAYA *embraces him and weeps quietly.*]

GAYEV [*Embarrassed.*]   Don't, don't, Luba.

VARYA [*Crying.*]   I told you, Petya, to wait until tomorrow.

MME. RANEVSKAYA   My Grisha . . . my little boy . . . Grisha . . . my son.

VARYA   What can one do, Mamma dear, it's God's will.

TROFIMOV [*Softly, through tears.*]   There . . . there.

MME. RANEVSKAYA [*Weeping quietly.*]   My little boy was lost . . . drowned.
Why? Why, my friend? [*More quietly.*] Anya's asleep in there, and here
I am talking so loudly . . . making all this noise. . . . But tell me, Petya,
why do you look so badly? Why have you aged so?

TROFIMOV   A mangy master, a peasant woman in the train called me.

MME. RANEVSKAYA   You were just a boy then, a dear little student, and now
your hair's thin—and you're wearing glasses! Is it possible you're still a
student? [*Goes toward the door.*]

TROFIMOV   I suppose I'm a perpetual student.

MME. RANEVSKAYA [*Kisses her brother, then* VARYA.]   Now, go to bed. . . .
You have aged, too, Leonid.

PISHCHIK [*Follows her.*]   So now we turn in. Oh, my gout! I'm staying the
night here . . . Lubov Andreyevna, my angel, tomorrow morning . . . I do
need 240 rubles.

GAYEV   He keeps at it.

PISHCHIK   I'll pay it back, dear . . . it's a trifling sum.

MME. RANEVSKAYA   All right, Leonid will give it to you. Give it to him,
Leonid.

GAYEV   Me give it to him! That's a good one!

MME. RANEVSKAYA   It can't be helped. Give it to him! He needs it. He'll pay
it back.

[MME. RANEVSKAYA, TROFIMOV, PISHCHIK, *and* FIRS *go out;* GAYEV, VARYA,
and YASHA *remain.*]

GAYEV   Sister hasn't got out of the habit of throwing money around. [*To*
YASHA.] Go away, my good fellow, you smell of the barnyard.

YASHA [*With a grin.*]   And you, Leonid Andreyevich, are just the same as
ever.

GAYEV   Who? [*To* VARYA.] What did he say?

VARYA [*To* YASHA.]   Your mother's come from the village; she's been sitting
in the servants' room since yesterday, waiting to see you.

YASHA   Botheration!

VARYA   You should be ashamed of yourself!

YASHA   She's all I needed! She could have come tomorrow. [*Exits.*]

VARYA   Mamma is just the same as ever; she hasn't changed a bit. If she
had her own way, she'd keep nothing for herself.

GAYEV   Yes . . . [*Pauses.*] If a great many remedies are offered for some
disease, it means it is incurable; I keep thinking and racking my brains;
I have many remedies, ever so many, and that really means none. It would
be fine if we came in for a legacy; it would be fine if we married off our

Anya to a very rich man; or we might go to Yaroslavl and try our luck
with our aunt, the Countess. She's very rich, you know . . .

VARYA [*Weeping.*]   If only God would help us!

GAYEV   Stop bawling. Aunt's very rich, but she doesn't like us. In the first
place, Sister married a lawyer who was no nobleman . . . [ANYA *appears
in the doorway.*] She married beneath her, and it can't be said that her
behavior has been very exemplary. She's good, kind, sweet, and I love
her, but no matter what extenuating circumstances you may adduce,
there's no denying that she has no morals. You sense it in her least gesture.

VARYA [*In a whisper.*]   Anya's in the doorway.

GAYEV   Who? [*Pauses.*] It's queer, something got into my right eye—my
eyes are going back on me. . . . And on Thursday, when I was in the
circuit court—

   [*Enter* ANYA.]

VARYA   Why aren't you asleep, Anya?

ANYA   I can't get to sleep, I just can't.

GAYEV   My little pet! [*Kisses* ANYA's *face and hands.*] My child! [*Weeps.*] You
are not my niece, you're my angel! You're everything to me. Believe me,
believe—

ANYA   I believe you, Uncle. Everyone loves you and respects you . . . but,
Uncle dear, you must keep still. . . . You must. What were you saying just
now about my mother? Your own sister? What made you say that?

GAYEV   Yes, yes . . . [*Covers his face with her hand.*] Really, that was awful!
Good God! Heaven help me! Just now I made a speech to the bookcase
. . . so stupid! And only after I was through, I saw how stupid it was.

VARYA   It's true, Uncle dear, you ought to keep still. Just don't talk, that's
all.

ANYA   If you could only keep still, it would make things easier for you, too.

GAYEV   I'll keep still. [*Kisses* ANYA's *and* VARYA's *hands.*] I will. But now about
business. On Thursday I was in court; well, there were a number of us
there, and we began talking of one thing and another, and this and that,
and do you know, I believe it will be possible to raise a loan on a promissory note to pay the interest at the bank.

VARYA   If only God would help us!

GAYEV   On Tuesday I'll go and see about it again. [*To* VARYA.] Stop bawling.
[*To* ANYA.] Your mamma will talk to lopahin, and he, of course, will not
refuse her . . . and as soon as you're rested, you'll go to Yaroslavl to the
Countess, your great-aunt. So we'll be working in three directions at
once, and the thing is in the bag. We'll pay the interest—I'm sure of it.
[*Puts a candy in his mouth.*] I swear on my honor, I swear by anything
you like, the estate shan't be sold. [*Excitedly.*] I swear by my own happiness! Here's my hand on it, you can call me a swindler and a scoundrel
if I let it come to an auction! I swear by my whole being.

ANYA [*Relieved and quite happy again.*]   How good you are, Uncle, and
how clever! [*Embraces him.*] Now I'm at peace, quite at peace, I'm happy.
   [*Enter* FIRS.]

FIRS [*Reproachfully.*]   Leonid Andreyevich, have you no fear of God?
When are you going to bed?

GAYEV   Directly, directly. Go away, Firs, I'll . . . yes, I will undress myself.
Now, children, 'nightie-'nightie. We'll consider details tomorrow, but

now go to sleep. [*Kisses* ANYA *and* VARYA.] I am a man of the eighties; they have nothing good to say of that period nowadays. Nevertheless, in the course of my life, I have suffered not a little for my convictions. It's not for nothing that the peasant loves me; one should know the peasant; one should know from which—

ANYA   There you go again, Uncle.

VARYA   Uncle dear, be quiet.

FIRS [*Angrily.*]   Leonid Andreyevich!

GAYEV   I'm coming, I'm coming! Go to bed! Double bank shot in the side pocket! Here goes a clean shot . . .

[*Exits,* FIRS *hobbling after him.*]

ANYA   I am at peace now. I don't want to go to Yaroslavl—I don't like my great-aunt, but still, I am at peace, thanks to Uncle. [*Sits down.*]

VARYA   We must get some sleep. I'm going now. While you were away, something unpleasant happened. In the old servants' quarters, there are only the old people as you know; Yefim, Polya, Yevstigney, and Karp, too. They began letting all sorts of rascals in to spend the night. . . . I didn't say anything. Then I heard they'd been spreading a report that I gave them nothing but dried peas to eat—out of stinginess, you know . . . and it was all Yevstigney's doing. . . . All right, I thought, if that's how it is, I thought, just wait. I sent for Yevstigney . . . [*Yawns.*] He comes. . . . "How's this, Yevstigney?" I say, "You fool . . ." [*Looking at* ANYA.] Anichka! [*Pauses.*] She's asleep. [*Puts her arm around* ANYA.] Come to your little bed. . . . Come . . . [*Leads her.*] My darling has fallen asleep. . . . Come.

[*They go out. Far away beyond the orchard, a shepherd is piping.* TRO-FIMOV *crosses the stage and, seeing* VARYA *and* ANYA, *stands still.*]

VARYA   Sh! She's asleep . . . asleep. . . . Come, darling.

ANYA [*Softly, half-asleep.*]   I'm so tired. Those bells . . . Uncle . . . dear. . . . Mamma and Uncle . . .

VARYA   Come, my precious, come along. [*They go into* ANYA's *room.*]

TROFIMOV [*With emotion.*]   My sunshine, my spring!

Act II

A meadow. An old, long-abandoned, lopsided little chapel; near it a well, large slabs, which had apparently once served as tombstones, and an old bench. In the background the road to the Gayev estate. To one side poplars loom darkly, where the cherry orchard begins. In the distance a row of telegraph poles, and far off, on the horizon, the faint outline of a large city which is seen only in fine, clear weather. The sun will soon be setting. CHARLOTTA, YASHA, *and* DUNYASHA *are seated on the bench.* YEPIHODOV *stands near and plays a guitar. All are pensive.* CHARLOTTA *wears an old peaked cap. She has taken a gun from her shoulder and is straightening the buckle on the strap.*

CHARLOTTA [*Musingly.*]   I haven't a real passport, I don't know how old I am, and I always feel that I am very young. When I was a little girl, my father and mother used to go from fair to fair and give performances, very good ones. And I used to do the *salto mortale*,[4] and all sorts of other

---

4. Somersault (Italian).

tricks. And when papa and mamma died, a German lady adopted me and began to educate me. Very good. I grew up and became a governess. But where I come from and who am I, I don't know. . . . Who were my parents? Perhaps they weren't even married. . . . I don't know . . . [*Takes a cucumber out of her pocket and eats it.*] I don't know a thing. [*Pause.*] One wants so much to talk, and there isn't anyone to talk to. . . . I haven't anybody.

YEPIHODOV [*Plays the guitar and sings.*] "What care I for the jarring world? What's friend or foe to me? . . ." How agreeable it is to play the mandolin.

DUNYASHA   That's a guitar, not a mandolin. [*Looks in a hand mirror and powders her face.*]

YEPIHODOV   To a madman in love it's a mandolin. [*Sings.*] "Would that the heart were warmed by the fire of mutual love!"
[YASHA *joins in.*]

CHARLOTTA   How abominably these people sing. Pfui! Like jackals!

DUNYASHA [*To* YASHA.]   How wonderful it must be though to have stayed abroad!

YASHA   Ah, yes, of course, I cannot but agree with you there. [*Yawns and lights a cigar.*]

YEPIHODOV   Naturally. Abroad, everything has long since achieved full perfection.

YASHA   That goes without saying.

YEPIHODOV   I'm a cultivated man, I read all kinds of remarkable books. And yet I can never make out what direction I should take, what is it that I want, properly speaking. Should I live, or should I shoot myself, properly speaking? Nevertheless, I always carry a revolver about me. . . . Here it is . . . [*Shows revolver.*]

CHARLOTTA   I've finished. I'm going. [*Puts the gun over her shoulder.*] You are a very clever man, Yepihodov, and a very terrible one; women must be crazy about you. Br-r-r! [*Starts to go.*] These clever men are all so stupid; there's no one for me to talk to . . . always alone, alone, I haven't a soul . . . and who I am, and why I am, nobody knows. [*Exits unhurriedly.*]

YEPIHODOV   Properly speaking and letting other subjects alone, I must say regarding myself, among other things, that fate treats me mercilessly, like a storm treats a small boat. If I am mistaken, let us say, why then do I wake up this morning, and there on my chest is a spider of enormous dimensions . . . like this . . . [*Indicates with both hands.*] Again, I take up a pitcher of kvass to have a drink, and in it there is something unseemly to the highest degree, something like a cockroach. [*Pause.*] Have you read Buckle?[5] [*Pause.*] I wish to have a word with you, Avdotya Fyodorovna, if I may trouble you.

DUNYASHA   Well, go ahead.

YEPIHODOV   I wish to speak with you alone. [*Sighs.*]

DUNYASHA [*Embarrassed.*]   Very well. Only first bring me my little cape. You'll find it near the wardrobe. It's rather damp here.

YEPIHODOV   Certainly, ma'am; I will fetch it, ma'am. Now I know what to do with my revolver. [*Takes the guitar and goes off playing it.*]

---

5. Henry Thomas Buckle (1821–1862) wrote a *History of Civilization in England* (1857–61), which was considered daringly materialistic and free thinking.

YASHA Two-and-Twenty Troubles! An awful fool, between you and me. [*Yawns.*]

DUNYASHA I hope to God he doesn't shoot himself! [*Pause.*] I've become so nervous, I'm always fretting. I was still a little girl when I was taken into the big house, I am quite unused to the simple life now, and my hands are white, as white as a lady's. I've become so soft, so delicate, so refined, I'm afraid of everything. It's so terrifying; and if you deceive me, yasha, I don't know what will happen to my nerves. [YASHA *kisses her.*]

YASHA You're a peach! Of course, a girl should never forget herself; and what I dislike more than anything is when a girl don't behave properly.

DUNYASHA I've fallen passionately in love with you; you're educated—you have something to say about everything. [*Pause.*]

YASHA [*Yawns.*] Yes, ma'am. Now the way I look at it, if a girl loves someone, it means she is immoral. [*Pause.*] It's agreeable smoking a cigar in the fresh air. [*Listens.*] Someone's coming this way. . . . It's our madam and the others. [DUNYASHA *embraces him impulsively.*] You go home, as though you'd been to the river to bathe; go to the little path, or else they'll run into you and suspect me of having arranged to meet you here. I can't stand that sort of thing.

DUNYASHA [*Coughing softly.*] Your cigar's made my head ache.

[*Exits.* YASHA *remains standing near the chapel. Enter* MME. RANEVSKAYA, GAYEV, *and* LOPAHIN.]

LOPAHIN You must make up your mind once and for all—there's no time to lose. It's quite a simple question, you know. Do you agree to lease your land for summer cottages or not? Answer in one word, yes or no; only one word!

MME. RANEVSKAYA Who's been smoking such abominable cigars here? [*Sits down.*]

GAYEV Now that the railway line is so near, it's made things very convenient. [*Sits down.*] Here we've been able to have lunch in town. Yellow ball in the side pocket! I feel like going into the house and playing just one game.

MME. RANEVSKAYA You can do that later.

LOPAHIN Only one word! [*Imploringly.*] Do give me an answer!

GAYEV [*Yawning.*] Who?

MME. RANEVSKAYA [*Looks into her purse.*] Yesterday I had a lot of money and now my purse is almost empty. My poor Varya tries to economize by feeding us just milk soup; in the kitchen the old people get nothing but dried peas to eat, while I squander money thoughtlessly. [*Drops the purse, scattering gold pieces.*] You see, there they go . . . [*Shows vexation.*]

YASHA Allow me—I'll pick them up. [*Picks up the money.*]

MME. RANEVSKAYA Be so kind. Yasha. And why did I go to lunch in town? That nasty restaurant, with its music and the tablecloth smelling of soap. . . . Why drink so much, Leonid? Why eat so much? Why talk so much? Today again you talked a lot, and all so inappropriately about the seventies, about the decadents.[6] And to whom? Talking to waiters about decadents!

6. A group of French poets of the 1880s (Mallarmé is today the most famous) were labeled "decadents" by their enemies and sometimes adopted the name themselves, proud of their refinement and sensitivity.

LOPAHIN Yes.

GAYEV [*Waving his hand.*] I'm incorrigible; that's obvious. [*Irritably, to* YASHA.] Why do you keep dancing about in front of me?

YASHA [*Laughs.*] I can't hear your voice without laughing—

GAYEV Either he or I—

MME. RANEVSKAYA Go away, Yasha; run along.

YASHA [*Handing* MME. RANEVSKAYA *her purse.*] I'm going at once. [*Hardly able to suppress his laughter.*] This minute. [*Exits.*]

LOPAHIN That rich man, Deriganov, wants to buy your estate. They say he's coming to the auction himself.

MME. RANEVSKAYA Where did you hear that?

LOPAHIN That's what they are saying in town.

GAYEV Our aunt in Yaroslavl has promised to help, but when she will send the money, and how much, no one knows.

LOPAHIN How much will she send? A hundred thousand? Two hundred?

MME. RANEVSKAYA Oh, well, ten or fifteen thousand; and we'll have to be grateful for that.

LOPAHIN Forgive me, but such frivolous people as you are, so queer and unbusinesslike—I never met in my life. One tells you in plain language that your estate is up for sale, and you don't seem to take it in.

MME. RANEVSKAYA What are we to do? Tell us what to do.

LOPAHIN I do tell you, every day; every day I say the same thing! You must lease the cherry orchard and the land for summer cottages, you must do it and as soon as possible—right away. The auction is close at hand. Please understand! Once you've decided to have the cottages, you can raise as much money as you like, and you're saved.

MME. RANEVSKAYA Cottages—summer people—forgive me, but it's all so vulgar.

GAYEV I agree with you absolutely.

LOPAHIN I shall either burst into tears or scream or faint! I can't stand it! You've worn me out! [*To* GAYEV.] You're an old woman!

GAYEV Who?

LOPAHIN An old woman! [*Gets up to go.*]

MME. RANEVSKAYA [*Alarmed.*] No, don't go! Please stay, I beg you, my dear. Perhaps we shall think of something.

LOPAHIN What is there to think of?

MME. RANEVSKAYA Don't go, I beg you. With you here it's more cheerful anyway. [*Pause.*] I keep expecting something to happen, it's as though the house were going to crash about our ears.

GAYEV [*In deep thought.*] Bank shot in the corner. . . . Three cushions in the side pocket. . . .

MME. RANEVSKAYA We have been great sinners . . .

LOPAHIN What sins could you have committed?

GAYEV [*Putting a candy in his mouth.*] They say I've eaten up my fortune in candy! [*Laughs.*]

MME. RANEVSKAYA Oh, my sins! I've squandered money away recklessly, like a lunatic, and I married a man who made nothing but debts. My husband drank himself to death on champagne, he was a terrific drinker. And then, to my sorrow, I fell in love with another man, and I lived with him. And just then—that was my first punishment—a blow on the head:

my little boy was drowned here in the river. And I went abroad, went away forever . . . never to come back, never to see this river again . . . I closed my eyes and ran, out of my mind. . . . But he followed me, pitiless, brutal. I bought a villa near Mentone, because he fell ill there; and for three years, day and night, I knew no peace, no rest. The sick man wore me out, he sucked my soul dry. Then last year, when the villa was sold to pay my debts, I went to Paris, and there he robbed me, abandoned me, took up with another woman, I tried to poison myself—it was stupid, so shameful—and then suddenly I felt drawn back to Russia, back, to my own country, to my little girl. [*Wipes her tears away.*] Lord, Lord! Be merciful, forgive me my sins—don't punish me anymore! [*Takes a telegram out of her pocket.*] This came today from Paris—he begs me to forgive him, implores me to go back . . . [*Tears up the telegram.*] Do I hear music? [*Listens.*]

GAYEV   That's our famous Jewish band, you remember? Four violins, a flute, and a double bass.

MME. RANEVSKAYA   Does it still exist? We ought to send for them some evening and have a party.

LOPAHIN [*Listens.*]   I don't hear anything. [*Hums softly.*] "The Germans for a fee will Frenchify a Russian."[7] [*Laughs.*] I saw a play at the theater yesterday—awfully funny.

MME. RANEVSKAYA   There was probably nothing funny about it. You shouldn't go to see plays, you should look at yourselves more often. How drab your lives are—how full of unnecessary talk.

LOPAHIN   That's true; come to think of it, we do live like fools. [*Pause.*] My pop was a peasant, an idiot; he understood nothing, never taught me anything, all he did was beat me when he was drunk, and always with a stick. Fundamentally, I'm just the same kind of blockhead and idiot. I was never taught anything—I have a terrible handwriting. I write so that I feel ashamed before people, like a pig.

MME. RANEVSKAYA   You should get married, my friend.

LOPAHIN   Yes . . . that's true.

MME. RANEVSKAYA   To our Varya, she's a good girl.

LOPAHIN   Yes.

MME. RANEVSKAYA   She's a girl who comes of simple people, she works all day long; and above all, she loves you. Besides, you've liked her for a long time now.

LOPAHIN   Well, I've nothing against it. She's a good girl. [*Pause.*]

GAYEV   I've been offered a place in the bank—6,000 a year. Have you heard?

MME. RANEVSKAYA   You're not up to it. Stay where you are.

[FIRS *enters, carrying an overcoat.*]

FIRS [*To* GAYEV.]   Please put this on, sir, it's damp.

GAYEV [*Putting it on.*]   I'm fed up with you, brother.

FIRS   Never mind. This morning you drove off without saying a word. [*Looks him over.*]

MME. RANEVSKAYA   How you've aged, Firs.

---

7. Satirical reference to Russian efforts, from the time of Peter the Great (1672–1725), to imitate Western Europe and particularly Parisian culture.

FIRS   I beg your pardon?

LOPAHIN   The lady says you've aged.

FIRS   I've lived a long time; they were arranging my wedding and your papa wasn't born yet. [*Laughs.*] When freedom came[8] I was already head footman. I wouldn't consent to be set free then; I stayed on with the master . . . [*Pause.*] I remember they were all very happy, but why they were happy, they didn't know themselves.

LOPAHIN   It was fine in the old days! At least there was flogging!

FIRS [*Not hearing.*]   Of course. The peasants kept to the masters, the masters kept to the peasants; but now they've all gone their own ways, and there's no making out anything.

GAYEV   Be quiet, Firs. I must go to town tomorrow. They've promised to introduce me to a general who might let us have a loan.

LOPAHIN   Nothing will come of that. You won't even be able to pay the interest, you can be certain of that.

MME. RANEVSKAYA   He's raving, there isn't any general.

[*Enter* TROFIMOV, ANYA, *and* VARYA.]

GAYEV   Here come our young people.

ANYA   There's Mamma, on the bench.

MME. RANEVSKAYA [*Tenderly.*]   Come here, come along, my darlings. [*Embraces* ANYA *and* VARYA.] If you only knew how I love you both! Sit beside me—there, like that. [*All sit down.*]

LOPAHIN   Our perpetual student is always with the young ladies.

TROFIMOV   That's not any of your business.

LOPAHIN   He'll soon be fifty, and he's still a student!

TROFIMOV   Stop your silly jokes.

LOPAHIN   What are you so cross about, you queer bird?

TROFIMOV   Oh, leave me alone.

LOPAHIN [*Laughs.*]   Allow me to ask you, what do you think of me?

TROFIMOV   What I think of you, Yermolay Alexeyevich, is this: you are a rich man who will soon be a millionaire. Well, just as a beast of prey, which devours everything that comes in its way, is necessary for the process of metabolism to go on, so you, too, are necessary. [*All laugh.*]

VARYA   Better tell us something about the planets, Petya.

MME. RANEVSKAYA   No, let's go on with yesterday's conversation.

TROFIMOV   What was it about?

GAYEV   About man's pride.

TROFIMOV   Yesterday we talked a long time, but we came to no conclusion. There is something mystical about man's pride in your sense of the word. Perhaps you're right, from your own point of view. But if you reason simply, without going into subtleties, then what call is there for pride? Is there any sense in it, if man is so poor a thing physiologically, and if, in the great majority of cases, he is coarse, stupid, profoundly unhappy? We should stop admiring ourselves. We should work, and that's all.

GAYEV   You die, anyway.

TROFIMOV   Who knows? And what does it mean—to die? Perhaps man has a hundred senses, and at his death only the five we know perish, while the other ninety-five remain alive.

8. Czar (or Tsar) Alexander II (ruled 1855–81) emancipated the serfs in 1861.

MME. RANEVSKAYA   How clever you are, Petya!

LOPAHIN [*Ironically.*]   Awfully clever!

TROFIMOV   Mankind goes forward, developing its powers. Everything that is now unattainable for it will one day come within man's reach and be clear to him; only we must work, helping with all our might those who seek the truth. Here among us in Russia only the very few work as yet. The great majority of the intelligentsia, as far as I can see, seek nothing, do nothing, are totally unfit for work of any kind. They call themselves the intelligentsia, yet they are uncivil to their servants, treat the peasants like animals, are poor students, never read anything serious, do absolutely nothing at all, only talk about science, and have little appreciation of the arts. They are all solemn, have grim faces, they all philosophize and talk of weighty matters. And meanwhile the vast majority of us, ninety-nine out of a hundred, live like savages. At the least provocation— a punch in the jaw, and curses. They eat disgustingly, sleep in filth and stuffiness, bedbugs everywhere, stench and damp and moral slovenliness. And obviously, the only purpose of all our fine talk is to hoodwink ourselves and others. Show me where the public nurseries are that we've heard so much about, and the libraries. We read about them in novels, but in reality they don't exist, there is nothing but dirt, vulgarity, and Asiatic backwardness. I don't like very solemn faces, I'm afraid of them, I'm afraid of serious conversations. We'd do better to keep quiet for a while.

LOPAHIN   Do you know, I get up at five o'clock in the morning, and I work from morning till night; and I'm always handling money, my own and other people's, and I see what people around me are really like. You've only to start doing anything to see how few honest, decent people there are. Sometimes when I lie awake at night, I think: "Oh, Lord, thou hast given us immense forests, boundless fields, the widest horizons, and living in their midst, we ourselves ought really to be giants."

MME. RANEVSKAYA   Now you want giants! They're only good in fairy tales; otherwise they're frightening.

[YEPIHODOV *crosses the stage at the rear, playing the guitar.*]

MME. RANEVSKAYA [*Pensively.*]   There goes Yepihodov.

GAYEV   Ladies and gentlemen, the sun has set.

TROFIMOV   Yes.

GAYEV [*In a low voice, declaiming as it were.*]   Oh, Nature, wondrous Nature, you shine with eternal radiance, beautiful and indifferent! You, whom we call our mother, unite within yourself life and death! You animate and destroy!

VARYA [*Pleadingly.*]   Uncle dear!

ANYA   Uncle, again!

TROFIMOV   You'd better bank the yellow ball in the side pocket.

GAYEV   I'm silent, I'm silent . . .

[*All sit plunged in thought. Stillness reigns. Only* FIRS's *muttering is audible. Suddenly a distant sound is heard, coming from the sky as it were, the sound of a snapping string, mournfully dying away.*]

MME. RANEVSKAYA   What was that?

LOPAHIN   I don't know. Somewhere far away, in the pits, a bucket's broken loose; but somewhere very far away.

GAYEV   Or it might be some sort of bird, perhaps a heron.

TROFIMOV   Or an owl . . .

MME. RANEVSKAYA [*Shudders.*]   It's weird, somehow. [*Pause.*]

FIRS   Before the calamity the same thing happened—the owl screeched, and the samovar hummed all the time.

GAYEV   Before what calamity?

FIRS   Before the Freedom. [*Pause.*]

MME. RANEVSKAYA   Come, my friends, let's be going. It's getting dark. [*To* ANYA.] You have tears in your eyes. What is it, my little one? [*Embraces her.*]

ANYA   I don't know, Mamma; it's nothing.

TROFIMOV   Somebody's coming.

[A TRAMP *appears, wearing a shabby white cap and an overcoat. He is slightly drunk.*]

TRAMP   Allow me to inquire, will this short cut take me to the station?

GAYEV   It will. Just follow that road.

TRAMP   My heartfelt thanks. [*Coughing.*] The weather is glorious. [*Recites.*] "My brother, my suffering brother. . . . Go down to the Volga!9 Whose groans . . . ?" [*To* VARYA.] Mademoiselle, won't you spare 30 kopecks for a hungry Russian?

[VARYA, *frightened, cries out.*]

LOPAHIN [*Angrily.*]   Even panhandling has its proprieties.

MME. RANEVSKAYA [*Scared.*]   Here, take this. [*Fumbles in her purse.*] I haven't any silver . . . never mind, here's a gold piece.

TRAMP   My heartfelt thanks. [*Exits. Laughter.*]

VARYA [*Frightened.*]   I'm leaving. I'm leaving. . . . Oh, Mamma dearest, at home the servants have nothing to eat, and you gave him a gold piece!

MME. RANEVSKAYA   What are you going to do with me? I'm such a fool. When we get home, I'll give you everything I have. Yermolay Alexeyevich, you'll lend me some more . . .

LOPAHIN   Yes, ma'am.

MME. RANEVSKAYA   Come, ladies and gentlemen, it's time to be going. Oh! Varya, we've settled all about your marriage. Congratulations!

VARYA [*Through tears.*]   Really, Mamma, that's not a joking matter.

LOPAHIN   "Aurelia, get thee to a nunnery, go . . ."

GAYEV   And do you know, my hands are trembling: I haven't played billiards in a long time.

LOPAHIN   "Aurelia, nymph, in your orisons, remember me!"1

MME. RANEVSKAYA   Let's go, it's almost suppertime.

VARYA   He frightened me! My heart's pounding.

LOPAHIN   Let me remind you, ladies and gentlemen, on the twenty-second of August the cherry orchard will be up for sale. Think about that! Think!

[All except TROFIMOV and ANYA *go out.*]

ANYA [*Laughs.*]   I'm grateful to that tramp, he frightened Varya and so we're alone.

---

9. Lines from poems by Semyon Nadson (1826–1878) and Nikolay Nekrasov (1821–1878).   1. Lopahin makes comic use of Hamlet's meeting with Ophelia. (Here *Aurelia* conveys the Russian text's distortion of "Ophelia" as "Okhmelia.") Hamlet, seeing her approaching, says: "Nymph, in thy orisons / Be all my sins remembered" (3.1.91–92), and later, suspecting her of spying for her father, sends her off with "Get thee to a nunnery" (3.1.122).

TROFIMOV Varya's afraid we'll fall in love with each other all of a sudden. She hasn't left us alone for days. Her narrow mind can't grasp that we're above love. To avoid the petty and illusory, everything that prevents us from being free and happy—that is the goal and meaning of our life. Forward! Do not fall behind, friends!

ANYA [Strikes her hands together.] How well you speak! [Pause.] It's wonderful here today.

TROFIMOV Yes, the weather's glorious.

ANYA What have you done to me, Petya? Why don't I love the cherry orchard as I used to? I loved it so tenderly. It seemed to me there was no spot on earth lovelier than our orchard.

TROFIMOV All Russia is our orchard. Our land is vast and beautiful, there are many wonderful places in it. [Pause.] Think of it, Anya, your grandfather, your great-grandfather and all your ancestors were serf owners, owners of living souls, and aren't human beings looking at you from every tree in the orchard, from every leaf, from every trunk? Don't you hear voices? Oh, it's terrifying! Your orchard is a fearful place, and when you pass through it in the evening or at night, the old bark on the trees gleams faintly, and the cherry trees seem to be dreaming of things that happened a hundred, two hundred years ago and to be tormented by painful visions. What is there to say? We're at least two hundred years behind, we've really achieved nothing yet, we have no definite attitude to the past, we only philosophize, complain of the blues, or drink vodka. It's all so clear: in order to live in the present, we should first redeem our past, finish with it, and we can expiate it only by suffering, only by extraordinary, unceasing labor. Realize that, Anya.

ANYA The house in which we live has long ceased to be our own, and I will leave it, I give you my word.

TROFIMOV If you have the keys, fling them into the well and go away. Be free as the wind.

ANYA [In ecstasy.] How well you put that!

TROFIMOV Believe me, Anya, believe me! I'm not yet thirty, I'm young, I'm still a student—but I've already suffered so much. In winter I'm hungry, sick, harassed, poor as a beggar, and where hasn't Fate driven me? Where haven't I been? And yet always, every moment of the day and night, my soul is filled with inexplicable premonitions. . . . I have a premonition of happiness, Anya. . . . I see it already!

ANYA [Pensively.] The moon is rising.

[YEPIHODOV is heard playing the same mournful tune on the guitar. The moon rises. Somewhere near the poplars VARYA is looking for ANYA and calling, "Anya, where are you?"]

TROFIMOV Yes, the moon is rising. [Pause.] There it is, happiness, it's approaching, it's coming nearer and nearer, I can already hear its footsteps. And if we don't see it, if we don't know it, what does it matter? Others will!

VARYA'S VOICE Anya! Where are you?

TROFIMOV That Varya again! [Angrily.] It's revolting!

ANYA Never mind, let's go down to the river. It's lovely there.

TROFIMOV Come on. [They go.]

VARYA'S VOICE Anya! Anya!

Act III

A drawing room separated by an arch from a ballroom. Evening. Chandelier burning. The Jewish band is heard playing in the anteroom. In the ballroom they are dancing the Grand Rond. PISHCHIK *is heard calling,* "Promenade à une paire!"[2] PISHCHIK *and* CHARLOTTA, TROFIMOV *and* MME. RANEVSKAYA, ANYA *and the* POST OFFICE CLERK, VARYA *and the* STATIONMASTER, *and others enter the drawing room in couples.* DUNYASHA *is in the last couple.* VARYA *weeps quietly, wiping her tears as she dances. All parade through drawing room,* PISHCHIK *calling,* "Grand rond, balancez!"[3] *and* "Les cavaliers à genoux et remerciez vos dames!"[4] FIRS, *wearing a dress coat, brings in soda water on a tray.* PISHCHIK *and* TROFIMOV *enter the drawing room.*

PISHCHIK   I have high blood pressure; I've already had two strokes. Dancing's hard work for me; but as they say, "If you run with the pack, you can bark or not, but at least wag your tail." Still, I'm as strong as a horse. My late lamented father, who would have his joke, God rest his soul, used to say, talking about our origin, that the ancient line of the Simeonov-Pishchiks was descended from the very horse that Caligula had made a senator.[5] [*Sits down.*] But the trouble is, I have no money. A hungry dog believes in nothing but meat. [*Snores, and wakes up at once.*] It's the same with me—I can think of nothing but money.

TROFIMOV   You know, there *is* something equine about your figure.

PISHCHIK   Well, a horse is a fine animal—one can sell a horse.

[*Sound of billiards being played in an adjoining room.* VARYA *appears in the archway.*]

TROFIMOV [*Teasing her.*]   Madam Lopahina! Madam Lopahina!

VARYA [*Angrily.*]   Mangy master!

TROFIMOV   Yes, I am a mangy master and I'm proud of it.

VARYA [*Reflecting bitterly.*]   Here we've hired musicians, and what shall we pay them with? [*Exits.*]

TROFIMOV [*To* PISHCHIK.]   If the energy you have spent during your lifetime looking for money to pay interest had gone into something else, in the end you could have turned the world upside down.

PISHCHIK   Nietzsche,[6] the philosopher, the greatest, most famous of men, that colossal intellect, says in his works that it is permissible to forge banknotes.

TROFIMOV   Have you read Nietzsche?

PISHCHIK   Well . . . Dashenka told me. . . . And now I've got to the point where forging banknotes is the only way out for me. . . . The day after tomorrow I have to pay 310 rubles—I already have 130 . . . [*Feels in his pockets. In alarm.*] The money's gone! I've lost my money! [*Through tears.*] Where's my money? [*Joyfully.*] Here it is! Inside the lining . . . I'm all in a sweat . . .

[*Enter* MME. RANEVSKAYA *and* CHARLOTTA.]

MME. RANEVSKAYA [*Hums the "Lezginka."*[7]]   Why isn't Leonid back yet?

---

2. Promenade with your partner! (French). *Grand Rond:* a ring dance.   3. Make a large circle, get set! (French).   4. Gentlemen, on your knees and thank your ladies! (French).5.The mad emperor Caligula (12–41 C.E.) brought his favorite horse into the Roman senate to make it a senator.   6. Friedrich Nietzsche (1844–1900), German philosopher.   7. The music that in the Caucasus mountains accompanies a courtship dance in which the man dances with abandon around the woman, who moves with grace and ease.

What is he doing in town? [*To* DUNYASHA.] Dunyasha, offer the musicians tea.

TROFIMOV   The auction hasn't taken place, most likely.

MME. RANEVSKAYA   It's the wrong time to have the band, and the wrong time to give a dance. Well, never mind. [*Sits down and hums softly.*]

CHARLOTTA [*Hands* PISHCHIK *a pack of cards.*]   Here is a pack of cards. Think of any card you like.

PISHCHIK   I've thought of one.

CHARLOTTA   Shuffle the pack now. That's right. Give it here, my dear Mr. Pishchik. *Eins, zwei, drei!*[8] Now look for it—it's in your side pocket.

PISHCHIK [*Taking the card out of his pocket.*]   The eight of spades! Perfectly right! Just imagine!

CHARLOTTA [*Holding the pack of cards in her hands. To* TROFIMOV.]   Quickly, name the top card.

TROFIMOV   Well, let's see—the queen of spades.

CHARLOTTA   Right! [*To* PISHCHIK.] Now name the top card.

PISHCHIK   The ace of hearts.

CHARLOTTA   Right! [*Claps her hands and the pack of cards disappears.*] Ah, what lovely weather it is today! [*A mysterious feminine* VOICE, *which seems to come from under the floor, answers her:* "Oh, yes, it's magnificent weather, madam."] You are my best ideal. [VOICE: "And I find you pleasing too, madam."]

STATIONMASTER [*Applauding.*]   The lady ventriloquist, bravo!

PISHCHIK [*Amazed.*]   Just imagine! Enchanting Charlotta Ivanovna, I'm simply in love with you.

CHARLOTTA   In love? [*Shrugs her shoulders.*] Are you capable of love? *Guter Mensch, aber schlechter Musikant!*[9]

TROFIMOV [*Claps* PISHCHIK *on the shoulder.*]   You old horse, you!

CHARLOTTA   Attention please! One more trick! [*Takes a plaid*[1] *from a chair.*] Here is a very good plaid; I want to sell it. [*Shaking it out.*] Does anyone want to buy it?

PISHCHIK [*In amazement.*]   Just imagine!

CHARLOTTA   *Eins, zwei, drei!* [*Raises the plaid quickly, behind it stands* ANYA. *She curtsies, runs to her mother, embraces her, and runs back into the ballroom, amid general enthusiasm.*]

MME. RANEVSKAYA [*Applauds.*]   Bravo! Bravo!

CHARLOTTA   Now again! *Eins, zwei, drei!* [*Lifts the plaid; behind it stands* VARYA, *bowing.*]

PISHCHIK [*In amazement.*]   Just imagine!

[CHARLOTTA *throws the plaid at* PISHCHIK, *curtsies, and runs into the ballroom.*]

PISHCHIK [*Running after her.*]   The rascal! What a woman, what a woman! [*Exits.*]

MME. RANEVSKAYA   And Leonid still isn't here. What is he doing in town so long? I don't understand. It must be all over by now. Either the estate has been sold, or the auction hasn't taken place. Why keep us in suspense so long?

8. One, two, three (German).   9. "A good man, but a bad musician" (German), usually quoted in the plural: *"Gute Leute, schlechte Musikanten."* It comes from *Das Buch le Grand* (1826) by the German poet Heinrich Heine (1799–1856). Here it suggests that Pishchik may be a good man but a bad lover.   1. A small plaid blanket or lap robe.

VARYA [*Trying to console her.*]   Uncle's bought it, I feel sure of that.

TROFIMOV [*Mockingly.*]   Oh, yes!

VARYA   Great-aunt sent him an authorization to buy it in her name, and to transfer the debt. She's doing it for Anya's sake. And I'm sure that God will help us, and Uncle will buy it.

MME. RANEVSKAYA   Great-aunt sent fifteen thousand to buy the estate in her name, she doesn't trust us, but that's not even enough to pay the interest. [*Covers her face with her hands.*] Today my fate will be decided, my fate—

TROFIMOV [*Teasing* VARYA.]   Madam Lopahina!

VARYA [*Angrily.*]   Perpetual student! Twice already you've been expelled from the university.

MME. RANEVSKAYA   Why are you so cross, Varya? He's teasing you about Lopahin. Well, what of it? If you want to marry Lopahin, go ahead. He's a good man, and interesting; if you don't want to, don't. Nobody's compelling you, my pet!

VARYA   Frankly, Mamma dear, I take this thing seriously; he's a good man and I like him.

MME. RANEVSKAYA   All right then, marry him. I don't know what you're waiting for.

VARYA   But, Mamma, I can't propose to him myself. For the last two years, everyone's been talking to me about him—talking. But he either keeps silent, or else cracks jokes. I understand; he's growing rich, he's absorbed in business—he has no time for me. If I had money, even a little, say, 100 rubles, I'd throw everything up and go far away—I'd go into a nunnery.

TROFIMOV   What a blessing . . .

VARYA   A student ought to be intelligent. [*Softly, with tears in her voice.*] How homely you've grown, Petya! How old you look! [*To* MME. RANEVSKAYA, *with dry eyes.*] But I can't live without work, Mamma dear; I must keep busy every minute.

[*Enter* YASHA.]

YASHA [*Hardly restraining his laughter.*]   Yepihodov has broken a billiard cue! [*Exits.*]

VARYA   Why is Yepihodov here? Who allowed him to play billiards? I don't understand these people! [*Exits.*]

MME. RANEVSKAYA   Don't tease her, Petya. She's unhappy enough without that.

TROFIMOV   She bustles so—and meddles in other people's business. All summer long she's given Anya and me no peace. She's afraid of a love affair between us. What business is it of hers? Besides, I've given no grounds for it, and I'm far from such vulgarity. We are above love.

MME. RANEVSKAYA   And I suppose I'm beneath love? [*Anxiously.*] What can be keeping Leonid? If I only knew whether the estate has been sold or not. Such a calamity seems so incredible to me that I don't know what to think—I feel lost. . . . I could scream. . . . I could do something stupid. . . . Save me, Petya, tell me something, talk to me!

TROFIMOV   Whether the estate is sold today or not, isn't it all one? That's all done with long ago—there's no turning back, the path is overgrown. Calm yourself, my dear. You mustn't deceive yourself. For once in your life you must face the truth.

MME. RANEVSKAYA   What truth? You can see the truth, you can tell it from falsehood, but I seem to have lost my eyesight, I see nothing. You settle every great problem so boldly, but tell me, my dear boy, isn't it because you're young, because you don't yet know what one of your problems means in terms of suffering? You look ahead fearlessly, but isn't it because you don't see and don't expect anything dreadful, because life is still hidden from your young eyes? You're bolder, more honest, more profound than we are, but think hard, show just a bit of magnanimity, spare me. After all, I was born here, my father and mother lived here, and my grandfather; I love this house. Without the cherry orchard, my life has no meaning for me, and if it really must be sold, then sell me with the orchard. [*Embraces* TROFIMOV, *kisses him on the forehead.*] My son was drowned here. [*Weeps.*] Pity me, you good, kind fellow!

TROFIMOV   You know, I feel for you with all my heart.

MME. RANEVSKAYA   But that should have been said differently, so differently! [*Takes out her handkerchief—a telegram falls on the floor.*] My heart is so heavy today—you can't imagine! The noise here upsets me—my inmost being trembles at every sound—I'm shaking all over. But I can't go into my own room; I'm afraid to be alone. Don't condemn me, Petya. . . . I love you as though you were one of us, I would gladly let you marry Anya—I swear I would—only, my dear boy, you must study—you must take your degree—you do nothing, you let yourself be tossed by Fate from place to place—it's so strange. It's true, isn't it? And you should do something about your beard, to make it grow somehow! [*Laughs.*] You're so funny!

TROFIMOV [*Picks up the telegram.*]   I've no wish to be a dandy.

MME. RANEVSKAYA   That's a telegram from Paris. I get one every day. One yesterday and one today. That savage is ill again—he's in trouble again. He begs forgiveness, implores me to go to him, and really I ought to go to Paris to be near him. Your face is stern, Petya; but what is there to do, my dear boy? What am I to do? He's ill, he's alone and unhappy, and who is to look after him, who is to keep him from doing the wrong thing, who is to give him his medicine on time? And why hide it or keep still about it—I love him! That's clear. I love him, love him! He's a millstone round my neck, he'll drag me to the bottom, but I love that stone, I can't live without it. [*Presses* TROFIMOV's *hand.*] Don't think badly of me. Petya, and don't say anything, don't say . . .

TROFIMOV [*Through tears.*]   Forgive me my frankness in heaven's name; but, you know, he robbed you!

MME. RANEVSKAYA   No, no, no, you mustn't say such things! [*Covers her ears.*]

TROFIMOV   But he's a scoundrel! You're the only one who doesn't know it. He's a petty scoundrel—a nonentity!

MME. RANEVSKAYA [*Controlling her anger.*]   You are twenty-six or twenty-seven years old, but you're still a schoolboy.

TROFIMOV   That may be.

MME. RANEVSKAYA   You should be a man at your age. You should understand people who love—and ought to be in love yourself. You ought to fall in love! [*Angrily.*] Yes, yes! And it's not purity in you, it's prudishness, you're simply a queer fish, a comical freak!

TROFIMOV [*Horrified.*]   What is she saying?

MME. RANEVSKAYA   "I am above love!" You're not above love, but simple, as
our Firs says, you're an addlehead. At your age not to have a mistress!

TROFIMOV [*Horrified.*]   This is frightful! What is she saying! [*Goes rapidly
into the ballroom, clutching his head.*] It's frightful—I can't stand it, I
won't stay! [*Exits, but returns at once.*] All is over between us! [*Exits into
anteroom.*]

MME. RANEVSKAYA [*Shouts after him.*]   Petya! Wait! You absurd fellow, I
was joking. Petya!

    [*Sound of somebody running quickly downstairs and suddenly falling
    down with a crash. ANYA and VARYA scream. Sound of laughter a moment
    later.*]

MME. RANEVSKAYA   What's happened?

    [ANYA *runs in.*]

ANYA [*Laughing.*]   Petya's fallen downstairs! [*Runs out.*]

MME. RANEVSKAYA   What a queer bird that Petya is!

    [STATIONMASTER, *standing in the middle of the ballroom, recites Alexey
    Tolstoy's "Magdalene,"*[2] *to which all listen, but after a few lines, the
    sound of a waltz is heard from the anteroom and the reading breaks
    off. All dance.* TROFIMOV, ANYA, VARYA *and* MME. RANEVSKAYA *enter from
    the anteroom.*]

MME. RANEVSKAYA   Petya, you pure soul, please forgive me. . . . Let's
dance.

    [*Dances with* PETYA, ANYA *and* VARYA *dance.* FIRS *enters, puts his stick
    down by the side door.* YASHA *enters from the drawing room and watches
    the dancers.*]

YASHA   Well, Grandfather?

FIRS   I'm not feeling well. In the old days it was generals, barons, and
admirals that were dancing at our balls, and now we have to send for the
post office clerk and the stationmaster, and even they aren't too glad to
come. I feel kind of shaky. The old master that's gone, their grandfather,
dosed everyone with sealing wax, whatever ailed 'em. I've been taking
sealing wax every day for twenty years or more. Perhaps that's what's kept
me alive.

YASHA   I'm fed up with you, Grandpop. [*Yawns.*] It's time you croaked.

FIRS   Oh, you addlehead! [*Mumbles.*]

    [TROFIMOV *and* MME. RANEVSKAYA *dance from the ballroom into the
    drawing room.*]

MME. RANEVSKAYA   Merci. I'll sit down a while. [*Sits down.*] I'm tired.

    [*Enter* ANYA.]

ANYA [*Excitedly.*]   There was a man in the kitchen just now who said the
cherry orchard was sold today.

MME. RANEVSKAYA   Sold to whom?

ANYA   He didn't say. He's gone. [*Dances off with* TROFIMOV.]

YASHA   It was some old man gabbing, a stranger.

FIRS   And Leonid Andreyevich isn't back yet, he hasn't come. And he's

---

2. Called *The Sinning Woman* in Russian, it begins: "A bustling crowd with happy laughter, / with twang-
ing lutes and clashing cymbals / with flowers and foliage all around / the colonnaded portico." Alexey
Tolstoy (1817–1875), popular in his time as a dramatist and poet, was a distant relative of Leo Tolstoy.

wearing his lightweight between-season overcoat; like enough, he'll catch cold. Ah, when they're young they're green.

MME. RANEVSKAYA   This is killing me. Go, Yasha, find out to whom it has been sold.

YASHA   But the old man left long ago. [*Laughs.*]

MME RANEVSKAYA   What are you laughing at? What are you pleased about?

YASHA   That Yepihodov is such a funny one. A funny fellow, Two-and-Twenty Troubles!

MME. RANEVSKAYA   Firs, if the estate is sold, where will you go?

FIRS   I'll go where you tell me.

MME. RANEVSKAYA   Why do you look like that? Are you ill? You ought to go to bed.

FIRS   Yes! [*With a snigger.*] Me go to bed, and who's to hand things round? Who's to see to things? I'm the only one in the whole house.

YASHA [*To* MME. RANEVSKAYA.]   Lubov Andreyevna, allow me to ask a favor of you, be so kind! If you go back to Paris, take me with you, I beg you. It's positively impossible for me to stay here. [*Looking around; sotto voce.*] What's the use of talking? You see for yourself, it's an uncivilized country, the people have no morals, and then the boredom! The food in the kitchen's revolting, and besides there's this Firs wanders about mumbling all sorts of inappropriate words. Take me with you, be so kind!

[*Enter* PISHCHIK.]

PISHCHIK   May I have the pleasure of a waltz with you, charming lady? [MME. RANEVSKAYA *accepts.*] All the same, enchanting lady, you must let me have 180 rubles. . . . You must let me have [*dancing*] just one hundred and eighty rubles. [*They pass into the ballroom.*]

YASHA [*Hums softly.*]   "Oh, wilt thou understand the tumult in my soul?"
[*In the ballroom a figure in a gray top hat and checked trousers is jumping about and waving its arms; shouts: "Bravo, Charlotta Ivanovna!"*]

DUNYASHA [*Stopping to powder her face; to* FIRS.]   The young miss has ordered me to dance. There are so many gentlemen and not enough ladies. But dancing makes me dizzy, my heart begins to beat fast, Firs Nikolayevich. The Post Office Clerk said something to me just now that quite took my breath away.

[*Music stops.*]

FIRS   What did he say?

DUNYASHA   "You're like a flower," he said.

YASHA [*Yawns.*]   What ignorance. [*Exits.*]

DUNYASHA   "Like a flower!" I'm such a delicate girl. I simply adore pretty speeches.

FIRS   You'll come to a bad end.

[*Enter* YEPIHODOV.]

YEPIHODOV [*To* DUNYASHA.]   You have no wish to see me, Avdotya Fyodorovna . . . as though I was some sort of insect. [*Sighs.*] Ah, life!

DUNYASHA   What is it you want?

YEPIHODOV   Indubitably you may be right. [*Sighs.*] But of course, if one looks at it from the point of view, if I may be allowed to say so, and apologizing for my frankness, you have completely reduced me to a state of mind. I know my fate. Every day some calamity befalls me, and I grew used to it long ago, so that I look upon my fate with a smile. You gave me your word, and though I—

DUNYASHA   Let's talk about it later, please. But just now leave me alone, I am daydreaming. [*Plays with a fan.*]

YEPIHODOV   A misfortune befalls me every day; and if I may be allowed to say so, I merely smile, I even laugh.

[*Enter* VARYA.]

VARYA [*To* YEPIHODOV.]   Are you still here? What an impertinent fellow you are really! Run along, Dunyasha. [*To* YEPIHODOV.] Either you're playing billiards and breaking a cue, or you're wandering about the drawing room as though you were a guest.

YEPIHODOV   You cannot, permit me to remark, penalize me.

VARYA   I'm not penalizing you; I'm just telling you. You merely wander from place to place, and don't do your work. We keep you as a clerk, but heaven knows what for.

YEPIHODOV [*Offended.*]   Whether I work or whether I walk, whether I eat or whether I play billiards, is a matter to be discussed only by persons of understanding and of mature years.

VARYA [*Enraged.*]   You dare say that to me—you dare? You mean to say I've no understanding? Get out of here at once! This minute!

YEPIHODOV [*Scared.*]   I beg you to express yourself delicately.

VARYA [*Beside herself.*]   Clear out this minute! Out with you!

[YEPIHODOV *goes toward the door,* VARYA *following.*]

VARYA   Two-and-Twenty Troubles! Get out—don't let me set eyes on you again!

[*Exit* YEPIHODOV. *His voice is heard behind the door:* "I shall lodge a complaint against you!"]

VARYA   Oh, you're coming back? [*She seizes the stick left near door by* FIRS.] Well, come then . . . come . . . I'll show you. . . . Ah, you're coming? You're coming? . . . Come . . . [*Swings the stick just as* LOPAHIN *enters.*]

LOPAHIN   Thank you kindly.

VARYA [*Angrily and mockingly.*]   I'm sorry.

LOPAHIN   It's nothing. Thank you kindly for your charming reception.

VARYA   Don't mention it. [*Walks away, looks back and asks softly.*] I didn't hurt you, did I?

LOPAHIN   Oh, no, not at all. I shall have a large bump, though.

[*Voices from the ballroom* "Lopahin is here! Lopahin!" *Enter* PISHCHIK.]

PISHCHIK   My eyes do see, my ears do hear! [*Kisses* LOPAHIN.] You smell of cognac, my dear friend. And we've been celebrating here, too.

[*Enter* MME. RANEVSKAYA.]

MME. RANEVSKAYA   Is that you, Yermolay Alexeyevich? What kept you so long? Where's Leonid?

LOPAHIN   Leonid Andreyevich arrived with me. He's coming.

MME. RANEVSKAYA   Well, what happened? Did the sale take place? Speak!

LOPAHIN [*Embarrassed, fearful of revealing his joy.*]   The sale was over at four o'clock. We missed the train—had to wait till half-past nine. [*Sighing heavily.*] Ugh. I'm a little dizzy.

[*Enter* GAYEV *In his right hand he holds parcels, with his left he is wiping away his tears.*]

MME. RANEVSKAYA   Well, Leonid? What news? [*Impatiently, through tears.*] Be quick, for God's sake!

GAYEV [*Not answering, simply waves his hand. Weeping, to* FIRS.]   Here, take these; anchovies, Kerch herrings . . . I haven't eaten all day. What

I've been through! [*The click of billiard balls comes through the open door of the billiard room and* YASHA's *voice is heard:* "Seven and eighteen!" GAYEV's *expression changes, he no longer weeps.*] I'm terribly tired. Firs, help me change. [*Exits, followed by* FIRS.]

PISHCHIK How about the sale? Tell us what happened.

MME. RANEVSKAYA Is the cherry orchard sold?

LOPAHIN Sold.

MME. RANEVSKAYA Who bought it?

LOPAHIN I bought it.

[*Pause,* MME. RANEVSKAYA *is overcome. She would fall to the floor, were it not for the chair and table near which she stands.* VARYA *takes the keys from her belt, flings them on the floor in the middle of the drawing room and goes out.*]

LOPAHIN I bought it. Wait a bit, ladies and gentlemen, please, my head is swimming, I can't talk. [*Laughs.*] We got to the auction and Deriganov was there already. Leonid Andreyevich had only 15,000 and straight off Deriganov bid 30,000 over and above the mortgage. I saw how the land lay, got into the fight, bid 40,000. He bid 45,000. I bid fifty-five. He kept adding five thousands, I ten. Well . . . it came to an end. I bid ninety above the mortgage and the estate was knocked down to me. Now the cherry orchard's mine! Mine! [*Laughs uproariously.*] Lord! God in Heaven! The cherry orchard's mine! Tell me that I'm drunk—out of my mind—that it's all a dream. [*Stamps his feet.*] Don't laugh at me! If my father and my grandfather could rise from their graves and see all that has happened—how their Yermolay, who used to be flogged, their half-literate Yermolay, who used to run about barefoot in winter, how that very Yermolay has bought the most magnificent estate in the world. I bought the estate where my father and grandfather were slaves, where they weren't even allowed to enter the kitchen. I am asleep—it's only a dream—I only imagine it. . . . It's the fruit of your imagination, wrapped in the darkness of the unknown! [*Picks up the keys, smiling genially.*] She threw down the keys, wants to show she's no longer mistress here. [*Jingles keys.*] Well, no matter. [*The band is warming up.*] Hey, musicians! Strike up! I want to hear you! Come, everybody, and see how Yermolay Lopahin will lay the ax to the cherry orchard and how the trees will fall to the ground. We will build summer cottages there, and our grandsons and great grandsons will see a new life here. Music! Strike up!

[*The band starts to play.* MME RANEVSKAYA *has sunk into a chair and is weeping bitterly.*]

LOPAHIN [*Reproachfully.*] Why, why didn't you listen to me? My dear friend, my poor friend, you can't bring it back now. [*Tearfully.*] Oh, if only this were over quickly! Oh, if only our wretched, disordered life were changed!

PISHCHIK [*Takes him by the arm; sotto voce.*] She's crying. Let's go into the ballroom. Let her be alone. Come. [*Takes his arm and leads him into the ballroom.*]

LOPAHIN What's the matter? Musicians, play so I can hear you! Let me have things the way I want them. [*Ironically.*] Here comes the new master, the owner of the cherry orchard. [*Accidentally he trips over a little table, almost upsetting the candelabra.*] I can pay for everything. [*Exits with* PISHCHIK.]

[MME. RANEVSKAYA, *alone, sits huddled up, weeping bitterly. Music plays softly. Enter* ANYA *and* TROFIMOV *quickly.* ANYA *goes to her mother and falls on her knees before her.* TROFIMOV *stands in the doorway.*]

ANYA   Mamma, Mamma, you're crying! Dear, kind, good Mamma, my precious, I love you, I bless you! The cherry orchard is sold, it's gone, that's true, quite true. But don't cry, Mamma, life is still before you, you still have your kind, pure heart. Let us go, let us go away from here, darling. We will plant a new orchard, even more luxuriant than this one. You will see it, you will understand, and like the sun at evening, joy—deep, tranquil joy—will sink into your soul, and you will smile, Mamma. Come, darling, let us go.

Act IV

Scene as in Act I. No window curtains or pictures, only a little furniture, piled up in a corner, as if for sale. A sense of emptiness. Near the outer door and at the back, suitcases, bundles, etc., are piled up. A door open on the left and the voices of VARYA *and* ANYA *are heard.* LOPAHIN *stands waiting.* YASHA *holds a tray with glasses full of champagne.* YEPIHODOV *in the anteroom is tying up a box. Behind the scene a hum of voices: peasants have come to say good-bye. Voice of* GAYEV: "Thanks, brothers, thank you."*

YASHA   The country folk have come to say good-bye. In my opinion, Yermolay Alexeyevich, they are kindly souls, but there's nothing in their heads.

    [*The hum dies away. Enter* MME. RANEVSKAYA *and* GAYEV: *She is not crying, but is pale, her face twitches and she cannot speak.*]

GAYEV   You gave them your purse, Luba. That won't do! That won't do!

MME. RANEVSKAYA   I couldn't help it! I couldn't! [*They go out.*]

LOPAHIN [*Calls after them.*]   Please, I beg you, have a glass at parting. I didn't think of bringing any champagne from town and at the station I could find only one bottle. Please, won't you? [*Pause.*] What's the matter, ladies and gentlemen, don't you want any? [*Moves away from the door.*] If I'd known, I wouldn't have bought it. Well, then I won't drink any, either. [YASHA *carefully sets the tray down on a chair.*] At least you have a glass, Yasha.

YASHA   Here's to the travelers! And good luck to those that stay! [*Drinks.*] This champagne isn't the real stuff, I can assure you.

LOPAHIN   Eight rubles a bottle. [*Pause.*] It's devilishly cold here.

YASHA   They didn't light the stoves today—it wasn't worth it, since we're leaving. [*Laughs.*]

LOPAHIN   Why are you laughing?

YASHA   It's just that I'm pleased.

LOPAHIN   It's October, yet it's as still and sunny as though it were summer. Good weather for building. [*Looks at his watch, and speaks off.*] Bear in mind, ladies and gentlemen, the train goes in forty-seven minutes, so you ought to start for the station in twenty minutes. Better hurry up!

    [*Enter* TROFIMOV, *wearing an overcoat.*]

TROFIMOV   I think it's time to start. The carriages are at the door. The devil only knows what's become of my rubbers; they've disappeared. [*Calling off.*] Anya! My rubbers are gone. I can't find them.

LOPAHIN   I've got to go to Kharkov. I'll take the same train you do. I'll
spend the winter in Kharkov. I've been hanging round here with you, till
I'm worn out with loafing. I can't live without work—I don't know what
to do with my hands, they dangle as if they didn't belong to me.

TROFIMOV   Well, we'll soon be gone, then you can go on with your useful
labors again.

LOPAHIN   Have a glass.

TROFIMOV   No, I won't.

LOPAHIN   So you're going to Moscow now?

TROFIMOV   Yes, I'll see them into town, and tomorrow I'll go on to Moscow.

LOPAHIN   Well, I'll wager the professors aren't giving any lectures, they're
waiting for you to come.

TROFIMOV   That's none of your business.

LOPAHIN   Just how many years have you been at the university?

TROFIMOV   Can't you think of something new? Your joke's stale and flat.
[Looking for his rubbers.] We'll probably never see each other again, so
allow me to give you a piece of advice at parting: don't wave your hands
about! Get out of the habit. And another thing: building bungalows, figuring that summer residents will eventually become small farmers, figuring like that is just another form of waving your hands about. . . . Never
mind, I love you anyway; you have fine, delicate fingers, like an artist;
you have a fine delicate soul.

LOPAHIN   [Embracing him.]   Good-bye, my dear fellow. Thank you for
everything. Let me give you some money for the journey, if you need it.

TROFIMOV   What for? I don't need it.

LOPAHIN   But you haven't any.

TROFIMOV   Yes, I have, thank you. I got some money for a translation—
here it is in my pocket. [Anxiously.] But where are my rubbers?

VARYA [From the next room.]   Here! Take the nasty things. [Flings a pair
of rubbers onto the stage.]

TROFIMOV   What are you so cross about, Varya? Hm . . . and these are not
my rubbers.

LOPAHIN   I sowed three thousand acres of poppies in the spring, and now
I've made 40,000 on them, clear profit; and when my poppies were in
bloom, what a picture it was! So, as I say, I made 40,000; and I am
offering you a loan because I can afford it. Why turn up your nose at it?
I am a peasant—I speak bluntly.

TROFIMOV   Your father was a peasant, mine was a druggist—that proves
absolutely nothing whatever. [LOPAHIN takes out his wallet.] Don't, put
that away! If you were to offer me two hundred thousand, I wouldn't
take it. I'm a free man. And everything that all of you, rich and poor alike,
value so highly and hold so dear hasn't the slightest power over me. It's
like so much fluff floating in the air. I can get on without you, I can pass
you by, I'm strong and proud. Mankind is moving toward the highest
truth, toward the highest happiness possible on earth, and I am in the
front ranks.

LOPAHIN   Will you get there?

TROFIMOV   I will. [Pause.] I will get there, or I will show others the way to
get there.

[The sound of axes chopping down trees is heard in the distance.]

LOPAHIN   Well, good-bye, my dear fellow. It's time to leave. We turn up our noses at one another, but life goes on just the same. When I'm working hard, without resting, my mind is easier, and it seems to me that I, too, know why I exist. But how many people are there in Russia, brother, who exist nobody knows why? Well, it doesn't matter. That's not what makes the wheels go round. They say Leonid Andreyevich has taken a position in the bank, 6,000 rubles a year. Only, of course, he won't stick to it, he's too lazy. . . .

ANYA [*In the doorway.*]   Mamma begs you not to start cutting down the cherry trees until she's gone.

TROFIMOV   Really, you should have more tact! [*Exits.*]

LOPAHIN   Right away—right away! Those men . . . [*Exits.*]

ANYA   Has Firs been taken to the hospital?

YASHA   I told them this morning. They must have taken him.

ANYA [*To* YEPIHODOV, *who crosses the room.*]   Yepihodov, please find out if Firs has been taken to the hospital.

YASHA [*Offended.*]   I told Yegor this morning. Why ask a dozen times?

YEPIHODOV   The aged Firs, in my definitive opinion, is beyond mending. It's time he was gathered to his fathers. And I can only envy him. [*Puts a suitcase down on a hat box and crushes it.*] There now, of course, I knew it! [*Exits.*]

YASHA [*Mockingly.*]   Two-and-Twenty Troubles!

VARYA [*Through the door.*]   Has Firs been taken to the hospital?

ANYA   Yes.

VARYA   Then why wasn't the note for the doctor taken too?

ANYA   Oh! Then someone must take it to him. [*Exits.*]

VARYA [*From adjoining room.*]   Where's Yasha? Tell him his mother's come and wants to say good-bye.

YASHA [*Waves his hand.*]   She tries my patience.

[DUNYASHA *has been occupied with the luggage. Seeing* YASHA *alone, she goes up to him.*]

DUNYASHA   You might just give me one little look, Yasha. You're going away. . . . You're leaving me . . . [*Weeps and throws herself on his neck.*]

YASHA   What's there to cry about? [*Drinks champagne.*] In six days I shall be in Paris again. Tomorrow we get into an express train and off we go, that's the last you'll see of us. . . . I can scarcely believe it. *Vive la France!*[3] It don't suit me here, I just can't live here. That's all there is to it. I'm fed up with the ignorance here, I've had enough of it. [*Drinks champagne.*] What's there to cry about? Behave yourself properly, and you'll have no cause to cry.

DUNYASHA [*Powders her face, looking in pocket mirror.*]   Do send me a letter from Paris. You know I loved you, Yasha, how I loved you! I'm a delicate creature, Yasha.

YASHA   Somebody's coming! [*Busies himself with the luggage; hums softly.*]
[*Enter* MME. RANEVSKAYA, GAYEV, ANYA, *and* CHARLOTTA.]

GAYEV   We ought to be leaving. We haven't much time. [*Looks at* YASHA.] Who smells of herring?

MME. RANEVSKAYA   In about ten minutes we should be getting into the

3. Long live France! (French).

carriages. [*Looks around the room.*] Good-bye, dear old home, good-bye, grandfather. Winter will pass, spring will come, you will no longer be here, they will have torn you down. How much these walls have seen! [*Kisses* ANYA *warmly.*] My treasure, how radiant you look! Your eyes are sparkling like diamonds. Are you glad? Very?

ANYA [*Gaily.*]   Very glad. A new life is beginning, Mamma.

GAYEV   Well, really, everything is all right now. Before the cherry orchard was sold, we all fretted and suffered; but afterward, when the question was settled finally and irrevocably, we all calmed down, and even felt quite cheerful. I'm a bank employee now, a financier. The yellow ball in the side pocket! And anyhow, you are looking better, Luba, there's no doubt of that.

MME. RANEVSKAYA   Yes, my nerves are better, that's true. [*She is handed her hat and coat.*] I sleep well. Carry out my things, Yasha. It's time. [*To* ANYA.] We shall soon see each other again, my little girl. I'm going to Paris, I'll live there on the money your great-aunt sent us to buy the estate with—long live Auntie! But that money won't last long.

ANYA   You'll come back soon, soon, Mamma, won't you? Meanwhile I'll study. I'll pass my high school examination, and then I'll go to work and help you. We'll read all kinds of books together, Mamma, won't we? [*Kisses her mother's hands.*] We'll read in the autumn evenings, we'll read lots of books, and a new wonderful world will open up before us. [*Falls into a revery.*] Mamma, do come back.

MME. RANEVSKAYA   I will come back, my precious.

> [*Embraces her daughter. Enter* LOPAHIN *and* CHARLOTTA, *who is humming softly.*]

GAYEV   Charlotta's happy: she's singing.

CHARLOTTA [*Picks up a bundle and holds it like a baby in swaddling clothes.*] Bye, baby, bye. [*A baby is heard crying: "Wah! Wah!"*] Hush, hush, my pet, my little one. ["*Wah! Wah!*"] I'm so sorry for you! [*Throws the bundle down.*] You will find me a position, won't you? I can't go on like this.

LOPAHIN   We'll find one for you, Charlotta Ivanovna, don't worry.

GAYEV   Everyone's leaving us. Varya's going away. We've suddenly become of no use.

CHARLOTTA   There's no place for me to live in town, I must go away. [*Hums.*]

> [*Enter* PISHCHIK.]

LOPAHIN   There's nature's masterpiece!

PISHCHIK [*Gasping.*]   Oh . . . let me get my breath . . . I'm in agony. . . . Esteemed friends . . . Give me a drink of water. . . .

GAYEV   Wants some money, I suppose. No, thank you . . . I'll keep out of harm's way. [*Exits.*]

PISHCHIK   It's a long while since I've been to see you, most charming lady. [*To* LOPAHIN.] So you are here . . . glad to see you, you intellectual giant . . . There . . . [*Gives* LOPAHIN *money.*] Here's 400 rubles, and I still owe you 840.

LOPAHIN [*Shrugging his shoulders in bewilderment.*]   I must be dreaming. . . . Where did you get it?

PISHCHIK   Wait a minute . . . it's hot. . . . A most extraordinary event!

Some Englishmen came to my place and found some sort of white clay on my land . . . [*To* MME. RANEVSKAYA.] And 400 for you . . . most lovely . . . most wonderful . . . [*Hands her the money.*] The rest later. [*Drinks water.*] A young man in the train was telling me just now that a great philosopher recommends jumping off roofs. "Jump!" says he; "that's the long and the short of it!" [*In amazement.*] Just imagine! Some more water!

LOPAHIN   What Englishmen?

PISHCHIK   I leased them the tract with the clay on it for twenty-four years. . . . And now, forgive me, I can't stay. . . . I must be dashing on. . . . I'm going over to Znoikov . . . to Kardamanov . . . I owe them all money . . . [*Drinks water.*] Good-bye, everybody . . . I'll look in on Thursday . . .

MME. RANEVSKAYA   We're just moving into town; and tomorrow I go abroad.

PISHCHIK [*Upset.*]   What? Why into town? That's why the furniture is like that . . . and the suitcases. . . . Well, never mind! [*Through tears.*] Never mind . . . men of colossal intellect, these Englishmen. . . . Never mind . . . Be happy. God will come to your help. . . . Never mind . . . everything in this world comes to an end. [*Kisses* MME. RANEVSKAYA'*s hand.*] If the rumor reaches you that it's all up with me, remember this old . . . horse, and say: "Once there lived a certain . . . Simeonov-Pishchik . . . the kingdom of Heaven be his. . . ." Glorious weather! . . . Yes . . . [*Exits, in great confusion, but at once returns and says in the doorway.*] My daughter Dashenka sends her regards. [*Exits.*]

MME. RANEVSKAYA   Now we can go. I leave with two cares weighing on me. The first is poor old Firs. [*Glancing at her watch.*] We still have about five minutes.

ANYA   Mamma, Firs has already been taken to the hospital. Yasha sent him there this morning.

MME. RANEVSKAYA   My other worry is Varya. She's used to getting up early and working; and now, with no work to do, she is like a fish out of water. She has grown thin and pale, and keeps crying, poor soul. [*Pause.*] You know this very well, Yermolay Alexeyevich; I dreamed of seeing her married to you, and it looked as though that's how it would be. [*Whispers to* ANYA, *who nods to* CHARLOTTA *and both go out.*] She loves you. You find her attractive. I don't know, I don't know why it is you seem to avoid each other; I can't understand it.

LOPAHIN   To tell you the truth, I don't understand it myself. It's all a puzzle. If there's still time, I'm ready now, at once. Let's settle it straight off, and have done with it! Without you, I feel I'll never be able to propose.

MME. RANEVSKAYA   That's splendid. After all, it will only take a minute. I'll call her at once. . . .

LOPAHIN   And luckily, here's champagne, too. [*Looks at the glasses.*] Empty! Somebody's drunk it all. [*Yasha coughs.*] That's what you might call guzzling . . .

MME. RANEVSKAYA [*Animatedly.*]   Excellent! We'll go and leave you alone. Yasha, *allez!*[4] I'll call her. [*At the door.*] Varya, leave everything and come here. Come! [*Exits with* YASHA.]

LOPAHIN [*Looking at his watch.*]   Yes . . . [*Pause behind the door, smothered laughter and whispering; at last, enter* VARYA.]

---

4. Go on! (French).

VARYA [*Looking over the luggage in leisurely fashion.*]   Strange, I can't find it . . .

LOPAHIN   What are you looking for?

VARYA   Packed it myself, and I don't remember . . . [*Pause.*]

LOPAHIN   Where are you going now, Varya?

VARYA   I? To the Ragulins'. I've arranged to take charge there—as house-keeper, if you like.

LOPAHIN   At Yashnevo? About fifty miles from here. [*Pause.*] Well, life in this house is ended!

VARYA [*Examining luggage.*]   Where is it? Perhaps I put it in the chest. Yes, life in this house is ended. . . . There will be no more of it.

LOPAHIN   And I'm just off to Kharkov—by this next train. I've a lot to do there. I'm leaving Yepihodov here . . . I've taken him on.

VARYA   Oh!

LOPAHIN   Last year at this time, it was snowing, if you remember, but now it's sunny and there's no wind. It's cold, though. . . . It must be three below.

VARYA   I didn't look. [*Pause.*] And besides, our thermometer's broken. [*Pause.* VOICE *from the yard:* "Yermolay Alexeyevich!"]

LOPAHIN [*As if he had been waiting for the call.*]   This minute! [*Exits quickly.*]

[VARYA *sits on the floor and sobs quietly, her head on a bundle of clothes. Enter* MME. RANEVSKAYA *cautiously.*]

MME. RANEVSKAYA   Well? [*Pause.*] We must be going.

VARYA [*Wiping her eyes.*]   Yes, it's time, Mamma dear. I'll be able to get to the Ragulins' today, if only we don't miss the train.

MME. RANEVSKAYA [*At the door.*]   Anya, put your things on.

[*Enter* ANYA, GAYEV, CHARLOTTA. GAYEV *wears a heavy overcoat with a hood. Enter servants and coachmen.* YEPIHODOV *bustles about the luggage.*]

MME. RANEVSKAYA   Now we can start on our journey.

ANYA [*Joyfully.*]   On our journey!

GAYEV   My friends, my dear, cherished friends, leaving this house forever, can I be silent? Can I, at leave-taking, refrain from giving utterance to those emotions that now fill my being?

ANYA [*Imploringly.*]   Uncle!

VARYA   Uncle, Uncle dear, don't.

GAYEV [*Forlornly.*]   I'll bank the yellow in the side pocket . . . I'll be silent . . .

[*Enter* TROFIMOV, *then* LOPAHIN.]

TROFIMOV   Well, ladies and gentlemen, it's time to leave.

LOPAHIN   Yepihodov, my coat.

MME. RANEVSKAYA   I'll sit down just a minute. It seems as though I'd never before seen what the walls of this house were like, the ceilings, and now I look at them hungrily, with such tender affection.

GAYEV   I remember when I was six years old sitting on that window sill on Whitsunday,[5] watching my father going to church.

MME. RANEVSKAYA   Has everything been taken?

---

5. Or Pentecost, a Christian festival occurring on the seventh Sunday after Easter.

LOPAHIN   I think so. [*Putting on his overcoat.*] Yepihodov, see that every-thing's in order.

YEPIHODOV [*In a husky voice.*]   You needn't worry, Yermolay Alexeyevich.

LOPAHIN   What's the matter with your voice?

YEPIHODOV   I just had a drink of water. I must have swallowed something.

YASHA [*Contemptuously.*]   What ignorance!

MME. RANEVSKAYA   When we're gone, not a soul will be left here.

LOPAHIN   Until the spring.

> [VARYA *pulls an umbrella out of a bundle, as though about to hit someone with it.* LOPAHIN *pretends to be frightened.*]

VARYA   Come, come, I had no such idea!

TROFIMOV   Ladies and gentlemen, let's get into the carriages—it's time. The train will be in directly.

VARYA   Petya, there they are, your rubbers, by that trunk. [*Tearfully.*] And what dirty old things, they are!

TROFIMOV [*Puts on rubbers.*]   Let's go, ladies and gentlemen.

GAYEV [*Greatly upset, afraid of breaking down.*]   The train . . . the station. . . . Three cushions in the side pocket, I'll bank this one in the corner . . .

MME. RANEVSKAYA   Let's go.

LOPAHIN   Are we all here? No one in there? [*Locks the side door on the left.*] There are some things stored here, better lock up. Let us go!

ANYA   Good-bye, old house! Good-bye, old life!

TROFIMOV   Hail to you, new life!

> [*Exits with* ANYA: VARYA *looks round the room and goes out slowly.* YASHA *and* CHARLOTTA *with her dog go out.*]

LOPAHIN   And so, until the spring. Go along, friends . . . Bye-bye! [*Exits.*]

> [MME. RANEVSKAYA *and* GAYEV *remain alone. As though they had been waiting for this, they throw themselves on each other's necks, and break into subdued, restrained sobs, afraid of being overheard.*]

GAYEV [*In despair.*]   My sister! My sister!

MME. RANEVSKAYA   Oh, my orchard—my dear, sweet, beautiful orchard! My life, my youth, my happiness—good-bye! Good-bye!

> [*Voice of* ANYA, *gay and summoning:* "Mamma!" *Voice of* TROFIMOV, *gay and excited:* "Halloo!"]

MME. RANEVSKAYA   One last look at the walls, at the windows. . . . Our poor mother loved to walk about this room . . .

GAYEV   My sister, my sister!

> [*Voice of* ANYA "Mamma!" *Voice of* TROFIMOV "Halloo!"]

MME. RANEVSKAYA   We're coming.

> [*They go out. The stage is empty. The sound of doors being locked, of carriages driving away. Then silence. In the stillness is heard the muffled sound of the ax striking a tree, a mournful, lonely sound.*
> *Footsteps are heard.* FIRS *appears in the doorway on the right. He is dressed as usual in a jacket and white waistcoat and wears slippers. He is ill.*]

FIRS [*Goes to the door, tries the handle.*]   Locked! They've gone . . . [*Sits down on the sofa.*] They've forgotten me. . . . Never mind . . . I'll sit here a bit . . . I'll wager Leonid Andreyevich hasn't put his fur coat on, he's gone off in his light overcoat . . . [*Sighs anxiously.*] I didn't keep an eye on him. . . . Ah, when they're young, they're green . . . [*Mumbles some-*

thing indistinguishable.] Life has gone by as if I had never lived. [*Lies down.*] I'll lie down a while . . . There's no strength left in you, old fellow; nothing is left, nothing. Ah, you addlehead!

[*Lies motionless. A distant sound is heard coming from the sky, as it were, the sound of a snapping string mournfully dying away. All is still again, and nothing is heard but the strokes of the ax against a tree far away in the orchard.*]

CHARLES BAUDELAIRE
1821–1867

Few writers have had such impact on succeeding generations as Charles Baudelaire, called both the "first modern poet" and the "father of modern criticism." Nor is his reputation confined to the West, for Baudelaire is the most widely read French poet around the globe. Yet for a long time Baudelaire's literary image was dominated by his reputation as a scandalous writer whose blatant eroticism and open fascination with evil outraged all right-thinking people. Both he and Flaubert were brought to trial in 1857 for "offenses against public and religious morals"—Flaubert for *Madame Bovary* and Baudelaire for his just-published book of poetry *Les Fleurs du Mal* (The Flowers of Evil). Some of this reputation is justified; the poet did intend to shock, and he displayed in painfully vivid scenes his own spiritual and sensual torment. Haunted by a religiously framed vision of human nature as fallen and corrupt, he lucidly analyzed his own weaknesses as well as the hypocrisy and sins he found in society. Lust, hatred, laziness, a disabling self-awareness that ironized all emotions, a horror of death and decay, and finally an apathy that swallowed up all other vices— all contrasted bitterly with the poet's dreams of a lost Eden, an ideal harmony of being. Perfection existed only in the distance: in scenes of erotic love, faraway voyages, or artistic beauty created often out of ugliness and crude reality. Baudelaire's ability to present realistic detail inside larger symbolic horizons, his constant use of imagery and suggestion, his consummate craftsmanship and the intense musicality of his verse made him a precursor of Symbolism and, in the words of T. S. Eliot, "the greatest exemplar in *modern* poetry in any language."

Baudelaire was born in Paris on April 9, 1821. His father died when the poet was six, and his widowed mother married Captain (later General) Jacques Aupick the following year. In 1832 the family moved to Lyons, and young Charles was placed in boarding school; in 1836 Aupick and his family were reassigned to Paris. Throughout his life Baudelaire remained greatly attached to his mother and detested his disciplinarian stepfather. He was a rebellious and difficult youth whom his parents sent on a long voyage to the Indies in 1841 to remove him from bad influences; but he cut short the trip at Réunion Island and insisted on returning home after ten months. Baudelaire's unconventional behavior and extravagant lifestyle continued to worry his family, especially after he turned twenty-one and received his father's inheritance. In 1844, they obtained a court order to supervise his finances, and from then on the poet subsisted on allowances paid by a notary.

In contrast to the Romantics with their love of nature and pastoral scenes, Baudelaire was a city poet fascinated by the variety and excitement of modern urban life. Living in Paris, he collaborated with other writers; published poems, translations, and criticism in different journals; and in 1842 began a lifelong liaison with Jeanne Duval, the "black Venus" of many poems. When he read Edgar Allan Poe for the first time, he was struck by the similarity of their ideas: by Poe's dedication to beauty, his fascination with bizarre images and death, and above all his emphasis on craftsmanship and perfectly controlled art. The French poet recognized in Poe "not only subjects I had dreamed of, but SENTENCES that I had thought and he had written twenty years earlier." Baudelaire's translations of Poe, collected in five volumes published from 1856 to 1865, were immensely popular and introduced the American writer to a broad European audience.

Public scandal greeted the appearance in 1857 of Baudelaire's major work, *The Flowers of Evil*. French authorities, already annoyed at Flaubert's acquittal, seized the book immediately. Less than two months later, the poet and his publisher were condemned to pay a fine and to delete six poems. A second edition with more poems appeared in 1861, and new lyrics were added to later printings. By now the poet was also well known as a critic. He championed the modern art of his time, interpreting and upholding the spirit of modernity in the art criticism of his 1845, 1846, and 1859 Salons; in remarkable studies of the painters Eugène Delacroix and Constantin Guys; and in a spirited defense of the German composer Richard Wagner. His literary criticism, although it included studies of *Madame Bovary,* Victor Hugo, and Théophile Gautier, was in general limited to brief journal reviews. Baudelaire started publishing prose poetry at the beginning of the 1860s, experimenting with a form that was almost unknown in France and in which he hoped to achieve "the miracle of a poetic prose, musical without rhythm or rhyme, able . . . to adapt itself to the soul's lyric movements, to the undulations of reverie, to the sudden starts of consciousness." A slim book of twenty prose poems appeared in 1862; the complete *Little Poems in Prose* (also called *Paris Spleen*) would contain fifty poems in all. Baudelaire's health was precarious during these years. In 1862, he had what was apparently a minor stroke, which he called a "warning" and described with characteristically vivid imagery: "I felt pass over me a draft of wind from imbecility's wing." Four years later, in Belgium, he was stricken with aphasia and hemiplegia; unable to speak, he was brought back to Paris where he died on August 31, 1867.

Baudelaire wished to shock, to startle, to make the reader rethink cherished ideas and values. In the prefatory poem to *The Flowers of Evil, To the Reader,* Baudelaire ends a catalog of human vices by insisting that both he and the reader are caught in a common guilt: "You—hypocrite Reader—my double—my brother!" The poet's insistent theme of ennui (pathological boredom or apathy) occurs here at the beginning of the book: it is the melancholy inertia that keeps human beings from acting either for good or for evil, placing them outside the realm of choice, much as Dante relegated to Limbo those who were unwilling to take a moral stand. (In Catholic theology, such spiritual inertia is termed *acedia*.) This *spleen*, as it is also called (from the part of the body governing a splenetic or bilious humor), appears throughout *The Flowers of Evil* as an insidious, debilitating force. In *To the Reader* Baudelaire argues that the devil's most terrifying weapon against humankind is not the litany of sins so colorfully described, but rather his ability to diminish the possibility of action: to evaporate— like a chemist in a laboratory—the precious metal of human will.

The Voyage, placed by Baudelaire at the end of the collection, describes the opposite of inertia: an active search for goals always out of reach. Written in a consciously Byronic tone and intended, according to the poet, to upset current faith in human progress, *The Voyage* describes "progress" as a series of temporary advances that end in disappointment and disgust. These smaller achievements—discovering new lands, inventing new luxuries, gaining fame and fortune, seeking ecstasy in sadism and sensuality—are all bound to deceive because they are merely symbols of a larger unending voyage: the quest for the infinite. Since human beings contain an "inner [spiritual] infinite" they cannot be satisfied with any limits and must constantly travel toward the unknown and the new. The "country" of earthly experience is not adequate for travelers impelled by an inner fire; their voyage ends, therefore, with a final plunge—

for answers—into the unfathomable obscurity of death. The last line, "In the depths of the Unknown, we'll discover the New!" became a famous rallying cry for generations who sought new insights by exploring such unmapped frontiers.

Baudelaire alternates between acid melancholy and glimpses of happiness. Not all voyages are unhappy; one of his rare contented and even tender poems is the lyrical *Invitation to the Voyage*, a lover's invitation to an exotic land of peace, beauty, and sensuous harmony. The voyage is imaginary, of course, implying two forms of escape from reality: an escape out of real time into a primeval accord of the senses, and an escape into another artistic vision—the glowing interiors painted by such Dutch masters as Jan Vermeer. A similar but more cynical voyage of escape occurs in *Her Hair*. Here the poet, abandoning himself to passion, buries his face in the dark tide of his mistress's hair as if to submerge himself in the dark ocean of dream. This escape is available only on a temporary basis, however; the woman remains his "oasis" only so long as he adorns her hair with jewels. In both poems, and probably in Baudelaire's poetry in general, we must admit that women do not exist as separate personalities even if there are specific historical figures behind the poems. They are foils for poetic inspiration, conventional images of beauty, coldness, vision, or vice given one or another form. The woman in *A Carcass* exists only as an appropriate listener in a poem that mocks Petrarchan ideals of feminine beauty. At the end, Baudelaire is even more clamped in his own solitude, registering repeatedly a personal experience from which he builds an amazingly complex imaginative universe.

Baudelaire was convinced that "every good poet has always been a realist," and he himself was a master of realistic details used for effects that go beyond conventional or photographic realism. The rhythmic thump of firewood being delivered is repeated throughout *Song of Autumn I*, where it coordinates ascending images of death. Imagery in *A Carcass* is more brutal. Even if the contrast between the language of courtly love ("star of my eyes") and crude and obscene descriptions no longer shocks in quite the same way, there remains the striking feat of imagination in which Baudelaire superimposes a swarming, vibrating new life onto the blurred outlines of a decaying animal carcass. The poem's ostensible theme is familiar—*carpe diem*, "seize the day" or "think of the future and love me now," since only a poet can preserve beauty—but one has only to compare Yeats's poem *When You Are Old* to recognize the harshness of this address to the beloved. The mixture of tones is more subtle in the *Spleen* poems, celebrated for their evocation of gray misery. Here Baudelaire inserts mundane items like bats, spiders, old-fashioned clothes, uncorked perfume bottles, and noisy rainspouts. Such down-to-earth details give substance to concurrent mythical or allegorical scenes. A chill revelation of mortality emerges from the sequence of thoroughly practical references to water in *Spleen LXXVIII*, beginning with the rain and fog in the city and including a cat twisting and turning uncomfortably on clammy tiles, the whine of a rainspout, the wheeze of wet wood and a damp clock pendulum, and finally a deck of cards left by an old woman who died of dropsy. If the sequence is interesting as a tour de force of linked images, it also serves cumulatively to evoke an atmosphere of lethargy and decay, climaxing in a tiny, altogether unrealistic final scene in which two face cards talk sinisterly of their past loves.

Similar themes are to be found in the prose poems (published as *Little Poems in Prose* or *Paris Spleen*), although with a more openly autobiographical tone and a more homely setting. This prose must also find its own way to be musical "without rhyme." Stanzas become paragraphs; rhythm is created through variations in sentence length, syntax, and sound patterns, and the juxtaposition of scenes and tones. Rhythm is undeniably present, however changed: it is audible in the triple cadence ending *Windows* (helping him "to live, to feel that I am, and what I am") or in the contrasting dialogue leading up to the soul's explosion at the end of *Anywhere out of the World*.

The realistic details that are often buried in the lyrics of *The Flowers of Evil* appear on the surface in the prose poems, where they are fused with poetic daydreams or flights of that speculative imagination Baudelaire calls elsewhere "The Queen of the

Faculties." Transforming an everyday urban scene in *Crowds*, he is able to imagine himself alone in "a bath of multitude," where he can be "himself or someone else, as he chooses." In *Windows*, after having deduced the life story of an old woman seen across the roofs, he ends by saying that her story is only a "legend"—or, at least, that he does not care whether it is true as long as it provides a point of departure for his own imagination. In each case the poet is visibly alone, experiencing either the melancholy of spleen or the joy of an artistic imagination that creates and populates its own world.

Baudelaire is a complex and ironic poet, an inheritor of that Romantic irony that wishes to embrace all the opposites of human existence: good and evil, love and hate, self and other, dream and reality. His is a universe of relationships, of echoes and correspondences, perceived only by the poetic imagination. His best-known poem, in fact, is the sonnet *Correspondences*. This poem describes a vision of the mystic unity of all nature, which is demonstrated by the reciprocity of our five senses (*synesthesia*). Nature, says the poet, is a system of perpetual analogies in which one thing always corresponds to another—physical objects to each other (colonnades in a temple, for example, to trees in the forest), spiritual reality to physical reality, and the five senses (taste, smell, touch, sight, and hearing) among themselves—to produce such combinations as "bitter green," a "soft look," or "a harsh sound." Human beings are not usually aware of the "universal analogy"—the forest of the first stanza watches us without our knowing it—but it is the role of the poet to act as seer and guide, urging us toward a state of awareness in which both mind and senses fuse in another dimension. *Correspondences* is no vaguely intuitive poem, however. Even though it describes a state of ecstatic awareness, it works through the stages of a logical argument. The thesis is set out in the first stanza, explained in the second, and illustrated with cumulative examples in the third and fourth. Baudelaire's yearning for mystic harmony does not make him neglect either a base in reality or a rigorous application of intellect. His fusion of idealist vision, realistic detail, and artistic discipline made him the most influential poet of the nineteenth century and the first poet of the modern age.

The selections printed here, from a range of Baudelaire's most influential lyric and prose poems, are translated by different modern poets. While remaining faithful to the original text, each translation necessarily stresses different aspects (for example, images, meter and rhyme, word order, tone, a particular set of associations when more than one is possible) to create a genuine English poem. The footnotes occasionally point out elements that are especially significant in the French text.

PRONOUNCING GLOSSARY

The following list uses common English syllables and stress accents to provide rough equivalents of selected words whose pronunciation may be unfamiliar to the general reader.

Baudelaire: *boh-d'lair'*

ennui: *on-wee'*

Pylades: *pill'-ah-deez*

Venustre: *ven-yew'-struh*

The Salon of 1859

FROM III

The Queen of the Faculties[1]

In recent times we have heard it said in a thousand different ways: "Copy nature; and nature only. No greater enjoyment, no more splendid triumph can exist than an outstanding copy of nature."[2] And this doctrine, which is hostile to art, claimed the right to be applied not only to painting but to all the arts, even to the novel, even to poetry. To these doctrinaires so satisfied with nature, an imaginative man would certainly have had the right to reply: "I regard it as useless and tedious to copy what is there in front of me, because nothing of that satisfies me. Nature is ugly, and I like the figments of my own fantasy better than the triviality of material reality." But it would have been more philosophical to ask the doctrinaires in question first whether they were quite certain of the existence of external nature; or, if that question seemed too likely to arouse their sarcasm, whether they were quite certain they knew nature in its entirety, nature and all it embodies? A "yes" would have been the most boastful and the most extravagant of answers. As far as I have been able to understand its strange and degrading utterances, the doctrine really meant, or at least I do it the honor of supposing it really meant: the artist, the true artist, the true poet, should paint only in accordance with what he sees and feels. He must be really faithful to his own nature. He must avoid, like death itself, the temptation of borrowing the eyes or the feelings of another man, however great, for in that case the production he gave us would be a pack of lies, relatively to himself, not realities. Now if the pedants I am speaking about (pedantry can be found even in meanness), who have their representatives everywhere, since this theory flatters both the uncreative and the lazy, did not intend the proposition to be understood in that way, we are entitled to assume that all they meant to say is: "We have no imagination, and we hereby decree that no one else shall have any."

What a mysterious faculty is this queen of the faculties! It touches all the others; it stimulates them, sends them forth to do battle. It sometimes resembles them so closely as to identify itself with them, and yet it never loses its own identity, and men in whom imagination is not active are easily recognizable by some nameless curse that dries up their work, like the fig tree of the Gospel.[3]

Imagination is analysis, imagination is synthesis; and yet men who are skillful in analysis and competent enough to sum up problems can well be devoid of imagination. Imagination is all that, and yet not entirely that. Imagination is sensitiveness, and yet there are some very sensitive people, too

---

1. Translated by P. E. Charvet. Published in the *Revue française, The Queen of the Faculties* is the third section of Baudelaire's review of the Salon of 1859, an exposition of painters that opened in Paris on April 15, 1859. The review took the form of a letter to the editor; the latter attached a statement that contributors expressed their own opinions and not necessarily those of the journal. *Faculties*: sense perceptions. 2. The realist movement in painting, represented by Gustave Courbet, had gained prestige in recent years. Baudelaire disliked realist painting, considering it (as he did the photography of his time) merely documentary reproduction, and he shifts quickly to philosophical questions of cognition, where he can argue that nature appears differently to each person. 3. In the New Testament, Mark 11.13–14 and 20–21.

sensitive perhaps, who have none. It is imagination that has taught man the moral significance of color, contour, sound and scent.[4] In the beginning of things, imagination created analogy and metaphor. It decomposes all creation, and, with the wealth of materials amassed and ordered according to rules whose origins can be found only in the deepest recesses of the soul, it creates a new world, it produces the sensation of something new. Since imagination created the world (I think we are entitled to say that much even in the religious sense), it is right that imagination should govern the world. What does opinion say about a soldier without imagination? That he may make a tough fighter, but that, if he is put in command of an army, he will make no conquests. An analogous case would be that of a poet or a novelist who removed imagination from command of the faculties, and gave it,[5] for example, to his knowledge of the language or to his observation of facts. What does opinion say of a diplomat without imagination? That he may well have a thorough knowledge of the history of treaties and alliances in the past, but he will never guess the treaties and alliances that lie hidden in the future. What does opinion say of a scholar without imagination? That he has learned all that can be learned, because it has been taught, but he will never discover laws as yet unsuspected of existing. Imagination is the queen of truth, and the possible is one of the provinces of truth. Imagination is positively related to the infinite. Without it, all the faculties, however firm and sharpened they may be, are as though they did not exist, whereas the weakness of some secondary faculties, provided these are stimulated by a vigorous imagination, is a secondary misfortune.[6] No faculties can do without imagination, but imagination can take the place of some. Often, proudly and simply, it goes straight to the heart of what these faculties have been seeking and finding only after successive efforts to apply a number of methods unsuited to the natural order of things. Finally, imagination plays a powerful part in ethics; for if you will allow me to go that far, what is virtue without imagination? * * *

---

4. The faculties of sight, touch, hearing, and smell.   5. Gave command.   6. Of secondary importance.

THE FLOWERS OF EVIL

To the Reader[1]

Infatuation, sadism, lust, avarice
possess our souls and drain the body's force;
we spoonfeed our adorable remorse,
like whores or beggars nourishing their lice.

---

1. Translated by Robert Lowell. The translation pays primary attention to the insistent rhythm of the original poetic language and keeps the *abba* rhyme scheme.

Our sins are mulish, our confessions lies;   5
we play to the grandstand with our promises,
we pray for tears to wash our filthiness,
importantly pissing hogwash through our styes.

The devil, watching by our sickbeds, hissed
old smut and folk-songs to our soul, until   10
the soft and precious metal of our will
boiled off in vapor for this scientist.

Each day his flattery[2] makes us eat a toad,
and each step forward is a step to hell,
unmoved, though previous corpses and their smell   15
asphyxiate our progress on this road.

Like the poor lush who cannot satisfy,
we try to force our sex with counterfeits,
die drooling on the deliquescent tits,
mouthing the rotten orange we suck dry.   20

Gangs of demons are boozing in our brain—
ranked, swarming, like a million warrior-ants,[3]
they drown and choke the cistern of our wants;
each time we breathe, we tear our lungs with pain.

If poison, arson, sex, narcotics, knives   25
have not yet ruined us and stitched their quick,
loud patterns on the canvas of our lives,
it is because our souls are still too sick.[4]

Among the vermin, jackals, panthers, lice,
gorillas and tarantulas that suck   30
and snatch and scratch and defecate and fuck
in the disorderly circus of our vice,

there's one more ugly and abortive birth.
It makes no gestures, never beats its breast,
yet it would murder for a moment's rest,[5]   35
and willingly annihilate the earth.

It's BOREDOM. Tears have glued its eyes together.
You know it well, my Reader. This obscene
beast chain-smokes yawning for the guillotine—
you—hypocrite Reader—my double—my brother!   40

2. The devil is literally described as a puppet master controlling our strings.   3. Literally, intestinal worms.   4. Literally, not bold enough.   5. Literally, swallow the world in a yawn.

Correspondences[1]

Nature is a temple whose living colonnades
Breathe forth a mystic speech in fitful sighs;
Man wanders among symbols in those glades
Where all things watch him with familiar eyes.

Like dwindling echoes gathered far away   5
Into a deep and thronging unison
Huge as the night or as the light of day,
All scents and sounds and colors meet as one.

Perfumes there are as sweet as the oboe's sound,
Green as the prairies, fresh as a child's caress,[2]   10
—And there are others, rich, corrupt, profound[3]

And of an infinite pervasiveness,
Like myrrh, or musk, or amber,[4] that excite
The ecstasies of sense, the soul's delight.

Correspondances

La Nature est un temple où de vivants piliers
Laissent parfois sortir de confuses paroles;
L'homme y passe à travers des forêts de symboles
Qui l'observent avec des regards familiers.

Comme de longs échos qui de loin se confondent   5
Dans une ténébreuse et profonde unité,
Vaste comme la nuit et comme la clarté,
Les parfums, les couleurs et les sons se répondent.

Il est des parfums frais comme des chairs d'enfants,
Doux comme les hautbois, verts comme les prairies,   10
—Et d'autres, corrompus, riches et triomphants,

Ayant l'expansion des choses infinies,
Comme l'ambre, le musc, le benjoin et l'encens,
Qui chantent les transports de l'esprit et des sens.

1. Translated by Richard Wilbur. The translation keeps the intricate melody of the sonnet's original rhyme scheme. 2. Literally, flesh. 3. Literally, triumphant. 4. Or ambergris, a substance secreted by whales. Ambergris and musk (a secretion of the male musk deer) are used in making perfume.

Her Hair[1]

O fleece, that down the neck waves to the nape!
O curls! O perfume nonchalant and rare!
O ecstacy! To fill this alcove[2] shape
With memories that in these tresses sleep,
I would shake them like pennons in the air!   5

Languorous Asia, burning Africa,
And a far world, defunct almost, absent,
Within your aromatic forest stay!
As other souls on music drift away,
Mine, o my love! still floats upon your scent.   10

I shall go there where, full of sap, both tree
And man swoon in the heat of southern climes;
Strong tresses, be the swell that carries me!
I dream upon your sea of ebony
Of dazzling sails, of oarsmen, masts and flames: 15

A sun-drenched and reverberating port,
Where I imbibe color and sound and scent;
Where vessels, gliding through the gold and moire,
Open their vast arms as they leave the shore
To clasp the pure and shimmering firmament.   20

I'll plunge my head, enamored of its pleasure,
In this black ocean where the other hides;
My subtle spirit then will know a measure
Of fertile idleness and fragrant leisure,
Lulled by the infinite rhythm of its tides!   25

Pavilion, of blue-shadowed tresses spun,
You give me back the azure from afar;
And where the twisted locks are fringed with down
Lurk mingled odors I grow drunk upon
Of oil of coconut, of musk and tar.   30

A long time! always! my hand in your hair
Will sow the stars of sapphire, pearl, ruby,
That you be never deaf to my desire,
My oasis and gourd whence I aspire
To drink deep of the wine of memory![3]   35

1. Translated by Doreen Bell. The translation emulates the French original's challenging *abaab* rhyme
pattern.   2. Bedroom.   3. The last two lines are a question: "Are you not . . . ?"

A Carcass[1]

Remember, my love, the item you saw
    That beautiful morning in June:
By a bend in the path a carcass reclined
    On a bed sown with pebbles and stones;

Her legs were spread out like a lecherous whore,   5
    Sweating out poisonous fumes,
Who opened in slick invitational style
    Her stinking and festering womb.

The sun on this rottenness focused its rays
    To cook the cadaver till done,   10
And render to Nature a hundredfold gift
    Of all she'd united in one.

And the sky cast an eye on this marvelous meat
    As over the flowers in bloom.
The stench was so wretched that there on the grass   15
    You nearly collapsed in a swoon.

The flies buzzed and droned on these bowels of filth
    Where an army of maggots arose,
Which flowed like a liquid and thickening stream
    On the animate rags of her clothes.[2]   20

And it rose and it fell, and pulsed like a wave,
    Rushing and bubbling with health.
One could say that this carcass, blown with vague breath,
    Lived in increasing itself.

And this whole teeming world made a musical sound   25
    Like babbling brooks and the breeze,
Or the grain that a man with a winnowing-fan
    Turns with a rhythmical ease.

The shapes wore away as if only a dream
    Like a sketch that is left on the page   30
Which the artist forgot and can only complete
    On the canvas, with memory's aid.

From back in the rocks, a pitiful bitch
    Eyed us with angry distaste,
Awaiting the moment to snatch from the bones   35
    The morsel she'd dropped in her haste.

---

1. Translated by James McGowan with special attention to imagery. The alternation of long and short lines in English emulates the French meter's rhythmic swing between twelve-syllable and eight-syllable lines in an *abab* rhyme scheme.   **2.** By extension. The torn flesh is described as "living rags."

—And you, in your turn, will be rotten as this:
    Horrible, filthy, undone,
Oh sun of my nature and star of my eyes,
    My passion, my angel[3] in one!   40

Yes, such will you be, oh regent of grace,
    After the rites have been read,
Under the weeds, under blossoming grass
    As you molder with bones of the dead.

Ah then, oh my beauty, explain to the worms   45
    Who cherish your body so fine,
That I am the keeper for corpses of love
    Of the form, and the essence divine![4]

Invitation to the Voyage[1]

    My child, my sister, dream
    How sweet all things would seem
Were we in that kind land to live together,
    And there love slow and long,
    There love and die among   5
Those scenes that image you, that sumptuous weather.
    Drowned suns that glimmer there
    Through cloud-disheveled air
Move me with such a mystery as appears
    Within those other skies   10
    Of your treacherous eyes
When I behold them shining through their tears.

There, there is nothing else but grace and measure,
Richness, quietness, and pleasure.

    Furniture that wears   15
    The lustre of the years
Softly would glow within our glowing chamber,
    Flowers of rarest bloom
    Proffering their perfume
Mixed with the vague fragrances of amber;   20
    Gold ceilings would there be,
    Mirrors deep as the sea,

---

3. Series of conventional Petrarchan images that idealize the beloved.   4. "Any form created by man is immortal. For form is independent of matter . . ." (from Baudelaire's journal *My Heart Laid Bare* 80). 1. Translated by Richard Wilbur. The translation maintains both the rhyme scheme and the rocking motion of the original meter, which follows an unusual pattern of two five-syllable lines followed by one seven-syllable line, and a seven-syllable couplet as refrain.

The walls all in an Eastern splendor hung—
　　Nothing but should address
　　The soul's loneliness,
Speaking her sweet and secret native tongue.　　　　　　　　　25

There, there is nothing else but grace and measure,
Richness, quietness, and pleasure.

　　See, sheltered from the swells
　　There in the still canals　　　　　　　　　　　　　　30
Those drowsy ships that dream of sailing forth;
　　It is to satisfy
　　Your least desire, they ply
Hither through all the waters of the earth.
　　The sun at close of day　　　　　　　　　　　　　　35
　　Clothes the fields of hay,
Then the canals, at last the town entire
　　In hyacinth and gold:
　　Slowly the land is rolled
Sleepward under a sea of gentle fire.　　　　　　　　　　40

There, there is nothing else but grace and measure,
Richness, quietness, and pleasure.

Song of Autumn I[2]

Soon we shall plunge into the chilly fogs;
Farewell, swift light! our summers are too short!
I hear already the mournful fall of logs
Re-echoing from the pavement of the court.

All of winter will gather in my soul:　　　　　　　　　　5
Hate, anger, horror, chills, the hard forced work;
And, like the sun in his hell by the north pole,
My heart will be only a red and frozen block.

I shudder, hearing every log that falls;
No scaffold could be built with hollower sounds.　　　　　10
My spirit is like a tower whose crumbling walls
The tireless battering-ram brings to the ground.

It seems to me, lulled by monotonous shocks,
As if they were hastily nailing a coffin today.
For whom?—Yesterday was summer. Now autumn knocks.　　15
That mysterious sound is like someone's going away.

2. Translated by C. F. MacIntyre to follow the original rhyme pattern.

Spleen LXXVIII[1]

Old Pluvius,[2] month of rains, in peevish mood
Pours from his urn chill winter's sodden gloom
On corpses fading in the near graveyard,
On foggy suburbs pours life's tedium.

My cat seeks out a litter on the stones,   5
Her mangy body turning without rest.
An ancient poet's soul in monotones
Whines in the rain-spouts like a chilblained ghost.

A great bell mourns, a wet log wrapped in smoke
Sings in falsetto to the wheezing clock,   10
While from a rankly perfumed deck of cards
(A dropsical old crone's fatal bequest)
The Queen of Spades, the dapper Jack of Hearts
Speak darkly of dead loves, how they were lost.

Spleen LXXIX[1]

I have more memories than if I had lived a thousand years.

Even a bureau crammed with souvenirs,
Old bills, love letters, photographs, receipts,
Court depositions, locks of hair in plaits,
Hides fewer secrets than my brain could yield.   5
It's like a tomb, a corpse-filled Potter's Field,[2]
A pyramid where the dead lie down by scores.
I am a graveyard that the moon abhors:
Like guilty qualms, the worms burrow and nest
Thickly in bodies that I loved the best.   10
I'm a stale boudoir where old-fashioned clothes
Lie scattered among wilted fern and rose,
Where only the Boucher girls[3] in pale pastels
Can breathe the uncorked scents and faded smells.

Nothing can equal those days for endlessness   15
When in the winter's blizzardy caress
Indifference expanding to Ennui[4]
Takes on the feel of Immortality.
O living matter, henceforth you're no more

---

1. Translated by Kenneth O. Hanson, with emphasis on the imagery. The French original uses identical *abab* rhymes in the two quatrains and shifts to *ccd, eed* in the tercets.   2. The rainy time (Latin, literal trans.); a period extending from January 20 to February 18 as the fifth month of the French Revolutionary calendar.   1. Translated by Anthony Hecht. The translation follows the original rhymed couplets, except for one technical impossibility: Baudelaire's repetition (in a poem about monotony) of an identical rhyme for eight lines (lines 11–18, the sound of long *a*).   2. A general term describing the common cemetery for those buried at public expense.   3. François Boucher (1703–1770), court painter for Louis XV of France, drew many pictures of young women clothed and nude.   4. Melancholy, paralyzing boredom.

Than a cold stone encompassed by vague fear   20
And by the desert, and the mist and sun;
An ancient Sphinx ignored by everyone,
Left off the map, whose bitter irony
Is to sing as the sun sets in that dry sea.[5]

Spleen LXXXI[1]

When the low heavy sky weighs like a lid
Upon the spirit aching for the light
And all the wide horizon's line is hid
By a black day sadder than any night;

When the changed earth is but a dungeon dank   5
Where batlike Hope goes blindly fluttering
And, striking wall and roof and mouldered plank,
Bruises his tender head and timid wing;

When like grim prison bars stretch down the thin,
Straight, rigid pillars of the endless rain,   10
And the dumb throngs of infamous spiders spin
Their meshes in the caverns of the brain,

Suddenly, bells leap forth into the air,
Hurling a hideous uproar to the sky
As 'twere a band of homeless spirits who fare   15
Through the strange heavens, wailing stubbornly.

And hearses, without drum or instrument,
File slowly through my soul; crushed, sorrowful,
Weeps Hope, and Grief, fierce and omnipotent,
Plants his black banner on my drooping skull.   20

The Voyage[1]

To Maxime du Camp[2]

I

The child, in love with prints and maps,
Holds the whole world in his vast appetite.
How large the earth is under the lamplight!
But in the eyes of memory, how the world is cramped!

---

5. Baudelaire combines two references to ancient Egypt, the Sphinx and the legendary statue of Memnon at Thebes, which was supposed to sing at sunset.   1. Translated by Sir John Squire in accord with the original rhyme scheme.   1. Translated by Charles Henri Ford. The French poem is written in the traditional twelve-syllable (alexandrine) line with an *abab* rhyme scheme.   2. A wry dedication to the progress-oriented author of *Modern Songs* (1855), which began "I was born a traveler."

We set out one morning, brain afire,   5
Hearts fat with rancor and bitter desires,
Moving along to the rhythm of wind and waves,
Lull the inner infinite on the finite of seas:

Some are glad, glad to leave a degraded home;
Others, happy to shake off the horror of their hearts,   10
Still others, astrologers drowned in the eyes of woman—
Oh the perfumes of Circe,[3] the power and the pig!—

To escape conversion to the Beast, get drunk
On space and light and the flames of skies;
The tongue of the sun and the ice that bites   15
Slowly erase the mark of the Kiss.

But the true voyagers are those who leave
Only to be going; hearts nimble as balloons,
They never diverge from luck's black sun,
And with or without reason, cry, Let's be gone!
                                                                   20
Desire to them is nothing but clouds,
They dream, as a draftee dreams of the cannon,
Of vast sensualities, changing, unknown,
Whose name the spirit has never pronounced!

II

We imitate—horrible!—the top and ball   25
In their waltz and bounce; even in sleep
We're turned and tormented by Curiosity,
Who, like a mad Angel, lashes the stars.

Peculiar fortune that changes its goal,
And being nowhere, is anywhere at all!   30
And Man, who is never untwisted from hope,
Scrambling like a madman to get some rest!

The soul's a three-master seeking Icaria;[4]
A voice on deck calls: "Wake up there!"
A voice from the mast-head, vehement, wild: 35
"Love . . . fame . . . happiness!" We're on the rocks!

Every island that the lookout hails
Becomes the Eldorado[5] foretold by Fortune;
Then Imagination embarks on its orgy
But runs aground in the brightness of morning.   40

---

3. In Homer's *Odyssey*, an island sorceress who changed visitors into beasts. Odysseus's men were transformed into pigs.   **4.** Greek island in the Aegean Sea named after the mythological Icarus, who, escaping from prison on wings made by his father, Daedalus, plunged into nearby waters and drowned when the wings gave way. His name was associated with utopian flights, as in Étienne Cabet's novel about a utopian community, *Voyage to Icaria* (1840). *Three-master:* a ship.   **5.** Fabled country of gold and abundance.

Poor little lover of visionary fields!
Should he be put in irons, dumped in the sea,
This drunken sailor, discoverer of Americas,
Mirage that makes the gulf more bitter?

So the old vagabond, shuffling in mud,   45
Dreams, nose hoisted, of a shining paradise,
His charmed eye lighting on Capua's[6] coast
At every candle aglow in a hovel.

III

Astounding voyagers! what noble stories
We read in your eyes, deeper than seas;   50
Show us those caskets, filled with rich memories,
Marvelous jewels, hewn from stars and aether.

Yes, we would travel, without sail or steam!
Gladden a little our jail's desolation,
Sail over our minds, stretched like a canvas,   55
All your memories, framed with gold horizons.

Tell us, what have you seen?

IV

                          "We have seen stars
And tides; we have seen sands, too,
And, despite shocks and unforeseen disasters,
We were often bored, just as we are here.   60

The glory of sun on a violet sea,
The glory of cities in the setting sun,
Kindled our hearts with torment and longing
To plunge into the sky's magnetic reflections.

Neither the rich cities nor sublime landscapes,   65
Ever possessed that mysterious attraction
Of Change and Chance having fun with the clouds.
And always Desire kept us anxious!

—Enjoyment adds force to Appetite!
Desire, old tree nurtured by pleasure,   70
Although your dear bark thicken and harden,
Your branches throb to hold the sun closer!

Great tree, will you outgrow the cypress?
Still we have gathered carefully
Some sketches for your hungry album,   75
Brothers, for whom all things from far away

6. City on the Volturno River in southern Italy, famous for its luxury and sensuality.

Are precious! We've bowed down to idols;
To thrones encrusted with luminous rocks;
To figured palaces whose magic pomp
Would ruin your bankers with a ruinous dream;   80

To costumes that intoxicate the eye,
To women whose teeth and nails are dyed,
To clever jugglers, fondled by the snake."[7]

V

And then, and what more?

VI

"O childish minds!

Not to forget the principal thing,   85
We saw everywhere, without looking for it,
From top to toe of the deadly scale,
The tedious drama of undying sin:

Woman, low slave, vain and stupid,
Without laughter self-loving, and without disgust,   90
Man, greedy despot, lewd, hard and covetous,
Slave of the slave, rivulet in the sewer;

The hangman exulting, the martyr sobbing;
Festivals that season and perfume the blood;[8]
The poison of power unnerving the tyrant,   95
The masses in love with the brutalizing whip;

Many religions, very like our own,
All climbing to heaven; and Holiness,
Like a delicate wallower in a feather bed,
Seeking sensation from hair shirts and nails.   100

Jabbering humanity, drunk with its genius,
As crazy now as it was in the past,
Crying to God in its raging agony:
'O master, fellow creature, I curse thee forever!'

And then the least stupid, brave lovers of Lunacy,   105
Fleeing the gross herd that Destiny pens in,
Finding release in the vast dreams of opium!
—Such is the story, the whole world over."

---

7. Snake charmers. The images in this stanza evoke India.   8. Literally, Festivals seasoned and perfumed by blood.

VII

Bitter knowledge that traveling brings!
The globe, monotonous and small, today,   110
Yesterday, tomorrow, always, throws us our image:
An oasis of horror in a desert of boredom!

Should we go? Or stay? If you can stay, stay;
But go if you must. Some run, some hide
To outwit Time, the enemy so vigilant and   115
Baleful. And many, alas, must run forever

Like the wandering Jew[9] and the twelve apostles,
Who could not escape his relentless net[1]
By ship or by wheel; while others knew how
To destroy him without leaving home.   120

When finally he places his foot on our spine,
May we be able to hope and cry, Forward!
As in days gone by when we left for China,
Eyes fixed on the distance, hair in the wind,

With heart as light as a young libertine's   125
We'll embark on the sea of deepening shadows.
Do you hear those mournful, enchanting voices[2]
That sing: "Come this way, if you would taste

The perfumed Lotus. Here you may pick
Miraculous fruits for which the heart hungers.   130
Come and drink deep of this strange,
Soft afternoon that never ends?"

Knowing his voice, we visualize the phantom—
It is our Pylades there, his arms outstretched.
While she whose knees we used to kiss cries out,   135
"For strength of heart, swim back to your Electra!"[3]

VIII

O Death, old captain, it is time! weigh anchor!
This country confounds us; hoist sail and away!
If the sky and sea are black as ink,
Our hearts, as you know them, burst with blinding rays.   140

Pour us your poison, that last consoling draft!
For we long, so the fire burns in the brain,
To sound the abyss, Hell or Heaven, what matter?
In the depths of the Unknown, we'll discover the New!

---

9. According to medieval legend, a Jew who mocked Christ on his way to the cross and was condemned
to wander unceasingly until Judgment Day.   1. These three stanzas describe Time (ultimately Death) as
a Roman gladiator, the *retiarius*, who used a net to trap his opponent.   2. The voices of the dead, luring
the sailor to the Lotus-land of ease and forgetfulness.   3. In Greek mythology, Orestes and Pylades were
close friends ready to sacrifice their lives for each other. Electra was Orestes' faithful sister, who saved him
from the Furies.

PARIS SPLEEN[1]

One o'Clock in the Morning

At last! I am alone! Nothing can be heard but the rumbling of a few belated and weary cabs. For a few hours at least silence will be ours, if not sleep. At last! The tyranny of the human face has disappeared, and now there will be no one but myself to make me suffer.

At last! I am allowed to relax in a bath of darkness! First a double turn of the key in the lock. This turn of the key will, it seems to me, increase my solitude and strengthen the barricades that, for the moment, separate me from the world.

Horrible life! Horrible city! Let us glance back over the events of the day: saw several writers, one of them asking me if you could go to Russia by land (he thought Russia was an island, I suppose); disagreed liberally with the editor of a review who to all my objections kept saying: "Here we are on the side of respectability," implying that all the other periodicals were run by rascals; bowed to twenty or more persons of whom fifteen were unknown to me; distributed hand shakes in about the same proportion without having first taken the precaution of buying gloves; to kill time during a shower, dropped in on a dancer who asked me to design her a costume of *Venustre*;[2] went to pay court to a theatrical director who in dismissing me said: "Perhaps you would do well to see Z. . . . ; he is the dullest, stupidest and most celebrated of our authors; with him you might get somewhere. Consult him and then we'll see": boasted (why?) of several ugly things I never did, and cravenly denied some other misdeeds that I had accomplished with the greatest delight; offense of fanfaronnade,[3] crime against human dignity; refused a slight favor to a friend and gave a written recommendation to a perfect rogue; Lord! let's hope that's all!

Dissatisfied with everything, dissatisfied with myself, I long to redeem myself and to restore my pride in the silence and solitude of the night. Souls of those whom I have loved, souls of those whom I have sung, strengthen me, sustain me, keep me from the vanities of the world and its contaminating fumes; and You, dear God! grant me grace to produce a few beautiful verses to prove to myself that I am not the lowest of men, that I am not inferior to those whom I despise.

Crowds

It is not given to every man to take a bath of multitude; enjoying a crowd is an art; and only he can relish a debauch of vitality at the expense of the human species, on whom, in his cradle, a fairy has bestowed the love of masks and masquerading, the hate of home, and the passion for roaming.

Multitude, solitude: identical terms, and interchangeable by the active and

---

1. Translated by Louis Varèse.   2. Venus. Baudelaire ironically reproduces the dancer's mispronunciation.   3. Boasting.

fertile poet. The man who is unable to people his solitude is equally unable to be alone in a bustling crowd.

The poet enjoys the incomparable privilege of being able to be himself or someone else, as he chooses. Like those wandering souls who go looking for a body, he enters as he likes into each man's personality. For him alone everything is vacant; and if certain places seem closed to him, it is only because in his eyes they are not worth visiting.

The solitary and thoughtful stroller finds a singular intoxication in this universal communion. The man who loves to lose himself in a crowd enjoys feverish delights that the egoist locked up in himself as in a box, and the slothful man like a mollusk in his shell, will be eternally deprived of. He adopts as his own all the occupations, all the joys and all the sorrows that chance offers.

What men call love is a very small, restricted, feeble thing compared with this ineffable orgy, this divine prostitution of the soul giving itself entire, all its poetry and all its charity, to the unexpected as it comes along, to the stranger as he passes.

It is a good thing sometimes to teach the fortunate of this world, if only to humble for an instant their foolish pride, that there are higher joys than theirs, finer and more uncircumscribed. The founders of colonies, shepherds of peoples, missionary priests exiled to the ends of the earth, doubtlessly know something of this mysterious drunkenness; and in the midst of the vast family created by their genius, they must often laugh at those who pity them because of their troubled fortunes and chaste lives.

Windows

Looking from outside into an open window one never sees as much as when one looks through a closed window. There is nothing more profound, more mysterious, more pregnant, more insidious, more dazzling than a window lighted by a single candle. What one can see out in the sunlight is always less interesting than what goes on behind a windowpane. In that black or luminous square life lives, life dreams, life suffers.

Across the ocean of roofs I can see a middle-aged woman, her face already lined, who is forever bending over something and who never goes out. Out of her face, her dress, and her gestures, out of practically nothing at all, I have made up this woman's story, or rather legend, and sometimes I tell it to myself and weep.

If it had been an old man I could have made up his just as well.

And I go to bed proud to have lived and to have suffered in some one besides myself.

Perhaps you will say "Are you sure that your story is the real one?" But what does it matter what reality is outside myself, so long as it has helped me to live, to feel that I am, and what I am?

Anywhere out of the World[1]

Life is a hospital where every patient is obsessed by the desire of changing beds. One would like to suffer opposite the stove, another is sure he would get well beside the window.

It always seems to me that I should be happy anywhere but where I am, and this question of moving is one that I am eternally discussing with my soul.

"Tell me, my soul, poor chilly soul, how would you like to live in Lisbon? It must be warm there, and you would be as blissful as a lizard in the sun. It is a city by the sea; they say that it is built of marble, and that its inhabitants have such a horror of the vegetable kingdom that they tear up all the trees. You see it is a country after my own heart; a country entirely made of mineral and light, and with liquid to reflect them."

My soul does not reply.

"Since you are so fond of being motionless and watching the pageantry of movement, would you like to live in the beatific land of Holland? Perhaps you could enjoy yourself in that country which you have so long admired in paintings on museum walls. What do you say to Rotterdam,[2] you who love forests of masts, and ships that are moored on the doorsteps of houses?"

My soul remains silent.

"Perhaps you would like Batavia[3] better? There, moreover, we should find the wit of Europe wedded to the beauty of the tropics."

Not a word. Can my soul be dead?

"Have you sunk into so deep a stupor that you are happy only in your unhappiness? If that is the case, let us fly to countries that are the counterfeits of Death. I know just the place for us, poor soul. We will pack up our trunks for Torneo.[4] We will go still farther, to the farthest end of the Baltic Sea; still farther from life if possible; we will settle at the Pole. There the sun only obliquely grazes the earth, and the slow alternations of daylight and night abolish variety and increase that other half of nothingness, monotony. There we can take deep baths of darkness, while sometimes for our entertainment, the Aurora Borealis will shoot up its rose-red sheafs like the reflections of the fireworks of hell!"

At last my soul explodes! "Anywhere! Just so it is out of the world!"

---

1. The title (given in English by Baudelaire) is based on a line from Thomas Hood's poem *Bridge of Sighs*: "Anywhere, anywhere—out of the world." Baudelaire probably found the reference in Poe's *Poetic Principle*.
2. Large Dutch seaport.   3. Former name of Jakarta, capital of the Dutch East Indies and now the capital city of Indonesia.   4. A city in Finland.

STÉPHANE MALLARMÉ
1842–1898

Of all the Symbolist writers, Mallarmé (*mahl-ahr-may'*) is the most compulsive vision-ary. He uses ordinary words and concrete images, but only as raw material for a wholly imaginary creation. Like Rimbaud, he seeks a way out of sordid reality through the liberating power of the imagination; but unlike the younger poet, he did not turn his back on literature, even though his lofty poetic ideals made it increasingly difficult for him to put words on paper. Mallarmé works to purify language; he avoids the direct approach because obliquely he can say more. Thus he suggests, rather than names; keeps several levels of meaning alive at the same time; complicates his syntax and sometimes even misleads us to prolong the pleasure of final discovery. Although Mallarmé's poems are immediately accessible on the level of visual imagery, they also offer the pleasure of a chess game for those who like to pursue intricate structures of thought. He constitutes another example of the poet adventuring on the frontiers of thought. By the second half of the twentieth century, Mallarmé's multileveled patterns of allusion and abstract theories of poetic language had found followers among not only poets but also philosophers of language.

Étienne (called Stéphane) Mallarmé was born in Paris on March 18, 1842, into a settled bourgeois family. His father was deputy clerk in the Registry, and ancestors on both sides of the family had been minor government bureaucrats as far back as the French Revolution. Mallarmé's mother died when he was five, and his sister in 1857: the pain of their loss recurs in images of his later poetry. After graduating from boarding school in 1860, he worked for two years in his grandfather's office before deciding to become a teacher of English. In 1863 he received a teaching position in the southeastern provincial town of Tournon and moved there with his new wife, a young German woman named Maria Gerhard. Their daughter, Geneviève, was born in 1864. A son, Anatole, was born in 1871 and died in 1879.

Mallarmé began publishing poems and articles in 1862, although his output was always meager and he did not produce a collection in book form until 1887. Much of his work was published separately in various journals. His first important group of poems was published in 1866 in the new literary magazine *Contemporary Parnassus,* and his translations of Edgar Allan Poe appeared in 1872. Mallarmé was eager to move to Paris, the capital of the arts, but as a young teacher in the state educational system he was dependent on governmental assignments. Sent in 1886 to Besançon and in 1867 to Avignon, he was finally able to move to Paris in 1871, and there he taught at the Lycée Fontanes. The poet was not a particularly good language teacher, had little aptitude for drills and discipline, and was often a figure of fun for his students. Nonetheless, he was an important and charismatic figure for the young writers, artists, and musicians who heard him talk about the nature of poetry at the "Tuesdays," gatherings held every Tuesday evening from 1880 until shortly before his death. Mallarmé's influence was widespread. In 1876 Édouard Manet illustrated *L'Après-midi d'un faune* (The Afternoon of a Faun), and in 1894 Claude Debussy composed a musical *Prélude*, inspired by the same text. Verlaine included Mallarmé in his account of the new poets, *The Accursed Poets,* and after Verlaine's death Mal-larmé was elected "Prince of Poets" by his colleagues in 1896.

He gave lectures and interviews on the nature of poetry, from which passages are printed here. Mallarmé also experimented with spatial and typographical arrange-ments in a long poem, *Dice Thrown Will Never Abolish Chance* (1897), that fore-shadowed modern concrete poetry. During the last part of his life, he devoted his energies to the concept of a comprehensive "Book" whose allusive structure would extend into all dimensions of the universe. Yet he himself finally felt that his vision had outstripped technical possibilities; and when he died on September 9, 1898, the "Book" remained incomplete.

The creative process itself is the central topic of Mallarmé's poetry, whether in the earlier autobiographical poems or in later impersonal scenes from which the narrator is excluded. Mallarmé's particular symbolism builds on allusion and suggestion to evoke a virtual reality, a richer dimension he prefers to ordinary limited realism. The poet is haunted by the difficulty of writing and describes himself as a grave digger excavating his thoughts from the "cold and niggard soil" of his brain, or as paralyzed by the blank whiteness of the paper on which he must write. Escaping into art, he wishes in one poem to imitate the spare perfection of painted Chinese porcelain. Even such a banal object as a fan, fluttering open and then lying closed against a bracelet, can evoke the desired realm of absolute beauty. A common characteristic of Mallarmé's evocations of beauty, and one that distinguishes them from scenes in Baudelaire, Rimbaud, and Verlaine, is his emphasis on absence and silence. An early poem, Saint, illustrates the way the poet plays with a sense of loss or absence while using concrete details to create a series of vivid—though intangible—images.

The saint of the poem (according to a previous title, St. Cecilia, the patron saint of music), is seen at—perhaps represented on—the window of a cabinet where musical instruments are kept. The cabinet's cedar-wood viol, which no longer gleams with gold as it did when formerly played with accompanying flute and mandolin, and the old book lying open at the Magnificat, together establish the idea of a real, historical music that is now stilled or absent. The poem's single sentence is divided into two contrasting scenes; in the last two stanzas, the saint plays an imaginary harp that suggests an ideal or soundless music. She, the "Musician of silences," has her finger poised on the shape of a golden harp implied by the outstretched wing of a sculptured angel, a "plumage instrumental" that receives from the evening sun all the gilding that was lost to the real instrument of the first stanza. By the end of the poem, the ideal music suggested by the saint's gesture is more present to the reader than the "real" music at the beginning.

The ideal music of this and other poems is created by refining and manipulating ordinary language: purifying "the language of the horde," as Mallarmé says in The Tomb of Edgar Poe. This "tomb" or epitaph poem was written for a Baltimore memorial ceremony at which a monument to Poe was erected. Mallarmé describes the American poet as a St. George confronting the dragon of mediocrity and slander (that is, critics who accused him of writing only drunken fantasies). Another allegory of the alienated poet, The Virginal, Vibrant, and Beautiful Dawn, is built around the image of a swan who—refusing to sing about life, warmth, and mundane reality—is finally frozen into the dazzling glacier of his ideal dreams. The sonnet emphasizes images of whiteness, arrested movement, sterility, and chill; the French text intensifies this bleakness by reiterating a shrill ee sound throughout all fourteen lines and piling up negative linguistic forms. Mallarmé's artist is a technician, coordinating different relationships among words to invent his "purer" poetic language

Mallarmé's best-known poem, the source of Claude Debussy's orchestral Prélude in 1894 and Nijinsky's ballet in 1912, is The Afternoon of a Faun. Here the familiar themes of artistic creation, dream, and loss—the doomed attempt to capture perfect form in mere words—underlie the warm and sensuous picture of a woodland satyr recounting his erotic pursuit of two nymphs. Was it a dream, he wonders, that he caught the two water nymphs—one passionate, one naïve—only to lose them on the brink of possession? The poem is framed by the faun's desire first to "perpetuate" these nymphs in memory and finally to follow them back into dream. It is famous for its vivid and sensual descriptions, for its intricate imagery, and for the extraordinary musicality of its classical verse (the French alexandrine, or twelve-syllable line). Turning to his pipes and to drunken dreams to celebrate a perfect union he could not hold, the faun illustrates once more Mallarmé's theme of poetic creation, describing an ideal beauty that is absent and a sensuously intuited love that remains perpetually not just out of reach but in fact a figment of the imagination.

From The Evolution of Literature[1]

* * *

"As far as content is concerned," Mallarmé answered, "I feel that the young poets are nearer than the Parnassians[2] to the poetic ideal. The latter still treat their subjects as the old philosophers and orators did: that is, they present things directly, whereas I think that they should be presented allusively. Poetry lies in the *contemplation* of things, in the image emanating from the reveries which things arouse in us. The Parnassians take something in its entirety and simply exhibit it; in so doing, they fall short of mystery; they fail to give our minds that exquisite joy which consists of believing that we are creating something. To *name* an object is largely to destroy poetic enjoyment, which comes from gradual divination. The ideal is to *suggest* the object. It is the perfect use of this mystery which constitutes symbol. An object must be gradually evoked in order to show a state of soul * * *."

From Crisis in Poetry[1]

* * * *

It is not *description* which can unveil the efficacy and beauty of monuments, seas, or the human face in all their maturity and native state, but rather evocation, *allusion, suggestion*. These somewhat arbitrary terms reveal what may well be a very decisive tendency in modern literature, a tendency which limits literature and yet sets it free. For what is the magic charm of art, if not this: that, beyond the confines of a fistful of dust or of all other reality, beyond the book itself, beyond the very text, it delivers up that volatile scattering which we call the Spirit, Who cares for nothing save universal musicality.

Speech is no more than a commercial approach to reality. In literature, allusion is sufficient: essences are distilled and then embodied in Idea.

* * *

If the poem is to be pure, the poet's voice must be stilled and the initiative taken by the words themselves, which will be set in motion as they meet unequally in collision. And in an exchange of gleams they will flame out like some glittering swath of fire sweeping over precious stones, and thus replace the audible breathing in lyric poetry of old—replace the poet's own personal and passionate control of verse.

1. Prose selections translated by Bradford Cook. *The Evolution of Literature* is the title given to an interview with Jules Huret in 1891, one of several that the journalist conducted with leading writers that year.   2. A school of poetry that flourished in the 1860s and 1870s in France, dedicating itself to art and emphasizing precise, formal beauty. In Greek myth, Mount Parnassus was the home of the Muses.   1. Published in 1896. Mallarmé returns to the concept of the "pure" poem, created as a structure of rhythmic patterns and interwoven allusions. Unlike the romantic poem, which emphasized its author's voice and personality, the pure poem transcends both author and specific references to create a new, poetic presence over and above the material from which it is made.

The inner structures of a book of verse must be inborn; in this way, chance will be totally eliminated and the poet will be absent. From each theme, itself predestined, a given harmony will be born somewhere in the parts of the total poem and take its proper place within the volume; because, for every sound, there is an echo. Motifs of like pattern will move in balance from point to point. There will be none of the sublime incoherence found in the page-settings of the Romantics, none of the artificial unity that used to be based on the square measurements of the book. Everything will be hesitation, disposition of parts, their alternations and relationships—all this contributing to the rhythmic totality, which will be the very silence of the poem, in its blank spaces, as that silence is translated by each structural element in its own way. * * *

One of the undeniable ideals of our time is to divide words into two different categories: first, for vulgar or immediate, second, for essential purposes.

The first is for narrative, instruction, or description (even though an adequate exchange of human thoughts might well be achieved through the silent exchange of money). The elementary use of language involves that universal *journalistic style* which characterizes all kinds of contemporary writing, with the exception of literature.

Why should we perform the miracle by which a natural object is almost made to disappear beneath the magic waving wand of the written word, if not to divorce that object from the direct and the palpable, and so conjure up its *essence* in all purity?

When I say: "a flower!" then from that forgetfulness to which my voice consigns all floral form, something different from the usual calyces arises, something all music, essence, and softness: the flower which is absent from all bouquets.

* * *

The Afternoon of a Faun[1]

Eclogue[2]

THE FAUN

These nymphs that I would perpetuate:
      so clear
And light, their carnation,[3] that it floats in the air
Heavy with leafy slumbers.

     Did I love a dream?
My doubt, night's ancient hoard, pursues its theme
In branching labyrinths, which, being still   5
The veritable woods themselves, alas, reveal

---

1. All poems translated by Henry Weinfield. In Greek mythology, a faun was a woodland satyr with goatlike hooves and horns. 2. A pastoral poem, usually in dialogue form, originating in Greek poetry. Here, italics indicate the divisions of the faun's internal dialogue. 3. A rosy flesh pink.

My triumph as the ideal fault of roses.
Consider . . .

        if the women of your glosses
Are phantoms of your fabulous[4] desires!
Faun, the illusion flees from the cold, blue eyes   10
Of the chaster nymph like a fountain gushing tears;
But the other, all in sighs, you say, compares
To a hot wind through the fleece that blows at noon?
No! through the motionless and weary swoon
Of stifling heat that suffocates the morning,   15
Save from my flute, no waters murmuring
In harmony flow out into the groves;
And the only wind on the horizon no ripple moves,
Exhaled from my twin pipes and swift to drain
The melody in arid drifts of rain,   20
Is the visible, serene and fictive air
Of inspiration rising as if in prayer.

RELATE, Sicilian shores,[5] whose tranquil fens
My vanity disturbs as do the suns,
Silent beneath the brilliant flowers of flame: 25
"That cutting hollow reeds my art would tame,
I saw far off, against the glaucous gold
Of foliage twined to where the springs run cold,
An animal whiteness languorously swaying;
To the slow prelude that the pipes were playing,   30
This flight of swans—no! naiads[6]—rose in a shower
Of spray . . ."

        Day burns inert in the tawny hour
And excess of hymen is escaped away—
Without a sign, from one who pined for the primal A:[7]
And so, beneath a flood of antique light,   35
As innocent as are the lilies white,
To my first ardors I awake alone.

Besides sweet nothings by their lips made known,
Kisses that only mark their perfidy,
My chest reveals an unsolved mystery . . .   40
The toothmarks of some strange, majestic creature:
Enough! Arcana such as these disclose their nature
Only through vast twin reeds played to the skies,
That, turning to music all that clouds the eyes,
Dream, in a long solo, that we amused   45
The beauty all around us by confused
Equations[8] with our credulous melody;

---

4. Fabled; i.e., both marvelous and narrated.   **5.** An invocation to the surrounding countryside, which recalls the openings of classical poems like the *Iliad* and the *Aeneid.*   **6.** Water nymphs.   **7.** The musical note A. In the French text it is *la* (from the do-re-mi scale), which is also the feminine article "the." *Hymen:* marriage or sexual union.   **8.** Playing his reed pipes, the faun creates a musical line that is equated with the nymphs' silhouette as he remembers it behind closed eyes.

And dream that the song can make love soar so high
That, purged of all ordinary fantasies
Of back or breast—incessant shapes that rise   50
In blindness—it distills sonorities
From every empty and monotonous line.[9]

Then, instrument of flights;[1] Syrinx malign,
At lakes where you attend me, bloom once more!
Long shall my discourse from the echoing shore   55
Depict those goddesses: by masquerades,[2]
I'll strip the veils that sanctify their shades;
And when I've sucked the brightness out of grapes,
To quell the flood of sorrow that escapes,
I'll lift the empty cluster to the sky,   60
Avidly drunk till evening has drawn nigh,
And blow in laughter through the luminous skins.

Let us inflate our MEMORIES, O nymphs.
"Piercing the reeds, my darting eyes transfix,
Plunged in the cooling waves, immortal necks,   65
And cries of fury echo through the air;
Splendid cascades of tresses disappear
In shimmering jewels. Pursuing them, I find
There, at my feet, two sleepers intertwined,
Bruised in the languor of duality,   70
Their arms about each other heedlessly.
I bear them, still entangled, to a height
Where frivolous shadow never mocks the light
And dying roses yield the sun their scent,
That with the day our passions might be spent."   75
I adore you, wrath of virgins—fierce delight
Of the sacred burden's writhing naked flight
From the fiery lightning of my lips that flash
With the secret terror of the thirsting flesh:
From the cruel one's feet to the heart of the shy,   80
Whom innocence abandons suddenly,
Watered in frenzied or less woeful tears.
"Gay with the conquest of those traitorous fears,
I sinned when I divided the dishevelled
Tuft of kisses that the gods had ravelled.   85
For hardly had I hidden an ardent moan
Deep in the joyous recesses of one
(Holding by a finger, that her swanlike pallor
From her sister's passion might be tinged with color,
The little one, unblushingly demure,   90
When from my arms, loosened[3] by death obscure,
This prey, ungrateful to the end, breaks free,
Spurning the sobs that still transported me."

---

9. Lines 51 and 52 are one line in the French text.   1. In Greek mythology, a nymph who fled from the god Pan and was changed into a reed, from which flutes, or panpipes, are made.   2. Literally, idolatrous pictures (of the nymphs).   3. I.e., his arms were momentarily weakened.

Others will lead me on to happiness,
Their tresses knotted round my horns, I guess.   95
You know, my passion, that, crimson with ripe seeds,
Pomegranates burst in a murmur of bees,
And that our blood, seized by each passing form,
Flows toward desire's everlasting swarm.
In the time when the forest turns ashen and gold   100
And the summer's demise in the leaves is extolled,
Etna![4] when Venus visits her retreat,
Treading your lava with innocent feet,
Though a sad sleep thunders and the flame burns cold,
I hold the queen!
               Sure punishment[5] . . .

                                 No, but the soul,   105
Weighed down by the body, wordless, struck dumb,
To noon's proud silence must at last succumb:
And so, let me sleep, oblivious of sin,
Stretched out on the thirsty sand, drinking in
The bountiful rays of the wine-growing star!   110

Couple, farewell; I'll see the shade that now you are.

The Tomb[1] of Edgar Poe

As to Himself at last eternity changes him
The Poet reawakens with a naked sword
His century appalled at never having heard
That in this voice triumphant death had sung its hymn.

They, like a writhing hydra, hearing seraphim[2]   5
Bestow a purer sense on the language of the horde,
Loudly proclaimed that the magic potion[3] had been poured
From the dregs of some dishonored mixture of foul slime.

From the war between earth and heaven, what grief!
If understanding cannot sculpt a bas-relief   10
To ornament the dazzling tomb of Poe:

Calm block here fallen from obscure disaster,[4]
Let this granite at least mark the boundaries evermore
To the dark flights of Blasphemy[5] hurled to the future.

4. A volcano in Sicily.   5. The faun imagines swift punishment when in his heightened desire he fantasizes seizing Venus, the goddess of love.   1. A *tomb* is also a funeral poem. The poem was written for a memorial ceremony honoring Edgar Allan Poe (1809–1849) in Baltimore, Maryland, and was first published in the 1877 memorial volume.   2. The Angel: the above said Poet [Mallarmé's note]. Mallarmé explained this in English to the memorial organizers. *Hydra*: a mythical many-headed serpent; here compared with those who slandered Poe when he was alive.   3. In plain prose: Charged him with always being drunk [Mallarmé's note]. Critics accused Poe of finding inspiration in drunken fantasies.   4. The memorial marker (*Calm block*) is seen as a meteorite fallen from a dark or negative star (*disaster*); a play on words: *aster* is Greek for "star."   5. Blasphemy: against poets, such as the charge of Poe being drunk [Mallarmé's note]. *Boundaries*: literally, the milestone along French roads, intended here to limit the batlike flights of slander.

Saint[1]

At the window frame concealing
The viol old and destitute
Whose gilded sandalwood, now peeling,
Once shone with mandolin or flute,

Is the Saint, pale, unfolding   5
The old, worn missal,[2] a divine
Magnificat[3] in rivers flowing
Once at vespers and compline:[4]

At the glass of this monstrance,[5] vessel
Touched by a harp that took its shape   10
From the evening flight of an Angel
For the delicate fingertip

Which, without the old, worn missal
Or sandalwood, she balances
On the plumage instrumental,   15
Musician of silences.

[The Virginal, Vibrant, and Beautiful Dawn]

II

The virginal, vibrant, and beautiful dawn,
Will a beat of its drunken wing[1] not suffice
To rend this hard lake haunted beneath the ice
By the transparent glacier of flights never flown?

A swan of former times remembers it's the one   5
Magnificent but hopelessly struggling to resist
For never having sung of a land in which to exist
When the boredom of the sterile winter has shone.

Though its quivering neck will shake free of the agonies
Inflicted on the bird by the space it denies,   10
The horror of the earth will remain where it lies.

Phantom whose pure brightness assigns it this domain,[2]
It stiffens in the cold dream of disdain
That clothes the useless exile of the Swan.[3]

1. The original title was "Saint Cecilia Playing on the Wing of an Angel."   2. Literally, an old book,
probably containing the music for the old instruments. Cecilia is the patron saint of music.   3. A
hymn of praise to God.   4. Evening church services. *Once:* formerly.   5. An altar receptacle to hold the Host,
with a small glass window in front.   1. A wild, impulsive gesture. The French *d'aile ivre* is a famous
extended rhyme with *délivre* ("free itself") in line 6.   2. "As far as I am concerned, a poet today, in the
midst of this society which refuses to let him live, is a man who seeks out solitude in order to sculpture his
own tomb" [Mallarmé, interview with Jules Huret].   3. The word *swan* rhymes with *sign* in French (*cygne/
signe*), and the capitalized Swan may be read as a symbol of the writer's futile quest for the absolute Sign.

PAUL VERLAINE
1844–1896

If the abstract Mallarmé and the flamboyant Rimbaud are better known to modern readers, it is Verlaine whose asymmetrical lines and fleeting images influenced the next generation of poets and helped shape twentieth-century free verse. Verlaine's love for the nuance that captures several dimensions of experience and his rejection of fixed categories as a kind of lesser vision are evoked in the mysterious figure of Pierrot, the mournful clown who stands slightly apart from society and recognizes his own alienation. It was an alienation Verlaine knew; he scandalized society by his irregular life and affair with Arthur Rimbaud, and by the time of his death he was both "Prince of Poets" and a symbol of decadence.

Paul-Marie Verlaine was born at Metz, France, in a well-to-do army family that indulged their only son. When Verlaine was seven, his father resigned his commission and the family moved to Paris, where Verlaine was educated, frequented the circles of the classically oriented Parnassian poets, and attended law school for a year before deciding to devote himself to poetry. Earning a living in a series of clerical positions, he published his first collection, *Saturnian Poems* (under the sign of Saturn, supposedly signaling a morbid imagination) in 1866; *Fêtes galantes* (Gallant Feasts; elegant pastoral festivities) appeared three years later. Verlaine at this time was already having problems with alcoholism and showing signs of the sudden rages that punctuated his later life; several times, he went so far as to attack his mother. In 1870, under pressure from his family and perhaps hoping to settle down, he married Mathilde Mauté, a devout Catholic and sister of a friend. Anticipations of peace and happiness dominate the poems of *The Good Song,* written shortly before his marriage and published the same year. The next year, however, he met Arthur Rimbaud, and relations with his wife deteriorated sharply; Mathilde left Verlaine in 1872 when he would not break with Rimbaud, and the couple was divorced in 1874. The two poets spent much of the following year in London, but their tempestuous relationship ended in Belgium in July 1873, when Verlaine shot Rimbaud after a quarrel and was imprisoned for two years. Poems from this period were published in 1874 as *Songs without Words,* a paradoxical title that recalls the poet's advice in his *Art of Poetry:* "You must have music first of all." (In fact, Verlaine's poetry has often been set to music.) While in prison, he turned for solace to his childhood Catholicism and wrote poems (later published in *Wisdom,* 1880) that evoke his pain, remorse, and renewed hope of salvation. Emerging from prison in 1875, Verlaine attempted to renew his relationship with Rimbaud but was rebuffed. The famous affair had ended, and with Rimbaud in Africa, Verlaine's only further connection was to edit the *Illuminations* in 1886 and a posthumous collection in 1895.

Verlaine's religious conversion in 1873 did not herald a life of peace and contemplation. After teaching French for a while in England, he returned to Paris and attempted unsuccessfully to regain his job with the city. He also tried farming with a former student, Lucien Létinois. After Létinois's death from typhoid fever, Verlaine moved in with his mother but was again imprisoned for violence. He moved to Paris in 1885, where he lived in poverty and ill health. His continued alcoholism was taking its toll, and he spent much of his life in hospitals until his death in 1896. During the last ten years, however, his literary reputation was on the rise. The next generation of poets in France and England looked to him as a master, admiring both his poetry and his anticonformist ways. Critical studies were written about him; he wrote prolifically, lectured in England, and was hailed as their leader by a new group of self-styled "Decadent" poets in France. In August 1894, Verlaine was elected "Prince of Poets" by his colleagues.

His later poetry is quite different from his early, ambivalent style: it stresses religious themes and a voice of absolute conviction. Some continuity is visible: previous images of the poet's vulnerability before life (*Autumn Song*) become a worshiper's humility before God; the sensuality and dissonances of earlier poems become examples of evil in the poet's battle against sin. On several occasions, Verlaine even parodies his former style. For many readers, however, the volumes of poetry and prose after *Yesteryear and Yesterday* (*Jadis et Naguère*; 1884) are less compelling precisely because they turn to more assertive, explicit, and often conventional forms of expression. Gone is the taste for nuance and ambiguity, the irony and self-conscious pathos, the half tones and the lilt of asymmetrical rhythms that seem peculiarly Verlaine and without which—as he says in *The Art of Poetry*—everything else is merely literary convention, or "literature."

The five poems printed here come from five different collections published from 1866 to 1884. *Autumn Song,* one of seven "Mournful Landscapes" in the *Saturnian Poems*, captures a moment of experience while displaying Verlaine's intense musicality in its short rhymed lines and gently rocking melody. (In the French, the indented lines have three syllables, the others four.) Dead leaves proclaim the end of the year, and the speaker—already disheartened by the melodious cry of the autumn wind—weeps quietly over the passage of time in his own life. In this acute evocation of a state of mind, the melancholy speaker is equated with a dead leaf blown helplessly on the wind (compare Shelley's *Ode to the West Wind*).

Another imaginary landscape, this time a painted one, appears in *Moonlight,* a poem from *Fêtes galantes* that evokes the dreamlike scenes in which the eighteenth-century French artist Antoine Watteau (1684–1721) portrayed aristocratic men and women playing at being romantic shepherds and shepherdesses. *Moonlight* is truly a poem of nuances and masks, of paradoxical images and elusive identity. The moon's half-light illuminates uncertain characters who dance dejectedly inside their fanciful costumes, sing in a sad minor key about love and good luck, and cannot believe in their own happiness; in this painted world, their song itself is part of the moonlight, and the whole scene an image of the addressee's (perhaps Verlaine's) soul.

Moonlight reappears in *The White Moonglow* (from *The Good Song*), one of the poems Verlaine gave his fiancée before their marriage. This "exquisite hour" celebrates a moment of intimacy between the two lovers walking at night; it is a swift, delicate sketch in which the human figures never actually appear. Instead, there are overheard voices, fragmentary or reflected images, and refracted moonlight.

Verlaine is not all moonlight and fading voices, however. In *Wooden Horses,* he depicts a busy merry-go-round in an amusement park peopled by pickpockets and by workers eager to make love on their day off. This time the music is harshly rhythmic, an insistent tempo that is echoed and reinforced by the poem's repetitions: the wooden horses gallop on and on, their riders drunk with dizziness in what begins to seem like a mindless pursuit of passion. Evening comes with velvet elegance in the last stanza, but here it is only a background for amorous couples pairing off to the beat of the drums. All four poems evoke a particular moment of experience, a fleeting subjective impression that is built out of a few telling details and associated rhythm patterns.

Such, in fact, is the recommendation of Verlaine's *Art of Poetry,* published in *Yesteryear and Yesterday.* This poem, which became the unofficial manifesto of the new Symbolist school, not only reflects Verlaine's own preferences in 1874 but also outlines a program of antitraditional poetic strategies. No more four-square rhythm; no more fixed images with clear outlines and colors; no wit, eloquence, or rhyme for its own sake; in short, none of the traditional poetic techniques intended to create beautiful and lasting images in explicit, rational verse. Instead, Verlaine proclaimed the joys of the *vers impair,* the "uneven" line whose odd number of syllables creates a floating effect. (*The Art of Poetry* uses a nine-syllable line.) Words are slightly inexact, perhaps containing suggestive overtones. Composite images express a state of mind; nuances invite a blurring of boundaries and release the imagination; and above all, music and emotion are the poet's guide until words become "soluble" and poetry a natural experience. Verlaine's opposition of "poetry" and "literature," and the example of his own poems, became a model for the young Symbolist poets—among them Jules Laforgue, much admired by the early T. S. Eliot—and helped shape European lyric tradition for many years.

PRONOUNCING GLOSSARY

The following list uses common English syllables and stress accents to provide rough equivalents of selected names whose pronunciation may be unfamiliar to the general reader.

Bois de la Cambre: *bwah-deu-lah-cawm'-br*   Verlaine: *vehr-len'*

Autumn Song[1]

With long sobs
the violin-throbs
    of autumn wound
my heart with languorous
and monotonous   5
    sound.

Choking and pale
when I mind the tale
    the hours keep,
my memory strays   10
down other days
    and I weep;

and I let me go
where ill winds blow,
    now here, now there,   15
harried and sped,
even as a dead
    leaf, anywhere.

Moonlight[1]

Your soul is like a painter's landscape[2] where
charming masks in shepherd mummeries
are playing lutes[3] and dancing with an air
of being sad in their fantastic guise.

Even while they sing, all in a minor key,   5
of love triumphant and life's careless boon,

---

1. All poems translated by C. F. MacIntyre. The poem is one of the "Mournful Landscapes" in *Saturnian Poems* (1866).   1. From *Fêtes galantes* (1869).   2. A reference to Antoine Watteau's (1684–1721) dreamlike paintings in which elegant men and women, costumed as shepherds and shepherdesses, play at being pastoral lovers.   3. Arab musical instrument associated with serenades that was fashionable in the 18th century.

they seem in doubt of their felicity,
their song melts in the calm light of the moon,

the lovely melancholy light that sets
the little birds to dreaming in the tree   10
and among the statues makes the jets
of slender fountains sob with ecstasy.

[The White Moonglow][1]

The white moonglow
shines on the trees;
from each bough
a voice flees
as the leaves move . . .   5

Oh, my love.

The pond reflects,
a mirror deep,
the black silhouette
of the willow tree   10
where the wind weeps . . .

Oh, reverie.

Now a tender
and vast appeasement
seems to descend
from the firmament   15
with the irised star[2] . . .

Ah, exquisite hour.

Wooden Horses[1]

By Saint-Gille
let's away,
my light-footed bay.
V. Hugo[2]

Turn, good wooden horses, round
a hundred turns, a thousand turns.
Forever turn till the axles burn,
turn, turn, to the oboes' sound.

---

1. From *The Good Song* (1870).   **2.** The multiple reflections of the moonlight.   **1.** From *Songs without Words* (1874).   **2.** French poet (1802–1885). Saint-Gilles is a suburb of Brussels, Belgium, with a public fairground.

The big soldier and the fattest maid   5
ride your backs as if in their chamber,
because their masters have also made
an outing today in the Bois de la Cambre.[3]

Turn, turn, horses of their hearts,
while all around your whirling there   10
are the clever sharpers[4] at their art;
turn to the cornet's bragging blare.

It's as much fun as getting dead
drunk, to ride in this silly ring!
Good for the belly, bad for the head,   15
a plenty good and a plenty bad thing.

Turn, turn, no need today
of any spurs to make you bound,
galloping around and round,
turn, turn, without hope of hay.   20

And hurry, horses of their love,
already night is falling here
and the pigeon flies to join the dove,
far from madame, far from the fair.

Turn! Turn! Slow evening comes,   25
in velvet, buttoned up with stars.
Away the lovers go, in pairs.
Turn to the beat of the joyous drums.

The Art of Poetry[1]

You must have music first of all,
and for that a rhythm uneven[2] is best,
vague in the air and soluble,
with nothing heavy and nothing at rest.

You must not scorn to do some wrong   5
in choosing the words to fill your lines:
nothing more dear than the tipsy song
where the Undefined and Exact combine.

It is the veiled and lovely eye,
the full noon quivering with light;   10
it is, in the cool of an autumn sky,
the blue confusion of stars at night!

3. An elegant park south of Brussels.   4. Literally, pickpockets.   1. From *Yesteryear and Yesterday* (1884), written in 1874.   2. The *vers impair* (line with an uneven number of syllables), which gives traditional French readers a sense of "nothing at rest." This poem uses a nine-syllable line and—as here—often illustrates its points.

Never the Color, always the Shade,
always the nuance is supreme!
Only by shade is the trothal made   15
between flute and horn, of dream with dream!

Epigram's an assassin! Keep
away from him, fierce Wit, and vicious
laughter that makes the Azure[3] weep,
and from all that garlic of vulgar dishes!   20

Take Eloquence and wring his neck!
You would do well, by force and care,
wisely to hold Rhyme in check,
or she's off—if you don't watch—God knows where!

Oh, who will tell the wrongs of Rhyme?   25
What crazy negro or deaf child
made this trinket for a dime,
sounding hollow and false when filed?

Let there be music, again and forever!
Let your verse be a quick-wing'd thing and light—   30
such as one feels when a new love's fervor
to other skies wings the soul in flight.

Happy-go-lucky, let your lines
disheveled run where the dawn winds lure,
smelling of wild mint, smelling of thyme . . .   35
and all the rest is literature.

3. The sky's unbroken azure was, for many Symbolists, an image of absolute poetry as opposed to vulgarity.

ARTHUR RIMBAUD
1854–1891

In a dazzlingly brief literary career, which he abandoned at the age of twenty, Arthur Rimbaud (*ram-boh'*) put his indelible stamp on the visionary and experimental aspects of modern poetry. Taking literally the ancient (and Romantic) notion of the poet as prophet, he determined to make himself a seer, or *voyant*, by whatever violent means were necessary. His writing reveals the mixture of idealism, hope, and faith in his own genius that led him to believe in the possibility of a self-produced apocalypse. It also recounts a futile search for love that permeates his poetic quest; a stormy relationship with the older poet Paul Verlaine; and finally, the bitterness and sense of defeat that drove him to abandon his former life and become a fortune hunter in Africa. Rimbaud was an especially strong model for the Surrealists and for others in twentieth-century literature who saw in him an example of complete dedication to a poetic ideal that surpassed mere written words: he exemplified a revolutionary reimagining of human experience that would open vistas, explode harmful patterns of thought, and thus bring about a better future. Despite—or perhaps because of—

Rimbaud's admission of defeat, he became a mythic figure whose brilliant poems and prose were markers on the way of a career that, in the words of one admirer, passed like a lightning bolt through French literature.

Jean-Nicolas-Arthur Rimbaud was born on October 20, 1854, in Charleville, a town in northeastern France. Rimbaud's father abandoned the family when Arthur was seven, and his embittered mother raised her children in a repressive and disciplinarian atmosphere. In 1870, Rimbaud made the first of his flights from home and spent ten days in jail as a vagrant. Yet he proved to be an unusually gifted student and was encouraged in his literary tastes and endeavors by a sympathetic teacher who intro-duced him to current poetry. It was this teacher, Georges Izambard, to whom Rim-baud first wrote of his poetic ambitions and his desire to make himself a seer by the systematic "derangement of all the senses." In 1871, the poet Paul Verlaine (to whom Rimbaud had sent some of his work) invited Rimbaud to Paris. It was the beginning of a stormy two-year relationship in Paris, London, and Brussels that ended in 1873 when Verlaine shot Rimbaud through the wrist and was sentenced to two years' impris-onment. In that year, at the age of nineteen, Rimbaud decided to give up writing and seek his fortune in commerce. He found his way to many parts of Europe, to Cyprus, to Java, and to Aden, where he worked for an exporting firm, later moving to Harar in Abys-sinia. As an independent trader he went on expeditions in Abyssinia and engaged in gun running; despite rumor, it does not appear that he trafficked in slaves. Falling ill with a cancerous tumor on one knee and unable to find adequate treatment, Rimbaud returned to France with a gangrenous leg in May 1891. His leg was amputated at a Mar-seille hospital, and he died six months later on November 10, 1891.

In a short and violent literary career—he wrote all his poetry between the ages of fifteen and twenty—Rimbaud combines an aggressive, cynical realism and attempts to transform both self and surroundings into a magically perfect whole. The visionary image sequences of his first major poem (a symbolic voyage entitled *The Drunken Boat*), the agonized and mocking autobiographical prose of *A Season in Hell*, and finally the transfigured scenes from real life called *Illuminations* together represent stages in this endeavor to discover—or create—a state of natural innocence and har-mony. For a while, Rimbaud believed that he could manipulate language to create the vision of an ideal world. "I have strung ropes from steeple to steeple; garlands from window to window; golden chains from star to star, and I dance."

The Drunken Boat, written when the poet was still sixteen and had never seen the sea, uses the traditional literary theme of the voyage to express his rebellion against guides and restraints. Speaking as a boat let loose on the high seas, the narrator describes a gradually intensifying series of encounters with a total reality—at once beautiful and terrifying—that goes beyond his individual power to sustain. Yet the concluding section is not a resolution of the original need for flight: Rimbaud's boat cannot accept the world of proud commercial shipping or of prison ships, and dreams of the childhood world of a solitary paper boat set adrift in a small pool. The poem ends in a clearer restatement of its original alienation and in an attitude that many have interpreted as prefiguring Rimbaud's eventual departure from Europe and his rejection of poetry.

Rimbaud's attempt to become a *voyant*, to transform his everyday reality by means of the re-creating power of poetry, is both summarized and mocked in the bitter autobiographical prose poem *A Season in Hell*. In an atmosphere of perpetual crisis, alternating between agonized idealism and cynical disbelief, he reviews his quest for perfect truth and love and vividly describes his effort to reach the unknown by pure hallucination. "I saw very plainly a mosque in place of a factory, a school of drummers composed of angels . . . a drawing room at the bottom of the lake . . . I became a fabulous opera." At the end of *A Season in Hell* he tells us that he has rejected these earlier illusions and embraced earth and rugged reality. Yet he never wrote poetry to celebrate his newly rediscovered realism (and may well have completed the *Illumi-nations* after that point), so that he remains best known for the passion and beauty of his apocalyptic vision.

The Illuminations offers a series of transformations that leave only traces of their varied points of departure: bridges in London, plowed fields, a park statue, dawn. They parade illusions and free association, and they cut short logical sequences to develop an almost musical organization of themes and images. Almost all are prose poems, intricately organized in complex rhythmic and visual patterns. Some echo autobiographical themes, but the scenes and allusions are transformed. *Bridges* recalls the London where Rimbaud lived for a time, but it is an impressionistic memory that transforms the real scene. *Barbarian* may echo a previous sea voyage and drug use, but the poem transcends the question of any single source in reality. Set outside normal time and space, "Long after the days and the seasons, and the creatures and the countries," it enacts a withdrawal that moves gradually from echoes of the real world to an elemental core of tenderness and beauty, completely inside the world of imagination.

Clearly the reader cannot approach *Barbarian* as if it were by Lamartine—or even by Baudelaire. Rimbaud's vision has leaped beyond the picturing of actual scenes and beyond the rational core that so often supports even a visionary poem. Instead, he cuts short all explanations and simply presents the vision for itself. *Barbarian* is not, however, merely an impressionistic, unstructured collection of words. It is carefully organized according to an almost musical development of themes and pattern of oppositions: red and white (raw meat and arctic flowers, embers and frost, fire and diamonds, flames and drift ice), heat and cold, subterranean volcanoes and starry sky. On a more fundamental level, it is a world that swings between the real and the ideal, from echoes of a former reality to an ideal world where there are ultimately no complete images, only "forms, sweats, eyes" that will be part of a new creation heralded by a feminine voice reaching into the very heart of this fiery, icy vortex. *Barbarian* ends on a note of openness and ambiguity, as the cyclical opposition of reality and imagination seem about to recommence with "The banner." The poem may foreshadow the future Symbolist doctrines: it disassembles scenes from recognizable reality to assemble a new transcendent vision, and it employs to this end a subtly nonrational language that emulates the patterns of music. Yet Rimbaud is even more closely associated with twentieth-century poetry and with those writers—including the Surrealists—who found in the explosion of poetic form a complete and often violent engagement of the self.

From Letter of the Seer [Letter to Paul Demeny][1]

Charleville
May 15, 1871

* * *

Here is some prose on the future of poetry:

All ancient poetry culminated in the poetry of the Greeks. Harmonious life. From Greece to the Romantic movement—the Middle Ages—there are writers and versifiers. From Ennius to Theroldus, from Theroldus to Casimir Delavigne, everything is rhymed prose, a game, the stupidity and glory of endless idiotic generations. Racine alone is pure, strong, and great. But had his rhymes been twisted, his hemistichs[2] messed up, the Divine Dumbhead would be as unknown today as the latest-come author of the *Origins*. . . . After Racine, the game gets moldy. It's been going on for two hundred years!

---

1. Translated by Paul Schmidt. Rimbaud had met the young poet Paul Demeny through his teacher, Georges Izambard. In this letter, called the *Lettre du Voyant* (Letter of the Seer), the sixteen-year-old poet alternates flippant remarks with a theory of the poet as impersonal visionary. Throughout, the word for *poet* is written without the customary accent, thus suggesting the ancient Greek word for "creator" or "maker."
2. Half a line of verse.

No joke, and no paradox. My reason inspires me with more certainty on the subject than a young radical has fits. Anyway, *newcomers* can swear at their ancestors; it's their house and they've got all the time in the world.

Romanticism has never been fairly judged. Who's to judge it? The Critics!! The Romantics? They illustrate perfectly the fact that the song is very rarely the work of the singer—that is, his thought, snug and understood.

For *I* is an *other*. If brass wakes as a bugle, it is not its fault at all. That is quite clear to me: I am a spectator at the flowering of my thought: I watch it, I listen to it: I draw a bow across a string: a symphony stirs in the depths, or surges onto the stage.

If those old idiots hadn't discovered only the false meaning of EGO, we wouldn't have to sweep away the millions of skeletons that have for ages and ages piled up the products of their one-eyed intelligence, and acclaimed themselves their authors!

In Greece, as I said, words and music gave a rhythm to Action. Afterward music and rhymes became toys, pastimes. Studying this past has a certain charm for the curious: some people delight in reworking these antiquities: that's their business. The universal intelligence has always cast off its ideas naturally; men would pick up some of these fruits of the mind: they were acted upon, they inspired books: and so it went; man didn't develop himself, not yet awake, or not yet aware of the great dream. Pen pushers, these writers: the author, the creator, the poet; that man has never existed!

The first task of the man who wants to be a poet is to study his own awareness of himself, in its entirety; he seeks out his soul, he inspects it, he tests it, he learns it. As soon as he knows it, he must cultivate it! That seems simple: every brain experiences a certain natural development; hundreds of *egoists* call themselves authors; there are many more who attribute their intellectual progress to themselves!—But the problem is to make the soul into a monster, like the comprachicos,[3] you know? Think of a man grafting warts onto his face and growing them there.

I say you have to be a visionary, make yourself a visionary.

A Poet makes himself a visionary through a long, boundless, and systematized *disorganization of all the senses*. All forms of love, of suffering, of madness; he searches himself, he exhausts within himself all poisons, and preserves their quintessences. Unspeakable torment, where he will need the greatest faith, a superhuman strength, where he becomes among all men the great invalid, the great criminal, the great accursed—and the Supreme Scientist! For he attains the *unknown!* Because he has cultivated his soul, already rich, more than anyone! He attains the unknown, and if, demented, he finally loses the understanding of his visions, he will at least have seen them! So what if he is destroyed in his ecstatic flight through things unheard of, unnameable: other horrible workers will come; they will begin at the horizons where the first one has fallen!

—Back in six minutes—

I interrupt my discourse with another psalm: be kind enough to lend a willing ear, and everybody will be delighted. Bow in hand, I begin:

MY LITTLE LOVELIES . . .

There. And please note that if I were not afraid of making you spend more than 60 centimes on postage due—poor starving me who hasn't had a single

3. Kidnappers who mutilated children to make money by exhibiting them as freaks; described in Victor Hugo's novel *The Man Who Laughs* (1869).

centime in the last seven months!—I would send you also my "Amant de Paris," one hundred hexameters, and my "Mort de Paris," two hundred hexameters!

Here we go again:

The poet, therefore, is truly the thief of fire.[4]

He is responsible for humanity, for *animals* even; he will have to make sure his visions can be smelled, fondled, listened to; if what he brings back from *beyond* has form, he gives it form; if it has none, he gives it none. A language must be found; besides, all speech being idea, a time of universal language will come! Only an academic—deader than a fossil—could compile a dictionary, in no matter what language. Weaklings who begin to *think* about the first letter of the alphabet would quickly go mad!

This language will be of the soul, for the soul, and will include everything: perfumes, sounds, colors, thought grappling with thought. The poet would make precise the quantity of the unknown arising in his time in the universal soul: he would provide more than the formula of his thought, the record *of his path to Progress!* Enormity becoming norm, absorbed into everything, he would truly become a *multiplier of progress!*

That future will be materialistic, as you see. Always full of *Number* and *Harmony*, these poems will be made to last. Essentially, it will again be Greek Poetry,[5] in a way.

This eternal art will be functional, since poets are citizens. Poetry will no longer give rhythm to action; it *will be in advance.*

And there will be poets like this! When the eternal slavery of Women is destroyed, when she lives for herself and through herself, when man—up till now abominable—will have set her free, she will be a poet as well! Woman will discover the unknown! Will her world of ideas differ from ours? She will discover strange things, unfathomable, repulsive, delightful; we will accept and understand them.

While we wait, let us ask the *poet* for *something new*—ideas and forms.

The Drunken Boat[1]

As I descended black, impassive Rivers,
I sensed that haulers[2] were no longer guiding me:
Screaming Redskins took them for their targets,
Nailed nude to colored stakes: barbaric trees.

I was indifferent to all my crews;   5
I carried English cottons, Flemish wheat.
When the disturbing din of haulers ceased,
The Rivers let me ramble where I willed.

Through the furious ripping of the sea's mad tides,
Last winter, deafer than an infant's mind,

---

4. In Greek myth, Prometheus stole fire from the gods to give to human beings, thus lifting them above the condition of animals.   5. Rimbaud has earlier praised ancient Greek poetry for the way it combined music and words, giving rhythm to action (probably an allusion to Homer).   1. Translated by Stephen Stepanchev.   2. The image is of a commercial barge being towed along a canal.

I ran! And drifting, green Peninsulas
Did not know roar more gleefully unkind.

A tempest blessed my vigils on the sea.
Lighter than a cork I danced on the waves,
Those endless rollers, as they say, of graves:[3]   15
Ten nights beyond a lantern's[4] silly eye!

Sweeter than sourest apple-flesh to children,
Green water seeped into my pine-wood hull
And washed away blue wine[5] stains, vomitings,
Scattering rudder, anchor, man's lost rule.   20

And then I, trembling, plunged into the Poem
Of the Sea,[6] infused with stars, milk-white,
Devouring azure greens; where remnants, pale
And gnawed, of pensive corpses fell from light;

Where, staining suddenly the blueness, delirium.   25
The slow rhythms of the pulsing glow of day,
Stronger than alcohol and vaster than our lyres,
The bitter reds of love ferment the way!

I know skies splitting into light, whirled spouts
Of water, surfs, and currents: I know the night,   30
The dawn exalted like a flock of doves, pure wing,
And I have seen what men imagine they have seen.

I saw the low sun stained with mystic horrors,
Lighting long, curdled clouds of violet,
Like actors in a very ancient play,   35
Waves rolling distant thrills like lattice[7] light!

I dreamed of green night, stirred by dazzling snows,
Of kisses rising to the sea's eyes, slowly,
The sap-like coursing of surprising currents,
And singing phosphors,[8] flaring blue and gold!   40

I followed, for whole months, a surge like herds
Of insane cattle in assault on the reefs,
Unhopeful that three Marys,[9] come on luminous feet,
Could force a muzzle on the panting seas!

Yes, I struck incredible Floridas[1]   45
That mingled flowers and the eyes of panthers
In skins of men! And rainbows bridled green
Herds beneath the horizon of the seas.

---

3. Victor Hugo's *Oceano nox* (Night on the ocean; Latin) describes the sea as a graveyard in which sailors' corpses roll eternally.   4. Port beacons.   5. A cheap, ordinary, bitter wine.   6. A play on words. *Poem* suggests "creation" (Greek *poiein*, "making"); *Sea*, the source or "mother" of life, sounds the same as "mother" in French (*mer / mère*).   7. Like the ripple of venetian blinds.   8. *Noctiluca*, tiny marine animals.   9. A legend that the three biblical Marys crossed the sea during a storm to land in Camargue, a region in southern France famous for its horses and bulls.   1. A name (plural) given to any exotic country.

I saw the ferment of enormous marshes, weirs
Where a whole Leviathan[2] lies rotting in the weeds!   50
Collapse of waters within calms at sea,
And distances in cataract toward chasms!

Glaciers, silver suns, pearl waves, and skies like coals,
Hideous wrecks at the bottom of brown gulfs
Where giant serpents eaten by red bugs   55
Drop from twisted trees and shed a black perfume!

I should have liked to show the young those dolphins
In blue waves, those golden fish, those fish that sing.
—Foam like flowers rocked my sleepy drifting,
And, now and then, fine winds supplied me wings.   60

When, feeling like a martyr, I tired of poles and zones,
The sea, whose sobbing made my tossing sweet,
Raised me its dark flowers, deep and yellow whirled,
And, like a woman, I fell on my knees . . . [3]

Peninsula, I tossed upon my shores   65
The quarrels and droppings of clamorous, blond-eyed birds.
I sailed until, across my rotting cords,
Drowned men, spinning backwards, fell asleep! . . .

Now I, a lost boat in the hair of coves,[4]
Hurled by tempest into a birdless air,   70
I, whose drunken carcass neither Monitors
Nor Hansa ships[5] would fish back for men's care;

Free, smoking, rigged with violet fogs,
I, who pierced the red sky like a wall
That carries exquisite mixtures for good poets,   75
Lichens of sun and azure mucus veils;

Who, spotted with electric crescents, ran
Like a mad plank, escorted by seashores,
When cudgel blows of hot Julys struck down
The sea-blue skies upon wild water spouts;   80

I, who trembled, feeling the moan at fifty leagues
Of rutting Behemoths[6] and thick Maelstroms, I,
Eternal weaver of blue immobilities,
I long for Europe with its ancient quays!

I saw sidereal archipelagoes! and isles   85
Whose delirious skies are open to the voyager:
—Is it in depthless nights you sleep your exile,
A million golden birds, O future Vigor?—

---

2. Vast biblical sea monster (Job 41.1–10).   **3.** The poet's ellipses; nothing has been omitted.   **4.** Sea-weed.   **5.** Vessels belonging to the German Hanseatic League of commercial maritime cities. *Monitors:* armored coast-guard ships, after the iron-clad Union warship *Monitor* of the American Civil War. **6.** Biblical animal resembling a hippopotamus (Job 40.15–24).

But, truly, I have wept too much! The dawns disturb.
All moons are painful, and all suns break bitterly: 90
Love has swollen me with drunken torpors.
Oh, that my keel might break and spend me in the sea!

Of European waters I desire
Only the black, cold puddle in a scented twilight
Where a child of sorrows squats and sets the sails   95
Of a boat as frail as a butterfly in May.

I can no longer, bathed in languors, O waves,
Cross the wake of cotton-bearers on long trips,
Nor ramble in a pride of flags and flares,
Nor swim beneath the horrible eyes of prison ships.[7]   100

A Season in Hell[1]

Night of Hell

I have swallowed a first-rate draught of poison.—Thrice blessed be the counsel that came to me!—My entrails are on fire. The violence of the venom wrings my limbs, deforms me, fells me. I am dying of thirst, I am suffocating, I cannot cry out. This is hell, the everlasting punishment! Mark how the fire surges up again! I am burning properly. There you are, demon!

I had caught a glimpse of conversion to righteousness and happiness, salvation. May I describe the vision; the atmosphere of hell does not permit hymns! It consisted of millions of charming creatures, a sweet sacred concert, power and peace, noble ambitions, and goodness knows what else.

Noble ambitions![2]

And yet this is life!—What if damnation is eternal! A man who chooses to mutilate himself is rightly damned, isn't he? I believe that I am in hell, consequently I am there.[3] This is the effect of the catechism. I am the slave of my baptism.[4] Parents, you have caused my affliction and you have caused your own. Poor innocent!—Hell cannot assail pagans.—This is life, nevertheless! Later, the delights of damnation will be deeper. A crime, quickly, that I may sink to nothingness, in accordance with human law.

Be silent, do be silent! . . . There is shame, reproof, in this place: Satan who says that the fire is disgraceful, that my wrath is frightfully foolish.— Enough! . . . The errors that are whispered to me, enchantments, false perfumes, childish melodies.[5]—And to say that I possess truth, that I understand justice: I have a sound and steady judgment, I am prepared for perfection . . . Pride.—The skin of my head is drying up. Pity! Lord, I am terrified. I am thirsty, so thirsty! Ah! childhood, the grass, the rain, the lake upon the

---

7. Portholes of ships tied at anchor and used as prisons.　1. Translated by Enid Rhodes Peschel. *Night of Hell* is the second section (after the preface) of the autobiographical *A Season in Hell*. The first section, *Bad Blood*, describes his solitary childhood and sense of being a member of an "inferior race." It also contrasts an authoritarian and hypocritical European society with African paganism, which is seen as a freer and more natural existence.　2. Mockery of his childhood idealism and attraction to traditional Catholicism.　3. A parody of French philosopher René Descartes's (1596–1650) phrase "I think, therefore I am," which had become a symbol of well-ordered thought.　4. Since baptism creates the possibility of both heaven and hell.　5. The poetic visions and harmonies that Rimbaud explored with Paul Verlaine.

stones, *the moonlight when the bell tower was striking twelve*[6] . . . the devil is in the bell tower, at that hour. Mary! Blessed Virgin! . . . —The horror of my stupidity.

Over there, are they not honest-souls, who wish me well? . . . Come . . . I have a pillow over my mouth, they don't hear me, they are phantoms. Besides, no one ever thinks of others. Let no one approach. I reek of burning, that's certain.

The hallucinations are countless. It's exactly what I've always had: no more faith in history, neglect of principles. I shall be silent about this: poets and visionaries would be jealous. I am a thousand times the richest, let us be avaricious like the sea.

Now then! the clock of life has just stopped. I am no longer in the world.— Theology is serious, hell is certainly *below*—and heaven above.—Ecstasy, nightmare, sleep in a nest of flames.

What pranks during my vigilance in the country . . . Satan, Ferdinand,[7] races with the wild seeds . . . Jesus walks on the purplish briers, without bending them . . . Jesus used to walk on the troubled waters.[8] The lantern revealed him to us, a figure standing, pale and with brown tresses, beside a wave of emerald. . . .

I am going to unveil all the mysteries: mysteries religious or natural, death, birth, futurity, antiquity, cosmogony, nothingness, I am a master of phantasmagories.

Listen! . . .

I have all the talents!—There is nobody here and there is somebody: I would not wish to scatter my treasure.—Do you wish for Negro chants, dances of houris?[9] Do you wish me to vanish, to dive in search of the *ring*?[1] Do you? I shall produce gold, cures.

Rely, then, upon me: faith comforts, guides, heals. All of you, come,— even the little children,[2]—that I may console you, that one may pour out his heart for you,—the marvelous heart!—Poor men, laborers! I do not ask for prayers; with your confidence alone, I shall be happy.

—And let's think of me. This makes me miss the world very little. I have the good fortune not to suffer any longer. My life was nothing but sweet follies, regrettably.

Bah! let's make all the grimaces imaginable.

Decidedly, we are out of the world. No more sound. My sense of touch has disappeared. Ah! my castle, my Saxony,[3] my forest of willows. The evenings, the mornings, the nights, the days . . . Am I weary!

I ought to have my hell for wrath, my hell for pride,—and the hell of the caress; a concert of hells.

I am dying of weariness. This is the tomb, I am going to the worms, horror of horrors! Satan, jester, you wish to undo me, with your spells. I protest. I protest! one jab of the pitchfork, one lick of fire.

Ah! to rise again to life! To cast eyes upon our deformities. And that poison, that kiss a thousand times accursed! My weakness, the cruelty of the world!

6. A collection of romanticized childhood memories. 7. Peasant name for the devil. 8. Jesus' disciples saw him walking on the sea at night (John 6.16–21). 9. Beautiful virgins in the Koranic paradise. 1. At the end of Wagner's opera *Götterdämmerung*, Hagen plunges into the river Rhine to recapture the golden ring of world power. 2. Parody of Jesus' words "Suffer little children, and forbid them not, to come unto me" (Matthew 19.14). 3. Germanic duchy, part of Rimbaud's visionary memories.

Dear God, your mercy, hide me, I regard myself too poorly!—I am hidden and I am not.

It is the fire that rises again with the soul condemned to it.

THE ILLUMINATIONS[1]

The Bridges[2]

Crystalline gray skies. A strange pattern of bridges, these straight, those arched, others descending obliquely at angles to the first, and these configurations repeating themselves in the other illuminated circuits of the canal,[3] but all so long and light that the shores, laden with domes, sink and diminish. Some of these bridges are still encumbered with hovels.[4] Others support masts, signals, frail parapets. Minor chords interweave, and flow smoothly; ropes rise from the steep banks. One detects a red jacket, perhaps other costumes and musical instruments. Are these popular tunes, fragments of manorial concerts, remnants of public anthems? The water is gray and blue, ample as an arm of the sea.

A white ray, falling from the summit of the sky, reduces to nothingness this theatrical performance.

Barbarian

Long after the days and the seasons, and the creatures and the countries,

The banner of bleeding meat[1] on the silk of the seas and of the arctic flowers; (they do not exist.)

Delivered from the old fanfares of heroism—that still attack our heart and our head—far from the former assassins.

—Oh! the banner of bleeding meat on the silk of the seas and of the arctic flowers; (they do not exist.)

Delights!

Blazing coals, raining in squalls of hoarfrost—Delights!—fires in the rain of the wind of diamonds, rain hurled down by the earthly heart eternally carbonized for us—O world!—

(Far from the old retreats and the old flames, that are known, that are felt,)

Blazing coals and froths. Music, veering of whirlpools and collisions of drift ice with the stars.

O Delights, oh world, oh music! And there, the forms, the sweats, the heads of hair and the eyes, floating. And the white tears, boiling—oh delights!—and the feminine voice borne down to the bottom of the volcanoes and the arctic grottoes.

The banner . . .

---

1. Translated by Enid Rhodes Peschel.   2. An impressionistic memory of London.   3. The river Thames as it winds through the city.   4. Houses were once built on London Bridge.   1. Perhaps a description of the Danish flag (a white cross on a red field), which Rimbaud would have seen on a visit to Iceland, then a Danish possession.

Perspectives on European Empire

European imperial expansion, which reaches back to sixteenth-century voyages of exploration and trade, took on a particularly frenzied pace in the nineteenth century, when it was fueled by nationalist ambitions and the desire for material resources. By 1878, European nations ruled 67 percent of the earth's land surface, and the competition among them was most intense in the scramble for Africa. The diverse territories of South Africa became an early bone of contention and ended in war between the British and the Afrikaners. In west central Africa, Great Britain, Germany, France, and Portugal (and, covertly, King Leopold II of Belgium) competed strenuously for pieces of the Dark Continent. If their rivalry was temporarily allayed by the Berlin Conference of 1884–85, which partitioned the Congo River basin, rejected slavery, and guaranteed free trade to all participants, international tensions remained. At home, a vocal minority raised humanitarian objections to the abuse of subject peoples but continued to support their nation's mission to liberate and civilize less "advanced" races. John Ruskin's famous lecture on British imperial duty distinguished in 1870 between the banners of civilization and greed—"the one that floats in heavenly fire" and the other that "hangs heavy with foul tissue of terrestrial gold"—and the missionary explorer David Livingstone recommended peaceful change through the "three Cs" of Commerce, Christianity, and Civilization. Tales of atrocities encompassing Rhodesia to King Leopold's Congo Free State made it clear, however, that the zeal to civilize was often a mask for brutal exploitation.

Individual voices offer their personal perspective on European empire. Not many are indigenous African voices, for until the turn of the century their words were most often preserved as part of colonial archives and investigative committee reports or, indirectly, in histories and explorers' journals. Chief Machemba's letter of protest to the German officer Hermann von Wissmann is one such document, a proud statement of independence that also tries to deal with the concrete threat of imperial aggression. The European voices differ among themselves but chiefly focus on ways to proceed *inside* an imperial society. With varying emphases, they stem from a similar vision of national pride and competitiveness; of the civilizing mission of Western society (and, by extension, the inferiority of non-European cultures); and of a desire for trade benefiting the home country. These are large issues, and they elicit passionate opinions.

The entire argument of Macaulay's *Minute on Indian Education* is based on the English historian's vision of the supremacy of Western civilization and of the English language as a treasure-house of civilized learning. Cecil Rhodes is less abstract, and the businessman-conqueror of Rhodesia speaks openly of England's imperial destiny: "the world is not quite big enough" for British expansion. Quite a different tone is struck by Giuseppe Garibaldi, the international revolutionary who tired of nationalist wars of aggression. Garibaldi proposes restructuring the imperial nation-states into a European confederation, whose energy could then turn to the development of global trade. Victorian explorer Mary Kingsley, whose travels took her through French, German, and British territory in West Africa, never really questions the existence of European control. Harshly criticizing the Crown colony's ignorance of African customs, she proposes replacing imperial bureaucracy with a council of British merchants. The English–South African feminist writer Olive Schreiner passionately defends the rights of colonial settlers against the European exploitation typified by Rhodes, all the while employing (perhaps for the sake of her audience) a colorful mix of nationalist, racist, and patriarchal rhetoric. Finally, Sol T. Plaatje, a young South African working his way up in the British civil service, writes a private diary during the Boer siege of Mafeking that demonstrates what can happen to European "civilized" principles under pressure and in a multicultural context. Not until the next century will the nature of this "civilization" be systematically called into question, both for itself and for its pragmatic links to empire.

THOMAS BABINGTON MACAULAY
1800–1859

Nowhere is the missionary spirit of European imperialism better expressed than in Thomas Babington Macaulay's paean to the advantages of English culture: the English language contains "the most profound speculations on metaphysics, morals, government, jurisprudence, and trade; with full and correct information respecting every experimental science which tends to preserve the health, to increase the comfort, or to expand the intellect of man." In other words, it is just what less fortunate parts of the world need, if they are to achieve the heights of Western progress and civilization. Macaulay's minute (memorandum) on Indian education is guided by the principle, popularized in an often quoted line from Rudyard Kipling, that the "white man's burden" is to civilize the farthest reaches of a backward world. Such a principle clearly coexists with less benevolent motives for conquest and can also be considered an agent of that conquest insofar as it serves to export Western models of thought. Whether seen as humanitarian vision or as nationalist pride, it defines a cultural perspective that had far-reaching consequences—as it did here, in a proposal that marked the beginning of Indian bilingualism in English.

The author of the minute, Thomas B. Macaulay, was a famous essayist, orator, and Whig member of Parliament whose powerful speeches in favor of the Reform Bill of 1832 had made him a respected public figure. Macaulay shared the Whigs' belief in progress, especially in the progress of modern Western history. An immensely cultured man, now known chiefly for his monumental *History of England* and for the heroic (and moral) poems *Lays of Ancient Rome,* he backed social reforms such as the Ten Hours' Bill in England, which reduced the hours that young people could work in the factories and suggested that the extra time be used for their education. In 1834, when he was only thirty-three, he accepted a position as legal member of the Board of Control of India and served on the Supreme Council, where he was made president of the Committee of Public Instruction. Here he listened to the arguments of those who favored a traditional education in the classical languages of Sanskrit and Arabic (the Orientalists) and of those who favored Western learning and the use of English. It was not a new debate, and both sides had already agreed on the need to introduce Western learning to Indian schools. The argument was over the language of instruction: whether such knowledge should be "engrafted" on Indian culture by an elite group of students who were thoroughly trained in Sanskrit and Arabic, or obtained from the beginning as part of an education in English. The many vernacular languages of India were not considered for this purpose, for both Orientalists and Anglicists agreed that there was not enough written in the vernacular to meet current needs. After both sides had submitted written arguments to the Supreme Council, Macaulay wrote a discursive memorandum on the subject to Lord William Bentinck, the governor-general of India.

Macaulay, with his customary rhetorical flair, frames the issue in terms of cultural progress and social utility. Which language, he asks, offers the most advanced level of civilization: the most up-to-date knowledge, the most sound and useful thoughts, and, incidentally, the greatest opportunity for employment and political influence? The answer is readily available. In addition, this fervent believer in the British Empire describes a corollary advantage: the creation of a new class of educated people, trained in English, who will understand the Western model of civilization and be able to implement it throughout India. The minute's famous conclusion, that this class should be "Indian in blood and color, but English in taste, in opinions, in morals, and in intellect," could not fail to impress Lord Bentinck, who gave it his Seal of Approval on March 17, 1835.

[*From* Minute on Indian Education, February 2, 1835][1]

* * * A sum is set apart "for the revival and promotion of literature and the encouragement of the learned natives of India, and for the introduction and promotion of a knowledge of the sciences among the inhabitants of the British territories."[2] It is argued, or rather taken for granted, that by literature, the Parliament can have meant only Arabic and Sanscrit literature, that they never would have given the honorable appellation of "a learned native" to a native who was familiar with the poetry of Milton, the metaphysics of Locke, and the physics of Newton; but that they meant to designate by that name only such persons as might have studied in the sacred books of the Hindoos all the uses of cusa-grass,[3] and all the mysteries of absorption into the Deity. This does not appear to be a very satisfactory interpretation. To take a parallel case; suppose that the Pacha of Egypt, a country once superior in knowledge to the nations of Europe, but now sunk far below them, were to appropriate a sum for the purpose of "reviving and promoting literature, and encouraging learned natives of Egypt," would anybody infer that he meant the youth of his pachalic[4] to give years to the study of hieroglyphics, to search into all the doctrines disguised under the fable of Osiris,[5] and to ascertain with all possible accuracy the ritual with which cats and onions were anciently adored? Would he be justly charged with inconsistency, if, instead of employing his young subjects in deciphering obelisks, he were to order them to be instructed in the English and French languages, and in all the sciences to which those languages are the chief keys?

* * *

We now come to the gist of the matter. We have a fund to be employed as government shall direct for the intellectual improvement of the people of this country. The simple question is, what is the most useful way of employing it?

All parties seem to be agreed on one point, that the dialects commonly spoken among the natives of this part of India, contain neither literary nor scientific information, and are, moreover, so poor and rude that, until they are enriched from some other quarter, it will not be easy to translate any valuable work into them. It seems to be admitted on all sides, that the intellectual improvement of those classes of the people who have the means of pursuing higher studies can at present be effected only by means of some language not vernacular amongst them.

What then shall that language be? One-half of the committee maintain that it should be the English. The other half strongly recommend the Arabic and Sanscrit. The whole question seems to me to be, which language is the best worth knowing?

I have no knowledge of either Sanscrit or Arabic.—But I have done what I could to form a correct estimate of their value. I have read translations of

---

1. A memorandum written by Macaulay, in his capacity as president of the Committee of Public Instruction, to Lord Bentinck, governor-general of India.   2. Macaulay cites an 1813 act of Parliament that established a fund for Indian education.   3. Also called *darbha*, a sacred grass required in various Hindu rituals.   4. The district over which the pacha or pasha rules.   5. In ancient Egypt, the god of the underworld.

the most celebrated Arabic and Sanscrit works. I have conversed both here and at home with men distinguished by their proficiency in the Eastern tongues. I am quite ready to take the oriental learning at the valuation of the orientalists themselves. I have never found one among them who could deny that a single shelf of a good European library was worth the whole native literature of India and Arabia. The intrinsic superiority of the Western literature is, indeed, fully admitted by those members of the committee who support the oriental plan of education.

It will hardly be disputed, I suppose, that the department of literature in which the Eastern writers stand highest is poetry. And I certainly never met with any orientalist who ventured to maintain that the Arabic and Sanscrit poetry could be compared to that of the great European nations. But when we pass from works of imagination to works in which facts are recorded, and general principles investigated, the superiority of the Europeans becomes absolutely immeasurable. It is, I believe, no exaggeration to say, that all the historical information which has been collected from all the books written in the Sanscrit language is less valuable than what may be found in the most paltry abridgments used at preparatory schools in England. In every branch of physical or moral philosophy, the relative position of the two nations is nearly the same.

How, then, stands the case? We have to educate a people who cannot at present be educated by means of their mother-tongue. We must teach them some foreign language. The claims of our own language it is hardly necessary to recapitulate. It stands pre-eminent even among the languages of the west. It abounds with works of imagination not inferior to the noblest which Greece has bequeathed to us; with models of every species of eloquence; with historical compositions, which, considered merely as narratives, have seldom been surpassed, and which, considered as vehicles of ethical and political instruction, have never been equaled; with just and lively representations of human life and human nature; with the most profound speculations on metaphysics, morals, government, jurisprudence, and trade; with full and correct information respecting every experimental science which tends to preserve the health, to increase the comfort, or to expand the intellect of man. Whoever knows that language has ready access to all the vast intellectual wealth, which all the wisest nations of the earth have created and hoarded in the course of ninety generations. It may safely be said, that the literature now extant in that language is of far greater value than all the literature which three hundred years ago was extant in all the languages of the world together. Nor is this all. In India, English is the language spoken by the ruling class. It is spoken by the higher class of natives at the seats of government. It is likely to become the language of commerce throughout the seas of the East. It is the language of two great European communities which are rising, the one in the south of Africa, the other in Australasia; communities which are every year becoming more important, and more closely connected with our Indian empire. Whether we look at the intrinsic value of our literature, or at the particular situation of this country, we shall see the strongest reason to think that, of all foreign tongues, the English tongue is that which would be the most useful to our native subjects.

The question now before us is simply whether, when it is in our power to teach this language, we shall teach languages in which, by universal confession, there are no books on any subject which deserve to be compared to our own; whether, when we can teach European science, we shall teach systems which, by universal confession, whenever they differ from those of Europe, differ for the worse; and whether, when we can patronize sound philosophy and true history, we shall countenance, at the public expense, medical doctrines, which would disgrace an English farrier[6]—astronomy, which would move laughter in girls at an English boarding school,—history, abounding with kings thirty feet high, and reigns thirty thousand years long,—and geography, made up of seas of treacle and seas of butter.

We are not without experience to guide us. History furnishes several analogous cases, and they all teach the same lesson. There are in modern times, to go no further, two memorable instances of a great impulse given to the mind of a whole society,—of prejudices overthrown,—of knowledge diffused,—of taste purified,—of arts and sciences planted in countries which had recently been ignorant and barbarous.

The first instance to which I refer, is the great revival of letters among the Western nations at the close of the fifteenth and the beginning of the sixteenth century. At that time almost every thing that was worth reading was contained in the writings of the ancient Greeks and Romans. Had our ancestors acted as the Committee of Public Instruction has hitherto acted; had they neglected the language of Cicero and Tacitus;[7] had they confined their attention to the old dialects of our own island; had they printed nothing and taught nothing at the universities but chronicles in Anglo-Saxon, and romances in Norman-French, would England have been what she now is? What the Greek and Latin were to the contemporaries of More and Ascham,[8] our tongue is to the people of India. The literature of England is now more valuable than that of classical antiquity. I doubt whether the Sanscrit literature be as valuable as that of our Saxon and Norman progenitors. In some departments,—in history, for example, I am certain that it is much less so.

Another instance may be said to be still before our eyes. Within the last hundred and twenty years, a nation which has previously been in a state as barbarous as that in which our ancestors were before the crusades, has gradually emerged from the ignorance in which it was sunk, and has taken its place among civilized communities.—I speak of Russia. There is now in that country a large educated class, abounding with persons fit to serve the state in the highest functions, and in no wise inferior to the most accomplished men who adorn the best circles of Paris and London. There is reason to hope that this vast empire, which in the time of our grandfathers was probably behind the Punjab,[9] may, in the time of our grandchildren, be pressing close on France and Britain in the career of improvement. And how was this change effected? Not by flattering national prejudices: not by feeding the mind of the young Muscovite with the old women's stories which his rude fathers had believed: not by filling his head with lying legends about St. Nicholas: not by encouraging him to study the great question, whether the

6. A person who shoes horses or, by extension, cares for them.   7. Gaius Cornelius Tacitus (ca. 56–120 C.E.), Roman historian and eminent prose stylist. Marcus Tullius Cicero (106–43 B.C.E.), Roman statesman, orator, and author whose "Ciceronian" style became a model for later writers.   8. Roger Ascham (1515–1568), humanist scholar and author of *The Scholemaster* (1570). Sir Thomas More (1477–1535), humanist and chancellor of England (1529–32).   9. A large region of the Indian subcontinent, currently divided between India and Pakistan.

world was or was not created on the 13th of September;[1] not by calling him "a learned native," when he has mastered all these points of knowledge: but by teaching him those foreign languages in which the greatest mass of information had been laid up, and thus putting all that information within his reach. The languages of Western Europe civilized Russia. I cannot doubt that they will do for the Hindoo what they have done for the Tartar.

* * *

To sum up what I have said, I think it clear that we are not fettered by the Act of Parliament of 1813; that we are not fettered by any pledge expressed or implied; that we are free to employ our funds as we choose; that we ought to employ them in teaching what is best worth knowing; that English is better worth knowing than Sanscrit or Arabic; that the natives are desirous to be taught English, and are not desirous to be taught Sanscrit or Arabic;[2] that neither as the languages of law, nor as the languages of religion, have the Sanscrit and Arabic any peculiar claim to our engagement; that it is possible to make natives of this country thoroughly good English scholars, and that to this end our efforts ought to be directed.

In one point I fully agree with the gentlemen to whose general views I am opposed. I feel with them, that it is impossible for us, with our limited means, to attempt to educate the body of the people. We must at present do our best to form a class who may be interpreters between us and the millions whom we govern; a class of persons, Indian in blood and color, but English in taste, in opinions, in morals, and in intellect. To that class we may leave it to refine the vernacular dialects of the country, to enrich those dialects with terms of science borrowed from the Western nomenclature, and to render them by degrees fit vehicles for conveying knowledge to the great mass of the population.

* * *

1. According to the Byzantine calendar, which the Russians accepted together with Christianity, the world was created on September 1, 5508 B.C.E. Peter the Great moved Russia to the Julian calendar (to be superseded by the current Gregorian calendar) in an attempt to reconcile discrepancies that had crept in over the centuries: By the 19th century, there was a difference of twelve days between the Byzantine and Julian calendars, so the Byzantine date of creation would appear as September 13 in the new reckoning. 2. Graduates of the Sanscrit (i.e., Sanskrit) and Arabic curriculum had complained that they could not find jobs.

GIUSEPPE GARIBALDI
1807–1882

In the midst of nineteenth-century images of European empire, which are commonly versions of national grandeur writ large, it is unusual to come across a truly international vision. That vision belonged to Giuseppe Garibaldi, the Italian revolutionary and "hero of two worlds" who had fought wars of liberation in South America and Italy. Even though he was an Italian nationalist before there was a nation of Italy, Garibaldi's main allegiance was to the common people and their struggles to free themselves from despotic and often foreign rule. A brilliant guerrilla leader and strategist, he was distrusted as an unpredictable revolutionary by the various heads of state to whom he offered his services. In Sicily, however, he was welcomed by the peasants as a liberator, when he landed there with his forces—the "One Thousand" or "Red Shirts"—on May 11, 1860, and proceeded to defeat the king of Naples' much larger army.

The conquest of Sicily was Garibaldi's most memorable exploit. For centuries, the island had been ruled by foreigners and linked with Naples on the mainland as the kingdom of the Two Sicilies. A succession of Spanish, Austrian, and French rulers down to the current Bourbon king, Francis II, governed the dual kingdom with a heavy hand and bloodily suppressed Sicilian nationalist rebellions. Naples, like Sicily, welcomed him as a hero. After the the final battle of the war at Volturno, Garibaldi held a plebiscite in Naples and Sicily and turned the enthusiastic region over to King Victor Emmanuel II of Sardinia-Piedmont, the man who would soon be the first king of the new nation of Italy. Garibaldi himself returned to his island home of Caprera, disillusioned by politics, tired of war, and unable to forget the atrocities he had witnessed in Sicily after the peasants took revenge on their oppressors. (Giovanni Verga's *Freedom*, printed in this volume, describes one such scene.) Taking advantage of his international fame, he sent a public letter, dated October 15, 1860, to all the heads of Europe, suggesting a plan to stop wars between nations and allow resources to be used for peaceful ends.

It is a surprising memorandum, one that was ignored at the time by its recipients but that anticipates in the twentieth century both the United Nations and the European Union. In making the case for peace, Garibaldi tries many avenues of persuasion. Like a diplomat, he flatters his addressees; like a businessman, he criticizes waste and proposes a new allocation of resources; like an entrepreneur, he plans for industrial growth and international trade. Unlike contemporary imperialists, however, he does not seek local solutions in foreign conquests, but imagines instead a reconfigured Europe and a totally different construction of empire.

Memorandum[1]

[Monte Tifata, Campania,
15 October 1860]

It is well known to all intelligent people that Europe is far from finding itself in a normal state and justifiable to its populations.

France, which undisputably occupies the first position among the European powers, maintains under arms six hundred thousand soldiers, one of the first fleets in the world, and an immense quantity of employees for its internal security.

Great Britain does not have the same number of soldiers, but a superior fleet, and perhaps a superior number of employees, for the security of its possessions abroad.

Russia and Prussia, in order to maintain themselves in equilibrium, also need to employ immense armies.

The secondary States, if for no other reason than their spirit of imitation

---

1. This document, translated here by Anthony P. Campanella, was sent by Garibaldi to the heads of all European governments.

and to show their presence, are obliged to maintain themselves proportionately at the same level.

I will not speak of Austria and the Ottoman Empire[2] both of which are damned to destruction for the good of the unfortunate peoples they oppress.

In sum, one may ask himself: why this agitated and violent state of Europe? Everyone speaks of civilization and progress . . . But to me it seems, excepting our elegance, that instead we do not differ much from primitive times, when men tore each other apart in order to possess themselves of another's prey. We pass our lives threatening each other continuously and reciprocally, while in Europe the large majority of the people, not only the intelligent, but also those of good sense, understand perfectly that we can also pass our poor lives without this perpetual state of threats and hostilities of some against the others, and without this necessity, which seems to be fatally imposed upon peoples by some secret and invisible enemy of mankind, by killing ourselves with so much science and finesse.

For example, let us suppose one thing:

Let us suppose that Europe should form a single State.

Who ever would think of disturbing it in its own domain? Who would ever consider, I ask you, disturbing the tranquility of this sovereign of the world?

And in such a supposition there would be no more armies, no more fleets, and the immense capital sums wrested almost always from the needs and misery of peoples in order to be squandered in the service of extermination, would be converted instead to the advantage of the people in one colossal development of industry, by improving roads, in the construction of bridges, in the excavation of canals, in founding public buildings, and in the erection of schools which would divert from misery and ignorance so many poor creatures in all countries of the world, regardless of their grade of civilization, now condemned by egoism, connivance and bad administration of privileged classes bent upon the bestialization and prostitution of mankind and its surroundings.

However, the realization of the social reforms to which I allude, rarely depends upon a sole initiative, regardless of its strength and exuberance. But when has Europe ever presented greater probabilities for success in achieving these humanitarian benefits than now?

Let us examine the situation. Alexander II in Russia proclaims the emancipation of slaves.[3]

Victor Emmanuel in Italy throws his scepter onto the battlefield and shows himself to be in favor of regenerating a noble race and great nation.[4]

In Great Britain there is a virtuous queen[5] and a generous and wise nation, which associates itself enthusiastically for the cause of oppressed nationalities.

Finally France, because of the mass of its concentrated population,

---

2. During the 19th century, both the Ottoman Turkish Empire and the Austrian Habsburg Empire suppressed, or tried to suppress, a series of nationalist revolts among their subject peoples. In addition, Austrian soldiers had put down numerous rebellions in Italy, and Austria declared war on Piedmont in 1859. **3.** Alexander II, czar of Russia, had announced a plan to abolish serfdom in 1856; the law was enacted in 1861 after extensive negotiations with the serfs' former owners. **4.** The king of Piedmont, Victor Emmanuel II (1820–1878), personally commanded his troops against Austrian forces in the battles of Magenta and Solferino (June 1859). He was proclaimed king of the new Kingdom of Italy on March 17, 1861. **5.** Queen Victoria (1819–1901).

because of the valor of its soldiers, and because of its recent prestige from the most brilliant period of its military history, is called upon to be the arbiter of Europe.[6]

But who shall initiate this great undertaking?

The nation which marches in the vanguard of the revolution! The idea of a European confederation, which would be placed ahead of the French Emperor and which would spread security and happiness in the world, would that not be better than all the political combinations which torment and make uneasy each day of this poor people?

Concerning the thought of atrocious destruction which a single battle among the great fleets of western powers could bring, he who would dare give such an order would be frightened with terror, and probably there will never be a man so vilely daring as to assume such a frightful responsibility.

The rivalry which has persisted between France and Great Britain from the fourteenth century to today exists still; but today we will show it to be for the glory of human progress, which is infinitely less intensive so that a compromise between the two greatest nations of Europe, that is a compromise which would have as its aim the welfare of humanity, could no longer figure among the dreams and utopias of serious men.

Therefore the foundation of a European Confederation is naturally based upon France and Great Britain. Then France and Great Britain should frankly and faithfully shake hands, while Italy, Spain, Portugal, Hungary, Belgium, Switzerland, Greece and Rumania will come along too, in fact they will instinctively group themselves around them.

In this manner all divided and oppressed nationalities, that is the Slavic, Celtic, Germanic, Scandinavian races, gigantic Russia included, will not want to remain outside of this political regeneration to which they are drawn by the genius of the century.

I realize that an objection arises naturally in opposition to the preceding project:

What is to be done with the innumerable mass of men now employed in the military armies and navies?

The answer is simple:

During the same time that these masses are discharged, we would also be getting rid of the cumbersome and damaging institutions; and the spirit of the sovereigns, no longer preoccupied with the ambition of conquest, war and destruction, would be turned instead towards the creation of useful institutions and would descend from the study of generalities to that of the families and also of individuals.

Furthermore with the growth of industry, with commerce protected, the merchant marine will reclaim from the military marine all the financial support from the latter at once, and the incalculable quantity of enterprises created by the peace, from our association and security, would swallow up all this armed population, perhaps even twice that which it is today.

War becoming practically impossible again, armies would become useless. But that which would not become useless is maintaining the soldierly and generous customs of the people by means of national militias, so that they

---

6. Napoleon III of France had earned the reputation of arbiter of Europe during the negotiations leading to the Treaty of Paris (1856), which concluded the Crimean War. *Military history*: a joint force of Piedmontese and French troops, commanded by Napoleon III, defeated the Austrians at the Battle of Solferino.

would be ready to suppress disorders and any ambitions which might attempt to destroy the European pact.

I strongly desire that my words become known to those to whom God confided the holy mission of doing well, and they will do it, certainly preferring instead of a false and ephemeral greatness, true greatness, that which has its foundation in love and in the gratitude of the people.

G. Garibaldi

MACHEMBA
late nineteenth century

One of the rare documents written by a tribal chief directly to the colonial invader is a letter in Swahili written by the Yao chief Machemba and addressed to Major Hermann von Wissmann, the German officer in command of subduing Tanganyika for the German East African Company and the German Empire. It is significant that the only copy of the document is a German translation preserved in the German Colonial Archives along with other records. And while it is undoubtedly a literal translation, the lost Swahili original comes to us filtered through the conqueror's language in a way that still raises questions.

What we do know is that Major von Wissmann, who had recently completed a bloody suppression of coastal resistance, was now turning his attention to the interior and requiring the submission of all the local chiefs. Those who submitted were given "protectorate" status that required them to obey officials of the German East African Company (upon which Kaiser Wilhelm recently bestowed an imperial charter) and to collect taxes for the Germans. Profitability was the motive, and the new taxes included a head tax, a burial tax, an inheritance tax, and road tolls. The company also sought to acquire land, confiscating African property when the owners could not produce written deeds.

Machemba was chief of the numerous Yao tribes and a wealthy trader, with headquarters on the Makonde Plateau and a vast commercial network inside and outside Tanganyika. He had no connections with the coastal Swahili (who moreover looked down upon the interior tribes as "uncivilized") and had not interfered in their struggle, being content to rule in the interior and leave the coast to the Germans. Yet he would not be exempt from attack. He had already displeased the Germans by giving asylum to escaped slaves, many of whom joined his armies, and by selling modern weapons rather than old flintlocks to his neighbors. Worse, his trading networks in the hinterland absorbed much of the business coming from neighboring Mozambique, and neither the profits nor customs duties reached the coast. Finally, the Germans had heard reports of large coal deposits in his territory but were turned back when, in the summer of 1890, they tried to lure him with promises of friendship.

Machemba was in a dangerous situation. The other inland chiefs had already begun to submit. For all his wealth and power and the advantage of guerrilla warfare on his own terrain, he would be vulnerable in the long term to the kind of scorch-and-burn attack that had reduced the coast. Swahili resistance had collapsed after a protracted struggle, during which the invaders burned crops and razed villages. In addition, the Germans also had cannons and a large military force that included hundreds of Sudanese mercenaries. No help could be expected from the British, even though they had a missionary station in the area: their officials had already helped intimidate the sultan of Zanzibar and had supported the German blockade of the coast.

Machemba is aware of all these factors when he responds to Wissmann's letter, which requires him to come to the German station at Lindi and submit. His response is a mixture of indignation, protest, and diplomacy. The chief's outraged pride is visible throughout, and translations of the letter are usually truncated to focus on his refusal to obey. The complete letter, however, shows Machemba also trying to preserve peace and avoiding anything that could be seen as a warlike challenge—unless he is attacked. Using reason and appeals to fairness and biblical morality, he insists that he and his family present no danger for the Germans, and he leaves the door open for friendship. Friendship is not, of course, what the Germans have in mind, and their forces invade the interior on three occasions to bring him to heel. Each time, he disappears and harasses them with guerrilla tactics until they finally return to the coast and report failure. In March 1891, however, persuaded by the destruction of his people's villages, Machemba did go to Lindi to accept the Germans' conditions. The peace did not last; he refused to collect their taxes and in 1899 was forced to flee to neighboring Mozambique, where he conducted a similar resistance against the Portuguese. Machemba's letter shows a proud and resourceful leader coping with impossible odds and is a dramatic and personal statement of the African resistance to colonial invasion.

[Letter to Major von Wissmann][1]

[undated—ca. Fall 1890]

Addressed to my friend and brother, the Commander-in-Chief:

I am informing you that your letter has arrived, and that I have read it and know everything it contains. Moreover, I have heard what you have to say;[2] but I find no reason that I should obey you. I would rather die. I have no relationship[3] to you, and I cannot recall that you ever gave me a paisa[4] or a quarter paisa or a needle or a thread. I look for a reason why I should obey you, and I find not the slightest. If it is only a matter of friendship, then I am not opposed, now or in the future. But to be your subject—that I cannot do. If it is only a matter of friendship, then we are agreed.

If you want to fight, I am ready. But to be your subject—never.

What you are hearing here is said without ambush. I will not fall at your feet, for you are a creature of God,[5] and I, too, am created. I am no God to be able to help you, and if you hear anything in my message, it is that we have no relationship.

I am sultan in my land. You are sultans in your land. Behold,[6] I am by no means saying to you that you should obey me. Not at all: indeed, I know that you are a free man. Not since I was born have I ever set foot on the coast; should I set foot on it now because you summon me? I will not come, and,

---

1. This letter was written by Chief Machemba of the Yao people to Major Hermann von Wissmann, commander of the German forces in Tanganyika and head of the station at Lindi. Translated from the German by Robert Sullivan and Sarah Lawall.   2. The spoken message accompanying the letter.   3. Literally, "relationships": personal, commercial, or diplomatic ties.   4. Also, pice, a small coin, one–sixty-fourth of the Indian rupee in the East India Company's currency system. Machemba lists a descending order of possible gifts. The colonial trading companies initially gave gifts to local rulers whom they wished to persuade.   5. In the German text, *creature of God* would be recognized as a phrase from the Lutheran Bible.   6. The word translated *Behold* echoes biblical language in German and is more than simply *Look* or *See*. *Sultan:* king or ruler. The sultan of Zanzibar—now displaced by the Germans—was the traditional ruler of the mainland peoples of Tanganyika.

if you are strong enough, then come get me. I would rather lose your respect [by being captured] than submit to you.

Besides, my child is called "Weakling,"[7] and, ever since he was born, has not known what war is. God willing, if you want to get me, then come: I will not come in person. Greetings.

This letter comes from your friend Machemba, son of M'chakama of the family of Masaninga, written in his own hand.

7. Literal translation from German. The lost Swahili term may have had special cultural significance, such as describing a youth who has not yet seen combat.

CECIL RHODES
1853–1902

The spread of European empire in Africa cannot be understood without reference to Cecil John Rhodes, a British businessman and imperialist whose wealth, energy, and manipulation of public opinion made him a force capable of overthrowing native rulers and bending colonial governments to his will. Rhodes was born in England and moved to South Africa in 1870; within ten years he had become wealthy as a diamond speculator, founded the De Beers diamond-mining company, and was elected to the Cape Parliament. In 1889, he engineered the creation of the British South Africa Company, which he controlled and whose royal charter gave it unlimited power to acquire lands and rule them in the name of the British Empire. Rhodes stopped at nothing to expand his holdings in the name of British imperialism, gaining the territory that became Rhodesia (modern Zimbabwe and Zambia) by deceiving the Ndebele ruler Lobengula in a contract through which the latter signed away all rights to the development and effective control of Matabeleland and Mashonaland. As prime minister of Cape Colony from 1890 to 1896, Rhodes maintained his power base with the Afrikaners by laws that restricted the rights of black Africans to vote, to own land, and to live where they wished. He left office only when forced to do so by the revelation of his complicity in an attempt to overthrow the Boer government of the Transvaal.

Rhodes was driven by a romantic nationalist vision of British imperial rule that is hard to imagine today. In a *Confession of Faith* written in his twenties, he dreamed of colonizing the world with an elite group of Anglo-Saxon settlers and even of bringing the United States back into the British Empire. (His Rhodes Scholarships are a philanthropic version of the same dream.) In the meantime, he dedicated himself to the political unification of South Africa as a federation of states under British influence. A charismatic speaker, he held out to his listeners in his 1899 speech at the Cape Town Drill Hall a picture of ever-expanding imperial horizons and limitless prosperity for "every civilized man." It is a sharp distinction: civilized = European; uncivilized = indigenous African. And, indeed, there is no mention of the African population in Rhodes's speech. He speaks instead of a country that has been "given to us" for profitable exploitation. Modern readers will be struck, therefore, by Rhodes's assertion that he is also working for the "union of the races"—until we realize that he means European races, who possess the mantle of empire. Those who are not mentioned—the missing factor in this political equation—are the "natives," a term that has lost its currency in the twenty-first century.

[*From* Speech at Drill Hall, Cape Town, South Africa][1]

* * *

"And, sir, my people have changed. I speak of the English people, with their marvelous common sense, coupled with their powers of imagination— all thoughts of a Little England are over. They are tumbling over each other, Liberals and Conservatives, to show which side are the greatest and most enthusiastic Imperialists. The people have changed, and so do all the parties, just like the Punch and Judy show at a country fair.[2] The people have found out that England is small, and her trade is large, and they have also found out that other people are taking their share of the world, and enforcing hostile tariffs. The people of England are finding out that "trade follows the flag," and they have all become Imperialists. They are not going to part with any territory. And the bygone ideas of nebulous republics are over. The English people intend to retain every inch of land they have got, and perhaps, sir, they intend to secure a few more inches. And so the thought of my country has changed. When I began this business of annexation, both sides were most timid. They would ask one to stop at Kimberley, then they asked one to stop at Khama's country. I remember Lord Salisbury's Chief Secretary imploring me to stop at the Zambesi.[3] Mr. Mayor, excuse me for using the word "I," but unfortunately I have been alone in these efforts. Now, sir, they won't stop anywhere; they have found out that the world is not quite big enough for British trade and the British flag; and that the operation of even conquering the planets is only something which has yet to be known. I have little doubt about the Colonial people, and in saying so, I cover in the Colonial people the Dutch as well as the English. Notwithstanding my past little temporary difficulty, if we were all to accept equal rights,[4] I feel convinced that we should all be united on the proposition that Africa is not, after all, big enough for us.

"And, gentlemen, with that comes the development of our own country. * * * You have the sheep, the wine, the gold, the diamonds, and the health, and a marvelous climate. There is no place in the world to touch this; there is no place to touch it for the beauty of its climate, and the variety of its products, and yet we stupid human mortals are quarreling over the equality of rights, instead of thinking of the great country that has been given to us. * * * That is what we are working for, not only union of the country but union of the races, and, if I may put it, that will come right once the principle of equal rights is accepted—equal rights for every civilized man south of the Zambesi.

1. Published in 1900. The speech was delivered on July 18, 1899. 2. A traditional puppet play that showed constant battles between a brutal husband and his nagging wife. *Parties*: i.e., political parties. 3. A large river flowing through south-central Africa. *Kimberley* is a city in the Northern Cape of Africa, known for its diamond mines. Rhodes's company (De Beers Consolidated Mines) took control of the mines in 1888. *Khama*: Khama III, ruler of Bechuanaland (now Botswana), which was a British protectorate. He made a journey to England in 1895 to confirm British protection for his country. *Chief Secretary*: the representative of Lord Salisbury, who was prime minister of Britain. 4. Equal rights specifically for settlers of Dutch ancestry (the Boers) and the English. *Temporary difficulty*: in January 1896, Rhodes was forced to resign as prime minister of the Cape after being implicated in the "Jameson Raid," an unsuccessful attempt to overthrow the government of the Transvaal (a neighboring Boer state). The following year, a committee of the British House of Commons condemned him for grave breaches of official duty.

OLIVE SCHREINER
1855–1920

As a war between Britain and the Boer republics seemed likely, one of the voices speaking out in opposition was that of Olive Schreiner, an English South African whose controversial first novel, *The Story of an African Farm* (1883), gave a realistic picture of African colonial life and established her both as a feminist thinker and as someone who could speak with authority about South African society.

Schreiner was born in the Cape Colony in 1855, the ninth child of parents who had moved to South Africa in 1838 to take up missionary activities among the heathen. She was taught at home and lacked the formal education given her brothers, one of whom became prime minister of Cape Colony in 1899. Because a young woman was expected to support herself by undertaking traditional feminine tasks, Schreiner worked as a family governess from 1874 to 1881, at which point she moved to London to be part of a more cosmopolitan environment. *The Story of an African Farm*, published under a pseudonym, was an immediate success for the vividness of its writing and the intellectual boldness with which it attacked the social, educational, and religious narrowness of colonial—and Victorian—society. She was not happy in London, however, and returned to South Africa in 1889 where she married and, along with her husband, became actively engaged in political affairs.

The man who symbolized everything that Schreiner disliked in South African politics was Cecil Rhodes, the British businessman whose charter company had taken control of vast parts of South Africa, from the Kimberly diamond mines to the newly annexed territories of Mashonaland and Matabeleland that became Rhodesia (modern Zimbabwe). His rise to power in Cape Colony coincided with Schreiner's return home, for he had managed, with the support of the conservative Afrikaner Bond, to become Cape prime minister in 1890. In order to keep that support, he passed laws that restricted the Africans' right to vote and established an early system of social segregation that later became apartheid. Rhodes is the chief figure in the "small knot of speculators" criticized here, and it is his company's ruthless exploitation of Mashonaland, and its internal war on the indigenous population, that Schreiner attacks in her novel, *Trooper Peter Halket of Mashonaland* (1897). He remained prime minister until 1896, when his complicity in the Jameson Raid (an attempt to overthrow the government of the Transvaal) was revealed.

The Jameson Raid consolidated and strengthened nationalist feelings in the Boer republics. It suggested that the British Empire would never recognize the autonomy of the Transvaal and thus contributed to an existing atmosphere of mistrust. Negotiations were already under way to resolve the status of the British nationals in the Transvaal—the Uitlanders, or foreigners who had come to work there and found they had few political rights. Boer fears about British motives now seemed justified, and the specter loomed even larger of a de facto takeover by a large British voting population that would reject Boer customs. President Paul Kruger, who had led a successful rebellion against the earlier annexation of 1877, wanted no binding ties to the "paramount power" in Africa, as Great Britain termed itself. Prime Minister Joseph Chamberlain of Great Britain was urged to use force on behalf of British nationals, and public opinion—intensified by fears of losing a world market—soared in favor of intervention. Neither side thought far into the future: Boer nationalists, remembering earlier successes, were convinced of winning a war on their own soil; while British nationalists burned to wipe out the disgrace of their defeat at Majuba in 1881.

It is at this point, when war seems (and soon will be) inevitable, that Schreiner writes a public letter to the British people, hoping to bring together two peoples who have, she says, much in common. She suggests that the real problem is the greed of European speculators, who see South Africa only as a source of plunder and war as an instrument of economic policy. It is a passionate statement in defense of the Boer settlers and, by extension, all settlers in South Africa who dream of a new African nation built by their own hands. Modern readers may be struck by the fact that Schreiner almost never mentions the plight of the indigenous Africans, whose soil the settlers occupy. Instead, this letter focuses on the pressing danger of the day and the risk of war between two colonial states whose image of a developed and "civilized" Africa is, in the long run, remarkably similar.

From An English–South African's View of the Situation[1]

* * *

* * * Amid all this chorus of opinion, there is one voice which, though heard, has not yet been heard with that distinctness and fullness which its authority demands—it is the voice of the African-born Englishman who loves England, the man who, born in South Africa, and loving it as all men, who are men, love their birth-land, is yet an Englishman, bound to England not only by ties of blood, but that much more intense passion which springs from personal contact alone. Our position is unique, and it would seem that we are marked out, at the present juncture of South African affairs, for an especial function, which imposes on us at whatever cost to ourselves the duty of making our voices heard and taking our share in the life of our two nations at their

Most Critical Juncture.[2]

For let us consider what exactly our position is.

Born in South Africa, our eyes first opened on these African hills and plains; around us, of other parentage, but born with us in the land, our birth-fellows, were men of another white race, and we grew up side by side with them. Is it strange that, like all men living who have the hearts of men, we learnt to love this land in which we first saw light? * * * Is it strange that when, after long years of absence, years it may be of success and the joy which springs from human fellowship and youth, our ship has cast its anchor in sight of Table Bay, and the great front of Table Mountain[3] has reared up before us, a cry of passionate joy has welled up within us; and when we saw the black men with their shining skins unloading in the docks, and the rugged faces of South Africans browned with our African sun, we put our foot on the dear old earth again, and our hearts have cried: "We are South Africans! We have come back again to our land and to our people"? * * * Side by side with us in South Africa are other South Africans whose position is not and cannot be exactly what ours is. Shading away from us by imperceptible degrees, stand on one side of us those English South Africans who, racially English, yet know nothing or little personally of her; the grandparents, and not the parents of such men, have left England; they are proud of being Englishmen; proud of England's great record and great names, as a man is proud of his grandmother's family; they are before all things essentially South

---

1. Published in 1899.   2. Typographical emphasis found in the original text.   3. Cape Town is situated on the harbor of Table Bay, on the western coast of South Africa, and at the foot of a flattop mountain called Table Mountain.

African. He desires to see England increase and progress, and to remain in harmony and union with her while she does not interfere with internal affairs of South Africa, but he does not and cannot feel to her as those of us do whose love is personal and whose intellectual sympathies center largely in England.

Yet further from us on the same side stand our oldest white fellow South Africans; who were, many, not of English blood originally, though among that body of early white settlers, men who preceded us in South Africa by three centuries, were a few with English names, and though by intermarriage Dutch and English South Africans are daily and hourly blending, the bulk of these folk were Dutchmen from Holland and Friesland,[4] with a few Swedes, Germans, and Danes, and later was intermingled with them a strong strain of Huguenot[5] blood from France. These men were mainly of that folk which, in the sixteenth century, held Philip and the Spanish Empire at bay,[6] and struck the first death-blow into the heart of that mighty Imperial system whose death-gasp we have witnessed to-day. A brave, free, fearless folk with the

Blood of the Old Sea Kings[7]

in their veins; a branch of that old Teutonic race which came with the Angles and Saxons into England and subdued the Britons, and who in the persons of the Franks entered Gaul,[8] and spread its blood across Europe. They are a people most nearly akin to the English of all European folk; in language, form, and feature resembling them, and in a certain dogged persistence, and an inalienable, indestructible air of personal freedom.

*   *   *

If it be asked, has the Dutch South African always dealt gently and generously with the native folks with whom he came into contact, we answer, "No, he has not"—neither has any other white race of whom we have record in history. He kept slaves in the early days! Yes, and a century ago the English wished to make war on her American subjects in Virginia for refusing to take the slaves she sent. There was a time when we might have vaunted some superiority in the English African method of dealing with the native.

That Day is Past.

The terrible events of the last five years in South Africa have left us silent. There is undoubtedly a score laid against us on this matter, Dutch and English South Africans alike; for the moment it is in abeyance; in fifty or a hundred years it will probably be presented for payment as other bills are, and the white man of Africa will have to settle it. It has been run up as heavily north of the Limpopo as south,[9] and when our sons stand up to settle

4. A region of northern Europe settled by Germanic peoples. Part of the original Friesland is now a province of the northern Netherlands.   5. In the 16th and 17th centuries, French Protestants. Many Huguenots were driven out of France by religious persecution.   6. In 1588, Philip II of Spain sent a fleet of large ships (the Armada) to invade England. It was destroyed in a memorable sea battle by a fleet of smaller but more maneuverable English ships.   7. I.e., Vikings, Norse sailors and explorers.   8. Ancient name for the part of western Europe that is now France and Belgium. *Franks*: Germanic tribes who invaded Gaul in the 5th century C.E., when it was part of the Roman Empire.   9. The Limpopo is a large river part of whose course separates South Africa from Zimbabwe—at that time, the Cape Colony from the northern territories owned by King Lobengula of the Ndebele. In 1880, Cecil Rhodes won power in the Cape Parliament by promising Afrikaners that he would support expansion north of the Limpopo River. His British South Africa Company first won concessions and then conquered Ndebeleland military in 1893–94.

it, it will be Dutchmen and Englishmen together who have to pay for the sins of their fathers.

* * *

We South Africans, Dutch and English alike, are a curious folk, strong, brave, with a terrible intensity and perseverance, but we are not a sharp people well versed in the movements of the speculative world. In a few years the entire wealth of South Africa, its mines of gold and diamonds, its coal-fields, and even its most intractable lands from the lovely Hex River Valley to Magaliesberg, had largely passed into the hands of a very small knot of speculators.[1] In hardly any instances are they South Africans. That they were not South Africans born would in itself matter less than nothing, had they thrown in their lot with us, if in sympathies, hopes, and fears they were one with us. They are not. It is not merely that the wealth which should have made us one of the richest peoples in the world has left us one of the poorest, and is exported to other countries, that it builds palaces in Park Lane, buys yachts in the Mediterranean, fills the bags of the croupiers at Monte Carlo,[2] decks foreign women with jewels, while our citizens toil in poverty; this is a small matter. But those men are not of us! That South Africa we love whose great future is dearer to us than our own interests, in the thought of whose great and noble destiny lies the source of our patriotism and highest inspiration, for whose good in a far-distant future we, Dutch and English alike, would sacrifice all in the present—this future is no more to them than the future of the Galapago Islands.[3] We are a hunting ground to them, a field for extracting wealth, for

Building up Fame and Fortune;

nothing more. This matter does not touch the Transvaal alone; from the lovely Hex River Valley, east, west, north, and south, our lands are being taken from us, and passing into the hands of men who not only care nothing for South Africa, but apply the vast wealth they have drawn from South Africa soil in an attempt to corrupt our public life, and put their own nominees into our parliaments, to grasp the reins of power, that their wealth may yet more increase. Is it strange that from the hearts of South Africans, English and Dutch alike, there is arising an exceedingly great and bitter cry, "We have sold our birthright for a mess of pottage![4] The lands, the mineral wealth which should have been ours to build up the great Africa of the future, has gone into strange hands! And they use the gold they gain out of us to enslave us; they strike at our hearts with a sword gilded with South African gold! While the gold and stones remained undiscovered in the bosom of our earth, it was saved up for us and for our grandchildren to build up the great future; it is going from us never to return; and when they have rifled our earth and picked the African bones

1. Chief among them Schreiner's archenemy, the diamond and gold magnate Cecil Rhodes and his British South Africa Company. *Hex River Valley:* the Cape wine lands, a picturesque grape-growing region. *Magaliesberg:* an ancient mountain range with rare geological formations, fauna, and flora. 2. A resort in Monaco on the French Riviera, known chiefly for its gambling casino. *Park Lane:* a fashionable shopping district in central London. 3. Volcanic islands in the Pacific Ocean, west of Ecuador, that are home to a variety of rare and endangered species. 4. In Genesis 25.29–34, Esau comes in hungry from the fields, and his younger twin brother, Jacob, offers him vegetable stew (pottage) in exchange for his birthright. Esau accepts but regrets it later (Genesis 27.36).

bare, as the vultures clear the carcase of their prey, they will leave us with a broken skeleton!"

* * *

South Africa has need of more citizens leal[5] and true. Whoever enters South Africa and desires to become one of us, to drink from our cup and sup from our platter, to mix his seed with ours and build up the South Africa of the future—him let us receive with open arms. From great mixtures of races spring great peoples. That scorned and oppressed Russian Jew, landing here to-day, vivified by our fresh South African breezes, may yet be the progenitor of the Spinoza and Maimonides[6] of the great future South Africa, who shall lead the world in philosophy and thought. The pale German cobbler who with his wife and children lands to-day, so he stays with us and becomes one with us, may yet be the father of the greater Hans Sachs[7] of Africa; and the half-starved Irish peasant become the forerunner of our future Burkes and William Porters. The rough Cornish[8] miner, who is looking out with surprised eyes at our new South African world to-day, may yet give to us our greatest statesman and noblest leader. The great African nation of the future will have its foundation laid on stones from many lands. Even to the Coolie[9] and the Chinaman, so he comes among us, we personally should say, Stretch forth the hand of brotherhood; we may not desire him, we may not intentionally bring him among us, but, so he comes to remain with us, let South Africa be home to him.

"Be not unmindful to entertain strangers, for some have thereby entertained angels unawares."[1]

* * *

Who Gains by War?

There are some who *think* they gain! In the background we catch sight of misty figures; we know the old tread; we hear the rustle of paper passing from hand to hand, and we know the fall of gold;[2] it is an old familiar sound in Africa; we know it now! There are some who *think* they gain! Will they gain?

* * *

Do not think that when imported soldiers walk across South African plains to take the lives of South African men and women that it is only African sand and African bushes that are cracking beneath their tread; at each step they are breaking the fibers, invisible as air but strong as steel, which bind

5. Loyal.   6. Baruch Spinoza (1632–1677) was a Dutch philosopher and theologian. Moses Maimonides (1135–1204) was a medieval Jewish scholar, philosopher, and physician, born in Spain.   7. A medieval German writer and Meistersinger (i.e., a master in a medieval guild that was devoted to the cultivation of music and poetry). Sachs (1494–1576), a shoemaker, is the subject of an opera by Richard Wagner (*Die Meistersinger von Nürnberg*, 1868).   8. From Cornwall, a province at the southwestern tip of Great Britain. *Edmund Burke* (1729–1797), born in Ireland, was a British politician and author of *Reflections on the Revolution in France* (1790). *William Porter:* i.e., William Porter of Limavady, an Irishman who became attorney general at the Cape and was responsible for giving the vote to educated blacks in the 1870s.   9. An Indian.   1. See Hebrews 13.2.   2. Rhodes had been implicated in the Jameson Raid of December 1895, an attempt to overthrow the government of the gold-rich Transvaal. Similarly (as later records show) the gold magnates Julius Wernher and Alfred Beit supported the plans of Alfred Milner, high commissioner for South Africa (1897–1903), to "work up a crisis" that would make war inevitable and allow the annexation of the Transvaal.

the hearts of South Africans to England. Once broken they can never be made whole again; they are living things; broken they will be dead. Each bullet which a soldier sends to the heart of a South African to take his life wakes up another who did not know he was an African. You will not kill us with your Lee-Metfords; you will make us. There are men who do not know they love a Dutchman,[3] but the first three hundred that fall, they will know it.

Do not say, "But you are English, you have nothing to fear; we have no war with you!" There are hundreds of us, men and women who have loved England; we would have given our lives for her; but rather than strike down one South African man fighting for freedom, we would take this right hand and hold it in the fire, till nothing was left of it but a charred and blackened bone.

* * *

3. I.e., a Boer settler of Dutch descent. *Lee-Metfords:* a magazine rifle, the equivalent of the German Mauser, that was accepted as the British main service rifle in December 1888.

MARY KINGSLEY
1862–1900

The Victorian audience that read Mary Kingsley's *Travels in West Africa* was already well acquainted with stories of the great explorers in Africa, whether newspaper accounts of Mungo Park and David Livingstone or book-length memoirs such as Richard F. Burton's *Two Trips to Gorilla Land and the Cataracts of the Congo* and Henry Morton Stanley's *In Darkest Africa*. They also devoured fictional explorations, including H. Rider Haggard's fantastic *King Solomon's Mines*. In Mary Kingsley, however, they found an intrepid explorer of a different stamp: a single woman traveling alone (with the usual porters) through uncharted jungles. Crossing swamps and fording rivers, falling into spiked pits and trading with cannibals, she was the stuff of legend—"a daring pioneer into the death-haunted unknown," according to one obituary. Her adventures also came in a colorful and entertaining package that combined travelogue, scientific research, and detailed ethnological observation.

Kingsley's travels occupied less than two years of her relatively short life, most of which was taken up with domestic responsibilities at home. She took care of the household from an early age—"from the day I could first carry a duster"—for her invalid mother, while her father traveled the globe during most of each year as attendant physician for one or another nobleman. Like many Victorian women, she was given no formal education, although her younger brother, a mediocre student, was sent to Cambridge University. Kingsley seems to have taught herself to read by watching him and by using his primers, and she subsequently obtained a formidable home schooling by working her way through her father's vast library of books on science and ethnology. She was fascinated by ancient and modern books on exploration and by her father's stories of his travels. At one point she did receive tutoring: her father let her learn German so that she could help him in his research on sacrificial rites. To these scholarly studies Kingsley added practical knowledge gleaned between the ages of sixteen and twenty from a handyman's magazine, the *English Mechanic,* which showed her how to repair their old house and fix the plumbing, and from the friendly advice of a neighbor who was an electrical engineer. In 1884, the family moved to Cambridge, where she read Charles Darwin, Thomas Huxley, and the ethnographer E. B. Tylor, heard about the Berlin conference that partitioned Africa among European states, and followed news accounts of competing explorers-entrepreneurs in the Congo. By the time both her parents died in 1892, she was almost thirty years old and superbly equipped to manage on her own. She was also ready and eager to travel in the Africa of which she dreamed, and when her brother (whose housekeeper she dutifully remained) left on a trip to the East, she packed and left for the Canary Islands. The journey lasted only a few months, but it convinced her to return to Africa as soon as possible, especially to the west Africa of her favorite explorers.

Kingsley made two trips in west Africa: the first, a five-month journey in 1893 that took her through French, German, and English-held territories; the second—part of which is described here—a ten-month expedition in 1895 whose most remarkable aspect was a hazardous journey up the Ogowé River in the French Congo (Gabon). Her ostensible aim in the second journey was to collect specimens of rare African fish for the British Museum. (She brought back sixty-five species of fish and eighteen species of reptiles.) Meanwhile, she took copious notes on the landscape and on local customs, all of which found their way into *Travels in West Africa* (1897) and *West African Studies* (1899). Kingsley insisted on her role as serious scientist, remarking in the Preface to *Travels in West Africa* that "I have written only on things that I know from personal experience and very careful observation. I have never accepted an explanation of a native custom from one person alone, nor have I set down things as being prevalent customs from having seen a single instance." She traveled very simply, "tentless and living on native food," and supported herself throughout as a trader. It was a calculated choice, although necessary to stretch her limited budget. As a trader, she occupied a familiar role in the local economy, gaining the villagers' confidence and much ethnological information she could not otherwise have obtained. Still, she must have seemed an alien figure, traveling the rain forest dressed in long black skirts with a corset and cummerbund, white blouse, black leather boots, and hat. An unflappable trader, resourceful and courageous in all circumstances, she once bargained for the release of a porter who was about to satisfy a local debt by ending up in the cook pot. Kingsley's success depended on her ability to work within local customs and on an ethnographer's perspective that put both European and African habits in cultural context.

She remains a complicated and even tragic figure, located both inside and outside Victorian imperial tradition. She was taught to consider women inferior and conformed to Victorian domestic conventions even after becoming a well-known and influential explorer. Although she strongly criticized British colonial policies and objected to the presence of missionaries, her idea of reform was merely an adjustment of the imperial system: she proposed replacing British colonial bureaucracy by a council of large merchants who would foster profitable trade while respecting African customs and local rulers. Yet Kingsley was sincere in her stated preference for African over European society, and she is credited with having revolutionized British attitudes toward Africa. Her books and lectures provided a wealth of new knowledge about west Africa's peoples and customs, and she argued strongly for "the real African that does exist and suffers" from imperial policy. The appeal of her journal comes partly from its detailed and appreciative observation of the people and land, and partly from the author's humorous yet vividly personal involvement in everything as it happens.

Travels in West Africa[1]

FROM CHAPTER XIII.

From Esoon to Agonjo

* * * All our paths took us during the early part of the day up and down hills, through swamps and little rivers, all flowing Rembwéwards. About the middle of the afternoon, when we had got up to the top of a high hill, after having had a terrible time on a timber fall of the first magnitude, into which four of us had fallen, I of course for one, I saw a sight that made my heart stand still. Stretching away to the west and north, winding in and out among the feet of the now isolated mound-like mountains, was that never to be mistaken black-green forest swamp of mangrove; doubtless the fringe of the River Rembwé, which evidently comes much further inland than the mangrove belt on the Ogowé.[2] * * * Cheered by this pleasing prospect, we marched on forgetful of our scratches, down the side of the hill, and down the foot slope of it, until we struck the edge of the swamp. We skirted this for some mile or so, going N.E. Then we struck into the swamp, to reach what we had regarded as the Rembwé river. * * * We found ourselves at the edge of that open line we had seen from the mountain. Not standing, because you don't so much as try to stand on mangrove roots unless you are a born fool, and then you don't stand long, but clinging, like so many monkeys, to the net of aërial roots which surrounded us, looking blankly at a lake of ink-black slime. It was half a mile across, and some miles long. We could not see either the west or east termination of it, for it lay like a rotten serpent twisted between the mangroves. It never entered into our heads to try to cross it, for when a swamp is too deep for mangroves to grow in it, "No bottom lib for them dam ting," as a Kruboy[3] once said to me, anent a small specimen of this sort of ornament to a landscape. But we just looked round to see which direction we had better take. Then I observed that the roots, aërial and otherwise, were coated in mud, and had no leaves on them, for a foot above our heads. Next I noticed that the surface of the mud before us had a sort of quiver running through it, and here and there it exhibited swellings on its surface, which rose in one place and fell in another. No need for an old coaster like me to look at that sort of thing twice to know what it meant, and feeling it was a situation more suited to Mr. Stanley[4] than myself, I attempted to emulate his methods and addressed my men. "Boys," said I, "this beastly hole is tidal, and the tide is coming in. As it took us two hours to get to this sainted swamp, it's time we started out, one time, and the nearest way. It's to be hoped the practice we have acquired in mangrove roots in coming, will enable us to get up sufficient pace to get out on to dry land before we are all drowned." The boys took the hint. Fortunately one of

---

1. Published in 1897. Kingsley's group has left the town of Esoon and is traveling toward the Rembwé River in Gabon.   2. I.e., the Ogowé River in west-central Africa: the greatest river between the Niger and the Congo, flowing for 683 miles, chiefly in Gabon. *Mangrove:* tropical swamp trees whose masses of shallow roots emerge from the water, spreading laterally and forming buttresses. Mangrove roots also grow downward into the mud from the trunk, branches, or from ripening fruit, ultimately creating a network of new trunks.   3. A servant hired from the Krumen tribe.   4. Henry Morton Stanley (1841–1904), whose *Through the Dark Continent* (1878) describes his exploration of uncharted lakes and rivers in west central Africa. *Coaster:* someone who has lived in one of Britain's west African protectorates.

the Ajumbas had been down in Ogowé, it was Gray Shirt, who "sabed them tide palaver." The rest of them, and the Fans,[5] did not know what tide meant, but Gray Shirt hustled them along and I followed, deeply regretting that my ancestors had parted prematurely with prehensile tails for four limbs,[6] particularly when two of them are done up in boots and are not sufficient to enable one to get through a mangrove swamp network of slimy roots rising out of the water, and swinging lines of aërial ones coming down to the water *à la* mangrove,[7] with anything approaching safety. Added to these joys were any quantity of mangrove flies, a broiling hot sun, and an atmosphere three quarters solid stench from the putrifying ooze all round us. For an hour and a half thought I, Why did I come to Africa, or why, having come, did I not know when I was well off and stay in Glass?[8] Before these problems were settled in my mind we were close to the true land again, with the water under us licking lazily among the roots and over our feet.

We did not make any fuss about it, but we meant to stick to dry land for some time, and so now took to the side of a hill that seemed like a great bubble coming out of the swamp, and bore steadily E. until we found a path. This path, according to the nature of paths in this country, promptly took us into another swamp, but of a different kind to our last—a knee-deep affair, full of beautiful palms and strange water plants, the names whereof I know not. There was just one part where that abomination, *pandanus,*[9] had to be got through, but, as swamps go, it was not at all bad. I ought to mention that there were leeches in it, lest I may be thought too enthusiastic over its charms. But the great point was that the mountains we got to on the other side of it, were a good solid ridge, running, it is true, E. and W., while we wanted to go N.; still on we went waiting for developments, and watching the great line of mangrove-swamp spreading along below us to the left hand, seeing many of the lines in its dark face, which betokened more of those awesome slime lagoons that we had seen enough of at close quarters.

About four o'clock we struck some more plantations, and passing through these, came to a path running north-east, down which we went. I must say the forest scenery here was superbly lovely. Along this mountain side cliff to the mangrove-swamp the sun could reach the soil, owing to the steepness and abruptness and the changes of curves of the ground; while the soft steamy air which came up off the swamp swathed everything, and although unpleasantly strong in smell to us, was yet evidently highly agreeable to the vegetation. Lovely wine palms and rafia palms, looking as if they had been grown under glass, so deliciously green and profuse was their feather-like foliage, intermingled with giant red woods, and lovely dark glossy green lianes, blooming in wreaths and festoons of white and mauve flowers, which gave a glorious wealth of beauty and color to the scene. Even the monotony of the mangrove-belt alongside gave an additional charm to it, like the frame round a picture.

As we passed on, the ridge turned N. and the mangrove line narrowed between the hills. Our path now ran east and more in the middle of the

---

5. Members of the dangerous and cannibalistic Fan (or Fang) tribe, hired recently for the trip; the Fans became Kingsley's favorite ethnic group. *Ajumbas:* members of the Ajumba tribe, hired at the beginning of the trip; *Gray Shirt* is their leader. *"Sabed them tide palaver":* Knew about tide talk (Ajumba).   **6.** A reference to Darwin's theories in *The Descent of Man* (1871).   **7.** As mangroves do (French).   **8.** A town about five miles outside Libreville, Gabon.   **9.** Screwpine (Latin). *E.:* east.

forest, and the cool shade was charming after the heat we had had earlier in the day. We crossed a lovely little stream coming down the hillside in a cascade; and then our path plunged into a beautiful valley. We had glimpses through the trees of an amphitheater of blue mist-veiled mountains coming down in a crescent before us, and on all sides, save due west where the mangrove-swamp came in. Never shall I forget the exceeding beauty of that valley, the foliage of the trees round us, the delicate wreaths and festoons of climbing plants, the graceful delicate plumes of the palm trees, interlacing among each other, and showing through all a background of soft, pale, purple-blue mountains and forest, not really far away, as the practiced eye knew, but only made to look so by the mist, which has this trick of giving suggestion of immense space without destroying the beauty of detail. Those African misty forests have the same marvelous distinctive quality that Turner[1] gives one in his greatest pictures. I am no artist, so I do not know exactly what it is, but I see it is there. I luxuriated in the exquisite beauty of that valley, little thinking or knowing what there was in it besides beauty, as Allah "in mercy hid the book of fate."[2] On we went among the ferns and flowers until we met a swamp, a different kind of swamp to those we had heretofore met, save the little one last mentioned. This one was much larger, and a gem of beauty; but we had to cross it. It was completely furnished with characteristic flora. Fortunately when we got to its edge we saw a woman crossing before us, but unfortunately she did not take a fancy to our appearance, and instead of staying and having a chat about the state of the roads, and the shortest way to N'dorko, she bolted away across the swamp. I noticed she carefully took a course, not the shortest, although that course immersed her to her arm-pits. In we went after her, and when things were getting unpleasantly deep, and feeling highly uncertain under foot, we found there was a great log of a tree under the water which, as we had seen the lady's care at this point, we deemed it advisable to walk on. All of us save one, need I say that one was myself, effected this with safety. As for me, when I was at the beginning of the submerged bridge, and busily laying about in my mind for a definite opinion as to whether it was better to walk on a slippy tree trunk bridge you could see, or on one you could not, I was hurled off by that inexorable fate that demands of me a personal acquaintance with fluvial and paludial ground deposits; whereupon I took a header, and am thereby able to inform the world, that there is between fifteen and twenty feet of water each side of that log. I conscientiously went in on one side, and came up on the other. The log, I conjecture, is dum or ebony, and it is some fifty feet long; anyhow it is some sort of wood that won't float. I really cannot be expected, by the most exigent of scientific friends, to go botanizing under water without a proper outfit. Gray Shirt says it is a bridge across an under-swamp river. Having survived this and reached the opposite bank, we shortly fell in with a party of men and women, who were taking, they said, a parcel of rubber to Holty's.[3] They told us N'dorko was quite close, and that the plantations we saw before us were its outermost ones, but spoke of a swamp,

---

1. Joseph Mallord William Turner (1775–1851), Romantic landscape painter known for expressionistic scenes that evoke an atmosphere through manipulation of light and color. (See the plate in this volume.) 2. Reference unknown; possibly an echo of Pope's line in the *Essay on Man* (Epistle I, line 77): "Heaven from all creatures hides the book of Fate." 3. Holty's (John Holt's) and Hatton and Cookson's were trading posts or "sub-factories" in the area.

a bad swamp. We knew it, we said, in the foolishness of our hearts thinking they meant the one we had just forded, and leaving them resting, passed on our way; half-a-mile further on we were wiser and sadder, for then we stood on the rim of one of the biggest swamps I have ever seen south of the Rivers. It stretched away in all directions, a great sheet of filthy water, out of which sprang gorgeous marsh plants, in islands, great banks of screw pine, and coppices of wine palm, with their lovely fronds reflected back by the still, mirror-like water, so that the reflection was as vivid as the reality, and above all remarkable was a plant[4] new and strange to me, whose pale-green stem came up out of the water and then spread out in a flattened surface, thin, and in a peculiarly graceful curve. This flattened surface had growing out from it leaves, the size, shape and color of lily of the valley leaves; until I saw this thing I had held the wine palm to be the queen of grace in the vegetable kingdom, but this new beauty quite surpassed her.

Our path went straight into this swamp over the black rocks forming its rim, in an imperative, no alternative, "Come-along-this-way" style. Singlet,[5] who was leading, carrying a good load of bottled fish and a gorilla specimen, went at it like a man, and disappeared before the eyes of us close following him, then and there down through the water. He came up, thanks be, but his load is down there now, worse luck. Then I said we must get the rubber carriers who were coming this way to show us the ford; and so we sat down on the bank a tired, disconsolate, dilapidated-looking row, until they arrived. When they came up they did not plunge in forthwith; but leisurely set about making a most nerve-shaking set of preparations, taking off their clothes, and forming them into bundles, which, to my horror, they put on the tops of their heads. The women carried the rubber on their backs still, but rubber is none the worse for being under water. The men went in first, each holding his gun high above his head. They skirted the bank before they struck out into the swamp, and were followed by the women and by our party, and soon we were all up to our chins.

We were two hours and a quarter passing that swamp. I was one hour and three-quarters; but I made good weather of it, closely following the rubber-carriers, and only going in right over head and all twice. Other members of my band were less fortunate. One finding himself getting out of his depth, got hold of a palm frond and pulled himself into deeper water still, and had to roost among the palms until a special expedition of the tallest men went and gathered him like a flower. Another got himself much mixed up and scratched because he thought to make a short cut through screw pines. He did not know the screw pine's little ways,[6] and he had to have a special relief expedition. One and all, we got horribly infested with leeches, having a frill of them round our necks like astrachan[7] collars, and our hands covered with them, when we came out. The depth of the swamp is very uniform, at its ford we went in up to our necks, and climbed up on to the rocks on the hither side out of water equally deep.

Knowing you do not like my going into details on such matters, I will

---

4. Specimen placed in Herbarium at Kew [Kingsley's note].   5. One of the Ajumbas.   6. *Pandanus candelabrum*—a marsh tree from 20 to 30 feet high growing in dense thickets. * * * Their leaves, which grow in clusters, are sword-shaped * * * with sharp spiney margins, and the whole affair is exceedingly tough and scratchy [Kingsley's note].   7. I.e., astrakhan: a curly gray fur from the karakul lamb of central Asia, often made into collars and caps for winter clothing.

confine my statement regarding our leeches, to the fact that it was for the best that we had some trade salt with us. It was most comic to see us salting each other; but in spite of the salt's efficacious action I was quite faint from loss of blood, and we all presented a ghastly sight as we made our way on into N'dorko. Of course the bleeding did not stop at once, and it attracted flies and—but I am going into details, so I forbear.

We had to pass across the first bit of open country I had seen for a long time—a real patch of grass on the top of a low ridge, which is fringed with swamp on all sides save the one we made our way to, the eastern. Shortly after passing through another plantation, we saw brown huts, and in a few minutes were standing in the middle of a ramshackle village, at the end of which, through a high stockade, with its gateway smeared with blood which hung in gouts, we saw our much longed for Rembwe River. I made for it, taking small notice of the hubbub our arrival occasioned, and passed through the gateway to its bank; then, setting its guarding bell ringing violently, I stood on the steep, black, mud slime bank, surrounded by a noisy crowd. It is a big river, but nothing to the Ogowé, either in breadth or beauty; what beauty it has is of the Niger delta type—black mud-laden water, with a mangrove swamp fringe to it in all directions. I soon turned back into the village and asked for Ugumu's[8] factory. "This is it," said an exceedingly dirty, good-looking, civil-spoken man in perfect English, though as pure blooded an African as ever walked. "This is it, sir," and he pointed to one of the huts on the right-hand side, indistinguishable in squalor from the rest. "Where's the Agent?" said I. "I'm the Agent," he answered. You could have knocked me down with a feather. "Where's John Holt's factory?" said I. "You have passed it; it is up on the hill." This showed Messrs. Holt's local factory to be no bigger than Ugumu's. At this point a big, scraggy, very black man with an irregularly formed face the size of a tea-tray and looking generally as if he had come out of a pantomime on the *Arabian Nights*, dashed through the crowd, shouting, "I'm for Holty, I'm for Holty." "This is my trade, you go 'way," says Agent number one. Fearing my two Agents would fight and damage each other, so that neither would be any good for me, I firmly said, "Have you got any rum?" Agent number one looked crestfallen, Holty's triumphant. "Rum, fur sure," says he; so I gave him a five-franc piece, which he regarded with great pleasure, and putting it in his mouth, he legged it like a lamp-lighter[9] away to his store on the hill. "Have you any tobacco?" said I to Agent number one. He brightened, "Plenty tobacco, plenty cloth," said he; so I told him to give me out twenty heads. I gave my men two heads apiece. I told them rum was coming, and ordered them to take the loads on to Hatton and Cookson's Agent's hut and then to go and buy chop[1] and make themselves comfortable. They highly approved of this plan, and grunted assent ecstatically; and just as the loads were stowed Holty's anatomy hove in sight with a bottle of rum under each arm, and one in each hand; while behind him came an acolyte, a fat, small boy, panting and puffing and doing his level best to keep up with his long-legged flying master. I gave my men some and put the rest in with my goods, and explained that I belonged to Hatton and Cookson's (it's the proper thing to belong to somebody), and that therefore

8. I.e., Hatton and Cookson's (*Ugumu* is the local pronunciation of the store's name when abbreviated to H & C).   9. Speedily, like a lamplighter making his rounds.   1. Food.

I must take up my quarters at their Store; but Holty's energetic agent hung about me like a vulture in hopes of getting more five franc-piece pickings. I sent Ngouta off to get me some tea, and had the hut cleared of an excited audience, and shut myself in with Hatton and Cookson's agent, and asked him seriously and anxiously if there was not a big factory of the firm's on the river, because it was self-evident he had not got anything like enough stuff to pay off my men with, and my agreement was to pay off on the Rembwé, hence my horror at the smallness of the firm's N'dorko store. "Besides," I said, "Mr. Glass (I knew the head Rembwé agent of Hatton and Cookson was a Mr. Glass), you have only got cloth and tobacco, and I have promised the Fans to pay off in whatever they choose, and I know for sure they want powder." "I am not Mr. Glass," said my friend; "he is up at Agonjo, I only do small trade for him here." Joy! ! ! ! but where's Agonjo? To make a long story short I found Agonjo was an hour's paddle up the Rembwé and the place we ought to have come out at. There was a botheration again about sending up a message, because of a war palaver; but I got a pencil note, with my letter of introduction from Mr. Cockshut to Sanga Glass, at last delivered to that gentleman; and down he came, in a state of considerable astonishment, not unmixed with alarm, for no white man of any kind had been across from the Ogowé for years, and none had ever come out at N'dorko. Mr. Glass I found an exceedingly neat, well-educated M'pongwe gentleman in irreproachable English garments, and with irreproachable, but slightly *floreate*,[2] English language. We started talking trade, with my band in the middle of the street; making a patch of uproar in the moonlit surrounding silence. * * *

2. Flowery. *M'pongwe:* a major ethnic group in Gabon, like the Fan.

SOL T. PLAATJE
1876–1932

The war diary of Sol T. Plaatje gave a new dimension to the so-called "white man's war" that took place in South Africa between 1899 and 1902. Plaatje, an eminent African politician, journalist, novelist, and activist for civil rights, kept a private diary for five months during the war, when he was twenty-three and employed as a court interpreter at Mafeking. The diary was never published and came to light only in 1969, when John Comaroff, a social anthropologist doing research in the area, found it in an old album of family papers that had been brought to him by Plaatje's grandson. In the meantime, the siege of Mafeking in 1899–1900 had become one of the most famous episodes in modern military history, a legend of heroic resistance by a heavily outnumbered group of British soldiers and settlers at a small outpost in South Africa during the Boer War of 1899–1902. The British commander, Colonel Robert Baden-Powell, became a national hero, and military histories dwelled on the strategies of Boer and British forces during a war that was called the Anglo-Boer War. The role of the African defenders and the disproportionate suffering of the Africans in Mafeking disappeared from historical record until Plaatje's diary emerged with its day-to-day account of the siege from the perspective of an educated black African participant.

Plaatje was born in the Orange Free State (a Boer republic) on October 9, 1876, but his parents moved to Pniel in Cape Colony when he was an infant. He was educated by German and English missionaries until age seventeen, at which point he found a job as messenger with the Post Office at Kimberley, where he worked for four and a half years. Here he was part of a larger mission-educated community and was able to continue his education in the new South African Improvement Society, whose members read and critiqued each others' writings in English. The support that this community gave to the British governmental system, with its promise of judicial equality and the right to vote for all literate male citizens possessing some property or income, remained with Plaatje later on as a sharp contrast to Boer society. The young Plaatje was bent on working his way up in a system that he associated with individual freedom and social mobility, and he took the first step when, in October 1898, he accepted a new post as clerk and court interpreter in Mafeking. Working for the court, he interpreted in Dutch, English, and Setswana (also known as Tswana), took notes of court proceedings, typed documents, and had other clerical duties. From a Barolong family himself (the name *Plaatje* was given by Dutch settlers), he became the intermediary between the British command and the leaders of the adjoining (and older) Barolong village of Mafikeng, which was included in Baden-Powell's defense perimeter. Energetic and ambitious, he also wrote articles for the local newspaper, the *Mafeking Mail,* and acted as typist and secretary to Vere Stent, the Reuters war correspondent, and for others on occasion.

Plaatje did not expect the war (he registered for Civil Service examinations shortly before the Boers began the siege), but he was in a unique position to observe it. As his mood moves from patriotic optimism to increasing gloom and stress, he records a broad spectrum of events: official news of the war along with an insider's perspective on the consequences of military strategy; court stories of rape, murder, robbery, and military disgrace; the daily reality of cannonballs bursting through houses and shredding people and animals; skirmishes with the enemy and the Barolong cattle raids on Boer flocks that helped stave off famine for a while; the imposition of passes and a rationing system that left many Africans to starve; and a series of personal and social anecdotes that give a complex picture of a diverse society under extreme pressure. It is also a picture of social and economic inequities that run along racial lines, from the initial refusal to arm Africans because they were not part of the white man's war to the expulsion of "superfluous" Africans into hostile territory as food supplies dwindled.

After the war, Plaatje became a vigorous critic of racial injustice, speaking out strongly against the South African government's move to deny rights to black Africans and documenting the harm done by the Natives' Land Act of 1913, which moved Africans off their traditional lands and into native reservations. He became the first secretary general of the South African Native National Congress (later the African National Congress) and visited Britain and the United States to arouse support, but the advent of World War I deflected attention elsewhere. The Mafeking diary, discovered seventy years later, is not only a reconstruction of the siege by a black African participant, but also a record of the young Sol Plaatje discovering his life's work.

Mafeking Diary[1]

FROM CHAPTER I

October–November 1899

Sunday, [October] 29th

Divine Services. No thunder. Haikonna[2] terror; and I have therefore got ample opportunity to sit down and think before I jot down anything about my experiences of the past week. I have discovered nearly everything about war and find that artillery in war is of no use. The Boers seem to have started hostilities, the whole of their reliance leaning on the strength and number of their cannons—and they are now surely discovering their mistake. I do not think that they will have more pluck to do anything better than what they did on Wednesday and we can therefore expect that they will either go away or settle round us until the troops arrive.[3]

To give a short account of what I found war to be, I can say: no music is as thrilling and as immensely captivating as to listen to the firing of the guns on your own side. It is like enjoying supernatural melodies in a paradise to hear one or two shots fired off the armored train; but no words can suitably depict the fascination of the music produced by the action of a Maxim, which to Boer[4] ears, I am sure, is an exasperation which not only disturbs the ear but also disorganizes the free circulation of the listener's blood. * * * The Maxim is everybody's favorite here. Whenever there is an almost sickening rattle of Mausers you can hear them enquiring amongst themselves when "makasono" is going to "kgalema."[5] Boers are fond of shooting. They do not wait until they see anything but let go at the rate of 100 rounds per minute at the least provocation. * * *

Monday, 30th

During this day we received another ultimatum[6] that if we did not surrender we would be bombarded early next day. We knew that the big gun had been with us for more than a week, and as she failed to shake us in eight days I am afraid that the Boers are merely fooling themselves to imagine that we entertain any fear in being bombarded—for so far from being alarmed, we are getting used to it. * * *

---

1. Published in 1973, *Mafeking Diary* is the private diary of African journalist and interpreter Sol T. Plaatje, which he kept during the most famous episode of the Boer War (1899–1902): the 217-day siege of Mafeking (modern Mafikeng) in South Africa. Boer forces bombarded the town daily, and the toll on the defenders was heavy.   2. A colloquial South African term meaning "no" or "not there." *Thunder*: i.e., the noise of guns.   3. Throughout the siege, the defenders of Mafeking looked for the arrival of British troops; hope waned in the later days. *Wednesday*: on October 25, the Boer general began shelling Mafeking with heavy artillery that included a 94-pound (cannonball) Creusot siege gun.   4. The Boers were African settlers of (chiefly) Dutch descent. The two Boer republics—the Transvaal (South African Republic) and the Orange Free State—fought Great Britain in the South African, or Boer, War. *Maxim*: the first fully automatic machine gun, developed in 1884 and soon used by all the major powers.   5. Scold, speak angrily (Tswana [Setswana] vernacular). *Mausers*: German five-shot bolt-action repeating rifles. *Makasono*: i.e., Maxim (Tswana vernacular).   6. On October 20, General Cronje had sent an initial warning that he would start shelling in two days; noncombatants were advised to leave.

FROM **CHAPTER 2**

December 1899

Tuesday, 12th

"Sanna"[7] never moved till 5 p.m. when she sent five shells into the location. The thinner artillery and Mausers were very mild.

We had a civil court today. A lot of boys[8] of the firm of Julius Weil are suing their employers for wages. Mr Spencer Minchin, LL.B., solicitor[9] now Lieutenant Minchin, Bechuanaland Rifles), appeared for all the plaintiffs, and Mr J. W. de Kock, attorney (now member of the Town Guard), appeared for the defense. It was a novel court: only the parties concerned looked as usual, but not the court. The plaintiffs' attorney was in military attire; lawyer for the defense, never shaved since the siege, all hairy and dressed in a third-hand suit without a collar, looked more like a farmer than an attorney. Myself in knickerbockers and without a jacket, looked more like a member of the football team or a village cyclist than a court interpreter. All of the natives, but one, carried their cases.

FROM **CHAPTER 3**

January 1900

Monday, 1st

The first day of the first week of the first month in 1900. Not at all a lovely morning. The distant pop of the Mauser distinctly shows that there is no holiday for poor beleaguered us. I tried to go to town but "Au Sanna," going strong, caused me to come back and take shelter. I wonder why some people call her "Grietje," as "Griet" for a thing of her potency would be nearer the mark. She was exceptionally "kwaai"[1] all day today. Goodness knows what provoked her.

* * *

One shell burst near Weil's this morning. The employers had a narrow escape and two mules which happened to be about were killed on the spot. One burst near the commissariat yard. A fragment came in contact with one of the laborers and eviscerated him which, in short, means killed him on the spot. A few broken walls completed the total for today. "Sanna" was very hot today, and so was a beastly new 7-pounder to the east of the town which at one time caused me to leave the Market Square post-haste—it was for dear life.

* * *

---

7. I.e., "Au Sanna": one of several names given to the 94-pound siege gun. Others are "Big Ben," "Long Tom," and the Boer "Grietje" (diminutive of "Griet," or "Gretchen"). 8. African employees. *Civil court* was held, as opposed to a military court. 9. One of two types of lawyer in the British system, the other being the barrister. *LL.B.*: Bachelor of Laws (British). 1. Hot-tempered (Dutch).

Wednesday, 3rd

* * *

They have turned their attention away from the Rooi-neks and have decided to knock spots out of the "verdomde Kaffers" this morning. They are shelling the stadt[2] from east and west. There is a miscellaneous collection of Natives from Johannesburg who thought that the war would last a month or less. They came here as they thought Mafeking was safe enough to spend the month, after which they would return to the revolutionized Rand. They are a miscellaneous collection and include Pondos, Shangaans, Barotse, Zambezian and South Central African breeds.[3] They are harmless lot of people—some of them live under the two trees on the space between the B.S.A. Police camp and the stadt. They do a little night's toil when they require a little cash to buy grain which they "nona"[4] with horseflesh. They are quiet and are waiting for the end of this trouble, and I am sure they would not do any harm to anybody.

This morning I was trying to go to town. I was just near the two trees when the bells rang. There was a horrible smash all round me and I could see the branches of one of the trees flying in the air in a cloud of dust. From under the tree all the men in the shade were raised from four to seven foot high.
* * *

Friday, 5th

* * *

* * * During the month of November the authorities, deeming it expedient in view of the approaching hard times, forbade the sale of grain of any sort by the storekeeper. All grain belonging to storekeepers was commandeered, and the government had it retailed cheaply—on economic lines—to the public.

For this purpose they have established a grain store in the stadt, one at the location, and Lippman's in town.[5] Early in December orders were issued to private owners as well that they were to state the amount of grain in their possession, as this drain got a grip of us; and it became imperative that all grain should be collected from private people, and everybody be allowed to buy so little as not to have the slightest chance of wasting anything. It is only by dint of a favor that I was allowed to buy a steen brood[6] per diem. Therefore it is criminal to have in your possession any quantity of grain beyond what

---

2. Town (Dutch). "Stadt" is used consistently for the established Tshidi Barolong village. The "town" is Mafeking itself (reserved for the whites), and the "location" (term for an African town) is a temporary village outside Mafeking inhabited by Africans of various tribes, many of whom had worked in the gold mines around Johannesburg. *Rooi-neks*: rednecks (Dutch), a name for the British, who sunburned easily. *Verdomde Kaffers* (Dutch): damned natives. Literally, the Kaffirs (Xhosa) were a group of related tribes who fought against European colonization of their lands in the Kaffir Wars (1779–1879). 3. Tribespeople from the Eastern Cape, Northern province, western Zambia, the floodplain of the Zambezi River, and south-central Africa. *Rand*: Witwatersrand, a large gold-mining region of South Africa that includes Johannesburg. 4. Literally, "become fat" (Tswana); the grain was enriched, or "fattened," by the addition of horse meal. *B.S.A. Police*: I.e., British South African Police, made up in large part of recruits from Great Britain. 5. In the Barolong village, at the multitribal African "location," and in the town of Mafeking. 6. A loaf (or "brick") of bread (Dutch). According to Colonel Baden-Powell's staff diary, meal and flour suitable for bread were reserved for "white" rations.

the regulations permit you to purchase from one of these stores run on economical lines.[7]

Rice, barley, oatmeal, and sugar have also been included and their sale is restricted unless one has an order which regulates the quantity he can purchase in a certain shop to last him a certain period. A common person would be enriched by this arrangement, as cash cannot procure whatever one requires—he being allowed to purchase so much worth and the balance all remaining in his till. But our[8] case is different: the regulation diet is cheap enough as the purchase price is also regulated, but it is too small to keep a decent man alive. One can only increase his diet by various unrestricted luxuries, the prices of which rule higher than the clouds.

From an official's viewpoint, this restriction is a wise policy, as it prevents the decrease of our supplies from passing faster than the days of the siege. To the merchant it is a boon, in as much as it enables him to demand whatever he desires for his unrestricted dainties. It is a curse, however, in that the money is circulated at the expense of the private individual's pocket.

From a Serolong[9] point of view this whole jumble is more annoying than comforting. For this they may be excused, as the arrangement is in the hands of young officers who know as little about Natives and their mode of living as they know about the man on the moon and *his* mode of living.

* * *

* * * The store has been shut for the last five days, because when the regulation was struck down to 6*d* a time,[1] Barolongali[2] told the storeman he could go to H. This was last Sunday. The store has since been shut. * * * I presume the truth is that the officers are either under the impression the Barolongs are able to purchase from a closer store, or that they can live a week without—for otherwise I cannot comprehend. This causes me to believe that they liken Barolongs to the man in the moon, who is at his place every time there is a full moon. The full moon is always at night, when the store is closed, and the man in the moon could not possibly come down for any grain; and it is their belief that Barolong can do the same: for while this "every-morsel-economical-collection" is in progress, the store shows no sign of reopening—God help these poor beleaguered people.

---

7. *Economy* was the watchword of the various rationing plans, which became more and more severe. From the announcement of January 5, 1900: "It has come to notice that several people who have small quantities of Mealie [Indian corn] Meal and Grain in their possession are in the habit of handing over to their servants certain bulk quantities in order that the servants may feed themselves. This causes unnecessary waste. Servants should be put on rations by their masters daily. The following quantities should amply suffice under present circumstances: 1 lb. to 1½ lbs. of Mealie Meal or Grain, proportionate deduction being made when Native women or children have to be fed, such as ½ to ¾ lb. per diem." 8. The Africans had a smaller food ration than the whites, so that while everyone paid the same low price for rationed food, the Africans were forced by hunger to purchase additional unregulated food at higher prices. Plaatje does not mention that whites were also permitted to obtain food on credit or from a special fund kept for that purpose. 9. I.e., Barolong, or, more specifically, the language spoken by the Barolong. 1. Purchases were limited to 6 pennies' worth of grain. 2. The Barolong women, who were by tradition the only makers of "kaffir beer," a dietary staple of Barolong culture. They insulted the storekeeper when they were told that they could not buy corn for the beer. Another explanation is given in Baden-Powell's staff diary for January 1, however: he believed that the Barolongs had "large stores of grain hidden away," and closed the shops "to see if there is any real want."

Wednesday, 24th

There is a proclamation by the Colonel R.S.S. Baden-Powell[3] that no food stores of any kind would in the future be sold to the public; and white people are now going to buy food in rations and be compelled to buy small quantities, the same as blacks. I have often heard the black folk say money is useless as you cannot eat it when you feel hungry, and now I have lived it and experienced it. The thing appears to be going from bad to worse. The big gun is still hammering away at us. It was particularly cruel today. One of its shells hit on the Market Square this morning. It bumped right up in the air and singled out old Moshweshwe's hut (one-and-a-half miles away); after its decline it entered the hut from the back, decapitating two women and wounding three brothers severely and one not dangerously. The old boy was not there.

* * *

FROM CHAPTER 4

February 1900

Thursday, 8th

There was a little rain about 4.00 this morning and the weather is very enjoyable this morning.

Runners came in from the north. They bring good news as far as concerns Plumer's forces up north;[4] but nothing fresh from east and south.

"Au Sanna" went off during the middle of the morning but was quiet all day. I hear they were working at her all day. From today no Natives are allowed in town without a pass. There are three classes of Natives, viz. permanent employees in town; permanent employees outside town; and stadt folk. The former (class one) are registered in the same manner as in Kimberley (the contract ticket) and walk about with a red ticket. I don't quite understand the procedure in class two. Class three receive a yellow ticket from Lekoko and hand it back every time they return from town.

* * *

The people are now receiving oatmeal for food instead of grain which, it is feared, will run short if sure steps are not taken to save it. The oats were intended for horses, but as the horses could eat grass when things grow serious, it is being thought of as human food. There is a general grumble all round here also. The pang has been felt all round, just at this time when folks had appetites. I have developed a marvelously strong appetite. I long for food every evening at 10.00 p.m. and after taking my supper at 7.00 I nearly die during the night if I do not take a cup of cocoa and a few biscuits before going to bed. Things are getting serious and I consider myself lucky

---

3. Colonel Robert Baden-Powell, who organized the defense of Mafeking. The food stores were all closed as of January 21, and remaining stocks were to be distributed by imperial authorities. Although there was a common rationing plan, Europeans still received much higher amounts. European children under fourteen were allotted 6 pennies' worth a day, the same amount as a full ration for Barolong men who were part of the defense.   4. Colonel Plumer's regiment had been stationed close to the Rhodesian border and was at this point fighting a Boer force 65 miles north of Mafeking at Crocodile Pools.

for having thought out the thing at the beginning and stuffed my pants with matches and such things as were likely to be called in when things grow serious. I trust I will not number among those who will eat horses if we are not relieved by the end of March.

* * *

Saturday, 10th

Things are looking mighty blue. Colonel Baden-Powell states he has received a message from Lord Roberts[5] that we will not be relieved for another three months yet and that he has not got any food for any but Barolongs, the white people and fixed residents of the place. He is therefore going to shut up the town grain store, which was only used for refugees, who came here from Johannesburg before the war, imagining that the war was going to be a matter of days.

He is going to give them only ten days grace after which he is going to close all stores, and also shut the door against their employment at the defense works, where gangs of hundreds of them are employed every day and night. These people include Bangwaketse, Bakwena, Zulus, Zambesians, Shangaan, and others too numerous to mention. The Civil Commissioner has suggested that letters be written to Bathoen and he be asked to communicate with Gnl. Snyman[6] requesting him to let his people come out of Mafeking, as he is on friendly terms with the Boers. By this means of course many people, including Barolongs, who will only be too pleased to go to Kanya can leave this beleaguered place. * * *

Friday, 16th

The stadt has [for] once changed from its usual appearance and assumed a sullen aspect. We have not experienced it yet, but if the long look for the greatest day is unequaled, today was undoubtedly a second study of judgment day. People were almost disinclined to talk to one another, and there was dead silence in the green shrubbery which almost gave one the impression that on other days they were talkative. I spent my day in old Watermann's garden, without food of any sort: it was only [when] she, grand lady, brought me several sweet cones [that I could] break my fast. I felt very stimulated after being invigorated by them and tired of novel reading and shorthand exercises. * * *

* * *

Wednesday, 21st

Myself, Philemon and Mr Gates are taking a census of the stadt. The latter and an assistant are taking it across the river. Phil starts at Tloung, myself

---

5. Field marshal and commander in chief of British forces in South Africa from December 1899 to November 1900. 6. General Cronje's successor as commander of Boer forces at Mafeking. *Bathoen:* Bathoen I, chief of the Bangkawetse people at Kanya (north of Mafeking, in modern Botswana). Nine hundred people left town on February 27.

at Bokone, and we'll meet in the center. It is a tedious, bothersome job. We commenced at 7.00 and at 10.00 I was knocked up. The people are vexing me exceedingly: one would ask me what I wished to do with the name of the owner of a place, another would object to a repetition of the census as they were counted (registered) twice already during the present siege. * * *

Mathakgon[7] left with nearly 30 men on another cattle-raiding expedition—his fourth during the present siege.

I have not seen my siege friends (the beggars) today. There were always scores of them every day at the residency and they were relieved by the soup kitchen. They are made up of the blackish races of this continent—mostly Zulus and Zambesians. * * * Last month one died in the Civil Commissioner's yard. It was a miserable scene to be surrounded by about 50 hungry beings, agitating the engagement of your pity and to see one of them succumb to his agonies and fall backwards with a dead thud. Surely these Transvaal Boers are abominable. * * *

Saturday, 24th

Morning dawned somewhat pleasantly. During the night the Boers were forced to leave their trenches in the brickfields[8] the nearest to Mafeking—and fall 1000 yards backwards. When our forces occupied the Dutch "marope"[9] they suddenly remembered that the place is most certainly mined with dynamite and immediately searched and discovered the spot where the mine is, then cut the chord which the enemy was going to pull in order to cause a destructive explosion. This must have caused the Boers to wonder why the thing refused to work—but such was the case. The mine was emptied and the dynamite brought into town.

* * *

Sunday, 25th

* * *

We get our rations—groceries (tea, coffee, sugar, pepper, and salt), vegetables (green mealies, beet, cabbage, turnips, carrots, etc., from the gardens and fields on the river beds) and preserved meat—from a government store provided for the purpose. These we draw weekly and have to call early for them, once every week, but the bread is a nuisance for this we have to call for once every day, and each time one gets a little bit—not fit to keep St Leger[1] alive more than a few hours. If the issuer likes, he can successfully cause us to do without it by telling our messenger that he was too late if he called at 7.00 in the morning and too early if he called at 3.00 in the afternoon; and when he comes at the right time, he would tell the messenger that I should have called personally, well knowing that this is an impossibility.

* * *

7. A Barolong cattle raider who daringly plundered Boer flock. He became a popular hero.   8. Disputed territory about a mile south of Mafeking.   9. Ruins (Tswana).   1. Plaatje's one-year-old son, Frederick York St. Leger (Sainty), who was living with his mother in Burghersdorp during the siege of Mafeking.

Tuesday, 27th

I woke at 5.00 to find a fine peaceful morning. One could even wish that a morning like that ought to find one in a peaceful neighborhood where one will partake of the sweet balmy air without any interference. I found I had nothing to do, so I lay down to slumber again. Just a little after 6.00 again the 9-pounder Krupp opened the ball from Game Tree. I was wondering at it when it was followed by what appeared to be a 15-pounder from Jackal Tree[2] by "Au Sanna," and several others. They kept it up all the morning. Every bomb-proof in the place was almost useless as shells were bursting from every direction.

It was a terrible morning. When I left home I was simply bewildered and hardly knew what to do. I was intending to go up to the rocks, which I had deserted since the middle of November, for since then we never had it half so hot. Even at New Year it was terrible; but nothing resembling this. I stopped at the rocks, which are much more comfortable than a dug-out, where one cannot see what goes on outside. I was wondering if this was going to be our future lot, or whether it was simply a one day's warming up. It is difficult to describe the scene, just as difficult as it is to tell how many guns there were against us. We are only sure of one thing, and that is that there were some big guns against us which have not been in Mafeking [before]. Since the big gun left its first position our house has always been out of its view so that it has not been in danger of being hit, but this morning they were mercilessly in our line. A fragment of shell that burst just at the Gape's dropped on the roof of the back house, but did not penetrate it. While I was going to the rocks, "Au Sanna" was firing in such rapid succession that three shells burst all about me before I got there. This is to say nothing at least of the smaller fry. I screwed up as much courage as I could and left the rocks to go to the Court of S.J.[3] in town. * * *

---

2. A nearby Boer fort and the usual position of the big cannon. *Krupp:* cannon made by the German manufacturer Krupp. *Game Tree:* a Boer fort about 1,000 yards north of Mafeking.   3. I.e., the Court of Summary Jurisdiction, usually responsible for civilian cases, as opposed to the courts martial, which handled military affairs. During the siege, these distinctions became blurred since the whole town had been placed under martial law. Plaatje was employed by the Court of Summary Jurisdiction, where he translated Dutch, English, and Setswana.

ICELAND
(Den.)

NORWAY

SWEDEN

Spitzbergen
(Nor.)

R U S S I A N   E M P I R E

GREAT
BRITAIN

IRELAND

ENGLAND

DENMARK
NETH.
BELG.

LUX.

GERMANY

FRANCE
SWITZ.

AUSTRIA
HUNGARY

MONT. SERB.
ROMANIA
BULGARIA

MONGOLIA

MANCHURIA

Azores
(Port.)

PORTUGAL

SPAIN

VAL.

GREECE

OTTOMAN
EMPIRE

AFGHANISTAN

C H I N A

KOREA (Jap.)

JAPAN

Madeira
(Port.)

Canary Is.
(Sp.)

RIO DE ORO

MOROCCO

ALGERIA

TUNISIA

LIBYA

EGYPT

ARABIA

PERSIA

I N D I A

BURMA

MACAO
(Port.)

HONG
KONG
(Br.)

Formosa
(Jap.)

Marianas

Cape
Verde Is.
(Port.)

SENEGAL

GAMBIA
PORT.
GUINEA

SIERRA LEONE
LIBERIA
IVORY COAST
GOLD COAST
TOGOLAND
NIGERIA
CAMEROONS
SP. GUINEA
FR. CONGO

FRENCH WEST AFRICA

ANGLO-
EGYPTIAN
SUDAN

ERITREA

FR. SOMALILAND
BR. SOMALILAND

ITALIAN
SOMALILAND

ABYSSINIA

Ceylon

SIAM

FRENCH
INDOCHINA

PHILIPPINES
(U.S.)

Guam
(U.S.)

Caroline Is.

MALAYA

BRUNEI

SARAWAK

BORNEO

SUMATRA

DUTCH EAST INDIES

JAVA

Maldives
(Br.)

Chagos
(Br.)

RUANDA
URUNDI

BELGIAN
CONGO

UGANDA
BRITISH EAST AFRICA
GERMAN EAST AFRICA
NYASALAND

Ascension
(Br.)

St. Helena
(Br.)

ANGOLA

RHODESIA

Coco Is.
(Br.)

NEW
GUINEA

PAPUA
(Aust.)

GERMAN
SOUTH-WEST
AFRICA

MADAGASCAR

Mauritius (Br.)

Réunion
(Fr.)

I N D I A N

O C E A N

A U S T R A L I A

MOZAMBIQUE

SWAZILAND
BECHUANALAND
BASUTOLAND

UNION OF
SOUTH AFRICA

Tristan da Cunha
(Br.)

A T L A N T I C

O C E A N

Tasmania

The World
ca. 1913

GREENLAND
(Den.)

ALASKA
(U.S.)

C A N A D A

PACIFIC

OCEAN

Hawaiian Islands
(U.S.)

Marshall Is.
German
Pacific
Islands

Bismarck
Archipelago

Solomon Is. (Br.)

New Hebrides
(Br. & Fr.)

New Caledonia
(Fr.)

Marquesas Is.

French Polynesia

Tahiti

NEW
ZEALAND

PACIFIC

OCEAN

U N I T E D
S T A T E S

ATLANTIC

OCEAN

Bermuda
(Br.)

Bahamas (Br.)

HAITI
DOMINICAN REPUBLIC
Puerto Rico (U.S.)

Guadeloupe (Fr.)
Martinique (Fr.)

MEXICO

BR.
HONDURAS

CUBA

JAMAICA

GUATEMALA
EL SALVADOR
HONDURAS
NICARAGUA
COSTA RICA

PANAMA

Grenada
(Br.)

Barbados (Br.)
Trinidad (Br.)

VENEZUELA

BR. GUIANA
DUTCH GUIANA
FR. GUIANA

COLOMBIA

Galapagos Is.

ECUADOR

PERU

BOLIVIA

B R A Z I L

PARAGUAY

CHILE

ARGENTINA

URUGUAY

Falkland Is.
(Br.)

Colonial Empires

British

French

German

Dutch

Italian

Portuguese

Chazaud

ARCTIC OCEAN

Spitzbergen

SIBERIA

ICELAND
Reykjavik

RUSSIA

Ob

Lena

Yenisey

Lake Baikal

NORWAY
Oslo
SWEDEN
FINLAND
Helsinki
ESTONIA
Stockholm
St. Petersburg
(Leningrad/Petrograd)
New

GREAT
BRITAIN
IRELAND
Dublin
Nottingham
Eastbourne
London
Albert
Paris
FRANCE
DENMARK
NETH.
BELG.
LUX.
GER.
POLAND
LATVIA
LITHUANIA
BELARUS
Moscow
Talnovo
Voronezh
KAZAKHSTAN
MONGOLIA
N. KOREA
S. KOREA
JAPAN

Fenton
Munich
SWITZ.
Venice
ITALY
Rome
Madrid
SPAIN
PORTUGAL
Azores

CZECH.
Prague
AUS.
SLOVA.
HUN.
SLO.
CRO.
BOS.
YUG.
ROM.
BUL.
Oświęcim
(Auschwitz)
UKRAINE
MOL.
GEORGIA
ARM.
AZER.
Baku
Caspian Sea
UZBEK.
TURKM.
KYRGYZ.
TAJIK.
XINJIANG
TIBET

Volga

Don

Black Sea
Istanbul
(Byzantium)
GREECE
TURKEY
SYRIA
LEB.
ISR.
JORD.
Damascus
IRAQ
Baghdad
IRAN
Tehran
AFGHAN.
PAKISTAN
Himalayas
NEPAL
Jumna
INDIA

CHINA
Yellow
Yangtse
Taiwan
Iwo Jima
MYANMAR
(BURMA)
LAOS
VIETNAM
PHILIPPINES
MICRONESIA
Caroline Is.

Algiers
Hauts
Plateaux
Canary Is.
MOROCCO
WESTERN
SAHARA
ALGERIA
TUN.
Tripoli
LIBYA
Cairo
EGYPT
Nile
Medina
Mecca
SAUDI
ARABIA
Riyadh
YEMEN
Sanaa
KUWAIT
QATAR
BAHRAIN
U.A.E.
OMAN
Muscat
Persian Gulf
Arabian Sea
BANGLADESH
THAILAND
CAMBODIA
BRUNEI
MALAYSIA
SINGAPORE
INDONESIA
PAPUA
NEW GUINEA

St. Louis
Dakar
CAPE
VERDE
SENEGAL
GAMBIA
GUINEA
BISSAU
GUINEA
SIERRA
LEONE
LIBERIA
CÔTE D'IVOIRE
BURKINA FASO
GHANA
Kumasi
Accra
Keta
MAURITANIA
MALI
Timbuktu
Senegal
Niger
TOGO
BENIN
NIGER
NIGERIA
Sokoto
Ibadan
Ife
Lagos
Benin City
IBO
CAMEROON
SÃO TOMÉ
AND
PRÍNCIPE
EQUAT.
GUINEA
GABON
CONGO
Matadi
CHAD
SUDAN
C. AFR. REP.
UGANDA
Entebbe
RWANDA
BURUNDI
CONGO
ERITREA
ETHIOPIA
Djibouti
SOMALIA
Mogadishu
KENYA
Mombasa
TANZANIA
SEYCHELLES
COMOROS
MALDIVES
SRI LANKA

St. Helena

ANGOLA
ZAMBIA
ZIMB.
Zambezi
NAMIBIA
BOTSWANA
Limpopo
MOZAMBIQUE
MADAGASCAR
MAURITIUS
SWAZILAND
Johannesburg
Durban
SOUTH
AFRICA
Cape Town
LESOTHO

INDIAN
OCEAN

ATLANTIC
OCEAN

AUSTRALIA

Tasmania

The World Today

GREENLAND

Nuuk

Labrador Sea

ALASKA

Bering Sea

Aleutian Islands

Hudson Bay

C A N A D A

N O R T H

P A C I F I C

O C E A N

Vancouver

U N I T E D

Missouri

Montreal
Ottawa
Toronto
Wingham

Colorado

San Francisco

S T A T E S

NAVAJO
ZUNI
LAGUNA

Taos

Chicago
Ohio

Mississippi

New York
Washington, D.C.

A T L A N T I C

Los Angeles

Rio Grande

O C E A N

H A W A I I
Honolulu

Key West
Havana
CUBA

MEXICO

Mexico City

DOMINICAN
REPUBLIC
HAITI

PUERTO RICO

Guadeloupe
Martinique
St. Lucia
Bridgetown
Barbados

MARSHALL
ISLANDS

NAURU

KIRIBATI

SOLOMON
ISLANDS

TUVALU

BELIZE
JAMAICA

GUATEMALA
EL SALVADOR
HONDURAS
NICARAGUA
COSTA RICA
PANAMA

Caribbean Sea

Caracas
VENEZUELA

GUYANA
SURINAME
FR. GUIANA

Bogotá
COLOMBIA

Samoa Is.

VANUATU

WESTERN
SAMOA

French Polynesia

FIJI

Tahiti

Quito
ECUADOR

Galapagos Is.

PERU
Lima

Amazon

B R A Z I L

Recife

NEW
CALEDONIA

TONGA

New Caledonia

S O U T H   P A C I F I C

O C E A N

La Paz
BOLIVIA

BORORO

Brasília

Paraná

Asunción

Rio de
Janeiro
São Paulo
PARAGUAY

NEW
ZEALAND

CHILE

Santiago

Buenos Aires
ARGENTINA

URUGUAY
Montevideo

Falkland Is.

*Antarctic
Peninsula*

Chazaud

The Twentieth Century: Modernisms and Modernity

The twentieth century is not the first age to consider itself modern. Other periods have made a point of being consciously new: the Renaissance, with the dawn of secular humanism and "modern" artistic perspectives; the Enlightenment, with its "quarrel of the ancients and moderns," or even the late fifth century B.C.E. in Athens, in the cultural battles celebrated by Aristophanes. The Victorians of the late nineteenth century believed that they ushered in a truly modern age, created by the achievements of science and the Industrial Revolution. Their faith in progress was echoed in art and literature that—although it often rejected industrial society—was intent on forcing open new horizons of thought. "One must be absolutely modern," proclaimed the poet Arthur Rimbaud.

There is, nonetheless, a particular stamp to the twentieth century's idea of modernity: it is not so much comparative as *interrogative*, and it inquires *how* we know *what* we know, rather than merely rejecting previous modes of thought (which it also did). Employing the tools of reason and scientific investigation, uncovering more and more complex structures of the natural universe, it also confronted the possibility that "knowledge" was not fixed or stable and that much of what we think we know reflects the questions we ask and the methods we use to obtain answers. Modernity in the twentieth century is not merely an opposition of old and new perspectives, but a philosophical interrogation of what it means to have a perspective at all. For writers and artists, this interrogation brought new insights as well as further questions about the means of expression available for representing them.

These insights did not remain static, nor did the literature related to them: the "modernism" that emerged as an innovative literary style early in the century evolved over many years before being absorbed into diverse approaches that emphasized cultural contexts rather than the implications of form. Its formal innovations were not lost, nor was their significance forgotten: they simply became part of the writer's trade. If the first half of the century became known as a period of modernist and then "high modernist" style, the second half extended the exploration of modernity into different fields with "postmodernist" thought that criticized the universalist assumptions of modernist thought or with "postcolonial" and related views that considered "postmodern" merely a label, an outgrowth of modernism, and turned to their own separately defined missions.

In science, philosophy, social theory, and the arts, the nineteenth century defined many of the issues that would become crucial in the twentieth. Unprecedented developments in science had encouraged people to believe that they would soon master all the secrets of the universe and revealed a faith in progress and rational solutions that had not been seen since the Enlightenment. The discovery of important underlying structures in chemistry (atomic theory, the periodic table of elements), physics (unified field theory), and astronomy seemed to make the universe more rational and, hence, predictable. Technological applications suggested that these discoveries would serve humanity, not master it: photography provided unique documentary records, for example, and locomotives and steamships exploited discoveries in thermodynamics to offer rapid transportation throughout the world. The history of living nature itself became an object of study when Charles Darwin (1809–1882) examined the evolution of species according to material evidence, without reference to divine laws or purpose, and proposed his enormously influential theories of natural selection and the mutability of species.

The appeal of large explanatory systems was seen in other fields as well, notably in the positivist philosophy of Auguste Comte (1798–1857) and in the economic and social theories of Karl Marx (1818–1883). Comte held that scientific method constituted a total world view by which everything would ultimately be explained, including human society. He outlined a science of humanity that would analyze and define the laws governing human society (the beginning of sociology). Comte's positivism has come to stand for an excessive faith in the power of science and rational inquiry to discover unambiguous answers for all problems. Twentieth-century writers pointed out that positivism's belief in the scientific "rightness" of certain ideas made it blind to its own bias and created inflexible attitudes with damaging consequences in real life. Marx's *Manifesto of the Communist Party* (1848) and *Capital* (1867) proposed that the most basic material needs—food, shelter, and the social relationships enabling group survival—provided an economic foundation from which all other aspects of human culture were derived. His vision of modern workers as alienated cogs in the industrial economic machine, no longer owning their own labor, expressed for many the antihuman aspect of modern technological progress. Yet he also believed in the power of rational systems to find answers for social ills; he described the division of modern industrial society into the two competing forces of capital and labor (the proletariat), and proposed the theory of dialectical materialism to explain the processes of history.

One of the strongest opponents of positivism and its faith in rational solutions was the German philosopher Friedrich Nietzsche (1844–1900). Nietzsche focused on the individual, not society, and admired only the *Übermensch*, the superhuman being who refuses to be bound by the prevailing social paradigms of nationalism, Christianity, faith in science, loyalty to the state, or bourgeois civilized comfort. Nietzsche's insistence on the individual's complete freedom (and responsibility) in a world that lacks transcendental law ("God is dead") and his attack on the unimaginative mediocrity of mass society in the modern industrial world made him a powerful influence in the early years of the twentieth century.

The shape and intensity of this debate as well as its impact on the world at large were dictated for many years by a historical event that turned the generations of the early twentieth century against everything inherited from the recent past: the Great War, World War I (1914–18). Despite the confident rationalism of the political leaders of "Papa's Europe" (a term of resentment used by many to describe an authoritarian, patriarchal society that claimed to have all the answers), World War I had for the first time involved the whole continent of Europe and the United States in battle and was the first "total war" in which modern weapons spared no one, including civilians. Clearly, something was wrong. A generation of European and American youth was lost in the trenches, and many of the survivors resolved to reexamine the bases of certainty, the structures of knowledge, the systems of belief, and the repositories of authority in a society that had allowed such a war to occur. Their reaction would also be reflected in literature—not only in subject matter but, for many, in a new use of language, in new ways of representing our knowledge of the world, and, most especially, in new hesitations about subscribing to any single mode of understanding. They drew on areas beyond the intellect and interrogated the whole of human consciousness.

Various thinkers helped formulate alternatives to positivist rationalism. The French philosopher Henri Bergson (1859–1941) criticized scientific rationality as a mode of knowledge because human experience, he felt, could only be apprehended by consciousness. Instead of quantitative and logical inquiry, Bergson proposed intuiting the "immediate data of consciousness" as an alternate, nonscientific means of knowledge. Sigmund Freud (1856–1939), the founder of psychoanalysis, studied subconscious motives and instinctual drives to gain insights into human behavior. His essays and case studies argued that dreams and manias contain their own networks of meaning and that human beings cannot properly be understood without taking into consideration both the irrational and the rational levels of their existence. All are caught up, he suggested, in the process of mediating the same sexual drives and civilizational repressions that caused neurosis in his own patients. Freud focused attention on the way that everyday, "rational" behavior is shaped by unconscious impulses and hidden motivations, and on the way human beings actually create (and modify) their images of self through engaging in dialogue with others. His influence is so widespread that it is probably impossible for any post-Freud poet, novelist, or playwright—whether or not the author has ever read the psychoanalyst—to write without taking into consideration the psychological undercurrents of human behavior.

Positivism had assumed that language was an unambiguous tool for representing reality (a view parodied in "The sun is called a sun because it *looks* like a sun"). In contrast, the Swiss linguist Ferdinand de Saussure (1857–1913) and the Austrian philosopher Ludwig Wittgenstein (1889–1951) emphasized that language does not give us the "real thing" but a series of labels—"signifiers" pointing to a "signified." What works in conversation is not the thing itself but the way the label—the word used to describe it—provides a recognizable common ground for different speakers. In this perspective, both literature and linguistic systems are seen as *games*, combinations of pieces (words) and rules (grammar, syntax, and other conventions). Twentieth-century writers stressing the gamelike nature of language combine words and word fragments to exhibit the play of relationships, instead of struggling to find the "right word" dear to Gustave Flaubert. Game theory can be frustrating in practice. Samuel Beckett's (1906–1989) tongue-tied characters in *Endgame* make brief conversational sense but finally express very little except, perhaps, the absurd inexpressibility of the human condition. Yet there are practical conclusions to be drawn from this frustrating prospect. If a work by Borges, Beckett, or Robbe-Grillet persuades us that language determines how we see the world (as well as our place in it), then we will recognize other shaping uses of language: in advertising or in political speeches. Not all language games are played by literature.

Ever since Plato, Western philosophers have struggled systematically to understand the relationship between appearance and reality. Such issues are the central concern of the twentieth-century philosophy phenomenology (phenomena are literally "things as they appear" and its offshoot, existentialism. Both approaches investigate the role of perception in establishing our ideas of what is real. The phenomenology proposed by Edmund Husserl (1859–1938) described all consciousness as consciousness *of* something *by* someone and concluded that every object of study should be imagined in "brackets"—not as a thing in itself, but as implicated in a relationship between perceiver and perceived.

The ethical implications of this view were taken up by the philosophers Martin Heidegger (1889–1976) and Jean-Paul Sartre (1905–1980), who questioned the meaning of existence in a world without preexisting truths, values, or general laws. Heidegger's profoundly somber vision defined the "absurd" condition of human beings "thrown into the world" without any understanding of their fate. Sartre, more interested in social activism, derived from the same "absurd" freedom an ideal of human authenticity that consists in choosing our actions at each point and avoiding the bad faith of pretending that others are responsible for our choices. Albert Camus (1913–1960), writing at the same time as Sartre, offers in *The Guest* a good example of existentialism's emphasis on freedom, responsibility, and social "engagement."

Existentialism's popular appeal in the 1940s and 1950s was undoubtedly enhanced by the fact that it was a philosophic attempt to recover clear vision—and a basis for action—in a confused and meaningless world. The notion of philosophical absurdity corresponded to a very real confusion caused by the radical historical changes taking place in the first half of the century. By 1950, there had been two world wars, the second of which was truly global, and a sweeping realignment of geopolitical forces that saw the flourishing of Marxism and the establishment of major Communist states. Almost all the old monarchies had been overthrown, and colonial empires were being dismantled as the emerging nations of Africa and Asia struggled for independence and self-definition. The wielders of authority became the enormous buck-passing bureaucracies of the modern state, multinational corporations, international governmental organizations, and ethnic alliances. Transportation and telecommunications progressed to an extent envisaged only in earlier ages' science fiction and effectively shrank the global community. The rise of the modern industrial state set up new political, cultural, and economic tensions, the most important of which was a widening gulf between the West and "less developed" countries.

These changes in historical conditions had visible effects on literature and art. Cultural parochialism—the belief that there is only one correct view of the world (one's own)—was much harder to maintain when people traveled widely and experienced different ways of life. Racial and ethnic stereotypes were challenged, and traditional ideas of identity and social class were broken down. Romantic heroism and aristocratic rank seemed irrelevant to soldiers who died anonymously in the trenches of World War I, or to civilians killed at a distance by bombing raids, or to the millions of refugees and displaced persons created by wars and political persecution throughout the century. The conventional roles of the sexes came under examination. Western women achieved civil rights that they had been denied for centuries: the right to vote (1920 in the United States), the right to have bank accounts and to own and control their own property, the right to be educated equally with men, and the right to enter professions not previously open to them. Technology became part of the modern literary consciousness, inspiring both enthusiasm and fear, and initiating all over again the question of human values in a society where so much could be done (and so many controlled) by the use of machines and mass media.

The literary and artistic movements of the twentieth century are part of this evolution; they were shaped by it and helped shape it for others. Many of these movements flourished in Europe or America and were exported to other parts of the globe, where they flourished or failed, according to their relevance for local conditions. Expressionism, Dadaism, Surrealism, and Futurism—each worth exploring—are all different ways of expressing the reality of the world.

Dada-Surrealism is the best-known and most influential twentieth-century movement, and the only one to have followers today. Dada began in Zürich, Switzerland, in 1916 as a movement of absolute revolt that set out to subvert authority and break all the rules (including those of art), hoping to liberate the creative imagination. Dada creations were attacks on the mind and emotions; both Dadaists and Surrealists emphasized a "revolution of the mind" that destabilized ordinary ways of looking at things. Freedom from conventional perspectives, they felt, was a first step in reforming society. Surrealists especially aimed to bring about a fuller awareness of human experience, including both conscious and unconscious states. In France, the *Surrealist Manifestoes* of 1924 and 1930 proclaimed that Surrealism was a means of expressing "the actual functioning of thought," "the total recuperation of our psychic force by a means that is nothing else than the dizzying descent into ourselves." The Surrealists experimented with various means to liberate the unconscious imagination and reach a sublime state they called "the marvelous": Dream writing, automatic writing (writing rapidly and continuously whatever comes to mind), riddle games, interruption and collage, and chiefly the creation of startling images opened the mind to new possibilities.

Known for its intensity, playfulness, and openness to change, Surrealism proved to be the most influential and enduring of these movements of revolt. By the end of the twentieth century, art and literature had absorbed the characteristic Surrealist themes of free play, antirationality, and the importance of the unconscious mind, and employed the preferred Surrealist techniques of collage, metamorphosis, and the blurring of dream and reality. In an ironic mark of success, commercial advertising also adopted Surrealist strategies, and the term *surrealist* became a convenient for unconventional or fantastic works whether or not they were connected to the movement.

Modernism is the usual term for a general change in attitudes and artistic strategy occurring at the beginning of the century, but there are many modernisms. Taken more narrowly, it refers to a group of Anglo-American writers (many associated with the Imagists of 1908–17) who favored clear, precise images and common speech and who thought of the work as an art object produced by consummate craft rather than as a statement of emotion. James Joyce, Ezra Pound, T. S. Eliot, William Faulkner, and Virginia Woolf are examples of Anglo-American modernism—and of the larger modernism, too. In its broader sense, modernism reconstructed conventional images of the world and of human nature by changing the forms in which reality was usually represented. Modernist writers played with shifting and contradictory appearances to suggest the changing and uncertain nature of reality (Pirandello); they broke up the logically developing plot typical of the nineteenth-century novel and offered instead unexpected connections or sudden changes of perspective (Woolf, Faulkner); they used interior monologues and free association to express the rhythms of consciousness (Joyce). They drew attention to style instead of trying to make it transparent and made much greater use of image clusters, thematic associations, and musical patterning to supply the basic structures of both fiction and poetry. Modernists blended fantasy with reality while representing real historical or psychological dilemmas (Kafka) and explored age-old questions of human identity in terms of contemporary philosophy and psychology. No one modernist did all these things, of course, and the writers differ substantially among themselves: Pirandello's image of human experience is not that of Proust or T. S. Eliot, and history is focused differently in Faulkner and Pablo Neruda. Yet there is another element that unites these figures: their experiments with perspective and language are still defined within the traditional concepts of individual psychological depth and the idea of the artwork as a coherent aesthetic whole. The combination of discontinuous, experimental style and a continuing belief in the wholeness of the human personality and of the artwork generally marks the early modernist tradition.

Modernism evolved after the mid-century, questioning—as "postmodernism"— some of its philosophical premises while continuing to explore the implications of language and linguistic form. Postmodernist writers viewed their recently canonized predecessors—Joyce, Proust, Eliot, Woolf, Mann, and Stevens, for example—as part of a conservative "high modernism" that championed formal innovation but preserved traditional roots in mainstream thought. In this view, the high-modernist quest for more profound insight and inclusive vision does not so much break with the past as it continues an idealist Western tradition reaching back to Homer and the Bible. In contrast, postmodernist writers created a network of allusions, interruptions, contradictions, and blurred reference as if to disorient a reader who seeks to reduce human events to one demonstrated meaning. Where high modernism wished to reveal a core of profound experience through innovative form, these rhetorical writers were suspicious of profundity: calling something "profound," after all, implies that it is especially true and valuable, and reflects the speaker's own value judgment. Modern authors who wished to avoid such judgments rejected images of depth and profundity, and limited themselves to inconclusive surface images. Thus, Alain Robbe-Grillet resists drawing conclusions when he gives conflicting versions of a single scene in *The Secret Room*, and obliges readers to find their own solutions; Italo Calvino's *Invisible Cities* openly plays with ambiguous versions of reality. In *Endgame*, Samuel Beckett uses spare dialogue and a nearly barren stage to provide openings for readers and playgoers to fill in the blanks of meaning. Such arbitrary constructions of meaning are a recurrent theme in *Endgame*, which, therefore, assumes the status of a text reflecting on its own nature—a prize postmodernist theme. Readers will find that certain easily identified strategies are at work in much of this literature, strategies whose general aim is to avoid creating any fixed reference point or sense of completeness. The line is not always easy to draw: Luigi Pirandello, Marcel Proust, Bertolt Brecht, and particularly Franz Kafka and James Joyce are experimental modernist writers who have also been called precursors of postmodernism.

Without diminishing the description of social reality in earlier twentieth-century literature, one may say that Western literature in the latter half of the twentieth century gave unprecedented recognition to different ethnic, sexual, and cultural identities, both depicted as subject matter and embodied in narrative perspective. In many ways, the pluralism of literary styles and the willingness to blur the boundaries of previous generic and descriptive conventions corresponded to the diversity of a new geopolitical age as well as the increasing sophistication of scientific theory. Late twentieth-century writers inhabited a world of shifting frontiers and massive waves of migration, of global markets and volatile economic conditions, of famines, continental epidemics, and terrorist attacks appearing in the daily news. The United Nations had 191 members, and about 6,800 languages were spoken around the globe: at the same time, English emerged as a medium of global communication. Postcolonial societies struggled with a mixed heritage of indigenous and colonial traditions, debating whether to reject (with difficulty) the colonizer's language and culture or to develop and control the rich hybridity of existing cultural consciousness. Cultural, racial, religious, and gender issues came to the forefront of political controversy, assuming different values in different parts of the world. Writers in the later twentieth century did not emulate the essentialism of earlier literature, therefore, but gave difference its due; instead of revealing the similarities among human beings, they were likely to represent a profusion of styles and perspectives that expressed the range and diversity of individual experience and contemporary cultural perspectives. Chinua Achebe has described this impulse to see life from different angles in terms of an old Igbo belief: "Wherever Something stands, Something Else will stand beside it. Nothing is absolute." Some—those as far apart as Alexander Solzhenitsyn and Chinua Achebe—chose to work in a more realistic vein; others, like Gabriel García Márquez, expanded into "magical realist" realms that blurred the frontiers between dreamlike visions and physical or political reality. Leslie Marmon Silko's *Yellow Woman* used its setting in the American Southwest as a point of departure for a (possibly) mystical meeting based on Laguna Indian legend. By the end of the century, contemporary writers continued to profit from modernist innovations in language and perspective at the same time that they found different ways to articulate the world of *their* experience. Modernism, as an exploration of literary and linguistic forms employed to express the twentieth-century's ongoing interrogation of reality, continued to exert its influence throughout the century and to change the contexts of modern experience.

THE TWENTIETH CENTURY:
MODERNISMS AND MODERNITY

TEXTS	CONTEXTS
1899 Joseph Conrad, ***Heart of Darkness***	**1899–1902** Boer War in South Africa
	1900 Max Planck proposes quantum theory, the first step in the discovery of the atom
1903 Henry James, ***The Ambassadors***	**1903** Wright brothers invent the powered airplane
1904 Max Weber, ***The Protestant Ethic and the Spirit of Capitalism*** • Private publication of poems by Constantine Cavafy	
1905 Sigmund Freud, *"Dora" (Fragment of an Analysis of a Case of Hysteria)*	**1905** Modern labor movement begins with the founding of the Industrial Workers of the World (IWW)
1907 August Strindberg, *The Ghost Sonata*	**1907** Japanese immigration to the United States prohibited
1908 Gertrude Stein, *Three Lives*	
1909 F. T. Marinetti, *Futurist Manifesto*	**1909** Commercial manufacture of plastic begins • NAACP founded in the United States
	1910 Mexican Revolution begins
1911 ***Encyclopaedia Britannica*** (eleventh edition)	
1912 Thomas Mann, ***Death in Venice***	**1912–1913** Balkan wars
1913 Marcel Proust, ***Swann's Way,*** first volume of *Remembrance of Things Past* (1913–27) • D. H. Lawrence, *Sons and Lovers*	
1914 James Joyce, *Dubliners*, which includes ***The Dead***	**1914–1918** World War I involves Europe, Turkey, the Middle East, Africa, the United States, and the Pacific
1915 Franz Kafka, ***The Metamorphosis*** • T. S. Eliot, ***The Love Song of J. Alfred Prufrock***	**1915** Albert Einstein formulates general theory of relativity • First transcontinental phone call in America
1916 James Joyce, *A Portrait of the Artist as a Young Man*	
	1917 Russian Revolution overthrows the Romanov dynasty
1918 Tristan Tzara, ***Dada Manifesto***	**1918–1919** Global influenza epidemic; more than 20 million die
1919 Oswald Spengler, ***The Decline of the West*** • Paul Valéry, ***The Crisis of the Mind*** • Alfonsina Storni, *Irremediably*	**1919** League of Nations formed (U.S. Senate rejects membership, 1920)

Boldface titles indicate works in the anthology.

THE TWENTIETH CENTURY:
MODERNISMS AND MODERNITY

TEXTS	CONTEXTS
1920 Edith Wharton, *The Age of Innocence*	**1920** Mahatma Gandhi leads India's struggle for independence from Britain • Women given the vote in the United States
1921 Luigi Pirandello, **Six Characters in Search of an Author**	**1921–1935** Harlem Renaissance, black literary and artistic movement
1922 T. S. Eliot, *The Waste Land* • Paris publication of James Joyce, *Ulysses* (imported copies burned in U.S. Post Office) • Rainer Maria Rilke, *Sonnets to Orpheus*	**1922** Irish Free State established • USSR formed • Discovery of Egyptian pharaoh Tutankhamen's tomb
1923 Rainer Maria Rilke, **Duino Elegies**	**1923** Turkey becomes a republic
1924 Thomas Mann, *The Magic Mountain* • André Breton, *First Surrealist Manifesto*	**1924** Insecticides first used
1926 Franz Kafka, *The Castle* • Paul Éluard, **Capital of Pain**	
1927 Virginia Woolf, *To the Lighthouse* • Sigmund Freud, **The Future of an Illusion**	
1928 William Butler Yeats, *The Tower* • André Breton, *Nadja*	**1928** Sixty-two nations sign the Kellogg-Briand antiwar pact in Paris • First Five-Year Plan in USSR • Penicillin discovered • First scheduled television broadcasts • Women given the vote in Great Britain
1929 William Faulkner, *The Sound and the Fury* • Virginia Woolf, **A Room of One's Own** • Sigmund Freud, **Civilization and Its Discontents**	**1929** Stock market crash heralds beginning of world economic crisis; Great Depression lasts until 1937
1930 Katherine Anne Porter, **Flowering Judas**	
1932 *Zuñi Ritual Poetry* published by anthropologist Ruth L. Bunzel	
1933 Federico García Lorca, *Blood Wedding*	**1933** Adolf Hitler given dictatorial powers in Germany • Nazis build first concentration camps
	1934 Stalin begins purges of Communist party
1937 Wallace Stevens, *The Man with the Blue Guitar*	
1938–1940 Bertolt Brecht, **The Good Woman of Setzuan**	
1939 Aimé Césaire, *Notebook of a Return to the Native Land*	**1939** Germany invades Poland; all Europe is drawn into World War II

THE TWENTIETH CENTURY:
MODERNISMS AND MODERNITY

TEXTS	CONTEXTS
1940 Richard Wright, *Native Son*	
1941 Jorge Luis Borges, **The Garden of Forking Paths**	1941 United States formally enters World War II
1942 Albert Camus, *The Stranger* • William Faulkner, **Go Down, Moses**	
1943 T. S. Eliot, **Four Quartets** • Jean-Paul Sartre, **Being and Nothingness**	
1944 Virginia Woolf, *A Haunted House and Other Short Stories,* which includes *An Unwritten Novel*	
1945 Hannah Arendt, **Organized Guilt and Universal Responsibility**	1945 World War II ends with the dropping of atomic bombs on Hiroshima and Nagasaki • United Nations and Arab League founded
1946 George Orwell, **The Prevention of Literature** • Tadeusz Borowski, **Ladies and Gentlemen, to the Gas Chamber**	1946 Churchill's "Iron Curtain" speech marks beginning of Cold War • Pan-African Federation formed
	1947 Religious massacres accompany partition of India and Pakistan into independent states • Transistor invented
1948 Ezra Pound, *Pisan Cantos*	1948 Creation of Jewish state in Palestine
1949 Simone de Beauvoir, **The Second Sex** • George Orwell, *Nineteen Eighty-four*	1949 Communist People's Republic of China established • Apartheid instituted in South Africa
1950 Pablo Neruda, **General Song**	1950–1953 Korean War involves North and South Korea, the United Nations, and China
1951 Doris Lessing, **The Old Chief Mshlanga**	
1952 Ralph Ellison, *Invisible Man*	1952 Revolution in Egypt, which becomes a republic in 1953 • First hydrogen bomb
1953 Joyce Mansour, *Screams*	1953 Discovery of DNA structure launches modern genetic science
1955 Alain Robbe-Grillet, *The Voyeur*	
	1956 First Congress of Black Writers meets in Paris
1957 Albert Camus, *Exile and the Kingdom,* which includes **The Guest** • Samuel Beckett, **Endgame**	
1958 Chinua Achebe, **Things Fall Apart**	1958 European Common Market established • Algerian War of Independence (ends in 1962)

THE TWENTIETH CENTURY:
MODERNISMS AND MODERNITY

TEXTS	CONTEXTS
1960 Marguerite Duras, *Hiroshima mon amour*	1960–1962 Independence for Belgian Congo, Nigeria, Tanganyika, and Uganda
1961 Frantz Fanon, **The Wretched of the Earth**	1961 Soviet astronaut orbits Earth
	1961–1973 United States engages in the Vietnam War
1962 Doris Lessing, *The Golden Notebook* • Alain Robbe-Grillet, *Snapshots*, which includes **The Secret Room**	
1963 Anna Akhmatova, **Requiem,** published • Alexander Solzhenitsyn, **Matryona's Home**	
	1966 First Dakar Arts Festival provides showcase for African culture
1967 Gabriel García Márquez, *One Hundred Years of Solitude*	
1968 Alice Munro, *Dance of the Happy Shades,* which includes **Walker Brothers Cowboy**	
	1969 American astronaut is first man on the moon
1970 Gabriel García Márquez, **Death Constant beyond Love**	
1972 Ingeborg Bachmann, *Three Paths to the Lake,* which includes **The Barking** • Italo Calvino, **Invisible Cities**	
	1973 Arab oil producers cut off shipments to nations supporting Israel; ensuing energy crisis reshapes global economy
1977 Leslie Marmon Silko, *Ceremony*	
1978 Edward Said, **Orientalism**	
1981 Salman Rushdie, *Midnight's Children* • Leslie Marmon Silko, *Storyteller,* which includes **Yellow Woman**	1981 AIDS virus identified and named; kills 6 million worldwide by 1996
1984 Audre Lorde, *Sister Outsider,* which includes **Age, Race, Class, and Sex**	
	1986 Nuclear disaster in Chernobyl spreads radiation contamination throughout Europe
	1987 World stock market crash
1989 Trinh T. Minh-ha, **Woman, Native, Other**	1989 Mikhail Gorbachev restructures the Soviet state • Berlin Wall demolished
1990 Derek Walcott, **Omeros**	1990 East and West Germany united

THE TWENTIETH CENTURY: MODERNISMS AND MODERNITY

TEXTS	CONTEXTS
	1991 United States and USSR agree to arms reduction • Economic chaos and nationalist unrest bring end of Soviet Union
	1992 Rio Earth Summit: 172 nations discuss global environmental damage and disagree on economic responsibility • Fighting between Christian Serbs and Muslim Croats marks beginning of ethnic wars in the former Yugoslavia; UN troops intervene and effect temporary peace
	1993 European Community, the West's largest trading unit, formed; talks begin on a common currency
	1994 Nelson Mandela becomes president of South Africa after first multiracial elections • Israel and PLO sign peace agreement and begin negotiating its conditions
	1996 Scientists in Scotland create Dolly, the clone of an adult sheep
	1997 Death of Mother Teresa
	2001 Terrorists attack the World Trade Center in New York and the Pentagon in Washington, D.C., on September 11
2002 Salman Rushdie, *Step across This Line*	**2002** Euro banknotes and coins introduced as legal tender for members of European Monetary Union
	2004 Death of Yasser Arafat

JOSEPH CONRAD
1857–1924

Born in Russia to Polish parents, learning English at twenty-one, and then serving as a sailor for sixteen years, Joseph Conrad nonetheless became a prolific writer of English fiction and, in his best work, a master of evocative modernist prose. His ability to suggest the vibration, color, and form of distant places as well as the complexity of human responses to moments of moral crisis stamped works like *Heart of Darkness* and *Lord Jim*, and made them permanent points of reference. Conrad's own sense of separation and exile, his yearning for the kinship and solidarity of the larger humanity he describes in the Preface to *The Nigger of the "Narcissus,"* permeates these works along with the despairing vision of a universe in which even the most ardent idealist finds no ultimate meaning or moral value.

He was born Jozef Teodor Konrad Korzeniowski on December 3, 1857, the only child of Polish patriots who were involved in Polish resistance to Russian rule. (He changed his name to Conrad, more pronounceable in English, for the publication of his first novel in 1895.) When his father was condemned for conspiracy in 1862, the family went together into exile in northern Russia, where Conrad's mother died three years later from tuberculosis. Conrad's father, who was a poet and translator, supported the small family by translating Shakespeare and Victor Hugo, and Conrad himself read novels by William Makepeace Thackeray, Walter Scott, and Charles Dickens in Polish and French. When his father died a few years later, in 1869, the eleven-year-old orphan went to live with his maternal uncle, Tadeusz Bobrowski, who sent him to school in Cracow (Poland) and Switzerland. Bobrowski supported his orphaned nephew both financially and emotionally, and, when Conrad asked to fulfill a long-standing dream of going to sea, gave him an annual allowance and helped him find a berth in the merchant marine.

During the next few years, he worked on French ships, traveling to the West Indies and participating in various activities—some of which were probably illegal—that would play a role in future novels of the sea. He also lost money at the casino in Monte Carlo, may have had an unhappy romance, and attempted suicide. Signing on to a British ship in 1878 to avoid conscription by the French (he had just turned twenty-one), Conrad visited England for the first time, knowing only a few words of English. He served for sixteen years on British merchant ships, earning his Master's Certificate in 1886 (the same year that he became a British subject) and learning English fast and well. Trips to the Far East and India gave him material for future novels, among them *The Nigger of the "Narcissus"* (1897) and *Typhoon* (1903), and two early novels set in Malaya, *Almayer's Folly* (1895) and *An Outcast of the Islands* (1896). For a long time, on the basis of these first works, Conrad was viewed as an exotic storyteller and a novelist of the sea. He turned his back on the sea as a profession when he married in 1896 and, buoyed by the publication of his first novel, chose writing as his career.

Among the various voyages that furnished material for his fiction, one stands out as the most intense, emotional, and subsequently controversial of them all: the trip up the Congo River that he made in 1890, straight into the heart of King Leopold's privately owned Congo Free State. Like many nineteenth-century explorers, Conrad was fascinated by the mystery of this dark (because uncharted by Europeans) continent, and he persuaded a relative to find him a job as pilot on a Belgian merchant steamer. Circumstances from then on are much as described by Marlow in *Heart of Darkness* (1899). The steamer that Conrad was supposed to pilot had been damaged, and while waiting for a replacement he was shifted to another one to help out and to learn about the river. This second trip is the journey recounted in *Heart of Darkness*: the boat traveled upstream to collect a seriously ill trader, Georges Antoine Klein (who died on the return trip), and Conrad, after speaking with Klein and observing the inhuman conditions imposed by slave labor and the ruthless search for ivory, returned seriously ill and traumatized by his journey. The experience marked him both physically and mentally. After a few years, he began to write about it with a moral rage that emerged openly at first and subsequently in more complex, ironic form. *An Outpost of Progress*. a harshly satirical story of two murderous incompetents in a jungle trading post, was published in 1897, and Conrad wrote *Heart of Darkness* two years later.

The "darkness" of the title is both a conventional metaphor for obscurity and evil, and a common cliché referring to Africa and the "unenlightened" state of its indigenous population. Leopold II of Belgium, who owned the trading company that effectively was the Congo Free State, gained a free hand in the area after calling an international conference in 1876 "to open to civilization the only part of our globe where Christianity has not penetrated and to pierce the darkness which envelops the entire population." Conrad plays on images of darkness and savagery throughout the novella and complicates any simple opposition by associating moral darkness, the evil that lurks in human beings and underlies their predatory idealism, with a white exterior, beginning with the town that is the headquarters of the Belgian firm and is described as a "whited sepulcher." It is not surprising, however, that Chinua Achebe should have criticized *Heart of Darkness* for its racist picture of Africans. Marlow's words and behavior—indeed, the selectivity of his narrative—are as distant and cruelly patronizing as those of any European colonialist. They constitute the background for the strange figure of Kurtz, the charismatic, once idealistic, and now totally corrupt trader whose report to the International Society for the Suppression of Savage Customs concludes seventeen pages of benevolent rhetoric with the scrawl "Exterminate all the brutes!" Marlow's strange bond with this soul gone mad stems initially from a desire to see a man described as a universal genius, an "emissary of pity, and science, and progress" and part of the "gang of virtue." It continues as a horrified fascination with someone who has explored moral extremes up to the end. Kurtz is, for Marlow, the "inconceivable mystery of a soul that knew no restraint," and his dying judgment—"The horror! The horror!"—encompasses a more than personal despair.

Heart of Darkness

1

The *Nellie*, a cruising yawl,[1] swung to her anchor without a flutter of the sails, and was at rest. The flood had made, the wind was nearly calm, and being bound down the river, the only thing for it was to come to and wait for the turn of the tide.

The sea-reach of the Thames stretched before us like the beginning of an interminable waterway. In the offing the sea and the sky were welded together without a joint, and in the luminous space the tanned sails of the barges drifting up with the tide seemed to stand still in red clusters of canvas sharply peaked, with gleams of varnished sprits. A haze rested on the low shores that ran out to sea in vanishing flatness. The air was dark above Gravesend,[2] and farther back still seemed condensed into a mournful gloom, brooding motionless over the biggest, and the greatest, town on earth.

The Director of Companies was our captain and our host. We four affectionately watched his back as he stood in the bows looking to seaward. On

---

1. A two-masted boat.   2. A port on the Thames River, the last major town in the estuary.

the whole river there was nothing that looked half so nautical. He resembled a pilot, which to a seaman is trustworthiness personified. It was difficult to realise his work was not out there in the luminous estuary, but behind him, within the brooding gloom.

Between us there was, as I have already said somewhere, the bond of the sea. Besides holding our hearts together through long periods of separation, it had the effect of making us tolerant of each other's yarns—and even convictions. The Lawyer—the best of old fellows—had, because of his many years and many virtues, the only cushion on deck, and was lying on the only rug. The Accountant had brought out already a box of dominoes, and was toying architecturally with the bones. Marlow sat cross-legged right aft, leaning against the mizzenmast. He had sunken cheeks, a yellow complexion, a straight back, an ascetic aspect, and, with his arms dropped, the palms of hands outwards, resembled an idol. The Director, satisfied the anchor had good hold, made his way aft and sat down amongst us. We exchanged a few words lazily. Afterwards there was silence on board the yacht. For some reason or other we did not begin that game of dominoes. We felt meditative, and fit for nothing but placid staring. The day was ending in a serenity of still and exquisite brilliance. The water shone pacifically; the sky, without a speck, was a benign immensity of unstained light; the very mist on the Essex marshes was like a gauzy and radiant fabric, hung from the wooded rises inland, and draping the low shores in diaphanous folds. Only the gloom to the west, brooding over the upper reaches, became more sombre every minute, as if angered by the approach of the sun.

And at last, in its curved and imperceptible fall, the sun sank low, and from glowing white changed to a dull red without rays and without heat, as if about to go out suddenly, stricken to death by the touch of that gloom brooding over a crowd of men.

Forthwith a change came over the waters, and the serenity became less brilliant but more profound. The old river in its broad reach rested unruffled at the decline of day, after ages of good service done to the race that peopled its banks, spread out in the tranquil dignity of a waterway leading to the uttermost ends of the earth. We looked at the venerable stream not in the vivid flush of a short day that comes and departs for ever, but in the august light of abiding memories. And indeed nothing is easier for a man who has, as the phrase goes, "followed the sea" with reverence and affection, than to evoke the great spirit of the past upon the lower reaches of the Thames. The tidal current runs to and fro in its unceasing service, crowded with memories of men and ships it has borne to the rest of home or to the battles of the sea. It had known and served all the men of whom the nation is proud, from Sir Francis Drake to Sir John Franklin, knights all, titled and untitled—the great knights-errant of the sea. It had borne all the ships whose names are like jewels flashing in the night of time, from the *Golden Hind* returning with her round flanks full of treasure, to be visited by the Queen's Highness and thus pass out of the gigantic tale, to the *Erebus* and *Terror*,[3] bound on other conquests—and that never returned. It had known the ships and the men. They had sailed from Deptford, from Greenwich, from Erith—the

3. The *Erebus* and the *Terror* were ships commanded by Arctic explorer Sir John Franklin (1786–1847) and lost in an attempt to find a passage from the Atlantic Ocean to the Pacific. *Golden Hind:* the ship that Elizabethan explorer Sir Francis Drake (1540–1596) used to sail around the world.

adventurers and the settlers; kings' ships and the ships of men on 'Change; captains, admirals, the dark "interlopers"[4] of the Eastern trade, and the commissioned "generals" of East India fleets. Hunters for gold or pursuers of fame, they all had gone out on that stream, bearing the sword, and often the torch, messengers of the might within the land, bearers of a spark from the sacred fire. What greatness had not floated on the ebb of that river into the mystery of an unknown earth! . . . The dreams of men, the seed of commonwealths, the germs of empires.

The sun set; the dusk fell on the stream, and lights began to appear along the shore. The Chapman lighthouse, a three-legged thing erect on a mudflat, shone strongly. Lights of ships moved in the fairway—a great stir of lights going up and going down. And farther west on the upper reaches the place of the monstrous town was still marked ominously on the sky, a brooding gloom in sunshine, a lurid glare under the stars.

"And this also," said Marlow suddenly, "has been one of the dark places of the earth."

He was the only man of us who still "followed the sea." The worst that could be said of him was that he did not represent his class. He was a seaman, but he was a wanderer too, while most seamen lead, if one may so express it, a sedentary life. Their minds are of the stay-at-home order, and their home is always with them—the ship; and so is their country—the sea. One ship is very much like another, and the sea is always the same. In the immutability of their surroundings the foreign shores, the foreign faces, the changing immensity of life, glide past, veiled not by a sense of mystery but by a slightly disdainful ignorance; for there is nothing mysterious to a seaman unless it be the sea itself, which is the mistress of his existence and as inscrutable as Destiny. For the rest, after his hours of work, a casual stroll or a casual spree on shore suffices to unfold for him the secret of a whole continent, and generally he finds the secret not worth knowing. The yarns of seamen have a direct simplicity, the whole meaning of which lies within the shell of a cracked nut. But Marlow was not typical (if his propensity to spin yarns be excepted), and to him the meaning of an episode was not inside like a kernel but outside, enveloping the tale which brought it out only as a glow brings out a haze, in the likeness of one of these misty halos that sometimes are made visible by the spectral illumination of moonshine.

His remark did not seem at all surprising. It was just like Marlow. It was accepted in silence. No one took the trouble to grunt even; and presently he said, very slow:

"I was thinking of very old times, when the Romans first came here, nineteen hundred years ago—the other day. . . . Light came out of this river since—you say Knights? Yes; but it is like a running blaze on a plain, like a flash of lightning in the clouds. We live in the flicker—may it last as long as the old earth keeps rolling! But darkness was here yesterday. Imagine the feelings of a commander of a fine—what d'ye call 'em?—trireme[5] in the Mediterranean, ordered suddenly to the north; run overland across the Gauls in a hurry; put in charge of one of these craft the legionaries—a wonderful lot of handy men they must have been too—used to build, apparently by the

---

4. Private ships intruding on the East India Company's monopoly of trade. *Deptford, Greenwich, Erith:* ports on the Thames between London and Gravesend. '*Change:* the stock exchange.   5. A Roman galley with three banks of oars.

hundred, in a month or two, if we may believe what we read. Imagine him here—the very end of the world, a sea the colour of lead, a sky the colour of smoke, a kind of ship about as rigid as a concertina—and going up this river with stores, or orders, or what you like. Sandbanks, marshes, forests, savages—precious little to eat fit for a civilised man, nothing but Thames water to drink. No Falernian wine[6] here, no going ashore. Here and there a military camp lost in a wilderness, like a needle in a bundle of hay—cold, fog, tempests, disease, exile, and death—death skulking in the air, in the water, in the bush. They must have been dying like flies here. Oh yes—he did it. Did it very well, too, no doubt, and without thinking much about it either, except afterwards to brag of what he had gone through in his time, perhaps. They were men enough to face the darkness. And perhaps he was cheered by keeping his eye on a chance of promotion to the fleet at Ravenna[7] by and by, if he had good friends in Rome and survived the awful climate. Or think of a decent young citizen in a toga—perhaps too much dice, you know—coming out here in the train of some prefect, or tax-gatherer, or trader, even, to mend his fortunes. Land in a swamp, march through the woods, and in some inland post feel the savagery, the utter savagery, had closed round him—all that mysterious life of the wilderness that stirs in the forest, in the jungles, in the hearts of wild men. There's no initiation either into such mysteries. He has to live in the midst of the incomprehensible, which is also detestable. And it has a fascination, too, that goes to work upon him. The fascination of the abomination—you know. Imagine the growing regrets, the longing to escape, the powerless disgust, the surrender, the hate."

He paused.

"Mind," he began again, lifting one arm from the elbow, the palm of the hand outwards, so that, with his legs folded before him, he had the pose of a Buddha preaching in European clothes and without a lotus-flower—"Mind, none of us would feel exactly like this. What saves us is efficiency—the devotion to efficiency. But these chaps were not much account, really. They were no colonists; their administration was merely a squeeze, and nothing more, I suspect. They were conquerors, and for that you want only brute force—nothing to boast of, when you have it, since your strength is just an accident arising from the weakness of others. They grabbed what they could get for the sake of what was to be got. It was just robbery with violence, aggravated murder on a great scale, and men going at it blind—as is very proper for those who tackle a darkness. The conquest of the earth, which mostly means the taking it away from those who have a different complexion or slightly flatter noses than ourselves, is not a pretty thing when you look into it too much. What redeems it is the idea only. An idea at the back of it; not a sentimental pretence but an idea; and an unselfish belief in the idea—something you can set up, and bow down before, and offer a sacrifice to. . . ."

He broke off. Flames glided in the river, small green flames, red flames, white flames, pursuing, overtaking, joining, crossing each other—then separating slowly or hastily. The traffic of the great city went on in the deepening night upon the sleepless river. We looked on, waiting patiently—there was nothing else to do till the end of the flood; but it was only after a long silence, when he said, in a hesitating voice, "I suppose you fellows remember I did

6. Wine from a famous wine-making district in southern Italy.   7. Once a major Roman port on the Adriatic Sea.

once turn fresh-water sailor for a bit," that we knew we were fated, before the ebb began to run, to hear about one of Marlow's inconclusive experiences.

"I don't want to bother you much with what happened to me personally," he began, showing in this remark the weakness of many tellers of tales who seem so often unaware of what their audience would best like to hear; "yet to understand the effect of it on me you ought to know how I got out there, what I saw, how I went up that river to the place where I first met the poor chap. It was the farthest point of navigation and the culminating point of my experience. It seemed somehow to throw a kind of light on everything about me—and into my thoughts. It was sombre enough too—and pitiful—not extraordinary in any way—not very clear either. No, not very clear. And yet it seemed to throw a kind of light.

"I had then, as you remember, just returned to London after a lot of Indian Ocean, Pacific, China Seas—a regular dose of the East—six years or so, and I was loafing about, hindering you fellows in your work and invading your homes, just as though I had got a heavenly mission to civilise you. It was very fine for a time, but after a bit I did get tired of resting. Then I began to look for a ship—I should think the hardest work on earth. But the ships wouldn't even look at me. And I got tired of that game too.

"Now when I was a little chap I had a passion for maps. I would look for hours at South America, or Africa, or Australia, and lose myself in all the glories of exploration. At that time there were many blank spaces on the earth, and when I saw one that looked particularly inviting on a map (but they all look that) I would put my finger on it and say, When I grow up I will go there. The North Pole was one of these places, I remember. Well, I haven't been there yet, and shall not try now. The glamour's off. Other places were scattered about the Equator, and in every sort of latitude all over the two hemispheres. I have been in some of them, and . . . well, we won't talk about that. But there was one yet—the biggest, the most blank, so to speak—that I had a hankering after.

"True, by this time it was not a blank space any more. It had got filled since my boyhood with rivers and lakes and names. It had ceased to be a blank space of delightful mystery—a white patch for a boy to dream gloriously over. It had become a place of darkness. But there was in it one river especially, a mighty big river, that you could see on the map, resembling an immense snake uncoiled, with its head in the sea, its body at rest curving afar over a vast country, and its tail lost in the depths of the land. And as I looked at the map of it in a shop-window, it fascinated me as a snake would a bird—a silly little bird. Then I remembered there was a big concern, a Company for trade on that river. Dash it all! I thought to myself, they can't trade without using some kind of craft on that lot of fresh water—steamboats! Why shouldn't I try to get charge of one? I went on along Fleet Street,[8] but could not shake off the idea. The snake had charmed me.

"You understand it was a Continental concern, that Trading Society;[9] but I have a lot of relations living on the Continent, because it's cheap and not so nasty as it looks, they say.

"I am sorry to own I began to worry them. This was already a fresh depar-

---

8. A major street in central London, famous as a publishing headquarter. 9. The trading company—specifically, a Belgian company that operated ships on the Congo River in the protectorate of King Leopold II of Belgium.

ture for me. I was not used to get things that way, you know. I always went my own road and on my own legs where I had a mind to go. I wouldn't have believed it of myself; but, then—you see—I felt somehow I must get there by hook or by crook. So I worried them. The men said, 'My dear fellow,' and did nothing. Then—would you believe it?—I tried the women. I, Charlie Marlow, set the women to work—to get a job. Heavens! Well, you see, the notion drove me. I had an aunt, a dear enthusiastic soul. She wrote: 'It will be delightful. I am ready to do anything, anything for you. It is a glorious idea. I know the wife of a very high personage in the Administration, and also a man who has lots of influence with,' etc. etc. She was determined to make no end of fuss to get me appointed skipper of a river steamboat, if such was my fancy.

"I got my appointment—of course; and I got it very quick. It appears the Company had received news that one of their captains had been killed in a scuffle with the natives. This was my chance, and it made me the more anxious to go. It was only months and months afterwards, when I made the attempt to recover what was left of the body, that I heard the original quarrel arose from a misunderstanding about some hens. Yes, two black hens. Fresleven—that was the fellow's name, a Dane—thought himself wronged somehow in the bargain, so he went ashore and started to hammer the chief of the village with a stick. Oh, it didn't surprise me in the least to hear this, and at the same time to be told that Fresleven was the gentlest, quietest creature that ever walked on two legs. No doubt he was; but he had been a couple of years already out there engaged in the noble cause, you know, and he probably felt the need at last of asserting his self-respect in some way. Therefore he whacked the old nigger mercilessly, while a big crowd of his people watched him, thunderstruck, till some man—I was told the chief's son—in desperation at hearing the old chap yell, made a tentative jab with a spear at the white man—and of course it went quite easy between the shoulder-blades. Then the whole population cleared into the forest, expecting all kinds of calamities to happen, while, on the other hand, the steamer Fresleven commanded left also in a bad panic, in charge of the engineer, I believe. Afterwards nobody seemed to trouble much about Fresleven's remains, till I got out and stepped into his shoes. I couldn't let it rest, though; but when an opportunity offered at last to meet my predecessor, the grass growing through his ribs was tall enough to hide his bones. They were all there. The supernatural being had not been touched after he fell. And the village was deserted, the huts gaped black, rotting, all askew within the fallen enclosures. A calamity had come to it, sure enough. The people had vanished. Mad terror had scattered them, men, women, and children, through the bush, and they had never returned. What became of the hens I don't know either. I should think the cause of progress got them, anyhow. However, through this glorious affair I got my appointment, before I had fairly begun to hope for it.

"I flew around like mad to get ready, and before forty-eight hours I was crossing the Channel to show myself to my employers, and sign the contract. In a very few hours I arrived in a city that always makes me think of a whited sepulchre. Prejudice no doubt. I had no difficulty in finding the Company's offices. It was the biggest thing in the town, and everybody I met was full of it. They were going to run an oversea empire, and make no end of coin by trade.

"A narrow and deserted street in deep shadow, high houses, innumerable windows with venetian blinds, a dead silence, grass sprouting between the stones, imposing carriage archways right and left, immense double doors standing ponderously ajar. I slipped through one of these cracks, went up a swept and ungarnished staircase, as arid as a desert, and opened the first door I came to. Two women, one fat and the other slim, sat on straw-bottomed chairs, knitting black wool. The slim one got up and walked straight at me—still knitting with downcast eyes—and only just as I began to think of getting out of her way, as you would for a somnambulist, stood still, and looked up. Her dress was as plain as an umbrella-cover, and she turned round without a word and preceded me into a waiting-room. I gave my name, and looked about. Deal table in the middle, plain chairs all round the walls, on one end a large shining map, marked with all the colours of a rainbow. There was a vast amount of red—good to see at any time, because one knows that some real work is done in there, a deuce of a lot of blue, a little green, smears of orange, and, on the East Coast, a purple patch, to show where the jolly pioneers of progress drink the jolly lager-beer. However, I wasn't going into any of these. I was going into the yellow. Dead in the centre. And the river was there—fascinating—deadly—like a snake. Ough! A door opened, a white-haired secretarial head, but wearing a compassionate expression, appeared, and a skinny forefinger beckoned me into the sanctuary. Its light was dim, and a heavy writing desk squatted in the middle. From behind that structure came out an impression of pale plumpness in a frockcoat. The great man himself. He was five feet six, I should judge, and had his grip on the handle-end of ever so many millions. He shook hands, I fancy, murmured vaguely, was satisfied with my French. *Bon voyage.*

"In about forty-five seconds I found myself again in the waiting-room with the compassionate secretary, who, full of desolation and sympathy, made me sign some document. I believe I undertook amongst other things not to disclose any trade secrets. Well, I am not going to.

"I began to feel slightly uneasy. You know I am not used to such ceremonies, and there was something ominous in the atmosphere. It was just as though I had been let into some conspiracy—I don't know—something not quite right; and I was glad to get out. In the outer room the two women knitted black wool feverishly. People were arriving, and the younger one was walking back and forth introducing them. The old one sat on her chair. Her flat cloth slippers were propped up on a foot-warmer, and a cat reposed on her lap. She wore a starched white affair on her head, had a wart on one cheek, and silver-rimmed spectacles hung on the tip of her nose. She glanced at me above the glasses. The swift and indifferent placidity of that look troubled me. Two youths with foolish and cheery countenances were being piloted over, and she threw at them the same quick glance of unconcerned wisdom. She seemed to know all about them and about me too. An eerie feeling came over me. She seemed uncanny and fateful. Often far away there I thought of these two, guarding the door of Darkness, knitting black wool as for a warm pall, one introducing, introducing continuously to the unknown, the other scrutinising the cheery and foolish faces with unconcerned old eyes. *Ave!* Old knitter of black wool. *Morituri te salutant.*[1] Not

1. "Those who are about to die salute you" (Latin): the greeting of gladiators to the Roman emperor before beginning combat in the arena.

many of those she looked at ever saw her again—not half, by a long way.

"There was yet a visit to the doctor. 'A simple formality,' assured me the secretary, with an air of taking an immense part in all my sorrows. Accordingly a young chap wearing his hat over the left eyebrow, some clerk I suppose—there must have been clerks in the business, though the house was as still as a house in a city of the dead—came from somewhere upstairs, and led me forth. He was shabby and careless, with ink-stains on the sleeves of his jacket, and his cravat was large and billowy, under a chin shaped like the toe of an old boot. It was a little too early for the doctor, so I proposed a drink, and thereupon he developed a vein of joviality. As we sat over our vermuths he glorified the Company's business, and by and by I expressed casually my surprise at him not going out there. He became very cool and collected all at once. 'I am not such a fool as I look, quoth Plato to his disciples,' he said sententiously, emptied his glass with great resolution, and we rose.

"The old doctor felt my pulse, evidently thinking of something else the while. 'Good, good for there,' he mumbled, and then with a certain eagerness asked me whether I would let him measure my head. Rather surprised, I said Yes, when he produced a thing like callipers and got the dimensions back and front and every way, taking notes carefully. He was an unshaven little man in a threadbare coat like a gaberdine, with his feet in slippers, and I thought him a harmless fool. 'I always ask leave, in the interests of science, to measure the crania of those going out there,' he said. 'And when they come back too?' I asked. 'Oh, I never see them,' he remarked; 'and, moreover, the changes take place inside, you know.' He smiled, as if at some quiet joke. 'So you are going out there. Famous. Interesting too.' He gave me a searching glance, and made another note. 'Ever any madness in your family?' he asked, in a matter-of-fact tone. I felt very annoyed. 'Is that question in the interests of science too?' 'It would be,' he said, without taking notice of my irritation, 'interesting for science to watch the mental changes of individuals, on the spot, but . . . ' 'Are you an alienist?' I interrupted. 'Every doctor should be—a little,' answered that original[2] imperturbably. 'I have a little theory which you Messieurs who go out there must help me to prove. This is my share in the advantages my country shall reap from the possession of such a magnificent dependency. The mere wealth I leave to others. Pardon my questions, but you are the first Englishman coming under my observation . . . ' I hastened to assure him I was not in the least typical. 'If I were,' said I, 'I wouldn't be talking like this with you.' 'What you say is rather profound, and probably erroneous,' he said, with a laugh. 'Avoid irritation more than exposure to the sun. Adieu. How do you English say, eh? Good-bye. Ah! Good-bye. Adieu. In the tropics one must before everything keep calm.' . . . He lifted a warning forefinger. . . . '*Du calme, du calme. Adieu.*'[3]

"One thing more remained to do—say good-bye to my excellent aunt. I found her triumphant. I had a cup of tea—the last decent cup of tea for many days—and in a room that most soothingly looked just as you would expect a lady's drawing-room to look, we had a long quiet chat by the fireside. In the course of these confidences it became quite plain to me I had been

---

2. Unusual or eccentric person. *Alienist:* an early term for a psychiatrist. 3. "Be calm, be calm. Good-bye" (French).

represented to the wife of the high dignitary, and goodness knows to how many more people besides, as an exceptional and gifted creature—a piece of good fortune for the Company—a man you don't get hold of every day. Good heavens! and I was going to take charge of a two-penny-halfpenny river-steamboat with a penny whistle attached! It appeared, however, I was also one of the Workers, with a capital—you know. Something like an emissary of light, something like a lower sort of apostle. There had been a lot of such rot let loose in print and talk just about that time, and the excellent woman, living right in the rush of all that humbug, got carried off her feet. She talked about 'weaning those ignorant millions from their horrid ways,' till, upon my word, she made me quite uncomfortable. I ventured to hint that the Company was run for profit.

" 'You forget, dear Charlie, that the labourer is worthy of his hire,' she said brightly. It's queer how out of touch with truth women are. They live in a world of their own, and there had never been anything like it, and never can be. It is too beautiful altogether, and if they were to set it up it would go to pieces before the first sunset. Some confounded fact we men have been living contentedly with ever since the day of creation would start up and knock the whole thing over.

"After this I got embraced, told to wear flannel, be sure to write often, and so on—and I left. In the street—I don't know why—a queer feeling came to me that I was an impostor. Odd thing that I, who used to clear out for any part of the world at twenty-four hours' notice, with less thought than most men give to the crossing of a street, had a moment—I won't say of hesitation, but of startled pause, before this commonplace affair. The best way I can explain it to you is by saying that, for a second or two, I felt as though, instead of going to the centre of a continent, I were about to set off for the centre of the earth.

"I left in a French steamer, and she called in every blamed port they have out there, for, as far as I could see, the sole purpose of landing soldiers and custom-house officers. I watched the coast. Watching a coast as it slips by the ship is like thinking about an enigma. There it is before you—smiling, frowning, inviting, grand, mean, insipid, or savage, and always mute with an air of whispering, Come and find out. This one was almost featureless, as if still in the making, with an aspect of monotonous grimness. The edge of a colossal jungle, so dark green as to be almost black, fringed with white surf, ran straight, like a ruled line, far, far away along a blue sea whose glitter was blurred by a creeping mist. The sun was fierce, the land seemed to glisten and drip with steam. Here and there greyish-whitish specks showed up clustered inside the white surf, with a flag flying above them perhaps—settlements some centuries old, and still no bigger than pin-heads on the untouched expanse of their background. We pounded along, stopped, landed soldiers; went on, landed custom-house clerks to levy toll in what looked like a God-forsaken wilderness, with a tin shed and a flag-pole lost in it; landed more soldiers—to take care of the custom-house clerks presumably. Some, I heard, got drowned in the surf; but whether they did or not, nobody seemed particularly to care. They were just flung out there, and on we went. Every day the coast looked the same, as though we had not moved; but we passed various places—trading places—with names like Gran' Bassam, Little Popo; names that seemed to belong to some sordid farce acted in front of a sinister back-cloth. The idleness of a passenger, my isolation amongst all these men with whom I had no point of contact, the oily and languid sea, the uniform sombreness of the coast, seemed to keep me away from the truth of things, within the toil of a mournful and senseless delusion. The voice of the surf heard now and then was a positive pleasure, like the speech of a brother. It was something natural, that had its reason, that had a meaning. Now and then a boat from the shore gave one a momentary contact with reality. It was paddled by black fellows. You could see from afar the white of their eyeballs glistening. They shouted, sang; their bodies streamed with perspiration; they had faces like grotesque masks—these chaps; but they had bone, muscle, a wild vitality, an intense energy of movement, that was as natural and true as the surf along their coast. They wanted no excuse for being there. They were a great comfort to look at. For a time I would feel I belonged still to a world of straightforward facts; but the feeling would not last long. Something would turn up to scare it away. Once, I remember, we came upon a man-of-war anchored off the coast. There wasn't even a shed there, and she was shelling the bush. It appears the French had one of their wars going on thereabouts. Her ensign dropped limp like a rag; the muzzles of the long six-inch guns stuck out all over the low hull; the greasy, slimy swell swung her up lazily and let her down, swaying her thin masts. In the empty immensity of earth, sky, and water, there she was, incomprehensible, firing into a continent. Pop, would go one of the six-inch guns; a small flame would dart and vanish, a little white smoke would disappear, a tiny projectile would give a feeble screech—and nothing happened. Nothing could happen. There was a touch of insanity in the proceeding, a sense of lugubrious drollery in the sight; and it was not dissipated by somebody on board assuring me earnestly there was a camp of natives—he called them enemies!—hidden out of sight somewhere.

"We gave her her letters (I heard the men in that lonely ship were dying of fever at the rate of three a day) and went on. We called at some more places with farcical names, where the merry dance of death and trade goes on in a still and earthy atmosphere as of an overheated catacomb; all along the formless coast bordered by dangerous surf, as if Nature herself had tried to ward off intruders; in and out of rivers, streams of death in life, whose banks were rotting into mud, whose waters, thickened into slime, invaded the contorted mangroves, that seemed to writhe at us in the extremity of an impotent despair. Nowhere did we stop long enough to get a particularised impression, but the general sense of vague and oppressive wonder grew upon me. It was like a weary pilgrimage amongst hints for nightmares.

"It was upward of thirty days before I saw the mouth of the big river. We anchored off the seat of the government. But my work would not begin till some two hundred miles farther on. So as soon as I could I made a start for a place thirty miles higher up.

"I had my passage on a little sea-going steamer. Her captain was a Swede, and knowing me for a seaman, invited me on the bridge. He was a young man, lean, fair, and morose, with lanky hair and a shuffling gait. As we left the miserable little wharf, he tossed his head contemptuously at the shore. 'Been living there?' he asked. I said, 'Yes.' 'Fine lot these government chaps—are they not?' he went on, speaking English with great precision and considerable bitterness. 'It is funny what some people will do for a few francs a month. I wonder what becomes of that kind when it goes up country?' I said to him I expected to see that soon. 'So-o-o!' he exclaimed. He shuffled athwart, keeping one eye ahead vigilantly. 'Don't be too sure,' he continued. 'The other day I took up a man who hanged himself on the road. He was a Swede, too.' 'Hanged himself! Why, in God's name?' I cried. He kept on looking out watchfully. 'Who knows? The sun too much for him, or the country perhaps.'

"At last we opened a reach. A rocky cliff appeared, mounds of turned-up earth by the shore, houses on a hill, others with iron roofs, amongst a waste of excavations, or hanging to the declivity. A continuous noise of the rapids above hovered over this scene of inhabited devastation. A lot of people, mostly black and naked, moved about like ants. A jetty projected into the river. A blinding sunlight drowned all this at times in a sudden recrudescence of glare. 'There's your Company's station,' said the Swede, pointing to three wooden barrack-like structures on the rocky slope. 'I will send your things up. Four boxes did you say? So. Farewell.'

"I came upon a boiler wallowing in the grass, then found a path leading up the hill. It turned aside for the boulders, and also for an undersized railway truck lying there on its back with its wheels in the air. One was off. The thing looked as dead as the carcass of some animal. I came upon more pieces of decaying machinery, a stack of rusty nails. To the left a clump of trees made a shady spot, where dark things seemed to stir feebly. I blinked, the path was steep. A horn tooted to the right, and I saw the black people run. A heavy and dull detonation shook the ground, a puff of smoke came out of the cliff, and that was all. No change appeared on the face of the rock. They were building a railway. The cliff was not in the way or anything; but this objectless blasting was all the work going on.

"A slight clinking behind me made me turn my head. Six black men advanced in a file, toiling up the path. They walked erect and slow, balancing small baskets full of earth on their heads, and the clink kept time with their footsteps. Black rags were wound round their loins, and the short ends behind waggled to and fro like tails. I could see every rib, the joints of their limbs were like knots in a rope; each had an iron collar on his neck, and all were connected together with a chain whose bights swung between them, rhythmically clinking. Another report from the cliff made me think suddenly of that ship of war I had seen firing into a continent. It was the same kind of ominous voice; but these men could by no stretch of imagination be called enemies. They were called criminals, and the outraged law, like the bursting shells, had come to them, an insoluble mystery from the sea. All their meagre breasts panted together, the violently dilated nostrils quivered, the eyes stared stonily uphill. They passed me within six inches, without a glance, with that complete, deathlike indifference of unhappy savages. Behind this raw matter one of the reclaimed, the product of the new forces at work, strolled despondently, carrying a rifle by its middle. He had a uniform jacket with one button off, and seeing a white man on the path, hoisted his weapon to his shoulder with alacrity. This was simple prudence, white men being so much alike at a distance that he could not tell who I might be. He was speedily reassured, and with a large, white, rascally grin, and a glance at his charge, seemed to take me into partnership in his exalted trust. After all, I also was a part of the great cause of these high and just proceedings.

"Instead of going up, I turned and descended to the left. My idea was to let that chain-gang get out of sight before I climbed the hill. You know I am not particularly tender; I've had to strike and to fend off. I've had to resist and to attack sometimes—that's only one way of resisting—without counting the exact cost, according to the demands of such sort of life as I had blundered into. I've seen the devil of violence, and the devil of greed, and the devil of hot desire; but, by all the stars! these were strong, lusty, red-eyed devils, that swayed and drove men—men, I tell you. But as I stood on this hillside, I foresaw that in the blinding sunshine of that land I would become acquainted with a flabby, pretending, weak-eyed devil of a rapacious and pitiless folly. How insidious he could be, too, I was only to find out several months later and a thousand miles farther. For a moment I stood appalled, as though by a warning. Finally I descended the hill, obliquely, towards the trees I had seen.

"I avoided a vast artificial hole somebody had been digging on the slope, the purpose of which I found it impossible to divine. It wasn't a quarry or a sandpit, anyhow. It was just a hole. It might have been connected with the philanthropic desire of giving the criminals something to do. I don't know. Then I nearly fell into a very narrow ravine, almost no more than a scar in the hillside. I discovered that a lot of imported drainage-pipes for the settlement had been tumbled in there. There wasn't one that was not broken. It was a wanton smash-up. At last I got under the trees. My purpose was to stroll into the shade for a moment; but no sooner within than it seemed to me I had stepped into the gloomy circle of some Inferno. The rapids were near, and an uninterrupted, uniform, headlong, rushing noise filled the mournful stillness of the grove, where not a breath stirred, not a leaf moved, with a mysterious sound—as though the tearing pace of the launched earth had suddenly become audible.

"Black shapes crouched, lay, sat between the trees, leaning against the trunks, clinging to the earth, half coming out, half effaced within the dim light, in all the attitudes of pain, abandonment, and despair. Another mine[4] on the cliff went off, followed by a slight shudder of the soil under my feet. The work was going on. The work! And this was the place where some of the helpers had withdrawn to die.

"They were dying slowly—it was very clear. They were not enemies, they were not criminals, they were nothing earthly now—nothing but black shadows of disease and starvation, lying confusedly in the greenish gloom. Brought from all the recesses of the coast in all the legality of time contracts, lost in uncongenial surroundings, fed on unfamiliar food, they sickened, became inefficient, and were then allowed to crawl away and rest. These moribund shapes were free as air—and nearly as thin. I began to distinguish the gleam of eyes under the trees. Then, glancing down, I saw a face near my hand. The black bones reclined at full length with one shoulder against the tree, and slowly the eyelids rose and the sunken eyes looked up at me, enormous and vacant, a kind of blind, white flicker in the depths of the orbs, which died out slowly. The man seemed young—almost a boy—but you know with them it's hard to tell. I found nothing else to do but to offer him one of my good Swede's ship's biscuits I had in my pocket. The fingers closed slowly

4. Explosive charge.

on it and held—there was no other movement and no other glance. He had tied a bit of white worsted[5] round his neck—Why? Where did he get it? Was it a badge—an ornament—a charm—a propitiatory act? Was there any idea at all connected with it? It looked startling round his black neck, this bit of white thread from beyond the seas.

"Near the same tree two more bundles of acute angles sat with their legs drawn up. One, with his chin propped on his knees, stared at nothing, in an intolerable and appalling manner: his brother phantom rested its forehead, as if overcome with a great weariness; and all about others were scattered in every pose of contorted collapse, as in some picture of a massacre or a pestilence. While I stood horror-struck, one of these creatures rose to his hands and knees, and went off on all-fours towards the river to drink. He lapped out of his hand, then sat up in the sunlight, crossing his shins in front of him, and after a time let his woolly head fall on his breastbone.

"I didn't want any more loitering in the shade, and I made haste towards the station. When near the buildings I met a white man, in such an unexpected elegance of get-up that in the first moment I took him for a sort of vision. I saw a high starched collar, white cuffs, a light alpaca[6] jacket, snowy trousers, a clear necktie, and varnished boots. No hat. Hair parted, brushed, oiled, under a green-lined parasol held in a big white hand. He was amazing, and had a penholder behind his ear.

"I shook hands with this miracle, and I learned he was the Company's chief accountant, and that all the book-keeping was done at this station. He had come out for a moment, he said, 'to get a breath of fresh air.' The expression sounded wonderfully odd, with its suggestion of sedentary desk-life. I wouldn't have mentioned the fellow to you at all, only it was from his lips that I first heard the name of the man who is so indissolubly connected with the memories of that time. Moreover, I respected the fellow. Yes; I respected his collars, his vast cuffs, his brushed hair. His appearance was certainly that of a hairdresser's dummy; but in the great demoralisation of the land he kept up his appearance. That's backbone. His starched collars and got-up shirt-fronts were achievements of character. He had been out nearly three years; and, later, I could not help asking him how he managed to sport such linen. He had just the faintest blush, and said modestly, 'I've been teaching one of the native women about the station. It was difficult. She had a distaste for the work.' Thus this man had verily accomplished something. And he was devoted to his books, which were in apple-pie order.

"Everything else in the station was in a muddle,—heads, things, buildings. Strings of dusty niggers with splay feet arrived and departed; a stream of manufactured goods, rubbishy cottons, beads, and brass-wire sent into the depths of darkness, and in return came a precious trickle of ivory.

"I had to wait in the station for ten days—an eternity. I lived in a hut in the yard, but to be out of the chaos I would sometimes get into the accountant's office. It was built of horizontal planks, and so badly put together that, as he bent over his high desk, he was barred from neck to heels with narrow strips of sunlight. There was no need to open the big shutter to see. It was hot there too; big flies buzzed fiendishly, and did not sting, but stabbed. I sat generally on the floor, while, of faultless appearance (and even slightly

5. Wool fabric.   6. An expensive fine wool that comes from a South American animal of the same name.

scented), perching on a high stool, he wrote, he wrote. Sometimes he stood up for exercise. When a truckle-bed[7] with a sick man (some invalided agent from up country) was put in there, he exhibited a gentle annoyance. 'The groans of this sick person' he said, 'distract my attention. And without that it is extremely difficult to guard against clerical errors in this climate.'

"One day he remarked, without lifting his head, 'In the interior you will no doubt meet Mr Kurtz.' On my asking who Mr Kurtz was, he said he was a first-class agent; and seeing my disappointment at this information, he added slowly, laying down his pen, 'He is a very remarkable person.' Further questions elicited from him that Mr Kurtz was at present in charge of a trading-post, a very important one, in the true ivory-country, at 'the very bottom of there. Sends in as much ivory as all the others put together . . .' He began to write again. The sick man was too ill to groan. The flies buzzed in a great peace.

"Suddenly there was a growing murmur of voices and a great tramping of feet. A caravan had come in. A violent babble of uncouth sounds burst out on the other side of the planks. All the carriers were speaking together, and in the midst of the uproar the lamentable voice of the chief agent was heard 'giving it up' tearfully for the twentieth time that day. . . . He rose slowly. 'What a frightful row,' he said. He crossed the room gently to look at the sick man, and returning, said to me, 'He does not hear.' 'What! Dead?' I asked, startled. 'No, not yet,' he answered, with great composure. Then, alluding with a toss of the head to the tumult in the station-yard, 'When one has got to make correct entries, one comes to hate those savages—hate them to the death.' He remained thoughtful for a moment. 'When you see Mr Kurtz,' he went on, 'tell him from me that everything here'—he glanced at the desk—'is very satisfactory. I don't like to write to him—with those messengers of ours you never know who may get hold of your letter—at that Central Station.' He stared at me for a moment with his mild, bulging eyes. 'Oh, he will go far, very far,' he began again. 'He will be a somebody in the Administration before long. They, above—the Council in Europe, you know—mean him to be.'

"He turned to his work. The noise outside had ceased, and presently in going out I stopped at the door. In the steady buzz of flies the homeward-bound agent was lying flushed and insensible; the other, bent over his books, was making correct entries of perfectly correct transactions; and fifty feet below the doorstep I could see the still tree-tops of the grove of death.

"Next day I left that station at last, with a caravan of sixty men, for a two-hundred-mile tramp.

"No use telling you much about that. Paths, paths, everywhere; a stamped-in network of paths spreading over the empty land, through long grass, through burnt grass, through thickets, down and up chilly ravines, up and down stony hills ablaze with heat; and a solitude, a solitude, nobody, not a hut. The population had cleared out a long time ago. Well, if a lot of mysterious niggers armed with all kinds of fearful weapons suddenly took to travelling on the road between Deal and Gravesend, catching the yokels right and left to carry heavy loads for them, I fancy every farm and cottage

---

7. I.e., trundle bed, a low portable bed that is on castors and that may be slid under a higher bed when it is not being used.

thereabouts would get empty very soon. Only here the dwellings were gone too. Still, I passed through several abandoned villages. There's something pathetically childish in the ruins of grass walls. Day after day, with the stamp and shuffle of sixty pair of bare feet behind me, each pair under a 60-lb. load. Camp, cook, sleep, strike camp, march. Now and then a carrier dead in harness, at rest in the long grass near the path, with an empty water-gourd and his long staff lying by his side. A great silence around and above. Perhaps on some quiet night the tremor of far-off drums, sinking, swelling, a tremor vast, faint; a sound weird, appealing, suggestive, and wild—and perhaps with as profound a meaning as the sound of bells in a Christian country. Once a white man in an unbuttoned uniform, camping on the path with an armed escort of lank Zanzibaris,[8] very hospitable and festive—not to say drunk. Was looking after the upkeep of the road, he declared. Can't say I saw any road or any upkeep, unless the body of a middle-aged negro, with a bullet-hole in the forehead, upon which I absolutely stumbled three miles farther on, may be considered as a permanent improvement. I had a white companion too, not a bad chap, but rather too fleshy and with the exasperating habit of fainting on the hot hillsides, miles away from the least bit of shade and water. Annoying, you know, to hold your own coat like a parasol over a man's head while he is coming-to. I couldn't help asking him once what he meant by coming there at all. 'To make money, of course. What do you think?' he said scornfully. Then he got fever, and had to be carried in a hammock slung under a pole. As he weighed sixteen stone[9] I had no end of rows with the carriers. They jibbed, ran away, sneaked off with their loads in the night— quite a mutiny. So, one evening, I made a speech in English with gestures, not one of which was lost to the sixty pairs of eyes before me, and the next morning I started the hammock off in front all right. An hour afterwards I came upon the whole concern wrecked in a bush—man, hammock, groans, blankets, horrors. The heavy pole had skinned his poor nose. He was very anxious for me to kill somebody, but there wasn't the shadow of a carrier near. I remembered the old doctor—'It would be interesting for science to watch the mental changes of individuals, on the spot.' I felt I was becoming scientifically interesting. However, all that is to no purpose. On the fifteenth day I came in sight of the big river again, and hobbled into the Central Station. It was on a back water surrounded by scrub and forest, with a pretty border of smelly mud on one side, and on the three others enclosed by a crazy fence of rushes. A neglected gap was all the gate it had, and the first glance at the place was enough to let you see the flabby devil was running that show. White men with long staves in their hands appeared languidly from amongst the buildings, strolling up to take a look at me, and then retired out of sight somewhere. One of them, a stout, excitable chap with black moustaches, informed me with great volubility and many digressions, as soon as I told him who I was, that my steamer was at the bottom of the river. I was thunderstruck. What, how, why? Oh, it was 'all right.' The 'manager himself' was there. All quite correct. 'Everybody had behaved splendidly! splendidly!'—'You must,' he said in agitation, 'go and see the general manager at once. He is waiting!'

8. Mercenary soldiers from the island of Zanzibar off the east African coast.   9. I.e., 224 pounds (1 stone equals 14 pounds).

"I did not see the real significance of that wreck at once. I fancy I see it now, but I am not sure—not at all. Certainly the affair was too stupid—when I think of it—to be altogether natural. Still . . . But at the moment it presented itself simply as a confounded nuisance. The steamer was sunk. They had started two days before in a sudden hurry up the river with the manager on board, in charge of some volunteer skipper, and before they had been out three hours they tore the bottom out of her on stones, and she sank near the south bank. I asked myself what I was to do there, now my boat was lost. As a matter of fact, I had plenty to do in fishing my command out of the river. I had to set about it the very next day. That, and the repairs when I brought the pieces to the station, took some months.

"My first interview with the manager was curious. He did not ask me to sit down after my twenty-mile walk that morning. He was commonplace in complexion, in feature, in manners, and in voice. He was of middle size and of ordinary build. His eyes, of the usual blue, were perhaps remarkably cold, and he certainly could make his glance fall on one as trenchant and heavy as an axe. But even at these times the rest of his person seemed to disclaim the intention. Otherwise there was only an indefinable, faint expression of his lips, something stealthy—a smile—not a smile—I remember it, but I can't explain. It was unconscious, this smile was, though just after he had said something it got intensified for an instant. It came at the end of his speeches like a seal applied on the words to make the meaning of the commonest phrase appear absolutely inscrutable. He was a common trader, from his youth up employed in these parts—nothing more. He was obeyed, yet he inspired neither love nor fear, nor even respect. He inspired uneasiness. That was it! Uneasiness. Not a definite mistrust—just uneasiness—nothing more. You have no idea how effective such a . . . a . . . faculty can be. He had no genius for organising, for initiative, or for order even. That was evident in such things as the deplorable state of the station. He had no learning, and no intelligence. His position had come to him—why? Perhaps because he was never ill . . . He had served three terms of three years out there . . . Because triumphant health in the general rout of constitutions is a kind of power in itself. When he went home on leave he rioted on a large scale—pompously. Jack ashore—with a difference—in externals only. This one could gather from his casual talk. He originated nothing, he could keep the routine going—that's all. But he was great. He was great by this little thing that it was impossible to tell what could control such a man. He never gave that secret away. Perhaps there was nothing within him. Such a suspicion made one pause—for out there there were no external checks. Once when various tropical diseases had laid low almost every 'agent' in the station, he was heard to say, 'Men who come out here should have no entrails.' He sealed the utterance with that smile of his, as though it had been a door opening into a darkness he had in his keeping. You fancied you had seen things—but the seal was on. When annoyed at meal-times by the constant quarrels of the white men about precedence, he ordered an immense round table to be made, for which a special house had to be built. This was the station's mess-room. Where he sat was the first place—the rest were nowhere. One felt this to be his unalterable conviction. He was neither civil nor uncivil. He was quiet. He allowed his 'boy'—an overfed young negro from the coast— to treat the white men, under his very eyes, with provoking insolence.

"He began to speak as soon as he saw me. I had been very long on the road. He could not wait. Had to start without me. The up-river stations had to be relieved. There had been so many delays already that he did not know who was dead and who was alive, and how they got on—and so on, and so on. He paid no attention to my explanations, and, playing with a stick of sealing-wax, repeated several times that the situation was 'very grave, very grave.' There were rumours that a very important station was in jeopardy, and its chief, Mr Kurtz, was ill. Hoped it was not true. Mr Kurtz was . . . I felt weary and irritable. Hang Kurtz, I thought. I interrupted him by saying I had heard of Mr Kurtz on the coast. 'Ah! So they talk of him down there,' he murmured to himself. Then he began again, assuring me Mr Kurtz was the best agent he had, an exceptional man, of the greatest importance to the Company; therefore I could understand his anxiety. He was, he said, 'very, very uneasy.' Certainly he fidgeted on his chair a good deal, exclaimed, 'Ah, Mr Kurtz!' broke the stick of sealing-wax and seemed dumbfounded by the accident. Next thing he wanted to know 'how long it would take to' . . . I interrupted him again. Being hungry, you know, and kept on my feet too, I was getting savage. 'How can I tell?' I said, 'I haven't even seen the wreck yet—some months, no doubt.' All this talk seemed to me so futile. 'Some months,' he said. 'Well, let us say three months before we can make a start. Yes. That ought to do the affair.' I flung out of his hut (he lived all alone in a clay hut with a sort of verandah) muttering to myself my opinion of him. He was a chattering idiot. Afterwards I took it back when it was borne in upon me startlingly with what extreme nicety he had estimated the time requisite for the 'affair.'

"I went to work the next day, turning, so to speak, my back on that station. In that way only it seemed to me I could keep my hold on the redeeming facts of life. Still, one must look about sometimes; and then I saw this station, these men strolling aimlessly about in the sunshine of the yard. I asked myself sometimes what it all meant. They wandered here and there with their absurd long staves in their hands, like a lot of faithless pilgrims bewitched inside a rotten fence. The word 'ivory' rang in the air, was whispered, was sighed. You would think they were praying to it. A taint of imbecile rapacity blew through it all, like a whiff from some corpse. By Jove! I've never seen anything so unreal in my life. And outside, the silent wilderness surrounding this cleared speck on the earth struck me as something great and invincible, like evil or truth, waiting patiently for the passing away of this fantastic invasion.

"Oh, these months! Well, never mind. Various things happened. One evening a grass shed full of calico, cotton prints, beads, and I don't know what else, burst into a blaze so suddenly that you would have thought the earth had opened to let an avenging fire consume all that trash. I was smoking my pipe quietly by my dismantled steamer, and saw them all cutting capers in the light, with their arms lifted high, when the stout man with moustaches came tearing down to the river, a tin pail in his hand, assured me that everybody was 'behaving splendidly, splendidly,' dipped about a quart of water and tore back again. I noticed there was a hole in the bottom of his pail.

"I strolled up. There was no hurry. You see the thing had gone off like a box of matches. It had been hopeless from the very first. The flame had leaped high, driven everybody back, lighted up everything—and collapsed.

The shed was already a heap of embers glowing fiercely. A nigger was being beaten near by. They said he had caused the fire in some way; be that as it may, he was screeching most horribly. I saw him, later, for several days, sitting in a bit of shade looking very sick and trying to recover himself: afterwards he arose and went out—and the wilderness without a sound took him into its bosom again. As I approached the glow from the dark I found myself at the back of two men, talking. I heard the name of Kurtz pronounced, then the words, 'take advantage of this unfortunate accident.' One of the men was the manager. I wished him a good evening. 'Did you ever see anything like it—eh? it is incredible,' he said, and walked off. The other man remained. He was a first-class agent, young, gentlemanly, a bit reserved, with a forked little beard and a hooked nose. He was standoffish with the other agents, and they on their side said he was the manager's spy upon them. As to me, I had hardly ever spoken to him before. We got into talk, and by and by we strolled away from the hissing ruins. Then he asked me to his room, which was in the main building of the station. He struck a match, and I perceived that this young aristocrat had not only a silver-mounted dressing-case but also a whole candle all to himself. Just at that time the manager was the only man supposed to have any right to candles. Native mats covered the clay walls; a collection of spears, assegais,[1] shields, knives, was hung up in trophies. The business entrusted to this fellow was the making of bricks—so I had been informed; but there wasn't a fragment of a brick anywhere in the station, and he had been there more than a year—waiting. It seems he could not make bricks without something, I don't know what—straw maybe. Anyway, it could not be found there, and as it was not likely to be sent from Europe, it did not appear clear to me what he was waiting for. An act of special creation perhaps. However, they were all waiting—all the sixteen or twenty pilgrims of them—for something; and upon my word it did not seem an uncongenial occupation, from the way they took it, though the only thing that ever came to them was disease—as far as I could see. They beguiled the time by backbiting and intriguing against each other in a foolish kind of way. There was an air of plotting about that station, but nothing came of it, of course. It was as unreal as everything else—as the philanthropic pretence of the whole concern, as their talk, as their government, as their show of work. The only real feeling was a desire to get appointed to a trading-post where ivory was to be had, so that they could earn percentages. They intrigued and slandered and hated each other only on that account—but as to effectually lifting a little finger—oh no. By heavens! there is something after all in the world allowing one man to steal a horse while another must not look at a halter. Steal a horse straight out. Very well. He has done it. Perhaps he can ride. But there is a way of looking at a halter that would provoke the most charitable of saints into a kick.

"I had no idea why he wanted to be sociable, but as we chatted in there it suddenly occurred to me the fellow was trying to get at something—in fact, pumping me. He alluded constantly to Europe, to the people I was supposed to know there—putting leading questions as to my acquaintances in the sepulchral city, and so on. His little eyes glittered like mica[2] discs—with curiosity—though he tried to keep up a bit of superciliousness. At first I was

1. Slender hardwood javelins used as weapons.   2. A mineral silicate that separates into glittering layers.

astonished, but very soon I became awfully curious to see what he would find out from me. I couldn't possibly imagine what I had in me to make it worth his while. It was very pretty to see how he baffled himself, for in truth my body was full only of chills, and my head had nothing in it but that wretched steamboat business. It was evident he took me for a perfectly shameless prevaricator. At last he got angry, and, to conceal a movement of furious annoyance, he yawned. I rose. Then I noticed a small sketch in oils, on a panel, representing a woman, draped and blindfolded, carrying a lighted torch. The background was sombre—almost black. The movement of the woman was stately, and the effect of the torchlight on the face was sinister.

"It arrested me, and he stood by civilly, holding an empty half-pint champagne bottle (medical comforts) with the candle stuck in it. To my question he said Mr Kurtz had painted this—in this very station more than a year ago—while waiting for means to go to his trading-post. 'Tell me, pray,' said I, 'who is this Mr Kurtz?'

" 'The chief of the Inner Station,' he answered in a short tone, looking away. 'Much obliged,' I said, laughing. 'And you are the brickmaker of the Central Station. Every one knows that.' He was silent for a while. 'He is a prodigy,' he said at last. 'He is an emissary of pity, and science, and progress, and devil knows what else. We want,' he began to declaim suddenly, 'for the guidance of the cause entrusted to us by Europe, so to speak, higher intelligence, wide sympathies, a singleness of purpose.' 'Who says that?' I asked. 'Lots of them,' he replied. 'Some even write that; and so *he* comes here, a special being, as you ought to know.' 'Why ought I to know?' I interrupted, really surprised. He paid no attention. 'Yes. To-day he is chief of the best station, next year he will be assistant-manager, two years more and . . . but I daresay you know what he will be in two years' time. You are of the new gang—the gang of virtue. The same people who sent him specially also recommended you. Oh, don't say no. I've my own eyes to trust.' Light dawned upon me. My dear aunt's influential acquaintances were producing an unexpected effect upon that young man. I nearly burst into a laugh. 'Do you read the Company's confidential correspondence?' I asked. He hadn't a word to say. It was great fun. 'When Mr Kurtz,' I continued severely, 'is General Manager, you won't have the opportunity.'

"He blew the candle out suddenly, and we went outside. The moon had risen. Black figures strolled about listlessly, pouring water on the glow, whence proceeded a sound of hissing; steam ascended in the moonlight; the beaten nigger groaned somewhere. 'What a row the brute makes!' said the indefatigable man with the moustaches, appearing near us. 'Serve him right. Transgression—punishment—bang! Pitiless, pitiless. That's the only way. This will prevent all conflagrations for the future. I was just telling the manager . . . ' He noticed my companion, and became crestfallen all at once. 'Not in bed yet,' he said, with a kind of servile heartiness; 'it's so natural. Ha! Danger—agitation.' He vanished. I went on to the river-side, and the other followed me. I heard a scathing murmur at my ear, 'Heap of muffs—go to.' The pilgrims could be seen in knots gesticulating, discussing. Several had still their staves in their hands. I verily believe they took these sticks to bed with them. Beyond the fence the forest stood up spectrally in the moonlight, and through the dim stir, through the faint sounds of that lamentable courtyard, the silence of the land went home to one's very heart—its mystery, its greatness, the amazing reality of its concealed life. The hurt nigger moaned feebly somewhere near by, and then fetched a deep sigh that made me mend my pace away from there. I felt a hand introducing itself under my arm. 'My dear sir,' said the fellow, 'I don't want to be misunderstood, and especially by you, who will see Mr Kurtz long before I can have that pleasure. I wouldn't like him to get a false idea of my disposition. . . .'

"I let him run on, this papier-mâché Mephistopheles, and it seemed to me that if I tried I could poke my forefinger through him, and would find nothing inside but a little loose dirt, maybe. He, don't you see, had been planning to be assistant-manager by and by under the present man, and I could see that the coming of that Kurtz had upset them both not a little. He talked precipitately, and I did not try to stop him. I had my shoulders against the wreck of my steamer, hauled up on the slope like a carcass of some big river animal. The smell of mud, of primeval mud, by Jove! was in my nostrils, the high stillness of primeval forest was before my eyes; there were shiny patches on the black creek. The moon had spread over everything a thin layer of silver—over the rank grass, over the mud, upon the wall of matted vegetation standing higher than the wall of a temple, over the great river I could see through a sombre gap glittering, glittering, as it flowed broadly by without a murmur. All this was great, expectant, mute, while the man jabbered about himself. I wondered whether the stillness on the face of the immensity looking at us two were meant as an appeal or as a menace. What were we who had strayed in here? Could we handle that dumb thing, or would it handle us? I felt how big, how confoundedly big, was that thing that couldn't talk and perhaps was deaf as well. What was in there? I could see a little ivory coming out from there, and I had heard Mr Kurtz was in there. I had heard enough about it too—God knows! Yet somehow it didn't bring any image with it—no more than if I had been told an angel or a fiend was in there. I believed it in the same way one of you might believe there are inhabitants in the planet Mars. I knew once a Scotch sailmaker who was certain, dead sure, there were people in Mars. If you asked him for some idea how they looked and behaved, he would get shy and mutter something about 'walking on all-fours.' If you as much as smiled, he would—though a man of sixty—offer to fight you. I would not have gone so far as to fight for Kurtz, but I went for him near enough to a lie. You know I hate, detest, and can't bear a lie, not because I am straighter than the rest of us, but simply because it appals me. There is a taint of death, a flavour of mortality in lies—which is exactly what I hate and detest in the world—what I want to forget. It makes me miserable and sick, like biting something rotten would do. Temperament, I suppose. Well, I went near enough to it by letting the young fool there believe anything he liked to imagine as to my influence in Europe. I became in an instant as much of a pretence as the rest of the bewitched pilgrims. This simply because I had a notion it somehow would be of help to that Kurtz whom at the time I did not see—you understand. He was just a word for me. I did not see the man in the name any more than you do. Do you see him? Do you see the story? Do you see anything? It seems to me I am trying to tell you a dream—making a vain attempt, because no relation of a dream can convey the dream-sensation, that commingling of absurdity, surprise, and bewilderment in a tremor of struggling revolt, that notion of being captured by the incredible which is of the very essence of dreams. . . ."

He was silent for a while.

". . . No, it is impossible; it is impossible to convey the life-sensation of any given epoch of one's existence—that which makes its truth, its meaning—its subtle and penetrating essence. It is impossible. We live, as we dream—alone. . . ."

He paused again as if reflecting, then added:

"Of course in this you fellows see more than I could then. You see me, whom you know. . . ."

It had become so pitch dark that we listeners could hardly see one another. For a long time already he, sitting apart, had been no more to us than a voice. There was not a word from anybody. The others might have been asleep, but I was awake. I listened, I listened on the watch for the sentence, for the word, that would give me the clue to the faint uneasiness inspired by this narrative that seemed to shape itself without human lips in the heavy night-air of the river.

". . . Yes—I let him run on," Marlow began again, "and think what he pleased about the powers that were behind me. I did! And there was nothing behind me! There was nothing but that wretched, old, mangled steamboat I was leaning against, while he talked fluently about 'the necessity for every man to get on.' 'And when one comes out here, you conceive, it is not to gaze at the moon.' Mr Kurtz was a 'universal genius,' but even a genius would find it easier to work with 'adequate tools—intelligent men.' He did not make bricks—why, there was a physical impossibility in the way—as I was well aware; and if he did secretarial work for the manager, it was because 'no sensible man rejects wantonly the confidence of his superiors.' Did I see it? I saw it. What more did I want? What I really wanted was rivets, by heaven! Rivets. To get on with the work—to stop the hole. Rivets I wanted. There were cases of them down at the coast—cases—piled up—burst—split! You kicked a loose rivet at every second step in that station yard on the hillside. Rivets had rolled into the grove of death. You could fill your pockets with rivets for the trouble of stooping down—and there wasn't one rivet to be found where it was wanted. We had plates that would do, but nothing to fasten them with. And every week the messenger, a lone negro, letter-bag on shoulder and staff in hand, left our station for the coast. And several times a week a coast caravan came in with trade goods—ghastly glazed calico that made you shudder only to look at it, glass beads value about a penny a quart, confounded spotted cotton handkerchiefs. And no rivets. Three carriers could have brought all that was wanted to set that steamboat afloat.

"He was becoming confidential now, but I fancy my unresponsive attitude must have exasperated him at last, for he judged it necessary to inform me he feared neither God nor devil, let alone any mere man. I said I could see that very well, but what I wanted was a certain quantity of rivets—and rivets were what really Mr Kurtz wanted, if he had only known it. Now letters went to the coast every week. . . . 'My dear sir,' he cried, 'I write from dictation.' I demanded rivets. There was a way—for an intelligent man. He changed his manner; became very cold, and suddenly began to talk about a hippopotamus; wondered whether sleeping on board the steamer (I stuck to my salvage night and day) I wasn't disturbed. There was an old hippo that had the bad habit of getting out on the bank and roaming at night over the station grounds. The pilgrims used to turn out in a body and empty every rifle they could lay hands on at him. Some even had sat up o' nights for him. All this energy was wasted, though. 'That animal has a charmed life,' he said; 'but you can say this only of brutes in this country. No man—you apprehend me?—no man here bears a charmed life.' He stood there for a moment in the moonlight with his delicate hooked nose set a little askew, and his mica eyes glittering without a wink, then, with a curt Good-night, he strode off. I could see he was disturbed and considerably puzzled, which made me feel more hopeful than I had been for days. It was a great comfort to turn from that chap to my influential friend, the battered, twisted, ruined, tinpot steamboat. I clambered on board. She rang under my feet like an empty Huntley & Palmer biscuit-tin kicked along a gutter; she was nothing so solid in make, and rather less pretty in shape, but I had expended enough hard work on her to make me love her. No influential friend would have served me better. She had given me a chance to come out a bit—to find out what I could do. No, I don't like work. I had rather laze about and think of all the fine things that can be done. I don't like work—no man does—but I like what is in the work— the chance to find yourself. Your own reality—for yourself, not for others— what no other man can ever know. They can only see the mere show, and never can tell what it really means.

"I was not surprised to see somebody sitting aft, on the deck, with his legs dangling over the mud. You see I rather chummed with the few mechanics there were in that station, whom the other pilgrims naturally despised—on account of their imperfect manners, I suppose. This was the foreman—a boiler-maker by trade—a good worker. He was a lank, bony, yellow-faced man, with big intense eyes. His aspect was worried, and his head was as bald as the palm of my hand; but his hair in falling seemed to have stuck to his chin, and had prospered in the new locality, for his beard hung down to his waist. He was a widower with six young children (he had left them in charge of a sister of his to come out there), and the passion of his life was pigeon-flying. He was an enthusiast and a connoisseur. He would rave about pigeons. After work hours he used sometimes to come over from his hut for a talk about his children and his pigeons; at work, when he had to crawl in the mud under the bottom of the steamboat, he would tie up that beard of his in a kind of white serviette[3] he brought for the purpose. It had loops to go over his ears. In the evening he could be seen squatted on the bank rinsing that wrapper in the creek with great care, then spreading it solemnly on a bush to dry.

"I slapped him on the back and shouted 'We shall have rivets!' He scrambled to his feet exclaiming 'No! Rivets!' as though he couldn't believe his ears. Then in a low voice, 'You . . . eh?' I don't know why we behaved like lunatics. I put my finger to the side of my nose and nodded mysteriously. 'Good for you!' he cried, snapped his fingers above his head, lifting one foot. I tried a jig. We capered on the iron deck. A frightful clatter came out of that hulk, and the virgin forest on the other bank of the creek sent it back in a thundering roll upon the sleeping station. It must have made some of the pilgrims sit up in their hovels. A dark figure obscured the lighted doorway of the manager's hut, vanished, then, a second or so after, the doorway itself vanished too. We stopped, and the silence driven away by the stamping of our feet flowed back again from the recesses of the land. The great wall of

3. Table napkin (French).

vegetation, an exuberant and entangled mass of trunks, branches, leaves, boughs, festoons, motionless in the moonlight, was like a rioting invasion of soundless life, a rolling wave of plants, piled up, crested, ready to topple over the creek, to sweep every little man of us out of his little existence. And it moved not. A deadened burst of mighty splashes and snorts reached us from afar, as though an ichthyosaurus[4] had been taking a bath of glitter in the great river. 'After all,' said the boiler-maker in a reasonable tone, 'why shouldn't we get the rivets?' Why not, indeed! I did not know of any reason why we shouldn't. 'They'll come in three weeks,' I said confidently.

"But they didn't. Instead of rivets there came an invasion, an infliction, a visitation. It came in sections during the next three weeks, each section headed by a donkey carrying a white man in new clothes and tan shoes, bowing from that elevation right and left to the impressed pilgrims. A quarrelsome band of footsore sulky niggers trod on the heels of the donkey; a lot of tents, camp-stools, tin boxes, white cases, brown bales would be shot down in the courtyard, and the air of mystery would deepen a little over the muddle of the station. Five such instalments came, with their absurd air of disorderly flight with the loot of innumerable outfit shops and provision stores, that, one would think, they were lugging, after a raid, into the wilderness for equitable division. It was an inextricable mess of things decent in themselves but that human folly made look like the spoils of thieving.

"This devoted band called itself the Eldorado[5] Exploring Expedition, and I believe they were sworn to secrecy. Their talk, however, was the talk of sordid buccaneers: it was reckless without hardihood, greedy without audacity, and cruel without courage; there was not an atom of foresight or of serious intention in the whole batch of them, and they did not seem aware these things are wanted for the work of the world. To tear treasure out of the bowels of the land was their desire, with no more moral purpose at the back of it than there is in burglars breaking into a safe. Who paid the expenses of the noble enterprise I don't know; but the uncle of our manager was leader of that lot.

"In exterior he resembled a butcher in a poor neighbourhood, and his eyes had a look of sleepy cunning. He carried his fat paunch with ostentation on his short legs, and during the time his gang infested the station spoke to no one but his nephew. You could see these two roaming about all day long with their heads close together in an everlasting confab.[6]

"I had given up worrying myself about the rivets. One's capacity for that kind of folly is more limited than you would suppose. I said Hang!—and let things slide. I had plenty of time for meditation, and now and then I would give some thought to Kurtz. I wasn't very interested in him. No. Still, I was curious to see whether this man, who had come out equipped with moral ideas of some sort, would climb to the top after all, and how he would set about his work when there."

2

"One evening as I was lying flat on the deck of my steamboat, I heard voices approaching—and there were the nephew and the uncle strolling

4. An extinct prehistoric marine animal combining aspects of a crocodile and a fish.   5. *El Dorado* (literally, "the gilded one," Spanish), the land of gold sought by the Spanish conquistadors in South America.
6. Conversation.

along the bank. I laid my head on my arm again, and had nearly lost myself in a doze, when somebody said in my ear, as it were: 'I am as harmless as a little child, but I don't like to be dictated to. Am I the manager—or am I not? I was ordered to send him there. It's incredible.' . . . I became aware that the two were standing on the shore alongside the forepart of the steamboat, just below my head. I did not move; it did not occur to me to move: I was sleepy. 'It *is* unpleasant,' grunted the uncle. 'He has asked the Administration to be sent there,' said the other, 'with the idea of showing what he could do; and I was instructed accordingly. Look at the influence that man must have. Is it not frightful?' They both agreed it was frightful, then made several bizarre remarks: 'Make rain and fine weather—one man—the Council—by the nose'—bits of absurd sentences that got the better of my drowsiness, so that I had pretty near the whole of my wits about me when the uncle said, 'The climate may do away with this difficulty for you. Is he alone there?' 'Yes,' answered the manager; 'he sent his assistant down the river with a note to me in these terms: "Clear this poor devil out of the country, and don't bother sending more of that sort. I had rather be alone than have the kind of men you can dispose of with me." It was more than a year ago. Can you imagine such impudence?' 'Anything since then?' asked the other hoarsely. 'Ivory,' jerked the nephew; 'lots of it—prime sort—lots—most annoying, from him.' 'And with that?' questioned the heavy rumble. 'Invoice,' was the reply fired out, so to speak. Then silence. They had been talking about Kurtz.

"I was broad awake by this time, but, lying perfectly at ease, remained still, having no inducement to change my position. 'How did that ivory come all this way?' growled the elder man, who seemed very vexed. The other explained that it had come with a fleet of canoes in charge of an English half-caste clerk Kurtz had with him; that Kurtz had apparently intended to return himself, the station being by that time bare of goods and stores, but after coming three hundred miles, had suddenly decided to go back, which he started to do alone in a small dugout with four paddlers, leaving the half-caste to continue down the river with the ivory. The two fellows there seemed astounded at anybody attempting such a thing. They were at a loss for an adequate motive. As for me, I seemed to see Kurtz for the first time. It was a distinct glimpse: the dugout, four paddling savages, and the lone white man turning his back suddenly on the headquarters, on relief, on thoughts of home—perhaps; setting his face towards the depths of the wilderness, towards his empty and desolate station. I did not know the motive. Perhaps he was just simply a fine fellow who stuck to his work for its own sake. His name, you understand, had not been pronounced once. He was 'that man.' The half-caste, who, as far as I could see, had conducted a difficult trip with great prudence and pluck, was invariably alluded to as 'that scoundrel.' The 'scoundrel' had reported that the 'man' had been very ill—had recovered imperfectly. . . . The two below me moved away then a few paces, and strolled back and forth at some little distance. I heard: 'Military post—doctor—two hundred miles—quite alone now—unavoidable delays—nine months—no news—strange rumours.' They approached again, just as the manager was saying, 'No one, as far as I know, unless a species of wandering trader—a pestilential fellow, snapping ivory from the natives.' Who was it they were talking about now? I gathered in snatches that this was some man supposed to be in Kurtz's district, and of whom the manager did not approve. 'We will not be free from unfair competition till one of these fellows is hanged for an example,' he said. 'Certainly,' grunted the other; 'get him hanged! Why not? Anything—anything can be done in this country. That's what I say; nobody here, you understand, *here*, can endanger your position. And why? You stand the climate—you outlast them all. The danger is in Europe; but there before I left I took care to—' They moved off and whispered, then their voices rose again. 'The extraordinary series of delays is not my fault. I did my possible.' The fat man sighed, 'Very sad.' 'And the pestiferous absurdity of his talk,' continued the other; 'he bothered me enough when he was here. "Each station should be like a beacon on the road towards better things, a centre for trade of course, but also for humanising, improving, instructing." Conceive you[7]—that ass! And he wants to be manager! No, it's—' Here he got choked by excessive indignation, and I lifted my head the least bit. I was surprised to see how near they were—right under me. I could have spat upon their hats. They were looking on the ground, absorbed in thought. The manager was switching his leg with a slender twig: his sagacious relative lifted his head. 'You have been well since you came out this time?' he asked. The other gave a start. 'Who? I? Oh! Like a charm—like a charm. But the rest—oh, my goodness! All sick. They die so quick, too, that I haven't the time to send them out of the country—it's incredible!' 'H'm. Just so,' grunted the uncle. 'Ah! my boy, trust to this—I say, trust to this.' I saw him extend his short flipper of an arm for a gesture that took in the forest, the creek, the mud, the river—seemed to beckon with a dishonouring flourish before the sunlit face of the land a treacherous appeal to the lurking death, to the hidden evil, to the profound darkness of its heart. It was so startling that I leaped to my feet and looked back at the edge of the forest, as though I had expected an answer of some sort to that black display of confidence. You know the foolish notions that come to one sometimes. The high stillness confronted these two figures with its ominous patience, waiting for the passing away of a fantastic invasion.

"They swore aloud together—out of sheer fright, I believe—then, pretending not to know anything of my existence, turned back to the station. The sun was low; and leaning forward side by side, they seemed to be tugging painfully uphill their two ridiculous shadows of unequal length, that trailed behind them slowly over the tall grass without bending a single blade.

"In a few days the Eldorado Expedition went into the patient wilderness, that closed upon it as the sea closes over a diver. Long afterwards the news came that all the donkeys were dead. I know nothing as to the fate of the less valuable animals. They, no doubt, like the rest of us, found what they deserved. I did not inquire. I was then rather excited at the prospect of meeting Kurtz very soon. When I say very soon I mean it comparatively. It was just two months from the day we left the creek when we came to the bank below Kurtz's station.

"Going up that river was like travelling back to the earliest beginnings of the world, when vegetation rioted on the earth and the big trees were kings. An empty stream, a great silence, an impenetrable forest. The air was warm,

7. "Just imagine." This phrase, like "I did my possible" (I did the best I could), above, and others throughout the novel, is a literal translation of the French spoken by Belgian traders. Conrad reminds us of the setting: the Belgian Congo was an international scandal for its brutal treatment of Africans.

thick, heavy, sluggish. There was no joy in the brilliance of sunshine. The long stretches of the waterway ran on, deserted, into the gloom of over-shadowed distances. On silvery sandbanks hippos and alligators sunned themselves side by side. The broadening waters flowed through a mob of wooded islands; you lost your way on that river as you would in a desert, and butted all day long against shoals, trying to find the channel, till you thought yourself bewitched and cut off for ever from everything you had known once—somewhere—far away—in another existence perhaps. There were moments when one's past came back to one, as it will sometimes when you have not a moment to spare to yourself; but it came in the shape of an unrestful and noisy dream, remembered with wonder amongst the over-whelming realities of this strange world of plants, and water, and silence. And this stillness of life did not in the least resemble a peace. It was the stillness of an implacable force brooding over an inscrutable intention. It looked at you with a vengeful aspect. I got used to it afterwards; I did not see it any more; I had no time. I had to keep guessing at the channel; I had to discern, mostly by inspiration, the signs of hidden banks; I watched for sunken stones; I was learning to clap my teeth smartly before my heart flew out, when I shaved by a fluke some infernal sly old snag that would have ripped the life out of the tin-pot steamboat and drowned all the pilgrims; I had to keep a look-out for the signs of dead wood we could cut up in the night for next day's steaming. When you have to attend to things of that sort, to the mere incidents of the surface, the reality—the reality, I tell you—fades. The inner truth is hidden—luckily, luckily. But I felt it all the same; I felt often its mysterious stillness watching me at my monkey tricks, just as it watches you fellows performing on your respective tight-ropes for—what is it? half a crown a tumble—"

"Try to be civil, Marlow," growled a voice, and I knew there was at least one listener awake besides myself.

"I beg your pardon. I forgot the heartache which makes up the rest of the price. And indeed what does the price matter, if the trick be well done? You do your tricks very well. And I didn't do badly either, since I managed not to sink that steamboat on my first trip. It's a wonder to me yet. Imagine a blindfolded man set to drive a van over a bad road. I sweated and shivered over that business considerably, I can tell you. After all, for a seaman, to scrape the bottom of the thing that's supposed to float all the time under his care is the unpardonable sin. No one may know of it, but you never forget the thump—eh? A blow on the very heart. You remember it, you dream of it, you wake up at night and think of it—years after—and go hot and cold all over. I don't pretend to say that steamboat floated all the time. More than once she had to wade for a bit, with twenty cannibals splashing around and pushing. We had enlisted some of these chaps on the way for a crew. Fine fellows—cannibals—in their place. They were men one could work with, and I am grateful to them. And, after all, they did not eat each other before my face: they had brought along a provision of hippo-meat which went rot-ten, and made the mystery of the wilderness stink in my nostrils. Phoo! I can sniff it now. I had the manager on board and three or four pilgrims with their staves—all complete. Sometimes we came upon a station close by the bank, clinging to the skirts of the unknown, and the white men rushing out of a tumble-down hovel, with great gestures of joy and surprise and welcome, seemed very strange—had the appearance of being held there captive by a spell. The word 'ivory' would ring in the air for a while—and on we went again into the silence, along empty reaches, round the still bends, between the high walls of our winding way, reverberating in hollow claps the ponderous beat of the stern-wheel. Trees, trees, millions of trees, massive, immense, running up high; and at their foot, hugging the bank against the stream, crept the little begrimed steamboat, like a sluggish beetle crawling on the floor of a lofty portico. It made you feel very small, very lost, and yet it was not altogether depressing, that feeling. After all, if you were small, the grimy beetle crawled on—which was just what you wanted it to do. Where the pilgrims imagined it crawled to I don't know. To some place where they expected to get something, I bet! For me it crawled towards Kurtz—exclusively; but when the steam-pipes started leaking we crawled very slow. The reaches opened before us and closed behind, as if the forest had stepped leisurely across the water to bar the way for our return. We penetrated deeper and deeper into the heart of darkness. It was very quiet there. At night sometimes the roll of drums behind the curtain of trees would run up the river and remain sustained faintly, as if hovering in the air high over our heads, till the first break of day. Whether it meant war, peace, or prayer we could not tell. The dawns were heralded by the descent of a chill stillness; the woodcutters slept, their fires burned low; the snapping of a twig would make you start. We were wanderers on a prehistoric earth, on an earth that wore the aspect of an unknown planet. We could have fancied ourselves the first of men taking possession of an accursed inheritance, to be subdued at the cost of profound anguish and of excessive toil. But suddenly, as we struggled round a bend, there would be a glimpse of rush walls, of peaked grass-roofs, a burst of yells, a whirl of black limbs, a mass of hands clapping, of feet stamping, of bodies swaying, of eyes rolling, under the droop of heavy and motionless foliage. The steamer toiled along slowly on the edge of a black and incomprehensible frenzy. The prehistoric man was cursing us, praying to us, welcoming us—who could tell? We were cut off from the comprehension of our surroundings; we glided past like phantoms, wondering and secretly appalled, as sane men would be before an enthusiastic outbreak in a madhouse. We could not understand because we were too far and could not remember, because we were travelling in the night of first ages, of those ages that are gone, leaving hardly a sign—and no memories.

"The earth seemed unearthly. We are accustomed to look upon the shackled form of a conquered monster, but there—there you could look at a thing monstrous and free. It was unearthly, and the men were—No, they were not inhuman. Well, you know, that was the worst of it—this suspicion of their not being inhuman. It would come slowly to one. They howled and leaped, and spun, and made horrid faces; but what thrilled you was just the thought of their humanity—like yours—the thought of your remote kinship with this wild and passionate uproar. Ugly. Yes, it was ugly enough; but if you were man enough you would admit to yourself that there was in you just the faintest trace of a response to the terrible frankness of that noise, a dim suspicion of there being a meaning in it which you—you so remote from the night of first ages—could comprehend. And why not? The mind of man is capable of anything—because everything is in it, all the past as well as all the future. What was there after all? Joy, fear, sorrow, devotion, valour, rage—who can tell?—but truth—truth stripped of its cloak of time. Let the fool gape and shudder—the man knows, and can look on without a wink. But he must at least be as much of a man as these on the shore. He must meet that truth with his own true stuff—with his own inborn strength. Principles? Principles won't do. Acquisitions, clothes, pretty rags—rags that would fly off at the first good shake. No; you want a deliberate belief. An appeal to me in this fiendish row—is there? Very well; I hear; I admit, but I have a voice too, and for good or evil mine is the speech that cannot be silenced. Of course, a fool, what with sheer fright and fine sentiments, is always safe. Who's that grunting? You wonder I didn't go ashore for a howl and a dance? Well, no—I didn't. Fine sentiments, you say? Fine sentiments be hanged! I had no time. I had to mess about with white-lead and strips of woollen blanket helping to put bandages on those leaky steam-pipes—I tell you. I had to watch the steering, and circumvent those snags, and get the tin-pot along by hook or by crook. There was surface-truth enough in these things to save a wiser man. And between whiles I had to look after the savage who was fireman. He was an improved specimen; he could fire up a vertical boiler.[8] He was there below me, and, upon my word, to look at him was as edifying as seeing a dog in a parody of breeches and a feather hat, walking on his hind legs. A few months of training had done for that really fine chap. He squinted at the steam-gauge and at the water-gauge with an evident effort of intrepidity—and he had filed teeth too, the poor devil, and the wool of his pate shaved into queer patterns, and three ornamental scars on each of his cheeks. He ought to have been clapping his hands and stamping his feet on the bank, instead of which he was hard at work, a thrall to strange witchcraft, full of improving knowledge. He was useful because he had been instructed; and what he knew was this—that should the water in that transparent thing disappear, the evil spirit inside the boiler would get angry through the greatness of his thirst, and take a terrible vengeance. So he sweated and fired up and watched the glass fearfully (with an impromptu charm, made of rags, tied to his arm, and a piece of polished bone, as big as a watch, stuck flatways through his lower lip), while the wooded banks slipped past us slowly, the short noise was left behind, the interminable miles of silence—and we crept on, towards Kurtz. But the snags were thick, the water was treacherous and shallow, the boiler seemed indeed to have a sulky devil in it, and thus neither that fireman nor I had any time to peer into our creepy thoughts.

"Some fifty miles below the Inner Station we came upon a hut of reeds, an inclined and melancholy pole, with the unrecognisable tatters of what had been a flag of some sort flying from it, and a neatly stacked wood-pile. This was unexpected. We came to the bank, and on the stack of firewood found a flat piece of board with some faded pencil-writing on it. When deciphered it said: 'Wood for you. Hurry up. Approach cautiously.' There was a signature, but it was illegible—not Kurtz—a much longer word. Hurry up. Where? Up the river? 'Approach cautiously.' We had not done so. But the warning could not have been meant for the place where it could be only found after approach. Something was wrong above. But what—and how much? That was the question. We commented adversely upon the imbecility of that telegraphic style. The bush around said nothing, and would not let

8. A simple and easily fired narrow boiler.

us look very far, either. A torn curtain of red twill hung in the doorway of the hut, and flapped sadly in our faces. The dwelling was dismantled; but we could see a white man had lived there not very long ago. There remained a rude table—a plank on two posts; a heap of rubbish reposed in a dark corner, and by the door I picked up a book. It had lost its covers, and the pages had been thumbed into a state of extremely dirty softness; but the back had been lovingly stitched afresh with white cotton thread, which looked clean yet. It was an extraordinary find. Its title was, *An Inquiry into some Points of Seamanship,* by a man Towser, Towson—some such name—Master in His Majesty's Navy. The matter looked dreary reading enough, with illustrative diagrams and repulsive tables of figures, and the copy was sixty years old. I handled this amazing antiquity with the greatest possible tenderness, lest it should dissolve in my hands. Within, Towson or Towser was inquiring earnestly into the breaking strain of ships' chains and tackle, and other such matters. Not a very enthralling book; but at the first glance you could see there a singleness of intention, an honest concern for the right way of going to work, which made these humble pages, thought out so many years ago, luminous with another than a professional light. The simple old sailor, with his talk of chains and purchases, made me forget the jungle and the pilgrims in a delicious sensation of having come upon something unmistakably real. Such a book being there was wonderful enough; but still more astounding were the notes pencilled in the margin, and plainly referring to the text. I couldn't believe my eyes! They were in cipher! Yes, it looked like cipher. Fancy a man lugging with him a book of that description into this nowhere and studying it—and making notes—in cipher at that! It was an extravagant mystery.

"I had been dimly aware for some time of a worrying noise, and when I lifted my eyes I saw the wood-pile was gone, and the manager, aided by all the pilgrims, was shouting at me from the river-side. I slipped the book into my pocket. I assure you to leave off reading was like tearing myself away from the shelter of an old and solid friendship.

"I started the lame engine ahead. 'It must be this miserable trader—this intruder,' exclaimed the manager, looking back malevolently at the place we had left. 'He must be English,' I said. 'It will not save him from getting into trouble if he is not careful,' muttered the manager darkly. I observed with assumed innocence that no man was safe from trouble in this world.

"The current was more rapid now, the steamer seemed at her last gasp, the stern-wheel flopped languidly, and I caught myself listening on tiptoe for the next beat of the float,[9] for in sober truth I expected the wretched thing to give up every moment. It was like watching the last flickers of a life. But still we crawled. Sometimes I would pick out a tree a little way ahead to measure our progress towards Kurtz by, but I lost it invariably before we got abreast. To keep the eyes so long on one thing was too much for human patience. The manager displayed a beautiful resignation. I fretted and fumed and took to arguing with myself whether or no I would talk openly with Kurtz; but before I could come to any conclusion it occurred to me that my speech or my silence, indeed any action of mine, would be a mere futility. What did it matter what any one knew or ignored? What did it matter who was man-

---

9. The sound of the paddle ("paddle float") as it hits the water.

ager? One gets sometimes such a flash of insight. The essentials of this affair lay deep under the surface, beyond my reach, and beyond my power of meddling.

"Towards the evening of the second day we judged ourselves about eight miles from Kurtz's station. I wanted to push on; but the manager looked grave, and told me the navigation up there was so dangerous that it would be advisable, the sun being very low already, to wait where we were till next morning. Moreover, he pointed out that if the warning to approach cautiously were to be followed, we must approach in daylight—not at dusk, or in the dark. This was sensible enough. Eight miles meant nearly three hours' steaming for us, and I could also see suspicious ripples at the upper end of the reach. Nevertheless, I was annoyed beyond expression at the delay, and most unreasonably too, since one night more could not matter much after so many months. As we had plenty of wood, and caution was the word, I brought up in the middle of the stream. The reach was narrow, straight, with high sides like a railway cutting. The dusk came gliding into it long before the sun had set. The current ran smooth and swift, but a dumb immobility sat on the banks. The living trees, lashed together by the creepers and every living bush of the undergrowth, might have been changed into stone, even to the slenderest twig, to the lightest leaf. It was not sleep—it seemed unnatural, like a state of trance. Not the faintest sound of any kind could be heard. You looked on amazed, and began to suspect yourself of being deaf—then the night came suddenly, and struck you blind as well. About three in the morning some large fish leaped, and the loud splash made me jump as though a gun had been fired. When the sun rose there was a white fog, very warm and clammy, and more blinding than the night. It did not shift or drive; it was just there, standing all round you like something solid. At eight or nine, perhaps, it lifted as a shutter lifts. We had a glimpse of the towering multitude of trees, of the immense matted jungle, with the blazing little ball of the sun hanging over it—all perfectly still—and then the white shutter came down again, smoothly, as if sliding in greased grooves. I ordered the chain, which we had begun to heave in, to be paid out again. Before it stopped running with a muffled rattle, a cry, a very loud cry, as of infinite desolation, soared slowly in the opaque air. It ceased. A complaining clamour, modulated in savage discords, filled our ears. The sheer unexpectedness of it made my hair stir under my cap. I don't know how it struck the others: to me it seemed as though the mist itself had screamed, so suddenly, and apparently from all sides at once, did this tumultuous and mournful uproar arise. It culminated in a hurried outbreak of almost intolerably excessive shrieking, which stopped short, leaving us stiffened in a variety of silly attitudes, and obstinately listening to the nearly as appalling and excessive silence. 'Good God! What is the meaning—?' stammered at my elbow one of the pilgrims—a little fat man, with sandy hair and red whiskers, who wore side-spring boots, and pink pyjamas tucked into his socks. Two others remained open-mouthed a whole minute, then dashed into the little cabin, to rush out incontinently and stand darting scared glances, with Winchesters[1] at 'ready' in their hands. What we could see was just the steamer we were on, her outlines blurred as though she had been on the point of dissolving, and a misty strip of water,

---

1. Breech-loading rifles.

perhaps two feet broad, around her—and that was all. The rest of the world was nowhere, as far as our eyes and ears were concerned. Just nowhere. Gone, disappeared; swept off without leaving a whisper or a shadow behind.

"I went forward, and ordered the chain to be hauled in short, so as to be ready to trip the anchor and move the steamboat at once if necessary. 'Will they attack?' whispered an awed voice. 'We will all be butchered in this fog,' murmured another. The faces twitched with the strain, the hands trembled slightly, the eyes forgot to wink. It was very curious to see the contrast of expressions of the white men and of the black fellows of our crew, who were as much strangers to that part of the river as we, though their homes were only eight hundred miles away. The whites, of course greatly discomposed, had besides a curious look of being painfully shocked by such an outrageous row. The others had an alert, naturally interested expression; but their faces were essentially quiet, even those of the one or two who grinned as they hauled at the chain. Several exchanged short, grunting phrases, which seemed to settle the matter to their satisfaction. Their headman, a young, broad-chested black, severely draped in dark-blue fringed cloths, with fierce nostrils and his hair all done up artfully in oily ringlets, stood near me. 'Aha!' I said, just for good fellowship's sake. 'Catch 'im,' he snapped, with a blood-shot widening of his eyes and a flash of sharp teeth—'catch 'im. Give 'im to us.' 'To you, eh?' I asked; 'what would you do with them?' 'Eat 'im!' he said curtly, and, leaning his elbow on the rail, looked out into the fog in a dignified and profoundly pensive attitude. I would no doubt have been properly horrified, had it not occurred to me that he and his chaps must be very hungry: that they must have been growing increasingly hungry for at least this month past. They had been engaged for six months (I don't think a single one of them had any clear idea of time, as we at the end of countless ages have. They still belonged to the beginnings of time—had no inherited experience to teach them, as it were), and of course, as long as there was a piece of paper written over in accordance with some farcical law or other made down the river, it didn't enter anybody's head to trouble how they would live. Certainly they had brought with them some rotten hippo-meat, which couldn't have lasted very long, anyway, even if the pilgrims hadn't, in the midst of a shocking hullabaloo, thrown a considerable quantity of it overboard. It looked like a high-handed proceeding; but it was really a case of legitimate self-defence. You can't breathe dead hippo waking, sleeping, and eating, and at the same time keep your precarious grip on existence. Besides that, they had given them every week three pieces of brass wire, each about nine inches long; and the theory was they were to buy their provisions with that currency in river-side villages. You can see how *that* worked. There were either no villages, or the people were hostile, or the director, who like the rest of us fed out of tins, with an occasional old he-goat thrown in, didn't want to stop the steamer for some more or less recondite reasons. So, unless they swallowed the wire itself, or made loops of it to snare the fishes with, I don't see what good their extravagant salary could be to them. I must say it was paid with a regularity worthy of a large and honourable trading company. For the rest, the only thing to eat—though it didn't look eatable in the least—I saw in their possession was a few lumps of some stuff like half-cooked dough, of a dirty lavender colour, they kept wrapped in leaves, and now and then swallowed a piece of, but so small that it seemed done more for the look of the thing than for any serious purpose of sustenance. Why in the name of all the gnawing devils of hunger they didn't go for us—they were thirty to five—and have a good tuck-in for once, amazes me now when I think of it. They were big powerful men, with not much capacity to weigh the consequences, with courage, with strength, even yet, though their skins were no longer glossy and their muscles no longer hard. And I saw that something restraining, one of those human secrets that baffle probability, had come into play there. I looked at them with a swift quickening of interest—not because it occurred to me I might be eaten by them before very long, though I own to you that just then I perceived—in a new light, as it were—how unwholesome the pilgrims looked, and I hoped, yes, I positively hoped, that my aspect was not so—what shall I say?—so—unappetising: a touch of fantastic vanity which fitted well with the dream-sensation that pervaded all my days at that time. Perhaps I had a little fever too. One can't live with one's finger everlastingly on one's pulse. I had often 'a little fever,' or a little touch of other things—the playful paw-strokes of the wilderness, the preliminary trifling before the more serious onslaught which came in due course. Yes; I looked at them as you would on any human being, with a curiosity of their impulses, motives, capacities, weaknesses, when brought to the test of an inexorable physical necessity. Restraint! What possible restraint? Was it superstition, disgust, patience, fear—or some kind of primitive honour? No fear can stand up to hunger, no patience can wear it out, disgust simply does not exist where hunger is; and as to superstition, beliefs, and what you may call principles, they are less than chaff in a breeze. Don't you know the devilry of lingering starvation, its exasperating torment, its black thoughts, its sombre and brooding ferocity? Well, I do. It takes a man all his inborn strength to fight hunger properly. It's really easier to face bereavement, dishonour, and the perdition of one's soul—than this kind of prolonged hunger. Sad, but true. And these chaps too had no earthly reason for any kind of scruple. Restraint! I would just as soon have expected restraint from a hyena prowling amongst the corpses of a battlefield. But there was the fact facing me—the fact dazzling, to be seen, like the foam on the depths of the sea, like a ripple on an unfathomable enigma, a mystery greater—when I thought of it—than the curious, inexplicable note of desperate grief in this savage clamour that had swept by us on the river-bank, behind the blind whiteness of the fog.

"Two pilgrims were quarrelling in hurried whispers as to which bank. 'Left.' 'No, no; how can you? Right, right, of course.' 'It is very serious,' said the manager's voice behind me; 'I would be desolated if anything should happen to Mr. Kurtz before we came up.' I looked at him, and had not the slightest doubt he was sincere. He was just the kind of man who would wish to preserve appearances. That was his restraint. But when he muttered something about going on at once, I did not even take the trouble to answer him. I knew, and he knew, that it was impossible. Were we to let go our hold of the bottom, we would be absolutely in the air—in space. We wouldn't be able to tell where we were going to—whether up or down stream, or across—till we fetched against one bank or the other—and then we wouldn't know at first which it was. Of course I made no move. I had no mind for a smash-up. You couldn't imagine a more deadly place for a shipwreck. Whether drowned at once or not, we were sure to perish speedily in one way or another. 'I authorise you to take all the risks,' he said, after a short silence.

'I refuse to take any,' I said shortly; which was just the answer he expected, though its tone might have surprised him. 'Well, I must defer to your judgment. You are captain,' he said, with marked civility. I turned my shoulder to him in sign of my appreciation, and looked into the fog. How long would it last? It was the most hopeless look-out. The approach to this Kurtz grubbing for ivory in the wretched bush was beset by as many dangers as though he had been an enchanted princess sleeping in a fabulous castle. 'Will they attack, do you think?' asked the manager, in a confidential tone.

"I did not think they would attack, for several obvious reasons. The thick fog was one. If they left the bank in their canoes they would get lost in it, as we would be if we attempted to move. Still, I had also judged the jungle of both banks quite impenetrable—and yet eyes were in it, eyes that had seen us. The river-side bushes were certainly very thick; but the undergrowth behind was evidently penetrable. However, during the short lift I had seen no canoes anywhere in the reach—certainly not abreast of the steamer. But what made the idea of attack inconceivable to me was the nature of the noise—of the cries we had heard. They had not the fierce character boding of immediate hostile intention. Unexpected, wild, and violent as they had been, they had given me an irresistible impression of sorrow. The glimpse of the steamboat had for some reason filled those savages with unrestrained grief. The danger, if any, I expounded, was from our proximity to a great human passion let loose. Even extreme grief may ultimately vent itself in violence—but more generally takes the form of apathy. . . .

"You should have seen the pilgrims stare! They had no heart to grin, or even to revile me; but I believe they thought me gone mad—with fright, maybe. I delivered a regular lecture. My dear boys, it was no good bothering. Keep a look-out? Well, you may guess I watched the fog for the signs of lifting as a cat watches a mouse; but for anything else our eyes were of no more use to us than if we had been buried miles deep in a heap of cotton-wool. It felt like it too—choking, warm, stifling. Besides, all I said, though it sounded extravagant, was absolutely true to fact. What we afterwards alluded to as an attack was really an attempt at repulse. The action was very far from being aggressive—it was not even defensive, in the usual sense: it was undertaken under the stress of desperation, and in its essence was purely protective.

"It developed itself, I should say, two hours after the fog lifted, and its commencement was at a spot, roughly speaking, about a mile and a half below Kurtz's station. We had just floundered and flopped round a bend, when I saw an islet, a mere grassy hummock of bright green, in the middle of the stream. It was the only thing of the kind; but as we opened the reach more, I perceived it was the head of a long sandbank, or rather of a chain of shallow patches stretching down the middle of the river. They were discoloured, just awash, and the whole lot was seen just under the water, exactly as a man's backbone is seen running down the middle of his back under the skin. Now, as far as I did see, I could go to the right or to the left of this. I didn't know either channel, of course. The banks looked pretty well alike, the depth appeared the same; but as I had been informed the station was on the west side, I naturally headed for the western passage.

"No sooner had we fairly entered it than I became aware it was much narrower than I had supposed. To the left of us there was the long uninterrupted shoal, and to the right a high steep bank heavily overgrown with bushes. Above the bush the trees stood in serried ranks. The twigs overhung the current thickly, and from distance to distance a large limb of some tree projected rigidly over the stream. It was then well on in the afternoon, the face of the forest was gloomy, and a broad strip of shadow had already fallen on the water. In this shadow we steamed up—very slowly, as you may imagine. I sheered her well inshore—the water being deepest near the bank, as the sounding-pole informed me.

"One of my hungry and forbearing friends was sounding in the bows just below me. This steamboat was exactly like a decked scow. On the deck there were two little teak-wood houses, with doors and windows. The boiler was in the fore-end, and the machinery right astern. Over the whole there was a light roof, supported on stanchions. The funnel projected through that roof, and in front of the funnel a small cabin built of light planks served for a pilot-house. It contained a couch, two camp-stools, a loaded Martini-Henry[2] leaning in one corner, a tiny table, and the steering-wheel. It had a wide door in front and a broad shutter at each side. All these were always thrown open, of course. I spent my days perched up there on the extreme fore-end of that roof, before the door. At night I slept, or tried to, on the couch. An athletic black belonging to some coast tribe, and educated by my poor predecessor, was the helmsman. He sported a pair of brass earrings, wore a blue cloth wrapper from the waist to the ankles, and thought all the world of himself. He was the most unstable kind of fool I had ever seen. He steered with no end of a swagger while you were by; but if he lost sight of you, he became instantly the prey of an abject funk, and would let that cripple of a steamboat get the upper hand of him in a minute.

"I was looking down at the sounding-pole, and feeling much annoyed to see at each try a little more of it stick out of that river, when I saw my poleman give up the business suddenly, and stretch himself flat on the deck, without even taking the trouble to haul his pole in. He kept hold on it though, and it trailed in the water. At the same time the fireman, whom I could also see below me, sat down abruptly before his furnace and ducked his head. I was amazed. Then I had to look at the river mighty quick, because there was a snag in the fairway. Sticks, little sticks, were flying about—thick; they were whizzing before my nose, dropping below me, striking behind me against my pilot-house. All this time the river, the shore, the woods, were very quiet—perfectly quiet. I could only hear the heavy splashing thump of the stern-wheel and the patter of these things. We cleared the snag clumsily. Arrows, by Jove! We were being shot at! I stepped in quickly to close the shutter on the land-side. That fool-helmsman, his hands on the spokes, was lifting his knees high, stamping his feet, champing his mouth, like a reined-in horse. Confound him! And we were staggering within ten feet of the bank. I had to lean right out to swing the heavy shutter, and I saw a face amongst the leaves on the level with my own, looking at me very fierce and steady; and then suddenly, as though a veil had been removed from my eyes, I made out, deep in the tangled gloom, naked breasts, arms, legs, glaring eyes—the bush was swarming with human limbs in movement, glistening, of bronze colour. The twigs shook, swayed, and rustled, the arrows flew out of them, and then the

2. A breech-loading rifle taking an especially powerful charge.

shutter came to. 'Steer her straight,' I said to the helmsman. He held his head rigid, face forward; but his eyes rolled, he kept on lifting and setting down his feet gently, his mouth foamed a little. 'Keep quiet!' I said in a fury. I might just as well have ordered a tree not to sway in the wind. I darted out. Below me there was a great scuffle of feet on the iron deck; confused exclamations; a voice screamed, 'Can you turn back?' I caught sight of a V-shaped ripple on the water ahead. What? Another snag! A fusillade burst out under my feet. The pilgrims had opened with their Winchesters, and were simply squirting lead into that bush. A deuce of a lot of smoke came up and drove slowly forward. I swore at it. Now I couldn't see the ripple or the snag either. I stood in the doorway, peering, and the arrows came in swarms. They might have been poisoned, but they looked as though they wouldn't kill a cat. The bush began to howl. Our wood-cutters raised a warlike whoop; the report of a rifle just at my back deafened me. I glanced over my shoulder, and the pilot-house was yet full of noise and smoke when I made a dash at the wheel. The fool-nigger had dropped everything, to throw the shutter open and let off that Martini-Henry. He stood before the wide opening, glaring, and I yelled at him to come back, while I straightened the sudden twist out of that steamboat. There was no room to turn even if I had wanted to, the snag was somewhere very near ahead in that confounded smoke, there was no time to lose, so I just crowded her into the bank—right into the bank, where I knew the water was deep.

"We tore slowly along the overhanging bushes in a whirl of broken twigs and flying leaves. The fusillade below stopped short, as I had foreseen it would when the squirts got empty. I threw my head back to a glinting whizz that traversed the pilot-house, in at one shutter-hole and out at the other. Looking past that mad helmsman, who was shaking the empty rifle and yelling at the shore, I saw vague forms of men running bent double, leaping, gliding, distinct, incomplete, evanescent. Something big appeared in the air before the shutter, the rifle went overboard, and the man stepped back swiftly, looked at me over his shoulder in an extraordinary, profound, familiar manner, and fell upon my feet. The side of his head hit the wheel twice, and the end of what appeared a long cane clattered round and knocked over a little camp-stool. It looked as though after wrenching that thing from somebody ashore he had lost his balance in the effort. The thin smoke had blown away, we were clear of the snag, and looking ahead I could see that in another hundred yards or so I would be free to sheer off, away from the bank; but my feet felt so very warm and wet that I had to look down. The man had rolled on his back and stared straight up at me; both his hands clutched that cane. It was the shaft of a spear that, either thrown or lunged through the opening, had caught him in the side just below the ribs; the blade had gone in out of sight, after making a frightful gash; my shoes were full; a pool of blood lay very still, gleaming dark-red under the wheel; his eyes shone with an amazing lustre. The fusillade burst out again. He looked at me anxiously, gripping the spear like something precious, with an air of being afraid I would try to take it away from him. I had to make an effort to free my eyes from his gaze and attend to the steering. With one hand I felt above my head for the line of the steam whistle, and jerked out screech after screech hurriedly. The tumult of angry and warlike yells was checked instantly, and then from the depths of the woods went out such a tremulous and prolonged wail of mournful fear and utter despair as may be imagined to follow the flight of the last hope from the earth. There was a great commotion in the bush; the shower of arrows stopped, a few dropping shots rang out sharply—then silence, in which the languid beat of the stern-wheel came plainly to my ears. I put the helm hard a-starboard at the moment when the pilgrim in pink pyjamas, very hot and agitated, appeared in the doorway. 'The manager sends me—' he began in an official tone, and stopped short. 'Good God!' he said, glaring at the wounded man.

"We two whites stood over him, and his lustrous and inquiring glance enveloped us both. I declare it looked as though he would presently put to us some question in an understandable language; but he died without uttering a sound, without moving a limb, without twitching a muscle. Only in the very last moment, as though in response to some sign we could not see, to some whisper we could not hear, he frowned heavily, and that frown gave to his black death-mask an inconceivably sombre, brooding, and menacing expression. The lustre of inquiring glance faded swiftly into vacant glassiness. 'Can you steer?' I asked the agent eagerly. He looked very dubious; but I made a grab at his arm, and he understood at once I meant him to steer whether or no. To tell you the truth, I was morbidly anxious to change my shoes and socks. 'He is dead,' murmured the fellow, immensely impressed. 'No doubt about it,' said I, tugging like mad at the shoe-laces. 'And by the way, I suppose Mr Kurtz is dead as well by this time.'

"For the moment that was the dominant thought. There was a sense of extreme disappointment, as though I had found out I had been striving after something altogether without a substance. I couldn't have been more disgusted if I had travelled all this way for the sole purpose of talking with Mr Kurtz. Talking with . . . I flung one shoe overboard, and became aware that that was exactly what I had been looking forward to—a talk with Kurtz. I made the strange discovery that I had never imagined him as doing, you know, but as discoursing. I didn't say to myself, 'Now I will never see him,' or 'Now I will never shake him by the hand,' but, 'Now I will never hear him.' The man presented himself as a voice. Not of course that I did not connect him with some sort of action. Hadn't I been told in all the tones of jealousy and admiration that he had collected, bartered, swindled, or stolen more ivory than all the other agents together? That was not the point. The point was in his being a gifted creature, and that of all his gifts the one that stood out pre-eminently, that carried with it a sense of real presence, was his ability to talk, his words—the gift of expression, the bewildering, the illuminating, the most exalted and the most contemptible, the pulsating stream of light, or the deceitful flow from the heart of an impenetrable darkness.

"The other shoe went flying unto the devil-god of that river. I thought, By Jove! it's all over. We are too late; he has vanished—the gift has vanished, by means of some spear, arrow, or club. I will never hear that chap speak after all—and my sorrow had a startling extravagance of emotion, even such as I had noticed in the howling sorrow of these savages in the bush. I couldn't have felt more of lonely desolation somehow, had I been robbed of a belief or had missed my destiny in life. . . . Why do you sigh in this beastly way, somebody? Absurd? Well, absurd. Good Lord! mustn't a man ever—Here, give me some tobacco." . . .

There was a pause of profound stillness, then a match flared, and Marlow's lean face appeared, worn, hollow, with downward folds and dropped eyelids, with an aspect of concentrated attention; and as he took vigorous draws at his pipe, it seemed to retreat and advance out of the night in the regular flicker of the tiny flame. The match went out.

"Absurd!" he cried. "This is the worst of trying to tell . . . Here you all are, each moored with two good addresses, like a hulk with two anchors, a butcher round one corner, a policeman round another, excellent appetites, and temperature normal—you hear—normal from year's end to year's end. And you say, Absurd! Absurd be—exploded! Absurd! My dear boys, what can you expect from a man who out of sheer nervousness had just flung overboard a pair of new shoes? Now I think of it, it is amazing I did not shed tears. I am, upon the whole, proud of my fortitude. I was cut to the quick at the idea of having lost the inestimable privilege of listening to the gifted Kurtz. Of course I was wrong. The privilege was waiting for me. Oh yes, I heard more than enough. And I was right, too. A voice. He was very little more than a voice. And I heard—him—it—this voice—other voices—all of them were so little more than voices—and the memory of that time itself lingers around me, impalpable, like a dying vibration of one immense jabber, silly, atrocious, sordid, savage, or simply mean, without any kind of sense. Voices, voices—even the girl herself—now—"

He was silent for a long time.

"I laid the ghost of his gifts at last with a lie," he began suddenly. "Girl! What? Did I mention a girl? Oh, she is out of it—completely. They—the women I mean—are out of it—should be out of it. We must help them to stay in that beautiful world of their own, lest ours gets worse. Oh, she had to be out of it. You should have heard the disinterred body of Mr Kurtz saying, 'My Intended.' You would have perceived directly then how completely she was out of it. And the lofty frontal bone of Mr Kurtz! They say the hair goes on growing sometimes, but this—ah—specimen was impressively bald. The wilderness had patted him on the head, and, behold, it was like a ball—an ivory ball; it had caressed him, and—lo!—he had withered; it had taken him, loved him, embraced him, got into his veins, consumed his flesh, and sealed his soul to its own by the inconceivable ceremonies of some devilish initiation. He was its spoiled and pampered favourite. Ivory? I should think so. Heaps of it, stacks of it. The old mud shanty was bursting with it. You would think there was not a single tusk left either above or below the ground in the whole country. 'Mostly fossil,' the manager had remarked disparagingly. It was no more fossil than I am; but they call it fossil when it is dug up. It appears these niggers do bury the tusks sometimes—but evidently they couldn't bury this parcel deep enough to save the gifted Mr Kurtz from his fate. We filled the steamboat with it, and had to pile a lot on the deck. Thus he could see and enjoy as long as he could see, because the appreciation of this favour had remained with him to the last. You should have heard him say, 'My ivory.' Oh yes, I heard him. 'My Intended, my ivory, my station, my river, my—' everything belonged to him. It made me hold my breath in expectation of hearing the wilderness burst into a prodigious peal of laughter that would shake the fixed stars in their places. Everything belonged to him—but that was a trifle. The thing was to know what he belonged to, how many powers of darkness claimed him for their own. That was the reflection that made you creepy all over. It was impossible—it was not good for one either—

trying to imagine. He had taken a high seat amongst the devils of the land—I mean literally. You can't understand. How could you?—with solid pavement under your feet, surrounded by kind neighbours ready to cheer you or to fall on you, stepping delicately between the butcher and the policeman, in the holy terror of scandal and gallows and lunatic asylums—how can you imagine what particular region of the first ages a man's untrammelled feet may take him into by the way of solitude—utter solitude without a policeman—by the way of silence—utter silence, where no warning voice of a kind neighbour can be heard whispering of public opinion? These little things make all the great difference. When they are gone you must fall back upon your own innate strength, upon your own capacity for faithfulness. Of course you may be too much of a fool to go wrong—too dull even to know you are being assaulted by the powers of darkness. I take it, no fool ever made a bargain for his soul with the devil: the fool is too much of a fool, or the devil too much of a devil—I don't know which. Or you may be such a thunderingly exalted creature as to be altogether deaf and blind to anything but heavenly sights and sounds. Then the earth for you is only a standing place—and whether to be like this is your loss or your gain I won't pretend to say. But most of us are neither one nor the other. The earth for us is a place to live in, where we must put up with sights, with sounds, with smells, too, by Jove!—breathe dead hippo, so to speak, and not be contaminated. And there, don't you see? your strength comes in, the faith in your ability for the digging of unostentatious holes to bury the stuff in—your power of devotion, not to yourself, but to an obscure, back-breaking business. And that's difficult enough. Mind, I am not trying to excuse or even explain—I am trying to account to myself for—for—Mr Kurtz—for the shade of Mr Kurtz. This initiated wraith from the back of Nowhere honoured me with its amazing confidence before it vanished altogether. This was because it could speak English to me. The original Kurtz had been educated partly in England, and—as he was good enough to say himself—his sympathies were in the right place. His mother was half-English, his father was half-French. All Europe contributed to the making of Kurtz; and by and by I learned that, most appropriately, the International Society for the Suppression of Savage Customs had entrusted him with the making of a report, for its future guidance. And he had written it too. I've seen it. I've read it. It was eloquent, vibrating with eloquence, but too high-strung, I think. Seventeen pages of close writing he had found time for! But this must have been before his—let us say—nerves went wrong, and caused him to preside at certain midnight dances ending with unspeakable rites, which—as far as I reluctantly gathered from what I heard at various times—were offered up to him—do you understand?—to Mr Kurtz himself. But it was a beautiful piece of writing. The opening paragraph, however, in the light of later information, strikes me now as ominous. He began with the argument that we whites, from the point of development we had arrived at, 'must necessarily appear to them [savages] in the nature of supernatural beings—we approach them with the might as of a deity,' and so on, and so on. 'By the simple exercise of our will we can exert a power for good practically unbounded,' etc. etc. From that point he soared and took me with him. The peroration was magnificent, though difficult to remember, you know. It gave me the notion of an exotic Immensity ruled by an august Benevolence. It made me tingle with enthusiasm. This was the unbounded power of eloquence—of words—of burning noble words. There were no practical hints to interrupt the magic current of phrases, unless a kind of note at the foot of the last page, scrawled evidently much later, in an unsteady hand, may be regarded as the exposition of a method. It was very simple, and at the end of that moving appeal to every altruistic sentiment it blazed at you, luminous and terrifying, like a flash of lightning in a serene sky: 'Exterminate all the brutes!' The curious part was that he had apparently forgotten all about that valuable postscriptum, because, later on, when he in a sense came to himself, he repeatedly entreated me to take good care of 'my pamphlet' (he called it), as it was sure to have in the future a good influence upon his career. I had full information about all these things, and, besides, as it turned out, I was to have the care of his memory. I've done enough for it to give me the indisputable right to lay it, if I choose, for an everlasting rest in the dust-bin of progress, amongst all the sweepings and, figuratively speaking, all the dead cats of civilisation. But then, you see, I can't choose. He won't be forgotten. Whatever he was, he was not common. He had the power to charm or frighten rudimentary souls into an aggravated witchdance in his honour; he could also fill the small souls of the pilgrims with bitter misgivings: he had one devoted friend at least, and he had conquered one soul in the world that was neither rudimentary nor tainted with self-seeking. No; I can't forget him, though I am not prepared to affirm the fellow was exactly worth the life we lost in getting to him. I missed my late helmsman awfully—I missed him even while his body was still lying in the pilot-house. Perhaps you will think it passing strange this regret for a savage who was no more account than a grain of sand in a black Sahara. Well, don't you see, he had done something, he had steered; for months I had him at my back—a help—an instrument. It was a kind of partnership. He steered for me—I had to look after him, I worried about his deficiencies, and thus a subtle bond had been created, of which I only became aware when it was suddenly broken. And the intimate profundity of that look he gave me when he received his hurt remains to this day in my memory—like a claim of distant kinship affirmed in a supreme moment.

"Poor fool! If he had only left that shutter alone. He had no restraint, no restraint—just like Kurtz—a tree swayed by the wind. As soon as I had put on a dry pair of slippers, I dragged him out, after first jerking the spear out of his side, which operation I confess I performed with my eyes shut tight. His heels leaped together over the little doorstep; his shoulders were pressed to my breast; I hugged him from behind desperately. Oh! he was heavy, heavy; heavier than any man on earth, I should imagine. Then without more ado I tipped him overboard. The current snatched him as though he had been a wisp of grass, and I saw the body roll over twice before I lost sight of it for ever. All the pilgrims and the manager were then congregated on the awning-deck about the pilot-house, chattering at each other like a flock of excited magpies, and there was a scandalised murmur at my heartless promptitude. What they wanted to keep that body hanging about for I can't guess. Embalm it, maybe. But I had also heard another, and a very ominous, murmur on the deck below. My friends the wood-cutters were likewise scandalised, and with a better show of reason—though I admit that the reason itself was quite inadmissible. Oh, quite! I had made up my mind that if my late helmsman was to be eaten, the fishes alone should have him. He had been a very second-rate helmsman while alive, but now he was dead he might have become a first-class temptation, and possibly cause some startling trouble. Besides, I was anxious to take the wheel, the man in pink pyjamas showing himself a hopeless duffer at the business.

"This I did directly the simple funeral was over. We were going half-speed, keeping right in the middle of the stream, and I listened to the talk about me. They had given up Kurtz, they had given up the station; Kurtz was dead, and the station had been burnt—and so on—and so on. The red-haired pilgrim was beside himself with the thought that at least this poor Kurtz had been properly revenged. 'Say! We must have made a glorious slaughter of them in the bush. Eh? What do you think? Say?' He positively danced, the bloodthirsty little gingery beggar.[3] And he had nearly fainted when he saw the wounded man! I could not help saying, 'You made a glorious lot of smoke, anyhow.' I had seen, from the way the tops of the bushes rustled and flew, that almost all the shots had gone too high. You can't hit anything unless you take aim and fire from the shoulder; but these chaps fired from the hip with their eyes shut. The retreat, I maintained—and I was right—was caused by the screeching of the steam-whistle. Upon this they forgot Kurtz, and began to howl at me with indignant protests.

"The manager stood by the wheel murmuring confidentially about the necessity of getting well away down the river before dark at all events, when I saw in the distance a clearing on the river-side and the outlines of some sort of building. 'What's this?' I asked. He clapped his hands in wonder. 'The station!' he cried. I edged in at once, still going half-speed.

"Through my glasses I saw the slope of a hill interspersed with rare trees and perfectly free from undergrowth. A long decaying building on the summit was half buried in the high grass; the large holes in the peaked roof gaped black from afar; the jungle and the woods made a background. There was no enclosure or fence of any kind; but there had been one apparently, for near the house half a dozen slim posts remained in a row, roughly trimmed, and with their upper ends ornamented with round carved balls. The rails, or whatever there had been between, had disappeared. Of course the forest surrounded all that. The river-bank was clear, and on the water side I saw a white man under a hat like a cart-wheel beckoning persistently with his whole arm. Examining the edge of the forest above and below, I was almost certain I could see movements—human forms gliding here and there. I steamed past prudently, then stopped the engines and let her drift down. The man on the shore began to shout, urging us to land. 'We have been attacked,' screamed the manager. 'I know—I know. It's all right,' yelled back the other, as cheerful as you please. 'Come along. It's all right. I am glad.'

"His aspect reminded me of something I had seen—something funny I had seen somewhere. As I manœuvred to get alongside, I was asking myself, 'What does this fellow look like?' Suddenly I got it. He looked like a harlequin. His clothes had been made of some stuff that was brown holland[4] probably, but it was covered with patches all over, with bright patches, blue, red, and yellow—patches on the back, patches on the front, patches on elbows, on knees; coloured binding round his jacket, scarlet edging at the

---

3. Red-haired rascal (British).   4. Unbleached linen fabric. *Harlequin:* a traditional clown figure known by his multicolored costume.

bottom of his trousers; and the sunshine made him look extremely gay and wonderfully neat withal, because you could see how beautifully all this patching had been done. A beardless, boyish face, very fair, no features to speak of, nose peeling, little blue eyes, smiles and frowns chasing each other over that open countenance like sunshine and shadow on a wind-swept plain. 'Look out, captain!' he cried; 'there's a snag lodged in here last night.' What! Another snag? I confess I swore shamefully. I had nearly holed my cripple, to finish off that charming trip. The harlequin on the bank turned his little pug nose up to me. 'You English?' he asked, all smiles. 'Are you?' I shouted from the wheel. The smiles vanished, and he shook his head as if sorry for my disappointment. Then he brightened up. 'Never mind!' he cried encouragingly. 'Are we in time?' I asked. 'He is up there,' he replied, with a toss of the head up the hill, and becoming gloomy all of a sudden. His face was like the autumn sky, overcast one moment and bright the next.

"When the manager, escorted by the pilgrims, all of them armed to the teeth, had gone to the house, this chap came on board. 'I say, I don't like this. These natives are in the bush,' I said. He assured me earnestly it was all right. 'They are simple people,' he added; 'well, I am glad you came. It took me all my time to keep them off.' 'But you said it was all right,' I cried. 'Oh, they meant no harm,' he said; and as I stared he corrected himself, 'Not exactly.' Then vivaciously, 'My faith, your pilot-house wants a clean up!' In the next breath he advised me to keep enough steam on the boiler to blow the whistle in case of any trouble. 'One good screech will do more for you than all your rifles. They are simple people,' he repeated. He rattled away at such a rate he quite overwhelmed me. He seemed to be trying to make up for lots of silence, and actually hinted, laughing, that such was the case. 'Don't you talk with Mr Kurtz?' I said. 'You don't talk with that man—you listen to him,' he exclaimed with severe exaltation. 'But now—' He waved his arm, and in the twinkling of an eye was in the uttermost depths of despondency. In a moment he came up again with a jump, possessed himself of both my hands, shook them continuously, while he gabbled: 'Brother sailor . . . honour . . . pleasure . . . delight . . . introduce   myself . . . Russian . . . son of an arch-priest . . . Government of Tambov . . . What? Tobacco! English tobacco; the excellent English tobacco! Now, that's brotherly. Smoke? Where's a sailor that does not smoke?'

"The pipe soothed him, and gradually I made out he had run away from school, had gone to sea in a Russian ship; ran away again; served some time in English ships; was now reconciled with the arch-priest. He made a point of that. 'But when one is young one must see things, gather experience, ideas; enlarge the mind.' 'Here!' I interrupted. 'You can never tell! Here I met Mr Kurtz,' he said, youthfully solemn and reproachful. I held my tongue after that. It appears he had persuaded a Dutch trading-house on the coast to fit him out with stores and goods, and had started for the interior with a light heart, and no more idea of what would happen to him than a baby. He had been wandering about that river for nearly two years alone, cut off from everybody and everything. 'I am not so young as I look. I am twenty-five,' he said. 'At first old Van Shuyten would tell me to go to the devil,' he narrated with keen enjoyment; 'but I stuck to him, and talked and talked, till at last he got afraid I would talk the hind-leg off his favourite dog, so he gave me some cheap things and a few guns, and told me he hoped he would never see my face again. Good old Dutchman, Van Shuyten. I sent him one small lot of ivory a year ago, so that he can't call me a little thief when I get back. I hope he got it. And for the rest I don't care. I had some wood stacked for you. That was my old house. Did you see?'

"I gave him Towson's book. He made as though he would kiss me, but restrained himself. 'The only book I had left, and I thought I had lost it,' he said, looking at it ecstatically. 'So many accidents happen to a man going about alone, you know. Canoes get upset sometimes—and sometimes you've got to clear out so quick when the people get angry.' He thumbed the pages. 'You made notes in Russian?' I asked. He nodded. 'I thought they were writ-ten in cipher,' I said. He laughed, then became serious. 'I had lots of trouble to keep these people off,' he said. 'Did they want to kill you?' I asked. 'Oh no!' he cried, and checked himself. 'Why did they attack us?' I pursued. He hesitated, then said shamefacedly, 'They don't want him to go.' 'Don't they?' I said curiously. He nodded a nod full of mystery and wisdom. 'I tell you,' he cried, 'this man has enlarged my mind.' He opened his arms wide, staring at me with his little blue eyes that were perfectly round."

3

"I looked at him, lost in astonishment. There he was before me, in motley, as though he had absconded from a troupe of mimes, enthusiastic, fabulous. His very existence was improbable, inexplicable, and altogether bewildering. He was an insoluble problem. It was inconceivable how he had existed, how he had succeeded in getting so far, how he had managed to remain—why he did not instantly disappear. 'I went a little farther,' he said, 'then still a little farther—till I had gone so far that I don't know how I'll ever get back. Never mind. Plenty time. I can manage. You take Kurtz away quick—quick—I tell you.' The glamour of youth enveloped his particoloured rags, his des-titution, his loneliness, the essential desolation of his futile wanderings. For months—for years—his life hadn't been worth a day's purchase; and there he was gallantly, thoughtlessly alive, to all appearance indestructible solely by the virtue of his few years and of his unreflecting audacity. I was seduced into something like admiration—like envy. Glamour urged him on, glamour kept him unscathed. He surely wanted nothing from the wilderness but space to breathe in and to push on through. His need was to exist, and to move onwards at the greatest possible risk, and with a maximum of privation. If the absolutely pure, uncalculating, unpractical spirit of adventure had ever ruled a human being, it ruled this be-patched youth. I almost envied him the possession of this modest and clear flame. It seemed to have consumed all thought of self so completely, that, even while he was talking to you, you forgot that it was he—the man before your eyes—who had gone through these things. I did not envy him his devotion to Kurtz, though. He had not meditated over it. It came to him, and he accepted it with a sort of eager fatalism. I must say that to me it appeared about the most dangerous thing in every way he had come upon so far.

"They had come together unavoidably, like two ships becalmed near each other, and lay rubbing sides at last. I suppose Kurtz wanted an audience, because on a certain occasion, when encamped in the forest, they had talked all night, or more probably Kurtz had talked. 'We talked of everything,' he said, quite transported at the recollection. 'I forgot there was such a thing as sleep. The night did not seem to last an hour. Everything! Everything! . . . Of love too.' 'Ah, he talked to you of love!' I said, much amused. 'It isn't what you think,' he cried, almost passionately. 'It was in general. He made me see things—things.'

"He threw his arms up. We were on deck at the time, and the head-man of my wood-cutters, lounging near by, turned upon him his heavy and glittering eyes. I looked around, and I don't know why, but I assure you that never, never before, did this land, this river, this jungle, the very arch of this blazing sky, appear to me so hopeless and so dark, so impenetrable to human thought, so pitiless to human weakness. 'And, ever since, you have been with him, of course?' I said.

"On the contrary. It appears their intercourse had been very much broken by various causes. He had, as he informed me proudly, managed to nurse Kurtz through two illnesses (he alluded to it as you would to some risky feat), but as a rule Kurtz wandered alone, far in the depths of the forest. 'Very often coming to this station, I had to wait days and days before he would turn up,' he said. 'Ah, it was worth waiting for!—sometimes.' 'What was he doing? exploring or what?' I asked. 'Oh yes, of course'; he had discovered lots of villages, a lake too—he did not know exactly in what direction; it was dangerous to inquire too much—but mostly his expeditions had been for ivory. 'But he had no goods to trade with by that time,' I objected. 'There's a good lot of cartridges left even yet,' he answered, looking away. 'To speak plainly, he raided the country,' I said. He nodded. 'Not alone, surely!' He muttered something about the villages round that lake. 'Kurtz got the tribe to follow him, did he?' I suggested. He fidgeted a little. 'They adored him,' he said. The tone of these words was so extraordinary that I looked at him searchingly. It was curious to see his mingled eagerness and reluctance to speak of Kurtz. The man filled his life, occupied his thoughts, swayed his emotions. 'What can you expect?' he burst out; 'he came to them with thunder and lightning, you know—and they had never seen anything like it—and very terrible. He could be very terrible. You can't judge Mr Kurtz as you would an ordinary man. No, no, no! Now—just to give you an idea—I don't mind telling you, he wanted to shoot me too one day—but I don't judge him.' 'Shoot you!' I cried. 'What for?' 'Well, I had a small lot of ivory the chief of that village near my house gave me. You see I used to shoot game for them. Well, he wanted it, and wouldn't hear reason. He declared he would shoot me unless I gave him the ivory and then cleared out of the country, because he could do so, and had a fancy for it, and there was nothing on earth to prevent him killing whom he jolly well pleased. And it was true too. I gave him the ivory. What did I care! But I didn't clear out. No, no. I couldn't leave him. I had to be careful, of course, till we got friendly again for a time. He had his second illness then. Afterwards I had to keep out of the way; but I didn't mind. He was living for the most part in those villages on the lake. When he came down to the river, sometimes he would take to me, and sometimes it was better for me to be careful. This man suffered too much. He hated all this, and somehow he couldn't get away. When I had a chance I begged him to try and leave while there was time; I offered to go back with him. And he would say yes, and then he would remain; go off on another ivory hunt; disappear for weeks; forget himself amongst these people—forget himself—you know.' 'Why! he's mad,' I said. He protested indignantly. Mr Kurtz couldn't be mad. If I had heard him talk, only two days ago, I wouldn't dare hint at such a thing. . . . I had taken up my binoculars while we talked, and was looking at the shore, sweeping the limit of the forest at each side and at the back of the house. The consciousness of there being people in that bush, so silent, so quiet—as silent and quiet as the ruined house on the hill—made me uneasy. There was no sign on the face of nature of this amazing tale that was not so much told as suggested to me in desolate exclamations, completed by shrugs, in interrupted phrases, in hints ending in deep sighs. The woods were unmoved, like a mask—heavy, like the closed door of a prison—they looked with their air of hidden knowledge, of patient expectation, of unapproachable silence. The Russian was explaining to me that it was only lately that Mr Kurtz had come down to the river, bringing along with him all the fighting men of that lake tribe. He had been absent for several months—getting himself adored, I suppose—and had come down unexpectedly, with the intention to all appearance of making a raid either across the river or down stream. Evidently the appetite for more ivory had got the better of the—what shall I say?—less material aspirations. However, he had got much worse suddenly. 'I heard he was lying helpless, and so I came up—took my chance,' said the Russian. 'Oh, he is bad, very bad.' I directed my glass to the house. There were no signs of life, but there was the ruined roof, the long mud wall peeping above the grass, with three little square window-holes, no two of the same size; all this brought within reach of my hand, as it were. And then I made a brusque movement, and one of the remaining posts of that vanished fence leaped up in the field of my glass. You remember I told you I had been struck at the distance by certain attempts at ornamentation, rather remarkable in the ruinous aspect of the place. Now I had suddenly a nearer view, and its first result was to make me throw my head back as if before a blow. Then I went carefully from post to post with my glass, and I saw my mistake. These round knobs were not ornamental but symbolic; they were expressive and puzzling, striking and disturbing—food for thought and also for the vultures if there had been any looking down from the sky; but at all events for such ants as were industrious enough to ascend the pole. They would have been even more impressive, those heads on the stakes, if their faces had not been turned to the house. Only one, the first I had made out, was facing my way. I was not so shocked as you may think. The start back I had given was really nothing but a movement of surprise. I had expected to see a knob of wood there, you know. I returned deliberately to the first I had seen—and there it was, black, dried, sunken, with closed eyelids—a head that seemed to sleep at the top of that pole, and, with the shrunken dry lips showing a narrow white line of the teeth, was smiling too, smiling continuously at some endless and jocose dream of that eternal slumber.

"I am not disclosing any trade secrets. In fact the manager said afterwards that Mr Kurtz's methods had ruined the district. I have no opinion on that point, but I want you clearly to understand that there was nothing exactly profitable in these heads being there. They only show that Mr Kurtz lacked restraint in the gratification of his various lusts, that there was something wanting in him—some small matter which, when the pressing need arose, could not be found under his magnificent eloquence. Whether he knew of this deficiency himself I can't say. I think the knowledge came to him at last—only at the very last. But the wilderness had found him out early, and had taken on him a terrible vengeance for the fantastic invasion. I think it had whispered to him things about himself which he did not know, things of which he had no conception till he took counsel with this great solitude—and the whisper had proved irresistibly fascinating. It echoed loudly within him because he was hollow at the core. . . . I put down the glass, and the head that had appeared near enough to be spoken to seemed at once to have leaped away from me into inaccessible distance.

"The admirer of Mr Kurtz was a bit crestfallen. In a hurried, indistinct voice he began to assure me he had not dared to take these—say, symbols—down. He was not afraid of the natives; they would not stir till Mr Kurtz gave the word. His ascendancy was extraordinary. The camps of these people surrounded the place, and the chiefs came every day to see him. They would crawl . . . 'I don't want to know anything of the ceremonies used when approaching Mr Kurtz,' I shouted. Curious, this feeling that came over me that such details would be more intolerable than those heads drying on the stakes under Mr Kurtz's windows. After all, that was only a savage sight, while I seemed at one bound to have been transported into some lightless region of subtle horrors, where pure, uncomplicated savagery was a positive relief, being something that had a right to exist—obviously—in the sunshine. The young man looked at me with surprise. I suppose it did not occur to him that Mr Kurtz was no idol of mine. He forgot I hadn't heard any of these splendid monologues on, what was it? on love, justice, conduct of life—or what not. If it had come to crawling before Mr Kurtz, he crawled as much as the veriest savage of them all. I had no idea of the conditions, he said: these heads were the heads of rebels. I shocked him excessively by laughing. Rebels! What would be the next definition I was to hear? There had been enemies, criminals, workers—and these were rebels. Those rebellious heads looked very subdued to me on their sticks. 'You don't know how such a life tries a man like Kurtz,' cried Kurtz's last disciple. 'Well, and you?' I said. 'I! I! I am a simple man. I have no great thoughts. I want nothing from anybody. How can you compare me to . . . ?' His feelings were too much for speech, and suddenly he broke down. 'I don't understand,' he groaned. 'I've been doing my best to keep him alive, and that's enough. I had no hand in all this. I have no abilities. There hasn't been a drop of medicine or a mouthful of invalid food for months here. He was shamefully abandoned. A man like this, with such ideas. Shamefully! Shamefully! I—I—haven't slept for the last ten nights. . . .'

"His voice lost itself in the calm of the evening. The long shadows of the forest had slipped down hill while we talked, had gone far beyond the ruined hovel, beyond the symbolic row of stakes. All this was in the gloom, while we down there were yet in the sunshine, and the stretch of the river abreast of the clearing glittered in a still and dazzling splendour, with a murky and overshadowed bend above and below. Not a living soul was seen on the shore. The bushes did not rustle.

"Suddenly round the corner of the house a group of men appeared, as though they had come up from the ground. They waded waist-deep in the grass, in a compact body, bearing an improvised stretcher in their midst. Instantly, in the emptiness of the landscape, a cry arose whose shrillness pierced the still air like a sharp arrow flying straight to the very heart of the land; and, as if by enchantment, streams of human beings—of naked human beings—with spears in their hands, with bows, with shields, with wild glances and savage movements, were poured into the clearing by the dark-faced and pensive forest. The bushes shook, the grass swayed for a time, and then everything stood still in attentive immobility.

" 'Now, if he does not say the right thing to them we are all done for,' said the Russian at my elbow. The knot of men with the stretcher had stopped too, half-way to the steamer, as if petrified. I saw the man on the stretcher sit up, lank and with an uplifted arm, above the shoulders of the bearers. 'Let us hope that the man who can talk so well of love in general will find some particular reason to spare us this time,' I said. I resented bitterly the absurd danger of our situation, as if to be at the mercy of that atrocious phantom had been a dishonouring necessity. I could not hear a sound, but through my glasses I saw the thin arm extended commandingly, the lower jaw moving, the eyes of that apparition shining darkly far in its bony head that nodded with grotesque jerks. Kurtz—Kurtz—that means 'short' in German—don't it? Well, the name was as true as everything else in his life—and death. He looked at least seven feet long. His covering had fallen off, and his body emerged from it pitiful and appalling as from a winding-sheet. I could see the cage of his ribs all astir, the bones of his arm waving. It was as though an animated image of death carved out of old ivory had been shaking its hand with menaces at a motionless crowd of men made of dark and glittering bronze. I saw him open his mouth wide—it gave him a weirdly voracious aspect, as though he had wanted to swallow all the air, all the earth, all the men before him. A deep voice reached me faintly. He must have been shouting. He fell back suddenly. The stretcher shook as the bearers staggered forward again, and almost at the same time I noticed that the crowd of savages was vanishing without any perceptible movement of retreat, as if the forest that had ejected these beings so suddenly had drawn them in again as the breath is drawn in a long aspiration.

"Some of the pilgrims behind the stretcher carried his arms—two shotguns, a heavy rifle, and a light revolver-carbine—the thunderbolts of that pitiful Jupiter. The manager bent over him murmuring as he walked beside his head. They laid him down in one of the little cabins—just a room for a bedplace and a camp-stool or two, you know. We had brought his belated correspondence, and a lot of torn envelopes and open letters littered his bed. His hand roamed feebly amongst these papers. I was struck by the fire of his eyes and the composed languor of his expression. It was not so much the exhaustion of disease. He did not seem in pain. This shadow looked satiated and calm, as though for the moment it had had its fill of all the emotions.

"He rustled one of the letters, and looking straight in my face said, 'I am glad.' Somebody had been writing to him about me. These special recommendations were turning up again. The volume of tone he emitted without effort, almost without the trouble of moving his lips, amazed me. A voice! a voice! It was grave, profound, vibrating, while the man did not seem capable of a whisper. However, he had enough strength in him—factitious no doubt—to very nearly make an end of us, as you shall hear directly.

"The manager appeared silently in the doorway; I stepped out at once and he drew the curtain after me. The Russian, eyed curiously by the pilgrims, was staring at the shore. I followed the direction of his glance.

"Dark human shapes could be made out in the distance, flitting indistinctly against the gloomy border of the forest, and near the river two bronze figures, leaning on tall spears, stood in the sunlight under fantastic head-dresses of spotted skins, warlike and still in statuesque repose. And from right to left along the lighted shore moved a wild and gorgeous apparition of a woman.

"She walked with measured steps, draped in striped and fringed cloths, treading the earth proudly, with a slight jingle and flash of barbarous orna-ments. She carried her head high; her hair was done in the shape of a helmet; she had brass leggings to the knee, brass wire gauntlets to the elbow, a crimson spot on her tawny cheek, innumerable necklaces of glass beads on her neck; bizarre things, charms, gifts of witch-men, that hung about her, glittered and trembled at every step. She must have had the value of several elephant tusks upon her. She was savage and superb, wild-eyed and magnif-icent; there was something ominous and stately in her deliberate progress. And in the hush that had fallen suddenly upon the whole sorrowful land, the immense wilderness, the colossal body of the fecund and mysterious life seemed to look at her, pensive, as though it had been looking at the image of its own tenebrous and passionate soul.

"She came abreast of the steamer, stood still, and faced us. Her long shadow fell to the water's edge. Her face had a tragic and fierce aspect of wild sorrow and of dumb pain mingled with the fear of some struggling, half-shaped resolve. She stood looking at us without a stir, and like the wilderness itself, with an air of brooding over an inscrutable purpose. A whole minute passed, and then she made a step forward. There was a low jingle, a glint of yellow metal, a sway of fringed draperies, and she stopped as if her heart had failed her. The young fellow by my side growled. The pilgrims murmured at my back. She looked at us all as if her life had depended upon the unswerving steadiness of her glance. Suddenly she opened her bared arms and threw them up rigid above her head, as though in an uncontrollable desire to touch the sky, and at the same time the swift shadows darted out on the earth, swept around on the river, gathering the steamer into a shadowy embrace. A formidable silence hung over the scene.

"She turned away slowly, walked on, following the bank, and passed into the bushes to the left. Once only her eyes gleamed back at us in the dusk of the thickets before she disappeared.

" 'If she had offered to come aboard I really think I would have tried to shoot her,' said the man of patches nervously. 'I had been risking my life every day for the last fortnight to keep her out of the house. She got in one day and kicked up a row about those miserable rags I picked up in the store-room to mend my clothes with. I wasn't decent. At least it must have been that, for she talked like a fury to Kurtz for an hour, pointing at me now and then. I don't understand the dialect of this tribe. Luckily for me, I fancy Kurtz felt too ill that day to care, or there would have been mischief. I don't understand. . . . No—it's too much for me. Ah, well, it's all over now.'

"At this moment I heard Kurtz's deep voice behind the curtain: 'Save me!—save the ivory, you mean. Don't tell me. Save *me*! Why, I've had to save you. You are interrupting my plans now. Sick! Sick! Not so sick as you would like to believe. Never mind. I'll carry my ideas out yet—I will return. I'll show you what can be done. You with your little peddling notions—you are inter-fering with me. I will return. I . . . '

"The manager came out. He did me the honour to take me under the arm and lead me aside. 'He is very low, very low,' he said. He considered it necessary to sigh, but neglected to be consistently sorrowful. 'We have done all we could for him—haven't we? But there is no disguising the fact, Mr Kurtz has done more harm than good to the Company. He did not see the time was not ripe for vigorous action. Cautiously, cautiously—that's my principle. We must be cautious yet. The district is closed to us for a time. Deplorable! Upon the whole, the trade will suffer. I don't deny there is a remarkable quantity of ivory—mostly fossil. We must save it, at all events—but look how precarious the position is—and why? Because the method is unsound.' 'Do you,' said I, looking at the shore, 'call it "unsound method"?' 'Without doubt,' he exclaimed hotly, 'Don't you?' . . . 'No method at all,' I murmured after a while. 'Exactly,' he exulted. 'I anticipated this. Shows a complete want of judgment. It is my duty to point it out in the proper quarter.' 'Oh,' said I, 'that fellow—what's his name?—the brickmaker, will make a readable report for you.' He appeared confounded for a moment. It seemed to me I had never breathed an atmosphere so vile, and I turned mentally to Kurtz for relief—positively for relief. 'Nevertheless, I think Mr Kurtz is a remarkable man,' I said with emphasis. He started, dropped on me a cold heavy glance, said very quietly, 'He *was*,' and turned his back on me. My hour of favour was over; I found myself lumped along with Kurtz as a partisan of methods for which the time was not ripe: I was unsound! Ah! but it was something to have at least a choice of nightmares.

"I had turned to the wilderness really, not to Mr Kurtz, who, I was ready to admit, was as good as buried. And for a moment it seemed to me as if I also were buried in a vast grave full of unspeakable secrets. I felt an intolerable weight oppressing my breast, the smell of the damp earth, the unseen presence of victorious corruption, the darkness of an impenetrable night. . . . The Russian tapped me on the shoulder. I heard him mumbling and stammering something about 'brother seaman—couldn't conceal—knowledge of matters that would affect Mr Kurtz's reputation.' I waited. For him evidently Mr Kurtz was not in his grave; I suspect that for him Mr Kurtz was one of the immortals. 'Well!' said I at last, 'speak out. As it happens, I am Mr Kurtz's friend—in a way.'

"He stated with a good deal of formality that had we not been 'of the same profession,' he would have kept the matter to himself without regard to consequences. He suspected 'there was an active ill-will towards him on the part of these white men that—' 'You are right,' I said, remembering a certain conversation I had overheard. 'The manager thinks you ought to be hanged.' He showed a concern at this intelligence which amused me at first. 'I had better get out of the way quietly,' he said earnestly. 'I can do no more for Kurtz now, and they would soon find some excuse. What's to stop them? There's a military post three hundred miles from here.' 'Well, upon my word,' said I, 'perhaps you had better go if you have any friends amongst the savages near by.' 'Plenty,' he said. 'They are simple people—and I want nothing, you know.' He stood biting his lip, then: 'I don't want any harm to happen to these whites here, but of course I was thinking of Mr Kurtz's reputation—but you are a brother seaman and—' 'All right,' said I, after a time. 'Mr Kurtz's reputation is safe with me.' I did not know how truly I spoke.

"He informed me, lowering his voice, that it was Kurtz who had ordered the attack to be made on the steamer. 'He hated sometimes the idea of being taken away—and then again . . . But I don't understand these matters. I am a simple man. He thought it would scare you away—that you would give it up, thinking him dead. I could not stop him. Oh, I had an awful time of it this last month.' 'Very well,' I said. 'He is all right now.' 'Ye-e-es,' he muttered, not very convinced apparently. 'Thanks,' said I; 'I shall keep my eyes open.' 'But quiet—eh?' he urged anxiously. 'It would be awful for his reputation if anybody here—' I promised a complete discretion with great gravity. 'I have a canoe and three black fellows waiting not very far. I am off. Could you give me a few Martini-Henry cartridges?' I could, and did, with proper secrecy. He helped himself, with a wink at me, to a handful of my tobacco. 'Between sailors—you know—good English tobacco.' At the door of the pilot-house he turned round—'I say, haven't you a pair of shoes you could spare?' He raised one leg. 'Look.' The soles were tied with knotted strings sandal-wise under his bare feet. I rooted out an old pair, at which he looked with admiration before tucking it under his left arm. One of his pockets (bright red) was bulging with cartridges, from the other (dark blue) peeped 'Towson's Inquiry,' etc. etc. He seemed to think himself excellently well equipped for a renewed encounter with the wilderness. 'Ah! I'll never, never meet such a man again. You ought to have heard him recite poetry—his own too it was, he told me. Poetry!' He rolled his eyes at the recollection of these delights. 'Oh, he enlarged my mind!' 'Good-bye,' said I. He shook hands and vanished in the night. Sometimes I ask myself whether I had ever really seen him— whether it was possible to meet such a phenomenon! . . .

"When I woke up shortly after midnight his warning came to my mind with its hint of danger that seemed, in the starred darkness, real enough to make me get up for the purpose of having a look round. On the hill a big fire burned, illuminating fitfully a crooked corner of the station-house. One of the agents with a picket of a few of our blacks, armed for the purpose, was keeping guard over the ivory; but deep within the forest, red gleams that wavered, that seemed to sink and rise from the ground amongst confused columnar shapes of intense blackness, showed the exact position of the camp where Mr Kurtz's adorers were keeping their uneasy vigil. The monotonous beating of a big drum filled the air with muffled shocks and a lingering vibration. A steady droning sound of many men chanting each to himself some weird incantation came out from the black, flat wall of the woods as the humming of bees comes out of a hive, and had a strange narcotic effect upon my half-awake senses. I believe I dozed off leaning over the rail, till an abrupt burst of yells, an overwhelming outbreak of a pent-up and mysterious frenzy, woke me up in a bewildered wonder. It was cut short all at once, and the low droning went on with an effect of audible and soothing silence. I glanced casually into the little cabin. A light was burning within, but Mr Kurtz was not there.

"I think I would have raised an outcry if I had believed my eyes. But I didn't believe them at first—the thing seemed so impossible. The fact is I was completely unnerved by a sheer blank fright, pure abstract terror, unconnected with any distinct shape of physical danger. What made this emotion so overpowering was—how shall I define it?—the moral shock I received, as if something altogether monstrous, intolerable to thought and odious to the soul, had been thrust upon me unexpectedly. This lasted of course the merest fraction of a second, and then the usual sense of commonplace, deadly danger, the possibility of a sudden onslaught and massacre, or something of the kind, which I saw impending, was positively welcome and composing. It pacified me, in fact, so much, that I did not raise an alarm.

"There was an agent buttoned up inside an ulster[5] and sleeping on a chair on deck within three feet of me. The yells had not awakened him; he snored very slightly; I left him to his slumbers and leaped ashore. I did not betray Mr Kurtz—it was ordered I should never betray him—it was written I should be loyal to the nightmare of my choice. I was anxious to deal with this shadow by myself alone—and to this day I don't know why I was so jealous of sharing with any one the peculiar blackness of that experience.

"As soon as I got on the bank I saw a trail—a broad trail through the grass. I remember the exultation with which I said to myself, 'He can't walk—he is crawling on all-fours—I've got him.' The grass was wet with dew. I strode rapidly with clenched fists. I fancy I had some vague notion of falling upon him and giving him a drubbing. I don't know. I had some imbecile thoughts. The knitting old woman with the cat obtruded herself upon my memory as a most improper person to be sitting at the other end of such an affair. I saw a row of pilgrims squirting lead in the air out of Winchesters held to the hip. I thought I would never get back to the steamer, and imagined myself living alone and unarmed in the woods to an advanced age. Such silly things—you know. And I remember I confounded the beat of the drum with the beating of my heart, and was pleased at its calm regularity.

"I kept to the track though—then stopped to listen. The night was very clear; a dark blue space, sparkling with dew and starlight, in which black things stood very still. I thought I could see a kind of motion ahead of me. I was strangely cocksure of everything that night. I actually left the track and ran in a wide semicircle (I verily believe chuckling to myself) so as to get in front of that stir, of that motion I had seen—if indeed I had seen anything. I was circumventing Kurtz as though it had been a boyish game.

"I came upon him, and, if he had not heard me coming, I would have fallen over him too, but he got up in time. He rose, unsteady, long, pale, indistinct, like a vapour exhaled by the earth, and swayed slightly, misty and silent before me; while at my back the fires loomed between the trees, and the murmur of many voices issued from the forest. I had cut him off cleverly; but when actually confronting him I seemed to come to my senses, I saw the danger in its right proportion. It was by no means over yet. Suppose he began to shout? Though he could hardly stand, there was still plenty of vigour in his voice. 'Go away—hide yourself,' he said, in that profound tone. It was very awful. I glanced back. We were within thirty yards of the nearest fire. A black figure stood up, strode on long black legs, waving long black arms, across the glow. It had horns—antelope horns, I think—on its head. Some sorcerer, some witch-man no doubt: it looked fiend-like enough. 'Do you know what you are doing?' I whispered. 'Perfectly,' he answered, raising his voice for that single word: it sounded to me far off and yet loud, like a hail through a speaking-trumpet. If he makes a row we are lost, I thought to myself. This clearly was not a case for fisticuffs, even apart from the very natural aversion I had to beat that Shadow—this wandering and tormented thing. 'You will be lost,' I said—'utterly lost.' One gets sometimes such a

5. A long, loose overcoat often with a belt.

flash of inspiration, you know. I did say the right thing, though indeed he could not have been more irretrievably lost than he was at this very moment, when the foundations of our intimacy were being laid—to endure—to endure—even to the end—even beyond.

" 'I had immense plans,' he muttered irresolutely. 'Yes,' said I; 'but if you try to shout I'll smash your head with—' There was not a stick or a stone near. 'I will throttle you for good,' I corrected myself. 'I was on the threshold of great things,' he pleaded, in a voice of longing, with a wistfulness of tone that made my blood run cold. 'And now for this stupid scoundrel—' 'Your success in Europe is assured in any case,' I affirmed steadily. I did not want to have the throttling of him, you understand—and indeed it would have been very little use for any practical purpose. I tried to break the spell—the heavy, mute spell of the wilderness—that seemed to draw him to its pitiless breast by the awakening of forgotten and brutal instincts, by the memory of gratified and monstrous passions. This alone, I was convinced, had driven him out to the edge of the forest, to the bush, towards the gleam of fires, the throb of drums, the drone of weird incantations; this alone had beguiled his unlawful soul beyond the bounds of permitted aspirations. And, don't you see, the terror of the position was not in being knocked on the head—though I had a very lively sense of that danger too—but in this, that I had to deal with a being to whom I could not appeal in the name of anything high or low. I had, even like the niggers, to invoke him—himself—his own exalted and incredible degradation. There was nothing either above or below him, and I knew it. He had kicked himself loose of the earth. Confound the man! he had kicked the very earth to pieces. He was alone, and I before him did not know whether I stood on the ground or floated in the air. I've been telling you what we said—repeating the phrases we pronounced—but what's the good? They were common everyday words—the familiar, vague sounds exchanged on every waking day of life. But what of that? They had behind them, to my mind, the terrific suggestiveness of words heard in dreams, of phrases spoken in nightmares. Soul! If anybody had ever struggled with a soul, I am the man. And I wasn't arguing with a lunatic either. Believe me or not, his intelligence was perfectly clear—concentrated, it is true, upon himself with horrible intensity, yet clear; and therein was my only chance—barring, of course, the killing him there and then, which wasn't so good, on account of unavoidable noise. But his soul was mad. Being alone in the wilderness, it had looked within itself, and, by heavens! I tell you, it had gone mad. I had—for my sins, I suppose, to go through the ordeal of looking into it myself. No eloquence could have been so withering to one's belief in mankind as his final burst of sincerity. He struggled with himself too. I saw it—I heard it. I saw the inconceivable mystery of a soul that knew no restraint, no faith, and no fear, yet struggling blindly with itself. I kept my head pretty well; but when I had him at last stretched on the couch, I wiped my forehead, while my legs shook under me as though I had carried half a ton on my back down that hill. And yet I had only supported him, his bony arm clasped round my neck—and he was not much heavier than a child.

"When next day we left at noon, the crowd, of whose presence behind the curtain of trees I had been acutely conscious all the time, flowed out of the woods again, filled the clearing, covered the slope with a mass of naked, breathing, quivering, bronze bodies. I steamed up a bit, then swung downstream, and two thousand eyes followed the evolutions of the splashing, thumping, fierce river-demon beating the water with its terrible tail and breathing black smoke into the air. In front of the first rank, along the river, three men, plastered with bright red earth from head to foot, strutted to and fro restlessly. When we came abreast again, they faced the river, stamped their feet, nodded their horned heads, swayed their scarlet bodies; they shook towards the fierce river-demon a bunch of black feathers, a mangy skin with a pendent tail—something that looked like a dried gourd; they shouted periodically together strings of amazing words that resembled no sounds of human language; and the deep murmurs of the crowd, interrupted suddenly, were like the responses of some satanic litany.

"We had carried Kurtz into the pilot-house: there was more air there. Lying on the couch, he stared through the open shutter. There was an eddy in the mass of human bodies, and the woman with helmeted head and tawny cheeks rushed out to the very brink of the stream. She put out her hands, shouted something, and all that wild mob took up the shout in a roaring chorus of articulated, rapid, breathless utterance.

" 'Do you understand this?' I asked.

"He kept on looking out past me with fiery, longing eyes, with a mingled expression of wistfulness and hate. He made no answer, but I saw a smile, a smile of indefinable meaning, appear on his colourless lips that a moment after twitched convulsively. 'Do I not?' he said slowly, gasping, as if the words had been torn out of him by a supernatural power.

"I pulled the string of the whistle, and I did this because I saw the pilgrims on deck getting out their rifles with an air of anticipating a jolly lark. At the sudden screech there was a movement of abject terror through that wedged mass of bodies. 'Don't! don't you frighten them away,' cried some one on deck disconsolately. I pulled the string time after time. They broke and ran, they leaped, they crouched, they swerved, they dodged the flying terror of the sound. The three red chaps had fallen flat, face down on the shore, as though they had been shot dead. Only the barbarous and superb woman did not so much as flinch, and stretched tragically her bare arms after us over the sombre and glittering river.

"And then that imbecile crowd down on the deck started their little fun, and I could see nothing more for smoke.

"The brown current ran swiftly out of the heart of darkness, bearing us down towards the sea with twice the speed of our upward progress; and Kurtz's life was running swiftly too, ebbing, ebbing out of his heart into the sea of inexorable time. The manager was very placid, he had no vital anxieties now, he took us both in with a comprehensive and satisfied glance: the 'affair' had come off as well as could be wished. I saw the time approaching when I would be left alone of the party of 'unsound method.' The pilgrims looked upon me with disfavour. I was, so to speak, numbered with the dead. It is strange how I accepted this unforeseen partnership, this choice of nightmares forced upon me in the tenebrous land invaded by these mean and greedy phantoms.

"Kurtz discoursed. A voice! a voice! It rang deep to the very last. It survived his strength to hide in the magnificent folds of eloquence the barren darkness of his heart. Oh, he struggled! he struggled! The wastes of his weary brain were haunted by shadowy images now—images of wealth and fame revolving obsequiously round his unextinguishable gift of noble and lofty expression. My Intended, my station, my career, my ideas—these were the subjects for the occasional utterances of elevated sentiments. The shade of the original Kurtz frequented the bedside of the hollow sham, whose fate it was to be buried presently in the mould of primeval earth. But both the diabolic love and the unearthly hate of the mysteries it had penetrated fought for the possession of that soul satiated with primitive emotions, avid of lying fame, of sham distinction, of all the appearances of success and power.

"Sometimes he was contemptibly childish. He desired to have kings meet him at railway stations on his return from some ghastly Nowhere, where he intended to accomplish great things. 'You show them you have in you something that is really profitable, and then there will be no limits to the recognition of your ability,' he would say. 'Of course you must take care of the motives—right motives—always.' The long reaches that were like one and the same reach, monotonous bends that were exactly alike, slipped past the steamer with their multitude of secular[6] trees looking patiently after this grimy fragment of another world, the forerunner of change, of conquest, of trade, of massacres, of blessings. I looked ahead—piloting. 'Close the shutter,' said Kurtz suddenly one day; 'I can't bear to look at this.' I did so. There was a silence. 'Oh, but I will wring your heart yet!' he cried at the invisible wilderness.

"We broke down—as I had expected—and had to lie up for repairs at the head of an island. This delay was the first thing that shook Kurtz's confidence. One morning he gave me a packet of papers and a photograph—the lot tied together with a shoe-string. 'Keep this for me,' he said. 'This noxious fool' (meaning the manager) 'is capable of prying into my boxes when I am not looking.' In the afternoon I saw him. He was lying on his back with closed eyes, and I withdrew quietly, but I heard him mutter, 'Live rightly, die, die . . . .' I listened. There was nothing more. Was he rehearsing some speech in his sleep, or was it a fragment of a phrase from some newspaper article? He had been writing for the papers and meant to do so again, 'for the furthering of my ideas. It's a duty.'

"His was an impenetrable darkness. I looked at him as you peer down at a man who is lying at the bottom of a precipice where the sun never shines. But I had not much time to give him, because I was helping the engine-driver to take to pieces the leaky cylinders, to straighten a bent connecting-rod, and in other such matters. I lived in an infernal mess of rust, filings, nuts, bolts, spanners, hammers, ratchet-drills—things I abominate, because I don't get on with them. I tended the little forge we fortunately had aboard; I toiled wearily in a wretched scrap-heap—unless I had the shakes too bad to stand.

"One evening coming in with a candle I was startled to hear him say a little tremulously, 'I am lying here in the dark waiting for death.' The light was within a foot of his eyes. I forced myself to murmur, 'Oh, nonsense!' and stood over him as if transfixed.

"Anything approaching the change that came over his features I have never seen before, and hope never to see again. Oh, I wasn't touched. I was fascinated. It was as though a veil had been rent. I saw on that ivory face the

6. Centuries old (from *séculaire*, French)

expression of sombre pride, of ruthless power, of craven terror—of an intense and hopeless despair. Did he live his life again in every detail of desire, temptation, and surrender during that supreme moment of complete knowledge? He cried in a whisper at some image, at some vision—he cried out twice, a cry that was no more than a breath:

"'The horror! The horror!'

"I blew the candle out and left the cabin. The pilgrims were dining in the mess-room, and I took my place opposite the manager, who lifted his eyes to give me a questioning glance, which I successfully ignored. He leaned back, serene, with that peculiar smile of his sealing the unexpressed depths of his meanness. A continuous shower of small flies streamed upon the lamp, upon the cloth, upon our hands and faces. Suddenly the manager's boy put his insolent black head in the doorway, and said in a tone of scathing contempt:

"'Mistah Kurtz—he dead.'

"All the pilgrims rushed out to see. I remained, and went on with my dinner. I believe I was considered brutally callous. However, I did not eat much. There was a lamp in there—light, don't you know—and outside it was so beastly, beastly dark. I went no more near the remarkable man who had pronounced a judgement upon the adventures of his soul on this earth. The voice was gone. What else had been there? But I am of course aware that next day the pilgrims buried something in a muddy hole.

"And then they very nearly buried me.

"However, as you see, I did not go to join Kurtz there and then. I did not. I remained to dream the nightmare out to the end, and to show my loyalty to Kurtz once more. Destiny. My destiny! Droll thing life is—that mysterious arrangement of merciless logic for a futile purpose. The most you can hope from it is some knowledge of yourself—that comes too late—a crop of unextinguishable regrets. I have wrestled with death. It is the most unexciting contest you can imagine. It takes place in an impalpable greyness, with nothing underfoot, with nothing around, without spectators, without clamour, without glory, without the great desire of victory, without the great fear of defeat, in a sickly atmosphere of tepid scepticism, without much belief in your own right, and still less in that of your adversary. If such is the form of ultimate wisdom, then life is a greater riddle than some of us think it to be. I was within a hair's-breadth of the last opportunity for pronouncement, and I found with humiliation that probably I would have nothing to say. This is the reason why I affirm that Kurtz was a remarkable man. He had something to say. He said it. Since I had peeped over the edge myself, I understand better the meaning of his stare, that could not see the flame of the candle, but was wide enough to embrace the whole universe, piercing enough to penetrate all the hearts that beat in the darkness. He had summed up—he had judged. 'The horror!' He was a remarkable man. After all, this was the expression of some sort of belief; it had candour, it had conviction, it had a vibrating note of revolt in its whisper, it had the appalling face of a glimpsed truth—the strange commingling of desire and hate. And it is not my own extremity I remember best—a vision of greyness without form filled with physical pain, and a careless contempt for the evanescence of all things— even of this pain itself. No! It is his extremity that I seem to have lived through. True, he had made that last stride, he had stepped over the edge, while I had been permitted to draw back my hesitating foot. And perhaps in this is the whole difference; perhaps all the wisdom, and all truth, and all sincerity, are just compressed into that inappreciable moment of time in which we step over the threshold of the invisible. Perhaps! I like to think my summing-up would not have been a word of careless contempt. Better his cry—much better. It was an affirmation, a moral victory paid for by innumerable defeats, by abominable terrors, by abominable satisfactions. But it was a victory! That is why I have remained loyal to Kurtz to the last, and even beyond, when a long time after I heard once more, not his own voice, but the echo of his magnificent eloquence thrown to me from a soul as translucently pure as a cliff of crystal.

"No, they did not bury me, though there is a period of time which I remember mistily, with a shuddering wonder, like a passage through some inconceivable world that had no hope in it and no desire. I found myself back in the sepulchral city resenting the sight of people hurrying through the streets to filch a little money from each other, to devour their infamous cookery, to gulp their unwholesome beer, to dream their insignificant and silly dreams. They trespassed upon my thoughts. They were intruders whose knowledge of life was to me an irritating pretence, because I felt so sure they could not possibly know the things I knew. Their bearing, which was simply the bearing of commonplace individuals going about their business in the assurance of perfect safety, was offensive to me like the outrageous flauntings of folly in the face of a danger it is unable to comprehend. I had no particular desire to enlighten them, but I had some difficulty in restraining myself from laughing in their faces, so full of stupid importance. I daresay I was not very well at that time. I tottered about the streets—there were various affairs to settle—grinning bitterly at perfectly respectable persons. I admit my behaviour was inexcusable, but then my temperature was seldom normal in these days. My dear aunt's endeavours to 'nurse up my strength' seemed altogether beside the mark. It was not my strength that wanted nursing, it was my imagination that wanted soothing. I kept the bundle of papers given me by Kurtz, not knowing exactly what to do with it. His mother had died lately, watched over, as I was told, by his Intended. A clean-shaven man, with an official manner and wearing gold-rimmed spectacles, called on me one day and made inquiries, at first circuitous, afterwards suavely pressing, about what he was pleased to denominate certain 'documents.' I was not surprised, because I had had two rows with the manager on the subject out there. I had refused to give up the smallest scrap out of that package, and I took the same attitude with the spectacled man. He became darkly menacing at last, and with much heat argued that the Company had the right to every bit of information about its 'territories.' And, said he, 'Mr Kurtz's knowledge of unexplored regions must have been necessarily extensive and peculiar—owing to his great abilities and to the deplorable circumstances in which he had been placed: therefore—' I assured him Mr Kurtz's knowledge, however extensive, did not bear upon the problems of commerce or administration. He invoked then the name of science. 'It would be an incalculable loss if,' etc. etc. I offered him the report on the 'Suppression of Savage Customs,' with the postscriptum torn off. He took it up eagerly, but ended by sniffing at it with an air of contempt. 'This is not what we had a right to expect,' he remarked. 'Expect nothing else,' I said. 'There are only private letters.' He withdrew upon some threat of legal proceedings, and I saw him no more; but another fellow, calling himself Kurtz's cousin, appeared two days later, and was anxious to hear all the details about his dear relative's last moments. Incidentally he gave me to understand that Kurtz had been essentially a great musician. 'There was the making of an immense success,' said the man, who was an organist, I believe, with lank grey hair flowing over a greasy coat-collar. I had no reason to doubt his statement; and to this day I am unable to say what was Kurtz's profession, whether he ever had any—which was the greatest of his talents. I had taken him for a painter who wrote for the papers, or else for a journalist who could paint—but even the cousin (who took snuff during the interview) could not tell me what he had been—exactly. He was a universal genius—on that point I agreed with the old chap, who thereupon blew his nose noisily into a large cotton handkerchief and withdrew in senile agitation, bearing off some family letters and memoranda without importance. Ultimately a journalist anxious to know something of the fate of his 'dear colleague' turned up. This visitor informed me Kurtz's proper sphere ought to have been politics 'on the popular side.' He had furry straight eyebrows, bristly hair cropped short, an eyeglass on a broad ribbon, and, becoming expansive, confessed his opinion that Kurtz really couldn't write a bit—'but heavens! how that man could talk! He electrified large meetings. He had faith—don't you see?—he had the faith. He could get himself to believe anything—anything. He would have been a splendid leader of an extreme party.' 'What party?' I asked. 'Any party,' answered the other. 'He was an—an—extremist.' Did I not think so? I assented. Did I know, he asked, with a sudden flash of curiosity, 'what it was that had induced him to go out there?' 'Yes,' said I, and forthwith handed him the famous Report for publication, if he thought fit. He glanced through it hurriedly, mumbling all the time, judged 'it would do,' and took himself off with this plunder.

"Thus I was left at last with a slim packet of letters and the girl's portrait. She struck me as beautiful—I mean she had a beautiful expression. I know that the sunlight can be made to lie too, yet one felt that no manipulation of light and pose could have conveyed the delicate shade of truthfulness upon those features. She seemed ready to listen without mental reservation, without suspicion, without a thought for herself. I concluded I would go and give her back her portrait and those letters myself. Curiosity? Yes; and also some other feeling perhaps. All that had been Kurtz's had passed out of my hands: his soul, his body, his station, his plans, his ivory, his career. There remained only his memory and his Intended—and I wanted to give that up too to the past, in a way—to surrender personally all that remained of him with me to that oblivion which is the last word of our common fate. I don't defend myself. I had no clear perception of what it was I really wanted. Perhaps it was an impulse of unconscious loyalty, or the fulfilment of one of those ironic necessities that lurk in the facts of human existence. I don't know. I can't tell. But I went.

"I thought his memory was like the other memories of the dead that accumulate in every man's life—a vague impress on the brain of shadows that had fallen on it in their swift and final passage; but before the high and ponderous door, between the tall houses of a street as still and decorous as a well-kept alley in a cemetery, I had a vision of him on the stretcher, opening his mouth voraciously, as if to devour all the earth with all its mankind. He lived then before me; he lived as much as he had ever lived—a shadow insatiable of splendid appearances, of frightful realities; a shadow darker than the shadow of the night, and draped nobly in the folds of a gorgeous eloquence. The vision seemed to enter the house with me—the stretcher, the phantom-bearers, the wild crowd of obedient worshippers, the gloom of the forests, the glitter of the reach between the murky bends, the beat of the drum, regular and muffled like the beating of a heart—the heart of a conquering darkness. It was a moment of triumph for the wilderness, an invading and vengeful rush which, it seemed to me, I would have to keep back alone for the salvation of another soul. And the memory of what I had heard him say afar there, with the horned shapes stirring at my back, in the glow of fires, within the patient woods, those broken phrases came back to me, were heard again in their ominous and terrifying simplicity. I remembered his abject pleading, his abject threats, the colossal scale of his vile desires, the meanness, the torment, the tempestuous anguish of his soul. And later on I seemed to see his collected languid manner, when he said one day, 'This lot of ivory now is really mine. The Company did not pay for it. I collected it myself at a very great personal risk. I am afraid they will try to claim it as theirs though. H'm. It is a difficult case. What do you think I ought to do—resist? Eh? I want no more than justice.' . . . He wanted no more than justice—no more than justice. I rang the bell before a mahogany door on the first floor, and while I waited he seemed to stare at me out of the glossy panel—stare with that wide and immense stare embracing, condemning, loathing all the universe. I seemed to hear the whispered cry, 'The horror! The horror!'

"The dusk was falling. I had to wait in a lofty drawing-room with three long windows from floor to ceiling that were like three luminous and bedraped columns. The bent gilt legs and backs of the furniture shone in indistinct curves. The tall marble fireplace had a cold and monumental whiteness. A grand piano stood massively in a corner; with dark gleams on the flat surfaces like a sombre and polished sarcophagus. A high door opened—closed. I rose.

"She came forward, all in black, with a pale head, floating towards me in the dusk. She was in mourning. It was more than a year since his death, more than a year since the news came; she seemed as though she would remember and mourn for ever. She took both my hands in hers and murmured, 'I had heard you were coming.' I noticed she was not very young—I mean not girlish. She had a mature capacity for fidelity, for belief, for suffering. The room seemed to have grown darker, as if all the sad light of the cloudy evening had taken refuge on her forehead. This fair hair, this pale visage, this pure brow, seemed surrounded by an ashy halo from which the dark eyes looked out at me. Their glance was guileless, profound, confident, and trustful. She carried her sorrowful head as though she were proud of that sorrow, as though she would say, I—I alone know how to mourn for him as he deserves. But while we were still shaking hands, such a look of awful desolation came upon her face that I perceived she was one of those creatures that are not the playthings of Time. For her he had died only yesterday. And, by Jove! the impression was so powerful that for me too he seemed to have died only yesterday—nay, this very minute. I saw her and him in the same instant of time—his death and her sorrow—I saw her sorrow in the very moment of his death. Do you understand? I saw them together—I heard them together. She had said, with a deep catch of the breath, 'I have survived'; while my strained ears seemed to hear distinctly, mingled with her tone of despairing regret, the summing-up whisper of his eternal condemnation. I asked myself what I was doing there, with a sensation of panic in my heart as though I had blundered into a place of cruel and absurd mysteries not fit for a human being to behold. She motioned me to a chair. We sat down. I laid the packet gently on the little table, and she put her hand over it. . . . 'You knew him well,' she murmured, after a moment of mourning silence.

" 'Intimacy grows quickly out there,' I said. 'I knew him as well as it is possible for one man to know another.'

" 'And you admired him,' she said. 'It was impossible to know him and not to admire him. Was it?'

" 'He was a remarkable man,' I said unsteadily. Then before the appealing fixity of her gaze, that seemed to watch for more words on my lips, I went on, 'It was impossible not to—'

" 'Love him,' she finished eagerly, silencing me into an appalled dumbness. 'How true! how true! But when you think that no one knew him so well as I! I had all his noble confidence. I knew him best.'

" 'You knew him best,' I repeated. And perhaps she did. But with every word spoken the room was growing darker, and only her forehead, smooth and white, remained illumined by the unextinguishable light of belief and love.

" 'You were his friend,' she went on. 'His friend,' she repeated, a little louder. 'You must have been, if he had given you this, and sent you to me. I feel I can speak to you—and oh! I must speak. I want you—you who have heard his last words—to know I have been worthy of him. . . . It is not pride. . . . Yes! I am proud to know I understood him better than any one on earth—he told me so himself. And since his mother died I have had no one—no one—to—to—'

"I listened. The darkness deepened. I was not even sure whether he had given me the right bundle. I rather suspect he wanted me to take care of another batch of his papers which, after his death, I saw the manager examining under the lamp. And the girl talked, easing her pain in the certitude of my sympathy; she talked as thirsty men drink. I had heard that her engagement with Kurtz had been disapproved by her people. He wasn't rich enough or something. And indeed I don't know whether he had not been a pauper all his life. He had given me some reason to infer that it was his impatience of comparative poverty that drove him out there.

" ' . . . Who was not his friend who had heard him speak once?' she was saying. 'He drew men towards him by what was best in them.' She looked at me with intensity. 'It is the gift of the great,' she went on, and the sound of her low voice seemed to have the accompaniment of all the other sounds, full of mystery, desolation, and sorrow, I had ever heard—the ripple of the river, the soughing of the trees swayed by the wind, the murmurs of the crowds, the faint ring of incomprehensible words cried from afar, the whisper of a voice speaking from beyond the threshold of an eternal darkness. 'But you have heard him! You know!' she cried.

" 'Yes, I know,' I said with something like despair in my heart, but bowing my head before the faith that was in her, before that great and saving illusion that shone with an unearthly glow in the darkness, in the triumphant darkness from which I could not have defended her—from which I could not even defend myself.

" 'What a loss to me—to us!'—she corrected herself with beautiful generosity; then added in a murmur, 'To the world.' By the last gleams of twilight I could see the glitter of her eyes, full of tears—of tears that would not fall.

" 'I have been very happy—very fortunate—very proud,' she went on. 'Too fortunate. Too happy for a little while. And now I am unhappy for—for life.'

"She stood up; her fair hair seemed to catch all the remaining light in a glimmer of gold. I rose too.

" 'And of all this,' she went on mournfully, 'of all his promise, and of all his greatness, of his generous mind, of his noble heart, nothing remains—nothing but a memory. You and I—'

" 'We shall always remember him,' I said hastily.

" 'No!' she cried. 'It is impossible that all this should be lost—that such a life should be sacrificed to leave nothing—but sorrow. You know what vast plans he had. I knew of them too—I could not perhaps understand—but others knew of them. Something must remain. His words, at least, have not died.'

" 'His words will remain,' I said.

" 'And his example,' she whispered to herself. 'Men looked up to him—his goodness shone in every act. His example—'

" 'True,' I said; 'his example too. Yes, his example. I forgot that.'

" 'But I do not. I cannot—I cannot believe—not yet. I cannot believe that I shall never see him again, that nobody will see him again, never, never, never.'

"She put out her arms as if after a retreating figure, stretching them black and with clasped pale hands across the fading and narrow sheen of the window. Never see him! I saw him clearly enough then. I shall see this eloquent phantom as long as I live, and I shall see her too, a tragic and familiar Shade, resembling in this gesture another one, tragic also, and bedecked with powerless charms, stretching bare brown arms over the glitter of the infernal stream, the stream of darkness. She said suddenly very low, 'He died as he lived.'

" 'His end,' said I, with dull anger stirring in me, 'was in every way worthy of his life.'

" 'And I was not with him,' she murmured. My anger subsided before a feeling of infinite pity.

" 'Everything that could be done—' I mumbled.

" 'Ah, but I believed in him more than any one on earth—more than his own mother, more than—himself. He needed me! Me! I would have treasured every sigh, every word, every sign, every glance.'

"I felt like a chill grip on my chest. 'Don't,' I said, in a muffled voice.

" 'Forgive me. I—I—have mourned so long in silence—in silence. . . . You were with him—to the last? I think of his loneliness. Nobody near to understand him as I would have understood. Perhaps no one to hear. . . . '

" 'To the very end,' I said shakily. 'I heard his very last words. . . . ' I stopped in a fright.

" 'Repeat them,' she murmured in a heart-broken tone. 'I want—I want—something—something—to—to live with.'

"I was on the point of crying at her, 'Don't you hear them?' The dusk was repeating them in a persistent whisper all around us, in a whisper that seemed to swell menacingly like the first whisper of a rising wind. 'The horror! The horror!'

" 'His last word—to live with,' she insisted. 'Don't you understand I loved him—I loved him—I loved him!'

"I pulled myself together and spoke slowly.

" 'The last word he pronounced was—your name.'

"I heard a light sigh and then my heart stood still, stopped dead short by an exulting and terrible cry, by the cry of inconceivable triumph and of unspeakable pain. 'I knew it—I was sure!' . . . She knew. She was sure. I heard her weeping; she had hidden her face in her hands. It seemed to me that the house would collapse before I could escape, that the heavens would fall upon my head. But nothing happened. The heavens do not fall for such a trifle. Would they have fallen, I wonder, if I had rendered Kurtz that justice which was his due? Hadn't he said he wanted only justice? But I couldn't. I could not tell her. It would have been too dark—too dark altogether. . . ."

Marlow ceased, and sat apart, indistinct and silent, in the pose of a meditating Buddha. Nobody moved for a time. "We have lost the first of the ebb," said the Director suddenly. I raised my head. The offing was barred by a black bank of clouds, and the tranquil waterway leading to the uttermost ends of the earth flowed sombre under an overcast sky—seemed to lead into the heart of an immense darkness.

CIVILIZATION ON TRIAL

Nineteenth-century writings on civilization tended to emphasize its evolution from barbarism to the pinnacle reached by modern industrial society. It was a linear ascent in which the moderns rose higher than their predecessors, even if, as the saying goes, they stood on the shoulders of giants. Darwin described the descent of man as an ascent in abilities and accomplishment, and Macaulay paid tribute to the achievements of Western culture and its exemplary accumulation of human knowledge. Both perspectives are echoed in the eleventh edition of the *Encyclopaedia Britannica* (1911), in an article on the progress of civilization. There were some disagreements—in discussions of the status of women, for example, or in measuring the treatment of colonized peoples against the ostensible civilizing mission of their exploiters—but these were disagreements about consistency and justice rather than an attack on the notion of progress itself.

Civilization is not as easily defined at the beginning of the twentieth century, or, rather, the two parts of its definition that had existed in uneasy parallelism during the nineteenth century now seem to work against each other. On the one hand, there is a consistent pride taken in the idea of human beings subduing and exploiting nature. Technological advancement made possible the Crystal Palace of the 1851 world's fair, and it underlay subsequent international expositions in which nations competed to display products and promote the national image. On the other hand, the achievements of art, literature, and philosophy were recognized as milestones in the history of civilization, with the best of them—the great works of the mind—still alive for later generations.

What if progress did not move relentlessly forward—if some of the choices were the wrong ones—if the technical prowess that was the most visible sign of an advanced society could also mean its doom? Max Weber's image of civilization is humanistic; he celebrates the inquiring mind and the development of all human abilities. Yet he finds that contemporary life is becoming less and less *civilized* as it accepts more and more constraints: the "iron cage" of the modern worker threatens to become a permanent shell, sign of a straitened and mechanized existence that has nothing to do with the larger claims of civilization. Oswald Spengler's view of the slow rise of civilization is more traditionally linear but with one disappointing exception: civilizations (plural) also die at the end of a predictable life cycle, and modern Western civilization has already begun to fall. His pessimism seemed reasonable, if unwelcome, at the end of World War I. It was shared by the French philosopher-poet Paul Valéry, who spoke for many in declaring that the achievements of Western civilization had been negated, and perhaps permanently destroyed, by their drawbacks: without an advanced civilization's knowledge, precision, logic, and discipline, the Great War's lethal destruction would not have been possible. To Valéry, bitterly, the life of the mind *was* civilization, and he had just found that its rise from an animal level could be reversed in a moment. Sigmund Freud saw the problem differently: civilization was a set of constraints entered into reluctantly by instinctively hostile and competitive individuals for the survival of the community (and, therefore, the individual). Understanding individual psychology was a key to understanding the larger patterns of behavior. In the long run, however, they were only patterns and not a finished stage of society: "civilization" as such was an illusion. From the heady optimism of earlier years to the disillusionment and cross-examination after World War I, the debate over civilization was also a struggle over ethical and (primarily European) cultural values. In succeeding years, the debate would continue but with broader horizons and more diverse cultural expectations.

SIGMUND FREUD

1856–1939

Freud is best known for his insights into individual behavior, both the exploration of human sexuality and the influence of unconscious impulses on conscious activity. He did not content himself with structural models of the individual mind, however, and, in the last decades of his life, adapted his theories of mental conflict to larger models of civilization. It is not the progress from barbarism to civilization that interests him, but the conflicting impulses that take place within human beings as they struggle to impose civilization on themselves. Civilization is an illusion, a temporary truce for survival that always masks hostile instincts. When achieved, it is a hard-won and not entirely pleasurable prize, obtained at the price of renunciation and control. The mass of men, Freud suggests, will always resist civilization because they are led by passion and the desire for instant gratification: when thwarted in personal ambition, they seek an outlet elsewhere for their aggressive instincts. Only benevolent coercion, carried out by wise leaders with the power to compel productive behavior, will reduce the pressures from a majority that is always hostile to the constraints of civilization. The political implications of this analysis are clear, and Freud emphasizes the need for strong leaders who can separate themselves from the community they must lead. It is not a democratic position, and Freud is both fascinated by and suspicious of the American example insofar as it puts checks on strong leaders in the name of the group (or groups). There is a salutary realism, however, in his observation that civilization is not a permanent achievement built on the progress from barbarism, but a negotiated relationship between human instincts and the institutions necessary for survival. When Freud was awarded the Goethe prize in 1930, the citation recognized that he had "opened access to the driving forces of the soul and thus created the possibility of recognizing the emergence and construction of cultural forms and of curing some of its illnesses."

From The Future of an Illusion[1]

* * *

Human civilization, by which I mean all those respects in which human life has raised itself above its animal status and differs from the life of beasts—and I scorn to distinguish between culture and civilization—,[2] presents, as we know, two aspects to the observer. It includes on the one hand all the knowledge and capacity that men have acquired in order to control the forces of nature and extract its wealth for the satisfaction of human needs, and, on the other hand, all the regulations necessary in order to adjust the relations of men to one another and especially the distribution of the available wealth. The two trends of civilization are not independent of each other: firstly, because the mutual relations of men are profoundly influenced by the amount of instinctual satisfaction which the existing wealth makes possible; secondly, because an individual man can himself come to function as wealth in relation to another one, in so far as the other person makes use of his capacity for work, or chooses him as a sexual object, and thirdly, moreover, because every individual is virtually an enemy of civilization, though civilization is supposed to be an object of universal human interest. It is remarkable that, little as men are able to exist in isolation, they should nevertheless feel as a heavy burden the sacrifices which civilization expects of them in order to make a communal life possible. Thus civilization has to be defended against the individual, and its regulations, institutions and commands are directed to that task. They aim not only at effecting a certain distribution of wealth but at maintaining that distribution; indeed, they have to protect everything that contributes to the conquest of nature and the production of wealth against men's hostile impulses. Human creations are easily destroyed, and science and technology, which have built them up, can also be used for their annihilation.

One thus gets an impression that civilization is something which was imposed on a resisting majority by a minority which understood how to obtain possession of the means to power and coercion. It is, of course, natural to assume that these difficulties are not inherent in the nature of civilization itself but are determined by the imperfections of the cultural forms which have so far been developed. And in fact it is not difficult to indicate those defects. While mankind has made continual advances in its control over nature and may expect to make still greater ones, it is not possible to

1. Printed in 1927. Translated by James Strachey. **2.** Freud refers to a debate of long standing. The founder of cultural anthropology, Edward Burnett Tylor (1832–1917), described culture as a complex whole, including "knowledge, belief, art, morals, law, custom, and any other capabilities and habits acquired by man as a member of society." By the middle of the 20th century, 164 separate definitions could be cited.

establish with certainty that a similar advance has been made in the management of human affairs; and probably at all periods, just as now once again, many people have asked themselves whether what little civilization has thus acquired is indeed worth defending at all. One would think that a re-ordering of human relations should be possible, which would remove the sources of dissatisfaction with civilization by renouncing coercion and the suppression of the instincts, so that, undisturbed by internal discord, men might devote themselves to the acquisition of wealth and its enjoyment. That would be the golden age, but it is questionable if such a state of affairs can be realized. It seems rather that every civilization must be built up on coercion and renunciation of instinct, it does not even seem certain that if coercion were to cease the majority of human beings would be prepared to undertake to perform the work necessary for acquiring new wealth. One has, I think, to reckon with the fact that there are present in all men destructive, and therefore anti-social and anti-cultural, trends and that in a great number of people these are strong enough to determine their behaviour in human society.

This psychological fact has a decisive importance for our judgment of human civilization. Whereas we might at first think that its essence lies in controlling nature for the purpose of acquiring wealth and that the dangers which threaten it could be eliminated through a suitable distribution of that wealth among men, it now seems that the emphasis has moved over from the material to the mental. The decisive question is whether and to what extent it is possible to lessen the burden of the instinctual sacrifices imposed on men, to reconcile men to those which must necessarily remain and to provide a compensation for them. It is just as impossible to do without control of the mass by a minority as it is to dispense with coercion in the work of civilization. For masses are lazy and unintelligent, they have no love for instinctual renunciation, and they are not to be convinced by argument of its inevitability, and the individuals composing them support one another in giving free rein to their indiscipline. It is only through the influence of individuals who can set an example and whom masses recognize as their leaders that they can be induced to perform the work and undergo the renunciations on which the existence of civilization depends. All is well if these leaders are persons who possess superior insight into the necessities of life and who have risen to the height of mastering their own instinctual wishes. But there is a danger that in order not to lose their influence they may give way to the mass more than it gives way to them, and it therefore seems necessary that they shall be independent of the mass by having means to power at their disposal. To put it briefly, there are two widespread human characteristics which are responsible for the fact that the regulations of civilization can only be maintained by a certain degree of coercion—namely, that men are not spontaneously fond of work and that arguments are of no avail against their passions.

I know the objections which will be raised against these assertions. It will be said that the characteristic of human masses depicted here, which is supposed to prove that coercion cannot be dispensed with in the work of civilization, is itself only the result of defects in the cultural regulations, owing to which men have become embittered, revengeful and inaccessible. New generations, who have been brought up in kindness and taught to have a high opinion of reason, and who have experienced the benefits of civilization at an early age, will have a different attitude to it. They will feel it as a possession of their very own and will be ready for its sake to make the sacrifices as regards work and instinctual satisfaction that are necessary for its preservation. They will be able to do without coercion and will differ little from their leaders. If no culture has so far produced human masses of such a quality, it is because no culture has yet devised regulations which will influence men in this way, and in particular from childhood onwards.

It may be doubted whether it is possible at all, or at any rate as yet, at the present stage of our control over nature, to set up cultural regulations of this kind. It may be asked where the number of superior, unswerving and disinterested leaders are to come from who are to act as educators of the future generations, and it may be alarming to think of the enormous amount of coercion that will inevitably be required before these intentions can be carried out. The grandeur of the plan and its importance for the future of human civilization cannot be disputed. It is securely based on the psychological discovery that man is equipped with the most varied instinctual dispositions, whose ultimate course is determined by the experiences of early childhood. But for the same reason the limitations of man's capacity for education set bounds to the effectiveness of such a transformation in his culture. One may question whether, and in what degree, it would be possible for a different cultural environment to do away with the two characteristics of human masses which make the guidance of human affairs so difficult. The experiment has not yet been made. Probably a certain percentage of mankind (owing to a pathological disposition or an excess of instinctual strength) will always remain asocial, but if it were feasible merely to reduce the majority that is hostile towards civilization to-day into a minority, a great deal would have been accomplished—perhaps all that *can* be accomplished.

I should not like to give the impression that I have strayed a long way from the line laid down for my enquiry. Let me therefore give an express assurance that I have not the least intention of making judgements on the great experiment in civilization that is now in progress in the vast country that stretches between Europe and Asia.[3] I have neither the special knowledge nor the capacity to decide on its practicability, to test the expediency of the methods employed or to measure the width of the inevitable gap between intention and execution. What is in preparation there is unfinished and therefore eludes an investigation for which our own long-consolidated civilization affords us material.

From Civilization and Its Discontents[1]

* * *

* * * Men are not gentle creatures who want to be loved, and who at the most can defend themselves if they are attacked; they are, on the contrary, creatures among whose instinctual endowments is to be reckoned a powerful share of aggressiveness. As a result, their neighbour is for them not only a potential helper or sexual object, but also someone who tempts them to

3. I.e., the United States.   1. Printed in 1929. Translated by James Strachey.

satisfy their aggressiveness on him, to exploit his capacity for work without compensation, to use him sexually without his consent, to seize his possessions, to humiliate him, to cause him pain, to torture and to kill him. *Homo homini lupus*.[2] Who, in the face of all his experience of life and of history, will have the courage to dispute this assertion? As a rule this cruel aggressiveness waits for some provocation or puts itself at the service of some other purpose, whose goal might also have been reached by milder measures. In circumstances that are favourable to it, when the mental counter-forces which ordinarily inhibit it are out of action, it also manifests itself spontaneously and reveals man as a savage beast to whom consideration towards his own kind is something alien. Anyone who calls to mind the atrocities committed during the racial migrations or the invasions of the Huns, or by the people known as Mongols under Jenghiz Khan and Tamerlane, or at the capture of Jerusalem by the pious Crusaders,[3] or even, indeed, the horrors of the recent World War—anyone who calls these things to mind will have to bow humbly before the truth of this view.

The existence of this inclination to aggression, which we can detect in ourselves and justly assume to be present in others, is the factor which disturbs our relations with our neighbour and which forces civilization into such a high expenditure [of energy]. In consequence of this primary mutual hostility of human beings, civilized society is perpetually threatened with disintegration. The interest of work in common would not hold it together; instinctual passions are stronger than reasonable interests. Civilization has to use its utmost efforts in order to set limits to man's aggressive instincts and to hold the manifestations of them in check by psychical reaction-formations. Hence, therefore, the use of methods intended to incite people into identifications and aim-inhibited relationships of love, hence the restriction upon sexual life, and hence too the ideal's commandment to love one's neighbour as oneself—a commandment which is really justified by the fact that nothing else runs so strongly counter to the original nature of man. In spite of every effort, these endeavours of civilization have not so far achieved very much. It hopes to prevent the crudest excesses of brutal violence by itself assuming the right to use violence against criminals, but the law is not able to lay hold of the more cautious and refined manifestations of human aggressiveness. The time comes when each one of us has to give up as illusions the expectations which, in his youth, he pinned upon his fellow-men, and when he may learn how much difficulty and pain has been added to his life by their ill-will. At the same time, it would be unfair to reproach civilization with trying to eliminate strife and competition from human activity. These things are undoubtedly indispensable. But opposition is not necessarily enmity; it is merely misused and made an *occasion* for enmity.

* * *

It is clearly not easy for men to give up the satisfaction of this inclination to aggression. They do not feel comfortable without it. The advantage which a comparatively small cultural group offers of allowing this instinct an outlet

---

2. "Man is a wolf to man"; from line 495 in *The Comedy of Asses* by the Roman playwright Plautus (254–181 B.C.E.).   3. In 1099, during the First Crusade, after Jerusalem had surrendered to the besieging Crusaders under a promise of protection, the latter slaughtered all the Muslim men, women, and children. *Huns*: fierce nomadic horsemen from Asia who invaded Europe between 370 and 455 C.E. *Mongols*: an Asiatic ethnographic group. Jenghiz Khan (1162?–1227) and Tamerlane (1336–1405) were Mongol and Turkic conquerors, respectively, known for destroying cities and massacring their inhabitants.

in the form of hostility against intruders is not to be despised. It is always possible to bind together a considerable number of people in love, so long as there are other people left over to receive the manifestations of their aggressiveness. I once discussed the phenomenon that it is precisely communities with adjoining territories, and related to each other in other ways as well, who are engaged in constant feuds and in ridiculing each other—like the Spaniards and Portuguese, for instance, the North Germans and South Germans, the English and Scotch, and so on. I gave this phenomenon the name of "the narcissism of minor differences," a name which does not do much to explain it. We can now see that it is a convenient and relatively harmless satisfaction of the inclination to aggression, by means of which cohesion between the members of the community is made easier. In this respect the Jewish people, scattered everywhere, have rendered most useful services to the civilizations of the countries that have been their hosts; but unfortunately all the massacres of the Jews in the Middle Ages did not suffice to make that period more peaceful and secure for their Christian fellows. When once the Apostle Paul had posited universal love between men as the foundation of his Christian community, extreme intolerance on the part of Christendom towards those who remained outside it became the inevitable consequence. To the Romans, who had not founded their communal life as a State upon love, religious intolerance was something foreign, although with them religion was a concern of the State and the State was permeated by religion. Neither was it an unaccountable chance that the dream of a Germanic world-dominion called for anti-semitism as its complement; and it is intelligible that the attempt to establish a new, communist civilization in Russia should find its psychological support in the persecution of the bourgeois. One only wonders, with concern, what the Soviets will do after they have wiped out their bourgeois.

If civilization imposes such great sacrifices not only on man's sexuality but on his aggressivity, we can understand better why it is hard for him to be happy in that civilization. In fact, primitive man was better off in knowing no restrictions of instinct. To counterbalance this, his prospects of enjoying this happiness for any length of time were very slender. Civilized man has exchanged a portion of his possibilities of happiness for a portion of security. We must not forget, however, that in the primal family only the head of it enjoyed this instinctual freedom; the rest lived in slavish suppression. In that primal period of civilization, the contrast between a minority who enjoyed the advantages of civilization and a majority who were robbed of those advantages was, therefore, carried to extremes. As regards the primitive peoples who exist to-day, careful researches have shown that their instinctual life is by no means to be envied for its freedom. It is subject to restrictions of a different kind but perhaps of greater severity than those attaching to modern civilized man.

When we justly find fault with the present state of our civilization for so inadequately fulfilling our demands for a plan of life that shall make us happy, and for allowing the existence of so much suffering which could probably be avoided—when, with unsparing criticism, we try to uncover the roots of its imperfection, we are undoubtedly exercising a proper right and are not showing ourselves enemies of civilization. We may expect gradually to carry through such alterations in our civilization as will better satisfy our needs and will escape our criticisms. But perhaps we may also familiarize ourselves with the idea that there are difficulties attaching to the nature of civilization which will not yield to any attempt at reform. Over and above the tasks of restricting the instincts, which we are prepared for, there forces itself on our notice the danger of a state of things which might be termed 'the psychological poverty of groups'.[4] This danger is most threatening where the bonds of a society are chiefly constituted by the identification of its members with one another, while individuals of the leader type do not acquire the importance that should fall to them in the formation of a group. The present cultural state of America would give us a good opportunity for studying the damage to civilization which is thus to be feared. But I shall avoid the temptation of entering upon a critique of American civilization; I do not wish to give an impression of wanting myself to employ American methods.

4. Literally, "psychological misery," a term used by Freud's teacher, the French physician and neurologist Pierre Janet (1859–1947), to suggest the neurotic's inability to synthesize ideas.

MAX WEBER
1864–1920

Among the many influential works of the German sociologist Max Weber, none has provoked as much debate—and had as many followers—as his description of the "Protestant ethic": a single-minded dedication to work as a moral, and hence religious, obligation. Weber, who wrote books on world religions as well as on more technical subjects, was always conscious of cultural contexts and proposed new methods of interpretive sociology that linked social and economic factors. From a study of medieval trading societies to *The Sociology of Religion* (first published in 1922 in German) and *The Theory of Social and Economic Organization* (first published in 1925 in German), published by his widow after his death, he pursued a sociological investigation that valued the rich variety of human thought and feelings, and attacked any mode of social or economic life that limited their development. Civilization at its best, he felt, nurtured a broadly inquiring mind and the development of all human faculties, including spontaneous pleasure in the arts. Such an attitude underlies Weber's critique of modern capitalism for the way it imprisons human beings in the joyless "iron cage" of a regimented and narrowly specialized existence. He observes a convergence between the early Puritans' notion of a calling—a religious duty to the successful stewardship of worldly goods—and capitalism's summoning of modern workers to specialized tasks for the benefit of a larger economic machine. Lacking the spiritual motivation of the early Puritans, however, work in the capitalist era tends to become a mere game, a competitive sport whose technical proficiency masks its true emptiness.

The Protestant Ethic and the Spirit of Capitalism[1]

From *Part V. Asceticism and the Spirit of Capitalism*

* * *

One of the fundamental elements of the spirit of modern capitalism, and not only of that but of all modern culture: rational conduct on the basis of the idea of the calling,[2] was born—that is what this discussion has sought to demonstrate—from the spirit of Christian asceticism.* * * The idea that modern labour has an ascetic character is of course not new. Limitation to specialized work, with a renunciation of the Faustian[3] universality of man which it involves, is a condition of any valuable work in the modern world; hence deeds and renunciation inevitably condition each other to-day. This fundamentally ascetic trait of middle-class life, if it attempts to be a way of life at all, and not simply the absence of any, was what Goethe wanted to teach, at the height of his wisdom, in the *Wanderjahre*, and in the end which he gave to the life of his *Faust*.[4] For him the realization meant a renunciation, a departure from an age of full and beautiful humanity, which can no more be repeated in the course of our cultural development than can the flower of the Athenian culture of antiquity.

The Puritan[5] wanted to work in a calling; we are forced to do so. For when asceticism was carried out of monastic cells into everyday life, and began to dominate worldly morality, it did its part in building the tremendous cosmos of the modern economic order. This order is now bound to the technical and economic conditions of machine production which to-day determine the lives of all the individuals who are born into this mechanism, not only those directly concerned with economic acquisition, with irresistible force. Perhaps it will so determine them until the last ton of fossilized coal is burnt. In Baxter's[6] view the care for external goods should only lie on the shoulders of the "saint like a light cloak, which can be thrown aside at any moment." But fate decreed that the cloak should become an iron cage.[7]

Since asceticism undertook to remodel the world and to work out its ideals in the world, material goods have gained an increasing and finally an inexorable power over the lives of men as at no previous period in history. To-day the spirit of religious asceticism—whether finally, who knows?—has escaped from the cage. But victorious capitalism, since it rests on mechanical foundations, needs its support no longer. The rosy blush of its laughing heir, the Enlightenment, seems also to be irretrievably fading, and the idea of duty

1. Published in 1904. Translated by Talcott Parsons. 2. A life-task, a definite field in which to work [Weber]; in a religious context, a vocation assumed in response to a perceived call from God. 3. Having a limitless striving for knowledge and great faith in progress; named for Johann Faust, a medieval seeker after knowledge and the chief character of Goethe's drama *Faust* (1808), printed in this anthology. 4. At the end of *Faust*, Part II (1832), the aging Faust is so pleased with his vision of the future progress of humanity that he exclaims, "Wait a bit; you are so beautiful!" This willingness to pause in his striving signals the moment of his death, according to his earlier pact with the devil. *Wanderjahre: Wilhelm Meisters Wanderjahre* (1821; translated as *Wilhelm Meister's Travels*) is a sequel to Goethe's novel *Wilhelm Meisters Lehrjahre* (1795–96) and was known for its observations on the state of European culture. 5. Strict Protestant, a member of an English religious and social movement that sought to purify the church, and everyday life, through strict observance of New Testament doctrine. Puritanism flourished in 17th-century New England and was the law of the Massachusetts Bay Colony. 6. I.e., in Chapter XII of *The Saints' Everlasting Rest* (1650) by Richard Baxter (1615–1691), an English Puritan who stressed the value of work for everyone, including the wealthy. 7. Literally, a steel casing or shell (*stahlhartes Gehäuse*), suggesting a cyborg. Parsons's translation of *iron cage*, which was widely taken up by social scientists as a striking metaphor, is derived from an image in the Puritan John Bunyan's *Pilgrim's Progress* (1678).

in one's calling prowls about in our lives like the ghost of dead religious beliefs. Where the fulfilment of the calling cannot directly be related to the highest spiritual and cultural values, or when, on the other hand, it need not be felt simply as economic compulsion, the individual generally abandons the attempt to justify it at all. In the field of its highest development, in the United States, the pursuit of wealth, stripped of its religious and ethical meaning, tends to become associated with purely mundane passions, which often actually give it the character of sport.[8]

No one knows who will live in this cage in the future, or whether at the end of this tremendous development entirely new prophets will arise, or there will be a great rebirth of old ideas and ideals, or, if neither, mechanized petrification, embellished with a sort of convulsive self-importance. For of the last stage of this cultural development, it might well be truly said: "Specialists without spirit, sensualists without heart; this nullity imagines that it has attained a level of civilization never before achieved."[9]

* * *

8. "Couldn't the old man be satisfied with his $75,000 a year and rest? No! The frontage of the store must be widened to 400 feet. Why? That beats everything, he says. In the evening, when his wife and daughter read together, he wants to go to bed. Sundays he looks at the clock every five minutes to see when the day will be over—what a futile life!" In these terms the son-in-law (who had emigrated from Germany) of the leading dry-goods man of an Ohio city expressed his judgment of the latter; a judgment which would undoubtedly have seemed simply incomprehensible to the old man. A symptom of German lack of energy [Weber's note].   9. From Goethe.

PAUL VALÉRY
1871–1945

Poet and philosopher, deeply immersed in the European literary and artistic tradition to which he belongs, Paul Valéry spoke with horror and dismay when he described the bitter lethargy permeating Europe at the end of World War I. The "Great War" of 1914–1918 had involved complete societies and many nations; it introduced new weapons with enormous killing power on land, on sea, and in air; and it sacrificed a generation in the trenches—8.5 million soldiers—as well as an estimated 13 million civilians. European economic infrastructure collapsed, leading to famine and riots. It was not necessary to be a poet to sense widespread psychological harm, and the young economist John Maynard Keynes reported that "our power of feeling or caring beyond the immediate questions of our own material well-being is temporarily eclipsed. . . . Never in the lifetime of men now living has the universal element in the soul of man burnt so dimly." Valéry responded to this collective sense of shock, and expressed his own, when he wrote *The Crisis of the Mind* in 1919. Unlike Spengler, whose reaction to World War I took the form of a scientific analysis of broad sociological patterns, the French poet brings his readers into personal identification with the continent-wide crisis. "We later civilizations . . ." he says, transforming history into a personal record and inviting his twentieth-century readers to think of themselves as partners in a shared and vulnerable enterprise. Whether personified as the consciousness of Europe or as Hamlet writ large, this central figure defines the dilemma as a crisis of the mind, the painful self-awareness of modern civilization facing its own mortality and, at the same time, a loss of faith in its guiding values. Hamlet wryly considers his options at the end, but his mocking reference to the "anthill" society of a civilization without intellectual ambitions makes it clear where his preferences lie. Throughout, Valéry reminds us that works of the human mind are the guideposts by which civilizations are measured—and that they are fragile.

The Crisis of the Mind[1]

From First Letter [1919]

We later civilizations . . .[2] we too now know that we are mortal.

We had long heard tell of whole worlds that had vanished, of empires sunk without a trace, gone down with all their men and all their machines into the unexplorable depths of the centuries, with their gods and their laws, their academies and their sciences pure and applied, their grammars and their dictionaries, their Classics, their Romantics, and their Symbolists, their critics and the critics of their critics. . . . We were aware that the visible earth is made of ashes, and that ashes signify something. Through the obscure depths of history we could make out the phantoms of great ships laden with riches and intellect; we could not count them. But the disasters that had sent them down were, after all, none of our affair.

Elam, Nineveh, Babylon[3] were but beautiful vague names, and the total ruin of those worlds had as little significance for us as their very existence. But France, England, Russia . . . these too would be beautiful names. *Lusitania*,[4] too, is a beautiful name. And we see now that the abyss of history is deep enough to hold us all. We are aware that a civilization has the same fragility as a life. The circumstances that could send the works of Keats and Baudelaire to join the works of Menander[5] are no longer inconceivable; they are in the newspapers.

That is not all. The searing lesson is more complete still. It was not enough for our generation to learn from its own experience how the most beautiful things and the most ancient, the most formidable and the best ordered, can perish *by accident*; in the realm of thought, feeling, and common sense, we witnessed extraordinary phenomena: paradox suddenly become fact, and obvious fact brutally belied.

I shall cite but one example: the great virtues of the German peoples have begotten more evils than idleness ever bred vices. With our own eyes, we have seen conscientious labor, the most solid learning, the most serious discipline and application adapted to appalling ends.

So many horrors could not have been possible without so many virtues. Doubtless, much science was needed to kill so many, to waste so much property, annihilate so many cities in so short a time; but *moral qualities* in like number were also needed. Are Knowledge and Duty, then, suspect?

1. Published in 1919. Translated by Jackson Mathews and Denise Folliot. The ellipses in the text appear in the original.   2. The ellipses have been placed here by the translators.   3. Ancient capital of southern Mesopotamia and, later, of the Chaldean Empire. *Elam*: ancient region with ties to Mesopotamia, Elam flourished in the 13th century B.C.E. *Nineveh*: oldest city in the Assyrian Empire, famous for its magnificent buildings and great library.   4. British passenger liner sunk by a German submarine on May 7, 1915. 5. When Valéry wrote, no works by Menander (342–292 B.C.E.), the leading dramatist of Greek New Comedy and a strong influence on later comic tradition, were thought to have survived.

So the Persepolis of the spirit is no less ravaged than the Susa[6] of material fact. Everything has not been lost, but everything has sensed that it might perish.

An extraordinary shudder ran through the marrow of Europe. She felt in every nucleus of her mind that she was no longer the same, that she was no longer herself, that she was about to lose consciousness, a consciousness acquired through centuries of bearable calamities, by thousands of men of the first rank, from innumerable geographical, ethnic, and historical coincidences.

So—as though in desperate defense of her own physiological being and resources—all her memory confusedly returned. Her great men and her great books came back pell-mell. Never has so much been read, nor with such passion, as during the war: ask the booksellers. . . . Never have people prayed so much and so deeply: ask the priests. All the saviors, founders, protectors, martyrs, heroes, all the fathers of their country, the sacred heroines, the national poets were invoked. . . .

And in the same disorder of mind, at the summons of the same anguish, all cultivated Europe underwent the rapid revival of her innumerable ways of thought: dogmas, philosophies, heterogeneous ideals; the three hundred ways of explaining the World, the thousand and one versions of Christianity, the two dozen kinds of positivism, the whole spectrum of intellectual light spread out its incompatible colors, illuminating with a strange and contradictory glow the death agony of the European soul. While inventors were feverishly searching their imaginations and the annals of former wars for the means of doing away with barbed wire, of outwitting submarines or paralyzing the flight of airplanes, her soul was intoning at the same time all the incantations it ever knew, and giving serious consideration to the most bizarre prophecies; she sought refuge, guidance, consolation throughout the whole register of her memories, past acts, and ancestral attitudes. Such are the known effects of anxiety, the disordered behavior of a mind fleeing from reality to nightmare and from nightmare back to reality, terrified, like a rat caught in a trap. . . .

The military crisis may be over. The economic crisis is still with us in all its force. But the intellectual crisis, being more subtle and, by its nature, assuming the most deceptive appearances (since it takes place in the very realm of dissimulation) . . . this crisis will hardly allow us to grasp its true extent, its *phase*.

No one can say what will be dead or alive tomorrow, in literature, philosophy, aesthetics; no one yet knows what ideas and modes of expression will be inscribed on the casualty list, what novelties will be proclaimed.

Hope, of course, remains—singing in an undertone:

> *Et cum vorandi vicerit libidinem*
> *Late triumphet imperator spiritus.*[7]

But hope is only man's mistrust of the clear foresight of his mind. Hope suggests that any conclusion unfavorable to us *must be* an error of the mind. And yet the facts are clear and pitiless: thousands of young writers and young

---

6. Capital of Elam. *Persepolis*: ancient capital of Persia.   7. "And when it has conquered the lust to devour / Let the mind triumph widely as ruler" (Latin).

artists have died; the illusion of a European culture has been lost, and knowledge has been proved impotent to save anything whatever; science is mortally wounded in its moral ambitions and, as it were, put to shame by the cruelty of its applications; idealism is barely surviving, deeply stricken, and called to account for its dreams; realism is hopeless, beaten, routed by its own crimes and errors; greed and abstinence are equally flouted; faiths are confused in their aim—cross against cross, crescent against crescent; and even the skeptics, confounded by the sudden, violent, and moving events that play with our minds as a cat with a mouse . . . even the skeptics lose their doubts, recover, and lose them again, no longer master of the motions of their thought.

The swaying of the ship has been so violent that the best-hung lamps have finally overturned.[8] . . .

* * *

And what made that disorder in the mind of Europe? The free coexistence, in all her cultivated minds, of the most dissimilar ideas, the most contradictory principles of life and learning. That is characteristic of a *modern* epoch.

I am not averse to generalizing the notion of "modern" to designate a certain way of life, rather than making it purely a synonym of *contemporary*. There are moments and places in history to which *we moderns* could return without too greatly disturbing the harmony of those times, without seeming objects infinitely curious and conspicuous . . . creatures shocking, dissonant, and unassimilable. Wherever our entrance would create the least possible sensation, that is where we should feel almost at home. It is clear that Rome in the time of Trajan, or Alexandria under the Ptolemies,[9] would take us in more easily than many places less remote in time but more specialized in a single type of manners and entirely given over to a single race, a single culture, and a single system of life.

Well then! Europe in 1914 had perhaps reached the limit of modernism in this sense. Every mind of any scope was a crossroads for all shades of opinion; every thinker was an international exposition[1] of thought. There were works of the mind in which the wealth of contrasts and contradictory tendencies was like the insane displays of light in the capitals of those days: eyes were fatigued, scorched. . . . How much material wealth, how much labor and planning it took, how many centuries were ransacked, how many heterogeneous lives were combined, to make possible such a carnival, and to set it up as the supreme wisdom and the triumph of humanity?

* * *

Standing, now, on an immense sort of terrace of Elsinore that stretches from Basel to Cologne, bordered by the sands of Nieuport, the marshes of the

---

8. The orator's traditional metaphor of the ship of state, here seen battered by storms until the ship's lanterns—and their guidance—go down.   9. A Greek dynasty that ruled Egypt between 323 and 30 B.C.E., from Ptolemy I to Cleopatra VII, bringing widespread prosperity and making Alexandria a great cultural center. *Trajan:* Roman emperor from 98 to 117 C.E., who embarked on many public works and refused to persecute the Christians.   1. International expositions (world's fairs) occurred regularly after London's famous Great Exhibition of 1851.

Somme, the limestone of Champagne, the granites of Alsace . . . our Hamlet of Europe is watching millions of ghosts.[2]

But he is an intellectual Hamlet, meditating on the life and death of truths; for ghosts, he has all the subjects of our controversies; for remorse, all the titles of our fame. He is bowed under the weight of all the discoveries and varieties of knowledge, incapable of resuming this endless activity; he broods on the tedium of rehearsing the past and the folly of always trying to innovate. He staggers between two abysses—for two dangers never cease threatening the world: order and disorder.

Every skull he picks up is an illustrious skull. *Whose was it?* This one was *Lionardo.*[3] He invented the flying man, but the flying man has not exactly served his inventor's purposes. We know that, mounted on his great swan (*il grande uccello sopra del dosso del suo magnio cecero*)[4] he has other tasks in our day than fetching snow from the mountain peaks during the hot season to scatter it on the streets of towns. And that other skull was *Leibnitz*, who dreamed of universal peace. And this one was *Kant . . . and Kant begat Hegel, and Hegel begat Marx, and Marx begat.*[5] . . .

Hamlet hardly knows what to make of so many skulls. But suppose he forgets them! Will he still be himself? . . . His terribly lucid mind contemplates the passage from war to peace: darker, more dangerous than the passage from peace to war; all peoples are troubled by it. . . . "What about Me," he says, "what is to become of Me, the European intellect? . . . And what is peace? . . . *Peace is perhaps that state of things in which the natural hostility between men is manifested in creation, rather than destruction as in war.* Peace is a time of creative rivalry and the battle of production; but am I not tired of producing? . . . Have I not exhausted my desire for radical experiment, indulged too much in cunning compounds? . . . Should I not perhaps lay aside my hard duties and transcendent ambitions? . . . Perhaps follow the trend and do like Polonius who is now director of a great newspaper; like Laertes, who is something in aviation; like Rosencrantz,[6] who is doing God knows what under a Russian name?

"Farewell, ghosts! The world no longer needs you—or me. By giving the name of progress to its own tendency to a fatal precision, the world is seeking to add to the benefits of life the advantages of death. A certain confusion still reigns; but in a little while all will be made clear, and we shall witness at last the miracle of an animal society, the perfect and ultimate anthill."

2. Shakespeare's Hamlet was an internationally known figure (like Faust or Don Juan) that represented a melancholy excess of consciousness. Here, his castle of Elsinore has become all of Europe: Basel (a city in Switzerland, bordering on France and Germany), Cologne (long a free imperial city, later occupied by France, and subsequently a great cultural center in Germany), Nieuport (a city close to Ypres in Belgian Flanders, one end of a 20-mile strip of land flooded to hold back German invasion), the Somme (a river in France and, with Ypres, the site of bloody battles in World War I), Champagne (a region in France and the site of a major German offensive in 1918, whose defeat marked a turning point in the war), and Alsace (a region in France also claimed by Germany).   3. I.e., Leonardo da Vinci (1452–1519), an Italian Renaissance artist and inventor. *Whose was it?*: Hamlet V.i. Valéry's text gives Hamlet's words in English. 4. From the last page of Leonardo's notebook on aviation: "The great bird [will take its first flight mounted] on the back of his great swan" (Italian).   5. A series of German philosophers and social theorists. Gottfried Wilhelm Leibnitz or Leibniz (1646–1716), Immanuel Kant (1724–1804), Georg Wilhelm Friedrich Hegel (1770–1831), and Karl Marx (1818–1883) are all linked in a sentence that echoes biblical genealogies.   6. Polonius, Laertes, and Rosencrantz are all characters in Shakespeare's *Hamlet*.

OSWALD SPENGLER
1880–1936

Alarmingly for his readers, Oswald Spengler's view of nineteenth- and twentieth-century Western culture was not an image of progress with better times yet to come. Instead, the German historian described contemporary society, with its great cities and global networks, as the symptom of an inevitable decline toward the extinction of Western civilization. Spengler did not base his diagnosis solely on the study of Western history, but on a global inquiry into the rise and fall of historical civilizations. He argued powerfully that Western thinkers had not only failed to take into consideration other cultural traditions, but also to recognize that their own patterns of thought were not universal. Cultures and civilizations, he proposed, followed cyclical patterns: they arose, they matured, and they died when their initial creative impulses were exhausted. In a way, Spengler's world-historical analysis foreshadows the global studies of our day. He sees Western civilization against the background of global history and recognizes that social and individual perspectives are strongly shaped by geographic and economic conditions. Yet his theoretical paradigm is not one that many would share: culture as pure creativity and struggle, and civilization as its doomed finale, are thought-provoking metaphors rather than laws of social science. As metaphors—especially joined to Spengler's reactionary political views—they lend themselves in ways that he could scarcely foresee. The Nazis adapted parts of his ideas to support their own agenda of destruction and rebirth, and, as a result, his works fell out of favor after World War II. Yet Spengler's emphasis on the multiplicity of world civilizations and his claim that civilization is a doom that falls on every mature society continue to provoke discussion in any era that considers itself "civilized."

The Decline of the West[1]

From *Introduction*

VIII

To-day we think in continents, and it is only our philosophers and historians who have not realized that we do so. Of what significance to us, then, are conceptions and purviews that they put before us as universally valid, when in truth their furthest horizon does not extend beyond the intellectual atmosphere of Western Man?

Examine, from this point of view, our best books. When Plato speaks of humanity, he means the Hellenes[2] in contrast to the barbarians, which is entirely consonant with the ahistoric mode of the Classical life and thought, and his premises take him to conclusions that *for Greeks* were complete and significant. When, however, Kant[3] philosophizes, say on ethical ideas, he maintains the validity of his theses for men of all times and places. He does not say this in so many words, for, for himself and his readers, it is something that goes without saying. In his æsthetics he formulates the principles, not of Phidias's art, or Rembrandt's[4] art, but of Art generally. But what he poses as necessary forms of thought are in reality only necessary forms of Western

---

1. Published in 1919. Translated by Charles Francis Atkinson.   2. Greeks (from *Hellas*, "Greece") (Greek).   3. The German philosopher Immanuel Kant (1724–1804).   4. Rembrandt van Rijn (1606–1669) was an important Dutch painter and artist. *Phidias* (490–430 B.C.E.), a famous sculptor of ancient Athens, was responsible for the sculptural decoration of the Parthenon.

thought, though a glance at Aristotle and his essentially different conclusions should have sufficed to show that Aristotle's intellect, not less penetrating than his own, was of different structure from it. The categories of the Westerner are just as alien to Russian thought as those of the Chinaman or the ancient Greek are to him. For us, the effective and complete comprehension of Classical root-words is just as impossible as that of Russian and Indian, and for the modern Chinese or Arab, with their utterly different intellectual constitutions, "philosophy from Bacon[5] to Kant" has only a curiosity-value.

It is *this* that is lacking to the Western thinker, the very thinker in whom we might have expected to find it—insight into the *historically relative* character of his data, which are expressions of one *specific existence and one only*; knowledge of the necessary limits of their validity; the conviction that his "unshakable" truths and "eternal" views are simply true for him and eternal for his world-view; the duty of looking beyond them to find out what the men of other Cultures have with equal certainty evolved out of themselves. That and nothing else will impart completeness to the philosophy of the future, and only through an understanding of the living world shall we understand the symbolism of history. Here there is nothing constant, nothing universal. We must cease to speak of the forms of "Thought," the principles of "Tragedy," the mission of "The State." Universal validity involves always the fallacy of arguing from particular to particular.

But something much more disquieting than a logical fallacy begins to appear when the centre of gravity of philosophy shifts from the abstract-systematic to the practical-ethical and our Western thinkers from Schopenhauer[6] onward turn from the problem of cognition to the problem of life (the will to life, to power, to action). Here it is not the ideal abstract "man" of Kant that is subjected to examination, but actual man as he has inhabited the earth during historical time, grouped, whether primitive or advanced, by peoples; and it is more than ever futile to define the structure of his highest ideas in terms of the "ancient-mediæval-modern" scheme with its local limitations. But it is done, nevertheless.

Consider the historical horizon of Nietzsche.[7] His conceptions of decadence, militarism, the transvaluation of all values, the will to power, lie deep in the essence of Western civilization and are for the analysis of that civilization of decisive importance. But what, do we find, was the foundation on which he built up his creation? Romans and Greeks, Renaissance and European present, with a fleeting and uncomprehending side-glance at Indian philosophy—in short "ancient, medæval and modern" history. Strictly speaking, he never once moved outside the scheme, nor did any other thinker of his time.

What correlation, then, is there or can there be of his idea of the "Dionysian" with the inner life of a highly-civilized Chinese or an up-to-date American? What is the significance of his type of the "Superman"—for the world of Islam? Can image-forming antitheses of Nature and Intellect, Heathen and Christian, Classical and Modern, have any meaning for the soul of

---

5. Sir Francis Bacon (1561–1626), author of the *Novum Organum* (1620), which systematically described patterns of human error in the pursuit of knowledge. 6. Arthur Schopenhauer (1788–1860), German philosopher and author of *The World as Will and Idea* (1819). 7. The German philosopher Friedrich Nietzsche (1844–1900), author of *Thus Spake Zarathustra* (1883–1885), which introduced the concept of the Superman (later misused by the Nazis for their own purposes), and whose *The Birth of Tragedy* (1871) distinguished between Dionysian and Apollonian elements in human nature.

the Indian or the Russian? What can Tolstoi—who from the depths of his humanity rejected the whole Western world-idea as something alien and distant—*do* with the "Middle Ages," with Dante, with Luther? What can a Japanese do with Parzeval and "Zarathustra," or an Indian with Sophocles?[8] And is the thought-range of Schopenhauer, Comte, Feuerbach, Hebbel or Strindberg[9] any wider? Is not their whole psychology, for all its intention of world-wide validity, one of purely West-European significance?

How comic seem Ibsen's woman-problems—which also challenge the attention of all "humanity"—when, for his famous Nora, the lady of the North-west European city with the horizon that is implied by a house-rent of £100 to £300 a year and a Protestant upbringing, we substitute Caesar's wife, Madame de Sévigné,[1] a Japanese or a Turkish peasant woman! But, for that matter, Ibsen's own circle of vision is that of the middle class in a great city of yesterday and to-day. His conflicts, which start from spiritual premisses that did not exist till about 1850 and can scarcely last beyond 1950, are neither those of the great world nor those of the lower masses, still less those of the cities inhabited by non-European populations.

All these are local and temporary values—most of them indeed limited to the momentary "intelligentsia" of cities of West-European type. World-historical or "eternal" values they emphatically are not. Whatever the substantial importance of Ibsen's and Nietzsche's generation may be, it infringes the very meaning of the word "world-history"—which denotes the totality and not a selected part—to subordinate, to undervalue, or to ignore the factors which lie outside "modern" interests. Yet in fact they are so undervalued or ignored to an amazing extent. What the West has said and thought, hitherto, on the problems of space, time, motion, number, will, marriage, property, tragedy, science, has remained narrow and dubious, because men were always looking for *the* solution of *the* question. It was never seen that many questioners implies many answers, that any philosophical question is really a veiled desire to get an explicit affirmation of what is implicit in the question itself, that the great questions of any period are fluid beyond all conception, and that therefore it is only by obtaining a *group of historically limited solutions* and measuring it by *utterly impersonal* criteria that the final secrets can be reached. The real student of mankind treats no standpoint as absolutely right or absolutely wrong. In the face of such grave problems as that of Time or that of Marriage, it is insufficient to appeal to personal experience, or an inner voice, or reason, or the opinion of ancestors or contemporaries. These may say what is true for the questioner himself and for his time, but that is not all. In other Cultures the phenomenon talks a different language, for other men there are different truths. The *thinker* must admit the validity of all, or of none.

How greatly, then, Western world-criticism can be widened and deepened! How immensely far beyond the innocent relativism of Nietzsche and his

8. Martin Luther (1483–1546), German pastor and scholar who attacked corruption in the Catholic Church and whose *Ninety-five Theses* mark the beginning of the Protestant Reformation. 9. August Strindberg (1849–1912), Swedish naturalist dramatist known for his psychological realism, also influenced Expressionist drama. *Comte:* Frenchman Auguste Comte (1798–1857), the founder of positivism. *Feuerbach:* the German moralist philosopher Ludwig Feuerbach (1804–1872). *Hebbel:* Friedrich Hebbel (1813–1863), German poet, dramatist, and author of historical tragedies. 1. Marie de Rabutin-Chantal, marquise de Sévigné (1626–1696), known for the lively letters that she wrote to her daughter between 1671 and 1677. *Nora:* the heroine of Ibsen's drama *A Doll's House* (1879).

generation one must look—how fine one's sense for form and one's psychological insight must become—how completely one must free oneself from
limitations of self, of practical interests, of horizon—before one dare assert
the pretension to understand world-history, the *world-as-history*.

* * *

XII

* * * The "Decline of the West" comprises nothing less than the problem
of *Civilization*. We have before us one of the fundamental questions of all
higher history. What is Civilization, understood as the organic-logical sequel,
fulfilment and finale of a culture?

For every Culture has *its own* Civilization. In this work, for the first time
the two words, hitherto used to express an indefinite, more or less ethical,
distinction, are used in a *periodic* sense, to express a strict and necessary
organic succession. The Civilization is the inevitable *destiny* of the Culture,
and in this principle we obtain the viewpoint from which the deepest and
gravest problems of historical morphology become capable of solution. Civilizations are the most external and artificial states of which a species of
developed humanity is capable. They are a conclusion, the thing-become
succeeding the thing-becoming, death following life, rigidity following
expansion, intellectual age and the stone-built, petrifying world-city following mother-earth and the spiritual childhood of Doric and Gothic.[2] They are
an end, irrevocable, yet by inward necessity reached again and again.

So, for the first time, we are enabled to understand the Romans as the
successors of the Greeks, and light is projected into the deepest secrets of the
late-Classical period. What, but this, can be the meaning of the fact—which
can only be disputed by vain phrases—that the Romans were barbarians who
did not *precede* but *closed* a great development? Unspiritual, unphilosophi-
cal, devoid of art, clannish to the point of brutality, aiming relentlessly at
tangible successes, they stand between the Hellenic Culture and nothingness. An imagination directed purely to practical objects—they had religious
laws governing godward relations as they had other laws governing human
relations, but there was no specifically Roman saga of gods—was something
which is not found at all in Athens. In a word, Greek *soul*—Roman *intellect*;
and this antithesis is the differentia between Culture and Civilization.[3] Nor
is it only to the Classical that it applies. Again and again there appears this
type of strong-minded, completely non-metaphysical man, and in the hands
of this type lies the intellectual and material destiny of each and every "late"
period. Such are the men who carried through the Babylonian, the Egyptian,
the Indian, the Chinese, the Roman Civilizations, and in such periods do
Buddhism, Stoicism, Socialism ripen into definitive world-conceptions
which enable a moribund humanity to be attacked and re-formed in its intimate structure. *Pure* Civilization, as a historical process, consists in a pro-

2. Early architectural styles in ancient Greece and medieval Europe, respectively. 3. An opposition that
was frequently debated, with culture generally reflecting human behavior and civilization found in human
institutions. For Spengler, culture is a "great soul," an organic totality that is born in a specific place and
evolves to maturity, when it dies or is transformed. "The aim once attained—the idea, the entire content
of inner possibilities, fulfilled and made externally actual—the Culture suddenly hardens, it mortifies, its
blood congeals, its force breaks down, and it becomes *Civilization*."

gressive *taking-down* of forms that have become inorganic or dead.

The transition from Culture to Civilization was accomplished for the Classical world in the 4th, for the Western in the 19th Century. From these periods onward the great intellectual decisions take place, not as in the days of the Orpheus-movement or the Reformation in the "whole world" where not a hamlet is too small to be unimportant, but in three or four world-cities that have absorbed into themselves the whole content of History, while the old wide landscape of the Culture, become merely provincial, serves only to feed the cities with what remains of its higher mankind.

* * *

XIII

* * *

Here, then, I lay it down that *Imperialism*, of which petrifacts such as the Egyptian empire, the Roman, the Chinese, the Indian may continue to exist for hundreds or thousands of years—dead bodies, amorphous and dispirited masses of men, scrap-material from a great history—is to be taken as the typical symbol of the passing away. Imperialism is Civilization unadulterated. In this phenomenal form the destiny of the West is now irrevocably set. The energy of culture-man is directed inwards, that of civilization-man outwards. And thus I see in Cecil Rhodes[4] the first man of a new age. He stands for the political style of a far-ranging, Western, Teutonic and especially German future, and his phrase "expansion is everything" is the Napoleonic reassertion of the indwelling tendency of *every* Civilization that has fully ripened— Roman, Arab or Chinese. It is not a matter of choice—it is not the conscious will of individuals, or even that of whole classes or peoples that decides. The expansive tendency is a doom, something daemonic and immense, which grips, forces into service, and uses up the late mankind of the world-city stage, willy-nilly, aware or unaware.* * *

4. The British businessman-imperialist (1853–1902) who was largely responsible for British expansion in South Africa (see p. 1593).

ENCYCLOPAEDIA BRITANNICA
(ELEVENTH EDITION)
1911

The eleventh edition of the *Encyclopaedia Britannica* (1911) has a special position in the history of encyclopedias. It is a collector's item, famous for the many searching articles written by leading scholars and authorities of the day: Edmund Gosse wrote on criticism, T. H. Huxley on amphibia, Prince Peter Kropotkin on anarchism, and Thomas Babington Macaulay on John Bunyan. Thirty-five women wrote signed entries, among them Agnes Clerke on Copernicus and Victoria Welby on significs. As a whole, the encyclopedia was entertaining and frequently argumentative, with articles often ten times the length of those in competing publications. It offered critical perspectives as well as information and was—in Sir Kenneth Clark's words—"the last encyclopaedia in the tradition of Diderot which assumes that information can be made memorable only when it is slightly coloured by prejudice." The "eleventh edition" is recognized, therefore, as a key to what many people thought about important issues just after the turn of the century.

One of the most popular topics was the nature of civilization, which had, for most readers, reached its apogee in contemporary Western culture. (An early example of this view can be found in Macaulay's *Minute on Indian Education* (1835, p. 1584.) Pride and excitement ruled, for a scientific paradigm seemed available to explain not only the history of human evolution, but projected future progress along rational lines. With a little more effort, guided by recent advances in science, technology, and the social sciences, human society would evolve to the next level of civilization. It is this tremendous optimism and complete confidence based on modern science and apparent patterns of historical evolution that emerge in the eleventh edition's article on civilization. Three years later, World War I would begin.

Encyclopaedia Britannica (Eleventh Edition)

Volume VI. Châtelet to Constantine

from CIVILIZATION[1]

CIVILIZATION. The word "civilization" is an obvious derivative of the Lat. *civis,* a citizen, and *civilis,* pertaining to a citizen. Etymologically speaking, then, it would be putting no undue strain upon the word to interpret it as having to do with the entire period of human progress since mankind attained sufficient intelligence and social unity to develop a system of government. But in select practice "civilization" is usually interpreted in a somewhat narrower sense, as having application solely to the most recent and comparatively brief period of time that has elapsed since the most highly developed races of men have used systems of writing. This restricted usage is probably explicable, in part at least, by the fact that the word, though distinctly modern in origin, is nevertheless older than the interpretation of social evolution that now finds universal acceptance. Only very recently has it come to be understood that primitive societies vastly antedating the historical period had attained relatively high stages of development and fixity, socially and politically. Now that this is understood, however, nothing but an arbitrary and highly inconvenient restriction of meanings can prevent us from speaking of the citizens of these early societies as having attained certain stages of civilization. It will be convenient, then, in outlining the successive stages of human progress here, to include under the comprehensive term "civilization" those long earlier periods of "savagery" and "barbarism"[2] as well as the more recent period of higher development to which the word "civilization" is sometimes restricted.

1. Written by Henry Smith Williams, a medical doctor who wrote *The Story of Nineteenth-Century Science* and *The Lesson of Heredity*, edited a multivolume *History of Science* (1904–1910) and *The Historians' History of the World* (1904–5), and lectured in the Hartford School of Sociology.   2. Terms derived from Lewis H. Morgan (1818–1881), the "Father of American Anthropology," in his *Ancient Society: or, Researches in the Lines of Human Progress from Savagery, through Barbarism to Civilization* (1877), an influential book whose evolutionary views inspired Friedrich Engels's *The Origins of the Family* (1884).

* * *

A recognition of the principle that, broadly speaking, progress has everywhere been achieved along the same lines and through the same sequence of changes, makes it possible to interpret the past history of the civilized races of to-day in the light of the present-day conditions of other races that are still existing under social and political conditions of a more primitive type.

* * *

To-day the thesis that all mankind are one brotherhood needs no defence. The most primitive of existing aborigines are regarded merely as brethren who, through some defect or neglect of opportunity, have lagged behind in the race. Similarly the defective and criminal classes that make up so significant a part of the population of even our highest present-day civilizations, are no longer regarded with anger or contempt, as beings who are suffering just punishment for wilful transgressions, but are considered as pitiful victims of hereditary and environmental influences that they could neither choose nor control. Insanity is no longer thought of as demoniac possession, but as the most lamentable of diseases.

The changed attitude towards savage races and defective classes affords tangible illustrations of a fundamental transformation of point of view which doubtless represents the most important result of the operation of new scientific knowledge in the course of the 19th century. It is a transformation that is only partially effected as yet, to be sure; but it is rapidly making headway, and when fully achieved it will represent, probably, the most radical metamorphosis of mental view that has taken place in the entire course of the historical period.

* * *

It is coming to be more and more widely recognized that all theologies are but the reflex of the more or less faulty knowledge of the times in which they originate; that the true and abiding purpose of religion should be the practical betterment of humanity—the advancement of civilization in the best sense of the word; and that this end may perhaps be best subserved by different systems of theology, adapted to the varied genius of different times and divers races. Wherefore there is not the same enthusiastic desire to-day that found expression a generation ago, to impose upon the cultured millions of the East a religion that seems to them alien to their manner of thought, unsuited to their needs and less distinctly ethical in teaching than their own religions.

* * *

At some time, after the first period of cosmopolitanism shall be ushered in as a tenth ethnic period, it will come to be recognized that there is a word fraught with fuller meanings even than the word patriotism. That word is humanitarianism. The enlightened generation that realizes the full implications of that word will doubtless marvel that their ancestors of the third period of civilization should have risen up as nations and slaughtered one another by thousands to settle a dispute about a geographical boundary.

Such a procedure will appear to have been quite as barbarous as the cannibalistic practices of their yet more remote ancestors, and distinctly less rational, since cannibalism might sometimes save its practiser from starvation, whereas warfare of the civilized type was a purely destructive agency.

* * *

It will be thought fitting that man should become the conscious arbiter of his own racial destiny to the extent of applying whatever laws of heredity he knows or may acquire in the interests of his own species, as he has long applied them in the case of domesticated animals.* * * It does not follow that all men will be brought to a dead level of equality of body and mind, nor that individual competition will cease; but the average physical mental status of the race will be raised immeasurably.* * * There are millions of men in Europe and America to-day whose whole mental equipment—despite the fact that they have been taught to read and write—is far more closely akin to the average of the Upper Period of Barbarism than to the highest standards of their own time.

* * *

But the citizen of the future, if the auguries of the present prove true, will be able to apply principles of right and wrong without reference to national boundaries. He will understand that the interests of the entire human family are, in the last analysis, common interests. The census through which he attempts to estimate "the greatest good of the greatest number" must include, not his own nation merely, but the remotest member of the human race. On this universal basis must be founded that absolute standard of ethics which will determine the relations of cosmopolite man with his fellows. When this ideal is attained, mankind will again represent a single family, as it did in the day when our primeval ancestors first entered on the pathway of progress; but it will be a family whose habitat has been extended from the narrow glade of some tropical forest to the utmost habitable confines of the globe. Each member of this family will be permitted to enjoy the greatest amount of liberty consistent with the like liberty of every other member; but the interests of the few will everywhere be recognized as subservient to the interests of the many, and such recognition of mutual interests will establish the practical criterion for the interpretation of international affairs.

But such an extension of the altruistic principle by no means presupposes the elimination of egoistic impulses—of individualism. On the contrary, we must suppose that man at the highest stages of culture will be, even as was the savage, a seeker after the greatest attainable degree of efficiency and comfort for the least necessary expenditure of energy. The pursuit of this ideal has been from first to last the ultimate impelling force in nature urging man forward. The only change has been a change in the interpretation of the ideal, an altered estimate as to what manner of things are most worth the purchase price of toil and self-denial. That the things most worth the having cannot, generally speaking, be secured without such toil and self-denial, is a lesson that began to be inculcated while man was a savage, and that has never ceased to be reiterated generation after generation. It is the final test of progressive civilization that a given effort shall produce a larger and larger modicum of average individual comfort.* * * The efforts of civilized man provide him, on the average, with a marvellous range of comforts, as contrasted with those that rewarded the most strenuous efforts of savage or barbarian, to whom present-day necessaries would have been undreamed-of luxuries. But the ideal ratio between effort and result has by no means been achieved; nor will it have been until the inventive brain of man has provided a civilization in which a far higher percentage of citizens will find the life-vocations to which they are best adapted by nature, and in which, therefore, the efforts of the average worker may be directed with such vigour, enthusiasm and interest as can alone make for true efficiency; a civilization adjusted to such an economic balance that the average man may live in reasonable comfort without heart-breaking strain, and yet accumulate a sufficient surplus to ensure ease and serenity for his declining days. Such, seemingly, should be the normal goal of progressive civilization. Doubtless mankind in advancing towards that goal will institute many changes that could by no possibility be foretold; but (to summarize the views just presented) it seems a safe augury from present-day conditions and tendencies that the important lines of progress will include (1) the organic betterment of the race through wise application of the laws of heredity; (2) the lessening of international jealousies and the consequent minimizing of the drain upon communal resources that attends a military régime; and (3) an ever-increasing movement towards the industrial and economic unification of the world.   (H.S. Wi)

CONSTANTINE CAVAFY
1863–1933

A private poet who circulated his work in folders to relatives and friends and never offered a book for sale, Constantine Cavafy became, almost in spite of himself, the most influential Greek poet of the twentieth century when a posthumous edition of 154 short poems was published in 1935. His precisely worded, obliquely evocative portraits link past and present in historical figures displayed with all their poignant desires and personal tragedies. The modern world is present, too: glimpses of contemporary Alexandria spark the recall of erotic memories, and forgotten landscapes resurge—like Proust's madeleine—with complex emotional and intellectual associations. Cavafy's poetry draws his readers into an astonishingly real personal universe, establishing a common bond between them and fictional characters in an immense variety of circumstances. The sense of participation comes not merely from the recognition of familiar emotional situations, but also from Cavafy's unique blend of such drama with an ironic and philosophical perspective that makes subtly different demands on the reader's imagination.

He was born in 1863 to Greek parents living in Alexandria, Egypt. The export-import firm of Cavafy Brothers had once been wealthy, but their fortunes declined and his father died in 1870. Two years later, Cavafy's mother took the family to England, where his parents had lived in the 1850s and where she hoped they would prosper again. Unfortunately, his two older brothers were inexperienced in business affairs, and the rest of their funds vanished, obliging them to return to Alexandria, where they lived in straitened circumstances. During the poet's seven years in England, however, he became bilingual and read widely in English literature. In 1882, Cavafy's mother returned to her father's house outside Constantinople with Cavafy and two brothers. They remained there for three years, during which time Cavafy discovered his homosexuality and had his first love affair. The young writer—who was now fluent in English, Greek, and French—began to write poems in all three languages. The family returned to Alexandria in 1885, where Cavafy settled for the rest of his life, living with his mother until 1899 and, after her death, sharing quarters with his unmarried brothers. Cavafy continued to write poetry and essays while working for an Alexandrian newspaper and for the Egyptian Stock Exchange before receiving the position he would hold from then on: an appointment as a special clerk in the Irrigation Service of the Ministry of Public Works. Although Cavafy shared his poetry with friends and relatives, he does not seem to have had any interest in seeking a wider audience. He had several pamphlets printed privately—an initial booklet of fourteen poems in 1904, enlarged with seven more in 1910—but otherwise restricted himself to folders of poems given to a few readers. In his later years, his reputation spread internationally through the efforts of British novelist E. M. Forster, who met him during World War I in Alexandria and remained a friend for the next twenty years. Cavafy's poem *Ithaka* was published in T. S. Eliot's journal *Criterion*, and occasionally European visitors to Alexandria came to meet its author. He was reportedly a sociable person and a fascinating conversationalist, but he lived to himself and his circle of friends. Forster described him as a Greek gentleman with a straw hat standing "at a slight angle to the universe," and he was virtually unknown in Greece when he died in 1933.

Cavafy observed that his works could be divided into three broad categories—historical, philosophical, and erotic—and he arranged his folders of poetry in thematic as well as chronological order. It is easy to see how a primary division could be made: of the poems printed here, *Kaisarion* is historical, *The Next Table* is erotic, and *Ithaka* is philosophical. But isn't that too simple? The young Kaisarion is "good-looking and sensitive," with a "dreamy, an appealing beauty"; *The Next Table* involves memory, self-deception, and a portrait of aging as much as the act of love; and *Ithaka* would not exist without its basis in historical legend. Moreover, Cavafy says that *Waiting for the Barbarians*, which seems clearly to depict a moment during the decadence of the Roman Empire, is symbolic and "not necessarily Roman." The primary categories are not only broad, but (as Cavafy undoubtedly knew) they overlap and leave room for others, whether political allusion (*When the Watchman Saw the Light*), psychological portrait (*The City* or, differently, *Sculptor of Tyana*), devotion to art (*Craftsman of Wine Bowls*) or something else. All poems seem to exist in a framework that could be called philosophical, from the fleeting imagery of *Ionic* to the heavy burden of memory in *In the Evening*.

History in these poems exists on several levels. It is not the better-known Homeric or Periclean ages of Greek history, but rather the Hellenistic period and Byzantine Empire, a history whose tangled politics, sophisticated art, social decadence, and vulnerability to invasion had their analogue in twentieth-century Alexandria. Cavafy's Alexandria is a modern metropolis with a glorious past, and the poet searches history for dramatic anecdotes that reveal the texture of life in that turbulent age. It is not merely the murdered Kaisarion—son of Caesar and Cleopatra—who interests him, but John Kantakuzinos, a minor and impoverished ruler forced to use glass jewels in his crown; or King Dimitrios, who in 288 B.C.E. disguised himself in simple clothes to escape capture after being deserted by his soldiers; or the scheming Anna Komnina, furious at seeing the Byzantine throne slip out of her hands in 1137. Ancient Greece appears primarily as a reference point in the distant past: the home of heroes like Patroklos or the god Hermes, who are both subjects for the vain sculptor of Tyana, of gods who appear for a moment in the streets of Alexandria or the landscape of

Ionia, or of Odysseus, whose epic voyage becomes a lesson that you can't go home again. From whatever era, Cavafy's precisely rendered narratives invite readers to enter, for a moment, the world of his poetic imagination and to draw their own connections to contemporary life and circumstances.

POEMS[1]

Waiting for the Barbarians[2]

What are we waiting for, assembled in the forum?[3]

    The barbarians are due here today.

Why isn't anything happening in the senate?
Why do the senators sit there without legislating?

    Because the barbarians are coming today.   5
    What laws can the senators make now?
    Once the barbarians are here, they'll do the legislating.

Why did our emperor get up so early,
and why is he sitting at the city's main gate
on his throne, in state, wearing the crown?   10

    Because the barbarians are coming today
    and the emperor is waiting to receive their leader.
    He has even prepared a scroll to give him,
    replete with titles, with imposing names.

Why have our two consuls and praetors[4] come out today   15
wearing their embroidered, their scarlet togas?
Why have they put on bracelets with so many amethysts,
and rings sparkling with magnificent emeralds?
Why are they carrying elegant canes
beautifully worked in silver and gold?   20

    Because the barbarians are coming today
    and things like that dazzle the barbarians.

Why don't our distinguished orators come forward as usual
to make their speeches, say what they have to say?

1. All poems are translated by Edmund Keeley and Philip Sherrard. 2. Written in 1898; published in 1910. The setting appears to be ancient Rome during the decadence of the empire, when the city was sacked by the Visigoth leader Alaric in 410. Cavafy has specified that there is no precise reference, however, noting that the barbarians are only a symbol in this poem and that "the emperor, the senators and the orators are not necessarily Roman." 3. A large public area in Rome, containing temples, shops, the Senate building, and the rostrum from which orators addressed the people. 4. Judicial officers who held preliminary hearings before cases were assigned to a judge. *Consuls*: the two chief administrative officers of the state who presided over the Senate. They were elected by the people under the Republic but named by the emperor during the empire.

Because the barbarians are coming today   25
and they're bored by rhetoric and public speaking.

Why this sudden restlessness, this confusion?
(How serious people's faces have become.)
Why are the streets and squares emptying so rapidly,
everyone going home so lost in thought?   30

Because night has fallen and the barbarians have not come.
And some who have just returned from the border say
there are no barbarians any longer.

And now, what's going to happen to us without barbarians?
They were, those people, a kind of solution.   35

The City[1]

You said: "I'll go to another country, go to another shore,
find another city better than this one.
Whatever I try to do is fated to turn out wrong
and my heart lies buried as though it were something dead.
How long can I let my mind moulder in this place?   5
Wherever I turn, wherever I happen to look,
I see the black ruins of my life, here,
where I've spent so many years, wasted them, destroyed them
       totally."

You won't find a new country, won't find another shore.
This city will always pursue you. You will walk   10
the same streets, grow old in the same neighborhoods,
will turn gray in these same houses.
You will always end up in this city. Don't hope for things elsewhere:
there is no ship for you, there is no road.
As you've wasted your life here, in this small corner,   15
you've destroyed it everywhere else in the world.

Sculptor of Tyana[1]

As you'll have heard, I'm no beginner.
I've handled a lot of stone in my time,
and in my own country, Tyana, I'm pretty well known.
Actually, senators here have also commissioned
a number of statues from me.

1. Written in 1894 under the title *Once More in the Same City* and listed under "Prisons." Published with
the current title in 1910.   1. First written in June 1893, entitled *A Sculptor's Studio*; rewritten in November 1903. Tyana was a city in Cappadocia, a district in Asia Minor, but the scene—set in Rome—is imaginary.

                                    Let me show you   5
a few of them. Notice this Rhea:[2]
reverential, all fortitude, very old.
Notice Pompey. And Marius here,
and Paulus Aemilius, and Scipio Africanus.[3]
The likeness as close as I could make it.   10
And Patroklos (I still have to touch him up a bit).
Near those pieces of yellowish marble there
stands Kaisarion.[4]

And for some time now I've been busy
working on a Poseidon.[5] I'm studying   15
his horses in particular: how to shape them exactly.
They have to be made so light
that it's clear their bodies, their legs,
are not touching the earth but galloping over water.

But here's my favorite work,   20
wrought with the utmost care and feeling.
This one—it was a summer day, very hot,
and my mind rose to ideal things—
this one came to me in a vision, this young Hermes.[6]

Ionic[1]

That we've broken their statues,
that we've driven them out of their temples,
doesn't mean at all that the gods are dead.
O land of Ionia, they're still in love with you,
their souls still keep your memory.   5
When an August dawn wakes over you,
your atmosphere is potent with their life,
and sometimes a young ethereal figure,
indistinct, in rapid flight,
wings across your hills.   10

---

2. Daughter of heaven and earth, and mother of the gods on Olympus.   3. Scipio Africanus the Younger (185–129 B.C.E.) led the army that destroyed Carthage in 146 B.C.E. *Pompey:* Gnaeus Pompeius Magnus (106–48 B.C.E.), Roman general and statesman who fled to Egypt after being defeated by Julius Caesar, was assassinated by King Ptolemy. Gaius Marius (157–86 B.C.E.), a popular general, was elected consul seven times. Lucius Aemilius Paulus (228–160 B.C.E.) was a Roman consul whose army was disastrously defeated by Hannibal at the Battle of Cannae (216 B.C.E.).   4. Or Caesarion ("Little Caesar," 47–30 B.C.E.), the son of Cleopatra and Julius Caesar. Co-ruler of Egypt with his mother, he was killed by Octavian (the future emperor Augustus Caesar) for political reasons after her death. *Patroklos:* Achilles' friend in Homer's *Iliad,* killed in battle.   5. Greek god of the sea.   6. Son of Zeus and messenger of the gods, often depicted as a nude youth bearing a herald's wand, or caduceus.   1. Belonging to Ionia, a strip of land on the west coast of Asia Minor where Greek settlers built important trading cities whose art and philosophy dominated Greek cultural life until the end of the 6th century B.C.E. *Ionic* can also mean "Greek," however, and the scene is characteristically vague. Originally entitled *Memory* (1886), the poem was rewritten in 1905 as *Thessaly* (a frequently invaded region of northern Greece), and only in 1911 was the final version published as *Ionic.*

Ithaka[1]

As you set out for Ithaka
hope the voyage is a long one,
full of adventure, full of discovery.
Laistrygonians and Cyclops,
angry Poseidon[2]—don't be afraid of them: 5
you'll never find things like that on your way
as long as you keep your thoughts raised high,
as long as a rare excitement
stirs your spirit and your body.
Laistrygonians and Cyclops,   10
wild Poseidon—you won't encounter them
unless you bring them along inside your soul,
unless your soul sets them up in front of you.

Hope the voyage is a long one.
May there be many a summer morning when,   15
with what pleasure, what joy,
you come into harbors seen for the first time;
may you stop at Phoenician trading stations[3]
to buy fine things,
mother of pearl and coral, amber and ebony,   20
sensual perfume of every kind—
as many sensual perfumes as you can;
and may you visit many Egyptian cities
to gather stores of knowledge from their scholars.

Keep Ithaka always in your mind.   25
Arriving there is what you are destined for.
But do not hurry the journey at all.
Better if it lasts for years,
so you are old by the time you reach the island,
wealthy with all you have gained on the way,   30
not expecting Ithaka to make you rich.

Ithaka gave you the marvelous journey.
Without her you would not have set out.
She has nothing left to give you now.

And if you find her poor, Ithaka won't have fooled you.   35
Wise as you will have become, so full of experience,
you will have understood by then what these Ithakas mean.

---

1. Published in 1911. Ithaka is the island kingdom of Odysseus and the goal of his homeward journey after the Trojan War. An early, quite different version of this poem was entitled *Second Odyssey*.   2. Greek god of the sea. Odysseus encounters both the Laistrygonians (fierce rock-throwing cannibal giants in *Odyssey* 10) and the Cyclops (a one-eyed cannibal giant in the *Odyssey* 9) on his voyage home.   3. The Phoenicians (from Phoenicia, now in modern Syria and Lebanon) were famous merchants and sailors who established trade routes throughout the Mediterranean.

In the Evening[1]

It wouldn't have lasted long anyway—
the experience of years makes that clear.
Even so, Fate did put an end to it a bit abruptly.
It was soon over, that wonderful life.
Yet how strong the scents were,   5
what a magnificent bed we lay in,
what pleasure we gave our bodies.

An echo from my days given to sensuality,
an echo from those days came back to me,
something of the fire of the young life we shared: 10
I picked up a letter again,
and I read it over and over till the light faded away.

Then, sad, I went out on to the balcony,
went out to change my thoughts at least by seeing
something of this city I love,   15
a little movement in the street and the shops.

Kaisarion[1]

Partly to throw light on a certain period,
partly to kill an hour or two,
last night I picked up and read
a volume of inscriptions about the Ptolemies.
The lavish praise and flattery are much the same   5
for each of them. All are brilliant,
glorious, mighty, benevolent;
everything they undertake is full of wisdom.
As for the women of their line, the Berenices and Cleopatras,[2]
they too, all of them, are marvelous.   10

When I'd verified the facts I wanted
I would have put the book away had not a brief
insignificant mention of King Kaisarion
suddenly caught my eye . . .

And there you were with your indefinable charm.   15
Because we know
so little about you from history,
I could fashion you more freely in my mind.

---

1. Published in 1917; written in 1916 as *Alexandrian* (a reference to the city of Alexandria, Egypt).
1. Published in 1918. See p. 1718, n. 4.   2. Cleopatra (69–30 B.C.E.) was queen of Egypt and mother
of Kaisarion. Berenice (ca. 273–221 B.C.E.) was the sister of Ptolemy III Euergetes (ca. 284–221 B.C.E.)
who married Antiochus II, king of Syria, and, after his death, would have married the emperor Titus if the
Romans had not objected.

I made you good-looking and sensitive.
My art gives your face   20
a dreamy, an appealing beauty.
And so completely did I imagine you
that late last night,
as my lamp went out—I let it go out on purpose—
it seemed you came into my room,   25
it seemed you stood there in front of me, looking just as you would
     have
in conquered Alexandria,
pale and weary, ideal in your grief,
still hoping they might take pity on you,
those scum who whispered: "Too many Caesars."[3]   30

The Next Table[1]

He[2] must be barely twenty-two years old—
yet I'm certain that almost that many years ago
I enjoyed the very same body.

It isn't erotic fever at all.
And I've been in the casino[3] for a few minutes only,   5
so I haven't had time to drink a great deal.
I enjoyed that very same body.

And if I don't remember where, this one lapse of memory doesn't
     mean a thing.

There, now that he's sitting down at the next table,
I recognize every motion he makes—and under his clothes   10
I see again the limbs I loved, naked.

Craftsman of Wine Bowls[1]

On this wine bowl—pure silver,
made for the house of Herakleidis,[2]
where good taste is the rule—
notice these graceful flowers, the streams, the thyme.
In the center I put this beautiful young man,   5
naked, erotic, one leg still dangling

---

3. The teenage Kaisarion was killed because, as the son of Julius Caesar and Cleopatra, he represented a
political threat to the future emperor Augustus (then Octavian). The reason for his execution was given in
a sentence modeled on a line from Homer's *Iliad* (2.204): "It is not a good thing to have too many Caesars."
1. Printed in 1919.   2. The language of the Greek original does not reveal the gender of the person
seated at the next table, but this calculated ambiguity is not possible in English translation.   3. Casinos
were respectable places of entertainment.   1. Printed in 1921; written in 1903 and twice revised.
2. Treasurer of Antiochus IV Epiphanus (ruled 175–163 B.C.E.).

in the water. O memory, I begged
for you to help me most in making
the young face I loved appear the way it was.
This proved very difficult because   10
some fifteen years have gone by since the day
he died as a soldier in the defeat at Magnesia.[3]

When the Watchman Saw the Light[1]

Winter, summer, the watchman sat there looking out
from the roof of Atreus' palace[2] Now he has
good news to report. In the distance[3] he saw the fire light up.
And he's happy; besides, the drudgery's over now.
It's hard to sit there night and day   5
in heat and cold, looking out for a fire to appear
on the peak of Arachnaion.[4] Now the longed-for signal
has appeared. Yet when happiness
comes, it brings less joy
than one expected.[5] But at least   10
this much has been gained: we've rid ourselves
of hope and expectation. Many things will happen
to the house of Atreus. No need to be wise
to guess this now the watchman
has seen the light. So let's not exaggerate.   15
The light is good; and those coming are good,
their words and actions also good.
And let's hope all goes well. But
Argos can do without the house
of Atreus. Ancient houses are not eternal.   20
Of course many people will have much to say.
We should listen. But we won't be deceived
by words such as Indispensable, Unique, and Great.
Someone else indispensable and unique and great
can always be found at a moment's notice.

---

3. In 190 B.C.E. at the battle of Magnesia, the Romans defeated Antiochus III the Great, the father of
Antiochus IV.   1. Written in 1900 and unpublished during the poet's lifetime. The title refers to the
prologue of Aeschylus's *Agamemnon* (printed in this anthology's first volume), a speech given by the watchman who is waiting for the signal that announces the king's return to Argos.   2. A reminder of the
hereditary curse on the family: King Atreus was Agamemnon's father, and Atreus himself was supposed to
have revenged himself on his brother Thyestes by serving his children to him for dinner.   3. A chain of
bonfires stretching from Troy to Greece had been prepared to announce the return of Agamemnon's ship
from the Trojan War.   4. A mountain in the Epidauros (Argeia) region of Greece.   5. A general statement but also a reminder that Agamemnon is coming home to his death at the hands of Queen Clytemnestra. Just as in Aeschylus's play, the watchman knows that all is not well at home.

WILLIAM BUTLER YEATS
1865–1939

The twentieth century's greatest poet in the English language, William Butler Yeats is also a major figure in the Irish literary renaissance. His sensuous imagery and fusion of historical references and metaphysical vision stir readers around the world. Years after the poet's death, the Nigerian Chinua Achebe borrowed three words from one of his lines as the title of a novel, *Things Fall Apart*—confident that his audience would immediately recognize the source. Often called a Symbolist, owing to his use of allusive imagery and large symbolic structures, Yeats has little in common with Baudelaire, Mallarmé, or other Continental Symbolists. Instead, the Irish poet was fascinated by occult theories and large historical patterns, adopting a cyclical model of history in which the rise and fall of civilizations are predetermined inside a series of interweaving evolutionary spirals. He created a private mythology that helped him come to terms with personal and cultural pain and allowed him to explain—as symptoms of Western civilization's declining spiral—the plight of contemporary Irish society and the chaos of European culture around World War I.

Yeats was born in a Dublin suburb on June 13, 1865, the oldest of four children born to John Butler and Susan Pollexfen Yeats. His father, a cosmopolitan Anglo-Irishman who had turned from law to painting, took over Yeats's education when he found that, at age nine, the boy could not read. J. B. Yeats was a highly argumentative religious skeptic who alternately terrorized his son and awakened his interest in poetry and the visual arts, inspiring at one and the same time both rebellion against scientific rationalism and belief in the higher knowledge of art. His mother's strong ties to her home in County Sligo (where Yeats spent many summers and school holidays) introduced him to the beauties of the Irish countryside and the Irish folklore and supernatural legends that appear throughout his work. Living alternately in Ireland and England for much of his youth, Yeats became part of literary society in both countries and—though an Irish nationalist—was unable to adopt a narrowly patriotic point of view. Even the failed Easter Rebellion of 1916, which he celebrated in *Easter 1916*, and the revolutionary figures who were beloved friends took their place in a larger mythic historical framework. By the end of his life, he had abandoned all practical politics and devoted himself to the reality of personal experience inside a mystic view of history.

For many, it is Yeats's mastery of images that defines his work. From his early use of symbols as private keys, or dramatic metaphors for complex personal emotions, to the immense cosmology of his last work, he continued to create a highly visual poetry whose power derives from the dramatic interweaving of specific images. Symbols such as the Tower, Byzantium, Helen of Troy, the opposition of sun and moon, birds of prey, the blind man, and the fool recur frequently and draw their meaning not from inner connections established inside the poem (as for the French Symbolists) but from an underlying myth based on occult tradition, Irish folklore, history, and Yeats's own personal experience. Symbols as Yeats used them, however, make sense in and among themselves: the "gyre," or spiral unfolding of history, is simultaneously the falcon's spiral flight; and the sphinxlike beast slouching blank-eyed toward Bethlehem in *The Second Coming* is a comprehensible horror capable of many explicit interpretations but resistant to all and, therefore, the more terrifying. Even readers unacquainted with Yeats's mythic system will respond to images precisely expressing a situation or state of mind (for example, golden Byzantium for intellect, art, wisdom—all that "body" cannot supply) and to a visionary organization that proposes shape and context for twenty-first-century anxieties.

The nine poems included here cover the range of Yeats's career, which embraced several periods and styles. Yeats had attended art school and planned to be an artist before he turned fully to literature in 1886, and his early works show the influence of the Pre-Raphaelite school in art and literature. Pre-Raphaelitism called for a return to the sensuous representation and concrete particulars found in Italian painting before Raphael (1483–1520), and Pre-Raphaelite poetry evoked a poetic realm of luminous supernatural beauty described in allusive and erotically sensuous detail. Rossetti's *Blessed Damozel,* yearning for her beloved "from the gold bar of heaven," has eyes "deeper than the depth / Of waters stilled at even; / She had three lilies in her hand, / And the stars in her hair were seven." The Pre-Raphaelite fascination with the medieval past (William Morris wrote a *Defense of Guenevere,* King Arthur's adulterous wife) combined with Yeats's own interest in Irish legend, and in 1889 a long poem describing a traveler in fairyland (*The Wanderings of Oisin*) established his reputation and won Morris's praise. The musical, evocative style of Yeats's Pre-Raphaelite period is well shown in *The Lake Isle of Innisfree* (1890), with its hidden "bee-loud glade" where "peace comes dropping slow" and evening, after the "purple glow" of noon, is "full of the linnet's wings." Another poem from the same period, *When You Are Old,* pleads his love for the beautiful actress and Irish nationalist Maud Gonne, whom he met in 1889 and who repeatedly refused to marry him. From the love poems of his youth to his old age, when *The Circus Animals' Desertion* described her as prey to fanaticism and hate, Yeats returned again and again to examine his feelings for this woman, who personified love, beauty, and Irish nationalism along with hope, frustration, and despair.

Yeats's family moved to London in 1887, where he continued an earlier interest in mystical philosophy by taking up theosophy under its Russian interpreter Madame Blavatsky. Madame Blavatsky claimed mystic knowledge from Tibetan monks and preached a doctrine of the Universal Oversoul, individual spiritual evolution through cycles of incarnation, and the world as a conflict of opposites. Yeats was taken with her grandiose cosmology, although he inconveniently wished to test it by experiment and analysis and was ultimately expelled from the society in 1890. He found a more congenial literary model in the works of William Blake, which he coedited in 1893 with F. J. Ellis. Yeats's interest in large mystical systems later waned but never altogether disappeared, and traces may be seen in the introduction that he wrote in 1916 for *Gitanjali,* a collection of poems by the Indian author Rabindranath Tagore.

Several collections of Irish folk and fairy tales and a book describing Irish traditions (*The Celtic Twilight,* 1893) demonstrated a corresponding interest in Irish national identity. In 1896 he had met Lady Gregory, an Irish nationalist who invited him to spend summers at Coole Park, her country house in Galway, and who worked closely with him (and later J. M. Synge) in founding the Irish National Theatre (later the Abbey Theatre). Along with other participants in what was once called the Irish literary renaissance, he aimed to create "a national literature that made Ireland beautiful in the memory . . . freed from provincialism by an exacting criticism." To this end, he wrote *Cathleen ni Houlihan* (1902), a play in which the title character personifies Ireland, which became immensely popular with Irish nationalists. He also established Irish literary societies in Ireland, promoted and reviewed Irish books, and lectured and wrote about the need for Irish community. In 1922 he was elected senator of the Irish Free State, serving until 1928.

Gradually, Yeats became embittered by the split between narrow Irish nationalism and the free expression of Irish culture. He was outraged at the attacks on Synge's *Playboy of the Western World* (1907) for its supposed derogatory picture of Irish culture, and he commented scathingly in *Poems Written in Discouragement* (1913, reprinted in *Responsibilities,* 1914) on the inability of the Irish middle class to appreciate art or literature. When he celebrates the abortive Easter uprisings of 1916, it is with a more universal, aesthetic view; "A terrible beauty is born" in the self-sacrifice that leads even a "drunken, vainglorious lout" to be "transformed utterly" by political martyrdom. Except for summers at Coole Park, Yeats in his middle age was spending more time in England than in Ireland. He began his *Autobiographies* in 1914, and wrote symbolic plays intended for small audiences on the model of the Japanese *nō* theater. There is a change in the tone of his works at this time, a new precision and epigrammatic quality that is partly owing to his disappointment with Irish nationalism and partly to the new tastes in poetry promulgated by his friend Ezra Pound and by T. S. Eliot after the example of John Donne and the metaphysical poets.

Yeats's marriage in 1917 to Georgie Hyde-Lees provided him with much-needed stability and also an impetus to work out a larger symbolic scheme. He interpreted his wife's experiments with automatic writing (writing whatever comes to mind, without correction or rational intent) as glimpses into a hidden cosmic order and gradually evolved a total system, which he explained in *A Vision* (1926). The wheel of history takes 26,000 years to turn; and inside that wheel civilizations evolve in roughly 2,000 year gyres, spirals expanding outward until they collapse at the beginning of a new gyre, which will reverse the direction of the old. Human personalities fall into different types within the system, and both gyres and types are related to the different phases of the moon. Yeats's later poems in *The Tower* (1928), *The Winding Stair* (1933), and *Last Poems* (1939) are set in the context of this system. Even when it is not literally present, it suggests an organizing pattern that resolves contraries inside an immense historical perspective. *Leda and the Swan,* on one level an erotic retelling of a mythic rape, also foreshadows the Trojan War—brute force mirroring brute force. In the two poems on the legendary city of Byzantium, Yeats admired an artistic civilization that "could answer all my questions" but that was also only a moment in history. Byzantine art, with its stylized perspectives and mosaics made by arranging tiny colored pieces of stone, was the exact opposite of the Western tendency to imitate nature, and it provided a kind of escape, or healing distance, for the poet. The idea of an inhuman, metallic, abstract beauty separated "out of nature" by art expresses a mystic and Symbolist quest for an invulnerable world distinct from the ravages of time. This world was to be found in an idealized Byzantium, where the poet's body would be transmuted into "such a form as Grecian goldsmiths make / Of hammered gold and gold enamelling / To keep a drowsy Emperor awake; / Or set upon a golden bough to sing / To lords and ladies of Byzantium / Of what is past, or passing, or to come." At the end of *Among School Children*, the sixty-year-old "public man" compensates for the passing of youth by dreaming of pure "Presences" that never fade. Yeats had often adopted the persona of the old man for whom the perspectives of age, idealized beauty, or history were ways to keep human agony at a distance. In *Lapis Lazuli,* the tragic figures of history transcend their roles by the calm "gaiety" with which they accept their fate; the ancient Chinamen carved in the poem's damaged blue stone climb toward a vantage point where they stare detachedly down on the world's tragedies: "Their eyes mid many wrinkles, their eyes, / Their ancient, glittering eyes, are gay."

But the world is still there, its tragedies still take place, and Yeats's poetry is always aware of the physical and emotional roots from which it sprang. Whatever the wished-for distance, his poems are full of passionate feelings, erotic desire and disappointment, delight in sensuous beauty, horror at civil war and anarchy, dismay at degradation and change. By the time of his death on January 28, 1939, Yeats had rejected his Byzantine identity as the golden songbird and sought out "the brutality, the ill breeding, the barbarism of truth." "The Wild Old Wicked Man" replaced earlier druids or ancient Chinamen as spokesman, and in *The Circus Animals' Desertion* Yeats described his former themes as so many circus animals put on display. No matter how much these themes embodied "pure mind," they were based in "a mound of refuse or the sweepings of a street . . . the foul rag-and-bone shop of the heart"— the rose springing from the dunghill. Yeats's poetry, which draws its initial power from the mastery of images and verbal rhythm, continues to resonate in the reader's mind for this attempt to come to terms with reality, to grasp and make sense of human experience in the transfiguring language of art.

PRONOUNCING GLOSSARY

The following list uses common English syllables and stress accents to provide rough equivalents of selected words whose pronunciation may be unfamiliar to the general reader.

Callimachus: *ca-li'-mah-cus*   gyre: *jai-er*

Cuchulain: *coo-hu'-lin*   Quattrocento: *kwah-troh-chen'-toh*

When You Are Old[1]

When you are old and gray and full of sleep,
And nodding by the fire, take down this book,
And slowly read, and dream of the soft look
Your eyes had once, and of their shadows deep;

How many loved your moments of glad grace,   5
And loved your beauty with love false or true,
But one man loved the pilgrim soul in you,
And loved the sorrows of your changing face;

And bending down beside the glowing bars,
Murmur, a little sadly, how Love fled   10
And paced upon the mountains overhead
And hid his face amid a crowd of stars.

Easter 1916[1]

I have met them at close of day
Coming with vivid faces
From counter or desk among grey
Eighteenth-century houses.
I have passed with a nod of the head   5
Or polite meaningless words,
Or have lingered awhile and said
Polite meaningless words,
And thought before I had done
Of a mocking tale or a gibe   10
To please a companion
Around the fire at the club,
Being certain that they and I
But lived where motley is worn:
All changed, changed utterly: 15
A terrible beauty is born.

---

1. An adaptation of a love sonnet by the French Renaissance poet Pierre de Ronsard (1524–1585), which begins similarly ("Quand vous serez bien vieille") but ends by asking the beloved to "pluck the roses of life today."   1. On Easter Sunday 1916, Irish nationalists began an unsuccessful rebellion against British rule, which lasted throughout the week and ended in the surrender and execution of its leaders.

That woman's[2] days were spent
In ignorant good-will,
Her nights in argument
Until her voice grew shrill.   20
What voice more sweet than hers
When, young and beautiful,
She rode to harriers?
This man had kept a school
And rode our wingèd horse;   25
This other his helper and friend[3]
Was coming into his force;
He might have won fame in the end,
So sensitive his nature seemed,
So daring and sweet his thought.   30
This other man[4] I had dreamed
A drunken, vainglorious lout.
He had done most bitter wrong
To some who are near my heart,
Yet I number him in the song;   35
He, too, has resigned his part
In the casual comedy;
He, too, has been changed in his turn,
Transformed utterly:
A terrible beauty is born.   40

Hearts with one purpose alone
Through summer and winter seem
Enchanted to a stone
To trouble the living stream.
The horse that comes from the road,   45
The rider, the birds that range
From cloud to tumbling cloud,
Minute by minute they change;
A shadow of cloud on the stream
Changes minute by minute;   50
A horse-hoof slides on the brim,
And a horse plashes within it;
The long-legged moor-hens dive,
And hens to moor-cocks call;
Minute by minute they live: 55
The stone's in the midst of all.

Too long a sacrifice
Can make a stone of the heart.
O when may it suffice?
That is Heaven's part, our part   60

2. Constance Gore-Booth (1868–1927), later Countess Markiewicz, an ardent nationalist.   **3.** Patrick Pearse (1879–1916) and his friend Thomas MacDonagh (1878–1916), both schoolmasters and leaders of the rebellion and both executed by the British. As a Gaelic poet, Pearse symbolically rode the winged horse of the Muses, Pegasus.   **4.** Major John MacBride (1865–1916), who had married and separated from Maud Gonne (1866–1953), Yeats's great love.

To murmur name upon name,
As a mother names her child
When sleep at last has come
On limbs that had run wild.
What is it but nightfall?   65
No, no, not night but death;
Was it needless death after all?
For England may keep faith
For all that is done and said.
We know their dream; enough   70
To know they dreamed and are dead;
And what if excess of love
Bewildered them till they died?
I write it out in a verse—
MacDonagh and MacBride   75
And Connolly⁵ and Pearse
Now and in time to be,
Wherever green is worn,
Are changed, changed utterly:
A terrible beauty is born.   80

The Second Coming¹

Turning and turning in the widening gyre²
The falcon cannot hear the falconer;
Things fall apart; the centre cannot hold;
Mere anarchy is loosed upon the world,
The blood-dimmed tide is loosed, and everywhere   5
The ceremony of innocence is drowned;
The best lack all conviction, while the worst
Are full of passionate intensity.

Surely some revelation is at hand;
Surely the Second Coming is at hand.   10
The Second Coming! Hardly are those words out
When a vast image out of *Spiritus Mundi*³
Troubles my sight: somewhere in sands of the desert
A shape with lion body and the head of a man
A gaze blank and pitiless as the sun,   15
Is moving its slow thighs, while all about it
Reel shadows of the indignant desert birds.
The darkness drops again; but now I know
That twenty centuries of stony sleep
Were vexed to nightmare by a rocking cradle,   20

---

5. James Connolly (1870–1916), labor leader and nationalist executed by the British.   1. The Second Coming of Christ, believed by Christians to herald the end of the world, is transformed here into the prediction of a new birth initiating a new era and terminating the two-thousand-year cycle of Christianity.   2. The cone pattern of the falcon's flight and of historical cycles, in Yeats's vision.   3. World-soul (Latin) or, as *Anima Mundi* in Yeats's *Per Amica Silentia Lunae*, a "great memory" containing archetypal images; recalls C. G. Jung's collective unconscious.

And what rough beast, its hour come round at last,
Slouches towards Bethlehem to be born?

Leda and the Swan[1]

A sudden blow: the great wings beating still
Above the staggering girl, her thighs caressed
By the dark webs, her nape caught in his bill,
He holds her helpless breast upon his breast.

How can those terrified vague fingers push   5
The feathered glory from her loosening thighs?
And how can body, laid in that white rush,
But feel the strange heart beating where it lies?

A shudder in the loins engenders there
The broken wall, the burning roof and tower   10
And Agamemnon dead.[2]
                            Being so caught up,
So mastered by the brute blood of the air,
Did she put on his knowledge with his power
Before the indifferent beak could let her drop?

Sailing to Byzantium[1]

1

That is no country for old men. The young
In one another's arms, birds in the trees
—Those dying generations—at their song,
The salmon-falls, the mackerel-crowded seas,
Fish, flesh, or fowl, commend all summer long   5
Whatever is begotten, born, and dies.
Caught in the sensual music all neglect
Monuments of unageing intellect.

2

An aged man is but a paltry thing,
A tattered coat upon a stick, unless   10
Soul clap its hands and sing, and louder sing
For every tatter in its mortal dress,

1. Zeus, ruler of the Greek gods, took the form of a swan to rape the mortal Leda; she gave birth to Helen of Troy, whose beauty caused the Trojan War. 2. The ruins of Troy and the death of Agamemnon, the Greek leader, whose sacrifice of his daughter Iphigenia to win the gods' favor caused his wife, Clytemnestra (also a daughter of Leda), to assassinate him on his return. 1. The ancient name for modern Istanbul, the capital of the Eastern Roman Empire, which represented for Yeats (who had seen Byzantine mosaics in Italy) a highly stylized and perfectly integrated artistic world where "religious, aesthetic, and practical life were one."

Nor is there singing school but studying
Monuments of its own magnificence;
And therefore I have sailed the seas and come   15
To the holy city of Byzantium.

3

O sages standing in God's holy fire
As in the gold mosaic of a wall,
Come from the holy fire, perne in a gyre,[2]
And be the singing-masters of my soul.   20
Consume my heart away; sick with desire
And fastened to a dying animal
It knows not what it is; and gather me
Into the artifice of eternity.

4

Once out of nature I shall never take   25
My bodily form from any natural thing,
But such a form as Grecian goldsmiths make
Of hammered gold and gold enamelling
To keep a drowsy Emperor awake;
Or set upon a golden bough to sing   30
To lords and ladies of Byzantium
Of what is past, or passing, or to come.

Among School Children

1

I walk through the long schoolroom questioning;
A kind old nun in a white hood replies;
The children learn to cipher and to sing,
To study reading-books and history,
To cut and sew, be neat in everything   5
In the best modern way—the children's eyes
In momentary wonder stare upon
A sixty-year-old smiling public man.[1]

2

I dream of a Ledaean[2] body, bent
Above a sinking fire, a tale that she   10
Told of a harsh reproof, or trivial event
That changed some childish day to tragedy—
Told, and it seemed that our two natures blent

2. I.e., come spinning down in a spiral. *Perne:* a spool or bobbin. *Gyre:* the cone pattern of the falcon's
flight and of historical cycles, in Yeats's vision.   1. Yeats was elected senator of the Irish Free State in
1922.   2. Beautiful as Leda or as her daughter, Helen of Troy.

Into a sphere from youthful sympathy,
Or else, to alter Plato's parable,   15
Into the yolk and white of the one shell.[3]

3

And thinking of that fit of grief or rage
I look upon one child or t'other there
And wonder if she stood so at that age—
For even daughters of the swan can share   20
Something of every paddler's heritage—
And had that color upon cheek or hair,
And thereupon my heart is driven wild:
She stands before me as a living child.

4

Her present image floats into the mind—   25
Did Quattrocento finger fashion it
Hollow of cheek[4] as though it drank the wind
And took a mess of shadows for its meat?
And I though never of Ledaean kind
Had pretty plumage once—enough of that,   30
Better to smile on all that smile, and show
There is a comfortable kind of old scarecrow.

5

What youthful mother, a shape upon her lap
Honey of generation had betrayed,
And that must sleep, shriek, struggle to escape   35
As recollection or the drug decide,[5]
Would think her son, did she but see that shape
With sixty or more winters on its head,
A compensation for the pang of his birth,
Or the uncertainty of his setting forth?   40

6

Plato thought nature but a spume that plays
Upon a ghostly paradigm of things;
Solider Aristotle played the taws
Upon the bottom of a king of kings;
World-famous golden-thighed Pythagoras[6]   45

3. In Plato's *Symposium*, Socrates explains love by telling how the gods split human beings into two
halves—like halves of an egg—so that each half seeks its opposite throughout life. Yeats compares the two
parts to the yolk and white of an egg.   4. Italian painters of the 15th century (the Quattrocento), such
as Botticelli (1444–1510), were known for their delicate figures.   5. Yeats's note to this poem recalls the
Greek scholar Porphyry (ca. 234–ca. 305), who associates "honey" with "the pleasure arising from copulation" that engenders children; the poet further describes honey as a drug that destroys the child's " 'recollection' of pre-natal freedom."   6. Three Greek philosophers. Plato (427–337 B.C.E.) believed that
nature was only a series of illusionistic reflections or appearances cast by abstract "forms" that were the
only true realities. Aristotle (384–322 B.C.E.), more pragmatic, was Alexander the Great's tutor and spanked
him with the "taws" (leather straps). Pythagoras (582–407 B.C.E.), a demigod to his disciples and thought
to have a golden thigh bone, pondered the relationship of music, mathematics, and the stars.

Fingered upon a fiddle-stick or strings
What a star sang and careless Muses heard:
Old clothes upon old sticks to scare a bird.

7

Both nuns and mothers worship images,
But those the candles light are not as those   50
That animate a mother's reveries,
But keep a marble or a bronze repose.
And yet they too break hearts—O Presences
That passion, piety, or affection knows,
And that all heavenly glory symbolize—   55
O self-born mockers of man's enterprise;

8

Labor is blossoming or dancing where
The body is not bruised to pleasure soul,
Nor beauty born out of its own despair,
Nor blear-eyed wisdom out of midnight oil.   60
O chestnut tree, great-rooted blossomer,
Are you the leaf,the blossom, or the bole?
O body swayed to music, O brightening glance,
How can we know the dancer from the dance?

Byzantium[1]

The unpurged images of day recede;
The Emperor's drunken soldiery are abed;
Night resonance recedes, night-walkers' song
After great cathedral gong;
A starlit or a moonlit dome[2] disdains   5
All that man is,
All mere complexities,
The fury and the mire of human veins.

Before me floats an image, man or shade,
Shade more than man, more image than a shade;   10
For Hades' bobbin bound in mummy-cloth
May unwind the winding path;[3]
A mouth that has no moisture and no breath
Breathless mouths may summon;

---

1. The holy city of *Sailing to Byzantium* (p. 1729), seen here as it resists and transforms the blood and mire of human life into its own transcendent world of art.   2. According to Yeat's system in *A Vision* (1925), the first "starlit" phase in which the moon does not shine and the fifteenth, opposing phase of the full moon represent complete objectivity (potential being) and complete subjectivity (the achievement of complete beauty). In between these absolute phases lie the evolving "mere complexities" of human life. 3. Unwinding the spool of fate that leads from mortal death to the superhuman. *Hades:* the realm of the dead in Greek mythology.

I hail the superhuman;   15
I call it death-in-life and life-in-death.

Miracle, bird or golden handiwork,
More miracle than bird or handiwork,
Planted on the starlit golden bough,
Can like the cocks of Hades crow,[4]   20
Or, by the moon embittered, scorn aloud
In glory of changeless metal
Common bird or petal
And all complexities of mire or blood.

At midnight on the Emperor's pavement flit   25
Flames that no faggot feeds, nor steel has lit,
Nor storm disturbs, flames begotten of flame,
Where blood-begotten spirits come
And all complexities of fury leave,
Dying into a dance,   30
An agony of trance,
An agony of flame that cannot singe a sleeve.

Astraddle on the dolphin's[5] mire and blood,
Spirit after spirit! The smithies break the flood,
The golden smithies of the Emperor!   35
Marbles of the dancing floor
Break bitter furies of complexity,
Those images that yet
Fresh images beget,
That dolphin-torn, that gong-tormented sea.   40

Lapis Lazuli[1]

For Harry Clifton

I have heard that hysterical women say
They are sick of the palette and fiddle-bow,
Of poets that are always gay,
For everybody knows or else should know
That if nothing drastic is done   5
Aeroplane and Zeppelin will come out,
Pitch like King Billy[2] bomb-balls in
Until the town lie beaten flat.

---

4. To mark the transition from death to the dawn of new life.   **5.** A dolphin rescued the famous singer Arion by carrying him on his back over the sea. Dolphins were associated with Apollo, Greek god of music and prophecy, and in ancient art they are often shown escorting the souls of the dead to the Isles of the Blessed. Here, the dolphin is also flesh and blood, a part of life.   **1.** A deep blue semiprecious stone. One of Yeats's letters (to Dorothy Wellesley, July 6, 1935) describes a Chinese carving in lapis lazuli that depicts an ascetic and pupil about to climb a mountain: "Ascetic, pupil, hard stone, eternal theme of the sensual east . . . the east has its solutions always and therefore knows nothing of tragedy."   **2.** A linkage of past and present. According to an Irish ballad, King William III of England "threw his bomb-balls in" and set fire to the tents of the deposed James II at the Battle of the Boyne in 1690. Also a reference to Kaiser Wilhelm II (King William II) of Germany, who sent zeppelins to bomb London during World War I. *Zeppelin:* a long, cylindrical airship, supported by internal gas chambers.

All perform their tragic play,
There struts Hamlet, there is Lear,
That's Ophelia, that Cordelia;[3]   10
Yet they, should the last scene be there,
The great stage curtain about to drop,
If worthy their prominent part in the play,
Do not break up their lines to weep.   15
They know that Hamlet and Lear are gay;
Gaiety transfiguring all that dread.
All men have aimed at, found and lost;
Black out; Heaven blazing into the head:[4]
Tragedy wrought to its uttermost.   20
Though Hamlet rambles and Lear rages,
And all the drop-scenes drop at once
Upon a hundred thousand stages,
It cannot grow by an inch or an ounce.

On their own feet they came, or on shipboard,   25
Camel-back, horse-back, ass-back, mule-back,
Old civilisations put to the sword.
Then they and their wisdom went to rack:
No handiwork of Callimachus[5]
Who handled marble as if it were bronze,   30
Made draperies that seemed to rise
When sea-wind swept the corner, stands;
His long lamp-chimney shaped like the stem
Of a slender palm, stood but a day;
All things fall and are built again,   35
And those that build them again are gay.
Two Chinamen, behind them a third,
Are carved in Lapis Lazuli,
Over them flies a long-legged bird,[6]
A symbol of longevity;   40
The third, doubtless a serving-man,
Carries a musical instrument.

Every discoloration of the stone,
Every accidental crack or dent,
Seems a water-course or an avalanche,   45
Or lofty slope where it still snows
Though doubtless plum or cherry-branch
Sweetens the little half-way house
Those Chinamen climb towards, and I
Delight to imagine them seated there;   50
There, on the mountain and the sky,
On all the tragic scene they stare.
One asks for mournful melodies;
Accomplished fingers begin to play.

3. Tragic figures in Shakespeare's plays.   4. The loss of rational consciousness making way for the blaze
of inner revelation or "mad" tragic vision. Also suggests the final curtain and an air raid curfew.   5. Athenian sculptor (5th century B.C.E.), famous for a gold lamp in the Erechtheum (temple on the Acropolis)
and for using drill lines in marble to give the effect of flowing drapery.   6. A crane.

Their eyes mid many wrinkles, their eyes,   55
Their ancient, glittering eyes, are gay.

The Circus Animals' Desertion

1

I sought a theme and sought for it in vain,
I sought it daily for six weeks or so.
Maybe at last, being but a broken man,
I must be satisfied with my heart, although
Winter and summer till old age began   5
My circus animals were all on show,
Those stilted boys, that burnished chariot,
Lion and woman[1] and the Lord knows what.

2

What can I but enumerate old themes?
First that sea-rider Oisin led by the nose   10
Through three enchanted islands, allegorical dreams,[2]
Vain gaiety, vain battle, vain repose,
Themes of the embittered heart, or so it seems,
That might adorn old songs or courtly shows;
But what cared I that set him on to ride,   15
I, starved for the bosom of his faery bride?
And then a counter-truth filled out its play,
The Countess Cathleen[3] was the name I gave it;
She, pity-crazed, had given her soul away,
But masterful Heaven had intervened to save it.   20
I thought my dear must her own soul destroy,
So did fanaticism and hate enslave it,
And this brought forth a dream and soon enough
This dream itself had all my thought and love.

And when the Fool and Blind Man stole the bread   25
Cuchulain[4] fought the ungovernable sea;
Heart-mysteries there, and yet when all is said
It was the dream itself enchanted me:
Character isolated by a deed
To engross the present and dominate memory.   30
Players and painted stage took all my love,
And not those things that they were emblems of.

---

1. Yeats enumerates images and themes from his earlier work; here, the sphinx of *The Double Vision of Michael Robartes*.   2. In *The Wanderings of Oisin* (1889), an early poem in which Yeats describes a legendary Irish hero who wandered in fairyland for 150 years.   3. A play (1892), dedicated to Maud Gonne, in which the countess is saved by heaven after having sold her soul to the devil in exchange for food for the poor. The figure of Cathleen comes up frequently in Yeats's work and is often taken as a personification of nationalist Ireland.   4. A legendary Irish hero. Yeats is referring to the play *On Baile's Strand* (1904).

3

Those masterful images because complete
Grew in pure mind, but out of what began?
A mound of refuse or the sweepings of a street,   35
Old kettles, old bottles, and a broken can,
Old iron, old bones, old rags, that raving slut
Who keeps the till. Now that my ladder's gone,
I must lie down where all the ladders start,
In the foul rag-and-bone shop of the heart.   40

LUIGI PIRANDELLO
1867–1936

"Who am I?" and "What is real?" are the persistent and even agonized questions that underlie Luigi Pirandello's novels, short stories, and plays. The term *Pirandellismo* or "Pirandellism"—coined from the author's name—suggests that there are as many truths as there are points of view. Here are already the basic issues of later existential philosophy as seen in writers like Jean-Paul Sartre and Albert Camus: the difficulty of achieving a sense of identity, the impossibility of authentic communication between people, and the overlapping frontiers of appearance and reality. These dilemmas are dramatic crises in self-knowledge and as such are particularly suited for demonstration in the theater. Indeed, Pirandello is best known as an innovative dramatist who revolutionized European stage techniques to break down comfortable illusions of compartmentalized, stable reality. Instead of the late nineteenth century's "well-made play"—with its neatly constructed plot that packaged real life into a conventional beginning, middle, and end, and its consistent characters remaining safely inaccessible on the other side of the footlights—he offers unpredictable plots and characters whose ambiguity puts into question the solidity of identities assumed in everyday life. It is not easy to know the truth, he suggests, or to make oneself known behind the face or "naked mask" that each of us wears in society. Pirandello's theater readily displays its nature as dramatic illusion: plays exist within plays until one is not sure where the "real" play begins or ends, and characters question their own reality and that of the audience. In their manipulation of ambiguous appearances and tragicomic effects, these plays foreshadow the absurdist theater of Samuel Beckett, Eugène Ionesco, and Harold Pinter, the cosmic irony of Antonin Artaud's "theater of cruelty," and the emphasis on spectacle and illusion in works by Jean Genet. Above all, they insist that the most "real" life is that which changes from moment to moment, exhibiting a fluidity that renders difficult and perhaps impossible any single formulation of either character or situation. This fluidity is a cause of existential anguish because it implies perpetual loss; readers may wish to contrast Pirandello's cosmos of uncertain boundaries with the sense of continuity throughout different dimensions of existence that informs, for example, Wole Soyinka's *Death and the King's Horseman*.

Pirandello was born in Girgenti (now Agrigento), Sicily, on June 28, 1867. His father was a sulfur merchant who intended his son to go into business like himself, but Pirandello preferred language and literature. After studying in Palermo and the University of Rome, he traveled to the University of Bonn in 1888, and in 1891 he received a doctorate in romance philology with a thesis on the dialect of his hometown. In 1894, Pirandello made an arranged marriage with the daughter of a rich sulfur merchant. They lived for ten years in Rome, where he wrote poetry and short stories, until the collapse of the sulfur mines destroyed the fortunes of both families, and he was suddenly forced to earn a living. To add to his misfortunes, his wife became insane with a jealous paranoia that lasted until her death in 1918. The author himself died on December 1, 1936.

Pirandello's early work shows a number of different influences. His poetry was indebted to nineteenth-century Italian predecessors like Giosuè Carducci (1835–1907), and in 1896 he translated Goethe's *Roman Elegies*. Soon, however, he turned to short stories or *novelle* under the influence of a narrative style called *verismo* (realism) exemplified in the work of the Sicilian writer Giovanni Verga (1840–1922). Pirandello wrote hundreds of stories of all lengths and—in his clarity, realism, and psychological acuteness (often including a taste for the grotesque)—is recognized as an Italian master of the story much as was Guy de Maupassant in France. Collections include the 1894 *Love without Love* and an anthology in 1922 titled *A Year's Worth of Stories*.

In such stories, and in his early novels, Pirandello begins to develop his character-istic themes: the questioning of appearance and reality, and problems of identity. In *The Outcast* (1901), an irate husband drives his innocent wife out of the house only to take her back when—without his knowing it—the supposed adultery has actually occurred. The hero of Pirandello's best-known novel, *The Late Mattia Pascal*, tries to create a fresh identity for himself and leave behind the old Mattia Pascal. When things become too difficult he returns to his "late" self and begins to write his life story, an early example of the tendency in Pirandello's works to comment on their own composition. The protagonists in these and other works are visibly commonplace, middle-class citizens, neither heroic nor villainous, but prototypes of the twentieth-century antihero who remains aggressively average while taking the center of the stage.

The questions of identity that obsessed Pirandello (he speaks of them as reflecting the "pangs of my spirit") are explored on social, psychological, and metaphysical levels. He was acquainted with the experimental psychology of his day and learned from works such as Alfred Binet's *Personality Alterations* (1892) about the existence of a subconscious personality beneath our everyday awareness (a theme Pirandello shares with Proust and Freud). Successive layers of personality, conflicts among the various parts, and the simultaneous existence of multiple perspectives shape an identity that is never fixed but always fluid and changing. This identity escapes the grasp of onlook-ers and subject alike, and expresses a basic incongruity in human existence that chal-lenges the most earnest attempts to create a unified self. The protagonist of a later novel, *One, None, and a Hundred Thousand* (1925–26), finds that what "he" is depends on the viewpoint of a great number of people. Such incongruity can be tragic or comic—or both at once—according to one's attitude, a topic that Pirandello explored in a 1908 essay, *On Humor*, and that is echoed in the double-edged humor of his plays. The "Pirandellian" themes of ambiguous identity, lack of communication, and deceptive appearance reappear in all the genres, however, reaching a particular intensity in his first dramatic success, *It Is So [If You Think So]* (1917), and in the play included here, *Six Characters in Search of an Author* (1921).

Six Characters in Search of an Author and *Henry IV* established Pirandello's stature as a major dramatist. He directed his own company (the Teatro d'Arte di Roma) from 1924 to 1928 and received the Nobel Prize for Literature in 1934. His later plays, featuring fantastic and grotesque elements, did not achieve the wide popularity of their predecessors. In 1936, he published a collection of forty-three plays as *Naked Masks*, a title conceived in 1918 after Luigi Chiarelli's "grotesque theater." Piran-dello's characters are "naked" and vulnerable inside the social roles or masks they put on to survive: Henry IV, trapped for life inside a pretense of insanity, or the Father in *Six Characters*, forced to play out a demeaning role in which, he insists, only part of his true nature is revealed. The term *naked mask* also suggests Pirandello's superb manipulation of theatrical ambiguity—the confusion between the actor and the character portrayed—that ultimately prolongs the confusion of appearance and reality, which is one of his chief themes. Pirandello is famous in twentieth-century theater for his use of the play within a play, a technique of embedded dramatic episodes that maintain a life of their own while serving as foil to the overall or governing plot. Dividing lines are sometimes hard to draw when stage dialogue can be taken as referring to either context—a situation that allows for double meanings at the same time that it reiterates the impossibility of real communication.

Six Characters in Search of an Author combines all these elements in an extraordinarily self-reflexive style. At the very beginning, the Stage Hand's interrupted hammering suggests that the audience has chanced on a rehearsal—of still another play by Pirandello—instead of coming to a finished performance; concurrently, Pirandello's stage dialogue pokes fun at his own reputation for obscurity. Just as the Actors are apparently set to rehearse *The Rules of the Game,* six unexpected persons come down the aisle seeking the Producer: they are Characters out of an unwritten novel who demand to be given dramatic existence. The play *Six Characters* is continually in the process of being composed: composed as the interwoven double plot we see on stage, written down in shorthand by the Prompter for the Actors to reproduce, and potentially composed as the Characters' inner drama finally achieves its rightful existence as a work of art. The conflicts between the different levels of the play finally prevent the completion of any but the first work, but it has created a convincing dramatic illusion in the meantime that incorporates the psychological drama of the "six characters" as well as a discussion of the relationship of life and art.

The initial absurdity of the play appears when the six admittedly fictional characters arrive with their claim to be "truer and more real" than the "real" characters they confront. (Of course, to the audience all the actors on stage are equally unreal.) Their greater "truth" is the truth of art with its profound but formally fixed glimpses into human nature. Each Character represents, specifically and in depth, a particular identity created by the author, who later suggested that the Characters should wear masks to distinguish them from the Actors. These masks are not the conventional masks of ancient Greek drama or the Japanese *nō* theater, nor do they function as the ceremonial masks representing spirits in African ritual, masks that temporarily invest the wearer with the spirit's identity and authority. Instead, they are a theatrical device, a symbol and visual reminder of each character's unchanging essence. The Six Characters are incapable of developing outside their roles and are condemned, in their search for existence, painfully to reenact their essential selves.

Conversely, the fictional characters have a more stable personality than "real" people who are still "nobody," incomplete, open to change and misinterpretation. Characters are "somebody" because their nature has been decided once and for all. Yet there is a further complication to this contrast between real and fictional characters: the Characters have real anxieties in that they want to play their own roles and are disturbed at the prospect of having Actors represent them incorrectly. All human beings, suggests Pirandello, whether fictional or real, are subject to misunderstanding. We even misunderstand ourselves when we think we are the same person in all situations. "We always have the illusion of being the same person for everybody," says the Father, "but it's not true!" When he explains himself as a very human philosopher driven by the Demon of Experiment, his self-image is quite different from the picture held by his vengeful Stepdaughter or the passive Mother who blames him for her expulsion from the house. The Stepdaughter, in turn, appears to love an innocent little sister because the sister reminds her of an earlier self. It is an entanglement of motives and deceit of mutual understanding that goes beyond the tabloid level of a sordid family scandal and claims a broader scope. Pirandello, in fact, does not intend merely to describe a particular setting or situation; that is the concern of what he calls "historical writers." He belongs to the opposite category of "philosophical writers" whose characters and situations embody "a particular sense of life and acquire from it a universal value."

Six Characters in Search of an Author underwent an interesting evolution to become the play that we see today. First performed in Rome in 1921, where its unsettling plot and characters already scandalized a traditionalist audience, it was reshaped in more radical theatrical form after the remarkable performance produced by Georges Pitoëff in Paris in 1923. Pirandello, who came to Paris somewhat wary of Pitoëff's innovations (he brought on the Characters in a green-lit stage elevator), was soon convinced that the Russian director's stagecraft suggested changes that would enhance the original text. Pitoëff had used his knowledge of technical effects to accentuate the interrelationships of appearance and reality: he extended the stage with several steps leading down into the auditorium (a break in the conventional stage's "fourth wall" that Pirandello was quick to exploit); he underscored the play within a play with rehearsal effects, showing the Stage Hand hammering and the Director arranging suitable props and lighting; he emphasized the division between Characters and Actors by separating groups on stage and dressing the Characters (all except the Little Girl) in black. Pirandello welcomed and expanded on many of these changes. To distinguish even further the Characters from the Actors, he proposed stylized masks as well as black clothes for the former and light-colored summery clothing for the latter. To bring out Madame Pace's grotesque fictionality, he changed her costume from a sober black gown to a garish red silk dress and carrot-colored wool wig. Most striking, however, is the dramatist's development of Pitoëff's steps into a real bridge between the world of the stage and the auditorium, a strategy that allows his Actors (and Characters) to come and go in the "real world" of the audience. Pirandello's revised ending to *Six Characters in Search of an Author* makes a final break with theatrical illusion: with the other characters immobilized on stage, the Stepdaughter races down the steps, through the auditorium, and out into the foyer from which the audience can still hear her distraught laughter.

Pirandello does not hold his audience by uttering grand philosophical truths. There is constant suspense and a process of discovery in *Six Characters*, from the moment that the rehearsal with its complaining Actors and Manager is interrupted and the initial hints of melodrama and family scandal catch our attention in the Stepdaughter's and Mother's complaints. It is a story that could be found in the most sensational papers: an adulterous wife thrust out of her home and supporting herself and her children after her lover's death by sewing, the daughter's turn to prostitution to support the family, the Father's unknowing attempt to seduce his Stepdaughter (interpreted by the latter as the continuation of an old and perverse impulse), and the final drowning and suicide of the two youngest children. Pirandello plays with the sensational aspect of his story by focusing the play on the characters' repeated attempts to portray the seduction scene; Actors and Manager perceive the salable quality of such "human-interest" events and are eager to let the story unfold. The Stepdaughter's protective fondness for her doomed baby sister and her enigmatic reproach to the little Boy ("instead of killing myself, I'd have killed one of those two") hint at the inner plot that is revealed only as the action continues. The interplay of illusion and reality persists to the very end, when the Actors argue about whether the Boy is dead or not, the Producer is terrified as the lights change eerily around the surviving Characters, and the Stepdaughter breaks away from the ending tableau to escape into the audience.

The translation by John Linstrum has been selected on the one hand for its accuracy to the Italian text and its fluent use of contemporary English idiom and on the other for its quality as a performance-oriented script, staged in London in 1979. Readers are encouraged to test the continued liveliness of Pirandello's dialogue by rehearsing their own selection of scenes—or perhaps by relocating them in a contemporary setting. According to director Robert Brustein, whose 1988 production of *Six Characters in Search of an Author* set the action in New York and replaced Madame Pace with a pimp, "Pirandello both encourages and stimulates a pluralism in theater because there can be dozens, hundreds, thousands of productions of *Six Characters*, and every one of them is going to be different."

PRONOUNCING GLOSSARY

The following list uses common English syllables and stress accents to provide rough equivalents of selected words whose pronunciation may be unfamiliar to the general reader.

commedia dell'arte: *com-may'-dee-ah del ar'-tay*

Luigi Pirandello: *loo-ee'-jee pee-ran-del'-oh*

Pace: *pah'-chay*

Pitoëff: *pee'-toh-eff*

Six Characters in Search of an Author[1]

A Comedy in the Making

THE CHARACTERS	THE COMPANY
FATHER	THE PRODUCER
MOTHER	THE STAGE STAFF
STEPDAUGHTER	THE ACTORS
SON	
LITTLE BOY	
LITTLE GIRL	
MADAME PACE	

Act One

When the audience enters, the curtain is already up and the stage is just as it would be during the day. There is no set; it is empty, in almost total darkness. This is so that from the beginning the audience will have the feeling of being present, not at a performance of a properly rehearsed play, but at a performance of a play that happens spontaneously. Two small sets of steps, one on the right and one on the left, lead up to the stage from the auditorium. On the stage, the top is off the PROMPTER's *box and is lying next to it. Downstage, there is a small table and a chair with arms for the* PRODUCER: *it is turned with its back to the audience.*

Also downstage there are two small tables, one a little bigger than the other, and several chairs, ready for the rehearsal if needed. There are more chairs scattered on both left and right for the ACTORS *to one side at the back and nearly hidden is a piano.*

When the houselights go down the STAGE HAND *comes on through the back door. He is in blue overalls and carries a tool bag. He brings some pieces of wood*

---

1. Translated by John Linstrum. In the Italian editions, Pirandello notes that he did not divide the play into formal acts or scenes. The translator has marked the divisions for clarity, however, according to the stage directions.

on, comes to the front, kneels down and starts to nail them together. The STAGE MANAGER *rushes on from the wings.*

STAGE MANAGER   Hey! What are you doing?

STAGE HAND   What do you think I'm doing? I'm banging nails in.

STAGE MANAGER   Now? [*He looks at his watch.*] It's half-past ten already. The Producer will be here in a moment to rehearse.

STAGE HAND   I've got to do my work some time, you know.

STAGE MANAGER   Right—but not now.

STAGE HAND   When?

STAGE MANAGER   When the rehearsal's finished. Come on, get all this out of the way and let me set for the second act of *The Rules of the Game.*[2]

[*The* STAGE HAND *picks up his tools and wood and goes off, grumbling and muttering. The* ACTORS *of the company come in through the door, men and women, first one then another, then two together and so on: there will be nine or ten, enough for the parts for the rehearsal of a play by Pirandello,* The Rules of the Game, *today's rehearsal. They come in, say their "Good-mornings" to the* STAGE MANAGER *and each other. Some go off to the dressing-rooms; others, among them the* PROMPTER *with the text rolled up under his arm, scatter about the stage waiting for the* PRODUCER *to start the rehearsal. Meanwhile, sitting or standing in groups, they chat together; some smoke, one complains about his part, another one loudly reads something from "The Stage." It would be as well if the* ACTORS *and* ACTRESSES *were dressed in colourful clothes, and this first scene should be improvised naturally and vivaciously. After a while somebody might sit down at the piano and play a song; the younger* ACTORS *and* ACTRESSES *start dancing.*]

STAGE MANAGER   [*Clapping his hands to call their attention.*]   Come on, everybody! Quiet please. The Producer's here.

[*The piano and the dancing both stop. The* ACTORS *turn to look out into the theatre and through the door at the back comes the* PRODUCER; *he walks down the gangway between the seats and, calling "Good-morning" to the* ACTORS, *climbs up one of the sets of stairs onto the stage. The* SECRETARY *gives him the post, a few magazines, a script. The* ACTORS *move to one side of the stage.*]

PRODUCER   Any letters?

SECRETARY   No. That's all the post there is. [*Giving him the script.*]

PRODUCER   Put it in the office. [*Then looking round and turning to the* STAGE MANAGER.] I can't see a thing here. Let's have some lights please.

STAGE MANAGER   Right. [*Calling.*] Workers please!

[*In a few seconds the side of the stage where the* ACTORS *are standing is brilliantly lit with white light. The* PROMPTER *has gone into his box and spread out his script.*]

PRODUCER   Good. [*Clapping hands.*] Well then, let's get started. Anybody missing?

STAGE MANAGER   [*Heavily ironic.*]   Our leading lady.

PRODUCER   Not again! [*Looking at his watch.*] We're ten minutes late

---

2. *Il giuoco delle parti*, written in 1918. The hero, Leone Gala, pretends to ignore his wife Silia's infidelity until the end, when he takes revenge by tricking her lover Guido Venanzi into taking his place in a fatal duel she had engineered to get rid of her husband.

already. Send her a note to come and see me. It might teach her to be on time for rehearsals. [*Almost before he has finished, the* LEADING ACTRESS's *voice is heard from the auditorium.*]

LEADING ACTRESS   Morning everybody. Sorry I'm late. [*She is very expensively dressed and is carrying a lap-dog. She comes down the aisle and goes up on to the stage.*]

PRODUCER   You're determined to keep us waiting, aren't you?

LEADING ACTRESS   I'm sorry. I just couldn't find a taxi anywhere. But you haven't started yet and I'm not on at the opening anyhow. [*Calling the* STAGE MANAGER, *she gives him the dog.*] Put him in my dressing-room for me will you?

PRODUCER   And she's even brought her lap-dog with her! As if we haven't enough lap-dogs here already. [*Clapping his hands and turning to the* PROMPTER.] Right then, the second act of *The Rules of the Game*. [*Sits in his arm-chair.*] Quiet please! Who's on?

[*The* ACTORS *clear from the front of the stage and sit to one side, except for three who are ready to start the scene—and the* LEADING ACTRESS. *She has ignored the* PRODUCER *and is sitting at one of the little tables.*]

PRODUCER   Are you in this scene, then?

LEADING ACTRESS   No—I've just told you.

PRODUCER [*Annoyed.*]   Then get off, for God's sake. [*The* LEADING ACTRESS *goes and sits with the others. To the* PROMPTER.] Come on then, let's get going.

PROMPTER [*Reading his script.*]   "The house of Leone Gala. A peculiar room, both dining-room and study."

PRODUCER [*To the* STAGE MANAGER.]   We'll use the red set.

STAGE MANAGER [*Making a note.*]   The red set—right.

PROMPTER [*Still reading.*]   "The table is laid and there is a desk with books and papers. Bookcases full of books and china cabinets full of valuable china. An exit at the back leads to Leone's bedroom. An exit to the left leads to the kitchen. The main entrance is on the right."

PRODUCER   Right. Listen carefully everybody: there, the main entrance, there, the kitchen. [*To the* LEADING ACTOR *who plays Socrates.*[3]] Your entrances and exits will be from there. [*To the* STAGE MANAGER.] We'll have the French windows there and put the curtains on them.

STAGE MANAGER [*Making a note.*]   Right.

PROMPTER [*Reading.*]   "Scene One. Leone Gala, Guido Venanzi, and Filippo, who is called Socrates." [*To* PRODUCER.] Have I to read the directions as well?

PRODUCER   Yes, you have! I've told you a hundred times.

PROMPTER [*Reading.*]   "When the curtain rises, Leone Gala, in a cook's hat and apron, is beating an egg in a dish with a little wooden spoon. Filippo is beating another and he is dressed as a cook too. Guido Venanzi is sitting listening."

LEADING ACTOR   Look, do I really have to wear a cook's hat?

PRODUCER [*Annoyed by the question.*]   I expect so! That's what it says in the script. [*Pointing to the script.*]

LEADING ACTOR   If you ask me it's ridiculous.

---

3. Nickname given to Gala's servant, Philip, in *The Rules of the Game*, the play they are rehearsing.

PRODUCER [*Leaping to his feet furiously.*] Ridiculous? It's ridiculous, is it? What do you expect me to do if nobody writes good plays any more[4] and we're reduced to putting on plays by Pirandello? And if you can understand them you must be very clever. He writes them on purpose so nobody enjoys them, neither actors nor critics nor audience. [*The* ACTORS *laugh. Then crosses to* LEADING ACTOR *and shouts at him.*] A cook's hat and you beat eggs. But don't run away with the idea that that's all you are doing—beating eggs. You must be joking! You have to be symbolic of the shells of the eggs you are beating. [*The* ACTORS *laugh again and start making ironical comments to each other.*] Be quiet! Listen carefully while I explain. [*Turns back to* LEADING ACTOR.] Yes, the shells, because they are symbolic of the empty form of reason, without its content, blind instinct! You are reason and your wife is instinct: you are playing a game where you have been given parts and in which you are not just yourself but the puppet of yourself.[5] Do you see?

LEADING ACTOR [*Spreading his hands.*] Me? No.

PRODUCER [*Going back to his chair.*] Neither do I! Come on, let's get going; you wait till you see the end! You haven't seen anything yet! [*Confidentially.*] By the way, I should turn almost to face the audience if I were you, about three-quarters face. Well, what with the obscure dialogue and the audience not being able to hear you properly in any case, the whole lot'll go to hell. [*Clapping hands again.*] Come on. Let's get going!

PROMPTER Excuse me, can I put the top back on the prompt-box? There's a bit of a draught.

PRODUCER Yes, yes, of course. Get on with it.

[*The* STAGE DOORKEEPER, *in a braided cap, has come into the auditorium, and he comes all the way down the aisle to the stage to tell the* PRODUCER *the* SIX CHARACTERS *have come, who, having come in after him, look about them a little puzzled and dismayed. Every effort must be made to create the effect that the* SIX CHARACTERS *are very different from the* ACTORS *of the company. The placings of the two groups, indicated in the directions, once the* CHARACTERS *are on the stage, will help this: so will using different coloured lights. But the most effective idea is to use masks for the* CHARACTERS, *masks specially made of a material that will not go limp with perspiration and light enough not to worry the actors who wear them: they should be made so that the eyes, the nose and the mouth are all free. This is the way to bring out the deep significance of the play. The* CHARACTERS *should not appear as ghosts, but as created realities, timeless creations of the imagination, and so more real and consistent than the changeable realities of the* ACTORS. *The masks are designed to give the impression of figures constructed by art, each one fixed forever in its own fundamental emotion; that is, Remorse for the* FATHER, *Revenge for the* STEPDAUGHTER, *Scorn for the* SON, *Sorrow for the* MOTHER. *Her mask should have wax tears in the corners of the*

---

4. The producer refers to the realistic, tightly constructed plays (often French) that were internationally popular in the late 19th century and a staple of Italian theaters at the beginning of the 20th. 5. Leone Gala is a rationalist and an aesthete—the opposite of his impulsive, passionate wife, Silia. By masking his feelings and constantly playing the role of gourmet cook, he chooses his own role and thus becomes his own "puppet."

eyes and down the cheeks like the sculptured or painted weeping Madonna in a church. Her dress should be of a plain material, in stiff folds, looking almost as if it were carved and not of an ordinary material you can buy in a shop and have made up by a dressmaker.

The FATHER is about fifty: his reddish hair is thinning at the temples, but he is not bald: he has a full moustache that almost covers his young-looking mouth, which often opens in an uncertain and empty smile. He is pale, with a high forehead: he has blue oval eyes, clear and sharp: he is dressed in light trousers and a dark jacket: his voice is sometimes rich, at other times harsh and loud.

The MOTHER appears crushed by an intolerable weight of shame and humiliation. She is wearing a thick black veil and is dressed simply in black; when she raises her veil she shows a face like wax, but not suffering, with her eyes turned down humbly.

The STEPDAUGHTER, who is eighteen years old, is defiant, even insolent. She is very beautiful, dressed in mourning as well, but with striking elegance. She is scornful of the timid, suffering, dejected air of her young brother, a grubby LITTLE BOY of fourteen, also dressed in black; she is full of a warm tenderness, on the other hand, for the LITTLE SISTER (GIRL), a girl of about four, dressed in white with a black silk sash round her waist.

The SON is twenty-two, tall, almost frozen in an air of scorn for the FATHER and indifference to the MOTHER: he is wearing a mauve overcoat and a long green scarf round his neck.]

DOORMAN   Excuse me, sir.

PRODUCER [*Angrily.*]   What the hell is it now?

DOORMAN   There are some people here—they say they want to see you, sir.

[*The PRODUCER and the ACTORS are astonished and turn to look out into the auditorium.*]

PRODUCER   But I'm rehearsing! You know perfectly well that no-one's allowed in during rehearsals. [*Turning to face out front.*] Who are you? What do you want?

FATHER [*Coming forward, followed by the others, to the foot of one of the sets of steps.*]   We're looking for an author.

PRODUCER [*Angry and astonished.*]   An author? Which author?

FATHER   Any author will do, sir.

PRODUCER   But there isn't an author here because we're not rehearsing a new play.

STEPDAUGHTER [*Excitedly as she rushes up the steps.*]   That's better still, better still! We can be your new play.

ACTORS [*Lively comments and laughter from the ACTORS.*]   Oh, listen to that, etc.

FATHER [*Going up on the stage after the STEPDAUGHTER.*]   Maybe, but if there isn't an author here . . .[*To the PRODUCER.*] Unless you'd like to be . . .

[*Hand in hand, the MOTHER and the LITTLE GIRL, followed by the LITTLE BOY, go up on the stage and wait. The SON stays sullenly behind.*]

PRODUCER   Is this some kind of joke?

FATHER   Now, how can you think that? On the contrary, we are bringing you a story of anguish.

STEPDAUGHTER   We might make your fortune for you!

PRODUCER   Do me a favour, will you? Go away. We haven't time to waste on idiots.

FATHER [*Hurt but answering gently.*]   You know very well, as a man of the theatre, that life is full of all sorts of odd things which have no need at all to pretend to be real because they are actually true.

PRODUCER   What the devil are you talking about?

FATHER   What I'm saying is that you really must be mad to do things the opposite way round: to create situations that obviously aren't true and try to make them seem to be really happening. But then I suppose that sort of madness is the only reason for your profession.

[*The* ACTORS *are indignant.*]

PRODUCER [*Getting up and glaring at him.*]   Oh, yes? So ours is a profession of madmen, is it?

FATHER   Well, if you try to make something look true when it obviously isn't, especially if you're not forced to do it, but do it for a game . . . Isn't it your job to give life on the stage to imaginary people?

PRODUCER [*Quickly answering him and speaking for the* ACTORS *who are growing more indignant.*]   I should like you to know, sir, that the actor's profession is one of great distinction. Even if nowadays the new writers only give us dull plays to act and puppets to present instead of men, I'd have you know that it is our boast that we have given life, here on this stage, to immortal works.

[*The* ACTORS, *satisfied, agree with and applaud the* PRODUCER.]

FATHER [*Cutting in and following hard on his argument.*]   There! You see? Good! You've given life! You've created living beings with more genuine life than people have who breathe and wear clothes! Less real, perhaps, but nearer the truth. We are both saying the same thing.

[*The* ACTORS *look at each other, astonished.*]

PRODUCER   But just a moment! You said before . . .

FATHER   I'm sorry, but I said that before, about acting for fun, because you shouted at us and said you'd no time to waste on idiots, but you must know better than anyone that Nature uses human imagination to lift her work of creation to even higher levels.

PRODUCER   All right then: but where does all this get us?

FATHER   Nowhere. I want to try to show that one can be thrust into life in many ways, in many forms: as a tree or a stone, as water or a butterfly—or as a woman. It might even be as a character in a play.

PRODUCER [*Ironic, pretending to be annoyed.*]   And you, and these other people here, were thrust into life, as you put it, as characters in a play?

FATHER   Exactly! And alive, as you can see.

[*The* PRODUCER *and the* ACTORS *burst into laughter as if at a joke.*]

FATHER   I'm sorry you laugh like that, because we carry in us, as I said before, a story of terrible anguish as you can guess from this woman dressed in black.

[*Saying this, he offers his hand to the* MOTHER *and helps her up the last steps and, holding her still by the hand, leads her with a sense of tragic solemnity across the stage which is suddenly lit by a fantastic light.*

The LITTLE GIRL *and the* (LITTLE) BOY *follow the* MOTHER: *then the* SON *comes up and stands to one side in the background: then the* STEP-

DAUGHTER *follows and leans against the proscenium arch: the* ACTORS *are astonished at first, but then, full of admiration for the "entrance," they burst into applause—just as if it were a performance specially for them.*]

PRODUCER [*At first astonished and then indignant.*]   My God! Be quiet all of you. [*Turns to the* CHARACTERS.] And you lot get out! Clear off! [*Turns to the* STAGE MANAGER.] Jesus! Get them out of here.

STAGE MANAGER [*Comes forward but stops short as if held back by something strange.*]   Go on out! Get out!

FATHER [*To* PRODUCER.]   Oh no, please, you see, we . . .

PRODUCER [*Shouting.*]   We came here to work, you know.

LEADING ACTOR   We really can't be messed about like this.

FATHER [*Resolutely, coming forward.*]   I'm astonished! Why don't you believe me? Perhaps you are not used to seeing the characters created by an author spring into life up here on the stage face to face with each other. Perhaps it's because we're not in a script? [*He points to the* PROMPTER'*s box.*]

STEPDAUGHTER [*Coming down to the* PRODUCER, *smiling and persuasive.*] Believe me, sir, we really are six of the most fascinating characters. But we've been neglected.

FATHER   Yes, that's right, we've been neglected. In the sense that the author who created us, living in his mind, wouldn't or couldn't make us live in a written play for the world of art.[6] And that really is a crime sir, because whoever has the luck to be born a character can laugh even at death. Because a character will never die! A man will die, a writer, the instrument of creation: but what he has created will never die! And to be able to live for ever you don't need to have extraordinary gifts or be able to do miracles. Who was Sancho Panza? Who was Prospero?[7] But they will live for ever because—living seeds—they had the luck to find a fruitful soil, an imagination which knew how to grow them and feed them, so that they will live for ever.

PRODUCER   This is all very well! But what do you want here?

FATHER   We want to live, sir.

PRODUCER [*Ironically.*]   For ever!

FATHER   No, no: only for a few moments—in you.

AN ACTOR   Listen to that!

LEADING ACTRESS   They want to live in us!

YOUNG ACTOR [*Pointing to the* STEPDAUGHTER.]   I don't mind . . . so long as I get her.

FATHER   Listen, listen: the play is all ready to be put together and if you and your actors would like to, we can work it out now between us.

PRODUCER [*Annoyed.*]   But what exactly do you want to do? We don't make up plays like that here! We present comedies and tragedies here.

FATHER   That's right, we know that of course. That's why we've come.

PRODUCER   And where's the script?

FATHER   It's in us, sir. [*The* ACTORS *laugh.*] The play is in us: we are the

---

6. In the 1925 preface to *Six Characters*, Pirandello explains that these characters came to him first as characters for a novel that he later abandoned. Haunted by their half-realized personalities, he decided to use the situation in a play.   7. The magician and exiled duke of Milan in Shakespeare's *The Tempest*. Sancho Panza was Don Quixote's servant in Cervantes's novel *Don Quixote* (1605–15).

play and we are impatient to show it to you: the passion inside us is driving us on.

STEPDAUGHTER [*Scornfully, with the tantalising charm of deliberate impudence.*] My passion, if only you knew! My passion for him! [*She points at the* FATHER *and suggests that she is going to embrace him: but stops and bursts into a screeching laugh.*]

FATHER [*With sudden anger.*] You keep out of this for the moment! And stop laughing like that!

STEPDAUGHTER Really? Then with your permission, ladies and gentlemen; even though it's only two months since I became an orphan, just watch how I can sing and dance.

[*The* ACTORS, *especially the younger, seem strangely attracted to her while she sings and dances and they edge closer and reach out their hands to catch hold of her.*[8] *She eludes them, and when the* ACTORS *applaud her and the* PRODUCER *speaks sharply to her she stays still quite removed from them all.*]

FIRST ACTOR Very good! etc.

PRODUCER [*Angrily.*] Be quiet! Do you think this is a nightclub? [*Turns to* FATHER *and asks with some concern.*] Is she a bit mad?

FATHER Mad? Oh no—it's worse than that.

STEPDAUGHTER [*Suddenly running to the* PRODUCER.] Yes. It's worse, much worse! Listen please! Let's put this play on at once, because you'll see that at a particular point I—when this darling little girl here—[*Taking the* LITTLE GIRL *by the hand from next to the* MOTHER *and crossing with her to the* PRODUCER.] Isn't she pretty? [*Takes her in her arms.*] Darling! Darling! [*Puts her down again and adds, moved very deeply but almost without wanting to.*] Well, this lovely little girl here, when God suddenly takes her from this poor Mother: and this little idiot here [*Turning to the* LITTLE BOY *and seizing him roughly by the sleeve.*] does the most stupid thing, like the half-wit he is,—then you will see me run away! Yes, you'll see me rush away! But not yet, not yet! Because, after all the intimate things there have been between him and me [*In the direction of the* FATHER, *with a horrible vulgar wink.*] I can't stay with them any longer, to watch the insult to this mother through that supercilious cretin over there. [*Pointing to the* SON.] Look at him! Look at him! Condescending, stand-offish, because he's the legitimate son, him! Full of contempt for me, for the boy and for the little girl: because we are bastards. Do you understand? Bastards. [*Running to the* MOTHER *and embracing her.*] And this poor mother—she—who is the mother of all of us—he doesn't want to recognise her as his own mother—and he looks down on her, he does, as if she were only the mother of the three of us who are bastards—the traitor. [*She says all this quickly, with great excitement, and after having raised her voice on the word "bastards" she speaks quietly, half-spitting the word "traitor."*]

MOTHER [*With deep anguish to the* PRODUCER.] Sir, in the name of these two little ones, I beg you . . .[*Feels herself grow faint and sways.*] Oh, my God.

---

8. Pirandello uses a contemporary popular song, "Chu-Chin-Chow" from the Ziegfeld Follies of 1917, for the Stepdaughter to display her talents.

FATHER [*Rushing to support her with almost all the* ACTORS *bewildered and concerned.*] Get a chair someone . . . quick, get a chair for this poor widow.

[*One of the* ACTORS *offers a chair: the others press urgently around. The* MOTHER, *seated now, tries to stop the* FATHER *lifting her veil.*]

ACTORS Is it real? Has she really fainted? etc.

FATHER Look at her, everybody, look at her.

MOTHER No, for God's sake, stop it.

FATHER Let them look?

MOTHER [*Lifting her hands and covering her face, desperately.*] Oh, please, I beg you, stop him from doing what he is trying to do; it's hateful.

PRODUCER [*Overwhelmed, astounded.*] It's no use, I don't understand this any more. [*To the* FATHER.] Is this woman your wife?

FATHER [*At once.*] That's right, she is my wife.

PRODUCER How is she a widow, then, if you're still alive?

[*The* ACTORS *are bewildered too and find relief in a loud laugh.*]

FATHER [*Wounded, with rising resentment.*] Don't laugh! Please don't laugh like that! That's just the point, that's her own drama. You see, she had another man. Another man who ought to be here.

MOTHER No, no![*Crying out.*]

STEPDAUGHTER Luckily for him he died. Two months ago, as I told you: we are in mourning for him, as you can see.

FATHER Yes, he's dead: but that's not the reason he isn't here. He isn't here because—well just look at her, please, and you'll understand at once—hers is not a passionate drama of the love of two men, because she was incapable of love, she could feel nothing—except, perhaps a little gratitude (but not to me, to him). She's not a woman; she's a mother. And her drama—and, believe me, it's a powerful one—her drama is focused completely on these four children of the two men she had.

MOTHER I had them? How dare you say that I had them, as if I wanted them myself? It was him, sir! He forced the other man on me. He made me go away with him!

STEPDAUGHTER [*Leaping up, indignantly.*] It isn't true!

MOTHER [*Bewildered.*] How isn't it true?

STEPDAUGHTER It isn't true, it just isn't true.

MOTHER What do you know about it?

STEPDAUGHTER It isn't true. [*To the* PRODUCER.] Don't believe it! Do you know why she said that? She said it because of him, over there. [*Pointing to the* SON.] She tortures herself, she exhausts herself with worry and all because of the indifference of that son of hers. She wants to make him believe that she abandoned him when he was two years old because the Father made her do it.

MOTHER [*Passionately.*] He did! He made me! God's my witness. [*To the* PRODUCER.] Ask him if it isn't true. [*Pointing to the* FATHER.] Make him tell our son it's true. [*Turning to the* STEPDAUGHTER.] You don't know anything about it.

STEPDAUGHTER I know that when my father was alive you were always happy and contented. You can't deny it.

MOTHER No, I can't deny it.

STEPDAUGHTER He was always full of love and care for you. [*Turning to the* LITTLE BOY *with anger.*] Isn't it true? Admit it. Why don't you say something, you little idiot?

MOTHER Leave the poor boy alone! Why do you want to make me appear ungrateful? You're my daughter. I don't in the least want to offend your father's memory. I've already told him that it wasn't my fault or even to please myself that I left his house and my son.

FATHER It's quite true. It was my fault.

LEADING ACTOR [*To other actors.*] Look at this. What a show!

LEADING ACTRESS And we're the audience.

YOUNG ACTOR For a change.

PRODUCER [*Beginning to be very interested.*] Let's listen to them! Quiet! Listen!

[*He goes down the steps into the auditorium and stands there as if to get an idea of what the scene will look like from the audience's viewpoint.*]

SON [*Without moving, coldly, quietly, ironically.*] Yes, listen to his little scrap of philosophy. He's going to tell you all about the Daemon of Experiment.

FATHER You're a cynical idiot, and I've told you so a hundred times. [*To the* PRODUCER *who is now in the stalls.*] He sneers at me because of this expression I've found to defend myself.

SON Words, words.

FATHER Yes words, words! When we're faced by something we don't understand, by a sense of evil that seems as if it's going to swallow us, don't we all find comfort in a word that tells us nothing but that calms us?

STEPDAUGHTER And dulls your sense of remorse, too. That more than anything.

FATHER Remorse? No, that's not true. It'd take more than words to dull the sense of remorse in me.

STEPDAUGHTER It's taken a little money too, just a little money. The money that he was going to offer as payment, gentlemen.

[*The* ACTORS *are horrified.*]

SON [*Contemptuously to his stepsister.*] That's a filthy trick.

STEPDAUGHTER A filthy trick? There it was in a pale blue envelope on the little mahogany table in the room behind the shop at Madame Pace's. You know Madame Pace, don't you? One of those Madames who sell "Robes et Manteaux" so that they can attract poor girls like me from decent families into their workroom.[9]

SON And she's bought the right to tyrannise over the whole lot of us with that money—with what he was going to pay her: and luckily—now listen carefully—he had no reason to pay it to her.

STEPDAUGHTER But it was close!

MOTHER [*Rising up angrily.*] Shame on you, daughter! Shame!

STEPDAUGHTER Shame? Not shame, revenge! I'm desperate, desperate to live that scene! The room . . . over here the showcase of coats, there the divan, there the mirror, and the screen, and over there in front of the

9. The implication is that Madame Pace (Italian for "peace") runs a call-girl operation under the guise of selling fashionable "dresses and coats."

window, that little mahogany table with the pale blue envelope and the money in it. I can see it all quite clearly. I could pick it up! But you should turn your faces away, gentlemen: because I'm nearly naked! I'm not blushing any longer—I leave that to him. [*Pointing at the* FATHER.] But I tell you he was very pale, very pale then. [*To the* PRODUCER.] Believe me.

PRODUCER   I don't understand any more.

FATHER   I'm not surprised when you're attacked like that! Why don't you put your foot down and let me have my say before you believe all these horrible slanders she's so viciously telling about me.

STEPDAUGHTER   We don't want to hear any of your long winded fairy-stories.

FATHER   I'm not going to tell any fairy-stories! I want to explain things to him.

STEPDAUGHTER   I'm sure you do. Oh, yes! In your own special way.

  [*The* PRODUCER *comes back up on stage to take control.*]

FATHER   But isn't that the cause of all the trouble? Words! We all have a world of things inside ourselves and each one of us has his own private world. How can we understand each other if the words I use have the sense and the value that I expect them to have, but whoever is listening to me inevitably thinks that those same words have a different sense and value, because of the private world he has inside himself too. We think we understand each other: but we never do. Look! All my pity, all my compassion for this woman [*Pointing to the* MOTHER.] she sees as ferocious cruelty.

MOTHER   But he turned me out of the house!

FATHER   There, do you hear? I turned her out! She really believed that I had turned her out.

MOTHER   You know how to talk. I don't . . . But believe me, sir, [*Turning to the* PRODUCER.] after he married me . . . I can't think why! I was a poor, simple woman.

FATHER   But that was the reason! I married you for your simplicity, that's what I loved in you, believing—[*He stops because she is making gestures of contradiction. Then, seeing the impossibility of making her understand, he throws his arms wide in a gesture of desperation and turns back to the* PRODUCER.] No, do you see? She says no! It's terrifying, sir, believe me, terrifying, her deafness, her mental deafness. [*He taps his forehead.*] Affection for her children, oh yes. But deaf, mentally deaf, deaf, sir, to the point of desperation.

STEPDAUGHTER   Yes, but make him tell you what good all his cleverness has brought us.

FATHER   If only we could see in advance all the harm that can come from the good we think we are doing.

  [*The* LEADING ACTRESS, *who has been growing angry watching the* LEADING ACTOR *flirting with the* STEPDAUGHTER, *comes forward and snaps at the* PRODUCER.]

LEADING ACTRESS   Excuse me, are we going to go on with our rehearsal?

PRODUCER   Yes, of course. But I want to listen to this first.

YOUNG ACTOR   It's such a new idea.

YOUNG ACTRESS   It's fascinating.

LEADING ACTRESS   For those who are interested. [*She looks meaningfully at the* LEADING ACTOR.]

PRODUCER [*To the* FATHER.]   Look here, you must explain yourself more clearly.[*He sits down.*]

FATHER   Listen then. You see, there was a rather poor fellow working for me as my assistant and secretary, very loyal: he understood her in everything. [*Pointing to the* MOTHER.] But without a hint of deceit, you must believe that: he was good and simple, like her: neither of them was capable even of thinking anything wrong, let alone doing it.

STEPDAUGHTER   So instead he thought of it for them and did it too!

FATHER   It's not true! What I did was for their good—oh yes and mine too, I admit it! The time had come when I couldn't say a word to either of them without there immediately flashing between them a sympathetic look: each one caught the other's eye for advice, about how to take what I had said, how not to make me angry. Well, that was enough, as I'm sure you'll understand, to put me in a bad temper all the time, in a state of intolerable exasperation.

PRODUCER   Then why didn't you sack this secretary of yours?

FATHER   Right! In the end I did sack him! But then I had to watch this poor woman wandering about in the house on her own, forlorn, like a stray animal you take in out of pity.

MOTHER   It's quite true.

FATHER [*Suddenly, turning to her, as if to stop her.*]   And what about the boy? Is that true as well?

MOTHER   But first he tore my son from me, sir.

FATHER   But not out of cruelty! It was so that he could grow up healthy and strong, in touch with the earth.

STEPDAUGHTER [*Pointing to the* SON *jeeringly.*]   And look at the result!

FATHER [*Quickly.*]   And is it my fault, too, that he's grown up like this? I took him to a nurse in the country, a peasant, because his mother didn't seem strong enough to me, although she is from a humble family herself. In fact that was what made me marry her. Perhaps it was superstitious of me; but what was I to do? I've always had this dreadful longing for a kind of sound moral healthiness.

[*The* STEPDAUGHTER *breaks out again into noisy laughter.*]
Make her stop that! It's unbearable.

PRODUCER   Stop it will you? Let me listen, for God's sake.

[*When the* PRODUCER *has spoken to her, she resumes her previous position . . . absorbed and distant, a half-smile on her lips. The* PRODUCER *comes down into the auditorium again to see how it looks from there.*]

FATHER   I couldn't bear the sight of this woman near me. [*Pointing to the* MOTHER.] Not so much because of the annoyance she caused me, you see, or even the feeling of being stifled, being suffocated that I got from her, as for the sorrow, the painful sorrow that I felt for her.

MOTHER   And he sent me away.

FATHER   With everything you needed, to the other man, to set her free from me.

MOTHER   And to set yourself free!

FATHER   Oh, yes, I admit it. And what terrible things came out of it. But I did it for the best, and more for her than for me: I swear it! [*Folds his arms: then turns suddenly to the* MOTHER.] I never lost sight of you did I? Until that fellow, without my knowing it, suddenly took you off to another town one day. He was idiotically suspicious of my interest in them, a genuine interest, I assure you, without any ulterior motive at all. I watched the new little family growing up round her with unbelievable tenderness, she'll confirm that. [*He points to the* STEPDAUGHTER.]

STEPDAUGHTER   Oh yes, I can indeed. I was a pretty little girl, you know, with plaits down to my shoulders and my little frilly knickers showing under my dress—so pretty—he used to watch me coming out of school. He came to see how I was maturing.

FATHER   That's shameful! It's monstrous.

STEPDAUGHTER   No it isn't! Why do you say it is?

FATHER   It's monstrous! Monstrous. [*He turns excitedly to the* PRODUCER *and goes on in explanation.*] After she'd gone away [*Pointing to the* MOTHER.] my house seemed empty. She'd been like a weight on my spirit but she'd filled the house with her presence. Alone in the empty rooms I wandered about like a lost soul. This boy here, [*Indicating the* SON.] growing up away from home—whenever he came back to the home—I don't know—but he didn't seem to be mine any more. We needed the mother between us, to link us together, and so he grew up by himself, apart, with no connection to me either through intellect or love. And then—it must seem odd, but it's true—first I was curious about and then strongly attracted to the little family that had come about because of what I'd done. And the thought of them began to fill all the emptiness that I felt around me. I needed, I really needed to believe that she was happy, wrapped up in the simple cares of her life, lucky because she was better off away from the complicated torments of a soul like mine. And to prove it, I used to watch that child coming out of school.

STEPDAUGHTER   Listen to him! He used to follow me along the street; he used to smile at me and when we came near the house he'd wave his hand—like this! I watched him, wide-eyed, puzzled. I didn't know who he was. I told my mother about him and she knew at once who it must be. [MOTHER *nods agreement.*] At first, she didn't let me go to school again, at any rate for a few days. But when I did go back, I saw him standing near the door again—looking ridiculous—with a brown paper bag in his hand. He came close and petted me: then he opened the bag and took out a beautiful straw hat with a hoop of rosebuds round it— for me!

PRODUCER   All this is off the point, you know.

SON [*Contemptuously.*]   Yes . . . literature, literature.

FATHER   What do you mean, literature? This is real life: real passions.

PRODUCER   That may be! But you can't put it on the stage just like that.

FATHER   That's right you can't. Because all this is only leading up to the main action. I'm not suggesting that this part should be put on the stage. In any case, you can see for yourself, [*Pointing at the* STEPDAUGHTER.] she isn't a pretty little girl any longer with plaits down to her shoulders.

STEPDAUGHTER   —and with frilly knickers showing under her frock.

FATHER   The drama begins now: and it's new and complex.

STEPDAUGHTER [*Coming forward, fierce and brooding.*]   As soon as my father died . . .

FATHER [*Quickly, not giving her time to speak.*]   They were so miserable. They came back here, but I didn't know about it because of the Mother's stubbornness. [*Pointing to the* MOTHER.] She can't really write you know; but she could have got her daughter to write, or the boy, or tell me that they needed help.

MOTHER   But tell me, sir, how could I have known how he felt?

FATHER   And hasn't that always been your fault? You've never known anything about how I felt.

MOTHER   After all the years away from him and after all that had happened.

FATHER   And was it my fault if that fellow took you so far away? [*Turning back to the* PRODUCER.] Suddenly, overnight, I tell you, he'd found a job away from here without my knowing anything about it. I couldn't possibly trace them; and then, naturally I suppose, my interest in them grew less over the years. The drama broke out, unexpected and violent, when they came back: when I was driven in misery by the needs of my flesh, still alive with desire . . . and it is misery, you know, unspeakable misery for the man who lives alone and who detests sordid, casual affairs; not old enough to do without women, but not young enough to be able to go and look for one without shame! Misery? Is that what I called it. It's horrible, it's revolting, because there isn't a woman who will give her love to him any more. And when he realises this, he should do without . . . It's easy to say though. Each of us, face to face with other men, is clothed with some sort of dignity, but we know only too well all the unspeakable things that go on in the heart. We surrender, we give in to temptation: but afterwards we rise up out of it very quickly, in a desperate hurry to rebuild our dignity, whole and firm as if it were a gravestone that would cover every sign and memory of our shame, and hide it from even our own eyes. Everyone's like that, only some of us haven't the courage to talk about it.

STEPDAUGHTER   But they've all got the courage to do it!

FATHER   Yes! But only in secret! That's why it takes more courage to talk about it! Because if a man does talk about it—what happens then?— everybody says he's a cynic. And it's simply not true; he's just like everybody else; only better perhaps, because he's not afraid to use his intelligence to point out the blushing shame of human bestiality, that man, the beast, shuts his eyes to, trying to pretend it doesn't exist. And what about woman—what is she like? She looks at you invitingly, teasingly. You take her in your arms. But as soon as she feels your arms round her she closes her eyes. It's the sign of her mission, the sign by which she says to a man, "Blind yourself—I'm blind!"

STEPDAUGHTER   And when she doesn't close her eyes any more? What then? When she doesn't feel the need to hide from herself any more, to shut her eyes and hide her own shame. When she can see instead, dispassionately and dry-eyed this blushing shame of a man who has blinded himself, who is without love. What then? Oh, then what disgust, what utter disgust she feels for all these intellectual complications, for all this philosophy that points to the bestiality of man and then tries to defend him, to excuse him . . . I can't listen to him, sir. Because when a man says he needs to "simplify" life like this—reducing it to bestiality—and throws away every human scrap of innocent desire, genuine feeling, idealism, duty, modesty, shame, then there's nothing more contemptible and nauseating than his remorse—crocodile tears!

PRODUCER Let's get to the point, let's get to the point. This is all chat.

FATHER Right then! But a fact is like a sack—it won't stand up if it's empty. To make it stand up, first you have to put in it all the reasons and feelings that caused it in the first place. I couldn't possibly have known that when that fellow died they'd come back here, that they were desperately poor and that the Mother had gone out to work as a dressmaker, nor that she'd gone to work for Madame Pace, of all people.

STEPDAUGHTER She's a very high-class dressmaker—you must understand that. She apparently has only high-class customers, but she has arranged things carefully so that these high-class customers in fact serve her—they give her a respectable front . . . without spoiling things for the other ladies at the shop who are not quite so high-class at all.

MOTHER Believe me, sir, the idea never entered my head that the old hag gave me work because she had an eye on my daughter . . .

STEPDAUGHTER Poor Mummy! Do you know what that woman would do when I took back the work that my mother had been doing? She would point out how the dress had been ruined by giving it to my mother to sew: she bargained, she grumbled. So, you see, I paid for it, while this poor woman here thought she was sacrificing herself for me and these two children, sewing dresses all night for Madame Pace.

[The ACTORS *make gestures and noises of disgust.*]

PRODUCER [*Quickly.*] And there one day, you met . . .

STEPDAUGHTER [*Pointing at the* FATHER.] Yes, him. Oh, he was an old customer of hers! What a scene that's going to be, superb!

FATHER With her, the mother, arriving—

STEPDAUGHTER [*Quickly, viciously.*] —Almost in time!

FATHER [*Crying out.*] —No, just in time, just in time! Because, luckily, I found out who she was in time. And I took them all back to my house, sir. Can you imagine the situation now, for the two of us living in the same house? She, just as you see her here: and I, not able to look her in the face.

STEPDAUGHTER It's so absurd! Do you think it's possible for me, sir, after what happened at Madame Pace's, to pretend that I'm a modest little miss, well brought up and virtuous just so that I can fit in with his damned pretensions to a "sound moral healthiness"?

FATHER This is the real drama for me; the belief that we all, you see, think of ourselves as one single person: but it's not true: each of us is several different people, and all these people live inside us. With one person we seem like this and with another we seem very different. But we always have the illusion of being the same person for everybody and of always being the same person in everything we do. But it's not true! It's not true! We find this out for ourselves very clearly when by some terrible chance we're suddenly stopped in the middle of doing something and we're left dangling there, suspended. We realise then, that every part of us was not involved in what we'd been doing and that it would be a dreadful injustice of other people to judge us only by this one action as we dangle there, hanging in chains, fixed for all eternity, as if the whole of one's personality were summed up in that single, interrupted action. Now do you understand this girl's treachery? She accidentally found me somewhere I shouldn't have been, doing something I shouldn't have been doing! She discovered a part of me that shouldn't have existed for her: and now she wants to fix on me a reality that I should never have had to assume for her: it came from a single brief and shameful moment in my life. This is what hurts me most of all. And you'll see that the play will make a tremendous impact from this idea of mine. But then, there's the position of the others. His . . .[*Pointing to the* SON.]

SON [*Shrugging his shoulders scornfully.*]   Leave me out of it. I don't come into this.

FATHER   Why don't you come into this?

SON   I don't come into it and I don't want to come into it, because you know perfectly well that I wasn't intended to be mixed up with you lot.

STEPDAUGHTER   We're vulgar, common people, you see! He's a fine gentleman. But you've probably noticed that every now and then I look at him contemptuously, and when I do, he lowers his eyes—he knows the harm he's done me.

SON [*Not looking at her.*]   I have?

STEPDAUGHTER   Yes, you. It's your fault, dearie, that I went on the streets! Your fault! [*Movement of horror from the* ACTORS.] Did you or didn't you, with your attitude, deny us—I won't say the intimacy of your home—but that simple hospitality that makes guests feel comfortable? We were intruders who had come to invade the country of your "legitimacy"! [*Turning to the* PRODUCER.] I'd like you to have seen some of the little scenes that went on between him and me, sir. He says that I tyrannised over everyone. But don't you see? It was because of the way he treated us. He called it "vile" that I should insist on the right we had to move into his house with my mother—and she's his mother too. And I went into the house as its mistress.

SON [*Slowly coming forward.*]   They're really enjoying themselves, aren't they, sir? It's easy when they all gang up against me. But try to imagine what happened: one fine day, there is a son sitting quietly at home and he sees arrive as bold as brass, a young woman like this, who cheekily asks for his father, and heaven knows what business she has with him. Then he sees her come back with the same brazen look in her eye accompanied by that little girl there: and he sees her treat his father—without knowing why—in a most ambiguous and insolent way—asking him for money in a tone that leads one to suppose he really ought to give it, because he is obliged to do so.

FATHER   But I was obliged to do so: I owed it to your mother.

SON   And how was I to know that? When had I ever seen her before? When had I ever heard her mentioned? Then one day I see her come in with her, [*Pointing at the* STEPDAUGHTER.] that boy and that little girl: they say to me, "Oh, didn't you know? This is your mother, too." Little by little I began to understand, mostly from her attitude. [*Points to* STEPDAUGHTER.] Why they'd come to live in the house so suddenly. I can't and I won't say what I feel, and what I think. I wouldn't even like to confess it to myself. So I can't take any active part in this. Believe me, sir, I am a character who has not been fully developed dramatically, and I feel uncomfortable, most uncomfortable, in their company. So please leave me out of it.

FATHER   What! But it's precisely because you feel like this . . .

SON [*Violently exasperated.*]   How do you know what I feel?

FATHER   All right! I admit it! But isn't that a situation in itself? This with-drawing of yourself, it's cruel to me and to your mother: when she came back to the house, seeing you almost for the first time, not recognising you, but knowing that you're her own son . . .[*Turning to point out the* MOTHER *to the* PRODUCER.] There, look at her: she's weeping.

STEPDAUGHTER [*Angrily, stamping her foot.*]   Like the fool she is!

FATHER [*Quickly pointing at the* STEPDAUGHTER *to the* PRODUCER.]   She can't stand that young man, you know. [*Turning and referring to the* SON.] He says that he doesn't come into it, but he's really the pivot of the action! Look here at this little boy, who clings to his mother all the time, fright-ened, humiliated. And it's because of him over there! Perhaps this little boy's problem is the worst of all: he feels an outsider, more than the others do; he feels so mortified, so humiliated just being in the house,— because it's charity, you see. [*Quietly.*] He's like his father: timid; he doesn't say anything . . .

PRODUCER   It's not a good idea at all, using him: you don't know what a nuisance children are on the stage.

FATHER   He won't need to be on the stage for long. Nor will the little girl— she's the first to go.

PRODUCER   That's good! Yes. I tell you all this interests me—it interests me very much. I'm sure we've the material here for a good play.

STEPDAUGHTER [*Trying to push herself in.*]   With a character like me you have!

FATHER [*Driving her off, wanting to hear what the* PRODUCER *has decided.*] You stay out of it!

PRODUCER [*Going on, ignoring the interruption.*]   It's new, yes.

FATHER   Oh, it's absolutely new!

PRODUCER   You've got a nerve, though, haven't you, coming here and throwing it at me like this?

FATHER   I'm sure you understand. Born as we are for the *stage* . . .

PRODUCER   Are you amateur actors?

FATHER   No! I say we are born for the stage because . . .

PRODUCER   Come on now! You're an old hand at this, at acting!

FATHER   No I'm not. I only act, as everyone does, the part in life that he's chosen for himself, or that others have chosen for him. And you can see that sometimes my own passion gets a bit out of hand, a bit theatrical, as it does with all of us.

PRODUCER   Maybe, maybe . . . But you do see, don't you, that without an author . . . I could give you someone's address . . .

FATHER   Oh no! Look here! You do it.

PRODUCER   Me? What are you talking about?

FATHER   Yes, you. Why not?

PRODUCER   Because I've never written anything!

FATHER   Well, why not start now, if you don't mind my suggesting it? There's nothing to it. Everybody's doing it. And your job is even easier, because we're here, all of us, alive before you.

PRODUCER   That's not enough.

FATHER   Why isn't it enough? When you've seen us live our drama . . .

PRODUCER   Perhaps so. But we'll still need someone to write it.

FATHER   Only to write it down, perhaps, while it happens in front of him—live—scene by scene. It'll be enough to sketch it out simply first and then run through it.

PRODUCER   [*Coming back up, tempted by the idea.*]   Do you know I'm almost tempted . . . just for fun . . . it might work.

FATHER   Of course it will. You'll see what wonderful scenes will come right out of it! I could tell you what they will be!

PRODUCER   You tempt me . . . you tempt me! We'll give it a chance. Come with me to the office. [*Turning to the* ACTORS.] Take a break: but don't go far away. Be back in a quarter of an hour or twenty minutes. [*To the* FATHER.] Let's see, let's try it out. Something extraordinary might come out of this.

FATHER   Of course it will! Don't you think it'd be better if the others came too? [*Indicating the other* CHARACTERS.]

PRODUCER   Yes, come on, come on. [*Going, then turning to speak to the* ACTORS.] Don't forget: don't be late: back in a quarter of an hour.

> [*The* PRODUCER *and the* SIX CHARACTERS *cross the stage and go. The* ACTORS *look at each other in astonishment.*]

LEADING ACTOR   Is he serious? What's he going to do?

YOUNG ACTOR   I think he's gone round the bend.

ANOTHER ACTOR   Does he expect to make up a play in five minutes?

YOUNG ACTOR   Yes, like the old actors in the commedia dell'arte![1]

LEADING ACTRESS   Well if he thinks I'm going to appear in that sort of nonsense . . .

YOUNG ACTOR   Nor me!

FOURTH ACTOR   I should like to know who they are.

THIRD ACTOR   Who do you think? They're probably escaped lunatics—or crooks.

YOUNG ACTOR   And is he taking them seriously?

YOUNG ACTRESS   It's vanity. The vanity of seeing himself as an author.

LEADING ACTOR   I've never heard of such a thing! If the theatre, ladies and gentlemen, is reduced to this . . .

FIFTH ACTOR   I'm enjoying it!

THIRD ACTOR   Really! We shall have to wait and see what happens next I suppose.

> [*Talking, they leave the stage. Some go out through the back door, some to the dressing-rooms.*
> *The curtain stays up.*
> *The interval lasts twenty minutes.*]

Act Two

The theatre warning-bell sounds to call the audience back. From the dressing-rooms, the door at the back and even from the auditorium, the ACTORS, *the* STAGE MANAGER, *the* STAGE HANDS, *the* PROMPTER, *the* PROPERTY MAN *and the* PRODUCER, *accompanied by the* SIX CHARACTERS *all come back on to the stage.*

The house lights go out and the stage lights come on again.

---

1. A form of popular theater beginning in 16th-century Italy; the actors improvised dialogue according to basic comic or dramatic plots and in response to the audience's reaction.

PRODUCER   Come on, everybody! Are we all here? Quiet now! Listen! Let's get started! Stage manager?

STAGE MANAGER   Yes, I'm here.

PRODUCER   Give me that little parlour setting, will you? A couple of plain flats and a door flat will do. Hurry up with it!

[*The* STAGE MANAGER *runs off to order someone to do this immediately and at the same time the* PRODUCER *is making arrangements with the* PROPERTY MAN, *the* PROMPTER, *and the* ACTORS: *the two flats and the door flat are painted in pink and gold stripes.*]

PRODUCER [*To* PROPERTY MAN.]   Go see if we have a sofa in stock.

PROPERTY MAN   Yes, there's that green one.

STEPDAUGHTER   No, no, not a green one! It was yellow, yellow velvet with flowers on it: it was enormous! And so comfortable!

PROPERTY MAN   We haven't got one like that.

PRODUCER   It doesn't matter! Give me whatever there is.

STEPDAUGHTER   What do you mean, it doesn't matter? It was Mme. Pace's famous sofa.

PRODUCER   It's only for a rehearsal! Please, don't interfere. [*To the* STAGE MANAGER.]   Oh, and see if there's a shop window, will you—preferably a long, low one.

STEPDAUGHTER   And a little table, a little mahogany table for the blue envelope.

STAGE MANAGER [*To the* PRODUCER.]   There's that little gold one.

PRODUCER   That'll do—bring it.

FATHER   A mirror!

STEPDAUGHTER   And a screen! A screen, please, or I won't be able to manage, will I?

STAGE MANAGER   All right. We've lots of big screens, don't you worry.

PRODUCER [*To* STEPDAUGHTER.]   Then don't you want some coat-hangers and some clothes racks?

STEPDAUGHTER   Yes, lots of them, lots of them.

PRODUCER [*To the* STAGE MANAGER.]   See how many there are and have them brought up.

STAGE MANAGER   Right, I'll see to it.

[*The* STAGE MANAGER *goes off to do it: and while the* PRODUCER *is talking to the* PROMPTER, *the* CHARACTERS *and the* ACTORS, *the* STAGE MANAGER *is telling the* SCENE SHIFTERS *where to set up the furniture they have brought.*]

PRODUCER [*To the* PROMPTER.]   Now you, go sit down, will you? Look, this is an outline of the play, act by act. [*He hands him several sheets of paper.*] But you'll need to be on your toes.

PROMPTER   Shorthand?

PRODUCER [*Pleasantly surprised.*]   Oh, good! You know shorthand?

PROMPTER   I don't know much about prompting, but I do know about shorthand.

PRODUCER   Thank God for that anyway! [*He turns to a* STAGE HAND.]   Go fetch me some paper from my office—lots of it—as much as you can find!

[*The* STAGE HAND *goes running off and then comes back shortly with a bundle of paper that he gives to the* PROMPTER.]

PRODUCER [*Crossing to the* PROMPTER.] Follow the scenes, one after another, as they are played and try to get the lines down . . . at least the most important ones. [*Then turning to the* ACTORS.] Get out of the way everybody! Here, go over to the prompt side [*Pointing to stage left.*] and pay attention.

LEADING ACTRESS But, excuse me, we . . .

PRODUCER [*Anticipating her.*] You won't be expected to improvise, don't worry!

LEADING ACTOR Then what are we expected to do?

PRODUCER Nothing! Just go over there, listen and watch. You'll all be given your parts later written out. Right now we're going to rehearse, as well as we can. And they will be doing the rehearsal. [*He points to the* CHARACTERS.]

FATHER [*Rather bewildered, as if he had fallen from the clouds into the middle of the confusion on the stage.*] We are? Excuse me, but what do you mean, a rehearsal?

PRODUCER I mean a rehearsal—a rehearsal for the benefit of the actors. [*Pointing to the* ACTORS.]

FATHER But if we are the characters . . .

PRODUCER That's right, you're "the characters": but characters don't act here, my dear chap. It's actors who act here. The characters are there in the script—[*Pointing to the* PROMPTER.] that's when there is a script.

FATHER That's the point! Since there isn't one and you have the luck to have the characters alive in front of you . . .

PRODUCER Great! You want to do everything yourselves, do you? To act your own play, to produce your own play!

FATHER Well yes, just as we are.

PRODUCER That would be an experience for us, I can tell you!

LEADING ACTOR And what about us? What would we be doing then?

PRODUCER Don't tell me you think you know how to act! Don't make me laugh! [*The* ACTORS *in fact laugh.*] There you are, you see, you've made them laugh. [*Then remembering.*] But let's get back to the point! We need to cast the play. Well, that's easy: it almost casts itself. [*To the* SECOND ACTRESS.] You, the mother. [*To the* FATHER.] You'll need to give her a name.

FATHER Amalia.

PRODUCER But that's the real name of your wife isn't it? We can't use her real name.

FATHER But why not? That is her name . . . But perhaps if this lady is to play the part . . .[*Indicating the* ACTRESS *vaguely with a wave of his hand.*] I don't know what to say . . . I'm already starting to . . . how can I explain it . . . to sound false, my own words sound like someone else's.

PRODUCER Now don't worry yourself about it, don't worry about it at all. We'll work out the right tone of voice. As for the name, if you want it to be Amalia, then Amalia it shall be: or we can find another. For the moment we'll refer to the characters like this: [*To the* YOUNG ACTOR, *the juvenile lead.*] you are The Son. [*To the* LEADING ACTRESS.] You, of course, are The Stepdaughter.

STEPDAUGHTER [*Excitedly.*] What did you say? That woman is me? [*Bursts into laughter.*]

PRODUCER [*Angrily.*] What are you laughing at?

LEADING ACTRESS [*Indignantly.*] Nobody has ever dared to laugh at me before! Either you treat me with respect or I'm walking out! [*Starting to go.*]

STEPDAUGHTER I'm sorry. I wasn't really laughing at you.

PRODUCER [*To the* STEPDAUGHTER.] You should feel proud to be played by . . .

LEADING ACTRESS [*Quickly, scornfully.*] . . . that woman!

STEPDAUGHTER But I wasn't thinking about her, honestly. I was thinking about me: I can't see myself in you at all . . . you're not a bit like me!

FATHER Yes, that's right: you see, our meaning . . .

PRODUCER What are you talking about, "our meaning"? Do you think you have exclusive rights to what you represent? Do you think it can only exist inside you? Not a bit of it!

FATHER What? Don't we even have our own meaning?

PRODUCER Not a bit of it! Whatever you mean is only material here, to which the actors give form and body, voice and gesture, and who, through their art, have given expression to much better material than what you have to offer: yours is really very trivial and if it stands up on the stage, the credit, believe me, will all be due to my actors.

FATHER I don't dare to contradict you. But you for your part, must believe me—it doesn't seem trivial to us. We are suffering terribly now, with these bodies, these faces . . .

PRODUCER [*Interrupting impatiently.*] Yes, well, the make-up will change that, make-up will change that, at least as far as the faces are concerned.

FATHER Yes, but the voices, the gestures . . .

PRODUCER That's enough! You can't come on the stage here as yourselves. It is our actors who will represent you here: and let that be the end of it!

FATHER I understand that. But now I think I see why our author who saw us alive as we are here now, didn't want to put us on the stage. I don't want to offend your actors. God forbid that I should! But I think that if I saw myself represented . . . by I don't know whom . . .

LEADING ACTOR [*Rising majestically and coming forward, followed by a laughing group of* YOUNG ACTRESSES.] By me, if you don't object.

FATHER [*Respectfully, smoothly.*] I shall be honoured, sir. [*He bows.*] But I think, that no matter how hard this gentleman works with all his will and all his art to identify himself with me . . .[*He stops, confused.*]

LEADING ACTOR Yes, go on.

FATHER Well, I was saying the performance he will give, even if he is made up to look like me . . . I mean with the difference in our appearance . . .[*All the* ACTORS *laugh.*] it will be difficult for it to be a performance of me as I really am. It will be more like—well, not just because of his figure—it will be more an interpretation of what I am, what he believes me to be, and not how I know myself to be. And it seems to me that this should be taken into account by those who are going to comment on us.

PRODUCER So you are already worrying about what the critics will say, are you? And I'm still waiting to get this thing started! The critics can say what they like: and we'll worry about putting on the play. If we can! [*Stepping out of the group and looking around.*] Come on, come on! Is the scene set for us yet? [*To the* ACTORS *and* CHARACTERS.] Out of the way! Let's have a look at it. [*Climbing down off the stage.*] Don't let's waste any more time. [*To the* STEPDAUGHTER.] Does it look all right to you?

SON   What! That? I don't recognise it at all.

PRODUCER   Good God! Did you expect us to reconstruct the room at the back of Mme. Pace's shop here on the stage? [*To the* FATHER.] Did you say the room had flowered wallpaper?

FATHER   White, yes.

PRODUCER   Well it's not white: it's striped. That sort of thing doesn't matter at all! As for the furniture, it looks to me as if we have nearly everything we need. Move that little table a bit further downstage. [*A* STAGE HAND *does it. To the* PROPERTY MAN.] Go and fetch an envelope, pale blue if you can find one, and give it to that gentleman there. [*Pointing to the* FATHER.]

STAGE HAND   An envelope for letters?

PRODUCER
FATHER   } Yes, an envelope for letters!

STAGE HAND   Right. [*He goes off.*]

PRODUCER   Now then, come on! The first scene is the young lady's. [*The* LEADING ACTRESS *comes to the centre.*] No, no, not yet. I said the young lady's. [*He points to the* STEPDAUGHTER.] You stay there and watch.

STEPDAUGHTER [*Adding quickly.*]   . . . how I bring it to life.

LEADING ACTRESS [*Resenting this.*]   I shall know how to bring it to life, don't you worry, when I am allowed to.

PRODUCER [*His head in his hands.*]   Ladies, please, no more arguments! Now then. The first scene is between the young lady and Mme. Pace. Oh! [*Worried, turning round and looking out into the auditorium.*] Where is Mme. Pace?

FATHER   She isn't here with us.

PRODUCER   So what do we do now?

FATHER   But she is real. She's real too!

PRODUCER   All right. So where is she?

FATHER   May I deal with this? [*Turns to the* ACTRESSES.] Would each of you ladies be kind enough to lend me a hat, a coat, a scarf or something?

ACTRESSES [*Some are surprised or amused.*]   What? My scarf? A coat? What's he want my hat for? What are you wanting to do with them? [*All the* ACTRESSES *are laughing.*]

FATHER   Oh, nothing much, just hang them up here on the racks for a minute or two. Perhaps someone would be kind enough to lend me a coat?

ACTORS   Just a coat? Come on, more! The man must be mad.

AN ACTRESS   What for? Only my coat?

FATHER   Yes, to hang up here, just for a moment. I'm very grateful to you. Do you mind?

ACTRESSES [*Taking off various hats, coats, scarves, laughing and going to hang them on the racks.*]   Why not? Here you are. I really think it's crazy. Is it to dress the set?

FATHER   Yes, exactly. It's to dress the set.

PRODUCER   Would you mind telling me what you are doing?

FATHER   Yes, of course: perhaps, if we dress the set better, she will be drawn by the articles of her trade and, who knows, she may even come to join us . . . [*He invites them to watch the door at the back of the set.*] Look! Look!

> [*The door at the back opens and* MME. PACE *takes a few steps downstage: she is a gross old harridan wearing a ludicrous carroty-coloured wig with a single red rose stuck in at one side, Spanish fashion: garishly made-up: in a vulgar but stylish red silk dress, holding an ostrich-feather fan in one hand and a cigarette between two fingers in the other. At the sight of this apparition, the* ACTORS *and the* PRODUCER *immediately jump off the stage with cries of fear, leaping down into the auditorium and up the aisles. The* STEPDAUGHTER, *however, runs across to* MME. PACE, *and greets her respectfully, as if she were the mistress.*]

STEPDAUGHTER [*Running across to her.*]   Here she is! Here she is!

FATHER [*Smiling broadly.*]   It's her! What did I tell you? Here she is!

PRODUCER [*Recovering from his shock, indignantly.*]   What sort of trick is this?

LEADING ACTOR [*Almost at the same time as the others.*]   What the hell is happening?

JUVENILE LEAD   Where on earth did they get that extra from?

YOUNG ACTRESS   They were keeping her hidden!

LEADING ACTRESS   It's a game, a conjuring trick!

FATHER   Wait a minute! Why do you want to spoil a miracle by being factual? Can't you see this is a miracle of reality, that is born, brought to life, lured here, reproduced, just for the sake of this scene, with more right to be alive here than you have? Perhaps it has more truth than you have yourselves. Which actress can improve on Mme. Pace there? Well? That is the real Mme. Pace. You must admit that the actress who plays her will be less true than she is herself—and there she is in person! Look! My daughter recognised her straight away and went to meet her. Now watch—just watch this scene.

> [*Hesitantly, the* PRODUCER *and the* ACTORS *move back to their original places on the stage.*
>
> *But the scene between the* STEPDAUGHTER *and* MME. PACE *had already begun while the* ACTORS *were protesting and the* FATHER *explaining: it is being played under their breaths, very quietly, very naturally, in a way that is obviously impossible on stage. So when the* ACTORS' *attention is recalled by the* FATHER *they turn and see that* MME. PACE *has just put her hand under the* STEPDAUGHTER's *chin to make her lift her head up: they also hear her speak in a way that is unintelligible to them. They watch and listen hard for a few moments, then they start to make fun of them.*]

PRODUCER   Well?

LEADING ACTOR   What's she saying?

LEADING ACTRESS   Can't hear a thing!

JUVENILE LEAD   Louder! Speak up!

STEPDAUGHTER [*Leaving* MME. PACE *who has an astonishing smile on her face, and coming down to the* ACTORS.]   Louder? What do you mean, "Louder"? What we're talking about you can't talk about loudly. I could shout about it a moment ago to embarrass him [*Pointing to the* FATHER.] to shame him and to get my own back on him! But it's a different matter for Mme. Pace. It would mean prison for her.

PRODUCER   What the hell are you on about? Here in the theatre you have to make yourself heard! Don't you see that? We can't hear you even from here, and we're on the stage with you! Imagine what it would be like with an audience out front! You need to make the scene go! And after all, you would speak normally to each other when you're alone, and you will be, because we shan't be here anyway. I mean we're only here because it's a rehearsal. So just imagine that there you are in the room at the back of the shop, and there's no one to hear you.

[*The* STEPDAUGHTER, *with a knowing smile, wags her finger and her head rather elegantly, as if to say no.*]

PRODUCER   Why not?

STEPDAUGHTER [*Mysteriously, whispering loudly.*]   Because there is some-one who will hear if she speaks normally. [*Pointing to* MME. PACE.]

PRODUCER [*Anxiously.*]   You're not going to make someone else appear are you?

[*The* ACTORS *get ready to dive off the stage again.*]

FATHER   No, no. She means me. I ought to be over there, waiting behind the door: and Mme. Pace knows I'm there, so excuse me will you: I'll go there now so that I shall be ready for my entrance.

[*He goes towards the back of the stage.*]

PRODUCER [*Stopping him.*]   No, no wait a minute! You must remember the stage conventions! Before you can go on to that part . . .

STEPDAUGHTER [*Interrupts him.*]   Oh yes, let's get on with that part. Now! Now! I'm dying to do that scene. If he wants to go through it now, I'm ready!

PRODUCER [*Shouting.*]   But before that we must have, clearly stated, the scene between you and her. [*Pointing to* MME. PACE.] Do you see?

STEPDAUGHTER   Oh God! She's only told me what you already know, that my mother's needlework is badly done again, the dress is spoilt and that I shall have to be patient if I want her to go on helping us out of our mess.

MME. PACE [*Coming forward, with a great air of importance.*]   Ah, yes, sir, for that I do not wish to make a profit, to make advantage.

PRODUCER [*Half frightened.*]   What? Does she really speak like that?

[*All the* ACTORS *burst out laughing.*]

STEPDAUGHTER [*Laughing too.*]   Yes, she speaks like that, half in Spanish, in the silliest way imaginable!

MME. PACE   Ah it is not good manners that you laugh at me when I make myself to speak, as I can, English, señor.

PRODUCER   No, no, you're right! Speak like that, please speak like that, madam. It'll be marvelous. Couldn't be better! It'll add a little touch of comedy to a rather crude situation. Speak like that! It'll be great!

STEPDAUGHTER   Great! Why not? When you hear a proposition made in that sort of accent, it'll almost seem like a joke, won't it? Perhaps you'll want to laugh when you hear that there's an "old señor"[2] who wants to "amuse himself with me"—isn't that right, Madame?

MME. PACE   Not so old . . . but not quite young, no? But if he is not to your taste . . . he is, how you say, discreet!

[*The* MOTHER *leaps up, to the astonishment and dismay of the* ACTORS

---

2. Old gentleman.

who had not been paying any attention to her, so that when she shouts out they are startled and then smilingly restrain her: however she has already snatched off MME. PACE's *wig and flung it on the floor.*]

MOTHER You witch! Witch! Murderess! Oh, my daughter!

STEPDAUGHTER [*Running across and taking hold of the* MOTHER.] No! No! Mother! Please!

FATHER [*Running across to her as well.*] Calm yourself, calm yourself! Come and sit down.

MOTHER Get her away from here!

STEPDAUGHTER [*To the* PRODUCER *who has also crossed to her.*] My mother can't bear to be in the same place with her.

FATHER [*Also speaking quietly to the* PRODUCER.] They can't possibly be in the same place! That's why she wasn't with us when we first came, do you see! If they meet, everything's given away from the very beginning.

PRODUCER It's not important, that's not important! This is only a first run-through at the moment! It's all useful stuff, even if it is confused. I'll sort it all out later. [*Turning to the* MOTHER *and taking her to sit down on her chair.*] Come on, my dear, take it easy; take it easy: come and sit down again.

STEPDAUGHTER Go on, Mme. Pace.

MME. PACE [*Offended.*] Oh no, thank-you! I no longer do nothing here with your mother present.

STEPDAUGHTER Get on with it, bring in this "old señor" who wants to "amuse himself with me"! [*Turning majestically to the others.*] You see, this next scene has got to be played out—we must do it now. [*To* MME. PACE.] Oh, you can go!

MME. PACE Ah, I go, I go—I go! Most probably! I go!

[*She leaves banging her wig back into place, glaring furiously at the* ACTORS *who applaud her exit, laughing loudly.*]

STEPDAUGHTER [*To the* FATHER.] Now you come on! No, you don't need to go off again! Come back! Pretend you've just come in! Look, I'm standing here with my eyes on the ground, modestly—well, come on, speak up! Use that special sort of voice, like somebody who has just come in. "Good afternoon, my dear."

PRODUCER [*Off the stage by now.*] Look here, who's the director here, you or me? [*To the* FATHER *who looks uncertain and bewildered.*] Go on, do as she says: go upstage—no, no don't bother to make an entrance. Then come down stage again.

[*The* FATHER *does as he is told, half mesmerised. He is very pale but already involved in the reality of his re-created life, smiles as he draws near the back of the stage, almost as if he genuinely is not aware of the drama that is about to sweep over him. The* ACTORS *are immediately intent on the scene that is beginning now.*]

THE SCENE

FATHER [*Coming forward with a new note in his voice.*] Good afternoon, my dear.

STEPDAUGHTER [*Her head down trying to hide her fright.*] Good afternoon.

FATHER [*Studying her a little under the brim of her hat which partly hides her face from him and seeing that she is very young, he exclaims to himself a little complacently and a little guardedly because of the danger of being compromised in a risky adventure.*]   Ah . . . but . . . tell me, this won't be the first time, will it? The first time you've been here?

STEPDAUGHTER   No, sir.

FATHER   You've been here before? [*And after the* STEPDAUGHTER *as nodded an answer.*] More than once? [*He waits for her reply: tries again to look at her under the brim of her hat: smiles: then says.*] Well then . . . it shouldn't be too . . . May I take off your hat?

STEPDAUGHTER [*Quickly, to stop him, unable to conceal her shudder of fear and disgust.*] No, don't! I'll do it!

[*She takes it off unsteadily.*

The MOTHER *watches the scene intently with the* SON *and the two smaller children who cling close to her all the time: they make a group on one side of the stage opposite the* ACTORS: *She follows the words and actions of the* FATHER *and the* STEPDAUGHTER *in this scene with a variety of expressions on her face—sadness, dismay, anxiety, horror: sometimes she turns her face away and sobs.*]

MOTHER   Oh God! Oh God!

FATHER [*He stops as if turned to stone by the sobbing: then he goes on in the same tone of voice.*]   Here, give it to me. I'll hang it up for you. [*He takes the hat in his hand.*] But such a pretty, dear little head like yours should have a much smarter hat than this! Would you like to help me choose one, then, from these hats of Madame's hanging up here? Would you?

YOUNG ACTRESS [*Interrupting.*]   Be careful! Those are our hats!

PRODUCER [*Quickly and angrily.*]   For God's sake, shut up! Don't try to be funny! We're rehearsing! [*Turns back to the* STEPDAUGHTER.] Please go on, will you, from where you were interrupted.

STEPDAUGHTER [*Going on.*]   No, thank you, sir.

FATHER   Oh, don't say no to me please! Say you'll have one—to please me. Isn't this a pretty one—look! And then it will please Madame too, you know. She's put them out here on purpose, of course.

STEPDAUGHTER   No, look, I could never wear it.

FATHER   Are you thinking of what they would say at home when you went in wearing a new hat? Goodness me! Don't you know what to do? Shall I tell you what to say at home?

STEPDAUGHTER [*Furiously, nearly exploding.*]   That's not why! I couldn't wear it because . . . as you can see: you should have noticed it before. [*Indicating her black dress.*]

FATHER   You're in mourning! Oh, forgive me. You're right, I see that now. Please forgive me. Believe me, I'm really very sorry.

STEPDAUGHTER [*Gathering all her strength and making herself overcome her contempt and revulsion.*]   That's enough. Don't go on, that's enough. I ought to be thanking you and not letting you blame yourself and get upset. Don't think any more about what I told you, please. And I should do the same. [*Forcing herself to smile and adding.*] I should try to forget that I'm dressed like this.

PRODUCER [*Interrupting, turning to the* PROMPTER *in the box and jumping up on the stage again.*]   Hold it, hold it! Don't put that last line down, leave it out. [*Turning to the* FATHER *and the* STEPDAUGHTER.] It's going well! It's going well! [*Then to the* FATHER *alone.*] Then we'll put in there the bit that we talked about. [*To the* ACTORS.] That scene with the hats is good, isn't it?

STEPDAUGHTER   But the best bit is coming now! Why can't we get on with it?

PRODUCER   Just be patient, wait a minute. [*Turning and moving across to the* ACTORS.] Of course, it'll all have to be made a lot more light-hearted.

LEADING ACTOR   We shall have to play it a lot quicker, I think.

LEADING ACTRESS   Of course: there's nothing particularly difficult in it. [*To the* LEADING ACTOR.] Shall we run through it now?

LEADING ACTOR   Yes right . . . Shall we take it from my entrance? [*He goes to his position behind the door upstage.*]

PRODUCER [*To the* LEADING ACTRESS.]   Now then, listen, imagine the scene between you and Mme. Pace is finished. I'll write it up myself properly later on. You ought to be over here I think—[*She goes the opposite way.*] Where are you going now?

LEADING ACTRESS   Just a minute, I want to get my hat—[*She crosses to take her hat from the stand.*]

PRODUCER   Right, good, ready now? You are standing here with your head down.

STEPDAUGHTER [*Very amused.*]   But she's not dressed in black!

LEADING ACTRESS   Oh, but I shall be, and I'll look a lot better than you do, darling.

PRODUCER [*To the* STEPDAUGHTER.]   Shut up, will you! Go over there and watch! You might learn something! [*Clapping his hands.*] Right! Come on! Quiet please! Take it from his entrance.

[*He climbs off stage so that he can see better. The door opens at the back of the set and the* LEADING ACTOR *enters with the lively, knowing air of an ageing roué.*[3] *The playing of the following scene by the* ACTORS *must seem from the very beginning to be something quite different from the earlier scene, but without having the faintest air of parody in it.*

Naturally the STEPDAUGHTER *and the* FATHER *unable to see themselves in the* LEADING ACTOR *and* LEADING ACTRESS, *hearing their words said by them, express their reactions in different ways, by gestures, or smiles or obvious protests so that we are aware of their suffering, their astonishment, their disbelief.*

The PROMPTER's *voice is heard clearly between every line in the scene, telling the* ACTORS *what to say next.*]

LEADING ACTOR   Good afternoon, my dear.

FATHER [*Immediately, unable to restrain himself.*]   Oh, no!

[*The* STEPDAUGHTER, *watching the* LEADING ACTOR *enter this way, bursts into laughter.*]

PRODUCER [*Furious.*]   Shut up, for God's sake! And don't you dare laugh like that! We're never going to get anywhere at this rate.

STEPDAUGHTER [*Coming to the front.*]   I'm sorry, I can't help it! The lady stands exactly where you told her to stand and she never moved. But if it were me and I heard someone say good afternoon to me in that way and with a voice like that I should burst out laughing—so I did.

---

3. Dissipated lover.

FATHER [*Coming down a little too.*]   Yes, she's right, the whole manner, the voice . . .

PRODUCER   To hell with the manner and the voice! Get out of the way, will you, and let me watch the rehearsal!

LEADING ACTOR [*Coming down stage.*]   If I have to play an old man who has come to a knocking shop—

PRODUCER   Take no notice, ignore them. Go on please! It's going well, it's going well! [*He waits for the* ACTOR *to begin again.*] Right, again!

LEADING ACTOR   Good afternoon, my dear.

LEADING ACTRESS   Good afternoon.

LEADING ACTOR [*Copying the gestures of the* FATHER, *looking under the brim of the hat, but expressing distinctly the two emotions, first, complacent satisfaction and then anxiety.*]   Ah! But tell me . . . this won't be the first time I hope.

FATHER [*Instinctively correcting him.*]   Not "I hope"—"will it," "will it."

PRODUCER   Say "will it"—and it's a question.

LEADING ACTOR [*Glaring at the* PROMPTER.]   I distinctly heard him say "I hope."

PRODUCER   So what? It's all the same, "I hope" or "isn't it." It doesn't make any difference. Carry on, carry on. But perhaps it should still be a little bit lighter; I'll show you—watch me! [*He climbs up on the stage again, and going back to the entrance, he does it himself.*] Good afternoon, my dear.

LEADING ACTRESS   Good afternoon.

PRODUCER   Ah, tell me . . .[*He turns to the* LEADING ACTOR *to make sure that he has seen the way he has demonstrated of looking under the brim of the hat.*] You see—surprise . . . anxiety and self-satisfaction. [*Then, starting again, he turns to the* LEADING ACTRESS.] This won't be the first time, will it? The first time you've been here? [*Again turns to the* LEADING ACTOR *questioningly.*] Right? [*To the* LEADING ACTRESS.] And then she says, "No, sir." [*Again to* LEADING ACTOR.] See what I mean? More subtlety. [*And he climbs off the stage.*]

LEADING ACTRESS   No, sir.

LEADING ACTOR   You've been here before? More than once?

PRODUCER   No, no, no! Wait for it, wait for it. Let her answer first. "You've been here before?"

[*The* LEADING ACTRESS *lifts her head a little, her eyes closed in pain and disgust, and when the* PRODUCER *says "Now" she nods her head twice.*]

STEPDAUGHTER [*Involuntarily.*]   Oh, my God! [*And she immediately claps her hand over her mouth to stifle her laughter.*]

PRODUCER   What now?

STEPDAUGHTER [*Quickly.*]   Nothing, nothing!

PRODUCER [*To* LEADING ACTOR.]   Come on, then, now it's you.

LEADING ACTOR   More than once? Well then, it shouldn't be too . . . May I take off your hat?

[*The* LEADING ACTOR *says this last line in such a way and adds to it such a gesture that the* STEPDAUGHTER, *even with her hand over her mouth trying to stop herself laughing, can't prevent a noisy burst of laughter.*]

LEADING ACTRESS [*Indignantly turning.*]   I'm not staying any longer to be laughed at by that woman!

LEADING ACTOR   Nor am I! That's the end—no more!

PRODUCER [*To* STEPDAUGHTER, *shouting.*]   Once and for all, will you shut up! Shut up!

STEPDAUGHTER   Yes, I'm sorry . . . I'm sorry.

PRODUCER   You're an ill-mannered little bitch! That's what you are! And you've gone too far this time!

FATHER [*Trying to interrupt.*]   Yes, you're right, she went too far, but please forgive her . . .

PRODUCER [*Jumping on the stage.*]   Why should I forgive her? Her behaviour is intolerable!

FATHER   Yes, it is, but the scene made such a peculiar impact on us . . .

PRODUCER   Peculiar? What do you mean peculiar? Why peculiar?

FATHER   I'm full of admiration for your actors, for this gentleman [*To the* LEADING ACTOR.] and this lady. [*To the* LEADING ACTRESS.] But, you see, well . . . they're not us!

PRODUCER   Right! They're not! They're actors!

FATHER   That's just the point—they're actors. And they are acting our parts very well, both of them. But that's what's different. However much they want to be the same as us, they're not.

PRODUCER   But why aren't they? What is it now?

FATHER   It's something to do with . . . being themselves, I suppose, not being us.

PRODUCER   Well we can't do anything about that! I've told you already. You can't play the parts yourselves.

FATHER   Yes, I know, I know . . .

PRODUCER   Right then. That's enough of that. [*Turning back to the* ACTORS.] We'll rehearse this later on our own, as we usually do. It's always a bad idea to have rehearsals with authors there! They're never satisfied.[*Turns back to the* FATHER *and the* STEPDAUGHTER.] Come on, let's get on with it; and let's see if it's possible to do it without laughing.

STEPDAUGHTER   I won't laugh any more, I won't really. My best bit's coming up now, you wait and see!

PRODUCER   Right: when you say "Don't think any more about what I told you, please. And I should do the same." [*Turning to the* FATHER.] Then you come in immediately with the line "I understand, ah yes, I understand" and then you ask . . .

STEPDAUGHTER [*Interrupting.*]   Ask what? What does he ask?

PRODUCER   Why you're in mourning.

STEPDAUGHTER   No! No! That's not right! Look: when I said that I should try not to think abut the way I was dressed, do you know what he said? "Well then, let's take it off, we'll take it off at once, shall we, your little black dress."

PRODUCER   That's great! That'll be wonderful! That'll bring the house down!

STEPDAUGHTER   But it's the truth!

PRODUCER   The truth! Do me a favour will you? This is the theatre you know! Truth's all very well up to a point but . . .

STEPDAUGHTER   What do you want to do then?

PRODUCER   You'll see! You'll see! Leave it all to me.

STEPDAUGHTER   No. No I won't. I know what you want to do! Out of my feeling of revulsion, out of all the vile and sordid reasons why I am what I am, you want to make a sugary little sentimental romance. You want him to ask me why I'm in mourning and you want me to reply with the tears running down my face that it is only two months since my father died. No. No. I won't have it! He must say to me what he really did say. "Well then, let's take it off, we'll take it off at once, shall we, your little black dress." And I, with my heart still grieving for my father's death only two months before, I went behind there, do you see? Behind that screen and with my fingers trembling with shame and loathing I took off the dress, unfastened my bra . . .

PRODUCER [*His head in his hands.*]   For God's sake! What are you saying!

STEPDAUGHTER [*Shouting excitedly.*]   The truth! I'm telling you the truth!

PRODUCER   All right then, Now listen to me. I'm not denying it's the truth. Right. And believe me I understand your horror, but you must see that we can't really put a scene like that on the stage.

STEPDAUGHTER   You can't? Then thanks very much. I'm not stopping here.

PRODUCER   No, listen . . .

STEPDAUGHTER   No, I'm going. I'm not stopping. The pair of you have worked it all out together, haven't you, what to put in the scene. Well, thank you very much! I understand everything now! He wants to get to the scene where he can talk about his spiritual torments but I want to show you my drama! Mine!

PRODUCER [*Shaking with anger.*]   Now we're getting to the real truth of it, aren't we? Your drama—yours! But it's not only yours, you know. It's drama for the other people as well! For him [*Pointing to the* FATHER.] and for your mother! You can't have one character coming on like you're doing, trampling over the others, taking over the play. Everything needs to be balanced and in harmony so that we can show what has to be shown! I know perfectly well that we've all got a life inside us and that we all want to parade it in front of other people. But that's the difficulty, how to present only the bits that are necessary in relation to the other characters: and in the small amount we show, to hint at all the rest of the inner life of the character! I agree, it would be so much simpler, if each character, in a soliloquy or in a lecture could pour out to the audience what's bubbling away inside him. But that's not the way we work. [*In an indulgent, placating tone.*] You must restrain yourself, you see. And believe me, it's in your own interests: because you could so easily make a bad impression, with all this uncontrollable anger, this disgust and exasperation. That seems a bit odd, if you don't mind my saying so, when you've admitted that you'd been with other men at Mme. Pace's and more than once.

STEPDAUGHTER   I suppose that's true. But you know, all the other men were all him as far as I was concerned.

PRODUCER [*Not understanding.*]   Uum—? What? What are you talking about?

STEPDAUGHTER   If someone falls into evil ways, isn't the responsibility for all the evil which follows to be laid at the door of the person who caused the first mistake? And in my case, it's him, from before I was even born. Look at him: see if it isn't true.

PRODUCER   Right then! What about the weight of remorse he's carrying?

Isn't that important? Then, give him the chance to show it to us.

STEPDAUGHTER But how? How on earth can he show all his long-suffering remorse, all his moral torments as he calls them, if you don't let him show his horror when he finds me in his arms one fine day, after he had asked me to take my dress off, a black dress for my father who had just died: and he finds that I'm the child he used to go and watch as she came out of school, me, a woman now, and a woman he could buy.[*She says these last words in a voice trembling with emotion.*]

[*The* MOTHER, *hearing her say this, is overcome and at first gives way to stifled sobs: but then she bursts out into uncontrollable crying. Everyone is deeply moved. There is a long pause.*]

STEPDAUGHTER [*As soon as the* MOTHER *has quietened herself she goes on, firmly and thoughtfully.*] At the moment we are here on our own and the public doesn't know about us. But tomorrow you will present us and our story in whatever way you choose, I suppose. But wouldn't you like to see the real drama? Wouldn't you like to see it explode into life, as it really did?

PRODUCER Of course, nothing I'd like better, then I can use as much of it as possible.

STEPDAUGHTER Then persuade my mother to leave.

MOTHER [*Rising and her quiet weeping changing to a loud cry.*] No! No! Don't let her! Don't let her do it!

PRODUCER But they're only doing it for me to watch—only for me, do you see?

MOTHER I can't bear it, I can't bear it!

PRODUCER But if it's already happened, I can't see what's the objection.

MOTHER No! It's happening now, as well: it's happening all the time. I'm not acting my suffering! Can't you understand that? I'm alive and here now but I can never forget that terrible moment of agony, that repeats itself endlessly and vividly in my mind. And these two little children here, you've never heard them speak have you? That's because they don't speak any more, not now. They just cling to me all the time: they help to keep my grief alive, but they don't really exist for themselves any more, not for themselves. And she [*Indicating the* STEPDAUGHTER.] . . . she has gone away, left me completely, she's lost to me, lost . . . you see her here for one reason only: to keep perpetually before me, always real, the anguish and the torment I've suffered on her account.

FATHER The eternal moment, as I told you, sir. She is here [*Indicating the* STEPDAUGHTER.] to keep me too in that moment, trapped for all eternity, chained and suspended in that one fleeting shameful moment of my life. She can't give up her role and you cannot rescue me from it.

PRODUCER But I'm not saying that we won't present that bit. Not at all! It will be the climax of the first act, when she [*He points to the* MOTHER.] surprises you.

FATHER That's right, because that is the moment when I am sentenced: all our suffering should reach a climax in her cry. [*Again indicating the* MOTHER.]

STEPDAUGHTER I can still hear it ringing in my ears! It was that cry that sent me mad! You can have me played just as you like: it doesn't matter! Dressed, too, if you want, so long as I can have at least an arm—only an arm—bare, because, you see, as I was standing like this [*She moves across* to the FATHER *and leans her head on his chest.*] with my head like this and my arms round his neck, I saw a vein, here in my arm, throbbing: and then it was almost as if that throbbing vein filled me with a shivering fear, and I shut my eyes tightly like this, like this and buried my head in his chest. [*Turning to the* MOTHER.] Scream, Mummy, scream. [*She buries her head in the* FATHER's *chest, and with her shoulders raised as if to try not to hear the scream, she speaks with a voice tense with suffering.*] Scream, as you screamed then!

MOTHER [*Coming forward to pull them apart.*]   No! She's my daughter! My daughter! [*Tearing her from him.*] You brute, you animal, she's my daughter! Can't you see she's my daughter?

PRODUCER [*Retreating as far as the footlights while the* ACTORS *are full of dismay.*]   Marvellous! Yes, that's great! And then curtain, curtain!

FATHER [*Running downstage to him, excitedly.*]   That's it, that's it! Because it really was like that!

PRODUCER [*Full of admiration and enthusiasm.*]   Yes, yes, that's got to be the curtain line! Curtain! Curtain!

[*At the repeated calls of the* PRODUCER, *the* STAGE MANAGER *lowers the curtain, leaving on the apron in front, the* PRODUCER *and the* FATHER.]

PRODUCER [*Looking up to heaven with his arms raised.*]   The idiots! I didn't mean now! The bloody idiots—dropping it in on us like that! [*To the* FATHER, *and lifting up a corner of the curtain.*] That's marvellous! Really marvellous! A terrific effect! We'll end the act like that! It's the best tag line I've heard for ages. What a First Act ending! I couldn't have done better if I'd written it myself!

[*They go through the curtain together.*]

Act Three

When the curtain goes up we see that the STAGE MANAGER *and* STAGE HANDS *have struck the first scene and have set another, a small garden fountain.*

From one side of the stage the ACTORS *come on and from the other the* CHARACTERS. *The* PRODUCER *is standing in the middle of the stage with his hand over his mouth, thinking.*

PRODUCER [*After a short pause, shrugging his shoulders.*]   Well, then: let's get on to the second act! Leave it all to me, and everything will work out properly.

STEPDAUGHTER   This is where we go to live at his house [*Pointing to the* FATHER.] In spite of the objections of him over there. [*Pointing to the* SON.]

PRODUCER [*Getting impatient.*]   All right, all right! But leave it all to me, will you?

STEPDAUGHTER   Provided that you make it clear that he objected!

MOTHER [*From the corner, shaking her head.*]   That doesn't matter. The worse it was for us, the more he suffered from remorse.

PRODUCER [*Impatiently.*]   I know, I know! I'll take it all into account. Don't worry!

MOTHER [*Pleading.*]   To set my mind at rest, sir, please do make sure it's clear that I tried all I could—

STEPDAUGHTER [*Interrupting her scornfully and going on.*]   —to pacify me, to persuade me that this despicable creature wasn't worth making trouble about! [*To the* PRODUCER.] Go on, set her mind at rest, because it's true, she tried very hard. I'm having a whale of a time now! You can see, can't you, that the meeker she was and the more she tried to worm her way into his heart, the more lofty and distant he became! How's that for a dramatic situation!

PRODUCER   Do you think that we can actually begin the Second Act?

STEPDAUGHTER   I won't say another word! But you'll see that it won't be possible to play everything in the garden, like you want to do.

PRODUCER   Why not?

STEPDAUGHTER [*Pointing to the* SON.]   Because to start with, he stays shut up in his room in the house all the time! And then all the scenes for this poor little devil of a boy happen in the house. I've told you once.

PRODUCER   Yes, I know that! But on the other hand we can't put up a notice to tell the audience where the scene is taking place, or change the set three or four times in each Act.

LEADING ACTOR   That's what they used to do in the good old days.

PRODUCER   Yes, when the audience was about as bright as that little girl over there!

LEADING ACTRESS   And it makes it easier to create an illusion.

FATHER [*Leaping up.*]   An illusion? For pity's sake don't talk about illusions! Don't use that word, it's especially hurtful to us!

PRODUCER [*Astonished.*]   And why, for God's sake?

FATHER   It's so hurtful, so cruel! You ought to have realised that!

PRODUCER   What else should we call it? That's what we do here—create an illusion for the audience . . .

LEADING ACTOR   With our performance . . .

PRODUCER   A perfect illusion of reality!

FATHER   Yes, I know that, I understand. But on the other hand, perhaps you don't understand us yet. I'm sorry! But you see, for you and for your actors what goes on here on the stage is, quite rightly, well, it's only a game.

LEADING ACTRESS [*Interrupting indignantly.*]   A game! How dare you! We're not children! What happens here is serious!

FATHER   I'm not saying that it isn't serious. And I mean, really, not just a game but an art, that tries, as you've just said, to create the perfect illusion of reality.

PRODUCER   That's right!

FATHER   Now try to imagine that we, as you see us here, [*He indicates himself and the other* CHARACTERS.] that we have no other reality outside this illusion.

PRODUCER [*Astonished and looking at the* ACTORS *with the same sense of bewilderment as they feel themselves.*]   What the hell are you talking about now?

FATHER [*After a short pause as he looks at them, with a faint smile.*]   Isn't it obvious? What other reality is there for us? What for you is an illusion you create, for us is our only reality. [*Brief pause. He moves towards the* PRODUCER *and goes on.*] But it's not only true for us, it's true for others as well, you know. Just think about it. [*He looks intently into the* PRODUCER's *eyes.*] Do you really know who you are? [*He stands pointing at the* PRODUCER.]

PRODUCER [*A little disturbed but with a half smile.*]   What? Who I am? I am me!

FATHER   What if I told you that that wasn't true: what if I told you that you were me?

PRODUCER   I would tell you that you were mad!

[*The* ACTORS *laugh.*]

FATHER   That's right, laugh! Because everything here is a game! [*To the* PRODUCER.] And yet you object when I say that it is only for a game that the gentleman there [*Pointing to the* LEADING ACTOR.] who is "himself" has to be "me," who, on the contrary, am "myself." You see, I've caught you in a trap.

[*The* ACTORS *start to laugh.*]

PRODUCER   Not again! We've heard all about this a little while ago.

FATHER   No, no. I didn't really want to talk about this. I'd like you to forget about your game. [*Looking at the* LEADING ACTRESS *as if to anticipate what she will say.*] I'm sorry—your artistry! Your art!—that you usually pursue here with your actors; and I am going to ask you again in all seriousness, who are you?

PRODUCER [*Turning with a mixture of amazement and annoyance, to the* ACTORS.]   Of all the bloody nerve! A fellow who claims he is only a character comes and asks me who I am!

FATHER [*With dignity but without annoyance.*]   A character, my dear sir, can always ask a man who he is, because a character really has a life of his own, a life full of his own specific qualities, and because of these he is always "someone." While a man—I'm not speaking about you personally, of course, but man in general—well, he can be an absolute "nobody."

PRODUCER   All right, all right! Well, since you've asked me, I'm the Director, the Producer—I'm in charge! Do you understand?

FATHER [*Half smiling, but gently and politely.*]   I'm only asking to try to find out if you really see yourself now in the same way that you saw yourself, for instance, once upon a time in the past, with all the illusions you had then, with everything inside and outside yourself as it seemed then—and not only seemed, but really was! Well then, look back on those illusions, those ideas that you don't have any more, on all those things that no longer seem the same to you. Don't you feel that not only this stage is falling away from under your feet but so is the earth itself, and that all these realities of today are going to seem tomorrow as if they had been an illusion?

PRODUCER   So? What does that prove?

FATHER   Oh, nothing much. I only want to make you see that if we [*Pointing to himself and the other* CHARACTERS.] have no other reality outside our own illusion, perhaps you ought to distrust your own sense of reality: because whatever is a reality today, whatever you touch and believe in and that seems real for you today, is going to be—like the reality of yesterday—an illusion tomorrow.

PRODUCER [*Deciding to make fun of him.*]   Very good! So now you're saying that you as well as this play you're going to show me here, are more real than I am?

FATHER [*Very seriously.*]   There's no doubt about that at all.

PRODUCER   Is that so?

FATHER   I thought you'd realised that from the beginning.

PRODUCER   More real than I am?

FATHER   If your reality can change between today and tomorrow—

PRODUCER   But everybody knows that it can change, don't they? It's always changing! Just like everybody else's!

FATHER [*Crying out.*]   But ours doesn't change! Do you see? That's the difference! Ours doesn't change, it can't change, it can never be different, never, because it is already determined, like this, for ever, that's what's so terrible! We are an eternal reality. That should make you shudder to come near us.

PRODUCER [*Jumping up, suddenly struck by an idea, and standing directly in front of the* FATHER.]   Then I should like to know when anyone saw a character step out of his part and make a speech like you've done, proposing things, explaining things. Tell me when, will you? I've never seen it before.

FATHER   You've never seen it because an author usually hides all the difficulties of creating. When the characters are alive, really alive and standing in front of their author, he has only to follow their words, the actions that they suggest to him: and he must want them to be what they want to be: and it's his bad luck if he doesn't do what they want! When a character is born he immediately assumes such an independence even of his own author that everyone can imagine him in scores of situations that his author hadn't even thought of putting him in, and he sometimes acquires a meaning that his author never dreamed of giving him.

PRODUCER   Of course I know all that.

FATHER   Well, then. Why are you surprised by us? Imagine what a disaster it is for a character to be born in the imagination of an author who then refuses to give him life in a written script. Tell me if a character, left like this, suspended, created but without a final life, isn't right to do what we are doing now, here in front of you. We spent such a long time, such a very long time, believe me, urging our author, persuading him, first me, then her, [*Pointing to the* STEPDAUGHTER.] then this poor Mother . . .

STEPDAUGHTER [*Coming down the stage as if in a dream.*]   It's true, I would go, would go and tempt him, time after time, in his gloomy study just as it was growing dark, when he was sitting quietly in an armchair not even bothering to switch a light on but leaving the shadows to fill the room: the shadows were swarming with us, we had come to tempt him. [*As if she could see herself there in the study and is annoyed by the presence of the* ACTORS.] Go away will you! Leave us alone! Mother there, with that son of hers—me with the little girl—that poor little kid always on his own—and then me with him [*Pointing to the* FATHER.] and then at last, just me, on my own, all on my own, in the shadows. [*She turns quickly as if she wants to cling on to the vision she has of herself, in the shadows.*] Ah, what scenes, what scenes we suggested to him! What a life I could have had! I tempted him more than the others!

FATHER   Oh yes, you did! And it was probably all your fault that he did nothing about it! You were so insistent, you made too many demands.

STEPDAUGHTER   But he wanted me to be like that! [*She comes closer to the* PRODUCER *to speak to him in confidence.*] I think it's more likely that he felt discouraged about the theatre and even despised it because the public only wants to see . . .

PRODUCER   Let's go on, for God's sake, let's go on. Come to the point will you?

STEPDAUGHTER   I'm sorry, but if you ask me, we've got too much happening already, just with our entry into his house. [*Pointing to the* FATHER.] You said that we couldn't put up a notice or change the set every five minutes.

PRODUCER   Right! Of course we can't! We must combine things, group them together in one continuous flowing action: not the way you've been wanting, first of all seeing your little brother come home from school and wander about the house like a lost soul, hiding behind the doors and brooding on some plan or other that would—what did you say it would do?

STEPDAUGHTER   Wither him . . . shrivel him up completely.

PRODUCER   That's good! That's a good expression. And then you "can see it there in his eyes, getting stronger all the time"—isn't that what you said?

STEPDAUGHTER   Yes, that's right. Look at him! [*Pointing to him as he stands next to his* MOTHER.]

PRODUCER   Yes, great! And then, at the same time, you want to show the little girl playing in the garden, all innocence. One in the house and the other in the garden—we can't do it, don't you see that?

STEPDAUGHTER   Yes, playing in the sun, so happy! It's the only pleasure I have left, her happiness, her delight in playing in the garden: away from the misery, the squalor of that sordid flat where all four of us slept and where she slept with me—with me! Just think of it! My vile, contaminated body close to hers, with her little arms wrapped tightly round my neck, so lovingly, so innocently. In the garden, wherever she saw me, she would run and take my hand. She never wanted to show me the big flowers, she would run about looking for the "little weeny" ones, so that she could show them to me; she was so happy, so thrilled! [*As she says this, tortured by the memory, she breaks out into a long desperate cry, dropping her head on her arms that rest on a little table. Everybody is very affected by her. The* PRODUCER *comes to her almost paternally and speaks to her in a soothing voice.*]

PRODUCER   We'll have the garden scene, we'll have it, don't worry: and you'll see, you'll be very pleased with what we do! We'll play all the scenes in the garden! [*He calls out to a* STAGE HAND *by name.*] Hey . . . , let down a few bits of tree, will you? A couple of cypresses will do, in front of the fountain. [*Someone drops in the two cypresses and a* STAGE HAND *secures them with a couple of braces and weights.*]

PRODUCER   [*To the* STEPDAUGHTER.]   That'll do for now, won't it? It'll just give us an idea. [*Calling out to a* STAGE HAND *by name again.*] Hey, . . . give me something for the sky will you?

STAGE HAND   What's that?

PRODUCER   Something for the sky! A small cloth to come in behind the fountain. [*A white cloth is dropped from the flies.*] Not white! I asked for a sky! Never mind: leave it! I'll do something with it. [*Calling out.*] Hey lights! Kill everything will you? Give me a bit of moonlight—the blues in the batten and a blue spot on the cloth . . .[*They do.*] That's it! That'll do! [*Now on the scene there is the light he asked for, a mysterious blue light that makes the* ACTORS *speak and move as if in the garden in the evening under a moon. To the* STEPDAUGHTER.] Look here now: the little boy can come out here in the garden and hide among the trees instead of hiding behind the doors in the house. But it's going to be difficult to find a little girl to play the scene with you where she shows you the flowers. [*Turning to the* LITTLE BOY.] Come on, come on, son, come across here. Let's see what it'll look like. [*But the (*LITTLE*) BOY doesn't move.*] Come on will you, come on. [*Then he pulls him forward and tries to make him hold his head up, but every time it falls down again on his chest.*] There's something very odd about this lad . . . What's wrong with him? My God, he'll have to say something sometime! [*He comes over to him again, puts his hand on his shoulder and pushes him between the trees.*] Come a bit nearer: let's have a look. Can you hide a bit more? That's it. Now pop your head out and look round. [*He moves away to look at the effect and as the* BOY *does what he has been told to do, the* ACTORS *watch impressed and a little disturbed.*] Ahh, that's good, very good . . .[*He turns to the* STEPDAUGHTER.] How about having the little girl, surprised to see him there, run across. Wouldn't that make him say something?

STEPDAUGHTER [*Getting up.*]   It's no use hoping he'll speak, not as long as that creature's there. [*Pointing to the* SON.] You'll have to get him out of the way first.

SON [*Moving determinedly to one of the sets of steps leading off the stage.*] With pleasure! I'll go now! Nothing will please me better!

PRODUCER [*Stopping him immediately.*]   Hey, no! Where are you going? Hang on!

>[*The* MOTHER *gets up, anxious at the idea that he is really going and instinctively raising her arms as if to hold him back, but without moving from where she is.*]

SON [*At the footlights, to the* PRODUCER *who is restraining him there.*] There's no reason why I should be here! Let me go will you? Let me go!

PRODUCER   What do you mean there's no reason for you to be here?

STEPDAUGHTER [*Calmly, ironically.*]   Don't bother to stop him. He won't go!

FATHER   You have to play that terrible scene in the garden with your mother.

SON [*Quickly, angry and determined.*]   I'm not going to play anything! I've said that all along! [*To the* PRODUCER.] Let me go will you?

STEPDAUGHTER [*Crossing to the* PRODUCER.]   It's all right. Let him go. [*She moves the* PRODUCER's *hand from the* SON. *Then she turns to the* SON *and says.*] Well, go on then! Off you go!

>[*The* SON *stays near the steps but as if pulled by some strange force he is quite unable to go down them: then to the astonishment and even the dismay of the* ACTORS, *he moves along the front of the stage towards the other set of steps down into the auditorium: but having got there, he again stays near and doesn't actually go down them. The* STEPDAUGHTER *who has watched him scornfully but very intently, bursts into laughter.*]

STEPDAUGHTER   He can't, you see? He can't! He's got to stay here! He must. He's chained to us for ever! No, I'm the one who goes, when what must happen does happen, and I run away, because I hate him, because I can't bear the sight of him any longer. Do you think it's possible for him to run away? He has to stay here with that wonderful father of his and his mother there. She doesn't think she has any other son but him. [*She turns to the* MOTHER.] Come on, come on, Mummy, come on! [*Turning back to the* PRODUCER *to point her out to him.*] Look, she's going to try to stop him . . .[*To the* MOTHER, *half compelling her, as if by some magic power.*] Come on, come on. [*Then to the* PRODUCER *again.*] Imagine how she must feel at showing her affection for him in front of your actors! But her longing to be near him is so strong that—look! She's going to go through that scene with him again! [*The* MOTHER *has now actually come close to the* SON *as the* STEPDAUGHTER *says the last line: she gestures to show that she agrees to go on.*]

SON [*Quickly.*]   But I'm not! I'm not! If I can't get away then I suppose I shall have to stay here; but I repeat that I will not have any part in it.

FATHER [*To the* PRODUCER, *excitedly.*]   You must make him!

SON   Nobody's going to make me do anything!

FATHER   I'll make you!

STEPDAUGHTER   Wait! Just a minute! Before that, the little girl has to go to the fountain. [*She turns to take the* LITTLE GIRL, *drops on her knees in front of her and takes her face between her hands.*] My poor little darling, those beautiful eyes, they look so bewildered. You're wondering where you are, aren't you? Well, we're on a stage, my darling! What's a stage? Well, it's a place where you pretend to be serious. They put on plays here. And now we're going to put on a play. Seriously! Oh, yes! Even you . . .[*She hugs her tightly and rocks her gently for a moment.*] Oh, my little one, my little darling, what a terrible play it is for you! What horrible things have been planned for you! The garden, the fountain . . . Oh, yes, it's only a pretend fountain, that's right. That's part of the game, my pretty darling: everything is pretends here. Perhaps you'll like a pretends fountain better than a real one: you can play here then. But it's only a game for the others; not for you, I'm afraid, it's real for you, my darling, and your game is in a real fountain, a big beautiful green fountain with bamboos casting shadows, looking at your own reflection, with lots of baby ducks paddling about, shattering the reflections. You want to stroke one! [*With a scream that electrifies and terrifies everybody.*] No, Rosetta, no! Your mummy isn't watching you, she's over there with that selfish bastard! Oh, God, I feel as if all the devils in hell were tearing me apart inside . . . And you . . .[*Leaving the* LITTLE GIRL *and turning to the* LITTLE BOY *in the usual way.*] What are you doing here, hanging about like a beggar? It'll be your fault too, if that little girl drowns; you're always like this, as if I wasn't paying the price for getting all of you into this house. [*Shaking his arm to make him take his hand out of his pocket.*] What have you got there? What are you hiding? Take it out, take your hand out! [*She drags his hand out of his pocket and to everyone's horror he is holding a revolver. She looks at him for a moment, almost with satisfaction: then she says, grimly.*] Where on earth did you get that? [*The* (LITTLE) BOY, *looking frightened, with his eyes wide and empty, doesn't answer.*] You idiot, if I'd been you, instead of killing myself, I'd have killed one of those two: either or both, the father and the son. [*She pushes him toward the cypress trees where he then stands watching: then she takes the* LITTLE GIRL *and helps her to climb in to the fountain, making her lie so that she is hidden: after that she kneels down and puts her head and arms on the rim of the fountain.*]

PRODUCER   That's good! It's good! [*Turning to the* STEPDAUGHTER.] And at the same time . . .

SON [*Scornfully.*]   What do you mean, at the same time? There was nothing at the same time! There wasn't any scene between her and me. [*Pointing to the* MOTHER.] She'll tell you the same thing herself, she'll tell you what happened.

> [*The* SECOND ACTRESS *and the* JUVENILE LEAD *have left the group of* ACTORS *and have come to stand nearer the* MOTHER *and the* SON *as if to study them so as to play their parts.*]

MOTHER   Yes, it's true. I'd gone to his room . . .

SON   Room, do you hear? Not the garden!

PRODUCER   It's not important! We've got to reorganize the events anyway. I've told you that already.

SON [*Glaring at the* JUVENILE LEAD *and the* SECOND ACTRESS.]   What do you want?

JUVENILE LEAD   Nothing. I'm just watching.

SON [*Turning to the* SECOND ACTRESS]   You as well! Getting ready to play her part are you? [*Pointing to the* MOTHER.]

PRODUCER   That's it. And I think you should be grateful—they're paying you a lot of attention.

SON   Oh, yes, thank you! But haven't you realised yet that you'll never be able to do this play? There's nothing of us inside you and you actors are only looking at us from the outside. Do you think we could go on living with a mirror held up in front of us that didn't only freeze our reflection for ever, but froze us in a reflection that laughed back at us with an expression that we didn't even recognise as our own?

FATHER   That's right! That's right!

PRODUCER [*To* JUVENILE LEAD *and* SECOND ACTRESS.]   Okay. Go back to the others.

SON   It's quite useless. I'm not prepared to do anything.

PRODUCER   Oh, shut up, will you, and let me listen to your mother. [*To the* MOTHER.] Well, you'd gone to his room, you said.

MOTHER   Yes, to his room. I couldn't bear it any longer. I wanted to empty my heart to him, tell him about all the agony that was crushing me. But as soon as he saw me come in . . .

SON   Nothing happened. I got away! I wasn't going to get involved. I never have been involved. Do you understand?

MOTHER   It's true! That's right!

PRODUCER   But we must make up the scene between you, then. It's vital!

MOTHER   I'm ready to do it! If only I had the chance to talk to him for a moment, to pour out all my troubles to him.

FATHER [*Going to the* SON *and speaking violently.*]   You'll do it! For your Mother! For your Mother!

SON [*More than ever determined.*]   I'm doing nothing!

FATHER [*Taking hold of his coat collar and shaking him.*]   For God's sake, do as I tell you! Do as I tell you! Do you hear what she's saying? Haven't you any feelings for her?

SON [*Taking hold of his* FATHER.]   No I haven't! I haven't! Let that be the end of it!

> [*There is a general uproar. The* MOTHER *frightened out of her wits, tries to get between them and separate them.*]

MOTHER   Please stop it! Please!

FATHER [*Hanging on.*]   Do as I tell you! Do as I tell you!

SON [*Wrestling with him and finally throwing him to the ground near the steps. Everyone is horrified.*]   What's come over you? Why are you so frantic? Do you want to parade our disgrace in front of everybody? Well, I'm having nothing to do with it! Nothing! And I'm doing what our author wanted as well—he never wanted to put us on the stage.

PRODUCER   Then why the hell did you come here?

SON [*Pointing to the* FATHER.]   He wanted to, I didn't.

PRODUCER   But you're here now, aren't you?

SON   He was the one who wanted to come and he dragged all of us here with him and agreed with you in there about what to put in the play: and that meant not only what had really happened, as if that wasn't bad enough, but what hadn't happened as well.

PRODUCER   All right, then, you tell me what happened. You tell me! Did you rush out of your room without saying anything?

SON [*After a moment's hesitation.*]   Without saying anything. I didn't want to make a scene.

PRODUCER [*Needling him.*]   What then? What did you do then?

SON [*He is now the centre of everyone's agonised attention and he crosses the stage.*]   Nothing . . . I went across the garden . . .[*He breaks off gloomy and absorbed.*]

PRODUCER [*Urging him to say more, impressed by his reluctance to speak.*]   Well? What then? You crossed the garden?

SON [*Exasperated, putting his face into the crook of his arm.*]   Why do you want me to talk about it? It's horrible! [*The* MOTHER *is trembling with stifled sobs and looking towards the fountain.*]

PRODUCER [*Quietly, seeing where she is looking and turning to the* SON *with growing apprehension.*]   The little girl?

SON [*Looking straight in front, out to the audience.*]   There, in the fountain . . .

FATHER [*On the floor still, pointing with pity at the* MOTHER.]   She was trailing after him!

PRODUCER [*To the* SON, *anxiously.*]   What did you do then?

SON [*Still looking out front and speaking slowly.*]   I dashed across. I was going to jump in and pull her out . . . But something else caught my eye: I saw something behind the tree that made my blood run cold: the little boy, he was standing there with a mad look in his eyes: he was standing looking into the fountain at his little sister, floating there, drowned.

> [*The* STEPDAUGHTER *is still bent at the fountain hiding the* LITTLE GIRL, *and she sobs pathetically, her sobs sounding like an echo. There is a pause.*]

SON [*Continued.*]   I made a move towards him: but then . . .

> [*From behind the trees where the* LITTLE BOY *is standing there is the sound of a shot.*]

MOTHER [*With a terrible cry she runs along with the* SON *and all the* ACTORS *in the midst of a great general confusion.*]   My son! My son! [*And then from out of the confusion and crying her voice comes out.*] Help! Help me!

PRODUCER [*Amidst the shouting he tries to clear a space whilst the* LITTLE BOY *is carried by his feet and shoulders behind the white skycloth.*]   Is he wounded? Really wounded?

[*Everybody except the* PRODUCER *and the* FATHER *who is still on the floor by the steps, has gone behind the skycloth and stays there talking anxiously. Then independently the* ACTORS *start to come back into view.*]

LEADING ACTRESS [*Coming from the right, very upset.*]   He's dead! The poor boy! He's dead! What a terrible thing!

LEADING ACTOR [*Coming back from the left and smiling.*]   What do you mean, dead? It's all make-believe. It's a sham! He's not dead. Don't you believe it!

OTHER ACTORS FROM THE RIGHT   Make-believe? It's real! Real! He's dead!

OTHER ACTORS FROM THE LEFT   No, he isn't. He's pretending! It's all make-believe.

FATHER [*Running off and shouting at them as he goes.*]   What do you mean, make-believe? It's real! It's real, ladies and gentlemen! It's reality! [*And with desperation on his face he too goes behind the skycloth.*]

PRODUCER [*Not caring any more.*]   Make-believe?! Reality?! Oh, go to hell the lot of you! Lights! Lights! Lights!

[*At once all the stage and auditorium is flooded with light. The* PRODUCER *heaves a sigh of relief as if he has been relieved of a terrible weight and they all look at each other in distress and with uncertainty.*]

PRODUCER God! I've never known anything like this! And we've lost a whole day's work! [*He looks at the clock.*] Get off with you, all of you! We can't do anything now! It's too late to start a rehearsal. [*When the* ACTORS *have gone, he calls out.*] Hey, lights! Kill everything! [*As soon as he has said this, all the lights go out completely and leave him in the pitch dark.*] For God's sake!! You might have left the workers![4] I can't see where I'm going! [*Suddenly, behind the skycloth, as if because of a bad connection, a green light comes up to throw on the cloth a huge sharp shadow of the* CHARACTERS, *but without the* LITTLE BOY *and the* LITTLE GIRL. *The* PRODUCER, *seeing this, jumps off the stage, terrified. At the same time the flood of light on them is switched off and the stage is again bathed in the same blue light as before. Slowly the* SON *comes on from the right, followed by the* MOTHER *with her arms raised towards him. Then from the left, the* FATHER *enters.*

They come together in the middle of the stage and stand there as if transfixed. Finally from the left the STEPDAUGHTER *comes on and moves towards the steps at the front: on the top step she pauses for a moment to look back at the other three and then bursts out in a raucous laugh, dashes down the steps and turns to look at the three figures still on the stage. Then she runs out of the auditorium and we can still hear her manic laughter out into the foyer and beyond.*

After a pause the curtain falls slowly.]

4. Working lights.

MARCEL PROUST
1871–1922

Proust's influence in twentieth-century letters is unequaled by that of any other writer. His massive novel sequence, *Remembrance of Things Past* (*À la recherche du temps perdu*), broke from nineteenth-century tradition to provide the example of a new kind of characterization and narrative line, a monumentally complex and precisely coordinated aesthetic structure, and a concept of the individual's cumulatively created profound identity—much of it buried in the experience of our senses—that has influenced writers everywhere modern Western literature is known. All of these innovations refer to an exploration of time in terms that parallel the influential work of Proust's contemporary, the philosopher Henri Bergson, with its emphasis on experience as duration, or *lived* time (rather than the artificial measurements of clock or calendar), and the importance of intuitive knowledge. Proust's plot refuses the immediate sense of direction given by traditional nineteenth-century novels: it acquires purpose gradually, through the relationship of different themes, and its collective intent appears only at the end, when Marcel's suddenly catalyzed memory grasps the relationship of all parts. Characters are not sketched in fully from the beginning but are revealed piece by piece, evolving inside the different perspectives of individual chapters; even the protagonist is not fully outlined before the end. Proust's novel is a monumental construction coordinated down to its smallest parts not by the development of traditional novel form but by a new structural vision; it suggested the availability of intuitive or nonrational elements as organizational principles in an example that continues to be a reference point for twentieth-century writers.

Marcel Proust was born on July 10, 1871, the older of two sons in a wealthy middle-class Parisian family. His father was a well-known doctor and professor of medicine, a Catholic from a small town outside Paris. His mother, a sensitive, scrupulous, and highly educated woman to whom Marcel was devoted, came from an urban Jewish family. Proust fell ill with severe asthma when he was nine and thereafter spent his childhood holidays at a seaside resort in Normandy that became the fictional model for Balbec. In spite of his illness, which limited what he could do, he graduated with honors from the Lycée Condorcet in Paris in 1889 and did a year's military service at Orléans (the fictional Doncières). As a student, Proust had met many young writers and composers, and he began to frequent the salons of the wealthy bourgeoisie and the aristocracy of the Faubourg Saint-Germain (an elegant area of Paris), from which he drew much of the material for his portraits of society. He wrote for Symbolist magazines such as *Le Banquet* and *La Revue blanche* and published a collection of essays, poems, and stories in an elegant book, *Pleasures and Days* (1896), with drawings by Madeleine Lemaire and music by Reynaldo Hahn. In 1899 (with his mother's help since he knew no English), he began to translate the English moralist and art critic John Ruskin.

Proust is known as the author of one work: the enormous, seven-volume exploration of time and consciousness called *Remembrance of Things Past*. As early as 1895, he had begun work on a shorter novel that traced the same themes and autobiographical awareness, but *Jean Santeuil* (published posthumously in 1952) never found a coherent structure for its numerous episodes and Proust abandoned it in 1899. Many episodes from the unfinished manuscript reflected Proust's interest in current events, especially the Dreyfus Affair (1894–1906) that was dividing France around issues of military honor, anti-Semitism, and national security. Themes, ideas, and some episodes from the earlier novel were absorbed into *Remembrance of Things Past*, and it is striking that the major difference (aside from length) between the two works is simply the extremely sophisticated and subtle structure that Proust devised for the later one.

Proust's health started seriously to decline in 1902, and to make matters worse, he lost both parents by 1905. The following year, his asthma worsening, he moved into a cork-lined, fumigated room at 102, boulevard Haussmann in Paris, where he stayed until forced to move in 1919. From 1907 to 1914, he spent summers in the seacoast town of Cabourg (another source of material for the fictional Balbec), but when in Paris emerged rarely from his apartment and then only late at night for dinners with friends. In 1909 he conceived the structure of his novel as a whole and wrote its first and last chapters together. A first draft was finished by September 1912, but Proust had difficulty finding a publisher and finally published the first volume at his own expense in 1913. Though *Swann's Way* (*Du côté de chez Swann*) was a success, World War I delayed publication of subsequent volumes, and Proust began the painstaking revision and enlargement of the whole manuscript (from 1,500 to 4,000 pages, and from three to seven parts) that was to occupy him until his death on November 18, 1922. *Within a Budding Grove* (*À l'ombre des jeunes filles en fleurs*, or "In the shadow of young girls in flower") won the prestigious Goncourt Prize in 1919, and *The Guermantes Way* (*Le Côté de Guermantes*) followed in 1920–21. The last volume published in Proust's lifetime was *Cities of the Plain II* (*Sodome et Gomorrhe II*, or "Sodom and Gomorrah II," 1922), and the remaining volumes—*The Captive* (*La Prisonnière*, 1923), *The Fugitive* (*Albertine disparue*, or "Albertine disappeared," 1925), and *Time Regained* (*Le Temps retrouvé*, 1927)—were published posthumously from manuscripts on which he had been working. Written almost completely in the first person and based on events in the author's life (although by no means purely autobiographical), the novel is famous both for its evocation of the closed world of Parisian society at the turn of the century and as a meditation on time and human emotions.

When *Swann's Way* appeared in 1913, it was immediately seen as a new kind of fiction. Unlike nineteenth-century novels such as Flaubert's *Madame Bovary*, *Remembrance of Things Past* has no clear and continuous plot line building to a dénouement, nor (until the last volume, published in 1927) could the reader detect a consistent development of the central character, Marcel. Only at the end does the narrator recognize the meaning and value of what has preceded, and when he retells his story it is not from an omniscient, explanatory point of view but rather as a reliving and gradual assessment of Marcel's lifelong experience. Most of the novel sets forth a roughly chronological sequence of events, yet its opening pages swing through recollections of many times and places before settling on the narrator's childhood in Combray. The second section, *Swann in Love* (*Un Amour de Swann*), is a story told about another character and in the third person. Thus the novel proceeds by apparently discontinuous blocks of recollection, all bound together by the central consciousness of the narrator. This was always Proust's plan: he insisted that he had from the beginning a fixed structure and goal for the whole novel that reached down to the "solidity of the smallest parts," and his substantial revisions of the shorter first draft enriched an already existing structure without changing the sequence of scenes and events.

The overall theme of the novel is suggested by a literal translation of its title: "In Search of Lost Time." The narrator, a "Marcel" who suggests but is not identical with the author, is an old man weakened by a long illness who puzzles over the events of his past, trying to find in them a significant pattern. He begins with his childhood, ordered within the comfortable security of accepted manners and ideals in the family home at Combray. In succeeding volumes he goes out into the world, experiences love and disappointment, discovers the disparity between idealized images of places and their crude, sometimes banal reality, and is increasingly overcome by disillusionment with himself and society. Until the end of the novel, Marcel remains a *grand nerveux* (nervous or high-strung person), an extremely sensitive person impelled by the major experiences of his life—love, betrayal, art, separation, and death—to discard his earlier naïve perspective and seek out a largely intuited meaning for life.

In the short ending chapter, things suddenly come into focus as Marcel reaches a new understanding of the role of time. Abruptly reliving a childhood experience when he sees a familiar book and recognizing the ravages of time in the aged and enfeebled figures of his old friends, Marcel faces the approach of death with a new sense of existential continuity and realizes that his vocation as an artist lies in giving form to this buried existence. Apparently lost, the past is still alive within us, a part of our being, and memory can recapture it to give coherence and depth to present identity. Marcel has not yet begun to write by the end of the last volume, *Time Regained*, but paradoxically the book that he plans to write is already there: Proust's *Remembrance of Things Past*.

The larger subject of the novel, penetrating its description of society and Marcel's experience, is "that invisible substance called time." Although neither ever claimed any direct connection (and Proust recognized more readily the influence of his philosophy professor, Darlu), Proust echoes the concerns of contemporary philosopher Bergson when he looks to intuition and a sense of lived experience for a way to represent reality. Bergson's opposition of intellect and intuition, his preference for *duration* (everyday lived time) as opposed to abstract or clock time as a means of knowledge, and his distinction between the interactive "social ego" and the individually "profound" or intuitive ego all correspond to themes in Proust. Marcel's awareness of his life in time is created through memory—not rational or "forced" but spontaneous or "involuntary" memory—the chance recollection that wells up from his subconscious mind when he repeats a previous action such as dipping cookies in lime-blossom tea, stumbling on a paving stone, hearing a spoon clatter, or glimpsing a familiar book. Involuntary memory is more powerful because it draws on a buried level of experience where the five senses are still linked. Life thus recalled comes to us in one piece, not separated into different categories for easier intellectual understanding. Sounds are connected with colors (the name *Brabant* with gold), and emotions with the settings in which they were experienced (sorrow with the smell of varnish on the stairway up to bed). Involuntary memory re-creates a whole past world in all its concrete reality—and so does art. When Proust attributes such an absolute metaphysical value to art, making it a special means of knowledge and the focus of his book, he joins a special French tradition of "moralist" writers: those who, from Michel de Montaigne to Albert Camus, strive for clear vision and a sense of universal human values.

Proust's style has a unique "architectural" design that coordinates large blocks of material: themes, situations, places, and events recur and are transformed across time. His long sentences and mammoth paragraphs reflect the slow and careful progression of thought among the changing objects of its perception. The ending paragraph of *Combray* is composed of two long sentences that encompass an enormous range of meditative detail as the narrator not only recalls his childhood world—the old gray house, garden, public square and country roads, Swann's park, the river, the villagers, and indeed the whole town of Combray—but simultaneously compares the suddenly arisen house to a stage set, and the unfolding village itself to the twists and turns of a Japanese flower taking on color and form inside a bowl of water—here, in the narrator's cup of lime-blossom tea. Characters are remembered in different settings and perspectives, creating a "multiple self" who is free to change and still remain the same. Thus Charles Swann appears first as the visitor who often delays the child Marcel's bedtime kiss from his mother, next as an anxious and disappointed lover, and finally as a tragic, dying man rejected by his friends, the Guermantes, in their haste to get to a ball. Marcel's grandmother appears throughout the scenes in Combray, later during a visit to the seaside resort of Balbec, still later in her death agonies when Marcel is unable truly to grieve, and finally as a sudden recollection when Marcel has trouble tying his shoelace in Balbec. Nor is it characters alone who undergo cumulative transformations. The little musical phrase that Marcel first hears as part of a sonata by the composer Vinteuil and that is associated with love in various settings recurs toward the end of the novel as part of a septet and becomes a revelation of the subtle constructions of art. Places overlap in the memory: the imagined and the real Balbec or Venice confront one another, and the church steeples of Vieuxvicq and Martinville are juxtaposed. On a linguistic level, Proust juxtaposes entire social roles and habits of mind through the interaction of different types of speech. When Charles and the Princesse de Guermantes meet in a bourgeois salon, their manner of speaking to each other creates a small "in-group" dialogue of the aristocracy and sets them off from everyone else. The flexibility of Proust's style, representing thought and habits of speech rather than following a superimposed common code, makes him an example of verbal and visionary innovation that is paralleled by other writers of the same period, such as James Joyce and Virginia Woolf, and is enormously influential on later writers of the "new novel" tradition.

The selection printed here, *Combray*, is the first chapter of *Swann's Way*, which is the first full volume of Proust's novel. "Swann's way" is one of the two directions in which Marcel's family used to take walks from their home in Combray, toward Tansonville, home of Charles Swann, and is associated with various scenes and anecdotes of love and private life. The longer walk toward the estate of the Guermantes (*The Guermantes Way*), a fictional family of the highest aristocracy appearing frequently in the novel, evokes an aura of high society and French history, a more public sphere. Fictional people and places mingle throughout with the real; names that are not annotated are Proust's inventions. The narrator of *Combray* is Marcel as an old man, and the French verb tense used in his recollections (here and throughout all but the final volume) is appropriately the imperfect, a tense of uncompleted action ("I used to . . . I would ask myself").

Combray introduces the work's themes and methods rather like the overture of an opera. All but one of the main characters appear or are mentioned, and the patterns of future encounters are set. Marcel, waiting anxiously for his beloved mother's response to a note sent down to her during dinner, suffers the same agony of separation as does Swann in his love for the promiscuous Odette, or the older Marcel himself for Albertine. The strange world of half-sleep, half-waking with which the novel begins prefigures later awakenings of memory. Long passages of intricate introspection and sudden shifts of time and space introduce us to the style and point of view of the rest of the book. The narrator shares the painful anxiety of little Marcel's desperate wait for his mother's bedtime kiss; for though his observations and judgments are tempered with mature wisdom, he is only at the beginning of his progress to full consciousness. The remembrance of things past is a key to further discovery but not an end in itself.

Combray ends with Proust's most famous image, summing up for many readers the world, the style, and the process of discovery of the Proustian vision. Nibbling at a madeleine (a small, rich cookielike pastry) that he has dipped in lime-blossom tea, Marcel suddenly has an overwhelming feeling of happiness. He soon associates this tantalizing, puzzling phenomenon with the memory of earlier times when he sipped tea with his Aunt Léonie. He realizes that there is something valuable about such passive, spontaneous, and sensuous memory, quite different from the abstract operations of reason. Although the Marcel of "Combray" does not yet know it, he will pursue the elusive significance of this moment of happiness until, in *Time Regained*, he can as a complete artist bring it to the surface and link past and present time in a fuller and richer identity.

PRONOUNCING GLOSSARY

The following list uses common English syllables and stress accents to provide rough equivalents of selected words whose pronunciation may be unfamiliar to the general reader.

Bathilde: *bah-teeld'*

Charlus: *shar-lews'*

Chartres: *shar'-tr*

Combray: *cohm-bray'*

Corot: *core-oh'*

Duc: *dewk*

Faubourg Saint-Germain: *foh-boor'*
    sanh zhair-manh'

George Sand: *zhorzh sond*

Maubant: *moh-bawnh'*

Maulévrier: *moh-lay'-vree-ay'*

Proust: *proost*

Quai d'Orleáns: *kay dor-lay-onh*

Saint-Cloud: *sanh—cloo'*

Saint-Loup: *sanh–loo'*

Sévigné: *say-veen-yay'*

Vinteuil: *van-teuh'-ee*

Swann's Way

Part 1. Combray[1]

I

For a long time, I went to bed early. Sometimes, my candle scarcely out, my eyes would close so quickly that I did not have time to say to myself: "I'm falling asleep." And, half an hour later, the thought that it was time to try to sleep would wake me; I wanted to put down the book I thought I still had in my hands and blow out my light; I had not ceased while sleeping to form reflections on what I had just read, but these reflections had taken a rather peculiar turn; it seemed to me that I myself was what the book was talking about: a church, a quartet, the rivalry between François I and Charles V.[2] This belief lived on for a few seconds after my waking; it did not shock my reason but lay heavy like scales on my eyes and kept them from realizing that the candlestick was no longer lit. Then it began to grow unintelligible to me, as after metempsychosis do the thoughts of an earlier existence; the subject of the book detached itself from me, I was free to apply myself to it or not; immediately I recovered my sight and I was amazed to find a darkness around me soft and restful for my eyes, but perhaps even more so for my mind, to which it appeared a thing without cause, incomprehensible, a thing truly dark. I would ask myself what time it might be; I could hear the whistling of the trains which, remote or nearby, like the singing of a bird in a forest, plotting the distances, described to me the extent of the deserted countryside where the traveler hastens toward the nearest station; and the little road he is following will be engraved on his memory by the excitement he owes to new places, to unaccustomed activities, to the recent conversation and the farewells under the unfamiliar lamp that follow him still through the silence of the night, to the imminent sweetness of his return.

    I would rest my cheeks tenderly against the lovely cheeks of the pillow, which, full and fresh, are like the cheeks of our childhood. I would strike a match to look at my watch. Nearly midnight. This is the hour when the invalid who has been obliged to go off on a journey and has had to sleep in

---

1. Translated by Lydia Davis.   2. Francis I (1496–1567), king of France, and Charles V (1500–1558), Holy Roman emperor and king of Spain, fought four wars over the empire's expansion in Europe.

an unfamiliar hotel, wakened by an attack, is cheered to see a ray of light under the door. How fortunate, it's already morning! In a moment the servants will be up, he will be able to ring, someone will come help him. The hope of being relieved gives him the courage to suffer. In fact he thought he heard footsteps; the steps approach, then recede. And the ray of light that was under his door has disappeared. It is midnight; they have just turned off the gas; the last servant has gone and he will have to suffer the whole night through without remedy.

I would go back to sleep, and would sometimes afterward wake again for brief moments only, long enough to hear the organic creak of the woodwork, open my eyes and stare at the kaleidoscope of the darkness, savor in a momentary glimmer of consciousness the sleep into which were plunged the furniture, the room, that whole of which I was only a small part and whose insensibility I would soon return to share. Or else while sleeping I had effortlessly returned to a period of my early life that had ended forever, rediscovered one of my childish terrors such as my great-uncle pulling me by my curls, a terror dispelled on the day—the dawn for me of a new era—when they were cut off. I had forgotten that event during my sleep, I recovered its memory as soon as I managed to wake myself up to escape the hands of my great-uncle, but as a precautionary measure I would completely surround my head with my pillow before returning to the world of dreams.

Sometimes, as Eve was born from one of Adam's ribs, a woman was born during my sleep from a cramped position of my thigh. Formed from the pleasure I was on the point of enjoying, she, I imagined, was the one offering it to me. My body, which felt in hers my own warmth, would try to find itself inside her, I would wake up. The rest of humanity seemed very remote compared with this woman I had left scarcely a few moments before; my cheek was still warm from her kiss, my body aching from the weight of hers. If, as sometimes happened, she had the features of a woman I had known in life, I would devote myself entirely to this end: to finding her again, like those who go off on a journey to see a longed-for city with their own eyes and imagine that one can enjoy in reality the charm of a dream. Little by little the memory of her would fade, I had forgotten the girl of my dream.

A sleeping man holds in a circle around him the sequence of the hours, the order of the years and worlds. He consults them instinctively as he wakes and reads in a second the point on the earth he occupies, the time that has elapsed before his waking; but their ranks can be mixed up, broken. If toward morning, after a bout of insomnia, sleep overcomes him as he is reading, in a position quite different from the one in which he usually sleeps, his raised arm alone is enough to stop the sun and make it retreat,[3] and, in the first minute of his waking, he will no longer know what time it is, he will think he has only just gone to bed. If he dozes off in a position still more displaced and divergent, after dinner sitting in an armchair for instance, then the confusion among the disordered worlds will be complete, the magic armchair will send him traveling at top speed through time and space, and, at the moment of opening his eyelids, he will believe he went to bed several months earlier in another country. But it was enough if, in my own bed, my sleep was deep and allowed my mind to relax entirely; then it would let go of the

---

3. If his uplifted arm prevents him from seeing the sunlight, he will think it is still night.

map of the place where I had fallen asleep and, when I woke in the middle of the night, since I did not know where I was, I did not even understand in the first moment who I was; I had only, in its original simplicity, the sense of existence as it may quiver in the depths of an animal; I was more destitute than a cave dweller; but then the memory—not yet of the place where I was, but of several of those where I had lived and where I might have been—would come to me like help from on high to pull me out of the void from which I could not have got out on my own; I crossed centuries of civilization in one second, and the image confusedly glimpsed of oil lamps, then of wing-collar shirts, gradually recomposed my self's original features.

Perhaps the immobility of the things around us is imposed on them by our certainty that they are themselves and not anything else, by the immobility of our mind confronting them. However that may be, when I woke thus, my mind restlessly attempting, without success, to discover where I was, everything revolved around me in the darkness, things, countries, years. My body, too benumbed to move, would try to locate, according to the form of its fatigue, the position of its limbs so as to deduce from this the direction of the wall, the placement of the furniture, so as to reconstruct and name the dwelling in which it found itself. Its memory, the memory of its ribs, its knees, its shoulders, offered in succession several of the rooms where it had slept, while around it the invisible walls, changing place according to the shape of the imagined room, spun through the shadows. And even before my mind, hesitating on the thresholds of times and shapes, had identified the house by reassembling the circumstances, it—my body—would recall the kind of bed in each one, the location of the doors, the angle at which the light came in through the windows, the existence of a hallway, along with the thought I had had as I fell asleep and that I had recovered upon waking. My stiffened side, trying to guess its orientation, would imagine, for instance, that it lay facing the wall in a big canopied bed and immediately I would say to myself: "Why, I went to sleep in the end even though Mama didn't come to say goodnight to me," I was in the country in the home of my grandfather, dead for many years; and my body, the side on which I was resting, faithful guardians of a past my mind ought never to have forgotten, recalled to me the flame of the night-light of Bohemian glass, in the shape of an urn, which hung from the ceiling by little chains, the mantelpiece of Siena marble,[4] in my bedroom at Combray, at my grandparents' house, in faraway days which at this moment I imagined were present without picturing them to myself exactly and which I would see more clearly in a little while when I was fully awake.

Then the memory of a new position would reappear; the wall would slip away in another direction: I was in my room at Mme. de Saint-Loup's,[5] in the country; good Lord! It's ten o'clock or even later, they will have finished dinner! I must have overslept during the nap I take every evening when I come back from my walk with Mme. de Saint-Loup, before putting on my evening clothes. For many years have passed since Combray, where, however late we returned, it was the sunset's red reflections I saw in the panes of my window. It is another sort of life one leads at Tansonville, at Mme. de Saint-

4. Marble from central Italy, mottled and reddish in color. *Bohemian glass:* likely to have been ornately engraved. Bohemia (now part of the Czech Republic) was a major center of the glass industry.   5. Charles Swann's daughter, Gilberte, who has married Robert de Saint-Loup, a nephew of the Guermantes.

Loup's, another sort of pleasure I take in going out only at night, in following by moonlight those lanes where I used to play in the sun; and the room where I fell asleep instead of dressing for dinner—from far off I can see it, as we come back, pierced by the flares of the lamp, a lone beacon in the night.

These revolving, confused evocations never lasted for more than a few seconds; often, in my brief uncertainty about where I was, I did not distinguish the various suppositions of which it was composed any better than we isolate, when we see a horse run, the successive positions shown to us by a kinetoscope.[6] But I had seen sometimes one, sometimes another, of the bedrooms I had inhabited in my life, and in the end I would recall them all in the long reveries that followed my waking: winter bedrooms in which, as soon as you are in bed, you bury your head in a nest braided of the most disparate things: a corner of the pillow, the top of the covers, a bit of shawl, the side of the bed and an issue of the *Débats roses*,[7] which you end by cementing together using the birds' technique of pressing down on it indefinitely; where in icy weather the pleasure you enjoy is the feeling that you are separated from the outdoors (like the sea swallow which makes its nest deep in an underground passage in the warmth of the earth) and where, since the fire is kept burning all night in the fireplace, you sleep in a great cloak of warm, smoky air, shot with the glimmers from the logs breaking into flame again, a sort of immaterial alcove, a warm cave dug out of the heart of the room itself, a zone of heat with shifting thermal contours, aerated by drafts which cool your face and come from the corners, from the parts close to the window or far from the hearth, and which have grown cold again: summer bedrooms where you delight in becoming one with the soft night, where the moonlight leaning against the half-open shutters casts its enchanted ladder to the foot of the bed, where you sleep almost in the open air, like a titmouse rocked by the breeze on the tip of a ray of light; sometimes the Louis XVI[8] bedroom, so cheerful that even on the first night I had not been too unhappy there and where the slender columns that lightly supported the ceiling stood aside with such grace to show and reserve the place where the bed was; at other times, the small bedroom with the very high ceiling, hollowed out in the form of a pyramid two stories high and partly paneled in mahogany, where from the first second I had been mentally poisoned by the unfamiliar odor of the vetiver,[9] convinced of the hostility of the violet curtains and the insolent indifference of the clock chattering loudly as though I were not there; where a strange and pitiless quadrangular cheval glass, barring obliquely one of the corners of the room, carved from deep inside the soft fullness of my usual field of vision a site for itself which I had not expected; where my mind, struggling for hours to dislodge itself, to stretch upward so as to assume the exact shape of the room and succeed in filling its gigantic funnel to the very top, had suffered many hard nights, while I lay stretched out in my bed, my eyes lifted, my ear anxious, my nostril restive, my heart pounding, until habit had changed the color of the curtains, silenced the clock, taught pity to the cruel oblique mirror, concealed, if not

6. An early moving-picture machine that showed photographs in rapid succession, giving the illusion of motion.   7. The evening edition of the daily newspaper *Le Journal des Débats*.   8. Furnished in late 18th-century style, named for the French king of the time and marked by great elegance.   9. The aromatic root of a tropical grass packaged as a moth repellent.

driven out completely, the smell of the vetiver and appreciably diminished the apparent height of the ceiling. Habit! That skillful but very slow house-keeper who begins by letting our mind suffer for weeks in a temporary arrangement; but whom we are nevertheless truly happy to discover, for without habit our mind, reduced to no more than its own resources, would be powerless to make a lodging habitable.

Certainly I was now wide-awake, my body had veered around one last time and the good angel of certainty had brought everything around me to a stand-still, laid me down under my covers, in my bedroom, and put approximately where they belonged in the darkness my chest of drawers, my desk, my fire-place, the window onto the street and the two doors. But even though I knew I was not in any of the houses of which my ignorance upon waking had instantly, if not presented me with the distinct picture, at least made me believe the presence possible, my memory had been stirred; generally I would not try to go back to sleep right away; I would spend the greater part of the night remembering our life in the old days, in Combray at my great-aunt's house, in Balbec,[1] in Paris, in Doncières, in Venice, elsewhere still, remem-bering the places, the people I had known there, what I had seen of them, what I had been told about them.

At Combray, every day, in the late afternoon, long before the moment when I would have to go to bed and stay there, without sleeping, far away from my mother and grandmother, my bedroom again became the fixed and painful focus of my preoccupations. They had indeed hit upon the idea, to distract me on the evenings when they found me looking too unhappy, of giving me a magic lantern,[2] which, while awaiting the dinner hour, they would set on top of my lamp; and, after the fashion of the first architects and master glaziers of the Gothic age, it replaced the opacity of the walls with impalpable iridescences, supernatural multicolored apparitions, where legends were depicted as in a wavering, momentary stained-glass window. But my sadness was only increased by this since the mere change in lighting destroyed the familiarity which my bedroom had acquired for me and which, except for the torment of going to bed, had made it tolerable to me. Now I no longer recognized it and I was uneasy there, as in a room in some hotel or "chalet" to which I had come for the first time straight from the railway train.

Moving at the jerky pace of his horse, and filled with a hideous design, Golo[3] would come out of the small triangular forest that velveted the hillside with dark green and advance jolting toward the castle of poor Geneviève de Brabant. This castle was cut off along a curved line that was actually the edge of one of the glass ovals arranged in the frame which you slipped between the grooves of the lantern. It was only a section of castle and it had a moor in front of it where Geneviève stood dreaming, wearing a blue belt. The castle and the moor were yellow, and I had not had to wait to see them to find out their color since, before the glasses of the frame did so, the bronze sonority of the name Brabant had shown it to me clearly. Golo would stop for a moment to listen sadly to the patter read out loud by my great-aunt,[4]

1. The narrator's room at the fictional seaside resort of Balbec, a setting in the later novel *Within a Budding Grove*. 2. A kind of slide projector. 3. Villain of a 5th-century legend. He falsely accuses Geneviève de Brabant of adultery. Brabant was a principality in what is now Belgium. 4. Marcel's great-aunt is reading the story to him as they wait for dinner.

which he seemed to understand perfectly, modifying his posture, with a meekness that did not exclude a certain majesty, to conform to the directions of the text; then he moved off at the same jerky pace. And nothing could stop his slow ride. If the lantern was moved, I could make out Golo's horse continuing to advance over the window curtains, swelling out with their folds, descending into their fissures. The body of Golo himself, in its essence as supernatural as that of his steed, accommodated every material obstacle, every hindersome object that he encountered by taking it as his skeleton and absorbing it into himself, even the doorknob he immediately adapted to and floated invincibly over with his red robe or his pale face as noble and as melancholy as ever, but revealing no disturbance at this transvertebration.

Certainly I found some charm in these brilliant projections, which seemed to emanate from a Merovingian[5] past and send out around me such ancient reflections of history. But I cannot express the uneasiness caused in me by this intrusion of mystery and beauty into a room I had at last filled with myself to the point of paying no more attention to the room than to that self. The anesthetizing influence of habit having ceased, I would begin to have thoughts, and feelings, and they are such sad things. That doorknob of my room, which differed for me from all other doorknobs in the world in that it seemed to open of its own accord, without my having to turn it, so unconscious had its handling become for me, was now serving as an astral body[6] for Golo. And as soon as they rang for dinner, I hastened to run to the dining room where the big hanging lamp, ignorant of Golo and Bluebeard,[7] and well acquainted with my family and beef casserole, shed the same light as on every other evening; and to fall into the arms of Mama, whom Geneviève de Brabant's misfortunes made all the dearer to me, while Golo's crimes drove me to examine my own conscience more scrupulously.

After dinner, alas, I soon had to leave Mama, who stayed there talking with the others, in the garden if the weather was fine, in the little drawing room to which everyone withdrew if the weather was bad. Everyone, except my grandmother, who felt that "it's a pity to shut oneself indoors in the country" and who had endless arguments with my father on days when it rained too heavily, because he sent me to read in my room instead of having me stay outdoors. "That's no way to make him strong and active," she would say sadly, "especially that boy, who so needs to build up his endurance and willpower." My father would shrug his shoulders and study the barometer, for he liked meteorology, while my mother, making no noise so as not to disturb him, watched him with a tender respect, but not so intently as to try to penetrate the mystery of his superior qualities. But as for my grandmother, in all weathers, even in a downpour when Françoise had rushed the precious wicker armchairs indoors so that they would not get wet, we would see her in the empty, rain-lashed garden, pushing back her disordered gray locks so that her forehead could more freely drink in the salubriousness of the wind and rain. She would say: "At last, one can breathe!" and would roam the soaked paths—too symmetrically aligned for her liking by the new gardener, who lacked all feeling for nature and whom my father had been asking since

---

5. The first dynasty of French kings (ca. 500–751).   6. Spiritual counterpart of the physical body. According to the doctrine of Theosophy (a spiritualist movement originating in 1875), the astral body survives the death of the physical body.   7. The legendary wife murderer, presumably shown on another set of slides.

morning if the weather would clear—with her jerky, enthusiastic little step, regulated by the various emotions excited in her soul by the intoxication of the storm, the power of good health, the stupidity of my upbringing, and the symmetry of the gardens, rather than by the desire, quite unknown to her, to spare her plum-colored skirt the spots of mud under which it would disappear up to a height that was always, for her maid, a source of despair and a problem.

When these garden walks of my grandmother's took place after dinner, one thing had the power to make her come inside again: this was—at one of the periodic intervals when her circular itinerary brought her back, like an insect, in front of the lights of the little drawing room where the liqueurs were set out on the card table—if my great-aunt called out to her: "Bathilde! Come and stop your husband from drinking cognac!" To tease her, in fact (she had brought into my father's family so different a mentality that everyone poked fun at her and tormented her), since liqueurs were forbidden to my grandfather, my great-aunt would make him drink a few drops. My poor grandmother would come in, fervently beg her husband not to taste the cognac; he would become angry, drink his mouthful despite her, and my grandmother would go off again, sad, discouraged, yet smiling, for she was so humble at heart and so gentle that her tenderness for others, and the lack of fuss she made over her own person and her sufferings, came together in her gaze in a smile in which, unlike what one sees in the faces of so many people, there was irony only for herself, and for all of us a sort of kiss from her eyes, which could not see those she cherished without caressing them passionately with her gaze. This torture which my great-aunt inflicted on her, the spectacle of my grandmother's vain entreaties and of her weakness, defeated in advance, trying uselessly to take the liqueur glass away from my grandfather, were the kinds of things which you later become so accustomed to seeing that you smile as you contemplate them and take the part of the persecutor resolutely and gaily enough to persuade yourself privately that no persecution is involved; at that time they filled me with such horror that I would have liked to hit my great-aunt. But as soon as I heard: "Bathilde, come and stop your husband from drinking cognac!," already a man in my cowardice, I did what we all do, once we are grown up, when confronted with sufferings and injustices: I did not want to see them; I went up to sob at the very top of the house next to the schoolroom,[8] under the roofs, in a little room that smelled of orris root[9] and was also perfumed by a wild blackcurrant bush which had sprouted outside between the stones of the wall and extended a branch of flowers through the half-open window. Intended for a more specialized and more vulgar use, this room, from which during the day you could see all the way to the keep[1] of Roussainville-le-Pin, for a long time served me as a refuge, no doubt because it was the only one I was permitted to lock, for all those occupations of mine that demanded an inviolable solitude: reading, reverie, tears, and sensuous pleasure. Alas! I did not know that, much more than her husband's little deviations from his regimen, it was my weak will, my delicate health, the uncertainty they cast on my future that so sadly preoccupied my grandmother in the course of those incessant

---

8. A room in the house dedicated to the children's schoolwork.   9. A powder then used as a room deodorizer.   1. The best-fortified tower of a medieval castle. *Vulgar use*: it was used as a toilet.

perambulations, afternoon and evening, when we would see, as it passed and then passed again, lifted slantwise toward the sky, her beautiful face with its brown furrowed cheeks, which with age had become almost mauve like the plowed fields in autumn, crossed, if she was going out, by a veil half raised, while upon them, brought there by the cold or some sad thought, an involuntary tear was always drying.

My sole consolation, when I went upstairs for the night, was that Mama would come and kiss me once I was in bed. But this goodnight lasted so short a time, she went down again so soon, that the moment when I heard her coming up, then the soft sound of her garden dress of blue muslin, hung with little cords of plaited straw, passing along the hallway with its double doors, was for me a painful one. It heralded the moment that was to follow it, when she had left me, when she had gone down again. So that I came to wish that this goodnight I loved so much would take place as late as possible, so as to prolong the time of respite in which Mama had not yet come. Sometimes when, after kissing me, she opened the door to go, I wanted to call her back, to say "kiss me one more time," but I knew that immediately her face would look vexed, because the concession she was making to my sadness and agitation by coming up to kiss me, by bringing me this kiss of peace, irritated my father, who found these rituals absurd, and she would have liked to try to induce me to lose the need for it, the habit of it, far indeed from allowing me to acquire that of asking her, when she was already on the doorstep, for one kiss more. And to see her vexed destroyed all the calm she had brought me a moment before, when she had bent her loving face down over my bed and held it out to me like a host[2] for a communion of peace from which my lips would draw her real presence and the power to fall asleep. But those evenings, when Mama stayed so short a time in my room, were still sweet compared to the ones when there was company for dinner and when, because of that, she did not come up to say goodnight to me. That company was usually limited to M. Swann, who, apart from a few acquaintances passing through, was almost the only person who came to our house at Combray, sometimes for a neighborly dinner (more rarely after that unfortunate marriage of his, because my parents did not want to receive his wife), sometimes after dinner, unexpectedly. On those evenings when, as we sat in front of the house under the large chestnut tree, around the iron table, we heard at the far end of the garden, not the copious high-pitched bell that drenched, that deafened in passing with its ferruginous,[3] icy, inexhaustible noise any person in the household who set it off by coming in "without ringing," but the shy, oval, golden double tinkling of the little visitors' bell, everyone would immediately wonder: "A visitor—now who can that be?" but we knew very well it could only be M. Swann; my great-aunt speaking loudly, to set an example, in a tone of voice that she strained to make natural, said not to whisper that way; that nothing is more disagreeable for a visitor just coming in who is led to think that people are saying things he should not hear; and they would send as a scout my grandmother, who was always glad to have a pretext for taking one more walk around the garden and who would profit from it by surreptitiously pulling up a few rose stakes on the way so as to make the roses look a little more natural, like a mother who runs her hand

2. Communion wafer.   3. Ironlike.

through her son's hair to fluff it up after the barber has flattened it too much.

We would all remain hanging on the news my grandmother was going to bring us of the enemy, as though there had been a great number of possible assailants to choose among, and soon afterward my grandfather would say: "I recognize Swann's voice." In fact one could recognize him only by his voice, it was difficult to make out his face, his aquiline nose, his green eyes under a high forehead framed by blond, almost red hair, cut Bressant-style,[4] because we kept as little light as possible in the garden so as not to attract mosquitoes, and I would go off, as though not going for that reason, to say that the syrups should be brought out; my grandmother placed a great deal of importance, considering it more amiable, on the idea that they should not seem anything exceptional, and for visitors only. M. Swann, though much younger, was very attached to my grandfather, who had been one of the closest friends of his father, an excellent man but peculiar, in whom, apparently, a trifle was sometimes enough to interrupt the ardor of his feelings, to change the course of his thinking. Several times a year I would hear my grandfather at the table telling anecdotes, always the same ones, about the behavior of old M. Swann upon the death of his wife, over whom he had watched day and night. My grandfather, who had not seen him for a long time, had rushed to his side at the estate the Swanns owned in the vicinity of Combray and, so that he would not be present at the coffining, managed to entice him for a while, all in tears, out of the death chamber. They walked a short way in the park, where there was a little sunshine. Suddenly M. Swann, taking my grandfather by the arm, cried out: "Oh, my old friend, what a joy it is to be walking here together in such fine weather! Don't you think it's pretty, all these trees, these hawthorns! And my pond—which you've never congratulated me on! You look as sad as an old nightcap. Feel that little breeze? Oh, say what you like, life has something to offer despite everything, my dear Amédée!" Suddenly the memory of his dead wife came back to him and, no doubt feeling it would be too complicated to try to understand how he could have yielded to an impulse of happiness at such a time, he confined himself, in a habitual gesture of his whenever a difficult question came into his mind, to passing his hand over his forehead, wiping his eyes and the lenses of his lorgnon. Yet he could not be consoled for the death of his wife, but, during the two years he survived her, would say to my grandfather: "It's odd, I think of my poor wife often, but I can't think of her for long at a time." "Often, but only a little at a time, like poor old Swann," had become one of my grandfather's favorite phrases, which he uttered apropos of the most different sorts of things. I would have thought Swann's father was a monster, if my grandfather, whom I considered a better judge and whose pronouncement, forming a legal precedent for me, often allowed me later to dismiss offenses I might have been inclined to condemn, had not exclaimed: "What! He had a heart of gold!"

For many years, even though, especially before his marriage, the younger M. Swann often came to see them at Combray, my great-aunt and my grandparents did not suspect that he had entirely ceased to live in the kind of society his family had frequented and that, under the sort of incognito which

4. Crew cut in front and longer in back: a hair style popularized by the actor Jean-Baptiste Bressant (1815–1886).

this name Swann gave him among us, they were harboring—with the perfect innocence of honest innkeepers who have under their roof, without knowing it, some celebrated highwayman—one of the most elegant members of the Jockey Club, a favorite friend of the Comte de Paris and the Prince of Wales, one of the men most sought after by the high society of the Faubourg Saint-Germain.[5]

Our ignorance of this brilliant social life that Swann led was obviously due in part to the reserve and discretion of his character, but also to the fact that bourgeois people in those days formed for themselves a rather Hindu notion of society and considered it to be made up of closed castes, in which each person, from birth, found himself placed in the station which his family occupied and from which nothing, except the accidents of an exceptional career or an unhoped-for marriage, could withdraw him in order to move him into a higher caste. M. Swann, the father, was a stockbroker; "Swann the son" would find he belonged for his entire life to a caste in which fortunes varied, as in a tax bracket, between such and such fixed incomes. One knew which had been his father's associations, one therefore knew which were his own, with which people he was "in a position" to consort. If he knew others, these were bachelor acquaintances on whom old friends of the family, such as my relatives, would close their eyes all the more benignly because he continued, after losing his parents, to come faithfully to see us; but we would have been ready to wager that these people he saw, who were unknown to us, were the sort he would not have dared greet had he encountered them when he was with us. If you were determined to assign Swann a social coefficient that was his alone, among the other sons of stockbrokers in a position equal to that of his parents, this coefficient would have been a little lower for him because, very simple in his manner and with a long-standing "craze" for antiques and painting, he now lived and amassed his collections in an old town house which my grandmother dreamed of visiting, but which was situated on the quai d'Orléans,[6] a part of town where my great-aunt felt it was ignominious to live. "But are you a connoisseur? I ask for your own sake, because you're likely to let the dealers unload some awful daubs on you," my great-aunt would say to him; in fact she did not assume he had any competence and even from an intellectual point of view had no great opinion of a man who in conversation avoided serious subjects and showed a most prosaic preciseness not only when he gave us cooking recipes, entering into the smallest details, but even when my grandmother's sisters talked about artistic subjects. Challenged by them to give his opinion, to express his admiration for a painting, he would maintain an almost ungracious silence and then, on the other hand, redeem himself if he could provide, about the museum in which it was to be found, about the date at which it had been painted, a pertinent piece of information. But usually he would content himself with trying to entertain us by telling a new story each time about something that had just happened to him involving people selected from among those we knew, the Combray pharmacist, our cook, our coachman. Certainly

5. A fashionable area of Paris on the left bank of the Seine; many of the French aristocracy lived there. *Jockey Club:* an exclusive men's club devoted to horse racing, opera, and other diversions. Louis-Philippe-Albert d'Orléans, comte de Paris (1838–1894), was the heir apparent to the French throne, should the monarchy ever be restored; the Prince of Wales became, in 1901, King Edward VII of England. 6. A beautiful though less fashionable section in the heart of Paris, along the Seine.

these tales made my great-aunt laugh, but she could not distinguish clearly if this was because of the absurd role Swann always assigned himself or because of the wit he showed in telling them: "You are quite a character, Monsieur Swann!" Being the only rather vulgar person in our family, she took care to point out to strangers, when they were talking about Swann, that, had he wanted to, he could have lived on the boulevard Haussmann or the avenue de l'Opéra, that he was the son of M. Swann, who must have left four or five million,[7] but that this was his whim. One that she felt moreover must be so amusing to others that in Paris, when M. Swann came on New Year's Day to bring her her bag of marrons glacés,[8] she never failed, if there was company, to say to him: "Well, Monsieur Swann! Do you still live next door to the wine warehouse, so as to be sure of not missing the train when you go to Lyon?"[9] And she would look out of the corner of her eye, over her lorgnon, at the other visitors.

But if anyone had told my great-aunt that this same Swann, who, as the son of old M. Swann, was perfectly "qualified" to be received by all the "best of the bourgeoisie," by the most respected notaries or lawyers of Paris (a hereditary privilege he seemed to make little use of), had, as though in secret, quite a different life; that on leaving our house, in Paris, after telling us he was going home to bed, he retraced his steps as soon as he had turned the corner and went to a certain drawing room that no eye of any broker or broker's associate would ever contemplate, this would have seemed to my aunt as extraordinary as might to a better-educated lady the thought of being personally on close terms with Aristaeus[1] and learning that, after having a chat with her, he would go deep into the heart of the realms of Thetis, into an empire hidden from mortal eyes, where Virgil shows him being received with open arms; or—to be content with an image that had more chance of occurring to her, for she had seen it painted on our petits-fours plates at Combray—of having had as a dinner guest Ali Baba,[2] who, as soon as he knows he is alone, will enter the cave dazzling with unsuspected treasure.

One day when he had come to see us in Paris after dinner apologizing for being in evening clothes, Françoise having said, after he left, that she had learned from the coachman that he had dined "at the home of a princess," "Yes, a princess of the demimonde!"[3] my aunt had responded, shrugging her shoulders without raising her eyes from her knitting, with serene irony.

Thus, my great-aunt was cavalier in her treatment of him. Since she believed he must be flattered by our invitations, she found it quite natural that he never came to see us in the summertime without having in his hand a basket of peaches or raspberries from his garden and that from each of his trips to Italy he would bring me back photographs of masterpieces.

They did not hesitate to send him off in search of it when they needed a recipe for gribiche[4] sauce or pineapple salad for large dinners to which they had not invited him, believing he did not have sufficient prestige for one to

---

7. I.e., francs—nearly $1 million in the currency of the day, about $17 million in 2004. *Boulevard Haussmann* and *avenue de l'Opéra*: large modern avenues where the wealthy bourgeoisie liked to live.   8. Candied chestnuts, a traditional Parisian New Year's gift.   9. The wine warehouse was close to the Gare de Lyon, the terminal from which trains left for the industrial city of Lyon and other destinations in southeastern France.   1. Son of the Greek god Apollo. In Virgil's *Fourth Georgic*, Aristaeus seeks help from the sea nymph Thetis.   2. Hero of an *Arabian Nights* tale, a poor youth who discovers a robbers' cave filled with treasure.   3. Literally, *half-world* (French): women of questionable reputation, not quite members of society.   4. A seasoned mayonnaise that includes chopped hard-boiled eggs.

be able to serve him up to acquaintances who were coming for the first time. If the conversation turned to the princes of the House of France:[5] "people you and I will never know, will we, and we can manage quite well without that, can't we," my great-aunt would say to Swann, who had, perhaps, a letter from Twickenham[6] in his pocket; she had him push the piano around and turn the pages on the evenings when my grandmother's sister sang, handling this creature, who was elsewhere so sought after, with the naive roughness of a child who plays with a collector's curio no more carefully than with some object of little value. No doubt the Swann who was known at the same time to so many clubmen was quite different from the one created by my great-aunt, when in the evening, in the little garden at Combray, after the two hesitant rings of the bell had sounded, she injected and invigorated with all that she knew about the Swann family the dark and uncertain figure who emerged, followed by my grandmother, from a background of shadows, and whom we recognized by his voice. But even with respect to the most insignificant things in life, none of us constitutes a material whole, identical for everyone, which a person has only to go look up as though we were a book of specifications or a last testament; our social personality is a creation of the minds of others. Even the very simple act that we call "seeing a person we know" is in part an intellectual one. We fill the physical appearance of the individual we see with all the notions we have about him, and of the total picture that we form for ourselves, these notions certainly occupy the greater part. In the end they swell his cheeks so perfectly, follow the line of his nose in an adherence so exact, they do so well at nuancing the sonority of his voice as though the latter were only a transparent envelope that each time we see this face and hear this voice, it is these notions that we encounter again, that we hear. No doubt, in the Swann they had formed for themselves, my family had failed out of ignorance to include a host of details from his life in the fashionable world that caused other people, when they were in his presence, to see refinements rule his face and stop at his aquiline nose as though at their natural frontier; but they had also been able to garner in this face disaffected of its prestige, vacant and spacious, in the depths of these depreciated eyes, the vague, sweet residue—half memory, half forgetfulness—of the idle hours spent together after our weekly dinners, around the card table or in the garden, during our life of good country neighborliness. The corporeal envelope of our friend had been so well stuffed with all this, as well as with a few memories relating to his parents, that this particular Swann had become a complete and living being, and I have the impression of leaving one person to go to another distinct from him, when, in my memory, I pass from the Swann I knew later with accuracy to that first Swann—to that first Swann in whom I rediscover the charming mistakes of my youth and who in fact resembles less the other Swann than he resembles the other people I knew at the time, as though one's life were like a museum in which all the portraits from one period have a family look about them, a single tonality—to that first Swann abounding in leisure, fragrant with the smell of the tall chestnut tree, the baskets of raspberries, and a sprig of tarragon.

5. The French royal family, headed by the comte de Paris. The political climate was antiroyalist, and all claimants to the French throne and their heirs were banished from France by law in 1886.   6. Fashionable London suburb. The French royal family had a house there, which was, for some time, the residence of the exiled comte de Paris.

Yet one day when my grandmother had gone to ask a favor from a lady she had known at the Sacré-Coeur[7] (and with whom, because of our notion of the castes, she had not wished to remain in close contact despite a reciprocal congeniality), this lady, the Marquise de Villeparisis of the famous de Bouillon family, had said to her: "I believe you know M. Swann very well; he is a great friend of my nephew and niece, the des Laumes."[8] My grandmother had returned from her visit full of enthusiasm for the house, which overlooked some gardens and in which Mme. de Villeparisis had advised her to rent a flat, and also for a waistcoat maker and his daughter, who kept a shop in the courtyard where she had gone to ask them to put a stitch in her skirt, which she had torn in the stairwell. My grandmother had found these people wonderful, she declared that the girl was a gem and the waistcoat maker was most distinguished, the finest man she had ever seen. Because for her, distinction was something absolutely independent of social position. She went into ecstasies over an answer the waistcoat maker had given her, saying to Mama: "Sévigné[9] couldn't have said it any better!" and, in contrast, of a nephew of Mme. de Villeparisis whom she had met at the house: "Oh, my dear daughter, how common he is!"

Now the remark about Swann had had the effect, not of raising him in my great-aunt's estimation, but of lowering Mme. de Villeparisis. It seemed that the respect which, on my grandmother's faith, we accorded Mme. de Villeparisis created a duty on her part to do nothing that would make her less worthy, a duty in which she had failed by learning of Swann's existence, by permitting relatives of hers to associate with him. "What! She knows Swann? A person you claim is a relation of the Maréchal de MacMahon?"[1] My family's opinion regarding Swann's associations seemed confirmed later by his marriage to a woman of the worst social station, practically a cocotte, whom, what was more, he never attempted to introduce, continuing to come to our house alone, though less and less, but from whom they believed they could judge—assuming it was there that he had found her—the social circle, unknown to them, that he habitually frequented.

But one time, my grandfather read in a newspaper that M. Swann was one of the most faithful guests at the Sunday lunches given by the Duc de X . . . , whose father and uncle had been the most prominent statesmen in the reign of Louis-Philippe.[2] Now, my grandfather was interested in all the little facts that could help him enter imaginatively into the private lives of men like Molé, the Duc Pasquier, the Duc de Broglie.[3] He was delighted to learn that Swann associated with people who had known them. My great-aunt, however, interpreted this news in a sense unfavorable to Swann: anyone who chose his associations outside the caste into which he had been born, outside his social "class," suffered in her eyes a regrettable lowering of his social

7. A convent school in Paris, attended by daughters of the aristocracy and the wealthy bourgeoisie. 8. A fictional family, like the Guermantes. Proust strengthens the apparent reality of the Guermantes family, including the Marquise de Villeparis, by relating them to the historical house of Bouillon, a famous aristocratic family that could trace its descent from the Middle Ages. 9. The Marquise de Sévigné (1626–1696), known for her lively style in letters that described contemporary events and the life of the aristocracy. 1. Marshal of France (1808–1893), elected president of the French Republic in 1873. 2. King of France from 1830 to 1848, father of the comte de Paris. 3. Achille-Charles-Léon-Victor, Duc de Broglie (1785–1870) had a busy public career that ended in 1851. Louis-Mathieu, Comte Molé (1781–1855) held various cabinet positions before becoming premier of France in 1836. Duc Étienne-Denis Pasquier (1767–1862) also held important public positions up to 1837. All three were active during the reign of Louis-Philippe.

position. It seemed to her that he gave up forthwith the fruit of all the good relations with well-placed people so honorably preserved and stored away for their children by foresightful families (my great-aunt had even stopped seeing the son of a lawyer we knew because he had married royalty and was therefore in her opinion demoted from the respected rank of lawyer's son to that of one of those adventurers, former valets or stableboys, on whom they say that queens sometimes bestowed their favors). She disapproved of my grandfather's plan to question Swann, the next evening he was to come to dinner, about these friends of his we had discovered. At the same time my grandmother's two sisters, old maids who shared her nobility of character, but not her sort of mind, declared that they could not understand what pleasure their brother-in-law could find in talking about such foolishness. They were women of lofty aspirations, who for that very reason were incapable of taking an interest in what is known as tittle-tattle, even if it had some historic interest, and more generally in anything that was not directly connected to an aesthetic or moral subject. The disinterestedness of their minds was such, with respect to all that, closely or distantly, seemed connected with worldly matters, that their sense of hearing—having finally understood its temporary uselessness when the conversation at dinner assumed a tone that was frivolous or merely pedestrian without these two old spinsters being able to lead it back to the subjects dear to them—would suspend the functioning of its receptive organs and allow them to begin to atrophy. If my grandfather needed to attract the two sisters' attention at such times, he had to resort to those bodily signals used by alienists with certain lunatics suffering from distraction: striking a glass repeatedly with the blade of a knife while speaking to them sharply and looking them suddenly in the eye, violent methods which these psychiatrists often bring with them into their ordinary relations with healthy people, either from professional habit or because they believe everyone is a little crazy.

They were more interested when, the day before Swann was to come to dinner, and had personally sent them a case of Asti wine, my aunt, holding a copy of the *Figaro*[4] in which next to the title of a painting in an exhibition of Corot,[5] these words appeared: "From the collection of M. Charles Swann," said: "Did you see this? Swann is 'front page news' in the *Figaro*." "But I've always told you he had a great deal of taste," said my grandmother. "Of course you would! Anything so long as your opinion is not the same as *ours*," answered my great-aunt, who, knowing that my grandmother was never of the same opinion as she, and not being quite sure that she herself was the one we always declared was right, wanted to extract from us a general condemnation of my grandmother's convictions against which she was trying to force us into solidarity with her own. But we remained silent. When my grandmother's sisters expressed their intention of speaking to Swann about this mention in the *Figaro*, my great-aunt advised them against it. Whenever she saw in others an advantage, however small, that she did not have, she persuaded herself that it was not an advantage but a detriment and she pitied them so as not to have to envy them. "I believe you would not be pleasing him at all; I am quite sure I would find it very unpleasant to see my name

4. A leading Parisian newspaper. *Asti:* an Italian white wine.   5. Jean-Baptiste-Camille Corot (1796–1875), a popular French landscape painter.

printed boldly like that in the newspaper, and I would not be at all gratified if someone spoke to me about it." But she did not persist in trying to convince my grandmother's sisters; for they in their horror of vulgarity had made such a fine art of concealing a personal allusion beneath ingenious circumlocutions that it often went unnoticed even by the person to whom it was addressed. As for my mother, she thought only of trying to persuade my father to agree to talk to Swann not about his wife but about his daughter, whom he adored and because of whom it was said he had finally entered into this marriage. "You might just say a word to him; just ask how she is: It must be so hard for him." But my father would become annoyed: "No, no; you have the most absurd ideas. It would be ridiculous."

But the only one of us for whom Swann's arrival became the object of a painful preoccupation was I. This was because on the evenings when strangers, or merely M. Swann, were present, Mama did not come up to my room. I had dinner before everyone else and afterward I came and sat at the table, until eight o'clock when it was understood that I had to go upstairs; the precious and fragile kiss that Mama usually entrusted to me in my bed when I was going to sleep I would have to convey from the dining room to my bedroom and protect during the whole time I undressed, so that its sweetness would not shatter, so that its volatile essence would not disperse and evaporate, and on precisely those evenings when I needed to receive it with more care, I had to take it, I had to snatch it brusquely, publicly, without even having the time and the freedom of mind necessary to bring to what I was doing the attention of those individuals controlled by some mania, who do their utmost not to think of anything else while they are shutting a door, so as to be able, when the morbid uncertainty returns to them, to confront it victoriously with the memory of the moment when they did shut the door. We were all in the garden when the two hesitant rings of the little bell sounded. We knew it was Swann; even so we all looked at one another questioningly and my grandmother was sent on reconnaissance. "Remember to thank him intelligibly for the wine, you know how delicious it is and the case is enormous," my grandfather exhorted his two sisters-in-law. "Don't start whispering," said my great-aunt. "How comfortable would you feel arriving at a house where everyone is speaking so quietly!" "Ah! Here's M. Swann. Let's ask him if he thinks the weather will be good tomorrow," said my father. My mother thought that one word from her would wipe out all the pain that we in our family might have caused Swann since his marriage. She found an opportunity to take him aside. But I followed her; I could not bring myself to part from her by even one step while thinking that very soon I would have to leave her in the dining room and that I would have to go up to my room without having the consolation I had on the other evenings, that she would come kiss me. "Now, M. Swann," she said to him, "do tell me about your daughter; I'm sure she already has a taste for beautiful things like her papa." "Here, come and sit with the rest of us on the veranda," said my grandfather, coming up to them. My mother was obliged to stop, but she derived from this very constraint one more delicate thought, like good poets forced by the tyranny of rhyme to find their most beautiful lines: "We can talk about her again when we're by ourselves," she said softly to Swann. "Only a mother is capable of understanding you. I'm sure her own mother would agree with me." We all sat down around the iron table. I would have preferred not to think about the hours of anguish I was going to endure that evening alone in my room without being able to go to sleep; I tried to persuade myself they were not at all important, since I would have forgotten them by tomorrow morning, and to fix my mind on ideas of the future that should have led me as though across a bridge beyond the imminent abyss that frightened me so. But my mind, strained by my preoccupation, convex like the glance which I shot at my mother, would not allow itself to be penetrated by any foreign impressions. Thoughts certainly entered it, but only on condition that they left outside every element of beauty or simply of playfulness that could have moved or distracted me. Just as a patient, by means of an anesthetic, can watch with complete lucidity the operation being performed on him, but without feeling anything, I could recite to myself some lines that I loved or observe the efforts my grandfather made to talk to Swann about the Duc d'Audiffret-Pasquier,[6] without the former making me feel any emotion, the latter any hilarity. Those efforts were fruitless. Scarcely had my grandfather asked Swann a question relating to that orator than one of my grandmother's sisters, in whose ears the question was resonating like a profound but untimely silence that should be broken for the sake of politeness, would address the other: "Just imagine, Céline,[7] I've met a young Swedish governess who has been telling me about cooperatives in the Scandinavian countries; the details are most interesting. We really must have her here for dinner one evening." "Certainly!" answered her sister Flora, "but I haven't been wasting my time either. At M. Vinteuil's I met a learned old man who knows Maubant[8] very well, and Maubant has explained to him in the greatest detail how he creates his parts. It's most interesting. He's a neighbor of M. Vinteuil's, I had no idea; and he's very nice." "M. Vinteuil isn't the only one who has nice neighbors," exclaimed my aunt Céline in a voice amplified by her shyness and given an artificial tone by her premeditation, while casting at Swann what she called a meaningful look. At the same time my aunt Flora, who had understood that this phrase was Céline's way of thanking Swann for the Asti, was also looking at Swann with an expression that combined congratulation and irony, either simply to emphasize her sister's witticism, or because she envied Swann for having inspired it, or because she could not help making fun of him since she thought he was being put on the spot. "I think we can manage to persuade the old gentleman to come for dinner," continued Flora; "when you get him started on Maubant or Mme. Materna,[9] he talks for hours without stopping." "That must be delightful," sighed my grandfather, in whose mind, unfortunately, nature had as completely failed to include the possibility of taking a passionate interest in Swedish cooperatives or the creation of Maubant's parts as it had forgotten to furnish those of my grandmother's sisters with the little grain of salt one must add oneself, in order to find some savor in it, to a story about the private life of Molé or the Comte de Paris. "Now, then," said Swann to my grandfather, "what I'm going to say has more to do than it might appear with what you were asking me, because in certain respects things haven't changed enormously. This

6. The Duc d'Audiffret-Pasquier (1823–1905) was president of the Chamber of Peers during the reign of Louis-Philippe.   7. A misprint—as the context makes clear, it is Céline who speaks and Flora who responds.   8. Henri-Polydore Maubant (1823–1902), an actor at the Comédie Française. *Vinteuil:* A fictitious composer.   9. Amalie Materna (1845–1918), Austrian soprano who took part in the premiere of Wagner's *Ring* cycle at Bayreuth in 1876.

morning I was rereading something in Saint-Simon[1] that would have amused you. It's in the volume about his mission to Spain; it's not one of the best, hardly more than a journal, but at least it's a marvelously well written one, which already makes it rather fundamentally different from the deadly boring journals we think we have to read every morning and evening." "I don't agree, there are days when reading the papers seems to me very pleasant indeed . . ." my aunt Flora interrupted, to show that she had read the sentence about Swann's Corot in Le Figaro. "When they talk about things or people that interest us!" said my aunt Céline, going one better. "I don't deny it," answered Swann with surprise. "What I fault the newspapers for is that day after day they draw our attention to insignificant things whereas only three or four times in our lives do we read a book in which there is something really essential. Since we tear the band off the newspaper so feverishly every morning, they ought to change things and put into the newspaper, oh, I don't know, perhaps . . . Pascal's Pensées![2] (He isolated this word with an ironic emphasis so as not to seem pedantic.) "And then, in the gilt-edged volume that we open only once in ten years," he added, showing the disdain for worldly matters affected by certain worldly men, "we would read that the Queen of Greece has gone to Cannes or that the Princesse de Léon has given a costume ball. This way, the proper proportions would be reestablished." But, feeling sorry he had gone so far as to speak even lightly of serious things: "What a lofty conversation we're having," he said ironically; "I don't know why we're climbing to such 'heights' "—and turning to my grandfather: "Well, Saint-Simon describes how Maulévrier[3] had the audacity to offer to shake hands with Saint-Simon's sons. You know, this is the same Maulévrier of whom he says: 'Never did I see in that thick bottle anything but ill-humor, vulgarity, and foolishness.' " "Thick or not, I know some bottles in which there is something quite different," said Flora vivaciously, determined that she too should thank Swann, because the gift of Asti was addressed to both of them. Céline laughed. Swann, disconcerted, went on: " 'I cannot say whether it was ignorance or a trap,' wrote Saint-Simon. 'He tried to shake hands with my children. I noticed it in time to prevent him.' " My grandfather was already in ecstasies over "ignorance or a trap," but Mlle. Céline, in whom the name of Saint-Simon—a literary man—had prevented the complete anesthesia of her auditory faculties, was already growing indignant: "What? You admire that? Well, that's a fine thing! But what can it mean; isn't one man as good as the next? What difference does it make whether he's a duke or a coachman, if he's intelligent and good-hearted? Your Saint-Simon had a fine way of raising his children, if he didn't teach them to offer their hands to all decent people. Why, it's quite abominable. And you dare to quote that?" And my grandfather, terribly upset and sensing how impossible it would be, in the face of this obstruction, to try to get Swann to tell the stories that would have amused him, said quietly to Mama: "Now remind me of the line you taught me that comforts me so much at times like this. Oh, yes!

1. The memoirs of the Duc de Saint-Simon (1675–1755) describe court life and intrigue during the reigns of Louis XIV and Louis XV. He was sent to Spain in 1721 to arrange the marriage of Louis XV to the daughter of the king of Spain.   2. The Thoughts of the religious philosopher Blaise Pascal (1623–1662) are comments on the human condition and one of the major works of French classicism (see vol. 1 of this anthology).   3. Jean-Baptiste-Louis Andrault, marquis de Maulévrier-Langeron (1677–1754), the French ambassador to Spain. Saint-Simon considered him of inferior birth and would not let his own children shake Maulévrier's hand (Memoirs, vol. 39).

'What virtues, Lord, Thou makest us abhor![4] Oh, how good that is!"

I did not take my eyes off my mother, I knew that when we were at the table, they would not let me stay during the entire dinner and that, in order not to annoy my father, Mama would not let me kiss her several times in front of the guests as though we were in my room. And so I promised myself that in the dining room, as they were beginning dinner and I felt the hour approaching, I would do everything I could do alone in advance of this kiss which would be so brief and furtive, choose with my eyes the place on her cheek that I would kiss, prepare my thoughts so as to be able, by means of this mental beginning of the kiss, to devote the whole of the minute Mama would grant me to feeling her cheek against my lips, as a painter who can obtain only short sittings prepares his palette and, guided by his notes, does in advance from memory everything for which he could if necessary manage without the presence of the model. But now before the dinner bell rang my grandfather had the unwitting brutality to say: "The boy looks tired, he ought to go up to bed. We're dining late tonight anyway." And my father, who was not as scrupulous as my grandmother and my mother about honoring treaties, said: "Yes, go on now, up to bed with you." I tried to kiss Mama, at that moment we heard the dinner bell. "No, really, leave your mother alone, you've already said goodnight to each other as it is, these demonstrations are ridiculous. Go on now, upstairs!" And I had to leave without my viaticum;[5] I had to climb each step of the staircase, as the popular expression has it, "against my heart,"[6] climbing against my heart which wanted to go back to my mother because she had not, by kissing me, given it license to go with me. That detested staircase which I always entered with such gloom exhaled an odor of varnish that had in some sense absorbed, fixated, the particular sort of sorrow I felt every evening and made it perhaps even crueler to my sensibility because, when it took that olfactory form, my intelligence could no longer share in it. When we are asleep and a raging toothache is as yet perceived by us only in the form of a girl whom we attempt two hundred times to pull out of the water or a line by Molière[7] that we repeat to ourselves incessantly, it is a great relief to wake up so that our intelligence can divest the idea of raging toothache of its disguise of heroism or cadence. It was the opposite of this relief that I experienced when my sorrow at going up to my room entered me in a manner infinitely swifter, almost instantaneous, at once insidious and abrupt, through the inhalation—far more toxic than the intellectual penetration—of the smell of varnish peculiar to that staircase. Once in my room, I had to stop up all the exits, close the shutters, dig my own grave by undoing my covers, put on the shroud of my nightshirt. But before burying myself in the iron bed which they had added to the room because I was too hot in the summer under the rep curtains of the big bed, I had a fit of rebelliousness, I wanted to attempt the ruse of a condemned man. I wrote to my mother begging her to come upstairs for something serious that I could not tell her in my letter. My fear was that Françoise, my aunt's cook who was charged with looking after me when I was at Combray, would refuse to convey my note. I suspected that, for her, delivering a mes-

---

4. Adaptation of a line from *Pompey's Death* (III.4), a tragedy by the French classical dramatist Pierre Corneille (1606–1684). 5. The communion wafer and wine given to the dying in Catholic rites. 6. The literal translation of a common phrase meaning "reluctantly" (French). 7. Jean-Baptiste Poquelin Molière (1622–1673), French classical dramatist (see p. 10).

sage to my mother when there was company would seem as impossible as for a porter to hand a letter to an actor while he was onstage. With respect to things that could or could not be done she possessed a code at once imperious, extensive, subtle, and intransigent about distinctions that were impalpable or otiose (which made it resemble those ancient laws which, alongside such fierce prescriptions as the massacre of children at the breast, forbid one with an exaggerated delicacy to boil a kid in its mother's milk, or to eat the sinew from an animal's thigh).[8] This code, to judge from her sudden obstinacy when she did not wish to do certain errands that we gave her, seemed to have anticipated social complexities and worldly refinements that nothing in Françoise's associations or her life as a village domestic could have suggested to her; and we had to say to ourselves that in her there was a very old French past, noble and ill understood, as in those manufacturing towns where elegant old houses testify that there was once a court life, and where the employees of a factory for chemical products work surrounded by delicate sculptures representing the miracle of Saint Théophile or the four sons of Aymon.[9] In this particular case, the article of the code which made it unlikely that except in case of fire Françoise would go bother Mama in the presence of M. Swann for so small a personage as myself simply betokened the respect she professed not only for the family—as for the dead, for priests, and for kings—but also for the visitor to whom one was offering one's hospitality, a respect that would perhaps have touched me in a book but that always irritated me on her lips, because of the solemn and tender tones she adopted in speaking of it, and especially so this evening when the sacred character she conferred on the dinner might have the effect of making her refuse to disturb its ceremonial. But to give myself a better chance, I did not hesitate to lie and tell her that it was not in the least I who had wanted to write to Mama, but that it was Mama who, as she said goodnight to me, had exhorted me not to forget to send her an answer concerning something she had asked me to look for; and she would certainly be very annoyed if this note was not delivered to her. I think Françoise did not believe me, for, like those primitive men whose senses were so much more powerful than ours, she could immediately discern, from signs imperceptible to us, any truth that we wanted to hide from her; she looked at the envelope for five minutes as if the examination of the paper and the appearance of the writing would inform her about the nature of the contents or tell her which article of her code she ought to apply. Then she went out with an air of resignation that seemed to signify: "If it isn't a misfortune for parents to have a child like that!" She came back after a moment to tell me that they were still only at the ice stage, that it was impossible for the butler to deliver the letter right away in front of everyone, but that, when the mouth-rinsing bowls[1] were put round, they would find a way to hand it to Mama. Instantly my anxiety subsided; it was now no longer, as it had been only a moment ago, until tomorrow that I had left my mother, since my little note, no doubt annoying her (and doubly because this stratagem would make me ridiculous in Swann's eyes), would at least allow me, invisible and enraptured, to enter the same room as

8. References to the strict dietary laws of Deuteronomy 14.21 and Genesis 31.32, respectively. 9. The four sons of Aymon, heroic knights who together rode the magic horse Bayard. *Théophile:* a cleric who was saved from damnation by the Virgin Mary after he repented for having signed a pact with the devil. 1. Bowls with warm water for rinsing were passed around at the end of the meal.

she, would whisper about me in her ear; since that forbidden, hostile dining room, where, just a moment before, the ice itself—the "*granité*"[2]—and the rinsing bowls seemed to me to contain pleasures noxious and mortally sad because Mama was enjoying them far away from me, was opening itself to me and, like a fruit that has turned sweet and bursts its skin, was about to propel, to project, all the way to my intoxicated heart, Mama's attention as she read my lines. Now I was no longer separated from her; the barriers were down, an exquisite thread joined us. And that was not all: Mama would probably come!

I thought Swann would surely have laughed at the anguish I had just suffered if he had read my letter and guessed its purpose; yet, on the contrary, as I learned later, a similar anguish[3] was the torment of long years of his life and no one, perhaps, could have understood me as well as he; in his case, the anguish that comes from feeling that the person you love is in a place of amusement where you are not, where you cannot join her, came to him through love, to which it is in some sense predestined, by which it will be hoarded, appropriated; but when, as in my case, this anguish enters us before love has made its appearance in our life, it drifts as it waits for it, vague and free, without a particular assignment, at the service of one feeling one day, of another the next, sometimes of filial tenderness or affection for a friend. And the joy with which I served my first apprenticeship when Françoise came back to tell me my letter would be delivered Swann too had known well, that deceptive joy given to us by some friend, some relative of the woman we love when, arriving at the house or theater where she is, for some dance, gala evening, or premiere at which he is going to see her, this friend notices us wandering outside, desperately awaiting some opportunity to communicate with her. He recognizes us, speaks to us familiarly, asks us what we are doing there. And when we invent the story that we have something urgent to say to his relative or friend, he assures us that nothing could be simpler, leads us into the hall, and promises to send her to us in five minutes. How we love him, as at that moment I loved Françoise—the well-intentioned intermediary who with a single word has just made tolerable, human, and almost propitious the unimaginable, infernal festivity into the thick of which we had been imagining that hostile, perverse, and exquisite vortices of pleasure were carrying away from us and inspiring with derisive laughter the woman we love! If we are to judge by him, the relative who has come up to us and is himself also one of the initiates in the cruel mysteries, the other guests at the party cannot have anything very demoniacal about them. Those inaccessible and excruciating hours during which she was about to enjoy unknown pleasures—now, through an unexpected breach, we are entering them; now, one of the moments which, in succession, would have composed those hours, a moment as real as the others, perhaps even more important to us, because our mistress is more involved in it, we can picture to ourselves, we possess it, we are taking part in it, we have created it, almost: the moment in which he will tell her we are here, downstairs. And no doubt the other moments of the party would not have been essentially very different from this one, would not have had anything more delectable about them that should make us

2. A sherbetlike ice served as a separate course or after dinner.   3. That is, his unhappy love for Odette de Crécy, described later in *Swann in Love*.

suffer so, since the kind friend has said to us: "Why, she'll be delighted to come down! It'll be much nicer for her to chat with you than to be bored up there." Alas! Swann had learned by experience that the good intentions of a third person have no power over a woman who is annoyed to find herself pursued even into a party by someone she does not love. Often, the friend comes back down alone.

My mother did not come, and with no consideration for my pride (which was invested in her not denying the story that she was supposed to have asked me to let her know the results of some search) asked Françoise to say these words to me: "There is no answer," words I have so often since then heard the doormen in grand hotels or the footmen in bawdy houses bring back to some poor girl who exclaims in surprise: "What, he said nothing? Why, that's impossible! Did you really give him my note? All right, I'll go on waiting." And—just as she invariably assures him she does not need the extra gas jet which the doorman wants to light for her, and remains there, hearing nothing further but the few remarks about the weather exchanged by the doorman and a lackey whom he sends off suddenly, when he notices the time, to put a customer's drink on ice—having declined Françoise's offer to make me some tea or to stay with me, I let her return to the servants' hall, I went to bed and closed my eyes, trying not to hear the voices of my family, who were having their coffee in the garden. But after a few seconds, I became aware that, by writing that note to Mama, by approaching, at the risk of angering her, so close to her that I thought I could touch the moment when I would see her again, I had shut off from myself the possibility of falling asleep without seeing her again, and the beating of my heart grew more painful each minute because I was increasing my agitation by telling myself to be calm, to accept my misfortune. Suddenly my anxiety subsided, a happiness invaded me as when a powerful medicine begins to take effect and our pain vanishes: I had just formed the resolution not to continue trying to fall asleep without seeing Mama again, to kiss her at all costs even though it was with the certainty of being on bad terms with her for a long time after, when she came up to bed. The calm that came with the end of my distress filled me with an extraordinary joy, quite as much as did my expectation, my thirst for and my fear of danger. I opened the window noiselessly and sat down on the foot of my bed; I hardly moved so that I would not be heard from below. Outdoors, too, things seemed frozen in silent attention so as not to disturb the moonlight which, duplicating and distancing each thing by extending its shadow before it, denser and more concrete than itself, had at once thinned and enlarged the landscape like a map that had been folded and was now opened out. What needed to move, some foliage of the chestnut tree, moved. But its quivering, minute, complete, executed even in its slightest nuances and ultimate refinements, did not spill over onto the rest, did not merge with it, remained circumscribed. Exposed against this silence, which absorbed nothing of them, the most distant noises, those that must have come from gardens that lay at the other end of town, could be perceived detailed with such "finish" that they seemed to owe this effect of remoteness only to their pianissimo, like those muted motifs so well executed by the orchestra of the Conservatoire[4] that, although you do not lose a single note,

4. The national music conservatory (academy) in Paris.

you nonetheless think you are hearing them far away from the concert hall and all the old subscribers—my grandmother's sisters too, when Swann had given them his seats—strained their ears as if they were listening to the distant advances of an army on the march that had not yet turned the corner of the rue de Trévise.[5]

I knew that the situation I was now placing myself in was the one that could provoke the gravest consequences of all for me, coming from my parents, much graver in truth than a stranger would have supposed, the sort he would have believed could be produced only by truly shameful misdeeds. But in my upbringing, the order of misdeeds was not the same as in that of other children, and I had become accustomed to placing before all the rest (because there were probably no others from which I needed to be more carefully protected) those whose common characteristic I now understand was that you lapse into them by yielding to a nervous impulse. But at the time no one uttered these words, no one revealed this cause, which might have made me believe I was excusable for succumbing to them or even perhaps incapable of resisting them. But I recognized them clearly from the anguish that preceded them as well as from the rigor of the punishment that followed them; and I knew that the one I had just committed was in the same family as others for which I had been severely punished, though infinitely graver. When I went and placed myself in my mother's path at the moment she was going up to bed, and when she saw that I had stayed up to say goodnight to her again in the hallway, they would not let me continue to live at home, they would send me away to school the next day, that much was certain. Well! Even if I had had to throw myself out of the window five minutes later, I still preferred this. What I wanted now was Mama, to say goodnight to her, I had gone too far along the road that led to the fulfillment of that desire to be able to turn back now.

I heard the footsteps of my family, who were seeing Swann out; and when the bell on the gate told me he had left, I went to the window. Mama was asking my father if he had thought the lobster was good and if M. Swann had had more coffee-and-pistachio ice. "I found it quite ordinary," said my mother; "I think next time we'll have to try another flavor." "I can't tell you how changed I find Swann," said my great-aunt, "he has aged so!" My great-aunt was so used to seeing Swann always as the same adolescent that she was surprised to find him suddenly not as young as the age she continued to attribute to him. And my family was also beginning to feel that in him this aging was abnormal, excessive, shameful, and more deserved by the unmarried, by all those for whom it seems that the great day that has no tomorrow is longer than for others, because for them it is empty and the moments in it add up from morning on without then being divided among children. "I think he has no end of worries with that wretched wife of his who is living with a certain Monsieur de Charlus,[6] as all of Combray knows. It's the talk of the town." My mother pointed out that in spite of this he had been looking much less sad for some time now. "He also doesn't make that gesture of his as often, so like his father, of wiping his eyes and running his hand across his forehead. I myself think that in his heart of hearts he no longer loves that woman." "Why, naturally he doesn't love her anymore," answered my grandfather. "I received a letter from him about it a long time ago, by now,

5. A street in Combray.   6. The brother of the duc de Guermantes.

a letter with which I hastened not to comply and which leaves no doubt about his feelings, at least his feelings of love, for his wife. Well now! You see, you didn't thank him for the Asti," added my grandfather, turning to his two sisters-in-law. "What? We didn't thank him? I think, just between you and me, that I put it quite delicately," answered my aunt Flora. "Yes, you managed it very well: quite admirable," said my aunt Céline. "But you were very good too." "Yes, I was rather proud of my remark about kind neighbors." "What? Is that what you call thanking him?" exclaimed my grandfather. "I certainly heard that, but devil take me if I thought it was directed at Swann. You can be sure he never noticed." "But see here, Swann isn't stupid, I'm sure he appreciated it. After all, I couldn't tell him how many bottles there were and what the wine cost!" My father and mother were left alone there, and sat down for a moment; then my father said: "Well, shall we go up to bed?" "If you like, my dear, even though I'm not the least bit sleepy; yet it couldn't be that perfectly harmless coffee ice that's keeping me so wide-awake; but I can see a light in the servants' hall, and since poor Françoise has waited up for me, I'll go and ask her to unhook my bodice while you're getting undressed." And my mother opened the latticed door that led from the vestibule to the staircase. Soon, I heard her coming upstairs to close her window. I went without a sound into the hallway; my heart was beating so hard I had trouble walking, but at least it was no longer pounding from anxiety, but from terror and joy. I saw the light cast in the stairwell by Mama's candle. Then I saw Mama herself; I threw myself forward. In the first second, she looked at me with astonishment, not understanding what could have happened. Then an expression of anger came over her face, she did not say a single word to me, and indeed for much less than this they would go several days without speaking to me. If Mama had said one word to me, it would have been an admission that they could talk to me again and in any case it would perhaps have seemed to me even more terrible, as a sign that, given the gravity of the punishment that was going to be prepared for me, silence, and estrangement, would have been childish. A word would have been like the calm with which you answer a servant when you have just decided to dismiss him; the kiss you give a son you are sending off to enlist, whereas you would have refused it if you were simply going to be annoyed with him for a few days. But she heard my father coming up from the dressing room where he had gone to undress and, to avoid the scene he would make over me, she said to me in a voice choked with anger: "Run, run, so at least your father won't see you waiting like this as if you were out of your mind!" But I repeated to her: "Come say goodnight to me," terrified as I saw the gleam from my father's candle already rising up the wall, but also using his approach as a means of blackmail and hoping that Mama, to avoid my father's finding me there still if she continued to refuse, would say: "Go back to your room, I'll come." It was too late, my father was there in front of us. Involuntarily, though no one heard, I murmured these words: "I'm done for!"

It was not so. My father was constantly refusing me permission for things that had been authorized in the more generous covenants granted by my mother and grandmother because he did not bother about "principles" and for him there was no "rule of law."[7] For a completely contingent reason, or

7. The "law of nations" (Latin) or natural law, supposed to govern international and public relations. Marcel sees his relationship with his mother and grandmother as a social contract; his father, who does not respect the rules, becomes the unpredictable tyrant.

even for no reason at all, he would at the last minute deny me a certain walk that was so customary, so consecrated that to deprive me of it was a violation, or, as he had done once again this evening, long before the ritual hour he would say to me: "Go on now, up to bed, no arguments!" But also, because he had no principles (in my grandmother's sense), he was not strictly speaking intransigent. He looked at me for a moment with an expression of surprise and annoyance, then as soon as Mama had explained to him with a few embarrassed words what had happened, he said to her: "Go along with him, then. You were just saying you didn't feel very sleepy, stay in his room for a little while, I don't need anything." "But my dear," answered my mother timidly, "whether I'm sleepy or not doesn't change anything, we can't let the child get into the habit . . . ." "But it isn't a question of habit," said my father, shrugging his shoulders, "you can see the boy is upset, he seems very sad; look, we're not executioners! You'll end by making him ill, and that won't do us much good! There are two beds in his room; go tell Françoise to prepare the big one for you and sleep there with him tonight. Now then, goodnight, I'm not as high-strung as the two of you, I'm going to bed."

It was impossible to thank my father; he would have been irritated by what he called mawkishness. I stood there not daring to move; he was still there in front of us, tall in his white nightshirt, under the pink and violet Indian cashmere shawl that he tied around his head now that he had attacks of neuralgia, with the gesture of Abraham in the engraving after Benozzo Gozzoli[8] that M. Swann had given me, as he told Sarah she must leave Issac's side. This was many years ago. The staircase wall on which I saw the rising glimmer of his candle has long since ceased to exist. In me, too, many things have been destroyed that I thought were bound to last forever and new ones have formed that have given birth to new sorrows and joys which I could not have foreseen then, just as the old ones have become difficult for me to understand. It was a very long time ago, too, that my father ceased to be able to say to Mama: "Go with the boy." The possibility of such hours will never be reborn for me. But for a little while now, I have begun to hear again very clearly, if I take care to listen, the sobs that I was strong enough to contain in front of my father and that broke out only when I found myself alone again with Mama. They have never really stopped; and it is only because life is now becoming quieter around me that I can hear them again, like those convent bells covered so well by the clamor of the town during the day that one would think they had ceased altogether but which begin sounding again in the silence of the evening.

Mama spent that night in my room; when I had just committed such a misdeed that I expected to have to leave the house, my parents granted me more than I could ever have won from them as a reward for any good deed. Even at the moment when it manifested itself through this pardon, my father's conduct toward me retained that arbitrary and undeserved quality that characterized it and was due to the fact that it generally resulted from fortuitous convenience rather than a premeditated plan. It may even be that what I called his severity, when he sent me to bed, deserved that name less than my mother's or my grandmother's, for his nature, in certain respects

---

8. Florentine painter (1420–1497) whose frescoes at Pisa contain scenes from the life of the biblical patriarch Abraham.

more different from mine than theirs was, had probably kept him from discovering until now how very unhappy I was every evening, something my mother and my grandmother knew well; but they loved me enough not to consent to spare me my suffering, they wanted to teach me to master it in order to reduce my nervous sensitivity and strengthen my will. As for my father, whose affection for me was of another sort, I do not know if he would have been courageous enough for that: the one time he realized that I was upset, he had said to my mother: "Go and comfort him." Mama stayed in my room that night and, as though not to allow any remorse to spoil those hours which were so different from what I had had any right to expect, when Françoise, realizing that something extraordinary was happening when she saw Mama sitting next to me, holding my hand and letting me cry without scolding me, asked her: "Why, madame, now what's wrong with Monsieur that he's crying so?" Mama answered her: "Why, even he doesn't know, Françoise, he's in a state; prepare the big bed for me quickly and then go on up to bed yourself." And so, for the first time, my sadness was regarded no longer as a punishable offense but as an involuntary ailment that had just been officially recognized, a nervous condition for which I was not responsible; I had the relief of no longer having to mingle qualms of conscience with the bitterness of my tears, I could cry without sin. I was also not a little proud, with respect to Françoise, of this turnabout in human affairs which, an hour after Mama had refused to come up to my room and had sent the disdainful answer that I should go to sleep, raised me to the dignity of a grown-up and brought me suddenly to a sort of puberty of grief, of emancipation from tears. I ought to have been happy: I was not. It seemed to me that my mother had just made me a first concession which must have been painful to her, that this was a first abdication on her part from the ideal she had conceived for me, and that for the first time she, who was so courageous, had to confess herself beaten. It seemed to me that, if I had just gained a victory, it was over her, that I had succeeded, as illness, affliction, or age might have done, in relaxing her will, in weakening her judgment, and that this evening was the beginning of a new era, would remain as a sad date. If I had dared, now, I would have said to Mama: "No, I don't want you to do this, don't sleep here." But I was aware of the practical wisdom, the realism as it would be called now, which in her tempered my grandmother's ardently idealistic nature, and I knew that, now that the harm was done, she would prefer to let me at least enjoy the soothing pleasure of it and not disturb my father. To be sure, my mother's lovely face still shone with youth that evening when she so gently held my hands and tried to stop my tears; but it seemed to me that this was precisely what should not have been, her anger would have saddened me less than this new gentleness which my childhood had not known before; it seemed to me that with an impious and secret hand I had just traced in her soul a first wrinkle and caused a first white hair to appear. At the thought of this my sobs redoubled, and then I saw that Mama, who never let herself give way to any emotion with me, was suddenly overcome by my own and was trying to suppress a desire to cry. When she saw that I had noticed, she said to me with a smile: "There now, my little chick, my little canary, he's going to make his mama as silly as himself if this continues. Look, since you're not sleepy and your mama isn't either, let's not go on upsetting each other, let's do something, let's get one of your books." But I had none there. "Would you enjoy it less if I took out the books your grandmother will be giving you on your saint's day? Think about it carefully: you mustn't be disappointed not to have anything the day after tomorrow." On the contrary, I was delighted, and Mama went to get a packet of books, of which I could not distinguish, through the paper in which they were wrapped, more than their shape, short and thick, but which, in this first guise, though summary and veiled, already eclipsed the box of colors from New Year's Day and the silk-worms from last year. They were *La Mare au Diable, François le Champi, La Petite Fadette,* and *Les Maîtres Sonneurs.*[9] My grandmother, as I learned afterward, had first chosen the poems of Musset, a volume of Rousseau, and *Indiana*;[1] for though she judged frivolous reading to be as unhealthy as sweets and pastries, it did not occur to her that a great breath of genius might have a more dangerous and less invigorating influence on the mind even of a child than would the open air and the sea breeze on his body. But as my father had nearly called her mad when he learned which books she wanted to give me, she had returned to the bookstore, in Jouy-le-Vicomte herself, so that I would not risk not having my present (it was a burning-hot day and she had come home so indisposed that the doctor had warned my mother not to let her tire herself out that way again) and she had resorted to the four pastoral novels of George Sand. "My dear daughter," she said to Mama, "I could not bring myself to give the boy something badly written."

In fact, she could never resign herself to buying anything from which one could not derive an intellectual profit, and especially that which beautiful things afford us by teaching us to seek our pleasure elsewhere than in the satisfactions of material comfort and vanity. Even when she had to make someone a present of the kind called "useful," when she had to give an armchair, silverware, a walking stick, she looked for "old" ones, as though, now that long desuetude had effaced their character of usefulness, they would appear more disposed to tell us about the life of people of other times than to serve the needs of our own life. She would have liked me to have in my room photographs of the most beautiful monuments or landscapes. But at the moment of buying them, and even though the thing represented had an aesthetic value, she would find that vulgarity and utility too quickly resumed their places in that mechanical mode of representation, the photograph. She would try to use cunning and, if not to eliminate commercial banality entirely, at least to reduce it, to substitute for the greater part of it more art, to introduce into it in a sense several "layers" of art: instead of photographs of Chartres Cathedral, the Fountains of Saint-Cloud, or Mount Vesuvius, she would make inquiries of Swann as to whether some great painter had not depicted them, and preferred to give me photographs of Chartres Cathedral by Corot, of the Fountains of Saint-Cloud by Hubert Robert, of Mount Vesuvius by Turner,[2] which made one further degree of art. But if the photographer had been removed from the representation of the masterpiece or of nature and replaced by a great artist, he still reclaimed

9. *The Devil's Pool, François the Foundling Discovered in the Fields, Little Fadette,* and *The Master Bell-ringers,* all novels of idealized country life by the French woman writer George Sand (1806–1876). 1. The works of Alfred de Musset (1810–1857) and Jean-Jacques Rousseau (1712–1778), often romantic and sometimes confessional, and George Sand's *Indiana* (1832), a novel of free love, would be thought unsuitable reading for a young child. 2. All photographs of paintings: the cathedral at Chartres, painted in 1830 by Corot; the fountains in the old park at Saint-Cloud, outside Paris, painted by Hubert Robert (1733–1809); and Vesuvius, a famous volcano near Naples, painted by J. M. W. Turner (1775–1851).

his rights to reproduce that very interpretation. Having deferred vulgarity as far as possible, my grandmother would try to move it back still further. She would ask Swann if the work had not been engraved, preferring, whenever possible, old engravings that also had an interest beyond themselves, such as those that represent a masterpiece in a state in which we can no longer see it today (like the engraving by Morghen of Leonardo's *Last Supper* before its deterioration).[3] It must be said that the results of this interpretation of the art of gift giving were not always brilliant. The idea I formed of Venice from a drawing by Titian[4] that is supposed to have the lagoon in the background was certainly far less accurate than the one I would have derived from simple photographs. We could no longer keep count, at home, when my great-aunt wanted to draw up an indictment against my grandmother, of the armchairs she had presented to young couples engaged to be married or old married couples which, at the first attempt to make use of them, had immediately collapsed under the weight of one of the recipients. But my grandmother would have believed it petty to be overly concerned about the solidity of a piece of wood in which one could still distinguish a small flower, a smile, sometimes a lovely invention from the past. Even what might, in these pieces of furniture, answer a need, since it did so in a manner to which we are no longer accustomed, charmed her like the old ways of speaking in which we see a metaphor that is obliterated, in our modern language, by the abrasion of habit. Now, in fact, the pastoral novels of George Sand that she was giving me for my saint's day were, like an old piece of furniture, full of expressions that had fallen into disuse and turned figurative again, the sort you no longer find anywhere but in the country. And my grandmother had bought them in preference to others just as she would sooner have rented an estate on which there was a Gothic dovecote or another of those old things that exercise such a happy influence on the mind by filling it with longing for impossible voyages through time.

Mama sat down by my bed; she had picked up *François le Champi*, whose reddish cover and incomprehensible title[5] gave it, in my eyes, a distinct personality and a mysterious attraction. I had not yet read a real novel. I had heard people say that George Sand was an exemplary novelist. This already predisposed me to imagine something indefinable and delicious in *François le Champi*. Narrative devices intended to arouse curiosity or emotion, certain modes of expression that make one uneasy or melancholy, and that a reader with some education will recognize as common to many novels, appeared to me—who considered a new book not as a thing having many counterparts, but as a unique person, having no reason for existing but in itself—simply as a disturbing emanation of *François le Champi*'s peculiar essence. Behind those events so ordinary, those things so common, those words so current, I sensed a strange sort of intonation, accentuation. The action began; it seemed to me all the more obscure because in those days, when I read, I often daydreamed, for entire pages, of something quite different. And in addition to the lacunae that this distraction left in the story, there was the fact, when Mama was the one reading aloud to me, that she skipped all the

---

3. Leonardo da Vinci's *Last Supper* was the subject of a famous engraving by Raphael Morghen (1758–1833). The paints in the original fresco had deteriorated rapidly, and a major restoration took place only in the 19th century.   4. Tiziano Vecellio (1488?–1576), Renaissance painter of the Venetian school.   5. *Champi* ("foundling") is an old French word that the child Marcel would not have known.

love scenes. Thus, all the bizarre changes that take place in the respective attitudes of the miller's wife and the child and that can be explained only by the progress of a nascent love seemed to me marked by a profound mystery whose source I readily imagined must be in that strange and sweet name "Champi," which gave the child, who bore it without my knowing why, its vivid, charming purplish color. If my mother was an unfaithful reader she was also, in the case of books in which she found the inflection of true feeling, a wonderful reader for the respect and simplicity of her interpretation, the beauty and gentleness of the sound of her voice. Even in real life, when it was people and not works of art which moved her to compassion or admiration, it was touching to see with what deference she removed from her voice, from her motions, from her words, any spark of gaiety that might hurt some mother who had once lost a child, any recollection of a saint's day or birthday that might remind some old man of his advanced age, any remark about housekeeping that might seem tedious to some young scholar. In the same way, when she was reading George Sand's prose, which always breathes that goodness, that moral distinction which Mama had learned from my grandmother to consider superior to all else in life, and which I was to teach her only much later not to consider superior to all else in books too, taking care to banish from her voice any pettiness, any affectation which might have prevented it from receiving that powerful torrent, she imparted all the natural tenderness, all the ample sweetness they demanded to those sentences which seemed written for her voice and which remained, so to speak, entirely within the register of her sensibility. She found, to attack them in the necessary tone, the warm inflection that preexists them and that dictated them, but that the words do not indicate; with this inflection she softened as she went along any crudeness in the tenses of the verbs, gave the imperfect and the past historic the sweetness that lies in goodness, the melancholy that lies in tenderness, directed the sentence that was ending toward the one that was about to begin, sometimes hurrying, sometimes slowing down the pace of the syllables so as to bring them, though their quantities were different, into one uniform rhythm, she breathed into this very common prose a sort of continuous emotional life.

My remorse was quieted, I gave in to the sweetness of that night in which I had my mother close to me. I knew that such a night could not be repeated; that the greatest desire I had in the world, to keep my mother in my room during those sad hours of darkness, was too contrary to the necessities of life and the wishes of others for its fulfillment, granted this night, to be anything other than artificial and exceptional. Tomorrow my anxieties would reawaken and Mama would not stay here. But when my anxieties were soothed, I no longer understood them; and then tomorrow night was still far away; I told myself I would have time to think of what to do, even though that time could not bring me any access of power, since these things did not depend on my will and seemed more avoidable to me only because of the interval that still separated them from me.

So it was that, for a long time, when, awakened at night, I remembered Combray again, I saw nothing of it but this sort of luminous panel, cut out among indistinct shadows, like those panels which the glow of a Bengal light[6]

---

6. A steady, blue-colored firework often used for signals.

or some electric projection will cut out and illuminate in a building whose other parts remain plunged in darkness: at the rather broad base, the small parlor, the dining room, the opening of the dark path by which M. Swann, the unconscious author of my sufferings, would arrive, the front hall where I would head toward the first step of the staircase, so painful to climb, that formed, by itself, the very narrow trunk of this irregular pyramid; and, at the top, my bedroom with the little hallway and its glass-paned door for Mama's entrance; in a word, always seen at the same hour, isolated from everything that might surround it, standing out alone against the darkness, the bare minimum of scenery (such as one sees prescribed at the beginnings of the old plays for performances in the provinces) needed for the drama of my undressing; as though Combray had consisted only of two floors connected by a slender staircase and as though it had always been seven o'clock in the evening there. The fact is, I could have answered anyone who asked me that Combray also included other things and existed at other times of day. But since what I recalled would have been supplied to me only by my voluntary memory, the memory of the intelligence, and since the information it gives about the past preserves nothing of the past itself, I would never have had any desire to think about the rest of Combray. It was all really quite dead for me.

Dead forever? Possibly.

There is a great deal of chance in all this, and a second sort of chance event, that of our own death, often does not allow us to wait long for the favors of the first.

I find the Celtic belief very reasonable, that the souls of those we have lost are held captive in some inferior creature, in an animal, in a plant, in some inanimate object, effectively lost to us until the day, which for many never comes, when we happen to pass close to the tree, come into possession of the object that is their prison.[7] Then they quiver, they call out to us, and as soon as we have recognized them, the spell is broken. Delivered by us, they have overcome death and they return to live with us.

It is the same with our past. It is a waste of effort for us to try to summon it, all the exertions of our intelligence are useless. The past is hidden outside the realm of our intelligence and beyond its reach, in some material object (in the sensation that this material object would give us) which we do not suspect. It depends on chance whether we encounter this object before we die, or do not encounter it.

For many years, already, everything about Combray that was not the theater and drama of my bedtime had ceased to exist for me, when one day in winter, as I returned home, my mother, seeing that I was cold, suggested that, contrary to my habit, I have a little tea. I refused at first and then, I do not know why, changed my mind. She sent for one of those squat, plump cakes called *petites madeleines* that look as though they have been molded in the grooved valve of a scallop shell. And soon, mechanically, oppressed by the gloomy day and the prospect of another sad day to follow, I carried to my lips a spoonful of the tea in which I had let soften a bit of madeleine. But at the very instant when the mouthful of tea mixed with cake crumbs touched my palate, I quivered, attentive to the extraordinary thing that was happening inside me. A delicious pleasure had invaded me, isolated me,

---

7. A belief attributed to Druids, the priests of the ancient Celtic peoples.

without my having any notion as to its cause. It had immediately rendered the vicissitudes of life unimportant to me, its disasters innocuous, its brevity illusory, acting in the same way that love acts, by filling me with a precious essence: or rather this essence was not merely inside me, it was me. I had ceased to feel mediocre, contingent, mortal. Where could it have come to me from—this powerful joy? I sensed that it was connected to the taste of the tea and the cake, but that it went infinitely far beyond it, could not be of the same nature. Where did it come from? What did it mean? How could I grasp it? I drink a second mouthful, in which I find nothing more than in the first, a third that gives me a little less than the second. It is time for me to stop, the virtue of the drink seems to be diminishing. Clearly, the truth I am seeking is not in the drink, but in me. The drink has awoken it in me, but does not know this truth, and can do no more than repeat indefinitely, with less and less force, this same testimony which I do not know how to interpret and which I want at least to be able to ask of it again and find again, intact, available to me, soon, for a decisive clarification. I put down the cup and turn to my mind. It is up to my mind to find the truth. But how? Such grave uncertainty, whenever the mind feels overtaken by itself; when it, the seeker, is also the obscure country where it must seek and where all its baggage will be nothing to it. Seek? Not only that: create. It is face-to-face with something that does not yet exist and that only it can accomplish, then bring into its light.

And I begin asking myself again what it could be, this unknown state which brought with it no logical proof, but only the evidence of its felicity, its reality, and in whose presence the other states of consciousness faded away. I want to try to make it reappear. I return in my thoughts to the moment when I took the first spoonful of tea. I find the same state again, without any new clarity. I ask my mind to make another effort, to bring back once more the sensation that is slipping away. And, so that nothing may interrupt the thrust with which it will try to grasp it again, I clear away every obstacle, every foreign idea, I protect my ears and my attention from the noises in the next room. But feeling my mind grow tired without succeeding, I now compel it to accept the very distraction I was denying it, to think of something else, to recover its strength before a supreme attempt. Then for a second time I create an empty space before it, I confront it again with the still recent taste of that first mouthful, and I feel something quiver in me, shift, try to rise, something that seems to have been unanchored at a great depth; I do not know what it is, but it comes up slowly; I feel the resistance and I hear the murmur of the distances traversed.

Undoubtedly what is palpitating thus, deep inside me, must be the image, the visual memory which is attached to this taste and is trying to follow it to me. But it is struggling too far away, too confusedly; I can just barely perceive the neutral glimmer in which the elusive eddying of stirred-up colors is blended; but I cannot distinguish the form, cannot ask it, as the one possible interpreter, to translate for me the evidence of its contemporary, its inseparable companion, the taste, ask it to tell me what particular circumstance is involved, what period of the past.

Will it reach the clear surface of my consciousness—this memory, this old moment which the attraction of an identical moment has come from so far to invite, to move, to raise up from the deepest part of me? I don't know.

Now I no longer feel anything, it has stopped, gone back down perhaps; who knows if it will ever rise up from its darkness again? Ten times I must begin again, lean down toward it. And each time, the laziness that deters us from every difficult task, every work of importance, has counseled me to leave it, to drink my tea and think only about my worries of today, my desires for tomorrow, upon which I may ruminate effortlessly.

And suddenly the memory appeared. That taste was the taste of the little piece of madeleine which on Sunday mornings at Combray (because that day I did not go out before it was time for Mass), when I went to say good morning to her in her bedroom, my aunt Léonie would give me after dipping it in her infusion of tea or lime blossom. The sight of the little madeleine had not reminded me of anything before I tasted it; perhaps because I had often seen them since, without eating them, on the shelves of the pastry shops, and their image had therefore left those days of Combray and attached itself to others more recent; perhaps because of these recollections abandoned so long outside my memory, nothing survived, everything had come apart; the forms and the form, too, of the little shell made of cake, so fatly sensual within its severe and pious pleating—had been destroyed, or, still half asleep, had lost the force of expansion that would have allowed them to rejoin my consciousness. But, when nothing subsists of an old past, after the death of people, after the destruction of things, alone, frailer but more enduring, more immaterial, more persistent, more faithful, smell and taste still remain for a long time, like souls, remembering, waiting, hoping, upon the ruins of all the rest, bearing without giving way, on their almost impalpable droplet, the immense edifice of memory.

And as soon as I had recognized the taste of the piece of madeleine dipped in lime-blossom tea that my aunt used to give me (though I did not yet know and had to put off to much later discovering why this memory made me so happy), immediately the old gray house on the street, where her bedroom was, came like a stage set to attach itself to the little wing opening onto the garden that had been built for my parents behind it (that truncated section which was all I had seen before then); and with the house the town, from morning to night and in all weathers, the Square, where they sent me before lunch, the streets where I went on errands, the paths we took if the weather was fine. And as in that game in which the Japanese amuse themselves by filling a porcelain bowl with water and steeping in it little pieces of paper until then undifferentiated which, the moment they are immersed in it, stretch and bend, take color and distinctive shape, turn into flowers, houses, human figures, firm and recognizable, so now all the flowers in our garden and in M. Swann's park, and the water lilies on the Vivonne,[8] and the good people of the village and their little dwellings and the church and all of Combray and its surroundings, all of this, acquiring form and solidity, emerged, town and gardens alike, from my cup of tea.

8. The local river.

THOMAS MANN
1875–1955

Thomas Mann's reputation as the great German novelist of the twentieth century represents only part of his stature; by the time of his death, he had become an international figure to whom people looked for statements on art, modern society, and the human condition. Continuing the great nineteenth-century tradition of psychological realism, Mann took as his subject the cultural and spiritual crises of Europe at the turn of the century. His career spanned a time of great change, including as it did the upheaval of two world wars and the visible disintegration of an entire society. Where other modern novelists, such as James Joyce, William Faulkner, and Virginia Woolf, stressed innovative language and style, Mann emphasized instead the society of his time and—inside that society—the universal human conflicts between art and life, sensuality and intellect, individual and social will.

Many of Mann's themes derive from the nineteenth-century German aesthetic tradition in which he grew up. The philosophers Schopenhauer and Nietzsche and the composer Wagner had the most influence on his work: Arthur Schopenhauer (1788–1860) for his vision of the artist's suffering and development; Friedrich Nietzsche (1844–1900) for his portrait of the diseased artist overcoming chaos and decay to produce, through discipline and will, artworks that justify existence; and Richard Wagner (1813–1883) for embodying the complete artist who controlled all aspects of his work: music, lyrics, the very staging of his operas. Mann's well-known use of the verbal *leitmotif* is also borrowed from Wagner, who would use in his operas a recurrent musical theme (the *leitmotif*) associated with a particular person, thing, action, or state of being. In Mann's literary adaptation, evocative phrases, repeated almost without change, link memories throughout the text and establish a cumulative emotional resonance. In the story *Tonio Kröger*, for example, Tonio's dual ancestry is repeatedly suggested by the contrasting phrases of the "dark, fiery mother, who played the piano and mandolin," and the father with his "thoughtful blue eyes" and "wild flower in the buttonhole." Inside the tradition of realistic narration, Mann created a highly organized literary structure with subtly interrelated themes and images that built up rich associations of ideas: in his own words, an "epic prose composition . . . understood by me as spiritual thematic pattern, as a musical complex of associations."

Mann was born in Lübeck, a historic seaport and commercial city in northern Germany, on June 6, 1875. His father was a grain merchant and head of the family firm; his mother came from a German-Brazilian family and was known for her beauty and musical talent. The contrast of Nordic and Latin that plays such a large part in Mann's work begins in his consciousness of his own heritage and is expanded to far-reaching symbolic levels. He disliked the scientific emphasis of his secondary education and left school in 1894 after repeating two years. Rejoining his family in Munich, where they had moved in 1891 after his father's death, he worked as an unpaid apprentice in a fire insurance business but found more interest in university lectures in history, political economy, and art. He decided against a business career after his first published story, *Fallen* (1896), received praise from the noted poet Richard Dehmel, and from 1896 to 1898 lived and wrote in Italy before returning to Munich for a two-year stint as manuscript reader for the satiric weekly *Simplicissimus*. In 1905, he married Katia Pringsheim, with whom he had six children. The short stories collected in *Little Herr Friedemann* (1899) were a success, and enabled Mann to find a publisher for his first major work, *Buddenbrooks* (1901).

Buddenbrooks describes the decline of a prosperous German family through four generations and is to some extent based on the history of the Mann family business. Nonetheless, the elements of autobiography are quickly absorbed into the more universal themes of the inner decay of the German burgher ("bourgeois," or middle-class) tradition and its growing isolation from other segments of society, a decline paralleled in the portrait of a developing artistic sensitivity and its relation to death. Children in the family of the self-confident, aggressive, and disciplined Consul Johann Buddenbrooks become increasingly introspective, hesitant, unhealthy, and artistic. The end of the family comes with young Hanno, a musical genius who is completely absorbed in his piano improvisations and thus prey to the fatal temptation of infinite beauty. In this novel, as in many later works, Mann's fictional world is governed by a tension or dualism between sensuous experience and intellect or will. A diseased and alienated imaginative soul is set against a healthy, gregarious, somewhat obtuse normal citizen; the erratic and poor artist against the disciplined and prosperous burgher; the dark, brown-eyed Latin against the blond, blue-eyed Nordic; warm, unself-conscious feelings against icy intellect; freedom against authority; immorality and decadence against moral respectability; a longing for the eternal and infinite against active participation in everyday life.

There is no recommended resolution of these polarities, for if either overwhelms the other, tragedy must follow. In the seemingly autobiographical *Tonio Kröger,* the protagonist is portrayed as sensitive to the claims of both, and his growing awareness of their combined importance is a sign of maturity. Ideally, the artist must live both extremes at once, in constant lucidity and pain. In *Death in Venice* (1912), the author Gustave Aschenbach suffers and dies for having been unable to keep the balance; in the novel *Doctor Faustus* (1947), the composer Adrian Leverkühn sells his soul to experience both poles. In *Mario and the Magician* (1929), the sadistic hypnotist Cipolla is an artist in his fashion, exercising a fatally corrupt art in which all his psychological insight, cutting intellect, and iron will produce only torment for himself and others. Mann's letters and essays show that he felt deeply involved in the relations of the artist's life to the artwork, but his protagonists have their own identity and symbolize much more than Mann's own artistic career. As artist and craftsman, he always insisted on distinguishing the work of art from its raw material, the emotions and experiences of life. He cultivated objectivity, distance, and irony in his own works, and no character—including the narrator—is immune from the author's critical eye.

Throughout his writings up to and during World War I, Mann established himself as an important spokesman for modern Germany. His early conservatism and defense of an authoritarian nationalist government (*Reflections of a Non-Political Man,* 1918) gave way to an ardent defense of democracy and liberal humanism as the Nazis came to power. Mann's most famous novel, *The Magic Mountain* (1924), is a bildungsroman (a novel of the protagonist's education and development) that uses the isolation of a mountaintop tuberculosis sanitorium to gain perspective on the philosophic issues of twentieth-century Europe. The hero, Hans Castorp, has to decide how to live as he listens to the competing dogmas of the humanist Settembrini and the fanatic antirationalist Naphta, and undergoes a double temptation of oblivion through eroticism (Clavdia Chauchat) and death (symbolized by the isolated sanitorium). The novel ends with Castorp choosing active participation in a world at war; whether or not he survives the trenches is left unresolved, but he has taken charge of his own destiny. *The Magic Mountain* was immensely popular, and its author received the Nobel Prize in 1929. He was so much an international figure when he went into voluntary exile in Switzerland as Hitler came to power in 1933 that the Nazis, stung by his criticism, revoked his citizenship. Moving to America in 1938, he wrote and lectured against Nazism, and in 1944 he became an American citizen.

Mann's later works cover a range of themes. *Joseph and His Brothers* (1933–45) is a tetralogy on the biblical tale of Joseph, who, abandoned for dead by his brothers, survives and comes to power in Egypt. *Doctor Faustus,* which Mann called "the novel of my epoch, dressed up in the story of a highly precarious and sinful artistic life," portrayed the composer Adrian Leverkühn as a modern Faust who personifies the temptation and corruption of contemporary Germany. Leverkühn makes a pact with the devil to become aware of the extremes of his own personality, thus enriching his experience and his music. His pieces are rationally composed by using intellectual patterns derived from the twelve-tone row, an avant-garde theory of composition based on a sequence of twelve tones with no previous harmonic relations, instead of the traditional musical scale. His *Lamentation of Doctor Faustus* is a direct challenge in theme and technique to the scale-based tonality of that earlier German masterpiece, Beethoven's Ninth Symphony with its concluding *Ode to Joy*. A somber and compelling work, *Doctor Faustus* symbolizes the negation of life Mann found inherent in Hitler's attempt to reshape German culture. Well after the war, when Mann had moved to Zurich, he published a final, comic picture of the artist-figure as a confidence man who uses his skill and ironic insight to manipulate society (*The Confessions of Felix Krull*, 1954). Mann's last work before his death on August 12, 1955, the *Confessions* recapitulates his familiar themes but in a lighthearted parody of traditional bildungsromans that is a far cry from the moral seriousness of earlier tales.

Mann's most famous novella, *Death in Venice*, was published in 1912, shortly after the writer's own vacation in Venice and two years before World War I. Its sense of impending doom involves the cultural disintegration of the "European soul" (soon to be expressed in the Great War) symbolized by the corruption and death of the writer Gustave Aschenbach during an epidemic. The story pictures a loss of psychological balance, a sickness of the artistic soul to match that of plague-ridden Venice masking its true condition before unsuspecting tourists. Erotic and artistic themes mingle as the respected Aschenbach, escaping a lifetime of laborious creation and self-discipline, allows himself to be swept away by the classical beauty of a young boy until he becomes a grotesque figure, dyeing his hair and rouging his cheeks in a vain attempt to appear young. The issue, however, is not Aschenbach's obsession with Tadzio but rather the way that this fatal love casts light on the artist's whole career.

Aschenbach has laboriously repressed emotions and spontaneity to achieve the disciplined, classical style of a master—and also to earn fame. Plagued by nervous exhaustion at the beginning of the story, he reacts to the sight of a foreign traveler with a "sudden, strange expansion of his inner space" and starts dreaming of exotic, dangerous landscapes. From the tropical swampland and tigers of the Ganges delta to the mountains of a later dream's Dionysiac revels, these visionary landscapes become a metaphor for all the subterranean impulses he has rejected in himself and for his art. Enigmatic figures guide Aschenbach's adventure of the emotions: the traveler, the grotesque old man on the boat, the gondolier, the street singer, and Tadzio himself interpreted as a godlike figure out of Greek myth or culture. Indeed, allusions to ancient myth and literature multiply rapidly as Aschenbach falls under Tadzio's spell and begins to rationalize his fascination as the artist's pursuit of divine beauty. Turning to Plato's *Phaedrus*, a dialogue that combines themes of love with the search for absolute beauty and truth, Aschenbach sketches his own "Platonic" argument as a meditation on the dual nature of the artist. It is the same dualism that was described by Nietzsche in *The Birth of Tragedy* (1872) as the complementary opposition of the Apollonian and Dionysian aspects of art. In serving Apollo, the god of clarity and light, Aschenbach has sacrificed an integral part of his artistic vision. He has developed an "official" note and been anthologized in textbooks, but he has lost spontaneity and joy; he lives with the tension of a clenched fist and suffers from repressed yearnings for freedom and mystic beauty. Aschenbach has betrayed the "dark god" Dionysus, who takes thorough and humiliating vengeance as the writer sinks into a passive, fatalistic acceptance of his feelings and remains to the end in the plague-stricken city. "Who can untangle the riddle of the artist's essence and character?" asks the narrator. *Death in Venice* is a crystallization of Mann's work at its best, displaying the penetrating detail of his social and psychological realism, the power of his tightly interwoven symbolic structure, and the cumulative impact of his artist-hero's fall.

The following list uses common English syllables and stress accents to provide rough equivalents of selected words whose pronunciation may be unfamiliar to the general reader.

Bildungsroman: *bil'-doongs-roh-mahn'*   Schwabing: *shva'-bing*

Föhringer Chaussée: *feuh-ring-er shoh-*   Wagner: *vahg'-ner*
    say'

Death in Venice[1]

CHAPTER 1

On a spring afternoon in 19—,[2] a year that for months glowered threateningly over our continent, Gustav Aschenbach—or von[3] Aschenbach, as he had been known officially since his fiftieth birthday—set off alone from his dwelling in Prinzregentenstrasse[4] in Munich on a rather long walk. He had been overstrained by the difficult and dangerous morning's work, which just now required particular discretion, caution, penetration, and precision of will: even after his midday meal the writer had not been able to halt the running on of the productive machinery within him, that "motus animi continuus" which Cicero[5] claims is the essence of eloquence, nor had he been able to obtain the relaxing slumber so necessary to him once a day to relieve the increasing demands on his resources. Thus, he sought the open air right after tea, hoping that fresh air and exercise would restore him and help him to have a profitable evening.

It was early May, and after weeks of cold, wet weather a premature summer had set in. The Englischer Garten,[6] although only beginning to come into leaf, was as muggy as in August and at the end near the city was full of vehicles and people out for a stroll. Increasingly quiet paths led Aschenbach toward Aumeister,[7] where he spent a moment surveying the lively crowd in the beer garden, next to which several hackneys and carriages were lingering; but then as the sun went down he took a route homeward outside the park over the open fields and, since he felt tired and thunder clouds now threatened over Föhring,[8] he waited at the North Cemetery stop for the tram that would take him directly back into the city.

As it happened he found the tram stop and the surrounding area deserted. Neither on the paved Ungererstrasse, whose streetcar-tracks stretched in glistening solitude toward Schwabing, nor on the Föhringer Chaussee[9] was there a vehicle to be seen, nothing stirred behind the fences of the stonemasons' shops, where the crosses, headstones, and monuments for sale

---

1. Translated by and some notes adapted from Clayton Koelb.   2. In 1911, when the story was written, the "Moroccan crisis" was precipitated when a German gunboat appeared off the coast of Agadir, prompting negotiations between France and Germany over their respective national interests. A series of similar diplomatic crises led to the outbreak of World War I in 1914.   3. From or of. *Von* appears in the names of only nobility. Aschenbach was made an honorary nobleman on his fiftieth birthday.   4. A street in Munich that forms the southern boundary of the Englischer Garten (English Garden). Mann lived in various apartments in this neighborhood.   5. Marcus Tullius Cicero (106–43 B.C.E.), Roman orator. *Motus animi continuus:* the continuous motion of the spirit (Latin, attributed to Cicero).   6. The English Garden, a 900-acre public park with diverse attractions that extended from the city to the water meadows of the Isar River.   7. A beer garden in the northern section.   8. A district in Munich.   9. A street. Ungererstrasse is a street that borders the North Cemetery. Schwabing is another district in Munich.

formed a second, untenanted graveyard, and the Byzantine architecture of the mortuary chapel across the way lay silent in the glow of the departing day. Its facade was decorated with Greek crosses and hieratic paintings in soft colors; in addition it displayed symmetrically arranged scriptural quotations in gold letters, such as, "They are entering the house of God," or, "May the eternal light shine upon them." Waiting, he found a few moments' solemn diversion in reading these formulations and letting his mind's eye bask in their radiant mysticism, when, returning from his reveries, he noticed a man in the portico, above the two apocalyptic beasts guarding the front steps. The man's not altogether ordinary appearance took his thoughts in a completely different direction.

It was not clear whether the man had emerged from the chapel through the bronze door or had climbed the steps up to the entry from the outside without being noticed. Aschenbach, without entering too deeply into the question, inclined to the first assumption. Moderately tall, thin, clean-shaven, and strikingly snub-nosed, the man belonged to the red-haired type and possessed a redhead's milky and freckled complexion. He was clearly not of Bavarian stock, and in any case the wide and straight-brimmed straw hat that covered his head lent him the appearance of a foreigner, of a traveler from afar. To be sure, he also wore the familiar native rucksack strapped to his shoulders and a yellowish Norfolk suit[1] apparently of loden cloth. He had a gray mackintosh over his left forearm, which he held supported against his side, and in his right hand he held a stick with an iron tip, which he propped obliquely against the ground, leaning his hip against its handle and crossing his ankles. With his head held up, so that his Adam's apple protruded nakedly from the thin neck that emerged from his loose sport shirt, he gazed intently into the distance with colorless, red-lashed eyes, between which stood two stark vertical furrows that went rather oddly with his short, turned-up nose. It may be that his elevated and elevating location had something to do with it, but his posture conveyed an impression of imperious surveillance, fortitude, even wildness. His lips seemed insufficient, perhaps because he was squinting, blinded, toward the setting sun or maybe because he was afflicted by a facial deformity—in any case they were retracted to such an extent that his teeth, revealed as far as the gums, menacingly displayed their entire white length.

It is entirely possible that Aschenbach had been somewhat indiscreet in his half-distracted, half-inquisitive survey of the stranger, for he suddenly realized that his gaze was being returned, and indeed returned so belligerently, so directly eye to eye, with such a clear intent to bring matters to a head and force the other to avert his eyes, that Aschenbach, with an awkward sense of embarrassment, turned away and began to walk along the fence, intending for the time being to pay no more attention to the fellow. In a moment he had forgotten about him. But perhaps the man had the look of the traveler about him, or perhaps because he exercised some physical or spiritual influence, Aschenbach's imagination was set working. He felt a sudden, strange expansion of his inner space, a rambling unrest, a youthful thirst for faraway places, a feeling so intense, so new—or rather so long unused and forgotten—that he stood rooted to the spot, his hands behind his back

---

1. A belted suit.

and his gaze to the ground, pondering the essence and direction of his emotion.

It was wanderlust and nothing more, but it was an overwhelming wanderlust that rose to a passion and even to a delusion. His desire acquired vision, and his imagination, not yet calmed down from the morning's work, created its own version of the manifold marvels and terrors of the earth, all of them at once now seeking to take shape within him. He saw, saw a landscape, a tropical swamp under a vaporous sky, moist, luxuriant, and monstrous, a sort of primitive wilderness of islands, morasses, and alluvial estuaries; saw hairy palm trunks rise up near and far out of rank fern brakes, out of thick, swollen, wildly blooming vegetation; saw wondrously formless trees sink their aerial roots into the earth through stagnant, green-shadowed pools, where exotic birds, their shoulders high and their bills shaped weirdly, stood motionless in the shallows looking askance amidst floating flowers that were white as milk and big as platters; saw the eyes of a lurking tiger sparkle between the gnarled stems of a bamboo thicket; and felt his heart pound with horror and mysterious desire. Then the vision faded, and with a shake of his head Aschenbach resumed his promenade along the fences bordering the headstone-makers' yard.

He had regarded travel, at least since he had commanded the financial resources to enjoy the advantages of global transportation at will, as nothing more than a measure he had to take for his health, no matter how much it went against his inclination. Too much taken up with the tasks that his problematic self and the European soul posed for him, too burdened with the obligation of productivity, too averse to distraction to be a success as a lover of the world's motley show, he had quite contented himself with the view of the earth's surface anyone could get without stirring very far from home. He had never even been tempted to leave Europe. Especially now that his life was slowly waning, now that his artist's fear of never getting finished—his concern that the sands might run out of the glass before he had done his utmost and given his all—could no longer be dismissed as pure fancy, his external existence had confined itself almost exclusively to the lovely city that had become his home and to the rustic country house he had built in the mountains where he spent the rainy summers.

Besides, even this impulse that had come over him so suddenly and so late in life was quickly moderated and set right by reason and a self-discipline practiced since early youth. He had intended to keep at the work to which he now devoted his life until he reached a certain point and then move out to the country. The thought of sauntering about the world, of thereby being seduced away from months of work, seemed all too frivolous, too contrary to plan, and ultimately impermissible. And yet he knew all too well why this temptation had assailed him so unexpectedly. He had to admit it to himself: it was the urge to escape that was behind this yearning for the far away and the new, this desire for release, freedom, and forgetfulness. It was the urge to get away from his work, from the daily scene of an inflexible, cold, and passionate service. Of course he loved this service and almost loved the enervating struggle, renewed each day, between his stubborn, proud, so-often-tested will and his growing lassitude, about which no one could be allowed to know and which the product of his toil could not be permitted to reveal in any way, by any sign of failure or of negligence. Yet it seemed reasonable not to overbend the bow and not to stifle obstinately the outbreak of such a vital need. He thought about his work, thought about the place where once again, today as yesterday, he had been forced to abandon it, a passage that would submit, it seemed, neither to patient care nor to surprise attack. He considered it again, sought once more to break through or untangle the logjam, then broke off the effort with a shudder of repugnance. The passage presented no extraordinary difficulty; what disabled him was the malaise of scrupulousness confronting him in the guise of an insatiable perfectionism. Even as a young man, to be sure, he had considered perfectionism the basis and most intimate essence of his talent, and for its sake he had curbed and cooled his emotions, because he knew that emotion inclines one to satisfaction with a comfortable approximation, a half of perfection. Was his enslaved sensitivity now avenging itself by leaving him, refusing to advance his project and give wings to his art, taking with it all his joy, all his delight in form and expression? It was not that he was producing bad work—that at least was the advantage of his advanced years; he felt every moment comfortably secure in his mastery. But, though the nation honored it, he himself was not pleased with his mastery, and indeed it seemed to him that his work lacked those earmarks of a fiery, playful fancy that, stemming from joy, gave more joy to his appreciative audience than did any inner content or weighty excellence. He was fearful of the summer in the country, all alone in the little house with the maid who prepared his meals and the servant who waited on him at table, fearful too of the familiar mountaintops and mountainsides that once more would surround him in his discontented, slow progress. And so what he needed was a respite, a kind of spur-of-the-moment existence, a way to waste some time, foreign air and an infusion of new blood, to make the summer bearable and productive. Travel it would be then—it was all right with him. Not too far, though, not quite all the way to the tigers. One night in a sleeping car and a siesta for three or maybe four weeks in some fashionable vacation spot in the charming south . . .

Such were his thoughts as the noise of the electric tram approached along the Ungererstrasse, and he decided as he got on to devote this evening to studying maps and time tables. Once aboard it occurred to him to look around for the man in the straw hat, his comrade in this excursion that had been, in spite of all, so consequential. But he could get no clear idea of the man's whereabouts; neither his previous location, nor the next stop, nor the tram car itself revealed any signs of his presence.

CHAPTER 2

Gustav Aschenbach, the author of the clear and vigorous prose epic on the life of Frederick the Great;[2] the patient artist who wove together with enduring diligence the novelistic tapestry *Maia*,[3] a work rich in characters and eminently successful in gathering together many human destinies under the shadow of a single idea; the creator of that powerful story bearing the title "A Man of Misery," which had earned the gratitude of an entire young generation by showing it the possibility for a moral resolution that passed

2. King Frederick II (1712–1786) started Prussia on its rise to domination of Germany and made his court a prominent European cultural center.   3. In Hindu religion, the illusory appearance of the world concealing a higher spiritual reality.

through and beyond the deepest knowledge; the author, finally (and this completes the short list of his mature works), of the passionate treatment of the topic "Art and Intellect,"[4] an essay whose power of organization and antithetical eloquence had prompted serious observers to rank it alongside Schiller's "On Naïve and Sentimental Poetry";[5] Gustav Aschenbach, then, was born the son of a career civil servant in the justice ministry in L., a district capital in the province of Silesia. His ancestors had been officers, judges, and government functionaries, men who had led upright lives of austere decency devoted to the service of king and country. A more ardent spirituality had expressed itself once among them in the person of a preacher; more impetuous and sensuous blood had entered the family line in the previous generation through the writer's mother, the daughter of a Bohemian music director. It was from her that he had in his features the traits of a foreign race. The marriage of sober conscientiousness devoted to service with darker, more fiery impulses engendered an artist and indeed this very special artist.

Since his entire being was bent on fame, he emerged early on as, perhaps not exactly precocious, but nonetheless, thanks to the decisiveness and peculiar terseness of his style, surprisingly mature and ready to go before the public. He was practically still in high school when he made a name for himself. Ten years later he learned how to keep up appearances, to manage his fame from his writing desk, to produce gracious and significant sentences for his necessarily brief letters (for many demands are made on such a successful and reliable man). By the age of forty, exhausted by the tortures and vicissitudes of his real work, he had to deal with a daily flood of mail bearing stamps from countries in every corner of the globe.

Tending neither to the banal nor to the eccentric, his talent was such as to win for his stories both the acceptance of the general public and an admiring, challenging interest from a more discerning audience. Thus he found himself even as a young man obliged in every way to achieve and indeed to achieve extraordinary things. He had therefore never known sloth, never known the carefree, laissez-faire attitude of youth. When he got sick in Vienna around the age of thirty-five, a canny observer remarked about him to friends, "You see, Aschenbach has always lived like this"—and the speaker closed the fingers of his left hand into a fist—"never like this"—and he let his open hand dangle comfortably from the arm of the chair. How right he was! And the morally courageous aspect of it was that, possessing anything but a naturally robust constitution, he was not so much born for constant exertion as he was called to it.

Medical concerns had prevented him from attending school as a child and compelled the employment of private instruction at home. He had grown up alone and without companions, and yet he must have realized early on that he belonged to a tribe in which talent was not so much a rarity as was the bodily frame talent needs to find its fulfillment, a tribe known for giving their best early in life but not for longevity. His watchword, however, was "Endure," and he saw in his novel about Frederick the Great precisely the apotheosis of this commandment, which seemed to him the essence of a

---

4. *Frederick, Maia, A Man of Misery*, and *Art and Intellect* are titles of projects Mann had worked on and abandoned.   5. An influential essay by the German Romantic writer Friedrich Schiller (1759–1805).

selflessly active virtue. He harbored, moreover, a keen desire to live to a ripe old age, for he had long believed that an artistic career could be called truly great, encompassing, indeed truly worthy of honor only if the artist were allotted sufficient years to be fruitful in his own way at all stages of human life.

Since he thus bore the burdens of his talent on slender shoulders and wished to carry those burdens far, he was in great need of discipline. Fortunately for him discipline was his heritage at birth from his paternal side. At forty, at fifty, even at an age when others squander and stray, content to put their great plans aside for the time being, he started his day at an early hour by dousing his chest and back with cold water. Then, placing two tall wax candles in silver candlesticks at the head of his manuscript, he would spend two or three fervently conscientious morning hours sacrificing on the altar of art the powers he had assembled during his sleep. It was forgivable— indeed it even indicated the victory of his moral force—that uninformed readers mistook the Maiaworld or the epic scroll on which unrolled Frederick's heroic life for the products of single sustained bursts of energy, whereas they actually grew into grandeur layer by layer, out of small daily doses of work and countless individual flashes of inspiration. These works were thoroughly excellent in every detail solely because their creator had endured for years under the pressure of a single project, bringing to bear a tenacity and perseverance similar to that which had conquered his home province,[6] and because he had devoted only his freshest and worthiest hours to actual composition.

If a work of the intellect is to have an immediate, broad, and deep effect, there must be a mysterious affinity, a correspondence between the personal fate of its originator and the more general fate of his contemporaries. People do not know why they accord fame to a particular work. Far from being experts, they suppose they see in it a hundred virtues that would justify their interest; but the real reason for their approval is something imponderable—it is sympathy. Aschenbach had actually stated forthrightly, though in a relatively inconspicuous passage, that nearly everything achieving greatness did so under the banner of "Despite"—despite grief and suffering, despite poverty, destitution, infirmity, affliction, passion, and a thousand obstacles. But this was more than an observation, it was the fruit of experience; no, it was the very formula for his life and his fame, the key to his work. Was it any wonder, then, that it was also the basis for the moral disposition and outward demeanor of his most original fictional characters?

Early on an observant critic had described the new type of hero that this writer preferred, a figure returning over and over again in manifold variation: it was based on the concept of "an intellectual and youthful manliness which grits its teeth in proud modesty and calmly endures the swords and spears as they pass through its body." It was a nice description, ingenious and precise, despite its seemingly excessive emphasis on passivity. For meeting one's fate with dignity, grace under pressure of pain, is not simply a matter of sufferance; it is an active achievement, a positive triumph, and the figure of St. Sebastian[7] is thus the most beautiful image, if not of art in general, then

6. As a result of the Seven Years' War (1759–63), Frederick the Great wrested Silesia from Austria. Today, most of Silesia has become a region in southwestern Poland.   7. A 3rd-century Roman martyr whose arrow-pierced body was a popular subject for Renaissance painters.

surely of the art under discussion here. Having looked at the characters in Aschenbach's narrated world, having seen the elegant self-discipline that managed right up to the last moment to hide from the eyes of the world the undermining process, the biological decline, taking place within; having seen the yellow, physically handicapped ugliness that nonetheless managed to kindle its smoldering ardor into a pure flame, managed even to catapult itself to mastery in the realm of beauty; or having seen the pale impotence that pulls out of the glowing depths of the spirit enough power to force a whole frivolous people to fall at the feet of the cross, at the feet of that very impotence; or the lovable charm that survives even the empty and rigorous service of pure form; or the false, dangerous life of the born deceiver, with the quick enervation of its longing and with its artfulness—having seen all these human destinies and many more besides, it was easy enough to doubt that there could be any other sort of heroism than that of weakness. In any case, what kind of heroism was more appropriate to the times than this? Gustav Aschenbach was the poet of all those who work on the edge of exhaustion, of the overburdened, worn down moralists of achievement who nonetheless still stand tall, those who, stunted in growth and short of means, use ecstatic feats of will and clever management to extract from themselves at least for a period of time the effects of greatness. Their names are legion, and they are the heroes of the age. And all of them recognized themselves in his work; they saw themselves justified, exalted, their praises sung. And they were grateful; they heralded his name.

He had been once as young and rough as the times and, seduced by them, had made public blunders and mistakes, had made himself vulnerable, had committed errors against tact and good sense in word and deed. But he had won the dignity toward which, in his opinion, every great talent feels an inborn urge and spur. One could say in fact that his entire development had been a conscious and defiant rise to dignity, beyond any twinge of doubt and of irony that might have stood in his way.

Pleasing the great mass of middle-class readers depends mainly on offering vividly depicted, intellectually undemanding characterizations, but passionately uncompromising youth is smitten only with what is problematic; and Aschenbach had been as problematic and uncompromising as any young man can be. He had pandered to the intellect, exhausted the soil of knowledge, milled flour from his seed corn, revealed secrets, put talent under suspicion, betrayed art. Indeed, while his portrayals entertained, elevated, invigorated the blissfully credulous among his readers, as a youthful artist it was his cynical observations on the questionable nature of art and of the artist's calling that had kept the twenty-year-old element fascinated.

But it seems that nothing so quickly or so thoroughly blunts a high-minded and capable spirit as the sharp and bitter charm of knowledge; and it is certain that the melancholy, scrupulous thoroughness characteristic of the young seems shallow in comparison with the solemn decision of masterful maturity to disavow knowledge, to reject it, to move beyond it with head held high, to forestall the least possibility that it could cripple, dishearten, or dishonor his will, his capacity for action and feeling, or even his passion. How else could one interpret the famous story "A Man of Misery" save as an outbreak of disgust at the indecent psychologism then current? This disgust was embodied in the figure of that soft and foolish semi-villain who, out of weakness, viciousness, and moral impotence, buys a black-market destiny for himself by driving his wife into the arms of a beardless boy, who imagines profundity can justify committing the basest acts. The weight of the words with which the writer of that work reviled the vile announced a decisive turn away from all moral skepticism, from all sympathy with the abyss, a rejection of the laxity inherent in the supposedly compassionate maxim that to understand everything is to forgive everything. What was coming into play here—or rather, what was already in full swing—was that "miracle of ingenuousness reborn" about which there was explicit discussion, not without a certain mysterious emphasis, in one of the author's dialogues published only slightly later. Strange relationships! Was it an intellectual consequence of this "rebirth," of this new dignity and rigor, that just then readers began to notice an almost excessive increase in his sense of beauty, a noble purity, simplicity, and sense of proportion that henceforth gave his works such a palpable, one might say deliberately classical and masterful quality? But moral determination that goes beyond knowledge, beyond analytic and inhibiting perception—would that not also be a reduction, a moral simplification of the world and of the human soul and therefore also a growing potential for what is evil, forbidden, and morally unacceptable? And does form not have two faces? Is it not moral and amoral at the same time—moral insofar as form is the product and expression of discipline, but amoral and indeed immoral insofar as it harbors within itself by nature a certain moral indifference and indeed is essentially bent on forcing the moral realm to stoop under its proud and absolute scepter?

That is as may be. Since human development is human destiny, how could a life led in public, accompanied by the accolades and confidence of thousands, develop as does one led without the glory and the obligations of fame? Only those committed to eternal bohemianism would be bored and inclined to ridicule when a great talent emerges from its libertine chrysalis, accustoms itself to recognizing emphatically the dignity of the spirit, takes on the courtly airs of solitude, a solitude full of unassisted, defiantly independent suffering and struggle, and ultimately achieves power and honor in the public sphere. And how much playfulness, defiance, and indulgence there is in the way talent develops! A kind of official, educative element began in time to appear in Aschenbach's productions. His style in later years dispensed with the sheer audacity, the subtle and innovative shadings of his younger days, and moved toward the paradigmatic, the polished and traditional, the conservative and formal, even formulaic. Like Louis XIV[8]—as report would have it—the aging writer banished from his vocabulary every base expression. About this time it came to pass that the educational authorities began using selected passages from his works in their prescribed textbooks.[9] He seemed to sense the inner appropriateness of it, and he did not refuse when a German prince, newly ascended to the throne, bestowed on the author of *Frederick*, on his fiftieth birthday, a nonhereditary title.

Relatively early on, after a few years of moving about, a few tries at living here and there, he chose Munich as his permanent residence and lived there in bourgeois respectability such as comes to intellectuals sometimes, in

---

8. King of France (1638–1715), the "great monarch" of the French classical period.   9. I.e., he received national recognition in the highly centralized German educational system.

exceptional cases. His marriage to a girl from a learned family, entered upon when still a young man, was terminated after only a short term of happiness by her death. A daughter, already married, remained to him. He never had a son.

Gustav Aschenbach was a man of slightly less than middle height, dark-haired and clean shaven. His head seemed a little too big for a body that was almost dainty. His hair, combed back, receding at the top, still very full at the temples, though quite gray, framed a high, furrowed, and almost embossed-looking brow. The gold frame of his rimless glasses cut into the bridge of his full, nobly curved nose. His mouth was large, sometimes relaxed and full, sometimes thin and tense; his cheeks were lean and hollow, and his well-proportioned chin was marked by a slight cleft. Important destinies seemed to have played themselves out on this long-suffering face, which he often held tilted somewhat to one side. And yet it was art alone, not a difficult and troubled life, that had taken over the task of chiseling these features. Behind this brow was born the scintillating repartee between Voltaire and King Frederick on the subject of war; these eyes, looking tiredly but pierc-ingly through the glasses, had seen the bloody inferno of the field hospitals during the Seven Years' War.[1] Indeed, even on the personal level art provides an intensified version of life. Art offers a deeper happiness, but it consumes one more quickly. It engraves upon the faces of its servants the traces of imaginary, mental adventures and over the long term, even given an external existence of cloistered quietude, engenders in them a nervous sensitivity, an over-refinement, a weariness and an inquisitiveness such as are scarcely ever produced by a life full of extravagant passions and pleasures.

CHAPTER 3

Several obligations of both a practical and a literary nature forced the eager traveler to remain in Munich for about two weeks after his walk in the park. Finally he gave instructions for his country house to be prepared for his moving in within a month's time and, on a day sometime between the middle and end of May, he took the night train to Trieste, where he remained only twenty-four hours and where he boarded the boat to Pola[2] on the morning of the next day.

What he sought was someplace foreign, someplace isolated, but someplace nonetheless easy to get to. He thus took up residence on an Adriatic island, a destination that had been highly spoken of in recent years and lay not far from the Istrian coast. It was populated by locals dressed in colorful rags who spoke in wildly exotic accents, and the landscape was graced by rugged cliffs on the coast facing the open sea. But the rain and oppressive air, the provincial, exclusively Austrian clientele at the hotel, and the lack of the peaceful, intimate relation with the sea that only a soft sandy beach can offer—these things irritated him, denied him a sense of having found the place he was looking for; he was troubled by a pressure within him pushing in a direction he could not quite grasp; he studied ship schedules, he sought

---

1. A global war (1756–63) fought in Europe, North America, and India between European powers. Fran-çois-Marie Arouet de Voltaire (1694–1778), French writer and philosopher, was a guest at the court of Frederick the Great from 1750 until 1753, when he found it wise to leave after a disagreement.   2. Tri-este (in Italy) and Pola (or Pula, in Croatia) are major ports at the head of the Adriatic Sea. Until 1919 they were Austrian possessions.

about for something; and suddenly the surprising but obvious destination came to him. If you wanted to reach in a single night someplace incomparable, someplace as out of the ordinary as a fairy tale, where did you go? The answer was clear. What was he doing here? He had gone astray. It was over there that he had wanted to go all along. He did not hesitate a moment in remedying his error and gave notice of his departure. A week and a half after his arrival on the island a swift motorboat carried him and his baggage through the early morning mist across the water to the military port, where he landed only long enough to find the gangway leading him onto the damp deck of a ship that was already getting up steam for a trip to Venice.[3]

It was an aged vessel, long past its prime, sooty, and gloomy, sailing under the Italian flag. In a cavernous, artificially lit cabin in the ship's interior—to which Aschenbach had been conducted with smirking politeness by a hunchbacked, scruffy sailor the moment he embarked—sat a goateed man behind a desk. With his hat cocked over his brow and a cigarette butt hanging from the corner of his mouth, his facial features were reminiscent of an old time ringmaster. He took down the passengers' personal information and doled out tickets with the grimacing, easy demeanor of the professional. "To Venice!" He repeated Aschenbach's request, stretching his arm to dip his pen in the congealed remains at the bottom of his slightly tilted inkwell. "To Venice, first class! There, sir, you're all taken care of." He inscribed great letters like crane's feet on a piece of paper, poured blue sand out of a box onto them, poured it back into an earthenware bowl, folded the paper with his yellow, bony fingers, and resumed writing. "What a fine choice for your destination!" he babbled in the meantime. "Ah, Venice, a wonderful city! A city that is irresistible to cultured people both for its history and for its modern charm!" The smooth swiftness of his movements and the empty chatter with which he accompanied them had an anesthetic and diversionary effect, as if he were concerned that the traveler should change his mind about his decision to go to Venice. He hastily took the money and dropped the change on the stained cloth covering the table with the practiced swiftness of a croupier.[4] "Enjoy yourself, sir!" he said with a theatrical bow. "It is an honor to be of service to you. . . . Next, please!" he cried with his arm raised, acting as if he were still doing a brisk business, though in fact there was no one else there to do business with. Aschenbach returned above deck.

With one arm resting on the rail, he observed the passengers on board and the idle crowd loitering on the pier to watch the ship depart. The second-class passengers, both men and women, crouched on the forward deck using boxes and bundles as seats. A group of young people, apparently employees of businesses in Pola, who had banded together in great excitement for an excursion to Italy, formed the social set of the first upper deck. They made no little fuss over themselves and their plans, chattered, laughed, and took complacent enjoyment in their own continual gesturing. Leaning over the railing they called out in fluent and mocking phrases to various friends going about their business, briefcases under their arms, along the dockside street below, while the latter in turn made mock-threatening gestures with their walking sticks at the celebrants above. One of the merrymakers, wearing a

---

3. An ancient city whose network of bridges and canals links 118 islands in the Gulf of Venice. The Republic of Venice was headed by a doge (duke) and was a cultural, commercial, and political center in Europe from the 14th century.   4. Attendant at a gambling table who handles bets and money.

bright yellow, overly fashionable summer suit, red tie, and a panama hat with a cockily turned-up brim, outdid all the others in his screeching gaiety. But scarcely had Aschenbach gotten a closer look at him when he realized with something like horror that this youth was not genuine. He was old, no doubt about it. There were wrinkles around his eyes and mouth. The faint carmine of his cheeks was rouge; the brown hair beneath the colorfully banded hat was a wig; his neck was shrunken and sinewy; his clipped mustache and goatee were dyed; the full, yellowish set of teeth he exposed when he laughed was a cheap set of dentures; and his hands, bedecked with signet rings on both forefingers, were those of an old man. With a shudder Aschenbach watched him and his interaction with his friends. Did they not know, had they not noticed that he was old, that he had no right to wear their foppish and colorful clothes, had no right to pretend to be one of their own? They apparently tolerated him in their midst as a matter of course, out of habit, and treated him as an equal, answering in kind without reluctance when he teasingly poked one of them in the ribs. But how could this be? Aschenbach covered his brow with his hand and closed his eyes, which were feeling inflamed from not getting enough sleep. It seemed to him that things were starting to take a turn away from the ordinary, as if a dreamy estrangement, a bizarre distortion of the world were setting in and would spread if he did not put a stop to it by shading his eyes a bit and taking another look around him. Just at this moment he experienced a sensation of motion and, looking up with an unreasoning terror, realized that the heavy and gloomy hulk of the ship was slowly parting company with the stone pier. The engines ran alternately forward and reverse, and inch by inch the band of oily, iridescent water between the pier and the hull of the ship widened. After a set of cumbersome maneuvers the steamer managed to point its bowsprit toward the open sea. Aschenbach went over to the starboard side, where the hunchback had set up a deck chair for him and a steward dressed in a stained tailcoat offered him service.

The sky was gray and the wind was moist. The harbor and the island were left behind, and soon all sight of land vanished beyond the misty horizon. Flakes of coal soot saturated with moisture fell on the scrubbed, never drying deck. No more than an hour later a canvas canopy was put up, since it had started to rain.

Wrapped in his cloak, a book on his lap, the traveler rested, and the hours passed by unnoticed. It stopped raining; the linen canopy was removed. The horizon was unobstructed. Beneath the overcast dome of the sky the immense disk of the desolate sea stretched into the distance all around. But in empty, undivided space our sense of time fails us, and we lose ourselves in the immeasurable. Strange and shadowy figures—the old fop, the goat-beard from below deck—invaded Aschenbach's mind as he rested. They gestured obscurely and spoke the confused speech of dreams. He fell asleep.

At noon they called him to lunch down in the corridorlike dining hall onto which opened the doors of all the sleeping quarters and in which stood a long table. He dined at one end, while at the other the business employees from Pola, including the old fop, had been carousing since ten o'clock with the jolly captain. The meal was wretched and he soon got up. He felt an urgent need to get out, to look at the sky, to see if it might not be brightening over Venice.

It had never occurred to him that anything else could happen, for the city had always received him in shining glory. But the sky and the sea remained overcast and leaden. From time to time a misty rain fell, and he came to the realization that he would approach a very different Venice by sea than the one he had previously reached by land. He stood by the foremast, gazing into the distance, awaiting the sight of land. He remembered the melancholy, enthusiastic poet of long ago who had furnished his dreams with the domes and bell towers rising from these waters. He softly repeated to himself some of those verses in which the awe, joy, and sadness of a former time had taken stately shape[5] and, easily moved by sensations thus already formed, looked into his earnest and weary heart to see if some new enthusiasm or entanglement, some late adventure of feeling might be in store for him, the idle traveler.

Then the flat coastline emerged on the right; the sea became populated with fishing boats; the barrier island with its beach appeared. The steamer soon left the island behind to the left, slipping at reduced speed through the narrow harbor named after it.[6] They came to a full stop in the lagoon in view of rows of colorfully wretched dwellings and awaited the arrival of the launch belonging to the health service.

An hour passed before it appeared. One had arrived and yet had not arrived; there was no great hurry and yet one felt driven by impatience. The young people from Pola had come up on deck, apparently yielding to a patriotic attraction to the military trumpet calls resounding across the water from the public garden. Full of excitement and Asti, they shouted cheers at the bersaglieri[7] conducting drills over there. It was disgusting, however, to see the state into which the made-up old coot's false fellowship with the young people had brought him. His aged brain had not been able to put up the same resistance to the wine as the younger and more vigorous heads, and he was wretchedly drunk. His vision blurred; a cigarette dangled from his shaking fingers; he stood swaying tipsily in place, pulled to and fro by intoxication, barely able to maintain his balance. Since he would have fallen over at the first step, he dared not move from the spot. Yet he maintained a woeful bravado, buttonholing everyone who came near; he stammered, blinked, giggled, raised his beringed, wrinkled forefinger in fatuous banter, and ran the tip of his tongue around the corners of his mouth in an obscenely suggestive manner. Aschenbach watched him from under a darkened brow and was once again seized by a feeling of giddiness, as if the world were displaying a slight but uncontrollable tendency to distort, to take on a bizarre and sneering aspect. It was a feeling, to be sure, that conditions prevented him from indulging, for just then the engine began anew its pounding, and the ship, interrupted so close to its destination, resumed its course through the canal of San Marco.[8]

Once more, then, it lay before him, that most astounding of landing places, that dazzling grouping of fantastic buildings that the republic presented to the awed gaze of approaching mariners: the airy splendor of the palace and

---

5. The lines are probably from *Sonnets on Venice* (1825) by the German classical poet August Graf Platen (1796–1835): "My eye left the high seas behind / as the temples of [the architect Andrea] Palladio rose from the waters."   **6.** Both the barrier island and the harbor are called Lido. The island is the site of a famous resort.   **7.** Elite Italian troops. *Asti:* or asti spumante, a sweet, sparkling Italian wine.   **8.** Saint Mark's Canal, named for the patron saint of Venice.

the Bridge of Sighs; the pillars on the water's edge bearing the lion and the saint; the showy projecting flank of the fairy tale cathedral; the view toward the gate and the great clock.[9] It occurred to him as he raised his eyes that to arrive in Venice by land, at the railway station, was like entering a palace by a back door; that one ought not to approach this most improbable of cities save as he now did, by ship, over the high seas.

The engine stopped, gondolas swarmed about, the gangway was lowered, customs officials boarded and haughtily went about their duties; disembarkation could begin. Aschenbach let it be known that he desired a gondola to take him and his luggage over to the landing where he could get one of the little steamboats that ran between the city and the Lido; for it was his intention to take up residence by the sea. His wishes met with acquiescence; a call went down with his request to the water's surface where the gondoliers were quarreling with each other in dialect. He was still prevented from disembarking; his trunk presented problems; only with considerable difficulty could it be pulled and tugged down the ladderlike gangway. He therefore found himself unable for several moments to escape from the importunities of the ghastly old impostor, who, driven by some dark drunken impulse, was determined to bid elaborate farewell to the foreign traveler. "We wish you the happiest of stays," he bleated, bowing and scraping. "Keeping a fond memory of us! Au revoir, excusez, and bonjour,[1] your excellency!" He drooled, he batted his eyes, he licked the corners of his mouth, and the dyed goatee on his elderly chin bristled. "Our compliments," he babbled, two fingertips at his mouth, "our compliments to your beloved, your dearly beloved, your lovely beloved . . ." And suddenly his uppers fell out of his jaw onto his lower lip. Aschenbach took his chance to escape. "Your beloved, your sweet beloved . . ." He heard the cooing, hollow, obstructed sounds behind his back as he descended the gangway, clutching at the rope handrail as he went.

Who would not need to fight off a fleeting shiver, a secret aversion and anxiety, at the prospect of boarding a Venetian gondola for the first time or after a long absence? This strange conveyance, surviving unchanged since legendary times and painted the particular sort of black[2] ordinarily reserved for coffins, makes one think of silent, criminal adventures in a darkness full of splashing sounds; makes one think even more of death itself, of biers and gloomy funerals, and of that final, silent journey. And has anyone noticed that the seat of one of these boats, this armchair painted coffin-black and upholstered in dull black cloth, is one of the softest, most luxurious, most sleep-inducing seats in the world? Aschenbach certainly realized this as he sat down at the gondolier's feet, opposite his luggage lying in a copious pile in the bow. The oarsmen were still quarreling in a rough, incomprehensible language punctuated by threatening gestures. The peculiar quiet of this city of water, however, seemed to soften their voices, to disembody them, to disperse them over the sea. It was warm here in the harbor. Stroked by the mild breath of the sirocco,[3] leaning back into the cushions as the yielding element carried him, the traveler closed his eyes in the pleasure of indulging

---

9. A large clock tower built in the late 15th century. *Bridge of Sighs:* condemned prisoners would walk over this bridge when proceeding to prison from the ducal palace. *Pillars:* one is surmounted by a statue of St. Theodore stepping on a crocodile; the second, by a winged lion, emblem of St. Mark. *Cathedral:* the Church of St. Mark.   1. Goodbye, excuse me, and good-day (French).   2. Legend explains the gondolas' traditional black through an ancient law forbidding ostentation.   3. A hot wind originating in the Sahara, which becomes humid as it picks up moisture over the Mediterranean.

in an indolence both unaccustomed and sweet. The trip will be short, he thought; if only it could last forever! The gondola rocked softly, and he felt himself slip away from the crowded ship and the clamoring voices.

How quiet, ever more quiet it grew around him! Nothing could be heard but the splashing of the oar, the hollow slap of the waves against the gondola's prow, rising rigid and black above the water with its halberdlike beak— and then a third thing, a voice, a whisper. It was the murmur of the gondolier, who was talking to himself through his clenched teeth in fits and starts, emitting sounds that were squeezed out of him by the labor of his arms. Aschenbach looked up and realized with some astonishment that the lagoon was widening about him and that he was traveling in the direction of the open sea. It seemed, then, that he ought not to rest quite so peacefully but instead make sure his wishes were carried out.

"I told you to take me to the steamer landing," he said with a half turn toward the stern. The murmur ceased. He received no answer.

"I told you to take me to the steamer landing!" he repeated, turning around completely and looking up into the face of the gondolier, whose figure, perched on the high deck and silhouetted against the dun sky, towered behind him. The man had a disagreeable, indeed brutal-looking appearance; he wore a blue sailor suit belted with a yellow sash, and a shapeless straw hat that was beginning to come unraveled and was tilted rakishly on his head. His facial features and the blond, curly mustache under his short, turned-up nose marked him as clearly not of Italian stock. Although rather slender of build, so that one would not have thought him particularly well suited to his profession, he plied his oar with great energy, putting his whole body into every stroke. Several times he pulled his lips back with the strain, baring his white teeth. His reddish eyebrows puckered, he looked out over his passenger's head and replied in a decisive, almost curt tone of voice: "You are going to the Lido."

Aschenbach responded, "Indeed. But I took the gondola only to get over to San Marco. I want to use the vaporetto."[4]

"You cannot use the vaporetto, sir."

"And why not?"

"Because the vaporetto does not accept luggage."

He was right about that; Aschenbach remembered. He said nothing. But the gruff, presumptuous manner of the man, so unlike the normal way of treating foreigners in this country, was not to be endured. He said, "That is my business. Perhaps I intend to put my luggage in storage. You will kindly turn back."

There was silence. The oar splashed, the waves slapped dully against the bow. And the murmuring and whispering began anew: the gondolier was talking to himself through his clenched teeth.

What to do? Alone at sea with this strangely insubordinate, uncannily resolute person, the traveler saw no way to enforce his wishes. And anyway, if he could just avoid getting angry, what a lovely rest he could have! Had he not wished the trip could last longer, could last forever? The smartest thing to do was to let matters take their course; more important, it was also the most pleasant thing to do. A magic circle of indolence seemed to surround

4. Little steamboat (Italian); used for public transport.

the place where he sat, this low armchair upholstered in black, so gently rocked by the rowing of the autocratic gondolier behind him. The idea that he might have fallen into the hands of a criminal rambled about dreamily in Aschenbach's mind, but it was incapable of rousing his thoughts to active resistance. More annoying was the possibility that all this was simply a device by which to extort money from him. A sense of duty or of pride, the memory, as it were, that one must prevent such things, induced him once more to pull himself together. He asked, "What do you want for the trip?"

And the gondolier, looking out over him, answered, "You will pay."

It was clear what reply was necessary here. Aschenbach said mechanically, "I will pay nothing, absolutely nothing, if you take me where I do not want to go."

"You want to go to the Lido."

"But not with you."

"I row you well."

True enough, thought Aschenbach, and relaxed. True enough, you row me well. Even if you are just after my money, even if you send me to the house of Aides[5] with a stroke of your oar from behind, you will have rowed me well.

But no such thing occurred. In fact, some company even happened by in the form of a boat filled with musicians, both men and women, who waylaid the gondola, sailing obtrusively right alongside. They sang to the accompaniment of guitars and mandolins and filled the quiet air over the lagoon with the strains of their mercenary tourist lyrics. Aschenbach threw some money in the hat they held out to him, whereupon they fell silent and sailed off. The murmur of the gondolier became perceptible once again as he talked to himself in fits and starts.

And so they arrived, bobbing in the wake of a steamer sailing back to the city. Two municipal officials walked up and down along the landing, their hands behind their backs and their faces turned to the lagoon. Aschenbach stepped from the gondola onto the dock assisted by one of those old men who seemed on hand, armed with a boathook, at every pier in Venice. Since he had no small coins with him, he crossed over to the hotel next to the steamer wharf to get change with which to pay the boatman an appropriate fee. His needs met in the lobby, he returned to find his baggage stowed on a cart on the dock. Gondola and gondolier had disappeared.

"He took off," said the old man with the boathook. "A bad man he was, sir, a man without a license. He's the only gondolier who doesn't have a license. The others telephoned over. He saw that we were on the lookout for him, so he took off."

Aschenbach shrugged his shoulders.

"You had a free ride, sir," the old man said, holding out his hat. Aschenbach threw some coins in it. He gave instructions that his luggage be taken to the Hotel des Bains[6] and then followed the cart along the boulevard of white blossoms, lined on both sides by taverns, shops, and boarding houses, that runs straight across the island to the beach.

He entered the spacious hotel from behind, from the garden terrace, and

5. A Greek spelling of *Hades*, the ruler of the world of the dead in Greek and Roman mythology. The newly dead entered the underworld by paying a coin to the boatman, Charon, who then ferried them across the river Styx. 6. Bathing hotel (French, literal trans.); a famous seaside hotel.

crossed the great lobby to reach the vestibule where the office was. Since he had a reservation, he was received with officious courtesy. A manager, a quiet, flatteringly polite little man with a black mustache and a French-style frock coat, accompanied him in the elevator to the third floor and showed him to his room. It was a pleasant place, furnished in cherry wood, decorated with highly fragrant flowers, and offering a view of the open sea through a set of tall windows. After the manager had withdrawn and while his luggage was being brought up and put in place in his room, he went up to one of the windows and looked out on the beach. It was nearly deserted in the afternoon lull, and the ocean, at high tide and bereft of sunshine, was sending long, low waves against the shore in a peaceful rhythm.

A lonely, quiet person has observations and experiences that are at once both more indistinct and more penetrating than those of one more gregarious; his thoughts are weightier, stranger, and never without a tinge of sadness. Images and perceptions that others might shrug off with a glance, a laugh, or a brief conversation occupy him unduly, become profound in his silence, become significant, become experience, adventure, emotion. Loneliness fosters that which is original, daringly and bewilderingly beautiful, poetic. But loneliness also fosters that which is perverse, incongruous, absurd, forbidden. Thus the events of the journey that brought him here—the ghastly old fop with his drivel about a beloved, the outlaw gondolier who was cheated of his reward—continued to trouble the traveler's mind. Though they did not appear contrary to reason, did not really give cause for second thoughts, the paradox was that they were nonetheless fundamentally and essentially odd, or so it seemed to him, and therefore troubling precisely because of this paradox. In the meantime his eyes greeted the sea, and he felt joy in knowing Venice to be in such comfortable proximity. He turned away at last, went to wash his face, gave some instructions to the maid with regard to completing arrangements to insure his comfort, and then put himself in the hands of the green-uniformed elevator operator, who took him down to the ground floor.

He took his tea on the terrace facing the sea, then went down to the shore and walked along the boardwalk for a good distance toward the Hotel Excelsior. When he got back it seemed about time to change for dinner. He did so slowly and precisely, the way he did everything, because he was used to working as he got dressed. Still, he found himself in the lobby a bit on the early side for dinner. There he found many of the hotel's guests gathered, unfamiliar with and affecting indifference to each other, sharing only the wait for the dinner bell. He picked up a newspaper from a table, sat down in a leather chair, and looked over the assembled company. It differed from that of his previous sojourn in a way that pleased him.

A broad horizon, tolerant and comprehensive, opened up before him. All the great languages of Europe melded together in subdued tones. Evening dress, the universal uniform of cultured society, provided a decorous external unity to the variety of humanity assembled here. There was the dry, long face of an American, a Russian extended family, English ladies, German children with French nannies. The Slavic component seemed to predominate. Polish was being spoken nearby.

It came from a group of adolescents and young adults gathered around a little wicker table under the supervision of a governess or companion. There were three young girls who looked to be fifteen to seventeen years old and a long-haired boy of maybe fourteen. Aschenbach noted with astonishment that the boy was perfectly beautiful. His face, pale and gracefully reserved, was framed by honey-colored curls. He had a straight nose and a lovely mouth and wore an expression of exquisite, divine solemnity. It was a face reminiscent of Greek statues from the noblest period of antiquity; it combined perfection of form with a unique personal charm that caused the onlooker to doubt ever having met with anything in nature or in art that could match its perfection. One could not help noticing, furthermore, that widely differing views on child-rearing had evidently directed the dress and general treatment of the siblings. The three girls, the eldest of whom was for all intents an adult, were got up in a way that was almost disfiguringly chaste and austere. Every grace of figure was suppressed and obscured by their uniformly habitlike half-length dresses, sober and slate-gray in color, tailored as if to be deliberately unflattering, relieved by no decoration save white, turned-down collars. Their smooth hair, combed tightly against their heads, made their faces appear nunnishly vacant and expressionless. It could only be a mother who was in charge here, one who never once considered applying to the boy the severity of upbringing that seemed required of her when it came to the girls. Softness and tenderness were the obvious conditions of the boy's existence. No one had yet been so bold as to take the scissors to his lovely hair, which curled about his brows, over his ears, and even further down the back of his neck—as it does on the statue of the "Boy Pulling a Thorn from his Foot."[7] His English sailor suit had puffy sleeves that narrowed at the cuff to embrace snugly the delicate wrists of his still childlike yet delicate hands. The suit made his slim figure seem somehow opulent and pampered with all its decoration, its bow, braidwork, and embroidery. He sat so that the observer saw him in profile. His feet were clad in black patent leather and arranged one in front of the other; one elbow was propped on the arm of his wicker chair with his cheek resting on his closed hand; his demeanor was one of careless refinement, quite without the almost submissive stiffness that seemed to be the norm for his sisters. Was he in poor health? Perhaps, for the skin of his face was white as ivory and stood out in sharp contrast to the darker gold of the surrounding curls. Or was he simply a coddled favorite, the object of a biased and capricious affection? Aschenbach was inclined to suppose the latter. There is inborn in every artistic disposition an indulgent and treacherous tendency to accept injustice when it produces beauty and to respond with complicity and even admiration when the aristocrats of this world get preferential treatment.

A waiter went about and announced in English that dinner was ready. Most of the company gradually disappeared through the glass door into the dining room. Latecomers passed by, arriving from the vestibule or from the elevators. Dinner was beginning to be served inside, but the young Poles still lingered by their wicker table. Aschenbach, comfortably seated in his deep armchair, his eyes captivated by the beautiful vision before him, waited with them.

The governess, a short, corpulent, rather unladylike woman with a red

---

7. A bronze Greco-Roman statue admired for the graceful pose and handsome appearance of the boy it depicts.

face, finally gave the sign to get up. With her brows raised she pushed back her chair and bowed as a tall lady, dressed in gray and white and richly bejeweled with pearls, entered the lobby. The demeanor of this woman was cool and measured; the arrangement of her lightly powdered hair and the cut of her clothes displayed the taste for simplicity favored by those who regard piety as an essential component of good breeding. She could have been the wife of a highly placed German official. Her jewelry was the only thing about her appearance that suggested fabulous luxury; it was priceless, consisting of earrings and a very long, triple strand of softly shimmering pearls, each as big as a cherry.

The boy and the girls had risen quickly. They bent to kiss their mother's hand while she, with a restrained smile on her well-preserved but slightly tired and rather pointy-nosed face, looked across the tops of their heads at the governess, to whom she directed a few words in French. Then she walked to the glass door. The young ones followed her, the girls in the order of their ages, behind them the governess, the boy last of all. For some reason he turned around before crossing the threshold. Since there was no one else left in the lobby, his strangely misty gray eyes met those of Aschenbach, who was sunk deep in contemplation of the departing group, his newspaper on his knees.

What he had seen was, to be sure, in none of its particulars remarkable. They did not go in to dinner before their mother; they had waited for her, greeted her respectfully when she came, and then observed perfectly normal manners going into the dining room. It was just that it had all happened so deliberately, with such a sense of discipline, responsibility, and self-respect, that Aschenbach felt strangely moved. He lingered a few moments more, then went along into the dining room himself. He was shown to his table, which, he noted with a brief twinge of regret, was very far away from that of the Polish family.

Tired but nonetheless mentally stimulated, he entertained himself during the tedious meal with abstract, even transcendent matters. He pondered the mysterious combination of regularity and individuality that is necessary to produce human beauty; proceeded then to the general problem of form and of art; and ultimately concluded that his thoughts and discoveries resembled those inspirations that come in dreams: they seem wonderful at the time, but in the sober light of day they show up as utterly shallow and useless. After dinner he spent some time smoking, sitting, and wandering about in the park, which was fragrant in the evening air. He went to bed early and passed the night in a sleep uninterruptedly deep but frequently enlivened by all sorts of dreams.

The next day the weather had gotten no better. There was a steady wind off the land. Under a pale overcast sky the sea lay in a dull calm, almost as if it had shriveled up, with a soberingly contracted horizon; it had receded so far from the beach that it uncovered several rows of long sandbars. When Aschenbach opened his window, he thought he could detect the stagnant smell of the lagoon.

He was beset by ill humor. He was already having thoughts of leaving. Once years ago, after several lovely weeks here in springtime, just such weather had been visited upon him and had made him feel so poorly that he had had to take flight from Venice like a fugitive. Was he not feeling once again the onset of the feverish listlessness he had felt then, the throbbing of his temples, the heaviness in his eyelids? To change his vacation spot yet again would be a nuisance; but if the wind did not shift soon, he simply could not remain here. He did not unpack everything, just in case. He ate at nine in the special breakfast room between the lobby and the dining room.

In this room prevailed the solemn stillness that great hotels aspire to. The waiters went about on tip-toe. The clink of the tea service and a half-whispered word were all one could hear. Aschenbach noticed the Polish girls and their governess at a table in the corner diagonally across from the door, two tables away. They sat very straight, their ash-blond hair newly smoothed down flat, their eyes red. They wore starched blue linen dresses with little white turned-down collars and cuffs, and they passed a jar of preserves to each other. They had almost finished their breakfast. The boy was not there.

Aschenbach smiled. Well, little Phaeacian, he thought. It seems you, and not they, have the privilege of sleeping to your heart's content. Suddenly cheered, he recited to himself the line:

"Changes of dress, warm baths, and downy beds."[8]

He ate his breakfast at a leisurely pace, received some mail that had been forwarded—delivered personally by the doorman, who entered the room with his braided hat in hand—and opened a few letters while he smoked a cigarette. Thus it happened that he was present for the entrance of the late sleeper they were waiting for over there in the corner.

He came through the glass door and traversed the silent room diagonally over to the table where his sisters sat. His carriage was extraordinarily graceful, not only in the way he held his torso but also in the way he moved his knees and set one white-shod foot in front of the other. He moved lightly, in a manner both gentle and proud, made more lovely still by the childlike bashfulness with which he twice lifted and lowered his eyelids as he went by, turning his face out toward the room. Smiling, he murmured a word in his soft, indistinct speech and took his place, showing his full profile to the observer. The latter was once more, and now especially, struck with amazement, indeed even alarm, at the truly godlike beauty possessed by this mortal child. Today the boy wore a lightweight sailor suit of blue and white striped cotton with a red silk bow on the chest, finished at the neck with a simple white upright collar. And above this collar, which did not even fit in very elegantly with the character of the costume, rose up that blossom, his face, a sight unforgettably charming. It was the face of Eros, with the yellowish glaze of Parian marble,[9] with delicate and serious brows, the temples and ears richly and rectangularly framed by soft, dusky curls.

Fine, very fine, thought Aschenbach with that professional, cool air of appraisal artists sometimes use to cover their delight, their enthusiasm when they encounter a masterpiece. He thought further: Really, if the sea and the sand were not waiting for me, I would stay here as long as you stay. With that, however, he departed, walking past the attentive employees through the lobby, down the terrace steps, and straight across the wooden walkway to the hotel's private beach. There he let a barefoot old man in linen pants, sailor shirt, and straw hat who managed affairs on the beach show him to

8. A reference to Homer's *Odyssey* 8.249. The Phaeacians were a peaceful, happy people who showed hospitality to the shipwrecked Odysseus.   9. White marble from the island of Paros was especially prized by sculptors in antiquity. Eros was the Greek god of love.

his rented beach cabana and arrange a table and chair on its sandy, wooden platform. Then he made himself comfortable in his beach chair, which he had pulled through the pale yellow sand closer to the sea.

The beach scene, this view of a carefree society engaged in purely sensual enjoyment on the edge of the watery element, entertained and cheered him as it always did. The gray, smooth ocean was already full of wading children, swimmers, and colorful figures lying on the sandbars with their arms crossed behind their heads. Others were rowing about in little flat-bottomed boats painted red and blue, capsizing to gales of laughter. People sat on the platforms of the cabanas, arranged in a long neat row along the beach, as if they were little verandas. In front of them people played games, lounged lazily, visited and chatted, some dressed in elegant morning clothes and others enjoying the nakedness sanctioned by the bold and easy freedom of the place. Down on the moist, hard sand there were a few individuals strolling about in white beach robes or in loose, brightly colored bathing dresses. To the right some children had built an elaborate sand castle and bedecked it with little flags in the colors of every country. Vendors of mussels, cakes, and fruit knelt and spread their wares before them. On the left, a Russian family was encamped in front of one of the cabanas that were set at a right angle between the others and the sea, thus closing that end of the beach. The family included men with beards and huge teeth; languid women past their prime; a young lady from a Baltic country, sitting at an easel and painting the ocean to the accompaniment of cries of frustration; two affable, ugly children; and an old maid in a babushka, displaying the affectionately servile demeanor of a slave. They resided there in grateful enjoyment, called out endlessly the names of their unruly, giddy children, exchanged pleasantries at surprising length in their few words of Italian with the jocular old man from whom they bought candy, kissed each other on the cheeks, and cared not a whit for anyone who might witness their scene of shared humanity.

Well, then, I will stay, thought Aschenbach. Where could things be better? His hands folded in his lap, he let his eyes roam the ocean's distances, let his gaze slip out of focus, grow hazy, blur in the uniform distances, mistiness of empty space. He loved the sea from the depth of his being: first of all because a hardworking artist needs his rest from the demanding variety of phenomena he works with and longs to take refuge in the bosom of simplicity and enormity; and, second, because he harbors an affinity for the undivided, the immeasurable, the eternal, the void. It was a forbidden affinity, directly contrary to his calling, and seductive precisely for that reason. To rest in the arms of perfection is what all those who struggle for excellence long to do; and is the void not a form of perfection? But while he was thus dreaming away toward the depths of emptiness, the horizontal line of the sea's edge was crossed by a human figure. When he had retrieved his gaze from the boundless realms and refocused his eyes, he saw it was the lovely boy who, coming from the left, was passing before him across the sand. He went barefoot, ready to go in wading, his slim legs bare from the knees down. He walked slowly but with a light, proud step, as if he were used to going about without shoes, and looked around at the row of cabanas that closed the end of the beach. The Russian family was still there, gratefully leading its harmonious existence, but no sooner had he laid eyes on them than a storm cloud of angry contempt crossed his face. His brow darkened, his lips began to curl, and from one side of his mouth emerged a bitter grimace that gouged a furrow in his cheek. He frowned so deeply that his eyes seemed pressed inward and sunken, seemed to speak dark and evil volumes of hatred from their depths. He looked down at the ground, cast one more threatening glance backward, and then, shrugging his shoulders as if to discard something and get away from it, he left his enemies behind.

A sort of delicacy or fright, something like a mixture of respect and shame, caused Aschenbach to turn away as if he had not seen anything; for it is repugnant to a chance witness, if he is a serious person, to make use of his observations, even to himself. But Aschenbach felt cheered and shaken at the same time—that is, happiness overwhelmed him. This childish fanaticism directed against the most harmless, good-natured target imaginable put into a human perspective something that otherwise seemed divinely indeterminate. It transformed a precious creation of nature that had before been no more than a feast for the eyes into a worthy object of deeper sympathy. It endowed the figure of the youngster, who had already shone with significance because of his beauty, with an aura that allowed him to be taken seriously beyond his years.

Still turned away, Aschenbach listened to the boy's voice, his clear, somewhat weak voice, by means of which he was trying to hail from afar his playmates at work on the sand castle. They answered him, calling again and again his name or an affectionate variation on his name. Aschenbach listened with a certain curiosity, unable to distinguish anything more than two melodious syllables—something like Adgio or more frequently Adgiu, with a drawn-out *u* at the end of the cry. The sound made him glad, it seemed to him that its harmony suited its object, and he repeated it softly to himself as he turned back with satisfaction to his letters and papers.

With his small traveling briefcase on his knees, he took his fountain pen and began to attend to various matters of correspondence. But after a mere quarter of an hour he was feeling regret that he should thus take leave in spirit and miss out on this, the most charming set of circumstances he knew of, for the sake of an activity he carried on with indifference. He cast his writing materials aside and turned his attention back to the sea; and not long after, distracted by the voices of the youngsters at the sand castle, he turned his head to the right and let it rest comfortably on the back of his chair, where he could once more observe the comings and goings of the exquisite Adgio.

His first glance found him; the red bow on his breast could not be missed. He was engaged with some others in setting up an old board as a bridge over the moat around the sand castle, calling out advice on proper procedure and nodding his head. There were about ten companions with him, boys and girls, most of an age with him but a few younger, chattering in a confusion of tongues—Polish, French, and even some Balkan languages. But it was his name that most often resounded through it all. He was evidently popular, sought after, admired. One companion, likewise a Pole, a sturdy boy called something like Yashu, who wore a belted linen suit and had black hair slicked down with pomade, seemed to be his closest friend and vassal. With the work on the sand castle finished for the time being, they went off together along the beach, arms about each other, and the one called Yashu gave his beautiful partner a kiss.

Aschenbach was tempted to shake his finger at him. "Let me give you a piece of advice, Kritobulos," he thought and smiled to himself. "Take a year's journey. You will need at least that much time for your recovery."[1] And then he breakfasted on large, fully ripe strawberries that he obtained from a peddler. It had gotten very warm, although the sun had not managed to pierce the layer of mist that covered the sky. Lassitude seized his spirit, while his senses enjoyed the enormous, lulling entertainment afforded by the quiet sea. The task of puzzling out what name it was that sounded like Adgio struck the serious man as a fitting, entirely satisfying occupation. With the help of a few Polish memories he determined that it was probably Tadzio he had heard, the nickname for Tadeusz. It was pronounced Tadziu in the form used for direct address.

Tadzio was taking a swim. Aschenbach, who had lost sight of him for a moment, spotted his head and then his arm, which rose as it stroked. He was very far out; the water apparently stayed shallow for a long way. But already his family seemed to be getting concerned about him, already women's voices were calling to him from the cabanas, shouting out once more this name that ruled over the beach almost like a watchword and that possessed something both sweet and wild in its soft consonants and drawn-out cry of *uuu* at the end. "Tadziu! Tadziu!" He turned back; he ran through the sea with his head thrown back, beating the resisting water into a foam with his legs. The sight of this lively adolescent figure, seductive and chaste, lovely as a tender young god, emerging from the depths of the sky and the sea with dripping locks and escaping the clutches of the elements—it all gave rise to mythic images. It was a sight belonging to poetic legends from the beginning of time that tell of the origins of form and of the birth of the gods. Aschenbach listened with his eyes closed to this mythic song reverberating within him, and once again he thought about how good it was here and how he wanted to stay.

Later on Tadzio lay on the sand, resting from his swim, wrapped in a white beach towel that was drawn up under his right shoulder, his head resting on his bare arm. Even when Aschenbach refrained from looking at him, instead reading a few pages in his book, he almost never forgot who was lying nearby or forgot that it would cost him only a slight turn of his head to the right to bring the adorable sight back into view. It almost seemed to him that he was sitting here with the express purpose of keeping watch over the resting boy. Busy as he might be with his own affairs, he maintained his vigilant care for the noble human figure not far away on his right. A paternal kindness, an emotional attachment filled and moved his heart, the attachment that someone who produces beauty at the cost of intellectual self-sacrifice feels toward someone who naturally possesses beauty.

After midday he left the beach, returned to the hotel, and took the elevator up to his room. There he spent a considerable length of time in front of the mirror looking at his gray hair and his severe, tired face. At the same time he thought about his fame and about the fact that many people recognized him on the street and looked at him with respect, all on account of those graceful, unerringly accurate words of his. He called the roll of the long list

---

1. Recalling Socrates' advice to Kritoboulos when the latter kissed Alcibiades' handsome son (Xenophon's *Memorabilia* 1.3).

of successes his talent had brought him, as many as he could think of, and even recalled his elevation to the nobility. He then retired to the dining room for lunch and ate at his little table. As he was entering the elevator when the meal was over, a throng of young people likewise coming from lunch crowded him to the back of the swaying little chamber. Tadzio was among them. He stood very close by, so close in fact that for the first time Aschenbach had the opportunity to view him not from a distance like a picture but minutely, scrutinizing every detail of his human form. Someone was talking to the boy, and while he was answering with his indescribably sweet smile they reached the second floor, where he got off, backing out, his eyes cast down. Beauty breeds modesty, Aschenbach thought and gave urgent consideration as to why. He had had occasion to notice, however, that Tadzio's teeth were not a very pleasing sight. They were rather jagged and pale and had no luster of health but rather a peculiar brittle transparency such as one sometimes sees in anemics. He is very sensitive, he is sickly, thought Aschenbach. He will probably not live long. And he refrained from trying to account for the feeling of satisfaction and reassurance that accompanied this thought.

He passed a couple of hours in his room and in the afternoon took the vaporetto across the stagnant-smelling lagoon to Venice. He got off at San Marco, took tea in the piazza,[2] and then, following his habitual routine in Venice, set off on a walk through the streets. It was this walk, however, that initiated a complete reversal of his mood and his plans.

The air in the little streets was odiously oppressive, so thick that the smells surging out of the dwellings, shops, and restaurants, a suffocating vapor of oil, perfume, and more, all hung about and failed to disperse. Cigarette smoke hovered in place and only slowly disappeared. The press of people in the small spaces annoyed rather than entertained him as he walked. The longer he went on, the more it became a torture. He was overwhelmed by that horrible condition produced by the sea air in combination with the sirocco, a state of both nervousness and debility at once. He began to sweat uncomfortably. His eyes ceased to function, his breathing was labored, he felt feverish, the blood pounded in his head. He fled from the crowded shop-lined streets across bridges into the poor quarter. There beggars molested him, and the evil emanations from the canals hindered his breathing. In a quiet piazza, one of those forgotten, seemingly enchanted little places in the interior of the city, he rested on the edge of a well, dried his forehead, and reached the conclusion that he would have to leave Venice.

For the second time, and this time definitively, it became clear that this city in this weather was particularly harmful to his health. To remain stubbornly in place obviously went against all reason, and the prospect of a change in the direction of the wind was highly uncertain. A quick decision had to be made. To return home this soon was out of the question. Neither his summer nor his winter quarters were prepared for his arrival. But this was not the only place with beaches on the ocean, and those other places did not have the noxious extra of the lagoon and its fever-inducing vapors. He recalled a little beach resort not far from Trieste that had been enthusiastically recommended to him. Why not go there and, indeed, without delay, so that yet another change of location would still be worthwhile? He

---

2. A famous public square in front of the church, lined by restaurants and cafés.

declared himself resolved and stood up. At the next gondola stop he boarded a boat to take him to San Marco through the dim labyrinth of canals, under graceful marble balconies flanked by stone lions, around corners of slippery masonry, past mournful palace facades affixed with business insignia[3] reflected in the garbage-strewn water. He had trouble getting to his destination, since the gondolier was in league with lace and glass factories and made constant efforts to induce him to stop at them to sightsee and buy; and so whenever the bizarre journey through Venice began to weave its magic, the mercenary lust for booty afflicting this sunken queen of cities[4] did what it could to bring the enchanted spirit back to unpleasant reality.

Upon returning to the hotel he did not even wait for dinner but went right to the office and declared that unforeseen circumstances compelled him to depart the next morning. With many expressions of regret the staff acknowledged the payment of his bill. He dined and then passed the mild evening reading magazines in a rocking chair on the rear terrace. Before going to bed he did all his packing for the morning's departure.

He did not sleep especially well, as the impending move made him restless. When he opened the windows the next morning the sky was still overcast, but the air seemed fresher and . . . he already started to have second thoughts. Had he been hasty or wrong to give notice thus? Was it a result of his sick and unreliable condition? If he had just put it off a bit, if he had just made an attempt to get used to the Venetian air or to hold out for an improvement in the weather instead of losing heart so quickly! Then, instead of this hustle and bustle, he would have a morning on the beach like the one yesterday to look forward to. Too late. Now he would have to go ahead with it, to wish today what he wished for yesterday. He got dressed and at eight o'clock took the elevator down to breakfast on the ground floor.

The breakfast room was still empty when he entered. A number of individual guests arrived while he sat waiting for his order. With his teacup at his lips he watched the Polish girls and their attendant come in. Severe and morning-fresh, eyes still red, they proceeded to their table in the corner by the window. Immediately thereafter the doorman approached him with hat in hand to tell him it was time to leave. The car was ready, he said, to take him and some other travelers to the Hotel Excelsior, and from there a motor boat would convey them through the company's private canal to the railroad station. Time was pressing, he said. Aschenbach found it not at all pressing. There was more than an hour until the departure of his train. He was annoyed at the habitual hotel practice of packing departing guests off earlier than necessary and informed the doorman that he wanted to finish his breakfast in peace. The man withdrew hesitatingly only to show up again five minutes later. The car simply could not wait longer, he said. Very well, let it go and take his trunks with it, Aschenbach replied with annoyance. As for himself, he preferred to take the public steamer at the proper time and asked that they let him take care of his own arrangements. The employee bowed. Aschenbach, happy to have fended off this nuisance, finished his meal without haste and even had the waiter bring him a newspaper. Time had become short indeed when at last he got up to leave. And it just so happened

---

3. Once-stately Renaissance homes that now lodge businesses.   4. A major sea power by the 15th century, Venice was called Queen of the Seas.

that at that very moment Tadzio came in through the glass door.

He crossed the path of the departing traveler on his way to his family's table. He lowered his eyes modestly before the gray-haired, high-browed gentleman, only to raise them again immediately in his own charming way, displaying their soft fullness to him. Then he was past. Adieu, Tadzio, thought Aschenbach. I saw you for such a short time. And enunciating his thought as it occurred to him, contrary to his every habit, he added under his breath the words: "Blessings on you." He then made his departure, dispensed tips, received a parting greeting from the quiet little manager in the French frock coat, and left the hotel on foot, as he had arrived. Followed by a servant with his hand luggage, he traversed the island along the boulevard, white with flowers, that led to the steamer landing. He arrived, he took his seat—and what followed was a journey of pain and sorrow through the uttermost depths of regret.

It was the familiar trip across the lagoon, past San Marco, up the Grand Canal. Aschenbach sat on the curved bench in the bow, his arm resting on the railing, his hand shading his eyes. They left the public gardens behind them; the Piazzetta once more revealed its princely splendor, and soon it too was left behind. Then came the great line of palaces, and as the waterway turned there appeared the magnificent marble arch of the Rialto.[5] The traveler looked, and his heart was torn. He breathed the atmosphere of the city, this slightly stagnant smell of sea and of swamp from which he had felt so strongly compelled to flee, breathed it now deeply, in tenderly painful draughts. Was it possible that he had not known, had not considered how desperately he was attached to all this? What this morning had been a partial regret, a slight doubt as to the rightness of his decision, now became affliction, genuine pain, a suffering in his soul so bitter that it brought tears to his eyes more than once. He told himself he could not possibly have foreseen such a reaction. What was so hard to take, actually sometimes down-right impossible to endure, was the thought that he would never see Venice again, that this was a parting forever. Since it had become evident for the second time that the city made him sick, since for the second time he had been forced to run head over heels away, he would have to regard it henceforth as an impossible destination, forbidden to him, something he simply was not up to, something it would be pointless for him to try for again. Yes, he felt that, should he go away now, shame and spite would certainly prevent him from ever seeing the beloved city again, now that it had twice forced him to admit physical defeat. This conflict between the inclination of his soul and the capacity of his body seemed to the aging traveler suddenly so weighty and so important, his physical defeat so ignominious, so much to be resisted at all cost, that he could no longer grasp the ease with which he had reached the decision yesterday, without serious struggle, to acquiesce.

Meanwhile, the steamer was approaching the railway station, and his pain and helplessness were rising to the level of total disorientation. His tortured mind found the thought of departure impossible, the thought of return no less so. In such a state of acute inner strife he entered the station. It was already very late, he had not a moment to lose if he was to catch his train. He wanted to, and he did not want to. But time was pressing, it goaded him

5. A famous, highly arched bridge over the Grand Canal.

onward; he made haste to obtain his ticket and looked about in the bustle of the station for the hotel employee stationed here. This person appeared and announced that the large trunk was already checked and on its way. Already on its way? Yes indeed—to Como.[6] To Como? After a frantic exchange, after angry questions and embarrassed answers, the fact emerged that the trunk had been put together with the baggage of other, unknown travelers in the luggage office at the Hotel Excelsior and sent off in precisely the wrong direction.

Aschenbach had difficulty maintaining the facial expression expected under such circumstances. An adventurous joy, an unbelievable cheerfulness seized his breast from within like a spasm. The hotel employee sped off to see if he could retrieve the trunk and returned, as one might have expected, with no success whatever. Only then did Aschenbach declare that he did not wish to travel without his luggage and that he had decided to return and await the recovery of the trunk at the Hotel des Bains. Was the company boat still here at the station? The man assured him it was waiting right at the door. With an impressive display of Italian cajolery he persuaded the agent to take back Aschenbach's ticket. He swore he would telegraph ahead, that no effort would be spared to get the trunk back with all due speed, and . . . thus came to pass something very odd indeed. The traveler, not twenty minutes after his arrival at the station, found himself once again on the Grand Canal on his way back to the Lido.

What a wondrous, incredible, embarrassing, odd and dreamlike adventure! Thanks to a sudden reversal of destiny, he was to see once again, within the very hour, places that he had thought in deepest melancholy he was leaving forever. The speedy little vessel shot toward its destination, foam flying before its bow, maneuvering with droll agility between gondolas and steamers, while its single passenger hid beneath a mask of annoyed resignation the anxious excitement of a boy playing hooky. Still from time to time his frame was shaken with laughter over this mischance, which he told himself could not have worked out better for the luckiest person in the world. Explanations would have to be made, amazed faces confronted, but then—so he told himself—all would be well again, a great disaster averted, a terrible error made right, and everything he thought he had left behind would be open to him once more, would be his to enjoy at his leisure. . . . And by the way, was it just the rapid movement of the boat, or could it really be that he felt a strong breeze off the ocean to complete his bliss?

The waves slapped against the concrete walls of the narrow canal that cut through the island to the Hotel Excelsior. A motor bus was waiting there for the returning traveler and conveyed him alongside the curling waves down the straight road to the Hotel des Bains. The little manager with the mustache and the cutaway frock coat came down the broad flight of steps to meet him.

With quiet cajolery the manager expressed his regret over the incident, declared it extremely embarrassing for himself personally and for the establishment, but expressed his emphatic approval of Aschenbach's decision to wait here for the return of his luggage. To be sure, his room was already taken, but another, by no means worse, stood ready. "Pas de chance, mon-

6. A large lake and resort area in northwest Italy.

sieur,"[7] said the elevator man with a smile as they glided upwards. And so the fugitive was billeted once again, and in a room that matched almost exactly his previous one in orientation and furnishings.

Tired, numb from the whirl of this strange morning, he distributed the contents of his small suitcase in his room and then sank down in an armchair by the open window. The sea had taken on a light green coloration, the air seemed thinner and purer, the beach with its cabanas and boats seemed more colorful, although the sky was still gray. Aschenbach looked out, his hands folded in his lap, content to be here once more, but shaking his head in reproach at his own fickle mood, his lack of knowledge of his own desires. He sat thus for perhaps an hour, resting and thoughtlessly dreaming. At noon he spied Tadzio, dressed in his striped linen suit with red bow, returning from the shore through the beach barrier and along the wooden walkway to the hotel. Aschenbach recognized him at once from his high vantage point even before he got a good look at him, and he was just about to form a thought something like: Look, Tadzio, you too have returned! But at that very moment he felt the casual greeting collapse and fall silent before the truth of his heart. He felt the excitement in his blood, the joy and pain in his soul, and recognized that it was because of Tadzio that his departure had been so difficult.

He sat quite still, quite unseen in his elevated location and looked into himself. His features were active; his brows rose; an alert, curious, witty smile crossed his lips. Then he raised his head and with both his arms, which were hanging limp over the arms of his chair, he made a slow circling and lifting movement that turned his palms forward, as if to signify an opening and extending of his embrace. It was a gesture of readiness, of welcome, and of relaxed acceptance.

CHAPTER 4

The god with fiery cheeks[8] now, naked, directed his horses, four-abreast, fire-breathing, day by day through the chambers of heaven, and his yellow curls fluttered along with the blast of the east wind. A silky-white sheen lay on the Pontos,[9] its broad stretches undulating languidly. The sands burned. Under the silvery shimmering blue of the ether there were rustcolored canvas awnings spread out in front of the beach cabanas, and one passed the morning hours in the sharply framed patch of shade they offered. But the evening was also delightful, when the plants in the park wafted balsamic perfumes, the stars above paced out their circuits, and the murmur of the night-shrouded sea, softly penetrating, cast a spell on the soul. Such an evening bore the joyful promise of another festive day of loosely ordered leisure, bejeweled with countless, thickly strewn possibilities of happy accidents.

The guest, whom accommodating mischance kept here, was far from disposed to see in the return of his belongings a reason to depart once more. He had been obliged to get along without a few things for a couple of days and to appear at meals in the great dining room wearing his traveling clothes. Then, when the errant baggage was finally set down once more in his room, he unpacked thoroughly and filled closets and drawers with his things, deter-

7. No luck, sir (French).   8. Helios, Greek god of the sun (later equated with Apollo).   9. The sea (Greek, literal trans.); a figurative reference to the Adriatic Sea.

mined for the time being to stay indefinitely, happy to be able to pass the morning's hours on the beach in his silk suit and to present himself once more at his little table at dinner time wearing proper evening attire.

The benevolent regularity of this existence had at once drawn him into its power; the soft and splendid calm of this lifestyle had him quickly ensnared. What a fine place to stay, indeed, combining the charms of a refined southern beach resort with the cozy proximity of the wondrous, wonder-filled city! Aschenbach was no lover of pleasure. Whenever and wherever it seemed proper to celebrate, to take a rest, to take a few days off, he soon had to get back—it was especially so in his younger days—anxiously and reluctantly back to the affliction of his high calling, the sacred, sober service of his day-to-day life. This place alone enchanted him, relaxed his will, made him happy. Sometimes in the morning, under the canopy of his beach cabana, dreaming away across the blue of the southern sea, or sometimes as well on a balmy night, leaning back under the great starry sky on the cushions of a gondola taking him back home to the Lido from the Piazza San Marco, where he had tarried long—and the bright lights and the melting sounds of the serenade were left behind—he remembered his country home in the mountains, the site of his summertime struggles, where the clouds drifted through the garden, where in the evening fearful thunderstorms extinguished the lights in the house and the ravens he fed soared to the tops of the spruce trees. Then it might seem to him that he had been transported to the land of Elysium[1] at the far ends of the earth, where a life of ease is bestowed upon mortals, where there is no snow, no winter, no storms or streaming rain, but rather always the cooling breath rising from Okeanos,[2] where the days run out in blissful leisure, trouble-free, struggle-free, dedicated only to the sun and its revels.

Aschenbach saw the boy Tadzio often, indeed almost continually; limited space and a regular schedule common to all the guests made it inevitable that the lovely boy was in his vicinity nearly all day, with brief interruptions. He saw, he met him everywhere: in the hotel's public places, on the cooling boat trips to the city and back, in the ostentation of the piazza itself; and often too in the streets and byways a chance encounter would take place. Chiefly, however, it was the mornings on the beach that offered him with delightful regularity an extended opportunity to study and worship the charming apparition. Yes, it was this narrow and constrained happiness, this regularly recurring good fortune that filled him with contentment and joy in life, that made his stay all the more dear to him and caused one sunny day after another to fall so agreeably in line.

He got up early, as he otherwise did under the relentless pressure of work, and was one of the first on the beach when the sun was still mild and the sea lay white in the glare of morning dreams. He gave a friendly greeting to the guard at the beach barrier, said a familiar hello to the barefoot old man who got his place ready, spreading the brown awning and arranging the cabana furniture on the platform, and settled in. Three hours or four were then his in which, as the sun rose to its zenith and grew fearsome in strength and the sea turned a deeper and deeper blue, he could watch Tadzio.

1. Located at the western edge of the Earth, a pleasant otherworld for those heroes favored by the gods.
2. According to Greek mythology, a river encircling the world.

He would see him coming from the left along the edge of the sea, would see him from the back as he appeared from between the cabanas, or sometimes would suddenly discover, not without a happy shudder, that he had missed his arrival and that he was already there, already in the blue and white bathing suit that was now his only article of attire on the beach, that he was already up to his usual doings in sand and sun—his charmingly trivial, lazily irregular life that was both recreation and rest, filled with lounging, wading, digging, catching, resting, and swimming, watched over by the women on the platform who called to him, making his name resound with their high voices: "Tadziu! Tadziu!" He would come running to them gesturing excitedly and telling them what he had done, showing them what he had found or caught: mussels and sea horses, jelly fish, crabs that ran off going sideways. Aschenbach understood not a single word he said, and though it may have been the most ordinary thing in the world it was all a vague harmony to his ear. Thus, foreignness raised the boy's speech to the level of music, a wanton sun poured unstinting splendor over him, and the sublime perspectives of the sea always formed the background and aura that set off his appearance.

Soon the observer knew every line and pose of this noble body that displayed itself so freely; he exulted in greeting anew every beauty, familiar though it had become, and his admiration, the discreet arousal of his senses, knew no end. They called the boy to pay his compliments to a guest who was attending the ladies at the cabana; he came running, still wet from the sea; he tossed his curls, and as he held out his hand he stood on one foot while holding the other up on tiptoe. His body was gracefully poised in the midst of a charming turning motion, while his face showed an embarrassed amiability, a desire to please that came from an aristocratic sense of duty. Sometimes he would lie stretched out with his beach towel wrapped about his chest, his delicately chiseled arm propped in the sand, his chin in the hollow of his hand. The one called Yashu sat crouching by him, playing up to him, and nothing could have been more enchanting than the smiling eyes and lips with which the object of this flattery looked upon his inferior, his vassal. Or he would stand at the edge of the sea, alone, separated from his friends, very near Aschenbach, erect, his hands clasped behind his neck, slowly rocking on the balls of his feet and dreaming off into the blue yonder, while little waves that rolled in bathed his toes. His honey-colored hair clung in circles to his temples and his neck; the sun made the down shine on his upper back; the subtle definition of the ribs and the symmetry of his chest stood out through the tight-fitting material covering his torso; his armpits were still as smooth as those of a statue, the hollows behind his knees shone likewise, and the blue veins showing through made his body seem to be made of translucent material. What discipline, what precision of thought was expressed in the stretch of this youthfully perfect body! But was not the rigorous and pure will that had been darkly active in bringing this divine form into the clear light of day entirely familiar to the artist in him? Was this same will not active in him, too, when he, full of sober passion, freed a slender form from the marble mass of language,[3] a form he had seen with

---

3. The Italian artist Michelangelo Buonarroti (1475–1564) explained that he created his statues by carving away the marble block until the figure within was set free.

his spiritual eye and that he presented to mortal men as image and mirror of spiritual beauty?

Image and mirror! His eyes embraced the noble figure there on the edge of the blue, and in a transport of delight he thought his gaze was grasping beauty itself, the pure form of divine thought, the universal and pure perfection that lives in the spirit and which here, graceful and lovely, presented itself for worship in the form of a human likeness and exemplar. Such was his intoxication; the aging artist welcomed the experience without reluctance, even greedily. His intellect was in labor, his educated mind set in motion. His memory dredged up ancient images passed on to him in the days of his youth, thoughts not until now touched by the spark of his personal involvement. Was it not written that the sun turns our attention from intellectual to sensuous matters?[4] It was said that the sun numbs and enchants our reason and memory to such an extent that the soul in its pleasure forgets its ordinary condition; its amazed admiration remains fixed on the loveliest of sun-drenched objects. Indeed, only with the help of a body can the soul rise to the contemplation of still higher things. Amor[5] truly did as mathematicians have always done by assisting slow-learning children with concrete pictures of pure forms: so, too, did the god like to make use of the figure and coloration of human youth in order to make the spiritual visible to us, furnishing it with the reflected glory of beauty and thus making of it a tool of memory, so that seeing it we might then be set aflame with pain and hope.

Those, at any rate, were the thoughts of the impassioned onlooker. He was capable of sustaining just such a high pitch of emotion. He spun himself a charming tapestry out of the roar of the sea and the glare of the sun. He saw the ancient plane tree not far from the walls of Athens,[6] that sacred, shadowy place filled with the scent of willow blossoms, decorated with holy images and votive offerings in honor of the nymphs and of Achelous.[7] The stream flowed in crystal clarity over smooth pebbles past the foot of the wide-branched tree. The crickets sang. Two figures reclined on the grass that gently sloped so that you could lie with your head held up; they were sheltered here from the heat of the day—an older man and a younger, one ugly and one handsome, wisdom at the side of charm. Amidst polite banter and wooing wit Socrates taught Phaedrus about longing and virtue. He spoke to him of the searing terror that the sensitive man experiences when his eye lights on an image of eternal beauty; spoke to him of the appetites of the impious, bad man who cannot conceive of beauty when he sees beauty's image and is incapable of reverence; spoke of the holy fear that overcomes a noble heart when a godlike face or a perfect body appears before him—how he then trembles and is beside himself and scarcely dares turn his eyes upon the sight and honors him who has beauty, indeed would even sacrifice to him as to a holy image, if he did not fear looking foolish in the eyes of others. For beauty, my dear Phaedrus, beauty alone is both worthy of love and visible at the same time; beauty, mark me well, is the only form of spirit that our senses can both grasp and endure. For what should become of us

---

4. In section 764E of the *Erotikos* (Dialogue on love) by the Greek essayist Plutarch (46–120).   5. The god of love (Latin).   6. A reference to the scene and some of the arguments in Plato's dialogue *Phaedrus*. Plato's school, or Academy, was located in a grove of plane trees outside Athens; in the dialogue, the young student Phaedrus tells Socrates of Lysias's speech on love, and Socrates responds with two speeches of his own.   7. A brook or small river in ancient Athens, here personified as a god.

if divinity itself, or reason and virtue and truth were to appear directly to our senses? Would we not be overcome and consumed in the flames of love, as Semele[8] was at the sight of Zeus? Thus beauty is the sensitive man's way to the spirit—just the way, just the means, little Phaedrus. . . . And then he said the subtlest thing of all, crafty wooer that he was: he said that the lover was more divine than the beloved, because the god was in the former and not in the latter—perhaps the tenderest, most mocking thought that ever was thought, a thought alive with all the guile and the most secret bliss of love's longing.

A writer's chief joy is that thought can become all feeling, that feeling can become all thought. The lonely author possessed and commanded at this moment just such a vibrant thought, such a precise feeling: namely, that nature herself would shiver with delight were intellect to bow in homage before beauty. He suddenly wanted to write. They say, to be sure, that Eros loves idleness; the god was made to engage in no other activity. But at this moment of crisis the excitement of the love-struck traveler drove him to productivity, and the occasion was almost a matter of indifference. The intellectual world had been challenged to profess its views on a certain great and burning problem of culture and of taste, and the challenge had reached him. The problem was well known to him, was part of his experience; the desire to illuminate it with the splendor of his eloquence was suddenly irresistible. And what is more, he wanted to work here in the presence of Tadzio, to use the boy's physical frame as the model for his writing, to let his style follow the lines of that body that seemed to him divine, to carry his beauty into the realm of intellect as once the eagle carried the Trojan shepherd into the ethereal heavens.[9] Never had his pleasure in the word seemed sweeter to him, never had he known so surely that Eros dwelt in the word as now in the dangerous and delightful hours he spent at his rough table under the awning. There with his idol's image in full view, the music of his voice resounding in his ear, he formed his little essay after the image of Tadzio's beauty—composed that page-and-a-half of choice prose that soon would amaze many a reader with its purity, nobility, and surging depth of feeling. It is surely for the best that the world knows only the lovely work and not also its origins, not the conditions under which it came into being; for knowledge of the origins from which flowed the artist's inspiration would surely often confuse the world, repel it, and thus vitiate the effects of excellence. Strange hours! Strangely enervating effort! Strangely fertile intercourse between a mind and a body! When Aschenbach folded up his work and left the beach, he felt exhausted, even unhinged, as if his conscience were indicting him after a debauch.

The next morning as he was about to leave the hotel he chanced to notice from the steps that Tadzio was already on his way to the shore, alone; he was just approaching the beach barrier. He felt first a suggestion, then a compulsion: the wish, the simple thought that he might make use of the opportunity to strike up a casual, cheerful acquaintanceship with this boy who unwittingly had caused such a stir in his mind and heart, speak with him

8. The mortal mother of Zeus's son Dionysus. She perished in flames when the king of the gods appeared (at her request) in his divine glory. 9. The young Trojan prince Ganymede was tending flocks when Zeus, in the form of an eagle, carried him off to Olympus where he became Zeus's lover and the cupbearer to the gods.

and enjoy his answer and his gaze. The lovely lad sauntered along; he could be easily caught up with; Aschenbach quickened his steps. He reached him on the walkway behind the cabanas, was about to put his hand on his head or on his shoulder, was about to let some word pass his lips, some friendly French phrase. But then he felt his heart beating like a hammer, perhaps only because of his rapid walk, so that he was short of breath and could only have spoken in a trembling gasp. He hesitated, tried to master himself, then suddenly feared he had been walking too long right behind the handsome boy, feared he might notice, might turn around with an inquiring look. He took one more run at him, but then he gave up, renounced his goal, and hung his head as he went by.

Too late! he thought at that moment. Too late! But was it really too late? This step he had failed to take might very possibly have led to something good, to something easy and happy, to a salutary return to reality. But it may have been that the aging traveler did not wish to return to reality, that he was too much in love with his own intoxication. Who can untangle the riddle of the artist's essence and character? Who can understand the deep instinctive fusion of discipline and a desire for licentiousness upon which that character is based? For it is licentiousness to be unable to wish for a salutary return to reality. Aschenbach was no longer inclined to self-criticism. The taste, the intellectual constitution that came with his years, his self-esteem, maturity, and the simplicity of age made him disinclined to analyze the grounds for his behavior or to decide whether it was conscience or debauchery and weakness that caused him not to carry out his plan. He was confused; he feared that someone, if only the custodian on the beach, might have observed his accelerated gait and his defeat; he feared very much looking foolish. And all the while he made fun of himself, of his comically solemn anxiety. "We've been quite confounded," he thought, "and now we're as crestfallen as a gamecock that lets its wings droop during a fight.[1] It must surely be the god himself who thus destroys our courage at the very sight of loveliness, who crushes our proud spirit so deeply in the dust. . . ." His thoughts roamed playfully: he was far too arrogant to be fearful of a mere emotion.

He had already ceased to pay much attention to the extent of time he was allowing himself for his holiday; the thought of returning home did not even cross his mind. He had had an ample amount of money sent to him by mail. His sole source of concern was the possible departure of the Polish family, but he had privately obtained information, thanks to casual inquiries at the hotel barber shop, that the Polish party had arrived only very shortly before he did. The sun tanned his face and hands, the bracing salt air stimulated his emotions. Just as he ordinarily used up all the resources he gathered from sleep, nourishment, or nature on literary work, so now he expended each contribution that sun, leisure, and sea air made to his daily increase in strength in a generous, extravagant burst of enthusiasm and sentiment.

He slept fitfully; the exquisitely uniform days were separated by short nights full of happy restlessness. To be sure he retired early, for at nine o'clock, when Tadzio had left the scene, the day was over as far as he was concerned. At the first glimmer of dawn, however, a softly penetrating pang of alarm awakened him, as his heart remembered its great adventure. No

---

1. From the Greek tragedian Phrynichus (512–476 B.C.E.), quoted in Plutarch's *Erotikos* (762E).

longer able to endure the pillow, he arose, wrapped himself in a light robe against the morning chill, and positioned himself at the open window to await the sunrise. This wonderful occurrence filled his sleep-blessed soul with reverence. Heaven, earth, and sea still lay in the ghostly, glassy pallor of dawn; a fading star still floated in the insubstantial distance. Then a breath of wind arose, a winged message from unapproachable abodes announcing that Eos was arising from the side of her spouse. There became visible on the furthest boundary between sea and sky that first sweet blush of red that reveals creation assuming perceptible form. The goddess was approaching, she who seduced young men, she who had stolen Kleitos and Kephalos and enjoyed the love of handsome Orion in defiance of all the envious Olympians.[2] A strewing of roses began there on the edge of the world, where all shone and blossomed in unspeakable purity. Childlike clouds, transfigured and luminous, hovered like attending Cupids in the rosy bluish fragrance. Purple light fell on the sea, then washed forward in waves. Golden spears shot up from below to the heights of the heavens, and the brilliance began to burn. Silently, with divine ascendancy, glow and heat and blazing flames spun upwards, as the brother-god's sacred chargers, hooves beating, mounted the heavens. The lonely, wakeful watcher sat bathed in the splendor of the god's rays; he closed his eyes and let the glory kiss his eyelids. With a confused, wondering smile on his lips he recognized feelings from long ago, early, exquisite afflictions of the heart that had withered in the severe service that his life had become and now returned so strangely transformed. He meditated, he dreamed. Slowly his lips formed a name, and still smiling, his face turned upward, his hands folded in his lap, he fell asleep once more in his armchair.

The whole day that had thus began in fiery celebration was strangely heightened and mythically transformed. Where did that breath of air come from, the one that suddenly played about his temples and ears so softly and significantly like a whisper from a higher realm? White feathery clouds stood in scattered flocks in the heavens like grazing herds that the gods tend. A stronger wind blew up; Poseidon's[3] steeds reared and ran, and the bulls obedient to the god with the blue-green locks lowered their horns and bellowed as they charged. But amid the boulders on the distant beach the waves hopped up like leaping goats. A magical world, sacred and animated by the spirit of Pan,[4] surrounded the beguiled traveler, and his heart dreamed tender fables. Often, as the sun set behind Venice, he would sit on a bench in the park to watch Tadzio, dressed in white with a colorful sash, delight in playing ball on the smooth, rolled gravel; and it was as if he were watching Hyacinthos, who had to die because two gods loved him.[5] Indeed he felt the painful envy Zephyros felt toward his rival in love, the god who abandoned his oracle, his bow, and his cithara to spend all his time playing with the beautiful boy. He saw the discus, directed by cruel jealousy, strike the lovely

2. Eos, the Greek goddess of dawn, was known for seducing handsome young men, including Kleitos and Kephalos. When she took the hunter Orion for her lover, Artemis, the jealous goddess of the hunt, killed him with her arrows. 3. God of the sea and brother of Zeus in Greek mythology, associated with the horse and the bull. 4. A Greek demigod, half man and half goat, associated with fertility and sexuality. 5. Apollo and Zephyr, god of the west wind, both loved the youth Hyacinthos. When Apollo accidentally killed him in a discus game—Zephyr blew the discus off course—a flower marked with the Greek syllables "ai ai" ("alas!") sprang from the boy's blood. Apollo is an archer and musician as well as the god of the Delphic oracle.

head; he too, turned pale as he received the stricken body; and the flower that sprang from that sweet blood bore the inscription of his unending lament. . . .

There is nothing stranger or more precarious than the relationship between people who know each other only by sight, who meet and watch each other every day, even every hour, yet are compelled by convention or their own whim to maintain the appearance of indifference and unfamiliarity, to avoid any word or greeting. There arises between them a certain restlessness and frustrated curiosity, the hysteria of an unsatisfied, unnaturally suppressed urge for acquaintanceship and mutual exchange, and in point of fact also a kind of tense respect. For people tend to love and honor other people so long as they are not in a position to pass judgment on them; and longing is the result of insufficient knowledge.

Some sort of relationship or acquaintance necessarily had to develop between Aschenbach and the young Tadzio, and with a pang of joy the older man was able to ascertain that his involvement and attentions were not altogether unrequited. For example, what impelled the lovely boy no longer to use the boardwalk behind the cabanas when he appeared on the beach in the morning but instead to saunter by toward his family's cabana on the front path, through the sand, past Aschenbach's customary spot, sometimes unnecessarily close by him, almost touching his table, his chair? Did Aschenbach's superior emotional energy exercise such an attraction, such a fascination on the tender, unreflecting object of those emotions? The writer waited daily for Tadzio's appearance; sometimes he would act as if he were busy when this event took place and let the lovely one pass by without seeming to notice. Sometimes, though, he would look up, and their eyes would meet. Both of them were gravely serious when it happened. In the refined and respectable bearing of the older man nothing betrayed his inner tumult; but in Tadzio's eyes there was the hint of an inquiry, of a thoughtful question. A hesitation became visible in his gait, he looked at the ground, he looked up again in his charming way, and when he was past there seemed to be something in his demeanor saying that only his good breeding prevented him from turning around.

One evening, however, something quite different happened. The Polish children and their governess were missing at the main meal in the large dining room. Aschenbach had taken note of it with alarm. Concerned about their absence, he was strolling in front of the hotel at the bottom of the terrace after dinner, dressed in his evening clothes and a straw hat, when he suddenly saw appear in the light of the arc lamps the nunlike sisters and their attendant, with Tadzio four steps behind. They were apparently returning from the steamer landing after having taken their meal for some reason in the city. It must have been cool on the water: Tadzio wore a dark blue sailor's coat with gold buttons and a sailor's hat to go with it. The sun and sea air had not browned him. His skin was the same marble-like yellow color it had been from the beginning. But today he seemed paler than usual, whether because of the cool temperature or because of the pallid moonglow cast by the lamps. His even brows showed in starker contrast, his eyes darkened to an even deeper tone. He was more beautiful than words could ever tell, and Aschenbach felt as he often had before the painful truth that words are capable only of praising physical beauty, not of rendering it visible.

He had not been expecting the exquisite apparition: it had come on unhoped for. He had not had time to fortify himself in a peaceful, respectable demeanor. Joy, surprise, and admiration might have been clearly displayed in the gaze that met that of the one he had so missed—and in that very second, it came to pass that Tadzio smiled. He smiled at Aschenbach, smiled eloquently, intimately, charmingly, and without disguise, with lips that began to open only as he smiled. It was the smile of Narcissus[6] leaning over the mirroring water, that deep, beguiled, unresisting smile that comes as he extends his arm toward the reflection of his own beauty—a very slightly distorted smile, distorted by the hopelessness of his desire to kiss the lovely lips of his shadow—a coquettish smile, curious and faintly pained, infatuated and infatuating.

He who had been the recipient of this smile rushed away with it as if it were a gift heavy with destiny. He was so thoroughly shaken that he was forced to flee the light of the terrace and the front garden and to seek with a hasty tread the darkness of the park in the rear. Strangely indignant and tender exhortations broke forth from him: "You must not smile so! Listen, no one is allowed to smile that way at anyone!" He threw himself on a bench; he breathed in the nocturnal fragrance of the plants, beside himself. Leaning back with his arms hanging at his sides, overpowered and shivering uncontrollably, he whispered the eternal formula of longing—impossible under these conditions, absurd, reviled, ridiculous, and yet holy and venerable even under these conditions—"I love you!"

CHAPTER 5

In the fourth week of his stay on the Lido Gustav Aschenbach made a number of disturbing discoveries regarding events in the outside world. In the first place it seemed to him that as the season progressed toward its height the number of guests at the hotel declined rather than increased. In particular it seemed that the German language ceased to be heard around him: lately his ear could detect only foreign sounds in the dining room and on the beach. He had taken to visiting the barbershop frequently, and in a conversation there one day he heard something that startled him. The barber had mentioned a German family that had just left after staying only a short time; then he added by way of flattering small talk, "But you're staying, sir, aren't you. You're not afraid of the disease." Aschenbach looked at him. "The disease?" he repeated. The man broke off his chatter, acted busy, ignored the question. When Aschenbach pressed the issue, he explained that he knew nothing and tried to change the subject with a stream of embarrassed eloquence.

That was at noon. In the afternoon Aschenbach sailed across to Venice in a dead calm and under a burning sun. He was driven by his mania to pursue the Polish children, whom he had seen making for the steamer landing along with their attendant. He did not find his idol at San Marco. But at tea, sitting at his round wrought-iron table on the shady side of the piazza, he suddenly smelled a peculiar aroma in the air, one that he now felt had been lurking

6. A beautiful Greek youth who fell in love with his own image in a pool and drowned trying to reach it. "Tadzio's smile is Narcissus', who sees his own reflection—he sees it in the face of another / he sees his beauty in its effects. Coquettishness and tenderness are also in this smile" [Mann's note].

at the edge of his consciousness for several days without his becoming fully aware of it. It was a medicinally sweet smell that put in mind thoughts of misery and wounds and ominous cleanliness. After a few moments' reflection he recognized it; then he finished his snack and left the piazza on the side opposite the cathedral. The odor became stronger in the narrow streets. At the street corners there were affixed printed posters in which the city fathers warned the population about certain illnesses of the gastric system that could be expected under these atmospheric conditions, advising that they should not eat oysters and mussels or use the water in the canals. The euphemistic nature of the announcement was obvious. Groups of local people stood together silently on the bridges and in the piazzas, and the foreign traveler stood among them, sniffing and musing.

There was a shopkeeper leaning in the doorway of his little vaulted quarters among coral necklaces and imitation amethyst trinkets, and Aschenbach asked him for some information about the ominous odor. The man took his measure with a heavy-lidded stare and then hastily put on a cheerful expression. "A precautionary measure, sir," he answered with many a gesture. "A police regulation that we must accept. The weather is oppressive, the sirocco is not conductive to good health. In short, you understand—perhaps they're being too careful. . . ." Aschenbach thanked him and went on. Even on the steamer that took him back to the Lido he could now detect the odor of disinfectant.

Once back at the hotel he went directly to the lobby to have a look at the newspapers. In the ones in foreign languages he found nothing. The German papers mentioned rumors, cited highly varying figures, quoted official denials, and offered doubts about their veracity. This explained the departure of the German and Austrian element. The citizens of other nations apparently knew nothing, suspected nothing, and were not yet concerned. "Best to keep quiet," thought Aschenbach anxiously, as he threw the papers back on the table. "Best to keep it under wraps." But at the same time his heart filled with a feeling of satisfaction over this adventure in which the outside world was becoming involved. For passion, like crime, does not sit well with the sure order and even course of everyday life; it welcomes every loosening of the social fabric, every confusion and affliction visited upon the world, for passion sees in such disorder a vague hope of finding an advantage for itself. Thus Aschenbach felt a dark satisfaction over the official cover-up of events in the dirty alleys of Venice. This heinous secret belonging to the city fused and became one with his own innermost secret, which he was likewise intent upon keeping. For the lovesick traveler had no concern other than that Tadzio might depart, and he recognized, not without a certain horror, that he would not know how to go on living were that to happen.

Recently he had not contented himself with allowing chance and the daily routine to determine his opportunities to see and be near the lovely lad; he pursued him, he lay in wait for him. On Sundays, for example, the Polish family never went to the beach. He guessed that they went to mass at San Marco. He followed speedily, entered the golden twilight of the sanctuary from the heat of the piazza, and found him, the one he had missed so, bent over a prie-dieu[7] taking part in the holy service. He stood in the background

7. Pray God (French, literal trans.); a low bench on which to kneel during prayers, with a raised shelf for elbows or book.

on the fissured mosaic floor, in the midst of a kneeling, murmuring crowd of people who kept crossing themselves, and felt the condensed grandeur of the oriental temple weigh voluptuously on his senses. Up in front the priest moved about, conducted his ritual, and chanted away, while incense billowed up and enshrouded the feeble flames of the altar candles. Mixed in with the sweet, heavy, ceremonial fragrance seemed to be another: the smell of the diseased city. But through all the haze and glitter Aschenbach saw how the lovely one up in front turned his head, looked for him, and found him.

When at last the crowd streamed out of the open portals into the shining piazza with its flocks of pigeons, the infatuated lover hid in the vestibule where he lay in wait, staking out his quarry. He saw the Polish family leave the church, saw the children take leave of their mother with great ceremony, saw her make for the Piazzetta on her way home. He ascertained that the lovely one, his cloisterly sisters, and the governess were on their way off to the right, through the clock tower gate, and into the Merceria,[8] and after giving them a reasonable head start he followed. He followed like a thief as they strolled through Venice. He had to stop when they lingered somewhere, had to flee into restaurants or courtyards to avoid them when they turned back. He lost them, got hot and tired as he searched for them over bridges and in dirty cul-de-sacs, and suffered long moments of mortal pain when he saw them coming toward him in a narrow passage where no escape was possible. And yet one cannot really say he suffered. He was intoxicated in head and heart, and his steps followed the instructions of the demon whose pleasure it is to crush under foot human reason and dignity.[9]

At some point or other Tadzio and his party would take a gondola, and Aschenbach, remaining hidden behind a portico or a fountain while they got in, did likewise shortly after they pulled away from the bank. He spoke quickly and in subdued tones to the gondolier, instructing him that a generous tip was in store for him if he would follow that gondola just now rounding the corner—but not too close, as unobtrusively as possible. Sweat trickled over his body as the gondolier, with the roguish willingness of a procurer, assured him in the same lowered tones that he would get service, that he would get conscientious service.

He leaned back in the soft black cushions and glided and rocked in pursuit of the other black, beak-prowed bark, to which his passion held him fastened as if by a chain. Sometimes he lost sight of it, and at those times he would feel worried and restless. But his boatman seemed entirely familiar with such assignments and always knew just how to bring the object of his desire back into view by means of clever maneuvers and quick passages and shortcuts. The air was still, and it smelled. The sun burned heavily through a haze that gave the sky the color of slate. Water gurgled against wood and stone. The cry of the gondolier, half warning and half greeting, received distant answer from out of the silent labyrinth as if by mysterious arrangement. Umbels of flowers hung down over crumbling walls from small gardens on higher ground. They were white and purple and smelled like almonds. Moorish window casings showed their forms in the haze. The marble steps of a church descended into the waters; a beggar crouching there and asserting his misery

---

8. Commercial district north of the Piazza San Marco.   9. Dionysus, originally an Eastern fertility god, worshipped with wild dances in ecstatic rites.

held out his hat and showed the whites of his eyes as if he were blind; a dealer in antiques stood before his cavelike shop and with fawning gestures invited the passerby to stop, hoping for a chance to swindle him. That was Venice, that coquettish, dubious beauty of a city, half fairy tale and half tourist trap, in whose noisome air the fine arts once thrived luxuriantly and where musicians were inspired to create sounds that cradle the listener and seductively rock him to sleep. To the traveler in the midst of his adventure it seemed as if his eyes were drinking in just this luxury, as if his ears were wooed by just such melodies. He remembered, too, that the city was sick and was keeping its secret out of pure greed, and he cast an even more licentious leer toward the gondola floating in the distance before him.

Entangled and besotted as he was, he no longer wished for anything else than to pursue the beloved object that inflamed him, to dream about him when he was absent and to speak amorous phrases, after the manner of lovers, to his mere shadow. His solitary life, the foreign locale, and his late but deep transport of ecstasy encouraged and persuaded him to allow himself the most bewildering transgressions without timidity or embarrassment. That is how it happened that on his return from Venice late in the evening he had stopped on the second floor of the hotel in front of the lovely one's door, leaned his brow against the hinge in complete intoxication, unable for a protracted period to drag himself away, heedless of the danger of being caught in such an outrageous position.

Still, there were moments when he paused and half came to his senses. How has this come to pass? he wondered in alarm. How did I come to this? Like everyone who has achieved something thanks to his natural talents, he had an aristocratic interest in his family background. At times when his life brought him recognition and success he would think about his ancestors and try to reassure himself that they would approve, that they would be pleased, that they would have had to admire him. Even here and now he thought about them, entangled as he was in such an illicit experience, seized by such exotic emotional aberrations. He thought about their rigorous self-possession, their manly respectability, and he smiled a melancholy smile. What would they say? But then what would they have said about his whole life, a life that had so diverged, one might say degenerated, from theirs, a life under the spell of art that he himself had mocked in the precocity of his youth, this life that yet so fundamentally resembled theirs? He too had done his service, he too had practiced a strict discipline; he too had been a soldier and a man of war, like many of them. For art was a war, a grinding battle that one was just no longer up to fighting for very long these days. It was a life of self-control and a life lived in despite, a harsh, steadfast, abstemious existence that he had made the symbol of a tender and timely heroism. He had every right to call it manly, call it courageous, and he wondered if the love-god who had taken possession of him might be particularly inclined and partial somehow to those who lived such a life. Had not that very god enjoyed the highest respect among the bravest nations of the earth? Did they not say that it was because of their courage that he had flourished in their cities? Numerous war heroes of ages past had willingly borne the yoke imposed by the god, for a humiliation imposed by the god did not count. Acts that would have been denounced as signs of cowardice when done in other circumstances and for other ends—prostrations, oaths, urgent pleas, and fawning behavior—none redounded to the shame of the lover, but rather he more likely reaped praise for them.[1]

Such was the infatuated thinker's train of thought; thus he sought to offer himself support; thus he attempted to preserve his dignity. But at the same time he stubbornly kept on the track of the dirty doings in the city's interior, that adventure of the outside world that darkly joined together with his heart's adventure and nourished his passion with vague, lawless hopes. Obsessed with finding out the latest and most reliable news about the status and progress of the disease, he went to the city's coffee houses and leafed through the German newspapers, which had long since disappeared from the table in the hotel lobby. He read alternating assertions and denials. The number of illnesses and deaths might be as high as twenty, forty, even a hundred or more; but then in the next article or next issue any outbreak of the epidemic, if not categorically denied, would be reported as limited to a few isolated cases brought in by foreigners. There were periodic doubts, warnings, and protests against the dangerous game being played by the Italian authorities. Reliable information was simply not available.

The solitary guest was nonetheless conscious of having a special claim on his share in the secret. Though he was excluded, he took a bizarre pleasure in pressing knowledgeable people with insidious questions and forcing those who were part of the conspiracy of silence to utter explicit lies. At breakfast one day in the main dining room, for example, he engaged the manager in conversation. This unobtrusive little person in his French frock coat was going about between the tables greeting everyone and supervising the help. He made a brief stop at Aschenbach's table, too, for a casual chat. Now then why, the guest just happened to ask very casually, why in the world had they been disinfecting Venice for all this time? "It's a police matter," the toady answered, "a measure intended to stop in due and timely fashion any and all unwholesome conditions, any disturbance of the public health that might come about owing to the brooding heat of this exceptionally warm weather." "The police are to be commended," replied Aschenbach. After the exchange of a few more meteorological observations the manager took his leave.

On that very same day, in the evening after dinner, it happened that a little band of street singers from the city performed in the hotel's front garden. They stood, two men and two women, next to the iron lamppost of an arc light and raised their faces, shining in the white illumination, toward the great terrace, where the guests were enjoying this traditional popular entertainment while drinking coffee and cooling beverages. Hotel employees—elevator boys, waiters, and office personnel—stood by listening at the entrances to the lobby. The Russian family, zealous and precise in taking their pleasure, had wicker chairs moved down into the garden so as to be nearer the performers. There they sat in a semi-circle, in their characteristically grateful attitude. Behind the ladies and gentlemen stood the old slave woman in her turbanlike headdress.

The low-life virtuosos were extracting sounds from a mandolin, a guitar, a harmonica, and a squeaky violin. Interspersed among the instrumental numbers were vocals in which the younger of the women blended her sharp,

1. A reference to the Athenian code of love as described by Pausanias in Plato's *Symposium*, sections 182d–e and 183b.

quavering voice with the sweet falsetto of the tenor in a love duet full of yearning. But the chief talent and real leader of the group was clearly the other man, the guitar player, who sang a kind of buffo[2] baritone while he played. Though his voice was weak, he was a gifted mime and projected remarkable comic energy. Often he would move away from the group, his great instrument under his arm, and advance toward the terrace with many a flourish. The audience rewarded his antics with rousing laughter. The Russians in particular, ensconced in their orchestra seats, displayed particular delight over all this southern vivacity and encouraged him with applause and cheers to ever bolder and more brazen behavior.

Aschenbach sat at the balustrade, cooling his lips from time to time with a mixture of pomegranate[3] juice and soda that sparkled ruby-red in his glass. His nerves greedily consumed the piping sounds, the vulgar, pining melodies; for passion numbs good taste and succumbs in all seriousness to enticements that a sober spirit would receive with humor or even reject scornfully. His features, reacting to the antics of the buffoon, had become fixed in a rigid and almost painful smile. He sat in an apparently relaxed attitude, and all the while he was internally tense and sharply attentive, for Tadzio stood no more than six paces away, leaning against the stone railing.

He stood there in the white belted suit that he sometimes wore to dinner, a figure of inevitable and innate grace, his left forearm on the railing, his ankles crossed, his right hand supported on his hip. He wore an expression that was not quite a smile but more an air of distant curiosity or polite receptivity as he looked down toward the street musicians. Sometimes he straightened up and, with a lovely movement of both arms that lifted his chest, he would pull his white blouse down through his leather belt. Occasionally, though—as the aging observer noted with triumph and even with horror, his reason staggering—Tadzio would turn his head to look across his left shoulder in the direction of the one who loved him, sometimes with deliberate hesitation, sometimes with sudden swiftness as if to catch him unawares. Their eyes never met, for an ignominious caution forced the errant lover to keep his gaze fearfully in check. The women guarding Tadzio were sitting in the back of the terrace, and things had reached the point that the smitten traveler had to take care lest his behavior should become noticeable and he fall under suspicion. Indeed his blood had nearly frozen on a number of occasions when he had been compelled to notice on the beach, in the hotel lobby, or in the Piazza San Marco that Tadzio was called away from his vicinity, that they were intent on keeping the boy away from him. He felt horribly insulted, and his pride flinched from unfamiliar tortures that his conscience prevented him from dismissing.

In the meantime the guitar player had begun singing a solo to his own accompaniment, a popular ditty in many verses that was quite the hit just then all over Italy. He was adept at performing it in a highly histrionic manner, and his band joined in the refrain each time, both with their voices and all their instruments. He was of a lean build, and even his face was thin to the point of emaciation. He stood there on the gravel in an attitude of impertinent bravura, apart from his fellow performers, his shabby felt hat so far

2. Comic. 3. A tropical fruit with many seeds, associated in Greek mythology both with Persephone, the queen of Hades, and with the world of the dead.

back on his head that a roll of red hair surged forth from beneath the brim, and as he thumped the guitar strings, he hurled his buffooneries toward the terrace above in an insistent recitative. The veins on his brow swelled in response to his exertions. He seemed not to be of Venetian stock, more likely a member of the race of Neapolitan comics, half pimp, half actor, brutal and daring, dangerous and entertaining. The lyrics of his song were as banal as could be, but in his mouth they acquired an ambiguous, vaguely offensive quality because of his facial expressions and his gestures, his suggestive winks and his manner of letting his tongue play lasciviously at the corner of his mouth. His strikingly large Adam's apple protruded nakedly from his scrawny neck, which emerged from the soft collar of a sport shirt worn in incongruous combination with more formal city clothes. His pale, snub-nosed face was beardless and did not permit an easy reckoning of his age; it seemed ravaged by grimaces and by vice. The two defiant, imperious, even wild-looking furrows that stood between his reddish eyebrows went rather oddly with the grin on his mobile lips. What particularly drew the attention of the lonely spectator, however, was his observation that this questionable figure seemed to carry with it its own questionable atmosphere. For every time the refrain began again the singer would commence a grotesque circular march, clowning and shaking the hands of his audience; every time his path would bring him directly underneath Aschenbach's spot, and every time that happened there wafted up to the terrace from his clothes and from his body a choking stench of carbolic acid.[4]

His song finished, he began collecting money. He started with the Russians, who produced a generous offering, and then ascended the steps. As bold as he had been during the performance, just so obsequious was he now. Bowing and scraping, he slithered about between the tables, a smile of crafty submissiveness laying bare his large teeth, and all the while the two furrows between his red eyebrows stood forth menacingly. The guests surveyed with curiosity and some revulsion this strange being who was gathering in his livelihood. They threw coins in his hat from a distance and were careful not to touch him. The elimination of the physical separation between the performer and his respectable audience always tends to produce a certain embarrassment, no matter how pleasurable the performance. The singer felt it and sought to excuse himself by acting servile. He came up to Aschenbach, and with him came the smell, though no one else in the vicinity seemed concerned about it.

"Listen," the lonely traveler said in lowered tones, almost mechanically. "They are disinfecting Venice. Why?" The jester answered hoarsely: "Because of the police. That, sir, is the procedure when it gets hot like this and when the sirocco comes. The sirocco is oppressive. It's not conducive to good health. . . ." He spoke as if he were amazed that anyone could ask such questions, and he demonstrated by pushing with his open palm just how oppressive the sirocco was. "So there is no disease in Venice?" Aschenbach asked very quietly through his closed teeth. The tense muscles in the comedian's face produced a grimace of comic perplexity. "A disease? What sort of disease? Is the sirocco a disease? Do you suppose our police force is a disease? You like to make fun, don't you? A disease! Why on earth? Some pre-

---

4. A chemical used as a disinfectant.

ventive measures, you understand. A police regulation to minimize the effects of the oppressive weather . . . ," he gesticulated. "Very well," Aschenbach said once again, briefly and quietly, and he dropped an indecently large coin into the hat. Then he indicated with a look that the man should go. He obeyed with a grin and a bow. But even before he reached the steps two hotel employees intercepted him and, putting their faces very close to his, cross-examined him in whispers. He shrugged, he protested, he swore that he had been circumspect. You could tell. Dismissed, he returned to the garden and, after making a few arrangements with his group by the light of the arc lamp, he stepped forward to offer one parting song.

It was a song the solitary traveler could not remember ever having heard before, an impudent Italian hit in an incomprehensible dialect embellished with a laughing refrain in which the whole group regularly joined, fortissimo. The refrain had neither words nor instrumental accompaniment; nothing was left but a certain rhythmically structured but still very natural-sounding laughter, which the soloist in particular was capable of producing with great talent and deceptive realism. Having reestablished a proper artistic distance between himself and his audience, he had regained all his former impudence. His artfully artificial laughter, directed impertinently up to the terrace, was the laughter of scorn. Even before the part of the song with actual lyrics had come to a close, one could see him begin to battle an irresistible itch. He would hiccup, his voice would catch, he would put his hand up to his mouth, he would twist his shoulders, and at the proper moment the unruly laughter would break forth, exploding in a hoot, but with such realism that it was infectious. It spread among the listeners so that even on the terrace an unfounded mirth set in, feeding on nothing but itself. This appeared only to double the singer's exuberance. He bent his knees, slapped his thighs, held his sides, fairly split with laughter; but he was no longer laughing, he was howling. He pointed his finger upwards, as if to say that there could be nothing funnier than the laughing audience up there, and soon everyone in the garden and on the veranda was laughing, including the waiters, elevator boys, and servants lingering in the doorways.

Aschenbach no longer reclined in his chair; he sat upright as if trying to defend himself or to flee. But the laughter, the rising smell of hospital sanitation, and the nearness of the lovely boy—all blended to cast a dreamy spell about him that held his mind and his senses in an unbreakable, inescapable embrace. In the general confusion of the moment he made so bold as to cast a glance at Tadzio, and when he did so he was granted the opportunity to see that the lovely lad answered his gaze with a seriousness equal to his own. It was as if the boy were regulating his behavior and attitude according to that of the man, as if the general mood of gaiety had no power over the boy so long as the man kept apart from it. This childlike and meaningful docility was so disarming, so overwhelming, that the gray-haired traveler could only with difficulty refrain from hiding his face in his hands. It had also seemed to him that Tadzio's habit of straightening up and taking a deep sighing breath suggested an obstruction in his breathing. "He is sickly; he will probably not live long," he thought once again with that sobriety that sometimes frees itself in some strange manner from intoxication and longing. Ingenuous solicitude mixed with a dissolute satisfaction filled his heart.

The Venetian singers had meanwhile finished their number and left, accompanied by applause. Their leader did not fail to adorn even his departure with jests. He bowed and scraped and blew kisses so that everyone laughed, which made him redouble his efforts. When his fellow performers were already gone, he pretended to back hard into a lamppost at full speed, then crept toward the gate bent over in mock pain. There at last he cast off the mask of the comic loser, unbent or rather snapped up straight, stuck his tongue out impudently at the guests on the terrace, and slipped into the darkness. The audience dispersed; Tadzio was already long gone from his place at the balustrade. But the lonely traveler remained sitting for a long time at his little table, nursing his pomegranate drink much to the annoyance of the waiters. The night progressed; time crumbled away. Many years ago in his parents' house there had been an hourglass. He suddenly could see the fragile and portentous little device once more, as though it were standing right in front of him. The rust-colored fine sand ran silently through the glass neck, and as it began to run out of the upper vessel a rapid little vortex formed.

In the afternoon of the very next day the obstinate visitor took a further step in his probing of the outside world, and this time he met with all possible success. What he did was to enter the English travel agency in the Piazza San Marco and, having changed some money at the cash register and having assumed the demeanor of a diffident foreigner, he directed his fateful question to the clerk who was taking care of him. The clerk was a wool-clad Briton, still young, his hair parted in the middle and eyes set close together, possessed of that steady, trustworthy bearing that stands out as so foreign and so remarkable among the roguishly nimble southerners. He began: "No cause for concern, sir. A measure of no serious importance. Such regulations are frequently imposed to ward off the ill effects of the heat and the sirocco. . . ." But when he raised his blue eyes he met the foreigner's gaze. It was a tired and rather sad gaze, and it was directed with an air of mild contempt toward his lips. The Englishman blushed. "That is," he continued in a low voice, somewhat discomfited, "the official explanation, which they see fit to stick to hereabouts. I can tell you, though, that there's a good deal more to it." And then, in his candid and comfortable language, he told the truth.

For some years now Asiatic cholera had shown an increasing tendency to spread and roam. The pestilence originated in the warm swamps of the Ganges delta,[5] rising on the foul-smelling air of that lushly uninhabitable primeval world, that wilderness of islands avoided by humankind where tigers lurk in bamboo thickets. It had raged persistently and with unusual ferocity throughout Hindustan; then it had spread eastwards to China and westwards to Afghanistan and Persia; and, following the great caravan routes, it had brought its horrors as far as Astrakhan and even Moscow. But while Europe was shaking in fear lest the specter should progress by land from Russia westward, it had emerged simultaneously in several Mediterranean port cities, having been carried in on Syrian merchant ships. It had raised its grisly head in Toulon and Malaga, shown its grim mask several times in Palermo and Naples, and seemed now firmly ensconced throughout Calabria and Apulia.[6] The northern half of the peninsula had so far been spared. On a

---

5. In India.   6. Regions in southern Italy. Astrakhan, Toulon, Málaga, Palermo, and Naples are seaports in Russia, France, Spain, Sicily, and southern Italy, respectively.

single day in mid-May of this year, however, the terrible vibrioid bacteria had been found on two emaciated, blackening corpses, that of a ship's hand and that of a woman who sold vegetables. These cases were hushed up. A week later, though, there were ten more, twenty more, thirty more, not localized but spread through various parts of the city. A man from the Austrian hinterlands who had come for a pleasant holiday of a few days in Venice died upon returning to his home town, exhibiting unmistakable symptoms. Thus it was that the first rumors of the affliction visited upon the city on the lagoon appeared in German newspapers. In response the Venetian authorities promulgated the assertion that matters of health had never been better in the city. They also immediately instituted the most urgent measures to counter the disease. But apparently the food supply—vegetables, meat, and milk—had been infected, for death, though denied and hushed up, devoured its way through the narrow streets. The early arrival of summer's heat made a lukewarm broth of the water in the canals and thus made conditions for the disease's spread particularly favorable. It almost seemed as though the pestilence had been reinvigorated, as if the tenacity and fecundity of its microscopic agitators had been redoubled. Cures were rare; out of a hundred infected eighty died, and in a particularly gruesome fashion, for the evil raged here with extreme ferocity. Often it took on its most dangerous form, commonly known as the "dry type." In such cases the body is unable to rid itself of the massive amounts of water secreted by the blood-vessels. In a few hours' time the patient dries up and suffocates, his blood as viscous as pitch, crying out hoarsely in his convulsions. It sometimes happened that a few lucky ones suffered only a mild discomfort followed by a loss of consciousness from which they would never again, or only rarely, awaken. At the beginning of June the quarantine wards of the Ospedale Civico quietly filled up, space became scarce in both of the orphanages, and a horrifyingly brisk traffic clogged the routes between the docks at the Fondamenta Nuove[7] and San Michele, the cemetery island. But the fear of adverse consequences to the city, concern for the newly opened exhibit of paintings in the public gardens, for the losses that the hotels, businesses, and the whole tourist industry would suffer in case of a panic or a boycott—these matters proved weightier in the city than the love of truth or respect for international agreements. They prompted the authorities stubbornly to maintain their policy of concealment and denial. The highest medical official in Venice, a man of considerable attainments, had angrily resigned his post and was surreptitiously replaced by a more pliable individual. The citizenry knew all about it, and the combination of corruption in high places with the prevailing uncertainty, the state of emergency in which the city was placed when death was striking all about, caused a certain demoralization of the lower levels of society. It encouraged those antisocial forces that shun the light, and they manifested themselves as immoderate, shameless, and increasingly criminal behavior. Contrary to the norm, one saw many drunks at evening time; people said that gangs of rogues made the streets unsafe at night; muggings and even murders multiplied. Already on two occasions it had come to light that alleged victims of the plague had in fact been robbed of their lives by their

7. New footings (Italian, literal trans.); the new piers. *Ospedale Civico:* city hospital.

own relatives who administered poison. Prostitution and lasciviousness took on brazen and extravagant forms never before seen here and thought to be at home only in the southern parts of the country and in the seraglios of the orient.

The Englishman explained the salient points of these developments. "You would do well," he concluded, "to depart today rather than tomorrow. The imposition of a quarantine cannot be more than a few days off." "Thank you," said Aschenbach and left the agency.

The piazza was sunless and sultry. Unsuspecting foreigners sat in the side-walk cafes or stood in front of the cathedral completely covered with pigeons. They watched as the swarming birds beat their wings and jostled each other for their chance to pick at the kernels of corn offered to them in an open palm. In feverish excitement, triumphant in his possession of the truth, but with a taste of gall in his mouth and a fantastic horror in his heart, the lonely traveler paced back and forth over the flagstones of the magnificent plaza. He considered doing the decent thing, the thing that would cleanse him. Tonight after dinner he could go up to the lady with the pearls and speak to her. He planned exactly what he would say: "Permit me, Madame, stranger though I may be, to be of service to you with a piece of advice, a word of warning concerning a matter that has been withheld from you by self-serving people. Depart at once, taking Tadzio and your daughters with you. There is an epidemic in Venice." He could then lay his hand in farewell on the head of that instrument of a scornful deity, turn away, and flee this swamp. But at the same time he sensed that he was infinitely far from seriously wanting to take such a step. It would bring him back to his senses, would make him himself again; but when one is beside oneself there is nothing more abhorrent than returning to one's senses. He remembered a white building decorated with inscriptions that gleamed in the evening light, inscriptions in whose radiant mysticism his mind's eye had become lost. He remembered too that strange figure of the wanderer who had awakened in the aging man a young man's longing to roam in faraway and exotic places. The thought of returning home, of returning to prudence and sobriety, toil and mastery, was so repugnant to him that his face broke out in an expression of physical disgust. "Let them keep quiet," he whispered vehemently. And: "I will keep quiet!" The consciousness of his guilty complicity intoxicated him, just as small amounts of wine will intoxicate a weary brain. The image of the afflicted and ravaged city hovered chaotically in his imagination, incited in him inconceivable hopes, beyond all reason, monstrously sweet. How could that tender happiness he had dreamed of a moment earlier compare with these expectations? What value did art and virtue hold for him when he could have chaos? He held his peace and stayed.

That night he had a terrifying dream—if indeed one can call "dream" an experience that was both physical and mental, one that visited him in the depths of his sleep, in complete isolation as well as sensuous immediacy, but yet such that he did not see himself as physically and spatially present apart from its action. Instead, its setting was in his soul itself, and its events burst in upon him from outside, violently crushing his resistance, his deep, intellectual resistance, passing through easily and leaving his whole being, the culmination of a lifetime of effort, ravaged and annihilated.

It began with fear, fear and desire and a horrified curiosity about what was to come. Night ruled, and his senses were attentive; for from afar there approached a tumult, a turmoil, a mixture of noises: rattling, clarion calls and muffled thunder, shrill cheering on top of it all, and a certain howl with a drawn-out *uuu* sound at the end. All this was accompanied and drowned out by the gruesomely sweet tones of a flute playing a cooing, recklessly persistent tune that penetrated to the very bowels, where it cast a shameless enchantment. But there was a phrase, darkly familiar, that named what was coming: *"The stranger god!"*[8] A smoky glow welled up, and he recognized a mountain landscape like the one around his summer house. And in the fragmented light he could see people, animals, a swarm, a roaring mob, all rolling and plunging and whirling down from the forested heights, past tree-trunks and great moss-covered fragments of rock, overflowing the slope with their bodies, flames, tumult, and reeling circular dance. Women, stumbling over the fur skirts that hung too long from their belts, moaned, threw their heads back, shook their tambourines on high, brandished naked daggers and torches that threw off sparks, held serpents with flickering tongues by the middle of their bodies, or cried out, lifting their breasts in both hands. Men with horns on their brows, girdled with hides, their own skins shaggy, bent their necks and raised their arms and thighs, clashed brazen cymbals and beat furiously on drums, while smooth-skinned boys used garlanded staves to prod their goats, clinging to the horns so they could be dragged along, shouting with joy, when the goats sprang. And the ecstatic band howled the cry with soft consonants in the middle and a drawn-out *uuu* sound on the end, a cry that was sweet and wild at the same time, like none ever heard before: here it rang in the air like the bellowing of stags in rut; and there many voices echoed it back in anarchic triumph, using it to goad each other to dance and shake their limbs, never letting it fall silent. But it was all suffused and dominated by the deep, beckoning melody of the flute. Was it not also beckoning him, the resisting dreamer, with shameless persistence to the festival, to its excesses, and to its ultimate sacrifice? Great was his loathing, great his fear, sincere his resolve to defend his own against the foreign invader, the enemy of self-controlled and dignified intellect. But the noise and the howling, multiplied by the echoing mountainsides, grew, gained the upper hand, swelled to a madness that swept everything along with it. Fumes oppressed the senses: the acrid scent of the goats, the emanation of panting human bodies, a whiff as of stagnant water—and another smell perceptible through it all, a familiar reek of wounds and raging sickness. His heart pounded with the rhythm of the drum beats, his mind whirled, rage took hold of him and blinded him, he was overcome by a numbing lust, and his soul longed to join in the reeling dance of the god. Their obscene symbol,[9] gigantic, wooden, was uncovered and raised on high, and they howled out their watchword all the more licentiously. With foam on their lips they raved; they stimulated each other with lewd gestures and fondling hands; laughing and wheezing, they pierced each other's flesh with their pointed staves and then licked the bleeding limbs. Now among them, now a part of them, the dreamer belonged to the stranger god. Yes, they were he, and he was they, when they threw themselves on the animals, tearing

8. Dionysus (also Bacchus), whose cult was brought to Greece from Thrace and Phrygia. The dream describes the orgiastic rites of his worship.   9. The phallus.

and killing, devouring steaming gobbets of flesh, when on the trampled moss-covered ground there began an unfettered rite of copulation in sacrifice to the god. His soul tasted the lewdness and frenzy of surrender.

The afflicted dreamer awoke unnerved, shattered, a powerless victim of the demon. He no longer shunned the observant glances of people about him; he no longer cared if he was making himself a target of their suspicions. And in any case they were all departing, fleeing the sickness. Many cabanas now stood empty, the population of the dining room was seriously depleted, and in the city one only rarely saw a foreigner. The truth seemed to have leaked out, and in spite of the stubborn conniving of those with vested interests at stake, panic could no longer be averted. The lady with the pearls nonetheless remained with her family, perhaps because the rumors did not reach her or perhaps because she was too proud and fearless to succumb to them. Tadzio remained, and to Aschenbach, blind to all but his own concerns, it seemed at times that death and departure might very well remove all the distracting human life around them and leave him alone with the lovely one on this island. Indeed, in the mornings on the beach when his gaze would rest heavily, irresponsibly, fixedly on the object of his desire; or at the close of day when he would take up his shameful pursuit of the boy through narrow streets where loathsome death did its hushed-up business; then everything monstrous seemed to him to have a prosperous future, the moral law to have none.

He wished, like any other lover, to please his beloved and felt a bitter concern that it would not be possible. He added youthfully cheerful touches to his dress, took to using jewelry and perfume. Several times a day he took lengthy care getting dressed and then came down to the dining room all bedecked, excited and expectant. His aging body disgusted him when he looked at the sweet youth with whom he was smitten; the sight of his gray hair and his sharp facial features overwhelmed him with shame and hopelessness. He felt a need to restore and revive his body. He visited the barbershop more and more frequently.

Leaning back in the chair under the protective cloth, letting the manicured hands of the chattering barber care for him, he confronted the tortured gaze of his image in the mirror.

"Gray," he said with his mouth twisted.

"A bit," the man replied. "It's all because of a slight neglect, an indifference to externals—quite understandable in the case of important people, but still not altogether praiseworthy, all the less so since just such people ought not to harbor prejudices in matters of the natural and the artificial. If certain people were to extend the moral qualms they have about the cosmetic arts to their teeth, as logic compels, they would give no little offense. And anyway, we're only as old we feel in our hearts and minds. Gray hair can in certain circumstances give more of a false impression than the dye that some would scorn. In your case, sir, you have a right to your natural hair color. Will you allow me to give you back what is rightfully yours?"

"How?" Aschenbach inquired.

So the glib barber washed his customer's hair with two liquids, one clear and one dark, and it turned as black as it had been in youth. Then he rolled it with the curling iron into soft waves, stepped back and admired his handiwork.

"All that's left," he said, "is to freshen up the complexion a bit."

He went about, with ever renewed solicitude, moving from one task to another the way a person does who can never finish anything and is never satisfied. Aschenbach, resting comfortably, was in any case quite incapable of fending him off. Actually he was rather excited about what was happening, watching in the mirror as his brows took on a more decisive and symmetrical arch and his eyes grew in width and brilliance with the addition of a little shadow on the lids. A little further down he could see his skin, previously brown and leathery, perk up with a light application of delicate carmine rouge, his lips, pale and bloodless only a moment ago, swell like raspberries, the furrows in his cheeks and mouth, the wrinkles around his eyes give way to a dab of cream and the glow of youth. His heart pounded as he saw in the mirror a young man in full bloom. The cosmetic artist finally pronounced himself satisfied and thanked the object of his ministrations with fawning politeness, the way such people do. "A minor repair job," he said as he put a final touch to Aschenbach's appearance. "Now, sir, you can go and fall in love without second thoughts." The beguiled lover went out, happy as in a dream, yet confused and timid. His tie was red, and his broad-brimmed straw hat was encircled by a band of many colors.

A tepid breeze had come up; it rained only seldom and then not hard, but the air was humid, thick, and full of the stench of decay. Rustling, rushing, and flapping sounds filled his ears. He burned with fever beneath his makeup, and it seemed to him that the air was filled with vile, evil wind-spirits, impure winged sea creatures who raked over, gnawed over, and de-filed with garbage the meals of their victim.[1] For the sultry weather ruined one's appetite, and one could not suppress the idea that all the food was poisoned with infection.

Trailing the lovely boy one afternoon, Aschenbach had penetrated deep into the maze in the heart of the diseased city. He had lost his sense of direction, for the little streets, canals, bridges, and piazzas in the labyrinth all looked alike. He could no longer even tell east from west, since his only concern had been not to lose sight of the figure he pursued so ardently. He was compelled to a disgraceful sort of discretion that involved clinging to walls and seeking protection behind the backs of passersby, and so he did not for some time become conscious of the fatigue, the exhaustion which a high pitch of emotion and continual tension had inflicted on his body and spirit. Tadzio walked behind the rest of his family. In these narrow streets he would generally let the governess and the nunlike sisters go first, while he sauntered along by himself, occasionally turning his head to assure him-self with a quick glance of his extraordinary dawn-gray eyes over his shoulder that his lover was still following. He saw him, and he did not betray him. Intoxicated by this discovery, lured onward by those eyes, tied to the apron string of his own passion, the lovesick traveler stole forth in pursuit of his unseemly hope—but ultimately found himself disappointed. The Polish fam-ily had gone across a tightly arched bridge, and the height of the arch had

1. "Harpies: hideously thin, they flew swiftly in, fell with insatiable greed on whatever food was there, ate without being satisfied, and *befouled* whatever they left with their filth" [Mann's note]. See Virgil's *Aeneid* 3.210–62.

hidden them from their pursuer. When he was at last able to cross, he could no longer find them. He searched for them in three directions—straight ahead and to both sides along the narrow, dirty landing—but in vain. He finally had to give up, too debilitated and unnerved to go on.

His head was burning hot, his body was sticky with sweat, the scruff of his neck was tingling, an unbearable thirst assaulted him, and he looked about for immediate refreshment of any sort. In front of a small greengrocer's shop he bought some fruit, strawberries that were overripe and soft, and he ate them while he walked. A little piazza that was quite deserted and seemed enchanted opened out before him. He recognized it, for it was here that weeks ago he had made his thwarted plan to flee the city. He collapsed on the steps of the well in the very middle of the plaza and rested his head on the stone rim. It was quiet, grass grew between the paving stones, refuse lay strewn about. Among the weathered buildings of varying heights around the periphery was one that looked rather palatial. It had Gothic-arched windows, now gaping emptily, and little balconies decorated with lions. On the ground floor of another there was a pharmacy. Warm gusts of wind from time to time carried the smell of carbolic acid.

He sat there, the master, the artist who had attained to dignity, the author of the "Man of Misery," that exemplary work which had with clarity of form renounced bohemianism and the gloomy murky depths, had condemned sympathy for the abyss, reviled the vile. There he sat, the great success who had overcome knowledge and outgrown every sort of irony, who had accustomed himself to the obligations imposed by the confidence of his large audience. There he sat, the author whose greatness had been officially recognized and whose name bore the title of nobility, the author whose style children were encouraged to emulate—sat there with his eyes shut, though from time to time a mocking and embarrassed look would slip sidelong out from underneath his lids, only to conceal itself again swiftly; and his slack, cosmetically enhanced lips formed occasional words that emerged out of the strange dream-logic engendered in his half-dozing brain.[2]

"For beauty, Phaedrus—mark me well—only beauty is both divine and visible at the same time, and thus it is the way of the senses, the way of the artist, little Phaedrus, to the spirit. But do you suppose, my dear boy, that anyone could ever attain to wisdom and genuine manly honor by taking a path to the spirit that leads through the senses? Or do you rather suppose (I leave the decision entirely up to you) that this is a dangerously delightful path, really a path of error and sin that necessarily leads astray? For you must know that we poets cannot walk the path of beauty without Eros joining our company and even making himself our leader; indeed, heroes though we may be after our own fashion, disciplined warriors though we may be, still we are as women, for passion is our exaltation, and our longing must ever be for love. That is our bliss and our shame. Do you see, then, that we poets can be neither wise nor honorable, that we necessarily go astray, that we necessarily remain dissolute adventurers of emotion? The masterly demeanor of

2. Aschenbach adopts the role of Socrates in Plato's *Phaedrus* to examine the role of the artist. Although the Platonic dialogue briefly contrasts inspired art with mere technical perfection, it is chiefly concerned with moral choices and absolute beauty.

our style is a lie and a folly, our fame and our honor a sham, the confidence accorded us by our public utterly ridiculous, the education of the populace and of the young by means of art a risky enterprise that ought not to be allowed. For how can a person succeed in educating others who has an inborn, irremediable, and natural affinity for the abyss? We may well deny it and achieve a certain dignity, but wherever we may turn that affinity abides. Let us say we renounce analytical knowledge; for knowledge, Phaedrus, has neither dignity nor discipline; it is knowing, understanding, forgiving, formless and unrestrained; it has sympathy for the abyss; it *is* the abyss. Let us therefore resolutely reject it, and henceforth our efforts will be directed only toward beauty, that is to say toward simplicity, grandeur, and a new discipline, toward reborn ingenuousness and toward form. But form and ingenuousness, Phaedrus, lead to intoxication and to desire, might lead the noble soul to horrible emotional outrages that his own lovely discipline would reject as infamous, lead him to the abyss. Yes, they too lead to the abyss. They lead us poets there, I say, because we are capable not of resolution but only of dissolution. And now I shall depart, Phaedrus; but you stay here until you can no longer see me, and then you depart as well."

A few days afterwards Gustav von Aschenbach left the hotel at a later hour than usual, since he was feeling unwell. He was struggling with certain attacks of dizziness that were only partly physical and were accompanied by a powerfully escalating sense of anxiety and indecision, a feeling of having no prospects and no way out. He was not at all sure whether these feelings concerned the outside world or his own existence. He noticed in the lobby a great pile of luggage prepared for departure, and when he asked the doorman who was leaving, he received for an answer the aristocratic Polish name he had in his heart been expecting to hear all along. He took it in with no change in the expression on his ravaged face, briefly raising his head as people do to acknowledge casually the receipt of a piece of information they do not need, and asked, "When?" The answer came: "After lunch." He nodded and went to the beach.

It was dreary there. Rippling tremors crossed from near to far on the wide, flat stretch of water between the beach and the first extended sandbar. Where so recently there had been color, life, and joy, it was now almost deserted, and an autumnal mood prevailed, a feeling that the season was past its prime. The sand was no longer kept clean. A camera with no photographer to operate it stood on its tripod at the edge of the sea, a black cloth that covered it fluttering with a snapping noise in a wind that now blew colder.

Tadzio and three or four playmates that still remained were active in front of his family's cabana to Aschenbach's right; and, resting in his beach chair approximately halfway between the ocean and the row of cabanas, with a blanket over his legs, Aschenbach watched him once more. Their play was unsupervised, since the women must have been busy with preparations for their departure. The game seemed to have no rules and quickly degenerated. The sturdy boy with the belted suit and the black, slicked-down hair who was called Yashu, angered and blinded by sand thrown in his face, forced Tadzio into a wrestling match, which ended swiftly with the defeat of the weaker, lovely boy. It seemed as if in the last moments before leave-taking the subservient feelings of the underling turned to vindictive cruelty as he sought to take revenge for a long period of slavery. The winner would not release his defeated opponent but instead kneeled on his back and pushed his face in the sand, persisting for so long that Tadzio, already out of breath from the fight, seemed in danger of suffocating. He made spasmodic attempts to shake off his oppressor, lay still for whole moments, then tried again with no more than a twitch. Horrified, Aschenbach wanted to spring to the rescue, but then the bully finally released his victim. Tadzio was very pale; he got up halfway and sat motionless for several minutes supported on one arm, his hair disheveled and his eyes darkening. Then he rose to his feet and slowly walked away. They called to him, cheerfully at first but then with pleading timidity. He paid no attention. The black-haired boy, apparently instantly regretting his transgression, caught up with him and tried to make up. A jerk of a lovely shoulder put him off. Tadzio crossed diagonally down to the water. He was barefoot and wore his striped linen suit with the red bow.

He lingered at the edge of the sea with his head hung down, drawing figures in the wet sand with his toe. Then he went into the shallows, which at their deepest point did not wet his knees, strode through them, and progressed idly to the sandbar. Upon reaching it he stood for a moment, his face turned to the open sea, then began to walk slowly to the left along the narrow stretch of uncovered ground. Separated from the mainland by the broad expanse of water, separated from his mates by a proud mood, he strode forth, a highly remote and isolated apparition with wind-blown hair, wandering about out there in the sea, in the wind, on the edge of the misty boundlessness. Once more he stopped to gaze outward. Suddenly, as if prompted by a memory or an impulse, he rotated his upper body in a lovely turn out of its basic posture, his hand resting on his hip, and looked over his shoulder toward the shore. The observer sat there as he had sat once before, when for the first time he had met the gaze of those dawn-gray eyes cast back at him from that threshold. His head, resting on the back of the chair, had slowly followed the movements of the one who was striding about out there; now his head rose as if returning the gaze, then sank on his chest so that his eyes looked out from beneath. His face took on the slack, intimately absorbed expression of deep sleep. It seemed to him, though, as if the pale and charming psychagogue[3] out there were smiling at him, beckoning to him; as if, lifting his hand from his hip, he were pointing outwards, hovering before him in an immensity full of promise. And, as so often before, he arose to follow him.

Minutes passed before anyone rushed to the aid of the man who had collapsed to one side in his chair. They carried him to his room. And later that same day a respectfully shaken world received the news of his death.

---

3. Leader of souls to the underworld (Greek); a title of the god Hermes.

RAINER MARIA RILKE
1875–1926

Rilke's intensely personal search to understand the "great mysteries" of the universe asks questions that are ordinarily thought of as religious. Whether his gaze is turned toward the objects and creatures of earth, which he describes with extraordinary clarity and affection, or toward a higher intuited realm whose enigma remains to be deciphered, he seeks throughout a comprehensive vision of cosmic unity. Like the existentialists after him, Rilke is haunted by the baffling incompleteness of human experience, by the passage of time, and by a need to situate himself inside some framework of reality. His response is to turn to art, as the Symbolists do, in order to reconcile the different dimensions of experience. When objects are represented artistically, they are drawn into a "human" world: they are infused with ideas, emotions, and value. The poet's role, according to Rilke, is to observe with a fresh sensitivity "this fleeting world, which in some strange way / keeps calling to us," and to bear witness, through language, to the transfiguration of its materiality in and by human emotions. Rilke's sharply focused yet visionary lyricism has made him the best-known and most influential German poet of the twentieth century.

Born in Prague on December 4, 1875, to German-speaking parents who separated when he was nine, Rilke had an unhappy childhood. His mother dressed him as a girl to compensate for the earlier loss of a baby daughter, and he was sent to military academies from 1886 to 1891, where he was lonely and miserable. After a year in business school, he worked in his uncle's law firm and studied at the University of Prague; but his heart was set on a literary career, and he published two books of poetry and wrote plays, stories, and reviews. In 1897, he moved to Munich and fell in love with Lou Andreas-Salomé, who would be a constant influence on him throughout his life. Accompanying Andreas-Salomé and her husband to Russia in 1899, he met Tolstoy and Pasternak and—swayed by Russian mysticism and the Russian landscape—wrote most of the poems in *The Book of Hours: The Book of Monastic Life* (1905) and a romantic verse tale, *The Tale of Love and Death of Cornet Christoph Rilke* (1906). Rilke met his future wife, the sculptor Clara Westhoff, when the two were living in the artists' colony Worpswede (northern Germany). They were married in March 1901 and settled in a cottage near the colony, where Rilke wrote the second part of *The Book of Hours: The Book of Pilgrimage*. He and Clara separated amicably at the end of the year, and Rilke moved to Paris to begin a commissioned study of the sculptor Rodin (*Auguste Rodin*, 1903), with whom his wife had studied.

Paris was an important city for Rilke, although he also felt lonely and isolated and fled at different times to other parts of Europe. He wrote the last section of *The Book of Hours: The Book of Poverty and Death* in Italy during 1903. In Paris, nonetheless, the German poet found a new kind of literary and artistic inspiration. In Rodin, who became his friend, he found a workmanlike dedication to the technical demands of his craft, an intense concentration on visible, tangible objects, and, above all, a belief in art as an essentially religious activity. Rilke was also struck by the poetry of Baudelaire, whose minutely realistic but strangely beautiful description of a rotting carcass (*A Carcass*) initiated, he felt, "the entire development toward objective expression, which we now recognize in Cézanne." Although he wrote in distress to his friend Lou Andreas-Salomé, complaining of nightmares and a sense of failure, it is at this time (and with her encouragement) that Rilke began his major work. The anguished, semi-autobiographical spiritual confessions of *The Notebook of Malte Laurids Brigge* (1910) date to this period, as do *New Poems* (1907–8), in which he abandoned his earlier Impressionistic and Romantic style and developed a more intense symbolic vision focused on objects. *New Poems* emphasized physical reality, the absolute otherness and "thing-like" nature of what was observed—be it fountain, panther, flower, human being, or the "Archaic Torso of Apollo," presented here. "Thing-poems" (*Ding-*

gedichte), in fact, is the term usually used when discussing Rilke's writing at this time. A letter to Lou Andreas-Salomé describes his feeling about how ancient art objects take on a peculiar luster once they are detached from history and are seen as "things" in and for themselves: "No subject matter is attached to them, no irrelevant voice interrupts the silence of their concentrated reality . . . no history casts a shadow over their naked clarity—: they *are*. That is all . . . one day one of them reveals itself to you, and shines like a first star."

Such "things" are not dead or inanimate but are supremely alive, filled with a strange vitality before the poet's glance: the charged sexuality of the marble torso, the metamorphosis of the Spanish dancer (*Spanish Dancer*), or the caged panther padding around his prison (*The Panther*). If "things" are not dead, neither is death unambiguous: when Rilke retells the ancient myth of Orpheus and his lost wife, Eurydice, the dead woman seems to achieve a new and fuller existence in the underworld. Themes of the interpenetration of life and death, the visible and invisible world, and creativity itself are taken up in Rilke's next major work, the sequence of ten poems called the *Duino Elegies* (1923). (An elegy is a mournful lyric poem, usually a lament for loss.)

The composition of the *Duino Elegies* came in two bursts of inspiration separated by ten years. Rilke found the quiet and isolation that he needed to write when a patron, Princess Marie von Thurn und Taxis-Hohenlohe, proposed that he stay by himself in her castle at Duino, near Trieste, during the winter of 1911–12. The story has been told many times of how Rilke, walking on the rocks above the sea and puzzling over how to answer a bothersome business letter, seemed to hear in the roar of the wind the first lines of his elegy: "Who, if I cried out, would hear me among the angels' / hierarchies?" By February, he had written the first and second elegies, and when he left Duino Castle in May, he had conceived the whole cycle and written fragments of the third, sixth, ninth, and tenth. Completion did not come easily in the following years. In 1913, because of the world war, Rilke's Paris apartment was confiscated, and his belongings were sold at auction. (He was considered an enemy alien.) Rilke himself was drafted into the German army and spent his days drawing precise vertical and horizontal lines on paper for the War Archives Office in Vienna. Released from military service in 1916, he composed little after this experience and feared that he would never be able to complete the Duino sequence. In 1922, however, a friend's purchase of the tiny Château de Muzot in Switzerland gave him a peaceful place to retire to and write. He not only completed the *Duino Elegies* in Muzot, but wrote— as a memorial for the young daughter of a friend—a two-part sequence of fifty-five sonnets, *Sonnets to Orpheus* (1922).

With *Duino Elegies* and *Sonnets to Orpheus*, Rilke's last great works were complete. The melancholy philosophic vision of the early elegies had described an angel of absolute reality, whose impersonal perfection was terrifyingly separate from mortal concerns. In the later elegies and the *Sonnets*, the idea of angelic remoteness is set off against the role of the poet, who functions as a bridge between material and human worlds. The defining symbolic figures of this poetry move from the dominant angel of the *Elegies* to the human poet Orpheus, who retires in turn before Eurydice, the woman who achieves fuller being when she passes into the realm of the dead. Affirming the essential unity of life and death, Rilke closed his two complementary sequences ("the little rust-colored sail of the Sonnets and the Elegies' gigantic white canvas") and wrote little—chiefly poems in French—over the next few years. Increasingly ill with leukemia, he died on December 29, 1926, as the result of a sudden infection after pricking himself on roses he cut for a friend in his garden.

The four selections from the *New Poems* printed here demonstrate Rilke's acutely visual imagination and the ambivalent objectivity of his "thing-poems." Whether it is a flamenco dancer, a caged panther, a swan entering the water, or the splendor of an ancient Greek statue, the subject is not only presented for itself, but is also suffused with human emotions. Keyed to a physical presence that transcends words, the viewer's response is challenged on an existential level. The "archaic torso of Apollo" is not a living being, but a fifth-century-B.C.E. Greek sculpture on display in the Louvre Museum in Paris. This headless marble torso is truly a "thing," a lifeless, even defaced chunk of stone. Yet such is the perfection of its luminous sensuality—descended, the speaker suggests, from the brilliant gaze of its missing head and "ripening" eyes—that it seems impossibly alive, and an inner radiance bursts starlike from the marble. The human vitality of this marble torso, a vitality achieved through artistic vision, challenges and puts to shame the observer's own puny existence. Nor is there any place to escape from the lesson, once it is recognized; instead, "You must change your life."

The ten *Duino Elegies* explore the same ambiguous relationship of life and art but in a more extended narrative style; they also take up one of Rilke's favorite themes: the complex tension between life and death in which human beings often appear as puppets on a falsely real stage, ephemeral beings whose greatest achievements are finally reduced to nothing. *The Ninth Elegy* begins by stressing the peculiar paradox of the human condition: Why, being mortal, do we not live serenely and happily as part of nature—like the laurel leaf? Why is it "human" to long for some further destiny? In *The First Elegy*, the answer was that the poet gives profundity to human lives, but in the *Ninth*, it turns out that the poet responds to a larger need. "Everything here / apparently needs us. . . . Us, the most fleeting of all." The poet's magic consists in finding some "pure word" that names things in their essence, says them "*more* intensely than the Things themselves / ever dreamed of existing." Ultimately, Rilke is celebrating the power of human creativity: like the "rope-maker in Rome or the potter along the Nile," he observes reality and creates from it a new being. For the poet, however, it is a process of making the visible angelically "invisible": he "delivers" Things by absorbing them into his imagination's inner dimension. "Earth, isn't this what you want: to arise within us, / *invisible*?" Rilke's poetic journey, in the *Elegies* as in the *Sonnets to Orpheus* that follow, was an inward journey that preserved what was most alive and valuable in human existence by subjecting it to the transfiguring perspective of art.

PRONOUNCING GLOSSARY

The following list uses common English syllables and stress accents to provide rough equivalents of selected words whose pronunciation may be unfamiliar to the general reader.

Dinggedichte: *ding'-ge-dikh-tuh*   Muzot: *moo-zoh'*

From NEW POEMS[1]

Archaic Torso of Apollo[2]

We cannot know his legendary head[3]
with eyes like ripening fruit. And yet his torso
is still suffused with brilliance from inside,
like a lamp, in which his gaze, now turned to low,

---

1. All selections are translated by Stephen Mitchell.   2. The first poem in the second volume of Rilke's *New Poems* (1908), which were dedicated "to my good friend, Auguste Rodin" (the French sculptor, 1840–1917), whose secretary Rilke was for a brief period and on whom he wrote two monographs, in 1903 and 1907). The poem itself was inspired by an ancient Greek statue discovered at Miletus (a Greek colony on the coast of Asia Minor) that was called simply the *Torso of a Youth from Miletus*; since the god Apollo was an ideal of youthful male beauty, his name was often associated with such statues.   3. In a torso, the head and limbs are missing.

gleams in all its power. Otherwise   5
the curved breast could not dazzle you so, nor could
a smile run through the placid hips and thighs
to that dark center where procreation flared.

Otherwise this stone would seem defaced
beneath the translucent cascade of the shoulders   10
and would not glisten like a wild beast's fur:

would not, from all the borders of itself,
burst like a star: for here there is no place
that does not see you. You must change your life.

Archaïscher Torso Apollos

Wir kannten nicht sein unerhörtes Haupt,
darin die Augenäpfel reiften. Aber
sein Torso glüht noch wie ein Kandelaber,
in dem sein Schauen, nur zurückgeschraubt,

sich hält und glänzt. Sonst könnte nicht der Bug   5
der Brust dich blenden, und im leisen Drehen
der Lenden könnte nicht ein Lächeln gehen
zu jener Mitte, die die Zeugung trug.

Sonst stünde dieser Stein entstellt und kurz
unter der Schultern durchsichtigem Sturz   10
und flimmerte nicht so wie Raubtierfelle;

und bräche nicht aus allen seinen Rändern
aus wie ein Stern: denn da ist keine Stelle,
die dich nicht sieht. Du mußt dein Leben ändern.

The Panther

In the Jardin des Plantes,[1] *Paris*

His vision, from the constantly passing bars,
has grown so weary that it cannot hold
anything else. It seems to him there are
a thousand bars; and behind the bars, no world.

As he paces in cramped circles, over and over,   5
the movement of his powerful soft strides
is like a ritual dance around a center
in which a mighty will stands paralyzed.

---

1. A zoo in Paris. Rilke also admired, at Rodin's studio, the plaster cast of an ancient statue of a panther.

Only at times, the curtain of the pupils
lifts, quietly—. An image enters in,   10
rushes down through the tensed, arrested muscles,
plunges into the heart and is gone.

The Swan

This laboring through what is still undone,
as though, legs bound, we hobbled along the way,
is like the awkward walking of the swan.

And dying—to let go, no longer feel
the solid ground we stand on every day—   5
is like his anxious letting himself fall

into the water, which receives him gently
and which, as though with reverence and joy,
draws back past him in streams on either side;
while, infinitely silent and aware,   10
in his full majesty and ever more
indifferent, he condescends to glide.

Spanish Dancer[1]

As on all its sides a kitchen-match darts white
flickering tongues before it bursts into flame:
with the audience around her, quickened, hot,
her dance begins to flicker in the dark room.

And all at once it is completely fire.   5

One upward glance and she ignites her hair
and, whirling faster and faster, fans her dress
into passionate flames, till it becomes a furnace
from which, like startled rattlesnakes, the long
naked arms uncoil, aroused and clicking.[2]   10

And then: as if the fire were too tight
around her body, she takes and flings it out
haughtily, with an imperious gesture,
and watches: it lies raging on the floor,
still blazing up, and the flames refuse to die—.   15
Till, moving with total confidence and a sweet
exultant smile, she looks up finally
and stamps it out with powerful small feet.

---

1. The dance described is the flamenco (from *flamear*, "to flame"). 2. The dancer accompanies herself
with the rhythmic clicking of castanets (worn on the fingers).

FROM DUINO ELEGIES

The Ninth Elegy

Why, if this interval of being can be spent serenely
in the form of a laurel,[1] slightly darker than all
other green, with tiny waves on the edges
of every leaf (like the smile of a breeze)—: why then
have to be human—and, escaping from fate,   5
keep longing for fate? . . . [2]
                Oh *not* because happiness *exists,*
that too-hasty profit snatched from approaching loss.
Not out of curiosity, not as practice for the heart, which
would exist in the laurel too. . . .   10

But because *truly* being here is so much; because everything here
apparently needs us, this fleeting world, which in some strange way
keeps calling to us. Us, the most fleeting of all.
Once for each thing. Just once; no more. And we too,
just once. And never again. But to have been   15
this once, completely, even if only once:
to have been at one with the earth, seems beyond undoing.

And so we keep pressing on, trying to achieve it,
trying to hold it firmly in our simple hands,
in our overcrowded gaze, in our speechless heart.   20
Trying to become it.—Whom can we give it to? We would
hold on to it all, forever . . . Ah, but what can we take along
into that other realm? Not the art of looking,
which is learned so slowly, and nothing that happened here. Nothing.
The sufferings, then. And, above all, the heaviness,   25
and the long experience of love,—just what is wholly
unsayable. But later, among the stars,
what good is it—*they* are *better* as they are: unsayable.
For when the traveler returns from the mountain-slopes into the valley,
he brings, not a handful of earth, unsayable to others, but instead   30
some word he has gained, some pure word, the yellow and blue
gentian. Perhaps we are *here* in order to say: house,
bridge, fountain, gate, pitcher, fruit-tree, window—
at most: column, tower. . . . But to *say* them, you must understand,
oh to say them *more* intensely than the Things themselves   35
ever dreamed of existing. Isn't the secret intent
of this taciturn earth, when it forces lovers together,
that inside their boundless emotion all things may shudder with joy?
Threshold: what it means for two lovers
to be wearing down, imperceptibly, the ancient threshold of their door—   40
they too, after the many who came before them
and before those to come. . . . , lightly.

1. The nymph Daphne, escaping from the pursuit of her would-be lover Apollo, was changed by that god into a laurel tree (Ovid, *Metamorphoses* I.548 ff.). 2. Here and elsewhere in the elegy, Rilke's ellipsis marks indicate a pause, not an omission.

Here is the time for the *sayable, here* is its homeland.
Speak and bear witness. More than ever
the Things that we might experience are vanishing, for   45
what crowds them out and replaces them is an imageless act.
An act under a shell, which easily cracks open as soon as
the business inside outgrows it and seeks new limits.
Between the hammers our heart
endures, just as the tongue does   50
between the teeth and, despite that,
still is able to praise.

Praise this world to the angel, not the unsayable one,
you can't impress *him* with glorious emotion; in the universe
where he feels more powerfully, you are a novice. So show him   55
something simple which, formed over generations,
lives as our own, near our hand and within our gaze.
Tell him of Things. He will stand astonished; as *you* stood
by the rope-maker in Rome or the potter along the Nile.
Show him how happy a Thing can be, how innocent and ours,   60
how even lamenting grief purely decides to take form,
serves as a Thing, or dies into a Thing—, and blissfully
escapes far beyond the violin.—And these Things,
which live by perishing, know you are praising them; transient,
they look to us for deliverance: us, the most transient of all.   65
They want us to change them, utterly, in our invisible heart,
within—oh endlessly—within us! Whoever we may be at last.

Earth, isn't this what you want: to arise within us,
invisible? Isn't it your dream
to be wholly invisible someday?—O Earth: invisible!   70
What, if not transformation, is your urgent command?
Earth, my dearest, I will. Oh believe me, you no longer
need your springtimes to win me over—one of them,
ah, even one, is already too much for my blood.
Unspeakably I have belonged to you, from the first.   75
You were always right, and your holiest inspiration
is our intimate companion, Death.

Look, I am living. On what? Neither childhood nor future
grows any smaller. . . . Superabundant being
wells up in my heart.   80

WALLACE STEVENS
1879–1955

"A bucket of sand and a wishing lamp," Wallace Stevens once said, was all he needed to "create a world in half a second that would make this one look like a hunk of mud." His poetry invites us into an imaginative world that fuses poignantly sensuous images with the most abstract metaphysics. Stevens himself embodied contrasts: a Hartford insurance executive as well as a major American poet, he was never a part of the contemporary literary scene with its movements and isms. He was acquainted with current New York writers and artists, he collected modern art (which is often reflected in his poems), and, later in his career, he wrote and lectured about poetry; but it is not through these associations that he joins the mainstream of modern European and American letters. In his work Stevens combines two aspects of modernist tradition. His musical free verse and sensuous, significant imagery recall Symbolism, which he especially admired in the French poet Paul Verlaine. His stress on concrete, physical descriptions inside a philosophical framework is characteristic of "existential" writers such as Jean-Paul Sartre and Albert Camus. More than any other modern poet, Stevens inherited the Symbolists' desire to balance the intertwined concepts of concrete reality and human imagination. Like the Symbolists, too, he finds an ultimate human value in the artist's freedom to create the world anew in a "supreme fiction": fiction, because "true" reality can never be ascertained or re-created; supreme, because it is the highest aspiration of human creativity. This fiction is not yet the ungraspable "fictionality" of postmodernist writers such as Samuel Beckett and Alain Robbe-Grillet, for it does not dissolve into a series of competing perspectives. Instead, Stevens's modernist poetry holds up the ideal of a supreme artistic transformation whose creation bestows meaning on an otherwise meaningless universe.

Stevens was born in Reading, Pennsylvania, on October 2, 1879, the second of five children. His father was a schoolteacher and then attorney with diverse interests; his mother taught school. He enrolled at Harvard in 1897 as a nondegree student and while at college contributed poems, stories, and sketches to the Harvard *Advocate* (of which he became president) and the Harvard *Monthly*. He also came to know the philosopher and writer George Santayana, whose assertion of a common imaginative essence in religion and poetry appealed greatly to him.

Stevens left Harvard in 1900 to try journalism and then law school in New York; he received his degree and was admitted to the bar in 1904. After working as an attorney for several firms he finally entered the insurance business in 1908. In 1916 he joined a subsidiary of the Hartford Accident and Indemnity Company, becoming vice president of the parent company in 1934 and remaining there until his death in 1955. He dictated business correspondence and poems to the same secretary. In 1922 business affairs took him to Florida, and until 1940 he returned frequently to its warm and lush landscape, which contrasted in his poetry—both physically and emotionally—with the chillier climate of the north.

Stevens married Elsie V. Kachel in 1909, and in 1924 his daughter, Holly, was born; she later edited her father's letters. He published individual poems in little magazines (small avant-garde literary magazines) and was a friend of *Poetry* editor Harriet Monroe and of the poets William Carlos Williams and Marianne Moore. *Harmonium*, his first collection of poetry, appeared in 1923. In following years, Stevens's insurance career occupied most of his time, and he published little poetry until 1935, when *Ideas of Order* appeared. Later volumes included *The Man with the Blue Guitar* (1937), *Parts of a World* (1942), and a collection of prose essays, *The Necessary Angel* (1951). Stevens kept the two parts of his career quite separate but gradually became a well-known and influential poet, winning the Bollingen Prize for poetry in 1949 and the National Book Award in 1951 (for *The Auroras of Autumn*) and 1955 (for *The Collected Poems of Wallace Stevens*). He died of cancer on August 2, 1955.

Stevens's poetry expresses the dualism between reality and imagination, between things as they really are and as we perceive and then shape them. For we can never know reality directly; our five senses see, touch, taste, smell, and hear what is outside us, constructing an image of the world in which we live, but this world also exists separate from us and beyond our image of it. This paradox underlies all Stevens's poetry, which swings between the two poles of the shaping, creative imagination and the material world of which we are only partly aware. The names of real Connecticut towns or the state of Tennessee, an inventory of the trash in a dump, descriptions of coffee and oranges at breakfast, and marred old pieces of furniture inhabit his poems side by side with the most abstract speculations, transformations of everyday scenes, and visions of the edge of space. Poetic artifice—the playful and imaginative use of language—clothes the most mundane observations, as if to assert a relationship between verbal style and the real subject about which it tries to speak. Stevens once said that "it is pleasant to hear the milkman, and yet . . . the imaginative world is the only real world after all," and this balancing of dualities continues throughout his work.

Sunday Morning, one of Stevens's earlier poems, already reflects this dualism on several levels. The opening lines present a contrast between the comfortable self-indulgence of the Sunday morning breakfast table, warmly alive with sun and bright colors, and the traditional Christian dedication of the day to thoughts of human mortality redeemed by Christ's death. The contrast continues in a quasi-dialogue between the poet, who protests any attempt to transcend this world or death, and the woman, who speaks of paradise and some "imperishable bliss." Earth itself is suffi-cient paradise, says the poet, and "friendlier" than the untouchable sky or super-natural explanations of different religions; death is a necessary part of life's constant renewal and sharpens our awareness of love and beauty while they exist. The wholly natural beauty of the New England landscape at the poem's end, with its acceptance of death and change, suggests to the speaker a more real and human ideal than the unchanging perfection of eternal life.

The soft, consolatory tone of *Sunday Morning* (which derives in part from Stevens's recollection of his mother's death in 1912), becomes bold and gaudier in *The Emperor of Ice-Cream*, which also deals—but more ironically—with the contrast of life and death. The scene is a wake: a dead woman lies covered with the same sheet on which she once embroidered fantail pigeons. Stevens, however, begins his poem in the kitchen with the festivities in which the survivors are taking part. For the day is devoted not only to the dead but to the living, in whose imperial court the ice cream server is emperor, and the women dressed in their best clothes are handmaidens. Words with erotic overtones (*concupiscent, wenches*) reinforce the scene's essential hedonism, in which the only reality that counts is the pleasure of the moment.

Yet there is another reality, that of the dead woman, who has now become a mere object much like her own furniture, and Stevens painstakingly registers its details. The dresser is made of pine wood and lacks three glass knobs; the dead woman's calloused feet protrude from the too-short embroidered sheet. Such close-up obser-vation puts the woman in a new imaginative context, in a world of lifeless inanimate things whose stillness comments with grim finality on the first stanza's boisterous celebration. The empire of ice cream contains both life and death; people, flowers, and yesterday's newspapers all ultimately come down to the same level of bare phys-icality. Wisdom lies in accepting the common outcome of all earthly appearances— "Let be be finale of seem"—and in celebrating life while it remains.

Stevens's juxtaposition of reality and our imaginative perception of it is echoed throughout his writing by a dialectic of other oppositions, one idea being raised seem-ingly only to be challenged and tested by another. Thus the jar on a hill in Tennessee juxtaposes human intellect and aesthetic imagination against the unshaped wilder-ness of nature, and *Peter Quince at the Clavier* celebrates the immortal presence— in the memory—of a long-dead woman's physical beauty. Such balancing or counterpoint rejects a single perspective and opens up avenues for continued meditation.

   Counterpoint is basically a musical term, and Stevens's work is filled with the imagery of musical performance: the harpsichord of *Peter Quince at the Clavier*, the singer in *The Idea of Order at Key West*, and the nightingale and even grackles of *The Man on the Dump*. Other poems speak of a blue guitar (the image taken from a painting by Pablo Picasso), an old horn, a lute, citherns, saxophones, not to mention the "tink and tank and tunk-a-tunk-tunk" of an unnamed instrument (perhaps a banjo). Musical images are used to describe events, such as the tambourinelike rhythm of Susanna's attendants arriving (with the additional musical end rhymes of *tambourines* and *Byzantines*), or emotions, like the erotic intensity of the elders' lustful glance ("The basses of their beings throb / In witching chords") and the comic counterpoint of their quivering nerves pulsing "pizzicati of Hosanna." Even the title of Stevens's book is the name of a musical instrument, *Harmonium*, and he had wanted to name his collected poems *The Whole of Harmonium*.

   Music for Stevens was not, however, merely musical images in a poem, or the notion of harmonizing the sounds of words or holding contrasted ideas in counterpoint. It implied for him a supreme, intuited language, the "foreign song" of the gold-feathered bird on the edge of space in *Of Mere Being*, perhaps the same bird that sang to the emperor in Yeats's *Sailing to Byzantium*. The singer, bird or human, is the type of the poet, the "one of fictive music" who creates the world anew through the incantatory power of imagination.

   The singer of *The Idea of Order at Key West* is such a poet, embodying imagination at its most ambitious: "She was the single artificer of the world / In which she sang." Nature itself cannot create such a world, for it lacks the igniting spark; while the sea may imitate human gestures and sounds, it cannot truly speak, and makes only "meaningless plungings of water and wind." Imagination is supreme; the singer has "the maker's rage to order words" (*poet* comes from a Greek word meaning "maker"), and her song creates for herself and for her listeners a world of imagination in which lights from the fishing boats seem to map out the night against which they shine.

   The luminous beauty of the singer's world is only one of many possible poetic worlds, all of which take their place on the accumulated heap of poetry where the latest artificer sits as *The Man on the Dump*. The trash heap of history is the place to find outworn poetic images, from dewy clichés to the nightingale as traditional symbol for poetry (see Keats's *Ode to a Nightingale*, p. 760). In a poem filled with the debris of modern times, from old tires to dead cats, Stevens suggests that poetry's philosophical quest to name the "the" of existence cannot employ previous ages' images and ideas but must develop its own, even if they appear only as the grating music of grackles or beatings on an old tin can. Yet all are engaged in the same enterprise, creating what he elsewhere called "supreme fictions" to give meaning to our lives.

   Stevens's poetry celebrates the ability of the individual imagination to conceive its own world. Broader social or political themes are pushed to the background, even in texts (such as *The Man on the Dump* or *The Emperor of Ice-Cream*) that derive power from their realistic descriptions. Consequently, the politically minded critics of the 1930s accused the poet of being an escapist, content to be the "single artificer of his own world of mannerism." Stevens responded that to do otherwise was to misunderstand "the spiritual role of the poet," for this role was not to make political statements but to clarify basic issues by illuminating the relations between human subjectivity and a world of objects. Such an explanation may have seemed too philosophical to those seeking an openly committed literature, and Stevens's early work was largely unappreciated. The gaudy exuberance of its images made it seem less serious than the poetry of political commitment and visionary mysticism that Yeats was then writing, or Eliot's evocation in *The Waste Land* of a universal and profound despair. Only after World War II did Americans, and Europeans, realize that Stevens, too, was a master worthy to stand beside his greatest contemporaries.

Sunday Morning[1]

I

Complacencies of the peignoir, and late
Coffee and oranges in a sunny chair,
And the green freedom of a cockatoo
Upon a rug mingle to dissipate
The holy hush of ancient sacrifice.   5
She dreams a little, and she feels the dark
Encroachment of that old catastrophe,
As a calm darkens among water-lights.
The pungent oranges and bright, green wings
Seem things in some procession of the dead,   10
Winding across wide water, without sound.
The day is like wide water, without sound,
Stilled for the passing of her dreaming feet
Over the seas, to silent Palestine,
Dominion of the blood and sepulchre.[2]   15

II

Why should she give her bounty to the dead?
What is divinity if it can come
Only in silent shadows and in dreams?
Shall she not find in comforts of the sun,
In pungent fruit and bright, green wings, or else   20
In any balm or beauty of the earth,
Things to be cherished like the thought of heaven?[3]
Divinity must live within herself:
Passions of rain, or moods in falling snow;
Grievings in loneliness, or unsubdued   25
Elations when the forest blooms; gusty
Emotions on wet roads on autumn nights;
All pleasures and all pains, remembering
The bough of summer and the winter branch.
These are the measures destined for her soul.   30

III

Jove[4] in the clouds had his inhuman birth.
No mother suckled him, no sweet land gave
Large-mannered motions to his mythy mind
He moved among us, as a muttering king,
Magnificent, would move among his hinds,[5]   35

---

1. Although the central figure of the poem is clearly a woman sitting over late breakfast on Sunday morning instead of going to church, Stevens comments that "this is not essentially a woman's meditation on religion and the meaning of life. It is anybody's meditation" (Stevens's *Letters*, p. 250). 2. Throughout the stanza there are hints of Christ's Crucifixion and the celebration of the Mass. 3. "The poem is simply an expression of paganism" (Stevens's *Letters*, p. 250). 4. Ruler of the gods in Roman mythology. Stevens softens the traditional story in which Jove's father, Cronus, swallows the infant shortly after birth.

Until our blood, commingling, virginal,[6]
With heaven, brought such requital to desire
The very hinds discerned it, in a star.[7]
Shall our blood fail? Or shall it come to be
The blood of paradise? And shall the earth   40
Seem all of paradise that we shall know?
The sky will be much friendlier then than now,
A part of labor and a part of pain,
And next in glory to enduring love,
Not this dividing and indifferent blue.   45

IV

She says, "I am content when wakened birds,
Before they fly, test the reality
Of misty fields, by their sweet questionings;
But when the birds are gone, and their warm fields
Return no more, where, then, is paradise?"   50
There is not any haunt of prophecy,[8]
Nor any old chimera of the grave,
Neither the golden underground, nor isle
Melodious, where spirits gat them home,[9]
Nor visionary south, nor cloudy palm   55
Remote on heaven's hill, that has endured
As April's green endures; or will endure
Like her remembrance of awakened birds,
Or her desire for June and evening, tipped
By the consummation of the swallow's wings.   60

V

She says, "But in contentment I still feel
The need of some imperishable bliss."
Death is the mother of beauty; hence from her,
Alone, shall come fulfilment to our dreams
And our desires. Although she strews the leaves   65
Of sure obliteration on our paths,
The path sick sorrow took, the many paths
Where triumph rang its brassy phrase, or love
Whispered a little out of tenderness,
She makes the willow shiver in the sun   70
For maidens who were wont to sit and gaze
Upon the grass, relinquished to their feet.
She causes boys to pile new plums and pears
On disregarded plate.[1] The maidens taste
And stray impassioned in the littering leaves.   75

---

6. An allusion to the conception of Jesus in the womb of the Virgin Mary.   7. The star over Bethlehem that marked Jesus' birth.   8. E.g., like the oracle at Delphi.   9. The Elysian Fields, or Isles of the Blessed, where the heroes of Greek myth went after death.   1. "Plate is used in the sense of so-called family plate. Disregarded refers to the disuse into which things fall that have been possessed for a long time. I mean, therefore, that death releases and renews. What the old have come to disregard, the young inherit and make use of" (Stevens's *Letters*, p. 183).

VI

Is there no change of death in paradise?
Does ripe fruit never fall? Or do the boughs
Hang always heavy in that perfect sky,
Unchanging, yet so like our perishing earth,
With rivers like our own that seek for seas   80
They never find, the same receding shores
That never touch with inarticulate pang?
Why set the pear upon those river-banks
Or spice the shores with odors of the plum?
Alas, that they should wear our colors there,   85
The silken weavings of our afternoons,
And pick the strings of our insipid lutes!
Death is the mother of beauty, mystical,
Within whose burning bosom we devise
Our earthly mothers waiting, sleeplessly.   90

VII

Supple and turbulent, a ring of men
Shall chant in orgy on a summer morn
Their boisterous devotion to the sun,
Not as a god, but as a god might be,
Naked among them, like a savage source.   95
Their chant shall be a chant of paradise,
Out of their blood, returning to the sky;
And in their chant shall enter, voice by voice,
The windy lake wherein their lord delights,
The trees, like serafin,[2] and echoing hills,   100
That choir among themselves long afterward.
They shall know well the heavenly fellowship
Of men that perish and of summer morn.
And whence they came and whither they shall go
The dew upon their feet shall manifest.[3]   105

VIII

She hears, upon that water without sound,
A voice that cries, "The tomb in Palestine
Is not the porch of spirits lingering.[4]
It is the grave of Jesus, where he lay."
We live in an old chaos of the sun,   110
Or old dependency of day and night,
Or island solitude, unsponsored, free,
Of that wide water, inescapable.
Deer walk upon our mountains, and the quail
Whistle about us their spontaneous cries;   115
Sweet berries ripen in the wilderness;

2. Angels of the highest rank.   3. "Life is as fugitive as dew upon the feet of men dancing in dew. Men do not either come from any direction or disappear in any direction. Life is as meaningless as dew" (Stevens's *Letters*, p. 250).   4. I.e., remaining on Earth after the body is dead.

And, in the isolation of the sky,
At evening, casual flocks of pigeons make
Ambiguous undulations as they sink.
Downward to darkness, on extended wings.   120

Peter Quince at the Clavier[1]

I

Just as my fingers on these keys
Make music, so the selfsame sounds
On my spirit make a music, too.

Music is feeling, then, not sound;
And thus it is that what I feel,   5
Here in this room, desiring you,

Thinking of your blue-shadowed silk,
Is music. It is like the strain
Waked in the elders by Susanna.[2]

Of a green evening, clear and warm,   10
She bathed in her still garden, while
The red-eyed elders watching, felt

The basses of their beings throb
In witching chords, and their thin blood
Pulse pizzicati of Hosanna.[3]   15

II

In the green water, clear and warm,
Susanna lay.
She searched
The touch of springs,
And found   20
Concealed imaginings.
She sighed,
For so much melody.

Upon the bank, she stood
In the cool   25
Of spent emotions.
She felt, among the leaves,
The dew
Of old devotions.

1. General term in the 16th century for a keyboard instrument, such as a harpsichord. In Shakespeare's
A Midsummer Night's Dream, Peter Quince is the carpenter-playwright who directs his own play about the
tragic lovers Pyramus and Thisbe. Both the play and the production amuse the noble audience.   2. In
the biblical Apocrypha, a Babylonian woman falsely accused of adultery by lecherous elders who spied on
her bathing.   3. A cry of praise to God. *Pizzicati*: notes sounded by plucking a string (as on a violin).

She walked upon the grass, 30
Still quavering.
The winds were like her maids,
On timid feet,
Fetching her woven scarves,
Yet wavering. 35

A breath upon her hand
Muted the night.
She turned—
A cymbal crashed,
And roaring horns. 40

III

Soon, with a noise like tambourines,
Came her attendant Byzantines.[4]

They wondered why Susanna cried
Against the elders by her side;

And as they whispered, the refrain 45
Was like a willow swept by rain.

Anon,[5] their lamps' uplifted flame
Revealed Susanna and her shame.

And then, the simpering Byzantines
Fled, with a noise like tambourines. 50

IV

Beauty is momentary in the mind—
The fitful tracing of a portal;
But in the flesh it is immortal.
The body dies; the body's beauty lives.
So evenings die, in their green going, 55
A wave, interminably flowing.
So gardens die, their meek breath scenting
The cowl of winter, done repenting.
So maidens die,[6] to the auroral
Celebration of a maiden's choral.[7] 60
Susanna's music touched the bawdy strings
Of those white elders; but, escaping,
Left only Death's ironic scraping.[8]
Now, in its immortality, it plays
On the clear viol[9] of her memory, 65
And makes a constant sacrament of praise.

---

4. Inhabitants of ancient Byzantium, a Christian empire of the Near East. "Somebody once called my attention to the fact that there were no Byzantines in Susanna's time. I hope that that bit of precious pedantry will seem as unimportant to you as it does to me" (Stevens's *Letters*, p. 250). **5.** Soon. **6.** As maidens, that is, become women. **7.** Choral song. **8.** Rasping fiddle music. **9.** A stringed instrument of the 16th and 17th centuries, played with a bow; also a pun on *violation*.

Anecdote of the Jar

I placed a jar in Tennessee.
And round it was, upon a hill.
It made the slovenly wilderness
Surround that hill.

The wilderness rose up to it,   5
And sprawled around, no longer wild.
The jar was round upon the ground
And tall and of a port[1] in air.

It took dominion everywhere.
The jar was gray and bare.   10
It did not give of bird or bush,
Like nothing else in Tennessee.

The Emperor of Ice-Cream[1]

Call the roller of big cigars,
The muscular one, and bid him whip
In kitchen cups concupiscent[2] curds.
Let the wenches dawdle in such dress
As they are used to wear, and let the boys   5
Bring flowers in last month's newspapers.
Let be be finale of seem.[3]
The only emperor is the emperor of ice-cream.

Take from the dresser of deal,[4]
Lacking the three glass knobs, that sheet   10
On which she embroidered fantails[5] once
And spread it so as to cover her face.
If her horny feet protrude, they come
To show how cold she is, and dumb.
Let the lamp affix its beam.   15
The only emperor is the emperor of ice-cream.

1. Dignified bearing, manner.   **1.** "I think I should select from my poems as my favorite 'The Emperor of Ice-Cream.' This wears a deliberately commonplace costume, and yet seems to me to contain something of the essential gaudiness of poetry; that is the reason why I like it" (Stevens's *Letters*, p. 263).   **2.** Lusty, sensual. "The words 'concupiscent curds' . . . express the concupiscence of life, but, by contrast with the things in relation to them in the poem they express or accentuate life's destitution" (Stevens's *Letters*, p. 500).   **3.** "The true sense of 'Let be be the finale of seem' is let being become the conclusion or denouement of appearing to be: in short, icecream is an absolute good. The poem is obviously not about icecream, but about being as distinguished from seeming to be" (Stevens's *Letters*, p. 341).   **4.** Fir or pine wood.   **5.** Fantail pigeons.

The Idea of Order at Key West[1]

She sang beyond the genius of the sea.[2]
The water never formed to mind or voice,
Like a body wholly body, fluttering
Its empty sleeves; and yet its mimic motion
Made constant cry, caused constantly a cry,   5
That was not ours although we understood,
Inhuman, of the veritable ocean.

The sea was not a mask.[3] No more was she.
The song and water were not medleyed sound
Even if what she sang was what she heard.   10
Since what she sang was uttered word by word.
It may be that in all her phrases stirred
The grinding water and the gasping wind;
But it was she and not the sea we heard.

For she was the maker of the song she sang.   15
The ever-hooded, tragic-gestured sea
Was merely a place by which she walked to sing.
Whose spirit is this? we said, because we knew
It was the spirit that we sought and knew
That we should ask this often as she sang.   20

If it was only the dark voice of the sea
That rose, or even colored by many waves;
If it was only the outer voice of sky
And cloud, of the sunken coral water-walled,
However clear, it would have been deep air,   25
The heaving speech of air, a summer sound
Repeated in a summer without end
And sound alone. But it was more than that,
More even than her voice, and ours, among
The meaningless plungings of water and the wind,   30
Theatrical distances, bronze shadows heaped
On high horizons, mountainous atmospheres
Of sky and sea.
              It was her voice that made
The sky acutest at its vanishing.   35
She measured to the hour its solitude.
She was the single artificer of the world
In which she sang. And when she sang, the sea,
Whatever self it had, became the self
That was her song, for she was the maker. Then we,   40

---

1. Published in *Ideas of Order* (1935). "In 'The Idea of Order at Key West' life has ceased to be a matter of chance. It may be that every man introduces his own order into the life about him. . . . But still there is order. . . . These are tentative ideas for the purposes of poetry" (Stevens's *Letters*, p. 293). Key West is the southernmost of the Florida keys, and Stevens spent midwinter vacations there for almost twenty years. 2. I.e., beyond the power of the sea to respond. 3. The movement of the waves, imitating fluttering sleeves, also emits an inhuman cry. The sea mimics the human body, but without a mind; it is not even as close as the mask worn by actors in ancient Greek drama.

As we beheld her striding there alone,
Knew that there never was a world for her
Except the one she sang and, singing, made.

Ramon Fernandez,⁴ tell me, if you know,
Why, when the singing ended and we turned   45
Toward the town, tell why the glassy lights,
The lights in the fishing boats at anchor there,
As the night descended, tilting in the air,
Mastered the night and portioned out the sea,
Fixing emblazoned zones and fiery poles,⁵   50
Arranging, deepening, enchanting night.

Oh! Blessed rage for order, pale Ramon,
The maker's rage to order words of the sea,
Words of the fragrant portals, dimly-starred,
And of ourselves and of our origins,   55
In ghostlier demarcations, keener sounds.

The Man on the Dump

Day creeps down. The moon is creeping up.
The sun is a corbeil of flowers the moon Blanche¹
Places there, a bouquet. Ho-ho . . . The dump is full
Of images. Days pass like papers² from a press.
The bouquets come here in the papers. So the sun,   5
And so the moon, both come, and the janitor's poems
Of every day, the wrapper on the can of pears,
The cat in the paper-bag, the corset, the box
From Esthonia:³ the tiger chest, for tea.

The freshness of night has been fresh a long time.   10
The freshness of morning, the blowing of day, one says
That it puffs as Cornelius Nepos⁴ reads, it puffs
More than, less than or it puffs like this or that.
The green smacks in the eye, the dew in the green
Smacks like fresh water in a can, like the sea   15

On a cocoanut—how many men have copied dew
For buttons, how many women have covered themselves
With dew, dew dresses, stones and chains of dew, heads
Of the floweriest flowers dewed with the dewiest dew.
One grows to hate these things except on the dump.   20
Now, in the time of spring (azaleas, trilliams,

4. French critic (1894–1944) who described the way impressionistic techniques in literature impose a
subjective order on reality. Stevens had read some of Fernandez's criticism but denied that he intended any
specific reference here.   5. As with the geographic zones and poles of the earth. *Emblazoned*: ornamented, usually with heraldic symbols.   1. A woman's name, etymologically signifying whiteness. *Corbeil*:
basket.   2. Newspapers.   3. Or Estonia; a Baltic republic, once part of the Soviet Union.   4. Roman
historian (1st century B.C.E.), now little read, the author of brief anecdotal and highly moralized *Lives of
Famous Men*.

Myrtle, viburnums, daffodils, blue phlox),[5]
Between that disgust and this, between the things
That are on the dump (azaleas and so on)
And those that will be (azaleas and so on).   25
One feels the purifying change. One rejects
The trash.

           That's the moment when the moon creeps up
To the bubbling of bassoons. That's the time
One looks at the elephant-colorings of tires.   30
Everything is shed; and the moon comes up as the moon
(All its images are in the dump) and you see
As a man (not like an image of a man),
You see the moon rise in the empty sky.

One sits and beats an old tin can, lard pail.   35
One beats and beats for that which one believes.
That's what one wants to get near. Could it after all
Be merely oneself, as superior as the ear
To a crow's voice? Did the nightingale[6] torture the ear,
Pack the heart and scratch the mind? And does the ear   40
Solace itself in peevish birds? Is it peace,
Is it a philosopher's honeymoon,[7] one finds
On the dump? Is it to sit among mattresses of the dead,
Bottles, pots, shoes and grass and murmur *aptest eve*:
Is it to hear the blatter of grackles[8] and say   45
Invisible priest; is it to eject, to pull
The day to pieces and cry *stanza my stone*?[9]
Where was it one first heard of the Truth? The the.[1]

---

5. Spring flowers.   6. Traditional image for lyric poetry—for example, in Keat's *Ode to a Nightingale*.
7. Like a busman's holiday—that is, no respite at all.   8. Noisy birds.   9. Suggests a Romantic, mystical, "nightingale" poetry that turns its back on material reality. "Invisible priest" may recall Rilke's proposed artistic transformation of reality into an invisible higher reality (see *The Ninth Elegy*).   1. "The truth" is an intangible absolute (like "*the* good"); what it specifies cannot be defined. The *the* itself however represents an urge to seek absolute meaning: to say *the*, not merely *a*.

JAMES JOYCE
1882–1941

Modernism is synonymous with James Joyce. An Irish writer who spent most of his
life outside Ireland and became an international figure, Joyce created a narrative style
that changed the way modern novelists were able to write about the world. Writers
as widely separated as the American William Faulkner, the Irishman Samuel Beckett,
the Colombian Gabriel García Márquez, and the French "new novelists" Alain Robbe-
Grillet, Marguerite Duras, and Nathalie Sarraute have learned from his literary and
linguistic innovations. From *Dubliners* to *Ulysses* and *Finnegans Wake*, Joyce found
new ways to explore the daily lives and fragmentary dreams of characters (including
his own youthful self) in the parochial Dublin society that he had fled. Although he
returned to Ireland as the starting point for all three works, he blamed Irish society
for its narrowness and "moral paralysis" and repeatedly evoked the broader horizons

of European culture and myth. Joyce's best-known contribution to modern literature is the stream-of-consciousness technique that attempts to reproduce the natural flow of thoughts and emotions. Stream-of-consciousness writing does not always seem logical, for thoughts tend to jump around in an arbitrary manner, but it can be very convincing since it gives the reader apparent access to the workings of a character's mind. The aim—and it is a characteristically modernist aim—is to obtain a fuller understanding of human experience by displaying subconscious associations along with conscious thoughts. Joyce's later work exploits these subterranean connections more and more, and his language becomes increasingly playful as he strives to create a newly meaningful form of writing and to "forge in the smithy of my soul the uncreated conscience of my race."

Born in Dublin on February 2, 1882, to May Murray and John Stanislaus Joyce, he was given the impressive name of James Augustine Aloysius Joyce. His father held a well-paid and easy post in the civil service, and the family was comfortable until 1891, when his job was eliminated with a small pension and he declined to take up more demanding work elsewhere. The Joyce family (there were ten children) moved steadily down the social and economic scale, and life became difficult under the improvident guidance of a man whom Joyce later portrayed as "a drinker, a good fellow, a storyteller, somebody's secretary, something in a distillery, a tax-gatherer, a bankrupt, and at present a praiser of his own past." Joyce attended the well-known Catholic preparatory school of Clongowes Wood College from six to nine years of age, leaving when his family could no longer afford the tuition; two years later, he was admitted as a scholarship student to Belvedere College in Dublin. Both were Jesuit schools and provided a rigorous Catholic training against which Joyce violently rebelled but which he was never able to forget. In Belvedere College, shaken by a dramatic hell-fire sermon shortly after his first experience with sex, he even thought of becoming a priest; the life of the senses and his vocation as an artist won out, however, and the sermon and his reaction to it became part of *A Portrait of the Artist as a Young Man.* After graduating from Belvedere in 1898, Joyce entered another Irish Catholic institution—University College, Dublin—where he consciously rebelled against Irish tradition and looked abroad for new values. Teaching himself Norwegian to read Henrik Ibsen in the original, he criticized the writers of the Irish Literary Renaissance as provincial and had no interest in joining their ranks. Like the hero of *Portrait,* Stephen Dedalus, he decided in 1902 to escape the stifling conventions of his native country and leave for the Continent.

This first trip did not last long. For six months, he supported himself in Paris by giving English lessons, but when his mother turned seriously ill he was called home. After her death, he taught school for a time in Dublin and then returned to the Continent with Nora Barnacle, a country woman from western Ireland with whom he had two children and whom he married in 1931. The young couple moved to Trieste, where Joyce taught English in a Berlitz school and where he started writing both the short stories collected as *Dubliners* (1914) and an early version (partially published as *Stephen Hero* in 1944) of *A Portrait of the Artist as a Young Man. Dubliners* sketches aspects of life in Dublin as Joyce knew it, which means that the parochiality, piety, and repressive conventions of Irish life are shown stifling artistic and psychological development. Whether it be the young boy who arrives too late at the fair in *Araby,* the poor-aunt laundress of *Clay,* or the frustrated writer Gabriel Conroy of *The Dead,* characters in *Dubliners* dream of a better life against a dismal and impoverishing background whose cumulative effect is one of despair. The style of *Dubliners* is more realistic than Joyce's later fiction, but he is already employing a structure of symbolic meanings and revelatory moments called "epiphanies." The all-blanketing white snow at the end of *The Dead* suggests the chill uniformity of death and Gabriel Conroy's alienation from (or, on another level, unity with) the rest of his world. It is Gabriel who observes the scene and whose suddenly expanded vision of the whole universe being swallowed up in oblivion constitutes an epiphany, a moment when everything fuses and makes sense in a larger spiritual perspective.

A Portrait of the Artist as a Young Man is based on Joyce's life until 1902, but the novel is clearly not a conventional autobiography and the reader recognizes in the first pages a radical experiment in fictional language. From the child's vocabulary and fragmented echoing of his parents' baby talk ("nicens little boy," "baby tuckoo") to the mature rhetoric of the end ("Old father, old artificer, stand me now and ever in good stead"), everything in *Portrait* is introduced sequentially and shaped to make the most powerful cumulative impact. Even Stephen's first naïve thoughts prepare for themes developed later on: the importance of sense impressions, from the clammy bed to his mother's smell; the political symbolism of Dante's green and maroon hairbrushes; the bird imagery and threat of punishment on high in Dante's reproach; and the small boy's habit of thinking over things and rephrasing them in poetic language. Events that stand out in the young boy's mind, such as the humiliation of receiving an unfair spanking in school, are described with their full impact because they are not simply first-person (subjective) or third-person (objective) accounts but an imaginative combination of the two. An outside observer with access to all Stephen's feelings follows the course of events. *Portrait*, like *Dubliners*, is still in the tradition of naturalist narrative and specifically of the *Künstlerroman*, or artist-novel, which follows chronologically the career of its artist hero. Its sophisticated symbolism, use of epiphanies, and stress on dramatic dialogue, however, hint at the radical break with narrative tradition that Joyce was preparing in *Ulysses*.

Ulysses (1922) is one of the most celebrated instances of literary censorship. Its serial publication in the New York *Little Review* from 1918 to 1920 was stopped as obscene by the U.S. Post Office after a complaint from the New York Society for the Prevention of Vice. The novel was banned, and all available copies were actually burned in England and America until a 1933 decision by Judge Woolsey in a U.S. district court lifted the ban in the United States. The problem was not new: Joyce's realistic descriptions of sensory experience from bedroom to bathroom, his playfully allusive use of language, and his antinationalist and antireligious attitudes had already offended many readers from *Dubliners* (which an Irish printer refused to print on the grounds that it was anti-Irish) to *Portrait* (which was refused as a "work of doubtful character even though it may be a classic"). While Joyce's descriptions have lost none of their pungency, it is hard to imagine a reader who would not be struck also by another side—by the "classical" density and enormous mythic scope of this complex, symbolic, and linguistically innovative novel. Openly referring to an ancient predecessor, the *Odyssey* of Homer ("Ulysses" is the Latin name for the hero Odysseus), *Ulysses* structures numerous episodes to suggest parallels with the Greek epic, and transforms the twenty-year Homeric journey home into the day-long wanderings through Dublin of an unheroic advertising man, Leopold Bloom, and a rebellious young teacher and writer from *Portrait*, Stephen Dedalus.

Bloom is in one sense a perfectly ordinary man, the "common man" of modern society. He comes to no great decisions (whereas Stephen decides to leave Ireland and dedicate himself to art), and his life will continue its uneventful and somewhat downtrodden way. Yet Bloom is the most fully developed character in the book, a man whose dimensions encompass the mythic overtones of the outcast (Ulysses or the Wandering Jew), the psychological tension of a father and husband cut off from family relationships, and (in bathroom, bedroom, and meat market) the most mundane domestic details. The ancient Ulysses was a man of many roles, and so is the modern Bloom. If the *Odyssey* has been described as one of the first voyages of Everyman, *Ulysses* shows Everyman in the twentieth century. According to T. S. Eliot, Joyce's paralleling of ancient myth and modern life is more than literary homage; it is "a way of controlling, of ordering, of giving a shape and significance to the immense panorama of futility and anarchy which is contemporary history."

There is no classical parallel, however, for the language of *Ulysses*, which has long been recognized as a paradigm of modernist style. Its quick shifts in points of view, changes of narrative voice, and blendings of the most exacting realism with hallucinatory scenes that combine memory and distorted current vision are the literary equivalent of cinematic montage. In addition, Joyce abandoned the regular syntax and logical sequences of traditional narrative for a style that tried to represent the flow of thought and emotion in a character's mind. A development of the "interior monologue," this stream of consciousness technique is far looser and freer in its fragmented, punning, freely associating representation of consciousness. Sometimes it is a sleepy jangle in which the relaxed mind lazily plays with sound associations: "Sinbad the Sailor and Tinbad the Tailor and Jinbad the Jailer and Whinbad the Whaler and Ninbad the Nailer and . . ." Sometimes it is more obscure, as in the introduction to a bar scene with its associative, fragmented vision and imitations of different sounds: "Bronze by gold heard the hoofirons, steelyringing Imperthnthn thnthnthn. Chips, picking chips off rocky thumbnail, chips. Horrid! And gold flushed more. A husky fifenote blew. Blew. Blue bloom in on the Gold pinnacled hair." In the famous ending to the novel, it combines passion and response in specific images called up from memory, as his wife, Molly, recalls her first yielding to Bloom: "O that awful deepdown torrent O and the sea the sea crimson sometimes like fire and the glorious sunsets and the figtrees in the Alameda gardens yes and all the queer little streets and pink and blue and yellow houses and the rosegardens and the jessamine and geraniums and cactuses . . . yes and then he asked me would I yes to say yes my mountain flower and first I put my arms around him yes and drew him down to me so he could feel my breasts all perfume yes and his heart was going like mad and yes I said yes I will Yes." The extraordinary thing about Joyce's stream-of-consciousness technique, as the perspicacious Judge Woolsey commented in his court decision, was that it represents the many layers of experience making up each individual's current consciousness: "Not only what is in the focus of each man's observation of the actual things about him, but also in a penumbral zone residua of past impressions, some recent and some drawn up by association from the domain of the subconscious." Taken to the extreme, it is so completely individualized that a reader who remains outside the personal code cannot break in; at its best, though, it can draw on echoes and clues already present in the text. The complicated inner reference in *Ulysses* provided a glimpse of unparalleled richness into human awareness and set a challenging example for narrative style after Joyce.

After the publication of *Ulysses*, Joyce spent the next seventeen years writing an even more complex work: *Finnegans Wake* (1939). Despite the title, which refers to a ballad in which the bricklayer Tim Finnegan is brought back to life at his wake when somebody spills whisky on him, the novel is the multivoiced, multidimensional dream of Humphrey Chimpden Earwicker: HCE, Here Comes Everybody, Haveth Childers Everywhere, Tristan, Humpty-Dumpty, and Allmen. HCE's dream includes his wife, Anna Earwicker, as Anna Livia Plurabelle, ALP, the voice of the river Liffey, or a suggestion of historical "holy wars," and together they constitute the originating pair of Adam and Eve. *Finnegans Wake* expands on the encyclopedic series of literary and cultural references underlying *Ulysses* and does so in language that has been even more radically broken apart and reassembled. Digressing exuberantly in all directions at once, with complex puns and hybrid words that mix languages, *Finnegans Wake* is—in spite of its cosmic symbolism—a game of language and reference by an artist "hoppy on akkant of his joyicity." It has not achieved the wide audience of *Portrait* or *Ulysses*, but when Joyce died in Zurich in 1941 he considered it the culmination of his career as a writer.

The Dead is the last and by far the fullest story in *Dubliners*, and it recapitulates many of the volume's themes. In 1906, Joyce had written to his publisher that the collection would be "a chapter of the moral history of my country," and he further explained that he had chosen Dublin because it was the "centre of paralysis" in Ireland. The city formed a background of blunted hopes and lost dreams: desperately poor, with large slums and many more people than jobs, it stagnated in political, religious, and cultural divisions that color the lives of characters in these stories. The book is arranged, Joyce explained, in an order that represents four aspects of life in the city: "childhood, adolescence, maturity and public life." Individual stories focus on one or a few characters, who may dream of a better life but are eventually frustrated by, or sink voluntarily back into, their shabby reality. Stories often end with a moment of special insight (an epiphany), visible to the reader but not always to the protagonist, that puts events in sharp and illuminating perspective.

Joyce's work draws heavily on real life, including his own; and several aspects of *The Dead* recall—and transmute—elements in his own life. As in other stories, the neighborhood setting is familiar from his youth. The real-life models for Miss Kate and Miss Julia were indeed music teachers (but they were married). Mr. Bartell d'Arcy evokes a contemporary tenor who performed under a similar name. The figure of Gabriel Conroy, who writes reviews for local journals, dislikes Irish nationalism, and prefers European culture, physically resembles photographs of Joyce—a lesser Joyce who might never have had the courage to leave home for Europe. The tale of Gretta's dead admirer, Michael Furey, echoes Nora Barnacle's similar experience. The sources of *Dubliners*, whether personal or social, are all inescapably real: so real, including coarse language and contemporary allusions, that publishers were unwilling to produce the volume for fear of libel or obscenity charges. An Irish publisher went so far as to print a censored version in 1909, but subsequently burned all the copies when he and Joyce had further disputes. In 1914, some nine years after its initial (later retracted) acceptance, *Dubliners* finally appeared.

The Dead is divided into three parts, chronicling the stages of the Misses Morkan's party and also the stages by which Gabriel Conroy moves from the rather pompous, insecure, and externally oriented figure of the beginning to a man who has been forced to reassess himself and human relationships at the end. The party is an annual dinner dance that takes place after the New Year, probably on January 6, the Catholic Feast of the Epiphany (which many have connected with Gabriel's personal epiphany at the end of the story). A jovial occasion, it brings together friends and acquaintances for an evening of music, dancing, sumptuous food, and a formal after-dinner speech that Gabriel delivers. The undercurrents are not always harmonious, however, for small anxieties and personal frictions crop up that both create a realistic picture and suggest tensions in contemporary Irish society: nationalism, religion, poverty, and class differences. Gabriel has a position to maintain, and he is determined to live up to his responsibilities: he is at once cultured speaker and intellectual, carver and master of ceremonies, and the man whom the Misses Morkan expect to take care of occasional problems like alcoholic guests. He is a complex character, both a writer of real imagination (or we would not have the ending scene) and a narcissistic figure who is so used to focusing on himself that he has drawn apart from other people.

Three times in the course of the story Gabriel's self-image is challenged, each time by a woman. Lily, the maidservant in the beginning scene, rebuffs his patronizing questions with a bitter comment about men; immediately, Gabriel worries about his mistake and whether his speech will likewise take the wrong tone for its audience—that is, be above their heads. In the second episode, Miss Ivors's attack on his ignorance of Irish culture shakes him again, for he interprets it as an attempt to make him look ridiculous. Finally, just as Gabriel is thoroughly aroused by watching his wife's graceful figure and hopes to recapture a long-lost intimacy, he finds that she is thinking of a long-dead suitor, Michael Furey. Michael died because, ill, he made her a farewell visit; and Gabriel realizes that his own colorless self will never rival the memory of Furey's passionate devotion. The jovial evening has lost its sparkle; once again, Gabriel looks back in frustration and unhappiness, and this time recognizes signs of death and delusion everywhere. By the end of *The Dead,* he feels his identity "fading out into a grey impalpable world," approaching—in his artistic imagination—a state in which both living and dead are one community, blanketed by the snow that falls throughout the universe in his final vision.

The Dead

Lily, the caretaker's daughter, was literally run off her feet. Hardly had she brought one gentleman into the little pantry behind the office on the ground floor and helped him off with his overcoat than the wheezy hall-door bell clanged again and she had to scamper along the bare hallway to let in another guest. It was well for her she had not to attend to the ladies also. But Miss Kate and Miss Julia had thought of that and had converted the bathroom upstairs into a ladies' dressing-room. Miss Kate and Miss Julia were there, gossiping and laughing and fussing, walking after each other to the head of the stairs, peering down over the banisters and calling down to Lily to ask her who had come.

It was always a great affair, the Misses Morkan's annual dance. Everybody who knew them came to it, members of the family, old friends of the family, the members of Julia's choir, any of Kate's pupils that were grown up enough and even some of Mary Jane's pupils too. Never once had it fallen flat. For years and years it had gone off in splendid style as long as anyone could remember; ever since Kate and Julia, after the death of their brother Pat, had left the house in Stoney Batter and taken Mary Jane, their only niece, to live with them in the dark gaunt house on Usher's Island,[1] the upper part of which they had rented from Mr. Fulham, the cornfactor on the ground floor. That was a good thirty years ago if it was a day. Mary Jane, who was then a little girl in short clothes, was now the main prop of the household for she had the organ[2] in Haddington Road. She had been through the Academy[3] and gave a pupils' concert every year in the upper room of the Antient Concert Rooms. Many of her pupils belonged to better-class families on the Kingstown and Dalkey line.[4] Old as they were, her aunts also did their share. Julia, though she was quite grey, was still the leading soprano in Adam and Eve's, and Kate, being too feeble to go about much, gave music lessons to beginners on the old square[5] piano in the back room. Lily, the caretaker's daughter, did housemaid's work for them. Though their life was modest they believed in eating well; the best of everything: diamond-bone sirloins, three-shilling tea and the best bottled stout.[6] But Lily seldom made a mistake in the orders so that she got on well with her three mistresses. They were fussy, that was all. But the only thing they would not stand was back answers.

Of course they had good reason to be fussy on such a night. And then it was long after ten o'clock and yet there was no sign of Gabriel and his wife. Besides they were dreadfully afraid that Freddy Malins might turn up screwed.[7] They would not wish for worlds that any of Mary Jane's pupils should see him under the influence; and when he was like that it was sometimes very hard to manage him. Freddy Malins always came late but they wondered what could be keeping Gabriel: and that was what brought them every two minutes to the banisters to ask Lily had Gabriel or Freddy come.

—O, Mr. Conroy, said Lily to Gabriel when she opened the door for him,

---

1. Not an island, but an area in western Dublin on the south bank of the river Liffey. Stoney Batter is a street of small shops and a few houses in Dublin.   2. I.e., earned money by playing the organ at church.   3. The Royal Academy of Music.   4. Railway to a fashionable section of Dublin.   5. I.e., upright. *Adam and Eve's:* popular name (taken from a nearby inn) for a Dublin Catholic church.   6. Strong beer.   7. Drunk.

Miss Kate and Miss Julia thought you were never coming. Good-night, Mrs. Conroy.

—I'll engage they did, said Gabriel, but they forgot that my wife here takes three mortal hours to dress herself.

He stood on the mat, scraping the snow from his goloshes, while Lily led his wife to the foot of the stairs and called out:

—Miss Kate, here's Mrs. Conroy.

Kate and Julia came toddling down the dark stairs at once. Both of them kissed Gabriel's wife, said she must be perished alive and asked was Gabriel with her.

—Here I am as right as the mail,[8] Aunt Kate! Go on up. I'll follow, called out Gabriel from the dark.

He continued scraping his feet vigorously while the three women went upstairs, laughing, to the ladies' dressing-room. A light fringe of snow lay like a cape on the shoulders of his overcoat and like toecaps on the toes of his goloshes; and, as the buttons of his overcoat slipped with a squeaking noise through the snow-stiffened frieze, a cold fragrant air from out-of-doors escaped from crevices and folds.

—Is it snowing again, Mr. Conroy? asked Lily.

She had preceded him into the pantry to help him off with his overcoat. Gabriel smiled at the three syllables she had given his surname and glanced at her. She was a slim, growing girl, pale in complexion and with hay-coloured hair. The gas in the pantry made her look still paler. Gabriel had known her when she was a child and used to sit on the lowest step nursing a rag doll.

—Yes, Lily, he answered, and I think we're in for a night of it.

He looked up at the pantry ceiling, which was shaking with the stamping and shuffling of feet on the floor above, listened for a moment to the piano and then glanced at the girl, who was folding his overcoat carefully at the end of a shelf.

—Tell me, Lily, he said in a friendly tone, do you still go to school?

—O no, sir, she answered. I'm done schooling this year and more.

—O, then, said Gabriel gaily, I suppose we'll be going to your wedding one of these fine days with your young man, eh?

The girl glanced back at him over her shoulder and said with great bitterness:

—The men that is now is only all palaver[9] and what they can get out of you.

Gabriel coloured as if he felt he had made a mistake and, without looking at her, kicked off his goloshes and flicked actively with his muffler at his patent-leather shoes.

He was a stout tallish young man. The high colour of his cheeks pushed upwards even to his forehead where it scattered itself in a few formless patches of pale red; and on his hairless face there scintillated restlessly the polished lenses and the bright gilt rims of the glasses which screened his delicate and restless eyes. His glossy black hair was parted in the middle and brushed in a long curve behind his ears where it curled slightly beneath the groove left by his hat.

8. Reliable as mail delivery.   9. Fancy talk.

When he had flicked lustre into his shoes he stood up and pulled his waistcoat down more tightly on his plump body. Then he took a coin rapidly from his pocket.

—O Lily, he said, thrusting it into her hands, it's Christmastime, isn't it? Just . . . here's a little.. . . .

He walked rapidly towards the door.

—O no, sir! cried the girl, following him. Really, sir, I wouldn't take it.

—Christmas-time! Christmas-time! said Gabriel, almost trotting to the stairs and waving his hand to her in deprecation.

The girl, seeing that he had gained the stairs, called out after him:

—Well, thank you, sir.

He waited outside the drawing-room door until the waltz should finish, listening to the skirts that swept against it and to the shuffling of feet. He was still discomposed by the girl's bitter and sudden retort. It had cast a gloom over him which he tried to dispel by arranging his cuffs and the bows of his tie. Then he took from his waistcoat pocket a little paper and glanced at the headings he had made for his speech. He was undecided about the lines from Robert Browning[1] for he feared they would be above the heads of his hearers. Some quotation that they could recognise from Shakespeare or from the Melodies[2] would be better. The indelicate clacking of the men's heels and the shuffling of their soles reminded him that their grade of culture differed from his. He would only make himself ridiculous by quoting poetry to them which they could not understand. They would think that he was airing his superior education. He would fail with them just as he had failed with the girl in the pantry. He had taken up a wrong tone. His whole speech was a mistake from first to last, an utter failure.

Just then his aunts and his wife came out of the ladies' dressing-room. His aunts were two small plainly dressed old women. Aunt Julia was an inch or so the taller. Her hair, drawn low over the tops of her ears, was grey; and grey also, with darker shadows, was her large flaccid face. Though she was stout in build and stood erect her slow eyes and parted lips gave her the appearance of a woman who did not know where she was or where she was going. Aunt Kate was more vivacious. Her face, healthier than her sister's, was all puckers and creases, like a shrivelled red apple, and her hair, braided in the same old-fashioned way, had not lost its ripe nut colour.

They both kissed Gabriel frankly. He was their favourite nephew, the son of their dead elder sister, Ellen, who had married T. J. Conroy of the Port and Docks.[3]

—Gretta tells me you're not going to take a cab back to Monkstown to-night, Gabriel, said Aunt Kate.

—No, said Gabriel, turning to his wife, we had quite enough of that last year, hadn't we? Don't you remember, Aunt Kate, what a cold Gretta got out of it? Cab windows rattling all the way, and the east wind blowing in after we passed Merrion.[4] Very jolly it was. Gretta caught a dreadful cold.

Aunt Kate frowned severely and nodded her head at every word.

—Quite right, Gabriel, quite right, she said. You can't be too careful.

1. English poet (1812–1889) who had a contemporary reputation for obscurity.   2. Thomas Moore's (1779–1852) immensely popular *Irish Melodies,* a collection of poems with many set to old Irish melodies.
3. The Dublin Port and Docks Board, which regulated customs and shipping.   4. A village on Dublin Bay.

—But as for Gretta there, said Gabriel, she'd walk home in the snow if she were let.

Mrs. Conroy laughed.

—Don't mind him, Aunt Kate, she said. He's really an awful bother, what with green shades for Tom's eyes at night and making him do the dumbbells, and forcing Eva to eat the stirabout.[5] The poor child! And she simply hates the sight of it! . . . O, but you'll never guess what he makes me wear now!

She broke out into a peal of laughter and glanced at her husband, whose admiring and happy eyes had been wandering from her dress to her face and hair. The two aunts laughed heartily too, for Gabriel's solicitude was a standing joke with them.

—Goloshes! said Mrs. Conroy. That's the latest. Whenever it's wet underfoot I must put on my goloshes. To-night even he wanted me to put them on, but I wouldn't. The next thing he'll buy me will be a diving suit.

Gabriel laughed nervously and patted his tie reassuringly while Aunt Kate nearly doubled herself, so heartily did she enjoy the joke. The smile soon faded from Aunt Julia's face and her mirthless eyes were directed towards her nephew's face. After a pause she asked:

—And what are goloshes, Gabriel?

—Goloshes, Julia! exclaimed her sister. Goodness me, don't you know what goloshes are? You wear them over your . . . over your boots, Gretta, isn't it?

—Yes, said Mrs. Conroy. Guttapercha[6] things. We both have a pair now. Gabriel says everyone wears them on the continent.

—O, on the continent, murmured Aunt Julia, nodding her head slowly.

Gabriel knitted his brows and said, as if he were slightly angered:

—It's nothing very wonderful but Gretta thinks it very funny because she says the word reminds her of Christy Minstrels.[7]

—But tell me, Gabriel, said Aunt Kate, with brisk tact. Of course, you've seen about the room. Gretta was saying . . .

—O, the room is all right, replied Gabriel. I've taken one in the Gresham.

—To be sure, said Aunt Kate, by far the best thing to do. And the children, Gretta, you're not anxious about them?

—O, for one night, said Mrs. Conroy. Besides, Bessie will look after them.

—To be sure, said Aunt Kate again. What a comfort it is to have a girl like that, one you can depend on! There's that Lily, I'm sure I don't know what has come over her lately. She's not the girl she was at all.

Gabriel was about to ask his aunt some questions on this point but she broke off suddenly to gaze after her sister who had wandered down the stairs and was craning her neck over the banisters.

—Now, I ask you, she said, almost testily, where is Julia going? Julia! Julia! Where are you going?

Julia, who had gone halfway down one flight, came back and announced blandly:

—Here's Freddy.

At the same moment a clapping of hands and a final flourish of the pianist

---

5. Porridge.   6. A rubberlike substance.   7. *Goloshes* sounds like "golly shoes," which reminds Gretta of the Christy Minstrels, a popular blackface minstrel show.

told that the waltz had ended. The drawing-room door was opened from within and some couples came out. Aunt Kate drew Gabriel aside hurriedly and whispered into his ear:

—Slip down, Gabriel, like a good fellow and see if he's all right, and don't let him up if he's screwed. I'm sure he's screwed. I'm sure he is.

Gabriel went to the stairs and listened over the banisters. He could hear two persons talking in the pantry. Then he recognised Freddy Malins' laugh. He went down the stairs noisily.

—It's such a relief, said Aunt Kate to Mrs. Conroy, that Gabriel is here. I always feel easier in my mind when he's here. . . . Julia, there's Miss Daly and Miss Power will take some refreshment. Thanks for your beautiful waltz, Miss Daly. It made lovely time.

A tall wizen-faced man, with a stiff grizzled moustache and swarthy skin, who was passing out with his partner said:

—And may we have some refreshment, too, Miss Morkan?

—Julia, said Aunt Kate summarily, and here's Mr. Browne and Miss Furlong. Take them in, Julia, with Miss Daly and Miss Power.

—I'm the man for the ladies, said Mr. Browne, pursing his lips until his moustache bristled and smiling in all his wrinkles. You know, Miss Morkan, the reason they are so fond of me is—

He did not finish his sentence, but, seeing that Aunt Kate was out of earshot, at once led the three young ladies into the back room. The middle of the room was occupied by two square tables placed end to end, and on these Aunt Julia and the caretaker were straightening and smoothing a large cloth. On the sideboard were arrayed dishes and plates, and glasses and bundles of knives and forks and spoons. The top of the closed square piano served also as a sideboard for viands and sweets. At a smaller sideboard in one corner two young men were standing, drinking hop-bitters.[8]

Mr. Browne led his charges thither and invited them all, in jest, to some ladies' punch, hot, strong and sweet. As they said they never took anything strong he opened three bottles of lemonade for them. Then he asked one of the young men to move aside, and, taking hold of the decanter, filled out for himself a goodly measure of whiskey. The young men eyed him respectfully while he took a trial sip.

—God help me, he said, smiling, it's the doctor's orders.

His wizened face broke into a broader smile, and the three young ladies laughed in musical echo to his pleasantry, swaying their bodies to and fro, with nervous jerks of their shoulders. The boldest said:

—O, now, Mr. Browne, I'm sure the doctor never ordered anything of the kind.

Mr. Browne took another sip of his whiskey and said, with sidling mimicry:

—Well, you see, I'm like the famous Mrs. Cassidy, who is reported to have said: *Now, Mary Grimes, if I don't take it, make me take it, for I feel I want it.*

His hot face had leaned forward a little too confidentially and he had assumed a very low Dublin accent so that the young ladies, with one instinct, received his speech in silence. Miss Furlong, who was one of Mary Jane's pupils, asked Miss Daly what was the name of the pretty waltz she had

8. Unfermented beer.

played; and Mr. Browne, seeing that he was ignored, turned promptly to the two young men who were more appreciative.

A red-faced young woman, dressed in pansy,[9] came into the room, excitedly clapping her hands and crying:

—Quadrilles![1] Quadrilles!

Close on her heels came Aunt Kate, crying:

—Two gentlemen and three ladies, Mary Jane!

—O, here's Mr. Bergin and Mr. Kerrigan, said Mary Jane. Mr. Kerrigan, will you take Miss Power? Miss Furlong, may I get you a partner, Mr. Bergin. O, that'll just do now.

—Three ladies, Mary Jane, said Aunt Kate.

The two young gentlemen asked the ladies if they might have the pleasure, and Mary Jane turned to Miss Daly.

—O, Miss Daly, you're really awfully good, after playing for the last two dances, but really we're so short of ladies to-night.

—I don't mind in the least, Miss Morkan.

—But I've a nice partner for you, Mr. Bartell D'Arcy, the tenor. I'll get him to sing later on. All Dublin is raving about him.

—Lovely voice, lovely voice! said Aunt Kate.

As the piano had twice begun the prelude to the first figure Mary Jane led her recruits quickly from the room. They had hardly gone when Aunt Julia wandered slowly into the room, looking behind her at something.

—What is the matter, Julia? asked Aunt Kate anxiously. Who is it?

Julia, who was carrying in a column of table-napkins turned to her sister and said, simply, as if the question had surprised her:

—It's only Freddy, Kate, and Gabriel with him.

In fact right behind her Gabriel could be seen piloting Freddy Malins across the landing. The latter, a young man of forty, was of Gabriel's size and build, with very round shoulders. His face was fleshy and pallid, touched with colour only at the thick hanging lobes of his ears and at the wide wings of his nose. He had coarse features, a blunt nose, a convex and receding brow, tumid and protruded lips. His heavy-lidded eyes and the disorder of his scanty hair made him look sleepy. He was laughing heartily in a high key at a story which he had been telling Gabriel on the stairs and at the same time rubbing the knuckles of his left fist backwards and forwards into his left eye.

—Good-evening, Freddy, said Aunt Julia.

Freddy Malins bade the Misses Morkan good-evening in what seemed an offhand fashion by reason of the habitual catch in his voice and then, seeing that Mr. Browne was grinning at him from the sideboard, crossed the room on rather shaky legs and began to repeat in an undertone the story he had just told to Gabriel.

—He's not so bad, is he? said Aunt Kate to Gabriel.

Gabriel's brows were dark but he raised them quickly and answered:

—O no, hardly noticeable.

—Now, isn't he a terrible fellow! she said. And his poor mother made him take the pledge on New Year's Eve. But come on, Gabriel, into the drawing-room.

9. Violet.   1. An intricate square dance for four couples.

Before leaving the room with Gabriel she signalled to Mr. Browne by frowning and shaking her forefinger in warning to and fro. Mr. Browne nodded in answer and, when she had gone, said to Freddy Malins:

—Now, then, Teddy, I'm going to fill you out a good glass of lemonade just to buck you up.

Freddy Malins, who was nearing the climax of his story, waved the offer aside impatiently but Mr. Browne, having first called Freddy Malins' attention to a disarray in his dress,[2] filled out and handed him a full glass of lemonade. Freddy Malins' left hand accepted the glass mechanically, his right hand being engaged in the mechanical readjustment of his dress. Mr. Browne, whose face was once more wrinkling with mirth, poured out for himself a glass of whisky while Freddy Malins exploded, before he had well reached the climax of his story, in a kink of high-pitched bronchitic laughter and, setting down his untasted and overflowing glass, began to rub the knuckles of his left fist backwards and forwards into his left eye, repeating words of his last phrase as well as his fit of laughter would allow him.

Gabriel could not listen while Mary Jane was playing her Academy piece, full of runs and difficult passages, to the hushed drawing-room. He liked music but the piece she was playing had no melody for him and he doubted whether it had any melody for the other listeners, though they had begged Mary Jane to play something. Four young men, who had come from the refreshment-room to stand in the doorway at the sound of the piano, had gone away quietly in couples after a few minutes. The only persons who seemed to follow the music were Mary Jane herself, her hands racing along the key-board or lifted from it at the pauses like those of a priestess in momentary imprecation, and Aunt Kate standing at her elbow to turn the page.

Gabriel's eyes, irritated by the floor, which glittered with beeswax under the heavy chandelier, wandered to the wall above the piano. A picture of the balcony scene in *Romeo and Juliet* hung there and beside it was a picture of the two murdered princes[3] in the Tower which Aunt Julia had worked in red, blue and brown wools when she was a girl. Probably in the school they had gone to as girls that kind of work had been taught, for one year his mother had worked for him as a birthday present a waistcoat of purple tabinet,[4] with little foxes' heads upon it, lined with brown satin and having round mulberry buttons. It was strange that his mother had had no musical talent though Aunt Kate used to call her the brains carrier of the Morkan family. Both she and Julia had always seemed a little proud of their serious and matronly sister. Her photograph stood before the pierglass.[5] She held an open book on her knees and was pointing out something in it to Constantine who, dressed in a man-o'-war suit,[6] lay at her feet. It was she who had chosen the names for her sons for she was very sensible of the dignity of family life. Thanks to her, Constantine was now senior curate in Balbriggan and, thanks to her, Gabriel himself had taken his degree in the Royal University. A shadow passed over his face as he remembered her sullen opposition to his marriage. Some slighting phrases she had used still rankled in his memory;

2. That his fly was open.   3. According to Shakespeare's *Richard III*, the young heirs to the British throne were murdered in the Tower of London by order of their uncle, King Richard III. *Balcony scene:* Shakespeare's *Romeo and Juliet* 2.2.   4. A damasklike fabric.   5. A large mirror.   6. A sailor suit.

she had once spoken of Gretta as being country cute[7] and that was not true of Gretta at all. It was Gretta who had nursed her during all her last long illness in their house at Monkstown.

He knew that Mary Jane must be near the end of her piece for she was playing again the opening melody with runs of scales after every bar and while he waited for the end the resentment died down in his heart. The piece ended with a trill of octaves in the treble and a final deep octave in the bass. Great applause greeted Mary Jane as, blushing and rolling up her music nervously, she escaped from the room. The most vigorous clapping came from the four young men in the doorway who had gone away to the refreshment-room at the beginning of the piece but had come back when the piano had stopped.

Lancers were arranged. Gabriel found himself partnered with Miss Ivors. She was a frank-mannered talkative young lady, with a freckled face and prominent brown eyes. She did not wear a low-cut bodice and the large brooch which was fixed in the front of her collar bore on it an Irish device.

When they had taken their places she said abruptly:

—I have a crow to pluck[8] with you.

—With me? said Gabriel.

She nodded her head gravely.

—What is it? asked Gabriel, smiling at her solemn manner.

—Who is G. C.? answered Miss Ivors, turning her eyes upon him.

Gabriel coloured and was about to knit his brows, as if he did not understand, when she said bluntly:

—O, innocent Amy! I have found out that you write for *The Daily Express*.[9] Now, aren't you ashamed of yourself?

—Why should I be ashamed of myself? asked Gabriel, blinking his eyes and trying to smile.

—Well, I'm ashamed of you, said Miss Ivors frankly. To say you'd write for a rag like that. I didn't think you were a West Briton.[1]

A look of perplexity appeared on Gabriel's face. It was true that he wrote a literary column every Wednesday in *The Daily Express*, for which he was paid fifteen shillings. But that did not make him a West Briton surely. The books he received for review were almost more welcome than the paltry cheque. He loved to feel the covers and turn over the pages of newly printed books. Nearly every day when his teaching in the college was ended he used to wander down the quays to the second-hand booksellers, to Hickey's on Bachelor's Walk, to Webb's or Massey's on Aston's Quay, or to O'Clohissey's in the by-street. He did not know how to meet her charge. He wanted to say that literature was above politics. But they were friends of many years' standing and their careers had been parallel, first at the University and then as teachers: he could not risk a grandiose phrase with her. He continued blinking his eyes and trying to smile and murmured lamely that he saw nothing political in writing reviews of books.

When their turn to cross[2] had come he was still perplexed and inattentive. Miss Ivors promptly took his hand in a warm grasp and said in a soft friendly tone:

—Of course, I was only joking. Come, we cross now.

7. Unintelligent (not acute). 8. A bone to pick; an argument. 9. Conservative Dublin newspaper opposed to Irish independence. 1. An Irishman who supports union with Britain (an insult). 2. A step in the square dance.

When they were together again she spoke of the University question,[3] and Gabriel felt more at ease. A friend of hers had shown her his review of Browning's poems. That was how she had found out the secret: but she liked the review immensely. Then she said suddenly:

—O, Mr. Conroy, will you come for an excursion to the Aran Isles[4] this summer? We're going to stay there a whole month. It will be splendid out in the Atlantic. You ought to come. Mr. Clancy is coming, and Mr. Kilkelly and Kathleen Kearney. It would be splendid for Gretta too if she'd come. She's from Connacht,[5] isn't she?

—Her people are, said Gabriel shortly.

—But you will come, won't you? said Miss Ivors, laying her warm hand eagerly on his arm.

—The fact is, said Gabriel, I have already arranged to go——

—Go where? asked Miss Ivors.

—Well, you know, every year I go for a cycling tour with some fellows and so——

—But where? asked Miss Ivors.

—Well, we usually go to France or Belgium or perhaps Germany, said Gabriel awkwardly.

—And why do you go to France and Belgium, said Miss Ivors, instead of visiting your own land?

—Well, said Gabriel, it's partly to keep in touch with the languages and partly for a change.

—And haven't you your own language to keep in touch with—Irish? asked Miss Ivors.

—Well, said Gabriel, if it comes to that, you know, Irish is not my language.

Their neighbours had turned to listen to the cross-examination. Gabriel glanced right and left nervously and tried to keep his good humour under the ordeal which was making a blush invade his forehead.

—And haven't you your own land to visit, continued Miss Ivors, that you know nothing of, your own people, and your own country?

—O, to tell you the truth, retorted Gabriel suddenly, I'm sick of my own country, sick of it!

—Why? asked Miss Ivors.

Gabriel did not answer for his retort had heated him.

—Why? repeated Miss Ivors.

They had to go visiting together[6] and, as he had not answered her, Miss Ivors said warmly:

—Of course, you've no answer.

Gabriel tried to cover his agitation by taking part in the dance with great energy. He avoided her eyes for he had seen a sour expression on her face. But when they met in the long chain[7] he was surprised to feel his hand firmly pressed. She looked at him from under her brows for a moment quizzically until he smiled. Then, just as the chain was about to start again, she stood on tiptoe and whispered into his ear:

—West Briton!

3. Controversy over the establishment of Irish Catholic universities to rival the dominant Protestant tradition of Oxford and Cambridge in England, and Trinity College in Dublin.   4. Off the west coast of Ireland, idealized by the nationalists as an example of unspoiled Irish culture and language.   5. The westernmost province of Ireland.   6. A square-dance step.   7. Another square-dance step.

When the lancers were over Gabriel went away to a remote corner of the room where Freddy Malins' mother was sitting. She was a stout feeble old woman with white hair. Her voice had a catch in it like her son's and she stuttered slightly. She had been told that Freddy had come and that he was nearly all right. Gabriel asked her whether she had had a good crossing. She lived with her married daughter in Glasgow and came to Dublin on a visit once a year. She answered placidly that she had had a beautiful crossing and that the captain had been most attentive to her. She spoke also of the beautiful house her daughter kept in Glasgow, and of all the nice friends they had there. While her tongue rambled on Gabriel tried to banish from his mind all memory of the unpleasant incident with Miss Ivors. Of course the girl or woman, or whatever she was, was an enthusiast but there was a time for all things. Perhaps he ought not to have answered her like that. But she had no right to call him a West Briton before people, even in joke. She had tried to make him ridiculous before people, heckling him and staring at him with her rabbit's eyes.

He saw his wife making her way towards him through the waltzing couples. When she reached him she said into his ear:

—Gabriel, Aunt Kate wants to know won't you carve the goose as usual. Miss Daly will carve the ham and I'll do the pudding.

—All right, said Gabriel.

—She's sending in the younger ones first as soon as this waltz is over so that we'll have the table to ourselves.

—Were you dancing? asked Gabriel.

—Of course I was. Didn't you see me? What words had you with Molly Ivors?

—No words. Why? Did she say so?

—Something like that. I'm trying to get that Mr. D'Arcy to sing. He's full of conceit, I think.

—There were no words, said Gabriel moodily, only she wanted me to go for a trip to the west of Ireland and I said I wouldn't.

His wife clasped her hands excitedly and gave a little jump.

—O, do go, Gabriel, she cried. I'd love to see Galway again.

—You can go if you like, said Gabriel coldly.

She looked at him for a moment, then turned to Mrs. Malins and said:

—There's a nice husband for you, Mrs. Malins.

While she was threading her way back across the room Mrs. Malins, without adverting to the interruption, went on to tell Gabriel what beautiful places there were in Scotland and beautiful scenery. Her son-in-law brought them every year to the lakes and they used to go fishing. Her son-in-law was a splendid fisher. One day he caught a fish, a beautiful big big fish, and the man in the hotel boiled it for their dinner.

Gabriel hardly heard what she said. Now that supper was coming near he began to think again about his speech and about the quotation. When he saw Freddy Malins coming across the room to visit his mother Gabriel left the chair free for him and retired into the embrasure of the window. The room had already cleared and from the back room came the clatter of plates and knives. Those who still remained in the drawing-room seemed tired of dancing and were conversing quietly in little groups. Gabriel's warm trembling fingers tapped the cold pane of the window. How cool it must be outside! How pleasant it would be to walk out alone, first along by the river and then through the park! The snow would be lying on the branches of the trees and forming a bright cap on the top of the Wellington Monument.[8] How much more pleasant it would be there than at the supper-table!

He ran over the headings of his speech: Irish hospitality, sad memories, the Three Graces, Paris,[9] the quotation from Browning. He repeated to himself a phrase he had written in his review: *One feels that one is listening to a thought-tormented music.* Miss Ivors had praised the review. Was she sincere? Had she really any life of her own behind all her propagandism? There had never been any ill-feeling between them until that night. It unnerved him to think that she would be at the supper-table, looking up at him while he spoke with her critical quizzing eyes. Perhaps she would not be sorry to see him fail in his speech. An idea came into his mind and gave him courage. He would say, alluding to Aunt Kate and Aunt Julia: *Ladies and Gentlemen, the generation which is now on the wane among us may have had its faults but for my part I think it had certain qualities of hospitality, of humour, of humanity, which the new and very serious and hypereducated generation that is growing up around us seems to me to lack.* Very good: that was one for Miss Ivors. What did he care that his aunts were only two ignorant old women?

A murmur in the room attracted his attention. Mr. Browne was advancing from the door, gallantly escorting Aunt Julia, who leaned upon his arm, smiling and hanging her head. An irregular musketry of applause escorted her also as far as the piano and then, as Mary Jane seated herself on the stool, and Aunt Julia, no longer smiling, half turned so as to pitch her voice fairly into the room, gradually ceased. Gabriel recognized the prelude. It was that of an old song of Aunt Julia's—*Arrayed for the Bridal.*[1] Her voice, strong and clear in tone, attacked with great spirit the runs which embellish the air and though she sang very rapidly she did not miss even the smallest of the grace notes. To follow the voice, without looking at the singer's face, was to feel and share the excitement of swift and secure flight. Gabriel applauded loudly with all the others at the close of the song and loud applause was borne in from the invisible supper-table. It sounded so genuine that a little colour struggled into Aunt Julia's face as she bent to replace in the music-stand the old leather-bound song-book that had her initials on the cover. Freddy Malins, who had listened with his head perched sideways to hear her better, was still applauding when everyone else had ceased and talking animatedly to his mother who nodded her head gravely and slowly in acquiescence. At last, when he could clap no more, he stood up suddenly and hurried across the room to Aunt Julia whose hand he seized and held in both his hands, shaking it when words failed him or the catch in his voice proved too much for him.

—I was just telling my mother, he said, I never heard you sing so well, never. No, I never heard your voice so good as it is to-night. Now! Would you believe that now? That's the truth. Upon my word and honour that's the truth. I never heard your voice sound so fresh and so . . . so clear and fresh, never.

---

8. A tall obelisk in Phoenix Park, celebrating the duke of Wellington (1769–1852). 9. The Trojan prince of Homer's *Iliad. Three Graces:* daughters of Zeus and Eurynome in Greek mythology; they embodied (and bestowed) charm. 1. An English lyric by George Linley, drawn from the first act of Vincenzo Bellini's 1835 opera *I Puritani* (The Puritans).

Aunt Julia smiled broadly and murmured something about compliments as she released her hand from his grasp. Mr. Browne extended his open hand towards her and said to those who were near him in the manner of a showman introducing a prodigy to an audience:

—Miss Julia Morkan, my latest discovery!

—He was laughing very heartily at this himself when Freddy Malins turned to him and said:

—Well, Browne, if you're serious you might make a worse discovery. All I can say is I never heard her sing half so well as long as I am coming here. And that's the honest truth.

—Neither did I, said Mr. Browne. I think her voice has greatly improved.

Aunt Julia shrugged her shoulders and said with meek pride:

—Thirty years ago I hadn't a bad voice as voices go.

—I often told Julia, said Aunt Kate emphatically, that she was simply thrown away in that choir. But she never would be said by me.

She turned as if to appeal to the good sense of the others against a refractory child while Aunt Julia gazed in front of her, a vague smile of reminiscence playing on her face.

—No, continued Aunt Kate, she wouldn't be said or led by anyone, slaving there in that choir night and day, night and day. Six o'clock on Christmas morning! And all for what?

—Well, isn't it for the honour of God, Aunt Kate? asked Mary Jane, twisting round on the piano-stool and smiling.

Aunt Kate turned fiercely on her niece and said:

—I know all about the honour of God, Mary Jane, but I think it's not at all honourable for the pope to turn out the women out of the choirs that have slaved there all their lives and put little whipper-snappers of boys over their heads.[2] I suppose it is for the good of the Church if the pope does it. But it's not just, Mary Jane, and it's not right.

She had worked herself into a passion and would have continued in defence of her sister for it was a sore subject with her but Mary Jane, seeing that all the dancers had come back, intervened pacifically:

—Now, Aunt Kate, you're giving scandal to Mr. Browne who is of the other persuasion.

Aunt Kate turned to Mr. Browne, who was grinning at this allusion to his religion, and said hastily:

—O, I don't question the pope's being right. I'm only a stupid old woman and I wouldn't presume to do such a thing. But there's such a thing as common everyday politeness and gratitude. And if I were in Julia's place I'd tell that Father Healy straight up to his face . . .

—And besides, Aunt Kate, said Mary Jane, we really are all hungry and when we are hungry we are all very quarrelsome.

—And when we are thirsty we are also quarrelsome, added Mr. Browne.

—So that we had better go to supper, said Mary Jane, and finish the discussion afterwards.

On the landing outside the drawing-room Gabriel found his wife and Mary Jane trying to persuade Miss Ivors to stay for supper. But Miss Ivors, who had put on her hat and was buttoning her cloak, would not stay. She did not feel in the least hungry and she had already overstayed her time.

2. In 1903, Pope Pius X decreed that all church singers be male.

—But only for ten minutes, Molly, said Mrs. Conroy. That won't delay you.

—To take a pick itself, said Mary Jane, after all your dancing.

—I really couldn't, said Miss Ivors.

—I am afraid you didn't enjoy yourself at all, said Mary Jane hopelessly.

—Ever so much, I assure you, said Miss Ivors, but you really must let me run off now.

—But how can you get home? asked Mrs. Conroy.

—O, it's only two steps up the quay.

Gabriel hesitated a moment and said:

—If you will allow me, Miss Ivors, I'll see you home if you really are obliged to go.

But Miss Ivors broke away from them.

—I won't hear of it, she cried. For goodness sake go in to your suppers and don't mind me. I'm quite well able to take care of myself.

—Well, you're the comical girl, Molly, said Mrs. Conroy frankly.

—*Beannacht libh*,[3] cried Miss Ivors, with a laugh, as she ran down the staircase.

Mary Jane gazed after her, a moody puzzled expression on her face, while Mrs. Conroy leaned over the banisters to listen for the hall-door. Gabriel asked himself was he the cause of her abrupt departure. But she did not seem to be in ill humour: she had gone away laughing. He stared blankly down the staircase.

At that moment Aunt Kate came toddling out of the supper-room, almost wringing her hands in despair.

—Where is Gabriel? she cried. Where on earth is Gabriel? There's everyone waiting in there, stage to let, and nobody to carve the goose!

—Here I am, Aunt Kate! cried Gabriel, with sudden animation, ready to carve a flock of geese, if necessary.

A fat brown goose lay at one end of the table and at the other end, on a bed of creased paper strewn with sprigs of parsley, lay a great ham, stripped of its outer skin and peppered over with crust crumbs, a neat paper frill round its shin and beside this was a round of spiced beef. Between these rival ends ran parallel lines of side-dishes: two little minsters[4] of jelly, red and yellow; a shallow dish full of blocks of blancmange and red jam, a large green leaf-shaped dish with a stalk-shaped handle, on which lay bunches of purple raisins and peeled almonds, a companion dish on which lay a solid rectangle of Smyrna figs, a dish of custard topped with grated nutmeg, a small bowl full of chocolates and sweets wrapped in gold and silver papers and a glass vase in which stood some tall celery stalks. In the center of the table there stood, as sentries to a fruit-stand which upheld a pyramid of oranges and American apples, two squat old-fashioned decanters of cut glass, one containing port and the other dark sherry. On the closed square piano a pudding in a huge yellow dish lay in waiting and behind it were three squads of bottles of stout and ale and minerals,[5] drawn up according to the colours of their uniforms, the first two black, with brown and red labels, the third and smallest squad white, with transverse green sashes.

Gabriel took his seat boldly at the head of the table and, having looked to

---

3. Farewell; blessings on you (Irish).   4. Confectioneries shaped to look like cathedrals.   5. Carbonated drinks.

the edge of the carver, plunged his fork firmly into the goose. He felt quite at ease now for he was an expert carver and liked nothing better than to find himself at the head of a well-laden table.

—Miss Furlong, what shall I send you? he asked. A wing or a slice of the breast?

—Just a small slice of the breast.

—Miss Higgins, what for you?

—O, anything at all, Mr. Conroy.

While Gabriel and Miss Daly exchanged plates of goose and plates of ham and spiced beef Lily went from guest to guest with a dish of hot floury potatoes wrapped in a white napkin. This was Mary Jane's idea and she had also suggested apple sauce for the goose but Aunt Kate had said that plain roast goose without apple sauce had always been good enough for her and she hoped she might never eat worse. Mary Jane waited on her pupils and saw that they got the best slices and Aunt Kate and Aunt Julia opened and carried across from the piano bottles of stout and ale for the gentlemen and bottles of minerals for the ladies. There was a great deal of confusion and laughter and noise, the noise of orders and counter-orders, of knives and forks, of corks and glass-stoppers. Gabriel began to carve second helpings as soon as he had finished the first round without serving himself. Everyone protested loudly so that he compromised by taking a long draught of stout for he had found the carving hot work. Mary Jane settled down quietly to her supper but Aunt Kate and Aunt Julia were still toddling round the table, walking on each other's heels, getting in each other's way and giving each other unheeded orders. Mr. Browne begged of them to sit down and eat their suppers and so did Gabriel but they said there was time enough so that, at last, Freddy Malins stood up and, capturing Aunt Kate, plumped her down on her chair amid general laughter.

When everyone had been well served Gabriel said, smiling:

—Now, if anyone wants a little more of what vulgar people call stuffing let him or her speak.

A chorus of voices invited him to begin his own supper and Lily came forward with three potatoes which she had reserved for him.

—Very well, said Gabriel amiably, as he took another preparatory draught, kindly forget my existence, ladies and gentlemen, for a few minutes.

He sat to his supper and took no part in the conversation with which the table covered Lily's removal of the plates. The subject of talk was the opera company which was then at the Theatre Royal. Mr. Bartell D'Arcy, the tenor, a dark-complexioned young man with a smart moustache, praised very highly the leading contralto of the company but Miss Furlong thought she had a rather vulgar style of production. Freddy Malins said there was a negro chieftain[6] singing in the second part of the Gaiety pantomime who had one of the finest tenor voices he had ever heard.

—Have you heard him? he asked Mr. Bartell D'Arcy across the table.

—No, answered Mr. Bartell D'Arcy carelessly.

—Because, Freddy Malins explained, now I'd be curious to hear your opinion of him. I think he has a grand voice.

—It takes Teddy to find out the really good things, said Mr. Browne familiarly to the table.

---

6. Actually, a blackface performer.

—And why couldn't he have a voice too? asked Freddy Malins sharply. Is it because he's only a black?

Nobody answered this question and Mary Jane led the table back to the legitimate opera. One of her pupils had given her a pass for *Mignon*.[7] Of course it was very fine, she said, but it made her think of poor Georgina Burns. Mr. Browne could go back farther still, to the old Italian companies that used to come to Dublin—Tietjens, Ilma de Murzka, Campanini, the great Trebelli, Giuglini, Ravelli, Aramburo.[8] Those were the days, he said, when there was something like singing to be heard in Dublin. He told too of how the top gallery of the old Royal used to be packed night after night, of how one night an Italian tenor had sung five encores to *Let Me Like a Soldier Fall*,[9] introducing a high C every time, and of how the gallery boys would sometimes in their enthusiasm unyoke the horses from the carriage of some great *prima donna* and pull her themselves through the streets to her hotel. Why did they never play the grand old operas now, he asked, *Dinorah, Lucrezia Borgia*?[1] Because they could not get the voices to sing them: that was why.

—O, well, said Mr. Bartell D'Arcy, I presume there are as good singers today as there were then.

—Where are they? asked Mr. Browne defiantly.

—In London, Paris, Milan, said Mr. Bartell D'Arcy warmly. I suppose Caruso,[2] for example, is quite as good, if not better than any of the men you have mentioned.

—Maybe so, said Mr. Browne. But I may tell you I doubt it strongly.

—O, I'd give anything to hear Caruso sing, said Mary Jane.

—For me, said Aunt Kate, who had been picking a bone, there was only one tenor. To please me, I mean. But I suppose none of you ever heard of him.

—Who was he, Miss Morkan? asked Mr. Bartell D'Arcy politely.

—His name, said Aunt Kate, was Parkinson. I heard him when he was in his prime and I think he had then the purest tenor voice that was ever put into a man's throat.

—Strange, said Mr. Bartell D'Arcy. I never even heard of him.

—Yes, yes, Miss Morkan is right, said Mr. Browne. I remember hearing of old Parkinson but he's too far back for me.

—A beautiful pure sweet mellow English tenor, said Aunt Kate with enthusiasm.

Gabriel having finished, the huge pudding was transferred to the table. The clatter of forks and spoons began again. Gabriel's wife served out spoonfuls of the pudding and passed the plates down the table. Midway down they were held up by Mary Jane, who replenished them with raspberry or orange jelly or with blancmange and jam. The pudding was of Aunt Julia's making and she received praises for it from all quarters. She herself said that it was not quite brown enough.

—Well, I hope, Miss Morkan, said Mr. Browne, that I'm brown enough for you because, you know, I'm all brown.

All the gentlemen, except Gabriel, ate some of the pudding out of compliment to Aunt Julia. As Gabriel never ate sweets the celery had been left

7. Popular French opera (1866) by Ambroise Thomas.   8. Famous opera singers.   9. From William V. Wallace's romantic light opera *Maritana* (1845).   1. Operas by Giacomo Meyerbeer (1859) and Gaetano Donizetti (1833), respectively.   2. Enrico Caruso (1873–1921).

for him. Freddy Malins also took a stalk of celery and ate it with his pudding. He had been told that celery was a capital thing for the blood and he was just then under doctor's care. Mrs. Malins, who had been silent all through the supper, said that her son was going down to Mount Melleray[3] in a week or so. The table then spoke of Mount Melleray, how bracing the air was down there, how hospitable the monks were and how they never asked for a penny-piece from their guests.

—And do you mean to say, asked Mr. Browne incredulously, that a chap can go down there and put up there as if it were a hotel and live on the fat of the land and then come away without paying a farthing?

—O, most people give some donation to the monastery when they leave, said Mary Jane.

—I wish we had an institution like that in our Church, said Mr. Browne candidly.

He was astonished to hear that the monks never spoke, got up at two in the morning and slept in their coffins.[4] He asked what they did it for.

—That's the rule of the order, said Aunt Kate firmly.

—Yes, but why? asked Mr. Browne.

Aunt Kate repeated that it was the rule, that was all. Mr. Browne still seemed not to understand. Freddy Malins explained to him, as best he could, that the monks were trying to make up for the sins committed by all the sinners in the outside world. The explanation was not very clear for Mr. Browne grinned and said:

—I like that idea very much but wouldn't a comfortable spring bed do them as well as a coffin?

—The coffin, said Mary Jane, is to remind them of their last end.

As the subject had grown lugubrious it was buried in a silence of the table during which Mrs. Malins could be heard saying to her neighbour in an indistinct undertone:

—They are very good men, the monks, very pious men.

The raisins and almonds and figs and apples and oranges and chocolates and sweets were now passed about the table and Aunt Julia invited all the guests to have either port or sherry. At first Mr. Bartell D'Arcy refused to take either but one of his neighbours nudged him and whispered something to him upon which he allowed his glass to be filled. Gradually as the last glasses were being filled the conversation ceased. A pause followed, broken only by the noise of the wine and by unsettlings of chairs. The Misses Morkan, all three, looked down at the tablecloth. Someone coughed once or twice and then a few gentlemen patted the table gently as a signal for silence. The silence came and Gabriel pushed back his chair and stood up.

The patting at once grew louder in encouragement and then ceased altogether. Gabriel leaned his ten trembling fingers on the tablecloth and smiled nervously at the company. Meeting a row of upturned faces he raised his eyes to the chandelier. The piano was playing a waltz tune and he could hear the skirts sweeping against the drawing-room door. People, perhaps, were standing in the snow on the quay outside, gazing up at the lighted windows and listening to the waltz music. The air was pure there. In the distance lay the park where the trees were weighted with snow. The Wellington Monu-

3. A Trappist abbey whose hospitality included the treatment of wealthy alcoholics.   4. The coffin story is a popular fiction.

ment wore a gleaming cap of snow that flashed westward over the white field of Fifteen Acres.[5]

He began:

—Ladies and Gentlemen.

—It has fallen to my lot this evening, as in years past, to perform a very pleasing task but a task for which I am afraid my poor powers as a speaker are all too inadequate.

—No, no! said Mr. Browne.

—But, however that may be, I can only ask you to-night to take the will for the deed and to lend me your attention for a few moments while I endeavour to express to you in words what my feelings are on this occasion.

—Ladies and Gentlemen. It is not the first time that we have gathered together under this hospitable roof, around this hospitable board. It is not the first time that we have been the recipients—or perhaps, I had better say, the victims—of the hospitality of certain good ladies.

He made a circle in the air with his arm and paused. Everyone laughed or smiled at Aunt Kate and Aunt Julia and Mary Jane who all turned crimson with pleasure. Gabriel went on more boldly:

—I feel more strongly with every recurring year that our country has no tradition which does it so much honour and which it should guard so jealously as that of its hospitality. It is a tradition that is unique as far as my experience goes (and I have visited not a few places abroad) among the modern nations. Some would say, perhaps, that with us it is rather a failing than anything to be boasted of. But granted even that, it is, to my mind, a princely failing, and one that I trust will long be cultivated among us. Of one thing, at least, I am sure. As long as this one roof shelters the good ladies aforesaid—and I wish from my heart it may do so for many and many a long year to come—the tradition of genuine warm-hearted courteous Irish hospitality, which our forefathers have handed down to us and which we in turn must hand down to our descendants, is still alive among us.

A hearty murmur of assent ran around the table. It shot through Gabriel's mind that Miss Ivors was not there and that she had gone away discourteously: and he said with confidence in himself:

—Ladies and Gentlemen.

—A new generation is growing up in our midst, a generation actuated by new ideas and new principles. It is serious and enthusiastic for these new ideas and its enthusiasm, even when it is misdirected, is, I believe, in the main sincere. But we are living in a skeptical and, if I may use the phrase, a thought-tormented age: and sometimes I fear that this new generation, educated or hypereducated as it is, will lack those qualities of humanity, of hospitality, of kindly humour which belonged to an older day. Listening to-night to the names of all those great singers of the past it seemed to me, I must confess, that we were living in a less spacious age. Those days might, without exaggeration, be called spacious days: and if they are gone beyond recall let us hope, at least, that in gatherings such as this we shall still speak of them with pride and affection, still cherish in our hearts the memory of those dead and gone great ones whose fame the world will not willingly let die.

—Hear, hear! said Mr. Browne loudly.

---

5. A section of Phoenix Park used for British military reviews.

—But yet, continued Gabriel, his voice falling into a softer inflection, there are always in gatherings such as this sadder thoughts that will recur to our minds: thoughts of the past, of youth, of changes, of absent faces that we miss here tonight. Our path through life is strewn with many such sad memories: and were we to brood upon them always we could not find the heart to go on bravely with our work among the living. We have all of us living duties and living affections which claim, and rightly claim, our strenuous endeavours.

—Therefore, I will not linger on the past. I will not let any gloomy moralising intrude upon us here to-night. Here we are gathered together for a brief moment from the bustle and rush of our everyday routine. We are met here as friends, in the spirit of good-fellowship, as colleagues, also to a certain extent, in the true spirit of *camaraderie*, and as the guests of—what shall I call them?—the Three Graces of the Dublin musical world.

The table burst into applause and laughter at this sally. Aunt Julia vainly asked each of her neighbours in turn to tell her what Gabriel had said.

—He says we are the Three Graces, Aunt Julia, said Mary Jane.

Aunt Julia did not understand but she looked up, smiling, at Gabriel, who continued in the same vein:

—Ladies and Gentlemen.

—I will not attempt to play to-night the part that Paris played on another occasion.[6] I will not attempt to choose between them. The task would be an invidious one and one beyond my poor powers. For when I view them in turn, whether it be our chief hostess herself, whose good heart, whose too good heart, has become a byword with all who know her, or her sister, who seems to be gifted with perennial youth and whose singing must have been a surprise and a revelation to us all to-night, or, last but not least, when I consider our youngest hostess, talented, cheerful, hard-working and the best of nieces, I confess, Ladies and Gentlemen, that I do not know to which of them I should award the prize.

Gabriel glanced down at his aunts and, seeing the large smile on Aunt Julia's face and the tears which had risen to Aunt Kate's eyes, hastened to his close. He raised his glass of port gallantly, while every member of the company fingered a glass expectantly, and said loudly:

—Let us toast them all three together. Let us drink to their health, wealth, long life, happiness and prosperity and may they long continue to hold the proud and self-won position which they hold in their profession and the position of honour and affection which they hold in our hearts.

All the guests stood up, glass in hand, and, turning towards the three seated ladies, sang in unison, with Mr. Browne as leader:

> *For they are jolly gay fellows,*
> *For they are jolly gay fellows,*
> *For they are jolly gay fellows,*
> *Which nobody can deny.*

Aunt Kate was making frank use of her handkerchief and even Aunt Julia seemed moved. Freddy Malins beat time with his pudding-fork and the sing-

---

6. Paris was required to judge a beauty contest between the Greek goddesses Hera, Athena, and Aphrodite; see n. 9, p. 1903.

ers turned towards one another, as if in melodious conference, while they sang, with emphasis:

> *Unless he tells a lie,*
> *Unless he tells a lie,*

Then, turning once more towards their hostesses, they sang:

> *For they are jolly gay fellows,*
> *For they are jolly gay fellows,*
> *For they are jolly gay fellows,*
> *Which nobody can deny.*

The acclamation which followed was taken up beyond the door of the supper-room by many of the other guests and renewed time after time, Freddy Malins acting as officer with his fork on high.

The piercing morning air came into the hall where they were standing so that Aunt Kate said:

—Close the door, somebody. Mrs. Malins will get her death of cold.

—Browne is out there, Aunt Kate, said Mary Jane.

—Browne is everywhere, said Aunt Kate, lowering her voice.

Mary Jane laughed at her tone.

—Really, she said archly, he is very attentive.

—He has been laid on here like the gas, said Aunt Kate in the same tone, all during the Christmas.

She laughed herself this time good-humouredly and then added quickly:

—But tell him to come in, Mary Jane, and close the door. I hope to goodness he didn't hear me.

At that moment the hall-door was opened and Mr. Browne came in from the doorstep, laughing as if his heart would break. He was dressed in a long green overcoat with mock astrakhan cuffs and collar and wore on his head an oval fur cap. He pointed down the snow-covered quay from where the sound of shrill prolonged whistling was borne in.

—Teddy will have all the cabs in Dublin out, he said.

Gabriel advanced from the little pantry behind the office, struggling into his overcoat and, looking round the hall, said:

—Gretta not down yet?

—She's getting on her things, Gabriel, said Aunt Kate.

—Who's playing up there? asked Gabriel.

—Nobody. They're all gone.

—O no, Aunt Kate, said Mary Jane. Bartell D'Arcy and Miss O'Callaghan aren't gone yet.

—Someone is strumming at the piano, anyhow, said Gabriel.

Mary Jane glanced at Gabriel and Mr. Browne and said with a shiver:

—It makes me feel cold to look at you two gentlemen muffled up like that. I wouldn't like to face your journey home at this hour.

—I'd like nothing better this minute, said Mr. Browne stoutly, than a rattling fine walk in the country or a fast drive with a good spanking goer between the shafts.

—We used to have a very good horse and trap at home, said Aunt Julia sadly.

—The never-to-be-forgotten Johnny, said Mary Jane, laughing.

Aunt Kate and Gabriel laughed too.

—Why, what was wonderful about Johnny? asked Mr. Browne.

—The late lamented Patrick Morkan, our grandfather, that is, explained Gabriel, commonly known in his later years as the old gentleman, was a glue-boiler.

—O, now, Gabriel, said Aunt Kate, laughing, he had a starch mill.

—Well, glue or starch, said Gabriel, the old gentleman had a horse by the name of Johnny. And Johnny used to work in the old gentleman's mill, walking round and round in order to drive the mill. That was all very well; but now comes the tragic part about Johnny. One fine day the old gentleman thought he'd like to drive out with the quality to a military review in the park.

—The Lord have mercy on his soul, said Aunt Kate compassionately.

—Amen, said Gabriel. So the old gentleman, as I said, harnessed Johnny and put on his very best tall hat and his very best stock collar and drove out in grand style from his ancestral mansion somewhere near Back Lane,[7] I think.

Everyone laughed, even Mrs. Malins, at Gabriel's manner and Aunt Kate said:

—O now, Gabriel, he didn't live in Back Lane, really. Only the mill was there.

—Out from the mansion of his forefathers, continued Gabriel, he drove with Johnny. And everything went on beautifully until Johnny came in sight of King Billy's[8] statue: and whether he fell in love with the horse King Billy sits on or whether he thought he was back again in the mill, anyhow he began to walk round the statue.

Gabriel paced in a circle round the hall in his goloshes amid the laughter of the others.

—Round and round he went, said Gabriel, and the old gentleman, who was a very pompous old gentleman, was highly indignant. *Go on, sir! What do you mean, sir? Johnny! Johnny! Most extraordinary conduct! Can't understand the horse!*

The peals of laughter which followed Gabriel's imitation of the incident were interrupted by a resounding knock at the hall-door. Mary Jane ran to open it and let in Freddy Malins. Freddy Malins, with his hat well back on his head and his shoulders humped with cold, was puffing and steaming after his exertions.

—I could only get one cab, he said.

—O, we'll find another along the quay, said Gabriel.

—Yes, said Aunt Kate. Better not keep Mrs. Malins standing in the draught.

Mrs. Malins was helped down the front steps by her son and Mr. Browne and, after many manœuvres, hoisted into the cab. Freddy Malins clambered in after her and spent a long time settling her on the seat, Mr. Browne helping him with advice. At last she was settled comfortably and Freddy Malins invited Mr. Browne into the cab. There was a good deal of confused

---

7. A shabby street in a run-down area of Dublin.　　8. William III, king of England from 1689 to 1702, defeated the Irish nationalists at the Battle of the Boyne.

talk, and then Mr. Browne got into the cab. The cabman settled his rug over his knees, and bent down for the address. The confusion grew greater and the cabman was directed differently by Freddy Malins and Mr. Browne, each of whom had his head out through a window of the cab. The difficulty was to know where to drop Mr. Browne along the route and Aunt Kate, Aunt Julia and Mary Jane helped the discussion from the doorstep with cross-directions and contradictions and abundance of laughter. As for Freddy Malins he was speechless with laughter. He popped his head in and out of the window every moment, to the great danger of his hat, and told his mother how the discussion was progressing till at last Mr. Browne shouted to the bewildered cabman above the din of everybody's laughter:

—Do you know Trinity College?

—Yes, sir, said the cabman.

—Well, drive bang up against Trinity College gates, said Mr. Browne, and then we'll tell you where to go. You understand now?

—Yes, sir, said the cabman.

—Make like a bird for Trinity College.

—Right, sir, cried the cabman.

The horse was whipped up and the cab rattled off along the quay amid a chorus of laughter and adieus.

Gabriel had not gone to the door with the others. He was in a dark part of the hall gazing up the staircase. A woman was standing near the top of the first flight, in the shadow also. He could not see her face but he could see the terracotta and salmonpink panels of her skirt which the shadow made appear black and white. It was his wife. She was leaning on the banisters, listening to something. Gabriel was surprised at her stillness and strained his ear to listen also. But he could hear little save the noise of laughter and dispute on the front steps, a few chords struck on the piano and a few notes of a man's voice singing.

He stood still in the gloom of the hall, trying to catch the air that the voice was singing and gazing up at his wife. There was grace and mystery in her attitude as if she were a symbol of something. He asked himself what is a woman standing on the stairs in the shadow, listening to distant music, a symbol of. If he were a painter he would paint her in that attitude. Her blue felt hat would show off the bronze of her hair against the darkness and the dark panels of her skirt would show off the light ones. *Distant Music* he would call the picture if he were a painter.

The hall-door was closed; and Aunt Kate, Aunt Julia and Mary Jane came down the hall, still laughing.

—Well, isn't Freddy terrible? said Mary Jane. He's really terrible.

Gabriel said nothing but pointed up the stairs towards where his wife was standing. Now that the hall-door was closed the voice and the piano could be heard more clearly. Gabriel held up his hand for them to be silent. The song seemed to be in the old Irish tonality[9] and the singer seemed uncertain both of his words and of his voice. The voice, made plaintive by distance and by the singer's hoarseness, faintly illuminated the cadence of the air with words expressing grief:

---

9. Based on five (and later seven) tones rather than the modern eight-tone scale.

> *O, the rain falls on my heavy locks*
> *And the dew wets my skin,*
> *My babe lies cold[1] . . .*

—O, exclaimed Mary Jane. It's Bartell D'Arcy singing and he wouldn't sing all the night. O, I'll get him to sing a song before he goes.

—O do, Mary Jane, said Aunt Kate.

Mary Jane brushed past the others and ran to the staircase but before she reached it the singing stopped and the piano was closed abruptly.

—O, what a pity! she cried. Is he coming down, Gretta?

Gabriel heard his wife answer yes and saw her come down towards them. A few steps behind her were Mr. Bartell D'Arcy and Miss O'Callaghan.

—O, Mr. D'Arcy, cried Mary Jane, it's downright mean of you to break off like that when we were all in raptures listening to you.

—I have been at him all the evening, said Miss O'Callaghan, and Mrs. Conroy too and he told us he had a dreadful cold and couldn't sing.

—O, Mr. D'Arcy, said Aunt Kate, now that was a great fib to tell.

—Can't you see that I'm as hoarse as a crow? said Mr. D'Arcy roughly.

He went into the pantry hastily and put on his overcoat. The others, taken aback by his rude speech, could find nothing to say. Aunt Kate wrinkled her brows and made signs to the others to drop the subject. Mr. D'Arcy stood swathing his neck carefully and frowning.

—It's the weather, said Aunt Julia, after a pause.

—Yes, everybody has colds, said Aunt Kate readily, everybody.

—They say, said Mary Jane, we haven't had snow like it for thirty years; and I read this morning in the newspapers that the snow is general all over Ireland.

—I love the look of snow, said Aunt Julia sadly.

—So do I, said Miss O'Callaghan. I think Christmas is never really Christmas unless we have the snow on the ground.

—But poor Mr. D'Arcy doesn't like the snow, said Aunt Kate, smiling.

Mr. D'Arcy came from the pantry, fully swathed and buttoned, and in a repentant tone told them the history of his cold. Everyone gave him advice and said it was a great pity and urged him to be very careful of his throat in the night air. Gabriel watched his wife who did not join in the conversation. She was standing right under the dusty fanlight and the flame of the gas lit up the rich bronze of her hair which he had seen her drying at the fire a few days before. She was in the same attitude and seemed unaware of the talk about her. At last she turned towards them and Gabriel saw that there was colour on her cheeks and that her eyes were shining. A sudden tide of joy went leaping out of his heart.

—Mr. D'Arcy, she said, what is the name of that song you were singing?

—It's called *The Lass of Aughrim*, said Mr. D'Arcy, but I couldn't remember it properly. Why? Do you know it?

—*The Lass of Aughrim*, she repeated. I couldn't think of the name.

—It's a very nice air, said Mary Jane. I'm sorry you were not in voice tonight.

---

1. From "The Lass of Aughrim," a ballad about a peasant girl seduced by a lord; when she brings her baby to the castle door, the lord's mother imitates his voice and sends her away. Mother and child are drowned at sea, and the repentant lord curses his mother.

—Now, Mary Jane, said Aunt Kate, don't annoy Mr. D'Arcy. I won't have him annoyed.

Seeing that all were ready to start she shepherded them to the door where good-night was said:

—Well, good-night, Aunt Kate, and thanks for the pleasant evening.

—Good-night, Gabriel. Good-night, Gretta!

—Good-night, Aunt Kate, and thanks ever so much. Good-night, Aunt Julia.

—O, good-night, Gretta, I didn't see you.

—Good-night, Mr. D'Arcy. Good-night, Miss O'Callaghan.

—Good-night, Miss Morkan.

—Good-night, again.

—Good-night, all. Safe home.

—Good-night. Good-night.

The morning was still dark. A dull yellow light brooded over the houses and the river; and the sky seemed to be descending. It was slushy underfoot; and only streaks and patches of snow lay on the roofs, on the parapets of the quay and on the area railings. The lamps were still burning redly in the murky air and, across the river, the palace of the Four Courts[2] stood out menacingly against the heavy sky.

She was walking on before him with Mr. Bartell D'Arcy, her shoes in a brown parcel tucked under one arm and her hands holding her skirt up from the slush. She had no longer any grace of attitude but Gabriel's eyes were still bright with happiness. The blood went bounding along his veins; and the thoughts went rioting through his brain, proud, joyful, tender, valorous.

She was walking on before him so lightly and so erect that he longed to run after her noiselessly, catch her by the shoulders and say something foolish and affectionate into her ear. She seemed to him so frail that he longed to defend her against something and then to be alone with her. Moments of their secret life together burst like stars upon his memory. A heliotrope envelope was lying beside his breakfast-cup and he was caressing it with his hand. Birds were twittering in the ivy and the sunny web of the curtain was shimmering along the floor: he could not eat for happiness. They were standing on the crowded platform and he was placing a ticket inside the warm palm of her glove. He was standing with her in the cold, looking in through a grated window at a man making bottles in a roaring furnace. It was very cold. Her face, fragrant in the cold air, was quite close to his; and suddenly she called out to the man at the furnace:

—Is the fire hot, sir?

But the man could not hear her with the noise of the furnace. It was just as well. He might have answered rudely.

A wave of yet more tender joy escaped from his heart and went coursing in warm flood along his arteries. Like the tender fires of stars moments of their life together, that no one knew of or would ever know of, broke upon and illumined his memory. He longed to recall to her those moments, to make her forget the years of their dull existence together and remember only their moments of ecstasy. For the years, he felt, had not quenched his soul or hers. Their children, his writing, her household cares had not quenched

2. The Irish law courts building.

all their souls' tender fire. In one letter that he had written to her then he had said: *Why is it that words like these seem to me so dull and cold? Is it because there is no word tender enough to be your name?*

Like distant music these words that he had written years before were borne towards him from the past. He longed to be alone with her. When the others had gone away, when he and she were in their room in the hotel, then they would be alone together. He would call her softly:

—Gretta!

Perhaps she would not hear at once: she would be undressing. Then something in his voice would strike her. She would turn and look at him.

At the corner of Winetavern Street they met a cab. He was glad of its rattling noise as it saved him from conversation. She was looking out of the window and seemed tired. The others spoke only a few words, pointing out some building or street. The horse galloped along wearily under the murky morning sky, dragging his old rattling box after his heels, and Gabriel was again in a cab with her, galloping to catch the boat, galloping to their honeymoon.

As the cab drove across O'Connell Bridge Miss O'Callaghan said:

—They say you never cross O'Connell Bridge without seeing a white horse.

—I see a white man this time, said Gabriel.

—Where? asked Mr. Bartell D'Arcy.

Gabriel pointed to the statue,[3] on which lay patches of snow. Then he nodded familiarly to it and waved his hand.

—Good-night, Dan, he said gaily.

When the cab drew up before the hotel Gabriel jumped out and, in spite of Mr. Bartell D'Arcy's protest, paid the driver. He gave the man a shilling over his fare. The man saluted and said:

—A prosperous New Year to you, sir.

—The same to you, said Gabriel cordially.

She leaned for a moment on his arm in getting out of the cab and while standing at the curbstone, bidding the others good-night. She leaned lightly on his arm, as lightly as when she had danced with him a few hours before. He had felt proud and happy then, happy that she was his, proud of her grace and wifely carriage. But now, after the kindling again of so many memories, the first touch of her body, musical and strange and perfumed, sent through him a keen pang of lust. Under cover of her silence he pressed her arm closely to his side; and, as they stood at the hotel door, he felt that they had escaped from their lives and duties, escaped from home and friends and run away together with wild and radiant hearts to a new adventure.

An old man was dozing in a great hooded chair in the hall. He lit a candle in the office and went before them to the stairs. They followed him in silence, their feet falling in soft thuds on the thickly carpeted stairs. She mounted the stairs behind the porter, her head bowed in the ascent, her frail shoulders curved as with a burden, her skirt girt tightly about her. He could have flung his arms about her hips and held her still for his arms were trembling with desire to seize her and only the stress of his nails against the palms of his hands held the wild impulse of his body in check. The porter halted on the stairs to settle his guttering candle. They halted too on the steps below him.

3. Of Daniel O'Connell (1775–1847), called "The Liberator" by the Irish independence movement.

In the silence Gabriel could hear the falling of the molten wax into the tray and the thumping of his own heart against his ribs.

The porter led them along a corridor and opened a door. Then he set his unstable candle down on a toilet-table and asked at what hour they were to be called in the morning.

—Eight, said Gabriel.

The porter pointed to the tap of the electric-light and began a muttered apology but Gabriel cut him short.

—We don't want any light. We have light enough from the street. And I say, he added, pointing to the candle, you might remove that handsome article, like a good man.

The porter took up his candle again, but slowly for he was surprised by such a novel idea. Then he mumbled good-night and went out. Gabriel shot the lock to.

A ghostly light from the street lamp lay in a long shaft from one window to the door. Gabriel threw his overcoat and hat on a couch and crossed the room towards the window. He looked down into the street in order that his emotion might calm a little. Then he turned and leaned against a chest of drawers with his back to the light. She had taken off her hat and cloak and was standing before a large swinging mirror, unhooking her waist.[4] Gabriel paused for a few moments, watching her, and then said:

—Gretta!

She turned away from the mirror slowly and walked along the shaft of light towards him. Her face looked so serious and weary that the words would not pass Gabriel's lips. No, it was not the moment yet.

—You looked tired, he said.

—I am a little, she answered.

—You don't feel ill or weak?

—No, tired: that's all.

She went on to the window and stood there, looking out. Gabriel waited again and then, fearing that diffidence was about to conquer him, he said abruptly:

—By the way, Gretta!

—What is it?

—You know that poor fellow Malins? he said quickly.

—Yes. What about him?

—Well, poor fellow, he's a decent sort of chap after all, continued Gabriel in a false voice. He gave me back that sovereign I lent him and I didn't expect it really. It's a pity he wouldn't keep away from that Browne, because he's not a bad fellow at heart.

He was trembling now with annoyance. Why did she seem so abstracted? He did not know how he could begin. Was she annoyed, too, about something? If she would only turn to him or come to him of her own accord! To take her as she was would be brutal. No, he must see some ardour in her eyes first. He longed to be master of her strange mood.

—When did you lend him the pound? she asked, after a pause.

Gabriel stove to restrain himself from breaking out into brutal language about the sottish Malins and his pound. He longed to cry to her from his

---

4. I.e., loosening her waistband.

soul, to crush her body against his, to overmaster her. But he said:

—O, at Christmas, when he opened that little Christmas-card shop in Henry Street.

He was in such a fever of rage and desire that he did not hear her come from the window. She stood before him for an instant, looking at him strangely. Then, suddenly raising herself on tiptoe and resting her hands lightly on his shoulders, she kissed him.

—You are a very generous person, Gabriel, she said.

Gabriel, trembling with delight at her sudden kiss and at the quaintness of her phrase, put his hands on her hair and began smoothing it back, scarcely touching it with his fingers. The washing had made it fine and brilliant. His heart was brimming over with happiness. Just when he was wishing for it she had come to him of her own accord. Perhaps her thoughts had been running with his. Perhaps she had felt the impetuous desire that was in him and then the yielding mood had come upon her. Now that she had fallen to him so easily he wondered why he had been so diffident.

He stood, holding her head between his hands. Then, slipping one arm swiftly about her body and drawing her towards him, he said softly:

—Gretta dear, what are you thinking about?

She did not answer nor yield wholly to his arm. He said again, softly:

—Tell me what it is, Gretta. I think I know what is the matter. Do I know?

She did not answer at once. Then she said in an outburst of tears:

—O, I am thinking about that song, *The Lass of Aughrim*.

She broke loose from him and ran to the bed and, throwing her arms across the bed-rail, hid her face. Gabriel stood stock-still for a moment in astonishment and then followed her. As he passed in the way of the cheval-glass he caught sight of himself in full length, his broad, well-filled shirt-front, the face whose expression always puzzled him when he saw it in a mirror and his glimmering gilt-rimmed eyeglasses. He halted a few paces from her and said:

—What about the song? Why does that make you cry?

She raised her head from her arms and dried her eyes with the back of her hand like a child. A kinder note than he had intended went into his voice.

—Why, Gretta? he asked.

—I am thinking about a person long ago who used to sing that song.

—And who was the person long ago? asked Gabriel, smiling.

—It was a person I used to know in Galway when I was living with my grandmother, she said.

The smile passed away from Gabriel's face. A dull anger began to gather again at the back of his mind and the dull fires of his lust began to glow angrily in his veins.

—Someone you were in love with? he asked ironically.

—It was a young boy I used to know, she answered, named Michael Furey. He used to sing that song, *The Lass of Aughrim*. He was very delicate.

Gabriel was silent. He did not wish her to think that he was interested in this delicate boy.

—I can see him so plainly, she said after a moment. Such eyes as he had: big dark eyes! And such an expression in them—an expression!

—O then, you were in love with him? said Gabriel.

—I used to go out walking with him,[5] she said, when I was in Galway. A thought flew across Gabriel's mind.

—Perhaps that was why you wanted to go to Galway with that Ivors girl? he said coldly.

She looked at him and asked in surprise:

—What for?

Her eyes made Gabriel feel awkward. He shrugged his shoulders and said:

—How do I know? To see him perhaps.

She looked away from him along the shaft of light towards the window in silence.

—He is dead, she said at length. He died when he was only seventeen. Isn't it a terrible thing to die so young as that?

—What was he? asked Gabriel, still ironically.

—He was in the gasworks,[6] she said.

Gabriel felt humiliated by the failure of his irony and by the evocation of this figure from the dead, a boy in the gasworks. While he had been full of memories of their secret life together, full of tenderness and joy and desire, she had been comparing him in her mind with another. A shameful consciousness of his own person assailed him. He saw himself as a ludicrous figure, acting as a pennyboy[7] for his aunts, a nervous well-meaning sentimentalist, orating to vulgarians and idealising his own clownish lusts, the pitiable fatuous fellow he had caught a glimpse of in the mirror. Instinctively he turned his back more to the light lest she might see the shame that burned upon his forehead.

He tried to keep up his tone of cold interrogation but his voice when he spoke was humble and indifferent.

—I suppose you were in love with this Michael Furey, Gretta, he said.

—I was great[8] with him at that time, she said.

Her voice was veiled and sad. Gabriel, feeling now how vain it would be to try to lead her whither he had purposed, caressed one of her hands and said, also sadly:

—And what did he die of so young, Gretta? Consumption, was it?

—I think he died for me, she answered.

A vague terror seized Gabriel at this answer as if, at that hour when he had hoped to triumph, some impalpable and vindictive being was coming against him, gathering forces against him in its vague world. But he shook himself free of it with an effort of reason and continued to caress her hand. He did not question her again for he felt that she would tell him of herself. Her hand was warm and moist: it did not respond to his touch but he continued to caress it just as he had caressed her first letter to him that spring morning.

—It was in the winter, she said, about the beginning of the winter when I was going to leave my grandmother's and come up here to the convent. And he was ill at the time in his lodgings in Galway and wouldn't be let out and his people in Oughterard[9] were written to. He was in decline, they said, or something like that. I never knew rightly.

5. I.e., she dated him.   6. A utilities plant that manufactured coal gas. Working there was an unhealthy occupation.   7. Errand boy.   8. Close friends.   9. A small village in western Ireland.

She paused for a moment and sighed.

—Poor fellow, she said. He was very fond of me and he was such a gentle boy. We used to go out together, walking, you know, Gabriel, like the way they do in the country. He was going to study singing only for his health. He had a very good voice, poor Michael Furey.

—Well; and then? asked Gabriel.

—And then when it came to the time for me to leave Galway and come up to the convent he was much worse and I wouldn't be let see him so I wrote a letter saying I was going up to Dublin and would be back in the summer and hoping he would be better then.

She paused for a moment to get her voice under control and then went on:

—Then the night before I left I was in my grandmother's house in Nun's Island,[1] packing up, and I heard gravel thrown up against the window. The window was so wet I couldn't see so I ran downstairs as I was and slipped out the back into the garden and there was the poor fellow at the end of the garden, shivering.

—And did you not tell him to go back? asked Gabriel.

—I implored of him to go home at once and told him he would get his death in the rain. But he said he did not want to live. I can see his eyes as well as well! He was standing at the end of the wall where there was a tree.

—And did he go home? asked Gabriel.

—Yes, he went home. And when I was only a week in the convent he died and he was buried in Oughterard where his people came from. O, the day I heard that, that he was dead!

She stopped, choking with sobs, and, overcome by emotion, flung herself face downward on the bed, sobbing in the quilt. Gabriel held her hand for a moment longer, irresolutely, and then, shy of intruding on her grief, let it fall gently and walked quietly to the window.

She was fast asleep.

Gabriel, leaning on his elbow, looked for a few moments unresentfully on her tangled hair and half-open mouth, listening to her deep-drawn breath. So she had had that romance in her life: a man had died for her sake. It hardly pained him now to think how poor a part he, her husband, had played in her life. He watched her while she slept as though he and she had never lived together as man and wife. His curious eyes rested long upon her face and on her hair: and, as he thought of what she must have been then, in that time of her first girlish beauty, a strange friendly pity for her entered his soul. He did not like to say even to himself that her face was no longer beautiful but he knew that it was no longer the face for which Michael Furey had braved death.

Perhaps she had not told him all the story. His eyes moved to the chair over which she had thrown some of her clothes. A petticoat string dangled to the floor. One boot stood upright, its limp upper fallen down: the fellow of it lay upon its side. He wondered at his riot of emotions of an hour before.

---

1. An island in the western city of Galway, on which is located the Convent of Poor Clares.

From what had it proceeded? From his aunt's supper, from his own foolish speech, from the wine and dancing, the merrymaking when saying good-night in the hall, the pleasure of the walk along the river in the snow. Poor Aunt Julia! She, too, would soon be a shade with the shade of Patrick Morkan and his horse. He had caught that haggard look upon her face for a moment when she was singing *Arrayed for the Bridal*. Soon, perhaps, he would be sitting in that same drawing-room, dressed in black, his silk hat on his knees. The blinds would be drawn down and Aunt Kate would be sitting beside him, crying and blowing her nose and telling him how Julia had died. He would cast about in his mind for some words that might console her, and would find only lame and useless ones. Yes, yes: that would happen very soon.

The air of the room chilled his shoulders. He stretched himself cautiously along under the sheets and lay down beside his wife. One by one they were all becoming shades. Better pass boldly into that other world, in the full glory of some passion, than fade and wither dismally with age. He thought of how she who lay beside him had locked in her heart for so many years that image of her lover's eyes when he had told her that he did not wish to live.

Generous tears filled Gabriel's eyes. He had never felt like that himself towards any woman but he knew that such a feeling must be love. The tears gathered more thickly in his eyes and in the partial darkness he imagined he saw the form of a young man standing under a dripping tree. Other forms were near. His soul had approached that region where dwell the vast hosts of the dead. He was conscious of, but could not apprehend, their wayward and flickering existence. His own identity was fading out into a grey impal-pable world: the solid world itself which these dead had one time reared and lived in was dissolving and dwindling.

A few light taps upon the pane made him turn to the window. It had begun to snow again. He watched sleepily the flakes, silver and dark, falling obliquely against the lamplight. The time had come for him to set out on his journey westward. Yes, the newspapers were right: snow was general all over Ireland. It was falling on every part of the dark central plain, on the treeless hills, falling softly upon the Bog of Allen and, farther westward, softly falling into the dark mutinous Shannon[2] waves. It was falling, too, upon every part of the lonely churchyard on the hill where Michael Furey lay buried. It lay thickly drifted on the crooked crosses and headstones, on the spears of the little gate, on the barren thorns. His soul swooned slowly as he heard the snow falling faintly through the universe and faintly falling, like the descent of their last end, upon all the living and the dead.

2. An estuary of the Shannon River, west-southwest of Dublin. The Bog of Allen is southwest of Dublin.

VIRGINIA WOOLF
1882–1941

Virginia Woolf did more than write innovative novels that stand on a par with those of Joyce and Proust; she also explained and exemplified a new kind of prose that she associated with feminine consciousness. Woolf is known for her precise evocations of states of mind—or of mind and body, since she refused to separate the two. She structures her novels according to her protagonists' moments of awareness, and in that way joins Proust and Joyce in their move away from the linear plots and objective descriptions of nineteenth-century realism. In novels like *Mrs. Dalloway* and *The Waves,* blocks of time are rearranged, different points of view juxtaposed, and incomplete perspectives set against each other to create a larger pattern. Alternating modes of narration prevent any single reference point and remind the reader that subjectivity is always at work, in literature and in everyday life. Woolf has an additional role in modernist literary history: she was an ardent feminist who explored—directly in her essays and indirectly in her novels and short stories—the situation of women in society, the construction of gender identity, and the predicament of the woman writer.

She was born Adeline Virginia Stephen on January 25, 1882, one of the four children of the eminent Victorian editor and historian Leslie Stephen and his wife, Julia. The family actively pursued intellectual and artistic interests, and Julia was admired and sketched by some of the most famous Pre-Raphaelite artists. Following the customs of the day, only the sons, Adrian and Thoby, were given formal and university education; Virginia and her sister, Vanessa (the painter Vanessa Bell), were instructed at home by their parents and depended for further education on their father's immense library. Virginia bitterly resented this unequal treatment and the systematic discouragement of women's intellectual development that it implied. Throughout her own work, themes of society's different attitudes toward men and women play a strong role, especially in *A Room of One's Own* (1929) and *Three Guineas* (1938). *A Room of One's Own* examines the history of literature written by women and also contains an impassioned plea that women writers be given conditions equal to those available for men: specifically, the privacy of a room in which to write and economic independence. (At the time Woolf wrote, it was unusual for women to have any money of their own or to be able to devote themselves to a career.) After her mother's death in 1895, Woolf was expected to take over the supervision of the family household, which she did until her father's death in 1904. Of fragile physical health after an attack of whooping cough when she was six, she suffered in addition a nervous breakdown after the death of each parent.

Woolf moved to central London with her sister and brother Adrian after their father's death and took a house in the Bloomsbury district. They soon became the focus of what was later called the Bloomsbury Group, a gathering of writers, artists, and intellectuals impatient with conservative Edwardian society, who met regularly to discuss new ideas. It was an eclectic group and included the novelist E. M. Forster, the historian Lytton Strachey, the economist John Maynard Keynes, and the art critics Clive Bell (who married Vanessa) and Roger Fry (who introduced the group to Postimpressionist painters as Édouard Manet and Paul Cézanne). Woolf was not yet writing fiction but contributed reviews to the *Times Literary Supplement,* taught literature and composition at Morley College (an institution with a volunteer faculty that provided educational opportunities for workers), and worked for the adult suffrage movement and a feminist group. In 1912 she married Leonard Woolf, who encouraged her to write and with whom she founded the Hogarth Press in 1917. The press became one of the most respected of the small literary presses and published works by such major authors as T. S. Eliot, Katherine Mansfield, Strachey, Forster, Maxim Gorky, and John Middleton Murry as well as Woolf's own novels and translations of Freud. Over the next two decades she produced her best-known work while coping with frequent bouts of physical and mental illness. Already depressed during World War II and exhausted after the completion of her last novel, *Between the Acts* (1941), she sensed the approach of a serious attack of insanity and the confinement it would entail: in such situations, she was obliged to "rest" and forbidden to read or write. In March 1941, she drowned herself in a river close to her Sussex home.

As a fiction writer, Woolf is best known for her poetic evocations of the way we think and feel. Like Proust and Joyce, she is superbly capable of evoking all the concrete, sensuous details of everyday experience; like them, she explores the structures of consciousness. Her rejection of nineteenth-century realism was not a criticism of the great realist novels like *Madame Bovary;* she turned her attention to more recent and derivative writers. What she really deplored was the microscopic, documentary realism that contemporaries like Arnold Bennett and John Galsworthy drew from the nineteenth-century masters. Their contemporary pretense of scientific objectivity was false, she felt: they claimed to stand outside the scene they described but refused to take into account the fact that there are no neutral observers. Worse, their goal of scientific objectivity often resulted in a mere chronological accumulation of details, the "appalling narrative business of . . . getting from lunch to dinner." Woolf had an explanation for this documentary style: she attributed it to a consciously masculine (or patriarchal) perspective that found security only in logic, order, and the accumulation of knowledge. She proposed, in contrast, a more subjective and, therefore, a more accurate account of experience. Her focus was not so much the object under observation as the way the observer perceived that object: "Let us record the atoms as they fall upon the mind in the order in which they fall, let us trace the pattern, however disconnected and incoherent in appearance, which each sight or incident scores upon the consciousness." Such writing, underwritten by a feminine creative consciousness, would open new avenues for modern literature.

Woolf's writing has been compared with Postimpressionist art in the way that it emphasizes the abstract arrangement of perspectives to suggest additional networks of meaning. After two relatively traditional novels, she began to develop a more flexible approach that openly manipulated fictional structure. The continuously developing plot gave way to an organization by juxtaposed points of view; the experience of "real" or chronological time was displaced (although not completely) by a mind ranging ambiguously among its memories; and an intricate pattern of symbolic themes connected otherwise unrelated characters in the same story. All these techniques made new demands on the reader's ability to synthesize and re-create a whole picture. In *Jacob's Room* (1922), a picture of the hero must be assembled from a series of partial points of view. In *The Waves* (1931), the multiple perspective of different characters soliloquizing on their relationship to the dead Percival is broken by ten interludes that together construct an additional, interacting perspective when they describe the passage of a single day from dawn to dusk. Her novels may expand or telescope the sense of time: *Mrs. Dalloway* (1925) focuses apparently on Clarissa Dalloway's preparations for a party that evening but at the same time calls up—at different times, and according to different contexts—her whole life from childhood to her present age of fifty. Problems of identity are a constant concern in these shifting perspectives, and Woolf often portrays the search of unfulfilled personalities for whatever will complete them. Her work is studded with moments of heightened awareness (comparable to Joyce's epiphanies) in which a character suddenly *sees into* a person or situation. With Woolf, this moment is less a matter of mystical insight (as it is with Joyce) than a creation of the mind using all its faculties.

No one can read Woolf without being struck by the importance she gives to the creative imagination. Her major characters display a sensitivity beyond rational logic, and her narrative style celebrates the aesthetic impulse to coordinate many dimensions inside one harmoniously significant whole. Human beings are not complete, Woolf suggests, without exercising their intuitive and imaginative faculties. Like other modernist writers, she is fascinated by the creative process and often makes reference to it in her work. Whether describing the struggles of a painter in *To the Lighthouse* (1927) or of a writer in the story *An Unwritten Novel,* she illustrates the exploratory and the creative work of human imagination. Not all this work is visible in the finished painting or novel: observing, sifting, coordinating, projecting different interpretations and relationships, the mind performs an enormous labor of coordinating consciousness that cannot be captured entirely in any fixed form.

A *Room of One's Own* itself does not conform to any one fixed form. At once lecture and essay, autobiography and fiction, it originated in a pair of lectures on women and fiction given at Newnham and Girton Colleges (for women) at Cambridge University in 1928. At the beginning, Woolf warns her audience that, instead of defining either women or fiction, she will use "all the liberties and licences of a novelist" to get at the matter obliquely and leave her auditors to sort out the truth from the "lies [that] will flow from my lips." She then retraces the days (that is, the narrator's days) preceding her visit, and lays bare the thought processes leading up to the lecture itself.

The lecture (or, in its written form, Chapter One), continues in the form of a meditative ramble through various parts of Oxbridge (a compound of Oxford and Cambridge universities) and London. It includes the famous, and apparently true, anecdote in which she is warned off the university lawn and forbidden entrance to the library because she is a woman, and a vivid contrast of the food and living quarters of women and men at Oxbridge. By the end of her visit, frustrated, furious, and puzzled, she decides that the subject needs research—and London's British Museum, at least, is open to all.

In Chapter Two, the narrator heads for the British Museum to locate a comprehensive definition of femininity. To her surprise and mounting anger, she discovers that the thousands of books on the subject—all written by fascinated men—define women as inferior animals, useful but alien in nature. Moreover, these same definitions have become prescriptions for generations of young women, who learn to submit and to accept their assigned role as the Victorian "Angel of the House." What they require, asserts the narrator, is the independence brought by an annual income of £500. (Woolf had recently inherited such an income.) Chapter Three pursues similar themes, adding to the £500 the need for "a room of one's own" and the privacy necessary to work out an idea. After a discouraging inspection of Professor Trevelyan's *History of England,* she crystallizes the issues by evoking the career of the "terribly gifted" Judith Shakespeare, William's imaginary sister, who has the same literary and dramatic ambitions as her brother but—as a woman—finds her way blocked at every turn. Woolf does not belittle William Shakespeare, but comments on his freedom: his work reveals an "incandescent, unimpeded mind."

The bleak portrayals in these chapters are lightened by a great deal of satirical wit and humor, often conveyed by calculated fictional distortion. Woolf uses her novelist's license to subvert and criticize the patriarchal message she describes. The Reading Room of the British Museum, august repository of masculine knowledge about women, is seen as a (bald-headed) dome crowned with the names of famous men. The narrator's scholarly seeming list of feminine characteristics is not only amusingly biased but contradictory and incoherent; it implies that the "masculine" passion for lists and documentation is not the best way to learn about human nature. Professor von X.'s portrait is an open caricature linked to suggestions that his scientific disdain hides repressed fear and anger. A *Room of One's Own* is still famous for its vivid, scathing, and occasionally humorous portrayal of women as objects of male definition and disapproval. Its model of a feminine literary history and its hypothesis of a separate feminine consciousness and manner of writing had substantial influence on writers and literary theory in the latter half of the twentieth century.

From A Room of One's Own[1]

CHAPTER ONE

But, you may say, we asked you to speak about women and fiction—what has that got to do with a room of one's own? I will try to explain. When you asked me to speak about women and fiction I sat down on the banks of a river and began to wonder what the words meant. They might mean simply a few remarks about Fanny Burney; a few more about Jane Austen; a tribute to the Brontës and a sketch of Haworth Parsonage under snow; some witticisms if possible about Miss Mitford; a respectful allusion to George Eliot; a reference to Mrs. Gaskell[2] and one would have done. But at second sight the words seemed not so simple. The title women and fiction might mean, and you may have meant it to mean, women and what they are like; or it might mean women and the fiction that they write; or it might mean women and the fiction that is written about them; or it might mean that somehow all three are inextricably mixed together and you want me to consider them in that light. But when I began to consider the subject in this last way, which seemed the most interesting, I soon saw that it had one fatal drawback. I should never be able to come to a conclusion. I should never be able to fulfil what is, I understand, the first duty of a lecturer—to hand you after an hour's discourse a nugget of pure truth to wrap up between the pages of your notebooks and keep on the mantelpiece for ever. All I could do was to offer you an opinion upon one minor point—a woman must have money and a room of her own if she is to write fiction; and that, as you will see, leaves the great problem of the true nature of woman and the true nature of fiction unsolved. I have shirked the duty of coming to a conclusion upon these two questions—women and fiction remain, so far as I am concerned, unsolved problems. But in order to make some amends I am going to do what I can to show you how I arrived at this opinion about the room and the money. I am going to develop in your presence as fully and freely as I can the train of thought which led me to think this. Perhaps if I lay bare the ideas, the prejudices, that lie behind this statement you will find that they have some bearing upon women and some upon fiction. At any rate, when a subject is highly controversial—and any question about sex is that—one cannot hope to tell the truth. One can only show how one came to hold whatever opinion one does hold. One can only give one's audience the chance of drawing their own conclusions as they observe the limitations, the prejudices, the idiosyncrasies of the speaker. Fiction here is likely to contain more truth than fact. Therefore I propose, making use of all the liberties and licences of a novelist, to tell you the story of the two days that preceded my coming here—how,

1. This essay is based upon two papers read to the Arts Society at Newnham and the Odtaa at Girton in October 1928. The papers were too long to be read in full, and have since been altered and expanded [Woolf's note]. Newnham and Girton are women's colleges at Cambridge University, and Odtaa ("One damn thing after another") is the acronym of a literary society. Woolf's talk was entitled *Women and Fiction*. 2. English novelist Elizabeth Gaskell (1810–1865) was the author of *Cranford* (1853). British writers: Fanny (Frances) Burney (1752–1840), author of *Evelina* (1778); Jane Austen (1775–1817), author of *Pride and Prejudice* (1813); the three Brontë sisters, who were raised in the Yorkshire parsonage of Haworth— Charlotte (1816–1855), author of *Jane Eyre* (1847); Emily (1818–1848), author of *Wuthering Heights* (1847); and Anne (1820–1849), author of *Agnes Grey* (1847); Mary Russell Mitford (1787–1855), author of the blank-verse tragedy *Rienzi* (1828); George Eliot (pen name of Mary Ann Evans; 1819–1880), author of *Middlemarch* (1871–72).

bowed down by the weight of the subject which you have laid upon my shoulders, I pondered it, and made it work in and out of my daily life. I need not say that what I am about to describe has no existence; Oxbridge[3] is an invention; so is Fernham; "I" is only a convenient term for somebody who has no real being. Lies will flow from my lips, but there may perhaps be some truth mixed up with them; it is for you to seek out this truth and to decide whether any part of it is worth keeping. If not, you will of course throw the whole of it into the wastepaper basket and forget all about it.

Here then was I (call me Mary Beton, Mary Seton, Mary Carmichael or by any name you please—it is not a matter of any importance) sitting on the banks of a river a week or two ago in fine October weather, lost in thought. That collar I have spoken of, women and fiction, the need of coming to some conclusion on a subject that raises all sorts of prejudices and passions, bowed my head to the ground. To the right and left bushes of some sort, golden and crimson, glowed with the colour, even it seemed burnt with the heat, of fire. On the further bank the willows wept in perpetual lamentation, their hair about their shoulders. The river reflected whatever it chose of sky and bridge and burning tree, and when the undergraduate had oared his boat through the reflections they closed again, completely, as if he had never been. There one might have sat the clock round lost in thought. Thought—to call it by a prouder name than it deserved—had let its line down into the stream. It swayed, minute after minute, hither and thither among the reflections and the weeds, letting the water lift it and sink it, until—you know the little tug—the sudden conglomeration of an idea at the end of one's line: and then the cautious hauling of it in, and the careful laying of it out? Alas, laid on the grass how small, how insignificant this thought of mine looked; the sort of fish that a good fisherman puts back into the water so that it may grow fatter and be one day worth cooking and eating. I will not trouble you with that thought now, though if you look carefully you may find it for yourselves in the course of what I am going to say.

But however small it was, it had, nevertheless, the mysterious property of its kind—put back into the mind, it became at once very exciting, and important; and as it darted and sank, and flashed hither and thither, set up such a wash and tumult of ideas that it was impossible to sit still. It was thus that I found myself walking with extreme rapidity across a grass plot. Instantly a man's figure rose to intercept me. Nor did I at first understand that the gesticulations of a curious-looking object, in a cut-away coat and evening shirt, were aimed at me. His face expressed horror and indignation. Instinct rather than reason came to my help; he was a Beadle;[4] I was a woman. This was the turf; there was the path. Only the Fellows and Scholars are allowed here; the gravel is the place for me. Such thoughts were the work of a moment. As I regained the path the arms of the Beadle sank, his face assumed its usual repose, and though turf is better walking than gravel, no very great harm was done. The only charge I could bring against the Fellows and Scholars of whatever the college might happen to be was that in protection of their turf, which has been rolled for 300 years in succession, they had sent my little fish into hiding.

---

3. A fictional university combining the names of Oxford and Cambridge.   4. A lower-ranked university officer, assistant to authority.

What idea it had been that had sent me so audaciously trespassing I could not now remember. The spirit of peace descended like a cloud from heaven, for if the spirit of peace dwells anywhere, it is in the courts and quadrangles of Oxbridge on a fine October morning. Strolling through those colleges past those ancient halls the roughness of the present seemed smoothed away; the body seemed contained in a miraculous glass cabinet through which no sound could penetrate, and the mind, freed from any contact with facts (unless one trespassed on the turf again), was at liberty to settle down upon whatever meditation was in harmony with the moment. As chance would have it, some stray memory of some old essay about revisiting Oxbridge in the long vacation brought Charles Lamb to mind—Saint Charles, said Thackeray,[5] putting a letter of Lamb's to his forehead. Indeed, among all the dead (I give you my thoughts as they came to me), Lamb is one of the most congenial; one to whom one would have liked to say, Tell me then how you wrote your essays? For his essays are superior even to Max Beerbohm's,[6] I thought, with all their perfection, because of that wild flash of imagination, that lightning crack of genius in the middle of them which leaves them flawed and imperfect, but starred with poetry. Lamb then came to Oxbridge perhaps a hundred years ago. Certainly he wrote an essay—the name escapes me— about the manuscript of one of Milton's poems which he saw here. It was *Lycidas* perhaps, and Lamb wrote how it shocked him to think it possible that any word in *Lycidas* could have been different from what it is. To think of Milton changing the words in that poem seemed to him a sort of sacrilege. This led me to remember what I could of *Lycidas* and to amuse myself with guessing which word it could have been that Milton had altered, and why. It then occurred to me that the very manuscript itself which Lamb had looked at was only a few hundred yards away, so that one could follow Lamb's footsteps across the quadrangle to that famous library[7] where the treasure is kept. Moreover, I recollected, as I put this plan into execution, it is in this famous library that the manuscript of Thackeray's *Esmond* is also preserved. The critics often say that *Esmond* is Thackeray's most perfect novel. But the affectation of the style, with its imitation of the eighteenth century, hampers one, so far as I remember; unless indeed the eighteenth-century style was natural to Thackeray—a fact that one might prove by looking at the manu- script and seeing whether the alterations were for the benefit of the style or of the sense. But then one would have to decide what is style and what is meaning, a question which—but here I was actually at the door which leads into the library itself. I must have opened it, for instantly there issued, like a guardian angel barring the way with a flutter of black gown instead of white wings, a deprecating, silvery, kindly gentleman, who regretted in a low voice as he waved me back that ladies are only admitted to the library if accom- panied by a Fellow of the College or furnished with a letter of introduction.

That a famous library has been cursed by a woman is a matter of complete indifference to a famous library. Venerable and calm, with all its treasures safe locked within its breast, it sleeps complacently and will, so far as I am

5. I.e., William Makepeace Thackeray (1811–1863), whose novels include *Vanity Fair* (1847–48) and *The History of Henry Esmond, Esq.* (1852). *Charles Lamb* (1775–1834): English essayist and letter writer, author of *Essays of Elia* (1823), which contains *Oxford in the Vacation*, mentioned in Woolf's text.   **6.** English caricaturist and writer (1872–1956).   **7.** Trinity College Library, in Cambridge, designed by Sir Chris- topher Wren and built from 1676 to 1684.

concerned, so sleep for ever. Never will I wake those echoes, never will I ask for that hospitality again, I vowed as I descended the steps in anger. Still an hour remained before luncheon, and what was one to do? Stroll on the meadows? sit by the river? Certainly it was a lovely autumn morning; the leaves were fluttering red to the ground; there was no great hardship in doing either. But the sound of music reached my ear. Some service or celebration was going forward. The organ complained magnificently as I passed the chapel door. Even the sorrow of Christianity sounded in that serene air more like the recollection of sorrow than sorrow itself; even the groanings of the ancient organ seemed lapped in peace. I had no wish to enter had I the right, and this time the verger might have stopped me, demanding perhaps my baptismal certificate, or a letter of introduction from the Dean. But the outside of these magnificent buildings is often as beautiful as the inside. Moreover, it was amusing enough to watch the congregation assembling, coming in and going out again, busying themselves at the door of the chapel like bees at the mouth of a hive. Many were in cap and gown; some had tufts of fur on their shoulders; others were wheeled in bath-chairs; others, though not past middle age, seemed creased and crushed into shapes so singular that one was reminded of those giant crabs and crayfish who heave with difficulty across the sand of an aquarium. As I leant against the wall the University indeed seemed a sanctuary in which are preserved rare types which would soon be obsolete if left to fight for existence on the pavement of the Strand.[8] Old stories of old deans and old dons came back to mind, but before I had summoned up courage to whistle—it used to be said that at the sound of a whistle old Professor ——— instantly broke into a gallop—the venerable congregation had gone inside. The outside of the chapel remained. As you know, its high domes and pinnacles can be seen, like a sailing-ship always voyaging never arriving, lit up at night and visible for miles, far away across the hills. Once, presumably, this quadrangle with its smooth lawns, its massive buildings, and the chapel itself was marsh too, where the grasses waved and the swine rooted. Teams of horses and oxen, I thought, must have hauled the stone in wagons from far countries, and then with infinite labour the grey blocks in whose shade I was now standing were poised in order one on top of another, and then the painters brought their glass for the windows, and the masons were busy for centuries[9] up on that roof with putty and cement, spade and trowel. Every Saturday somebody must have poured gold and silver out of a leathern purse into their ancient fists, for they had their beer and skittles presumably of an evening. An unending stream of gold and silver, I thought, must have flowed into this court perpetually to keep the stones coming and the masons working; to level, to ditch, to dig and to drain. But it was then the age of faith, and money was poured liberally to set these stones on a deep foundation, and when the stones were raised, still more money was poured in from the coffers of kings and queens and great nobles to ensure that hymns should be sung here and scholars taught. Lands were granted; tithes were paid. And when the age of faith was over and the age of reason had come, still the same flow of gold and silver

8. One of the busiest streets in London, the main artery between the city and the West End.   9. Just over one century: King's College Chapel at Cambridge was built from 1446 to 1547. The college guidebook attributes its superb craftsmanship to the work of four master masons: Reginald Ely, John Wolrich, Simon Clerk, and John Wastell.

went on; fellowships were founded; lectureships endowed; only the gold and silver flowed now, not from the coffers of the king, but from the chests of merchants and manufacturers, from the purses of men who had made, say, a fortune from industry, and returned, in their wills, a bounteous share of it to endow more chairs, more lectureships, more fellowships in the university where they had learnt their craft. Hence the libraries and laboratories; the observatories; the splendid equipment of costly and delicate instruments which now stands on glass shelves, where centuries ago the grasses waved and the swine rooted. Certainly, as I strolled round the court, the foundation of gold and silver seemed deep enough; the pavement laid solidly over the wild grasses. Men with trays on their heads went busily from staircase to staircase. Gaudy blossoms flowered in window-boxes. The strains of the gramophone blared out from the rooms within. It was impossible not to reflect—the reflection whatever it may have been was cut short. The clock struck. It was time to find one's way to luncheon.

It is a curious fact that novelists have a way of making us believe that luncheon parties are invariably memorable for something very witty that was said, or for something very wise that was done. But they seldom spare a word for what was eaten. It is part of the novelist's convention not to mention soup and salmon and ducklings, as if soup and salmon and ducklings were of no importance whatsoever, as if nobody ever smoked a cigar or drank a glass of wine. Here, however, I shall take the liberty to defy that convention and to tell you that the lunch on this occasion began with soles, sunk in a deep dish, over which the college cook had spread a counterpane of the whitest cream, save that it was branded here and there with brown spots like the spots on the flanks of a doe. After that came the partridges, but if this suggests a couple of bald, brown birds on a plate you are mistaken. The partridges, many and various, came with all their retinue of sauces and salads, the sharp and the sweet, each in its order; their potatoes, thin as coins but not so hard; their sprouts, foliated as rosebuds but more succulent. And no sooner had the roast and its retinue been done with than the silent serving-man, the Beadle himself perhaps in a milder manifestation, set before us, wreathed in napkins, a confection which rose all sugar from the waves. To call it pudding and so relate it to rice and tapioca would be an insult. Meanwhile the wineglasses had flushed yellow and flushed crimson; had been emptied; had been filled. And thus by degrees was lit, halfway down the spine, which is the seat of the soul, not that hard little electric light which we call brilliance, as it pops in and out upon our lips, but the more profound, subtle and subterranean glow, which is the rich yellow flame of rational intercourse. No need to hurry. No need to sparkle. No need to be anybody but oneself. We are all going to heaven and Vandyck[1] is of the company—in other words, how good life seemed, how sweet its rewards, how trivial this grudge or that grievance, how admirable friendship and the society of one's kind, as, lighting a good cigarette, one sunk among the cushions in the window-seat.

If by good luck there had been an ash-tray handy, if one had not knocked the ash out of the window in default, if things had been a little different

1. The Flemish portrait painter Sir Anthony Van Dyck (1599–1641), who was appointed court painter by Charles I of England in 1632 and painted many portraits of the royal family and the nobility.

from what they were, one would not have seen, presumably, a cat without a tail. The sight of that abrupt and truncated animal padding softly across the quadrangle changed by some fluke of the subconscious intelligence the emotional light for me. It was as if some one had let fall a shade. Perhaps the excellent hock was relinquishing its hold. Certainly, as I watched the Manx cat pause in the middle of the lawn as if it too questioned the universe, something seemed lacking, something seemed different. But what was lacking, what was different, I asked myself, listening to the talk. And to answer that question I had to think myself out of the room, back into the past, before the war indeed, and to set before my eyes the model of another luncheon party held in rooms not very far distant from these; but different. Everything was different. Meanwhile the talk went on among the guests, who were many and young, some of this sex, some of that; it went on swimmingly, it went on agreeably, freely, amusingly. And as it went on I set it against the background of that other talk, and as I matched the two together I had no doubt that one was the descendant, the legitimate heir of the other. Nothing was changed; nothing was different save only—here I listened with all my ears not entirely to what was being said, but to the murmur or current behind it. Yes, that was it—the change was there. Before the war at a luncheon party like this people would have said precisely the same things but they would have sounded different, because in those days they were accompanied by a sort of humming noise, not articulate, but musical, exciting, which changed the value of the words themselves. Could one set that humming noise to words? Perhaps with the help of the poets one could. A book lay beside me and, opening it, I turned casually enough to Tennyson.[2] And here I found Tennyson was singing:

> There has fallen a splendid tear
> From the passion-flower at the gate.
> She is coming, my dove, my dear;
> She is coming, my life, my fate;
> The red rose cries, "She is near, she is near";
> And the white rose weeps, "She is late";
> The larkspur listens, "I hear, I hear";
> And the lily whispers, "I wait."

Was that what men hummed at luncheon parties before the war? And the women?

> My heart is like a singing bird
> Whose nest is in a water'd shoot;
> My heart is like an apple tree
> Whose boughs are bent with thick-set fruit;
> My heart is like a rainbow shell
> That paddles in a halcyon sea;
> My heart is gladder than all these
> Because my love is come to me.[3]

Was that what women hummed at luncheon parties before the war?
There was something so ludicrous in thinking of people humming such

---

2. Alfred, Lord Tennyson (1809–1892); a passage from his long poem, *Maud* (1855), follows.   3. The first stanza of *A Birthday*, a short poem by Christina Rossetti (1830–1894).

things even under their breath at luncheon parties before the war that I burst out laughing, and had to explain my laughter by pointing at the Manx cat, who did look a little absurd, poor beast, without a tail, in the middle of the lawn. Was he really born so, or had he lost his tail in an accident? The tailless cat, though some are said to exist in the Isle of Man, is rarer than one thinks. It is a queer animal, quaint rather than beautiful. It is strange what a difference a tail makes—you know the sort of things one says as a lunch party breaks up and people are finding their coats and hats.

This one, thanks to the hospitality of the host, had lasted far into the afternoon. The beautiful October day was fading and the leaves were falling from the trees in the avenue as I walked through it. Gate after gate seemed to close with gentle finality behind me. Innumerable beadles were fitting innumerable keys into well-oiled locks; the treasure-house was being made secure for another night. After the avenue one comes out upon a road—I forget its name—which leads you, if you take the right turning, along to Fernham. But there was plenty of time. Dinner was not till half-past seven. One could almost do without dinner after such a luncheon. It is strange how a scrap of poetry works in the mind and makes the legs move in time to it along the road. Those words—

> There has fallen a splendid tear
> From the passion-flower at the gate.
> She is coming, my dove, my dear—

sang in my blood as I stepped quickly along towards Headingley.[4] And then, switching off into the other measure, I sang, where the waters are churned up by the weir:

> My heart is like a singing bird
> Whose nest is in a water'd shoot;
> My heart is like an apple tree . . .

What poets, I cried aloud, as one does in the dusk, what poets they were!

In a sort of jealousy, I suppose, for our own age, silly and absurd though these comparisons are, I went on to wonder if honestly one could name two living poets now as great as Tennyson and Christina Rossetti were then. Obviously it is impossible, I thought, looking into those foaming waters, to compare them. The very reason why the poetry excites one to such abandonment, such rapture, is that it celebrates some feeling that one used to have (at luncheon parties before the war perhaps), so that one responds easily, familiarly, without troubling to check the feeling, or to compare it with any that one has now. But the living poets express a feeling that is actually being made and torn out of us at the moment. One does not recognize it in the first place; often for some reason one fears it; one watches it with keenness and compares it jealously and suspiciously with the old feeling that one knew. Hence the difficulty of modern poetry; and it is because of this difficulty that one cannot remember more than two consecutive lines of any good modern poet. For this reason—that my memory failed me—the argument flagged for want of material. But why, I continued, moving on towards Headingley, have we stopped humming under our breath at luncheon parties? Why has Alfred ceased to sing

4. In Leeds (Yorkshire).

She is coming, my dove, my dear?

Why has Christina ceased to respond

My heart is gladder than all these
Because my love is come to me?

Shall we lay the blame on the war? When the guns fired in August 1914, did the faces of men and women show so plain in each other's eyes that romance was killed? Certainly it was a shock (to women in particular with their illusions about education, and so on) to see the faces of our rulers in the light of the shell-fire. So ugly they looked—German, English, French—so stupid. But lay the blame where one will, on whom one will, the illusion which inspired Tennyson and Christina Rossetti to sing so passionately about the coming of their loves is far rarer now than then. One has only to read, to look, to listen, to remember. But why say "blame"? Why, if it was an illusion, not praise the catastrophe, whatever it was, that destroyed illusion and put truth in its place? For truth . . . those dots mark the spot where, in search of truth, I missed the turning up to Fernham. Yes indeed, which was truth and which was illusion, I asked myself. What was the truth about these houses, for example, dim and festive now with their red windows in the dusk, but raw and red and squalid, with their sweets and their boot-laces, at nine o'clock in the morning? And the willows and the river and the gardens that run down to the river, vague now with the mist stealing over them, but gold and red in the sunlight—which was the truth, which was the illusion about them? I spare you the twists and turns of my cogitations, for no conclusion was found on the road to Headingley, and I ask you to suppose that I soon found out my mistake about the turning and retraced my steps to Fernham.

As I have said already that it was an October day, I dare not forfeit your respect and imperil the fair name of fiction by changing the season and describing lilacs hanging over garden walls, crocuses, tulips and other flowers of spring. Fiction must stick to facts, and the truer the facts the better the fiction—so we are told. Therefore it was still autumn and the leaves were still yellow and falling, if anything, a little faster than before, because it was now evening (seven twenty-three to be precise) and a breeze (from the southwest to be exact) had risen. But for all that there was something odd at work:

My heart is like a singing bird
Whose nest is in a water'd shoot;
My heart is like an apple tree
Whose boughs are bent with thick-set fruit—

perhaps the words of Christina Rossetti were partly responsible for the folly of the fancy—it was nothing of course but a fancy—that the lilac was shaking its flowers over the garden walls, and the brimstone butterflies were scudding hither and thither, and the dust of the pollen was in the air. A wind blew, from what quarter I know not, but it lifted the half-grown leaves so that there was a flash of silver grey in the air. It was the time between the lights when colours undergo their intensification and purples and golds burn in windowpanes like the beat of an excitable heart; when for some reason the beauty of the world revealed and yet soon to perish (here I pushed into the garden, for, unwisely, the door was left open and no beadles seemed about), the beauty of the world which is so soon to perish, has two edges, one of laughter, one of anguish, cutting the heart asunder. The gardens of Fernham lay before me in the spring twilight, wild and open, and in the long grass, sprinkled and carelessly flung, were daffodils and bluebells, not orderly perhaps at the best of times, and now wind-blown and waving as they tugged at their roots. The windows of the building, curved like ships' windows among generous waves of red brick, changed from lemon to silver under the flight of the quick spring clouds. Somebody was in a hammock, somebody, but in this light they were phantoms only, half guessed, half seen, raced across the grass—would no one stop her?—and then on the terrace, as if popping out to breathe the air, to glance at the garden, came a bent figure, formidable yet humble, with her great forehead and her shabby dress—could it be the famous scholar, could it be J—— H—— herself?[5] All was dim, yet intense too, as if the scarf which the dusk had flung over the garden were torn asunder by star or sword—the flash of some terrible reality leaping, as its way is, out of the heart of the spring. For youth——

Here was my soup. Dinner was being served in the great dining-hall. Far from being spring it was in fact an evening in October. Everybody was assembled in the big dining-room. Dinner was ready. Here was the soup. It was a plain gravy soup. There was nothing to stir the fancy in that. One could have seen through the transparent liquid any pattern that there might have been on the plate itself. But there was no pattern. The plate was plain. Next came beef with its attendant greens and potatoes—a homely trinity, suggesting the rumps of cattle in a muddy market, and sprouts curled and yellowed at the edge, and bargaining and cheapening, and women with string bags on Monday morning. There was no reason to complain of human nature's daily food, seeing that the supply was sufficient and coal-miners doubtless were sitting down to less. Prunes and custard followed. And if any one complains that prunes, even when mitigated by custard, are an uncharitable vegetable (fruit they are not), stringy as a miser's heart and exuding a fluid such as might run in misers' veins who have denied themselves wine and warmth for eighty years and yet not given to the poor, he should reflect that there are people whose charity embraces even the prune. Biscuits and cheese came next, and here the water-jug was liberally passed round, for it is the nature of biscuits to be dry, and these were biscuits to the core. That was all. The meal was over. Everybody scraped their chairs back; the swing-doors swung violently to and fro; soon the hall was emptied of every sign of food and made ready no doubt for breakfast next morning. Down corridors and up staircases the youth of England went banging and singing. And was it for a guest, a stranger (for I had no more right here in Fernham than in Trinity or Somerville or Girton or Newnham or Christchurch), to say, "The dinner was not good," or to say (we were now, Mary Seton and I, in her sitting-room), "Could we not have dined up here alone?" for if I had said anything of the kind I should have been prying and searching into the secret economies of a house which to the stranger wears so fine a front of gaiety and courage. No, one could say nothing of the sort. Indeed, conversation for a moment flagged. The human frame being what it is, heart, body and brain all mixed together, and

5. Jane Harrison (1850–1928), English classical scholar, fellow, and lecturer at Newnham College, and author of *Prolegomena to the Study of Greek Religion* (1903) and *Ancient Art and Ritual* (1913).

not contained in separate compartments as they will be no doubt in another million years, a good dinner is of great importance to good talk. One cannot think well, love well, sleep well, if one has not dined well. The lamp in the spine does not light on beef and prunes. We are all *probably* going to heaven, and Vandyck is, we *hope,* to meet us round the next corner—that is the dubious and qualifying state of mind that beef and prunes at the end of the day's work breed between them. Happily my friend, who taught science, had a cupboard where there was a squat bottle and little glasses—(but there should have been sole and partridge to begin with)—so that we were able to draw up to the fire and repair some of the damages of the day's living. In a minute or so we were slipping freely in and out among all those objects of curiosity and interest which form in the mind in the absence of a particular person, and are naturally to be discussed on coming together again—how somebody has married, another has not; one thinks this, another that; one has improved out of all knowledge, the other most amazingly gone to the bad—with all those speculations upon human nature and the character of the amazing world we live in which spring naturally from such beginnings. While these things were being said, however, I became shamefacedly aware of a current setting in of its own accord and carrying everything forward to an end of its own. One might be talking of Spain or Portugal, of book or racehorse, but the real interest of whatever was said was none of those things, but a scene of masons on a high roof some five centuries ago. Kings and nobles brought treasure in huge sacks and poured it under the earth. This scene was for ever coming alive in my mind and placing itself by another of lean cows and a muddy market and withered greens and the stringy hearts of old men—these two pictures, disjointed and disconnected and nonsensical as they were, were for ever coming together and combating each other and had me entirely at their mercy. The best course, unless the whole talk was to be distorted, was to expose what was in my mind to the air, when with good luck it would fade and crumble like the head of the dead king when they opened the coffin at Windsor.[6] Briefly, then, I told Miss Seton about the masons who had been all those years on the roof of the chapel, and about the kings and queens and nobles bearing sacks of gold and silver on their shoulders, which they shovelled into the earth; and then how the great financial magnates of our own time came and laid cheques and bonds, I suppose, where the others had laid ingots and rough lumps of gold. All that lies beneath the colleges down there, I said; but this college, where we are now sitting, what lies beneath its gallant red brick and the wild unkempt grasses of the garden? What force is behind the plain china off which we dined, and (here it popped out of my mouth before I could stop it) the beef, the custard and the prunes?

Well, said Mary Seton, about the year 1860—Oh, but you know the story, she said, bored, I suppose, by the recital. And she told me—rooms were hired. Committees met. Envelopes were addressed. Circulars were drawn up. Meetings were held; letters were read out; so-and-so has promised so much; on the contrary, Mr. —— won't give a penny. The *Saturday Review* has been very rude. How can we raise a fund to pay for offices? Shall we

6. At the royal residence of Windsor Castle, nine English kings are buried in two chapels serving as royal mausoleums.

hold a bazaar? Can't we find a pretty girl to sit in the front row? Let us look up what John Stuart Mill said on the subject. Can any one persuade the editor of the —— to print a letter? Can we get Lady —— to sign it? Lady —— is out of town. That was the way it was done, presumably, sixty years ago, and it was a prodigious effort, and a great deal of time was spent on it. And it was only after a long struggle and with the utmost difficulty that they got thirty thousand pounds together.[7] So obviously we cannot have wine and partridges and servants carrying tin dishes on their heads, she said. We cannot have sofas and separate rooms. "The amenities," she said, quoting from some book or other, "will have to wait."[8]

At the thought of all those women working year after year and finding it hard to get two thousand pounds together, and as much as they could do to get thirty thousand pounds, we burst out in scorn at the reprehensible poverty of our sex. What had our mothers been doing then that they had no wealth to leave us? Powdering their noses? Looking in at shop windows? Flaunting in the sun at Monte Carlo? There were some photographs on the mantel-piece. Mary's mother—if that was her picture—may have been a wastrel in her spare time (she had thirteen children by a minister of the church), but if so her gay and dissipated life had left too few traces of its pleasures on her face. She was a homely body; an old lady in a plaid shawl which was fastened by a large cameo; and she sat in a basket-chair, encouraging a spaniel to look at the camera, with the amused, yet strained expression of one who is sure that the dog will move directly the bulb is pressed. Now if she had gone into business; had become a manufacturer of artificial silk or a magnate on the Stock Exchange; if she had left two or three hundred thousand pounds to Fernham, we could have been sitting at our ease tonight and the subject of our talk might have been archaeology, botany, anthropology, physics, the nature of the atom, mathematics, astronomy, relativity, geography. If only Mrs Seton and her mother and her mother before her had learnt the great art of making money and had left their money, like their fathers and their grandfathers before them, to found fellowships and lectureships and prizes and scholarships appropriated to the use of their own sex, we might have dined very tolerably up here alone off a bird and a bottle of wine; we might have looked forward without undue confidence to a pleasant and honourable lifetime spent in the shelter of one of the liberally endowed professions. We might have been exploring or writing; mooning about the venerable places of the earth; sitting contemplative on the steps of the Parthenon, or going at ten to an office and coming home comfortably at half-past four to write a little poetry. Only, if Mrs Seton and her like had gone into business at the age of fifteen, there would have been—that was the snag in the argument—no Mary. What, I asked, did Mary think of that? There between the curtains was the October night, calm and lovely, with a star or two caught in the yellowing trees. Was she ready to resign her share of it and her memories (for they had been a happy family, though a large one) of games and quarrels up in Scotland, which she is never tired of praising for

7. "We are told that we ought to ask for £30,000 at least. . . . It is not a large sum, considering that there is to be but one college of this sort for Great Britain, Ireland and the Colonies, and considering how easy it is to raise immense sums for boys' schools. But considering how few people really wish women to be educated, it is a good deal."—Lady Stephen, *Life of Miss Emily Davis* [Woolf's note].   8. "Every penny which could be scraped together was set aside for building, and the amenities had to be postponed."—R. Strachey, *The Cause* [Woolf's note].

the fineness of its air and the quality of its cakes, in order that Fernham might have been endowed with fifty thousand pounds or so by a stroke of the pen? For, to endow a college would necessitate the suppression of families altogether. Making a fortune and bearing thirteen children—no human being could stand it. Consider the facts, we said. First there are nine months before the baby is born. Then the baby is born. Then there are three or four months spent in feeding the baby. After the baby is fed there are certainly five years spent in playing with the baby. You cannot, it seems, let children run about the streets. People who have seen them running wild in Russia say that the sight is not a pleasant one. People say, too, that human nature takes its shape in the years between one and five. If Mrs Seton, I said, had been making money, what sort of memories would you have had of games and quarrels? What would you have known of Scotland, and its fine air and cakes and all the rest of it? But it is useless to ask these questions, because you would never have come into existence at all. Moreover, it is equally useless to ask what might have happened if Mrs Seton and her mother and her mother before her had amassed great wealth and laid it under the foundations of college and library, because, in the first place, to earn money was impossible for them, and in the second, had it been possible, the law denied them the right to possess what money they earned. It is only for the last forty-eight years that Mrs Seton has had a penny of her own. For all the centuries before that it would have been her husband's property—a thought which, perhaps, may have had its share in keeping Mrs Seton and her mothers off the Stock Exchange. Every penny I earn, they may have said, will be taken from me and disposed of according to my husband's wisdom—perhaps to found a scholarship or to endow a fellowship in Balliol or Kings,[9] so that to earn money, even if I could earn money, is not a matter that interests me very greatly. I had better leave it to my husband.

At any rate, whether or not the blame rested on the old lady who was looking at the spaniel, there could be no doubt that for some reason or other our mothers had mismanaged their affairs very gravely. Not a penny could be spared for "amenities"; for partridges and wine, beadles and turf, books and cigars, libraries and leisure. To raise bare walls out of the bare earth was the utmost they could do.

So we talked standing at the window and looking, as so many thousands look every night, down on the domes and towers of the famous city beneath us. It was very beautiful, very mysterious in the autumn moonlight. The old stone looked very white and venerable. One thought of all the books that were assembled down there; of the pictures of old prelates and worthies hanging in the panelled rooms; of the painted windows that would be throwing strange globes and crescents on the pavement; of the tablets and memorials and inscriptions; of the fountains and the grass; of the quiet rooms looking across the quiet quadrangles. And (pardon me the thought) I thought, too, of the admirable smoke and drink and the deep armchairs and the pleasant carpets: of the urbanity, the geniality, the dignity which are the offspring of luxury and privacy and space. Certainly our mothers had not provided us with anything comparable to all this—our mothers who found

9. I.e., King's College, Cambridge. *Balliol:* Balliol College, Oxford.

it difficult to scrape together thirty thousand pounds, our mothers who bore thirteen children to ministers of religion at St Andrews.[1]

So I went back to my inn, and as I walked through the dark streets I pondered this and that, as one does at the end of the day's work. I pondered why it was that Mrs Seton had no money to leave us; and what effect poverty has on the mind; and what effect wealth has on the mind; and I thought of the queer old gentlemen I had seen that morning with tufts of fur upon their shoulders; and I remembered how if one whistled one of them ran; and I thought of the organ booming in the chapel and of the shut doors of the library; and I thought how unpleasant it is to be locked out; and I thought how it is worse perhaps to be locked in; and, thinking of the safety and prosperity of the one sex and of the poverty and insecurity of the other and of the effect of tradition and of the lack of tradition upon the mind of a writer, I thought at last that it was time to roll up the crumpled skin of the day, with its arguments and its impressions and its anger and its laughter, and cast it into the hedge. A thousand stars were flashing across the blue wastes of the sky. One seemed alone with an inscrutable society. All human beings were laid asleep—prone, horizontal, dumb. Nobody seemed stirring in the streets of Oxbridge. Even the door of the hotel sprang open at the touch of an invisible hand—not a boots was sitting up to light me to bed, it was so late.

CHAPTER TWO

The scene, if I may ask you to follow me, was now changed. The leaves were still falling, but in London now, not Oxbridge; and I must ask you to imagine a room, like many thousands, with a window looking across people's hats and vans and motor-cars to other windows, and on the table inside the room a blank sheet of paper on which was written in large letters WOMEN AND FICTION, but no more. The inevitable sequel to lunching and dining at Oxbridge seemed, unfortunately, to be a visit to the British Museum. One must strain off what was personal and accidental in all these impressions and so reach the pure fluid, the essential oil of truth. For that visit to Oxbridge and the luncheon and the dinner had started a swarm of questions. Why did men drink wine and women water? Why was one sex so prosperous and the other so poor? What effect has poverty on fiction? What conditions are necessary for the creation of works of art?—a thousand questions at once suggested themselves. But one needed answers, not questions; and an answer was only to be had by consulting the learned and the unprejudiced, who have removed themselves above the strife of tongue and the confusion of body and issued the result of their reasoning and research in books which are to be found in the British Museum. If truth is not to be found on the shelves of the British Museum, where, I asked myself, picking up a notebook and a pencil, is truth?

Thus provided, thus confident and enquiring, I set out in the pursuit of truth. The day, though not actually wet, was dismal, and the streets in the neighborhood of the Museum were full of open coal-holes, down which sacks

1. Probably St. Andrew's in Holborn, an old London church rebuilt under the famous architect Sir Christopher Wren during 1683–95.

were showering; four-wheeled cabs were drawing up and depositing on the pavement corded boxes containing, presumably, the entire wardrobe of some Swiss or Italian family seeking fortune or refuge or some other desirable commodity which is to be found in the boarding-houses of Bloomsbury[2] in the winter. The usual hoarse-voiced men paraded the streets with plants on barrows. Some shouted; others sang. London was like a workshop. London was like a machine. We were all being shot backwards and forwards on this plain foundation to make some pattern. The British Museum was another department of the factory. The swing-doors swung open; and there one stood under the vast dome, as if one were a thought in the huge bald forehead which is so splendidly encircled by a band of famous names.[3] One went to the counter; one took a slip of paper; one opened a volume of the catalogue, and . . . . . the five dots here indicate five separate minutes of stupefaction, wonder and bewilderment. Have you any notion how many books are written about women in the course of one year? Have you any notion how many are written by men? Are you aware that you are, perhaps, the most discussed animal in the universe? Here had I come with a notebook and a pencil proposing to spend a morning reading, supposing that at the end of the morning I should have transferred the truth to my notebook. But I should need to be a herd of elephants, I thought, and a wilderness of spiders, desperately referring to the animals that are reputed longest lived and most multitudinously eyed, to cope with all this. I should need claws of steel and beak of brass even to penetrate the husk. How shall I ever find the grains of truth embedded in all this mass of paper, I asked myself, and in despair began running my eye up and down the long list of titles. Even the names of the books gave me food for thought. Sex and its nature might well attract doctors and biologists; but what was surprising and difficult of explanation was the fact that sex—woman, that is to say—also attracts agreeable essayists, light-fingered novelists, young men who have taken the M.A. degree; men who have taken no degree; men who have no apparent qualification save that they are not women. Some of these books were, on the face of it, frivolous and facetious; but many, on the other hand, were serious and prophetic, moral and hortatory. Merely to read the titles suggested innumerable schoolmasters, innumerable clergymen mounting their platforms and pulpits and holding forth with a loquacity which far exceeded the hour usually allotted to such discourse on this one subject. It was a most strange phenomenon; and apparently—here I consulted the letter M—one confined to male sex. Women do not write books about men—a fact that I could not help welcoming with relief, for if I had first to read all that men have written about women, then all that women have written about men, the aloe that flowers once in a hundred years would flower twice before I could set pen to paper. So, making a perfectly arbitrary choice of a dozen volumes or so, I sent my slips of paper to lie in the wire tray, and waited in my stall, among the other seekers for the essential oil of truth.

What could be the reason, then, of this curious disparity, I wondered,

2. A residential and academic borough in London, site of the British Museum and various educational institutions.   3. The names of famous men, including Chaucer, Spenser, Shakespeare, Milton, Pope, Wordsworth, Byron, Carlyle, and Tennyson, are painted in a circle around the dome of the Reading Room at the British Museum.

drawing cart-wheels on the slips of paper provided by the British taxpayer for other purposes. Why are women, judging from this catalogue, so much more interesting to men than men are to women? A very curious fact it seemed, and my mind wandered to picture the lives of men who spend their time in writing books about women; whether they were old or young, married or unmarried, red-nosed or humpbacked—anyhow, it was flattering, vaguely, to feel oneself the object of such attention, provided that it was not entirely bestowed by the crippled and the infirm—so I pondered until all such frivolous thoughts were ended by an avalanche of books sliding down on to the desk in front of me. Now the trouble began. The student who has been trained in research at Oxbridge has no doubt some method of shepherding his question past all distractions till it runs into its answer as a sheep runs into its pen. The student by my side, for instance, who was copying assiduously from a scientific manual was, I felt sure, extracting pure nuggets of the essential ore every ten minutes or so. His little grunts of satisfaction indicated so much. But if, unfortunately, one has had no training in a university, the question far from being shepherded to its pen flies like a frightened flock hither and thither, helter-skelter, pursued by a whole pack of hounds. Professors, schoolmasters, sociologists, clergymen, novelists, essayists, journalists, men who had no qualification save that they were not women, chased my simple and single question—Why are women poor?—until it became fifty questions; until the fifty questions leapt frantically into mid-stream and were carried away. Every page in my notebook was scribbled over with notes. To show the state of mind I was in, I will read you a few of them, explaining that the page was headed quite simply, WOMEN AND POVERTY, in block letters; but what followed was something like this:

> *Condition in Middle Ages of,*
> *Habits in the Fiji Islands of,*
> *Worshipped as goddesses by,*
> *Weaker in moral sense than,*
> *Idealism of,*
> *Greater conscientiousness of,*
> *South Sea Islanders, age of puberty among,*
> *Attractiveness of,*
> *Offered as sacrifice to,*
> *Small size of brain of,*
> *Profounder sub-consciousness of,*
> *Less hair on the body of,*
> *Mental, moral and physical inferiority of,*
> *Love of children of,*
> *Greater length of life of,*
> *Weaker muscles of,*
> *Strength of affections of,*
> *Vanity of,*
> *Higher education of,*
> *Shakespeare's opinion of,*
> *Lord Birkenhead's opinion of,*
> *Dean Inge's opinion of,*

La Bruyère's opinion of,
Dr. Johnson's opinion of,
Mr. Oscar Browning's[4] opinion of, . . .

Here I drew breath and added, indeed, in the margin, Why does Samuel Butler[5] say, "Wise men never say what they think of women"? Wise men never say anything else apparently. But, I continued, leaning back in my chair and looking at the vast dome in which I was a single but by now somewhat harassed thought, what is so unfortunate is that wise men never think the same thing about women. Here is Pope:[6]

Most women have no character at all.

And here is La Bruyère:

Les femmes sont extrêmes; elles sont meilleures ou pires que les hommes—[7]

a direct contradiction by keen observers who were contemporary. Are they capable of education or incapable? Napoleon thought them incapable.[8] Dr. Johnson thought the opposite.[9] Have they souls or have they not souls? Some savages say they have none. Others, on the contrary, maintain that women are half divine and worship them on that account.[1] Some sages hold that they are shallow in the brain; others that they are deeper in the consciousness. Goethe honoured them; Mussolini[2] despises them. Wherever one looked men thought about women and thought differently. It was impossible to make head or tail of it all, I decided, glancing with envy at the reader next door who was making the neatest abstracts, headed often with an A or a B or a C, while my own notebook rioted with the wildest scribble of contradictory jottings. It was distressing, it was bewildering, it was humiliating. Truth had run through my fingers. Every drop had escaped.

I could not possibly go home, I reflected, and add as a serious contribution to the study of women and fiction that women have less hair on their bodies than men, or that the age of puberty among the South Sea Islanders[3] is

4. A schoolmaster and later fellow of King's College, Cambridge (1837–1923); anecdotes about his strong opinions (see p. 1954) were published in a 1927 biography. The first earl of Birkenhead, F. E. Smith (1872–1930), a conservative politician who opposed women's suffrage and praised the domestic "true functions of womanhood." William Ralph Inge (1860–1954), dean of St. Paul's Cathedral in London and a religious writer. Jean de La Bruyère (1645–1696), French moralist and author of satirical *Characters* (1688), imitating the Greek writer Theophrastus. Samuel Johnson (1709–1784), author of moral essays and of the famous *A Dictionary of the English Language* (1747).   5. Satirical author (1835–1902) who wrote *Erewhon* (1872) and *The Way of All Flesh* (1903); his *Notebooks* are the source of this statement.   6. Alexander Pope (1688–1744), translator of Homer and author of *An Essay on Man* (1733–34) and the satirical *The Rape of the Lock* (1712–14).   7. Women are extreme; they are better or worse than men (French).   8. Napoleon wrote: "What we ask of education is not that girls should think, but that they should believe. The weakness of women's brains, the instability of their ideas, the place they will fill in society, their need for perpetual resignation, and for an easy and generous type of charity—all this can only be met by religion" (notes written on May 15, 1807, concerning the establishment of a girl's school at Écouen).   9. " 'Men know that women are an overmatch for them, and therefore they choose the weakest or the most ignorant. If they did not think so, they never could be afraid of women knowing as much as themselves.' . . . Injustice to the sex, I think it but candid to acknowledge that, in a subsequent conversation, he told me that he was serious in what he said."—BOSWELL, *The Journal of a Tour to the Hebrides* [Woolf's note].   1. "The ancient Germans believed that there was something holy in women, and accordingly consulted them as oracles."—FRAZER, *Golden Bough* [Woolf's note].   2. Benito Mussolini (1883–1945), Fascist dictator of Italy between 1922 and 1943. Johann Wolfgang von Goethe (1749–1832), German author of *Faust*. "The eternal feminine draws us along" is the last line of *Faust*, Part 2.   3. The native peoples of the islands in the south-central Pacific Ocean were the subject of several anthropological studies in the early 20th century, including Margaret Mead's widely read *Coming of Age in Samoa* (1928).

nine—or is it ninety?—even the handwriting had become in its distraction indecipherable. It was disgraceful to have nothing more weighty or respectable to show after a whole morning's work. And if I could not grasp the truth about W. (as for brevity's sake I had come to call her) in the past, why bother about W. in the future? It seemed pure waste of time to consult all those gentlemen who specialise in woman and her effect on whatever it may be— politics, children, wages, morality—numerous and learned as they are. One might as well leave their books unopened.

But while I pondered I had unconsciously, in my listlessness, in my desperation, been drawing a picture where I should, like my neighbour, have been writing a conclusion. I had been drawing a face, a figure. It was the face and the figure of Professor von X. engaged in writing his monumental work entitled *The Mental, Moral, and Physical Inferiority of the Female Sex*.[4] He was not in my picture a man attractive to women. He was heavily built; he had a great jowl; to balance that he had very small eyes; he was very red in the face. His expression suggested that he was labouring under some emotion that made him jab his pen on the paper as if he were killing some noxious insect as he wrote, but even when he had killed it that did not satisfy him; he must go on killing it; and even so, some cause for anger and irritation remained. Could it be his wife, I asked, looking at my picture. Was she in love with a cavalry officer? Was the cavalry officer slim and elegant and dressed in astrachan?[5] Had he been laughed at, to adopt the Freudian theory, in his cradle by a pretty girl? For even in his cradle the professor, I thought, could not have been an attractive child. Whatever the reason, the professor was made to look very angry and very ugly in my sketch, as he wrote his great book upon the mental, moral and physical inferiority of women. Drawing pictures was an idle way of finishing an unprofitable morning's work. Yet it is in our idleness, in our dreams, that the submerged truth sometimes comes to the top. A very elementary exercise in psychology, not to be dignified by the name of psycho-analysis, showed me, on looking at my notebook, that the sketch of the angry professor had been made in anger. Anger had snatched my pencil while I dreamt. But what was anger doing there? Interest, confusion, amusement, boredom—all these emotions I could trace and name as they succeeded each other throughout the morning. Had anger, the black snake, been lurking among them? Yes, said the sketch, anger had. It referred me unmistakably to the one book, to the one phrase, which had roused the demon; it was the professor's statement about the mental, moral and physical inferiority of women. My heart had leapt. My cheeks had burnt. I had flushed with anger. There was nothing specially remarkable, however foolish, in that. One does not like to be told that one is naturally the inferior of a little man— I looked at the student next me—who breathes hard, wears a ready-made tie, and has not shaved this fortnight. One has certain foolish vanities. It is only human nature, I reflected, and began drawing cart-wheels and circles over the angry professor's face till he looked like a burning bush or a flaming comet—anyhow, an apparition without human semblance or significance. The professor was nothing now but a faggot burning on the top of Hampstead

4. A fictional portrait, probably based on Otto Weininger's *Sex and Character* (1906), that distinguished between male (productive and moral) and female (negative and amoral) characteristics.   5. Curly lambskin.

Heath.[6] Soon my own anger was explained and done with; but curiosity remained. How explain the anger of the professors? Why were they angry? For when it came to analysing the impression left by these books there was always an element of heat. This heat took many forms; it showed itself in satire, in sentiment, in curiosity, in reprobation. But there was another element which was often present and could not immediately be identified. Anger, I called it. But it was anger that had gone underground and mixed itself with all kinds of other emotions. To judge from its odd effects, it was anger disguised and complex, not anger simple and open.

Whatever the reason, all these books,[7] I thought, surveying the pile on the desk, are worthless for my purposes. They were worthless scientifically, that is to say, though humanly they were full of instruction, interest, boredom, and very queer facts about the habits of the Fiji Islanders. They had been written in the red light of emotion and not in the white light of truth. Therefore they must be returned to the central desk and restored each to his own cell in the enormous honeycomb. All that I had retrieved from that morning's work had been the one fact of anger. The professors—I lumped them together thus—were angry. But why, I asked myself, having returned the books, why, I repeated, standing under the colonnade among the pigeons and the prehistoric canoes, why are they angry? And, asking myself this question, I strolled off to find a place for luncheon. What is the real nature of what I call for the moment their anger? I asked. Here was a puzzle that would last all the time that it takes to be served with food in a small restaurant somewhere near the British Museum. Some previous luncher had left the lunch edition of the evening paper on a chair, and, waiting to be served, I began idly reading the headlines. A ribbon of very large letters ran across the page. Somebody had made a big score in South Africa. Lesser ribbons announced that Sir Austen Chamberlain was at Geneva.[8] A meat axe with human hair on it had been found in a cellar. Mr. Justice —— commented in the Divorce Courts upon the Shamelessness of Women. Sprinkled about the paper were other pieces of news. A film actress had been lowered from a peak in California and hung suspended in mid-air. The weather was going to be foggy. The most transient visitor to this planet, I thought, who picked up this paper could not fail to be aware, even from this scattered testimony, that England is under the rule of a patriarchy. Nobody in their senses could fail to detect the dominance of the professor. His was the power and the money and the influence. He was the proprietor of the paper and its editor and sub-editor. He was the Foreign Secretary and the Judge. He was the cricketer; he owned the race-horses and the yachts. He was the director of the company that pays two hundred per cent to its shareholders. He left millions to charities and colleges that were ruled by himself. He suspended the film actress in mid-air. He will decide if the hair on the meat axe is human; he it is who will acquit or convict the murderer, and hang him, or let him go free. With the exception of the fog he seemed to control every-

6. A public open space in the village of Hampstead, in London. *Faggot:* a bundle of sticks. 7. E.g., *Fijian Society, or the Sociology and Psychology of the Fijians* (1921), by Reverend W. Deane, principal of a teachers' training college in Ndávuilévu, Fiji; and *The Hill Tribes of Fiji* (1922), by A. B. Brewster, a colonial functionary, mixed facts with interpretation. Reverend Deane remarks that "the amount of sexual immorality and promiscuous intercourse during the past forty years is appalling." Fiji is an island in the South Pacific (see n. 3, p. 1940). 8. The site of the League of Nations. Chamberlain was the British foreign secretary between 1924 and 1929.

thing. Yet he was angry. I knew that he was angry by this token. When I read what he wrote about women I thought, not of what he was saying, but of himself. When an arguer argues dispassionately he thinks only of the argument; and the reader cannot help thinking of the argument too. If he had written dispassionately about women, had used indisputable proofs to establish his argument and had shown no trace of wishing that the result should be one thing rather than another, one would not have been angry either. One would have accepted the fact, as one accepts the fact that a pea is green or a canary yellow. So be it, I should have said. But I had been angry because he was angry. Yet it seemed absurd, I thought, turning over the evening paper, that a man with all this power should be angry. Or is anger, I wondered, somehow, the familiar, the attendant sprite on power? Rich people, for example, are often angry because they suspect that the poor want to seize their wealth. The professors, or patriarchs, as it might be more accurate to call them, might be angry for that reason partly, but partly for one that lies a little less obviously on the surface. Possibly they were not "angry" at all; often, indeed, they were admiring, devoted, exemplary in the relations of private life. Possibly when the professor insisted a little too emphatically upon the inferiority of women, he was concerned not with their inferiority, but with his own superiority. That was what he was protecting rather hot-headedly and with too much emphasis, because it was a jewel to him of the rarest price. Life for both sexes—and I looked at them, shouldering their way along the pavement—is arduous, difficult, a perpetual struggle. It calls for gigantic courage and strength. More than anything, perhaps, creatures of illusion as we are, it calls for confidence in oneself. Without self-confidence we are as babes in the cradle. And how can we generate this imponderable quality, which is yet so invaluable, most quickly? By thinking that other people are inferior to oneself. By feeling that one has some innate superiority—it may be wealth, or rank, a straight nose, or the portrait of a grandfather by Romney[9]—for there is no end to the pathetic devices of the human imagination—over other people. Hence the enormous importance to a patriarch who has to conquer, who has to rule, of feeling that great numbers of people, half the human race indeed, are by nature inferior to himself. It must indeed be one of the chief sources of his power. But let me turn the light of this observation on to real life, I thought. Does it help to explain some of those psychological puzzles that one notes in the margin of daily life? Does it explain my astonishment the other day when Z, most humane, most modest of men, taking up some book by Rebecca West[1] and reading a passage in it, exclaimed, "The arrant feminist! She says that men are snobs!" The exclamation, to me so surprising—for why was Miss West an arrant feminist for making a possibly true if uncomplimentary statement about the other sex?—was not merely the cry of wounded vanity; it was a protest against some infringement of his power to believe in himself. Women have served all these centuries as looking-glasses possessing the magic and delicious power of reflecting the figure of man at twice its natural size. Without that power probably the earth would still be swamp and jungle. The glories of all our wars would be unknown. We should still be scratching the outlines of

9. George Romney (1734–1802), portrait painter of 18th-century British society.   1. Pseudonym of Cicily Isabel Andrews (1892–1983), British novelist and journalist.

deer on the remains of mutton bones and bartering flints for sheepskins or whatever simple ornament took our unsophisticated taste. Supermen[2] and Fingers of Destiny would never have existed. The Czar and the Kaiser would never have worn their crowns or lost them. Whatever may be their use in civilized societies, mirrors are essential to all violent and heroic action. That is why Napoleon and Mussolini both insist so emphatically upon the inferiority of women, for if they were not inferior, they would cease to enlarge. That serves to explain in part the necessity that women so often are to men. And it serves to explain how restless they are under her criticism; how impossible it is for her to say to them this book is bad, this picture is feeble, or whatever it may be, without giving far more pain and rousing far more anger than a man would do who gave the same criticism. For if she begins to tell the truth, the figure in the looking-glass shrinks; his fitness for life is diminished. How is he to go on giving judgment, civilising natives, making laws, writing books, dressing up and speechifying at banquets, unless he can see himself at breakfast and at dinner at least twice the size he really is? So I reflected, crumbling my bread and stirring my coffee and now and again looking at the people in the street. The looking-glass vision is of supreme importance because it charges the vitality; it stimulates the nervous system. Take it away and man may die, like the drug fiend deprived of his cocaine. Under the spell of that illusion, I thought, looking out of the window, half the people on the pavement are striding to work. They put on their hats and coats in the morning under its agreeable rays. They start the day confident, braced, believing themselves desired at Miss Smith's tea party; they say to themselves as they go into the room, I am the superior of half the people here, and it is thus that they speak with that self-confidence, that self-assurance, which have had such profound consequences in public life and lead to such curious notes in the margin of the private mind.

But these contributions to the dangerous and fascinating subject of the psychology of the other sex—it is one, I hope, that you will investigate when you have five hundred a year of your own—were interrupted by the necessity of paying the bill. It came to five shillings and ninepence. I gave the waiter a ten-shilling note and he went to bring me change. There was another ten-shilling note in my purse; I noticed it, because it is a fact that still takes my breath away—the power of my purse to breed ten-shilling notes automatically. I open it and there they are. Society gives me chicken and coffee, bed and lodging, in return for a certain number of pieces of paper which were left me by an aunt, for no other reason than that I share her name.

My aunt, Mary Beton, I must tell you, died by a fall from her horse when she was riding out to take the air in Bombay. The news of my legacy reached me one night about the same time that the act was passed that gave votes to women.[3] A solicitor's letter fell into the post-box and when I opened it I found that she had left me five hundred pounds[4] a year for ever. Of the

---

2. Fascist politicians, such as Adolf Hitler (1889–1945) in Germany and Mussolini (1883–1945) in Italy, rationalized their aggressive policies by exploiting and distorting Friedrich Nietzsche's (1844–1900) concept of the *Übermensch*, or superior being (in *Thus Spake Zarathustra*, 1883–85). **3.** Women were given the vote in 1918; the voting age was lowered from thirty to twenty-one in 1928. **4.** Roughly $29,000 today, calculating inflation and exchange rates between the pound and the dollar in 1918 and 2003. Such calculations are never perfectly reliable, however, since the relative cost of specific items (such as bread or rent) varies.

two—the vote and the money—the money, I own, seemed infinitely the more important. Before that I had made my living by cadging odd jobs from news-papers, by reporting a donkey show here or a wedding there; I had earned a few pounds by addressing envelopes, reading to old ladies, making artificial flowers, teaching the alphabet to small children in a kindergarten. Such were the chief occupations that were open to women before 1918. I need not, I am afraid, describe in any detail the hardness of the work, for you know perhaps women who have done it; nor the difficulty of living on the money when it was earned, for you may have tried. But what still remains with me as a worse infliction than either was the poison of fear and bitterness which those days bred in me. To begin with, always to be doing work that one did not wish to do, and to do it like a slave, flattering and fawning, not always necessarily perhaps, but it seemed necessary and the stakes were too great to run risks; and then the thought of that one gift which it was death to hide[5]—a small one but dear to the possessor—perishing and with it myself, my soul—all this became like a rust eating away the bloom of the spring, destroying the tree at its hearts. However, as I say, my aunt died; and when-ever I change a ten-shilling note a little of that rust and corrosion is rubbed off; fear and bitterness go. Indeed, I thought, slipping the silver into my purse, it is remarkable, remembering the bitterness of those days, what a change of temper a fixed income will bring about. No force in the world can take from me my five hundred pounds. Food, house and clothing are mine for ever. Therefore not merely do effort and labour cease, but also hatred and bitterness. I need not hate any man; he cannot hurt me. I need not flatter any man; he has nothing to give me. So imperceptibly I found myself adopting a new attitude towards the other half of the human race. It was absurd to blame any class or any sex, as a whole. Great bodies of people are never responsible for what they do. They are driven by instincts which are not within their control. They too, the patriarchs, the professors, had endless difficulties, terrible drawbacks to contend with. Their education had been in some ways as faulty as my own. It had bred in them defects as great. True, they had money and power, but only at the cost of harbouring in their breasts an eagle, a vulture, for ever tearing the liver out and plucking at the lungs— the instinct for possession, the rage for acquisition which drives them to desire other people's fields and goods perpetually; to make frontiers and flags; battleships and poison gas; to offer up their own lives and their children's lives. Walk through the Admiralty Arch[6] (I had reached that monument), or any other avenue given up to trophies and cannon, and reflect upon the kind of glory celebrated there. Or watch in the spring sunshine the stockbroker and the great barrister going indoors to make money and more money and more money when it is a fact that five hundred pounds a year will keep one alive in the sunshine. These are unpleasant instincts to harbour, I reflected. They are bred of the conditions of life; of the lack of civilisation, I thought, looking at the statue of the Duke of Cambridge,[7] and in particular at the feathers in his cocked hat, with a fixity that they have scarcely ever received

5. From *When I Consider How My Light Is Spent* by John Milton (1608–1673): "And that one talent which is death to hide, / Lodged with me useless."   6. A triple arch in Trafalgar Square (London) at the entrance to the Mall, erected in 1910.   7. An equestrian statue of the second duke of Cambridge (1819–1904), cousin of Queen Victoria, in the full dress uniform of a field marshal.

before. And, as I realised these drawbacks, by degrees fear and bitterness modified themselves into pity and toleration; and then in a year or two, pity and toleration went, and the greatest release of all came, which is freedom to think of things in themselves. That building, for example, do I like it or not? Is that picture beautiful or not? Is that in my opinion a good book or a bad? Indeed my aunt's legacy unveiled the sky to me, and substituted for the large and imposing figure of a gentleman, which Milton recommended for my perpetual adoration, a view of the open sky.

So thinking, so speculating, I found my way back to my house by the river. Lamps were being lit and an indescribable change had come over London since the morning hour. It was as if the great machine after labouring all day had made with our help a few yards of something very exciting and beautiful—a fiery fabric flashing with red eyes, a tawny monster roaring with hot breath. Even the wind seemed flung like a flag as it lashed the houses and rattled the hoardings.

In my little street, however, domesticity prevailed. The house painter was descending his ladder; the nursemaid was wheeling the perambulator carefully in and out back to nursery tea; the coal-heaver was folding his empty sacks on top of each other; the woman who keeps the green-grocer's shop was adding up the day's takings with her hands in red mittens. But so engrossed was I with the problem you have laid upon my shoulders that I could not see even these usual sights without referring them to one centre. I thought how much harder it is now than it must have been even a century ago to say which of these employments is the higher, the more necessary. Is it better to be a coal-heaver or a nursemaid; is the charwoman who has brought up eight children of less value to the world than the barrister who has made a hundred thousand pounds? It is useless to ask such questions; for nobody can answer them. Not only do the comparative values of charwoman and lawyers rise and fall from decade to decade, but we have no rods with which to measure them even as they are at the moment. I had been foolish to ask my professor to furnish me with "indisputable proofs" of this or that in his argument about women. Even if one could state the value of any one gift at the moment, those values will change; in a century's time very possibly they will have changed completely. Moreover, in a hundred years, I thought, reaching my own doorstep, women will have ceased to be the protected sex. Logically they will take part in all the activities and exertions that were once denied them. The nursemaid will heave coal. The shop-woman will drive an engine. All assumptions founded on the facts observed when women were the protected sex will have disappeared—as, for example (here a squad of soldiers marched down the street), that women and clergymen and gardeners live longer than other people. Remove that protection, expose them to the same exertions and activities, make them soldiers and sailors and engine-drivers and dock labourers, and will not women die off so much younger, so much quicker, than men that one will say, "I saw a woman today," as one used to say, "I saw an aeroplane." Anything may happen when womanhood has ceased to be a protected occupation, I thought, opening the door. But what bearing has all this upon the subject of my paper, Women and Fiction? I asked, going indoors.

CHAPTER THREE

It was disappointing not to have brought back in the evening some important statement, some authentic fact. Women are poorer than men because—this or that. Perhaps now it would be better to give up seeking for the truth, and receiving on one's head an avalanche of opinion hot as lava, discoloured as dish-water. It would be better to draw the curtains; to shut out distractions; to light the lamp; to narrow the enquiry and to ask the historian, who records not opinions but facts, to describe under what conditions women lived, not throughout the ages, but in England, say in the time of Elizabeth.[8]

For it is a perennial puzzle why no woman wrote a word of that extraordinary literature when every other man, it seemed, was capable of song or sonnet. What were the conditions in which women lived, I asked myself; for fiction, imaginative work that is, is not dropped like a pebble upon the ground, as science may be; fiction is like a spider's web, attached ever so lightly perhaps, but still attached to life at all four corners. Often the attachment is scarcely perceptible; Shakespeare's plays, for instance, seem to hang there complete by themselves. But when the web is pulled askew, hooked up at the edge, torn in the middle, one remembers that these webs are not spun in mid-air by incorporeal creatures, but are the work of suffering human beings, and are attached to grossly material things, like health and money and the houses we live in.

I went, therefore, to the shelf where the histories stand and took down one of the latest, Professor Trevelyan's *History of England*.[9] Once more I looked up Women, found "position of," and turned to the pages indicated. "Wife-beating," I read, "was a recognised right of man, and was practised without shame by high as well as low. . . . Similarly," the historian goes on, "the daughter who refused to marry the gentleman of her parents' choice was liable to be locked up, beaten and flung about the room, without any shock being inflicted on public opinion. Marriage was not an affair of personal affection, but of family avarice, particularly in the 'chivalrous' upper classes. . . . Betrothal often took place while one or both of the parties was in the cradle, and marriage when they were scarcely out of the nurses' charge." That was about 1470, soon after Chaucer's[1] time. The next reference to the position of women is some two hundred years later, in the time of the Stuarts.[2] "It was still the exception for women of the upper and middle class to choose their own husbands, and when the husband had been assigned, he was lord and master, so far at least as law and custom could make him. Yet even so," Professor Trevelyan concludes, "neither Shakespeare's women nor those of authentic seventeenth-century memoirs, like the Verneys and the Hutchinsons,[3] seem wanting in personality and character." Certainly, if we consider it, Cleopatra must have had a way with her; Lady Macbeth,[4] one would suppose, had a will of her own; Rosalind, one might conclude, was an attractive girl. Professor Trevelyan is speaking no

---

8. Queen of England from 1558 to 1603.   9. Published in London in 1926. References are to pages 260–61 and, later, to pages 436–37.   1. Geoffrey Chaucer (1340?–1400), author of *The Canterbury Tales* (1390–1400).   2. The British royal house from 1603–1714 (except for the Commonwealth interregnum of 1649–60).   3. F. P. Verney compiled *The Memoirs of the Verney Family during the Seventeenth Century* (1892–99), and Lucy Hutchinson recounted her husband's life in *Memoirs of the Life of Colonel Hutchinson* (1806).   4. Heroine of Shakespeare's *Macbeth*. Cleopatra (69–30 B.C.E.), queen of Egypt and heroine of Shakespeare's *Antony and Cleopatra*.

more than the truth when he remarks that Shakespeare's women do not seem wanting in personality and character. Not being a historian, one might go even further and say that women have burnt like beacons in all the works of all the poets from the beginning of time—Clytemnestra, Antigone, Cleopatra, Lady Macbeth, Phèdre, Cressida, Rosalind, Desdemona, the Duchess of Malfi,[5] among the dramatists; then among the prose writers: Millamant, Clarissa,larissa, Becky Sharp, Anna Karenina, Emma Bovary, Madame de Guermantes[6]—the names flock to mind, nor do they recall women "lacking in personality and character." Indeed, if woman had no existence save in the fiction written by men, one would imagine her a person of the utmost importance; very various; heroic and mean; splendid and sordid; infinitely beautiful and hideous in the extreme; as great as a man, some think even greater.[7] But this is woman in fiction. In fact, as Professor Trevelyan points out, she was locked up, beaten and flung about the room.

A very queer, composite being thus emerges. Imaginatively she is of the highest importance; practically she is completely insignificant. She pervades poetry from cover to cover; she is all but absent from history. She dominates the lives of kings and conquerors in fiction; in fact she was the slave of any boy whose parents forced a ring upon her finger. Some of the most inspired words, some of the most profound thoughts in literature fall from her lips; in real life she could hardly read, could scarcely spell, and was the property of her husband.

It was certainly an odd monster that one made up by reading the historians first and the poets afterwards—a worm winged like an eagle; the spirit of life and beauty in a kitchen chopping up suet. But these monsters, however amusing to the imagination, have no existence in fact. What one must do to bring her to life was to think poetically and prosaically at one and the same moment, thus keeping in touch with fact—that she is Mrs. Martin, aged thirty-six, dressed in blue, wearing a black hat and brown shoes; but not losing sight of fiction either—that she is a vessel in which all sorts of spirits and forces are coursing and flashing perpetually. The moment, however, that one tries this method with the Elizabethan woman, one branch of illumination fails; one is held up by the scarcity of facts. One knows nothing detailed, nothing perfectly true and substantial about her. History scarcely mentions her. And I turned to Professor Trevelyan again to see what history

5. Doomed heroine of John Webster's *The Duchess of Malfi* (ca. 1613). Clytemnestra is the heroine of Aeschylus's *Agamemnon* (458 B.C.E.). Antigone is the eponymous heroine of a 442 B.C.E. play by Sophocles. Phèdre is the heroine of Jean Racine's *Phèdre* (in this anthology, *Phaedra*, 1677). Cressida, Rosalind, and Desdemona are heroines of Shakespeare's *Troilus and Cressida*, *As You Like It*, and *Othello*, respectively. 6. A character in Marcel Proust's *Remembrance of Things Past* (*The Guermantes Way*, 1920–21). Millamant is the heroine of William Congreve's satirical comedy *The Way of the World* (1700). Clarissa is the eponymous heroine of Samuel Richardson's seven-volume epistolary novel (1747–48). Becky Sharp appears in William Thackeray's *Vanity Fair* (1847–48). Anna Karenina is the title character in a Leo Tolstoy novel (1875–77). Emma Bovary is the heroine of Gustave Flaubert's *Madame Bovary* (1856). 7. "It remains a strange and almost inexplicable fact that in Athena's city, where women were kept in almost Oriental suppression as odalisques or drudges, the stage should yet have produced figures like Clytemnestra and Cassandra, Atossa and Antigone, Phèdre and Medea, and all the other heroines who dominate play after play of the 'misogynist' Euripides. But the paradox of this world where in real life a respectable woman could hardly show her face alone in the street, and yet on the stage woman equals or surpasses man, has never been satisfactorily explained. In modern tragedy the same predominance exists. At all events, a very cursory survey of Shakespeare's work (similarly with Webster, though not with Marlowe or Jonson) suffices to reveal how this dominance, this initiative of women, persists from Rosalind to Lady Macbeth. So too in Racine; six of his tragedies bear their heroines' names; and what male characters of his shall we set against Hermione and Andromaque, Bérénice and Roxane, Phèdre and Athalie? So again with Ibsen; what men shall we match with Solveig and Nora, Hedda and Hilda Wangel and Rebecca West?"—F. L. LUCAS, *Tragedy*, pp. 114–15 [Woolf's note].

meant to him. I found by looking at his chapter headings that it meant—
"The Manor Court and the Methods of Open-field Agriculture . . . The
Cistercians and Sheep-farming . . . The Crusades . . . The University . . .
The House of Commons . . . The Hundred Years' War . . . The Wars of the
Roses . . . The Renaissance Scholars . . . The Dissolution of the Monasteries
. . . Agrarian and Religious Strife . . . The Origin of English Sea-power . . .
The Armada . . ." and so on. Occasionally an individual woman is mentioned,
an Elizabeth, or a Mary; a queen or a great lady. But by no possible means
could middle-class women with nothing but brains and character at their
command have taken part in any one of the great movements which, brought
together, constitute the historian's view of the past. Nor shall we find her in
any collection of anecdotes. Aubrey[8] hardly mentions her. She never writes
her own life and scarcely keeps a diary; there are only a handful of her letters
in existence. She left no plays or poems by which we can judge her. What
one wants, I thought—and why does not some brilliant student at Newnham
or Girton[9] supply it?—is a mass of information; at what age did she marry;
how many children had she as a rule; what was her house like; had she a
room to herself; did she do the cooking; would she be likely to have a servant?
All these facts lie somewhere, presumably, in parish registers and account
books; the life of the average Elizabethan woman must be scattered about
somewhere, could one collect it and make a book of it. It would be ambitious
beyond my daring, I thought, looking about the shelves for books that were
not there, to suggest to the students of those famous colleges that they should
re-write history, though I own that it often seems a little queer as it is, unreal,
lop-sided; but why should they not add a supplement to history? calling it,
of course, by some inconspicuous name so that women might figure there
without impropriety? For one often catches a glimpse of them in the lives of
the great, whisking away into the background, concealing, I sometimes think,
a wink, a laugh, perhaps a tear. And, after all, we have lives enough of Jane
Austen; it scarcely seems necessary to consider again the influence of the
tragedies of Joanna Baillie[1] upon the poetry of Edgar Allan Poe; as for myself,
I should not mind if the homes and haunts of Mary Russell Mitford were
closed to the public for a century at least. But what I find deplorable, I
continued, looking about the bookshelves again, is that nothing is known
about women before the eighteenth century. I have no model in my mind to
turn about this way and that. Here am I asking why women did not write
poetry in the Elizabethan age, and I am not sure how they were educated;
whether they were taught to write; whether they had sitting-rooms to themselves; how many women had children before they were twenty-one; what,
in short, they did from eight in the morning till eight at night. They had no
money evidently; according to Professor Trevelyan they were married
whether they liked it or not before they were out of the nursery, at fifteen or
sixteen very likely. It would have been extremely odd, even upon this showing, had one of them suddenly written the plays of Shakespeare, I concluded,
and I thought of that old gentleman, who is dead now, but was a bishop, I
think, who declared that it was impossible for any woman, past, present, or

8. John Aubrey (1626–1697), author of *Brief Lives*, which includes sketches of his famous contemporaries.
9. Woolf delivered her lectures at Newnham and Girton Colleges for women, part of Cambridge University
in 1880 and 1873, respectively.   1. Joanna Baillie (1762–1851) was a poet and dramatist whose *Plays
on the Passions* (1798–1812) were famous in her day.

to come, to have the genius of Shakespeare. He wrote to the papers about it. He also told a lady who applied to him for information that cats do not as a matter of fact go to heaven, though they have, he added, souls of a sort. How much thinking those old gentlemen used to save one! How the borders of ignorance shrank back at their approach! Cats do not go to heaven. Women cannot write the plays of Shakespeare.

Be that as it may, I could not help thinking, as I looked at the works of Shakespeare on the shelf, that the bishop was right at least in this; it would have been impossible, completely and entirely, for any woman to have written the plays of Shakespeare in the age of Shakespeare. Let me imagine, since facts are so hard to come by, what would have happened had Shakespeare had a wonderfully gifted sister, called Judith,[2] let us say. Shakespeare himself went, very probably—his mother was an heiress—to the grammar school, where he may have learnt Latin—Ovid, Virgil and Horace[3]—and the elements of grammar and logic. He was, it is well known, a wild boy who poached rabbits, perhaps shot a deer, and had, rather sooner than he should have done, to marry a woman in the neighbourhood, who bore him a child rather quicker than was right. That escapade sent him to seek his fortune in London. He had, it seemed, a taste for the theatre; he began by holding horses at the stage door. Very soon he got work in the theatre, became a successful actor, and lived at the hub of the universe, meeting everybody, knowing everybody, practising his art on the boards, exercising his wits in the streets, and even getting access to the palace of the queen. Meanwhile his extraordinarily gifted sister, let us suppose, remained at home. She was as adventurous, as imaginative, as agog to see the world as he was. But she was not sent to school. She had no chance of learning grammar and logic, let alone of reading Horace and Virgil. She picked up a book now and then, one of her brother's perhaps, and read a few pages. But then her parents came in and told her to mend the stockings or mind the stew and not moon about with books and papers. They would have spoken sharply but kindly, for they were substantial people who knew the conditions of life for a woman and loved their daughter—indeed, more likely than not she was the apple of her father's eye. Perhaps she scribbled some pages up in an apple loft on the sly, but was careful to hide them or set fire to them. Soon, however, before she was out of her teens, she was to be betrothed to the son of a neighbouring wool-stapler.[4] She cried out that marriage was hateful to her, and for that she was severely beaten by her father. Then he ceased to scold her. He begged her instead not to hurt him, not to shame him in this matter of her marriage. He would give her a chain of beads or a fine petticoat, he said; and there were tears in his eyes. How could she disobey him? How could she break his heart? The force of her own gift alone drove her to it. She made up a small parcel of her belongings, let herself down by a rope one summer's night and took the road to London. She was not seventeen. The birds that sang in the hedge were not more musical than she was. She had the quickest fancy, a gift like her brother's, for the tune of words. Like him, she had a taste for the theatre. She stood at the stage door; she wanted to act, she said.

---

2. The name of Shakespeare's younger daughter. 3. Roman authors. Publius Ovidius Naso (43 B.C.E.–17 C.E.), author of the *Metamorphoses*. Publius Vergilius Maro (70–19 B.C.E.), author of the *Aeneid*. Quintus Horatius Flaccus (65–8 B.C.E.), author of *Odes* and satires. 4. A dealer in woolen goods, which were a "staple" or established type of merchandise.

Men laughed in her face. The manager—a fat, loose-lipped man—guffawed. He bellowed something about poodles dancing and women acting—no woman, he said, could possibly be an actress. He hinted—you can imagine what. She could get no training in her craft. Could she even seek her dinner in a tavern or roam the streets at midnight? Yet her genius was for fiction and lusted to feed abundantly upon the lives of men and women and the study of their ways. At last—for she was very young, oddly like Shakespeare the poet in her face, with the same grey eyes and rounded brows—at last Nick Greene[5] the actor-manager took pity on her; she found herself with child by that gentleman and so—who shall measure the heat and violence of the poet's heart when caught and tangled in a woman's body?—killed herself one winter's night and lies buried at some cross-roads where the omnibuses now stop outside the Elephant and Castle.[6]

That, more or less, is how the story would run, I think, if a woman in Shakespeare's day had had Shakespeare's genius. But for my part, I agree with the deceased bishop, if such he was—it is unthinkable that any woman in Shakespeare's day should have had Shakespeare's genius. For genius like Shakespeare's is not born among labouring, uneducated, servile people. It was not born in England among the Saxons and the Britons. It is not born today among the working classes. How, then, could it have been born among women whose work began, according to Professor Trevelyan, almost before they were out of the nursery, who were forced to it by their parents and held to it by all the power of law and custom? Yet genius of a sort must have existed among women as it must have existed among the working classes. Now and again an Emily Brontë or a Robert Burns[7] blazes out and proves its presence. But certainly it never got itself on to paper. When, however, one reads of a witch being ducked, of a woman possessed by devils, of a wise woman selling herbs, or even of a very remarkable man who had a mother, then I think we are on the track of a lost novelist, a suppressed poet, of some mute and inglorious[8] Jane Austen, some Emily Brontë who dashed her brains out on the moor or mopped and mowed about the highways crazed with the torture that her gift had put her to. Indeed, I would venture to guess that Anon, who wrote so many poems without signing them, was often a woman. It was a woman Edward Fitzgerald,[9] I think, suggested who made the ballads and the folk-songs, crooning them to her children, beguiling her spinning with them, or the length of the winter's night.

This may be true or it may be false—who can say?—but what is true in it, so it seemed to me, reviewing the story of Shakespeare's sister as I had made it, is that any woman born with a great gift in the sixteenth century would certainly have gone crazed, shot herself, or ended her days in some lonely cottage outside the village, half witch, half wizard, feared and mocked at. For it needs little skill in psychology to be sure that a highly gifted girl who had tried to use her gift for poetry would have been so thwarted and hindered by other people, so tortured and pulled asunder by her own contrary instincts, that she must have lost her health and sanity to a certainty. No

---

5. A fictional character based on Shakespeare's contemporary Robert Greene (1558–1592) and appearing in Woolf's *Orlando*.   6. A popular London pub. *Cross-roads*: suicides were commonly buried at cross-roads.   7. Scottish poet (1759–1796).   8. A reference to Thomas Grey's line in *Elegy Written in a Country Churchyard* (1751): "Some mute inglorious Milton here may rest."   9. British author (1809–1883), known for his translation from the Persian of the *Rubáiyát of Omar Khayyám* (1859).

girl could have walked to London and stood at a stage door and forced her way into the presence of actor-managers without doing herself a violence and suffering an anguish which may have been irrational—for chastity may be a fetish invented by certain societies for unknown reasons—but were none the less inevitable. Chastity had then, it has even now, a religious importance in a woman's life, and has so wrapped itself round with nerves and instincts that to cut it free and bring it to the light of day demands courage of the rarest. To have lived a free life in London in the sixteenth century would have meant for a woman who was poet and playwright a nervous stress and dilemma which might well have killed her. Had she survived, whatever she had written would have been twisted and deformed, issuing from a strained and morbid imagination. And undoubtedly, I thought, looking at the shelf where there are no plays by women, her work would have gone unsigned. That refuge she would have sought certainly. It was the relic of the sense of chastity that dictated anonymity to women even so late as the nineteenth century. Currer Bell, George Eliot, George Sand,[1] all the victims of inner strife as their writings prove, sought ineffectively to veil themselves by using the name of a man. Thus they did homage to the convention, which if not implanted by the other sex was liberally encouraged by them (the chief glory of a woman is not to be talked of, said Pericles,[2] himself a much-talked-of man), that publicity in women is detestable. Anonymity runs in their blood. The desire to be veiled still possesses them. They are not even now as concerned about the health of their fame as men are, and, speaking generally, will pass a tombstone or a signpost without feeling an irresistible desire to cut their names on it, as Alf, Bert or Chas. must do in obedience to their instinct, which murmurs if it sees a fine woman go by, or even a dog, Ce chien est à moi.[3] And, of course, it may not be a dog, I thought, remembering Parliament Square, the Sièges Allée[4] and other avenues; it may be a piece of land or a man with curly black hair. It is one of the great advantages of being a woman that one can pass even a very fine negress without wishing to make an Englishwoman of her.

That woman, then, who was born with a gift of poetry in the sixteenth century, was an unhappy woman, a woman at strife against herself. All the conditions of her life, all her own instincts, were hostile to the state of mind which is needed to set free whatever is in the brain. But what is the state of mind that is most propitious to the act of creation, I asked. Can one come by any notion of the state that furthers and makes possible that strange activity? Here I opened the volume containing the Tragedies of Shakespeare. What was Shakespeare's state of mind, for instance, when he wrote *Lear* and *Antony and Cleopatra*? It was certainly the state of mind most favourable to poetry that there has ever existed. But Shakespeare himself said nothing about it. We only know casually and by chance that he "never blotted a line."[5] Nothing indeed was ever said by the artist himself about his state of mind

1. Pseudonyms of Charlotte Brontë, Mary Ann Evans (1819–1880), and Lucile-Aurore Dupin (1804–1876), author of *Lélia* (1833), respectively.   2. From the Greek leader Pericles' funeral oration (431 B.C.E.), as reported in Thucydides' history of the Peloponnesian War (2.35–46).   3. This dog is mine (French); from the philosopher Blaise Pascal's *Thoughts* (1657–58). He uses an anecdote about poor children to illustrate a universal impulse to assert property claims.   4. An avenue in Berlin containing statues of Hohenzollern rulers. Parliament Square is in London next to the Houses of Parliament and Westminster Abbey.   5. Ben Jonson's (1572–1637) description of Shakespeare.

until the eighteenth century perhaps. Rousseau[6] perhaps began it. At any rate, by the nineteenth century self-consciousness had developed so far that it was the habit for men of letters to describe their minds in confessions and autobiographies. Their lives also were written, and their letters were printed after their deaths. Thus, though we do not know what Shakespeare went through when he wrote *Lear*, we do know what Carlyle went through when he wrote the *French Revolution*; what Flaubert went through when he wrote *Madame Bovary*; what Keats[7] was going through when he tried to write poetry against the coming of death and the indifference of the world.

And one gathers from this enormous modern literature of confession and self-analysis that to write a work of genius is almost always a feat of prodigious difficulty. Everything is against the likelihood that it will come from the writer's mind whole and entire. Generally material circumstances are against it. Dogs will bark; people will interrupt; money must be made; health will break down. Further, accentuating all these difficulties and making them harder to bear is the world's notorious indifference. It does not ask people to write poems and novels and histories; it does not need them. It does not care whether Flaubert finds the right word or whether Carlyle scrupulously verifies this or that fact. Naturally, it will not pay for what it does not want. And so the writer, Keats, Flaubert, Carlyle, suffers, especially in the creative years of youth, every form of distraction and discouragement. A curse, a cry of agony, rises from those books of analysis and confession. "Mighty poets in their misery dead"[8]—that is the burden of their song. If anything comes through in spite of all this, it is a miracle, and probably no book is born entire and uncrippled as it was conceived.

But for women, I thought, looking at the empty shelves, these difficulties were infinitely more formidable. In the first place, to have a room of her own, let alone a quiet room or a sound-proof room, was out of the question, unless her parents were exceptionally rich or very noble, even up to the beginning of the nineteenth century. Since her pin money, which depended on the good will of her father, was only enough to keep her clothed, she was debarred from such alleviations as came even to Keats or Tennyson or Carlyle, all poor men, from a walking tour, a little journey to France, from the separate lodging which, even if it were miserable enough, sheltered them from the claims and tyrannies of their families. Such material difficulties were formidable; but much worse were the immaterial. The indifference of the world which Keats and Flaubert and other men of genius have found so hard to bear was in her case not indifference but hostility. The world did not say to her as it said to them, Write if you choose; it makes no difference to me. The world said with a guffaw, Write? What's the good of your writing? Here the psychologists of Newnham and Girton might come to our help, I thought, looking again at the blank spaces on the shelves. For surely it is time that the effect of discouragement upon the mind of the artist should be measured, as I have seen a dairy company measure the effect of ordinary milk and Grade A milk upon the body of the rat. They set two rats in cages side by side, and of the two one was furtive, timid and small, and the other was glossy, bold and big. Now what food do we feed women as artists upon?

6. Jean-Jacques Rousseau (1712–1778), French author of the *Confessions* (1781).   7. John Keats (1795–1821), British poet. Thomas Carlyle (1795–1881), essayist and historian, translator of Goethe and author of *The French Revolution* (1837).   8. From Wordsworth's *Resolution and Independence* (1807).

I asked, remembering, I suppose, that dinner of prunes and custard. To answer that question I had only to open the evening paper and to read that Lord Birkenhead is of opinion—but really I am not going to trouble to copy out Lord Birkenhead's opinion upon the writing of women. What Dean Inge says I will leave in peace. The Harley Street specialist may be allowed to rouse the echoes of Harley Street[9] with his vociferations without raising a hair on my head. I will quote, however, Mr. Oscar Browning, because Mr. Oscar Browning was a great figure in Cambridge at one time, and used to examine the students at Girton and Newnham. Mr. Oscar Browning was wont to declare "that the impression left on his mind, after looking over any set of examination papers, was that, irrespective of the marks he might give, the best woman was intellectually the inferior of the worst man." After saying that Mr. Browning went back to his rooms—and it is this sequel that endears him and makes him a human figure of some bulk and majesty—he went back to his rooms and found a stable-boy lying on the sofa—"a mere skeleton, his cheeks were cavernous and sallow, his teeth were black, and he did not appear to have the full use of his limbs. . . . 'That's Arthur' [said Mr. Browning]. 'He's a dear boy really and most high-minded.' " The two pictures always seem to me to complete each other. And happily in this age of biography the two pictures often do complete each other, so that we are able to interpret the opinions of great men not only by what they say, but by what they do.

But though this is possible now, such opinions coming from the lips of important people must have been formidable enough even fifty years ago. Let us suppose that a father from the highest motives did not wish his daughter to leave home and become writer, painter or scholar. "See what Mr. Oscar Browning says," he would say; and there was not only Mr. Oscar Browning; there was the *Saturday Review*; there was Mr. Greg[1]—the "essentials of a woman's being," said Mr. Greg emphatically, "are that *they are supported by, and they minister to, men*"—there was an enormous body of masculine opinion to the effect that nothing could be expected of women intellectually. Even if her father did not read out loud these opinions, any girl could read them for herself; and the reading, even in the nineteenth century, must have lowered her vitality, and told profoundly upon her work. There would always have been that assertion—you cannot do this, you are incapable of doing that—to protest against, to overcome. Probably for a novelist this germ is no longer of much effect; for there have been women novelists of merit. But for painters it must still have some sting in it; and for musicians, I imagine, is even now active and poisonous in the extreme. The woman composer stands where the actress stood in the time of Shakespeare. Nick Greene, I thought, remembering the story I had made about Shakespeare's sister, said that a woman acting put him in mind of a dog dancing. Johnson repeated the phrase two hundred years later of women preaching. And here, I said, opening a book about music, we have the very words used again in this year of grace, 1928, of women who try to write music. "Of Mlle. Germaine Tailleferre one can only repeat Dr. Johnson's dictum concerning a woman preacher, transposed into terms of music. 'Sir, a woman's composing is like a dog's walking

9. A London street known for its many prominent physicians.   1. William Rathbone Greg (1809–1891), cited from a *Saturday Review* essay entitled *Why Are Women Redundant* (1873).

on his hind legs. It is not done well, but you are surprised to find it done at all.' "[2] So accurately does history repeat itself.

Thus, I concluded, shutting Mr. Oscar Browning's life and pushing away the rest, it is fairly evident that even in the nineteenth century a woman was not encouraged to be an artist. On the contrary, she was snubbed, slapped, lectured and exhorted. Her mind must have been strained and her vitality lowered by the need of opposing this, of disproving that. For here again we come within range of that very interesting and obscure masculine complex which has had so much influence upon the woman's movement; that deep-seated desire, not so much that *she* shall be inferior as that *he* shall be superior, which plants him wherever one looks, not only in front of the arts, but barring the way to politics too, even when the risk to himself seems infinitesimal and the suppliant humble and devoted. Even Lady Bessborough,[3] I remembered, with all her passion for politics, must humbly bow herself and write to Lord Granville Leveson-Gower: ". . . notwithstanding all my violence in politics and talking so much on that subject, I perfectly agree with you that no woman has any business to meddle with that or any other serious business, farther than giving her opinion (if she is ask'd)." And so she goes on to spend her enthusiasm where it meets with no obstacle whatsoever upon that immensely important subject, Lord Granville's maiden speech in the House of Commons. The spectacle is certainly a strange one, I thought. The history of men's opposition to women's emancipation is more interesting perhaps than the story of that emancipation itself. An amusing book might be made of it if some young student at Girton or Newnham would collect examples and deduce a theory—but she would need thick gloves on her hands, and bars to protect her of solid gold.

But what is amusing now, I recollected, shutting Lady Bessborough, had to be taken in desperate earnest once. Opinions that one now pastes in a book labelled cock-a-doodle-dum and keeps for reading to select audiences on summer nights once drew tears, I can assure you. Among your grandmothers and great-grandmothers there were many that wept their eyes out. Florence Nightingale shrieked aloud in her agony.[4] Moreover, it is all very well for you, who have got yourselves to college and enjoy sitting-rooms—or is it only bed-sitting-rooms?—of your own to say that genius should disregard such opinions; that genius should be above caring what is said of it. Unfortunately, it is precisely the men or women of genius who mind most what is said of them. Remember Keats. Remember the words he had cut on his tombstone.[5] Think of Tennyson; think—but I need hardly multiply instances of the undeniable, if very, unfortunate, fact that it is the nature of the artist to mind excessively what is said about him. Literature is strewn with the wreckage of men who have minded beyond reason the opinions of others.

And this susceptibility of theirs is doubly unfortunate, I thought, returning again to my original enquiry into what state of mind is most propitious for creative work, because the mind of an artist, in order to achieve the prodi-

2. *A Survey of Contemporary Music*, Cecil Gray, p. 246 [Woolf's note]. The statement is originally found in James Boswell's *Life of Johnson* (1791). 3. Henrietta, Countess of Bessborough (1761–1821), who corresponded with Lord Granville George Leveson-Gower (1815–1891), British foreign secretary in William Gladstone's administrations and after him the leader of the Liberal Party. 4. See *Cassandra*, by Florence Nightingale, printed in *The Cause*, by R. Strachey [Woolf's note]. Nightingale (1820–1910) was an English nurse and founder of nursing as a profession for women. 5. "Here lies one whose name was writ in water."

gious effort of freeing whole and entire the work that is in him, must be incandescent, like Shakespeare's mind, I conjectured, looking at the book which lay open at *Antony and Cleopatra*. There must be no obstacle in it, no foreign matter unconsumed.

For though we say that we know nothing about Shakespeare's state of mind, even as we say that, we are saying something about Shakespeare's state of mind. The reason perhaps why we know so little of Shakespeare—compared with Donne or Ben Jonson or Milton—is that his grudges and spites and antipathies are hidden from us. We are not held up by some "revelation" which reminds us of the writer. All desire to protest, to preach, to proclaim an injury, to pay off a score, to make the world the witness of some hardship or grievance was fired out of him and consumed. Therefore his poetry flows from him free and unimpeded. If ever a human being got his work expressed completely, it was Shakespeare. If ever a mind was incandescent, unimpeded, I thought, turning again to the bookcase, it was Shakespeare's mind.

An Unwritten Novel

Such an expression of unhappiness was enough by itself to make one's eyes slide above the paper's edge to the poor woman's face—insignificant without that look, almost a symbol of human destiny with it. Life's what you see in people's eyes; life's what they learn, and, having learnt it, never, though they seek to hide it, cease to be aware of—what? That life's like that, it seems. Five faces opposite—five mature faces—and the knowledge in each face. Strange though, how people want to conceal it! Marks of reticence are on all those faces: lips shut, eyes shaded, each one of the five doing something to hide or stultify his knowledge. One smokes; another reads; a third checks entries in a pocket book; a fourth stares at the map of the line framed opposite; and the fifth—the terrible thing about the fifth is that she does nothing at all. She looks at life. Ah, but my poor, unfortunate woman, do play the game—do, for all our sakes, conceal it!

As if she heard me, she looked up, shifted slightly in her seat and sighed. She seemed to apologize and at the same time to say to me, "If only you knew!" Then she looked at life again. "But I do know," I answered silently, glancing at the *Times*[1] for manners' sake. "I know the whole business. 'Peace between Germany and the Allied Powers was yesterday officially ushered in at Paris—Signor Nitti, the Italian Prime Minister—a passenger train at Doncaster was in collision with a goods train . . . ' We all know—the *Times* knows—but we pretend we don't." My eyes had once more crept over the paper's rim. She shuddered, twitched her arm queerly to the middle of her back and shook her head. Again I dipped into my great reservoir of life. "Take what you like," I continued, "births, deaths, marriages, Court Circular, the habits of birds, Leonardo da Vinci, the Sandhills murder, high wages and the cost of living—oh, take what you like," I repeated, "it's all in the *Times*!"

1. Major London newspaper, reputed to cover everything from international and royal news (the Court Circular) to a variety of local topics.

Again with infinite weariness she moved her head from side to side until, like a top exhausted with spinning, it settled on her neck.

The *Times* was no protection against such sorrow as hers. But other human beings forbade intercourse. The best thing to do against life was to fold the paper so that it made a perfect square, crisp, thick, impervious even to life. This done, I glanced up quickly, armed with a shield of my own. She pierced through my shield; she gazed into my eyes as if searching any sediment of courage at the depths of them and damping it to clay. Her twitch alone denied all hope, discounted all illusion.

So we rattled through Surrey and across the border into Sussex.[2] But with my eyes upon life I did not see that the other travellers had left, one by one, till, save for the man who read, we were alone together. Here was Three Bridges station. We drew slowly down the platform and stopped. Was he going to leave us? I prayed both ways—I prayed last that he might stay. At that instant he roused himself, crumpled his paper contemptuously, like a thing done with, burst open the door, and left us alone.

The unhappy woman, leaning a little forward, palely and colourlessly addressed me—talked of stations and holidays, of brothers at Eastbourne,[3] and the time of year, which was, I forget now, early or late. But at last looking from the window and seeing, I knew, only life, she breathed, "Staying away—that's the drawback of it—" Ah, now we approached the catastrophe.[4] "My sister-in-law"—the bitterness of her tone was like lemon on cold steel, and speaking, not to me, but to herself, she muttered, "Nonsense, she would say—that's what they all say," and while she spoke she fidgeted as though the skin on her back were as a plucked fowl's in a poulterer's shop-window.

"Oh, that cow!" she broke off nervously, as though the great wooden cow in the meadow had shocked her and saved her from some indiscretion. Then she shuddered, and then she made the awkward angular movement that I had seen before, as if, after the spasm, some spot between the shoulders burnt or itched. Then again she looked the most unhappy woman in the world, and I once more reproached her, though not with the same conviction, for if there were a reason, and if I knew the reason, the stigma was removed from life.

"Sisters-in-law," I said—

Her lips pursed as if to spit venom at the word; pursed they remained. All she did was to take her glove and rub hard at a spot on the windowpane. She rubbed as if she would rub something out for ever—some stain, some indelible contamination. Indeed, the spot remained for all her rubbing, and back she sank with the shudder and the clutch of the arm I had come to expect. Something impelled me to take my glove and rub my window. There, too, was a little speck on the glass. For all my rubbing it remained. And then the spasm went through me; I crooked my arm and plucked at the middle of my back. My skin, too, felt like the damp chicken's skin in the poulterer's shop-window; one spot between the shoulders itched and irritated, felt clammy, felt raw. Could I reach it? Surreptitiously I tried. She saw me. A smile of infinite irony, infinite sorrow, flitted and faded from her face. But she had communicated, shared her secret, passed her poison; she would speak no

<hr />

2. The train is passing through the southeastern English countryside, headed away from London.   3. A seaside resort.   4. In the literary sense: a dénouement or crucial revelation.

more. Leaning back in my corner, shielding my eyes from her eyes, seeing only the slopes and hollows, greys and purples, of the winter's landscape, I read her message, deciphered her secret, reading it beneath her gaze.

Hilda's the sister-in-law. Hilda? Hilda? Hilda Marsh—Hilda the blooming, the full bosomed, the matronly. Hilda stands at the door as the cab draws up, holding a coin. "Poor Minnie, more of a grasshopper than ever—old cloak she had last year. Well, well, with two children these days one can't do more. No, Minnie, I've got it; here you are, cabby—none of your ways with me. Come in, Minnie. Oh, I could carry *you*, let alone your basket!" So they go into the dining-room. "Aunt Minnie, children."

Slowly the knives and forks sink from the upright. Down they get (Bob and Barbara), hold out hands stiffly; back again to their chairs, staring between the resumed mouthfuls. [But this we'll skip; ornaments, curtains, trefoil china plate, yellow oblongs of cheese, white squares of biscuit—skip, oh, but wait! Halfway through luncheon one of those shivers; Bob stares at her, spoon in mouth. "Get on with your pudding, Bob"; but Hilda disapproves. "Why *should* she twitch?" Skip, skip, till we reach the landing on the upper floor; stairs brass-bound; linoleum worn; oh, yes! little bedroom looking out over the roofs of Eastbourne—zigzagging roofs like the spines of caterpillars, this way, that way, striped red and yellow, with blue-black slating.] Now, Minnie, the door's shut; Hilda heavily descends to the basement; you unstrap the straps of your basket, lay on the bed a meagre nightgown, stand side by side furred felt slippers. The looking-glass—no, you avoid the looking-glass. Some methodical disposition of hat-pins. Perhaps the shell box has something in it? You shake it; it's the pearl stud there was last year—that's all. And then the sniff, the sigh, the sitting by the window. Three o'clock on a December afternoon; the rain drizzling! one light low in the skylight of a drapery emporium; another high in a servant's bedroom—this one goes out. That gives her nothing to look at. A moment's blankness—then, what are you thinking? (Let me peep across at her opposite; she's asleep or pretending it; so what would she think about sitting at the window at three o'clock in the afternoon? Health, money, bills, her God?) Yes, sitting on the very edge of the chair looking over the roofs of Eastbourne, Minnie Marsh prays to God. That's all very well; and she may rub the pane too, as though to see God better; but what God does she see? Who's the God of Minnie Marsh, the God of the back streets of Eastbourne, the God of three o'clock in the afternoon? I, too, see roofs, I see sky; but, oh, dear—this seeing of Gods! More like President Kruger than Prince Albert[5]—that's the best I can do for him; and I see him on a chair, in a black frock-coat, not so very high up either; I can manage a cloud or two for him to sit on; and then his hand trailing in the cloud holds a rod, a truncheon is it?—black, thick, thorned—a brutal old bully—Minnie's God! Did he send the itch and the patch and the twitch? Is that why she prays? What she rubs on the window is the stain of sin. Oh, she committed some crime!

I have my choice of crimes. The woods flit and fly—in summer there are bluebells; in the opening there, when spring comes, primroses. A parting,

---

5. Prince Albert (1819–1861), husband of the British queen Victoria, was a popular figure known for political moderation. Paul Kruger (1825–1904), Transvaal statesman strongly opposed to British influence in South Africa, president of the Boer Republic for twenty years. Contemporary pictures show him in formal frock coat with a severe, bearded face.

was it, twenty years ago? Vows broken? Not Minnie's! . . . She was faithful.
How she nursed her mother! All her savings on the tombstone—wreaths
under glass—daffodils in jars. But I'm off the track. A crime. . . . They would
say she kept her sorrow, suppressed her secret—her sex, they'd say—the
scientific people. But what flummery to saddle *her* with sex! No—more like
this. Passing down the streets of Croydon twenty years ago, the violet loops
of ribbon in the draper's window spangled in the electric light catch her eye.
She lingers—past six. Still by running she can reach home. She pushes
through the glass wing door. It's sale-time. Shallow trays brim with ribbons.
She pauses, pulls this, fingers that with the raised roses on it—no need to
choose, no need to buy, and each tray with its surprises. "We don't shut till
seven," and then it *is* seven. She runs, she rushes, home she reaches, but
too late. Neighbours—the doctor—baby brother—the kettle—scalded—hospital—dead—or only the shock of it, the blame? Ah, but the detail matters
nothing! It's what she carries with her; the spot, the crime, the thing to
expiate, always there between her shoulders. "Yes," she seems to nod to me,
"it's the thing I did."

Whether you did, or what you did, I don't mind; it's not the thing I want.
The draper's window looped with violet—that'll do; a little cheap perhaps, a
little commonplace—since one has a choice of crimes, but then so many (let
me peep across again—still sleeping, or pretending sleep! white, worn, the
mouth closed—a touch of obstinacy, more than one would think—no hint
of sex)—so many crimes aren't *your* crime; your crime was cheap, only the
retribution solemn; for now the church door opens, the hard wooden pew
receives her; on the brown tiles she kneels; every day, winter, summer, dusk,
dawn (here she's at it) prays. All her sins fall, fall, for ever fall. The spot
receives them. It's raised, it's red, it's burning. Next she twitches. Small boys
point. "Bob at lunch today"—But elderly women are the worst.

Indeed now you can't sit praying any longer. Kruger's sunk beneath the
clouds—washed over as with a painter's brush of liquid grey, to which he
adds a tinge of black—even the tip of the truncheon gone now. That's what
always happens! Just as you've seen him, felt him, someone interrupts. It's
Hilda now.

How you hate her! She'll even lock the bathroom door overnight, too,
though it's only cold water you want, and sometimes when the night's been
bad it seems as if washing helped. And John at breakfast—the children—
meals are worst, and sometimes there are friends—ferns don't altogether
hide 'em—they guess, too; so out you go along the front,[6] where the waves
are grey, and the papers blow, and the glass shelters green and draughty, and
the chairs cost tuppence—too much—for there must be preachers along the
sands. Ah, that's a nigger—that's a funny man—that's a man with parakeets—poor little creatures! Is there no one here who thinks of God?—just
up there, over the pier, with his rod—but no—there's nothing but grey in
the sky or if it's blue the white clouds hide him, and the music—it's military
music—and what are they fishing for? Do they catch them? How the children
stare! Well, then home a back way—"Home a back way!" The words have
meaning; might have been spoken by the old man with whiskers—no, no, he
didn't really speak; but everything has meaning—placards leaning against

---

6. Waterfront; chairs were available for rent.

doorways—names above shop-windows—red fruit in baskets—women's heads in the hairdresser's—all say "Minnie Marsh!" But here's a jerk. "Eggs are cheaper!"[7] That's what always happens! I was heading her over the waterfall, straight for madness, when, like a flock of dream sheep, she turns t'other way and runs between my fingers. Eggs are cheaper. Tethered to the shores of the world, none of the crimes, sorrows, rhapsodies, or insanities for poor Minnie Marsh; never late for luncheon; never caught in a storm without a mackintosh; never utterly unconscious of the cheapness of eggs. So she reaches home—scrapes her boots.

Have I read you right? But the human face—the human face at the top of the fullest sheet of print holds more, withholds more. Now, eyes open, she looks out; and in the human eye—how d'you define it?—there's a break—a division—so that when you've grasped the stem the butterfly's off— the moth that hangs in the evening over the yellow flower—move, raise your hand, off, high, away. I won't raise my hand. Hang still, then, quiver, life, soul, spirit, whatever you are of Minnie Marsh—I, too, on my flower—the hawk over the down—alone, or what were the worth of life? To rise, hang still in the evening, in the midday; hang still over the down. The flicker of a hand—off, up! then poised again. Alone, unseen; seeing all so still down there, all so lovely. None seeing none caring. The eyes of others our prisons; their thoughts our cages. Air above, air below. And the moon and immortality. . . . Oh, but I drop to the turf! Are you down too, you in the corner, what's your name—woman—Minnie Marsh; some such name as that? There she is, tight to her blossom; opening her hand-bag, from which she takes a hollow shell—an egg—who was saying that eggs were cheaper? You or I? Oh, it was you who said it on the way home, you remember, when the old gentleman, suddenly opening his umbrella—or sneezing was it? Anyhow, Kruger went, and you came "home a back way," and scraped your boots. Yes. And now you lay across your knees a pocket-handkerchief into which drop little angular fragments of eggshell—fragments of a map—a puzzle. I wish I could piece them together! If you would only sit still. She's moved her knees—the map's in bits again. Down the slopes of the Andes the white blocks of marble go bounding and hurtling, crushing to death a whole troop of Spanish muleteers, with their convoy—Drake's booty, gold and silver.[8] But to return—

To what, to where? She opened the door, and, putting her umbrella in the stand—that goes without saying: so, too, the whiff of beef from the basement; dot, dot, dot. But what I cannot thus eliminate, what I must, head down, eyes shut, with the courage of a battalion and the blindness of a bull; charge and disperse are, indubitably, the figures behind the ferns, commercial travelers. There, I've hidden them all this time in the hope that somehow they'd disappear, or better still emerge, as indeed they must, if the story's to go on gathering richness and rotundity, destiny and tragedy, as stories should, rolling along with it two, if not three, commercial travellers and a whole grove of aspidistra. "The fronds of the aspidistra only partly concealed

7. The narrator's silent imaginings are interrupted and brought down to earth when "Minnie Marsh," preparing to eat her snack of hard-boiled egg, comments out loud that "Eggs are cheaper!" 8. The yellow and white fragments of egg inspire another series of images. Sir Francis Drake (1540?–1596) was an English explorer and sea captain who captured Spanish ships returning from South America laden with gold and silver stolen from the Indians: the Indians are imagined as rolling blocks of marble down the Andes mountains to crush the invaders.

the commercial traveller—" Rhododendrons would conceal him utterly, and into the bargain give me my fling of red and white, for which I starve and strive; but rhododendrons in Eastbourne—in December—on the Marshes' table—no, no. I dare not;[9] it's all a matter of crusts and cruets, frills and ferns. Perhaps there'll be a moment later by the sea. Moreover, I feel, pleasantly pricking through the green fretwork and over the glacis of cut glass, a desire to peer and peep at the man opposite—one's as much as I can manage. James Moggridge is it, whom the Marshes call Jimmy? [Minnie, you must promise not to twitch till I've got this straight.] James Moggridge travels in[1]— shall we say buttons?—but the time's not come for bringing *them* in—the big and the little on the long cards, some peacock-eyed, others dull gold; cairngorms some, and others coral sprays—but I say the time's not come. He travels, and on Thursdays, his Eastbourne day, takes his meals with the Marshes. His red face, his little steady eyes—by no means altogether commonplace—his enormous appetite (that's safe; he won't look at Minnie till the bread's swamped the gravy dry), napkin tucked diamond-wise—but this is primitive, and, whatever it may do the reader, don't take me in. Let's dodge to the Moggridge household, set that in motion. Well, the family boots are mended on Sundays by James himself. He reads *Truth*.[2] But his passion? Roses—and his wife a retired hospital nurse—interesting—for God's sake let me have one woman with a name I like! But no; she's of the unborn children of the mind, illicit, none the less loved, like my rhododendrons. How many die in every novel that's written—the best, the dearest, while Moggridge lives. It's life's fault. Here's Minnie eating her egg at the moment opposite and at t'other end of the line—are we past Lewes?[3]—there must be Jimmy—or what's her twitch for?

There must be Moggridge—life's fault. Life imposes her laws; life blocks the way; life's behind the fern; life's the tyrant; oh, but not the bully! No, for I assure you I come willingly; I come wooed by Heaven knows what compulsion across ferns and cruets, table splashed and bottles smeared. I come irresistibly to lodge myself somewhere on the firm flesh, in the robust spine, wherever I can penetrate or find foothold on the person, in the soul, of Moggridge the man. The enormous stability of the fabric; the spine tough as whalebone, straight as oaktree; the ribs radiating branches; the flesh taut tarpaulin; the red hollows; the suck and regurgitation of the heart; while from above meat falls in brown cubes and beer gushes to be churned to blood again—and so we reach the eyes. Behind the aspidistra they see something: black, white, dismal; now the plate again; behind the aspidistra they see an elderly woman; "Marsh's sister. Hilda's more my sort"; the tablecloth now. "Marsh would know what's wrong with Morrises . . ." talk that over; cheese has come; the plate again; turn it round—the enormous fingers; now the woman opposite. "Marsh's sister—not a bit like Marsh; wretched, elderly female. . . . You should feed your hens. . . . God's truth, what's set her twitching? Not what *I* said? Dear, dear, dear! these elderly women. Dear, dear!"

---

9. Aspidistra (a long-leaved, common house plant) is more appropriate for the imagined story's middle-class setting than rhododendron, which would not fit the season or context.   1. The commercial traveler (traveling salesman) given the name James Moggridge is imagined as selling buttons; there follows a brief description of his merchandise on its display cards. *Cairngorm*: A yellow quartz.   2. A popular weekly magazine.   3. County town in East Sussex.

[Yes, Minnie; I know you've twitched, but one moment—James Moggridge.]

"Dear, dear, dear!" How beautiful the sound is! like the knock of a mallet on seasoned timber, like the throb of the heart of an ancient whaler when the seas press thick and the green is clouded. "Dear, dear!" what a passing bell for the souls of the fretful to soothe them and solace them, lap them in linen, saying, "So long. Good luck to you!" and then, "What's your pleasure?" for though Moggridge would pluck his rose for her, that's done, that's over. Now what's the next thing? "Madam, you'll miss your train," for they don't linger.

That's the man's way; that's the sound that reverberates; that's St. Paul's,[4] and the motor-omnibuses. But we're brushing the crumbs off. Oh, Moggridge, you won't stay? You must be off? Are you driving through Eastbourne this afternoon in one of those little carriages? Are you the man who's walled up in green cardboard boxes, and sometimes sits so solemn staring like a sphinx; and always there's a look of the sepulchral, something of the undertaker, the coffin, and the dusk about horse and driver? Do tell me—but the doors slammed. We shall never meet again. Moggridge, farewell!

Yes, yes, I'm coming. Right up to the top of the house. One moment I'll linger. How the mud goes round in the mind—what a swirl these monsters leave, the waters rocking, the weeds waving and green here, black there, striking to the sand, till by degrees the atoms reassemble, the deposit sifts itself, and again through the eyes one sees clear and still, and there comes to the lips some prayer for the departed, some obsequy for the souls of those one nods to, the people one never meets again.

James Moggridge is dead now, gone for ever. Well, Minnie—"I can face it no longer." If she said that—(Let me look at her. She is brushing the eggshell into deep declivities). She said it certainly, leaning against the wall of the bedroom, and plucking at the little balls which edge the claret-coloured curtain. But when the self speaks to the self, who is speaking?— the entombed soul, the spirit driven in, in, in to the central catacomb; the self that took the veil[5] and left the world—a coward perhaps, yet somehow beautiful, as it flits with its lantern restlessly up and down the dark corridors. "I can bear it no longer," her spirit says. "That man at lunch—Hilda—the children." Oh, heavens, her sob! It's the spirit wailing its destiny, the spirit driven hither, thither, lodging on the diminishing carpets—meagre footholds—shrunken shreds of all the vanishing universe—love, life, faith, husband, children, I know not what splendours and pageantries glimpsed in girlhood. "Not for me—not for me."

But then—the muffins, the bald elderly dog? Bead mats I should fancy and the consolation of underlinen. If Minnie Marsh were run over and taken to hospital, nurses and doctors themselves would exclaim.[6] . . . There's the vista and the vision—there's the distance—the blue blot at the end of the avenue, while, after all, the tea is rich, the muffin hot, and the dog—"Benny, to your basket, sir, and see what mother's brought you!" So, taking the glove with the worn thumb, defying once more the encroaching demon of what's called going in holes, you renew the fortifications, threading the grey wool, running it in and out.

4. St. Paul's Cathedral in London.   5. Became a nun.   6. The hospital attendants are to exclaim at the neatness of Minnie Marsh's underwear. Immaculate and well-kept clothing—both inside and out— were the signs of a proper lady.

Running it in and out, across and over, spinning a web through which God himself—hush, don't think of God! How firm the stitches are! You must be proud of your darning. Let nothing disturb her. Let the light fall gently, and the clouds show an inner vest of the first green leaf. Let the sparrow perch on the twig and shake the raindrop hanging to the twig's elbow. . . . Why look up? Was it a sound, a thought? Oh, heavens! Back again to the thing you did, the plate glass with the violet loops? But Hilda will come. Ignominies, humiliations, oh! Close the breach.

Having mended her glove, Minnie Marsh lays it in the drawer. She shuts the drawer with decision. I catch sight of her face in the glass. Lips are pursed. Chin held high. Next she laces her shoes. Then she touches her throat. What's your brooch? Mistletoe or merrythought?[7] And what is happening? Unless I'm much mistaken, the pulse's quickened, the moment's coming, the threads are racing, Niagara's ahead. Here's the crisis! Heaven be with you! Down she goes. Courage, courage! Face it, be it! For God's sake don't wait on the mat now! There's the door! I'm on your side. Speak! Confort her, confound her soul![8]

"Oh, I beg your pardon! Yes, this is Eastbourne. I'll reach it down for you. Let me try the handle." [But Minnie, though we keep up pretences, I've read you right—I'm with you now.]

"That's all your luggage?"

"Much obliged, I'm sure."

(But why do you look about you? Hilda won't come to the station, nor John; and Moggridge is driving at the far side of Eastbourne.)

"I'll wait by my bag, ma'am, that's safest. He said he'd meet me. . . . Oh, there he is! That's my son."

So they walk off together.

Well, but I'm confounded. . . . Surely, Minnie, you know better! A strange young man. . . . Stop! I'll tell him—Minnie!—Miss Marsh!—I don't know though. There's something queer in her cloak as it blows. Oh, but it's untrue, it's indecent. . . . Look how he bends as they reach the gateway. She finds her ticket. What's the joke? Off they go, down the road, side by side. . . . Well, my world's done for! What do I stand on? What do I know? That's not Minnie. There never was Moggridge. Who am I? Life's bare as bone.

And yet the last look of them—he stepping from the kerb and she following him round the edge of the big building brims me with wonder—floods me anew. Mysterious figures! Mother and son. Who are you? Why do you walk down the street? Where tonight will you sleep, and then, tomorrow? Oh, how it whirls and surges—floats me afresh! I start after them. People drive this way and that. The white light splutters and pours. Plate-glass windows. Carnations; chrysanthemums. Ivy in dark gardens. Milk carts at the door. Wherever I go, mysterious figures, I see you, turning the corner, mothers and sons; you, you, you. I hasten, I follow. This, I fancy, must be the sea. Grey is the landscape; dim as ashes; the water murmurs and moves. If I fall on my knees, if I go through the ritual, the ancient antics, it's you, unknown figures, you I adore; if I open my arms, it's you I embrace, you I draw to me—adorable world!

---

7. Wishbone.   8. The narrator imagines a major confrontation between the poor spinster "Minnie Marsh" and "Hilda."

FRANZ KAFKA
1883–1924

The predicament of Franz Kafka's writing is, for many, the predicament of modern civilization. Nowhere is the anxiety and alienation of twentieth-century society more visible than in his stories of individuals struggling to prevail against a vast, meaningless, and apparently hostile system. Identifying that system as bureaucracy, family, religion, language, or the invisible network of social habit is less important than recognizing the protagonists' bewilderment at being placed in impossible situations. Kafka's heroes are driven to find answers in an unresponsive world, and they are required to act according to incomprehensible rules administered by an inaccessible authority; small wonder that they fluctuate among fear, hope, anger, resignation, and despair. Kafka's fictional world has long fascinated contemporary writers, who find in it an extraordinary blend of prosaic realism and nightmarish, infinitely interpretable symbolism. Whether evoking the multilayered bureaucracy of the modern state, the sense of guilt felt by those facing the accusations of authority, or the vulnerability of characters who cannot make themselves understood, Kafka's descriptions are believable because of their scrupulous attention to detail: the flea on a fur collar, the dust under an unmade bed, the creases and yellowing of an old newspaper, or the helplessness of a beetle turned upside down. The sheer *ordinariness* of these details grounds the entire narrative, giving the reader a continuing expectation of reality even when events escape all logic and the situation is at its most hallucinatory. This paradoxical combination has appealed to a range of contemporary writers—each different from the other—who have read and absorbed Kafka's lesson: Samuel Beckett, Harold Pinter, Alain Robbe-Grillet, Gabriel García Márquez.

Kafka was born into cultural alienation: Jewish (though not truly part of the Jewish community) in Catholic Czechoslovakia, son of a German-speaking shopkeeper when German was the language of the imposed Austro-Hungarian government, and drawn to literature when his father—a domineering, self-made man—pushed him toward success in business. Nor was he happier at home. Resenting his father's overbearing nature and feeling deprived of maternal love, he nonetheless lived with his parents for most of his life and complained in long letters about his coldness and inability to love (despite numerous liaisons). Kafka took a degree in law to qualify himself for a position in a large accident-insurance corporation, where he worked until illness forced his retirement in 1922. By the time of his death from tuberculosis two years later, he had published a number of short stories and two novellas (*The Metamorphosis*, 1915; *In the Penal Colony*, 1919), but left behind him the manuscripts of three near-complete novels that—considering himself a failure—he asked to have burned. Instead, Kafka's executor, Max Brod, published the novels (*The Trial*, 1925; *The Castle*, 1926; *Amerika*, 1927) and a biography celebrating the genius of his tormented, guilt-ridden friend.

Despite the indubitable fact that Franz Kafka became a respected senior executive, handling claims, litigations, public relations, and his institute's annual reports, and was one of the few top German executives retained when Czechoslovakia finally gained independence in 1918, his image in the modern imagination is derived from the portraits of inner anguish given in his fiction, diaries, and letters. This "Kafka" is a tormented and sensitive soul, guiltily resentful of his job in a giant bureaucracy, unable to free himself from his family or to cope with the demands of love, physically feeble, and constantly beset by feelings of inferiority and doom in an existence whose laws he can never quite understand. *Before the Law,* a parable published in Kafka's lifetime and included in *The Trial*, recounts the archetypal setting of the "Kafka" character: a countryman waits and waits throughout his lifetime for permission to enter a crucial Gate, where the doorkeeper (the first of many) repeatedly refuses him entrance. He tries everything from good behavior to bribes without success. Finally, as the now-aged countryman dies in frustration, he is told that the gate existed only for him, and that it is now being closed. For the countryman (as for Vladimir and Estragon in Beckett's *Waiting for Godot*, and indeed for much modern literature), there is no response. The Law that governs our existence is all-powerful but irrational; at least it is not to be understood by its human suppliants, a lesson that Kafka could have derived equally well from his readings in the Danish philosopher Søren Kierkegaard, in Friedrich Nietzsche, or in the Talmud.

The combination of down-to-earth, matter-of-fact setting and unreal or nightmarish events is the hallmark of Kafka's style. His characters speak prosaically and react in a commonsense way when such a response (given the situation) is utterly grotesque. A young businessman is changed overnight into a giant beetle (*The Metamorphosis*) or charged with undefined crimes and finally executed (*The Trial*); a would-be land surveyor is unable to communicate with the castle that employs him and that keeps sending incomprehensible messages (*The Castle*); a visitor to a penal colony observes a gigantic machine whose function is to execute condemned criminals by inscribing their sentence deeper and deeper into their flesh (*In the Penal Colony*). The term *surrealist* is often attached to this blend of everyday reality and dream configuration, with its implication of psychic undercurrents and cosmic significance stirring beneath the most ordinary-seeming existence. Kafka, however, had no connection with the Surrealists, whose vision of a miraculous level of existence hidden behind everyday life is the obverse of his heroes' vain attempts to maintain control over the impossible and the absurd.

Kafka's stories are not allegories, although many readers have been tempted to find in them an underlying message. A political reading sees them as indictments of faceless bureaucracy controlling individual lives in the modern totalitarian state. The sense of being found guilty by an entire society recalls the traditional theme of the Wandering Jew and predicts for many the Holocaust of World War II (in fact, Kafka's three sisters died in concentration camps). His heroes' self-conscious quest to fit into some meaningful structure, their ceaseless attempts to do the right thing when there is no rational way of knowing what that is, is the very picture of absurdity and alienation that existentialist philosophers and writers examined during and after World War II. The assumption that there is a Law and the presence of protagonists who die in search for purity (*The Hunger Artist*) or in a humble admission of guilt (*The Trial*) allow the stories to be taken as religious metaphors. Kafka's desperately lucid analysis of the way his parents' influence shaped an impressionable child into an unhappy adult (*Letter to My Father*) articulates emotional tangles and parent-child rivalry with an openness and detail that recalls decades of psychoanalytical criticism following Freud. The picture of a sick society where individual rights and sensitivity no longer count and unreasoning torment is visited on the ignorant has been read as an indictment of disintegrating modern culture. Yet no one allegorical interpretation is finally possible, for all these potential meanings overlap as they expand toward social, familial, political, philosophical, and religious dimensions and constitute the richly allusive texture of separate tales by a master storyteller.

The Metamorphosis, Kafka's longest complete work published in his lifetime, is first of all a consummate narrative: the question "What happens next?" never disappears from the moment that Gregory Samsa wakes up to find himself transformed into a giant bug. It was no dream, no nightmarish fantasy in which Gregory temporarily identified himself with other downtrodden vermin of society. Instead, this grotesque transformation is permanent, a single unshakable fact that renders almost comic his family's calculations and attempts to adjust. "The terror of art," said Kafka in a conversation about *The Metamorphosis*, is that "the dream reveals the reality." This artistic dream, become Gregory's reality, sheds light on the intolerable nature of his former daily existence. The other side of his job is its mechanical rigidity, personal rivalries, and threatening suspicion of any deviation from the norm. Gregory himself is part of this world, as he shows when he fawns on the chief clerk and tries to manipulate him by criticizing their boss.

More disturbing is the transformation that takes place in Gregory's family, where the expected love and support turns into shamed acceptance and animal resentment now that Gregory has let the family down. Mother and sister are ineffectual, and their sympathy is slowly replaced by disgust. Gregory's father quickly reassumes his position of authority and beats the beetle back into his room: first with the businesslike newspaper and chief clerk's cane, and later with a barrage of apples from the family table. Just before his death, Gregory has become an "it" whose death is warmly wished by the whole family—and perhaps they are right, in one of Kafka's ironies. The beetle's death brings not remorse but a new lease on life to his family. Weak and passive when Gregory took care of them, they regain strength and vitality under the pressure of earning a living. Mother, father, and sister celebrate Gregory's death with a holiday trip out of town, into the sunshine and open air, where they make plans for the future.

Gregory Samsa may be a pathetic figure, but he is not a tragic one. In his passiveness and unvoiced resentment, his willingness to exist at a surface level of adjustment to job and family, he has become an accomplice in his own fate. His descent into animal consciousness is not a true pilgrimage to inner awareness, even though it involves letting go the trappings of civilization. Rather, it is an obscuring of consciousness that is perfectly represented when he is swept out onto the dustheap at the end. From that point on, it is the family's story, continuing a career that has meant death for Gregory and joyous survival for his family, but in which both are reduced to existence on an animal level.

The Metamorphosis[1]

I

Gregory Samsa woke from uneasy dreams one morning to find himself changed into a giant bug. He was lying on his back, which was of a shell-like hardness, and when he lifted his head a little he could see his dome-shaped brown belly, banded with what looked like reinforcing arches, on top of which his quilt, while threatening to slip off completely at any moment, still maintained a precarious hold. His many legs, pitifully thin in relation to the rest of him, threshed ineffectually before his eyes.

'What's happened to me?' he thought. This was no dream. His room, a normal human room except that it was rather too small, lay peacefully between the four familiar walls. Above the table, which was littered with a collection of drapery samples—Samsa was a traveller—hung the picture that he had recently cut out of a magazine and mounted in an attractive gilt frame. It showed a lady in a fur hat and boa, sitting up straight and holding out an enormous fur muff that entirely concealed her forearms.

Gregory's gaze shifted to the window, and the murky weather—raindrops beat audibly on the zinc windowsill—made him feel quite melancholy. 'Why don't I go back to sleep for a bit and forget all the fooling about?' he thought, but this was impossible: he liked to sleep on his right side, and in his present state he was unable to assume that position. Try as he might to throw himself over to the right, he always rocked back into his previous position. He must

---

1. Translated by J. A. Underwood.

have made a hundred attempts; he shut his eyes to keep out the sight of all those toiling legs; and he gave up only when he became aware of a faint, dull ache in his side of a kind he had never felt before.

'God,' he thought, 'what a gruelling job I chose! On the go day in and day out. The business side of it is much more hectic than in the office itself, and on top of that there's the wretched travelling, the worry about train connections, the awful meals eaten at all hours, and the constant chopping and changing as far as human relationships are concerned, never knowing anyone for long, never making friends. Oh, to hell with the whole thing!' He felt a slight itch high up on his belly; pushed himself, on his back, slowly closer to the bedpost, the better to lift his head; located the itchy place, which was covered with a lot of tiny white spots he did not know what to make of; and tried to touch the place with a leg, withdrawing it immediately, however, because the contact sent cold shivers through him.

He slid back into his original position. 'These early mornings,' he thought, 'are enough to drive one round the bend. A man needs his sleep. Other travellers live like kept women. I mean, when I go back to the hotel during the morning to write up my orders, some fellows are just sitting down to their breakfast. If I tried that on with my boss I'd be out on my ear immediately. Might not be a bad thing for me, at that. If it weren't for my parents I'd have handed in my notice long ago; I'd have gone to see the boss and given him a piece of my mind. Why, he'd have fallen off his desk! Funny habit, that, his sitting on the desk and talking down to his employees from a great height, especially since you have to step right up close because of his deafness. Ah well, there's still hope; once I've got the money together to pay off my parents' debt to him—that might take another five or six years—I'll definitely do it. I'll take the plunge. Meanwhile, though, I'd better get up; my train leaves at five.'

And he looked across at the alarm clock that stood ticking on the wardrobe. 'Heavens above!' he thought. It was half past six, and the hands were moving steadily onwards; in fact it was after half past, it was almost a quarter to. Had the alarm not rung? He could see from the bed that it had been set correctly for four o'clock; it must have rung. Yes, but—how could he have slept calmly through a ring so loud it shook the furniture? Well, not calmly, he hadn't slept calmly, but probably all the more soundly for that. What was he to do now, though? The next train left at seven; to catch that would have meant a frantic rush, and there were the samples to be packed, and he was not feeling particularly spry to start with, far from it. And even if he did catch the train he was in for a rocket from the boss because the office boy would have been at the station at five and would have reported his absence long ago, the office boy being a tool of the boss and a spineless, mindless creature. What if he were to report sick? No, that would be highly embarrassing as well as suspicious, Gregory not having had a day's illness in his five years with the firm. The boss would be sure to bring the health-insurance company's doctor round and blame his parents for having an idle son, cutting short all their protests by quoting the doctor's view that people were invariably in perfect health, just work-shy. And would he in fact be so wrong in this case? Aside from a certain drowsiness, quite superfluous after his long sleep, Gregory really felt very fit and was even aware of having an unusually robust appetite.

He laments his life's dullness.

His parents are all that's keeping his job and his temper.

As he was rapidly considering all this, though without managing to make up his mind to get out of bed—the alarm clock was just striking a quarter to seven—there came a cautious knock on the door at the head of his bed. 'Gregory,'—it was his mother speaking—'it's a quarter to seven. Weren't you going off this morning?' That gentle voice! Gregory gave a start when he heard his own voice in reply; it was unmistakably his, but blended with it, as if welling up irrepressibly from below, was a distressing squeak that allowed the words to retain their clarity only for a moment, afterwards distorting their resonance to the point where one wondered whether one had heard correctly. Gregory had wanted to answer at length and explain everything, but in the circumstances he confined himself to saying, 'Yes, yes—thank you, mother, I'm just getting up.' Because of the wooden door the alteration in Gregory's voice was presumably not noticeable outside, for his mother, reassured by his words, went shuffling off. Their brief exchange, however, had alerted the other members of the family to the fact that Gregory, unexpectedly, was still at home, and soon his father was knocking at the door on one side, not hard, but with his fist. 'Gregory, Gregory,' he called, 'what is it?' And after a little while he repeated his admonishment in a deeper voice: 'Gregory! Gregory!' At the door on the other side his sister was quietly plaintive: 'Gregory? Are you all right? Can I get you anything?' 'Just coming,' Gregory replied to them both, trying by means of the most careful enunciation and by leaving long pauses between the words to remove any conspicuous quality from his voice. His father did indeed go back to his breakfast, but his sister whispered, 'Gregory, open the door, *please*.' Nothing was further from Gregory's mind, however; in fact he was congratulating himself on his cautious habit, adopted from his travels, of locking all the doors of his room at night even when he was at home.

He first wanted to get up in peace and quiet, dress, and above all have breakfast, and only then contemplate the future, because as he knew full well he would never think things through to a sensible conclusion as long as he remained in bed. He recalled having quite often felt some slight pain in bed, possibly as a result of having lain awkwardly, which had turned out to be purely imaginary once he was up, and he was curious to see how this morning's imaginings would gradually evaporate. Not for a moment did he doubt that the alteration in his voice was merely an early symptom of that occupational affliction of commercial travellers, the streaming cold.

Getting rid of the quilt was quite simple; all he needed to do was to puff himself up a little and it fell to the floor. After that, however, things became difficult, particularly since he was so extraordinarily broad. He would have needed arms and hands to lift himself up, but instead he had only a large number of legs that were in continuous, multifarious motion and in any case quite beyond his control. Whenever he tried to bend one it promptly stretched out straight; and if he did eventually manage to make the leg execute the desired movement all the others, left as it were to their own devices, went on working away in a state of the most acute and painful excitement. 'Right—that's enough dawdling in bed!' Gregory told himself.

First he tried to get the lower part of his body out of bed, but this lower part, which incidentally he had not yet seen and of which he could form no very clear idea, proved too unwieldy; progress was so slow; and when finally, in a kind of rage, he summoned all his strength and recklessly thrust himself forward he had mistaken the direction, striking the lower bedpost a violent blow, and the sharp pain he felt informed him that it was this lower part of his body that was perhaps the most sensitive at the moment.

So he tried to get his upper body out of bed first, carefully twisting his head round towards the edge of the mattress. He managed this without difficulty, and despite its width and great weight his body did eventually begin to follow the movement of his head. But when at length he had his head out beyond the edge of the bed in mid air he suddenly thought better of continuing, afraid that if in the end he let himself fall like that it would take a miracle to prevent his sustaining a head injury. And the last thing he wanted to do just then was to lose consciousness; he would rather stay in bed.

But when after a similar struggle he lay back with a sigh in his first position and again saw his legs locked in what seemed if anything even fiercer combat than before, powerless to bring any kind of order into their chaos, he again told himself that he could not possibly stay where he was and that the only sensible thing was to risk all for even the faintest hope of somehow freeing himself from his bed. At the same time he was careful to remind himself at intervals that desperate decisions were no substitute for cool, calm thought. At such moments he focused as sharply as his eyes would allow on the window; unfortunately the sight of the morning mist, which even shrouded the other side of the narrow street, had little to offer in the way of brisk reassurance. 'Seven o'clock already,' he said to himself as the alarm clock struck again, 'seven o'clock and still such a mist.' And for a while he lay quiet, hardly breathing, hoping perhaps that total silence might bring about a return to normal, everyday reality.

But then he said to himself, 'Before a quarter past seven strikes I simply must be out of bed—right out. Anyway, someone will be here from the office by then to ask about me, because the office opens before seven o'clock.' And he set about rocking the whole length of his body evenly out of bed. If he allowed himself to fall out in this way his head, which he intended to lift smartly as he fell, would presumably remain unhurt. His back appeared to be hard; probably falling onto the carpet would do no damage to that. What worried him most was the thought of the loud crash that would inevitably accompany his fall and in all likelihood occasion if not alarm, at least concern beyond the various doors. But he would have to take that risk.

When Gregory was already leaning half out of bed—the new method was not so much work as play, since all he had to do was to keep rocking to and fro—it occurred to him how simple everything would be if someone were to come to his assistance. Two strong people—he had in mind his father and the maid—would have been quite sufficient; they need only have slid their arms under his arched back, eased him out of bed, bent down with him, and simply waited with patient vigilance until he had swung himself over onto the floor, where his legs would then, he hoped, acquire some purpose. So, quite apart from the fact that the doors were locked, should he really have called for help? In spite of his predicament he was unable to suppress a smile at the thought.

He had reached the stage where, if he rocked a little harder, he almost lost his balance, and he was very soon going to have to make up his mind once and for all because in five minutes it would be a quarter past seven— when the doorbell rang. 'That'll be someone from the office,' he said to himself and almost froze, except that his legs started dancing about all the more frantically. There was a moment's silence. 'They're not letting him in,' Gregory said to himself, caught up in some absurd hope. But then of course, as always, the maid strode purposefully to the door and opened it. The visitor's first word of greeting sufficed to tell Gregory who it was—the chief clerk himself. Why was Gregory of all people fated to work for a firm where the least little omission promptly aroused the greatest suspicion? Were all employees without exception knaves; was there not one single loyal and devoted person among them who, having failed to turn a mere couple of hours one morning to the firm's advantage, was driven so distracted by qualms of conscience as to become incapable of getting out of bed? Would it not have been enough to send an apprentice round to inquire, assuming this whole inquisition to be necessary in the first place? Did the chief clerk really have to come in person, so demonstrating to the entire, innocent family that the investigation of this suspicious affair could be entrusted only to a person of his discernment. And it was more in consequence of the state of agitation into which Gregory was thrown by these reflections than as a result of a genuine decision that he now swung himself out of bed with all his might. There was a loud thump, though not in fact a crash. To some extent his fall had been softened by the carpet, and also his back was more resilient than Gregory had thought—hence the muffled and really quite unremarkable sound. But he had not been careful enough about his head and had banged it; he twisted it round and rubbed it on the carpet in anger and pain.

'Something just fell down in there,' said the chief clerk in the room on the left. Gregory tried to imagine whether something similar might not happen to the chief clerk one day as had happened to him this morning. One had to admit it was possible. But as if in brusque reply to this question the chief clerk, in the next room, now took several resolute steps that made his patent-leather boots creak. From the room on the right Gregory's sister informed him in a whisper, 'Gregory, the chief clerk's here.' 'I know,' Gregory said under his breath, not daring to raise his voice to the point where his sister could have heard his reply.

'Gregory,' came his father's voice from the room on the left, 'the chief clerk has come round to ask why you didn't leave on the early train. We don't know what to tell him. In any case he'd like a word with you personally. So please will you open the door. He'll have the goodness, I'm sure, to overlook the mess in your room.' Meanwhile the chief clerk put in a friendly, 'Good morning, Mr Samsa.' 'He's not well,' Gregory's mother told the chief clerk as his father was still talking through the door. 'He's not well, sir, you can take it from me. What else would make Gregory miss his train? Why, the boy thinks of nothing but his work! It makes me quite cross that he never goes out in the evening; now he's just had a whole week in town, but every evening he spent at home. He sits there with us at the table and quietly reads the paper or pores over timetables. His only amusement is when he does his fretwork. He made a little picture frame, for instance, which took him two or three evenings; you'll be surprised how pretty it is; it's hanging up in his room; you'll see it in a moment, when Gregory opens the door. I'm glad you're here, sir, by the way; we'd never have got Gregory to unlock the door by ourselves, he's so stubborn; and I'm sure he's unwell, although he said he wasn't this morning.' 'Won't be a moment,' Gregory said slowly and deliberately, keeping quite still in order not to miss a word of this exchange. 'I likewise, madam, can think of no other explanation,' said the chief clerk. 'Let us hope it's nothing serious. On the other hand I am bound to say that those of us who are in business are—unfortunately or if you like fortunately—very often obliged simply to shrug off minor indispositions for business reasons.' 'Can the chief clerk come in, then?' asked his father impatiently, knocking on the door again. 'No,' said Gregory. In the room on the left an embarrassed silence fell; in the room on the right his sister began to sob.

Why did his sister not go round and join the others? Probably she had only just got out of bed and had not even begun dressing yet. And whyever was she crying? Was it because he did not get up and let the chief clerk in, because he was in danger of losing his job and because the boss would then start pestering his parents again about those old debts? Worries of that kind were surely quite superfluous for the present. Gregory was still around and had not the slightest intention of abandoning his family. Just at the moment he happened to be lying on the carpet, and no one who was aware of his condition would seriously have expected him to let the chief clerk into the room. But this minor discourtesy, for which a suitable excuse could easily be found at a later stage, hardly constituted grounds for firing Gregory on the spot. And to Gregory's way of thinking it would have been far more sensible to leave him in peace now instead of plaguing him with tears and exhortations. But of course it was the uncertainty that was upsetting the others and that accounted for their behavior.

'Mr Samsa,' the chief clerk now called out in a louder voice, 'what is going on? You barricade yourself in your room, answer in monosyllables, are causing your parents grave and unnecessary concern, and are in addition—this merely by the by—neglecting your professional duties in a quite outrageous manner. On behalf of your parents and your superior I ask you most earnestly for an immediate and unequivocal explanation. I am astonished, I really am. I knew and believed you to be a clam and reasonable person, and suddenly you seem bent on manifesting these freakish whims. Your superior in fact intimated to me this morning a possible explanation for your absences—it had to do with the cash-up recently entrusted to you—but I assure you I gave him virtually my word of honour that that could not possibly be the true explanation. Now, however, having witnessed your incredible obstinacy, I find myself losing all inclination to plead your cause in any way whatsoever. I would add that your position is very far from assured. It was my original intention to tell you all this in private but, since you choose to make me waste my time here in this fruitless fashion, I see no reason why your good parents should not hear it too. Your figures recently have been most unsatisfactory; this is not of course the season for doing a lot of business, we recognize that; but a season for doing no business at all does not exist and cannot, Mr Samsa, be allowed to exist.'

'But, sir,' cried Gregory, most upset and forgetting everything else in his excitement, 'I'm just going to open the door, this very moment. A slight indisposition, a dizzy spell, prevented me from getting up. I'm still in bed. But I already feel perfectly fit again. I'm getting out of bed now. Just be patient for a moment. Things aren't going quite as well as I expected. I'm all right, though. Funny how something like that can hit you. Yesterday evening

I was fine, my parents will tell you, or rather, I already had a sort of feeling then that something might be wrong. You'd think it would have shown on my face. Whyever didn't I send word to the office! One always thinks, doesn't one, that one can get over these things without staying at home. Sir, spare my parents this ordeal, please! All these reproaches you've levelled against me are quite unfounded; no one's ever said a word to me about any of this. You may not have seen the latest batch of orders I sent in. Incidentally I'll be on my way by the eight o'clock train; the few hours' rest has done me good. Don't let me keep you, sir; I'll be in the office myself directly; would you be so kind as to tell the boss so with my compliments?'

And while Gregory was blurting all this out, barely aware of what he was saying, he had managed to reach the wardrobe without difficulty, no doubt as a result of the practice already acquired in bed, and was now trying to use it to pull himself upright. He really did intend to open the door; he intended to let himself be seen and have a word with the chief clerk; he was eager to find out what the others, wanting him as they now did, would say when they saw him. If they panicked, Gregory would be absolved of responsibility and could relax. If on the other hand they reacted calmly, then he too would have no call to get excited and could indeed, if he hurried, be at the station by eight. At first he kept slipping on the wardrobe's smooth surface, but in the end, after one final heave, he was standing erect; he had completely forgotten about the pains in his lower region, acute though they were. Next he let himself fall against the back of a nearby chair, gripping it around the edge with his legs. Having got himself under control in this way, he stopped talking; now he could listen to what the chief clerk had to say.

'Did you understand a word of that?' the chief clerk was asking Gregory's parents. 'I suppose he's not trying to make complete fools of us?' 'Heavens,' cried his mother, already in tears, 'he may be seriously ill and here we are, tormenting him. Meg!' she shouted then, 'Meg!' 'Yes, Mother?' cried his sister from the other side. They were communicating through Gregory's room. 'You must go round to the doctor this minute. Gregory's ill. Quickly, now—fetch the doctor. Did you hear Gregory talking just then?' 'That sounded like an animal,' said the chief clerk in a quiet voice that contrasted sharply with the mother's yelling. 'Anna! Anna!' his father shouted down the hall in the direction of the kitchen, clapping his hands as he did so, 'fetch a locksmith immediately!' In a moment the two girls were running down the hall with a rustle of skirts—how had his sister got dressed so quickly?—and pulling open the door. There was no sound of it being slammed shut behind them; probably they had left it open, as so often happens in homes visited by a major calamity.

Gregory, however, felt much calmer. So they could no longer understand what he said, although his words had seemed to him quite clear, clearer than before; perhaps his ear had made the necessary adjustment. Still, they were now convinced that all was not well with him, and they were prepared to help. The confidence and assurance with which the first instructions had been issued had done him good. He felt involved once more in the body of mankind and expected both men, the doctor and the locksmith, without in fact distinguishing in any precise way between them, to achieve great and surprising things. In order to make his voice as clear as possible for the coming decisive discussion he gave a little cough, though taking great care to muffle it lest this sound too should turn out different from human cough-ing, which was an issue he no longer felt competent to judge. Meanwhile silence had fallen in the adjoining room. Possibly his parents were sitting around the table with the chief clerk and whispering; possibly they were all leaning against the door, listening.

Using the chair, Gregory slowly pushed himself towards the door, let go of it when he got there, threw himself against the door, used this to support himself in an upright position—the balls of his feet had a small amount of adhesive on them—and there took a moment's rest from his labours. Then he set about trying to use his mouth to turn the key in the lock. Unfortunately it seemed he had no proper teeth—how was he to grip the key?—although admittedly his jaws were very strong; and indeed with their help he actually managed to move the key, ignoring the fact that in doing so he was clearly damaging himself in some way since a brown fluid began to pour from his mouth, run down over the key, and drip onto the floor. 'Listen,' the chief clerk said in the adjoining room, 'he's turning the key.' This was an enormous encouragement to Gregory; but they should all have called out to him, including his father and mother: 'Go to it, Gregory,' they should have called, 'go on—turn that key!' And in the belief that they were all following his efforts in great excitement he bit down blindly on the key with all the strength he could muster. As the key gradually rotated in the lock he shuffled round in an arc; he was now supporting himself with his mouth alone, either hang-ing from the key or, if pressing was in order, pressing down on it once more with the whole weight of his body. The sharper sound as the bolt finally snapped back was literally a tonic to Gregory. With a sigh of relief he said to himself, 'I didn't need the locksmith, then.' And he laid his head on the door handle to finish opening the door.

His having to open the door in this way meant that he himself could still not be seen when the door was already open quite wide. He first had to work himself slowly round his leaf of the door, and he had to do it very carefully if he did not want to fall flat on his back before entering the other room. He was engaged in this difficult manoeuvre, too busy to notice anything else, when he heard the chief clerk suddenly utter a loud 'Oh!'—it sounded like a gust of wind—and then he saw too, because the chief clerk had been nearest to the door, how he pressed a hand to his gaping mouth and started slowly giving ground as if an invisible force had been driving him steadily backwards. His mother, who despite the presence of the chief clerk was standing there with her hair all undone and still tousled from the night, looked first with clasped hands at his father, then took two steps towards Gregory and sank down, her skirts billowing in circles around her, her face lowered to her bosom and quite invisible. His father looked hostile and clenched a fist as if to force Gregory back into his room; then, with a diffident glance round the living-room, he shaded his eyes with his hands and wept until his great chest shook.

Gregory did not in fact enter the room now but leant against the inside of the other, still bolted leaf of the door in such a way that only half his body could be seen, and above it his head, tilted to one side, peering out at them. It had grown much lighter meanwhile; clearly visible across the street was a section of the endless, grey-black building opposite—it was a hospital—with its hard, regular windows punched in the façade; rain was still falling, but only in huge, individually visible drops that were also being hurled to earth literally one by one. A superabundance of breakfast things littered the table, because for Gregory's father breakfast was the main meal of the day, which he used to sit over for hours, reading a variety of newspapers. Hanging on the wall opposite was a photograph of Gregory taken when he was in the army, showing him as a lieutenant: one hand on his sword, a carefree smile on his lips, his whole bearing and uniform commanding respect. The door to the hall was open, and since the front door stood open too one could see out onto the landing and the top of the stairs.

'Right,' said Gregory, well aware that he was the only one to have retained his composure, 'I shall now get dressed, pack my samples, and be off. You will let me go, won't you? You see, sir, I am not a stubborn person and I like my work; it's a wearisome business, travelling, but I couldn't live without it. Where are you off to, sir? Back to the office? Are you? Will you make a faithful report of all this? One may find oneself temporarily incapacitated as far as work is concerned, but that is precisely the time to look back on one's previous achievements and bear in mind that afterwards, once the hindrance has been overcome, one will undoubtedly work all the harder and with even greater application. I'm so deeply beholden to the boss, as you well know. On the other hand I have my responsibility towards my parents and my sister. I'm in a tight spot, but I shall work my way out of it. Only don't make it more difficult for me than it is already. Stick up for me in the office! We travellers are not liked, I know. People think we earn a mint of money and have a great life into the bargain. That is their preconception, and they have no particular occasion to review it. But you, sir, have a better grasp of the circumstances than the rest of the staff—indeed, between you and me, a better grasp than the boss himself, who in his capacity as employer readily allows his judgement to err to an employee's disadvantage. You also appreciate how easily the traveller, who spends almost the entire year away from the office, can fall victim to gossip, ill luck, and unjustified complaints—with not the slightest chance of defending himself, since he usually hears nothing whatever about them and it is only when he returns exhausted from a trip that he reaps the appalling consequences, the root causes of which can by then no longer be unravelled. Sir, before you go, just give me some indication that you agree with at least a small part of what I have said!'

But the chief clerk had turned away with a shrug at Gregory's first words although he continued to look back at Gregory over his shoulder with pursed lips. And during the whole of Gregory's speech he was not still for a moment but kept moving, without taking his eyes off Gregory, towards the door— very slowly, though, inch by inch, as if there existed some secret injunction against leaving the room. He had reached the hall already, and from the sharp movement with which he withdrew his foot from the living-room for the last time one might have thought he had just scorched his sole. Once in the hall, he stretched his right hand out in front of him towards the stairs as if some almost supernatural deliverance awaited him there.

Gregory realized that he could under no circumstances allow the chief clerk to leave in this frame of mind if he did not want his position with the firm to be very seriously jeopardized. His parents did not understand these things too well; they had formed the conviction over the years that with this job Gregory was taken care of for life; moreover they were now so preoccupied with their immediate worries as to have quite lost the faculty of fore-sight. Gregory, however, had not. The chief clerk must be detained, mollified, persuaded, and ultimately won over; Gregory's future and that of his family depended on it! If only his sister had been there! She was clever; she had already been in tears when Gregory was still lying quietly on his back. Undoubtedly the chief clerk, who was quite a lady's man, would have allowed himself to be swayed by her; she would have closed the front door and talked him out of his panic in the hall. But his sister was not there, and Gregory must do something himself. So, forgetting that he was still quite unfamiliar with his present capabilities as far as moving about was concerned, forgetting too that his last speech had possibly if not probably been understood as little as the previous one, he let go of the door; thrust himself through the doorway; tried to go to the chief clerk, who was already—absurdly—clutching the landing banister with both hands; but promptly fell, giving a little cry as he groped for a hold, onto his many legs. No sooner had this happened than, for the first time that morning, he experienced a feeling of physical well-being; his legs, with firm ground under them, responded perfectly, as he discovered to his delight; indeed they strove impatiently to carry him where he wanted to go; and he was immediately convinced that an end to all the agony was at hand. But even as he lay there, swaying with pent-up movement, on the floor not far from his mother, just opposite where she knelt in a state of seemingly total self-absorption, she suddenly sprang up, arms out-stretched, fingers splayed, cried, 'Help, for the love of God, help!'; craned her head forward as if trying to see Gregory better while on the contrary she was taking frenzied steps backwards; forgot the breakfast table behind her and, when she reached it, hopped distractedly up on it and sat on the edge; and seemed quite unaware of the fact that the overturned coffee pot beside her was emptying itself copiously onto the carpet.

'Mother, mother,' said Gregory softly, looking up at her. He had forgotten all about the chief clerk for the moment, though at the sight of the coffee pouring out he could not stop himself snapping at the air several times with his jaws. At this his mother let out another yell, fell off the table, and fled into the arms of his father as he hurried towards her. But Gregory had no time for his parents now; the chief clerk, already on the stairs, had laid his chin on the banister for one last look back. Gregory took a run to make doubly sure of catching him; the chief clerk must have suspected something then because he leapt down several steps at once and disappeared, his parting cry of 'Shoo!' echoing back up the stairwell. Unfortunately Gregory's father, who until now had been relatively composed, appeared to find the chief clerk's flight thoroughly unsettling, because instead of going after the man himself or at least not obstructing Gregory in his pursuit he seized the chief clerk's stick, which the latter had left behind on a chair together with his hat and coat, took a large newspaper from the table in his other hand, and with much stamping of his feet and brandishing of the stick and newspaper started to drive Gregory back into his room. None of Gregory's pleas availed, none were even understood; bend his head as meekly as he might, his father only stamped the louder. Across the room his mother, despite the cold weather, had thrown open a window and was leaning out, a long way out, pressing her face into her hands. This caused a powerful draught between street and stairwell that made the curtains billow, the newspapers rustle on the table, and one or two sheets even go floating across the floor. His father kept up the relentless pressure, hissing like a madman. Gregory, however, had had no practice at walking backwards and really could not go very fast. If only he could have turned round he would have been back in his room in an instant, but he was afraid of taxing his father's patience by so time-consuming a manoeuvre, with the stick in his father's hand threatening at any moment to deliver a mortal blow to his back or head. In the end, though, Gregory had no alternative, for he found to his dismay that he could not even control his direction in reverse; so with repeated anxious glances at his father he began to turn himself round as quickly as possible, which in the event was very slowly indeed. His father, perhaps realizing that he meant well, did not hinder him in this but even, from a distance, directed the rotation process intermittently with the end of his stick. If only it had not been for that unbearable hissing from his father! It threw Gregory into utter confusion. He was already nearly half-way round when, through continually listening for the hiss, he made a mistake and started turning the other way. But when, happily, he was facing the doorway at last, it became clear that his body was too wide to pass through just like that. His father, of course, given his state of mind at that moment, did not even begin to think of, for example, opening the other leaf of the door to provide Gregory with sufficient width of passage. His one and only idea was that Gregory must be got back into his room as quickly as possible. Nor would he ever have permitted the elaborate preparations Gregory would have had to make in order to assume an upright position and possibly get through the door that way. Instead he acted as if there had been no obstacle, urging Gregory on even more noisily than before; it no longer sounded like the voice of just one father behind him; things were really in earnest now, and Gregory thrust himself at the opening, come what might. One side of his body lifted up, he lay at an angle in the doorway, his flank was rubbed quite raw, some nasty-looking stains appeared on the white door, soon he was stuck fast and couldn't have moved another inch unaided, his legs on one side hanging quivering in mid air while those on the other were squashed painfully against the floor—at which point his father gave him a truly liberating shove from behind and he went flying right into his room, bleeding profusely. The door was banged to with the stick, and at last there was silence.

II

Not until dusk did Gregory wake from a sleep so deep it had been like a coma. He would undoubtedly have woken before long even without being disturbed, because he felt quite rested and no longer sleepy, but his impression was that he had been roused by a quick footstep and by the door to the hall being carefully shut. The light of the electric street lamps shone wanly on the ceiling in places and on the upper parts of the various pieces of furniture, but down below, where Gregory lay, it was dark. Probing still rather awkwardly with his feelers, which he was only now beginning to appreciate, he pushed himself slowly over to the door to see what had happened there. His left side seemed to be one long scar; it pulled unpleasantly, and he was reduced to limping on his twin rows of legs. Moreover one leg had suffered severe damage during the course of the morning's events—it was almost a miracle that only the one had been damaged—and trailed lifelessly behind.

Not until he had reached the door did he notice what had in fact drawn him in that direction, namely the smell of something to eat. For there stood a bowl of sweetened milk with little slices of white bread floating in it. He could have laughed for joy, because he felt even hungrier than he had in the morning, and he promptly plunged almost his whole head into the milk. But he soon drew it out again in disappointment; it was not only that eating was difficult for him on account of his tender left side—and he could only eat if his whole body panted systematically—but also that he did not at all like the taste, although ordinarily milk was his favourite drink, which would have been why his sister had brought it for him; indeed it was with a feeling almost of disgust that he turned aside from the bowl and crawled back into the middle of the room.

In the living-room the gas had been lit, as Gregory could see through the gap between the doors, but whereas usually at this time Gregory's father liked to read the afternoon paper aloud to his mother and sometimes to his sister, too, now there was not a sound to be heard. Well, perhaps the reading aloud, which his sister was always telling him about in her letters, had dropped out of use in recent weeks. But the whole flat was so quiet, though it was surely not empty. 'What a peaceful life the family was leading!' Gregory said to himself, and as he stared fixedly into the darkness he felt enormously proud of having been able to provide his parents and his sister with such a life in so pleasant a flat. But what if all this peace, all this prosperity, all this satisfied contentment were to end in terror? Rather than risk losing himself in such thoughts Gregory preferred to move about, and he began crawling back and forth across the room.

Once during the long evening the door on one side and once the door on the other were opened a crack and then quickly closed again; someone had presumably felt the urge to come in but had had too many misgivings. Gregory stationed himself right by the door to the living-room, determined to get his diffident visitor into the room somehow or other or at least find out who it was; but from then on the door was not opened again, and Gregory waited in vain. In the morning, with the doors locked, everyone had wanted to come in; now that he had opened one door and the others had clearly been opened during the day no one came any more, and the keys had even been taken and put back in the locks from outside.

It was late into the night before the living-room light went out, and then it quickly became clear that his parents and his sister had in fact stayed up all that time, because the three of them could quite distinctly be heard tiptoeing away. Now no one would be coming into Gregory's room until morning, surely, so he had a long while in which to consider in peace and quiet how best to reorganize his life. But the tall, spacious room, in which he was obliged to lie flat on the floor, frightened him without his being able to discover why, because after all it was his room and he had been living in it for five years—and with a half-unconscious change of direction, and not without a slight feeling of shame, he went scuttling under the couch, where despite the fact that his back was a little squeezed and he could no longer lift his head he immediately felt very much at home, his only regret being that his body was too wide to be accommodated under the couch in its entirety.

Gregory provides for the family

There he spent the whole night, some of it in a doze from which his stomach kept waking him with a start, but some of it a prey to worries and obscure hopes, all of which, however, led him to the conclusion that for the time being he must keep calm and try, by being patient and exercising great consideration, to make it easier for his family to bear the inconvenience to which he was in his present state quite frankly obliged to put them.

Early the next morning, almost before it was light, Gregory had an opportunity to test the firmness of his new resolutions when his sister, almost fully dressed, opened the door from the living-room and nervously peered in. She did not spot Gregory straight away, but when she noticed him under the couch—God, he must be somewhere, he couldn't just have flown away—she got such a fright that she involuntarily slammed the door shut again. But as if thinking better of her action she opened it again immediately and tiptoed into the room, rather as if she were in the presence of a chronic invalid or even a stranger. Gregory, his head pushed forward to the edge of the couch, watched her. Would she notice that he had left the milk—though not because he had no appetite, far from it—and would she bring some other food that suited him better? If she did not do so of her own accord he would rather starve than tell her, despite what was really a terrible urge to dart out from under the couch, hurl himself at his sister's feet, and beg her to bring him something good to eat. His sister, however, noticing immediately and with some surprise that the bowl was still full, with only a little milk spilt around it, picked it up—not, admittedly, with her bare hands but with a rag—and carried it out. Gregory was extremely curious to know what she would bring in its stead, and he devoted a great deal of thought to it. But never could he have guessed what his sister, in the goodness of her heart, actually did. She brought him a whole selection of things, all laid out on an old newspaper, to see what he liked. There were some old, half-rotten vegetables; the bones from supper, covered with congealed white sauce; some raisins and almonds; a piece of cheese that Gregory had pronounced inedible two days previously; a slice of dry bread, another spread with butter, and another spread with butter and salted. As well as all this she brought back the bowl, which it had probably been decided once and for all should be Gregory's, this time with water in it. Very tactfully, knowing that Gregory would not eat in her presence, she then withdrew and even turned the key in the lock to let Gregory know that he could set to as he pleased. Gregory's legs whirred as he crossed to where the food was. His wounds must incidentally have healed up completely by now, for he felt no further impediment; he was astonished at this and remembered how he had nicked his finger with a knife more than a month ago and how the wound had still been quite painful the day before yesterday. 'Have I perhaps become less sensitive?' he thought, sucking greedily at the piece of cheese, to which of all the things available he had been most immediately and emphatically drawn. With tears of contentment in his eyes, he demolished in quick succession the cheese, the vegetables, and the sauce. The fresh food did not appeal to him; in fact, finding even the smell of it intolerable, he went so far as to drag the things he wanted to eat a little way off. He had long finished all the food and was simply lazing about when, as a sign that he should withdraw, his sister began slowly turning the key. This roused him immediately, although he had been more than half asleep, and he hurried back beneath the couch. But it required enormous strength of mind for him to stay under the couch even for the short time his sister spent in the room, because as a result of his copious meal his body had swollen slightly and in that narrow space he could hardly breathe. Between bouts of near-suffocation he watched with somewhat protruding eyes as his unsuspecting sister swept together with a broom not only the scraps but even the food Gregory had left untouched, as if realizing that it too was no longer needed, and hurriedly threw everything into a pail that she covered with a wooden lid before carrying it out. Hardly was her back turned before Gregory emerged from beneath the couch to stretch and distend himself.

This was how Gregory now received his food each day, once in the morning when his parents and the maid were still asleep, and a second time after the family's lunch, because then his parents had another little sleep and the maid was sent off on some errand or other by his sister. Doubtless they no more wished Gregory to starve than she did, but perhaps it would have been too much for them to learn about his eating habits other than by hearsay, perhaps his sister was concerned to spare them even what might have been only a minor sorrow, for in all conscience they could be said to be suffering enough.

What excuses had been used on that first morning to get the doctor and the locksmith out of the flat again Gregory was never able to discover, because since there was no understanding him it did not occur to anyone, not even to his sister, that he might be able to understand other people, so that when his sister was in his room he had to content himself with her intermittent sighs and invocations of the saints. It was only later, when she had grown accustomed to things to a certain extent—there could never of course be any question of her becoming fully accustomed—Gregory occasionally caught a remark that was meant well enough or could be so interpreted. 'He enjoyed his food today,' she would comment if Gregory had scoffed the lot, whereas if the opposite was the case, and by degrees it came more and more often to be so, she would say almost sadly, 'Oh, he's left everything again.'

But while Gregory was unable to learn any news directly he did pick up a certain amount from the adjoining rooms, and as soon as he heard voices he would run to the door concerned and press his whole body up against it. Particularly in the early days there was no conversation that did not in some way, if only obliquely, have to do with him. For two days there were discussions at every meal as to how they should now conduct themselves, but between mealtimes, too, the same subject kept coming up, because there were always at least two members of the family at home; presumably no one wanted to stay at home on his or her own, and there could be no question of leaving the flat completely deserted. Also the maid had come to his mother on the very first day—it was not clear how much she knew of what had happened—and asked on bended knee to be discharged immediately, and when a quarter of an hour later she came back to say goodbye she expressed thanks for her discharge with tears in her eyes, as if it had been the greatest blessing ever bestowed on her in that house, and spontaneously delivered herself of a fearful oath to the effect that she would never breathe a word to anyone.

This meant that Gregory's sister, together with his mother, now had to do the cooking as well, although there was not much work involved as they were hardly eating anything. Again and again Gregory heard one of them vainly exhorting the others to eat, only to receive the inevitable reply, 'No, thank you, I've had enough,' or words to that effect. No drinking went on either. His sister was always asking his father if he wanted a beer, generously offering to go out for it herself, and when he said nothing she suggested, with a view to removing any misgivings he might have, that she could even send the janitor, but eventually Gregory's father told her firmly, 'No,' and the subject was not mentioned again.

In the course of the very first day his father gave both his mother and his sister a comprehensive account of the family's financial circumstances and prospects. Every now and then he got up from the table and went over to the small patent safe that he had retrieved from the collapse of his business five years before to fetch a receipt or a notebook or whatever it might be. He could be heard unlocking it—a complicated process—and, having removed what he wanted, locking it again. In part these elucidations of his father's were the first gratifying communications to have reached Gregory's ears since his captivity began. He had always assumed that his father had been left with nothing whatsoever from that business; at least, his father had never said anything to him to the contrary, nor as a matter of fact had Gregory ever asked him about it. The catastrophe had plunged them all into utter despair, and Gregory's sole concern at that time had been to do everything to erase it from the family's memory as swiftly as possible. That was when he had begun to work with quite exceptional enthusiasm and from being a minor clerk had become a traveller virtually overnight, as such of course enjoying an entirely different earning potential since his results, if he was successful, were immediately convertible, in terms of commission, into cash that could be taken home and laid on the table before the astonished and delighted eyes of the family. Those had been marvellous times, and they had never recurred since, at least not with the same splendour, although subsequently Gregory was earning so much money that he was in a position to meet the expenses of the entire family and indeed did so. They had simply started taking it for granted, not just the family but Gregory himself; they accepted the money gratefully, Gregory provided it willingly, but no special warmth seemed to be engendered any more. Only his sister had remained close to Gregory in spite of everything, and since unlike himself she was very fond of music and could play the violin most movingly it was his secret ambition, regardless of the expense that would inevitably be involved—he'd manage to cover that in some other way—to send her to the Conservatory in the following year. During his brief stays in the city the Conservatory often cropped up in conversation with his sister, but never as anything more than a beautiful dream that could not possibly come true, and even those innocent references were unwelcome to their parents' ears; Gregory, however, had quite definite ideas on the subject and meant to make his announcement with some solemnity on Christmas Eve.

Such were the thoughts—quite futile in his present condition—that passed through his head as he stood glued to the door, listening. Once or twice, too tired to take in any more, he inadvertently let his head droop and knock against the door, but he lifted it again immediately because even the tiny sound it made had been heard in the next room, and they had all stopped talking. 'What's he up to now?' his father said after a while, obviously looking towards the door, and only then was the interrupted conversation gradually resumed.

Gregory now became thoroughly acquainted—for his father tended to be very repetitive, partly because he had not concerned himself with these matters for some time, partly too because Gregory's mother did not always grasp everything on first hearing—with the fact that, the catastrophe notwithstanding, an admittedly very small amount of capital still survived from the old days, now of course slightly swollen by the interest that had been allowed to accumulate in the mean time. Furthermore the money that Gregory had brought home each month—he had kept only the loose change for himself—had not all been used up and had itself accumulated to form a modest capital. Behind his door Gregory nodded enthusiastically, delighted to hear of this unexpected prudence and thrift. He could in fact have used the money to clear some more of his father's debt to the boss, and the day when he could write that item off completely would have been very much nearer, but as things were his father's arrangement was undoubtedly the better one.

The fact remained that the sum was nowhere near enough for the family to be able, for example, to live off the interest; it might be enough to support them for one or at most two years, but that was all. In other words it was money that ought not in fact to be touched at all but ought to be put aside for an emergency; the money for day-to-day expenses had to be earned. Now Gregory's father, though in good health, was an old man who had not worked for the past five years and in any case could not take on very much; during those five years, which had been the first holiday of his arduous yet unsuccessful life, he had put on a great deal of weight and become very clumsy in his movements as a result. And was Gregory's old mother to start going out to work when, crippled as she was by asthma, she found it an effort to walk round the flat and spent every other day lying on the sofa with the window open, gasping for breath? And was his sister to go out to work, a child of only seventeen whose life until then surely no one would have begrudged her, consisting as it had of dressing prettily, sleeping long hours, lending a hand with the housework, indulging in a few modest pleasures, and above all playing the violin? Whenever the talk turned to this necessity for earning money Gregory let go of the door and threw himself down on the cool leather sofa beside it, burning with shame and grief.

Often he lay there right through the night, not sleeping a wink but simply scratching at the leather for hours on end. Or he embarked on the laborious task of pushing a chair over to the window and crawling up the wall to the sill in order to brace himself in the chair and lean against the glass, obviously in response to some memory of the feeling of freedom it had once given him to look out of the window. Because the fact of the matter was that, as the days went by, even things that were quite close he saw less and less clearly; the hospital opposite, the all-too-frequent sight of which he had formerly cursed, he could not see at all now, and had he not known full well that he lived in the quiet but entirely urban Charlotte Street he might have thought his window overlooked a wilderness in which the grey sky and the grey earth merged indistinguishably. His thoughtful sister needed to see the chair standing there on only two occasions before she began, each time she had tidied up his room, pushing it carefully back beneath the window and even, from then on, leaving the inner casement open.

If only Gregory had been able to speak to his sister and thank her for everything she was having to do for him he could have borne her attentions more easily; as it was they pained him. Admittedly she tried to cover up the awkwardness of the situation as much as possible, and of course as time went by she became better and better at doing so, but in time, too, Gregory acquired a keener perception of things. Even her entrance was terrible for him. As soon as she had stepped over the threshold, and without even pausing to shut the door, for all her usual concern to spare everyone the sight of Gregory's room, she ran straight to the window, tore it open with fumbling hands as if she were on the point of suffocating, and stood by it for a while, no matter how cold the weather, taking deep breaths. She terrified Gregory twice daily with this running and banging; he spent the whole time trembling under the couch, yet he was perfectly sure she would have spared him the experience had she anyhow found it in her power to remain in a room occupied by Gregory with the window closed.

Once—this must have been a month after Gregory's metamorphosis, by which time his sister no longer had any particular reason to be astonished at his appearance—she came a little earlier than usual and found Gregory, motionless and at his most terrifying, still looking out of the window. Gregory would not have been surprised had she not come in, because his position made it impossible for her to open the window immediately, but not only did she not come in, she even withdrew smartly and shut the door; a stranger might almost have thought Gregory had been lying in wait for her with the intention of biting her. Gregory, of course, hid under the couch immediately, but he had to wait until noon before his sister returned, and when she did she seemed much more agitated than usual. He realized from this that she still found the sight of him unbearable and would inevitably go on finding it unbearable, and that it probably cost her a great effort of self-control not to run at the sight of even the small portion of his body that stuck out from beneath the couch. To spare her even this sight he one day took his sheet, carried it over to the couch on his back—the job took him four hours—and there arranged it in such a way as to cover him completely, so that his sister could not see him even when she bent down. Had she considered the sheet unnecessary she could after all have removed it, because surely it was obvious that it could not be Gregory's idea of fun to cut himself off so utterly and completely, yet she left the sheet as it was, and Gregory even thought he detected a look of gratitude when at one point, to see how his sister was taking the new arrangement, he carefully lifted the sheet a little with his head.

For the first fortnight his parents could not bring themselves to enter his room, and he often heard them expressing unqualified approval of his sister's present efforts, whereas before they had thought her a fairly ineffectual sort of girl and had frequently lost patience with her. Now, however, both his father and his mother often waited outside Gregory's room while his sister cleaned it out, and no sooner had she emerged than she had to give them a detailed account of the state of the room, what Gregory had eaten, how he had behaved this time, and whether perhaps some slight improvement were noticeable. His mother in fact wanted to visit Gregory relatively early on, but his father and sister restrained her, initially using arguments based on common sense to which Gregory listened attentively and in full agreement. Subsequently they had to restrain her by force, and when she then cried out,

'Let me go to Gregory, my poor, unfortunate son! Don't you see that I must go to him?' Gregory thought it might not be a bad idea if his mother did come in, not every day of course but perhaps once a week; she understood things so much better than his sister, who for all her pluck was still a mere child and, when all was said and done, had perhaps only taken on so hard a task in a fit of childish exuberance.

Gregory's wish to see his mother was soon fulfilled. He did not like to show himself at the window during the day, if only for his parents' sake; he could not move about much in the few square metres of floor space; lying still he found difficult enough at night; eating no longer gave him the slightest pleasure; so to amuse himself he adopted the habit of crawling all over the walls and ceiling. He was particularly partial to hanging from the ceiling; this was quite different from lying on the floor; one could breathe more freely; gentle vibrations went coursing through the body; and in the almost blissful state of abstraction that Gregory found himself in up there it sometimes happened that, much to his own astonishment, he let go and went crashing to the floor. But of course he now had his body under much better control than before, and even a fall like that did not harm him. Gregory's sister noticed his new pastime straight away—he left traces of adhesive behind when he crawled— and took it into her head to give Gregory as much crawling-space as possible by removing such items of furniture, chiefly the wardrobe and the desk, as precluded it. She could not, however, do this on her own; she dared not ask her father to help; the maid would certainly not have lent a hand because, although for her sixteen or so years of age she had stuck it out bravely since the departure of the previous cook, she had asked as a special dispensation to be allowed to keep the kitchen permanently locked and to be obliged to open it only on receipt of a specific signal; so his sister had no alternative but to take advantage of one of the father's absences to fetch Gregory's mother. And along his mother promptly came, uttering cries of pleasure and excitement, though she fell silent at the door of Gregory's room. First, of course, his sister checked whether everything was all right in the room, only then letting the mother enter. Gregory had very hastily pulled the sheet down even lower and made more folds, and the whole arrangement really did look as if a sheet had simply been thrown over the couch at random. Gregory also refrained from stealing a glance under the sheet this time; he was prepared to forgo seeing his mother on this occasion, content with the fact that she had come at last. 'Come on, you can't see him,' said his sister, obviously leading his mother by the hand. Gregory listened as the two frail women started to shift the old, rather heavy wardrobe; he could tell that his sister was deliberately doing most of the work herself the whole time, ignoring the anxious warnings of the mother, who was afraid she was going to strain herself. It took a very long time. After they had been at it for perhaps a quarter of an hour his mother said they should leave the wardrobe where it was: for one thing it was too heavy, they would not be finished before father came back, and with the wardrobe in the middle of the room they would be blocking Gregory's every move; for another thing it was by no means certain that in removing his furniture they were doing Gregory a favour. It seemed to her that the opposite was the case; she found the sight of the bare walls downright depressing; and who was to say that Gregory's reaction would not be the same, since he had had the furniture for ages, was used to it, and would feel lonely in the empty room. 'And isn't it,' his mother concluded in a low voice—in fact she had been virtually whispering the whole time as if to make sure that Gregory, of whose exact whereabouts she was unaware, should not even hear the sound of her voice, since she was already convinced he would not understand the words—'isn't it as if by removing the furniture we were showing that we had given up all hope of improvement and were callously leaving him to his own devices? I believe the best thing would be to try to keep the room exactly as it was, then when Gregory returns to us he will find everything the same and it will be that much easier for him to forget the time between.'

Hearing his mother's words, Gregory realized that the fact that no one had addressed him directly in the past two months, coupled with the monotony of life in the bosom of the family, must have considerably muddled his wits; this was the only explanation he could find of his seriously having wanted his room cleared. Did he really wish to have his warm, friendly room, cosily furnished as it was with family heirlooms, transformed into a cave in which he would admittedly be able to crawl all over the place unimpeded but at the price of rapidly and completely forgetting his human past? Why, he was on the verge of forgetting already, and he had been rallied only by hearing his mother's voice again after all this time. Nothing was to be removed; it must all stay; the positive influence that the furniture had on his condition was something he could not do without; and if the furniture prevented him from indulging in his stupid crawling, that was no disadvantage but a very good thing.

Unfortunately his sister thought otherwise; in discussions of Gregory's affairs she had taken to presenting herself, not without some justification, as something of an expert compared with her parents, so that on this occasion too the mother's advice was sufficient reason as far as the daughter was concerned for insisting on the removal not only of the wardrobe and the desk, which was all she had had in mind originally, but of every piece of furniture in the room, the indispensable couch excepted. It was of course more than mere childish defiance and the self-confidence she had so unexpectedly and laboriously acquired in recent weeks that impelled her to make this demand; she had also observed with her own eyes how Gregory required a great deal of space for crawling, whereas he did not, so far as one could see, have the slightest use for the furniture. But perhaps another contributory factor was the highly romantic nature of girls of that age, which, seeking gratification at every turn, had in the present instance led Meg into the temptation of trying to make Gregory's plight even more horrific, thereby putting herself in a position to render him even greater services. Because in a room in which Gregory patrolled empty walls probably no one but Meg would ever dare to set foot.

And so it was that she would not allow her resolve to be shaken by her mother, who even with the room as it was appeared to be nervous and unsure of herself, soon falling silent and giving the sister what help she could to move the wardrobe out. Well, Gregory could manage without the wardrobe at a pinch, but the desk must stay. And no sooner had the women left the room with the wardrobe, groaning as they flattened themselves against it, than Gregory poked his head out from under the couch to see how he might prudently and as far as possible tactfully intervene. As luck would have it, however, his mother came back first, leaving Meg in the other room with her arms around the wardrobe, rocking it to and fro without of course moving it an inch. Now his mother was not used to the sight of him; it might make her ill; so Gregory scurried backwards in some alarm until he was right at the far end of the couch, though he was too late to prevent the sheet at the front from swaying slightly, just enough to catch his mother's eye. She stopped short, stood quite still for a moment, then went back to Meg.

Although Gregory kept telling himself that nothing out of the ordinary was happening, it was only a few bits of furniture being moved about, he was soon forced to admit that the women's to-ing and fro-ing, their muttered cries, and the scraping of the furniture on the floor were affecting him like a great turmoil that was being fuelled from all sides, and however firmly he drew in his head and legs and pressed his body to the floor the conclusion was inescapable that he was not going to be able to put up with it for long. They were clearing his room out, taking away everything that was dear to him; the wardrobe, which contained his fret-saw and the other tools, was already gone; now they were freeing his desk from the holes it had dug in the floor, the desk at which as a student of commerce and before that as a schoolboy, in fact ever since his junior-school days, he had sat and laboured over his essays—no, he simply hadn't time to scrutinize the good intentions of the two women, whose existence he had in any case almost forgotten since they were now toiling in exhausted silence, and all that could be heard was the heavy tramp of their feet.

The upshot was that he darted from his hiding-place—the women happened to be leaning against the desk in the next room, getting their breath back—changed direction four times, quite unable to decide what to salvage first, then, spotting the picture of the lady all in furs where it hung conspicuously on the otherwise bare wall, quickly crawled up to it and pressed himself against the glass, which offered a firm purchase and did his hot belly good. This picture at least, which Gregory was now completely covering, surely no one would take away from him. He twisted his head round towards the living-room door to observe the women's return.

They had not given themselves much of a rest and were already coming back; Meg had her arm around her mother and was virtually carrying her. 'All right, what shall we take next?' she said, looking about her. Then her eyes met Gregory's up on the wall. Probably only because her mother was there she retained her composure, bent her head closer to her mother to prevent her from looking about her, and said, if with somewhat tremulous haste, 'Come, let's go back in the living-room for a moment, shall we?' It was clear to Gregory what Meg was up to: she meant to get her mother out of harm's way and then chase him down from the wall. Well, just let her try! He was sitting on his picture and was not going to part with it. He'd leap off in Meg's face first.

But Meg's words had served only to increase the mother's agitation; she now stepped to one side, saw the huge brown blotch on the flowered wall-paper, cried out, before she had really registered the fact that it was Gregory she was looking at, in a shrill, strident voice, 'Oh God, oh God!' and with arms outstretched as if giving up altogether fell back on the couch and lay still. 'Gregory!' cried his sister, shaking her fist and glaring at him. It was the first time she had addressed him directly since the metamorphosis. She ran

↑ In her anger, she addresses
Gregory by name.

into the next room for some sort of essence that might revive her unconscious mother; Gregory wanted to help—time enough later to save the picture—but he was stuck fast to the glass and had to tear himself free; then he too ran into the next room as if there were some advice he could give his sister, like in the old days, but had to stand behind her doing nothing while she rummaged among various bottles, and gave her a fright when she turned round; one bottle fell to the floor and broke; a sliver of glass flew in Gregory's face, wounding him, and some pungent medicament swirled round him; Meg wasted no more time but gathered up as many bottles as she could and ran with them back to her mother, slamming the door behind her with her foot. Gregory was now cut off from his mother, who—and it was his fault—might be on the point of death; he could not open the door without frightening away his sister, and she must stay with their mother; there was nothing he could do except wait; and in an agony of anxiety and self-reproach he began to crawl about, all over everything, walls, furniture, ceiling, until eventually, in his despair, with the whole room starting to spin round him, he fell right in the middle of the big table.

For a while Gregory lay there weakly; around him all was silence; possibly that was a good sign. Then there came a ring at the door. The maid was of course locked in her kitchen, so Meg had to go. It was Gregory's father. 'What's happened?' was the first thing he said; presumably Meg's appearance had given the game away. Meg answered in a muffled voice, obviously with her face buried against her father's chest, 'Mother fainted but she's all right now. Gregory's got out.' 'I knew it,' said the father, 'I kept telling you it would happen, but you women never listen.' It was clear to Gregory that his father had misinterpreted Meg's all-too-brief report and assumed that he had been responsible for some act of violence. He must now attempt to placate his father, having neither the time nor the means to put him right. Accordingly he made a run for the door of his room and pressed himself against it in order that his father should see as soon as he entered the living-room that his intentions were of the best, that he was prepared to go back into his room immediately, and that it was not necessary to drive him there but only to open the door, when he would promptly disappear.

His father, however, was in no mood to spot such niceties; 'Ah!' he cried on entering, and his tone of voice suggested simultaneous rage and delight. Gregory pulled his head back from the door and swung it round towards his father. The man who stood there bore no resemblance to the mental image Gregory had had of him; admittedly he had neglected of late, through his new-found interest in crawling, to concern himself to the same extent as previously with events in the rest of the flat, and he ought in fact to have been quite prepared to find that things had changed. Yes, but, even so, could this really be his father? The same man as had lain wearily in bed, buried in his pillows, when Gregory left on a business trip; had greeted him from an armchair in his dressing-gown when Gregory returned home in the evening; had even found it beyond him to rise to his feet, merely raising his arms to indicate that he was pleased; and had, on the rare occasions when they went for a walk together, on a couple of Sundays a year and on the principal public holidays, shuffled along between Gregory and his mother, managing, though they were pretty slow walkers themselves, to go a little more slowly still, wrapped in his old overcoat, always placing his walking-stick with great care, and when he wanted to say something had almost invariably come to a complete halt and gathered his escort about him? Now, however, he was drawn up to his full height; dressed in a severe blue uniform with gilt buttons of the kind worn by bank commissionaires; the high, stiff collar of his jacket was topped by a powerful double chin; beneath the bushy eyebrows his piercing dark eyes had a fresh, alert look; the usually dishevelled white hair had been meticulously combed down, parted, and brilliantined. Tossing his cap, which bore a gold monogram, probably that of a bank, in an arc that took it right across the room onto the couch and pushing back the long flaps of his uniform jacket to thrust his hands into his trouser pockets, he bore down on Gregory with a look of grim determination on his face. Probably he did not know himself what he meant to do; nevertheless he raised his feet to an unusual height, and Gregory was amazed at the enormous size of the soles of his boots. Not that he dwelt on his amazement, remembering as he did from the very first day of his new life that his father believed the only way to treat him was with the utmost severity; no, he fled from his father's advance, stopping whenever his father came to a halt and hurrying on again the moment his father moved. They made several circuits of the room like this without anything decisive happening, indeed without the whole performance, so slowly was it enacted, even having the appearance of a chase. For this reason Gregory also kept to the floor for the time being, especially since he was afraid his father might look upon a retreat to the walls or ceiling as evidence of conspicuous ill will. But he had to admit to himself that he would not be able to keep up even this kind of running for long, because where his father took one step he had to make a whole host of movements. He was beginning to experience difficulty in breathing, and it was a fact that even in his previous life his lungs had never been wholly reliable. As he staggered on, barely keeping his eyes open in order to save all his strength for his legs, not even, in his lethargy, considering any other escape than by running, having already almost forgotten that the walls were at his disposal, though in this room they were cluttered with elaborately carved furniture, all notches and protruberances—something was lobbed gently over his shoulder, struck the floor just in front of him, and rolled away. It was an apple; another went flying after it; Gregory came to a terrified halt, further running being pointless now that his father had decided to bombard him. He had filled his pockets from the fruit bowl on the sideboard and was throwing one apple after another without even taking aim first. The small, red apples rolled around the floor as if electrified, bumping into one another. One feebly tossed apple struck Gregory a glancing blow on the back, doing no damage. But another that came flying after it hit him on the back and sank right in; Gregory tried to drag himself forward as though the shocking, unbelievable pain might go away if he moved; but it was like being pinned to the ground, and he stretched himself out, all his senses a complete blur. The last thing he saw was the door of his room being wrenched open and his mother rushing out past his shrieking sister, in her chemise because his sister had started undressing her to ease her breathing while she was unconscious, rushing up to his father with her tucked-up skirts spilling to the floor one by one as she ran, stumbling over the skirts as she fell upon his father and, with her arms around him, in absolute union with him—but Gregory's sight was already failing at this point—her hands cupping the back of his father's head, begged him to spare Gregory's life.

III

The severity of Gregory's wound, from which he suffered for more than a month—no one daring to remove the apple, it remained lodged in his flesh as a visible reminder—seemed to have brought home even to his father that, for all his present deplorable and repugnant appearance, Gregory was a member of the family and was therefore not to be treated as an enemy; on the contrary, family duty required them to swallow their loathing and simply grin and bear it.

And if in all likelihood Gregory had now, as a result of his injury, permanently lost some of his mobility and for the present resembled an elderly invalid in that it took him endless minutes to cross from one side of his room to the other—crawling on the walls and ceiling being out of the question—he felt fully compensated for this deterioration in his condition by the fact that every evening the door to the living-room, which he was in the habit of keeping a sharp eye on for as much as an hour or two beforehand, was thrown open and he was allowed to lie in the darkness of his room, invisible from next door, and observe the whole family around the brightly-lit table and listen to their conversation—all this as it were by general consent, in other words under very different circumstances from before.

Gone, of course, were the lively exchanges of earlier days, which Gregory had always recalled with a certain nostalgia in those tiny hotel rooms as he threw his weary body down on yet another damp bed. Now it was mostly a very peaceful time. His father fell asleep in his chair soon after supper; his mother and sister kept reminding each other to be quiet; his mother, leaning forward into the light, sewed lingerie for a fashion shop; his sister, who had taken a job as a shop assistant, spent her evenings learning shorthand and French with a view, possibly, to securing a better position later on. Occasionally his father would wake up, and as if unaware that he had been asleep he would say to the mother, 'You're doing a lot of sewing again today!' and go straight back to sleep, while mother and sister exchanged tired smiles.

With an almost mulish obstinacy Gregory's father refused to take off his commissionaire's uniform even in the house; and while his dressing-gown hung idle on the peg he slept fully dressed in his place at table as if permanently ready for duty, all ears, even here, for the dictates of his superior. As a result the uniform, which had not been new to start with, defied all Gregory's mother's and sister's efforts to keep it clean, and Gregory often spent whole evenings gazing at the appallingly stained garment, bright with its ever-polished buttons, in which the old man slept in great discomfort and yet at his ease.

As soon as the clock struck ten Gregory's mother tried by quietly talking to his father to wake him up and coax him into going to bed, because it was not proper sleep that he was getting where he was and sleep was something that, having to report for duty at six o'clock, he needed very badly. But with the wilfulness that had characterized him since he had taken this humble job he invariably insisted on staying up longer, although he regularly dozed off and afterwards it was only with the greatest difficulty that he could be persuaded to exchange chair for bed. No matter how much Gregory's mother and sister urged him with mild reproaches, for a quarter of an hour he went on slowly shaking his head with his eyes firmly closed, refusing to stand up. Gregory's mother plucked at his sleeve, whispering blandishments in his ear, and his sister left her work to go to her mother's aid, but the effect on Gregory's father was nil. He only slumped deeper into his chair. Not until the women grasped him under the armpits did he open his eyes, look from mother to sister, and say, 'What a life! So much for a quiet old age!' Then, leaning on the two women, he would rise awkwardly to his feet as if he were an enormous burden even to himself, allow the women to escort him to the door, and there wave them away to continue on his own, while Gregory's mother quickly put down her sewing and his sister her pen in order to run after him and offer further assistance.

Who in this overworked and exhausted family had time to give Gregory any more attention than was absolutely necessary? The housekeeping budget was progressively curtailed; the maid was dismissed after all; a big, raw-boned cleaning-woman with wispy white hair came in mornings and evenings to do the heaviest work; everything else Gregory's mother took care of, on top of all her sewing. It even reached the point where various pieces of family jewellery, formerly worn with great delight by Gregory's mother and sister on evenings out and other festive occasions, were sold, as Gregory learnt the same evening when the family discussed the prices fetched. But the main complaint was always that, while the flat was far too big for their present circumstances, they could not leave it because of the insoluble problem of how to move Gregory. Gregory, however, fully appreciated that he was not the only consideration in the way of a move, since it would have been a simple matter to transport him in a suitable crate fitted with a few air-holes; no, what chiefly held the family back from finding a new flat was their feeling of utter despair and the idea that they had been struck by a misfortune exceeding anything ever experienced within their entire circle of friends and relations. What the world requires of poor people they were fulfilling to the last degree; the father fetched breakfast for minor bank officials; the mother sacrificed herself for the underwear of total strangers; the sister ran back and forth behind the counter at her customers' beck and call; to do any more was beyond the family's power. And the wound in Gregory's back began to hurt all over again when his mother and sister, having put his father to bed, came back, left their work where they had dropped it, moved their chairs closer together until they were sitting cheek to cheek; and when his mother, indicating Gregory's room, said, 'Shut the door now, Meg,' and he was in darkness again, while in the other room the women wept together or possibly sat dry-eyed, staring at the table-top.

Gregory's nights and days passed almost entirely without sleep. He thought intermittently of taking the affairs of the family in hand again just as before, the very next time the door opened; after a long interval the boss and the chief clerk reappeared in his thoughts together with the other clerks and the apprentices, the dim-witted errand boy, two or three friends from other firms, a provincial hotel chamber-maid of brief, fond memory, a cashier in a hat shop whom he had courted in earnest but rather too slowly—they all appeared, interspersed with strangers or people he had forgotten, but instead of helping him and his family they were without exception unapproachable and he was glad to see them go. Afterwards, however, he was again in no mood to bother about his family; he was merely angry at the appalling service, and although he could think of nothing he might have felt like eating he began to plan ways of gaining access to the larder, there to help himself to what, even if he was not hungry, was after all no more than his due. With no thought any longer of how she might particularly please Gregory, his sister now hurriedly shoved any old thing into his room with her foot before leaving for work in the morning and again after lunch, and in the evening, regardless of whether the food had perhaps merely been picked at or—as was usually the case—left completely untouched, she swept it out again with a whisk of her broom. The cleaning, which she now always did in the evenings, could not have taken less time. The walls of Gregory's room were streaked with dirt, and balls of dust and little heaps of excrement dotted the floor. At the beginning Gregory used to position himself, when his sister arrived, in corners that were particularly bad in this respect, intending his action as a sort of reproach to her. But he could have stayed there for weeks without his sister mending her ways; the fact was, she could see the dirt as clearly as he could, only she had made up her mind to leave it. At the same time she watched with, for her, a quite novel sensitivity—it had come over the whole family, in fact—that the cleaning of Gregory's room should remain her prerogative. On one occasion Gregory's mother had subjected his room to a major spring-clean, which had taken several buckets of water to complete successfully—all the humidity upsetting Gregory too, of course, so that he flopped down on the couch in a sulk and lay still—but she did not go unpunished. As soon as Gregory's sister saw the change in his room that evening she ran into the living-room, deeply hurt, and despite her mother's imploringly upraised hands burst into a paroxysm of tears of which her parents— the father had of course started up out of his chair in alarm—were at first astonished and helpless witnesses; until they too began to get excited; father upbraiding mother to his right for not leaving the cleaning of the room to Gregory's sister; and to his left yelling at the sister that she would never be allowed to clean Gregory's room again; while Gregory's mother tried to drag his father, who was beside himself with rage, into the bedroom; his sister, shaking with sobs, pounded the table with her little fists; and Gregory himself hissed aloud in his fury at the fact that no one thought of shutting the door and sparing him this noisy scene.

But even if his sister, exhausted from her day's work, had had enough of looking after Gregory as she had once done, there was still no need for Gregory's mother to have taken her place and still no reason why Gregory should be neglected. For now the cleaning-woman was there. This elderly widow, whose powerful build had presumably helped her to weather the worst in the course of her long life, had no particular horror of Gregory. Without as it were being nosy she had once inadvertently opened the door of Gregory's room, and at the sight of Gregory, who was taken completely by surprise and began running to and fro although no one was chasing him, she had stood there in amazement with her hands clasped before her. Since then she had not let a day go by without, morning and evening, opening the door a crack and peeping in at Gregory. The first few times she had also called him to her, using words she probably regarded as affable, such as 'Come on, you old dung beetle, come over here!' or 'Look at the old dung beetle!' Addressed in this fashion, Gregory had made no reply but stayed where he was without moving as though the door had never been opened. If only, instead of letting the woman plague him to no purpose as the mood took her, they had told her to clean his room out every day! One early morning— heavy rain, possibly in token of the coming of spring, was beating at the window-panes—Gregory felt so bitter when the cleaning-woman started using those words again that he turned, though very slowly and rather decrepitly, as if to attack her. Instead of taking fright, however, the cleaning-woman merely picked up a nearby chair and raised it high in the air, and from the way in which she stood there with her mouth wide open it was clear that she would shut her mouth only when the chair in her hand had come crashing down on Gregory's back. 'You keep your distance, all right?' she asked as Gregory turned away again; then she calmly put the chair back in the corner.

Gregory was now eating almost nothing. Only when he happened to walk past the food put down for him did he aimlessly take a bite, which he kept in his mouth for hours and then usually spat out again. At first he thought it was sadness at the state of his room that had spoilt his appetite, but in fact the changes in his room were something to which he became reconciled very quickly. They had got into the habit of putting in with him things that could not be accommodated elsewhere, and there were now a great many such things because they had let one room of the flat to three lodgers. These earnest gentlemen—all three wore full beards, as Gregory discovered on one occasion through a crack in the door—were sticklers for order, not only in their room but also, now that they were installed as lodgers, as far as the whole household was concerned, which meant particularly the kitchen. They had no time for useless junk and even less if it was dirty. Moreover they had brought most of their furniture with them. As a result, many things had become superfluous for which there was no market but which on the other hand no one wanted to throw away. All of them found their way into Gregory's room, as did the ash bucket and the rubbish bin from the kitchen. Everything that was temporarily out of use the cleaning-woman, who was always in a great hurry, simply flung into Gregory's room; Gregory was usually lucky enough to see only the object in question and the hand holding it. The cleaning-woman may have meant to fetch the things again when she had a moment or throw them all out at one go; in fact they stayed where they had landed, except when Gregory forced a path through the stuff and shifted it, at first because he had to, there being no other space for crawling, but subsequently with ever-increasing pleasure, although the aftermath of such expeditions was that he relapsed, dead-tired and in a mood of deep gloom, into hours of lying without moving.

As the lodgers sometimes had supper at home as well, eating in the communal living-room, there were evenings when the living-room door stayed shut, but Gregory found it quite easy to forgo the opening of the door; there had already been evenings when, with the door open, he had not taken advantage of the fact but had lain motionless in the darkest corner of his room, unnoticed by the family. On one occasion, however, the cleaning-woman having left the door to the living-room ajar, it stayed that way and was still ajar when the lodgers came home in the evening and the lamp was lit. They sat down at the head of the table, where Gregory's father and mother and Gregory himself had formerly eaten, unfolded their napkins, and picked up their knives and forks. Promptly Gregory's mother appeared in the doorway with a dish of meat and right behind her his sister with another dish piled high with potatoes. Steam rose thickly from both. The lodgers bent over the dishes as they were placed in front of them; it was as if they wanted to inspect the food before eating it, and indeed the one in the middle, evidently an authority in the eyes of the other two, actually cut through a piece of meat while it was still on the dish, clearly in order to establish whether it was done or whether it should perhaps be sent back to the kitchen. He was satisfied, and Gregory's mother and sister, who had been watching apprehensively, broke into relieved smiles.

The family ate in the kitchen. Gregory's father, however, before going to the kitchen, came into the living-room and with a bow, cap in hand, made a tour of the table. The lodgers rose as one man and mumbled something into their beards. Afterwards, when they were alone, they ate in almost complete silence. It struck Gregory as odd that, of all the multifarious sounds of eating, the one that stood out most persistently was the champing of their teeth; it was as if they meant to show him that one needed teeth to eat and that even the finest of toothless jaws were good for nothing. 'I do feel like eating,' Gregory said worriedly to himself, 'but not these things. The way these lodgers stuff themselves—and I'm starving!'

That same evening—and Gregory could not remember hearing it once during the whole time—the sound of the violin came from the kitchen. The lodgers had finished their supper, the middle one had produced a newspaper and given the other two a page each, and they were now leaning back in their chairs, reading and smoking. When the violin began to play they looked up, got to their feet, and tiptoed to the hall doorway, where they stood huddled together. Their movements must have been audible in the kitchen because Gregory's father called out, 'Would the gentlemen perhaps rather not have the violin played? It can be stopped immediately.' 'On the contrary,' said the middle lodger, 'would the young lady not like to come in here and play in the living-room where it's much cosier and more relaxed?' 'Why, certainly!' cried Gregory's father as if he had been the violinist. The lodgers came back into the room and waited. Soon Gregory's father entered with the music stand, his mother with the music, and his sister with the violin. His sister calmly got everything ready to play; his parents, who had never let rooms before and consequently overdid the politeness towards their lodgers, dared not even sit in their own chairs; Gregory's father leant against the door, his right hand inserted between two buttons of his livery jacket; his mother, however, offered a chair by one of the lodgers, sat down where the gentleman had happened to put it, which was tucked away in a corner.

Gregory's sister began to play, while his father and mother, one on each side of her, followed the movements of her hands with close attention. Drawn by her playing, Gregory ventured forward a little way until his head was inside the living-room. He gave scarcely a thought to the fact that he had been showing so little regard for others recently, whereas before he had prided himself on his altruism. And now there was even more reason for his staying out of sight because, as a result of the dust that lay everywhere in his room and blew about at the slightest disturbance, he too was covered in dust; he dragged lengths of thread, hairs, and scraps of left-over food around with him on his back and flanks; he was far too apathetic altogether to do as he had previously done several times a day, which was to lie on his back and rub himself on the carpet. Yet in spite of it all he had no inhibitions about edging forward onto the spotless floor of the living-room.

Not that anyone paid any attention to him. The family was completely absorbed in the violin-playing; the lodgers, however, having begun by stationing themselves, hands in pockets, much too close behind his sister's music stand where they could all see the score, which must surely have bothered his sister, soon retired muttering to the window and stood there with heads lowered, watched anxiously by Gregory's father. It now looked very much as if, disappointed in their expectation of hearing some beautiful or entertaining violin-playing, they were fed up with the whole performance and were allowing their peace to be disturbed further only out of politeness. Particularly the way in which they all blew their cigar smoke into the air out of nose and mouth together suggested a high degree of irritation. Yet his sister was playing so beautifully. Her face was titled to one side; her eyes had a sad, searching look as they followed the lines of the score. Gregory crawled a little farther into the room and pressed his head to the floor in the hope of perhaps meeting her gaze. Could he really be an animal, if music affected him so deeply? He felt as if he were being shown the way to that food he so longed for without knowing what it was. He was determined to reach his sister and suggest by tugging at her skirt that she should bring her violin and come into his room, because no one here was rewarding her playing as he wished to reward it. He wanted to keep her in his room and not let her go, at least not while he lived; for the first time his nightmarish appearance would serve some useful purpose; he meant to be at all the doors of his room simultaneously and spit in his attackers' faces; his sister, though, must not be coerced but must stay with him of her own free will; she should sit beside him on the couch and lower her ear to his mouth, and he would then confide to her that it had been his firm intention to send her to the Conservatory and that if this mishap had not intervened he would have told everyone so at Christmas—presumably Christmas had already passed—and would have turned a deaf ear to any objections. Following this declaration his sister would burst into tears of emotion and Gregory would lift himself up to the level of her shoulder and kiss her bare neck, for since she had been going out to work she had worn neither neckband nor collars.

'Mr Samsa!' the middle lodger cried, addressing Gregory's father and pointing, without another word, at the slowly advancing Gregory. The music stopped; the middle lodger looked at his friends with a smile and a shake of the head before turning back to Gregory. Gregory's father seemed to feel that getting rid of Gregory was less urgent for the moment than reassuring the lodgers, although the lodgers, far from being upset, appeared to be deriving more amusement from Gregory than they had from the violin-playing. He hurried over to them and tried by spreading his arms to drive them into their room, at the same time using his body in an attempt to block their view of Gregory. At this they did in fact turn a little nasty, though there was no knowing whether it was because of the father's behaviour or because of the realization now dawning on them that they had unwittingly had such a creature as Gregory for a next-door neighbour. They demanded explanations of

[handwritten marginal note: He wants to hear more music]

Gregory's father, their own arms flew up, they plucked nervously at their beards and only slowly gave ground in the retreat to their room. Meanwhile his sister had recovered from the forlorn mood into which she had lapsed following the abrupt interruption of her playing; after dangling violin and bow loosely in her hands for a while and continuing to gaze at the score as if she were still playing, she had suddenly pulled herself together, laid the instrument in her mother's lap where she sat fighting for breath with labouring lungs, and run into the next room, which the lodgers, driven on by Gregory's father, were now approaching more rapidly. Quilts and pillows could be seen flying into the air and falling back into place, guided by his sister's practised hands. Before the lodgers even reached the room she had finished making the beds and slipped out again. Gregory's father appeared to have fallen a prey to his own obstinacy once more, this time to the point of forgetting completely the respect that, after all, he owed his paying guests. He kept driving them on and driving them on until, right in the doorway of the room, the middle lodger stamped his foot with a sound like thunder and stopped Gregory's father in his tracks. 'I hereby give notice,' he said with upraised hand, looking round to include Gregory's mother and sister as well, 'that in view of the disgusting circumstances obtaining in this flat and in this family—here he suddenly decided to spit on the floor—'I intend to quit my room immediately. I shall not of course pay a thing for the days I have already spent in residence here; on the contrary, I shall be considering whether to lodge a—believe me—very easily justifiable claim against you for damages.' He stopped talking and looked straight ahead of him as if waiting for something. And indeed his two friends chimed in promptly with the words, 'We too give notice as of now.' At that he seized the door handle and slammed the door.

Gregory's father groped his way to his chair and slumped into it; he might have been stretching out for his customary evening nap, except that the violent nodding of his head, almost as though it had come loose, showed that he was anything but asleep. All this time Gregory had been lying motionless where the lodgers had first spotted him. Disappointment at the failure of his plan but perhaps also the weakness brought on by prolonged starvation had robbed him of all possibility of movement. Dreading with a kind of certainty that a general state of collapse was about to break over him at any moment, he waited. Not even the violin alarmed him when, having slipped from his mother's trembling fingers, it fell from her lap and hit the floor with a loud, ringing sound.

'My dear parents,' said Gregory's sister, banging her hand down on the table by way of an introduction, 'we can't go on like this. I see that even if you perhaps don't. I refuse to utter my brother's name in front of this creature, so all I say is: we must try to get rid of it. We've tried our level best to look after it and put up with it, and I believe no one can reproach us in the slightest.'

'She's right, by God,' Gregory's father said to himself. His mother, who had still not managed to get her breath back, now put a hand to her mouth and with a crazed look in her eyes began coughing hollowly.

His sister hurried over to her and put a hand on her forehead. His father appeared to have been set thinking along more specific lines by the girl's words; he had sat up in his chair and was playing with his cap among the plates that still lay on the table from the lodgers' supper, casting occasional glances at the motionless Gregory.

'We must somehow get rid of it,' said Gregory's sister, now addressing only his father because the mother could hear nothing above her coughing, 'or it will be the death of you both, I can see it coming. When people have to work as hard as we do they cannot take this everlasting worry at home as well. I can't either.' And she burst into such floods of tears that they splashed down onto her mother's face, from which she wiped them with perfunctory movements of her hands.

'But, my child,' said her father pityingly and with evident understanding, 'what are we to do?'

Gregory's sister merely shrugged her shoulders in token of the perplexity that had come over her with her tears, contrasting with her earlier assurance.

'If he understood what we said,' Gregory's father began half wonderingly, but his sister, still weeping, waved a hand violently to show that it was out of the question.

'If he understood what we said,' Gregory's father repeated as, by closing his eyes, he took in the girl's conviction that this was impossible, 'we might perhaps be able to come to an arrangement with him. But as things are . . . .'

'It has to go,' his sister cried. 'It's the only way, Father. You must just try to get out of the habit of thinking it's Gregory. That's been our undoing, in fact, that we've believed it for so long. But how can it be Gregory? If it were he would long ago have seen the impossibility of people living in the same house as such an animal and would have gone away of his own accord. In which case we would have no brother but could at least go on living and could honour his memory. As it is, the brute persecutes us, drives away the lodgers, and clearly means to take over the whole flat and have us sleeping out on the street. Look, Father,' she screamed suddenly, 'there he goes again!' And in a state of panic that Gregory found quite incomprehensible she even left her mother's side, actually using the back of the chair to push herself off as thought she would rather sacrifice her mother than remain in Gregory's vicinity, and dashed behind her father, who then, prompted purely by her reaction, also stood up and half raised his arms in front of the girl as though to protect her.

But of course nothing was further from Gregory's mind than to try to inspire fear in anyone, let alone his sister. He had simply begun to turn himself round in order to make his way back to his room, only it looked rather spectacular because in his ailing condition he had to help this difficult process along with his head by repeatedly lifting it in the air and bringing it down on the floor with a bang. He stopped and looked round. Apparently they had recognized that he meant well; the alarm had been only a momentary one. Now they were looking at him in sad-eyed silence. His mother was lying in her chair with her legs outstretched and pressed together, so exhausted that she could barely keep her eyes open; his father and sister were sitting together, she with one arm draped round his father's neck.

'I suppose it's all right to turn round now,' thought Gregory, and he went back to work. He could not help panting with the effort, and every now and then he had to pause for a rest. Not that anyone put him under pressure: it was all left to him. As soon as he had completed his turn he set off in a straight line. He was amazed at the enormous distance separating him from his room and could not understand how in his enfeebled state he had made the same journey almost without realizing it a short while before. Concentrating entirely on crawling fast, he hardly noticed the fact that not a word, not a cry from any member of his family disturbed his progress. Not until he had reached the doorway did he turn his head, and then not completely because he could feel his neck becoming stiff; nevertheless he saw that behind him nothing had changed except that his sister had risen to her feet. His last glimpse was of his mother, now fast asleep.

Almost before he was inside his room the door was hurriedly pushed to, bolted, and locked. The sudden noise behind him frightened Gregory so much that his legs gave way. It was his sister who had been in such a hurry. She had been on her feet already, waiting; she had then sprung forward nimbly—Gregory had not even heard her coming—and, with a cry of 'At last!' for her parents' benefit, she had turned the key in the lock.

'Now what?' Gregory asked himself as he looked about him in the darkness. He quite soon discovered that he could no longer move at all. He was not surprised; in fact what struck him as unnatural was that he had actually been able to get about until then on such thin legs. Otherwise he felt comparatively comfortable. Admittedly he hurt all over, but he had the impression that the pains were gradually becoming fainter and fainter and would eventually go away together. The rotten apple in his back and the inflamed area around it, now completely covered with a soft dust, were almost forgotten. He recalled his family with sympathy and love. His own belief that he must go was if possible even firmer than his sister's. He remained in this state of vacant and peaceable reflection until the church clock struck three in the morning. He lived to see the first signs of the general brightening outside the window. Then, independently of his will, his head sank to the floor and his last breath streamed feebly from his nostrils.

When the cleaning-woman arrived in the early morning—out of sheer, bustling energy she slammed all the doors, no matter how often she had been asked not to, so hard that throughout the flat, from the moment of her arrival onwards, peaceful sleep was an impossibility—she noticed nothing out of the ordinary about Gregory at first on her customary brief visit. She thought he was deliberately lying so still, playing the injured party; she credited him with boundless intelligence. Happening to have the long-handled broom in her hand, she tried to tickle Gregory with it from the door. When even this was unsuccessful she lost patience and gave Gregory a little prod, and it was only when she had shifted him from his place without encountering any resistance that her attention was aroused. She was quick to grasp the true state of affairs, reacting with a look of surprise and a low whistle; then, without wasting any more time, she tore open the bedroom door and bellowed into the darkness within, 'Take a look at this—the thing's snuffed it! It's lying here dead as a doornail!'

The Samsas were sitting up in the matrimonial bed and had first to overcome their alarm at the cleaning-woman's irruption before there was any question of registering her announcement. Then, however, Mr and Mrs Samsa got quickly out of bed, one on each side, Mr Samsa throwing the quilt round his shoulders, Mrs Samsa wearing only her nightdress; thus attired, they entered Gregory's room. Meanwhile the door to the living-room, where Meg had been sleeping since the lodgers moved in, had also opened; Meg was fully dressed as thought she had not even been to bed, an impression her pale face seemed to confirm. 'Dead?' said Mrs Samsa, looking inquiringly up at the cleaning-woman although she could verify everything herself and even see for herself without verification. 'I reckon so,' said the cleaning-woman, and to prove it she gave Gregory's corpse another great sideways shove with the broom. Mrs Samsa made as if to put a restraining hand on the broom but did not do so. 'Well,' said Mr Samsa, 'thanks be to God.' He crossed himself, and the three women followed his example. Meg, her eyes fixed on the corpse, said, 'See how thin he was. Well, he hadn't eaten anything for ages, had he? The food used to come out exactly as it had gone in.' Gregory's body was indeed completely flat and dried out, as could be seen only now that it was no longer raised on its legs and there was nothing else about it to distract the eye.

'Meg, come into our room for a moment,' said Mrs Samsa, smiling wistfully, and Meg, not without a backward glance at the corpse, followed her parents into their bedroom. The cleaning-woman closed the door and opened the window wide. Despite the earliness of the hour the fresh air already held a trace of mildness, for by this time it was the end of March.

The three lodgers emerged from their room and stared about them in astonishment, looking for their breakfast; they had been forgotten. 'Where's our breakfast?' the middle lodger gruffly demanded of the cleaning-woman. But she put a finger to her lips and in silence gestured quickly to the lodgers to come into Gregory's room. They came, and in the already quite bright room, with their hands in the pockets of their somewhat threadbare jackets, they stood around Gregory's corpse.

Then the bedroom door opened and Mr Samsa appeared in his livery, his wife on one arm and his daughter on the other. They were all slightly red-eyed from crying, Meg occasionally pressing her face against her father's arm.

'Get out of my flat this instant,' said Mr Samsa, pointing to the door without letting go of the women. 'How do you mean?' said the middle lodger, stunned but managing a honeyed smile. The other two had their hands behind their backs and were rubbing them together as if in delighted anticipation of a major row that, moreover, promised to turn out in their favour. 'I mean precisely what I say,' replied Mr Samsa, and with his two escorts he began to walk straight towards the middle lodger. The latter made no move at first but stood looking at the floor as if things were falling into a fresh pattern in his mind. 'All right, we'll go,' he concluded, looking up at Mr Samsa as though, in a sudden access of humility, he were even seeking fresh approval for this decision. Mr Samsa merely nodded curtly several times, glaring at him. Sure enough, the lodger promptly turned and strode out into the hall. His two friends, who had stopped rubbing their hands and started listening intently some time ago, now went literally scurrying after him as if afraid that Mr Samsa might reach the hall before them and cut them off from their leader. Out in the hall all three of them took their hats from the hat stand, drew their sticks from the stick rack, bowed silently, and left the flat. Prompted by what turned out to be a quite unfounded distrust, Mr Samsa stepped out onto the landing with the two women; there they leant on the banister and watched the three gentlemen slowly but surely descending the long stairwell, disappearing at a particular turn of the staircase between each floor and reemerging a moment or two later; the lower they went, the more the Samsa family lost interest in them, and as a butcher's man passed them coming up and then climbed high above them, proudly bearing his tray on his head, Mr Samsa soon left the landing with the women, and they went back into their flat as though relieved.

They decided to spend the day resting and going for a walk. They had not only earned this break from work; they needed it, and needed it badly. So they sat down at the table and wrote three letters of apology, Mr Samsa to his superiors, Mrs Samsa to the man who sent her needlework, and Meg to the proprietor of the shop she served in. While they were writing, the cleaning-woman came in to say that she was going since her morning work was done. The three letter-writers merely nodded at first without looking up; only when the cleaning-woman continued to show no sign of leaving did they look up in some irritation. 'Well?' Mr Samsa asked. The cleaning-woman stood smiling in the doorway as though she had some excellent news to announce to the family but would surrender it only on being quizzed at length. The little ostrich feather that stood up almost vertically from her hat and had been a source of irritation to Mr Samsa throughout her period of service bobbed and dipped in all directions. 'What was it you wanted?' asked Mrs Samsa, who was the person for whom the cleaning-woman still had most respect. 'Yes, well,' the cleaning-woman replied before a peal of amiable laughter prevented her from continuing for a moment, 'if you were worrying about how to get rid of that rubbish next door, you needn't. It's already dealt with.' Mrs Samsa and Meg bent over their letters as if to go on writing; Mr Samsa, realizing that the cleaning-woman now intended to launch into a full description, countered with a resolutely outstretched hand. Prevented from telling her story, she recalled the great hurry she was in, and with a clearly offended ' 'Bye, all,' she whirled round and left the flat amid a fearful banging of doors.

'She'll be getting her notice this evening,' said Mr Samsa, but neither his wife nor his daughter offered any response, the cleaning-woman having apparently shattered their so recently acquired peace of mind once more. They got up, crossed to the window, and stood with their arms around each other. Mr Samsa turned in his chair to face them and watched them in silence for a while. Then he called out, 'Look, come over here. Forget about the past, can't you? And have a bit of consideration for me.' The women obeyed him immediately, hurrying over to him, caressing him, and quickly finishing their letters.

Afterwards the three of them left the flat together, which was something they had not done for months, and took the tram out into the country. They had the carriage to themselves, and it was full of warmth and sunlight. Leaning back comfortably in their seats, they discussed their prospects, which closer examination revealed to be not at all bad, because all three employments—and they had never really questioned one another about this before—were most advantageous and, particularly as far as the future was concerned, very promising indeed. The chief immediate improvement in their situation could of course be expected from a simple change of accommodation; they now wanted to take a smaller, less expensive flat that was at the same time better located and altogether more practical than their present one, which Gregory had found. As they discussed these things Mr and Mrs

Samsa, watching their daughter become increasingly animated, were struck almost simultaneously by the realization that in recent months, despite all the troubles that had drained the colour from her cheeks, she had blossomed into a beautiful, full-bosomed girl. Speaking more quietly now, and communicating almost unconsciously through glances, they thought about how the time was also coming when they must start looking round for a nice husband for her. And they saw it as a sort of confirmation of their new-found dreams and good intentions when, at the end of the journey, their daughter was the first to stand up, stretching her young body.

T. S. ELIOT
1888–1965

In poetry and in literary criticism, Thomas Stearns Eliot has a unique position as a writer who not only expressed but helped to define modernist taste and style. He rejected the narrative, moralizing, and frequently "noble" style of late Victorian poetry, employing instead precisely focused and often startling images and an elliptical, allusive, and ironic voice that had enormous influence on modern American poetry. His early essays on literature and literary history helped bring about not only a new appreciation of seventeenth-century "metaphysical" poetry but also a different understanding of the text, no longer seen as the inspired overflow of spontaneous emotion but as a carefully made aesthetic object. Yet much of Eliot's immediate impact was not merely formal but spiritual or philosophical. The search for meaning that pervades his work created a famous picture of the barrenness of modern culture in *The Waste Land* (1922), which juxtaposed images of past nobility and present decay, civilizations near and far, and biblical, mythical, and Buddhist allusions to evoke the dilemma of a composite, anxious, and infinitely vulnerable modern soul. Readers in different countries who know nothing of Eliot's other works are often familiar with *The Waste Land* as a literary-historical landmark representing the cultural crisis in European society after World War I. In many ways, Eliot's combination of spiritual insight and technical innovation carries on the tradition of the Symbolist poet who was both visionary artist and consummate craftsman.

Two countries, England and the United States, claim Eliot as part of their national literature. Born September 26, 1888, to a prosperous and educated family in St. Louis, Eliot went to Harvard University for his undergraduate and graduate education and moved to England only in 1915, where he became a British citizen in 1927. While at Harvard, Eliot was influenced by the anti-Romantic humanist Irving Babbitt and the philosopher and aesthetician George Santayana. He later wrote a doctoral dissertation on the philosophy of F. H. Bradley, whose examination of private consciousness (*Appearance and Reality*) appears in Eliot's own later essays and poems. Eliot also found literary examples that would be important for him in future years: the poetry of Dante and John Donne, and the plays of Elizabethan and Jacobean dramatists. In 1908 he read Arthur Symons's *The Symbolist Movement in Literature* and became acquainted with the French Symbolist poets, whose richly allusive images—as well as highly self-conscious, ironic, and craftsmanlike technique—he would adopt for his own. Eliot began writing poetry while in college and published his first major poem, *The Love Song of J. Alfred Prufrock*, in Chicago's *Poetry* magazine in 1915. When he moved to England, however, he began a many-sided career as poet, reviewer, essayist, editor, and, later, playwright. By the time he received the Nobel Prize for literature in 1948, Eliot was recognized as one of the most influential twentieth-century writers in English.

Eliot's first poems, in 1915, already displayed the evocative yet startling images, abrupt shifts in focus, and combination of human sympathy and ironic wit that would attract and puzzle his readers. The *Preludes* linked the "notion of some infinitely gentle / Infinitely suffering thing" with a harsh fatalism in which "The worlds revolve like ancient women / Gathering fuel in vacant lots." Prufrock's dramatic monologue openly tried to startle readers by asking them to imagine the evening spread out "like a patient etherised upon a table" and by changing focus abruptly among imaginary landscapes, metaphysical questions, drawing-room chatter, literary and biblical allusions, and tones of high seriousness set against the most banal and even singsong speech. "I grow old . . . I grow old . . . / I shall wear the bottoms of my trousers rolled." The individual stanzas of *Prufrock* are individual scenes, each with its own coherence (for example, the third stanza's yellow fog as a cat). Together, they compose a symbolic landscape sketched in the narrator's mind as a combination of factual observation and subjective feelings: the delicately stated eroticism of the arm "downed with light brown hair," and the frustrated aggression in "I should have been a pair of ragged claws / Scuttling across the floors of silent seas." In its discontinuity, precise yet evocative imagery, mixture of romantic and everyday reference, formal and conversational speech, and in the complex and ironic self-consciousness of its most unheroic hero, *The Love Song of J. Alfred Prufrock* already displays many of the modernist traits typical of Eliot's entire work. Also typical is the theme of spiritual void and of a disoriented protagonist who—at least at this point—does not know how to cope with a crisis that is as much that of modern Western culture as it is his own personal tragedy.

Once established in London, Eliot married, taught briefly before taking a job in the foreign department of Lloyd's Bank (1917–25), and in 1925 joined the publishing firm of Faber & Faber. He wrote a number of essays and book reviews that were published in *The Sacred Wood* (1920) and *Homage to Dryden* (1924), and enjoyed a great deal of influence as assistant editor of the *Egoist* (1917–19) and founding editor of the quarterly *Criterion* from 1922 until it folded in 1939. Eliot helped shape changing literary tastes as much by his essays and literary criticism as by his poetry. Influenced himself by T. E. Hulme's proposal that the time had come for a classical literature of "hard, dry wit" after Romantic vagueness and religiosity and following Imagism's goal of clear, precise physical images phrased in everyday language, he outlined his own definitions of literature and literary history and contributed to a theoretical approach later known as the New Criticism. In his essay *Tradition and the Individual Talent* (1919), Eliot proclaimed that there existed a special level of great works—"masterpieces"—that formed among themselves an "ideal order" of quality even though, as individual works, they expressed the characteristic sensibility of their age. The best poets were aware of fitting into the cumulative "mind of Europe" (for Eliot, the humanistic tradition of Homer, Dante, and Shakespeare) and thus of being to some extent depersonalized in their works. Eliot's "impersonal theory of poetry" emphasizes the medium in which a writer works, rather than his or her inner state; craft and control rather than the Romantic ideal of a spontaneous overflow of private emotion. In a famous passage that compares the creative mind to the untouched catalyst of a chemistry experiment, he insists that the writer makes the art object out of language and the experience of any number of people. "The poet's mind is in fact a receptacle for seizing and storing up numberless feelings, phrases, images, which remain there until all the particles which can unite to form a new compound are present together." Poetry can and should express the whole being—intellectual and emotional, conscious and unconscious. In a review of Herbert Grierson's edition of the seventeenth-century Metaphysical poets (1921), Eliot praised the complex mixture of intellect and passion that characterized John Donne and the other Meta-physicals (and that characterized Eliot himself) and criticized the tendency of English literature after the seventeenth century to separate the language of analysis from that of feeling. His criticism of this "dissociation of sensibility" implied a change in literary tastes: from Milton to Donne, from Tennyson to Gerard Manley Hopkins, from Romanticism to classicism, from simplicity to complexity.

The great poetic example of this change came with *The Waste Land* in 1922. Eliot dedicated the poem to Ezra Pound, who had helped him revise the first draft, with a quotation from Dante praising the "better craftsman." Quotations from, or allusions to, a wide range of sources, including Shakespeare, Dante, Charles Baudelaire, Rich-ard Wagner, Ovid, St. Augustine, Buddhist sermons, folk songs, and the anthropol-ogists Jessie Weston and James Frazer, punctuate this lengthy poem, to which Eliot added explanatory notes when it was first published in book form. *The Waste Land* describes modern society in a time of cultural and spiritual crisis and sets off the fragmentation of modern experience against references (some in foreign languages) to a more stable cultural heritage. The ancient Greek prophet Tiresias is juxtaposed with the contemporary charlatan Madame Sosostris; celebrated lovers like Antony and Cleopatra with a house-agent's clerk who mechanically seduces an uninterested typist at the end of her day; the religious vision of St. Augustine and Buddhist sermons with a sterile world of rock and dry sand where "one can neither stand nor lie nor sit." The modern wasteland could be redeemed if it learned to answer (or perhaps, to ask) the right questions: a situation Eliot symbolized by oblique references to the legend of a knight passing an evening of trial in a Chapel Perilous, and healing a Fisher King by asking the right questions about the Holy Grail and its lance. The series of references (many from literary masterworks) that Eliot integrated into his poem were so many "fragments I have shored against my ruins," pieces of a puzzle whose resolution would bring "shantih," or the peace that passes understanding, but that is still out of reach, as the poem's final lines in a foreign language suggest.

The most influential technical innovation in *The Waste Land* was the deliberate use of fragmentation and discontinuity. Eliot pointedly refused to supply any transi-tional passages or narrative thread and expected the reader to construct a pattern whose implications would make sense as a whole. This was a direct attack on linear habits of reading, which are here broken up with sudden introductions of a different scene or unexplained literary references, shifts in perspective, interpolation of a for-eign language, changes from elegant description to barroom gossip, from Elizabethan to modern scenes, from formal to colloquial language. Eliot's rupture of traditional expectations served several functions. It contributed to the general picture of cultural disintegration that the poem expressed, it allowed him to exploit the Symbolist or allusive powers of language inasmuch as they now carried the burden of meaning, and finally—by drawing attention to its own technique—it exemplified modernist "self-reflexive" or self-conscious style. It is impossible to read a triple shift such as "I remember / Those are pearls that were his eyes. / 'Are you alive, or not? Is there nothing in your head?' "—moving from the narrator's meditative recall to a quotation from Shakespeare and the woman's blunt attack—without noticing the abrupt changes in style and tone. Eliot's "heap of broken images" and "fragments shored against my ruins" also took the shape of fragments of thought and speech, and as such embodied a new tradition of literary language.

The spiritual search of *Prufrock, Gerontion* (1919), and *The Waste Land* entered a new phase for Eliot in 1927, when he became a member of the Anglican Church. *Ash Wednesday* (1930) and a verse play on the death of the English St. Thomas à Becket (*Murder in the Cathedral*, 1935) display the same distress over the human condition but now within a framework of hope for those who have accepted religious discipline. Eliot began writing plays to reach a larger audience, of which the best known are *The Family Reunion* (1939), which recasts the Orestes story from Greek tragedy, and *The Cocktail Party* (1949), a drawing-room comedy that also explored its characters' search for salvation. He is still best known for his poetry, however, and his last major work in that genre is the *Four Quartets*, begun in 1934 and published in its entirety in 1943.

As their title suggests, the *Four Quartets* are divided into sections much like the movement of a musical quartet. Each has five sections, inside which themes are introduced, developed, and resolved, and each has the title of a place. *Little Gidding* is a village in Huntingdonshire, England, that was the home of a seventeenth-century Anglican Catholic religious community of which only a chapel (rebuilt after the English Civil Wars) remained. All the *Quartets* use varying forms of free verse, ranging from the most intense short lyrics to—for the first time—continuous narrative passages of the kind Eliot once disdained. Throughout, the poet ponders the relationship of historical change and eternal order.

Eliot's experiences in World War II as a watchman checking for fires during bombing raids enter into *Little Gidding,* and he uses the chapel in that village as the point of departure for a meditation on the meaning of strife and change in a universe that the mind strives to structure, always imperfectly, by the timeless truths of religion. The *Quartet* opens with a section that is itself divided into three separate movements, first establishing the season of "midwinter spring" with the sun blazing on ice, then the chapel as the goal of any season's journey, and finally the chapel as a place so consecrated by prayer that the dead may communicate with the living. The lyrics opening the second section mourn the place's present decay by all four elements of earth, air, fire, and water and pass on to an imaginary conversation between the poet, wandering after the last bomb and before the all-clear signal, and an anonymous "dead master." The mood is pessimistic, and the dead master (a "compound ghost" with elements of Eliot, the Virgil of Dante's *Divine Comedy*, and W. B. Yeats) prophesies a bitter old age full of remorse and impotent rage at human folly. Their conversation suggests a comparison between the air-raid scene and Dante's *Inferno*, for it echoes the triple-line stanzaic form of *The Divine Comedy* and recalls the Italian poet's own encounter with his former master, Brunetto Latini, in Hell (*Inferno* 15.22–124). The rest of the poem, however, moves forward to a kind of resolution out of time. The third section's beginning rhetoric of logical persuasion ("There are three conditions") introduces the concept of memory expanding our perspectives and enabling us to transcend the narrow commitments of history and civil war. The intense lyrics of the short fourth section propose that the flames of the annunciatory dove (or bomb) may be purgation as well as destruction; and in the final section, as the afternoon draws to a close, the poet ends his meditation on past and present, time and eternity, by asserting his faith in a condition of mind and spirit that combines both *now* and *always*, a transcendental vision that is a "condition of complete simplicity" and "crowned knot of fire."

The poem's conclusion is thus a religious one, moving from the agony of history to an eternal, purifying flame that may recall a similar mystic vision of all-penetrating light at the end of Dante's *Paradiso*. It may seem paradoxical that the poet who is known for expressing the dilemma of modern consciousness and for developing a new poetic style appropriate to twentieth-century experience should resolve that experience in a metaphor of transcendence. From his earliest work, however, Eliot was preoccupied with the spiritual implications of the most mundane reality, and the yoking of concrete with transcendental vision defines at once the range and depth of his modernist style.

The Love Song of J. Alfred Prufrock

S'io credesse che mia risposta fosse
A persona che mai tornasse al mondo,
Questa fiamma staria senza piu scosse.
Ma perciocche giammai di questo fondo
Non torno vivo alcun, s'i'odo il vero,
Senza tema d'infamia ti rispondo.[1]

Let us go then, you and I,
When the evening is spread out against the sky
Like a patient etherised upon a table;
Let us go, through certain half-deserted streets,
The muttering retreats   5
Of restless nights in one-night cheap hotels
And sawdust restaurants with oyster-shells:
Streets that follow like a tedious argument
Of insidious intent
To lead you to an overwhelming question . . .   10
Oh, do not ask, "What is it?"
Let us go and make our visit.

In the room the women come and go
Talking of Michelangelo.[2]

The yellow fog that rubs its back upon the window-panes,   15
The yellow smoke that rubs its muzzle on the window-panes
Licked its tongue into the corners of the evening,
Lingered upon the pools that stand in drains,
Let fall upon its back the soot that falls from chimneys,
Slipped by the terrace, made a sudden leap,   20
And seeing that it was a soft October night,
Curled once about the house, and fell asleep.

And indeed there will be time[3]
For the yellow smoke that slides along the street,
Rubbing its back upon the window-panes;   25
There will be time, there will be time
To prepare a face to meet the faces that you meet;
There will be time to murder and create,
And time for all the works and days of hands[4]
That lift and drop a question on your plate;   30
Time for you and time for me,
And time yet for a hundred indecisions,

---

1. From Dante's *Inferno* 27.61–66, in which the false counselor Guido da Montefeltro, enveloped in flame, explains that he would never reveal his past if he thought the traveler could report it: "If I thought my reply were meant for one / who ever could return into the world, / this flame would stir no more; and yet, since none—/ if what I hear is true—ever returned / alive from this abyss, then without fear / of facing infamy, I answer you." 2. Michelangelo Buonarroti (1475–1564), famous Italian Renaissance sculptor, painter, architect, and poet; here, merely a topic of fashionable conversation. 3. Echo of a love poem by Andrew Marvell (1621–1678), *To His Coy Mistress:* "Had we but world enough and time." 4. An implied contrast with the more productive agricultural labor of hands in the *Works and Days* of the Greek poet Hesiod (8th century B.C.E.).

And for a hundred visions and revisions,
Before the taking of a toast and tea.

    In the room the women come and go 35
Talking of Michelangelo.

    And indeed there will be time
To wonder, "Do I dare?" and, "Do I dare?"
Time to turn back and descend the stair,
With a bald spot in the middle of my hair— 40
(They will say: "How his hair is growing thin!")
My morning coat, my collar mounting firmly to the chin,
My necktie rich and modest, but asserted by a simple pin—
(They will say: "But how his arms and legs are thin!")
Do I dare 45
Disturb the universe?
In a minute there is time
For decisions and revisions which a minute will reverse.

    For I have known them all already, known them all—
Have known the evenings, mornings, afternoons, 50
I have measured out my life with coffee spoons;
I know the voices dying with a dying fall[5]
Beneath the music from a farther room.
    So how should I presume?

    And I have known the eyes already, known them all— 55
The eyes that fix you in a formulated phrase,
And when I am formulated, sprawling on a pin,
When I am pinned and wriggling on the wall,
Then how should I begin
To spit out all the butt-ends of my days and ways? 60
    And how should I presume?

    And I have known the arms already, known them all—
Arms that are braceleted and white and bare
(But in the lamplight, downed with light brown hair!)
Is it perfume from a dress 65
That makes me so digress?
Arms that lie along a table, or wrap about a shawl.
    And should I then presume?
    And how should I begin?

          . . .

    Shall I say, I have gone at dusk through narrow streets 70
And watched the smoke that rises from the pipes
Of lonely men in shirt-sleeves, leaning out of windows? . . .

    I should have been a pair of ragged claws
Scuttling across the floors of silent seas.

5. Recalls Duke Orsino's description of a musical phrase in Shakespeare's *Twelfth Night* (1.1.4): "It has a dying fall."

. . .

And the afternoon, the evening, sleeps so peacefully!   75
Smoothed by long fingers,
Asleep . . . tired . . . or it malingers,
Stretched on the floor, here beside you and me.
Should I, after tea and cakes and ices,
Have the strength to force the moment to its crisis?   80
But though I have wept and fasted, wept and prayed,
Though I have seen my head (grown slightly bald) brought in upon a
    platter,
I am no prophet[6]—and here's no great matter;
I have seen the moment of my greatness flicker,
And I have seen the eternal Footman hold my coat, and snicker,   85
And in short, I was afraid.

And would it have been worth it, after all,
After the cups, the marmalade, the tea,
Among the porcelain, among some talk of you and me,
Would it have been worth while,   90
To have bitten off the matter with a smile,
To have squeezed the universe into a ball
To roll it toward some overwhelming question,[7]
To say: "I am Lazarus, come from the dead,[8]
Come back to tell you all, I shall tell you all"—   95
If one, settling a pillow by her head,
  Should say: "That is not what I meant at all.
  That is not it, at all."

And would it have been worth it, after all,
Would it have been worth while,
After the sunsets and the dooryards and the sprinkled streets,   100
After the novels, after the teacups, after the skirts that trail along the
    floor—
And this, and so much more?—
It is impossible to say just what I mean!
But as if a magic lantern[9] threw the nerves in patterns on a screen: 105
Would it have been worth while
If one, settling a pillow or throwing off a shawl,
And turning toward the window, should say:
  "That is not it at all,
  That is not what I meant, at all."   110

. . .

No! I am not Prince Hamlet, nor was meant to be;
Am an attendant lord, one that will do
To swell a progress,[1] start a scene or two,

---

6. Salome obtained the head of the prophet John the Baptist on a platter as a reward for dancing before the tetrarch Herod (Matthew 14.3–11).   7. Another echo of Marvell's *To His Coy Mistress*, when the lover suggests rolling "all our strength and all / our sweetness up into one ball" to send against the "iron gates of life."   8. The story of Lazarus, raised from the dead, is told in John 11.1–44.   9. A slide projector.   1. A procession of attendants accompanying a king or nobleman across the stage, as in Elizabethan drama.

Advise the prince; no doubt, an easy tool,
Deferential, glad to be of use, 115
Politic, cautious, and meticulous;
Full of high sentence, but a bit obtuse;
At times, indeed, almost ridiculous—
Almost, at times, the Fool.

    I grow old . . . I grow old . . . 120
I shall wear the bottoms of my trousers rolled.

    Shall I part my hair behind? Do I dare to eat a peach?
I shall wear white flannel trousers, and walk upon the beach.
I have heard the mermaids singing, each to each.

    I do not think that they will sing to me. 125

    I have seen them riding seaward on the waves
Combing the white hair of the waves blown back
When the wind blows the water white and black.

    We have lingered in the chambers of the sea
By sea-girls wreathed with seaweed red and brown 130
Till human voices wake us, and we drown.

The Waste Land[1]

"Nam Sibyllam quidem Cumis ego ipse oculis meis vidi in ampulla
pendere, et cum illi pueri dicerent: Σίβυλλα τί θέλεις; respondebat
illa: ἀποθανεῖν θέλω."[2]

      For Ezra Pound
      il miglior fabbro.[3]

I. The Burial of the Dead[4]

    April is the cruellest month, breeding
Lilacs out of the dead land, mixing
Memory and desire, stirring
Dull roots with spring rain.
Winter kept us warm, covering 5
Earth in forgetful snow, feeding

---

1. Eliot provided footnotes for *The Waste Land* when it was first published in book form; these notes are included here. A general note at the beginning referred readers to the religious symbolism described in Jessie L. Weston's study of the Grail legend, *From Ritual to Romance* (1920), and to fertility myths and vegetation ceremonies (especially those involving Adonis, Attis, and Osiris) as described in the *The Golden Bough* (1890–1918) by the anthropologist Sir James Frazer. 2. Lines from Petronius's *Satyricon* (ca. 60 C.E.) describing the Sibyl, a prophetess shriveled with age and suspended in a bottle. "For indeed I myself have seen with my own eyes the Sibyl at Cumae, hanging in a bottle, and when those boys would say to her: 'Sibyl, what do you want?' she would reply: 'I want to die.'" 3. The dedication to Pound, who suggested cuts and changes in the first manuscript of *The Waste Land,* borrows words used by Guido Guinizelli to describe his predecessor, the Provençal poet Arnaut Daniel, in Dante's *Purgatorio* (26.117): he is "the better craftsman." 4. From the burial service of the Anglican Church.

A little life with dried tubers.
Summer surprised us, coming over the Starnbergersee[5]
With a shower of rain; we stopped in the colonnade,
And went on in sunlight, into the Hofgarten,[6]   10
And drank coffee, and talked for an hour.
Bin gar keine Russin, stamm' aus Litauen, echt deutsch.[7]
And when we were children, staying at the archduke's,
My cousin's, he took me out on a sled,
And I was frightened. He said, Marie,   15
Marie, hold on tight. And down we went.[8]
In the mountains, there you feel free.
I read, much of the night, and go south in the winter.

　　What are the roots that clutch, what branches grow
Out of this stony rubbish? Son of man,[9]   20
You cannot say, or guess, for you know only
A heap of broken images, where the sun beats,
And the dead tree gives no shelter, the cricket no relief,[1]
And the dry stone no sound of water. Only
There is shadow under this red rock,   25
(Come in under the shadow of this red rock),
And I will show you something different from either
Your shadow at morning striding behind you
Or your shadow at evening rising to meet you;
I will show you fear in a handful of dust.   30
　　　　　　　　Frisch weht der Wind
　　　　　　　　Der Heimat zu
　　　　　　　　Mein Irisch Kind,
　　　　　　　　Wo weilest du?[2]
"You gave me hyacinths first a year ago;   35
"They called me the hyacinth girl."
—Yet when we came back, late, from the Hyacinth garden,
Your arms full, and your hair wet, I could not
Speak, and my eyes failed, I was neither
Living nor dead, and I knew nothing,   40
Looking into the heart of light, the silence.
Oed' und leer das Meer.[3]

　　Madame Sosostris,[4] famous clairvoyante,
Had a bad cold, nevertheless
Is known to be the wisest woman in Europe,   45

---

5. A lake near Munich.　6. A public park.　7. "I am certainly no Russian, I come from Lithuania and am pure German." German settlers in Lithuania considered themselves superior to the Baltic natives. 8. Lines 8–16 recall *My Past*, the memoirs of Countess Marie Larisch.　9. "Cf. Ezekiel II, i" [Eliot's note]. The passage reads "Son of man, stand upon thy feet, and I will speak unto thee."　1. "Cf. Ecclesiastes XII, v" [Eliot's note]. "Also when they shall be afraid of that which is high, and fears shall be in the way, . . . the grasshopper shall be a burden, and desire shall fail."　2. "V. *Tristan und Isolde*, I, verses 5–8" [Eliot's note]. A sailor in Richard Wagner's opera sings, "The wind blows fresh / Towards the homeland / My Irish child / Where are you waiting?" (German)　3. "Id. III, verse 24" [Eliot's note]. "Barren and empty is the sea" (German) is the erroneous report the dying Tristan hears as he waits for Isolde's ship in the third act of Wagner's opera.　4. A fortune-teller with an assumed Egyptian name, possibly suggested by a similar figure in a novel by Aldous Huxley (*Crome Yellow*, 1921).

With a wicked pack of cards.[5] Here, said she,
Is your card, the drowned Phoenician Sailor,
(Those are pearls that were his eyes.[6] Look!)
Here is Belladonna, the Lady of the Rocks,
The lady of situations.   50
Here is the man with three staves, and here the Wheel,
And here is the one-eyed merchant, and this card,
Which is blank, is something he carries on his back,
Which I am forbidden to see. I do not find
The Hanged Man. Fear death by water.   55
I see crowds of people, walking round in a ring.
Thank you. If you see dear Mrs. Equitone,
Tell her I bring the horoscope myself:
One must be so careful these days.

Unreal City,[7]   60
Under the brown fog of a winter dawn,
A crowd flowed over London Bridge, so many,
I had not thought death had undone so many.[8]
Sighs, short and infrequent, were exhaled,[9]
And each man fixed his eyes before his feet.   65
Flowed up the hill and down King William Street,
To where Saint Mary Woolnoth kept the hours
With a dead sound on the final stroke of nine.[1]
There I saw one I knew, and stopped him, crying: "Stetson!
"You who were with me in the ships at Mylae![2]   70
"That corpse you planted last year in your garden,
"Has it begun to sprout? Will it bloom this year?
"Or has the sudden frost disturbed its bed?

---

5. "I am not familiar with the exact constitution of the Tarot pack of cards, from which I have obviously departed to suit my own convenience. The Hanged Man, a member of the traditional pack, fits my purpose in two ways: because he is associated in my mind with the Hanged God of Frazer, and because I associate him with the hooded figure in the passage of the disciples to Emmaus in Part V. The Phoenician Sailor and the Merchant appear later; also the 'crowds of people,' and Death by Water is executed in Part IV. The Man with Three Staves (an authentic member of the Tarot pack) I associate, quite arbitrarily, with the Fisher King himself" [Eliot's note]. Tarot cards are used for telling fortunes; the four suits (cup, lance, sword, and coin) are life symbols related to the Grail legend; and, as Eliot suggests, various figures on the cards are associated with different characters and situations in *The Waste Land.* For example, the *drowned Phoenician Sailor* (line 47) recurs in the merchant from Smyrna (III) and Phlebas the Phoenician (IV). *Belladonna* (line 49)—a poison, hallucinogen, medicine, and cosmetic (in Italian, "beautiful lady"); also an echo of Leonardo da Vinci's painting of the Virgin, *Madonna of the Rocks*—heralds the neurotic society woman amid her jewels and perfumes (II). *The Wheel* (line 51) is the wheel of fortune. The Hanged Man (line 55) becomes the sacrificed fertility god whose death ensures resurrection and new life for his people.
6. A line from Ariel's song in Shakespeare's *The Tempest* (1.2.398), which describes the transformation of a drowned man.   7. "Cf. Baudelaire: 'Fourmillante cité, cité pleine de rêves, / Où le spectre en plein jour raccroche le passant' " [Eliot's note]. "Swarming city, city full of dreams, / Where the specter in broad daylight accosts the passerby"; a description of Paris from "The Seven Old Men" in *The Flowers of Evil* (1857).   8. "Cf. *Inferno* III, 55–57: 'si lunga tratta / di gente, ch'io non avrei mai creduto / che morte tanta n'avesse disfatta' " [Eliot's note]. "Behind that banner trailed so long a file / of people—I should never have believed / that death could have unmade so many souls"; not only is Dante amazed at the number of people who have died but he is also describing a crowd of people who were neither good nor bad—nonentities denied even the entrance to hell.   9. "Cf. *Inferno* IV, 25–27: 'Quivi, secondo che per ascoltare, / non avea pianto, ma' che di sospiri, / che l'aura eterna facevan tremare' " [Eliot's note]. "Here, so far as I could tell by listening, there was no weeping but so many sighs that they caused the everlasting air to tremble"; the first circle of hell, or limbo, contained the souls of virtuous people who lived before Christ or had not been baptized.   1. "A phenomenon which I have often noticed" [Eliot's note]. The church is in the financial district of London, where King William Street is also located.   2. An "average" modern name (with business associations) linked to the ancient battle of Mylae (260 B.C.E.), where Rome was victorious over its commercial rival, Carthage.

"Oh keep the Dog far hence, that's friend to men,[3]
"Or with his nails he'll dig it up again!   75
"You! hypocrite lecteur!—mon semblable,—mon frère!"[4]

II. A Game of Chess[5]

The Chair she sat in, like a burnished throne,[6]
Glowed on the marble, where the glass
Held up by standards wrought with fruited vines
From which a golden Cupidon peeped out   80
(Another hid his eyes behind his wing)
Doubled the flames of sevenbranched candelabra
Reflecting light upon the table as
The glitter of her jewels rose to meet it,
From satin cases poured in rich profusion.   85
In vials of ivory and coloured glass
Unstoppered, lurked her strange synthetic perfumes,
Unguent, powdered, or liquid—troubled, confused
And drowned the sense in odours; stirred by the air
That freshened from the window, these ascended   90
In fattening the prolonged candle-flames,
Flung their smoke into the laquearia,[7]
Stirring the pattern on the coffered ceiling.
Huge sea-wood fed with copper
Burned green and orange, framed by the coloured stone,   95
In which sad light a carvèd dolphin swam.
Above the antique mantel was displayed
As though a window gave upon the sylvan scene[8]
The change of Philomel,[9] by the barbarous king
So rudely forced; yet there the nightingale[1]   100
Filled all the desert with inviolable voice
And still she cried, and still the world pursues,
"Jug Jug"[2] to dirty ears.
And other withered stumps of time
Were told upon the walls; staring forms   105

3. "Cf. the Dirge in Webster's *White Devil*" [Eliot's note]. The dirge, or song of lamentation, sung by Cornelia in John Webster's play (1625), asks to "keep the wolf far thence, that's foe to men," so that the wolf's nails may not dig up the bodies of her murdered relatives. Eliot's reversal of dog for wolf, and friend for foe, domesticates the grotesque scene; it may also foreshadow rebirth since (according to Weston's book), the rise of the Dog Star, Sirius, announced the flooding of the Nile and the consequent return of fertility to Egyptian soil.   4. "V. Baudelaire, Preface to *Fleurs du Mal*" [Eliot's note]. Baudelaire's poem preface, titled "To the Reader," ended "Hypocritical reader!—my likeness!—my brother!" The poet challenges the reader to recognize that both are caught up in the worst sin of all—the moral wasteland of *ennui* ("boredom") as lack of will, the refusal to care one way or the other.   5. Reference to a play, *A Game of Chess* (1627) by Thomas Middleton (1580–1627); see n. 5, p. 2010. Part II juxtaposes two scenes of modern sterility: an initial setting of wealthy boredom, neurosis, and lack of communication, and a pub scene in which similar concerns of appearance, sexual attraction, and thwarted childbirth are brought out more visibly, and in more vulgar language.   6. "Cf. *Antony and Cleopatra*, II, ii, 1.190" [Eliot's note]. A paler version of Cleopatra's splendor as she met her future lover, Antony: "The barge she sat in, like a burnished throne, / Burned on the water."   7. "Laquearia. V. *Aeneid*, I, 726: dependent lychni laquearibus aureis incensi, et noctem flammis funalia vincunt" [Eliot's note]. "Glowing lamps hang from the gold-paneled ceiling, and the torches conquer night with their flames"; the banquet setting of another classical love scene, in which Dido is inspired with a fatal passion for Aeneas.   8. "Sylvan scene. V. Milton, *Paradise Lost*, IV, 140" [Eliot's note]. Eden as first seen by Satan.   9. "V. Ovid, *Metamorphoses*, VI, Philomela" [Eliot's note]. Philomela was raped by her brother-in-law, King Tereus, who cut out her tongue so that she could not tell her sister, Procne. Later Procne is changed into a swallow and Philomela into a nightingale to save them from the king's rage after they have revenged themselves by killing his son.   1. "Cf. Part III, l.204" [Eliot's note].   2. Represents the nightingale's song in Elizabethan poetry.

Leaned out, leaning, hushing the room enclosed.
Footsteps shuffled on the stair.
Under the firelight, under the brush, her hair
Spread out in fiery points
Glowed into words, then would be savagely still.   110

   "My nerves are bad to-night. Yes, bad. Stay with me.
Speak to me. Why do you never speak. Speak.
    What are you thinking of? What thinking? What?
I never know what you are thinking. Think."

    I think we are in rats' alley[3]   115
Where the dead men lost their bones.

   "What is that noise?"
                The wind under the door.[4]
"What is that noise now? What is the wind doing?"
                  Nothing again nothing.   120
                      "Do
"You know nothing? Do you see nothing? Do you remember
"Nothing?"

    I remember
Those are pearls that were his eyes.   125
"Are you alive, or not? Is there nothing in your head?"
                           But

O O O O that Shakespeherian Rag—
It's so elegant
So intelligent   130
"What shall I do now? What shall I do?"
"I shall rush out as I am, and walk the street
"With my hair down, so. What shall we do to-morrow?
"What shall we ever do?"
                    The hot water at ten.   135
And if it rains, a closed car at four.
And we shall play a game of chess,[5]
Pressing lidless eyes and waiting for a knock upon the door.

    When Lil's husband got demobbed,[6] I said—
I didn't mince my words, I said to her myself,   140
HURRY UP PLEASE ITS TIME[7]
Now Albert's coming back, make yourself a bit smart.
He'll want to know what you done with that money he gave you
To get yourself some teeth. He did, I was there.
You have them all out, Lil, and get a nice set,   145
He said, I swear, I can't bear to look at you.
And no more can't I, I said, and think of poor Albert,
He's been in the army four years, he wants a good time,

---

3. "Cf. Part III, l.195" [Eliot's note].   4. "Cf. Webster: 'Is the wind in that door still?'" [Eliot's note].
From *The Devil's Law Case* (1623), 3.2.162, with the implied meaning "is there still breath in him?"
5. "Cf. the game of chess in Middleton's *Women Beware Women*" [Eliot's note]. In this scene, a woman
is seduced in a series of strategic steps that parallel the moves of a chess game, which is occupying her
mother-in-law at the same time.   6. Demobilized, discharged from the army.   7. The British bar-
tender's warning that the pub is about to close.

And if you don't give it him, there's others will, I said.
Oh is there, she said. Something o' that, I said. 150
Then I'll know who to thank, she said, and give me a straight look.
HURRY UP PLEASE ITS TIME
If you don't like it you can get on with it, I said.
Others can pick and choose if you can't.
But if Albert makes off, it won't be for lack of telling. 155
You ought to be ashamed, I said, to look so antique.
(And her only thirty-one.)
I can't help it, she said, pulling a long face,
It's them pills I took, to bring it off, she said.
(She's had five already, and nearly died of young George.) 160
The chemist[8] said it would be all right, but I've never been the same.
You are a proper fool, I said.
Well, if Albert won't leave you alone, there it is, I said,
What you get married for if you don't want children?
HURRY UP PLEASE ITS TIME 165
Well, that Sunday Albert was home, they had a hot gammon,[9]
And they asked me in to dinner, to get the beauty of it hot—
HURRY UP PLEASE ITS TIME
HURRY UP PLEASE ITS IME
Goonight Bill. Goonight Lou. Goonight May. Goonight. 170
Ta ta. Goonight. Goonight.
Good night, ladies, good night, sweet ladies, good night, good night.[1]

III. *The Fire Sermon*[2]

The river's tent is broken: the last fingers of leaf
Clutch and sink into the wet bank. The wind
Crosses the brown land, unheard. The nymphs are departed. 175
Sweet Thames, run softly, till I end my song.[3]
The river bears no empty bottles, sandwich papers,
Silk handkerchiefs, cardboard boxes, cigarette ends
Or other testimony of summer nights. The nymphs are departed.
And their friends, the loitering heirs of city directors; 180
Departed, have left no addresses.
By the waters of Leman I sat down and wept[4] . . .
Sweet Thames, run softly till I end my song,
Sweet Thames, run softly, for I speak not loud or long.
But at my back in a cold blast I hear[5] 185
The rattle of the bones, and chuckle spread from ear to ear.

A rat crept softly through the vegetation
Dragging its slimy belly on the bank

---

8. The druggist, who gave her pills to cause a miscarriage. 9. Ham. 1. The popular song for a party's end ("Good Night, Ladies") shifts into Ophelia's last words in *Hamlet* (4.5.72) as she goes off to drown herself. 2. Reference to the Buddha's Fire Sermon (see n. 2, p. 2015), in which he denounced the fiery lusts and passions of earthly experience. "All things are on fire . . . with the fire of passion . . . of hatred . . . of infatuation." Part III describes the degeneration of even these passions in the sterile decadence of the modern Waste Land. 3. "V. Spenser, *Prothalamion*" [Eliot's note]. The line is the refrain of a marriage song by the Elizabethan poet Edmund Spenser (1552?–1599) and evokes a river of unpolluted pastoral beauty. 4. In Psalms 137.1, the exiled Hebrews sit by the rivers of Babylon and weep for their lost homeland. *Waters of Leman*: Lake Geneva (where Eliot wrote much of *The Waste Land*). A *leman* is a mistress or lover. 5. Distorted echo of Andrew Marvell's (1621–1678) poem *To His Coy Mistress*: "But at my back I always hear / Time's wingèd chariot hurrying near."

While I was fishing in the dull canal
On a winter evening round behind the gashouse   190
Musing upon the king my brother's wreck
And on the king my father's death before him.[6]
White bodies naked on the low damp ground
And bones cast in a little low dry garret,
Rattled by the rat's foot only, year to year.   195
But at my back from time to time I hear[7]
The sound of horns and motors, which shall bring[8]
Sweeney to Mrs. Porter in the spring.
O the moon shone bright on Mrs. Porter[9]
And on her daughter   200
They wash their feet in soda water
Et O ces voix d'enfants, chantant dans la coupole![1]

Twit twit twit
Jug jug jug jug jug jug
So rudely forc'd.   205
Tereu[2]

    Unreal City
Under the brown fog of a winter noon
Mr. Eugenides, the Smyrna merchant
Unshaven, with a pocket full of currants   210
C.i.f. London: documents at sight,[3]
Asked me in demotic French
To luncheon at the Cannon Street Hotel
Followed by a weekend at the Metropole.[4]

    At the violet hour, when the eyes and back   215
Turn upward from the desk, when the human engine waits
Like a taxi throbbing waiting,
I Tiresias,[5] though blind, throbbing between two lives,

---

6. "Cf. *The Tempest* I.ii" [Eliot's note]. Ferdinand, the king's son, believing his father drowned and mourning his death, hears in the air a song containing the line that Eliot quotes earlier at lines 48 and 126. 7. "Cf. Marvell, 'To His Coy Mistress' " [Eliot's note]. 8. "Cf. Day, *Parliament of Bees*: 'When of the sudden, listening, you shall hear, / A noise of horns and hunting, which shall bring / Actaeon to Diana in the spring, / Where all shall see her naked skin' " [Eliot's note]. The young hunter Actaeon was changed into a stag, hunted down, and killed when he came upon the goddess Diana bathing. Sweeney is in no such danger from his visit to Mrs. Porter. 9. "I do not know the origin of the ballad from which these lines are taken: it was reported to me from Sydney, Australia" [Eliot's note]. A song popular among Allied troops during World War I. One version continues lines 199–201 as follows: "And so they oughter / To keep them clean." 1. "V. Verlaine, *Parsifal*" [Eliot's note]. "And O these children's voices, singing in the dome!" (French); the last lines of a sonnet by Paul Verlaine (1844–1896), which ambiguously celebrates the Grail hero's chaste restraint. In Richard Wagner's opera, Parsifal's feet are washed to purify him before entering the presence of the Grail. 2. Tereus, who raped Philomela (see line 99); also the nightingale's song. 3. "The currants were quoted at a price 'carriage and insurance free to London'; and the Bill of Lading etc. were to be handed to the buyer upon payment of the sight draft" [Eliot's note]. 4. Smyrna is an ancient Phoenician seaport, and early Smyrna merchants spread the Eastern fertility cults. In contrast, their descendant Mr. Eugenides ("Well-born") invites the poet to lunch in a large commercial hotel and a weekend at a seaside resort in Brighton. 5. "Tiresias, although a mere spectator and not indeed a 'character,' is yet the most important personage in the poem, uniting all the rest. Just as the one-eyed merchant, seller of currants, melts into the Phoenician Sailor, and the latter is not wholly distinct from Ferdinand Prince of Naples, so all the women are one woman, and the two sexes meet in Tiresias. What Tiresias *sees*, in fact, is the substance of the poem. The whole passage from Ovid is one of great anthropological interest" [Eliot's note]. The passage then quoted from Ovid's *Metamorphoses* (3.320–38) describes how Tiresias spent seven years of his life as a woman and thus experienced love from the point of view of both sexes. Blinded by Juno, he was recompensed by Jove with the gift of prophecy.

Old man with wrinkled female breasts, can see
At the violet hour, the evening hour that strives   220
Homeward, and brings the sailor home from sea,[6]
The typist home at teatime, clears her breakfast, lights
Her stove, and lays out food in tins.
Out of the window perilously spread
Her drying combinations touched by the sun's last rays,   225
On the divan are piled (at night her bed)
Stockings, slippers, camisoles, and stays.
I Tiresias, old man with wrinkled dugs
Perceived the scene, and foretold the rest—
I too awaited the expected guest.   230
He, the young man carbuncular, arrives,
A small house agent's clerk, with one bold stare,
One of the low on whom assurance sits
As a silk hat on a Bradford[7] millionaire.
The time is now propitious, as he guesses,   235
The meal is ended, she is bored and tired,
Endeavours to engage her in caresses
Which still are unreproved, if undesired.
Flushed and decided, he assaults at once;
Exploring hands encounter no defence;   240
His vanity requires no response,
And makes a welcome of indifference.
(And I Tiresias have foresuffered all
Enacted on this same divan or bed;
I who have sat by Thebes below the wall   245
And walked among the lowest of the dead.)[8]
Bestows one final patronising kiss,
And gropes his way, finding the stairs unlit . . .

    She turns and looks a moment in the glass,
Hardly aware of her departed lover;   250
Her brain allows one half-formed thought to pass:
"Well now that's done: and I'm glad it's over."
When lovely woman stoops to folly and[9]
Paces about her room again, alone,
She smoothes her hair with automatic hand,   255
And puts a record on the gramophone.

    "This music crept by me upon the waters"[1]
And along the Strand, up Queen Victoria Street.

---

6. "This may or may not appear as exact as Sappho's lines, but I had in mind the 'longshore' or 'dory' fisherman, who returns at nightfall" [Eliot's note]. The Greek poet Sappho's poem describes how the evening star brings home those whom dawn has sent abroad; there is also an echo of Robert Louis Stevenson's (1850–1894) *Requiem* 1.221: "Home is the sailor, home from the sea."   7. A manufacturing town in Yorkshire that prospered greatly during World War I.   8. Tiresias prophesied in the marketplace at Thebes for many years before dying and continuing to prophesy in Hades.   9. "V. Goldsmith, the song in *The Vicar of Wakefield*" [Eliot's note]. "When lovely woman stoops to folly / And finds too late that men betray / What charm can soothe her melancholy, / What art can wash her guilt away?" Oliver Goldsmith (ca. 1730–1774), *The Vicar of Wakefield* (1766).   1. "V. *The Tempest*, as above" [Eliot's note, referring to line 191]. Spoken by Ferdinand as he hears Ariel sing of his father's transformation by the sea, his eyes turning to pearls, his bones to coral, and everything else he formerly was into "something rich and strange."

O City city,[2] I can sometimes hear
Beside a public bar in Lower Thames Street,   260
The pleasant whining of a mandoline
And a clatter and a chatter from within
Where fishmen lounge at noon: where the walls
Of Magnus Martyr[3] hold
Inexplicable splendour of Ionian white and gold.   265

    The river sweats[4]
    Oil and tar
    The barges drift
    With the turning tide
    Red sails   270
    Wide
    To leeward, swing on the heavy spar.
    The barges wash
    Drifting logs
    Down Greenwich reach   275
    Past the Isle of Dogs.[5]
        Weialala leia
        Wallala leialala
    Elizabeth and Leicester[6]
    Beating oars   280
    The stern was formed
    A gilded shell
    Red and gold
    The brisk swell
    Rippled both shores   285
    Southwest wind
    Carried down stream
    The peal of bells
    White towers
        Weialala leia   290
        Wallala leialala

"Trams and dusty trees.
Highbury bore me. Richmond and Kew
Undid me.[7] By Richmond I raised my knees
Supine on the floor of a narrow canoe."   295

---

2. A double invocation: the city of London and the City as London's central financial district (see lines 60 and 207). See also lines 375–76, the great cities of Western civilization. 3. "The interior of St. Magnus Martyr is to my mind one of the finest among Wren's interiors. See *The Proposed Demolition of Nineteen City Churches*: (P. S. King & Son, Ltd)" [Eliot's note]. The architect was Christopher Wren (1632–1723), and the church is located just below London Bridge on Lower Thames Street. 4. "The Song of the (three) Thames-daughters begins here. From line 292 to 306 inclusive they speak in turn. V. *Götterdämmerung* III.i.: the Rhine-daughters" [Eliot's note]. In Wagner's opera *The Twilight of the Gods* (1876), the three Rhine-maidens mourn the loss of their gold, which gave the river its sparkling beauty; lines 277–78 here echo the Rhine-maidens' refrain. 5. A peninsula opposite Greenwich on the Thames. 6. "V. Froude, *Elizabeth*, vol. I, ch. iv, letter of De Quadra to Philip of Spain: 'In the afternoon we were in a barge, watching the games on the river. (The queen) was alone with Lord Robert and myself on the poop, when they began to talk nonsense, and went so far that Lord Robert at last said, as I was on the spot there was no reason why they should not be married if the queen pleased" [Eliot's note]. Sir Robert Dudley (1532–1588), the earl of Leicester, was a favorite of Queen Elizabeth and at one point hoped to marry her. 7. "Cf. *Purgatorio*, V, 133: 'Ricorditi di me, che son la Pia, / Siena mi fe', disfecemi Maremma'" [Eliot's note]. La Pia, in Purgatory, recalls her seduction: "Remember me, who am La Pia. / Siena made me, Maremma undid me." Eliot's parody substitutes Highbury (a London suburb) and Richmond and Kew, popular excursion points on the Thames.

"My feet are at Moorgate,[8] and my heart
Under my feet. After the event
He wept. He promised 'a new start.'
I made no comment. What should I resent?'

"On Margate Sands.[9]   300
I can connect
Nothing with nothing.
The broken fingernails of dirty hands.
My people humble people who expect
Nothing.'   305
            la la

To Carthage then I came[1]

Burning burning burning burning[2]
O Lord Thou pluckest me out[3]
O Lord Thou pluckest   310

burning

IV. *Death by Water*

Phlebas the Phoenician, a fortnight dead,
Forgot the cry of gulls, and the deep sea swell
And the profit and loss.
                        A current under sea   315
Picked his bones in whispers. As he rose and fell
He passed the stages of his age and youth
Entering the whirlpool.
                        Gentile or Jew
O you who turn the wheel and look to windward,   320
Consider Phlebas, who was once handsome and tall as you.

V. *What the Thunder Said*[4]

After the torchlight red on sweaty faces
After the frosty silence in the gardens
After the agony in stony places
The shouting and the crying   325

8. A London slum.   9. A seaside resort on the Thames.   1. "V. St. Augustine's *Confessions*: 'to Carthage then I came, where a cauldron of unholy loves sang all about mine ears' " [Eliot's note]. The youthful Augustine is described. Carthage is also the scene of Dido's faithful love for Aeneas, referred to in line 92. 2. "The complete text of the Buddha's Fire Sermon (which corresponds in importance to the Sermon on the Mount) from which these words are taken, will be found translated in the late Henry Clarke Warren's *Buddhism in Translation* (Harvard Oriental Studies). Mr. Warren was one of the great pioneers of Buddhist studies in the Occident" [Eliot's note]. The Sermon on the Mount is in Matthew 5–7.   3. "From St. Augustine's *Confessions* again. The collocation of these two representatives of eastern and western asceticism, as the culmination of this part of the poem is not an accident" [Eliot's note]. See also Zechariah 3.2, where the high priest Joshua is described as a "brand plucked out of the fire."   4. "In the first part of Part V three themes are employed: the journey to Emmaus, the approach to the Chapel Perilous (see Miss Weston's book) and the present decay of eastern Europe" [Eliot's note]. On their journey to Emmaus (Luke 24.13–34), Jesus' disciples were joined by a stranger who later revealed himself to be the crucified and resurrected Christ. The *thunder* of the title is a divine voice in the Hindu *Upanishads* (see n. 3, p. 2017).

Prison and palace and reverberation
Of thunder of spring over distant mountains
He who was living is now dead[5]
We who were living are now dying
With a little patience   330

    Here is no water but only rock
Rock and no water and the sandy road
The road winding above among the mountains
Which are mountains of rock without water
If there were water we should stop and drink   335
Amongst the rock one cannot stop or think
Sweat is dry and feet are in the sand
If there were only water amongst the rock
Dead mountain mouth of carious teeth that cannot spit
Here one can neither stand nor lie nor sit   340
There is not even silence in the mountains
But dry sterile thunder without rain
There is not even solitude in the mountains
But red sullen faces sneer and snarl
From doors of mudcracked houses   345
                                  If there were water

    And no rock
    If there were rock
    And also water
    And water   350
    A spring
    A pool among the rock
    If there were the sound of water only
    Not the cicada[6]
    And dry grass singing   355
    But sound of water over a rock
    Where the hermit-thrush[7] sings in the pine trees
    Drip drop drip drop drop drop drop
    But there is no water

    Who is the third who walks always beside you?   360
When I count, there are only you and I together[8]
But when I look ahead up the white road
There is always another one walking beside you
Gliding wrapt in a brown mantle, hooded
I do not know whether a man or a woman   365
—But who is that on the other side of you?

---

5. Allusions to stages in Christ's Passion: the betrayal, prayer in the garden of Gethsemane, imprisonment, trial, crucifixion, and burial. Despair reigns, for this is death before the Resurrection. **6.** Grasshopper or cricket; see line 23. **7.** "The hermit-thrush which I have heard in Quebec Province. . . . Its 'water-dripping song' is justly celebrated" [Eliot's note]. **8.** "The following lines were stimulated by the account of one of the Antarctic expeditions (I forget which, but I think one of Shackleton's): it was related that the party of explorers, at the extremity of their strength, had the constant delusion that there was *one more member* than could actually be counted" [Eliot's note]. See also n. 4, p. 2015.

What is that sound high in the air⁹
Murmur of maternal lamentation
Who are those hooded hordes swarming
Over endless plains, stumbling in cracked earth   370
Ringed by the flat horizon only
What is the city over the mountains
Cracks and reforms and bursts in the violet air
Falling towers
Jerusalem Athens Alexandria   375
Vienna London
Unreal

    A woman drew her long black hair out tight
And fiddled whisper music on those strings
And bats with baby faces in the violet light   380
Whistled, and beat their wings
And crawled head downward down a blackened wall
And upside down in air were towers
Tolling reminiscent bells, that kept the hours
And voices singing out of empty cisterns and exhausted wells.   385

    In this decayed hole among the mountains
In the faint moonlight, the grass is singing
Over the tumbled graves, about the chapel
There is the empty chapel, only the wind's home.
It has no windows, and the door swings,   390
Dry bones can harm no one.
Only a cock stood on the rooftree
Co co rico co co rico¹
In a flash of lightning. Then a damp gust
Bringing rain   395

    Ganga was sunken, and the limp leaves
Waited for rain, while the black clouds
Gathered far distant, over Himavant.²
The jungle crouched, humped in silence.
Then spoke the thunder   400
Da
Datta: what have we given?³
My friend, blood shaking my heart

---

9. Eliot's note to lines 367–77 refers to Hermann Hesse's *Blick ins Chaos* (Glimpse into Chaos) and a passage that reads, translated, "Already half of Europe, already at least half of Eastern Europe is on the way to Chaos, drives drunk in holy madness on the edge of the abyss and sings at the same time, sings drunk and hymn-like, as Dimitri Karamazov sang [in Dostoevsky's *The Brothers Karamazov*]. The offended bourgeois laughs at the songs; the saint and the seer hear them with tears."   1. European version of the cock's crow: *cock-a-doodle-doo.* The cock crowed in Matthew 26.34 and 74, after Peter had denied Jesus three times.   2. A mountain in the Himalayas. *Ganga:* the river Ganges in India.   3. " 'Datta, dayadh-vam, damyata' (Give, sympathise, control). The fable of the meaning of the Thunder is found in the *Bri-hadaranyaka*—Upanishad 5,1" [Eliot's note]. In the fable, the word *DA*, spoken by the supreme being Prajapati, is interpreted as *Datta* ("to give alms"), *Dayadhvam* ("to sympathize or have compassion"), and *Damyata* ("to have self-control") by gods, human beings, and demons respectively. The conclusion is that when the thunder booms DA DA DA, Prajapati is commanding that all three virtues be practiced simultaneously.

The awful daring of a moment's surrender
Which an age of prudence can never retract 405
By this, and this only, we have existed
Which is not to be found in our obituaries
Or in memories draped by the beneficent spider[4]
Or under seals broken by the lean solicitor
In our empty rooms 410
Da
Dayadhvam:[5] I have heard the key
Turn in the door once and turn once only
We think of the key, each in his prison
Thinking of the key, each confirms a prison 415
Only at nightfall, aethereal rumours
Revive for a moment a broken Coriolanus[6]
Da
Damyata: The boat responded
Gaily, to the hand expert with sail and oar 420
The sea was calm, your heart would have responded
Gaily, when invited, beating obedient
To controlling hands

                       I sat upon the shore
Fishing,[7] with the arid plain behind me 425
Shall I at least set my lands in order?
London Bridge is falling down falling down falling down

Poi s'ascose nel foco che gli affina[8]
Quando fiam uti chelidon[9]—O swallow swallow
Le Prince d'Aquitaine à la tour abolie[1] 430
These fragments I have shored against my ruins
Why then Ile fit you. Hieronymo's mad againe.[2]
Datta. Dayadhvam. Damyata.
      Shantih   shantih   shantih[3]

---

4. "Cf. Webster, *The White Devil*, V, vi: '. . . they'll remarry / Ere the worm pierce your winding-sheet, ere the spider / Make a thin curtain for your epitaphs' " [Eliot's note]. 5. Eliot's note on the command "to sympathize" or reach outside the self, cites two descriptions of helpless isolation. The first comes from Dante's *Inferno* 33.46: as Ugolino, imprisoned in a tower with his children to die of starvation, says, "And I heard below the door of the horrible tower being locked up". The second is a modern description by the English philosopher F. H. Bradley (1846–1924) of the inevitably self-enclosed or private nature of consciousness: "My external sensations are no less private to myself than are my thoughts or my feelings. In either case my experience falls within my own circle, a circle closed on the outside; and, with all its elements alike, every sphere is opaque to the others which surround it. . . . In brief, regarded as an existence which appears in a soul, the whole world for each is peculiar and private to that soul" (*Appearance and Reality*). 6. A proud Roman patrician who was exiled and led an army against his homeland. In Shakespeare's play, both his grandeur and his downfall come from a desire to be ruled only by himself. 7. "V. Weston: *From Ritual to Romance*; chapter on the Fisher King" [Eliot's note]. 8. Eliot's note quotes a passage in the *Purgatorio* in which Arnaut Daniel (see n. 3, p. 2006) asks Dante to remember his pain. The line cited here, "then he hid himself in the fire which refines them" (*Purgatorio* 26.148), shows Daniel departing in fire which—in Purgatory—exists as a purifying rather than a destructive element. 9. "V. *Pervigilium Veneris*. Cf. Philomela in Parts II and III" [Eliot's note]. "When shall I be as a swallow?" A line from the *Vigil of Venus*, an anonymous late Latin poem, that asks for the gift of song; here associated with Philomela as a swallow, not the nightingale of lines 99–103 and 203–06. 1. "V. Gerard de Nerval, Sonnet *El Desdichado*" [Eliot's note]. The Spanish title means "The Disinherited One," and the sonnet is a monologue describing the speaker as a melancholy, ill-starred dreamer: "the Prince of Aquitaine in his ruined tower." Another line recalls the scene at the end of *The Love Song of J. Alfred Prufrock* (p. 2003): "I dreamed in the grotto where sirens swim." 2. "V. Kyd's *Spanish Tragedy*" [Eliot's note]. Thomas Kyd's revenge play (1594) is subtitled *Hieronymo's Mad Againe*. The protagonist "fits" his son's murderers into appropriate roles in a court entertainment so that they may all be killed. 3. "Shantih. Repeated as here, a formal ending to an Upanishad. 'The Peace which passeth understanding' is our equivalent to this word" [Eliot's note]. The *Upanishads* comment on the sacred Hindu scriptures, the *Vedas*.

The Hollow Men

Mistah Kurtz—he dead.[1]

The Hollow Men

A penny for the Old Guy[2]

I

We are the hollow men
We are the stuffed men
Leaning together
Headpiece filled with straw. Alas!
Our dried voices, when   5
We whisper together
Are quiet and meaningless
As wind in dry glass
Or rats' feet[3] over broken glass
In our dry cellar   10

    Shape without form, shade without colour,
Paralysed force, gesture without motion;

    Those who have crossed
With direct eyes, to death's other Kingdom[4]
Remember us—if at all—not as lost   15
Violent souls, but only
As the hollow men
The stuffed men.

II

Eyes I dare not meet in dreams
In death's dream kingdom[5]   20
These do not appear:
There, the eyes are
Sunlight on a broken column
There, is a tree swinging
And voices are   25
In the wind's singing
More distant and more solemn
Than a fading star.

---

1. Contemptuous words that announce the death of the mysterious Kurtz in Conrad's *Heart of Darkness*.
2. Guy Fawkes, who tried to blow up Parliament in 1605. Each November, British schoolchildren collect
pennies for a celebration to burn him in scarecrow effigy.   **3.** Similar images appear in *The Waste Land*,
lines 115 and 195.   **4.** In Greco-Roman mythology, Sleep is the brother of Death; sleep's children bring
images in dreams.   **5.** In his essay on Dante (1929), Eliot will remark that the poet is overwhelmed and
cannot meet Beatrice's eyes (*Purgatorio* 30; *Paradiso* 4).

Let me be no nearer
In death's dream kingdom   30
Let me also wear
Such deliberate disguises[6]
Rat's coat, crowskin, crossed staves
In a field
Behaving as the wind behaves   35
No nearer—

    Not that final meeting
In the twilight kingdom

III

This is the dead land
This is cactus land   40
Here the stone images[7]
Are raised, here they receive
The supplication of a dead man's hand
Under the twinkle of a fading star.

    Is it like this   45
In death's other kingdom
Waking alone
At the hour when we are
Trembling with tenderness
Lips that would kiss   50
Form prayers to broken stone.

IV

The eyes are not here
There are no eyes here
In this valley of dying stars
In this hollow valley   55
This broken jaw of our lost kingdoms

    In this last of meeting places
We grope together
And avoid speech
Gathered on this beach of the tumid river[8]   60

    Sightless, unless
The eyes reappear
As the perpetual star

---

6. The speaker will disguise himself as a scarecrow, using crossed sticks covered with old clothes and sometimes dead vermin. **7.** Compare lines 22–24 of *The Waste Land.* **8.** The Acheron, one of five mythological rivers separating the underworld from the living, surrounds Hell in Dante's *Inferno;* also a suggestion of the Congo River in Conrad's *Heart of Darkness.*

Multifoliate rose[9]
Of death's twilight kingdom   65
The hope only
Of empty men.

                                   V

Here we go round the prickly pear
Prickly pear prickly pear
Here we go round the prickly pear   70
At five o'clock in the morning.[1]

  Between the idea
And the reality
Between the motion
And the act   75
Falls the Shadow
                    For Thine is the Kingdom[2]

  Between the conception
And the creation
Between the emotion   80
And the response
Falls the Shadow

                    Life is very long

  Between the desire
And the spasm   85
Between the potency
And the existence
Between the essence
And the descent
Falls the Shadow   90
                    For Thine is the Kingdom

  For Thine is
Life is
For Thine is the

  This is the way the world ends   95
This is the way the world ends
This is the way the world ends
Not with a bang but a whimper.

9. In Dante's *Paradiso* 32, an image of heaven.   1. Parody of the children's dance rhyme "Here we go round the mulberry bush . . . On a cold and frosty morning."   2. From the Lord's Prayer.

From Four Quartets

Little Gidding[1]

Midwinter spring is its own season
Sempiternal though sodden towards sundown,
Suspended in time, between pole and tropic.
When the short day is brightest, with frost and fire,
The brief sun flames the ice, on pond and ditches,   5
In windless cold that is the heart's heat,
Reflecting in a watery mirror
A glare that is blindness in the early afternoon.
And glow more intense than blaze of branch, or brazier,
Stirs the dumb spirit: no wind, but pentecostal fire[2]   10
In the dark time of the year. Between melting and freezing
The soul's sap quivers. There is no earth smell
Or smell of living thing. This is the spring time
But not in time's covenant. Now the hedgerow
Is blanched for an hour with transitory blossom   15
Of snow, a bloom more sudden
Than that of summer, neither budding nor fading,
Not in the scheme of generation.
Where is the summer, the unimaginable
Zero summer?   20
          If you came this way,
Taking the route you would be likely to take
From the place you would be likely to come from,
If you came this way in may time,[3] you would find the hedges
White again, in May, with voluptuary sweetness.   25
It would be the same at the end of the journey,
If you came at night like a broken king,[4]
If you came by day not knowing what you came for,
It would be the same, when you leave the rough road
And turn behind the pig-sty to the dull façade   30
And the tombstone. And what you thought you came for
Is only a shell, a husk of meaning
From which the purpose breaks only when it is fulfilled
If at all. Either you had no purpose
Or the purpose is beyond the end you figured   35
And is altered in fulfilment. There are other places
Which also are the world's end, some at the sea jaws,
Or over a dark lake, in a desert or a city—
But this is the nearest, in place and time,
Now and in England.   40
          If you came this way,
Taking any route, starting from anywhere,
At any time or at any season,

---

1. A village in Huntingdonshire that housed a religious community in the 17th century. Eliot visited the (rebuilt) chapel on a midwinter day.   2. On the Pentecost day after Christ's resurrection, the apostles saw "cloven tongues like as of fire" (Acts 2.3) and were "filled with the Holy Ghost" (Acts 2.4).   3. When the May (Hawthorne) is in bloom.   4. Charles I, king of England (1600–1649), visited the religious community several times and went there secretly after his final defeat in the English Civil War.

It would always be the same: you would have to put off
Sense and notion. You are not here to verify,   45
Instruct yourself, or inform curiosity
Or carry report. You are here to kneel
Where prayer has been valid. And prayer is more
Than an order of words, the conscious occupation
Of the praying mind, or the sound of the voice praying.   50
And what the dead had no speech for, when living,
They can tell you, being dead: the communication
Of the dead is tongued with fire beyond the language of the living.
Here, the intersection of the timeless moment
Is England and nowhere. Never and always.   55

II

Ash on an old man's sleeve
Is all the ash the burnt roses leave.
Dust in the air suspended
Marks the place where a story ended.
Dust inbreathed was a house—   60
The wall, the wainscot and the mouse.
The death of hope and despair,
    This is the death of air.[5]

There are flood and drouth
Over the eyes and in the mouth,   65
Dead water and dead sand
Contending for the upper hand.
The parched eviscerate soil
Gapes at the vanity of toil,
Laughs without mirth.   70
    This is the death of earth.

Water and fire succeed
The town, the pasture and the weed.
Water and fire deride
The sacrifice that we denied.   75
Water and fire shall rot
The marred foundations we forgot,
Of sanctuary and choir.
    This is the death of water and fire.

In the uncertain hour before the morning[6]   80
  Near the ending of interminable night
    At the recurrent end of the unending
After the dark dove[7] with the flickering tongue

5. Allusion to "Fire lives in the death of air," a phrase from the pre-Socratic philosopher Heraclitus (535–475 B.C.E.) describing how one element (here, fire) lives at the expense of another (here, air).   6. The narrative passage from here to the end of Part II is written in tercets, a form that recalls Dante's use of *terza rima* (triple rhyme) in *The Divine Comedy*. Eliot later commented that this section was "the nearest equivalent to a canto of the *Inferno* or *Purgatorio*" that he could create.   7. A play on the emblem of the Holy Spirit that descended to the apostles at Pentecost and on the then-current German slang for bomb, *Taube* ("dove").

Had passed below the horizon of his homing
    While the dead leaves still rattled on like tin   85
Over the asphalt where no other sound was
    Between three districts whence the smoke arose
    I met one walking, loitering and hurried
As if blown towards me like the metal leaves
    Before the urban dawn wind unresisting.   90
    And as I fixed upon the down-turned face
That pointed scrutiny with which we challenge
    The first-met stranger in the waning dusk
    I caught the sudden look of some dead master
Whom I had known, forgotten, half recalled   95
    Both one and many; in the brown baked features
    The eyes of a familiar compound ghost
Both intimate and unidentifiable.
    So I assumed a double part,[8] and cried
    And heard another's voice cry: "What! are *you* here?"   100
Although we were not. I was still the same,
    Knowing myself yet being someone other—
    And he a face still forming; yet the words sufficed
To compel the recognition they preceded.
    And so, compliant to the common wind,   105
    Too strange to each other for misunderstanding,
In concord at this intersection time
    Of meeting nowhere, no before and after,
    We trod the pavement in a dead patrol.
I said: "The wonder that I feel is easy,   110
    Yet ease is cause of wonder. Therefore speak:
    I may not comprehend, may not remember."
And he: "I am not eager to rehearse
    My thought and theory which you have forgotten.
    These things have served their purpose: let them be.   115
So with your own, and pray they be forgiven
    By others, as I pray you to forgive
    Both bad and good. Last season's fruit is eaten
And the fullfed beast shall kick the empty pail.
    For last year's words belong to last year's language   120
    And next year's words await another voice.
But, as the passage now presents no hindrance
    To the spirit unappeased and peregrine
    Between two worlds become much like each other,
So I find words I never thought to speak   125
    In streets I never thought I should revisit
    When I left my body on a distant shore.
Since our concern was speech, and speech impelled us
    To purify the dialect of the tribe[9]
    And urge the mind to aftersight and foresight,   130
Let me disclose the gifts reserved for age

---

8. The role of questioner of souls (after Dante in *The Divine Comedy*) and the role of one interrogating himself.   9. In his epitaph-sonnet for Edgar Allan Poe, *The Tomb of Edgar Poe*, the French poet Stéphane Mallarmé (1842–1898) defines the poet's role as purifying speech by using ordinary language (*the dialect of the tribe*) in a more precise and yet complex way, creating a new structure of interlocking or multiple meanings (see lines 221–24.)

To set a crown upon your lifetime's effort.
First, the cold friction of expiring sense
Without enchantment, offering no promise
    But bitter tastelessness of shadow fruit 135
    As body and soul begin to fall asunder.
Second, the conscious impotence of rage
    At human folly, and the laceration
    Of laughter at what ceases to amuse.
And last, the rending pain of re-enactment 140
    Of all that you have done, and been; the shame
    Of motives late revealed, and the awareness
Of things ill done and done to others' harm
    Which once you took for exercise of virtue.
    Then fools' approval stings, and honour stains. 145
From wrong to wrong the exasperated spirit
    Proceeds, unless restored by that refining fire
    Where you must move in measure, like a dancer.'[1]
The day was breaking. In the disfigured street
    He left me, with a kind of valediction, 150
    And faded on the blowing of the horn.[2]

III

There are three conditions which often look alike
Yet differ completely, flourish in the same hedgerow:
Attachment to self and to things and to persons; detachment
From self and from things and from persons; and, growing between
    them, indifference 155
Which resembles the others as death resembles life,
Being between two lives—unflowering, between
The live and the dead nettle. This is the use of memory:
For liberation—not less of love but expanding
Of love beyond desire, and so liberation 160
From the future as well as the past. Thus, love of a country
Begins as attachment to our own field of action
And comes to find that action of little importance
Though never indifferent. History may be servitude,
History may be freedom. See, now they vanish, 165
The faces and places, with the self which, as it could, loved them,
To become renewed, transfigured, in another pattern.

Sin is Behovely,[3] but
All shall be well, and
All manner of thing shall be well. 170
If I think, again, of this place,
And of people, not wholly commendable,
Of no immediate kin or kindness,
But some of peculiar genius,
All touched by a common genius, 175

---

1. In Dante's *Purgatorio* (26.148), fire is seen as a purgative or refining element, and characters are enveloped in flames that move in accord with their bodies.   **2.** The horn that marks the all-clear signal after an air raid; also the disappearance of Hamlet's father's ghost (*Hamlet* 1.2.157): "It faded on the crowing of the cock."   **3.** Inevitable. Lines 168–70 repeat the consoling words of Dame Julian of Norwich, a 14th-century English mystic: "Sin is behovabil, but all shall be well and all manner of thing shall be well."

United in the strife which divided them;
If I think of a king at nightfall,
Of three men, and more, on the scaffold[4]
And a few who died forgotten
In other places, here and abroad,   180
And of one who died blind and quiet,[5]
Why should we celebrate
These dead men more than the dying?
It is not to ring the bell backward
Nor is it an incantation   185
To summon the spectre of a Rose.
We cannot revive old factions[6]
We cannot restore old policies
Or follow an antique drum.
These men, and those who opposed them   190
And those whom they opposed
Accept the constitution of silence
And are folded in a single party.
Whatever we inherit from the fortunate
We have taken from the defeated   195
What they had to leave us—a symbol:
A symbol perfected in death.
And all shall be well and
All manner of thing shall be well
By the purification of the motive   200
In the ground of our beseeching.

IV

The dove descending breaks the air
With flame of incandescent terror
Of which the tongues declare
The one discharge from sin and error.   205
The only hope, or else despair
    Lies in the choice of pyre or pyre—
    To be redeemed from fire by fire.

Who then devised the torment? Love.
Love is the unfamiliar Name   210
Behind the hands that wove
The intolerable shirt of flame[7]
Which human power cannot remove.
    We only live, only suspire
    Consumed by either fire or fire.   215

4. Charles I and his chief advisers were executed on the scaffold after the English Civil War.   5. The
poet John Milton (1608–1674), who supported Parliament and the Commonwealth in the English Civil
War.   6. Alluding to the factionalisms of history exemplified here in the Wars of the Roses (1555–85),
when Yorkists, whose badge was the white rose, fought Lancastrians, whose badge was a red rose, for the
English throne. The struggle ended in the strong centralized monarchy of the Tudors, whose Tudor Rose
"in-folded" (cf. line 259) the other two. There is also allusion to the discovery, beyond history, of the vast
rose of pure light seen by Dante in the *Paradiso* (30.112 ff), evoked in line 261.   7. The shirt, poisoned
with the blood of Nessus the centaur, that Deianeira (unknowingly) gave her husband, Hercules, to
strengthen his love for her. Instead, the shirt so burned Hercules' flesh that he chose death on a funeral
pyre to escape the agony.

V

What we call the beginning is often the end
And to make an end is to make a beginning.
The end is where we start from. And every phrase
And sentence that is right (where every word is at home,
Taking its place to support the others,   220
The word neither diffident nor ostentatious,
An easy commerce of the old and the new,
The common word exact without vulgarity,
The formal word precise but not pedantic,
The complete consort[8] dancing together)   225
Every phrase and every sentence is an end and a beginning,
Every poem an epitaph. And any action
Is a step to the block, to the fire, down the sea's throat
Or to an illegible stone: and that is where we start.
We die with the dying: 230
See, they depart, and we go with them.
We are born with the dead:
See, they return, and bring us with them.
The moment of the rose and the moment of the yew-tree
Are of equal duration. A people without history   235
Is not redeemed from time, for history is a pattern
Of timeless moments. So, while the light fails
On a winter's afternoon, in a secluded chapel
History is now and England.

With the drawing of this Love and the voice of this Calling[9]   240
We shall not cease from exploration
And the end of all our exploring
Will be to arrive where we started
And know the place for the first time.
Through the unknown, remembered gate   245
When the last of earth left to discover
Is that which was the beginning;
At the source of the longest river
The voice of the hidden waterfall
And the children in the apple-tree   250
Not known, because not looked for
But heard, half-heard, in the stillness
Between two waves of the sea.
Quick now, here, now, always[1]—
A condition of complete simplicity   255
(Costing not less than everything)
And all shall be well and
All manner of thing shall be well
When the tongues of flame are in-folded
Into the crowned knot of fire   260
And the fire and the rose are one.

8. Both "harmony" and "company."   9. Line from *The Cloud of Unknowing*, a 14th-century book of
Christian mysticism.   1. This same line occurs toward the end of *Burnt Norton*, the first of the *Four
Quartets*, where it also follows voices of children hidden in foliage; there is a suggestion of sudden insight
gained in a moment of passive openness to illumination.

ANNA AKHMATOVA
1889–1966

The voice of Anna Akhmatova is intensely personal, whether she speaks as lover, wife, and mother or as a national poet commemorating the mute agony of millions. From the subjective love lyrics of her earliest work to the communal mourning of *Requiem* and the many-layered drama of *Poem without a Hero,* she expresses universal themes in terms of individual experience, and historical events through the filter of basic emotions like fear, love, hope, and pain. Akhmatova is one of the great Russian poets of the twentieth century, but she retains a broad sense of European culture, both past and present, and fills her later works with references to Western music, literature, and art that give a startling breadth and scope to her very personalized poetry. Too cosmopolitan and too independent to be tolerated by the authorities, Akhmatova was viciously attacked and her books suppressed (1922–40) because they did not fit the government-approved model of literature: they were too "individualistic" and were not "socially useful." Although she was rehabilitated in the 1960s and eventually achieved recognized status as national poet, Akhmatova was read in secret for a long time, chiefly for the perfection of her early love lyrics. After the death of Joseph Stalin in 1953, however, her collected poems—including poems of the war years and unknown texts written during the periods of enforced silence—brought the full range of her work to public attention.

She was born Anna Andreevna Gorenko on June 11, 1889, in a suburb of the Black Sea port of Odessa and in a traditional society that she described as "Dostoevsky's Russia." Her father was a maritime engineer and her mother an independent woman of populist sympathies who belonged to an early revolutionary group called People's Will. The poet took the pen name of Akhmatova (accented on the second syllable) from her maternal great-grandmother, who was of Tatar descent. Her family soon moved to Tsarskoe Selo ("the Czar's Village"), a small town outside St. Petersburg that had been for centuries the site of the summer palace of the czars, and also—perhaps more important for Akhmatova—a place where the great Romantic poet Alexander Pushkin wrote his youthful works. She attended the local school at Tsarskoe Selo but completed her degree in Kiev; in 1907, she briefly studied law at the Kiev College for Women before moving to St. Petersburg to study literature.

In Tsarskoe Selo, Akhmatova met Nikolai Gumilyov, whom she married in April 1910. After their marriage, the couple visited Paris during the spring of 1910 and in 1911, meeting many writers and artists, including Amedeo Modigliani, who sketched Akhmatova several times and with whom she recalled wandering around Paris and reading aloud the poetry of Paul Verlaine. It was a time of change in the arts, and when the couple returned to St. Petersburg, Gumilyov helped organize a Poets' Guild that became the core of a new small literary movement, Acmeism, which rejected the romantic, quasi-religious aims of Russian Symbolism and (like Imagism) valued clarity and concreteness and a closeness to things of this Earth. The Symbolist–Acmeist debate went on inside a lively literary and social life, while the three main figures of Acmeism—Akhmatova, Gumilyov, and Osip Mandelstam—gained a reputation as important poets.

Akhmatova's first collection of poems, *Evening,* was published in the spring of 1912; it is an intensely personal collection of lyrics in which the poet describes evening as a time of awakening to love—and grief. There is a new clarity and directness to these traditionally romantic subjects, however, as for the first time in Russian poetry a woman in love expresses and analyzes her own emotions. In October of the same year, her son, Lev Gumilyov, was born; it was his arrest and imprisonment in 1935 that inspired the first poems of the cycle that would become *Requiem.* Lev was ultimately imprisoned for a total of fourteen years as the government sought a way to punish his mother, who would not or could not write according to the approved socialist realist style praising the government. Even after she had become a national poet known for her patriotic poetry during World War II, Akhmatova was still criticized by the Stalinist regime as a reactionary "half-harlot, half-nun" who wrote subjective love lyrics without social significance: the love poetry of *Evening, Rosary* (1914), and *The White Flock* (1917, published a month before the start of the Russian Revolution).

The White Flock was published during World War I, the destruction of which so shocked Akhmatova that she wrote, "This untimely death is so terrible / I cannot look at God's world." Yet more bloodshed was to follow in the civil war following the Revolution of 1917. Akhmatova refused to flee abroad, as many Russians were doing. Her marriage with Gumilyov was breaking up, and they divorced in 1918; she remarried an Assyriologist, Vladimir Shileiko, who did not approve of his wife's writing poetry and burned some of her poems (she divorced him in 1928). Akhmatova's political difficulties began in 1922. Although she and Gumilyov were divorced, his arrest and execution for counterrevolutionary activities in 1921 put her own status into question. After 1922 and the publication of *Anno Domini*, she was no longer allowed to publish and was forced into the unwilling withdrawal from public activity that Russians call "internal emigration." Officially forgotten, she was not forgotten in fact; in the schools, her poems were copied out by hand and circulated among students who would never hear her name mentioned in a literature class.

Depending on a meager and irregular pension, Akhmatova prepared essays on the life and works of Pushkin and wrote poems that would not appear until much later. Stalin's "Great Purge" of 1935–38 sent millions of people to prison camps and made the 1930s a time of terror and uncertainty for everyone. It is this fear and misery that is expressed in *Requiem,* as the poet blends references to her own life with an awareness of the common plight. The art critic Nikolai Punin, with whom she lived from 1926 to 1940, was arrested briefly in 1935; Osip Mandelstam, her great friend, was exiled to Voronezh in May 1934 and then sent to a prison camp in 1938, where he died the same year; her son, Lev, was arrested briefly in 1935 and again in 1938, remaining imprisoned until 1941, when he was allowed to enlist in the military. Composing *Requiem* itself was a risky act carried out over several years, and Akhmatova and her friend Lidia Chukovskaya memorized the stanzas to preserve the poem in the absence of written copy. Akhmatova wrote of Mandelstam (but perhaps of them all) that "in the room of the poet in disgrace / Fear and the Muse keep watch by turns / And the night comes on / That knows no dawn." A temporary lifting of the ban against her works in 1940 did not last; although she was allowed to pubish a new collection, *From Six Books,* the edition was recalled by officials after six months.

It was in 1940 that Akhmatova became interested in larger musical forms and began thinking in terms of cycles of poems instead of her accustomed separate lyrics. She envisaged a larger framework for the core poems of *Requiem* in this year, and wrote the "Dedication" and two epilogues. She also began work on the *Poem without a Hero,* a long and complex verse narrative in three parts that sums up many of her earlier themes: love, death, creativity, the unity of European culture, and the suffering of her people. During World War II the poet was allowed a partial return to public life, addressing women on the radio during the siege of Leningrad (St. Petersburg) in 1941 and writing patriotic lyrics such as the famous *Courage* (published in *Pravda* in 1942), which rallied the Russian people to defend their homeland (and national language) from enslavement. Despite her patriotic activities, she was subject to vicious official attacks after the war. Stalin's minister of culture, Andrei Zhdanov, in the famous Report of 1946 proclaimed the doctrine of socialist realism as the official style and attacked Akhmatova's "individualistic" writing as the "poetry of an overwrought upper-class lady who frantically races back and forth between boudoir and chapel." Akhmatova was immediately expelled from the Writer's Union, which meant that she was not officially recognized as a professional writer (and hence could not earn her living in that career).

Unable once more to publish her work, she supported herself between 1946 and

1958 by translating poetry from a number of foreign languages. Her son was arrested again in 1949; hoping to obtain his release, she wrote the kind of adulatory poetry in praise of Stalin that the regime required. The attempt was unsuccessful, and her son remained in prison until 1956. The Stalinist cycle, *In Praise of Peace* (1950), contains such clumsy imitations of socialist-realist poetry that it has been considered a parody: "Where a tank rumbled, there is now a peaceful tractor." Akhmatova later directed that it be omitted from her collected works.

During the slow thaw that followed Stalin's death in 1953, Akhmatova was rehabilitated. Gradually her poems were allowed back into print; an edition of selected poems with added texts was published in 1958, and in the same year she was even elected to an honorary position on the executive council of the Writer's Union. In 1965 a larger collection appeared, *The Flight of Time,* which contained a new series called *The Seventh Book* as well as part of the still-unfinished *Poem without a Hero*. She took an interest in the young writers who flocked to her and supported those who—like Josif Brodsky—were accused by the new order of being a "parasite on the state." Akhmatova's work was already recognized internationally: Robert Frost visited her on his trip to the Soviet Union in 1962, *Requiem* was first published "without her consent" in Munich in 1963 (not until 1987 was the full text published in the Soviet Union), and in 1964 she traveled to Italy to receive the Taormina poetry prize. She was surrounded by admirers when she visited England in 1965 to receive an honorary degree from Oxford University. Her death in 1966 signaled the end of an era in modern Russian poetry, for she was the last of the famous "quartet" that also included Mandelstam, Tsvetaeva, and Pasternak.

Requiem is a lyrical cycle, a series of poems written on a common theme, but it is also a short epic narrative. The story it tells is acutely personal, even autobiographical, but like an epic it also transcends personal significance and describes (as in *The Song of Roland*) a moment in the history of a nation. Akhmatova, who had seen her husband and son arrested and her friends die in prison camps, was only one of millions who had suffered similar losses in the purges of the 1930s. The "Preface," "Dedication," and two epilogues to *Requiem* constitute a framework examining this image of a common fate, while the core of numbered poems develops a more subjective picture and the stages of an individual drama. In the inner poems, Akhmatova blends her separate personal losses—husband, son, and friends—to create a single focus, the figure of a mother grieving for her condemned son. In the frame, the poet identifies herself with the crowd of women with whom she waited for seventeen months outside the Leningrad prison—women who, in turn, represent bereaved women throughout the Soviet Union. The "I" of the speaker throughout remains anonymous, in spite of the fact that she describes her personal emotions in the central poems; her identity is that of a sorrowing mother, and she is distinguished from her fellow-sufferers only by the poetic gift that makes her the "exhausted mouth, / Through which a hundred million scream." *Requiem* is at once a public and a private poem, a picture of individual grief simultaneously linked to a national disaster, and a vision of community suffering that extends past even national disaster into medieval Russian history and Greek mythology. The martyrdom of the Soviet people is consistently pictured in religious terms, from the recurrent mention of crosses and crucifixion to the culminating image of maternal suffering in Mary, the mother of Christ.

The "Dedication" and "Prologue" establish the context for the poem as a whole: the mass arrests in the 1930s after the assassination on December 1, 1934, of Sergei Kirov, the top Communist Party official in Leningrad. The women waiting outside the Kresty ("Crosses") prison of Leningrad arrive at dawn in the coldest of weather, waiting for news of their loved ones, hoping to be allowed to pass them a parcel or a letter, and fearing the sentence of death or exile to the prison camps of frozen Siberia. Instead of living a natural life where "for someone the sunset luxuriates," these women and the prisoners are forced into a suspended existence of separation and uncertainty in which all values are inverted and the city itself has become only the setting for its prisons. It is a situation before which the great forces of nature bow in silent horror.

With the numbered poems, Akhmatova recounts the growing anguish of a bereaved mother as her son is arrested and sentenced to death. The speaker describes her husband's arrest at dawn, in the midst of the family. Her son was arrested later, and in the rest of the poem she relives her numbed incomprehension as she struggles against the increasing likelihood that he will be condemned to death. Recalling her own carefree adolescence in contrast to her current situation as she weeps outside the prison walls or pleads with Stalin to relent, the mother has a premonition of her son's fate that pushes her into the temporary relief of insanity and forgetting, and to a desire for her own arrest and death. After sentence is passed, the traumatized mother can speak of his execution only in oblique terms that are at once universal and potentially consoling: by shifting the image of death onto the plane of the Crucifixion and God's will. It is a tragedy that cannot be comprehended or looked at directly, just as, she suggests, at the Crucifixion "No one glanced and no one would have dared" to look at the grieving Mary. In the two epilogues, the grieving speaker returns from religious transcendence to Earth and current history. Here she takes on a newly composite identity, seeing herself not as an isolated sufferer but as reciprocally identified with the women whose fate she has shared. It is their memory she perpetuates by writing *Requiem*, and it is in their memory that she herself lives on. No longer the victim of purely personal tragedy, she has become a bronze statue commemorating a community of suffering, a figure shaped by circumstances into a monument of public and private grief.

Requiem[1]

1935–1940

No, not under the vault of alien skies,[2]
And not under the shelter of alien wings—
I was with my people then,
There, where my people, unfortunately, were.

1961

Instead of a Preface

In the terrible years of the Yezhov terror,[3] I spent seventeen months in the prison lines of Leningrad. Once, someone "recognized" me. Then a woman with bluish lips standing behind me, who, of course, had never heard me called by name before, woke up from the stupor to which every one had succumbed and whispered in my ear (everyone spoke in whispers there):

"Can you describe this?"

And I answered: "Yes, I can."

Then something that looked like a smile passed over what had once been her face.

April 1, 1957
Leningrad[4]

---

1. Translated by Judith Hemschemeyer.   **2.** A phrase borrowed from *Message to Siberia* by the Russian poet Pushkin (1799–1837).   **3.** In 1937–38, mass arrests were carried out by the secret police, headed by Nikolai Yezhov.   **4.** The prose preface was written after her son had been released from prison and it was possible to think of editing the poem for publication.

Dedication

Mountains bow down to this grief,
Mighty rivers cease to flow,
But the prison gates hold firm,
And behind them are the "prisoners' burrows"
And mortal woe.   5
For someone a fresh breeze blows,
For someone the sunset luxuriates—
We[5] wouldn't know, we are those who everywhere
Hear only the rasp of the hateful key
And the soldiers' heavy tread.   10
We rose as if for an early service,
Trudged through the savaged capital
And met there, more lifeless than the dead;
The sun is lower and the Neva[6] mistier,
But hope keeps singing from afar.   15
The verdict . . . And her tears gush forth,
Already she is cut off from the rest,
As if they painfully wrenched life from her heart,
As if they brutally knocked her flat,
But she goes on . . . Staggering . . . Alone . . . 20
Where now are my chance friends
Of those two diabolical years?
What do they imagine is in Siberia's storms,[7]
What appears to them dimly in the circle of the moon?
I am sending my farewell greeting to them.   25

March 1940

Prologue

That was when the ones who smiled
Were the dead, glad to be at rest.
And like a useless appendage, Leningrad
Swung from its prisons.
And when, senseless from torment,   5
Regiments of convicts marched,
And the short songs of farewell
Were sung by locomotive whistles.
The stars of death stood above us
And innocent Russia writhed   10
Under bloody boots
And under the tires of the Black Marias.[8]

---

5. The women waiting in line before the prison gates.   6. The large river that flows through St. Petersburg.   7. Victims of the purges who were not executed were condemned to prison camps in Siberia. Their wives were allowed to accompany them into exile, although they had to live in towns at a distance from the camps.   8. Police cars for conveying those arrested.

I

They led you away at dawn,
I followed you, like a mourner,
In the dark front room the children were crying,[9]
By the icon shelf the candle was dying.
On your lips was the icon's chill.[1]   5
The deathly sweat on your brow . . . Unforgettable!—
I will be like the wives of the Streltsy,[2]
Howling under the Kremlin towers.

1935

II

Quietly flows the quiet Don,[3]
Yellow moon slips into a home.

He slips in with cap askew,
He sees a shadow, yellow moon.

This woman is ill,   5
This woman is alone,

Husband in the grave,[4] son in prison,
Say a prayer for me.

III

No, it is not I, it is somebody else who is suffering.
I would not have been able to bear what happened,
Let them shroud it in black,
And let them carry off the lanterns . . .
                                                              Night.   5

1940

IV

You should have been shown, you mocker,
Minion of all your friends,
Gay little sinner of Tsarskoye Selo,[5]
What would happen in your life—
How three-hundredth in line, with a parcel,   5
You would stand by the Kresty prison,

9. Akhmatova's third husband, the art historian Nikolai Punin, was arrested at dawn while the children (his daughter and her cousin) cried.   1. The icon—a small religious painting—was set on a shelf before which a candle was kept lit. Punin had kissed the icon before being taken away.   2. Elite troops organized by Ivan the Terrible around 1550. They rebelled and were executed by Peter the Great in 1698. Pleading in vain, their wives and mothers saw the men killed under the towers of the Kremlin.   3. The great Russian river, often celebrated in folk songs. This poem is modeled on a simple, rhythmic short folk song known as a *chastuska*.   4. Akhmatova's first husband, the poet Nikolai Gumilyov, was shot in 1921.
5. Akhmatova recalls her early, carefree, and privileged life in Tsarskoe Selo outside St. Petersburg.

Your tempestuous tears
Burning through the New Year's ice.
Over there the prison poplar bends,
And there's no sound—and over there how many   10
Innocent lives are ending now . . .

V

For seventeen months I've been crying out,
Calling you home.
I flung myself at the hangman's[6] feet,
You are my son and my horror.
Everything is confused forever,   5
And it's not clear to me
Who is a beast now, who is a man,
And how long before the execution.
And there are only dusty flowers,
And the chinking of the censer, and tracks   10
From somewhere to nowhere.
And staring me straight in the eyes,
And threatening impending death,
Is an enormous star.[7]

1939

VI

The light weeks will take flight,
I won't comprehend what happened.
Just as the white nights[8]
Stared at you, dear son, in prison

So they are staring again,   5
With the burning eyes of a hawk,
Talking about your lofty cross,
And about death.

1939

VII

THE SENTENCE

And the stone word fell
On my still-living breast.
Never mind, I was ready.
I will manage somehow.

6. Stalin's. Akhmatova wrote a letter to him pleading for the release of her son.   7. The *star*, the *censer*,
the foliage, and the confusion between beast and man recall apocalyptic passages in the Book of Revelation
(8.5, 7, 10–11 and 9.7–10).   8. In St. Petersburg, because it is so far north, the nights around the
summer solstice are never totally dark.

Today I have so much to do: 5
I must kill memory once and for all,
I must turn my soul to stone,
I must learn to live again—

Unless . . . Summer's ardent rustling
Is like a festival outside my window. 10
For a long time I've foreseen this
Brilliant day, deserted house.

June 22, 1939[9]
Fountain House

VIII

TO DEATH

You will come in any case—so why not now?
I am waiting for you—I can't stand much more.
I've put out the light and opened the door
For you, so simple and miraculous.
So come in any form you please, 5
Burst in as a gas shell
Or, like a gangster, steal in with a length of pipe,
Or poison me with typhus fumes.
Or be that fairy tale you've dreamed up,[1]
So sickeningly familiar to everyone— 10
In which I glimpse the top of a pale blue cap[2]
And the house attendant white with fear.
Now it doesn't matter anymore. The Yenisey[3] swirls,
The North Star shines.
And the final horror dims 15
The blue luster of beloved eyes.

August 19, 1939
Fountain House

IX

Now madness half shadows
My soul with its wing,
And makes it drunk with fiery wine
And beckons toward the black ravine.

And I've finally realized 5
That I must give in,
Overhearing myself
Raving as if it were somebody else.

---

9. The date that her son was sentenced to labor camp.　1. A denunciation to the police for imaginary crimes, common during the purges as people hastened to protect themselves by accusing their neighbors. 2. The NKVD (secret police) wore blue caps.　3. A river in Siberia along which there were many prison camps.

And it does not allow me to take
Anything of mine with me   10
(No matter how I plead with it,
No matter how I supplicate):

Not the terrible eyes of my son—
Suffering turned to stone,
Not the day of the terror,   15
Not the hour I met with him in prison,

Not the sweet coolness of his hands,
Not the trembling shadow of the lindens,
Not the far-off, fragile sound—
Of the final words of consolation.   20

May 4, 1940
Fountain House

X

CRUCIFIXION

"Do not weep for Me, Mother,
I am in the grave."

1

A choir of angels sang the praises of that momentous hour,
And the heavens dissolved in fire.
To his Father He said: "Why hast Thou forsaken me!"[4]
And to his Mother: "Oh, do not weep for Me . . ."[5]

1940
Fountain House

2

Mary Magdalene beat her breast and sobbed,
The beloved disciple[6] turned to stone,
But where the silent Mother stood, there
No one glanced and no one would have dared.

1943
Tashkent

Epilogue I

I learned how faces fall,
How terror darts from under eyelids,
How suffering traces lines

---

4. Jesus' last words from the Cross (Matthew 27.46).   5. These words and the epigraph refer to a line from the Russian Orthodox prayer sung at services on Easter Saturday: "Weep not for Me, Mother, when you look upon the grave." Jesus is comforting Mary with the promise of his resurrection.   6. The apostle John.

Of stiff cuneiform on cheeks,
How locks of ashen-blonde or black   5
Turn silver suddenly,
Smiles fade on submissive lips
And fear trembles in a dry laugh.
And I pray not for myself alone,
But for all those who stood there with me   10
In cruel cold, and in July's heat,
At that blind, red wall.

Epilogue II

Once more the day of remembrance[7] draws near.
I see, I hear, I feel you:

The one they almost had to drag at the end,
And the one who tramps her native land no more,

And the one who, tossing her beautiful head,   5
Said: "Coming here's like coming home."

I'd like to name them all by name,
But the list[8] has been confiscated and is nowhere to be found.

I have woven a wide mantle for them
From their meager, overheard words.   10

I will remember them always and everywhere,
I will never forget them no matter what comes.

And if they gag my exhausted mouth
Through which a hundred million scream,

Then may the people remember me   15
On the eve of my remembrance day.

And if ever in this country
They decide to erect a monument to me,

I consent to that honor
Under these conditions—that it stand   20

Neither by the sea, where I was born:
My last tie with the sea is broken,

Nor in the tsar's garden near the cherished pine stump,[9]
Where an inconsolable shade[1] looks for me,

---

7. In the Russian Orthodox Church, a memorial service is held on the anniversary of a death.   8. Of prisoners.   9. The gardens and park surrounding the summer palace in Tsarskoe Selo. Akhmatova writes elsewhere of the stump of a favorite tree in the gardens and of the poet Pushkin, whom she describes as walking in the park.   1. A ghost; probably the restless spirit of Akhmatova's executed husband, Gumilyov, who had courted her in Tsarskoe Selo.

But here, where I stood for three hundred hours,   25
And where they never unbolted the doors for me.

This, lest in blissful death
I forget the rumbling of the Black Marias,

Forget how that detested door slammed shut
And an old woman howled like a wounded animal.   30

And may the melting snow stream like tears
From my motionless lids of bronze,

And a prison dove coo in the distance,
And the ships of the Neva sail calmly on.

March 1940

KATHERINE ANNE PORTER
1890–1980

Her stories are finely constructed models of psychological analysis, but it is their moral dimension that predominates in Katherine Anne Porter's world. She situates her protagonists at crucial moments when issues of life and death, or love, betrayal, and disappointment are involved: when their spiritual identity expands or when it seems suddenly to have been frozen for all time. Even though she is a regional writer in the sense that she comes from and often writes about the American South, she does not construct (like Faulkner) a mythical southern community but instead uses her southern background to provide characters and situations that also have broader significance. Porter remains within the realist tradition, with its linear chronology, consistent characters, and development of historical context, but she employs in addition modern techniques of interior monologue, symbolic association, and networks of inner reference to create a compact, densely interconnected artistic structure. She describes individual subjective worlds with an ironic awareness of their complexity and a verbal spareness and precision that have come to represent her mastery of the modern short story.

Porter was born on May 15, 1890, in Indian Creek, Texas, the third of five children and the descendant of a family that remembered "solid wealth and property in Kentucky, Louisiana, and Virginia" but had fallen on poorer days in Texas after the Civil War. She was educated in convent schools in Louisiana but was a rebellious student, running away from school at sixteen to marry. At nineteen, she was divorced; at twenty-one, she worked on a Chicago newspaper and briefly as an extra in the movies; at twenty-four, she returned to Texas and supported herself as a ballad singer; and at twenty-eight, she became a reporter for the *Rocky Mountain News* in Denver, where she nearly died during the influenza epidemic of 1918. Porter used material in her life as the basis for much of her fiction: stories like *Old Mortality, The Grave,* and *Noon Wine* reflect the experience of a young southern girl named Miranda, and an older Miranda in the novella *Pale Horse, Pale Rider* encounters love, sickness, and death during the Great Epidemic. Her one novel, *Ship of Fools* (1962), derives partly from a cruise she took from Veracruz, Mexico, to Bremerhaven, Germany, in 1931.

Yet Porter's writing must not be taken as purely autobiographical: the heroine of *Flowering Judas,* for example, shares aspects of the author's own background but is also based on a friend, an American schoolteacher living in Mexico at the same time. Porter's experience is a vantage point from which she can observe people reacting to a variety of situations, all of them integrated into a larger and more complex interpersonal perspective. She is much concerned with the relations between people, especially within the family, and probes the ambiguous and often self-deluding attitudes inherent in the closest emotional ties. "My whole attempt," she has said, "has been to discover and understand human motives, human feelings, to make a distillation of what human relations and experiences my mind has been able to absorb."

She lived briefly in New York after World War I and then moved to Mexico, where she played a small part in revolutionary politics during the Obregón revolution in 1919–20. Porter was sympathetic toward revolutionary or liberal causes: anything that promised help for the "anguish that human beings inflict on each other—the never-ending wrong, forever incurable." This sympathy did not prevent her taking a realistic view of various revolutionary groups and individuals, as is shown by her description of Braggioni in *Flowering Judas.* In 1921, Porter left Mexico for Fort Worth, and over the next ten years she wrote stories, reviews, and articles on Mexican culture while acting in amateur theater and traveling as often as she could. Many of the stories published during the 1920s and collected in *Flowering Judas* draw on her Mexican experience. Some characters are based on actual persons—Uspensky in *Hacienda* suggests the film director Sergei Eisenstein, who made a massive documentary about Mexico—and some are unknown people, glimpsed for a moment, whose lives are then imagined (as in her first published story, *Maria Concepcion*). Reality is crucial raw material for Porter's fiction, and she has described the way that scattered memories of different people and scenes observed over the years combine into a new tale with a structure all its own: "Now and again thousands of memories converge, harmonize, arrange themselves around a central idea in a coherent form, and I write a story."

In Porter's stories, individuals are caught within the broad movements of history. Ordinary people act out their destinies inside a culture and society—whether the American South or West, Mexico, Europe, or an ocean liner—that shape much of what they can be. Often the protagonist is an inquiring, independent, yet vulnerable young woman, like Miranda in *Pale Horse, Pale Rider,* who rejects the oversimplifications of wartime propaganda and seeks refuge from its pressures in a love affair about which she is nonetheless fearfully hesitant. Yet these apparently simple and straightforward stories of personal experience open out upon larger historical and metaphysical planes. The setting for *Pale Horse, Pale Rider* is World War I, a context that influences what the characters can do, say, and think. Beyond history, there is spiritual anguish, the natural human condition in Porter's profoundly pessimistic religious vision. This view of human life as painful and incomplete is accompanied by a dedication to art as a "true testimony" that outlives its own society and civilization. "The arts," Porter said, "represent the substance of faith and the only reality. They are what we find again when the ruins are cleared away." Many of her protagonists are artists or have artistic sensibilities, and the clarity, balance, and fine discriminations of her own style may be considered a way of ordering reality into art.

Porter was a perfectionist who published only a small part of her writings before her death in 1980. A collection of three novellas—*Old Mortality, Noon Wine,* and *Pale Horse, Pale Rider*—appeared in 1939, and her second collection of stories, *The Leaning Tower,* was published in 1944. In 1962, she gained a wider audience with a novel, *Ship of Fools,* a picture of modern society that was modeled on Sebastian Brant's fifteenth-century allegory of the same name. *Collected Stories* followed in 1965 and *Collected Essays* in 1970. She received a number of awards during her lifetime, including the Pulitzer Prize and the National Book Award for fiction, and was recognized as a consummate stylist. Her world is distinguished by a precise, thoughtful style that seeks the exact word (Flaubert's *mot juste*) to render each detail of physical reality, each shade of perception, and by a darkly pessimistic view of human life. Both elements are present in *Flowering Judas,* the title story from her first collection.

The Flowering Judas is a tree, the redbud tree, whose flowers Laura eats in a dream at the end of the story; but it is clearly more than that. The name of Judas, the betrayer of Christ, immediately evokes themes of betrayal and faith, and these religious overtones are confirmed when the dream ends with the words from the Mass that assert the physical presence of Christ in the Communion wafer and wine: "This is my body and my blood." Laura cries "No!" to Eugenio's accusation, a phrase that has characterized her response to life throughout the story. Unlike Braggioni, who loves the world "profitably," Laura refuses human ties on an emotional level and is "not at home in the world" at all. "No. No. No" is the "holy talismanic word" that keeps her safe and apart, but in the end it has led her to the disaster of complicity in Eugenio's suicide and to the desolation symbolized by a desert of crumbling stone. This barren landscape recalls T. S. Eliot's *The Waste Land* and *The Hollow Men*, and Eliot's *Gerontion* describes further a depraved springtime with "dogwood and chestnut, flowering judas / To be eaten, to be divided, to be drunk / Among whispers." In Laura's guilty dream, Eugenio accuses her of murder—worse: of cannibalism, according to this negative image of a Communion without faith. Porter's heroine awakens into a fearful consciousness of alienation and loss that goes beyond the particular historical moment to a vision of human existence denied all underlying principles of faith and love.

Flowering Judas

Braggioni sits heaped upon the edge of a straight-backed chair much too small for him, and sings to Laura in a furry, mournful voice. Laura has begun to find reasons for avoiding her own house until the latest possible moment, for Braggioni is there almost every night. No matter how late she is, he will be sitting there with a surly, waiting expression, pulling at his kinky yellow hair, thumbing the strings of his guitar, snarling a tune under his breath. Lupe the Indian maid meets Laura at the door, and says with a flicker of a glance towards the upper room, "He waits."

Laura wishes to lie down, she is tired of her hairpins and the feel of her long tight sleeves, but she says to him, "Have you a new song for me this evening?" If he says yes, she asks him to sing it. If he says no, she remembers his favorite one, and asks him to sing it again. Lupe brings her a cup of chocolate and a plate of rice, and Laura eats at the small table under the lamp, first inviting Braggioni, whose answer is always the same: "I have eaten, and besides, chocolate thickens the voice."

Laura says, "Sing, then," and Braggioni heaves himself into song. He scratches the guitar familiarly as though it were a pet animal, and sings passionately off key, taking the high notes in a prolonged painful squeal. Laura, who haunts the markets listening to the ballad singers, and stops every day to hear the blind boy playing his need-flute in Sixteenth of September Street,[1] listens to Braggioni with pitiless courtesy, because she dares not

---

1. On September 16, 1810, revolt broke out against Spanish rule; the date has become a common street name in Mexico.

smile at his miserable performance. Nobody dares to smile at him. Braggioni is cruel to everyone, with a kind of specialized insolence, but he is so vain of his talents, and so sensitive to slights, it would require a cruelty and vanity greater than his own to lay a finger on the vast cureless wound of his self-esteem. It would require courage, too, for it is dangerous to offend him, and nobody has this courage.

Braggioni loves himself with such tenderness and amplitude and eternal charity that his followers—for he is a leader of men, a skilled revolutionist, and his skin has been punctured in honorable warfare—warm themselves in the reflected glow, and say to each other: "He has a real nobility, a love of humanity raised above mere personal affections." The excess of this self-love has flowed out, inconveniently for her, over Laura, who, with so many others, owes her comfortable situation and her salary to him. When he is in a very good humor, he tells her, "I am tempted to forgive you for being a *gringa*. *Gringita!*"[2] and Laura, burning, imagines herself leaning forward suddenly, and with a sound back-handed slap wiping the suety smile from his face. If he notices her eyes at these moments he gives no sign.

She knows what Braggioni would offer her, and she must resist tenaciously without appearing to resist, and if she could avoid it she would not admit even to herself the slow drift of his intention. During these long evenings which have spoiled a long month for her, she sits in her deep chair with an open book on her knees, resting her eyes on the consoling rigidity of the printed page when the sight and sound of Braggioni singing threaten to identify themselves with all her remembered afflictions and to add their weight to her uneasy premonitions of the future. The gluttonous bulk of Braggioni has become a symbol of her many disillusions, for a revolutionist should be lean, animated by heroic faith, a vessel of abstract virtues. This is nonsense, she knows it now and is ashamed of it. Revolution must have leaders, and leadership is a career for energetic men. She is, her comrades tell her, full of romantic error, for what she defines as cynicism in them is merely "a developed sense of reality." She is almost too willing to say, "I am wrong, I suppose I don't really understand the principles," and afterward she makes a secret truce with herself, determined not to surrender her will to such expedient logic. But she cannot help feeling that she has been betrayed irreparably by the disunion between her way of living and her feeling of what life should be, and at times she is almost contented to rest in this sense of grievance as a private store of consolation. Sometimes she wishes to run away, but she stays. Now she longs to fly out of this room, down the narrow stairs, and into the street where the houses lean together like conspirators under a single mottled lamp, and leave Braggioni singing to himself.

Instead she looks at Braggioni, frankly and clearly, like a good child who understands the rules of behavior. Her knees cling together under sound blue serge, and her round white collar is not purposely nun-like. She wears the uniform of an idea, and has renounced vanities. She was born Roman Catholic, and in spite of her fear of being seen by someone who might make a scandal of it, she slips now and again into some crumbling little church, kneels on the chilly stone, and says a Hail Mary on the gold rosary she bought in Tehuantepec.[3] It is no good and she ends by examining the altar with its

2. Feminine diminutive of *gringo*, a contemptuous Latin-American term for foreigner (especially North American).   3. Town in southern Mexico. *Hail Mary*: Roman Catholic prayer, the "Ave Maria."

tinsel flowers and ragged brocades, and feels tender about the battered doll-shape of some male saint whose white, lace-trimmed drawers hang limply around his ankles below the hieratic dignity of his velvet robe. She has encased herself in a set of principles derived from her early training, leaving no detail of gesture or of personal taste untouched, and for this reason she will not wear lace made on machines. This is her private heresy, for in her special group the machine is sacred, and will be the salvation of the workers. She loves fine lace, and there is a tiny edge of fluted cobweb on this collar, which is one of twenty precisely alike, folded in blue tissue paper in the upper drawer of her clothes chest.

Braggioni catches her glance solidly as if he had been waiting for it, leans forward, balancing his paunch between his spread knees, and sings with tremendous emphasis, weighing his words. He has, the song relates, no father and no mother, nor even a friend to console him; lonely as a wave of the sea he comes and goes, lonely as a wave. His mouth opens round and yearns sideways, his balloon cheeks grow oily with the labor of song. He bulges marvelously in his expensive garments. Over his lavender collar, crushed upon a purple necktie, held by a diamond hoop: over his ammunition belt of tooled leather worked in silver, buckled cruelly around his gasping middle: over the tops of his glossy yellow shoes Braggioni swells with ominous ripeness, his mauve silk hose stretched taut, his ankles bound with the stout leather thongs of his shoes.

When he stretches his eyelids at Laura she notes again that his eyes are the true tawny yellow cat's eyes. He is rich, not in money, he tells her, but in power, and this power brings with it the blameless ownership of things, and the right to indulge his love of small luxuries. "I have a taste for the elegant refinements," he said once, flourishing a yellow silk handkerchief before her nose. "Smell that? It is Jockey Club,[4] imported from New York." Nonetheless he is wounded by life. He will say so presently. "It is true everything turns to dust in the hand, to gall on the tongue." He sighs and his leather belt creaks like a saddle girth. "I am disappointed in everything as it comes. Everything." He shakes his head. "You, poor thing, you will be disappointed too. You are born for it. We are more alike than you realize in some things. Wait and see. Some day you will remember what I have told you, you will know that Braggioni was your friend."

Laura feels a slow chill, a purely physical sense of danger, a warning in her blood that violence, mutilation, a shocking death, wait for her with lessening patience. She has translated this fear into something homely, immediate, and sometimes hesitates before crossing the street. "My personal fate is nothing, except as the testimony of a mental attitude," she reminds herself, quoting from some forgotten philosophic primer, and is sensible enough to add, "Anyhow, I shall not be killed by an automobile if I can help it."

"It may be true I am as corrupt, in another way, as Braggioni," she thinks in spite of herself, "as callous, as incomplete," and if this is so, any kind of death seems preferable. Still she sits quietly, she does not run. Where could she go? Uninvited she has promised herself to this place; she can no longer imagine herself as living in another country, and there is no pleasure in remembering her life before she came here.

---

4. Expensive cologne.

Precisely what is the nature of this devotion, its true motives, and what are its obligations? Laura cannot say. She spends part of her days in Xochimilco,[5] near by, teaching Indian children to say in English, "The cat is on the mat." When she appears in the classroom they crowd about her with smiles on their wise, innocent, clay-colored faces, crying, "Good morning, my titcher!" in immaculate voices, and they make of her desk a fresh garden of flowers every day.

During her leisure she goes to union meetings and listens to busy important voices quarreling over tactics, methods, internal politics. She visits the prisoners of her own political faith in their cells, where they entertain themselves with counting cockroaches, repenting of their indiscretions, composing their memoirs, writing out manifestoes and plans for their comrades who are still walking about free, hands in pockets, sniffing fresh air. Laura brings them food and cigarettes and a little money, and she brings messages disguised in equivocal phrases from the men outside who dare not set foot in the prison for fear of disappearing into the cells kept empty for them. If the prisoners confuse night and day, and complain, "Dear little Laura, time doesn't pass in this infernal hole, and I won't know when it is time to sleep unless I have a reminder," she brings them their favorite narcotics, and says in a tone that does not wound them with pity, "Tonight will really be night for you," and though her Spanish amuses them, they find her comforting, useful. If they lose patience and all faith, and curse the slowness of their friends in coming to their rescue with money and influence, they trust her not to repeat everything, and if she inquires, "Where do you think we can find money, or influence?" they are certain to answer, "Well, there is Braggioni, why doesn't he do something?"

She smuggles letters from headquarters to men hiding from firing squads in back streets in mildewed houses, where they sit in tumbled beds and talk bitterly as if all Mexico were at their heels, when Laura knows positively they might appear at the band concert in the Alameda[6] on Sunday morning, and no one would notice them. But Braggioni says, "Let them sweat a little. The next time they may be careful. It is very restful to have them out of the way for a while." She is not afraid to knock on any door in any street after midnight, and enter in the darkness, and say to one of these men who is really in danger: "They will be looking for you—seriously—tomorrow morning after six. Here is some money from Vicente. Go to Vera Cruz and wait."

She borrows money from the Roumanian agitator to give to his bitter enemy the Polish agitator. The favor of Braggioni is their disputed territory, and Braggioni holds the balance nicely, for he can use them both. The Polish agitator talks love to her over café tables, hoping to exploit what he believes is her secret sentimental preference for him, and he gives her misinformation which he begs her to repeat as the solemn truth to certain persons. The Roumanian is more adroit. He is generous with his money in all good causes, and lies to her with an air of ingenuous candor, as if he were her good friend and confidant. She never repeats anything they may say. Braggioni never asks questions. He has other ways to discover all that he wishes to know about them.

Nobody touches her, but all praise her gray eyes, and the soft, round under

5. Suburb of Mexico City (the Indian word means "flower plantation"). 6. Public mall.

lip which promises gayety, yet is always grave, nearly always firmly closed: and they cannot understand why she is in Mexico. She walks back and forth on her errands, with puzzled eyebrows, carrying her little folder of drawings and music and school papers. No dancer dances more beautifully than Laura walks, and she inspires some amusing, unexpected ardors, which cause little gossip, because nothing comes of them. A young captain who had been a soldier in Zapata's army attempted, during a horseback ride near Cuernavaca,[7] to express his desire for her with the noble simplicity befitting a rude folk-hero: but gently, because he was gentle. This gentleness was his defeat, for when he alighted, and removed her foot from the stirrup, and essayed to draw her down into his arms, her horse, ordinarily a tame one, shied fiercely, reared and plunged away. The young hero's horse careered blindly after his stable-mate, and the hero did not return to the hotel until rather late that evening. At breakfast he came to her table in full charro[8] dress, gray buckskin jacket and trousers with strings of silver buttons down the leg, and he was in a humorous, careless mood. "May I sit with you?" and "You are a wonderful rider. I was terrified that you might be thrown and dragged. I should never have forgiven myself. But I cannot admire you enough for your riding!"

"I learned to ride in Arizona," said Laura.

"If you will ride with me again this morning, I promise you a horse that will not shy with you," he said. But Laura remembered that she must return to Mexico City at noon.

Next morning the children made a celebration and spent their playtime writing on the blackboard, "We lov ar ticher," and with tinted chalks they drew wreaths of flowers around the words. The young hero wrote her a letter: "I am a very foolish, wasteful, impulsive man. I should have first said I love you, and then you would not have run away. But you shall see me again." Laura thought, "I must send him a book of colored crayons," but she was trying to forgive herself for having spurred her horse at the wrong moment.

A brown, shock-haired youth came and stood in her patio one night and sang like a lost soul for two hours, but Laura could think of nothing to do about it. The moonlight spread a wash of gauzy silver over the clear spaces of the garden, and the shadows were cobalt blue. The scarlet blossoms of the Judas tree[9] were dull purple, and the names of the colors repeated themselves automatically in her mind, while she watched not the boy, but his shadow, fallen like a dark garment across the fountain rim, trailing in the water. Lupe came silently and whispered expert counsel in her ear: "If you will throw him one little flower, he will sing another song or two and go away." Laura threw the flower, and he sang a last song and went away with the flower tucked in the band of his hat. Lupe said, "He is one of the organizers of the Typographers Union, and before that he sold corridos[1] in the Merced market, and before that, he came from Guanajuato, where I was born. I would not trust any man, but I trust least those from Guanajuato."

She did not tell Laura that he would be back again the next night, and the next, nor that he would follow her at a certain fixed distance around the Merced market, through the Zócolo, up Francisco I. Madero[2] Avenue, and so along the Paseo de la Reforma to Chapultepec Park, and into the Philos-

7. In southern Mexico. Emiliano Zapata (1879–1919), Mexican revolutionary and agrarian reformer of Indian descent.   8. A flamboyant traditional costume, often worn at festivals.   9. The redbud tree; in legend, the tree from which Judas Iscariot hanged himself after betraying Jesus.   1. Popular ballads that also passed along news.   2. Mexican statesman and reformer (1873–1913); president 1911–1913.

opher's Footpath, still with that flower withering in his hat, and an indivisible attention in his eyes.

Now Laura is accustomed to him, it means nothing except that he is nineteen years old and is observing a convention with all propriety, as though it were founded on a law of nature, which in the end it might well prove to be. He is beginning to write poems which he prints on a wooden press, and he leaves them stuck like handbills in her door. She is pleasantly disturbed by the abstract, unhurried watchfulness of his black eyes which will in time turn easily towards another object. She tells herself that throwing the flower was a mistake, for she is twenty-two years old and knows better; but she refuses to regret it, and persuades herself that her negation of all external events as they occur is a sign that she is gradually perfecting herself in the stoicism she strives to cultivate against that disaster she fears, though she cannot name it.

She is not at home in the world. Every day she teaches children who remain strangers to her, though she loves their tender round hands and their charming opportunist savagery. She knocks at unfamiliar doors not knowing whether a friend or a stranger shall answer, and even if a known face emerges from the sour gloom of that unknown interior, still it is the face of a stranger. No matter what this stranger says to her, nor what her message to him, the very cells of her flesh reject knowledge and kinship in one monotonous word. No. No. No. She draws her strength from this one holy talismanic word which does not suffer her to be led into evil. Denying everything, she may walk anywhere in safety, she looks at everything without amazement.

No, repeats this firm unchanging voice of her blood; and she looks at Braggioni without amazement. He is a great man, he wishes to impress this simple girl who covers her great round breasts with thick dark cloth, and who hides long, invaluably beautiful legs under a heavy skirt. She is almost thin except for the incomprehensible fullness of her breasts, like a nursing mother's, and Braggioni, who considers himself a judge of women, speculates again on the puzzle of her notorious virginity, and takes the liberty of speech which she permits without a sign of modesty, indeed, without any sort of sign, which is disconcerting.

"You think you are so cold, *gringita!* Wait and see. You will surprise yourself some day! May I be there to advise you!" He stretches his eyelids at her, and his ill-humored cat's eyes waver in a separate glance for the two points of light marking the opposite ends of a smoothly drawn path between the swollen curve of her breasts. He is not put off by that blue serge, nor by her resolutely fixed gaze. There is all the time in the world. His cheeks are bellying with the wind of song. "O girl with the dark eyes," he sings, and reconsiders. "But yours are not dark. I can change all that. O girl with the green eyes, you have stolen my heart away!" then his mind wanders to the song, and Laura feels the weight of his attention being shifted elsewhere. Singing thus, he seems harmless, he is quite harmless, there is nothing to do but sit patiently and say "No," when the moment comes. She draws a full breath, and her mind wanders also, but not far. She dares not wander too far.

Not for nothing has Braggioni taken pains to be a good revolutionist and a professional lover of humanity. He will never die of it. He has the malice, the cleverness, the wickedness, the sharpness of wit, the hardness of heart, stipulated for loving the world profitably. *He will never die of it.* He will live to see himself kicked out from his feeding trough by other hungry world-saviors. Traditionally he must sing in spite of his life which drives him to bloodshed, he tells Laura, for his father was a Tuscany peasant who drifted to Yucatan[3] and married a Maya woman: a woman of race, an aristocrat. They gave him the love and knowledge of music, thus: and under the rip of his thumbnail, the strings of the instrument complain like exposed nerves.

Once he was called Delgadito[4] by all the girls and married women who ran after him; he was so scrawny all his bones showed under his thin cotton clothing, and he could squeeze his emptiness to the very backbone with his two hands. He was a poet and the revolution was only a dream then; too many women loved him and sapped away his youth, and he could never find enough to eat anywhere, anywhere! Now he is a leader of men, crafty men who whisper in his ear, hungry men who wait for hours outside his office for a word with him, emaciated men with wild faces who waylay him at the street gate with a timid, "Comrade, let me tell you . . ." and they blow the foul breath from their empty stomachs in his face.

He is always sympathetic. He gives them handfuls of small coins from his own pocket, he promises them work, there will be demonstrations, they must join the unions and attend the meetings, above all they must be on the watch for spies. They are closer to him than his own brothers, without them he can do nothing—until tomorrow, comrade!

Until tomorrow. "They are stupid, they are lazy, they are treacherous, they would cut my throat for nothing," he says to Laura. He has good food and abundant drink, he hires an automobile and drives in the Paseo on Sunday morning, and enjoys plenty of sleep in a soft bed beside a wife who dares not disturb him; and he sits pampering his bones in easy billows of fat, singing to Laura, who knows and thinks these things about him. When he was fifteen, he tried to drown himself because he loved a girl, his first love, and she laughed at him. "A thousand women have paid for that," and his tight little mouth turns down at the corners. Now he perfumes his hair with Jockey Club, and confides to Laura: "One woman is really as good as another for me, in the dark. I prefer them all."

His wife organizes unions among the girls in the cigarette factories, and walks in picket lines, and even speaks at meetings in the evening. But she cannot be brought to acknowledge the benefits of true liberty. "I tell her I must have my freedom, net.[5] She does not understand my point of view." Laura has heard this many times. Braggioni scratches the guitar and meditates. "She is an instinctively virtuous woman, pure gold, no doubt of that. If she were not, I should lock her up, and she knows it."

His wife, who works so hard for the good of the factory girls, employs part of her leisure lying on the floor weeping because there are so many women in the world, and only one husband for her, and she never knows where nor when to look for him. He told her: "Unless you can learn to cry when I am not here, I must go away for good." That day he went away and took a room at the Hotel Madrid.

It is this month of separation for the sake of higher principles that has been spoiled not only for Mrs. Braggioni, whose sense of reality is beyond criticism, but for Laura, who feels herself bogged in a nightmare. Tonight Laura envies Mrs. Braggioni, who is alone, and free to weep as much as she

3. A state in southeastern Mexico, home of the ancient Maya civilization, which flourished from approximately 1000 B.C.E. *Tuscany:* from central Italy. 4. Skinny. 5. "And that's that."

pleases about a concrete wrong. Laura has just come from a visit to the prison, and she is waiting for tomorrow with a bitter anxiety as if tomorrow may not come, but time may be caught immovably in this hour, with herself transfixed, Braggioni singing on forever, and Eugenio's body not yet discovered by the guard.

Braggioni says: "Are you going to sleep?" Almost before she can shake her head, he begins telling her about the May-day disturbances coming on in Morelia,[6] for the Catholics hold a festival in honor of the Blessed Virgin, and the Socialists celebrate their martyrs on that day. "There will be two independent processions, starting from either end of town, and they will march until they meet, and the rest depends . . ." He asks her to oil and load his pistols. Standing up, he unbuckles his ammunition belt, and spreads it laden across her knees. Laura sits with the shells slipping through the cleaning cloth dipped in oil, and he says again he cannot understand why she works so hard for the revolutionary idea unless she loves some man who is in it. "Are you not in love with someone?" "No," says Laura. "And no one is in love with you?" "No." "Then it is your own fault. No woman need go begging. Why, what is the matter with you? The legless beggar woman in the Alameda has a perfectly faithful lover. Did you know that?"

Laura peers down the pistol barrel and says nothing, but a long, slow faintness rises and subsides in her; Braggioni curves his swollen fingers around the throat of the guitar and softly smothers the music out of it, and when she hears him again he seems to have forgotten her, and is speaking in the hypnotic voice he uses when talking in small rooms to a listening, close-gathered crowd. Some day this world, now seemingly so composed and eternal, to the edges of every sea shall be merely a tangle of gaping trenches, of crashing walls and broken bodies. Everything must be torn from its accustomed place where it has rotted for centuries, hurled skyward and distributed, cast down again clean as rain, without separate identity. Nothing shall survive that the stiffened hands of poverty have created for the rich and no one shall be left alive except the elect spirits destined to procreate a new world cleansed of cruelty and injustice, ruled by benevolent anarchy: "Pistols are good, I love them, cannon are even better, but in the end I pin my faith to good dynamite," he concludes, and strokes the pistol lying in her hands. "Once I dreamed of destroying this city, in case it offered resistance to General Ortíz, but it fell into his hands like an overripe pear."

He is made restless by his own words, rises and stands waiting. Laura holds up the belt to him: "Put that on, and go kill somebody in Morelia, and you will be happier," she says softly. The presence of death in the room makes her bold. "Today, I found Eugenio going into a stupor. He refused to allow me to call the prison doctor. He had taken all the tablets I brought him yesterday. He said he took them because he was bored."

"He is a fool, and his death is his own business," says Braggioni, fastening his belt carefully.

"I told him if he had waited only a little while longer, you would have got him set free," says Laura. "He said he did not want to wait."

"He is a fool and we are well rid of him," says Braggioni, reaching for his hat.

He goes away. Laura knows his mood has changed, she will not see him

---

6. Capital of Michoacan state in western Mexico and home of a 17th-century Spanish cathedral.

any more for a while. He will send word when he needs her to go on errands into strange streets, to speak to the strange faces that will appear, like clay masks with the power of human speech, to mutter their thanks to Braggioni for his help. Now she is free, and she thinks, I must run while there is time. But she does not go.

Braggioni enters his own house where for a month his wife has spent many hours every night weeping and tangling her hair upon her pillow. She is weeping now, and she weeps more at the sight of him, the cause of all her sorrows. He looks about the room. Nothing is changed, the smells are good and familiar, he is well acquainted with the woman who comes toward him with no reproach except grief on her face. He says to her tenderly: "You are so good, please don't cry any more, you dear good creature." She says, "Are you tired, my angel? Sit here and I will wash your feet." She brings a bowl of water, and kneeling, unlaces his shoes, and when from her knees she raises her sad eyes under her blackened lids, he is sorry for everything, and bursts into tears. "Ah, yes, I am hungry, I am tired, let us eat something together," he says, between sobs. His wife leans her head on his arm and says, "Forgive me!" and this time he is refreshed by the solemn, endless rain of her tears.

Laura takes off her serge dress and puts on a white linen nightgown and goes to bed. She turns her head a little to one side, and lying still, reminds herself that it is time to sleep. Numbers tick in her brain like little clocks, soundless doors close of themselves around her. If you would sleep, you must not remember anything, the children will say tomorrow, good morning, my teacher, the poor prisoners who come every day bringing flowers to their jailor. 1-2-3-4-5—it is monstrous to confuse love with revolution, night with day, life with death—ah, Eugenio!

The tolling of the midnight bell is a signal, but what does it mean? Get up, Laura, and follow me: come out of your sleep, out of your bed, out of this strange house. What are you doing in this house? Without a word, without fear she rose and reached for Eugenio's hand, but he eluded her with a sharp, sly smile and drifted away. This is not all, you shall see—Murderer, he said, follow me, I will show you a new country, but it is far away and we must hurry. No, said Laura, not unless you take my hand, no; and she clung first to the stair rail, and then to the topmost branch of the Judas tree that bent down slowly and set her upon the earth, and then to the rocky ledge of a cliff, and then to the jagged wave of a sea that was not water but a desert of crumbling stone. Where are you taking me, she asked in wonder but without fear. To death, and it is a long way off, and we must hurry, said Eugenio. No, said Laura, not unless you take my hand. Then eat these flowers, poor prisoner, said Eugenio in a voice of pity, take and eat: and from the Judas tree he stripped the warm bleeding flowers, and held them to her lips. She saw that his hand was fleshless, a cluster of small white petrified branches, and his eye sockets were without light, but she ate the flowers greedily for they satisfied both hunger and thirst. Murderer! said Eugenio, and Cannibal! This is my body and my blood.[7] Laura cried No! and at the sound of her own voice, she awoke trembling, and was afraid to sleep again.

---

7. Jesus words to his disciples at the Last Supper as he gave them bread and wine (Matthew 26; Mark 14; Luke 22.1); a transubstantiation and participation in divine essence that is supposed to take place during the Christian Sacrament of Communion.

ALFONSINA STORNI
1892–1938

Alfonsina Storni is a unique voice in Latin American literature. Independent and outspoken, an international literary figure who was the first woman to be accepted by Argentina's male-dominated literary establishment, her reputation as a feminist has almost overshadowed her work as a poet. The two aspects are strongly connected. She drew on her own life for the substance of her poems, plays, articles, and lectures, and made herself a voice for women's experience. Obliged from a young age to be totally self-supporting, an unwed mother at the age of nineteen, she possessed both a realistic perspective and a sense of outrage at the treatment of women. Her sarcastic indictment of male vanity scandalized many readers. Storni is best known for intensely subjective and emotional lyrics, and for her skill at creating dramatic situations in conversational language.

She was born on May 29, 1892, in the small town of Sala Capriasca, Switzerland, where her family had journeyed for her father's health; the family returned to Argentina in 1896. The family business collapsed in 1900, and their attempts to run a restaurant, the Swiss Café, fared no better. Leaving school in 1906 to help her mother support the family by sewing, Storni took a better-paying job in a hat factory after her father's death later that year. From that time on, she supported herself in a range of positions as actress, cashier, secretary, market researcher, lecturer, teacher at various levels, and poet and essayist. Looking back in 1934, Storni remarked that being forced to earn her own living (like a man, she explained, and certainly not like the sheltered women of her time) gave her an intellectual and emotional independence that colored everything she wrote. "My writing has inevitably reflected this, which is my personal truth: I have had to live as a man, so I demand to live by male standards. . . . What I am doing is anticipating the woman of the future, because female standards all depend on the economic system."

After a year with a traveling acting company, she decided that she did not want to become a professional actress and earned a limited teaching degree working as a chorus girl on weekends. She returned to her home town of Rosario to teach in a rural elementary school but fell in love with a married man and became pregnant, leaving for Buenos Aires to avoid scandal after the birth of her child. Her son, Alejandro, was born when Storni was just nineteen years old, and she cautiously concealed his existence to keep her job. When her first book of poetry was published in 1916, however, she was nonetheless dismissed: *La Inquietud del rosal* (The Restlessness of the Rosebush) was too openly based in her own situation, with its descriptions of erotic love and loss and its defiance of social conventions. "I am like the she-wolf./ I broke with the pack," proclaims its best-known poem. But Storni was beginning to make a name for herself as a writer: she received a literary prize, published articles in various journals and newspapers, and became the first woman in Argentina to be part of a literary circle when she joined the group Nosotros. She supported herself by teaching while writing articles on women's rights, lectured on Spanish American women poets, and published books of poetry that earned her a reputation for lyricism, emotional intensity, and wit.

Storni's next two collections, *El dulce daño* (The Sweet Pain, 1918) and *Irremediablemente* (Irremediably, 1919), use everyday language and images of daily life to express broad disillusionment and outrage. Rows of identical houses in *Squares and Angles* illustrate the poet's contempt for the conformity of bourgeois life—a life that gives prepackaged shape to souls, ideas, and even a tear. One of her best-known poems, *You Want Me White*, scornfully addresses a lover who accepts the double standard by which a woman must be "white" (that is, chaste, pure, inexperienced) while a man pursues a more colorful existence, his soul "entangled/In all the bedrooms." Underlying the rebellion of these poems is a recurrent theme that human beings act according to preset cultural images and fail, therefore, to communicate: in *Little Bitty Man*, "you don't understand me/and never will./Nor do I understand you." Storni speaks out for women because, unlike men, they have not been permitted to speak for themselves: in *Ancestral Burden*, she evokes the repressed bitterness of generations of women who have mutely endured their assigned roles.

Storni was by now a well-known poet and received two important literary prizes when she published her next collection, *Languidez* (Languor, 1920). Its prologue announced that she would henceforth abandon subjective poetry, having said all she wished to say about her own life. The year 1920 was a busy one in many ways: she became an Argentinian citizen, wrote the novel *La Golondrina* (The Swallow), and joined Anaconda, a literary group associated with the noted Uruguayan novelist Horacio Quiroga, who became a close friend. The following decade was difficult: Argentina experienced an economic depression, mass social unrest, and a military coup in 1930. Thanks to a friend, however, Storni obtained a permanent teaching position in 1921, and she began to participate in several literary and artistic circles, where she met the visiting Federico García Lorca and other international figures. She wrote and produced plays for children and adults, traveled and lectured in Europe, and was treated several times for fatigue and nervous depression.

The new poetry she foresaw in *Languor* did not appear until 1925, with the publication of *Ocre* (Ocher), a collection of complex, sensuous, and occasionally humorous poems that revel in the use of her craft but observe life—and the poet herself—from an ironic distance. "I am useless," proclaims a sonnet that begins with resignation at her failure to bring about change; the poem ends, however, in a powerful evocation of the voluptuous pleasure felt by a warm body in the summer sun. Storni's next major work, *Mundo de siete pozos* (The World of Seven Wells), appeared nine years later and confirmed the poet's shift toward more objective and abstract descriptions. For the first time, she employs free verse and structures poems according to fantastic or dreamlike associations. The last collection, *Mascarilla y trébol* (Mask and Clover, 1938), published a few months before her death, moves even further from her initial subjective lyricism. Its fifty-two poems are all "antisonnets"—that is, poems that preserve the Petrarchan sonnet's two quatrains and two tercets but lack rhymes. Storni foresaw that readers would find these poems harsh and obscure after her earlier emotional lyricism, and she was right. Recent critics, however, have come to prize the poems' tight construction, use of abstract imagery, and innovative perspectives.

The final years of her life were clouded with pain and the knowledge of terminal illness. She had been diagnosed with cancer in 1935 and had a mastectomy the same year. The operation left her shattered; when the disease recurred and spread in 1938, she was unwilling to undergo further operations. Images of death and of the sea had permeated *The World of Seven Wells*, and they reappear in *Departure*, given here from an anthology of her poetry that Storni compiled in 1938. On October 25 of that year, in considerable pain, she took her own life by walking into the sea at Mar del Plata, Argentina.

[Poems]

Squares and Angles[1]

Houses in a row, houses in a row,
Houses in a row.
Squares, squares, squares.
Houses in a row.
People now have square souls,   5
Ideas in a row
And an angle on the back.
Yesterday I myself cried a tear.
My God—square.

You Want Me White[1]

You'd like me to be white as dawn,
You'd like me to be made of foam,
You wish I were mother of pearl,
A lily
Chaste above all others.   5
Of delicate perfume.
A closed bud.

Not one ray of the moon
Should have filtered me,
Not one daisy   10
Should have called me sister.
You want me to be snowy,
You want me to be white,
You want me to be like dawn.

You who have held all the wineglasses   15
In your hand,
Your lips stained purple
With fruit and honey
You who in the banquet
Crowned with young vines   20
Made toasts with your flesh to Bacchus.[2]
You who in the gardens
Black with Deceit
Dressed in red
Ran to your Ruin.   25

---

1. Translated by Florence Williams Talamantes.   1. Translated by Marion Freeman and Mary Crow.
White here does not refer to race; it means colorless and pure.   2. In Greek and Roman mythology, the
god of wine.

You who keep your skeleton
Well preserved, intact,
I don't know yet
Through what miracles
You want to make me white   30
(God forgive you),
You want to make me chaste
(God forgive you),
You want to make me like dawn!

Run away to the woods;   35
Go to the mountain;
Wash your mouth;
Get to know the wet earth
With your hands;
Feed your body   40
With bitter roots;
Drink from the rocks;
Sleep on the white frost;
Renew your tissue
With the salt of rocks and water;   45
Talk to the birds
And get up at dawn.
And when your flesh
Has returned to you,
And when you have put   50
Your soul back into it,
Your soul which was left entangled
In all the bedrooms,
Then, my good man,
Ask me to be white,   55
Ask me to be snowy,
Ask me to be chaste.

Little-Bitty Man[1]

Little bitty man, little bitty man,
let your canary loose that wants to fly away.
I'm that canary, little bitty man,
let me go free.

I was in your cage, little bitty man,   5
little bitty man who gives me a cage.
I say little bitty because you don't understand me
and never will.

Nor do I understand you, but meanwhile
open up the cage, for I want to be free.   10
Little bitty man, I loved you half an hour.
Ask no more of me.

1. Translated by Mary Crow and Marion Freeman.

Ancestral Burden[1]

You once told me my father never wept;
You once told me my grandfather never wept;
The men of my race have not wept;
They were of steel.

Speaking thus you cried a tear   5
And it fell into my mouth . . . More poison
I have never drunk in another glass
So small.

Weak woman, poor woman who understands,
The pain of centuries I knew upon drinking it;   10
Oh, my soul cannot bear
All its burden.

Departure[2]

A road
to the limit:
high golden doors
close it off;
deep galleries;   5
arcades . . .

The air has no weight;
the doors stand by themselves
in the emptiness;
they disintegrate into golden dust;   10
they close, they open;
they go down to the algae
tombs;
they come up loaded with coral.

Patrols,   15
there are patrols of columns;
the doors hide
behind the blue parapets;
water bursts into fields of forget-me-nots;
it tosses up deserts of purple crystals;   20
it incubates great emerald worms;
it plaits its innumerable arms.

1. Translated by Florence Williams Talamantes.   2. Translated by Marion Freeman.

A rain of wings,
now;
pink angels   25
dive like arrows
into the sea.
I could walk on them
without sinking.
A path of ciphers   30
for my feet;
columns of numbers
for each step—
submarine.

They carry me: 35
invisible vines
stretch out their hooks
from the horizon.
My neck creaks.
I walk.   40
The water holds its own.
My shoulders open into wings.
I touch the ends of the sky
with their tips.
I wound it.   45
The sky's blood
bathing the sea . . .
poppies, poppies,
there is nothing but poppies.

I grow light: 50
the flesh falls from my bones.
Now.
The sea rises through the channels
of my spine.
Now.   55
The sky rolls through the bed
of my veins.
Now.
The sun! The sun!
Its last rays   60
envelop me,
push me:
I am a spindle
I spin, spin, spin, spin!

DADA-SURREALIST POETRY: A SELECTION

Dada-Surrealistic poetry was written for the intuitions. Not that it lacks structure or its own inner logic, but it appeals directly to the impulsive, irrational, and unconscious layers of human experience. Part of a social and artistic revolution that began during World War I and flourished as a group movement until World War II, Dada-Surrealism exploded literary and artistic conventions to liberate the human imagination and catalyze in each reader or spectator an unending process of growth. Dada-Surrealist writers sought to present desire, not discipline; automatic writing, not rational prose; dream worlds, not common sense; marvels, not realism; joyous pursuit of error; and art and poetry as living experience. They hoped to awaken minds that had been numbed by habit—by the day-to-day routine of work, respectability, and reverence for authority. Games (and they invented many) were the most authentic expression of Dada-Surrealist attitudes, for games required the live interaction of several people and an exchange of ideas that always opened new horizons.

It is thus paradoxical that Dada-Surrealism has become an influential part of literary history, its works reprinted and anthologized like any other. This potential paradox was not lost on the group and caused many quarrels. Yet the major Dada-Surrealist writers were still artists, and they found in the movement a fresh vision and different concepts of poetic language. By proposing startling combinations of images and ideas, and making these combinations attractive, Dada-Surrealist poets guided readers into trying new modes of thought. They created beautiful, unexpected combinations that were rationally impossible but made a strange, intuitive sense in terms of unconscious emotions or desires. In the earlier stages of the movement, they experimented with "automatic" writing—that is, they wrote without exerting conscious or rational control over the free flow of speech, to bring subterranean impulses to the surface. (The genuine automatism of Surrealist poetry is much debated, and some works printed as automatic poems were in fact edited for publication.) Some writers—like Tristan Tzara and Paul Éluard—eventually moved past Surrealism to other styles; others, like Kurt Schwitters and Aimé Césaire, were already working inside a larger framework. Only André Breton, the founding figure of Parisian Surrealism, remained true to its principles (which he usually defined) throughout his life. His own work strongly influenced Joyce Mansour, a younger writer whose macabre work is in many ways an ironic comment on the glorious visions of early Surrealism. Selections from the six writers presented here constitute a brief introduction to Dada-Surrealism but are only a small part of a movement whose influence has been felt worldwide in art and literature.

Tristan Tzara (born in Romania as Samuel Rosenstock) is the best-known figure of Dadaism. His celebrity is in part owing to his own efforts since Dadaism itself was a decentered movement and early Dada groups existed in Berlin, Cologne, Hanover (Germany), Zürich, and New York, each with its distinguishing characteristics. In 1916, the German poet Hugo Ball had received permission to set up a literary cabaret in a Zürich bar; called the Cabaret Voltaire, it attracted a group of writers, artists, and performers who were fleeing the war and who were eager to attack conservative cultural institutions. The Cabaret Voltaire was the scene of raucous performances with masks, costumes, simultaneous readings, nonsense poetry, "sound" poetry, and chants with African drums—to mention only a few. (Modern "happenings" descend from Dadaist performance art.)

Tzara was part of the group, and when the Cabaret closed he became the most aggressive Dada publicist. The *Dada Manifesto 1918*, his first (he published seven, one of which is the *Proclamation without Pretention*), is a violent, nihilist, ironic attack on ready-made ideas ("I am against systems, the most acceptable system is the one of not having any system, on principle"). Throughout the manifesto, Tzara uses nonsense words and aggressive attacks to counteract conventional images of discipline and order: after "IDEAL IDEAL IDEAL" and "KNOWLEDGE KNOWLEDGE KNOWLEDGE," he shouts "BOOMBOOM BOOMBOOM BOOMBOOM." Yet there is both method and artistry in his madness, as can be seen in the concluding section of the first *Dada Manifesto*, *DADAIST DISGUST*. Tzara has just proclaimed "the opposition of all cosmic faculties" to the causes of this disgust, and he proceeds with a cumulative summary of such opposition. Dada will abolish conventional ideas and social hierarchies; it will abolish the long view of chronological perspective and live for the spontaneous joy of momentary madness; Dada unites contraries because definitions do not matter; and Dada reaches for freedom, which, in a burst of irrational images, turns out to be LIFE itself. It is "life" that is the goal and substance of Dadaist poetry, life that opposes any artificial and socially engineered restraints. Tzara's ironically titled *Proclamation without Pretension* contrasts Dadaist spontaneity and willingness to embrace living contradictions with academic "Art," which is concocted by an artistic "druggist" using formulas and logic. (Like Verlaine in his *Art of Poetry*, the Dadaist and Surrealist poets were suspicious of Art and Literature insofar as they evoked self-reproducing traditions: poetry, in its etymological sense as *creativity*, was far more important.) The wit and humor of this *Proclamation*, and its playful typography, make it far more than a conventional manifesto.

Kurt Schwitters, who lived in Hanover, Germany, until the Nazis forced him to flee to England, is best known for his collages and "Merz" constructions. *Merz*, a nonsense word he extracted from a German bank sign, *Commerzbank*, became the artist's term for the small and large artworks he constructed out of objects collected at random or obtained as personal mementos. His home in Hanover contained an enormous Merz column that grew outward and up through the ceiling over the years; it was destroyed during World War II. Schwitters's poetry includes, in addition to *Anna Blume*, the *Sonata in Vowels*, a startling and impressive sound poem in which a series of vowels is arranged in sonata form and performed by the artist as a piece of music. *Anna Blume* itself is a happily delirious love lyric that expresses the speaker's delight in both Anna's person and her first name (a palindrome: it is the same forward and backward). A conversational sequence of associations and contradictions, and the humorous parody of a logical syllogism, together create a gently sensual portrait.

When Tzara moved to Paris in 1920, he was welcomed enthusiastically by a group of young French poets that included Paul Éluard (born Eugène Grindel) and André Breton. Both are central figures in French Surrealism. Éluard reached a particularly wide audience with his love lyrics, magical evocations of transfigured landscapes that teach, in the poet's words, "how to see" and "to see otherwise, other things." Poems from *Capital of Pain* (1926) reshape familiar images into new subjective creations: the speaker is so close to his beloved that they seem to be somehow identical; elsewhere, she permeates the natural landscape, and they are again indistinguishable. Various images achieve the shock that the Surrealists prized for its ability to jolt readers out of their habitual ways of seeing: "She is standing on my eyelids," for example, may ultimately evoke the poet dreaming of his beloved but is first of all a startling image. Yet there is usually a kind of inner logic: the irrational (but imaginable) pictures of the second stanza are explained in the last lines, when the poet comments that her effect is to make him speak lyrical nonsense. Éluard's "seeing otherwise" is implicit in variously transfigured scenes that depict, on the one hand, the poet leaving everyday reality behind as he drifts into the rich inner life of dream and, on the other, a subjective moment that is constructed as a fleeting yet inexorable mirror. His visionary poetry, full of metamorphoses, points toward the "marvelous" state that was the Surrealists' poetic goal.

Breton, often called the Pope of Surrealism for his dedication to Surrealist principles and his insistence on doctrinal purity, outlined a series of core beliefs in the first Surrealist *Manifesto* (1924): absolute freedom of imagination, respect for mad-

ness as special inner vision, a belief in the revelatory power of dreams and the unconscious, a hatred of clichéd or predictable thinking (and a related fascination with
chance), and the power of "mad love" to transcend rationality and project the lover
to a sublime or marvelous state *beyond*. Breton is always alert for the moment when
reality metamorphoses into Surrealist experience, and in *Vigilance* this alertness is
rewarded: the dreaming poet sets his everyday surroundings on fire and observes a
gradual change of state in which he himself finally participates. Another version of
metamorphosis occurs in *Free Union*, a poem celebrating his wife in a cumulative
series of associations that extend, finally, to the four basic elements: earth, air, fire,
and water. *Free Union* means both free love and the free union or association of
images: this series of apparently random associations with the woman (in imitation
of the medieval *blason* or poem of extended comparison) is in fact organized by visual
and sonorous associations, one sound or image suggesting another.

With Aimé Césaire and Joyce Mansour, Surrealist poetry takes on a new cast.
Césaire is best known for his long poem *Notebook of a Return to the Native Land*
(1939), several plays, and the *Discourse on Colonialism* (1950), and as a founder of
Négritude. His Surrealist decade begins officially in 1941, when Breton, coming
across Césaire's poetry in the journal *Tropiques*, arranges to meet him and becomes
a fervent supporter. Césaire's *Miraculous Weapons* (1946) employs Surrealist verbal
techniques in explosive scenes that emphasize processes of destruction, liberation,
and new birth, all the while evoking the varied landscape of his native Martinique.
These poems proceed by sequences of association and opposition, juxtaposing local
and cosmic images. A chameleon, a child diving for coins, or a tropical tree appear
simultaneously with the voice of thunderbolts, the mythic serpent sun, and a poet-
prophet who is an organic part of the miracles he describes. Césaire was interested
in liberating unconscious patterns of thought through the Surrealist tactic of automatic writing: *The Virgin Forest* is one such experiment, later separated into three
shorter prose poems, one of which, *Day and Night*, is printed here.

Joyce Mansour, an Egyptian who lived much of her adult life in Paris, was one of
three contemporary poets praised by Breton in a 1960 interview, and she herself
dedicated three books to Breton, recognizing his influence. Her work, however,
reverses many of the traditional Surrealist themes and attitudes. Where the founding
(male) Surrealist poets experience the marvelous through the mad love of a woman,
Mansour develops the same visionary erotics in terms of men, and its horizons are
not so celebratory. Her materialist, visceral, and predatory vision is focused in terms
of this world and its images, not on an expanding, infinitely multiplied cosmos. Mansour's eyes may close, like Éluard's, in a dreamlike vision that contains impossible
images, and she too may imagine identity with her partner, but the result is a self-
conscious (and, therefore, faintly humorous) landscape of nightmare.

"Surrealism," says Breton, "is based on the belief in the superior reality of certain
forms of previously neglected associations, in the omnipotence of dream, in the disinterested play of thought." The Dada-Surrealist attempt to uncover and reproduce
such associations, and to use the free play of thought as a model for literary creation,
is still with us at the beginning of the twenty-first century.

KURT SCHWITTERS
1887–1948

Anna Blume[1]

O beloved of my twenty-seven senses, I
love your!—you ye you your, I your, you my.
—We?
This belongs (by the way) elsewhere.
Who are you, uncounted female? You are   5
—are you? People say you are,—let
them say on, they don't know a hawk from a handsaw.[2]
You wear your hat upon your feet and walk round
on your hands, upon your hands you walk.
Halloo, your red dress, sawn up in white pleats.   10
Red I love Anna Blume, red I love your!—You
ye you your, I your, you my.—We?
This belongs (by the way) in icy fire.
Red bloom, red Anna Blume, what do people say?
Prize question: 1.) Anna Blume has a bird.
           2.) Anna Blume is red.   15
           3.) What colour is the bird?
Blue is the colour of your yellow hair.
Red is the cooing of your green bird.
You simple girl in a simple dress, you dear   20
green beast, I love your! You ye you your,
I your, you my.—We?
This belongs (by the way) in the chest of fires.
Anna Blume! Anna, a-n-n-a, I trickle your
name. Your name drips like softest tallow.   25
Do you know, Anna, do you know already?
You can also be read from behind, and you, you
the loveliest of all, are from behind, as you are from
before: "a-n-n-a".
Tallow trickles caressingly down my back.   30
Anna Blume, you trickle beast, I love your!

---

1. Translated from the German by David Britt. Published in 1919.   2. They don't know how the church tower stands (literally); i.e., they don't know the simplest things.

PAUL ÉLUARD
1895–1952

Woman in Love[1]

She is standing on my eyelids
And her hair is in mine,
She has the shape of my hands,
She has the color of my eyes,
She is engulfed in my shadow   5
Like a stone against the sky.

Her eyes are always open
She does not let me sleep.
Her dreams in broad daylight
Make suns evaporate,   10
Make me laugh, weep and laugh,
And speak without anything to say.

To Be Caught in One's Own Trap

It is a restaurant like the others. Must I believe I resemble no one? Next to me a great woman is beating eggs with her fingers. A passenger places his clothing on a table and avoids me. He is wrong, I don't know any mystery, I don't even know the meaning of the word. I have never looked for anything, never found anything, he is wrong to insist.

The storm that, off and on, leaves the fog turns my eyes and shoulders. Space then has doors and windows. The passenger announces to me I am not the same anymore. Not the same anymore! I gather the fragments of all my wonders. It is the great woman who told me that these are fragments of wonders, these fragments. I throw them in the healthy streams full of birds. The sea, the calm sea is between them like the sky in the light. Colors too, if someone talks to me of colors, I don't look anymore. Talk to me about shapes, I really need cause for concern.

Great woman, talk to me about shapes, or I fall asleep and I lead a rich life, my hands caught in my head and my head in my mouth, in my closed mouth, inward language.

1. All Éluard selections are translated from the French by R. M. Weisman, except for *Woman in Love*, which is translated by Lloyd Alexander. The Éluard selections are taken from *Capital of Pain* (1926).

[Nature Was Caught in the Nets of Your Life]

Nature was caught in the nets of your life.
The tree, your shadow, shows its naked flesh: the sky.
It has the voice of the sand and the gestures of the wind.
And everything you say moves behind you.

[She Is Always Unwilling to Understand]

She is always unwilling to understand, to listen,
She laughs to hide her fear of herself.
She has always walked beneath the arches of nights
And wherever she went
She left   5
The mark of broken things.

[Unknown, She Was My Favorite Shape]

Unknown, she was my favorite shape,
She who relieved me of the worry of being a man,
And I see her and I lose her and I suffer
My pain, like a little sunlight in cold water.

The Mirror of a Moment

It dissipates day,
It shows men the thin images of appearance,
It robs men of the possibility of amusement.
It is as hard as stone,
Formless stone,   5
The stone of movement and sight,
And its brilliance deforms all armor, all masks.
What the hand has taken does not deign to take the shape of the hand,
What has been understood no longer exists,
The bird was confused with the wind,   10
The sky with its truth,
Man with his reality.

TRISTAN TZARA
1896–1963

From Dada Manifesto 1918

DADAIST DISGUST[1]

Every product of disgust capable of becoming a negation of the family is *dada*; the whole being protesting in its destructive force with clenched fists: **DADA**; knowledge of all the means rejected up to this point by the timid sex of easy compromise and sociability: DADA; abolition of logic, dance of all those impotent to create: **DADA**; of all hierarchy and social equation installed for the preservation of values by our valets: DADA; each and every object, feelings and obscurities, apparitions and the precise shock of parallel lines, can be means for the combat: DADA; abolition of memory: **DADA**; abolition of archeology: *DADA*; abolition of the prophets: *DADA*; abolition of the future: DADA; an absolute indisputable belief in each god immediate product of spontaneity: **DADA**; elegant and unprejudicial leap from one harmony to the other sphere; trajectory of a word tossed like a sonorous cry of phonograph record; respecting all individualities in their momentary madness: serious, fearful, timid, ardent, vigorous, determined, enthusiastic; stripping its chapel of every useless awkward accessory; spitting out like a luminous waterfall any unpleasant or amorous thought, or coddling it—with the lively satisfaction of knowing that it doesn't matter—with the same intensity in the bush of his soul, free of insects for the aristocrats, and gilded with archangels' bodies. Freedom: *DADA DADA DADA*, shrieking of contracted pains, intertwining of contraries and of all contradictions, grotesqueries, nonsequiturs: LIFE.

Proclamation without Pretension[2]

Art goes to sleep for the birth of a new world
"ART"—a *parrot word*—replaced by **DADA**
PLESIAUSAURUS,[3] or handkerchief
The talent WHICH YOU CAN LEARN *makes the poet a druggist*
TODAY *criticism balances no longer launches resemblances*   5
Hypertrophic painters hyperestheticized and hypnotized by the hyacinths of muezzins of hypocritical appearance
CONSOLIDATE THE EXACT HARVEST OF CALCULATIONS
HYPERDROME[4] OF IMMORTAL GUARANTEES: *There is no importance there is no transparency or apparency*   10
MUSICIANS BREAK YOUR BLIND INSTRUMENTS on the stage
The **SYRINGE** *is only for my understanding.* **I am writing because**

---

1. Both Tzara selections translated from the French by Mary Ann Caws. This is the last section of Tzara's *Dada Manifesto 1918*.   2. Published in 1918.   3. A large prehistoric marine reptile.   4. A play on *hyper* (above) and *hippodrome* (a racetrack for horses).

it is as natural as pissing as being sick
Art needs an operation
Art is a ***PRETENTION*** heated in the TIMIDITY of the urinary   15
basin, **Hysteria** born in the **Studio**

We are seeking **upright pure sober unique** strength we are
seeking **NOTHING** we affirm the **VITALITY** of each instant
the anti-philosophy of **Spontaneous** acrobatic
In this moment I hate the man who whispers before intermission—   20
eau de cologne—bitter theater. CHEERY WIND.
IF EVERYBODY SAYS THE OPPOSITE IT IS BECAUSE THEY ARE RIGHT.
Prepare the geyser actions of our blood—submarine formation
of transchromatic airplanes, cellular metals numbered in the
leap of images
               above the regulations of the   25
BEAUTIFUL and its control
**It is not for the runts who are still worshipping
their navel**

ANDRÉ BRETON
1896–1966

Free Union[1]

My wife whose hair is a forest fire
Her thoughts that are hot lightning
Her hourglass waist
My wife with the waist of an otter in the teeth of a tiger
My wife with the mouth of a cockade and a bouquet of stars of the
     greatest magnitude   5
Her teeth are prints of white mice on white earth
Her tongue of polished amber and glass
My wife with the tongue of a stabbed host[2]
The tongue of a doll that opens and closes its eyes
A tongue of unbelievable stone   10
My wife whose eyelashes are children's first letters
Eyebrows the edge of a swallow's nest
My wife with temples the slates of a greenhouse roof
And steam on the panes
My wife with shoulders of champagne   15
And a spring with heads of dolphins under ice
My wife with wrists of matches

---

1. Translated by Louis Simpson. Published in 1931.   2. Communion host. In *Nadja* (1928), Breton
describes a striking postcard that depicts a section of Uccello's painting, *The Desecration of the Host*.

My wife with fingers of chance and the ace of hearts
Her fingers of cut hay
My wife with armpits of sable and berries[3]   20
And Midsummer Night
Of privet and a nest of angel fish
Whose arms are sea foam and a flood gate
And a mixture of wheat and a mill
My wife with legs that are rockets   25
With movements of clockwork[4] and despair
My wife with calves the core of an elderberry tree
My wife whose feet are initials[5]
Her feet are bunches of keys and caulkers drinking
My wife with a neck of unhulled barley[6]   30
Her throat is the Valley of Gold[7]
A rendez-vous in the very bed of the flood
With her breasts of night
My wife with breasts a molehill by the sea
My wife with breasts a crucible of ruby   35
Breasts the specter of the rose[8] covered with dew
My wife whose belly is the opening of a fan of days
Her belly a giant claw
My wife with the back of a bird in vertical flight
A back of quicksilver   40
A back of light
The back of her neck crushed stone and wet chalk
And the fall of a glass from which you have just drunk
My wife with her gondola[9] hips
Chandelier hips and arrow feathers   45
And shafts of white peacock feathers
Untrembling scales
My wife with buttocks of sandstone and asbestos
My wife with swansback buttocks
Buttocks of springtime   50
With her gladiola sex
Sex of a mine and the duck-billed platypus
My wife with her sex of seaweed and ancient candy
My wife with her sex mirror
My wife with her eyes filled with tears   55
Her eyes of violet armor and a magnetic needle
My wife with her savanna eyes
My wife's eyes are water to be drunk in prison
Eyes of wood always under the axe
Her eyes are the level of water of air and earth and fire   60

---

3. The French word is suggested by the similar sound of the word for "cut hay" in the previous line.
4. Word play added to the independent similes of lines 25–26, "rockets/with movements of clockwork,"
suggests a time fuse.   5. Also a botanical term for fast-multiplying cells at the tips of roots and branches.
6. In French, "unhulled" is a word resembling *pearlike* and, with *"barley,"* suggests pearl barley; by extension
a necklace of pearls. The next line extends the association to include gold.   7. A reference to Val-d'Or,
a place in St.-Cloud near Paris, or, it has been suggested, a town in southwestern Quebec (Canada) where
gold was discovered in 1909.   8. *The Specter of the Rose,* a poem by Théophile Gautier (1811–1872),
was also the subject of a ballet created in 1911 by Sergey Diaghilev (1872–1929).   9. A long, narrow,
flat-bottomed boat that traditionally ferries from two to six passengers on the Venetian canals. It has a
raised prow and stern, and is propelled by a gondolier using a single long oar.

Vigilance[1]

In Paris the tower of Saint-Jacques[2] swaying
Like a sunflower
Sometimes runs its brow against the Seine and its shadow glides
    imperceptibly among the tugs
At that moment on tiptoe in my sleep
I head for the room where I am lying   5
And set fire to it
So that nothing will remain of the consent wrung from me
The furniture then makes way for animals of the same size looking at
    me fraternally
Lions in whose manes the chairs are now burning out
Sharks whose white bellies absorb the last quivering of the sheets   10
At the hour of love and of blue eyelids
I see myself burning in turn I see that solemn hiding place of nothings
Which was once my body
Probed by the patient beaks of the fire-ibises
When all is finished I enter invisible into the ark   15
Taking no heed of the passersby of life whose shuffling steps are heard
    far off
I see the ridges of the sun
Through the hawthorn of the rain
I hear human linen tearing like a great leaf
Under the fingernails of absence and presence who are in collusion   20
All the looms are withering only a piece of perfumed lace remains of
    them
A shell of lace in the perfect shape of a breast
I touch nothing but the heart of things I hold the thread

---

1. Translated by Mary Ann Caws. Published in 1932.   2. Only the tower remains of the Parisian church
of Saint-Jacques-de-la-Boucherie, one of whose patrons was the medieval alchemist Nicolas Flamel (1330–
1418). The tower was cherished by the Surrealists for its associations with alchemy.

AIMÉ CÉSAIRE
born 1913

Do Not Have Pity[1]

Smoke on, salt swamps

Rock-painted icons of the unknown
deflect towards me the muted nightfall
of their laughter

smoke on, salt marshes, sea-needle heart   5
dead stars coaxed by marvellous hands dart forth
from the pulp of my eyes
Smoke on smoke on
the thin penumbra of my voice cracks with
flaming red cities   10
and my pure hands irresistibly call forth
at a very far remove from the ancestral heritage
the invincible zeal of acid in the flesh of
life—sea swamps—

like a viper sprung from the blond force of a blinding light.   15

Sun Serpent

Sun serpent: eye beguiling my eye
and the sea squalid with islands, finger joints cracking flame-
        throwing
roses, and my body lightning-blasted, unharmed,
the water hoists up carcasses of light lost in the gangway without ceremony
haloes of whirling ice encircle the smoking heart of crows   5
our hearts—
the voice of muffled thunderbolts rolling on their forked hinges
diffused by anolis lizards[1] through a landscape of broken glasses
vampire flowers relieving orchids of their spell
elixir of fire at the core   10
fire righteous fire, mango tree of night swaddled with bees
my desire: a contingent of tigers surprised amidst the sulphur
but at its arousal the tin is gilded with childhood layers
and my pebbled body gobbling fish gobbling doves gobbling slumbers . . .
the word Brazil is sugar in the depth of the swamp.   15

---

1. All Césaire selections translated from the French by Gregson Davis. From *Miraculous Weapons* (1946). The original title was "Do Not Have Pity for Me," a rebellious echo of the French poet Guillaume Apollinaire's (1880–1918) line "Have pity on me," which ends a description of the modern poet caught between old and new orders (*The Pretty Redhead*).   1. Antillean lizards related to iguanas.

Day and Night

the sun the executioner the press of the masses the routine of dying and my
cry of wounded beast—and so it goes even unto the infinity of fevers, the
awesome floodgate of death bombarded by my very own aleutian eyes that
from wormy earth search amid earth and worms your eyes of flesh, of sun,
like the black urchin for the coin in the water where flows the never-failing
song of the virgin forest sprung from the silence of the earth, of my very own
aleutian eyes, and so it goes: the lewd leapfrog of hermaphrodite thoughts,
the calls of jaguars, of water-hole, of antelopes, of savannahs with their
branches plucked in the course of their first great adventure: the exquisite
cyathus subtending a beautiful nymph stripped of her leaves amid the milk
of manchineel[1] trees and the accolades of brotherhood leeches.

1. Manzanilla.

JOYCE MANSOUR
1928–1986

[I Saw You through My Closed Eye][1]

I saw you through my closed eye
Climbing the wall frightened of your dreams.
Your feet were losing their footing on the sleepy moss.
Your eyes were holding onto hanging nails.
While I screamed without opening my mouth   5
To open your head to the night.

[I Opened Your Head]

I opened your head
To read your thoughts.
I devoured your eyes
To taste your sight.
I drank your blood   5
To know your wants
And made of your shivering body
My nourishment.

1. All Mansour selections translated from the French by Serge Gavronsky. From *Screams* (1953).

[Men's Vices]

Men's vices
are my domain
Their wounds my sweet desserts
I love to chew on their vile thoughts
For their ugliness makes my beauty.   5

[Empty Black Haunted House]

Empty black haunted house
Our steps precede and follow us.
Rooms crowded with unfinished visions
Of objects beyond reach
Empty empty perverted house.   5
Your head walled in your eyes
That burn indecently blue
Haunt us call us
Fill our mouths.
Eternal inedible bread.   10

WILLIAM FAULKNER
1897–1962

Chronicler of the American South, William Faulkner's inventive imagination and innovative use of language brought him an international reputation and influenced writers in Europe, Latin America, and China. His account of the historical change between the Old and the New South transcends regional issues or the mythical community of Yoknapatawpha, Mississippi, where most of his work is situated. Faulkner writes about broader themes: the clash of generations and ways of life, racial and family tragedies, and, in almost archetypal terms, the opposition of good and evil. Adapting James Joyce's stream-of-consciousness technique, he lets his characters reveal themselves in brilliantly extended narrative sentences that have become famous as "Faulknerian" style; and his fantastic, sometimes allegorical, depictions of events anticipate "magical realist" fiction. With Faulkner's novels, the nineteenth-century Balzacian tradition of the human comedy—the novel as a panorama of society— acquires a new vocabulary and a renewed place in literary history.

William Cuthbert Falkner was born on September 25, 1897, in New Albany, Mississippi, to a prosperous family with many ties to southern history. The eldest of four sons, Faulkner (he adopted this spelling in 1924 for his first book) was named for a great-grandfather who commanded a Confederate regiment in the Civil War, built railroads, and wrote novels. Faulkner's father worked for the family railroad until it was sold in 1902, afterward moving the family to Oxford and eventually becoming business manager of the University of Mississippi. Faulkner's close acquaintance with southern customs and attitudes, his own experience as the descendant of a once-prosperous and influential family, and his attachment to Lafayette County and the town of Oxford (Yoknapatawpha County and Jefferson in the novels) help to shape themes and setting in his fiction.

Young Faulkner read widely in his grandfather's library and borrowed books from an older friend, Philip Stone. Leaving high school after two years to work as a bookkeeper in his grandfather's bank, he continued reading and discussing literature with Stone, who encouraged his writing and introduced him to novels of the nineteenth-century French realist writer Honoré de Balzac. In the last six months of 1918, he trained in Canada as a fighter pilot—then a common way of getting more quickly into combat in the First World War—but the war ended, and he returned to Oxford to enroll at the University of Mississippi as a special student. Leaving the university in 1920 to work in a New York bookstore, he returned in 1921 and became postmaster for three years at the university. During this period, he wrote poetry and seems to have been influenced by the French Symbolists: his first published poem, *L'Après-midi d'un faune*, takes its title from Stéphane Mallarmé. Faulkner's first book, a collection of lyrics called *The Marble Faun*, appeared in 1924.

In 1925, the young writer spent six months in New Orleans, where he was attracted to a literary group associated with *The Double Dealer*, a magazine in which he published poems, essays, and prose sketches. The group's chief figure was the novelist Sherwood Anderson, author of a series of regional stories published as *Winesburg, Ohio*, who encouraged Faulkner to make fictional use of his southern background and who recommended Faulkner's first novel to his New York publisher. After completing *Soldier's Pay* (1926), Faulkner took a freighter to Europe, where he bicycled and hiked through Italy and France, and lived for a short while in Paris. He returned to Mississippi at the end of the year, where he wrote his second novel, *Mosquitoes* (1927), a satire on the New Orleans group.

Taking up Anderson's earlier suggestion, Faulkner now embarked on the regional "Yoknapatawpha" (*yok-na-pa-taw'-pha*) series with *Sartoris* (1929), an account of the return home, marriage, and death of wounded veteran Bayard Sartoris. In Yoknapatawpha County, Faulkner created a whole fictional world with characters who reappear from novel to novel (a technique he would have encountered in Balzac's *Comédie humaine*). Here imaginary families such as the Sartorises, Compsons, Sutpens, McCaslins, and Snopeses rise to prosperity or fall into various kinds of weakness, degradation, and death. Individual characters work out destinies that are already half-shaped by family tradition and invisible community pressures. They are caught in close, often incestuous blood relationships and make their way in a world where the values, traditions, and privileges of an old plantation society are yielding to the values of a new mercantile class. A network of family dynasties illustrates this picture of a changing society: the decaying and impoverished Compson family (*The Sound and the Fury*, 1929); two generations of Sutpens rising to great wealth and dying in madness and isolation (*Absalom, Absalom!*, 1936); the McCaslin family with its history of incest, miscegenation, and guilt (*Go Down, Moses*, 1942); and the viciously grasping and ambitious "poor white" Snopes family (*The Hamlet*, 1940; *The Town*, 1957; *The Mansion*, 1959), who appear in the stories printed here. These are violent works, and the murders, lynchings, and bestialities of all kinds that appear in them account for Faulkner's early American reputation as a lurid local writer. European critics, however, especially the French, who recognized his ability as early as 1931, were quick to recognize mythic overtones and classical and biblical prototypes in these tales of twisted family relationships.

Faulkner, in *The Sound and the Fury*, experimented with the stream-of-consciousness technique. Here the Compson family's tragedy is told through several different points of view, the first of which is the disconnected and emotionally skewed world of the idiot Benjy. Both *Sartoris* and *The Sound and the Fury* were rejected several times before being published in 1929, and Faulkner supported himself during these years by working at odd jobs (on a shrimp trawler, in a lumber mill and a power plant, and as a carpenter, painter, and paperhanger) and then from his short stories, of which he sold thirty between 1930 and 1932. In 1929, he married Estelle Oldham Franklin, with whom he had one child, Jill, in 1933. Irritated at the difficulty of finding publishers for his serious or experimental works, the novelist set out to write a best seller—and succeeded. *Sanctuary* (1931), a novel of the Deep South that described the rape and prostitution of a schoolgirl as well as murder, perjury, and the lynching of an innocent man, was made into a movie (*The Story of Temple Drake*, 1933) and brought its author invitations to work on movie scripts for a variety of Hollywood studios. From 1932 to 1955, the novelist added to his income by working as a film doctor, revising and collaborating on scripts for films such as *To Have and Have Not* and *The Big Sleep*. Although his works continued to receive critical praise, he did not have any commercial successes after *Sanctuary*; in 1945, when he was, according to the French writer and philosopher Jean-Paul Sartre, the idol of young French readers, almost all his novels were out of print. It took an anthology, *The Portable Faulkner*, to reintroduce Faulkner to a wide audience in 1946. In 1950, he won the Nobel Prize for literature and used the prize money to establish the William Faulkner Foundation to assist Latin American writers and award educational scholarships to Mississippi blacks. Five years later he received the Pulitzer Prize and the National Book Award for *A Fable* (1954). Faulkner's last book was a comedy set in Yoknapatawpha County, *The Reivers* (1962). He died of a heart attack in Oxford, Mississippi, on July 6, 1962.

In Faulkner's world, men and women are measured by the breadth of their compassion or the quality of their endurance. Although there are villains, few wholly negative characters appear, and these are seen as grotesque distortions of humanity, like the cruel and frustrated Jason Compson or the impotent rapist Popeye of *Sanctuary*, who "had that vicious depthless quality of stamped tin." Heroes tend to be larger than life. They have the moral endurance of Bayard Sartoris II, who as a boy kills his grandmother's murderer and as a man faces down his father's killer—unarmed—in order to break the pattern of "honorable revenge"; or the physical endurance of the tall convict in *Old Man*, whose "whole purpose," according to Faulkner, was "to prove . . . just how much the human body could bear, stand, endure." Yet Faulkner's world is by no means unrelievedly somber. The everyday realism and earthy humor of his works have led to his being called a "comic" writer in the broad sense that implies a universal vision encompassing the pettiness as well as the grandeur of human existence. Not all of his characters are heroes. Some are ordinary people whose perseverance and dedication to an idea, a person, or a way of life give them larger significance; some are thoughtful people driven by circumstances to question their own identity and values; some are idiots able only to feel a succession of emotions; some are simply confidence men. Faulkner generally describes such figures from the outside. We see them act, and we may even follow their thoughts in interior monologues; but these are only traces of an inner personality that has already been defined and to which we have no real access.

The "truth" of the novels comes to us through a variety of perspectives and rhetorical strategies. Three different narrators in *Absalom, Absalom!* tell the story of Thomas Sutpen. The four points of view in *The Sound and the Fury* move from Benjy's imagined inner monologue to the monologues of his suicidal and psychopathic brothers, and finally to a third-person narrative focusing on Dilsey, who "endures." The convict in *Old Man* possesses a doggedly limited view of things modeled on simplistic cops-and-robbers stories and adventure tales. In *Go Down, Moses*, six pages of ledger reading explore McCaslin family relationships. Chronology may be broken; details are exaggerated or distorted; and dialect speech emphasizes the presence of the storyteller's art. Throughout, Faulkner's fluid style escapes rigid categories; it is a style of tensions and contradictions, tragedy and humor, realism and mythic outreach, now short and laconic, now rambling.

The two stories paired here, both of which recur in altered form in *The Hamlet* (1940), exhibit the range of Faulkner's art—from the dehumanized menace of Abner Snopes in *Barn Burning* to the comic wonder and dismay of V. K. Ratliff in *Spotted Horses*, describing how Flem Snopes cheated the whole community into buying wild horses from Texas. The Snopes family and Snopesism are at the center of both stories. Just as the Sartoris family represents southern aristocratic tradition in all its romanticism and humanity, the Snopeses originate as the society's shiftless "poor whites" and come to embody the cold, calculating, exploitative side of human nature that is working its way to the fore in a modern, commercially oriented age. Although members of the Snopes family take on individuality and human traits (generally perverse) when described separately, together they become allegorized into "Snopesism," a vision of evil that is openly diabolical and calls up its own counterforce. In Faulkner's view of the eternal battle between good and evil, "There is always someone that will never stop trying to cope with Snopes, that will never stop trying to get rid of Snopes." Abner Snopes, father of Flem (unnamed in this story) and Colonel Sartoris Snopes, is such a personification of inhuman, two-dimensional evil: "without face or depth—a shape black, flat, and bloodless as though cut from tin . . . , the voice harsh like tin and without heat like tin." His human qualities are purely destructive: a ferocious independence and conviction of his own rectitude, linked to deep jealousy and rage against others' prosperity or authority; a vicious paranoia that creates opportunities for revenge; an arsonist's love for the destructive element of fire that speaks to "some deep mainspring" of his being. Young Colonel Sartoris Snopes is torn between two loyalties, as his name implies. Dependent on his family and fiercely defensive of his father whenever the "enemy" threatens, he nonetheless dislikes lying, takes joy in imagining Major de Spain's mansion as a sanctuary his father cannot touch, wishes his father would change even as he recognizes he will not, and finally cuts himself off completely from his family by warning Major de Spain about the arson. To the psychological realism of individual portraits, and the struggle between father and son, Faulkner adds a struggle between right and wrong—both sides inextricably related to each other and, at the end, both left with an unknown future.

The picture of pure destruction that plays such a large role in *Barn Burning* returns in comic vein in *Spotted Horses*, as the horses bursting out of their pen run wild over the countryside and defy their new owners' best attempts to catch them. Literally an unbridled force of nature (and spotted horses are often demonic in folklore), they invade a house, force one of the inhabitants to jump out the window in his underwear, run over a mule-drawn wagon and its inhabitants, and in general upset the normal order of things. Adding to the ridiculousness of the situation is the fact that the townspeople are caught empty-handed through their own greed, having bought the horses against their better judgment when they knew or suspected that Flem Snopes was behind the sale. V. K. Ratliff, the sewing-machine agent who narrates the story, cannot help admiring the monumental craftiness with which Snopes manipulates events to his own profit, although Ratliff is also opposed to everything that Snopes stands for and tries to shame him into returning Mrs. Armstid's money. For this comedy also has somber overtones: Henry Armstid is driven further into madness, his family pushed further into desperate poverty, as Snopes refuses to return the money. Snopes is out of sight for most of the story, and when he appears toward the end and sends Mrs. Armstid on her way with a bag of candy for the children, the comedy turns bitter—an example of Snopesism in all its callous greed. Only a return to the level of storytelling, with Ratliff as a teller of tall tales who can appreciate the scale of Snopes's successful trickery, allows the story to maintain its character as one of Faulkner's most farcical tales.

Barn Burning

The store in which the Justice of the Peace's court was sitting smelled of cheese. The boy, crouched on his nail keg at the back of the crowded room, knew he smelled cheese, and more: from where he sat he could see the ranked shelves close-packed with the solid, squat, dynamic shapes of tin cans whose labels his stomach read, not from the lettering which meant nothing to his mind but from the scarlet devils and the silver curve of fish—this, the cheese which he knew he smelled and the hermetic[1] meat which his intestines believed he smelled coming in intermittent gusts momentary and brief between the other constant one, the smell and sense just a little of fear because mostly of despair and grief, the old fierce pull of blood. He could not see the table where the Justice sat and before which his father and his father's enemy (*our enemy* he thought in that despair; *ourn! mine and hisn both! He's my father!*) stood, but he could hear them, the two of them that is, because his father had said no word yet:

"But what proof have you, Mr. Harris?"

"I told you. The hog got into my corn. I caught it up and sent it back to him. He had no fence that would hold it. I told him so, warned him. The next time I put the hog in my pen. When he came to get it I gave him enough wire to patch up his pen. The next time I put the hog up and kept it. I rode down to his house and saw the wire I gave him still rolled on to the spool in his yard. I told him he could have the hog when he paid me a dollar pound fee. That evening a nigger came with the dollar and got the hog. He was a strange nigger. He said, 'He say to tell you wood and hay kin burn.' I said, 'What?' 'That whut he say to tell you,' the nigger said. 'Wood and hay kin burn.' That night my barn burned. I got the stock out but I lost the barn."

"Where is the nigger? Have you got him?"

"He was a strange nigger, I tell you. I don't know what became of him."

"But that's not proof. Don't you see that's not proof?"

"Get that boy up here. He knows." For a moment the boy thought too that the man meant his older brother until Harris said, "Not him. The little one. The boy," and, crouching, small for his age, small and wiry like his father, in patched and faded jeans even too small for him, with straight, uncombed, brown hair and eyes gray and wild as storm scud, he saw the men between himself and the table part and become a lane of grim faces, at the end of which he saw the Justice, a shabby, collarless, graying man in spectacles, beckoning him. He felt no floor under his bare feet; he seemed to walk beneath the palpable weight of the grim turning faces. His father, stiff in his black Sunday coat donned not for the trial but for the moving, did not even look at him. *He aims for me to lie*, he thought, again with that frantic grief and despair. *And I will have to do hit.*

"What's your name, boy?" the Justice said.

"Colonel Sartoris Snopes,"[2] the boy whispered.

"Hey?" the Justice said. "Talk louder. Colonel Sartoris? I reckon anybody named for Colonel Sartoris in this country can't help but tell the truth, can

---

1. Sealed-in, canned, in tins whose labels display scarlet devils and the silver curve of fish.   2. The Snopes boy is named for Colonel [John] Sartoris, legendary founder of the aristocratic Sartoris family.

they?" The boy said nothing. *Enemy! Enemy!* he thought; for a moment he could not even see, could not see that the Justice's face was kindly nor discern that his voice was troubled when he spoke to the man named Harris: "Do you want me to question this boy?" But he could hear, and during those subsequent long seconds while there was absolutely no sound in the crowded little room save that of quiet and intent breathing it was as if he had swung outward at the end of a grape vine, over a ravine, and at the top of the swing had been caught in a prolonged instant of mesmerized gravity, weightless in time.

"No!" Harris said violently, explosively. "Damnation! Send him out of here!" Now time, the fluid world, rushed beneath him again, the voices coming to him again through the smell of cheese and sealed meat, the fear and despair and the old grief of blood:

"This case is closed. I can't find against you, Snopes, but I can give you advice. Leave this country and don't come back to it."

His father spoke for the first time, his voice cold and harsh, level, without emphasis: "I aim to. I don't figure to stay in a country among people who . . ." he said something unprintable and vile, addressed to no one.

"That'll do," the Justice said. "Take your wagon and get out of this country before dark. Case dismissed."

His father turned, and he followed the stiff black coat, the wiry figure walking a little stiffly from where a Confederate provost's man's[3] musket ball had taken him in the heel on a stolen horse thirty years ago, followed the two backs now, since his older brother had appeared from somewhere in the crowd, no taller than the father but thicker, chewing tobacco steadily, between the two lines of grim-faced men and out of the store and across the worn gallery and down the sagging steps and among the dogs and half-grown boys in the mild May dust, where as he passed a voice hissed:

"Barn burner!"

Again he could not see, whirling; there was a face in a red haze, moonlike, bigger than the full moon, the owner of it half again his size, he leaping in the red haze toward the face, feeling no blow, feeling no shock when his head struck the earth, scrabbling up and leaping again, feeling no blow this time either and tasting no blood, scrabbling up to see the other boy in full flight and himself already leaping into pursuit as his father's hand jerked him back, the harsh, cold voice speaking above him: "Go get in the wagon."

It stood in a grove of locusts and mulberries across the road. His two hulking sisters in their Sunday dresses and his mother and her sister in calico and sunbonnets were already in it, sitting on and among the sorry residue of the dozen and more movings which even the boy could remember—the battered stove, the broken beds and chairs, the clock inlaid with mother-of-pearl, which would not run, stopped at some fourteen minutes past two o'clock of a dead and forgotten day and time, which had been his mother's dowry. She was crying, though when she saw him she drew her sleeve across her face and began to descend from the wagon. "Get back," the father said.

"He's hurt. I got to get some water and wash his . . ."

"Get back in the wagon," his father said. He got in too, over the tailgate. His father mounted to the seat where the older brother already sat and struck

3. Military policeman.

the gaunt mules two savage blows with the peeled willow, but without heat. It was not even sadistic; it was exactly that same quality which in later years would cause his descendants to over-run the engine before putting a motor car into motion, striking and reining back in the same movement. The wagon went on, the store with its quiet crowd of grimly watching men dropped behind; a curve in the road hid it. *Forever* he thought. *Maybe he's done satisfied now, now that he has . . .* stopping himself, not to say it aloud even to himself. His mother's hand touched his shoulder.

"Does hit hurt?" she said.

"Naw," he said. "Hit don't hurt. Lemme be."

"Can't you wipe some of the blood off before hit dries?"

"I'll wash to-night," he said. "Lemme be, I tell you."

The wagon went on. He did not know where they were going. None of them ever did or ever asked, because it was always somewhere, always a house of sorts waiting for them a day or two days or even three days away. Likely his father had already arranged to make a crop on another farm before he . . . Again he had to stop himself. He (the father) always did. There was something about his wolflike independence and even courage when the advantage was at least neutral which impressed strangers, as if they got from his latent ravening ferocity not so much a sense of dependability as a feeling that his ferocious conviction in the rightness of his own actions would be of advantage to all whose interest lay with his.

That night they camped, in a grove of oaks and beeches where a spring ran. The nights were still cool and they had a fire against it, of a rail lifted from a nearby fence and cut into lengths—a small fire, neat, niggard almost, a shrewd fire; such fires were his father's habit and custom always, even in freezing weather. Older, the boy might have remarked this and wondered why not a big one; why should not a man who had not only seen the waste and extravagance of war, but who had in his blood an inherent voracious prodigality with material not his own, have burned everything in sight? Then he might have gone a step farther and thought that that was the reason: that niggard blaze was the living fruit of nights passed during those four years in the woods hiding from all men, blue or gray,[4] with his strings of horses (captured horses, he called them). And older still, he might have divined the true reason: that the element of fire spoke to some deep mainspring of his father's being, as the element of steel or of powder spoke to other men, as the one weapon for the preservation of integrity, else breath were not worth the breathing, and hence to be regarded with respect and used with discretion.

But he did not think this now and he had seen those same niggard blazes all his life. He merely ate his supper beside it and was already half asleep over his iron plate when his father called him, and once more he followed the stiff back, the stiff and ruthless limp, up the slope and on to the starlit road where, turning, he could see his father against the stars but without face or depth—a shape black, flat, and bloodless as though cut from tin in the iron folds of the frockcoat which had not been made for him, the voice harsh like tin and without heat like tin:

"You were fixing to tell them. You would have told him." He didn't answer.

4. In the Civil War (1861–65), Union soldiers wore blue and Confederate soldiers gray uniforms.

His father struck him with the flat of his hand on the side of the head, hard but without heat, exactly as he had struck the two mules at the store, exactly as he would strike either of them with any stick in order to kill a horse fly, his voice still without heat or anger: "You're getting to be a man. You got to learn. You got to learn to stick to your own blood or you ain't going to have any blood to stick to you. Do you think either of them, any man there this morning, would? Don't you know all they wanted was a chance to get at me because they knew I had them beat? Eh?" Later, twenty years later, he was to tell himself, "If I had said they wanted only truth, justice, he would have hit me again." But now he said nothing. He was not crying. He just stood there. "Answer me," his father said.

"Yes," he whispered. His father turned.

"Get on to bed. We'll be there tomorrow."

To-morrow they were there. In the early afternoon the wagon stopped before a paintless two-room house identical almost with the dozen others it had stopped before even in the boy's ten years, and again, as on the other dozen occasions, his mother and aunt got down and began to unload the wagon, although his two sisters and his father and brother had not moved.

"Likely hit ain't fitten for hawgs," one of the sisters said.

"Nevertheless, fit it will and you'll hog it and like it," his father said. "Get out of them chairs and help your Ma unload."

The two sisters got down, big, bovine, in a flutter of cheap ribbons; one of them drew from the jumbled wagon bed a battered lantern, the other a worn broom. His father handed the reins to the older son and began to climb stiffly over the wheel. "When they get unloaded, take the team to the barn and feed them." Then he said, and at first the boy thought he was still speaking to his brother: "Come with me."

"Me?" he said.

"Yes," his father said. "You."

"Abner," his mother said. His father paused and looked back—the harsh level stare beneath the shaggy, graying, irascible brows.

"I reckon I'll have a word with the man that aims to begin to-morrow owning me body and soul for the next eight months."

They went back up the road. A week ago—or before last night, that is—he would have asked where they were going, but not now. His father had struck him before last night but never before had he paused afterward to explain why; it was as if the blow and the following calm, outrageous voice still rang, repercussed, divulging nothing to him save the terrible handicap of being young, the light weight of his few years, just heavy enough to prevent his soaring free of the world as it seemed to be ordered but not heavy enough to keep him footed solid in it, to resist it and try to change the course of its events.

Presently he could see the grove of oaks and cedars and the other flowering trees and shrubs where the house would be, though not the house yet. They walked beside a fence massed with honeysuckle and Cherokee roses[5] and came to a gate swinging open between two brick pillars, and now, beyond a sweep of drive, he saw the house for the first time and at that instant he forgot his father and the terror and despair both, and even when he remem-

5. An evergreen climbing rose with white flowers.

bered his father again (who had not stopped) the terror and despair did not return. Because, for all the twelve movings, they had sojourned until now in a poor country, a land of small farms and fields and houses, and he had never seen a house like this before. *Hit's big as a courthouse* he thought quietly, with a surge of peace and joy whose reason he could not have thought into words, being too young for that: *They are safe from him. People whose lives are a part of this peace and dignity are beyond his touch, he no more to them than a buzzing wasp: capable of stinging for a little moment but that's all; the spell of this peace and dignity rendering even the barns and stable and cribs which belong to it impervious to the puny flames he might contrive . . .* this, the peace and joy, ebbing for an instant as he looked again at the stiff black back, the stiff and implacable limp of the figure which was not dwarfed by the house, for the reason that it had never looked big anywhere and which now, against the serene columned backdrop, had more than ever that impervious quality of something cut ruthlessly from tin, depthless, as though, sidewise to the sun, it would cast no shadow. Watching him, the boy remarked the absolutely undeviating course which his father held and saw the stiff foot come squarely down in a pile of fresh droppings where a horse had stood in the drive and which his father could have avoided by a simple change of stride. But it ebbed only for a moment, though he could not have thought this into words either, walking on in the spell of the house, which he could even want but without envy, without sorrow, certainly never with that ravening and jealous rage which unknown to him walked in the ironlike black coat before him: *Maybe he will feel it too. Maybe it will even change him now from what maybe he couldn't help but be.*

They crossed the portico. Now he could hear his father's stiff foot as it came down on the boards with clocklike finality, a sound out of all proportion to the displacement of the body it bore and which was not dwarfed either by the white door before it, as though it had attained to a sort of vicious and ravening minimum not to be dwarfed by anything—the flat, wide, black hat, the formal coat of broadcloth which had once been black but which had now that friction-glazed greenish cast of the bodies of old house flies, the lifted sleeve which was too large, the lifted hand like a curled claw. The door opened so promptly that the boy knew the Negro must have been watching them all the time, an old man with neat grizzled hair, in a linen jacket, who stood barring the door with his body, saying, "Wipe you foots, white man, fo you come in here. Major ain't home nohow."

"Get out of my way, nigger," his father said, without heat too, flinging the door back and the Negro also and entering, his hat still on his head. And now the boy saw the prints of the stiff foot on the doorjamb and saw them appear on the pale rug behind the machinelike deliberation of the foot which seemed to bear (or transmit) twice the weight which the body compassed. The Negro was shouting "Miss Lula! Miss Lula!"[6] somewhere behind them, then the boy, deluged as though by a warm wave by a suave turn of carpeted stair and a pendant glitter of chandeliers and a mute gleam of gold frames, heard the swift feet and saw her too, a lady—perhaps he had never seen her like before either—in a gray, smooth gown with lace at the throat and an apron tied at the waist and the sleeves turned back, wiping cake or biscuit

---

6. "Miss" is a traditional Southern form of respectful address used also for married women.

dough from her hands with a towel as she came up the hall, looking not at his father at all but at the tracks on the blond rug with an expression of incredulous amazement.

"I tried," the Negro cried. "I tole him to . . ."

"Will you please go away?" she said in a shaking voice. "Major de Spain is not at home. Will you please go away?"

His father had not spoken again. He did not speak again. He did not even look at her. He just stood stiff in the center of the rug, in his hat, the shaggy iron-gray brows twitching slightly above the pebble-colored eyes as he appeared to examine the house with brief deliberation. Then with the same deliberation he turned; the boy watched him pivot on the good leg and saw the stiff foot drag round the arc of the turning, leaving a final long and fading smear. His father never looked at it, he never once looked down at the rug. The Negro held the door. It closed behind them, upon the hysteric and indistinguishable woman-wail. His father stopped at the top of the steps and scraped his boot clean on the edge of it. At the gate he stopped again. He stood for a moment, planted stiffly on the stiff foot, looking back at the house. "Pretty and white, ain't it?" he said. "That's sweat. Nigger sweat. Maybe it ain't white enough yet to suit him. Maybe he wants to mix some white sweat with it."

Two hours later the boy was chopping wood behind the house within which his mother and aunt and the two sisters (the mother and aunt, not the two girls, he knew that; even at this distance and muffled by walls the flat loud voices of the two girls emanated an incorrigible idle inertia) were setting up the stove to prepare a meal, when he heard the hooves and saw the linen-clad man on a fine sorrel mare, whom he recognized even before he saw the rolled rug in front of the Negro youth following on a fat bay carriage horse—a suffused, angry face vanishing, still at full gallop, beyond the corner of the house where his father and brother were sitting in the two tilted chairs; and a moment later, almost before he could have put the axe down, he heard the hooves again and watched the sorrel mare go back out of the yard, already galloping again. Then his father began to shout one of the sisters' names, who presently emerged backward from the kitchen door dragging the rolled rug along the ground by one end while the other sister walked behind it.

"If you ain't going to tote, go on and set up the wash pot," the first said.

"You, Sarty!" the second shouted. "Set up the wash pot!" His father appeared at the door, framed against that shabbiness, as he had been against that other bland perfection, impervious to either, the mother's anxious face at his shoulder.

"Go on," the father said. "Pick it up." The two sisters stooped, broad, lethargic; stooping, they presented an incredible expanse of pale cloth and a flutter of tawdry ribbons.

"If I thought enough of a rug to have to git hit all the way from France I wouldn't keep hit where folks coming in would have to tromp on hit," the first said. They raised the rug.

"Abner," the mother said. "Let me do it."

"You go back and git dinner," his father said. "I'll tend to this."

From the woodpile through the rest of the afternoon the boy watched them, the rug spread flat in the dust beside the bubbling wash-pot, the two sisters stooping over it with that profound and lethargic reluctance, while the father stood over them in turn, implacable and grim, driving them though never raising his voice again. He could smell the harsh homemade lye[7] they were using; he saw his mother come to the door once and look toward them with an expression not anxious now but very like despair; he saw his father turn, and he fell to with the axe and saw from the corner of his eye his father raise from the ground a flattish fragment of field stone and examine it and return to the pot, and this time his mother actually spoke: "Abner. Abner. Please don't. Please, Abner."

Then he was done too. It was dusk; the whippoorwills had already begun. He could smell coffee from the room where they would presently eat the cold food remaining from the mid-afternoon meal, though when he entered the house he realized they were having coffee again probably because there was a fire on the hearth, before which the rug now lay spread over the backs of the two chairs. The tracks of his father's foot were gone. Where they had been were now long, water-cloudy scoriations resembling the sporadic course of a lilliputian[8] mowing machine.

It still hung there while they ate the cold food and then went to bed, scattered without order or claim up and down the two rooms, his mother in one bed, where his father would later lie, the older brother in the other, himself, the aunt, and the two sisters on pallets on the floor. But his father was not in bed yet. The last thing the boy remembered was the depthless, harsh silhouette of the hat and coat bending over the rug and it seemed to him that he had not even closed his eyes when the silhouette was standing over him, the fire almost dead behind it, the stiff foot prodding him awake. "Catch up the mule," his father said.

When he returned with the mule his father was standing in the black door, the rolled rug over his shoulder. "Ain't you going to ride?" he said.

"No. Give me your foot."

He bent his knee into his father's hand, the wiry, surprising power flowed smoothly, rising, he rising with it, on to the mule's bare back (they had owned a saddle once; the boy could remember it though not when or where) and with the same effortlessness his father swung the rug up in front of him. Now in the starlight they retraced the afternoon's path, up the dusty road rife with honeysuckle, through the gate and up the black tunnel of the drive to the lightless house, where he sat on the mule and felt the rough warp of the rug drag across his thighs and vanish.

"Don't you want me to help?" he whispered. His father did not answer and now he heard again that stiff foot striking the hollow portico with that wooden and clocklike deliberation, that outrageous overstatement of the weight it carried. The rug, hunched, not flung (the boy could tell that even in the darkness) from his father's shoulder struck the angle of wall and floor with a sound unbelievably loud, thunderous, then the foot again, unhurried and enormous; a light came on in the house and the boy sat, tense, breathing steadily and quietly and just a little fast, though the foot itself did not increase its beat at all, descending the steps now; now the boy could see him.

"Don't you want to ride now?" he whispered. "We kin both ride now," the

---

7. A caustic cleanser made from leaching ashes, certain to damage any delicate material. 8. Miniature, after the tiny inhabitants of Lilliput described in Jonathan Swift's *Gulliver's Travels* (1726).

light within the house altering now, flaring up and sinking. *He's coming down the stairs now,* he thought. He had already ridden the mule up beside the horse block; presently his father was up behind him and he doubled the reins over and slashed the mule across the neck, but before the animal could begin to trot the hard, thin arm came round him, the hard, knotted hand jerking the mule back to a walk.

In the first red rays of the sun they were in the lot, putting plow gear on the mules. This time the sorrel mare was in the lot before he heard it at all, the rider collarless and even bareheaded, trembling, speaking in a shaking voice as the woman in the house had done, his father merely looking up once before stooping again to the hame he was buckling, so that the man on the mare spoke to his stooping back:

"You must realize you have ruined that rug. Wasn't there anybody here, any of your women . . ." he ceased, shaking, the boy watching him, the older brother leaning now in the stable door, chewing, blinking slowly and steadily at nothing apparently. "It cost a hundred dollars. But you never had a hundred dollars. You never will. So I'm going to charge you twenty bushels of corn against your crop. I'll add it in your contract and when you come to the commissary you can sign it. That won't keep Mrs. de Spain quiet but maybe it will teach you to wipe your feet off before you enter her house again."

Then he was gone. The boy looked at his father, who still had not spoken or even looked up again, who was now adjusting the logger-head in the hame.

"Pap," he said. His father looked at him—the inscrutable face, the shaggy brows beneath which the gray eyes glinted coldly. Suddenly the boy went toward him, fast, stopping as suddenly. "You done the best you could!" he cried. "If he wanted hit done different why didn't he wait and tell you how? He won't git no twenty bushels! He won't git none! We'll gether hit and hide hit! I kin watch . . ."

"Did you put the cutter back in that straight stock like I told you?"

"No, sir," he said.

"Then go do it."

That was Wednesday. During the rest of that week he worked steadily, at what was within his scope and some which was beyond it, with an industry that did not need to be driven nor even commanded twice; he had this from his mother, with the difference that some at least of what he did he liked to do, such as splitting wood with the half-size axe which his mother and aunt had earned, or saved money somehow, to present him with at Christmas. In company with the two older women (and on one afternoon, even one of the sisters), he built pens for the shoat and the cow which were a part of his father's contract with the landlord, and one afternoon, his father being absent, gone somewhere on one of the mules, he went to the field.

They were running a middle buster[9] now, his brother holding the plow straight while he handled the reins, and walking beside the straining mule, the rich black soil shearing cool and damp against his bare ankles, he thought *Maybe this is the end of it. Maybe even that twenty bushels that seems hard to have to pay for just a rug will be a cheap price for him to stop forever and always from being what he used to be;* thinking, dreaming now, so that his brother had to speak sharply to him to mind the mule: *Maybe he even won't*

---

9. A double moldboard plow that throws a ridge of earth both ways.

collect the twenty bushels. Maybe it will all add up and balance and vanish—corn, rug, fire; the terror and grief, the being pulled two ways like between two teams of horses—gone, done with for ever and ever.

Then it was Saturday; he looked up from beneath the mule he was harnessing and saw his father in the black coat and hat. "Not that," his father said. "The wagon gear." And then, two hours later, sitting in the wagon bed behind his father and brother on the seat, the wagon accomplished a final curve, and he saw the weathered paintless store with its tattered tobacco- and patent-medicine posters and the tethered wagons and saddle animals below the gallery. He mounted the gnawed steps behind his father and brother, and there again was the lane of quiet, watching faces for the three of them to walk through. He saw the man in spectacles sitting at the plank table and he did not need to be told this was a Justice of the Peace; he sent one glare of fierce, exultant, partisan defiance at the man in collar and cravat now, whom he had seen but twice before in his life, and that on a galloping horse, who now wore on his face an expression not of rage but of amazed unbelief which the boy could not have known was at the incredible circumstance of being sued by one of his own tenants, and came and stood against his father and cried at the Justice: "He ain't done it! He ain't burnt . . ."

"Go back to the wagon," his father said.

"Burnt?" the Justice said. "Do I understand this rug was burned too?"

"Does anybody here claim it was?" his father said. "Go back to the wagon." But he did not, he merely retreated to the rear of the room, crowded as that other had been, but not to sit down this time, instead, to stand pressing among the motionless bodies, listening to the voices:

"And you claim twenty bushels of corn is too high for the damage you did to the rug?"

"He brought the rug to me and said he wanted the tracks washed out of it. I washed the tracks out and took the rug back to him."

"But you didn't carry the rug back to him in the same condition it was in before you made the tracks on it."

His father did not answer, and now for perhaps half a minute there was no sound at all save that of breathing, the faint, steady suspiration of complete and intent listening.

"You decline to answer that, Mr. Snopes?" Again his father did not answer. "I'm going to find against you, Mr. Snopes. I'm going to find that you were responsible for the injury to Major de Spain's rug and hold you liable for it. But twenty bushels of corn seems a little high for a man in your circumstances to have to pay. Major de Spain claims it cost a hundred dollars. October corn will be worth about fifty cents. I figure that if Major de Spain can stand a ninety-five dollar loss on something he paid cash for, you can stand a five-dollar loss you haven't earned yet. I hold you in damages to Major de Spain to the amount of ten bushels of corn over and above your contract with him, to be paid to him out of your crop at gathering time. Court adjourned."

It had taken no time hardly, the morning was but half begun. He thought they would return home and perhaps back to the field, since they were late, far behind all other farmers. But instead his father passed on behind the wagon, merely indicating with his hand for the older brother to follow with it, and crossed the road toward the blacksmith shop opposite, pressing on after his father, overtaking him, speaking, whispering up at the harsh, calm face beneath the weathered hat: "He won't git no ten bushels neither. He won't git one. We'll . . ." until his father glanced for an instant down at him, the face absolutely calm, the grizzled eyebrows tangled above the cold eyes, the voice almost pleasant, almost gentle:

"You think so? Well, we'll wait till October anyway."

The matter of the wagon—the setting of a spoke or two and the tightening of the tires—did not take long either, the business of the tires accomplished by driving the wagon into the spring branch behind the shop and letting it stand there, the mules nuzzling into the water from time to time, and the boy on the seat with the idle reins, looking up the slope and through the sooty tunnel of the shed where the slow hammer rang and where his father sat on an upended cypress bolt, easily, either talking or listening, still sitting there when the boy brought the dripping wagon up out of the branch and halted it before the door.

"Take them on to the shade and hitch," his father said. He did so and returned. His father and the smith and a third man squatting on his heels inside the door were talking, about crops and animals; the boy, squatting too in the ammoniac dust and hoof-parings and scales of rust, heard his father tell a long and unhurried story out of the time before the birth of the older brother even when he had been a professional horsetrader. And then his father came up beside him where he stood before a tattered last year's circus poster on the other side of the store, gazing rapt and quiet at the scarlet horses, the incredible poisings and convolutions of tulle and tights and the painted leers of comedians, and said, "It's time to eat."

But not at home. Squatting beside his brother against the front wall, he watched his father emerge from the store and produce from a paper sack a segment of cheese and divide it carefully and deliberately into three with his pocket knife and produce crackers from the same sack. They all three squatted on the gallery and ate, slowly, without talking; then in the store again, they drank from a tin dipper tepid water smelling of the cedar bucket and of living beech trees. And still they did not go home. It was a horse lot this time, a tall rail fence upon and along which men stood and sat and out of which one by one horses were led, to be walked and trotted and then cantered back and forth along the road while the slow swapping and buying went on and the sun began to slant westward, they—the three of them—watching and listening, the older brother with his muddy eyes and his steady, inevitable tobacco, the father commenting now and then on certain of the animals, to no one in particular.

It was after sundown when they reached home. They ate supper by lamplight, then, sitting on the doorstep, the boy watched the night fully accomplish, listening to the whippoorwills and the frogs, when he heard his mother's voice: "Abner! No! No! Oh, God. Oh, God. Abner!" and he rose, whirled, and saw the altered light through the door where a candle stub now burned in a bottle neck on the table and his father, still in the hat and coat, at once formal and burlesque as though dressed carefully for some shabby and ceremonial violence, emptying the reservoir of the lamp back into the five-gallon kerosene can from which it had been filled, while the mother tugged at his arm until he shifted the lamp to the other hand and flung her back, not savagely or viciously, just hard, into the wall, her hands flung out against the wall for balance, her mouth open and in her face the same quality of hopeless despair as had been in her voice. Then his father saw him standing in the door.

"Go to the barn and get that can of oil we were oiling the wagon with," he said. The boy did not move. Then he could speak.

"What . . ." he cried. "What are you . . ."

"Go get that oil," his father said. "Go."

Then he was moving, running, outside the house, toward the stable: this the old habit, the old blood which he had not been permitted to choose for himself, which had been bequeathed him willy nilly and which had run for so long (and who knew where, battening on what of outrage and savagery and lust) before it came to him. *I could keep on*, he thought. *I could run on and on and never look back, never need to see his face again. Only I can't. I can't*, the rusted can in his hand now, the liquid sploshing in it as he ran back to the house and into it, into the sound of his mother's weeping in the next room, and handed the can to his father.

"Ain't you going to even send a nigger?" he cried. "At least you sent a nigger before!"

This time his father didn't strike him. The hand came even faster than the blow had, the same hand which had set the can on the table with almost excruciating care flashing from the can toward him too quick for him to follow it, gripping him by the back of his shirt and on to tiptoe before he had seen it quit the can, the face stooping at him in breathless and frozen ferocity, the cold, dead voice speaking over him to the older brother, who leaned against the table, chewing with that steady, curious, sidewise motion of cows:

"Empty the can into the big one and go on. I'll catch up with you."

"Better tie him up to the bedpost," the brother said.

"Do like I told you," the father said. Then the boy was moving, his bunched shirt and the hard, bony hand between his shoulder-blades, his toes just touching the floor, across the room and into the other one, past the sisters sitting with spread heavy thighs in the two chairs over the cold hearth, and to where his mother and aunt sat side by side on the bed, the aunt's arms about his mother's shoulders.

"Hold him," the father said. The aunt made a startled movement. "Not you," the father said. "Lennie. Take hold of him. You'll hold him better than that. If he gets loose don't you know what he is going to do? He will go up yonder." He jerked his head toward the road. "Maybe I'd better tie him."

"I'll hold him," his mother whispered.

"See you do then." Then his father was gone, the stiff foot heavy and measured upon the boards, ceasing at last.

Then he began to struggle. His mother caught him in both arms, he jerking and wrenching at them. He would be stronger in the end, he knew that. But he had no time to wait for it. "Lemme go!" he cried. "I don't want to have to hit you!"

"Let him go!" the aunt said. "If he don't go, before God, I am going up there myself!"

"Don't you see I can't?" his mother cried. "Sarty! Sarty! No! No! Help me, Lizzie!"

Then he was free. His aunt grasped at him but it was too late. He whirled, running, his mother stumbled forward on to her knees behind him, crying to the nearer sister: "Catch him, Net! Catch him!" But that was too late too, the sister (the sisters were twins, born at the same time, yet either of them now gave the impression of being, encompassing as much living meat and volume and weight as any other two of the family) not yet having begun to rise from the chair, her head, face, alone merely turned, presenting to him in the flying instant an astonishing expanse of young female features untroubled by any surprise even, wearing only an expression of bovine interest. Then he was out of the room, out of the house, in the mild dust of the starlit road and the heavy rifeness of honeysuckle, the pale ribbon unspooling with terrific slowness under his running feet, reaching the gate at last and turning in, running, his heart and lungs drumming, on up the drive toward the lighted house, the lighted door. He did not knock, he burst in, sobbing for breath, incapable for the moment of speech; he saw the astonished face of the Negro in the linen jacket without knowing when the Negro had appeared.

"De Spain!" he cried, panted. "Where's . . . ." then he saw the white man too emerging from a white door down the hall. "Barn!" he cried. "Barn!"

"What?" the white man said. "Barn?"

"Yes!" the boy cried. "Barn!"

"Catch him!" the white man shouted.

But it was too late this time too. The Negro grasped his shirt, but the entire sleeve, rotten with washing, carried away, and he was out that door too and in the drive again, and had actually never ceased to run even while he was screaming into the white man's face.

Behind him the white man was shouting, "My horse! Fetch my horse!" and he thought for an instant of cutting across the park and climbing the fence into the road, but he did not know the park nor how high the vine-massed fence might be and he dared not risk it. So he ran on down the drive, blood and breath roaring; presently he was in the road again though he could not see it. He could not hear either: the galloping mare was almost upon him before he heard her, and even then he held his course, as if the very urgency of his wild grief and need must in a moment more find his wings, waiting until the ultimate instant to hurl himself aside and into the weed-choked roadside ditch as the horse thundered past and on, for an instant in furious silhouette against the stars, the tranquil early summer night sky which, even before the shape of the horse and rider vanished, stained abruptly and violently upward: a long, swirling roar incredible and soundless, blotting the stars, and he springing up and into the road again, running again, knowing it was too late yet still running even after he heard the shot and, an instant later, two shots, pausing now without knowing he had ceased to run, crying "Pap! Pap!", running again before he knew he had begun to run, stumbling, tripping over something and scrabbling up again without ceasing to run, looking backward over his shoulder at the glare as he got up, running on among the invisible trees, panting, sobbing, "Father! Father!"

At midnight he was sitting on the crest of a hill. He did not know it was midnight and he did not know how far he had come. But there was no glare behind him now and he sat now, his back toward what he had called home for four days anyhow, his face toward the dark woods which he would enter when breath was strong again, small, shaking steadily in the chill darkness, hugging himself into the remainder of his thin, rotten shirt, the grief and despair now no longer terror and fear but just grief and despair. *Father. My father*, he thought. "He was brave!" he cried suddenly, aloud but not loud, no more than a whisper: "He was! He was in the war! He was in Colonel Sartoris' cav'ry!" not knowing that his father had gone to that war a private in the fine old European sense, wearing no uniform, admitting the authority of and giving fidelity to no man or army or flag, going to war as Malbrouck[1] himself did: for booty—it meant nothing and less than nothing to him if it were enemy booty or his own.

The slow constellations wheeled on. It would be dawn and then sun-up after a while and he would be hungry. But that would be to-morrow and now he was only cold, and walking would cure that. His breathing was easier now and he decided to get up and go on, and then he found that he had been asleep because he knew it was almost dawn, the night almost over. He could tell that from the whippoorwills. They were everywhere now among the dark trees below him, constant and inflectioned and ceaseless, so that, as the instant for giving over to the day birds drew nearer and nearer, there was no interval at all between them. He got up. He was a little stiff, but walking would cure that too as it would the cold, and soon there would be the sun. He went on down the hill, toward the dark woods within which the liquid silver voices of the birds called unceasing—the rapid and urgent beating of the urgent and quiring heart of the late spring night. He did not look back.

Spotted Horses

I

Yes, sir. Flem Snopes[2] has filled that whole country full of spotted horses. You can hear folks running them all day and all night, whooping and hollering, and the horses running back and forth across them little wooden bridges ever now and then kind of like thunder. Here I was this morning pretty near halfway to town, with the team ambling along and me setting in the buckboard about half asleep, when all of a sudden something come swurging up outen the bushes and jumped the road clean, without touching hoof to it. It flew right over my team, big as a billboard and flying through the air like a hawk. It taken me thirty minutes to stop my team and untangle the harness and the buckboard and hitch them up again.

That Flem Snopes. I be dog[3] if he ain't a case, now. One morning about ten years ago, the boys was just getting settled down on Varner's porch for a little talk and tobacco, when here come Flem out from behind the counter, with his coat off and his hair all parted like he might have been clerking for Varner for ten years already. Folks all knowed him; it was a big family of them about five miles down the bottom. That year, at least. Sharecropping. They never stayed on any place over a year. Then they would move on to another place, with the chap or maybe the twins of that year's litter. It was a regular nest of them. But Flem. The rest of them stayed tenant farmers, moving ever year, but here come Flem one day, walking out from behind

---

1. The Duke of Marlborough (1650–1722), an English general whose name became distorted as Malbrouck and Malbrouck in English and French popular songs celebrating his exploits.   2. The now-grown older brother from *Barn Burning*.   3. "I'll be darned."

Jody Varner's counter like he owned it. And he wasn't there but a year or two before folks knowed that, if him and Jody was both still in that store in ten years more, it would be Jody clerking for Flem Snopes. Why, that fellow could make a nickel where it wasn't but four cents to begin with. He skun me in two trades, myself, and the fellow that can do that, I just hope he'll get rich before I do; that's all.

All right. So here Flem was, clerking at Varner's, making a nickel here and there and not telling nobody about it. No, sir. Folks never knowed when Flem got the better of somebody lessen the fellow he beat told it. He'd just set there in the store-chair, chewing his tobacco and keeping his own business to hisself, until about a week later we'd find out it was somebody else's business he was keeping to hisself—provided the fellow he trimmed was mad enough to tell it. That's Flem.

We give him ten years to own everything Jody Varner had. But he never waited no ten years. I reckon you-all know that gal of Uncle Billy Varner's, the youngest one; Eula. Jody's sister. Ever Sunday ever yellow-wheeled buggy and curried riding horse in that country would be hitched to Bill Varner's fence, and the young bucks setting on the porch, swarming around Eula like bees around a honey pot. One of these here kind of big, soft-looking gals that could giggle richer than plowed newground. Wouldn't none of them leave before the others, and so they would set there on the porch until time to go home, with some of them with nine and ten miles to ride and then get up tomorrow and go back to the field. So they would all leave together and they would ride in a clump down to the creek ford and hitch them curried horses and yellow-wheeled buggies and get out and fight one another. Then they would get in the buggies again and go on home.

Well, one day about a year ago, one of them yellow-wheeled buggies and one of them curried saddle-horses quit this country. We heard they was heading for Texas. The next day Uncle Billy and Eula and Flem come into town in Uncle Bill's surrey, and when they come back, Flem and Eula was married. And on the next day we heard that two more of them yellow-wheeled buggies had left the country. They mought have gone to Texas, too. It's a big place.

Anyway, about a month after the wedding, Flem and Eula went to Texas, too. They was gone pretty near a year. Then one day last month, Eula come back, with a baby. We figgered up, and we decided that it was as well-growed a three-months-old baby as we ever see. It can already pull up on a chair. I reckon Texas makes big men quick, being a big place. Anyway, if it keeps on like it started, it'll be chewing tobacco and voting time it's eight years old.

And so last Friday here come Flem himself. He was on a wagon with another fellow. The other fellow had one of these two-gallon hats and a ivory-handled pistol and a box of gingersnaps sticking out of his hind pocket, and tied to the tailgate of the wagon was about two dozen of them Texas ponies, hitched to one another with barbed wire. They was colored like parrots and they was quiet as doves, and ere[4] a one of them would kill you quick as a rattlesnake. Nere a one of them had two eyes the same color, and nere a one of them had ever see a bridle, I reckon; and when that Texas man got down offen the wagon and walked up to them to show how gentle they was, one of them cut his vest clean offen him, same as with a razor.

4. Any.

Flem had done already disappeared; he had went on to see his wife, I reckon, and to see if that ere baby had done gone on to the field to help Uncle Billy plow, maybe. It was the Texas man that taken the horses on to Mrs. Littlejohn's lot. He had a little trouble at first, when they come to the gate, because they hadn't never see a fence before, and when he finally got them in and taken a pair of wire cutters and unhitched them and got them into the barn and poured some shell corn into the trough, they durn nigh tore down the barn. I reckon they thought that shell corn was bugs, maybe. So he left them in the lot and he announced that the auction would begin at sunup tomorrow.

That night we was setting on Mrs. Littlejohn's porch. You-all mind the moon was nigh full that night, and we would watch them spotted varmints swirling along the fence and back and forth across the lot same as minnows in a pond. And then now and then they would all kind of huddle up against the barn and rest themselves by biting and kicking one another. We would hear a squeal, and then a set of hoofs would go Bam! against the barn, like a pistol. It sounded just like a fellow with a pistol, in a nest of cattymounts,[5] taking his time.

II

It wasn't ere a man knowed yet if Flem owned them things or not. They just knowed one thing: that they wasn't never going to know for sho if Flem did or not, or if maybe he didn't just get on that wagon at the edge of town, for the ride or not. Even Eck Snopes didn't know, Flem's own cousin. But wasn't nobody surprised at that. We knowed that Flem would skin Eck quick as he would ere a one of us.

They was there by sunup next morning, some of them come twelve and sixteen miles, with seed-money tied up in tobacco sacks in their overalls, standing along the fence, when the Texas man come out of Mrs. Littlejohn's after breakfast and clumb onto the gate post with that ere white pistol butt sticking outen his hind pocket. He taken a new box of gingersnaps outen his pocket and bit the end offen it like a cigar and spit out the paper, and said the auction was open. And still they was coming up in wagons and a horse-and-mule-back and hitching the teams across the road and coming to the fence. Flem wasn't nowhere in sight.

But he couldn't get them started. He begun to work on Eck, because Eck holp him last night to get them into the barn and feed them that shell corn. Eck got out jist in time. He come outen that barn like a chip of the crest on a busted dam of water, and clumb into the wagon just in time.

He was working on Eck when Henry Armstid come up in his wagon. Eck was saying he was skeered to bid on one of them, because he might get it, and the Texas man says, "Them ponies? Them little horses?" He clumb down offen the gate post and went toward the horses. They broke and run, and him following them, kind of chirping to them, with his hand out like he was fixing to catch a fly, until he got three or four of them cornered. Then he jumped into them, and then we couldn't see nothing for a while because of the dust. It was a big cloud of it, and them blare-eyed, spotted things swoaring outen it twenty foot to a jump, in forty directions without counting up.

5. Catamounts, wildcats.

Then the dust settled and there they was, that Texas man and the horse. He had its head twisted clean around like a owl's head. Its legs was braced and it was trembling like a new bride and groaning like a saw mill, and him holding its head wrung clean around on its neck so it was snuffing sky. "Look it over," he says, with his heels dug too and that white pistol sticking outen his pocket and his neck swole up like a spreading adder's until you could just tell what he was saying, cussing the horse and talking to us all at once: "Look him over, the fiddle-headed son of fourteen fathers. Try him, buy him; you will get the best—" Then it was all dust again, and we couldn't see nothing but spotted hide and mane, and that ere Texas man's boot-heels like a couple of walnuts on two strings, and after a while that two-gallon hat come sailing out like a fat old hen crossing a fence.

When the dust settled again, he was just getting outen the far fence corner, brushing himself off. He come and got his hat and brushed it off and come and clumb onto the gate post again. He was breathing hard. He taken the gingersnap box outen his pocket and et one, breathing hard. The hammer-head horse was still running round and round the lot like a merry-go-round at a fair. That was when Henry Armstid come shoving up to the gate in them patched overalls and one of them dangle-armed shirts of hisn. Hadn't nobody noticed him until then. We was all watching the Texas man and the horses. Even Mrs. Littlejohn; she had done come out and built a fire under the washpot in her back yard, and she would stand at the fence a while and then go back into the house and come out again with a armful of wash and stand at the fence again. Well, here come Henry shoving up, and then we see Mrs. Armstid right behind him, in that ere faded wrapper and sunbonnet and them tennis shoes. "Git on back to that wagon," Henry says.

"Henry," she says.

"Here, boys," the Texas man says; "make room for missus to git up and see. Come on, Henry," he says; "here's your chance to buy that saddle-horse missus has been wanting. What about ten dollars, Henry?"

"Henry," Mrs. Armstid says. She put her hand on Henry's arm. Henry knocked her hand down.

"Git on back to that wagon, like I told you," he says.

Mrs. Armstid never moved. She stood behind Henry, with her hands rolled into her dress, not looking at nothing. "He hain't no more despair[6] than to buy one of them things," she says. "And us not five dollars ahead of the porehouse, he hain't no more despair." It was the truth, too. They ain't never made more than a bare living offen that place of theirs, and them with four chaps and the very clothes they wears she earns by weaving by the firelight at night while Henry's asleep.

"Shut your mouth and git on back to that wagon," Henry says. "Do you want I taken a wagon stake to you here in the big road?"

Well, that Texas man taken one look at her. Then he begun on Eck again, like Henry wasn't even there. But Eck was skeered. "I can git me a snapping turtle or a water moccasin for nothing. I ain't going to buy none."

So the Texas man said he would give Eck a horse. "To start the auction, and because you holp me last night. If you'll start the bidding on the next horse," he says, "I'll give you that fiddle-head horse."

6. To spare.

I wish you could have seen them, standing there with their seed-money in their pockets, watching that Texas man give Eck Snopes a live horse, all fixed to call him a fool if he taken it or not. Finally Eck says he'll take it. "Only I just starts the bidding," he says. "I don't have to buy the next one lessen I ain't overtopped." The Texas man said all right, and Eck bid a dollar on the next one, with Henry Armstid standing there with his mouth already open, watching Eck and the Texas man like a mad dog or something. "A dollar," Eck says.

The Texas man looked at Eck. His mouth was already open too, like he had started to say something and what he was going to say had up and died on him. "A dollar?" he says. "One dollar? You mean, *one* dollar, Eck?"

"Durn it," Eck says; "Two dollars, then."

Well, sir, I wish you could a seen that Texas man. He taken out that gingersnap box and held it up and looked into it, careful, like it might have been a diamond ring in it, or a spider. Then he throwed it away and wiped his face with a bandanna. "Well," he says. "Well. Two dollars. Two dollars. Is your pulse all right, Eck?" he says. "Do you have ager-sweats[7] at night, maybe?" he says. "Well," he says, "I got to take it. But are you boys going to stand there and see Eck get two horses at a dollar a head?"

That done it. I be dog if he wasn't nigh as smart as Flem Snopes. He hadn't no more than got the words outen his mouth before here was Henry Armstid, waving his hand. "Three dollars," Henry says. Mrs. Armstid tried to hold him again. He knocked her hand off, shoving up to the gate post.

"Mister," Mrs. Armstid says, "we got chaps in the house and not corn to feed the stock. We got five dollars I earned my chaps a-weaving after dark, and him snoring in the bed. And he hain't no more despair."

"Henry bids three dollars," the Texas man says. "Raise him a dollar, Eck, and the horse is yours."

"Henry," Mrs. Armstid says.

"Raise him, Eck," the Texas man says.

"Four dollars," Eck says.

"Five dollars," Henry says, shaking his fist. He shoved up right under the gate post. Mrs. Armstid was looking at the Texas man too.

"Mister," she says, "if you take that five dollars I earned my chaps a-weaving for one of them things, it'll be a curse onto you and yourn during all the time of man."

But it wasn't no stopping Henry. He had shoved up, waving his first at the Texas man. He opened it; the money was in nickels and quarters, and one dollar bill that looked like a cow's cud. "Five dollars," he says. "And the man that raises it'll have to beat my head off, or I'll beat hisn."

"All right," the Texas man says. "Five dollars is bid. But don't you shake your hand at me."

III

It taken till nigh sundown before the last one was sold. He got them hotted up once and the bidding got up to seven dollars and a quarter, but most of them went around three or four dollars, him setting on the gate post and

---

7. Ague; chills and fever with sweating.

picking the horses out one at a time by mouthword, and Mrs. Littlejohn pumping up and down at the tub and stopping and coming to the fence for a while and going back to the tub again. She had done got done too, and the wash was hung on the line in the back yard, and we could smell supper cooking. Finally they was all sold; he swapped the last two and the wagon for a buckboard.

We was all kind of tired, but Henry Armstid looked more like a mad dog than ever. When he bought, Mrs. Armstid had went back to the wagon, setting in it behind them two rabbit-sized, bone-pore mules, and the wagon itself looking like it would fall all to pieces soon as the mules moved. Henry hadn't even waited to pull it outen the road; it was still in the middle of the road and her setting in it, not looking at nothing, ever since this morning.

Henry was right up against the gate. He went up to the Texas man. "I bought a horse and I paid cash," Henry says. "And yet you expect me to stand around here until they are all sold before I can get my horse. I'm going to take my horse outen that lot."

The Texas man looked at Henry. He talked like he might have been asking for a cup of coffee at the table. "Take your horse," he says.

Then Henry quit looking at the Texas man. He begun to swallow, holding onto the gate. "Ain't you going to help me?" he says.

"It ain't my horse," the Texas man says.

Henry never looked at the Texas man again, he never looked at nobody. "Who'll help me catch my horse?" he says. Never nobody said nothing. "Bring the plowline," Henry says. Mrs. Armstid got outen the wagon and brought the plowline. The Texas man got down offen the post. The woman made to pass him, carrying the rope.

"Don't you go in there, missus," the Texas man says.

Henry opened the gate. He didn't look back. "Come on here," he says.

"Don't you go in there, missus," the Texas man says.

Mrs. Armstid wasn't looking at nobody, neither, with her hands across her middle, holding the rope. "I reckon I better," she says. Her and Henry went into the lot. The horses broke and run. Henry and Mrs. Armstid followed.

"Get him into the corner," Henry says. They got Henry's horse cornered finally, and Henry taken the rope, but Mrs. Armstid let the horse get out. They hemmed it up again, but Mrs. Armstid let it get out again, and Henry turned and hit her with the rope. "Why didn't you head him back?" Henry says. He hit her again. "Why didn't you?" It was about that time I looked around and see Flem Snopes standing there.

It was the Texas man that done something. He moved fast for a big man. He caught the rope before Henry could hit the third time, and Henry whirled and made like he would jump at the Texas man. But he never jumped. The Texas man went and taken Henry's arm and led him outen the lot. Mrs. Armstid come behind them and the Texas man taken some money outen his pocket and he give it into Mrs. Armstid's hand. "Get him into the wagon and take him on home," the Texas man says, like he might have been telling them he enjoyed his supper.

Then here comes Flem. "What's that for, Buck?" Flem says.

"Thinks he bought one of them ponies," the Texas man says. "Get him on away, missus."

But Henry wouldn't go. "Give him back that money," he says. "I bought that horse and I aim to have him if I have to shoot him."

And there was Flem, standing there with his hands in his pockets, chewing, like he had just happened to be passing.

"You take your money and I take my horse," Henry says. "Give it back to him," he says to Mrs. Armstid.

"You don't own no horse of mine," the Texas man says. "Get him on home, missus."

Then Henry seen Flem. "You got something to do with these horses," he says. "I bought one. Here's the money for it." He taken the bill outen Mrs. Armstid's hand. He offered it to Flem. "I bought one. Ask him. Here. Here's the money," he says, giving the bill to Flem.

When Flem taken the money, the Texas man dropped the rope he had snatched outen Henry's hand. He had done sent Eck Snopes's boy up to the store for another box of gingersnaps, and he taken the box of ginger-snaps, and he taken the box outen his pocket and looked into it. It was empty and he dropped it on the ground. "Mr. Snopes will have your money for you tomorrow," he says to Mrs. Armstid. "You can get it from him tomorrow. He don't own no horse. You get him into the wagon and get him on home." Mrs. Armstid went back to the wagon and got in. "Where's that ere buckboard I bought?" the Texas man says. It was after sundown then. And then Mrs. Littlejohn come out on the porch and rung the supper bell.

IV

I come on in and et supper. Mrs. Littlejohn would bring in a pan of bread or something, then she would go out to the porch a minute and come back and tell us. The Texas man had hitched his team to the buckboard he had swapped them last two horses for, and him and Flem had gone, and then she told that the rest of them that never had ropes had went back to the store with I. O. Snopes to get some ropes, and wasn't nobody at the gate but Henry Armstid, and Mrs. Armstid setting in the wagon in the road, and Eck Snopes and that boy of hisn. "I don't care how many of them fool men gets killed by them things," Mrs. Littlejohn says, "but I ain't going to let Eck Snopes take that boy into that lot again." So she went down to the gate, but she come back without the boy or Eck neither.

"It ain't no need to worry about that boy," I says. "He's charmed." He was right behind Eck last night when Eck went to help feed them. The whole drove of them jumped clean over that boy's head and never touched him. It was Eck that touched him. Eck snatched him into the wagon and taken a rope and frailed the tar outen him.

So I had done et and went to my room and was undressing, long as I had a long trip to make next day; I was trying to sell a machine[8] to Mrs. Bundren up past Whiteleaf; when Henry Armstid opened that gate and went in by hisself. They couldn't make him wait for the balance of them to get back with their ropes. Eck Snopes said he tried to make Henry wait, but Henry wouldn't do it. Eck said Henry walked right up to them and that when they broke, they run clean over Henry like a hay-mow breaking down. Eck said he snatched that boy of hisn out of the way just in time and that them things went through that gate like a creek flood and into the wagons and teams hitched side the road, busting wagon tongues and snapping harness like it

---

8. The narrator, V. K. Ratliff, is a traveling salesman who sells sewing machines.

was fishing line, with Mrs. Armstid still setting in their wagon in the middle of it like something carved outen wood. Then they scattered, wild horses and tame mules with pieces of harness and single trees dangling offen them, both ways up and down the road.

"There goes ourn, paw!" Eck says his boy said. "There it goes, into Mrs. Littlejohn's house." Eck says it run right up the steps and into the house like a boarder late for supper. I reckon so. Anyway, I was in my room, in my underclothes, with one sock on and one sock in my hand, leaning out the window when the commotion busted out, when I heard something run into the melodeon[9] in the hall; it sounded like a railroad engine. Then the door to my room come sailing in like when you throw a tin bucket top into the wind and I looked over my shoulder and see something that looked like a fourteen-foot pinwheel a-blaring its eyes at me. It had to blare them fast, because I was already done jumped out the window.

I reckon it was anxious, too. I reckon it hadn't never seen barbed wire or shell corn before, but I know it hadn't never seen underclothes before, or maybe it was a sewing-machine agent it hadn't never seen. Anyway, it swirled and turned to run back up the hall and outen the house, when it met Eck Snopes and that boy just coming in, carrying a rope. It swirled again and run down the hall and out the back door just in time to meet Mrs. Littlejohn. She had just gathered up the clothes she had washed, and she was coming onto the back porch with a armful of washing on one hand and a scrubbing board in the other, when the horse skidded up to her, trying to stop and swirl again. It never taken Mrs. Littlejohn no time a-tall.

"Git outen here, you son," she says. She hit it across the face with the scrubbing board; that ere scrubbing board split as neat as ere a axe could have done it, and when the horse swirled to run back up the hall, she hit it again with what was left of the scrubbing board, not on the head this time. "And stay out," she says.

Eck and that boy was halfway down the hall by this time. I reckon that horse looked like a pinwheel to Eck too. "Git to hell outen here, Ad!" Eck says. Only there wasn't time. Eck dropped flat on his face, but the boy never moved. The boy was about a yard tall maybe, in overhalls just like Eck's; that horse swoared over his head without touching a hair. I saw that, because I was just coming back up the front steps, still carrying that ere sock and still in my underclothes, when the horse come onto the porch again. It taken one look at me and swirled again and run to the end of the porch and jumped the banisters and the lot fence like a hen-hawk and lit in the lot running and went out the gate again and jumped eight or ten upside-down wagons and went on down the road. It was a full moon then. Mrs. Armstid was still setting in the wagon like she had done been carved outen wood and left there and forgot.

That horse. It ain't never missed a lick. It was going about forty miles a hour when it come to the bridge over the creek. It would have had a clear road, but it so happened that Vernon Tull was already using the bridge when it got there. He was coming back from town; he hadn't heard about the auction; him and his wife and three daughters and Mrs. Tull's aunt, all setting in chairs in the wagon bed, and all asleep, including the mules. They waked up when the horse hit the bridge one time, but Tull said the first he

9. A small keyboard organ.

knew was when the mules tried to turn the wagon around in the middle of the bridge and he seen that spotted varmint run right twixt the mules and run up the wagon tongue like a squirrel. He said he just had time to hit it across the face with his whip-stock, because about that time the mules turned the wagon around on that ere one-way bridge and that horse clumb across one of the mules and jumped down onto the bridge again and went on, with Vernon standing up in the wagon and kicking at it.

Tull said the mules turned in the harness and clumb back into the wagon too, with Tull trying to beat them out again, with the reins wrapped around his wrist. After that he says all he seen was over-turned chairs and women-folks' legs and white drawers shining in the moonlight, and his mules and that spotted horse going on up the road like a ghost.

The mules jerked Tull outen the wagon and drug him a spell on the bridge before the reins broke. They thought at first that he was dead, and while they was kneeling around him, picking the bridge splinters outen him, here comes Eck and that boy, still carrying the rope. They was running and breathing a little hard. "Where'd he go?" Eck says.

V

I went back and got my pants and shirt and shoes on just in time to go and help get Henry Armstid outen the trash in the lot. I be dog if he didn't look like he was dead, with his head hanging back and his teeth showing in the moonlight, and a little rim of white under his eyelids. He could still hear them horses, here and there; hadn't none of them got more than four-five miles away yet, not knowing the country, I reckon. So we could hear them and folks yelling now and then: "Whooey. Head him!"

We toted Henry into Mrs. Littlejohn's. She was in the hall; she hadn't put down the armful of clothes. She taken one look at us, and she laid down the busted scrubbing board and taken up the lamp and opened a empty door. "Bring him in here," she says.

We toted him in and laid him on the bed. Mrs. Littlejohn set the lamp on the dresser, still carrying the clothes. "I'll declare, you men," she says. Our shadows was way up the wall, tiptoeing too; we could hear ourselves breathing. "Better get his wife," Mrs. Littlejohn says. She went out, carrying the clothes.

"I reckon we had," Quick says. "Go get her, somebody."

"Whyn't you go?" Winterbottom says.

"Let Ernest git her," Durley says. "He lives neighbors with them."

Ernest went to fetch her. I be dog if Henry didn't look like he was dead. Mrs. Littlejohn come back, with a kettle and some towels. She went to work on Henry, and then Mrs. Armstid and Ernest come in. Mrs. Armstid come to the foot of the bed and stood there, with her hands rolled into her apron, watching what Mrs. Littlejohn was doing, I reckon.

"You men get outen the way," Mrs. Littlejohn says. "Git outside," she says. "See if you can't find something else to play with that will kill some more of you."

"Is he dead?" Winterbottom says.

"It ain't your fault if he ain't," Mrs. Littlejohn says. "Go tell Will Varner to come up here. I reckon a man ain't so different from a mule, come long come short. Except maybe a mule's got more sense."

We went to get Uncle Billy. It was a full moon. We could hear them, now and then, four mile away: "Whooey. Head him." The country was full of them, one on ever wooden bridge in the land, running across it like thunder: "Whooey. There he goes. Head him."

We hadn't got far before Henry begun to scream. I reckon Mrs. Littlejohn's water had brung him to; anyway, he wasn't dead. We went on to Uncle Billy's. The house was dark. We called to him, and after a while the window opened and Uncle Billy put his head out, peart as a peckerwood,[1] listening. "Are they still trying to catch them durn rabbits?" he says.

He come down, with his britches on over his nightshirt, and his suspenders dangling, carrying his horse-doctoring grip. "Yes, sir," he says, cocking his head like a woodpecker; "they're still a-trying."

We could hear Henry before we reached Mrs. Littlejohn's. He was going Ah-Ah-Ah. We stopped in the yard. Uncle Billy went on in. We could hear Henry. We stood in the yard, hearing them on the bridges, this-a-way and that: "Whooey. Whooey."

"Eck Snopes ought to caught hisn," Ernest says.

"Looks like he ought," Winterbottom said.

Henry was going Ah-Ah-Ah steady in the house; then he begun to scream. "Uncle Billy's started," Quick says. We looked into the hall. We could see the light where the door was. Then Mrs. Littlejohn come out.

"Will needs some help," she says. "You, Ernest. You'll do." Ernest went into the house.

"Hear them?" Quick said. "That one was on Four Mile bridge." We could hear them; it sounded like thunder a long way off; it didn't last long: "Whooey."

We could hear Henry: "Ah-Ah-Ah-Ah-Ah."

"They are both started now," Winterbottom says. "Ernest too."

That was early in the night. Which was a good thing, because it taken a long night for folks to chase them things right and for Henry to lay there and holler, being as Uncle Billy never had none of this here chloryfoam to set Henry's leg with. So it was considerate in Flem to get them started early. And what do you reckon Flem's comment was?

That's right. Nothing. Because he wasn't there. Hadn't nobody see him since that Texas man left.

VI

That was Saturday night. I reckon Mrs. Armstid got home about daylight, to see about the chaps. I don't know where they thought her and Henry was. But lucky the oldest one was a gal, about twelve, big enough to take care of the little ones. Which she did for the next two days. Mrs. Armstid would nurse Henry all night and work in the kitchen for hern and Henry's keep, and in the afternoon she would drive home (it was about four miles) to see to the chaps. She would cook up a pot of victuals and leave it on the stove, and the gal would bar the house and keep the little ones quiet. I would hear Mrs. Littlejohn and Mrs. Armstid talking in the kitchen. "How are the chaps making out?" Mrs. Littlejohn says.

"All right," Mrs. Armstid says.

"Don't they git skeered at night?" Mrs. Littlejohn says.

1. Pert as a woodpecker.

"Ina May bars the door when I leave," Mrs. Armstid says. "She's got the axe in bed with her. I reckon she can make out."

I reckon they did. And I reckon Mrs. Armstid was waiting for Flem to come back to town; hadn't nobody seen him until this morning; to get her money the Texas man said Flem was keeping for her. Sho. I reckon she was.

Anyway, I heard Mrs. Armstid and Mrs. Littlejohn talking in the kitchen this morning while I was eating breakfast. Mrs. Littlejohn had just told Mrs. Armstid that Flem was in town. "You can ask him for that five dollars," Mrs. Littlejohn says.

"You reckon he'll give it to me?" Mrs. Armstid says.

Mrs. Littlejohn was washing dishes, washing them like a man, like they was made out of iron. "No," she says. "But asking him won't do no hurt. It might shame him. I don't reckon it will, but it might."

"If he wouldn't give it back, it ain't no use to ask," Mrs. Armstid says.

"Suit yourself," Mrs. Littlejohn says. "It's your money."

I could hear the dishes.

"Do you reckon he might give it back to me?" Mrs. Armstid says. "That Texas man said he would. He said I could get it from Mr. Snopes later."

"Then go and ask him for it," Mrs. Littlejohn says.

I could hear the dishes.

"He won't give it back to me," Mrs. Armstid says.

"All right," Mrs. Littlejohn says. "Don't ask him for it, then."

I could hear the dishes; Mrs. Armstid was helping. "You don't reckon he would, do you?" she says. Mrs. Littlejohn never said nothing. It sounded like she was throwing the dishes at one another. "Maybe I better go and talk to Henry about it," Mrs. Armstid says.

"I would," Mrs. Littlejohn says. I be dog if it didn't sound like she had two plates in her hands, beating them together. "Then Henry can buy another five-dollar horse with it. Maybe he'll buy one next time that will out and out kill him. If I thought that, I'd give you back the money, myself."

"I reckon I better talk to him first," Mrs. Armstid said. Then it sounded like Mrs. Littlejohn taken up all the dishes and throwed them at the cookstove, and I come away.

That was this morning. I had been up to Bundren's and back, and I thought that things would have kind of settled down. So after breakfast, I went up to the store. And there was Flem, setting in the store chair and whittling, like he might not have ever moved since he come to clerk for Jody Varner. I. O. was leaning in the door, in his shirt sleeves and with his hair parted too, same as Flem was before he turned the clerking job over to I. O. It's a funny thing about them Snopes: they all looks alike, yet there ain't ere a two of them that claims brothers. They're always just cousins, like Flem and Eck and Flem and I. O. Eck was there too, squatting against the wall, him and that boy, eating cheese and crackers outen a sack; they told me that Eck hadn't been home a-tall. And that Lon Quick hadn't got back to town, even. He followed his horse clean down to Samson's Bridge, with a wagon and a camp outfit. Eck finally caught one of hisn. It run into a blind lane at Freeman's and Eck and the boy taken and tied their rope across the end of the lane, about three foot high. The horse come to the end of the lane and whirled and run back without ever stopping. Eck says it never seen the rope a-tall. He says it looked just like one of these here Christmas pinwheels. "Didn't it try to run again?" I says.

"No," Eck says, eating a bit of cheese offen his knife blade. "Just kicked some."

"Kicked some?" I says.

"It broke its neck," Eck says.

Well, they was squatting there, about six of them, talking, talking at Flem; never nobody knowed yet if Flem had ere a interest in them horses or not. So finally I come right out and asked him. "Flem's done skun all of us so much," I says, "that we're proud of him. Come on, Flem," I says, "how much did you and that Texas man make offen them horses? You can tell us. Ain't nobody here but Eck that bought one of them; the others ain't got back to town yet, and Eck's your own cousin; he'll be proud to hear, too. How much did you-all make?"

They was all whittling, not looking at Flem, making like they was studying. But you could a heard a pin drop. And I. O. He had been rubbing his back up and down on the door, but he stopped now, watching Flem like a pointing dog. Flem finished cutting the sliver offen his stick. He spit across the porch, into the road. " 'Twarn't none of my horses," he says.

I. O. cackled, like a hen, slapping his legs with both hands. "You boys might just as well quit trying to get ahead of Flem," he said.

Well, about that time I see Mrs. Armstid come outen Mrs. Littlejohn's gate, coming up the road. I never said nothing. I says, "Well, if a man can't take care of himself in a trade, he can't blame the man that trims him."

Flem never said nothing, trimming at the stick. He hadn't seen Mrs. Armstid. "Yes, sir," I says. "A fellow like Henry Armstid ain't got nobody but hisself to blame."

"Course he ain't," I. O. says. He ain't seen her, neither. "Henry Armstid's a born fool. Always is been. If Flem hadn't a got his money, somebody else would."

We looked at Flem. He never moved. Mrs. Armstid come on up the road.

"That's right," I says. "But, come to think of it, Henry never bought no horse." We looked at Flem; you could a heard a match drop. "That Texas man told her to get that five dollars back from Flem next day. I reckon Flem's done already taken that money to Mrs. Littlejohn's and give it to Mrs. Armstid."

We watched Flem. I. O. quit rubbing his back against the door again. After a while Flem raised his head and spit across the porch, into the dust. I. O. cackled, just like a hen. "Ain't he a beating fellow, now?" I. O. says.

Mrs. Armstid was getting closer, so I kept on talking, watching to see if Flem would look up and see her. But he never looked up. I went on talking about Tull, about how he was going to sue Flem, and Flem setting there, whittling his stick, not saying nothing else after he said they wasn't none of his horses.

Then I. O. happened to look around. He seen Mrs. Armstid. "Pssst!" he says. Flem looked up. "Here she comes!" I. O. says. "Go out the back. I'll tell her you done went in to town today."

But Flem never moved. He just set there, whittling, and we watched Mrs. Armstid come up onto the porch, in that ere faded sunbonnet and wrapper and them tennis shoes that made a kind of hissing noise on the porch. She come onto the porch and stopped, her hands rolled into her dress in front, not looking at nothing.

"He said Saturday," she says, "that he wouldn't sell Henry no horse. He said I could get the money from you."

Flem looked up. The knife never stopped. It went on trimming off a sliver same as if he was watching it. "He taken that money off with him when he left," Flem says.

Mrs. Armstid never looked at nothing. We never looked at her, neither, except the boy of Eck's. He had a half-et cracker in his hand, watching her, chewing.

"He said Henry hadn't bought no horse," Mrs. Armstid says. "He said for me to get the money from you today."

"I reckon he forgot about it," Flem said. "He taken that money off with him Saturday." He whittled again. I. O. kept on rubbing his back, slow. He licked his lips. After a while the woman looked up the road, where it went on up the hill, toward the graveyard. She looked up that way for a while, with that boy of Eck's watching her and I. O. rubbing his back slow against the door. Then she turned back toward the steps.

"I reckon it's time to get dinner started," she says.

"How's Henry this morning, Mrs. Armstid?" Winterbottom says.

She looked at Winterbottom; she almost stopped. "He's resting, I thank you kindly," she says.

Flem got up, outen the chair, putting his knife away. He spit across the porch. "Wait a minute, Mrs. Armstid," he says. She stopped again. She didn't look at him. Flem went on into the store, with I. O. done quit rubbing his back now, with his head craned after Flem, and Mrs. Armstid standing there with her hands rolled into her dress, not looking at nothing. A wagon come up the road and passes; it was Freeman, on the way to town. Then Flem come out again, with I. O. still watching him. Flem had one of these little striped sacks of Jody Varner's candy; I bet he still owes Jody that nickel, too. He put the sack into Mrs. Armstid's hand, like he would have put it into a hollow stump. He spit again across the porch. "A little sweetening for the chaps," he says.

"You're right kind," Mrs. Armstid says. She held the sack of candy in her hand, not looking at nothing. Eck's boy was watching the sack, the half-et cracker in his hand; he wasn't chewing now. He watched Mrs. Armstid roll the sack into her apron. "I reckon I better get on back and help with dinner," she says. She turned and went back across the porch. Flem set down in the chair again and opened his knife. He spit across the porch again, past Mrs. Armstid where she hadn't went down the steps yet. Then she went on, in that ere sunbonnet and wrapper all the same color, back down the road toward Mrs. Littlejohn's. You couldn't see her dress move, like a natural woman walking. She looked like a old snag[2] still standing up and moving along on a high water. We watched her turn in at Mrs. Littlejohn's and go outen sight. Flem was whittling. I. O. begun to rub his back on the door. Then he begun to cackle, just like a durn hen.

"You boys might just as well quit trying," I. O. says. "You can't git ahead of Flem. You can't touch him. Ain't he a sight, now?"

I be dog if he ain't. If I had brung a herd of wild cattymounts into town and sold them to my neighbors and kinfolks, they would have lynched me. Yes, sir.

2. Drifting tree.

FREEDOM AND RESPONSIBILITY AT MID-CENTURY

Amid the ruins of World War II, a global war of unprecedented proportions and viciousness, it is not surprising that public attention focused on questions of responsibility, perhaps of revenge, certainly of justice and reparations for the long struggle and millions of innocent deaths. The trials at Nuremberg provided a visible forum for many issues, but other questions raised by individual actions during the war—some heroic, some contemptible—remained alive. The former Nazi official Adolf Eichmann was tried and executed in Israel in 1962, and lawsuits persist today over the restitution of stolen property, including bank accounts and works of art. Small wonder, then, that individual freedom and responsibility—two concepts that define a human being, according to philosopher Jean-Paul Sartre—are at the center of much philosophical and political debate at mid-century.

"Freedom" and "responsibility" are large and abstract ideas: they are part of an ambitious rethinking of human existence, and of the relationship of individual and society, that characterizes mid-century thought. In their breadth, they interrogate fundamental assumptions about human nature and lay claim to universal significance. The existential condition, according to Sartre, is the condition of all humanity; the "essential plurality" of human beings, their inescapable connectedness, is a given for Hannah Arendt; and the power of language to crystallize and to shape thought, described by George Orwell, exists wherever speech is found. Selections in this group demonstrate the importance each writer attributes to intellectual freedom and the urgency of thinking through our actions in the world. For Sartre, trying to avoid intellectual responsibility is the ultimate self-deception, a "bad faith" that diminishes our human presence in the world. For Arendt, remembering the mass murders of Nazi Germany, and for Orwell, examining the thought control of Soviet communism, the great enemy is the totalitarian state, which tries to stamp out even the notion of individual freedom or responsibility in order to serve an all-absorbing purpose. If Arendt is correct that elements of totalitarianism exist in all modern societies, then the corresponding antidote, as defined by all three writers, is the preservation of intellectual freedom and the exercise of that freedom in recognizing our similarity with, and responsibility for, all other human beings around the globe.

GEORGE ORWELL
1903–1950

"Big Brother is watching you"—George Orwell's image of totalitarian thought control—has become part of our modern political vocabulary, along with "doublethink" ("War Is Peace," "Freedom Is Slavery," "Ignorance Is Strength"), "thoughtcrime," and "Thought Police." The power to determine language use is the power to control thought processes, as the writer knew when he described "Newspeak," a fictional language that simplified English to reduce thought-provoking complexities and eliminate challenging ideas. A prolific journalist and observer of contemporary society, Orwell is most widely known for two works: *Nineteen Eighty-Four* (1949), a bleak novel about a future totalitarian state that is always at war so as to ensure governmental control of private life, and *Animal Farm* (1945), a satirical fable that uses barnyard animals to parody dictator Joseph Stalin's assumption of power after the Russian Revolution. The writer's keen ear for the political subversion of language is nowhere more evident than in the victorious pigs' slogan: "All Animals Are Equal, But Some Animals Are More Equal Than Others."

He was born Eric Arthur Blair in Bengal, India, the child of a minor official in the civil service. Educated in England, he attended Eton on a scholarship but chose not to enter Cambridge University and went instead to Burma in 1922 as an assistant district superintendent of police. Orwell's first novel, *Burmese Days* (1934), and two widely read autobiographical pieces, *Shooting an Elephant* and *The Hanging*, are drawn from this period and express his discomfort at the role of police officer in a despotic colonial society. Resigning after five years and still troubled by guilt over his privileged position, he took various menial and poorly paid jobs in France and England before heading for Spain to fight Fascists during the Spanish Civil War. He was severely wounded in 1937 and fled for his life later that year when the radical group with which he was fighting was betrayed to the enemy by rival Communist forces. Orwell's lifelong hatred of Communist as well as Fascist totalitarianism dates particularly to this period, which he describes vividly in his report on the war, *Homage to Catalonia* (1938).

A defiant individualist, champion of the underdog and of individual freedom everywhere, Orwell found himself at odds with established opinion on the Right and Left. He criticized British imperialism and called for the British to withdraw from India; he attacked Stalin and Soviet Communism at a time when Stalin was a military ally and the USSR was widely considered a socialist utopia; he criticized capitalism for its dumbing down of cultural experience and for the systematic exploitation of its workers. Most of all, Orwell—a writer whose essays are celebrated for their lucidity and verve—despised the misuse of language to obscure the truth and to rewrite history for political gain. In *The Politics of the English Language* (1950), he argued that slovenly language "makes it easier for us to have foolish thoughts" and that "the present political chaos is connected with the decay of language." He particularly attacked totalitarianism because it denied the concept of objective truth and manipulated language to impose its own view of reality while suppressing personal and intellectual liberty. Modern writers, Orwell claims, are not energetic enough in recognizing and repelling the danger to their own profession; they are too wrapped up in their own work and too afraid of challenging currently fashionable ideas. *The Prevention of Literature* begins by recalling the bland speeches at a meeting of the P.E.N. Club the previous year, in which political liberty was never mentioned although the occasion was the tercentenary of Milton's *Areopagitica*, a famous defense of freedom of the press. Yet, as Orwell argues in the same essay, both history and literature depend on the possibility of free expression and the objective reporting of facts, if they are to represent the complexity of human experience.

From The Prevention of Literature[1]

* * *

* * * In our age, the idea of intellectual liberty is under attack from two directions. On the one side are its theoretical enemies, the apologists of totalitarianism, and on the other its immediate, practical enemies, monopoly and bureaucracy. Any writer or journalist who wants to retain his integrity finds himself thwarted by the general drift of society rather than by active persecution. The sort of things that are working against him are the concentration of the Press in the hands of a few rich men, the grip of monopoly on radio and the films, the unwillingness of the public to spend money on books, making it necessary for nearly every writer to earn part of his living by hack-

1. Dated November 12, 1945; first published in *Polemic* (January 1946).

work, the encroachment of official bodies like the M.O.I.[2] and the British Council, which help the writer to keep alive abut also waste his time and dictate his opinions, and the continuous war atmosphere of the past ten years, whose distorting effects no one has been able to escape. Everything in our age conspires to turn the writer, and every other kind of artist as well, into a minor official, working on themes handed to [him] from above and never telling what seems to him the whole of the truth. But in struggling against this fate he gets no help from his own side: that is, there is no large body of opinion which will assure him that he is in the right. In the past, at any rate throughout the Protestant centuries,[3] the idea of rebellion and the idea of intellectual integrity were mixed up. A heretic—political, moral, religious, or aesthetic—was one who refused to outrage his own conscience. His outlook was summed up in the words of the Revivalist hymn:

> Dare to be a Daniel,[4]
> Dare to stand alone;
> Dare to have a purpose firm,
> Dare to make it known.

To bring this hymn up to date one would have to add a "Don't" at the beginning of each line. For it is the peculiarity of our age that the rebels against the existing order, at any rate the most numerous and characteristic of them, are also rebelling against the idea of individual integrity. "Daring to stand alone" is ideologically criminal as well as practically dangerous. The independence of the writer and the artist is eaten away by vague economic forces, and at the same time it is undermined by those who should be its defenders. It is with the second process that I am concerned here.

Freedom of speech and of the Press are usually attacked by arguments which are not worth bothering about. Anyone who has experience in lecturing and debating knows them backwards. Here I am not trying to deal with the familiar claim that freedom is an illusion, or with the claim that there is more freedom in totalitarian countries than in democratic ones, but with the much more tenable and dangerous proposition that freedom is undesirable and that intellectual honesty is a form of anti-social selfishness. Although other aspects of the question are usually in the foreground, the controversy over freedom of speech and of the Press is at bottom a controversy over the desirability, or otherwise, of telling lies. What is really at issue is the right to report contemporary events truthfully, or as truthfully as is consistent with the ignorance, bias and self-deception from which every observer necessarily suffers. In saying this I may seem to be saying that straightforward 'reportage' is the only branch of literature that matters: but I will try to show later that at every literary level, and probably in every one of the arts, the same issue arises in more or less subtilised forms. Meanwhile, it is necessary to strip away the irrelevancies in which this controversy is usually wrapped up.

The enemies of intellectual liberty always try to present their case as a

---

2. The British Ministry of Information. In an unpublished preface to his satirical fable *Animal Farm* (1945), Orwell noted that an official from the Ministry of Information had discouraged a publisher from printing the book in 1943 for fear that it might offend the Russians, whose leaders were depicted as rival pigs. 3. The centuries after the Protestant Reformation, usually dated to October 31, 1517, when German theologian Martin Luther (1483–1546) issued his Ninety-five Theses protesting the sale of papal indulgences.   4. According to the Book of Daniel (167–164 B.C.E.), the Jewish prophet Daniel was thrown into a den of lions for continuing to pray despite a royal edict; miraculously, he survived.

plea for discipline versus individualism. The issue truth-versus-untruth is as far as possible kept in the background. Although the point of emphasis may vary, the writer who refuses to sell his opinions is always branded as a mere egoist. He is accused, that is, either of wanting to shut himself up in an ivory tower, or of making an exhibitionist display of his own personality, or of resisting the inevitable current of history in an attempt to cling to unjustified privileges. The Catholic and the Communist are alike in assuming that an opponent cannot be both honest and intelligent. Each of them tacitly claims that 'the truth' has already been revealed, and that the heretic, if he is not simply a fool, is secretly aware of 'the truth' and merely resists it out of selfish motives. In Communist literature the attack on intellectual liberty is usually masked by oratory about "petty-bourgeois individualism", "the illusions of nineteenth-century liberalism", etc., and backed up by words of abuse such as "romantic" and "sentimental", which, since they do not have any agreed meaning, are difficult to answer. In this way the controversy is manoeuvred away from its real issue. One can accept, and most enlightened people would accept, the Communist thesis that pure freedom will only exist in a classless society, and that one is most nearly free when one is working to bring about such a society. But slipped in with this is the quite unfounded claim that the Communist party is itself aiming at the establishment of the classless society, and that in the U.S.S.R. this aim is actually on the way to being realised. If the first claim is allowed to entail the second, there is almost no assault on common sense and common decency that cannot be justified. But meanwhile, the real point has been dodged. Freedom of the intellect means the freedom to report what one has seen, heard, and felt, and not to be obliged to fabricate imaginary facts and feelings. The familiar tirades against "escapism", "individualism", "romanticism" and so forth, are merely a forensic device, the aim of which is to make the perversion of history seem respectable.

* * *

* * * But after all, how is it that books ever come to be written? Above a quite low level, literature is an attempt to influence the views of one's contemporaries by recording experience. And so far as freedom of expression is concerned, there is not much difference between a mere journalist and the most 'unpolitical' imaginative writer. The journalist is unfree, and is conscious of unfreedom, when he is forced to write lies or suppress what seems to him important news: the imaginative writer is unfree when he has to falsify his subjective feelings, which from his point of view are facts. He may distort and caricature reality in order to make his meaning clearer, but he cannot misrepresent the scenery of his own mind: he cannot say with any conviction that he likes what he dislikes, or believes what he disbelieves. If he is forced to do so, the only result is that his creative faculties dry up. Nor can the imaginative writer solve the problem by keeping away from controversial topics. There is no such thing as genuinely non-political literature, and least of all in an age like our own, when fears, hatreds, and loyalties of a directly political kind are near to the surface of everyone's consciousness. Even a single tabu[5] can have an all-round crippling effect upon the mind, because

5. I.e., Taboo, forbidden thought or behavior.

there is always the danger that any thought which is freely followed up may lead to the forbidden thought. It follows that the atmosphere of totalitarianism is deadly to any kind of prose writer, though a poet, at any rate a lyric poet, might possibly find it breathable. And in any totalitarian society that survives for more than a couple of generations, it is probable that prose literature, of the kind that has existed during the past four hundred years, must actually *come to an end.*

Literature has sometimes flourished under despotic regimes, but, as has often been pointed out, the despotisms of the past were not totalitarian. Their repressive apparatus was always inefficient, their ruling classes were usually either corrupt or apathetic or half-liberal in outlook, and the prevailing religious doctrines usually worked against perfectionism and the notion of human infallibility. Even so it is broadly true that prose literature has reached its highest levels in periods of democracy and free speculation. What is new in totalitarianism is that its doctrines are not only unchallengeable but also unstable. They have to be accepted on pain of damnation, but on the other hand they are always liable to be altered at a moment's notice. Consider, for example, the various attitudes, completely incompatible with one another, which an English Communist or 'fellow traveller' has had to adopt towards the war between Britain and Germany. For years before September 1939 he was expected to be in a continuous stew about "the horrors of Nazism" and to twist everything he wrote into a denunciation of Hitler; after September 1939, for twenty months, he had to believe that Germany was more sinned against than sinning, and the word 'Nazi', at least so far as print went, had to drop right out of his vocabulary. Immediately after hearing the 8 o'clock news bulletin on the morning of June 22, 1941, he had to start believing once again that Nazism was the most hideous evil the world had ever seen.[6] Now, it is easy for a politician to make such changes: for a writer the case is somewhat different. If he is to switch his allegiance at exactly the right moment, he must either tell lies about his subjective feelings, or else suppress them altogether. In either case he has destroyed his dynamo. Not only will ideas refuse to come to him, but the very words he uses will seem to stiffen under his touch. Political writing in our time consists almost entirely of prefabricated phrases bolted together like the pieces of a child's Meccano set.[7] It is the unavoidable result of self-censorship. To write in plain, vigorous language one has to think fearlessly, and if one thinks fearlessly one cannot be politically orthodox. It might be otherwise in an 'age of faith', when the prevailing orthodoxy has been long established and is not taken too seriously. In that case it would be possible, or might be possible, for large areas of one's mind to remain unaffected by what one officially believed. Even so, it is worth noticing that prose literature almost disappeared during the only age of faith that Europe has ever enjoyed. Throughout the whole of the Middle Ages there was almost no imaginative prose literature and very little in the way of historical writing: and the intel-

---

6. Orwell points out that international Communist policy, which was supposed to transcend national interests, in fact reflected the foreign policies of Soviet Russia. On August 23, 1939, Nazi Germany and the USSR signed a far-reaching nonaggression pact, and Communist attacks on Nazism ceased; on June 22, 1941, Nazi Germany attacked Soviet Russia without warning, and the criticism resumed.   7. Developed by 1901 by Frank Hornby of Liverpool, England, this construction toy, made of perforated metal pieces, was similar to the later American-made Erector set.

lectual leaders of society expressed their most serious thoughts in a dead language[8] which barely altered during a thousand years.

Totalitarianism, however, does not so much promise an age of faith as an age of schizophrenia. A society becomes totalitarian when its structure becomes flagrantly artificial: that is, when its ruling class has lost its function but succeeds in clinging to power by force or fraud. Such a society, no matter how long it persists, can never afford to become either tolerant or intellectually stable. It can never permit either the truthful recording of facts, or the emotional sincerity, that literary creation demands. * * *

* * * Prose literature as we know it is the product of rationalism, of the Protestant centuries, of the autonomous individual. And the destruction of intellectual liberty cripples the journalist, the sociological writer, the historian, the novelist, the critic, and the poet, in that order. In the future it is possible that a new kind of literature, not involving individual feeling or truthful observation, may arise, but no such thing is at present imaginable. It seems much likelier that if the liberal culture that we have lived in since the Renaissance actually comes to an end, the literary art will perish with it.

Of course, print will continue to be used, and it is interesting to speculate what kinds of reading matter would survive in a rigidly totalitarian society. Newspapers will presumably continue until television technique reaches a higher level, but apart from newspapers it is doubtful even now whether the great mass of people in the industrialised countries feel the need for any kind of literature. They are unwilling, at any rate, to spend anywhere near as much on reading matter as they spend on several other recreations. Probably novels and stories will be completely superseded by film and radio productions. Or perhaps some kind of low-grade sensational fiction will survive, produced by a sort of conveyor-belt process that reduces human initiative to the minimum.

It would probably not be beyond human ingenuity to write books by machinery. But a sort of mechanising process can already be seen at work in the film and radio, in publicity and propaganda, and in the lower reaches of journalism. The Disney films, for instance, are produced by what is essentially a factory process, the work being done partly mechanically and partly by teams of artists who have to subordinate their individual style. Radio features are commonly written by tired hacks to whom the subject and the manner of treatment are dictated beforehand: even so, what they write is merely a kind of raw material to be chopped into shape by producers and censors. So also with the innumerable books and pamphlets commissioned by government departments. Even more machine-like is the production of short stories, serials, and poems for the very cheap magazines. Papers such as the *Writer* abound with advertisements of Literary Schools, all of them offering you readymade plots at a few shillings a time. Some, together with the plot, supply the opening and closing sentences of each chapter. Others furnish you with a sort of algebraical formula by the use of which you can construct your plots for yourself. Others offer packs of cards marked with characters and situations, which have only to be shuffled and dealt in order

---

8. I.e., Latin, the medium of expression for scholars and intellectuals throughout Europe during the Middle Ages.

to produce ingenious stories automatically. It is probably in some such way that the literature of a totalitarian society would be produced, if literature were still felt to be necessary. Imagination—even consciousness, so far as possible—would be eliminated from the process of writing. Books would be planned in their broad lines by bureaucrats, and would pass through so many hands that when finished they would be no more an individual product than a Ford car at the end of the assembly line. It goes without saying that anything so produced would be rubbish; but anything that was not rubbish would endanger the structure of the state. As for the surviving literature of the past, it would have to be suppressed or at least elaborately rewritten.

*   *   *

But however it may be with the physical sciences, or with music, painting, and architecture, it is—as I have tried to show—certain that literature is doomed if liberty of thought perishes. Not only is it doomed in any country which retains a totalitarian structure; but any writer who adopts the totalitarian outlook, who finds excuses for persecution and the falsification of reality, thereby destroys himself as a writer. There is no way out of this. No tirades against "individualism" and "the ivory tower", no pious platitudes to the effect that "true individuality is only attained through identification with the community", can get over the fact that a bought mind is a spoiled mind. Unless spontaneity enters at some point or another, literary creation is impossible, and language itself becomes ossified. At some time in the future, if the human mind becomes something totally different from what it now is, we may learn to separate literary creation from intellectual honesty. At present we know only that the imagination, like certain wild animals, will not breed in captivity. Any writer or journalist who denies that fact—and nearly all the current praise of the Soviet Union contains or implies such a denial— is, in effect, demanding his own destruction.

JEAN-PAUL SARTRE
1905–1980

We are all "condemned to be free," according to the existentialist philosopher Jean-Paul Sartre: *free* because we live in a universe without meaning or laws, and *condemned* because we alone are responsible for all our actions. In *Being and Nothingness: An Essay on Phenomenological Ontology*, the French thinker proposed a theory of human existence that found eager adherents in a postwar society tired of authoritarian structures and ready to experience the pleasures of freedom. The other aspect of freedom—the burden of total responsibility—was less easily grasped. According to one anecdote, a young man, dazzled by the prospect of absolute liberty, asked Sartre, "You mean that everything is permitted?" to which the philosopher responded: "On the contrary: nothing is permitted." Permission is only possible where there are rules, and, for Sartre, there is no transcendent authority to provide rules or guarantee decisions. It is precisely the absence of such authority that defines human freedom and brings about the anguish of having to choose one's way without a verifiable standard of value.

Sartre remains the best-known existentialist thinker (more than his former teacher, Martin Heidegger, for example) because he consistently linked abstract ideas to their pragmatic consequences for individuals and for society. A novelist, dramatist, essayist, and political activist as well as a teacher of philosophy, he produced literary works that illustrated existential principles, such as the novel *Nausea* (1938), the trilogy *The Roads of Freedom* (1945–49), and the play *No Exit* (1944), as well as essays and book-length studies of literature that include *What Is Literature?* (1948), *Baudelaire* (1947) and *The Family Idiot: Gustave Flaubert, 1821–1857* (1971). A believer in "engaged" literature (literature that speaks out on contemporary political issues), he wrote numerous essays espousing the struggle for human freedom that he found in Marxism, Négritude, Algerian independence, Maoism, the antiwar movement, and anticolonialism. Sartre's image of freedom derives from a model of individual consciousness, and after *Being and Nothingness* he worked to extend that model into the realm of political theory. From the early drama *Dirty Hands* (1946) to the *Critique of Dialectical Reason* (1960), he explored the relationship between absolute freedom for the individual and a moral responsibility for collective action. For some, Sartre lost sight of his all-important focus on individual liberty when he supported totalitarian régimes that he believed to be at the forefront of social revolution; hence, in 1952, his much-publicized break with the novelist Albert Camus. The paradigm of an individual consciousness coming to grips with its situation in the world remains, however, the indispensable route for understanding Sartre's work.

Existence precedes essence is a famous statement of that paradigm: our actions are constantly determining the person we *will have been* at the end. There is no pre-existing essential identity—no Wordsworthian child who is born "trailing clouds of glory" and remains essentially the same person from infancy to old age. Instead, the existential self is always in process. Nor is there any explanation of why we are alive to give meaning to existence: instead, we are "abandoned" in the world with nothing more than an awareness of our surroundings and a need to cope with them in order to survive. Constraints always apply—material conditions, actions by other people, disease, war—but we are free to choose the way that we recognize these constraints, and free to choose between various possible actions. The only thing that is not possible is not to choose, for remaining passive is a choice in itself and also shapes our final identity. The existential self is thus a *potential* identity that comes into being through a series of conscious choices; its "essential" or fixed form is achieved only at the moment of death, when no further action is possible. Two terms recur frequently in this argument: the *pour-soi* ("for itself"), an active principle that projects imaginary worlds of "what if?" and chooses to act in one or another way, and the *en-soi* ("in itself"), a retreat into passivity that refuses to contemplate different possibilities or to choose for oneself. Refusing to choose, accepting the deathlike status of the *en-soi*, is often disguised by accepting conventional ideas, dogma, or other people's opinions: it constitutes, in Sartre's eyes, a move toward artificial stability and a refusal of existential freedom, which he names "bad faith." Exercising choice is an anguishing burden, for there are no guarantees that the choice is valid (Sartre's short story *The Wall* describes a wrong decision), but only by choosing does one remain fully alive, authentically human. It is not surprising that Sartre described his existentialism as a humanism or that others have described it as a tragic mode of being.

Being and Nothingness: An Essay on
Phenomenological Ontology[1]

III. Freedom and Responsibility

Although the considerations which are about to follow are of interest primarily to the ethicist, it may nevertheless be worthwhile after these descriptions and arguments to return to the freedom of the for-itself[2] and to try to understand what the fact of this freedom represents for human destiny.

The essential consequence of our earlier remarks is that man being condemned to be free carries the weight of the whole world on his shoulders; he is responsible for the world and for himself as a way of being. We are taking the word "responsibility" in its ordinary sense as "consciousness (of) being the incontestable author of an event or of an object." In this sense the responsibility of the for-itself is overwhelming since he[3] is the one by whom it happens that *there is* a world; since he is also the one who makes himself be, then whatever may be the situation in which he finds himself, the for-itself must wholly assume this situation with its peculiar coefficient of adversity, even though it be insupportable. He must assume the situation with the proud consciousness of being the author of it, for the very worst disadvantages or the worst threats which can endanger my person have meaning only in and through my project; and it is on the ground of the engagement which I am that they appear. It is therefore senseless to think of complaining since nothing foreign has decided what we feel, what we live, or what we are.

Furthermore this absolute responsibility is not resignation; it is simply the logical requirement of the consequences of our freedom. What happens to me happens through me, and I can neither affect myself with it nor revolt against it nor resign myself to it. Moreover everything which happens to me is *mine*. By this we must understand first of all that I am always equal to what happens to me *qua* man, for what happens to a man through other men and through himself can be only human. The most terrible situations of war, the worst tortures do not create a non-human state of things; there is no non-human situation. It is only through fear, flight, and recourse to magical types of conduct that I shall decide on the non-human, but this decision is human, and I shall carry the entire responsibility for it. But in addition the situation is *mine* because it is the image of my free choice of myself, and everything which it presents to me is *mine* in that this represents me and symbolizes me. Is it not I who decide the coefficient of adversity in things and even their unpredictability by deciding myself?

Thus there are no *accidents* in a life; a community event which suddenly bursts forth and involves me in it does not come from the outside. If I am mobilized in a war, this war is *my* war; it is in my image and I deserve it. I deserve it first because I could always get out of it by suicide or by desertion; these ultimate possibles are those which must always be present for us when there is a question of envisaging a situation. For lack of getting out of it, I

---

1. First published in 1943. Translated by Hazel E. Barnes.　2. *Pour-soi* in the French, a nongendered reflexive phrase meaning "for oneself ("himself, herself, itself, myself."　3. I am shifting to the personal pronoun here since Sartre is describing the for-itself in concrete personal terms rather than as a metaphysical entity. Strictly speaking, of course, this is his position throughout, and the French "il" is indifferently "he" or "it" [Barnes's note.]

have *chosen* it. This can be due to inertia, to cowardice in the face of public opinion, or because I prefer certain other values to the value of the refusal to join in the war (the good opinion of my relatives, the honor of my family, etc.). Anyway you look at it, it is a matter of a choice. This choice will be repeated later on again and again without a break until the end of the war. Therefore we must agree with the statement by J. Romains, "In war there are no innocent victims."[4] If therefore I have preferred war to death or to dishonor, everything takes place as if I bore the entire responsibility for this war. Of course others have declared it, and one might be tempted perhaps to consider me as a simple accomplice. But this notion of complicity has only a juridical sense, and it does not hold here. For it depended on me that for me and by me this war should not exist, and I have decided that it does exist. There was no compulsion here, for the compulsion could have got no hold on a freedom. I did not have any excuse; for as we have said repeatedly in this book, the peculiar character of human-reality is that it is without excuse. Therefore it remains for me only to lay claim to this war.

But in addition the war is *mine* because by the sole fact that it arises in a situation which I cause to be and that I can discover it there only by engaging myself for or against it, I can no longer distinguish at present the choice which I make of myself from the choice which I make of the war. To live this war is to choose myself through it and to choose it through my choice of myself. There can be no question of considering it as "four years of vacation" or as a "reprieve," as a "recess," the essential part of my responsibilities being elsewhere in my married, family, or professional life. In this war which I have chosen I choose myself from day to day, and I make it mine by making myself. If it is going to be four empty years, then it is I who bear the responsibility for this.

Finally, as we pointed out earlier, each person is an absolute choice of self from the standpoint of a world of knowledges and of techniques which this choice both assumes and illumines; each person is an absolute upsurge at an absolute date and is perfectly unthinkable at another date. It is therefore a waste of time to ask what I should have been if this war had not broken out, for I have chosen myself as one of the possible meanings of the epoch which imperceptibly led to war. I am not distinct from this same epoch; I could not be transported to another epoch without contradiction. Thus *I am* this war which restricts and limits and makes comprehensible the period which preceded it. In this sense we may define more precisely the responsibility of the for-itself if to the earlier quoted statement, "There are no innocent victims," we add the words, "We have the war we deserve." Thus, totally free, undistinguishable from the period for which I have chosen to be the meaning, as profoundly responsible for the war as if I had myself declared it, unable to live without integrating it in *my* situation, engaging myself in it wholly and stamping it with my seal, I must be without remorse or regrets as I am without excuse; for from the instant of my upsurge into being, I carry the weight of the world by myself alone without anything or any person being able to lighten it.

Yet this responsibility is of a very particular type. Someone will say, "I did

---

4. From *Verdun: The Prelude* (1938), vol. 15 of *Men of Good Will*, 27 vols. (1932–46) by the French novelist Jules Romains (1885–1972).

not ask to be born." This is a naive way of throwing greater emphasis on our facticity.[5] I am responsible for everything, in fact, except for my very responsibility, for I am not the foundation of my being. Therefore everything takes place as if I were compelled to be responsible. I am *abandoned* in the world,[6] not in the sense that I might remain abandoned and passive in a hostile universe like a board floating on the water, but rather in the sense that I find myself suddenly alone and without help, engaged in a world for which I bear the whole responsibility without being able, whatever I do, to tear myself away from this responsibility for an instant. For I am responsible for my very desire of fleeing responsibilities. To make myself passive in the world, to refuse to act upon things and upon Others[7] is still to choose myself, and suicide is one mode among others of being-in-the-world. Yet I find an absolute responsibility for the fact that my facticity (here the fact of my birth) is directly inapprehensible and even inconceivable, for this fact of my birth never appears as a brute fact but always across a projective reconstruction of my for-itself. I am ashamed of being born or I am astonished at it or I rejoice over it, or in attempting to get rid of my life I affirm that I live and I assume this life as bad. Thus in a certain sense I *choose* being born. This choice itself is integrally affected with facticity since I am not able not to choose, but this facticity in turn will appear only in so far as I surpass it toward my ends. Thus facticity is everywhere but inapprehensible; I never encounter anything except my responsibility. That is why I can not ask, "*Why* was I born?" or curse the day of my birth or declare that I did not ask to be born, for these various attitudes toward my birth—*i.e.*, toward the *fact* that I realize a presence in the world—are absolutely nothing else but ways of assuming this birth in full responsibility and of making it *mine*. Here again I encounter only myself and my projects so that finally my abandonment— *i.e.*, my facticity—consists simply in the fact that I am condemned to be wholly responsible for myself. I am the being which *is* in such a way that in its being its being is in question. And this "is" of my being *is* as present and inapprehensible.

Under these conditions since every event in the world can be revealed to me only as an *opportunity* (an opportunity made use of, lacked, neglected, *etc.*), or better yet since everything which happens to us can be considered as a *chance* (*i.e.*, can appear to us only as a way of realizing this being which is in question in our being) and since others as transcendences-transcended[8] are themselves only *opportunities* and *chances*, the responsibility of the for-itself extends to the entire world as a peopled-world. It is precisely thus that the for-itself apprehends itself in anguish;[9] that is, as a being which is neither the foundation of its own being nor of the Other's being nor of the in-itselfs which form the world, but a being which is compelled to decide the meaning of being—within it and everywhere outside of it. The one who realizes in anguish his condition as *being* thrown into a responsibility which extends to

---

5. On our inescapably material existence.   6. Recalling the concept of German existentialist philosopher Martin Heidegger (1889–1976) that we are "thrown" into the world.   7. The recurrent capitalization of Other and Others emphasizes absolute difference: whatever is outside myself is unknowable or Other.   8. The Other, insofar as the Other is another *for-itself* that I perceive as an object.   9. Intense anxiety that comes from realizing that one is condemned at each moment to be free and to make choices that determine one's essence without having any assurance of the validity of one's values. A similar description of *angst* was proposed in *The Concept of Dread* (1844) by Danish philosopher Søren Kierkegaard (1813–1855).

his very abandonment has no longer either remorse or regret or excuse; he is no longer anything but a freedom which perfectly reveals itself and whose being resides in this very revelation. But as we pointed out at the beginning of this work, most of the time we flee anguish in bad faith.[1]

1. The self-deception by which one attempts to deny his or her existential freedom and the personal responsibility that follows.

HANNAH ARENDT
1906–1975

"What is important for me is to understand." Trained as a philosopher, Hannah Arendt turned to political theory when conditions in Nazi Germany forced her to reassess the ability of pure philosophy to address political reality and everyday human affairs. Henceforth, she examined the underlying principles of modern political activity and pursued philosophical explanations for the isolation of the "mob man," for revolution, lying in politics, violence, and what she called "the banality of evil" in twentieth-century society. Most of all, in *The Origins of Totalitarianism* (1951) and related essays, she sought to understand a new form of political organization that threatened to destroy Western culture as a community of laws and human dignity. Totalitarianism, with its dependence on all-pervasive systematic terror for total domination, "exploded our categories of political thought and our standards for moral judgment."

Arendt was raised as a privileged and exceptional child in an old German Jewish family of Königsberg, East Prussia. She was given a secular upbringing and was not particularly aware of her Jewishness until anti-Semitism became public policy under Adolf Hitler. Studying at Marburg and Heidelberg universities with the existentialist philosophers Martin Heidegger and Karl Jaspers, she devoted herself to the abstract analysis of perceptions and consciousness. A turning point came with the burning of the German Reichstag (parliament building) on February 27, 1933, which the government used as an excuse to arrest and persecute Jews. From that moment, Arendt said, she felt responsible: "That is, I was no longer of the opinion that one can simply be a bystander."

Fleeing Germany later that year, she worked in Paris with an organization that helped Jewish teenagers emigrate to Palestine from Germany and Poland. Part of Arendt's disenchantment with abstract philosophy stemmed from seeing former friends and acquaintances deny the reality of what was happening and rationalize their support for Nazi policies. She described it as a time in which "an empty space formed around one" and recalled that she was more shocked by the intellectual dishonesty than by anti-Semitism itself. In response to this abandonment of intellectual responsibility, she decided never again to get involved "in any kind of intellectual business," refusing to be called a philosopher and describing herself as a political scientist or as someone doing work in political theory.

Despite her dislike of the term, Arendt is generally referred to as a political philosopher. She herself called for a new political philosophy that would reformulate the relationship between thought and action. Her studies of totalitarianism are broadly conceptual, going beyond the physical description of centrally organized terrorist states to ask how these states acquire complete control over the thought processes of their citizens. Racism, anti-Semitism, and imperialism, asserts *The Origins of Total-*

itarianism, have combined over preceding centuries to encourage a state-sponsored machinery that isolates individuals from one another and from any concept of common humanity. Arendt's immediate examples are Hitler's Germany and Stalin's Soviet Russia, but she insists that elements of totalitarianism exist in all modern societies and will surface given the proper conditions. Modern society—an atomized mass society—produces loneliness; with loneliness comes a fear of being weak and a corresponding desire for power; violence and terror provide that power. Totalitarian terror is uniquely threatening because it depends not on people or laws, but on a presumed logic of history or a "natural law" that supersedes civic institutions and absorbs human beings into one faceless mass. Under a totalitarian system, the lonely individual of mass society has not only lost a sense of connectedness with other human beings but has been reduced to the status of an interchangeable piece in the larger movement of history.

In *Organized Guilt and Universal Responsibility,* Arendt singles out Gestapo chief Heinrich Himmler as a prominent example of totalitarianism's separation of the public and private spheres of existence. In private life a respectable, middle-class father upholding traditional family values, Himmler filled a different role as a Nazi official, organizing a police state that played on the insecurities of other "family men" to turn their attention inward, dehumanizing external relationships and making mass murder acceptable. He illustrates the aspects of totalitarianism that most appall Arendt: the transformation of human relationships into the impersonal machinery of the state, and the corruption of thought processes by a logic that denies the inherent responsibility of each human being for human beings generally.

PRONOUNCING GLOSSARY

The following list uses common English syllables and stress accents to provide rough equivalents of selected words whose pronunciation may be unfamiliar to the general reader.

Gleichschaltung: *glaikh-shahl'-toong*

Péguy: *pay-gee'*

Buchenwald: *boo'-khen-vahld*

citoyen: *see-twai-yonh'*

From Organized Guilt and Universal Responsibility[1]

III

In trying to understand what were the real motives which caused people to act as cogs in the mass-murder machine, we shall not be aided by speculations about German history and the so-called German national character, of whose potentialities those who knew Germany most intimately had not the slightest idea fifteen years ago. There is more to be learned from the characteristic personality of the man who can boast that he was the organizing spirit of the murder. Heinrich Himmler[2] is not one of those intellectuals stemming from the dim No Man's Land between the Bohemian and the Pimp, whose significance in the composition of the Nazi élite has been

---

1. First published as "German Guilt" in *Jewish Frontier*, no. 12 (1945).   2. Himmler (1900–1945) was chief of the SS (*Schutzstaffel*, or "Protection Echelon"—the elite corps of the Nazi Party) and head of the Gestapo ("Secret State Police") under Hitler. He was responsible for executing Hitler's Final Solution (the extermination of the Jews) and establishing the death camps in Poland. (See *Ladies and Gentlemen, to the Gas Chamber*, pp. 2307–20).

repeatedly stressed of late. He is neither a Bohemian like Goebbels, nor a sex criminal like Streicher, nor a perverted fanatic like Hitler, nor an adventurer like Goering.[3] He is a "bourgeois" with all the outer aspect of respectability, all the habits of a good *paterfamilias*[4] who does not betray his wife and anxiously seeks to secure a decent future for his children; and he has consciously built up his newest terror organization, covering the whole country, on the assumption that most people are not Bohemians nor fanatics, nor adventurers, nor sex maniacs, nor sadists, but first and foremost jobholders, and good family men.

It was Péguy, I believe, who called the family man the "grand aventurier du 20e siècle."[5] He died too soon to learn that he was also the great criminal of the century. We had been so accustomed to admire or gently ridicule the family man's kind concern and earnest concentration on the welfare of his family, his solemn determination to make life easy for his wife and children, that we hardly noticed how the devoted *paterfamilias*, worried about nothing so much as his security, was transformed under the pressure of the chaotic economic conditions of our time into an involuntary adventurer, who for all his industry and care could never be certain what the next day would bring. The docility of this type was already manifest in the very early period of Nazi "Gleichschaltung."[6] It became clear that for the sake of his pension, his life insurance, the security of his wife and children, such a man was ready to sacrifice his beliefs, his honor, and his human dignity. It needed only the Satanic genius of Himmler to discover that after such degradation he was entirely prepared to do literally anything when the ante was raised and the bare existence of his family was threatened. The only condition he put was that he should be fully exempted from responsibility for his acts. Thus that very person, the average German, whom the Nazis notwithstanding years of the most furious propaganda could not induce to kill a Jew on his own account (not even when they made it quite clear that such a murder would go unpunished) now serves the machine of destruction without opposition. In contrast to the earlier units of the SS men and Gestapo, Himmler's over-all organization relies not on fanatics, nor on congenital murderers, nor on sadists; it relies entirely upon the normality of jobholders and family men.

We need not specially mention the sorry reports about Latvians, Lithuanians, or even Jews who have participated in Himmler's murder organization in order to show that it requires no particular national character in order to supply this new type of functionary. They are not even all natural murderers or traitors out of perversity. It is not even certain that they would do the work if it were only their own lives and future that were at stake. They felt (after they no longer needed to fear God, their conscience cleared through

---

3. Hermann Goering (1893–1946) was head of Hitler's armed forces and, with Himmler, set up concentration camps in Germany. Joseph Goebbels (1897–1945) was Hitler's minister of propaganda and established an almost religious cult of the *Führer* ("Leader"). Julius Streicher (1885–1946) was a violent anti-Semite whose newspaper, *Der Stürmer*, incited anti-Jewish sentiments throughout Germany. Adolf Hitler (1889–1945), leader of the National Socialist German Workers' Party (the Nazis), was dictator of Germany from 1933 until his suicide in 1945. A gifted orator and mass psychologist, he gained and retained power by inflaming racial hatred and violently suppressing dissent; his invasion of Czechoslovakia and Poland brought on World War II.   4. "Father of the family" (Latin): the head of the household in ancient Roman law.   5. "The great adventurer of the twentieth century" (French). Péguy: the French poet Charles Péguy (1873–1914).   6. Coordination (German): the political coordination of all activities in society to correspond to Nazi policies. Here, it means "going along" to preserve a job or special status. Eventually, *Gleichschaltung* would transform all social groups into Nazi organizations (youth groups into Hitler Youth, for example).

the bureaucratic organization of their acts) only the responsibility toward their own families. The transformation of the family man from a responsible member of society, interested in all public affairs, to a "bourgeois" concerned only with his private existence and knowing no civic virtue, is an international modern phenomenon. The exigencies of our time—"Bedenkt den Hunger und die grosse Kälte in diesem Tale, das von Jammer schallt" (Brecht)[7]— can at any moment transform him into the mob man and make him the instrument of whatsoever madness and horror. Each time society, through unemployment, frustrates the small man in his normal functioning and normal self-respect, it trains him for that last stage in which he will willingly undertake any function, even that of hangman. A Jew released from Buchenwald[8] once discovered among the SS men who gave him the certificates of release a former schoolmate, whom he did not address but yet stared at. Spontaneously the man stared at remarked: You must understand, I have five years of unemployment behind me. They can do anything they want with me.

It is true that the development of this modern type of man, who is the exact opposite of the "citoyen"[9] and whom for lack of a better name we have called the "bourgeois," enjoyed particularly favorable conditions in Germany. Hardly another country of Occidental culture was so little imbued with the classic virtues of civic behavior. In no other country did private life and private calculations play so great a role. This is a fact which the Germans in time of national emergency disguised with great success, but never altered. Behind the façade of proclaimed and propagandized national virtues, such as "love of the Fatherland," "German courage," "German loyalty," etc., there lurked corresponding real national vices. There is hardly another country where on the average there is so little patriotism as Germany; and behind the chauvinistic claims of loyalty and courage, a fatal tendency to disloyalty and betrayal for opportunistic reasons is hidden.[1]

The mob man, however, the end-result of the "bourgeois," is an international phenomenon; and we would do well not to submit him to too many temptations in the blind faith that only the German mob man is capable of such frightful deeds. What we have called the "bourgeois" is the modern man of the masses, not in his exalted moments of collective excitement, but in the security (today one should say the insecurity) of his own private domain. He has driven the dichotomy of private and public functions, of family and occupation, so far that he can no longer find in his own person any connection between the two. When his occupation forces him to murder people he does not regard himself as a murderer because he has not done it out of inclination but in his professional capacity. Out of sheer passion he would never do harm to a fly.

If we tell a member of this new occupational class which our time has produced that he is being held to account for what he did, he will feel nothing

---

7. "Think of the hunger and the great cold in this valley that rings with lamentations." "Hunger" is substituted for "darkness" in these lines, cited from the end of *The Threepenny Opera* by the German playwright Bertolt Brecht (1898–1956). (See his *The Good Woman of Setzuan*, pp. 2116–69.)   8. One of the biggest concentration camps on German soil, established in 1937.   9. Citizen (French): a title given equally to all French citizens by the French Revolution's *Declaration of the Rights of Man and Citizen* (August 1789); it replaced all other titles and signified social equality. Arendt refers elsewhere to Montesquieu's description (in *The Spirit of Laws*, 1748) of three forms of government—republic, monarchy, tyranny—in which the *citoyen* of the Republic is motivated characteristically by civic virtue (as opposed to fear under tyranny and honor under a monarchy).   1. It should be remembered that Arendt wrote this blanket denunciation shortly after the end of World War II.

except that he has been betrayed. But if in the shock of the catastrophe he really becomes conscious that in fact he was not only a functionary but also a murderer, then his way out will not be that of rebellion, but suicide—just as so many have already chosen the way of suicide in Germany, where it is plain that there has been one wave of self-destruction after another. And that too would be of little use to us.

IV

For many years now we have met Germans who declare that they are ashamed of being Germans. I have often felt tempted to answer that I am ashamed of being human. This elemental shame, which many people of the most various nationalities share with one another today, is what finally is left of our sense of international solidarity; and it has not yet found an adequate political expression. Our fathers' enchantment with humanity was of a sort which not only light-mindedly ignored the national question; what is far worse, it did not even conceive of the terror of the idea of humanity and of the Judeo-Christian faith in the unitary origin of the human race. It was not very pleasant even when we had to bury our false illusions about "the noble savage," having discovered that men were capable of being cannibals. Since then peoples have learned to know one another better and learned more and more about the evil potentialities in men. The result has been that they have recoiled more and more from the idea of humanity and become more susceptible to the doctrine of race, which denies the very possibility of a common humanity. They instinctively felt that the idea of humanity, whether it appears in a religious or humanistic form, implies the obligation of a general responsibility which they do not wish to assume. For the idea of humanity, when purged of all sentimentality, has the very serious consequence that in one form or another men must assume responsibility for all crimes committed by men and that all nations share the onus of evil committed by all others. Shame at being a human being is the purely individual and still non-political expression of this insight.

In political terms, the idea of humanity, excluding no people and assigning a monopoly of guilt to no one, is the only guarantee that one "superior race" after another may not feel obligated to follow the "natural law" of the right of the powerful, and exterminate "inferior races unworthy of survival"; so that at the end of an "imperialistic age" we should find ourselves in a stage which would make the Nazis look like crude precursors of future political methods. To follow a non-imperialistic policy and maintain a non-racist faith becomes daily more difficult because it becomes daily clearer how great a burden mankind is for man.

Perhaps those Jews, to whose forefathers we owe the first conception of the idea of humanity, knew something about that burden when each year they used to say "Our Father and King, we have sinned before you," taking not only the sins of their own community but all human offenses upon themselves. Those who today are ready to follow this road in a modern version do not content themselves with the hypocritical confession "God be thanked, I am not like that," in horror at the undreamed-of potentialities of the German national character. Rather, in fear and trembling, have they finally realized of what man is capable—and this is indeed the precondition of any modern political thinking. Such persons will not serve very well as functionaries of vengeance. This, however, is certain: Upon them and only upon them, who are filled with a genuine fear of the inescapable guilt of the human race, can there be any reliance when it comes to fighting fearlessly, uncompromisingly, everywhere against the incalculable evil that men are capable of bringing about.

BERTOLT BRECHT
1898–1956

Bertolt Brecht is a dominant figure in modern drama not only as the author of half a dozen plays that rank as modern classics, but as the first master of a powerful new concept of theater. He disagreed with the traditional notion, derived from Aristotle's *Poetics,* that drama should draw its spectators into identification with and sympathy for the characters, and he rejected the realist aesthetic of naturalness and psychological credibility. Brecht saw only harm in such uncritical submission to illusions. Like Pirandello, he believed that the modern stage should break with the dramatic conventions of writers such as Ibsen and Chekhov, who depicted action from a distance, as if it were a slice of real life going on behind an invisible "fourth wall." Unlike Pirandello, however, Brecht did not stress the anguish of individuals in society; his focus was the community at large and a recognition of social responsibility. For Brecht, a political activist, the modern audience must not be allowed to indulge in passive emotional identification at a safe distance or in a whirlpool of existential identity crises. His characters are first of all members of society, and his audience must be educated and moved to action. The movement called "epic theater" suited his needs well, and he developed its basic ideas in plays, theoretical writings, and dramatic productions until it became one of the most powerful theatrical styles of the century.

Eugen Berthold Brecht was born in the medieval town of Augsburg, Bavaria, on February 10, 1898. His father was a respected town citizen, director of a paper mill, and a Catholic. His mother, the daughter of a civil servant from the Black Forest, was a Protestant who raised young Berthold in her own faith. (The spelling *Bertolt* was adopted later.) Brecht attended local schools until 1917, when he enrolled in Munich University to study natural science and medicine. He continued his studies while acting as drama critic for an Augsburg newspaper and writing his own plays: *Drums in the Night* (1918) won the Kleist prize in 1922. In 1918 Brecht was mobilized for a year as an orderly in a military hospital, and he pursued medical studies at Munich until 1921.

Moving to Berlin in 1924, Brecht worked briefly with the directors Max Reinhardt and Erwin Piscator but was chiefly interested in his own writing. In this pre-Marxist period he is especially concerned with the plight of the individual "common man," pushed around by social and economic forces beyond his control until he loses both identity and humanity. In *A Man's a Man* (1924–25), the timid dock worker Galy Gay is transformed by fright and persuasion into another person, the ferociously successful soldier Jeriah Jip. When the actual Jip turns up at the end of the play, he is given Gay's former papers and forced to assume Gay's old identity. The play teaches that human personalities can be broken down and reassembled like a machine; the only weapon against such mindless manipulation is awareness, an awareness that enables people to understand and control their destiny.

In 1929 he married Helene Weigel, an actress who worked closely with him and for whom he wrote many leading roles. Together they would direct and make famous the theater group founded for them in 1949 in East Berlin: the Berliner Ensemble.

Most of Brecht's plays are didactic, either openly or by implication. After he became a fervent Marxist in the mid-1920s, he considered it even more his moral and artistic duty to encourage the audience to remedy social ills. *The Threepenny Opera* (1928), a ballad opera written with composer Kurt Weill (1900–1950) and modeled on John Gay's *The Beggar's Opera* (1728), satirizes capitalist society from the point of view of outcasts and romantic thieves. Brecht also wrote a number of "lesson" plays intended to set forth Communist doctrine and to instruct the workers of Germany in the meaning of social revolution. The lesson is particularly harsh in *The Measures Taken* (1930), which describes the necessary execution of a young party member who has broken discipline and helped the local poor, thus postponing the revolution. Such drama, however doctrinally pure, was not likely to win adherents to the cause, and the lesson plays were condemned as unattractive and "intellectualist" by the Communist press in Berlin and Moscow.

Brecht's unorthodoxy, his pacifism, his enthusiasm for Marx, and his desire to create an activist popular theater that would embody a Marxist view of art all put him at odds with the rising power of Hitler's National Socialism. He fled Germany for Denmark in 1933 before the Nazis could include him in their purge of left-wing intellectuals; in 1935 he was deprived of his German citizenship. Brecht was to flee several more times as the Nazi invasions expanded throughout Europe: in 1939 he went to Sweden, in 1940 to Finland, and in 1941 to the United States, where he joined a colony of German expatriates in Santa Monica, California, working for the film industry. This was the period of some of his greatest plays: *The Life of Galileo* (1938–39), which attacks society for suppressing Galileo's discovery that the Earth revolves around the sun but also condemns the scientist for not insisting openly on the truth; *Mother Courage and Her Children* (1939), which describes an avaricious peddler who doggedly pursues the profits to be made from war even though her own three children are victims of it; *The Good Woman of Setzuan* (1938–40), printed here, which shows how an instinctively good and generous person can survive in this world only by putting on a mask of hardness and calculation; and *The Caucasian Chalk Circle* (1944–45), which adapts the legendary choice of Solomon between two mothers who claim the same infant and decides in favor of the servant girl—who cared for the child—over the wealthy mother (the implied comparison is between those who do the work of society and those who merely profit from their possessions). In America, Brecht arranged for the translation of his work into English, and *Galileo*, with Charles Laughton in the title role, was produced in 1947. In the same year, Brecht was questioned by the House Un-American Activities Committee as part of a wide-ranging inquiry into possible Communist activity in the entertainment business. No charges were brought, but he left for Europe the day after being brought before the committee.

After leaving the United States, Brecht worked for a year in Zurich before going to Berlin with his wife, Helene Weigel, to stage *Mother Courage*. The East Berlin government offered the couple positions as directors of their own troupe, the Berliner Ensemble, and Brecht—who had just finished a theoretical work on the theater, *A Little Organon for the Theater* (1949)—turned his attention to the professional role of director. Although the East Berliners subsidized Brecht's work and advertised the artist's presence among them as a tribute to their own political system, they also obliged him to defend some of his plays against charges of political unorthodoxy and indeed to revise them. After 1934, the prevailing Communist Party view had upheld a style called "socialist realism," whose goal was to offer simple messages and to foster identification with revolutionary heroes. Brecht's mind was too keen and questioning, too attracted by irony and paradox, for him to provide the simplistic drama desired or to have a comfortable relation with authority, either of the Right or of the Left. After settling in East Berlin, he wrote no major new plays but only minor propaganda pieces and adaptations of classical works such as Molière's *Don Juan* and Shakespeare's *Coriolanus*. As an additional measure of protection, he took out Austrian citizenship through his wife's nationality. Brecht died in Berlin on August 14, 1956. Presumably, he would have taken ironic pleasure in the fact that, on February 10, 1998, the one hundredth anniversary of his birth was celebrated throughout Germany and included a presidential speech at the Berlin Academy of Arts.

The "epic theater" for which Brecht is known derives its name from a famous essay, *On Epic and Dramatic Poetry*, by Goethe and Schiller, who in 1797 described *dramatic* poetry as pulling the audience into emotional identification, in contrast to *epic* poetry, which by being distanced in the time, place, and nature of the action could be absorbed in calm contemplation. The idea of an epic theater is a paradox: how can a play engage an audience that is still held at a distance? Brecht's solution was to employ many "alienation effects" that were genuinely dramatic but that prevented total identification with the characters and forced spectators to think critically about what was taking place. In this, he echoed the work of the revolutionary Soviet director Vsevolod Meyerhold, whose antirealistic use of masks, pantomime, posters and film projections, song interludes, and direct address to the audience was well known to German audiences in the 1920s. These alienation effects have since become standard production techniques in the modern theater. In spite of Brecht's intentions and frequent revisions, however, the characters and situations of his plays remain emotionally engrossing, especially in his best-known works, such as *The Good Woman of Setzuan*.

Brecht's concept of an epic theater touches on all aspects of the form: dramatic structure, stage setting, music, and the actor's performance. The structure is to be open, episodic, and broken by dramatic or musical interludes. It is a "chronicle" that recounts events in an epic or distanced perspective. Episodes may also be performed independently as self-contained dramatic parables, instead of being organically tied to a centrally developing plot. Skits appear between scenes: in *A Man's a Man*, there is a fantastic interlude in which an elephant is accused of having murdered its mother. Songs break dramatic action and yet crystallize important themes: in *The Good Woman of Setzuan*, "The Song of Defenselessness" presents an outraged Shen Te masking herself and turning into Shui Ta; Yang Sun's lording it over his coworkers is satirized in "The Song of the Eighth Elephant." Sometimes a narrator comments on the action (as in *The Threepenny Opera* and *A Man's a Man*). The alienation effects are also heightened by setting most of the plays in faraway lands (China in *The Good Woman of Setzuan*, India in *A Man's a Man*, England in *The Threepenny Opera*, the Soviet Union in *The Caucasian Chalk Circle*, Chicago in *Saint Joan of the Stockyards* and *The Resistible Rise of Arturo Ui*) or distant times (the seventeenth century in *Mother Courage*, Renaissance Italy in *Galileo*, or an imagined ghostly afterlife in *The Trial of Lucullus*).

Stagecraft and performance further support Brecht's concept of a critical, intellectualized theater. Events on stage may be announced beforehand by signs or accompanied by projected images during the action itself. Place-names printed on signs are suspended over the actors, and footlights and stage machinery are openly displayed. Masks are used for wicked people (for example, the Shui Ta personality in *The Good Woman of Setzuan*), or soldiers' faces are chalked white to suggest a stylized fear. Songs that interrupt the dramatic action are addressed directly to the audience, sometimes heralded by a sign that Brecht called a "musical emblem." In addition, Brecht described a special kind of acting: actors should "demonstrate" their parts instead of being submerged in them. At rehearsals, Brecht often asked actors to speak their parts in the third person instead of the first. Such constant artificiality injected into all aspects of the performance makes it difficult for the audience to identify completely and unself-consciously with the characters on stage.

Audiences may react emotionally to Brecht's plays and characters, but their reactions are never simple. Brecht's characters are complex and inhabit complex situations. Galileo is both a dedicated scientist who sacrifices his reputation for honesty so as to complete his work, and a weak sensualist who fails to realize how his recantation will affect others' pursuit of scientific knowledge. In *The Good Woman of Setzuan,* the overgenerous Shen Te can survive only by periodically adopting the mask of a harshly practical "cousin," Shui Ta. Mother Courage is both a tragic mother figure and a small-time profiteer who loses her children as she battens on war. Brecht's work teems with such paradoxes at all levels. He is a cynic who deflates religious zeal, militant patriotism, and heroic example as delusions that lead the masses on to futile sacrifice; but he is also a preacher who makes prominent use of traditional biblical language and imagery, and themes of individual sacrifice.

The Good Woman of Setzuan was written between 1938 and 1940, with the collaboration of Margarete Steffin and Ruth Berlau, and with music by Paul Dessau. Painfully drafted while Brecht, his family, Steffin, and Berlau sought refuge in Scandinavia from the Nazis' conquest of Europe, the play is stamped with bitter disillusionment at a world in which it is impossible to be good and survive. The "good woman," Shen Te, is forced to disguise herself as her male "cousin" and alter ego, the cruel Shui Ta, to save herself from a swarm of parasites and opportunists who will not leave her a roof over her head. Appearing alternately as the ruthless Shui Ta and the generous Shen Te, she embodies different ways of being, encounters different responses from the people around her, is gradually contaminated, and recognizes despairingly that she will always need to call on her wicked cousin to survive. The play's setting in China was probably suggested by a 1935 visit to Moscow, where Brecht was impressed by the highly stylized performances of the Chinese actor Mei Lan-fang, one of whose traditional roles was that of the woman warrior who must disguise herself as a man. Brecht had already written a short play and a story that described the way women were subordinated and exploited in traditional patriarchal society, a theme that returns strongly in *The Good Woman of Setzuan.* The opposition of men and women is not absolute, however, for the play contains both good and bad male and female characters. Indeed, the Woman of the English title may be misleading, even if Shen Te represents goodness, for the German title's *Mensch* means literally "person" or "human being" and embraces both genders. For Brecht, the problem of good and evil, and the need to reform a corrupt world, confronts both women and men. As the Epilogue tells the audience: "*You* write the happy ending to the play!"

Shen Te's story has a larger frame: the state of the universe or, more mundanely, the question of whether the world is so corrupt that affairs cannot be allowed to continue. Her situation arises from a good deed whose counterpart recurs in various world mythologies and also in the Bible: hospitality offered to disguised divine messengers, who reward the giver accordingly. Three Chinese gods visiting Earth in search of good people give Shen Te, a penniless prostitute, a thousand silver dollars in recompense for being the only person in Setzuan to give them lodging. Brecht borrows (as so often) from the Bible: specifically, from the Old Testament story of Sodom and Gomorrah, in which God sends angels down to find ten good people in the debauched city of Sodom so that it may be saved from destruction. Yet these modern gods are somewhat comic and certainly ineffectual. Wearing old-fashioned clothes and dusty shoes, they have been delegated as the result of a bureaucratic Resolution on high (whose terms they debate); they ignore inconvenient questions and merely repeat the conventional, inapplicable regulations; they are terrified of complications that would disturb the status quo and—in an echo of Nazi slogans about proper order—they persuade themselves at the end that "everything is in order" and leave on a pink cloud despite Shen Te's despairing cries. These caricatured godlets represent the bureaucratic state more than anything else. Their refusal to be involved only reinforces Brecht's underlying thesis that "good" and "evil" are not divine but rather social issues and that the way to reform a corrupt world is for people to unite in common action focused on the common good.

The current translation, by Eric Bentley, Brecht's early translator and collaborator, is a performance-oriented version of the original text of 1940, undertaken with Brecht's approval.

PRONOUNCING GLOSSARY

The following list uses common English syllables and stress accents to provide rough equivalents of selected words whose pronunciation may be unfamiliar to the general reader.

Lin To: *lin taw*   Shu Fu: *shoo foo*

Mi Tzu: *mee'-dz*   Shui Ta: *shway tah*

Setzuan: *sets-wan'*   Yang Sun: *yahng sun*

Shen Te: *shun-teu*   Wong: *wahng*

The Good Woman of Setzuan[1]

CHARACTERS

WONG, *a water seller*
THREE GODS
SHEN TE, *a prostitute, later a shopkeeper*
MRS. SHIN, *former owner of Shen Te's shop*
A *family of eight* (HUSBAND, WIFE, BROTHER, SISTER-IN-LAW, GRANDFATHER, NEPHEW, NIECE, BOY)
An UNEMPLOYED MAN
A CARPENTER

MRS. MI TZU, *Shen Te's landlady*
Mr. SHUI TA
YANG SUN, *an unemployed pilot, later a factory manager*
An OLD WHORE
A POLICEMAN
An OLD MAN
An OLD WOMAN, *his wife*
Mr. SHU FU, *a barber*
MRS. YANG, *mother of Yang Sun*
GENTLEMEN, VOICES, PRIEST, WAITER, *children (three), etc.*

Prologue

At the gates of the half-Westernized city of Setzuan. Evening. WONG *the water seller*[2] *introduces himself to the audience.*

WONG I sell water here in the city of Setzuan. It isn't easy. When water is scarce, I have long distances to go in search of it, and when it is plentiful, I have no income. But in our part of the world there is nothing unusual about poverty. Many people think only the gods can save the situation. And I hear from a cattle merchant—who travels a lot—that some of the highest gods are on their way here at this very moment. Informed sources have it that heaven is quite disturbed at all the complaining.[3] I've been coming out here to the city gates for three days now to bid these gods welcome. I want to be the first to greet them. What about those fellows over there? No, no, they *work*. And that one there has ink on his fingers,

---

1. Translated by Eric Bentley. Setzuan is a province in China; the play's setting is both the capital of Setzuan and, according to a later statement in the play, a generalized location: "wherever man is exploited by man." 2. Water peddlers were common in ancient China. 3. Heaven, in Chinese philosophy, was identical with absolute and transcendental order.

he's no god, he must be a clerk from the cement factory. *Those* two are another story. They look as though they'd like to beat you. But gods don't need to beat you, do they? [THREE GODS *appear.*] What about those three? Old-fashioned clothes—dust on their feet—they *must* be gods! [*He throws himself at their feet.*] Do with me what you will, illustrious ones!

FIRST GOD [*With an ear trumpet.*] Ah! [*He is pleased.*] So we were expected?

WONG [*Giving them water.*] Oh, yes. And I *knew* you'd come.

FIRST GOD We need somewhere to stay the night. You know of a place?

WONG The whole town is at your service, illustrious ones! What sort of a place would you like?

[*The* GODS *eye each other.*]

FIRST GOD Just try the first house you come to, my son.

WONG That would be Mr. Fo's place.

FIRST GOD Mr. Fo.

WONG One moment! [*He knocks at the first house.*]

VOICE FROM MR. FO'S. No!

[WONG *returns a little nervously.*]

WONG It's too bad. Mr. Fo isn't in. And his servants don't dare do a thing without his consent. He'll have a fit when he finds out who they turned away, won't he?

FIRST GOD [*Smiling.*] He will, won't he?

WONG One moment! The next house is Mr. Cheng's. Won't he be thrilled!

FIRST GOD Mr. Cheng

[WONG *knocks.*]

VOICE FROM MR. CHENG'S Keep your gods. We have our own troubles!

WONG [*Back with the* GODS.] Mr. Cheng is very sorry, but he has a house-ful of relations. I think some of them are a bad lot, and naturally, he wouldn't like you to see them.

THIRD GOD Are we so terrible?

WONG Well, only with bad people, of course. Everyone knows the province of Kwan is always having floods.

SECOND GOD Really? How's that?

WONG Why, because they're so irreligious.

SECOND GOD Rubbish. It's because they neglected the dam.

FIRST GOD [*To* SECOND.] Sh! [*To* WONG.] You're still in hopes, aren't you, my son?

WONG Certainly. All Setzuan is competing for the honor! What happened up to now is pure coincidence. I'll be back. [*He walks away, but then stands undecided.*]

SECOND GOD What did I tell you?

THIRD GOD It *could* be pure coincidence.

SECOND GOD The same coincidence in Shun, Kwan, and Setzuan? People just aren't religious any more, let's face the fact. Our mission has failed!

FIRST GOD Oh come, we might run into a good person any minute.

THIRD GOD How did the resolution read? [*Unrolling a scroll and reading from it.*] "The word can stay as it is if enough people are found [*At the word "found" he unrolls it a little more*] living lives worthy of human beings." Good people, that is. Well, what about this water seller himself? *He's* good, or I'm very much mistaken.

SECOND GOD You're very much mistaken. When he gave us a drink, I had the impression there was something odd about the cup. Well, look! [*He shows the cup to the* FIRST GOD.]

FIRST GOD A false bottom!

SECOND GOD The man is a swindler.

FIRST GOD Very well, count *him* out. That's one man among millions. And as a matter of fact, we only need one on *our* side. These atheists are saying, "The world must be changed because no one can *be* good and *stay* good." No one, eh? I say: let us find one—just one—and we have those fellows where we want them!

THIRD GOD [*To* WONG.] Water seller, is it so hard to find a place to stay?

WONG Nothing could be easier. It's just me. I don't go about it right.

THIRD GOD Really?

[*He returns to the others. A* GENTLEMAN *passes by.*]

WONG Oh dear, they're catching on. [*He accosts the* GENTLEMAN.] Excuse the intrusion, dear sir, but three gods have just turned up. Three of the very highest. They need a place for the night. Seize this rare opportunity—to have real gods as your guests!

GENTLEMAN [*laughing*]. A new way of finding free rooms for a gang of crooks. [*Exit* GENTLEMAN.]

WONG [*shouting at him.*] Godless rascal! Have you no religion, gentlemen of Setzuan? [*Pause*]. Patience, illustrious ones! [*Pause.*] There's only one person left. Shen Te, the prostitute. She *can't* say no. [*Calls up to a window.*] Shen Te!

[SHEN TE *opens the shutters and looks out.*]

WONG Shen Te, it's Wong. *They're* here, and nobody wants them. Will you take them?

SHEN TE Oh, no, Wong, I'm expecting a gentleman.

WONG Can't you forget about him for tonight?

SHEN TE The rent has to be paid by tomorrow or I'll be out on the street.

WONG This is no time for calculation, Shen Te.

SHEN TE Stomachs rumble even on the Emperor's birthday, Wong.

WONG Setzuan is one big dung hill!

SHEN TE Oh, very well! I'll hide till my gentleman has come and gone. Then I'll take them. [*She disappears.*]

WONG They mustn't see her gentleman or they'll know what she is.

FIRST GOD [*Who hasn't heard any of this.*] I think it's hopeless.

[*They approach* WONG.]

WONG [*Jumping, as he finds them behind him.*] A room has been found, illustrious ones! [*He wipes sweat off his brow.*]

SECOND GOD Oh, good.

THIRD GOD Let's see it.

WONG [*Nervously.*] Just a minute. It has to be tidied up a bit.

THIRD GOD Then we'll sit down here and wait.

WONG [*Still more nervous.*] No, no! [*Holding himself back.*] Too much traffic, you know.

THIRD GOD [*With a smile.*] Of course, if you *want* us to move.

[*They retire a little. They sit on a doorstep.* WONG *sits on the ground.*]

WONG [*After a deep breath.*] You'll be staying with a single girl—the finest human being in Setzuan!

THIRD GOD That's nice.

WONG [*To the audience.*]   They gave me such a look when I picked up my cup just now.

THIRD GOD   You're worn out, Wong.

WONG   A little, maybe.

FIRST GOD   Do people here have a hard time of it?

WONG   The good ones do.

FIRST GOD   What about yourself!

WONG   You mean I'm not good. That's true. And I don't have an easy time either!

[*During this dialogue, a* GENTLEMAN *has turned up in front of Shen Te's House, and has whistled several times. Each time* WONG *has given a start.*]

THIRD GOD [*To* WONG, *softly.*]   Psst! I think he's gone now.

WONG [*Confused and surprised.*]   Ye-e-es.

[*The* GENTLEMAN *has left now, and* SHEN TE *has come down to the street.*]

SHEN TE [*softly.*]   Wong!

[*Getting no answer, she goes off down the street.* WONG *arrives just too late, forgetting his carrying pole.*]

WONG [*Softly.*]   Shen Te! Shen Te! [*To himself.*]   So she's gone off to earn the rent. Oh dear, I can't go to the gods *again* with no room to offer them. Having failed in the service of the gods, I shall run to my den in the sewer pipe down by the river and hide from their sight!

[*He rushes off.* SHEN TE *returns, looking for him, but finding the* GODS. *She stops in confusion.*]

SHEN TE   You are the illustrious ones? My name is Shen Te. It would please me very much if my simple room could be of use to you.

THIRD GOD   Where is the water seller, Miss . . . Shen Te?

SHEN TE   I missed him, somehow.

FIRST GOD   Oh, he probably thought you weren't coming, and was afraid of telling us.

THIRD GOD [*Picking up the carrying pole.*]   We'll leave this with you. He'll be needing it.

[*Led by* SHEN TE, *they go into the house. It grows dark, then light. Dawn. Again escorted by* SHEN TE, *who leads them through the half-light with a little lamp, the* GODS *take their leave.*]

FIRST GOD   Thank you, thank you, dear Shen Te, for your elegant hospitality! We shall not forget! And give our thanks to the water seller—he showed us a good human being.

SHEN TE   Oh, *I'm* not good. Let me tell you something: when Wong asked me to put you up, I hesitated.

FIRST GOD   It's all right to hesitate if you then go ahead! And in giving us that room you did much more than you knew. You proved that good people still exist, a point that has been disputed of late—even in heaven. Farewell!

SECOND GOD   Farewell!

THIRD GOD   Farewell!

SHEN TE   Stop, illustrious ones! I'm not sure you're right. I'd like to be good, it's true, but there's the rent to pay. And that's not all: I sell myself for a living. Even so I can't make ends meet, there's too much competition. I'd like to honor my father and mother and speak nothing but the truth and not covet my neighbor's house. I should love to stay with one man. But how? How is it done? Even breaking a few of your commandments,[4] I can hardly manage.

FIRST GOD [*Clearing his throat.*]   These thoughts are but, um, the misgivings of an unusually good woman!

THIRD GOD   Good-bye, Shen Te! Give our regards to the water seller!

SECOND GOD   And above all: be good! Farewell!

FIRST GOD   Farewell!

THIRD GOD   Farewell!

[*They start to wave good-bye.*]

SHEN TE   But everything is so expensive, I don't feel sure I can do it!

SECOND GOD   That's not in our sphere. We never meddle with economics.

THIRD GOD   One moment. [*They stop.*] Isn't it true she might do better if she had more money?

SECOND GOD   Come, come! How could we ever account for it Up Above?

FIRST GOD   Oh, there are ways. [*They put their heads together and confer in dumb show. To* SHEN TE, *with embarrassment.*] As you say you can't pay your rent, well, um, we're not paupers, so of course we *insist* on paying for our room. [*Awkwardly thrusting money into her hands.*] There! [*Quickly.*] But don't tell anyone! The incident is open to misinterpretation.

SECOND GOD   It certainly is!

FIRST GOD [*Defensively.*]   But there's no law against it! It was never decreed that a god mustn't pay hotel bills!

[*The* GODS *leave.*]

1

A small tobacco shop. The shop is not as yet completely furnished and hasn't started doing business.

SHEN TE [*To the audience.*]   It's three days now since the gods left. When they said they wanted to pay for the room, I looked down at my hand, and there was more than a thousand silver dollars![5] I bought a tobacco shop with the money, and moved in yesterday. I don't own the building, of course, but I can pay the rent, and I hope to do a lot of good here. Beginning with Mrs. Shin, who's just coming across the square with her pot. She had the shop before me, and yesterday she dropped in to ask for rice for her children. [*Enter* MRS. SHIN. *Both women bow.*] How do you do, Mrs. Shin.

MRS. SHIN   How do you do, Miss Shen Te. You like your new home?

SHEN TE   Indeed, yes. Did your children have a good night?

MRS. SHIN   In that hovel? The youngest is coughing already.

SHEN TE   Oh, dear!

MRS. SHIN   You're going to learn a thing or two in these slums.

SHEN TE   Slums? That's not what you said when you sold me the shop!

MRS. SHIN   Now don't start nagging! Robbing me and my innocent children of their home and then calling it a slum! That's the limit!

4. An allusion to the Decalogue of the Old Testament and specifically to Commandments 4, 6, 8, 9, and 10 (Exodus 20).   5. Either official Chinese silver dollars (yuan) or coins from one of the foreign currencies in circulation.

[*She weeps.*]

SHEN TE [*Tactfully.*] I'll get your rice.

MRS. SHIN And a little cash while you're at it.

SHEN TE I'm afraid I haven't sold anything yet.

MRS. SHIN [*Screeching.*] I've got to have it. Strip the clothes from my back
and then cut my throat, will you? I know what I'll do: I'll dump my
children on your doorstep! [*She snatches the pot out of* SHEN TE'*s hands.*]

SHEN TE Please don't be angry. You'll spill the rice.

     [*Enter an elderly* HUSBAND *and* WIFE *with their shabbily dressed*
     NEPHEW.]

WIFE Shen Te, dear! You've come into money, they tell me. And we haven't
a roof over our heads! A tobacco shop. We had one too. But it's gone.
Could we spend the night here, do you think?

NEPHEW [*Appraising the shop.*] Not bad!

WIFE He's our nephew. We're inseparable!

MRS. SHIN And who are these . . . ladies and gentlemen?

SHEN TE They put me up when I first came in from the country. [*To the
audience.*] Of course, when my small purse was empty, they put me out
on the street, and they may be afraid I'll do the same to them [*To the
newcomers, kindly.*] Come in, and welcome, though I've only one little
room for you—it's behind the shop.

HUSBAND That'll do. Don't worry.

WIFE [*Bringing* SHEN TE *some tea.*] We'll stay over here, so we won't be in
your way. Did you make it a tobacco shop in memory of your first real
home? We can certainly give you a hint or two! That's one reason we
came.

MRS SHIN [*To* SHEN TE.] Very nice! As long as you have a few customers
too!

HUSBAND Sh! A customer!

     [*Enter an* UNEMPLOYED MAN, *in rags.*]

UNEMPLOYED MAN Excuse me. I'm unemployed.

     [MRS. SHIN *laughs.*]

SHEN TE Can I help you?

UNEMPLOYED MAN Have you any damaged cigarettes? I thought there
might be some damage when you're unpacking.

WIFE What nerve, begging for tobacco! [*Rhetorically.*] Why don't they ask
for bread?

UNEMPLOYED MAN Bread is expensive. One cigarette butt and I'll be a new
man.

SHEN TE [*Giving him cigarettes.*] That's very important—to be a new man.
You'll be my first customer and bring me luck.

     [*The* UNEMPLOYED MAN *quickly lights a cigarette, inhales, and goes off,
coughing.*]

WIFE Was that right, Shen Te, dear?

MRS. SHIN If this is the opening of a shop, you can hold the closing at the
end of the week.

HUSBAND I bet he had money on him.

SHEN TE Oh, no, he said he hadn't!

NEPHEW How d'you know he wasn't lying?

SHEN TE [*Angrily.*] How do you know he was?

WIFE [*Wagging her head.*]   You're too good, Shen Te, dear. If you're going to keep this shop, you'll have to learn to say no.

HUSBAND   Tell them the place isn't yours to dispose of. Belongs to . . . some relative who insists on all accounts being strictly in order . . .

MRS. SHIN   That's right! What do you think you are—a philanthropist?

SHEN TE [*Laughing.*]   Very well, suppose I ask you for my rice back, Mrs. Shin?

WIFE [*Combatively, at* MRS. SHIN.]   So that's *her* rice?

[*Enter the* CARPENTER, *a small man.*]

MRS. SHIN [*Who, at the sight of him, starts to hurry away.*]   See you tomorrow, Miss Shen Te! [*Exit* MRS. SHIN.]

CARPENTER   Mrs. Shin, it's you I want!

WIFE [*To* SHEN TE.]   Has she some claim on you?

SHEN TE   She hungry. That's a claim.

CARPENTER   Are you the new tenant? And filling up the shelves already? Well, they're not yours till they're paid for, ma'am. I'm the carpenter, so I should know.

SHEN TE   I took the shop "furnishings included."

CARPENTER   You're in league with that Mrs. Shin, of course. All right. I demand my hundred silver dollars.

SHEN TE   I'm afraid I haven't got a hundred silver dollars.

CARPENTER   Then you'll find it. Or I'll have you arrested.

WIFE [*Whispering to* SHEN TE.]   That relative: make it a cousin.

SHEN TE   Can't it wait till next month?

CARPENTER   No!

SHEN TE   Be a little patient, Mr. Carpenter, I can't settle all claims at once.

CARPENTER   Who's patient with me? [*He grabs a shelf from the wall.*] Pay up—or I take the shelves back!

WIFE   Shen Te! Dear! Why don't you let your . . . cousin settle this affair? [*To* CARPENTER.] Put your claim in writing. Shen Te's cousin will see you get paid.

CARPENTER [*Derisively.*]   Cousin, eh?

HUSBAND   Cousin, yes.

CARPENTER   I know these cousins!

NEPHEW   Don't be silly. He's a personal friend of mine.

HUSBAND   What a man! Sharp as a razor!

CARPENTER   All right. I'll put my claim in writing. [*Puts shelf on floor, sits on it, writes out bill.*]

WIFE [*To* SHEN TE.]   He'd tear the dress off your back to get his shelves. Never recognize a claim! That's my motto.

SHEN TE   He's done a job, and wants something in return. It's shameful that I can't give it to him. What will the gods say?

HUSBAND   You did your bit when you took *us* in.

[*Enter the* BROTHER, *limping, and the* SISTER-IN-LAW, *pregnant.*]

BROTHER [*To* HUSBAND *and* WIFE.]   So this is where you're hiding out! There's family feeling for you! Leaving us on the corner!

WIFE [*Embarrassed, to* SHEN TE.]   It's my brother and his wife. [*To them.*] Now stop grumbling, and sit quietly in that corner. [*To* SHEN TE.] It can't be helped. She's in her fifth month.

SHEN TE   Oh yes. Welcome!

WIFE [*To the couple.*]   Say thank you. [*They mutter something.*] The cups
are there. [*To* SHEN TE.] Lucky you bought this shop when you did!

SHEN TE [*Laughing and bringing tea.*]   Lucky indeed!
      [*Enter* MRS. MI TZU, *the landlady.*]

MRS. MI TZU   Miss Shen Te? I am Mrs. Mi Tzu, your landlady. I hope our
relationship will be a happy one. I like to think I give my tenants modern,
personalized service. Here is your lease. [*To the others, as* SHEN TE *reads
the lease.*] There's nothing like the opening of a little shop, is there? A
moment of true beauty! [*She is looking around.*] Not very much on the
shelves, of course. But everything in the gods' good time! Where are your
references, Miss Shen Te?

SHEN TE   Do I *have* to have references?

MRS. MI TZU   After all, I haven't a notion who you are!

HUSBAND   Oh, *we'd* be glad to vouch for Miss Shen Te! We'd go through
fire for her!

MRS. MI TZU   And who may *you* be?

HUSBAND [*Stammering.*]   Ma Fu, tobacco dealer.

MRS. MI TZU   Where is your shop, Mr. . . . Ma Fu?

HUSBAND   Well, um, I haven't got a shop—I've just sold it.

MRS. MI TZU   I see. [*To* SHEN TE.] Is there no one else that knows you?

WIFE [*Whispering to* SHEN TE.]   Your cousin! Your cousin!

MRS. MI TZU   This is a respectable house, Miss Shen Te. I never sign a
lease without certain assurances.

SHEN TE [*Slowly, her eyes downcast.*]   I have . . . a cousin.

MRS. MI TZU   On the square? Let's go over and see him. What does he do?

SHEN TE [*As before.*]   He lives . . . in another city.

WIFE [*Prompting.*]   Didn't you say he was in Shung?

SHEN TE   That's right. Shung.

HUSBAND [*Prompting.*]   I had his name on the tip of my tongue, Mr. . . .

SHEN TE [*With an effort.*]   Mr. . . . Shui . . . Ta.

HUSBAND   That's it! Tall, skinny fellow!

SHEN TE   Shui Ta!

NEPHEW [*To* CARPENTER.]   *You* were in touch with him, weren't you? About
the shelves?

CARPENTER [*Surlily.*]   Give him this bill. [*He hands it over.*] I'll be back in
the morning. [*Exit* CARPENTER.]

NEPHEW [*Calling after him, but with his eyes on* MRS. MI TZU.]   Don't worry!
Mr. Shui Ta pays on the nail!

MRS. MI TZU [*Looking closely at* SHEN TE.]   I'll be happy to make his
acquaintance, Miss Shen Te. [*Exit* MRS. MI TZU.]
      [*Pause.*]

WIFE   By tomorrow morning she'll know more about you than you do yourself.

SISTER-IN-LAW [*To* NEPHEW.]   This thing isn't built to last.
      [*Enter* GRANDFATHER.]

WIFE   It's Grandfather! [*To* SHEN TE.] Such a good old soul!
      [*The* BOY *enters.*]

BOY [*Over his shoulder.*]   Here they are!

WIFE   And the boy, how he's grown! But he always could eat enough for
ten.

[*Enter the* NIECE.]

WIFE [*To* SHEN TE.] Our little niece from the country. There are more of us now than in your time. The less we had, the more there were of us; the more there were of us, the less we had. Give me the key. We must protect ourselves from unwanted guests. [*She takes the key and locks the door.*] Just make yourself at home. I'll light the little lamp.

NEPHEW [*A big joke.*] I hope her cousin doesn't drop in tonight! The strict Mr. Shui Ta!

[SISTER-IN-LAW *laughs.*]

BROTHER [*Reaching for a cigarette.*] One cigarette more or less . . .

HUSBAND One cigarette more or less.

[*They pile into the cigarettes. The* BROTHER *hands a jug of wine round.*]

NEPHEW Mr. Shui Ta'll pay for it!

GRANDFATHER [*Gravely, to* SHEN TE.] How do you do?

[SHEN TE, *a little taken aback by the belatedness of the greeting, bows. She has the carpenter's bill in one hand, the landlady's lease in the other.*]

WIFE How about a bit of a song? To keep Shen Te's spirits up?

NEPHEW Good idea. Grandfather: you start!

SONG OF THE SMOKE

GRANDFATHER
I used to think (before old age beset me)
That brains could fill the pantry of the poor.
But where did all my cerebration get me?
I'm just as hungry as I was before.
So what's the use?
See the smoke float free
Into ever colder coldness!
It's the same with me[6]

HUSBAND The straight and narrow path leads to disaster
And so the crooked path I tried to tread.
That got me to disaster even faster.
(They say we shall be happy when we're dead.)
So what's the use?
See the smoke float free
Into ever colder coldness!
It's the same with me

NIECE You older people, full of expectation,
At any moment now you'll walk the plank!
The future's for the younger generation!
Yes, even if that future is a blank.
So what's the use?
See the smoke float free
Into ever colder coldness!
It's the same with me.

NEPHEW [*To the* BROTHER.] Where'd you get that wine?

6. The refrain in this song is taken from a poem Brecht wrote in the 1920s entitled *The Song of the Opium Den.*

SISTER-IN-LAW [*Answering for the* BROTHER.] He pawned the sack of tobacco.

HUSBAND [*Stepping in.*] What? That tobacco was all we had to fall back on! You pig!

BROTHER *You'd* call a man a pig because your wife was frigid! Did you refuse to drink it?

[*They fight. The shelves fall over.*]

SHEN TE [*Imploringly.*] Oh don't! Don't break everything! Take it, take it all, but don't destroy a gift from the gods!

WIFE [*Disparagingly.*] This shop isn't big enough. I should never have mentioned it to Uncle and the others. When *they* arrive, it's going to be disgustingly overcrowded.

SISTER-IN-LAW And did you hear our gracious hostess? She cools off quick!

[*Voices outside. Knocking at the door.*]

UNCLE'S VOICE Open the door!

WIFE Uncle? Is that you, Uncle?

UNCLE'S VOICE Certainly, it's me. Auntie says to tell you she'll have the children here in ten minutes.

WIFE [*To* SHEN TE.] I'll have to let him in.

SHEN TE [*Who scarcely hears her.*]

> The little lifeboat is swiftly sent down
> Too many men too greedily
> Hold on to it as they drown.

1a

Wong's den in a sewer pipe.

WONG [*Crouching there.*] All quiet! It's four days now since I left the city. The gods passed this way on the second day. I heard their steps on the bridge over there. They must be a long way off by this time, so I'm safe. [*Breathing a sigh of relief, he curls up and goes to sleep. In his dream the pipe becomes transparent, and the* GODS *appear. Raising an arm, as if in self-defense.*] I know, I know, illustrious ones! I found no one to give you a room—not in all Setzuan! There, it's out. Please continue on your way!

FIRST GOD [*Mildly.*] But you did find someone. Someone who took us in for the night, watched over us in our sleep, and in the early morning lighted us down to the street with a lamp.

WONG It was . . . Shen Te that took you in?

THIRD GOD Who else?

WONG And I ran away! "She isn't coming," I thought, "she just can't afford it."

GODS [*Singing.*]

> O you feeble, well-intentioned, and yet feeble chap
> Where there's need the fellow thinks there is no goodness!
> When there's danger he thinks courage starts to ebb away!
> Some people only see the seamy side!
> What hasty judgment! What premature desperation!

WONG I'm *very* ashamed, illustrious ones.

FIRST GOD Do us a favor, water seller. Go back to Setzuan. Find Shen Te, and give us a report on her. We hear that she's come into a little money. Show interest in her goodness—for no one can be good for long if goodness is not in demand. Meanwhile we shall continue the search, and find other good people. After which, the idle chatter about the impossibility of goodness will stop!

[*The* GODS *vanish.*]

2

A knocking.

WIFE   Shen Te! Someone at the door. Where is she anyway?

NEPHEW   She must be getting the breakfast. Mr. Shui Ta will pay for it.
[*The* WIFE *laughs and shuffles to the door. Enter Mr.* SHUI TA *and the* CARPENTER.]

WIFE   Who is it?

SHUI TA   I am Miss Shen Te's cousin.

WIFE   What??

SHUI TA   My name is Shui Ta.

WIFE   Her cousin?

NEPHEW   Her cousin?

NIECE   But that was a joke. She hasn't got a cousin.

HUSBAND   So early in the morning?

BROTHER   What's all the noise?

SISTER-IN-LAW   This fellow says he's her cousin.

BROTHER   Tell him to prove it.

NEPHEW   Right. If you're Shen Te's cousin, prove it by getting the breakfast.

SHUI TA [*Whose regime begins as he puts out the lamp to save oil; loudly, to all present, asleep or awake.*]   Would you all please get dressed! Customers will be coming! I wish to open my shop!

HUSBAND   *Your* shop? Doesn't it belong to our good friend Shen Te?
[SHUI TA *shakes his head.*]

SISTER-IN-LAW   So we've been cheated. Where *is* the little liar?

SHUI TA   Miss Shen Te has been delayed. She wishes me to tell you there will be nothing she can do—now I am here.

WIFE [*Bowled over.*]   I thought she was good!

NEPHEW   Do you have to believe *him?*

HUSBAND   I don't.

NEPHEW   Then do something.

HUSBAND   Certainly! I'll send out a search party at once. You, you, you, and you, go out and look for Shen Te. [*As the* GRANDFATHER *rises and makes for the door*] Not you, Grandfather, you and I will hold the fort.

SHUI TA   You won't find Miss Shen Te. She has suspended her hospitable activity for an unlimited period. There are too many of you. She asked me to say: this is a tobacco shop, not a gold mine.

HUSBAND   Shen Te never said a thing like that. Boy, food! There's a bakery on the corner. Stuff your shirt full when they're not looking!

SISTER-IN-LAW   Don't overlook the raspberry tarts.

HUSBAND   And don't let the policeman see you.
[*The* BOY *leaves.*]

SHUI TA   Don't you depend on this shop now? Then why give it a bad name by stealing from the bakery?

NEPHEW   Don't listen to him. Let's find Shen Te. She'll give him a piece of her mind.

SISTER-IN-LAW   Don't forget to leave us some breakfast.

[BROTHER, SISTER-IN-LAW and NEPHEW *leave*.]

SHUI TA [*To the* CARPENTER.]   You see, Mr. Carpenter, nothing has changed since the poet, eleven hundred years ago, penned these lines:

> A governor was asked what was needed
> To save the freezing people in the city.
> He replied:
> "A blanket ten thousand feet long
> To cover the city and all its suburbs."[7]

[*He starts to tidy up the shop.*]

CARPENTER   Your cousin owes me money. I've got witnesses. For the shelves.

SHUI TA   Yes, I have your bill. [*He takes it out of his pocket.*] Isn't a hundred silver dollars rather a lot?

CARPENTER   No deductions! I have a wife and children.

SHUI TA   How many children?

CARPENTER   Three.

SHUI TA   I'll make you an offer. Twenty silver dollars.

[*The* HUSBAND *laughs*.]

CARPENTER   You're crazy. Those shelves are real walnut.

SHUI TA   Very well, Take them away.

CARPENTER   What?

SHUI TA   They cost too much. Please take them away.

WIFE   Not bad! [*And she, too, is laughing.*]

CARPENTER [*A little bewildered.*]   Call Shen Te, someone! [*To* SHUI TA.] She's good!

SHUI TA   Certainly. She's ruined.

CARPENTER [*Provoked into taking some of the shelves.*]   All right, you can keep your tobacco on the floor.

SHUI TA [*to the* HUSBAND.]   Help him with the shelves.

HUSBAND [*Grins and carries one shelf over to the door where the* CARPENTER *now is.*]   Good-bye, shelves!

CARPENTER [*To the* HUSBAND.]   You dog! You want my family to starve?

SHUI TA   I repeat my offer. I have no desire to keep my tobacco on the floor. Twenty silver dollars.

CARPENTER [*With desperate aggressiveness.*]   One hundred!

[SHUI TA *shows indifference, looks through the window. The* HUSBAND *picks up several shelves.*]

CARPENTER [*To* HUSBAND.]   You needn't smash them against the doorpost, you idiot! [*To* SHUI TA.] These shelves were made to measure. They're no use anywhere else!

SHUI TA   Precisely.

[*The* WIFE *squeals with pleasure.*]

---

7. Reference to a poem, *The Big Rug*, by the classical Chinese poet Po Chü-i (772–846 C.E.).

CARPENTER [*Giving up, sullenly.*]   Take the shelves. Pay what you want to pay.
SHUI TA [*Smoothly.*]   Twenty silver dollars.
　　　[*He places two large coins on the table. The* CARPENTER *picks them up.*]
HUSBAND [*Brings the shelves back in.*]   And quite enough too!
CARPENTER [*Slinking off.*]   Quite enough to get drunk on.
HUSBAND [*Happily.*]   Well, we got rid of *him*!
WIFE [*Weeping with fun, gives a rendition of the dialogue just spoken.*]   "Real walnut," says he. "Very well, take them away," says his lordship. "I have three children," says he. "Twenty silver dollars," says his lordship. "They're no use anywhere else," says he. "Pre-cisely," said his lordship! [*She dissolves into shrieks of merriment.*]
SHUI TA   And now: go!
HUSBAND   What's that?
SHUI TA   You're thieves, parasites. I'm giving you this chance. Go!
HUSBAND [*Summoning all his ancestral dignity.*]   That sort deserves no answer. Besides, one should never shout on an empty stomach.
WIFE   Where's that boy?
SHUI TA   Exactly. The boy. I want no stolen goods in this shop. [*Very loudly.*] I strongly advise you to leave! [*But they remain seated, noses in the air. Quietly.*] As you wish. [SHUI TA *goes to the door. A* POLICEMAN *appears.* SHUI TA *bows.*] I am addressing the officer in charge of this precinct?
POLICEMAN   That's right, Mr., um, what was the name, sir?
SHUI TA   Mr. Shui Ta.
POLICEMAN   Yes, of course, sir.
　　　[*They exchange a smile.*]
SHUI TA   Nice weather we're having.
POLICEMAN   A little on the warm side, sir.
SHUI TA   Oh, a little on the warm side.
HUSBAND [*Whispering to the* WIFE.]   If he keeps it up till the boy's back, we're done for. [*Tries to signal* SHUI TA.]
SHUI TA [*Ignoring the signal.*]   Weather, of course, is one thing indoors, another out on the dusty street!
POLICEMAN   Oh, quite another, sir!
WIFE [*To the* HUSBAND.]   It's all right as long as he's standing in the doorway—the boy will see him.
SHUI TA   Step inside for a moment! It's quite cool indoors. My cousin and I have just opened the place. And we attach the greatest importance to being on good terms with the, um, authorities.
POLICEMAN [*Entering.*]   Thank you, Mr. Shui Ta. It *is* cool!
HUSBAND [*Whispering to the* WIFE.]   And now the boy *won't* see him.
SHUI TA [*Showing* HUSBAND *and* WIFE *to the* POLICEMAN.]   Visitors, I think my cousin knows them. They were just leaving.
HUSBAND [*Defeated.*]   Ye-e-es, we were . . . just leaving.
SHUI TA   I'll tell my cousin you couldn't wait.
　　　[*Noise from the street. Shouts of* "Stop, Thief!"]
POLICEMAN   What's that?
　　　[*The* BOY *is in the doorway with cakes and buns and rolls spilling out of his shirt. The* WIFE *signals desperately to him to leave. He gets the idea.*]

POLICEMAN No, you don't. [*He grabs the* BOY *by the collar.*] Where's all this from?

BOY [*Vaguely pointing.*] Down the street.

POLICEMAN [*Grimly.*] So that's it. [*Prepares to arrest the* BOY.]

WIFE [*Stepping in.*] And *we* knew nothing about it. [*To the* BOY.] Nasty little thief!

POLICEMAN [*Dryly.*] Can you clarify the situation, Mr. Shui Ta?

[SHUI TA *is silent.*]

POLICEMAN [*Who understands silence.*] Aha. You're all coming with me—to the station.

SHUI TA I can hardly say how sorry I am that *my* establishment . . .

WIFE Oh, he saw the boy leave not ten minutes ago!

SHUI TA And to conceal the theft asked a policeman in?

POLICEMAN Don't listen to her, Mr. Shui Ta, I'll be happy to relieve you of their presence one and all! [*To all three.*] Out!

[*He drives them before him.*]

GRANDFATHER [*Leaving last, gravely.*] Good morning!

POLICEMAN Good morning!

[SHUI TA, *left alone, continues to tidy up.* MRS. MI TZU *breezes in.*]

MRS. MI TZU You're her cousin, are you? Then have the goodness to explain what all this means—police dragging people from a respectable house! By what right does your Miss Shen Te turn my property into a house of assignation?—Well, as you see, I know all!

SHUI TA Yes. My cousin has the worst possible reputation: that of being poor.

MRS. MI TZU No sentimental rubbish, Mr. Shui Ta. Your cousin was a common . . .

SHUI TA Pauper. Let's use the uglier word.

MRS. MI TZU I'm speaking of her conduct, not her earnings. But there must have *been* earnings, or how did she buy all this? Several elderly gentlemen took care of it, I suppose. I repeat: this is a respectable house! I have tenants who prefer not to live under the same roof with such a person.

SHUI TA [*Quietly.*] How much do you want?

MRS. MI TZU [*He is ahead of her now.*] I beg your pardon.

SHUI TA To reassure yourself. To reassure your tenants. How much will it cost?

MRS. MI TZU You're a cool customer.

SHUI TA [*Picking up the lease.*] The rent is high. [*He reads on.*] I assume it's payable by the month?

MRS. MI TZU Not in her case.

SHUI TA [*Looking up.*] What?

MRS. MI TZU Six months' rent payable in advance. Two hundred silver dollars.

SHUI TA Six . . . ! Sheer usury! And where am I to find it?

MRS. MI TZU You should have thought of that before.

SHUI TA Have you no heart, Mrs. Mi Tzu? It's true Shen Te acted foolishly, being kind to all those people, but she'll improve with time. I'll see to it she does. She'll work her fingers to the bone to pay her rent, and all the time be as quiet as a mouse, as humble as a fly.

MRS. MI TZU Her social background . . .

SHUI TA   Out of the depths! She came out of the depths! And before she'll
go back there, she'll work, sacrifice, shrink from nothing. . . . Such a
tenant is worth her weight in gold, Mrs. Mi Tzu.

MRS. MI TZU   It's silver we were talking about, Mr. Shui Ta. Two hundred
silver dollars or . . .

[Enter the POLICEMAN.]

POLICEMAN   Am I intruding, Mr. Shui Ta?

MRS. MI TZU   This tobacco shop is well known to the police, I see.

POLICEMAN   Mr. Shui Ta has done us a service, Mrs. Mi Tzu. I am here
to present our official felicitations!

MRS. MI TZU   That means less than nothing to me, sir. Mr. Shui Ta, all I
can say is: I hope your cousin will find my terms acceptable. Good day,
gentlemen. [Exit.]

SHUI TA   Good day, ma'am.

[Pause.]

POLICEMAN   Mrs. Mi Tzu a bit of a stumbling block, sir?

SHUI TA   She wants six months' rent in advance.

POLICEMAN   And you haven't got it, eh? [SHUI TA is silent.] But surely you
can get it, sir? A man like you?

SHUI TA   What about a woman like Shen Te?

POLICEMAN   You're not staying, sir?

SHUI TA   No, and I won't be back. Do you smoke?

POLICEMAN   [Taking two cigars, and placing them both in his pocket.]
Thank you, sir—I see your point, Miss Shen Te—let's mince no words—
Miss Shen Te lived by selling herself. "What else could she have done?"
you ask. "How else was she to pay the rent?" True. But the fact remains,
Mr. Shui Ta, it is not respectable. Why not? A very deep question. But,
in the first place, love—love isn't bought and sold like cigars, Mr. Shui
Ta. In the second place, it isn't respectable to go waltzing off with someone that's paying his way, so to speak—it must be for love! Thirdly and
lastly, as the proverb has it: not for a handful of rice but for love! [Pause.
He is thinking hard.] "Well," you may say, "and what good is all this
wisdom if the milk's already spilt?" Miss Shen Te is what she is. Is where
she is. We have to face the fact that if she doesn't get hold of six months'
rent pronto, she'll be back on the streets. The question then as I see it—
everything in this world is a matter of opinion—the question as I see it
is: how is she to get hold of this rent? How? Mr. Shui Ta: I don't know.
[Pause.] I take that back, sir. It's just come to me. A husband. We must
find her a husband!

[Enter a little OLD WOMAN.]

OLD WOMAN   A good cheap cigar for my husband, we'll have been married
forty years tomorrow and we're having a little celebration.

SHUI TA   Forty years? And you still want to celebrate?

OLD WOMAN   As much as we can afford to. We have the carpet shop across
the square. We'll be good neighbors, I hope?

SHUI TA   I hope so too.

POLICEMAN   [Who keeps making discoveries.]   Mr. Shui Ta, you know what
we need? We need capital. And how do we acquire capital? We get married.

SHUI TA   [To OLD WOMAN.]   I'm afraid I've been pestering this gentleman
with my personal worries.

POLICEMAN [*Lyrically.*] We can't pay six months' rent, so what do we do? We marry money.

SHUI TA That might not be easy.

POLICEMAN Oh, I don't know. She's a good match. Has a nice, growing business. [*To the* OLD WOMAN.] What do you think?

OLD WOMAN [*Undecided.*] Well—

POLICEMAN Should she put an ad in the paper?

OLD WOMAN [*Not eager to commit herself.*] Well, if *she* agrees—

POLICEMAN I'll write it for her. *You* lend us a hand, and *we* write an ad for you! [*He chuckles away to himself, takes out his notebook, wets the stump of a pencil between his lips, and writes away.*]

SHUI TA [*Slowly.*] Not a bad idea.

POLICEMAN "What . . . respectable . . . man . . . with small capital . . . widower . . . not excluded . . . desires . . . marriage . . . into flourishing . . . tobacco shop?" And now let's add: "Am . . . pretty . . ." No! . . . "Prepossessing appearance."

SHUI TA If you don't think that's an exaggeration?

OLD WOMAN Oh, not a bit. I've seen her.

> [*The* POLICEMAN *tears the page out of his notebook, and hands it over to* SHUI TA.]

SHUI TA [*With horror in his voice.*] How much luck we need to keep our heads above water! How many ideas! How many friends! [*To the* POLICEMAN.] Thank you, sir, I think I see my way clear.

3

Evening in the municipal park. Noise of a plane overhead. YANG SUN, *a young man in rags, is following the plane with his eyes: one can tell that the machine is describing a curve above the park.* YANG SUN *then takes a rope out of his pocket, looking anxiously about him as he does so. He moves toward a large willow. Enter two prostitutes, one old, the other the* NIECE *whom we have already met.*

NIECE Hello. Coming with me?

YANG SUN [*Taken aback.*] If you'd like to buy me a dinner.

OLD WHORE Buy you a dinner! [*To the* NIECE.] Oh, we know him—it's the unemployed pilot. Waste no time on him!

NIECE But he's the only man left in the park. And it's going to rain.

OLD WHORE Oh, how do you know?

> [*And they pass by.* YANG SUN *again looks about him, again takes his rope, and this time throws it round a branch of the willow tree. Again he is interrupted. It is the two prostitutes returning—and in such a hurry they don't notice him.*]

NIECE It's going to pour!

> [*Enter* SHEN TE.]

OLD WHORE There's that *gorgon* Shen Te! That *drove* your family out into the cold!

NIECE It wasn't her. It was that cousin of hers. She offered to pay for the cakes. I've nothing against her.

OLD WHORE I have, though. [*So that* SHEN TE *can hear.*] Now where could the little lady be off to? She may be rich now but that won't stop her snatching our young men, will it?

SHEN TE   I'm going to the tearoom by the pond.

NIECE   Is it true what they say? You're marrying a widower—with three children?

SHEN TE   Yes. I'm just going to see him.

YANG SUN [*His patience at breaking point.*]   Move on there! This is a park, not a whorehouse!

OLD WHORE   Shut your mouth!

[*But the two prostitutes leave.*]

YANG SUN   Even in the farthest corner of the park, even when it's raining, you can't get rid of them! [*He spits.*]

SHEN TE [*Overhearing this.*]   And what right have you to scold them? [*But at this point she sees the rope.*] Oh!

YANG SUN   Well, what are you staring at?

SHEN TE   That rope. What is it for?

YANG SUN   Think! Think! I haven't a penny. Even if I had, I wouldn't spend it on you. I'd buy a drink of water.

[*The rain starts.*]

SHEN TE [*Still looking at the rope.*]   What is the rope for? You mustn't!

YANG SUN   What's it to you? Clear out!

SHEN TE [*Irrelevantly.*]   It's raining.

YANG SUN   Well, don't try to come under this tree.

SHEN TE   Oh, no. [*She stays in the rain.*]

YANG SUN   Now go away. [*Pause.*] For one thing, I don't like your looks, you're bowlegged.

SHEN TE [*Indignantly.*]   That's not true!

YANG SUN   Well, don't show 'em to me. Look, it's raining. You better come under this tree.

[*Slowly, she takes shelter under the tree.*]

SHEN TE   Why did you want to do it?

YANG SUN   You really want to know? [*Pause.*] To get rid of you! [*Pause.*] You know what a flyer is?

SHEN TE   Oh yes, I've met a lot of pilots. At the tearoom.

YANG SUN   You call *them* flyers? Think they know what a machine is? Just 'cause they have leather helmets? They gave the airfield director a bribe, that's the way *those* fellows got up in the air! Try one of them out sometime. "Go up to two thousand feet," tell him, "then let it fall, then pick it up again with a flick of the wrist at the last moment." Know what he'll say to that? "It's not in my contract." Then again, there's the landing problem. It's like landing on your own backside. It's no different, planes are human. Those fools don't understand. [*Pause.*] And I'm the biggest fool for reading the book on flying in the Peking school and skipping the page where it says: "We've got enough flyers and we don't need you." I'm a mail pilot with no mail. You understand that?

SHEN TE [*Shyly.*]   Yes, I do.

YANG SUN   No, you don't. You'd never understand that.

SHEN TE   When we were little we had a crane with a broken wing. He made friends with us and was very good-natured about our jokes. He would strut along behind us and call out to stop us going too fast for him. But every spring and autumn when the cranes flew over the villages in great swarms, he got quite restless. [*Pause.*] I understand that.

[*She bursts out crying.*]

YANG SUN   Don't!

SHEN TE [*Quieting down.*]   No.

YANG SUN   It's bad for the complexion.

SHEN TE [*Sniffing.*]   I've stopped.

   [*She dries her tears on her big sleeve. Leaning against the tree, but not looking at her, he reaches for her face.*]

YANG SUN   You can't even wipe your own face. [*He is wiping it for her with his handkerchief. Pause.*]

SHEN TE [*Still sobbing.*]   I don't know *anything*!

YANG SUN   You interrupted me! What for?

SHEN TE   It's such a rainy day. You only wanted to do . . . *that* because it's such a rainy day. [*To the audience.*]

> In our country
> The evenings should never be somber
> High bridges over rivers
> The gray hour between night and morning
> And the long, long winter:
> Such things are dangerous
> For, with all the misery,
> A very little is enough
> And men throw away an unbearable life.

   [*Pause.*]

YANG SUN   Talk about yourself for a change.

SHEN TE   What about me? I have a shop.

YANG SUN [*Incredulous.*]   You have a shop, have you? Never thought of walking the streets?

SHEN TE   I did walk the streets. Now I have a shop.

YANG SUN [*Ironically.*]   A gift of the gods, I suppose!

SHEN TE   How did you know?

YANG SUN [*Even more ironical.*]   One fine evening the gods turned up saying: here's some money!

SHEN TE [*Quickly.*]   One fine morning.

YANG SUN [*Fed up.*]   This isn't much of an entertainment.

   [*Pause.*]

SHEN TE   I can play the zither a little. [*Pause.*] And I can mimic men. [*Pause.*] I got the shop, so the first thing I did was to give my zither away. I can be as stupid as a fish now, I said to myself, and it won't matter.

> I'm rich now, I said
> I walk alone, I sleep alone
> For a whole year, I said
> I'll have nothing to do with a man.

YANG SUN   And now you're marrying one! The one at the tearoom by the pond?

   [SHEN TE *is silent.*]

YANG SUN   What do you know about love?

SHEN TE   Everything.

YANG SUN   Nothing. [*Pause.*] Or d'you just mean you enjoyed it?

SHEN TE   No.

YANG SUN [*Again without turning to look at her, he strokes her cheek with his hand.*]   You like that?

SHEN TE   Yes.

YANG SUN [*Breaking off.*]   You're easily satisfied, I must say. [*Pause.*] What a town!

SHEN TE   You have no friends?

YANG SUN [*Defensively.*]   Yes, I have! [*Change of tone.*] But they don't want to hear I'm still unemployed. "What?" they ask. "Is there still water in the sea?" You have friends?

SHEN TE [*Hesitating.*]   Just a . . . cousin.

YANG SUN   Watch him carefully.

SHEN TE   He only came once. Then he went away. He won't be back. [YANG SUN *is looking away.*] But to be without hope, they say, is to be without goodness!
    [*Pause.*]

YANG SUN   Go on talking. A voice is a voice.

SHEN TE   Once, when I was a little girl, I fell, with a load of brushwood. An old man picked me up. He gave me a penny too. Isn't it funny how people who don't have very much like to give some of it away? They must like to show what they can do, and how could they show it better than by being kind? Being wicked is just like being clumsy. When we sing a song, or build a machine, or plant some rice, we're being kind. You're kind.

YANG SUN   You make it sound easy.

SHEN TE   Oh, no. [*Little pause.*] Oh! A drop of rain!

YANG SUN   Where'd you feel it?

SHEN TE   Between the eyes.

YANG SUN   Near the right eye? Or the left?

SHEN TE   Near the left eye.

YANG SUN   Oh, good. [*He is getting sleepy.*] So you're through with men, eh?

SHEN TE [*With a smile.*]   But I'm not bowlegged.

YANG SUN   Perhaps not.

SHEN TE   Definitely not.
    [*Pause.*]

YANG SUN [*Leaning wearily against the willow.*]   I haven't had a drop to drink all day, I haven't eaten anything for *two* days. I couldn't love you if I tried.
    [*Pause.*]

SHEN TE   I like it in the rain.
    [*Enter* WONG *the water seller, singing.*]

THE SONG OF THE WATER SELLER IN THE RAIN

"Buy my water," I am yelling
And my fury restraining
For no water I'm selling
'Cause it's raining, 'cause it's raining!
I keep yelling: "Buy my water!"
But no one's buying

Athirst and dying
And drinking and paying!
Buy water!
Buy water, you dogs!

Nice to dream of lovely weather!
Think of all the consternation
Were there no precipitation
Half a dozen years together!
    Can't you hear them shrieking: "Water!"
    Pretending they adore me?
    They all would go down on their knees before me!
    Down on your knees!
    Go down on your knees, you dogs!

What are lawns and hedges thinking?
What are fields and forests saying?
"At the cloud's breast we are drinking!
And we've no idea who's paying!"
    I keep yelling: "Buy my water!"
    But no one's buying
    Athirst and dying
    And drinking and paying!
    Buy water!
    Buy water, you dogs!

[*The rain has stopped now.* SHEN TE *sees* WONG *and runs toward him.*]

SHEN TE   Wong! You're back! Your carrying pole's at the shop.

WONG   Oh, thank you, Shen Te. And how is life treating *you*?

SHEN TE   I've just met a brave and clever man. And I want to buy him a cup of your water.

WONG [*Bitterly.*]   Throw back your head and open your mouth and you'll have all the water you need—

SHEN TE [*Tenderly.*]
        I want *your* water, Wong
        The water that has tired you so
        The water that you carried all this way
        The water that is hard to sell because it's been raining.
        I need it for the young man over there—he's a flyer!

                A flyer is a bold man:
                Braving the storms
                In company with the clouds
                He crosses the heavens
                And brings to friends in faraway lands
                The friendly mail!

[*She pays* WONG, *and runs over to* YANG SUN *with the cup. But* YANG SUN *is fast asleep.*]

SHEN TE [*Calling to* WONG, *with a laugh.*]   He's fallen asleep! Despair and rain and I have worn him out!

3a

Wong's den. The sewer pipe is transparent, and the GODS *again appear to* WONG
in a dream.

WONG [*Radiant*] I've seen her, illustrious ones! And she hasn't changed!
FIRST GOD That's good to hear.
WONG She loves someone.
FIRST GOD Let's hope the experience gives her the strength to stay good!
WONG It does. She's doing good deeds all the time.
FIRST GOD Ah? What sort? What sort of good deeds, Wong?
WONG Well, she has a kind word for everybody.
FIRST GOD [*Eagerly.*] And then?
WONG Hardly anyone leaves her shop without tobacco in his pocket—
    even if he can't pay for it.
FIRST GOD Not bad at all. Next?
WONG She's putting up a family of eight.
FIRST GOD [*Gleefully, to the* SECOND GOD.] Eight! [*To* WONG.] And that's
    not all, of course!
WONG She bought a cup of water from me even thought it was raining.
FIRST GOD Yes, yes, yes, all these smaller good deeds!
WONG Even they run into money. A little tobacco shop doesn't make so
    much.
FIRST GOD [*Sententiously.*] A prudent gardener works miracles on the
    smallest plot.
WONG She hands out rice every morning. That eats up half her earnings.
FIRST GOD [*A little disappointed.*] Well, as a beginning . . .
WONG They call her the Angel of the Slums—whatever the carpenter may
    say!
FIRST GOD What's this? A carpenter speaks ill of her?
WONG Oh, he only says her shelves weren't paid for in full.
SECOND GOD [*Who has a bad cold and can't pronounce his n's and m's.*]
    What's this? Not paying a carpenter? Why was that?
WONG I suppose she didn't have the money.
SECOND GOD [*Severely.*] One pays what one owes, that's in our book of
    rules! First the letter of the law, then the spirit.
WONG But it wasn't Shen Te, illustrious ones, it was her cousin. She called
    him in to help.
SECOND GOD Then her cousin must never darken her threshold again!
WONG Very well, illustrious ones! But in fairness to Shen Te, let me say
    that her cousin is a businessman.
FIRST GOD Perhaps we should inquire what is customary? I find business
    quite unintelligible. But everybody's doing it. Business! Did the Seven
    Good Kings do business? Did Kung the Just[8] sell fish?
SECOND GOD In any case, such a thing must not occur again!
    [*The* GODS *start to leave.*]
THIRD GOD Forgive us for taking this tone with you, Wong, we haven't

---

8. The philosopher Confucius (551–479 B.C.E.). *Seven Good Kings*: legendary wise kings who personified
the old order and traditional values.

been getting enough sleep. The rich recommend us to the poor, and the poor tell us they haven't enough room.

SECOND GOD Feeble, feeble, the best of them!

FIRST GOD No great deeds! No heroic daring!

THIRD GOD On such a *small* scale!

SECOND GOD Sincere, yes, but what is actually *achieved*?

[*One can no longer hear them.*]

WONG [*Calling after them.*] I've thought of something, illustrious ones: Perhaps you shouldn't ask—too—much—all—at—once!

4

The square in front of Shen Te's tobacco shop. Besides Shen Te's place, two other shops are seen: the carpet shop and a barber's. Morning. Outside Shen Te's the GRANDFATHER, *the* SISTER-IN-LAW, *the* UNEMPLOYED MAN, *and* MRS. SHIN *stand waiting.*

SISTER-IN-LAW She's been out all night again.

MRS. SHIN No sooner did we get rid of that crazy cousin of hers than Shen Te herself starts carrying on! Maybe she does give us an ounce of rice now and then, but can you depend on her? Can you depend on her?

[*Loud voices from the barber's.*]

VOICE OF SHU FU What are you doing in my shop? Get out—at once!

VOICE OF WONG But sir. They all let me sell . . .

[WONG *comes staggering out of the barber's shop pursued by Mr.* SHU FU, *the barber, a fat man carrying a heavy curling iron.*]

SHU FU Get out, I said! Pestering my customers with your slimy old water! Get out! Take your cup!

[*He holds out the cup.* WONG *reaches out for it. Mr.* SHU FU *strikes his hand with the curling iron, which is hot.* WONG *howls.*]

SHU FU You had it coming my man!

[*Puffing, he returns to his shop. The* UNEMPLOYED MAN *picks up the cup and gives it to* WONG.]

UNEMPLOYED MAN You can report that to the police.

WONG My hand! It's smashed up!

UNEMPLOYED MAN Any bones broken?

WONG I can't move my fingers.

UNEMPLOYED MAN Sit down. I'll put some water on it.

[WONG *sits.*]

MRS. SHIN The water won't cost you anything.

SISTER-IN-LAW You might have got a bandage from Miss Shen Te till she took to staying out all night. It's a scandal.

MRS. SHIN [*Despondently.*] If you ask me, she's forgotten we ever existed!

[*Enter* SHEN TE *down the street, with a dish of rice.*]

SHEN TE [*To the audience.*] How wonderful to see Setzuan in the early morning! I always used to stay in bed with my dirty blanket over my head afraid to wake up. This morning I saw the newspapers being delivered by little boys, the streets being washed by strong men, and fresh vegetables coming in from the country on ox carts. It's a long walk from where Yang Sun lives, but I feel lighter at every step. They say you walk on air when you're in love, but it's even better walking on the rough earth, on the hard cement. In the early morning, the old city looks like a great heap of rubbish! Nice, though, with all its little lights. And the sky, so pink, so transparent, before the dust comes and muddies it! What a lot you miss if you never see your city rising from its slumbers like an honest old craftsman pumping his lungs full of air and reaching for his tools, as the poet says! [*Cheerfully, to her waiting guests.*] Good morning, everyone, here's your rice! [*Distributing the rice, she comes upon* WONG.] Good morning, Wong, I'm quite lightheaded today. On my way over, I looked at myself in all the shop windows. I'd love to be beautiful.

> [*She slips into the carpet shop. Mr.* SHU FU *has just emerged from his shop.*]

SHU FU [*To the audience.*]   It surprises me how beautiful Miss Shen Te is looking today! I never gave her a passing thought before. But now I've been gazing upon her comely form for exactly three minutes! I begin to suspect I am in love with her. She is overpoweringly attractive! [*Crossly, to* WONG.] Be off with you rascal!

> [*He returns to his shop.* SHEN TE *comes back out of the carpet shop with the* OLD MAN, *its proprietor, and his wife—whom we have already met— the* OLD WOMAN. SHEN TE *is wearing a shawl. The* OLD MAN *is holding up a looking glass for her.*]

OLD WOMAN   Isn't it lovely? We'll give you a reduction because there's a little hole in it.

SHEN TE [*Looking at another shawl on the old woman's arm.*]   The other one's nice too.

OLD WOMAN [*Smiling.*]   Too bad there's no hole in that!

SHEN TE   That's right. My shop doesn't make very much.

OLD WOMAN   And your deeds eat it all up! Be more careful, my dear . . .

SHEN TE [*Trying on the shawl with the hole.*]   Just now, I'm lightheaded! Does the color suit me?

OLD WOMAN   You'd better ask a man.

SHEN TE [*To the* OLD MAN.]   Does the color suit me?

OLD MAN   You'd better ask your young friend.

SHEN TE   I'd like to have your opinion.

OLD MAN   It suits you very well. But wear it this way: the dull side out.

> [SHEN TE *pays up.*]

OLD WOMAN   If you decide you don't like it, you can exchange it. [*She pulls* SHEN TE *to one side.*] Has he got money?

SHEN TE [*With a laugh*]   Yang Sun? Oh, no.

OLD WOMAN   Then how're you going to pay your rent?

SHEN TE   I'd forgotten about that.

OLD WOMAN   And next Monday is the first of the month! Miss Shen Te, I've got something to say to you. After we [*Indicating her husband.*] got to know you, we had our doubts about that marriage ad. We thought it would be better if you'd let *us* help you. Out of our savings. We reckon we could lend you two hundred silver dollars. We don't need anything in writing—you could pledge us your tobacco stock.

SHEN TE   You're prepared to lend money to a person like me?

OLD WOMAN   It's folks like you that need it. We'd think twice about lending anything to your cousin.

OLD MAN [*Coming up.*]   All settled, my dear?

SHEN TE   I wish the gods could have heard what your wife was just saying,
Mr. Ma. They're looking for good people who're happy—and helping me
makes you happy because you know it was love that got me into diffi-
culties!
   [The old couple smile knowingly at each other.]
OLD MAN   And here's the money, Miss Shen Te.
   [He hands her an envelope. SHEN TE takes it. She bows. They bow back.
   They return to their shop.]
SHEN TE [Holding up her envelope.]   Look, Wong, here's six months' rent!
Don't you believe in miracles now? And how do you like my new shawl?
WONG   For the young fellow I saw you with in the park?
   [SHEN TE nods.]
MRS. SHIN   Never mind all that. It's time you took a look at this hand!
SHEN TE   Have you hurt your hand?
MRS. SHIN   That barber smashed it with his hot curling iron. Right in front
of our eyes.
SHEN TE [Shocked at herself.]   And I never noticed! We must get you to a
doctor this minute or who knows what will happen?
UNEMPLOYED MAN   It's not a doctor he should see, it's a judge. He can ask
for compensation. The barber's filthy rich.
WONG   You think I have a chance?
MRS. SHIN [With relish.]   If it's really good and smashed. But is it?
WONG   I think so. It's very swollen. Could I get a pension?
MRS. SHIN   You'd need a witness.
WONG   Well, you all saw it. You could all testify.
   [He looks round. The UNEMPLOYED MAN, the GRANDFATHER, and the SIS-
   TER-IN-LAW are all sitting against the wall of the shop eating rice. Their
   concentration on eating is complete.]
SHEN TE [To MRS. SHIN.]   You saw it yourself.
MRS. SHIN   I want nothing to do with the police. It's against my principles.
SHEN TE [To SISTER-IN-LAW.]   What about you?
SISTER-IN-LAW   Me? I wasn't looking.
SHEN TE [To the GRANDFATHER, coaxingly.]   Grandfather, you'll testify,
won't you?
SISTER-IN-LAW   And a lot of good that will do. He's simple-minded.
SHEN TE [To the UNEMPLOYED MAN.]   You seem to be the only witness left.
UNEMPLOYED MAN   My testimony would only hurt him. I've been picked
up twice for begging.
SHEN TE
   Your brother is assaulted, and you shut your eyes?
   He is hit, cries out in pain, and you are silent?
   The beast prowls, chooses and seizes his victim, and you say:
   "Because we showed no displeasure, he has spared us."
If no one present will be a witness, I will. I'll say I saw it.
MRS. SHIN [Solemnly.]   The name for that is perjury.
WONG   I don't know if I can accept that. Though maybe I'll have to. [Look-
ing at his hand.] Is it swollen enough, do you think? The swelling's not
going down.
UNEMPLOYED MAN   No, no, the swelling's holding up well.
WONG   Yes. It's more swollen if anything. Maybe my wrist is broken after
all. I'd better see a judge at once.

[*Holding his hand very carefully, and fixing his eyes on it, he runs off.*
MRS. SHIN *goes quickly into the barber's shop.*]

UNEMPLOYED MAN [*Seeing her.*]   She is getting on the right side of Mr. Shu Fu.

SISTER-IN-LAW   You and I can't change the world, Shen Te.

SHEN TE   Go away! Go away all of you! [*The* UNEMPLOYED MAN, *the* SISTER-IN-LAW, *and the* GRANDFATHER *stalk off, eating and sulking. To the audience.*]

> They've stopped answering
> They stay put
> They do as they're told
> They don't care
> Nothing can make them look up
> But the smell of food.

[*Enter* MRS. YANG, *Yang Sun's mother, out of breath.*]

MRS. YANG   Miss Shen Te. My son has told me everything. I am Mrs. Yang, Sun's mother. Just think. He's got an offer. Of a job as a pilot. A letter has just come. From the director of the airfield in Peking!

SHEN TE   So he can fly again! Isn't that wonderful!

MRS. YANG [*Less breathlessly all the time.*]   They won't give him the job for nothing. They want five hundred silver dollars.

SHEN TE   We can't let money stand in his way, Mrs. Yang!

MRS. YANG   If only you could help him out!

SHEN TE   I have the shop. I can try! [*She embraces* MRS. YANG.] I happen to have two hundred with me now. Take it. [*She gives her the old couple's money.*] It was a loan but they said I could repay it with my tobacco stock.

MRS. YANG   And they were calling Sun the Dead Pilot of Setzuan! A friend in need!

SHEN TE   We must find another three hundred.

MRS. YANG   How?

SHEN TE   Let me think. [*Slowly.*] I know someone who can help. I didn't want to call on his services again, he's hard and cunning. But a flyer must fly. And I'll make this the last time.

[*Distant sound of a plane.*]

MRS. YANG   If the man you mentioned can do it . . . . Oh, look, there's the morning mail plane, heading for Peking!

SHEN TE   The pilot can see us, let's wave!

[*They wave. The noise of the engine is louder.*]

MRS. YANG   You know that pilot up there?

SHEN TE   Wave, Mrs. Yang! I know the pilot who will be up there. He gave up hope. But he'll do it now. One man to raise himself above the misery, above us all. [*To the audience.*]

> Yang Sun, my lover:
> Braving the storms
> In company with the clouds
> Crossing the heavens
> And bringing to friends in faraway lands
> The friendly mail!

4a

In front of the inner curtain. Enter SHEN TE, *carrying Shui Ta's mask. She sings.*

THE SONG OF DEFENSELESSNESS

In our country
A useful man needs luck
Only if he finds strong backers
Can he prove himself useful.
The good can't defend themselves and
Even the gods are defenseless.

Oh, why don't the gods have their own ammunition
And launch against badness their own expedition
Enthroning the good and preventing sedition
And bringing the world to a peaceful condition?

Oh, why don't the gods do the buying and selling
Injustice forbidding, starvation dispelling
Give bread to each city and joy to each dwelling?
Oh, why don't the gods do the buying and selling?

[*She puts on Shui Ta's mask and sings in his voice.*]

You can only help one of your luckless brothers
By trampling down a dozen others.

Why is it the gods do not feel indignation
And come down in fury to end exploitation
Defeat all defeat and forbid desperation
Refusing to tolerate such toleration?

Why is it?

5

Shen Te's tobacco shop. Behind the counter, Mr. SHUI TA, *reading the paper.*
MRS. SHIN *is cleaning up. She talks and he takes no notice.*

MRS. SHIN And when certain rumors get about, what *happens* to a little
place like this? It goes to pot. *I* know. So, if you want my advice, Mr.
Shui Ta, find out just what has been going on between Miss Shen Te
and that Yang Sun from Yellow Street. And remember: a certain interest
in Miss Shen Te has been expressed by the barber next door, a man with
twelve houses and only one wife,[9] who, for that matter, is likely to drop
off at any time. A certain interest has been expressed. He was even
inquiring about her means and, if *that* doesn't prove a man is getting
serious, what would?

[*Still getting no response, she leaves with her bucket.*]

YANG SUN'S VOICE Is that Miss Shen Te's tobacco shop?
MRS. SHIN'S VOICE Yes, it is, but it's Mr. Shui Ta who's here today.

9. Ancient Chinese law permitted a man to have more than one wife.

[SHUI TA *runs to the mirror with the short, light steps of* SHEN TE, *and is just about to start primping, when he realizes his mistake, and turns away, with a short laugh. Enter* YANG SUN. MRS. SHIN *enters behind him and slips into the back room to eavesdrop.*]

YANG SUN   I am Yang Sun. [SHUI TA *bows.*] Is Shen Te in?

SHUI TA   No.

YANG SUN   I guess you know our relationship? [*He is inspecting the stock.*] Quite a place! And I thought she was just talking big. I'll be flying again, all right. [*He takes a cigar, solicits and receives a light from* SHUI TA.] You think we can squeeze the other three hundred out of the tobacco stock?

SHUI TA   May I ask if it is your intention to sell at once?

YANG SUN   It was decent of her to come out with the two hundred but they aren't much use with the other three hundred still missing.

SHUI TA   Shen Te was overhasty promising so much. She might have to sell the shop itself to raise it. Haste, they say, is the wind that blows the house down.

YANG SUN   Oh, she isn't a girl to keep a man waiting. For one thing or the other, if you take my meaning.

SHUI TA   I take your meaning

YANG SUN [*Leering.*]   Uh, huh.

SHUI TA   Would you explain what the five hundred silver dollars are for?

YANG SUN   Want to sound me out? Very well. The director of the Peking airfield is a friend of mine from flying school. I give him five hundred: he gets me the job.

SHUI TA   The price is high.

YANG SUN   Not as these things go. He'll have to fire one of the present pilots—for negligence. Only the man he has in mind isn't negligent. Not easy, you understand. You needn't mention that part of it to Shen Te.

SHUI TA [*Looking intently at* YANG SUN.]   Mr. Yang Sun, you are asking my cousin to give up her possessions, leave her friends, and place her entire fate in your hands. I presume you intend to marry her?

YANG SUN   I'd be prepared to.

[*Slight pause.*]

SHUI TA   Those two hundred silver dollars would pay the rent here for six months. If you were Shen Te wouldn't you be tempted to continue in business?

YANG SUN   What? Can you imagine Yang Sun the flyer behind a counter? [*In an oily voice.*] "A strong cigar or a mild one, worthy sir?" Not in this century!

SHUI TA   My cousin wishes to follow the promptings of her heart, and, from her own point of view, she may even have what is called the right to love. Accordingly, she has commissioned me to help you to this post. There is nothing here that I am not empowered to turn immediately into cash. Mrs. Mi Tzu, the landlady, will advise me about the sale.

[*Enter* MRS. MI TZU.]

MRS. MI TZU   Good morning, Mr. Shui Ta, you wish to see me about the rent? As you know it falls due the day after tomorrow.

SHUI TA   Circumstances have changed, Mrs. Mi Tzu: my cousin is getting married. Her future husband here, Mr. Yang Sun, will be taking her to Peking. I am interested in selling the tobacco stock.

MRS. MI TZU   How much are you asking, Mr. Shui Ta?

YANG SUN   Three hundred sil—

SHUI TA   Five hundred silver dollars.

MRS. MI TZU   How much did she pay for it, Mr. Shui Ta?

SHUI TA   A thousand. And very little has been sold.

MRS. MI TZU   She was robbed. But I'll make you a special offer if you'll promise to be out by the day after tomorrow. Three hundred silver dollars.

YANG SUN   [Shrugging.]   Take it, man, take it.

SHUI TA   It is not enough.

YANG SUN   Why not? Why not? Certainly, it's enough.

SHUI TA   Five hundred silver dollars.

YANG SUN   But why? We only need three!

SHUI TA   [To MRS. MI TZU.]   Excuse me. [Takes YANG SUN on one side.] The tobacco stock is pledged to the old couple who gave my cousin the two hundred.

YANG SUN   Is it in writing?

SHUI TA   No.

YANG SUN   [To MRS. MI TZU.]   Three hundred will do.

MRS. MI TZU   Of course, I need an assurance that Miss Shen Te is not in debt.

YANG SUN   Mr. Shui Ta?

SHUI TA   She is not in debt.

YANG SUN   When can you let us have the money?

MRS. MI TZU   The day after tomorrow. And remember: I'm doing this because I have a soft spot in my heart for young lovers! [Exit.]

YANG SUN   [Calling after her.]   Boxes, jars and sacks—three hundred for the lot and the pain's over! [To SHUI TA.] Where else can we raise money by the day after tomorrow?

SHUI TA   Nowhere. Haven't you enough for the trip and the first few weeks?

YANG SUN   Oh, certainly.

SHUI TA   How much, exactly.

YANG SUN   Oh, I'll dig it up, even if I have to steal it.

SHUI TA   I see.

YANG SUN   Well, don't fall off the roof. I'll get to Peking somehow.

SHUI TA   Two people can't travel for nothing.

YANG SUN   [Not giving SHUI TA a chance to answer.]   I'm leaving her behind. No millstones round my neck!

SHUI TA   Oh.

YANG SUN   Don't look at me like that!

SHUI TA   How precisely is my cousin to live?

YANG SUN   Oh, you'll think of something.

SHUI TA   A small request, Mr. Yang Sun. Leave the two hundred silver dollars here until you can show me two tickets for Peking.

YANG SUN   You learn to mind your own business, Mr. Shui Ta.

SHUI TA   I'm afraid Miss Shen Te may not wish to sell the shop when she discovers that . . .

YANG SUN   You don't know women. She'll want to. Even then.

SHUI TA   [A slight outburst.]   She is a human being, sir! And not devoid of common sense!

YANG SUN   Shen Te is a woman: she *is* devoid of common sense. I only
have to lay my hand on her shoulder, and church bells ring.

SHUI TA [*With difficulty.*]   Mr. Yang Sun!

YANG SUN   Mr. Shui Whatever-it-is!

SHUI TA   My cousin is devoted to you . . . because . . .

YANG SUN   Because I have my hands on her breasts. Give me a cigar. [*He
takes one for himself, stuffs a few more in his pocket, then changes his
mind and takes the whole box.*] Tell her I'll marry her, then bring me the
three hundred. Or let her bring it. One or the other. [*Exit.*]

MRS. SHIN [*Sticking her head out of the back room.*]   Well, he has your
cousin under his thumb, and doesn't care if all Yellow Street knows it!

SHUI TA [*Crying out.*]   I've lost my shop! And he doesn't love me! [*He runs
berserk through the room, repeating these lines incoherently. Then stops
suddenly, and addresses* MRS. SHIN.] Mrs. Shin, you grew up in the gutter,
like me. Are we lacking in hardness? I doubt it. If you steal a penny from
me, I'll take you by the throat till you spit it out! You'd do the same to
me. The times are bad, this city is hell, but we're like ants, we keep
coming, up and up the walls, however smooth! Till bad luck comes. Being
in love, for instance. One weakness is enough, and love is the deadliest.

MRS. SHIN [*Emerging from the back room.*]   You should have a little talk
with Mr. Shu Fu, the barber. He's a real gentleman and just the thing
for your cousin. [*She runs off.*]

SHUI TA

>   A caress becomes a stranglehold
>   A sigh of love turns to a cry of fear
>   Why are there vultures circling in the air?
>   A girl is going to meet her lover.

[SHUI TA *sits down and Mr.* SHU FU *enters with* MRS. SHIN.]

SHUI TA   Mr. Shu Fu?

SHU FU   Mr. Shui Ta.

[*They both bow.*]

SHUI TA   I am told that you have expressed a certain interest in my cousin
Shen Te. Let me set aside all propriety and confess: she is at this moment
in grave danger.

SHU FU   Oh, dear!

SHUI TA   She has lost her shop, Mr. Shu Fu.

SHU FU   The charm of Miss Shen Te, Mr. Shui Ta, derives from the goodness, not of her shop, but of her heart. Men call her the Angel of the
Slums.

SHUI TA   Yet her goodness has cost her two hundred silver dollars in a
single day: we must put a stop to it.

SHU FU   Permit me to differ, Mr. Shui Ta. Let us, rather, open wide the
gates to such goodness! Every morning, with pleasure tinged by affection,
I watch her charitable ministrations. For they are hungry, and she giveth
them to eat! Four of them, to be precise. Why only four? I ask. Why not
four hundred?[1] I hear she has been seeking shelter for the homeless.
What about my humble cabins behind the cattle run? They are at her

---

1. An allusion to the biblical miracle of loaves and fishes, when Christ fed five thousand people (Matthew
14.13–21).

disposal. And so forth. And so on. Mr. Shui Ta, do you think Miss Shen
Te could be persuaded to listen to certain ideas of mine? Ideas like these?

SHUI TA   Mr. Shu Fu, she would be honored.

    [*Enter* WONG *and the* POLICEMAN. *Mr.* SHU FU *turns abruptly away and
studies the shelves.*]

WONG   Is Miss Shen Te here?

SHUI TA   No.

WONG   I am Wong the water seller. You are Mr. Shui Ta?

SHUI TA   I am.

WONG   I am a friend of Shen Te's.

SHUI TA   An intimate friend, I hear.

WONG [*To the* POLICEMAN.]   You see? [*To* SHUI TA.] It's because of my hand.

POLICEMAN   He hurt his hand, sir, that's a fact.

SHUI TA [*Quickly.*]   You need a sling, I see. [*He takes a shawl from the back
room, and throws it to* WONG.]

WONG   But that's her new shawl!

SHUI TA   She has no more use for it.

WONG   But she bought it to please someone!

SHUI TA   It happens to be no longer necessary.

WONG [*Making the sling.*]   She is my only witness.

POLICEMAN   Mr. Shui Ta, your cousin is supposed to have seen the barber
hit the water seller with a curling iron.

SHUI TA   I'm afraid my cousin was not present at the time.

WONG   But she was, sir! Just ask her! Isn't she in?

SHUI TA [*Gravely.*]   Mr. Wong, my cousin has her own troubles. You
wouldn't wish her to add to them by committing perjury?

WONG   But it was she that told me to go to the judge!

SHUI TA   Was the judge supposed to heal your hand?

    [*Mr.* SHU FU *turns quickly around.* SHUI TA *bows to* SHU FU, *and vice
versa.*]

WONG [*Taking the sling off, and putting it back.*]   I see how it is.

POLICEMAN   Well, I'll be on my way. [*To* WONG.] And you be careful. If Mr.
Shu Fu wasn't a man who tempers justice with mercy, as the saying is,
you'd be in jail for libel. Be off with you!

    [*Exit* WONG *followed by* POLICEMAN.]

SHUI TA   Profound apologies, Mr. Shu Fu.

SHU FU   Not at all, Mr. Shui Ta. [*Pointing to the shawl.*] The episode is
over?

SHUI TA   It may take her time to recover. There are some fresh wounds.

SHUI FU   We shall be discreet. Delicate. A short vacation could be
arranged . . .

SHUI TA   First of course, you and she would have to talk things over.

SHU FU   At a small supper in a small, but high-class, restaurant.

SHUI TA   I'll go and find her. [*Exit into back room.*]

MRS. SHIN [*Sticking her head in again.*]   Time for congratulations, Mr. Shu
Fu?

SHU FU   Ah, Mrs. Shin! Please inform Miss Shen Te's guests they may take
shelter in the cabins behind the cattle run!

    [MRS. SHIN *nods, grinning.*]

SHU FU [*To the audience.*]   Well? What do you think of me, ladies and gentlemen? What could a man do more? Could he be less selfish? More farsighted? A small supper in a small but . . . Does that bring rather vulgar and clumsy thoughts into your mind? Ts, ts, ts. Nothing of the sort will occur. She won't even be touched. Not even accidentally while passing the salt. An exchange of ideas only. Over the flowers on the table— white chrysanthemums, by the way [He writes down a note of this.]—yes, over the white chrysanthemums, two young souls will . . . shall I say "find each other"? We shall NOT exploit the misfortune of others. Understanding? Yes. An offer of assistance? Certainly. But quietly. Almost inaudibly. Perhaps with a single glance. A glance that could also—mean more.

MRS. SHIN [Coming forward.]   Everything under control, Mr. Shu Fu?

SHU FU   Oh, Mrs. Shin, what do you know about this worthless rascal Yang Sun?

MRS. SHIN   Why, he's the most worthless rascal . . .

SHU FU   Is he really? You're sure? [As she opens her mouth.] From now on, he doesn't exist! Can't be found anywhere!

[Enter YANG SUN.]

YANG SUN   What's been going on here?

MRS. SHIN   Shall I call Mr. Shui Ta, Mr. Shu Fu? He wouldn't want strangers in here!

SHU FU   Mr. Shui Ta is in conference with Miss Shen Te. Not to be disturbed!

YANG SUN   Shen Te here? I didn't see her come in. What kind of conference?

SHU FU [Not letting him enter the back room.]   Patience, dear sir! And if by chance I have an inkling who you are, pray take note that Miss Shen Te and I are about to announce our engagement.

YANG SUN   What?

MRS. SHIN   You didn't expect that, did you?

[YANG SUN is trying to push past the barber into the back room when SHEN TE comes out.]

SHU FU   My dear Shen Te, ten thousand apologies! Perhaps you . . .

YANG SUN   What is it, Shen Te? Have you gone crazy?

SHEN TE [Breathless.]   My cousin and Mr. Shu Fu have come to an understanding. They wish me to hear Mr. Shu Fu's plans for helping the poor.

YANG SUN   Your cousin wants to part us.

SHEN TE   Yes.

YANG SUN   And you've agreed to it?

SHEN TE   Yes.

YANG SUN   They told you I was bad. [SHEN TE is silent.] And suppose I am. Does that make me need you less? I'm low, Shen Te, I have no money, I don't do the right thing but at least I put up a fight! [He is near her now, and speaks in an undertone.] Have you no eyes? Look at him. Have you forgotten already?

SHEN TE   No.

YANG SUN   How it was raining?

SHEN TE   No.

YANG SUN   How you cut me down from the willow tree? Bought me water? Promised me money to fly with?

SHEN TE [Shakily.]   Yang Sun, what do you want?

YANG SUN   I want you to come with me

SHEN TE [*In a small voice.*]   Forgive me, Mr. Shu Fu, I want to go with Mr. Yang Sun.

YANG SUN   We're lovers, you know. Give me the key to the shop. [SHEN TE *takes the key from around her neck.* YANG SUN *puts it on the counter. To* MRS. SHIN.] Leave it under the mat when you're through. Let's go, Shen Te.

SHU FU   But this is rape! Mr. Shui Ta!!

YANG SUN [*To* SHEN TE.]   Tell him not to shout.

SHEN TE   Please don't shout for my cousin, Mr. Shu Fu. He doesn't agree with me, I know, but he's wrong. [*To the audience.*]

> I want to go with the man I love
> I don't want to count the cost
> I don't want to consider if it's wise
> I don't want to know if he loves me
> I want to go with the man I love.

YANG SUN   That's the spirit.

[*And the couple leave.*]

5a

In front of the inner curtain. SHEN TE, *in her wedding clothes, on the way to her wedding.*

SHEN TE   Something terrible has happened. As I left the shop with Yang Sun, I found the old carpet dealer's wife waiting on the street, trembling all over. She told me her husband had taken to his bed—sick with all the worry and excitement over the two hundred silver dollars they lent me. She said it would be best if I gave it back now. Of course, I had to say I would. She said she couldn't quite trust my cousin Shui Ta or even my fiancé, Yang Sun. There were tears in her eyes. With my emotions in an uproar, I threw myself into Yang Sun's arms, I couldn't resist him. The things he'd said to Shui Ta had taught Shen Te nothing. Sinking into his arms, I said to myself:

> To let no one perish, not even oneself
> To fill everyone with happiness, even oneself
> Is so good

How could I have forgotten those two old people? Yang Sun swept me away like a small hurricane. But he's not a bad man, and he loves me. He'd rather work in the cement factory than owe his flying to a crime. Though, of course, flying *is* a great passion with Sun. Now, on the way to my wedding, I waver between fear and joy.

6

The "private dining room" on the upper floor of a cheap restaurant in a poor section of town. With SHEN TE: *the* GRANDFATHER, *the* SISTER-IN-LAW, *the* NIECE, MRS. SHIN, *the* UNEMPLOYED MAN. *In a corner, alone, a* PRIEST.[2] *A* WAITER *pouring wine. Downstage,* YANG SUN *talking to his mother. He wears a dinner jacket.*

---

2. A Buddhist monk or priest.

YANG SUN   Bad news, Mamma. She came right out and told me she can't
   sell the shop for me. Some idiot is bringing a claim because he lent her
   the two hundred she gave you.

MRS. YANG   What did you say? Of course, you can't marry her now.

YANG SUN   It's no use saying anything to *her*. I've sent for her cousin, Mr.
   Shui Ta. He said there was nothing in writing.

MRS. YANG   Good idea. I'll go out and look for him. Keep an eye on things.
   [*Exit* MRS. YANG. SHEN TE *has been pouring wine.*]

SHEN TE [*To the audience, pitcher in hand.*]   I wasn't mistaken in him. He's
   bearing up well. Though it must have been an awful blow—giving up
   flying. I do love him so. [*Calling across the room to him.*] Sun, you haven't
   drunk a toast with the bride!

YANG SUN   What do we drink to?

SHEN TE   Why, to the future!

YANG SUN   When the bridegroom's dinner jacket won't be a hired one!

SHEN TE   But when the bride's dress will still get rained on sometimes!

YANG SUN   To everything we ever wished for!

SHEN TE   May all our dreams come true!
   [*They drink.*]

YANG SUN [*With loud conviviality.*]   And now, friends, before the wedding
   gets under way, I have to ask the bride a few questions. I've no idea what
   kind of a wife she'll make, and it worries me. [*Wheeling on* SHEN TE.] For
   example. Can you make five cups of tea with three tea leaves?

SHEN TE   No.

YANG SUN   So I won't be getting very much tea. Can you sleep on a straw
   mattress the size of that book? [*He points to the large volume the* PRIEST
   is reading.]

SHEN TE   The two of us?

YANG SUN   The one of you.

SHEN TE   In that case, no.

YANG SUN   What a wife! I'm shocked!
   [*While the audience is laughing, his mother returns. With a shrug of her
   shoulders, she tells* SUN *the expected guest hasn't arrived. The* PRIEST
   shuts the book with a bang, and makes for the door.]

MRS. YANG   Where are *you* off to? It's only a matter of minutes.

PRIEST [*Watch in hand.*]   Time goes on, Mrs. Yang, and I've another wedding to attend to. Also a funeral.

MRS. YANG [*Irately.*]   D'you think we planned it this way? I was hoping to
   manage with one pitcher of wine, and we've run through two already.
   [*Points to empty pitcher. Loudly.*] My dear Shen Te, I don't know where
   your cousin can be keeping himself!

SHEN TE   My cousin?!

MRS. YANG   Certainly. I'm old-fashioned enough to think such a close relative should attend the wedding.

SHEN TE   Oh, Sun, is it the three hundred silver dollars?

YANG SUN [*Not looking her in the eye.*]   Are you deaf? Mother says she's old-
   fashioned. And I say I'm considerate. We'll wait another fifteen minutes.

HUSBAND   Another fifteen minutes.

MRS. YANG [*Addressing the company.*]   Now you all know, don't you, that
   my son is getting a job as a mail pilot?

SISTER-IN-LAW   In Peking, too, isn't it?

MRS. YANG   In Peking, too! The two of us are moving to Peking!

SHEN TE   Sun, tell your mother Peking is out of the question now.

YANG SUN   Your cousin'll tell her. If he agrees. I don't agree.

SHEN TE [*Amazed, and dismayed.*]   Sun!

YANG SUN   I hate this godforsaken Setzuan. What people! Know what they look like when I half close my eyes? Horses! Whinnying, fretting, stamping, screwing their necks up! [*Loudly.*] And what is it the thunder says? They are su-per-flu-ous! [*He hammers out the syllables.*] They've run their last race! They can go trample themselves to death! [*Pause.*] I've got to get out of here.

SHEN TE   But I've promised the money to the old couple.

YANG SUN   And since you always do the wrong thing, it's lucky your cousin's coming. Have another drink.

SHEN TE [*Quietly.*]   My cousin can't be coming.

YANG SUN   How d'you mean?

SHEN TE   My cousin can't be where I am.

YANG SUN   Quite a conundrum!

SHEN TE [*Desperately.*]   Sun, I'm the one that loves you. Not my cousin. He was thinking of the job in Peking when he promised you the old couple's money—

YANG SUN   Right. And that's why he's bringing the three hundred silver dollars. Here—to my wedding.

SHEN TE   He is not bringing the three hundred silver dollars.

YANG SUN   Huh? What makes you think that?

SHEN TE [*Looking into his eyes.*]   He says you only bought one ticket to Peking.

[*Short pause.*]

YANG SUN   That was yesterday. [*He pulls two tickets part way out of his inside pocket, making her look under his coat.*] Two tickets. I don't want Mother to know. She'll get left behind. I sold her furniture to buy these tickets, so you see . . .

SHEN TE   But what's to become of the old couple?

YANG SUN   What's to become of me? Have another drink. Or do you believe in moderation? If I drink, I fly again. And if you drink, you may learn to understand me.

SHEN TE   You want to fly. But I can't help you.

YANG SUN   "Here's a plane, my darling—but it's only got one wing!"

[*The* WAITER *enters.*]

WAITER   Mrs. Yang!

MRS. YANG   Yes?

WAITER   Another pitcher of wine, ma'am?

MRS. YANG   We have enough, thanks. Drinking makes me sweat.

WAITER   Would you mind paying, ma'am?

MRS. YANG [*To everyone.*]   Just be patient a few moments longer, everyone, Mr. Shui Ta is on his way over! [*To the* WAITER.] Don't be a spoilsport.

WAITER   I can't let you leave till you've paid your bill, ma'am.

MRS. YANG   But they know me here!

WAITER   That's just it.

PRIEST [*Ponderously getting up.*]   I humbly take my leave. [*And he does.*]

MRS. YANG [*To the others, desperately.*]   Stay where you are, everybody! The priest says he'll be back in two minutes!

YANG SUN   It's no good Mamma. Ladies and gentlemen, Mr. Shui Ta still hasn't arrived and the priest has gone home. We won't detain you any longer.

[*They are leaving now*]

GRANDFATHER [*In the doorway, having forgotten to put his glass down.*]   To the bride! [*He drinks, puts down the glass, and follows the others.*]

[*Pause.*]

SHEN TE   Shall I go too?

YANG SUN   You? Aren't you the bride? Isn't this your wedding? [*He drags her across the room, tearing her wedding dress.*] If we can wait, you can wait. Mother calls me her falcon. She wants to see me in the clouds. But I think it may be St. Nevercome's Day before she'll go to the door and see my plane thunder by. [*Pause. He pretends the guests are still present.*] Why such a lull in the conversation, ladies and gentlemen? Don't you like it here? The ceremony is only slightly postponed—because an important guest is expected at any moment. Also because the bride doesn't know what love is. While we're waiting, the bridegroom will sing a little song. [*He does so.*]

THE SONG OF ST. NEVERCOME'S DAY

On a certain day, as is generally known,
    One and all will be shouting: Hooray, hooray!
For the beggar maid's son has a solid-gold throne
And the day is St. Nevercome's Day
On St. Nevercome's, Nevercome's, Nevercome's Day
    He'll sit on his solid-gold throne

Oh, hooray, hooray! That day goodness will pay!
    That day badness will cost you your head!
And merit and money will smile and be funny
    While exchanging salt and bread
On St. Nevercome's, Nevercome's, Nevercome's Day
    While exchanging salt and bread

And the grass, oh, the grass will look down at the sky
    And the pebbles will roll up the stream
And all men will be good without batting an eye
    They will make of our earth a dream
On St. Nevercome's, Nevercome's, Nevercome's Day
    They will make of our earth a dream

And as for me, that's the day I shall be
    A flyer and one of the best
Unemployed man, you will have work to do
    Washerwoman, you'll get your rest
On St. Nevercome's, Nevercome's, Nevercome's Day
    Washerwoman, you'll get your rest

MRS. YANG   It looks like he's not coming.

[*The three of them sit looking at the door.*]

6a

Wong's den. The sewer pipe is again transparent and again the GODS *appear to* WONG *in a dream.*

WONG   I'm so glad you've come, illustrious ones. It's Shen Te. She's in great trouble from following the rule about loving thy neighbor. Perhaps she's *too* good for this world!

FIRST GOD   Nonsense! You are eaten up by lice and doubts!

WONG   Forgive me, illustrious one, I only meant you might deign to intervene.

FIRST GOD   Out of the question! My colleague here intervened in some squabble or other only yesterday. [*He points to the* THIRD GOD, *who has a black eye.*] The results are before us!

WONG   She had to call on her cousin again. But not even he could help. I'm afraid the shop is done for.

THIRD GOD [*A little concerned.*]   Perhaps we should help after all?

FIRST GOD   The gods help those that help themselves.

WONG   What if we *can't* help ourselves, illustrious ones?

[*Slight pause.*]

SECOND GOD   Try, anyway! Suffering ennobles!

FIRST GOD   Our faith in Shen Te is unshaken!

THIRD GOD   We certainly haven't found any *other* good people. You can see where we spend our nights from the straw on our clothes.

WONG   You might help her find her way by—

FIRST GOD   The good man finds his own way here below!

SECOND GOD   The good woman too.

FIRST GOD   The heavier the burden, the greater her strength!

THIRD GOD   We're only onlookers, you know.

FIRST GOD   And everything will be all right in the end, O ye of little faith!

[*They are gradually disappearing through these last lines.*]

7

The yard behind Shen Te's shop. A few articles of furniture on a cart. SHEN TE *and* MRS. SHIN *are taking the washing off the line.*

MRS. SHIN   If you ask me, you should fight tooth and nail to keep the shop.

SHEN TE   How can I? I have to sell the tobacco to pay back the two hundred silver dollars today.

MRS. SHIN   No husband, no tobacco, no house and home! What are you going to live on?

SHEN TE   I can work. I can sort tobacco.

MRS. SHIN   Hey, look, Mr. Shui Ta's trousers! He must have left here stark naked!

SHEN TE   Oh, he may have another pair, Mrs. Shin.

MRS. SHIN   But if he's gone for good as you say, why has he left his pants behind?

SHEN TE   Maybe he's thrown them away.

MRS. SHIN   Can I take them?

SHEN TE   Oh, no.

    [*Enter Mr.* SHU FU, *running.*]

SHU FU   Not a word! Total silence! I know all. You have sacrificed your own love and happiness so as not to hurt a dear old couple who had put their trust in you! Not in vain does this district—for all its malevolent tongues—call you the Angel of the Slums! That young man couldn't rise to your level, so you left him. And now, when I see you closing up the little shop, that veritable haven of rest for the multitude, well, I cannot, I cannot let it pass. Morning after morning I have stood watching in the doorway not unmoved—while you graciously handed out rice to the wretched. Is that never to happen again? Is the good woman of Setzuan to disappear? If only you would allow *me* to assist you! Now don't say anything! No assurances, no exclamations of gratitude! [*He has taken out his checkbook.*] Here! A blank check. [*He places it on the cart.*] Just my signature. Fill it out as you wish. Any sum in the world. I herewith retire from the scene, quietly, unobtrusively, making no claims, on tiptoe, full of veneration, absolutely selflessly . . . [*He has gone.*]

MRS. SHIN   Well! You're saved. There's always some idiot of a man. . . . Now hurry! Put down a thousand silver dollars and let me fly to the bank before he comes to his senses.

SHEN TE   I can pay you for the washing without any check.

MRS. SHIN   What? You're not going to cash it just because you might have to marry him? Are you crazy? Men like him *want* to be led by the nose! Are you still thinking of that flyer? All Yellow Street knows how he treated you!

SHEN TE

    When I heard his cunning laugh, I was afraid

    But when I saw the holes in his shoes, I loved him dearly.

MRS. SHIN   Defending that good-for-nothing after all that's happened!

SHEN TE [*Staggering as she holds some of the washing.*]   Oh!

MRS. SHIN [*Taking the washing from her, dryly.*]   So you feel dizzy when you stretch and bend? There couldn't be a little visitor on the way? If that's it, you can forget Mr. Shu Fu's blank check: it wasn't meant for a christening present!

    [*She goes to the back with a basket. Shen Te's eyes follow* MRS. SHIN *for a moment. Then she looks down at her own body, feels her stomach, and a great joy comes into her eyes.*]

SHEN TE   O joy! A new human being is on the way. The world awaits him. In the cities the people say: he's got to be reckoned with, this new human being! [*She imagines a little boy to be present, and introduces him to the audience.*] This is my son, the well-known flyer!

    Say: Welcome

    To the conqueror of unknown mountains and unreachable regions

    Who brings us our mail across the impassable deserts!

    [*She leads him up and down by the hand.*]

Take a look at the world, my son. That's a tree. Tree, yes. Say: "Hello, tree!" And bow. Like this. [*She bows.*] Now you know each other. And, look, here comes the water seller. He's a friend, give him your hand. A cup of fresh water for my little son, please. Yes, it *is* a warm day. [*Handing the cup.*] Oh dear, a policeman, we'll have to make a circle round *him*. Perhaps we can pick a few cherries over there in the rich Mr. Pung's garden. But we mustn't be seen. You want cherries? Just like children with fathers. No, no, you can't go straight at them like that. Don't pull. We must learn to be reasonable. Well, have it your own way. [*She has let him make for the cherries.*] Can you reach? Where to put them? Your mouth is the best place. [*She tries one herself.*] Mmm, they're good. But the policeman, we must run! [*They run.*] Yes, back to the street. Calm now, so no one will notice us. [*Walking the street with her child, she sings.*]

> Once a plum—'twas in Japan—
> Made a conquest of a man
> But the man's turn soon did come
> For he gobbled up the plum

[*Enter* WONG, *with a child by the hand. He coughs.*]

SHEN TE Wong!

WONG It's about the carpenter, Shen Te. He's lost his shop, and he's been drinking. His children are on the streets. This is one. Can you help?

SHEN TE [*To the child.*] Come here, little man. [*Takes him down to the footlights. To the audience.*]

> You there! A man is asking you for shelter!
> A man of tomorrow says: what about today?
> His friend the conqueror, whom you know,
> Is his advocate!

[*To* WONG.] He can live in Mr. Shu Fu's cabins. I may have to go there myself. I'm going to have a baby. That's a secret—don't tell Yang Sun—we'd only be in his way. Can you find the carpenter for me?

WONG I knew you'd think of something. [*To the child.*] Good-bye, son, I'm going for your father.

SHEN TE What about your hand, Wong? I wanted to help, but my cousin . . .

WONG Oh, I can get along with one hand, don't worry. [*He shows how he can handle his pole with his left hand alone.*]

SHEN TE But your right hand! Look, take this cart, sell everything that's on it, and go to the doctor with the money . . .

WONG She's still good. But first I'll bring the carpenter. I'll pick up the cart when I get back [*Exit* WONG.]

SHEN TE [*To the child.*] Sit down over here, son, till your father comes.

[*The child sits crosslegged on the ground. Enter the* HUSBAND *and* WIFE, *each dragging a large, full sack.*]

WIFE [*Furtively.*] You're alone, Shen Te, dear?

[SHEN TE *nods. The* WIFE *beckons to the* NEPHEW *offstage. He comes on with another sack.*]

WIFE Your cousin's away? [SHEN TE *nods.*] He's not coming back?

SHEN TE No. I'm giving up the shop.

WIFE That's why we're here. We want to know if we can leave these things in your new home. Will you do us this favor?

SHEN TE Why, yes, I'd be glad to.

HUSBAND [*Cryptically.*] And if anyone asks about them, say they're yours.

SHEN TE   Would anyone ask?
WIFE   [*With a glance back at her husband.*]   Oh, someone might. The
   police, for instance. They don't seem to like us. Where can we put it?
SHEN TE   Well, I'd rather not get in any more trouble . . .
WIFE   Listen to her! The good woman of Setzuan!
      [SHEN TE *is silent.*]
HUSBAND   There's enough tobacco in those sacks to give us a new start in
   life. We could have our own tobacco factory!
SHEN TE [*Slowly.*]   You'll have to put them in the back room
      [*The sacks are taken offstage, while the child is alone. Shyly glancing
      about him, he goes to the garbage can, starts playing with the contents,
      and eating some of the scraps. The others return.*]
WIFE   We're counting on you, Shen Te!
SHEN TE   Yes. [*She sees the child and is shocked.*]
HUSBAND   We'll see you in Mr. Shu Fu's cabins.
NEPHEW   The day after tomorrow.
SHEN TE   Yes. Now, go. Go! I'm not feeling well.
      [*Exeunt all three, virtually pushed off.*]
         He is eating the refuse in the garbage can!
         Only look at his little gray mouth!
      [*Pause. Music.*]
         As this is the world *my* son will enter
         I will study to defend him.
         To be good to you, my son,
         I shall be a tigress to all others
         If I have to.
         And I shall have to.
      [*She starts to go.*]
         One more time, then. I hope really the last.
      [*Exit* SHEN TE, *taking Shui Ta's trousers.* MRS. SHIN *enters and watches
      her with marked interest. Enter the* SISTER-IN-LAW *and the* GRANDFA-
      THER.*]
SISTER-IN-LAW   So it's true, the shop has closed down. And the furniture's
   in the back yard. It's the end of the road!
MRS. SHIN [*Pompously.*]   The fruit of high living, selfishness, and sensu-
   ality! Down the primrose path to Mr. Shu Fu's cabins—with you!
SISTER-IN-LAW   Cabins? Rat holes! He gave them to us because his soap
   supplies only went moldy there!
      [*Enter the* UNEMPLOYED MAN.]
UNEMPLOYED MAN   Shen Te is moving?
SISTER-IN-LAW   Yes, She was sneaking away.
MRS. SHIN   She's ashamed of herself, and no wonder!
UNEMPLOYED MAN   Tell her to call Mr. Shui Ta or she's done for this time!
SISTER-IN-LAW   Tell her to call Mr. Shui Ta or *we're* done for this time!
      [*Enter* WONG *and* CARPENTER, *the latter with a child on each hand.*]
CARPENTER   So we'll have a roof over our heads for a change!
MRS. SHIN   Roof? Whose roof?
CARPENTER   Mr. Shu Fu's cabins. And we have little Feng to thank for it.
   [*Feng, we find, is the name of the child already there; his father now takes
   him. To the other two.*] Bow to your little brother, you two!

[*The* CARPENTER *and the two new arrivals bow to Feng. Enter* SHUI TA.]

UNEMPLOYED MAN   Sst! Mr. Shui Ta!

[*Pause.*]

SHUI TA   And what is this crowd here for, may I ask?

WONG   How do you do, Mr. Shui Ta. This is the carpenter. Miss Shen Te promised him space in Mr. Shu Fu's cabins.

SHUI TA   That will not be possible.

CARPENTER   We can't go there after all?

SHUI TA   All the space is needed for other purposes.

SISTER-IN-LAW   You mean we have to get out? But we've got nowhere to go.

SHUI TA   Miss Shen Te finds it possible to provide employment. If the proposition interests you, you may stay in the cabins.

SISTER-IN-LAW [*With distaste.*]
You mean *work*? Work for Miss Shen Te?

SHUI TA   Making tobacco, yes. There are three bales here already. Would you like to get them?

SISTER-IN-LAW [*Trying to bluster.*]   We have our own tobacco! We were in the tobacco business before you were born!

SHUI TA [*To the* CARPENTER *and the* UNEMPLOYED MAN]   You *don't* have your own tobacco. What about you?

[*The* CARPENTER *and the* UNEMPLOYED MAN *get the point, and go for the sacks. Enter* MRS. MI TZU.]

MRS. MI TZU   Mr. Shui Ta? I've brought you your three hundred silver dollars.

SHUI TA   I'll sign your lease instead. I've decided not to sell.

MRS. MI TZU   What? You don't need the money for that flyer?

SHUI TA   No.

MRS. MI TZU   And you can pay six months' rent?

SHUI TA [*Takes the barber's blank check from the cart and fills it out.*]   Here is a check for ten thousand silver dollars. On Mr. Shu Fu's account. Look. [*He shows her the signature on the check.*] Your six months' rent will be in your hands by seven this evening. And now, if you'll excuse me.

MRS. MI TZU   So it's Mr. Shu Fu now. The flyer has been given his walking papers. These modern girls! In my day they'd have said she was flighty. That poor, deserted Mr. Yang Sun!

[*Exit* MRS. MI TZU. *The* CARPENTER *and the* UNEMPLOYED MAN *drag the three sacks back on the stage.*]

CARPENTER [*To* SHUI TA.]   I don't know why I'm doing this for you.

SHUI TA   Perhaps your children want to eat, Mr. Carpenter.

SISTER-IN-LAW [*Catching sight of the sacks.*]   Was my brother-in-law here?

MRS. SHIN   Yes, he was.

SISTER-IN-LAW   I thought as much. I know those sacks! That's our tobacco!

SHUI TA   Really? I thought it came from my back room! Shall we consult the police on the point?

SISTER-IN-LAW [*Defeated.*]   No.

SHUI TA   Perhaps you will show me the way to Mr. Shu Fu's cabins?

[*Taking Feng by the hand,* SHUI TA *goes off, followed by the* CARPENTER *and his two older children, the* SISTER-IN-LAW, *the* GRANDFATHER, *and*

the UNEMPLOYED MAN. *Each of the last three drags a sack. Enter* OLD
    MAN *and* OLD WOMAN.]

MRS. SHIN   A pair of pants—missing from the clothes line one minute—
    and next minute on the honorable backside of Mr. Shui Ta.

OLD WOMAN   We thought Miss Shen Te was here.

MRS. SHIN [*Preoccupied.*]   Well, she's not.

OLD MAN   There was something she was going to give us.

WONG   She was going to help me too. [*Looking at his hand.*] It'll be too
    late soon. But she'll be back. This cousin has never stayed long.

MRS. SHIN [*Approaching a conclusion.*]   No, he hasn't, has he?

7a

The Sewer Pipe: WONG *asleep. In his dream, he tells the* GODS *his fears. The* GODS
seem tired from all their travels. They stop for a moment and look over their
shoulders at the water seller.

WONG   Illustrious ones. I've been having a bad dream. Our beloved Shen
    Te was in great distress in the rushes down by the river—the spot where
    the bodies of suicides are washed up. She kept staggering and holding
    her head down as if she was carrying something and it was dragging her
    down into the mud. When I called out to her, she said she had to take
    your Book of Rules[3] to the other side, and not get it wet, or the ink would
    all come off. You had talked to her about the virtues, you know, the time
    she gave you shelter in Setzuan.

THIRD GOD   Well, but what do you suggest, my dear Wong?

WONG   Maybe a little relaxation of the rules, Benevolent One, in view of
    the bad times.

THIRD GOD   As for instance?

WONG   Well, um, good-will, for instance, might do instead of love?

THIRD GOD   I'm afraid that would create new problems.

WONG   Or, instead of justice, good sportsmanship?

THIRD GOD   That would only mean more work.

WONG   Instead of honor, outward propriety?

THIRD GOD   Still more work! No, no! The rules will have to stand, my dear
    Wong!
        [*Wearily shaking their heads, all three journey on.*]

8

Shui Ta's tobacco factory in Shu Fu's cabins. Huddled together behind bars,
several families, mostly women and children. Among these people the SISTER-IN-
LAW, *the* GRANDFATHER, *the* CARPENTER, *and his three children. Enter* MRS. YANG
followed by YANG SUN.

MRS. YANG [*To the audience.*]   There's something I just *have* to tell you:
    strength and wisdom are wonderful things. The strong and wise Mr. Shui
    Ta has transformed my son from a dissipated good-for-nothing into a

---

3. Reference to neo-Confucianist commentators' rigid and prescriptive interpretation of Confucius's *Ana-
lects*, especially regarding the role of women.

model citizen. As you may have heard, Mr. Shui Ta opened a small tobacco factory near the cattle runs. It flourished. Three months ago— I shall never forget it—I asked for an appointment, and Mr. Shui Ta agree to see us—me and my son. I can see him now as he came through the door to meet us. . . .

[*Enter* SHUI TA, *from a door.*]

SHUI TA What can I do for you, Mrs. Yang?

MRS. YANG This morning the police came to the house. We find you've brought an action for breach of promise of marriage. In the name of Shen Te. You also claim that Sun came by two hundred silver dollars by improper means.

SHUI TA That is correct.

MRS. YANG Mr. Shui Ta, the money's all gone. When the Peking job didn't materialize, he ran through it all in three days. I know he's a good-for-nothing. He sold my furniture. He was moving to Peking without me. Miss Shen Te thought highly of him at one time.

SHUI TA What do *you* say, Mr. Yang Sun?

YANG SUN The money's gone.

SHUI TA [*To* MRS. YANG.] Mrs. Yang, in consideration of my cousin's incomprehensible weakness for your son, I am prepared to give him another chance. He can have a job—here. The two hundred silver dollars will be taken out of his wages.

YANG SUN So it's the factory or jail?

SHUI TA Take your choice.

YANG SUN May I speak with Shen Te?

SHUI TA You may not.

[*Pause.*]

YANG SUN [*Sullenly.*] Show me where to go.

MRS. YANG Mr. Shui Ta, you are kindness itself: the gods will reward you! [*To* YANG SUN.] And honest work will make a man of you, my boy. [YANG SUN *follows* SHUI TA *into the factory.* MRS. YANG *comes down again to the footlights.*] Actually, honest work didn't agree with him—at first. And he got no opportunity to distinguish himself till—in the third week—when the wages were being paid . . .

[SHUI TA *has a bag of money. Standing next to his foreman—the former* UNEMPLOYED MAN—*he counts out the wages. It is Yang Sun's turn.*]

UNEMPLOYED MAN [*Reading.*] Carpenter, six silver dollars. Yang Sun, six silver dollars.

YANG SUN [*Quietly.*] Excuse me, sir. I don't think it can be more than five. May I see? [*He takes the foreman's list.*] It says six working days. But that's a mistake, sir. I took a day off for court business. And I won't take what I haven't earned, however miserable the pay is!

UNEMPLOYED MAN Yang Sun. Five silver dollars. [*To* SHUI TA.] A rare case, Mr. Shui Ta!

SHUI TA How is it the book says six when it should say five?

UNEMPLOYED MAN I must've made a mistake, Mr. Shui Ta. [*With a look at* YANG SUN.] It won't happen again.

SHUI TA [*Taking* YANG SUN *aside.*] You don't hold back, do you? You give your all to the firm. You're even honest. Do the foreman's mistakes always favor the workers?

YANG SUN   He does have . . . friends.

SHUI TA   Thank you. May I offer you any little recompense?

YANG SUN   Give me a trial period of one week, and I'll prove my intelligence is worth more to you than my strength.

MRS. YANG [*Still down at the footlights.*]   Fighting words, fighting words! That evening, I said to Sun: "If you're a flyer, then fly, my falcon! Rise in the world!" And he got to be foreman. Yes, in Mr. Shui Ta's tobacco factory, he worked real miracles.

[*We see* YANG SUN *with his legs apart standing behind the workers, who are handing along a basket of raw tobacco above their heads.*]

YANG SUN   Faster! Faster! You, there, d'you think you can just stand around, now you're not foreman any more? It'll be your job to lead us in song. Sing!

[UNEMPLOYED MAN *starts singing. The others join in the refrain.*]

SONG OF THE EIGHTH ELEPHANT

Chang had seven elephants—all much the same—
But then there was Little Brother
The seven, they were wild, Little Brother, he was tame
And to guard them Chang chose Little Brother
    Run faster!
    Mr. Chang has a forest park
    Which must be cleared before tonight
    And already it's growing dark!

When the seven elephants cleared that forest park
    Mr. Chang rode high on Little Brother
While the seven toiled and moiled till dark
    On his big behind sat Little Brother
    Dig faster!
    Mr. Chang has a forest park
    Which must be cleared before tonight
    And already it's growing dark!

And the seven elephants worked many an hour
    Till none of them could work another
Old Chang, he looked sour, on the seven he did glower
    But gave a pound of rice to Little Brother
    What was that?
    Mr. Chang has a forest park
    Which must be cleared before tonight
    And already it's growing dark!

And the seven elephants hadn't any tusks
    The one that had the tusks was Little Brother
Seven are no match for one, if the one has a gun!
    How old Chang did laugh at Little Brother!
    Keep on digging!
    Mr. Chang has a forest park
    Which must be cleared before tonight
    And already it's growing dark!

[*Smoking a cigar,* SHUI TA *strolls by.* YANG SUN, *laughing, has joined in the refrain of the third stanza and speeded up the tempo of the last stanza by clapping his hands.*]

MRS. YANG And that's why I say: strength and wisdom are wonderful things. It took the strong and wise Mr. Shui Ta to bring out the best in Yang Sun. A real superior man is like a bell. If you ring it, it rings, and if you don't, it don't, as the saying is.[4]

9

Shen Te's shop, now an office with club chairs and fine carpets. It is raining. SHUI TA, *now fat, is just dismissing the* OLD MAN *and* OLD WOMAN. MRS. SHIN, *in obviously new clothes, looks on, smirking.*

SHUI TA No! I canNOT tell you when we expect her back.
OLD WOMAN The two hundred silver dollars came today. In an envelope. There was no letter, but it must be from Shen Te. We want to write and thank her. May we have her address?
SHUI TA I'm afraid I haven't got it.
OLD MAN [*Pulling Old Woman's sleeve.*] Let's be going.
OLD WOMAN She's got to come back some time!
[*They move off, uncertainly, worried.* SHUI TA *bows.*]
MRS. SHIN They lost the carpet shop because they couldn't pay their taxes. The money arrived too late.
SHUI TA They could have come to me.
MRS. SHIN People don't like coming to you.
SHUI TA [*Sits suddenly, one hand to his head.*] I'm dizzy.
MRS. SHIN After all, you *are* in your seventh month. But old Mrs. Shin will be there in your hour of trial! [*She cackles feebly.*]
SHUI TA [*In a stifled voice.*] Can I count on that?
MRS. SHIN We all have our price, and mine won't be too high for the great Mr. Shui Ta! [*She opens Shui Ta's collar.*]
SHUI TA It's for the child's sake. All of this.
MRS. SHIN "All for the child," of course.
SHUI TA I'm so fat. People must notice.
MRS. SHIN Oh no, they think it's 'cause you're rich.
SHIU TA [*More feelingly.*] What will happen to the child?
MRS. SHIN You ask that nine times a day. Why, it'll have the best that money can buy!
SHUI TA He must never see Shui Ta.
MRS. SHIN Oh, no. Always Shen Te.
SHUI TA What about the neighbors? There are rumors, aren't there?
MRS. SHIN As long as Mr. Shu Fu doesn't find out, there's nothing to worry about. Drink this.
[*Enter* YANG SUN *in a smart business suit, and carrying a businessman's briefcase.* SHUI TA *is more or less in Mrs. Shin's arms.*]
YANG SUN [*Surprised.*] I guess I'm in the way.
SHUI TA [*Ignoring this, rises with an effort.*] Till tomorrow, Mrs. Shin.

---

4. A saying by the Chinese philosopher Mo-tzu (470–391 B.C.E.).

[MRS. SHIN *leaves with a smile, putting on her new gloves.*]

YANG SUN   Gloves now! She couldn't be fleecing you? And since when did *you* have a private life? [*Taking a paper from the briefcase.*] You haven't been at your best lately, and things are getting out of hand. The police want to close us down. They say that at the most they can only permit twice the lawful number of workers.

SHUI TA [*Evasively.*]   The cabins are quite good enough.

YANG SUN   For the workers maybe, not for the tobacco. They're too damp. We must take over some of Mrs. Mi Tzu's buildings.

SHUI TA   Her price is double what I can pay.

YANG SUN   Not unconditionally. If she has me to stroke her knees she'll come down.

SHUI TA   I'll never agree to that.

YANG SUN   What's wrong? Is it the rain? You get so irritable whenever it rains.

SHUI TA   Never! I will never . . .

YANG SUN   Mrs. Mi Tzu'll be here in five minutes. *You* fix it. And Shu Fu will be with her. . . . What's all that noise?

[*During the above dialogue,* WONG *is heard offstage, calling:* "The good Shen Te, where is she? Which of you has seen Shen Te, good people? Where is Shen Te?" *A knock. Enter* WONG.]

WONG   Mr. Shui Ta, I've come to ask when Miss Shen Te will be back, it's six months now. . . . There are rumors. People say something's happened to her.

SHUI TA   I'm busy. Come back next week.

WONG [*Excited.*]   In the morning there was always rice on her doorstep— for the needy. It's been there again lately!

SHUI TA   And what do people conclude from this?

WONG   That Shen Te is still in Setzuan! She's been . . . [*He breaks off.*]

SHUI TA   She's been what? Mr. Wong, if you're Shen Te's friend, talk a little less about her, that's my advice to you.

WONG   I don't want your advice! Before she disappeared, Miss Shen Te told me something very important—she's pregnant!

YANG SUN   What? What was that?

SHUI TA [*Quickly.*]   The man is lying.

WONG   A good woman isn't so easily forgotten, Mr. Shui Ta.

[*He leaves.* SHUI TA *goes quickly into the back room.*]

YANG SUN [*To the audience.*]   Shen Te pregnant? So that's why. Her cousin sent her away, so I wouldn't get wind of it. I have a son, a Yang appears on the scene, and what happens? Mother and child vanish into thin air! That scoundrel, that unspeakable . . . [*The sound of sobbing is heard from the back room.*] What was that? Someone sobbing? Who was it? Mr. Shui Ta the Tobacco King doesn't weep his heart out. And where does the rice come from that's on the doorstep in the morning? [SHUI TA *returns. He goes to the door and looks out into the rain.*] Where is she?

SHUI TA   Sh! It's nine o'clock. But the rain's so heavy, you can't hear a thing.

YANG SUN   What do you want to hear?

SHUI TA   The mail plane.

YANG SUN   What?!

SHUI TA I've been told *you* wanted to fly at one time. Is that all forgotten?

YANG SUN Flying mail is night work. I prefer the daytime. And the firm is very dear to me—after all it belongs to my ex-fiancée, even if she's not around. And she's not, is she?

SHUI TA What do you mean by that?

YANG SUN Oh, well, let's say I haven't altogether—lost interest.

SHUI TA My cousin might like to know that.

YANG SUN I might not be indifferent—if I found she was being kept under lock and key.

SHUI TA By whom?

YANG SUN By you.

SHUI TA What could you do about it?

YANG SUN I could submit for discussion—my position in the firm.

SHUI TA You are now my manager. In return for a more . . . . appropriate position, you might agree to drop the inquiry into your ex-fiancée's whereabouts?

YANG SUN I might.

SHUI TA What position *would* be more appropriate?

YANG SUN The one at the top.

SHUI TA My own? [*Silence.*] And if I preferred to throw you out on your neck?

YANG SUN I'd come back on my feet. With suitable escort.

SHUI TA The police?

YANG SUN The police.

SHUI TA And when the police found no one?

YANG SUN I might ask them not to overlook the back room. [*Ending the pretense.*] In short, Mr. Shui Ta, my interest in this young woman has not been officially terminated. I should like to see more of her. [*Into Shui Ta's face.*] Besides, she's pregnant and needs a friend. [*He moves to the door.*] I shall talk about it with the water seller.

> [*Exit.* SHUI TA *is rigid for a moment, then he quickly goes into the back room. He returns with Shen Te's belongings: underwear, etc. He takes a long look at the shawl of the previous scene. He then wraps the things in a bundle, which, upon hearing a noise, he hides under the table. Enter* MRS. MI TZU *and Mr.* SHU FU. *They put away their umbrellas and galoshes.*]

MRS. MI TZU I thought your manager was here, Mr. Shui Ta. He combines charm with business in a way that can only be to the advantage of all of us.

SHU FU You sent for us, Mr. Shui Ta?

SHUI TA The factory is in trouble.

SHU FU It always is.

SHUI TA The police are threatening to close us down unless I can show that the extension of our facilities is imminent.

SHU FU Mr. Shui Ta, I'm sick and tired of your constantly expanding projects. I place cabins at your cousin's disposal; you make a factory of them. I hand your cousin a check; you present it. Your cousin disappears; you find the cabins too small and start talking of yet more—

SHUI TA Mr. Shu Fu, I'm authorized to inform you that Miss Shen Te's return is now imminent.

SHU FU   Imminent? It's becoming his favorite word.

MRS. MI TZU   Yes, what does it mean?

SHUI TA   Mrs. Mi Tzu, I can pay you exactly half what you asked for your buildings. Are you ready to inform the police that I am taking them over?

MRS. MI TZU   Certainly, if I can take over your manager.

SHU FU   What?

MRS. MI TZU   He's so efficient.

SHUI TA   I'm afraid I need Mr. Yang Sun.

MRS. MI TZU   So do I.

SHUI TA   He will call on you tomorrow.

SHU FU   So much the better. With Shen Te likely to turn up at any moment, the presence of that young man is hardly in good taste.

SHUI TA   So we have reached a settlement. In what was once the good Shen Te's little shop we are laying the foundations for the great Mr. Shui Ta's twelve magnificent super tobacco markets. You will bear in mind that though they call me the Tobacco King of Setzuan, it is my cousin's interests that have been served . . .

VOICES [Off.]   The police, the police! Going to the tobacco shop! Something must have happened!

   [Enter YANG SUN, WONG, and the POLICEMAN.]

POLICEMAN   Quiet there, quiet, quiet! [They quiet down.] I'm sorry, Mr. Shui Ta, but there's a report that you've been depriving Miss Shen Te of her freedom. Not that I believe all I hear, but the whole city's in an uproar.

SHUI TA   That's a lie.

POLICEMAN   Mr. Yang Sun has testified that he heard someone sobbing in the back room.

SHU FU   Mrs. Mi Tzu and myself will testify that no one here has been sobbing.

MRS. MI TZU   We have been quietly smoking our cigars.

POLICEMAN   Mr. Shui Ta, I'm afraid I shall have to take a look at that room. [He does so. The room is empty.] No one there, of course, sir.

YANG SUN   But I heard sobbing. What's that?

   [He finds the clothes.]

WONG   Those are Shen Te's things. [To crowd.] Shen Te's clothes are here!

VOICES [Off, in sequence.]   Shen Te's clothes!
   —They've been found under the table!
   —Body of murdered girl still missing!
   —Tobacco King suspected!

POLICEMAN   Mr. Shui Ta, unless you can tell us where the girl is, I'll have to ask you to come along.

SHUI TA   I do not know.

POLICEMAN   I can't say how sorry I am, Mr. Shui Ta. [He shows him the door.]

SHUI TA   Everything will be cleared up in no time. There are still judges in Setzuan.

YANG SUN   I heard sobbing!

9a

Wong's den. For the last time, the GODS *appear to the water seller in his dream. They have changed and show signs of a long journey, extreme fatigue, and plenty of mishaps. The* FIRST *no longer has a hat; the* THIRD *has lost a leg; all three are barefoot.*

WONG Illustrious ones, at last you're here. Shen Te's been gone for months and today her cousin's been arrested. They think he murdered her to get the shop. But I had a dream and in this dream Shen Te said her cousin was keeping her prisoner. You must find her for us, illustrious ones!

FIRST GOD We've found very few good people anywhere, and even they didn't keep it up. Shen Te is still the only one that stayed good.

SECOND GOD If she *has* stayed good.

WONG Certainly she has. But she's vanished.

FIRST GOD That's the last straw. All is lost!

SECOND GOD A little moderation, dear colleague!

FIRST GOD [*Plaintively.*] What's the good of moderation now? If she can't be found, we'll have to resign! The world is a terrible place! Nothing but misery, vulgarity, and waste! Even the countryside isn't what it used to be. The trees are getting their heads chopped off by telephone wires, and there's such a noise from all the gunfire, and I can't stand those heavy clouds of smoke, and—

THIRD GOD The place is absolutely unlivable! Good intentions bring people to the brink of the abyss, and good deeds push them over the edge. I'm afraid our book of rules is destined for the scrap heap—

SECOND GOD It's people! They're a worthless lot!

THIRD GOD The world is too cold!

SECOND GOD It's people! They're too weak!

FIRST GOD Dignity, dear colleagues, dignity! Never despair! As for this world, didn't we agree that we only have to find one human being who can stand the place? Well, we found her. True, we lost her again. We must find her again, that's all! And at once!

  [*They disappear.*]

10

Courtroom. Groups: SHU FU *and* MRS. MI TZU; YANG SUN *and* MRS. YANG; WONG, *the* CARPENTER, *the* GRANDFATHER, *the* NIECE, *the* OLD MAN, *the* OLD WOMAN; MRS. SHIN, *the* POLICEMAN; *the* UNEMPLOYED MAN, *the* SISTER-IN-LAW.

OLD MAN So much power isn't good for one man.

UNEMPLOYED MAN And he's going to open twelve super tobacco markets!

WIFE One of the judges is a friend of Mr. Shu Fu's.

SISTER-IN-LAW Another one accepted a present from Mr. Shui Ta only last night. A great fat goose.

OLD WOMAN [*To* WONG] And Shen Te is nowhere to be found.

WONG Only the gods will ever know the truth.

POLICEMAN Order in the court! My lords the judges!

  [*Enter the* THREE GODS *in judges' robes. We overhear their conversation as they pass along the footlights to their bench.*]

THIRD GOD   We'll never get away with it, our certificates were so badly
   forged.
SECOND GOD   My predecessor's "sudden indigestion" will certainly cause
   comment.
FIRST GOD   But he *had* just eaten a whole goose.
UNEMPLOYED MAN   Look at that! *New* judges.
WONG   New judges. And what good ones!
   [*The* THIRD GOD *hears this, and turns to smile at* WONG. *The* GODS *sit.
   The* FIRST GOD *beats on the bench with his gavel. The* POLICEMAN *brings
   in* SHUI TA, *who walks with lordly steps. He is whistled[5] at.*]
POLICEMAN [*To* SHUI TA.]   Be prepared for a surprise. The judges have been
   changed.
   [SHUI TA *turns quickly round, looks at them, and staggers.*]
NIECE   What's the matter now?
WIFE   The great Tobacco King nearly fainted.
HUSBAND   Yes, as soon as he saw the new judges.
WONG   Does *he* know who they are?
   [SHUI TA *picks himself up, and the proceedings open.*]
FIRST GOD   Defendant Shui Ta, you are accused of doing away with your
   cousin Shen Te in order to take possession of her business. Do you plead
   guilty or not guilty?
SHUI TA   Not guilty, my lord.
FIRST GOD [*Thumbing through the documents of the case.*]   The first witness
   is the policeman. I shall ask him to tell us something of the respective
   reputations of Miss Shen Te and Mr. Shui Ta.
POLICEMAN   Miss Shen Te was a young lady who aimed to please, my lord.
   She liked to live and let live, as the saying goes. Mr. Shui Ta, on the
   other hand, is a man of principle. Though the generosity of Miss Shen
   Te forced him at times to abandon half measures, unlike the girl he was
   always on the side of the law, my lord. One time, he even unmasked a
   gang of thieves to whom his too trustful cousin had given shelter. The
   evidence, in short, my lord, proves that Mr. Shui Ta was *incapable* of the
   crime of which he stands accused!
FIRST GOD   I see. And are there others who could testify along, shall we
   say, the same lines?
   [SHU FU *rises.*]
POLICEMAN [*Whispering to* GODS.]   Mr. Shu Fu—a very important person.
FIRST GOD [*Inviting him to speak.*]   Mr. Shu Fu!
SHU FU   Mr. Shui Ta is a businessman, my lord. Need I say more?
FIRST GOD   Yes.
SHU FU   Very well, I will. He is Vice President of the Council of Commerce
   and is about to be elected a Justice of the Peace. [*He returns to his seat.*
   MRS. MI TZU *rises.*]
WONG   Elected! *He* gave him the job!
   [*With a gesture the* FIRST GOD *asks who* MRS. MI TZU *is.*]
POLICEMAN   Another very important person. Mrs. Mi Tzu.
FIRST GOD [*Inviting her to speak.*]   Mrs. Mi Tzu!
MRS. MI TZU   My lord, as Chairman of the Committee on Social Work, I
   wish to call attention to just a couple of eloquent facts: Mr. Shui Ta not

5. Hissed.

only has erected a model factory with model housing in our city, he is a regular contributor to our home for the disabled. [*She returns to her seat.*]

POLICEMAN [*Whispering.*] And she's a great friend of the judge that ate the goose!

FIRST GOD [*To the* POLICEMAN.] Oh, thank you. What next? [*To the Court, genially.*] Oh, yes. We should find out if any of the evidence is less favorable to the defendant.

    [WONG, *the* CARPENTER, *the* OLD MAN, *the* OLD WOMAN, *the* UNEMPLOYED MAN, *the* SISTER-IN-LAW, *and the* NIECE *come forward.*]

POLICEMAN [*Whispering.*] Just the riffraff, my lord.

FIRST GOD [*Addressing the "riffraff."*] Well, um, riffraff—do you know anything of the defendant, Mr. Shui Ta?

WONG Too much, my lord.

UNEMPLOYED MAN What don't we know, my lord.

CARPENTER He ruined us.

SISTER-IN-LAW He's a cheat.

NIECE Liar.

WIFE Thief.

BOY Blackmailer.

BROTHER Murderer.

FIRST GOD Thank you. We should now let the defendant state his point of view.

SHUI TA I only came on the scene when Shen Te was in danger of losing what I had understood was a gift from the gods. Because I did the filthy jobs which someone had to do, they hate me. My activities were restricted to the minimum, my lord.

SISTER-IN-LAW He had us arrested!

SHUI TA Certainly. You stole from the bakery!

SISTER-IN-LAW Such concern for the bakery! You didn't want the shop for yourself, I suppose!

SHUI TA I didn't want the shop overrun with parasites.

SISTER-IN-LAW We had nowhere else to go.

SHUI TA There were too many of you.

WONG What about this old couple: Were *they* parasites?

OLD MAN We lost our shop because of you!

OLD WOMAN And we gave your cousin money!

SHUI TA My cousin's fiancé was a flyer. The money had to go to *him*.

WONG Did you care whether he flew or not? Did you care whether she married him or not? You wanted her to marry someone else! [*He points to* SHU FU.]

SHUI TA The flyer unexpectedly turned out to be a scoundrel.

YANG SUN [*Jumping up.*] Which was the reason you made him your manager?

SHUI TA Later on he improved.

WONG And when he improved, you sold him to her? [*He points out* MRS. MI TZU.]

SHUI TA She wouldn't let me have her premises unless she had him to stroke her knees!

MRS. MI TZU What? The man's a pathological liar. [*To him.*] Don't mention my property to me as long as you live! Murderer! [*She rustles off, in high dudgeon.*]

YANG SUN [*Pushing in.*]   My lord, I wish to speak for the defendant.

SISTER-IN-LAW   Naturally. He's your employer.

UNEMPLOYED MAN   And the worst slave driver in the country.

MRS. YANG   That's a lie! My lord, Mr. shui ta is a great man. He . . .

YANG SUN   He's this and he's that, but he is not a murderer, my lord. Just fifteen minutes before his arrest I heard Shen Te's voice in his own back room.

FIRST GOD   Oh? Tell us more!

YANG SUN   I heard sobbing, my lord!

FIRST GOD   But lots of women sob, we've been finding.

YANG SUN   Could I fail to recognize her voice?

SHU FU   No, you made her sob so often yourself, young man!

YANG SUN   Yes. But I also made her happy. Till he [*Pointing at* SHUI TA.] decided to sell her to you!

SHUI TA   Because you didn't love her.

WONG   Oh, no: it was for the money, my lord!

SHUI TA   And what was the money for, my lord? For the poor! And for Shen Te so she could go on being good!

WONG   For the poor? That he sent to his sweatshops? And why didn't you let Shen Te be good when you signed the big check?

SHUI TA   For the child's sake, my lord.

CARPENTER   What about *my* children? What did he do about them?

    [SHUI TA *is silent.*]

WONG   The shop was to be a fountain of goodness. That was the gods' idea. You came and spoiled it!

SHUI TA   If I hadn't, it would have run dry!

MRS. SHIN   There's a lot in that, my lord.

WONG   What have you done with the good Shen Te, bad man? She *was* good, my lords, she was, I swear it! [*He raises his hand in an oath.*]

THIRD GOD   What's happened to your hand, water seller?

WONG [*Pointing to* SHUI TA.]   It's all his fault, my lord, *she* was going to send me to a doctor—[*To* SHUI TA.] You were her worst enemy!

SHUI TA   I was her only friend!

WONG   Where is she then? Tell us where your good friend is!

    [*The excitement of this exchange has run through the whole crowd.*]

ALL   Yes, where is she? Where is Shen Te? [*Etc.*]

SHUI TA   Shen Te . . . had to go.

WONG   Where? Where to?

SHUI TA   I cannot tell you! I cannot tell you!

ALL   Why? Why did she have to go away? [*Etc.*]

WONG [*Into the din with the first words, but talking on beyond the others.*]   Why not, why not? Why did she have to go away?

SHUI TA [*Shouting.*]   Because you'd all have torn her to shreds, that's why! My lords, I have a request. Clear the court! When only the judges remain, I will make a confession.

ALL [*Except* WONG, *who is silent, struck by the new turn of events.*]   So he's guilty? He's confessing! [*Etc.*]

FIRST GOD [*Using the gavel.*]   Clear the court!

POLICEMAN   Clear the court!

WONG   Mr. Shui Ta has met his match this time.

MRS. SHIN [*With a gesture toward the judges.*]   You're in for a little surprise.

[*The court is cleared. Silence.*]

SHUI TA   Illustrious ones!

[*The* GODS *look at each other, not quite believing their ears.*]

SHUI TA   Yes, I recognize you!

SECOND GOD [*Taking matters in hand, sternly.*]   What have you done with our good woman of Setzuan?

SHUI TA   I have a terrible confession to make: I am she! [*He takes off his mask, and tears away his clothes.* SHEN TE *stands there.*]

SECOND GOD   Shen Te!

SHEN TE   Shen Te, yes. Shui Ta *and* Shen Te. Both.

> Your injunction
> To be good and yet to live
> Was a thunderbolt:
> It has torn me in two
> I can't tell how it was
> But to be good to others
> And myself at the same time
> I could not do it
> Your world is not an easy one, illustrious ones!
> When we extend our hand to a beggar, he tears it off for us
> When we help the lost, we are lost ourselves
> And so
> Since not to eat is to die
> Who can long refuse to be bad?
> As I lay prostrate beneath the weight of good intentions
> Ruin stared me in the face
> It was when I was unjust that I ate good meat
> And hobnobbed with the mighty
> Why?
> Why are bad deeds rewarded?
> Good ones punished?
> I enjoyed giving
> I truly wished to be the Angel of the Slums
> But washed by a foster-mother in the water of the gutter
> I developed a sharp eye
> The time came when pity was a thorn in my side
> And, later, when kind words turned to ashes in my mouth
> And anger took over
> I became a wolf
> Find me guilty, then, illustrious ones,
> But know:
> All that I have done I did
> To help my neighbor
> To love my lover
> And to keep my little one from want
> For your great, godly deeds, I was too poor, too small.

[*Pause.*]

FIRST GOD [*Shocked.*]   Don't go on making yourself miserable, Shen Te!
We're overjoyed to have found you!

SHEN TE I'm telling you I'm the bad man who committed all those crimes!

FIRST GOD [*Using—or failing to use—his ear trumpet.*] The good woman who did all those good deeds?

SHEN TE Yes, but the bad man too!

FIRST GOD [*As if something had dawned.*] Unfortunate coincidences! Heartless neighbors!

THIRD GOD [*Shouting in his ear.*] But how is she to continue?

FIRST GOD Continue? Well, she's a strong, healthy girl . . .

SECOND GOD You didn't hear what she said!

FIRST GOD I heard every word! She is confused, that's all! [*He begins to bluster.*] And what about this book of rules—we can't renounce our rules, can we? [*More quietly.*] Should the world be changed? How? By whom? The world should *not* be changed! [*At a sign from him, the lights turn pink, and music plays.*]

> And now the hour of parting is at hand.
> Dost thou behold, Shen Te, yon fleecy cloud?
> It is our chariot. At a sign from me
> 'Twill come and take us back from whence we came
> Above the azure vault and silver stars. . . .

SHEN TE No! Don't go, illustrious ones!

FIRST GOD

> Our cloud has landed now in yonder field
> From which it will transport us back to heaven.
> Farewell, Shen Te, let not thy courage fail thee. . . .
> [*Exeunt* GODS.]

SHEN TE What about the old couple? They've lost their shop! What about the water seller and his hand? And I've got to defend myself against the barber, because I don't love him! And against Sun, because I do love him! How? How?

> [*Shen Te's eyes follow the* GODS *as they are imagined to step into a cloud, which rises and moves forward over the orchestra and up beyond the balcony.*]

FIRST GOD [*From on high.*] We have faith in you, Shen Te!

SHEN TE There'll be a child. And he'll have to be fed. I can't stay here. Where shall I go?

FIRST GOD Continue to be good, good woman of Setzuan!

SHEN TE I need my bad cousin!

FIRST GOD But not very often!

SHEN TE Once a week at least!

FIRST GOD Once a month will be quite enough!

SHEN TE [*Shrieking.*] No, no! Help!

> [*But the cloud continues to recede as the* GODS *sing.*]

VALEDICTORY HYMN

> What rapture, oh, it is to know
> A good thing when you see it
> And having seen a good thing, oh,
> What rapture 'tis to flee it

> Be good, sweet maid of Setzuan
> Let Shui Ta be clever
> Departing, we forget the man
> Remember your endeavor
>
> Because through all the length of days
> Her goodness faileth never
> Sing hallelujah! Make Shen Te's
> Good name live on forever!

SHEN TE   Help!

Epilogue

> You're thinking, aren't you, that this is no right
> Conclusion to the play you've seen tonight?
> After a tale, exotic, fabulous,
> A nasty ending was slipped up on us.
> We feel deflated too. We too are nettled
> To see the curtain down and nothing settled.
> How could a better ending be arranged?
> Could one change people? Can the world be changed?
> Would new gods do the trick? Will atheism?
> Moral rearmament? Materialism?
> It is for you to find a way, my friends,
> To help good men arrive at happy ends.
> *You* write the happy ending to the play!
> There must, there must, there's got to be a way!

FEDERICO GARCÍA LORCA
1898–1936

Although he died young, the poet and playwright Federico García Lorca is the best-known writer of modern Spain and perhaps the most famous Spanish writer since Cervantes. A member of the brilliant "Generation of 1927"—along with Jorge Guillén, Vicente Aleixandre, Pedro Salinas, and Rafael Alberti—and known for the striking imagery and lyric musicality of his work, Lorca is both classical and modern, traditional and innovative, difficult and popular, a voice combining regional and universal themes. The poetry and plays that began as personal statements took on larger significance first as the expression of tragic conflicts in Spanish culture and then as poignant laments for an anguished humanity. When Lorca was dragged from a friend's house and executed by a Fascist squad on August 19, 1936, his murder outraged the whole European and American literary and artistic community, and seemed to symbolize the mindless destruction of humane and cultural values that loomed with the approach of World War II.

Lorca was born on June 5, 1898, in the small village of Fuentevaqueros, near the Andalusian city of Granada. (Despite the Spanish practice of using both paternal and maternal last names—correctly "García Lorca"—the author is generally called "Lorca.") His father was a prosperous farmer, and his mother, who had been a schoolteacher, encouraged him to read widely and develop his musical talent. The composer Manuel de Falla befriended the young musician, who became an expert pianist and guitar player. Lorca began law studies at the University of Granada, where—after several years' absence—he received a degree in 1923. He published a book called *Impressions and Landscapes* (1918) after a trip through Spain but left Granada in 1919 for Madrid, where he entered the Residencia de Estudiantes, a modern college established to provide a cosmopolitan education for Spanish youth. Madrid was not only the capital of Spain but also the center of intellectual and artistic ferment, and the Residencia attracted many of those who would become the most influential writers and artists of their generation (among the latter the artist Salvador Dalí and the film director Luis Buñuel). From poetry readings and the publication of a few poems in magazines, Lorca quickly gained the reputation of a rising young poet, even before the appearance of his first collection of verse, the *Book of Poems* of 1921. Although he lived at the Residencia almost continuously until 1928, he never seriously pursued a degree but spent his time reading, writing, improvising music and poetry in company with his friends, and producing his first plays.

In these early years, before his departure for New York in 1929, Lorca concentrated on writing poetry, although he was clearly interested in the theater as well. *The Butterfly's Evil Spell* (1920), a fantasy about a cockroach that is hopelessly enchanted by the beauty of a butterfly, was staged in Barcelona; in 1923 Lorca wrote, designed sets for, and directed a puppet play on a theme from Andalusian folklore, *The Girl Who Waters the Sweet Basil Flower and the Inquisitive Prince,* for which de Falla himself arranged the music. Yet the major achievement of this period is the composition of several books of poetry, not all of which were published at the time: the *Book of Poems*; most of the *Songs* (1927); early versions of the poems in the *Poem of the Deep Song,* which was not published as a book until 1931, although several poems were recited at a 1922 Andalusian festival; and the *Gypsy Ballads* (1928), which was an immediate popular success.

The first collection, the *Book of Poems,* introduces themes that will become familiar in later works: death, an innocent or childlike point of view, a closeness to nature that takes the form of animal fables or symbolic meanings attached to images like the pomegranate ("the idea of blood enclosed / In a hard and bitter globe"), and overall a certain witty or ironic distance from the situations he describes. The playful tone never quite covers Lorca's constant preoccupation with death, however: death as the common fate that shadows our most vivid experiences. Speaking to a chorus of questioning children in *The Ballad of the Little Square,* the poet answers that he feels in his mouth only "the savor of the bones / of my great skull."

The *Poem of the Deep Song* marked a return to the gypsy themes and ballads of Lorca's home province of Andalusia, a region known for its mixture of Arab and Spanish culture and for a tradition of wandering gypsy singers who improvised, to guitar accompaniment, rhythmic laments on themes of love and death. The *cante jondo* ("deep song") was an ancient Andalusian ballad form that centered on repeated notes or phrases, and Lorca took full advantage (as he would in the *Lament for Ignacio Sánchez Mejías*) of the haunting quality that could be obtained through this obsessive refrain. The *Songs* written subsequently are noted for their lyricism and for the moments of experience they capture; however, many reach beyond the sensuously precise description of real objects to encompass abstract concepts, psychological states, and clusters of associations—as does the Symbolist poetry Lorca knew. Lorca describes how "the ear of grain keeps intact / its hard yellow laughter," how a little mute boy looks for his voice in a drop of water, and how Narcissus (both youth and flower) is mirrored in a double image in which "over your white eyes flicker / shadows and sleeping fish."

Lorca's next collection, the *Gypsy Ballads,* marks the beginning of his mature verse.

Blending classical ballad form with scenes taken directly from contemporary life, the poet expresses, with images of violence and eroticism, the tragic struggle in which innocence, spontaneity, creativity, and freedom are repressed by society and by the inevitable limitations of human nature. In the famous *Ballad of the Spanish Civil Guard*, the militia with their "patent-leather souls" and heads filled with "a vague astronomy / of shapeless pistols" cut down the gypsies in their fantastic city with its banners and "cinnamon towers." The unsuspecting populace, caught in the midst of their festival, are helpless to prevent absolute destruction—the tile roofs become "furrows in the soil," and the burned city itself persists only in the sterile "play of moon and sand" on the poet's brow. A hostile, violent world is pictured here, in which even the wind pursues a young girl with lustful breath and "hot sword," and St. Eulalia's martyrdom and mutilation are described with a mixture of eroticism and horror. These themes are not restricted to poetry: they reoccur in a contemporary play, *Mariana Pineda* (1928), in which Lorca's heroine is executed for refusing to identify a group of revolutionaries (among them the lover who abandoned her).

Impelled by an emotional crisis, Lorca left Spain for New York in 1929 and there wrote a series of poems later published as *Poet in New York* (1940). The collection does not focus exclusively on the city, however, and moves from the poet's youth in Europe to scenes of rural New York and northern Vermont as Lorca tries to come to terms with his own complex personality against a background of psychological, artistic, and social tensions. Blended with the familiar theme of doomed love and death is a tentative exploration of homosexuality, which Lorca could not admit to inside traditional Spanish society and which he expressed only with hesitation and anxiety in this and later works. A large part of the ten-section *Poet in New York* does, however, focus primarily on the city, which is seen as a frightening symbol of the modern industrial West. In a richly varied and densely metaphorical apocalyptic vision, Lorca juxtaposes two ways of life and creates a vision of contrast that, he said, "puts my poetic world in contact with the poetic world of New York." Beginning with a denunciation of the dehumanized commercial city-world of sterile concrete and glass, he moves on to celebrate the only area where the natural world survives: Harlem, with its "garnet violence deaf and dumb in the shadows," and its "great king a prisoner in a janitor's uniform." In the face of this universal despair there are foreshadowings of a coming upheaval when "the Stock Market will be a pyramid of moss" and the oppressed and deprived will unite to proclaim "the reign of the ear of corn." The book's ending sections mark an escape from New York to Havana and (in spite of a continued sense of alienation) to the dancelike harmony of a more primitive life.

From 1930 to his death in 1936, Lorca was extremely active in the theater both as writer and as director (after 1931) of a traveling theatrical group (La Barraca) subsidized by the Spanish Republic. After a series of farces that mixed romantically tragic and comic themes, he presented the tragedies for which he is best known: *Blood Wedding* (1933) and *Yerma* (1934). In 1936 he wrote the posthumously published *The House of Bernarda Alba* (1945). All Lorca's theater, from the early fantasy of *The Butterfly's Evil Spell* to the puppet plays, farces, and last tragedies, rejects the conventionally realistic nineteenth-century drama and employs an openly poetic form that suggests musical patterns, includes choruses, songs, and stylized movement, and may even (as in the fragmentary surrealist drama, *The Audience*) attack the audience itself. The tragic themes of Lorca's poetry emerge here in dramatic form, usually centering on the suffering of individual women whose instinctual fulfillment (through love or children) is denied by fate or social circumstance. In *Blood Wedding*, the Mother's last remaining son dies in a moonlit struggle with Leonardo, who has run away with the son's bride (Leonardo's former betrothed) on their wedding day. Leonardo (who also dies) is a member of the family that has killed the Mother's husband and other sons, and images of approaching death and sensual, frustrated love permeate the whole play. In *Yerma* (the title name also means desert or sterility), the heroine is caught between her own passionate, sensual nature, yearning to love and bear children, and the need—for honor's sake—to remain with a husband who cares only for a well-regulated house. When Yerma realizes the extent of Juan's spiritual as well as sexual sterility, she strangles him and (because she will not remarry) simultaneously kills her only chance to fulfill her natural instincts through bearing children. *The House of Bernarda Alba* (subtitled "A Drama about Women in the Villages of Spain") revolves around the same themes of sterility and frustrated love, as the repressed spinster daughters of the stern matriarch Bernarda Alba (and even the mad grandmother) reveal their common desire to marry a young man. Bernarda, however, upholds the proprieties that hedge in Spanish society; she refuses to let her daughters have visitors, ignores their rivalry over young Pepe el Romano (engaged to the wealthy oldest daughter, Angustias), recommends a painful death for an unwed mother being dragged through the streets, and—when the youngest daughter, Adela, commits suicide over Pepe, who has become her lover—seems chiefly concerned that Adela's body be dressed "as though she were a virgin." The conflict between social custom and individual need takes on mythic proportions in *The House of Bernarda Alba*, where only women appear on a stage that is strangely quarantined and painted white, and where the disturbing male principle represented by Pepe el Romano is reiterated by the noise of a stallion's hooves banging against stable walls.

In 1936, the year of his death, Lorca was revising a series of short lyric poems based on the Arabic forms of *casida* and the *gacela,* a collection eventually published in 1940 as *The Divan at Tamarit* (a "divan" is a poetic collection and Lorca wrote the poems at a country house called after the ancient place-name of Tamarit). In the previous year, he had published a long elegiac poem on the death of his good friend, the famous bullfighter Ignacio Sánchez Mejías, who had been fatally gored by a bull on August 11, 1934, in Manzanares and died two days later in Madrid. Sánchez Mejías was a cultured man, well known in literary circles and himself the author of a play, and Lorca's *Lament for Ignacio Sánchez Mejías* celebrates both his friend and the value of human grace and courage in a world where everything ends in death.

Lorca's *Lament* is not only cast as an elegy (a medium-length poem that mourns a death), but also recalls one of the most famous poems of Spanish literature: the *Verses on the Death of His Father* written by the medieval poet Jorge Manrique (1440–1479). Manrique's catalog of his father's noble qualities ("What a friend to his friends!") and his description of individual lives as flowing into the sea of death are echoed by passages in the modern elegy. Yet there is a fundamental difference between the two: while Manrique's elegy stresses religious themes and the prospect of eternal life, Lorca—in grim contrast—rejects such consolation and insists that his friend's death is permanent.

The four parts of the *Lament* incorporate a variety of forms and perspectives, all working together to suggest a progression from the report of death in the precise first line—"At five in the afternoon"—to the end where the dead man's nobility and elegance survive in "a sad breeze through the olive trees." The "deep song" technique of an insistent refrain coloring the whole organizes the first section, *Cogida* [the bull's toss] *and Death,* with its throbbing return to the moment of death. The scene in the arena wavers between an objective report—the boy with the shroud, the coffin on wheels—and the shared agony of the bull's bellowing and wounds burning like suns. Lorca moves in the next ballad section to a personal refusal of Sánchez Mejías's death ("I will not see it!") and a request that images of whiteness cover up this spilled blood; instead, he imagines Ignacio climbing steps to seek dawn and a mystic meeting with his true self but encountering, bewildered, only his broken body. After a tribute to his princely friend, the poet finally admits what he cannot force himself to see: the finality of physical dissolution as moss and grass invade the buried bullfighter's skull.

In *The Laid Out Body,* a series of somber quatrains in regular meter recognizes the inevitability of death and dissolution (Ignacio's "pure shape which had nightingales" is now "filled with depthless holes"), and the fact that the bullfighter will be entombed in unyielding, lifeless stone. In this and the final section, with its rhythmic free verse, Lorca accepts physical death ("even the sea dies!") but preserves, in his poetry, a vision of his noble countryman that surpasses such obliteration. For those who exist only on the unthinking, physical level (the bull, fig tree, household ants, the black satin of his funeral suit), Ignacio has indeed "died for ever." Yet human beings recognize other qualities beyond the physical and in fact shape their estimate of an individual according to these qualities. In life, Sánchez Mejías was known to his friends for "the signal maturity of your understanding . . . your appetite for death and the taste of its mouth." These qualities survive, for a while, in memory. Lorca, echoing the pride with which the Latin poet Horace claimed to perpetuate his subjects in a "monument of lasting bronze," sings of his friend "for posterity" and captures the life and death of Sánchez Mejías in his *Lament*.

Lament for Ignacio Sánchez Mejías[1]

1. Cogida[2] and Death

At five in the afternoon.
It was exactly five in the afternoon.
A boy brought the white sheet
at five in the afternoon.
A frail of lime[3] ready prepared   5
at five in the afternoon.
The rest was death, and death alone
at five in the afternoon.

The wind carried away the cottonwool[4]
at five in the afternoon.   10
And the oxide scattered crystal and nickel
at five in the afternoon.
Now the dove and the leopard[5] wrestle
at five in the afternoon.
And a thigh with a desolate horn   15
at five in the afternoon.
The bass-string struck up
at five in the afternoon.
Arsenic bells[6] and smoke
at five in the afternoon.   20
Groups of silence in the corners
at five in the afternoon.
And the bull alone with a high heart!
At five in the afternoon.
When the sweat of snow was coming   25
at five in the afternoon,
when the bull ring was covered in iodine
at five in the afternoon,

1. Translated by Stephen Spender and J. L. Gili.   2. Harvesting (Spanish, literal trans.); the toss when the bull catches the bullfighter.   3. A disinfectant that was sprinkled on the body after death. *Frail:* a basket.   4. To stop the blood; the beginning of a series of medicinal, chemical, and inhuman images that emphasize the presence of death.   5. Traditional symbols for peace and violence; they wrestle with one another as the bullfighter's thigh struggles with the bull's horn.   6. Bells are rung to announce a death. The *bass-string* of the guitar strums a lament.

death laid eggs in the wound
at five in the afternoon.
At five in the afternoon.
Exactly at five o'clock in the afternoon.   30

A coffin on wheels is his bed
at five in the afternoon.
Bones and flutes resound in his ears[7]
at five in the afternoon.   35
Now the bull was bellowing through his forehead
at five in the afternoon.
The room[8] was iridescent with agony
at five in the afternoon.   40
In the distance the gangrene now comes
at five in the afternoon.
Horn of the lily through green[9] groins
at five in the afternoon.
The wounds were burning like suns   45
at five in the afternoon,
and the crowd was breaking the windows[1]
at five in the afternoon.
At five in the afternoon.
Ah, that fatal five in the afternoon!   50
It was five by all the clocks!
It was five in the shade of the afternoon!

2. *The Spilled Blood*

I will not see it!

Tell the moon to come
for I do not want to see the blood   55
of Ignacio on the sand.
I will not see it!

The moon wide open.
Horse of still clouds,
and the grey bull ring of dreams   60
with willows in the barreras.[2]
I will not see it!

Let my memory kindle![3]
Warn the jasmines[4]
of such minute whiteness!   65
I will not see it!

The cow of the ancient world
passed her sad tongue

7. A suggestion of the medieval dance of death.   8. The room adjoining the arena where wounded
bullfighters are taken for treatment.   9. Gangrene turns flesh a greenish color. *Lily:* the shape of the
wound resembles this flower.   1. A Spanish idiom for the crowd's loud roar.   2. The barriers around
the ring within which the fight takes place and over which a fighter may escape the bull's charge. *Willows:*
symbols of mourning.   3. My memory burns within me (literal trans.).   4. The poet calls on (*warn* as
"notify") the small white jasmine flowers to come and cover the blood.

over a snout of blood
spilled on the sand,
and the bulls of Guisando,[5]   70
partly death and partly stone,
bellowed like two centuries
sated with treading the earth.
No.
I do not want to see it!   75
I will not see it!

Ignacio goes up the tiers[6]
with all his death on his shoulders.
He sought for the dawn
but the dawn was no more.   80
He seeks for his confident profile
and the dream bewilders him.
He sought for his beautiful body
and encountered his opened blood.   85
Do not ask me to see it!
I do not want to hear it spurt
each time with less strength:
that spurt that illuminates
the tiers of seats, and spills   90
over the corduroy and the leather
of a thirsty multitude.
Who shouts that I should come near!
Do not ask me to see it!

His eyes did not close   95
when he saw the horns near,
but the terrible mothers
lifted their heads.[7]
And across the ranches,[8]
an air of secret voices rose,   100
shouting to celestial bulls,
herdsmen of pale mist.
There was no prince in Seville[9]
who could compare with him,
nor sword like his sword   105
nor heart so true.
Like a river of lions
was his marvellous strength,
and like a marble torso
his firm drawn moderation.   110
The air of Andalusian Rome
gilded his head[1]
where his smile was a spikenard[2]
of wit and intelligence.

---

5. Carved stone bulls from the Celtic past, a tourist attraction in the province of Madrid.   6. An imaginary scene in which the bullfighter mounts the stairs of the arena.   7. The three Fates traditionally raised their heads when the thread of life was cut.   8. Fighting bulls are raised on the ranches of Lorca's home province of Andalusia.   9. Leading city of Andalusia.   1. The image suggests a statue from Roman times, when Andalusia was part of the Roman Empire.   2. A small, white, fragrant flower common in Andalusia; by extension, the bullfighter's white teeth.

What a great torero[3] in the ring! 115
What a good peasant in the sierra![4]
How gentle with the sheaves!
How hard with the spurs!
How tender with the dew!
How dazzling in the fiesta! 120
How tremendous with the final
banderillas[5] of darkness!

But now he sleeps without end.
Now the moss and the grass
open with sure fingers 125
the flower of his skull.
And now his blood comes out singing;
singing along marshes and meadows,
sliding on frozen horns,
faltering soulless in the mist, 130
stumbling over a thousand hoofs
like a long, dark, sad tongue,
to form a pool of agony
close to the starry Guadalquivir.[6]
Oh, white wall of Spain! 135
Oh, black bull of sorrow!
Oh, hard blood of Ignacio!
Oh, nightingale of his veins!
No.
I will not see it! 140
No chalice can contain it,
no swallows[7] can drink it,
no frost of light can cool it,
nor song nor deluge of white lilies,
no glass can cover it with silver. 145
No.
I will not see it!

3. *The Laid Out Body*[8]

Stone is a forehead where dreams grieve
without curving waters and frozen cypresses.
Stone is a shoulder on which to bear Time 150
with trees formed of tears and ribbons and planets.[9]

I have seen grey showers move towards the waves
raising their tender riddled arms,
to avoid being caught by the lying stone
which loosens their limbs without soaking the blood. 155

---

3. Bullfighter.   4. Mountainous country. Sánchez Mejías is seen as a good *serrano* or "man of the hills."
5. The multicolored short spears that are thrust in the bull's shoulders to provoke him to attack.   6. A
great river that passes through all the major cities of Andalusia. The singing stream of the bullfighter's
blood suggests both the river and a nightingale.   7. According to a Spanish legend of the Crucifixion,
swallows—a symbol of innocence—drank the blood of Christ on the Cross. The poet is seeking ways of
concealing the dead man's blood.   8. Present body (literal trans.); the Spanish expression for a funeral
wake, when the body is laid out for public mourning. The title contrasts with that of the next section:
Absent Soul.   9. Traditional funeral imagery carved on gravestones.

For stone gathers seed and clouds,
skeleton larks and wolves of penumbra:
but yields not sounds nor crystals nor fire,
only bull rings and bull rings and more bull rings without walls.

Now Ignacio the well born lies on the stone.   160
All is finished. What is happening? Contemplate his face:
death has covered him with pale sulphur
and has placed on him the head of a dark minotaur.[1]

All is finished. The rain penetrates his mouth.
The air, as if mad, leaves his sunken chest,   165
and Love, soaked through with tears of snow,
warms itself on the peak of the herd.[2]

What are they saying? A stenching silence settles down.
We are here with a body laid out which fades away,
with a pure shape which had nightingales   170
and we see it being filled with depthless holes.

Who creases the shroud? What he says is not true![3]
Nobody sings here, nobody weeps in the corner,
nobody pricks the spurs, nor terrifies the serpent.
Here I want nothing else but the round eyes   175
to see this body without a chance of rest.

Here I want to see those men of hard voice.
Those that break horses and dominate rivers;
those men of sonorous skeleton who sing
with a mouth full of sun and flint.   180

Here I want to see them. Before the stone.
Before this body with broken reins.
I want to know from them the way out
for this captain strapped down by death.

I want them to show me a lament like a river   185
which will have sweet mists and deep shores,
to take the body of Ignacio where it loses itself
without hearing the double panting of the bulls.

Loses itself in the round bull ring of the moon
which feigns in its youth a sad quiet bull: 190
loses itself in the night without song of fishes
and in the white thicket of frozen smoke.

I don't want them to cover his face with handkerchiefs
that he may get used to the death he carries.
Go, Ignacio; feel not the hot bellowing.   195
Sleep, fly, rest: even the sea dies!

---

1. A monster from Greek myth: half man, half bull.   2. Of the ranch (literal trans.).   3. Lorca criticizes the conventional pieties voiced by someone standing close to the shrouded body; the poet prefers a clear-eyed, realistic view of death.

4. Absent Soul

The bull does not know you, nor the fig tree,
nor the horses, nor the ants in your own house.
The child and the afternoon do not know you
because you have died for ever.   200

The back of the stone does not know you,
nor the black satin in which you crumble.
Your silent memory does not know you
because you have died for ever.

The autumn will come with small white snails,[4]   205
misty grapes and with clustered hills,
but no one will look into your eyes
because you have died for ever.

Because you have died for ever,
like all the death of the Earth,   210
like all the dead who are forgotten
in a heap of lifeless dogs.[5]

Nobody knows you. No. But I sing of you.
For posterity I sing of your profile and grace.
Of the signal maturity of your understanding.   215
Of your appetite for death and the taste of its mouth.
Of the sadness of your once valiant gaiety.

It will be a long time, if ever, before there is born
an Andalusian so true, so rich in adventure.
I sing of his elegance with words that groan,   220
and I remember a sad breeze through the olive trees.

From Llanto por Ignacio Sánchez Mejías

4. Alma Ausente

No te conoce el toro ni la higuera,
ni caballos ni hormigas de tu casa.
No te conoce el niño ni la tarde
porque te has muerto para siempre.

No te conoce el lomo de la piedra,   5
ni el raso negro donde te destrozas.
No te conoce tu recuerdo mudo
porque te has muerto para siempre.

---

4. Actually, conch shell–shaped horns; the shepherds' horns that sound in the hills each fall as the sheep
are driven to new pastures.   5. Dogs as a (typically Continental) image for undignified, inferior creatures.

El otoño vendrá con caracolas,
uva de niebla y montes agrupados, 10
pero nadie querrá mirar tus ojos
porque te has muerto para siempre.

Porque te has muerto para siempre,
como todos los muertos de la Tierra,
como todos los muertos que se olvidan 15
en un montón de perros apagados.

No te conoce nadie. No. Pero yo te canto.
Yo canto para luego tu perfil y tu gracia.
La madurez insigne de tu conocimiento.
Tu apetencia de muerte y el gusto de su boca. 20
La tristeza que tuvo tu valiente alegría.

Tardará mucho tiempo en nacer, si es que nace,
un andaluz tan claro, tan rico de aventura.
Yo canto su elegancia con palabras que gimen
y recuerdo una brisa triste por los olivos. 25

JORGE LUIS BORGES
1899–1986

Argentinian Jorge Luis Borges represents above all other modernist writers the game-like or playful aspect of literary creation. The "real world" is only one of the possible realities in Borges's multiple universe, which treats history and fantasy as equally real. Borges creates a world of pure thought in which abstract fictional games are played out by pushing an initial situation or concept to its elegantly logical extreme. If everything is possible, there is no need for psychological consistency, for a realistic setting, or for a story that unfolds in ordinary time and space. Consequently, the voice telling the story becomes lost inside the setting it creates, just as a drawing by Saul Steinberg or Maurits Escher depicts the pen that is drawing the rest of the landscape in which it (the pen) appears. This thorough immersion in the play of subjective imagination appealed to writers like the French "new novelists," who were experimenting with shifting perspectives and a refusal of objective reality, and for a long time Borges's honored reputation in Europe outstripped his prestige in his native land.

Borges was born in Buenos Aires on August 24, 1899, to a prosperous family whose ancestors were distinguished in Argentinian history. The family moved early to a large house whose library and garden were to form an essential part of his literary imagination. His paternal grandmother was English, and young Borges knew English as well as Spanish; he was educated by an English tutor until he was nine. The family was traveling in Europe at the outbreak of World War I, and Borges learned French and German while attending secondary school in Switzerland during the war. After the war, they moved to Spain, where he associated with a group of young experimental poets known as the Ultraists. When Borges returned home in 1921, he founded his own group of Argentinian Ultraists: their mural-review, *Prisma*, was printed on sign paper and plastered on walls. He also became close friends with the philosopher

Macedonio Fernández, whose dedication to pure thought and linguistic intricacies greatly influenced his own attitudes; and contributed regularly to the avant-garde review *Martin Fierro*. Although devoted to pure art, Borges consistently opposed the military dictatorship of Juan Perón and made his political views plain in speeches and nonliterary writings, even if they were not included in his fiction. His attitude did not go unnoticed: in 1946, the Perón regime removed him from the librarian's post that he had held since 1937 and offered him a job as a chicken inspector.

During the 1930s, Borges turned to short narrative pieces and in 1935 published a collection of sketches entitled *Universal History of Infamy*. His more mature stories—brief metaphysical fictions whose density and elegance at times approach poetry—came as an experiment after a head injury and operation in 1938. *The Garden of Forking Paths* (1941), his first major collection, introduced him to a wider public as an intellectual and idealist writer, whose short stories subordinated familiar techniques of character, scene, plot, and narrative voice to a central idea, which was often a philosophical concept. This concept was used not as a lesson or dogma but as the starting point of fantastic elaborations to entertain readers within the game of literature.

Borges's imaginative world is an immense labyrinth, a "garden of forking paths," in which images of mazes and infinite mirroring, cyclical repetition and recall illustrate the effort of an elusive narrative voice to understand its own significance and that of the world. In *Borges and I,* he comments on the parallel existence of two Borgeses: the one who exists in his work (the one his readers know) and the living, fleshly identity felt by the man who sets pen to paper. "Little by little, I yield him ground. . . . I don't know which one of the two of us is writing this page." Borges has written on the idea (derived from the British philosophers David Hume and George Berkeley) of the individual self as a cluster of different perceptions, and he further elaborates this notion in his fictional proliferation of identities and alternate realities. Disdaining the "psychological fakery" of realistic novels (the "draggy novel of characters"), he prefers writing that is openly artful, concerned with technique for its own sake, and invents its own multidimensional reality.

Stories in *The Garden of Forking Paths, Fictions* (1944), and *The Aleph* (1949) develop these themes in a variety of styles. Borges is fond of detective stories (and has written a number of them) in which the search for an elusive explanation, given carefully planted clues, matters more than how recognizable the characters may be. In *Death and the Compass,* a mysterious murderer leaves tantalizing traces that refer to points of the compass and lead the detective into a fatal trap that closes on him at a fourth compass point, symbolized by the architectural lozenges of the house in which he dies. The author composes an art of puzzles and discovery, a grand code that treats our universe as a giant library where meaning is locked away in endless hexagonal galleries (*The Library of Babel*), as an enormous lottery whose results are all the events of our lives (*The Lottery in Babylon*), as a series of dreams within dreams (*The Circular Ruins*), or as a small iridescent sphere containing all of the points in space (*The Aleph*). In *Pierre Menard, Author of the "Quixote,"* the narrator is a scholarly reviewer of a certain fictitious Menard, whose masterwork has been to rewrite *Don Quixote* as if it were created today: not revise it or yet transcribe it, but actually *reinvent* it word for word. He has succeeded; the two texts are "verbally identical" although Menard's modern version is "more ambiguous" than Cervantes's and thus "infinitely richer."

The imaginary universe of *Tlön, Uqbar, Orbis Tertius* exemplifies the mixture of fact and fiction with which Borges invites us to speculate on the solidity of our own world. The narrator is engaged in tracking down mysterious references to a country called Tlön, whose language, science, and literature are exactly opposite (and perhaps related to) our own. For example, the Tlönians use verbs or adjectives instead of nouns, since they have no concept of objects in space, and their science consists of an association of ideas in which the most astounding theory becomes the truth. In a postscript, the narrator reveals that the encyclopedia has turned out to be an immense scholarly hoax, yet also mentions that strange and unearthly objects—recognizably from Tlön—have recently been found.

The intricate, riddling, mazelike ambiguity of Borges's stories earned him international reputation and influence, to the point that a "style like Borges" has become a recognized term. In Argentina, he was given the prestigious post of director of the National Library after the fall of Perón in 1955, and in 1961 he shared the International Publishers' Prize with Samuel Beckett. Always nearsighted, he grew increasingly blind in the mid-1950s and was forced to dictate his work. Nonetheless, he continued to travel, teach, and lecture in the company of his wife, Else Astete Millán, whom he married in 1967. Until his death Borges lived in his beloved Buenos Aires, the city that he celebrated in his first volume of poetry.

The Garden of Forking Paths begins as a simple spy story purporting to reveal the hidden truth about a German bombing raid during World War I. Borges alludes to documented facts: the geographic setting of the town of Albert and the Ancre River; a famous Chinese novel as Ts'ui Pên's proposed model; the *History of the World War (1914–1918)* published by B. H. Liddell Hart in 1934. Official history is undermined on the first page, however, both by the newly discovered confession of Dr. Yu Tsun and by his editor's suspiciously defensive footnote. Ultimately, Yu Tsun will learn from his ancestor's novel that history is a labyrinth of alternate possibilities (much like the "alternate worlds" of science fiction).

Borges executes his detective story with the traditional carefully planted clues. We know from the beginning that Yu Tsun—even though arrested—has successfully outwitted his rival, Captain Richard Madden; that his problem was to convey the name of a bombing target to his chief in Berlin; that he went to the telephone book to locate someone capable of transmitting his message; and that he had one bullet in his revolver. The cut-off phone call, the chase at the railroad station, and Madden's hasty arrival at Dr. Albert's house provide the excitement and pressure expected in a straightforward detective plot. Quite different spatial and temporal horizons open up halfway through, however. Coincidences—those chance relationships that might well have happened differently—introduce the idea of forking paths or alternate possible routes for history. Both Yu Tsun and Richard Madden are aliens trying to prove their worth inside their respective bureaucracies; the road to Stephen Albert's house turns mazelike always to the left; the only suitable name in the phone book—the man Yu Tsun must kill—is a Sinologist who has reconstructed the labyrinthine text written long ago by Yu Tsun's ancestor. This text, Ts'ui Pên's *The Garden of Forking Paths,* describes the universe as an infinite series of alternative versions of experience. In different versions of the story (taking place at different times), Albert and Yu Tsun are enemies—or friends—or not even there. The war and Richard Madden appear diminished (although no less real) in such a kaleidoscopic perspective, for they exist in only one of many possible dimensions. Yet Madden hurries up the walk, and current reality returns to demand Albert's death. It may seem as though the vision of other worlds in which Albert continues to exist (or is Yu Tsun's enemy) would soften the murderer's remorse for his deed. Instead, it makes more poignant the narrator's realization that in this dimension no other way could be found.

PRONOUNCING GLOSSARY

The following list uses common English syllables and stress accents to provide rough equivalents of selected words whose pronunciation may be unfamiliar to the general reader.

Borges: *bore'-hess*

Hsi P'êng: *shee pung*

Hung Lu Meng: *hoong low mung*

Ts'ui Pên: *tsoo-ay pun*

Yu Tsun: *yew tsoo-en*

The Garden of Forking Paths[1]

On page 22 of Liddell Hart's *History of World War I* you will read that an attack against the Serre-Montauban line by thirteen British divisions (supported by 1,400 artillery pieces), planned for the 24th of July, 1916, had to be postponed until the morning of the 29th. The torrential rains, Captain Liddell Hart comments, caused this delay, an insignificant one, to be sure.

The following statement, dictated, reread and signed by Dr. Yu Tsun, former professor of English at the *Hochschule* at Tsingtao,[2] throws an unsuspected light over the whole affair. The first two pages of the document are missing.

". . . and I hung up the receiver. Immediately afterwards, I recognized the voice that had answered in German. It was that of Captain Richard Madden. Madden's presence in Viktor Runeberg's apartment meant the end of our anxieties and—but this seemed, *or should have seemed,* very secondary to me—also the end of our lives. It meant that Runeberg had been arrested or murdered.[3] Before the sun set on that day, I would encounter the same fate. Madden was implacable. Or rather, he was obliged to be so. An Irishman at the service of England, a man accused of laxity and perhaps of treason, how could he fail to seize and be thankful for such a miraculous opportunity: the discovery, capture, maybe even the death of two agents of the German Reich?[4] I went up to my room; absurdly I locked the door and threw myself on my back on the narrow iron cot. Through the window I saw the familiar roofs and the cloud-shaded six o'clock sun. It seemed incredible to me that that day without premonitions or symbols should be the one of my inexorable death. In spite of my dead father, in spite of having been a child in a symmetrical garden of Hai Feng, was I—now—going to die? Then I reflected that everything happens to a man precisely, precisely *now*. Centuries of centuries and only in the present do things happen; countless men in the air, on the face of the earth and the sea, and all that really is happening is happening to me . . . The almost intolerable recollection of Madden's horselike face banished these wanderings. In the midst of my hatred and terror (it means nothing to me now to speak of terror, now that I have mocked Richard Madden, now that my throat yearns for the noose) it occurred to me that that tumultuous and doubtless happy warrior did not suspect that I possessed the Secret. The name of the exact location of the new British artillery park on the River Ancre. A bird streaked across the gray sky and blindly I translated it into an airplane and that airplane into many (against the French sky) annihilating the artillery station with vertical bombs. If only my mouth, before a bullet shattered it, could cry out that secret name so it could be heard in Germany . . . My human voice was very weak. How might I make it carry to the ear of the Chief? To the ear of that sick and hateful man who knew nothing of Runeberg and me save that we were in Stafford-

---

1. Translated by Donald A. Yates.   2. Or Ch'ing-tao; a major port in east China, part of territory leased to (and developed by) Germany in 1898. *Hochschule:* university (German).   3. "A hypothesis both hateful and odd. The Prussian spy Hans Rabener, alias Viktor Runeberg, attacked with drawn automatic the bearer of the warrant for his arrest, Captain Richard Madden. The latter, in self-defense, inflicted the wound which brought about Runeberg's death [Editor's note]." This entire note is by Borges as "Editor." 4. Empire (German).

shire[5] and who was waiting in vain for our report in his arid office in Berlin, endlessly examining newspapers . . . I said out loud: *I must flee.* I sat up noiselessly, in a useless perfection of silence, as if Madden were already lying in wait for me. Something—perhaps the mere vain ostentation of proving my resources were nil—made me look through my pockets. I found what I knew I would find. The American watch, the nickel chain and the square coin, the key ring with the incriminating useless keys to Runeberg's apartment, the notebook, a letter which I resolved to destroy immediately (and which I did not destroy), a crown, two shillings and a few pence, the red and blue pencil, the handkerchief, the revolver with one bullet. Absurdly, I took it in my hand and weighed it in order to inspire courage within myself. Vaguely I thought that a pistol report can be heard at a great distance. In ten minutes my plan was perfected. The telephone book listed the name of the only person capable of transmitting the message; he lived in a suburb of Fenton,[6] less than a half hour's train ride away.

I am a cowardly man. I say it now, now that I have carried to its end a plan whose perilous nature no one can deny. I know its execution was terrible. I didn't do it for Germany, no. I care nothing for a barbarous country which imposed upon me the abjection of being a spy. Besides, I know of a man from England—a modest man—who for me is no less great than Goethe.[7] I talked with him for scarcely an hour, but during that hour he was Goethe . . . I did it because I sensed that the Chief somehow feared people of my race—for the innumerable ancestors who merge within me. I wanted to prove to him that a yellow man could save his armies. Besides, I had to flee from Captain Madden. His hands and his voice could call at my door at any moment. I dressed silently, bade farewell to myself in the mirror, went downstairs, scrutinized the peaceful street and went out. The station was not far from my home, but I judged it wise to take a cab. I argued that in this way I ran less risk of being recognized; the fact is that in the deserted street I felt myself visible and vulnerable, infinitely so. I remember that I told the cab driver to stop a short distance before the main entrance. I got out with voluntary, almost painful slowness; I was going to the village of Ashgrove but I bought a ticket for a more distant station. The train left within a very few minutes, at eight-fifty. I hurried; the next one would leave at nine-thirty. There was hardly a soul on the platform. I went through the coaches; I remember a few farmers, a woman dressed in mourning, a young boy who was reading with fervor the *Annals* of Tacitus,[8] a wounded and happy soldier. The coaches jerked forward at last. A man whom I recognized ran in vain to the end of the platform. It was Captain Richard Madden. Shattered, trembling, I shrank into the far corner of the seat, away from the dreaded window.

From this broken state I passed into an almost abject felicity. I told myself that the duel had already begun and that I had won the first encounter by frustrating, even if for forty minutes, even if by a stroke of fate, the attack of my adversary. I argued that this slightest of victories foreshadowed a total victory. I argued (no less fallaciously) that my cowardly felicity proved that

5. County in west-central England.   6. In Lincolnshire, a county in east England.   7. Johann Wolfgang von Goethe (1749–1832), German poet, novelist, and dramatist; author of *Faust*; often taken as representing the peak of German cultural achievement.   8. Cornelius Tacitus (55–117), Roman historian whose *Annals* give a vivid picture of the decadence and corruption of the Roman Empire under Tiberius, Claudius, and Nero.

I was a man capable of carrying out the adventure successfully. From this weakness I took strength that did not abandon me. I foresee that man will resign himself each day to more atrocious undertakings; soon there will be no one but warriors and brigands; I give them this counsel: *The author of an atrocious undertaking ought to imagine that he has already accomplished it, ought to impose upon himself a future as irrevocable as the past.* Thus I proceeded as my eyes of a man already dead registered the elapsing of that day, which was perhaps the last, and the diffusion of the night. The train ran gently along, amid ash trees. It stopped, almost in the middle of the fields. No one announced the name of the station. "Ashgrove?" I asked a few lads on the platform. "Ashgrove," they replied. I got off.

A lamp enlightened the platform but the faces of the boys were in shadow. One questioned me, "Are you going to Dr. Stephen Albert's house?" Without waiting for my answer, another said, "The house is a long way from here, but you won't get lost if you take this road to the left and at every crossroads turn again to your left." I tossed them a coin (my last), descended a few stone steps and started down the solitary road. It went downhill, slowly. It was of elemental earth; overhead the branches were tangled; the low, full moon seemed to accompany me.

For an instant, I thought that Richard Madden in some way had penetrated my desperate plan. Very quickly, I understood that that was impossible. The instructions to turn always to the left reminded me that such was the common procedure for discovering the central point of certain labyrinths. I have some understanding of labyrinths: not for nothing am I the great grandson of that Ts'ui Pên who was governor of Yunnan and who renounced worldly power in order to write a novel that might be even more populous than the *Hung Lu Meng*[9] and to construct a labyrinth in which all men would become lost. Thirteen years he dedicated to these heterogeneous tasks, but the hand of a stranger murdered him—and his novel was incoherent and no one found the labyrinth. Beneath English trees I meditated on that lost maze: I imagined it inviolate and perfect at the secret crest of a mountain; I imagined it erased by rice fields or beneath the water; I imagined it infinite, no longer composed of octagonal kiosks and returning paths, but of rivers and provinces and kingdoms . . . I thought of a labyrinth of labyrinths, of one sinuous spreading labyrinth that would encompass the past and the future and in some way involve the stars. Absorbed in these illusory images, I forgot my destiny of one pursued. I felt myself to be, for an unknown period of time, an abstract perceiver of the world. The vague, living countryside, the moon, the remains of the day worked on me, as well as the slope of the road which eliminated any possibility of weariness. The afternoon was intimate, infinite. The road descended and forked among the now confused meadows. A high-pitched, almost syllabic music approached and receded in the shifting of the wind, dimmed by leaves and distance. I thought that a man can be an enemy of other men, of the moments of other men, but not of a country: not of fireflies, words, gardens, streams of water, sunsets. Thus I arrived before a tall, rusty gate. Between the iron bars I made out a poplar grove and a pavilion. I understood suddenly two things, the first trivial, the second almost

---

9. *The Dream of the Red Chamber* (1791) by Ts'ao Hsüeh-ch'in; the most famous Chinese novel, a love story and panorama of Chinese family life involving more than 430 characters.

unbelievable: the music came from the pavilion, and the music was Chinese. For precisely that reason I had openly accepted it without paying it any heed. I do not remember whether there was a bell or whether I knocked with my hand. The sparkling of the music continued.

From the rear of the house within a lantern approached: a lantern that the trees sometimes striped and sometimes eclipsed, a paper lantern that had the form of a drum and the color of the moon. A tall man bore it. I didn't see his face for the light blinded me. He opened the door and said slowly, in my own language: "I see that the pious Hsi P'êng persists in correcting my solitude. You no doubt wish to see the garden?"

I recognized the name of one of our consuls and I replied, disconcerted, "The garden?"

"The garden of forking paths."

Something stirred in my memory and I uttered with incomprehensible certainty, "The garden of my ancestor Ts'ui Pên."

"Your ancestor? Your illustrious ancestor? Come in."

The damp path zigzagged like those of my childhood. We came to a library of Eastern and Western books. I recognized bound in yellow silk several volumes of the Lost Encyclopedia, edited by the Third Emperor of the Luminous Dynasty but never printed.[1] The record on the phonograph revolved next to a bronze phoenix. I also recall a *famille rose*[2] vase and another, many centuries older, of that shade of blue which our craftsmen copied from the potters of Persia . . .

Stephen Albert observed me with a smile. He was, as I have said, very tall, sharp-featured, with gray eyes and a gray beard. He told me that he had been a missionary in Tientsin "before aspiring to become a Sinologist."

We sat down—I on a long, low divan, he with his back to the window and a tall circular clock. I calculated that my pursuer, Richard Madden, could not arrive for at least an hour. My irrevocable determination could wait.

"An astounding fate, that of Ts'ui Pên," Stephen Albert said. "Governor of his native province, learned in astronomy, in astrology and in the tireless interpretation of the canonical books, chess player, famous poet and calligrapher—he abandoned all this in order to compose a book and a maze. He renounced the pleasures of both tyranny and justice, of his populous couch, of his banquets and even of erudition—all to close himself up for thirteen years in the Pavilion of the Limpid Solitude. When he died, his heirs found nothing save chaotic manuscripts. His family, as you may be aware, wished to condemn them to the fire; but his executor—a Taoist or Buddhist monk—insisted on their publication."

"We descendants of Ts'ui Pên," I replied, "continue to curse that monk. Their publication was senseless. The book is an indeterminate heap of contradictory drafts. I examined it once: in the third chapter the hero dies, in the fourth he is alive. As for the other undertaking of Ts'ui Pên, his labyrinth . . ."

"Here is Ts'ui Pên's labyrinth," he said, indicating a tall lacquered desk.

1. The Yung-lo emperor of the Ming ("bright") dynasty commissioned a massive encyclopedia between 1403 and 1408. A single copy of the 11,095 manuscript volumes was made in the mid-1500s; the original was later destroyed, and only 370 volumes of the copy remain today.   2. Pink family (French); refers to a Chinese decorative enamel ranging in color from an opaque pink to purplish rose. *Famille rose* pottery was at its best during the reign of Yung Chên (1723–1735).

"An ivory labyrinth!" I exclaimed. "A minimum labyrinth."

"A labyrinth of symbols," he corrected. "An invisible labyrinth of time. To me, a barbarous Englishman, has been entrusted the revelation of this diaphanous mystery. After more than a hundred years, the details are irretrievable; but it is not hard to conjecture what happened. Ts'ui Pên must have said once: *I am withdrawing to write a book.* And another time: *I am withdrawing to construct a labyrinth.* Every one imagined two works; to no one did it occur that the book and the maze were one and the same thing. The Pavilion of the Limpid Solitude stood in the center of a garden that was perhaps intricate; that circumstance could have suggested to the heirs a physical labyrinth. Ts'ui Pên died; no one in the vast territories that were his came upon the labyrinth; the confusion of the novel suggested to me that *it* was the maze. Two circumstances gave me the correct solution of the problem. One: the curious legend that Ts'ui Pên had planned to create a labyrinth which would be strictly infinite. The other: a fragment of a letter I discovered."

Albert rose. He turned his back on me for a moment; he opened a drawer of the black and gold desk. He faced me and in his hands he held a sheet of paper that had once been crimson, but was now pink and tenuous and cross-sectioned. The fame of Ts'ui Pên as a calligrapher had been justly won. I read, uncomprehendingly and with fervor, these words written with a minute brush by a man of my blood: *I leave to the various futures (not to all) my garden of forking paths.* Wordlessly, I returned the sheet. Albert continued:

"Before unearthing this letter, I had questioned myself about the ways in which a book can be infinite. I could think of nothing other than a cyclic volume, a circular one. A book whose last page was identical with the first, a book which had the possibility of continuing indefinitely. I remembered too that night which is at the middle of the Thousand and One Nights when Scheherazade[3] (through a magical oversight of the copyist) begins to relate word for word the story of the Thousand and One Nights, establishing the risk of coming once again to the night when she must repeat it, and thus on to infinity. I imagined as well a Platonic, hereditary work, transmitted from father to son, in which each new individual adds a chapter or corrects with pious care the pages of his elders. These conjectures diverted me; but none seemed to correspond, not even remotely, to the contradictory chapters of Ts'ui Pên. In the midst of this perplexity, I received from Oxford the manuscript you have examined. I lingered, naturally, on the sentence: *I leave to the various futures (not to all) my garden of forking paths.* Almost instantly, I understood: 'The garden of forking paths' was the chaotic novel; the phrase 'the various futures (not to all)' suggested to me the forking in time, not in space. A broad rereading of the work confirmed the theory. In all fictional works, each time a man is confronted with several alternatives, he chooses one and eliminates the others; in the fiction of Ts'ui Pên, he chooses—simultaneously—all of them. *He creates,* in this way, diverse futures, diverse times which themselves also proliferate and fork. Here, then, is the explanation of the novel's contradictions. Fang, let us say, has a secret; a stranger calls at his door; Fang resolves to kill him. Naturally, there are several possible outcomes: Fang can kill the intruder, the intruder can kill Fang, they

3. The narrator of the collection also known as the *Arabian Nights*, a thousand and one tales supposedly told by Scheherazade to her husband, Shahrayar, king of Samarkand, to postpone her execution.

both can escape, they both can die, and so forth. In the work of Ts'ui Pên, all possible outcomes occur; each one is the point of departure for other forkings. Sometimes, the paths of this labyrinth converge: for example, you arrive at this house, but in one of the possible pasts you are my enemy, in another, my friend. If you will resign yourself to my incurable pronunciation, we shall read a few pages."

His face, within the vivid circle of the lamplight, was unquestionably that of an old man, but with something unalterable about it, even immortal. He read with slow precision two versions of the same epic chapter. In the first, an army marches to a battle across a lonely mountain; the horror of the rocks and shadows makes the men undervalue their lives and they gain an easy victory. In the second, the same army traverses a palace where a great festival is taking place; the resplendent battle seems to them a continuation of the celebration and they win the victory. I listened with proper veneration to these ancient narratives, perhaps less admirable in themselves than the fact that they had been created by my blood and were being restored to me by a man of a remote empire, in the course of a desperate adventure, on a Western isle. I remember the last words, repeated in each version like a secret commandment: *Thus fought the heroes, tranquil their admirable hearts, violent their swords, resigned to kill and to die.*

From that moment on, I felt about me and within my dark body an invisible, intangible swarming. Not the swarming of the divergent, parallel and finally coalescent armies, but a more inaccessible, more intimate agitation that they in some manner prefigured. Stephen Albert continued:

"I don't believe that your illustrious ancestor played idly with these variations. I don't consider it credible that he would sacrifice thirteen years to the infinite execution of a rhetorical experiment. In your country, the novel is a subsidiary form of literature; in Ts'ui Pên's time it was a despicable form. Ts'ui Pên was a brilliant novelist, but he was also a man of letters who doubtless did not consider himself a mere novelist. The testimony of his contemporaries proclaims—and his life fully confirms—his metaphysical and mystical interests. Philosophic controversy usurps a good part of the novel. I know that of all problems, none disturbed him so greatly nor worked upon him so much as the abysmal problem of time. Now then, the latter is the only problem that does not figure in the pages of the *Garden*. He does not even use the word that signifies *time*. How do you explain this voluntary omission?"

I proposed several solutions—all unsatisfactory. We discussed them. Finally, Stephen Albert said to me:

"In a riddle whose answer is chess, what is the only prohibited word?"

I thought a moment and replied, "The word *chess*."

"Precisely," said Albert. "*The Garden of Forking Paths* is an enormous riddle, or parable, whose theme is time; this recondite cause prohibits its mention. To omit a word always, to resort to inept metaphors and obvious periphrases, is perhaps the most emphatic way of stressing it. That is the tortuous method preferred, in each of the meanderings of his indefatigable novel, by the oblique Ts'ui Pên. I have compared hundreds of manuscripts, I have corrected the errors that the negligence of the copyists has introduced, I have guessed the plan of this chaos, I have re-established—I believe I have re-established—the primordial organization, I have translated the entire work: it is clear to me that not once does he employ the word 'time.' The explanation is obvious: *The Garden of Forking Paths* is an incomplete, but not false, image of the universe as Ts'ui Pên conceived it. In contrast to Newton and Schopenhauer,[4] your ancestor did not believe in a uniform, absolute time. He believed in an infinite series of times, in a growing, dizzying net of divergent, convergent and parallel times. This network of times which approached one another, forked, broke off, or were unaware of one another for centuries, embraces *all* possibilities of time. We do not exist in the majority of these times; in some you exist, and not I; in others I, and not you; in others, both of us. In the present one, which a favorable fate has granted me, you have arrived at my house; in another, while crossing the garden, you found me dead; in still another, I utter these same words, but I am a mistake, a ghost."

"In every one," I pronounced, not without a tremble to my voice, "I am grateful to you and revere you for your re-creation of the garden of Ts'ui Pên."

"Not in all," he murmured with a smile. "Time forks perpetually toward innumerable futures. In one of them I am your enemy."

Once again I felt the swarming sensation of which I have spoken. It seemed to me that the humid garden that surrounded the house was infinitely saturated with invisible persons. Those persons were Albert and I, secret, busy and multiform in other dimensions of time. I raised my eyes and the tenuous nightmare dissolved. In the yellow and black garden there was only one man; but this man was as strong as a statue . . . this man was approaching along the path and he was Captain Richard Madden.

"The future already exists," I replied, "but I am your friend. Could I see the letter again?"

Albert rose. Standing tall, he opened the drawer of the tall desk; for the moment his back was to me. I had readied the revolver. I fired with extreme caution. Albert fell uncomplainingly, immediately. I swear his death was instantaneous—a lightning stroke.

The rest is unreal, insignificant. Madden broke in, arrested me. I have been condemned to the gallows. I have won out abominably; I have communicated to Berlin the secret name of the city they must attack. They bombed it yesterday; I read it in the same papers that offered to England the mystery of the learned Sinologist Stephen Albert who was murdered by a stranger, one Yu Tsun. The Chief had deciphered this mystery. He knew my problem was to indicate (through the uproar of the war) the city called Albert, and that I had found no other means to do so than to kill a man of that name. He does not know (no one can know) my innumerable contrition and weariness.

For Victoria Ocampo

---

4. Arthur Schopenhauer (1788–1860) was a German philosopher whose concept of will proceeded from a concept of the self as enduring through time. In *Seven Conversations with Jorge Luis Borges*, Borges also comments on Schopenhauer's interest in the "oneiric [dreamlike] essence of life." Isaac Newton (1642–1727) was an English mathematician and philosopher best known for his formulation of laws of gravitation and motion.

Borges and I[1]

Things happen to him, the other one, to Borges. I stroll about Buenos Aires and stop, almost mechanically now perhaps, to look at the arch of an entranceway and the ironwork gate; news of Borges reaches me in the mail and I see his name on an academic ballot or in a biographical dictionary. I like hourglasses, maps, eighteenth-century typography, etymologies, the taste of coffee, and Robert Louis Stevenson's[2] prose; he shares these preferences, but with a vanity that turns them into the attributes of an actor. It would be an exaggeration to say that our relationship is a hostile one; I live, I go on living, so that Borges may contrive his literature; and that literature justifies me. I do not find it hard to admit that he has achieved some valid pages, but these pages can not save me, perhaps because what is good no longer belongs to anyone, not even to him, the other one, but to the language or to tradition. In any case, I am destined to perish, definitively, and only some instant of me may live on in him. Little by little, I yield him ground, the whole terrain, though I am quite aware of his perverse habit of magnifying and falsifying. Spinoza[3] realized that all things strive to persist in their own nature: the stone eternally wishes to be stone and the tiger a tiger. I shall subsist in Borges, not in myself (assuming I am someone), and yet I recognize myself less in his books than in many another, or than in the intricate flourishes played on a guitar. Years ago I tried to free myself from him, and I went from the mythologies of the city suburbs to games with time and infinity,[4] but now those games belong to Borges, and I will have to think up something else. Thus is my life a flight, and I lose everything, and everything belongs to oblivion, or to him.

I don't know which one of the two of us is writing this page.

1. Translated by Anthony Kerrigan.   2. Scottish author (1850–1894) whose novels include *Treasure Island* (1883) and *The Strange Case of Dr. Jekyll and Mr. Hyde* (1886).   3. Baruch Spinoza (1632–1677), an eminent Rationalist philosopher.   4. From early poetry such as *Fervor of Buenos Aires* (1923) to the fantastic tales in *The Garden of Forking Paths* (1941) and *Fictions* (1944).

PABLO NERUDA
1904–1973

Love poet, nature poet, political poet, and poet of common things, the Nobel Prize winner Pablo Neruda is known equally as Latin America's most important twentieth-century poet and an advocate of justice and equality for the masses. His audience was humanity itself, and he engaged himself as poet and activist in the great issues of the day. Neruda's influence on the younger generation of Spanish and Spanish-American literature was immense: for them, as Julio Cortázar wrote, he exemplified not only a newly materialist style and awareness, but also an *American* way of seeing. His America is not the "Saxon America" of the North (much as he admired Walt Whitman), but Latin America, which he saw as the essence of humanity and seed of the future. Whatever Neruda's styles or subjects (and there are many), he evoked the most basic levels of human emotions and experience. In later life, he took on the role of public poet, emphasizing the common people's struggle for survival and freedom in both ancient and modern times. His faith in the power of language—both to represent reality and to communicate it—is diametrically opposed to the linguistic skepticism of a Samuel Beckett. For Neruda, "the word fills with meaning" and his *General Song* was to be the "common book of mankind."

He was born Neftalí Ricardo Reyes y Basoalto, on July 12, 1904, in the small town of Parral, in southern Chile. His mother, a schoolteacher, died a month after his birth, and his father, a railroad worker, moved in 1906 to another town, Temuco, where he remarried and where Neruda had his early schooling. The boy's stepmother was a kind peasant woman whom he loved and called his "guardian angel," but his father was a more distant figure. Their family was among the first white settlers to open up the indigenous lands of the Araucanian Mapuche tribe, a fact that Neruda—who had both Spanish and Indian blood—would recall with mixed feelings.

The young Neftalí Reyes attended school in Temuco, wrote poems in his arithmetic notebook, and read voraciously. Temuco, however, was a frontier town, and the boy's love of literature was not encouraged either at home or at school—with one exception. That exception was the poet Gabriela Mistral, principal of the girls' school at Temuco, who would herself win the Nobel Prize in literature in 1945. She encouraged the young writer and loaned him books: Russian novels, Symbolist poetry, and science-fiction by Jules Verne. Already beginning the prolific production that marked his career, he published an article and fourteen poems between 1917 and 1919, and began to win local literary prizes. At fifteen, seeking a pen name that would not be tied to the provinces, he chose the surname of a Czech writer, Jan Neruda, and the given name Pablo, which some have associated with the Evangelist Saint Paul.

In 1921, Neruda traveled to Santiago, the capital of Chile, where he made a small income by translating and by writing articles for newspapers, but he was constantly hungry. In 1924, *Twenty Love Poems and a Song of Despair* was immediately popular and brought him a national reputation. Two women dominate these sensual and erotic poems, women who are concurrently equated with natural forces: "Body of woman, white hills, white thighs." It is a continuation of the Romantic fusion of woman and nature, and ends in Romantic separation and loneliness: "My voice tried to find the wind to touch her hearing" (*Tonight I Can Write . . .*). *Twenty Love Poems* established Neruda's reputation as both a love poet and a poet of nature, a reputation he would reinforce in later collections.

The impoverished poet benefited, like Rubén Darío, from the Latin American tradition of awarding diplomatic posts to talented artists and in 1927 was appointed Chile's consul to Rangoon, Burma. The next five years, during which he also served in Ceylon, Java, and Singapore, were not comfortable ones, for the poet had only a sketchy knowledge of English and needed to supplement his income by writing articles for the Santiago newspaper *La Nación*. Lonely and isolated, appalled at the misery brought by colonial occupation, Neruda started writing the somber poems of *Residence on Earth (1925–1931)* (1933). The volume had an enormous impact on the younger generation of Spanish-American writers: according to the Argentinian novelist Julio Cortázar, "It required a different dimension of language and, after that, an *American* way of seeing that had not been seen until then." *Walking Around*, a poem from the second volume of *Residence on Earth (1925–1935)* (1935), conveys the collection's existential anguish and the poet's awareness of his surroundings—"It happens that I am tired of being a man"—but later in the poem, the speaker rebels at the scene through which he strides "with fury, with forgetfulness."

Neruda returned to Chile in 1932 and was sent as consul to Buenos Aires the following year. Although he did not care for bureaucratic work, he entered happily into the literary circles of the Argentinian capital, where he also became a friend of the visiting Spanish poet Federico García Lorca (see p. 2169). Their friendship was renewed in 1934, when Neruda went as consul to Spain, and Lorca introduced him to the Madrid audience in 1935 as "an authentic poet, one of those who has tuned his sense to a world which is not ours, and which few people perceive . . . [one of] the great ones." Neruda's fame grew with the publication of the second volume of *Residence on Earth*. It was a time of struggle between the established tradition of "pure poetry," represented by Juan Ramón Jiménez, and a new mode of "impure poetry," in which the poetic "I" was less controlling and remained open to the chaos of external phenomena. Neruda became a founding editor of a new poetry journal, *Green Horse for Poetry*, and published a combative manifesto, *Towards an Impure Poetry*, in the first issue of October 1935. "It is useful, at certain hours of the day and night, to look closely at the world of objects at rest. . . . From them flow the contacts of man with the earth, like an object lesson for all troubled lyricists." The battle continues in *Walking Around*, where he mocks the pure poet's traditional image of the poetic swan (developed by Baudelaire and Mallarmé in this volume) and describe himself as "a felt swan / navigating on a water of origin and ash"—that is, the urban landscape. The poem's list of randomly encountered objects ("forgotten sets of teeth in a coffee-pot . . . stores full of orthopaedic appliances") contrasts with pure poetry's carefully arranged landscapes and suggests the Surrealists' enthusiasm for unpredictable reality.

Walking Around also demonstrates the poet's conversion to a more activist political stance, influenced by his friends, the radical poets Rafael Alberti and Miguel Hernández. In 1936, civil war broke out in Spain between the Republic and the forces of General Francisco Franco, and Neruda, like artists all over Europe, supported the side of the Republic; he lost his consul's post in consequence. His friend Lorca was dragged from home by Fascist guards and murdered. Neruda traveled, lectured, and set up various organizations (including a review, *Poets of the World Defend the Spanish People*) to aid the Spanish Republic. Maintaining close ties with the Communist Party, which had joined the fight against Spanish Fascism, he published in 1937 a new collection of poems, *Spain in My Heart*, that heralded a change in his literary stance. From now on, he would be a public poet, reading his poems aloud and addressing not individuals but a larger community—a community that could be either contemporary (*I'm Explaining a Few Things*) or far removed (the Inca laborers of *The Heights of Macchu Picchu*). In *I'm Explaining a Few Things*, Neruda tells his listeners, who are presumably looking for beauty, philosophy, or an exotic portrait of the Chilean landscape, that things have changed in Spain and there are other topics for poetry. Flames, molten metal, dead children, and the blood of victims have replaced the house, flowers, and thriving marketplace that he once knew. Neruda's repeated exhortation "Come and see the blood in the streets!" illustrates the poet's intention to speak directly to his audience and to articulate great issues instead of private feelings.

Further consular appointments took Neruda to Paris in 1939, where he was charged with helping refugees from Spain, and to Mexico, where he lived until 1943. Traveling throughout Central and South America, he absorbed images of people and places, and began to imagine a poem that would delineate Latin American identity. The gradual evolution of this plan is illustrated by the career of *The Song of Chile* (1943), which Neruda began in 1938 as a national epic but which was later incorporated as canto 7 of the broader *General Song (Canto General)* (1950). The *General Song* celebrates both Latin American identity and human beings generally, while describing Latin American history—a history that, after October 22, 1943, was anchored for Neruda in the lost Inca city of Macchu Picchu in Peru. (The usual spelling is "Machu Picchu," but Neruda uses "Macchu" throughout.) Climbing the mountain to its stone ruins on that day, the poet had an almost mystical vision of the past linked with vast natural forces and the progress of humanity, a vision that he expressed two years later in the crucial second canto of the *General Song: The Heights of Macchu Picchu*.

The *General Song* is divided into fifteen cantos, each with its own subdivisions. It begins with a description of the land's first inhabitants, focuses on the ancient mountain fortress of Macchu Picchu, continues with a thematic account of subsequent centuries of foreign invaders (including both Spanish conquistadors and twentieth-century United States corporations), and denounces Latin American leaders who have betrayed their people. At this point, the linear history of Latin America gives way to seven thematically related but otherwise disparate cantos. Neruda now speaks in prophetic tones, invoking America (meaning Latin America) as a whole, and he focuses on a variety of topics that include his own memories (*The Fugitive*), exhortations of others (*Let the Railsplitter Awake,* addressing the people of the United States), and a vision of all-embracing elemental life (*The Great Ocean*). The *General Song*'s violent criticism of North American commercial aggression has limited its audience in the United States, but the poem is internationally recognized as a major work of Latin American literature and a remarkable plea for universal justice and equality.

The second canto of the *General Song, The Heights of Macchu Picchu* was published as a separate poem in 1946 and only later integrated into the larger work. Its twelve sections (also called cantos) are divided into two broad movements that express different philosophical attitudes and a turning point in the poet's thought. Throughout the first five cantos, Neruda struggles with a sense of loss and alienation; beginning with Canto VI, he describes his ascent to Macchu Picchu and the vision of a larger community of struggling, suffering human beings that now gives meaning to his existence. The portion printed here, the second half of *The Heights of Macchu Picchu,* begins with the poet's invocation of the abandoned city after having climbed to its perch on a precipice in the Andes. He invokes the "mother of stone" and of the Latin American people, and bears witness to a lost civilization. In Canto IX, the city is described in fused images of nature and daily life, of the passage of time as well as intuitions that transcend chronology. In Cantos X through XII, Neruda imagines the experience of the people who interest him most: everyday people, the laborers who built Macchu Picchu and knew hunger and fatigue. The geometry of Macchu Picchu's impressive architecture shapes, for him, a "hypotenuse of rough blood and sackcloth," and he calls out for the workers, his brothers, to speak to him of their long-gone suffering. Though they are dead, he imagines their experiences and voice coming to reside in his own flesh and blood, reborn in a brotherhood of the people.

Neruda lived as an exile during much of the time he wrote the *General Song*. He had returned to Chile in 1943 and was elected to the Chilean Senate in 1945, but he was forced to flee two years later after criticizing the president, Gabriel González Videla, in an open letter. The conclusion of the *General Song* speaks bitterly of this period, and of "my Canto general, written / on the run, singing beneath / the clandestine wings of my country." Celebrated internationally, officially honored in Latin America, Europe, India, and China, Neruda was unable to return to Chile until 1952.

In that year, he turned to a different style of writing: an unadorned, direct expression with everyday subject matter such as fire, rain, bread, clothes, a bee, or tomatoes. This new simplicity stemmed from Neruda's commitment to his role as public poet; he felt a responsibility to write for simple people, including those who were just learning to read. "We must go back to what is simply human," he said, and the *Elemental Odes* (1954) respond to this need. The short lines, vivid, realistic images, humorous narrative, and cheerful preparations for a feast in *Ode to the Tomato,* printed here, create an attractive scene of joyful abundance whose subtle artistry is concealed. He continued to write prolifically in various styles, publishing one or more books a year, and he traveled around the world, lecturing and reading his poetry. He continued to be politically active and was appointed ambassador to Paris after the election of Salvador Allende as president of Chile in 1970. In 1971, Neruda was awarded the Nobel Prize for literature but returned to Isla Negra in 1972, gravely ill. The news at home was not good: political tensions were mounting in Chile, and

Neruda watched the rising unrest daily on television. His friend, President Allende, was assassinated in a military coup on September 11, 1973, and the poet died twelve days later. The first public demonstration against Pinochet's military government took place at Neruda's funeral, a gesture that proved dangerous (his house was sacked afterward) but a fitting tribute to this national poet and representative of the people.

PRONOUNCING GLOSSARY

The following list uses common English syllables and stress accents to provide rough equivalents of selected words whose pronunciation may be unfamiliar to the general reader.

Argüelles: *ar-hweh'-jes*

Castile: *cah-stee'*

Macchu Picchu: *mah'-choo peek'-choo*

Mantur: *mahn-toor*

Pablo Neruda: *pah'-bloh nay-roo'-dah*

Raúl: *rah-ool'*

Urubamba: *oo-roo-bahm'-ba*

Wilkamayu: *vill-kah-mah'-yoo*

Wiracocha: *veer-ah-coch'-ah*

Tonight I Can Write . . .[1]

Tonight I can write the saddest lines.

Write, for example, 'The night is shattered
and the blue stars shiver in the distance.'

The night wind revolves in the sky and sings.

Tonight I can write the saddest lines.   5
I loved her, and sometimes she loved me too.

Through nights like this one I held her in my arms.
I kissed her again and again under the endless sky.

She loved me, sometimes I loved her too.
How could one not have loved her great still eyes.   10

Tonight I can write the saddest lines.
To think that I do not have her. To feel that I have lost her.

To hear the immense night, still more immense without her.
And the verse falls to the soul like dew to the pasture.

What does it matter that my love could not keep her.   15
The night is shattered and she is not with me.

This is all. In the distance someone is singing. In the distance.
My soul is not satisfied that it has lost her.

1. Translated by W. S. Merwin.

My sight searches for her as though to go to her.
My heart looks for her, and she is not with me.   20

The same night whitening the same trees.
We, of that time, are no longer the same.

I no longer love her, that's certain, but how I loved her.
My voice tried to find the wind to touch her hearing.

Another's. She will be another's. Like my kisses before.   25
Her voice. Her bright body. Her infinite eyes.

I no longer love her, that's certain, but maybe I love her.
Love is so short, forgetting is so long.

Because through nights like this one I held her in my arms
my soul is not satisfied that it has lost her.   30

Though this be the last pain that she makes me suffer
and these the last verses that I write for her.

Walking Around[1]

It happens that I am tired of being a man.
It happens that I go into the tailor's shops and the movies
all shrivelled up, impenetrable, like a felt swan
navigating on a water of origin and ash.

The smell of barber shops makes me sob out loud.   5
I want nothing but the repose either of stones or of wool,
I want to see no more establishments, no more gardens,
nor merchandise, nor glasses, nor elevators.

It happens that I am tired of my feet and my nails
and my hair and my shadow.   10
It happens that I am tired of being a man.

Just the same it would be delicious
to scare a notary with a cut lily
or knock a nun stone dead with one blow of an ear.

It would be beautiful   15
to go through the streets with a green knife
shouting until I died of cold.

I do not want to go on being a root in the dark,
hesitating, stretched out, shivering with dreams,
downwards, in the wet tripe of the earth,   20
soaking it up and thinking, eating every day.

---

1. Translated by W. S. Merwin.

I do not want to be the inheritor of so many misfortunes.
I do not want to continue as a root and as a tomb,
as a solitary tunnel, as a cellar full of corpses,
stiff with cold, dying with pain.   25

For this reason Monday burns like oil
at the sight of me arriving with my jail-face,
and it howls in passing like a wounded wheel,
and its footsteps towards nightfall are filled with hot blood.

And it shoves me along to certain corners, to certain damp houses,   30
to hospitals where the bones come out of the windows,
to certain cobblers' shops smelling of vinegar,
to streets horrendous as crevices.

There are birds the colour of sulphur, and horrible intestines
hanging from the doors of the houses which I hate,   35
there are forgotten sets of teeth in a coffee-pot,
there are mirrors
which should have wept with shame and horror,
there are umbrellas all over the place, and poisons, and navels.

I stride along with calm, with eyes, with shoes,   40
with fury, with forgetfulness,
I pass, I cross offices and stores full of orthopaedic appliances,
and courtyards hung with clothes on wires,
underpants, towels and shirts which weep
slow dirty tears.   45

I'm Explaining a Few Things[1]

You are going to ask: and where are the lilacs?
and the poppy-petalled metaphysics?
and the rain repeatedly spattering
its words and drilling them full
of apertures and birds?   5

I'll tell you all the news.

I lived in a suburb,
a suburb of Madrid,[2] with bells,
and clocks, and trees.

From there you could look out   10
over Castile's[3] dry face:
a leather ocean.
        My house was called
the house of flowers, because in every cranny
geraniums burst: it was

---

1. Translated by Nathaniel Tarn.   2. The capital of Spain.   3. Spain.

a good-looking house   15
with its dogs and children.
                    Remember, Raúl?
Eh, Rafael?
            Federico,[4] do you remember
from under the ground
my balconies on which
the light of June drowned flowers in your mouth?
                                        Brother, my brother! 20
Everything
loud with big voices, the salt of merchandises,
pile-ups of palpitating bread,
the stalls of my suburb of Argüelles with its statue
like a drained inkwell in a swirl of hake:[5]   25
oil flowed into spoons,
a deep baying
of feet and hands swelled in the streets,
metres, litres, the sharp
measure of life,
                    stacked-up fish,   30
the texture of roofs with a cold sun in which
the weather vane falters,
the fine, frenzied ivory of potatoes,
wave on wave of tomatoes rolling down to the sea.

And one morning all that was burning,   35
one morning the bonfires
leapt out of the earth
devouring human beings—
and from then on fire,
gunpowder from then on,   40
and from then on blood.
Bandits with planes and Moors,
bandits with finger-rings and duchesses,
bandits with black friars[6] spattering blessings
came through the sky to kill children   45
and the blood of children ran through the streets
without fuss, like children's blood.

Jackals that the jackals would despise,
stones that the dry thistle would bite on and spit out,
vipers that the vipers would abominate!   50

Face to face with you I have seen the blood
of Spain tower like a tide
to drown you in one wave
of pride and knives!

4. I.e., the poet Federico García Lorca, who was murdered by the Fascists on August 19, 1936. *Rafael:* his
friend, the poet Rafael Alberti.   5. A fish similar to the cod. *Argüelles:* a busy shopping area in Madrid,
near the university.   6. *Finger-rings, duchesses, friars* imply a collusion of the wealthy, the aristocracy,
and the Church to suppress the people. *Bandits:* Neruda lists categories of invaders. *Moors:* probably an
analogy between the early Muslim invaders of Spain and German and Italian pilots who bombed the village
of Guernica in April 1937.

Treacherous   55
generals:
see my dead house,
look at broken Spain:
from every house burning metal flows
instead of flowers,   60
from every socket of Spain
Spain emerges
and from every dead child a rifle with eyes,
and from every crime bullets are born
which will one day find   65
the bull's eye of your hearts.

And you will ask: why doesn't his poetry
speak of dreams and leaves
and the great volcanoes of his native land?

Come and see the blood in the streets.   70
Come and see
the blood in the streets.
Come and see the blood
in the streets!

General Song (Canto General)[1]

From *Canto II. The Heights of Macchu Picchu*[2]

VI

And so I scaled the ladder of the earth
amid the atrocious maze of lost jungles
up to you, Macchu Picchu.
High citadel of terraced stones,
at long last the dwelling of him whom the earth   5
did not conceal in its slumbering vestments.
In you, as in two parallel lines,
the cradle of lightning and man
was rocked in a wind of thorns.

Mother of stone, sea spray of the condors.   10

Towering reef of the human dawn.

Spade lost in the primal sand.

This was the dwelling, this is the site:
here the full kernels of corn rose
and fell again like red hailstones.   15

---

1. Translated by Jack Schmitt.   2. Ancient city of the Incas, situated on a remote precipice in the Andes
mountains of Peru; the city escaped the Spanish invaders and was rediscovered in 1911. The Inca empire
flourished in the 14th century and was destroyed by Francisco Pizarro in 1532.

Here the golden fiber emerged from the vicuña[3]
to clothe love, tombs, mothers,
the king, prayers, warriors.

Here man's feet rested at night
beside the eagle's feet, in the high gory   20
retreats, and at dawn
they trod the rarefied mist with feet of thunder
and touched lands and stones
until they recognized them in the night or in death.

I behold vestments and hands,   25
the vestige of water in the sonorous void,
the wall tempered by the touch of a face
that beheld with my eyes the earthen lamps,
that oiled with my hands the vanished
wood: because everything—clothing, skin, vessels,   30
words, wine, bread—
is gone, fallen to earth.

And the air flowed with orange-blossom
fingers over all the sleeping:
a thousand years of air, months, weeks of air,   35
of blue wind, of iron cordillera,[4]
like gentle hurricanes of footsteps
polishing the solitary precinct of stone.

VII

O remains of a single abyss, shadows of one gorge—
the deep one—the real, most searing death
attained the scale
of your magnitude,
and from the quarried stones,   5
from the spires,
from the terraced aqueducts
you tumbled as in autumn
to a single death.
Today the empty air no longer weeps,   10
no longer knows your feet of clay,
has now forgotten your pitchers that filtered the sky
when the lightning's knives emptied it,
and the powerful tree was eaten away
by the mist and felled by the wind.   15
It sustained a hand that fell suddenly
from the heights to the end of time.
You are no more, spider hands, fragile
filaments, spun web:
all that you were has fallen: customs, frayed   20
syllables, masks of dazzling light.

---

3. A llama-like animal, found in the Andes, that possesses a fine soft fleece.   4. Mountain range.

But a permanence of stone and word:
the citadel was raised like a chalice in the hands
of all, the living, the dead, the silent, sustained
by so much death, a wall, from so much life a stroke   25
of stone petals: the permanent rose, the dwelling:
this Andean reef of glacial colonies.

When the clay-colored hand
turned to clay, when the little eyelids closed,
filled with rough walls, brimming with castles,   30
and when the entire man was trapped in his hole,
exactitude remained hoisted aloft:
this high site of the human dawn:
the highest vessel that has contained silence:
a life of stone after so many lives.   35

VIII

Rise up with me, American[5] love.

Kiss the secret stones with me.
The torrential silver of the Urubamba[6]
makes the pollen fly to its yellow cup.
It spans the void of the grapevine,   5
the petrous plant, the hard wreath
upon the silence of the highland casket.
Come, minuscule life, between the wings
of the earth, while—crystal and cold, pounded air
extracting assailed emeralds—   10
O, wild water, you run down from the snow.

Love, love, even the abrupt night,
from the sonorous Andean flint
to the dawn's red knees,
contemplates the snow's blind child.   15

O, sonorous threaded Wilkamayu,
when you beat your lineal thunder
to a white froth, like wounded snow,
when your precipitous storm
sings and batters, awakening the sky,   20
what language do you bring to the ear recently
wrenched from your Andean froth?

Who seized the cold's lightning
and left it shackled in the heights,
dispersed in its glacial tears,   25
smitten in its swift swords,
hammering its embattled stamens,

---

5. For Neruda (and for many Latin Americans), *America* refers to Latin America; North America is called "Saxon America."   6. The river flowing through the valley below Macchu Picchu, called Wilkamayu by the Indians.

borne on its warrior's bed,
startled in its rocky end?

What are your tormented sparks saying?   30
Did your secret insurgent lightning
once journey charged with words?
Who keeps on shattering frozen syllables,
black languages, golden banners,
deep mouths, muffled cries,   35
in your slender arterial waters?

Who keeps on cutting floral eyelids
that come to gaze from the earth?
Who hurls down the dead clusters
that fell in your cascade hands   40
to strip the night stripped
in the coal of geology?

Who flings the branch down from its bonds?
Who once again entombs farewells?

Love, love, never touch the brink   45
or worship the sunken head:
let time attain its stature
in its salon of shattered headsprings,
and, between the swift water and the walls,
gather the air from the gorge,   50
the parallel sheets of the wind,
the cordilleras' blind canal,
the harsh greeting of the dew,
and, rise up, flower by flower, through the dense growth,
treading the hurtling serpent.   55

In the steep zone—forest and stone,
mist of green stars, radiant jungle—
Mantur explodes like a blinding lake
or a new layer of silence.

Come to my very heart, to my dawn,   60
up to the crowned solitudes.
The dead kingdom is still alive.

And over the Sundial the sanguinary shadow
of the condor[7] crosses like a black ship.

IX

Sidereal eagle, vineyard of mist.
Lost bastion, blind scimitar.

7. The heights of Macchu Picchu and the smaller Huayna Picchu were said to form the shape of a condor,
a large vulturelike bird seen as the messenger of humanity. *Sundial:* the *intihuatana*, or "hitching post of
the sun," a large altar carved directly out of the granite; its shape and position served to predict the date
of the winter solstice and other periods of importance to agriculture.

Spangled waistband, solemn bread.
Torrential stairway, immense eyelid.
Triangular tunic, stone pollen.   5
Granite lamp, stone bread.
Mineral serpent, stone rose.
Entombed ship, stone headspring.
Moonhorse, stone light.
Equinoctial square, stone vapor.   10
Ultimate geometry, stone book.
Tympanum fashioned amid the squalls.
Madrepore[8] of sunken time.
Rampart tempered by fingers.
Ceiling assailed by feathers.   15
Mirror bouquets, stormy foundations.
Thrones toppled by the vine.
Regime of the enraged claw.
Hurricane sustained on the slopes.
Immobile cataract of turquoise.   20
Patriarchal bell of the sleeping.
Hitching ring of the tamed snows.
Iron recumbent upon its statues.
Inaccessible dark tempest.
Puma hands, bloodstained rock.   25
Towering sombrero, snowy dispute.
Night raised on fingers and roots.
Window of the mists, hardened dove.
Nocturnal plant, statue of thunder.
Essential cordillera, searoof.   30
Architecture of lost eagles.
Skyrope, heavenly bee.
Bloody level, man-made star.
Mineral bubble, quartz moon.
Andean serpent, brow of amaranth.[9]   35
Cupola of silence, pure land.
Seabride, tree of cathedrals.
Cluster of salt, black-winged cherry tree.
Snow-capped teeth, cold thunderbolt.
Scored moon, menacing stone.   40
Headdresses of the cold, action of the air.
Volcano of hands, obscure cataract.
Silver wave, pointer of time.

X

Stone upon stone, and man, where was he?
Air upon air, and man, where was he?
Time upon time, and man, where was he?
Were you too a broken shard
of inconclusive man, of empty raptor,   5
who on the streets today, on the trails,
on the dead autumn leaves, keeps

8. Coral.   9. An annual plant with flowers and highly nutritious edible seeds.

tearing away at the heart right up to the grave?
Poor hand, foot, poor life . . .
Did the days of light   10
unraveled in you, like raindrops
on the banners of a feast day,
give petal by petal of their dark food
to the empty mouth?
                              Hunger, coral of mankind,
hunger, secret plant, woodcutters' stump,   15
hunger, did the edge of your reef rise up
to these high suspended towers?

I want to know, salt of the roads,
show me the spoon—architecture, let me
scratch at the stamens of stone with a little stick,   20
ascend the rungs of the air up to the void,
scrape the innards until I touch mankind.

Macchu Picchu, did you put
stone upon stone and, at the base, tatters?
Coal upon coal and, at the bottom, tears?   25
Fire in gold and, within it, the trembling
drop of red blood?
Bring me back the slave that you buried!
Shake from the earth the hard bread
of the poor wretch, show me   30
the slave's clothing and his window.
Tell me how he slept when he lived.
Tell me if his sleep was
harsh, gaping, like a black chasm
worn by fatigue upon the wall.   35
The wall, the wall! If upon his sleep
each layer of stone weighed down, and if he fell beneath it
as beneath a moon, with his dream!
Ancient America, sunken bride,
your fingers too,   40
on leaving the jungle for the high void of the gods,
beneath the nuptial standards of light and decorum,
mingling with the thunder of drums and spears,
your fingers, your fingers too,
which the abstract rose, the cold line, and   45
the crimson breast of the new grain transferred
to the fabric of radiant substance, to the hard cavities—
did you, entombed America, did you too store in the depths
of your bitter intestine, like an eagle, hunger?

                              XI

Through the hazy splendor,
through the stone night, let me plunge my hand,
and let the aged heart of the forsaken beat in me
like a bird captive for a thousand years!

Let me forget, today, this joy, which is greater than the sea,   5
because man is greater than the sea and its islands,
and we must fall into him as into a well to emerge from the bottom
with a bouquet of secret water and sunken truths.
Let me forget, great stone, the powerful proportion,
the transcendent measure, the honeycombed stones,   10
and from the square let me today run
my hand over the hypotenuse of rough blood and sackcloth.
When, like a horseshoe of red elytra,[1] the frenzied condor
beats my temples in the order of its flight,
and the hurricane of cruel feathers sweeps the somber dust   15
from the diagonal steps, I do not see the swift brute,
I do not see the blind cycle of its claws,
I see the man of old, the servant, asleep in the fields,
I see a body, a thousand bodies, a man, a thousand women,
black with rain and night, beneath the black squall,   20
with the heavy stone of the statue:
Juan Stonecutter, son of Wiracocha[2]
Juan Coldeater, son of a green star,
Juan Barefoot, grandson of turquoise,
rise up to be born with me, my brother.   25

XII

Rise up to be born with me, my brother.

Give me your hand from the deep
zone of your disseminated sorrow.
You'll not return from the bottom of the rocks.
You'll not return from subterranean time.   5
Your stiff voice will not return.
Your drilled eyes will not return.
Behold me from the depths of the earth,
laborer, weaver, silent herdsman:
tamer of the tutelary guanacos:[3]   10
mason of the defied scaffold:
bearer of the Andean tears:
jeweler with your fingers crushed:
tiller trembling in the seed:
potter spilt in your clay: 15
bring to the cup of this new life, brothers,
all your timeless buried sorrows.
Show me your blood and your furrow,
tell me: I was punished here,
because the jewel did not shine or the earth   20
did not surrender the gemstone or kernel on time:
show me the stone on which you fell
and the wood on which you were crucified,
strike the old flintstones,
the old lamps, the whips sticking   25

1. An insect's wing cases.   2. Inca rain god who taught the arts of civilization to humanity.   3. Reddish-brown grazing animals related to the llama.

throughout the centuries to your wounds
and the war clubs glistening red.
I've come to speak through your dead mouths.
Throughout the earth join all
the silent scattered lips   30
and from the depths speak to me all night long,
as if I were anchored with you,
tell me everything, chain by chain,
link by link, and step by step,
sharpen the knives that you've kept,   35
put them in my breast and in my hand,
like a river of yellow lightning,
like a river of buried jaguars,
and let me weep hours, days, years,
blind ages, stellar centuries.   40

Give me silence, water, hope.

Give me struggle, iron, volcanoes.

Cling to my body like magnets.

Hasten to my veins and to my mouth.

Speak through my words and my blood.   45

Ode to the Tomato[1]

The street
drowns in tomatoes:
noon,
summer,
light   5
breaks
in two
tomato
halves,
and the streets   10
run
with juice.
In December[2]
the tomato
cuts loose,   15
invades
kitchens,
takes over lunches,
settles
at rest   20

1. Translated by Nathaniel Tarn.   2. Summer in Chile.

on sideboards,
with the glasses,
butter dishes,
blue salt-cellars.
It has   25
its own radiance,
a goodly majesty.
Too bad we must
assassinate:
a knife   30
plunges
into its living pulp,
red
viscera,
a fresh,   35
deep,
inexhaustible
sun
floods the salads
of Chile,   40
beds cheerfully
with the blonde onion,
and to celebrate
oil
the filial essence   45
of the olive tree
lets itself fall
over its gaping hemispheres,
the pimento
adds   50
its fragrance,
salt its magnetism—
we have the day's
wedding:
parsley   55
flaunts
its little flags,
potatoes
thump to a boil,
the roasts   60
beat
down the door
with their aromas:
it's time!
let's go!   65
and upon
the table,
belted by summer,
tomatoes,
stars of the earth,   70
stars multiplied
and fertile

show off
their convolutions,
canals   75
and plenitudes
and the abundance
boneless,
without husk,
or scale or thorn,   80
grant us
the festival
of ardent colour
and all-embracing freshness.

SAMUEL BECKETT
1906–1989

The sparest, starkest representation of the human condition in all its "absurd" emptiness fills Samuel Beckett's novels and plays. Not that other authors do not concern themselves with the problem of representing reality, but where Pirandello plays with allusions to an elusive identity, Joyce with the stream of consciousness, and Proust with layers of the self reconstituted through affective memory, Beckett's world is haunted—like that of Kafka—by an absence of meaning at the core. Whether expressed by the protagonist's ramblings in the novels *Molloy* (1951), *Malone Dies* (1951), or *The Unnamable* (1953), by the stripped-down dialogue of the plays *Waiting for Godot* (1952) and *Endgame* (1957), or by the telegraphic style of a late novel, *How It Is* (1961), Beckett's characters engage in a desperate attempt to find or to create meaning for themselves. Born into a world without reason, they live out their lives waiting for an explanation that never comes and whose existence may be only a figment of their imagination. In the meantime, human relationships are reduced to the most elemental tensions of cruelty, hope, frustration, and disillusionment around themes of birth, death, human emotions, material obstacles, and unending consciousness. Beckett's comedy of errors is a bitter one and, even in its puns and parodies, draws heavily on what the author has described as "the power of the text to claw."

Like Joyce and Yeats, Beckett was born in Ireland; like Joyce, he chose to live abroad for most of his life. Born near Dublin on April 13, 1906, he was educated in Ireland and received a B.A. from Trinity College in 1927. From 1928 to 1930, he taught English at the École Normale Supérieure in Paris, where he met James Joyce and was for a while influenced by the older novelist's exuberant and punning use of language. Beckett wrote an essay on the early stages of Joyce's *Finnegans Wake* and later helped in the French translation of part of the book. In 1930 he entered a competition for a poem on the subject of time and won first prize with a ninety-eight-line (and seventeen-footnote) monologue, *Whoroscope*, spoken by the seventeenth-century French physicist and philosopher René Descartes. Beckett returned to Trinity College, where he took an M.A. in 1931, published an essay on Proust, and stayed on the following year to teach French. It was a brief academic career, for he gave up teaching in 1932 and, after living in England, France, and Germany, made Paris his permanent home in 1937. Although two early novels, *Murphy* (1938) and *Watt* (1953), were written in English, Beckett was already turning to French as his preferred language for original composition; in the years after World War II, he wrote almost exclusively in French and only later translated (often with substantial changes) the same texts into English. He said that he wrote in French because it was easier to write "without style"—without the native speaker's temptation to elegance and virtuoso display. Although no generalization holds true for all cases, comparing the French and English versions of the same work often suggests just such a contrast, with the French text closer to basic grammatical forms and, therefore, possessing a harsher, less nuanced focus.

Whether comic or despairing (often both), Beckett's characters ring changes on the Cartesian image of the Rational Man that has been at the base of Western cultural attitudes ever since the philosopher René Descartes moved from specific questions about the physical sciences to the larger question of human existence. Descartes, like Beckett, went back to zero in order not to be led astray by any preconceived assumptions or doctrines. He doubted everything—except that he doubted, which in itself indicated that he was thinking and that if "I think, therefore I am" (*Cogito, ergo sum*). Upon that certainty Descartes erected a logical system for exploring the natural universe and explaining the human condition. Beckett is not so sure that logic allows us to know what we are looking at or to match up our terminology with reality at all. In *Watt*, the protagonist is caught in a peculiar hesitation inasmuch as things, "if they consented to be named, did so as it were with reluctance." He looks at a pot, but "it was not a pot, the more he looked, the more he reflected, the more he felt sure of that, that it was not a pot at all. It resembled a pot, it was almost a pot, but it was not a pot of which one could say, Pot, pot and be comforted." The gentle bewilderment that Watt feels turns bitter and more dangerous in later novels such as the famous trilogy (*Molloy, Malone Dies,* and *The Unnamable*) or in *How It Is*, which refuses to present any image of rational control as it murmurs, free of punctuation, the monologue of an unstructured consciousness inside an accompanying "quaqua [bzzz bzzz] on all sides."

The narrative perspective in the trilogy moves from a series of related monologue stories, in which narrators come more and more to resemble one another, to the ramblings of an "unnamable" speaker who seems to represent them all at the end. In *Molloy*, there are two interlocking points of view as, first Molloy tells of setting out on a bicycle to visit his bedridden mother, a search that takes him months and leads him all over (with many echoes of Homer's *Odyssey*). The last we hear of Molloy is that he is crippled and has lost his bicycle but is determined still to proceed if only by rolling; Moran takes over at that point and describes a corresponding search for Molloy in the course of which he loses his bicycle, is crippled, and ends up frustrated back home. The next novel, *Malone Dies*, is similarly divided between protagonists, even if in the mind of a single narrator: a dying and bedridden Malone writes the diary of his last days and also composes the story of Macmann, who is to die at the same moment as Malone and apparently does so as the novel ends. The last in the trilogy, *The Unnamable*, has no fixed authorial perspective or claim to responsibility. "I'm in words, made of words." Someone (unnamed and—by now—clearly unnamable) is seated in an undefined gray space and time, writing a series of stories that may be the tales of Malone, Malloy, and Moran, or of a new Mahood who also becomes Worm, who may in turn be the narrator writing stories about himself; or it may simply evoke the act of storytelling as it creates fictions of life to establish some mode of reality. In 1949, when the trilogy was just complete, Beckett published a dialogue on modern art that described the artist's disgust with traditional art's "puny exploits . . . doing a little better the same old thing" and his preference for "the expression that there is nothing to express, nothing with which to express, nothing from which to express, no power to express, no desire to express, together with the obligation to express." The disintegration of narrative perspective in Beckett's fiction is one means of denying that there is a knowable "something to express" or an author-itative point of view from which to express "nothing."

How can one possibly make a convincing stage play out of "nothing"? The popu-larity of Beckett's first performed play, *Waiting for Godot* (French version presented 1953; English, 1955), showed that absurdist theater—with its empty, repetitive dia-logue, its grotesquely bare yet apparently symbolic settings, and its refusal to build to a dramatic climax—had meaning even for audiences used to theatrical realism and logically developing plots. These audiences found two clownlike tramps, Vladimir and Estragon (Didi and Gogo), talking, quarreling, falling down, contemplating suicide, and generally filling up time with conversation that ranges from vaudeville patter to metaphysical speculation as they wait under a tree for a Godot who never comes. Instead, the two are joined in the middle of each act by another grotesque pair: the rich Pozzo and his brutally abused servant Lucky, whom he leads around by a rope tied to his neck. The popular interpretation of "Godot" as a diminutive for "God," and of the play as a statement of existential anguish at the inexplicable human condition, is scarcely defused by Beckett's caution that "If by Godot I had meant God, I would have said God." Yet identifying Godot is less important than identifying the ignomin-ious plight on stage as symbolically our own and identifying *with* the characters as they express the anxious, often repugnant, but also comic picture of human relation-ships in an absurd universe.

After the popular success of *Waiting for Godot*, Beckett wrote *Endgame* (French version performed 1957; English, 1958) and a series of stage plays and brief pieces for the radio. The stage plays have the same bare yet striking settings: *Krapp's Last Tape* (1958) presents an old man sitting at a table with his tape recorder, recalling a love affair thirty years past; and *Happy Days* (1961) portrays a married couple, the wife of which chatters ceaselessly about her possessions although she is buried up to her waist in the first act and up to her neck in the second. When Beckett received the Nobel Prize for literature in 1969, he was recognized as the purest exponent of the twentieth century's chief philosophical dilemma: the notion of the "absurd," or the grotesque contradiction between human attempts to discover meaning in life and the simultaneous conviction that there is no "meaning" available that we have not created ourselves. *Endgame*, often called Beckett's major achievement, is a prime example of this dilemma.

When the curtain rises on *Endgame*, it is as though the world were awakening from sleep. The sheets draping the furniture and central character are taken off, and Hamm sets himself in motion like an actor or chess pawn: "Me . . . to play." Yet we are also near the end for, as the title implies, nothing new will happen; an "endgame" is the final phase of a chess game, the stage at which the end is predictably in sight although the play must still be completed. Throughout, the theme of "end," "finish," "no more" is sounded, even while Hamm notes the passage of time: "Something is taking its course." But time does not lead anywhere; it is either past or present and always barren. The past exists as Nagg's and Nell's memories, as Hamm's story, which may or may not describe Clov's entry into the home, and as a period in which Clov once loved Hamm. The present shows four characters dwindling away, alone in a dead world, caught between visions of dusty hell and dreams of life reborn. In one of the biblical echoes that permeate the play, Hamm and Clov repeatedly evoke the last words of the crucified Jesus in the Gospel according to St. John: "It is finished." But this is not a biblical morality play, and *Endgame* describes a world not of divine but of self-creation. Hamm may be composing and directing the entire performance: a storyteller and playwright with "asides" and "last soliloquy" whose "dialogue" keeps Clov on stage against his will, a mad artist who (when looking out the window onto a flourishing world) can see only dust and ashes, or a magician presiding over an imaginary kingdom who concludes an inner story and unavailing prayer with

Prospero's line from Shakespeare's *The Tempest* (4.1.148): "Our revels now are ended." Or he may simply be aware of their lives *as* a performance without any other meaning: Shakespeare's passage continues later: "We are such stuff / As dreams are made on, and our little life / Is rounded with a sleep." The situation at the end of the play is little changed—only barer, as Hamm discards his stick, whistle, and dog, "reckoning closed and story ended." Yet Clov is still waiting to leave as Hamm covers his face, and it is not impossible that the play will resume in precisely the same terms tomorrow.

Endgame, like *Waiting for Godot* (and like Kafka's stories), has been given a number of symbolic interpretations. Some refer to Beckett's love of wordplay: Hamm as Hamm-actor, Hammlet, Hammer, and Nag and Nell as shortened forms of *Nägel* and *nello*, German and Italian words for "nail," which are invoked as crucifixion themes suggesting the martyrdom of humanity. The setting of a boxlike room with two windows is seen as a skull, the seat of consciousness, or (emphasizing the bloody handkerchief and the reference to fontanelles—the soft spot in the skull of a newborn child) as a womb. The characters' isolation in a dead world after an unnamed catastrophe (which may be Hamm's fault) suggests the world after atomic holocaust; or, for those who recall Beckett's fascination with the apathetic figure of Belacqua waiting, in the Purgatory of Dante's *Divine Comedy*, for his punishment to begin, it evokes an image of pre-Purgatorial consciousness. The ash cans in which Hamm has "bottled" his parents, and the general cruelty between characters, are to represent the dustbin of modern Western civilized values. Hamm and Clov represent the uneasy adjustment of soul and body, the class struggle of rich and poor, or the master-slave relationship in all senses (including the slave's acceptance of his victimization). Clearly Beckett has created a structure that accommodates all these readings while authorizing none. He himself said to director Alan Schneider that he was less interested in symbolism than in describing a "local situation," an interaction of four characters in a given set of circumstances, and that the audience's interpretation was its own responsibility.

Beckett both authorized and denied these interpretations. He pruned down an earlier, more anecdotal two-act play to achieve *Endgame*'s skeletal plot and almost anonymous characters, and in doing so created a structure that immediately elicits the reader's instinct to "fill in the blanks." His puns and allusions openly point to a further meaning that *may* be contained in the implied reference, but may also be part of an infinite regress of meaning—expressing the "absurd" itself. Working against too heavy an insistence on symbolic meanings is the fact that the play is also funny—especially when performed on stage. The characters popping out of ash cans, the jerky, repetitive motions with which Clov carries out his master's commands, and the often obscene vaudeville patter accompanied by appropriate gestures, all provide a comic perspective that keeps *Endgame* from sinking into tragic despair. The intellectual distance offered by comedy is entirely in keeping with the more somber side of the play, which rejects pathos and constantly drags its characters' escapist fancies down to the minimal facts of survival: food, shelter, sleep, painkiller. Thus it is possible to say that *Endgame* describes—but only among many other things—what it is like to be alive, declining toward death in a world without meaning.

Endgame[1]

For Roger Blin

CHARACTERS

NAGG
NELL
HAMM
CLOV

Bare interior.
Gray light.
Left and right back, high up, two small windows, curtains drawn.
Front right, a door. Hanging near door, its face to wall, a picture.
Front left, touching each other, covered with an old sheet, two ashbins.
Center, in an armchair on castors, covered with an old sheet, HAMM.
Motionless by the door, his eyes fixed on HAMM, CLOV. *Very red face.*
Brief tableau.

[CLOV *goes and stands under window left. Stiff, staggering walk. He looks up at window left. He turns and looks at window right. He goes and stands under window right. He looks up at window right. He turns and looks at window left. He goes out, comes back immediately with a small step-ladder, carries it over and sets it down under window left, gets up on it, draws back curtain. He gets down, takes six steps (for example) towards window right, goes back for ladder, carries it over and sets it down under window right, gets up on it, draws back curtain. He gets down, takes three steps towards window left, goes back for ladder, carries it over and sets it down under window left, gets up on it, looks out of window. Brief laugh. He gets down, takes one step towards window right, goes back for ladder, carries it over and sets it down under window right, gets up on it, looks out of window. Brief laugh. He gets down, goes with ladder towards ashbins, halts, turns, carries back ladder and sets it down under window right, goes to ashbins, removes sheet covering them, folds it over his arm. He raises one lid, stoops and looks into bin. Brief laugh. He closes lid. Same with other bin. He goes to* HAMM, *removes sheet covering him, folds it over his arm. In a dressing-gown, a stiff toque[2] on his head, a large blood-stained handkerchief over his face, a whistle hanging from his neck, a rug over his knees, thick socks on his feet,* HAMM *seems to be asleep.* CLOV *looks him over. Brief laugh. He goes to door, halts, turns towards auditorium.*]

CLOV [*Fixed gaze, tonelessly.*] Finished, it's finished, nearly finished, it must be nearly finished. [*Pause.*] Grain upon grain, one by one, and one day, suddenly, there's a heap, a little heap, the impossible heap. [*Pause.*] I can't be punished any more. [*Pause.*] I'll go now to my kitchen, ten feet by ten feet by ten feet, and wait for him to whistle me. [*Pause.*] Nice dimensions, nice proportions, I'll lean on the table, and look at the wall, and wait for him to whistle me.

[*He remains a moment motionless, then goes out. He comes back imme-*

---

1. Translated by the author.   2. A fitted cloth hat with little or no brim, sometimes indicating official status, as with a judge's toque.

diately, goes to window right, takes up the ladder and carries it out. Pause. HAMM *stirs. He yawns under the handkerchief. He removes the handkerchief from his face. Very red face. Black glasses.*]

HAMM Me—[*He yawns.*]—to play.[3] [*He holds the handkerchief spread out before him.*] Old Stancher![4] [*He takes off his glasses, wipes his eyes, his face, the glasses, puts them on again, folds the handkerchief and puts it back neatly in the breast-pocket of his dressing-gown. He clears his throat, joins the tips of his fingers.*] Can there be misery—[*He yawns.*]—loftier than mine? No doubt. Formerly. But now? [*Pause.*] My father? [*Pause.*] My mother? [*Pause.*] My . . . dog? [*Pause.*] Oh I am willing to believe they suffer as much as such creatures can suffer. But does that mean their sufferings equal mine? No doubt. [*Pause.*] No, all is a—[*He yawns.*]—bsolute, [*Proudly.*] the bigger a man is the fuller he is. [*Pause. Gloomily.*] And the emptier. [*He sniffs.*] Clov! [*Pause.*] No, alone. [*Pause.*] What dreams! Those forests! [*Pause.*] Enough, it's time it ended, in the shelter too. [*Pause.*] And yet I hesitate, I hesitate to . . . to end. Yes, there it is, it's time it ended and yet I hesitate to—[*He yawns.*]—to end. [*Yawns.*] God, I'm tired, I'd be better off in bed. [*He whistles. Enter* CLOV *immediately. He halts beside the chair.*] You pollute the air! [*Pause.*] Get me ready, I'm going to bed.

CLOV I've just got you up.

HAMM And what of it?

CLOV I can't be getting you up and putting you to bed every five minutes, I have things to do. [*Pause.*]

HAMM Did you ever see my eyes?

CLOV No.

HAMM Did you never have the curiosity, while I was sleeping, to take off my glasses and look at my eyes?

CLOV Pulling back the lids? [*Pause.*] No.

HAMM One of these days I'll show them to you. [*Pause.*] It seems they've gone all white. [*Pause.*] What time is it?

CLOV The same as usual.

HAMM [*Gesture towards window right.*] Have you looked?

CLOV Yes.

HAMM Well?

CLOV Zero.

HAMM It'd need to rain.

CLOV It won't rain. [*Pause.*]

HAMM Apart from that, how do you feel?

CLOV I don't complain.

HAMM You feel normal?

CLOV [*Irritably.*] I tell you I don't complain.

HAMM I feel a little queer. [*Pause.*] Clov!

CLOV Yes.

HAMM Have you not had enough?

CLOV Yes! [*Pause.*] Of what?

HAMM Of this . . . this . . . thing.

---

3. Hamm announces that it is his move at the beginning of *Endgame*: the comparison is with a game of chess, of which the "endgame" is the final stage. 4. The handkerchief that stanches his blood.

CLOV   I always had. [*Pause.*] Not you?

HAMM   [*Gloomily.*]   Then there's no reason for it to change.

CLOV   It may end. [*Pause.*] All life long the same questions, the same answers.

HAMM   Get me ready. [CLOV *does not move.*] Go and get the sheet. [CLOV *does not move.*] Clov!

CLOV   Yes.

HAMM   I'll give you nothing more to eat.

CLOV   Then we'll die.

HAMM   I'll give you just enough to keep you from dying. You'll be hungry all the time.

CLOV   Then we won't die. [*Pause.*] I'll go and get the sheet. [*He goes towards the door.*]

HAMM   No! [CLOV *halts.*] I'll give you one biscuit per day. [*Pause.*] One and a half. [*Pause.*] Why do you stay with me?

CLOV   Why do you keep me?

HAMM   There's no one else.

CLOV   There's nowhere else. [*Pause.*]

HAMM   You're leaving me all the same.

CLOV   I'm trying.

HAMM   You don't love me.

CLOV   No.

HAMM   You loved me once.

CLOV   Once!

HAMM   I've made you suffer too much. [*Pause.*] Haven't I?

CLOV   It's not that.

HAMM   [*Shocked.*]   I haven't made you suffer too much?

CLOV   Yes!

HAMM   [*Relieved.*]   Ah you gave me a fright! [*Pause. Coldly.*] Forgive me. [*Pause. Louder.*] I said, Forgive me.

CLOV   I heard you. [*Pause.*] Have you bled?

HAMM   Less. [*Pause.*] Is it not time for my pain-killer?

CLOV   No. [*Pause.*]

HAMM   How are your eyes?

CLOV   Bad.

HAMM   How are your legs?

CLOV   BAD.

HAMM   But you can move.

CLOV   Yes.

HAMM   [*Violently.*]   Then move! [CLOV *goes to back wall, leans against it with his forehead and hands.*] Where are you?

CLOV   Here.

HAMM   Come back! [CLOV *returns to his place beside the chair.*] Where are you?

CLOV   Here.

HAMM   Why don't you kill me?

CLOV   I don't know the combination of the cupboard. [*Pause.*]

HAMM   Go and get two bicycle-wheels.

CLOV   There are no more bicycle-wheels.

HAMM   What have you done with your bicycle?

CLOV   I never had a bicycle.

HAMM   The thing is impossible.

CLOV   When there were still bicycles I wept to have one. I crawled at your feet. You told me to go to hell. Now there are none.

HAMM   And your rounds? When you inspected my paupers. Always on foot?

CLOV   Sometimes on horse. [*The lid of one of the bins lifts and the hands of* NAGG *appear, gripping the rim. Then his head emerges. Nightcap. Very white face.* NAGG *yawns, then listens.*] I'll leave you, I have things to do.

HAMM   In your kitchen?

CLOV   Yes.

HAMM   Outside of here it's death. [*Pause.*] All right, be off. [*Exit* CLOV. *Pause.*] We're getting on.

NAGG   Me pap![5]

HAMM   Accursed progenitor!

NAGG   Me pap!

HAMM   The old folks at home! No decency left! Guzzle, guzzle, that's all they think of. [*He whistles. Enter* CLOV. *He halts beside the chair.*] Well! I thought you were leaving me.

CLOV   Oh not just yet, not just yet.

NAGG   Me pap!

HAMM   Give him his pap.

CLOV   There's no more pap.

HAMM   [*To* NAGG.]   Do you hear that? There's no more pap. You'll never get any more pap.

NAGG   I want me pap!

HAMM   Give him a biscuit. [*Exit* CLOV.] Accursed fornicator! How are your stumps?

NAGG   Never mind me stumps.

[*Enter* CLOV *with biscuit.*]

CLOV   I'm back again, with the biscuit. [*He gives biscuit to* NAGG *who fingers it, sniffs it.*]

NAGG   [*Plaintively.*]   What is it?

CLOV   Spratt's medium.[6]

NAGG   [*As before.*]   It's hard! I can't!

HAMM   Bottle him!

[CLOV *pushes* NAGG *back into the bin, closes the lid.*]

CLOV   [*Returning to his place beside the chair.*]   If age but knew!

HAMM   Sit on him!

CLOV   I can't sit.

HAMM   True. And I can't stand.

CLOV   So it is.

HAMM   Every man his speciality. [*Pause.*] No phone calls? [*Pause.*] Don't we laugh?

CLOV   [*After reflection.*]   I don't feel like it.

HAMM   [*After reflection.*]   Nor I. [*Pause.*] Clov!

CLOV   Yes.

HAMM   Nature has forgotten us.

5. Food, mush.   6. A common plain cookie.

CLOV There's no more nature.

HAMM No more nature! You exaggerate.

CLOV In the vicinity.

HAMM But we breathe, we change! We lose our hair, our teeth! Our bloom! Our ideals!

CLOV Then she hasn't forgotten us.

HAMM But you say there is none.

CLOV [Sadly.] No one that ever lived ever thought so crooked as we.

HAMM We do what we can.

CLOV We shouldn't. [Pause.]

HAMM You're a bit of all right, aren't you?[7]

CLOV A smithereen.[8] [Pause.]

HAMM This is slow work. [Pause.] Is it not time for my pain-killer?

CLOV No. [Pause.] I'll leave you, I have things to do.

HAMM In your kitchen?

CLOV Yes.

HAMM What, I'd like to know.

CLOV I look at the wall.

HAMM The wall! And what do you see on your wall? Mene, mene?[9] Naked bodies?

CLOV I see my light dying.

HAMM Your light dying! Listen to that! Well, it can die just as well here, your light. Take a look at me and then come back and tell me what you think of your light. [Pause.]

CLOV You shouldn't speak to me like that. [Pause.]

HAMM [Coldly.] Forgive me. [Pause. Louder.] I said, Forgive me.

CLOV I heard you.

[The lid of NAGG's bin lifts. His hands appear, gripping the rim. Then his head emerges. In his mouth the biscuit. He listens.]

HAMM Did your seeds come up?

CLOV No.

HAMM Did you scratch round them to see if they had sprouted?

CLOV They haven't sprouted.

HAMM Perhaps it's still too early.

CLOV If they were going to sprout they would have sprouted. [Violently.] They'll never sprout!

[Pause. NAGG takes biscuit in his hand.]

HAMM This is not much fun. [Pause.] But that's always the way at the end of the day, isn't it, Clov?

CLOV Always.

HAMM It's the end of the day like any other day, isn't it, Clov?

CLOV Looks like it. [Pause.]

HAMM [Anguished.] What's happening, what's happening?

CLOV Something is taking its course. [Pause.]

HAMM All right, be off. [He leans back in his chair, remains motionless. CLOV does not move, heaves a great groaning sigh. HAMM sits up.] I thought I told you to be off.

---

7. You're pretty good, aren't you? (British slang).   8. A tiny bit.   9. From Daniel 5.25: "Mene, mene, tekel, upharsin"; words written by a divine hand on the wall during the feast of Belshazzar, king of Babylon. They predict doom and tell the king "Thou art weighed in the balances, and art found wanting" (Daniel 5.27).

CLOV I'm trying. [*He goes to door, halts.*] Ever since I was whelped.
      [*Exit* CLOV.]

HAMM We're getting on.
      [*He leans back in his chair, remains motionless.* NAGG *knocks on the lid
      of the other bin. Pause. He knocks harder. The lid lifts and the hands of*
      NELL *appear, gripping the rim. Then her head emerges. Lace cap. Very
      white face.*]

NELL What is it, my pet? [*Pause.*] Time for love?

NAGG Were you asleep?

NELL Oh no!

NAGG Kiss me.

NELL We can't.

NAGG Try.
      [*Their heads strain towards each other, fail to meet, fall apart again.*]

NELL Why this farce, day after day? [*Pause.*]

NAGG I've lost me tooth.

NELL When?

NAGG I had it yesterday.

NELL [*Elegiac.*] Ah yesterday!
      [*They turn painfully towards each other.*]

NAGG Can you see me?

NELL Hardly. And you?

NAGG What?

NELL Can you see me?

NAGG Hardly.

NELL So much the better, so much the better.

NAGG Don't say that. [*Pause.*] Our sight has failed.

NELL Yes.
      [*Pause. They turn away from each other.*]

NAGG Can you hear me?

NELL Yes. And you?

NAGG Yes. [*Pause.*] Our hearing hasn't failed.

NELL Our what?

NAGG Our hearing.

NELL No. [*Pause.*] Have you anything else to say to me?

NAGG Do you remember—

NELL No.

NAGG When we crashed on our tandem[1] and lost our shanks.
      [*They laugh heartily.*]

NELL It was in the Ardennes.
      [*They laugh less heartily.*]

NAGG On the road to Sedan.[2] [*They laugh still less heartily.*] Are you cold?

NELL Yes, perished. And you?

NAGG [*Pause.*] I'm freezing. [*Pause.*] Do you want to go in?

NELL Yes.

NAGG Then go in. [NELL *does not move.*] Why don't you go in?

NELL I don't know. [*Pause.*]

NAGG Has he changed your sawdust?

---

1. A bicycle built for two.   2. Town in northern France where the French were defeated in the Franco-Prussian War (1870). Ardennes is a forest in northern France, the scene of bitter fighting in both world wars.

NELL It isn't sawdust. [*Pause. Wearily.*] Can you not be a little accurate, Nagg?

NAGG Your sand then. It's not important.

NELL It is important. [*Pause.*]

NAGG It was sawdust once.

NELL Once!

NAGG And now it's sand. [*Pause.*] From the shore. [*Pause. Impatiently.*] Now it's sand he fetches from the shore.

NELL Now it's sand.

NAGG Has he changed yours?

NELL No.

NAGG Nor mine. [*Pause.*] I won't have it! [*Pause. Holding up the biscuit.*] Do you want a bit?

NELL No. [*Pause.*] Of what?

NAGG Biscuit. I've kept you half. [*He looks at the biscuit. Proudly.*] Three quarters. For you. Here. [*He proffers the biscuit.*] No? [*Pause.*] Do you not feel well?

HAMM [*Wearily.*] Quiet, quiet, you're keeping me awake. [*Pause.*] Talk softer. [*Pause.*] If I could sleep I might make love. I'd go into the woods. My eyes would see . . . the sky, the earth. I'd run, run, they wouldn't catch me. [*Pause.*] Nature! [*Pause.*] There's something dripping in my head. [*Pause.*] A heart, a heart in my head. [*Pause.*]

NAGG [*Soft.*] Do you hear him? A heart in his head! [*He chuckles cautiously.*]

NELL One mustn't laugh at those things, Nagg. Why must you always laugh at them?

NAGG Not so loud!

NELL [*Without lowering her voice.*] Nothing is funnier than unhappiness, I grant you that. But—

NAGG [*Shocked.*] Oh!

NELL Yes, yes, it's the most comical thing in the world. And we laugh, we laugh, with a will, in the beginning. But it's always the same thing. Yes, it's like the funny story we have heard too often, we still find it funny, but we don't laugh any more. [*Pause.*] Have you anything else to say to me?

NAGG No.

NELL Are you quite sure? [*Pause.*] Then I'll leave you.

NAGG Do you not want your biscuit? [*Pause.*] I'll keep it for you. [*Pause.*] I thought you were going to leave me.

NELL I am going to leave you.

NAGG Could you give me a scratch before you go?

NELL No. [*Pause.*] Where?

NAGG In the back.

NELL No. [*Pause.*] Rub yourself against the rim.

NAGG It's lower down. In the hollow.

NELL What hollow?

NAGG The hollow! [*Pause.*] Could you not? [*Pause.*] Yesterday you scratched me there.

NELL [*Elegiac.*] Ah yesterday!

NAGG Could you not? [*Pause.*] Would you like me to scratch you? [*Pause.*] Are you crying again?

NELL   I was trying. [*Pause.*]

HAMM   Perhaps it's a little vein. [*Pause.*]

NAGG   What was that he said?

NELL   Perhaps it's a little vein.

NAGG   What does that mean? [*Pause.*] That means nothing. [*Pause.*] Will I tell you the story of the tailor?

NELL   No. [*Pause.*] What for?

NAGG   To cheer you up.

NELL   It's not funny.

NAGG   It always made you laugh. [*Pause.*] The first time I thought you'd die.

NELL   It was on Lake Como.³ [*Pause.*] One April afternoon. [*Pause.*] Can you believe it?

NAGG   What?

NELL   That we once went out rowing on Lake Como. [*Pause.*] One April afternoon.

NAGG   We had got engaged the day before.

NELL   Engaged!

NAGG   You were in such fits that we capsized. By rights we should have been drowned.

NELL   It was because I felt happy.

NAGG   [*Indignant.*]   It was not, it was not, it was my story and nothing else. Happy! Don't you laugh at it still? Every time I tell it. Happy!

NELL   It was deep, deep. And you could see down to the bottom. So white. So clean.

NAGG   Let me tell it again. [*Raconteur's voice.*] An Englishman, needing a pair of striped trousers in a hurry for the New Year festivities, goes to his tailor who takes his measurements. [*Tailor's voice.*] "That's the lot, come back in four days, I'll have it ready." Good. Four days later. [*Tailor's voice.*] "So sorry, come back in a week, I've made a mess of the seat." Good, that's all right, a neat seat can be very ticklish. A week later. [*Tailor's voice.*] "Frightfully sorry, come back in ten days. I've made a hash of the crotch." Good, can't be helped, a snug crotch is always a teaser. Ten days later. [*Tailor's voice.*] "Dreadfully sorry, come back in a fortnight, I've made a balls of the fly." Good, at a pinch, a smart fly is a stiff proposition. [*Pause. Normal voice.*] I never told it worse. [*Pause. Gloomy.*] I tell this story worse and worse. [*Pause. Raconteur's voice.*] Well, to make it short, the bluebells are blowing and he ballockses⁴ the buttonholes. [*Customer's voice.*] "God damn you to hell, Sir, no, it's indecent, there are limits! In six days, do you hear me, six days, God made the world. Yes Sir, no less Sir, the WORLD! And you are not bloody well capable of making me a pair of trousers in three months!" [*Tailor's voice, scandalized.*] "But my dear Sir, my dear Sir, look—[*Disdainful gesture, disgustedly.*]—at the world—[*Pause.*] and look—[*Loving gesture, proudly.*]—at my TROUSERS!"

>   [*Pause. He looks at* NELL *who has remained impassive, her eyes unseeing, breaks into a high forced laugh, cuts it short, pokes his head towards* NELL, *launches his laugh again.*]

HAMM   Silence!

---

3. A large lake and tourist resort in northern Italy, near the Swiss border.   4. "Bollixes," botches.

[NAGG *starts, cuts short his laugh.*]

NELL   You could see down to the bottom.

HAMM [*Exasperated.*]   Have you not finished? Will you never finish? [*With sudden fury.*] Will this never finish? [NAGG *disappears into his bin, closes the lid behind him.* NELL *does not move. Frenziedly.*] My kingdom for a nightman![5] [*He whistles. Enter* CLOV.] Clear away this muck! Chuck it in the sea!

[CLOV *goes to bins, halts.*]

NELL   So white.

HAMM   What? What's she blathering about?

[CLOV *stoops, takes* NELL's *hand, feels her pulse.*]

NELL [*To* CLOV.]   Desert!

[CLOV *lets go her hand, pushes her back in the bin, closes the lid.*]

CLOV [*Returning to his place beside the chair.*]   She has no pulse.

HAMM   What was she drivelling about?

CLOV   She told me to go away, into the desert.

HAMM   Damn busybody! Is that all?

CLOV   No.

HAMM   What else?

CLOV   I didn't understand.

HAMM   Have you bottled her?

CLOV   Yes.

HAMM   Are they both bottled?

CLOV   Yes.

HAMM   Screw down the lids. [CLOV *goes towards door.*] Time enough. [CLOV *halts.*] My anger subsides, I'd like to pee.

CLOV [*With alacrity.*]   I'll go and get the catheter. [*He goes towards door.*]

HAMM   Time enough. [CLOV *halts.*] Give me my pain-killer.

CLOV   It's too soon. [*Pause.*] It's too soon on top of your tonic, it wouldn't act.

HAMM   In the morning they brace you up and in the evening they calm you down. Unless it's the other way round. [*Pause.*] That old doctor, he's dead naturally?

CLOV   He wasn't old.

HAMM   But he's dead?

CLOV   Naturally. [*Pause.*] You ask me that? [*Pause.*]

HAMM   Take me for a little turn. [CLOV *goes behind the chair and pushes it forward.*] Not too fast! [CLOV *pushes chair.*] Right round the world! [CLOV *pushes chair.*] Hug the walls, then back to the center again. [CLOV *pushes chair.*] I was right in the center, wasn't I?

CLOV [*Pushing.*]   Yes.

HAMM   We'd need a proper wheel-chair. With big wheels. Bicycle wheels! [*Pause.*] Are you hugging?

CLOV [*Pushing.*]   Yes.

HAMM [*Groping for wall.*]   It's a lie! Why do you lie to me?

CLOV [*Bearing closer to wall.*]   There! There!

HAMM   Stop! [CLOV *stops chair close to back wall.* HAMM *lays his hand against wall.*] Old wall! [*Pause.*] Beyond is the . . . other hell. [*Pause. Violently.*] Closer! Closer! Up against!

CLOV Take away your hand. [HAMM *withdraws his hand.* CLOV *rams chair against wall.*] There!

[HAMM *leans towards wall, applies his ear to it.*]

HAMM Do you hear? [*He strikes the wall with his knuckles.*] Do you hear? Hollow bricks! [*He strikes again.*] All that's hollow! [*Pause. He straightens up. Violently.*] That's enough. Back!

CLOV We haven't done the round.

HAMM Back to my place! [CLOV *pushes chair back to center.*] Is that my place?

CLOV Yes, that's your place.

HAMM Am I right in the center?

CLOV I'll measure it.

HAMM More or less! More or less!

CLOV [*Moving chair slightly.*] There!

HAMM I'm more or less in the center?

CLOV I'd say so.

HAMM You'd say so! Put me right in the center!

CLOV I'll go and get the tape.

HAMM Roughly! Roughly! [CLOV *moves chair slightly.*] Bang in the center!

CLOV There! [*Pause.*]

HAMM I feel a little too far to the left. [CLOV *moves chair slightly.*] Now I feel a little too far to the right. [CLOV *moves chair slightly.*] I feel a little too far forward. [CLOV *moves chair slightly.*] Now I feel a little too far back. [CLOV *moves chair slightly.* Don't stay there, [*i.e., behind the chair*] you give me the shivers.

[CLOV *returns to his place beside the chair.*]

CLOV If I could kill him I'd die happy. [*Pause.*]

HAMM What's the weather like?

CLOV As usual.

HAMM Look at the earth.

CLOV I've looked.

HAMM With the glass?

CLOV No need of the glass.

HAMM Look at it with the glass.

CLOV I'll go and get the glass.

[*Exit* CLOV.]

HAMM No need of the glass!

[*Enter* CLOV *with telescope.*]

CLOV I'm back again, with the glass. [*He goes to window right, looks up at it.*] I need the steps.

HAMM Why? Have you shrunk? [*Exit* CLOV *with telescope.*] I don't like that, I don't like that.

[*Enter* CLOV *with ladder, but without telescope.*]

CLOV I'm back again, with the steps. [*He sets down ladder under window right, gets up on it, realizes he has not the telescope, gets down.*] I need the glass. [*He goes towards door.*]

HAMM [*Violently.*] But you have the glass!

CLOV [*Halting, violently.*] No, I haven't the glass!

[*Exit* CLOV.]

HAMM   This is deadly.

[*Enter* CLOV *with telescope. He goes towards ladder.*]

CLOV   Things are livening up. [*He gets up on ladder, raises the telescope, lets it fall.*] I did it on purpose. [*He gets down, picks up the telescope, turns it on auditorium.*] I see . . . a multitude . . . in transports . . . of joy.[6] [*Pause.*] That's what I call a magnifier. [*He lowers the telescope, turns towards* HAMM.] Well? Don't we laugh?

HAMM   [*After reflection.*]   I don't.

CLOV   [*After reflection.*]   Nor I. [*He gets up on ladder, turns the telescope on the without.*] Let's see. [*He looks, moving the telescope.*] Zero . . . [*he looks*] . . . zero . . . [*he looks*] . . . and zero.

HAMM   Nothing stirs. All is—

CLOV   Zer—

HAMM   [*Violently.*]   Wait till you're spoke to! [*Normal voice.*] All is . . . all is . . . all is what? [*Violently.*] All is what?

CLOV   What all is? In a word? Is that what you want to know? Just a moment. [*He turns the telescope on the without, looks, lowers the telescope, turns towards* HAMM.] Corpsed. [*Pause.*] Well? Content?

HAMM   Look at the sea.

CLOV   It's the same.

HAMM   Look at the ocean!

[CLOV *gets down, takes a few steps towards window left, goes back for ladder, carries it over and sets it down under window left, gets up on it, turns the telescope on the without, looks at length. He starts, lowers the telescope, examines it, turns it again on the without.*]

CLOV   Never seen anything like that!

HAMM   [*Anxious.*]   What? A sail? A fin? Smoke?

CLOV   [*Looking.*]   The light is sunk.

HAMM   [*Relieved.*]   Pah! We all knew that.

CLOV   [*Looking.*]   There was a bit left.

HAMM   The base.

CLOV   [*Looking.*]   Yes.

HAMM   And now?

CLOV   [*Looking.*]   All gone.

HAMM   No gulls?

CLOV   [*Looking.*]   Gulls!

HAMM   And the horizon? Nothing on the horizon?

CLOV   [*Lowering the telescope, turning towards* HAMM, *exasperated.*]   What in God's name could there be on the horizon? [*Pause.*]

HAMM   The waves, how are the waves?

CLOV   The waves? [*He turns the telescope on the waves.*] Lead.

HAMM   And the sun?

CLOV   [*Looking.*]   Zero.

HAMM   But it should be sinking. Look again.

CLOV   [*Looking.*]   Damn the sun.

HAMM   Is it night already then?

6. Echo of Revelation 7.9–10: "After this I beheld, and, lo, a great multitude, which . . . cried with a loud voice, saying, Salvation."

CLOV [*Looking.*] No.

HAMM Then what is it?

CLOV [*Looking.*] Gray. [*Lowering the telescope, turning towards* HAMM, *louder.*] Gray! [*Pause. Still louder.*] GRRAY! [*Pause. He gets down, approaches* HAMM *from behind, whispers in his ear.*]

HAMM [*Starting.*] Gray! Did I hear you say gray?

CLOV Light black. From pole to pole.

HAMM You exaggerate. [*Pause.*] Don't stay there, you give me the shivers.

[CLOV *returns to his place beside the chair.*]

CLOV Why this farce, day after day?

HAMM Routine. One never knows. [*Pause.*] Last night I saw inside my breast. There was a big sore.

CLOV Pah! You saw your heart.

HAMM No, it was living. [*Pause. Anguished.*] Clov!

CLOV Yes.

HAMM What's happening?

CLOV Something is taking its course. [*Pause.*]

HAMM Clov!

CLOV [*Impatiently.*] What is it?

HAMM We're not beginning to . . . to . . . mean something?

CLOV Mean something! You and I, mean something! [*Brief laugh.*] Ah that's a good one!

HAMM I wonder. [*Pause.*]. Imagine if a rational being came back to earth, wouldn't he be liable to get ideas into his head if he observed us long enough. [*Voice of rational being.*] Ah, good, now I see what it is, yes, now I understand what they're at! [CLOV *starts, drops the telescope and begins to scratch his belly with both hands. Normal voice.*] And without going so far as that, we ourselves . . . [*With emotion.*] . . . we ourselves . . . at certain moments . . . [*Vehemently.*] To think perhaps it won't all have been for nothing!

CLOV [*Anguished, scratching himself.*] I have a flea!

HAMM A flea! Are there still fleas?

CLOV On me there's one. [*Scratching.*] Unless it's a crablouse.

HAMM [*Very perturbed.*] But humanity might start from there all over again! Catch him, for the love of God!

CLOV I'll go and get the powder.

[*Exit* CLOV.]

HAMM A flea! This is awful! What a day!

[*Enter* CLOV *with a sprinkling-tin.*]

CLOV I'm back again, with the insecticide.

HAMM Let him have it!

[CLOV *loosens the top of his trousers, pulls it forward and shakes powder into the aperture. He stoops, looks, waits, starts, frenziedly shakes more powder, stoops, looks, waits.*]

CLOV The bastard!

HAMM Did you get him?

CLOV Looks like it. [*He drops the tin and adjusts his trousers.*] Unless he's laying doggo.

HAMM Laying! Lying you mean. Unless he's *lying* doggo.

CLOV Ah? One says lying? One doesn't say laying?

HAMM Use your head, can't you. If he was laying we'd be bitched.

CLOV Ah. [*Pause.*] What about that pee?

HAMM I'm having it.

CLOV Ah that's the spirit, that's the spirit! [*Pause.*]

HAMM [*With ardour.*] Let's go from here, the two of us! South! You can make a raft and the currents will carry us away, far away, to other . . . mammals!

CLOV God forbid!

HAMM Alone, I'll embark alone! Get working on that raft immediately. Tomorrow I'll be gone for ever.

CLOV [*Hastening towards door.*] I'll start straight away.

HAMM Wait! [CLOV *halts.*] Will there be sharks, do you think?

CLOV Sharks? I don't know. If there are there will be. [*He goes towards door.*]

HAMM Wait! [CLOV *halts.*] Is it not yet time for my pain-killer?

CLOV [*Violently.*] No! [*He goes towards door.*]

HAMM Wait! [CLOV *halts.*] How are your eyes?

CLOV Bad.

HAMM But you can see.

CLOV All I want.

HAMM How are your legs?

CLOV Bad.

HAMM But you can walk.

CLOV I come . . . and go.

HAMM In my house. [*Pause. With prophetic relish.*] One day you'll be blind, like me. You'll be sitting there, a speck in the void, in the dark, for ever, like me. [*Pause.*] One day you'll say to yourself, I'm tired, I'll sit down, and you'll go and sit down. Then you'll say, I'm hungry, I'll get up and get something to eat. But you won't get up. You'll say, I shouldn't have sat down, but since I have I'll sit on a little longer, then I'll get up and get something to eat. But you won't get up and you won't get anything to eat. [*Pause.*] You'll look at the wall awhile, then you'll say, I'll close my eyes, perhaps have a little sleep, after that I'll feel better, and you'll close them. And when you open them again there'll be no wall any more. [*Pause.*] Infinite emptiness will be all around you, all the resurrected dead of all the ages wouldn't fill it, and there you'll be like a little bit of grit in the middle of the steppe. [*Pause.*] Yes, one day you'll know what it is, you'll be like me, except that you won't have anyone with you, because you won't have had pity on anyone and because there won't be anyone left to have pity on. [*Pause.*]

CLOV It's not certain. [*Pause.*] And there's one thing you forget.

HAMM Ah?

CLOV I can't sit down.

HAMM [*Impatiently.*] Well you'll lie down then, what the hell! Or you'll come to a standstill, simply stop and stand still, the way you are now. One day you'll say, I'm tired, I'll stop. What does the attitude matter? [*Pause.*]

CLOV So you all want me to leave you.

HAMM Naturally.

CLOV Then I'll leave you.

HAMM   You can't leave us.

CLOV   Then I won't leave you. [*Pause.*]

HAMM   Why don't you finish us? [*Pause.*] I'll tell you the combination of the cupboard if you promise to finish me.

CLOV   I couldn't finish you.

HAMM   Then you won't finish me. [*Pause.*]

CLOV   I'll leave you, I have things to do.

HAMM   Do you remember when you came here?

CLOV   No. Too small, you told me.

HAMM   Do you remember your father?

CLOV   [*Wearily.*]   Same answer. [*Pause.*] You've asked me these questions millions of times.

HAMM   I love the old questions. [*With fervor.*] Ah the old questions, the old answers, there's nothing like them! [*Pause.*] It was I was a father to you.

CLOV   Yes. [*He looks at* HAMM *fixedly.*] You were that to me.

HAMM   My house a home for you.

CLOV   Yes. [*He looks about him.*] This was that for me.

HAMM [*Proudly.*]   But for me, [*Gesture towards himself.*] no father. But for Hamm, [*Gesture towards surroundings.*] no home. [*Pause.*]

CLOV   I'll leave you.

HAMM   Did you ever think of one thing?

CLOV   Never.

HAMM   That here we're down in a hole. [*Pause.*] But beyond the hills? Eh? Perhaps it's still green. Eh? [*Pause.*] Flora! Pomona! [*Ecstatically.*] Ceres![7] [*Pause.*] Perhaps you won't need to go very far.

CLOV   I can't go very far. [*Pause.*] I'll leave you.

HAMM   Is my dog ready?

CLOV   He lacks a leg.

HAMM   Is he silky?

CLOV   He's a kind of Pomeranian.

HAMM   Go and get him.

CLOV   He lacks a leg.

HAMM   Go and get him! [*Exit* CLOV.] We're getting on.

[*Enter* CLOV *holding by one of its three legs a black toy dog.*]

CLOV   Your dogs are here. [*He hands the dog to* HAMM *who feels it, fondles it.*]

HAMM   He's white, isn't he?

CLOV   Nearly.

HAMM   What do you mean, nearly? Is he white or isn't he?

CLOV   He isn't. [*Pause.*]

HAMM   You've forgotten the sex.

CLOV [*Vexed.*]   But he isn't finished. The sex goes on at the end. [*Pause.*]

HAMM   You haven't put on his ribbon.

CLOV [*Angrily.*]   But he isn't finished, I tell you! First you finish your dog and then you put on his ribbon! [*Pause.*]

HAMM   Can he stand?

CLOV   I don't know.

___

7. In Roman mythology, the goddesses of flowers, fruits, and fertility.

HAMM   Try. [*He hands the dog to* CLOV *who places it on the ground.*] Well?

CLOV   Wait! [*He squats down and tries to get the dog to stand on its three legs, fails, lets it go. The dog falls on its side.*]

HAMM [*Impatiently.*]   Well?

CLOV   He's standing.

HAMM [*Groping for the dog.*]   Where? Where is he?
          [CLOV *holds up the dog in a standing position.*]

CLOV   There. [*He takes* HAMM'S *hand and guides it towards the dog's head.*]

HAMM [*His hand on the dog's head.*]   Is he gazing at me?

CLOV   Yes.

HAMM [*Proudly.*]   As if he were asking me to take him for a walk?

CLOV   If you like.

HAMM [*As before.*]   Or as if he were begging me for a bone. [*He withdraws his hand.*] Leave him like that, standing there imploring me.
          [CLOV *straightens up. The dog falls on its side.*]

CLOV   I'll leave you.

HAMM   Have you had your visions?

CLOV   Less.

HAMM   Is Mother Pegg's light on?

CLOV   Light! How could anyone's light be on?

HAMM   Extinguished!

CLOV   Naturally it's extinguished. If it's not on it's extinguished.

HAMM   No, I mean Mother Pegg.

CLOV   But naturally she's extinguished! [*Pause.*] What's the matter with you today?

HAMM   I'm taking my course. [*Pause.*] Is she buried?

CLOV   Buried! Who would have buried her?

HAMM   You.

CLOV   Me! Haven't I enough to do without burying people?

HAMM   But you'll bury me.

CLOV   No I won't bury you. [*Pause.*]

HAMM   She was bonny once, like a flower of the field. [*With reminiscent leer.*] And a great one for the men!

CLOV   We too were bonny—once. It's a rare thing not to have been bonny—once. [*Pause.*]

HAMM   Go and get the gaff.
          [CLOV *goes to door, halts.*]

CLOV   Do this, do that, and I do it. I never refuse. Why?

HAMM   You're not able to.

CLOV   Soon I won't do it any more.

HAMM   You won't be able to any more. [*Exit* CLOV.] Ah the creatures, the creatures, everything has to be explained to them.
          [*Enter* CLOV *with gaff.*]

CLOV   Here's your gaff. Stick it up. [*He gives the gaff to* HAMM *who, wielding it like a puntpole, tries to move his chair.*]

HAMM   Did I move?

CLOV   No.
          [HAMM *throws down the gaff.*]

HAMM   Go and get the oilcan.

CLOV   What for?

HAMM   To oil the castors.

CLOV I oiled them yesterday.

HAMM Yesterday! What does that mean? Yesterday!

CLOV [*Violently.*] That means that bloody awful day, long ago, before this bloody awful day. I use the words you taught me. If they don't mean anything any more, teach me others. Or let me be silent. [*Pause.*]

HAMM I once knew a madman who thought the end of the world had come. He was a painter—and engraver. I had a great fondness for him. I used to go and see him, in the asylum. I'd take him by the hand and drag him to the window. Look! There! All that rising corn! And there! Look! The sails of the herring fleet! All that loveliness! [*Pause.*] He'd snatch away his hand and go back into his corner. Appalled. All he had seen was ashes. [*Pause.*] He alone had been spared. [*Pause.*] Forgotten. [*Pause.*] It appears the case is . . . was not so . . . so unusual.

CLOV A madman! When was that?

HAMM Oh way back, way back, you weren't in the land of the living.

CLOV God be with the days!

[*Pause. HAMM raises his toque.*]

HAMM I had a great fondness for him. [*Pause. He puts on his toque again.*] He was a painter—and engraver.

CLOV There are so many terrible things.

HAMM No, no, there are not so many now. [*Pause.*] Clov!

CLOV Yes.

HAMM Do you not think this has gone on long enough?

CLOV Yes! [*Pause.*] What?

HAMM This . . . this . . . thing.

CLOV I've always thought so. [*Pause.*] You not?

HAMM [*Gloomily.*] Then it's a day like any other day.

CLOV As long as it lasts. [*Pause.*] All life long the same inanities.

HAMM I can't leave you.

CLOV I know. And you can't follow me. [*Pause.*]

HAMM If you leave me how shall I know?

CLOV [*Briskly.*] Well you simply whistle me and if I don't come running it means I've left you. [*Pause.*]

HAMM You won't come and kiss me goodbye?

CLOV Oh I shouldn't think so. [*Pause.*]

HAMM But you might be merely dead in your kitchen.

CLOV The result would be the same.

HAMM Yes, but how would I know, if you were merely dead in your kitchen?

CLOV Well . . . sooner or later I'd start to stink.

HAMM You stink already. The whole place stinks of corpses.

CLOV The whole universe.

HAMM [*Angrily.*] To hell with the universe. [*Pause.*] Think of something.

CLOV What?

HAMM An idea, have an idea. [*Angrily.*] A bright idea!

CLOV Ah good. [*He starts pacing to and fro, his eyes fixed on the ground, his hands behind his back. He halts.*] The pains in my legs! It's unbelievable! Soon I won't be able to think any more.

HAMM You won't be able to leave me. [CLOV *resumes his pacing.*] What are you doing?

CLOV Having an idea. [*He paces.*] Ah! [*He halts.*]

HAMM   What a brain! [*Pause.*] Well?

CLOV   Wait! [*He meditates. Not very convinced.*] Yes . . . [*Pause. More convinced.*] Yes! [*He raises his head.*] I have it! I set the alarm. [*Pause.*]

HAMM   This is perhaps not one of my bright days, but frankly—

CLOV   You whistle me. I don't come. The alarm rings. I'm gone. It doesn't ring. I'm dead. [*Pause.*]

HAMM   Is it working? [*Pause. Impatiently.*] The alarm, is it working?

CLOV   Why wouldn't it be working?

HAMM   Because it's worked too much.

CLOV   But it's hardly worked at all.

HAMM   [*Angrily.*]   Then because it's worked too little!

CLOV   I'll go and see. [*Exit* CLOV. *Brief ring of alarm off. Enter* CLOV *with alarm-clock. He holds it against* HAMM's *ear and releases alarm. They listen to it ringing to the end. Pause.*] Fit to wake the dead! Did you hear it?

HAMM   Vaguely.

CLOV   The end is terrific!

HAMM   I prefer the middle. [*Pause.*] Is it not time for my pain-killer?

CLOV   No! [*He goes to door, turns.*] I'll leave you.

HAMM   It's time for my story. Do you want to listen to my story.

CLOV   No.

HAMM   Ask my father if he wants to listen to my story.
   [CLOV *goes to bins, raises the lid of* NAGG's, *stoops, looks into it. Pause. He straightens up.*]

CLOV   He's asleep.

HAMM   Wake him.
   [CLOV *stoops, wakes* NAGG *with the alarm. Unintelligible words.* CLOV *straightens up.*]

CLOV   He doesn't want to listen to your story.

HAMM   I'll give him a bon-bon.
   [CLOV *stoops. As before.*]

CLOV   He wants a sugar-plum.

HAMM   He'll get a sugar-plum.
   [CLOV *stoops. As before.*]

CLOV   It's a deal. [*He goes towards door.* NAGG's *hands appear, gripping the rim. Then the head emerges.* CLOV *reaches door, turns.*] Do you believe in the life to come?

HAMM   Mine was always that. [*Exit* CLOV.] Got him that time!

NAGG   I'm listening.

HAMM   Scoundrel! Why did you engender me?

NAGG   I didn't know.

HAMM   What? What didn't you know?

NAGG   That it'd be you. [*Pause.*] You'll give me a sugar-plum?

HAMM   After the audition.

NAGG   You swear?

HAMM   Yes.

NAGG   On what?

HAMM   My honor.
   [*Pause. They laugh heartily.*]

NAGG   Two.

HAMM   One.

NAGG One for me and one for—

HAMM One! Silence! [*Pause.*] Where was I? [*Pause. Gloomily.*] It's finished, we're finished. [*Pause.*] Nearly finished. [*Pause.*] There'll be no more speech. [*Pause.*] Something dripping in my head, ever since the fontanelles. [*Stifled hilarity of* NAGG.] Splash, splash, always on the same spot. [*Pause.*] Perhaps it's a little vein. [*Pause.*] A little artery. [*Pause. More animated.*] Enough of that, it's story time, where was I? [*Pause. Narrative tone.*] The man came crawling towards me, on his belly. Pale, wonderfully pale and thin, he seemed on the point of—[*Pause. Normal tone.*] No, I've done that bit. [*Pause. Narrative tone.*] I calmly filled my pipe—the meerschaum, lit it with . . . let us say a vesta, drew a few puffs. Aah! [*Pause.*] Well, what is it *you* want? [*Pause.*] It was an extraordinarily bitter day, I remember, zero by the thermometer. But considering it was Christmas Eve there was nothing . . . extra-ordinary about that. Season able weather, for once in a way. [*Pause.*] Well, what ill wind blows you my way? He raised his face to me, black with mingled dirt and tears. [*Pause. Normal tone.*] That should do it. [*Narrative tone.*] No, no, don't look at me, don't look at me. He dropped his eyes and mumbled something, apologies I presume. [*Pause.*] I'm a busy man, you know, the final touches, before the festivities, you know what it is. [*Pause. Forcibly.*] Come on now, what is the object of this invasion? [*Pause.*] It was a glorious bright day, I remember, fifty by the heliometer,[8] but already the sun was sinking down into the . . . down among the dead. [*Normal tone.*] Nicely put, that. [*Narrative tone.*] Come on now, come on, present your petition and let me resume my labors. [*Pause. Normal tone.*] There's English for you. Ah well . . . [*Narrative tone.*] It was then he took the plunge. It's my little one, he said. Tsstss, a little one, that's bad. My little boy, he said, as if the sex mattered. Where did he come from? He named the hole. A good half-day, on horse. What are you insinuating? That the place is still inhabited? No no, not a soul, except himself and the child— assuming he existed. Good. I enquired about the situation at Kov, beyond the gulf. Not a sinner. Good. And you expect me to believe you have left your little one back there, all alone, and alive into the bargain? Come now! [*Pause.*] It was a howling wild day, I remember, a hundred by the anemometer.[9] The wind was tearing up the dead pines and sweeping them . . . away. [*Pause. Normal tone.*] A bit feeble, that. [*Narrative tone.*] Come on, man, speak up, what is you want from me, I have to put up my holly. [*Pause.*] Well to make it short it finally transpired that what he wanted from me was . . . bread for his brat? Bread? But I have no bread, it doesn't agree with me. Good. Then perhaps a little corn? [*Pause. Normal tone.*] That should do it. [*Narrative tone.*] Corn, yes, I have corn, it's true, in my granaries. But use your head. I give you some corn, a pound, a pound and a half, you bring it back to your child and you make him—if he's still alive—a nice pot of porridge, [NAGG *reacts.*] a nice pot and a half of porridge, full of nourishment. Good. The colors come back into his little cheeks—perhaps. And then? [*Pause.*] I lost patience. [*Violently.*] Use your head, can't you, use your head, you're on earth, there's no cure

---

8. Literally, a "sun meter." Ordinarily, a telescope used to measure distances between celestial bodies.
9. A wind meter.

for that! [*Pause.*] It was an exceedingly dry day, I remember, zero by the hygrometer.[1] Ideal weather, for my lumbago. [*Pause. Violently.*] But what in God's name do you imagine? That the earth will awake in spring? That the rivers and seas will run with fish again? That there's manna in heaven still for imbeciles like you? [*Pause.*] Gradually I cooled down, sufficiently at least to ask him how long he had taken on the way. Three whole days. Good. In what condition he had left the child. Deep in sleep. [*Forcibly.*] But deep in what sleep, deep in what sleep already? [*Pause.*] Well to make it short I finally offered to take him into my service. He had touched a chord. And then I imagined already that I wasn't much longer for this world. [*He laughs. Pause.*] Well? [*Pause.*] Well? Here if you were careful you might die a nice natural death, in peace and comfort. [*Pause.*] Well? [*Pause.*] In the end he asked me would I consent to take in the child as well—if he were still alive. [*Pause.*] It was the moment I was waiting for. [*Pause.*] Would I consent to take in the child . . . [*Pause.*] I can see him still, down on his knees, his hands flat on the ground, glaring at me with his mad eyes, in defiance of my wishes. [*Pause. Normal tone.*] I'll soon have finished with this story. [*Pause.*] Unless I bring in other characters. [*Pause.*] But where would I find them? [*Pause.*] Where would I look for them? [*Pause. He whistles. Enter* CLOV.] Let us pray to God.

NAGG Me sugar-plum!

CLOV There's a rat in the kitchen!

HAMM A rat! Are there still rats?

CLOV In the kitchen there's one.

HAMM And you haven't exterminated him?

CLOV Half. You disturbed us.

HAMM He can't get away?

CLOV No.

HAMM You'll finish him later. Let us pray to God.

CLOV Again!

NAGG Me sugar-plum!

HAMM God first! [*Pause.*] Are you right?

CLOV [*Resigned.*] Off we go.

HAMM [*To* NAGG.] And you?

NAGG [*Clasping his hands, closing his eyes, in a gabble.*] Our Father which art—

HAMM Silence! In silence! Where are your manners? [*Pause.*] Off we go. [*Attitudes of prayer. Silence. Abandoning his attitude, discouraged.*] Well?

CLOV [*Abandoning his attitude.*] What a hope! And you?

HAMM Sweet damn all! [*To* NAGG.] And you?

NAGG Wait! [*Pause. Abandoning his attitude.*] Nothing doing!

HAMM The bastard! He doesn't exist!

CLOV Not yet.

NAGG Me sugar-plum!

HAMM There are no more sugar-plums! [*Pause.*]

NAGG It's natural. After all I'm your father. It's true if it hadn't been me it would have been someone else. But that's no excuse. [*Pause.*] Turkish Delight,[2] for example, which no longer exists, we all know that, there is

1. A moisture meter. 2. A sticky sweet candy.

nothing in the world I love more. And one day I'll ask you for some, in return for a kindness, and you'll promise it to me. One must live with the times. [*Pause.*] Whom did you call when you were a tiny boy, and were frightened, in the dark? Your mother? No. Me. We let you cry. Then we moved you out of earshot, so that we might sleep in peace. [*Pause.*] I was asleep, as happy as a king, and you woke me up to have me listen to you. It wasn't indispensable, you didn't really need to have me listen to you. [*Pause.*] I hope the day will come when you'll really need to have me listen to you, and need to hear my voice, any voice. [*Pause.*] Yes, I hope I'll live till then, to hear you calling me like when you were a tiny boy, and were frightened, in the dark, and I was your only hope. [*Pause. NAGG knocks on lid of NELL's bin. Pause.*] Nell! [*Pause. He knocks louder. Pause. Louder.*] Nell! [*Pause. NAGG sinks back into his bin, closes the lid behind him. Pause.*]

HAMM   Our revels now are ended.[3] [*He gropes for the dog.*] The dog's gone.
CLOV   He's not a real dog, he can't go.
HAMM   [*Groping.*]   He's not there.
CLOV   He's lain down.
HAMM   Give him up to me. [CLOV *picks up the dog and gives it to* HAMM. HAMM *holds it in his arms. Pause.* HAMM *throws away the dog.*] Dirty brute! [CLOV *begins to pick up the objects lying on the ground.*] What are you doing?
CLOV   Putting things in order. [*He straightens up. Fervently.*] I'm going to clear everything away! [*He starts picking up again.*]
HAMM   Order!
CLOV   [*Straightening up.*]   I love order. It's my dream. A world where all would be silent and still and each thing in its last place, under the last dust. [*He starts picking up again.*]
HAMM   [*Exasperated.*]   What in God's name do you think you are doing?
CLOV   [*Straightening up.*]   I'm doing my best to create a little order.
HAMM   Drop it!
        [CLOV *drops the objects he has picked up.*]
CLOV   After all, there or elsewhere. [*He goes towards door.*]
HAMM   [*Irritably.*]   What's wrong with your feet?
CLOV   My feet?
HAMM   Tramp! Tramp!
CLOV   I must have put on my boots.
HAMM   Your slippers were hurting you? [*Pause.*]
CLOV   I'll leave you.
HAMM   No!
CLOV   What is there to keep me here?
HAMM   The dialogue. [*Pause.*] I've got on with my story. [*Pause.*] I've got on with it well. [*Pause. Irritably.*] Ask me where I've got to.
CLOV   Oh, by the way, your story?
HAMM   [*Surprised.*]   What story?
CLOV   The one you've been telling yourself all your days.
HAMM   Ah you mean my chronicle?
CLOV   That's the one. [*Pause.*]

---

3. Lines spoken by Prospero in Shakespeare's *The Tempest* 4.1.148.

HAMM [*Angrily.*]   Keep going, can't you, keep going!

CLOV   You've got on with it, I hope.

HAMM [*Modestly.*]   Oh not very far, not very far. [*He sighs.*] There are days like that, one isn't inspired. [*Pause.*] Nothing you can do about it, just wait for it to come. [*Pause.*] No forcing, no forcing, it's fatal. [*Pause.*] I've got on with it a little all the same. [*Pause.*] Technique, you know. [*Pause. Irritably.*] I say I've got on with it a little all the same.

CLOV [*Admiringly.*]   Well I never! In spite of everything you were able to get on with it!

HAMM [*Modestly.*]   Oh not very far, you know, not very far, but nevertheless, better than nothing.

CLOV   Better than nothing! Is it possible?

HAMM   I'll tell you how it goes. He comes crawling on his belly—

CLOV   Who?

HAMM   What?

CLOV   Who do you mean, he?

HAMM   Who do I mean! Yet another.

CLOV   Ah him! I wasn't sure.

HAMM   Crawling on his belly, whining for bread for his brat. He's offered a job as gardener. Before—[CLOV *bursts out laughing.*] What is there so funny about that?

CLOV   A job as gardener!

HAMM   Is that what tickles you?

CLOV   It must be that.

HAMM   It wouldn't be the bread?

CLOV   Or the brat. [*Pause.*]

HAMM   The whole thing is comical, I grant you that. What about having a good guffaw the two of us together?

CLOV [*After reflection.*]   I couldn't guffaw again today.

HAMM [*After reflection.*]   Nor I. [*Pause.*] I continue then. Before accepting with gratitude he asks if he may have his little boy with him.

CLOV   What age?

HAMM   Oh tiny.

CLOV   He would have climbed the trees.

HAMM   All the little odd jobs.

CLOV   And then he would have grown up.

HAMM   Very likely. [*Pause.*]

CLOV   Keep going, can't you, keep going!

HAMM   That's all. I stopped there. [*Pause.*]

CLOV   Do you see how it goes on.

HAMM   More or less.

CLOV   Will it not soon be the end?

HAMM   I'm afraid it will.

CLOV   Pah! You'll make up another.

HAMM   I don't know. [*Pause.*] I feel rather drained. [*Pause.*] The prolonged creative effort. [*Pause.*] If I could drag myself down to the sea! I'd make a pillow of sand for my head and the tide would come.

CLOV   There's no more tide. [*Pause.*]

HAMM   Go and see is she dead.

[CLOV *goes to bins, raises the lid of* NELL's, *stoops, looks into it. Pause.*]

CLOV   Looks like it.
       [*He closes the lid, straightens up.* HAMM *raises his toque. Pause. He puts it on again.*]
HAMM   [*With his hand to his toque.*]   And Nagg?
       [CLOV *raises lid of* NAGG's *bin, stoops, looks into it. Pause.*]
CLOV   Doesn't look like it. [*He closes the lid, straightens up.*]
HAMM   [*Letting go his toque.*]   What's he doing? [CLOV *raises lid of* NAGG's *bin, stoops, looks into it. Pause.*]
CLOV   He's crying. [*He closes lid, straightens up.*]
HAMM   Then he's living. [*Pause.*] Did you ever have an instant of happiness?
CLOV   Not to my knowledge. [*Pause.*]
HAMM   Bring me under the window. [CLOV *goes towards chair.*] I want to feel the light on my face. [CLOV *pushes chair.*] Do you remember, in the beginning, when you took me for a turn? You used to hold the chair too high. At every step you nearly tipped me out. [*With senile quaver.*] Ah great fun, we had, the two of us, great fun. [*Gloomily.*] And then we got into the way of it. [CLOV *stops the chair under window right.*] There already? [*Pause. He tilts back his head.*] Is it light?
CLOV   It isn't dark.
HAMM   [*Angrily.*]   I'm asking you is it light.
CLOV   Yes. [*Pause.*]
HAMM   The curtain isn't closed?
CLOV   No.
HAMM   What window is it?
CLOV   The earth.
HAMM   I knew it! [*Angrily.*] But there's no light there! The other! [CLOV *stops the chair under window left.* HAMM *tilts back his head.*] That's what I call light! [*Pause.*] Feels like a ray of sunshine. [*Pause.*] No?
CLOV   No.
HAMM   It isn't a ray of sunshine I feel on my face?
CLOV   No. [*Pause.*]
HAMM   Am I very white? [*Pause. Angrily.*] I'm asking you am I very white!
CLOV   Not more so than usual. [*Pause.*]
HAMM   Open the window.
CLOV   What for?
HAMM   I want to hear the sea.
CLOV   You wouldn't hear it.
HAMM   Even if you opened the window?
CLOV   No.
HAMM   Then it's not worth while opening it?
CLOV   No.
HAMM   [*Violently.*]   Then open it! [CLOV *gets up on the ladder, opens the window. Pause.*] Have you opened it?
CLOV   Yes. [*Pause.*]
HAMM   You swear you've opened it?
CLOV   Yes. [*Pause.*]
HAMM   Well . . . ! [*Pause.*] It must be very calm. [*Pause. Violently.*] I'm asking you is it very calm!
CLOV   Yes.

HAMM   It's because there are no more navigators. [*Pause.*] You haven't much conversation all of a sudden. Do you not feel well?

CLOV   I'm cold.

HAMM   What month are we? [*Pause.*] Close the window, we're going back. [CLOV *closes the window, gets down, pushes the chair back to its place, remains standing behind it, head bowed.*] Don't stay there, you give me the shivers! [CLOV *returns to his place beside the chair.*] Father! [*Pause. Louder.*] Father! [*Pause.*] Go and see did he hear me.

> [CLOV *goes to* NAGG's *bin, raises the lid, stoops. Unintelligible words.* CLOV *straightens up.*]

CLOV   Yes.

HAMM   Both times?

> [CLOV *stoops. As before.*]

CLOV   Once only.

HAMM   The first time or the second?

> [CLOV *stoops. As before.*]

CLOV   He doesn't know.

HAMM   It must have been the second.

CLOV   We'll never know. [*He closes lid.*]

HAMM   Is he still crying?

CLOV   No.

HAMM   The dead go fast. [*Pause.*] What's he doing?

CLOV   Sucking his biscuit.

HAMM   Life goes on. [CLOV *returns to his place beside the chair.*] Give me a rug. I'm freezing.

CLOV   There are no more rugs. [*Pause.*]

HAMM   Kiss me. [*Pause.*] Will you not kiss me?

CLOV   No.

HAMM   On the forehead.

CLOV   I won't kiss you anywhere. [*Pause.*]

HAMM   [*Holding out his hand.*]   Give me your hand at least. [*Pause.*] Will you not give me your hand?

CLOV   I won't touch you. [*Pause.*]

HAMM   Give me the dog. [CLOV *looks round for the dog.*] No!

CLOV   Do you not want your dog?

HAMM   No.

CLOV   Then I'll leave you.

HAMM   [*Head bowed, absently.*]   That's right.

> [CLOV *goes to door, turns.*]

CLOV   If I don't kill that rat he'll die.

HAMM   [*As before.*]   That's right. [*Exit* CLOV. *Pause.*] Me to play. [*He takes out his handkerchief, unfolds it, holds it spread out before him.*] We're getting on. [*Pause.*] You weep, and weep, for nothing, so as not to laugh, and little by little . . . you begin to grieve. [*He folds the handkerchief, puts it back in his pocket, raises his head.*] All those I might have helped. [*Pause.*] Helped! [*Pause.*] Saved. [*Pause.*] Saved! [*Pause.*] The place was crawling with them! [*Pause. Violently.*] Use your head, can't you, use your head, you're on earth, there's no cure for that! [*Pause.*] Get out of here and love one another! Lick your neighbor as yourself![4] [*Pause.*

---

4. Parody of Jesus' words in the Bible: "Thou shalt love thy neighbor as thyself" (Matthew 19.19).

Calmer.] When it wasn't bread they wanted it was crumpets. [*Pause. Violently.*] Out of my sight and back to your petting parties! [*Pause.*] All that, all that! [*Pause.*] Not even a real dog! [*Calmer.*] The end is in the beginning and yet you go on. [*Pause.*] Perhaps I could go on with my story, end it and begin another. [*Pause.*] Perhaps I could throw myself out on the floor. [*He pushes himself painfully off his seat, falls back again.*] Dig my nails into the cracks and drag myself forward with my fingers. [*Pause.*] It will be the end and there I'll be, wondering what can have brought it on and wondering what can have . . . [*He hesitates.*] . . . why it was so long coming. [*Pause.*] There I'll be, in the old shelter, alone against the silence and . . . [*He hesitates.*] . . . the stillness. If I can hold my peace, and sit quiet, it will be all over with sound, and motion, all over and done with. [*Pause.*] I'll have called my father and I'll have called my . . . [*He hesitates.*] . . . my son. And even twice, or three times, in case they shouldn't have heard me, the first time, or the second. [*Pause.*] I'll say to myself, He'll come back. [*Pause.*] And then? [*Pause.*] And then? [*Pause.*] He couldn't, he has gone too far. [*Pause.*] And then? [*Pause. Very agitated.*] All kinds of fantasies! That I'm being watched! A rat! Steps! Breath held and then . . . [*He breathes out.*] Then babble, babble, words, like the solitary child who turns himself into children, two, three, so as to be together, and whisper together, in the dark. [*Pause.*] Moment upon moment, pattering down, like the millet grains of . . . [*He hesitates.*] . . . that old Greek,[5] and all life long you wait for that to mount up to a life. [*Pause. He opens his mouth to continue, renounces.*] Ah let's get it over! [*He whistles. Enter* CLOV *with alarm-clock. He halts beside the chair.*] What? Neither gone nor dead?

CLOV   In spirit only.

HAMM   Which?

CLOV   Both.

HAMM   Gone from me you'd be dead.

CLOV   And vice versa.

HAMM   Outside of here it's death! [*Pause.*] And the rat?

CLOV   He's got away.

HAMM   He can't go far. [*Pause. Anxious.*] Eh?

CLOV   He doesn't need to go far. [*Pause.*]

HAMM   Is it not time for my pain-killer?

CLOV   Yes.

HAMM   Ah! At last! Give it to me! Quick! [*Pause.*]

CLOV   There's no more pain-killer. [*Pause.*]

HAMM [*Appalled.*]   Good . . . ! [*Pause.*] No more pain-killer!

CLOV   No more pain-killer. You'll never get any more pain-killer. [*Pause.*]

HAMM   But the little round box. It was full!

CLOV   Yes. But now it's empty.

[*Pause.* CLOV *starts to move about the room. He is looking for a place to put down the alarm-clock.*]

HAMM [*Soft.*]   What'll I do? [*Pause. In a scream.*] What'll I do? [CLOV *sees the picture, takes it down, stands it on the floor with its face to the wall,*

5. Zeno of Elea, a Greek philosopher active around 450 B.C.E., known for logical paradoxes that reduce to absurdity various attempts to define *Being*. Aristotle reports that Zeno's paradox on sound questioned: If a grain of millet falling makes no sound, how can a bushel of grains make any sound? (Aristotle's *Physics* 5.250a.19).

hangs up the alarm-clock in its place.] What are you doing?

CLOV   Winding up.

HAMM   Look at the earth.

CLOV   Again!

HAMM   Since it's calling to you.

CLOV   Is your throat sore? [*Pause.*] Would you like a lozenge? [*Pause.*] No. [*Pause.*] Pity. [*He goes, humming, towards window right, halts before it, looks up at it.*]

HAMM   Don't sing.

CLOV   [*Turning towards* HAMM.]   One hasn't the right to sing any more?

HAMM   No.

CLOV   Then how can it end?

HAMM   You want it to end?

CLOV   I want to sing.

HAMM   I can't prevent you.

[*Pause.* CLOV *turns towards window right.*]

CLOV   What did I do with that steps? [*He looks around for ladder.*] You didn't see that steps? [*He sees it.*] Ah, about time. [*He goes towards window left.*] Sometimes I wonder if I'm in my right mind. Then it passes over and I'm as lucid as before. [*He gets up on ladder, looks out of window.*] Christ, she's under water! [*He looks.*] How can that be? [*He pokes forward his head, his hand above his eyes.*] It hasn't rained. [*He wipes the pane, looks. Pause.*] Ah what a fool I am! I'm on the wrong side! [*He gets down, takes a few steps towards window right.*] Under water! [*He goes back for ladder.*] What a fool I am! [*He carries ladder towards window right.*] Sometimes I wonder if I'm in my right senses. Then it passes off and I'm as intelligent as ever. [*He sets down ladder under window right, gets up on it, looks out of window. He turns towards* HAMM.] Any particular sector you fancy? Or merely the whole thing?

HAMM   Whole thing.

CLOV   The general effect? Just a moment. [*He looks out of window. Pause.*]

HAMM   Clov.

CLOV   [*Absorbed.*]   Mmm.

HAMM   Do you know what it is?

CLOV   [*As before.*]   Mmm.

HAMM   I was never there. [*Pause.*] Clov!

CLOV   [*Turning towards* HAMM, *exasperated.*]   What is it?

HAMM   I was never there.

CLOV   Lucky for you. [*He looks out of window.*]

HAMM   Absent, always. It all happened without me. I don't know what's happened. [*Pause.*] Do you know what's happened? [*Pause.*] Clov!

CLOV   [*Turning towards* HAMM, *exasperated.*]   Do you want me to look at this muckheap, yes or no?

HAMM   Answer me first.

CLOV   What?

HAMM   Do you know what's happened?

CLOV   When? Where?

HAMM   [*Violently.*]   When! What's happened? Use your head, can't you! What has happened?

CLOV   What for Christ's sake does it matter? [*He looks out of window.*]

HAMM   I don't know. [*Pause.* CLOV *turns towards* HAMM.]

CLOV [*Harshly.*]   When old Mother Pegg asked you for oil for her lamp and you told her to get out to hell, you knew what was happening then, no? [*Pause.*] You know what she died of, Mother Pegg? Of darkness.

HAMM [*Feebly.*]   I hadn't any.

CLOV [*As before.*]   Yes, you had. [*Pause.*]

HAMM   Have you the glass?

CLOV   No, it's clear enough as it is.

HAMM   Go and get it. [*Pause.* CLOV *casts up his eyes, brandishes his fists. He loses balance, clutches on to the ladder. He starts to get down, halts.*]

CLOV   There's one thing I'll never understand. [*He gets down.*] Why I always obey you. Can you explain that to me?

HAMM   No. . . . Perhaps it's compassion. [*Pause.*] A kind of great compassion. [*Pause.*] Oh you won't find it easy, you won't find it easy. [*Pause.* CLOV *begins to move about the room in search of the telescope.*]

CLOV   I'm tired of our goings on, very tired. [*He searches.*] You're not sitting on it? [*He moves the chair, looks at the place where it stood, resumes his search.*]

HAMM [*Anguished.*]   Don't leave me there! [*Angrily* CLOV *restores the chair to its place.*] Am I right in the center?

CLOV   You'd need a microscope to find this—[*He sees the telescope.*] Ah, about time. [*He picks up the telescope, gets up on the ladder, turns the telescope on the without.*]

HAMM   Give me the dog.

CLOV [*Looking.*]   Quiet!

HAMM [*Angrily.*]   Give me the dog! [CLOV *drops the telescope, clasps his hands to his head. Pause. He gets down precipitately, looks for the dog, sees it, picks it up, hastens towards* HAMM *and strikes him violently on the head with the dog.*]

CLOV   There's your dog for you! [*The dog falls to the ground. Pause.*]

HAMM   He hit me!

CLOV   You drive me mad, I'm mad!

HAMM   If you must hit me, hit me with the axe. [*Pause.*] Or with the gaff, hit me with the gaff. Not with the dog. With the gaff. Or with the axe. [CLOV *picks up the dog and gives it to* HAMM *who takes it in his arms.*]

CLOV [*Imploringly.*]   Let's stop playing!

HAMM   Never! [*Pause.*] Put me in my coffin.

CLOV   There are no more coffins.

HAMM   Then let it end! [CLOV *goes towards ladder.*] With a bang! [CLOV *gets up on ladder, gets down again, looks for telescope, sees it, picks it up, gets up ladder, raises telescope.*] Of darkness! And me? Did anyone ever have pity on me?

CLOV [*Lowering the telescope, turning towards* HAMM.]   What? [*Pause.*] Is it me you're referring to?

HAMM [*Angrily.*]   An aside, ape! Did you never hear an aside before? [*Pause.*] I'm warming up for my last soliloquy.

CLOV   I warn you. I'm going to look at this filth since it's an order. But it's the last time. [*He turns the telescope on the without.*] Let's see. [*He moves the telescope.*] Nothing . . . nothing . . . good . . . good . . . nothing . . . goo—[*He starts, lowers the telescope, examines it, turns it again on the without. Pause.*] Bad luck to it!

HAMM More complications! [CLOV *gets down.*] Not an underplot, I trust.
    [CLOV *moves ladder nearer window, gets up on it, turns telescope on the without.*]

CLOV [*Dismayed.*] Looks like a small boy!

HAMM [*Sarcastic.*] A small . . . boy!

CLOV I'll go and see. [*He gets down, drops the telescope, goes towards door, turns.*] I'll take the gaff. [*He looks for the gaff, sees it, picks it up, hastens towards door.*]

HAMM No! [CLOV *halts.*]

CLOV No? A potential procreator?

HAMM If he exists he'll die there or he'll come here. And if he doesn't . . . [*Pause.*]

CLOV You don't believe me? You think I'm inventing? [*Pause.*]

HAMM It's the end, Clov, we've come to the end. I don't need you any more. [*Pause.*]

CLOV Lucky for you. [*He goes towards door.*]

HAMM Leave me the gaff.
    [CLOV *gives him the gaff, goes towards door, halts, looks at alarm-clock, takes it down, looks round for a better place to put it, goes to bins, puts it on lid of* NAGG's *bin. Pause.*]

CLOV I'll leave you. [*He goes towards door.*]

HAMM Before you go . . . [CLOV *halts near door.*] . . . say something.

CLOV There is nothing to say.

HAMM A few words . . . to ponder . . . in my heart.

CLOV Your heart!

HAMM Yes. [*Pause Forcibly.*] Yes! [*Pause.*] With the rest, in the end, the shadows, the murmurs, all the trouble, to end up with. [*Pause.*] Clov. . . . He never spoke to me. Then, in the end, before he went, without my having asked him, he spoke to me. He said . . .

CLOV [*Despairingly.*] Ah . . . !

HAMM Something . . . from your heart.

CLOV My heart!

HAMM A few words . . . from your heart. [*Pause.*]

CLOV [*Fixed gaze, tonelessly, towards auditorium.*] They said to me, That's love, yes, yes, not a doubt, now you see how—

HAMM Articulate!

CLOV [*As before.*] How easy it is. They said to me, That's friendship, yes, yes, no question, you've found it. They said to me, Here's the place, stop, raise your head and look at all that beauty. That order! They said to me. Come now, you're not a brute beast, think upon these things and you'll see how all becomes clear. And simple! They said to me, What skilled attention they get, all these dying of their wounds.

HAMM Enough!

CLOV [*As before.*] I say to myself—sometimes, Clov, you must learn to suffer better than that if you want them to weary of punishing you—one day. I say to myself—sometimes, Clov, you must be there better than that if you want them to let you go—one day. But I feel too old, and too far, to form new habits. Good, it'll never end, I'll never go. [*Pause.*] Then one day, suddenly, it ends, it changes, I don't understand, it dies, or it's me, I don't understand, that either. I ask the words that remain—sleeping, waking, morning, evening. They have nothing to say. [*Pause.*] I open the door of the cell and go. I am so bowed I only see my feet, if I open my eyes, and between my legs a little trail of black dust. I say to myself that the earth is extinguished, though I never saw it lit. [*Pause.*] It's easy going. [*Pause.*] When I fall I'll weep for happiness. [*Pause. He goes towards door.*]

HAMM   Clov! [CLOV *halts, without turning.*] Nothing. [CLOV *moves on.*] Clov!

        [CLOV *halts, without turning.*]

CLOV   This is what we call making an exit.

HAMM   I'm obliged to you, Clov. For your services.

CLOV [*Turning, sharply.*]   Ah pardon, it's I am obliged to you.

HAMM   It's we are obliged to each other. [*Pause.* CLOV *goes towards door.*] One thing more. [CLOV *halts.*] A last favor. [*Exit* CLOV.] Cover me with the sheet. [*Long pause.*] No? Good. [*Pause.*] Me to play. [*Pause. Wearily.*] Old endgame lost of old, play and lose and have done with losing. [*Pause. More animated.*] Let me see. [*Pause.*] Ah yes! [*He tries to move the chair, using the gaff as before. Enter* CLOV, *dressed for the road. Panama hat, tweed coat, raincoat over his arm, umbrella, bag. He halts by the door and stands there, impassive and motionless, his eyes fixed on* HAMM, *till the end.* HAMM *gives up.*] Good. [*Pause.*] Discard. [*He throws away the gaff, makes to throw away the dog, thinks better of it.*] Take it easy. [*Pause.*] And now? [*Pause.*] Raise hat. [*He raises his toque.*] Peace to our . . . arses. [*Pause.*] And put on again. [*He puts on his toque.*] Deuce. [*Pause. He takes off his glasses.*] Wipe. [*He takes out his handkerchief and, without unfolding it, wipes his glasses.*] And put on again. [*He puts on his glasses, puts back the handkerchief in his pocket.*] We're coming. A few more squirms like that and I'll call. [*Pause.*] A little poetry. [*Pause.*] You prayed—[*Pause. He corrects himself.*] You CRIED for night; it comes—[*Pause. He corrects himself.*] It FALLS: now cry in darkness. [*He repeats, chanting.*] You cried for night; it falls: now cry in darkness.[6] [*Pause.*] Nicely put, that. [*Pause.*] And now? [*Pause.*] Moments for nothing, now as always, time was never and time is over, reckoning closed and story ended. [*Pause. Narrative tone.*] If he could have his child with him. . . . [*Pause.*] It was the moment I was waiting for. [*Pause.*] You don't want to abandon him? You want him to bloom while you are withering? Be there to solace your last million last moments? [*Pause.*] He doesn't realize, all he knows is hunger, and cold, and death to crown it all. But you! You ought to know what the earth is like, nowadays. Oh I put him before his responsibilities! [*Pause. Normal tone.*] Well, there we are, there I am, that's enough. [*He raises the whistle to his lips, hesitates, drops it. Pause.*] Yes, truly! [*He whistles. Pause. Louder. Pause.*] Good. [*Pause.*] Father! [*Pause. Louder.*] Father! [*Pause.*] Good. [*Pause.*] We're coming. [*Pause.*] And to end up with?

---

6. Parody of a line from the poem *Meditation*, by Baudelaire: "You were calling for evening; it falls; here it is."

[*Pause.*] Discard. [*He throws away the dog. He tears the whistle from his neck.*] With my compliments. [*He throws whistle towards auditorium. Pause. He sniffs. Soft.*] Clov! [*Long pause.*] No? Good. [*He takes out the handkerchief.*] Since that's the way we're playing it . . . [*He unfolds handkerchief.*] . . . let's play it that way . . . [*He unfolds.*] . . . and speak no more about it . . . [*He finishes unfolding.*] . . . speak no more. [*He holds handkerchief spread out before him.*] Old stancher! [*Pause.*] You . . . remain.

> [*Pause. He covers his face with handkerchief, lowers his arms to armrests, remains motionless.*]
> [*Brief tableau.*]

CURTAIN

RICHARD WRIGHT
1908–1960

Richard Wright is internationally known for powerful naturalist fiction that describes alienated protagonists trapped in a materialistic and repressive society. He is equally well known for another reason: his novels, short stories, autobiography, and essays made him the twentieth century's most forceful exponent of African-American consciousness. From his explosive first novel, *Native Son* (1940), to the political essays of his later years, Wright explored the phenomenon of racism in modern society. Concurrently, he pursued questions of existential identity, wrote about economic inequities, and maintained that his characters' struggle transcended any purely racial or gender definition. Realistic settings, an often hallucinatory narrative, and the violent protest embedded in his works opened new horizons for contemporary readers and new possibilities for young African-American writers. Wright himself left the United States during the anti-Communist witch hunts of the late 1940s, and spent the last fifteen years of his life in Paris. There he was welcomed by writers and intellectuals like the existentialist philosopher Jean-Paul Sartre, the modernist writer Gertrude Stein, and the Swedish sociologist Gunnar Myrdal. He continued to write fiction but devoted much of his time to political and cultural issues, giving lectures and writing polemic essays based on travels in Africa, Asia, and Spain.

Wright was born in 1908 on a farm near Natchez, Mississippi. His father was a poor and illiterate sharecropper, and his mother taught in black country schools. When Wright was five years old, his father deserted the family, and the family moved several times to be with relatives while Wright's mother worked. A brief period of prosperity in Arkansas ended when they had to flee town after the saloon-keeper uncle with whom they were living was shot by envious whites. After Wright's mother suffered a paralytic stroke in 1919, the family was forced to move to her parents' house in Jackson, Mississippi. Wright's education was irregular, and in many ways he was self-taught: attending segregated black public schools and a Seventh-Day Adventist school until ninth grade, he was frequently absent because of family illness or inability to buy books and clothes. The future novelist learned about the larger world from library books that he not only had to acquire by subterfuge but also had to conceal. His grandmother and aunt, strict Seventh-Day Adventists, believed fiction immoral and burned any novels or magazines he brought home. The privations and violence of those early years, his rebellion against a fanatically strict religious upbringing, and his long puzzlement over racism—his grandmother appeared white, and as a child he did not feel a part of racial divisions—are described in *Uncle Tom's Children* (1938) and in the autobiographical *Black Boy* (1945).

After graduating from junior high school in 1925, Wright worked two years for an optical company in Memphis. He read widely, exploring many of the European authors praised by contemporary editor and satirist H. L. Mencken, whose scathing critique of American culture astonished and impressed him. Like other black writers of his generation, Wright found in the naturalist tradition of Europe and America a style congenial to what he had to say. He was particularly struck by the direct, factual, and seemingly objective manner of the American novelists Theodore Dreiser and Sinclair Lewis: "All my life had shaped me for the realism, the naturalism of the modern novel." His first-written, posthumously published novel, *Lawd Today* (1963), contains pages of dialogue that read like transcriptions of overheard speech. Later works go beyond this documentary style, as Wright finds affinities with the prose styles of Marcel Proust and the expatriate writer Gertrude Stein, and as he comes into contact with other American writers who show him diverse literary techniques adaptable to his own vision.

In 1927, eager to escape the South, Wright moved to Chicago, one of the northern cities that southern blacks saw as havens of opportunity and acceptance. Life was not easy in Chicago: he supported himself as a porter, dishwasher, and postal clerk; and when he lost his job in the Depression, he went on relief sweeping streets. Soon he found work with the WPA Federal Writers' Project, one of many federal projects created to help jobless people through the Depression. He wrote guidebooks for the WPA and poems, fiction, and essays on his own; in addition, he read authors like Dostoevsky, Gogol, Baudelaire, Mann, Proust, and T. S. Eliot and works in psychology and sociology. A friend introduced him to the John Reed Club, a Communist literary group, and he became a member of the party in 1933. He withdrew from the party in 1942, however, after becoming disillusioned with its emphasis on international political objectives and concurrent disregard for Wright's chief concerns: individualism, black civil rights, and artistic freedom.

Wright's first short-story collection, *Uncle Tom's Children* (1938), is set in the South, and all four stories are concerned with racism. (A new edition in 1940 included a fifth story and an autobiographical essay, *The Ethics of Living Jim Crow*.) The stories are tense with terror, beatings, and murder, and only one (*Fire and Cloud*) gives any sense of even momentary triumph. *Big Boy Leaves Home*, the often-reprinted first story, describes a teenager's flight after three of his friends are killed—one in a horrific scene of tarring, feathering, and burning alive. *Uncle Tom's Children* won first prize in a Federal Writers' Project competition sponsored by *Story* magazine and was named one of the ten best books of the year. Still, Wright was dissatisfied. He felt that something was lacking: "I found that I had written a book which even bankers' daughters could read and weep over and feel good about. I swore that if I ever wrote another book, no one would weep over it; that it would be so hard and deep that they would face it without the consolation of tears." Perhaps he had in mind the philosophical and political dimension of his later novels, starting with *Native Son*; perhaps, like Bertolt Brecht, he felt he could not teach his audience unless he prevented them from identifying too closely with his characters.

With *Native Son*, the account of a black chauffeur in Chicago who kills two women (one white and the other his black girlfriend) and is brought to trial after a lengthy manhunt, Wright finds the "hard and deep" tone he sought. The novel is, on one level, a lurid drama of murder, futile attempts to hide evidence, and eventual discovery; but it is also a dramatic account of poverty in the black ghetto and a psychological portrait of the hatred, fear, and confusion that characterize its violent protagonist, Bigger Thomas. In the lengthy third section, Wright presents a sociological analysis in the words of Bigger's Communist defense lawyer, who almost abandons any effective defense of his client for a lengthy denunciation of the society that made him a criminal. The ending of the novel shows a condemned Bigger surrounded by people who have their own interpretations of his condition, and Bigger himself just beginning to attain a sense of his own identity: "what I wanted, what I am." The novel appeared in 1940 as a Book-of-the-Month Club selection (with some deletions required by the publisher); it quickly broke sales records, and the novelist became a national figure.

Wright's style combines naturalism—that is, realistic description governed by "scientific" principles of environmental influence—and a poetic or symbolic style. Obsessive themes and color associations imply extended networks of meaning: the color white, for example, is always vaguely threatening and recurs in nightmares. The famous opening scene of *Native Son,* in which Bigger kills a monstrous rat invading his family kitchen, establishes a violent, doom-laden atmosphere that prefigures Bigger's own destiny to be hunted like an animal and killed. Realistic narrative often shifts into obsessed imaginings and fantastic dreams that suggest the action of larger psychological or cultural forces.

After his move to Paris in the mid-1940s, Wright's work developed more global and universal themes. Now openly anti-Communist, he continued to push for revolutionary reform in *Black Power* (1954, an essay on Ghana), *Pagan Spain* (1957), and the lectures of *White Man, Listen!* (1957). His model for reform, however, was Western and industrial, a perspective that did not appeal to many African writers of the Négritude (black identity) movement. The new novels became more philosophical and even didactic. *Savage Holiday* (1954), using Freudian symbolism (and white characters); *The Outsider* (1953), dramatizing existential themes in a collapsing society; and *The Long Dream* (1958), the first volume of a projected trilogy on black experience, move beyond racial questions to explore the human condition. Some critics have argued that Wright's exile in Europe cut him off from his roots and that the later novels are comparatively weak. Yet all share Wright's great theme in which a protagonist passes through violent crises that force a coming to terms with his or her identity and role in society. This subject, he asserted, is "the main burden of all serious fiction . . . character-destiny and the items, social, political, and personal, of that character-destiny." When Wright died of a heart attack on November 28, 1960, he was in the midst of many unfinished projects, including a book of haiku.

The Man Who Was Almost a Man is drawn from the posthumously published *Eight Men* (1961), a collection of five stories, two radio plays, and an autobiographical essay that were written at different periods. An early version of the story, *Almos' a Man,* was published in 1941 and itself stems from a projected novel about a black boxer, *Tarbaby's Dawn.* Like much of Wright's fiction, *The Man Who Was Almost a Man* derives its setting and themes from the author's experience even though events are altered to fit the requirements of the story. Here racial issues are only hinted at as part of the background, while emphasis is put on the difficult passage from adolescence to maturity and on the vulnerability of fragile personalities to being defined from outside.

Seventeen-year-old Dave Saunders is desperate to be considered a man: his family, coworkers, employer, and the store owner all call him "boy" and remind him that he is only a child. He comes from a strict family that guides his every step. Treated like a child, he responds by seeing adulthood as a matter of power: and power, to Dave, means a gun. With a gun, people would have to respect him; he could "kill anybody, black or white." When Dave's attempts at gun practice turn sour, his adolescent vulnerability is badly hurt as he is ridiculed by his coworkers, betrayed—as he sees it—by his mother, promised a beating by his father, and required to pay for the dead mule with his wages for the next two years. Humiliation tips the balance between accepting responsibility for his actions and running away. It is not as a man that he flees, however, but as an adolescent whose whole sense of identity is now locked up with the gun. Like the railroad tracks stretching ahead, "away to somewhere, somewhere where he could be a man," Dave's escape is presented not as a solution but as a continuation of the same problem.

The Man Who Was Almost a Man is a good example of Wright's ability to combine realistic description with modernist techniques expressing a state of mind. His skillful use of dialect and his knowledgeable description of local scenes and attitudes place the story firmly in its sociohistorical setting. A more poetic approach is used to convey Dave's emotional turmoil: sensual images suggest his quasi-erotic response to the revolver, and an internalized point of view reproduces his startled pain when he shoots the gun and his horror when he realizes that he has just shot Jenny. Time slows down while Dave ineffectually plugs the mule's wounds with earth and watches her die; time slows again, and faces blur, when he is the humiliated focus of the crowd's attention. This blend of narrative realism and modernist manipulation of language typifies Wright's best work and makes *The Man Who Was Almost a Man* one of his most popular stories.

The Man Who Was Almost a Man

Dave struck out across the fields, looking homeward through paling light. Whut's the use talkin wid em niggers in the field? Anyhow, his mother was putting supper on the table. Them niggers can't understan nothing. One of these days he was going to get a gun and practice shooting, then they couldn't talk to him as though he were a little boy. He slowed, looking at the ground. Shucks, Ah ain scareda them even ef they are biggern me! Aw, Ah know whut Ahma do. Ahm going by ol Joe's sto n git that Sears Roebuck catlog n look at them guns. Mebbe Ma will lemme buy one when she gits mah pay from ol man Hawkins. Ahma beg her t gimme some money. Ahm ol ernough to hava gun. Ahm seventeen. Almost a man. He strode, feeling his long loose-jointed limbs. Shucks, a man oughta hava little gun aftah he done worked hard all day.

He came in sight of Joe's store. A yellow lantern glowed on the front porch. He mounted steps and went through the screen door, hearing it bang behind him. There was a strong smell of coal oil and mackerel fish. He felt very confident until he saw fat Joe walk in through the rear door, then his courage began to ooze.

"Howdy, Dave! Whutcha want?"

"How yuh, Mistah Joe? Aw, Ah don wanna buy nothing. Ah jus wanted t see ef yuhd lemme look at tha catlog erwhile."

"Sure! You wanna see it here?"

"Nawsuh. Ah wans t take it home wid me. Ah'll bring it back termorrow when Ah come in from the fiels."

"You plannin on buying something?"

"Yessuh."

"Your ma lettin you have your own money now?"

"Shucks. Mistah Joe, Ahm gittin t be a man like anybody else!"

Joe laughed and wiped his greasy white face with a red bandanna.

"Whut you plannin on buyin?"

Dave looked at the floor, scratched his head, scratched his thigh, and smiled. Then he looked up shyly.

"Ah'll tell yuh, Mistah Joe, ef yuh promise yuh won't tell."

"I promise."

"Waal, Ahma buy a gun."

"A gun? Whut you want with a gun?"

"Ah wanna keep it."

"You ain't nothing but a boy. You don't need a gun."

"Aw, lemme have the catlog, Mistah Joe. Ah'll bring it back."

Joe walked through the rear door. Dave was elated. He looked around at barrels of sugar and flour. He heard Joe coming back. He craned his neck to see if he were bringing the book. Yeah, he's got it. Gawddog, he's got it!

"Here, but be sure you bring it back. It's the only one I got."

"Sho, Mistah Joe."

"Say, if you wanna buy a gun, why don't you buy one from me? I gotta gun to sell."

"Will it shoot?"

"Sure it'll shoot."

"Whut kind is it?"

"Oh, it's kinda old . . . a left-hand Wheeler.[1] A pistol. A big one."

"Is it got bullets in it?"

"It's loaded."

"Kin Ah see it?"

"Where's your money?"

"Whut yuh wan fer it?"

"I'll let you have it for two dollars."

"Just two dollahs? Shucks, Ah could buy tha when Ah git mah pay."

"I'll have it here when you want it."

"Awright, suh. Ah be in fer it."

He went through the door, hearing it slam again behind him. Ahma git some money from Ma n buy me a gun! Only two dollahs! He tucked the thick catalogue under his arm and hurried.

"Where yuh been, boy?" His mother held a steaming dish of black-eyed peas.

"Aw, Ma, Ah jus stopped down the road t talk wid the boys."

"Yuh know bettah t keep suppah waitin."

He sat down, resting the catalogue on the edge of the table.

"Yuh git up from there and git to the well n wash yosef! Ah ain feedin no hogs in mah house!"

She grabbed his shoulder and pushed him. He stumbled out of the room, then came back to get the catalogue.

"Whut this?"

"Aw, Ma, it's jusa catlog."

"Who yuh git it from?"

"From Joe, down at the sto."

"Waal, thas good. We kin use it in the outhouse."

"Naw, Ma." He grabbed for it. "Gimme ma catlog, Ma."

She held onto it and glared at him.

"Quit hollerin at me! Whut's wrong wid yuh? Yuh crazy?"

"But Ma, please. It ain mine! It's Joe's! He tol me t bring it back t im termorrow."

---

1. The first revolving pistol, patented by Captain Artemus Wheeler in 1818; it was superseded by the Colt revolver after 1830.

She gave up the book. He stumbled down the back steps, hugging the thick book under his arm. When he had splashed water on his face and hands, he groped back to the kitchen and fumbled in a corner for the towel. He bumped into a chair; it clattered to the floor. The catalogue sprawled at his feet. When he had dried his eyes he snatched up the book and held it again under his arm. His mother stood watching him.

"Now, ef yuh gonna act a fool over that ol book, Ah'll take it n burn it up."

"Naw, Ma, please."

"Waal, set down n be still!"

He sat down and drew the oil lamp close. He thumbed page after page, unaware of the food his mother set on the table. His father came in. Then his small brother.

"Whutcha got there, Dave?" his father asked.

"Jusa catlog," he answered, not looking up.

"Yeah, here they is!" His eyes glowed at blue-and-black revolvers. He glanced up, feeling sudden guilt. His father was watching him. He eased the book under the table and rested it on his knees. After the blessing was asked, he ate. He scooped up peas and swallowed fat meat without chewing. Buttermilk helped to wash it down. He did not want to mention money before his father. He would do much better by cornering his mother when she was alone. He looked at his father uneasily out of the edge of his eye.

"Boy, how come yuh don quit foolin wid tha book n eat yo suppah?"

"Yessuh."

"How you n ol man Hawkins gitten erlong?"

"Suh?"

"Can't yuh hear? Why don yuh lissen? Ah ast yu how wuz yuh n ol man Hawkins gittin erlong?"

"Oh, swell, Pa. Ah plows mo lan than anybody over there."

"Waal, yuh oughta keep yo mind on whut yuh doin."

"Yessuh."

He poured his plate full of molasses and sopped it up slowly with a chunk of cornbread. When his father and brother had left the kitchen, he still sat and looked again at the guns in the catalogue, longing to muster courage enough to present his case to his mother. Lawd, ef Ah only had tha pretty one! He could almost feel the slickness of the weapon with his fingers. If he had a gun like that he would polish it and keep it shining so it would never rust. N Ah'd keep it loaded, by Gawd!

"Ma?" His voice was hesitant.

"Hunh?"

"Ol man Hawkins give yuh mah money yit?"

"Yeah, but ain no usa yuh thinking bout throwin nona it erway. Ahm keepin tha money sos yuh kin have cloes t go to school this winter."

He rose and went to her side with the open catalogue in his palms. She was washing dishes, her head bent low over a pan. Shyly he raised the book. When he spoke, his voice was husky, faint.

"Ma, Gawd knows Ah wans one of these."

"One of whut?" she asked, not raising her eyes.

"One of these," he said again, not daring even to point. She glanced up at the page, then at him with wide eyes.

"Nigger, is yuh gone plumb crazy?"

"Aw, Ma—"

"Git outta here! Don yuh talk t me bout no gun! Yuh a fool!"

"Ma, Ah kin buy one fer two dollahs."

"Not ef Ah knows it, yuh ain!"

"But yuh promised me one—"

"Ah don care whut Ah promised! Yuh ain nothing but a boy yit!"

"Ma, ef yuh lemme buy one Ah'll *never* ast yuh fer nothing no mo."

"Ah tol yuh t git outta here! Yuh ain gonna toucha penny of tha money fer no gun! Thas how come Ah has Mistah Hawkins t pay yo wages t me, cause Ah knows yuh ain got no sense."

"But, Ma, we needa gun. Pa ain got no gun. We needa gun in the house. Yuh kin never tell whut might happen."

"Now don yuh try to maka fool outta me, boy! Ef we did hava gun, yuh wouldn't have it!"

He laid the catalogue down and slipped his arm around her waist.

"Aw, Ma, Ah done worked hard alla summer n ain ast yuh fer nothin, is Ah, now?"

"Thas whut yuh spose t do!"

"But Ma, Ah wans a gun. Yuh kin lemme have two dollahs outta mah money. Please, Ma. I kin give it to Pa . . . Please, Ma! Ah loves yuh, Ma."

When she spoke her voice came soft and low.

"Whut yu wan wida gun, Dave? Yuh don need no gun. Yuh'll git in trouble. N ef yo pa jus thought Ah let yuh have money t buy a gun he'd hava fit."

"Ah'll hide it, Ma. It ain but two dollahs."

"Lawd, chil, whut's wrong wid yuh?"

"Ain nothin wrong, Ma. Ahm almos a man now. Ah wans a gun."

"Who gonna sell yuh a gun?"

"Ol Joe at the sto."

"N it don cos but two dollahs?"

"Thas all, Ma. Jus two dollahs. Please, Ma."

She was stacking the plates away; her hands moved slowly, reflectively. Dave kept an anxious silence. Finally, she turned to him.

"Ah'll let yuh git tha gun ef yuh promise me one thing."

"Whut's tha, Ma?"

"Yuh bring it straight back t me, yuh hear? It be fer Pa."

"Yessum! Lemme go now, Ma."

She stooped, turned slightly to one side, raised the hem of her dress, rolled down the top of her stocking, and came up with a slender wad of bills.

"Here," she said. "Lawd knows yuh don need no gun. But yer pa does. Yuh bring it right back t me, yuh hear? Ahma put it up. Now ef yuh don, Ahma have yuh pa lick yuh so hard yuh won fergit it."

"Yessum."

He took the money, ran down the steps, and across the yard.

"Dave! Yuuuuuh Daaaaave!"

He heard, but he was not going to stop now. "Naw, Lawd!"

The first movement he made the following morning was to reach under his pillow for the gun. In the gray light of dawn he held it loosely, feeling a sense of power. Could kill a man with a gun like this. Kill anybody, black or white. And if he were holding his gun in his hand, nobody could run over him; they would have to respect him. It was a big gun, with a long barrel and a heavy handle. He raised and lowered it in his hand, marveling at its weight.

He had not come straight home with it as his mother had asked; instead he had stayed out in the fields, holding the weapon in his hand, aiming it now and then at some imaginary foe. But he had not fired it; he had been afraid that his father might hear. Also he was not sure he knew how to fire it.

To avoid surrendering the pistol he had not come into the house until he knew that they were all asleep. When his mother had tiptoed to his bedside late that night and demanded the gun, he had first played possum; then he had told her that the gun was hidden outdoors, that he would bring it to her in the morning. Now he lay turning it slowly in his hands. He broke it, took out the cartridges, felt them, and then put them back.

He slid out of bed, got a long strip of old flannel from a trunk, wrapped the gun in it, and tied it to his naked thigh while it was still loaded. He did not go in to breakfast. Even though it was not yet daylight, he started for Jim Hawkins' plantation. Just as the sun was rising he reached the barns where the mules and plows were kept.

"Hey! That you, Dave?"

He turned. Jim Hawkins stood eying him suspiciously.

"What're yuh doing here so early?"

"Ah didn't know Ah wuz gittin up so early, Mistah Hawkins. Ah wuz fixin t hitch up ol Jenny n take her t the fiels."

"Good. Since you're so early, how about plowing that stretch down by the woods?"

"Suits me, Mistah Hawkins."

"O.K. Go to it!"

He hitched Jenny to a plow and started across the fields. Hot dog! This was just what he wanted. If he could get down by the woods, he could shoot his gun and nobody would hear. He walked behind the plow, hearing the traces creaking, feeling the gun tied tight to his thigh.

When he reached the woods, he plowed two whole rows before he decided to take out the gun. Finally, he stopped, looked in all directions, then untied the gun and held it in his hand. He turned to the mule and smiled.

"Know whut this is, Jenny? Naw, yuh wouldn know! Yuhs jusa ol mule! Anyhow, this is a gun, n it kin shoot, by Gawd!"

He held the gun at arm's length. Whut t hell, Ahma shoot this thing! He looked at Jenny again.

"Lissen here, Jenny! When Ah pull this ol trigger, Ah don wan yuh t run n acka fool now!"

Jenny stood with head down, her short ears pricked straight. Dave walked off about twenty feet, held the gun far out from him at arm's length, and turned his head. Hell, he told himself, Ah ain afraid. The gun felt loose in his fingers; he waved it wildly for a moment. Then he shut his eyes and tightened his forefinger. Bloom! A report half deafened him and he thought his right hand was torn from his arm. He heard Jenny whinnying and galloping over the field, and he found himself on his knees, squeezing his fingers hard between his legs. His hand was numb; he jammed it into his mouth, trying to warm it, trying to stop the pain. The gun lay at his feet. He did not quite know what had happened. He stood up and stared at the gun as though it were a living thing. He gritted his teeth and kicked the gun. Yuh almos broke mah arm! He turned to look for Jenny; she was far over the fields, tossing her head and kicking wildly.

"Hol on there, ol mule!"

When he caught up with her she stood trembling, walling her big white eyes at him. The plow was far away; the traces had broken. Then Dave stopped short, looking, not believing. Jenny was bleeding. Her left side was red and wet with blood. He went closer. Lawd, have mercy! Wondah did Ah shoot this mule? He grabbed for Jenny's mane. She flinched, snorted, whirled, tossing her head.

"Hol on now! Hol on."

Then he saw the hole in Jenny's side, right between the ribs. It was round, wet, red. A crimson stream streaked down the front leg, flowing fast. Good Gawd! Ah wuzn't shootin at tha mule. He felt panic. He knew he had to stop that blood, or Jenny would bleed to death. He had never seen so much blood in all his life. He chased the mule for half a mile, trying to catch her. Finally she stopped, breathing hard, stumpy tail half arched. He caught her mane and led her back to where the plow and gun lay. Then he stooped and grabbed handfuls of damp black earth and tried to plug the bullet hole. Jenny shuddered, whinnied, and broke from him.

"Hol on! Hol on now!"

He tried to plug it again, but blood came anyhow. His fingers were hot and sticky. He rubbed dirt into his palms, trying to dry them. Then again he attempted to plug the bullet hole, but Jenny shied away, kicking her heels high. He stood helpless. He had to do something. He ran at Jenny; she dodged him. He watched a red stream of blood flow down Jenny's leg and form a bright pool at her feet.

"Jenny . . . Jenny," he called weakly.

His lips trembled. She's bleeding t death! He looked in the direction of home, wanting to go back, wanting to get help. But he saw the pistol lying in the damp black clay. He had a queer feeling that if he only did something, this would not be; Jenny would not be there bleeding to death.

When he went to her this time, she did not move. She stood with sleepy, dreamy eyes; and when he touched her she gave a low-pitched whinny and knelt to the ground, her front knees slopping in blood.

"Jenny . . . Jenny . . ." he whispered.

For a long time she held her neck erect; then her head sank, slowly. Her ribs swelled with a mighty heave and she went over.

Dave's stomach felt empty, very empty. He picked up the gun and held it gingerly between his thumb and forefinger. He buried it at the foot of a tree. He took a stick and tried to cover the pool of blood with dirt—but what was the use? There was Jenny lying with her mouth open and her eyes walled and glassy. He could not tell Jim Hawkins he had shot his mule. But he had to tell something. Yeah, Ah'll tell em Jenny started gittin wil n fell on the joint of the plow. . . . But that would hardly happen to a mule. He walked across the field slowly, head down.

It was sunset. Two of Jim Hawkins' men were over near the edge of the woods digging a hole in which to bury Jenny. Dave was surrounded by a knot of people, all of whom were looking down at the dead mule.

"I don't see how in the world it happened," said Jim Hawkins for the tenth time.

The crowd parted and Dave's mother, father, and small brother pushed into the center.

"Where Dave?" his mother called.

"There he is," said Jim Hawkins.

His mother grabbed him.

"Whut happened, Dave? Whut yuh done?"

"Nothin."

"C'mon, boy, talk," his father said.

Dave took a deep breath and told the story he knew nobody believed.

"Waal," he drawled. "Ah brung ol Jenny down here sos Ah could do mah plowin. Ah plowed bout two rows, just like yuh see." He stopped and pointed at the long rows of upturned earth. "Then somethin musta been wrong wid ol Jenny. She wouldn ack right a-tall. She started snortin n kickin her heels. Ah tried t hol her, but she pulled erway, rearin n goin in. Then when the point of the plow was stickin up in the air, she swung erroun n twisted herself back on it . . . She stuck herself n started t bleed. N fo Ah could do anything, she wuz dead."

"Did you ever hear of anything like that in all your life?" asked Jim Hawkins.

There were white and black standing in the crowd. They murmured. Dave's mother came close to him and looked hard into his face. "Tell the truth, Dave," she said.

"Looks like a bullet hole to me," said one man.

"Dave, whut yuh do wid the gun?" his mother asked.

The crowd surged in, looking at him. He jammed his hands into his pockets, shook his head slowly from left to right, and backed away. His eyes were wide and painful.

"Did he hava gun?" asked Jim Hawkins.

"By Gawd, Ah tol yuh tha wuz a gun wound," said a man, slapping his thigh.

His father caught his shoulders and shook him till his teeth rattled.

"Tell whut happened, yuh rascal! Tell whut . . ."

Dave looked at Jenny's stiff legs and began to cry.

"Whut yuh do wid tha gun?" his mother asked.

"Whut wuz he doin wida gun?" his father asked.

"Come on and tell the truth," said Hawkins. "Ain't nobody going to hurt you . . ."

His mother crowded close to him.

"Did yuh shoot tha mule, Dave?"

Dave cried, seeing blurred white and black faces.

"Ahh ddinn gggo tt sshooot hher . . . Ah ssswear ffo Gawd Ahh ddin . . . Ah wuz a-tryin t sssee ef the old gggun would sshoot—"

"Where yuh git the gun from?" his father asked.

"Ah got it from Joe, at the sto."

"Where yuh git the money?"

"Ma give it t me."

"He kept worryin me, Bob. Ah had t. Ah tol im t bring the gun right back t me . . . It was fer yuh, the gun."

"But how yuh happen to shoot that mule?" asked Jim Hawkins.

"Ah wuzn shootin at the mule, Mistah Hawkins. The gun jumped when Ah pulled the trigger . . . N fo Ah knowed anythin Jenny was there a-bleedin."

Somebody in the crowd laughed. Jim Hawkins walked close to Dave and looked into his face.

"Well, looks like you have bought you a mule, Dave."

"Ah swear fo Gawd, Ah didn go t kill the mule, Mistah Hawkins!"

"But you killed her!"

All the crowd was laughing now. They stood on tiptoe and poked heads over one another's shoulders.

"Well, boy, looks like yuh done bought a dead mule! Hahaha!"

"Ain tha ershame."

"Hohohohoho."

Dave stood, head down, twisting his feet in the dirt.

"Well, you needn't worry about it, Bob," said Jim Hawkins to Dave's father. "Just let the boy keep on working and pay me two dollars a month."

"Whut yuh wan fer yo mule, Mistah Hawkins?"

Jim Hawkins screwed up his eyes.

"Fifty dollars."

"Whut yuh do wid tha gun?" Dave's father demanded.

Dave said nothing.

"Yuh wan me t take a tree n beat yuh till yuh talk!"

"Nawsuh!"

"Whut yuh do wid it?"

"Ah throwed it erway."

"Where?"

"Ah . . . Ah throwed it in the creek."

"Waal, c mon home. N firs thing in the mawnin git to tha creek n fin tha gun."

"Yessuh."

"Whut yuh pay fer it?"

"Two dollahs."

"Take tha gun n git yo money back n carry it t Mistah Hawkins, yuh hear? N don fergit Ahma lam you black bottom good fer this! Now march yosef on home, suh!"

Dave turned and walked slowly. He heard people laughing. Dave glared, his eyes welling with tears. Hot anger bubbled in him. Then he swallowed and stumbled on.

That night Dave did not sleep. He was glad that he had gotten out of killing the mule so easily, but he was hurt. Something hot seemed to turn over inside him each time he remembered how they had laughed. He tossed on his bed, feeling his hard pillow. N Pa says he's gonna beat me . . . He remembered other beatings, and his back quivered. Naw, naw, Ah sho don wan im t beat me tha way no mo. Dam em all! Nobody ever gave him anything. All he did was work. They treat me like a mule, n then they beat me. He gritted his teeth. N Ma had t tell on me.

Well, if he had to, he would take old man Hawkins that two dollars. But that meant selling the gun. And he wanted to keep that gun. Fifty dollars for a dead mule.

He turned over, thinking how he had fired the gun. He had an itch to fire it again. *Ef other men kin shoota gun, by Gawd, Ah kin!* He was still, listening. *Mebbe they all sleepin now.* The house was still. He heard the soft breathing of his brother. *Yes, now!* He would go down and get that gun and see if he could fire it! He eased out of bed and slipped into overalls.

The moon was bright. He ran almost all the way to the edge of the woods. He stumbled over the ground, looking for the spot where he had buried the gun. *Yeah, here it is.* Like a hungry dog scratching for a bone, he pawed it up. He puffed his black cheeks and blew dirt from the trigger and barrel. He broke it and found four cartridges unshot. He looked around; the fields were filled with silence and moonlight. He clutched the gun stiff and hard in his fingers. But, as soon as he wanted to pull the trigger, he shut his eyes and turned his head. *Naw, Ah can't shoot wid mah eyes closed n mah head turned.* With effort he held his eyes open; then he squeezed. *Blooooom!* He was stiff, not breathing. The gun was still in his hands. *Dammit, he'd done it!* He fired again. *Blooooom!* He smiled. *Blooooom! Blooooom! Click, click.* There! It was empty. If anybody could shoot a gun, he could. He put the gun into his hip pocket and started across the fields.

When he reached the top of a ridge he stood straight and proud in the moonlight, looking at Jim Hawkins' big white house, feeling the gun sagging in his pocket. *Lawd, ef Ah had just one mo bullet Ah'd taka shot at tha house. Ah'd like t scare ol man Hawkins jusa little . . . Jusa enough t let im know Dave Saunders is a man.*

To his left the road curved, running to the tracks of the Illinois Central. He jerked his head, listening. From far off came a faint *hoooof-hoooof; hoooof-hoooof; hoooof-hoooof.* . . . He stood rigid. *Two dollahs a mont. Les see now . . . Tha means it'll take bout two years. Shucks! Ah'll be dam!*

He started down the road, toward the tracks. *Yeah, here she comes!* He stood beside the track and held himself stiffly. *Here she comes, erroun the ben . . . C mon, yuh slow poke! C mon!* He had his hand on his gun; something quivered in his stomach. Then the train thundered past, the gray and brown box cars rumbling and clinking. He gripped the gun tightly; then he jerked his hand out of his pocket. *Ah betcha Bill wouldn't do it! Ah betcha . . .* The cars slid past, steel grinding upon steel. *Ahm ridin yuh ternight, so hep me Gawd!* He was hot all over. He hesitated just a moment; then he grabbed, pulled atop of a car, and lay flat. He felt his pocket; the gun was still there. Ahead the long rails were glinting in the moonlight, stretching away, away to somewhere, somewhere where he could be a man . . .

ALBERT CAMUS
1913–1960

Albert Camus is often linked with the contemporary philosopher Jean-Paul Sartre as an "existentialist" writer, and indeed—as novelist, playwright, and essayist—he is widely known for his analysis of two concerns basic to existentialism: its distinctive assessment of the human condition and its search for authentic values. Yet Camus rejected doctrinaire labels, and Sartre himself suggested that the author was better placed in the tradition of French "moralist" writers such as Michel de Montaigne and René Pascal, who analyzed human behavior inside an implied ethical context with its own standards of good and evil. For Camus, liberty, justice, brotherhood, and happiness were some of these standards, along with the terms *revolt* and *absurd* that described human nonacceptance of a world without meaning or value. From his childhood among the very poor in Algiers to his later roles as journalist, Resistance fighter, internationally famous literary figure, and winner of the Nobel Prize in 1957, Camus never strayed from an intense awareness of the most basic levels of human existence or from a sympathy with those—often poor and oppressed—who lived at that level. "I can understand only in human terms. I understand the things I touch, things that offer me resistance." He describes the raw experience of life as it is shared by all human beings, and provides a bond between them. Camus's reaction to the "absurd," the human condition stripped bare, is, therefore, quite different from Samuel Beckett's retreat into agonized subjectivity; where Beckett is haunted by the fictionality of experience, Camus asserts human consciousness and human solidarity as the only values there are.

Camus was born on November 7, 1913, into a "world of poverty and light" in Mondavi, Algeria (then a colony of France). He was the second son in a poor family of mixed Alsatian-Spanish descent, and his father died in one of the first battles of World War I. The two boys lived together with their mother, uncle, and grandmother in a two-room apartment in the working-class section of the capital city, Algiers. Camus and his brother, Lucien, were raised by their strict grandmother while their mother worked as a cleaning woman to support the family. Images of the Mediterranean landscape, with its overwhelming, sensual closeness of sea and blazing sun, recur throughout his work, as does a profound compassion for those who—like his mother—labor unrecognized and in silence. (Camus's mother was illiterate and was left deaf and with a speech impediment by an untreated childhood illness.)

A passionate athlete as well as scholarship student, Camus completed his secondary education and enrolled as a philosophy student at the University of Algiers before contracting, at seventeen, the tuberculosis that undermined his health and shocked him with its demonstration of the human body's vulnerability to disease and death. Camus later finished his degree, but in the meantime he had gained from his illness a metaphor for everything that opposes and puts limits to human fulfillment and happiness: something he was later to term (after Antonin Artaud) the "plague" that infects bodies, minds, cities, and society. (*The Plague* is the title of his second novel.)

Camus lived and worked as a journalist in Algeria until 1940. He then moved to France when his political commentary (including a famous report on administrative mismanagement during a famine of Berber tribesmen) so embroiled him with the local government that his paper was suspended and he himself refused a work permit. Then as later, however, his work extended far beyond journalism. He published two collections of essays, *The Wrong Side and the Right Side* (1937) and *Nuptials* (1939), started a novel (*A Happy Death*), and founded a collective theater, Le Théâtre du Travail (The Labor Theater), for which he wrote and adapted a number of plays. The theater always fascinated Camus, possibly because it involved groups of people and live interaction between actors and audience. He not only continued to write plays after leaving Algeria (*Cross Purposes*, 1944; *The Just Assassins*, 1949) but was considering directing a new theater shortly before his death. The Labor Theater was a popular theater with performances on the docks in Algiers and was sponsored by the Communist Party, which Camus had joined in 1934. Like many intellectuals of his day, Camus found in the party a promising vehicle for social protest; he was unwilling to abandon either his independence or his convictions, however, and resigned in 1935 when the party line changed and he was asked to give up his support for Algerian nationalism. He left the Labor Theater in 1937 and, with a group of young Algerian intellectuals associated with the publishing house of Charlot, founded a similar but politically independent Team Theater (Théâtre de l'Équipe). During this decade, Camus also began work on his most famous novel, *The Stranger* (1942), the play *Caligula* (1944), and a lengthy essay defining his concept of the "absurd" hero, *The Myth of Sisyphus* (1942).

These three works established Camus's reputation as a philosopher of the absurd: the absurdly grotesque discrepancy between human beings' brief, material existence and their urge to believe in larger meanings—to "make sense" of a world that has no discernible sense. In *The Stranger,* Camus described a thirty-year-old clerk named Meursault who lives a series of "real" events: he attends his mother's funeral, makes love to his mistress, goes swimming, shoots an Arab on the beach, and is tried for murder. These events are described through Meursault's mind, and yet they appear without any connection, as if each one began a new world. They are simply a series of concrete, sensuous *facts* separated from each other and from any kind of human or social meaning. Meursault is finally condemned to death not for murder but for this alienation and for its failure to respond to society's expectations of proper behavior. Just before his execution, when he is infuriated by the prison chaplain's attempt to console him with thoughts of an afterlife, he rises to a new level of existential awareness and an ardent affirmation of life in the here and now, the only truly human field of action. Stylistically, much of *The Stranger*'s impact comes from the contrast between the immediacy of the physical experience described and the objective meaninglessness of that experience. On all levels, the novel reaffirms the importance of life lived moment by moment, in a total awareness that creates whatever meaning exists: the same awareness of his own activity that brings the mythological Sisyphus happiness when eternally pushing uphill the rock that will only roll down again, or the same search for an absolute honesty free of human pretenses that characterizes the mad emperor Caligula.

During World War II, Camus worked in Paris as a reader for the publishing firm of Gallimard, a post that he kept until his death in 1960. At the same time, he was part of the French Resistance and helped edit the underground journal *Combat*. His friendship with the existentialist philosopher Jean-Paul Sartre began in 1944, and after the war he and Sartre were internationally known as uncompromising analysts of the modern conscience. Camus's second novel, *The Plague* (1947), used a description of plague in a quarantined city, the Algerian Oran, to symbolize the spread of evil during World War II ("the feeling of suffocation from which we all suffered, and the atmosphere of threat and exile") and also to show the human struggle against physical and spiritual death in all its forms. Not content merely to symbolize his views in fiction, Camus also spoke out in philosophical essays and political statements, and his independent mind and refusal of doctrinaire positions brought him attacks from all sides. In the bitter struggle that brought independence to Algeria in 1962, Camus recognized the claims of both French and Arab Algerians to the land in which they were born. In the quest for social reform, he rejected any ideology that subordinated individual freedom and singled out Communism—the doctrine most reformist intellectuals saw as the only active hope—as a particular danger with its emphasis on the deindividualized and inevitable march of history. Camus's open anti-Communism led to a spectacular break with Sartre, whose review *Les Temps Modernes* (Modern Times) condemned *The Rebel* (1951) in bitter personal attacks. The concept of revolt that Camus outlined in *The Rebel* was more ethical than political: he defined revolt as a basic nonacceptance of preestablished limits (whether by death or by oppression) that was shared by all human beings and, therefore, required a reciprocal acceptance and balancing of each person's rights. Such "revolt" was directly opposed to revolutionary nihilism in that it made the rebellious impulse a basis for social tolerance inside the individual's self-assertion; it had no patience for master plans that prescribed patterns of thought or action.

Five years after *The Rebel* was published, Camus produced a very different book in *The Fall* (1956). This novel is a rhetorical tour de force spoken by a fallen lawyer who uses all the tricks of language to confess his weaknesses and yet emerge triumphant, the omniscient judge of his fellow creatures. If Camus's *Notebooks* reveal in his early works a cycle of Sisyphus or the absurd, and his middle ones a Promethean cycle of revolt, *The Fall* inaugurates a third cycle, that of Nemesis, or judgment. It offers a complex, ironic picture that combines a yearning toward purity with a cynical debunking of all such attempts. The narrator, Clamence, is a composite personality including (among other things) satirized aspects of both Sartre and Camus, but it is impossible to get to the bottom of his character behind the layers of self-consciously manipulated language. The style itself challenges and disorients the reader, who is both included and excluded from a narration that presents Clamence's half of a dialogue in which "you," the reader, are presumed to be present as the other half.

Camus was a consummate artist as well as moralist, well aware of the opportunities as well as the illusions of his craft. When he received the Nobel Prize in 1957, his acceptance speech emphasized the artificial but necessary "human" order imposed by art on the chaos of immediate experience. The artist is important as *creator* because he or she shapes a human perspective, allows understanding in human terms, and therefore provides a basis for action. By stressing the gap between art and reality, Camus in effect provides a bridge between them as two poles of human understanding. His own works illustrate this act of bridging through their juxtaposition of realistic detail and almost mythic allegorization of human destiny. The symbolism of his titles, from *The Stranger* to the last collection of stories, *Exile and the Kingdom* (1957), repeatedly interprets human destiny in terms of a thematic opposition between the individual's sense of alienation and exile in the world, and simultaneous search for the true realm of human happiness and action.

With *The Guest*, taken from *Exile and the Kingdom*, Camus returns to the landscape of his native Algeria. The colonial context is crucial in this story, not only to explain the real threat of guerrilla reprisal at the end (Camus may be recalling the actual killing of rural schoolteachers in 1954) but to establish the dimensions of a political situation in which the government, police, educational system, and economic welfare of Algeria are all controlled by France. A similar colonial (or newly postcolonial) setting is used to indicate a charged political atmosphere in works by Nadine Gordimer, Naguib Mahfouz, Chinua Achebe, and Wole Soyinka. The beginning of Camus's story illustrates how French colonial education reproduces French, not local concerns: the schoolteacher's geography lesson outlines the four main rivers of France. The Arab is led along like an animal behind the gendarme Balducci, who rides a horse (here too, Camus may be recalling a humiliation reported two decades before and used to inspire Algerian nationalists). Within this political context, however, he concentrates on quite different issues: freedom, brotherhood, responsibility, and the ambiguity of actions along with the inevitability of choice.

The remote desert landscape establishes a total physical and moral isolation for events in the story. "No one, in this desert . . . mattered," and the schoolteacher and his guest must each decide on his own what to do. When Balducci invades Daru's monastic solitude and tells him that he must deliver the Arab to prison, Daru is outraged to be involved and, indeed, to have responsibility for another's fate. Cursing both the system that tries to force him into complicity and the Arab who has not had enough sense to get away, Daru tries in every way possible to avoid taking a stand. In the morning, however, when the Arab has not in fact run away, the schoolteacher makes up a package of food and money and passes on to the Arab his own freedom of choice. We cannot underestimate the quiet heroism of this act, by which Daru alienates himself from his own people and—unexpectedly—from the Arab's compatriots too; he is, he believes, conveying to a fellow human being the freedom of action, which all people require. This level of common humanity is strongly underlined throughout the whole story as a "sort of brotherhood" and "strange alliance" that comes from having shared food and drink, and slept as equals under the same roof. Such hospitality is also the nomadic "law of the desert" that establishes fellowship between guest and host (a law that Daru refers to when he points out the second road at the end). The host's humane hospitality has placed a new burden and reciprocal responsibility on his guest, one that may explain why the Arab chooses—in apparent freedom—the road to prison. Camus considered "Cain" and "The Law" as titles for this story before settling on *The Guest* (and the title word *l'hôte*, is identical for "guest" and "host" in French). Both guest and host are obliged to shoulder the ambiguous, and potentially fatal, burden of freedom.

The Guest[1]

The schoolmaster was watching the two men climb toward him. One was on horseback, the other on foot. They had not yet tackled the abrupt rise leading to the schoolhouse built on the hillside. They were toiling onward, making slow progress in the snow, among the stones, on the vast expanse of the high, deserted plateau. From time to time the horse stumbled. Without hearing anything yet, he could see the breath issuing from the horse's nostrils. One of the men, at least, knew the region. They were following the trail although it had disappeared days ago under a layer of dirty white snow. The schoolmaster calculated that it would take them half an hour to get onto the hill. It was cold; he went back into the school to get a sweater.

He crossed the empty, frigid classroom. On the blackboard the four rivers of France,[2] drawn with four different colored chalks, had been flowing toward their estuaries for the past three days. Snow had suddenly fallen in mid-October after eight months of drought without the transition of rain, and the twenty pupils, more or less, who lived in the villages scattered over the plateau had stopped coming. With fair weather they would return. Daru now heated only the single room that was his lodging, adjoining the classroom and giving also onto the plateau to the east. Like the class windows, his window looked to the south too. On that side the school was a few kilometers from the point where the plateau began to slope toward the south. In clear weather could be seen the purple mass of the mountain range where the gap opened onto the desert.

Somewhat warmed, Daru returned to the window from which he had first seen the two men. They were no longer visible. Hence they must have tackled the rise. The sky was not so dark, for the snow had stopped falling during the night. The morning had opened with a dirty light which had scarcely become brighter as the ceiling of clouds lifted. At two in the afternoon it seemed as if the day were merely beginning. But still this was better than those three days when the thick snow was falling amidst unbroken darkness

---

1. Translated by Justin O'Brien.   2. The Seine, Loire, Rhône, and Gironde rivers. French geography was taught in the French colonies.

with little gusts of wind that rattled the double door of the classroom. Then Daru had spent long hours in his room, leaving it only to go to the shed and feed the chickens or get some coal. Fortunately the delivery truck from Tadjid, the nearest village to the north, had brought his supplies two days before the blizzard. It would return in forty-eight hours.

Besides, he had enough to resist a siege, for the little room was cluttered with bags of wheat that the administration left as a stock to distribute to those of his pupils whose families had suffered from the drought. Actually they had all been victims because they were all poor. Every day Daru would distribute a ration to the children. They had missed it, he knew, during these bad days. Possibly one of the fathers or big brothers would come this afternoon and he could supply them with grain. It was just a matter of carrying them over to the next harvest. Now shiploads of wheat were arriving from France and the worst was over. But it would be hard to forget that poverty, that army of ragged ghosts wandering in the sunlight, the plateaus burned to a cinder month after month, the earth shriveled up little by little, literally scorched, every stone bursting into dust under one's foot. The sheep had died then by thousands and even a few men, here and there, sometimes without anyone's knowing.

In contrast with such poverty, he who lived almost like a monk in his remote schoolhouse, nonetheless satisfied with the little he had and with the rough life, had felt like a lord with his whitewashed walls, his narrow couch, his unpainted shelves, his well, and his weekly provision of water and food. And suddenly this snow, without warning, without the foretaste of rain. This is the way the region was, cruel to live in, even without men—who didn't help matters either. But Daru had been born here. Everywhere else, he felt exiled.

He stepped out onto the terrace in front of the schoolhouse. The two men were now halfway up the slope. He recognized the horseman as Balducci, the old gendarme he had known for a long time. Balducci was holding on the end of a rope an Arab who was walking behind him with hands bound and head lowered. The gendarme waved a greeting to which Daru did not reply, lost as he was in contemplation of the Arab dressed in a faded blue jellaba, his feet in sandals but covered with socks of heavy raw wool, his head surmounted by a narrow, short chèche.[3] They were approaching. Balducci was holding back his horse in order not to hurt the Arab, and the group was advancing slowly.

Within earshot, Balducci shouted: "One hour to do the three kilometers from El Ameur!" Daru did not answer. Short and square in his thick sweater, he watched them climb. Not once had the Arab raised his head. "Hello," said Daru when they got up onto the terrace. "Come in and warm up." Balducci painfully got down from his horse without letting go the rope. From under his bristling mustache he smiled at the schoolmaster. His little dark eyes, deep-set under a tanned forehead, and his mouth surrounded with wrinkles made him look attentive and studious. Daru took the bridle, led the horse to the shed, and came back to the two men, who were now waiting for him in the school. He led them into his room. "I am going to heat up the classroom," he said. "We'll be more comfortable there." When he entered the room again,

3. Scarf; here wound as a turban around the head. *Jellaba:* a long hooded robe worn by Arabs in North Africa.

Balducci was on the couch. He had undone the rope tying him to the Arab, who had squatted near the stove. His hands still bound, the *chèche* pushed back on his head, he was looking toward the window. At first Daru noticed only his huge lips, fat, smooth, almost Negroid; yet his nose was straight, his eyes were dark and full of fever. The *chèche* revealed an obstinate forehead and, under the weathered skin now rather discolored by the cold, the whole face had a restless and rebellious look that struck Daru when the Arab, turning his face toward him, looked him straight in the eyes. "Go into the other room," said the schoolmaster, "and I'll make you some mint tea." "Thanks," Balducci said. "What a chore! How I long for retirement." And addressing his prisoner in Arabic: "Come on, you." The Arab got up and, slowly, holding his bound wrists in front of him, went into the classroom.

With the tea, Daru brought a chair. But Balducci was already enthroned on the nearest pupil's desk and the Arab had squatted against the teacher's platform facing the stove, which stood between the desk and the window. When he held out the glass of tea to the prisoner, Daru hesitated at the sight of his bound hands. "He might perhaps be untied." "Sure," said Balducci. "That was for the trip." He started to get to his feet. But Daru, setting the glass on the floor, had knelt beside the Arab. Without saying anything, the Arab watched him with his feverish eyes. Once his hands were free, he rubbed his swollen wrists against each other, took the glass of tea, and sucked up the burning liquid in swift little sips.

"Good," said Daru. "And where are you headed?"

Balducci withdrew his mustache from the tea. "Here, son."

"Odd pupils! And you're spending the night?"

"No. I'm going back to El Ameur. And you will deliver this fellow to Tinguit. He is expected at police headquarters."

Balducci was looking at Daru with a friendly little smile.

"What's this story?" asked the schoolmaster. "Are you pulling my leg?"

"No, son. Those are the orders."

"The orders? I'm not . . ." Daru hesitated, not wanting to hurt the old Corsican.[4] "I mean, that's not my job."

"What! What's the meaning of that? In wartime people do all kinds of jobs."

"Then I'll wait for the declaration of war!"

Balducci nodded.

"O.K. But the orders exist and they concern you too. Things are brewing, it appears. There is talk of a forthcoming revolt. We are mobilized, in a way."

Daru still had his obstinate look.

"Listen, son," Balducci said. "I like you and you must understand. There's only a dozen of us at El Ameur to patrol throughout the whole territory of a small department[5] and I must get back in a hurry. I was told to hand this guy over to you and return without delay. He couldn't be kept there. His village was beginning to stir; they wanted to take him back. You must take him to Tinguit tomorrow before the day is over. Twenty kilometers shouldn't faze a husky fellow like you. After that, all will be over. You'll come back to your pupils and your comfortable life."

Behind the wall the horse could be heard snorting and pawing the earth.

---

4. Balducci is a native of Corsica, a French island north of Sardinia.   5. French administrative and territorial division; like a country.

Daru was looking out the window. Decidedly, the weather was clearing and the light was increasing over the snowy plateau. When all the snow was melted, the sun would take over again and once more would burn the fields of stone. For days, still, the unchanging sky would shed its dry light on the solitary expanse where nothing had any connection with man.

"After all," he said, turning around toward Balducci, "what did he do?" And, before the gendarme had opened his mouth, he asked: "Does he speak French?"

"No, not a word. We had been looking for him for a month, but they were hiding him. He killed his cousin."

"Is he against us?"[6]

"I don't think so. But you can never be sure."

"Why did he kill?"

"A family squabble, I think. One owed the other grain, it seems. It's not at all clear. In short, he killed his cousin with a billhook. You know, like a sheep, *kreezk!*"

Balducci made the gesture of drawing a blade across his throat and the Arab, his attention attracted, watched him with a sort of anxiety. Daru felt a sudden wrath against the man, against all men with their rotten spite, their tireless hates, their blood lust.

But the kettle was singing on the stove. He served Balducci more tea, hesitated, then served the Arab again, who, a second time, drank avidly. His raised arms made the jellaba fall open and the schoolmaster saw his thin, muscular chest.

"Thanks, kid," Balducci said. "And now, I'm off."

He got up and went toward the Arab, taking a small rope from his pocket.

"What are you doing?" Daru asked dryly.

Balducci, disconcerted, showed him the rope.

"Don't bother."

The old gendarme hesitated. "It's up to you. Of course, you are armed?"

"I have my shotgun."

"Where?"

"In the trunk."

"You ought to have it near your bed."

"Why? I have nothing to fear."

"You're crazy, son. If there's an uprising, no one is safe, we're all in the same boat."

"I'll defend myself. I'll have time to see them coming."

Balducci began to laugh, then suddenly the mustache covered the white teeth.

"You'll have time? O.K. That's just what I was saying. You have always been a little cracked. That's why I like you, my son was like that."

At the same time he took out his revolver and put it on the desk.

"Keep it; I don't need two weapons from here to El Ameur."

The revolver shone against the black paint of the table. When the gendarme turned toward him, the schoolmaster caught the smell of leather and horseflesh.

"Listen, Balducci," Daru said suddenly, "every bit of this disgusts me, and

---

6. I.e., against the French colonial government.

first of all your fellow here. But I won't hand him over. Fight, yes, if I have to. But not that."

The old gendarme stood in front of him and looked at him severely.

"You're being a fool," he said slowly. "I don't like it either. You don't get used to putting a rope on a man even after years of it, and you're even ashamed—yes, ashamed. But you can't let them have their way."

"I won't hand him over," Daru said again.

"It's an order, son, and I repeat it."

"That's right. Repeat to them what I've said to you: I won't hand him over."

Balducci made a visible effort to reflect. He looked at the Arab and at Daru. At last he decided.

"No, I won't tell them anything. If you want to drop us, go ahead; I'll not denounce you. I have an order to deliver the prisoner and I'm doing so. And now you'll just sign this paper for me."

"There's no need. I'll not deny that you left him with me."

"Don't be mean with me. I know you'll tell the truth. You're from hereabouts and you are a man. But you must sign, that's the rule."

Daru opened his drawer, took out a little square bottle of purple ink, the red wooden penholder with the "sergeant-major" pen he used for making models of penmanship, and signed. The gendarme carefully folded the paper and put it into his wallet. Then he moved toward the door.

"I'll see you off," Daru said.

"No," said Balducci. "There's no use being polite. You insulted me."

He looked at the Arab, motionless in the same spot, sniffed peevishly, and turned away toward the door. "Good-by, son," he said. The door shut behind him. Balducci appeared suddenly outside the window and then disappeared. His footsteps were muffled by the snow. The horse stirred on the other side of the wall and several chickens fluttered in fright. A moment later Balducci reappeared outside the window leading the horse by the bridle. He walked toward the little rise without turning around and disappeared from sight with the horse following him. A big stone could be heard bouncing down. Daru walked back toward the prisoner, who, without stirring, never took his eyes off him. "Wait," the schoolmaster said in Arabic and went toward the bedroom. As he was going through the door, he had a second thought, went to the desk, took the revolver, and stuck it in his pocket. Then, without looking back, he went into his room.

For some time he lay on his couch watching the sky gradually close over, listening to the silence. It was this silence that had seemed painful to him during the first days here, after the war. He had requested a post in the little town at the base of the foothills separating the upper plateaus from the desert. There, rocky walls, green and black to the north, pink and lavender to the south, marked the frontier of eternal summer. He had been named to a post farther north, on the plateau itself. In the beginning, the solitude and the silence had been hard for him on these wastelands peopled only by stones. Occasionally, furrows suggested cultivation, but they had been dug to uncover a certain kind of stone good for building. The only plowing here was to harvest rocks. Elsewhere a thin layer of soil accumulated in the hollows would be scraped out to enrich paltry village gardens. This is the way it was: bare rock covered three quarters of the region. Towns sprang up, flourished, then disappeared; men came by, loved one another or fought bitterly, then died. No one in this desert, neither he nor his guest, mattered. And yet, outside this desert neither of them, Daru knew, could have really lived.

When he got up, no noise came from the classroom. He was amazed at the unmixed joy he derived from the mere thought that the Arab might have fled and that he would be alone with no decision to make. But the prisoner was there. He had merely stretched out between the stove and the desk. With eyes open, he was staring at the ceiling. In that position, his thick lips were particularly noticeable, giving him a pouting look. "Come," said Daru. The Arab got up and followed him. In the bedroom, the schoolmaster pointed to a chair near the table under the window. The Arab sat down without taking his eyes off Daru.

"Are you hungry?"

"Yes," the prisoner said.

Daru set the table for two. He took flour and oil, shaped a cake in a frying-pan, and lighted the little stove that functioned on bottled gas. While the cake was cooking, he went out to the shed to get cheese, eggs, dates, and condensed milk. When the cake was done he set it on the window sill to cool, heated some condensed milk diluted with water, and beat up the eggs into an omelette. In one of his motions he knocked against the revolver stuck in his right pocket. He set the bowl down, went into the classroom, and put the revolver in his desk drawer. When he came back to the room, night was falling. He put on the light and served the Arab. "Eat," he said. The Arab took a piece of the cake, lifted it eagerly to his mouth, and stopped short.

"And you?" he asked.

"After you. I'll eat too."

The thick lips opened slightly. The Arab hesitated, then bit into the cake determinedly.

The meal over, the Arab looked at the schoolmaster. "Are you the judge?"

"No, I'm simply keeping you until tomorrow."

"Why do you eat with me?"

"I'm hungry."

The Arab fell silent. Daru got up and went out. He brought back a folding bed from the shed, set it up between the table and the stove, perpendicular to his own bed. From a large suitcase which, upright in a corner, served as a shelf for papers, he took two blankets and arranged them on the camp bed. Then he stopped, felt useless, and sat down on his bed. There was nothing more to do or to get ready. He had to look at this man. He looked at him, therefore, trying to imagine his face bursting with rage. He couldn't do so. He could see nothing but the dark yet shining eyes and the animal mouth.

"Why did you kill him?" he asked in a voice whose hostile tone surprised him.

The Arab looked away.

"He ran away. I ran after him."

He raised his eyes to Daru again and they were full of a sort of woeful interrogation. "Now what will they do to me?"

"Are you afraid?"

He stiffened, turning his eyes away.

"Are you sorry?"

The Arab stared at him openmouthed. Obviously he did not understand.

Daru's annoyance was growing. At the same time he felt awkward and self-conscious with his big body wedged between the two beds.

"Lie down there," he said impatiently. "That's your bed."

The Arab didn't move. He called to Daru:

"Tell me!"

The schoolmaster looked at him.

"Is the gendarme coming back tomorrow?"

"I don't know."

"Are you coming with us?"

"I don't know. Why?"

The prisoner got up and stretched out on top of the blankets, his feet toward the window. The light from the electric bulb shone straight into his eyes and he closed them at once.

"Why?" Daru repeated, standing beside the bed.

The Arab opened his eyes under the blinding light and looked at him, trying not to blink.

"Come with us," he said.

In the middle of the night, Daru was still not asleep. He had gone to bed after undressing completely; he generally slept naked. But when he suddenly realized that he had nothing on, he hesitated. He felt vulnerable and the temptation came to him to put his clothes back on. Then he shrugged his shoulders; after all, he wasn't a child and, if need be, he could break his adversary in two. From his bed he could observe him, lying on his back, still motionless with his eyes closed under the harsh light. When Daru turned out the light, the darkness seemed to coagulate all of a sudden. Little by little, the night came back to life in the window where the starless sky was stirring gently. The schoolmaster soon made out the body lying at his feet. The Arab still did not move, but his eyes seemed open. A faint wind was prowling around the schoolhouse. Perhaps it would drive away the clouds and the sun would reappear.

During the night the wind increased. The hens fluttered a little and then were silent. The Arab turned over on his side with his back to Daru, who thought he heard him moan. Then he listened for his guest's breathing, become heavier and more regular. He listened to that breath so close to him and mused without being able to go to sleep. In this room where he had been sleeping alone for a year, this presence bothered him. But it bothered him also by imposing on him a sort of brotherhood he knew well but refused to accept in the present circumstances. Men who share the same rooms, soldiers or prisoners, develop a strange alliance as if, having cast off their armor with their clothing, they fraternized every evening, over and above their differences, in the ancient community of dream and fatigue. But Daru shook himself; he didn't like such musings, and it was essential to sleep.

A little later, however, when the Arab stirred slightly, the schoolmaster was still not asleep. When the prisoner made a second move, he stiffened, on the alert. The Arab was lifting himself slowly on his arms with almost the motion of a sleepwalker. Seated upright in bed, he waited motionless without turning his head toward Daru, as if he were listening attentively. Daru did not stir; it had just occurred to him that the revolver was still in the drawer of his desk. It was better to act at once. Yet he continued to observe the prisoner, who, with the same slithery motion, put his feet on the ground, waited again, then began to stand up slowly. Daru was about to call out to him when the Arab began to walk, in a quite natural but extraordinarily silent way. He was heading toward the door at the end of the room that opened into the shed. He lifted the latch with precaution and went out, pushing the door behind him but without shutting it. Daru had not stirred. "He is running away," he merely thought. "Good riddance!" Yet he listened attentively. The hens were not fluttering; the guest must be on the plateau. A faint sound of water reached him, and he didn't know what it was until the Arab again stood framed in the doorway, closed the door carefully, and came back to bed without a sound. Then Daru turned his back on him and fell asleep. Still later he seemed, from the depths of his sleep, to hear furtive steps around the schoolhouse. "I'm dreaming! I'm dreaming!" he repeated to himself. And he went on sleeping.

When he awoke, the sky was clear; the loose window let in a cold, pure air. The Arab was asleep, hunched up under the blankets now, his mouth open, utterly relaxed. But when Daru shook him, he started dreadfully, staring at Daru with wild eyes as if he had never seen him and such a frightened expression that the schoolmaster stepped back. "Don't be afraid. It's me. You must eat." The Arab nodded his head and said yes. Calm had returned to his face, but his expression was vacant and listless.

The coffee was ready. They drank it seated together on the folding bed as they munched their pieces of the cake. Then Daru led the Arab under the shed and showed him the faucet where he washed. He went back into the room, folded the blankets and the bed, made his own bed and put the room in order. Then he went through the classroom and out onto the terrace. The sun was already rising in the blue sky; a soft, bright light was bathing the deserted plateau. On the ridge the snow was melting in spots. The stones were about to reappear. Crouched on the edge of the plateau, the schoolmaster looked at the deserted expanse. He thought of Balducci. He had hurt him, for he had sent him off in a way as if he didn't want to be associated with him. He could still hear the gendarme's farewell and, without knowing why, he felt strangely empty and vulnerable. At that moment, from the other side of the schoolhouse, the prisoner coughed. Daru listened to him almost despite himself and then, furious, threw a pebble that whistled through the air before sinking into the snow. That man's stupid crime revolted him, but to hand him over was contrary to honor. Merely thinking of it made him smart with humiliation. And he cursed at one and the same time his own people who had sent him this Arab and the Arab too who had dared to kill and not managed to get away. Daru got up, walked in a circle on the terrace, waited motionless, and then went back into the schoolhouse.

The Arab, leaning over the cement floor of the shed, was washing his teeth with two fingers. Daru looked at him and said: "Come." He went back into the room ahead of the prisoner. He slipped a hunting-jacket on over his sweater and put on walking-shoes. Standing, he waited until the Arab had put on his chèche and sandals. They went into the classroom and the schoolmaster pointed to the exit, saying: "Go ahead." The fellow didn't budge. "I'm coming," said Daru. The Arab went out. Daru went back into the room and made a package of pieces of rusk, dates, and sugar. In the classroom, before going out, he hesitated a second in front of his desk, then crossed the threshold and locked the door. "That's the way," he said. He started toward the east, followed by the prisoner. But, a short distance from the schoolhouse, he thought he heard a slight sound behind them. He retraced his steps and examined the surroundings of the house, there was no one there. The Arab watched him without seeming to understand. "Come on," said Daru.

They walked for an hour and rested beside a sharp peak of limestone. The snow was melting faster and faster and the sun was drinking up the puddles at once, rapidly cleaning the plateau, which gradually dried and vibrated like the air itself. When they resumed walking, the ground rang under their feet. From time to time a bird rent the space in front of them with a joyful cry. Daru breathed in deeply the fresh morning light. He felt a sort of rapture before the vast familiar expanse, now almost entirely yellow under its dome of blue sky. They walked an hour more, descending toward the south. They reached a level height made up of crumbly rocks. From there on, the plateau sloped down, eastward, toward a low plain where there were a few spindly trees and, to the south, toward outcroppings of rock that gave the landscape a chaotic look.

Daru surveyed the two directions. There was nothing but the sky on the horizon. Not a man could be seen. He turned toward the Arab, who was looking at him blankly. Daru held out the package to him. "Take it," he said. "There are dates, bread, and sugar. You can hold out for two days. Here are a thousand francs too." The Arab took the package and the money but kept his full hands at chest level as if he didn't know what to do with what was being given him. "Now look," the schoolmaster said as he pointed in the direction of the east, "there's the way to Tinguit. You have a two-hour walk. At Tinguit you'll find the administration and the police. They are expecting you." The Arab looked toward the east, still holding the package and the money against his chest. Daru took his elbow and turned him rather roughly toward the south. At the foot of the height on which they stood could be seen a faint path. "That's the trail across the plateau. In a day's walk from here you'll find pasturelands and the first nomads. They'll take you in and shelter you according to their law." The Arab had now turned toward Daru and a sort of panic was visible in his expression. "Listen," he said. Daru shook his head: "No, be quiet. Now I'm leaving you." He turned his back on him, took two long steps in the direction of the school, looked hesitantly at the motionless Arab, and started off again. For a few minutes he heard nothing but his own step resounding on the cold ground and did not turn his head. A moment later, however, he turned around. The Arab was still there on the edge of the hill, his arms hanging now, and he was looking at the schoolmaster. Daru felt something rise in his throat. But he swore with impatience, waved vaguely, and started off again. He had already gone some distance when he again stopped and looked. There was no longer anyone on the hill.

Daru hesitated. The sun was now rather high in the sky and was beginning to beat down on his head. The schoolmaster retraced his steps, at first somewhat uncertainly, then with decision. When he reached the little hill, he was bathed in sweat. He climbed it as fast as he could and stopped, out of breath, at the top. The rock-fields to the south stood out sharply against the blue sky, but on the plain to the east a steamy heat was already rising. And in that slight haze, Daru, with heavy heart, made out the Arab walking slowly on the road to prison.

A little later, standing before the window of the classroom, the school-master was watching the clear light bathing the whole surface of the plateau, but he hardly saw it. Behind him on the blackboard, among the winding French rivers, sprawled the clumsily chalked-up words he had just read: "You handed over our brother. You will pay for this." Daru looked at the sky, the plateau, and, beyond, the invisible lands stretching all the way to the sea. In this vast landscape he had loved so much, he was alone.

ALEXANDER SOLZHENITSYN
born 1918

The reputation of Russian novelist Alexander Solzhenitsyn is divided almost equally between two complementary aspects: he continues the tradition of the realistic nine-teenth-century novel (following the example of his compatriots Tolstoy and Dostoev-sky), and he has assumed the role of moral conscience in a modern society where both East and West are fatally flawed. Expelled from the Soviet Union in 1974 and stripped of his citizenship until a new regime restored it in 1990, Solzhenitsyn pro-claims the virtues of an older, religious way of life as the only salvation for a civilization that has been dehumanized by political oppression and materialist greed. Art and literature, he feels, are "endowed with the miraculous power to communicate" and thus make it possible for people to experience situations that they have not lived. This basis of common communication erases divisions and allows us to have "a single system of evaluation for evil deeds and for good ones." Solzhenitsyn tries to encom-pass both the historian's and the moralist's aims when he writes about the history of his own country in the twentieth century and paints a picture of human suffering and moral endurance under oppression. Like Thomas Mann, he includes a range of characters and diverse social types in novels that allude to larger social issues; unlike Mann, his tone is overtly moral and even didactic, especially in his later works. Sol-zhenitsyn is impelled to testify for all those who cannot speak: for the woman in *Cancer Ward* (1968), for example, who says, "Where can I read about us? Will that be only in a hundred years?" His testimony ranges from the more personal account of a day in a concentration camp (*One Day in the Life of Ivan Denisovich*, 1962) to broad historical panoramas such as *August 1914* (1971), which focuses on the defeat of the Russian Second Army in East Prussia during World War I, and *Gulag Archi-pelago* (1973–75), a description of the Soviet concentration-camp system. Clearly he finds the form of the realistic novel—expanded, in *August 1914,* with documents and imitation film scripts—the most appropriate method for representing the truth of history. Solzhenitsyn has little patience with avant-garde literature, which, he says, "has been thought up by empty-headed people." Instead, he tries to render the essence of history by blending documented fact and narrative fiction in his creative works and, in recent years, by editing and publishing (in Russian) historical documents from pre-Revolutionary Russia.

He was born Alexander Isayevich Solzhenitsyn on December 11, 1918, in Kislo-vodsk, in the northern Caucasus. His father had died six months earlier, and his mother supported them in Rostov-on-Don by working as a typist. The family was extremely poor, and—although Solzhenitsyn would have preferred studying literature in Moscow—he was obliged upon graduation from high school to enroll in the local Department of Mathematics at Rostov University. The choice, he says, was a lucky one, for his double degree in mathematics and physics allowed him to spend four years of his prison-camp sentence in a relatively privileged *sharashka,* or research institute, instead of at hard manual labor. During 1939–41 he also took correspondence courses from the Institute of History, Philosophy, and Literature in Moscow. When Solzhenitsyn graduated in 1941, in the middle of World War II, he was immediately inducted into the army, where he drove horse-drawn transport vehicles until he was sent to artillery school in 1942. That November he was put in charge of an artillery reconnaissance battery at the front, a position he held until his sudden arrest in February 1945.

The military censor had found passages in his letters to a friend that were—even under a pseudonym—visibly disrespectful of Stalin, and Solzhenitsyn was sentenced in July to eight years in the prison camps. From 1946 to 1950 he worked as a mathematician in research institutes staffed by prisoners (such as that described in *The First Circle*) but in 1950 was taken to a new kind of camp for political prisoners only, where he worked as a manual laborer. After his sentence was ostensibly over, an administrative order sent him into perpetual exile in southern Kazakhstan. Solzhenitsyn spent the years of exile teaching physics and mathematics in a rural school and wrote prose in secret. The tumor that had developed in his first labor camp grew worse, and in 1954 the author received treatment in a clinic in Tashkent (recalled in the novel *Cancer Ward*). He returned to exile in 1955 (the year he wrote *The First Circle*) and was not released until June 1956. Official rehabilitation came in 1957, and the author moved to Ryazan in European Soviet Union, where he continued to teach physics and mathematics, while secretly writing fiction, until 1962. *Matryona's Home* and *One Day in the Life of Ivan Denisovich* were written during this period.

At the age of forty-two, Solzhenitsyn had written a great deal but published nothing. In 1961, however, it looked as though the climate of political censorship might change. Nikita Khrushchev had just publicly attacked the "cult of personality" and hero worship that had surrounded Stalin, and the poet and editor Alexander Tvardovsky called on writers to portray "truth," not the artificial picture of perfect Soviet society that Stalin preferred. Solzhenitsyn was encouraged to submit *One Day in the Life of Ivan Denisovich*, which appeared (with Khrushchev's approval) in the November 1962 issue of Tvardovsky's journal *Novy Mir*. In January 1963 Tvardovsky published the stories *Matryona's Home* and *Incident at Krechetovka Station* but—with the exception of two short stories and an article on style—Solzhenitsyn would not be allowed to publish anything more in his native land. Even the highly praised *One Day in the Life of Ivan Denisovich* was removed from candidacy for the Lenin Prize in 1963. Khrushchev himself was forced into retirement in October 1964, and the temporary loosening of censorship came to an end. The novel *The First Circle* (already accepted by *Novy Mir*) and two plays (*The Lovegirl and the Innocent,* written 1954; *Candle in the Wind,* written 1960) were prohibited during 1964–65, and *Cancer Ward*, after the type was already partially set, was refused publication permission by the Writers' Union in 1966. Solzhenitsyn protested both the censorship and the fact that the Writers' Union did not defend its members before official attacks; he himself was expelled from the Writers' Union in 1969, after *The First Circle* and *Cancer Ward* had appeared in the West. The only means of publishing officially unacceptable works was to convey them abroad to a Western publishing house or to circulate them in *samizdat* ("self-publishing") form by circulating copies of typewritten manuscripts. Solzhenitsyn made arrangements to have his works published in the West and continued work on the larger historical novels: *The Gulag Archipelago*, which he had begun earlier, and *August 1914*, which he wrote in 1969–70. In 1970 he was awarded the Nobel Prize in literature, which he accepted in absentia because he was afraid that he would not be permitted to re-enter the Soviet Union once he left. After the publication abroad of the first volume of *The Gulag Archipelago*, however, he was arrested in February 1974 and expelled from the country. From 1974 to 1976 Solzhenitsyn lived in Zurich, and in 1976 he moved to the United States, where he lived in seclusion on a farm in Vermont. The expulsion remained in effect until the new president of the Soviet Union, Mikhail S. Gorbachev, offered in 1990 to restore Solzhenitsyn's citizenship as part of an attempt to rehabilitate artists and writers disgraced during previous regimes. Solzhenitsyn did not accept the offer, and later in the year he refused a prize awarded him by the Russian Republic for *The Gulag Archipelago*, noting that the book was not widely available in the Soviet Union and that the "phenomenon of the Gulag" had not been overcome. In September 1991, however, the old charge of treason was officially dropped, and the writer returned to Russia in May 1994 to widespread public acclaim. The novelist expected, and was expected, to be a prominent voice in contemporary Russian society—for a while, he even had a television program. His moral strictures and nostalgia for a simpler past, however, proved alien to a post-Soviet society intent on prosperity. Still a respected moral authority, Solzhenitsyn seems nowadays fated to speak from the margin.

Solzhenitsyn's first three novels have in common the themes of imprisonment, of personal suffering, and of the moral purity to be gained by those who endure and learn from their suffering. *One Day in the Life of Ivan Denisovich* is the story, told at a very basic level of hunger, cold, and brutally demanding work, of one fairly good day in the life of a prison-camp inmate, the peasant Ivan Denisovich Shukhov. When the book appeared, it was the first public recognition of Stalin's prison-camp system, and Solzhenitsyn's matter-of-fact narration of the prisoners' day-to-day struggle to survive and retain their humanity shocked readers in Russia and in the West. Shukhov is not a heroic figure, or even portrayed as particularly intelligent, but in his deprivation he has found a core of inner spiritual strength that might well be envied, Solzhenitsyn suggests, by those outside prison who compromise their principles, and accede to injustices, for fear of losing what they have.

The worlds of *Cancer Ward* and *The First Circle* are more privileged than that of *One Day in the Life of Ivan Denisovich*, but each retains the atmosphere of imprisonment and imminent death, and each composes a picture of society by juxtaposing characters with different backgrounds and different points of view. Solzhenitsyn calls this technique of juxtaposition "polyphonic" or many-voiced: he writes a "polyphonic novel with concrete details specifying the time and place of action. A novel without a central hero. . . . Each character becomes central when the action reverts to him." In *Cancer Ward*, thirteen patients representing different social and political classes are brought together in a ward at the cancer clinic in Tashkent; this microcosm of Soviet society is faced with sickness, suffering, death, and an authoritarian medical system that administers treatment without explaining it (or its side effects) to the patient. The ward becomes a metaphor for Soviet society, a metaphor given further dimensions when the inmates articulate their different values in response to a story by Tolstoy: *What Men Live By*. The ultimate question is not collective but individual, says Kostoglotov: a man may be a member of a collective, "but only while he's alive. . . . He has to die alone."

The same emphasis on the testing of individual values occurs in *The First Circle*, a novel whose title refers to the least painful circle of Hell in Dante's *Inferno* and indicates here the *sharashka*, or prisoner-staffed research section of the Mavrino Institute. The prisoners working in the *sharashka* are under pressure from their superiors (who are under pressure from Stalin) to produce spying devices, including a method for identifying voices on taped telephone calls, and an impregnable telephone coding system for Stalin. If they do not produce satisfactory work, they are sent back to almost-certain death in the labor camps (the lower circles of this Hell); if they do, they become part of the police state. No one is free, not even the dictator who is imprisoned by his own suspicions. The whole society of *The First Circle* is an Inferno, and only by sacrificing everything can one hope to retain spiritual freedom.

Solzhenitsyn turned next to a larger panoramic scope, where the authorial voice would dominate and interpret a mass of historical information. *August 1914* is the first volume of a planned trilogy inquiring into the course of modern Russian history: later volumes (of which a few chapters have appeared in journals and in the fictional portrait *Lenin in Zurich*) are titled *October 1916* and *March 1917*, after famous dates in the Russian Revolution. *August 1914* describes the defeat of the Second Russian Army in East Prussia during World War I and—in a consciously fragmented style that moves from scene to scene, includes extracts of documents, newspapers, proverbs, and songs, and provides sections marked "Screen" that imitate film scripts— attempts to depict a broad social panorama with characters from all classes, thus recording a moment in history from an epic point of view.

The second broad panorama is *The Gulag Archipelago*, a three-volume, seven- section account of Stalin's widespread prison camp system. (*Gulag* stands for "Chief Administration of Corrective Labor Camps," camps that were scattered across the Soviet Union like islands in a sea [the archipelago].) Solzhenitsyn describes the horror of these camps in quasi-anecdotal form, using personal experience, oral testimony, excerpts of documents, written eyewitness reports, and altogether a massive collection of evidence accumulated inside *An Attempt at Artistic Investigation* (the subtitle). In this book, perhaps even more than in *August 1914*, there is a tension between the bare facts that Solzhenitsyn transmits and the spiritual interpretation of history into which they fit. The author is overtly present, commenting, guessing intuititively from context when particular facts are missing, and stressing in his own voice the theme that has pervaded all his work: the purification of the soul through suffering. The title of the fourth section, "The Soul and Barbed Wire," symbolizes the recurrent opposition of soul and imprisoning society that has become familiar to his readers.

Since Solzhenitsyn is such a dedicated anti-Communist and anti-Marxist, many Westerners have jumped to the conclusion that he is in favor of the Western demo- cratic system. Such is not the case. He looks back to an earlier, more nationalist and spiritual authoritarianism represented for him by the image of Holy Russia: "For a thousand years Russia lived with an authoritarian order . . . that authoritarian order possessed a strong moral foundation . . . Christian Orthodoxy." In a speech given at Harvard in 1978, *A World Split Apart,* he criticized Western democracy's "herd instinct" and "need to accommodate mass standards," its emphasis on "well-being" and "constant desire to have still more things," its "spiritual exhaustion" in which "mediocrity triumphs under the guise of democratic restraints." Once again, he returns to the theme of purification by suffering that permeates his fiction: "We have been through a spiritual training far in advance of Western experience. The complex and deadly crush of life has produced stronger, deeper, and more interesting person- alities than those generated by standardized Western well-being."

One of those strong and deep personalities is surely Matryona in *Matryona's Home.* Solzhenitsyn's story, which is probably modeled on the old Russian literary form of the saint's life, is a testimony to Matryona's absolute simplicity, her refusal to possess anything more than the basic necessities (she will not raise a pig to kill for food), her willingness to help others without promise of reward, and finally to let her greedy in- laws tear down part of her own home and cart it off. The narrator of the story, like Solzhenitsyn an ex-convict and mathematics teacher, has buried himself deep in the country to avoid signs of modern Soviet society and to find—if it still exists—an image of the Old Russia. The town of Talnovo itself is tainted, not just by the *kolkhoz* (collective farm) system, which ceases to consider Matryona part of the collective as soon as she becomes ill, but also by the laziness, selfishness, and predatory greed of its inhabitants. Yet there remains Matryona. Her life has been filled with disappoint- ment and deprivation, and she remains an outsider in a materialist society that despises her lack of acquisitive instinct, but she seems to live in a dimension of spiritual contentment and love that is unknown to those around her. Only the nar- rator, who has learned to value essential qualities from his own experience in the concentration camps, is able finally to recognize her as "the righteous one," one of those whose spiritual merit seems alien to modern society yet is needed to save society from divine retribution (Genesis 18.23–33).

PRONOUNCING GLOSSARY

The following list uses common English syllables and stress accents to provide rough equivalents of selected words whose pronunciation may be unfamiliar to the general reader.

Matryona Vasilyevna: *mah-tryaw'-nuh*   Vysokoe Polye: *vi-saw'-kuh-yuh*
    vah-seel'-yev-nuh   *pawl'-yuh*

Matryona's Home[1]

1

A hundred and fifteen miles from Moscow trains were still slowing down to a crawl a good six months after it happened. Passengers stood glued to the windows or went out to stand by the doors. Was the line under repair, or what? Would the train be late?

It was all right. Past the crossing the train picked up speed again and the passengers went back to their seats.

Only the engine drivers knew what it was all about.

The engine drivers and I.

In the summer of 1953 I was coming back from the hot and dusty desert, just following my nose—so long as it led me back to European Russia. Nobody waited or wanted me at my particular place, because I was a little matter of ten years overdue. I just wanted to get to the central belt, away from the great heat, close to the leafy muttering of forests. I wanted to efface myself, to lose myself in deepest Russia . . . if it was still anywhere to be found.

A year earlier I should have been lucky to get a job carrying a hod this side of the Urals.[2] They wouldn't have taken me as an electrician on a decent construction job. And I had an itch to teach. Those who knew told me that it was a waste of money buying a ticket, that I should have a journey for nothing.

But things were beginning to move.[3] When I went up the stairs of the N—— Regional Education Department and asked for the Personnel Section, I was surprised to find Personnel sitting behind a glass partition, like in a chemist's shop, instead of the usual black leather-padded door. I went timidly up to the window, bowed, and asked, "Please, do you need any mathematicians somewhere where the trains don't run? I should like to settle there for good."

They passed every dot and comma in my documents through a fine comb, went from one room to another, made telephone calls. It was something out of the ordinary for them too—people always wanted the towns, the bigger

---

1. Translated by H. T. Willetts.   2. Mountain chain separating European Russia from (Asiatic) Siberia.
3. Stalin's death, on March 5, 1953, brought a gradual relaxation of the Soviet state's repressive policies.

the better. And lo and behold, they found just the place for me—Vysokoe Polye.[4] The very sound of it gladdened my heart.

Vysokoe Polye did not belie its name. It stood on rising ground, with gentle hollows and other little hills around it. It was enclosed by an unbroken ring of forest. There was a pool behind a weir. Just the place where I wouldn't mind living and dying. I spent a long time sitting on a stump in a coppice and wishing with all my heart that I didn't need breakfast and dinner every day but could just stay here and listen to the branches brushing against the roof in the night, with not a wireless anywhere to be heard and the whole world silent.

Alas, nobody baked bread in Vysokoe Polye. There was nothing edible on sale. The whole village lugged its victuals in sacks from the big town.

I went back to the Personnel Section and raised my voice in prayer at the little window. At first they wouldn't even talk to me. But then they started going from one room to another, made a telephone call, scratched with their pens, and stamped on my orders the word "Torfoprodukt."

Torfoprodukt? Turgenev[5] never knew that you can put words like that together in Russian.

On the station building at Torfoprodukt, an antiquated temporary hut of gray wood, hung a stern notice, BOARD TRAINS ONLY FROM THE PASSENGERS' HALL. A further message had been scratched on the boards with a nail, *And Without Tickets.* And by the booking office, with the same melancholy wit, somebody had carved for all time the words, *No Tickets.* It was only later that I fully appreciated the meaning of these addenda. Getting to Torfoprodukt was easy. But not getting away.

Here too, deep and trackless forests had once stood and were still standing after the Revolution. Then they were chopped down by the peat cutters and the neighboring kolkhoz.[6] Its chairman, Shashkov, had razed quite a few hectares of timber and sold it at a good profit down in the Odessa region.

The workers' settlement sprawled untidily among the peat bogs—monotonous shacks from the thirties, and little houses with carved façades and glass verandas, put up in the fifties. But inside these houses I could see no partitions reaching up to the ceilings, so there was no hope of renting a room with four real walls.

Over the settlement hung smoke from the factory chimney. Little locomotives ran this way and that along narrow-gauge railway lines, giving out more thick smoke and piercing whistles, pulling loads of dirty brown peat in slabs and briquettes. I could safely assume that in the evening a loudspeaker would be crying its heart out over the door of the club and there would be drunks roaming the streets and, sooner or later, sticking knives in each other.

This was what my dream about a quiet corner of Russia had brought me to—when I could have stayed where I was and lived in an adobe hut looking out on the desert, with a fresh breeze at night and only the starry dome of the sky overhead.

I couldn't sleep on the station bench, and as soon as it started getting light

---

4. High meadow.   **5.** A master of Russian prose style (1818–1883), best known for the novel *Fathers and Sons* (1861) and for a series of sympathetic sketches of peasant life published as *A Sportsman's Sketches* (1882). *Torfoprodukt:* peat product; a new word made by combining two words of Germanic origin: *torf* ("peat") and *produckt.*   **6.** Collective farm.

I went for another stroll round the settlement. This time I saw a tiny marketplace. Only one woman stood there at that early hour, selling milk, and I took a bottle and started drinking it on the spot.

I was struck by the way she talked. Instead of a normal speaking voice, she used an ingratiating singsong, and her words were the ones I was longing to hear when I left Asia for this place.

"Drink, and God bless you. You must be a stranger round here?"

"And where are you from?" I asked, feeling more cheerful.

I learnt that the peat workings weren't the only thing, that over the railway lines there was a hill, and over the hill a village, that this village was Talnovo, and it had been there ages ago, when the "gipsy woman" lived in the big house and the wild woods stood all round. And farther on there was a whole countryside full of villages—Chaslitsy, Ovintsy, Spudni, Shevertni, Shestimirovo, deeper and deeper into the woods, farther and farther from the railway, up towards the lakes.

The names were like a soothing breeze to me. They held a promise of backwoods Russia. I asked my new acquaintance to take me to Talnovo after the market was over and find a house for me to lodge in.

It appeared that I was a lodger worth having: in addition to my rent, the school offered a truckload of peat for the winter to whoever took me. The woman's ingratiating smile gave way to a thoughtful frown. She had no room herself, because she and her husband were "keeping" her aged mother, so she took me first to one lot of relatives then to another. But there wasn't a separate room to be had and both places were crowded and noisy.

We had come to a dammed-up stream that was short of water and had a little bridge over it. No other place in all the village took my fancy as this did: there were two or three willows, a lopsided house, ducks swimming on the pond, geese shaking themselves as they stepped out of the water.

"Well, perhaps we might just call on Matryona," said my guide, who was getting tired of me by now. "Only it isn't so neat and cozy-like in her house, neglects things she does. She's unwell."

Matryona's house stood quite near by. Its row of four windows looked out on the cold backs, the two slopes of the roof were covered with shingles, and a little attic window was decorated in the old Russian style. But the shingles were rotting, the beam ends of the house and the once mighty gates had turned gray with age, and there were gaps in the little shelter over the gate.

The small gate was fastened, but instead of knocking my companion just put her hand under and turned the catch, a simple device to prevent animals from straying. The yard was not covered, but there was a lot under the roof of the house. As you went through the outer door a short flight of steps rose to a roomy landing, which was open, to the roof high overhead. To the left, other steps led up to the top room, which was a separate structure with no stove, and yet another flight led down to the basement. To the right lay the house proper, with its attic and its cellar.

It had been built a long time ago, built sturdily, to house a big family, and now one lonely woman of nearly sixty lived in it.

When I went into the cottage she was lying on the Russian stove[7] under

___

7. A large stove built of masonry, used for both heating and cooking.

a heap of those indeterminate dingy rags which are so precious to a working man or woman.

The spacious room, and especially the big part near the windows, was full of rubber plants in pots and tubs standing on stools and benches. They peopled the householder's loneliness like a speechless but living crowd. They had been allowed to run wild, and they took up all the scanty light on the north side. In what was left of the light, and half-hidden by the stovepipe, the mistress of the house looked yellow and weak. You could see from her clouded eyes that illness had drained all the strength out of her.

While we talked she lay on the stove face downward, without a pillow, her head toward the door, and I stood looking up at her. She showed no pleasure at getting a lodger, just complained about the wicked disease she had. She was just getting over an attack; it didn't come upon her every month, but when it did, "It hangs on two or three days so as I shan't manage to get up and wait on you. I've room and to spare, you can live here if you like."

Then she went over the list of other housewives with whom I should be quieter and cozier and wanted me to make the round of them. But I had already seen that I was destined to settle in this dimly lit house with the tarnished mirror, in which you couldn't see yourself, and the two garish posters (one advertising books, the other about the harvest), bought for a ruble each to brighten up the walls.

Matryona Vasilyevna made me go off round the village again, and when I called on her the second time she kept trying to put me off, "We're not clever, we can't cook, I don't know how we shall suit. . . ." But this time she was on her feet when I got there, and I thought I saw a glimmer of pleasure in her eyes to see me back. We reached an agreement about the rent and the load of peat which the school would deliver.

Later on I found out that, year in year out, it was a long time since Matryona Vasilyevna had earned a single ruble. She didn't get a pension. Her relatives gave her very little help. In the kolkhoz she had worked not for money but for credits; the marks recording her labor days in her well-thumbed workbook.

So I moved in with Matryona Vasilyevna. We didn't divide the room. Her bed was in the corner between the door and the stove, and I unfolded my camp bed by one window and pushed Matryona's beloved rubber plants out of the light to make room for a little table by another. The village had electric light, laid on back in the twenties, from Shatury. The newspapers were writing about "Ilyich's little lamps," but the peasants talked wide-eyed about "Tsar Light."[8]

Some of the better-off people in the village might not have thought Matryona's house much of a home, but it kept us snug enough that autumn and winter. The roof still held the rain out, and the freezing winds could not blow the warmth of the stove away all at once, though it was cold by morning, especially when the wind blew on the shabby side.

In addition to Matryona and myself, a cat, some mice, and some cockroaches lived in the house.

8. The newspapers reflect the new order. *Ilyich:* i.e., Vladimir Ilyich Lenin (1870–1924), leader of the 1917 Russian Revolution and first head of the new state. The peasants still think in terms of the emperor (*Tsar,* or czar).

The cat was no longer young, and was gammy-legged as well. Matryona had taken her in out of pity, and she had stayed. She walked on all four feet but with a heavy limp: one of her feet was sore and she favored it. When she jumped from the stove she didn't land with the soft sound a cat usually makes, but with a heavy thud as three of her feet struck the floor at once— such a heavy thud that until I got used to it, it gave me a start. This was because she stuck three feet out together to save the fourth.

It wasn't because the cat couldn't deal with them that there were mice in the cottage: she would pounce into the corner like lightning and come back with a mouse between her teeth. But the mice were usually out of reach because somebody, back in the good old days, had stuck embossed wallpaper of a greenish color on Matryona's walls, and not just one layer of it but five. The layers held together all right, but in many places the whole lot had come away from the wall, giving the room a sort of inner skin. Between the timber of the walls and the skin of wallpaper the mice had made themselves runs where they impudently scampered about, running at times right up to the ceiling. The cat followed their scamperings with angry eyes, but couldn't get at them.

Sometimes the cat ate cockroaches as well, but they made her sick. The only thing the cockroaches respected was the partition which screened the mouth of the Russian stove and the kitchen from the best part of the room. They did not creep into the best room. But the kitchen at night swarmed with them, and if I went in late in the evening for a drink of water and switched on the light the whole floor, the big bench, and even the wall would be one rustling brown mass. From time to time I brought home some borax from the school laboratory and we mixed it with dough to poison them. There would be fewer cockroaches for a while, but Matryona was afraid that we might poison the cat as well. We stopped putting down poison and the cockroaches multiplied anew.

At night, when Matryona was already asleep and I was working at my table, the occasional rapid scamper of mice behind the wallpaper would be drowned in the sustained and ceaseless rustling of cockroaches behind the screen, like the sound of the sea in the distance. But I got used to it because there was nothing evil in it, nothing dishonest. Rustling was life to them.

I even got used to the crude beauty on the poster, forever reaching out from the wall to offer me Belinsky, Panferov,[9] and a pile of other books— but never saying a word. I got used to everything in Matryona's cottage.

Matryona got up at four or five o'clock in the morning. Her wall clock was twenty-seven years old and had been bought in the village shop. It was always fast, but Matryona didn't worry about that—just as long as it didn't lose and make her late in the morning. She switched on the light behind the kitchen screen and moving quietly, considerately, doing her best not to make a noise, she lit the stove, went to milk the goat (all the livestock she had was this one dirty-white goat with twisted horns), fetched water and boiled it in three iron pots: one for me, one for herself, and one for the goat. She fetched potatoes from the cellar, picking out the littlest for

---

9. Fedor Ivanovich Panferov (1896–1960), socialist-realist writer popular in the 1920s, best known for his novel *The Iron Flood*. Vissarion Grigoryevich Belinsky (1811–1848), Russian literary critic who emphasized social and political ideas.

the goat, little ones for herself and egg-sized ones for me. There were no big ones, because her garden was sandy, had not been manured since the war, and she always planted with potatoes, potatoes, and potatoes again, so that it wouldn't grow big ones.

I scarcely heard her about her morning tasks. I slept late, woke up in the wintry daylight, stretched a bit, and stuck my head out from under my blanket and my sheepskin. These, together with the prisoner's jerkin round my legs and a sack stuffed with straw underneath me, kept me warm in bed even on nights when the cold wind rattled our wobbly windows from the north. When I heard the discreet noises on the other side of the screen I spoke to her, slowly and deliberately:

"Good morning, Matryona Vasilyevna!"

And every time the same good-natured words came to me from behind the screen. They began with a warm, throaty gurgle, the sort of sound grandmothers make in fairy tales.

"M-m-m . . . same to you too!"

And after a little while, "Your breakfast's ready for you now."

She didn't announce what was for breakfast, but it was easy to guess: taters in their jackets or tatty soup (as everybody in the village called it), or barley gruel (no other grain could be bought in Torfoprodukt that year, and even the barley you had to fight for, because it was the cheapest and people bought it up by the sack to fatten their pigs on it). It wasn't always salted as it should be, it was often slightly burnt, it furred the palate and the gums, and it gave me heartburn.

But Matryona wasn't to blame: there was no butter in Torfoprodukt either, margarine was desperately short, and only mixed cooking fat was plentiful, and when I got to know it, I saw that the Russian stove was not convenient for cooking: the cook cannot see the pots and they are not heated evenly all round. I suppose the stove came down to our ancestors from the Stone Age, because you can stoke it up once before daylight, and food and water, mash and swill will keep warm in it all day long. And it keeps you warm while you sleep.

I ate everything that was cooked for me without demur, patiently putting aside anything uncalled-for that I came across: a hair, a bit of peat, a cockroach's leg. I hadn't the heart to find fault with Matryona. After all, she had warned me herself.

"We aren't clever, we can't cook—I don't know how we shall suit. . . ."

"Thank you," I said quite sincerely.

"What for? For what is your own?" she answered, disarming me with a radiant smile. And, with a guileless look of her faded blue eyes, she would ask, "And what shall I cook you for just now?"

For just now meant for supper. I ate twice a day, like at the front. What could I order for just now? It would have to be one of the same old things, taters or tater soup.

I resigned myself to it, because I had learned by now not to look for the meaning of life in food. More important to me was the smile on her roundish face, which I tried in vain to catch when at last I had earned enough to buy a camera. As soon as she saw the cold eye of the lens upon her, Matryona assumed a strained or else an exaggeratedly severe expression.

Just once I did manage to get a snap of her looking through the window into the street and smiling at something.

Matryona had a lot of worries that winter. Her neighbors put it into her head to try and get a pension. She was all alone in the world, and when she began to be seriously ill she had been dismissed from the kolkhoz as well. Injustices had piled up, one on top of another. She was ill, but was not regarded as a disabled person. She had worked for a quarter of a century in the kolkhoz, but it was a kolkhoz and not a factory, so she was not entitled to a pension for herself. She could only try and get one for her husband, for the loss of her breadwinner. But she had had no husband for twelve years now, not since the beginning of the war, and it wasn't easy to obtain all the particulars from different places about his length of service and how much he had earned. What a bother it was getting those forms through! Getting somebody to certify that he'd earned, say, three hundred rubles a month; that she lived alone and nobody helped her; what year she was born in. Then all this had to be taken to the Pension Office. And taken somewhere else to get all the mistakes corrected. And taken back again. Then you had to find out whether they would give you a pension.

To make it all more difficult the Pension Office was twelve miles east of Talnovo, the Rural Council Offices six miles to the west, the Factory District Council an hour's walk to the north. They made her run around from office to office for two months on end, to get an *i* dotted or a *t* crossed. Every trip took a day. She goes down to the Rural District Council—and the secretary isn't there today. Secretaries of rural councils often aren't here today. So come again tomorrow. Tomorrow the secretary is in, but he hasn't got his rubber stamp. So come again the next day. And the day after that back she goes yet again, because all her papers are pinned together and some cockeyed clerk has signed the wrong one.

"They shove me around, Ignatich," she used to complain to me after these fruitless excursions. "Worn out with it I am."

But she soon brightened up. I found that she had a sure means of putting herself in a good humor. She worked. She would grab a shovel and go off to pull potatoes. Or she would tuck a sack under her arm and go after peat. Or take a wicker basket and look for berries deep in the woods. When she'd been bending her back to bushes instead of office desks for a while, and her shoulders were aching from a heavy load, Matryona would come back cheerful, at peace with the world and smiling her nice smile.

"I'm on to a good thing now, Ignatich. I know where to go for it (peat she meant), a lovely place it is."

"But surely my peat is enough, Matryona Vasilyevna? There's a whole truckload of it."

"Pooh! Your peat! As much again, and then as much again, that might be enough. When the winter gets really stiff and the wind's battling at the windows, it blows the heat out of the house faster than you can make the stove up. Last year we got heaps and heaps of it. I'd have had three loads in by now. But they're out to catch us. They've summoned one woman from our village already."

That's how it was. The frightening breath of winter was already in the air. There were forests all round, and no fuel to be had anywhere. Excavators roared away in the bogs, but there was no peat on sale to the villagers. It was delivered, free, to the bosses and to the people round the bosses, and teachers, doctors, and workers got a load each. The people of Talnovo were not supposed to get any peat, and they weren't supposed to ask about it. The chairman of the kolkhoz walked about the village looking people in the eye while he gave his orders or stood chatting and talked about anything you liked except fuel. He was stocked up. Who said anything about winter coming?

So just as in the old days they used to steal the squire's wood, now they pinched peat from the trust. The women went in parties of five or ten so that they would be less frightened. They went in the daytime. The peat cut during the summer had been stacked up all over the place to dry. That's the good thing about peat, it can't be carted off as soon as it's cut. It lies around drying till autumn, or, if the roads are bad, till the snow starts falling. This was when the women used to come and take it. They could get six peats in a sack if it was damp, or ten if it was dry. A sackful weighed about half a hundredweight and it sometimes had to be carried over two miles. This was enough to make the stove up once. There were two hundred days in the winter. The Russian stove had to be lit in the mornings, and the "Dutch"[1] stove in the evenings.

"Why beat about the bush?" said Matryona angrily to someone invisible. "Since there've been no more horses, what you can't have around yourself you haven't got. My back never heals up. Winter you're pulling sledges, summer it's bundles on your back, it's God's truth I'm telling you."

The women went more than once in a day. On good days Matryona brought six sacks home. She piled my peat up where it could be seen and hid her own under the passageway, boarding up the hole every night.

"If they don't just happen to think of it, the devils will never find it in their born days," said Matryona smiling and wiping the sweat from her brow.

What could the peat trust do? Its establishment didn't run to a watchman for every bog. I suppose they had to show a rich haul in their returns, and then write off so much for crumbling, so much washed away by the rain. Sometimes they would take it into their heads to put out patrols and try to catch the women as they came into the village. The women would drop their sacks and scatter. Or somebody would inform and there would be a house-to-house search. They would draw up a report on the stolen peat and threaten a court action. The women would stop fetching it for a while, but the approach of winter drove them out with sledges in the middle of the night.

When I had seen a little more of Matryona I noticed that, apart from cooking and looking after the house, she had quite a lot of other jobs to do every day. She kept all her jobs, and the proper times for them, in her head and always knew when she woke up in the morning how her day would be occupied. Apart from fetching peat and stumps which the tractors unearthed in the bogs, apart from the cranberries which she put to soak in big jars for the winter ("Give your teeth an edge, Ignatich," she used to say when she offered me some), apart from digging potatoes and all the coming and going to do

---

1. Not a real tiled Dutch stove, but a cheap small stove (probably made from an oil barrel) that provided heat with less fuel than a big Russian stove.

with her pension, she had to get hay from somewhere for her one and only dirty-white goat.

"Why don't you keep a cow, Matryona?"

Matryona stood there in her grubby apron, by the opening in the kitchen screen, facing my table, and explained to me.

"Oh, Ignatich, there's enough milk from the goat for me. And if I started keeping a cow she'd eat me out of house and home in no time. You can't cut the grass by the railway track, because it belongs to the railway, and you can't cut any in the woods, because it belongs to the foresters, and they won't let me have any at the kolkhoz because I'm not a member any more, they reckon. And those who are members have to work there every day till the white flies swarm and make their own hay when there's snow on the ground—what's the good of grass like that? In the old days they used to be sweating to get the hay in at midsummer, between the end of June and the end of July, while the grass was sweet and juicy."

So it meant a lot of work for Matryona to gather enough hay for one skinny little goat. She took her sickle and a sack and went off early in the morning to places where she knew there was grass growing—round the edges of fields, on the roadside, on hummocks in the bog. When she had stuffed her sack with heavy fresh grass she dragged it home and spread it out in her yard to dry. From a sackful of grass she got one forkload of dry hay.

The farm had a new chairman, sent down from the town not long ago, and the first thing he did was to cut down the garden plots for those who were not fit to work. He left Matryona a third of an acre of sand—when there was over a thousand square yards just lying idle on the other side of the fence. Yet when they were short of working hands, when the women dug in their heels and wouldn't budge, the chairman's wife would come to see Matryona. She was from the town as well, a determined woman whose short gray coat and intimidating glare gave her a somewhat military appearance. She walked into the house without so much as a good morning and looked sternly at Matryona. Matryona was uneasy.

"Well now, Comrade Vasilyevna," said the chairman's wife, drawing out her words. "You will have to help the kolkhoz! You will have to go and help cart manure out tomorrow!"

A little smile of forgiveness wrinkled Matryona's face—as though she understood the embarrassment which the chairman's wife must feel at not being able to pay her for her work.

"Well—er," she droned. "I'm not well, of course, and I'm not attached to you any more . . . ," then she hurried to correct herself, "What time should I come then?"

"And bring your own fork!" the chairman's wife instructed her. Her stiff skirt crackled as she walked away.

"Think of that!" grumbled Matryona as the door closed. "Bring your own fork! They've got neither forks nor shovels at the kolkhoz. And I don't have a man who'll put a handle on for me!"

She went on thinking about it out loud all evening.

"What's the good of talking, Ignatich. I must help, of course. Only the way they work it's all a waste of time—don't know whether they're coming or going. The women stand propped up on their shovels and waiting for the factory whistle to blow twelve o'clock. Or else they get on to adding up who's earned what and who's turned up for work and who hasn't. Now what I call work, there isn't a sound out of anybody, only—oh dear, dear—dinner time's soon rolled round—what, getting dark already."

In the morning she went off with her fork.

But it wasn't just the kolkhoz—any distant relative, or just a neighbor, could come to Matryona of an evening and say, "Come and give me a hand tomorrow, Matryona. We'll finish pulling the potatoes."

Matryona couldn't say no. She gave up what she should be doing next and went to help her neighbor, and when she came back she would say without a trace of envy, "Ah, you should see the size of her potatoes, Ignatich! It was a joy to dig them up. I didn't want to leave the allotment, God's truth I didn't."

Needless to say, not a garden could be plowed without Matryona's help. The women of Talnovo had got it neatly worked out that it was a longer and harder job for one woman to dig her garden with a spade than for six of them to put themselves in harness and plow six gardens. So they sent for Matryona to help them.

"Well—did you pay her?" I asked sometimes.

"She won't take money. You have to try and hide it on her when she's not looking."

Matryona had yet another troublesome chore when her turn came to feed the herdsmen. One of them was a hefty deaf mute, the other a boy who was never without a cigaret in his drooling mouth. Matryona's turn came round only every six weeks, but it put her to great expense. She went to the shop to buy canned fish and was lavish with sugar and butter, things she never ate herself. It seems that the housewives showed off in this way, trying to outdo one another in feeding the herdsmen.

"You've got to be careful with tailors and herdsmen," Matryona explained. "They'll spread your name all round the village if something doesn't suit them."

And every now and then attacks of serious illness broke in on this life that was already crammed with troubles. Matryona would be off her feet for a day or two, lying flat out on the stove. She didn't complain and didn't groan, but she hardly stirred either. On these days Masha, Matryona's closest friend from her earliest years, would come to look after the goat and light the stove. Matryona herself ate nothing, drank nothing, asked for nothing. To call in the doctor from the clinic at the settlement would have seemed strange in Talnovo and would have given the neighbors something to talk about—what does she think she is, a lady? They did call her in once, and she arrived in a real temper and told Matryona to come down to the clinic when she was on her feet again. Matryona went, although she didn't really want to; they took specimens and sent them off to the district hospital—and that's the last anybody heard about it. Matryona was partly to blame herself.

But there was work waiting to be done, and Matryona soon started getting up again, moving slowly at first and then as briskly as ever.

"You never saw me in the old days, Ignatich. I'd lift any sack you liked, I didn't think a hundredweight was too heavy. My father-in-law used to say, 'Matryona, you'll break your back.' And my brother-in-law didn't have to come and help me lift on the cart. Our horse was a warhorse, a big strong one."

"What do you mean, a warhorse?"

"They took ours for the war and gave us this one instead—he'd been wounded. But he turned out a bit spirited. Once he bolted with the sledge right into the lake, the men folk hopped out of the way, but I grabbed the bridle, as true as I'm here, and stopped him. Full of oats that horse was. They liked to feed their horses well in our village. If a horse feels his oats he doesn't know what heavy means."

But Matryona was a long way from being fearless. She was afraid of fire, afraid of "the lightning," and most of all she was for some reason afraid of trains.

"When I had to go to Cherusti,[2] the train came up from Nechaevka way with its great big eyes popping out and the rails humming away—put me in a regular fever. My knees started knocking. God's truth I'm telling you!" Matryona raised her shoulders as though she surprised herself.

"Maybe it's because they won't give people tickets, Matryona Vasilyevna?"

"At the window? They try to shove only first-class tickets on to you. And the train was starting to move. We dashed about all over the place, 'Give us tickets for pity's sake.' "

"The men folk had climbed on top of the carriages. Then we found a door that wasn't locked and shoved straight in without tickets—and all the carriages were empty, they were all empty, you could stretch out on the seat if you wanted to. Why they wouldn't give us tickets, the hardhearted parasites, I don't know. . . ."

Still, before winter came, Matryona's affairs were in a better state than ever before. They started paying her at last a pension of eighty rubles. Besides this she got just over one hundred from the school and me.

Some of her neighbors began to be envious.

"Hm! Matryona can live forever now! If she had any more money, she wouldn't know what to do with it at her age."

Matryona had some new felt boots made. She bought a new jerkin. And she had an overcoat made out of the worn-out railwayman's greatcoat given to her by the engine driver from Cherusti who had married Kira, her foster daughter. The hump-backed village tailor put a padded lining under the cloth and it made a marvelous coat, such as Matryona had never worn before in all her sixty years.

In the middle of winter Matryona sewed two hundred rubles into the lining of this coat for her funeral. This made her quite cheerful.

"Now my mind's a bit easier, Ignatich."

December went by, January went by—and in those two months Matryona's illness held off. She started going over to Masha's house more often in the evening, to sit chewing sunflower seeds with her. She herself didn't invite guests in the evening out of consideration for my work. Once, on the feast of the Epiphany, I came back from school and found a party going on and was introduced to Matryona's three sisters, who called her "nan-nan" or "nanny" because she was the oldest. Until then not much had been heard of

2. About 100 miles east of Moscow and some 250 miles northwest of Nechaevka.

the sisters in our cottage—perhaps they were afraid that Matryona might ask them for help.

But one ominous event cast a shadow on the holiday for Matryona. She went to the church three miles away for the blessing of the water and put her pot down among the others. When the blessing was over, the women went rushing and jostling to get their pots back again. There were a lot of women in front of Matryona and when she got there her pot was missing, and no other vessel had been left behind. The pot had vanished as though the devil had run off with it.

Matryona went round the worshipers asking them, "Have any of you girls accidentally mistook somebody else's holy water? In a pot?"

Nobody owned up. There had been some boys there, and boys got up to mischief sometimes. Matryona came home sad.

No one could say that Matryona was a devout believer. If anything, she was a heathen, and her strongest beliefs were superstitious: you mustn't go into the garden on the fast of St. John or there would be no harvest next year. A blizzard meant that somebody had hanged himself. If you pinched your foot in the door, you could expect a guest. All the time I lived with her I didn't once see her say her prayers or even cross herself. But, whatever job she was doing, she began with a "God bless us," and she never failed to say "God bless you," when I set out for school. Perhaps she did say her prayers, but on the quiet, either because she was shy or because she didn't want to embarrass me. There were icons[3] on the walls. Ordinary days they were left in darkness, but for the vigil of a great feast, or on the morning of a holiday, Matryona would light the little lamp.

She had fewer sins on her conscience than her gammy-legged cat. The cat did kill mice.

Now that her life was running more smoothly, Matryona started listening more carefully to my radio. (I had, of course, installed a speaker, or as Matryona called it, a peeker.)[4]

When they announced on the radio that some new machine had been invented, I heard Matryona grumbling out in the kitchen, "New ones all the time, nothing but new ones. People don't want to work with the old ones any more, where are we going to store them all?"

There was a program about the seeding of clouds from airplanes. Matryona, listening up on the stove, shook her head, "Oh, dear, dear, dear, they'll do away with one of the two—summer or winter."

Once Shalyapin[5] was singing Russian folk songs. Matryona stood listening for a long time before she gave her emphatic verdict, "Queer singing, not our sort of singing."

"You can't mean that, Matryona Vasilyevna—just listen to him."

She listened a bit longer and pursed her lips, "No, it's wrong. It isn't our sort of tune, and he's tricky with his voice."

She made up for this another time. They were broadcasting some of

---

3. Religious images or portraits, usually painted on wood. A small lamp was set in front of the icons to illuminate them.   4. The translator is imitating Solzhenitsyn's wordplay. In the original, the narrator calls the speaker *razvedka* ("scout," literal trans. a military term); Matryona calls it *rozetka* (an electric plug).
5. Feodor Ivanovich Shalyapin (or Chaliapin, 1873–1938), Russian operatic bass with an international reputation as a great singer and actor; he included popular Russian music in his song recitals.

Glinka's[6] songs. After half a dozen of these drawing-room ballads, Matryona suddenly came from behind the screen clutching her apron, with a flush on her face and a film of tears over her dim eyes.

"That's our sort of singing," she said in a whisper.

2

So Matryona and I got used to each other and took each other for granted. She never pestered me with questions about myself. I don't know whether she was lacking in normal female curiosity or just tactful, but she never once asked if I had been married. All the Talnovo women kept at her to find out about me. Her answer was, "You want to know—you ask him. All I know is he's from distant parts."

And when I got round to telling her that I had spent a lot of time in prison, she said nothing but just nodded, as though she had already suspected it.

And I thought of Matryona only as the helpless old woman she was now and didn't try to rake up her past, didn't even suspect that there was anything to be found there.

I knew that Matryona had got married before the Revolution and had come to live in the house I now shared with her, and she had gone "to the stove" immediately. (She had no mother-in-law and no older sister-in-law, so it was her job to put the pots in the oven on the very first morning of her married life.) I knew that she had had six children and that they had all died very young, so that there were never two of them alive at once. Then there was a sort of foster daughter, Kira. Matryona's husband had not come back from the last war. She received no notification of his death. Men from the village who had served in the same company said that he might have been taken prisoner, or he might have been killed and his body not found. In the eight years that had gone by since the war Matryona had decided that he was not alive. It was a good thing that she thought so. If he was still alive he was probably in Brazil or Australia and married again. The village of Talnovo and the Russian language would be fading from his memory.

One day when I got back from school, I found a guest in the house. A tall, dark man, with his hat on his lap, was sitting on a chair which Matryona had moved up to the Dutch stove in the middle of the room. His face was completely surrounded by bushy black hair with hardly a trace of gray in it. His thick black moustache ran into his full black beard, so that his mouth could hardly be seen. Black side-whiskers merged with the black locks which hung down from his crown, leaving only the tips of his ears visible; his broad black eyebrows met in a wide double span. But the front of his head as far as the crown was a spacious bald dome. His whole appearance made an impression of wisdom and dignity. He sat squarely on his chair, with his hands folded on his stick, and his stick resting vertically on the floor, in an attitude of patient expectation, and he obviously hadn't much to say to Matryona, who was busy behind the screen.

When I came in, he eased his majestic head round toward me and suddenly

---

6. Mikhail Ivanovich Glinka (1804–1857), Russian composer who was instrumental in developing a "Russian" style of music, including the two operas *A Life for the Czar* and *Ruslan and Ludmila*.

addressed me, "Schoolmaster, I can't see you very well. My son goes to your school. Grigoryev, Antoshka."

There was no need for him to say any more. However strongly inclined I felt to help this worthy old man, I knew and dismissed in advance all the pointless things he was going to say. Antoshka Grigoryev was a plump, red-faced lad in 8-D who looked like a cat that's swallowed the cream. He seemed to think that he came to school for a rest and sat at his desk with a lazy smile on his face. Needless to say, he never did his homework. But the worst of it was that he had been put up into the next class from year to year because our district, and indeed the whole region and the neighboring region were famous for the high percentage of passes they obtained; the school had to make an effort to keep its record up. So Antoshka had got it clear in his mind that however much the teachers threatened him they would promote him in the end, and there was no need for him to learn anything. He just laughed at us. There he sat in the eighth class, and he hadn't even mastered his decimals and didn't know one triangle from another. In the first two terms of the school year I had kept him firmly below the passing line and the same treatment awaited him in the third.

But now this half-blind old man, who should have been Antoshka's grandfather rather than his father, had come to humble himself before me—how could I tell him that the school had been deceiving him for years, and that I couldn't go on deceiving him, because I didn't want to ruin the whole class, to become a liar and a fake, to start despising my work and my profession.

For the time being I patiently explained that his son had been very slack, that he told lies at school and at home, that his record book must be checked frequently, and that we must both take him severely in hand.

"Severe as you like, Schoolmaster," he assured me, "I beat him every week now. And I've got a heavy hand."

While we were talking I remembered that Matryona had once interceded for Antoshka Grigoryev, but I hadn't asked what relation of hers he was and I had refused to do what she wanted. Matryona was standing in the kitchen doorway like a mute suppliant on this occasion too. When Faddey Miron-ovich left, saying that he would call on me to see how things were going, I asked her, "I can't make out what relation this Antoshka is to you, Matryona Vasilyevna."

"My brother-in-law's son," said Matryona shortly, and went out to milk the goat.

When I'd worked it out, I realized that this determined old man with the black hair was the brother of the missing husband.

The long evening went by, and Matryona didn't bring up the subject again. But late at night, when I had stopped thinking about the old man and was working in a silence broken only by the rustling of the cockroaches and the heavy tick of the wall-clock, Matryona suddenly spoke from her dark corner, "You know, Ignatich, I nearly married him once."

I had forgotten that Matryona was in the room. I hadn't heard a sound from her—and suddenly her voice came out of the darkness, as agitated as if the old man were still trying to win her.

I could see that Matryona had been thinking about nothing else all evening.

She got up from her wretched rag bed and walked slowly toward me, as though she were following her own words. I sat back in my chair and caught my first glimpse of a quite different Matryona.

There was no overhead light in our big room with its forest of rubber plants. The table lamp cast a ring of light round my exercise books, and when I tore my eyes from it the rest of the room seemed to be half-dark and faintly tinged with pink. I thought I could see the same pinkish glow in her usually sallow cheeks.

"He was the first one who came courting me, before Efim did—he was his brother—the older one—I was nineteen and Faddey was twenty-three. They lived in this very same house. Their house it was. Their father built it."

I looked round the room automatically. Instead of the old gray house rotting under the faded green skin of wallpaper where the mice had their playground, I suddenly saw new timbers, freshly trimmed, not yet discolored, and caught the cheerful smell of pine tar.

"Well, and what happened then?"

"That summer we went to sit in the woods together," she whispered. "There used to be a woods where the stable yard is now. They chopped it down. I was just going to marry him, Ignatich. Then the German war started. They took Faddey into the army."

She let fall these few words—and suddenly the blue and white and yellow July of the year 1914 burst into flower before my eyes: the sky still peaceful, the floating clouds, the people sweating to get the ripe corn in. I imagined them side by side, the black-haired Hercules with a scythe over his shoulder, and the red-faced girl clasping a sheaf. And there was singing out under the open sky, such songs as nobody can sing nowadays, with all the machines in the fields.

"He went to the war—and vanished. For three years I kept to myself and waited. Never a sign of life did he give."

Matryona's round face looked out at me from an elderly threadbare headscarf. As she stood there in the gentle reflected light from my lamp, her face seemed to lose its slovenly workday wrinkles, and she was a scared young girl again with a frightening decision to make.

Yes . . . I could see it. The trees shed their leaves, the snow fell and melted. They plowed and sowed and reaped again. Again the trees shed their leaves, and the snow fell. There was a revolution. Then another revolution. And the whole world was turned upside down.

"Their mother died and Efim came to court me. 'You wanted to come to our house,' he says, 'so come.' He was a year younger than me, Efim was. It's a saying with us—sensible girls get married after Michaelmas, and silly ones at midsummer. They were shorthanded. I got married. . . . The wedding was on St. Peter's day, and then about St. Nicholas' day[7] in the winter he came back—Faddey, I mean, from being a prisoner in Hungary."

Matryona covered her eyes.

I said nothing.

She turned toward the door as though somebody were standing there. "He stood there at the door. What a scream I let out! I wanted to throw myself

---

7. December 19 (December 6, old style). *Michaelmas:* October 12 (September 29, old style). *St. Peter's Day:* probably July 12 (June 29, old style), Sts. Peter and Paul's Day.

at his feet! . . . but I couldn't. 'If it wasn't my own brother,' he says, 'I'd take my ax to the both of you.' "

I shuddered. Matryona's despair, or her terror, conjured up a vivid picture of him standing in the dark doorway and raising his ax to her.

But she quieted down and went on with her story in a sing-song voice, leaning on a chairback, "Oh dear, dear me, the poor dear man! There were so many girls in the village—but he wouldn't marry. I'll look for one with the same name as you, a second Matryona, he said. And that's what he did—fetched himself a Matryona from Lipovka. They built themselves a house of their own and they're still living in it. You pass their place every day on your way to school."

So that was it. I realized that I had seen the other Matryona quite often. I didn't like her. She was always coming to my Matryona to complain about her husband—he beat her, he was stingy, he was working her to death. She would weep and weep, and her voice always had a tearful note in it. As it turned out, my Matryona had nothing to regret, with Faddey beating his Matryona every day of his life and being so tightfisted.

"Mine never beat me once," said Matryona of Efim. "He'd pitch into another man in the street, but me he never hit once. Well, there was one time—I quarreled with my sister-in-law and he cracked me on the forehead with a spoon. I jumped up from the table and shouted at them, 'Hope it sticks in your gullets, you idle lot of beggars, hope you choke!' I said. And off I went into the woods. He never touched me any more."

Faddey didn't seem to have any cause for regret either. The other Matryona had borne him six children (my Antoshka was one of them, the littlest, the runt) and they had all lived, whereas the children of Matryona and Efim had died, every one of them, before they reached the age of three months, without any illness.

"One daughter, Elena, was born and was alive when they washed her, and then she died right after. . . . My wedding was on St. Peter's day, and it was St. Peter's day I buried my sixth, Alexander."

The whole village decided that there was a curse on Matryona.

Matryona still nodded emphatic belief when she talked about it. "There was a *course*[8] on me. They took me to a woman who used to be a nun to get cured, she set me off coughing and waited for the *course* to jump out of me like a frog. Only nothing jumped out."

And the years had run by like running water. In 1941 they didn't take Faddey into the army because of his poor sight, but they took Efim. And what had happened to the elder brother in the First World War happened to the younger in the Second—he vanished without a trace. Only he never came back at all. The once noisy cottage was deserted, it grew old and rotten, and Matryona, all alone in the world, grew old in it.

So she begged from the other Matryona, the cruelly beaten Matryona, a child of her womb (or was it a drop of Faddey's blood?), the youngest daughter, Kira.

For ten years she brought the girl up in her own house, in place of the children who had not lived. Then, not long before I arrived, she had married

---

8. *Curse/course* reflects wordplay in the Russian original, where a similar misuse of language indicates Matryona's lack of formal education.

her off to a young engine driver from Cherusti. The only help she got from anywhere came in dribs and drabs from Cherusti: a bit of sugar from time to time, or some of the fat when they killed a pig.

Sick and suffering, and feeling that death was not far off, Matryona had made known her will: the top room, which was a separate frame joined by tie beams to the rest of the house, should go to Kira when she died.[9] She said nothing about the house itself. Her three sisters had their eyes on it too.

That evening Matryona opened her heart to me. And, as often happens, no sooner were the hidden springs of her life revealed to me than I saw them in motion.

Kira arrived from Cherusti. Old Faddey was very worried. To get and keep a plot of land in Cherusti the young couple had to put up some sort of building. Matryona's top room would do very well. There was nothing else they could put up, because there was no timber to be had anywhere. It wasn't Kira herself so much, and it wasn't her husband, but old Faddey who was consumed with eagerness for them to get their hands on the plot at Cherusti.

He became a frequent visitor, laying down the law to Matryona and insisting that she should hand over the top room right away, before she died. On these occasions I saw a different Faddey. He was no longer an old man propped up by a stick, whom a push or a harsh word would bowl over. Although he was slightly bent by backache, he was still a fine figure; in his sixties he had kept the vigorous black hair of a young man; he was hot and urgent.

Matryona had not slept for two nights. It wasn't easy for her to make up her mind. She didn't grudge them the top room, which was standing there idle, any more than she ever grudged her labor or her belongings. And the top room was willed to Kira in any case. But the thought of breaking up the roof she had lived under for forty years was torture to her. Even I, a mere lodger, found it painful to think of them stripping away boards and wrenching out beams. For Matryona it was the end of everything.

But the people who were so insistent knew that she would let them break up her house before she died.

So Faddey and his sons and sons-in-law came along one February morning, the blows of five axes were heard and boards creaked and cracked as they were wrenched out. Faddey's eyes twinkled busily. Although his back wasn't quite straight yet, he scrambled nimbly up under the rafters and bustled about down below, shouting at his assistants. He and his father had built this house when he was a lad, a long time ago. The top room had been put up for him, the oldest son, to move into with his bride. And now he was furiously taking it apart, board by board, to carry it out of somebody else's yard.

After numbering the beam ends and the ceiling boards, they dismantled the top room and the storeroom underneath it. The living room and what was left of the landing they boarded up with a thin wall of deal. They did nothing about the cracks in the wall. It was plain to see that they were wreckers, not builders, and that they did not expect Matryona to be living there very long.

---

9. Lumber was scarce and valuable, and old houses were well built. Moving houses or sections of houses is still common in the country.

While the men were busy wrecking, the women were getting the drink ready for moving day—vodka would cost too much. Kira brought forty pounds of sugar from the Moscow region, and Matryona carried the sugar and some bottles to the distiller under cover of night.

The timbers were carried out and stacked in front of the gates, and the engine-driver son-in-law went off to Cherusti for the tractor.

But the very same day a blizzard, or "a blower," as Matryona once called it, began. It howled and whirled for two days and nights and buried the road under enormous drifts. Then, no sooner had they made the road passable and a couple of trucks had gone by, than it got suddenly warmer. Within a day everything was thawing out, damp mist hung in the air and rivulets gurgled as they burrowed into the snow, and you could get stuck up to the top of your jackboots.

Two weeks passed before the tractor could get at the dismantled top room. All this time Matryona went around like someone lost. What particularly upset her was that her three sisters came, with one voice called her a fool for giving the top room away, said they didn't want to see her any more, and went off. At about the same time the lame cat strayed and was seen no more. It was just one thing after another. This was another blow to Matryona.

At last the frost got a grip on the slushy road. A sunny day came along, and everybody felt more cheerful. Matryona had had a lucky dream the night before. In the morning she heard that I wanted to take a photograph of somebody at an old-fashioned handloom. (There were looms still standing in two cottages in the village; they wove coarse rugs on them.) She smiled shyly and said, "You just wait a day or two, Ignatich, I'll just send off the top room there and I'll put my loom up, I've still got it, you know, and then you can snap me. Honest to God!"

She was obviously attracted by the idea of posing in an old-fashioned setting. The red frosty sun tinged the window of the curtailed passageway with a faint pink, and this reflected light warmed Matryona's face. People who are at ease with their consciences always have nice faces.

Coming back from school before dusk I saw some movement near our house. A big new tractor-drawn sledge was already fully loaded, and there was no room for a lot of the timbers, so old Faddey's family and the helpers they had called in had nearly finished knocking together another homemade sledge. They were all working like madmen, in the frenzy that comes upon people when there is a smell of good money in the air or when they are looking forward to some treat. They were shouting at one another and arguing.

They could not agree on whether the sledges should be hauled separately or both together. One of Faddey's sons (the lame one) and the engine-driver son-in-law reasoned that the sledges couldn't both be taken at once because the tractor wouldn't be able to pull them. The man in charge of the tractor, a hefty fat-faced fellow who was very sure of himself, said hoarsely that he knew best, he was the driver, and he would take both at once. His motives were obvious: according to the agreement, the engine driver was paying him for the removal of the upper room, not for the number of trips he had to make. He could never have made two trips in a night—twenty-five kilometers each way, and one return journey. And by morning he had to get the tractor back in the garage from which he had sneaked it out for this job on the side.

Old Faddey was impatient to get the top room moved that day, and at a nod from him his lads gave in. To the stout sledge in front they hitched the one they had knocked together in such a hurry.

Matryona was running about among the men, fussing and helping them to heave the beams on the sledge. Suddenly I noticed that she was wearing my jacket and had dirtied the sleeves on the frozen mud round the beams. I was annoyed and told her so. That jacket held memories for me: it had kept me warm in the bad years.

This was the first time that I was ever angry with Matryona Vasilyevna.

Matryona was taken aback. "Oh dear, dear me," she said. "My poor head. I picked it up in a rush, you see, and never thought about it being yours. I'm sorry, Ignatich."

And she took it off and hung it up to dry.

The loading was finished, and all the men who had been working, about ten of them, clattered past my table and dived under the curtain into the kitchen. I could hear the muffled rattle of glasses and, from time to time, the clink of a bottle, the voices got louder and louder, the boasting more reckless. The biggest braggart was the tractor driver. The stink of hooch floated in to me. But they didn't go on drinking long. It was getting dark and they had to hurry. They began to leave. The tractor driver came out first, looking pleased with himself and fierce. The engine-driver son-in-law, Faddey's lame son, and one of his nephews were going to Cherusti. The others went off home. Faddey was flourishing his stick, trying to overtake somebody and put him right about something. The lame son paused at my table to light up and suddenly started telling me how he loved Aunt Matryona, and that he had got married not long ago, and his wife had just had a son. Then they shouted for him and he went out. The tractor set up a roar outside.

After all the others had gone, Matryona dashed out from behind the screen. She looked after them, anxiously shaking her head. She had put on her jacket and her headscarf. As she was going through the door, she said to me, "Why ever couldn't they hire two? If one tractor had cracked up, the other would have pulled them. What'll happen now, God only knows!"

She ran out after the others.

After the boozing and the arguments and all the coming and going, it was quieter than ever in the deserted cottage, and very chilly because the door had been opened so many times. I got into my jacket and sat down to mark exercise books. The noise of the tractor died away in the distance.

An hour went by. And another. And a third. Matryona still hadn't come back, but I wasn't surprised. When she had seen the sledge off, she must have gone round to her friend Masha.

Another hour went by. And yet another. Darkness, and with it a deep silence had descended on the village. I couldn't understand at the time why it was so quiet. Later, I found out that it was because all evening not a single train had gone along the line five hundred yards from the house. No sound was coming from my radio, and I noticed that the mice were wilder than ever. Their scampering and scratching and squeaking behind the wallpaper was getting noisier and more defiant all the time.

I woke up. It was one o'clock in the morning, and Matryona still hadn't come home.

Suddenly I heard several people talking loudly. They were still a long way off, but something told me that they were coming to our house. And sure enough, I heard soon afterward a heavy knock at the gate. A commanding voice, strange to me, yelled out an order to open up. I went out into the pitch darkness with a torch. The whole village was asleep, there was no light in the windows, and the snow had started melting in the last week so that it gave no reflected light. I turned the catch and let them in. Four men in greatcoats went on toward the house. It's a very unpleasant thing to be visited at night by noisy people in greatcoats.

When we got into the light though, I saw that two of them were wearing railway uniforms. The older of the two, a fat man with the same sort of face as the tractor driver, asked, "Where's the woman of the house?"

"I don't know."

"This is the place the tractor with a sledge came from?"

"This is it."

"Had they been drinking before they left?"

All four of them were looking around, screwing up their eyes in the dim light from the table lamp. I realized that they had either made an arrest or wanted to make one.

"What's happened then?"

"Answer the question!"

"But . . ."

"Were they drunk when they went?"

"Were they drinking here?"

Had there been a murder? Or hadn't they been able to move the top room? The men in greatcoats had me off balance. But one thing was certain: Matryona could do time for making hooch.

I stepped back to stand between them and the kitchen door. "I honestly didn't notice. I didn't see anything." (I really hadn't seen anything—only heard.) I made what was supposed to be a helpless gesture, drawing attention to the state of the cottage: a table lamp shining peacefully on books and exercises, a crowd of frightened rubber plants, the austere couch of a recluse, not a sign of debauchery.

They had already seen for themselves, to their annoyance, that there had been no drinking in that room. They turned to leave, telling each other this wasn't where the drinking had been then, but it would be a good thing to put in that it was. I saw them out and tried to discover what had happened. It was only at the gate that one of them growled. "They've all been cut to bits. Can't find all the pieces."

"That's a detail. The nine o'clock express nearly went off the rails. That would have been something." And they walked briskly away.

I went back to the hut in a daze. Who were "they"? What did "all of them" mean? And where was Matryona?

I moved the curtain aside and went into the kitchen. The stink of hooch rose and hit me. It was a deserted battlefield: a huddle of stools and benches, empty bottles lying around, one bottle half-full, glasses, the remains of pick-led herring, onion, and sliced fat pork.

Everything was deathly still. Just cockroaches creeping unperturbed about the field of battle.

They had said something about the nine o'clock express. Why? Perhaps I should have shown them all this? I began to wonder whether I had done right. But what a damnable way to behave—keeping their explanations for official persons only.

Suddenly the small gate creaked. I hurried out on to the landing. "Matryona Vasilyevna?"

The yard door opened, and Matryona's friend Masha came in, swaying and wringing her hands. "Matryona—our Matryona, Ignatich—"

I sat her down, and through her tears she told me the story.

The approach to the crossing was a steep rise. There was no barrier. The tractor and the first sledge went over, but the towrope broke and the second sledge, the homemade one, got stuck on the crossing and started falling apart—the wood Faddey had given them to make the second sledge was no good. They towed the first sledge out of the way and went back for the second. They were fixing the towrope—the tractor driver and Faddey's lame son, and Matryona (heaven knows what brought her there) were with them, between the tractor and the sledge. What help did she think she could be to the men? She was forever meddling in men's work. Hadn't a bolting horse nearly tipped her into the lake once, through a hole in the ice? Why did she have to go to the damned crossing? She had handed over the top room and owed nothing to anybody. The engine driver kept a lookout in case the train from Cherusti rushed up on them. Its headlamps would be visible a long way off. But two engines coupled together came from the other direction, from our station, backing without lights. Why they were without lights nobody knows. When an engine is backing, coal dust blows into the driver's eyes from the tender and he can't see very well. The two engines flew into them and crushed the three people between the tractor and the sledge to pulp. The tractor was wrecked, the sledge was matchwood, the rails were buckled, and both engines turned over.

"But how was it they didn't hear the engines coming?"

"The tractor engine was making such a din."

"What about the bodies?"

"They won't let anybody in. They've roped them off."

"What was that somebody was telling me about the express?"

"The nine o'clock express goes through our station at a good clip and on to the crossing. But the two drivers weren't hurt when their engines crashed, they jumped out and ran back along the line waving their hands, and they managed to stop the train. The nephew was hurt by a beam as well. He's hiding at Klavka's now so that they won't know he was at the crossing. If they find out they'll drag him in as a witness. . . . 'Don't know lies up, and do know gets tied up.' Kira's husband didn't get a scratch. He tried to hang himself, they had to cut him down. It's all because of me, he says, my aunty's killed and my brother. Now he's gone and given himself up. But the madhouse is where he'll be going, not prison. Oh, Matryona, my dearest Matryona. . . ."

Matryona was gone. Someone close to me had been killed. And on her last day I had scolded her for wearing my jacket.

The lovingly drawn red and yellow woman in the book advertisement smiled happily on.

Old Masha sat there weeping a little longer. Then she got up to go. And suddenly she asked me, "Ignatich, you remember, Matryona had a gray shawl. She meant it to go to my Tanya when she died, didn't she?"

She looked at me hopefully in the half-darkness—surely I hadn't forgotten?

No, I remembered. "She said so, yes."

"Well, listen, maybe you could let me take it with me now. The family will be swarming in tomorrow and I'll never get it then." And she gave me another hopeful, imploring look. She had been Matryona's friend for half a century, the only one in the village who truly loved her.

No doubt she was right.

"Of course—take it."

She opened the chest, took out the shawl, tucked it under her coat, and went out.

The mice had gone mad. They were running furiously up and down the walls, and you could almost see the green wallpaper rippling and rolling over their backs.

In the morning I had to go to school. The time was three o'clock. The only thing to do was to lock up and go to bed.

Lock up, because Matryona would not be coming.

I lay down, leaving the light on. The mice were squeaking, almost moaning, racing and running. My mind was weary and wandering, and I couldn't rid myself of an uneasy feeling that an invisible Matryona was flitting about and saying good-bye to her home.

And suddenly I imagined Faddey standing there, young and black-haired, in the dark patch by the door, with his ax uplifted. "If it wasn't my own brother, I'd chop the both of you to bits."

The threat had lain around for forty years, like an old broad sword in a corner, and in the end it had struck its blow.

3

When it was light the women went to the crossing and brought back all that was left of Matryona on a hand sledge with a dirty sack over it. They threw off the sack to wash her. There was just a mess . . . no feet, only half a body, no left hand. One woman said, "The Lord has left her her right hand. She'll be able to say her prayers where she's going."

Then the whole crowd of rubber plants were carried out of the cottage—these plants that Matryona had loved so much that once when smoke woke her up in the night she didn't rush to save her house but to tip the plants onto the floor in case they were suffocated. The women swept the floor clean. They hung a wide towel of old homespun over Matryona's dim mirror. They took down the jolly posters. They moved my table out of the way. Under the icons, near the windows, there stood a rough unadorned coffin on a row of stools.

In the coffin lay Matryona. Her body, mangled and lifeless, was covered with a clean sheet. Her head was swathed in a white kerchief. Her face was almost undamaged, peaceful, more alive than dead.

The villagers came to pay their last respects. The women even brought their small children to take a look at the dead. And if anyone raised a lament, all the women, even those who had looked in out of idle curiosity, always joined in, wailing where they stood by the door or the wall, as though they were providing a choral accompaniment. The men stood stiff and silent with their caps off.

The formal lamentation had to be performed by the women of Matryona's family. I observed that the lament followed a coldly calculated, age-old ritual. The more distant relatives went up to the coffin for a short while and made low wailing noises over it. Those who considered themselves closer kin to the dead woman began their lament in the doorway and when they got as far as the coffin, bowed down and roared out their grief right in the face of the departed. Every lamenter made up her own melody. And expressed her own thoughts and feelings.

I realized that a lament for the dead is not just a lament, but a kind of politics. Matryona's three sisters swooped, took possession of the cottage, the goat, and the stove, locked up the chest, ripped the two hundred rubles for the funeral out of the coat lining, and drummed it into everybody who came that only they were near relatives. Their lament over the coffin went like this, "Oh, nanny, nanny! Oh nan-nan! All we had in the world was you! You could have lived in peace and quiet, you could. And we should always have been kind and loving to you. Now your top room's been the death of you. Finished you off, it has, the cursed thing! Oh, why did you have to take it down? Why didn't you listen to us?"

Thus the sisters' laments were indictments of Matryona's husband's family: they shouldn't have made her take the top room down. (There was an underlying meaning, too: you've taken the top room, all right, but we won't let you have the house itself!)

Matryona's husband's family, her sisters-in-law, Efim and Faddey's sisters, and the various nieces lamented like this, "Oh poor auntie, poor auntie! Why didn't you take better care of yourself! Now they're angry with us for sure. Our own dear Matryona you were, and it's your own fault! The top room is nothing to do with it. Oh why did you go where death was waiting for you? Nobody asked you to go there. And what a way to die! Oh why didn't you listen to us?" (Their answer to the others showed through these laments: we are not to blame for her death, and the house we'll talk about later.)

But the "second" Matryona, a coarse, broad-faced woman, the substitute Matryona whom Faddey had married so long ago for the sake of her name, got out of step with family policy, wailing and sobbing over the coffin in her simplicity, "Oh my poor dear sister! You won't be angry with me, will you now? Oh-oh-oh! How we used to talk and talk, you and me! Forgive a poor miserable woman! You've gone to be with your dear mother, and you'll come for me some day, for sure! Oh-oh-oh-oh! . . ."

At every "oh-oh-oh" it was as though she were giving up the ghost. She writhed and gasped, with her breast against the side of the coffin. When her lament went beyond the ritual prescription, the women, as though acknowledging its success, all started saying, "Come away now, come away."

Matryona came away, but back she went again, sobbing with even greater abandon. Then an ancient woman came out of a corner, put her hand on Matryona's shoulder, and said, "There are two riddles in this world: how I was born, I don't remember, how I shall die, I don't know."

And Matryona fell silent at once, and all the others were silent, so that there was an unbroken hush.

But the old woman herself, who was much older than all the other old women there and didn't seem to belong to Matryona at all, after a while started wailing, "Oh, my poor sick Matryona! Oh my poor Vasilyevna! Oh what a weary thing it is to be seeing you into your grave!"

There was one who didn't follow the ritual, but wept straight-forwardly, in the fashion of our age, which has had plenty of practice at it. This was Matryona's unfortunate foster daughter, Kira, from Cherusti, for whom the top room had been taken down and moved. Her ringlets were pitifully out of curl. Her eyes looked red and bloodshot. She didn't notice that her headscarf was slipping off out in the frosty air and that her arm hadn't found the sleeve of her coat. She walked in a stupor from her foster mother's coffin in one house to her brother's in another. They were afraid she would lose her mind, because her husband had to go on trial as well.

It looked as if her husband was doubly at fault: not only had he been moving the top room, but as an engine driver, he knew the regulations about unprotected crossings and should have gone down to the station to warn them about the tractor. There were a thousand people on the Urals express that night, peacefully sleeping in the upper and lower berths of their dimly lit carriages, and all those lives were nearly cut short. All because of a few greedy people, wanting to get their hands on a plot of land, or not wanting to make a second trip with a tractor.

All because of the top room, which had been under a curse ever since Faddey's hands had started itching to take it down.

The tractor driver was already beyond human justice. And the railway authorities were also at fault, both because a busy crossing was unguarded and because the coupled engines were traveling without lights. That was why they had tried at first to blame it all on the drink, and then to keep the case out of court.

The rails and the track were so twisted and torn that for three days, while the coffins were still in the house, no trains ran—they were diverted onto another line. All Friday, Saturday, and Sunday, from the end of the investigation until the funeral, the work of repairing the line went on day and night. The repair gang was frozen, and they made fires to warm themselves and to light their work at night, using the boards and beams from the second sledge, which were there for the taking, scattered around the crossing.

The first sledge just stood there, undamaged and still loaded, a little way beyond the crossing.

One sledge, tantalizingly ready to be towed away, and the other perhaps still to be plucked from the flames—that was what harrowed the soul of black-bearded Faddey all day Friday and all day Saturday. His daughter was going out of her mind, his son-in-law had a criminal charge hanging over him, in his own house lay the son he had killed, and along the street the woman he had killed and whom he had once loved. But Faddey stood by the coffins, clutching his beard, only for a short time, and went away again. His high forehead was clouded by painful thoughts, but what he was thinking about was how to save the timbers of the top room from the flames and from Matryona's scheming sisters.

Going over the people of Talnovo in my mind, I realized that Faddey was not the only one like that.

Property, the people's property, or my property, is strangely called our "goods." If you lose your goods, people think you disgrace yourself and make yourself look foolish.

Faddey dashed about, never stopping to sit down, from the settlement to the station, from one official to another, there he stood with his bent back, leaning heavily on his stick, and begged them all to take pity on an old man and give him permission to recover the top room.

Somebody gave permission. And Faddey gathered together his surviving sons, sons-in-law, and nephews, got horses from the kolkhoz and from the other side of the wrecked crossing, by a roundabout way that led through three villages, brought the remnants of the top room home to his yard. He finished the job in the early hours of Sunday morning.

On Sunday afternoon they were buried. The two coffins met in the middle of the village, and the relatives argued about which of them should go first. Then they put them side by side on an open sledge, the aunt and the nephew, and carried the dead over the damp snow, with a gloomy February sky above, to the churchyard two villages away. There was an unkind wind, so the priest and the deacon waited inside the church and didn't come out to Talnovo to meet them.

A crowd of people walked slowly behind the coffins, singing in chorus. Outside the village they fell back.

When Sunday came the women were still fussing around the house. An old woman mumbled psalms by the coffin, Matryona's sisters flitted about, popping things into the oven, and the air round the mouth of the stove trembled with the heat of red-hot peats, those Matryona had carried in a sack from a distant bog. They were making unappetizing pies with poor flour.

When the funeral was over and it was already getting on toward evening, they gathered for the wake. Tables were put together to make a long one, which hid the place where the coffin had stood in the morning. To start with, they all stood round the table, and an old man, the husband of a sister-in-law, said the Lord's Prayer. Then they poured everybody a little honey and warm water,[1] just enough to cover the bottom of the bowl. We spooned it up without bread or anything, in memory of the dead. Then we ate something and drank vodka and the conversation became more animated. Before the jelly they all stood up and sang "Eternal remembrance" (they explained to me that it had to be sung before the jelly). There was more drinking. By now they were talking louder than ever, and not about Matryona at all. The sister-in-law's husband started boasting, "Did you notice, brother Christians, that they took the funeral service slowly today? That's because Father Mikhail noticed me. He knows I know the service. Other times, it's saints defend us, homeward wend us, and that's all."

At last the supper was over. They all rose again. They sang "Worthy Is She." Then again, with a triple repetition of "Eternal Remembrance."[2] But the voices were hoarse and out of tune, their faces drunken, and nobody put any feeling into this "eternal memory."

Then most of the guests went away, and only the near relatives were left. They pulled out their cigarets and lit up, there were jokes and laughter. There was some mention of Matryona's husband and his disappearance. The sister-in-law's husband, striking himself on the chest, assured me and the cobbler who was married to one of Matryona's sisters, "He was dead, Efim was dead! What could stop him coming back if he wasn't? If I knew they were going to

---

1. Traditionally Russians have *kutiia*, a wheat pudding with honey and almonds, at funerals and memorial gatherings; the villagers are too poor to have the main ingredients and their honey and water are symbolic of the *kutiia*.   2. Dirges, religious hymns sung to honor the dead. The village still follows religious rituals in time of crisis and does not use the civil ceremony proposed by the Soviet government.

hang me when I got to the old place, I'd come back just the same!"

The cobbler nodded in agreement. He was a deserter and had never left the old place. All through the war he was hiding in his mother's cellar.

The stern and silent old woman who was more ancient than all the ancients was staying the night and sat high up on the stove. She looked down in mute disapproval on the indecently animated youngsters of fifty and sixty.

But the unhappy foster daughter, who had grown up within these walls, went away behind the kitchen screen to cry.

Faddey didn't come to Matryona's wake—perhaps because he was holding a wake for his son. But twice in the next few days he walked angrily into the house for discussions with Matryona's sisters and the deserting cobbler.

The argument was about the house. Should it go to one of the sisters or to the foster daughter? They were on the verge of taking it to court, but they made peace because they realized that the court would hand over the house to neither side, but to the Rural District Council. A bargain was struck. One sister took the goat, the cobbler and his wife got the house, and to make up Faddey's share, since he had "nursed every bit of timber here in his arms," in addition to the top room which had already been carried away, they let him have the shed which had housed the goat and the whole of the inner fence between the yard and the garden.

Once again the insatiable old man got the better of sickness and pain and became young and active. Once again he gathered together his surviving sons and sons-in-law, they dismantled the shed and the fence, he hauled the timbers himself, sledge by sledge, and only toward the end did he have Antoshka of 8-D, who didn't slack this time, to help him.

They boarded Matryona's house up till the spring, and I moved in with one of her sisters-in-law, not far away. This sister-in-law on several occasions came out with some recollection of Matryona and made me see the dead woman in a new light. "Efim didn't love her. He used to say, 'I like to dress in an educated way, but she dresses any old way, like they do in the country.' Well then, he thinks, if she doesn't want anything, he might as well drink whatever's to spare. One time I went with him to the town to work, and he got himself a madam there and never wanted to come back to Matryona."

Everything she said about Matryona was disapproving. She was slovenly, she made no effort to get a few things about her. She wasn't the saving kind. She didn't even keep a pig, because she didn't like fattening them up for some reason. And the silly woman helped other people without pay. (What brought Matryona to mind this time was that the garden needed plowing, and she couldn't find enough helpers to pull the plow.)

Matryona's sister-in-law admitted that she was warmhearted and straightforward, but pitied and despised her for it.

It was only then, after these disapproving comments from her sister-in-law, that a true likeness of Matryona formed before my eyes, and I understood her as I never had when I lived side by side with her.

Of course! Every house in the village kept a pig. But she didn't. What can be easier than fattening a greedy piglet that cares for nothing in the world but food! You warm his swill three times a day, you live for him—then you cut his throat and you have some fat.

But she had none.

She made no effort to get things round her. She didn't struggle and strain to buy things and then care for them more than life itself.

She didn't go all out after fine clothes. Clothes, that beautify what is ugly and evil.

She was misunderstood and abandoned even by her husband. She had lost six children, but not her sociable ways. She was a stranger to her sisters and sisters-in-law, a ridiculous creature who stupidly worked for others without pay. She didn't accumulate property against the day she died. A dirty-white goat, a gammy-legged cat, some rubber plants. . . .

We had all lived side by side with her and had never understood that she was the righteous one without whom, as the proverb says, no village can stand.[3]

Nor any city.

Nor our whole land.

3. See Genesis 18.23–33, the story of Sodom.

DORIS LESSING
born 1919

The clash between cultures, between attitudes within cultures, and between elements of one's own personality, as well as the attempt to integrate opposing elements into a higher level of consciousness, are all fundamental to Doris Lessing's work and are explored in a style that ranges from the detailed realism of her earliest stories to the fantasies and "inner-space fiction" of her novels of the 1970s. Lessing herself has lived in the midst of such conflicts: brought up in the British colony of Rhodesia, she has written harsh indictments of colonial society and its cruel blindness to black culture and rights; living in London, she has described political and social issues and the way they determine interpersonal relationships; as a woman pursuing independence and the right to shape her own identity, she has investigated the psychology of the self in both sexual and intellectual terms and pondered the relations of the individual to the community. Lessing's social realism, her description of the frustrated and incomplete relationships between human beings, and her yearning (especially evident in the later novels) for a higher plane of awareness in which there is perfect understanding recall D. H. Lawrence's criticism of society and his vision of perfect harmony in tune with nature. Yet there are important differences, including Lessing's refusal to accept the archetypal roles of the sexes that Lawrence found the key to natural harmony. Her own experience could not be content with such answers, and her stories and novels have never ceased to explore the layers of consciousness that make up individual identity and social interaction.

She was born Doris May Tayler in Persia (now Iran), on October 22, 1919. Her parents were British—her mother a nurse and her father a clerk in the Imperial Bank of Persia who had been crippled in World War I and whose horror-filled memories of the "war to end war" punctuate her recollections of childhood. In 1925 her father decided to start a new life in British Africa, where the colonial government of Rhodesia (now Zimbabwe) was offering economic incentives to encourage the immigration of white settlers. For ten shillings an acre, he bought three thousand acres of farming land in Mashonaland, a section of Southern Rhodesia that was the homeland of the Matabele tribe but from which the government had evicted most of the population. The farm never prospered. Lessing attended a convent school in the capital city of Salisbury (now Harare) until fourteen, but considers herself largely self-educated from her avid reading of classics of European and American literature. She especially loved the nineteenth-century novel, and Tolstoy, Dostoevsky, Stendhal, and the other great realists impressed her with their "climate of ethical judgement" in which she felt "the warmth, the compassion, the humanity, the love of people" that are so important in her own works. Gradually she became aware of the problems of racial injustice in her new home and of the fact that she was one of a privileged class of white immigrants who had displaced the previous owners of the land. As she later noted, she was "a member of the white minority, pitted against a black majority that was abominably treated and still is." Themes of this early awakening, which combines a strong attachment to the land itself with horror at racial inequities and the sterility of white civilization in Rhodesia, run through much of her work: in particular, her first novel *The Grass Is Singing* (1949) and the collected *African Stories* (1964). To Lessing, "literature should be committed" in the face of all forms of tyranny. She herself was politically active in Rhodesia and a member of the British Communist Party from 1952 until 1956, the year of the intervention in Hungary. Much of her writing describes the painful clash of two ideals—individual conscience and collective good—as they were embodied for Lessing in her experience of communism. Her political activism and descriptions of racial injustice made their mark, and in 1956 she was declared a prohibited alien in both Southern Rhodesia and South Africa.

While still in Rhodesia, Lessing worked in several office jobs in Salisbury and made two unsuccessful marriages (Lessing is the surname of her second husband). In 1949 she moved to England with the son of her second marriage and published *The Grass Is Singing*. It was an immediate success, and she was henceforth able to make her living as a writer. She began the five-volume series *Children of Violence* (1952–69), which follows the life of a symbolically named heroine, Martha Quest, whose career in many instances parallels Lessing's own. *Children of Violence* is the portrait of an age and two cultures, and it explores with Lessing's characteristic energy a series of moral and intellectual issues for the time: the (female) protagonist's pursuit of individual freedom and the right to achieve her own identity, parent-child relationships, race relations, the hopes and frustrations of political idealism, reason versus irrationality, the shaping influence of culture and historical events. It follows the form of the nineteenth-century bildungsroman, or "education novel": Martha Quest moves toward greater understanding of the cultural forces acting on her, but it cannot be said that she controls the process of her development as consciously as will Lessing's later protagonists.

The Golden Notebook (1962), Lessing's most famous novel, makes a sharp break with the linear style of narrative found in *Children of Violence* and in the bildungsroman tradition. Once again, a protagonist (Anna Wulf) is struggling to build a unified identity from the multiple selves that constitute her fragmented personality. Linear narrative, however, cannot do justice to these many dimensions, or to the exploratory process by which Anna finally creates a free, integrated personality. "The point of that book was the relation of its parts to each other," said Lessing, and this relation (although framed by a conventional short novel called *Free Women*) is essentially that of an overlapping series of differently colored notebooks that contain Anna's different versions of her experience: black for Africa, red for politics, yellow for a fictionalized version with herself as a character named Ella, and blue for a factual diary. By analyzing her life from these different perspectives, Anna is able to understand and synthesize their interaction: to write, ultimately, the "Golden Notebook," which is "all of me in one book." A chronological account of the events would start with Anna's breakdown and inability to write and end with her regained equilibrium after a tangled love affair with a similarly split character, Saul Green. Such an account would miss the core of the book, however, or the process by which it all happens: Lessing's detailed description of a mind healing itself by recalling and assessing its relationships with other people, adjusting earlier views according to new insights, weighing (and sometimes rejecting) the explanations of psychoanalysis, comparing different ways of interpreting experience, and measuring the constantly changing whole against the test of each new encounter.

Although *The Golden Notebook* is now taken as one of the major novels of the twentieth century, it was seen at the time chiefly as a feminist manifesto—a one-sided appraisal that infuriated the author. To accusations of being "unfeminine" and a "man-hater" for putting into print emotions of female aggression, hostility, and resentment, she responded dryly, "apparently what many women were thinking, feeling, experiencing came as a great surprise." Yet, she notes, when at the same time novels and plays caustically attacked women as underminers and betrayers, "these attitudes in male writers were taken for granted, accepted as sound philosophical bases, as quite normal, certainly not as woman-hating, aggressive, or neurotic." Lessing's feminism is often a matter of establishing balances and an insistence on honesty of emotions and critical self-awareness in all her protagonists, whether male (*The Temptation of Jack Orkney*, 1972) or female (Anna Wulf).

The newly integrated "all of me" at the end of *The Golden Notebook* has broken beyond intellectualized understanding and reached "beyond the region where words could be made to have sense." In the "inner-space fiction" written during the 1970s and early 1980s, Lessing took up these themes of quasi-mystical insight: first with a schizophrenic hero whose cosmic imaginings are closer to psychic wholeness than his normal life (*Briefing for a Descent into Hell*, 1971), later in the dream exploration of other "bizarre" dimensions beyond the "ordinary" living-room wall (*The Memoirs of a Survivor*, 1974), and then in a science-fiction series, *Canopus in Argos: Archives* (1979–83), which describes the different protagonists' consciousness evolving under pressure to a higher plane of existence. These later books, as Lessing states, are influenced by Sufi mysticism, with its insistence on detached perception and the evolution of consciousness and on learning as a process of discovering the right questions. The wordless moment of understanding that comes when the right question is asked may seem a long way from Lessing's first novels about race relations in Southern Rhodesia or Martha Quest's awakening to emotional, intellectual, and political maturity. In each case, however, a process of listening to experience is required. The focus has not changed when she writes in the "Afterword" to the fourth Canopus novel: "It seems to me that we do not know nearly enough about ourselves." The attempt to know about ourselves, to grow through such knowledge, and to achieve harmony in this world or "in worlds or dimensions elsewhere" pervades her entire work.

Annoyed at criticism of her shift to science fiction, Lessing published two realistic novels under the name of Jane Somers: *The Diary of a Good Neighbour* (1983), a novel that gave graphic descriptions of the difficulties of aging and illness, and its sequel *If the Old Could . . .* (1984). Sales were respectable but not outstanding; and when both were reprinted in 1984 as *The Diaries of Jane Somers*, Lessing announced that she had published them under a pseudonym to test whether the critics who had disliked her new style would recognize the "realistic" Lessing under another name. They did not. Since then, she has produced realistic stories with a satirical or symbolic twist: *The Good Terrorist* (1985), a satire of naïve British terrorists who arrange a homey atmosphere in a London squat while carrying out bombing raids, and *The Fifth Child* (1988), which recounts the gradual destruction of a London family by their "alien" and uncontrollably savage fifth child. Lectures reprinted in *Prisons We Choose to Live Inside* (1987) reject the savagery that has dominated human history and that persists in wars such as the Afghan resistance, which Lessing documents in *The Wind Blows Away Our Words* (1987). The writer's role, she asserts, is to be both committed and detached, clarifying issues and suggesting remedies for those who are caught up in "mass emotions and social conditions." As both novelist and nonfiction writer, Lessing upholds the concept of the writer as a moral figure, whether the "moralist" of the French tradition who awakens our conscience to ethical issues (Albert Camus), or the polemic voice sounded in novels and essays by Alexander Solzhenitsyn.

The Old Chief Mshlanga is one of Lessing's earliest African stories, written during the period from 1950 to 1958, when she wrote most of her African fiction and published in *This Was the Old Chief's Country* (1951). This collection, together with five novellas set in Africa in *Five* (1953) and her best-selling novel *The Grass Is Singing*, established Lessing as an important interpreter of modern Africa—or, rather, of the colonial experience in Africa. She herself draws the distinction between the African experience as it can be understood by African whites and as it is felt by the black Africans whose heritage has been forcibly displaced. Lessing writes in the preface to her 1973 *Collected African Stories*:

> It can be said of all white-dominated Africa that it was—and indeed still is—the Old Chief's Country. So all the stories I write of a certain kind, I think of as belonging under that heading: tales about white people, sometimes about black people, living in a landscape that not so very long ago was settled by black tribes, living in complex societies that the white people are only just beginning to study, let alone understand. . . .
>
> I am not able to write about what has been lost, which was and still is recorded orally. As a writer that is my biggest regret, as it is of all the white writers from Africa I have known. The tribal life that was broken seems now to have had more real dignity, more responsibility for what is important in people—their self-respect, more tolerance of individuality, than our way of living has. The breakup of that society, the time of chaos that followed it, is as dramatic a story as any; but if you are a white writer, it is a story that you are told by others.

The dispossession that underlies the plot of *The Old Chief Mshlanga* began with the economic infiltration of the country by white colonizers, soon formalized in Chartered Company policies that divided land into categories of "alienated" (owned by white settlers) and "unalienated" (occupied by natives, including the Reserves whose inhabitants paid a head tax). The official Land Apportionment Act of 1930 confirmed this arrangement by separating the territory into areas called Native and European. The figure of the old Chief bridges past and present, a proud era fifty years earlier when his people owned the entire country and the diminished present in which they can be forcibly relocated on a Reserve after disagreeing with a white settler. Yet it is not the old Chief who is the protagonist; significantly, his situation is pushed into the background until the middle of the story, when it intrudes on the consciousness of a young white settler girl. Only gradually does the "vein of richness" that he and his people represent come to light. By the end of the story the tribe has disappeared. The girl visits their village to find it disintegrating into the riotously fertile landscape, and the richness of their existence is preserved mainly as an obscure recognition in her mind.

Yet in spite of her comment that "there was nothing there," the girl's close description of the lush scene shows that her eyes have been opened to an African presence that initially she could not see. The gain, however, is one-sided: even now it cannot bring her closer to the experience of the tribespeople but is restricted to a feeling for the landscape. There is no advantage for the old Chief: he and his people have disappeared into a symbolic essence, buried in a "richness" that inheres in the land even when it is turned over to a new settler—as it will be. Lessing's observant young girl has been changed by the encounter with the old Chief, but hers is a bleak awakening that includes a sense of loss and indirect responsibility. Perhaps, one day, she will write about it.

The Old Chief Mshlanga

They were good, the years of ranging the bush over her father's farm which, like every white farm, was largely unused, broken only occasionally by small patches of cultivation. In between, nothing but trees, the long sparse grass, thorn and cactus and gully, grass and outcrop and thorn. And a jutting piece of rock which had been thrust up from the warm soil of Africa unimaginable eras of time ago, washed into hollows and whorls by sun and wind that had travelled so many thousands of miles of space and bush, would hold the weight of a small girl whose eyes were sightless for anything but a pale willowed river, a pale gleaming castle—a small girl singing: "Out flew the web and floated wide, the mirror cracked from side to side . . ."[1]

Pushing her way through the green aisles of the mealie[2] stalks, the leaves arching like cathedrals veined with sunlight far overhead, with the packed red earth underfoot, a fine lace of red starred witchweed would summon up a black bent figure croaking premonitions: the Northern witch, bred of cold Northern forests, would stand before her among the mealie fields, and it was the mealie fields that faded and fled, leaving her among the gnarled roots of an oak, snow falling thick and soft and white, the woodcutter's fire glowing red welcome through crowding tree trunks.

A white child, opening its eyes curiously on a sun-suffused landscape, a gaunt and violent landscape, might be supposed to accept it as her own, to make the msasa trees and the thorn trees as familiars, to feel her blood running free and responsive to the swing of the seasons.

This child could not see a msasa tree,[3] or the thorn, for what they were. Her books held tales of alien fairies, her rivers ran slow and peaceful, and she knew the shape of the leaves of an ash or an oak, the names of the little creatures that lived in English streams, when the words "the veld"[4] meant strangeness, though she could remember nothing else.

Because of this, for many years, it was the veld that seemed unreal; the sun was a foreign sun, and the wind spoke a strange language.

The black people on the farm were as remote as the trees and the rocks. They were an amorphous black mass, mingling and thinning and massing like tadpoles, faceless, who existed merely to serve, to say "Yes, Baas,"[5] take their money and go. They changed season by season, moving from one farm to the next, according to their outlandish needs, which one did not have to understand, coming from perhaps hundreds of miles north or east, passing on after a few months—where? Perhaps even as far away as the fabled gold mines of Johannesburg,[6] where the pay was so much better than the few shillings a month and the double handful of mealie meal twice a day which they earned in that part of Africa.

The child was taught to take them for granted: the servants in the house would come running a hundred yards to pick up a book if she dropped it. She was called "Nkosikaas"—Chieftainess, even by the black children her own age.

---

1. The child is reciting lines 114–15 from Tennyson's *The Lady of Shalott*.   2. Maize; corn.   3. A large tree of central Africa, notable for the vivid colorings (pink through copper) of its spring foliage and for the fragrance of its white flowers.   4. Unenclosed country, open grassland.   5. Boss.   6. The largest city in the Union (now Republic) of South Africa.

Later, when the farm grew too small to hold her curiosity, she carried a gun in the crook of her arm and wandered miles a day, from vlei to vlei, from kopje[7] to kopje, accompanied by two dogs: the dogs and the gun were an armour against fear. Because of them she never felt fear.

If a native came into sight along the kaffir[8] paths half a mile away, the dogs would flush him up a tree as if he were a bird. If he expostulated (in his uncouth language which was by itself ridiculous) that was cheek. If one was in a good mood, it could be a matter for laughter. Otherwise one passed on, hardly glancing at the angry man in the tree.

On the rare occasions when white children met together they could amuse themselves by hailing a passing native in order to make a buffoon of him; they could set the dogs on him and watch him run; they could tease a small black child as if he were a puppy—save that they would not throw stones and sticks at a dog without a sense of guilt.

Later still, certain questions presented themselves in the child's mind; and because the answers were not easy to accept, they were silenced by an even greater arrogance of manner.

It was even impossible to think of the black people who worked about the house as friends, for if she talked to one of them, her mother would come running anxiously: "Come away; you mustn't talk to natives."

It was this instilled consciousness of danger, of something unpleasant, that made it easy to laugh out loud, crudely, if a servant made a mistake in his English or if he failed to understand an order—there is a certain kind of laughter that is fear, afraid of itself.

One evening, when I was about fourteen, I was walking down the side of a mealie field that had been newly ploughed, so that the great red clods showed fresh and tumbling to the vlei beyond, like a choppy red sea; it was that hushed and listening hour, when the birds send long sad calls from tree to tree, and all the colours of earth and sky and leaf are deep and golden. I had my rifle in the curve of my arm, and the dogs were at my heels.

In front of me, perhaps a couple of hundred yards away, a group of three Africans came into sight around the side of a big antheap. I whistled the dogs close in to my skirts and let the gun swing in my hand, and advanced, waiting for them to move aside, off the path, in respect for my passing. But they came on steadily, and the dogs looked up at me for the command to chase. I was angry. It was "cheek"[9] for a native not to stand off a path, the moment he caught sight of you.

In front walked an old man, stooping his weight on to a stick, his hair grizzled white, a dark red blanket slung over his shoulders like a cloak. Behind him came two young men, carrying bundles of pots, assegais,[1] hatchets.

The group was not a usual one. They were not natives seeking work. These had an air of dignity, of quietly following their own purpose. It was the dignity that checked my tongue. I walked quietly on, talking softly to the growling dogs, till I was ten paces away. Then the old man stopped, drawing his blanket close.

7. A small hill (Afrikaans). Vlei: a shallow pool or swamp (Afrikaans).   8. A black African; usually used disparagingly.   9. Impudence.   1. Spears.

"Morning, Nkosikaas," he said, using the customary greeting for any time of the day.

"Good morning," I said. "Where are you going?" My voice was a little truculent.

The old man spoke in his own language, then one of the young men stepped forward politely and said in careful English: "My Chief travels to see his brothers beyond the river."

A Chief! I thought, understanding the pride that made the old man stand before me like an equal—more than an equal, for he showed courtesy, and I showed none.

The old man spoke again, wearing dignity like an inherited garment, still standing ten paces off, flanked by his entourage, not looking at me (that would have been rude) but directing his eyes somewhere over my head at the trees.

"You are the little Nkosikaas from the farm of Baas Jordan?"

"That's right," I said.

"Perhaps your father does not remember," said the interpreter for the old man, "but there was an affair with some goats. I remember seeing you when you were . . ." The young man held his hand at knee level and smiled.

We all smiled.

"What is your name?" I asked.

"This is Chief Mshlanga," said the young man.

"I will tell my father that I met you," I said.

The old man said: "My greetings to your father, little Nkosikaas."

"Good morning," I said politely, finding the politeness difficult, from lack of use.

"Morning, little Nkosikaas," said the old man, and stood aside to let me pass.

I went by, my gun hanging awkwardly, the dogs sniffing and growling, cheated of their favourite game of chasing natives like animals.

Not long afterwards I read in an old explorer's book the phrase: "Chief Mshlanga's country." It went like this: "Our destination was Chief Mshlanga's country, to the north of the river; and it was our desire to ask his permission to prospect for gold in his territory."

The phrase "ask his permission" was so extraordinary to a white child, brought up to consider all natives as things to use, that it revived those questions, which could not be suppressed: they fermented slowly in my mind.

On another occasion one of those old prospectors who still move over Africa looking for neglected reefs, with their hammers and tents, and pans for sifting gold from crushed rock, came to the farm and, in talking of the old days, used that phrase again: "This was the Old Chief's country," he said. "It stretched from those mountains over there way back to the river, hundreds of miles of country." That was his name for our district: "The Old Chief's Country"; he did not use our name for it—a new phrase which held no implication of usurped ownership.

As I read more books about the time when this part of Africa was opened up, not much more than fifty years before, I found Old Chief Mshlanga had been a famous man, known to all the explorers and prospectors. But then he had been young; or maybe it was his father or uncle they spoke of—I never found out.

During that year I met him several times in the part of the farm that was traversed by natives moving over the country. I learned that the path up the side of the big red field where the birds sang was the recognized highway for migrants. Perhaps I even haunted it in the hope of meeting him: being greeted by him, the exchange of courtesies, seemed to answer the questions that troubled me.

Soon I carried a gun in a different spirit; I used it for shooting food and not to give me confidence. And now the dogs learned better manners. When I saw a native approaching, we offered and took greetings; and slowly that other landscape in my mind faded, and my feet struck directly on the African soil, and I saw the shapes of tree and hill clearly, and the black people moved back, as it were, out of my life: it was as if I stood aside to watch a slow intimate dance of landscape and men, a very old dance, whose steps I could not learn.

But I thought: this is my heritage, too; I was bred here; it is my country as well as the black man's country; and there is plenty of room for all of us, without elbowing each other off the pavements and roads.

It seemed it was only necessary to let free that respect I felt when I was talking with old Chief Mshlanga, to let both black and white people meet gently, with tolerance for each other's differences: it seemed quite easy.

Then, one day, something new happened. Working in our house as servants were always three natives: cook, houseboy, garden boy. They used to change as the farm natives changed: staying for a few months, then moving on to a new job, or back home to their kraals.[2] They were thought of as "good" or "bad" natives; which meant: how did they behave as servants? Were they lazy, efficient, obedient, or disrespectful? If the family felt good-humoured, the phrase was: "What can you expect from raw black savages?" If we were angry, we said: "These damned niggers, we would be much better off without them."

One day, a white policeman was on his rounds of the district, and he said laughingly: "Did you know you have an important man in your kitchen?"

"What!" exclaimed my mother sharply. "What do you mean?"

"A Chief's son." The policeman seemed amused. "He'll boss the tribe when the old man dies."

"He'd better not put on a Chief's son act with me," said my mother.

When the policeman left, we looked with different eyes at our cook: he was a good worker, but he drank too much at week-ends—that was how we knew him.

He was a tall youth, with very black skin, like black polished metal, his tightly growing black hair parted white man's fashion at one side, with a metal comb from the store stuck into it; very polite, very distant, very quick to obey an order. Now that it had been pointed out, we said: "Of course, you can see. Blood always tells."

My mother became strict with him now she knew about his birth and prospects. Sometimes, when she lost her temper, she would say: "You aren't the Chief yet, you know." And he would answer her very quietly, his eyes on the ground: "Yes, Nkosikaas."

One afternoon he asked for a whole day off, instead of the customary half-day, to go home next Sunday.

"How can you go home in one day?"

---

2. Native villages; collections of huts surrounding a central space.

"It will take me half an hour on my bicycle," he explained.

I watched the direction he took; and the next day I went off to look for this kraal; I understood he must be Chief Mshlanga's successor: there was no other kraal near enough our farm.

Beyond our boundaries on that side the country was new to me. I followed unfamiliar paths past *kopjes* that till now had been part of the jagged horizon, hazed with distance. This was Government land, which had never been cultivated by white men; at first I could not understand why it was that it appeared, in merely crossing the boundary, I had entered a completely fresh type of landscape. It was a wide green valley, where a small river sparkled, and vivid water-birds darted over the rushes. The grass was thick and soft to my calves, the trees stood tall and shapely.

I was used to our farm, whose hundreds of acres of harsh eroded soil bore trees that had been cut for the mine furnaces and had grown thin and twisted, where the cattle had dragged the grass flat, leaving innumerable criss-crossing trails that deepened each season into gullies, under the force of the rains.

This country had been left untouched, save for prospectors whose picks had struck a few sparks from the surface of the rocks as they wandered by; and for migrant natives whose passing had left, perhaps, a charred patch on the trunk of a tree where their evening fire had nestled.

It was very silent: a hot morning with pigeons cooing throatily, the midday shadows lying dense and thick with clear yellow spaces of sunlight between and in all that wide green park-like valley, not a human soul but myself.

I was listening to the quick regular tapping of a woodpecker when slowly a chill feeling seemed to grow up from the small of my back to my shoulders, in a constricting spasm like a shudder, and at the roots of my hair a tingling sensation began and ran down over the surface of my flesh, leaving me goose-fleshed and cold, though I was damp with sweat. Fever? I thought; then uneasily, turned to look over my shoulder; and realized suddenly that this was fear. It was extraordinary, even humiliating. It was a new fear. For all the years I had walked by myself over this country I had never known a moment's uneasiness; in the beginning because I had been supported by a gun and the dogs, then because I had learnt an easy friendliness for the Africans I might encounter.

I had read of this feeling, how the bigness and silence of Africa, under the ancient sun, grows dense and takes shape in the mind, till even the birds seem to call menacingly, and a deadly spirit comes out of the trees and the rocks. You move warily, as if your very passing disturbs something old and evil, something dark and big and angry that might suddenly rear and strike from behind. You look at groves of entwined trees, and picture the animals that might be lurking there; you look at the river running slowly, dropping from level to level through the vlei, spreading into pools where at night the bucks come to drink, and the crocodiles rise and drag them by their soft noses into underwater caves. Fear possessed me. I found I was turning round and round, because of that shapeless menace behind me that might reach out and take me; I kept glancing at the files of *kopjes* which, seen from a different angle, seemed to change with every step so that even known landmarks, like a big mountain that had sentinelled my world since I first became conscious of it, showed an unfamiliar sunlit valley among its foothills. I did not know where I was. I was lost. Panic seized me. I found I was spinning round and round, staring anxiously at this tree and that, peering up at the sun which appeared to have moved into an eastern slant, shedding the sad yellow light of sunset. Hours must have passed! I looked at my watch and found that this state of meaningless terror had lasted perhaps ten minutes.

The point was that it was meaningless. I was not ten miles from home: I had only to take my way back along the valley to find myself at the fence; away among the foothills of the *kopjes* gleamed the roof of a neighbour's house, and a couple of hours' walking would reach it. This was the sort of fear that contracts the flesh of a dog at night and sets him howling at the full moon. It had nothing to do with what I thought or felt; and I was more disturbed by the fact that I could become its victim than of the physical sensation itself: I walked steadily on, quietened, in a divided mind, watching my own pricking nerves and apprehensive glances from side to side with a disgusted amusement. Deliberately I set myself to think of this village I was seeking, and what I should do when I entered it—if I could find it, which was doubtful, since I was walking aimlessly and it might be anywhere in the hundreds of thousands of acres of bush that stretched about me. With my mind on that village, I realized that a new sensation was added to the fear: loneliness. Now such a terror of isolation invaded me that I could hardly walk; and if it were not that I came over the crest of a small rise and saw a village below me, I should have turned and gone home. It was a cluster of thatched huts in a clearing among trees. There were neat patches of mealies and pumpkins and millet, and cattle grazed under some trees at a distance. Fowls scratched among the huts, dogs lay sleeping on the grass, and goats friezed a *kopje* that jutted up beyond a tributary of the river lying like an enclosing arm around the village.

As I came close I saw the huts were lovingly decorated with patterns of yellow and red and ochre mud on the walls; and the thatch was tied in place with plaits of straw.

This was not at all like our farm compound, a dirty and neglected place, a temporary home for migrants who had no roots in it.

And now I did not know what to do next. I called a small black boy, who was sitting on a lot playing a stringed gourd, quite naked except for the strings of blue beads round his neck, and said: "Tell the Chief I am here." The child stuck his thumb in his mouth and stared shyly back at me.

For minutes I shifted my feet on the edge of what seemed a deserted village, till at last the child scuttled off, and then some women came. They were draped in bright cloths, with brass glinting in their ears and on their arms. They also stared, silently; then turned to chatter among themselves.

I said again: "Can I see Chief Mshlanga?" I saw they caught the name; they did not understand what I wanted. I did not understand myself.

At last I walked through them and came past the huts and saw a clearing under a big shady tree, where a dozen old men sat crosslegged on the ground, talking. Chief Mshlanga was leaning back against the tree, holding a gourd in his hand, from which he had been drinking. When he saw me, not a muscle of his face moved, and I could see he was not pleased: perhaps he was afflicted with my own shyness, due to being unable to find the right forms of courtesy for the occasion. To meet me, on our own farm, was one thing; but I should not have come here. What had I expected? I could not join them socially: the thing was unheard of. Bad enough that I, a white girl, should be walking the veld alone as a white man might: and in this part of the bush where only Government officials had the right to move.

Again I stood, smiling foolishly, while behind me stood the groups of brightly clad, chattering women, their faces alert with curiosity and interest, and in front of me sat the old men, with old lined faces, their eyes guarded, aloof. It was a village of ancients and children and women. Even the two young men who kneeled beside the Chief were not those I had seen with him previously: the young men were all away working on the white men's farms and mines, and the Chief must depend on relatives who were temporarily on holiday for his attendants.

"The small white Nkosikaas is far from home," remarked the old man at last.

"Yes," I agreed, "it is far." I wanted to say: "I have come to pay you a friendly visit, Chief Mshlanga." I could not say it. I might now be feeling an urgent helpless desire to get to know these men and women as people, to be accepted by them as a friend, but the truth was I had set out in a spirit of curiosity: I had wanted to see the village that one day our cook, the reserved and obedient young man who got drunk on Sundays, would one day rule over.

"The child of Nkosi Jordan is welcome," said Chief Mshlanga.

"Thank you," I said, and could think of nothing more to say. There was a silence, while the flies rose and began to buzz around my head; and the wind shook a little in the thick green tree that spread its branches over the old men.

"Good morning," I said at last. "I have to return now to my home."

"Morning, little Nkosikaas," said Chief Mshlanga.

I walked away from the indifferent village, over the rise past the staring amber-eyed goats, down through the tall stately trees into the great rich green valley where the river meandered and the pigeons cooed tales of plenty and the woodpecker tapped softly.

The fear had gone; the loneliness had set into stiff-necked stoicism; there was now a queer hostility in the landscape, a cold, hard, sullen indomitability that walked with me, as strong as a wall, as intangible as smoke; it seemed to say to me: you walk here as a destroyer. I went slowly homewards, with an empty heart: I had learned that if one cannot call a country to heel like a dog, neither can one dismiss the past with a smile in an easy gush of feeling, saying: I could not help it, I am also a victim.

I only saw Chief Mshlanga once again.

One night my father's big red land was trampled down by small sharp hooves, and it was discovered that the culprits were goats from Chief Mshlanga's kraal. This had happened once before, years ago.

My father confiscated all the goats. Then he sent a message to the old Chief that if he wanted them he would have to pay for the damage.

He arrived at our house at the time of sunset one evening, looking very old and bent now, walking stiffly under his regally-draped blanket, leaning on a big stick. My father sat himself down in his big chair below the steps of the house; the old man squatted carefully on the ground before him, flanked by his two young men.

The palaver was long and painful, because of the bad English of the young man who interpreted, and because my father could not speak dialect, but only kitchen kaffir.

From my father's point of view, at least two hundred pounds' worth of damage had been done to the crop. He knew he could not get the money from the old man. He felt he was entitled to keep the goats. As for the old Chief, he kept repeating angrily: "Twenty goats! My people cannot lose twenty goats! We are not rich, like the Nkosi Jordan, to lose twenty goats at once."

My father did not think of himself as rich, but rather as very poor. He spoke quickly and angrily in return, saying that the damage done meant a great deal to him, and that he was entitled to the goats.

At last it grew so heated that the cook, the Chief's son, was called from the kitchen to be interpreter, and now my father spoke fluently in English, and our cook translated rapidly so that the old man could understand how very angry my father was. The young man spoke without emotion, in a mechanical way, his eyes lowered, but showing how he felt his position by a hostile uncomfortable set of the shoulders.

It was now in the late sunset, the sky a welter of colours, the birds singing their last songs, and the cattle, lowing peacefully, moving past us towards their sheds for the night. It was the hour when Africa is most beautiful; and here was this pathetic, ugly scene, doing no one any good.

At last my father stated finally: "I'm not going to argue about it. I am keeping the goats."

The old Chief flashed back in his own language: "That means that my people will go hungry when the dry season comes."

"Go to the police, then," said my father, and looked triumphant.

There was, of course, no more to be said.

The old man sat silent, his head bent, his hands dangling helplessly over his withered knees. Then he rose, the young men helping him, and he stood facing my father. He spoke once again, very stiffly; and turned away and went home to his village.

"What did he say?" asked my father of the young man, who laughed uncomfortably and would not meet his eyes.

"What did he say?" insisted my father.

Our cook stood straight and silent, his brows knotted together. Then he spoke. "My father says: All this land, this land you call yours, is his land, and belongs to our people."

Having made this statement, he walked off into the bush after his father, and we did not see him again.

Our next cook was a migrant from Nyasaland, with no expectations of greatness.

Next time the policeman came on his rounds he was told this story. He remarked: "That kraal has no right to be there; it should have been moved long ago. I don't know why no one has done anything about it. I'll have a chat with the Native Commissioner next week. I'm going over for tennis on Sunday, anyway."

Some time later we heard that Chief Mshlanga and his people had been moved two hundred miles east, to a proper Native Reserve; the Government land was going to be opened up for white settlement soon.

I went to see the village again, about a year afterwards. There was nothing there. Mounds of red mud, where the huts had been, had long swathes of rotting thatch over them, veined with the red galleries of the white ants. The pumpkin vines rioted everywhere, over the bushes, up the lower branches of trees so that the great golden balls rolled underfoot and dangled overhead: it was a festival of pumpkins. The bushes were crowding up, the new grass sprang vivid green.

The settler lucky enough to be allotted the lush warm valley (if he chose to cultivate this particular section) would find, suddenly, in the middle of a mealie field, the plants were growing fifteen feet tall, the weight of the cobs dragging at the stalks, and wonder what unsuspected vein of richness he had struck.

TADEUSZ BOROWSKI
1922–1951

Incarcerated in the extermination camps of Auschwitz-Birkenau, Dautmergen, and Dachau-Allach between the ages of twenty and twenty-two, a tormented suicide by gas at twenty-nine, Tadeusz Borowski wrote stories of life in the camps that have made him the foremost writer of the "literature of atrocity." The stories' brutal realism and matter-of-fact tone convey, as passionate declamations could never do, the mind-numbing horror of a situation in which systematic slaughter was the background for everyday life. The narrator of these stories, modeled on Borowski but also a composite figure, has become part of the concentration-camp system, a survivor. He assists the Kapos, or senior prisoners who organize the camp; has a job in the system; and carries a burden of guilt that cannot quite be suppressed by his adopted impersonal attitude. Borowski's stories shocked their postwar audience by their uncompromising honesty: here were no saintly victims and demoniacally evil executioners, but human beings going about the business of extermination or, reduced to near-animal level, cooperating in their own and others' destruction. Any belief in civilization, in common humanity, or in divine Providence is sorely tested; Borowski's bleak picture questions everything and does not pretend to offer encouragement. His fiction is still read for its powerful evocation of the death camps, for its analysis of human relationships under pressure, and for an agonizing portrayal of individuals forced to choose between physical or spiritual survival.

Tadeusz Borowski was born on November 12, 1922, in the Polish city of Żytomierz, part of the then-Soviet Ukraine. When he was three years old, his father was sent to a labor camp in Siberia as a suspected dissident; four years later, his mother was deported as well, and Tadeusz and his twelve-year-old brother were separated. He was raised by an aunt and educated in a Soviet school until a prisoner exchange in 1932 brought his father home and his mother's release in 1934 reunited the family. Money was scarce, however, and the young boy was sent away to a Franciscan boarding school, where he could be educated inexpensively. Much later, he commented that he had never had a family life: "Either my father was sitting in Murmansk or my mother was in Siberia, or I was in a boarding school, on my own or in a camp." World War II began when he was still sixteen, and—since the Nazis did not permit higher education for Poles—Borowski continued his studies at Warsaw University via illegal underground classes. Unlike his fellow students, he refused to join political groups and did not become involved in the resistance; he wanted merely to write poetry, continue his literary studies, and write a master's thesis on the poetry of Leopold Staff. Polish publications were illegal, however, and his first poetry collection, *Wherever the Earth* (1942)—run off in 165 copies on a clandestine mimeograph machine— was enough to condemn him. *Wherever the Earth* prefigures the bleak perspective of the concentration camp stories: prophesying the end of the human race, it sees the world as a gigantic labor camp and the sky as a "low, steel lid" or "a factory ceiling" (an oppressive image he may have adapted from Baudelaire's *Spleen LXXXI*; see p. 1551). Borowski and his fiancée, Maria Rundo, were arrested in late February 1943 and sent to Auschwitz two months later. In the meantime, he was able to see from his cell window both the Jewish uprising in the Warsaw ghetto and the ghetto's fiery destruction by Nazi soldiers.

Borowski's camp experiences are reproduced in the 1946 collection *We Were in Auschwitz*, which he wrote with two other former Auschwitz prisoners, Janusz Nel Siedlecki and Krystyn Olszewski, and from which *Ladies and Gentlemen, to the Gas Chamber* is taken. Arriving in Auschwitz, he was put to hard labor with the other prisoners; but after a bout with pneumonia, he learned to survive by taking a position as an orderly in the Auschwitz hospital—which was not just a clinic but a place where prisoners were used as experimental subjects. Maria had been sent to the women's barracks at the same camp, and he wrote her daily letters that were smuggled in. The story *Auschwitz, Our Home* contains a series of such letters and conveys, in addition to reassurances of his love, the writer's succeeding moods of hope, anger, cynicism, and despair ("We remain as numb as trees when they are being cut down"). Love lyrics written to Maria in 1942, published by his friends in 1944, display the sensuous softness of dream and contrast sharply with the camp stories' harsh illumination.

> I'm dreamy today. Noise from the street,
> the sky-curtain's rustlings, every
> sound comes in like the horizon's smoke
> through a mist.
> . . . It's how at night
> I take your hair in my hand, let its
> waves flow through my palm and
> stay quiet, full of you,
> as sleep is quiet now in me.
> (trans. Addison Bross)

The narrator's dispassionate tone in the stories, as he describes senseless cruelty and mass murder, individual scenes of desperation, or the eccentric emotions of people about to die, continue to shock many readers. Borowski is certainly describing a world of antiheroes, those who survive by accommodating themselves to things as they are and avoiding acts of heroism. His second collection of stories, *The World of Stone* (1948), uses the same tone to describe life in postwar Germany (he spent two years in Munich before returning to Poland) and the writer's disgust at the false normalcy of postwar society. Yet his impersonality is chiefly a shield; vulnerable, he finds a way to cope with overwhelming events by holding them at a distance. Borowski is recording events for future testimony, and he writes to his fiancée, "I do not know whether we shall survive, but I like to think that one day we shall have the courage to tell the world the whole truth and call it by its proper name." At the end of *The World of Stone*, his ambition is "to grasp the true significance of the events, things, and people I have seen. For I intend to write."

Upon his return to Poland after the war, Borowski's searing talent was recognized; the stories *Ladies and Gentlemen, to the Gas Chamber* and *A Day at Harmensee* (a subcamp of Auschwitz) had been published, and he became a prominent writer. He married Maria and was courted by Poland's Stalinist government. At the government's urging, he wrote journalism and weekly stories that followed political lines and employed a newly strident tone. The Cold War had begun, and Borowski was persuaded that he had joined a popular revolution that would prevent any more horrors like Auschwitz. He went so far as to do intelligence work in Berlin for the Polish secret police in 1949. The revelation of Soviet prison camps, however, and political purges in Poland gradually disillusioned him: once more, he was part of a concentration-camp system and complicit with the oppressors. He committed suicide by gas on July 1, 1951.

Ladies and Gentlemen, to the Gas Chamber was written in Munich in an apartment shared with Nel Siedlecki and Olszewski; the three men had been transferred from Dachau-Allach to the Freimann repatriation camp outside Munich, which they soon left when the Polish artist and publisher Anatol Girs located them and found them jobs. (Many Birkenau prisoners were transferred to the repatriation camp as the Allied armies moved farther into Germany.) Narrated in an impersonal tone by one of the prisoners, the story describes the extermination camp of Birkenau, the second and largest of three concentration camps at Auschwitz (Polish: *Oświęcim*), an enclosed world of hierarchical authority and desperate struggles to survive. Food, shoes, shirts, underwear: this vital currency of the camp is obtained when new prisoners are stripped of their belongings as they arrive in railway cattle cars. The story could equally well have been entitled *A Day with Canada*, for it follows the narrator's first trip to the railroad station with the labor battalion "Canada." The trip will salvage goods from a train bringing fifteen thousand Polish Jews, former inhabitants of the cities Sosnowiec and Będzin. By the end of the day, most of the travelers will be burning in the crematorium, and the camp will live for a few more days on the loot from "a good, rich transport."

Borowski suggests the systematic dehumanization of the camps from the beginning: people are equated with lice, and they mill around by naked thousands in blocked-off sections. Lice and people are poisoned with the same gas, sealed tightly into the camp or expelled from a section by the delousing process. People will later be equated with sick horses (the converted stables retain their old signs), lumber and concrete trucked in from the railroad station, and insects whose jaws work away on moldy pieces of bread. Constantly supervised, subject to arbitrary rules and punishment, malnourished and pushed to exhaustion, their identities reduced to numbers tattooed on the arm, the prisoners live in the shadow of a hierarchical authority that is to be feared and placated. Paradoxically, their common vulnerability leads to alienation and rage at their fellow victims rather than at the executioners. The Nazis have foreseen everything, explains the narrator's friend Henri, including the fact that helplessness needs to vent itself on someone weaker. The only way to cope is to distance oneself from what is happening, to become a cog in the machine so that one does not really experience what is happening—to suspend, for the moment, one's humanity.

Borowski emphasizes the range of cultures and languages brought together in Birkenau, and that variety is contrasted with the rigid narrowness of their jailers. French, Russian, and German phrases appear in this Polish-language story, as well as the camp "Esperanto" spoken by the Greeks. Separate scenes focus on the suffering of individual men, women, and children; and the narrator mentions the chaotic, multicolored appearance of the crowds in their rags and variously striped uniforms. Over and against this cultural multiplicity is set the narrowly homogeneous model of the Nazi authorities: a lock-step "one mass, one will," bred from "Aryan" genes and trained in obedience to the Führer. The soldier with his blond hair and blue eyes, or the blonde woman commandant who wears her hair in a "Nordic" knot, offer images of the proposed master race. The SS officers are sleek, clean-shaven, and well fed; they dress in identical uniforms with silver insignia, shiny boots, whips and revolvers, and briefcases to keep records in order. It is a picture of prosperity and efficient organization, all the more chilling in its pretense of normalcy and civilized behavior. The same officer who urges prisoners ("Gentlemen") to be orderly and show goodwill suddenly whips a woman stooping to pick up a handbag. Sharp contrasts emphasize the hollowness of their civilized image: a group of officers shake hands and share news from home and family pictures while the train of deportees rolls into the station; an officer fumbles with a balky cigarette lighter as he orders the labor detail to remove infants' corpses from the cattle car; another officer superciliously refers to a desperate woman who tries to escape being condemned with her child as an "unnatural mother."

It is the narrator's first experience with the Canada salvage team, and he expects that his carefully cultivated impersonality will work as well here as it has in the camp. This day will test his defenses, however, and his ability to survive through willful alienation. For a while, he registers events intellectually, noting the dimensions of the camp and crematoria. Soon, however, unforeseen emotional challenges arise, and his control becomes shaky.

Words of sympathy from a condemned woman strike home: his vision blurs, and he asks Henri, "Are we good people?" It is only the first in a series of shocks, however, culminating when an apparently dead body grasps his hand. Vomiting from the cumulative horror, the narrator finds that the two dimensions he has tried to keep apart have temporarily fused—and he retreats once more to a dream of alienation. The narrator's utter defeat and despair are underlined when the returning labor battalion moves aside for an SS detachment singing lustily about conquering the world. Borowski's story was written after the Nazi downfall, but for the moment the picture is one of a spiritual desolation that not only illustrates a shameful moment in modern history but raises questions about what it means to be civilized, or even "human."

PRONOUNCING GLOSSARY

The following list uses common English syllables and stress accents to provide rough equivalents of selected words whose pronunciation may be unfamiliar to the general reader.

Auschwitz: *ow'-shvits*

Birkenau: *beer'-ken-ow*

Katowice: *kah-toh-veet'-seh*

Sosnowiec-Będzin: *sos-nawv'-yets ben-jin*

Tadeusz Borowski: *tah-day'-oosh baw-raw'-skee*

Ladies and Gentlemen, to the Gas Chamber[1]

The whole camp[2] went about naked. True, we had already passed through the delousing process and received our clothing back from the tanks filled with a dilution of cyclone[3] in water which so excellently poisoned lice in clothing and people in gas chambers—and only the blocks separated from us by trestles had not yet been issued clothing, nonetheless both the former and the latter went about naked: the heat was terrific. The camp was sealed up tight. Not a prisoner, not a louse could venture beyond its gates. The work of the commandos[4] had stopped. Thousands of naked people milled about all day on the roads and roll-call grounds; they siestaed under walls and on the roofs. People slept on bare boards, for the straw mattresses and blankets were being disinfected. The FKL[5] could be seen from the last blocks; delousing was going on there, too. Twenty-eight thousand women had been

1. Translated by Jadwiga Zwolska.　2. Auschwitz II, or Birkenau, the largest of the Nazi extermination camps, established in October 1941 near the town of Birkenau, Poland. Its death toll is usually estimated between 1 million and 2.5 million people.　3. Cyclone-B, the extermination gas.　4. Labor battalions.　5. Frauen Konzentration Lager: Women's concentration camp (German).

stripped and turned out of the blocks; they could be seen right now scrambling on the meadows, roads and roll-call grounds.

The morning is spent in waiting for dinner, contents of food parcels are being eaten, friends visited. The hours pass slowly as they do in extreme heat. Even the usual recreation is lacking: the wide roads to the crematoria are empty. There have been no transports for some days. Part of "Canada"[6] has been liquidated and assigned to a commando. Being well-fed and rested they chanced on the hardest one: the Harmensee.[7] For envious justice rules in the camp: when a mighty one falls, his friends make every effort that he may fall as low as possible. Canada, our Canada, is not like Fiedler's,[8] fragrant with resin, only with French perfume, but fewer tall pines probably grow there than the number of diamonds and coins—collected from all Europe—cached here.

Several of us are sitting right now on a top bunk swinging our legs in a carefree manner. We take out white, extravagantly baked bread: crumbly, falling to pieces, a little provoking in taste, but, for all that, bread that had not been moulding for weeks. Bread sent from Warsaw.[9] Barely a week ago, my mother had it in her hands. Good God . . .

We get out bacon and onions, open a tin of condensed milk. Huge, dripping with sweat, Henri yearns aloud for French wine brought by the transports from Strasbourg, from the vicinities of Paris, from Marseilles[1] . . .

"Listen, *mon ami*,[2] when we go on the loading platform again, I'll bring you real champagne. You've never drunk it, have you?"

"No. But you won't be able to smuggle it across the gate, so don't string me along. You'd better 'organize' a pair of shoes—you know, perforated leather, with a double sole.[3] And I'm not mentioning a sports shirt, you've promised me one long ago."

"Patience, patience. When the transports come I'll bring you everything. We'll go on the loading platform again."

"What if there won't be any more transports for the smokestack?"[4] I threw in maliciously. "You see how things eased up in the camp: unlimited food parcels, flogging not allowed. You've written home, haven't you? . . . People say all sorts of things about the regulations, you yourself do a lot of gabbing. Anyhow, damn it, they'll run out of people."

"Don't talk nonsense," says the plump Marseillaise, his face spiritual like a Cosway[5] miniature (he's my friend, and yet I don't know his name). His mouth filled with a sardine sandwich, he repeated, "don't talk nonsense," swallowing with difficulty ('it went down, damn it,') "don't talk nonsense, they can't run out of people or we'd all be finished in the camp. We all live on what they bring."

"Well, not all. We have food parcels . . ."

"You have, and a pal of yours has, and tens of your pals have them. You Poles have them, and not all of you at that. But we, the Jews, the Russkis?

and what then? If we, the transport 'organization,' had nothing to eat, would you be eating these food parcels of yours so calmly? We wouldn't let you."

"You'd let us, or you'd die of starvation like the Greeks. Whoever in the camp has food, has power."

"You've got them and we've got them, so why quarrel?"

That is true, no use quarreling. You have them and I have them, we eat together, sleep in one bunk. Henri cuts the bread, makes a tomato salad. It has a marvellous taste with the mustard from the camp canteen.

Under us, in the block, naked, sweating people mill about. They move here and there in the passages between the bunks, alongside the huge, ingeniously built stove, amidst the improvements which change the stables (there is still a sign on the door saying that *verseuchte Pferde*[6]—infected horses, should be sent to such and such a place) into a cozy home for more than half a thousand men. They nest on the lower bunks by eights and nines: stinking of sweat and excrement, their cheeks emaciated, they lie naked and bony. Under me, on the very bottom bunk—a rabbi; he has covered his head[7] with a bit of rag torn from the blanket and is reading a Hebrew prayer book (there's plenty of that kind of reading here . . .) in a loud and monotonous lament.

"Maybe we could shut him up? He yells as though he had caught God by the feet."

"I don't feel like getting down from the bunk. Let him yell; he'll go all the quicker to the smokestack."

"Religion is the opium of the people.[8] I like to smoke opium," the Marseillaise to my left, who is a communist and a *rentier*,[9] adds sententiously.

"If they did not believe in God and in a life beyond they'd have wrecked the crematorium long ago."

"And why don't you do it?"

The sense of the question is metaphoric, however, the Marseillaise replies, "Idiot," stuffs his mouth with a tomato and gestures as though he would say something, but he munches and keeps silent. We just finished stuffing ourselves when a bigger hubbub started near the door of the block: the Mussulmen[1] jumped back and scurried off among the bunks. A messenger ran into the block leader's cubbyhole. After a moment the block leader emerged[2] majestically.

"Canada! Fall in! Snappy now! A transport's coming!"

"Good God," shouted Henri, leaping down from the bunk.

The Marseillaise choked on the tomato, grabbed his coat, shouted *"raus"*[3] to those who sat below him, and in a moment they were already in the doorway. Everything seethed on the other bunks. Canada was going to the loading platform.

"Henri, shoes!" I shouted as a farewell. "*Keine Angst*,"[4] he shouted back, already outside.

I packed up the food and tied the satchel with string. In it, cheek by jowl with Portuguese sardines, lay onions and tomatoes from my father's garden

6. Infected horses (German).　7. Jews are expected to keep their heads covered while at prayer.　8. A quotation from the German political philosopher Karl Marx (1818–1883).　9. Someone with unearned income, a stockholder (French).　1. Or Muslim; people who had given up, considered the camp pariahs.　2. A Kapo, or senior prisoner in charge of a group of prisoners.　3. Outside (German).　4. Don't panic (German).

in Warsaw, and the bacon from the "Bacutil" in Lublin (from my brother) mingled with genuine candied fruit from Salonika.[5] I tied it all up, pulled my trousers on and climbed down from the bunk.

"*Platz!*"[6] I shouted, shouldering my way through the Greeks. They drew aside. In the door I came upon Henri.

"*Allez, allez, vite, vite!*"

"*Was ist los?*"[7]

"Do you want to go to the loading platform with us?"

"Can do."

"Then hurry, take your coat. They're a few men short, I spoke to the kapo," and he pushed me out of the block.

We lined up, someone wrote down our numbers, someone at the head shouted: "march, march" and we ran up to the gates accompanied by the babel of the multitude already being driven back to the block with thongs. It was not everyone that could go to the loading platform . . . . Good-byes said, we are already at the gate.

"*Links, zwei, drei, vier! Mützen ab!*"[8] Straightened up, with arms held stiffy at hips, we pass through the gate with a brisk, springy step—almost gracefully. Holding a huge tablet in his hand, a sleepy SS[9]-man counts drowsily, separating with his finger in the air every five men.

"*Hundert!*"[1] he shouted when the last five had passed him.

"*Stimmt!*"[2] a hoarse voice calls back from the head.

We march rapidly, almost at a run. Many outposts: youngsters with automatics. We pass all the sectors of Camp II B: the untenanted *Lager*[3] C, Czech and quarantine, and plunge deep among the apple and pear trees of the military hospital; amidst the exotic verdure, as though out of the moon, strangely exuberant these few sunny days, we pass in an arc some sort of wooden sheds, pass the big *Postenkette* lines and in a run reach the highway—we are there. A few score metres more, and among the trees—the loading platform.

It was an idyllic platform, as is usual with rural stations lost in remote areas. A square, bordered with the green of tall trees, was strewn with gravel. A tiny wooden shack squatted down at one side of the road, uglier and more jerry-built than the ugliest and flimsiest station shack. Farther away lay great stacks of rails, railway sleepers, piles of deal boards, parts of wooden sheds, bricks, stones and concrete well-rings. It is here that goods are unloaded for Birkenau: material for the expansion of the camp and people for the gas chambers. An ordinary work day: trucks drive up, take lumber, cement, people . . . .

Guards take their places on the rails, on the lumber, under the green shade of the Silesian[4] chestnuts, they surround the loading platform with a tight

5. Major port city in northeast Greece. Lublin is a city in eastern Poland. *Bacutil*: a meat-products company with branches in many Polish cities.   6. Make room (German).   7. What's the matter? (German). *Allez, allez, vite, vite!*: Come on, come on, quickly, quickly! (French).   8. Left, two, three, four! Caps off! (German).   9. Abbreviation for *Schutzstaffel* (Protective echelon, German), the Nazi police system that began as Hitler's private guard and grew, by 1939, to a powerful 250,000-member military and political organization that administered all state security functions. The SS was divided into many bureaucratic units, one of which, the Death's Head Battalions, managed the concentration camps. Selected for physical perfection and (Aryan) racial purity, SS members wore black or gray-green uniforms decorated with silver insignia.   1. A hundred! (German).   2. Right! (German).   3. Camp (German).   4. Probably local chestnuts. Silesia, in central Europe, was partitioned among Poland, Czechoslovakia, and Germany after World War I; Germany occupied Polish Silesia in 1939.

circle. They wipe perspiration from their foreheads and drink from their canteens. The heat is terrific, the sun stands motionless in the zenith. "Fall out!" We sit in patches of shade under the stacked rails. The hungry Greeks (a few of them have managed, the devil knows how, to slip out with us) ferret among the rails; someone finds a tin of food, mouldy buns, an unfinished tin of sardines. They eat.

"*Schweinedreck*,"[5] a tall, young guard with abundant blond hair and dreamy blue eyes, spits at them. "After all, you'll have so much grub in a moment that you won't be able to gobble it all. You'll have your fill for a long time." He adjusts his automatic and wipes his face with a handkerchief.

"Swine," we confirm in unison.

"Hey you, fatty," the guard's shoe touches lightly the back of Henri's neck. "*Pass mal auf*,[6] want a drink?"

"I'm thirsty, but I've no marks," the Frenchman replies in a business-like manner.

"Too bad."

"But, *Herr*[7] Guard, doesn't my word mean anything any more? Hasn't *Herr* Guard done business with me? How much?"

"A hundred. A deal?"

"A deal."

We drink the insipid and tasteless water on tick against the money and people not yet here.

"Look here, you," the Frenchman says throwing away the empty bottle which crashes somewhere away on the rails, "take no money, for there may be a search. And, anyway, what the hell d'you need money for, you've got enough to eat. Don't take a suit either, for that's suspicious, and might look like a get-away. Take a shirt, but only a silk one and with a collar. Underneath, a gym vest. And if you find anything to drink, don't call me. I can take care of myself. And look out you don't get walloped."

"Do they whip you?"

"That's normal. One has to have eyes in the back. *Arschaugen*."[8]

All around us sit the Greeks; like huge, inhuman insects they move their jaws greedily and voraciously devour mouldy chunks of bread. They are uneasy because they do not know what they're going to do. They are alarmed by the lumber and the rails. They don't like lifting heavy loads.

"*Was wir arbeiten?*"[9] they ask.

"*Nix. Transport kommen, alles Krematorium, compris?*"[1]

"*Alles verstehen*," they reply in the crematorium Esperanto.[2] They calm down; they won't have to load the rails on trucks or carry the lumber.

In the meantime the loading platform has become more and more noisy and crowded. The foremen are dividing up the groups, assigning some to opening and unloading the railway cars that are to arrive; others they assign to the wooden steps and explain to them how to work properly. These were wide, portable steps like those to mount a rostrum. Roaring motorcycles arrived bringing non-commissioned SS officers, hefty, well fed men in glossy

---

5. Dirty pigs (German).   6. See here (German).   7. Mister (German).   8. Eyes in your ass (German, literal trans.).   9. What are we working on? (German).   1. Nothing. Transport coming, everything crematorium, understood? (German; *compris* is French).   2. An artificial language created in 1887 by L. L. Zamenhof to simplify communication between different nationalities. *Alles verstehen:* Everything understood.

top-boots, with bespangled silver insignia, their faces churly and shiny. Some arrived with brief cases, others had flexible reed canes. This gave them an official and efficient air. They entered the canteen—for that miserable shack was their canteen where in summer they drank mineral water, *Sudeten-quelle*,[3] and in winter warmed themselves with hot wine.

They greeted one another in stately fashion: the arm stretched out in the Roman manner[4] and then, cordially shaking hands, they smiled warmly at one another, talked about letters, news from home, their children; they showed one another photographs. Some of them promenaded in the square with dignity, the gravel crunched, the boots crunched, the silver distinctions gleamed on the collars and the bamboo canes swished impatiently.

The throng in vari-coloured camp stripes lay in the narrow strips of shade under the rails, breathed heavily and unevenly, chattered in their own tongue, gazed lazily and indifferently at the majestic people in the green uniforms, at the green of the trees—near and unattainable, at the spires of a distant church from which a belated Angelus[5] was just being rung.

"The transport's coming," said someone, and all of them rose expectantly. The freight cars were coming around the bend, the locomotive driving from behind. The brakeman standing on the tender, leaned out, waved his arm and whistled. The locomotive whistled screechingly in reply, panted, and the train chugged slowly along the station. In the small, barred windows could be seen human faces, pale and crumpled, dishevelled as though they had not had enough sleep; terrified women, and men who, strange to say, had hair. They passed slowly and looked at the station in silence. And then, inside the cars there began a seething and a pounding on the wooden walls.

"Water! Air!" rose dull, despairing shrieks.

Human faces leaned out of windows, mouths desperately gasped for air. Having drawn a few gulps of air the people left the windows and others stormed their places and then also disappeared. The screams and the rattling grew louder and louder.

A man in a green uniform more bespangled with silver than that of the others, frowned with disgust. He puffed on his cigarette, then threw it away with a sudden motion, transferred his brief case from his right to his left hand and beckoned to a guard. The latter slowly removed his automatic from his shoulder, took aim and fired a round at the railway cars. Silence fell. In the meantime trucks backed up to the train, stools were placed at the back of each, and the camp workers took positions expertly at the cars. The giant with the brief case made a sign with his hand.

"Whoever takes gold or anything else but food will be shot as a thief of *Reich*property. Understood? *Verstanden?*"

"*Jawohl!*"[6] came the shout, discordant but expressing good will.

"*Also loos!*[7] To work!"

The bolts clattered, the freight cars were opened. A wave of fresh air rushed inside, stunning people as though with monoxide gas. Packed to the limit, overwhelmed by a fantastic amount of luggage: suitcases, satchels,

---

3. Water from the Sudetenland or Sudeten Mountains; a narrow strip of land on the northern and western borders of the Czech Republic. The Sudeten was annexed by Hitler in 1938.   4. The official "Heil Hitler!" (Hail Hitler!) salute, with the straight right arm abruptly raised in imitation of ancient Roman military salutes. Adolf Hitler was chancellor of Germany under Nazism (1933–45).   5. A call to prayer, rung three times a day in the Catholic Church. *Green uniforms*: i.e., the regular gray-green army uniforms. 6. Yes! (German). *Verstanden*: understand? (German).   7. Then get going!

gladstone bags, rucksacks and bundles of every description (for they were bringing everything that had constituted their former life and was to start their future) they were squeezed into terribly cramped quarters, fainting from the heat, being suffocated and smothering others. Now they had clustered around the open door, panting like fish thrown on sand.

"Attention! Get down with your luggage. Take everything. Place all your duds in a pile near the car. Hand over your coats. It's summer. March to the left. Understand?"

"Sir, what's going to happen to us?"—uneasy, nerves quivering, they are already jumping down onto the gravel.

"Where are you from?"

"Sosnowiec, Będzin.[8] Sir, what'll happen?" They stubbornly repeat the questions, gazing fervently into strange, tired eyes.

"I don't know, I don't understand Polish."

There is the law of the camp that people going to their death must be deceived to the last moment. It is the only permissible form of pity. The heat is sweltering. The sun has reached its zenith, the burnished sky trembles, the air shimmers; the wind, which blows through us intermittently, is merely hot, moist air. Lips are already cracked, the mouth savours the salty taste of blood. The body is weak and stiff from lying long in the sun. To drink, oh, to drink!

Like a stupefied, blind river that seeks a new bed, the motley throng, heavily laden, pours out of the car. But before they regain consciousness after being stunned by the fresh air and the smell of verdure, their baggage is torn from their hands, coats pulled off them, handbags snatched from the women's hands, sunshades taken away.

"But, mister, that's my sunshade, I can't . . ."

"*Verboten*,"[9] a guard barks through his teeth, hissing loud. In the back stands an SS-man: calm, self-possessed, expert.

"*Meine Herrschaften*,[1] don't throw your things about like that. You must show a little good will." He speaks kindly, and the thin cane bends with the nervous movement of his hands.

"Yes, sir, yes, sir," they reply in unison passing by, and walk at a brisker pace alongside the train cars. A woman bends down and quickly picks up a handbag. The cane swished, the woman cried out, stumbled and fell under the feet of the crowd. A child running behind her squeaked: "*Mamele!*"— just a tousled little girl . . .

The heap of things grows: suitcases, bundles, rucksaks, travel rugs, clothes, and handbags which open in falling and spill rainbow-coloured banknotes, gold, watches; in front of the car doors there rise piles of bread, collections of jars with multi-coloured jams and marmalades; pyramids of hams and sausages swell out, sugar spills on the gravel. Trucks packed with people drive away with an infernal racket amidst the lamentations and the shrieks of women wailing for their children separated from them, while the men, in stupefied silence, suddenly remain alone. They are the ones who went to the right: the young and healthy, they will go to the camp. They will not escape gassing, but first they will be put to work.

The trucks drive away and return continuously like some monstrous

---

8. Two cities in Katowice province (southern Poland). Będzin was also the site of a concentration camp, and more than ten thousand of its inhabitants were exterminated.   9. Forbidden (German).   1. Gentlemen (German).

assembly line. The Red-Cross[2] ambulance goes back and forth ceaselessly. The huge, blood-red cross on the radiator cover melts in the sun. The Red-Cross ambulance travels tirelessly: it is precisely this car that carries that gas, the gas which will poison these people.

Those from "Canada" who are near the steps have not a moment's rest: they separate the people for gassing from those who go to the camp; they push the former on to the steps and pack them in the trucks: sixty, more or less, to a truck.

A young, clean-shaven gentleman, an SS-man, stands at the side with a notebook in his hand; each truck means a check mark—when sixteen trucks pass, it means a thousand, more or less. The gentleman is poised and accurate. No truck will leave without his knowledge and his check mark. *Ordnung muss sein.*[3] The check marks swell into thousands, the thousands swell into whole transports of which brief mention is made: "From Salonika," "from Strasbourg," "from Rotterdam."[4] Today's transport will be referred to as "from Będzin." But it will receive the permanent name of "Będzin–Sosnowiec." Those who will go to the work camp from this transport will receive numbers 131–132. Thousands, of course, but abbreviated they will be referred to just like that: 131–132.

The transports grow with the passing of weeks, months, years. When the war is over, the cremated will be counted. There will be four and a half million of them. The bloodiest battle of the war, the greatest victory of Germany united in solidarity. *Ein Reich, ein Volk, ein Führer*[5] and—four crematoria. But in Oświęcim there will be sixteen crematoria capable of incinerating fifty thousand bodies daily. The camp is being expanded until its electrified wire fence will reach the Vistula;[6] it will be inhabited by 300,000 people in camp stripes, it will be called *Verbrecher-Stadt*—the City of Criminals. No, they will not run short of people. Jews will be cremated, Poles will be cremated, Russians will be cremated; people will come from the West and from the South, from the continent and from islands. People in prison stripes will come, they will rebuild ruined German towns, plough the fallow soil and when they weaken from pitiless toil, from an eternal *Bewegung!*[7] *Bewegung!* the doors of the gas chambers will open. The chambers will be improved, more economical, more cleverly camouflaged. They will be like those in Dresden about which legends were already rife.

The cars are already empty. A thin, pock-marked SS-man calmly glances inside, nods his head with disgust, encompasses us with his glance and points inside:

"*Rein.*[8] Clean it out!"

We jump inside. Babies, naked monsters with huge heads and bloated bellies, lie scattered about in corners amidst human excrement and lost watches. They are carried out like chickens: a few of them making a handful.

"Don't take them to the truck. Let the women have them," says the SS-man lighting a cigarette. His lighter has stuck, he is extremely busy with it.

"For God's sake, take these babies," I burst out, for the women run away from me in terror, drawing in their heads between lifted shoulders.

2. Ordinary trucks were painted with Red Cross insignia to quiet incoming prisoners by suggesting that they would receive humane treatment and medical care.   3. Order in everything (German).   4. Large port city in the Netherlands.   5. One State, One People, One Leader! (the slogan of Nazi Germany).   6. A river running through central Poland.   7. Hurry up! (German).   8. Clean (German).

The name of God is strangely unnecessary, for the women with the children go to the trucks, all of them—there is no exception. We all know what that means and look at one another with hate and horror.

"What's that, you don't want them?" The pock-marked SS-man asked as though surprised and reproachful, and starts to ready his revolver.

"No need to shoot, I'll take them."

A grey-haired, tall lady took the infants from me and for a while looked straight into my eyes.

"You poor child," she whispered smiling. Stumbling on the gravel she walked away.

I leaned on the side of a railway car. I was extremely tired. Someone is tugging my arm.

"*En avant*,[9] under the rails, come on!"

I gaze: the face flickers before my eyes, it melts—it huge and transparent—it becomes confused with the trees, immobile and strangely black, with the pouring throngs . . . I blink my eyes sharply: Henri.

"Look here, Henri, are we good people?"

"Why ask stupid questions?"

"You see, my friend, an unreasonable rage at these people wells up in me that I must be here on their account. I am not in the least sorry for them, that they're going to the gas chambers. May the ground open under them all. I'd throw myself on them with my fists. This must be pathological, I can't understand it."

"Oh, no, quite the contrary, it's normal, foreseen and taken into account. You are tired with this unloading business, you're rebellious, and rage can best be vented on someone weaker. It's even desirable that you should vent it. That's common sense, *compris?*" says the Frenchman somewhat ironically, placing himself comfortably under the rails. "Look at the Greeks, they know how to make the best of it. They gobble up everything they lay their hands on; I saw one of them finish a whole jar of jam."

"Cattle. Half of them will die tomorrow of the trots."

"Cattle? You, too, were hungry."

"Cattle," I repeat obstinately. I close my eyes, hear the shrieks, feel the trembling of the ground and the humid air on my lips. My throat is completely dry.

The flow of people is endless, the trucks growl like enraged dogs. Corpses are brought out of the cars before my eyes; trampled children, cripples laid out with the corpses, and crowds, crowds . . . . Railway cars are brought alongside the loading platform, the piles of rags, suitcases and rucksacks grow, people get out, look at the sun, breathe, beg for water, enter the trucks, drive away. Again cars are rolled up, again people . . . I feel the pictures become confused within me, I don't know if all this is really happening, or if I'm dreaming. I suddenly see the green of trees rocking with an entire street, with a motley crowd: but yes, it's the Avenue![1] My head is whirring. I feel that in a moment I will vomit.

Henri tugs at my arm.

"Don't sleep, we're going to load the stuff."

9. Forward (French).   1. A famous boulevard in the center of Warsaw that used to be the Polish king's route from the current Old Town to outside the city.

There are no more people. Stirring up huge clouds of dust, the last trucks move along the highway in the distance, the train has left, the SS-men walk stiff-necked on the emptied loading platform, the silver on their collars sparkling. Their boots gleam, their bloated red faces shine. There is a woman among them. Only now do I realize that she been here all the time, this dried-up, bosomless, bony woman. Sparse, colourless hair combed smoothly back and tied in a "Nordic"[2] knot, her hands in the pockets of her wide trouser-skirt. She strides from one end of the loading platform to the other, a rat-like, rancorous smile on her dry lips. She hates feminine beauty with the hatred of a repulsive woman aware of her repulsiveness. Yes, I have seen her many times and well remember her; she's the commandant of the FKL; she has come to look over her acquisitions, for some of the women have been stood aside and will walk to the camp. Our boys, hairdressers from Zaune,[3] will shave their heads completely and will have no end of fun at the sight of their humiliation, so alien to camp life.

So we load the stuff. We drag the heavy valises, spacious, well stocked, and with an effort throw them on the truck. There they are stacked, rammed down, crammed; anything that can be cut is carved up with a knife for the pleasure of it and in search of alcohol and perfume; the latter is poured right over oneself. One of the valises opens up: clothing, shirts, books tumble out . . . I grab a bundle, it is heavy, I open it: gold, two good handfuls—watch cases, bracelets, rings, necklaces, diamonds . . .

"*Gib her*,"[4]—an SS-man says calmly, holding up an open brief case full of gold and coloured foreign banknotes. He closes it, gives it to an officer, takes another empty one and stands on guard at another truck. The gold will go to the *Reich*.[5]

Heat, sweltering heat. The air stands like an immobile, white-hot column. Throats are parched, every spoken word causes pain. Oh, for a drink! We work feverishly: faster and faster, if only to get into shade, if only to rest. We finish loading, the last trucks leave; we pick up every bit of paper lying on the railway track, dig out of the fine gravel the alien rubbish of the transport, "so that no trace of that filth is left," and at the moment when the last truck disappears beyond the trees and we finally go towards the rails to rest and drink (maybe the Frenchman will again buy it from the guard?), the whistle of the railway man is heard from beyond the bend. Slowly, extremely slowly cars roll up, the locomotive whistles back screechingly, from the windows human faces look out, pale and crumpled and flattened like paper cut-outs, their eyes huge and feverish. The trucks are here already, and the calm gentleman with his notebook; the SS-men with brief cases for the gold and money come out of the canteen. We open the cars.

No, self-control is no longer possible. Valises are brutally jerked out of people's hands, overcoats torn off. "Go on, go on, move on!" They go, they pass on. Men, women, children. Some of them know . . .

Here is a woman walking quickly, hurrying imperceptibly but feverishly. A small child only a few years old, with the rosy, chubby face of a cherub, runs after her; it cannot catch up with her and holds out its little arms crying: "Mummy, mummy!"

---

2. A northern (especially Scandinavian) style, encouraged by the Nazis to establish an image of Teutonic racial purity.   3. The "sauna" barracks, in front of Canada, where prisoners were bathed, shaved, and deloused.   4. Give it to me (German).   5. The German state.

"You, woman, pick up the child!"

"It isn't mine, sir, it isn't mine!" the woman shouts hysterically and, covering her face with her hands, runs away. She wants to hide, she wants to catch up with the other women who will not go by truck, who will walk, who will live. She is young, healthy and pretty, she wants to live.

But the child follows her, complaining loudly:

"Mummy, mummy, don't run away!"

"It isn't mine, no, it isn't!"

Finally, Andrei, a sailor from Sevastopol,[6] caught up with her. His eyes were bleary from vodka and the heat. He caught up with her, knocked her off her feet with one wide swing of his arm, grabbed her by the hair when she was falling and put her on her feet her again. His face is livid with rage.

"Oh, you, *yebi tvoyu mat' blad' jevreyskaya!*[7] So you'd run away from your child! I'll fix you, you whore!" He caught her round her waist, choked down her shriek with a huge paw and with a swing threw her like a heavy sack of grain on the truck.

"That's for you! Take it, you bitch!" and threw the child at her feet.

"*Gut gemacht,* that's how unnatural mothers should be punished," said the SS-man who stood at the truck. "*Gut, gut Russki.*"[8]

"Shut up!" Andrei growled through his teeth and walked up to the railway cars. He drew out a canteen hidden under a pile of rags, unscrewed it, put it to his mouth and then to mine. Raw alcohol. It burns the throat. A roar in the head, my legs wobble under me, my gorge rises.

Suddenly, from this tide of humanity which, like a river driven by an invisible force, blindly pushes on toward the trucks, a girl emerged, jumped lightly from the car onto the gravel, and looked about her with a searching glance like one surprised at something.

Thick blond hair has spilled in a soft wave on her shoulders; she tossed it back impatiently. She instinctively passed her hands over her blouse, furtively adjusted her skirt. She stood like that for a moment. Finally, she tore her eyes away from the crowd and her gaze moved over our faces as though searching for someone. Unconsciously I sought to catch her glance, until our eyes met.

"Listen, tell me, where are they taking us?"

I looked at her. Here, before me, stood a girl with beautiful blond hair, wonderful breasts in an organdy summer blouse, her look wise and mature. Here she stood looking straight into my face and waited. Here, the gas chamber: mass death, loathsome and revolting. Here, the camp: a shaved head, quilted Soviet trousers in all that heat, the obnoxious, sickly odour of dirty, overheated feminine body; the animal hunger, inhuman toil, and the same gas chamber, only the death still more disgusting, more revolting, more horrible. Whoever has once entered here will never again pass the sentry post, not even as a handful of ashes, will never return to his former life.

"Why did she ever bring it here, they'll take it away from her," I thought automatically, seeing on her wrist a wonderful watch on a fine, gold bracelet. Tuśka had one like it, but hers was on a narrow, black ribbon.

"Listen, answer me."

6. A Soviet (now Russian) port on the Black Sea.   7. An untranslatable, extremely vulgar Russian expression.   8. Good, good, Russky (German). *Gut gemacht*: well done (German).

I remained silent. She set her mouth.

"I already know," she said with a shade of haughty contempt in her voice, throwing her head back; boldly she walked up to the trucks. Someone wanted to stop her, but she boldly moved him aside and ran up the steps into the nearly filled truck. In the distance I saw only the thick, blond hair tousled by the speed.

I went into cars, carried out the infants, threw out the luggage. I touched corpses but could not overcome the wild terror welling up within me. I ran away from them but they lay everywhere: placed side by side on the gravel, on the edge of the concrete platform, in the cars. Babies, repulsive, naked women, men twisted by convulsions. I ran away as far as I could. Someone caned me across the back, out of the corner of my eye I notice a cursing SS-man, I slip away from him and mix with the stripe-clad "Canada." Finally, I again crawl under the rails. The sun has gone down over the horizon and bathes the loading platform with its bloody, waning light. The shadows of the trees grow monstrously long; in the silence that settles on nature with the coming of evening, human cries soar skywards ever louder, ever more insistently.

It was only from here, from under the rails, that the entire inferno seething on the platform can be seen. Here is a couple fallen on the ground, locked in a desperate embrace. He has dug his fingers convulsively into her flesh and caught her dress in his teeth. She is shrieking hysterically, swearing, blaspheming until, trampled down by a boot, she gurgles and is still. Torn apart like pieces of wood, they are driven like animals into a truck. Here, four men from "Canada" strain under the weight of a corpse: a huge, swollen old woman: they swear and sweat with the effort, kick out of the way stray children who get underfoot all over the platform and howl horribly like dogs. They catch the children by the neck, by the head and arms and throw them in a pile on the trucks. Those four cannot manage to lift the woman to the truck, they call others and with a collective heave push the mountain of flesh on the floor of the truck. Huge, bloated, swollen corpses are carried from the whole ramp. Thrown among these are cripples, paralyzed, smothered and unconscious people. The mountain of corpses seethes, whines and howls. The driver starts the motor and drives away.

"*Halt, halt!*" the SS-man shrieks from a distance. "Stop, stop, damn you!"

They are dragging an old man in a full dress suit with an armband on his sleeve. His head is knocked about on the gravel and the stones, he groans and laments incessantly and monotonously: "*Ich will mit dem Herrn Kommendanten sprechen,*[9] I want to speak to the commandant." He repeats this with senile doggedness all the way. Thrown into the truck, trampled down by someone's foot, smothered, he continues to rattle: "*Ich will mit dem . . .*"

"Calm down, man!" calls out a young SS-man to him, laughing boisterously, "in half an hour you will speak to the supreme commandant! Only don't forget to say '*Heil Hitler*' to him."

Others carry a little girl who has only one leg, they hold her by the arms and that leg. Tears stream down her cheeks, and she whimpers pitifully: "Gentlemen, it hurts, it hurts . . ." They throw her on the truck with the corpses. She will be cremated alive with them.

Night falls, cool and starlit. We lie on the rails. It is immensely quiet. On

9. I want to speak with the commandant (German).

tall posts anemic lamps throw out circles of light into the impenetrable darkness. A step into it and a man disappears irretrievably. But the eyes of the
guards watch carefully. The automatics are ready to fire.

"Have you changed your shoes?" Henri asks me.

"No."

"Why not?"

"Man, I've had enough, completely enough."

"So soon, after the first transport? Just think, I . . . since Christmas, probably a million people have passed through my hands. The transports from
around Paris are the worst ones, a man always comes upon acquaintances."

"And what do you tell them?"

"That they're going to have a bath and then we'll meet in the camp, And
what would you say?"

I remain silent. We drink coffee spiked with alcohol; someone opens a tin
of cocoa, mixes it with sugar. This is ladled up with the hand; the cocoa
pastes up the mouth. Again coffee, again alcohol.

"What are we waiting for, Henri?"

"There'll be another transport. But no one knows."

"If there's another, I'm not going to unload it. I can't do it."

"It's got hold of you, yes? A fine 'Canada!' " Henri smiles benevolently and
disappears in the dark. He returns shortly.

"Very well. But be careful that the SS-man doesn't catch you. You'll stay
here all the time. And I'll fix you up with a pair of shoes."

"Don't bother me with the shoes."

I am sleepy. It is deep night.

Again *antreten*, again a transport. Cars emerge from the dark, pass the
strip of light and again disappear in the gloom. The loading platform is small
but the circle of light is still smaller. We will unload the cars as they come,
one by one. Trucks growl somewhere, they back up to the steps, spectrally
black, their reflectors light up the trees. *Wasser! Luft!*[1] The same all over
again, a late showing of the same film: they discharge a volley from their
automatics; the railway cars calm down. Only a little girl has leaned down
to her waist from the little window of the car and losing her balance fell to
the gravel. For a while she lay stunned, finally got up and started walking
around in a circle, faster and faster, waving her arms stiffly as if at calis-
thenics, drawing her breath in noisily, and monotonously and howling shrilly.
Suffocating—she has gone mad. She set the nerves on edge, so an SS-man
ran up to her and kicked her with a hobbled boot in the small of the back;
she fell. He pressed her down with his foot, took his revolver out and fired
once and then again; she lay, kicking the ground with her feet until she
stiffened. The cars begin to be opened.

I was again at the cars. A warm, sweetish odour gushed out. The car is
filled to half its height with a mound of humanity: immobile, horribly tangled
up but still steaming.

"*Ausladen!*"[2] sounded the voice of the SS-man who emerged out of the
dark. On his breast hung a portable reflector. He lighted up the inside of the
car.

"Why are you standing so stupidly? Unload!" and he swished his cane
across my back. I grabbed the arm of a corpse, his hand closed convulsively

1. Water! Air! (German).   2. Unload! (German).

around mine. I jerked away with a shriek and ran off. My heart pounded, my gorge rose. Nausea suddenly doubled me up. Crouching under the car I vomited. Staggering, I stole away under the stack of rails.

I lay on the kind, cool iron and dreamed of returning to the camp, about my bunk on which there is no straw mattress, about a bit of sleep among comrades who will not go to the gas chambers in the night. All at once the camp seemed like some haven of quiet; others are constantly dying and somehow one is still alive, has something to eat, strength to work, has a fatherland, a home, a girl . . .

The lights twinkle spectrally, the wave of humanity flows endlessly—turbid, feverish, stupefied. It seems to these people that they are beginning a new life in the camp and they prepare themselves psychologically for a hard struggle for existence. They do not know that they will immediately die and that the gold, the money, the diamonds which they providently conceal in the folds and seams of their clothing, in the heels of their shoes, in recesses of their bodies, will no longer be needed by them. Efficient, business-like people will rummage in their intestines, pull gold from under the tongue, diamonds from the placenta and the rectum. They will pull out their gold teeth and send them in tightly nailed-up cases to Berlin.[3]

The black figures of the SS-men walk about calm and proficient. The gentleman with the notebook in hand puts down the last check marks, adds up the figures; fifteen thousand.

Many, many trucks have driven off to the crematorium.

They are finishing up. The corpses spread on the ramp will be taken by the last truck, the luggage is all loaded. "Canada," loaded with bread, jams, sugar, smelling of perfume and clean underwear, lines up to march away. The "kapo" finishes packing the tea cauldron with gold, silk, and coffee. That's for the guards at the gates, they will let the commando pass without a search. For a few days the camp will live off that transport: eat its hams and its sausages, its preserved and fresh fruit, drink its brandies and liqueurs, wear its underwear, trade in its gold and luggage. Much will be taken out of the camp by civilians to Silesia, to Cracow and points beyond. They will bring cigarettes, eggs, vodka and letters from home.

For a few days the camp will speak about the "Sosnowiec-Będzin" transport. It was a good, rich transport.

When we return to the camp, the stars begin to pale, the sky becomes more and more transparent, rises higher up above us: the night clears. It foretells a fine, hot day.

Mighty columns of smoke rise up from the crematoria and merge into a huge, black river which rolls very slowly across the sky over Birkenau and disappears beyond the forests in the direction of Trzebinia.[4] The Sosnowiec transport is already being cremated.

We pass an SS detachment marching with machine guns to change the guard. They walk in step, shoulder to shoulder, one mass, one will.

"*Und morgen die ganze Welt . . .*"[5] they sing lustily.

"*Rechts ran!*[6] To the right march!" comes the order from up front. We move out of their way.

3. The capital of Germany.   4. A town west of Auschwitz, near Kraków.   5. And tomorrow the whole world (German); the last line of the Nazi song "The Rotten Bones Are Shaking," written by Hans Baumann. The previous line reads "for today Germany belongs to us."   6. To the right, get going! (German).

ALAIN ROBBE-GRILLET
born 1922

More than anyone else, Alain Robbe-Grillet represents in his novels, *ciné-romans* (film-novels), and theoretical statements the rejection of the nineteenth-century realistic tradition and the exploration of a new "mental realism." Terms such as *antinovel* and *new novel*, early applied to his works, reflect both the turning away from older models (like Balzac and Flaubert) and the notion that a new experiment with form is under way. Not that it is completely new; clearly there are links to other twentieth-century works in the modernist tradition. Robbe-Grillet himself mentions the influence of Kafka, Camus, and Faulkner (as well as *Alice in Wonderland*), and other readers will note parallel experimentation in Pirandello, Woolf, Beckett, and Joyce. Moreover, Robbe-Grillet calls on some of the same sources of fascination as his nineteenth-century predecessors. He may not use a linear plot, but he writes ambiguous, circular detective stories where erotic and violent crimes *seem* to have been committed. He may refuse to portray a consistently developing character, but his minute descriptions of objects and gestures impel the reader to imagine an underlying psychology and to speculate on the meaning of the observer's repetition and distortion of details.

Nonetheless, with Robbe-Grillet, we move to a particular phenomenon of mid-twentieth-century literature and a prime example of what has been called the post-modernist tradition. To the breakdown of conventional storytelling models familiar from literary modernism, he adds an insistence on the artificiality of all writing and representation. Readers are faced with cumulative uncertainty, with a self-contained "text" in which there is no stable narrative voice or "authorized" explanation. Here is not the abstractly intellectual puzzle of Borges but an often terrifying evocation of a sensuous reality that will not stay in place. This literature has become a "game" (as it is for Borges), but it is a deadly game. Playing with erotic and murderous images, with the treacherous undercurrents of an apparently familiar reality, Robbe-Grillet fascinates and sometimes repels his readers. At the same time that he reminds us that we cannot know what we see and that we share the world with a host of objects different from ourselves, he entices us to figure out the meaning of events—only to reestablish, at every turn, the absolute subjectivity of our most "objective" perceptions. Because they make a direct appeal to our senses, we cannot be disengaged from Robbe-Grillet's descriptions; they manipulate our awareness of physical experience. Throughout his career, Robbe-Grillet has explored the limits of representation with a collagelike technique that remains more true to life, he feels, than the planned coherence of a conventionally "realistic" novel.

Robbe-Grillet was born in Brittany, in northwestern France, to a family of scientists and engineers. His early training was not at all literary: in 1939 and 1941 the future writer took baccalaureate degrees in mathematics and natural science, and in 1946 (his career interrupted by forced labor in a German factory) a further degree from the National Agronomy Institute. He began work with the National Institute of Statistics and published an article on livestock possibilities before deciding to work part-time in his sister's biology laboratory and write a novel. This novel, *A Regicide*, was completed in 1949 but not published until 1978, well after Robbe-Grillet had become a successful novelist. In the meantime he took a position with an agricultural institute that sent him to Martinique, in the West Indies, to supervise banana plantations. Falling ill in 1951, Robbe-Grillet took advantage of the leisure time in the hospital and on the voyage home to write his second novel, *The Erasers*, which was immediately accepted and appeared in 1953.

The Erasers is a puzzling detective story involving confused identities, an abortive assassination carried out exactly twenty-four hours later by the muddled detective sent to investigate the original attempt, repeated allusions to the Oedipus myth, changing perspectives, and an overwhelming copiousness of detail about the most mundane natural objects. The novel became famous for its meticulous description of a tomato wedge cataloged with such scientific precision that it took on an objective existence of its own and implicitly challenged the human-centered orientation of a perspective that would see it only as part of a salad. "The flesh on the periphery, compact and uniform, of a fine chemical red, is evenly thick between a strip of shiny skin and the compartment where the seeds are lined up, yellow, well sized, held in place by a thin layer of greenish jelly alongside a swelling of the heart. This latter, of a faded and slightly grainy pink, begins, on the side of the depression below, in a cluster of white veins, one of which extends up to the seeds—in, perhaps, a somewhat uncertain manner." While minutely detailed descriptions are not new in literature, this catalog of physical properties had additional significance for its readers because it correlated so well with the notion, in contemporary phenomenological or existential philosophy, that we should recognize that things have their own existence separate from ourselves, their own "being-in-the-world."

The Erasers received the Fénéon Prize in 1954 but was not widely known; it was not until the scandal caused by The Voyeur (1955) that Robbe-Grillet reached a wide audience. Although The Voyeur was awarded the Critics' Prize in 1955, the jury was split between those who believed that it was not a "novel" at all (and was immoral and insane to boot) and those who admired its formal innovations. Mathias, the "voyeur" of the title, is a traveling watch salesman who may or may not have murdered a young girl during a sales trip on an island. The reader must piece together a version of what happened from a fragmented time span during which Mathias neglects to describe certain crucial hours, from actions and anxieties that suggest a guilty conscience, from a schizophrenic crisis when the crime is described in a café, and from obsessive erotic imaginings that may be just that—imaginings—or may be traces of the crime.

With the controversy over The Voyeur, Robbe-Grillet and his new mode of writing became the focus of critical debate in France. In Objective Literature, the influential critic Roland Barthes proposed that Robbe-Grillet had discovered a truer "neutral" writing by focusing on objects instead of repeating traditional socially inspired interpretations of reality. In 1955 Robbe-Grillet began a series of articles on modern literature, which he collected in 1963 as For a New Novel. The term new novel became popular; and although not all those described as "new novelists" wrote in the same way, they all rejected the traditional novel's assumption of a core of meaning—with a logically developing plot and psychologically consistent characters—that claimed to reflect a similar core of meaning in society. His next two novels, Jealousy (1957) and In the Labyrinth (1959), as well as the separate short pieces collected in Snapshots (1962), exploit the ideas developed in these articles, seeking patterns of potential meaning behind extended, objective description. In 1959 he temporarily abandoned novels to experiment with films, writing the script for Last Year at Marienbad (1961, filmed by Alain Resnais) and writing and directing The Immortal One (1963). Films, like novels, allowed Robbe-Grillet to manipulate visions of reality as he insistently focused on surfaces and shapes, presented different versions of the same scene, composed a sound track that contradicted or commented on photographed action and—in recent works—challenged his own imagination by including unexpected incidents that occurred on location. Robbe-Grillet published the scenarios of Last Year at Marienbad and The Immortal One, and a more documentary account of The Progressing Slippages of Pleasure (1974) as ciné-romans, which represent his pluralistic, decentered view of reality in audiovisual as well as verbal form.

Novels up to and including In the Labyrinth could still be interpreted as the subterranean story of a single protagonist. Later novels eliminated that anchoring center to display the presence of many centers—each a competing version of reality. Here emphasis is on the writer's freedom to create different and even mutually contradictory worlds and on the readers' freedom to choose and arrange their own version of events. Some passages do not fit into any of the story lines; the action progresses according to the suggestions of wordplay or verbal echoes; the same narrative persona may appear grammatically as "he" or "she"; or books are composed in collage fashion. Robbe-Grillet has been taught in the classroom for many years as a master of formal experimentation and only recently challenged on the quarantined atmosphere and obsessive sadism of his work. Women, for example, are repeatedly victimized, and terror and death are constant themes. Uncomfortable, perhaps, at this change in critical perspective, he has justified sadistic fantasies in his work partly as reflecting popular themes in a correspondingly sadistic and dehumanized world and partly as the therapeutic expression of his own obsessions (therapeutic for Robbe-Grillet because they are brought to a conscious level and thereby subject to change).

Therapeutic or not, there is no mistaking the basic images of Robbe-Grillet's world or the disturbing angles from which they are presented. *The Secret Room*, reprinted here from *Snapshots*, arranges in an artistic homage to the Symbolist painter Gustave Moreau (1826–98) many of Robbe-Grillet's most obsessive images: the spreading bloodstain; the young woman stretched out erotically in chains and stabbed under the left breast; the ascending staircase; the different points of view directed down on the victim; the mysterious, anonymous criminal; and even the figure eight of smoke coiling upward from the incense burner. The scene is bound to shock for its overt sadism, for the artistic savoring of human sacrifice, and for the erotic pleasure it suggests in female victimization. It would not be appropriate to ignore or repress this response, for the subject matter is not neutral or intended as such. Robbe-Grillet has presented an additional challenge, however, by insisting on the stylized *unreality* of the scene and by displacing the reader's attention to the technical triumph in which verbal art emulates a painterly style. The text imitates the oriental luxury and morbid eroticism of a famous painter so convincingly that one could almost name the artist even without the dedication. Yet this verbal art goes beyond its painterly model when Robbe-Grillet adds to it the passage of time, thus bringing a strange life to the subject seen paradoxically both as a finished canvas and as re-created stages of the same murderous event. It is a bizarre and disturbing scene, made to unsettle readers who try to reconcile its various aspects: its manipulation of stereotypes of the victimized woman, the horror of the helpless sacrifice, and an alienated perspective that is attributed to art but at the same time suggests sadistic impersonality.

PRONOUNCING GLOSSARY

The following list uses common English syllables and stress accents to provide rough equivalents of selected words whose pronunciation may be unfamiliar to the general reader.

Alain Robbe-Grillet: *ah-lanh′ rob–gree-*   Gustave Moreau: *gyew-stahv′ mor-oh′*
    yay′

The Secret Room[1]

To Gustave Moreau[2]

The first thing to be seen is a red stain, of a deep, dark, shiny red, with almost black shadows. It is in the form of an irregular rosette, sharply outlined, extending in several directions in wide outflows of unequal length, dividing and dwindling afterward into single sinuous streaks. The whole stands out

---

1. Translated by Bruce Morrissette.   2. French Symbolist painter (1826–1898) known for exotic, luminous scenes with subtly erotic and morbid overtones, such as *The Death of Darius* and *Dance of Salome*.

against a smooth, pale surface, round in shape, at once dull and pearly, a hemisphere joined by gentle curves to an expanse of the same pale color— white darkened by the shadowy quality of the place: a dungeon, a sunken room, or a cathedral—glowing with a diffused brilliance in the semidarkness.

Farther back, the space is filled with the cylindrical trunks of columns, repeated with progressive vagueness in their retreat toward the beginning of a vast stone stairway, turning slightly as it rises, growing narrower and narrower as it approaches the high vaults where it disappears.

The whole setting is empty, stairway and colonnades. Alone, in the foreground, the stretched-out body gleams feebly, marked with the red stain—a white body whose full, supple flesh can be sensed, fragile, no doubt, and vulnerable. Alongside the bloody hemisphere another identical round form, this one intact, is seen at almost the same angle of view; but the haloed point at its summit, of darker tint, is in this case quite recognizable, whereas the other one is entirely destroyed, or at least covered by the wound.

In the background, near the top of the stairway, a black silhouette is seen fleeing, a man wrapped in a long, floating cape, ascending the last steps without turning around, his deed accomplished. A thin smoke rises in twisting scrolls from a sort of incense burner placed on a high stand of ironwork with a silvery glint. Nearby lies the milkwhite body, with wide streaks of blood running from the left breast, along the flank and on the hip.

It is a fully rounded woman's body, but not heavy, completely nude, lying on its back, the bust raised up somewhat by thick cushions thrown down on the floor, which is covered with Oriental rugs. The waist is very narrow, the neck long and thin, curved to one side, the head thrown back into a darker area where, even so, the facial features may be discerned, the partly opened mouth, the wide-staring eyes, shining with a fixed brilliance, and the mass of long, black hair spread out in a complicated wavy disorder over a heavily folded cloth, of velvet perhaps, on which also rest the arm and shoulder.

It is a uniformly colored velvet of dark purple, or which seems so in this lighting. But purple, brown, blue also seem to dominate in the colors of the cushions—only a small portion of which is hidden beneath the velvet cloth, and which protrude noticeably, lower down, beneath the bust and waist— as well as in the Oriental patterns of the rugs on the floor. Farther on, these same colors are picked up again in the stone of the paving and the columns, and vaulted archways, the stairs, and the less discernible surfaces that disappear into the farthest reaches of the room.

The dimensions of this room are difficult to determine exactly; the body of the young sacrificial victim seems at first glance to occupy a substantial portion of it, but the vast size of the stairway leading down to it would imply rather that this is not the whole room, whose considerable space must in reality extend all around, right and left, as it does toward the faraway browns and blues among the columns standing in line, in every direction, perhaps toward other sofas, thick carpets, piles of cushions and fabrics, other tortured bodies, other incense burners.

It is also difficult to say where the light comes from. No clue, on the columns or on the floor, suggests the direction of the rays. Nor is any window or torch visible. The milkwhite body itself seems to light the scene, with its full breasts, the curve of its thighs, the rounded belly, the full buttocks, the

stretched-out legs, widely spread, and the black tuft of the exposed sex, provocative, proffered, useless now.

The man has already moved several steps back. He is now on the first steps
of the stairs, ready to go up. The bottom steps are wide and deep, like the
steps leading up to some great building, a temple or theater; they grow
smaller as they ascend, and at the same time describe a wide, helical curve,
so gradually that the stairway has not yet made a half-turn by the time it
disappears near the top of the vaults, reduced then to a steep, narrow flight
of steps without handrail, vaguely outlined, moreover, in the thickening darkness beyond.

But the man does not look in this direction, where his movement nonetheless carries him; his left foot on the second step and his right foot already
touching the third, with his knee bent, he has turned around to look at the
spectacle for one last time. The long, floating cape thrown hastily over his
shoulders, clasped in one hand at his waist, has been whirled around by the
rapid circular motion that has just caused his head and chest to turn in the
opposite direction, and a corner of the cloth remains suspended in the air
as if blown by a gust of wind; this corner, twisting around upon itself in the
form of a loose S, reveals the red silk lining with its gold embroidery.

The man's features are impassive, but tense, as if in expectation—or perhaps fear—of some sudden event, or surveying with one last glance the total
immobility of the scene. Though he is looking backward, his whole body is
turned slightly forward, as if he were continuing up the stairs. His right
arm—not the one holding the edge of the cape—is bent sharply toward the
left, toward a point in space where the balustrade should be, if this stairway
had one, an interrupted gesture, almost incomprehensible, unless it arose
from an instinctive movement to grasp the absent support.

As to the direction of his glance, it is certainly aimed at the body of the
victim lying on the cushions, its extended members stretched out in the form
of a cross, its bust raised up, its head thrown back. But the face is perhaps
hidden from the man's eyes by one of the columns, standing at the foot of
the stairs. The young woman's right hand touches the floor just at the foot
of this column. The fragile wrist is encircled by an iron bracelet. The arm is
almost in darkness, only the hand receiving enough light to make the thin,
outspread fingers clearly visible against the circular protrusion at the base
of the stone column. A black metal chain running around the column passes
through a ring affixed to the bracelet, binding the wrist tightly to the column.

At the top of the arm a rounded shoulder, raised up by the cushions, also
stands out well lighted, as well as the neck, the throat, and the other shoulder, the armpit with its soft hair, the left arm likewise pulled back with its
wrist bound in the same manner to the base of another column, in the
extreme foreground; here the iron bracelet and the chain are fully displayed,
represented with perfect clarity down to the slightest details.

The same is true, still in the foreground but at the other side, for a similar
chain, but not quite as thick, wound directly around the ankle, running twice
around the column and terminating in a heavy iron embedded in the floor.
About a yard farther back, or perhaps slightly farther, the right foot is identically chained. But it is the left foot, and its chain, that are the most minutely
depicted.

The foot is small, delicate, finely modeled. In several places the chain has broken the skin, causing noticeable if not extensive depressions in the flesh. The chain links are oval, thick, the size of an eye. The ring in the floor resembles those used to attach horses; it lies almost touching the stone pavement to which it is riveted by a massive iron peg. A few inches away is the edge of a rug; it is grossly wrinkled at this point, doubtless as a result of the convulsive, but necessarily very restricted, movements of the victim attempting to struggle.

The man is still standing about a yard away, half leaning over her. He looks at her face, seen upside down, her dark eyes made larger by their surrounding eyeshadow, her mouth wide open as if screaming. The man's posture allows his face to be seen only in a vague profile, but one senses in it a violent exaltation, despite the rigid attitude, the silence, the immobility. His back is slightly arched. His left hand, the only one visible, holds up at some distance from the body a piece of cloth, some dark-colored piece of clothing, which drags on the carpet, and which must be the long cape with its gold-embroidered lining.

This immense silhouette hides most of the bare flesh over which the red stain, spreading from the globe of the breast, runs in long rivulets that branch out, growing narrower, upon the pale background of the bust and the flank. One thread has reached the armpit and runs in an almost straight, thin line along the arm; others have run down toward the waist and traced out, along one side of the belly, the hip, the top of the thigh, a more random network already starting to congeal. Three or four tiny veins have reached the hollow between the legs, meeting in a sinuous line, touching the point of the V formed by the outspread legs, and disappearing into the black tuft.

Look, now the flesh is still intact: the black tuft and the white belly, the soft curve of the hips, the narrow waist, and, higher up, the pearly breasts rising and falling in time with the rapid breathing, whose rhythm grows more accelerated. The man, close to her, one knee on the floor, leans farther over. The head, with its long, curly hair, which alone is free to move somewhat, turns from side to side, struggling; finally the woman's mouth twists open, while the flesh is torn open, the blood spurts out over the tender skin, stretched tight, the carefully shadowed eyes grow abnormally large, the mouth opens wider, the head twists violently, one last time, from right to left, then more gently, to fall back finally and become still, amid the mass of black hair spread out on the velvet.

Afterward, the whole setting is empty, the enormous room with its purple shadows and its stone columns proliferating in all directions, the monumental staircase with no handrail that twists upward, growing narrower and vaguer as it rises into the darkness, toward the top of the vaults where it disappears.

Near the body, whose wound has stiffened, whose brilliance is already growing dim, the thin smoke from the incense burner traces complicated scrolls in the still air: first a coil turned horizontally to the left, which then straightens out and rises slightly, then returns to the axis of its point of origin, which it crosses as it moves to the right, then turns back in the first direction, only to wind back again, thus forming an irregular sinusoidal[3] curve, more and more flattened out, and rising, vertically, toward the top of the canvas.

3. S-shaped.

ITALO CALVINO
1923–1985

Italo Calvino is a marvelously entertaining storyteller whose tales, read by young and old, bring a lightness and fanciful imagination to pictures of everyday life—even though that "every day" may take place on the moon, or among the first invertebrates, or in a world where space and time obey different laws. Whether writing novels and short stories or openly retelling fables (and, for Calvino, all narrative was a *fabula*, a fable), he is at once simple and complex, humorous and profound. He narrates events in a deceptively matter-of-fact way while creating extended allegories of human behavior and experimenting with avant-garde literary structures. Calvino's fantastic works raise implicitly the same questions about human identity that are found in the major European moralists: they ask what it means to be human, how we ought to live, and what our relationship is to the universe. These questions are raised, however, as images, as imaginary sequences of "what if," whose logic is pursued extensively—even mathematically—to its ironic conclusion. For Calvino, the art of literature adds another way of seeing to the existing perspective of science: art helps us explore possibilities that can be conceived only by the imagination, and it shows us how to break free of old habits of thought.

He was born in a town near Havana, Cuba, in 1923, to Mario and Eva Calvino, Italian citizens who had lived in Cuba for many years. Both parents were botanists, and they returned to the family farm in San Remo (a picturesque town on the north Italian coast) two years after Italo's birth. Calvino's father joined the science faculty at the University of Turin, and his parents conducted plant experiments on the farm. Their interest in science and their independent and anticlerical frame of mind contributed to young Calvino's own independent outlook and to his ironic perspective. It was a difficult period for freethinkers: the Fascists were in power, and Benito Mussolini was dictator of Italy from 1922 until his fall in 1943. Mussolini's militarist nationalism was the order of the day, and Calvino—like others his age—was required to join a Fascist youth group. Calvino felt isolated from his peers and, when he was drafted into the national army in 1943, he deserted and joined a Resistance group.

Initially, Calvino followed his parents' footsteps by studying agronomy at the University of Turin. After the war, he decided to follow his real wishes, changed his major to English literature, and began to write fiction. His wartime experiences formed the basis for his first novel, *The Path to the Nest of Spiders* (1947), and for stories published as early as 1946 and reprinted in *The Crow Comes Last* (translated in *Adam, One Afternoon*) (1949). Both volumes were a success and assured Calvino's reputation as a talented young writer. He had graduated from the university in 1947, and the publishing firm of Einaudi gave him a job in which he met many leading authors, among them the neorealists Elio Vittorini and Cesare Pavese. Calvino's work was to take a different turn, however, and he embarked in the 1950s on a series of fantastic tales and fables that brought him an international audience.

For the next two decades, he wrote and published prolifically. His next three novels, collected in *Our Ancestors* (1960), are fantastic historical fictions. *The Cloven Viscount* (1952) tells the story of a man who is sheared in half on the battlefield by a cannonball: the two halves (one good, one bad) go on living their separate and melodramatically different lives until a duel reunites them. The protagonist of *The Baron in the Trees* (1957) climbs out the dining-room window at age twelve and devotes the rest of his life to living freely and fully—without ever touching the ground. *The Nonexistent Knight* (1959) follows the career of a perfect eighth-century Crusader in white armor, who happens not to have a body. Echoes of Ariosto's *Orlando Furioso* and Cervantes's *Don Quixote* (printed in the first volume of this anthology) abound in the twentieth-century narrative, whose humor is entirely modern.

These historical fantasies are matched by a series of fables that begin with Calvino's edition of two hundred Italian folktales from the sixteenth to the eighteenth century (1956) and continue through the new pieces in *Stories* (1958) and the science-fiction tales *Ti con zero* (1967) and *Cosmicomics* (1965). The protagonist/narrator of *Cosmicomics* is an epistemic cell named Qfwfq, who lives and observes life from the first protozoan age to future space colonies. Qfwfq's wry comments on his experiences (as a young, status-conscious amphibian in *The Aquatic Uncle*, he loses his lizard fiancée to his uncle, the patriarch of the family and a fish) and the paradoxical adventures of *Ti con zero* contain the indirect allusions to contemporary life that characterize Calvino's later fantasy. A semirealist style dominates in the stories *Marcovaldo; or, The Seasons in the City* (1963), where Calvino contrasts the escapist dreams of his protagonist, Marcovaldo, with the harsh reality and economic exploitation of a bleak industrial city. Sometimes those dreams take on life, as in *The City Lost in the Snow*, where an all-engulfing snowfall transforms relationships and blurs the distinction between real and imaginary objects. Throughout, the unreal atmosphere of dream, folktale, and fable enables the writer to comment indirectly on human tendencies and the ills of modern urban society.

In 1964, Calvino married the Argentinian translator Judith Esther (Chichita) Singer and moved to Paris, where he lived until he returned to Rome in 1980. Parisian cultural life in the 1960s was dominated by structuralist thinkers, and Calvino not only met many of them but participated for a while in Raymond Queneau's postmodern OuLiPo group. His subsequent fiction shows a marked predilection for working out intricate patterns of allusion and internal reference, starting with *The Castle of Crossed Destinies* (1969–1973), a variation on Boccaccio's *Decameron*, in which the gathered storytellers cannot speak and must represent their tales through a dwindling deck of tarot cards, whose images are also reproduced in the margins.

Invisible Cities (1972), which some consider Calvino's best work, is structured as an imaginary dialogue between the thirteenth-century Venetian explorer Marco Polo and the Mongol emperor Kublai Khan. According to Marco Polo's *Travels,* he remained for seventeen years in China and was sent on several occasions to bring back news of distant regions. In this imaginary account, the Khan has also asked Polo to report on the various cities throughout the realm, and the traveler brings back exemplary objects ("a helmet, a seashell, a coconut, a fan") on the basis of which he delivers his reports. Kublai Khan soon recognizes that the cities (all fifty-five of them) are imaginary and that Marco Polo's travels are equally unreal. In the meantime, the individual reports have established themselves as brilliantly ambiguous prose poems, both real and unreal, which lead the Khan to ponder the "invisible order that sustains cities" and ultimately to question reality.

Calvino's last fictional works, *If on a Winter's Night a Traveler* (1979) and *Mr. Palomar* (1983), employ increasingly allusive structures. *If on a Winter's Night a Traveler* begins and ends with references to its being read and to the narrator's search for a missing second chapter, which leads him on a frustrating chase through the beginnings of ten different (imaginary) novels, each of which is written in a radically different modern style and is, coincidentally, entitled *If on a winter's night a traveler*. *Mr. Palomar* is structured like a cube—that is, the mathematical cube of the number 3. Mr. Palomar's wanderings are separated into three major sections, each of which has three subsections and subsequently three other subsections, all of which are indexed and related to three thematic areas and related philosophical considerations. What is, on the one hand, an amusing parody of ponderous philosophical structures is, on the other, an intimate portrait of the self-reflexive Mr. Palomar (Calvino, according to his friend Gore Vidal) observing the minutiae of everyday life and asking what they mean—what it all means.

Invisible Cities pursues the same question, stated more and more openly by the Khan as the reports proceed. Like all nine chapters, Chapter 8 is framed by a brief dialogue between Marco Polo and Kublai Khan. The Khan, who has sent Polo to report on the farthest reaches of his empire, is eager to gain the knowledge that will mean mastery of his dominions. The sequence of his questions and the richly evocative reports delivered in answer take on the character of a chess game, whether the board be the tiles on which Polo spreads out his samples, a traditional chessboard, or a briefly glimpsed metaphysical plane. Throughout, the Khan seeks to discern a pattern of relationships that will let him grasp the game (and his empire), while Marco Polo's "essential landscapes," at once concretely real and bafflingly fabulous, refuse to be contained within a system. Moving deeper into understanding the game's principles, the Khan encounters only a checkmate—but one that carries with it the promise of another beginning.

Invisible Cities[1]

CHAPTER 8

From the foot of the Great Khan's[2] throne a majolica pavement extended. Marco Polo, mute informant,[3] spread out on it the samples of the wares he had brought back from his journeys to the ends of the empire: a helmet, a seashell, a coconut, a fan. Arranging the objects in a certain order on the black and white tiles, and occasionally shifting them with studied moves, the ambassador tried to depict for the monarch's eyes the vicissitudes of his travels, the conditions of the empire, the prerogatives of the distant provincial seats.

Kublai was a keen chess player; following Marco's movements, he observed that certain pieces implied or excluded the vicinity of other pieces and were shifted along certain lines. Ignoring the objects' variety of form, he could grasp the system of arranging one with respect to the others on the majolica floor. He thought: "If each city is like a game of chess, the day when I have learned the rules, I shall finally possess my empire, even if I shall never succeed in knowing all the cities it contains."

Actually, it was useless for Marco's speeches to employ all this bric-a-brac: a chessboard would have sufficed, with its specific pieces. To each piece, in turn, they could give an appropriate meaning: a knight could stand for a real horseman, or for a procession of coaches, an army on the march, an equestrian monument: a queen could be a lady looking down from her balcony, a fountain, a church with a pointed dome, a quince tree.

Returning from his last mission, Marco Polo found the Khan awaiting him, seated at a chessboard. With a gesture he invited the Venetian[4] to sit opposite him and describe, with the help only of the chessmen, the cities he had visited. Marco did not lose heart. The Great Khan's chessmen were huge pieces of polished ivory: arranging on the board looming rooks and sulky knights, assembling swarms of pawns, drawing straight or oblique avenues like a queen's

---

1. Translated by William Weaver. Published in 1972.   2. I.e., Kublai Khan (1215–1294), grandson of Genghis Khan, emperor of China (which he had conquered as a Mongol general) and ruler of the Mongolian dominions, which stretched from Mongolia to southern Russia and Persia. He welcomed foreign travelers and their information.   3. Initially, Marco Polo, who did not know either Chinese or Tartar, communicated with the Khan "with gestures, leaps, cries of wonder and of horror . . . or with objects he took from his knapsacks—ostrich plumes, pea-shooters, quartzes—which he arranged in front of him like chessmen" (Chapter 1).   4. The Polos were a family of Venetian merchants who traveled throughout the Middle East and Asia.

progress, Marco recreated the perspectives and the spaces of black and white cities on moonlit nights.

Contemplating these essential landscapes, Kublai reflected on the invisible order that sustains cities, on the rules that decreed how they rise, take shape and prosper, adapting themselves to the seasons, and then how they sadden and fall in ruins. At times he thought he was on the verge of discovering a coherent, harmonious system underlying the infinite deformities and discords, but no model could stand up to the comparison with the game of chess. Perhaps, instead of racking one's brain to suggest with the ivory pieces' scant help visions which were anyway destined to oblivion, it would suffice to play a game according to the rules, and to consider each successive state of the board as one of the countless forms that the system of forms assembles and destroys.

Now Kublai Khan no longer had to send Marco Polo on distant expeditions: he kept him playing endless games of chess. Knowledge of the empire was hidden in the pattern drawn by the angular shifts of the knight, by the diagonal passages opened by the bishop's incursions, by the lumbering, cautious tread of the king and the humble pawn, by the inexorable ups and downs of every game.

The Great Khan tried to concentrate on the game: but now it was the game's purpose that eluded him. Each game ends in a gain or a loss: but of what? What were the true stakes? At checkmate, beneath the foot of the king, knocked aside by the winner's hand, a black or a white square remains. By disembodying his conquests to reduce them to the essential, Kublai had arrived at the extreme operation: the definitive conquest, of which the empire's multiform treasures were only illusory envelopes. It was reduced to a square of planed wood: nothingness. . . .

Cities & Names 5[5]

Irene is the city visible when you lean out from the edge of the plateau at the hour when the lights come on, and in the limpid air, the pink of the settlement can be discerned spread out in the distance below: where the windows are more concentrated, where it thins out in dimly lighted alleys, where it collects the shadows of gardens, where it raises towers with signal fires; and if the evening is misty, a hazy glow swells like a milky sponge at the foot of the gulleys.

Travelers on the plateau, shepherds shifting their flocks, bird-catchers watching their nets, hermits gathering greens: all look down and speak of Irene. At times the wind brings a music of bass drums and trumpets, the bang of firecrackers in the light-display of a festival; at times the rattle of guns, the explosion of a powder magazine in the sky yellow with the fires of civil war. Those who look down from the heights conjecture about what is happening in the city; they wonder if it would be pleasant or unpleasant to be in Irene that evening. Not that they have any intention of going there (in any case the roads winding down to the valley are bad), but Irene is a magnet for the eyes and thoughts of those who stay up above.

At this point Kublai Khan expects Marco to speak of Irene as it is seen from within. But Marco cannot do this: he has not succeeded in discovering

---

5. The five section titles in Chapter 8 are selected from eleven thematic titles appearing throughout the different chapters: the others are "Cities & Memory," "Cities & Desire," "Cities & Signs," "Thin Cities," "Trading Cities," and "Cities & Eyes."

which is the city that those of the plateau call Irene. For that matter, it is of slight importance: if you saw it, standing in its midst, it would be a different city; Irene is a name for a city in the distance, and if you approach, it changes.

For those who pass it without entering, the city is one thing; it is another for those who are trapped by it and never leave. There is the city where you arrive for the first time; and there is another city which you leave never to return. Each deserves a different name; perhaps I have already spoken of Irene under other names; perhaps I have spoken only of Irene.

Cities & the Dead 4

What makes Argia different from other cities is that it has earth instead of air. The streets are completely filled with dirt, clay packs the rooms to the ceiling, on every stair another stairway is set in negative, over the roofs of the houses hang layers of rocky terrain like skies with clouds. We do not know if the inhabitants can move about the city, widening the worm tunnels and the crevices where roots twist: the dampness destroys people's bodies and they have scant strength; everyone is better off remaining still, prone; anyway, it is dark.

From up here, nothing of Argia can be seen; some say, "It's down below there," and we can only believe them. The place is deserted. At night, putting your ear to the ground, you can sometimes hear a door slam.

Cities & the Sky 3

Those who arrive at Thekla can see little of the city, beyond the plank fences, the sackcloth screens, the scaffoldings, the metal armatures, the wooden catwalks hanging from ropes or supported by sawhorses, the ladders, the trestles. If you ask, "Why is Thekla's construction taking such a long time?" the inhabitants continue hoisting sacks, lowering leaded strings, moving long brushes up and down, as they answer, "So that its destruction cannot begin." And if asked whether they fear that, once the scaffoldings are removed, the city may begin to crumble and fall to pieces, they add hastily, in a whisper, "Not only the city."

If, dissatisfied with the answers, someone puts his eye to a crack in a fence, he sees cranes pulling up other cranes, scaffoldings that embrace other scaffoldings, beams that prop up other beams. "What meaning does your construction have?" he asks. "What is the aim of a city under construction unless it is a city? Where is the plan you are following, the blueprint?"

"We will show it to you as soon as the working day is over; we cannot interrupt our work now," they answer.

Work stops at sunset. Darkness falls over the building site. The sky is filled with stars. "There is the blueprint," they say.

Continuous Cities 2

If on arriving at Trude I had not read the city's name written in big letters, I would have thought I was landing at the same airport from which I had taken off. The suburbs they drove me through were no different from the others, with the same little greenish and yellowish houses. Following the same signs we swung around the same flower beds in the same squares. The downtown streets displayed goods, packages, signs that had not changed at all. This was the first time I had come to Trude, but I already knew the hotel where I happened to be lodged; I had already heard and spoken my dialogues with the buyers and sellers of hardware; I had ended other days identically, looking through the same goblets at the same swaying navels.

Why come to Trude? I asked myself. And I already wanted to leave.

"You can resume your flight whenever you like," they said to me, "but you will arrive at another Trude, absolutely the same, detail by detail. The world is covered by a sole Trude which does not begin and does not end. Only the name of the airport changes."

Hidden Cities 1

In Olinda, if you go out with a magnifying glass and hunt carefully, you may find somewhere a point no bigger than the head of a pin which, if you look at it slightly enlarged, reveals within itself the roofs, the antennas, the skylights, the gardens, the pools, the streamers across the streets, the kiosks in the squares, the horse-racing track. That point does not remain there: a year later you will find it the size of half a lemon, then as large as a mushroom, then a soup plate. And then it becomes a full-size city, enclosed within the earlier city: a new city that forces its way ahead in the earlier city and presses it toward the outside.

Olinda is certainly not the only city that grows in concentric circles, like tree trunks which each year add one more ring. But in other cities there remains, in the center, the old narrow girdle of the walls from which the withered spires rise, the towers, the tiled roofs, the domes, while the new quarters sprawl around them like a loosened belt. Not Olinda: the old walls expand bearing the old quarters with them, enlarged, but maintaining their proportions on a broader horizon at the edges of the city; they surround the slightly newer quarters, which also grew up on the margins and became thinner to make room for still more recent ones pressing from inside; and so, on and on, to the heart of the city, a totally new Olinda which, in its reduced dimensions retains the features and the flow of lymph of the first Olinda and of all the Olindas that have blossomed one from the other; and within this innermost circle there are already blossoming—though it is hard to discern them—the next Olinda and those that will grow after it.

. . . *The Great Khan tried to concentrate on the game: but now it was the game's reason that eluded him. The end of every game is a gain or a loss: but of what? What were the real stakes? At checkmate, beneath the foot of the king, knocked aside by the winner's hand, nothingness remains: a black square, or a white one. By disembodying his conquests to reduce them to the essential, Kublai had arrived at the extreme operation: the definitive conquest, of which the empire's multiform treasures were only illusory envelopes; it was reduced to a square of planed wood.*

Then Marco Polo spoke: "Your chessboard, sire, is inlaid with two woods: ebony and maple. The square on which your enlightened gaze is fixed was cut from the ring of a trunk that grew in a year of drought: you see how its fibers are arranged? Here a barely hinted knot can be made out: a bud tried to burgeon on a premature spring day, but the night's frost forced it to desist."

Until then the Great Khan had not realized that the foreigner knew how to express himself fluently in his language, but it was not this fluency that amazed him.

"Here is a thicker pore: perhaps it was a larvum's nest; not a woodworm, because, once born, it would have begun to dig, but a caterpillar that gnawed the leaves and was the cause of the tree's being chosen for chopping down . . . This edge was scored by the wood carver with his gouge so that it would adhere to the next square, more protruding. . . ."

The quantity of things that could be read in a little piece of smooth and empty wood overwhelmed Kublai; Polo was already talking about ebony forests, about rafts laden with logs that come down the rivers, of docks, of women at the windows. . . .

INGEBORG BACHMANN
1926–1973

Ingeborg Bachmann's reputation as one of the most significant postwar writers in the German language is almost overshadowed by her image as an interpreter of women's experience and a critic of fascism. Winning early fame as a brilliant young poet whose vivid yet philosophical lyrics brought her prize after prize, she abandoned poetry in mid-career to write fiction that would say what "needed to be said" and speak for those who could not speak for themselves. Women in particular became the protagonists of her later work. Bachmann described the complex and frequently unrecognized forces that shape women's social experience and constitute "ways of death" as often as ways of life. Her powerful intellect and gift for precise description fused with a lyric tendency and strong ethical concerns to create a remarkable body of work that has been translated into twenty-two languages and continues to influence contemporary writers.

Bachmann was born on June 25, 1926, in Klagenfurt, a city in southern Austria close to the Italian and Yugoslavian borders. She was the oldest of three children; her father was a teacher and later school principal, and her mother's family operated a knitwear firm. Although she lived outside Austria for most of her adult life, moving permanently to Rome in 1963, much of her work is dominated by the image of a spiritual "Austria," whose fluctuating borders and multiethnic heritage create a unique view of the world. Several languages are spoken in her home province of Carinthia, and the valley in which she lived had two names, German and Slovene. Austria itself, although politically powerless, was the former center of the multinational Hapsburg empire and still participated in many cultures. The notion of physical and psychological boundaries permeates all levels of her writing, along with glimpses of an ideal freedom to move beyond artificial frontiers. Bachmann's own experience of political borders was sharpened when the Nazis marched into Klagenfurt in 1938. She was twelve years old, and that moment, she said, marked the end of her childhood. Attending schools in Klagenfurt throughout the war, she graduated in 1944 and studied briefly in Innsbruck and Graz before entering the University of Vienna in 1946.

Bachmann's first story, "The Ferryboat," was published in 1946, and other stories as well as her first poems appeared over the next few years. While earning recognition as a creative writer, she also pursued a degree in philosophy with minors in psychology and German literature. She prized the analytical philosophy of the Vienna school (proscribed under Hitler) and rejected the "German irrationalism" represented by existential philosopher Martin Heidegger (1889–1976). Her doctoral dissertation in 1950 was openly critical in analyzing the reception of Heidegger's philosophy. Three years later she published a major appreciative essay on the Viennese linguistic philosopher Ludwig Wittgenstein (1889–1951). What fascinated her about Wittgenstein was *"his despairing attempt to chart the limits of linguistic expression,"* an attempt that is paralleled in her own poetry and fiction.

In the years following her doctorate, Bachmann traveled to Paris and London, gave poetry readings, held a series of jobs ranging from scriptwriter to newspaper correspondent, and began to write in different genres. She worked briefly in the office of the American occupation authorities in Vienna and was a member of the broadcasting group Red/White/Red/ between 1951 and 1953. For Red/White/Red she wrote a number of radio plays, including adaptations of works by Thomas Wolfe and Louis Mac-Neice. Her translation of MacNeice's radio script "The Dark Tower" was produced with music by British composer Benjamin Britten, and Bachmann's interest in mixed genres continued after she left Red/White/Red. Her second radio play, "The Cicadas," was produced in 1954 with music by composer Hans Werner Henze, who later set several of her poems to music. Bachmann collaborated with Henze on other occasions and wrote the libretti for two of his operas as well as a ballet scenario. During the fifties, she also wrote a novel, *City without a Name,* only to have it rejected by five publishers. Her early reputation was clearly based on the poetry, and recognition came quickly for her extraordinary combination of striking natural images and abstract argument. Addressing the constellation Ursa Major, she began "Great Bear, come down, shaggy night, / cloud-coated beast with the old eyes, star eyes. / Through the thickets your paws break / shimmering with their claws, / star claws . . ." Her first volume, *Mortgaged Time,* appeared in 1953, and in the same year she received the prestigious annual prize awarded by "Group 47" (a group of Austrian writers who banded together in 1947 in an effort to establish new directions for German literature). A second collection, *Invocation of the Great Bear,* was published in 1956, by which time she had moved to Rome, published poems in the international poetry journal *Botteghe oscure,* received a second prize, and been the subject of a cover story in the popular German magazine *Der Spiegel.*

Bachmann's work took a sharp turn in the sixties, so that critics have often spoken of the "two Bachmanns," the first a more hermetic writer aiming at formal beauty, and the second a socially engaged writer of prose who once proclaimed: "I no longer try to make each sentence a work of art. The only thing that matters is what needs to be said." While there is a visible change in emphasis from poetry to prose (her last poem, "No More Delicacies," was written in 1964 as she began the novel sequence *Ways of Death*), Bachmann's later fiction makes great use of lyrical elements. Unlike Alexander Solzhenitsyn, she never attempted to emulate the linear style of the nineteenth-century realist novel. The prose writers who interest her are those who take a modernist perspective on problems of identity, communication, and narrative discourse: Marcel Proust, Italo Svevo (1861–1928), James Joyce, Franz Kafka, Robert Musil (1880–1942), William Faulkner, and Samuel Beckett, all of whom she discusses at length in her 1959–1960 lectures on "Questions of Contemporary Poetry" at the University of Frankfurt. She related their exploratory style to the problem of the self in modern society, a focus that she adapted to her own circumstances in later work.

Even during the fifties, Bachmann had been concerned with political issues. As "R. K." in Rome, she wrote political articles for a West German newspaper from 1954 to 1955, and she later joined a committee that opposed equipping the German army with atomic weapons. In the 1960s, she wrote a public letter to Simon Wiesenthal that protested reducing the statute of limitations for Nazi war crimes, and she later marched and signed declarations against the Vietnam war. She used her influence with a major publisher to block a translation of Anna Akhmatova's poems by a former leader of the Hitler Youth (she had met Akhmatova in Rome). The change in her writing was not a sudden affirmation of social responsibility, therefore, but a new way of understanding how her writing could be an instrument of social change. Stories such as "Youth in an Austrian Town" and "Among Murderers and Madmen," from her prizewinning collection, *The Thirtieth Year* (1961), already depicted the historical context of German fascism. Their style, however, is relatively picturesque, their conflicts inner and individual, and their situations symbolic or extraordinary. One story in the collection is narrated by a water nymph; in another, a trial judge breaks down when attempting to ascertain the truth about a defendant who has the same name.

Shifting to broader social themes, Bachmann concentrated on women's experience. Instead of choosing unusual situations, she lingered over the implications of everyday scenes, describing the daily life of Austrian women who were, individually and collectively, victims of a patriarchal society. Readers accustomed to Bachmann's elegantly precise poetry were disconcerted by the presence, in the story collection *Three Paths to the Lake* (1972), of a prosaic "women's literature" that presented not only mundane topics but also rambling narrators and a diffuse awareness. Yet Bachmann's skill was still evident in the way she orchestrated inner references into a structure of cumulative significance or employed an apparently undisciplined stream of consciousness to reveal repressed thoughts and thought patterns in women who had never been allowed to develop their own voice and identity.

There is a strong link between the writer's earlier preoccupation with fascism and her later studies of women. Fascism must begin somewhere, she said, before it becomes a political movement and an agent of mass destruction. She located the principles of fascism—the oppression of the weak and a sadistic desire for dominance and control—uncomfortably close to home, in the subordination of women by men. "Fascism is the first thing in the relationship between a man and a woman," she declared in an interview. Such repression permeates society in many forms. Bachmann's character Franziska Jordan (the victimized wife of her unfinished novel, *The Franza Case*) compares her situation to that of aborigines or preindustrial cultures in modern society: "I am a Papuan woman." In this view, the social structures of a patriarchal society gather all control into a central point dominated by white men, who in turn reinforce their power by pushing to the margins any other cultural or psychological identity. These newly marginalized figures, moreover, are kept in their place by being defined as childlike and primitive. Discouraged from developing a voice of their own, unable to put their experience into words, they lose control of their identity. Like modern philosophers of language and psychoanalysts, Bachmann realized that language is crucial to a sense of self. Experience that cannot be expressed is unrecognizable and soon *unspeakable*. The moral task of a writer, she felt, was to find the right words for that experience. By bringing the unspeakable into the light of consciousness, Bachmann hoped to operate a change in social consciousness itself.

She envisaged a novel cycle, *Ways of Death*, that would illuminate women's experience through the linked stories of individual figures appearing and reappearing in major or minor roles. Two projected novels, *The Franza Case* and *Requiem for Fanny Goldmann*, remained unfinished and have been published only as posthumous fragments. In 1966, however, Bachmann gave readings from a novel that would be published as *Malina* (1971), a challenging modernist work that includes a variety of forms and techniques: fairy tale, letters, dream sequences, dramatic dialogue, and finally the inexplicable disappearance of the narrator from a story that previously depended on her. The violent dreams in the second chapter, including a vision of Malina's father as a Nazi murderer, and a "cemetery of murdered daughters," give symbolic expression to Bachmann's horror of fascism as a consistent pattern of violence directed first against individual women and leading to mass destruction.

The Franza Case presents similar themes even more directly. Franziska Jordan (who also appears in The Barking) is married to the respected Viennese psychiatrist Leo Jordan, a man with sadistic tendencies and a fascination with Nazism. Franziska ("Franza") is his third wife, and he is systematically driving her mad as he did the others. He destroys her sanity by leaving notes on her "case" around the house for her to find, and in a desperate attempt to save herself she flees the clinic in which she had been placed and travels to Egypt with her brother. In the purity of a desert setting remote from the Viennese society where Dr. Jordan rules, she hopes to understand "who I am, where I come from, what is wrong with me, and what I am looking for in this waste"—in short, to reconstruct her violated identity. She never has a chance to recover from the damage inflicted by Dr. Jordan's psychological torture, for violence catches up with her again when she is attacked and raped. After Franziska's death, her brother Martin returns home alive but unable to explain what has happened. The cumulative effect is of a series of little murders, different in scale from the genocide of World War II but remarkably similar in the exercise of power to control, to suppress, and to kill.

Bachmann was still working on Ways of Death when she herself died in Rome on October 17, 1973, three weeks after the night her apartment caught fire and she was badly burned. Her second collection of stories, Three Paths to the Lake, had appeared the previous year, with characters and themes growing directly out of Ways of Death. In the spring of 1973 she had traveled to Poland to give a series of readings, during which time she also visited the concentration camps at Auschwitz and Birkenau. The camps were a reminder of the destructive arrogance of power and of a fascist mentality whose presence and cost she made it her task to describe.

The Barking, taken from Three Paths to the Lake, chronicles another aspect of The Franza Case. The major figure is Leo Jordan's mother, now old and in failing health, who is befriended by her daughter-in-law Franziska. In a series of conversations, the topic of which is invariably the brilliant Leo, the two women inadvertently bring to light his real selfishness and cruelty. Old Frau Jordan is unable to admit her fear and dislike of Leo and has lived a devoted lie all her life. Rather than recognize the truth emerging from these conversations, she escapes into hallucinations of barking dogs. The barking that barricades her from her son and removes "the fear of an entire lifetime" merely suggests rebellion, and yet it does recall the resentment voiced earlier by her pet dog, Nuri, who was given away because he barked at Dr. Jordan.

Franziska, in contrast, becomes more critical of Leo's behavior even though she also cannot bring herself to blame him openly. Her relationship with Leo disintegrates during the course of the story, although we are never told exactly why. There is no indication here of the systematic attempt to drive Franziska mad that governs The Franza Case, but certainly the picture of a homophobic, control-obsessed psychiatrist who belittles human relationships and specializes in concentration-camp psychoses implies, for Bachmann, an essentially Nazi mentality. Much of the story's strength lies in its subtly indirect depiction of this mentality and its simultaneous analysis of the roots of power. Leo Jordan is described obliquely, through the eyes of his dependent mother and wife. He instills fear in them and controls their lives, but this control also depends on their willingness to obliterate their own personalities to appease him. Bachmann leaves open the possibility of other modes of being: Frau Jordan's truly maternal relationship with another child, Kiki; Franziska's care for her mother-in-law; and Franziska's brother's generosity in paying the taxi bills his dead sister had incurred for Frau Jordan. The fate of the story's two main characters, however, bleakly illustrates Bachmann's conviction that the oppressive power relationships of fascism begin at an insidiously personal level, in the relationships of men and women, and in a systematic disrespect for human individuality.

PRONOUNCING GLOSSARY

The following list uses common English syllables and stress accents to provide rough equivalents of selected words whose pronunciation may be unfamiliar to the general reader.

Bachmann: *bakh'-mahn*

Frau: *frow*

Franziska: *frahn-tsis'-kah*

Johannes: *yoh-hah'-nes*

The Barking[1]

Old Frau[2] Jordan had been called "old Frau Jordan" for the past three decades because there had been first one and now another young Frau Jordan, and although she did live in Hietzing,[3] she had only a one-room apartment in a dilapidated villa, with a tiny kitchen and no more than half a tub in the bathroom. From her distinguished son Leo, the professor, she received 1,000 schillings[4] per month, and somehow she managed to make do, although those 1,000 schillings had depreciated so much over the last twenty years that she was just barely able to pay an older woman, a certain Frau Agnes, who "looked in" on her twice a week, to tidy up a little, just "the bare minimum." She even saved some of the money for birthday and Christmas presents for her son and grandson from her son's first marriage, whom the first young wife sent over punctually every Christmas to pick up his present. Leo on the other hand was too busy to notice, and since he had become famous and his local prestige had blossomed into international renown, he was busier than ever. Things only changed when the latest young Frau Jordan began to visit the old woman as often as she could, a really nice, likable girl, as the old woman soon admitted to herself, but at each visit she said only: But Franziska, it's not right, you shouldn't come so often, it's such a waste. You two surely have enough expenses as it is, but Leo is just such a good son!

Franziska always brought something with her, delicacies and sherry, some pastries, because she had guessed that the old woman liked to take a sip now and then and, moreover, attached great importance to having something in the house "for the company." After all, Leo might drop by, and he mustn't notice how much she was missing and that all day long she wondered how to allocate her money and how much she could put aside for presents. Her apartment was meticulously clean, but gave off a faint "old-woman" smell which she was not aware of and which put Leo Jordan to flight, apart from the fact that he had no time to lose and no idea what to talk about with his eighty-five-year-old mother. Sometimes, seldom, he had been amused—that much Franziska knew—namely, when he was having a relationship with a married woman, because then old Frau Jordan had gone without sleep and made strange, convoluted allusions, trembling for his safety: she believed that the married men whose wives Leo Jordan was living with were dangerous and jealous and bloodthirsty, and she wasn't able to calm down until he married Franziska, who did not have a jealous husband lurking in the bushes

---

1. Translated by Mary Fran Gilbert.   2. Mrs. (German).   3. A suburb west of Vienna, Austria.
4. The basic Austrian unit of currency.

but was young and cheerful, an orphan, admittedly not from an educated family, but at least with a brother who had gone to college. Families of the educated classes and educated men in general carried great weight with Frau Jordan, although she didn't do much socializing; she only heard about things. But her son had the right to marry into an educated family. The old woman and Franziska talked almost exclusively about Leo, because he was the only productive topic the two of them had, and Franziska was shown the photo album over and over again, Leo in a stroller, Leo at the beach, and Leo through the years, taking hikes, pasting stamps in his collection, and so on until his military service.

The Leo she came to know through the old woman was a completely different Leo from the man she had married, and when the two women sat drinking their sherry the old woman would say: He was a complicated child, a strange boy, actually you could tell all along that he was destined for great things.

For a while Franziska was happy to hear these assertions, that Leo was so good to his mother and had always done everything conceivable to help her, but then she noticed that something was wrong, and with dismay she realized—the old woman was afraid of her son. It began with the old woman saying, sometimes hastily and parenthetically (she believed it to be a clever tactic that Franziska would never see through because she was blinded by admiration for her husband): But please don't mention a word of it to Leo, you know how concerned he is, it might upset him, whatever you do, please don't tell him that something is wrong with my knee, it's such a little thing, he might get upset about it.

Although Franziska had since learned that Leo never got upset at all, certainly not because of his mother, and only listened to her reports with half an ear, she suppressed this first realization. Unfortunately she had already told him about the knee but swore to the old woman she wouldn't say a word. Leo had reacted with annoyance and then, to placate her, had explained that he really couldn't drive out to Hietzing because of such a trifle. Just tell her— he rattled off some medical terminology—she should buy this and that and do and walk as little as possible. Franziska bought the medication without further comment and claimed in Hietzing that she had secretly spoken with one of her husband's assistants without mentioning any names and that he had given her this advice, although she was at a loss as to how to keep the old woman in bed without the help of a nurse. But she no longer had enough courage to approach Leo about it, because a nurse cost money, and now she was caught in the middle. On the one hand Frau Jordan didn't want anything to do with it, and on the other Leo Jordan—albeit for completely different reasons—simply didn't want to hear about it. When Frau Jordan's knee was swollen, Franziska lied to her husband several times; she drove quickly to Hietzing, allegedly to the hairdresser's, and straightened up the little apartment, bringing all sorts of things with her. She purchased a radio but was uneasy afterward: Leo was bound to notice the expenditure, so she quickly transferred the money back and broke into the meager savings she had set aside for some sort of emergency which would hopefully never arise and could only be a minor emergency at any rate. She and her brother had divided what little remained after the death of their entire family, with the exception of a cottage in southern Carinthia[5] which was slowly falling into disrepair. In the end she called a general practitioner in the neighborhood and asked him to treat the old woman for a while, paying him out of her own savings. More importantly, she didn't dare reveal to the doctor who she was and who the old woman was, because that would only have hurt Leo's reputation, and protecting Leo's reputation was also in Franziska's best interest. But the old woman thought much more selflessly: there was no way she could ask her famous son to go so far as to come and take a look at her knee. She had used a cane before on occasion, but after this knee problem she really needed it, so Franziska sometimes drove her to town. Shopping with the old woman was a somewhat laborious undertaking: once she had only needed a comb, but there were no combs like the ones "in her day," and although the old woman was polite, standing in the store with erect dignity, she annoyed the little saleswoman by eyeing the price tags suspiciously, unable to refrain from telling Franziska in a clearly audible whisper that the prices here were outrageous, they'd better go somewhere else. The saleswoman, who was in no position to judge how important buying this comb was to the old woman, replied rudely that they wouldn't find this comb cheaper anywhere in town. Franziska launched into embarrassed negotiations with the mother, took the comb the old woman wanted but looked on as costing a fortune and quickly paid for it, saying: Just consider it a Christmas present from us, a present in advance. Prices have really gone up horrendously everywhere. The old woman didn't say a word, she sensed her defeat, but still, if prices really were so outrageous—a comb like this used to cost two schillings and nowadays it cost sixty—well then there wasn't much left for her to understand in this world.

After a while the topic "the good son" had been exhausted and Franziska repeatedly steered the conversation to the old woman herself, because the only thing she knew was that Leo's father had died young of a heart attack or stroke, quite suddenly, on a staircase, and that must have been a long time ago, because if you stopped to figure it out this woman had been a widow for almost half a century. First she had worked for years to raise her only child, and then she was suddenly an old woman nobody cared about anymore. She never spoke about her marriage, only in connection with Leo who had had a very difficult life, without a father, and she was so preoccupied with Leo that she failed to see the parallel to Franziska, who had lost both her parents when she was young. Her son was the only one who could have had a difficult time, and then it turned out that it hadn't been so bad after all, because a distant cousin had paid for his education, a certain Johannes about whom Franziska had heard very little, merely a few derogatory, critical references to some eternal—now aging—loafer who was swimming in money and supposedly led a life of idleness with all its ridiculous affectations. He dabbled a little in art, collected Chinese lacquerware, and was just another one of those freeloaders found in every family. Franziska knew also that he was homosexual, but she was really amazed how someone like Leo, whose very profession obliged him to uphold a neutral and scientific attitude toward homosexuality and phenomena of a quite different magnitude, could go on

5. A southwestern province of Austria.

and on about this cousin as though he had somehow, through his own negligence, fallen prey to works of art, homosexuality, and an inheritance to boot, but at that time Franziska still admired her husband too much to be more than irritated and hurt. With relief she heard from the old woman, in discussing those hard times, that Leo was infinitely grateful and had been a big help to this Johannes, who was then in the throes of a number of personal crises—which were better left untold. The old woman hesitated and then added, because she was, after all, sitting opposite the wife of a psychiatrist: I think you should know that Johannes is sexual.

Franziska controlled herself and suppressed a laugh, it was surely the most daring revelation the old woman had roused herself to in years, but with Franziska she was opening up more and more. She told her how Leo had often given Johannes advice, naturally free of charge, but Johannes was a hopeless case, and if a person didn't have the willpower to change it was understandable that he would be at his wits' end, and from what she heard, Johannes just kept on with it, the same as always. Franziska carefully translated this naive story into reality and understood even less why Leo talked about this cousin in such a disparaging and malicious way. At that time the obvious reason escaped her, namely, that Leo was reluctant to be reminded of his mother and his former wives and lovers who were nothing to him but a conspiracy of creditors from whom he could escape only by belittling them to himself and others. His tirades about his first wife were similar: she had been the epitome of everything diabolical, unappreciative and spiteful, traits that had not been revealed in depth until the divorce when her aristocratic father had hired a lawyer for her to secure some of the money for the child, money she'd given him when he was a young doctor and hard times had struck again. It was an alarmingly large sum to Franziska but, as she was told, one could expect nothing less from the "baroness," as Leo ironically called her, because the family had always treated him like an upstart, without having the slightest idea who was dwelling in their midst. It amused him to note that the "baroness" had never remarried and lived in total seclusion. After him she hadn't been able to find another fool—young and gullible and poor, as he had been—who would have married such a deserving Fräulein. She had understood nothing about his work, absolutely nothing, and although she behaved fairly in respect to the agreement about their son, sending him for regular visits and teaching him to respect his father, she obviously did it for no other reason than to prove to the world how generous she was.

The brilliant doctor's rise to fame along the thorny path of suffering had already become Franziska's religion at that time, and again and again she reproached herself with the image of him making his way, against indescribable odds and despite the obstacle that dreadful marriage posed, all the way to the top. And the cross he was forced to bear because of his mother, the financial and moral burden, was no light one for him, but that at least Franziska could take off his shoulders. Although it otherwise might not have occurred to her to spend her free hours with an old woman the time became something special when she thought of Leo: a helping hand, evidence of her love for him, allowing him to devote his undivided attention to his work.

Leo was just too good to her, he told her that she was overdoing it, the way she took care of his mother, a telephone call now and again would have sufficed. For the past few years the old woman had had a telephone which she feared more than loved: she didn't like to talk on the phone and always shouted into the mouthpiece and couldn't hear what the other party said, and besides that, the phone was too expensive, but of course Franziska wasn't to mention that to Leo. Once the old woman—prompted by Franziska and a second glass of sherry—did in fact begin to talk about the old days, the very old days, and it turned out that she wasn't from an educated family, her father had knit gloves and socks in a small factory in Lower Austria and she had been the oldest of eight children, but then she'd had a wonderful time when she took up employment with a Greek family, immensely rich people with a little boy, the most beautiful child she had ever laid eyes on, and she was his nursemaid. Being a nursemaid was a really good job, nothing degrading about it, and the Greek's young wife had had servants aplenty, oh yes, she'd had a real stroke of luck, such a good position had been hard to find back then. The child's name was Kiki, at least everyone had called him Kiki. When the old woman began talking about Kiki more and more frequently, remembering every detail—what Kiki had said, how cute and affectionate he was, the walks they'd taken together—her eyes lit up as they never did when she spoke of her own child. Kiki had simply been a little angel, never naughty, she stressed, never naughty at all, and the separation must have been terrible, they hadn't told Kiki that the Fräulein was leaving, and she had cried all night long, and once, years later, she had tried to find out what had become of the family. First she'd heard that they were traveling, then that they were back in Greece, and now she had no idea whatsoever what had happened to Kiki, who must be over sixty by now, yes, over sixty she said pensively, and she had been forced to leave because the Greek family had planned their first major trip and couldn't take her along, and when they left the young wife had given her a wonderful present. The old woman stood up and rummaged in a jewelry box, then showed her the brooch from Kiki's mother, it was the real thing, with diamonds, but she still asked herself today if they hadn't let her go because the wife had noticed that Kiki was more attached to her than to his own mother, she could understand that all right, but it had been the hardest blow of all, and she had never completely recovered from it. Franziska regarded the brooch thoughtfully; perhaps it really was quite valuable, she didn't know much about jewelry, but she was beginning to realize something else: this Kiki must have meant more to the old woman than Leo. She often hesitated to talk about Leo's childhood, or she began only to break off in fright saying abruptly: It was just childish nonsense, you know boys are so hard to raise, he didn't do it on purpose, he was just having such a bad time and it was all I could do to make ends meet. But you get everything back a hundredfold when a child has grown up and made his own way and become so famous, he takes after his father more than me, you know.

Franziska carefully handed back the brooch, and once again the old woman started in fear. Please Franziska, don't mention a word of this to Leo, it could annoy him. I have my plans, you know, if I get sick I could sell it so that I won't become even more of a burden to him. Franziska embraced the old woman with a hug that was both timid and fierce. Don't ever do that, promise me you'll never sell this brooch. You're not a burden to us at all!

On the way home she made one detour after the other, in a state of inner turmoil, this poor woman shouldn't sell her brooch while she and Leo spent money freely, went on trips, entertained. She kept debating what she should say to Leo, but a first, faint alarm sounded inside her, because even though the old woman had her quirks and exaggerated things, she must be right about something, and so in the end she didn't say a word about it at home and only reported cheerfully that his mother was doing very well. But before they left for a conference in London she arranged a contract with a garage which ran a private taxi service, made a downpayment, and said to the old woman: An idea has occurred to us, because you shouldn't walk too far by yourself. Just call a taxi when you want to go out, it hardly costs a thing, it's just a favor from an old patient, but don't say anything about it, especially not to Leo, you know how he is, he doesn't like it when you thank him and everything, and you just ride to town when you need something, and have the taxi wait, but always have Herr Pineider take you, the young one. He doesn't know that his father was one of Leo's patients though, that comes under professional secrecy, you know, I was just there and talked to him, and you have to promise me, for Leo's sake, that you'll take the taxi, it would ease our minds. In the beginning, the old woman made little use of the taxi, and Franziska scolded her for it when she returned from England; her leg had worsened and the old woman had naturally done all her shopping on foot, once even going so far as to take the streetcar into town because one could hardly get anything in Hietzing, and Franziska said firmly, as if to a stubborn child: This is definitely not to happen again.

They exhausted one topic after another: Kiki, the life of a young nursemaid in Vienna before the First World War and before her marriage, and sometimes it was only Franziska who talked, especially when she had just returned from a trip with Leo, a brilliant talk he'd delivered at the conference, and that he had given her this offprint for his mother. The old woman labored through the title with an effort: "The Significance of Endogenous and Exogenous Factors in Connection with the Occurrence of Paranoid and Depressive Psychoses in Former Concentration Camp Inmates and Refugees." Franziska assured her it was merely the groundwork for a much larger study he was working on, and he was even letting her help him with it. It would probably become the most significant and the first really important book in the field. A work of incalculable impact.

The old woman was strangely mute, surely she didn't understand the implications of these studies, maybe nothing at all of what her son was doing. Then she said, surprisingly: I hope he won't make too many enemies with it, here in Vienna, and then there's that other thing . . .

Franziska grew agitated: But that's exactly the point, that would be a very good thing, it's a provocation, too, and Leo isn't afraid of anyone, for him it's the only thing that counts, that has a purpose far beyond its scientific significance.

Yes, of course, the old woman said quickly, and he knows how to defend himself, and if you're famous you always have enemies. I was just thinking about Johannes, but that's so long ago now. Did you know that he was in a concentration camp for a year and a half before the war ended? Franziska was surprised, she hadn't known, but she failed to see the connection. The old woman didn't want to say any more but then continued: It meant a certain amount of danger for Leo, having a relative who, well, you know what

I mean. Yes, of course, said Franziska, still somewhat confused; sometimes the old woman had such a roundabout way of saying things without really saying them, and she couldn't make head or tail of it, although suddenly she was bursting with pride that a member of Leo's family had been through something so terrible and that Leo, in his tactful, modest way, had never said anything about it to her, not even about the danger he must have faced as a young doctor. That afternoon the old woman didn't want to go on talking; she merely asked disjointedly: Do you hear it, too?

What?

The dogs, the old woman said. There were never so many dogs in Hietzing, I've heard them barking again, and they bark at night, too. Frau Schönthal next door has a poodle now. It doesn't bark much though, it's such a nice dog, I see her almost every day when I go shopping, but we only say hello, her husband doesn't have much of an education.

Franziska drove home as quickly as she could; this time she wanted to ask Leo if there was anything to the fact that his mother had suddenly begun talking about dogs, if it was an alarming symptom, maybe it had something to do with her age. She had also noticed that the old woman had been upset once about ten schillings which had been lying on the table and then disappeared when Frau Agnes left, all this excitement about ten missing schillings, certainly she had only imagined it anyway, weren't those all signs of the process of aging? It couldn't possibly have been the cleaning woman, she was what people in certain circles—that is, in better circles—called a "God-fearing" woman who came more out of pity than for the money, which she didn't need anyway—she did it as a favor and nothing more. And old Frau Jordan's pitiful presents—an ancient, threadbare purse or some other useless paraphernalia—would hardly have induced Frau Agnes to come; she had realized long ago that she had nothing to expect from the old woman or from her son, and she knew nothing of Franziska's enthusiastic plans for improving the situation; Franziska had chided the old woman as though she were a child, because she didn't want to lose this valuable help over a bout of senile obstinacy and an unfounded suspicion.

More and more often she found the old woman at the window when she arrived, and they no longer sat together when Franziska came to drink sherry and nibble on pastries. The business with the dogs continued, although at the same time her hearing problem grew worse, and Franziska was at a loss. Something had to be done, and Leo, whom she bothered with none of this, was not going to avoid devoting some attention to his mother one of these days. Only then things started becoming complicated between Leo and herself, and she discovered that he had so intimidated her that she was afraid of him. But at least once, in a fit of her old courage, she overcame her inexplicable fear and suggested at dinner: Why don't we invite your mother to come and stay with us, we have enough room, and then our Rosi could always be with her and you would never have to worry, besides, she's so quiet and undemanding, she would never disturb you, and certainly not me, I'm suggesting it for your sake because I know how much you worry. Leo was in a good mood that evening and secretly happy about something. She didn't realize what it was but had decided to make use of the opportunity, and he answered, laughing: What an idea, you have no feel for the situation, my dear, you can't uproot an elderly person after a while, it would only depress her and she needs her freedom, she's a strong woman who has lived alone for decades. You don't know her the way I do, she would die of fright here, just from the kind of people who come over. She'd probably debate for hours on end whether to use the bathroom, out of fear that one of us just might want to use it. Come on, my little Franziska, please don't make such a face, I think your impulse is touching and admirable, but that wonderful idea of yours would be the death of her. Believe me, it's just that I happen to know more about these things.

But this business with the dogs . . . ? Franziska began to stutter, she hadn't wanted to talk about it and would gladly have immediately taken back what she'd said. She was no longer capable of putting her apprehension into words.

What, her husband asked in a completely different tone of voice, she doesn't still want a mutt, does she? I don't understand, Franziska answered. Why should she—you don't mean she wants to have a dog, do you?

Of course I do, and I'm more than glad that this childish interlude has blown over so quickly, at her age she just couldn't handle a dog, she should take care of herself, that's more important to me, a dog is such a nuisance, she has no idea what they would mean, with her advancing senility. She never said anything about it, Franziska replied half-heartedly, I don't think she wants a dog. I wanted to say something entirely different, but it's not important, sorry. Would you like a cognac, are you going to work later, should I type anything for you?

At her next visit Franziska didn't know how to persuade the old woman, who was always on the alert, to give her answers she needed to know. She approached the subject in a roundabout way, remarking casually: Incidentally, I saw Frau Schönthal's dog today, really a cute dog, I like poodles a lot, actually all animals, because I grew up in the country, you know, we always had dogs, I mean my grandparents and everyone in the village, and cats, too, of course. Wouldn't it be good for you to have a dog or a cat, now that you have trouble reading. I mean, certainly that kind of thing passes, but I for one would absolutely love to have a dog. But you know, in the city it's just a bother and not really fair to the dog, but here in Hietzing, where it can frisk around in the yard and you can go for walks . . .

The old woman exclaimed in agitation: A dog, no, no, I don't want a dog! Franziska realized she had done something wrong, but felt at the same time that she hadn't offended the old woman as she might have had she suggested a parrot or canaries: it must have been something else entirely that had put her in such a state of agitation. After a while the old woman said very quietly: Nuri was a really nice dog, and I got along well with him, that was, let me think, it must have been five years ago, but then I had to give him away, to a home or a place where they resell them. Leo doesn't like dogs. No, what am I saying, it was different, there was something in that dog I can't really understand, he couldn't stand Leo, he always jumped at him and barked madly whenever Leo made the slightest move toward the door, and then once he almost bit him, and Leo was so indignant, of course that's understandable, when a dog is that wild, but he was never like that otherwise, not even with strangers, and then naturally I gave him away. I couldn't let Leo be barked at and bitten by Nuri, no, that would have been too much, Leo should be able to feel at home when he visits me and not have to get angry about some poorly trained dog.

Franziska thought that, although there was no longer a dog who jumped at him and disliked him, Leo came seldom enough as it was, and even less often since Franziska came instead. How long had it been anyway since his last visit? Once the three of them had gone for a short ride along the Weinstrasse and into the Helenenthal and lunched at an inn with his mother; otherwise Franziska always came alone.

Be sure not to say anything to Leo, though, that business with Nuri really hurt his feelings, he's very sensitive, you know, and to this day I can't forgive myself for being so selfish as to want to have Nuri, but old people are very selfish, dear Franziska, you can't understand that yet, you're still so young and good, but when you're very old you get all these selfish desires, and you can't just let yourself give in to them. What would have become of me if Leo hadn't taken care of me, his father died all of a sudden like that and there was no time to make any arrangements, and there wasn't any money, either, my husband was a little careless, no, not a spendthrift, but he had a hard time of it and didn't have much of a knack with money, Leo doesn't take after him in that respect. In those days I could still work, the boy was a reason to keep going, and I was still young, but what would I do nowadays? My one fear has always been having to go to an old people's home, but Leo would never stand for that, and if I didn't have this apartment I'd have to go to some home, and I guess a dog isn't worth all that. Franziska listened to her, clenched up inside, and she said to herself: So that's it, that's it, she gave her dog away for his sake. And she asked herself: What kind of people are we?—because she was incapable of thinking: What kind of a man is my husband!—we're just so cruel, and she thinks she's selfish, and all the time we have everything we want! In order to hide her tears she quickly unpacked a small package from Meinl, little things, and acted as though she hadn't understood. Oh, by the way, I'm so scatterbrained today, I've only brought you the tea and coffee and a little smoked salmon and Russian salad. Actually it doesn't go together all that well, but I was really flustered at the store because Leo is leaving and one of the manuscripts isn't finished yet. But he'll give you a call tonight, and he'll be back in a week anyway.

He needs a break, the old woman said, see to it that he gets one if you can, you two haven't had any vacation at all yet this year. Franziska said brightly: That's a good idea, I'll convince him some way or another, I just need to think of a strategy, but thanks a lot, that's really a good piece of advice, he's constantly overworked, you know, and at some point I have to make him slow down.

What Franziska did not know was that this was her last visit to the old woman and she no longer needed the strategy, because other things came to pass, events of such hurricane force that she almost forgot the old woman and a great many other things as well.

In her fear, the old woman didn't ask her son on the phone why Franziska had stopped coming. She was worried, but her son sounded cheerful and unconcerned, and once he even came over and stayed for twenty minutes. He didn't touch the pastries, he didn't finish the sherry and he didn't talk about Franziska, but he did talk quite a bit about himself, and that made her ecstatic because it had been such a long time since he had spoken about himself. So he was leaving on vacation now, he needed a break, but the word "Mexico" gave the old woman a mild shock, wasn't that the place where they had scorpions and revolutions and savages and earthquakes, but he laughed reassuringly, kissed her and promised to write. He sent a few postcards, which she read religiously. Franziska hadn't added her regards. Once Franziska called her from Carinthia. Really, the money these young people throw out the window! Franziska had only called to ask if everything was okay. Then they talked about Leo, but the old woman kept shouting at the most inappropriate times: It's getting too expensive, child, but Franziska kept talking, yes, she had finally succeeded, he was finally taking a break, and she had had to go to her brother's, there was something to settle here, that was why she hadn't been able to accompany Leo. Family matters in Carinthia. Because of the house. Then the old woman received a strange envelope with a few lines from Franziska. She didn't say anything, just sent her regards and wrote that she would like her to have this photo she had taken herself, the photograph was of Leo, apparently on the Semmering Pass,[6] laughing in a snowy landscape in front of a large hotel. The old woman decided not to say anything to Leo; he wouldn't have asked her anyway. She hid the photograph under the brooch in her jewelry box.

She could no longer read books and was bored by the radio; newspapers were all she wanted, and Frau Agnes got them for her. It took her hours to decipher them, she read the obituaries and always felt a certain satisfaction when someone younger than herself had passed away. Well, look at that, Professor Haderer too, he could hardly have been more than seventy. Frau Schönthal's mother had died, too, of cancer, she wasn't even sixty-five. The old woman stiffly offered her condolences in the grocery store and didn't even look at the poodle, and then she went home and stood at the window. She slept more than old people are said to sleep, but she often awoke, only to hear the dogs again. She was startled whenever the cleaning woman came: since Franziska's visits had ended, it bothered her when anyone came over, and she had the impression that she was changing. Now she actually was frightened of suddenly collapsing in the street or losing control of herself when she had to go to town for something, and so she obediently called young Herr Pineider, who drove her around. And she became accustomed to this small precaution for her own safety. She completely lost her sense of time, and when Leo once came by to see her, deeply tanned, she no longer knew if he was returning from Mexico or when he had been there at all. But she was careful not to ask, and gathered from something he said that he had just arrived from Ischia,[7] back from a trip to Italy. Confused, she said: Good, good. That was good for you. And while he was telling her something the dogs began to bark, several of them, all at once, very near, and she was so completely encircled by the barking and a very gentle, gentle terror that she was no longer afraid of her son. The fear of an entire lifetime suddenly left her.

When he said on his way out: Next time I'll bring Elfi over, you have to meet her one of these days! she had no idea what he was talking about. Wasn't he married to Franziska anymore, how long had it been, how many wives was that now anyway, she could no longer remember how long he had

6. In the Alps in southern Austria, known as a tourist resort and center for winter sports.   7. An island vacation spot north of the Bay of Naples.

lived with Franziska and when, and she said: Go ahead and bring her over. Fine. Whatever is best for you. The barking was so close now that for an instant she was certain that Nuri was with her again and would jump at him and bark. She wished he would finally leave, she wanted to be alone. She thanked him out of habit, just in case, and he asked in astonishment: Whatever for? Now I really did go and forget to bring you my book after all. A phenomenal success. I'll have it sent.

Well then, thank you so much my child. Send it over, but unfortunately your dumb old mother can hardly read anymore and doesn't understand much anyway.

She let him embrace her and found herself alone again surrounded by the barking. It came from every garden and house in Hietzing, an invasion of the beasts had begun, the dogs came closer, barking to her, and she stood erect, as always, no longer dreaming of the time with Kiki and the Greeks, no longer thinking of the day when the last ten schillings had disappeared and Leo had lied to her. Instead she redoubled her efforts to hide things better, wishing she could throw them away, especially the brooch and the photograph, so that Leo wouldn't find anything after she died. But she couldn't think of a good hiding place, maybe the bucket with the scraps, but she trusted Frau Agnes less and less, too, because she would have had to give her the rubbish, and she suspected that the woman would rummage through it and find the brooch. Once she said, a little too harshly: At least you could give the bones and the leftovers to the dogs.

The cleaning woman looked at her in amazement and asked: What dogs? To the dogs, of course, insisted the old woman in an imperious tone, I want the dogs to have them!

She was a suspicious looking creature, a thief. She probably took the bones home with her.

To the dogs, I said. Can't you understand me, are you deaf or something? No wonder, at your age.

Then the barking diminished, and she thought: someone has chased the dogs off or given them away, because now it was no longer that same powerful, recurrent, barking. The fainter the barking, the more adamant she became: she was only biding her time until the louder barking resumed. One had to be able to wait, and she could wait. All at once it was no longer a barking sound, although there was no doubt it came from the dogs in the neighborhood. It wasn't a growling either, just now and again the great, wild, triumphant howling of a single dog, then a whimpering, the faint barking of all the others fading into the distance.

One day nearly two years after the death of his sister Franziska, Dr. Martin Ranner received a bill from a company by the name of Pineider for taxi services listed separately by date, for which Frau Franziska Jordan had made a downpayment and signed a contract. But because only very few trips had been made while Franziska was alive and the majority after her death he called the company for an explanation of this mysterious bill. Although the explanation actually explained very little, he had no desire to call his former brother-in-law or ever see him again, so he paid the fares, in installments, for a woman he had never known and never had anything to do with. He came to the conclusion that the old Frau Jordan must have passed away some time ago; the company had let several months go by since her last trip, perhaps out of reverence, before asserting its claims.

GABRIEL GARCÍA MÁRQUEZ
born 1928

One of the great novelists and prose stylists of the twentieth century, Gabriel García Márquez possesses both the technical virtuosity of the French "new novelists" and the breadth and historical scope of the traditional realistic writer. His most famous work, *One Hundred Years of Solitude* (1967), is also the best-known novel from the amazing literary explosion of the 1960s and 1970s called the Latin American "Boom," and embodies the mixture of fantasy and realism called "magical realism." In this novel and related stories, he follows the rise and fall of the Buendía family fortunes in a mythical town called Macondo, and sketches at the same time an echoing, intricate pattern of social, cultural, and psychological themes that become a symbolic picture of Latin American society. Not all of García Márquez's works are about Macondo, but the same themes and images reappear throughout: the contrast of dreamlike and everyday reality and the "magical" aspect of fictional creation, mythic overtones often rooted in local folklore, the representation of broader social and psychological conflicts through regional tales, the essential solitude of individuals facing love and death in a society of which they never quite seem a part. García Márquez is a political novelist in that many of his fictional situations are openly drawn from conditions in Latin American history, so that local readers will recognize current history in the change from prosperity to misery in Macondo that accompanies the presence and withdrawal of the banana company, the massacre of striking banana workers by government forces in 1928, the extreme separation of rich and poor, and the grotesquely oppressive power of political dictators pictured most recently in *The Autumn of the Patriarch* (1975). Yet his fiction achieves its impact not because of its base in real events but because these events are transformed and interpreted inside an artistic vision that—experimenting with many forms—creates a fictional universe all its own.

García Márquez was born in the small town of Aracataca in the "banana zone" of Colombia on March 6, 1928, to Gabriel Eligio García and Maria Márquez Iguarán. The first of twelve children, he was raised by his maternal grandparents until his grandfather died in 1936. He attributes his love of fantasy to his grandmother, who would tell him fantastic tales whenever she did not want to answer his questions. The recurring image of an old military man battered by circumstances (the grandfather of *Leaf Storm*, 1955; the protagonist of *No One Writes to the Colonel*, 1958; and in his younger days, Colonel Aureliano Buendía of *One Hundred Years of Solitude*, 1967) likewise recalls his grandfather, a retired colonel who had served on the Liberal side of a civil war at the beginning of the century. A scholarship student at the National Colegio in Zipaquirá, García Márquez received his bachelor's degree in 1946 and studied law at universities in Bogotá and Cartagena from 1947 to 1950. In 1947 he published his first story, *The Third Resignation,* a Kafkaesque tale of a man who continued to grow and retain consciousness in his coffin for seventeen years after his death. García Márquez had worked as a journalist while studying law, and in 1950 he abandoned his legal studies for journalism in order to have more time as a writer. His first novel, *Leaf Storm,* was published in 1955 and—in its use of interior monologue and juxtaposition of different perspectives—shows the strong influence of Faulkner. He would soon abandon the more subjective Faulknerian style for an objective manner derived both from his experience in journalism and from Ernest Hemingway. In *Leaf Storm*, we may perceive reality through the mind of a ten-year-old boy: "The heat won't let you breathe in the closed room. You can hear the sun buzzing in the streets, but that's all. The air is stagnant, like concrete; you get the feeling that it could get all twisted like a sheet of steel." In his next novel, *No One Writes to the Colonel*, an impersonal narrator catalogues the actions of the colonel about to make coffee: "He removed the pot from the fire, poured half the water onto the earthen floor, and scraped the inside of the can with a knife until the last scrapings of the ground coffee, mixed with bits of rust, fell into the pot."

In 1954 García Márquez had joined the newspaper *El Espectador* (The Spectator) in Bogotá; a report he wrote in 1955 that indirectly revealed corruption in the navy irritated the Rojas Pinilla dictatorship, and the paper was shut down. Working in Paris as *El Espectador*'s foreign correspondent when he learned that his job had been abolished, he lived in extreme poverty for the next year while beginning *The Evil Hour* (1962) and *No One Writes to the Colonel*. In 1957, after traveling in Eastern Europe, he returned to Latin America. Here he worked for several different newspapers in Venezuela, and later for the international press agency, Prensa Latina, in Cuba and New York, and for the Mexican periodicals *La Familia* and *Sucesos* (a sensationalist magazine) before beginning to write film scripts in 1963. A collection of short stories, *Big Mama's Funeral*, was published in 1962 along with the first edition of *The Evil Hour*, which, printed in Spain, was later repudiated by the author because of tampering by proofreaders. In 1965 the various themes and characters he had been developing throughout his earlier novels and short stories came together as the fully developed concept of a new book, and García Márquez shut himself up in his study for a year and a half to write *One Hundred Years of Solitude*. Published in 1967, the novel was a best-seller, immediately translated into numerous (now twenty-five) languages; it received prizes in Italy and France in 1969, and—when published in English in 1970—was chosen by American critics as one of the dozen best books of the year.

Layers of meaning accumulate around a core story in *One Hundred Years*, as the history of the doomed Buendía family takes on different and intertwined shades of significance. The family is cursed from the moment that its founder, José Arcadio Buendía, kills a friend who had insulted him and consummates an incestuous marriage; he then sets out in search of the sea and stops to settle in Macondo. Throughout a hundred years of family history in the nineteenth and twentieth centuries, the Buendías are soldiers, scholars, merchants, explorers, revolutionaries, inventors, lovers, ascetics, labor organizers, and above all stubborn individuals. Yet these individuals are caught up in, and defined by, a larger family history of which they sometimes appear only interrelated, component parts: names echo one another, and parallel situations evoke a feeling of half recognition inside a mirrorlike pattern of structural oppositions. The Buendía story is set in history but also exists on a mythic level: Remedios the Beauty is lifted up into heaven clutching her sheets when she dies, and when José Arcadio is killed, blood runs from his ear down the street all the way to his mother in her kitchen. The last Buendía is born with the sign of the curse—a pig's tail—and dies eaten by ants at the end. Yet this is not really the end, for in the very last pages, after his son's death and as a whirlwind gathers to destroy Macondo, Aureliano Babilonia reads the manuscript left by the dead magician Melquíades. At last able to decipher a text that could not be read until one hundred years had passed, Aureliano Babilonia finds that this text is the story of his own family; thus he is learning about his own existence, predicted and described a century ago. "It was the history of the family, written by Melquíades, down to the most trivial details, one hundred years ahead of time. He had written it in Sanskrit, which was his mother tongue, and he had encoded the even lines in the private cipher of the Emperor

Augustus and the odd ones in a Lacedemonian military code." Behind García Márquez there is yet another author—Melquíades—who has written *One Hundred Years of Solitude*, a novel whose complexity and self-contained referentiality recall the circular fictions of Borges.

The magical realism of *One Hundred Years of Solitude* depends on the juxtaposition of real and fantastic worlds, and it elicits a series of interpretations whose variety can be emulated only by interpretations of Kafka. For some readers, the novel is an allegory of the human condition and its fall from innocence; for others, it recounts the destructive, alienating influence on Latin American society of the aggressive individualism in Western culture; for others, it depicts essential human loneliness and the failure to communicate—even in love; for still others, it is a "total fiction" peculiarly valid for intricate repetitive patterns that refer to folklore and real life but finally create only a fictional universe. Each interpretation draws on the novel's blurring of real and unreal worlds, so that historical facts become the basis for fiction and fictional manipulation liberates our perspective on reality—a typically modernist method of using the imagination to encourage historical change.

After *One Hundred Years of Solitude*, García Márquez found new ways to combine magical-realist techniques and social commentary. In 1972, he published a collection of seven stories, *The Incredible and Sad Story of Innocent Eréndira and Her Heartless Grandmother*, which contains the story printed here, *Death Constant beyond Love*. From the title story, in which Eréndira's monstrously fat, tattooed, green-blooded grandmother is finally murdered after prostituting her grandchild to the entire countryside to repay a debt, to symbolic fantasies such as *A Very Old Man with Enormous Wings* (in which a castaway angel is exhibited in a chicken coop until his feathers grow back and he can fly away), the author presents tales in which the substance is incredible but the details themselves are highly realistic. The winged man smells bad and his wings are infested with parasites; the farm truck in which Eréndira tries to escape with her lover has an old motor and cannot outrun the military patrol summoned by her grandmother. The mixture of fantasy and realism is not easily interpretable in a single symbolic sense: Eréndira's prostitution may be political and cultural as well as personal, and larger social relationships may be symbolized in the town's attitude toward the angel. Throughout, the narrative line can easily be followed but also interpreted in several ways.

Increasingly preoccupied with contemporary political events, he next published *The Autumn of the Patriarch*, an intricate study of the idea of dictatorship embodied in reactions to a first, false death of the patriarch (his double was assassinated instead), and a second, apparently real death, on which new authorities are already gathering to divide up the power. García Márquez is aiming at more than a specific political situation: he points to a habit of mind, a social lethargy in which there is no apparent connection between the passive acceptance of life as it always has been and the manipulation of society by a succession of dictators. In his next novel, *Chronicle of a Death Foretold* (1981), he describes the same inertia in a small town where everyday life continues its ordinary gossipy routine around two life-shattering events: the rejection of Angela Vicario by her new husband when he finds she is not a virgin, and her brothers' murder of the local dandy whom she names (probably falsely) as her seducer. Against the background of a whole society's passive complicity in a murder that everyone knows will happen, it is death and love that are the two overriding realities.

In recent years—questioning the effectiveness of literature to remedy the social ills he so often describes—García Márquez has been more and more active politically, speaking out for revolutionary governments in Latin America and organizing assistance for political prisoners. Living in Mexico City, he continues to write, including a number of stories that are still unpublished and an account of Cuba under the U.S. blockade. He received the Nobel Prize for literature in 1982.

The story printed here, *Death Constant beyond Love* (1970), also has a political background although its protagonist, Senator Onésimo Sánchez, is seen chiefly as he struggles with his elemental problem of death. He is no hero: in *Innocent Eréndira* he writes a letter vouching for the grandmother's morality, and in this story he is clearly a corrupt politician who accepts bribes and stays in power by helping the local property owners avoid reform. His electoral train is a traveling circus with carnival wagons, fireworks, a ready-made audience of hired Indians, and a cardboard village with imitation brick houses and a painted ocean liner to offer the illusion of future prosperity; he uses carefully placed gifts to encourage support and a feeling of dependence.

Yet the background of poverty and corruption, the entertaining spectacle of the senator's "fictional world," and the political campaign itself fade into insignificance before broader themes of life and death. Forty-two, happily married, in full control of his own and others' lives as a successful politician in mid-career, he is made to feel suddenly helpless, vulnerable, and alone when told that all this will stop and he will be dead "forever" by next Christmas. Theoretically, he knows that death is inevitable and nature cannot be defeated. He has read the Stoic philosopher Marcus Aurelius (121–180 c.e.) and even refers to the *Meditations*, which recommends the cheerful acceptance of natural order (including death and oblivion), criticizes the delusions of those "who have tenaciously stuck to life," and stresses both the tranquil "ordering of the mind" and the idea that human beings are all "fellow-citizens" of a shared "political community." The example of the philosopher is not mere chance: Marcus Aurelius was also a political figure, a Roman emperor who wrote his *Meditations* as personal guidelines in a time of plague and political unrest.

The senator does gain some Stoic insight into the illusions of his career: he notices how similar are the dusty village and the worn cardboard facade that represents its hopes, and he is fed up with what he recognizes to be background maneuverings that keep him in power by prolonging the exploitation of the poor. But he also loses sympathy for the barefoot Indians standing in the square, and his newly alienated perspective is not accompanied by the Stoic injunction to maintain a just and ordered mind and to accept everything that happens as necessary and good. In this crisis, the senator is reduced to a basic and instinctual existence, expressed in García Márquez's recurrent themes of solitude, love, and death. The beautiful Laura provides an opportunity for him to sublimate his fear of death in erotic passion (inextricably intertwined, according to Freud). His choice means scandal and the destruction of his political career, but by now Onésimo Sánchez has felt the emptiness of his earlier activities and is engaged in a struggle to cheat death.

He does not succeed, of course, and dies weeping with rage that death separates him from Laura Farina. *Death Constant beyond Love* has reversed the ambitious claim of a famous sonnet by the Spanish Golden Age writer Quevedo (1580–1645), according to which there is "Love Constant beyond Death." Such love is an illusion, for it is death that awaits us beyond everything else. García Márquez repeatedly plays on these oppositions and inversions when he describes the real village and the cardboard version created by false political promises, the paper birds that magically take on life and fly out to sea, the paper butterfly that seems to fly and lands on the wall, the bribery money that flaps around like butterflies, the grotesquely padlocked chastity belt that Laura Farina wears, and even the initial opposition between the senator's living rose (symbol of womanhood and love) and the roseless town (named "The Viceroy's Rosebush"), where he encounters his destiny. His destiny is to be liberated from some illusions but not all: his final delusion is to try to hide from death in erotic love. The senator's defeat at the end, which is clearly emphasized as a defeat, suggests that his response was a futile retreat and—at the same time that it evokes pity for his loneliness, terror, and rage—puts in question what that response should be.

Death Constant beyond Love[1]

Senator Onésimo Sánchez had six months and eleven days to go before his death when he found the woman of his life. He met her in Rosal del Virrey,[2] an illusory village which by night was the furtive wharf for smugglers' ships, and on the other hand, in broad daylight looked like the most useless inlet on the desert, facing a sea that was arid and without direction and so far from everything no one would have suspected that someone capable of changing the destiny of anyone lived there. Even its name was a kind of joke, because the only rose in that village was being worn by Senator Onésimo Sánchez himself on the same afternoon when he met Laura Farina.

It was an unavoidable stop in the electoral campaign he made every four years. The carnival wagons had arrived in the morning. Then came the trucks with the rented Indians[3] who were carried into the towns in order to enlarge the crowds at public ceremonies. A short time before eleven o'clock, along with the music and rockets and jeeps of the retinue, the ministerial automobile, the color of strawberry soda, arrived. Senator Onésimo Sánchez was placid and weatherless inside the air-conditioned car, but as soon as he opened the door he was shaken by a gust of fire and his shirt of pure silk was soaked in a kind of light-colored soup and he felt many years older and more alone than ever. In real life he had just turned forty-two, had been graduated from Göttingen[4] with honors as a metallurgical engineer, and was an avid reader, although without much reward, of badly translated Latin classics. He was married to a radiant German woman who had given him five children and they were all happy in their home, he the happiest of all until they told him, three months before, that he would be dead forever by next Christmas.

While the preparations for the public rally were being completed, the senator managed to have an hour alone in the house they had set aside for him to rest in. Before he lay down he put in a glass of drinking water the rose he had kept alive all across the desert, lunched on the diet cereals that he took with him so as to avoid the repeated portions of fried goat that were waiting for him during the rest of the day, and he took several analgesic pills before the time prescribed so that he would have the remedy ahead of the pain. Then he put the electric fan close to the hammock and stretched out naked for fifteen minutes in the shadow of the rose, making a great effort at mental distraction so as not to think about death while he dozed. Except for the doctors, no one knew that he had been sentenced to a fixed term, for he had decided to endure his secret all alone, with no change in his life, not because of pride but out of shame.[5]

He felt in full control of his will when he appeared in public again at three in the afternoon, rested and clean, wearing a pair of coarse linen slacks and a floral shirt, and with his soul sustained by the anti-pain pills. Nevertheless, the erosion of death was much more pernicious than he had supposed, for as he went up onto the platform he felt a strange disdain for those who were

---

1. Translated by Gregory Rabassa. 2. "The rosebush of the Viceroy (governor)." 3. People descended from the original inhabitants of the continent, generally poorer and less privileged than those descended from Spanish or Portuguese colonists. 4. A well-known German university. 5. "Death is such as generation is, a mystery of nature . . . altogether not a thing of which any man should be ashamed." [Marcus Aurelius, *Meditations*, IV.5.]

fighting for the good luck to shake his hand, and he didn't feel sorry as he had at other times for the groups of barefoot Indians who could scarcely bear the hot saltpeter coals of the sterile little square. He silenced the applause with a wave of his hand, almost with rage, and he began to speak without gestures, his eyes fixed on the sea, which was sighing with heat. His measured, deep voice had the quality of calm water, but the speech that had been memorized and ground out so many times had not occurred to him in the nature of telling the truth, but, rather, as the opposite of a fatalistic pronouncement by Marcus Aurelius in the fourth book of his *Meditations*.

"We are here for the purpose of defeating nature," he began, against all his convictions. "We will no longer be foundlings in our own country, orphans of God in a realm of thirst and bad climate, exiles in our own land. We will be different people, ladies and gentlemen, we will be a great and happy people."

There was a pattern to his circus. As he spoke his aides threw clusters of paper birds into the air and the artificial creatures took on life, flew about the platform of planks, and went out to sea. At the same time, other men took some prop trees with felt leaves out of the wagons and planted them in the saltpeter soil behind the crowd. They finished by setting up a cardboard façade with make-believe houses of red brick that had glass windows, and with it they covered the miserable real-life shacks.

The senator prolonged his speech with two quotations in Latin in order to give the farce more time. He promised rainmaking machines, portable breeders for table animals, the oils of happiness which would make vegetables grow in the saltpeter and clumps of pansies in the window boxes. When he saw that his fictional world was all set up, he pointed to it. "That's the way it will be for us, ladies and gentlemen," he shouted. "Look! That's the way it will be for us."

The audience turned around. An ocean liner made of painted paper was passing behind the houses and it was taller than the tallest houses in the artificial city. Only the senator himself noticed that since it had been set up and taken down and carried from one place to another the superimposed cardboard town had been eaten away by the terrible climate and that it was almost as poor and dusty as Rosal del Virrey.

For the first time in twelve years, Nelson Farina didn't go to greet the senator. He listened to the speech from his hammock amidst the remains of his siesta, under the cool bower of a house of unplaned boards which he had built with the same pharmacist's hands with which he had drawn and quartered his first wife. He had escaped from Devil's Island[6] and appeared in Rosal del Virrey on a ship loaded with innocent macaws, with a beautiful and blasphemous black woman he had found in Paramaribo[7] and by whom he had a daughter. The woman died of natural causes a short while later and she didn't suffer the fate of the other, whose pieces had fertilized her own cauliflower patch, but was buried whole and with her Dutch name in the local cemetery. The daughter had inherited her color and her figure along with her father's yellow and astonished eyes, and he had good reason to imagine that he was rearing the most beautiful woman in the world.

6. A former French penal colony off the coast of French Guiana in northern South America.   7. Capital of Surinam (formerly Dutch Guiana) and a large port.

Ever since he had met Senator Onésimo Sánchez during his first electoral campaign, Nelson Farina had begged for his help in getting a false identity card which would place him beyond the reach of the law. The senator, in a friendly but firm way, had refused. Nelson Farina never gave up, and for several years, every time he found the chance, he would repeat his request with a different recourse. But this time he stayed in his hammock, condemned to rot alive in that burning den of buccaneers. When he heard the final applause, he lifted his head, and looking over the boards of the fence, he saw the back side of the farce: the props for the buildings, the framework of the trees, the hidden illusionists who were pushing the ocean liner along. He spat without rancor.

"*Merde,*" he said. "*C'est le Blacamán de la politique.*"[8]

After the speech, as was customary, the senator took a walk through the streets of the town in the midst of the music and the rockets and was besieged by the townspeople, who told him their troubles. The senator listened to them good-naturedly and he always found some way to console everybody without having to do them any difficult favors. A woman up on the roof of a house with her six youngest children managed to make herself heard over the uproar and the fireworks.

"I'm not asking for much, Senator," she said. "Just a donkey to haul water from Hanged Man's Well."

The senator noticed the six thin children. "What became of your husband?" he asked.

"He went to find his fortune on the island of Aruba,"[9] the woman answered good-humoredly, "and what he found was a foreign woman, the kind that put diamonds on their teeth."

The answer brought on a roar of laughter.

"All right," the senator decided, "you'll get your donkey."

A short while later an aide of his brought a good pack donkey to the woman's house and on the rump it had a campaign slogan written in indelible paint so that no one would ever forget that it was a gift from the senator.

Along the short stretch of street he made other, smaller gestures, and he even gave a spoonful of medicine to a sick man who had had his bed brought to the door of his house so he could see him pass. At the last corner, through the boards of the fence, he saw Nelson Farina in his hammock, looking ashen and gloomy, but nonetheless the senator greeted him, with no show of affection.

"Hello, how are you?"

Nelson Farina turned in his hammock and soaked him in the sad amber of his look.

"*Moi, vous savez,*"[1] he said.

His daughter came out into the yard when she heard the greeting. She was wearing a cheap, faded Guajiro Indian[2] robe, her head was decorated with colored bows, and her face was painted as protection against the sun, but even in that state of disrepair it was possible to imagine that there had

---

8. "Shit. He's the Blacamán of politics." (French. Blacamán is a charlatan and huckster who appears in several stories, including "Blacamán the Good, Vendor of Miracles.")   9. Off the coast of Venezuela, famous as a tourist resort.   1. "Oh, well, as for me, you know . . ."   2. Inhabitant of the rural Guajira Peninsula of northern Colombia; the figure of Laura Farina is thus connected with the rustic poor, with earthy reality (*farina* means flour), and with erotic inspiration (*Laura* was the beloved celebrated by the Italian Renaissance poet Francesco Petrarch, 1304–1374).

never been another so beautiful in the whole world. The senator was left breathless. "I'll be damned!" he breathed in surprise. "The Lord does the craziest things!"

That night Nelson Farina dressed his daughter up in her best clothes and sent her to the senator. Two guards armed with rifles who were nodding from the heat in the borrowed house ordered her to wait on the only chair in the vestibule.

The senator was in the next room meeting with the important people of Rosal del Virrey, whom he had gathered together in order to sing for them the truths he had left out of his speeches. They looked so much like all the ones he always met in all the towns in the desert that even the senator himself was sick and tired of that perpetual nightly session. His shirt was soaked with sweat and he was trying to dry it on his body with the hot breeze from an electric fan that was buzzing like a horse fly in the heavy heat of the room.

"We, of course, can't eat paper birds," he said. "You and I know that the day there are trees and flowers in this heap of goat dung, the day there are shad instead of worms in the water holes, that day neither you nor I will have anything to do here, do I make myself clear?"

No one answered. While he was speaking, the senator had torn a sheet off the calendar and fashioned a paper butterfly out of it with his hands. He tossed it with no particular aim into the air current coming from the fan and the butterfly flew about the room and then went out through the half-open door. The senator went on speaking with a control aided by the complicity of death.

"Therefore," he said, "I don't have to repeat to you what you already know too well: that my reelection is a better piece of business for you than it is for me, because I'm fed up with stagnant water and Indian sweat, while you people, on the other hand, make your living from it."

Laura Farina saw the paper butterfly come out. Only she saw it because the guards in the vestibule had fallen asleep on the steps, hugging their rifles. After a few turns, the large lithographed butterfly unfolded completely, flattened against the wall, and remained stuck there. Laura Farina tried to pull it off with her nails. One of the guards, who woke up with the applause from the next room, noticed her vain attempt.

"It won't come off," he said sleepily. "It's painted on the wall."

Laura Farina sat down again when the men began to come out of the meeting. The senator stood in the doorway of the room with his hand on the latch, and he only noticed Laura Farina when the vestibule was empty.

"What are you doing here?"

"*C'est de la part de mon père,*"[3] she said.

The senator understood. He scrutinized the sleeping guards, then he scrutinized Laura Farina, whose unusual beauty was even more demanding than his pain, and he resolved then that death had made his decision for him.

"Come in," he told her.

Laura Farina was struck dumb standing in the doorway to the room: thousands of bank notes were floating in the air, flapping like the butterfly. But the senator turned off the fan and the bills were left without air and alighted on the objects in the room.

3. My father sent me (French)

"You see," he said, smiling, "even shit can fly."

Laura Farina sat down on a schoolboy's stool. Her skin was smooth and firm, with the same color and the same solar density as crude oil, her hair was the mane of a young mare, and her huge eyes were brighter than the light. The senator followed the thread of her look and finally found the rose, which had been tarnished by the saltpeter.

"It's a rose," he said.

"Yes," she said with a trace of perplexity. "I learned what they were in Riohacha."[4]

The senator sat down on an army cot, talking about roses as he unbuttoned his shirt. On the side where he imagined his heart to be inside his chest he had a corsair's tattoo of a heart pierced by an arrow. He threw the soaked shirt to the floor and asked Laura Farina to help him off with his boots.

She knelt down facing the cot. The senator continued to scrutinize her, thoughtfully, and while he was untying the laces he wondered which one of them would end up with the bad luck of that encounter.

"You're just a child," he said.

"Don't you believe it," she said. "I'll be nineteen in April."

The senator became interested.

"What day?"

"The eleventh," she said.

The senator felt better. "We're both Aries,"[5] he said. And smiling, he added:

"It's the sign of solitude."

Laura Farina wasn't paying attention because she didn't know what to do with the boots. The senator, for his part, didn't know what to do with Laura Farina, because he wasn't used to sudden love affairs and, besides, he knew that the one at hand had its origins in indignity. Just to have some time to think, he held Laura Farina tightly between his knees, embraced her about the waist, and lay down on his back on the cot. Then he realized that she was naked under her dress, for her body gave off the dark fragrance of an animal of the woods, but her heart was frightened and her skin disturbed by a glacial sweat.

"No one loves us," he sighed.

Laura Farina tried to say something, but there was only enough air for her to breathe. He laid her down beside him to help her, he put out the light and the room was in the shadow of the rose. She abandoned herself to the mercies of her fate. The senator caressed her slowly, seeking her with his hand, barely touching her, but where he expected to find her, he came across something iron that was in the way.

"What have you got there?"

"A padlock,"[6] she said.

"What in hell!" the senator said furiously and asked what he knew only too well. "Where's the key?"

Laura Farina gave a breath of relief.

"My papa has it," she answered. "He told me to tell you to send one of your people to get it and to send along with him a written promise that you'll straighten out his situation."

---

4. A port on the Guajira Peninsula.   5. The first sign in the zodiac; people born from March 21 to April 19 are said to be under the sign of Aries.   6. She is wearing a chastity belt, a medieval device worn by women to prevent sexual intercourse.

The senator grew tense. "Frog[7] bastard," he murmured indignantly. Then he closed his eyes in order to relax and he met himself in the darkness. *Remember,* he remembered, *that whether it's you or someone else, it won't be long before you'll be dead and it won't be long before your name won't even be left.*[8]

He waited for the shudder to pass.

"Tell me one thing," he asked then. "What have you heard about me?"

"Do you want the honest-to-God truth?"

"The honest-to-God truth."

"Well," Laura Farina ventured, "they say you're worse than the rest because you're different."

The senator didn't get upset. He remained silent for a long time with his eyes closed, and when he opened them again he seemed to have returned from his most hidden instincts.

"Oh, what the hell," he decided. "Tell your son of a bitch of a father that I'll straighten out his situation."

"If you want, I can go get the key myself," Laura Farina said.

The senator held her back.

"Forget about the key," he said, "and sleep awhile with me. It's good to be with someone when you're so alone."

Then she laid his head on her shoulder with her eyes fixed on the rose. The senator held her about the waist, sank his face into woods-animal armpit, and gave in to terror. Six months and eleven days later he would die in that same position, debased and repudiated because of the public scandal with Laura Farina and weeping with rage at dying without her.

---

7. Epithet for "French."   8. A direct translation of a sentence from Marcus Aurelius in the fourth book of the *Meditations* (IV.6).

DEREK WALCOTT
born 1930

From the beginning of his career at the age of eighteen, Derek Walcott has situated his work firmly within the broad perspective of Afro-Caribbean experience as it derives from and relates to what constitute for him its main areas of reference: Europe, Africa, and the Americas. For although the Asian connection forms part of the social and cultural configuration of the Caribbean, his work as a writer engages principally these three areas as they determine his self-awareness as a West Indian of mixed African and European ancestry. An early poem, *A Far Cry from Africa,* from the volume *In a Green Night* (1962), alludes to events in Africa during the violent uprising in Kenya against British colonialism and gives poignant expression, in lines that have often been quoted, to the conflicting allegiances entailed by his situation:

> I who am poisoned with the blood of both
> Where shall I turn, divided to the vein?
> I who have cursed
> The drunken officer of British rule, how choose
> Between this Africa and the English tongue I love?

> Betray them both or give back what they give?
> How can I face such slaughter and be cool?
> How can I turn from Africa and live?

Walcott's entire imaginative work is marked by a dual impulse: it registers both the Afro-Caribbean quest for an established sense of place and of community and, at the same time, the compulsion to move toward wider horizons presented to the Caribbean personality and imagination by the background of historical events and cultural encounters of which the West Indies have been a living theater. Walcott's expression is thus posited on the idea of a creative potential inherent in the Caribbean situation by virtue of the possibilities it offers of shaping a distinctive mode of being.

Derek Walcott was born, along with his twin brother, Roderick, in Castries, the capital of the island of St. Lucia, on January 23, 1930. Shortly after their first birthday, their father, who was a government functionary and a talented artist, suddenly died, and the two boys were brought up by their mother, a schoolteacher who later became headmistress of the Methodist elementary school where they began their education. Both inherited their father's creative gift, Derek primarily in language, Roderick in the pictorial arts, and they remained intellectual and artistic companions until Roderick's death in 1999. Their mother provided an environment in which their talents could be nurtured, an essential factor in Walcott's development as a poet that he acknowledges in the tribute to her memory in the title poem of the collection *The Bounty* (1997).

He acquired early on a sense of his singularity from the fact that he was of pronounced mixed parentage in a predominantly black society as well as being a Protestant and member of the educated middle class in a peasant and Catholic community. Moreover, although he was brought up to speak standard English as his first language, his exposure to the local French creole—both languages the result of the island's successive occupations, first by the French and then by the English—reinforced his sense of his ambiguous relation to the communal life around him. But far from unsettling Walcott, these factors of personal history become in his work a source of strength. For the special quality of stance and tone in his writings springs from his having to work through the varied implications of his peculiar marginality within his own society and in the wider world—as a West Indian, product of a colonial history—toward the inauguration, in symbolic terms, of a new and integral self.

The university years in Jamaica were crucial for Walcott's subsequent development. They enabled him to acquire an expanded view of the Caribbean as an area unified by a common experience and a common legacy of history. Equally important, his literary studies familiarized him with the great works of Western literature and led him to appreciate their role in a cultural heritage integral to his own status as a product of the European imperial adventure. This wider range became apparent in *Poems* (1953), which demonstrates the efforts of a young writer still dependent on recognized literary models—the influence of T. S. Eliot is especially pronounced in the idiom and imagery—and undergoing a strenuous apprenticeship to his craft as a preliminary to finding his true voice. After his graduation in 1953, Walcott taught school for a while in Kingston, while also doing occasional work in journalism, before moving to Port of Spain, Trinidad, where he became a feature writer for a major local newspaper, the *Sunday Guardian*. In 1957, he was awarded a Rockefeller Fellowship to study theater at New York University. His encounter with the problems of race during his American sojourn gave further definition to his self-awareness as a West Indian; the experience confirmed for him the inescapable connection between race and history with which black people in the New World have to contend. On his return two years later to Port of Spain, he founded the Trinidad Theatre Workshop, to which he devoted his energies for nearly two decades.

The publication in England of *In a Green Night* (1962) brought Walcott's work to the attention of an international public and established his reputation beyond the Caribbean region. The poems in the volume are marked by a striking eloquence of diction and a rich tapestry of imagery. They center on his multiple heritage as a West Indian and indicate besides a determined wrestling with form: "I seek / As climate seeks its style to write / Verse crisp as sand, clear as sunlight / Cold as the curled wave, ordinary / As a tumbler of island water." With this volume, Walcott consciously assumes the weight of English literary tradition by translating its references and resources into a new poetic register determined by his Caribbean experience and sensibility.

It is in *The Castaway* (1969), his next volume, that Walcott attained full maturity as a poet. A cluster of poems devoted to the figure of Robinson Crusoe brings into prominence the presiding idea of the volume: its celebration of the heroic or creative individual in the shaping of history. *Crusoe's Journal* lends a poetic grandeur to the figure of the castaway, the lonely and bold adventurer who assumes the burden of pathfinder, creating a new reality—and, indeed, a new world—out of the unpromising materials at hand. In consonance with this special valuation of the castaway figure, Walcott situates the poet as the node of consciousness in the larger community. The theme is pursued again in *The Gulf* (1969), which turns on the poet's need to cultivate his singularity as a condition for the shaping of a redeeming vision for his people.

This preoccupation with the poetic vocation leads to the extended self-scrutiny in *Another Life* (1973), an autobiography in verse tracing Walcott's artistic development and the growth of his mind as he encounters the wider world of events and individuals. He does not lose sight, however, of the ironies involved in the relation between poet and community, as attested by the theme of the artist as doomed hero, already broached in an early poem, *Epitaph for Youth,* and elaborated anew in the homage to a fellow poet, Federico García Lorca, built into his evocation of the city of Granada in *The Bounty* (1997).

With *The Star-Apple Kingdom* (1977), Walcott brought to the fore the political and social themes that served in the previous volumes as the broad canvas to his meditations on the self in relation to history. The opening poem, *The Schooner Flight*, sets the pathetic tone of the entire volume, which is a long and anxious questioning of the destiny of the Caribbean, now being corrupted by tourism and commerce ("this chain store of islands").

The broader context of this interrogation emerges more fully in *The Fortunate Traveller* (1981), where Walcott's perception of the racial divide between the affluent North and the impoverished South dictates the ironic posture indicated by the title. In the poem *North and South,* Walcott evokes America in its quotidian ordinariness but against a background of a landscape that has served as the theater for a historical drama of immense proportions and tragic human implications. The epic scale of the evocation barely intimated in the poem is given a succinct and powerful statement in *Sea Cranes* and is developed in the work that has come to be regarded as Walcott's masterpiece, *Omeros.*

All Walcott's poetry flows into *Omeros,* which is best grasped as the imaginative summation of human history as seen from his Caribbean perspective. Its retrospective vision assumes an especial emotional value for the poet for whom, as he says, "Art is History's nostalgia." In an expansive recollection of his previous themes, *Omeros* sums up the West Indian experience through the adventures of Achille, a humble St. Lucian fisherman, whose travels take him to the points of compass of the West Indian consciousness. Homer's great epics, the *Iliad* and the *Odyssey,* serve as obvious references for the work, and the figure of Homer himself, in his modern Greek rendering of "Omeros," is evoked in a key passage of the poem in which he is represented as the quintessential exile. Moreover, Walcott's recourse to the image of the blind poet, of which Demokodos in Homer's *Odyssey* is the original model, reproduced in the character of Seven Seas in *Omeros* and that of Billy Blue in Walcott's *The Odyssey,* reinforce these references anticipated in earlier work but newly sustained by the scale of *Omeros*. The poem also employs some of the standard tropes of the classical epic, such as descent into the underworld and conflict and contest. Above all, the conflation of the poet's persona with Homer's hero lends a truly epic dimension and mythical significance to his quest for meaning in history.

Despite these connections, *Omeros* is not a mere rehash of Homer, with whose works there are few direct correlations in terms of content. Although the poem contains stretches of narration, they do not build up into a dramatic progression of events such as we find in the conventional epic. The rivalry between Achille and another local fisherman, Hector, over Helen (who is hardly idealized in the poem and remains, for all her beauty, an ordinary village woman) is presented as part of a strictly mundane local history that features other actors such as the white settler couple, Major Plunkett and his wife, Maud, as well as minor characters who move in and out of the narrative. Thus, the poem does not unfold in a linear fashion in the development of a plot, but represents rather a vast kaleidoscope, a series of tableaux presenting scenes, always evoked in striking visual terms, episodes that bear a relation to Caribbean experience, and incidents in the collective life of the folk, all woven around the figure of its major protagonist, and the whole framed by personal reminiscences and reflections that ground the poet's reconstruction of collective memory.

Achilles' descent into the underworld recounted in Chapter VIII can be seen in this light to extend the significance of the sea as the arena and graveyard of history to suggest a plumbing of the Caribbean unconscious, a reaching into the deep impulses embedded by centuries of a turbulent history. This plunge into a violent past has an obvious connection with the poet's recollection, in Chapter XXXV, of the Native Americans' experience and condition, the pathos of a "tribal sorrow" that originates in the tragic confrontation with the white race.

Walcott's exploration of the African element in Caribbean life, dramatized in Chapter XXV in the dream sequence that takes Achille back to the ancestral homeland, also arises from his preoccupation with the collective memory and its relation to identity. The theme is developed in the dialogue between Achille and his mythic progenitor, Afolabe, in terms that are less ambivalent than Walcott's previous handling of the African question in *Dream on Monkey Mountain*. In *Omeros*, the reconnection with Africa occurs through a recognition of the cultural continuum that links the West Indians to the continent of their forbears and becomes instrumental in the process of self-acceptance essential to the West Indians' repossession of their island home.

The journey motif links Walcott's *Omeros* with the work of other West Indian poets such as St. John Perse, Aimé Césaire, and Kamau Brathwaite. The motif underlies Walcott's meditations on the work of the painter Camille Pissarro in *Tiepolo's Hound* (1999), attesting again to a restlessness rendered native to the Caribbean spirit by its living environment, dominated by the vast expanse of sea and sky by which it is encircled. It conditions a charged naturalism that forms a powerful undercurrent to Walcott's evocations and that occasionally surfaces, as in these lines:

> O Sun, the one eye of heaven, O Force, O Light,
> my heart kneels to you, my shadow has never changed
> since the salt-fresh mornings of encircling delight
>
> across whose cities the wings of the frigate ranged
> freer than any republic, gliding with ancient
> ease! I praise you not for my eyes. That other sight.

Omeros is Walcott's triumphant affirmation of the vitality of the Caribbean soul. The poem illustrates the poet's genius in its full scope, his gift of language by which he gives sensuous embodiment to that other life of the intellect and of the imagination that he intimates in his autobiographical poem. The award in 1992 of the Nobel Prize for literature came as a fitting recognition of a work as rich in its abundance and variety as in its human import.

The following list uses common English syllables and stress accents to provide rough equivalents of selected words whose pronunciation may be unfamiliar to the general reader.

Achille: *ah-shee'l*

Afolabe: *ah-foh-lah'-be*

Bois-campêche: *bwah-cahm-pesh'*

Bois-flot: *bwah–floh'*

Choiseul: *shwah-zeuhl'*

Laurier-cannelle: *loh-reeay'–cah-nel'*

Ville de Paris: *veel deu pah-ree'*

OMEROS

Book One

From *Chapter I*

II

Achille looked up at the hole[1] the laurel had left.
He saw the hole silently healing with the foam
of a cloud like a breaker. Then he saw the swift[2]

crossing the cloud-surf, a small thing, far from its home,
confused by the waves of blue hills. A thorn vine gripped   5
his heel. He tugged it free. Around him, other ships

were shaping from the saw. With his cutlass he made
a swift sign of the cross, his thumb touching his lips
while the height rang with axes. He swayed back the blade,

and hacked the limbs from the dead god,[3] knot after knot,   10
wrenching the severed veins from the trunk as he prayed:
"Tree! You can be a canoe! Or else you cannot!"

The bearded elders endured the decimation
of their tribe without uttering a syllable
of the language they had uttered as one nation,[4]   15

the speech taught their saplings: from the towering babble
of the cedar to green vowels of *bois-campêche*.
The *bois-flot* held its tongue with the *laurier-cannelle*,[5]

---

1. The opening stanza describes the ritual felling of a laurel tree from which a dugout canoe is to be made. This refers to the hole in the ground where the tree had stood. The section that follows describes the making of the canoe.   2. A small, plainly colored bird, related to the swallow, that serves as a guide to the wandering hero.   3. The laurel tree, venerated as nature.   4. The flora as part of the total living environment.   5. *Bois-campêche, bois-flot, laurier-cannelle:* French for logwood, timber, and laurel, respectively.

the red-skinned logwood endured the thorns in its flesh,
while the Aruacs' patois[6] crackled in the smell
of a resinous bonfire that turned the leaves brown   20

with curling tongues, then ash, and their language was lost.
Like barbarians striding columns they have brought down,
the fishermen shouted. The gods were down at last.

Like pygmies they hacked the trunks of wrinkled giants   25
for paddles and oars. They were working with the same
concentration as an army of fire-ants.[7]

But vexed by the smoke for defaming their forest,
blow-darts of mosquitoes kept needling Achille's trunk.
He frotted white rum on both forearms that, at least,   30

those that he flattened to asterisks would die drunk.
They went for his eyes. They circled them with attacks
that made him weep blindly. Then the host retreated

to high bamboo like the archers of Aruacs
running from the muskets of cracking logs,[8] routed   35
by the fire's banner and the remorseless axe

hacking the branches. The men bound the big logs first
with new hemp[9] and, like ants, trundled them to a cliff
to plunge through tall nettles.[1] The logs gathered that thirst

for the sea which their own vined bodies were born with.   40
Now the trunks in eagerness to become canoes
ploughed into breakers of bushes, making raw holes

of boulders, feeling not death inside them, but use—
to roof the sea, to be hulls. Then, on the beach, coals[2]
were set in their hollows that were chipped with an adze.   45

A flat-bed truck had carried their rope-bound bodies.
The charcoals, smouldering, cored the dugouts for days
till heat widened the wood enough for ribbed gunwales.[3]

Under his tapping chisel Achille felt their hollows
exhaling to touch the sea, lunging towards the haze   50
of bird-printed islets, the beaks of their parted bows.

Then everything fit. The pirogues[4] crouched on the sand
like hounds with sprigs in their teeth. The priest
sprinkled them with a bell, then he made the swift's sign.[5]

---

6. Dialect. *Aruacs*: The original inhabitants of the Caribbean; also Arawaks.   7. Omnivorous ants with powerful stingers in their tails.   8. Log houses from which white men shot at the Aruacs.   9. The vine is excellent for making ropes.   1. A plant that stings.   2. They are used to fire the hollowed-out logs. 3. That is, the heat expanded the wood so that metal strips could be inserted to reinforce the sides of the boat.   4. French for dugout canoes.   5. The swift's wings are shaped like a cross.

When he smiled at Achille's canoe, *In God We Troust,*[6]   55
Achille said: "Leave it! Is God' spelling and mine."
After Mass one sunrise the canoes entered the troughs[7]

of the surpliced[8] shallows, and their nodding prows
agreed with the waves to forget their lives as trees;
one would serve Hector and another, Achilles.   60

From *Chapter VIII*

I

In the islet's museum there is a twisted
wine-bottle, crusted with fool's gold[1] from the iron-
cold depth below the redoubt. It has been listed

variously by experts; one, that a galleon
blown by a hurricane out of Cartagena,[2]   5
this far east, had bled a trail of gold bullion

and wine from its hold (a view held by many a
diver lowering himself); the other was nonsense
and far too simple: that the gold-crusted bottle

came from a flagship in the Battle of the Saints,[3]   10
but the glass was so crusted it was hard to tell.
Still, the myth widened its rings every century:[4]

that the *Ville de Paris*[5] sank there, not a galleon
crammed with imperial coin, and for her sentry,
an octopus-cyclops,[6] its one eye like the moon.   15

Deep as a diver's faith but never discovered,
their trust in the relic converted the village,
who came to believe that circling frigates hovered

over the relic, that gulls attacked them in rage.
They kept their faith when the experts' ended in doubt.   20
The galleon's shadow rode over the ruled page

where Achille, rough weather coming, counted his debt
by the wick of his kerosene lamp; the dark ship
divided his dreams, while the moon's octopus eye

---

6. The boat's name. The phrase "In God We Trust" is found on American money.   7. Sea channels.
8. The canoes make a lacelike pattern on the water, resembling the surplice worn by Catholic priests at
Mass.   1. Pyrite or, by extension, any pyritic material that resembles gold.   2. I.e., Cartagena, a seaport
on the northwest coast of Colombia.   3. Naval battle fought off the coast of Martinique on April 12,
1782, between the French fleet commanded by Admiral de Grasset and a British fleet under Admiral Sir
George Bridges Rodney. The French were routed, their fleet annihilated.   4. Like rings on a tree as it
ages.   5. The flagship of the French fleet.   6. Here Walcott conflates an octopus—a mollusk that has
eight arms, each with two rows of suckers—with Greek mythology's Cyclops, a one-eyed giant who, in
Homer's *Odyssey*, holds Odysseus and his men captive until they escape by blinding him.

climbed from the palms that lifted their tentacles' shape.   25
It glared like a shilling.[7] Everything was money.
Money will change her, he thought. Is this bad living

that make her come wicked. He had mocked the belief
in a wrecked ship out there. Now he began diving
in a small shallop[8] beyond the line of the reef,   30

with spear-gun[9] and lobster-pot.[1] He had to make sure
no sail would surprise him, feathering the oars back
without clicking the oarlocks. He fed the anchor

carefully overside. He tied the cinder-block
to one heel with a slip-knot[2] for faster descent,   35
then slipped the waterproof bag around his shoulders

for a money-pouch. She go get every red cent,
he swore, crossing himself as he dived. Wedged in boulders
down there was salvation and change. The concrete, tied

to his heel, pulled him down faster than a lead-   40
weighted, canvas-bound carcass, the stone heart inside
his chest added its poundage. What if love was dead

inside her already? What good lay in pouring
silver coins on a belly that had warmed him once?
This weighed him down even more, so he kept falling   45

for fathoms towards his fortune: moidores, doubloons,[3]
while the slow-curling fingers of weeds kept calling;
he felt the cold of the drowned entering his loins.

II

Why was he down here, from their coral palaces.
pope-headed turtles asked him, waving their paddles[4]   50
crusted with rings, nudged by curious porpoises

with black friendly skins. Why? asked the glass sea-horses,[5]
curling like questions. What on earth had he come for,
when he had a good life up there? The sea-mosses[6]

shook their beards angrily, like submarine cedars,   55
while he trod the dark water. Wasn't love worth more
than the coins of light pouring from the galleon's doors?

---

7. An English coin worth one-twentieth of a pound. Its use was discontinued when Britain adopted the decimal currency in 1969.   8. A small boat (from French *chaloupe*).   9. A gun that has a forked end on which fish are speared.   1. A basket for trapping lobsters.   2. A knot that moves along the rope on which it is tied.   3. These are Portuguese and Spanish gold coins, respectively.   4. The turtles propel themselves using their flippers as paddles.   5. Small bony fishes that have a horse-shaped head and the body of a fish with a curved tail (hence "curling like questions").   6. Any of certain frondlike red algae that look like moss (and hence "shook their beards").

In the corals' bone kingdom his skin calcifies.[7]
In that wavering garden huge fans on hinges
swayed, while fingers of seaweed pocketed the eyes[8]   60

of coins with the profiles of Iberian kings;[9]
here the sea-floor was mud, not corrugating sand
that showed you its ribs; here, the mutating fishes

had goggling eye-bulbs; in that world without sound,
they sucked the white coral, draining it like leeches,   65
and what looked like boulders sprung the pincers of crabs.

This was not a world meant for the living, he thought.
The dead didn't need money, like him, but perhaps
they hated surrendering things their hands had brought.

The shreds of the ocean's floor passed him from corpses   70
that had perished in the crossing, their hair like weeds,
their bones were long coral fingers, bubbles of eyes

watched him, a brain-coral[1] gurgled their words,
and every bubble englobed a biography,
no less than the wine-bottle's mouth, but for Achille,   75

treading the mulch floor of the Caribbean Sea,
no coins were enough to repay its deep evil.
The ransom of centuries shone through the mossy doors

that the moon-blind Cyclops counted, every tendril
raked in the guineas[2] it tested with its soft jaws.   80
Light paved the ceiling with silver with every swell.

Then he saw the galleon. Her swaying cabin-doors
fanned vaults of silvery mackerel. He caught the glint
of their coin-packed scales,[3] then the tentacle-shadows

whose motion was a miser's harvesting his mint.   85
He loosened the block[4] and shot up. Next day, her stealth
increased, her tentacles calling, until the wreck

vanished with all hope of Helen. Once more the whelk[5]
was his coin, his bank the sea-conch's.[6] Now, every day
he was clear-headed as the sea, wrenching lace fans   90

from the forbidden reef, or tailing a sting-ray[7]
floating like a crucifix when it sensed his lance,
and saving the conch-shells he himself had drowned.

---

7. Hardens. 8. Here, covered completely. 9. Relating to Iberia, the peninsula made up of Spain and Portugal. 1. A reef coral with its surface covered by ridges and furrows. 2. English coins, supposedly struck from gold from the Guinea coast in West Africa. 3. The fishes' scales are like silver coins. 4. Concrete (referred to in lines 39–42). 5. A large marine snail with a spiral shell. 6. A large spiral-shelled marine mollusk. Its shell resonates when blown into; runaway slaves often sent messages to each other this way. 7. A ray with a flat body and whiplike tail with spines near its base capable of inflicting severe wounds.

And though he lost faith[8] in any fictional ship,
an anchor still forked his brow whenever he frowned,   95
for she was a spectre now, in her ribbed shape,

he did not know where she was. She'd never be found.
He thought of the white skulls rolling out there like dice
rolled by the hand of the swell, their luck was like his;

he saw drowned Portuguese captains, their coral eyes   100
entered by minnows,[9] as he hauled the lobster-pot,
bearded with moss, in the cold shade of the redoubt.[1]

Book Three

Chapter XXV

I

Mangroves,[1] their ankles in water, walked with the canoe.
The swift, racing its browner shadow, screeched, then veered
into a dark inlet. It was the last sound Achille knew

from the other world. He feathered the paddle,[2] steered
away from the groping mangroves, whose muddy shelves   5
slipped warted crocodiles,[3] slitting the pods of their eyes;

then the horned river-horses[4] rolling over themselves
could capsize the keel. It was like the African movies
he had yelped at in childhood. The endless river unreeled

those images that flickered into real mirages: 10
naked mangroves walking beside him, knotted logs
wriggling into the water, the wet, yawning boulders

of oven-mouthed hippopotami. A skeletal[5] warrior
stood up straight in the stern and guided his shoulders,
clamped his neck in cold iron,[6] and altered the oar.   15

Achille wanted to scream, he wanted the brown water
to harden into a road, but the river widened ahead
and closed behind him. He heard screeching laughter

in a swaying tree, as monkeys swung from the rafter
of their tree-house, and the bared sound rotted the sky   20
like their teeth. For hours the river gave the same show

---

8. See line 16, above.   9. Tiny fish.   1. A small, usually temporary fort.   1. Tropical trees that grow
in lagoons and waterways.   2. Turned the oar so that it was horizontal when lifted from the water at the
end of a stroke. This reduces air resistance.   3. The skin of the crocodiles seems to be covered with
hardened protuberances.   4. I.e., hippopotami.   5. Here, ghostly, which is appropriate to the character of the passage as a dream sequence.   6. Reminiscent of the chains with which slaves were
bound.

for nothing, the canoe's mouth muttered its lie.
The deepest terror was the mud. The mud with no shadow
like the clear sand. Then the river coiled into a bend.

He saw the first signs of men, tall sapling fishing-stakes;   25
he came into his own beginning and his end,
for the swiftness of a second is all that memory takes.

Now the strange, inimical river surrenders its stealth
to the sunlight. And a light inside him wakes,[7]   30
skipping centuries, ocean and river, and Time itself.

And God said to Achille, "Look, I giving you permission
to come home. Is I send the sea-swift as a pilot,
the swift whose wings is the sign of my crucifixion.

And thou shalt have no God should in case you forgot
my commandments." And Achille felt the homesick shame   35
and pain of his Africa. His heart and his bare head

were bursting as he tried to remember the name
of the river- and the tree-god in which he steered,
whose hollow body carried him to the settlement ahead.

II

He remembered this sunburnt river with its spindly
stakes and the peaked huts platformed above the spindles
where thin, naked figures as he rowed past looked unkindly

or kindly in their silence. The silence an old fence kindles
in a boy's heart. They walked with his homecoming
canoe past bonfires in a scorched clearing near the edge   45

of the soft-lipped shallows whose noise hurt his drumming
heart as the pirogue slid its raw, painted wedge
towards the crazed sticks of a vine-fastened pier.

The river was sloughing[8] its old skin like a snake
in wrinkling sunshine; the sun resumed its empire   50
over this branch of the Congo; the prow found its stake

in the river and nuzzled it the way that a piglet
finds its favourite dug[9] in the sweet-grunting sow,
and now each cheek ran with its own clear rivulet

of tears, as Achille, weeping, fastened the bow   55
of the dugout, wiped his eyes with one dry palm,
and felt a hard hand help him up the shaking pier.

7. I.e., awakens ancestral memory.   8. Shedding.   9. The nipple of a pig from which the young suck milk.

Half of me was with him. One half with the midshipman
by a Dutch canal.[1] But now, neither was happier
or unhappier than the other. An old man put an arm   60

around Achille, and the crowd, chattering, followed both.
They touched his trousers, his undershirt, their hands
scrabbling[2] the texture, as a kitten does with cloth,

till they stood before an open hut. The sun stands
with expectant silence. The river stops talking,   65
the way silence sometimes suddenly turns off a market.

The wind squatted low in the grass. A man kept walking
steadily towards him, and he knew by that walk it
was himself in his father, the white teeth, the widening hands.

III

He sought his own features in those of their life-giver,   70
and saw two worlds mirrored there: the hair was surf
curling round a sea-rock, the forehead a frowning river,

as they swirled in the estuary of a bewildered love,
and Time stood between them. The only interpreter
of their lips' joined babble, the river with the foam,   75

and the chuckles of water under the sticks of the pier,
where the tribe stood like sticks themselves, reversed
by reflection.[3] Then they walked up to the settlement,

and it seemed, as they chattered, everything was rehearsed
for ages before this. He could predict the intent   80
of his father's gestures; he was moving with the dead.

Women paused at their work, then smiled at the warrior
returning from his battle with smoke,[4] from the kingdom
where he had been captured, they cried and were happy.

Then the fishermen sat near a large tree under whose dome   85
stones sat in a circle. His father said:
                                        "Afo-la-be,"[5]
touching his own heart.
                                        "In the place you have come from

what do they call you?"
                                        Time translates.   90
                                        Tapping his chest,
the son answers:
                    "Achille." The tribe rustles, "Achille."
Then, like cedars at sunrise, the mutterings settle.

1. Spoken in the author's own voice, this passage expresses the split in Walcott's heritage—half African,
half Dutch.   2. Scraping.   3. Mirrored upside down in the river.   4. Of an ordeal, in the dim past.
5. A Yoruba name meaning "born with honor."

AFOLABE
Achille. What does the name mean? I have forgotten the one   95
that I gave you. But it was, it seems, many years ago.
What does it mean?

ACHILLE
Well, I too have forgotten.

Everything was forgotten. You also. I do not know.
The deaf sea has changed around every name that you gave   100
us; trees, men, we yearn for a sound that is missing.

AFOLABE
A name means something.[6] The qualities desired in a son,
and even a girl-child; so even the shadows who called
you expected one virtue, since every name is a blessing,

since I am remembering the hope I had for you as a child.   105
Unless the sound means nothing. Then you would be nothing.
Did they think you were nothing in that other kingdom?[7]

ACHILLE
I do not know what the name means. It means something,
maybe. What's the difference? In the world I come from
we accept the sounds we were given. Men, trees, water.   110

AFOLABE
And therefore, Achille, if I pointed and I said, There
is the name of that man, that tree, and this father,
would every sound be a shadow that crossed your ear,

without the shape of a man or a tree? What would it be?
(And just as branches sway in the dusk from their fear   115
of amnesia,[8] of oblivion, the tribe began to grieve.)

ACHILLE
What would it be? I can only tell you what I believe,
or had to believe. It was prediction, and memory,
to bear myself back, to be carried here by a swift,

or the shadow of a swift making its cross on water,   120
with the same sign I was blessed with[9] with the gift
of this sound whose meaning I still do not care to know.

AFOLABE
No man loses his shadow except it is in the night,
and even then his shadow is hidden, not lost. At the glow
of sunrise, he stands on his own in that light.   125

---

6. African names always have a meaning of great social significance.   7. I.e., the New World.   8. Loss
of memory.   9. Baptized as a Christian, with possibly a pun on the French *blessé*, "wounded."

When he walks down to the river with the other fishermen
his shadow stretches in the morning, and yawns, but you,
if you're content with not knowing what our names mean,

then I am not Afolabe, your father, and you look through
my body as the light looks through a leaf. I am not here   130
or a shadow. And you, nameless son, are only the ghost

of a name. Why did I never miss you until you returned?
Why haven't I missed you, my son, until you were lost?
Are you the smoke from a fire that never burned?

There was no answer to this, as in life.[1] Achille nodded,   135
the tears glazing his eyes, where the past was reflected
as well as the future. The white foam lowered its head.

From *Chapter XXVI*

I

In a language as brown[1] and leisurely as the river,
they muttered about a future Achille already knew
but which he could not reveal even to his breath-giver

or in the council of elders. But he learned to chew
in the ritual of the kola nut,[2] drain gourds of palm-wine,[3]   5
to listen to the moan of the tribe's triumphal sorrow

in a white-eyed storyteller[4] to a balaphon's whine,[5]
who perished in what battle, who was swift with the arrow,
who mated with a crocodile,[6] who entered a river-horse

and lived in its belly, who was the thunder's favourite,   10
who the serpent-god[7] conducted miles off his course
for some blasphemous offence and how he would pay for it

by forgetting his parents, his tribe, and his own spirit
for an albino god,[8] and how that warrior was scarred
for innumerable moons so badly that he would disinherit   15

himself. And every night the seed-eyed, tree-wrinkled[9] bard,
the crooked tree who carried the genealogical leaves[1]
of the tribe in his cave-throated moaning,

---

1. Which is filled with unresolved questions.   1. Muddy, alluvial, and therefore fertile.   2. The bitter,
caffeine-laden seed of the kola tree; it is chewed on ceremonial occasions.   3. The natural sap of the
tropical palm, which, when drawn, ferments and becomes alcoholic.   4. The bard, or griot, whose function was to preserve the community's history (see lines 16–20).   5. An African instrument with flat
wooden keys like the xylophone that is played to accompany the griot's narrative.   6. In myths, heroes
were often said to descend from mixed parentage of humans and animals; in other instances, certain animals
are held to be ancestors or relatives of members of the tribe and thus function as their totem.   7. The
cult of the serpent is central to many African religions and to their derivatives in the New World.
8. Lacking in pigment, white, and therefore an alien god.   9. Gaunt, like an old tree.   1. I.e., the
leaves of the family tree.

traced the interlacing branches of their river-rooted lives
as intricately as the mangrove roots. Until morning   20
he sang, till the river was the only one to hear it.

Achille did not go down to the fishing stakes one dawn,
but left the hut door open, the hut he had been given
for himself and any woman he chose as his companion,

and he climbed a track of huge yams, to find that heaven   25
of soaring trees, that sacred circle of clear ground
where the gods assembled. He stood in the clearing

and recited the gods' names. The trees within hearing
ignored his incantation. He heard only the cool sound
of the river. He saw a tree-hole, raw in the uprooted ground.[2]   30

* * *

III

He walked the ribbed sand under the flat keels of whales,
under the translucent belly of the snaking current,
the tiny shadows of tankers passed over him like snails

as he breathed water, a walking fish in its element.
He floated in stride, his own shadow over his eyes   35
like a grazing shark, through vast meadows of coral,

over barnacled[3] cannons whose hulks sprouted anemones[4]
like Philoctete's shin; he walked for three hundred years
in the silken wake like a ribbon of the galleons,

their bubbles fading like the transparent men-o'-wars   40
with their lilac dangling tendrils, bursting like aeons,[5]
like phosphorous galaxies; he saw the huge cemeteries

of bone and the huge crossbows of the rusted anchors,
and groves of coral with hands as massive as trees
like calcified ferns and the greening gold ingots of bars   45

whose value had outlasted that of the privateers.[6]
Then, one afternoon, the ocean lowered and clarified
its ceiling, its emerald net, and after three centuries

of walking, he thought he could hear the distant quarrel
of breaker with shore; then his head broke clear,[7] and   50
his neck; then he could see his own shadow in the coral

---

2. See n. 1, p. 2361.   **3.** A barnacle is a type of marine crustacean with feathery appendages for gathering food; as adults, they affix themselves permanently to objects.   **4.** A reference to sea anemones, marine coelenterates whose form, bright colors, and clusters of tentacles resemble flowers.   **5.** Vast stretches of time.   **6.** Armed ships and their crew commissioned by governments to attack enemy ships on the open sea.   **7.** As he resurfaced.

grove, ribbed and rippling with light on the clear sand,
as his fins spread their toes, and he saw the leaf
of his own canoe far out, the life he had left behind

and the white line of surf around low Barrel of Beef[8]   55
with its dead lantern. The salt glare left him blind
for a minute, then the shoreline returned in relief.[9]

He woke to the sound of sunlight scratching at the door
of the hut, and he smelt not salt but the sluggish odour
of river. Fingers of light rethatched the roof's straw.   60

On the day of his feast they wore the same plantain trash
like Philoctete at Christmas. A bannered mitre[1]
of bamboo was placed on his head, a calabash

mask, and skirts that made him both woman and fighter.
That was how they danced at home, to fifes and tambours,   65
the same berries round their necks and the small mirrors

flashing from their stuffed breasts. One of the warriors
mounted on stilts walked like lightning over the thatch
of the peaked village. Achille saw the same dances

that the mitred warriors did with their bamboo stick   70
as they scuttered around him, lifting, dipping their lances
like divining rods turning the earth to music,

the same chac-chac and ra-ra,[2] the drumming the same,
and the chant of the seed-eyed prophet to the same
response from the blurring ankles. The same, the same.[3]   75

Book Four

From *Chapter XXXV*

I

"Somewhere over there," said my guide, "the Trail of Tears
started." I leant towards the crystalline creek. Pines
shaded it. Then I made myself hear the water's

language around the rocks in its clear-running lines
and its small shelving falls with their eddies, "Choctaws,"   5
"Creeks," "Choctaws,"[1] and I thought of the Greek revival

---

8. A rocky site off the coast of St. Lucia, a prominent landmark on the island.   9. In the double sense
of being sharply outlined and of bringing a sense of relief.   1. A ritual headdress, but more usually applied
to the liturgical headdress worn by bishops and abbots.   2. Dance forms in the Caribbean. *Ra-ra* is
derived from a Yoruba genre of chanted poetry.   3. Walcott registers the protagonist's recognition of his
cultural connection to Africa.   1. Native American nations expelled from their original homes and forced
to march to reservations in Oklahoma (see line 17).

carried past the names of towns with columned porches,
and how Greek it was, the necessary evil
of slavery, in the catalogue of Georgia's

marble past, the Jeffersonian ideal[2] in   10
plantations with its Hectors and Achilleses,
its foam in the dogwood's spray, past towns named Helen,

Athens, Sparta, Troy. The slave shacks, the rolling peace
of the wave-rolling meadows, oak, pine, and pecan,
and a creek like this one. From the window I saw   15

the bundles of women moving in ragged bands
like those on the wharf,[3] headed for Oklahoma;
then I saw Seven Seas,[4] a rattle in his hands.

A huge thunderhead[5] was unclenching its bruised fist
over the county. Shadows escaped through the pines   20
and the pecan groves and hounds[6] were closing in fast

deep into Georgia, where history happens
to be the baying echoes of brutality,
and terror in the oaks along red country roads,

or the gibbet[7] branches of a silk-cotton tree   25
from which Afolabes hung like bats. Hooded clouds[8]
guarded the town squares with their calendar churches,

whose white, peaked belfries asserted that pastoral
of brooks with leisurely accents. On their verges,
like islands reflected on windscreens, Negro shacks   30

moved like a running wound, like the rusty anchor
that scabbed Philoctete's shin,[9] I imagined the backs
moving through the foam of pods, one arm for an oar,

one for the gunny sack.[1] Brown streams tinkled in chains.
Bridges arched their spines. Led into their green pasture,[2]   35
horses sagely grazed or galloped the plantations.

---

2. "Life, liberty and the pursuit of happiness," belied by the institution of slavery. 3. Captured Africans waiting to be shipped to America. This passage establishes a parallel between the fate of Native Americans and that of African slaves. 4. A blind poet and singer in St. Lucia who features prominently in Walcott's play *The Odyssey*, a stage adaptation of Homer's epic. 5. A large mass of dark cumulus clouds pressing a thunderstorm. 6. Dogs were used to recapture runaway slaves; they were also set upon black protesters during the civil rights movement. 7. Gallows. The reference here is to the lynching in the Deep South of blacks, usually by hanging. 8. The Ku Klux Klan. 9. The companion of Achille in his Caribbean home and, like him, a fisherman. 1. A bag made from coarse, heavy material. 2. Conveying an impression of blessed peace, but deceptive.

II

"Life is so fragile. It trembles like the aspens.[3]
All its shadows are seasonal, including pain.
In drizzling dusk the rain enters the lindens

with its white lances, then lindens enclose the rain.   40
So that day isn't far when they will say, 'Indians
bowed under those branches, which tribe is not certain.'

Nor am I certain I lived. I breathed what the farm
exhaled. Its soils, its seasons. The swayed goldenrod,
the corn where summer hid me, pollen on my arm,   45

sweat tickling my armpits. The Plains were fierce as God
and wide as His mind. I enjoyed diminishing,
I exalted in insignificance after

the alleys of Boston, in the unfinishing
chores of the farm, alone. Once, from the barn's rafter   50
a swift or a swallow shot out, taking with it

my son's brown, whirring soul,[4] and I knew that its aim
was heaven. More and more we learn to do without
those we still love. With my father it was the same.

The bounty of God pursued me over the Plains   55
of the Dakotas, the pheasants, the quick-volleyed
arrows of finches; smoke bound me to the Indians

from morning to sunset when I have watched its veiled
rising, because I am a widow, barbarous
and sun-cured in the face, I loved them ever since   60

I worked as a hand in Colonel Cody's[5] circus,
under a great canvas larger than all their tents,
when they were paid to ride round in howling circles,

with a dime for their glory, and boys screamed in fright
at the galloping braves. Now the aspens enclose   65
the lances of rain, and the wet leaves shake with light."

*   *   *

3. A type of poplar tree whose leaves flutter in the slightest breeze. The speaker here is Catherine Weldon, a historical figure that Walcott has woven into the poem.   4. Perhaps a reference to an aspect of Native American beliefs.   5. I.e., William F. Cody, also called Buffalo Bill (1846–1917), who founded a circus and a traveling show that featured Native Americans in various humiliating roles. "A dime for their glory" (line 64) is an ironic comment on this.

Book Six

From *Chapter LII*

II

Provinces, Protectorates, Colonies, Dominions,
Governors-General, black Knights, ostrich-plumed[1] Viceroys,
deserts, jungles, hill-stations, all an empire's zones,

lay spilled from a small tea-chest; felt-footed houseboys
on fern-soft verandahs, hearty Toby-jugged[2] Chiefs   5
of Police, Girl-Guide Commissioners, Secretaries,

poppies on cenotaphs,[3] green-spined Remembrance wreaths,
cornets, kettledrums, gum-chewing dromedaries[4]
under Lawrence,[5] parasols, palm-striped pavilions,

dhows[6] and feluccas,[7] native-draped paddle-ferries   10
on tea-brown rivers, statue-rehearsing lions,
sandstorms seaming their eyes, horizontal monsoons,

rank odour of a sea-chest, mimosa memories
touched by a finger, lead soldiers, clopping Dragoons.[8]
Breadfruit hands on a wall. The statues close their eyes.   15

Mosquito nets, palm-fronds, scrolled Royal Carriages,
dacoits,[9] gun-bearers,[1] snarling apes on Gibraltar,[2]
sermons to sweat-soaked kerchiefs, the Rock of Ages[3]

pumped by a Zouave[4] band, lilies light the altar,
soldiers and doxies[5] by a splashing esplanade,   20
waves turning their sheet music, the yellowing teeth

of the parlour piano, *Airs from Erin*[6] played
to the whistling kettle, and on the teapot's head
the cozy's bearskin shako,[7] biscuits break with grief,

gold-braid laburnums,[8] lilac whiff of lavender,
columned poplars marching to Mafeking's relief.[9]   25
Naughty seaside cards, the sepia surrender

---

1. The ceremonial uniform of British colonial governors was topped by a cap with ostrich feathers.   2. A Toby jug is a small vessel—a mug, for instance—shaped like a fat man wearing a cocked hat.   3. Flowers atop tombs or monuments.   4. Camels, which constantly chew their cud.   5. A reference to T. E. Lawrence (1888–1935), also known as Lawrence of Arabia, who served as liaison officer between the British forces and Arab guerrillas fighting against Turkish rule during the First World War.   6. Arab sailboats.   7. Small, fast sailing vessels common to the Mediterranean. They are equipped with both masts and oars.   8. Heavily armed cavalry unit.   9. A gang of robbers of (Hindi).   1. Armored vehicles.   2. A reference to the Barbary macaques that live in Gibraltar, a British enclave at the southern tip of Spain, long a tourist attraction.   3. A well-known Judeo-Christian hymn.   4. The Zouaves were Algerian infantry units in the French and American Confederate armies.   5. Prostitutes.   6. Ireland.   7. The tea cozy, a cushioned cover draped over a teapot to keep the contents warm, resembles a *shako*, a stiff military hat with a high crown, in this case made from bearskin.   8. A shrub with bright yellow flowers (i.e., "gold-braid").   9. A town in South Africa relieved by British forces after a long siege by Afrikaners during the Boer War.

of Gordon[1] on the mantel, the steps of Khartoum,
The World's Classics[2] condensed, Clive[3] as brown as India
bathers in Benares,[4] an empire in costume.

His will be done, O Maud, His kingdom come,   30
as the sunflower turns,[5] and the white eyes widen
in the ebony faces, the sloe-eyes, the bent smoke

where a pig totters across a village midden[6]
over the sunset's shambles, Rangoon to Malta,[7]
the regimental button of the evening star.   35

Solace of laudanum, menstrual cramps, the runnings,
tinkles in the jordan, at dusk the zebra shade
of louvres on the quilt, the maps spread their warnings

and the tribal odour of the second chambermaid.
And every fortnight, ten sharp on Sunday mornings,   40
shouts and wheeling patterns from our Cadet Brigade.[8]

All spilt from a tea-chest, a studded souvenir,
props for an opera, Victoria Regina,[9]
for a bolster-plump Queen the pillbox sentries stamp,

piss, straw and saddle-soap, heaume[1] and crimson feather,   45
post-red double-deckers,[2] spit-and-polished leather,
and iron dolphins leaping round an Embankment[3] lamp.

*   *   *

Book Seven

From Chapter LXIV

I

I sang[1] of quiet Achille, Afolabe's son,
who never ascended in an elevator,
who had no passport, since the horizon needs none,

---

1. Charles Gordon (1833–1885), British governor-general in the Sudan who was killed on the steps of his residence at Khartoum during an uprising by the local population.   2. A famous collection of great literature published by Oxford University Press.   3. Robert Clive (1725–1774), an agent of the East India Company considered to have secured India for the British by thwarting the French and by defeating the local Bengali ruler at the Battle of Plassey in 1757.   4. Holy Hindu city situated on the northern bank of the Ganges in India and associated with Buddha.   5. Fragment of an Irish song beginning "Believe me if all those endearing young charms."   6. Rubbish heap.   7. Rangoon is a city in Myanmar (formerly Burma), a former British colony; Malta, an island in the Mediterranean off the Italian coast, was also a British colony.   8. A company of schoolboys selected and groomed to be future officers in the colonial army.   9. I.e., Queen Victoria (Latin); the insignia of Queen Victoria on English coins.   1. Helmet worn by armored men in the Middle Ages.   2. London buses.   3. Area in London where the Houses of Parliament and the main government offices are located.   1. The invocation, usually placed at the beginning of an epic poem, is here put at the end and expressed in the past tense.

never begged nor borrowed, was nobody's waiter,
whose end, when it comes, will be a death by water   5
(which is not for this book, which will remain unknown

and unread by him). I sang the only slaughter
that brought him delight, and that from necessity—
of fish, sang the channels of his back[2] in the sun.

I sang our wide country, the Caribbean Sea.   10
Who hated shoes, whose soles were as cracked as a stone,
who was gentle with ropes, who had one suit alone,

whom no man dared insult and who insulted no one,
whose grin was a white breaker cresting, but whose frown
was a growing thunderhead, whose fist of iron   15

would do me a greater honour if it held on
to my casket's oarlocks[3] than mine lifting his own
when both anchors are lowered in the one island,

but now the idyll dies, the goblet is broken,
and rainwater trickles down the brown cheek of a jar   20
from the clay of Choiseul. So much left unspoken

by my chirping nib![4] And my earth-door lies ajar.
I lie wrapped in a flour-sack sail. The clods thud
on my rope-lowered canoe. Rasping shovels scrape

a dry rain of dirt on its hold, but turn your head   25
when the sea-almond rattles or the rust-leaved grape
from the shells of my unpharaonic pyramid[5]

towards paper shredded by the wind and scattered
like white gulls that separate their names from the foam
and nod to a fisherman[6] with his khaki dog   30

that the skitters from the wave-crash, then frown at his form
for one swift second. In its earth-trough, my pirogue
with its brass-handled oarlocks is sailing. Not from

but with them, with Hector, with Maud[7] in the rhythm
of her beds[8] trowelled over, with a swirling log   35
lifting its mossed head from the swell; let the deep hymn

2. The ripples of muscles, denoting strength. The human frame represented as a furrowed landscape.
3. At the poet's own funeral.   4. The point of a pen dipped in ink often makes a rasping noise on the paper.   5. Modest, without the monumental grandeur of Egypt's pyramids.   6. I.e., Philoctete.
7. The wife of an English colonial officer, Major Plunkett, whose adventures, intertwined with the life of the St. Lucians, are narrated in earlier passages of the poem. *Hector:* rival of Achille who was killed in a car accident.   8. A reference to the flowerbeds tended by Maud. The image evokes her final resting place in the earth.

of the Caribbean continue my epilogue;
may waves remove their shawls as my mourners walk home
to their rusted villages, good shoes in one hand,

passing a boy who walked through the ignorant foam,   40
and saw a sail going out or else coming in,
and watched asterisks of rain[9] puckering the sand.

*   *   *

---

9. Which is life-giving.

ON BEING A CULTURAL OTHER

Cross-cultural perspectives generally move from *we* to *they,* from the perceiving *subject* to the perceived *other* people or land. World histories are written from the point of view of the writer, travel accounts from the perspective of a traveler away from home; analyses of gender, race, or class reflect the status of the speaker. Even discussions that try to be equally balanced tend to explain "others" in terms that "we" can understand—a process that is logically inevitable but one that also reinforces the original point of view. It is a wrenching reversal to consider oneself as both subject and object, as a cultural other in the midst of one's own society. A few writers have been able to speak from such a dual perspective (Frederick Douglass and Mona Caird earlier in this volume), but not until the twentieth century has there been such widespread and consistent attention paid to cross-cultural perspectives as a philosophical and anthropological phenomenon.

The following eight writers have all experienced what it means to be a cultural other and have used their experience as a basis for larger theoretical discussions. Topics and approach differ, and the tone ranges from abstract to conversational. Some writers immediately engage broad themes of philosophical or historical analysis, while others begin with personal anecdotes and gradually explore their wider implications. It is noticeable, however, that issues raised in the middle of the century tend to be more broadly conceived, emphasizing large unitary distinctions of self and other that will become more fragmented and multifaceted later on. René Ménil discusses the way that colonial exoticism projects a single image of colonized blacks, and Frantz Fanon investigates the way that colonialist oppression damages the cultural psyche of colonized peoples. Simone de Beauvoir writes about woman as a "second sex," defined by men, in a far-reaching study that contributed powerfully to feminist awareness; later feminist writers like Audre Lorde and Trinh T. Minh-ha move past the generic image of woman and describe further distinctions of race, class, sexual preference, and economic and political constraints. In another influential study, Edward Said investigates a broad category of "Orientalist" thought that tacitly defines Eastern culture as the diametric opposite of Western civilization. Chinua Achebe refuses stark oppositions but describes a linked and reciprocal awareness between "African" and English cultural identities. Finally, Salman Rushdie—whose sentence of death must be the most extreme expression of "otherness" in a cultural context—reminds us of the real fluidity of cultural identity in the twenty-first century, when displacement or migrancy is a fact of life for millions of people and a hybrid consciousness promises to become the normal state of mind.

RENÉ MÉNIL
born 1907

From Herodotus's tales of the Nile to Stanley's memoir of travels *In Darkest Africa*, explorers and world travelers have returned with tales of fascinatingly different, or "exotic," peoples, creatures, and customs encountered in various parts of the globe. As long as more accurate information was lacking, these reports—often fantastic—became the truth for their audiences, establishing an image of mysterious foreign parts, where, as mapmakers once wrote, "there be dragons." Civilization and normalcy were associated with home; barbarism and excesses of every kind were presumed to flourish elsewhere. Much of this dual perspective was repeated in the colonial situation, as the colonizers imported their own sets of ideas and imposed them as a new "normal" standard for the local population. What was barbarous, pagan, and exotic was to be tamed, converted, and civilized, and this could only happen if everyone shared the same beliefs.

Thus colonial exoticism, according to philosopher-critic René Ménil, was not merely the perspective of colonialist rulers; in addition, these exotic images permeated colonial society and tended to determine the self-image of the colonized. The problem did not go unnoted. Concepts of cultural identity were a crucial topic for black diasporic intellectuals in Paris during the 1920s and 1930s, for the French capital was the educational and cultural focus of France's African and Caribbean colonies. Ménil was part of a group of radical students in Paris at the time and helped publish the sole issue of a Surrealist revolutionary journal, *Légitime Défense*. He also associated with other intellectuals, including Léopold Sédar Senghor from Senegal and Aimé Césaire from Martinique, who were beginning to develop the concept of Négritude (black identity) in reaction to colonial theories of European (white) superiority.

Ménil was not uncritical of Négritude, which he considered a kind of racial mysticism that merely inverted European attitudes. As a philosopher, he believed in a more critical analysis of racial theories and political systems, including a thorough critique of colonial perspectives. Returning from Paris to Martinique, where he taught philosophy at the Victor Schoelcher School in Fort-de-France, Ménil cofounded the journal *Tropiques* and remained its editor until it ceased publishing in 1945. France was then controlled by the fascist Vichy government, and its representatives in Martinique attacked *Tropiques*—which published Surrealist literature and material with a clear anticolonial message, including Césaire's *Notebook of a Return to Native Land*—for being a "revolutionary, racial, and sectarian" journal. Despite official disapproval, however, and even a suspension in 1943, *Tropiques* managed to publish throughout the war.

Ménil's discussion of exoticism begins on a philosophical level. There is a "normal exoticism" whenever there is displacement: travelers are exotic to local inhabitants, and the "locals" are exotic to travelers. This moderate alienation is (or should be) overcome by more detailed knowledge of the other person. A less benign situation occurs in colonial countries, where the colonizer imposes not only a government but also a way of seeing that, over time, affects all aspects of life. In looking over French Caribbean poetry published during the previous twenty years, Ménil is struck by the way that its style and imagery derive from the same colonialist model. Even celebrations of black identity depict the same exotic stereotype, although now it is represented as an opposite and more authentic value. Both images, he notes, are derived from the same external and colonialist reference point, and, as long as this artificial point of departure is accepted as true, both render their readers incapable of real self-knowledge.

From Concerning Colonial Exoticism[1]

There is an exoticism founded in nature resulting from a particular form of human relation. Finding myself in a foreign land, I am disoriented and perceive the manners, practices and customs of the native as picturesque and marked with signs of alienness. And as the relation is reciprocal, the native of the land will have a similar, if inverse, vision of me. For him I am as alien as he is for me: he has an exotic vision of me and I have an exotic vision of him. Things cannot be otherwise. Montaigne in Italy, the Marquis de Custine[2] in Russia, Leiris in the Caribbean were moved and amazed as they stumbled upon manners new to them. The Italians, the Russians and the Caribbeans saw them as travellers 'from somewhere else'. Human relations in exoticism are those of two different consciousnesses brought face to face and seized with a sense of the difference between their respective customs. The exotic vision is a view of man taken 'from the other side', from outside and beyond geographical frontiers.

Unfortunately, the natural tendency in exoticism is to miss the 'seriousness' and authenticity of the drama (of the other) and to confine oneself to an idyllic and superficial vision. This is because the first impulse of consciousness surprised in a new situation is to examine the scenery, external picturesqueness, and people as part of the scenery, as objects and as decor (landscapes and costumes).

It is only through breaking the bounds of this idyllic consciousness that the stranger can approach the stranger in his own circumstances, as a profound and rich subject. Exoticism is thus a first movement in the relation between countries and peoples. But this moment needs to be overcome and negated to reach the truth of the person who until then had been perceived only in the exotic vision.

But besides this normal exoticism, there exists another form of exoticism which constitutes the object of the present examination—colonial exoticism. Next to that kind of exoticism resulting from the very nature of a particular form of human relationship—'I am exotic for a foreigner and he is exotic for me'—there looms the monstrosity of an exoticism unique of its kind. It is not without stupefaction, in fact, that upon analysis we notice that, in poetry as in painting, the Caribbean people have an exotic vision of themselves and offer up an exotic expression of themselves. It is not someone from abroad—such as the mainland French person—who portrays the Caribbean as picturesque and ornamental. He himself is the one who describes himself from a distance—externally and superficially—without involving his personal circumstances.

Let's think about this: for there to be exoticism, there needs to be two humanities facing one another in which one party appears alien to the other—in other words, *exotic*.

What conditions could have caused Caribbean society to become exotic—in other words foreign—to itself? The condition for such an aberration can be nothing but the colonial situation.

---

1. Translated by Michael Richardson and Krzysztof Fijałkowski; printed in 1959.　2. Astolphe, marquis de Custine (1790–1857), whose *Letters from Russia* describe his trip there in 1839 and include a satirical portrait of Czar Nicholas I.

The fundamental characteristic of human existence in colonial society is separation from oneself, exile from oneself, alienation from oneself. This phenomenon of cultural oppression, inseparable from colonialism, will determine within each colonial country a suppression of its particular national soul (its history, religion and customs) to introduce into this collectivity what we can call the 'soul-of-the-mainland-other'. Depersonalization and alienation follow. I perceive myself as a foreigner, as being exotic. Why? Because 'I' is consciousness, 'the other' becomes the self. I am 'exotic-to-myself' because my view of myself is the view of the white person having become mine after three centuries of colonial conditioning. Exoticism—a means of expression for the Caribbean person when he recounts his life in literature and painting—expresses separation and exile. This expression is superficial and false: it belongs to the psychopathology of colonial life. Vision, instead of springing from a genuine West Indian consciousness (to be conquered or re-conquered) is imposed from outside by white colonialist consciousness. This exoticism results from the distance our society finds in relation to itself within the colonial system.

Do not, therefore, be amazed by the tenacity of Caribbean exoticism—it is a phoenix eternally reborn from its own ashes. After the old exoticism of the period of ascendent imperialism (Duquesnay and Thaly[3] in Martinique), there now appears a rejuvenated and preened—surrealist—exoticism which is an aspect of the current anti-colonialist struggle.

But if we consider it without complacency, we see the wrinkles of a familiar old age behind the newness of form. In spite of the poet's resolute intention to escape the insignificance of exoticism, he is inevitably and despite himself tempted to return to it for the simple reason that the basis of the poetic process is the very structure of the colonial regime. *Exoticism is a constant of colonial consciousness centred—economically, socially and culturally—outside itself, on the mainland.* The embellishments of colonial poetry, despite an attempted humanism discernible among our best poets today, are woven on a similar canvas: a collective consciousness that, even in revolt, suffers from a tragic dispossession. For the historian, exoticism (whether it be of renunciation or revolt) remains exoticism—the literature of the colonial period. The sickness within Caribbean poetic consciousness, which desperately aims to assume possession of itself but is drawn outwards by a cultural system founded on the negation of individual characteristics, will vanish only when the colonial system itself is shattered and the colonial structures are replaced with human structures.

* * *

3. Osman Duquesnay, mayor of the city of Marin from 1908 to 1924, and Dr. Daniel Thaly (1879–1950) both wrote poetry in the Parnassian and French Symbolist tradition. Thaly's poetry was widely read and taught in school. He was also known as the "shepherd" for having brought a group of Carib Indians from Dominica to be put on display as native history during an exposition in Fort-de-France that celebrated the three-hundredth anniversary of the arrival of the French. (Martinican Caribs had disappeared by that time.)

SIMONE DE BEAUVOIR
1908–1986

"One is not born, but rather becomes a woman." With this statement, Simone de Beauvoir, in *The Second Sex*, argues that a female infant has no gendered identity but will be taught by society to recognize and accept the role of "woman." The French existentialist writer does more than simply affirm the philosophical principle that we choose our own identity but are also bound by the image others have of us. For Beauvoir, the harsh truth is that women learn who they are by growing up in a male-dominated society that sees them as the Others, the "second sex."

The Second Sex made Beauvoir a controversial figure and established her reputation as one of the earliest feminist thinkers. Like others (Mona Caird or Virginia Woolf in this volume), she describes various ways in which men have historically defined women, prescribing both their role in life and the approved attitudes toward it. Beauvoir's approach is different, however. At the time the book was published, she was already well known as an essayist, novelist, and existentialist thinker (and a close friend of the existentialist philosopher Jean-Paul Sartre), and she approaches the topic within the general framework of existential psychology. Here, an individual's sense of self does not exist in a vacuum, but is constantly being constructed in a social context and in interaction with others. One is more "authentic" when choosing each act "for oneself" (*pour soi*)—that is, after thinking through the act's implications—and less alive when refusing choice and living passively ("in oneself": *en soi*) according to other people's opinions. For women, she suggest, the obstacles to creating an authentic self in such circumstances are clear: women live in a society where ideas are largely dictated by a dominant group (men, the "first sex"), and that group looks on women as a different species, a categorical Other. Beauvoir proceeds to itemize some of the ways that the male view of women has been worked out and suggests that men generally link Woman with other concepts—Nature, Myth, and Mystery—that can be discussed while avoiding a more difficult dialogue with women themselves. Even though *The Second Sex* contains some factual information that is incomplete or out of date (especially in the second volume), Beauvoir's ideas remain pertinent and her discussion of cultural otherness foreshadows modern studies of cultural relations.

The Second Sex: Facts and Myths[1]
From *Myths: Dreams, Fears, Idols*

* * *

It is always difficult to describe a myth; it cannot be grasped or encompassed; it haunts the human consciousness without ever appearing before it in fixed form. The myth is so various, so contradictory, that at first its unity is not discerned: Delilah and Judith, Aspasia and Lucretia, Pandora and Athena[2]—woman is at once Eve and the Virgin Mary. She is an idol, a servant, the source of life, a power of darkness; she is the elemental silence of

---

1. Translated by H. M. Parshley; published in 1949.   2. Athena, daughter of Zeus, is the Greek goddess of wisdom. Delilah, in the Hebrew Bible, weakened the hero Samson by cutting off his hair (Judges 16). In Jewish tradition, Judith of Bethulia seduced the besieging general Holofernes and cut off his head while he slept. Aspasia, reputed to be a fascinating and cultured woman, was the mistress of the fifth-century-B.C.E. Athenian statesman Pericles. According to Roman legend, the rape of the virtuous wife Lucretia by the king's son caused a revolution that marked the beginning of the Roman Republic. In Greek mythology, Pandora released a host of evils into the world when she opened a mysterious box.

truth, she is artifice, gossip, and falsehood; she is healing presence and sorceress; she is man's prey, his downfall, she is everything that he is not and that he longs for, his negation and his *raison d'être*.[3]

"To be a woman," says Kierkegaard in *Stages on the Road of Life*,[4] "is something so strange, so confused, so complicated, that no one predicate comes near expressing it and that the multiple predicates that one would like to use are so contradictory that only a woman could put up with it." This comes from not regarding woman positively, such as she seems to herself to be, but negatively, such as she appears to man. For if woman is not the only *Other*, it remains none the less true that she is always defined as the Other. And her ambiguity is just that of the concept of the Other: it is that of the human situation in so far as it is defined in its relation with the Other. As I have already said, the Other is Evil; but being necessary to the Good, it turns into the Good; through it I attain to the Whole, but it also separates me therefrom; it is the gateway to the infinite and the measure of my finite nature. And here lies the reason why woman incarnates no stable concept; through her is made unceasingly the passage from hope to frustration, from hate to love, from good to evil, from evil to good. Under whatever aspect we may consider her, it is this ambivalence that strikes us first.

Man seeks in woman the Other as Nature and as his fellow being. But we know what ambivalent feelings Nature inspires in man. He exploits her, but she crushes him, he is born of her and dies in her; she is the source of his being and the realm that he subjugates to his will; Nature is a vein of gross material in which the soul is imprisoned, and she is the supreme reality; she is contingence and Idea, the finite and the whole; she is what opposes the Spirit, and the Spirit itself. Now ally, now enemy, she appears as the dark chaos from whence life wells up, as this life itself, and as the over-yonder toward which life tends. Woman sums up nature as Mother, Wife, and Idea; these forms now mingle and now conflict, and each of them wears a double visage.

* * *

Of all these myths, none is more firmly anchored in masculine hearts than that of the feminine "mystery." It has numerous advantages. And first of all it permits an easy explanation of all that appears inexplicable; the man who "does not understand" a woman is happy to substitute an objective resistance for a subjective deficiency of mind; instead of admitting his ignorance, he perceives the presence of a "mystery" outside himself: an alibi, indeed, that flatters laziness and vanity at once. A heart smitten with love thus avoids many disappointments: if the loved one's behavior is capricious, her remarks stupid, then the mystery serves to excuse it all. And finally, thanks again to the mystery, that negative relation is perpetuated which seemed to Kierkegaard infinitely preferable to positive possession;[5] in the company of a living enigma man remains alone—alone with his dreams, his hopes, his fears, his

3. Reason for being (French). 4. The first part of Danish philosopher Søren Kierkegaard's *Stages on Life's Way* (1845) contained a scathing attack on women. Coincidentally, his former fiancée had recently married someone else. 5. Kierkegaard broke his engagement to Regine Olsen in November 1841 because of complex feelings of guilt and religious anxiety. In *Fear and Trembling* (1843), he referred to the break as a sacrifice to a higher authority.

love, his vanity. This subjective game, which can go all the way from vice to mystical ecstasy, is for many a more attractive experience than an authentic relation with a human being. What foundations exist for such a profitable illusion?

Surely woman is, in a sense, mysterious, "mysterious as is all the world," according to Maeterlinck.[6] Each is *subject* only for himself; each can grasp in immanence only himself, alone: from this point of view the *other* is always a mystery. To men's eyes the opacity of the self-knowing self, of the *pour-soi*,[7] is denser in the *other* who is feminine; men are unable to penetrate her special experience through any working of sympathy: they are condemned to ignorance of the quality of woman's erotic pleasure, the discomfort of menstruation, and the pains of childbirth. The truth is that there is mystery on both sides: as the *other* who is of masculine sex, every man, also, has within him a presence, an inner self impenetrable to woman; she in turn is in ignorance of the male's erotic feeling. But in accordance with the universal rule I have stated, the categories in which men think of the world are established *from their point of view, as absolute*: they misconceive reciprocity, here as everywhere. A mystery for man, woman is considered to be mysterious in essence.

To tell the truth, her situation makes woman very liable to such a view. Her physiological nature is very complex; she herself submits to it as to some rigmarole from outside; her body does not seem to her to be a clear expression of herself; within it she feels herself a stranger. Indeed, the bond that in every individual connects the physiological life and the psychic life—or better the relation existing between the contingence of an individual and the free spirit that assumes it—is the deepest enigma implied in the condition of being human, and this enigma is presented in its most disturbing form in woman.

But what is commonly referred to as the mystery is not the subjective solitude of the conscious self, nor the secret organic life. It is on the level of communication that the word has its true meaning: it is not a reduction to pure silence, to darkness, to absence; it implies a stammering presence that fails to make itself manifest and clear. To say that woman is mystery is to say, not that she is silent, but that her language is not understood; she is there, but hidden behind veils; she exists beyond these uncertain appearances. What is she? Angel, demon, one inspired, an actress? It may be supposed either that there are answers to these questions which are impossible to discover, or, rather, that no answer is adequate because a fundamental ambiguity marks the feminine being; and perhaps in her heart she is even for herself quite indefinable: a sphinx.

* * *

* * * It is a vain question. If man fails to discover that secret essence of femininity, it is simply because it does not exist.

* * *

In the same way it is true that, beyond the secrecy created by their dissembling, there is mystery in the Black, the Yellow, in so far as they are

6. Maurice Maeterlinck (1862–1949), Belgian Symbolist playwright, author of *Pelléas et Mélisande* (1892)
7. An existentialist term meaning, literally, "for oneself," the self that chooses to act in full consciousness.

considered absolutely as the inessential Other. It should be noted that the American citizen, who profoundly baffles the average European, is not, however, considered as being "mysterious": one states more modestly that one does not understand him. And similarly woman does not always "understand" man; but there is no such thing as a masculine mystery. The point is that rich America, and the male, are on the Master side and that Mystery belongs to the slave.

To be sure, we can only muse in the twilight byways of bad faith[8] upon the positive reality of the Mystery; like certain marginal hallucinations, it dissolves under the attempt to view it fixedly. Literature always fails in attempting to portray "mysterious" women; they can appear only at the beginning of a novel as strange, enigmatic figures; but unless the story remains unfinished they give up their secret in the end and they are then simply consistent and transparent persons. The heroes in Peter Cheyney's[9] books, for example, never cease to be astonished at the unpredictable caprices of women: no one can ever guess how they will act, they upset all calculations. The fact is that once the springs of their action are revealed to the reader, they are seen to be very simple mechanisms: this woman was a spy, that one a thief; however clever the plot, there is always a key; and it could not be otherwise, had the author all the talent and imagination in the world. Mystery is never more than a mirage that vanishes as we draw near to look at it.

We can see now that the myth is in large part explained by its usefulness to man. The myth of woman is a luxury. It can appear only if man escapes from the urgent demands of his needs; the more relationships are concretely lived, the less they are idealized. The fellah[1] of ancient Egypt, the Bedouin peasant, the artisan of the Middle Ages, the worker of today has in the requirements of work and poverty relations with his particular woman companion which are too definite for her to be embellished with an aura either auspicious or inauspicious. The epochs and the social classes that have been marked by the leisure to dream have been the ones to set up the images, black and white, of femininity. But along with luxury there was utility; these dreams were irresistibly guided by interests. Surely most of the myths had roots in the spontaneous attitude of man toward his own existence and toward the world around him. But going beyond experience toward the transcendent Idea was deliberately used by patriarchal society for purposes of self-justification; through the myths this society imposed its laws and customs upon individuals in a picturesque, effective manner; it is under a mythical form that the group-imperative is indoctrinated into each conscience. Through such intermediaries as religions, traditions, language, tales, songs, movies, the myths penetrate even into such existences as are most harshly enslaved to material realities. Here everyone can find sublimation of his drab experiences: deceived by the woman he loves, one declares that she is a Crazy Womb; another, obsessed by his impotence, calls her a Praying Mantis; still another enjoys his wife's company: behold, she is Harmony, Rest, the Good Earth! The taste for eternity at a bargain, for a pocket-sized absolute, which is shared by a majority of men, is satisfied by myths. The smallest emotion, a slight annoyance, becomes the reflection of a timeless Idea—an illusion agreeably flattering to the vanity.

8. An existentialist term meaning "self-deception," the refusal to accept responsibility for one's acts (to "choose to be free") in order to avoid anxiety.   9. A British writer of hard-boiled detective fiction (1896–1951).   1. Peasant.

The myth is one of those snares of false objectivity into which the man who depends on ready-made valuations rushes headlong. Here again we have to do with the substitution of a set idol for actual experience and the free judgments it requires. For an authentic relation with an autonomous existent, the myth of Woman substitutes the fixed contemplation of a mirage. "Mirage! Mirage!" cries Laforgue.[2] "We should kill them since we cannot comprehend them; or better tranquilize them, instruct them, make them give up their taste for jewels, make them our genuinely equal comrades, our intimate friends, real associates here below, dress them differently, cut their hair short, say anything and everything to them." Man would have nothing to lose, quite the contrary, if he gave up disguising woman as a symbol. When dreams are official community affairs, clichés, they are poor and monotonous indeed beside the living reality; for the true dreamer, for the poet, woman is a more generous fount than is any down-at-heel marvel. The times that have most sincerely treasured women are not the period of feudal chivalry nor yet the gallant nineteenth century. They are the times—like the eighteenth century—when men have regarded women as fellow creatures; then it is that women seem truly romantic, as the reading of *Liaisons dangereuses, Le Rouge et le noir, Farewell to Arms,* is sufficient to show. The heroines of Laclos, Stendhal, Hemingway[3] are without mystery, and they are not the less engaging for that. To recognize in woman a human being is not to impoverish man's experience: this would lose none of its diversity, its richness, or its intensity if it were to occur between two subjectivities. To discard the myths is not to destroy all dramatic relation between the sexes, it is not to deny the significance authentically revealed to man through feminine reality; it is not to do away with poetry, love, adventure, happiness, dreaming. It is simply to ask that behavior, sentiment, passion be founded upon the truth.

"Woman is lost. Where are the women? The women of today are not women at all!" We have seen what these mysterious slogans mean. In men's eyes—and for the legion of women who see through men's eyes—it is not enough to have a woman's body nor to assume the female function as mistress or mother in order to be a "true woman." In sexuality and maternity woman as subject can claim autonomy; but to be a "true woman" she must accept herself as the Other. The men of today show a certain duplicity of attitude which is painfully lacerating to women; they are willing on the whole to accept woman as a fellow being, an equal; but they still require her to remain the inessential. For her these two destinies are incompatible; she hesitates between one and the other without being exactly adapted to either, and from this comes her lack of equilibrium. With man there is no break between public and private life: the more he confirms his grasp on the world in action and in work, the more virile he seems to be; human and vital values are combined in him. Whereas woman's independent successes are in contradiction with her femininity, since the "true woman" is required to make herself object, to be the Other.

* * *

2. Jules Laforgue (1860–1887), French Symbolist poet and essayist who influenced the early T. S. Eliot.
3. Ernest Hemingway (1899–1961), American author of *A Farewell to Arms* (1929). *Laclos:* Pierre-Ambroise-François Choderlos de Laclos (1741–1803), author of *Les Liaisons dangereuses* (Dangerous Relationships) (1782). *Stendhal:* pseudonym of Marie-Henri Beyle (1783–1842), author of *The Red and the Black* (1830).

What is certain is that today it is very difficult for women to accept at the same time their status as autonomous individuals and their womanly destiny; this is the source of the blundering and restlessness which sometimes cause them to be considered a "lost sex." And no doubt it is more comfortable to submit to a blind enslavement than to work for liberation: the dead, for that matter, are better adapted to the earth than are the living. In all respects a return to the past is no more possible than it is desirable. What must be hoped for is that the men for their part will unreservedly accept the situation that is coming into existence; only then will women be able to live in that situation without anguish. Then Laforgue's prayer will be answered: "Ah, young women, when will you be our brothers, our brothers in intimacy without ulterior thought of exploitation? When shall we clasp hands truly?" Then Breton's "Mélusine, no longer under the weight of the calamity let loose upon her by man alone, Mélusine set free . . ." will regain "her place in humanity." Then she will be a full human being, "when," to quote a letter of Rimbaud, "the infinite bondage of woman is broken, when she will live in and for herself, man—hitherto detestable—having let her go free."[4]

4. See Arthur Rimbaud's (1854–1891) letter of May 15, 1871, to Paul Demeny, printed in this volume. *Breton:* from *Arcane 17,* by the Surrealist poet André Breton (1896–1966), whose poetry is represented in this volume.

FRANTZ FANON
1925–1961

Psychiatrist and revolutionary, a supporter of the Algerian struggle for independence from France, Frantz Fanon also dedicated himself to a larger battle: to free the minds of the dispossessed—those he called "the wretched of the earth"—from the psychological bonds left by decades of colonialism. Born in the French protectorate of Martinique, he had seen the effects of those bonds in several contexts. In 1944, while serving with the Free French forces fighting in North Africa, he observed the different treatment given white and colonial troops. After the war, studying medicine in Paris, he associated with other members of the black diaspora at a time when Négritude (black consciousness) was being widely discussed. His first medical assignment took him to the hospital at Blida (outside Algiers), where he served as head of psychiatric services from 1953 to 1956 and again saw the results of discrimination. Nor was the damage only to the colonized: after the Algerians declared their independence in October 1954 and the guerrilla war intensified, Fanon saw many shattered patients on both the French and Algerian sides. By 1957 he had become a thorough anticolonialist. He lost his job at Blida that year for being involved with the FLN (National Liberation Front) and moved to Tunisia, where he continued writing and working with the rebels.

The Wretched of the Earth is Fanon's last book, published months before his death of leukemia. In it he describes how colonial rule leaves a destructive imprint on the minds of the colonized that goes far beyond physical occupation. The argument, developed beyond the black self-hatred that the psychiatrist analyzed in *Black Skin, White Masks* (1952), now takes up the psychological and political consequences of colonial domination. Fanon writes that colonialism's insistence on the racial inferiority of subject peoples inspires a cultural neurosis that expresses itself in humiliation, alienation, and inevitable violence. He documents the effects of this psychological destruction on both French and Algerian patients in brief case histories at the end of the book and suggests that the solution—which can only be reached by violent struggle—is to be found in the independence and dignity of separate African states. (*The Wretched of the Earth* was advertised by its American publisher as a "handbook of revolution.") Only a nationalist culture can counteract the chilling effect of the universalist model of civilization proposed (in their own image) by colonial powers. The colonialist model identifies Africans as subject peoples and barbarians in need of enlightenment, he notes, and a countermodel—rooted in the discovery of precolonial civilizations of great power and elegance—is needed to support both cultural and personal pride. Fanon is not a blind nationalist: in another chapter he examines the pitfalls of nationalist consciousness, and he knows that extreme nationalism and mystic Négritude can become merely instruments of a second oppression. He is, however, a passionate anticolonialist who believes that the mental and physical shackles of colonialism can be broken only by violent struggle and that such struggle is necessary to reestablish personal freedom and psychological equilibrium.

The Wretched of the Earth

From *On National Culture*[1]

Each generation must out of relative obscurity discover its mission, fulfill it, or betray it. In underdeveloped countries the preceding generations have both resisted the work or erosion carried by colonialism and also helped on the maturing of the struggles of today. We must rid ourselves of the habit, now that we are in the thick of the fight, of minimizing the action of our fathers or of feigning incomprehension when considering their silence and passivity. They fought as well as they could, with the arms that they possessed then; and if the echoes of their struggle have not resounded in the international arena, we must realize that the reason for this silence lies less in their lack of heroism than in the fundamentally different international situation of our time. It needed more than one native to say "We've had enough"; more than one peasant rising crushed, more than one demonstration put down before we could today hold our own, certain in our victory. As for we who have decided to break the back of colonialism, our historic mission is to sanction all revolts, all desperate actions, all those abortive attempts drowned in rivers of blood.

In this chapter we shall analyze the problem, which is felt to be fundamental, of the legitimacy of the claims of a nation. It must be recognized that the political party which mobilizes the people hardly touches on this problem of legitimacy. The political parties start from living reality and it is in the name of this reality, in the name of the stark facts which weigh down the present and the future of men and women, that they fix their line of action. The political party may well speak in moving terms of the nation, but what it is concerned with is that the people who are listening understand the need to take part in the fight if, quite simply, they wish to continue to exist.

1. Translated by Constance Farrington; published in 1961.

* * *

Inside the political parties, and most often in offshoots from these parties, cultured individuals of the colonized race make their appearance. For these individuals, the demand for a national culture and the affirmation of the existence of such a culture represent a special battlefield. While the politicians situate their action in actual present-day events, men of culture take their stand in the field of history. Confronted with the native intellectual who decides to make an aggressive response to the colonialist theory of precolonial barbarism, colonialism will react only slightly, and still less because the ideas developed by the young colonized intelligentsia are widely professed by specialists in the mother country. It is in fact a commonplace to state that for several decades large numbers of research workers have, in the main, rehabilitated the African, Mexican, and Peruvian civilizations. The passion with which native intellectuals defend the existence of their national culture may be a source of amazement; but those who condemn this exaggerated passion are strangely apt to forget that their own psyche and their own selves are conveniently sheltered behind a French or German culture which has given full proof of its existence and which is uncontested.

I am ready to concede that on the plane of factual being the past existence of an Aztec civilization does not change anything very much in the diet of the Mexican peasant of today. I admit that all the proofs of a wonderful Songhai civilization[2] will not change the fact that today the Songhais are underfed and illiterate, thrown between sky and water with empty heads and empty eyes. But it has been remarked several times that this passionate search for a national culture which existed before the colonial era finds its legitimate reason in the anxiety shared by native intellectuals to shrink away from that Western culture in which they all risk being swamped. Because they realize they are in danger of losing their lives and thus becoming lost to their people, these men, hotheaded and with anger in their hearts, relentlessly determine to renew contact once more with the oldest and most precolonial springs of life of their people.

Let us go further. Perhaps this passionate research and this anger are kept up or at least directed by the secret hope of discovering beyond the misery of today, beyond self-contempt, resignation, and abjuration, some very beautiful and splendid era whose existence rehabilitates us both in regard to ourselves and in regard to others. I have said that I have decided to go further. Perhaps unconsciously, the native intellectuals, since they could not stand wonderstruck before the history of today's barbarity, decided to back further and to delve deeper down; and, let us make no mistake, it was with the greatest delight that they discovered that there was nothing to be ashamed of in the past, but rather dignity, glory, and solemnity. The claim to a national culture in the past does not only rehabilitate that nation and serve as a justification for the hope of a future national culture. In the sphere of psycho-affective equilibrium it is responsible for an important change in the native. Perhaps we have not sufficiently demonstrated that colonialism is not simply content to impose its rule upon the present and the future of a dominated country. Colonialism is not satisfied merely with holding a people in its grip and emptying the native's brain of all form and content. By a kind of

2. A great trading empire, based in central Mali, that flourished in the 15th and 16th centuries.

perverted logic, it turns to the past of the oppressed people, and distorts, disfigures, and destroys it. This work of devaluing pre-colonial history takes on a dialectical significance today.

When we consider the efforts made to carry out the cultural estrangement so characteristic of the colonial epoch, we realize that nothing has been left to chance and that the total result looked for by colonial domination was indeed to convince the natives that colonialism came to lighten their darkness. The effect consciously sought by colonialism was to drive into the natives' heads the idea that if the settlers were to leave, they would at once fall back into barbarism, degradation, and bestiality.

On the unconscious plane, colonialism therefore did not seek to be considered by the native as a gentle, loving mother who protects her child from a hostile environment, but rather as a mother who unceasingly restrains her fundamentally perverse offspring from managing to commit suicide and from giving free rein to its evil instincts. The colonial mother protects her child from itself, from its ego, and from its physiology, its biology, and its own unhappiness which is its very essence.

In such a situation the claims of the native intellectual are not a luxury but a necessity in any coherent program. The native intellectual who takes up arms to defend his nation's legitimacy and who wants to bring proofs to bear out that legitimacy, who is willing to strip himself naked to study the history of his body, is obliged to dissect the heart of his people.

Such an examination is not specifically national. The native intellectual who decides to give battle to colonial lies fights on the field of the whole continent. The past is given back its value. Culture, extracted from the past to be displayed in all its splendor, is not necessarily that of his own country. Colonialism, which has not bothered to put too fine a point on its efforts, has never ceased to maintain that the Negro is a savage; and for the colonist, the Negro was neither an Angolan nor a Nigerian, for he simply spoke of "the Negro." For colonialism, this vast continent was the haunt of savages, a country riddled with superstitions and fanaticism, destined for contempt, weighed down by the curse of God, a country of cannibals—in short, the Negro's country. Colonialism's condemnation is continental in its scope. The contention by colonialism that the darkest night of humanity lay over pre-colonial history concerns the whole of the African continent. The efforts of the native to rehabilitate himself and to escape from the claws of colonialism are logically inscribed from the same point of view as that of colonialism. The native intellectual who has gone far beyond the domains of Western culture and who has got it into his head to proclaim the existence of another culture never does so in the name of Angola or of Dahomey. The culture which is affirmed is African culture. The Negro, never so much a Negro as since he has been dominated by the whites, when he decides to prove that he has a culture and to behave like a cultured person, comes to realize that history points out a well-defined path to him: he must demonstrate that a Negro culture exists.

And it is only too true that those who are most responsible for this racialization of thought, or at least for the first movement toward that thought, are and remain those Europeans who have never ceased to set up white culture to fill the gap left by the absence of other cultures. Colonialism did not dream of wasting its time in denying the existence of one national culture after another. Therefore the reply of the colonized peoples will be straight away continental in its breadth. In Africa, the native literature of the last twenty years is not a national literature but a Negro literature. The concept of negritude, for example, was the emotional if not the logical antithesis of that insult which the white man flung at humanity.

* * *

CHINUA ACHEBE
born 1930

Chinua Achebe has often emphasized the value of the Igbo dual vision of the world in which "Wherever Something stands, Something Else will stand beside it." From his childhood in Ogidi, Nigeria, he has existed at the intersection of two cultures: African and English, Christian and non-Christian, indigenous and colonial. Each finds a place in his writings, whether in the five novels, in his poetry, or in numerous political essays. Achebe cherishes a broad canvas that is able to represent not only both perspectives but also the reciprocal awareness in which each portrays the other as an alien element—a cultural other.

The writer's bicultural existence began officially from the moment he received two names at his baptism: Albert, the name of Queen Victoria's husband, and Chinualu- mogu, an Igbo name meaning "My spirit come fight for me." He grew up bilingual and continued to write novels in English despite the insistence of a group of writers in the 1960s that "colonial" languages should be abandoned. His response was char- acteristically inclusive: "The African writer should . . . aim at fashioning out an English which is at once universal and able to carry his peculiar experience." Achebe's own literary language blends Igbo vocabulary and speech patterns with English to arrive at a new composite that expresses modern Africa in all its rich hybridity.

As he shows in the autobiographical essay *Named for Victoria, Queen of England,* a time came when the dual vision that had seemed curiously balanced between two ways of life shifted proportions. With the new nationalisms emerging in Africa after World War II, Achebe cast a different eye on the harmonious balance that had seemed to exist in Ogidi. Moreover, as he studied literature and history at University College in Ibadan, he found little recognition of African contributions to history as well as distorted pictures of African culture in British imperial literature. The worst exces- ses—pictures of ferocious, simpleminded savages—could be attributed to ignorance and ill will, but such was not the case in *Mister Johnson* (1939), a patronizing picture of Africa by a well-meaning Anglo-Irish novelist, Joyce Cary, who had spent some years in the Nigerian civil service and tried diligently to depict the African way of life. Suddenly, Achebe found himself a cultural other. The balance was deceptive, after all: it existed, but in a more complex way. As the writer has often said, it was the example of Joyce Cary that set him to writing a more realistic picture of African society. His novels will explore the destructive possibilities of cultural interaction and transform (for example) the religious divisions of Ogidi from mere differences of social custom into the tragic family histories of *Things Fall Apart* (1958) and *Arrow of God* (1964).

From Named for Victoria, Queen of England[1]

I was born in Ogidi in Eastern Nigeria of devout Christian parents. The line between Christian and non-Christian was much more definite in my village forty years ago than it is today. When I was growing up I remember we tended to look down on the others. We were called in our language 'the people of the church' or 'the association of God'. The others were called, with the conceit appropriate to followers of the true religion, the heathen or even 'the people of nothing.'

Thinking about it today I am not so sure that it isn't they who should have been looking down on us for our apostasy. And perhaps they did. But the bounties of the Christian God were not to be taken lightly—education, paid jobs and many other advantages that nobody in his right senses could underrate. And in fairness we should add that there was more than naked opportunism in the defection of many to the new religion. For in some ways and in certain circumstances it stood firmly on the side of humane behaviour.* * *

* * *

I was baptized Albert Chinualumogu. I dropped the tribute to Victorian England when I went to the university although you might find some early acquaintances still calling me by it. The earliest of them all—my mother—certainly stuck to it to the bitter end. So if anyone asks you what Her Britannic Majesty Queen Victoria had in common with Chinua Achebe, the answer is: They both lost their Albert![2] As for the second name, which in the manner of my people is a full-length philosophical statement, I simply cut it in two, making it more businesslike without, I hope, losing the general drift of its meaning.

I have always been fond of stories and intrigued by language—first Igbo, spoken with such eloquence by the old men of the village, and later English which I began to learn at about the age of eight. I don't know for certain but I have probably spoken more words in Igbo than English but I have definitely written more words in English than Igbo. Which I think makes me perfectly bilingual. Some people have suggested that I should be better off writing in Igbo. Sometimes they seek to drive the point home by asking me in which language I dream. When I reply that I dream in both languages they seem not to believe it. More recently I have heard an even more potent and metaphysical version of the question: In what language do you have an orgasm? That should settle the matter if I knew.

We lived at the crossroads of cultures. We still do today; but when I was a boy one could see and sense the peculiar quality and atmosphere of it more clearly. I am not talking about all that rubbish we hear of the spiritual void and mental stresses that Africans are supposed to have, or the evil forces and irrational passions prowling through Africa's heart of darkness. We know the racist mystique behind a lot of that stuff and should merely point out that those who prefer to see Africa in those lurid terms have not themselves

---

1. Published in 1973.   2. Queen Victoria's husband, Prince Albert, died in 1861, and she mourned him for the rest of her life.

demonstrated any clear superiority in sanity or more competence in coping with life.

But still the crossroads does have a certain dangerous potency; dangerous because a man might perish there wrestling with multiple-headed spirits, but also he might be lucky and return to his people with the boon of prophetic vision.

On one arm of the cross we sang hymns and read the Bible night and day. On the other my father's brother and his family, blinded by heathenism, offered food to idols. That was how it was supposed to be anyhow. But I knew without knowing why that it was too simple a way to describe what was going on. Those idols and that food had a strange pull on me in spite of my being such a thorough little Christian that often at Sunday services at the height of the grandeur of 'Te Deum Laudamus'[3] I would have dreams of a mantle of gold falling on me as the choir of angels drowned our mortal song and the voice of God Himself thundering: This is my beloved son in whom I am well pleased. Yet, despite those delusions of divine destiny I was not past taking my little sister to our neighbour's house when our parents were not looking and partaking of heathen festival meals. I never found their rice and stew to have the flavour of idolatry. I was about ten then. If anyone likes to believe that I was torn by spiritual agonies or stretched on the rack of my ambivalence, he certainly may suit himself. I do not remember any undue distress. What I do remember is a fascination for the ritual and the life on the other arm of the crossroads. And I believe two things were in my favour—that curiosity, and the little distance imposed between me and it by the accident of my birth. The distance becomes not a separation but a bringing together like the necessary backward step which a judicious viewer may take in order to see a canvas steadily and fully.

* * *

I did not know that I was going to be a writer because I did not really know of the existence of such creatures until fairly late. The folk-stories my mother and elder sister told me had the immemorial quality of the sky and the forests and the rivers. Later, when I got to know that the European stories I read were written by known people it still didn't help much. It was the same Europeans who made all the other marvellous things like the motor car. We did not come into it at all. We made nothing that wasn't primitive and heathenish.

The nationalist movement in British West Africa after the Second World War brought about a mental revolution which began to reconcile us to ourselves. It suddenly seemed that we too might have a story to tell. 'Rule Britannia!' to which we had marched so unselfconsciously on Empire Day[4] now stuck in our throat.

At the university I read some appalling novels about Africa (including Joyce Cary's much praised *Mister Johnson*)[5] and decided that the story we

---

3. "We Praise God," a Latin hymn of public rejoicing.   **4.** A public holiday celebrated on May 24, the anniversary of Queen Victoria's birth; it is now celebrated as Commonwealth Day. *Rule Britannia*: a popular patriotic song composed by Thomas Arne (1710–1778) in 1740 to an ode by James Thomson (1700–1748). Britannia is a personification of England.   **5.** Achebe has frequently criticized novelist Joyce Cary's *Mister Johnson* (1939) for its unrealistic images of African life.

had to tell could not be told for us by anyone else no matter how gifted or well intentioned.

Although I did not set about it consciously in that solemn way, I now know that my first book, *Things Fall Apart*, was an act of atonement with my past, the ritual return and homage of a prodigal son. * * *

AUDRE LORDE
1934–1992

From her vantage point as Sister Outsider—a member of the community of women but nonetheless marginalized—the poet Audre Lorde interrogates the role of difference in modern American society. "Age, race, class, and sex" are not abstract concepts for her, but dimensions of her daily existence that distinguish who she is and also who she is *not*. As a middle-aged black working woman who is also a lesbian mother of two, Lorde does not correspond to the image of mainstream femininity held by the contemporary women's movement. Yet that image, she protests, also does not correspond to the diverse reality of contemporary society. Instead, it merely reflects the self-image of white heterosexual women active in the feminist movement: preoccupied with opposing male dominance, they emphasize a unified model of womanhood and fail to recognize how it undermines the idea of sisterhood itself. Throughout, the main culprit is the idea of the *norm*: the implied standard of appearance and behavior that in practice acts as a standard for exclusion.

Norms, Lorde suggests, are linked to a socioeconomic system that profits by marginalizing some groups of people—generally those weaker and less capable of defending themselves—in order to preserve the power and privilege of the dominant group. They regularize social behavior by providing an image toward which everyone is supposed to aspire: in American society, someone who is "white, thin, male, young, heterosexual, christian, and financially secure." The poet scathingly describes the ways that many women unthinkingly accept everything but the "male" part of this mythical norm, instead of reflecting on their own experience of being excluded from power. The challenge for women, she concludes, is to change society by redefining difference so that it cannot be used as a politically divisive instrument, separating superior from inferior.

Lorde was born in New York City of West Indian parents and began writing poetry in the eighth grade. While studying for her undergraduate degree and a master's degree in library science, she took various jobs that included ghost writer, social worker, factory worker, and X-ray technician and provided a range of experience that reappears in her writing. After working as a librarian from 1961 to 1968, she received a grant from the National Endowment for the Arts and was named poet-in-residence at Tougaloo College; later, she became a professor of English at Hunter College in New York. Lorde's poetry is known for its intense personal engagement, whether in the role of lover, mother, or exponent of black pride, or in the broader political issues that engaged her attention from 1973's *From a Land Where Other People Live* to *The Black Unicorn* (1978). The summer riots in Detroit and San Francisco are linked, in 1973, with images of war in Angola and Vietnam; in 1983, she reported bitterly on the invasion of Grenada (her mother's birthplace) and described the island as a victim of international politics. According to poet Adrienne Rich, it is impossible to simplify

Lorde's range and multifaceted identity: "Audre Lorde writes as a Black woman, a mother, a daughter, a Lesbian, a feminist, a visionary; poems of elemental wildness and healing, nightmare and lucidity." Lorde's own description was shorter and more personal: "My poetry comes from the intersection of me and my worlds."

From Age, Race, Class, and Sex: Women Redefining Difference[1]

Much of Western European history conditions us to see human differences in simplistic opposition to each other: dominant/subordinate, good/bad, up/down, superior/inferior. In a society where the good is defined in terms of profit rather than in terms of human need, there must always be some group of people who, through systematized oppression, can be made to feel surplus, to occupy the place of the dehumanized inferior. Within this society, that group is made up of Black and Third World people, working-class people, older people, and women.

As a forty-nine-year-old Black lesbian feminist socialist mother of two, including one boy, and a member of an interracial couple, I usually find myself a part of some group defined as other, deviant, inferior, or just plain wrong. Traditionally, in american society, it is the members of oppressed, objectified groups who are expected to stretch out and bridge the gap between the actualities of our lives and the consciousness of our oppressor. For in order to survive, those of us for whom oppression is as american as apple pie have always had to be watchers, to become familiar with the language and manners of the oppressor, even sometimes adopting them for some illusion of protection. Whenever the need for some pretense of communication arises, those who profit from our oppression call upon us to share our knowledge with them. In other words, it is the responsibility of the oppressed to teach the oppressors their mistakes. I am responsible for educating teachers who dismiss my children's culture in school. Black and Third World people are expected to educate white people as to our humanity. Women are expected to educate men. Lesbians and gay men are expected to educate the heterosexual world. The oppressors maintain their position and evade responsibility for their own actions. There is a constant drain of energy which might be better used in redefining ourselves and devising realistic scenarios for altering the present and constructing the future.

Institutionalized rejection of difference is an absolute necessity in a profit economy which needs outsiders as surplus people. As members of such an economy, we have *all* been programmed to respond to the human differences between us with fear and loathing and to handle that difference in one of three ways: ignore it, and if that is not possible, copy it if we think it is dominant, or destroy it if we think it is subordinate. But we have no patterns for relating across our human differences as equals. As a result, those differences have been misnamed and misused in the service of separation and confusion.

---

1. Paper delivered at the Copeland Colloquium, Amherst College, April 1980.

Certainly there are very real differences between us of race, age, and sex. But it is not those differences between us that are separating us. It is rather our refusal to recognize those differences, and to examine the distortions which result from our misnaming them and their effects upon human behavior and expectation.

Racism, the belief in the inherent superiority of one race over all others and thereby the right to dominance. Sexism, the belief in the inherent superiority of one sex over the other and thereby the right to dominance. Ageism. Heterosexism. Elitism. Classism.

It is a lifetime pursuit for each one of us to extract these distortions from our living at the same time as we recognize, reclaim, and define those differences upon which they are imposed. For we have all been raised in a society where those distortions were endemic within our living. Too often, we pour the energy needed for recognizing and exploring difference into pretending those differences are insurmountable barriers, or that they do not exist at all. This results in a voluntary isolation, or false and treacherous connections. Either way, we do not develop tools for using human difference as a springboard for creative change within our lives. We speak not of human difference, but of human deviance.

Somewhere, on the edge of consciousness, there is what I call a *mythical norm*, which each one of us within our hearts knows "that is not me." In america, this norm is usually defined as white, thin, male, young, heterosexual, christian, and financially secure. It is with this mythical norm that the trappings of power reside within this society. Those of us who stand outside that power often identify one way in which we are different, and we assume that to be the primary cause of all oppression, forgetting other distortions around difference, some of which we ourselves may be practising. By and large within the women's movement today, white women focus upon their oppression as women and ignore differences of race, sexual preference, class, and age. There is a pretense to a homogeneity of experience covered by the word *sisterhood* that does not in fact exist.

Unacknowledged class differences rob women of each others' energy and creative insight. Recently a women's magazine collective made the decision for one issue to print only prose, saying poetry was a less "rigorous" or "serious" art form. Yet even the form our creativity takes is often a class issue. Of all the art forms, poetry is the most economical. It is the one which is the most secret, which requires the least physical labor, the least material, and the one which can be done between shifts, in the hospital pantry, on the subway, and on scraps of surplus paper. Over the last few years, writing a novel on tight finances, I came to appreciate the enormous differences in the material demands between poetry and prose. As we reclaim our literature, poetry has been the major voice of poor, working class, and Colored women. A room of one's own may be a necessity for writing prose,[2] but so are reams of paper, a typewriter, and plenty of time. The actual requirements to produce the visual arts also help determine, along class lines, whose art is whose. In this day of inflated prices for material, who are our sculptors, our painters, our photographers? When we speak of a broadly based women's culture, we

---

2. Reference to Virginia Woolf's *A Room of One's Own* (1929), printed earlier in this volume.

need to be aware of the effect of class and economic differences on the supplies available for producing art.

As we move toward creating a society within which we can each flourish, ageism is another distortion of relationship which interferes without vision. By ignoring the past, we are encouraged to repeat its mistakes. The "generation gap" is an important social tool for any repressive society. If the younger members of a community view the older members as contemptible or suspect or excess, they will never be able to join hands and examine the living memories of the community, nor ask the all important question, "Why?" This gives rise to a historical amnesia that keeps us working to invent the wheel every time we have to go to the store for bread.

We find ourselves having to repeat and relearn the same old lessons over and over that our mothers did because we do not pass on what we have learned, or because we are unable to listen. For instance, how many times has this all been said before? For another, who would have believed that once again our daughters are allowing their bodies to be hampered and purgatoried by girdles and high heels and hobble skirts?

Ignoring the differences of race between women and the implications of those differences presents the most serious threat to the mobilization of women's joint power.

As white women ignore their built-in privilege of whiteness and define *woman* in terms of their own experience alone, then women of Color become "other," the outsider whose experience and tradition is too "alien" to comprehend. An example of this is the signal absence of the experience of women of Color as a resource for women's studies courses. The literature of women of Color is seldom included in women's literature courses and almost never in other literature courses, nor in women's studies as a whole. All too often, the excuse given is that the literatures of women of Color can only be taught by Colored women, or that they are too difficult to understand, or that classes cannot "get into" them because they come out of experiences that are "too different." I have heard this argument presented by white women of otherwise quite clear intelligence, women who seem to have no trouble at all teaching and reviewing work that comes out of the vastly different experiences of Shakespeare, Molière, Dostoyefsky, and Aristophanes. Surely there must be some other explanation.

This is a very complex question, but I believe one of the reasons white women have such difficulty reading Black women's work is because of their reluctance to see Black women as women and different from themselves. To examine Black women's literature effectively requires that we be seen as whole people in our actual complexities—as individuals, as women, as human—rather than as one of those problematic but familiar stereotypes provided in this society in place of genuine images of Black women. And I believe this holds true for the literatures of other women of Color who are not Black.

The literatures of all women of Color recreate the textures of our lives, and many white women are heavily invested in ignoring the real differences. For as long as any difference between us means one of us must be inferior, then the recognition of any difference must be fraught with guilt. To allow women of Color to step out of stereotypes is too guilt provoking, for it threatens the complacency of those women who view oppression only in terms of sex.

Refusing to recognize difference makes it impossible to see the different problems and pitfalls facing us as women.

* * *

Although elements of these attitudes exist for all women, there are particular resonances of heterosexism and homophobia among Black women. Despite the fact that woman-bonding has a long and honorable history in the African and African-american communities, and despite the knowledge and accomplishments of many strong and creative women-identified Black women in the political, social and cultural fields, heterosexual Black women often tend to ignore or discount the existence and work of Black lesbians. Part of this attitude has come from an understandable terror of Black male attack within the close confines of Black society, where the punishment for any female self-assertion is still to be accused of being a lesbian and therefore unworthy of the attention or support of the scarce Black male. But part of this need to misname and ignore Black lesbians comes from a very real fear that openly women-identified Black women who are no longer dependent upon men for their self-definition may well reorder our whole concept of social relationships.

Black women who once insisted that lesbianism was a white woman's problem now insist that Black lesbians are a threat to Black nationhood, are consorting with the enemy, are basically un-Black. These accusations, coming from the very women to whom we look for deep and real understanding, have served to keep many Black lesbians in hiding, caught between the racism of white women and the homophobia of their sisters. Often, their work has been ignored, trivialized, or misnamed, as with the work of Angelina Grimke, Alice Dunbar-Nelson, Lorraine Hansberry.[3] Yet women-bonded women have always been some part of the power of Black communities, from our unmarried aunts to the amazons of Dahomey.

And it is certainly not Black lesbians who are assaulting women and raping children and grandmothers on the streets of our communities.

Across this country, as in Boston during the spring of 1979 following the unsolved murders of twelve Black women, Black lesbians are spearheading movements against violence against Black women.

What are the particular details within each of our lives that can be scrutinized and altered to help bring about change? How do we redefine difference for all women? It is not our difference which separate women, but our reluctance to recognize those differences and to deal effectively with the distortions which have resulted from the ignoring and misnaming of those differences.

As a tool of social control, women have been encouraged to recognize only one area of human difference as legitimate, those differences which exist between women and men. And we have learned to deal across those differ-

---

3. Hansberry (1930–1965), the first African American woman to have a play produced on Broadway, is best known for *A Raisin in the Sun* (1959), a psychological drama about a working-class black family in Chicago. Angelina Weld Grimké (1880–1958) was an African American poet and playwright and a forerunner of the Harlem Renaissance. Alice Dunbar-Nelson (1875–1935) wrote poetry and short stories with a Creole setting and was active in women's causes.

ences with the urgency of all oppressed subordinates. All of us have had to learn to live or work or coexist with men, from our fathers on. We have recognized and negotiated these differences, even when this recognition only continued the old dominant/subordinate mode of human relationship, where the oppressed must recognize the masters' difference in order to survive.

But our future survival is predicated upon our ability to relate within equality. As women, we must root our internalized patterns of oppression within ourselves if we are to move beyond the most superficial aspects of social change. Now we must recognize differences among women who are our equals, neither inferior nor superior, and devise ways to use each others' difference to enrich our visions and our joint struggles.

The future of our earth may depend upon the ability of all women to identify and develop new definitions of power and new patterns of relating across difference. The old definitions have not served us, nor the earth that supports us. The old patterns, no matter how cleverly rearranged to imitate progress, still condemn us to cosmetically altered repetitions of the same old exchanges, the same old guilt, hatred, recrimination, lamentation, and suspicion.

For we have, built into all of us, old blueprints of expectation and response, old structures of oppression, and these must be altered at the same time as we alter the living conditions which are a result of those structures. For the master's tools will never dismantle the master's house.

As Paulo Freire[4] shows so well in *The Pedagogy of the Oppressed*, the true focus of revolutionary change is never merely the oppressive situations which we seek to escape, but that piece of the oppressor which is planted deep within each of us, and which knows only the oppressors' tactics, the oppressors' relationships.

Change means growth, and growth can be painful. But we sharpen self-definition by exposing the self in work and struggle together with those whom we define as different from ourselves, although sharing the same goals. For Black and white, old and young, lesbian and heterosexual women alike, this can mean new paths to our survival.

> We have chosen each other
> and the edge of each others battles
> the war is the same
> if we lose
> someday women's blood will congeal
> upon a dead planet
> if we win
> there is no telling
> we seek beyond history
> for a new and more possible meeting.[5]

---

4. Brazilian educator (1921–1997) who pioneered an influential system of progressive education that emphasized nonhierarchical dialogue, social awareness, and a developing consciousness of one's ability to transform reality. *Pedagogy of the Oppressed* (1968; English translation, 1970) is his major work.   5. From "Outlines," unpublished poem [Lorde's note].

EDWARD SAID
1935–2003

Orientalism, in Edward Said's view, is a mental operation, a way of seeing a different culture (in this instance, the Middle East) through the lens of local experience. Speaking generally, it is a form of exoticism—a fascination with the alien qualities of another culture and a first step in learning to bridge differences. When speaking specifically, however—as Said does—Orientalism represents a centuries-old pattern of thought that defines the Orient as the generic opposite of Western civilization: a hostile other world and the home of mysterious powers. Fueled at one time by fears of actual invasion, whether from ancient Persia or the Ottoman Empire, the vaguely menacing image of the East gradually became a cultural myth, a product of Western anxieties that was reproduced in popular art and literature, and that also took its toll in the religious, economic, and political spheres. Instead of being a bridge to understanding, the myth gave permanent form to a negative first impression. It depicted a way of life that was innately irrational, violent, and morally degenerate, and that, because it was supposed to be innate, would never change.

Said goes on to describe how the Orientalist myth has for centuries guided public policy. Such policy has been reinforced by academic research into the Middle East that is itself informed by Orientalist assumptions and collects information to fill out a preexisting image. (Readers may want to consult the references to "Orientalists" in the selection from Macaulay printed earlier in this volume.) Understandably, many modern Orientalist scholars were outraged by his critique and attacked him bitterly; some, however, felt that he had provided a corrective lens for research already in place. His description of the way that a cultural site (in this instance, the West) tends to domesticate images of other regions in accord with its own needs and anxieties has become fundamental to modern theories of reading and a staple of postcolonial literary and political criticism. It is echoed in critiques of the representation of Africa, India, and Latin America in the popular press and on television, and, of course, in the discussion of Palestine—a discussion to which Said, as a bicultural American writer born in Jerusalem and a member of the Palestine National Council from 1977 to 1991, actively contributed.

Orientalism

From *The Scope of Orientalism*[1]

* * *

Almost from earliest times in Europe the Orient was something more than what was empirically known about it. At least until the early eighteenth century, as R. W. Southern[2] has so elegantly shown, European understanding of one kind of Oriental culture, the Islamic, was ignorant but complex. For certain associations with the East—not quite ignorant, not quite informed—always seem to have gathered around the notion of an Orient. Consider first the demarcation between Orient and West. It already seems bold by the time of the *Iliad*. Two of the most profoundly influential qualities associated with the East appear in Aeschylus's *The Persians*, the earliest Athenian play extant, and in *The Bacchae* of Euripides, the very last one extant.

---

1. Published in 1978.　　2. R. W. Southern, *Western Views of Islam in the Middle Ages* (1962).

Aeschylus portrays the sense of disaster overcoming the Persians when they learn that their armies, led by King Xerxes, have been destroyed by the Greeks. The chorus sings the following ode:

> Now all Asia's land
> Moans in emptiness.
> Xerxes led forth, oh oh!
> Xerxes destroyed, woe woe!
> Xerxes' plans have all miscarried
> In ships of the sea.
> Why did Darius then
> Bring no harm to his men
> When he led them into battle,
> That beloved leader of men from Susa?[3]

What matters here is that Asia speaks through and by virtue of the European imagination, which is depicted as victorious over Asia, that hostile "other" world beyond the seas. To Asia are given the feelings of emptiness, loss, and disaster that seem thereafter to reward Oriental challenges to the West; and also, the lament that in some glorious past Asia fared better, was itself victorious over Europe.

In *The Bacchae*, perhaps the most Asiatic of all the Attic dramas, Dionysus is explicitly connected with his Asian origins and with the strangely threatening excesses of Oriental mysteries. Pentheus,[4] king of Thebes, is destroyed by his mother, Agave, and her fellow bacchantes. Having defied Dionysus by not recognizing either his power or his divinity, Pentheus is thus horribly punished, and the play ends with a general recognition of the eccentric god's terrible power.* * *

The two aspects of the Orient that set it off from the West in this pair of plays will remain essential motifs of European imaginative geography. A line is drawn between two continents. Europe is powerful and articulate; Asia is defeated and distant. Aeschylus *represents* Asia, makes her speak in the person of the aged Persian queen, Xerxes' mother. It is Europe that articulates the Orient; this articulation is the prerogative, not of a puppet master, but of a genuine creator, whose life-giving power represents, animates, constitutes the otherwise silent and dangerous space beyond familiar boundaries. There is an analogy between Aeschylus's orchestra, which contains the Asiatic world as the playwright conceives it, and the learned envelope of Orientalist scholarship, which also will hold in the vast, amorphous Asiatic sprawl for sometimes sympathetic but always dominating scrutiny. Secondly, there is the motif of the Orient as insinuating danger. Rationality is undermined by Eastern excesses, those mysteriously attractive opposites to what seem to be normal values. The difference separating East from West is symbolized by the sternness with which, at first, Pentheus rejects the hysterical bacchantes. When later he himself becomes a bacchant, he is destroyed not so much for having given in to Dionysus as for having incorrectly assessed Dionysus's menace in the first place. The lesson that Euripides intends is

---

3. Administrative capital of the Achaemenid Empire under Darius I (522–486 B.C.E.), father of Xerxes.
4. King of Thebes. In Euripides' *The Bacchae*, he is torn to pieces by the bacchantes for spying on them during their orgies. *Dionysus:* another name for Bacchus (hence *Bacchae*, the female followers of Bacchus). He is the Greek god of wine, ecstasy, and nature, a deity introduced to Greco-Roman religion from Asia Minor.

dramatized by the presence in the play of Cadmus and Tiresias, knowledgeable older men who realize that "sovereignty" alone does not rule men; there
is such a thing as judgment, they say, which means sizing up correctly the
force of alien powers and expertly coming to terms with them. Hereafter
Oriental mysteries will be taken seriously, not least because they challenge
the rational Western mind to new exercises of its enduring ambition and
power.

But one big division, as between West and Orient, leads to other smaller
ones, especially as the normal enterprises of civilization provoke such outgoing activities as travel, conquest, new experiences. In classical Greece and
Rome geographers, historians, public figures like Caesar, orators, and poets
added to the fund of taxonomic lore separating races, regions, nations, and
minds from each other; much of that was self-serving, and existed to prove
that Romans and Greeks were superior to other kinds of people. But concern
with the Orient had its own tradition of classification and hierarchy. From
at least the second century B.C. on, it was lost on no traveler or eastward-
looking and ambitious Western potentate that Herodotus—historian, traveler, inexhaustibly curious chronicler—and Alexander[5]—king warrior,
scientific conqueror—had been in the Orient before. The Orient was therefore subdivided into realms previously known, visited, conquered, by Herodotus and Alexander as well as their epigones, and those realms not previously
known, visited, conquered. Christianity completed the setting up of main
intra-Oriental spheres: there was a Near Orient and a Far Orient, a familiar
Orient, which René Grousset calls "l'empire du Levant,"[6] and a novel Orient.
The Orient therefore alternated in the mind's geography between being an
Old World to which one returned, as to Eden or Paradise, there to set up a
new version of the old, and being a wholly new place to which one came as
Columbus came to America, in order to set up a New World (although,
ironically, Columbus himself thought that he discovered a new part of the
Old World). Certainly neither of these Orients was purely one thing or the
other: it is their vacillations, their tempting suggestiveness, their capacity for
entertaining and confusing the mind, that are interesting.

Consider how the Orient, and in particular the Near Orient, became
known in the West as its great complementary opposite since antiquity.
There were the Bible and the rise of Christianity; there were travelers like
Marco Polo who charted the trade routes and patterned a regulated system
of commercial exchange, and after him Lodovico di Varthema and Pietro
della Valle; there were fabulists like Mandeville,[7] there were the redoubtable
conquering Eastern movements, principally Islam, of course; there were the
militant pilgrims, chiefly the Crusaders. Altogether an internally structured
archive is built up from the literature that belongs to these experiences. Out

---

5. I.e., Alexander the Great, king of Macedonia (336–323 B.C.E.), who conquered the Persian Empire and
invaded India. *Herodotus:* the first great Western historian (ca. 483–430/420 B.C.E.), a Greek born in Asia
Minor and author of the *History of the Greco-Persian Wars.*   6. *The Empire of the Levant: History of the
Oriental Question* (1946), by the French Orientalist historian René Grousset (1885–1952). The Levant is
the coastal countries, from Egypt to Turkey, in the eastern Mediterranean.   7. Sir John Mandeville was
the author of *The Voyage and Travel of Sir John Mandeville, Knight* (1356–57), a group of tales from actual
world travelers as edited by a purported English knight who added his own adventures. *Marco Polo:* Polo
(1254–1324), Italian merchant explorer and author of the *Travels of Marco Polo,* spent seventeen years in
China at the court of Kublai Khan. *Lodovico di Varthema:* Italian traveler (ca. 1465–1517) who wrote a
widely read account of his experiences in and observations of the Middle East and Asia. *Pietro della Valle*
(1586–1652) was the Italian discoverer of the ruins of ancient Babylon, sixty miles south of Baghdad. He
brought back specimens of cuneiform writing to Europe.

of this comes a restricted number of typical encapsulations: the journey, the history, the fable, the stereotype, the polemical confrontation. These are the lenses through which the Orient is experienced, and they shape the language, perception, and form of the encounter between East and West. What gives the immense number of encounters some unity, however, is the vacillation I was speaking about earlier. Something patently foreign and distant acquires, for one reason or another, a status more rather than less familiar. One tends to stop judging things either as completely novel or as completely well known; a new median category emerges, a category that allows one to see new things, things seen for the first time, as versions of a previously known thing. In essence such a category is not so much a way of receiving new information as it is a method of controlling what seems to be a threat to some established view of things. If the mind must suddenly deal with what it takes to be a radically new form of life—as Islam appeared to Europe in the early Middle Ages—the response on the whole is conservative and defensive. Islam is judged to be a fraudulent new version of some previous experience, in this case Christianity. The threat is muted, familiar values impose themselves, and in the end the mind reduces the pressure upon it by accommodating things to itself as either "original" or "repetitious." Islam thereafter is "handled": its novelty and its suggestiveness are brought under control so that relatively nuanced discriminations are now made that would have been impossible had the raw novelty of Islam been left unattended. The Orient at large, therefore, vacillates between the West's contempt for what is familiar and its shivers of delight in—or fear of—novelty.

Yet where Islam was concerned, European fear, if not always respect, was in order. After Mohammed's death in 632, the military and later the cultural and religious hegemony of Islam grew enormously. First Persia, Syria, and Egypt, then Turkey, then North Africa fell to the Muslim armies; in the eighth and ninth centuries Spain, Sicily, and parts of France were conquered. By the thirteenth and fourteenth centuries Islam ruled as far east as India, Indonesia, and China. And to this extraordinary assault Europe could respond with very little except fear and a kind of awe. Christian authors witnessing the Islamic conquests had scant interest in the learning, high culture, and frequent magnificence of the Muslims, who were, as Gibbon[8] said, "coeval with the darkest and most slothful period of European annals." (But with some satisfaction he added, "since the sum of science has risen in the West, it should seem that the Oriental studies have languished and declined.") What Christians typically felt about the Eastern armies was that they had "all the appearance of a swarm of bees, but with a heavy hand . . . they devastated everything": so wrote Erchembert, a cleric in Monte Cassino in the eleventh century.[9]

Not for nothing did Islam come to symbolize terror, devastation, the demonic, hordes of hated barbarians. For Europe, Islam was a lasting trauma. Until the end of the seventeenth century the "Ottoman peril" lurked alongside Europe to represent for the whole of Christian civilization a constant danger, and in time European civilization incorporated that peril and

---

8. British historian Edward Gibbon (1737–1794), author of the monumental *The History of the Decline and Fall of the Roman Empire* (1776–88), from which the following citation is taken.   9. Actually, 9th century. Erchembert continued an earlier *History of the Lombards* to 889.

its lore, its great events, figures, virtues, and vices, as something woven into the fabric of life. In Renaissance England alone, as Samuel Chew recounts in his classic study *The Crescent and the Rose*, "a man of average education and intelligence" had at his fingertips, and could watch on the London stage, a relatively large number of detailed events in the history of Ottoman Islam and its encroachments upon Christian Europe.[1] The point is that what remained current about Islam was some necessarily diminished version of those great dangerous forces that it symbolized for Europe. Like Walter Scott's[2] Saracens, the European representation of the Muslim, Ottoman, or Arab was always a way of controlling the redoubtable Orient, and to a certain extent the same is true of the methods of contemporary learned Orientalists, whose subject is not so much the East itself as the East made known, and therefore less fearsome, to the Western reading public.

There is nothing especially controversial or reprehensible about such domestications of the exotic; they take place between all cultures, certainly, and between all men. My point, however, is to emphasize the truth that the Orientalist, as much as anyone in the European West who thought about or experienced the Orient, performed this kind of mental operation. But what is more important still is the limited vocabulary and imagery that impose themselves as a consequence. The reception of Islam in the West is a perfect case in point, and has been admirably studied by Norman Daniel. One constraint acting upon Christian thinkers who tried to understand Islam was an analogical one; since Christ is the basis of Christian faith, it was assumed— quite incorrectly—that Mohammed was to Islam as Christ was to Christianity. Hence the polemic name "Mohammedanism" given to Islam, and the automatic epithet "imposter" applied to Mohammed. Out of such and many other misconceptions "there formed a circle which was never broken by imaginative exteriorisation. . . . The Christian concept of Islam was integral and self-sufficient."[3] Islam became an image—the word is Daniel's but it seems to me to have remarkable implications for Orientalism in general— whose function was not so much to represent Islam in itself as to represent it for the medieval Christian.

* * *Our initial description of Orientalism as a learned field now acquires a new concreteness. A field is often an enclosed space. The idea of representation is a theatrical one: the Orient is the stage on which the whole East is confined. On this stage will appear figures whose role it is to represent the larger whole from which they emanate. The Orient then seems to be, not an unlimited extension beyond the familiar European world, but rather a closed field, a theatrical stage affixed to Europe. An Orientalist is but the particular specialist in knowledge for which Europe at large is responsible, in the way that an audience is historically and culturally responsible for (and responsive to) dramas technically put together by the dramatist. In the depths of this Oriental stage stands a prodigious cultural repertoire whose individual items evoke a fabulously rich world: the Sphinx, Cleopatra, Eden, Troy, Sodom and Gomorrah, Astarte, Isis and Osiris, Sheba, Babylon, the Genii, the Magi,

1. Samuel C. Chew, *The Crescent and the Rose: Islam and England during the Renaissance* (1937).
2. Sir Walter Scott (1771–1832). English historical novelist, author of *The Talisman* (1825), set in Palestine during the Crusades.   3. Citing Norman Daniel, *Islam and the West: The Making of an Image* (1960).

Nineveh, Prester John, Mahomet,[4] and dozens more; settings, in some cases names only, half-imagined, half-known; monsters, devils, heroes; terrors, pleasures, desires. The European imagination was nourished extensively from this repertoire: between the Middle Ages and the eighteenth century such major authors as Ariosto, Milton, Marlowe, Tasso, Shakespeare, Cervantes, and the authors of the *Chanson de Roland* and the *Poema del Cid*[5] drew on the Orient's riches for their productions, in ways that sharpened the outlines of imagery, ideas, and figures populating it. In addition, a great deal of what was considered learned Orientalist scholarship in Europe pressed ideological myths into service, even as knowledge seemed genuinely to be advancing.

* * * The Orientalist stage, as I have been calling it, becomes a system of moral and epistemological rigor. As a discipline representing institutionalized Western knowledge of the Orient, Orientalism thus comes to exert a three-way force, on the Orient, on the Orientalist, and on the Western "consumer" of Orientalism. It would be wrong, I think, to underestimate the strength of the three-way relationship thus established. For the Orient ("out there" towards the East) is corrected, even penalized, for lying outside the boundaries of European society, "our" world; the Orient is thus *Orientalized,* a process that not only marks the Orient as the province of the Orientalist but also forces the uninitiated Western reader to accept Orientalist codifications (like d'Herbelot's alphabetized *Bibliothèque*)[6] as the *true* Orient. Truth, in short, becomes a function of learned judgment, not of the material itself, which in time seems to owe even its existence to the Orientalist.

This whole didactic process is neither difficult to understand nor difficult to explain. One ought again to remember that all cultures impose corrections upon raw reality, changing it from free-floating objects into units of knowledge. The problem is not that conversion takes place. It is perfectly natural for the human mind to resist the assault on it of untreated strangeness; therefore cultures have always been inclined to impose complete transformations on other cultures, receiving these other cultures not as they are but as, for the benefit of the receiver, they ought to be. To the Westerner, however, the Oriental was always *like* some aspect of the West; to some of the German Romantics, for example, Indian religion was essentially an Oriental

---

4. I.e., Muhammad (ca. 570–632 C.E.), founder of Islam. *Sphinx:* a colossal stone statue of a recumbent winged lion with a human head, near the pyramids of El Giza in Egypt (ca. 2575–ca. 2465 B.C.E.). *Cleopatra:* i.e., Cleopatra VII (69–30 B.C.E.), queen of Egypt and the last of the Ptolemy rulers. *Eden:* i.e., the Garden of Eden in Genesis (Hebrew Bible). *Troy:* or *Ilium,* ancient city in Asia Minor and the site of Homer's *Iliad.* *Sodom and Gomorrah:* sinful cities in the Hebrew Bible (Genesis 19.1–24), destroyed by God. *Astarte:* goddess of war and sexual love in the ancient Middle East. *Isis and Osiris:* gods of ancient Egypt. *Sheba:* rich kingdom in pre-Islamic southern Arabia, mentioned in the Hebrew Bible. *Babylon:* ancient capital of the Chaldean Empire. *Genii:* guardian spirits. *Magi:* noble pilgrims from the East who, according to the New Testament (Matthew 2.1–12), came to pay homage to the infant Jesus. *Nineveh:* the oldest city of the ancient Assyrian Empire. *Prester John:* legendary Christian ruler of the East, supposedly a descendant of the Magi. He was rumored in the 12th century to be ready to aid the Crusaders. 5. *The Song of the Cid* [Lord] is a 12th-century Spanish epic poem describing the life of Rodrigo Díaz de Vivar (1043–1099), a military leader who became Spain's national hero. Renaissance authors Ludovico Ariosto (1474–1533), John Milton (1608–1674), William Shakespeare (1564–1616), and Miguel de Cervantes Saavedra (1547–1616) are all represented in the first volume of this anthology, as is the medieval French *Song of Roland.* Marlowe: i.e., Christopher Marlowe (1564–1593), Elizabethan poet and dramatist. *Tasso:* i.e., Torquato Tasso (1544–1595), Italian author of the epic poem *Jerusalem Delivered* (1581), set during the First Crusade. 6. I.e., *Oriental Library; or, Universal Dictionary, Containing Everything That Has to Do with Knowledge of the Peoples of the Orient. Their History and Authentic Traditions,* by Barthélemy d'Herbelot de Molainville (1625–1695). It was published posthumously in 1697 with a preface by Antoine Galland, translator of *The Thousand and One Nights* (1704–17).

version of Germano-Christian pantheism. Yet the Orientalist makes it his work to be always converting the Orient from something into something else: he does this for himself, for the sake of his culture, in some cases for what he believes is the sake of the Oriental. This process of conversion is a disciplined one: it is taught, it has its own societies, periodicals, traditions, vocabulary, rhetoric, all in basic ways connected to and supplied by the prevailing cultural and political norms of the West. And * * * it tends to become more rather than less total in what it tries to do, so much so that as one surveys Orientalism in the nineteenth and twentieth centuries the overriding impression is of Orientalism's insensitive schematization of the entire Orient.

*　　*　　*

TRINH T. MINH-HA
born 1952

Much in demand as a speaker on "Third World" and "Women's" issues, the Vietnamese filmmaker and essayist Trinh T. Minh-ha questions the usefulness of both terms. Like Audre Lorde, she is suspicious of categories that can be used simply to set aside groups of people and cut short further discussion of difference. Categories always exist in context, she reminds us, and contexts are part of historical change: *Third World* arose in a particularly political and economic perspective, evolved over time, and is now situated in a very different relation to the *First World*—which itself is no longer the same. Trinh is also a feminist whose films *Reassemblage* (1982), *Surname Viet, Given Name Nam* (1989), and *When the Moon Waxes Red* (1989) describe differing cultural images of feminine identity. She rejects essentialized images of women and argues that identity, whether gendered or cultural, is multi-oriented and always in process: it cannot be reduced to fixed terms.

Trinh explores what it means to be aware of each word as a crossroad of possibilities. The same expression means something different to speakers in different situations, so that it is not merely words but also the speaker's (and listener's) relative position that must be examined. Recalling her own experience as a Vietnamese artist asked to lecture about postcolonial perspectives, she notes that *Third World* has different implications for those who view themselves as Westerners compared to those who view themselves as non-Westerners. Even that reference point is anchored in the West; imagine, she says, a world in which all whites would be designated as non–Afro-Asian. These differences would be a matter of philosophical curiosity were it not for their ultimate effect on global priorities. When I speak, I situate myself in relation to someone else, and it is easiest to project that relationship as one of *self* and *other* across a binary divide of two fixed identities in which my own self is unconsciously privileged as the norm. Thus, Trinh argues, the real issue is one of power relationships: of the self–other discourse that underlies colonialism and patriarchy, and is undermined by further distinctions and connections. In the modern world, even after the disappearance of colonies, the vocabulary and images of the dominant West permeate global culture and continue to influence the way in which people represent themselves.

Trinh illustrates her argument by describing the linguistic and physical control exerted by Western culture during an event that ostensibly celebrates difference: the annual Chinese New Year parade in San Francisco. From the language of tourist guides, advertising the parade in a flurry of Western stereotypes, to the reality of crowds regulated by mounted police and divided into performers and spectators, she sketches out a modern mingling of cultural worlds that is also dominated by continuing patterns of power.

Woman, Native, Other: Writing Postcoloniality and Feminism

From Chapter 3. Difference: "A Special Third World Women Issue"[1]

* * *

THIRD WORLD?

To survive, "Third World" must necessarily have negative *and* positive connotations: negative when viewed in a vertical ranking system—"underdeveloped" compared to over-industrialized, "underprivileged" within the already Second sex[2]—and positive when understood sociopolitically as a subversive, "non-aligned" force. Whether "Third World" sounds negative or positive also depends on *who* uses it. Coming from you Westerners, the word can hardly mean the same as when it comes from Us members of the Third World. Quite predictably, you/we who condemn it most are both we who buy in and they who deny any participation in the bourgeois mentality of the West. For it was in the context of such mentality that "Third World" stood out as a new semantic finding to designate what was known as "the savages" before the Independences. Today, hegemony is much more subtle, much more pernicious than the form of blatant racism once exercised by the colonial West. I/i always find myself asking, in this one-dimensional society, where I/i should draw the line between tracking down the oppressive mechanisms of the system and aiding their spread. "Third World" commonly refers to those states in Africa, Asia and Latin America which called themselves "non-aligned," that is to say, affiliated with neither the Western (capitalist) nor the Eastern (communist) power blocs. Thus, if "Third World" is often rejected for its judged-to-be-derogative connotations, it is not so much because of the hierarchical, first-second-third order implied, as some invariably repeat, but because of the growing threat "Third World" consistently presents to the Western bloc the last few decades. The emergence of repressed voices into the worldwide political arena has already prompted her (Julia Kristeva)[3] to ask: "How will the West greet the awakening of the 'third world' as the Chinese call it? Can we [Westerners] participate, actively and lucidly, in this awakening when the center of the planet is in the process of moving toward the East?"[4] Exploited, looked down upon, and lumped together in a conven-

1. Published in 1989. 2. I.e., women: a reference to Simone de Beauvoir's *The Second Sex* (1949). 3. French poststructuralist theoretician, psychoanalyst, and feminist (b. 1941). Her works in translation include *Desire in Language: A Semiotic Approach to Literature and Art* (1980), *About Chinese Women* (1974), and *Strangers to Ourselves* (1988). 4. From Julia Kristeva, "Woman Can Never Be Defined," trans. Marilyn A. August, in *New French Feminisms: An Anthology* ed. E. Marks and I. de Courtivron (1980), p. 139.

ient term that denies their individualities, a group of "poor" (nations), having once sided with neither of the dominating forces, has slowly learned to turn this denial to the best account. "The Third World to Third World peoples" thus becomes an empowering tool, and one which politically includes all non-whites in their solidarist struggle against all forms of Western dominance. And since "Third World" now refers to more than the geographically and economically determined nations of the "South" (versus "North"), since the term comprises such "developed" countries as Japan and those which have opted for socialist reconstruction of their system (China, Cuba, Ethiopia, Angola, Mozambique) as well as those which have favored a capitalist mode of development (Nigeria, India, Brazil), there no longer exists such a thing as a unified unaligned Third World bloc. Moreover, Third World has moved West (or North, depending on where the dividing line falls) and has expanded so as to include even the remote parts of the First World. What is at stake is not only the hegemony of Western cultures, but also their identities as unified cultures. Third World dwells on diversity; so does First World. This is our strength and our misery. The West is painfully made to realize the existence of a Third World in the First World, and vice versa. The Master is bound to recognize that His Culture is not as homogeneous, as monolithic as He believed it to be. He discovers, with much reluctance, He is just an other among others.

* * *

Should you visit San Francisco one day, be sure to be there sometime in late January or February, for you will be witnessing one of the most spectacular festivals celebrated in America. Chinatown, which until recently was the "wickedest thoroughfare in the States," the taint of "America's dream town," a vice-ridden and overcrowded ghetto where tourists rarely venture, is now the not-to-be-missed tourist attraction, an exotica famed for its packed restaurants, its Oriental delicacies, its glittering souvenir-crammed shops and, above all, its memorable Chinese New Year celebration. Over and over again, the (off-)scene repeats itself as if time no longer changes. How is the parade born? Where and in what circumstances was it invented? "Back home"—whose spirit this parade pretends to perpetuate—did the Chinese celebrate their New Year squeezed up along the sidewalks with several dozen hefty policemen (American and Chinese looking almost alike) on foot, on horseback, and on motor bikes (no Chinese policeman, however, has been seen on horseback or on a motor bike) to guard (what is supposed to be) their parade, shoo them, push them back, or call them to order if they happen to get off the line while watching the procession? What do you think the motives are behind such an ostentatious display of folklore, of arrogance and coercive power (besides the invariable it-is-for-your-own-good answer Order usually provides you with)? For I myself fail to see any sign of "celebration" in this segregated masquerade, where feasters are forcibly divided into actors and spectators, while participation exclusively consists in either exhibiting oneself exotically on the scene or watching the object of exhibition distantly off the scene. Chinese New Year thus takes on a typical dualistic Western face. Preserve the form of the old in the context-content of the new; this is what decoration means. Power arrogates to itself the right to interfere in every mass event that takes place, and the feast no longer belongs to the people, whose joint merrymaking cannot be viewed other than as a potential threat to Power. Tell me, where are those public celebrations described in tourist guides, that "spill onto every street in Chinatown and transform the squares into fairgrounds"?

* * *

SALMAN RUSHDIE
born 1947

"Migrant consciousness," states Salman Rushdie, is now a major part of modern life, challenging and complicating established patterns of nationalist allegiance. The twentieth century's great waves of immigration have meant that large numbers of people are living "in between," adapting to a new cultural tradition while retaining much of the old. As a group, they represent a multilingual, multicultural perspective that embraces diverse ways of life and is potentially more unsettling to fixed views than any move across a physical frontier. Rushdie himself is an example of such a consciousness. Born in India of Pakistani parents, educated in England, a writer of cosmopolitan fiction living in London, he draws on European, Hindu, and Islamic traditions and cannot be limited to any one of them. He is also an example of the dangers attendant on overstepping traditional beliefs: in 1989, the writer was sentenced to death from abroad by an influential Muslim cleric who disapproved of one of his novels. When Iranian Ayatollah Ruhollah Khomeini issued a *fatwa* condemning *The Satanic Verses* for its parody of the prophet Muhammad, he appealed to Muslims everywhere to execute Rushdie and also anyone associated with the novel, an extension that led to the fatal stabbing of Rushdie's Japanese translator. It was a lethal example of the gap between reading literally and reading literature: however offensive the image of Muhammad may have been to strict believers, it appeared in the novel as part of the hallucinations of a suicidal madman.

Rushdie was not new to controversy or to public disapproval of political satire. At the beginning of his career, he left Pakistan when officials there censored both a television script and a magazine article. His first successful novel, *Midnight's Children* (1980), included such an unflattering portrait of India's prime minister Indira Gandhi that she sued, and both Rushdie and his publisher were obliged to issue a public apology. The following novel, *Shame* (1983), used pseudonyms in satirizing the murderous rivalry of Pakistan's leading political families. Nor did Rushdie change his approach during the seven years when he was in hiding from the *fatwa* and protected by the British Secret Service. His next novel, *The Moor's Last Sigh* (1995), often taken as an allegory of the history of India, enraged many Hindus with its satirical picture of an extreme right-wing revivalist leader.

Throughout, Rushdie has believed that writers have an obligation to take up major issues and enter into public debate. He himself has been an active political journalist, from his attacks on Tory government policies in England during the 1980s to *The Jaguar Smile: A Nicaraguan Journey* (1987) and the essays collected in *Imaginary Homelands* (1991) and *Step across This Line* (2002). The writer seems not to have foreseen, however, that the line between fact and fiction would be so blurred in the reception of *The Satanic Verses*: that the novel's complex artistic structure would be ignored while the work was evaluated on very different grounds. In essays written after the shock of the *fatwa*, including the title essay in *Step across This Line*, Rushdie asks if artistic freedom is possible in modern society and explores the permeable borders between imagination and reality in everyday experience.

The reference point for his exploration is the terrorist attack on the World Trade Center towers on September 11, 2001, which crossed the "invisible boundary between the imaginable and the unimaginable." How can art help us *understand* what happened; how does it permit one to grasp the human and moral dimensions of this crime without retreating into blind anger and dismay? Our first need, says Rushdie, is to recognize that the attack was a human act, planned and carried out by human beings, and is, therefore, comprehensible on some level. It was in fact a "monstrous act of the imagination," a political message spelled out on a large stage for the world to read. The planners were individuals with their own personalities and a shared historical context; they, and not some mystical purpose, bear the responsibility for what they did. Using an abstract term such as "evil" to describe them actually impedes understanding, for it dehistoricizes their attack and lifts it out of the realm of human affairs. Art, by contrast (and Rushdie uses examples from Shakespeare), repositions "unimaginable" events in a human context and gives us—as human beings—the insight to deal with them. Herein lies art's value and the reason that artistic expression must not be limited by preexisting ideas or censored by the official Thought Policemen whose mental horizons are already set. Rushdie's concern at today's shrinking acceptance of intellectual and artistic freedom reaches beyond anxiety for his own situation; if we dehumanize our opponents, he suggests, we diminish and dehumanize ourselves.

From Step across This Line[1]

* * *

The crossing of borders, of language, geography, and culture, the examination of the permeable frontier between the universe of things and deeds and the universe of the imagination; the lowering of the intolerable frontiers created by the world's many different kinds of Thought Policemen: these matters have been at the heart of the literary project that was given to me by the circumstances of my life, rather than chosen by me for intellectual or "artistic" reasons. Born into one language, Urdu, I've made my life and work in another. Anyone who has crossed a language frontier will readily understand that such a journey involves a form of shape-shifting or self-translation. The change of language changes us. All languages permit slightly varying forms of thought, imagination, and play. I find my tongue doing slightly different things with Urdu than I do "with," to borrow the title of a story by Hanif Kureishi, "your tongue down my throat."[2]

The greatest writer ever to make a successful journey across the language frontier, Vladimir Nabokov,[3] enumerated, in his "Note on Translation," the "three grades of evil [that] can be discerned in the strange world of verbal transmigration." He was talking about the translation of books and poems, but when as a young writer I was thinking about how to "translate" the great subject of India into English, how to allow India itself to perform the act of "verbal transmigration," the Nabokovian "grades of evil" seemed to apply.

"The first, and lesser one, comprises obvious errors due to ignorance or misguided knowledge," Nabokov wrote. "This is mere human frailty and thus

1. Published in 2002. *Step across This Line* collects the Tanner Lectures on Human Values, given at Yale University in 2002.   2. Hanif Kureishi (b. 1954), of British and Pakistani descent, is a well-known British novelist, film director, and writer for stage and screen.   3. Russian-born American novelist and critic (1899–1977), a multilingual writer and master of intricately patterned English prose; his best-known novel is *Lolita* (1955).

excusable." Western works of art that dealt with India were riddled with such mistakes. To name just two: the scene in David Lean's film of *A Passage to India*[4] in which he makes Dr. Aziz leap onto Fielding's bed and cross his legs *while keeping his shoes on,* a solecism that would make any Indian wince; and the even more unintentionally hilarious scene in which Alec Guinness, as Godbole, sits by the edge of the sacred tank in a Hindu temple *and dangles his feet in the water.*

"The next step to Hell," Nabokov says, "is taken by the translator who skips words or passages that he does not bother to understand or that might seem obscure or obscene to vaguely imagined readers." For a long time, or so I felt, almost the whole of the multifarious Indian reality was "skipped" in this way by writers who were uninterested in anything except Western experiences of India—English girls falling for maharajas, or being assaulted, or not being assaulted, by non-maharajas, in nocturnal gardens, or mysteriously echoing caves—written up in a coolly classical Western manner. But of course most experiences of India are Indian experiences of it, and if there is one thing India is not, it is cool and classical. India is hot and vulgar, I thought, and it needed a literary "translation" in keeping with its true nature.

The third and worst crime of translation, in Nabokov's opinion, was that of the translator who sought to improve on the original, "vilely beautifying" it "in such a fashion as to conform to the notions and prejudices of a given public." The exoticization of India, its "vile beautification," is what Indians have disliked most. Now, at last, this kind of fake glamorizing is coming to an end, and the India of elephants, tigers, peacocks, emeralds, and dancing girls is being laid to rest. A generation of gifted Indian writers in English is bringing into English their many different versions of the Indian reality, and these many versions, taken together, are beginning to add up to something that one might call the truth.

In dreams begin responsibilities. The way we see the world affects the world we see. As our ideas of female beauty change, so we see different sorts of women as beautiful. As our ideas of healthy living change, so we begin to look at the things we eat differently. Our dreams of our own and our children's future shape the everyday judgments we make, about work, about people, about the world that either enables or obstructs those dreams. Daily life in the real world is also an imagined life. The creatures of our imagination crawl out from our heads, cross the frontier between dream and reality, between shadow and act, and become actual.

Imagination's monsters do the same thing. The attack on the World Trade Center was essentially a monstrous act of the imagination, intended to act upon all our imaginations, to shape our own imaginings of the future. It was an iconoclastic act, in which the defining icons of the modern, the world-shrinking airplanes and those soaring secular cathedrals, the tall buildings, were rammed into each other in order to send a message: that the modern world itself was the enemy, and would be destroyed. It may seem unimaginable to us, but to those who perpetrated this crime, the deaths of many thousands of innocent people were a side issue. Murder was not the point. The creation of a meaning was the point. The terrorists of September 11, and the planners of that day's events, behaved like perverted, but in another way brilliantly transgressive, performance artists: hideously innovative,

---

4. Lean's film (1984) is based on E. M. Forster's 1924 novel of the same name.

shockingly successful, using a low-tech attack to strike at the very heart of our high-tech world. In dreams begin responsibilities, too.

I am trying to talk about literature and ideas, but you see that I keep being dragged back to catastrophe. Like every writer in the world, I am trying to find a way of writing after September 11, 2001, a day that has become something like a borderline. Not only because the attacks were a kind of invasion but because we all crossed a frontier that day, an invisible boundary between the imaginable and the unimaginable, and it turned out to be the unimaginable that was real. On the other side of that frontier, we find ourselves facing a moral problem: how should a civilized society—in which, as in all civilizations, there are limits, things we will not do, or allow to be done in our name, because we consider them beyond the pale, unacceptable—respond to an attack by people for whom there are no limits at all, people who will, quite literally, do anything—blow off their own feet, or tilt the wings of an airplane just before it hits a tower, so that it takes out the maximum number of floors?

> The evil that men to do lives after them,
> the good is oft interred with their bones.[5]

It is not surprising that the word "evil" has been used a great deal these past months; perhaps too often. The terrorists become "the evildoers," their leader became "the evil one," and now comes the discovery of that unusual phenomenon, an "axis of evil," on which the president of the United States is threatening to make war. It's an oddly contradictory word, "evil," too freighted with absolute meaning to be an appropriate description of the messy relativity of actuality, too debased by over-use to mean as much as it should. Thus the comedy web site SatireWire.com reveals that.

> bitter after being snubbed for membership in the Axis of Evil, Libya, China, and Syria today announced that they had formed the Axis of Just as Evil, which they said would be way eviler than that stupid Iran-Iraq-North Korea axis. Cuba, Sudan, and Serbia said they had formed the Axis of Somewhat Evil, forcing Somalia to join with Uganda and Myanmar in the Axis of Occasionally Evil, while Bulgaria, Indonesia, and Russia established the Axis of Not So Much Evil Really as Just Generally Disagreeable. Sierra Leone, El Salvador, and Rwanda applied to be called the Axis of Countries That Aren't the Worst but Certainly Won't Be Asked to Host the Olympics; Canada, Mexico, and Australia formed the Axis of Nations That Are Actually Quite Nice but Secretly Have Nasty Thoughts About America, while Spain, Scotland, and New Zealand established the Axis of Countries That Sometimes Ask Sheep to Wear Lipstick.
>
> "That's not a threat, really, just something we like to do," said Scottish Executive First Minister Jack McConnell.

I wish, myself that the president had not promised to "rid the world of evil"—that's a big project, a war he probably can't win. "Evil" is a term that can obscure as well as clarify. For me, the greatest difficulty with it is that it dehistoricizes these events, depoliticizes, and even depersonalizes them. If evil is the devil's work, and in this deeply religious administration one must assume that many people in high places think it is, then that, to my unbe-

---

5. Mark Antony speaks in Shakespeare's *Julius Caesar* 3.2.

liever's way of thinking, actually lets the terrorists off the hook. If evil is external to us, a force working upon us from outside ourselves, then our moral responsibility for its effects is diminished.

The most attractive thing about the Shakespearean attitude to evil is its emphasis on human, not divine, responsibility for it. "The evil *that men do*," Mark Antony says, and that's the only kind that interests Shakespeare. The conspirators in *Julius Caesar* are obsessed with omens and auguries. "Never till now," says Casca,

> Did I go through a tempest dropping first.
> Either there is a civil strife in heaven,
> Or else the world, too saucy with the gods,
> Incenses them to send destruction.

And that's not all.

> Men all in fire walk up and down the streets.
> And yesterday the bird of night did sit,
> Even at noon-day, upon the market-place,
> Hooting and shrieking. When these prodigies
> Do so conjointly meet, let not men say
> "These are their reasons, they are natural";
> For, I believe, they are portentous things
> Unto the climate that they point upon.

The conspirators talk themselves into believing that the omens and portents, the signs from the gods, justify, even necessitate, their crime. To read the transcript of the so-called smoking-gun bin Laden videotape, the notorious "giggling" video in which he laughs about his crimes and the deaths of his own men, is to be struck by the similarities between the mind-set of Al-Qaida and that of Caesar's murderers. The tape is full of talk about prophetic dreams and visions. Bin Laden himself says: "Abu al-Hasan al-Masri told me a year ago: 'I saw in a dream, we were playing a soccer game against the Americans. When our team showed up in the field, they were all pilots!' He said the game went on and we defeated them. So that was a good omen for us." Or, again: "This brother came close and told me that he saw, in a dream, a tall building in America. . . . I was worried that maybe the secret would be revealed if everyone starts seeing it in their dream." At this point, on the tape, another person's voice is heard recounting yet another dream about two planes hitting a big building.

Dreams and omens are murderers' exculpations. Shakespeare knew better. It is again Casca, portent-ridden Casca, who speaks: "The fault, dear Brutus, lies not in the stars, / but in ourselves, that we are underlings." He's talking about the need for a coup. But after the assassination, we forget the final clause; it is the first part of the couplet, the part about responsibility for one's own actions, whose truth we are made to feel. "The fault, dear Brutus, lies not in the stars, / but in ourselves." It is Shakespeare's genius to put in the mouth of an assassin the very thought that will damn him afterward. Shakespeare doesn't believe in the devil's work. In the last scene of *Othello*, when the Moor finally learns how he has been duped by Iago, he says, "I look down towards his feet; but that's a fable." No cloven hoofs protrude from the villain's hose. "If that thou be'st a devil, I cannot kill thee." The world is real. There are no demons. Men are demonic enough.

The evil that men do, in Shakespeare, is always a kind of excess. It has to do with the denial of limits, the willingness to cross any moral frontier. Goneril and Regan, Lady Macbeth, Iago: for them, the end justifies everything. *By any means necessary*. Whereas Hamlet is the opposite: a man so beset by moral qualms that it takes him an eternity to act. The great question of action and the frontiers of action—how far can we go? How far is too far, how far is not far enough?—is at the heart of Shakespeare's world; also, now, of ours.

The problem of limits is made awkward for artists and writers, including myself, by our own adherence to, and insistence upon, a no-limits position in our own work. The frontierlessness of art has been and remains our heady ideology. The concept of transgressive art is so widely accepted—"if it isn't transgressive, it isn't underground"—as to constitute, in the eyes of conservative critics, a new orthodoxy. Once the new was shocking not because it set out to shock but because it set out to be new. Now, all too often, the shock *is* the new; and shock, in our jaded culture, wears off easily. Like the children in the Disney movie *Monsters, Inc.*, we don't scare as easily as we used to. So the artist who seeks to shock must try harder and harder, go further and further, and this escalation may now have become the worst kind of artistic self-indulgence. And now, in the aftermath of horror, of the iconoclastically transgressive image-making of the terrorists, do artists and writers still have the right to insist on the supreme, unfettered freedoms of art? Is it time, instead of endlessly pushing the envelope, stepping into forbidden territory, and generally causing trouble, to start discovering what frontiers might be necessary to art, rather than an affront to it?

The British writer (and lawyer) Anthony Julius addresses such questions in a new book, *Transgressions: The Offences of Art*. Dealing mainly, but not only, with the visual arts, he valuably reminds us of the word's arrival in English in the sixteenth century, "freighted with negative scriptural overtones," and its rapid acquisition of other layers of meaning: "rule-breaking, including the violation of principles, conventions, pieties, or taboos; the giving of serious offence; and the exceeding, erasing or disordering of physical or conceptual boundaries." He examines the transgressive art of Edouard Manet in the 1860s; in *Olympia*, a picture of a whore to which Manet gave a name often used by the whores of the period, he visited the frontier between art and "pornography"—which literally means "whore-painting," and is another new word hailing from the same epoch—crossing the boundaries between the nude (an aesthetic, unerotic idea) and the naked woman, gazing out of the picture with frankly erotic intent. In *Dead Christ with Angels*, Manet questioned the resurrection, and the painting caused great offense. Even *Le Déjeuner sur l'herbe* was accused of "transgressing the laws both of perspective and morality." Now that time has installed Manet and his great contemporaries as the art world's blue-chip masterworkers, we have one answer to those who would reimpose limits on art: which is, that one age's pornography is another's masterpiece. In 1857, after all, *Madame Bovary* so outraged conventional, decent people that Flaubert was prosecuted for writing it. Guardians of the frontiers of public morality should always beware, lest history make them look like fools.

Julius rightly credits the twentieth-century French writer Georges Bataille with the formulation of much of our modern idea of the transgressive. It is interesting, however, that Bataille believed that the breaking of taboos was both a necessity and a "reinscription" of the violated border. "Transgressions suspend taboos without suppressing them." Julia Kristeva[6] amplifies this: "The issue of ethics crops up wherever a code must be shattered in order to give way to the free play of negativity, need, desire, pleasure, and jouissance, before being put together again, although temporarily." Here, then, is a second possible answer to the would-be censors in our new, more timorous age: artworks, unlike terrorists, change nothing.

On the five defenses of art, Julius is excellent: the First Amendment defense; the "aesthetic alibi"—"art is a privileged zone in which the otherwise unsayable can be said"; the "estrangement defence" (it is the job of art . . . to alienate us from our preconceptions, by making the familiar strange and the unquestioned problematic); the "canonic defence" (works of art exist in a tradition of such works and must be judged and understood in relation to that tradition); and the "formalist defence" (that art has its own distinct mode of existence and is not to be confused with cognate but distinct works of the imagination, such as propaganda and polemic). As someone who has had some experience of transgression and its consequences, I have at different times employed all these defenses, as Julius is kind enough to note. He concludes, however, that "the aesthetic potential of the transgressive has been exhausted." In this I am not sure he is right.

Even before the attacks on America, I was concerned that, in Britain and Europe as well as America, the pressures on artistic and even intellectual freedoms were growing—that cautious, conservative political and institutional forces were gaining the upper hand, and that many social groups were deliberately fostering a new, short-fuse culture of easy offendedness, so that less and less was becoming sayable all the time, and more and more kinds of speech were being categorized as transgressive. Outside the Western world—across the Arab world, in many African countries, in Iran, China, North Korea, and elsewhere—writers and intellectuals are everywhere under attack, and more and more of them are being forced into exile. If it was important to resist this cultural closing-in before 9/11, it's twice as important now. The freedoms of art and the intellect are closely related to the general freedoms of society as a whole. The struggle for artistic freedom serves to crystallize the larger question that we were all asked when the planes hit the buildings: how should we live now? How uncivilized are we going to allow our own world to become in response to so barbaric an assault?

We are living, I believe, in a frontier time, one of the great hinge periods in human history, in which great changes are coming about at great speed. On the plus side, the end of the Cold War, the revolution in communications technology, great scientific achievements such as the completion of the Human Genome Project; in the minus column, a new kind of war against new kinds of enemies fighting with terrible new weapons. We will all be judged by how we handle ourselves in this time. What will be the spirit of this frontier? Will we give the enemy the satisfaction of changing ourselves into something like his hate-filled, illiberal mirror-image, or will we, as the guardians of the modern world, as the custodians of freedom and the occupants of the privileged lands of plenty, go on trying to increase freedom and decrease injustice? Will we become the suits of armor our fear makes us put on, or will we continue to be ourselves? The frontier both shapes our character and tests our mettle. I hope we pass the test.

6. A French poststructuralist theoretician and psychoanalyst (b. 1941), author of *Desire in Language: A Semiotic Approach to Literature and Art* (1980) and other works.

CHINUA ACHEBE
born 1930

The best-known African writer today is the Nigerian Chinua Achebe, whose first novel, *Things Fall Apart,* exploded the colonialist image of Africans as childlike people living in a primitive society. Achebe's novels, stories, poetry, and essays have made him a respected and prophetic figure in Africa. In Western countries, where he has traveled, taught, and lectured widely, he is admired as a major writer who has given an entirely new direction to the English-language novel. Achebe has created not only the African postcolonial novel with its new themes and characters but also a complex narrative point of view that questions cultural images—including its own—with a subtle irony and compassion born from bicultural experience. His vantage point is different from that of Doris Lessing or Albert Camus, two authors whose work is also concerned with African experience: Achebe writes, as he says, "from the inside." For him, as for many other writers in this volume, literature is important because it liberates the human imagination; it "begins as an adventure in self-discovery and ends in wisdom and human conscience."

Chinua Achebe was born in Ogidi, an Igbo-speaking town of Eastern Nigeria, on November 16, 1930. He was the fifth of six children in the family of Isaiah Okafor Achebe, a teacher for the Church Missionary Society, and his wife, Janet. Achebe's parents christened him Albert after Prince Albert, husband of Queen Victoria. When he entered the university, the author rejected his British name in favor of his indigenous name, Chinua, which abbreviates Chinualumogu, or "My spirit come fight for me." Achebe's novels offer a picture of Igbo society, with its fierce egalitarianism and "town meeting" debates. Two cultures coexisted in Ogidi: on the one hand, African social customs and traditional religion, and, on the other, British colonial authority and Christianity. Instead of being torn between the two, Achebe found himself curious about both ways of life and fascinated with the dual perspective that came from living "at the crossroads of cultures."

He attended Church schools in Ogidi, where instruction was carried out in English after the first two years. Achebe read the various books in his father's library, most of them primers or Church-related, but he also listened eagerly to his mother and sister when they told traditional Igbo stories. Entering a prestigious government college (secondary school) in Umuahia, he immediately took advantage of its well-stocked library. Achebe later commented on the crucial importance of books in creating writers and committed readers, noting that private secondary schools had few, if any, books and that almost all the first generation of Nigerian writers—including himself and Wole Soyinka (born 1934)—had gone to a government college.

After graduating in 1948, Achebe entered University College, Ibadan, on a scholarship to study medicine. In the following year he changed to a program in liberal arts that combined English, history, and religious studies. Research in the last two fields deepened his knowledge of Nigerian history and culture; the assigned literary texts, however, brought into sharp focus the distorted image of African culture offered by British colonial literature. Reading Joyce Cary's *Mister Johnson* (1939), a novel recommended for its depiction of life in Nigeria, he was shocked to find Nigerians described as violent savages with passionate instincts and simple minds: "and so I thought if this was famous, then perhaps someone ought to try and look at this from the inside." He began writing while at the university, contributing articles and sketches to several campus papers and publishing four stories in the *University Herald,* a magazine whose editor he became in his third year.

Upon receiving his B.A. in 1953, Achebe joined the Nigerian Broadcasting Service, working in the Talks Section and traveling to London in 1956 to attend the British Broadcasting Corporation Staff School. Promotions came quickly; he was named head of the Talks Section in 1957, controller of the Eastern Region Stations in 1959, and in 1961 director of External Services in charge of the Voice of Nigeria. The radio position was more than a merely administrative post, for Achebe and his colleagues were working to create a sense of shared national identity through broadcasting national news and information about Nigerian culture. Ever since the end of World War II, Nigeria had been torn by intellectual and political rivalries that overlaid the common struggle for independence (achieved in 1960). The three major ethnolinguistic groups—Yoruba, Hausa-Fulani, and Igbo (once spelled Ibo)—were increasingly locked in economic and political rivalry at the same time they were fighting to erase the vestiges of British colonial rule. These problems eventually boiled over in the Nigerian Civil War (1967–70). The persistence of political corruption is depicted in *A Man of the People* (1966) and *Anthills of the Savannah* (1987).

Achebe is convinced of the writer's social responsibility, and he draws frequent contrasts between the European "art for art's sake" tradition and an African belief in the indivisibility of art and society. His favorite example is the Owerri Igbo custom of *mbari*, a communal art project in which villagers selected by the priest of the earth goddess Ala live in a forest clearing for a year or more, working under the direction of master artists to prepare a temple of images in the goddess's honor. This creative communal enterprise and its culminating festival are diametrically opposed, he says, to the European custom of secluding art objects in museums or private collections. Instead, *mbari* celebrates art as a cultural process, affirming that "art belongs to all and is a 'function' of society." Achebe's own practice as novelist, poet, essayist, founder and editor of two journals, lecturer, and active representative of African letters exemplifies this commitment to the community.

His first novel, *Things Fall Apart* (1958), was a conscious attempt to counteract the distortions of Cary's *Mister Johnson* by describing the richness and complexity of traditional African society before the colonial and missionary invasion. It was important, Achebe said, to "teach my readers that their past—with all its imperfections—was not one long night of savagery from which the first Europeans acting on God's behalf delivered them." The novel was recognized immediately as an extraordinary work of literature in English. It also became the first classic work of modern African fiction, translated into nine languages, and Achebe became for many readers and writers the teacher of a whole generation. In 1959 he received the Margaret Wrong Memorial Prize, and in 1960—after the publication of a sequel, *No Longer at Ease*—he received the Nigerian National Trophy for literature. His later novels continue to examine the individual and cultural dilemmas of Nigerian society, although their background varies from the traditional religious society of *Arrow of God* (1964) to thinly disguised accounts of contemporary political strife.

Achebe's reputation as the "father of the African novel in English" does not depend solely on his accounts of Nigerian society. In contrast with writers such as Ngugi wa Thiong'o (b. 1938), who insist that the contemporary African writer has a moral obligation to write in one of the tribal languages, Achebe maintains his right to compose in the English he has used since his school days. His literary language is an English skillfully blended with Igbo vocabulary, proverbs, images, and speech patterns to create a new voice embodying the linguistic pluralism of modern African experience. By including standard English, Igbo, and pidgin in different contexts, Achebe demonstrates the existence of a diverse society that is otherwise concealed behind language barriers—a culture, he suggests, that escaped colonial officials who wrote about African character without ever understanding the language. He also thereby acknowledges that his primary African audience is composed of younger, schooled readers who are relatively fluent in English.

It is hard to overestimate the influence of Nigerian politics on Achebe's life after 1966. In January, a military coup d'état led by young Igbo officers overthrew the government; six months later, a second coup led by non-Igbo officers took power.

Ethnic rivalries intensified: thousands of Igbos were killed and driven out of the north. Achebe and his family fled the capital of Lagos when soldiers were sent to find him, and the novelist became a senior research fellow at the University of Nigeria, Nsukka (in Eastern Nigeria). In May 1967 the eastern region, mainly populated by Igbo-speakers, seceded as the new nation of Biafra. From then on until the defeat of Biafra in January 1970, a bloody civil war was waged with high civilian casualties and widespread starvation. Achebe traveled in Europe, North America, and Africa to win support for Biafra, proclaiming that "no government, black or white, has the right to stigmatize and destroy groups of its own citizens without undermining the basis of its own existence." A group of his poems about the war won the Commonwealth Poetry Prize in 1972, the same year that he published a volume of short stories, *Girls at War,* and left Nigeria to take up a three-year position at the University of Massachusetts at Amherst. Returning to Nsukka as professor of literature in 1976, Achebe continued to participate in his country's political life. He published an attack on the corrupt leadership in *The Trouble with Nigeria* (1983) and—drawing on circumstances surrounding a fifth military coup in 1985—produced his fifth novel, *Anthills of the Savannah,* in 1987. Although it reiterates Achebe's familiar indictment of ruthless politicians, alienated intellectuals, and those who accept dictatorship as a route to reform, this novel offers hope for the future through a return to the people and a symbolic child born at the end: a girl child with a boy's name, "May the Path Never Close." Badly hurt in a car accident the year after *Anthills* was published, Achebe slowly recovered and returned to his writing. He currently teaches at Bard College.

A predominant theme in Achebe's novels and essays is the notion of balance or interdependence: balance between earth and sky, individual and community, man and woman, or different perspectives on the same situation. Igbo thought is fundamentally dualistic, the novelist explains: "Wherever Something stands, Something Else will stand beside it. Nothing is absolute." Extremes carry the seeds of destruction. Indeed, destruction follows in Achebe's novels whenever balance is disturbed: when Okonkwo in *Things Fall Apart* represses any signs of "female" softness; when the priest Ezeulu in *Arrow of God* is imprisoned and refuses to authorize the feast of the New Yam, without which his people cannot plant their crops; and when, in later books, the lust for power and possessions blinds Nigerian leaders to the needs of the people.

The fundamental image of this balance is contained in the Igbo concept of *chi,* which recurs throughout Achebe's work. *Chi* is a personal deity, a fragment of the supreme being unique for each individual. A person's *chi,* says Achebe, may be visualized "as his other identity in spirit-land—his *spirit being* complementing his terrestrial *human being.*" It is both all-powerful and subject to persuasion: "When a man says yes his *chi* says yes also," but at the same time "a man does not challenge his *chi* to a wrestling match." *Chi* is simultaneously destiny and an internal commitment that cannot be denied, a religious concept and also a picture of psychic harmony. Both aspects are linked throughout Achebe's novels, beginning with *Things Fall Apart.* In killing Ikemefuna, whom he loves and who calls him father, Okonkwo sins not only against the earth goddess, protector of family relations, but also against his inmost feelings and thus against his *chi.* If Okonkwo's destiny (*chi*) is marked by bad luck, one reason may be that—driven by fear of resembling his father—he struggles to repress part of his personality (*chi*), with predictably ill results. In the final assessment, no one can fully explain *chi:* it is mysteriously uncertain, the element of fate over which we have no real control.

Things Fall Apart is both Okonkwo's tragedy and that of his society. The title (taken from William Butler Yeats's *The Second Coming*) introduces a narrative in which a complex and dignified traditional society disintegrates before foreign invaders who assault its political, economic, and religious institutions. The setting is eastern Nigeria around the turn of the century in the clan of Umuofia, which is composed of nine interrelated villages. One of these villages, Iguedo, is the home of the protagonist Okonkwo, an ambitious and powerful man who is driven by the memory of his father's failure and weakness.

During the first two-thirds of the book, Achebe paints the picture of a rich and coherent society, establishing an image of traditional African culture into which the final chapters' missionaries, court messengers, and district commissioner intrude as alien and disruptive elements. In sharp contrast to the simplified vision of African life given by European novelists Joyce Cary, Joseph Conrad, or Graham Greene, he explores the complex feelings and interpersonal relationships of diverse villagers seen as men, women, parents, children, friends, neighbors, or priests of the local deities. The intricate patterns of Umuofia's economic and social customs also emerge, belying European images of African "primitive" simplicity. No one who has read about Obierika's intricate marriage negotiations, the etiquette of *kola* hospitality, the religious "week of peace," Ezeudu's elaborate funeral rites, the domestic arbitration conducted by the *egwugwu* court, the female kinship customs linking families and villages, or indeed Umuofia's entire set of taboos and punishments will find this a simple society. The title system itself, which plays such a large part in the novel, is an ingenious social strategy for redistributing wealth throughout the community. The four honorific *ozo* titles (*Ozo, Idemili, Omalo,* and *Erulu*), through which a man enters the spiritual community of his ancestors and achieves increasing levels of prestige, are acquired in festivities during which the candidate divests himself of excess material wealth. There is a dignity and purpose to this society despite inner tensions that—as Achebe shows—create pain as well as vulnerability to attack from outside. The moderate Obierika disapproves of killing Ikemefuna and begins to question the practice of throwing away twins; one of the first converts to Christianity is a woman who gave birth to several sets of twins, all of whom were exposed (left in the wild) at birth. The general subordination of women is another source of tensions that have taken longer to surface. Whatever its cultural differences from European society, however, this is a highly organized and complex society that offers a great deal of continuity and coherence to its members.

Igbo names, like names throughout black Africa, consist of whole phrases or sentences. Some names are dictated by circumstance (referring to the day of birth, for example) and some (the "given" name selected by the child's father, for example) reflect the family situation or a child's expected destiny. Adults may earn additional titles of honor. Achebe uses the connotations of personal names to reinforce important themes in *Things Fall Apart*. Okonkwo's father's character as a lazy, artistic, and improvident man is suggested by the name Unoka, signifying "the home is supreme." Okonkwo's son Nwoye, who has inherited his grandfather's peace-loving nature and artistic qualities, is named after the second day of the Igbo week (*Oye*); unlike Okonkwo, Nwoye lacks a prefix specifying adulthood or even gender, for *Nwa* means "child." Ikemefuna, who is condemned to death by the Oracle and will be killed by his adoptive father, is named "My strength should not be dissipated." Although all names have significance, only those with some relevance to the story will be annotated in this edition.

Okonkwo's character and career suggest epic dimensions. He is a hero of enormous energy and determination, "one of the greatest men in Umuofia" as his friend Obierika says, but his particular mode of greatness also causes his downfall. Like Achilles in Homer's *Iliad*, Okonkwo clings to traditionally respected values of pride and warlike aggression, and he will die to preserve those values. His unwillingness to change sets him apart from the community and eventually isolates him from the clan with its emphasis on group decisions. Okonkwo is a passionate man who counts on physical strength, hard work, and courage to make his way. Humiliated by his father's laziness, shameful death, and lack of title, compelled early to support the entire family, he struggles desperately to root out any sign of inherited "feminine" weakness in himself or his son Nwoye. By cultivating strength and valor, he finds a way to surpass his father and become one of the village leaders. Okonkwo is not without tender feelings: he loves his wife Ekwefi; his daughter, Ezinma; and the youth Ikemefuna who is given to him to foster. When he cuts down Ikemefuna so as not to appear weak, he is shattered for days thereafter. Nonetheless, his obsession with fierce masculinity and his open disrespect for "womanly" qualities of gentleness, compassion, and peace separate him not only from other members of his clan such as the more balanced Obierika but also from the earth goddess herself. This imbalance leads to disaster.

PRONOUNCING GLOSSARY

The following list uses common English syllables and stress accents to provide rough equivalents of selected words whose pronunciation may be unfamiliar to the general reader. Most of the names in *Things Fall Apart* are pronounced basically as they would be in English (for example, Okonkwo as *oh-kon'-kwo*), except that Igbo (like other African languages and Chinese) is a tonal language and also uses high or low tones for individual syllables.

Chielo: *chee'-ay-loh*

Chinua Achebe: *chin'-oo-ah ah-chay'-bay*

egwugwu: *eg-woog'-woo*

Erulu: *air-oo'-loo*

Ezeani: *ez-ah'-nee*

Ezeugo: *e'-zoo-goh*

Idemili: *ee-day-mee'-lee*

Igbo: *ee'-boh*

Ikemefuna: *ee-kay-may'-foo-na*

mbari: *mbah'-ree*

Ndulue: *in'-doo-loo'-eh*

Nwakibie: *nwa'-kee-ee'-bee-yay*

Nwayieke: *nwah'-ee-eh'-kay*

Umuofia: *oo'-moo-off'-yah*

Things Fall Apart

Turning and turning in the widening gyre
The falcon cannot hear the falconer;
Things fall apart; the centre cannot hold;
Mere anarchy is loosed upon the world . . .
—W. B. Yeats, "The Second Coming"

Part One

1

Okonkwo[1] was well known throughout the nine villages and even beyond. His fame rested on solid personal achievements. As a young man of eighteen he had brought honor to his village by throwing Amalinze the Cat. Amalinze was the great wrestler who for seven years was unbeaten, from Umuofia to Mbaino.[2] was called the Cat because his back would never touch the earth. It was this man that Okonkwo threw in a fight which the old men agreed was one of the fiercest since the founder of their town engaged a spirit of the wild for seven days and seven nights.

The drums beat and the flutes sang and the spectators held their breath.

---

1. Man (*oko*) born on Nkwo Day; the name also suggests stubborn male pride.　2. Four settlements. *Umuofia* means children of the forest (literal trans.); but *ofia* ("forest") also means "bush" or land untouched by European influence.

Amalinze was a wily craftsman, but Okonkwo was as slippery as a fish in water. Every nerve and every muscle stood out on their arms, on their backs and their thighs, and one almost heard them stretching to breaking point. In the end Okonkwo threw the Cat.

That was many years ago, twenty years or more, and during this time Okonkwo's fame had grown like a bush-fire in the harmattan.[3] He was tall and huge, and his bushy eyebrows and wide nose gave him a very severe look. He breathed heavily, and it was said that, when he slept, his wives and children in their houses could hear him breathe. When he walked, his heels hardly touched the ground and he seemed to walk on springs, as if he was going to pounce on somebody. And he did pounce on people quite often. He had a slight stammer and whenever he was angry and could not get his words out quickly enough, he would use his fists. He had no patience with unsuccessful men. He had had no patience with his father.

Unoka,[4] for that was his father's name, had died ten years ago. In his day he was lazy and improvident and was quite incapable of thinking about tomorrow. If any money came his way, and it seldom did, he immediately bought gourds of palm-wine, called round his neighbors and made merry. He always said that whenever he saw a dead man's mouth he saw the folly of not eating what one had in one's lifetime. Unoka was, of course, a debtor, and he owed every neighbor some money, from a few cowries[5] to quite substantial amounts.

He was tall but very thin and had a slight stoop. He wore a haggard and mournful look except when he was drinking or playing on his flute. He was very good on his flute, and his happiest moments were the two or three moons after the harvest when the village musicians brought down their instruments, hung above the fireplace. Unoka would play with them, his face beaming with blessedness and peace. Sometimes another village would ask Unoka's band and their dancing *egwugwu*[6] to come and stay with them and teach them their tunes. They would go to such hosts for as long as three or four markets,[7] making music and feasting. Unoka loved the good fare and the good fellowship, and he loved this season of the year, when the rains had stopped and the sun rose every morning with dazzling beauty. And it was not too hot either, because the cold and dry harmattan wind was blowing down from the north. Some years the harmattan was very severe and a dense haze hung on the atmosphere. Old men and children would then sit round log fires, warming their bodies. Unoka loved it all, and he loved the first kites[8] that returned with the dry season, and the children who sang songs of welcome to them. He would remember his own childhood, how he had often wandered around looking for a kite sailing leisurely against the blue sky. As soon as he found one he would sing with his whole being, welcoming it back from its long, long journey, and asking it if it had brought home any lengths of cloth.

That was years ago, when he was young. Unoka, the grown-up, was a failure. He was poor and his wife and children had barely enough to eat.

---

3. A dusty wind from the Sahara.　4. Home is supreme.　5. Glossy half-inch-long tan-and-white shells, collected in strings and used as money. A bag of twenty-four thousand cowries weighed about sixty pounds and, at the time of the story, was worth approximately one British pound.　6. Here, masked performers as part of musical entertainment.　7. Counting one important market day a week, roughly two English weeks. The Igbo week has four days: Eke, Oye, Afo, and Nkwo. Eke is a rest day and the main market day; Afo, a half day on the farm; and Oye and Nkwo, full work days.　8. A kind of hawk.

People laughed at him because he was a loafer, and they swore never to lend him any more money because he never paid back. But Unoka was such a man that he always succeeded in borrowing more, and piling up his debts.

One day a neighbor called Okoye[9] came in to see him. He was reclining on a mud bed in his hut playing on the flute. He immediately rose and shook hands with Okoye, who then unrolled the goatskin which he carried under his arm, and sat down. Unoka went into an inner room and soon returned with a small wooden disc containing a kola nut, some alligator pepper and a lump of white chalk.[1]

"I have kola," he announced when he sat down, and passed the disc over to his guest.

"Thank you. He who brings kola brings life. But I think you ought to break it," replied Okoye, passing back the disc.

"No, it is for you, I think," and they argued like this for a few moments before Unoka accepted the honor of breaking the kola. Okoye, meanwhile, took the lump of chalk, drew some lines on the floor, and then painted his big toe.[2]

As he broke the kola, Unoka prayed to their ancestors for life and health, and for protection against their enemies. When they had eaten they talked about many things: about the heavy rains which were drowning the yams, about the next ancestral feast and about the impending war with the village of Mbaino. Unoka was never happy when it came to wars. He was in fact a coward and could not bear the sight of blood. And so he changed the subject and talked about music, and his face beamed. He could hear in his mind's ear the blood-stirring and intricate rhythms of the *ekwe* and the *udu* and the *ogene,*[3] and he could hear his own flute weaving in and out of them, decorating them with a colorful and plaintive tune. The total effect was gay and brisk, but if one picked out the flute as it went up and down and then broke up into short snatches, one saw that there was sorrow and grief there.

Okoye was also a musician. He played on the *ogene*. But he was not a failure like Unoka. He had a large barn full of yams and he had three wives. And now he was going to take the Idemili title,[4] the third highest in the land. It was a very expensive ceremony and he was gathering all his resources together. That was in fact the reason why he had come to see Unoka. He cleared his throat and began:

"Thank you for the kola. You may have heard of the title I intend to take shortly."

Having spoken plainly so far, Okoye said the next half a dozen sentences in proverbs. Among the Ibo the art of conversation is regarded very highly, and proverbs are the palm-oil with which words are eaten. Okoye was a great talker and he spoke for a long time, skirting round the subject and then

9. Man born on Oye Day; a generic "Everyman" name. 1. Signifies coolness and peace, and is offered in rituals of hospitality so that the guest may draw his personal emblem on the floor. *Kola nut:* a bitter, caffeine-rich nut that is broken and eaten ceremonially; it indicates life or vitality. *Alligator pepper:* black pepper, known as the "pepper for kola" to distinguish it from cooking pepper, or chilies. 2. If the guest has taken the first title, he marks his big toe. Higher titles require different facial markings. 3. A bell-shaped gong made from two pieces of sheet iron. *Ekwe:* a wooden drum, about three feet long, that produces high and low tones (as does the Igbo language). *Udu:* a clay pot with a hole to one side of the neck opening; various resonant tones are produced when the hole is struck with one hand while the other hand covers or uncovers the top. 4. A title of honor named after the river god Idemili, to whom the python is sacred. *Barn:* not a building, but a walled enclosure for the yam stacks (frames on which individual yams are tied, shaded with palm leaves, and exposed to circulating air).

hitting it finally. In short, he was asking Unoka to return the two hundred cowries he had borrowed from him more than two years before. As soon as Unoka understood what his friend was driving at, he burst out laughing. He laughed loud and long and his voice rang out clear as the *ogene*, and tears stood in his eyes. His visitor was amazed, and sat speechless. At the end, Unoka was able to give an answer between fresh outbursts of mirth.

"Look at that wall," he said, pointing at the far wall of his hut, which was rubbed with red earth so that it shone. "Look at those lines of chalk;" and Okoye saw groups of short perpendicular lines drawn in chalk. There were five groups, and the smallest group had ten lines. Unoka had a sense of the dramatic and so he allowed a pause, in which he took a pinch of snuff and sneezed noisily, and then he continued: "Each group there represents a debt to someone, and each stroke is one hundred cowries. You see, I owe that man a thousand cowries. But he has not come to wake me up in the morning for it. I shall pay you, but not today. Our elders say that the sun will shine on those who stand before it shines on those who kneel under them. I shall pay my big debts first." And he took another pinch of snuff, as if that was paying the big debts first. Okoye rolled his goatskin and departed.

When Unoka died he had taken no title at all and he was heavily in debt. Any wonder then that his son Okonkwo was ashamed of him? Fortunately, among these people a man was judged according to his worth and not according to the worth of his father. Okonkwo was clearly cut out for great things. He was still young but he had won fame as the greatest wrestler in the nine villages. He was a wealthy farmer and had two barns full of yams, and had just married his third wife. To crown it all he had taken two titles and had shown incredible prowess in two inter-tribal wars. And so although Okonkwo was still young, he was already one of the greatest men of his time. Age was respected among his people, but achievement was revered. As the elders said, if a child washed his hands he could eat with kings. Okonkwo had clearly washed his hands and so he ate with kings and elders. And that was how he came to look after the doomed lad who was sacrificed to the village of Umuofia by their neighbors to avoid war and bloodshed. The ill-fated lad was called Ikemefuna.[5]

2

Okonkwo had just blown out the palm-oil lamp and stretched himself on his bamboo bed when he heard the *ogene* of the town crier piercing the still night air. *Gome, gome, gome, gome,* boomed the hollow metal. Then the crier gave his message, and at the end of it beat his instrument again. And this was the message. Every man of Umuofia was asked to gather at the market place tomorrow morning. Okonkwo wondered what was amiss, for he knew certainly that something was amiss. He had discerned a clear overtone of tragedy in the crier's voice, and even now he could still hear it as it grew dimmer and dimmer in the distance.

The night was very quiet. It was always quiet except on moonlight nights. Darkness held a vague terror for these people, even the bravest among them. Children were warned not to whistle at night for fear of evil spirits. Danger-

---

5. My strength should not be dissipated.

ous animals became even more sinister and uncanny in the dark. A snake was never called by its name at night, because it would hear. It was called a string. And so on this particular night as the crier's voice was gradually swallowed up in the distance, silence returned to the world, a vibrant silence made more intense by the universal trill of a million million forest insects.

On a moonlight night it would be different. The happy voices of children playing in open fields would then be heard. And perhaps those not so young would be playing in pairs in less open places, and old men and women would remember their youth. As the Ibo say: "When the moon is shining the cripple becomes hungry for a walk."

But this particular night was dark and silent. And in all the nine villages of Umuofia a town crier with his *ogene* asked every man to be present tomorrow morning. Okonkwo on his bamboo bed tried to figure out the nature of the emergency—war with a neighboring clan? That seemed the most likely reason, and he was not afraid of war. He was a man of action, a man of war. Unlike his father he could stand the look of blood. In Umuofia's latest war he was the first to bring home a human head. That was his fifth head; and he was not an old man yet. On great occasions such as the funeral of a village celebrity he drank his palm-wine from his first human head.

In the morning the market place was full. There must have been about ten thousand men there, all talking in low voices. At last Ogbuefi Ezeugo stood up in the midst of them and bellowed four times, "*Umuofia kwenu,*"[6] and on each occasion he faced a different direction and seemed to push the air with a clenched fist. And ten thousand men answered "*Yaa!*" each time. Then there was perfect silence. Ogbuefi Ezeugo was a powerful orator and was always chosen to speak on such occasions. He moved his hand over his white head and stroked his white beard. He then adjusted his cloth, which was passed under his right armpit and tied above his left shoulder.

"*Umuofia kwenu,*" he bellowed a fifth time, and the crowd yelled in answer. And then suddenly like one possessed he shot out his left hand and pointed in the direction of Mbaino, and said through gleaming white teeth firmly clenched: "Those sons of wild animals have dared to murder a daughter of Umuofia." He threw his head down and gnashed his teeth, and allowed a murmur of suppressed anger to sweep the crowd. When he began again, the anger on his face was gone and in its place a sort of smile hovered, more terrible and more sinister than the anger. And in a clear unemotional voice he told Umuofia how their daughter had gone to market at Mbaino and had been killed. That woman, said Ezeugo, was the wife of Ogbuefi Udo,[7] and he pointed to a man who sat near him with a bowed head. The crowd then shouted with anger and thirst for blood.

Many others spoke, and at the end it was decided to follow the normal course of action. An ultimatum was immediately dispatched to Mbaino asking them to choose between war on the one hand, and on the other the offer of a young man and a virgin as compensation.

Umuofia was feared by all its neighbors. It was powerful in war and in magic, and its priests and medicine men were feared in all the surrounding

---

6. United Umuofia! An orator's call on the audience to respond as a group. *Ogbuefi*: cow killer (literal trans.); indicates someone who has taken a high title (e.g., the Idemili title) for which the celebration ceremony requires the slaughter of a cow. *Ezeugo*: a name denoting a priest or high initiate, someone who wears the eagle feather.   7. Peace.

country. Its most potent war-medicine was as old as the clan itself. Nobody knew how old. But on one point there was general agreement—the active principle in that medicine had been an old woman with one leg. In fact, the medicine itself was called *agadi-nwayi*, or old woman. It had its shrine in the center of Umuofia, in a cleared spot. And if anybody was so foolhardy as to pass by the shrine after dusk he was sure to see the old woman hopping about.

And so the neighboring clans who naturally knew of these things feared Umuofia, and would not go to war against it without first trying a peaceful settlement. And in fairness to Umuofia it should be recorded that it never went to war unless its case was clear and just and was accepted as such by its Oracle—the Oracle of the Hills and the Caves. And there were indeed occasions when the Oracle had forbidden Umuofia to wage a war. If the clan had disobeyed the Oracle they would surely have been beaten, because their dreaded *agadi-nwayi* would never fight what the Ibo call *a fight of blame*.

But the war that now threatened was a just war. Even the enemy clan knew that. And so when Okonkwo of Umuofia arrived at Mbaino as the proud and imperious emissary of war, he was treated with great honor and respect, and two days later he returned home with a lad of fifteen and a young virgin. The lad's name was Ikemefuna, whose sad story is still told in Umuofia unto this day.

The elders, or *ndichie,* met to hear a report of Okonkwo's mission. At the end they decided, as everybody knew they would, that the girl should go to Ogbuefi Udo to replace his murdered wife. As for the boy, he belonged to the clan as a whole, and there was no hurry to decide his fate. Okonkwo was, therefore, asked on behalf of the clan to look after him in the interim. And so for three years Ikemefuna lived in Okonkwo's household.

Okonkwo ruled his household with a heavy hand. His wives, especially the youngest, lived in perpetual fear of his fiery temper, and so did his little children. Perhaps down in his heart Okonkwo was not a cruel man. But his whole life was dominated by fear, the fear of failure and of weakness. It was deeper and more intimate than the fear of evil and capricious gods and of magic, the fear of the forest, and of the forces of nature, malevolent, red in tooth and claw. Okonkwo's fear was greater than these. It was not external but lay deep within himself. It was the fear of himself, lest he should be found to resemble his father. Even as a little boy he had resented his father's failure and weakness, and even now he still remembered how he had suffered when a playmate had told him that his father was *agbala*. That was how Okonkwo first came to know that *agbala* was not only another name for a woman, it could also mean a man who had taken no title. And so Okonkwo was ruled by one passion—to hate everything that his father Unoka had loved. One of those things was gentleness and another was idleness.

During the planting season Okonkwo worked daily on his farms from cock-crow until the chickens went to roost. He was a very strong man and rarely felt fatigue. But his wives and young children were not as strong, and so they suffered. But they dared not complain openly. Okonkwo's first son, Nwoye,[8] was then twelve years old but was already causing his father great anxiety

---

8. Child born on Oye day.

for his incipient laziness. At any rate, that was how it looked to his father, and he sought to correct him by constant nagging and beating. And so Nwoye was developing into a sad-faced youth.

Okonkwo's prosperity was visible in his household. He had a large compound enclosed by a thick wall of red earth. His own hut, or *obi*, stood immediately behind the only gate in the red walls. Each of his three wives had her own hut, which together formed a half moon behind the *obi*. The barn was built against one end of the red walls, and long stacks of yam stood out prosperously in it. At the opposite end of the compound was a shed for the goats, and each wife built a small attachment to her hut for the hens. Near the barn was a small house, the "medicine house" or shrine where Okonkwo kept the wooden symbols of his personal god and of his ancestral spirits. He worshiped them with sacrifices of kola nut, food and palm-wine, and offered prayers to them on behalf of himself, his three wives and eight children.

So when the daughter of Umuofia was killed in Mbaino, Ikemefuna came into Okonkwo's household. When Okonkwo brought him home that day he called his most senior wife and handed him over to her.

"He belongs to the clan," he told her. "So look after him."

"Is he staying long with us?" she asked.

"Do what you are told, woman," Okonkwo thundered, and stammered. "When did you become one of the *ndichie* of Umuofia?"

And so Nwoye's mother took Ikemefuna to her hut and asked no more questions.

As for the boy himself, he was terribly afraid. He could not understand what was happening to him or what he had done. How could he know that his father had taken a hand in killing a daughter of Umuofia? All he knew was that a few men had arrived at their house, conversing with his father in low tones, and at the end he had been taken out and handed over to a stranger. His mother had wept bitterly, but he had been too surprised to weep. And so the stranger had brought him, and a girl, a long, long way from home, through lonely forest paths. He did not know who the girl was, and he never saw her again.

3

Okonkwo did not have the start in life which many young men usually had. He did not inherit a barn from his father. There was no barn to inherit. The story was told in Umuofia, of how his father, Unoka, had gone to consult the Oracle of the Hills and the Caves to find out why he always had a miserable harvest.

The Oracle was called Agbala,[9] and people came from far and near to consult it. They came when misfortune dogged their steps or when they had a dispute with their neighbors. They came to discover what the future held for them or to consult the spirits of their departed fathers.

The way into the shrine was a round hole at the side of a hill, just a little bigger than the round opening into a henhouse. Worshipers and those who

---

9. The Oracle is masculine, but his priestess, or Voice, is feminine.

came to seek knowledge from the god crawled on their belly through the hole and found themselves in a dark, endless space in the presence of Agbala. No one had ever beheld Agbala, except his priestess. But no one who had ever crawled into his awful shrine had come out without the fear of his power. His priestess stood by the sacred fire which she built in the heart of the cave and proclaimed the will of the god. The fire did not burn with a flame. The glowing logs only served to light up vaguely the dark figure of the priestess.

Sometimes a man came to consult the spirit of his dead father or relative. It was said that when such a spirit appeared, the man saw it vaguely in the darkness, but never heard its voice. Some people even said that they had heard the spirits flying and flapping their wings against the roof of the cave.

Many years ago when Okonkwo was still a boy his father, Unoka, had gone to consult Agbala. The priestess in those days was a woman called Chika.[1] She was full of the power of her god, and she was greatly feared. Unoka stood before her and began his story.

"Every year," he said sadly, "before I put any crop in the earth, I sacrifice a cock to Ani, the owner of all land. It is the law of our fathers. I also kill a cock at the shrine of Ifejioku, the god of yams. I clear the bush and set fire to it when it is dry. I sow the yams when the first rain has fallen, and stake them when the young tendrils appear. I weed—"

"Hold your peace!" screamed the priestess, her voice terrible as it echoed through the dark void. "You have offended neither the gods nor your fathers. And when a man is at peace with his gods and his ancestors, his harvest will be good or bad according to the strength of his arm. You, Unoka, are known in all the clan for the weakness of your machete and your hoe. When your neighbors go out with their ax to cut down virgin forests, you sow your yams on exhausted farms that take no labor to clear. They cross seven rivers to make their farms; you stay at home and offer sacrifices to a reluctant soil. Go home and work like a man."

Unoka was an ill-fated man. He had a bad *chi* or personal god, and evil fortune followed him to the grave, or rather to his death, for he had no grave. He died of the swelling which was an abomination to the earth goddess. When a man was afflicted with swelling in the stomach and the limbs he was not allowed to die in the house. He was carried to the Evil Forest and left there to die. There was the story of a very stubborn man who staggered back to his house and had to be carried again to the forest and tied to a tree. The sickness was an abomination to the earth, and so the victim could not be buried in her bowels. He died and rotted away above the earth, and was not given the first or the second burial. Such was Unoka's fate. When they carried him away, he took with him his flute.

With a father like Unoka, Okonkwo did not have the start in life which many young men had. He neither inherited a barn nor a title, nor even a young wife. But in spite of these disadvantages, he had begun even in his father's lifetime to lay the foundations of a prosperous future. It was slow and painful. But he threw himself into it like one possessed. And indeed he was possessed by the fear of his father's contemptible life and shameful death.

1. Sky is supreme.

There was a wealthy man in Okonkwo's village who had three huge barns, nine wives and thirty children. His name was Nwakibie[2] and he had taken the highest but one title which a man could take in the clan. It was for this man that Okonkwo worked to earn his first seed yams.

He took a pot of palm-wine and a cock to Nwakibie. Two elderly neighbors were sent for, and Nwakibie's two grown-up sons were also present in his *obi*. He presented a kola nut and an alligator pepper, which were passed round for all to see and then returned to him. He broke the nut saying: "We shall all live. We pray for life, children, a good harvest and happiness. You will have what is good for you and I will have what is good for me. Let the kite perch and let the eagle perch too. If one says no to the other, let his wing break."

After the kola nut had been eaten Okonkwo brought his palm-wine from the corner of the hut where it had been placed and stood it in the center of the group. He addressed Nwakibie, calling him "Our father."

"*Nna ayi,*" he said. "I have brought you this little kola. As our people say, a man who pays respect to the great paves the way for his own greatness. I have come to pay you my respects and also to ask a favor. But let us drink the wine first."

Everybody thanked Okonkwo and the neighbors brought out their drinking horns from the goatskin bags they carried. Nwakibie brought down his own horn, which was fastened to the rafters. The younger of his sons, who was also the youngest man in the group, moved to the center, raised the pot on his left knee and began to pour out the wine. The first cup went to Okonkwo, who must taste his wine before anyone else.[3] Then the group drank, beginning with the eldest man. When everyone had drunk two or three horns, Nwakibie sent for his wives. Some of them were not at home and only four came in.

"Is Anasi not in?" he asked them. They said she was coming. Anasi[4] was the first wife and the others could not drink before her, and so they stood waiting.

Anasi was a middle-aged woman, tall and strongly built. There was authority in her bearing and she looked every inch the ruler of the womenfolk in a large and prosperous family. She wore the anklet of her husband's titles, which the first wife alone could wear.

She walked up to her husband and accepted the horn from him. She then went down on one knee, drank a little and handed back the horn. She rose, called him by his name and went back to her hut. The other wives drank in the same way, in their proper order, and went away.

The men then continued their drinking and talking. Ogbuefi Idigo was talking about the palm-wine tapper, Obiako, who suddenly gave up his trade.

"There must be something behind it," he said, wiping the foam of wine from his mustache with the back of his left hand. "There must be a reason for it. A toad does not run in the daytime for nothing."

"Some people say the Oracle warned him that he would fall off a palm tree and kill himself," said Akukalia.

"Obiako has always been a strange one," said Nwakibie. "I have heard that

---

2. The child surpasses his neighbors.   3. A ceremonial gesture; one who gives wine tastes it first to show that it is not poisoned.   4. First or favorite wife—not always the same.

many years ago, when his father had not been dead very long, he had gone to consult the Oracle. The Oracle said to him, 'Your dead father wants you to sacrifice a goat to him.' Do you know what he told the Oracle? He said, 'Ask my dead father if he ever had a fowl when he was alive.' " Everybody laughed heartily except Okonkwo, who laughed uneasily because, as the saying goes, an old woman is always uneasy when dry bones are mentioned in a proverb. Okonkwo remembered his own father.

At last the young man who was pouring out the wine held up half a horn of the thick, white dregs and said, "What we are eating is finished." "We have seen it," the others replied. "Who will drink the dregs?" he asked. "Whoever has a job in hand," said Idigo, looking at Nwakibie's elder son Igwelo with a malicious twinkle in his eye.

Everyone agreed that Igwelo should drink the dregs. He accepted the half-full horn from his brother and drank it. As Idigo had said, Igwelo had a job in hand because he had married his first wife a month or two before. The thick dregs of palm-wine were supposed to be good for men who were going in to their wives.

After the wine had been drunk Okonkwo laid his difficulties before Nwakibie.

"I have come to you for help," he said. "Perhaps you can already guess what it is. I have cleared a farm but have no yams to sow. I know what it is to ask a man to trust another with his yams, especially these days when young men are afraid of hard work. I am not afraid of work. The lizard that jumped from the high iroko tree to the ground said he would praise himself if no one else did. I began to fend for myself at an age when most people still suck at their mothers' breasts. If you give me some yam seeds I shall not fail you."

Nwakibie cleared his throat. "It pleases me to see a young man like you these days when our youth has gone so soft. Many young men have come to me to ask for yams but I have refused because I knew they would just dump them in the earth and leave them to be choked by weeds. When I say no to them they think I am hard-hearted. But it is not so. Eneke the bird[5] says that since men have learned to shoot without missing, he has learned to fly without perching. I have learned to be stingy with my yams. But I can trust you. I know it as I look at you. As our fathers said, you can tell a ripe corn by its look. I shall give you twice four hundred yams. Go ahead and prepare your farm."

Okonkwo thanked him again and again and went home feeling happy. He knew that Nwakibie would not refuse him, but he had not expected he would be so generous. He had not hoped to get more than four hundred seeds. He would now have to make a bigger farm. He hoped to get another four hundred yams from one of his father's friends at Isiuzo.[6]

Sharecropping was a very slow way of building up a barn of one's own. After all the toil one only got a third of the harvest. But for a young man whose father had no yams, there was no other way. And what made it worse in Okonkwo's case was that he had to support his mother and two sisters from his meager harvest. And supporting his mother also meant supporting his father. She could not be expected to cook and eat while her husband starved. And so at a very early age when he was striving desperately to build

5. Proverbial.   6. Head of the road; a small town.

a barn through sharecropping Okonkwo was also fending for his father's house. It was like pouring grains of corn into a bag full of holes. His mother and sisters worked hard enough, but they grew women's crops, like coco-yams, beans and cassava. Yam, the king of crops, was a man's crop.[7]

The year that Okonkwo took eight hundred seed-yams from Nwakibie was the worst year in living memory. Nothing happened at its proper time; it was either too early or too late. It seemed as if the world had gone mad. The first rains were late, and, when they came, lasted only a brief moment. The blazing sun returned, more fierce than it had ever been known, and scorched all the green that had appeared with the rains. The earth burned like hot coals and roasted all the yams that had been sown. Like all good farmers, Okonkwo had begun to sow with the first rains. He had sown four hundred seeds when the rains dried up and the heat returned. He watched the sky all day for signs of rain clouds and lay awake all night. In the morning he went back to his farm and saw the withering tendrils. He had tried to protect them from the smoldering earth by making rings of thick sisal leaves around them. But by the end of the day the sisal rings were burned dry and gray. He changed them every day, and prayed that the rain might fall in the night. But the drought continued for eight market weeks and the yams were killed.

Some farmers had not planted their yams yet. They were the lazy easygoing ones who always put off clearing their farms as long as they could. This year they were the wise ones. They sympathized with their neighbors with much shaking of the head, but inwardly they were happy for what they took to be their own foresight.

Okonkwo planted what was left of his seed-yams when the rains finally returned. He had one consolation. The yams he had sown before the drought were his own, the harvest of the previous year. He still had the eight hundred from Nwakibie and the four hundred from his father's friend. So he would make a fresh start.

But the year had gone mad. Rain fell as it had never fallen before. For days and nights together it poured down in violent torrents, and washed away the yam heaps. Trees were uprooted and deep gorges appeared everywhere. Then the rain became less violent. But it went from day to day without a pause. The spell of sunshine which always came in the middle of the wet season did not appear. The yams put on luxuriant green leaves, but every farmer knew that without sunshine the tubers would not grow.

That year the harvest was sad, like a funeral, and many farmers wept as they dug up the miserable and rotting yams. One man tied his cloth to a tree branch and hanged himself.

Okonkwo remembered that tragic year with a cold shiver throughout the rest of his life. It always surprised him when he thought of it later that he did not sink under the load of despair. He knew that he was a fierce fighter, but that year had been enough to break the heart of a lion.

"Since I survived that year," he always said, "I shall survive anything." He put it down to his inflexible will.

His father, Unoka, who was then an ailing man, had said to him during

---

7. Yams, a staple food in western Africa, were a sacred crop generally cultivated only by men, and eaten either roasted or boiled. Coco-yams (a brown root also called taro) and cassava (or manioc, which is fermented to remove natural arsenic): Low-status root vegetables prepared for eating by boiling and pounding.

that terrible harvest month: "Do not despair. I know you will not despair. You have a manly and a proud heart. A proud heart can survive a general failure because such a failure does not prick its pride. It is more difficult and more bitter when a man fails *alone*."

Unoka was like that in his last days. His love of talk had grown with age and sickness. It tried Okonkwo's patience beyond words.

4

"Looking at a king's mouth," said an old man, "one would think he never sucked at his mother's breast." He was talking about Okonkwo, who had risen so suddenly from great poverty and misfortune to be one of the lords of the clan. The old man bore no ill will towards Okonkwo. Indeed he respected him for his industry and success. But he was struck, as most people were, by Okonkwo's brusqueness in dealing with less successful men. Only a week ago a man had contradicted him at a kindred meeting which they held to discuss the next ancestral feast. Without looking at the man Okonkwo had said: "This meeting is for men." The man who had contradicted him had no titles. That was why he had called him a woman. Okonkwo knew how to kill a man's spirit.

Everybody at the kindred meeting took sides with Osugo[8] when Okonkwo called him a woman. The oldest man present said sternly that those whose palm-kernels were cracked for them by a benevolent spirit should not forget to be humble. Okonkwo said he was sorry for what he had said, and the meeting continued.

But it was really not true that Okonkwo's palm-kernels had been cracked for him by a benevolent spirit. He had cracked them himself. Anyone who knew his grim struggle against poverty and misfortune could not say he had been lucky. If ever a man deserved his success, that man was Okonkwo. An an early age he had achieved fame as the greatest wrestler in all the land. That was not luck. At the most one could say that his *chi* or personal god was good. But the Ibo people have a proverb that when a man says yes his *chi* says yes also. Okonkwo said yes very strongly; so his *chi* agreed. And not only his *chi* but his clan too, because it judged a man by the work of his hands. That was why Okonkwo had been chosen by the nine villages to carry a message of war to their enemies unless they agreed to give up a young man and a virgin to atone for the murder of Udo's wife. And such was the deep fear that their enemies had for Umuofia that they treated Okonkwo like a king and brought him a virgin who was given to Udo as wife, and the lad Ikemefuna.

The elders of the clan had decided that Ikemefuna should be in Okonkwo's care for a while. But no one thought it would be as long as three years. They seemed to forget all about him as soon as they had taken the decision.

At first Ikemefuna was very much afraid. Once or twice he tried to run away, but he did not know where to begin. He thought of his mother and his three-year-old sister and wept bitterly. Nwoye's mother was very kind to him and treated him as one of her own children. But all he said was: "When shall I go home?" When Okonkwo heard that he would not eat any food he

---

8. Low-status (*osu*) person.

came into the hut with a big stick in his hand and stood over him while he swallowed his yams, trembling. A few moments later he went behind the hut and began to vomit painfully. Nwoye's mother went to him and placed her hands on his chest and on his back. He was ill for three market weeks, and when he recovered he seemed to have overcome his great fear and sadness.

He was by nature a very lively boy and he gradually became popular in Okonkwo's household, especially with the children. Okonkwo's son, Nwoye, who was two years younger, became quite inseparable from him because he seemed to know everything. He could fashion out flutes from bamboo stems and even from the elephant grass. He knew the names of all the birds and could set clever traps for the little bush rodents. And he knew which trees made the strongest bows.

Even Okonkwo himself became very fond of the boy—inwardly of course. Okonkwo never showed any emotion openly, unless it be the emotion of anger. To show affection was a sign of weakness; the only thing worth demonstrating was strength. He therefore treated Ikemefuna as he treated everybody else—with a heavy hand. But there was no doubt that he liked the boy. Sometimes when he went to big village meetings or communal ancestral feasts he allowed Ikemefuna to accompany him, like a son, carrying his stool and his goatskin bag. And, indeed, Ikemefuna called him father.

Ikemefuna came to Umuofia at the end of the carefree season between harvest and planting. In fact he recovered from his illness only a few days before the Week of Peace began. And that was also the year Okonkwo broke the peace, and was punished, as was the custom, by Ezeani, the priest of the earth goddess.

Okonkwo was provoked to justifiable anger by his youngest wife, who went to plait her hair at her friend's house and did not return early enough to cook the afternoon meal. Okonkwo did not know at first that she was not at home. After waiting in vain for her dish he went to her hut to see what she was doing. There was nobody in the hut and the fireplace was cold.

"Where is Ojiugo?" he asked his second wife, who came out of her hut to draw water from a gigantic pot in the shade of a small tree in the middle of the compound.

"She has gone to plait her hair."

Okonkwo bit his lips as anger welled up within him.

"Where are her children? Did she take them?" he asked with unusual coolness and restraint.

"They are here," answered his first wife, Nwoye's mother. Okonkwo bent down and looked into her hut. Ojiugo's children were eating with the children of his first wife.

"Did she ask you to feed them before she went?"

"Yes," lied Nwoye's mother, trying to minimize Ojiugo's thoughtlessness.

Okonkwo knew she was not speaking the truth. He walked back to his *obi* to await Ojiugo's return. And when she returned he beat her very heavily. In his anger he had forgotten that it was the Week of Peace. His first two wives ran out in great alarm pleading with him that it was the sacred week. But Okonkwo was not the man to stop beating somebody half-way through, not even for fear of a goddess.

Okonkwo's neighbors heard his wife crying and sent their voices over the compound walls to ask what was the matter. Some of them came over to see for themselves. It was unheard of to beat somebody during the sacred week.

Before it was dusk Ezeani, who was the priest of the earth goddess, Ani, called on Okonkwo in his *obi*. Okonkwo brought out kola nut and placed it before the priest.

"Take away your kola nut. I shall not eat in the house of a man who has no respect for our gods and ancestors."

Okonkwo tried to explain to him what his wife had done, but Ezeani seemed to pay no attention. He held a short staff in his hand which he brought down on the floor to emphasize his points.

"Listen to me," he said when Okonkwo had spoken. "You are not a stranger in Umuofia. You know as well as I do that our forefathers ordained that before we plant any crops in the earth we should observe a week in which a man does not say a harsh word to his neighbor. We live in peace with our fellows to honor our great goddess of the earth without whose blessing our crops will not grow. You have committed a great evil." He brought down his staff heavily on the floor. "Your wife was at fault, but even if you came into your *obi* and found her lover on top of her, you would still have committed a great evil to beat her." His staff came down again. "The evil you have done can ruin the whole clan. The earth goddess whom you have insulted may refuse to give us her increase, and we shall all perish." His tone now changed from anger to command. "You will bring to the shrine of Ani tomorrow one she-goat, one hen, a length of cloth and a hundred cowries." He rose and left the hut.

Okonkwo did as the priest said. He also took with him a pot of palm-wine. Inwardly, he was repentant. But he was not the man to go about telling his neighbors that he was in error. And so people said he had no respect for the gods of the clan. His enemies said his good fortune had gone to his head. They called him the little bird *nza* who so far forgot himself after a heavy meal that he challenged his *chi*.[9]

No work was done during the Week of Peace. People called on their neighbors and drank palm-wine. This year they talked of nothing else but the *nso-ani*[1] which Okonkwo had committed. It was the first time for many years that a man had broken the sacred peace. Even the oldest men could only remember one or two other occasions somewhere in the dim past.

Ogbuefi Ezeudu, who was the oldest man in the village, was telling two other men who came to visit him that the punishment for breaking the Peace of Ani had become very mild in their clan.

"It has not always been so," he said. "My father told me that he had been told that in the past a man who broke the peace was dragged on the ground through the village until he died. But after a while this custom was stopped because it spoiled the peace which it was meant to preserve."

"Somebody told me yesterday," said one of the younger men, "that in some clans it is an abomination for a man to die during the Week of Peace."

"It is indeed true," said Ogbuefi Ezeudu. "They have that custom in Obo-doani.[2] If a man dies at this time he is not buried but cast into the Evil

---

9. The one that talks back (literal trans.); a small aggressive bird. In the story, it is easily defeated (alternatively, caught by a hawk) when it becomes foolish enough to challenge its personal god.   1. Sin, abomination against the earth goddess Ani.   2. The town of the land (literal trans.); i.e., Anytown, Nigeria.

Forest. It is a bad custom which these people observe because they lack understanding. They throw away large numbers of men and women without burial. And what is the result? Their clan is full of the evil spirits of these unburied dead, hungry to do harm to the living."

After the Week of Peace every man and his family began to clear the bush to make new farms. The cut bush was left to dry and fire was then set to it. As the smoke rose into the sky kites appeared from different directions and hovered over the burning field in silent valediction. The rainy season was approaching when they would go away until the dry season returned.

Okonkwo spent the next few days preparing his seed-yams. He looked at each yam carefully to see whether it was good for sowing. Sometimes he decided that a yam was too big to be sown as one seed and he split it deftly along its length with his sharp knife. His eldest son, Nwoye, and Ikemefuna helped him by fetching the yams in long baskets from the barn and in counting the prepared seeds in groups of four hundred. Sometimes Okonkwo gave them a few yams each to prepare. But he always found fault with their effort, and he said so with much threatening.

"Do you think you are cutting up yams for cooking?" he asked Nwoye. "If you split another yam of this size, I shall break your jaw. You think you are still a child. I began to own a farm at your age. And you," he said to Ikemefuna, "do you not grow yams where you come from?"

Inwardly Okonkwo knew that the boys were still too young to understand fully the difficult art of preparing seed-yams. But he thought that one could not begin too early. Yam stood for manliness, and he who could feed his family on yams from one harvest to another was a very great man indeed. Okonkwo wanted his son to be a great farmer and a great man. He would stamp out the disquieting signs of laziness which he thought he already saw in him.

"I will not have a son who cannot hold up his head in the gathering of the clan. I would sooner strangle him with my own hands. And if you stand staring at me like that," he swore, "Amadiora[3] will break your head for you!"

Some days later, when the land had been moistened by two or three heavy rains, Okonkwo and his family went to the farm with baskets of seed-yams, their hoes and machetes, and the planting began. They made single mounds of earth in straight lines all over the field and sowed the yams in them.

Yam, the king of crops, was a very exacting king. For three or four moons it demanded hard work and constant attention from cock-crow till the chickens went back to roost. The young tendrils were protected from earth-heat with rings of sisal leaves. As the rains became heavier the women planted maize, melons and beans between the yam mounds. The yams were then staked, first with little sticks and later with tall and big tree branches. The women weeded the farm three times at definite periods in the life of the yams, neither early nor late.

And now the rains had really come, so heavy and persistent that even the village rain-maker no longer claimed to be able to intervene. He could not stop the rain now, just as he would not attempt to start it in the heart of the dry season, without serious danger to his own health. The personal dynamism

3. God of thunder and lightning.

required to counter the forces of these extremes of weather would be far too great for the human frame.

And so nature was not interfered with in the middle of the rainy season. Sometimes it poured down in such thick sheets of water that earth and sky seemed merged in one gray wetness. It was then uncertain whether the low rumbling of Amadiora's thunder came from above or below. At such times, in each of the countless thatched huts of Umuofia, children sat around their mother's cooking fire telling stories, or with their father in his *obi* warming themselves from a log fire, roasting and eating maize. It was a brief resting period between the exacting and arduous planting season and the equally exacting but light-hearted month of harvests.

Ikemefuna had begun to feel like a member of Okonkwo's family. He still thought about his mother and his three-year-old sister, and he had moments of sadness and depression. But he and Nwoye had become so deeply attached to each other that such moments became less frequent and less poignant. Ikemefuna had an endless stock of folk tales. Even those which Nwoye knew already were told with a new freshness and the local flavor of a different clan. Nwoye remembered this period very vividly till the end of his life. He even remembered how he had laughed when Ikemefuna told him that the proper name for a corn cob with only a few scattered grains was *eze-agadi-nwayi*, or the teeth of an old woman. Nwoye's mind had gone immediately to Nwayieke, who lived near the udala[4] tree. She had about three teeth and was always smoking her pipe.

Gradually the rains became lighter and less frequent, and earth and sky once again became separate. The rain fell in thin, slanting showers through sunshine and quiet breeze. Children no longer stayed indoors but ran about singing:

> The rain is falling, the sun is shining,
> Alone Nnadi[5] is cooking and eating.

Nwoye always wondered who Nnadi was and why he should live all by himself, cooking and eating. In the end he decided that Nnadi must live in that land of Ikemefuna's favorite story where the ant holds his court in splendor and the sands dance forever.

5

The Feast of the New Yam was approaching and Umuofia was in a festival mood. It was an occasion for giving thanks to Ani, the earth goddess and the source of all fertility. Ani played a greater part in the life of the people than any other deity. She was the ultimate judge of morality and conduct. And what was more, she was in close communion with the departed fathers of the clan whose bodies had been committed to earth.

The Feast of the New Yam was held every year before the harvest began, to honor the earth goddess and the ancestral spirits of the clan. New yams could not be eaten until some had first been offered to these powers. Men and women, young and old, looked forward to the New Yam Festival because

---

4. African star apple tree. *Nwayieke*: Woman born on Eke Day.　5. Father is there, or Father exists.

it began the season of plenty—the new year. On the last night before the festival, yams of the old year were all disposed of by those who still had them. The new year must begin with tasty, fresh yams and not the shriveled and fibrous crops of the previous year. All cooking pots, calabashes and wooden bowls were thoroughly washed, especially the wooden mortar in which yam was pounded. Yam foo-foo[6] and vegetable soup was the chief food in the celebration. So much of it was cooked that, no matter how heavily the family ate or how many friends and relatives they invited from neighboring villages, there was always a large quantity of food left over at the end of the day. The story was always told of a wealthy man who set before his guests a mound of foo-foo so high that those who sat on one side could not see what was happening on the other, and it was not until late in the evening that one of them saw for the first time his in-law who had arrived during the course of the meal and had fallen to on the opposite side. It was only then that they exchanged greetings and shook hands over what was left of the food.

The New Yam Festival was thus an occasion for joy throughout Umuofia. And every man whose arm was strong, as the Ibo people say, was expected to invite large numbers of guests from far and wide. Okonkwo always asked his wives' relations, and since he now had three wives his guests would make a fairly big crowd.

But somehow Okonkwo could never become as enthusiastic over feasts as most people. He was a good eater and he could drink one or two fairly big gourds of palm-wine. But he was always uncomfortable sitting around for days waiting for a feast or getting over it. He would be very much happier working on his farm.

The festival was now only three days away. Okonkwo's wives had scrubbed the walls and the huts with red earth until they reflected light. They had then drawn patterns on them in white, yellow and dark green. They then set about painting themselves with cam wood and drawing beautiful black patterns on their stomachs and on their backs. The children were also decorated, especially their hair, which was shaved in beautiful patterns. The three women talked excitedly about the relations who had been invited, and the children reveled in the thought of being spoiled by these visitors from the motherland. Ikemefuna was equally excited. The New Yam Festival seemed to him to be a much bigger event here than in his own village, a place which was already becoming remote and vague in his imagination.

And then the storm burst. Okonkwo, who had been walking about aimlessly in his compound in suppressed anger, suddenly found an outlet.

"Who killed this banana tree?" he asked.

A hush fell on the compound immediately.

"Who killed this tree? Or are you all deaf and dumb?"

As a matter of fact the tree was very much alive. Okonkwo's second wife had merely cut a few leaves off it to wrap some food, and she said so. Without further argument Okonkwo gave her a sound beating and left her and her only daughter weeping. Neither of the other wives dared to interfere beyond an occasional and tentative, "It is enough, Okonkwo," pleaded from a reasonable distance.

6. A mashed, edible base that is shaped into balls with the fingers and then indented for cupping and eating soup.

His anger thus satisfied, Okonkwo decided to go out hunting. He had an old rusty gun made by a clever blacksmith who had come to live in Umuofia long ago. But although Okonkwo was a great man whose prowess was universally acknowledged, he was not a hunter. In fact he had not killed a rat with his gun. And so when he called Ikemefuna to fetch his gun, the wife who had just been beaten murmured something about guns that never shot. Unfortunately for her, Okonkwo heard it and ran madly into his room for the loaded gun, ran out again and aimed at her as she clambered over the dwarf wall of the barn. He pressed the trigger and there was a loud report accompanied by the wail of his wives and children. He threw down the gun and jumped into the barn, and there lay the woman, very much shaken and frightened but quite unhurt. He heaved a heavy sigh and went away with the gun.

In spite of this incident the New Yam Festival was celebrated with great joy in Okonkwo's household. Early that morning as he offered a sacrifice of new yam and palm-oil to his ancestors he asked them to protect him, his children and their mothers in the new year.

As the day wore on his in-laws arrived from three surrounding villages, and each party brought with them a huge pot of palm-wine. And there was eating and drinking till night, when Okonkwo's in-laws began to leave for their homes.

The second day of the new year was the day of the great wrestling match between Okonkwo's village and their neighbors. It was difficult to say which the people enjoyed more—the feasting and fellowship of the first day or the wrestling contest of the second. But there was one woman who had no doubt whatever in her mind. She was Okonkwo's second wife, Ekwefi, whom he nearly shot. There was no festival in all the seasons of the year which gave her as much pleasure as the wrestling match. Many years ago when she was the village beauty Okonkwo had won her heart by throwing the Cat in the greatest contest within living memory. She did not marry him then because he was too poor to pay her bride-price. But a few years later she ran away from her husband and came to live with Okonkwo. All this happened many years ago. Now Ekwefi[7] was a woman of forty-five who had suffered a great deal in her time. But her love of wrestling contests was still as strong as it was thirty years ago.

It was not yet noon on the second day of the New Yam Festival. Ekwefi and her only daughter, Ezinma,[8] sat near the fireplace waiting for the water in the pot to boil. The fowl Ekwefi had just killed was in the wooden mortar. The water began to boil, and in one deft movement she lifted the pot from the fire and poured the boiling water over the fowl. She put back the empty pot on the circular pad in the corner, and looked at her palms, which were black with soot. Ezinma was always surprised that her mother could lift a pot from the fire with her bare hands.

"Ekwefi," she said, "is it true that when people are grown up, fire does not burn them?" Ezinma, unlike most children, called her mother by her name.

"Yes," replied Ekwefi, too busy to argue. Her daughter was only ten years old but she was wiser than her years.

7. An abbreviation of "Do you have a cow?"; the cow being a symbol of wealth. Okonkwo would presumably have repaid Ekwefi's bride-price to her first husband.   8. True beauty (literal trans.), or goodness.

"But Nwoye's mother dropped her pot of hot soup the other day and it broke on the floor."

Ekwefi turned the hen over in the mortar and began to pluck the feathers.

"Ekwefi," said Ezinma, who had joined in plucking the feathers, "my eyelid is twitching."

"It means you are going to cry," said her mother.

"No," Ezinma said, "it is this eyelid, the top one."

"That means you will see something."

"What will I see?" she asked.

"How can I know?" Ekwefi wanted her to work it out herself.

"Oho," said Ezinma at last. "I know what it is—the wrestling match."

At last the hen was plucked clean. Ekwefi tried to pull out the horny beak but it was too hard. She turned round on her low stool and put the beak in the fire for a few moments. She pulled again and it came off.

"Ekwefi!" a voice called from one of the other huts. It was Nwoye's mother, Okonkwo's first wife.

"Is that me?" Ekwefi called back. That was the way people answered calls from outside. They never answered yes for fear it might be an evil spirit calling.

"Will you give Ezinma some fire to bring to me?" Her own children and Ikemefuna had gone to the stream.

Ekwefi put a few live coals into a piece of broken pot and Ezinma carried it across the clean swept compound to Nwoye's mother.

"Thank you, Nma," she said. She was peeling new yams, and in a basket beside her were green vegetables and beans.

"Let me make the fire for you," Ezinma offered.

"Thank you, Ezigbo," she said. She often called her Ezigbo, which means "the good one."

Ezinma went outside and brought some sticks from a huge bundle of firewood. She broke them into little pieces across the sole of her foot and began to build a fire, blowing it with her breath.

"You will blow your eyes out," said Nwoye's mother, looking up from the yams she was peeling. "Use the fan." She stood up and pulled out the fan which was fastened into one of the rafters. As soon as she got up, the troublesome nanny goat, which had been dutifully eating yam peelings, dug her teeth into the real thing, scooped out two mouthfuls and fled from the hut to chew the cud in the goats' shed. Nwoye's mother swore at her and settled down again to her peeling. Ezinma's fire was now sending up thick clouds of smoke. She went on fanning it until it burst into flames. Nwoye's mother thanked her and she went back to her mother's hut.

Just then the distant beating of drums began to reach them. It came from the direction of the *ilo*, the village playground. Every village had its own *ilo* which was as old as the village itself and where all the great ceremonies and dances took place. The drums beat the unmistakable wrestling dance—quick, light and gay, and it came floating on the wind.

Okonkwo cleared his throat and moved his feet to the beat of the drums. It filled him with fire as it had always done from his youth. He trembled with the desire to conquer and subdue. It was like the desire for a woman.

"We shall be late for the wrestling," said Ezinma to her mother.

"They will not begin until the sun goes down."

"But they are beating the drums."

"Yes. The drums begin at noon but the wrestling waits until the sun begins to sink. Go and see if your father has brought out yams for the afternoon."

"He has. Nwoye's mother is already cooking."

"Go and bring our own, then. We must cook quickly or we shall be late for the wrestling."

Ezinma ran in the direction of the barn and brought back two yams from the dwarf wall.

Ekwefi peeled the yams quickly. The troublesome nanny goat sniffed about, eating the peelings. She cut the yams into small pieces and began to prepare a pottage, using some of the chicken.

At that moment they heard someone crying just outside their compound. It was very much like Obiageli,[9] Nwoye's sister.

"Is that not Obiageli weeping?" Ekwefi called across the yard to Nwoye's mother.

"Yes," she replied. "She must have broken her waterpot."

The weeping was now quite close and soon the children filed in, carrying on their heads various sizes of pots suitable to their years. Ikemefuna came first with the biggest pot, closely followed by Nwoye and his two younger brothers. Obiageli brought up the rear, her face streaming with tears. In her hand was the cloth pad on which the pot should have rested on her head.

"What happened?" her mother asked, and Obiageli told her mournful story. Her mother consoled her and promised to buy her another pot.

Nwoye's younger brothers were about to tell their mother the true story of the accident when Ikemefuna looked at them sternly and they held their peace. The fact was that Obiageli had been making *inyanga*[1] with her pot. She had balanced it on her head, folded her arms in front of her and began to sway her waist like a grown-up young lady. When the pot fell down and broke she burst out laughing. She only began to weep when they got near the iroko tree outside their compound.

The drums were still beating, persistent and unchanging. Their sound was no longer a separate thing from the living village. It was like the pulsation of its heart. It throbbed in the air, in the sunshine, and even in the trees, and filled the village with excitement.

Ekwefi ladled her husband's share of the pottage into a bowl and covered it. Ezinma took it to him in his *obi*.

Okonkwo was sitting on a goatskin already eating his first wife's meal. Obiageli, who had brought it from her mother's hut, sat on the floor waiting for him to finish. Ezinma placed her mother's dish before him and sat with Obiageli.

"Sit like a woman!" Okonkwo shouted at her. Ezinma brought her two legs together and stretched them in front of her.

"Father, will you go to see the wrestling?" Ezinma asked after a suitable interval.

"Yes," he answered. "Will you go?"

"Yes." And after a pause she said: "Can I bring your chair for you?"

"No, that is a boy's job." Okonkwo was specially fond of Ezinma. She looked very much like her mother, who was once the village beauty. But his fondness only showed on very rare occasions.

"Obiageli broke her pot today," Ezinma said.

---

9. Born to eat (born into prosperity).   1. Showing off.

"Yes, she has told me about it," Okonkwo said between mouthfuls.

"Father," said Obiageli, "people should not talk when they are eating or pepper may go down the wrong way."

"That is very true. Do you hear that, Ezinma? You are older than Obiageli but she has more sense."

He uncovered his second wife's dish and began to eat from it. Obiageli took the first dish and returned to her mother's hut. And then Nkechi came in, bringing the third dish. Nkechi was the daughter of Okonkwo's third wife.

In the distance the drums continued to beat.

6

The whole village turned out on the *ilo*, men, women and children. They stood round in a huge circle leaving the center of the playground free. The elders and grandees of the village sat on their own stools brought there by their young sons or slaves. Okonkwo was among them. All others stood except those who came early enough to secure places on the few stands which had been built by placing smooth logs on forked pillars.

The wrestlers were not there yet and the drummers held the field. They too sat just in front of the huge circle of spectators, facing the elders. Behind them was the big and ancient silk-cotton tree which was sacred. Spirits of good children lived in that tree waiting to be born. On ordinary days young women who desired children came to sit under its shade.

There were seven drums and they were arranged according to their sizes in a long wooden basket. Three men beat them with sticks, working feverishly from one drum to another. They were possessed by the spirit of the drums.

The young men who kept order on these occasions dashed about, consulting among themselves and with the leaders of the two wrestling teams, who were still outside the circle, behind the crowd. Once in a while two young men carrying palm fronds ran round the circle and kept the crowd back by beating the ground in front of them or, if they were stubborn, their legs and feet.

At last the two teams danced into the circle and the crowd roared and clapped. The drums rose to a frenzy. The people surged forward. The young men who kept order flew around, waving their palm fronds. Old men nodded to the beat of the drums and remembered the days when they wrestled to its intoxicating rhythm.

The contest began with boys of fifteen or sixteen. There were only three such boys in each team. They were not the real wrestlers; they merely set the scene. Within a short time the first two bouts were over. But the third created a big sensation even among the elders who did not usually show their excitement so openly. It was as quick as the other two, perhaps even quicker. But very few people had ever seen that kind of wrestling before. As soon as the two boys closed in, one of them did something which no one could describe because it had been as quick as a flash. And the other boy was flat on his back. The crowd roared and clapped and for a while drowned the frenzied drums. Okonkwo sprang to his feet and quickly sat down again. Three young men from the victorious boy's team ran forward, carried him shoulder high and danced through the cheering crowd. Everybody soon knew who the boy was. His name was Maduka, the son of Obierika.[2]

2. The heart eats (enjoys) more.

The drummers stopped for a brief rest before the real matches. Their bodies shone with sweat, and they took up fans and began to fan themselves. They also drank water from small pots and ate kola nuts. They became ordinary human beings again, talking and laughing among themselves and with others who stood near them. The air, which had been stretched taut with excitement, relaxed again. It was as if water had been poured on the tightened skin of a drum. Many people looked around, perhaps for the first time, and saw those who stood or sat next to them.

"I did not know it was you," Ekwefi said to the woman who had stood shoulder to shoulder with her since the beginning of the matches.

"I do not blame you," said the woman. "I have never seen such a large crowd of people. Is it true that Okonkwo nearly killed you with his gun?"

"It is true indeed, my dear friend. I cannot yet find a mouth with which to tell the story."

"Your *chi* is very much awake, my friend. And how is my daughter, Ezinma?"

"She has been very well for some time now. Perhaps she has come to stay."

"I think she has. How old is she now?"

"She is about ten years old."

"I think she will stay. They usually stay if they do not die before the age of six."

"I pray she stays," said Ekwefi with a heavy sigh.

The woman with whom she talked was called Chielo.[3] She was the priestess of Agbala, the Oracle of the Hills and the Caves. In ordinary life Chielo was a widow with two children. She was very friendly with Ekwefi and they shared a common shed in the market. She was particularly fond of Ekwefi's only daughter, Ezinma, whom she called "my daughter." Quite often she bought beancakes and gave Ekwefi some to take home to Ezinma. Anyone seeing Chielo in ordinary life would hardly believe she was the same person who prophesied when the spirit of Agbala was upon her. The drummers took up their sticks and the air shivered and grew tense like a tightened bow.

The two teams were ranged facing each other across the clear space. A young man from one team danced across the center to the other side and pointed at whomever he wanted to fight. They danced back to the center together and then closed in.

There were twelve men on each side and the challenge went from one side to the other. Two judges walked around the wrestlers and when they thought they were equally matched, stopped them. Five matches ended in this way. But the really exciting moments were when a man was thrown. The huge voice of the crowd then rose to the sky and in every direction. It was even heard in the surrounding villages.

The last match was between the leaders of the teams. They were among the best wrestlers in all the nine villages. The crowd wondered who would throw the other this year. Some said Okafo was the better man; others said he was not the equal of Ikezue.[4] Last year neither of them had thrown the other even though the judges had allowed the contest to go on longer than was the custom. They had the same style and one saw the other's plans beforehand. It might happen again this year.

Dusk was already approaching when their contest began. The drums went

3. Chi who plants.   4. Strength is complete (a boastful name).

mad and the crowds also. They surged forward as the two young men danced
into the circle. The palm fronds were helpless in keeping them back.

Ikezue held out his right hand. Okafo seized it, and they closed in. It was
a fierce contest. Ikezue strove to dig in his right heel behind Okafo so as to
pitch him backwards in the clever *ege* style. But the one knew what the other
was thinking. The crowd had surrounded and swallowed up the drummers,
whose frantic rhythm was no longer a mere disembodied sound but the very
heartbeat of the people.

The wrestlers were now almost still in each other's grip. The muscles on
their arms and their thighs and on their backs stood out and twitched. It
looked like an equal match. The two judges were already moving forward to
separate them when Ikezue, now desperate, went down quickly on one knee
in an attempt to fling his man backwards over his head. It was a sad miscalculation. Quick as the lightning of Amadiora, Okafo raised his right leg and
swung it over his rival's head. The crowd burst into a thunderous roar. Okafo
was swept off his feet by his supporters and carried home shoulder high.
They sang his praise and the young women clapped their hands:

> Who will wrestle for our village?
> Okafo will wrestle for our village.
> Has he thrown a hundred men?
> He has thrown four hundred men.
> Has he thrown a hundred Cats?
> He has thrown four hundred Cats.
> Then send him word to fight for us.

7

For three years Ikemefuna lived in Okonkwo's household and the elders
of Umuofia seemed to have forgotten about him. He grew rapidly like a yam
tendril in the rainy season, and was full of the sap of life. He had become
wholly absorbed into his new family. He was like an elder brother to Nwoye,
and from the very first seemed to have kindled a new fire in the younger boy.
He made him feel grown-up; and they no longer spent the evenings in
mother's hut while she cooked, but now sat with Okonkwo in his *obi,* or
watched him as he tapped his palm tree for the evening wine. Nothing
pleased Nwoye now more than to be sent for by his mother or another of his
father's wives to do one of those difficult and masculine tasks in the home,
like splitting wood, or pounding food. On receiving such a message through
a younger brother or sister, Nwoye would feign annoyance and grumble aloud
about women and their troubles.

Okonkwo was inwardly pleased at his son's development, and he knew it
was due to Ikemefuna. He wanted Nwoye to grow into a tough young man
capable of ruling his father's household when he was dead and gone to join
the ancestors. He wanted him to be a prosperous man, having enough in his
barn to feed the ancestors with regular sacrifices. And so he was always happy
when he heard him grumbling about women. That showed that in time he
would be able to control his women-folk. No matter how prosperous a man
was, if he was unable to rule his women and his children (and especially his
women) he was not really a man. He was like the man in the song who had
ten and one wives and not enough soup for his foo-foo.

So Okonkwo encouraged the boys to sit with him in his *obi,* and he told them stories of the land—masculine stories of violence and bloodshed. Nwoye knew that it was right to be masculine and to be violent, but somehow he still preferred the stories that his mother used to tell, and which she no doubt still told to her younger children—stories of the tortoise and his wily ways, and of the bird *eneke-nti-oba*[5] who challenged the whole world to a wrestling contest and was finally thrown by the cat. He remembered the story she often told of the quarrel between Earth and Sky long ago, and how Sky withheld rain for seven years, until crops withered and the dead could not be buried because the hoes broke on the stony Earth. At last Vulture was sent to plead with Sky, and to soften his heart with a song of the suffering of the sons of men. Whenever Nwoye's mother sang this song he felt carried away to the distant scene in the sky where Vulture, Earth's emissary, sang for mercy. At last Sky was moved to pity, and he gave to Vulture rain wrapped in leaves of coco-yam. But as he flew home his long talon pierced the leaves and the rain fell as it had never fallen before. And so heavily did it rain on Vulture that he did not return to deliver his message but flew to a distant land, from where he had espied a fire. And when he got there he found it was a man making a sacrifice. He warmed himself in the fire and ate the entrails.

That was the kind of story that Nwoye loved. But he now knew that they were for foolish women and children, and he knew that his father wanted him to be a man. And so he feigned that he no longer cared for women's stories. And when he did this he saw that his father was pleased, and no longer rebuked him or beat him. So Nwoye and Ikemefuna would listen to Okonkwo's stories about tribal wars, or how, years ago, he had stalked his victim, overpowered him and obtained his first human head. And as he told them of the past they sat in darkness or the dim glow of logs, waiting for the women to finish their cooking. When they finished, each brought her bowl of foo-foo and bowl of soup to her husband. An oil lamp was lit and Okonkwo tasted from each bowl, and then passed two shares to Nwoye and Ikemefuna.

In this way the moons and the seasons passed. And then the locusts came. It had not happened for many a long year. The elders said locusts came once in a generation, reappeared every year for seven years and then disappeared for another lifetime. They went back to their caves in a distant land, where they were guarded by a race of stunted men. And then after another lifetime these men opened the caves again and the locusts came to Umuofia.

They came in the cold harmattan season after the harvests had been gathered, and ate up all the wild grass in the fields.

Okonkwo and the two boys were working on the red outer walls of the compound. This was one of the lighter tasks of the after-harvest season. A new cover of thick palm branches and palm leaves was set on the walls to protect them from the next rainy season. Okonkwo worked on the outside of the wall and the boys worked from within. There were little holes from one side to the other in the upper levels of the wall, and through these Okonkwo passed the rope, or *tie-tie*,[6] to the boys and they passed it round the wooden stays and then back to him; and in this way the cover was strengthened on the wall.

The women had gone to the bush to collect firewood, and the little children

---

5. The swallow with the ear of a crocodile (who is deaf) (literal trans.); a bird who proverbially flies without perching.   **6.** A creeper used as a rope to lash sections in building (pidgin English from "to tie").

to visit their playmates in the neighboring compounds. The harmattan was in the air and seemed to distill a hazy feeling of sleep on the world. Okonkwo and the boys worked in complete silence, which was only broken when a new palm frond was lifted on to the wall or when a busy hen moved dry leaves about in her ceaseless search for food.

And then quite suddenly a shadow fell on the world, and the sun seemed hidden behind a thick cloud. Okonkwo looked up from his work and wondered if it was going to rain at such an unlikely time of the year. But almost immediately a shout of joy broke out in all directions, and Umuofia, which had dozed in the noon-day haze, broke into life and activity.

"Locusts are descending," was joyfully chanted everywhere, and men, women and children left their work or their play and ran into the open to see the unfamiliar sight. The locusts had not come for many, many years, and only the old people had seen them before.

At first, a fairly small swarm came. They were the harbingers sent to survey the land. And then appeared on the horizon a slowly moving mass like a boundless sheet of black cloud drifting towards Umuofia. Soon it covered half the sky, and the solid mass was now broken by tiny eyes of light like shining star dust. It was a tremendous sight, full of power and beauty.

Everyone was now about, talking excitedly and praying that the locusts should camp in Umuofia for the night. For although locusts had not visited Umuofia for many years, everybody knew by instinct that they were very good to eat. And at last the locusts did descend. They settled on every tree and on every blade of grass; they settled on the roofs and covered the bare ground. Mighty tree branches broke away under them, and the whole country became the brown-earth color of the vast, hungry swarm.

Many people went out with baskets trying to catch them, but the elders counseled patience till nightfall. And they were right. The locusts settled in the bushes for the night and their wings became wet with dew. Then all Umuofia turned out in spite of the cold harmattan, and everyone filled his bags and pots with locusts. The next morning they were roasted in clay pots and then spread in the sun until they became dry and brittle. And for many days this rare food was eaten with solid palm-oil.

Okonkwo sat in his *obi* crunching happily with Ikemefuna and Nwoye, and drinking palm-wine copiously, when Ogbuefi Ezeudu came in. Ezeudu was the oldest man in this quarter of Umuofia. He had been a great and fearless warrior in his time, and was now accorded great respect in all the clan. He refused to join in the meal, and asked Okonkwo to have a word with him outside. And so they walked out together, the old man supporting himself with his stick. When they were out of earshot, he said to Okonkwo:

"That boy calls you father. Do not bear a hand in his death." Okonkwo was surprised, and was about to say something when the old man continued:

"Yes, Umuofia has decided to kill him. The Oracle of the Hills and the Caves has pronounced it. They will take him outside Umuofia as is the custom, and kill him there. But I want you to have nothing to do with it. He calls you his father."

The next day a group of elders from all the nine villages of Umuofia came to Okonkwo's house early in the morning, and before they began to speak in low tones Nwoye and Ikemefuna were sent out. They did not stay very long, but when they went away Okonkwo sat still for a very long time supporting his chin in his palms. Later in the day he called Ikemefuna and told him that he was to be taken home the next day. Nwoye overheard it and burst into tears, whereupon his father beat him heavily. As for Ikemefuna, he was at a loss. His own home had gradually become very faint and distant. He still missed his mother and his sister and would be very glad to see them. But somehow he knew he was not going to see them. He remembered once when men had talked in low tones with his father; and it seemed now as if it was happening all over again.

Later, Nwoye went to his mother's hut and told her that Ikemefuna was going home. She immediately dropped her pestle with which she was grinding pepper, folded her arms across her breast and sighed, "Poor child."

The next day, the men returned with a pot of wine. They were all fully dressed as if they were going to a big clan meeting or to pay a visit to a neighboring village. They passed their cloths under the right arm-pit, and hung their goatskin bags and sheathed machetes over their left shoulders. Okonkwo got ready quickly and the party set out with Ikemefuna carrying the pot of wine. A deathly silence descended on Okonkwo's compound. Even the very little children seemed to know. Throughout that day Nwoye sat in his mother's hut and tears stood in his eyes.

At the beginning of their journey the men of Umuofia talked and laughed about the locusts, about their women, and about some effeminate men who had refused to come with them. But as they drew near to the outskirts of Umuofia silence fell upon them too.

The sun rose slowly to the center of the sky, and the dry, sandy footway began to throw up the heat that lay buried in it. Some birds chirruped in the forests around. The men trod dry leaves on the sand. All else was silent. Then from the distance came the faint beating of the *ekwe*. It rose and faded with the wind—a peaceful dance from a distant clan.

"It is an *ozo* dance,"[7] the men said among themselves. But no one was sure where it was coming from. Some said Ezimili, others Abame or Aninta. They argued for a short while and fell into silence again, and the elusive dance rose and fell with the wind. Somewhere a man was taking one of the titles of his clan, with music and dancing and a great feast.

The footway had now become a narrow line in the heart of the forest. The short trees and sparse undergrowth which surrounded the men's village began to give way to giant trees and climbers which perhaps had stood from the beginning of things, untouched by the ax and the bush-fire. The sun breaking through their leaves and branches threw a pattern of light and shade on the sandy footway.

Ikemefuna heard a whisper close behind him and turned round sharply. The man who had whispered now called out aloud, urging the others to hurry up.

"We still have a long way to go," he said. Then he and another man went before Ikemefuna and set a faster pace.

Thus the men of Umuofia pursued their way, armed with sheathed machetes, and Ikemefuna, carrying a pot of palm-wine on his head, walked in their midst. Although he had felt uneasy at first, he was not afraid now. Okonkwo walked behind him. He could hardly imagine that Okonkwo was

7. Part of the *ozo* rituals, the spiritual ceremonies that accompanied the taking of titles.

not his real father. He had never been fond of his real father, and at the end of three years he had become very distant indeed. But his mother and his three-year-old sister . . . of course she would not be three now, but six. Would he recognize her now? She must have grown quite big. How his mother would weep for joy, and thank Okonkwo for having looked after him so well and for bringing him back. She would want to hear everything that had happened to him in all these years. Could he remember them all? He would tell her about Nwoye and his mother, and about the locusts. . . . Then quite suddenly a thought came upon him. His mother might be dead. He tried in vain to force the thought out of his mind. Then he tried to settle the matter the way he used to settle such matters when he was a little boy. He still remembered the song:

> *Eze elina, elina!*
> *Sala*
> *Eze ilikwa ya*
> *Ikwaba akwa oligholi*
> *Ebe Danda nechi eze*
> *Ebe Uzuzu nete egwu*
> *Sala*[8]

He sang it in his mind, and walked to its beat. If the song ended on his right foot, his mother was alive. If it ended on his left, she was dead. No, not dead, but ill. It ended on the right. She was alive and well. He sang the song again, and it ended on the left. But the second time did not count. The first voice gets to Chukwu, or God's house. That was a favorite saying of children. Ikemefuna felt like a child once more. It must be the thought of going home to his mother.

One of the men behind him cleared his throat. Ikemefuna looked back, and the man growled at him to go on and not stand looking back. The way he said it sent cold fear down Ikemefuna's back. His hands trembled vaguely on the black pot he carried. Why had Okonkwo withdrawn to the rear? Ikemefuna felt his legs melting under him. And he was afraid to look back.

As the man who had cleared his throat drew up and raised his machete, Okonkwo looked away. He heard the blow. The pot fell and broke in the sand. He heard Ikemefuna cry, "My father, they have killed me!" as he ran towards him. Dazed with fear, Okonkwo drew his machete and cut him down. He was afraid of being thought weak.

As soon as his father walked in, that night, Nwoye knew that Ikemefuna had been killed, and something seemed to give way inside him, like the snapping of a tightened bow. He did not cry. He just hung limp. He had had the same kind of feeling not long ago, during the last harvest season. Every child loved the harvest season. Those who were big enough to carry even a few yams in a tiny basket went with grown-ups to the farm. And if they could not help in digging up the yams, they could gather firewood together for roasting the ones that would be eaten there on the farm. This roasted yam soaked in red palm-oil and eaten in the open farm was sweeter than any meal

---

8. King don't eat, don't eat / Sala / King if you eat it / You will weep for the abomination / Where Danda installs a king / Where Uzuzu dances / Sala. *Sala:* meaningless refrain. *Danda:* the ant. *Uzuzu:* sand. Ikemefuna reassures himself by singing his favorite song about the country where the "sands dance forever" (see p. 2435).

at home. It was after such a day at the farm during the last harvest that Nwoye had felt for the first time a snapping inside him like the one he now felt. They were returning home with baskets of yams from a distant farm across the stream when they heard the voice of an infant crying in the thick forest. A sudden hush had fallen on the women, who had been talking, and they had quickened their steps. Nwoye had heard that twins were put in earthenware pots and thrown away in the forest, but he had never yet come across them. A vague chill had descended on him and his head had seemed to swell, like a solitary walker at night who passes an evil spirit on the way. Then something had given way inside him. It descended on him again, this feeling, when his father walked in, that night after killing Ikemefuna.

8

Okonkwo did not taste any food for two days after the death of Ikemefuna. He drank palm-wine from morning till night, and his eyes were red and fierce like the eyes of a rat when it was caught by the tail and dashed against the floor. He called his son, Nwoye, to sit with him in his *obi*. But the boy was afraid of him and slipped out of the hut as soon as he noticed him dozing.

He did not sleep at night. He tried not to think about Ikemefuna, but the more he tried the more he thought about him. Once he got up from bed and walked about his compound. But he was so weak that his legs could hardly carry him. He felt like a drunken giant walking with the limbs of a mosquito. Now and then a cold shiver descended on his head and spread down his body.

On the third day he asked his second wife, Ekwefi, to roast plantains for him. She prepared it the way he liked—with slices of oil-bean and fish.

"You have not eaten for two days," said his daughter Ezinma when she brought the food to him. "So you must finish this." She sat down and stretched her legs in front of her. Okonkwo ate the food absent-mindedly. 'She should have been a boy,' he thought as he looked at his ten-year-old daughter. He passed her a piece of fish.

"Go and bring me some cold water," he said. Ezinma rushed out of the hut, chewing the fish, and soon returned with a bowl of cool water from the earthen pot in her mother's hut.

Okonkwo took the bowl from her and gulped the water down. He ate a few more pieces of plantain and pushed the dish aside.

"Bring me my bag," he asked, and Ezinma brought his goatskin bag from the far end of the hut. He searched in it for his snuff-bottle. It was a deep bag and took almost the whole length of his arm. It contained other things apart from his snuff-bottle. There was a drinking horn in it, and also a drinking gourd, and they knocked against each other as he searched. When he brought out the snuff-bottle he tapped it a few times against his knee-cap before taking out some snuff on the palm of his left hand. Then he remembered that he had not taken out his snuff-spoon. He searched his bag again and brought out a small, flat, ivory spoon, with which he carried the brown snuff to his nostrils.

Ezinma took the dish in one hand and the empty water bowl in the other and went back to her mother's hut. "She should have been a boy," Okonkwo said to himself again. His mind went back to Ikemefuna and he shivered. If only he could find some work to do he would be able to forget. But it was the season of rest between the harvest and the next planting season. The only work that men did at this time was covering the walls of their compound with new palm fronds. And Okonkwo had already done that. He had finished it on the very day the locusts came, when he had worked on one side of the wall and Ikemefuna and Nwoye on the other.

"When did you become a shivering old woman," Okonkwo asked himself, "you, who are known in all the nine villages for your valor in war? How can a man who has killed five men in battle fall to pieces because he has added a boy to their number? Okonkwo, you have become a woman indeed."

He sprang to his feet, hung his goatskin bag on his shoulder and went to visit his friend, Obierika.

Obierika was sitting outside under the shade of an orange tree making thatches from leaves of the raffia-palm. He exchanged greetings with Okonkwo and led the way into his *obi.*

"I was coming over to see you as soon as I finished that thatch," he said, rubbing off the grains of sand that clung to his thighs.

"Is it well?" Okonkwo asked.

"Yes," replied Obierika. "My daughter's suitor is coming today and I hope we will clinch the matter of the bride-price. I want you to be there."

Just then Obierika's son, Maduka, came into the *obi* from outside, greeted Okonkwo and turned towards the compound.

"Come and shake hands with me," Okonkwo said to the lad. "Your wrestling the other day gave me much happiness." The boy smiled, shook hands with Okonkwo and went into the compound.

"He will do great things," Okonkwo said. "If I had a son like him I should be happy. I am worried about Nwoye. A bowl of pounded yams can throw him in a wrestling match. His two younger brothers are more promising. But I can tell you, Obierika, that my children do not resemble me. Where are the young suckers that will grow when the old banana tree dies? If Ezinma had been a boy I would have been happier. She has the right spirit."

"You worry yourself for nothing," said Obierika. "The children are still very young."

"Nwoye is old enough to impregnate a woman. At his age I was already fending for myself. No, my friend, he is not too young. A chick that will grow into a cock can be spotted the very day it hatches. I have done my best to make Nwoye grow into a man, but there is too much of his mother in him."

"Too much of his grandfather," Obierika thought, but he did not say it. The same thought also came to Okonkwo's mind. But he had long learned how to lay that ghost. Whenever the thought of his father's weakness and failure troubled him he expelled it by thinking about his own strength and success. And so he did now. His mind went to his latest show of manliness.

"I cannot understand why you refused to come with us to kill that boy," he asked Obierika.

"Because I did not want to," Obierika replied sharply. "I had something better to do."

"You sound as if you question the authority and the decision of the Oracle, who said he should die."

"I do not. Why should I? But the Oracle did not ask me to carry out its decision."

"But someone had to do it. If we were all afraid of blood, it would not be done. And what do you think the Oracle would do then?"

"You know very well, Okonkwo, that I am not afraid of blood; and if anyone tells you that I am, he is telling a lie. And let me tell you one thing, my friend. If I were you I would have stayed at home. What you have done will not please the Earth. It is the kind of action for which the goddess wipes out whole families."

"The Earth cannot punish me for obeying her messenger," Okonkwo said. "A child's fingers are not scalded by a piece of hot yam which its mother puts into its palm."

"That is true," Obierika agreed. "But if the Oracle said that my son should be killed I would neither dispute it nor be the one to do it."

They would have gone on arguing had Ofoedu[9] not come in just then. It was clear from his twinkling eyes that he had important news. But it would be impolite to rush him. Obierika offered him a lobe of the kola nut he had broken with Okonkwo. Ofoedu ate slowly and talked about the locusts. When he finished his kola nut he said:

"The things that happen these days are very strange."

"What has happened?" asked Okonkwo.

"Do you know Ogbuefi Ndulue?"[1] Ofoedu asked.

"Ogbuefi Ndulue of Ire village," Okonkwo and Obierika said together.

"He died this morning," said Ofoedu.

"That is not strange. He was the oldest man in Ire," said Obierika.

"You are right," Ofoedu agreed. "But you ought to ask why the drum has not beaten to tell Umuofia of his death."

"Why?" asked Obierika and Okonkwo together.

"That is the strange part of it. You know his first wife who walks with a stick?"

"Yes. She is called Ozoemena."[2]

"That is so," said Ofoedu. "Ozoemena was, as you know, too old to attend Ndulue during his illness. His younger wives did that. When he died this morning, one of these women went to Ozoemena's hut and told her. She rose from her mat, took her stick and walked over to the *obi*. She knelt on her knees and hands at the threshold and called her husband, who was laid on a mat. 'Ogbuefi Ndulue,' she called, three times, and went back to her hut. When the youngest wife went to call her again to be present at the washing of the body, she found her lying on the mat, dead."

"That is very strange, indeed," said Okonkwo. "They will put off Ndulue's funeral until his wife has been buried."[3]

"That is why the drum has not been beaten to tell Umuofia."

"It was always said that Ndulue and Ozoemena had one mind," said Obierika. "I remember when I was a young boy there was a song about them. He could not do anything without telling her."

"I did not know that," said Okonkwo. "I thought he was a strong man in his youth."

"He was indeed," said Ofoedu.

---

9. The ancestors are our guide.   1. Life has arrived.   2. Another bad thing will not happen.   3. A wife dying shortly after her husband was sometimes considered guilty of his death, so the village preserves appearances by burying Ozoemena before announcing Ogbuefi Ndule's death.

Okonkwo shook his head doubtfully.

"He led Umuofia to war in those days," said Obierika.

Okonkwo was beginning to feel like his old self again. All that he required was something to occupy his mind. If he had killed Ikemefuna during the busy planting season or harvesting it would not have been so bad; his mind would have been centered on his work. Okonkwo was not a man of thought but of action. But in absence of work, talking was the next best.

Soon after Ofoedu left, Okonkwo took up his goatskin bag to go.

"I must go home to tap my palm trees for the afternoon," he said.

"Who taps your tall trees for you?" asked Obierika.

"Umezulike," replied Okonkwo.

"Sometimes I wish I had not taken the *ozo* title," said Obierika. "It wounds my heart to see these young men killing palm trees in the name of tapping."

"It is so indeed," Okonkwo agreed. "But the law of the land must be obeyed."

"I don't know how we got that law," said Obierika. "In many other clans a man of title is not forbidden to climb the palm tree. Here we say he cannot climb the tall tree but he can tap the short ones standing on the ground. It is like Dimaragana, who would not lend his knife for cutting up dogmeat because the dog was taboo to him, but offered to use his teeth."

"I think it is good that our clan holds the *ozo* title in high esteem," said Okonkwo. "In those other clans you speak of, *ozo* is so low that every beggar takes it."

"I was only speaking in jest," said Obierika. "In Abame and Aninta the title is worth less than two cowries. Every man wears the thread of title on his ankle, and does not lose it even if he steals."

"They have indeed soiled the name of *ozo*," said Okonkwo as he rose to go.

"It will not be very long now before my in-laws come," said Obierika.

"I shall return very soon," said Okonkwo, looking at the position of the sun.

There were seven men in Obierika's hut when Okonkwo returned. The suitor was a young man of about twenty-five, and with him were his father and uncle. On Obierika's side were his two elder brothers and Maduka, his sixteen-year-old son.

"Ask Akueke's mother to send us some kola nuts," said Obierika to his son. Maduka vanished into the compound like lightning. The conversation at once centered on him, and everybody agreed that he was as sharp as a razor.

"I sometimes think he is too sharp," said Obierika, somewhat indulgently. "He hardly ever walks. He is always in a hurry. If you are sending him on an errand he flies away before he has heard half of the message."

"You were very much like that yourself," said his eldest brother. "As our people say, 'When mother-cow is chewing grass its young ones watch its mouth.' Maduka has been watching your mouth."

As he was speaking the boy returned, followed by Akueke,[4] his half-sister,

---

4. Wealth of Eke (a divinity). Similar names built on *Ako* (wealth) connote riches and are associated with the idea of women as a form of exchangeable material wealth.

carrying a wooden dish with three kola nuts and alligator pepper. She gave the dish to her father's eldest brother and then shook hands, very shyly, with her suitor and his relatives. She was about sixteen and just ripe for marriage. Her suitor and his relatives surveyed her young body with expert eyes as if to assure themselves that she was beautiful and ripe.

She wore a coiffure which was done up into a crest in the middle of the head. Cam wood was rubbed lightly into her skin, and all over her body were black patterns drawn with *uli.*[5] She wore a black necklace which hung down in three coils just above her full, succulent breasts. On her arms were red and yellow bangles, and on her waist four or five rows of *jigida,* or waist beads.

When she had shaken hands, or rather held out her hand to be shaken, she returned to her mother's hut to help with the cooking.

"Remove your *jigida* first," her mother warned as she moved near the fire-place to bring the pestle resting against the wall. "Every day I tell you that *jigida* and fire are not friends. But you will never hear. You grew your ears for decoration, not for hearing. One of these days your *jigida* will catch fire on your waist, and then you will know."

Akueke moved to the other end of the hut and began to remove the waist-beads. It had to be done slowly and carefully, taking each string separately, else it would break and the thousand tiny rings would have to be strung together again. She rubbed each string downwards with her palms until it passed the buttocks and slipped down to the floor around her feet.

The men in the *obi* had already begun to drink the palm-wine which Akueke's suitor had brought. It was a very good wine and powerful, for in spite of the palm fruit hung across the mouth of the pot to restrain the lively liquor, white foam rose and spilled over.

"That wine is the work of a good tapper," said Okonkwo.

The young suitor, whose name was Ibe, smiled broadly and said to his father: "Do you hear that?" He then said to the others: "He will never admit that I am a good tapper."

"He tapped three of my best palm trees to death," said his father, Ukegbu.

"That was about five years ago," said Ibe, who had begun to pour out the wine, "before I learned how to tap." He filled the first horn and gave to his father. Then he poured out for the others. Okonkwo brought out his big horn from the goatskin bag, blew into it to remove any dust that might be there, and gave it to Ibe to fill.

As the men drank, they talked about everything except the thing for which they had gathered. It was only after the pot had been emptied that the suitor's father cleared his voice and announced the object of their visit.

Obierika then presented to him a small bundle of short broomsticks. Ukegbu counted them.

"They are thirty?" he asked.

Obierika nodded in agreement.

"We are at last getting somewhere," Ukegbu said, and then turning to his brother and his son he said: "Let us go out and whisper together." The three rose and went outside. When they returned Ukegbu handed the bundle of

5. A liquid made from crushed seeds, which caused the skin to pucker temporarily. It was used to create black tattoolike decorations. *Cam wood:* a shrub. The powdered red heartwood of the camwood shrub was used as a cosmetic and dye.

sticks back to Obierika. He counted them; instead of thirty there were now only fifteen. He passed them over to his eldest brother, Machi, who also counted them and said:

"We had not thought to go below thirty. But as the dog said, 'If I fall down for you and you fall down for me, it is play.' Marriage should be a play and not a fight; so we are falling down again." He then added ten sticks to the fifteen and gave the bundle to Ukegbu.

In this way Akuke's bride-price was finally settled at twenty bags of cowries. It was already dusk when the two parties came to this agreement.

"Go and tell Akueke's mother that we have finished," Obierika said to his son, Maduka. Almost immediately the women came in with a big bowl of foo-foo. Obierika's second wife followed with a pot of soup, and Maduka brought in a pot of palm-wine.

As the men ate and drank palm-wine they talked about the customs of their neighbors.

"It was only this morning," said Obierika, "that Okonkwo and I were talking about Abame and Aninta, where titled men climb trees and pound foo-foo for their wives."

"All their customs are upside-down. They do not decide bride-price as we do, with sticks. They haggle and bargain as if they were buying a goat or a cow in the market."

"That is very bad," said Obierika's eldest brother. "But what is good in one place is bad in another place. In Umunso they do not bargain at all, not even with broomsticks. The suitor just goes on bringing bags of cowries until his in-laws tell him to stop. It is a bad custom because it always leads to a quarrel."

"The world is large," said Okonkwo. "I have even heard that in some tribes a man's children belong to his wife and her family."

"That cannot be," said Machi. "You might as well say that the woman lies on top of the man when they are making the children."

"It is like the story of white men who, they say, are white like this piece of chalk," said Obierika. He held up a piece of chalk, which every man kept in his *obi* and with which his guests drew lines on the floor before they ate kola nuts. "And these white men, they say, have no toes."[6]

"And have you never seen them?" asked Machi.

"Have you?" asked Obierika.

"One of them passes here frequently," said Machi. "His name is Amadi."

Those who knew Amadi laughed. He was a leper, and the polite name for leprosy was "the white skin."

9

For the first time in three nights, Okonkwo slept. He woke up once in the middle of the night and his mind went back to the past three days without making him feel uneasy. He began to wonder why he had felt uneasy at all. It was like a man wondering in broad daylight why a dream had appeared so terrible to him at night. He stretched himself and scratched his thigh where a mosquito had bitten him as he slept. Another one was wailing near his

6. They wear shoes.

right ear. He slapped the ear and hoped he had killed it. Why do they always go for one's ears? When he was a child his mother had told him a story about it. But it was as silly as all women's stories. Mosquito, she had said, had asked Ear to marry him, whereupon Ear fell on the floor in uncontrollable laughter. "How much longer do you think you will live?" she asked. "You are already a skeleton." Mosquito went away humiliated, and any time he passed her way he told Ear that he was still alive.

Okonkwo turned on his side and went back to sleep. He was roused in the morning by someone banging on his door.

"Who is that?" he growled. He knew it must be Ekwefi. Of his three wives Ekwefi was the only one who would have the audacity to bang on his door.

"Ezinma is dying," came her voice, and all the tragedy and sorrow of her life were packed in those words.

Okonkwo sprang from his bed, pushed back the bolt on his door and ran into Ekwefi's hut.

Ezinma lay shivering on a mat beside a huge fire that her mother had kept burning all night.

"It is *iba*,"[7] said Okonkwo as he took his machete and went into the bush to collect the leaves and grasses and barks of trees that went into making the medicine for *iba*.

Ekwefi knelt beside the sick child, occasionally feeling with her palm the wet, burning forehead.

Ezinma was an only child and the center of her mother's world. Very often it was Ezinma who decided what food her mother should prepare. Ekwefi even gave her such delicacies as eggs, which children were rarely allowed to eat because such food tempted them to steal. One day as Ezinma was eating an egg Okonkwo had come in unexpectedly from his hut. He was greatly shocked and swore to beat Ekwefi if she dared to give the child eggs again. But it was impossible to refuse Ezinma anything. After her father's rebuke she developed an even keener appetite for eggs. And she enjoyed above all the secrecy in which she now ate them. Her mother always took her into their bedroom and shut the door.

Ezinma did not call her mother *Nne* like all children. She called her by her name, Ekwefi, as her father and other grown-up people did. The relationship between them was not only that of mother and child. There was something in it like the companionship of equals, which was strengthened by such little conspiracies as eating eggs in the bedroom.

Ekwefi had suffered a good deal in her life. She had borne ten children and nine of them had died in infancy, usually before the age of three. As she buried one child after another her sorrow gave way to despair and then to grim resignation. The birth of her children, which should be a woman's crowning glory, became for Ekwefi mere physical agony devoid of promise. The naming ceremony after seven market weeks became an empty ritual. Her deepening despair found expression in the names she gave her children. One of them was a pathetic cry, Onwumbiko—"Death, I implore you." But Death took no notice; Onwumbiko died in his fifteenth month. The next child was a girl, Ozoemena—"May it not happen again." She died in her eleventh month, and two others after her. Ekwefi then became defiant and

---

7. A fever accompanied by jaundice, probably caused by malaria.

called her next child Onwuma—"Death may please himself." And he did.

After the death of Ekwefi's second child, Okonkwo had gone to a medicine man, who was also a diviner of the Afa Oracle,[8] to inquire what was amiss. This man told him that the child was an *ogbanje,* one of those wicked children who, when they died, entered their mothers' wombs to be born again.

"When your wife becomes pregnant again," he said, "let her not sleep in her hut. Let her go and stay with her people. In that way she will elude her wicked tormentor and break its evil cycle of birth and death."

Ekwefi did as she was asked. As soon as she became pregnant she went to live with her old mother in another village. It was there that her third child was born and circumcised on the eighth day. She did not return to Okonkwo's compound until three days before the naming ceremony. The child was called Onwumbiko.

Onwumbiko was not given proper burial when he died. Okonkwo had called on another medicine man who was famous in the clan for his great knowledge about *ogbanje* children. His name was Okagbue Uyanwa. Okagbue was a very striking figure, tall, with a full beard and a bald head. He was light in complexion and his eyes were red and fiery. He always gnashed his teeth as he listened to those who came to consult him. He asked Okonkwo a few questions about the dead child. All the neighbors and relations who had come to mourn gathered round them.

"On what market-day was it born?" he asked.

"*Oye,*" replied Okonkwo.

"And it died this morning?"

Okonkwo said yes, and only then realized for the first time that the child had died on the same market-day as it had been born. The neighbors and relations also saw the coincidence and said among themselves that it was very significant.

"Where do you sleep with your wife, in your *obi* or in her own hut?" asked the medicine man.

"In her hut."

"In future call her into your *obi.*"

The medicine man then ordered that there should be no mourning for the dead child. He brought out a sharp razor from the goatskin bag slung from his left shoulder and began to mutilate the child. Then he took it away to bury in the Evil Forest, holding it by the ankle and dragging it on the ground behind him. After such treatment it would think twice before coming again, unless it was one of the stubborn ones who returned, carrying the stamp of their mutilation—a missing finger or perhaps a dark line where the medicine man's razor had cut them.

By the time Onwumbiko died Ekwefi had become a very bitter woman. Her husband's first wife had already had three sons, all strong and healthy. When she had borne her third son in succession, Okonkwo had gathered a goat for her, as was the custom. Ekwefi had nothing but good wishes for her. But she had grown so bitter about her own *chi* that she could not rejoice with others over their good fortune. And so, on the day that Nwoye's mother celebrated the birth of her three sons with feasting and music, Ekwefi was

8. One who comunicates with the clients' ancestors by reading patterns made by objects (e.g., seeds, teeth, shells) thrown on a flat surface.

the only person in the happy company who went about with a cloud on her brow. Her husband's wife took this for malevolence, as husbands' wives were wont to. How could she know that Ekwefi's bitterness did not flow outwards to others but inwards into her own soul; that she did not blame others for their good fortune but her own evil *chi* who denied her any?

At last Ezinma was born, and although ailing she seemed determined to live. At first Ekwefi accepted her, as she had accepted others—with listless resignation. But when she lived on to her fourth, fifth and sixth years, love returned once more to her mother, and, with love, anxiety. She determined to nurse her child to health, and she put all her being into it. She was rewarded by occasional spells of health during which Ezinma bubbled with energy like fresh palm-wine. At such times she seemed beyond danger. But all of a sudden she would go down again. Everybody knew she was an *ogbanje*. These sudden bouts of sickness and health were typical of her kind. But she had lived so long that perhaps she had decided to stay. Some of them did become tired of their evil rounds of birth and death, or took pity on their mothers, and stayed. Ekwefi believed deep inside her that Ezinma had come to stay. She believed because it was that faith alone that gave her own life any kind of meaning. And this faith had been strengthened when a year or so ago a medicine man had dug up Ezinma's *iyi-uwa*. Everyone knew then that she would live because her bond with the world of *ogbanje* had been broken. Ekwefi was reassured. But such was her anxiety for her daughter that she could not rid herself completely of her fear. And although she believed that the *iyi-uwa* which had been dug up was genuine, she could not ignore the fact that some really evil children sometimes misled people into digging up a specious one.

But Ezinma's *iyi-uwa* had looked real enough. It was a smooth pebble wrapped in a dirty rag. The man who dug it up was the same Okagbue who was famous in all the clan for his knowledge in these matters. Ezinma had not wanted to cooperate with him at first. But that was only to be expected. No *ogbanje* would yield her secrets easily, and most of them never did because they died too young—before they could be asked questions.

"Where did you bury your *iyi-uwa*?" Okagbue had asked Ezinma. She was nine then and was just recovering from a serious illness.

"What is *iyi-uwa*?" she asked in return.

"You know what it is. You buried it in the ground somewhere so that you can die and return again to torment your mother."

Ezinma looked at her mother, whose eyes, sad and pleading, were fixed on her.

"Answer the question at once," roared Okonkwo, who stood beside her. All the family were there and some of the neighbors too.

"Leave her to me," the medicine man told Okonkwo in a cool, confident voice. He turned again to Ezinma. "Where did you bury your *iyi-uwa*?"

"Where they bury children," she replied, and the quiet spectators murmured to themselves.

"Come along then and show me the spot," said the medicine man.

The crowd set out with Ezinma leading the way and Okagbue following closely behind her. Okonkwo came next and Ekwefi followed him. When she came to the main road, Ezinma turned left as if she was going to the stream.

"But you said it was where they bury children?" asked the medicine man.

"No," said Ezinma, whose feeling of importance was manifest in her sprightly walk. She sometimes broke into a run and stopped again suddenly. The crowd followed her silently. Women and children returning from the stream with pots of water on their heads wondered what was happening until they saw Okagbue and guessed that it must be something to do with *ogbanje*. And they all knew Ekwefi and her daughter very well.

When she got to the big udala tree Ezinma turned left into the bush, and the crowd followed her. Because of her size she made her way through trees and creepers more quickly than her followers. The bush was alive with the tread of feet on dry leaves and sticks and the moving aside of tree branches. Ezinma went deeper and deeper and the crowd went with her. Then she suddenly turned round and began to walk back to the road. Everybody stood to let her pass and then filed after her.

"If you bring us all this way for nothing I shall beat sense into you," Okonkwo threatened.

"I have told you to let her alone. I know how to deal with them," said Okagbue.

Ezinma led the way back to the road, looked left and right and turned right. And so they arrived home again.

"Where did you bury your *iyi-uwa*?" asked Okagbue when Ezinma finally stopped outside her father's *obi*. Okagbue's voice was unchanged. It was quiet and confident.

"It is near that orange tree," Ezinma said.

"And why did you not say so, you wicked daughter of Akalogoli?" Okonkwo swore furiously. The medicine man ignored him.

"Come and show me the exact spot," he said quietly to Ezinma.

"It is here," she said when they got to the tree.

"Point at the spot with your finger," said Okagbue.

"It is here," said Ezinma touching the ground with her finger. Okonkwo stood by, rumbling like thunder in the rainy season.

"Bring me a hoe," said Okagbue.

When Ekwefi brought the hoe, he had already put aside his goatskin bag and his big cloth and was in his underwear, a long and thin strip of cloth wound round the waist like a belt and then passed between the legs to be fastened to the belt behind. He immediately set to work digging a pit where Ezinma had indicated. The neighbors sat around watching the pit becoming deeper and deeper. The dark top soil soon gave way to the bright red earth with which women scrubbed the floors and walls of huts. Okagbue worked tirelessly and in silence, his back shining with perspiration. Okonkwo stood by the pit. He asked Okagbue to come up and rest while he took a hand. But Okagbue said he was not tired yet.

Ekwefi went into her hut to cook yams. Her husband had brought out more yams than usual because the medicine man had to be fed. Ezinma went with her and helped in preparing the vegetables.

"There is too much green vegetable," she said.

"Don't you see the pot is full of yams?" Ekwefi asked. "And you know how leaves become smaller after cooking."

"Yes," said Ezinma, "that was why the snake-lizard killed his mother."

"Very true," said Ekwefi.

"He gave his mother seven baskets of vegetables to cook and in the end there were only three. And so he killed her," said Ezinma.

"That is not the end of the story."

"Oho," said Ezinma. "I remember now. He brought another seven baskets and cooked them himself. And there were again only three. So he killed himself too."

Outside the *obi* Okagbue and Okonkwo were digging the pit to find where Ezinma had buried her *iyi-uwa*. Neighbors sat around, watching. The pit was now so deep that they no longer saw the digger. They only saw the red earth he threw up mounting higher and higher. Okonkwo's son, Nwoye, stood near the edge of the pit because he wanted to take in all that happened.

Okagbue had again taken over the digging from Okonkwo. He worked, as usual, in silence. The neighbors and Okonkwo's wives were now talking. The children had lost interest and were playing.

Suddenly Okagbue sprang to the surface with the agility of a leopard.

"It is very near now," he said. "I have felt it."

There was immediate excitement and those who were sitting jumped to their feet.

"Call your wife and child," he said to Okonkwo. But Ekwefi and Ezinma had heard the noise and run out to see what it was.

Okagbue went back into the pit, which was now surrounded by spectators. After a few more hoe-fuls of earth he struck the *iyi-uwa*. He raised it carefully with the hoe and threw it to the surface. Some women ran away in fear when it was thrown. But they soon returned and everyone was gazing at the rag from a reasonable distance. Okagbue emerged and without saying a word or even looking at the spectators he went to his goatskin bag, took out two leaves and began to chew them. When he had swallowed them, he took up the rag with his left hand and began to untie it. And then the smooth, shiny pebble fell out. He picked it up.

"Is this yours?" he asked Ezinma.

"Yes," she replied. All the women shouted with joy because Ekwefi's troubles were at last ended.

All this had happened more than a year ago and Ezinma had not been ill since. And then suddenly she had begun to shiver in the night. Ekwefi brought her to the fireplace, spread her mat on the floor and built a fire. But she had got worse and worse. As she knelt by her, feeling with her palm the wet, burning forehead, she prayed a thousand times. Although her husband's wives were saying that it was nothing more than *iba*, she did not hear them.

Okonkwo returned from the bush carrying on his left shoulder a large bundle of grasses and leaves, roots and barks of medicinal trees and shrubs. He went into Ekwefi's hut, put down his load and sat down.

"Get me a pot," he said, "and leave the child alone."

Ekwefi went to bring the pot and Okonkwo selected the best from his bundle, in their due proportions, and cut them up. He put them in the pot and Ekwefi poured in some water.

"Is that enough?" she asked when she had poured in about half of the water in the bowl.

"A little more . . . I said a *little*. Are you deaf?" Okonkwo roared at her.

She set the pot on the fire and Okonkwo took up his machete to return to his *obi*.

"You must watch the pot carefully," he said as he went, "and don't allow it to boil over. If it does its power will be gone." He went away to his hut and Ekwefi began to tend the medicine pot almost as if it was itself a sick child. Her eyes went constantly from Ezinma to the boiling pot and back to Ezinma.

Okonkwo returned when he felt the medicine had cooked long enough. He looked it over and said it was done.

"Bring me a low stool for Ezinma," he said, "and a thick mat."

He took down the pot from the fire and placed it in front of the stool. He then roused Ezinma and placed her on the stool, astride the steaming pot. The thick mat was thrown over both. Ezinma struggled to escape from the choking and overpowering steam, but she was held down. She started to cry.

When the mat was at last removed she was drenched in perspiration. Ekwefi mopped her with a piece of cloth and she lay down on a dry mat and was soon asleep.

10

Large crowds began to gather on the village *ilo* as soon as the edge had worn off the sun's heat and it was no longer painful on the body. Most communal ceremonies took place at that time of the day, so that even when it was said that a ceremony would begin "after the midday meal" everyone understood that it would begin a long time later, when the sun's heat had softened.

It was clear from the way the crowd stood or sat that the ceremony was for men. There were many women, but they looked on from the fringe like outsiders. The titled men and elders sat on their stools waiting for the trials to begin. In front of them was a row of stools on which nobody sat. There were nine of them. Two little groups of people stood at a respectable distance beyond the stools. They faced the elders. There were three men in one group and three men and one woman in the other. The woman was Mgbafo and the three men with her were her brothers. In the other group were her husband, Uzowulu, and his relatives. Mgbafo and her brothers were as still as statues into whose faces the artist has molded defiance. Uzowulu and his relatives, on the other hand, were whispering together. It looked like whispering, but they were really talking at the top of their voices. Everybody in the crowd was talking. It was like the market. From a distance the noise was a deep rumble carried by the wind.

An iron gong sounded, setting up a wave of expectation in the crowd. Everyone looked in the direction of the *egwugwu*[9] house. *Gome, gome, gome* went the gong, and a powerful flute blew a high-pitched blast. Then came the voices of the *egwugwu,* guttural and awesome. The wave struck the women and children and there was a backward stampede. But it was momentary. They were already far enough where they stood and there was room for running away if any of the *egwugwu* should go towards them.

The drum sounded again and the flute blew. The *egwugwu* house was now a pandemonium of quavering voices: *Aru oyim de de de dei!*[1] filled the air as

9. Here the term refers to the village's highest spiritual and judicial authority, prominent men who, after putting on elaborate ceremonial costumes, embody the village's ancestral spirits.   1. Body of my friend, greetings!

the spirits of the ancestors, just emerged from the earth, greeted themselves in their esoteric language. The *egwugwu* house into which they emerged faced the forest, away from the crowd, who saw only its back with the many-colored patterns and drawings done by specially chosen women at regular intervals. These women never saw the inside of the hut. No woman ever did. They scrubbed and painted the outside walls under the supervision of men. If they imagined what was inside, they kept their imagination to themselves. No woman ever asked questions about the most powerful and the most secret cult in the clan.

Aru oyim de de de dei! flew around the dark, closed hut like tongues of fire. The ancestral spirits of the clan were abroad. The metal gong beat continuously now and the flute, shrill and powerful, floated on the chaos.

And then the *egwugwu* appeared. The women and children sent up a great shout and took to their heels. It was instinctive. A woman fled as soon as an *egwugwu* came in sight. And when, as on that day, nine of the greatest masked spirits in the clan came out together it was a terrifying spectacle. Even Mgbafo took to her heels and had to be restrained by her brothers.

Each of the nine *egwugwu* represented a village of the clan. Their leader was called Evil Forest. Smoke poured out of his head.

The nine villages of Umuofia had grown out of the nine sons of the first father of the clan. Evil Forest represented the village of Umueru, or the children of Eru, who was the eldest of the nine sons.

"Umuofia kwenu!" shouted the leading *egwugwu*, pushing the air with his raffia arms. The elders of the clan replied, "Yaa!"

"Umuofia kwenu!"

"Yaa!"

"Umuofia kwenu!"

"Yaa!"

Evil Forest then thrust the pointed end of his rattling staff into the earth. And it began to shake and rattle, like something agitating with a metallic life. He took the first of the empty stools and the eight other *egwugwu* began to sit in order of seniority after him.

Okonkwo's wives, and perhaps other women as well, might have noticed that the second *egwugwu* had the springy walk of Okonkwo. And they might also have noticed that Okonkwo was not among the titled men and elders who sat behind the row of *egwugwu*. But if they thought these things they kept them within themselves. The *egwugwu* with the springy walk was one of the dead fathers of the clan. He looked terrible with the smoked raffia body, a huge wooden face painted white except for the round hollow eyes and the charred teeth that were as big as a man's fingers. On his head were two powerful horns.

When all the *egwugwu* had sat down and the sound of the many tiny bells and rattles on their bodies had subsided, Evil Forest addressed the two groups of people facing them.

"Uzowulu's body, I salute you," he said. Spirits always addressed humans as "bodies." Uzowulu bent down and touched the earth with his right hand as a sign of submission.

"Our father, my hand has touched the ground," he said.

"Uzowulu's body, do you know me?" asked the spirit.

"How can I know you, father? You are beyond our knowledge."

Evil Forest then turned to the other group and addressed the eldest of the three brothers.

"The body of Odukwe, I greet you," he said, and Odukwe bent down and touched the earth. The hearing then began.

Uzowulu stepped forward and presented his case.

"That woman standing there is my wife, Mgbafo. I married her with my money and my yams. I do not owe my in-laws anything. I owe them no yams. I owe them no coco-yams. One morning three of them came to my house, beat me up and took my wife and children away. This happened in the rainy season. I have waited in vain for my wife to return. At last I went to my in-laws and said to them, 'You have taken back your sister. I did not send her away. You yourselves took her. The law of the clan is that you should return her bride-price.' But my wife's brothers said they had nothing to tell me. So I have brought the matter to the fathers of the clan. My case is finished. I salute you."

"Your words are good," said the leader of the *egwugwu*. "Let us hear Odukwe. His words may also be good."

Odukwe was short and thickset. He stepped forward, saluted the spirits and began his story.

"My in-law has told you that we went to his house, beat him up and took our sister and her children away. All that is true. He told you that he came to take back her bride-price and we refused to give it him. That also is true. My in-law, Uzowulu, is a beast. My sister lived with him for nine years. During those years no single day passed in the sky without his beating the woman. We have tried to settle their quarrels time without number and on each occasion Uzowulu was guilty—"

"It is a lie!" Uzowulu shouted.

"Two years ago," continued Odukwe, "when she was pregnant, he beat her until she miscarried."

"It is a lie. She miscarried after she had gone to sleep with her lover."

"Uzowulu's body, I salute you," said Evil Forest, silencing him. "What kind of lover sleeps with a pregnant woman?" There was a loud murmur of approbation from the crowd. Odukwe continued:

"Last year when my sister was recovering from an illness, he beat her again so that if the neighbors had not gone in to save her she would have been killed. We heard of it, and did as you have been told. The law of Umuofia is that if a woman runs away from her husband her bride-price is returned. But in this case she ran away to save her life. Her two children belong to Uzowulu. We do not dispute it, but they are too young to leave their mother. If, in the other hand, Uzowulu should recover from his madness and come in the proper way to beg his wife to return she will do so on the understanding that if he ever beats her again we shall cut off his genitals for him."

The crowd roared with laughter. Evil Forest rose to his feet and order was immediately restored. A steady cloud of smoke rose from his head. He sat down again and called two witnesses. They were both Uzowulu's neighbors, and they agreed about the beating. Evil Forest then stood up, pulled out his staff and thrust it into the earth again. He ran a few steps in the direction of the women; they all fled in terror, only to return to their places almost immediately. The nine *egwugwu* then went away to consult together in their house. They were silent for a long time. Then the metal gong sounded and the flute was blown. The *egwugwu* had emerged once again from their underground home. They saluted one another and then reappeared on the *ilo*.

"*Umuofia kwenu!*" roared Evil Forest, facing the elders and grandees of the clan.

"*Yaa!*" replied the thunderous crowd; then silence descended from the sky and swallowed the noise.

Evil Forest began to speak and all the while he spoke everyone was silent. The eight other *egwugwu* were as still as statues.

"We have heard both sides of the case," said Evil Forest. "Our duty is not to blame this man or to praise that, but to settle the dispute." He turned to Uzowulu's group and allowed a short pause.

"Uzowulu's body, I salute you," he said.

"Our father, my hand has touched the ground," replied Uzowulu, touching the earth.

"Uzowulu's body, do you know me?"

"How can I know you, father? You are beyond our knowledge," Uzowulu replied.

"I am Evil Forest. I kill a man on the day that his life is sweetest to him."

"That is true," replied Uzowulu.

"Go to your in-laws with a pot of wine and beg your wife to return to you. It is not bravery when a man fights with a woman." He turned to Odukwe, and allowed a brief pause.

"Odukwe's body, I greet you," he said.

"My hand is on the ground," replied Odukwe.

"Do you know me?"

"No man can know you," replied Odukwe.

"I am Evil Forest, I am Dry-meat-that-fills-the-mouth, I am Fire-that-burns-without-faggots. If your in-law brings wine to you, let your sister go with him. I salute you." He pulled his staff from the hard earth and thrust it back.

"*Umuofia kwenu!*" he roared, and the crowd answered.

"I don't know why such a trifle should come before the *egwugwu*," said one elder to another.

"Don't you know what kind of man Uzowulu is? He will not listen to any other decision," replied the other.

As they spoke two other groups of people had replaced the first before the *egwugwu*, and a great land case began.

11

The night was impenetrably dark. The moon had been rising later and later every night until now it was seen only at dawn. And whenever the moon forsook evening and rose at cock-crow the nights were as black as charcoal.

Ezinma and her mother sat on a mat on the floor after their supper of yam foo-foo and bitter-leaf soup. A palm-oil lamp gave out yellowish light. Without it, it would have been impossible to eat; one could not have known where one's mouth was in the darkness of that night. There was an oil lamp in all the four huts on Okonkwo's compound, and each hut seen from the others looked like a soft eye of yellow half-light set in the solid massiveness of night.

The world was silent except for the shrill cry of insects, which was part of the night, and the sound of wooden mortar and pestle as Nwayieke pounded her foo-foo. Nwayieke lived four compounds away, and she was notorious for her late cooking. Every woman in the neighborhood knew the sound of Nwayieke's mortar and pestle. It was also part of the night.

Okonkwo had eaten from his wives' dishes and was now reclining with his back against the wall. He searched his bag and brought out his snuff-bottle. He turned it on to his left palm, but nothing came out. He hit the bottle against his knee to shake up the tobacco. That was always the trouble with Okeke's snuff. It very quickly went damp, and there was too much saltpeter in it. Okonkwo had not bought snuff from him for a long time. Idigo was the man who knew how to grind good snuff. But he had recently fallen ill.

Low voices, broken now and again by singing, reached Okonkwo from his wives' huts as each woman and her children told folk stories. Ekwefi and her daughter, Ezinma, sat on a mat on the floor. It was Ekwefi's turn to tell a story.

"Once upon a time," she began, "all the birds were invited to a feast in the sky. They were very happy and began to prepare themselves for the great day. They painted their bodies with red cam wood and drew beautiful patterns on them with *uli*.

"Tortoise saw all these preparations and soon discovered what it all meant. Nothing that happened in the world of the animals ever escaped his notice; he was full of cunning. As soon as he heard of the great feast in the sky his throat began to itch at the very thought. There was a famine in those days and Tortoise had not eaten a good meal for two moons. His body rattled like a piece of dry stick in his empty shell. So he began to plan how he would go to the sky."

"But he had no wings," said Ezinma.

"Be patient," replied her mother. "That is the story. Tortoise had no wings, but he went to the birds and asked to be allowed to go with them.

" 'We know you too well,' said the birds when they had heard him. 'You are full of cunning and you are ungrateful. If we allow you to come with us you will soon begin your mischief.'

" 'You do not know me,' said Tortoise. 'I am a changed man. I have learned that a man who makes trouble for others is also making it for himself.'

"Tortoise had a sweet tongue, and within a short time all the birds agreed that he was a changed man, and they each gave him a feather, with which he made two wings.

"At last the great day came and Tortoise was the first to arrive at the meeting place. When all the birds had gathered together, they set off in a body. Tortoise was very happy and voluble as he flew among the birds, and he was soon chosen as the man to speak for the party because he was a great orator.

" 'There is one important thing which we must not forget,' he said as they flew on their way. 'When people are invited to a great feast like this, they take new names for the occasion. Our hosts in the sky will expect us to honor this age-old custom.'

"None of the birds had heard of this custom but they knew that Tortoise, in spite of his failings in other directions, was a widely traveled man who knew the customs of different peoples. And so they each took a new name.

When they had all taken, Tortoise also took one. He was to be called *All of you*.

"At last the party arrived in the sky and their hosts were very happy to see them. Tortoise stood up in his many-colored plumage and thanked them for their invitation. His speech was so eloquent that all the birds were glad they had brought him, and nodded their heads in approval of all he said. Their hosts took him as the king of the birds, especially as he looked somewhat different from the others.

"After kola nuts had been presented and eaten, the people of the sky set before their guests the most delectable dishes Tortoise had ever seen or dreamed of. The soup was brought out hot from the fire and in the very pot in which it had been cooked. It was full of meat and fish. Tortoise began to sniff aloud. There was pounded yam and also yam pottage cooked with palm-oil and fresh fish. There were also pots of palm-wine. When everything had been set before the guests, one of the people of the sky came forward and tasted a little from each pot. He then invited the birds to eat. But Tortoise jumped to his feet and asked: 'For whom have you prepared this feast?'

" 'For all of you,' replied the man.

"Tortoise turned to the birds and said: 'You remember that my name is *All of you*. The custom here is to serve the spokesman first and the others later. They will serve you when I have eaten.'

"He began to eat and the birds grumbled angrily. The people of the sky thought it must be their custom to leave all the food for their king. And so Tortoise ate the best part of the food and then drank two pots of palm-wine, so that he was full of food and drink and his body filled out in his shell.

"The birds gathered round to eat what was left and to peck at the bones he had thrown all about the floor. Some of them were too angry to eat. They chose to fly home on an empty stomach. But before they left each took back the feather he had lent to Tortoise. And there he stood in his hard shell full of food and wine but without any wings to fly home. He asked the birds to take a message for his wife, but they all refused. In the end Parrot, who had felt more angry than the others, suddenly changed his mind and agreed to take the message.

" 'Tell my wife,' said Tortoise, 'to bring out all the soft things in my house and cover the compound with them so that I can jump down from the sky without very great danger.'

"Parrot promised to deliver the message, and then flew away. But when he reached Tortoise's house he told his wife to bring out all the hard things in the house. And so she brought out her husband's hoes, machetes, spears, guns and even his cannon. Tortoise looked down from the sky and saw his wife bringing things out, but it was too far to see what they were. When all seemed ready he let himself go. He fell and fell and fell until he began to fear that he would never stop falling. And then like the sound of his cannon he crashed on the compound."

"Did he die?" asked Ezinma.

"No," replied Ekwefi. "His shell broke into pieces. But there was a great medicine man in the neighborhood. Tortoise's wife sent for him and he gathered all the bits of shell and stuck them together. That is why Tortoise's shell is not smooth."

"There is no song in the story," Ezinma pointed out.

"No," said Ekwefi. "I shall think of another one with a song. But it is your turn now."

"Once upon a time," Ezinma began, "Tortoise and Cat went to wrestle against Yams—no, that is not the beginning. Once upon a time there was a great famine in the land of animals. Everybody was lean except Cat, who was fat and whose body shone as if oil was rubbed on it . . ."

She broke off because at that very moment a loud and high-pitched voice broke the outer silence of the night. It was Chielo, the priestess of Agbala, prophesying. There was nothing new in that. Once in a while Chielo was possessed by the spirit of her god and she began to prophesy. But tonight she was addressing her prophecy and greetings to Okonkwo, and so everyone in his family listened. The folk stories stopped.

"*Agbala do-o-o-o! Agbala ekeneo-o-o-o,*"[2] came the voice like a sharp knife cutting through the night. "*Okonkwo! Agbala ekene gio-o-o-o! Agbala cholu ifu ada ya Ezinmao-o-o-o!*"[3]

At the mention of Ezinma's name Ekwefi jerked her head sharply like an animal that had sniffed death in the air. Her heart jumped painfully within her.

The priestess had now reached Okonkwo's compound and was talking with him outside his hut. She was saying again and again that Agbala wanted to see his daughter, Ezinma. Okonkwo pleaded with her to come back in the morning because Ezinma was now asleep. But Chielo ignored what he was trying to say and went on shouting that Agbala wanted to see his daughter. Her voice was as clear as metal, and Okonkwo's women and children heard from their huts all that she said. Okonkwo was still pleading that the girl had been ill of late and was asleep. Ekwefi quickly took her to their bedroom and placed her on their high bamboo bed.

The priestess screamed. "Beware, Okonkwo!" she warned. "Beware of exchanging words with Agbala. Does a man speak when a god speaks? Beware!"

She walked through Okonkwo's hut into the circular compound and went straight toward Ekwefi's hut. Okonkwo came after her.

"Ekwefi," she called, "Agbala greets you. Where is my daughter, Ezinma? Agbala wants to see her."

Ekwefi came out from her hut carrying her oil lamp in her left hand. There was a light wind blowing, so she cupped her right hand to shelter the flame. Nwoye's mother, also carrying an oil lamp, emerged from her hut. The children stood in the darkness outside their hut watching the strange event. Okonkwo's youngest wife also came out and joined the others.

"Where does Agbala want to see her?" Ekwefi asked.

"Where else but in his house in the hills and the caves?" replied the priestess.

"I will come with you, too," Ekwefi said firmly.

"*Tufia-a!*"[4] the priestess cursed, her voice cracking like the angry bark of thunder in the dry season. "How dare you, woman, to go before the mighty Agbala of your own accord? Beware, woman, lest he strike you in his anger. Bring me my daughter."

Ekwefi went into her hut and came out again with Ezinma.

---

2. Agbala wants something! Agbala greets.   3. Agbala greets you! Agbala wants to see his daughter Ezinma!   4. A curse in words meaning "spitting" or "clearing out," often accompanied by spitting.

"Come, my daughter," said the priestess. "I shall carry you on my back. A baby on its mother's back does not know that the way is long."

Ezinma began to cry. She was used to Chielo calling her "my daughter." But it was a different Chielo she now saw in the yellow half-light.

"Don't cry, my daughter," said the priestess, "lest Agbala be angry with you."

"Don't cry," said Ekwefi, "she will bring you back very soon. I shall give you some fish to eat." She went into the hut again and brought down the smoke-black basket in which she kept her dried fish and other ingredients for cooking soup. She broke a piece in two and gave it to Ezinma, who clung to her.

"Don't be afraid," said Ekwefi, stroking her head, which was shaved in places, leaving a regular pattern of hair. They went outside again. The priestess bent down on one knee and Ezinma climbed on her back, her left palm closed on her fish and her eyes gleaming with tears.

"*Agbala do-o-o-o! Agbala ekeneo-o-o-o!* . . ." Chielo began once again to chant greetings to her god. She turned round sharply and walked through Okonkwo's hut, bending very low at the eaves. Ezinma was crying loudly now, calling on her mother. The two voices disappeared into the thick darkness.

A strange and sudden weakness descended on Ekwefi as she stood gazing in the direction of the voices like a hen whose only chick has been carried away by a kite. Ezinma's voice soon faded away and only Chielo was heard moving farther and farther into the distance.

"Why do you stand there as though she had been kidnapped?" asked Okonkwo as he went back to his hut.

"She will bring her back soon," Nwoye's mother said.

But Ekwefi did not hear these consolations. She stood for a while, and then, all of a sudden, made up her mind. She hurried through Okonkwo's hut and went outside. "Where are you going?" he asked.

"I am following Chielo," she replied and disappeared in the darkness. Okonkwo cleared his throat, and brought out his snuff-bottle from the goat-skin bag by his side.

The priestess's voice was already growing faint in the distance. Ekwefi hurried to the main footpath and turned left in the direction of the voice. Her eyes were useless to her in the darkness. But she picked her way easily on the sandy footpath hedged on either side by branches and damp leaves. She began to run, holding her breasts with her hands to stop them flapping noisily against her body. She hit her left foot against an outcropped root, and terror seized her. It was an ill omen. She ran faster. But Chielo's voice was still a long way away. Had she been running too? How could she go so fast with Ezinma on her back? Although the night was cool, Ekwefi was beginning to feel hot from her running. She continually ran into the luxuriant weeds and creepers that walled in the path. Once she tripped up and fell. Only then did she realize, with a start, that Chielo had stopped her chanting. Her heart beat violently and she stood still. Then Chielo's renewed outburst came from only a few paces ahead. But Ekwefi could not see her. She shut her eyes for a while and opened them again in an effort to see. But it was useless. She could not see beyond her nose.

There were no stars in the sky because there was a rain-cloud. Fireflies went about with their tiny green lamps, which only made the darkness more profound. Between Chielo's outbursts the night was alive with the shrill tremor of forest insects woven into the darkness.

"*Agbala do-o-o-o! . . . . Agbala ekeneo-o-o-o! . . .*" Ekwefi trudged behind, neither getting too near nor keeping too far back. She thought they must be going towards the sacred cave. Now that she walked slowly she had time to think. What would she do when they got to the cave? She would not dare to enter. She would wait at the mouth, all alone in that fearful place. She thought of all the terrors of the night. She remembered that night, long ago, when she had seen *Ogbu-agali-odu,* one of those evil essences loosed upon the world by the potent "medicines" which the tribe had made in the distant past against its enemies but had now forgotten how to control. Ekwefi had been returning from the stream with her mother on a dark night like this when they saw its glow as it flew in their direction. They had thrown down their water-pots and lain by the roadside expecting the sinister light to descend on them and kill them. That was the only time Ekwefi ever saw *Ogbu-agali-odu.* But although it had happened so long ago, her blood still ran cold whenever she remembered that night.

The priestess's voice came at longer intervals now, but its vigor was undiminished. The air was cool and damp with dew. Ezinma sneezed. Ekwefi muttered, "Life to you." At the same time the priestess also said, "Life to you, my daughter." Ezinma's voice from the darkness warmed her mother's heart. She trudged slowly along.

And then the priestess screamed. "Somebody is walking behind me!" she said. "Whether you are spirit or man, may Agbala shave your head with a blunt razor! May he twist your neck until you see your heels!"

Elkwefi stood rooted to the spot. One mind said to her: "Woman, go home before Agbala does you harm." But she could not. She stood until Chielo had increased the distance between them and she began to follow again. She had already walked so long that she began to feel a slight numbness in the limbs and in the head. Then it occurred to her that they could not have been heading for the cave. They must have by-passed it long ago; they must be going towards Umuachi, the farthest village in the clan. Chielo's voice now came after long intervals.

It seemed to Ekwefi that the night had become a little lighter. The cloud had lifted and a few stars were out. The moon must be preparing to rise, its sullenness over. When the moon rose late in the night, people said it was refusing food, as a sullen husband refuses his wife's food when they have quarrelled.

"*Agbala do-o-o-o! Umuachi! Agbala ekene unuo-o-o!*" It was just as Ekwefi had thought. The priestess was now saluting the village of Umuachi. It was unbelievable, the distance they had covered. As they emerged into the open village from the narrow forest track the darkness was softened and it became possible to see the vague shape of trees. Ekwefi screwed her eyes up in an effort to see her daughter and the priestess, but whenever she thought she saw their shape it immediately dissolved like a melting lump of darkness. She walked numbly along.

Chielo's voice was now rising continuously, as when she first set out. Ekwefi had a feeling of spacious openness, and she guessed they must be on the village *ilo,* or playground. And she realized too with something like a jerk that Chielo was no longer moving forward. She was, in fact, returning. Ekwefi quickly moved away from her line of retreat. Chielo passed by, and they began to go back the way they had come.

It was a long and weary journey and Ekwefi felt like a sleepwalker most of the way. The moon was definitely rising, and although it had not yet appeared on the sky its light had already melted down the darkness. Ekwefi could now discern the figure of the priestess and her burden. She slowed down her pace so as to increase the distance between them. She was afraid of what might happen if Chielo suddenly turned round and saw her.

She had prayed for the moon to rise. But now she found the half-light of the incipient moon more terrifying than darkness. The world was now peopled with vague, fantastic figures that dissolved under her steady gaze and then formed again in new shapes. At one stage Ekwefi was so afraid that she nearly called out to Chielo for companionship and human sympathy. What she had seen was the shape of a man climbing a palm tree, his head pointing to the earth and his legs skywards. But at that very moment Chielo's voice rose again in her possessed chanting, and Ekwefi recoiled, because there was no humanity there. It was not the same Chielo who sat with her in the market and sometimes bought bean-cakes for Ezinma, whom she called her daughter. It was a different woman—the priestess of Agbala, the Oracle of the Hills and Caves. Ekwefi trudged along between two fears. The sound of her benumbed steps seemed to come from some other person walking behind her. Her arms were folded across her bare breasts. Dew fell heavily and the air was cold. She could no longer think, not even about the terrors of night. She just jogged along in a half-sleep, only waking to full life when Chielo sang.

At last they took a turning and began to head for the caves. From then on, Chielo never ceased in her chanting. She greeted her god in a multitude of names—the owner of the future, the messenger of earth, the god who cut a man down when his life was sweetest to him. Ekwefi was also awakened and her benumbed fears revived.

The moon was now up and she could see Chielo and Ezinma clearly. How a woman could carry a child of that size so easily and for so long was a miracle. But Ekwefi was not thinking about that. Chielo was not a woman that night.

"Agbala do-o-o-o! Agbala ekeneo-o-o-o! *Chi negbu madu ubosi ndu ya nato ya uto daluo-o-o! . . .*"[5]

Ekwefi could already see the hills looming in the moonlight. They formed a circular ring with a break at one point through which the foot-track led to the center of the circle.

As soon as the priestess stepped into this ring of hills her voice was not only doubled in strength but was thrown back on all sides. It was indeed the shrine of a great god. Ekwefi picked her way carefully and quietly. She was already beginning to doubt the wisdom of her coming. Nothing would happen to Ezinma, she thought. And if anything happened to her could she stop it? She would not dare to enter the underground caves. Her coming was quite useless, she thought.

5. Agbala wants something! Agbala greets . . . God who kills a man on the day his life is so pleasant he give thanks!

As these things went through her mind she did not realize how close they were to the cave mouth. And so when the priestess with Ezinma on her back disappeared through a hole hardly big enough to pass a hen, Ekwefi broke into a run as though to stop them. As she stood gazing at the circular darkness which had swallowed them, tears gushed from her eyes, and she swore within her that if she heard Ezinma cry she would rush into the cave to defend her against all the gods in the world. She would die with her.

Having sworn that oath, she sat down on a stony ledge and waited. Her fear had vanished. She could hear the priestess's voice, all its metal taken out of it by the vast emptiness of the cave. She buried her face in her lap and waited.

She did not know how long she waited. It must have been a very long time. Her back was turned on the footpath that led out of the hills. She must have heard a noise behind her and turned round sharply. A man stood there with a machete in his hand. Ekwefi uttered a scream and sprang to her feet.

"Don't be foolish," said Okonkwo's voice. "I thought you were going into the shrine with Chielo," he mocked.

Ekwefi did not answer. Tears of gratitude filled her eyes. She knew her daughter was safe.

"Go home and sleep," said Okonkwo. "I shall wait here."

"I shall wait too. It is almost dawn. The first cock has crowed."

As they stood there together, Ekwefi's mind went back to the days when they were young. She had married Anene because Okonkwo was too poor then to marry. Two years after her marriage to Anene she could bear it no longer and she ran away to Okonkwo. It had been early in the morning. The moon was shining. She was going to the stream to fetch water. Okonkwo's house was on the way to the stream. She went in and knocked at his door and he came out. Even in those days he was not a man of many words. He just carried her into his bed and in the darkness began to feel around her waist for the loose end of her cloth.

12

On the following morning the entire neighborhood wore a festive air because Okonkwo's friend, Obierika, was celebrating his daughter's *uri*. It was the day on which her suitor (having already paid the greater part of her bride-price) would bring palm-wine not only to her parents and immediate relatives but to the wide and extensive group of kinsmen called *umunna*. Everybody had been invited—men, women and children. But it was really a woman's ceremony and the central figures were the bride and her mother.

As soon as day broke, breakfast was hastily eaten and women and children began to gather at Obierika's compound to help the bride's mother in her difficult but happy task of cooking for a whole village.

Okonkwo's family was astir like any other family in the neighborhood. Nwoye's mother and Okonkwo's youngest wife were ready to set out for Obierika's compound with all their children. Nwoye's mother carried a basket of coco-yams, a cake of salt and smoked fish which she would present to Obierika's wife. Okonkwo's youngest wife, Ojiugo, also had a basket of plantains and coco-yams and a small pot of palm-oil. Their children carried pots of water.

Ekwefi was tired and sleepy from the exhausting experiences of the previous night. It was not very long since they had returned. The priestess, with Ezinma sleeping on her back, had crawled out of the shrine on her belly like a snake. She had not as much as looked at Okonkwo and Ekwefi or shown any surprise at finding them at the mouth of the cave. She looked straight ahead of her and walked back to the village. Okonkwo and his wife followed at a respectful distance. They thought the priestess might be going to her house, but she went to Okonkwo's compound, passed through his *obi* and into Ekwefi's hut and walked into her bedroom. She placed Ezinma carefully on the bed and went away without saying a word to anybody.

Ezinma was still sleeping when everyone else was astir, and Ekwefi asked Nwoye's mother and Ojiugo to explain to Obierika's wife that she would be late. She had got ready her basket of coco-yams and fish, but she must wait for Ezinma to wake.

"You need some sleep yourself," said Nwoye's mother. "You look very tired."

As they spoke Ezinma emerged from the hut, rubbing her eyes and stretching her spare frame. She saw the other children with their water-pots and remembered that they were going to fetch water for Obierika's wife. She went back to the hut and brought her pot.

"Have you slept enough?" asked her mother.

"Yes," she replied, "Let us go."

"Not before you have had your breakfast," said Ekwefi. And she went into her hut to warm the vegetable soup she had cooked last night.

"We shall be going," said Nwoye's mother. "I will tell Obierika's wife that you are coming later." And so they all went to help Obierika's wife—Nwoye's mother with her four children and Ojiugo with her two.

As they trooped through Okonkwo's *obi* he asked: "Who will prepare my afternoon meal?"

"I shall return to do it," said Ojiugo.

Okonkwo was also feeling tired, and sleepy, for although nobody else knew it, he had not slept at all last night. He had felt very anxious but did not show it. When Ekwefi had followed the priestess, he had allowed what he regarded as a reasonable and manly interval to pass and then gone with his machete to the shrine, where he thought they must be. It was only when he had got there that it had occurred to him that the priestess might have chosen to go round the villages first. Okonkwo had returned home and sat waiting. When he thought he had waited long enough he again returned to the shrine. But the Hills and the Caves were as silent as death. It was only on his fourth trip that he had found Ekwefi, and by then he had become gravely worried.

Obierika's compound was as busy as an anthill. Temporary cooking tripods were erected on every available space by bringing together three blocks of sun-dried earth and making a fire in their midst. Cooking pots went up and down the tripods, and foo-foo was pounded in a hundred wooden mortars. Some of the women cooked the yams and the cassava, and others prepared vegetable soup. Young men pounded the foo-foo or split firewood. The children made endless trips to the stream.

Three young men helped Obierika to slaughter the two goats with which the soup was made. They were very fat goats, but the fattest of all was tethered to a peg near the wall of the compound. It was as big as a small cow. Obierika had sent one of his relatives all the way to Umuike to buy that goat. It was the one he would present alive to his in-laws.

"The market of Umuike is a wonderful place," said the young man who had been sent by Obierika to buy the giant goat. "There are so many people on it that if you threw up a grain of sand it would not find a way to fall to earth again."

"It is the result of a great medicine," said Obierika. "The people of Umuike wanted their market to grow and swallow up the markets of their neighbors. So they made a powerful medicine. Every market day, before the first cock-crow, this medicine stands on the market ground in the shape of an old woman with a fan. With this magic fan she beckons to the market all the neighboring clans. She beckons in front of her and behind her, to her right and to her left."

"And so everybody comes," said another man, "honest men and thieves. They can steal your cloth from off your waist in that market."

"Yes," said Obierika. "I warned Nwankwo to keep a sharp eye and a sharp ear. There was once a man who went to sell a goat. He led it on a thick rope which he tied round his wrist. But as he walked through the market he realized that people were pointing at him as they do to a madman. He could not understand it until he looked back and saw that what he led at the end of the tether was not a goat but a heavy log of wood."

"Do you think a thief can do that kind of thing single-handed?" asked Nwankwo.

"No," said Obierika. "They use medicine."

When they had cut the goats' throats and collected the blood in a bowl, they held them over an open fire to burn off the hair, and the smell of burning hair blended with the smell of cooking. Then they washed them and cut them up for the women who prepared the soup.

All this anthill activity was going smoothly when a sudden interruption came. It was a cry in the distance: *Oji odu achu ijiji-o-o!* (*The one that uses its tail to drive flies away!*) Every woman immediately abandoned whatever she was doing and rushed out in the direction of the cry.

"We cannot all rush out like that, leaving what we are cooking to burn in the fire," shouted Chielo, the priestess. "Three or four of us should stay behind."

"It is true," said another woman. "We will allow three or four women to stay behind."

Five women stayed behind to look after the cooking-pots, and all the rest rushed away to see the cow that had been let loose. When they saw it they drove it back to its owner, who at once paid the heavy fine which the village imposed on anyone whose cow was let loose on his neighbors' crops. When the women had exacted the penalty they checked among themselves to see if any woman had failed to come out when the cry had been raised.

"Where is Mgbogo?" asked one of them.

"She is ill in bed," said Mgbogo's next-door neighbor. "She has *iba.*"

"The only other person is Udenkwo," said another woman, "and her child is not twenty-eight days yet."

Those women whom Obierika's wife had not asked to help her with the cooking returned to their homes, and the rest went back, in a body, to Obierika's compound.

"Whose cow was it?" asked the women who had been allowed to stay behind.

"It was my husband's," said Ezelagbo. "One of the young children had opened the gate of the cowshed."

Early in the afternoon the first two pots of palm-wine arrived from Obierika's in-laws. They were duly presented to the women, who drank a cup or two each, to help them in their cooking. Some of it also went to the bride and her attendant maidens, who were putting the last delicate touches of razor to her coiffure and cam wood on her smooth skin.

When the heat of the sun began to soften, Obierika's son, Maduka, took a long broom and swept the ground in front of his father's *obi*. And as if they had been waiting for that, Obierika's relatives and friends began to arrive, every man with his goatskin bag hung on one shoulder and a rolled goatskin mat under his arm. Some of them were accompanied by their sons bearing carved wooden stools. Okonkwo was one of them. They sat in a half-circle and began to talk of many things. It would not be long before the suitors came.

Okonkwo brought out his snuff-bottle and offered it to Ogbuefi Ezenwa, who sat next to him. Ezenwa[6] took it, tapped it on his kneecap, rubbed his left palm on his body to dry it before tipping a little snuff into it. His actions were deliberate, and he spoke as he performed them:

"I hope our in-laws will bring many pots of wine. Although they come from a village that is known for being closefisted, they ought to know that Akueke is the bride for a king."

"They dare not bring fewer than thirty pots," said Okonkwo. "I shall tell them my mind if they do."

At that moment Obierika's son, Maduka, led out the giant goat from the inner compound, for his father's relatives to see. They all admired it and said that that was the way things should be done. The goat was then led back to the inner compound.

Very soon after, the in-laws began to arrive. Young men and boys in single file, each carrying a pot of wine, came first. Obierika's relatives counted the pots as they came. Twenty, twenty-five. There was a long break, and the hosts looked at each other as if to say, "I told you." Then more pots came. Thirty, thirty-five, forty, forty-five. The hosts nodded in approval and seemed to say, "Now they are behaving like men." Altogether there were fifty pots of wine. After the pot-bearers came Ibe, the suitor, and the elders of his family. They sat in a half-moon, thus completing a circle with their hosts. The pots of wine stood in their midst. Then the bride, her mother and a half a dozen other women and girls emerged from the inner compound, and went round the circle shaking hands with all. The bride's mother led the way, followed by the bride and the other women. The married women wore their best cloths and the girls wore red and black waist-beads and anklets of brass.

When the women retired, Obierika presented kola nuts to his in-laws. His eldest brother broke the first one. "Life to all of us," he said as he broke it. "And let there be friendship between your family and ours."

The crowd answered: *"Ee-e-e!"*

"We are giving you our daughter today. She will be a good wife to you.

6. King from childhood (strong praise).

She will bear you nine sons like the mother of our town."

"Ee-e-e!"

The oldest man in the camp of the visitors replied: "It will be good for you and it will be good for us."

"Ee-e-e!"

"This is not the first time my people have come to marry your daughter. My mother was one of you."

"Ee-e-e!"

"And this will not be the last, because you understand us and we understand you. You are a great family."

"Ee-e-e!"

"Prosperous men and great warriors." He looked in the direction of Okonkwo. "Your daughter will bear us sons like you."

"Ee-e-e!"

The kola was eaten and the drinking of palm-wine began. Groups of four or five men sat round with a pot in their midst. As the evening wore on, food was presented to the guests. There were huge bowls of foo-foo and steaming pots of soup. There were also pots of yam pottage. It was a great feast.

As night fell, burning torches were set on wooden tripods and the young men raised a song. The elders sat in a big circle and the singers went round singing each man's praise as they came before him. They had something to say for every man. Some were great farmers, some were orators who spoke for the clan; Okonkwo was the greatest wrestler and warrior alive. When they had gone round the circle they settled down in the center, and girls came from the inner compound to dance. At first the bride was not among them. But when she finally appeared holding a cock in her right hand, a loud cheer rose from the crowd. All the other dancers made way for her. She presented the cock to the musicians and began to dance. Her brass anklets rattled as she danced and her body gleamed with cam wood in the soft yellow light. The musicians with their wood, clay and metal instruments went from song to song. And they were all gay. They sang the latest song in the village:

> If I hold her hand
> She says, "Don't touch!"
> If I hold her foot
> She says, "Don't touch!"
> But when I hold her waist-beads
> She pretends not to know.

The night was already far spent when the guests rose to go, taking their bride home to spend seven market weeks with her suitor's family. They sang songs as they went, and on their way they paid short courtesy visits to prominent men like Okonkwo, before they finally left for their village. Okonkwo made a present of two cocks to them.

13

Go-di-di-go-go-di-go. Di-go-go-di-go. It was the *ekwe* talking to the clan. One of the things every man learned was the language of the hollowed-out wooden instrument. Diim! Diim! Diim! boomed the cannon at intervals.

The first cock had not crowed, and Umuofia was still swallowed up in sleep and silence when the *ekwe* began to talk, and the cannon shattered the silence. Men stirred on their bamboo beds and listened anxiously. Somebody was dead. The cannon seemed to rend the sky. Di-go-go-di-go-di-di-go-go floated in the message-laden night air. The faint and distant wailing of women settled like a sediment of sorrow on the earth. Now and again a full-chested lamentation rose above the wailing whenever a man came into the place of death. He raised his voice once or twice in manly sorrow and then sat down with the other men listening to the endless wailing of the women and the esoteric language of the *ekwe*. Now and again the cannon boomed. The wailing of the women would not be heard beyond the village, but the *ekwe* carried the news to all the nine villages and even beyond. It began by naming the clan: *Umuofia obodo dike,* "the land of the brave." *Umuofia obodo dike! Umuofia obodo dike!* It said this over and over again, and as it dwelt on it, anxiety mounted in every heart that heaved on a bamboo bed that night. Then it went nearer and named the village: *Iguedo of the yellow grinding-stone!*[7] It was Okonkwo's village. Again and again Iguedo was called and men waited breathlessly in all the nine villages. At last the man was named and people sighed "E-u-u, Ezeudu is dead." A cold shiver ran down Okonkwo's back as he remembered the last time the old man had visited him. "That boy calls you father," he had said. "Bear no hand in his death."

Ezeudu was a great man, and so all the clan was at his funeral. The ancient drums of death beat, guns and cannon were fired, and men dashed about in frenzy, cutting down every tree or animal they saw, jumping over walls and dancing on the roof. It was a warrior's funeral, and from morning till night warriors came and went in their age groups. They all wore smoked raffia skirts and their bodies were painted with chalk and charcoal. Now and again an ancestral spirit or *egwugwu* appeared from the underworld, speaking in a tremulous, unearthly voice and completely covered in raffia. Some of them were very violent, and there had been a mad rush for shelter earlier in the day when one appeared with a sharp machete and was only prevented from doing serious harm by two men who restrained him with the help of a strong rope tied round his waist. Sometimes he turned round and chased those men, and they ran for their lives. But they always returned to the long rope he trailed behind. He sang, in a terrifying voice, that Ekwensu, or Evil Spirit, had entered his eye.

But the most dreaded of all was yet to come. He was always alone and was shaped like a coffin. A sickly odor hung in the air wherever he went, and flies went with him. Even the greatest medicine men took shelter when he was near. Many years ago another *egwugwu* had dared to stand his ground before him and had been transfixed to the spot for two days. This one had only one hand and it carried a basket full of water.

But some of the *egwugwu* were quite harmless. One of them was so old and infirm that he leaned heavily on a stick. He walked unsteadily to the place where the corpse was laid, gazed at it a while and went away again—to the underworld.

The land of the living was not far removed from the domain of the ances-

7. The yellow grindstone.

tors. There was coming and going between them, especially at festivals and also when an old man died, because an old man was very close to the ancestors. A man's life from birth to death was a series of transition rites which brought him nearer and nearer to his ancestors.

Ezeudu had been the oldest man in his village, and at his death there were only three men in the whole clan who were older, and four or five others in his own age group. Whenever one of these ancient men appeared in the crowd to dance unsteadily the funeral steps of the tribe, younger men gave way and the tumult subsided.

It was a great funeral, such as befitted a noble warrior. As the evening drew near, the shouting and the firing of guns, the beating of drums and the brandishing and clanging of machetes increased.

Ezeudu had taken three titles in his life. It was a rare achievement. There were only four titles in the clan, and only one or two men in any generation ever achieved the fourth and highest. When they did, they became the lords of the land. Because he had taken titles, Ezeudu was to be buried after dark with only a glowing brand to light the sacred ceremony.

But before this quiet and final rite, the tumult increased tenfold. Drums beat violently and men leaped up and down in frenzy. Guns were fired on all sides and sparks flew out as machetes clanged together in warriors' salutes. The air was full of dust and the smell of gunpowder. It was then that the one-handed spirit came, carrying a basket full of water. People made way for him on all sides and the noise subsided. Even the smell of gunpowder was swallowed in the sickly smell that now filled the air. He danced a few steps to the funeral drums and then went to see the corpse.

"Ezeudu!" he called in his guttural voice. "If you had been poor in your last life I would have asked you to be rich when you come again. But you were rich. If you had been a coward, I would have asked you to bring courage. But you were a fearless warrior. If you had died young, I would have asked you to get life. But you lived long. So I shall ask you to come again the way you came before. If your death was the death of nature, go in peace. But if a man caused it, do not allow him a moment's rest." He danced a few more steps and went away.

The drums and the dancing began again and reached fever-heat. Darkness was around the corner, and the burial was near. Guns fired the last salute and the cannon rent the sky. And then from the center of the delirious fury came a cry of agony and shouts of horror. It was as if a spell had been cast. All was silent. In the center of the crowd a boy lay in a pool of blood. It was the dead man's sixteen-year-old son, who with his brothers and half-brothers had been dancing the traditional farewell to their father. Okonkwo's gun had exploded and a piece of iron had pierced the boy's heart.

The confusion that followed was without parallel in the tradition of Umuofia. Violent deaths were frequent, but nothing like this had ever happened.

The only course open to Okonkwo was to flee from the clan. It was a crime against the earth goddess to kill a clansman, and a man who committed it must flee from the land. The crime was of two kinds, male and female. Okonkwo had committed the female, because it had been inadvertent. He could return to the clan after seven years.

That night he collected his most valuable belongings into head-loads. His wives wept bitterly and their children wept with them without knowing why. Obierika and half a dozen other friends came to help and to console him. They each made nine or ten trips carrying Okonkwo's yams to store in Obierika's barn. And before the cock crowed Okonkwo and his family were fleeing to his motherland. It was a little village called Mbanta,[8] just beyond the borders of Mbaino.

As soon as the day broke, a large crowd of men from Ezeudu's quarter stormed Okonkwo's compound, dressed in garbs of war. They set fire to his houses, demolished his red walls, killed his animals and destroyed his barn. It was the justice of the earth goddess, and they were merely her messengers. They had no hatred in their hearts against Okonkwo. His greatest friend, Obierika, was among them. They were merely cleansing the land which Okonkwo had polluted with the blood of a clansman.

Obierika was a man who thought about things. When the will of the goddess had been done, he sat down in his *obi* and mourned his friend's calamity. Why should a man suffer so grievously for an offense he had committed inadvertently? But although he thought for a long time he found no answer. He was merely led into greater complexities. He remembered his wife's twin children, whom he had thrown away. What crime had they committed? The Earth had decreed that they were an offense on the land and must be destroyed. And if the clan did not exact punishment for an offense against the great goddess, her wrath was loosed on all the land and not just on the offender. As the elders said, if one finger brought oil it soiled the others.

Part Two

14

Okonkwo was well received by his mother's kinsmen in Mbanta. The old man who received him was his mother's younger brother, who was now the eldest surviving member of that family. His name was Uchendu,[9] and it was he who had received Okonkwo's mother twenty and ten years before when she had been brought home from Umuofia to be buried with her people. Okonkwo was only a boy then and Uchendu still remembered him crying the traditional farewell: "Mother, mother, mother is going."

That was many years ago. Today Okonkwo was not bringing his mother home to be buried with her people. He was taking his family of three wives and their children to seek refuge in his motherland. As soon as Uchendu saw him with his sad and weary company he guessed what had happened, and asked no questions. It was not until the following day that Okonkwo told him the full story. The old man listened silently to the end and then said with some relief: "It is a female *ochu*."[1] And he arranged the requisite rites and sacrifices.

Okonkwo was given a plot of ground on which to build his compound, and two or three pieces of land on which to farm during the coming planting season. With the help of his mother's kinsmen he built himself an *obi* and three huts for his wives. He then installed his personal god and the symbols of his departed fathers. Each of Uchendu's five sons contributed three hun-

8. Small town.　　9. The thought created by life.　　1. Murder, manslaughter.

dred seed-yams to enable their cousin to plant a farm, for as soon as the first rain came farming would begin.

At last the rain came. It was sudden and tremendous. For two or three moons the sun had been gathering strength till it seemed to breathe a breath of fire on the earth. All the grass had long been scorched brown, and the sands felt like live coals to the feet. Evergreen trees wore a dusty coat of brown. The birds were silenced in the forests, and the world lay panting under the live, vibrating heat. And then came the clap of thunder. It was an angry, metallic and thirsty clap, unlike the deep and liquid rumbling of the rainy season. A mighty wind arose and filled the air with dust. Palm trees swayed as the wind combed their leaves into flying crests like strange and fantastic coiffure.

When the rain finally came, it was in large, solid drops of frozen water which the people called "the nuts of the water of heaven." They were hard and painful on the body as they fell, yet young people ran about happily picking up the cold nuts and throwing them into their mouths to melt.

The earth quickly came to life and the birds in the forests fluttered around and chirped merrily. A vague scent of life and green vegetation was diffused in the air. As the rain began to fall more soberly and in smaller liquid drops, children sought for shelter, and all were happy, refreshed and thankful.

Okonkwo and his family worked very hard to plant a new farm. But it was like beginning life anew without the vigor and enthusiasm of youth, like learning to become left-handed in old age. Work no longer had for him the pleasure it used to have, and when there was no work to do he sat in a silent half-sleep.

His life had been ruled by a great passion—to become one of the lords of the clan. That had been his life-spring. And he had all but achieved it. Then everything had been broken. He had been cast out of his clan like a fish onto a dry, sandy beach, panting. Clearly his personal god or *chi* was not made for great things. A man could not rise beyond the destiny of his *chi*. The saying of the elders was not true—that if a man said yea his *chi* also affirmed. Here was a man whose *chi* said nay despite his own affirmation.

The old man, Uchendu, saw clearly that Okonkwo had yielded to despair and he was greatly troubled. He would speak to him after the *isa-ifi*[2] ceremony.

The youngest of Uchendu's five sons, Amikwu, was marrying a new wife. The bride-price had been paid and all but the last ceremony had been performed. Amikwu and his people had taken palm-wine to the bride's kinsmen about two moons before Okonkwo's arrival in Mbanta. And so it was time for the final ceremony of confession.

The daughters of the family were all there, some of them having come a long way from their homes in distant villages. Uchendu's eldest daughter had come from Obodo, nearly half a day's journey away. The daughters of Uchendu's brothers were also there. It was a full gathering of *umuada*,[3] in the same way as they would meet if a death occurred in the family. There were twenty-two of them.

2. A ceremony to ascertain that a wife (here, a promised bride) had been faithful to her husband during a separation. 3. The daughters, who, according to Igbo custom, married outside the clan, perform a special initiation upon returning home for important gatherings.

They sat in a big circle on the ground and the bride sat in the center with a hen in her right hand. Uchendu sat by her, holding the ancestral staff of the family. All the other men stood outside the circle, watching. Their wives watched also. It was evening and the sun was setting.

Uchendu's eldest daughter, Njide, asked the questions.

"Remember that if you do not answer truthfully you will suffer or even die at childbirth," she began. "How many men have lain with you since my brother first expressed the desire to marry you?"

"None," she answered simply.

"Answer truthfully," urged the other women.

"None?" asked Njide.

"None," she answered.

"Swear on this staff of my fathers," said Uchendu.

"I swear," said the bride.

Uchendu took the hen from her, slit its throat with a sharp knife and allowed some of the blood to fall on his ancestral staff.

From that day Amikwu took the young bride to his hut and she became his wife. The daughters of the family did not return to their homes immediately but spent two or three days with their kinsmen.

On the second day Uchendu called together his sons and daughters and his nephew, Okonkwo. The men brought their goatskin mats, with which they sat on the floor, and the women sat on a sisal mat spread on a raised bank of earth. Uchendu pulled gently at his gray beard and gnashed his teeth. Then he began to speak, quietly and deliberately, picking his words with great care:

"It is Okonkwo that I primarily wish to speak to," he began. "But I want all of you to note what I am going to say. I am an old man and you are all children. I know more about the world than any of you. If there is any one among you who thinks he knows more let him speak up." He paused, but no one spoke.

"Why is Okonkwo with us today? This is not his clan. We are only his mother's kinsmen. He does not belong here. He is an exile, condemned for seven years to live in a strange land. And so he is bowed with grief. But there is just one question I would like to ask him. Can you tell me, Okonkwo, why it is that one of the commonest names we give our children is Nneka, or "Mother is Supreme?" We all know that a man is the head of the family and his wives do his bidding. A child belongs to its father and his family and not to its mother and her family. A man belongs to his fatherland and not to his motherland. And yet we say Nneka—'Mother is Supreme.' Why is that?"

There was silence. "I want Okonkwo to answer me," said Uchendu.

"I do not know the answer," Okonkwo replied.

"You do not know the answer? So you see that you are a child. You have many wives and many children—more children than I have. You are a great man in your clan. But you are still a child, *my* child. Listen to me and I shall tell you. But there is one more question I shall ask you. Why is it that when a woman dies she is taken home to be buried with her own kinsmen? She is not buried with her husband's kinsmen. Why is that? Your mother was brought home to me and buried with my people. Why was that?"

Okonkwo shook his head.

"He does not know that either," said Uchendu, "and yet he is full of sorrow because he has come to live in his motherland for a few years." He laughed a mirthless laughter, and turned to his sons and daughters. "What about you? Can you answer my question?"

They all shook their heads.

"Then listen to me," he said and cleared his throat. "It's true that a child belongs to its father. But when a father beats his child, it seeks sympathy in its mother's hut. A man belongs to his fatherland when things are good and life is sweet. But when there is sorrow and bitterness he finds refuge in his motherland. Your mother is there to protect you. She is buried there. And that is why we say that mother is supreme. Is it right that you, Okonkwo, should bring to your mother a heavy face and refuse to be comforted? Be careful or you may displease the dead. Your duty is to comfort your wives and children and take them back to your fatherland after seven years. But if you allow sorrow to weigh you down and kill you, they will all die in exile." He paused for a long while. "These are now your kinsmen." He waved at his sons and daughters. "You think you are the greatest sufferer in the world? Do you know that men are sometimes banished for life? Do you know that men sometimes lose all their yams and even their children? I had six wives once. I have none now except that young girl who knows not her right from her left. Do you know how many children I have buried—children I begot in my youth and strength? Twenty-two. I did not hang myself, and I am still alive. If you think you are the greatest sufferer in the world ask my daughter, Akueni, how many twins she has borne and thrown away. Have you not heard the song they sing when a woman dies?

> For whom is it well, for whom is it well?
> There is no one for whom it is well.

"I have no more to say to you."

15

It was in the second year of Okonkwo's exile that his friend, Obierika, came to visit him. He brought with him two young men, each of them carrying a heavy bag on his head. Okonkwo helped them put down their loads. It was clear that the bags were full of cowries.

Okonkwo was very happy to receive his friend. His wives and children were very happy too, and so were his cousins and their wives when he sent for them and told them who his guest was.

"You must take him to salute our father," said one of the cousins.

"Yes," replied Okonkwo. "We are going directly." But before they went he whispered something to his first wife. She nodded, and soon the children were chasing one of their cocks.

Uchendu had been told by one of his grandchildren that three strangers had come to Okonkwo's house. He was therefore waiting to receive them. He held out his hands to them when they came into his *obi,* and after they had shaken hands he asked Okonkwo who they were.

"This is Obierika, my great friend. I have already spoken to you about him."

"Yes," said the old man, turning to Obierika. "My son has told me about you, and I am happy you have come to see us. I knew your father, Iweka. He was a great man. He had many friends here and came to see them quite often. Those were good days when a man had friends in distant clans. Your generation does not know that. You stay at home, afraid of your next-door neighbor. Even a man's motherland is strange to him nowadays." He looked at Okonkwo. "I am an old man and I like to talk. That is all I am good for now." He got up painfully, went into an inner room and came back with a kola nut.

"Who are the young men with you?" he asked as he sat down again on his goatskin. Okonkwo told him.

"Ah," he said. "Welcome, my sons." He presented the kola nut to them, and when they had seen it and thanked him, he broke it and they ate.

"Go into that room," he said to Okonkwo, pointing with his finger. "You will find a pot of wine there."

Okonkwo brought the wine and they began to drink. It was a day old, and very strong.

"Yes," said Uchendu after a long silence. "People traveled more in those days. There is not a single clan in these parts that I do not know very well. Aninta, Umuazu, Ikeocha, Elumelu, Abame—I know them all."

"Have you heard," asked Obierika, "that Abame is no more?"

"How is that?" asked Uchendu and Okonkwo together.

"Abame has been wiped out," said Obierika. "It is a strange and terrible story. If I had not seen the few survivors with my own eyes and heard their story with my own ears, I would not have believed. Was it not on an Eke day that they fled into Umuofia?" he asked his two companions, and they nodded their heads.

"Three moons ago," said Obierika, "on an Eke market day a little band of fugitives came into our town. Most of them were sons of our land whose mothers had been buried with us. But there were some too who came because they had friends in our town, and others who could think of nowhere else open to escape. And so they fled into Umuofia with a woeful story." He drank his palm-wine, and Okonkwo filled his horn again. He continued:

"During the last planting season a white man had appeared in their clan."

"An albino," suggested Okonkwo.

"He was not an albino. He was quite different." He sipped his wine. "And he was riding an iron horse.[4] The first people who saw him ran away, but he stood beckoning to them. In the end the fearless ones went near and even touched him. The elders consulted their Oracle and it told them that the strange man would break their clan and spread destruction among them." Obierika again drank a little of his wine. "And so they killed the white man and tied his iron horse to their sacred tree because it looked as if it would run away to call the man's friends. I forgot to tell you another thing which the Oracle said. It said that other white men were on their way. They were locusts, it said, and that first man was their harbinger sent to explore the terrain. And so they killed him."

"What did the white man say before they killed him?" asked Uchendu.

"He said nothing," answered one of Obierika's companions.

"He said something, only they did not understand him," said Obierika. "He seemed to speak through his nose."

4. Bicycle.

"One of the men told me," said Obierika's other companion, "that he repeated over and over again a word that resembled Mbaino. Perhaps he had been going to Mbaino and had lost his way."

"Anyway," resumed Obierika, "they killed him and tied up his iron horse. This was before the planting season began. For a long time nothing happened. The rains had come and yams had been sown. The iron horse was still tied to the sacred silk-cotton tree. And then one morning three white men led by a band of ordinary men like us came to the clan. They saw the iron horse and went away again. Most of the men and women of Abame had gone to their farms. Only a few of them saw these white men and their followers. For many market weeks nothing else happened. They have a big market in Abame on every other Afo day and, as you know, the whole clan gathers there. That was the day it happened. The three white men and a very large number of other men surrounded the market. They must have used a powerful medicine to make themselves invisible until the market was full. And they began to shoot. Everybody was killed, except the old and the sick who were at home and a handful of men and women whose *chi* were wide awake and brought them out of that market."[5] He paused.

"Their clan is now completely empty. Even the sacred fish in their mysterious lake have fled and the lake has turned the color of blood. A great evil has come upon their land as the Oracle had warned."

There was a long silence. Uchendu ground his teeth together audibly. Then he burst out:

"Never kill a man who says nothing. Those men of Abame were fools. What did they know about the man?" He ground his teeth again and told a story to illustrate his point. "Mother Kite once sent her daughter to bring food. She went, and brought back a duckling. 'You have done very well,' said Mother Kite to her daughter, 'but tell me, what did the mother of this duckling say when you swooped and carried its child away?' 'It said nothing,' replied the young kite. It just walked away.' 'You must return the duckling,' said Mother Kite. 'There is something ominous behind the silence.' And so Daughter Kite returned the duckling and took a chick instead. 'What did the mother of this chick do?' asked the old kite. 'It cried and raved and cursed me,' said the young kite. 'Then we can eat the chick,' said her mother. 'There is nothing to fear from someone who shouts.' Those men of Abame were fools."

"They were fools," said Okonkwo after a pause. "They had been warned that danger was ahead. They should have armed themselves with their guns and their machetes even when they went to market."

"They have paid for their foolishness," said Obierika. "But I am greatly afraid. We have heard stories about white men who made the powerful guns and the strong drinks and took slaves away across the seas, but no one thought the stories were true."

"There is no story that is not true," said Uchendu. "The world has no end, and what is good among one people is an abomination with others. We have albinos among us. Do you not think that they came to our clan by mistake, that they have strayed from their way to a land where everybody is like them?"

---

5. Achebe bases his account on a similar incident in 1905 when British troops massacred the town of Ahiara in reprisal for the death of a missionary.

Okonkwo's first wife soon finished her cooking and set before their guests a big meal of pounded yams and bitter-leaf soup. Okonkwo's son, Nwoye, brought in a pot of sweet wine tapped from the raffia palm.

"You are a big man now," Obierika said to Nwoye. "Your friend Anene asked me to greet you."

"Is he well?" asked Nwoye.

"We are all well," said Obierika.

Ezinma brought them a bowl of water with which to wash their hands. After that they began to eat and to drink the wine.

"When did you set out from home?" asked Okonkwo.

"We had meant to set out from my house before cock-crow," said Obierika. "But Nweke did not appear until it was quite light. Never make an early morning appointment with a man who has just married a new wife." They all laughed.

"Has Nweke married a wife?" asked Okonkwo.

"He has married Okadigbo's second daughter," said Obierika.

"That is very good," said Okonkwo. "I do not blame you for not hearing the cock crow."

When they had eaten, Obierika pointed at the two heavy bags.

"That is the money from your yams," he said. "I sold the big ones as soon as you left. Later on I sold some of the seed-yams and gave out others to sharecroppers. I shall do that every year until you return. But I thought you would need the money now and so I brought it. Who knows what may happen tomorrow? Perhaps green men will come to our clan and shoot us."

"God will not permit it," said Okonkwo. "I do not know how to thank you."

"I can tell you," said Obierika. "Kill one of your sons for me."

"That will not be enough," said Okonkwo.

"Then kill yourself," said Obierika.

"Forgive me," said Okonkwo, smiling. "I shall not talk about thanking you any more."

16

When nearly two years later Obierika paid another visit to his friend in exile the circumstances were less happy. The missionaries had come to Umuofia. They had built their church there, won a handful of converts and were already sending evangelists to the surrounding towns and villages. That was a source of great sorrow to the leaders of the clan; but many of them believed that the strange faith and the white man's god would not last. None of his converts was a man whose word was heeded in the assembly of the people. None of them was a man of title. They were mostly the kind of people that were called *efulefu*, worthless, empty men. The imagery of an *efulefu* in the language of the clan was a man who sold his machete and wore the sheath to battle. Chielo, the priestess of Agbala, called the converts the excrement of the clan, and the new faith was a mad dog that had come to eat it up.

What moved Obierika to visit Okonkwo was the sudden appearance of the latter's son, Nwoye, among the missionaries in Umuofia.

"What are you doing here?" Obierika had asked when after many difficulties the missionaries had allowed him to speak to the boy.

"I am one of them," replied Nwoye.

"How is your father?" Obierika asked, not knowing what else to say.

"I don't know. He is not my father," said Nwoye, unhappily.

And so Obierika went to Mbanta to see his friend. And he found that Okonkwo did not wish to speak about Nwoye. It was only from Nwoye's mother that he heard scraps of the story.

The arrival of the missionaries had caused a considerable stir in the village of Mbanta. There were six of them and one was a white man. Every man and woman came out to see the white man. Stories about these strange men had grown since one of them had been killed in Abame and his iron horse tied to the sacred silk-cotton tree. And so everybody came to see the white man. It was the time of the year when everybody was at home. The harvest was over.

When they had all gathered, the white man began to speak to them. He spoke through an interpreter who was an Ibo man, though his dialect was different and harsh to the ears of Mbanta. Many people laughed at his dialect and the way he used words strangely. Instead of saying "myself" he always said "my buttocks."[6] But he was a man of commanding presence and the clansmen listened to him. He said he was one of them, as they could see from his color and his language. The other four black men were also their brothers, although one of them did not speak Ibo. The white man was also their brother because they were all sons of God. And he told them about this new God, the Creator of all the world and all the men and women. He told them that they worshipped false gods, gods of wood and stone. A deep murmur went through the crowd when he said this. He told them that the true God lived on high and that all men when they died went before Him for judgment. Evil men and all the heathen who in their blindness bowed to wood and stone were thrown into a fire that burned like palm-oil. But good men who worshipped the true God lived forever in His happy kingdom. "We have been sent by this great God to ask you to leave your wicked ways and false gods and turn to Him so that you may be saved when you die," he said.

"Your buttocks understand our language," said someone light-heartedly and the crowd laughed.

"What did he say?" the white man asked his interpreter. But before he could answer, another man asked a question: "Where is the white man's horse?" he asked. The Ibo evangelists consulted among themselves and decided that the man probably meant bicycle. They told the white man and he smiled benevolently.

"Tell them," he said, "that I shall bring many iron horses when we have settled down among them. Some of them will even ride the iron horse themselves." This was interpreted to them but very few of them heard. They were talking excitedly among themselves because the white man had said he was going to live among them. They had not thought about that.

At this point an old man said he had a question. "Which is this god of yours," he asked, "the goddess of the earth, the god of the sky, Amadiora of the thunderbolt, or what?"

The interpreter spoke to the white man and he immediately gave his

6. The Igbo language has high and low tones so that the same word may have different meanings according to its pronunciation. Here, Achebe is probably referring to a famous pair of near-homonyms: *íké* ("strength") and *íkè* ("buttocks").

answer. "All the gods you have named are not gods at all. They are gods of deceit who tell you to kill your fellows and destroy innocent children. There is only one true God and He has the earth, the sky, you and me and all of us."

"If we leave our gods and follow your god," asked another man, "who will protect us from the anger of our neglected gods and ancestors?"

"Your gods are not alive and cannot do you any harm," replied the white man. "They are pieces of wood and stone."

When this was interpreted to the men of Mbanta they broke into derisive laughter. These men must be mad, they said to themselves. How else could they say that Ani and Amadiora were harmless? And Idemili and Ogwugwu too? And some of them began to go away.

Then the missionaries burst into song. It was one of those gay and rollicking tunes of evangelism which had the power of plucking at silent and dusty chords in the heart of an Ibo man. The interpreter explained each verse to the audience, some of whom now stood enthralled. It was a story of brothers who lived in darkness and in fear, ignorant of the love of God. It told of one sheep out on the hills, away from the gates of God and from the tender shepherd's care.

After the singing the interpreter spoke about the Son of God whose name was Jesu Kristi. Okonkwo, who only stayed in the hope that it might come to chasing the men out of the village or whipping them, now said:

"You told us with your own mouth that there was only one god. Now you talk about his son. He must have a wife, then." The crowd agreed.

"I did not say He had a wife," said the interpreter, somewhat lamely.

"Your buttocks said he had a son," said the joker. "So he must have a wife and all of them must have buttocks."

The missionary ignored him and went on to talk about the Holy Trinity. At the end of it Okonkwo was fully convinced that the man was mad. He shrugged his shoulders and went away to tap his afternoon palm-wine.

But there was a young lad who had been captivated. His name was Nwoye, Okonkwo's first son. It was not the mad logic of the Trinity that captivated him. He did not understand it. It was the poetry of the new religion, something felt in the marrow. The hymn about brothers who sat in darkness and in fear seemed to answer a vague and persistent question that haunted his young soul—the question of the twins crying in the bush and the question of Ikemefuna who was killed. He felt a relief within as the hymn poured into his parched soul. The words of the hymn were like the drops of frozen rain melting on the dry palate of the panting earth. Nwoye's callow mind was greatly puzzled.

17

The missionaries spent their first four or five nights in the marketplace, and went into the village in the morning to preach the gospel. They asked who the king of the village was, but the villagers told them that there was no king. "We have men of high title and the chief priests and the elders," they said.

It was not very easy getting the men of high title and the elders together after the excitement of the first day. But the missionaries persevered, and in the end they were received by the rulers of Mbanta. They asked for a plot of land to build their church.

Every clan and village had its "evil forest." In it were buried all those who died of the really evil diseases, like leprosy and smallpox. It was also the dumping ground for the potent fetishes of great medicine men when they died. An "evil forest" was, therefore, alive with sinister forces and powers of darkness. It was such a forest that the rulers of Mbanta gave to the missionaries. They did not really want them in their clan, and so they made them that offer which nobody in his right senses would accept.

"They want a piece of land to build their shrine," said Uchendu to his peers when they consulted among themselves. "We shall give them a piece of land." He paused, and there was a murmur of surprise and disagreement. "Let us give them a portion of the Evil Forest. They boast about victory over death. Let us give them a real battlefield in which to show their victory." They laughed and agreed, and sent for the missionaries, whom they had asked to leave them for a while so that they might "whisper together." They offered them as much of the Evil Forest as they cared to take. And to their greatest amazement the missionaries thanked them and burst into song.

"They do not understand," said some of the elders. "But they will understand when they go to their plot of land tomorrow morning." And they dispersed.

The next morning the crazy men actually began to clear a part of the forest and to build their house. The inhabitants of Mbanta expected them all to be dead within four days. The first day passed and the second and third and fourth, and none of them died. Everyone was puzzled. And then it became known that the white man's fetish had unbelievable power. It was said that he wore glasses on his eyes so that he could see and talk to evil spirits. Not long after, he won his first three converts.

Although Nwoye had been attracted to the new faith from the very first day, he kept it secret. He dared not go too near the missionaries for fear of his father. But whenever they came to preach in the open marketplace or the village playground, Nwoye was there. And he was already beginning to know some of the simple stories they told.

"We have now built a church," said Mr. Kiaga, the interpreter, who was now in charge of the infant congregation. The white man had gone back to Umuofia, where he built his headquarters and from where he paid regular visits to Mr. Kiaga's congregation at Mbanta.

"We have now built a church," said Mr. Kiaga, "and we want you all to come in every seventh day to worship the true God."

On the following Sunday, Nwoye passed and repassed the little red-earth and thatch building without summoning enough courage to enter. He heard the voice of singing and although it came from a handful of men it was loud and confident. Their church stood on a circular clearing that looked like the open mouth of the Evil Forest. Was it waiting to snap its teeth together? After passing and re-passing by the church, Nwoye returned home.

It was well known among the people of Mbanta that their gods and ancestors were sometimes long-suffering and would deliberately allow a man to go on defying them. But even in such cases they set their limit at seven market weeks or twenty-eight days. Beyond that limit no man was suffered to go. And so excitement mounted in the village as the seventh week approached since the impudent missionaries built their church in the Evil Forest. The villagers were so certain about the doom that awaited these men that one or two converts thought it wise to suspend their allegiance to the new faith.

At last the day came by which all the missionaries should have died. But they were still alive, building a new red-earth and thatch house for their teacher, Mr. Kiaga. That week they won a handful more converts. And for the first time they had a woman. Her name was Nneka, the wife of Amadi, who was a prosperous farmer. She was very heavy with child.

Nneka had had four previous pregnancies and childbirths. But each time she had borne twins, and they had been immediately thrown away. Her husband and his family were already becoming highly critical of such a woman and were not unduly perturbed when they found she had fled to join the Christians. It was a good riddance.

One morning Okonkwo's cousin, Amikwu, was passing by the church on his way from the neighboring village, when he saw Nwoye among the Christians. He was greatly surprised, and when he got home he went straight to Okonkwo's hut and told him what he had seen. The women began to talk excitedly, but Okonkwo sat unmoved.

It was late afternoon before Nwoye returned. He went into the *obi* and saluted his father, but he did not answer. Nwoye turned round to walk into the inner compound when his father, suddenly overcome with fury, sprang to his feet and gripped him by the neck.

"Where have you been?" he stammered.

Nwoye struggled to free himself from the choking grip.

"Answer me," roared Okonkwo, "before I kill you!" He seized a heavy stick that lay on the dwarf wall and hit him two or three savage blows.

"Answer me!" he roared again. Nwoye stood looking at him and did not say a word. The women were screaming outside, afraid to go in.

"Leave that boy at once!" said a voice in the outer compound. It was Okonkwo's uncle, Uchendu. "Are you mad?"

Okonkwo did not answer. But he left hold of Nwoye, who walked away and never returned.

He went back to the church and told Mr. Kiaga that he had decided to go to Umuofia where the white missionary had set up a school to teach young Christians to read and write.

Mr. Kiaga's joy was very great. "Blessed is he who forsakes his father and his mother for my sake," he intoned. "Those that hear my words are my father and my mother."

Nwoye did not fully understand. But he was happy to leave his father. He would return later to his mother and his brothers and sisters and convert them to the new faith.

As Okonkwo sat in his hut that night, gazing into a log fire, he thought over the matter. A sudden fury rose within him and he felt a strong desire to take up his machete, go to the church and wipe out the entire vile and miscreant gang. But on further thought he told himself that Nwoye was not worth fighting for. Why, he cried in his heart, should he, Okonkwo, of all people, be cursed with such a son? He saw clearly in it the finger of his personal god or *chi*. For how else could he explain his great misfortune and exile and now his despicable son's behavior? Now that he had time to think of it, his son's crime stood out in its stark enormity. To abandon the gods of one's father and go about with a lot of effeminate men clucking like old hens was the very depth of abomination. Suppose when he died all his male children decided to follow Nwoye's steps and abandon their ancestors? Okonkwo felt a cold shudder run through him at the terrible prospects, like the prospect of annihilation. He saw himself and his fathers crowding round their ancestral shrine waiting in vain for worship and sacrifice and finding nothing but ashes of bygone days, and his children the while praying to the white man's god. If such a thing were ever to happen, he, Okonkwo, would wipe them off the face of the earth.

Okonkwo was popularly called the "Roaring Flame." As he looked into the log fire he recalled the name. He was a flaming fire. How then could he have begotten a son like Nwoye, degenerate and effeminate? Perhaps he was not his son. No! he could not be. His wife had played him false. He would teach her! But Nwoye resembled his grandfather, Unoka, who was Okonkwo's father. He pushed the thought out of his mind. He, Okonkwo, was called a flaming fire. How could he have begotten a woman for a son? At Nwoye's age Okonkwo had already become famous throughout Umuofia for his wrestling and his fearlessness.

He sighed heavily, and as if in sympathy the smoldering log also sighed. And immediately Okonkwo's eyes were opened and he saw the whole matter clearly. Living fire begets cold, impotent ash. He sighed again, deeply.

18

The young church in Mbanta had a few crises early in its life. At first the clan had assumed that it would not survive. But it had gone on living and gradually becoming stronger. The clan was worried, but not overmuch. If a gang of *efulefu* decided to live in the Evil Forest it was their own affair. When one came to think of it, the Evil Forest was a fit home for such undesirable people. It was true they were rescuing twins from the bush, but they never brought them into the village. As far as the villagers were concerned, the twins still remained where they had been thrown away. Surely the earth goddess would not visit the sins of the missionaries on the innocent villagers?

But on one occasion the missionaries had tried to overstep the bounds. Three converts had gone into the village and boasted openly that all the gods were dead and impotent and that they were prepared to defy them by burning all their shrines.

"Go and burn your mothers' genitals," said one of the priests. The men were seized and beaten until they streamed with blood. After that nothing happened for a long time between the church and the clan.

But stories were already gaining ground that the white man had not only brought a religion but also a government. It was said that they had built a place of judgment in Umuofia to protect the followers of their religion. It was even said that they had hanged one man who killed a missionary.

Although such stories were now often told they looked like fairy-tales in Mbanta and did not as yet affect the relationship between the new church and the clan. There was no question of killing a missionary here, for Mr. Kiaga, despite his madness, was quite harmless. As for his converts, no one could kill them without having to flee from the clan, for in spite of their worthlessness they still belonged to the clan. And so nobody gave serious thought to the stories about the white man's government or the consequences of killing the Christians. If they became more troublesome than they already were they would simply be driven out of the clan.

And the little church was at that moment too deeply absorbed in its own troubles to annoy the clan. It all began over the question of admitting outcasts.

These outcasts, or *osu*, seeing that the new religion welcomed twins and such abominations, thought that it was possible that they would also be received. And so one Sunday two of them went into the church. There was an immediate stir; but so great was the work the new religion had done among the converts that they did not immediately leave the church when the outcasts came in. Those who found themselves nearest to them merely moved to another seat. It was a miracle. But it only lasted till the end of the service. The whole church raised a protest and was about to drive these people out, when Mr. Kiaga stopped them and began to explain.

"Before God," he said, "there is no slave or free. We are all children of God and we must receive these our brothers."

"You do not understand," said one of the converts. "What will the heathen say of us when they hear that we receive *osu* into our midst? They will laugh."

"Let them laugh," said Mr. Kiaga. "God will laugh at them on the judgment day. Why do the nations rage and the peoples imagine a vain thing? He that sitteth in the heavens shall laugh. The Lord shall have them in derision."

"You do not understand," the convert maintained. "You are our teacher, and you can teach us the things of the new faith. But this is a matter which we know." And he told him what an *osu* was.

He was a person dedicated to a god, a thing set apart—a taboo for ever, and his children after him. He could neither marry nor be married by the free-born. He was in fact an outcast, living in a special area of the village, close to the Great Shrine. Wherever he went he carried with him the mark of his forbidden caste—long, tangled and dirty hair. A razor was taboo to him. An *osu* could not attend an assembly of the free-born, and they, in turn, could not shelter under his roof. He could not take any of the four titles of the clan, and when he died he was buried by his kind in the Evil Forest. How could such a man be a follower of Christ?

"He needs Christ more than you and I," said Mr. Kiaga.

"Then I shall go back to the clan," said the convert. And he went. Mr. Kiaga stood firm, and it was his firmness that saved the young church. The wavering converts drew inspiration and confidence from his unshakable faith. He ordered the outcasts to shave off their long, tangled hair. At first they were afraid they might die.

"Unless you shave off the mark of your heathen belief I will not admit you into the church," said Mr. Kiaga. "You fear that you will die. Why should that be? How are you different from other men who shave their hair? The same God created you and them. But they have cast you out like lepers. It is against the will of God, who has promised everlasting life to all who believe in His holy name. The heathen say you will die if you do this or that, and you are afraid. They also said I would die if I built my church on this ground. Am I dead? They said I would die if I took care of twins. I am still alive. The heathen speak nothing but falsehood. Only the word of our God is true."

The two outcasts shaved off their hair, and soon they were the strongest adherents of the new faith. And what was more, nearly all the *osu* in Mbanta followed their example. It was in fact one of them who in his zeal brought the church into serious conflict with the clan a year later by killing the sacred python, the emanation of the god of water.

The royal python was the most revered animal in Mbanta and all the surrounding clans. It was addressed as "Our Father," and was allowed to go wherever it chose, even into people's beds. It ate rats in the house and sometimes swallowed hens' eggs. If a clansman killed a royal python accidentally, he made sacrifices of atonement and performed an expensive burial ceremony such as was done for a great man. No punishment was prescribed for a man who killed the python knowingly. Nobody thought that such a thing could ever happen.

Perhaps it never did happen. That was the way the clan at first looked at it. No one had actually seen the man do it. The story had arisen among the Christians themselves.

But, all the same, the rulers and elders of Mbanta assembled to decide on their action. Many of them spoke at great length and in fury. The spirit of wars was upon them. Okonkwo, who had begun to play a part in the affairs of his motherland, said that until the abominable gang was chased out of the village with whips there would be no peace.

But there were many others who saw the situation differently, and it was their counsel that prevailed in the end.

"It is not our custom to fight for our gods," said one of them. "Let us not presume to do so now. If a man kills the sacred python in the secrecy of his hut, the matter lies between him and the god. We did not see it. If we put ourselves between the god and his victim we may receive blows intended for the offender. When a man blasphemes, what do we do? Do we go and stop his mouth? No. We put our fingers into our ears to stop us hearing. That is a wise action."

"Let us not reason like cowards," said Okonkwo. "If a man comes into my hut and defecates on the floor, what do I do? Do I shut my eyes? No! I take a stick and break his head. That is what a man does. These people are daily pouring filth over us, and Okeke says we should pretend not to see." Okonkwo made a sound full of disgust. This was a womanly clan, he thought. Such a thing could never happen in his fatherland, Umuofia.

"Okonkwo has spoken the truth," said another man. "We should do something. But let us ostracize these men. We would then not be held accountable for their abominations."

Everybody in the assembly spoke, and in the end it was decided to ostracize the Christians. Okonkwo ground his teeth in disgust.

That night a bell-man went through the length and breadth of Mbanta proclaiming that the adherents of the new faith were thenceforth excluded from the life and privileges of the clan.

The Christians had grown in number and were now a small community of men, women and children, self-assured and confident. Mr. Brown, the white missionary, paid regular visits to them. "When I think that it is only eighteen months since the Seed was first sown among you," he said, "I marvel at what the Lord hath wrought."

It was Wednesday in Holy Week and Mr. Kiaga had asked the women to bring red earth and white chalk and water to scrub the church for Easter; and the women had formed themselves into three groups for this purpose. They set out early that morning, some of them with their water-pots to the stream, another group with hoes and baskets to the village red-earth pit, and the others to the chalk quarry.

Mr. Kiaga was praying in the church when he heard the women talking excitedly. He rounded off his prayer and went to see what it was all about. The women had come to the church with empty water-pots. They said that some young men had chased them away from the stream with whips. Soon after, the women who had gone for red earth returned with empty baskets. Some of them had been heavily whipped. The chalk women also returned to tell a similar story.

"What does it all mean?" asked Mr. Kiaga, who was greatly perplexed.

"The village has outlawed us," said one of the women. "The bell-man announced it last night. But it is not our custom to debar anyone from the stream or the quarry."

Another woman said, "They want to ruin us. They will not allow us into the markets. They have said so."

Mr. Kiaga was going to send into the village for his men-converts when he saw them coming on their own. Of course they had all heard the bell-man, but they had never in all their lives heard of women being debarred from the stream.

"Come along," they said to the women. "We will go with you to meet those cowards." Some of them had big sticks and some even machetes.

But Mr. Kiaga restrained them. He wanted first to know why they had been outlawed.

"They say that Okoli killed the sacred python," said one man.

"It is false," said another. "Okoli told me himself that it was false."

Okoli was not there to answer. He had fallen ill on the previous night. Before the day was over he was dead. His death showed that the gods were still able to fight their own battles. The clan saw no reason then for molesting the Christians.

19

The last big rains of the year were falling. It was the time for treading red earth with which to build walls. It was not done earlier because the rains were too heavy and would have washed away the heap of trodden earth; and it could not be done later because harvesting would soon set in, and after that the dry season.

It was going to be Okonkwo's last harvest in Mbanta. The seven wasted and weary years were at last dragging to a close. Although he had prospered in his motherland Okonkwo knew that he would have prospered even more in Umuofia, in the land of his fathers where men were bold and warlike. In these seven years he would have climbed to the utmost heights. And so he regretted every day of his exile. His mother's kinsmen had been very kind to him, and he was grateful. But that did not alter the facts. He had called the first child born to him in exile Nneka—"Mother is Supreme"—out of politeness to his mother's kinsmen. But two years later when a son was born he called him Nwofia—"Begotten in the Wilderness."

As soon as he entered his last year in exile Okonkwo sent money to Obierika to build him two huts in his old compound where he and his family would live until he built more huts and the outside wall of his compound. He could not ask another man to build his own *obi* for him, nor the walls of his compound. Those things a man built for himself or inherited from his father.

As the last heavy rains of the year began to fall, Obierika sent word that the two huts had been built and Okonkwo began to prepare for his return, after the rains. He would have liked to return earlier and build his compound that year before the rains stopped, but in doing so he would have taken something from the full penalty of seven years. And that could not be. So he waited impatiently for the dry season to come.

It came slowly. The rain became lighter and lighter until it fell in slanting showers. Sometimes the sun shone through the rain and a light breeze blew. It was a gay and airy kind of rain. The rainbow began to appear, and sometimes two rainbows, like a mother and her daughter, the one young and beautiful, and the other an old and faint shadow. The rainbow was called the python of the sky.

Okonkwo called his three wives and told them to get things together for a great feast. "I must thank my mother's kinsmen before I go," he said.

Ekwefi still had some cassava left on her farm from the previous year. Neither of the other wives had. It was not that they had been lazy, but that they had many children to feed. It was therefore understood that Ekwefi would provide cassava for the feast. Nwoye's mother and Ojiugo would provide the other things like smoked fish, palm-oil and pepper for the soup. Okonkwo would take care of meat and yams.

Ekwefi rose early on the following morning and went to her farm with her daughter, Ezinma, and Ojiugo's daughter, Obiageli, to harvest cassava tubers. Each of them carried a long cane basket, a machete for cutting down the soft cassava stem, and a little hoe for digging out the tuber. Fortunately, a light rain had fallen during the night and the soil would not be very hard.

"It will not take us long to harvest as much as we like," said Ekwefi.

"But the leaves will be wet," said Ezinma. Her basket was balanced on her head, and her arms folded across her breasts. She felt cold. "I dislike cold water dropping on my back. We should have waited for the sun to rise and dry the leaves."

Obiageli called her "Salt" because she said that she disliked water. "Are you afraid you may dissolve?"

The harvesting was easy, as Ekwefi had said. Ezinma shook every tree violently with a long stick before she bent down to cut the stem and dig out the tuber. Sometimes it was not necessary to dig. They just pulled the stump, and earth rose, roots snapped below, and the tuber was pulled out.

When they had harvested a sizable heap they carried it down in two trips to the stream, where every woman had a shallow well for fermenting her cassava.

"It should be ready in four days or even three," said Obiageli. "They are young tubers."

"They are not all that young," said Ekwefi. "I planted the farm nearly two years ago. It is a poor soil and that is why the tubers are so small."

Okonkwo never did things by halves. When his wife Ekwefi protested that two goats were sufficient for the feast he told her that it was not her affair.

"I am calling a feast because I have the wherewithal. I cannot live on the bank of a river and wash my hands with spittle. My mother's people have been good to me and I must show my gratitude."

And so three goats were slaughtered and a number of fowls. It was like a wedding feast. There was foo-foo and yam pottage, egusi[7] soup and bitter-leaf soup and pots and pots of palm-wine.

All the *umunna*[8] were invited to the feast, all the descendants of Okolo, who had lived about two hundred years before. The oldest member of this extensive family was Okonkwo's uncle, Uchendu. The kola nut was given him to break, and he prayed to the ancestors. He asked them for health and children. "We do not ask for wealth because he that has health and children will also have wealth. We do not pray to have more money but to have more kinsmen. We are better than animals because we have kinsmen. An animal rubs its itching flank against a tree, a man asks his kinsman to scratch him." He prayed especially for Okonkwo and his family. He then broke the kola nut and threw one of the lobes on the ground for the ancestors.

As the broken kola nuts were passed round, Okonkwo's wives and children and those who came to help them with the cooking began to bring out the food. His sons brought out the pots of palm-wine. There was so much food and drink that many kinsmen whistled in surprise. When all was laid out, Okonkwo rose to speak.

"I beg you to accept this little kola," he said. "It is not to pay you back for all you did for me in these seven years. A child cannot pay for its mother's milk. I have only called you together because it is good for kinsmen to meet."

Yam pottage was served first because it was lighter than foo-foo and because yam always came first. Then the foo-foo was served. Some kinsmen ate it with egusi soup and others with bitter-leaf soup. The meat was then shared so that every member of the *umunna* had a portion. Every man rose in order of years and took a share. Even the few kinsmen who had not been able to come had their shares taken out for them in due term.

As the palm-wine was drunk one of the oldest members of the *umunna* rose to thank Okonkwo:

"If I say that we did not expect such a big feast I will be suggesting that we did not know how open-handed our son, Okonkwo, is. We all know him, and we expected a big feast. But it turned out to be even bigger than we expected. Thank you. May all you took out return again tenfold. It is good in these days when the younger generation consider themselves wiser than their sires to see a man doing things in the grand, old way. A man who calls his kinsmen to a feast does not do so to save them from starving. They all have food in their own homes. When we gather together in the moonlit village ground it is not because of the moon. Every man can see it in his own compound. We come together because it is good for kinsmen to do so. You may ask why I am saying all this. I say it because I fear for the younger generation, for you people." He waved his arm where most of the young men sat. "As for me, I have only a short while to live, and so have Uchendu and

---

7. Melon seed, which is roasted, ground, and cooked in soup.   8. Children of the father (literal trans.); the clan (male).

Unachukwu and Emefo. But I fear for you young people because you do not understand how strong is the bond of kinship. You do not know what it is to speak with one voice. And what is the result? An abominable religion has settled among you. A man can now leave his father and his brothers. He can curse the gods of his fathers and his ancestors, like a hunter's dog that suddenly goes mad and turns on his master. I fear for you; I fear for the clan." He turned again to Okonkwo and said, "Thank you for calling us together."

Part Three

20

Seven years was a long time to be away from one's clan. A man's place was not always there, waiting for him. As soon as he left, someone else rose and filled it. The clan was like a lizard; if it lost its tail it soon grew another.

Okonkwo knew these things. He knew that he had lost his place among the nine masked spirits who administered justice in the clan. He had lost the chance to lead his warlike clan against the new religion, which, he was told, had gained ground. He had lost the years in which he might have taken the highest titles in the clan. But some of these losses were not irreparable. He was determined that his return should be marked by his people. He would return with a flourish, and regain the seven wasted years.

Even in his first year in exile he had begun to plan for his return. The first thing he would do would be to rebuild his compound on a more magnificent scale. He would build a bigger barn than he had had before and he would build huts for two new wives. Then he would show his wealth by initiating his sons into the *ozo* society. Only the really great men in the clan were able to do this. Okonkwo saw clearly the high esteem in which he would be held, and he saw himself taking the highest title in the land.

As the years of exile passed one by one it seemed to him that his *chi* might now be making amends for the past disaster. His yams grew abundantly, not only in his motherland but also in Umuofia, where his friend gave them out year by year to sharecroppers.

Then the tragedy of his first son had occurred. At first it appeared as if it might prove too great for his spirit. But it was a resilient spirit, and in the end Okonkwo overcame his sorrow. He had five other sons and he would bring them up in the way of the clan.

He sent for the five sons and they came and sat in his *obi*. The youngest of them was four years old.

"You have all seen the great abomination of your brother. Now he is no longer my son or your brother. I will only have a son who is a man, who will hold his head up among my people. If any one of you prefers to be a woman, let him follow Nwoye now while I am alive so that I can curse him. If you turn against me when I am dead I will visit you and break your neck."

Okonkwo was very lucky in his daughters. He never stopped regretting that Ezinma was a girl. Of all his children she alone understood his every mood. A bond of sympathy had grown between them as the years had passed.

Ezinma grew up in her father's exile and became one of the most beautiful girls in Mbanta. She was called Crystal of Beauty, as her mother had been called in her youth. The young ailing girl who had caused her mother so much heartache had been transformed, almost overnight, into a healthy, buoyant maiden. She had, it was true, her moments of depression when she would snap at everybody like an angry dog. These moods descended on her suddenly and for no apparent reason. But they were very rare and short-lived. As long as they lasted, she could bear no other person but her father.

Many young men and prosperous middle-aged men of Mbanta came to marry her. But she refused them all, because her father had called her one evening and said to her: "There are many good and prosperous people here, but I shall be happy if you marry in Umuofia when we return home."

That was all he had said. But Ezinma had seen clearly all the thought and hidden meaning behind the few words. And she had agreed.

"Your half-sister, Obiageli, will not understand me," Okonkwo said. "But you can explain to her."

Although they were almost the same age, Ezinma wielded a strong influence over her half-sister. She explained to her why they should not marry yet, and she agreed also. And so the two of them refused every offer of marriage in Mbanta.

"I wish she were a boy," Okonkwo thought within himself. She understood things so perfectly. Who else among his children could have read his thoughts so well? With two beautiful grown-up daughters his return to Umuofia would attract considerable attention. His future sons-in-law would be men of authority in the clan. The poor and unknown would not dare to come forth.

Umuofia had indeed changed during the seven years Okonkwo had been in exile. The church had come and led many astray. Not only the low-born and the outcast but sometimes a worthy man had joined it. Such a man was Ogbuefi Ugonna,[9] who had taken two titles, and who like a madman had cut the anklet of his titles and cast it away to join the Christians. The white missionary was very proud of him and he was one of the first men in Umuofia to receive the sacrament of Holy Communion, or Holy Feast as it was called in Ibo. Ogbuefi Ugonna had thought of the Feast in terms of eating and drinking, only more holy than the village variety. He had therefore put his drinking-horn into his goatskin bag for the occasion.

But apart from the church, the white men had also brought a government. They had built a court where the District Commissioner judged cases in ignorance. He had court messengers who brought men to him for trial. Many of these messengers came from Umuru on the bank of the Great River, where the white men first came many years before and where they had built the center of their religion and trade and government. These court messengers were greatly hated in Umuofia because they were foreigners and also arrogant and high-handed. They were called kotma,[1] and because of their ash-colored shorts they earned the additional name of Ashy-Buttocks. They guarded the prison, which was full of men who had offended against the white man's law. Some of these prisoners had thrown away their twins and some had molested the Christians. They were beaten in the prison by the kotma and made to work every morning clearing the government compound and fetching wood for the white Commissioner and the court messengers.

9. Father's honor (with the eagle feather). 1. Court messenger (pidgin English).

Some of these prisoners were men of title who should be above such mean occupation. They were grieved by the indignity and mourned for their neglected farms. As they cut grass in the morning the younger men sang in time with the strokes of their machetes:

> *Kotma* of the ash buttocks,
> He is fit to be a slave.
> The white man has no sense,
> He is fit to be a slave.

The court messengers did not like to be called Ashy-Buttocks, and they beat the men. But the song spread in Umuofia.

Okonkwo's head was bowed in sadness as Obierika told him these things.

"Perhaps I have been away too long," Okonkwo said, almost to himself. "But I cannot understand these things you tell me. What is it that has happened to our people? Why have they lost the power to fight?"

"Have you not heard how the white man wiped out Abame?" asked Obierika.

"I have heard," said Okonkwo. "But I have also heard that Abame people were weak and foolish. Why did they not fight back? Had they no guns and machetes? We would be cowards to compare ourselves with the men of Abame. Their fathers had never dared to stand before our ancestors. We must fight these men and drive them from the land."

"It is already too late," said Obierika sadly. "Our own men and our sons have joined the ranks of the stranger. They have joined his religion and they help to uphold his government. If we should try to drive out the white men in Umuofia we should find it easy. There are only two of them. But what of our own people who are following their way and have been given power? They would go to Umuru and bring the soldiers, and we would be like Abame." He paused for a long time and then said: "I told you on my last visit to Mbanta how they hanged Aneto."

"What has happened to that piece of land in dispute?" asked Okonkwo.

"The white man's court has decided that it should belong to Nnama's family, who had given much money to the white man's messengers and interpreter."

"Does the white man understand our custom about land?"

"How can he when he does not even speak our tongue? But he says that our customs are bad; and our own brothers who have taken up his religion also say that our customs are bad. How do you think we can fight when our own brothers have turned against us? The white man is very clever. He came quietly and peaceably with his religion. We were amused at his foolishness and allowed him to stay. Now he has won our brothers, and our clan can no longer act like one. He has put a knife on the things that held us together and we have fallen apart."

"How did they get hold of Aneto to hang him?" asked Okonkwo.

"When he killed Oduche in the fight over the land, he fled to Aninta to escape the wrath of the earth. This was about eight days after the fight, because Oduche had not died immediately from his wounds. It was on the seventh day that he died. But everybody knew that he was going to die and Aneto got his belongings together in readiness to flee. But the Christians had told the white man about the accident, and he sent his *kotma* to catch

Aneto. He was imprisoned with all the leaders of his family. In the end Oduche died and Aneto was taken to Umuru and hanged. The other people were released, but even now they have not found the mouth with which to tell of their suffering."

The two men sat in silence for a long while afterwards.

21

There were many men and women in Umuofia who did not feel as strongly as Okonkwo about the new dispensation. The white man had indeed brought a lunatic religion, but he had also built a trading store and for the first time palm-oil and kernel[2] became things of great price, and much money flowed into Umuofia.

And even in the matter of religion there was a growing feeling that there might be something in it after all, something vaguely akin to method in the overwhelming madness.

This growing feeling was due to Mr. Brown, the white missionary, who was very firm in restraining his flock from provoking the wrath of the clan. One member in particular was very difficult to restrain. His name was Enoch and his father was the priest of the snake cult. The story went around that Enoch had killed and eaten the sacred python, and that his father had cursed him.

Mr. Brown preached against such excess of zeal. Everything was possible, he told his energetic flock, but everything was not expedient. And so Mr. Brown came to be respected even by the clan, because he trod softly on its faith. He made friends with some of the great men of the clan and on one of his frequent visits to the neighboring villages he had been presented with a carved elephant tusk, which was a sign of dignity and rank. One of the great men in that village was called Akunna[3] and he had given one of his sons to be taught the white man's knowledge in Mr. Brown's school.

Whenever Mr. Brown went to that village he spent long hours with Akunna in his *obi* talking through an interpreter about religion. Neither of them succeeded in converting the other but they learned more about their different beliefs.

"You say that there is one supreme God who made heaven and earth," said Akunna on one of Mr. Brown's visits. "We also believe in Him and call Him Chukwu. He made all the world and the other gods."

"There are no other gods," said Mr. Brown. "Chukwu is the only God and all others are false. You carve a piece of wood—like that one" (he pointed at the rafters from which Akunna's carved *Ikenga*[4] hung), "and you call it a god. But it is still a piece of wood."

"Yes," said Akunna. "It is indeed a piece of wood. The tree from which it came was made by Chukwu, as indeed all minor gods were. But He made them for His messengers so that we could approach Him through them. It is like yourself. You are the head of your church."

"No," protested Mr. Brown. "The head of my church is God Himself."

2. The red fleshy husk of the palm nut is crushed manually to produce cooking oil, leaving a fibrous residue along with hard kernels. The Europeans bought both the red oil and the kernels, from which they could extract a very fine oil by using machines.   3. Father's wealth.   4. A carved wooden figure with the horns of a ram that symbolized the strength of a man's right hand. Every adult male kept an *Ikenga* in his personal shrine.

"I know," said Akunna, "but there must be a head in this world among men. Somebody like yourself must be the head here."

"The head of my church in that sense is in England."

"That is exactly what I am saying. The head of your church is in your country. He has sent you here as his messenger. And you have also appointed your own messengers and servants. Or let me take another example, the District Commissioner. He is sent by your king."

"They have a queen," said the interpreter on his own account.

"Your queen sends her messenger, the District Commissioner. He finds that he cannot do the work alone and so he appoints *kotma* to help him. It is the same with God, or Chukwu. He appoints the smaller gods to help Him because His work is too great for one person."

"You should not think of Him as a person," said Mr. Brown. "It is because you do so that you imagine He must need helpers. And the worst thing about it is that you give all the worship to the false gods you have created."

"That is not so. We make sacrifices to the little gods, but when they fail and there is no one else to turn to we go to Chukwu. It is right to do so. We approach a great man through his servants. But when his servants fail to help us, then we go to the last source of hope. We appear to pay greater attention to the little gods but that is not so. We worry them more because we are afraid to worry their Master. Our fathers knew that Chukwu was the Overlord and that is why many of them gave their children the name Chukwuka—"Chukwu is Supreme.""

"You said one interesting thing," said Mr. Brown. "You are afraid of Chukwu. In my religion Chukwu is a loving Father and need not be feared by those who do His will."

"But we must fear Him when we are not doing His will," said Akunna. "And who is to tell His will? It is too great to be known."

In this way Mr. Brown learned a good deal about the religion of the clan and he came to the conclusion that a frontal attack on it would not succeed. And so he built a school and a little hospital in Umuofia. He went from family to family begging people to send their children to his school. But at first they only sent their slaves or sometimes their lazy children. Mr. Brown begged and argued and prophesied. He said that the leaders of the land in the future would be men and women who had learned to read and write. If Umuofia failed to send her children to the school, strangers would come from other places to rule them. They could already see that happening in the Native Court, where the D.C. was surrounded by strangers who spoke his tongue. Most of these strangers came from the distant town of Umuru on the bank of the Great River where the white man first went.

In the end Mr. Brown's arguments began to have an effect. More people came to learn in his school, and he encouraged them with gifts of singlets[5] and towels. They were not all young, these people who came to learn. Some of them were thirty years old or more. They worked on their farms in the morning and went to school in the afternoon. And it was not long before the people began to say that the white man's medicine was quick in working. Mr. Brown's school produced quick results. A few months in it were enough to make one a court messenger or even a court clerk. Those who stayed

5. Undershirts, T-shirts.

longer became teachers; and from Umuofia laborers went forth into the Lord's vineyard. New churches were established in the surrounding villages and a few schools with them. From the very beginning religion and education went hand in hand.

Mr. Brown's mission grew from strength to strength, and because of its link with the new administration it earned a new social prestige. But Mr. Brown himself was breaking down in health. At first he ignored the warning signs. But in the end he had to leave his flock, sad and broken.

It was in the first rainy season after Okonkwo's return to Umuofia that Mr. Brown left for home. As soon as he had learned of Okonkwo's return five months earlier, the missionary had immediately paid him a visit. He had just sent Okonkwo's son, Nwoye, who was now called Isaac,[6] to the new training college for teachers in Umuru. And he had hoped that Okonkwo would be happy to hear of it. But Okonkwo had driven him away with the threat that if he came into his compound again, he would be carried out of it.

Okonkwo's return to his native land was not as memorable as he had wished. It was true his two beautiful daughters aroused great interest among suitors and marriage negotiations were soon in progress, but, beyond that, Umuofia did not appear to have taken any special notice of the warrior's return. The clan had undergone such profound change during his exile that it was barely recognizable. The new religion and government and the trading stores were very much in the people's eyes and minds. There were still many who saw these new institutions as evil, but even they talked and thought about little else, and certainly not about Okonkwo's return.

And it was the wrong year too. If Okonkwo had immediately initiated his two sons into the *ozo* society as he had planned he would have caused a stir. But the initiation rite was performed once in three years in Umuofia, and he had to wait for nearly two years for the next round of ceremonies.

Okonkwo was deeply grieved. And it was not just a personal grief. He mourned for the clan, which he saw breaking up and falling apart, and he mourned for the warlike men of Umuofia, who had so unaccountably become soft like women.

22

Mr. Brown's successor was the Reverend James Smith, and he was a different kind of man. He condemned openly Mr. Brown's policy of compromise and accommodation. He saw things as black and white. And black was evil. He saw the world as a battlefield in which the children of light were locked in mortal conflict with the sons of darkness. He spoke in his sermons about sheep and goats and about wheat and tares. He believed in slaying the prophets of Baal.

Mr. Smith was greatly distressed by the ignorance which many of his flock showed even in such things as the Trinity and the Sacraments. It only showed that they were seeds sown on a rocky soil. Mr. Brown had thought of nothing but numbers. He should have known that the kingdom of God did not depend on large crowds. Our Lord Himself stressed the importance of fewness. Nar-

6. Son of Abraham, offered to God as a sacrifice (Genesis 22).

row is the way and few the number. To fill the Lord's holy temple with an idolatrous crowd clamoring for signs was a folly of everlasting consequence. Our Lord used the whip only once in His life—to drive the crowd away from His church.

Within a few weeks of his arrival in Umuofia Mr. Smith suspended a young woman from the church for pouring new wine into old bottles. This woman had allowed her heathen husband to mutilate her dead child. The child had been declared an *ogbanje*, plaguing its mother by dying and entering her womb to be born again. Four times this child had run its evil round. And so it was mutilated to discourage it from returning.

Mr. Smith was filled with wrath when he heard of this. He disbelieved the story which even some of the most faithful confirmed, the story of really evil children who were not deterred by mutilation, but came back with all the scars. He replied that such stories were spread in the world by the Devil to lead men astray. Those who believed such stories were unworthy of the Lord's table.

There was a saying in Umuofia that as a man danced so the drums were beaten for him. Mr. Smith danced a furious step and so the drums went mad. The over-zealous converts who had smarted under Mr. Brown's restraining hand now flourished in full favor. One of them was Enoch, the son of the snake-priest who was believed to have killed and eaten the sacred python. Enoch's devotion to the new faith had seemed so much greater than Mr. Brown's that the villagers called him the outsider who wept louder than the bereaved.

Enoch was short and slight of build, and always seemed in great haste. His feet were short and broad, and when he stood or walked his heels came together and his feet opened outwards as if they had quarreled and meant to go in different directions. Such was the excessive energy bottled up in Enoch's small body that it was always erupting in quarrels and fights. On Sundays he always imagined that the sermon was preached for the benefit of his enemies. And if he happened to sit near one of them he would occasionally turn to give him a meaningful look, as if to say, "I told you so." It was Enoch who touched off the great conflict between church and clan in Umuofia which had been gathering since Mr. Brown left.

It happened during the annual ceremony which was held in honor of the earth deity. At such times the ancestors of the clan who had been committed to Mother Earth at their death emerged again as *egwugwu* through tiny ant-holes.

One of the greatest crimes a man could commit was to unmask an *egwugwu* in public, or to say or do anything which might reduce its immortal prestige in the eyes of the uninitiated. And this was what Enoch did.

The annual worship of the earth goddess fell on a Sunday, and the masked spirits were abroad. The Christian women who had been to church could not therefore go home. Some of their men had gone out to beg the *egwugwu* to retire for a short while for the women to pass. They agreed and were already retiring, when Enoch boasted aloud that they would not dare to touch a Christian. Whereupon they all came back and one of them gave Enoch a good stroke of the cane, which was always carried. Enoch fell on him and tore off his mask. The other *egwugwu* immediately surrounded their dese-crated companion, to shield him from the profane gaze of women and children, and led him away. Enoch had killed an ancestral spirit, and Umuofia was thrown into confusion.

That night the Mother of the Spirits walked the length and breadth of the clan, weeping for her murdered son. It was a terrible night. Not even the oldest man in Umuofia had ever heard such a strange and fearful sound, and it was never to be heard again. It seemed as if the very soul of the tribe wept for a great evil that was coming—its own death.

On the next day all the masked *egwugwu* of Umuofia assembled in the marketplace. They came from all the quarters of the clan and even from the neighboring villages. The dreaded Otakagu came from Imo, and Ekwensu, dangling a white cock, arrived from Uli. It was a terrible gathering. The eerie voices of countless spirits, the bells that clattered behind some of them, and the clash of machetes as they ran forwards and backwards and saluted one another, sent tremors of fear into every heart. For the first time in living memory the sacred bull-roarer was heard in broad daylight.

From the marketplace the furious band made for Enoch's compound. Some of the elders of the clan went with them, wearing heavy protections of charms and amulets. These were men whose arms were strong in *ogwu*, or medicine. As for the ordinary men and women, they listened from the safety of their huts.

The leaders of the Christians had met together at Mr. Smith's parsonage on the previous night. As they deliberated they could hear the Mother of Spirits wailing for her son. The chilling sound affected Mr. Smith, and for the first time he seemed to be afraid.

"What are they planning to do?" he asked. No one knew, because such a thing had never happened before. Mr. Smith would have sent for the District Commissioner and his court messengers, but they had gone on tour on the previous day.

"One thing is clear," said Mr. Smith. "We cannot offer physical resistance to them. Our strength lies in the Lord." They knelt down together and prayed to God for delivery.

"O Lord, save Thy people," cried Mr. Smith.

"And bless Thine inheritance," replied the men.

They decided that Enoch should be hidden in the parsonage for a day or two. Enoch himself was greatly disappointed when he heard this, for he had hoped that a holy war was imminent; and there were a few other Christians who thought like him. But wisdom prevailed in the camp of the faithful and many lives were thus saved.

The band of *egwugwu* moved like a furious whirlwind to Enoch's compound and with machete and fire reduced it to a desolate heap. And from there they made for the church, intoxicated with destruction.

Mr. Smith was in his church when he heard the masked spirits coming. He walked quietly to the door which commanded the approach to the church compound, and stood there. But when the first three or four *egwugwu* appeared on the church compound he nearly bolted. He overcame this impulse and instead of running away he went down the two steps that led up to the church and walked towards the approaching spirits.

They surged forward, and a long stretch of the bamboo fence with which the church compound was surrounded gave way before them. Discordant bells clanged, machetes clashed and the air was full of dust and weird sounds.

Mr. Smith heard a sound of footsteps behind him. He turned round and saw Okeke, his interpreter. Okeke had not been on the best of terms with his master since he had strongly condemned Enoch's behavior at the meeting of the leaders of the church during the night. Okeke had gone as far as to say that Enoch should not be hidden in the parsonage, because he would only draw the wrath of the clan on the pastor. Mr. Smith had rebuked him in very strong language, and had not sought his advice that morning. But now, as he came up and stood by him confronting the angry spirits, Mr. Smith looked at him and smiled. It was a wan smile, but there was deep gratitude there.

For a brief moment the onrush of the *egwugwu* was checked by the unexpected composure of the two men. But it was only a momentary check, like the tense silence between blasts of thunder. The second onrush was greater than the first. It swallowed up the two men. Then an unmistakable voice rose above the tumult and there was immediate silence. Space was made around the two men, and Ajofia began to speak.

Ajofia was the leading *egwugwu* of Umuofia. He was the head and spokesman of the nine ancestors who administered justice in the clan. His voice was unmistakable and so he was able to bring immediate peace to the agitated spirits. He then addressed Mr. Smith, and as he spoke clouds of smoke rose from his head.

"The body of the white man, I salute you," he said, using the language in which immortals spoke to men.

"The body of the white man, do you know me?" he asked.

Mr. Smith looked at his interpreter, but Okeke, who was a native of distant Umuru, was also at a loss.

Ajofia laughed in his guttural voice. It was like the laugh of rusty metal. "They are strangers," he said, "and they are ignorant. But let that pass." He turned round to his comrades and saluted them, calling them the fathers of Umuofia. He dug his rattling spear into the ground and it shook with metallic life. Then he turned once more to the missionary and his interpreter.

"Tell the white man that we will not do him any harm," he said to the interpreter. "Tell him to go back to his house and leave us alone. We liked his brother who was with us before. He was foolish, but we liked him, and for his sake we shall not harm his brother. But this shrine which he built must be destroyed. We shall no longer allow it in our midst. It has bred untold abominations and we have come to put an end to it." He turned to his comrades. "Fathers of Umuofia, I salute you"; and they replied with one guttural voice. He turned again to the missionary. "You can stay with us if you like our ways. You can worship your own god. It is good that a man should worship the gods and the spirits of his fathers. Go back to your house so that you may not be hurt. Our anger is great but we have held it down so that we can talk to you."

Mr. Smith said to his interpreter: "Tell them to go away from here. This is the house of God and I will not live to see it desecrated."

Okeke interpreted wisely to the spirits and leaders of Umuofia: "The white man says he is happy you have come to him with your grievances, like friends. He will be happy if you leave the matter in his hands."

"We cannot leave the matter in his hands because he does not understand our customs, just as we do not understand his. We say he is foolish because he does not know our ways, and perhaps he says we are foolish because we do not know his. Let him go away."

Mr. Smith stood his ground. But he could not save his church. When the *egwugwu* went away the red-earth church which Mr. Brown had built was a pile of earth and ashes. And for the moment the spirit of the clan was pacified.

23

For the first time in many years Okonkwo had a feeling that was akin to happiness. The times which had altered so unaccountably during his exile seemed to be coming round again. The clan which had turned false on him appeared to be making amends.

He had spoken violently to his clansmen when they had met in the marketplace to decide on their action. And they had listened to him with respect. It was like the good old days again, when a warrior was a warrior. Although they had not agreed to kill the missionary or drive away the Christians, they had agreed to do something substantial. And they had done it. Okonkwo was almost happy again.

For two days after the destruction of the church, nothing happened. Every man in Umuofia went about armed with a gun or a machete. They would not be caught unawares, like the men of Abame.

Then the District Commissioner returned from his tour. Mr. Smith went immediately to him and they had a long discussion. The men of Umuofia did not take any notice of this, and if they did, they thought it was not important. The missionary often went to see his brother white man. There was nothing strange in that.

Three days later the District Commissioner sent his sweet-tongued messenger to the leaders of Umuofia asking them to meet him in his headquarters. That also was not strange. He often asked them to hold such palavers, as he called them. Okonkwo was among the six leaders he invited.

Okonkwo warned the others to be fully armed. "An Umuofia man does not refuse a call," he said. "He may refuse to do what he is asked; he does not refuse to be asked. But the times have changed, and we must be fully prepared."

And so the six men went to see the District Commissioner, armed with their machetes. They did not carry guns, for that would be unseemly. They were led into the courthouse where the District Commissioner sat. He received them politely. They unslung their goatskin bags and their sheathed machetes, put them on the floor, and sat down.

"I have asked you to come," began the Commissioner, "because of what happened during my absence. I have been told a few things but I cannot believe them until I have heard your own side. Let us talk about it like friends and find a way of ensuring that it does not happen again."

Ogbuefi Ekwueme[7] rose to his feet and began to tell the story.

"Wait a minute," said the Commissioner. "I want to bring in my men so that they too can hear your grievances and take warning. Many of them come from distant places and although they speak your tongue they are ignorant

---

7. A person who does what he says (a praise name).

of your customs. James! Go and bring in the men." His interpreter left the courtroom and soon returned with twelve men. They sat together with the men of Umuofia, and Ogbuefi Ekwueme began to tell the story of how Enoch murdered an *egwugwu*.

It happened so quickly that the six men did not see it coming. There was only a brief scuffle, too brief even to allow the drawing of a sheathed machete. The six men were handcuffed and led into the guardroom.

"We shall not do you any harm," said the District Commissioner to them later, "if only you agree to cooperate with us. We have brought a peaceful administration to you and your people so that you may be happy. If any man ill-treats you we shall come to your rescue. But we will not allow you to ill-treat others. We have a court of law where we judge cases and administer justice just as it is done in my own country under a great queen. I have brought you here because you joined together to molest others, to burn people's houses and their place of worship. That must not happen in the dominion of our queen, the most powerful ruler in the world. I have decided that you will pay a fine of two hundred bags of cowries. You will be released as soon as you agree to this and undertake to collect that fine from your people. What do you say to that?"

The six men remained sullen and silent and the Commissioner left them for a while. He told the court messengers, when he left the guardroom, to treat the men with respect because they were the leaders of Umuofia. They said, "Yes, sir," and saluted.

As soon as the District Commissioner left, the head messenger, who was also the prisoners' barber, took down his razor and shaved off all the hair on the men's heads. They were still handcuffed, and they just sat and moped.

"Who is the chief among you?" the court messengers asked in jest. "We see that every pauper wears the anklet of title in Umuofia. Does it cost as much as ten cowries?"

The six men ate nothing throughout that day and the next. They were not even given any water to drink, and they could not go out to urinate or go into the bush when they were pressed. At night the messengers came in to taunt them and to knock their shaven heads together.

Even when the men were left alone they found no words to speak to one another. It was only on the third day, when they could no longer bear the hunger and the insults, that they began to talk about giving in.

"We should have killed the white man if you had listened to me," Okonkwo snarled.

"We could have been in Umuru now waiting to be hanged," someone said to him.

"Who wants to kill the white man?" asked a messenger who had just rushed in. Nobody spoke.

"You are not satisfied with your crime, but you must kill the white man on top of it." He carried a strong stick, and he hit each man a few blows on the head and back. Okonkwo was choked with hate.

As soon as the six men were locked up, court messengers went into Umuofia to tell the people that their leaders would not be released unless they paid a fine of two hundred and fifty bags of cowries.

"Unless you pay the fine immediately," said their head-man, "we will take your leaders to Umuru before the big white man, and hang them."

This story spread quickly through the villages, and was added to as it went. Some said that the men had already been taken to Umuru and would be hanged on the following day. Some said that their families would also be hanged. Others said that soldiers were already on their way to shoot the people of Umuofia as they had done in Abame.

It was the time of the full moon. But that night the voice of children was not heard. The village *ilo* where they always gathered for a moon-play was empty. The women of Iguedo did not meet in their secret enclosure to learn a new dance to be displayed later to the village. Young men who were always abroad in the moonlight kept to their huts that night. Their manly voices were not heard on the village paths as they went to visit their friends and lovers. Umuofia was like a startled animal with ears erect, sniffing the silent, ominous air and not knowing which way to run.

The silence was broken by the village crier beating his sonorous *ogene*. He called every man in Umuofia, from the Akakanma age group upwards, to a meeting in the marketplace after the morning meal. He went from one end of the village to the other and walked all its breadth. He did not leave out any of the main footpaths.

Okonkwo's compound was like a deserted homestead. It was as if cold water had been poured on it. His family was all there, but everyone spoke in whispers. His daughter Ezinma had broken her twenty-eight-day visit to the family of her future husband, and returned home when she heard that her father had been imprisoned, and was going to be hanged. As soon as she got home she went to Obierika to ask what the men of Umuofia were going to do about it. But Obierika had not been home since morning. His wives thought he had gone to a secret meeting. Ezinma was satisfied that something was being done.

On the morning after the village crier's appeal the men of Umuofia met in the marketplace and decided to collect without delay two hundred and fifty bags of cowries to appease the white man. They did not know that fifty bags would go to the court messengers, who had increased the fine for that purpose.

24

Okonkwo and his fellow prisoners were set free as soon as the fine was paid. The District Commissioner spoke to them again about the great queen, and about peace and good government. But the men did not listen. They just sat and looked at him and at his interpreter. In the end they were given back their bags and sheathed machetes and told to go home. They rose and left the courthouse. They neither spoke to anyone nor among themselves.

The courthouse, like the church, was built a little way outside the village. The footpath that linked them was a very busy one because it also led to the stream, beyond the court. It was open and sandy. Footpaths were open and sandy in the dry season. But when the rains came the bush grew thick on either side and closed in on the path. It was now dry season.

As they made their way to the village the six men met women and children going to the stream with their waterpots. But the men wore such heavy and fearsome looks that the women and children did not say "*nno*" or "welcome" to them, but edged out of the way to let them pass. In the village little groups of men joined them until they became a sizable company. They walked silently. As each of the six men got to his compound, he turned in, taking some of the crowd with him. The village was astir in a silent, suppressed way.

Ezinma had prepared some food for her father as soon as news spread that the six men would be released. She took it to him in his *obi*. He ate absent-mindedly. He had no appetite; he only ate to please her. His male relations and friends had gathered in his *obi*, and Obierika was urging him to eat. Nobody else spoke, but they noticed the long stripes on Okonkwo's back where the warder's whip had cut into his flesh.

The village crier was abroad again in the night. He beat his iron gong and announced that another meeting would be held in the morning. Everyone knew that Umuofia was at last going to speak its mind about the things that were happening.

Okonkwo slept very little that night. The bitterness in his heart was now mixed with a kind of childlike excitement. Before he had gone to bed he had brought down his war dress, which he had not touched since his return from exile. He had shaken out his smoked raffia skirt and examined his tall feather head-gear and his shield. They were all satisfactory, he had thought.

As he lay on his bamboo bed he thought about the treatment he had received in the white man's court, and he swore vengeance. If Umuofia decided on war, all would be well. But if they chose to be cowards he would go out and avenge himself. He thought about wars in the past. The noblest, he thought, was the war against Isike. In those days Okudo[8] was still alive. Okudo sang a war song in a way that no other man could. He was not a fighter, but his voice turned every man into a lion.

"Worthy men are no more," Okonkwo sighed as he remembered those days. "Isike will never forget how we slaughtered them in that war. We killed twelve of their men and they killed only two of ours. Before the end of the fourth market week they were suing for peace. Those were days when men were men."

As he thought of these things he heard the sound of the iron gong in the distance. He listened carefully, and could just hear the crier's voice. But it was very faint. He turned on his bed and his back hurt him. He ground his teeth. The crier was drawing nearer and nearer until he passed by Okonkwo's compound.

"The greatest obstacle in Umuofia," Okonkwo thought bitterly, "is that coward, Egonwanne.[9] His sweet tongue can change fire into cold ash. When he speaks he moves our men to impotence. If they had ignored his womanish wisdom five years ago, we would not have come to this." He ground his teeth. "Tomorrow he will tell them that our fathers never fought a 'war of blame.' If they listen to him I shall leave them and plan my own revenge."

The crier's voice had once more become faint, and the distance had taken the harsh edge off his iron gong. Okonkwo turned from one side to the other and derived a kind of pleasure from the pain his back gave him. "Let Egonwanne talk about a 'war of blame' tomorrow and I shall show him my back and head." He ground his teeth.

8. Great eagle feather (a praise name).   9. Wealth of a sibling.

The marketplace began to fill as soon as the sun rose. Obierika was waiting in his *obi* when Okonkwo came along and called him. He hung his goatskin bag and his sheathed machete on his shoulder and went out to join him. Obierika's hut was close to the road and he saw every man who passed to the marketplace. He had exchanged greetings with many who had already passed that morning.

When Okonkwo and Obierika got to the meeting place there were already so many people that if one threw up a grain of sand it would not find its way to the earth again. And many more people were coming from every quarter of the nine villages. It warmed Okonkwo's heart to see such strength of numbers. But he was looking for one man in particular, the man whose tongue he dreaded and despised so much.

"Can you see him?" he asked Obierika.

"Who?"

"Egonwanne," he said, his eyes roving from one corner of the huge marketplace to the other. Most of the men sat on wooden stools they had brought with them.

"No," said Obierika, casting his eyes over the crowd. "Yes, there he is, under the silk-cotton tree. Are you afraid he would convince us not to fight?"

"Afraid? I do not care what he does to *you.* I despise him and those who listen to him. I shall fight alone if I choose."

They spoke at the top of their voices because everybody was talking, and it was like the sound of a great market.

"I shall wait till he has spoken," Okonkwo thought. "Then I shall speak."

"But how do you know he will speak against war?" Obierika asked after a while.

"Because I know he is a coward," said Okonkwo. Obierika did not hear the rest of what he said because at that moment somebody touched his shoulder from behind and he turned round to shake hands and exchange greetings with five or six friends. Okonkwo did not turn round even though he knew the voices. He was in no mood to exchange greetings. But one of the men touched him and asked about the people of his compound.

"They are well," he replied without interest.

The first man to speak to Umuofia that morning was Okika, one of the six who had been imprisoned. Okika was a great man and an orator. But he did not have the booming voice which a first speaker must use to establish silence in the assembly of the clan. Onyeka[1] had such a voice; and so he was asked to salute Umuofia before Okika began to speak.

"*Umuofia kwenu!*" he bellowed, raising his left arm and pushing the air with his open hand.

"*Yaa!*" roared Umuofia.

"*Umuofia kwenu!*" he bellowed again, and again and again, facing a new direction each time. And the crowd answered, "*Yaa!*"

There was immediate silence as though cold water had been poured on a roaring flame.

Okika sprang to his feet and also saluted his clansmen four times. Then he began to speak:

"You all know why we are here, when we ought to be building our barns or mending our huts, when we should be putting our compounds in order.

1. "Who surpasses [God]?" (a rhetorical question).

My father used to say to me: 'Whenever you see a toad jumping in broad daylight, then know that something is after its life.' When I saw you all pouring into this meeting from all the quarters of our clan so early in the morning, I knew that something was after our life." He paused for a brief moment and then began again:

"All our gods are weeping. Idemili is weeping, Ogwugwu is weeping, Agbala is weeping, and all the others. Our dead fathers are weeping because of the shameful sacrilege they are suffering and the abomination we have all seen with our eyes." He stopped again to steady his trembling voice.

"This is a great gathering. No clan can boast of greater numbers or greater valor. But are we all here? I ask you: Are all the sons of Umuofia with us here?" A deep murmur swept through the crowd.

"They are not," he said. "They have broken the clan and gone their several ways. We who are here this morning have remained true to our fathers, but our brothers have deserted us and joined a stranger to soil their fatherland. If we fight the stranger we shall hit our brothers and perhaps shed the blood of a clansman. But we must do it. Our fathers never dreamed of such a thing, they never killed their brothers. But a white man never came to them. So we must do what our fathers would never have done. Eneke the bird was asked why he was always on the wing and he replied: 'Men have learned to shoot without missing their mark and I have learned to fly without perching on a twig.' We must root out this evil. And if our brothers take the side of evil we must root them out too. And we must do it *now*. We must bail this water now that it is only ankle-deep. . . ."

At this point there was a sudden stir in the crowd and every eye was turned in one direction. There was a sharp bend in the road that led from the marketplace to the white man's court, and to the stream beyond it. And so no one had seen the approach of the five court messengers until they had come round the bend, a few paces from the edge of the crowd. Okonkwo was sitting at the edge.

He sprang to his feet as soon as he saw who it was. He confronted the head messenger, trembling with hate, unable to utter a word. The man was fearless and stood his ground, his four men lined up behind him.

In that brief moment the world seemed to stand still, waiting. There was utter silence. The men of Umuofia were merged into the mute backcloth of trees and giant creepers, waiting.

The spell was broken by the head messenger. "Let me pass!" he ordered.

"What do you want here?"

"The white man whose power you know too well has ordered this meeting to stop."

In a flash Okonkwo drew his machete. The messenger crouched to avoid the blow. It was useless. Okonkwo's machete descended twice and the man's head lay beside his uniformed body.

The waiting backcloth jumped into tumultuous life and the meeting was stopped. Okonkwo stood looking at the dead man. He knew that Umuofia would not go to war. He knew because they had let the other messengers escape. They had broken into tumult instead of action. He discerned fright in that tumult. He heard voices asking: "Why did he do it?"

He wiped his machete on the sand and went away.

25

When the District Commissioner arrived at Okonkwo's compound at the head of an armed band of soldiers and court messengers he found a small crowd of men sitting wearily in the *obi*. He commanded them to come outside, and they obeyed without a murmur.

"Which among you is called Okonkwo?" he asked through his interpreter.

"He is not here," replied Obierika.

"Where is he?"

"He is not here!"

The Commissioner became angry and red in the face. He warned the men that unless they produced Okonkwo forthwith he would lock them all up. The men murmured among themselves, and Obierika spoke again.

"We can take you where he is, and perhaps your men will help us."

The Commissioner did not understand what Obierika meant when he said, "Perhaps your men will help us." One of the most infuriating habits of these people was their love of superfluous words, he thought.

Obierika with five or six others led the way. The Commissioner and his men followed, their firearms held at the ready. He had warned Obierika that if he and his men played any monkey tricks they would be shot. And so they went.

There was a small bush behind Okonkwo's compound. The only opening into this bush from the compound was a little round hole in the red-earth wall through which fowls went in and out in their endless search for food. The hole would not let a man through. It was to this bush that Obierika led the Commissioner and his men. They skirted round the compound, keeping close to the wall. The only sound they made was with their feet as they crushed dry leaves.

Then they came to the tree from which Okonkwo's body was dangling, and they stopped dead.

"Perhaps your men can help us bring him down and bury him," said Obierika. "We have sent for strangers from another village to do it for us, but they may be a long time coming."

The District Commissioner changed instantaneously. The resolute administrator in him gave way to the student of primitive customs.

"Why can't you take him down yourselves?" he asked.

"It is against our custom," said one of the men. "It is an abomination for a man to take his own life. It is an offense against the Earth, and a man who commits it will not be buried by his clansmen. His body is evil, and only strangers may touch it. That is why we ask your people to bring him down, because you are strangers."

"Will you bury him like any other man?" asked the Commissioner.

"We cannot bury him. Only strangers can. We shall pay your men to do it. When he has been buried we will then do our duty by him. We shall make sacrifices to cleanse the desecrated land."

Obierika, who had been gazing steadily at his friend's dangling body, turned suddenly to the District Commissioner and said ferociously: "That man was one of the greatest men in Umuofia. You drove him to kill himself; and now he will be buried like a dog. . . ." He could not say any more. His voice trembled and choked his words.

"Shut up!" shouted one of the messengers, quite unnecessarily.

"Take down the body," the Commissioner ordered his chief messenger, "and bring it and all these people to the court."

"Yes, sah," the messenger said, saluting.

The Commissioner went away, taking three or four of the soldiers with him. In the many years in which he had toiled to bring civilization to different parts of Africa he had learned a number of things. One of them was that a District Commissioner must never attend to such undignified details as cutting a hanged man from the tree. Such attention would give the natives a poor opinion of him. In the book which he planned to write he would stress that point. As he walked back to the court he thought about that book. Every day brought him some new material. The story of this man who had killed a messenger and hanged himself would make interesting reading. One could almost write a whole chapter on him. Perhaps not a whole chapter but a reasonable paragraph, at any rate. There was so much else to include, and one must be firm in cutting out details. He had already chosen the title of the book, after much thought: *The Pacification of the Primitive Tribes of the Lower Niger.*

ALICE MUNRO
born 1931

"I don't take up a story and follow it as if it were a road, taking me somewhere, with views and neat diversions along the way," writes Alice Munro in her essay *What Is Real?* "I go into it and move back and forth and settle here and there, and stay in it for a while." This description of Munro the reader applies equally to Munro the writer. Munro's stories join the familiar to the enigmatic in a style that, like Virginia Woolf's, savors the nuances and subtleties of human relationships. Combining this writerly style with a keen attention to physical and psychological detail that places her in the realist tradition of Tolstoy and Chekhov, Munro's short fiction is marked by compassion and the awareness of multiple points of view. Whether focused on fox farming, high school dances, chance sexual encounters, marriage and divorce, or discovery and self-discovery, Munro's vision frequently centers on the lives of girls and women and on their introspective responses to the world around them. This writing is less concerned with "getting somewhere" than with settling here and there to reveal the mystery and complexity of seemingly simple day-to-day realities.

Born Alice Anne Laidlaw in the Scots-Irish community of Wingham, Ontario, Munro began writing stories in her teens—tales of romance and adventure far removed from her rural Canadian home. Her parents, Robert Eric Laidlaw and Ann Chamney Laidlaw, struggled throughout their marriage to make ends meet—fox farming during the Depression, selling wares door to door, raising turkeys—but no venture was successful enough to lift the family out of poverty. In 1949, Munro enrolled at the University of Western Ontario, leaving school in 1951 to marry James Munro and moving with him to Vancouver, British Columbia. While raising three daughters and managing a bookshop there during the 1950s and 1960s, Munro honed her storytelling skills. When, in 1968, *Dance of the Happy Shades* (from which the story printed here is taken) introduced her to the reading public, the response was overwhelming. Praised by critics, recipient also of the prestigious Governor General's Literary Award for fiction (the first of three), she had found a place for herself in the world of professional writers. In 1971 she published *Lives of Girls and Women*, a novel composed of a series of linked stories, all recounting the emergence of the character Del Jordan from her confined childhood to a career and an adult identity far transcending the borders of her hometown of Jubilee. This was followed in 1974 by a third book of stories, *Something I've Been Meaning to Tell You*. Munro's first marriage ended in divorce in 1972, after which she remarried and moved to the central Canadian town of Clinton, Ontario. Since then, she has published seven other collections of short fiction: *Who Do You Think You Are?: Stories* (1978; published outside Canada as *The Beggar Maid*, 1979), *The Moons of Jupiter* (1982), *The Progress of Love* (1986), *Friend of My Youth* (1990), *Open Secrets* (1994), a cumulative *Selected Stories* in 1996, and a new volume, *The Love of a Good Woman* (1998), which received the Giller Prize. She continues to receive prizes and awards.

The vagaries of life in rural Canada figure prominently in Munro's writing, and because of this some critics have labeled her a "regionalist." Her characters often inhabit small fictional towns similar to the Wingham of her youth, and the area of *Walker Brothers Cowboy* recalls just such a region in southwestern Ontario. Yet the worlds of human relationships that they create for themselves are more expansive and universal than the term *regionalist* implies. In this, she resembles James Joyce in *Dubliners*, William Faulkner writing about his mythic Yoknapatawpha County, and writers of the modern American South for whom she feels a marked affinity: Flannery O'Connor, Eudora Welty, Carson McCullers, and Walker Percy. Munro too focuses on interconnected lives in small communities and on the puzzles and discoveries of growing up. Her most memorable characters—Del Jordan of *Lives of Girls and Women*, and Rose of the story cycle *The Beggar Maid*—though distinct in their circumstances and personalities, share a breadth of vision and an openness to life's inconstancies that makes them seem larger and more significant than their surroundings. Through their eyes, we see a world not of heroic resolutions and tragic ends or of a linear progression from "here" to "there" but rather of moments and of details; of disappointments and small victories; and above all, of the inevitable swoop and sway between intimacy and alienation. What we see most powerfully is the masks we all wear, "the faces we put on to meet the faces that we meet" (to paraphrase T. S. Eliot). Munro's characters disguise themselves from themselves and from others but seek at the same time to be unmasked, discovered, and more fully human. Describing her fondness for the short-story form, Munro says: "I like looking at people's lives over a number of years, without continuity. Like catching them in snapshots. And I like the way people relate, or don't relate, to the people they were earlier." Like Munro's later work, *Walker Brothers Cowboy* catches a snapshot of the relationship between a character's present and past lives. The same story also illustrates the way the writer manipulates the boundaries between autobiography and fiction, basing her stories in personal experience but also radically changing historical facts. Thus there actually was a Nora who loved dancing and clothes with flowered prints; and Nora did give a dance lesson to the nine-year-old Alice Laidlaw, whose father was a traveling salesman; and Alice was impressed by Nora's vitality and joy. The romantic nostalgia that is so crucial to *Walker Brothers Cowboy*, however, is complete fiction; according to Munro, Nora would have been fifteen when her father married at twenty-five. Using memory, introspection, and a supreme gift for adapting reality to her ends, Munro the storyteller creates characters who struggle to understand and accept the vicissitudes of human relationships and, correspondingly, of life itself.

One of Munro's best-known stories, *Walker Brothers Cowboy* is the first story of her first collection, *Dance of the Happy Shades* (1968), and it already reveals the mixture of realistic observation and overtones of mystery that permeate her work. The small towns with their cracking sidewalks, the isolated farmhouses, the pricks of sunlight that come through a straw hat: such details not only confirm the solid reality of these scenes but also establish an atmosphere of awareness and discovery that will be important later on. Here, two children accompany their father, a door-to-door salesman, on a sales trip around the back country roads of southwest Ontario. The narrator, a solitary young girl, reports the day's events in a matter-of-fact tone, sketching in the process a picture of the family and its everyday existence. Their disappointed, plaintive, somewhat snobbish mother strives to maintain appearances and cannot resign herself to having come down in the world; their father copes cheerfully, telling the children stories as they walk by the lake or making up funny songs as they drive from place to place; the narrator and her younger brother, usually required to stay in their yard, find the sales trip a chance for adventure. It is a settled existence, with small frictions and disappointments but no surprises. An unscheduled trip to Nora's home, however, opens up other dimensions by hinting at an unforgotten romance in their father's past. The contrasts between the cheerless mother and Nora—full of warmth and vitality—are quietly implied, and the father's unaccustomed silence as they drive back home suggests emotional undercurrents that were previously invisible. The narrator's life—once so familiar and ordinary—has been changed into a different kind of landscape: "into something you will never know, with all kinds of weathers, and distances you cannot imagine."

Walker Brothers Cowboy[1]

After supper my father says, "Want to go down and see if the Lake's still there?" We leave my mother sewing under the dining-room light, making clothes for me against the opening of school. She has ripped up for this purpose an old suit and an old plaid wool dress of hers, and she has to cut and match very cleverly and also make me stand and turn for endless fittings, sweaty, itching from the hot wool, ungrateful. We leave my brother in bed in the little screened porch at the end of the front veranda, and sometimes he kneels on his bed and presses his face against the screen and calls mournfully, "Bring me an ice-cream cone!" but I call back, "You will be asleep," and do not even turn my head.

Then my father and I walk gradually down a long, shabby sort of street, with Silverwoods Ice Cream signs standing on the sidewalk, outside tiny, lighted stores. This is in Tuppertown, an old town on Lake Huron,[2] an old grain port. The street is shaded, in some places, by maple trees whose roots have cracked and heaved the sidewalk and spread out like crocodiles into the bare yards. People are sitting out, men in shirtsleeves and undershirts and women in aprons—not people we know but if anybody looks ready to nod and say, "Warm night," my father will nod too and say something the same. Children are still playing. I don't know them either because my mother

---

1. A traveling salesman for a Canadian door-to-door sales company that is probably modeled on the still-operating Watkins Products firm.   2. One of the Great Lakes, bordering on Ontario (Canada) and eastern Michigan. Place names are both real and invented. Real places mentioned in the story include Sunshine, a small town close to Munro's childhood home in Wingham; Dungannon, a small town close to Goderich; Fort William, which merged with Port Arthur in 1970 to become the city of Thunder Bay; and Brantford, a city in southeastern Ontario. Other place names, like Tuppertown, Turnaround, and Boylesbridge, are adapted or fictitious.

keeps my brother and me in our own yard, saying he is too young to leave it and I have to mind him. I am not so sad to watch their evening games because the games themselves are ragged, dissolving. Children, of their own will, draw apart, separate into islands of two or one under the heavy trees, occupying themselves in such solitary ways as I do all day, planting pebbles in the dirt or writing in it with a stick.

Presently we leave these yards and houses behind; we pass a factory with boarded-up windows, a lumberyard whose high wooden gates are locked for the night. Then the town falls away in a defeated jumble of sheds and small junkyards, the sidewalk gives up and we are walking on a sandy path with burdocks, plantains, humble nameless weeds all around. We enter a vacant lot, a kind of park really, for it is kept clear of junk and there is one bench with a slat missing on the back, a place to sit and look at the water. Which is generally gray in the evening, under a lightly overcast sky, no sunsets, the horizon dim. A very quiet, washing noise on the stones of the beach. Further along, towards the main part of town, there is a stretch of sand, a water slide, floats bobbing around the safe swimming area, a lifeguard's rickety throne. Also a long dark-green building, like a roofed veranda, called the Pavilion, full of farmers and their wives, in stiff good clothes, on Sundays. That is the part of the town we used to know when we lived at Dungannon and came here three or four times a summer, to the Lake. That, and the docks where we would go and look at the grain boats, ancient, rusty, wallowing, making us wonder how they got past the breakwater let alone to Fort William.

Tramps hang around the docks and occasionally on these evenings wander up the dwindling beach and climb the shifting, precarious path boys have made, hanging on to dry bushes, and say something to my father which, being frightened of tramps, I am too alarmed to catch. My father says he is a bit hard up himself. "I'll roll you a cigarette if it's any use to you," he says, and he shakes tobacco out carefully on one of the thin butterfly papers, flicks it with his tongue, seals it and hands it to the tramp, who takes it and walks away. My father also rolls and lights and smokes one cigarette of his own.

He tells me how the Great Lakes came to be. All where Lake Huron is now, he says, used to be flat land, a wide flat plain. Then came the ice, creeping down from the North, pushing deep into the low places. Like *that*— and he shows me his hand with his spread fingers pressing the rock-hard ground where we are sitting. His fingers make hardly any impression at all and he says, "Well, the old ice cap had a lot more power behind it than this hand has." And then the ice went back, shrank back towards the North Pole where it came from, and left its fingers of ice in the deep places it had gouged, and ice turned to lakes and there they were today. They were *new*, as time went. I try to see that plain before me, dinosaurs walking on it, but I am not able even to imagine the shore of the Lake when the Indians were there, before Tuppertown. The tiny share we have of time appalls me, though my father seems to regard it with tranquillity. Even my father, who sometimes seems to me to have been at home in the world as long as it has lasted, has really lived on this earth only a little longer than I have, in terms of all the time there has been to live in. He has not known a time, any more than I, when automobiles and electric lights did not at least exist. He was not alive when this century started. I will be barely alive—old, old—when it ends. I do not like to think of it. I wish the Lake to be always just a lake, with the safe-swimming floats marking it, and the breakwater and the lights of Tuppertown.

My father has a job, selling for Walker Brothers. This is a firm that sells almost entirely in the country, the back country. Sunshine, Boylesbridge, Turnaround—that is all his territory. Not Dungannon where we used to live, Dungannon is too near town and my mother is grateful for that. He sells cough medicine, iron tonic, corn plasters, laxatives, pills for female disorders, mouthwash, shampoo, liniment, salves, lemon and orange and raspberry concentrate for making refreshing drinks, vanilla, food coloring, black and green tea, ginger, cloves, and other spices, rat poison. He has a song about it, with these two lines:

> And have all liniments and oils,
> For everything from corns to boils. . . .

Not a very funny song, in my mother's opinion. A peddler's song, and that is what he is, a peddler knocking at backwoods kitchens. Up until last winter we had our own business, a fox farm. My father raised silver foxes and sold their pelts to the people who make them into capes and coats and muffs. Prices fell, my father hung on hoping they would get better next year, and they fell again, and he hung on one more year and one more and finally it was not possible to hang on anymore, we owed everything to the feed company. I have heard my mother explain this, several times, to Mrs. Oliphant, who is the only neighbor she talks to. (Mrs. Oliphant also has come down in the world, being a schoolteacher who married the janitor.) We poured all we had into it, my mother says, and we came out with nothing. Many people could say the same thing, these days, but my mother has no time for the national calamity, only ours. Fate has flung us onto a street of poor people (it does not matter that we were poor before; that was a different sort of poverty), and the only way to take this, as she sees it, is with dignity, with bitterness, with no reconciliation. No bathroom with a claw-footed tub and a flush toilet is going to comfort her, nor water on tap and sidewalks past the house and milk in bottles, not even the two movie theatres and the Venus Restaurant and Woolworths so marvellous it has live birds singing in its fan-cooled corners and fish as tiny as fingernails, as bright as moons, swimming in its green tanks. My mother does not care.

In the afternoons she often walks to Simon's Grocery and takes me with her to help carry things. She wears a good dress, navy blue with little flowers, sheer, worn over a navy-blue slip. Also a summer hat of white straw, pushed down on the side of the head, and white shoes I have just whitened on a newspaper on the back steps. I have my hair freshly done in long damp curls which the dry air will fortunately soon loosen, a stiff large hair ribbon on top of my head. This is entirely different from going out after supper with my father. We have not walked past two houses before I feel we have become objects of universal ridicule. Even the dirty words chalked on the sidewalk are laughing at us. My mother does not seem to notice. She walks serenely like a lady shopping, like a *lady* shopping, past the housewives in loose belt-less dresses torn under the arms. With me her creation, wretched curls and flaunting hair bow, scrubbed knees and white socks—all I do not want to be. I loathe even my name when she says it in public, in a voice so high, proud, and ringing, deliberately different from the voice of any other mother on the street.

My mother will sometimes carry home, for a treat, a brick of ice cream—pale Neapolitan; and because we have no refrigerator in our house we wake my brother and eat it at once in the dining room, always darkened by the wall of the house next door. I spoon it up tenderly, leaving the chocolate till last, hoping to have some still to eat when my brother's dish is empty. My mother tries then to imitate the conversations we used to have at Dungannon, going back to our earliest, most leisurely days before my brother was born, when she would give me a little tea and a lot of milk in a cup like hers and we would sit out on the step facing the pump, the lilac tree, the fox pens beyond. She is not able to keep from mentioning those days. "Do you remember when we put you in your sled and Major pulled you?" (Major our dog, that we had to leave with neighbors when we moved.) "Do you remember your sandbox outside the kitchen window?" I pretend to remember far less than I do, wary of being trapped into sympathy or any unwanted emotion.

My mother has headaches. She often has to lie down. She lies on my brother's narrow bed in the little screened porch, shaded by heavy branches. "I look up at that tree and I think I am at home," she says.

"What you need," my father tells her, "is some fresh air and a drive in the country." He means for her to go with him, on his Walker Brothers route.

That is not my mother's idea of a drive in the country.

"Can I come?"

"Your mother might want you for trying on clothes."

"I'm beyond sewing this afternoon," my mother says.

"I'll take her then. Take both of them, give you a rest."

What is there about us that people need to be given a rest from? Never mind. I am glad enough to find my brother and make him go to the toilet and get us both into the car, our knees unscrubbed, my hair unringleted. My father brings from the house his two heavy brown suitcases, full of bottles, and sets them on the back seat. He wears a white shirt, brilliant in the sunlight, a tie, light trousers belonging to his summer suit (his other suit is black, for funerals, and belonged to my uncle before he died), and a creamy straw hat. His salesman's outfit, with pencils clipped in the shirt pocket. He goes back once again, probably to say goodbye to my mother, to ask her if she is sure she doesn't want to come, and hear her say, "No. No thanks, I'm better just to lie here with my eyes closed." Then we are backing out of the driveway with the rising hope of adventure, just the little hope that takes you over the bump into the street, the hot air starting to move, turning into a breeze, the houses growing less and less familiar as we follow the shortcut my father knows, the quick way out of town. Yet what is there waiting for us all afternoon but hot hours in stricken farmyards, perhaps a stop at a country store and three ice-cream cones or bottles of pop, and my father singing? The one he made up about himself has a title—"The Walker Brothers Cowboy"—and it starts out like this:

> Old Ned Fields, he now is dead,
> So I am ridin' the route instead. . . .

Who is Ned Fields? The man he has replaced, surely, and if so he really is dead; yet my father's voice is mournful-jolly, making his death some kind of nonsense, a comic calamity. "Wisht I was back on the Rio Grande,[3] plungin' through the dusky sand." My father sings most of the time while driving the car. Even now, heading out of town, crossing the bridge and taking the sharp turn onto the highway, he is humming something, mumbling a bit of a song to himself, just tuning up, really, getting ready to improvise, for out along the highway we pass the Baptist Camp, the Vacation Bible Camp, and he lets loose:

> Where are the Baptists, where are the Baptists,
>   where are all the Baptists today?
> They're down in the water, in Lake Huron water,
>   with their sins all a-gittin' washed away."

My brother takes this for straight truth and gets up on his knees trying to see down to the Lake. "I don't see any Baptists," he says accusingly. "Neither do I, son," says my father. "I told you, they're down in the Lake."

No roads paved when we left the highway. We have to roll up the windows because of dust. The land is flat, scorched, empty. Bush lots at the back of the farms hold shade, black pine-shade like pools nobody can ever get to. We bump up a long lane and at the end of it what could look more unwelcoming, more deserted than the tall unpainted farmhouse with grass growing uncut right up to the front door, green blinds down, and a door upstairs opening on nothing but air? Many houses have this door, and I have never yet been able to find out why. I ask my father and he says they are for walking in your sleep. *What?* Well, if you happen to be walking in your sleep and you want to step outside. I am offended, seeing too late that he is joking, as usual, but my brother says sturdily, "If they did that they would break their necks."

The 1930s. How much this kind of farmhouse, this kind of afternoon seem to me to belong to that one decade in time, just as my father's hat does, his bright flared tie, our car with its wide running board (an Essex, and long past its prime). Cars somewhat like it, many older, none dustier, sit in the farmyards. Some are past running and have their doors pulled off, their seats removed for use on porches. No living things to be seen, chickens or cattle. Except dogs. There are dogs lying in any kind of shade they can find, dreaming, their lean sides rising and sinking rapidly. They get up when my father opens the car door, he has to speak to them. "Nice boy, there's a boy, nice old boy." They quiet down, go back to their shade. He should know how to quiet animals, he has held desperate foxes with tongs around their necks. One gentling voice for the dogs and another, rousing, cheerful, for calling at doors. "Hello there, missus, it's the Walker Brothers man and what are you out of today?" A door opens, he disappears. Forbidden to follow, forbidden even to leave the car, we can just wait and wonder what he says. Sometimes trying to make my mother laugh, he pretends to be himself in a farm kitchen, spreading out his sample case. "Now then, missus, are you troubled with parasitic life? Your children's scalps, I mean. All those crawly little things we're too polite to mention that show up on the heads of the best of families? Soap alone is useless, kerosene is not too nice a perfume, but I

3. A large river that begins in Colorado and flows south, becoming the border between Mexico and the United States.

have here—" Or else, "Believe me, sitting and driving all day the way I do I *know* the value of these fine pills. Natural relief. A problem common to old folks too, once their days of activity are over—How about you, Grandma?" He would wave the imaginary box of pills under my mother's nose and she would laugh finally, unwillingly. "He doesn't say that really, does he?" I said, and she said no of course not, he was too much of a gentleman.

One yard after another, then, the old cars, the pumps, dogs, views of gray barns and falling-down sheds and unturning windmills. The men, if they are working in the fields, are not in any fields that we can see. The children are far away, following dry creek beds or looking for blackberries, or else they are hidden in the house, spying at us through cracks in the blinds. The car seat has grown slick with our sweat. I dare my brother to sound the horn, wanting to do it myself but not wanting to get the blame. He knows better. We play I Spy, but it is hard to find many colors. Gray for the barns and sheds and toilets and houses, brown for the yard and fields, black or brown for the dogs. The rusting cars show rainbow patches, in which I strain to pick out purple or green; likewise I peer at doors for shreds of old peeling paint, maroon or yellow. We can't play with letters, which would be better, because my brother is too young to spell. The game disintegrates anyway. He claims my colors are not fair, and wants extra turns.

In one house no door opens, though the car is in the yard. My father knocks and whistles, calls, "Hullo there ! Walker Brothers man!" but there is not a stir of reply anywhere. This house has no porch, just a bare, slanting slab of cement on which my father stands. He turns around, searching the barnyard, the barn whose mow must be empty because you can see the sky through it, and finally he bends to pick up his suitcases. Just then a window is opened upstairs, a white pot appears on the sill, is tilted over and its contents splash down the outside wall. The window is not directly above my father's head, so only a stray splash would catch him. He picks up his suitcases with no particular hurry and walks, no longer whistling, to the car. "Do you know what that was?" I say to my brother. "*Pee.*" He laughs and laughs.

My father rolls and lights a cigarette before he starts the car. The window has been slammed down, the blind drawn, we never did see a hand or face. "Pee, pee," sings my brother ecstatically. "Somebody dumped down pee!" "Just don't tell your mother that," my father says. "She isn't liable to see the joke." "Is it in your song?" my brother wants to know. My father says no but he will see what he can do to work it in.

I notice in a little while that we are not turning in any more lanes, though it does not seem to me that we are headed home. "Is this the way to Sunshine?" I ask my father, and he answers, "No, ma'am, it's not." "Are we still in your territory?" He shakes his head. "We're going *fast*," my brother says approvingly, and in fact we are bouncing along through dry puddle-holes so that all the bottles in the suitcases clink together and gurgle promisingly.

Another lane, a house, also unpainted, dried to silver in the sun.

"I thought we were out of your territory."

"We are."

"Then what are we going in here for?"

"You'll see."

In front of the house a short, sturdy woman is picking up washing, which had been spread on the grass to bleach and dry. When the car stops she stares at it hard for a moment, bends to pick up a couple more towels to add to the bundle under her arm, comes across to us and says in a flat voice, neither welcoming nor unfriendly, "Have you lost your way?"

My father takes his time getting out of the car. "I don't think so," he says. "I'm the Walker Brothers man."

"George Golley is our Walker Brothers man," the woman says, "and he was out here no more than a week ago. Oh, my Lord God," she says harshly, "it's you."

"It was, the last time I looked in the mirror," my father says.

The woman gathers all the towels in front of her and holds on to them tightly, pushing them against her stomach as if it hurt. "Of all the people I never thought to see. And telling me you were the Walker Brothers man."

"I'm sorry if you were looking forward to George Golley," my father says humbly.

"And look at me, I was prepared to clean the henhouse. You'll think that's just a excuse but it's true. I don't go round looking like this every day." She is wearing a farmer's straw hat, through which pricks of sunlight penetrate and float on her face, a loose, dirty print smock, and canvas shoes. "Who are those in the car, Ben? They're not yours?"

"Well, I hope and believe they are," my father says, and tells our names and ages. "Come on, you can get out. This is Nora, Miss Cronin. Nora, you better tell me, is it still Miss, or have you got a husband hiding in the wood-shed?"

"If I had a husband that's not where I'd keep him, Ben," she says, and they both laugh, her laugh abrupt and somewhat angry. "You'll think I got no manners, as well as being dressed like a tramp," she says. "Come on in out of the sun. It's cool in the house."

We go across the yard ("Excuse me taking you in this way but I don't think the front door has been opened since Pap's funeral, I'm afraid the hinges might drop off"), up the porch steps, into the kitchen, which really is cool, high-ceilinged, the blinds of course down, a simple, clean, threadbare room with waxed worn linoleum, potted geraniums, drinking-pail and dipper, a round table with scrubbed oilcloth. In spite of the cleanness, the wiped and swept surfaces, there is a faint sour smell—maybe of the dishrag or the tin dipper or the oilcloth, or the old lady, because there is one, sitting in an easy chair under the clock shelf. She turns her head slightly in our direction and says, "Nora? Is that company?"

"Blind," says Nora in a quick explaining voice to my father. Then, "You won't guess who it is, Momma. Hear his voice."

My father goes to the front of her chair and bends and says hopefully, "Afternoon, Mrs. Cronin."

"Ben Jordan," says the old lady with no surprise. "You haven't been to see us in the longest time. Have you been out of the country?"

My father and Nora look at each other.

"He's married, Momma," says Nora cheerfully and aggressively. "Married and got two children and here they are." She pulls us forward, makes each of us touch the old lady's dry, cool hand while she says our names in turn. Blind! This is the first blind person I have ever seen close up. Her eyes are closed, the eyelids sunk away down, showing no shape of the eyeball, just hollows. From one hollow comes a drop of silver liquid, a medicine, or a miraculous tear.

"Let me get into a decent dress," Nora says. "Talk to Momma. It's a treat for her. We hardly ever see company, do we, Momma?"

"Not many makes it out this road," says the old lady placidly. "And the ones that used to be around here, our old neighbors, some of them have pulled out."

"True everywhere," my father says.

"Where's your wife then?"

"Home. She's not too fond of the hot weather, makes her feel poorly."

"Well." This is a habit of country people, old people, to say "well," meaning, "Is that so?" with a little extra politeness and concern.

Nora's dress, when she appears again—stepping heavily on Cuban heels down the stairs in the hall—is flowered more lavishly than anything my mother owns, green and yellow on brown, some sort of floating sheer crêpe, leaving her arms bare. Her arms are heavy, and every bit of her skin you can see is covered with little dark freckles like measles. Her hair is short, black, coarse and curly, her teeth very white and strong. "It's the first time I knew there was such a thing as green poppies," my father says, looking at her dress.

"You would be surprised all the things you never knew," says Nora, sending a smell of cologne far and wide when she moves and displaying a change of voice to go with the dress, something more sociable and youthful. "They're not poppies anyway, they're just flowers. You go and pump me some good cold water and I'll make these children a drink." She gets down from the cupboard a bottle of Walker Brothers Orange syrup.

"You telling me you were the Walker Brothers man!"

"It's the truth, Nora. You go and look at my sample cases in the car if you don't believe me. I got the territory directly south of here."

"Walker Brothers? Is that a fact? You selling for Walker Brothers?"

"Yes, ma'am."

"We always heard you were raising foxes over Dungannon way."

"That's what I was doing, but I kind of run out of luck in that business."

"So where're you living? How long've you been out selling?"

"We moved into Tuppertown. I been at it, oh, two, three months. It keeps the wolf from the door. Keeps him as far away as the back fence."

Nora laughs. "Well, I guess you count yourself lucky to have the work. Isabel's husband in Brantford, he was out of work the longest time. I thought if he didn't find something soon I was going to have them all land in here to feed, and I tell you I was hardly looking forward to it. It's all I can manage with me and Momma."

"Isabel married," my father says. "Muriel married too?"

"No, she's teaching school out West. She hasn't been home for five years. I guess she finds something better to do with her holidays. I would if I was her." She gets some snapshots out of the table drawer and starts showing him. "That's Isabel's oldest boy, starting school. That's the baby sitting in her carriage. Isabel and her husband. Muriel. That's her roommate with her. That's a fellow she used to go around with, and his car. He was working in a bank out there. That's her school, it has eight rooms. She teaches Grade Five." My father shakes his head. "I can't think of her any way but when she was going to school, so shy I used to pick her up on the road—I'd be on my way to see you—and she would not say one word, not even to agree it was a nice day."

"She's got over that."

"Who are you talking about?" says the old lady.

"Muriel. I said she's got over being shy."

"She was here last summer."

"No, Momma, that was Isabel. Isabel and her family were here last summer. Muriel's out West."

"I meant Isabel."

Shortly after this the old lady falls asleep, her head on the side, her mouth open. "Excuse her manners," Nora says. "It's old age." She fixes an afghan over her mother and says we can all go into the front room where our talking won't disturb her.

"You two," my father says. "Do you want to go outside and amuse yourselves?"

Amuse ourselves how? Anyway, I want to stay. The front room is more interesting than the kitchen, though barer. There is a gramophone and a pump organ and a picture on the wall of Mary, Jesus' mother—I know that much—in shades of bright blue and pink with a spiked band of light around her head. I know that such pictures are found only in the homes of Roman Catholics and so Nora must be one. We have never known any Roman Catholics at all well, never well enough to visit in their houses. I think of what my grandmother and my Aunt Tena, over in Dungannon, used to always say to indicate that somebody was a Catholic. *So-and-so digs with the wrong foot*, they would say. *She digs with the wrong foot.* That was what they would say about Nora.[4]

Nora takes a bottle, half full, out of the top of the organ and pours some of what is in it into the two glasses that she and my father have emptied of the orange drink.

"Keep it in case of sickness?" my father says.

"Not on your life," says Nora. "I'm never sick. I just keep it because I keep it. One bottle does me a fair time, though, because I don't care for drinking alone. Here's luck!" She and my father drink and I know what it is. Whisky. One of the things my mother has told me in our talks together is that my father never drinks whisky. But I see he does. He drinks whisky and he talks of people whose names I have never heard before. But after a while he turns to a familiar incident. He tells about the chamberpot that was emptied out the window. "Picture me there," he says, "hollering my heartiest. *Oh, lady, it's your Walker Brothers man, anybody home?*" He does himself hollering, grinning absurdly, waiting, looking up in pleased expectation, and then—oh, ducking, covering his head with his arms, looking as if he begged for mercy (when he never did anything like that, I was watching), and Nora laughs, almost as hard as my brother did at the time.

"That isn't true! That's not a word true!"

"Oh, indeed it is, ma'am. We have our heroes in the ranks of Walker Brothers. I'm glad you think it's funny," he says sombrely.

I ask him shyly, "Sing the song."

"What song? Have you turned into a singer on top of everything else?"

Embarrassed, my father says, "Oh, just this song I made up while I was driving around, it gives me something to do, making up rhymes."

But after some urging he does sing it, looking at Nora with a droll, apol-

4. Protestant–Catholic feuds were transplanted to southern Ontario by Irish settlers.

ogetic expression, and she laughs so much that in places he has to stop and wait for her to get over laughing so he can go on, because she makes him laugh too. Then he does various parts of his salesman's spiel. Nora when she laughs squeezes her large bosom under her folded arms. "You're crazy," she says. "That's all you are." She sees my brother peering into the gramophone and she jumps up and goes over to him. "Here's us sitting enjoying ourselves and not giving you a thought, isn't it terrible?" she says. "You want me to put a record on, don't you? You want to hear a nice record? Can you dance? I bet your sister can, can't she?"

I say no. "A big girl like you and so good-looking and can't dance!" says Nora. "It's high time you learned. I bet you'd make a lovely dancer. Here, I'm going to put on a piece I used to dance to and even your daddy did, in his dancing days. You didn't know your daddy was a dancer, did you? Well, he is a talented man, your daddy!"

She puts down the lid and takes hold of me unexpectedly around the waist, picks up my other hand, and starts making me go backwards. "This is the way, now, this is how they dance. Follow me. This foot, see. One and one-two. One and one-two. That's fine, that's lovely, don't look at your feet! Follow me, that's right, see how easy? You're going to be a lovely dancer! One and one-two. One and one-two. Ben, see your daughter dancing!" *Whispering while you cuddle near me, Whispering so no one can hear me . . .* [5]

Round and round the linoleum, me proud, intent, Nora laughing and moving with great buoyancy, wrapping me in her strange gaiety, her smell of whisky, cologne, and sweat. Under the arms her dress is damp, and little drops form along her upper lip, hang in the soft black hairs at the corners of her mouth. She whirls me around in front of my father—causing me to stumble, for I am by no means so swift a pupil as she pretends—and lets me go, breathless.

"Dance with me, Ben."

"I'm the world's worst dancer, Nora, and you know it."

"I certainly never thought so."

"You would now."

She stands in front of him, arms hanging loose and hopeful, her breasts, which a moment ago embarrassed me with their warmth and bulk, rising and falling under her loose flowered dress, her face shining with the exercise, and delight.

"Ben."

My father drops his head and says quietly, "Not me, Nora."

So she can only go and take the record off. "I can drink alone but I can't dance alone," she says. "Unless I am a whole lot crazier than I think I am."

"Nora," says my father, smiling. "You're not crazy."

"Stay for supper."

"Oh, no. We couldn't put you to the trouble."

"It's no trouble. I'd be glad of it."

"And their mother would worry. She'd think I'd turned us over in a ditch."

"Oh, well. Yes."

"We've taken a lot of your time now."

5. From the popular song *Whispering*, lyrics and music by John Schonberger, Vincent Rose, and Richard Coburn. The original 1920 recording by Paul Whiteman's band was one of the first records to sell 1 million copies.

"Time," says Nora bitterly. "Will you come by ever again?"

"I will if I can," says my father.

"Bring the children. Bring your wife."

"Yes, I will," says my father. "I will if I can."

When she follows us to the car he says, "You come to see us too, Nora. We're right on Grove Street, left-hand side going in, that's north, and two doors this side—east—of Baker Street."

Nora does not repeat these directions. She stands close to the car in her soft, brilliant dress. She touches the fender, making an unintelligible mark in the dust there.

On the way home my father does not buy any ice cream or pop, but he does go into a country store and get a package of licorice, which he shares with us. She digs with the wrong foot, I think, and the words seem sad to me as never before, dark, perverse. My father does not say anything to me about not mentioning things at home, but I know, just from the thoughtfulness, the pause when he passes the licorice, that there are things not to be mentioned. The whisky, maybe the dancing. No worry about my brother, he does not notice enough. At most he might remember the blind lady, the picture of Mary.

"Sing," my brother commands my father, but my father says gravely, "I don't know, I seem to be fresh out of songs. You watch the road and let me know if you see any rabbits."

So my father drives and my brother watches the road for rabbits and I feel my father's life flowing back from our car in the last of the afternoon, darkening and turning strange, like a landscape that has an enchantment on it, making it kindly, ordinary and familiar while you are looking at it, but changing it, once your back is turned, into something you will never know, with all kinds of weathers, and distances you cannot imagine.

When we get closer to Tuppertown the sky becomes gently overcast, as always, nearly always, on summer evenings by the Lake.

LESLIE MARMON SILKO
born 1948

Novelist, poet, memoirist, and writer of short fiction, Leslie Marmon Silko, within the confines of a single work, can comfortably alternate between prose and poetry in a manner reminiscent of the traditional Native American narrators from whom she descends. Among her primary concerns as an artist are the continuity of native tradition and the power of ancient forces to govern modern life. The people of whom she writes draw vitality from the mysterious personifications that represent the land; and reciprocally, the land maintains, or regains, its freshness through prescribed contact with its human tenants. Conflict, illness, and despair are traced to a disharmony between people and nature, sometimes recognizable in the form of witchcraft. Such trouble is as old as time itself and perhaps ineradicable. For healing to take place, at least temporarily, the disharmony and its perpetrators must be removed. It follows that modern evils are neither caused nor cured by Western civilization. The West simply does not have that power. Control, then, rests in the hands of those who harness the energies of native thought. The techniques involve ritual and, especially, storytelling. Since the latter implies a mixture of humor and detachment, it is understandable that Silko's work, for all its seriousness and its lyricism, is marked by a touch of irreverence. She is well acquainted with the proverbial trickster, Coyote, and has demonstrated that she herself is an accomplished live teller of Coyote tales. But storytelling holds more than amusement. "I will tell you something about stories," protests an unnamed voice in one of her novels. "They aren't just entertainment. Don't be fooled."

Storytelling has deep roots. But if a story is to be viable it must be constantly reshaped; and Silko is an unabashed reshaper. Her view of tradition as an ever-shifting body of knowledge, responsive to new influences even if deeply planted, is objectively correct, yet it may also be said to emerge from her personal background. She has written:

> My family are the Marmons at Old Laguna on the Laguna Pueblo Reservation where I grew up. We are mixed bloods—Laguna, Mexican, white—but the way we live is like Marmons, and if you are from Laguna Pueblo you will understand what I mean. All those languages, all those ways of living are combined, and we live somewhere on the fringes of all three. But I don't apologize for this any more—not to whites, not to full bloods—our origin is unlike any other. My poetry, my storytelling rise out this source.

She has also written: "I grew up at Laguna Pueblo. I am of mixed-breed ancestry, but what I know is Laguna. This place I am from is everything I am as a writer and human being."

Situated on a knoll above the San José River, forty miles west of the Rio Grande, Laguna Pueblo, like its near neighbor Acoma, is one of the Keresan-speaking communities of northern New Mexico. In existence at its present site since the 1400s, it has absorbed migrants from other Keresan towns and from among the Zuni, Hopi, and Navajo. In the 1860s and 1870s, two surveyors from Ohio, first Walter Marmon and, a little later, his brother, Robert, both government employees, settled in Laguna and married Laguna women. The Marmons wrote a constitution for Laguna, modeled after the U.S. Constitution, and each served a term as governor of the pueblo, an office never before held by a nonnative. The second of the two Marmons to arrive in Laguna, Robert Gunn Marmon, was the great-grandfather of Leslie Marmon Silko.

Born in Albuquerque on March 5, 1948, Silko spent her early years at Laguna, attending Laguna Day School until fifth grade, when she was transferred to Manzano Day School, a small private school in Albuquerque. Between 1964 and 1969 she attended the University of New Mexico (where she earned a B.A. in English), married, and gave birth to the first of her two sons, Cazimir Silko. During these years she published her first story, *Tony's Story*, a provocative tale of witchery and renewal that foreshadowed her masterwork, *Ceremony*, which would not appear for another decade.

Following graduation, she stayed on at the university and taught courses in creative writing and oral literature. After giving birth to her second son, Robert William Chapman, she studied for three semesters in the university's American Indian Law Program, with the intention of filing native land claims. In 1971 a National Endowment for the Arts Discovery Grant changed her mind about law school, and she quit to devote herself to writing. Seven of her stories, including *Yellow Woman*, were published in 1974 in a collection edited by Kenneth Rosen—*The Man to Send Rain Clouds: Contemporary Stories by American Indians*. It was from this that her reputation began to build.

The novel *Ceremony,* her first large-scale work, appeared in 1977. Widely hailed, it propelled her into the front rank of a growing legion of indigenous writers in the United States whose combined activity would now be recognized as a Native American renaissance. This group's success in winning critical attention and a broad audience would be comparable to the earlier "boom" in Latin American letters that had brought acclaim to such writers as Jorge Luis Borges and Gabriel García Márquez. The Kiowa novelist N. Scott Momaday, whose *House Made of Dawn* had won the Pulitzer Prize in 1969, was already being viewed as the father of the new movement; and the prolific, talented Louise Erdrich, of Chippewa descent, would eventually be accorded its greatest commercial success. But it was Silko—and *Ceremony*—that enabled the movement to come of age.

Though of average length, *Ceremony* is an extremely complex novel; it has two casts of characters, one predominantly male and human, the other female-dominated and intimately connected to the landscape. It is a story of illness and healing, witchery and exorcism, drought and revivification, with political overtones that acknowledge the influence of nonnative society without permitting this to overwhelm or even direct the inner core of native experience. *Ceremony* is a love story but of a special Native American kind that connects the human and nonhuman worlds, transferring power from nature to culture. With a sure grasp of its material, the novel rolls to its conclusion, sweeping up smaller, parablelike stories along the way, creating a many-chambered vehicle that energizes subplots as well as the larger story.

On the strength of *Ceremony,* Silko in 1981 was awarded a MacArthur Fellowship. That same year she brought out a second large work, *Storyteller,* combining previously published poems and short stories (including *Yellow Woman*) with new material in an arrangement one critic has called an autobiography. It is at least partly that, partly a tribute to Laguna, and partly a showcase in which her earlier work, contextualized, takes on a deeper significance.

Another result of *Ceremony* had been the opportunity to teach at the University of Arizona in Tucson. But with the MacArthur grant Silko was able to withdraw from teaching and (while continuing to live in Tucson) concentrate on an ambitious new writing project. Virtually silent for ten years, as rumors of a major new novel kept building, Silko in due course brought forth *Almanac of the Dead* (1991). An ocean of story, spreading far beyond Laguna Pueblo to embrace all of North America, including Mexico, Silko's largest work documents the imagined history of an American apocalypse. Inspired by prophetic texts ranging from the Maya Books of Chilam Balam to the songs of the Plains Ghost Dance, native people in league with the spirits of their ancestors conspire to heal the American land and rid it of alien influence. As the various stories converge and the millennium draws near, an irresistible army led by twin heroes, newly emerged from ancient Native American tradition, marches northward out of Mexico to reclaim the continent. In the words of one critic, the novel is a "wild, jarring, graphic, mordant, prodigious book" with "genius in the sheer, tireless variousness of its interconnecting tales."

Over the years, as Silko's work has expanded and deepened, one of her shortest and earliest pieces, *Yellow Woman,* has continued to grow in esteem. Often reprinted, it became the subject of a volume of critical essays published in 1993. In traditional Laguna lore Yellow Woman is either the heroine or a minor character in a wide range of tales. Occasionally Yellow Woman is mentioned together with her three sisters, Blue Woman, Red Woman, and White Woman, thus completing the four colors of corn. But although she may originally have been a corn spirit, she eventually became a kind of Everywoman. In fact, a traditional Laguna prayer-song, recited at the naming ceremony for a newborn daughter, begins, "Yellow Woman is born, Yellow Woman is born." In narrative lore, however, Yellow Woman most frequently appears in tales of abduction, where she is said to have been captured by a strange man at a stream while she is fetching water. Her captor, who carries her off to another world, is sometimes a kachina, or ancestral spirit; and when at last she returns to her home she is imbued with new power that proves of value for her people. In Silko's version, these traditional elements are constantly in the foreground. Or are they merely in the background? The story's ambiguity, frequently commented on by critics, is the source of its fascination.

PRONOUNCING GLOSSARY

The following list uses common English syllables and stress accents to provide rough equivalents of selected words whose pronunciation may be unfamiliar to the general reader.

kachina: *kuh-chee'-nuh*   Keres: *kay'-ruhs*
ka'tsina: *kuht-see'-nuh*

Yellow Woman

My thigh clung to his with dampness, and I watched the sun rising up through the tamaracks and willows. The small brown water birds came to the river and hopped across the mud, leaving brown scratches in the alkali-white crust. They bathed in the river silently. I could hear the water, almost at our feet where the narrow fast channel bubbled and washed green ragged moss and fern leaves. I looked at him beside me, rolled in the red blanket on the white river sand. I cleaned the sand out of the cracks between my toes, squinting because the sun was above the willow trees. I looked at him for the last time, sleeping on the white river sand.

I felt hungry and followed the river south the way we had come the afternoon before, following our footprints that were already blurred by lizard tracks and bug trails. The horses were still lying down, and the black one whinnied when he saw me but he did not get up—maybe it was because the corral was made out of thick cedar branches and the horses had not yet felt the sun like I had. I tried to look beyond the pale red mesas to the pueblo. I knew it was there, even if I could not see it, on the sandrock hill above the river, the same river that moved past me now and had reflected the moon last night.

The horse felt warm underneath me. He shook his head and pawed the sand. The bay whinnied and leaned against the gate trying to follow, and I remembered him asleep in the red blanket beside the river. I slid off the horse and tied him close to the other horse, I walked north with the river again, and the white sand broke loose in footprints over footprints.

"Wake up."

He moved in the blanket and turned his face to me with his eyes still closed. I knelt down to touch him.

"I'm leaving."

He smiled now, eyes still closed. "You are coming with me, remember?" He sat up now with his bare dark chest and belly in the sun.

"Where?"

"To my place."

"And will I come back?"

He pulled his pants on. I walked away from him, feeling him behind me and smelling the willows.

"Yellow Woman," he said.

I turned to face him. "Who are you?" I asked.

He laughed and knelt on the low, sandy bank, washing his face in the river. "Last night you guessed my name, and you knew why I had come."

I stared past him at the shallow moving water and tried to remember the night, but I could only see the moon in the water and remember his warmth around me.

"But I only said that you were him and that I was Yellow Woman—I'm not really her—I have my own name and I come from the pueblo on the other side of the mesa. Your name is Silva and you are a stranger I met by the river yesterday afternoon."

He laughed softly. "What happened yesterday has nothing to do with what you will do today, Yellow Woman."

"I know—that's what I'm saying—the old stories about the ka'tsina[1] spirit and Yellow Woman can't mean us."

My old grandpa liked to tell those stories best. There is one about Badger and Coyote who went hunting and were gone all day, and when the sun was going down they found a house. There was a girl living there alone, and she had light hair and eyes and she told them that they could sleep with her. Coyote wanted to be with her all night so he sent Badger into a prairie-dog hole, telling him he thought he saw something in it. As soon as Badger crawled in, Coyote blocked up the entrance with rocks and hurried back to Yellow Woman.

"Come here," he said gently.

He touched my neck and I moved close to him to feel his breathing and to hear his heart. I was wondering if Yellow Woman had known who she was—if she knew that she would become part of the stories. Maybe she'd had another name that her husband and relatives called her so that only the ka'tsina from the north and the storytellers would know her as Yellow Woman. But I didn't go on; I felt him all around me, pushing me down into the white river sand.

Yellow Woman went away with the spirit from the north and lived with him and his relatives. She was gone for a long time, but then one day she came back and she brought twin boys.

"Do you know the story?"

"What story?" He smiled and pulled me close to him as he said this. I was afraid lying there on the red blanket. All I could know was the way he felt, warm, damp, his body beside me. This is the way it happens in the stories, I was thinking, with no thought beyond the moment she meets the ka'tsina spirit and they go.

"I don't have to go. What they tell in stories was real only then, back in time immemorial, like they say."

He stood up and pointed at my clothes tangled in the blanket. "Let's go," he said.

I walked beside him, breathing hard because he walked fast, his hand around my wrist. I had stopped trying to pull away from him, because his

1. Kachina, an ancestral spirit.

hand felt cool and the sun was high, drying the river bed into alkali. I will see someone, eventually I will see someone, and then I will be certain that he is only a man—some man from nearby—and I will be sure that I am not Yellow Woman. Because she is from out of time past and I live now and I've been to school and there are highways and pickup trucks that Yellow Woman never saw.

It was an easy ride north on horseback. I watched the change from the cottonwood trees along the river to the junipers that brushed past us in the foothills, and finally there were only piñons, and when I looked up at the rim of the mountain plateau I could see pine trees growing on the edge. Once I stopped to look down, but the pale sandstone had disappeared and the river was gone and the dark lava hills were all around. He touched my hand, not speaking, but always singing softly a mountain song and looking into my eyes.

I felt hungry and wondered what they were doing at home now—my mother, my grandmother, my husband, and the baby. Cooking breakfast, saying, "Where did she go?—maybe kidnapped." And Al going to the tribal police with the details: "She went walking along the river."

The house was made with black lava rock and red mud. It was high above the spreading miles of arroyos and long mesas. I smelled a mountain smell of pitch and buck brush. I stood there beside the black horse, looking down on the small, dim country we had passed, and I shivered.

"Yellow Woman, come inside where it's warm."

He lit a fire in the stove. It was an old stove with a round belly and an enamel coffeepot on top. There was only the stove, some faded Navajo blankets, and a bedroll and cardboard box. The floor was made of smooth adobe plaster, and there was one small window facing east. He pointed at the box.

"There's some potatoes and the frying pan." He sat on the floor with his arms around his knees pulling them close to his chest and he watched me fry the potatoes. I didn't mind him watching me because he was always watching me—he had been watching me since I came upon him sitting on the river bank trimming leaves from a willow twig with his knife. We ate from the pan and he wiped the grease from his fingers on his Levi's.

"Have you brought women here before?" He smiled and kept chewing, so I said, "Do you always use the same tricks?"

"What tricks?" He looked at me like he didn't understand.

"The story about being a ka'tsina from the mountains. The story about Yellow Woman."

Silva was silent; his face was calm.

"I don't believe it. Those stories couldn't happen now," I said.

He shook his head and said softly, "But someday they will talk about us, and they will say, 'Those two lived long ago when things like that happened.' "

He stood up and went out. I ate the rest of the potatoes and thought about things—about the noise the stove was making and the sound of the mountain wind outside. I remembered yesterday and the day before, and then I went outside.

I walked past the corral to the edge where the narrow trail cut through the black rim rock. I was standing in the sky with nothing around me but the wind that came down from the blue mountain peak behind me. I could see faint mountain images in the distance miles across the vast spread of mesas and valleys and plains. I wondered who was over there to feel the mountain wind on those sheer blue edges—who walks on the pine needles in those blue mountains.

"Can you see the pueblo?" Silva was standing behind me.

I shook my head. "We're too far away."

"From here I can see the world." He stepped out on the edge. "The Navajo reservation begins over there." He pointed to the east. "The Pueblo boundaries are over here." He looked below us to the south, where the narrow trail seemed to come from. "The Texans have their ranches over there, starting with that valley, the Concho Valley. The Mexicans run some cattle over there too."

"Do you ever work for them?"

"I steal from them," Silva answered. The sun was dropping behind us and the shadows were filling the land below. I turned away from the edge that dropped forever into the valleys below.

"I'm cold," I said, "I'm going inside." I started wondering about this man who could speak the Pueblo language so well but who lived on a mountain and rustled cattle. I decided that this man Silva must be Navajo, because Pueblo men didn't do things like that.

"You must be a Navajo."

Silva shook his head gently. "Little Yellow Woman," he said, "you never give up, do you? I have told you who I am. The Navajo people know me, too." He knelt down and unrolled the bedroll and spread the extra blankets out on a piece of canvas. The sun was down, and the only light in the house came from outside—the dim orange light from sundown.

I stood there and waited for him to crawl under the blankets.

"What are you waiting for?" he said, and I lay down beside him. He undressed me slowly like the night before beside the river—kissing my face gently and running his hands up and down my belly and legs. He took off my pants and then he laughed.

"Why are you laughing?"

"You are breathing so hard."

I pulled away from him and turned my back to him.

He pulled me around and pinned me down with his arms and chest. "You don't understand, do you, little Yellow Woman? You will do what I want."

And again he was all around me with his skin slippery against mine, and I was afraid because I understood that his strength could hurt me. I lay underneath him and I knew that he could destroy me. But later, while he slept beside me, I touched his face and I had a feeling—the kind of feeling for him that overcame me that morning along the river. I kissed him on the forehead and he reached out for me.

When I woke up in the morning he was gone. It gave me a strange feeling because for a long time I sat there on the blankets and looked around the little house for some object of his—some proof that he had been there or maybe that he was coming back. Only the blankets and the cardboard box remained. The .30-30 that had been leaning in the corner was gone, and so was the knife I had used the night before. He was gone, and I had my chance to go now. But first I had to eat, because I knew it would be a long walk home.

I found some dried apricots in the cardboard box, and I sat down on a rock at the edge of the plateau rim. There was no wind and the sun warmed me. I was surrounded by silence. I drowsed with apricots in my mouth, and I didn't believe that there were highways or railroads or cattle to steal.

When I woke up, I stared down at my feet in the black mountain dirt. Little black ants were swarming over the pine needles around my foot. They must have smelled the apricots. I thought about my family far below me. They would be wondering about me, because this had never happened to me before. The tribal police would file a report. But if old Grandpa weren't dead he would tell them what happened—he would laugh and say, "Stolen by a ka'tsina, a mountain spirit. She'll come home—they usually do." There are enough of them to handle things. My mother and grandmother will raise the baby like they raised me. Al will find someone else, and they will go on like before, except that there will be a story about the day I disappeared while I was walking along the river. Silva had come for me; he said he had. I did not decide to go. I just went. Moonflowers blossom in the sand hills before dawn, just as I followed him. That's what I was thinking as I wandered along the trail through the pine trees.

It was noon when I got back. When I saw the stone house I remembered that I had meant to go home. But that didn't seem important any more, maybe because there were little blue flowers growing in the meadow behind the stone house and the gray squirrels were playing in the pines next to the house. The horses were standing in the corral, and there was a beef carcass hanging on the shady side of a big pine in front of the house. Flies buzzed around the clotted blood that hung from the carcass. Silva was washing his hands in a bucket full of water. He must have heard me coming because he spoke to me without turning to face me.

"I've been waiting for you."

"I went walking in the big pine trees."

I looked into the bucket full of bloody water with brown-and-white animal hairs floating in it. Silva stood there letting his hand drip, examining me intently.

"Are you coming with me?"

"Where?" I asked him.

"To sell the meat in Marquez."

"If you're sure it's O.K."

"I wouldn't ask you if it wasn't," he answered.

He sloshed the water around in the bucket before he dumped it out and set the bucket upside down near the door. I followed him to the corral and watched him saddle the horses. Even beside the horses he looked tall, and I asked him again if he wasn't Navajo. He didn't say anything; he just shook his head and kept cinching up the saddle.

"But Navajos are tall."

"Get on the horse," he said, "and let's go."

The last thing he did before we started down the steep trail was to grab the .30-30 from the corner. He slid the rifle into the scabbard that hung from his saddle.

"Do they ever try to catch you?" I asked.

"They don't know who I am."

"Then why did you bring the rifle?"

"Because we are going to Marquez where the Mexicans live."

The trail leveled out on a narrow ridge that was steep on both sides like an animal spine. On one side I could see where the trail went around the rocky gray hills and disappeared into the southeast where the pale sandrock mesas stood in the distance near my home. On the other side was a trail that went west, and as I looked far into the distance I thought I saw the little town. But Silva said no, that I was looking in the wrong place, that I just thought I saw houses. After that I quit looking off into the distance; it was hot and the wildflowers were closing up their deep-yellow petals. Only the waxy cactus flowers bloomed in the bright sun, and I saw every color that a cactus blossom can be; the white ones and the red ones were still buds, but the purple and the yellow were blossoms, open full and the most beautiful of all.

Silva saw him before I did. The white man was riding a big gray horse, coming up the trail towards us. He was traveling fast and the gray horse's feet sent rocks rolling off the trail into the dry tumbleweeds. Silva motioned for me to stop and we watched the white man. He didn't see us right away, but finally his horse whinnied at our horses and he stopped. He looked at us briefly before he lapped the gray horse across the three hundred yards that separated us. He stopped his horse in front of Silva, and his young fat face was shadowed by the brim of his hat. He didn't look mad, but his small, pale eyes moved from the blood-soaked gunny sacks hanging from my saddle to Silva's face and then back to my face.

"Where did you get the fresh meat?" the white man asked.

"I've been hunting," Silva said, and when he shifted his weight in the saddle the leather creaked.

"The hell you have, Indian. You've been rustling cattle. We've been looking for the thief for a long time."

The rancher was fat, and sweat began to soak through his white cowboy shirt and the wet cloth stuck to the thick rolls of belly fat. He almost seemed to be panting from the exertion of talking, and he smelled rancid, maybe because Silva scared him.

Silva turned to me and smiled. "Go back up the mountain, Yellow Woman."

The white man got angry when he heard Silva speak in a language he couldn't understand. "Don't try anything, Indian. Just keep riding to Marquez. We'll call the state police from there."

The rancher must have been unarmed because he was very frightened and if he had a gun he would have pulled it out then. I turned my horse around and the rancher yelled, "Stop!" I looked at Silva for an instant and there was something ancient and dark—something I could feel in my stomach—in his eyes, and when I glanced at his hand I saw his finger on the trigger of the .30-30 that was still in the saddle scabbard. I slapped my horse across the flank and the sacks of raw meat swung against my knees as the horse leaped up the trail. It was hard to keep my balance, and once I thought I felt the saddle slipping backward; it was because of this that I could not look back.

I didn't stop until I reached the ridge where the trail forked. The horse was breathing deep gasps and there was a dark film of sweat on its neck. I looked down in the direction I had come from, but I couldn't see the place.

I waited. The wind came up and pushed warm air past me. I looked up at the sky, pale blue and full of thin clouds and fading vapor trails left by jets.

I think four shots were fired—I remember hearing four hollow explosions that reminded me of deer hunting. There could have been more shots after that, but I couldn't have heard them because my horse was running again and the loose rocks were making too much noise as they scattered around his feet.

Horses have a hard time running downhill, but I went that way instead of uphill to the mountain because I thought it was safer. I felt better with the horse running southeast past the round gray hills that were covered with cedar trees and black lava rock. When I got to the plain in the distance I could see the dark green patches of tamaracks that grew along the river; and beyond the river I could see the beginning of the pale sandrock mesas. I stopped the horse and looked back to see if anyone was coming; then I got off the horse and turned the horse around, wondering if it would go back to its corral under the pines on the mountain. It looked back at me for a moment and then plucked a mouthful of green tumbleweeds before it trotted back up the trail with its ears pointed forward, carrying its head daintily to one side to avoid stepping on the dragging reins. When the horse disappeared over the last hill, the gunny sacks full of meat were still swinging and bouncing.

I walked toward the river on a wood-hauler's road that I knew would eventually lead to the paved road. I was thinking about waiting beside the road for someone to drive by, but by the time I got to the pavement I had decided it wasn't very far to walk if I followed the river back the way Silva and I had come.

The river water tasted good, and I sat in the shade under a cluster of silvery willows. I thought about Silva, and I felt sad at leaving him; still, there was something strange about him, and I tried to figure it out all the way back home.

I came back to the place on the river bank where he had been sitting the first time I saw him. The green willow leaves that he had trimmed from the branch were still lying there, wilted in the sand. I saw the leaves and I wanted to go back to him—to kiss him and to touch him—but the mountains were too far away now. And I told myself, because I believe it, he will come back sometime and be waiting again by the river.

I followed the path up from the river into the village. The sun was getting low, and I could smell supper cooking when I got to the screen door of my house. I could hear their voices inside—my mother was telling my grandmother how to fix the Jell-O and my husband, Al, was playing with the baby. I decided to tell them that some Navajo had kidnaped me, but I was sorry that old Grandpa wasn't alive to hear my story because it was the Yellow Woman stories he liked to tell best.

A Note on Translation

Reading literature in translation is a pleasure on which it is fruitless to frown. The purist may insist that we ought always read in the original languages, and we know ideally that this is true. But it is a counsel of perfection, quite impractical even for the purist, since no one in a lifetime can master all the languages whose literatures it would be a joy to explore. Master languages as fast as we may, we shall always have to read to some extent in translation, and this means we must be alert to what we are about: if in reading a work of literature in translation we are not reading the "original," what precisely are we reading? This is a question of great complexity, to which justice cannot be done in a brief note, but the following sketch of some of the considerations may be helpful.

One of the memorable scenes of ancient literature is the meeting of Hector and Andromache in book 6 of Homer's *Iliad*. Hector, leader and mainstay of the armies defending Troy, is implored by his wife, Andromache, to withdraw within the city walls and carry on the defense from there, where his life will not be constantly at hazard. In Homer's text her opening words to him are these: δαιμόνιε, φθίσει σε τὸ σὸν μένος (daimonie, phthisei se to son menos). How should they be translated into English?

Here is how they have actually been translated into English by capable translators, at various periods, in verse and prose:

1. George Chapman, 1598:

> O noblest in desire,
> Thy mind, inflamed with others' good, will set thy self on fire.

2. John Dryden, 1693:

> Thy dauntless heart (which I foresee too late),
> Too daring man, will urge thee to thy fate.

3. Alexander Pope, 1715:

> Too daring Prince! . . .
> For sure such courage length of life denies,
> And thou must fall, thy virtue's sacrifice.

4. William Cowper, 1791:

> Thy own great courage will cut short thy days,
> My noble Hector . . .

5. Lang, Leaf, and Myers, 1883 (prose):

> Dear my lord, this thy hardihood will undo thee. . . .

6. A. T. Murray, 1924 (prose):

> Ah, my husband, this prowess of thine will be thy doom. . . .

7. E. V. Rieu, 1950 (prose):

> "Hector," she said, "you are possessed. This bravery of yours will be your end."

2531

8. I. A. Richards, 1950 (prose):

"Strange man," she said, "your courage will be your destruction."

9. Richmond Lattimore, 1951:

Dearest,
Your own great strength will be your death. . . .

10. Robert Fitzgerald, 1979:

O my wild one, your bravery will be
Your own undoing!

11. Robert Fagles, 1990:

reckless one,
Your own fiery courage will destroy you!

From these strikingly different renderings of the same six words, certain facts about the nature of translation begin to emerge. We notice, for one thing, that Homer's word μένος (menos) is diversified by the translators into "mind," "dauntless heart," "such courage," "great courage," "hardihood," "prowess," "bravery," "courage," "great strength," "bravery," and "fiery courage." The word has in fact all these possibilities. Used of things, it normally means "force"; of animals, "fierceness" or "brute strength" or (in the case of horses) "mettle"; of men and women, "passion" or "spirit" or even "purpose." Homer's application of it in the present case points our attention equally— whatever particular sense we may imagine Andromache to have uppermost—to Hector's force, strength, fierceness in battle, spirited heart and mind. But since English has no matching term of like inclusiveness, the passage as the translators give it to us reflects this lack and we find one attribute singled out to the exclusion of the rest.

Here then is the first and most crucial fact about any work of literature read in translation. It cannot escape the linguistic characteristics of the language into which it is turned: the grammatical, syntactical, lexical, and phonetic boundaries that constitute collectively the individuality or "genius" of that language. A Greek play or a Russian novel in English will be governed first of all by the resources of the English language, resources that are certain to be in every instance very different, as the efforts with μένος show, from those of the original.

Turning from μένος to δαιμόνιε (daimonie) in Homer's clause, we encounter a second crucial fact about translations. Nobody knows exactly what shade of meaning δαιμονιε had for Homer. In later writers the word normally suggests divinity, something miraculous, wondrous; but in Homer it appears as a vocative of address for both chieftain and commoner, man and wife. The coloring one gives it must, therefore, be determined either by the way one thinks a Greek wife of Homer's era might actually address her husband (a subject on which we have no information whatever) or in the way one thinks it suitable for a hero's wife to address her husband in an epic poem, that is to say, a highly stylized and formal work. In general, the translators of our century have abandoned formality to stress the intimacy; the wifeliness; and, especially in Lattimore's case, a certain chiding tenderness, in Andromache's appeal: (6) "Ah, my husband," (7) "Hector" (with perhaps a hint, in "you are possessed," of the alarmed distaste with which wives have so often viewed their husbands' bellicose moods), (8) "Strange man," (9) "Dearest," (10) "O my wild one" (mixing an almost motherly admiration with reproach and concern), and (11) "reckless one." On the other hand, the older translators have obviously removed Andromache to an epic or heroic distance from her beloved, whence she sees and kindles to his selfless courage, acknowledging, even in the moment of pleading with him to be otherwise, his moral grandeur and the tragic destiny this too certainly implies: (1) "O noblest in desire, . . . inflamed by others' good"; (2) "Thy dauntless heart (which I foresee too late), / Too daring man"; (3) "Too daring Prince! . . . / And thou must fall, thy virtue's sacrifice"; (4) "My noble Hector." Even the less specific "Dear my lord" of Lang, Leaf, and Myers looks in the same direction because of its echo of the speech of countless Shakespearean men and women who have shared this powerful moral sense: "Dear my lord, make me acquainted with your cause of grief"; "Perseverance, dear my lord, keeps honor bright"; etc.

The fact about translation that emerges from all this is that just as the translated work reflects the individuality of the language it is turned into, so it reflects the individuality of the age in which it is made, and the age will permeate it everywhere like yeast in dough. We think of one kind of permeation when we think of the governing verse forms and attitudes toward verse at a given epoch. In Chapman's time, experiments seeking an "heroic" verse form for English were widespread, and accordingly he tries a "fourteener" couplet (two rhymed lines of seven stresses each) in his *Iliad* and a pentameter couplet in his *Odyssey*. When Dryden and Pope wrote, a closed pentameter couplet had become established as the heroic form par excellence. By Cowper's day, thanks largely to the prestige of *Paradise Lost*, the couplet had gone out of fashion for narrative poetry in favor of blank verse. Our age, inclining to prose and in verse to proselike informalities and relaxations, has, predictably, produced half a dozen excellent prose translations of the *Iliad* but only three in verse (by Fagles, Lattimore, and Fitzgerald), all relying on rhythms that are much of the time closer to the verse of William Carlos Williams and some of the prose of novelists like Faulkner than to the swift firm tread of Homer's Greek. For if it is true that what we translate from a given work is what, wearing the spectacles of our time, we see in it, it is also true that we see in it what we have the power to translate.

Of course, there are other effects of the translator's epoch on a translation besides those exercised by contemporary taste in verse and verse forms. Chapman writes in a great age of poetic metaphor and, therefore, almost instinctively translates his understanding of Homer's verb φθίσει (phthisei, "to cause to wane, consume, waste, pine") into metaphorical terms of flame, presenting his Hector to us as a man of burning generosity who will be consumed by his very ardor. This is a conception rooted in large part in the psychology of the Elizabethans, who had the habit of speaking of the soul as "fire," of one of the four temperaments as "fiery," of even the more material bodily processes, like digestion, as if they were carried on by the heat of fire ("concoction," "decoction"). It is rooted too in that characteristic Renaissance élan so unforgettably expressed in characters such as Tamburlaine and Dr. Faustus, the former of whom exclaims to the stars above:

> . . . I, the chiefest lamp of all the earth,
> First rising in the East with mild aspect,
> But fixèd now in the meridian line,
> Will send up fire to your turning spheres,
> And cause the sun to borrow light of you. . . .

Pope and Dryden, by contrast, write to audiences for whom strong metaphor has become suspect. They, therefore, reject the fire image (which we must recall is not present in the Greek) in favor of a form of speech more congenial to their age, the *sententia* or aphorism, and give it extra vitality by making it the scene of a miniature drama: in Dryden's case, the hero's dauntless heart "urges" him (in the double sense of physical as well as moral pressure) to his fate; in Pope's, the hero's courage, like a judge, "denies" continuance of life, with the consequence that he "falls"—and here Pope's second line suggests analogy to the sacrificial animal—the victim of his own essential nature, of what he is.

To pose even more graphically the pressures that a translator's period brings, consider the following lines from Hector's reply to Andromache's appeal that he withdraw, first in Chapman's Elizabethan version, then in Lattimore's twentieth-century one:

Chapman, 1598:

> The spirit I did first breathe
> Did never teach me that—much less since the contempt of death
> Was settled in me, and my mind knew what a Worthy was,
> Whose office is to lead in fight and give no danger pass
> Without improvement. In this fire must Hector's trial shine.
> Here must his country, father, friends be in him made divine.

Lattimore, 1951:

> and the spirit will not let me, since I have learned to be valiant
> and to fight always among the foremost ranks of the Trojans,
> winning for my own self great glory, and for my father.

If one may exaggerate to make a necessary point, the world of Henry V and Othello suddenly gives way here to our own, a world whose discomfort with any form of heroic self-assertion is remarkably mirrored in the burial of Homer's key terms (*spirit, valiant, fight, foremost, glory*)—five out of twenty-two words in the original, five out of thirty-six in the translation—in a cushioning huddle of harmless sounds.

Besides the two factors so far mentioned (language and period) as affecting the character of a translation, there is inevitably a third—the translator, with a particular degree of talent; a personal way of regarding the work to be translated; a special hierarchy of values, moral, aesthetic, metaphysical (which may or may not be summed up in a "worldview"); and a unique style or lack of it. But this influence all readers are likely to bear in mind, and it needs no laboring here. That, for example, two translators of Hamlet, one a Freudian, the other a Jungian, will produce impressively different translations is obvious from the fact that when Freudian and Jungian argue about the play in English they often seem to have different plays in mind.

We can now return to the question from which we started. After all allowances have been made for language, age, and individual translator, is anything of the original left? What, in short, does the reader of translations read? Let it be said at once that in utility prose—prose whose function is mainly referential—the reader who reads a translation reads everything that matters. "Nicht Rauchen," "Défense de Fumer," and "No Smoking," posted in a railway car, make their point, and the differences between them in sound and form have no significance for us in that context. Since the prose of a treatise and of most fiction is preponderantly referential, we rightly feel, when we have paid close attention to Cervantes or Montaigne or Machiavelli or Tolstoy in a good English translation, that we have had roughly the same experience as a native Spaniard, Frenchman, Italian, or Russian. But *roughly* is the correct word; for good prose points iconically *to* itself as well as referentially beyond itself, and everything that it points to in itself in the original (rhythms, sounds, idioms, wordplay, etc.) must alter radically in being translated. The best analogy is to imagine a van Gogh painting reproduced in the medium of tempera, etching, or engraving: the "picture" remains, but the intricate interanimation of volumes with colorings with brushstrokes has disappeared.

When we move on to poetry, even in its longer narrative and dramatic forms— plays like *Oedipus,* poems like the *Iliad* or *The Divine Comedy*—our situation as English readers worsens appreciably, as the many unlike versions of Andromache's appeal to Hector make very clear. But, again, only appreciably. True, this is the point at which the fact that a translation is *always* an interpretation explodes irresistibly on our attention; but if it is the best translation of its time, like Robert Fagles's translation of the *Iliad* for our time, the result will be not only a sensitive interpretation but also a work with intrinsic interest in its own right—at very best, a true work of art, a new poem. In these longer works, moreover, even if the translation is uninspired, many distinctive structural features—plot, setting, characters, meetings, partings, confrontations, and specific episodes generally—survive virtually unchanged. It is only when the shorter, primarily lyrical forms of poetry are presented that the reader of translations faces insuperable disadvantage. In these forms, the referential aspect of language has a tendency to disappear into, or, more often, draw its real meaning and accreditation from, the iconic aspect. Let us look for just a moment at a brief poem by Federico García Lorca and its English translation (by Stephen Spender and J. L. Gili):

> ¡Alto pinar!
> Cuatro palomas por el aire van.
>
> Cuatro palomas
> vuelan y tornan.
> Llevan heridas
> sus cuatro sombras.
>
> ¡Bajo pinar!
> Cuatro palomas en la tierra están.

> the pine trees:
> Four pigeons go through the air.
>
> Four pigeons
> fly and turn round.
> They carry wounded
> their four shadows.
>
> Below the pine trees:
> Four pigeons lie on the earth.

In this translation the referential sense of the English words follows with remarkable exactness the referential sense of the Spanish words they replace. But the life of Lorca's poem does not lie in that sense. It lies in such matters as the abruptness, like an intake of breath at a sudden revelation, of the two exclamatory lines (1 and 7), which then exhale musically in images of flight and death; or as the echoings of *palomas* in *heridas* and *sombras,* bringing together (as in fact the hunter's gun has done) these unrelated nouns and the unrelated experiences they stand for in a sequence that seems, momentarily, to have all the logic of a tragic action, in which *doves* become *wounds* become *shadows,* or as the external and internal rhyming among the five verbs, as though all motion must (as in fact it must) end with *están.*

Since none of this can be brought over into another tongue (least of all Lorca's rhythms), the translator must decide between leaving a reader to wonder why Lorca is a poet to be bothered about at all and making a new but true poem, whose merit will almost certainly be in inverse ratio to its likeness to the original. Samuel Johnson made such a poem in translating Horace's famous *Diffugere nives,* and so did A. E. Housman. If we juxtapose the last two stanzas of each translation, and the corresponding Latin, we can see at a glance that each has the consistency and inner life of a genuine poem and that neither of them (even if we consider only what is obvious to the eye, the line-lengths) is very close to Horace:

> Cum semel occideris, et de te splendida Minos
>   fecerit arbitria,
> non, Torquate, genus, non te facundia, non te
>   restituet pietas.

> Infernis neque enim tenebris Diana pudicum
>   liberat Hippolytum
> nec Lethaea valet Theseus abrumpere caro
>   vincula Pirithoo.

Johnson:

> Not you, Torquatus, boast of Rome,
> When Minos once has fixed your doom,
> Or eloquence, or splendid birth,
> Or virtue, shall restore to earth.
> Hippolytus, unjustly slain,
> Diana calls to life in vain;
> Nor can the might of Theseus rend
> The chains of hell that hold his friend.

Housman:

> When thou descendest once the shades among,
>   The stern assize and equal judgment o'er,
> Not thy long lineage nor thy golden tongue,
>   No, nor thy righteousness, shall friend thee more.
>
> Night holds Hippolytus the pure of stain,
>   Diana steads him nothing, he must stay;
> And Theseus leaves Pirithous in the chain
>   The love of comrades cannot take away.

The truth of the matter is that when the translator of short poems chooses to be literal, most or all of the poetry is lost; and when the translator succeeds in forging a new poetry, most or all of the original author is lost.

The best practical advice for those of us who must read poems in English translations is to focus intently on the images and dramatic scenes these poems evoke and ask ourselves what there is in them or in their effect on each other that produces each poem's particular electricity. To that extent, we can compensate for a part of our losses, learn something positive about the immense explosive powers of imagery, and rest easy in the secure knowledge that translation even in the mode of the short poem brings us (despite losses) closer to the work itself than not reading it at all. "To a thousand cavils," said Samuel Johnson, "one answer is sufficient; the purpose of a writer is to be read, and the criticism which would destroy the power of pleasing must be blown aside." Johnson was defending Pope's Homer for those marks of its own time and place that make it the great interpretation it is, but Johnson's exhilarating common sense applies equally to the problem we are considering here. Literature is to be read, and the criticism that would destroy the reader's power to make some form of contact with much of the world's great writing must indeed be blown aside.

MAYNARD MACK

Selected Bibliographies

THE ENLIGHTENMENT

Useful books on the Enlightenment include, for English background, H. Nicolson, *The Age of Reason: The Eighteenth Century* (1960), and, for an opposed view, D. Greene, *The Age of Exuberance: Backgrounds to Eighteenth-Century English Literature* (1970). For the intellectual and social situation in France, L. G. Crocker, *An Age of Crisis: Man and World in Eighteenth-Century French Thought* (1959); L. Gossman, *French Society and Culture: Background for Eighteenth-Century Literature* (1972); and A. Adam, *Grandeur and Illusion: French Literature and Society, 1600–1715* (1972). An excellent treatment of the period's literature in England is M. Price, *To the Palace of Wisdom: Studies in Order and Energy from Dryden to Blake* (1964). M. L. Williamson, *Raising Their Voices: British Women Writers 1650–1750* (1990), discusses women's contributions to the English Enlightenment. For the artistic situation of France, see T. M. Kavanaugh, *Esthetics of the Moment: Literature and Art in the French Enlightenment* (1996). For the philosophic background and its implications, see M. Losonsky, *Enlightenment and Action from Descartes to Kant: Passionate Thought* (2001). An unusual perspective on the meaning of the eighteenth century to our own time is provided by N. Postman, *Building a Bridge to the Eighteenth Century: How the Past Can Improve Our Future* (1999). R. A. Barney, *Plots of Enlightenment: Education and the Novel in Eighteenth-Century England* (1999), examines important issues of education (particularly relevant to the situation of women), especially as they are refracted through the novel.

Olympe de Gouges

Although there have been studies of de Gouges in French and in German, no book about her exists in English. Useful essays include J. Vampée, "Taking the Podium: Olympe de Gouges' Revolutionary Discourse," in *Women Writers in Pre-Revolutionary France: Strategies of Emancipation*, ed. C. H. Winn and D. Kuizenga (1977), pp. 299–312, and B. Woshinsky, "Olympe de Gouges' Declaration of the Rights of Women (1791)," *Mary Wollstonecraft Journal* 2, no. 1 (1973): 3–6.

Marie de la Vergne de La Fayette

The best general introduction to de La Fayette is S. Haig's biographical and critical study, *Madame de Lafayette* (1970). M. Turnell, *The Novel in France* (1950), contains a short treatment of *The Princess of Clèves*. More sophisticated is L. A. Gregorio, *Order in the Court: History and Society in La Princesse de Clèves* (1986). Important recent studies include Michael G. Paulson, *A Critical Analysis of de La Fayette's La princesse de Clèves as a Royal Exemplary Novel: Kings, Queens, and Splendor* (1991), John Campbell, *Questions of Interpretation in La Princesse de Clèves* (1996), and H. K. Kaps, *Moral Perspective in La Princesse de Clèves* (2001). Michael G. Paulson's most recent book on the subject is *Facets of a Princess: Multiple Readings of Madame de la Fayette's "La princesse de Clèves"* (1998).

Samuel Johnson

J. Boswell, *The Life of Samuel Johnson* (1791), remains a brilliant account of its subject. Important modern biographies are W. J. Bate, *Samuel Johnson* (1977), and L. Lipking, *Samuel Johnson: The Life of an Author* (1998). Bate's earlier, shorter book, *The Achievement of Samuel Johnson* (1955), provides an excellent introduction. Twentieth-century essays on Johnson are collected in P. J. Korshin, ed., *Johnson after Two Hundred Years* (1986), and P. Nath, ed., *Fresh Reflections on Samuel Johnson: Essays in Criticism* (1987). A more specialized collection of essays is *Samuel Johnson in Historical Context*, ed. J. Clark and H. Erskine-Hill (2001). Two recent studies are G. Clingham, *Johnson, Writing, and Memory* (2002), and N. Hudson, *Samuel Johnson and the Making of Modern England* (2003).

Sor Juana Inés de la Cruz

A volume in the Twayne series by Gerard Flynn, *Sor Juana Inés de la Cruz* (1971), provides a biographical, critical, and bibliographical introduction to Sister Juana. She is also treated in histories of Latin American literature: for example, J. Franco, *An Introduction to Spanish-American Literature*, 3rd ed. (1994). An important critical work, belatedly translated into English, is Octavio Paz, *Sor Juana; or, The Traps of Faith* (1988). Other studies include Stephanie Merrim, ed., *Feminist Perspectives on Sor Juana Inés de la Cruz* (1991); F. Royer, *The Tenth Muse: Sor Juana Inés de la Cruz* (1952); P. Kirk, *Sor Juana Inés de la Cruz: Religion, Art, and Feminism* (1998); and S. Merrim, *Early Modern Women's Writing and Sor Juana Inés de la Cruz* (1999).

Jean de La Fontaine

A useful introduction to La Fontaine's life and work is M. O. Sweetser's *La Fontaine* (1987). Other valuable recent studies include D. L. Rubin's *A Pact with Silence: Art and Thought in the Fables of Jean de La Fontaine* (1991); A. L. Birberick's *Reading Undercover: Audience and Author in Jean de La Fontaine* (1998); *Refiguring La Fontaine: Tercentenary Essays*, a collection by various authors, edited by A. L. Birberick; and M. Slater's *The Craft of La Fontaine* (2001).

Jean-Baptiste Poquelin Molière

K. Mantzius, *Molière* (1908), provides a good biographical introduction to Molière. Useful critical studies include J. D. Hubert, *Molière and the Comedy of Intellect* (1962); L. Gossman, *Men and Masks: A Study of Molière* (1963); Jacques Guicharnaud, ed., *Molière: A Collection of Critical Essays* (1964); and N. Gross, *From Gesture to Idea: Esthetics and Ethics in Molière's Comedy* (1982). An excellent treatment of Molière in his historical context is W. D. Howarth, *Molière: A Playwright and His Audience* (1984). Martin Turnell, *The Classical Moment: Studies of Corneille, Molière, and Racine* (1975), offers useful insight into French dramatic tradition. More specialized studies include L. F. Norman, *The Public Mirror: Molière and the Social Commerce of Depiction* (1999), and R. D. Lalande, *Intruders in the Play World: The Dynamics of Gender in Molière's Comedies* (1996). For stage history, see G. McCarthy, *The Theatres of Molière* (2002).

Hannah More

Studies that place More's work on education in context include P. Demers, *The World of Hannah More* (1996), and S. Pedersen, *Hannah More Meets Simple Simon: Tracts, Chapbooks, and Popular Culture in Late Eighteenth-Century England* (1984).

Alexander Pope

Pope has been the subject of a great deal of writing. Biographies include G. Sherburn, *The Early Career of Alexander Pope* (1934), and M. Mack, *Alexander Pope: A Life* (1985). A range of responses is represented in M. Mack and J. A. Winn, eds., *Pope: Recent Essays by Several Hands* (1980); H. Bloom, ed., *Alexander Pope* (1986); and W. Jackson and R. P. Yoder, eds.,

Critical Essays on Alexander Pope (1993). Perceptive critical books include R. A. Brower, *Alexander Pope: The Poetry of Allusion* (1959), and T. R. Edwards, *This Dark Estate: A Reading of Pope* (1963). Other useful studies include D. B. Morris, *Alexander Pope, The Genius of Sense* (1984); L. Damrosch, Jr., *The Imaginative World of Alexander Pope* (1987); Helen Deutsch, *Resemblance and Disgrace: Alexander Pope and the Deformation of Culture* (1996); and N. M. Goldsmith, *Alexander Pope: The Evolution of a Poet* (2002). F. Parker, *Scepticism and Literature: An Essay on Pope, Hume, Sterne, and Johnson* (2003), locates Pope's thought in relation to the ideas of other important eighteenth-century thinkers, as does J. D. Morillo, *Uneasy Feelings: Literature, the Passions, and Class from Neoclassicism to Romanticism* (2001), on Wordsworth, Adam Smith, and *An Essay on Man*. For *The Rape of the Lock* specifically, see the Bedford Critical Edition of the poem, edited by C. Wall (1998).

Jean Racine

A useful biography of Racine is G. Brereton, *Jean Racine: A Critical Biography*, rev. repr. (1973), which combines biography with literary criticism. Valuable critical insight is provided by O. de Mourgues, *Racine; or, The Triumph of Relevance* (1967); Richard Parish, *Racine: The Limits of Tragedy* (1993); and P. J. Yarrow, *Racine* (1977). A treatment of French tragic drama that includes extensive and valuable material on Racine is Albert Cook, *French Tragedy: The Power of Enactment* (1981). For an interpretation that includes the stage history of Racine's plays, see D. Maskell, *Racine: A Theatrical Reading* (1991). Intended especially for students is Philip Butler, *A Student's Guide to Racine* (1974). Special perspectives are provided by V. Desnain, *Hidden Tragedies: The Social Construction of Gender in Racine* (2002), and the collection of essays entitled *Racine: The Power and the Pleasure*, ed. E. Caldicott and D. Conroy (2001). A recent general treatment is R. W. Tobin, *Jean Racine Revisited* (1999).

Mary Robinson

Robinson has been the subject of some critical discussion, almost entirely in relation to her fiction and her memoir. Important essays bearing on her polemical work include A. J. Crane, "He-She Philosophers and Other Literary Bugbears: Mary Robinson's A Letter to the Women of England," *Women's Writing* 9, no. 1 (2002): 53–68, and Crane's " 'The Strongest but Most Undecorated Language': Mary Robinson's Rhetorical Strategy in *Letter to the Women of England*," *Women's Writing* 9, no. 1 (2002): 87–105.

Jean-Jacques Rousseau

Works that bear on *Émile* and on Rousseau's thought generally include R. Wokler, *Rousseau:*

A Very Short Introduction (2001); J. Bloch, *Rousseauism and Education in Eighteenth-Century France* (1995); and A. M. Melzer, *The Natural Goodness of Man: On the System of Rousseau's Thought* (1990).

"Sophia"
A general study of feminist thought in eighteenth-century England is A. Browne, *The Eighteenth Century Feminist Mind* (1987).

Jonathan Swift
A good introduction to Swift's life and character is I. Ehrenpreis, *The Personality of Jonathan Swift* (1958). For a more recent biography see J. McMinn, *Jonathan Swift: A Literary Life* (1991). An interpretation of the writer in his intellectual context is K. Williams, *Jonathan Swift and the Age of Compromise* (1958). E. Zimmerman, *Swift's Narrative Satires: Author and Authority* (1983), provides acute interpretation of the prose satires. Useful and varied collections of essays about Swift include C. T. Probyn, ed., *Jonathan Swift: The Contemporary Background* (1978); C. Rawson, ed., *The Character of Swift's Satire: A Revised Focus* (1983); C. Rawson, ed., *Jonathan Swift: A Collection of Critical Essays* (1995); and J. Kelly, *Critical Approaches to Swift: The Yahoos and A Modest Proposal* (1997). Two studies that offer provocative material are R. Knowles, *Gulliver's Travels: The Politics of Satire* (1997), and C. Rawson,

God, Gulliver, and Genocide: Barbarism and the European Imagination, 1492–1945 (2001).

François-Marie Arouet de Voltaire
Biographies and critical studies of Voltaire include R. Aldington, *Voltaire* (1934); G. Brandes, *The Life of Voltaire* (undated); I. O. Wade, *Voltaire and "Candide": A Study in the Fusion of History, Art, and Philosophy* (1959); and T. Besterman, *Voltaire*, 3rd ed. (1976). A good general introduction is P. E. Richter and Ilona Ricardo, *Voltaire* (1980). A work placing Voltaire in a broad context is F. M. Keener, *The Chain of Becoming: The Philosophical Tale, the Novel, and a Neglected Realism of the Enlightenment—Swift, Montesquieu, Voltaire, Johnson, and Austen* (1983), on Voltaire and his English contemporaries. Two useful works specifically about *Candide* are William Bottiglia, *Voltaire's Candide: Analysis of a Classic* (1964), and Haydn Mason, *Candide: Optimism Demolished* (1992). A useful survey of Voltaire's thought and writing is B. L. Knappe's *Voltaire Revisited* (2000). J. Gray's *Voltaire* (1999) focuses specifically on Voltaire's philosophical ideas.

Theodor Gottlieb von Hippel
Von Hippel has not been the subject of any books in English. A useful essay is R. P. Dasson, "The Feminist Manifesto of Theodor Gottlieb von Hippel (1741–96)," *Amsterdamer Beitrage zur Neuren Germanistik* 10 (1980):13–32.

THE NINETEENTH CENTURY: ROMANTICISM

Useful introductions to the Romantic period include L. R. Furst, *Romanticism in Perspective: A Comparative Study of Aspects of the Romantic Movements in England, France, and Germany*, 2nd ed. (1979); R. F. Gleckner and G. E. Enscoe, eds., *Romanticism: Points of View*, 2nd ed. (1970), a collection of essays by various contributors; Charles E. Larmore, *The Romantic Legacy* (1996); and M. Cranston, *The Romantic Movement* (1994). On French Romanticism, see P. T. Comeau, *Diehards and Innovators: The French Romantic Struggle, 1800–1830* (1988); on Germany, T. Ziolkowski, *German Romanticism and Its Institutions* (1990); on English and American developments, B. Taylor, R. Bain, and M. H. Abrams, *The Cast of Consciousness: Concepts of the Mind in British and American Romanticism* (1987); on the English and German situation, C. Jacobs, *Uncontainable Romanticism: Shelley, Brontë, and Kleist* (1989). A comparative study of European Romantic poetry appears in *Romantic Poetry*, ed. A. Esterhammer (2002). More specialized studies include M. Redfield, *The Politics of Aesthetics: Nationalism, Gender, Romanticism* (2003); R. M. Turley, *The Politics*

of Language in Romantic Literature (2002); and H. Thomas, *Romanticism and Slave Narratives: Transatlantic Testimonies* (2000).

John Adams and Abigail Adams
On John Adams, there is a commanding biography by D. G. McCullough: *John Adams* (2001). See also J. P. Diggins, *John Adams* (2003), and R. A. Ryerson, ed., *John Adams and the Founding of the Republic* (2001). On Abigail Adams, see P. E. Schloesser, *The Fair Sex: White Women and Racial Patriarchy in the Early American Republic* (2002; the book deals also with Mercy Otis Warren), and E. B. Gelles, *First Thoughts: Life and Letters of Abigail Adams* (1998).

Gustavo Adolfo Bécquer
Although Bécquer has been the subject of much literary analysis in Spanish, little has been written about him in English. One useful study is E. L. King, *Gustavo Adolfo Bécquer* (1953). For more recent views, see B. B. Bynum, *The Romantic Imagination in the Works of Gustavo Adolfo Bécquer* (1993).

William Blake
Blake has provided material for an enormous outpouring of critical work. Particularly useful for the student are N. Frye, ed., *Blake: A Collection of Critical Essays* (1966), and H. Adams, ed., *Critical Essays on William Blake* (1991). Valuable longer studies include M. Schorer, *William Blake: The Politics of Vision* (1946); H. Adams, *William Blake: A Reading of the Shorter Poems* (1963); E. D. Hirsch, *Innocence and Experience: An Introduction to Blake,* 2nd. ed. (1975); D. G. Gillham, *William Blake* (1973); and S. Gardner, *Blake's Innocence and Experience Retraced* (1986). A useful recent volume is *The Cambridge Companion to William Blake,* ed. M. Eaves (2003). Two full-length studies explore special aspects of the poet: K. D. Hutchings, *Imagining Nature: Blake's Environmental Poetics* (2002), and S. Makdisi, *William Blake and the Impossible History of the 1790s* (2003), on the political implications of Blake's poetry.

Robert Browning
A useful biography of Browning is C. de L. Ryals, *The Life of Robert Browning: A Critical Biography* (1993). W. C. DeVane, *A Browning Handbook,* 2nd ed. (1935), provides indispensable guidance. Valuable criticism includes I. Jack, *Browning's Major Poetry* (1973); L. Erickson, *Robert Browning: His Poetry and His Audiences* (1984); J. Woolford, *Browning the Revisionary* (1988); S. Hawlin, *The Complete Critical Guide to Robert Browning* (2002); and E. Loehndorf, *The Master's Voice: Robert Browning, the Dramatic Monologue and Modern Poetry* (1997).

Anna Petrovna Bunina
The only study in English about Bunina is W. Rosslyn's *Anna Bunina (1774–1829) and the Origins of Women's Poetry in Russia* (1997).

George Gordon, Lord Byron
A useful introduction to Byron's life and work is P. W. Graham, *Lord Byron* (1998). There have been many biographies; one is C. Franklin, *Byron: A Literary Life* (2000). I. Gilmour, *The Making of the Poets: Byron and Shelley in Their Time* (2002), treats two Romantic poets together. A collection of essays by one of the greatest living Byron scholars is J. J. McGann's *Byron and Romanticism* (2002).

Samuel Taylor Coleridge
There are two important recent biographies: R. Holmes, *Coleridge: Early Visions* (1989), the first part of a projected two-part biography; and R. Ashton, *The Life of Samuel Taylor Coleridge: A Critical Biography* (1996). J. L. Lowes, *The Road to Xanadu: A Study in the Ways of the Imagination* (1927), provides a fascinating study of the sources of *Kubla Khan.* For criticism, see also J. Cornwell, *Coleridge* (1973); J. Beer, *Coleridge's Poetic Intelligence* (1977); G. Davidson, *Coleridge's Career* (1990); and D. Sultana, ed.,

New Approaches to Coleridge: Biographical and Critical Essays (1981). Useful works that treat Coleridge in conjunction with Wordsworth are G. W. Ruoff, *Wordsworth and Coleridge: The Making of the Major Lyrics, 1802–1804* (1989), and P. Magnuson, *Coleridge and Wordsworth: A Lyrical Dialogue* (1988). *The Cambridge Companion to Coleridge,* ed. L. Newlyn (2002), provides a useful guide through essays by various authors. Works that place Coleridge in the context of Romanticism include J. R. Barth, *The Symbolic Imagination: Coleridge and the Romantic Tradition,* 2nd ed. (2001), and D. Vallins, *Coleridge and the Psychology of Romanticism: Feeling and Thought* (2000).

Rosalía de Castro
De Castro is the subject of a volume in the Twayne series: K. Kulp-Hill, *Rosalía de Castro* (1977). See also S. Stevens, *Rosalía de Castro and the Galician Revival* (1986), and M. C. Geoffrion-Vinci, *Between the Maternal Aegis and the Abyss: Woman as Symbol in the Poetry of Rosalía de Castro* (2002).

Germaine de Staël
Two works of use in understanding de Staël are G. R. Besser, *Germaine de Staël Revisited* (1994), and a collection of essays by various authors, *Germaine de Staël: Crossing the Borders,* ed. M. Gutwirth, A. Goldberger, and K. Szmurlo (1991).

Emily Dickinson
Emily Dickinson: An Interpretive Biography (1955), by T. H. Johnson, Dickinson's editor, is indispensable. Useful critical sources include C. Blake and C. F. Wells, eds., *The Recognition of Emily Dickinson: Selected Criticism since 1890* (1964), Albert J. Gelpi, *Emily Dickinson: The Mind of the Poet* (1965); P. Bennett, *Emily Dickinson: Woman Poet* (1990); S. Juhasz, ed., *Feminist Critics Read Emily Dickinson* (1983), a collection with a specifically feminist orientation; and J. Dobson, *Dickinson and the Strategies of Reticence: The Woman Writer in Nineteenth-Century America* (1989). Other critical studies are K. Stocks, *Emily Dickinson and the Modern Consciousness: A Poet of Our Time* (1988), and M. N. Smith, *Rowing in Eden: Rereading Emily Dickinson* (1992). A study that emphasizes formal aspects of Dickinson's work is C. L. Cooley, *The Music of Emily Dickinson's Poems and Letters: A Study of Imagery and Form* (2003). Useful for providing multiple views is *The Cambridge Companion to Emily Dickinson,* ed. Wendy Martin (2002).

Frederick Douglass
An illuminating biography of Douglass, which elaborates on the information of the *Narrative,* is N. I. Huggins, *Slave and Citizen: The Life of Frederick Douglass* (1980). A biography placing Douglass in the context of the nineteenth-century antislavery movement is W. S. McFeely,

Frederick Douglass (1991). For critical approaches, see W. E. Martin, *The Mind of Frederick Douglass* (1984); W. B. Rogers, *"We Are All Together Now": Frederick Douglass, William Lloyd Garrison, and the Prophetic Tradition* (1995); W. L. Andrews, ed., *Critical Essays on Frederick Douglass* (1991); and J. Stauffer, *The Black Hearts of Men: Radical Abolitionists and the Transformation of Race* (2002).

Johann Wolfgang von Goethe
E. Ludwig, *Goethe, The History of a Man, 1749–1832* (1928), is a solid biography. Also useful are V. Lange, ed., *Goethe: A Collection of Critical Essays* (1968); and the essays contained in the critical edition of W. Arndt, trans., and C. Hamlin, ed., *Faust* (1976). See also H. Hatfield, *Goethe: A Critical Introduction* (1963); M. Bidney, *Blake and Goethe: Psychology, Ontology, Imagination* (1988); and specifically for *Faust*, L. Dieckmann, *Goethe's Faust: A Critical Reading* (1972). A study relating Goethe's play to other versions of the Faust legend is A. Hoelzel, *The Paradoxical Quest: A Study of Faustian Vicissitudes* (1988). A varied group of essays appears in Reinhold Grimm and Jost Hermand, eds., *Our Faust? Roots and Ramifications of a Modern German Myth* (1987). An ongoing, ambitious study of Goethe's life and work in their historical context is N. Boyle, *Goethe: The Poet and the Age*, I: *The Poetry of Desire: 1749–1790*, II: *Revolution and Renunciation: 1790–1803* (1991). For a less complicated approach, see I. Wagner, *Goethe* (1999).

Heinrich Heine
Biographies of Heine include Philip Kossoff, *Valiant Heart: A Biography of Heinrich Heine* (1983). Valuable critical studies are Jeffrey L. Sammons, *Heinrich Heine, the Elusive Poet* (1969); Ursula Franklin, *Exiles and Ironists: Essays on the Kinship of Heine and Laforgue* (1988); G. F. Peters, *The Poet as Provocateur: Heinrich Heine and His Critics* (2000); and R. F. Cook, *By the Rivers of Babylon: Heinrich Heine's Late Songs and Reflections* (1998). See also R. F. Cook, ed., *A Companion to the Works of Heinrich Heine* (2002).

Friedrich Hölderlin
A valuable biographical and critical study is L. S. Salzberger, *Hölderlin* (1952). Also useful is E. L. Stahl, *Hölderlin's Symbolism, an Essay* (1945). Interpretations by various critics are supplied in *The Solid Letter; Readings of Friedrich Hölderlin*, ed. A. Fioretos (1999).

Victor Hugo
A. Maurois, *Victor Hugo and His World* (1966), trans. O. Bernard, provides a useful introduction. S. Guerlac, *The Impersonal Sublime: Hugo, Baudelaire, Lautréamont* (1990), and the collection of critical essays edited by H. Bloom, *Victor Hugo* (1988), are also valuable. R. Graham, *Victor Hugo* (1997), supplies a biographical interpretation; L. M. Porter, *Victor Hugo* (1999), examines the life and work. J. C. Ireson, *Victor Hugo* (1997), offers a companion to the poetry.

Thomas Hutchinson
For insight into Hutchinson and his political role, see W. Pencak, *America's Burke: The Mind of Thomas Hutchinson* (1982); M. Freiberg, *Prelude to Purgatory: Thomas Hutchinson in Provincial Massachusetts Politics, 1760–1770* (1990); and A. S. Walmsley, *Thomas Hutchinson and the Origins of the American Revolution* (1999).

John Keats
A first-rate critical biography is A. Ward, *John Keats: The Making of a Poet*, rev. ed. (1986). Also useful are W. J. Bate, *John Keats* (1963); S. Coote, *John Keats: A Life* (1995); T. Hilton, *Keats and His World* (1971); C. T. Watts, *A Preface to Keats* (1985); J. Barnard, *John Keats* (1987); H. Bloom, ed., *The Odes of Keats* (1987), a collection of essays; and H. de Almeida, *Critical Essays on John Keats* (1990). S. Hebron, *John Keats* (2002), and *The Cambridge Companion to Keats*, ed. S. Wolfson (2001), contain valuable material.

Alphonse de Lamartine
The standard biography of Lamartine is H. Remsen Whitehouse, *The Life of Lamartine* (1918; reprinted 1969). M. E. Birkett, *Lamartine and the Poetics of Landscape* (1982), examines the poet's transformation of landscape to convey human thoughts and emotions. L. M. Porter, *The Renaissance of the Lyric in French Romanticism: Elegy, "Poème," and Ode* (1978), treats both Hugo and Lamartine.

Giacomo Leopardi
The best biography of Leopardi is I. Origo, *Leopardi: A Biography* (1935), revised and enlarged as *Leopardi: A Study in Solitude* (1999). A study of Leopardi in relation to contemporaries from other countries is R. R. Fleming, *Keats, Leopardi, and Hölderlin: The Poet as Priest of the Absolute* (1976, 1987). For critical insight, see the commentary in O. M. Casale, ed. and trans., *A Leopardi Reader* (1981); J. P. Barricelli, *Giacomo Leopardi* (1986); and D. Bini, *A Fragrance from the Desert: Poetry and Philosophy in Giacomo Leopardi* (1983).

Mikhail Yuryevich Lermontov
Little has been written in English about Lermontov's poetry. Available studies include W. N. Vickery, *M. I. Lermontov: His Life and Work* (2001); B. M. Eikhenbaum, *Lermontov: A Study in Literary-Historical Evaluation*, trans. R. Parrott and H. Weber (1981); and *Mikhail Lermontov: Commemorative Essays (1991)*, ed. A. D. P. Briggs (1992).

Jean-Paul Marat
Valuable studies include L. R. Gottschalk, *Jean Paul Marat: A Study in Radicalism* (1967), and

C. D. Conner, *Jean Paul Marat: Scientist and Revolutionary* (1998).

Herman Melville
N. Arvin's *Herman Melville* (1950) is an excellent biographical study. Also valuable is D. K. Kirby, *Herman Melville* (1993). Important critical works include L. Thompson, *Melville's Quarrel with God* (1952); W. Berthoff, *The Example of Melville* (1962); and H. Parker, *Reading Billy Budd* (1990). Useful collections of critical essays include A. R. Lee, ed., *Herman Melville: Reassessments* (1984), R. Milder, ed., *Critical Essays on Melville's Billy Budd, Sailor* (1989); and D. Yanella, ed., *New Essays on Billy Budd* (2002). A general guide is J. Bryant, ed., *A Companion to Melville Studies* (1986).

Gérard de Nerval
Nerval has not been the subject of much commentary in English. A biography is N. Rinsler, *Gérard de Nerval* (1973). Critical treatments include P. Winston, *Nerval's Magic Alphabet* (1989), and J. Strauss, *Subjects of Terror: Nerval, Hegel, and the Modern Self* (1998).

Novalis (Friedrich von Hardenberg)
Useful studies of Novalis include F. Hiehal, *Novalis: German Poet, European Thinker, Christian Mystic*, 2nd ed., rev. (1954); B. Haywood, *Novalis, the Veil of Imagery: A Study of the Poetic Works of Friedrich von Hardenberg, 1772–1801* (1959); and W. A. O'Brien, *Novalis, Signs of Revolution* (1995). C. Appleby, *German Romantic Poetry: Goethe, Novalis, Heine, Hölderlin, Schlegel, Schiller* (2003), treats Novalis among others.

Thomas Paine
Two biographies that also deal with Paine's political views are J. Fruchtman, *Thomas Paine: Apostle of Freedom* (1994), and J. Keane, *Tom Paine: A Political Life* (1995). See also B. Woodcock and J. Coates, *Combative Styles: Romantic Writing and Ideology—Two Contrasting Interpretations* (1995), which considers William Blake, Thomas De Quincey, and Edmund Burke as well as Paine.

Alexander Sergeyevich Pushkin
Henri Troyat, *Pushkin*, trans. N. Amphoux (1970), is an excellent biography. For biography and criticism, the student might also consult Walter Arndt, *Pushkin Threefold: Narrative, Lyric, Polemic and Ribald Verse* (1972); John Bayley, *Pushkin: A Comparative Commentary* (1971); Paul Debreczeny, *The Other Pushkin: A Study of Alexander Pushkin's Prose Fiction* (1983); John Oliver Killens, *Great Black Russian: A Novel on the Life and Times of Alexander Pushkin* (1989); and D. M. Bethea, ed., *Puškin Today* (1993), an ambitious collection of essays. A useful biography is Stephanie Sandler, *Distant Pleasures: Alexander Pushkin and The Writing of*

Exile (1989). See also Brett Cooke, *Pushkin and the Creative Process* (1998).

Jean-Jacques Rousseau
F. C. Green, *Jean-Jacques Rousseau: A Critical Study of His Life and Writings* (1955), provides biography and criticism. Thomas McFarland, *Romanticism and the Heritage of Rousseau* (1995), examines the relation of Rousseau's assumptions to those of the Romantic movement. A thorough evaluation of Rousseau's achievement is L. G. Crocker, *Jean-Jacques Rousseau: A New Interpretative Analysis of His Works* (1973). More directly focused on the *Confessions* is H. Williams, *Rousseau and Romantic Autobiography* (1983). More recent studies include T. M. Kavanagh, *Writing the Truth: Authority and Desire in Rousseau* (1987); M. Morgenstern, *Rousseau and the Politics of Ambiguity: Self, Culture, and Society* (1996); and C. Kelly, *Rousseau's Exemplary Life: The Confessions as Political Philosophy* (1987). Special perspectives are provided by E. L. Stelzig, *The Romantic Subject in Autobiography: Rousseau and Goethe* (2000), and L. Lange, ed., *Feminist Interpretations of Jean-Jacques Rousseau* (2002). A good starting point for understanding Rousseau is R. Wokler, *Rousseau: A Very Short Introduction*, 2nd ed. (2001).

Percy Bysshe Shelley
E. Blunden, *Shelley: A Life Story* (1946), provides a useful biography. A critically oriented biography is P. Hodgart, *A Preface to Shelley* (1985). For criticism, see C. Baker, *Shelley's Major Poetry: The Fabric of a Vision* (1948); E. Wasserman, *Shelley: A Critical Reading* (1971); R. Holmes, *Shelley: The Pursuit*, new ed. (2003); J. Hall, *The Transforming Image: A Study of Shelley's Major Poetry* (1980); S. M. Sperry, *Shelley's Major Verse: The Narrative and Dramatic Poetry* (1988); M. O'Neill, *The Human Mind's Imaginings: Conflict and Achievement in Shelley's Poetry* (1989) and S. Haines, *Shelley's Poetry: The Divided Self* (1997). The Norton Critical Edition *Shelley's Poetry and Prose: Authoritative Texts, Criticism*, ed. D. H. Reiman and N. Fraistat, 2nd ed. (2002), contains valuable material.

Alfred, Lord Tennyson
For useful biography, see L. Ormond, *Alfred Tennyson: A Literary Life* (1993). Important criticism includes J. Buckley, *Tennyson: The Growth of a Poet* (1960); C. B. Ricks, *Tennyson* (1972); M. Shaw, *Alfred Lord Tennyson* (1988); H. F. Tucker, *Tennyson and the Doom of Romanticism* (1988); H. F. Tucker, ed., *Critical Essays on Alfred Lord Tennyson* (1993); J. W. Hood, *Divining Desire: Tennyson and the Poetics of Transcendence* (2000); and W. D. Shaw, *Alfred Lord Tennyson: The Poet in an Age of Theory* (1996). A valuable general guide is F. B. Pin-

ion, *Tennyson Companion: Life and Works* (1984).

Mercy Otis Warren
For further information on Warren, see, in addition to the Schloesser book cited for Abigail Adams, R. Zagarri, *A Woman's Dilemma: Mercy Otis Warren and the American Revolution* (1995), and J. H. Richards, *Mercy Otis Warren* (1995).

Walt Whitman
G. W. Allen, *The Solitary Singer: A Critical Biography of Walt Whitman* (1985), provides both biography and criticism. An important recent study is D. S. Reynolds, *Walt Whitman's America: A Cultural Biography* (1995). M. Hindus, ed., *Walt Whitman: The Critical Heritage* (1971), contains nineteenth- and twentieth-century essays; J. E. Miller, Jr., *A Critical Guide to Leaves of Grass* (1957), is helpful. Also valuable are R. V. Chase, *Walt Whitman Reconsidered* (1955); M. J. Killingsworth, *Whitman's Poetry of the Body: Sexuality, Politics, and the Text* (1989); B. Erkkila, *Whitman the Political Poet* (1989); M. W. Thomas, *The Lunar Light of Whitman's Poetry* (1987); and J. E. Miller, Jr., *Leaves of Grass: America's Lyric-Epic of Self and Democracy* (1992). A general guide is G. W. Allen, *The New Walt Whitman Handbook* (1986). A recent exploration of Whitman's poetry in relation to his contemporaries is D. Wardrop, *Word, Birth, and Culture: The Poetry of Poe, Whitman, and Dickinson* (2002). Investigating the bearing of Whitman's sexuality on his poetry is M. Maslan, *Whitman Possessed: Poetry, Sexuality, and Popular Authority* (2001).

Dorothy Wordsworth
Biographies of Dorothy Wordsworth include R. Gittings and J. Manton, *Dorothy Wordsworth* (1985), and E. Gunn, *A Passion for the Particular: Dorothy Wordsworth, a Portrait* (1981). A useful study placing Dorothy and William Wordsworth in political and intellectual context is A. M. Ellis, *Rebels and Conservatives: Dorothy and William Wordsworth and Their Circle* (1967). Two recent studies that focus on Dorothy's relationship to her brother and to others are R. E. Matlak, *The Poetry of Relationship: The Wordsworths and Coleridge, 1797–1800* (1997), and J. Worthen, *The Gang: Coleridge, the Hutchinsons and the Wordsworths in 1802* (2001). S. M. Zimmerman, *Romanticism, Lyricism, and History* (1999), treats both Wordsworths in the context of their period.

William Wordsworth
G. M. Harper, *Wordsworth: His Life, Works and Influence*, 3rd ed. (1929), remains the standard biography. A more recent biographical study is S. C. Gill, *William Wordsworth: A Life* (1989). Other important works (critical in emphasis) include R. D. Havens, *The Mind of a Poet*, 2 vols. (1962); G. Hartman, *Wordsworth's Poetry, 1787–1814* (1971); Thomas McFarland, *William Wordsworth: Intensity and Achievement* (1992); and J. H. Alexander, *Reading Wordsworth* (1987). A useful collection of critical essays is G. H. Gilpin, ed., *Critical Essays on William Wordsworth* (1990). Valuable contextualization is provided by P. Fletcher and J. Murphy, eds., *Wordsworth in Context* (1992). Recent years have seen the publication of several biographies, of which the best is K. R. Johnston, *The Hidden Wordsworth: Poet, Lover, Rebel, Spy* (1998). Also provocative is D. Wu, *Wordsworth: An Inner Life* (2002). A useful compendium is *The Cambridge Companion to Wordsworth*, ed. S. Gill (2003). Among the many works concerning Wordsworth and other Romantic poets, a valuable collection of essays is *Inventing the Individual: Romanticism and the Idea of individualism*, ed. L. H. Peer (2002), which includes essays on Keats and Goethe as well as Wordsworth.

THE NINETEENTH CENTURY: REALISM AND SYMBOLISM

E. Auerbach, *Mimesis: The Representation of Reality in Western Literature* (1953), is a wide-ranging book (from Homer to Proust) with chapters on nineteenth-century realism. G. J. Becker, ed., *Documents of Modern Literary Realism* (1963), surveys the development of modern realism and offers documents and essays from 1835 to 1955. H. Levin, *The Gates of Horn: A Study of Five French Realists* (1963), contains much on realism in general as well as specifically dealing with Stendhal, Balzac, Flaubert, Zola, and Proust. Linda Nochlin, *Realism* (1971), discusses realism in the visual arts. Naomi Schor, *Breaking the Chain: Women, The-ory, and French Realists Fiction* (1985), discusses the realist fiction of Flaubert, Zola, Balzac, and others in terms of feminist and psychoanalytic theory. Also helpful is R. Wellek, "The Concept of Realism in Literary Scholarship," in R. Wellek, *Concepts of Criticism: Essays* (1963). Nicholas Boyle and Martin Swales, eds., *Realism in European Literature: Essays in Honour of J. P. Stern* (1986), is a varied and useful collection that includes a discussion of realism as it relates to modernism and language consciousness. Elise Boulding, *The Underside of History: A View of Women through Time*, rev. ed. (1992), arranged by periods and sociological categories, contains much pertinent information about the role of women that is omitted from traditional histories. John Rignall, *Realist Fiction and the Strolling Spectator* (1992), indebted to Nietzsche and Walter Benjamin, analyzes realism's distanced point of view in eight nineteenth-century and three twentieth-century novelists.

Marcel Raymond, *From Baudelaire to Surrealism* (1933; trans. 1949, 1950), is a fundamental study of the evolution of the new poetry. Laurence M. Porter, *The Crisis of French Symbolism* (1990), situates the poetry of Baudelaire, Mallarmé, Verlaine, and Rimbaud between neo-classicism and the Symbolist school. An influential and still valuable presentation is found in *The Symbolist Movement in Literature* (1899; repr. 1980), by the English Symbolist Arthur Symons. P. Mansell Jones, *The Background of Modern French Poetry: Essays and Interviews* (1951; repr. 1968), describes the influence of Poe, Baudelaire, Mallarmé, and Whitman on modern free verse. Georges Poulet, *Exploding Poetry: Baudelaire/Rimbaud*, trans. Françoise Meltzer (1984), interprets the poetry of the two poets.

Charles Baudelaire

Lois Boe Hyslop, *Charles Baudelaire Revisited* (1992), is a useful introductory survey. F. W. Leakey, *Baudelaire, Les Fleurs du Mal* (1992), is a short guide to the poet's major work. Enid Starkie, *Baudelaire* (1957), is the fullest biography in English. Henri Peyre, ed., *Baudelaire: A Collection of Critical Essays* (1962), contains eleven essays on *The Flowers of Evil*, with selections by major writers. Harold Bloom, ed., *Charles Baudelaire* (1987), presents ten contemporary critics on Baudelaire's themes, literary and artistic criticism, selected texts, and relation to Poe. Patricia Clements, *Baudelaire and the English Tradition* (1985), is a penetrating analysis of Baudelaire's influence on English literature from Swinburne to T. S. Eliot; it includes comparisons and contrasts with late Symbolist tradition. Edward K. Kaplan, *Baudelaire's Prose Poems* (1990), studies the prose poems as a many-sided but coherent ensemble of "fables of modern life." Baudelaire's criticism of literature and art are discussed in Rosemary Lloyd, *Baudelaire's Literary Criticism* (1981), David Carrier, *High Art: Charles Baudelaire and the Origins of Modernist Painting* (1996). Lloyd's *Selected Letters of Charles Baudelaire: The Conquest of Solitude* (1986) contains personal and literary letters. Laurence M. Porter, *The Crisis of French Symbolism* (1990), has an interesting chapter on Baudelaire's relation to his imagined audience.

Mona Caird

Carolyn Christensen Nelson discusses Caird in *British Women Fiction Writers of the 1890s*

(1996). See also the pages in Ann L. Ardis's *New Women, New Novels: Feminism and Early Modernism* (1990) and in Gail Cunningham's *The New Woman and the Victorian Novel* (1978).

Anton Chekhov

Donald Rayfield, *The Cherry Orchard: Catastrophe and Comedy* (1994), presents an extended discussion of the play; good chapters are also found in Beverly Hahn, *Chekhov: A Study of the Major Stories and Plays* (1977); Harvey Pitcher, *The Chekhov Play: A New Interpretation* (1973); and Richard Pearce, *Chekhov: A Study of the Four Major Plays* (1983). Francis Fergusson compares Ibsen and Chekhov in "*Ghosts* and *The Cherry Orchard*," in *The Idea of a Theater, a Study of Ten Plays: The Art of Drama in Changing Perspective* (1949). There is helpful critical analysis in R. L. Jackson, ed., *Chekhov: A Collection of Critical Essays* (1967), and *Reading Chekhov's Text* (1993); in Donald Rayfield, *Chekhov: The Evolution of His Art* (1975); and in René Wellek and N. D. Wellek, eds., *Chekhov: New Perspectives* (1984); which includes a sketch of Chekhov criticism in England and America. Laurence Senelick, *The Chekhov Theatre: A Century of the Plays in Performance* (1997), presents a different perspective. Ralph E. Matlaw, ed., *Anton Chekhov's Short Stories: Texts of the Stories, Backgrounds, Criticism* (1979), includes eight valuable essays on aspects of the short stories and selections from Chekhov's letters. Virginia Llewellyn Smith, *Anton Chekhov and the Lady with the Dog* (1973), argues for autobiographical elements in Gurov's portrayal. Nick Worrall, *Chekhov on File* (1986), offers an introductory survey with useful cited passages and suggestions for further study. Donald Rayfield, *Anton Chekhov: A Life* (1998), is a revisionary biography that evokes a more complex personality based on newly discovered evidence.

Charles Darwin

Useful readings include biographies by John Bowlby, *Charles Darwin: A New Life* (1990), and Adrian Desmond and James Moore, *Darwin* (1991), as well as Robert J. Richards, *Darwin and the Emergence of Evolutionary Theories of Mind and Behavior* (1987), and a collection, *Darwin: Texts Commentary*, ed. Philip Appleman (2001), that contains many critical essays in addition to selections from Darwin's work and the work of his predecessors.

Fyodor Dostoevsky

Monroe C. Beardsley, "Dostoevsky's Metaphor of the 'Underground,'" *Journal of the History of Ideas* 3 (June 1942), is a subtle interpretation of the central metaphor of the *Notes*. Joseph Frank, "Nihilism and *Notes from Underground*," *Sewanee Review*, 69 (1961), interprets the *Notes* in the context of the history of the times. Robert L.

Jackson, *Dostoevsky's Underground Man in Russian Literature* (1981), traces the impact of the *Notes* on Russian literature. Konstantin Mochulsky, *Dostoevsky: His Life and Work*, trans. Michael A. Minihan (1967), is the best general work translated from Russian, the work of an emigré in Paris. René Wellek, ed., *Dostoevsky: A Collection of Critical Essays* (1962), contains an essay by the editor on the history of Dostoevsky criticism. Alba della Fazia Amoia, *Feodor Dostoevsky* (1993), is a general introduction to Dostoevsky's work aimed at a student audience. Joseph Frank, *Dostoevsky* (1976–2002), is an impressive biographical study in five volumes. Frank's *Through the Russian Prism: Essays on Literature and Culture* (1990) includes review essays that examine various approaches to Dostoevsky. Louis Breger, *Dostoevsky: The Author as Psychoanalyst* (1989), takes a psychoanalytic approach in analyzing levels of meaning in Dostoevsky's work as a new sensibility that anticipates the modern novel; he includes a chapter on *Notes*. Malcolm V. Jones, *Dostoyevsky after Bakhtin: Readings in Dostoyevsky's Fantastic Realism* (1990), examines Dostoevsky's "higher realism" in various perspectives and includes a chapter on *Notes*. Nina Pelikan Straus, *Dostoevsky and the Woman Question: Rereadings at the End of a Century* (1994), examines the presence of women and Dostoevsky's construction of the feminine.

Gustave Flaubert
William J. Berg and Laurey K. Martin, *Gustave Flaubert* (1997), is a general introduction to Flaubert's life and work. Victor H. Brombert, *The Novels of Flaubert: A Study of Themes and Techniques* (1966), has an excellent chapter on *Madame Bovary*; Raymond D. Giraud, ed., *Flaubert: A Collection of Critical Essays* (1964), and Harold Bloom, ed., *Emma Bovary* (1994), provide a range of short studies. Paul de Man, ed., *Gustave Flaubert: Madame Bovary. Backgrounds and Sources: Essays in Criticism* (1965), will help the reader, as will Alison Fairlie, *Flaubert: Madame Bovary* (1962), a good discussion of problems, structures, people, and values addressed to students. The chapter on *Madame Bovary* in Anthony Thorlby, *Gustave Flaubert and the Art of Realism* (1957), is still to be recommended, as is Margaret Lowe, *Towards the Real Flaubert: A Study of Madame Bovary* (1984).

Giuseppe Garibaldi
Jasper Ridley, *Garibaldi* (1974), is a full bibliography; also useful is the shorter *Garibaldi: A Great Life in Brief* (1956), by Denis Mack Smith. G. M. Trevelyan, *Garibaldi and the Thousand* (1909: repr. 1979), and *Garibaldi and the Making of Italy* (1911: repr. 1948) are important earlier studies. *Pages from the Garibaldian Epic*, ed. Anthony P. Campanella (1984), collects seven essays offering an international perspective on Garibaldi's career.

Nikolai Gogol
David Magarshack's *Gogol: A Life* (1957) is a detailed and readable biography of Gogol's development that contains many passages from his writing; an early short biography is Janko Lavrin's *Gogol* (1926). Thais S. Lindstrom's *Nikolay Gogol* (1974) is a clear, concise, and documented discussion of Gogol's life and work, including a discussion of individual works, a chronology, and an annotated bibliography. Vasilii Vasil'evich Gippius's *Gogol*, ed. and trans. Robert A. Maguire (1981), is an excellent annotated study of Gogol's work by an eminent Russian editor of his works. F. C. Driessen's *Gogol as a Short-Story Writer: A Study of His Technique of Composition*, trans. Ian F. Finlay (1965), offers a perceptive discussion of selected stories, including a substantial analysis of *The Overcoat*, and a biographical study that emphasizes Gogol's constant anxiety. *Gogol's "Overcoat": An Anthology of Critical Essays*, ed. Elizabeth Welt Trahan (1982), collects five important essays on *The Overcoat* in a slim but useful volume. Victor Erlich's *Gogol* (1969) is a readable thematic study of Gogol's work that examines his imagery and realism, and includes a discussion of *The Overcoat*. Other aspects of Gogol's work are discussed in Donald Fanger's *Dostoevsky and Romantic Realism: A Study of Dostoevsky in Relation to Balzac, Dickens, and Gogol* (1965), which contains an interesting examination of romantic and realistic traits in various nineteenth-century European novelists, including Gogol; Robert A. Maguire's *Exploring Gogol* (1994), a critical analysis of the role of space and place, vision and language in Gogol's work; and *Gogol from the Twentieth Century: Eleven Essays*, comp. by Robert A. Maguire (1974), which collects important essays on aspects of Gogol's work, the introduction of which includes a history of critical views of Gogol.

Henrik Ibsen
Michael Meyer, *Ibsen: A Biography* (1971), is a general work. J. W. McFarlane, ed., *Discussions of Henrik Ibsen* (1962), contains Henry James's "On the Occasion of 'Hedda Gabler.'" Rolf Fjelde, ed., *Ibsen: A Collection of Critical Essays* (1965), has a good essay on *Hedda Gabler*; and James McFarlane, ed., *The Cambridge Companion to Ibsen* (1994), offers sixteen essays on a wide variety of topics. Joan Templeton, *Ibsen's Women* (2001), is an excellent study that includes a chapter on *Hedda Gabler* and a discussion of Ibsen's modernism. Michael Goldman, *Ibsen: The Dramaturgy of Fear* (1999), discusses the plays from a different perspective, and Frederick J. Marker and Lise-Lone Marker, *Ibsen's Lively Art: A Performance Study of the Major Plays* (1989), use descriptions of the var-

ious performances of *Hedda Gabler* to examine differing interpretations of the main characters.

Mary Kingsley
Detailed and useful biographies are Katherine Frank, *A Voyager Out: The Life of Mary Kingsley* (1986), and Dea Birkett, *Mary Kingsley: Imperial Adventuress* (1992). Also recommended are the discussions of Kingsley in Catherine Barnes Stevenson, *Victorian Women Travel Writers in Africa* (1982), and in Sara Mills, *Discourses of Difference: An Analysis of Women's Travel Writing and Colonialism*, new ed. (1993).

Thomas Babington Macaulay
John Leonard Clive's *Macaulay: The Shaping of The Historian* (1973) and Jane Millgate's *Macaulay* (1973) are excellent biographies that also include useful discussions of the *Minute* in historical context.

Machemba
The most pertinent study is Robert D. Jackson's excellent "Resistance to the German Invasion of the Tanganyikan Coast, 1888–1891" in *Protest and Power in Black Africa*, ed. Robert I. Rotberg and Ali A. Mazrui (1970). John Iliffe, *A Modern History of Tanganyika* (1979), is also recommended as a useful history that includes a discussion of the resistance to colonial invasion.

Stéphane Mallarmé
Frederic C. St. Aubyn, *Stéphane Mallarmé*, updated ed. (1989), provides a brief biography and thematically arranged discussions of Mallarmé's work. Harold Bloom, ed., *Stéphane Mallarmé* (1987), collects thirteen challenging essays on Mallarmé's work and its implications for poetic practice. Hans-Jost Frey, *Studies in Poetic Discourse: Mallarmé, Baudelaire, Rimbaud, Hölderlin* trans. William Whobrey (1996), offers perceptive essays.

Karl Marx and Friedrich Engels
Good book-length studies of the life and work include Franz Mehring, *Karl Marx: The Story of His Life*, trans. Edward Fitzgerald (1962), Isaiah Berlin, *Karl Marx: His Life and Environment*, 4th ed. (1978), and Gustav Mayer, *Friedrich Engels: A Biography* (1937). The useful collection edited by Robert C. Tucker, *The Marx-Engels Reader*, 2nd ed. (1978), also includes a chronology and a bibliography of recommended readings organized by topic.

Guy de Maupassant
Francis Steegmuller's *Maupassant: A Lion in the Path* (1949) is a readable and informative biography that includes archival information as well as many passages from Maupassant's work and a list of sixty-five fake "Maupassant" stories published in America. Michael G. Lerner, *Maupassant* (1975), is a useful later biography. Charles J. Stivale, *The Art of Rupture: Narrative Desire and Duplicity in the Tales of Guy de Maupassant* (1994), examines the implications, for feminist theory and theories of realism, of the gender relationships in Maupassant's stories. Mary Donaldson-Evans discusses the role of women in *A Woman's Revenge: The Chronology of Dispossession in Maupassant's Fiction* (1986). An insightful early essay on Maupassant appears in Henry James, *Partial Portraits* (1888), and Richard Fusco's *Maupassant and the American Short Story: The Influence of Form at the Turn of the Century* (1994) is an interesting and well-documented discussion that includes comparisons with Bierce, O. Henry, Chopin, and James.

Friedrich Nietzsche
Studies of Nietzsche include Ronald Hayman, *Nietzsche: A Critical Life* (1980), R. J. Hollingdale, *Nietzsche* (1973), and Walter Kaufmann, *Nietzsche: Philosopher, Psychologist, Antichrist*, 4th ed. (1974). Copious selections are edited in Kaufmann's *The Portable Nietzsche* (1954) and *Basic Writings of Nietzsche* (1968).

Sol T. Plaatje
Useful further readings include a biography by Brian P. Willan, *Sol Plaatje: South African Nationalist 1876–1932* (1984), and a broadly informative chapter devoted to the siege of Mafeking in Thomas Pakenham's detailed study, *The Boer War* (1979).

Cecil Rhodes
Modern discussions of Rhodes include Brian Roberts, *Cecil Rhodes: Flawed Colossus* (1988), and Robert I. Rotberg, *The Founder: Cecil Rhodes and the Pursuit of Power* (1988). Extensive contextual information is available in Thomas Pakenham's *The Scramble for Africa. 1876–1912* (1991), a detailed study of the colonization of Africa by all five major colonial powers: Britain, Germany, France, Italy, and Portugal.

Arthur Rimbaud
Frederic C. St. Aubyn, *Arthur Rimbaud* (1988), is a useful biography that also treats Rimbaud's work. Wallace Fowlie, *Rimbaud* (1965), discusses the *Illuminations* and the myth of childhood in Rimbaud. Harold Bloom, ed., *Arthur Rimbaud* (1988), collects eleven essays on various aspects of Rimbaud's work. Georges Poulet, *Exploding Poetry: Baudelaire/Rimbaud*, trans. Françoise Meltzer, (1984), examines poetic worldviews in the work of the two poets.

Olive Schreiner
Ruth First and Ann Scott's *Olive Schreiner* (1980) is a useful full biography. Karel Schoeman focuses on the South African historical context, including the aftermath of the war, in *Only an Anguish to Live Here: Olive Schreiner and the Anglo-Boer War, 1899–1902* (1992). For a broader historical context, Thomas Pakenham's *The Boer War* (1979) and *The Scramble for Africa* (1991) are recommended.

Leo Tolstoy

R. F. Christian, *Tolstoy: A Critical Introduction* (1969), is clear, instructive, and informative. E. B. Greenwood, *Tolstoy: The Comprehensive Vision* (1975), is helpful in placing *The Death of Ivan Ilyich* in the perspective of Tolstoy's work as a whole. Some good analysis is found in H. Gifford, ed., *Leo Tolstoy: A Critical Anthology* (1971). Ralph E. Matlaw, ed., *Tolstoy: A Collection of Critical Essays* (1967), and Philip Rahv, *Image and Idea: Fourteen Essays on Literary Themes* (1949), both present essays on *The Death of Ivan Ilyich*. Theodore Redpath, *Tolstoy*, 2nd ed. (1969), provides a brief introduction with good criticism of ideas. Ernest J. Simmons, *Leo Tolstoy* (1946), and A. N. Wilson, *Tolstoy* (1988), are both excellent biographies. Rimvydas Šilbajoris, *Tolstoy's Aesthetics and His Art* (1991), includes accounts of reactions to the author at home and abroad as well as many substantial quotations.

Giovanni Verga

Thomas Goddard Bergin's *Giovanni Verga* (1931; repr. 1969) is an excellent early study of Verga's work, still readable and insightful. Alfred Alexander's *Giovanni Verga: A Great Writer and His World* (1972) is an interesting and readable account of Verga's life and work based on a wealth of material from the family archives; much information about historical and political contexts. Giovanni Cecchetti's *Giovanni Verga* (1978), intended as a critical guide to Verga's life and work, includes biographical material, a chronology, an annotated bibliography, and many critical analyses and judgments. Discussions of Verga's realism are found in D. Woolf, *The Art of Verga: A Study in Objectivity* (1977), S. B. Chandler, "The Primitive World of Giovanni Verga," *Mosaic* 5 (1972), and Giovanni Carsaniga, "Literary Realism in Italy: Verga, Capuana, and Verismo," in *The Cambridge Companion to the Italian Novel*, ed. Peter Bondanella and Andrea Ciccarelli (2003).

Paul Verlaine

Joanna Richardson, *Verlaine* (1971), is a useful biography. Stefan Zweig, *Paul Verlaine* (1913), trans. O. F. Theis (1980), discusses the poet and his work.

Émile Zola

Informative and readable biographies of Zola are F. W. J. Hemmings's *The Life and Times of Émile Zola* (1977) and Philip Walker's *Zola* (1985). An excellent resource on the affair itself is *The Dreyfus Affair: "J'accuse" and Other Writings*, ed. Alain Pagès and trans. Eleanor Levieux (1996), which collects Zola's writings related to the affair; it also includes an introduction, chronology, bibliography, and capsule biographies of leading figures.

THE TWENTIETH CENTURY: MODERNISMS AND MODERNITY

The Modern Tradition: Backgrounds of Modern Literature, ed. Richard Ellmann and Charles Feidelson, Jr. (1965), is a valuable collection of statements by writers, artists, philosophers, and scientists, arranged by themes. Monique Chefdor, Ricardo Quinones, and Albert Wachtel, eds., *Modernism: Challenges and Perspectives* (1986), offers many valuable essays on international modernism, ranging from definitions to historical practice in art, music, literature, and politics. David Hayman, *Re-forming the Narrative: Toward a Mechanics of Modernist Fiction* (1987), proposes five tactics that distinguish modernist narrative from earlier fiction; examples include Robbe-Grillet, Kafka, Rilke, Joyce, Beckett, and Borges. Cultural background is provided in Wilson H. Coates and Hayden V. White, *The Ordeal of Liberal Humanism: An Intellectual History of Western Europe* (1970), an excellent intellectual history of Western Europe after the French Revolution, and David Harvey, *Paris: Capital of Modernity* (2003), a copiously documented and illustrated study of the rise of social, economic, and literary modernism in late nineteenth-century Paris. Harry Levin, "What Was Modernism?" (1962), in *Refractions: Essays in Comparative Literature* (1966), is an influential survey of modernist writers as humanists and inheritors of the Enlightenment. Renato Poggioli, *The Theory of the Avant-Garde*, trans. Gerald Fitzgerald (1968), locates basic categories of attitudes toward society inside the different arts of the twentieth-century American avant-garde. William S. Rubin, *Dada, Surrealism and Their Heritage* (1968), gives a detailed history of Surrealist art with many superb illustrations. John D. Erickson, *Dada: Performance, Poetry, and Art* (1984), and Herbert S. Gershman, *The Surrealist Revolution in France* (1974), are valuable surveys. Matei Călinescu, *Five Faces of Modernity: Modernism, Avant-Garde, Decadence, Kitsch, Postmodernism* (1987), is a subtly argued, informative collection of essays on the aesthetics of five modern movements. Morton P. Levitt, *Modernist Survivors: The Contemporary Novel in England, the United States, France, and Latin America* (1987), illustrates the impact of literary modernism and the continuity of humanist values. James F. Knapp, *Literary Modernism and the Transformation of Work* (1988), examines work-related themes in English and

American modernist literature, and modernism's contradictory attitudes toward a changing economic order. Harry R. Garvin, ed., *Romanticism, Modernism, Postmodernism* (1980), is a useful collection of essays that attempts to define changing views of the artistic imagination and its place in society.

Daniel R. Schwarz, *Reconfiguring Modernism: Explorations in the Relationships between Modern Art and Modern Literature* (1997), is a comparative study. Ihab Hassan and Sally Hassan, eds., *Innovation/Renovation: New Perspectives on the Humanities* (1983), explores change in contemporary Western culture. Marjorie Perloff, *The Poetics of Indeterminacy: Rimbaud to Cage* (1981), has significance beyond its primary focus on contemporary English and American poetry stemming from the French tradition. See also Perloff, ed., *Postmodern Genres* (1989), for a collection of essays on postmodernism in art and literature. Susan Rubin Suleiman, *Subversive Intent: Gender, Politics, and the Avant-Garde* (1990), analyzes the cultural implications of avant-garde artistic practices. Jean-Michel Rabaté, *The Ghosts of Modernity* (1996), uses poststructural methods to reread the history of modernity; it includes references to Symbolist writers. Nancy K. Miller, ed., *The Poetics of Gender* (1986), presents essays on various aspects of feminist criticism. Elise Boulding, *The Underside of History: A View of Women through Time*, rev. ed. (1992), complements traditional histories by drawing attention to the position and contributions of women. *Freedom Dreams: The Black Radical Imagination*, by Robin Kelley (2002), includes a discussion of modern African-American arts and Surrealism.

Chinua Achebe

A recent and full biography is Ezenwa-Ohaeto, *Chinua Achebe: A Biography* (1997). C. L. Innes, *Chinua Achebe* (1990), is a comprehensive study of Achebe's work through 1988 that emphasizes his literary techniques and Africanization of the novel. Simon Gikandi, *Reading Chinua Achebe: Language and Ideology in Fiction* (1991), is also recommended. Robert M. Wren, *Achebe's World: The Historical and Cultural Context of the Novels of Chinua Achebe* (1980), provides historical background and cultural context for Achebe's novels and includes glossary and bibliography. Studies of *Things Fall Apart* include Kate Turkington, *Chinua Achebe: Things Fall Apart* (1977), a concise introductory study; and the nine essays in Solomon Ogbede Iyasere, ed., *Understanding Things Fall Apart: Selected Essays and Criticism* (1998). C. L. Innes and Bernth Lindfors, eds., *Critical Perspectives on Chinua Achebe* (1978), collect twenty-one essays on Achebe's work (almost exclusively the novels) through 1973. G. D. Killam, *The Writings of Chinua Achebe*, rev. ed.

(1977), is a commentary on Achebe's work through the mid-1970s, concentrating on the first four novels. Also of interest is *Conversations with Chinua Achebe*, ed. Bernth Lindfors (1977). Further information may be found in Ezenwa-Ohaeto, *Chinua Achebe: A Biography* (1997); *Conversations with Chinua Achebe*, ed. Bernth Lindfors (1997); and Robert M. Wren, *Achebe's World: The Historical and Cultural Context of the Novels of Chinua Achebe* (1980).

Anna Akhmatova

Sam N. Driver, *Anna Akhmatova* (1972), is an excellent introduction to Akhmatova's work and its historical context that stresses the years up to 1922, and Roberta Reeder, *Anna Akhmatova: Poet and Prophet* (1995), is a good recent biography. David Wells, *Anna Akhmatova: Her Poetry* (1996), is a readable, well-documented study that discusses works in chronological order. Amanda Haight, *Anna Akhmatova: A Poetic Pilgrimage* (1976, 1990), and Susan Amert, *In a Shattered Mirror: The Later Poetry of Anna Akhmatova* (1992), are perceptive book-length studies. Ronald Hingley, *Nightingale Fever: Russian Poets in Revolution* (1981), discusses Akhmatova, Pasternak, Tsvetaeva, and Mandelstam in the context of Russian literary history and Soviet politics up to the early years of World War II. Wendy Rosslyn, ed., *The Speech of Unknown Eyes: Akhmatova's Readers on Her Poetry* (1990), collects a range of different responses. Sharon Leiter, *Akhmatova's Petersburg* (1983), examines the image of St. Petersburg as a focus for spiritual and historical themes in Akhmatova's poetry. Anna Akhmatova, *My Half Century: Selected Prose*, ed. Ronald Meyer (1992), includes autobiographical material, correspondence, short pieces on other writers, and an essay on Akhmatova's prose.

Hannah Arendt

The biography by Elisabeth Young-Bruehl, *Hannah Arendt: For Love of the World* (1982), includes material from oral sources. Recommended book-length studies are Margaret Canovan, *Hannah Arendt: A Reinterpretation of Her Political Thought* (1992), and John McGowan, *Hannah Arendt: An Introduction* (1998). Also of interest are the diverse perspectives collected in Larry May and Jerome Kohn, eds., *Hannah Arendt: Twenty Years Later* (1996).

Ingeborg Bachmann

Karen R. Achberger, *Understanding Ingeborg Bachmann* (1995), is a good overview of Bachmann's work; it includes a short biography and bibliographic references. Introductions by Mark Anderson to Bachmann's *In the Storm of Roses: Selected Poems*, trans. and ed. Mark Anderson (1986), and *Three Paths to the Lake: Stories*, trans. Mary Fran Gilbert (1989), provide an excellent short overview of the writer's poetry and prose. Gudrun Brokoph-Mauch, ed., *Thunder Rumbling at My Heels: Tracing Ingeborg Bachmann* (1998), may also be consulted. Juliet Wigmore, "Ingeborg Bachmann" in Keith Bullivant, ed., *The Modern German Novel* (1987), discusses *Malina* and the *Ways of Death* cycle. Inta Ezergailis, *Women Writers—The Divided Self* (1982), has chapters on Bachmann and Doris Lessing, among others. A special issue of *Modern Austrian Literature* (1979) devoted to Austrian women writers contains several essays on Bachmann.

Simone de Beauvoir
Catharine Savage Brosman, *Simone de Beauvoir Revisited* (1991), is a detailed biographical study. Also recommended is the series of essays in *Feminist Interpretations of Simone de Beauvoir*, ed. Margaret A. Simons (1995).

Samuel Beckett
Samuel Beckett; *Endgame: With a Revised Text*, ed. S. E. Gontarski (1992), is a revised text based on productions directed or supervised by Beckett; the attached theatrical notebooks often clarify situations and settings. Arthur N. Athanason, *Endgame: The Ashbin Play* (1993), is a brief introduction; and Alan Astro, *Understanding Samuel Beckett* (1990), discusses the complete work with interpretations emphasizing cultural and linguistic aspects. Andrew K. Kennedy, *Samuel Beckett* (1989), provides a compact, comprehensive overview of Beckett's work with separate chapters on the major plays and novels. Richard Begam, *Samuel Beckett and the End of Modernity* (1996), discusses Beckett in the context of postmodernism. Useful biographies are Deirdre Bair, *Samuel Beckett: A Biography* (1990); Anthony Cronin, *Samuel Beckett: The Last Modernist* (1997); Lois G. Gordon, *The World of Samuel Beckett, 1906–1946* (1996); and James Knowlson, *Damned to Fame: The Life of Samuel Beckett* (1996). Hugh Kenner, *Samuel Beckett: A Critical Study* (1968), is an earlier but still valuable discussion of Beckett's work, and Steven Connor, ed., *Waiting for Godot and Endgame—Samuel Beckett* (1992), which includes eleven essays, of which seven are wholly or partially on *Endgame*.

Jorge Luis Borges
Useful biographies are James Woodall, *The Man in the Mirror of the Book: A Life of Jorge Luis Borges* (1996), and his *Borges: A Life* (1996). Martin S. Stabb, *Borges Revisited* (1991), is a general introduction to the man and his work. Jaime Alazraki, ed., *Critical Essays on Jorge Luis Borges* (1987), assembles articles and reviews (including the 1970 *Autobiographical Essay*), four comparative essays, and a general introduction that offer valuable perspectives on Borges's

writing as well as his impact on American writers and critics. Linda S. Maier, *Borges and the European Avant-garde* (1996), focuses on the European scene. Edna Aizenberg, ed., *Borges and His Successors: The Borgesian Impact on Literature and the Arts* (1990), is a wide-ranging collection of essays describing Borges as the precursor of postmodern fiction and criticism. Ana María Barrenechea, *Borges, the Labyrinth Maker*, trans. Robert Lima (1965), discusses Borges's intricate style, while Daniel Balderston, *Out of Context: Historical Reference and the Representation of Reality in Borges* (1993), focuses on the texts' manipulation of fictional and historical reality. Fernando Sorrentino, *Seven Conversations with Jorge Luis Borges*, trans. Clark M. Zlotchew (1982), is a series of informal, widely ranging interviews from 1972 with a prefaced list of the topics of each conversation.

Tadeusz Borowski
Brief discussions of Borowski are found in Czesław Miłosz, *The History of Polish Literature* (1969); and from a different perspective, Sidra DeKoven Ezrahi, *By Words Alone: The Holocaust in Literature* (1980). Jan Kott, "Introduction" to *This Way for the Gas, Ladies and Gentlemen* (1967), and Jan Walc, "When the Earth Is No Longer a Dream and Cannot Be Dreamed through to the End," *Polish Review* (1987), combine biography and literary analysis. Selections from the poetry are available in *Selected Poems: Tadeusz Borowski*, trans. Tadeusz Pióro with Larry Rafferty and Meryl Natchez (1990), and "Five Poems by Tadeusz Borowski," trans. Addison Bross, *Polish Review* (1983). Also pertinent are the *Historical Atlas of the Holocaust* (1996) and psychiatrist Bruno Bettelheim's analysis of different responses to genocide in *Surviving the Holocaust* (1986).

Bertolt Brecht
Martin Esslin, *Brecht: The Man and His Work* (1974), John Fuegi, *Brecht and Company: Sex, Politics, and the Making of the Modern Drama* (1994; repr. 2002), and John Willett, *The Theatre of Bertolt Brecht: A Study from Eight Aspects*, 3rd ed. (1975), offer biographical and critical perspectives on the author and his work. John Willett, ed. and trans., *Brecht on Theatre: The Development of an Aesthetic* (1964; repr. 1978), contains Brecht's own essays and lectures on his theater. Ronald Hayman, *Brecht: A Biography* (1983), offers a detailed view of Brecht's life. Eric Bentley, *The Brecht Commentaries 1943–1986*, 2nd ed., rev. (1987), offers lively essays on the major plays, on Brecht's stagecraft, and on his place in modern culture by a friend and sometime colleague. The essays in Walter Benjamin, *Understanding Brecht*, trans. Anna Bostock (1983), provide important insights into Brecht's work and modern thought

by a close friend and major intellectual figure. *A Bertolt Brecht Reference Companion* (1997), ed. Siegfried Mews, offers seventeen diverse essays with an introduction and bibliography. *The Cambridge Companion to Brecht*, ed. Peter Thomson and Glendyr Sacks (1994), contains an essay on *The Good Person of Szechwan*. Katherine Bliss Eaton, *The Theater of Meyerhold and Brecht* (1985), Antony Tatlow, *The Mask of Evil: Brecht's Response to the Poetry, Theatre and Thought of China and Japan—a Comparative and Critical Evaluation* (1977), and Renata Berg-Pan, *Bertolt Brecht and China* (1979), are valuable comparative studies.

Italo Calvino

Sara Maria Adler, *Calvino: The Writer as Fablemaker* (1979), is a book-length biography in English. Beno Weiss's *Understanding Italo Calvino* (1993), is a useful introductory guide to Calvino's life and writings. Discussions of *Invisible Cities* may be found in Kathryn Hume's *Calvino's Fictions: Cogito and Cosmos* (1992) and *Italo Calvino: Metamorphoses of Fantasy* (1987) by Albert Howard Carter III. See also Lucia Re, *Calvino and the Age of Neorealism: Fables of Estrangement* (1990), and I. T. Olken, *With Pleated Eye and Garnet Wing: Symmetries of Italo Calvino* (1984).

Albert Camus

Germaine Brée, *Camus*, rev. ed. (1972), is an excellent general study; see also by Brée *Camus: A Collection of Critical Essays* (1962). Phillip Rhein, *Albert Camus*, rev. ed. (1989), is a brief introduction and biography. Herbert Lottman, *Albert Camus: A Biography* (1979; repr. 1997), and Olivier Todd, *Albert Camus: A Life*, trans. Benjamin Ivry (1997), are detailed biographies. English Showalter, *Exiles and Strangers: A Reading of Camus's Exile and the Kingdom* (1984), offers essays on the six stories of Camus's collection and separate comments on translations.

Constantine Cavafy

Biographical information is available in Peter Bien, *Constantine Cavafy* (1964), and Robert Liddell, *Cavafy: A Critical Biography* (1974; repr. 2000), which also contains a bibliography. C. E. Bowra's "Constantine Cavafy and the Greek Past," in his *The Creative Experiment* (1949), is an important early essay. Separate discussions appear in Edmund Keeley, *Cavafy's Alexandria* (1996), which contains a bibliography, and in a chapter by Keeley in *Modern Greek Writers: Solomos, Calvos, Matesis, Palamas, Cavafy, Kazantzakis*, ed. Edmund Keeley and Peter Bien (1972).

Joseph Conrad

Among the many sources of biographical information are Conrad's *The Mirror of the Sea* (1906) and *A Personal Record* (1912), and Jocelyn Baines, *Joseph Conrad: A Critical Biography* (1960). Albert J. Guérard's critical study *Conrad*

the Novelist (1958) is also recommended, and Ian Watt's *Conrad in the Nineteenth Century* (1979) contains an interesting discussion of Impressionist techniques in Conrad. Chinua Achebe's essay "An Image of Africa: Racism in Conrad's *Heart of Darkness*" is published in his *Hopes and Impediments: Selected Essay, 1965–1987* (1988). Recent works focusing on *Heart of Darkness* include Peter Edgerly Firchow, *Envisioning Africa: Racism and Imperialism in Conrad's "Heart of Darkness"* (2000) and *Conrad in Africa: New Essays on "Heart of Darkness,"* ed. Attie de Lange and Gail Fincham, with Wieslaw Krajka (2002). Adam Hochschild, *King Leopold's Ghost: A Story of Greed, Terror, and Heroism in Colonial Africa* (1998), is a detailed and informative study of the Congo setting of Conrad's novella.

Dada-Surrealist Poetry

Valuable discussions of Dada include Alan Young, *Dada and After: Extremist Modernism and English Literature* (1981), and John D. Erickson, *Dada: Performance, Poetry, and Art* (1984). Studies of Surrealist poets include Mary Ann Caws, *The Poetry of Dada and Sur-realism* (1970), and J. H. Matthews, *Surrealist Poetry in France* (1969), which has a chapter on Mansour. Maurice Nadeau, *The History of Surrealism*, trans. Richard Howard (1954), is an early and authoritative history of Surrealism to 1939; it includes an extensive chronology and a selection of Surrealist documents. Herbert S. Gershman, *The Surrealist Revolution in France* (1974), is a good shorter account that also contains a chronology. William S. Rubin, *Dada, Surrealism, and Their Heritage* (1968), gives a detailed history of Surrealist art with many superb illustrations; a shorter history is available in Dawn Ades, *Dada and Surrealism* (1974). Marcel Raymond, *From Baudelaire to Surrealism*, trans. G. M. (1950), and Anna Balakian, *The Literary Origins of Surrealism*, new ed. (1966), trace Surrealism's roots in European Romantic and Symbolist poetry. Discussions of Aimé Césaire include Gregson Davis, *Aimé Césaire* (1997), and A. James Arnold, *Modernism and Negritude: The Poetry and Poetics of Aimé Césaire* (1981).

T. S. Eliot

Bernard Bergonzi, *T. S. Eliot*, 2nd ed. (1978), and Tony Sharpe, *T. S. Eliot: A Literary Life* (1991), are brief and readable introductions to the life and works. Martin Scofield, *T. S. Eliot: The Poems* (1988), offers a concise, balanced discussion of the evolution of Eliot's poetry. *The Waste Land* is discussed in Jay Martin, ed., *A Collection of Critical Essays on The Waste Land* (1968); Lois A. Cuddy and David H. Hirsch, eds., *Critical Essays on T. S. Eliot's The Waste Land* (1991); and as part of John T. Mayer, *T. S. Eliot's Silent Voices* (1989), which analyzes themes of awareness and self-consciousness in the early poetry. *Little Gidding* is examined in Steve Ellis, *The English Eliot: Design, Language, and Landscape in Four Quartets* (1991), and Edward Lobb, ed., *Words in Time: New Essays on Eliot's Four Quartets* (1993). John Paul Riquelme, *Harmony of Dissonances: T. S. Eliot, Romanticism, and Imagination* (1991), links Eliot's response to Romanticism with postmodern views. Useful general collections are Linda W. Wagner, ed., *T. S. Eliot: A Collection of Criticism* (1974), and Ronald Bush, ed., *T. S. Eliot: The Modernist in History* (1991).

Encyclopaedia Britannica (Eleventh Edition)
Further information on the eleventh edition and its place in intellectual history may be found in Harvey Einbinder's *The Myth of the Britannica* (1964), Herman Kogan's *The Great EB: The Story of the Encyclopaedia Britannica* (1958), and Gillian Thomas's *A Position to Command Respect: Women and the Eleventh Britannica* (1992).

Frantz Fanon
Biographies include David Caute, *Fanon* (1970); Irene L. Gendzier, *Frantz Fanon: A Critical Study* (1973); and David Macey, *Frantz Fanon: A Biography* (2001). See also Lewis R. Gordon, *Fanon and the Crisis of European Man: An Essay on Philosophy and the Human Sciences* (1995); Nigel C. Gibson, *Fanon: The Postcolonial Imagination* (2003); and a valuable series of collected essays in *Frantz Fanon: Critical Perspectives*, ed. Anthony C. Alessandrini (1999).

William Faulkner
Suggested studies include Michael Millgate, *The Achievement of William Faulkner* (1963; repr. 1989), a critical study of the novels and stories with a brief biography in the first chapter; Cleanth Brooks, *William Faulkner: The Yoknapatawpha Country* (1963), a basic literary analysis and study of Faulkner's mythical South in the Yoknapatawpha stories, with a list of Faulkner's fictional characters; James B. Carothers, *William Faulkner's Short Stories* (1985), an examination of the short stories in the context of the novels; Linda Wagner-Martin, ed., *William Faulkner: Four Decades of Criticism* (1973), a collection of essays. *William Faulkner, the Man and the Artist: A Biography* (1987), is vividly written by historian Stephen B. Oates. Joseph Blotner is the author of *Faulkner: A Biography*, 2 vols. (1974; repr. in 1 vol., 1984, 2005), the authorized and immensely detailed biography. Doreen Fowler and Ann J. Abadie, eds., *Faulkner and the Craft of Fiction: Faulkner and Yoknapatawpha* (1989), collects useful essays on themes and narrative structures.

Sigmund Freud
Peter Gay, *Freud: A Life for Our Time* (1988), is a full and readable biography by a major cultural historian and Freud scholar; the well-documented recent biography by Louis Breger,

Freud: Darkness in the Midst of Vision (2000), includes a discussion of Freud in relation to various movements and figures of his time. Michael Kahn, *Basic Freud: Psychoanalytic Thought for the Twenty-first Century* (2002), is a useful review of basic concepts in Freud.

James Joyce
Harry Levin, *James Joyce: A Critical Introduction*, 2nd rev. ed. (1968), is an excellent and readable general introduction. The standard and detailed biography, with illustrations, is Richard Ellmann, *James Joyce* (1982). Morris Beja, *James Joyce: A Literary Life* (1992), includes recent scholarship. Derek Attridge, ed., *The Cambridge Companion to James Joyce*, 2nd ed. (2004), and Mary T. Reynolds, ed., *James Joyce: A Collection of Critical Essays* (1993), treat various aspects of the work. Daniel R. Schwarz, ed., *The Dead* (1994), is a useful short book that includes the text and some contextual material, an account of *Dubliners'* history and criticism from the 1950s, and analyses by different authors using five modern critical perspectives. Diverse critical approaches are represented in Alan Roughley, *James Joyce and Critical Theory: An Introduction* (1991) and Suzette A. Henke's feminist study *James Joyce and the Politics of Desire* (1990). John Wyse Jackson and Bernard McGinley, eds., *Dubliners: An Illustrated Edition with Annotations* (1995), is a fascinating, copiously illustrated and documented edition that includes allusions to other works and a capsule essay after each story. David Pierce, *James Joyce's Ireland* (1992), includes contemporary photographs by Dan Harper and uses documents, photographs, and copious quotation to reconstruct Joyce's biography in historical context.

Franz Kafka
Anthony Thorlby, *Kafka: A Study* (1972), is a brief general introduction. Heinz Politzer, *Franz Kafka: Parable and Paradox* (1966), presents an interesting, readable study of symbolic relationships. Ernst Pawel, *The Nightmare of Reason: A Life of Franz Kafka* (1984), is an excellent contemporary biography with penetrating descriptions of his family and friends. Max Brod, *Franz Kafka: A Biography* (1960), is an early, admiring biography by a close friend and Kafka's executor. Ronald Gray, ed., *Kafka: A Collection of Critical Essays* (1962), is a useful early collection of essays on different works. Harold Bloom, ed., *Franz Kafka's The Metamorphosis* (1988), collects essays on spiritual, metaphorical, formal, social, and psychoanalytic aspects of *The Metamorphosis*. Jack Murray analyzes the sense of space in *The Landscapes of Alienation: Ideological Subversion in Kafka, Céline, and Onetti* (1991). Kurt Fickert, *End of a Mission: Kafka's Search for Truth in His Last Stories* (1993), interprets the stories as metaphors for an autobiographical quest to resolve personal problems. Walter H. Sokel, *The Myth of Power and the Self:*

Essays on Franz Kafka (2002), collects penetrating essays written over four decades by a leading Kafka scholar.

Doris Lessing

Ruth Whittaker, *Doris Lessing* (1988), is a concise, informative discussion of Lessing's fiction to 1985; it includes biographical contexts and selective bibliography. Two volumes of Lessing's autobiography are published as *Under My Skin* (1994) and *Walking in the Shade: Volume Two of My Autobiography, 1949–1962* (1997). Michael Thorpe, *Doris Lessing's Africa* (1978), is a valuable historical and critical commentary on Lessing's writings about Africa. Claire Sprague and Virginia Tiger, *Critical Essays on Doris Lessing* (1986), offers diverse perspectives on the range of Lessing's work; numerous interviews on a range of subjects are collected in Earl G. Ingersoll, *Putting Questions Differently: Interviews with Doris Lessing, 1964–1994* (1996). A good critical study of the novels is Roberta Rubenstein, *The Novelistic Vision of Doris Lessing: Breaking the Forms of Consciousness* (1979). Perspectives on women and literature are the focus of Gayle Greene, *Doris Lessing: The Poetics of Change* (1994).

Federico García Lorca

Ian Gibson, *Federico García Lorca: A Life* (1989), is an extensive and detailed biography. Carl W. Cobb, *Federico García Lorca* (1967), is a good general biography. Candelas Newton, *Understanding Federico García Lorca* (1995), is a brief general discussion of the work; Edwin Honig, *García Lorca* (1981), provides a critical introduction in literary historical context; and C. Brian Morris, *Son of Andalusia: The Lyrical Landscapes of Federico García Lorca* (1997), offers a more specialized view, with illustrations. Manuel Durán, ed., *Lorca: A Collection of Critical Essays* (1962), is a valuable collection of essays on the poet and his work (mainly the poetry). Manuel Durán and Francesca Colecchia, eds., *Lorca's Legacy: Essays on Lorca's Life, Poetry, and Theatre* (1991), offer a range of essays and a recent bibliography.

Audre Lorde

There is no book-length autobiography, but autobiographical material is available in Lorde's *The Cancer Journals* (1980) and *Zami: A New Spelling of My Name* (1982) as well as in *Bearing Witness: Selections from African-American Autobiography in the Twentieth Century*, ed. Henry Louis Gates, Jr. (1991), and *Revising the Word and the World: Essays in Feminist Literary Criticism*, ed. VèVè A. Clark, Ruth-Ellen B. Joeres, and Madelon Sprengnether (1993), which contains an interview with Lorde. See also Carmen Birkle, *Women's Stories of the Looking Glass: Autobiographical Reflections and Self-Representations in the Poetry of Sylvia Plath,* *Adrienne Rich, and Audre Lorde* (1996), and Zofia Burr, *Of Women, Poetry, and Power: Strategies of Address in Dickinson, Miles, Brooks, Lorde, and Angelou* (2002).

Thomas Mann

Ignace Feuerlicht, *Thomas Mann* (1968), provides a general biographical introduction. Henry Hatfield, ed., *Thomas Mann: A Collection of Critical Essays* (1964), and Harold Bloom, ed., *Thomas Mann* (2002), present essays on different works and brief biographical information. Terence J. Reed, *Thomas Mann: The Uses of Tradition*, 2nd ed. (1996), is an excellent, well-written general study incorporating recent material. Richard Winston, *Thomas Mann: The Making of an Artist, 1875–1911* (1981), the first volume of an unfinished study, is a detailed and authoritative presentation by the translator of Mann's diaries and letters.

Gabriel García Márquez

Gabriel García Márquez, *Living to Tell the Tale*, trans. Edith Grossman (2003), is the first volume of a projected three-volume autobiography Regina Janes, *Gabriel García Márquez: Revolutions in Wonderland* (1981), is an excellent general study on García Márquez in a Latin American context. Other useful introductions to the writer and his work are George R. McMurray, *Gabriel García Márquez* (1977), and Robin W. Fiddian, ed., *García Márquez* (1995). The summer 1972 issue of *Books Abroad* is dedicated to García Márquez. Harley D. Oberhelman, ed., *Gabriel García Márquez: A Study of the Short Fiction* (1991), includes a bibliography.

René Ménil

Additional essays by Ménil, as well as other writing from the period of *Tropiques*, may be found in *Refusal of the Shadow : Surrealism and the Caribbean*, ed. Michael Richardson, trans. Michael Richardson and Krzysztof Fijałkowski (1996).

Alice Munro

Catherine S. Ross, *Alice Munro: A Double Life* (1991), is a compact, readable biography that highlights the sources of Munro's writing; it includes a bibliography, photographs, maps, and interview comments about Nora. E. D. Blodgett, *Alice Munro* (1988), and Coral Ann Howells, *Alice Munro* (1998), introduce the writer and her work. Robert Thacker, ed., *The Rest of the Story: Critical Essays on Alice Munro* (1999), assembles eleven essays, including a discussion of Munro's correspondence with her literary agent; J. R. Struthers, "Alice Munro and the American South," in John Moss, ed., *The Canadian Novel: A Critical Anthology*, vol. 1: *Here and Now* (1983), is also recommended. Louis MacKendrick, ed., *Probable Fictions: Alice Munro's Narrative Acts* (1983), is an excellent survey of critical essays and of interviews with the author herself. For more on Munro's approach to gender issues and male/female relationships, see Beverly Rasporich, *Dance of the Sexes: Art and Gender in the Fiction of Alice Munro* (1990).

Pablo Neruda
Pablo Neruda, *Memoirs*, trans. Hardie St. Martin (1977), contains much biographical information; Manuel Durán and Margery Safir, *Earth Tones: The Poetry of Pablo Neruda* (1981), is an excellent thematic study that also offers a short biography; *Pablo Neruda*, ed. Harold Bloom (1989), contains nineteen valuable essays and reminiscences by scholars, translators, and those who knew Neruda; John Felstiner, *Translating Neruda: The Way to Macchu Picchu* (1980), describes in detail the process of translating *The Heights of Macchu Picchu* in terms of Neruda's life and perspectives; Luis Poirot, *Pablo Neruda: Absence and Presence* (1990), matches photographs of Neruda, his friends, and his homes with related passages from the poet, his wife, and friends. Also recommended are James Nolan, *Poet-Chief: The Native American Poetics of Walt Whitman and Pablo Neruda* (1994), Salvatore Bizzarro, *Pablo Neruda: All Poets the Poet* (1979), and Enrico Mario Santí, *Pablo Neruda: The Poetics of Prophecy* (1982).

George Orwell
Biographical studies include the authorized biographies *Orwell* by Michael Shelden (1991), *George Orwell: A Life* by Bernard Crick (1980), and *The Unknown Orwell* (1972) and *Orwell: The Transformation* (1979) by Peter Stansky and William Abrahams. See also Richard Rees, *George Orwell: Fugitive from the Camp of Victory* (1961); Keith Alldritt, *The Making of George Orwell: An Essay in Literary History* (1969); Alex Zwerdling, *Orwell and the Left* (1974); and a volume compiled by Raymond Williams, *George Orwell: A Collection of Critical Essays* (1974).

Luigi Pirandello
A good biography and general introduction is found in Susan Bassnett-McGuire, *Pirandello* (1983). Useful introductions are Fiora A. Bassanese, *Understanding Luigi Pirandello* (1997), and Walter Starkie, *Luigi Pirandello, 1867–1936*, 3rd ed. (1965). Glauco Cambon, comp., *Pirandello: A Collection of Critical Essays* (1967), emphasizes the plays. A. Richard Sogliuzzo, *Luigi Pirandello, Director: The Playwright in the Theatre* (1982), deals with Pirandello's dramatic theories and practices; it contains a discussion of *Six Characters*. John Louis DiGaetani, ed., *A Companion to Pirandello Studies* (1991), is an excellent collection of twenty-seven essays and four appendices on diverse aspects of Pirandello's thought and work; many essays take up *Six Characters*. Luigi Pirandello, *Pirandello's Love Letters to Marta*

Abba, ed. and trans. Benito Ortonolani (1994), illuminates the author's personal life in 1925–36 and his plans to reform the Italian theater.

Katherine Anne Porter
Joan Givner's *Katherine Anne Porter: A Life*, rev. ed. (1991), a lengthy study, is the only complete biography. For Porter's essays, see Robert Penn Warren, ed., *Katherine Anne Porter: A Collection of Critical Essays* (1979). Katherine Anne Porter, *The Collected Essays and Occasional Writings of Katherine Anne Porter* (1970), contains discussions of her own reading tastes and concept of art. Jane Krause DeMouy, *Katherine Anne Porter's Women: The Eye of Her Fiction* (1983), analyzes Porter's fiction.

Marcel Proust
Roger Shattuck, *Proust* (1974), is a general study that includes advice on "how to read" Proust; it is still useful although it predates the revised translation used here; George D. Painter, *Marcel Proust: A Biography* (rev. 1996), offers a comprehensive biography. An excellent general study is Germaine Brée, *Marcel Proust and Deliverance from Time*, trans. C. J. Richards and A. D. Truitt (1969). Terence Kilmartin, comp., *A Reader's Guide to Remembrance of Things Past* (1984), is a handbook guide to Proust's characters, to persons referred to in the text, to places, and to themes, all keyed to the revised translation by the translator. Julia Kristeva, *Proust and the Sense of Time*, trans. Stephen Bann (1993), takes a broadly psychoanalytic approach. René Girard, ed., *Proust: A Collection of Critical Essays* (1962; repr. 1977); Harold Bloom, ed., *Marcel Proust's Remembrance of Things Past* (1987); and Barbara J. Bucknall, ed., *Critical Essays on Marcel Proust* (1987), are also recommended.

Rainer Maria Rilke
J. F. Hendry, *The Sacred Threshold: A Life of Rainer Maria Rilke* (1983), is a brief and readable biography with numerous citations from Rilke's letters and work. Heinz F. Peters, *Rainer Maria Rilke: Masks and the Man* (1977), is a biographical and thematic study of Rilke's work and influence. Romano Guardini examines the elegies in *Rilke's Duino Elegies: An Interpretation* (1961). Donald Prater, *A Ringing Glass: The Life of Rainer Maria Rilke* (1993), is an excellent account of the poet's life and the conditions in which his work developed; it includes extensive quotations from many unpublished letters. *Rainer Maria Rilke: Aspects of His Mind and Poetry*, ed. William Rose and G. Craig Houston (1973), contains an excellent essay by C. M. Bowra on the *New Poems*. William H. Gass, *Reading Rilke: Reflections on the Problems of Translation* (1999), combines biography, philosophy, and reflections on specific translation problems in the *Duino Elegies*.

Alain Robbe-Grillet

Ilona Leki, *Alain Robbe-Grillet* (1983), is a good biography and survey of Robbe-Grillet's work in historical context, discussing each work, with a last chapter on the films. Introductory essays to Alain Robbe-Grillet, *Two Novels* trans. Richard Howard (1965, 1993), discuss the author's descriptive strategies. Bruce Morrissette, *The Novels of Robbe-Grillet* (1975), provides a valuable critical study that takes the works and films in chronological order. Morrissette, *Novel and Film: Essays in Two Genres* (1985), makes Robbe-Grillet the chief example in a discussion of modern cinematic vision. Ben Stoltzfus, *Alain Robbe-Grillet and the New French Novel* (1964), is an earlier introduction to Robbe-Grillet in the context of the emerging new novel form. Raylene L. Ramsay, *Robbe-Grillet and Modernity: Science, Sexuality, and Subversion* (1992), interrogates contemporary culture and the thematics of sexual violence.

Salman Rushdie

Useful studies of Rushdie include Timothy Brennan, *Salman Rushdie and the Third World: Myths of the Nation* (1989), James Harrison, *Salman Rushdie* (1992), and the thirteen essays on diverse subjects collected in *Critical Essays on Salman Rushdie*, ed. M. Keith Booker (1999). Rushdie's own views are available in his *Imaginary Homelands: Essays and Criticism, 1981–1991* (1991) and *Step across This Line: Collected Nonfiction 1992–2002* (2002), as well as in *Salman Rushdie Interviews: A Sourcebook of His Ideas*, ed. Pradyumna S. Chauhan (2001), and *Conversations with Salman Rushdie*, ed. Michael Reder (2000). For a broader historical perspective, see *Intellectuals in Politics: From the Dreyfus Affair to Salman Rushdie*, ed. Jeremy Jennings and Anthony Kemp-Welch (1997).

Edward Said

In addition to Said's many critical works, the following volumes may be consulted for autobiographical information: Edward Said, *Out of Place: A Memoir* (1999) and *Power, Politics, and Culture: Interviews with Edward W. Said* (2001), a collection of interviews and panel discussions from the years 1976 to 2000. See also the selection of readings in *Edward Said: A Critical Reader*, ed. Michael Sprinker (1992), and *Cultural Readings of Imperialism: Edward Said and the Gravity of History*, ed. Keith Ansell-Pearson, Benita Parry, and Judith Squires (1997).

Jean-Paul Sartre

Useful readings on Sartre are his autobiography, *The Words*, trans. Bernard Frechtman (1964), and selections from the ten-volume essay collection *Situations: Literary and Philosophical Essays* (vols. 1 and 3), trans. Annette Michelson

(1962), and *Situations: Colonialism and Neocolonialism* (vol. 5), trans. Azzedine Haddour, Steve Brewer, and Terry McWilliams (2001). An early study by a major translator and interpreter of Sartre is Hazel E. Barnes, *An Existentialist Ethics* (1967); see also the essays in Hugh J. Silverman and Frederick A. Elliston, eds., *Jean-Paul Sartre: Contemporary Approaches to His Philosophy* (1980).

Leslie Marmon Silko

Gregory Salyer, *Leslie Marmon Silko* (1997), is a brief introduction to the author and her work; Helen Jaskoski, *Leslie Marmon Silko: A Study of the Short Fiction* (1998), focuses on the stories. Leslie Silko, *Sacred Water: Narratives and Pictures* (1993), is an autobiographical narrative. Melody Graulich, ed., *"Yellow Woman": Leslie Marmon Silko* (1993), is a collection of pertinent critical essays. The story itself is profitably read, or reread, in Silko's *Storyteller* (1981), where it appears in context with several of her other short pieces on the Yellow Woman theme. For traditional texts on Yellow Woman and other figures in Laguna mythology, the best source is Franz Boas, *Keresan Texts* (1928); the stories in Boas's volume were obtained in 1919–21 from several Laguna informants, including Leslie Silko's great-grandfather, Robert Marmon.

Alexander Solzhenitsyn

Andrej Kodjak, *Alexander Solzhenitsyn* (1978), provides a biographical and critical introduction to Solzhenitsyn up to his deportation from the Soviet Union in 1974; it includes a discussion of Russian terms. Michael Scammell's detailed *Solzhenitsyn: A Biography* (1984) is complemented by D. M. Thomas, *Alexander Solzhenitsyn: A Century in His Life* (1998), which adds new information and a discussion of the writer's work after his return to Russia. Kathryn B. Feuer, ed., *Solzhenitsyn: A Collection of Critical Essays* (1976), and Harold Bloom, ed., *Alexander Solzhenitsyn* (2000), contain a range of essays on aspects and particular works, including *Matryona's Home*. John B. Dunlop, Richard S. Haugh, and Michael Nicholson, eds., *Solzhenitsyn in Exile: Critical Essays and Documentary Materials* (1985), offer critical essays and discussions of Solzhenitsyn's reception in different countries. John Dunlop, Richard Haugh, and Alexis Klimoff, eds., *Aleksandr Solzhenitsyn: Critical Essays and Documentary Materials* (1973), is a useful collection with a wide range of essays and reprinted texts, including a short autobiography by Solzhenitsyn and his Nobel Prize lecture.

Oswald Spengler

Various perspectives on Spengler's work are available in Klaus P. Fischer, *History and Prophecy: Oswald Spengler and the Decline of the West*

(1989), H. Stuart Hughes, *Oswald Spengler, a Critical Estimate* (1952), Jacinta O'Hagan, *Conceptualizing the West in International Relations: From Spengler to Said* (2002), and Werner J. Dannhauser, "Nietzsche and Spengler on Progress and Decline," in *History and the Idea of Progress*, ed. Arthur M. Melzer, Jerry Weinberger, and M. Richard Zinman (1995).

Wallace Stevens
A good general introduction is Robert Pack, *Wallace Stevens: An Approach to His Poetry and Thought* (1968); Robert Buttel, *Wallace Stevens: The Making of Harmonium* (1967), discusses Stevens's early and middle work. Many views on Stevens are presented in Marie Borroff, ed., *Wallace Stevens: A Collection of Critical Essays* (1963). Michel Benamou, *Wallace Stevens and the Symbolist Imagination* (1972), is an interesting study of Stevens's themes and style compared with those of French Symbolist poets. Albert Gelpi, *Wallace Stevens: The Poetics of Modernism* (1985), presents seven essays situating Stevens's work in the context of twentieth-century modernism in English; historical, philosophical, and artistic perspectives are discussed as well as Stevens's influence on contemporary poets. Janet McCann, *Wallace Stevens Revisited: "The Celestial Possible"* (1995), stresses metaphysical themes. John T. Newcomb, *Wallace Stevens and Literary Canons* (1992), examines the way Stevens's "canonical" reputation evolves in tandem with critical perspectives on American modernism. Glen MacLeod, *Wallace Stevens and Modern Art: From the Armory Show to Abstract Expressionism* (1993), traces the relations between Stevens's poetics and his understanding of issues in modern art.

Alfonsina Storni
Sonia Jones, *Alfonsina Storni* (1979), is a useful survey of Storni's life and work. Rachel Phillips, *Alfonsina Storni: From Poetess to Poet* (1975), analyzes the evolution of Storni's poetry. Florence Williams Talamantes, ed., *Alfonsina Storni: Argentina's Feminist Poet* (1975), Dorothy Scott Loos, ed., *Alfonsina Storni: Selected Poems* (1986), and Marion Freeman, ed., *Selected Poems: Alfonsina Storni* (1987), offer a range of selections and brief introductions. Gwen Kirkpatrick's "The Creation of Alfonsina Storni," in *A Dream of Light and Shadow: Portraits of Latin American Women Writers*, ed. Marjorie Agosín (1995), is also recommended.

Trinh T. Minh-ha
Further information may be found in the interviews of Trinh T. Minh-ha, *Framer Framed: Film Scripts and Interviews* (1992) and her *Cinema Interval* (1999). See also E. Ann Kaplan,

"Trinh T. Minh-ha," in *Postmodernism: The Key Figures,* ed. Hans Bertens and Joseph Natoli (2002); Herman Rapaport, "Deconstruction's Others: Trinh T. Minh-Ha and Jacques Derrida," *Diacritics* (Summer 1995); and Harriet A. Hirshorn, "Interview: Trinh T. Minh-ha," *Heresies* 6:2 (1987).

Paul Valéry
Recommended readings are Walter C. Putnam, *Paul Valéry Revisited* (1995), a general study of Valéry, and Paul Fussell, *The Great War and Modern Memory* (1975; repr. 2000).

Derek Walcott
Walcott's collection of essays, *What the Twilight Says* (1998), is an indispensable compendium of his social and aesthetic ideas. Robert Hamner, *Derek Walcott,* rev. ed. (1993), is a comprehensive and accessible full-length study of the writer's work; John Thieme, *Derek Walcott* (1999), is more up to date and provides commentaries on the key poems in Walcott's various collections and on the dramatic works. Lloyd W. Brown, *West Indian Poetry,* 2nd ed. (1984), contains a helpful chapter on Walcott's poetry in the context of the development of West Indian poetry in English. Edward Baugh, *Derek Walcott: Memory as Vision* (1978), provides an extended exegesis on *Another Life;* Rei Terada, *Derek Walcott's Poetry: American Mimicry* (1992), examines Walcott's creative integration within his poetry of influences from various sources. Bruce King, *Derek Walcott and West Indian Drama* (1995), is a history of the Trinidad Theatre Workshop and a study of the development of Walcott's dramatic art; the work is complemented by the same author's *Derek Walcott: A Caribbean Life* (2000), the first major biography of the writer. Robert D. Hamner, *Epic of the Dispossessed: Derek Walcott's "Omeros"* (1997), provides a detailed discussion of *Omeros* that considers its adaptation of epic idiom to the experience and life dilemmas of the common folk. *The Art of Derek Walcott,* ed. Stewart Brown (1991), and *Critical Perspectives on Derek Walcott,* ed. Robert D. Hamner (1993), are collective volumes that, though somewhat dated, can still be recommended for their coverage of Walcott's work up to their respective dates of their publication.

Max Weber
Biographical information is available in Marianne Weber's *Max Weber: A Biography,* trans. Harry Zohn (1975; repr. 1988) and Paul Honigsheim's *On Max Weber,* trans. Joan Rytina (1968). Stephen Kalberg's *Max Weber's Comparative-Historical Sociology* (1994) discusses Weber's approach, and *Weber's "Protestant Ethic": Origins, Evidence, Contexts,* ed. Hartmut Lehmann and Guenther Roth (1993), contains

eighteen essays by different writers on aspects of the book and its reception.

Virginia Woolf
Phyllis Rose, *Woman of Letters: A Life of Virginia Woolf* (1978), is a valuable biography; Edward Bishop, *Virginia Woolf* (1991), is a recent brief introduction. Two valuable collections of essays on Woolf's writing and her position in the modernist/postmodernist tradition are Patricia Clements and Isobel Grundy, eds., *Virginia Woolf: New Critical Essays* (1983), and Margaret Homans, ed., *Virginia Woolf: A Collection of Critical Essays* (1993). Jane Marcus, *Virginia Woolf and the Languages of Patriarchy* (1987), and Rachel Bowlby, *Feminist Destinations and Further Essays on Virginia Woolf* (1997), offer perceptive feminist analyses that include discussion of *A Room of One's Own*. Mark Hussey and Vara Neverow, eds., *Virginia Woolf: Emerging Perspectives* (1994), contains several essays on *A Room of One's Own*. S. P. Rosenbaum, ed., *Women and Fiction: The Manuscript Versions of "A Room of One's Own"* (1992), transcribes and edits two draft manuscripts that are the basis for *A Room of One's Own*. Gillian Beer, *Virginia Woolf: The Common Ground* (1996), offers four useful general essays and four discussions of specific novels. Patricia Ondek Laurence situates Woolf in *The Reading of Silence: Virginia Woolf in the English Tradition* (1991); comparative studies include Richard Pearce, *The Politics of Narration: James Joyce, William Faulkner, and Virginia Woolf* (1991).

Richard Wright
Michel Fabre, *The Unfinished Quest of Richard Wright*, trans. Isabel Barzun, 2nd ed. (1993), is an excellent and readable biography. Useful essay collections that reprint reviews of Wright's work are Robert J. Butler, ed., *The Critical Response to Richard Wright* (1995), and Henry Louis Gates, Jr. and K. A. Appiah, eds., *Richard Wright: Critical Perspectives Past and Present* (1993), which contains an essay specifically on the short stories. In addition are Harold Bloom, ed., *Richard Wright* (1987); Arnold Rampersad, ed., with Bruce Simon and Jeffrey Tucker, *Richard Wright: A Collection of Critical Essays* (1995); and Richard Macksey and Frank E. Moorer, eds., *Richard Wright, a Collection of Critical Essays* (1984).

William Butler Yeats
Edward Malins presents a brief introduction with biography, illustrations, and maps in *A Preface to Yeats*, 2nd ed. (1994). Richard Ellmann, *The Identity of Yeats*, 2nd ed. (1970), is an excellent discussion of Yeats's work as a whole. A. Norman Jeffares has revised his major study, *A New Commentary on the Poems of W. B. Yeats* (1984); a useful reference work is Lester I. Conner, *A Yeats Dictionary: Persons and Places in the Poetry of William Butler Yeats* (1998). Jeffares's *W. B. Yeats: A New Biography* (1989) takes into account new information about the poet. Elizabeth Cullingford, *Gender and History in Yeats's Love Poetry* (1993), examines aesthetic form and cultural perspectives in the love lyrics; Deirdre Toomey, *Yeats and Women*, 2nd ed. (1997), discusses Yeats's relations with women and the women in his poetry; and Marjorie Elizabeth Howes, *Yeats's Nations: Gender, Class, and Irishness* (1996), stresses political and social views. Essay collections include Harold Bloom, ed., *William Butler Yeats* (1986), and Richard J. Finneran, ed., *Critical Essays on W. B. Yeats* (1986). Essays in Deborah Fleming, ed., *Learning the Trade: Essays on W. B. Yeats and Contemporary Poetry* (1993), discuss Yeats's imprint on various contemporary poets; and contributions to Leonard Orr, ed., *Yeats and Postmodernism* (1991), approach Yeats from different postmodernist perspectives.

sing. Reprinted by kind permission of Jonathan Clowes Ltd, London, on behalf of Doris Lessing, and Simon & Schuster.

Audre Lorde: From SISTER OUTSIDER by Audre Lorde. Copyright © 1984. Used by permission of Ten Speed Press.

Stéphane Mallarmé: Poems from COLLECTED POEMS OF STÉPHANE MALLARMÉ, translated/edited by Henry Weinfield. Copyright © 1994 by The Regents of the University of California. Reprinted by permission of the publisher, the University of California Press. From *The Evolution of Literature* and *Crisis in Poetry* from PROSE, POEMS, ESSAYS AND LETTERS translated by Bradford Cook. Copyright © 1956 Johns Hopkins University Press. Reprinted by permission of Johns Hopkins University Press.

Thomas Mann: *Death in Venice* from DEATH IN VENICE: A NORTON CRITICAL EDITION by Thomas Mann, translated by Clayton Koelb. Translation copyright © 1994 by W. W. Norton & Company, Inc. Reprinted by permission of W. W. Norton & Company, Inc.

Joyce Mansour: Poems from SCREAMS, translated by Serge Gavronsky. Copyright © 1995. Reprinted by permission of The Post-Apollo Press.

Jean-Paul Marat: *Speech for the Trial of Louis XVI [Address to the Convention on the Crimes of King Louis XVI]* from REGICIDE AND REVOLUTION translated by Marian Rothstein, edited by Michael Walzer. Used by permission of Columbia University Press.

Karl Marx and Friedrich Engels: "Bourgeois and Proletarians" from THE MARX-ENGLES READER, SECOND EDITION by Karl Marx and Friedrich Engels, edited by Robert G. Tucker. Copyright © 1978, 1972 by W. W. Norton & Company, Inc. Used by permission of W. W. Norton & Company, Inc.

Herman Melville: BILLY BUDD, SAILOR, edited by Heyford and Sealts. Copyright © 1962 by the University of Chicago Press. Reprinted by permission of The University of Chicago Press.

René Ménil: From *Concerning Colonial Exoticism* from REFUSAL OF THE SHADOW edited by Michael Richardson, translated by K. Fijałkowski. Used by permission of Verso.

Jean-Baptiste Poquelin Molière: TARTUFFE, translated by Richard Wilbur. Copyright © 1963, 1962, 1961 and renewed 1991, 1990, 1989 by Richard Wilbur. Reprinted by permission of Harcourt Brace & Company. CAUTION: Professionals and amateurs are hereby warned that this translation, being fully protected under the copyright laws of the United States of America, the British Empire, including the Dominion of Canada, and all other countries which are signatories to the Universal Copyright Convention and the International Copyright Union, is subject to royalty. All rights, including professional, amateur, motion picture, recitation, lecturing, public reading, radio broadcasting and television, are strictly reserved. Particular emphasis is laid on the question of readings, permission for which must be secured from the author's agent in writing. Inquiries on professional rights (except for amateur rights) should be addressed to Mr. Gilbert Parker, Curtis Brown, Ltd., 10 Astor Place, New York, NY 10003; inquiries on translation rights should be addressed to Harcourt Brace & Company, Publishers, Orlando, FL 32887. The amateur acting rights of *Tartuffe* are controlled exclusively by the Dramatist's Play Service, Inc., 440 Park Ave. South, New York, NY 10016. No amateur performance of the play may be given without obtaining in advance the written performance of the Dramatist's Play Service and paying the requisite fee.

Alice Munro: *Walker Brothers Cowboy* from DANCE OF THE HAPPY SHADES by Alice Munro. Copyright © 1968 by Alice Munro. Originally published by McGraw-Hill Ryerson. Reprinted by permission of the Virginia Barber Literary Agency, Inc. and McGraw-Hill Ryerson. All rights reserved.

Pablo Neruda: *I'm Explaining a Few Things,* and *Ode to the Tomato* translated by Nathaniel Tarn and *Tonight I Can Write . . . ,* and *Walking Around* translated by W. S. Merwin from SELECTED POEMS BY PABLO NERUDA, edited by Nathaniel Tarn and published by Jonathan Cape. Used by permission of The Random House Group Ltd. *The Heights of Macchu Picchu* from CANTO GENERAL FIFTH ANNIVERSARY EDITION translated and edited by Jack Schmitt. Copyright © 1991 Fundación Pablo Neruda, Regents of the University of California. Used by permission of The University of California Press.

Gérard de Nerval: From SELECTED READINGS by Gérard de Nerval, translated by Geoffrey Wagner. Copyright © 1970.

Friedrich Nietzsche: From *Books Three* and *Five* from THE GAY SCIENCE, WITH A PRELUDE IN GERMAN RHYMES AND AN APPENDIX OF SONGS edited by Bernard Williams, translated

Edward Said: From ORIENTALISM by Edward W. Said. Copyright © 1978 by Edward W. Said. Used by permission of Pantheon Books, A division of Random House, Inc.

Jean-Paul Sarte: From *Freedom and Responsibility* from BEING AND NOTHINGNESS translated by Hazel E. Barnes. Used by permission of the Philosophical Library of New York.

Kurt Schwitters: *Anna Blume* translated by David Britt from DADA ART AND ANTI-ART, edited by Hans Richter. Copyright © 1965. Reprinted by permission of Thames & Hudson Ltd.

Leslie Marmon Silko: *Yellow Woman* from STORYTELLER. Copyright © 1981 by Leslie Marmon Silko. Published by Seaver Books, NY, NY. Reprinted by permission of the publisher.

Alexander Solzhenitsyn: *Matyrona's Home*, translated by H. T. Willetts. First published in May 1963 issue of *Encounter*.

Oswald Spengler: From THE DECLINE OF THE WEST: VOLUME 1 by Oswald Spengler, translated by C. F. Atkinson. Copyright © 1926 by Alfred A. Knopf, A division of Random House, Inc. Used by permission of Alfred A. Knopf, A division of Random House, Inc.

Madame de Staël: From MADAME DE STAËL ON POLITICS, LITERATURE AND NATIONAL CULTURE translated by Morroe Berger.

Wallace Stevens: *Anecdote of the Jar, The Emperor of Ice Cream, Peter Quince at the Clavier,* and *Sunday Morning,* copyright © 1923, copyright renewed 1951 by Wallace Stevens. *The Idea of Order at Key West,* copyright © 1936 by Wallace Stevens, copyright renewed 1964 by Holly Stevens. *The Man on the Dump,* copyright © 1942 by Wallace Stevens, copyright renewed 1970 by Holly Stevens. All from THE COLLECTED POEMS OF WALLACE STEVENS. Reprinted by permission of Alfred A. Knopf, Inc.

Alfonsina Storni: *Departure* translated by Marion Freeman, *Little-Bitty Man* translated by Mary Crow and Marion Freeman, and *You Want Me White,* translated by Mary Crow and Marion Freeman, from SELECTED POEMS, edited by Marion Freeman. Copyright © 1987 by Marion Freeman and Mary Crow. Reprinted by permission of White Pine Press, Buffalo, New York.

Jonathan Swift: *A Modest Proposal* from IRISH TRACTS 1727–1733, edited by Herbert Davis. Copyright © 1955. Reprinted by permission of Basil Blackwell.

Trinh T. Minh-ha: From WOMAN, NATIVE, OTHER: WRITING POSTCOLONIALITY AND FEMINISM by Trinh T. Minh-ha. Copyright © 1989 by Trinh T. Minh-ha. Used by permission of Indiana University Press.

Tristan Tzara: Excerpt from *Dada Manifesto 1918* and *Proclamation without Pretension* reprinted by permission of the translator, Mary Ann Caws.

Paul Valéry: From *Crisis of the Mind* from PAUL VALÉRY: AN ANTHOLOGY edited by Jackson Mathews. Copyright © 1977 Princeton University Press, renewed 2005 Princeton University Press. *La crise de l'esprit (in Variété I)* by Paul Valéry. Copyright Éditions Gallimard Press. Used by permission.

Giovanni Verga: From CAVALLERIA RUSTICANA AND OTHER STORIES translation and introduction by G. H. McWilliam (Penguin Classic 1999). Copyright © 1999 by G. H. McWilliam. Used by permission of Penguin Group (UK).

Paul Verlaine: Poems from PAUL VERLAINE: SELECTED POEMS, translated/edited by C. F. MacIntyre. Copyright © 1948 by The Regents of the University of California. Reprinted by permission of the University of California Press.

François-Marie Arouet de Voltaire: *Candide* from CANDIDE, OR OPTIMISM: A NORTON CRITICAL EDITION, SECOND EDITION by Voltaire, translated by Robert M. Adams. Translation copyright © 1991, 1966 by W. W. Norton & Company, Inc. Reprinted by permission of W. W. Norton & Company, Inc.

Theodor Gottlieb von Hippel: *Suggestions for Improvement* from ON IMPROVING THE STATUS OF WOMEN translated by Timothy F. Sellner. Copyright © 2003 by T. F. Sellner. Reprinted by permission of the translator.

Derek Walcott: Excerpts from chapters *I, VIII, XXV, XXVI, XXXIII, LII,* and *LXIV* from OMEROS by Derek Walcott. Copyright © 1990 by Derek Walcott. Reprinted by permission of Farrar, Straus and Giroux, LLC.

Index